Thy word is a lamp unto my feet, and a light unto my path

TO ______________________________

BY ______________________________

____

THE NEW PILGRIM BIBLE

KJV Student Edition

THE NEW PILGRIM BIBLE

KJV Student Edition

OXFORD
UNIVERSITY PRESS

Oxford NewYork
Auckland Bangkok Buenos Aires Cape Town Chennai
Dar esSalaam Delhi HongKong Istanbul Karachi Kolkata
Kuala Lumpur Madrid Melbourne Mexico City Mumbai Nairobi
São Paulo Shanghai Taipei Tokyo Toronto
and an associated company in Berlin

Produced with the assistance of The Livingstone Corporation (www.LivingstoneCorp.com).
Project staff includes Christopher Hudson, Joy Easton, Kathy Ristow, Tom Ristow,
Ashley Taylor, Rosalie Krusemark, and Peter Gregory.

Published by Oxford University Press, Inc.
198 Madison Avenue, New York, NY 10016
Printed in Korea
3 5 7 9 8 6 4 2

To the memory of Ruth Hill Munce
(1898—2001)

We hereby express our gratitude for the life and ministry of this woman, at whose suggestion the concept of the original edition of the Pilgrim Study Bible came to be. It was under her direction, and with her invaluable contributions as an editor, that after ten years the project was published in 1948.

CONTRIBUTORS

1948 EDITION

E. Schuyler English, *Editor-in-Chief*

Marion Bishop Bower, *Associate Editor*

Contributing and Consulting Editors

Archer E. Anderson
Alma Bailey
Paul. W. Beckwith
Frances E. Bennett
Miriam G. Cadman
Lewis Sperry Chafer
Mildred M. Cook
William Culbertson
Josephine M. Davies
William Allan Dean
Emily Dick
Mary V. Eberwein
G.A. Field
Frank E. Gaebelein
Helen Wright Gregg
Homer Hammontree
Philip E. Howard, Jr.
Donald M. Hunter
Louise R. Hunter
Harry A. Ironside
Edna Sorrell Kruse
Thomas G. Lawrence
Herbert Lockyer
Marie D. Loizeaux
Allan A. MacRae
Clarence E. Mason, Jr.
Esther A. Meyer
Ruth Hill Munce
Howard Oursler
J. Irvin Overholtzer
Isaac Page
Kathleen Sinclair Pollock
Leonard Sale-Harrison
William C. Thomas
Lehman Strauss
Reginald Wallis
G.R. Harding Wood

2002 EDITION

Contributing Editor
Doris W. Rikkers

Consulting Editors
Jerry L. Rockwell
Douglas D. Stauffer

Associate Editor
Joy Easton

Proofreaders
Peachtree Editorial & Proofreading Service

Developed with the assistance of
The Livingstone Corporation

Contents

Dedication vii
Contributors ix
Introduction xvii
About the Bible and Its Author xix
How We Got Our English Bible xxiii

Italic type indicates a chart.
Bold type indicates a map.
Roman type indicates an article.

The Old Testament

Concerning the Old Testament xxix

GENESIS (Gen.)
- Introduction 1
- The Days of Creation 3
- Dispensations in the Bible 4
- Covenants in the Bible 5
- The First Dispensation 5
- The Edenic Covenant 6
- The Adamic Covenant 9
- The Second Dispensation 10
- The Third Dispensation 18
- The Noahic Covenant 19
- The Fourth Dispensation 23
- The Abrahamic Covenant 28
- **The Journeys of Abraham 32**
- *The Family Tree of Abraham 40*
- **The Journeys of Jacob 55**
- **Joseph and His Brothers Go to Egypt 69**

EXODUS (Exod.)
- Introduction 87
- *The Ten Plagues 101*
- *The Gods and Goddesses of Egypt 105*
- **The Exodus from Egypt 110**
- The Fifth Dispensation 117
- The Mosaic Covenant 118
- *The Tabernacle and Its Furnishings 130*

LEVITICUS (Lev.)
- Introduction 153
- *Clean and Unclean Animals 170*

NUMBERS (Num.)
- Introduction 199
- *Israel's Complaints 220*
- *Offerings for the Altar 228*
- **Journey from the Wilderness to Canaan 259**

DEUTERONOMY (Deut.)
Introduction 265
The Palestinian Covenant 308
Songs of the Bible *313*

JOSHUA (Josh.)
Introduction 318
Miracles in Israel's Early History *323*
The Conquest of Southern Canaan 329
The Conquest of Northern Canaan 338
Division of the Land 344

JUDGES (Judg.)
Introduction 358
Resisting God's Call *368*
Battles of Gideon 370

RUTH
Introduction 396
Meaning of Names in Ruth *397*
The Book of Ruth 399

1 SAMUEL (1 Sam.)
Introduction 404
David's Travels in the Service of Saul 440
The Encounters of Saul and David *447*

2 SAMUEL (2 Sam.)
Introduction 453
David's Family Tree *457*
The Davidic Covenant 463
David's Conquests 466
Plagues in the Old Testament *491*

1 KINGS
Introduction 492
King David's Accomplishments *496*
The Divided Kingdom 515
Accomplishments of King Solomon *517*
Places in the Ministry of Elijah 530

2 KINGS
Introduction 542
Births Divinely Announced *549*
Passover Observances in the Bible *587*
Nebuchadnezzar's Campaigns Against Judah 590

1 CHRONICLES (1 Chron.)
Introduction 592
Literature of the Hebrew People *635*

2 CHRONICLES (2 Chron.)
Introduction 636
Heathen Gods Worshipped in Israel and Judah *666*
Exile of Northern Kingdom 677
Exile of Southern Kingdom 685

EZRA
Introduction 687
The Return from Exile 691

NEHEMIAH (Neh.)
Introduction 703
Public Readings of the Book of the Law 714

ESTHER
Introduction 724
The Persian Empire 727

JOB
Introduction 736
Job's Losses and Restoration 776

PSALMS (Ps.)
Introduction 777
Historical Connections of the Psalms 822
Shepherds in the Bible 837

PROVERBS (Prov.)
Introduction 882
Wise People 890

ECCLESIASTES (Eccles.)
Introduction 916

THE SONG OF SOLOMON (Song)
Introduction 930

ISAIAH (Isa.)
Introduction 941
Old Testament Prophets and Their Messages 965
The Assyrian Empire 982
Popular Readings from Isaiah 1006

JEREMIAH (Jer.)
Introduction 1019
Famines in the Bible 1041
Temple Plunderers 1101

LAMENTATIONS (Lam.)
Introduction 1103

EZEKIEL (Ezek.)
Introduction 1111

DANIEL (Dan.)
Introduction 1185
The Neo-Babylonian Empire 1186

HOSEA (Hos.)
Introduction 1210
Jerusalem During the Time of the Prophets 1221

JOEL
Introduction 1223

AMOS
Introduction 1229

OBADIAH (Obad.)
Introduction 1241

JONAH (Jon.)
Introduction 1244
The Book of Jonah 1247

MICAH (Mic.)
Introduction 1250

NAHUM (Nah.) 1259
Introduction

HABAKKUK (Hab.)
Introduction 1264

ZEPHANIAH (Zeph.)
Introduction 1270

HAGGAI (Hag.)
Introduction 1275

ZECHARIAH (Zech.)
Introduction 1278

MALACHI (Mal.)
Introduction 1299

Between the Old and New Testaments 1305

THE NEW TESTAMENT

Concerning the New Testament 1311

MATTHEW (Matt.)
Introduction 1313
The Journeys of Jesus' Birth 1317
Jesus' Baptism and Temptation 1319

MARK
Introduction 1375
Jesus' Ministry Beyond Galilee 1385
The Seven Cries from the Cross 1416

LUKE
Introduction 1419
Jerusalem During the Ministry of Jesus 1464

JOHN
Introduction 1478
Jesus in Galilee 1490

ACTS
Introduction 1521
The Sixth Dispensation: The Church Age 1524
Countries of the People Mentioned at Pentecost 1525

Philip's and Peter's Missionary Journeys **1536**
Paul's First Missionary Journey **1545**
Paul's Second Missionary Journey **1553**
Earthquakes in the Bible *1554*
Paul's Third Missionary Journey **1559**
Paul's Journey to Rome **1572**

ROMANS (Rom.)
Introduction 1576

1 CORINTHIANS (1 Cor.)
Introduction 1602
False Gods in New Testament Times *1612*

2 CORINTHIANS (2 Cor.)
Introduction 1626

GALATIANS (Gal.)
Introduction 1641

EPHESIANS (Eph.)
Introduction 1651
The Seventh Dispensation 1652

PHILIPPIANS (Phil.)
Introduction 1660

COLOSSIANS (Col.)
Introduction 1667

1 THESSALONIANS (1 Thess.)
Introduction 1674

2 THESSALONIANS (2 Thess.)
Introduction 1680

1 TIMOTHY (1 Tim.)
Introduction 1684

2 TIMOTHY (2 Tim.)
Introduction 1693

TITUS
Introduction 1699

PHILEMON (Philem.)
Introduction 1704

HEBREWS (Heb.)
Introduction 1707
The New Covenant 1718
Great Heroes of the Faith *1726*

JAMES
Introduction 1731

1 PETER (1 Pet.)
Introduction 1740

2 PETER (2 Pet.)
Introduction 1750

1 JOHN
Introduction 1756

2 JOHN
Introduction 1765

3 JOHN
Introduction 1767

JUDE
Introduction 1769

REVELATION (Rev.)
Introduction 1772
The Seven Churches of the Revelation 1776
The Seven Churches 1778
Outline for Revelation 6 to 20 1783

SUBJECT INDEX 1807

CONCORDANCE 1843

MAP INDEX 2049

MISCELLANEOUS ABBREVIATIONS

A.D.	*Anno Domini* (in the year of [our] Lord)
B.C.	Before Christ
c.	about
chap.	chapter
chaps.	chapters
cf.	compare
e.g.	for example
etc.	et cetera *(and so forth)*
i.e.	that is
N.T.	New Testament
O.T.	Old Testament
p.	page
Pss.	psalms
vs.	verse
vss.	verses

INTRODUCTION

The New Pilgrim Bible is an updated and enhanced edition of the original work first released in 1948. It continues to reflect the intent of the original editors and contributors: to create a study Bible with a doctrinal emphasis similar to that of *The Scofield© Study Bible,* and one that would be appreciated and used by students.

The original editors held to the "dispensational viewpoint" in the interpretation of Scripture. Although they recognized that this viewpoint may be criticized by those who do not hold this view, they were convinced that when a person has a clear understanding of God's program through the ages, and appreciates the clear distinction between His various dealings with mankind in the different dispensations, the Bible opens up in a new way so that it delineates a clear picture as to the holiness, the justice, the mercy, the love, and the grace of God to sinful men and women, through God's Son, our Lord Jesus Christ.

FEATURES

The notes and features in this Bible have been designed to aid your study and understanding of God's Word. To make the most of this Bible, you should be aware of its features and how to use them.

TEXT

The beautiful King James Version (also known as the Authorized Version) has been selected for this edition of *The New Pilgrim Bible*. Many of the notes include helpful descriptions and cross-references in order to assist the student in his or her Bible study.

Italicized words in the text indicate that these words were not found in the original languages, but were inserted by the translators to make the sense of the verse clear in English.

ASTERISKS *

Many words or terms within the Bible text are asterisked. This indicates that the word or phrase is explained in a note(s) and is included in the Subject Index at the back of the Bible. This list of important subjects guides further study by indicating all of the related references for which there are notes. For example, if you find that the term "Altar" is asterisked in the text, you may wish to consult the Subject Index to find other important verses related to Altar for which there are study notes. The Subject Index is also good place to begin your study if you ever need to research a biblical or theological term.

IN-TEXT OUTLINES

The Bible text of each book is divided by section headings and outline entries. Since each book of the Bible varies in content, the outline entries vary as well. Some books contain very detailed outlines within the text while others remain very simple. The book of Matthew also has numbered the parables, miracles and Old Testament prophecies to show the reader how numerous they are.

BOOK INTRODUCTIONS

Before each book is an introduction that provides additional information to aid the reader in understanding the book. The information varies slightly from book to book, but most contain author, date, theme, summary, and outline.

ARTICLES

The articles provide information on large sections of the Bible or on certain general topics.

STUDY NOTES

Thousands of detailed notes have been composed on a variety of significant terms, phrases, people, concepts, and events that appear in the Bible text. These notes are located directly within the text, in articles and at the bottom of the page. All are tied to the chapter and verse of the relevant text. Those located at the bottom of the page include the word or phrase from the text. The in-text notes contain a more general title. All study notes, no matter where they are located, are set apart from the inspired Word of God by lines and rules, or shading and should be recognized as being separate from the words of the actual Bible text.

MAPS AND CHARTS

There are 35 black and white maps and 32 charts located within the Scripture text. This new feature to *The New Pilgrim Bible* will aid the reader in studying and understanding God's Word.

DATES

The dates used throughout this Bible are those of Ussher's chronology and are generally correct beginning with 3000 B.C. Bishop James Ussher (1602–1675) was a highly respected scholar and theologian of the Irish Protestant church during the seventeenth century. He is best known for composing *The Annals of the World (1650–1654)* in which he systematically calculated the date of the creation of the world, using the genealogies found in the book of Genesis. From this chronology, he deduced the dates of later biblical events, many of which are included in the notes of this volume.

SUBJECT INDEX

This entirely new index of topics will guide the reader to the content of the text and the study notes throughout this study Bible.

CONCORDANCE

A concise concordance to the King James Version is included to help the reader locate key verses of Scripture.

We are grateful to the many editors who contributed to the original notes and to those who assisted in the development of this updated and enhanced edition. We pray that the contents of *The New Pilgrim Bible* will bring a new generation of readers to a saving knowledge of our Lord and Saviour, Jesus Christ.

The Editor
April, 2003

ABOUT THE BIBLE AND ITS AUTHOR

Those of us who have attempted to put a jig-saw puzzle together have been confronted with hundreds of little pieces, and have been puzzled in our effort to fit them into the right places. Sometimes we have forced a piece into a place where it did not belong, and therefore, other pieces have been kept from their correct spots. But when we have finished the puzzle, we have found that together all the small pieces have made a complete picture—none of the pieces has been out of place.

Certainly we do not think of the Bible as a jig-saw puzzle. But we can make a comparison. Sometimes we think the Bible is hard to understand. A single sentence or even a whole book is often puzzling by itself. But when we read each book carefully, comparing it with the others, being sure not to force our own ideas into the meaning, we soon begin to see that all together it makes a wonderful picture, the picture of the Lord Jesus Christ, the Son of God, saving sinful human beings. For the Bible tells "the story of man's complete ruin in sin, and God's perfect remedy in Christ."

In the background of the picture, we are each quite likely to find our own selves. But the hero of the book, from beginning to end, is the Lord Jesus Christ. The Old Testament writers kept saying, "He is coming!" The four Gospel writers said, "He has come!" And in the rest of the New Testament, there is the glad cry, "He is coming again!"

Almost every page of the Bible speaks of Him. The Bible is the written Word of God, but He is the living Word of God. The whole book is about Him, and we will be able to find Him everywhere as we read.

FORTY WRITERS

About forty different men wrote the sixty-six books of the Bible. It took nearly sixteen hundred years to complete the writing of it. The forty men, of course, were not all alive at the same time, and so could not possibly talk over what they would write, yet they all agree perfectly in what they say. When at times they do not seem to agree, and again we think of the picture puzzle, we shall always find that the mistake is ours, not theirs. While each does his part in his own way, and from his own point of view, they all write about the same God, the same Saviour from sin, and everything they say is true no matter what subject they touch upon.

ONE AUTHOR

With so many writers there must have been one all-wise person who planned the book and told each one what to write. That person is God's spirit, called the Holy Spirit, or the Holy Ghost. Although, like God the Father, He does not have a body of flesh like ours, He is not what we think of as a ghost. He is a real person. He speaks; He acts; He prays; He lives in some people's hearts; and He can

be grieved. These things could never be said of a ghost, or of a mere "influence." Therefore, we must believe that the Holy Spirit is a person. He is the third person of the Godhead; for God is a Trinity, that is, three persons in one.

TYPES

We cannot understand how three persons can be one, and one can be three, but we can believe it. If we could understand all about God, it would mean that He is not greater than ourselves, and who would want to worship such a God? But when we come to something that is difficult for us to understand, the author of the Bible very often helps us by using something we do understand to picture it. These word-pictures He uses are called "types." A type can be an object, a person, a custom, or a happening. It is real itself, but it pictures something far greater than itself.

TRINITY

And so now when we cannot understand about the Trinity, a "type" comes in to help us. A type of the Trinity is the sun. Let us see how it pictures for us God the Father, God the Son, and God the Holy Spirit.

The great ball called the sun, ninety million miles away, no one has ever seen—not even astronomers. All we see is the light from it; for it is only the light and the chemical power of the sun that come to earth.

In the same way, no man has seen God the Father at any time. But as astronomers have learned a great deal about the sun by studying the sunlight, so we can learn a great deal about God the Father by getting to know God the Son, Jesus Christ who came to earth. Like the sunshine, He is called the brightness (outshining) of God's glory (Hebrews 1:3).

And just as the sunlight *is* the sun, so Jesus Christ *is* God. For example: On a cloudy day when the sun suddenly comes out from behind a cloud everyone cries, "There's the sun!" They do not mean that the great ball in the sky has come into the yard or the room. That would be absurd. It is the sunlight that they see. But the sunlight and the sun are one, and we call them both, "the sun." So God the Father, and God the Son are one. We call both "God," for both are God.

But there is a third element in the sun—its chemical power. On bright spring days everyone eagerly checks the garden for green shoots and new growth. We all say that the sun makes the plants grow, but we really mean the chemical power in the sunshine does the work. That power is distinct from the sun and from the sunlight, yet it is one with them. And we speak of it, too, as "the sun," for it *is* the sun.

The Holy Spirit is like that. He is a distinct person, yet He is one with God the Father and God the Son. He is God the Holy Spirit. He quietly works in our hearts, unseen, and unknown except by the wonders that He does in giving life, the life of God, to those who will receive it.

This Holy Spirit is the wonderful person who is the author of the Bible. He chose the forty writers and told them what to write. He did not tell them as a president might dictate a letter to an assistant; it was more as if God poured His Spirit through the writers so that the words they wrote exactly expressed His thought in the writing style natural to the writer. For instance, Luke, being a doctor, has called attention in his Gospel especially to things which would be of interest to a doctor. But David, the shepherd boy who later became a king, often wrote about his sheep, comparing the way of the people in his kingdom to the silly ways of the sheep. (See also *inspiration.)

Of course the Bible was not written in the English language in which we have it, but the original writings, called manuscripts, were penned, for the most part, in Hebrew (Old Testament) and Greek (New Testament), with some smaller portions in Chaldee or Aramaic. It was a number of years before any versions were obtainable in the English language.

How We Got Our English Bible

No book in the world has a more fascinating history than the English Bible. Transmitted down through the ages by great men, some of whom paid their life's blood for its preservation, it is a living witness to God's providential care of His written revelation to the world. The story of this wonderful book, going back to the distant past and marching on to the present, quickens our appreciation of Scripture and strengthens our faith in its unique authority.

AUTHOR AND WRITERS

Who wrote the Bible? The only satisfying answer is a two-fold one. In the first place, we must not fail to recognize the true author of the Bible as God, for He inspired every portion of the book. This is made very plain in these words of the apostle Paul, "All Scripture is given by inspiration of God . . ." (2 Timothy 3:16). And what Paul so clearly affirms Peter confirms (2 Peter 1:21), and the Lord Jesus Christ seals by His own testimony (Matthew 5:17-18; John 10:35). In the second place, there is the part played by men in the origin of the Bible. While God through His Holy Spirit was indeed behind every page of Scripture, it must be freely acknowledged that in writing it He used men as His actual instruments. Thus we are reminded that the Bible, though coming from the divine author, had various human authors who were guided to set down its message of redemption. No one knows in detail how God used or inspired these men. However, we may be certain that He guided them in such a way as to enable them fully to reveal His grace, and also to keep them from making mistakes and at the same time to allow them the use of their human individuality and talent. Whatever the exact process of inspiration, that it was spiritual and not mechanical is clear.

Among the forty or so men whom God used in writing the Bible were Moses, David, Solomon, Isaiah, Matthew, Mark, Luke, John, Paul, Peter, James, and Jude. Over a period of about 1600 years, they labored until finally their great task, begun by Moses around 1500 B.C., was complete in the latter days of John, about A.D. 90.

THE ORIGINAL MANUSCRIPTS

As we read and study our English Bible, we must always remember that it is a translated book, going back many years to the original manuscripts which for the Old Testament were written in Hebrew and for the New Testament in Greek. Hebrew was the language of ancient Israel, while Greek was the world tongue of the first century.

"But," some ask, "where are the original manuscripts of the Bible—the first copies of the Psalms of David, the visions of Ezekiel, the letters of Paul, the four Gospels, and all the other portions of Scripture?" No one knows the answer to that question, because the original manuscripts of God's Word have disappeared from human sight. Yet this fact does not weaken faith in the Bible, if one only remembers that every original manuscript of every other piece of ancient literature has also disappeared. Moreover, there have been found many more ancient manuscripts of the Bible than of any other book of antiquity; and some of these manuscripts go back, in the case of the New Testament, almost to the first century.

Further, no other manuscripts, ancient or modern, have been copied and studied, letter by letter, with the care devoted to the Bible by learned men and women over thousands of years. We may therefore confidently affirm that the Bible rests upon a more solid textual foundation than any other ancient book.

BIBLE TRANSLATION

Very early in its history men began to translate God's Word into tongues other than those in which it was originally written. In fact the first translation was actually made before a single New Testament book had been written. Known as the Septuagint, it is the Old Testament put into Greek and, though made between 285 and 130 B.C., is used by scholars today. The translators of the King James Version, while taking note that the Septuagint "was not so sound and so perfect, but that it needed in many places correction," nevertheless said that it "prepared the way for our Saviour among the Gentiles by written preaching." Later, when the New Testament had been written and put together, the first complete translation, made by St. Jerome, appeared early in the fifth century A.D. Written in Latin and known as the Vulgate, it is used especially by the Roman Catholic Church. The King James translators called Jerome "the best linguist without controversy of his age, or of any other that went before him." They point out that he translated "the Old Testament out of the very fountains themselves," that is, the Hebrew language, "which he performed with that evidence of great learning, judgment, industry, and faithfulness, that he hath forever bound the Church unto him in a debt of special remembrance and thankfulness."

THE SIXTY-SIX BOOKS

Often questions like these are asked: "How does it happen that our Bible contains just sixty-six books? Were there not other sacred writings and why were they not given a place in Scripture?" Such queries have to do with what scholars call the canon, the word "canon" meaning a rule or measure. Few biblical questions are more complicated than that of the canon, yet we may reduce it to some key facts.

First, the selection of the sixty-six books was a long process, covering several centuries at least.

Second, the rival sacred books are all of later date than the canonical Old and New Testament books.

Third, these rival books, called The Apocrypha, are of inferior spiritual quality to the true Scriptures.

Fourth, even before the canon was closed—i.e., our present Bible accepted as the Word of God—the books which comprise it were regarded as Holy Scripture.

Fifth, the fires of persecution endeared the sixty-six canonical books to God's people.

Although no exact date may be given for the closing of the canon, it is safe to say that by about 100 B.C. the Old Testament was definitely established as being made up of the thirty-nine books now recognized. As for the New Testament, the twenty-seven books were generally accepted by A.D. 397, the chief standard being apostolicity—whether or not the books came from an apostle or had behind them true apostolic authority.

THE COMING OF THE ENGLISH BIBLE

The story of our English Bible takes us from these scholarly questions to a slave market in Rome of the sixth century. History records that one day a young man

was witnessing the sale of some fair-haired youths. Impressed by their beauty, he inquired as to who they were. "Angles," he was told, and was informed that they came from an island in the great sea. The young man, later to become Pope Gregory the Great, replied that the youths were so fair as to be called "angels," and resolved, if ever he obtained power in the church, to send their island a missionary. Thus did Augustine, the first missionary to England, arrive in A.D. 596. And when he landed, he had with him some copies of the Old Latin Bible. From that time Christianity took firm root in England, with the result that portions of the Latin Bible began to be translated into Anglo-Saxon by such men as the poet Caedmon, the Venerable Bede, and King Alfred. These portions were our first English Scriptures.

Languages, however, change. And, as the years flowed on, Anglo-Saxon, the parent of our English tongue, could no longer be understood by the common people. The only available Bibles were in Latin, a fact which meant that the priests alone could read them. The need for the Scriptures in the language of the people was urgent, and it was met through a man of God's appointment, John Wyclif, the great forerunner of the English Reformation. His translation of the Bible into Middle English, probably made about 1380-82, was revised by his follower, John Purvey, about 1388.

But English again changed, with the result that the common people were once more unable to read God's Word in their own tongue. Meanwhile, a hundred years after Wyclif 's time, Gutenberg over in Germany had invented the printing press and published as his first book the Latin Bible (1455-1456). To overestimate the importance of Gutenberg's work would be difficult; the inventing of printing unlocked the realm of books for the masses and was a prime factor in the revival of learning that closed the middle ages and ushered in our modern era. And one of the providential fruits of the revival of learning was our English Bible. For, in times of great opportunity, God always has a man ready to do His work.

Such a man was William Tyndale (c. 1490-1536). Like Wyclif he had the vision of giving the Word of God to every man, desiring, as he himself expressed it, to "cause the boy that driveth the plow" to know more of the Scriptures than the clergy of his time. Working under Luther's influence in Germany, he published at Worms in A.D. 1525 the first English New Testament. Those were stirring Reformation days, and Tyndale's New Testament had to be smuggled into England. But he persevered, and in 1530 his translation of the first five Old Testament books appeared. And then his work stopped, for in 1536 he was publicly strangled at Vilvorde, near Brussels, and his body later burned. So perished a great literary genius and a great Christian martyr, whose last words are reported to be: "Lord, open the King of England's eyes."

The seed, however, had been sown, and Tyndale's life bore immediate fruit. His work was finished by Miles Coverdale, and in 1535 there appeared the first complete printed English Bible, followed shortly by other notable versions, among them: the Great Bible (1539) and the Geneva or "Breeches" Bible (1557-1560).* Thus was fulfilled Tyndale's life purpose; and even "the boy that driveth the plow" had access to the Word of God.

THE KING JAMES VERSION

All the other translations, great as some of them are, will always be subordinate to the one which appeared in 1611. In that year there was published the Word of God in the form in which it is commonly read, even today over four hundred years later, throughout the English-speaking world. Known as the Authorized or King

James Version, from King James I, who interested himself in its beginnings, it was made by forty-seven great scholars of the time. The translation they produced is conceded by competent literary critics, Christian or otherwise, to be the greatest single piece of English literature and to be unsurpassed in power and beauty of expression even by Milton and Shakespeare. No book in the history of the world has ever been beloved by so many people as this Authorized Version; none has more profoundly affected the life and literature of the world.

Since the appearance of the King James Version in 1611, there have been many other translators of the Bible into English. Some are aimed at special audiences, like young people of those whose native tongue is not English; some are for specialists and scholars; some have been adopted in various Christian groups for use in study and teaching. But in spite of the multiplicity of versions available—and there seems to be no sign that the flood of new translations is ebbing—the King James Version has not been equalled, let alone surpassed, in the combination of accuracy of translation and beauty of expression. And as a translation whose words reside in the hearts and minds of millions of Christian people, the King James Version will always hold the highest place. For the work of the Bible is not completed until the word of the prophet Jeremiah, quoted by the Apostle Paul to the Hebrews, is fulfilled, "I will put my law in their inward parts, and write it in their hearts" (Jer. 31:33; Heb. 8:10). For as the Apostle reminds us in that same epistle (4:12), "The word of God *is* quick, and powerful, and sharper than any twoedged sword, piercing even to the dividing asunder of soul and spirit, and of the joints and marrow, and *is* a discerner of the thoughts and intents of the heart."

*Note: Prior to 1551, there were no verse divisions in the Bible. The original manuscripts of both the Old and the New Testament were not divided into chapters and verses. Chapter divisions did not appear until A.D. 1250 when Hugo de Sancto Caro (Cardinal Hugo) arranged the whole Bible by chapters for simplification of reference. Since even that helpful step was not sufficient for quick reference, in 1551 the complete Bible was divided into verses.

The Old Testament

Concerning the Old Testament

The Old Testament, containing thirty-nine books, is that portion of Scripture which came into the hands of men (See *About the Bible and Its Author,* p. xix) before the incarnation of the Son of God, our Lord Jesus Christ. It records the history of the human race and of the nation of Israel from their beginnings until about 425 B.C., as well as the poetic and prophetic expressions of inspired penmen during those many years. It was in Old Testament times that the first five *dispensations, concluding with the age of the Law, ran their course; but with the earthly manifestation, crucifixion, resurrection, and ascension of God in Christ a new dispensation and a new covenant came into being, and it is of this new covenant that the last twenty-seven books of the Bible are concerned, as written in what we call the New Testament.

It has been said that in the Old Testament the Lord Jesus Christ is concealed, while in the New Testament He is revealed, and this is very true. Throughout all the Bible, Old and New Testament, there is the witness of Christ, who Himself said: "Search the scriptures; for in them ye think ye have eternal life: and they are they which testify of me" (John 5:39). The Old Testament, in *type and in promise, looks forward to the advent and sacrificial suffering of Israel's Messiah, the Saviour, and to His reign of righteousness upon the throne of David. The blood is a silken thread which runs through the pages of the Old Testament, always pointing ahead to the blood of the Lamb of God which, as determined in the counsels and foreknowledge of God, was to be poured out on the Cross of Calvary for man's redemption. As early as the third chapter of Genesis a Redeemer is promised (Genesis 3:15), the seed of the woman, and henceforth the Word of God is occupied with His own program of man's salvation through Himself in the person of His Son. No one will ever wholly understand the Old Testament unless he looks for and finds Christ in its pages. Bear that in mind in all your reading.

The books of the Old Testament are generally divided into four classifications:

1. The Pentateuch, or The Books of the Law

The word "Pentateuch," from two Greek words, means *five books*, and refers, of course, to the first five books of the Bible, Genesis to Deuteronomy, which our Lord Himself ascribed to Moses. In these books the Law of Moses is found, and so they are often referred to collectively as the Law, as for example, "the law and the prophets" (Matthew 7:12). The Pentateuch introduces that which is taught in all God's Word—it shows man's fallen condition and his need of redemption, and it reveals the loving grace of God to provide a covering for sin through the blood of the altar and His assurance of a Redeemer.

Genesis is the book of beginnings;

Exodus, the book of deliverance;
Leviticus, the book of worship;
Numbers, the book of experience; and
Deuteronomy, the book of instruction, or exhortation.

2. The Books of History

While the whole of the Old Testament is, in a sense, historical, there are twelve books in particular, namely, Joshua to Esther, which record the history of the nation of Israel during approximately 1000 years, from about 1450 to 445 B.C. In this period the nation entered Palestine, the promised land of blessing; Israel was ruled by judges and by kings in this era; she was divided into two kingdoms, Israel and Judah; because of sin Israel was conquered by Assyria; Judah fell into captivity to Babylon and thus began "the times of the Gentiles" (Luke 21:24); and though a remnant was later restored to the land, this was not the fulfillment of the covenant of Deuteronomy 30, for the nation was dispersed again in A.D. 70. The final national regathering is still future.

3. The Books of Poetry

There are six poetical books, Job to Song of Solomon, and Lamentations. This does not mean that the writers made the lines rhyme with each other, or that the lines of the original writings can be scanned rhythmically. The writings referred to are rather the expressions, under the leading of the Holy Spirit, of the spiritual experiences of their penmen. Many of these writings are in lyric style, that is, they are songs, and in the Revised Versions all of these books, excepting two and one-half chapters in Job and the book of Ecclesiastes, are printed in poetic rather than prose form.

4. The Books of Prophecy

There are sixteen prophetic books in the Old Testament. They begin at Isaiah and continue (omitting Lamentations already mentioned) to the end of the Old Testament with the book of Malachi. Some of the writers, namely, Isaiah, Jeremiah, Ezekiel, and Daniel, are known as *major* prophets in contrast with the others, often called the *minor* prophets. But these terms do not have to do so much with the importance of the events prophesied; rather, the words *major* and *minor* simply distinguish the longer books from the shorter ones. Every message of the Word of God is of major importance.

The nature of the prophecies varies, though almost without exception they have to do with the Jewish people. Sometimes they specifically refer to Judah and sometimes to Israel, but most often to the nation as a whole, and her relationships to the Gentile nations. In some cases the prophecies are purely local; in other instances, they have a near as well as a distant meaning, the former symbolic of the latter; while in still others the predictions are wholly distant and are not yet fulfilled. A reading of the context and a knowledge of Bible history are the keys to understanding. Thus, some of the predictive writings were future when penned and are history now, while others are still future.

As to the prophets themselves, some lived and wrote before the Babylonian captivity, some during it, and others after the remnant returned. They may be classified, then as follows: *Pre-exilic:* Isaiah, Jeremiah, Hosea, Joel, Amos, Obadiah, Jonah, Micah, Nahum, Habakkuk, and Zephaniah; *Exilic:* Jeremiah (whose predictive utterances extended from pre-exilic days), Ezekiel, and Daniel; and *Post-exilic:* Haggai, Zechariah, and Malachi.

The Old Testament concludes with the words of Malachi the prophet looking forward to the coming of Israel's Messiah and Deliverer, both in His first (Malachi 3:1) and second advents (Malachi 4:2)—our Lord Jesus Christ, the Servant-Son and the Sun of Righteousness. Following these promises, the very Word of God, God was silent for four centuries.

The First Book of Moses, called

GENESIS

THEME

Genesis means *beginning.* Genesis is the book that tells about the beginnings of things. It tells of the beginning of this world, the beginning of man, the beginning of sin, of civilization, of nations, of agriculture, of machinery, of music, of poetry. It tells of the first marriage, the first child born, the first murder, the first drunkenness, the first kingdom, the first heathen temple; but most wonderful of all, it tells of the beginning of God's work of saving sinful man through the death of His Son, the Lord Jesus Christ. The story of His death, beginning in Genesis, runs like a scarlet thread through the whole Bible. The seeds of all truth are in Genesis. The rest of the Bible unfolds them.

THE BEGINNING OF THE WORLD

Genesis 1:1 gives the beginning of what we call time. It states the activity of God and places the focus on this earth and its relation to heaven. We know that when God first created the earth, it was perfect (Isaiah 45:18).

BACKGROUND

Genesis begins what we might call the parenthesis of time. It assumes that God exists and contradicts the evolutionary and Greek philosophical position that matter is eternal, because *God created* and only God is eternal. Its purpose is to bring the believer face to face with the living God and His plan for the earth and its residents. Genesis focuses on man and his role in the drama called redemption that culminates in the cross of Jesus Christ and the salvation He purchased with His own blood (Acts 20:28). This drama has a major person that is often overlooked—Lucifer, called Satan. He at one time occupied an important place in the economy of God as the "anointed cherub" (Ezekiel 28:14) and sought to take the place of God (Isaiah 14:12-15). Satan's attack in Genesis 3 against the man and woman God placed in the Garden is the first in an "invisible war" that still rages. This battle is for a kingdom, which will be ruled by the King of Kings and Lord of Lords, the Lord Jesus Christ (Revelation 17:14; 19:16) and will manifest itself in the Millennium (Revelation 20:4-6).

GENESIS' BEGINNING AND ENDING

Genesis begins with creation and ends with a coffin in Egypt; begins with glory and ends with a grave; begins with the living God and ends with a dead man; begins with the Spirit of God moving on the face of the deep and ends with a box of bones moving across the desert. Genesis is a book of life and of death. Something went wrong—Romans 5:12, "Wherefore, as by one man sin entered into the world, and death by sin; and so death passed upon all men, for that all have sinned."

OUTLINE OF GENESIS

I.	The First Creation, "In the Beginning"	Genesis 1:1-2
II.	Re-creation	Genesis 1:3—2:25
III.	Man's Fall into Sin	Genesis 3:1-7
IV.	God's Way of Salvation	Genesis 3:8-24
V.	Man's History to the Flood	Genesis 4:1—7:24
VI.	God's Dealing with the Nations	Genesis 8:1—11:9
VII.	Early History of God's Chosen Nation, from the Call of Abram to the Death of Joseph	Genesis 11:10—50:26

I. The First Creation (1:1-2)

1 In the beginning *God created the
heaven and the earth.
2 And the earth was without form, and
void; and darkness *was* upon the face of
the deep. And the *Spirit of God moved
upon the face of the waters.

II. Re-Creation. First day: light (1:3—2:25)

3 And God said, Let there be light: and
there was light.
4 And God saw the light, that *it was*
good: and God divided the light from
the darkness.
5 And God called the light Day,
and the darkness he called Night. And
the evening and the morning were the
first day.

Second day: firmament

¶ 6 And God said, Let there be a
firmament in the midst of the waters,
and let it divide the waters from the
waters.
7 And God made the firmament, and

1:6 The Firmament
God made the firmament and divided the waters above and below it. God calls this "Heaven" in 1:8. This is the atmosphere where the birds fly and clouds form. It is the first heaven. The second heaven is where the stars and planets make up the universe. When Paul spoke of the "third heaven" (2 Cor. 12:2), he was not thinking of the spaces into which we gaze through telescopes, but of God's dwelling place that far surpasses our universe (see 1 Kings 8:27).

1:1 God. Neither God the Father, God the Son, nor God the Holy Spirit had to be born or created. God always was. "God" (when printed in the Old Testament with only "G" a capital letter) is usually a translation of the Hebrew word *Elohim,* which is a plural noun and suggests the Trinity. It means *the strong, faithful One.* See *names of God.

1:2 was without form, and void. *Became* gives the meaning better than *was* in this case. Compare Genesis 19:26 where it is stated that Lot's wife "became a pillar of salt." She was not a pillar of salt in the first place, and neither was the earth without form and void in the first place.

1:2 *was*. See "Introduction," page xvii, for the meaning of words in italics throughout the Bible.

1:2 Spirit of God. The Holy Spirit, one of the three persons of the Godhead, each a distinct personality, yet all one. The Holy Spirit should never be spoken of as "It," but as "He." For further information about Father, Son, and Holy Spirit see *Trinity.

1:3 light. See verse 14 note. This could have been a dim light from the already created sun, moon, and stars.

1:5 Note the "Day" and "Night" are capitalized. The sun is not made until day four (vss. 14-19). Light here is the presence of God (see Rev. 21:23; 22:5). It is a type of the Lord Jesus Christ, who is the "light of the world" (John 8:12; 9:5). These are personifications of: God=Day, Evil=Night.

divided the waters which *were* under the
firmament from the waters which *were*
above the firmament: and it was so.
8 And God called the firmament
Heaven. And the evening and the
morning were the second day.

Third day: land, sea, plant life

¶9 And God said, Let the waters under
the heaven be gathered together
unto one place, and let the dry *land*
appear: and it was so.

1:19 The Days of Creation

Day one	= light
Day two	= heaven above, water below
Day three	= earth and sea/vegetation
Day four	= sun, moon and stars
Day five	= living creatures of water and sky
Day six	= living creatures on land/humans
Day seven	= rest

10 And God called the dry *land* Earth;
and the gathering together of the waters
called he Seas: and God saw that *it
was* good.
11 And God said, Let the earth bring
forth grass, the herb yielding seed, *and*
the fruit tree yielding fruit after his
kind, whose seed *is* in itself, upon the
earth: and it was so.
12 And the earth brought forth grass,
and herb yielding seed after his kind,
and the tree yielding fruit, whose seed
was in itself, after his kind: and God saw
that *it was* good.
13 And the evening and the morning
were the third day.

Fourth day: sun, moon, and stars

¶14 And God said, Let there be lights
in the firmament of the heaven to divide
the day from the night; and let them be
for signs, and for seasons, and for days,
and years:
15 And let them be for lights in the firmament
of the heaven to give light
upon the earth: and it was so.
16 And God made two great lights; the
greater light to rule the day, and the
lesser light to rule the night: *he made*
the stars also.
17 And God set them in the firmament
of the heaven to give light upon the
earth,
18 And to rule over the day and over
the night, and to divide the light from
the darkness: and God saw that *it was*
good.
19 And the evening and the morning
were the fourth day.

Fifth day: animal life

¶20 And God said, Let the waters
bring forth abundantly the moving creature
that hath life, and fowl *that* may fly
above the earth in the open firmament
of heaven.
21 And God created great whales, and
every living creature that moveth,
which the waters brought forth abundantly,
after their kind, and every
winged fowl after his kind: and God saw
that *it was* good.
22 And God blessed them, saying, Be
fruitful, and multiply, and fill the waters
in the seas, and let fowl multiply in the
earth.
23 And the evening and the morning
were the fifth day.

Sixth day: creation of man

¶24 And God said, Let the earth
bring forth the living creature after his
kind, cattle, and creeping thing, and
beast of the earth after his kind: and it
was so.
25 And God made the beast of the
earth after his kind, and cattle after
their kind, and every thing that creepeth

1:11 after his kind. A limit was put upon every created thing so that it could never become or produce any other kind of creature. From only two chickens many varieties of chickens can be produced, but never anything else than chickens. Apple seeds will never grow into peach trees, nor a monkey into a man.

1:14 lights. God created the "lights" in the firmament for the purpose of marking the twenty-four hour period of the "day and night." This is clearly the sun, moon, and stars (v.16).

upon the earth after his kind: and God
saw that *it was* good.
¶26 And God said, Let us make man in
our image, after our likeness: and let
them have dominion over the fish of the
sea, and over the fowl of the air, and
over the cattle, and over all the earth,
and over every creeping thing that
creepeth upon the earth.
27 So God created man in his *own*
image, in the image of God created
he him; male and female created he
them.

First Dispensation: Innocence
(Gen. 1:28—3:22)

First Covenant: Edenic

¶28 And God blessed them, and God
said unto them, Be fruitful, and multiply, and replenish the earth, and subdue
it: and have dominion over the fish of
the sea, and over the fowl of the air, and
over every living thing that moveth
upon the earth.
29 And God said, Behold, I have given
you every herb bearing seed, which *is*

1:27 IN GOD'S IMAGE

Of all the creation, only man was created like God, a trinity. Plants have only a body. Animals have a body and a soul. Man is a trinity who has a body, a soul, and spirit (1 Thess. 5:23). Someone has likened the body to sense-consciousness, the soul to self-consciousness, and the spirit to God-consciousness. Plants have life; they have bodies, a sense-consciousness which is evident by the fact that certain plants are affected by a touch of the hand, but plants have no self-consciousness. Animals have bodies and souls, sense-consciousness and self-consciousness; by the latter we mean only that an animal knows itself from some other animal. A dog does not confuse himself with another dog. But no animal has a spirit, or God-consciousness. You've never heard of an altar to God that was built by an animal. But man has all these characteristics: body, soul, and spirit. We must remember, however, that "God is a Spirit" (John 4:24). It is in His spiritual image that Adam was created—not in His physical image. God has infinite intellect, sensibilities, and volition, and these attributes were bestowed upon Adam in creation, but in lesser degree.

1:28 DISPENSATIONS IN THE BIBLE

A dispensation is a period of time, or an age, on the present earth during which God tests man's obedience to His will by means of some specific standard of conduct.

The seven dispensations are:

1. the Age of Innocence, beginning at Genesis 1:28 and ending at Genesis 3:22;
2. the Age of Conscience, beginning at Genesis 3:23 and ending at Genesis 8:22;
3. the Age of Human Government, beginning at Genesis 9:1 and ending at Genesis 11:9;
4. the Age of Promise, beginning at Genesis 12:1 and ending at Exodus 19:2;
5. the Age of Law, beginning at Exodus 19:3 and ending at the Cross (Matt. 27:35);
6. the Age of Grace, the church age, commissioned at *Pentecost (Acts 2:1-4), and ending at the return of the Lord Jesus Christ. The *Tribulation will be a time of judgment between the *Rapture and the Lord's return in glory (1 Thess. 4:13-17; Rev. 19:11-16);
7. the Age of the Kingdom, the *Millennium, beginning with the Lord's return in power to the earth (Rev. 20:4) and ending after the completion of the one thousand years, the doom of Satan, and the judgment of the *Great White Throne (Rev. 20:7-15), when the Lord Jesus Christ will deliver up the kingdom to God (1 Cor. 15:24), and there will be a new heaven and a new earth (Rev. 21:1).

1:26 us. God is three persons in One. See Genesis 11:7 note, "The Trinity."

1:27 created. The word "created" is used here for the third time. It is used of God's production of something new. It would be inaccurate to say that the Hebrew word *bara,* translated "created," only means *to create out of nothing,* since it denotes *to cut down* or *to divide;* however, it also has the connotation of *to create* or *to fashion*. It is important to observe its use in the Bible. It is employed forty-five times. Not once is *bara* in

3:1 THE ROLE OF THE SERPENT

Immediately "the serpent" (Gen. 3:1) is introduced. Note it does not talk about a "snake." "The serpent" is a proper name and easily connected with Satan. Revelation 12:9 says, "And the great dragon was cast out, that old serpent, called the Devil and Satan which deceiveth the whole world" (compare Rev. 20:2). This connects "the serpent" with Satan. He is called "Lucifer" in Isaiah 14:12, which means "light bearer." In 2 Corinthians 11:14 he appears as "an angel of light." There is no doubt who is being identified. His goal is to deceive. Note the strategy he uses with Eve.

Satan sows doubt in Eve's mind about what God has said. He challenges the *authorship* of God's Word, "Yea hath God said?" (3:1). He challenges the *accuracy* of God's Word, "Yea hath God said, ye shall not eat of *every* tree of the garden?" (3:1). God said they could eat from *all the trees* in the garden except one (Gen. 2:16-17). It's as if he is saying, "Eve, is it really fair that God has prohibited your eating from *every* tree?" Satan takes away from God's Word. Notice that Genesis 2:16 has "freely" and Satan leaves this out of his version in 3:1. Eve quotes Genesis 2:16 in 3:2 and leaves "every" out and just says "trees." Notice Eve tries the dynamic translation in Genesis 3:3, "Ye shall not eat of it, neither shall ye touch it, lest ye die." No, God said, "Ye shall surely die" (Gen. 2:17). Satan did the same with Jesus (Matt. 4:1-11). He came to him quoting the Bible. Note Jesus' defense, "It is written" (Matt. 4:4,6-7,10). Today the believer must stand with the shield of faith (Eph. 6:16) and say "it is written."

opened, and ye shall be as gods, knowing good and evil.

The Actual Fall

6And when the woman saw that the
tree *was* good for food, and that it *was*
pleasant to the eyes, and a tree to be
desired to make *one* wise, she took of
the fruit thereof, and did eat, and gave
also unto her husband with her; and he
did eat.
7And the eyes of them both were
opened, and they knew that they *were*
naked; and they sewed fig leaves together, and made themselves aprons.

3:6 The Fall of Man
This act of disobedience to God's command, "took of the fruit," is called the Fall of Man. It separated Adam and Eve from communion with God. It admitted Satan to influence within human affairs so that he is called god and prince of this world (see John 14:30; 16:11; 2 Cor. 4:4). On the cross the Lord Jesus Christ conquered this power of Satan over individual human hearts (1 Cor. 15:56, 57), but he is still in office because the time has not yet come for the Lord Jesus to take His *kingdom and rule over the whole earth.

IV. God's Way of Salvation (3:8-24)

¶8And they heard the voice of the
LORD God walking in the garden in the
cool of the day: and Adam and his wife
hid themselves from the presence of
the LORD God amongst the trees of the
garden.
9And the LORD God called unto Adam,
and said unto him, Where *art* thou?
10And he said, I heard thy voice in the
garden, and I was afraid, because I *was*
naked; and I hid myself.
11And he said, Who told thee that
thou *wast* naked? Hast thou eaten of the

was his sin described in Isaiah 14:12-15, "I will be like the most High." Here is the offer. Satan tempted Eve to be like God without God..

3:7 fig leaves. Having sinned, Adam and Eve tried to conceal themselves from God. Their fig leaves were like the beautiful clothes and jewels and possessions, or like the good works with which people try to cover up the evil in their hearts and lives. God looks at what we are, not at what we seem to be (see 1 Sam. 16:7).

3:8 hid themselves. Adam and Eve knew that they had sinned. That is why they hid themselves. A child doesn't hide from his father when he has been good, but only when he knows that he has been disobedient. We cannot ever hide from God, who knows all and sees all. Read Psalm 139 to find out that God is truly everywhere.

2:16 The LORD's Command
God's command was a simple test for man, but it was extremely necessary, because God created human beings to be His own companions and friends. He does not desire as companions those who must obey Him, like toy soldiers that are moved about and cannot help themselves. He wants those who love and obey Him of their own free will. Man was created innocent; that is, he had never yet sinned. But he was not created righteous; for righteousness implies choosing not to sin. Before he could be considered righteous, he had to prove that he would refuse sin if it were presented to him.

A good way to understand and remember the different states of man in different ages in relation to sin is to learn the following: Man in Eden was *able to sin*. After the Fall, man was *not able not to sin*. After he is saved, a man is *able not to sin*. When he is glorified, man will *not be able to sin*.

16 And the LORD God commanded the
man, saying, Of every tree of the garden thou mayest freely eat:
17 But of the tree of the knowledge of
good and evil, thou shalt not eat of it:
for in the day that thou eatest thereof
thou shalt surely die.
¶ 18 And the LORD God said, *It is* not
good that the man should be alone; I will
make him an help meet for him.
19 And out of the ground the LORD
God formed every beast of the field, and
every fowl of the air; and brought *them*
unto Adam to see what he would call
them: and whatsoever Adam called
every living creature, that *was* the
name thereof.
20 And Adam gave names to all cattle,
and to the fowl of the air, and to every
beast of the field; but for Adam there
was not found an help meet for him.
21 And the LORD God caused a deep
sleep to fall upon Adam and he slept:
and he took one of his ribs, and closed
up the flesh instead thereof;
22 And the rib, which the LORD God
had taken from man, made he a woman,
and brought her unto the man.
23 And Adam said, This *is* now bone
of my bones, and flesh of my flesh: she
shall be called Woman, because she was
taken out of Man.
24 Therefore shall a man leave his father and his mother, and shall cleave
unto his wife: and they shall be one
flesh.
25 And they were both naked, the man
and his wife, and were not ashamed.

*III. Man's Fall into *Sin (3:1-7)*

3 Now the serpent was more subtil
than any beast of the field which
the LORD God had made. And he
said unto the woman, Yea, hath God
said, Ye shall not eat of every tree of the
garden?
2 And the woman said unto the serpent, We may eat of the fruit of the trees
of the garden:
3 But of the fruit of the tree which *is*
in the midst of the garden, God hath
said, Ye shall not eat of it, neither shall
ye touch it, lest ye die.

Satan's lie

4 And the serpent said unto the woman, Ye shall not surely die:
5 For God doth know that in the day
ye eat thereof, then your eyes shall be

2:24 cleave. Adhere; remain faithful.
2:25 naked. God, who "is light" (1 John 1:5), whose brightness is "as the light" (Hab. 3:4), dwells in a glorious light so bright that no eye can see Him. Since Adam and Eve were made in the likeness of God, it is possible that such a light shone from their bodies. This, of course, took the place of clothing. They were clothed in light (Ps. 104:2).
3:1 Yea, hath God said? Satan questioned the word of God. See *temptation.
3:2 the woman said. Notice that she misquoted God's commandment by adding to His word. God did not say, "Neither shall ye touch it."
3:4 Ye shall not surely die. This is Satan's lie. They did die. See 5:5 and *death.
3:5 Satan challenged Eve's intellect. "Wouldn't you like to know what God knows?" This

tree, whereof I commanded thee that
thou shouldest not eat?
12And the man said, The woman
whom thou gavest *to be* with me, she
gave me of the tree, and I did eat.
13And the LORD God said unto the
woman, What *is* this *that* thou hast
done? And the woman said, The serpent beguiled me, and I did eat.

Second Covenant: Adamic

¶14And the LORD God said unto the
serpent, Because thou hast done this,
thou *art* *cursed above all cattle, and
above every beast of the field; upon thy
belly shalt thou go, and dust shalt thou
eat all the days of thy life:

3:14 The Adamic Covenant
The Adamic covenant gives the conditions under which fallen man must live. The elements of the covenant are:
1. The serpent, Satan's tool, is cursed (vs. 14).
2. A Saviour is promised (vs. 15).
3. The state of the woman is changed (vs. 16).
4. Life will be full of sorrow (vs. 17).
5. Man will toil on the earth (vss. 18-19).
6. Life will end in death (vs. 19).

15And I will put enmity between
thee and the woman, and between thy
seed and her seed; it shall bruise thy
head, and thou shalt bruise his heel.
16Unto the woman he said, I will
greatly multiply thy sorrow and thy
conception; in sorrow thou shalt bring

3:15 The Promise of a Saviour
Verse 15 contains the first promise of a Saviour. The promise said that:
1. A woman would have a Son.
2. The Son would destroy Satan. We have the sure promise of this destruction in Christ's death and resurrection, though Satan is still active. Note, however, Revelation 20:10.
3. Satan would bruise the heel of the woman's Son. *Christ's body—not His mind or soul—was bruised on the cross.

forth children; and thy desire *shall be*
to thy husband, and he shall rule over
thee.
17And unto Adam he said, Because
thou hast hearkened unto the voice of
thy wife, and hast eaten of the tree, of
which I commanded thee, saying, Thou
shalt not eat of it: cursed *is* the ground
for thy sake; in sorrow shalt thou eat *of*
it all the days of thy life;
18Thorns also and thistles shall it
bring forth to thee; and thou shalt eat
the herb of the field;
19In the sweat of thy face shalt thou
eat bread, till thou return unto the
ground; for out of it wast thou taken: for
dust thou *art,* and unto dust shalt thou
return.
¶20And Adam called his wife's name
Eve; because she was the mother of all
living.
21Unto Adam also and to his wife did
the LORD God make coats of skins, and
clothed them.

3:11 Who told thee? God asked these questions, not because He did not know, but to make Adam and Eve confess their sin.

3:16 rule. God placed the man as head of the household. Ephesians 5 and 1 Corinthians 11:1-3 explain more about this.

3:17 cursed is the ground. In their state of innocence, Adam and Eve had enjoyed the Garden of Eden as a gift without work on their part. They now had to accept the toil of life. The "curse," which is the result of sin, leads to the labor with which produce like corn and potatoes are raised, and metals, for instance, are drawn from the soil.

3:20 Eve. This name means *life giver* or *mother*. Adam believed God, and thus called his wife "mother" before their children were born. This is a beautiful example of faith.

3:21 coats of skins. Adam and Eve could not be clothed with skins unless animals had first been killed. The blood of the animal was shed and it became a substitute for the sinner (see Heb. 9:22). God Himself killed animals and made coats of skin to picture how the Lord Jesus, as the Lamb of God, should die for sin, that we might be clothed with the righteousness of God in Him (see Isa. 64:6, where the fading leaf is actually mentioned, and Ps. 132:9).

First Dispensation Ends

¶22And the LORD God said, Behold, the man is become as one of us, to know good and evil: and now, lest he put forth his hand, and take also of the tree of life, and eat, and live for ever:

Second Dispensation: Conscience (Gen. 3:23—8:22)

23Therefore the LORD God sent him forth from the garden of Eden, to till the ground from whence he was taken.

3:23 The Second Dispensation: The Age of Conscience
A new *dispensation, the second, is about to begin. Man had now sinned and was placed by God under the stewardship of moral responsibility whereby he was accountable to do all known good, to abstain from all known evil, and to approach God only through blood sacrifice. This era ended with the Flood, but man continued in his moral responsibility as God added further revelation concerning Himself and His will in succeeding ages.

24So he drove out the man; and he placed at the east of the garden of Eden Cherubim, and a flaming sword which turned every way, to keep the way of the tree of life.

V. Man's History to the Flood (4:1—7:24)

4 And Adam knew Eve his wife; and she conceived, and bare Cain, and said, I have gotten a man from the LORD.
2And she again bare his brother Abel. And Abel was a keeper of sheep, but Cain was a tiller of the ground.
3And in process of time it came to pass, that Cain brought of the fruit of the ground an offering unto the LORD.
4And Abel, he also brought of the firstlings of his flock and of the fat thereof. And the LORD had respect unto Abel and to his offering:
5But unto Cain and to his offering he had not respect. And Cain was very wroth, and his countenance fell.
6And the LORD said unto Cain, Why

3:22 lest . . . live for ever. God's whole provision here (vss. 22-24) was not to keep man from having something good, but to prevent his obtaining eternal life in his sinful condition. It would have been horrible if all men should have had to live forever in sin. Dr. Arno C. Gaebelein has said that it would be like wandering forever in a dark, filthy swamp filled with reptiles and monsters.

3:24 Cherubim. The cherubim (plural of cherub) were a very special kind of angel. Ezekiel 1:5-14 will tell you something about how they looked. Read the Ezekiel 10:8 note, "Cherubim." God placed the cherubim at the gate of the Garden of Eden to keep man from taking of the Tree of Life before he was ready to eat of it (see Rev. 2:7).

3:24 flaming sword. The flame revealed the holy presence of God shutting Adam out of Eden with a sword of justice. They evidently can approach the gate to the garden but not enter (Gen. 4:3-4,16). Adam and Eve having already died spiritually, now wait for physical death.

4:1 Cain. This name means *acquisition*. Cain was the son of parents who were sinners, and he too was a sinner. He was perfectly satisfied with himself; his "religion" was one of self-sufficiency. He was the first baby ever born and he was a murderer.

4:1 man. Male child.

4:2 Abel. This name means *that which ascends*. Abel is a picture of all those who recognize their own sinfulness and their need of God's salvation, and who are willing to approach God in His way, through the blood sacrifice, which speaks of the later death of Christ on the cross. Sin cannot be atoned for unless blood is shed. Read Hebrews 9:22.

4:3 an offering. There is no record that Adam and Eve told their children of the need for a sacrifice. The Holy Spirit has always been able to speak to hearts and convict them of sin and judgment. It is probable, however, that He used the parents to explain to the boys the meaning of the coats of skins they wore. See also Genesis 3:21 note.

4:6 LORD said unto Cain. God did not punish Cain without giving him plenty of chances

2:4 Some of the Names of God

God	=	Genesis 1:1
LORD God	=	Genesis 2:4
LORD	=	Genesis 4:4
Most High God	=	Genesis 14:18
Lord GOD	=	Genesis 15:2
Thou God seest me	=	Genesis 16:13
Almighty God	=	Genesis 17:1
Everlasting God	=	Genesis 21:33
God of Beth-el	=	Genesis 31:13

the field before it grew: for the LORD
God had not caused it to rain upon the
earth, and *there was* not a man to till the
ground.
6But there went up a mist from
the earth, and watered the whole face
of the ground.
¶7And the LORD God formed man *of*
the dust of the ground, and breathed
into his nostrils the breath of life; and
man became a living soul.

More about the Covenant in Eden

8And the LORD God planted a garden
eastward in Eden; and there he put the
man whom he had formed.
9And out of the ground made the
LORD God to grow every tree that is
pleasant to the sight, and good for food;
the tree of life also in the midst of the
garden, and the tree of knowledge of
good and evil.
10And a river went out of Eden to
water the garden; and from thence it
was parted, and became into four heads.
11The name of the first *is* Pison: that

2:8 The Edenic Covenant

This first of the eight covenants made between God and man required Adam to fulfill these responsibilities:

1. propagate the human race;
2. subdue the earth for man;
3. have dominion over the animals;
4. care for the garden and eat the fruits and herbs;
5. abstain from eating from the tree of the knowledge of good and evil.

(See also Genesis 1:28 note, "Covenants in the Bible.")

is it which compasseth the whole land
of Havilah, where *there is* gold;
12And the gold of that land *is* good:
there *is* bdellium and the onyx stone.
13And the name of the second river
is Gihon: the same *is* it that compasseth
the whole land of Ethiopia.
14And the name of the third river *is*
Hiddekel: that *is* it which goeth toward
the east of Assyria. And the fourth river
is Euphrates.
¶15And the LORD God took the man,
and put him into the garden of Eden to
dress it and to keep it.

2:9 Types in the Bible

Many concepts in the Bible are difficult to understand without the help of word pictures, which give us something we do understand. These word pictures are called "types." A type can be an object, a person, a custom, or a happening. It is real itself, but it pictures something far greater than itself.

---

need is. The Lord Jesus Christ is also "I AM" (see John 10:9,11; 14:6). *Jehovah Elohim* is the name used all through the second and third chapters of Genesis. These chapters tell the story of man's sin. *Jehovah Elohim* hates sin but loves the sinner, and He says, "I AM your Saviour." See *names of God.

2:9 tree of life. This was no doubt a real tree with real fruit. God meant it to be a *type of the Lord Jesus Christ, who alone gives life. Read more about this wonderful tree in Revelation 2:1-7; 22:1-2,14.

2:9 tree of knowledge. God indicates here that every tree was good for two reasons: they were pleasant to the sight, and they are good for food. Yet two trees are to be distinguished from all other trees: the tree of life and the tree of the knowledge of good and evil. This verse prepares us to better understand what God expected of Adam. (See Gen. 2:16 note.)

2:14 Hiddekel. Today this river is called the Tigris.

2:15 man. This word in Hebrew is *Adam* and means *man*.

2:15 dress. To trim, till.

1:28 Covenants in the Bible
A covenant is an agreement between two or more parties that may be conditional–it will continue only if any or all of the participants abide by certain or all of its stipulations–or it may be unconditional.
There are eight major covenants in the Bible:
1. the Edenic Covenant, Genesis 1:28;
2. the Adamic Covenant, Genesis 3:14-15;
3. the Noahic Covenant, Genesis 9:8-17;
4. the Abramic Covenant, Genesis 12:1-3 (compare 15:1-18);
5. the Mosaic Covenant, Exodus 20:1–31:18 (compare 19:3);
6. the Palestinian Covenant, Deuteronomy 29:1–30:20;
7. the Davidic Covenant, 2 Samuel 7:4-16;
8. the New Covenant, Hebrews 8:7-13 (compare 10:16-17).

upon the face of all the earth, and every
tree, in the which *is* the fruit of a tree
yielding seed; to you it shall be for
meat.
30And to every beast of the earth, and
to every fowl of the air, and to every
thing that creepeth upon the earth,
wherein *there is* life, *I have given* every
green herb for meat: and it was so.
31And God saw every thing that he
had made, and, behold, *it was* very good.
And the evening and the morning were
the sixth day.

1:28 The First Dispensation: The Age of Innocence
The first of the seven dispensations begins. Man was created in innocence and placed in a perfect environment. God presented him with a simple test and warned him of the consequences of disobedience. Man was not compelled to sin but when tempted by Satan, he chose to disobey God. The first dispensation ended with the expulsion from Eden.

*Sabbath rest of God

2 Thus the heavens and the earth
were finished, and all the host of
them.
2And on the seventh day God ended
his work which he had made; and he
rested on the seventh day from all his
work which he had made.
3And God blessed the seventh day,
and *sanctified it: because that in it he
had rested from all his work which God
created and made.
¶4These *are* the generations of the
heavens and of the earth when they
were created, in the day that the
LORD God made the earth and the
heavens,
5And every plant of the field before
it was in the earth, and every herb of

its various forms used to denote any act of man, but always, without exception, it has to do with a creative act of God.

1:29–30 meat. Food of any kind.

2:1 Chapter and verse divisions were made by man, not by God. They were inserted for purposes of reference only. See *How We Got Our English Bible,* p. xxiii. Thus, the thought in chapter 2 really begins with verse 4. There ends the first account of Creation, and a second account begins. This is not merely a summary of what went before, nor is it a contradiction of the record in Genesis 1:26. It is a detailed story of the same thing.

2:2 rested. God did not rest because He was tired, but the work of creation was finished, and He was delighting in it. It was complete.

2:3 sanctified. When the Bible speaks of something as being "sanctified," it means that it was *set apart to be used by or for God*. People in their worship of God have set apart certain things as holy, or sanctified; they are to be used for God. Exodus 29:37 is an example of this. Exodus 29:44 gives examples of a building and of people who were sanctified by God. Sometimes the same Hebrew word is translated "consecrate," "dedicate," or "holy."

2:4 LORD God. When "LORD" is printed in all capital letters, it stands for the wonderful name *Jehovah,* which is the Hebrew for "I AM." Read about the name in Exodus 3:13-15. The name *Elohim* ("God," see Gen. 1:1 note) refers especially to God as Creator; but *Jehovah* is the name that God uses for Himself when He wants to remind us that He cares about the people whom He has created. It shows Him to be a God who delights in making promises or covenants with His people. He is to His people whatever their

eight hundred and seven years, and
begat sons and daughters:
8And all the days of Seth were nine
hundred and twelve years: and he died.
¶9And Enos lived ninety years, and
begat Cainan:
10And Enos lived after he begat Cainan eight hundred and fifteen years, and
begat sons and daughters:
11And all the days of Enos were nine
hundred and five years: and he died.
¶12And Cainan lived seventy years,
and begat Mahalaleel:
13And Cainan lived after he begat
Mahalaleel eight hundred and forty
years, and begat sons and daughters:
14And all the days of Cainan were nine
hundred and ten years: and he died.
¶15And Mahalaleel lived sixty and
five years, and begat Jared:
16And Mahalaleel lived after he begat
Jared eight hundred and thirty years,
and begat sons and daughters:
17And all the days of Mahalaleel were
eight hundred ninety and five years:
and he died.
¶18And Jared lived an hundred sixty
and two years, and he begat Enoch:
19And Jared lived after he begat
Enoch eight hundred years, and begat
sons and daughters:
20And all the days of Jared were nine
hundred sixty and two years: and he died.
¶21And Enoch lived sixty and five
years, and begat Methuselah:
22And Enoch walked with God after
he begat Methuselah three hundred
years, and begat sons and daughters:
23And all the days of Enoch were
three hundred sixty and five years:
24And Enoch walked with God: and
he *was* not; for God took him.
25And Methuselah lived an hundred
eighty and seven years, and begat Lamech:
26And Methuselah lived after he
begat Lamech seven hundred eighty
and two years, and begat sons and
daughters:
27And all the days of Methuselah
were nine hundred sixty and nine years:
and he died.
¶28And Lamech lived an hundred
eighty and two years, and begat a son:
29And he called his name Noah, saying, This *same* shall comfort us concerning our work and toil of our hands,
because of the ground which the LORD
hath cursed.
30And Lamech lived after he begat
Noah five hundred ninety and five
years, and begat sons and daughters:
31And all the days of Lamech were
seven hundred seventy and seven
years: and he died.
32And Noah was five hundred years
old: and Noah begat Shem, Ham, and
Japheth.
6 And it came to pass, when men began to multiply on the face of the
earth, and daughters were born unto
them,

5:5 DEATH COMES TO ALL MEN

The proof of every man's *sin is that he dies. The surest thing about every child that comes into the world is that he or she will die, in spite of what Satan said, recorded in Genesis 3:4. There is only one hope of escaping physical death. The Lord Jesus Christ conquered *death, and the proof that He did is that He Himself arose, and someday He is going to take a great number of people to heaven without their dying. We read about this in 1 Corinthians 15:20-28 and 1 Thessalonians 4:13-18. Enoch, the one man in this list of whom it is not said "and he died," is a picture for us of that group of people. As Enoch was taken up to heaven without dying, before the judgment of the Flood, so believers in Jesus Christ as their Saviour will be taken up before judgment again falls upon the earth at the time of the coming *Tribulation (Matt. 24:15-22; Rev. 11–18, inclusive) when God is going to pour out His wrath on sin. Noah and his sons, who passed safely through the Flood in the ark, are a picture of Israel, who will put their faith in Christ during the period of the Tribulation and be saved. Methuselah, by the meaning of his name, *when he is dead, it shall be sent* (see Gen. 5:21-27), was a walking warning of judgment to come.

2 That the sons of God saw the daughters of men that they *were* fair; and they
took them wives of all which they
chose.
3 And the LORD said, My spirit shall
not always strive with man, for that he
also *is* flesh: yet his days shall be an
hundred and twenty years.
4 There were giants in the earth in
those days; and also after that, when
the sons of God came in unto the
daughters of men, and they bare *children* to them, the same *became* mighty
men which *were* of old, men of renown.
¶5 And *GOD saw that the wickedness
of man *was* great in the earth, and *that*
every imagination of the thoughts of his
heart *was* only evil continually.
6 And it repented the LORD that he
had made man on the earth, and it
grieved him at his heart.
7 And the LORD said, I will destroy
man whom I have created from the face
of the earth; both man, and beast, and
the creeping thing, and the fowls of the
air; for it repenteth me that I have made
them.

The Grace of the LORD

8 But Noah found grace in the eyes of
the LORD.
¶9 These *are* the generations of Noah:
Noah was a just man *and* *perfect in his
generations, *and* Noah walked with
God.
10 And Noah begat three sons, Shem,
Ham, and Japheth.
11 The earth also was corrupt before
God, and the earth was filled with violence.
12 And God looked upon the earth,
and, behold, it was corrupt; for all
flesh had corrupted his way upon the
earth.
13 And God said unto Noah, The end
of all flesh is come before me; for the
earth is filled with violence through
them; and, behold, I will destroy them
with the earth.
¶14 Make thee an ark of gopher wood;
rooms shalt thou make in the ark, and

6:2 THE SONS OF GOD

This verse shows the terribly sinful condition in the world. It is thought by many scholars that these "sons of God" were fallen angels who fell with Satan. These scholars say:

1. The phrase "sons of God" in the Bible always stands for beings directly created by God, as Adam, angels, or born-again believers in Christ (these last according to John 1:13 and 2 Cor. 5:17). The only beings at the time of Genesis 6 directly created by God were angels.
2. Here the phrase "sons of God" is in contrast to the phrase "daughters of men."
3. The Hebrew word translated "giants" means *fallen ones*. Jude 6 may refer to them.

On the other hand, many scholars do not believe that angels are meant by the phrase "sons of God." Matthew 22:30 tells us that angels do not marry. These scholars believe that this verse is telling us that the descendants of Seth, who had been worshippers of God and believers in Him, began to take wives from the descendants of Cain, who were wicked and did not fear God.

6:3 spirit. Holy Spirit; see *Trinity.

6:4 mighty men. The feats of these giants may well have been the basis for the ancient stories about mythical Atlas, Hercules, and the many gods and goddesses.

6:5 only evil continually. Here is an answer to the belief that there is some good in every man (see Rom. 7:18). Even after only a few generations, the heart of man was so wicked "that every imagination of the thoughts of his heart was only evil continually."

6:6 it repented the LORD. See Zechariah 8:14 note, "Repentance."

6:14 ark. The ark is a wonderful *type of the Lord Jesus Christ. It pictures for us the only way in which people can be saved from the awful judgment that God will surely bring on sin. Only those who were in the ark were saved then, and only those who are "in" the Lord Jesus Christ by having put their trust in Him will be saved when God again destroys sinners out of the earth. It is interesting and helpful to read Hebrews 11:7 in connection with this passage.

shalt pitch it within and without with
pitch.
15And this *is the fashion* which thou
shalt make it *of:* The length of the ark
shall be three hundred *cubits, the
breadth of it fifty cubits, and the height
of it thirty cubits.
16A window shalt thou make to the
ark, and in a cubit shalt thou finish it
above; and the door of the ark shalt
thou set in the side thereof; *with*
lower, second, and third *stories* shalt
thou make it.
17And, behold, I, even I, do bring a
flood of waters upon the earth, to destroy all flesh, wherein *is* the breath of
life, from under heaven; *and* every
thing that *is* in the earth shall die.
18But with thee will I establish my
covenant; and thou shalt come into the
ark, thou, and thy sons, and thy wife,
and thy sons' wives with thee.
19And of every living thing of all
flesh, two of every *sort* shalt thou
bring into the ark, to keep *them* alive
with thee; they shall be male and female.
20Of fowls after their kind, and of cattle after their kind, of every creeping
thing of the earth after his kind, two of
every *sort* shall come unto thee, to keep
them alive.
21And take thou unto thee of all food
that is eaten, and thou shalt gather *it* to
thee; and it shall be for food for thee,
and for them.
22Thus did Noah; according to all that
God commanded him, so did he.

7 And the LORD said unto Noah,
Come thou and all thy house into
the ark; for thee have I seen righteous
before me in this generation.
2Of every clean beast thou shalt take
to thee by sevens, the male and his female: and of beasts that *are* not clean by
two, the male and his female.
3Of fowls also of the air by sevens,
the male and the female; to keep seed
alive upon the face of all the earth.
4For yet seven days, and I will cause
it to rain upon the earth forty days and
forty nights; and every living substance
that I have made will I destroy from off
the face of the earth.
5And Noah did according unto all that
the LORD commanded him.
6And Noah *was* six hundred years old
when the flood of waters was upon the
earth.
¶7And Noah went in, and his sons,
and his wife, and his sons' wives with
him, into the ark, because of the waters
of the flood.
8Of clean beasts, and of beasts that

6:15 length. Shipbuilders, long after Noah's time, discovered what God told Noah, that the ideal proportions of a big ship are: length, six times the width and ten times the height. One cubit equals eighteen inches.

6:16 a window shalt thou make. The ark was well ventilated, for this window doubtless was actually a gallery open around the top.

6:19 two . . . male and female. Not every kind of fowl, nor every kind of animal, was needed to start animal life again after the Flood. For example, it is possible to breed every kind of chicken from just two of any kind. It has been figured out that there was a space of about 180 cubic feet for each animal. Only one half the area of the ark, then, was needed for living things. The other half could very well have been used as storage space for food.

7:1 have I seen. Noah was not sinless, and men probably saw many faults in him. But because he had put his trust in God to save him, God, looking ahead almost 2,500 years, counted all his sin as on His Son, the Lord Jesus Christ, and all His righteousness in His Son as on Noah. What wonderful love and grace! Read in Romans 4:20-24 how God is willing to do this for us too.

7:2 clean. Some of these were for sacrifices; God would not have accepted "unclean" animals, because the sacrifice represented His sinless Son. Only ten kinds of animals were clean. Leviticus 11 describes some unclean animals. Only two each of these were taken into the ark, as none would be needed for sacrifice.

are not clean, and of fowls, and of
every thing that creepeth upon the
earth,
[9]There went in two and two unto
Noah into the ark, the male and the female, as God had commanded Noah.
[10]And it came to pass after seven
days, that the waters of the flood were
upon the earth.
¶[11]In the six hundredth year of
Noah's life, in the second month, the seventeenth day of the month, the same day were all the fountains of the great deep broken up, and the windows of heaven were opened.
[12]And the rain was upon the earth
forty days and forty nights.
[13]In the selfsame day entered Noah,
and Shem, and Ham, and Japheth, the sons of Noah, and Noah's wife, and the three wives of his sons with them, into the ark;
[14]They, and every beast after his
kind, and all the cattle after their kind, and every creeping thing that creepeth upon the earth after his kind, and every fowl after his kind, every bird of every sort.
[15]And they went in unto Noah into
the ark, two and two of all flesh, wherein *is* the breath of life.
[16]And they that went in, went in male
and female of all flesh, as God had commanded him: and the LORD shut him in.
[17]And the flood was forty days upon
the earth; and the waters increased, and bare up the ark, and it was lift up above the earth.

7:11 THE HEBREW CALENDAR

The Hebrew months were lunar months. That means that they were counted from one new moon to the next. The new moon was always the beginning of the month, and the first day was called new-moon day or new month. The months were not thirty and thirty-one days as ours are, but were first thirty, then twenty-nine days, then thirty again, then twenty-nine, all through the year. Because of this difference in days, their months do not exactly agree with ours. At first they called them first month, second month, third month, and so forth. When the children of Israel went out of Egypt, God told them to count that month as their first month (Exod. 12:2). Their first month is about the time that we call April. When they began to give their months names, they called the first month Abib or Nisan.

This table will show you how their months compare with ours:

ORDER	HEBREW NAME	OUR NAME
1st	Abib or Nisan	April
2nd	Iyar or Zif	May
3rd	Sivan	June
4th	Tammuz	July
5th	Ab	August
6th	Elul	September
7th	Ethanim or Tishri	October
8th	Marcheshvan or Bul	November
9th	Chisleu	December
10th	Tebeth	January
11th	Shebat	February
12th	Adar	March

7:16 shut. "The LORD shut him in." Typically (see *type) this suggests our safety in Christ (John 10:28-29).

7:17 forty days. It rained for forty days (see vs. 12). However, the flood rose higher and higher for five months, then began to go down. The water was actually on the earth from May 17 to April 1 of the next year (see 8:13). Noah was not allowed to come out until the ground was thoroughly dry, May 27 (see 8:14-16).

18 And the waters prevailed, and were
increased greatly upon the earth; and
the ark went upon the face of the waters.
19 And the waters prevailed exceedingly upon the earth; and all the high
hills, that *were* under the whole heaven,
were covered.
20 Fifteen cubits upward did the waters prevail; and the mountains were
covered.
21 And all flesh died that moved upon
the earth, both of fowl, and of cattle, and
of beast, and of every creeping thing
that creepeth upon the earth, and every
man:
22 All in whose nostrils *was* the breath
of life, of all that *was* in the dry *land,*
died.
23 And every living substance was
destroyed which was upon the face of
the ground, both man, and cattle, and
the creeping things, and the fowl of the
heaven; and they were destroyed from
the earth: and Noah only remained
alive, and they that *were* with him in the
ark.
24 And the waters prevailed upon the
earth an hundred and fifty days.

VI. God's Dealing with Nations (8:1—11:9)

8 And God remembered Noah, and
every living thing, and all the cattle
that *was* with him in the ark: and God
made a wind to pass over the earth, and
the waters asswaged;
2 The fountains also of the deep and
the windows of heaven were stopped,
and the rain from heaven was restrained;
3 And the waters returned from off
the earth continually: and after the end
of the hundred and fifty days the waters
were abated.
4 And the ark rested in the seventh
month, on the seventeenth day of
the month, upon the mountains of
Ararat.
5 And the waters decreased continually until the tenth month: in the
tenth *month,* on the first *day* of the
month, were the tops of the mountains
seen.
¶6 And it came to pass at the end of
forty days, that Noah opened the window of the ark which he had made:
7 And he sent forth a raven, which
went forth to and fro, until the waters
were dried up from off the earth.
8 Also he sent forth a dove from him,
to see if the waters were abated from
off the face of the ground;
9 But the dove found no rest for the
sole of her foot, and she returned unto
him into the ark, for the waters *were* on
the face of the whole earth: then he put
forth his hand, and took her, and pulled
her in unto him into the ark.
10 And he stayed yet other seven
days; and again he sent forth the dove
out of the ark;
11 And the dove came in to him in the
evening; and, lo, in her mouth *was* an
olive leaf pluckt off: so Noah knew that
the waters were abated from off the
earth.
12 And he stayed yet other seven
days; and sent forth the dove; which
returned not again unto him any more.
¶13 And it came to pass in the six hundredth and first year, in the first *month,*
the first *day* of the month, the waters
were dried up from off the earth: and
Noah removed the covering of the ark,
and looked, and, behold, the face of the
ground was dry.
14 And in the second month, on the
seven and twentieth day of the month,
was the earth dried.
¶15 And God spake unto Noah, saying,
16 Go forth of the ark, thou, and thy

7:20 cubits. One cubit equals about eighteen inches. The water was twenty-two and a half feet above the mountains.
8:1 asswaged. Subsided.
8:4 Ararat. Ararat means *holy ground.*

wife, and thy sons, and thy sons' wives
with thee.
17 Bring forth with thee every living
thing that *is* with thee, of all flesh, *both*
of fowl, and of cattle, and of every
creeping thing that creepeth upon the
earth; that they may breed abundantly
in the earth, and be fruitful, and multiply upon the earth.
18 And Noah went forth, and his sons,
and his wife, and his sons' wives with
him:
19 Every beast, every creeping thing,
and every fowl, *and* whatsoever
creepeth upon the earth, after their
kinds, went forth out of the ark.
¶20 And Noah builded an altar unto
the LORD; and took of every clean
beast, and of every clean fowl, and offered burnt-offerings on the altar.
21 And the LORD smelled a sweet
savour; and the LORD said in his heart,
I will not again curse the ground any
more for man's sake; for the imagination of man's heart *is* evil from his
youth; neither will I again smite any
more every thing living, as I have done.
22 While the earth remaineth, seed-
time and harvest, and cold and heat, and
summer and winter, and day and night
shall not cease.

Third Dispensation:
Human Government (Gen. 9:1—11:9)
*Third *Covenant: Noahic*

9 And God blessed Noah and his
sons, and said unto them, Be fruitful, and multiply, and replenish the
earth.
2 And the fear of you and the dread of
you shall be upon every beast of the
earth, and upon every fowl of the air,
upon all that moveth *upon* the earth,
and upon all the fishes of the sea; into
your hand are they delivered.
3 Every moving thing that liveth shall
be meat for you; even as the green herb
have I given you all things.
4 But flesh with the life thereof, *which*
is the blood thereof, shall ye not
eat.
5 And surely your blood of your lives
will I require; at the hand of every beast
will I require it, and at the hand of man;
at the hand of every man's brother will
I require the life of man.
6 Whoso sheddeth man's blood, by

9:1 THE THIRD DISPENSATION: THE AGE OF HUMAN GOVERNMENT

A new *dispensation, the third, is about to begin, and God explains to Noah his new responsibility and also just what Noah may expect God to do. Under the terms of this *covenant, man's responsibility to God was to:

1. repeople the earth again;
2. recognize the right of animals, birds, and fishes to protect themselves, in return for the new privilege given to man of eating their flesh;
3. respect the natural right of animals to live, and as a reminder, not to drink their blood; for the "life" of an animal (or man) is in the blood (see Lev. 17:11);
4. establish human government. All government is included in the meaning of verses 5 and 6, for the power of life and death is mentioned. See *kingdom.

8:20 builded an altar. Very often we read in the Old Testament that someone "built an altar and sacrificed to the LORD." Sometimes the same man did it many times. It meant that the man wanted either to say "Thank You" to God for something or to tell Him, "I've sinned and wandered away, but now I want to come back and walk with Thee again," or perhaps, "I'm still trusting Thee as my Saviour." Sometimes he wanted to say all three!

8:21 a sweet savour. The burning meat was sweet because of what it represented. It was a *type of our Lord as the sacrifice for the sin of the world.

man shall his blood be shed: for in the
image of God made he man.
[7]And you, be ye fruitful, and multiply;
bring forth abundantly in the earth, and
multiply therein.
¶[8]And God spake unto Noah, and to
his sons with him, saying,

9:8 The Noahic Covenant
God promised never to send a flood again that would destroy the whole inhabited earth. The rainbow, He said, would be a sign of His promise. He has kept this promise. It stirs our hearts to notice in verses 14 and 15 that God said He would put the bow in the sky—not so we will remember His covenant—but so He will remember the promise when He sees the rainbow.

[9]And I, behold, I establish my covenant with you, and with your *seed
after you;
[10]And with every living creature that
is with you, of the fowl, of the cattle, and
of every beast of the earth with you;
from all that go out of the ark, to every
beast of the earth.
[11]And I will establish my covenant
with you; neither shall all flesh be cut
off any more by the waters of a flood;
neither shall there any more be a flood
to destroy the earth.
[12]And God said, This *is* the token of
the *covenant which I make between
me and you and every living creature
that *is* with you, for perpetual generations:
[13]I do set my bow in the cloud, and it
shall be for a token of a covenant between me and the earth.
[14]And it shall come to pass, when I
bring a cloud over the earth, that the
bow shall be seen in the cloud:
[15]And I will remember my covenant,
which *is* between me and you and every
living creature of all flesh; and the waters shall no more become a flood to
destroy all flesh.
[16]And the bow shall be in the cloud;
and I will look upon it, that I may remember the everlasting covenant between God and every living creature of
all flesh that *is* upon the earth.
[17]And God said unto Noah, This *is* the
token of the covenant, which I have
established between me and all flesh
that *is* upon the earth.
¶[18]And the sons of Noah, that went
forth of the ark, were Shem, and Ham,
and Japheth: and Ham *is* the father of
Canaan.
[19]These *are* the three sons of Noah:
and of them was the whole earth over-
spread.
[20]And Noah began *to be* an husbandman, and he planted a vineyard:
[21]And he drank of the wine, and was
drunken; and he was uncovered within
his tent.
[22]And Ham, the father of Canaan, saw
the nakedness of his father, and told his
two brethren without.
[23]And Shem and Japheth took a garment, and laid *it* upon both their shoulders, and went backward, and covered
the nakedness of their father; and their
faces *were* backward, and they saw not
their father's nakedness.
[24]And Noah awoke from his *wine,
and knew what his younger son had
done unto him.
[25]And he said, Cursed *be* Canaan; a

9:20 husbandman. A farmer.
9:21 drunken. Even Noah was not perfect, though he walked with God. The Lord Jesus Christ is the only One who has ever lived a perfect life on this earth. The Bible is so true that it even tells us the sinful things that people did so that we shall not be rendered hopeless when we sin, and so that we shall look to the Lord Jesus to keep us from sinning (see Jude 24).
9:22 saw the nakedness. Nakedness, in the Bible, suggests the shame of sin in the sight of God. (See Gen. 3:21 note.)
9:23 saw not their father's nakedness. Shem and Japheth showed respect for their father even in his weakness. Ham told of his father's weakness as if it were news.

9:25 The Curse on Canaan
Many people used to think that all the black races were under a curse, simply because they were descended from Ham–his name means *black*. This is by no means true. It is only Canaan and his descendants who were cursed. However, Noah did give a prophecy–far different from a curse–that Canaan's brothers, would be servants. He said that Canaan was to be a "servant of servants" to his brothers; they serve, but Canaan's descendants were to be counted still lower and serve them. This prophecy was fulfilled when the Israelites conquered the land of Canaan, as recorded in the book of Joshua.

servant of servants shall he be unto his
brethren.
26And he said, Blessed *be* the LORD
God of Shem; and Canaan shall be his
servant.
27God shall enlarge Japheth, and he
shall dwell in the tents of Shem; and
Canaan shall be his servant.
¶28And Noah lived after the flood
three hundred and fifty years.
29And all the days of Noah were nine
hundred and fifty years: and he died.

10 Now these *are* the generations
of the sons of Noah, Shem,
Ham, and Japheth: and unto them were
sons born after the flood.
2The sons of Japheth; Gomer, and
Magog, and Madai, and Javan, and Tubal, and Meshech, and Tiras.
3And the sons of Gomer; Ashkenaz,
and Riphath, and Togarmah.
4And the sons of Javan; Elishah, and
Tarshish, Kittim, and Dodanim.
5By these were the isles of the Gentiles divided in their lands; every one
after his tongue, after their families, in
their nations.
¶6And the sons of Ham; Cush, and
Mizraim, and Phut, and Canaan.
7And the sons of Cush; Seba, and
Havilah, and Sabtah, and Raamah, and
Sabtechah: and the sons of Raamah;
Sheba, and Dedan.
8And Cush begat Nimrod: he began
to be a mighty one in the earth.
9He was a mighty hunter before the
LORD: wherefore it is said, Even as
Nimrod the mighty hunter before the
LORD.
10And the beginning of his kingdom
was Babel, and Erech, and Accad, and
Calneh, in the land of Shinar.
11Out of that land went forth Asshur,
and builded Nineveh, and the city Rehoboth, and Calah,
12And Resen between Nineveh and
Calah: the same *is* a great city.
13And Mizraim begat Ludim, and
Anamim, and Lehabim, and Naphtuhim,
14And Pathrusim, and Casluhim, (out
of whom came Philistim,) and Caph-
torim.
¶15And Canaan begat Sidon his firstborn, and Heth,
16And the Jebusite, and the Amorite,
and the Girgasite,
17And the Hivite, and the Arkite, and
the Sinite,
18And the Arvadite, and the Zema-

9:26 Blessed. Notice that Shem has no importance of his own. It is only because Jehovah (see *names of God) is his God that he is mentioned. Jehovah was the God of Shem in a very special sense. A descendant of Shem was Abraham, whom God called to become the head of His own nation Israel, and a far greater descendant called was the Lord Jesus Christ Himself!

10:2 Madai, and Javan. It is believed that Madai became the people we call the Medes and that Javan is related to the Ionians of Greece.

10:5 isles. The offshore islands of the Archipelago.

10:6 sons of Ham. Cush, Mizraim, and Phut probably settled Egypt and Ethiopia, while Ham's other son Canaan, of course, occupied the land of Canaan, or Palestine.

10:8 Nimrod. The first leader of the dispensation of human government, the builder of the tower of Babel. His name means *rebel*.

rite, and the Hamathite: and afterward were the families of the Canaanites spread abroad.

19And the border of the Canaanites was from Sidon, as thou comest to Gerar, unto Gaza; as thou goest, unto Sodom, and Gomorrah, and Admah, and Zeboim, even unto Lasha.

20These *are* the sons of Ham, after their families, after their tongues, in their countries, *and* in their nations.

¶21Unto Shem also, the father of all the children of Eber, the brother of Japheth the elder, even to him were *children* born.

22The children of Shem; Elam, and Asshur, and Arphaxad, and Lud, and Aram.

23And the children of Aram; Uz, and Hul, and Gether, and Mash.

24And Arphaxad begat Salah; and Salah begat Eber.

25And unto Eber were born two sons: the name of one *was* Peleg; for in his days was the earth divided; and his brother's name *was* Joktan.

26And Joktan begat Almodad, and Sheleph, and Hazarmaveth, and Jerah,

27And Hadoram, and Uzal, and Diklah,

28And Obal, and Abimael, and Sheba,

29And Ophir, and Havilah, and Jobab: all these *were* the sons of Joktan.

30And their dwelling was from Mesha, as thou goest unto Sephar a mount of the east.

31These *are* the sons of Shem, after their families, after their tongues, in their lands, after their nations.

32These *are* the families of the sons of Noah, after their generations, in their nations: and by these were the nations divided in the earth after the flood.

Man fails under third covenant

11 And the whole earth was of one language, and of one speech.

2And it came to pass, as they journeyed from the east, that they found a plain in the land of Shinar; and they dwelt there.

3And they said one to another, Go to, let us make brick, and burn them throughly. And they had brick for stone, and slime had they for morter.

4And they said, Go to, let us build us a city and a tower, whose top *may reach* unto heaven; and let us make us a name, lest we be scattered abroad upon the face of the whole earth.

5And the LORD came down to see the city and the tower, which the children of men builded.

6And the LORD said, Behold, the people *is* one, and they have all one language; and this they begin to do: and now nothing will be restrained from them, which they have imagined to do.

10:21 Eber. It is from this name that the word "Hebrew" comes.

10:25 was the earth divided. There is considerable speculation as to what this refers to. Some say the continents were divided by an earthquake and drifted to their present position (Continental Drift Theory). Scripture does not support this and there is no evidence it took place at the Flood of Noah. The Bible says something about the division of the land in Deuteronomy 32:7-9. To place these verses in Genesis 11:7-8 would be compatable with the Tower of Babel and its place in scripture.

10:32 by these. Every person living has descended from one of Noah's three sons.

11:3 Go to. "Come now!"

11:3 slime. A type of mud.

11:4 whose top. They knew better than to try to build a tower up to heaven. Man-made religion has never been successful in reaching heaven. It is thought that this was to be a temple in which to worship the sun, moon, and stars! Such temples are still found in Egypt and *Babylon (Babel), with the signs of the zodiac pictured around the top.

11:4 let us make us a name. Ambition, a desire to glorify self rather than to live for God's glory, is sin.

[7]Go to, let us go down, and there confound their language, that they may not
understand one another's speech.
[8]So the LORD scattered them
abroad from thence upon the face of
all the earth: and they left off to build
the city.
[9]Therefore is the name of it called
Babel; because the LORD did there confound the language of all the earth: and
from thence did the LORD scatter them
abroad upon the face of all the earth.

VII. Early History
(11:10—50:26)

¶[10]These *are* the generations of
Shem: Shem *was* an hundred years old,
and begat Arphaxad two years after the
flood:
[11]And Shem lived after he begat Arphaxad five hundred years, and begat
sons and daughters.
[12]And Arphaxad lived five and thirty
years, and begat Salah:
[13]And Arphaxad lived after he begat
Salah four hundred and three years, and
begat sons and daughters.
[14]And Salah lived thirty years, and
begat Eber:
[15]And Salah lived after he begat Eber
four hundred and three years, and begat
sons and daughters.
[16]And Eber lived four and thirty
years, and begat Peleg:

11:7 THE TRINITY

God is a Trinity, that is, three persons in one: God the Father, God the Son, and God the Holy Spirit. God the Father is a Spirit; He does not have a body of flesh like ours. He is the Creator (Gen. 1:1). Through God the Son, we can see what God is like. God the Son is the Lord Jesus Christ who took on a human body and lived in the world. Through His perfect life, His love, and His goodness, He has revealed God to us (John 1:1,14). God the Holy Spirit is the third person of the Godhead. He is a real person, but He does not have a body of flesh like ours. He speaks; He acts; He prays; He lives in some people's hearts; and He can be grieved (Eph. 4:30; 1 Cor. 6:14-20).

No one of the persons acts independently of the other persons, but there is always mutual concurrence. The three divine persons are *one* God, not three gods. With respect to His being or essence, God is *one.* With respect to His personality, God is *three.*

11:10 THE GENERATIONS OF SHEM

The story goes on immediately to tell how God chose one man, Abraham (the name his father gave him was Abram, but God changed it to Abraham; see Gen. 17:5), from whom to start a new nation that would belong to Him in a special way and would be His witness among all the other nations that had turned their backs on Him. A witness knows and sees the acts of someone and tells others about those acts.

From this time on there were two groups of people in the world:

1. the nation called Israel, later called Jews. This new nation was to know and tell others about God; and
2. all other peoples, called Gentiles. The word "Gentiles" is often translated "heathen" in the Bible.

Abraham's story begins with his family tree to show that he came from the line of Shem, the son of Noah whose God was Jehovah. Abraham, as a boy, probably learned his history at the knees of Shem, his grandfather of ten generations back, for Shem did not die until Abraham was 150 years old! The length of men's lives grew shorter and shorter after the Flood, as sin and disease took more and more of a toll on their bodies.

11:7 let us go down. The Trinity—Father, Son, and Holy Spirit—speak here. Remember the same use of the plural in Genesis 1:26.

11:9 Babel. Babel means *confusion.*

11:9 scatter them abroad. God uses His name Jehovah (LORD) here. (See Gen. 2:4 note.) It is the name by which God enters into a relationship with man. The scattering was because of the Tower of Babel and disobedience to Genesis 9:1.

17And Eber lived after he begat Peleg four hundred and thirty years, and
begat sons and daughters.
18And Peleg lived thirty years, and
begat Reu:
19And Peleg lived after he begat Reu
two hundred and nine years, and begat
sons and daughters.
20And Reu lived two and thirty years,
and begat Serug:
21And Reu lived after he begat Serug
two hundred and seven years, and begat
sons and daughters.
22And Serug lived thirty years, and
begat Nahor:
23And Serug lived after he begat Nahor two hundred years, and begat sons
and daughters.
24And Nahor lived nine and twenty
years, and begat Terah:
25And Nahor lived after he begat Terah an hundred and nineteen years, and
begat sons and daughters.
26And Terah lived seventy years, and
begat Abram, Nahor, and Haran.
¶27Now these *are* the generations of
Terah: Terah begat Abram, Nahor, and
Haran; and Haran begat Lot.
28And Haran died before his father
Terah in the land of his nativity, in Ur
of the Chaldees.
29And Abram and Nahor took them
wives: the name of Abram's wife *was*
Sarai; and the name of Nahor's wife,
Milcah, the daughter of Haran, the father of Milcah, and the father of Iscah.
30But Sarai was barren; she *had* no
child.
31And Terah took Abram his son,
and Lot the son of Haran his son's son,
and Sarai his daughter in law, his son
Abram's wife; and they went forth with
them from Ur of the Chaldees, to go
into the land of Canaan; and they came
unto Haran, and dwelt there.
32And the days of Terah were two
hundred and five years: and Terah died
in Haran.

Fourth Dispensation: Promise
(Gen. 12:1—Ex. 19:2)

Fourth Covenant: Abrahamic

12 Now the LORD had said unto
Abram, Get thee out of thy
country, and from thy kindred, and from
thy father's house, unto a land that I will
shew thee:

12:1 The Fourth Dispensation:
The Age of Promise
A new *dispensation, the fourth, is about to begin, and God explains to Abraham, as He did to Noah and to Adam, the terms of the covenant He is about to make. All that Abraham and his descendants had to do was to stay in the land where God had put them, and He would have given them every blessing.

2And I will make of thee a great nation,
and I will bless thee, and make thy name
great; and thou shalt be a *blessing:
3And I will bless them that bless
thee, and curse him that curseth thee:
and in thee shall all families of the earth
be blessed.
4So Abram departed, as the LORD had
spoken unto him; and Lot went with
him: and Abram *was* seventy and five
years old when he departed out of
Haran.

11:28 Ur. Men, digging in the ruins of ancient cities, have discovered the city of Ur. It was a fairly large city, and there was evidently a great deal of business carried on there. Machinery, musical instruments, books, and even vanity cases have been unearthed! These things were not made just like ours, but they remind us that Abraham was accustomed to city life and luxuries as much as anyone today.

12:1 The Abrahamic Covenant. The covenant God made with Abraham is given more fully in Genesis 15:1-18. Turn there to find its other promises.

12:3 in thee shall all families of the earth be blessed. God is promising here that the Messiah, the Lord Jesus Christ, would be descended from, or born into, the family of Abraham. See Matthew 1:1. This is the second time that the Messiah has been promised. See Genesis 3:15 for the first promise.

Abram in the land of promise

5 And Abram took Sarai his wife, and Lot his brother's son, and all their substance that they had gathered, and the souls that they had gotten in Haran; and they went forth to go into the land of Canaan; and into the land of Canaan they came.

¶6 And Abram passed through the land unto the place of Sichem, unto the plain of Moreh. And the Canaanite *was* then in the land.

7 And the LORD appeared unto Abram, and said, Unto thy seed will I give this land: and there builded he an *altar unto the LORD, who appeared unto him.

> **12:7 The LORD appeared**
> We read several times in the Old Testament of God's appearing in human form to give a message to someone. Men speak of His appearance as a *theophany (see Gen. 35:9 note).

8 And he removed from thence unto a mountain on the east of Beth-el, and pitched his tent, *having* Beth-el on the west, and Hai on the east: and there he builded an altar unto the LORD, and called upon the name of the LORD.

9 And Abram journeyed, going on still toward the south.

Abram leaves the place of blessing

¶10 And there was a famine in the land: and Abram went down into Egypt to sojourn there; for the famine *was* grievous in the land.

11 And it came to pass, when he was come near to enter into Egypt, that he said unto Sarai his wife, Behold now, I know that thou *art* a fair woman to look upon:

12 Therefore it shall come to pass, when the Egyptians shall see thee, that they shall say, This *is* his wife: and they will kill me, but they will save thee alive.

13 Say, I pray thee, thou *art* my sister: that it may be well with me for thy sake; and my soul shall live because of thee.

¶14 And it came to pass, that, when Abram was come into Egypt, the Egyptians beheld the woman that she *was* very fair.

15 The princes also of Pharaoh saw her, and commended her before Pharaoh: and the woman was taken into Pharaoh's house.

16 And he entreated Abram well for her sake: and he had sheep, and oxen, and he asses, and menservants, and maidservants, and she asses, and camels.

17 And the LORD plagued Pharaoh and

12:8 Beth-el. Beth-el means *house of God*. It is one of the sacred places of Canaan, for both Abraham and Jacob built altars there (Gen. 35:7), and there God appeared to Jacob (Gen. 28:1-22). Years later, Jeroboam, the wicked king of Israel, set up an idol in this sacred place (1 Kings 12:28-29). Because of this sin God said that Beth-el should be destroyed (1 Kings 13:1-5; 2 Kings 23:15-17; Amos 3:14).

12:10 famine. God often allows a testing like this to come to His people to see if they will trust Him in spite of everything. Sometimes they forget to trust Him and turn to the world for comfort or relief (Egypt is a *type of the world). That only brings trouble, as it did for Abraham in this case. Then the only thing to do is confess the sin and go back and start afresh with God, as Abraham did. (Read on through the beginning of the next chapter to verse 4.)

12:10 sojourn. To dwell for a time.

12:13 Say, I pray thee, thou art my sister. This was a lie. Even a man like Abraham, who was the father of the Jewish race, sinned and needed a Saviour.

12:15 Pharaoh. This name is similar to "Caesar" during Roman rule. He was an absolute ruler, seldom benevolent.

12:17 plagued Pharaoh. A child of God, out of the will of God, can bring awful trouble even to those who are not God's people.

his house with great plagues because of
Sarai Abram's wife.
18 And Pharaoh called Abram, and
said, What *is* this *that* thou hast done
unto me? why didst thou not tell me
that she *was* thy wife?
19 Why saidst thou, She *is* my sister?
so I might have taken her to me to wife:
now therefore behold thy wife, take *her,*
and go thy way.
20 And Pharaoh commanded *his* men
concerning him: and they sent him
away, and his wife, and all that he had.

Abram returns to the land

13 And Abram went up out of
Egypt, he, and his wife, and all
that he had, and Lot with him, into the
south.
2 And Abram *was* very rich in cattle,
in silver, and in gold.
3 And he went on his journeys from
the south even to Beth-el, unto the
place where his tent had been at the
beginning, between Beth-el and Hai;
4 Unto the place of the *altar, which
he had made there at the first: and there
Abram called on the name of the LORD.
¶5 And Lot also, which went with
Abram, had flocks, and herds, and
tents.
6 And the land was not able to bear
them, that they might dwell together:
for their substance was great, so that
they could not dwell together.
7 And there was a strife between the
herdmen of Abram's cattle and the
herdmen of Lot's cattle: and the Canaanite and the Perizzite dwelled then
in the land.

Abram and Lot separate

8 And Abram said unto Lot, Let there
be no strife, I pray thee, between me
and thee, and between my herdmen and
thy herdmen; for we *be* brethren.
9 *Is* not the whole land before thee?
separate thyself, I pray thee, from me:
if *thou wilt take* the left hand, then I will
go to the right; or if *thou depart* to the
right hand, then I will go to the left.

Lot begins to backslide

10 And Lot lifted up his eyes, and beheld all the plain of Jordan, that it
was well watered every where, before
the LORD destroyed Sodom and Gomorrah, *even* as the garden of the LORD,

13:10 LOT'S SEPARATION FROM GOD

Abram and Lot were equally blessed in material abundance. For this reason, they had to choose different districts for their cattle. It was Lot's duty as the younger man to give Abram first choice. But Abram, being the greater and godlier man, allowed the first choice to his nephew. Lot's choice of the valley with its cities was "well watered" and had potential for greater success and wealth.

Note the seven steps by which the world drew Lot away from God:

1. In verse 10 he looked with desire at the sinful pleasure and success of this world, for that is what Sodom and Gomorrah represented.
2. In verse 11 he chose it.
3. In verse 12 he dwelt near it, and "pitched his tent toward Sodom."
4. In chapter 19:1 he "sat in the gate," which means that he had accepted the office of judge in the city.
5. He settled down and built a house (19:2).
6. He so neglected to walk with God that even his family had no respect for him (19:14).
7. He would not even trust God to keep him after He had saved him (19:19).

12:18 What is this that thou hast done unto me? The world cannot help seeing the sins (faults, we like to call them) in the lives of God's people, and the world is quick to judge our sins.

13:1 And Abram went up out of Egypt. Abram lost his fellowship with God when he went out of the land into Egypt. Now he returns to Beth-el, the house of God, and to the altar, and the fellowship is restored. The *covenant relationship was never broken.

like the land of Egypt, as thou comest
unto Zoar.
[11]Then Lot chose him all the plain of
Jordan; and Lot journeyed east: and
they separated themselves the one
from the other.
[12]Abram dwelled in the land of Canaan,
and Lot dwelled in the cities of
the plain, and pitched *his* tent toward
Sodom.
[13]But the men of Sodom *were* wicked
and sinners before the LORD exceedingly.
¶[14]And the LORD said unto Abram,
after that Lot was separated from him,
Lift up now thine eyes, and look from
the place where thou art northward, and
southward, and eastward, and westward:

The land given to Abram and his children

[15]For all the land which thou seest, to
thee will I give it, and to thy seed for
ever.
[16]And I will make thy *seed as the
dust of the earth: so that if a man can
number the dust of the earth, *then* shall
thy seed also be numbered.
[17]Arise, walk through the land in the
length of it and in the breadth of it; for
I will give it unto thee.
[18]Then Abram removed *his* tent, and
came and dwelt in the plain of Mamre,
which *is* in Hebron, and built there an
*altar unto the LORD.

14 And it came to pass in the days
of Amraphel king of Shinar, Arioch
king of Ellasar, Chedorlaomer king
of Elam, and Tidal king of nations;
[2]*That these* made war with Bera king
of Sodom, and with Birsha king of Gomorrah,
Shinab king of Admah, and
Shemeber king of Zeboiim, and the king
of Bela, which is Zoar.
[3]All these were joined together in the
vale of Siddim, which is the salt sea.
[4]Twelve years they served Chedorlaomer,
and in the thirteenth year they
rebelled.
[5]And in the fourteenth year came
Chedorlaomer, and the kings that *were*
with him, and smote the Rephaims in
Ashteroth Karnaim, and the Zuzims in
Ham, and the Emims in Shaveh Kiriathaim,
[6]And the Horites in their mount Seir,
unto El-paran, which *is* by the wilderness.
[7]And they returned, and came to Enmishpat,
which *is* Kadesh, and smote all
the country of the Amalekites, and also
the Amorites that dwelt in Hazezontamar.
[8]And there went out the king of
Sodom, and the king of Gomorrah, and
the king of Admah, and the king of Zeboiim,
and the king of Bela (the same
is Zoar;) and they joined battle with
them in the vale of Siddim;
[9]With Chedorlaomer the king of
Elam, and with Tidal king of nations,
and Amraphel king of Shinar, and
Arioch king of Ellasar; four kings with
five.
[10]And the vale of Siddim *was full of*
slimepits; and the kings of Sodom and
Gomorrah fled, and fell there; and they
that remained fled to the mountain.
[11]And they took all the goods of

13:18 which is in Hebron. Mature means *fatness,* that is, rich blessing; Hebron means *fellowship.* Blessing is always to be found in fellowship with God. Notice in Genesis 14:13-16 that because Abraham lived in a place of fellowship with God, he could defeat the enemy when no one else could.

14:1 Amraphel. This is another name for the Hammurabi of ancient history who drew up the first code of laws. His laws were very often unjust, deliberately favoring rich men and oppressing the poor. Though there are many parallels between this code and the law which God gave later to Israel through Moses, there are also many contrasts, and the latter law is far superior. See *Law of Moses.

14:3 vale of Siddim. The Dead Sea (Salt Sea) covers part of what was once the Vale of Siddim.

4:4-5 The Offerings of Cain and Abel
The reason why God accepted Abel's offering and did not accept Cain's is an extremely important thing to know. It is a life-and-death matter. It was not because Abel lived a better life than Cain. Both were sinners. The reason is that Abel offered a lamb, which was a picture of God's Son, the Lord Jesus Christ, who is the Lamb of God (John 1:29). Cain offered only the fruit of his own toil, his own achievement. God would not, never has, and never will accept anything or anyone but His own Son, because all that God counts as real righteousness is in His Son. Anyone outside of Christ is unrighteous in God's sight.

art thou wroth? and why is thy countenance fallen?
7If thou doest well, shalt thou not be
accepted? and if thou doest not well,
sin lieth at the door. And unto thee
shall be his desire, and thou shalt rule
over him.
¶8And Cain talked with Abel his
brother: and it came to pass, when they
were in the field, that Cain rose up against
Abel his brother, and slew him.
9And the LORD said unto Cain, Where
is Abel thy brother? And he said, I know
not: *Am* I my brother's keeper?
10And he said, What hast thou done?
the voice of thy brother's blood crieth
unto me from the ground.
11And now *art* thou cursed from the
earth, which hath opened her mouth to
receive thy brother's blood from thy
hand;
12When thou tillest the ground, it
shall not henceforth yield unto thee her
strength; a fugitive and a vagabond shalt
thou be in the earth.
13And Cain said unto the LORD, My
punishment *is* greater than I can bear.
14Behold, thou hast driven me out
this day from the face of the earth; and
from thy face shall I be hid; and I shall
be a fugitive and a vagabond in the
earth; and it shall come to pass, *that*
every one that findeth me shall slay me.
15And the LORD said unto him, Therefore whosoever slayeth Cain, vengeance
shall be taken on him sevenfold. And
the LORD set a mark upon Cain, lest any
finding him should kill him.
¶16And Cain went out from the presence of the LORD, and dwelt in the land
of Nod, on the east of Eden.
17And Cain knew his wife; and she
conceived, and bare Enoch: and he
builded a city, and called the name of

to repent, that is, to change his mind. God must surely have explained to him carefully the way of salvation. Cain was trusting his religion to enable him to be right with God. All Cain needed to do was ask Abel for a lamb to offer.

4:7 sin. The word used for "sin" in Hebrew means not only sin, but sin offering, because when a sinner brought his lamb as a sin offering, he always placed his hands on the lamb's head, saying, "I lay all my sin on this lamb." In this way the sin offering actually became the sinner's sin. When the lamb was killed the sin was gone! In 2 Corinthians 5:21, read how the Lord Jesus Christ became the sin offering for us.

4:15 whosoever slayeth. God did not give man the right to govern other men until after the time of the Flood. (See *dispensations.)

4:15 mark upon Cain. We are reading of a *dispensation before the making of laws. Cain was thus protected by God's care from private vengeance by an individual. In due course, laws were made (see Gen. 9:6), and the community received from God the authority to punish murder. Even today it is by this authority that crime is dealt with by courts of law.

4:16 Nod. Nod means *wandering.* It is as if we said that Cain was lost (see Luke 15:4). Jesus came "to seek and to save that which was lost" (Luke 19:10), and He takes away the mark of Cain and substitutes His own name on the forehead (Rev. 22:4).

4:17 wife. By this time Adam and Eve had many sons and daughters and even grandchildren. There was as yet no law against a man's marrying his near relatives, and Cain, of course, married one of his sisters. In these early days of man, when the bloodstream was fairly pure, there was no harm in close relatives marrying and having children.

4:17 The Dawn of Civilization
We now read of the dawn of civilization. There has been much research into the past, and nothing has been found to upset the scriptural story. Tools and mechanical devices are an endeavor to lessen hard work. Music and the arts are expressive of man's ability to appreciate the beautiful world around him. None of these things, if rightly used, is wrong, but Christ taught us to put first the things that come first (see Matt. 6:33).

In the first civilization there were cities (vs. 17), farming and ranching (vs. 20), music (vs. 21), foundries (vs. 22), poetry (vss. 23-24), but no government. Each man lived according to his own conscience, for as yet there was no code of laws, and no kings or rulers.

the city, after the name of his son,
Enoch.
18And unto Enoch was born Irad:
and Irad begat Mehujael: and Mehujael
begat Methusael: and Methusael begat
Lamech.
¶19And Lamech took unto him two
wives: the name of the one *was* Adah,
and the name of the other Zillah.
20And Adah bare Jabal: he was the
father of such as dwell in tents, and *of
such as have* cattle.
21And his brother's name *was* Jubal:
he was the father of all such as handle
the harp and organ.
22And Zillah, she also bare Tubal-cain,
an instructer of every artificer in brass
and iron: and the sister of Tubal-cain
was Naamah.
23And Lamech said unto his wives,
Adah and Zillah, Hear my voice; ye
wives of Lamech, hearken unto my
speech: for I have slain a man to my
wounding, and a young man to my hurt.
24If Cain shall be avenged sevenfold,
truly Lamech seventy and sevenfold.
¶25And Adam knew his wife again;
and she bare a son, and called his name
Seth: For God, *said she,* hath appointed
me another seed instead of Abel, whom
Cain slew.
26And to Seth, to him also there was
born a son; and he called his name
Enos: then began men to call upon the
name of the LORD.

5 This *is* the book of the generations
of Adam. In the day that God created man, in the likeness of God made
he him;
2Male and female created he them;
and blessed them, and called their name
Adam, in the day when they were created.
¶3And Adam lived an hundred and
thirty years, and begat *a son* in his own
likeness, after his image; and called his
name Seth:
4And the days of Adam after he had
begotten Seth were eight hundred
years: and he begat sons and daughters:
5And all the days that Adam lived
were nine hundred and thirty years: and
he died.
6And Seth lived an hundred and five
years, and begat Enos:
7And Seth lived after he begat Enos

4:23 to my wounding. That is, "who wounded me." Cain was protected by God, although he had killed his brother Abel, who had done him no harm. Lamech had slain in self-defense, so he argued that he might expect even fuller protection from God. This passage beginning with "Adah and Zillah" is one of the earliest Hebrew poems.

4:25 another seed. The word "seed," very common in the Bible, often means descendants. Three sons of Adam are mentioned and each is a spiritual *type. Cain symbolizes the people who depend on themselves alone for success in life and are jealous of others. Abel was one who sought help from another—God—through his slain lamb, and so Abel was justified. Seth is a beautiful type of resurrection. Though Abel was slain, Seth lived as Abel would have lived had he not died. These types are all fulfilled in the Lord Jesus Christ.

5:3 own likeness. Read Matthew 7:18. Adam had been created in the image and likeness of God (see Gen. 1:26), but Adam had become by his sin a "corrupt tree," and therefore, his descendants were in his likeness, having a sin nature like his own.

5:5 years. These were actual years. Increase of disease has shortened men's lives.

Sodom and Gomorrah, and all their victuals, and went their way.
[12]And they took Lot, Abram's
brother's son, who dwelt in Sodom, and
his goods, and departed.
¶[13]And there came one that had escaped, and told Abram the Hebrew; for
he dwelt in the plain of Mamre the Amorite, brother of Eshcol, and brother of
Aner: and these *were* confederate with
Abram.
[14]And when Abram heard that his
brother was taken captive, he armed his
trained *servants,* born in his own house,
three hundred and eighteen, and pursued *them* unto Dan.
[15]And he divided himself against
them, he and his servants, by night, and
smote them, and pursued them unto
Hobah, which *is* on the left hand of
*Damascus.
[16]And he brought back all the goods,
and also brought again his brother Lot,
and his goods, and the women also, and
the people.
¶[17]And the king of Sodom went out
to meet him after his return from the
slaughter of Chedorlaomer, and of the
kings that *were* with him, at the valley
of Shaveh, which *is* the king's dale.
[18]And Melchizedek king of Salem
brought forth bread and wine: and he
was the priest of the most high God.
[19]And he blessed him, and said,
Blessed *be* Abram of the most high God,
possessor of heaven and earth:
[20]And blessed be the most high God,
which hath delivered thine enemies
into thy hand. And he gave him tithes
of all.
[21]And the king of Sodom said unto
Abram, Give me the persons, and take
the goods to thyself.
[22]And Abram said to the king of Sodom, I have lift up mine hand unto the
LORD, the most high God, the possess-
or of heaven and earth,
[23]That I will not *take* from a thread
even to a shoelatchet, and that I will not
take any thing that *is* thine, lest thou
shouldest say, I have made Abram rich:
[24]Save only that which the young men
have eaten, and the portion of the men
which went with me, Aner, Eshcol, and
Mamre; let them take their portion.

God again promises blessing to Abram

15 After these things the word of
the LORD came unto Abram in
a vision, saying, Fear not, Abram: I *am*

14:18 MELCHIZEDEK

This great man, a king-priest, is a wonderful *type of the Lord Jesus Christ. Melchizedek is only mentioned three times in the whole Bible—here and in Psalm 110 and Hebrews, chapters 5 through 7. Though very little is told of him—we do not know of his birth nor his death nor his family, so that as far as any record goes he had no father or mother nor any beginning nor ending (Heb. 7:3)—yet in that very way too, he pictures for us Jesus Christ, the eternal Son. (See Gen. 1:1 and John 1:1 notes.)

Melchizedek brought bread and wine to Abraham to refresh him, the very things that represent to us the body and blood of our Lord and Saviour, Jesus Christ. Melchizedek's name means *king of righteousness*. Salem means *peace*. The city Salem was Jerusalem, where Christ will reign someday as King-Priest.

14:18 most high God. In Hebrew this is *El Elyon,* another name for God. As *El Elyon,* God is the owner of the universe—the world and everything that is in it. When Abraham realized that his God owned all things, he suddenly saw that he need not grasp at any earthly gain (Heb. 11:10). See *names of God.

14:20 tithes. A tithe means a tenth part or ten percent. Abraham was giving this to God—not because he felt that that was all he needed to give—but as a sign that he believed that everything that he possessed really belonged to God.

14:23 shoelatchet. Lace, strap, or fastening of a shoe.

thy shield, *and* thy exceeding great reward.
2 And Abram said, Lord GOD, what
wilt thou give me, seeing I go childless,
and the steward of my house *is* this
Eliezer of Damascus?
3 And Abram said, Behold, to me thou
hast given no seed: and, lo, one born in
my house is mine heir.
4 And, behold, the word of the LORD
came unto him, saying, This shall not be
thine heir; but he that shall come forth
out of thine own *bowels shall be thine
heir.
5 And he brought him forth abroad,
and said, Look now toward heaven, and
tell the stars, if thou be able to number
them: and he said unto him, So shall thy
seed be.
6 And he believed in the LORD; and he
counted it to him for *righteousness.
¶ 7 And he said unto him, I *am* the
LORD that brought thee out of Ur of the
Chaldees, to give thee this land to inherit it.
8 And he said, Lord GOD, whereby
shall I know that I shall inherit it?
9 And he said unto him, Take me an

15:6 Abraham's Faith
It was not possible, humanly speaking, for Abraham to have a son, for he and his wife were very old. That makes it all the more thrilling to read about his faith in Romans 4:18-24. The minute Abraham took God at His word, God put to Abraham's credit all of His own righteousness, and He will do the same for us.

heifer of three years old, and a she goat
of three years old, and a ram of three
years old, and a turtledove, and a young
pigeon.
10 And he took unto him all these, and
divided them in the midst, and laid each
piece one against another: but the birds
divided he not.
11 And when the fowls came down upon
the carcases, Abram drove them away.
12 And when the sun was going down,
a deep sleep fell upon Abram; and, lo, an
horror of great darkness fell upon him.
13 And he said unto Abram, Know of
a surety that thy seed shall be a stranger in a land *that is* not theirs, and shall
serve them; and they shall afflict them
four hundred years;

15:1–18 THE ABRAHAMIC COVENANT

Here we have the full description of the *covenant God made with Abraham. Covenants were often ratified in those days by this ceremony. The man who made the covenant would lay out the pieces of a sacrifice and walk between them as if to say, "May it be done to me as it was to this animal if I do not keep my word of this covenant." This is a confirmation of the covenant formed in Genesis 12:1-4. The key elements of the covenant were:

1. the promise of a great nation (Gen. 12:2);
2. the promise of land (Gen. 15:18);
3. the promise of a long life and peaceful death (Gen. 15:15);
4. the promise of blessings from God (Gen. 12:2).

15:2 Lord GOD. In Hebrew, this is *Adonai Jehovah,* still another name for God. *Adonai* means *master*. Abraham had so learned to trust God that he desired to serve Him as His slave. *Adonai* also means *husband.* Abraham meant that he was going to count on God for love and protection as a wife would on her husband. See *names of God.

15:2 what wilt thou give me? Abraham is reminding God of His promise to bless his descendants. Ten years have passed. Abraham is nearly eighty-five and still he has no son. He suggests that perhaps God means him to adopt one of his servants, as that was a common custom in those days if a wealthy man had no son. Abraham had yet to learn that God keeps His promises just exactly as they are made.

15:5 tell. To count, number.

15:9 heifer. A heifer is a young cow.

15:13 land that is not theirs. Abraham's descendants were to become slaves in Egypt.

14 And also that nation, whom they shall serve, will I judge: and afterward shall they come out with great substance.

15 And thou shalt go to thy fathers in *peace; thou shalt be buried in a good old age.

16 But in the fourth generation they shall come hither again: for the iniquity of the Amorites *is* not yet full.

17 And it came to pass, that, when the sun went down, and it was dark, behold a smoking furnace, and a burning lamp that passed between those pieces.

18 In the same day the LORD made a *covenant with Abram, saying, Unto thy seed have I given this land, from the river of Egypt unto the great river, the river Euphrates:

19 The Kenites, and the Kenizzites, and the Kadmonites,

20 And the Hittites, and the Perizzites, and the Rephaims,

21 And the Amorites, and the Canaanites, and the Girgashites, and the Jebusites.

Ishmael is born

16 Now Sarai Abram's wife bare him no children: and she had an handmaid, an Egyptian, whose name *was* Hagar.

2 And Sarai said unto Abram, Behold now, the LORD hath restrained me from bearing: I pray thee, go in unto my maid; it may be that I may obtain children by her. And Abram hearkened to the voice of Sarai.

3 And Sarai Abram's wife took Hagar her maid the Egyptian, after Abram had dwelt ten years in the land of Canaan, and gave her to her husband Abram to be his wife.

16:2 Abraham's Other Wife
Having a child by the wife's maid was a common custom in that country, according to Hammurabi's code of laws (see Gen. 14:1 note). But Abraham's faith was wavering, or he would have realized that he should not follow mere human reason nor try by his own efforts to help God fulfill His promises. The son born to Hagar made much trouble later. In fact, there is still trouble because he was born. In the land of Palestine there is quarreling between the Arabs (many of whose tribes are descendants of Ishmael) and the Jews (descendants of Isaac) over the question of which ones have the right to the land.

¶4 And he went in unto Hagar, and she conceived: and when she saw that she had conceived, her mistress was despised in her eyes.

5 And Sarai said unto Abram, My wrong *be* upon thee: I have given my maid into thy bosom; and when she saw that she had conceived, I was despised in her eyes: the LORD judge between me and thee.

6 But Abram said unto Sarai, Behold, thy maid *is* in thy hand; do to her as it pleaseth thee. And when Sarai dealt hardly with her, she fled from her face.

¶7 And the *angel of the LORD found her by a fountain of water in the wilderness, by the fountain in the way to Shur.

8 And he said, Hagar, Sarai's maid, whence camest thou? and whither wilt thou go? And she said, I flee from the face of my mistress Sarai.

9 And the angel of the LORD said unto her, Return to thy mistress, and submit thyself under her hands.

10 And the angel of the LORD said unto

15:14 that nation . . . will I judge. God always punishes those who afflict His people. Look again at Genesis 12:3 to see the promise that God made to Abraham.

15:16 iniquity of the Amorites. It was God's purpose to punish the Amorites by the hand of Israel when His time came. See Joshua 5:1 and 12:1-2.

15:17 burning lamp. This was the same Shekinah glory-fire that Adam and Eve saw after they left Eden (Gen. 3:24). It was a sign of the presence of the LORD.

15:18 this land. Israel has never yet possessed all this great tract from Egypt's Nile River to the Euphrates. But God will surely keep His promise as He kept His other promises to Abraham.

her, I will multiply thy seed exceedingly, that it shall not be numbered for multitude.

11 And the angel of the LORD said unto her, Behold, thou *art* with child, and shalt bear a son, and shalt call his name Ishmael; because the LORD hath heard thy affliction.

12 And he will be a wild man; his hand *will be* against every man, and every man's hand against him; and he shall dwell in the presence of all his brethren.

13 And she called the name of the LORD that spake unto her, Thou God seest me: for she said, Have I also here looked after him that seeth me?

14 Wherefore the well was called Beer-lahai-roi; behold, *it is* between Kadesh and Bered.

¶15 And Hagar bare Abram a son: and Abram called his son's name, which Hagar bare, Ishmael.

16 And Abram *was* fourscore and six years old, when Hagar bare Ishmael to Abram.

The Almighty God reveals Himself

17 And when Abram was ninety years old and nine, the LORD appeared to Abram, and said unto him, I *am* the Almighty God; walk before me, and be thou *perfect.

2 And I will make my covenant between me and thee, and will multiply thee exceedingly.

3 And Abram fell on his face: and God talked with him, saying,

4 As for me, behold, my covenant *is* with thee, and thou shalt be a father of many nations.

5 Neither shall thy name any more be called Abram, but thy name shall be Abraham; for a father of many nations have I made thee.

6 And I will make thee exceeding fruitful, and I will make nations of thee, and kings shall come out of thee.

7 And I will establish my covenant between me and thee and thy seed after thee in their generations for an everlasting covenant, to be a God unto thee, and to thy seed after thee.

8 And I will give unto thee, and to thy seed after thee, the land wherein thou art a stranger, all the land of Canaan, for an everlasting possession; and I will be their God.

¶9 And God said unto Abraham, Thou shalt keep my covenant therefore, thou, and thy seed after thee in their generations.

10 This *is* my covenant, which ye shall keep, between me and you and thy seed after thee; Every man child among you shall be circumcised.

11 And ye shall circumcise the flesh of your foreskin; and it shall be a token of the covenant betwixt me and you.

12 And he that is eight days old shall be circumcised among you, every man child in your generations, he that is born in the house, or bought with money of any stranger, which *is* not of thy seed.

16:11 Ishmael. This name means *God shall hear.*

16:14 Beer-lahai-roi. The Hebrew word *Beer* means *a well. Lahai-roi* means *He that liveth and seeth me.*

17:1 Almighty God. In Hebrew *El* (the strong One) *Shaddai* (the breasted One). Abraham now learns that God is not only *El,* the strong mighty Creator who can do wonders, but the One who cares for him as a mother would, for He is the all-sufficient One. As mothers do, *El Shaddai* reproves Abraham for obeying someone else. Abraham had followed Sarah's advice instead of "walking before" God only. See *names of God.

17:1 perfect. No man on earth can be perfectly sinless, but God meant that Abraham's heart was to be wholly and sincerely devoted to Him.

17:5 Abram. Abram means *high father.* Abraham means *father of many nations.* Instead of making only Abraham important, God intended to give blessing to many others through him.

17:10 Circumcision
In repeating His *covenant for the fourth time, God tells Abraham to cut a mark in the flesh of every male (Gen. 17:11) who is a descendant of Abraham as a sign that the circumcised man believes in the covenant. God intended that the mark should be the sign of a man's distrust of himself and his real trust in God, but later men whose hearts were not right at all with God used the mark as something in which they might boast; they considered that because they had the mark, they had special favor with God. (See Rom. 2:28-29.)

13He that is born in thy house, and he
that is bought with thy money, must
needs be circumcised: and my covenant
shall be in your flesh for an everlasting
covenant.
14And the uncircumcised man child
whose flesh of his foreskin is not circumcised, that soul shall be cut off from
his people; he hath broken my covenant.

Isaac is promised

¶15And God said unto Abraham, As
for Sarai thy wife, thou shalt not call
her name Sarai, but Sarah *shall* her
name *be*.
16And I will bless her, and give thee
a son also of her: yea, I will bless her,
and she shall be *a mother* of nations;
kings of people shall be of her.
17Then Abraham fell upon his face,
and laughed, and said in his heart, Shall
a child be born unto him that is an hundred years old? and shall Sarah, that is
ninety years old, bear?
18And Abraham said unto God,
O that Ishmael might live before thee!
19And God said, Sarah thy wife shall
bear thee a son indeed; and thou shalt
call his name Isaac: and I will establish
my covenant with him for an everlasting covenant, *and* with his seed after him.
20And as for Ishmael, I have heard
thee: Behold, I have blessed him, and
will make him fruitful, and will multiply him exceedingly; twelve princes
shall he beget, and I will make him a
great nation.
21But my *covenant will I establish
with Isaac, which Sarah shall bear unto
thee at this set time in the next year.
22And he left off talking with him, and
God went up from Abraham.
¶23And Abraham took Ishmael his
son, and all that were born in his house,
and all that were bought with his money,
every male among the men of Abraham's house; and circumcised the flesh
of their foreskin in the selfsame day, as
God had said unto him.
24And Abraham *was* ninety years old
and nine, when he was circumcised in
the flesh of his foreskin.
25And Ishmael his son *was* thirteen
years old, when he was circumcised in
the flesh of his foreskin.
26In the selfsame day was Abraham
circumcised, and Ishmael his son.
27And all the men of his house, born
in the house, and bought with money of
the stranger, were circumcised with
him.

18 And the LORD appeared unto
him in the plains of Mamre: and
he sat in the tent door in the heat of the
day;
2And he lift up his eyes and looked,
and, lo, three men stood by him: and
when he saw *them*, he ran to meet them
from the tent door, and bowed himself
toward the ground,
3And said, My Lord, if now I have
found favour in thy sight, pass not away,
I pray thee, from thy servant:

17:13 needs. Of necessity.
17:15 Sarai. Sarai means *contentious*, and Sarah means *princess*. God entered into a different relationship here—direct authority.
17:19 an everlasting covenant. This looks forward to the first coming of Christ.
18:1 the LORD appeared. See Genesis 35:9 note, "Theophany."

4Let a little water, I pray you, be
fetched, and wash your feet, and rest
yourselves under the tree:
5And I will fetch a morsel of bread,
and comfort ye your hearts; after that
ye shall pass on: for therefore are ye
come to your servant. And they said, So
do, as thou hast said.
6And Abraham hastened into the tent
unto Sarah, and said, Make ready quickly
three measures of fine meal, knead *it*,
and make cakes upon the hearth.
7And Abraham ran unto the herd, and
fetcht a calf tender and good, and gave
it unto a young man; and he hasted to
dress it.
8And he took butter, and milk, and the
calf which he had dressed, and set *it*
before them; and he stood by them under the tree, and they did eat.
¶9And they said unto him, Where *is*
Sarah thy wife? And he said, Behold, in
the tent.
10And he said, I will certainly return
unto thee according to the time of life;
and, lo, Sarah thy wife shall have a son.
And Sarah heard *it* in the tent door,
which *was* behind him.
11Now Abraham and Sarah *were* old
and well stricken in age; *and* it ceased
to be with Sarah after the manner of
women.
12Therefore Sarah laughed within
herself, saying, After I am waxed old
shall I have pleasure, my lord being old
also?
13And the LORD said unto Abraham,
Wherefore did Sarah laugh, saying,
Shall I of a surety bear a child, which am
old?
14Is any thing too hard for the LORD?
At the time appointed I will return unto

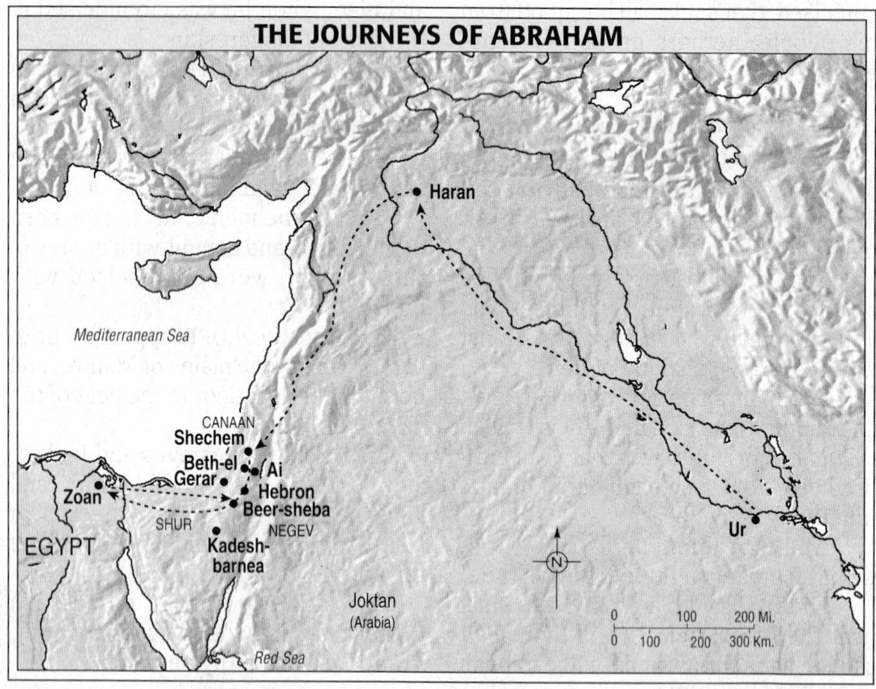

18:4 wash your feet. Because leather sandals were the only foot-covering people wore, it was the courteous thing, upon the arrival of guests, for a servant to wash their feet or to offer them water that they might do this themselves. About 1,900 years later when the Lord Jesus was on this earth, it was still polite to wash the feet of guests (see Luke 7:36-48 and John 13:2-10).

thee, according to the time of life, and
Sarah shall have a son.
15Then Sarah denied, saying, I
laughed not; for she was afraid. And he
said, Nay; but thou didst laugh.
¶16And the men rose up from thence,
and looked toward Sodom: and Abraham went with them to bring them on
the way.
17And the LORD said, Shall I hide from
Abraham that thing which I do;
18Seeing that Abraham shall surely
become a great and mighty nation, and
all the nations of the earth shall be
blessed in him?
19For I know him, that he will command
his children and his household after
him, and they shall keep the way of the
LORD, to do justice and judgment; that
the LORD may bring upon Abraham that
which he hath spoken of him.
20And the LORD said, Because the cry
of Sodom and Gomorrah is great, and
because their *sin is very grievous;
21I will go down now, and see whether they have done altogether according
to the cry of it, which is come unto me;
and if not, I will know.
22And the men turned their faces
from thence, and went toward Sodom:
but Abraham stood yet before the
LORD.
¶23And Abraham drew near, and said,
Wilt thou also destroy the righteous
with the wicked?
24Peradventure there be fifty righteous within the city: wilt thou also destroy and not spare the place for the
fifty righteous that *are* therein?
25That be far from thee to do after
this manner, to slay the righteous with
the wicked: and that the righteous
should be as the wicked, that be far from
thee: Shall not the Judge of all the earth
do right?
26And the LORD said, If I find in Sodom fifty righteous within the city, then
I will spare all the place for their sakes.
27And Abraham answered and said,
Behold now, I have taken upon me to
speak unto the Lord, which *am but* dust
and ashes:
28Peradventure there shall lack five
of the fifty righteous: wilt thou destroy
all the city for *lack of* five? And he said,
If I find there forty and five, I will not
destroy *it.*
29And he spake unto him yet again,
and said, Peradventure there shall be
forty found there. And he said, I will not
do *it* for forty's sake.
30And he said *unto him,* Oh let not the
Lord be angry, and I will speak: Peradventure there shall thirty be found
there. And he said, I will not do *it,* if I
find thirty there.
31And he said, Behold now, I have
taken upon me to speak unto the Lord:
Peradventure there shall be twenty
found there. And he said, I will not destroy *it* for twenty's sake.
32And he said, Oh let not the Lord be
angry, and I will speak yet but this once:
Peradventure ten shall be found there.
And he said, I will not destroy *it* for
ten's sake.
33And the LORD went his way, as soon
as he had left communing with Abraham: and Abraham returned unto his
place.

19

And there came two *angels to
Sodom at even; and *Lot sat in
the gate of Sodom: and Lot seeing
them rose up to meet them; and he
bowed himself with his face toward the
ground;
2And he said, Behold now, my lords,
turn in, I pray you, into your servant's
house, and tarry all night, and wash
your feet, and ye shall rise up early,
and go on your ways. And they said,
Nay; but we will abide in the street all
night.
3And he pressed upon them greatly;

18:24 Peradventure. Suppose or perhaps.
19:3 unleavened bread. Leaven is a kind of yeast used in baking. It is used as a *type of evil in the Bible. See Matthew 13:33 note.

and they turned in unto him, and entered into his house; and he made them
a feast, and did bake unleavened bread,
and they did eat.
¶4 But before they lay down, the
men of the city, *even* the men of Sodom, compassed the house round, both
old and young, all the people from
every quarter:
5 And they called unto Lot, and said
unto him, Where *are* the men which
came in to thee this night? bring them
out unto us, that we may know them.
6 And Lot went out at the door unto
them, and shut the door after him,
7 And said, I pray you, brethren, do
not so wickedly.
8 Behold now, I have two daughters
which have not known man; let me, I
pray you, bring them out unto you, and
do ye to them as *is* good in your eyes:
only unto these men do nothing; for
therefore came they under the shadow
of my roof.
9 And they said, Stand back. And they
said *again,* This one *fellow* came in to
sojourn, and he will needs be a judge:
now will we deal worse with thee, than
with them. And they pressed sore upon
the man, *even* Lot, and came near to
break the door.
10 But the men put forth their hand,
and pulled Lot into the house to them,
and shut to the door.
11 And they smote the men that *were*
at the door of the house with blindness,
both small and great: so that they wearied themselves to find the door.
¶12 And the men said unto Lot, Hast
thou here any besides? son in law, and
thy sons, and thy daughters, and whatsoever thou hast in the city, bring *them*
out of this place:
13 For we will destroy this place, because the cry of them is waxen great
before the face of the LORD; and the
LORD hath sent us to destroy it.
14 And Lot went out, and spake unto
his sons in law, which married his
daughters, and said, Up, get you out of
this place; for the LORD will destroy this
city. But he seemed as one that mocked
unto his sons in law.
¶15 And when the morning arose,
then the angels hastened Lot, saying,
Arise, take thy wife, and thy two daughters, which are here; lest thou be consumed in the iniquity of the city.
16 And while he lingered, the men laid
hold upon his hand, and upon the hand
of his wife, and upon the hand of his two
daughters; the LORD being merciful
unto him: and they brought him forth,
and set him without the city.
¶17 And it came to pass, when they
had brought them forth abroad, that he
said, Escape for thy life; look not behind
thee, neither stay thou in all the plain;
escape to the mountain, lest thou be
consumed.
18 And Lot said unto them, Oh, not so,
my Lord:
19 Behold now, thy servant hath found
grace in thy sight, and thou hast magnified thy mercy, which thou hast
shewed unto me in saving my life; and
I cannot escape to the mountain, lest
some evil take me, and I die:
20 Behold now, this city *is* near to flee
unto, and it *is* a little one: Oh, let me
escape thither, (*is* it not a little one?)
and my soul shall live.
21 And he said unto him, See, I have
accepted thee concerning this thing
also, that I will not overthrow this city,
for the which thou hast spoken.
22 Haste thee, escape thither; for I
cannot do any thing till thou be come
thither. Therefore the name of the city
was called Zoar.
¶23 The sun was risen upon the earth
when Lot entered into Zoar.
24 Then the LORD rained upon Sodom
and upon Gomorrah brimstone and
*fire from the LORD out of heaven;
25 And he overthrew those cities, and

19:9 sojourn. To dwell for a time.
19:9 sore. Greatly, severely.

19:24 Sodom and Gomorrah Destroyed
Those who have been studying the land near the Dead Sea believe that there was a tremendous volcanic eruption that spread brimstone and all manner of mineral salts, and that possibly an earthquake caused the water to come in and cover the whole area where the cities were. Since then, chemical companies have made much money from the deposits of salts which they have taken from the Dead Sea. The sea is called "Dead" because the great quantities of salts and sulphur make it impossible for any fish to live there.

all the plain, and all the inhabitants of
the cities, and that which grew upon the
ground.
¶26But his wife looked back from behind him, and she became a pillar of salt.
¶27And Abraham gat up early in the
morning to the place where he stood
before the LORD:
28And he looked toward Sodom and
Gomorrah, and toward all the land of
the plain, and beheld, and, lo, the smoke
of the country went up as the smoke of
a furnace.
¶29And it came to pass, when God
destroyed the cities of the plain, that
God remembered Abraham, and sent
Lot out of the midst of the overthrow,
when he overthrew the cities in the
which Lot dwelt.
¶30And Lot went up out of Zoar, and
dwelt in the mountain, and his two
daughters with him; for he feared to
dwell in Zoar: and he dwelt in a cave,
he and his two daughters.
31And the firstborn said unto the
younger, Our father *is* old, and *there is*
not a man in the earth to come in unto
us after the manner of all the earth:
32Come, let us make our father drink
*wine, and we will lie with him, that we
may preserve seed of our father.
33And they made their father drink
wine that night: and the firstborn went
in, and lay with her father; and he perceived not when she lay down, nor
when she arose.
34And it came to pass on the morrow,
that the firstborn said unto the younger,
Behold, I lay yesternight with my father: let us make him drink wine this
night also; and go thou in, *and* lie with
him, that we may preserve seed of our
father.
35And they made their father drink
wine that night also: and the younger
arose, and lay with him; and he perceived not when she lay down, nor
when she arose.
36Thus were both the daughters of
Lot with child by their father.
37And the firstborn bare a son, and
called his name Moab: the same *is*
the father of the Moabites unto this
day.
38And the younger, she also bare a
son, and called his name Ben-ammi: the
same *is* the father of the children of
Ammon unto this day.

20 And Abraham journeyed from
thence toward the south country, and dwelled between Kadesh and
Shur, and sojourned in Gerar.
2And Abraham said of Sarah his wife,
She *is* my sister: and Abimelech king of
Gerar sent, and took Sarah.
3But God came to Abimelech in a
dream by night, and said to him, Behold,
thou *art but* a dead man, for the woman
which thou hast taken; for she *is* a
man's wife.

19:26 looked back. The words mean *lingered.* Her longing for lost luxuries made her hang back so far that she shared in the destruction.
19:37 Moab. As a result of the horrible, incestuous sin in which Lot's daughters got him drunk and conceived children by him (vss. 31-36), Israel was troubled by the Moabites and Ammonites for centuries.
20:2 She is my sister. This is the second time that Abraham has lied in this way. See Genesis 12:13 note. It was a half-truth, for Sarah was Abraham's half sister (see vs. 12), but half-truths which are intended to deceive are lies.

20:2 Abraham's Sin
Gerar was the chief city of the Philistines. Abraham sinned again, as he had before, by going out of the land (read Gen. 12:10). The record of his failures is a strong proof that the Bible is God's own Book. If, as some people say, Genesis was written by a man who was just writing Jewish history, he would certainly not have told of the sins of the great Jewish father, Abraham! See Genesis 9:21 note.

4 But Abimelech had not come near
her: and he said, Lord, wilt thou slay
also a righteous nation?
5 Said he not unto me, She *is* my sister? and she, even she herself said, He
is my brother: in the integrity of my
heart and innocency of my hands have
I done this.
6 And God said unto him in a dream,
Yea, I know that thou didst this in the
integrity of thy heart; for I also withheld thee from sinning against me:
therefore suffered I thee not to touch
her.
7 Now therefore restore the man *his*
wife; for he *is* a *prophet, and he shall
pray for thee, and thou shalt live: and if
thou restore *her* not, know thou that
thou shalt surely die, thou, and all that
are thine.
8 Therefore Abimelech rose early in
the morning, and called all his servants,
and told all these things in their ears:
and the men were sore afraid.
9 Then Abimelech called Abraham,
and said unto him, What hast thou done
unto us? and what have I offended thee,
that thou hast brought on me and on my
kingdom a great sin? thou hast done
deeds unto me that ought not to be
done.
10 And Abimelech said unto Abraham,
What sawest thou, that thou hast done
this thing?
11 And Abraham said, Because I
thought, Surely the *fear of God *is* not
in this place; and they will slay me for
my wife's sake.
12 And yet indeed *she is* my sister; she
is the daughter of my father, but not the
daughter of my mother; and she became my wife.
13 And it came to pass, when God
caused me to wander from my father's
house, that I said unto her, This *is* thy
kindness which thou shalt shew unto
me; at every place whither we shall
come, say of me, He *is* my brother.
14 And Abimelech took sheep, and
oxen, and menservants, and womenservants, and gave *them* unto Abraham, and restored him Sarah his
wife.
15 And Abimelech said, Behold, my
land *is* before thee: dwell where it
pleaseth thee.
16 And unto Sarah he said, Behold, I
have given thy brother a thousand
pieces of silver: behold, he *is* to thee a
covering of the eyes, unto all that *are*
with thee, and with all *other:* thus she
was reproved.
¶17 So Abraham prayed unto God: and
God healed Abimelech, and his wife,
and his maidservants; and they bare
children.
18 For the LORD had fast closed up all
the wombs of the house of Abimelech,
because of Sarah Abraham's wife.

Isaac is born

21 And the LORD visited Sarah as
he had said, and the LORD did
unto Sarah as he had spoken.
2 For Sarah conceived, and bare
Abraham a son in his old age, at
the set time of which God had spoken
to him.
3 And Abraham called the name of his
son that was born unto him, whom Sarah bare to him, Isaac.

20:8 told all these things. Sometimes, if a child of God persists in sin, God has to bring him into public shame by allowing that sin to be told openly.
21:1 as he had said. See Genesis 17:15-16.

[4]And Abraham circumcised his son
Isaac being eight days old, as God had
commanded him.
[5]And Abraham was an hundred years
old, when his son Isaac was born unto
him.
¶[6]And Sarah said, God hath made me
to laugh, *so that* all that hear will laugh
with me.
[7]And she said, Who would have said
unto Abraham, that Sarah should have
given children suck? for I have born
him a son in his old age.
[8]And the child grew, and was
weaned: and Abraham made a great
feast the *same* day that Isaac was
weaned.
¶[9]And Sarah saw the son of Hagar the
Egyptian, which she had born unto
Abraham, mocking.
[10]Wherefore she said unto Abraham, Cast out this bondwoman and
her son: for the son of this bondwoman shall not be heir with my son,
even with Isaac.
[11]And the thing was very grievous in
Abraham's sight because of his son.
¶[12]And God said unto Abraham, Let
it not be grievous in thy sight because
of the lad, and because of thy bondwoman; in all that Sarah hath said
unto thee, hearken unto her voice; for
in Isaac shall thy seed be called.
[13]And also of the son of the bondwoman will I make a nation, because he
is thy seed.
[14]And Abraham rose up early in the
morning, and took bread, and a bottle
of water, and gave *it* unto Hagar, putting
it on her shoulder, and the child, and
sent her away: and she departed, and
wandered in the wilderness of Beer-
sheba.
[15]And the water was spent in the
bottle, and she cast the child under one
of the shrubs.
[16]And she went, and sat her down
over against *him* a good way off, as it
were a bowshot: for she said, Let me not
see the death of the child. And she sat
over against *him,* and lift up her voice,
and wept.
[17]And God heard the voice of the lad;
and the *angel of God called to Hagar
out of *heaven, and said unto her, What
aileth thee, Hagar? fear not; for God
hath heard the voice of the lad where
he *is.*
[18]Arise, lift up the lad, and hold him
in thine hand; for I will make him a great
nation.
[19]And God opened her eyes, and she

21:3 ISAAC: A TYPE OF CHRIST

We shall want to follow the story of Isaac carefully, for his life up to the time of his marriage is one of the most wonderful *types of the Lord Jesus Christ.

Notice how he reminds us of the Lord Jesus:

1. His miraculous birth. He was not born of a virgin as the Lord Jesus was, but his birth pictures that of the Lord, because it was humanly impossible, for his mother and father were very old.
2. His name. Isaac means *laughter,* and suggests the joy that the Lord Jesus Christ alone can give.
3. His sacrifice (described in chap. 22). While Abraham did not actually put Isaac to death, as God did His own Son, yet he was willing to, so, in a sense, Isaac was raised from the dead.
4. His marriage (described in chap. 24).
   a. The bride was one of his own relatives or kindred; she represents the true *church, those born of God.
   b. She had never seen him, yet she was willing to take the word of an unnamed servant about him. The servant represents the Holy Spirit.
   c. She traveled a long way to him across a desert; this world seems a desert to those who are eager to see the Lord Jesus.
   d. At last Isaac came to meet her and they were married; someday the Lord Jesus Christ will come in the air to meet His own people—who are called His bride—who will be taken to be with Him forever.

saw a well of water; and she went, and filled the bottle with water, and gave the lad drink.

20 And God was with the lad; and he grew, and dwelt in the wilderness, and became an archer.

21 And he dwelt in the wilderness of Paran: and his mother took him a wife out of the land of *Egypt.

¶22 And it came to pass at that time, that Abimelech and Phichol the chief captain of his host spake unto Abraham, saying, God *is* with thee in all that thou doest:

23 Now therefore swear unto me here by God that thou wilt not deal falsely with me, nor with my son, nor with my son's son: *but* according to the kindness that I have done unto thee, thou shalt do unto me, and to the land wherein thou hast sojourned.

24 And Abraham said, I will swear.

25 And Abraham reproved Abimelech because of a well of water, which Abimelech's servants had violently taken away.

26 And Abimelech said, I wot not who hath done this thing: neither didst thou tell me, neither yet heard I *of it,* but to day.

27 And Abraham took sheep and oxen, and gave them unto Abimelech; and both of them made a covenant.

28 And Abraham set seven ewe lambs of the flock by themselves.

29 And Abimelech said unto Abraham, What *mean* these seven ewe lambs which thou hast set by themselves?

30 And he said, For *these* seven ewe lambs shalt thou take of my hand, that they may be a witness unto me, that I have digged this well.

31 Wherefore he called that place Beer-sheba; because there they sware both of them.

32 Thus they made a covenant at Beer-sheba: then Abimelech rose up, and Phichol the chief captain of his host, and they returned into the land of the Philistines.

¶33 And *Abraham* planted a grove in Beer-sheba, and called there on the name of the LORD, the everlasting God.

34 And Abraham sojourned in the Philistines' land many days.

Isaac is offered to the LORD

22 And it came to pass after these things, that God did tempt Abraham, and said unto him, Abraham: and he said, Behold, *here* I *am.*

2 And he said, Take now thy son, thine only *son* Isaac, whom thou lovest, and get thee into the land of Moriah; and offer him there for a *burnt-offering upon one of the mountains which I will tell thee of.

¶3 And Abraham rose up early in the morning, and saddled his ass, and took two of his young men with him, and Isaac his son, and clave the wood for the burnt-offering, and rose up, and went

---

21:22 Abimelech. This man may or may not have been the same as the one in chapter 20. Abimelech was not a man's name, but a ruler's title, like Pharaoh, Caesar, King, or Emperor.

21:22 God is with thee. Abraham, the man who was wholly set apart to God, commands such respect from this king that he begs Abraham to be kind to him. The promise Abraham made and sealed by the gift of seven lambs (see vs. 30) pictures for us the way in which God shows kindness (see *grace of God) even to the unbelievers in the world because of the perfect work of the Lord Jesus Christ, the Lamb of God, whom He gave to the world.

21:26 wot. To know.

21:31 Beer-sheba. This means *well of the oath.*

21:33 the everlasting God. This is a translation from the Hebrew *El Olam*. He is the everlasting God, and He is the God of everlasting things. See *names of God.

22:3 clave. Split.

unto the place of which God had told
him.
4 Then on the third day Abraham lifted up his eyes, and saw the place afar
off.
5 And Abraham said unto his young
men, Abide ye here with the ass; and I
and the lad will go yonder and worship,
and come again to you.
6 And Abraham took the wood of the
burnt-offering, and laid *it* upon Isaac his
son; and he took the fire in his hand, and
a knife; and they went both of them together.
7 And Isaac spake unto Abraham his
father, and said, My father: and he said,
Here *am* I, my son. And he said, Behold
the fire and the wood: but where *is* the
lamb for a burnt-offering?
8 And Abraham said, My son, God will
provide himself a lamb for a burnt-offering: so they went both of them together.
9 And they came to the place which
God had told him of; and Abraham built
an *altar there, and laid the wood in order, and bound Isaac his son, and laid
him on the altar upon the wood.
10 And Abraham stretched forth his
hand, and took the knife to slay his
son.
11 And the *angel of the LORD called
unto him out of heaven, and said,
Abraham, Abraham: and he said, Here
am I.
12 And he said, Lay not thine hand upon
the lad, neither do thou any thing unto
him: for now I know that thou *fearest
God, seeing thou hast not withheld thy
son, thine only *son* from me.
13 And Abraham lifted up his eyes, and
looked, and behold behind *him* a ram
caught in a thicket by his horns: and
Abraham went and took the ram, and
offered him up for a burnt-offering in the
stead of his son.
14 And Abraham called the name of
that place Jehovah-jireh: as it is said *to*

22:1 TESTING VERSUS TEMPTING

Tempt has the idea of test; God never "tempted" anyone in the sense in which we use that word today. James 1:13-14 explains this. Abraham had been learning from God all these years, and from time to time God gave him a test. One of his first simple tests was the famine in the land (Gen. 12:10).

There were four very difficult tests:

1. leaving his country and home and relatives;
2. separating from Lot;
3. giving up has own plan for Ishmael;
4. sacrificing Isaac. This last was like a "final examination." Isaac was the dearest thing in the world to Abraham. Also, God's promises depended on Isaac's staying alive at least until he had children of his own. Along with this wonderful story of how Abraham passed his test of faith, read Hebrews 11:17-19.

22:5 I and the lad will . . . come again to you. Abraham's faith in God was very strong. He knew that, if necessary, God could raise Isaac from the dead.

22:6 they went both of them. This story pictures the unquestioning obedience of God's own Son, the Lord Jesus Christ, to His Father's will. We must always remember that it was really God who sent His Son to die on the cross; although, of course, Gentiles and Jews, rulers, soldiers, and priests—in fact, every person who ever lived—had a part in crucifying the Lord Jesus Christ, for everyone must confess, "It was my sin that nailed Him there." Read John 3:16 and Isaiah 53.

22:12 fearest God. Abraham had reverent trust in God. See Psalm 19:9 note on fear.

22:13 behold behind him a ram. A *type of Christ as the substitute.

22:14 Jehovah-jireh. *The LORD will provide* is the meaning of this name for God (see vs. 8). This phrase became a proverb with the Jewish people, for they said, "In the mount (as God provided for Abraham in his great need) Jehovah will provide" (for us too in our every need). See Philippians 4:19 and *names of God.

this day, In the mount of the LORD it
shall be seen.

Covenant with Abraham again

¶ 15 And the angel of the LORD called
unto Abraham out of heaven the second
time,
16 And said, By myself have I sworn,
saith the LORD, for because thou hast
done this thing, and hast not withheld
thy son, thine only *son:*
17 That in blessing I will bless thee,
and in multiplying I will multiply thy
seed as the stars of the heaven, and as
the sand which *is* upon the sea shore;
and thy seed shall possess the gate of
his enemies;
18 And in thy seed shall all the nations
of the earth be blessed; because thou
hast obeyed my voice.
19 So Abraham returned unto his
young men, and they rose up and went
together to Beer-sheba; and Abraham
dwelt at Beer-sheba.
¶ 20 And it came to pass after these
things, that it was told Abraham, saying, Behold, Milcah, she hath also born
children unto thy brother Nahor;
21 Huz his firstborn, and Buz his
brother, and Kemuel the father of Aram,
22 And Chesed, and Hazo, and Pil-
dash, and Jidlaph, and Bethuel.
23 And Bethuel begat Rebekah: these
eight Milcah did bear to Nahor, Abraham's brother.
24 And his concubine, whose name
was Reumah, she bare also Tebah, and
Gaham, and Thahash, and Maachah.

Sarah dies

23 And Sarah was an hundred
and seven and twenty years
old: *these were* the years of the life of
Sarah.
2 And Sarah died in Kirjath-arba; the
same *is* Hebron in the land of Canaan:
and Abraham came to mourn for Sarah,
and to weep for her.
¶ 3 And Abraham stood up from before
his dead, and spake unto the sons of
Heth, saying,
4 I *am* a stranger and a sojourner with
you: give me a possession of a buryingplace with you, that I may bury my dead
out of my sight.
5 And the children of Heth answered
Abraham, saying unto him,
6 Hear us, my lord: thou *art* a mighty
prince among us: in the choice of our
sepulchres bury thy dead; none of us

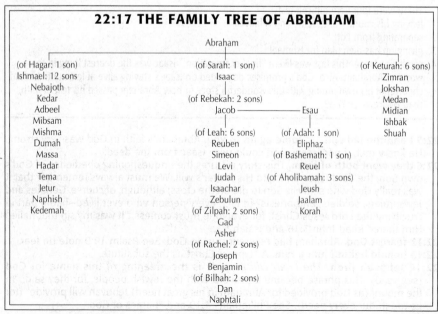

22:17 THE FAMILY TREE OF ABRAHAM

Abraham

- (of Hagar: 1 son) Ishmael: 12 sons
  - Nebajoth
  - Kedar
  - Adbeel
  - Mibsam
  - Mishma
  - Dumah
  - Massa
  - Hadar
  - Tema
  - Jetur
  - Naphish
  - Kedemah
- (of Sarah: 1 son) Isaac
  - (of Rebekah: 2 sons) Jacob — Esau
    - Jacob
      - (of Leah: 6 sons) Reuben, Simeon, Levi, Judah, Isaachar, Zebulun
      - (of Zilpah: 2 sons) Gad, Asher
      - (of Rachel: 2 sons) Joseph, Benjamin
      - (of Bilhah: 2 sons) Dan, Naphtali
    - Esau
      - (of Adah: 1 son) Eliphaz
      - (of Bashemath: 1 son) Reuel
      - (of Aholibamah: 3 sons) Jeush, Jaalam, Korah
- (of Keturah: 6 sons)
  - Zimran
  - Jokshan
  - Medan
  - Midian
  - Ishbak
  - Shuah

shall withhold from thee his sepulchre,
but that thou mayest bury thy dead.
7 And Abraham stood up, and bowed
himself to the people of the land, *even*
to the children of Heth.
8 And he communed with them, saying, If it be your mind that I should bury
my dead out of my sight; hear me,
and intreat for me to Ephron the son of
Zohar,
9 That he may give me the cave of
Machpelah, which he hath, which *is* in
the end of his field; for as much money
as it is worth he shall give it me for a
possession of a buryingplace amongst
you.
10 And Ephron dwelt among the children of Heth: and Ephron the Hittite
answered Abraham in the audience of
the children of Heth, *even* of all that
went in at the gate of his city, saying,
11 Nay, my lord, hear me: the field give
I thee, and the cave that *is* therein, I give
it thee; in the presence of the sons of my
people give I it thee: bury thy dead.
12 And Abraham bowed down himself
before the people of the land.
13 And he spake unto Ephron in the
audience of the people of the land, saying, But if thou *wilt give it,* I pray thee,
hear me: I will give thee money for the
field; take *it* of me, and I will bury my
dead there.
14 And Ephron answered Abraham,
saying unto him,
15 My lord, hearken unto me: the land
is worth four hundred shekels of silver;
what *is* that betwixt me and thee? bury
therefore thy dead.
16 And Abraham hearkened unto
Ephron; and Abraham weighed to
Ephron the silver, which he had named
in the audience of the sons of Heth, four
hundred shekels of silver, current
money with the merchant.
¶ 17 And the field of Ephron, which
was in Machpelah, which *was* before
Mamre, the field, and the cave which
was therein, and all the trees that *were*
in the field, that *were* in all the borders
round about, were made sure
18 Unto Abraham for a possession in the
presence of the children of Heth, before
all that went in at the gate of his city.
19 And after this, Abraham buried Sarah his wife in the cave of the field of
Machpelah before Mamre: the same *is*
Hebron in the land of Canaan.
20 And the field, and the cave that
is therein, were made sure unto

23:1-19 BURIAL OF THE DEAD

Burial of the dead was practiced by the Hebrews from the earliest times, and three of their most ancient cemeteries still remain: Machpelah, Shechem, and the Valley of Jehoshaphat. Cremation was practiced by the nations who didn't know God. "The burning of the dead" (2 Chron. 16:14) is not cremation but a burning for King Asa.

Burial places were usually outside the city or village, and the dead were carried to the grave on biers, amid the wailing of their friends, especially the women. In general, there were thirty days of mourning. Burial was refused to criminals, [and the "burial of an ass" was exposure to birds and beasts of prey.]

Some ancient tombs had heavy stone superstructures over them, as did the tomb of Hiram the king of Tyre. Israelite tombs were usually in caves in the limestone rock, the hard stratum being left as a roof, and the softer which is below being cut into. Jerusalem is surrounded by large caves connecting several chambers or vaults for bodies, somewhat resembling the Roman catacombs. It is the custom in hot countries for the burial to take place a few hours after death. The Babylonians and Assyrians are thought to have burnt their dead. The ancient Egyptians hewed tombs in the mountains and in the rocky ground; they also built pyramids to hold the bodies of some of their kings.

23:15 shekels of silver. This was ten pounds of silver, a very high price to pay for a piece of land. Compare Jeremiah 32:9.

Abraham for a possession of a buryingplace by the sons of Heth.

A bride for Isaac

24 And Abraham was old, *and*
well stricken in age: and the
LORD had blessed Abraham in all things.
2And Abraham said unto his eldest
servant of his house, that ruled over all
that he had, Put, I pray thee, thy hand
under my thigh:
3And I will make thee swear by the
LORD, the *God of heaven, and the God
of the earth, that thou shalt not take a
wife unto my son of the daughters of the
Canaanites, among whom I dwell:
4But thou shalt go unto my country,
and to my kindred, and take a wife unto
my son Isaac.
5And the servant said unto him, Peradventure the woman will not be willing to follow me unto this land: must I
needs bring thy son again unto the land
from whence thou camest?
6And Abraham said unto him, Beware thou that thou bring not my son
thither again.
¶7The LORD God of heaven, which
took me from my father's house, and
from the land of my kindred, and which
spake unto me, and that sware unto me,
saying, Unto thy seed will I give this
land; he shall send his *angel before
thee, and thou shalt take a wife unto my
son from thence.
8And if the woman will not be willing
to follow thee, then thou shalt be clear
from this my oath: only bring not my
son thither again.
9And the servant put his hand under
the thigh of Abraham his master, and
sware to him concerning that matter.
¶10And the servant took ten camels
of the camels of his master, and departed; for all the goods of his master *were*
in his hand: and he arose, and went to
Mesopotamia, unto the city of Nahor.
11And he made his camels to kneel
down without the city by a well of water at the time of the evening, *even*
the time that women go out to draw
water.
12And he said, O LORD God of my
master Abraham, I pray thee, send me
good speed this day, and shew kindness
unto my master Abraham.
13Behold, I stand *here* by the well of
water; and the daughters of the men of
the city come out to draw water:
14And let it come to pass, that the
damsel to whom I shall say, Let down
thy pitcher, I pray thee, that I may
drink; and she shall say, Drink, and I will
give thy camels drink also: *let the same*
be she *that* thou hast appointed for thy
servant Isaac; and thereby shall I know
that thou hast shewed kindness unto
my master.
¶15And it came to pass, before he had
done speaking, that, behold, Rebekah
came out, who was born to Bethuel, son
of Milcah, the wife of Nahor, Abraham's
brother, with her pitcher upon her
shoulder.
16And the damsel *was* very fair to
look upon, a virgin, neither had any man
known her: and she went down to the
well, and filled her pitcher, and came up.
17And the servant ran to meet her,
and said, Let me, I pray thee, drink a
little water of thy pitcher.
18And she said, Drink, my lord: and
she hasted, and let down her pitcher
upon her hand, and gave him drink.
19And when she had done giving him
drink, she said, I will draw *water* for

24:4 a wife unto my son. This is one of the most beautiful stories in the Bible. Of course, it is more than a story; it actually happened to Isaac, but the Spirit of God records it in the way He does so that we today may understand how God has chosen the *church to be the bride of His Son, the Lord Jesus Christ. Turn back to the Genesis 21:3 note, and read the four main points about this story of Isaac and his bride.

24:8 clear. To be innocent.

24:12 speed. Success. Hasten.

thy camels also, until they have done drinking.

20 And she hasted, and emptied her pitcher into the trough, and ran again unto the well to draw *water,* and drew for all his camels.

21 And the man wondering at her held his peace, to wit whether the LORD had made his journey prosperous or not.

22 And it came to pass, as the camels had done drinking, that the man took a golden earring of half a shekel weight, and two bracelets for her hands of ten *shekels* weight of gold;

24:22 Jewels
Precious stones are nowhere mentioned in the Bible as personal ornaments, except in connection with religious worship, but jewels of gold and silver were worn, mainly bracelets, anklets, chains, earrings, but even nose rings, brooches, and medallions on the forehead by women, which was displeasing to God (Isa. 3:16-23). The Ishmaelites wore earrings, and the Amalekites adorned the necks of their camels with gold chains.

23 And said, Whose daughter *art* thou? tell me, I pray thee: is there room *in* thy father's house for us to lodge in?

24 And she said unto him, I *am* the daughter of Bethuel the son of Milcah, which she bare unto Nahor.

25 She said moreover unto him, We have both straw and provender enough, and room to lodge in.

26 And the man bowed down his head, and worshipped the LORD.

27 And he said, Blessed *be* the LORD God of my master Abraham, who hath not left destitute my master of his mercy and his truth: I *being* in the way, the LORD led me to the house of my master's brethren.

28 And the damsel ran, and told *them of* her mother's house these things.

¶29 And Rebekah had a brother, and his name *was* Laban: and Laban ran out unto the man, unto the well.

30 And it came to pass, when he saw the earring and bracelets upon his sister's hands, and when he heard the words of Rebekah his sister, saying, Thus spake the man unto me; that he came unto the man; and, behold, he stood by the camels at the well.

31 And he said, Come in, thou blessed of the LORD; wherefore standest thou without? for I have prepared the house, and room for the camels.

¶32 And the man came into the house: and he ungirded his camels, and gave straw and provender for the camels, and water to *wash his feet, and the men's feet that *were* with him.

33 And there was set *meat* before him to eat: but he said, I will not eat, until I have told mine errand. And he said, Speak on.

34 And he said, I *am* Abraham's servant.

35 And the LORD hath blessed my master greatly; and he is become great: and he hath given him flocks, and herds, and silver, and gold, and menservants, and maidservants, and camels, and asses.

36 And Sarah my master's wife bare a son to my master when she was old: and unto him hath he given all that he hath.

37 And my master made me swear, saying, Thou shalt not take a wife to my son of the daughters of the Canaanites, in whose land I dwell:

38 But thou shalt go unto my father's house, and to my kindred, and take a wife unto my son.

39 And I said unto my master,

24:22 ten shekels weight of gold. A gold shekel was a weight equal to about two-fifths of an ounce.

24:36 unto him. The servant, who pictures the Holy Spirit, delighted to speak about his master's son just as the Holy Spirit delights to speak about the Lord Jesus Christ. Read John 16:13-15.

Peradventure the woman will not
follow me.
[40]And he said unto me, The LORD,
before whom I walk, will send his angel with thee, and prosper thy way; and
thou shalt take a wife for my son of my
kindred, and of my father's house:
[41]Then shalt thou be clear from *this*
my oath, when thou comest to my kindred; and if they give not thee *one,* thou
shalt be clear from my oath.
[42]And I came this day unto the well,
and said, O LORD God of my master
Abraham, if now thou do prosper my
way which I go;
[43]Behold, I stand by the well of water; and it shall come to pass, that when
the virgin cometh forth to draw *water,*
and I say to her, Give me, I pray thee, a
little water of thy pitcher to drink;
[44]And she say to me, Both drink
thou, and I will also draw for thy camels: *let* the same *be* the woman whom
the LORD hath appointed out for my
master's son.
[45]And before I had done speaking in
mine heart, behold, Rebekah came
forth with her pitcher on her shoulder;
and she went down unto the well, and
drew *water:* and I said unto her, Let me
drink, I pray thee.
[46]And she made haste, and let down
her pitcher from her *shoulder,* and said,
Drink, and I will give thy camels drink
also: so I drank, and she made the camels drink also.
[47]And I asked her, and said, Whose
daughter *art* thou? And she said, The
daughter of Bethuel, Nahor's son,
whom Milcah bare unto him: and I put
the earring upon her face, and the
bracelets upon her hands.
[48]And I bowed down my head, and
worshipped the LORD, and blessed the
LORD God of my master Abraham,
which had led me in the right way to
take my master's brother's daughter
unto his son.
[49]And now if ye will deal kindly and
truly with my master, tell me: and if not,
tell me; that I may turn to the right
hand, or to the left.
[50]Then Laban and Bethuel answered
and said, The thing proceedeth from the
LORD: we cannot speak unto thee bad
or good.
[51]Behold, Rebekah *is* before thee, take
her, and go, and let her be thy master's
son's wife, as the LORD hath spoken.
[52]And it came to pass, that, when
Abraham's servant heard their words,
he worshipped the LORD, *bowing him-*
self to the earth.
[53]And the servant brought forth jewels of silver, and jewels of gold, and raiment, and gave *them* to Rebekah: he
gave also to her brother and to her
mother precious things.
[54]And they did eat and drink, he and
the men that *were* with him, and tarried
all night; and they rose up in the morning, and he said, Send me away unto my
master.
[55]And her brother and her mother
said, Let the damsel abide with us *a few*
days, at the least ten; after that she
shall go.
[56]And he said unto them, Hinder me
not, seeing the LORD hath prospered
my way; send me away that I may go to
my master.
[57]And they said, We will call the damsel, and inquire at her mouth.
[58]And they called Rebekah, and said
unto her, Wilt thou go with this man?
And she said, I will go.
[59]And they sent away Rebekah their
sister, and her nurse, and Abraham's
servant, and his men.
[60]And they blessed Rebekah, and said
unto her, Thou *art* our sister, be thou *the*
mother of thousands of millions, and let
thy seed possess the gate of those
which hate them.
¶[61]And Rebekah arose, and her damsels, and they rode upon the camels,
and followed the man: and the servant
took Rebekah, and went his way.

24:49 deal. To act.

[62]And Isaac came from the way of the
well Lahai-roi; for he dwelt in the south
country.
[63]And Isaac went out to meditate in
the field at the eventide: and he lifted
up his eyes, and saw, and, behold, the
camels *were* coming.
[64]And Rebekah lifted up her eyes,
and when she saw Isaac, she lighted off
the camel.
[65]For she *had* said unto the servant,
What man *is* this that walketh in the
field to meet us? And the servant *had*
said, It *is* my master: therefore she took
a vail, and covered herself.
[66]And the servant told Isaac all things
that he had done.
[67]And Isaac brought her into his
mother Sarah's tent, and took Rebekah, and she became his wife; and he
loved her: and Isaac was comforted after his mother's **death.*

Abraham's new wife

25 Then again Abraham took a
wife, and her name *was* Keturah.
[2]And she bare him Zimran, and Jokshan, and Medan, and Midian, and Ishbak, and Shuah.
[3]And Jokshan begat Sheba, and Dedan.
And the sons of Dedan were Asshurim,
and Letushim, and Leummim.
[4]And the sons of Midian; Ephah, and
Epher, and Hanoch, and Abidah, and
Eldaah. All these *were* the children of
Keturah.
¶[5]And Abraham gave all that he had
unto Isaac.
[6]But unto the sons of the concubines,
which Abraham had, Abraham gave
gifts, and sent them away from Isaac his
son, while he yet lived, eastward, unto
the east country.
[7]And these *are* the days of the years
of Abraham's life which he lived, an
hundred threescore and fifteen years.

Abraham dies

[8]Then *Abraham gave up the ghost,
and died in a good old age, an old man,
and full *of years;* and was gathered to his
people.
[9]And his sons Isaac and Ishmael buried him in the cave of Machpelah, in the
field of Ephron the son of Zohar the
Hittite, which *is* before Mamre;
[10]The field which Abraham purchased of the sons of Heth: there was
Abraham buried, and Sarah his wife.
¶[11]And it came to pass after the death
of Abraham, that God blessed his son
Isaac; and Isaac dwelt by the well Lahai-roi.
¶[12]Now these *are* the generations of
Ishmael, Abraham's son, whom Hagar
the Egyptian, Sarah's handmaid, bare
unto Abraham:
[13]And these *are* the names of the
sons of Ishmael, by their names, according to their generations: the firstborn of Ishmael, Nebajoth; and *Kedar,
and Adbeel, and Mibsam,
[14]And Mishma, and Dumah, and
Massa,
[15]Hadar, and Tema, Jetur, Naphish,
and Kedemah:
[16]These *are* the sons of Ishmael, and
these *are* their names, by their towns,
and by their castles; twelve princes
according to their nations.
[17]And these *are* the years of the life of
Ishmael, an hundred and thirty and seven
years: and he gave up the ghost and
died; and was gathered unto his people.
[18]And they dwelt from Havilah unto
Shur, that *is* before Egypt, as thou goest
toward Assyria: *and* he died in the presence of all his brethren.

24:62 the well Lahai-roi. This was "the well of Him that liveth and seeth me" (see Gen. 16:14 and 25:11).

24:65 vail. The bride's wedding veil, in the Eastern countries, was generally a present from the bridegroom. This veil pictures to us the righteousness of God in our Lord Jesus Christ which covers us completely (Rom. 4:5-7) and is the "best robe" that God could provide.

¶ 19 And these *are* the generations of
Isaac, Abraham's son: Abraham begat
Isaac:
20 And Isaac was forty years old when
he took Rebekah to wife, the daughter
of Bethuel the Syrian of Padan-aram,
the sister to Laban the Syrian.
21 And Isaac intreated the LORD for
his wife, because she *was* barren: and
the LORD was intreated of him, and
Rebekah his wife conceived.
22 And the children struggled together
within her; and she said, If *it be* so, why
am I thus? And she went to enquire of
the LORD.
23 And the LORD said unto her, Two
nations *are* in thy womb, and two manner of people shall be separated from
thy bowels; and *the one* people shall be
stronger than *the other* people; and the
elder shall serve the younger.
¶ 24 And when her days to be delivered
were fulfilled, behold, *there were* twins
in her womb.
25 And the first came out red, all over
like an hairy garment; and they called
his name Esau.
26 And after that came his brother out,
and his hand took hold on Esau's heel;
and his name was called Jacob: and
Isaac *was* threescore years old when
she bare them.
¶ 27 And the boys grew: and Esau was
a cunning hunter, a man of the field;
and Jacob *was* a plain man, dwelling in
tents.
28 And Isaac loved Esau, because he
did eat of *his* venison: but Rebekah
loved Jacob.
29 And Jacob sod pottage: and Esau
came from the field, and he *was* faint:
30 And Esau said to Jacob, Feed me, I
pray thee, with that same red *pottage;*
for I *am* faint: therefore was his name
called Edom.
31 And Jacob said, Sell me this day thy
birthright.
32 And Esau said, Behold, I *am* at the
point to die: and what profit shall this
birthright do to me?
33 And Jacob said, Swear to me this
day; and he sware unto him: and he sold
his birthright unto Jacob.
34 Then Jacob gave Esau bread and
pottage of lentiles; and he did eat and
drink, and rose up, and went his way:
thus Esau despised *his* birthright.

25:25-27 Jacob and Esau
In many ways Esau was more manly and attractive than Jacob, but he lacked the one important thing in God's sight: faith. It was not just that Esau cared more for earthly things than for heavenly; Jacob did too during the first part of his life. It was that Esau did not believe God's promises; if he had, he could not have thrown them away so lightly. Jacob believed them. He went after them in the wrong way, and for selfish reasons, yet he took God at His word. God honored his faith, and though He had to discipline Jacob, He gave him the blessings.

25:31 THE PRIVILEGES OF THE BIRTHRIGHT

In Eastern countries, certain privileges always belonged to the firstborn son of a family. These were called the "birthright."

They were:

1. the right to a double share of the father's wealth at his death; and
2. the right to be priest in the family after the father's death, for women or children were not expected to have direct contact with God.

In Abraham's family, the birthright included one more right–the most important of all:

3. to be in the direct line of the coming Saviour. For all that they knew then, Esau might have been that Promised One.

25:27 cunning. Skillful.
25:28 venison. The flesh of hunted animals.
25:29 Jacob sod pottage. Sod means *boiled*. Jacob was boiling lentils (vs. 34).
25:30 Edom. This means *red.*

26 And there was a famine in the
land, beside the first famine that
was in the days of Abraham. And Isaac
went unto Abimelech king of the *Philistines unto Gerar.
2 And the LORD appeared unto him,
and said, Go not down into Egypt; dwell
in the land which I shall tell thee of:
3 Sojourn in this land, and I will be
with thee, and will bless thee; for unto
thee, and unto thy seed, I will give all
these countries, and I will perform the
oath which I sware unto Abraham thy
father;
4 And I will make thy seed to multiply as the stars of heaven, and will give
unto thy seed all these countries; and
in thy seed shall all the nations of the
earth be blessed;
5 Because that Abraham obeyed my
voice, and kept my charge, my commandments, my statutes, and my laws.
¶6 And Isaac dwelt in Gerar:
7 And the men of the place asked *him*
of his wife; and he said, She *is* my sister: for he feared to say, *She is* my wife;
lest, *said he,* the men of the place
should kill me for Rebekah; because
she *was* fair to look upon.
8 And it came to pass, when he had
been there a long time, that Abimelech
king of the Philistines looked out at a
window, and saw, and, behold, Isaac *was*
sporting with Rebekah his wife.
9 And Abimelech called Isaac, and
said, Behold, of a surety she *is* thy wife:
and how saidst thou, She *is* my sister?
And Isaac said unto him, Because I said,
Lest I die for her.
10 And Abimelech said, What *is* this
thou hast done unto us? one of the people might lightly have lien with thy
wife, and thou shouldest have brought
guiltiness upon us.
11 And Abimelech charged all *his* people, saying, He that toucheth this man
or his wife shall surely be put to death.
12 Then Isaac sowed in that land, and
received in the same year an hundredfold: and the LORD blessed him.
13 And the man waxed great, and went
forward, and grew until he became very
great:
14 For he had possession of flocks, and
possession of herds, and great store of
servants: and the Philistines envied
him.
15 For all the wells which his father's
servants had digged in the days of Abraham his father, the Philistines had
stopped them, and filled them with
earth.
16 And Abimelech said unto Isaac, Go
from us; for thou art much mightier
than we.
¶17 And Isaac departed thence, and
pitched his tent in the valley of Gerar,
and dwelt there.
18 And Isaac digged again the wells of
water, which they had digged in the
days of Abraham his father; for the
Philistines had stopped them after
the death of Abraham: and he called
their names after the names by which
his father had called them.
19 And Isaac's servants digged in the
valley, and found there a well of springing water.
20 And the herdmen of Gerar did
strive with Isaac's herdmen, saying,

26:2 Go not down. Gerar, where Isaac was and where his father had often stayed, was not actually in Egypt but "on the fence," we might say, between the two countries. God clearly warned Isaac not to fall into his father's sin, of going out of the Land of Promise, but Isaac apparently paid no attention.

26:7 She is my sister. Isaac sinned as his father had done. See Genesis 12:13 and 20:2 notes.

26:10 lien. Lain (past perfect of "lie").

26:12 blessed. God keeps His promises whether man is faithful or not. But it is also true that God will punish those of His own who are disobedient. Isaac's punishment was constant trouble from the Philistines as long as he stayed in their country.

26:20 Esek. The name of the well means *contention* or *quarreling.*

The water *is* ours: and he called the
name of the well Esek; because they
strove with him.
21 And they digged another well, and
strove for that also: and he called the
name of it Sitnah.
22 And he removed from thence, and
digged another well; and for that they
strove not: and he called the name of it
Rehoboth; and he said, For now the
LORD hath made room for us, and we
shall be fruitful in the land.
23 And he went up from thence to
Beer-sheba.
24 And the LORD appeared unto him
the same night, and said, I *am* the God
of Abraham thy father: fear not, for I
am with thee, and will bless thee, and
multiply thy seed for my servant
Abraham's sake.
25 And he builded an altar there, and
called upon the name of the LORD, and
pitched his tent there: and there Isaac's
servants digged a well.
¶ 26 Then Abimelech went to him from
Gerar, and Ahuzzath one of his friends,
and Phichol the chief captain of his army.
27 And Isaac said unto them, Wherefore come ye to me, seeing ye hate me,
and have sent me away from you?
28 And they said, We saw certainly
that the LORD was with thee: and we
said, Let there be now an oath betwixt
us, *even* betwixt us and thee, and let us
make a covenant with thee;
29 That thou wilt do us no hurt, as we
have not touched thee, and as we have
done unto thee nothing but good, and
have sent thee away in *peace: thou *art*
now the blessed of the LORD.
30 And he made them a feast, and they
did eat and drink.
31 And they rose up betimes in the
morning, and sware one to another: and
Isaac sent them away, and they departed from him in peace.
32 And it came to pass the same day,
that Isaac's servants came, and told him
concerning the well which they had
digged, and said unto him, We have
found water.
33 And he called it Shebah: therefore
the name of the city *is* Beer-sheba unto
this day.
¶ 34 And Esau was forty years old
when he took to wife Judith the daughter of Beeri the Hittite, and Bashemath
the daughter of Elon the Hittite:
35 Which were a grief of mind unto
Isaac and to Rebekah.

27 And it came to pass, that when
Isaac was old, and his eyes were
dim, so that he could not see, he called
Esau his eldest son, and said unto him,
My son: and he said unto him, Behold,
here am I.
2 And he said, Behold now, I am old, I
know not the day of my death:
3 Now therefore take, I pray thee, thy
weapons, thy quiver and thy bow, and
go out to the field, and take me *some*
venison;
4 And make me savoury meat, such
as I love, and bring *it* to me, that I may
eat; that my soul may bless thee before
I die.

26:21 Sitnah. This name means *hatred.*
26:22 Rehoboth. This means *enlargement.*
26:23 he went up from thence to Beer-sheba. Just as soon as Isaac went back to God's own place for him, the quarreling stopped and God made Himself known to him. It is plain that Isaac's heart was now right with God as it was not when God spoke before, for now Isaac built an altar. He did not do this when God warned him in verse 2. (Go back to the Gen. 8:20 note to see why men built altars.)
26:31 betimes. Early.
26:33 Shebah. Shebah means *oath.* Beer means *well.* Beer-sheba is the "well of the oath."
26:35 grief of mind. Isaac and Rebekah understood very well that the reason Abraham had been so careful to not let Isaac marry a Gentile was that practically all Gentiles in those days were ignorant of the true God. They had their religion, of course, but it was a false one.

[5]And Rebekah heard when Isaac
spake to Esau his son. And Esau went
to the field to hunt *for* venison, *and* to
bring *it*.

¶[6]And Rebekah spake unto Jacob her
son, saying, Behold, I heard thy father
speak unto Esau thy brother, saying,

[7]Bring me venison, and make me
savoury meat, that I may eat, and bless
thee before the LORD before my death.

[8]Now therefore, my son, obey my
voice according to that which I command thee.

[9]Go now to the flock, and fetch me
from thence two good kids of the goats;
and I will make them savoury meat for
thy father, such as he loveth:

[10]And thou shalt bring *it* to thy father,
that he may eat, and that he may bless
thee before his death.

[11]And Jacob said to Rebekah his
mother, Behold, Esau my brother *is* a
hairy man, and I *am* a smooth man:

[12]My father peradventure will feel
me, and I shall seem to him as a deceiver; and I shall bring a curse upon
me, and not a blessing.

[13]And his mother said unto him,
Upon me *be* thy curse, my son: only
obey my voice, and go fetch me *them*.

[14]And he went, and fetched, and
brought *them* to his mother: and his
mother made savoury meat, such as his
father loved.

[15]And Rebekah took goodly raiment
of her eldest son Esau, which *were* with
her in the house, and put them upon
Jacob her younger son:

[16]And she put the skins of the kids of
the goats upon his hands, and upon the
smooth of his neck:

[17]And she gave the savoury meat and
the bread, which she had prepared, into
the hand of her son Jacob.

¶[18]And he came unto his father, and
said, My father: and he said, Here *am*
I; who *art* thou, my son?

[19]And Jacob said unto his father, I *am*
Esau thy firstborn; I have done according as thou badest me: arise, I pray
thee, sit and eat of my venison, that thy
soul may bless me.

[20]And Isaac said unto his son, How *is*
it that thou hast found *it* so quickly, my
son? And he said, Because the LORD
thy God brought *it* to me.

[21]And Isaac said unto Jacob, Come
near, I pray thee, that I may feel thee,
my son, whether thou *be* my very son
Esau or not.

[22]And Jacob went near unto Isaac his
father; and he felt him, and said, The
voice *is* Jacob's voice, but the hands *are*
the hands of Esau.

[23]And he discerned him not, because
his hands were hairy, as his brother
Esau's hands: so he blessed him.

[24]And he said, *Art* thou my very son
Esau? And he said, I *am*.

[25]And he said, Bring *it* near to me,
and I will eat of my son's venison, that
my soul may bless thee. And he brought
it near to him, and he did eat: and he
brought him *wine, and he drank.

[26]And his father Isaac said unto him,
Come near now, and kiss me, my son.

[27]And he came near, and kissed him:
and he smelled the smell of his raiment,
and blessed him, and said, See, the
smell of my son *is* as the smell of a field
which the LORD hath blessed:

[28]Therefore God give thee of the dew
of heaven, and the fatness of the earth,
and plenty of corn and wine:

27:6 Rebekah spake. It is no wonder that Jacob was deceitful when his mother set him such a wrong example. God had to show them both, through much trouble and sorrow, that He could keep His promises without their scheming, and that they were not pleasing Him when they tried to get His blessings just for their own selfish use.

27:27 and blessed him. Isaac is speaking here out of the natural desires of his heart. He thinks he is giving Esau the blessing, but he does not realize that all he speaks of is earthly wealth and power. It is only in chapter 28:3-4 that he remembers that "the blessing of Abraham" is the thing to be prized, for that means the promise of the Saviour.

29 Let people serve thee, and nations
bow down to thee: be lord over thy
brethren, and let thy mother's sons bow
down to thee: cursed *be* every one that
curseth thee, and blessed *be* he that
blesseth thee.
¶30 And it came to pass, as soon as
Isaac had made an end of blessing Jacob,
and Jacob was yet scarce gone out from
the presence of Isaac his father, that
Esau his brother came in from his hunting.
31 And he also had made savoury
meat, and brought it unto his father, and
said unto his father, Let my father arise,
and eat of his son's venison, that thy
soul may bless me.
32 And Isaac his father said unto him,
Who *art* thou? And he said, I *am* thy
son, thy firstborn Esau.
33 And Isaac trembled very exceedingly, and said, Who? where *is* he that
hath taken venison, and brought *it* me,
and I have eaten of all before thou
camest, and have blessed him? yea, *and*
he shall be blessed.

Essau's remorse

34 And when Esau heard the words of
his father, he cried with a great and exceeding bitter cry, and said unto his father, Bless me, *even* me also, O my
father.
35 And he said, Thy brother came
with subtilty, and hath taken away thy
blessing.
36 And he said, Is not he rightly named
Jacob? for he hath supplanted me these
two times: he took away my *birthright;
and, behold, now he hath taken away my
blessing. And he said, Hast thou not
reserved a blessing for me?
37 And Isaac answered and said unto
Esau, Behold, I have made him thy lord,
and all his brethren have I given to him
for servants; and with corn and wine
have I sustained him: and what shall I
do now unto thee, my son?
38 And Esau said unto his father, Hast
thou but one blessing, my father? bless
me, *even* me also, O my father. And Esau
lifted up his voice, and wept.
39 And Isaac his father answered and
said unto him, Behold, thy dwelling
shall be the fatness of the earth, and of
the dew of heaven from above;
40 And by thy sword shalt thou live,
and shalt serve thy brother; and it shall
come to pass when thou shalt have the
dominion, that thou shalt break his yoke
from off thy neck.
¶41 And Esau hated Jacob because of
the blessing wherewith his father
blessed him: and Esau said in his heart,
The days of *mourning for my father
are at hand; then will I slay my brother
Jacob.
42 And these words of Esau her elder
son were told to Rebekah: and she sent
and called Jacob her younger son, and
said unto him, Behold, thy brother
Esau, as touching thee, doth comfort
himself, *purposing* to kill thee.
43 Now therefore, my son, obey my
voice; and arise, flee thou to Laban my
brother to Haran;
44 And tarry with him a few days, until thy brother's fury turn away;
45 Until thy brother's anger turn away
from thee, and he forget *that* which
thou hast done to him: then I will send,
and fetch thee from thence: why should
I be deprived also of you both in one
day?

27:29 cursed . . . blessed. This is all that Isaac seemed to remember of the blessing that had been passed to him from his father, Abraham, which he had received from God (Gen. 12:3; 25:5; 26:3-4).

27:33 yea, and he shall be blessed. Suddenly Isaac sees how he has sinned in wanting something other than God's will for his sons.

27:36 Jacob. This name means *supplanter,* or someone who takes another's place.

27:38 Esau lifted up his voice, and wept. Esau cried, not because of his sin in lightly selling his birthright (see Gen. 25:29-34), but because the chief blessing went to Jacob (see Heb. 12:16-17).

[46]And Rebekah said to Isaac, I am weary of my life because of the daughters of Heth: if Jacob take a wife of the daughters of Heth, such as these *which are* of the daughters of the land, what good shall my life do me?

Jacob at Beth-el

28 And Isaac called Jacob, and blessed him, and charged him, and said unto him, Thou shalt not take a wife of the daughters of Canaan.

[2]Arise, go to Padan-aram, to the house of Bethuel thy mother's father; and take thee a wife from thence of the daughters of Laban thy mother's brother.

[3]And God Almighty bless thee, and make thee fruitful, and multiply thee, that thou mayest be a multitude of people;

[4]And give thee the blessing of Abraham, to thee, and to thy seed with thee; that thou mayest inherit the land wherein thou art a stranger, which God gave unto Abraham.

[5]And Isaac sent away Jacob: and he went to Padan-aram unto Laban, son of Bethuel the Syrian, the brother of Rebekah, Jacob's and Esau's mother.

¶[6]When Esau saw that Isaac had blessed Jacob, and sent him away to Padan-aram, to take him a wife from thence; and that as he blessed him he gave him a charge, saying, Thou shalt not take a wife of the daughters of Canaan;

[7]And that Jacob obeyed his father and his mother, and was gone to Padan-aram;

[8]And Esau seeing that the daughters of Canaan pleased not Isaac his father;

[9]Then went Esau unto Ishmael, and took unto the wives which he had Mahalath the daughter of Ishmael Abraham's son, the sister of Nebajoth, to be his wife.

Jacob's dream

¶[10]And Jacob went out from Beersheba, and went toward Haran.

[11]And he lighted upon a certain place, and tarried there all night, because the sun was set; and he took of the stones of that place, and put *them for* his

28:10 JACOB: A TYPE OF ISRAEL

Jacob's whole life and character are a clear picture of the nation of Israel, which is descended from him. The following outline will show the likenesses:

1. Although Jacob was not the firstborn, he got the rights of a firstborn son because Esau did not want them. Although Israel did not come into being as a nation as soon as Gentile nations, it has a place in God's favor that Gentiles do not have because they did not want it.
2. For many years Jacob was out of the land God gave him, because of his own sin and weak faith. For many years, the nation, Israel, was out of their land because of their sin and lack of faith. They became a nation again in 1948.
3. All the time Jacob was away, he still tried to get God's blessing by his own efforts. He became very rich during that time, as many Israelites/Jews have been in the past.
4. Going back to the land, he was still the same old Jacob, but God met him there and changed his character and even his name. Forever after that he was conscious of his own weakness but also of his trust in the mighty God. Jews have been going back to their land. They still continue in unbelief and sin, but God will surely change their hearts and even their name, so that the nation shall forever after be a praise and a glory to Him. See Isaiah 60:21 and Jeremiah 31:33.

27:46 the daughters of Heth. Heth was the ancestor of the Hittites. Esau had married two of these girls (Gen. 26:34-35).

28:9 Mahalath. It is evident that Esau had more than one wife since this verse indicates he "took unto the wives which he had Mahalath." This one was added to the others. Esau had only three wives who bore him children (Gen. 36:2-5). Yet he had two wives named Bashemath (1) daughter of Elon the Hittite, the sister of Mahalath (Gen. 26:34); (2) the daughter of Ishmael (Gen 36:3).

pillows, and lay down in that place to
sleep.
12 And he dreamed, and behold a lad-
der set up on the earth, and the top of
it reached to heaven: and behold the
*angels of God ascending and descend-
ing on it.
13 And, behold, the LORD stood above
it, and said, I *am* the LORD God of Abraham thy father, and the God of Isaac: the
land whereon thou liest, to thee will I
give it, and to thy seed;
14 And thy seed shall be as the dust of
the earth, and thou shalt spread abroad
to the west, and to the east, and to the
north, and to the south: and in thee and
in thy seed shall all the families of the
earth be blessed.
15 And, behold, I *am* with thee, and
will keep thee in all *places* whither thou
goest, and will bring thee again into this
land; for I will not leave thee, until I
have done *that* which I have spoken to
thee of.
¶16 And Jacob awaked out of his sleep,
and he said, Surely the LORD is in this
place; and I knew *it* not.
17 And he was afraid, and said, How
dreadful *is* this place! this *is* none other
but the house of God, and this *is* the
gate of heaven.
18 And Jacob rose up early in the morning, and took the stone that he had put
for his pillows, and set it up *for* a pillar,
and poured oil upon the top of it.
19 And he called the name of that place
*Beth-el: but the name of that city *was
called* Luz at the first.
20 And Jacob vowed a vow, saying, If
God will be with me, and will keep me
in this way that I go, and will give me
bread to eat, and raiment to put on,
21 So that I come again to my father's
house in peace; then shall the LORD be
my God:
22 And this stone, which I have set *for*
a pillar, shall be God's house: and of all
that thou shalt give me I will surely give
the tenth unto thee.

29 Then Jacob went on his journey, and came into the land of
the people of the east.
2 And he looked, and behold a well in
the field, and, lo, there *were* three flocks
of sheep lying by it; for out of that well
they watered the flocks: and a great
stone *was* upon the well's mouth.
3 And thither were all the flocks gathered: and they rolled the stone from the
well's mouth, and watered the sheep,
and put the stone again upon the well's
mouth in his place.
4 And Jacob said unto them, My brethren, whence *be* ye? And they said, Of
Haran *are* we.
5 And he said unto them, Know ye
Laban the son of Nahor? And they said,
We know *him*.
6 And he said unto them, *Is* he well?
And they said, *He is* well: and, behold,
Rachel his daughter cometh with the
sheep.
7 And he said, Lo, *it is* yet high day,
neither *is it* time that the cattle should
be gathered together: water ye the
sheep, and go *and* feed *them*.
8 And they said, We cannot, until all
the flocks be gathered together, and *till*
they roll the stone from the well's
mouth; then we water the sheep.
¶9 And while he yet spake with them,
Rachel came with her father's sheep:
for she kept them.
10 And it came to pass, when Jacob
saw Rachel the daughter of Laban his
mother's brother, and the sheep of La-

28:14 in thy seed. God was telling Jacob that the promise He gave to Abraham of the Messiah's birth (see Gen. 12:3 note) will be in his line rather than in Esau's, where it naturally would have been.

28:20 If God. Jacob had faith in a far-off God who had made great promises, but he had no real intimate knowledge of that God. God had said (vss. 13-15), "I will," "I will," "I will," in blessing. Now Jacob says, "*If* God really will." Also, all of Jacob's ideas of blessing so far are of his own personal needs and wants.

ban his mother's brother, that Jacob
went near, and rolled the stone from the
well's mouth, and watered the flock of
Laban his mother's brother.

11And Jacob kissed Rachel, and lifted
up his voice, and wept.

12And Jacob told Rachel that he *was*
her father's brother, and that he *was*
Rebekah's son: and she ran and told her
father.

13And it came to pass, when Laban
heard the tidings of Jacob his sister's
son, that he ran to meet him, and embraced him, and kissed him, and
brought him to his house. And he told
Laban all these things.

14And Laban said to him, Surely thou
art my bone and my flesh. And he abode
with him the space of a month.

¶15And Laban said unto Jacob, Because thou *art* my brother, shouldest
thou therefore serve me for nought?
tell me, what *shall* thy wages *be?*

16And Laban had two daughters: the
name of the elder *was* Leah, and the
name of the younger *was* Rachel.

17Leah *was* tender eyed; but Rachel
was beautiful and well favoured.

18And Jacob loved Rachel; and said, I
will serve thee seven years for Rachel
thy younger daughter.

19And Laban said, *It is* better that I
give her to thee, than that I should give
her to another man: abide with me.

20And Jacob served seven years for
Rachel; and they seemed unto him
but a few days, for the love he had to
her.

¶21And Jacob said unto Laban, Give
me my wife, for my days are fulfilled,
that I may go in unto her.

22And Laban gathered together all
the men of the place, and made a feast.

23And it came to pass in the evening,
that he took Leah his daughter,
and brought her to him; and he went in
unto her.

24And Laban gave unto his daughter
Leah Zilpah his maid *for* an handmaid.

25And it came to pass, that in the
morning, behold, it *was* Leah: and he
said to Laban, What *is* this thou hast
done unto me? did not I serve with thee
for Rachel? wherefore then hast thou
beguiled me?

26And Laban said, It must not be so
done in our country, to give the younger before the firstborn.

27Fulfil her week, and we will give
thee this also for the service which thou
shalt serve with me yet seven other
years.

28And Jacob did so, and fulfilled her
week: and he gave him Rachel his
daughter to wife also.

29And Laban gave to Rachel his
daughter Bilhah his handmaid to be her
maid.

30And he went in also unto Rachel,
and he loved also Rachel more than
Leah, and served with him yet seven
other years.

¶31And when the LORD saw that Leah
was hated, he opened her womb: but
Rachel *was* barren.

32And Leah conceived, and bare a
son, and she called his name Reuben:
for she said, Surely the LORD hath
looked upon my affliction; now therefore my husband will love me.

29:32 Names of Jacob's Children

Jacob's children were all given names with meanings.
Reuben means *see, a son*.
Simeon means *hearing*.
Levi means *joined*.
Judah means *praise*.
Dan means *judging*.
Naphtali means *wrestling*.
Gad means *a troop*.
Asher means *happy*.
Issachar means *hire*.
Zebulun means *dwelling*.
Dinah means *judgment*.
Joseph means *adding*.

33And she conceived again, and bare
a son; and said, Because the LORD hath
heard that I *was* hated, he hath therefore given me this *son* also: and she
called his name Simeon.

34And she conceived again, and bare

a son; and said, Now this time will my
husband be joined unto me, because I
have born him three sons: therefore
was his name called Levi.
35 And she conceived again, and bare
a son: and she said, Now will I praise
the LORD: therefore she called his name
Judah; and left bearing.

30

And when Rachel saw that she
bare Jacob no children, Rachel
envied her sister; and said unto Jacob,
Give me children, or else I die.
2 And Jacob's anger was kindled
against Rachel: and he said, *Am* I in
God's stead, who hath withheld from
thee the fruit of the womb?
3 And she said, Behold my maid Bilhah, go in unto her; and she shall bear
upon my knees that I may also have
children by her.
4 And she gave him Bilhah her
handmaid to wife: and Jacob went in
unto her.
5 And Bilhah conceived, and bare Jacob a son.
6 And Rachel said, God hath judged
me, and hath also heard my voice, and
hath given me a son: therefore called
she his name Dan.
7 And Bilhah Rachel's maid conceived
again, and bare Jacob a second son.
8 And Rachel said, With great wres-
tlings have I wrestled with my sister,
and I have prevailed: and she called his
name Naphtali.
9 When Leah saw that she had left
bearing, she took Zilpah her maid, and
gave her Jacob to wife.
10 And Zilpah Leah's maid bare Jacob
a son.
11 And Leah said, A troop cometh: and
she called his name Gad.
12 And Zilpah Leah's maid bare Jacob
a second son.
13 And Leah said, Happy am I, for the
daughters will call me blessed: and she
called his name Asher.
¶ 14 And Reuben went in the days of
wheat harvest, and found mandrakes in
the field, and brought them unto his
mother Leah. Then Rachel said to Leah,
Give me, I pray thee, of thy son's mandrakes.
15 And she said unto her, *Is it* a small
matter that thou hast taken my husband? and wouldest thou take away my
son's mandrakes also? And Rachel said,
Therefore he shall lie with thee to night
for thy son's mandrakes.
16 And Jacob came out of the field in
the evening, and Leah went out to meet
him, and said, Thou must come in unto
me; for surely I have hired thee with my
son's mandrakes. And he lay with her
that night.
17 And God hearkened unto Leah, and
she conceived, and bare Jacob the fifth
son.
18 And Leah said, God hath given
me my hire, because I have given my
maiden to my husband: and she called
his name Issachar.
19 And Leah conceived again, and bare
Jacob the sixth son.
20 And Leah said, God hath endued
me *with* a good dowry; now will my
husband dwell with me, because I have
born him six sons: and she called his
name Zebulun.
21 And afterwards she bare a daughter, and called her name Dinah.
¶ 22 And God remembered Rachel,
and God hearkened to her, and opened
her womb.
23 And she conceived, and bare a son;
and said, God hath taken away my reproach:
24 And she called his name Joseph;
and said, The LORD shall add to me another son.
¶ 25 And it came to pass, when Rachel
had born Joseph, that Jacob said unto
Laban, Send me away, that I may go unto
mine own place, and to my country.
26 Give *me* my wives and my children,
for whom I have served thee, and let
me go: for thou knowest my service
which I have done thee.

30:20 endued. To endow, furnish with.

27 And Laban said unto him, I pray
thee, if I have found favour in thine
eyes, *tarry: for* I have learned by experience that the LORD hath blessed me
for thy sake.
28 And he said, Appoint me thy wages,
and I will give *it.*
29 And he said unto him, Thou
knowest how I have served thee, and
how thy cattle was with me.

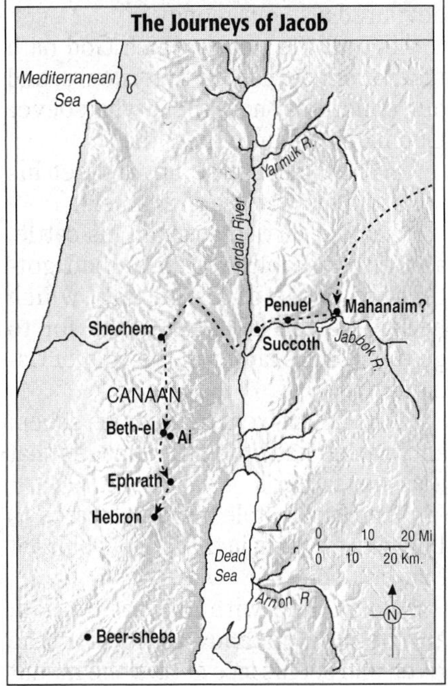

The Journeys of Jacob

30 For *it was* little which thou hadst
before I *came,* and it is *now* increased
unto a multitude; and the LORD hath
blessed thee since my coming: and now
when shall I provide for mine own
house also?
31 And he said, What shall I give thee?
And Jacob said, Thou shalt not give me
any thing: if thou wilt do this thing for
me, I will again feed *and* keep thy flock.
32 I will pass through all thy flock to
day, removing from thence all the
speckled and spotted cattle, and all the
brown cattle among the sheep, and
the spotted and speckled among the
goats: and *of such* shall be my hire.
33 So shall my *righteousness answer
for me in time to come, when it shall
come for my hire before thy face: every
one that *is* not speckled and spotted
among the goats, and brown among
the sheep, that shall be counted stolen
with me.
34 And Laban said, Behold, I would it
might be according to thy word.
35 And he removed that day the he
goats that were ringstraked and spotted, and all the she goats that were
speckled and spotted, *and* every one
that had *some* white in it, and all the
brown among the sheep, and gave *them*
into the hand of his sons.
36 And he set three days' journey betwixt himself and Jacob: and Jacob fed
the rest of Laban's flocks.
¶37 And Jacob took him rods of green
poplar, and of the hazel and chesnut
tree; and pilled white strakes in them,
and made the white appear which *was*
in the rods.
38 And he set the rods which he had
pilled before the flocks in the gutters in
the watering troughs when the flocks
came to drink, that they should conceive when they came to drink.
39 And the flocks conceived before the
rods, and brought forth cattle ringstraked, speckled, and spotted.
40 And Jacob did separate the lambs,
and set the faces of the flocks toward
the ringstraked, and all the brown in the
flock of Laban; and he put his own
flocks by themselves, and put them not
unto Laban's cattle.
41 And it came to pass, whensoever
the stronger cattle did conceive, that
Jacob laid the rods before the eyes of
the cattle in the gutters, that they might
conceive among the rods.
42 But when the cattle were feeble, he

30:35 ringstraked. Streaked with rings.
30:37 strake. A streak.
30:37-38 pilled. To strip off the bark, to peel.

put *them* not in: so the feebler were
Laban's, and the stronger Jacob's.
43And the man increased exceedingly, and had much cattle, and maidservants, and menservants, and camels,
and asses.

31 And he heard the words of
Laban's sons, saying, Jacob hath
taken away all that *was* our father's; and
of *that* which *was* our father's hath he
gotten all this glory.
2And Jacob beheld the countenance
of Laban, and, behold, it *was* not toward
him as before.
3And the LORD said unto Jacob, Return unto the land of thy fathers, and to
thy kindred; and I will be with thee.
4And Jacob sent and called Rachel
and Leah to the field unto his flock,
5And said unto them, I see your
father's countenance, that it *is* not toward me as before; but the God of my
father hath been with me.
6And ye know that with all my power
I have served your father.
7And your father hath deceived
me, and changed my wages ten times;
but God suffered him not to hurt me.
8If he said thus, The speckled shall
be thy wages; then all the cattle bare
speckled: and if he said thus, The
ringstraked shall be thy hire; then bare
all the cattle ringstraked.
9Thus God hath taken away the cattle of your father, and given *them* to me.
10And it came to pass at the time that
the cattle conceived, that I lifted up
mine eyes, and saw in a dream, and,
behold, the rams which leaped upon the
cattle *were* ringstraked, speckled, and
grisled.
11And the *angel of God spake unto
me in a dream, *saying,* Jacob: And I said,
Here *am* I.
12And he said, Lift up now thine eyes,
and see, all the rams which leap upon
the cattle *are* ringstraked, speckled, and
grisled: for I have seen all that Laban
doeth unto thee.
13I *am* the God of Beth-el, where thou
anointedst the pillar, *and* where thou
vowedst a vow unto me: now arise, get
thee out from this land, and return unto
the land of thy kindred.
14And Rachel and Leah answered and
said unto him, *Is there* yet any portion
or inheritance for us in our father's
house?
15Are we not counted of him strangers? for he hath sold us, and hath quite
devoured also our money.
16For all the riches which God hath
taken from our father, that *is* ours, and
our children's: now then, whatsoever
God hath said unto thee, do.
¶17Then Jacob rose up, and set his
sons and his wives upon camels;
18And he carried away all his cattle,
and all his goods which he had gotten, the cattle of his getting, which
he had gotten in Padan-aram, for to
go to Isaac his father in the land of Canaan.
19And Laban went to shear his sheep:
and Rachel had stolen the images that
were her father's.
20And Jacob stole away unawares to
Laban the Syrian, in that he told him not
that he fled.
21So he fled with all that he had;
and he rose up, and passed over the
river, and set his face *toward* the mount
*Gilead.
22And it was told Laban on the third
day that Jacob was fled.
23And he took his brethren with him,
and pursued after him seven days' journey; and they overtook him in the
mount Gilead.
24And God came to Laban the Syrian
in a dream by night, and said unto him,
Take heed that thou speak not to Jacob
either good or bad.
¶25Then Laban overtook Jacob. Now
Jacob had pitched his tent in the mount:
and Laban with his brethren pitched in
the mount of Gilead.
26And Laban said to Jacob, What hast

31:10 grisled. Of a gray color, or mixed with gray.

thou done, that thou hast stolen away
unawares to me, and carried away my
daughters, as captives *taken* with the
sword?
27 Wherefore didst thou flee away secretly, and steal away from me; and
didst not tell me, that I might have sent
thee away with mirth, and with songs,
with tabret, and with harp?
28 And hast not suffered me to kiss my
sons and my daughters? thou hast now
done foolishly in *so* doing.
29 It is in the power of my hand to do
you hurt: but the God of your father
spake unto me yesternight, saying,
Take thou heed that thou speak not to
Jacob either good or bad.
30 And now, *though* thou wouldest
needs be gone, because thou sore
longedst after thy father's house, *yet*
wherefore hast thou stolen my gods?
31 And Jacob answered and said to
Laban, Because I was afraid: for I said,
Peradventure thou wouldest take by
force thy daughters from me.
32 With whomsoever thou findest thy
gods, let him not live: before our brethren discern thou what *is* thine with me,
and take *it* to thee. For Jacob knew not
that Rachel had stolen them.
33 And Laban went into Jacob's tent,
and into Leah's tent, and into the two
maidservants' tents; but he found *them*
not. Then went he out of Leah's tent,
and entered into Rachel's tent.
34 Now Rachel had taken the images,
and put them in the camel's furniture,
and sat upon them. And Laban searched
all the tent, but found *them* not.
35 And she said to her father, Let it not
displease my lord that I cannot rise up
before thee; for the custom of women
is upon me. And he searched, but found
not the images.
¶ 36 And Jacob was wroth, and chode
with Laban: and Jacob answered and
said to Laban, What *is* my trespass?
what *is* my sin, that thou hast so hotly
pursued after me?
37 Whereas thou hast searched all
my stuff, what hast thou found of all thy
household stuff? set *it* here before my
brethren and thy brethren, that they
may judge betwixt us both.
38 This twenty years *have* I *been* with
thee; thy ewes and thy she goats have
not cast their young, and the rams of
thy flock have I not eaten.
39 That which was torn *of beasts* I
brought not unto thee; I bare the loss
of it; of my hand didst thou require it,
whether stolen by day, or stolen by
night.
40 *Thus* I was; in the day the drought
consumed me, and the frost by night;
and my sleep departed from mine eyes.
41 Thus have I been twenty years in
thy house; I served thee fourteen years
for thy two daughters, and six years for
thy cattle: and thou hast changed my
wages ten times.
42 Except the God of my father, the
God of Abraham, and the fear of Isaac,
had been with me, surely thou hadst
sent me away now empty. God hath
seen mine affliction and the labour of
my hands, and rebuked *thee* yesternight.
¶ 43 And Laban answered and said
unto Jacob, *These* daughters *are* my
daughters, and *these* children *are* my
children, and *these* cattle *are* my cattle,
and all that thou seest *is* mine: and what
can I do this day unto these my daughters, or unto their children which they
have born?
44 Now therefore come thou, let us
make a *covenant, I and thou; and let
it be for a witness between me and
thee.

31:27 tabret. A small drum or tambourine.
31:31 Peradventure. Perhaps.
31:34 furniture. Harness.
31:36 wroth. Intensely angry.
31:36 chode. Disputed.

45 And Jacob took a stone, and set it up *for* a pillar.

46 And Jacob said unto his brethren, Gather stones; and they took stones, and made an heap: and they did eat there upon the heap.

47 And Laban called it Jegar-sahadutha: but Jacob called it Galeed.

48 And Laban said, This heap *is* a witness between me and thee this day. Therefore was the name of it called Galeed;

49 And Mizpah; for he said, The LORD watch between me and thee, when we are absent one from another.

50 If thou shalt afflict my daughters, or if thou shalt take *other* wives beside my daughters, no man *is* with us; see, God *is* witness betwixt me and thee.

51 And Laban said to Jacob, Behold this heap, and behold *this* pillar, which I have cast betwixt me and thee;

52 This heap *be* witness, and *this* pillar *be* witness, that I will not pass over this heap to thee, and that thou shalt not pass over this heap and this pillar unto me, for harm.

53 The God of Abraham, and the God of Nahor, the God of their father, judge betwixt us. And Jacob sware by the fear of his father Isaac.

54 Then Jacob offered *sacrifice upon the mount, and called his brethren to eat bread: and they did eat bread, and tarried all night in the mount.

55 And early in the morning Laban rose up, and kissed his sons and his daughters, and blessed them: and Laban departed, and returned unto his place.

32

And Jacob went on his way, and the *angels of God met him.

2 And when Jacob saw them, he said, This *is* God's host: and he called the name of that place Mahanaim.

3 And Jacob sent messengers before him to Esau his brother unto the land of Seir, the country of Edom.

4 And he commanded them, saying, Thus shall ye speak unto my lord Esau; Thy servant Jacob saith thus, I have sojourned with Laban, and stayed there until now:

5 And I have oxen, and asses, flocks, and menservants, and womenservants: and I have sent to tell my lord, that I may find grace in thy sight.

¶ 6 And the messengers returned to Jacob, saying, We came to thy brother Esau, and also he cometh to meet thee, and four hundred men with him.

7 Then Jacob was greatly afraid and distressed: and he divided the people that *was* with him, and the flocks, and herds, and the camels, into two bands;

8 And said, If Esau come to the one company, and smite it, then the other company which is left shall escape.

¶ 9 And Jacob said, O God of my father Abraham, and God of my father Isaac, the LORD which saidst unto me, Return unto thy country, and to thy kindred, and I will deal well with thee:

10 I am not worthy of the least of all the mercies, and of all the truth, which thou hast shewed unto thy servant; for with my staff I passed over this Jordan; and now I am become two bands.

11 Deliver me, I pray thee, from the hand of my brother, from the hand of Esau: for I fear him, lest he will come and smite me, *and* the mother with the children.

12 And thou saidst, I will surely do thee good, and make thy seed as the sand of the sea, which cannot be numbered for multitude.

¶ 13 And he lodged there that same night; and took of that which came to his hand a present for Esau his brother;

14 Two hundred she goats, and twenty

31:47 Jegar-sahadutha. This means *the heap of witness* in the Chaldean language. *Galeed* means the same thing in Hebrew.

31:49 Mizpah. This word means *beacon,* that is, a kind of watchtower or lookout tower.

32:2 Mahanaim. The word means *two hosts* or *bands*. One was the band that could be seen—Jacob and his servants; the other band could not be seen—God's angels.

he goats, two hundred ewes, and
twenty rams,
15 Thirty milch camels with their
colts, forty kine, and ten bulls, twenty
she asses, and ten foals.
16 And he delivered *them* into the
hand of his servants, every drove by
themselves; and said unto his servants,
Pass over before me, and put a space
betwixt drove and drove.
17 And he commanded the foremost,
saying, When Esau my brother meeteth
thee, and asketh thee, saying, Whose
art thou? and whither goest thou? and
whose *are* these before thee?
18 Then thou shalt say, *They be* thy
servant Jacob's; it *is* a present sent unto
my lord Esau: and, behold, also he *is*
behind us.
19 And so commanded he the second,
and the third, and all that followed the
droves, saying, On this manner shall ye
speak unto Esau, when ye find him.
20 And say ye moreover, Behold, thy
servant Jacob *is* behind us. For he said,
I will appease him with the present that
goeth before me, and afterward I will
see his face; peradventure he will accept of me.
21 So went the present over before
him: and himself lodged that night in
the company.
22 And he rose up that night, and took
his *two wives, and his two womenservants, and his eleven sons, and
passed over the ford Jabbok.
23 And he took them, and sent them
over the brook, and sent over that he
had.

Jacob becomes Israel

¶24 And Jacob was left alone; and
there wrestled a man with him until the
breaking of the day.
25 And when he saw that he prevailed
not against him, he touched the hollow
of his thigh; and the hollow of Jacob's
thigh was out of joint, as he wrestled
with him.
26 And he said, Let me go, for the day
breaketh. And he said, I will not let thee
go, except thou bless me.
27 And he said unto him, What *is* thy
name? And he said, Jacob.
28 And he said, Thy name shall be
called no more Jacob, but Israel: for as
a prince hast thou power with God and
with men, and hast prevailed.
29 And Jacob asked *him,* and said, Tell
me, I pray thee, thy name. And he
said, Wherefore *is* it *that* thou dost
ask after my name? And he blessed him
there.
30 And Jacob called the name of the
place Peniel: for I have seen God face
to face, and my life is preserved.

32:25 GOD'S TOUCH ON JACOB

God had been working with Jacob all these years. He wanted Jacob to be humble and to depend on Him, for only when Jacob depended on God could he be of any use to God or have any power or real blessing from God. Now God put His final touch on His work in Jacob by bringing what seems like a terrible trouble into his life. He made Jacob crippled! Because Jacob had been stubborn and had always wanted his own way, God knew that there was no other way to bring him to his knees. God had already given Jacob wonderful blessings–riches in cattle and sheep–but Jacob did not really begin to trust God as he should have done until God crippled him. The lameness actually turned out to be a blessing!

32:15 milch. Giving milk.

32:28 no more Jacob, but Israel. No man has spiritual power for God until he knows himself to be utterly weak, and finds God to be all powerful. Jacob, the "supplanter," became Israel, "a prince with God."

32:30 Peniel. Peniel means *the face of God*. God is a Spirit and cannot be seen by mortal eyes (John 1:18), but when He wanted to appear, at various times He took a body so that He might be seen. God, in angelic form, and in the person of Jesus Christ has been seen by human beings. This was a *theophany; see Genesis 35:9 note.

31 And as he passed over Penuel the sun rose upon him, and he halted upon his thigh.

32 Therefore the children of Israel eat not *of* the sinew which shrank, which *is* upon the hollow of the thigh, unto this day: because he touched the hollow of Jacob's thigh in the sinew that shrank.

Jacob meets Esau

33 And Jacob lifted up his eyes, and looked, and, behold, Esau came, and with him four hundred men. And he divided the children unto Leah, and unto Rachel, and unto the two handmaids.

2 And he put the handmaids and their children foremost, and Leah and her children after, and Rachel and Joseph hindermost.

3 And he passed over before them, and bowed himself to the ground seven times, until he came near to his brother.

4 And Esau ran to meet him, and embraced him, and fell on his neck, and kissed him: and they wept.

5 And he lifted up his eyes, and saw the women and the children; and said, Who *are* those with thee? And he said, The children which God hath graciously given thy servant.

6 Then the handmaidens came near, they and their children, and they bowed themselves.

7 And Leah also with her children came near, and bowed themselves: and after came Joseph near and Rachel, and they bowed themselves.

8 And he said, What *meanest* thou by all this drove which I met? And he said, *These are* to find grace in the sight of my lord.

9 And Esau said, I have enough, my brother; keep that thou hast unto thyself.

10 And Jacob said, Nay, I pray thee, if now I have found grace in thy sight, then receive my present at my hand: for therefore I have seen thy face, as though I had seen the face of God, and thou wast pleased with me.

11 Take, I pray thee, my blessing that is brought to thee; because God hath dealt graciously with me, and because I have enough. And he urged him, and he took *it*.

12 And he said, Let us take our journey, and let us go, and I will go before thee.

13 And he said unto him, My lord knoweth that the children *are* tender, and the flocks and herds with young *are* with me: and if men should overdrive them one day, all the flock will die.

14 Let my lord, I pray thee, pass over before his servant: and I will lead on softly, according as the cattle that goeth before me and the children be able to endure, until I come unto my lord unto *Seir.

15 And Esau said, Let me now leave with thee *some* of the folk that *are* with me. And he said, What needeth it? let me find grace in the sight of my lord.

¶ 16 So Esau returned that day on his way unto Seir.

17 And Jacob journeyed to Succoth, and built him an house, and made booths for his cattle: therefore the name of the place is called Succoth.

¶ 18 And Jacob came to Shalem, a city of *Shechem, which *is* in the land of Canaan, when he came from Padan-aram; and pitched his tent before the city.

19 And he bought a parcel of a field, where he had spread his tent, at the

---

33:17 Succoth. The name means *booths* or *branches*.

33:19 he bought. This is the same field that Abraham had bought more than eighty years before. But in the meantime, while Jacob was out of the land, the former owners had taken it back, and rather than quarrel over it, Jacob bought it over again. This shows the change in Jacob.

hand of the children of Hamor, Shechem's father, for an hundred pieces of
money.
20 And he erected there an *altar, and
called it El-elohe-Israel.

34 And Dinah the daughter of
Leah, which she bare unto Jacob, went out to see the daughters of
the land.
2 And when Shechem the son of Hamor the Hivite, prince of the country,
saw her, he took her, and lay with her,
and defiled her.
3 And his soul clave unto Dinah the
daughter of Jacob, and he loved
the damsel, and spake kindly unto the
damsel.
4 And Shechem spake unto his father
Hamor, saying, Get me this damsel to
wife.
5 And Jacob heard that he had defiled
Dinah his daughter: now his sons were
with his cattle in the field: and Jacob
held his peace until they were come.
¶6 And Hamor the father of Shechem
went out unto Jacob to commune with
him.
7 And the sons of Jacob came out of
the field when they heard *it:* and the
men were grieved, and they were very
wroth, because he had wrought folly in
Israel in lying with Jacob's daughter;
which thing ought not to be done.
8 And Hamor communed with them,
saying, The soul of my son Shechem
longeth for your daughter: I pray you
give her him to wife.
9 And make ye marriages with us, *and*
give your daughters unto us, and take
our daughters unto you.
10 And ye shall dwell with us: and the
land shall be before you; dwell and trade
ye therein, and get you possessions
therein.
11 And Shechem said unto her father
and unto her brethren, Let me find
grace in your eyes, and what ye shall
say unto me I will give.
12 Ask me never so much dowry and
gift, and I will give according as ye shall
say unto me: but give me the damsel to
wife.
13 And the sons of Jacob answered
Shechem and Hamor his father deceitfully, and said, because he had defiled
Dinah their sister:
14 And they said unto them, We cannot do this thing, to give our sister
to one that is uncircumcised; for that
were a reproach unto us:
15 But in this will we consent unto
you: If ye will be as we *be,* that every
male of you be *circumcised;
16 Then will we give our daughters
unto you, and we will take your daughters to us, and we will dwell with you,
and we will become one people.
17 But if ye will not hearken unto us,
to be circumcised; then will we take our
daughter, and we will be gone.
18 And their words pleased Hamor,
and Shechem Hamor's son.
19 And the young man deferred not to
do the thing, because he had delight in
Jacob's daughter: and he *was* more
honourable than all the house of his father.
¶20 And Hamor and Shechem his son
came unto the gate of their city, and
communed with the men of their city,
saying,
21 These men *are* peaceable with
us; therefore let them dwell in the land,
and trade therein; for the land,
behold, *it is* large enough for them;
let us take their daughters to us for
wives, and let us give them our daughters.
22 Only herein will the men consent
unto us for to dwell with us, to be one
people, if every male among us be circumcised, as they *are* circumcised.
23 *Shall* not their cattle and their substance and every beast of theirs *be*
ours? only let us consent unto them,
and they will dwell with us.

33:19 parcel. A piece, portion.
33:20 El-elohe-Israel. This means *God, the God of Israel.*

24 And unto Hamor and unto Shechem
his son hearkened all that went out of
the gate of his city; and every male was
circumcised, all that went out of the
gate of his city.
¶ 25 And it came to pass on the third
day, when they were sore, that two of
the sons of Jacob, Simeon and Levi,
Dinah's brethren, took each man his
sword, and came upon the city boldly,
and slew all the males.
26 And they slew Hamor and Shechem
his son with the edge of the
sword, and took Dinah out of Shechem's
house, and went out.
27 The sons of Jacob came upon the
slain, and spoiled the city, because they
had defiled their sister.
28 They took their sheep, and their
oxen, and their asses, and that which
was in the city, and that which *was* in
the field,
29 And all their wealth, and all their
little ones, and their wives took they
captive, and spoiled even all that *was* in
the house.
30 And Jacob said to Simeon and Levi,
Ye have troubled me to make me to
stink among the inhabitants of the land,
among the Canaanites and the Perizzites:
and I *being* few in number, they
shall gather themselves together
against me, and slay me; and I shall be
destroyed, I and my house.
31 And they said, Should he deal with
our sister as with an harlot?

Jacob returns to Beth-el

35 And God said unto Jacob,
Arise, go up to Beth-el, and
dwell there: and make there an altar
unto God, that appeared unto thee
when thou fleddest from the face of
Esau thy brother.
2 Then Jacob said unto his household,
and to all that *were* with him, Put away
the strange gods that *are* among you,
and be clean, and change your garments:
3 And let us arise, and go up to Beth-el;
and I will make there an altar unto
God, who answered me in the day of my
distress, and was with me in the way
which I went.
4 And they gave unto Jacob all the
strange gods which *were* in their hand,
and *all their* earrings which *were* in their
ears; and Jacob hid them under the oak
which *was* by Shechem.
5 And they journeyed: and the terror
of God was upon the cities that *were*
round about them, and they did not pursue
after the sons of Jacob.
¶ 6 So Jacob came to Luz, which *is* in
the land of Canaan, that *is*, Beth-el, he
and all the people that *were* with him.
7 And he built there an altar, and called
the place El-beth-el: because there God
appeared unto him, when he fled from
the face of his brother.
8 But Deborah Rebekah's nurse died,
and she was buried beneath Beth-el
under an oak: and the name of it was
called Allon-bachuth.
¶ 9 And God appeared unto Jacob
again, when he came out of Padan-aram,
and blessed him.
10 And God said unto him, Thy name
is Jacob: thy name shall not be called any
more Jacob, but Israel shall be thy name:
and he called his name Israel.
11 And God said unto him, I *am* God

35:1 Beth-el. Jacob had gone from the house of God when he left the land of blessing (see Gen. 12:8 note). God often sends His disobedient children back to the place where they started on the wrong path.

35:7 El-beth-el. It is not the place, but the God of the place whom Jacob worships. *El-Beth-el* is "the God, the house of God."

35:8 Allon-bachuth. The name means *the oak of weeping*.

35:9 God appeared. Jacob had at last confessed all of his sin and had made his family do the same thing. Now there was nothing to keep him from having fellowship with God. God came near to him and talked with him as a friend to a friend. This was a *theophany; see verse 9 note, "Theophany," on next page.

35:9 Theophany
The appearances that God Himself made as He came to men as the divine messenger are called theophanies. Often God appeared as "the angel of the LORD." There are about a dozen such occurrences throughout the Old Testament.

Almighty: be fruitful and multiply; a
nation and a company of nations shall be
of thee, and kings shall come out of thy
loins;
12And the land which I gave Abraham
and Isaac, to thee I will give it, and to
thy seed after thee will I give the land.
13And God went up from him in the
place where he talked with him.
14And Jacob set up a pillar in the
place where he talked with him, *even*
a pillar of stone: and he poured a
drink-offering thereon, and he poured
oil thereon.

35:14 The Drink-Offering
The drink-offering was always an offering poured out to the LORD. It was never drunk. Numbers 15:5-7 gives some instructions for the drink offering. It is a *type of the Lord Jesus Christ who "poured out his soul unto death" as a sacrifice for sinful man. (Read Ps. 22:14; Isa. 53:12.)

15And Jacob called the name of the
place where God spake with him, Beth-
el.
¶16And they journeyed from Beth-el;
and there was but a little way to come
to Ephrath: and Rachel travailed, and
she had hard labour.
17And it came to pass, when she was
in hard labour, that the midwife said
unto her, Fear not; thou shalt have this
son also.
18And it came to pass, as her soul was
in departing, (for she died) that she
called his name Ben-oni: but his father
called him Benjamin.

Rachel dies

19And Rachel died, and was buried in
the way to Ephrath, which *is* Beth-lehem.
20And Jacob set a pillar upon her
grave: that *is* the pillar of Rachel's
grave unto this day.
¶21And Israel journeyed, and spread
his tent beyond the tower of Edar.
22And it came to pass, when Israel
dwelt in that land, that Reuben went
and lay with Bilhah his father's concubine: and Israel heard *it*. Now the sons
of Jacob were twelve:
23The sons of Leah; Reuben, Jacob's
firstborn, and Simeon, and Levi, and
Judah, and Issachar, and Zebulun:
24The sons of Rachel; Joseph, and
Benjamin:
25And the sons of Bilhah, Rachel's
handmaid; Dan, and Naphtali:
26And the sons of Zilpah, Leah's
handmaid; Gad, and Asher: these *are*
the sons of Jacob, which were born to
him in Padan-aram.
¶27And Jacob came unto Isaac his father unto Mamre, unto the city of
Arbah, which *is* Hebron, where Abraham and Isaac sojourned.
28And the days of Isaac were an hundred and fourscore years.

Isaac dies

29And Isaac gave up the ghost, and
died, and was gathered unto his people,
being old and full of days: and his sons
Esau and Jacob buried him.

36 Now these *are* the generations
of Esau, who *is* *Edom.

35:11 God Almighty. This is *El Shaddai*. See Genesis 17:1 note. See also *names of God.

35:18 Ben-oni. Rachel called her baby Ben-oni, "son of sorrow," but Jacob called him Benjamin, "son of my right hand." As a *type of the Lord Jesus Christ, he was both.

36:1 generations of Esau. It is interesting to notice that one of Esau's descendants was Amalek, whose tribe kept making trouble for the nation of Israel just as Esau had troubled Jacob.

2 Esau took his wives of the daughters of Canaan; Adah the daughter of Elon the Hittite, and Aholibamah the daughter of Anah the daughter of Zibeon the Hivite;

3 And Bashemath Ishmael's daughter, sister of Nebajoth.

4 And Adah bare to Esau Eliphaz; and Bashemath bare Reuel;

5 And Aholibamah bare Jeush, and Jaalam, and Korah: these *are* the sons of Esau, which were born unto him in the land of Canaan.

6 And Esau took his wives, and his sons, and his daughters, and all the persons of his house, and his cattle, and all his beasts, and all his substance, which he had got in the land of Canaan; and went into the country from the face of his brother Jacob.

7 For their riches were more than that they might dwell together; and the land wherein they were strangers could not bear them because of their cattle.

8 Thus dwelt Esau in mount Seir: Esau *is* Edom.

¶ 9 And these *are* the generations of Esau the father of the Edomites in mount Seir:

10 These *are* the names of Esau's sons; Eliphaz the son of Adah the wife of Esau, Reuel the son of Bashemath the wife of Esau.

11 And the sons of Eliphaz were Teman, Omar, Zepho, and Gatam, and Kenaz.

12 And Timna was concubine to Eliphaz Esau's son; and she bare to Eliphaz Amalek: these *were* the sons of Adah Esau's wife.

13 And these *are* the sons of Reuel; Nahath, and Zerah, Shammah, and Mizzah: these were the sons of Bashemath Esau's wife.

¶ 14 And these were the sons of Aholibamah, the daughter of Anah the daughter of Zibeon, Esau's wife: and she bare to Esau Jeush, and Jaalam, and Korah.

¶ 15 These *were* dukes of the sons of Esau: the sons of Eliphaz the firstborn *son* of Esau; duke Teman, duke Omar, duke Zepho, duke Kenaz,

16 Duke Korah, duke Gatam, *and* duke Amalek: these *are* the dukes *that came* of Eliphaz in the land of Edom; these *were* the sons of Adah.

¶ 17 And these *are* the sons of Reuel Esau's son; duke Nahath, duke Zerah, duke Shammah, duke Mizzah: these *are* the dukes *that came* of Reuel in the land of Edom; these *are* the sons of Bashemath Esau's wife.

¶ 18 And these *are* the sons of Aholibamah Esau's wife; duke Jeush, duke Jaalam, duke Korah: these *were* the dukes *that came* of Aholibamah the daughter of Anah, Esau's wife.

19 These *are* the sons of Esau, who *is* Edom, and these *are* their dukes.

¶ 20 These *are* the sons of Seir the Horite, who inhabited the land; Lotan, and Shobal, and Zibeon, and Anah,

21 And Dishon, and Ezer, and Dishan: these *are* the dukes of the Horites, the children of Seir in the land of Edom.

22 And the children of Lotan were Hori and Hemam; and Lotan's sister *was* Timna.

23 And the children of Shobal *were* these; Alvan, and Manahath, and Ebal, Shepho, and Onam.

24 And these *are* the children of Zibeon; both Ajah, and Anah: this *was that* Anah that found the mules in the wilderness, as he fed the asses of Zibeon his father.

25 And the children of Anah *were* these; Dishon, and Aholibamah the daughter of Anah.

26 And these *are* the children of Dishon; Hemdan, and Eshban, and Ithran, and Cheran.

27 The children of Ezer *are* these; Bilhan, and Zaavan, and Akan.

28 The children of Dishan *are* these: Uz, and Aran.

29 These *are* the dukes *that came* of the Horites; duke Lotan, duke Shobal, duke Zibeon, duke Anah,

---

36:15 dukes. These were chiefs of thousands.

30Duke Dishon, duke Ezer, duke Dishan: these *are* the dukes *that came* of
Hori, among their dukes in the land of
Seir.
¶31And these *are* the kings that
reigned in the land of Edom, before
there reigned any king over the children
of Israel.
32And Bela the son of Beor reigned
in Edom: and the name of his city *was*
Dinhabah.
33And Bela died, and Jobab the son
of Zerah of Bozrah reigned in his
stead.
34And Jobab died, and Husham of the
land of Temani reigned in his stead.
35And Husham died, and Hadad the
son of Bedad, who smote Midian in the
field of Moab, reigned in his stead: and
the name of his city *was* Avith.
36And Hadad died, and Samlah of
Masrekah reigned in his stead.
37And Samlah died, and Saul of Rehoboth *by* the river reigned in his stead.
38And Saul died, and Baal-hanan the
son of Achbor reigned in his stead.
39And Baal-hanan the son of Achbor
died, and Hadar reigned in his stead:
and the name of his city *was* Pau; and
his wife's name *was* Mehetabel, the
daughter of Matred, the daughter of
Mezahab.
40And these *are* the names of the
dukes *that came* of Esau, according to
their families, after their places, by
their names; duke Timnah, duke Alvah,
duke Jetheth,
41Duke Aholibamah, duke Elah, duke
Pinon,
42Duke Kenaz, duke Teman, duke
Mibzar,
43Duke Magdiel, duke Iram: these *be*
the dukes of Edom, according to their
habitations in the land of their possession: he *is* Esau the father of the
Edomites.

37 And Jacob dwelt in the land
wherein his father was a
stranger, in the land of Canaan.
2These *are* the generations of Jacob.
Joseph, *being* seventeen years old, was
feeding the flock with his brethren; and
the lad *was* with the sons of Bilhah, and
with the sons of Zilpah, his father's
wives: and Joseph brought unto his father their evil report.

37:2 JOSEPH: A TYPE OF CHRIST

The life of Joseph is one of the clearest of all *types of the Lord Jesus Christ. As you read the story, keep in mind these main points of likeness: Like the Lord Jesus Christ, Joseph

1. was his father's beloved son (Gen. 37:3; John 5:20);
2. was hated and rejected by his brothers so that they planned to kill him (Gen. 37:4; John 15:25);
3. saved the people of Egypt (Gen. 41:33-45; Acts 7:14). The Lord Jesus came to save the world and there He found His bride (Eph. 5:25-32—see the Eph. 5:25-32 note, which tells of the church, the bride of the Lord Jesus Christ);
4. saved his brothers (Israelites) and then revealed his identity to them (Gen. 45:1-9; Hos. 2:14-18);
5. was a ruler, and exalted his brethren (Gen. 47:5-12). The Lord Jesus will rule the whole world when He comes to earth again (Rev. 19:11-16) and will make Israel the chief nation of the world (Isa. 2:1-5).

36:31 before there reigned any king over the children of Israel. God Himself reigned over Israel, and He had promised to send His own Son someday to be their King. We read later on, however, that Israel rejected God as King and wanted a king like the other nations around them. (See 1 Sam. 8 and 9.) Edom was one of these nations.

37:1 stranger. The people of the land God gave Abraham never called him or Isaac anything but foreigners. They did not know that God had promised the land to Abraham and Isaac. Besides, Abraham had had a vision of a heavenly city, and he had his eyes on that. As a sign that he was not expecting anything from earth during his lifetime, he lived in a tent all his life and taught Isaac and Jacob to do so (read Heb. 11:9-10). Someday, however, he will enjoy the very land God promised (Gen. 12:1-3).

Joseph, his father's beloved son

3 Now Israel loved Joseph more than all his children, because he *was* the son of his old age: and he made him a coat of *many* colours.

4 And when his brethren saw that their father loved him more than all his brethren, they hated him, and could not speak peaceably unto him.

¶ 5 And Joseph dreamed a dream, and he told *it* his brethren: and they hated him yet the more.

6 And he said unto them, Hear, I pray you, this dream which I have dreamed:

7 For, behold, we *were* binding sheaves in the field, and, lo, my sheaf arose, and also stood upright; and, behold, your sheaves stood round about, and made obeisance to my sheaf.

Joseph hated by his brothers

8 And his brethren said to him, Shalt thou indeed reign over us? or shalt thou indeed have dominion over us? And they hated him yet the more for his dreams, and for his words.

¶ 9 And he dreamed yet another dream, and told it his brethren, and said, Behold, I have dreamed a dream more; and, behold, the sun and the moon and the eleven stars made obeisance to me.

10 And he told *it* to his father, and to his brethren: and his father rebuked him, and said unto him, What *is* this dream that thou hast dreamed? Shall I and thy mother and thy brethren indeed come to bow down ourselves to thee to the earth?

11 And his brethren envied him; but his father observed the saying.

¶ 12 And his brethren went to feed their father's flock in Shechem.

13 And Israel said unto Joseph, Do not thy brethren feed *the flock* in Shechem? come, and I will send thee unto them. And he said to him, Here *am I.*

14 And he said to him, Go, I pray thee, see whether it be well with thy brethren, and well with the flocks; and bring me word again. So he sent him out of the vale of Hebron, and he came to Shechem.

¶ 15 And a certain man found him, and, behold, *he was* wandering in the field: and the man asked him, saying, What seekest thou?

16 And he said, I seek my brethren: tell me, I pray thee, where they feed *their flocks.*

17 And the man said, They are departed hence; for I heard them say, Let us go to Dothan. And Joseph went after his brethren, and found them in Dothan.

18 And when they saw him afar off, even before he came near unto them, they conspired against him to slay him.

19 And they said one to another, Behold, this dreamer cometh.

Joseph cast into the pit

20 Come now therefore, and let us slay him, and cast him into some pit, and we will say, Some evil beast hath devoured him: and we shall see what will become of his dreams.

21 And Reuben heard *it,* and he delivered him out of their hands; and said, Let us not kill him.

22 And Reuben said unto them, Shed no blood, *but* cast him into this pit that *is* in the wilderness, and lay no hand upon him; that he might rid him out of their hands, to deliver him to his father again.

¶ 23 And it came to pass, when Joseph was come unto his brethren, that they stript Joseph out of his coat, *his* coat of *many* colours that *was* on him;

24 And they took him, and cast him into a pit: and the pit *was* empty, *there was* no water in it.

25 And they sat down to eat bread: and they lifted up their eyes and looked,

---

37:7 obeisance. An outward act of homage and respect.

37:25 Ishmeelites. These were descendants of Ishmael, the son of Abraham. Joseph and his brothers were descendants of Isaac, the son of Abraham.

and, behold, a company of Ishmeelites
came from Gilead with their camels
bearing spicery and balm and myrrh,
going to carry *it* down to Egypt.
26 And Judah said unto his brethren,
What profit *is it* if we slay our brother,
and conceal his blood?
27 Come, and let us sell him to the
Ishmeelites, and let not our hand be
upon him; for he *is* our brother *and* our
flesh. And his brethren were content.

Joseph drawn up from the pit
He goes to the Gentiles

28 Then there passed by Midianites
merchantmen; and they drew and lifted up Joseph out of the pit, and sold
Joseph to the Ishmeelites for twenty
pieces of silver: and they brought Joseph
into Egypt.
¶29 And Reuben returned unto the pit;
and, behold, Joseph *was* not in the pit;
and he rent his clothes.
30 And he returned unto his brethren,
and said, The child *is* not; and I, whither
shall I go?
31 And they took Joseph's coat, and
killed a kid of the goats, and dipped the
coat in the blood;
32 And they sent the coat of *many*
colours, and they brought *it* to their father; and said, This have we found:
know now whether it *be* thy son's coat
or no.
33 And he knew it, and said, *It is* my
son's coat; an evil beast hath devoured
him; Joseph is without doubt rent in
pieces.
34 And Jacob rent his clothes, and put
sackcloth upon his loins, and mourned
for his son many days.
35 And all his sons and all his daughters rose up to comfort him; but he refused to be comforted; and he said, For
I will go down into the grave unto my
son mourning. Thus his father wept for
him.
36 And the Midianites sold him into
Egypt unto Potiphar, an officer of Pharaoh's, *and* captain of the guard.

38 And it came to pass at that
time, that Judah went down
from his brethren, and turned in to a
certain Adullamite, whose name *was*
Hirah.
2 And Judah saw there a daughter of a
certain Canaanite, whose name *was*
Shuah; and he took her, and went in
unto her.
3 And she conceived, and bare a son;
and he called his name Er.
4 And she conceived again, and bare
a son; and she called his name Onan.
5 And she yet again conceived, and
bare a son; and called his name Shelah:
and he was at Chezib, when she bare
him.
6 And Judah took a wife for Er his
firstborn, whose name *was* Tamar.
7 And Er, Judah's firstborn, was wicked in the sight of the LORD; and the
LORD slew him.
8 And Judah said unto Onan, Go in
unto thy brother's wife, and marry her,
and raise up seed to thy brother.
9 And Onan knew that the seed
should not be his; and it came to pass,
when he went in unto his brother's
wife, that he spilled *it* on the ground,
lest that he should give seed to his
brother.
10 And the thing which he did displeased the LORD: wherefore he slew
him also.
11 Then said Judah to Tamar his
daughter in law, Remain a widow at thy
father's house, till Shelah my son be
grown: for he said, Lest peradventure
he die also, as his brethren *did*. And
Tamar went and dwelt in her father's
house.
¶12 And in process of time the daughter of Shuah Judah's wife died; and Judah was comforted, and went up unto
his sheepshearers to Timnath, he and
his friend Hirah the Adullamite.

37:28 twenty pieces of silver. This was the price of a boy; thirty pieces was the price of a full-grown man. Read Matthew 26:15.

13 And it was told Tamar, saying, Behold thy father in law goeth up to Timnath to shear his sheep.

14 And she put her widow's garments
off from her, and covered her with a vail,
and wrapped herself, and sat in an open
place, which *is* by the way to Timnath;
for she saw that Shelah was grown, and
she was not given unto him to wife.

15 When Judah saw her, he thought
her *to be* an harlot; because she had
covered her face.

16 And he turned unto her by the way,
and said, Go to, I pray thee, let me come
in unto thee; (for he knew not that she
was his daughter in law.) And she said,
What wilt thou give me, that thou
mayest come in unto me?

17 And he said, I will send *thee* a kid
from the flock. And she said, Wilt thou
give *me* a pledge, till thou send *it?*

18 And he said, What pledge shall I
give thee? And she said, Thy signet,
and thy bracelets, and thy staff that
is in thine hand. And he gave *it* her,
and came in unto her, and she conceived
by him.

19 And she arose, and went away, and
laid by her vail from her, and put on the
garments of her widowhood.

20 And Judah sent the kid by the hand
of his friend the Adullamite, to receive
his pledge from the woman's hand: but
he found her not.

21 Then he asked the men of that
place, saying, Where *is* the harlot,
that *was* openly by the way side? And
they said, There was no harlot in this
place.

22 And he returned to Judah, and said,
I cannot find her; and also the men of
the place said, *that* there was no harlot
in this *place.*

23 And Judah said, Let her take *it* to
her, lest we be shamed: behold, I sent
this kid, and thou hast not found her.

¶24 And it came to pass about three
months after, that it was told Judah,
saying, Tamar thy daughter in law hath
played the harlot; and also, behold, she
is with child by whoredom. And Judah
said, Bring her forth, and let her be
burnt.

25 When she *was* brought forth, she
sent to her father in law, saying, By the
man, whose these *are, am* I with child:
and she said, Discern, I pray thee,
whose *are* these, the signet, and bracelets, and staff.

26 And Judah acknowledged *them,* and
said, She hath been more righteous
than I; because that I gave her not to
Shelah my son. And he knew her again
no more.

¶27 And it came to pass in the time of
her travail, that, behold, twins *were* in
her womb.

28 And it came to pass, when she travailed, that *the one* put out *his* hand: and
the midwife took and bound upon his
hand a scarlet thread, saying, This came
out first.

29 And it came to pass, as he drew
back his hand, that, behold, his brother
came out: and she said, How hast thou
broken forth? *this* breach *be* upon thee:
therefore his name was called Pharez.

30 And afterward came out his
brother, that had the scarlet thread
upon his hand: and his name was called
Zarah.

Joseph is tested

39 And Joseph was brought down
to Egypt; and Potiphar, an officer of Pharaoh, captain of the guard, an
Egyptian, bought him of the hands of
the Ishmeelites, which had brought him
down thither.

2 And the LORD was with Joseph,
and he was a prosperous man; and he
was in the house of his master the
Egyptian.

3 And his master saw that the LORD
was with him, and that the LORD made
all that he did to prosper in his hand.

4 And Joseph found grace in his sight,
and he served him: and he made him

38:18 signet. A seal.

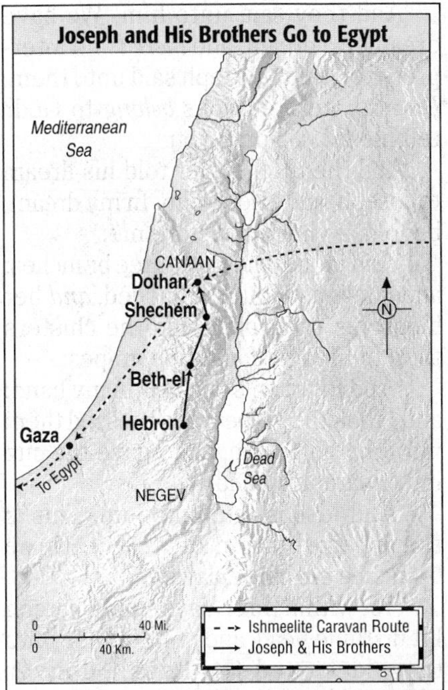

overseer over his house, and all *that* he
had he put into his hand.

5And it came to pass from the time
that he had made him overseer in his
house, and over all that he had, that the
LORD blessed the Egyptian's house for
Joseph's sake; and the blessing of the
LORD was upon all that he had in the
house, and in the field.

6And he left all that he had in Joseph's
hand; and he knew not ought he had,
save the bread which he did eat. And
Joseph was a goodly *person,* and well
favoured.

¶7And it came to pass after these
things, that his master's wife cast her
eyes upon Joseph; and she said, Lie
with me.

8But he refused, and said unto his
master's wife, Behold, my master
wotteth not what *is* with me in the
house, and he hath committed all that
he hath to my hand;

9*There is* none greater in this house
than I; neither hath he kept back any
thing from me but thee, because thou
art his wife: how then can I do this great
wickedness, and sin against God?

10And it came to pass, as she spake
to Joseph day by day, that he hearkened
not unto her, to lie by her, *or* to be with
her.

11And it came to pass about this time,
that *Joseph* went into the house to do his
business; and *there was* none of the men
of the house there within.

12And she caught him by his garment,
saying, Lie with me: and he left his
garment in her hand, and fled, and got
him out.

13And it came to pass, when she saw
that he had left his garment in her hand,
and was fled forth,

14That she called unto the men of her
house, and spake unto them, saying,
See, he hath brought in an Hebrew unto
us to mock us; he came in unto me to
lie with me, and I cried with a loud
voice:

15And it came to pass, when he heard
that I lifted up my voice and cried, that
he left his garment with me, and fled,
and got him out.

16And she laid up his garment by her,
until his lord came home.

17And she spake unto him according
to these words, saying, The Hebrew
servant, which thou hast brought unto
us, came in unto me to mock me:

18And it came to pass, as I lifted up
my voice and cried, that he left his garment with me, and fled out.

19And it came to pass, when his master heard the words of his wife, which
she spake unto him, saying, After this
manner did thy servant to me; that his
wrath was kindled.

20And Joseph's master took him, and
put him into the prison, a place where

39:8 wotteth. To know.

39:20 prison. Like the Lord Jesus Christ, Joseph was put into prison—not for wrongdoing, but because he was righteous. The prison into which the Lord Jesus went was the prison of death! Yet just as God did not leave Joseph in prison but raised him up to a place of

the king's prisoners *were* bound: and he
was there in the prison.
¶21But the LORD was with Joseph,
and shewed him mercy, and gave him
favour in the sight of the keeper of the
prison.
22And the keeper of the prison committed to Joseph's hand all the prisoners that *were* in the prison; and
whatsoever they did there, he was the
doer *of it.*
23The keeper of the prison looked not
to any thing *that was* under his hand;
because the LORD was with him, and
that which he did, the LORD made *it* to
prosper.

40 And it came to pass after these
things, *that* the butler of the
king of *Egypt and *his* baker had offended their lord the king of *Egypt.
2And Pharaoh was wroth against two
of his officers, against the chief of the
butlers, and against the chief of the bakers.
3And he put them in ward in the
house of the captain of the guard, into
the prison, the place where Joseph *was*
bound.
4And the captain of the guard charged
Joseph with them, and he served them:
and they continued a season in ward.
¶5And they dreamed a dream both of
them, each man his dream in one night,
each man according to the interpretation of his dream, the butler and the
baker of the king of Egypt, which *were*
bound in the prison.
6And Joseph came in unto them in
the morning, and looked upon them,
and, behold, they *were* sad.
7And he asked Pharaoh's officers that
were with him in the ward of his lord's
house, saying, Wherefore look ye *so*
sadly to day?
8And they said unto him, We have
dreamed a dream, and *there is* no interpreter of it. And Joseph said unto them,
Do not interpretations *belong* to God?
tell me *them,* I pray you.
9And the chief butler told his dream
to Joseph, and said to him, In my dream,
behold, a vine *was* before me;
10And in the vine *were* three branches:
and it *was* as though it budded, *and* her
blossoms shot forth; and the clusters
thereof brought forth ripe grapes:
11And Pharaoh's cup *was* in my hand:
and I took the grapes, and pressed them
into Pharaoh's cup, and I gave the cup
into Pharaoh's hand.
12And Joseph said unto him, This *is*
the interpretation of it: The three
branches *are* three days:
13Yet within three days shall Pharaoh
lift up thine head, and restore thee unto
thy place: and thou shalt deliver
Pharaoh's cup into his hand, after the
former manner when thou wast his
butler.
14But think on me when it shall be
well with thee, and shew kindness, I
pray thee, unto me, and make mention
of me unto Pharaoh, and bring me out
of this house:
15For indeed I was stolen away out of
the land of the Hebrews: and here also
have I done nothing that they should
put me into the dungeon.
16When the chief baker saw that the
interpretation was good, he said unto
Joseph, I also *was* in my dream, and,
behold, *I had* three white baskets on my
head:
17And in the uppermost basket *there*
was of all manner of bakemeats for Pharaoh; and the birds did eat them out of
the basket upon my head.
18And Joseph answered and said,

---

honor, so He did not leave His Holy One in the place of the dead, but God raised Him from the dead and gave Him a place on His own throne with Him far above all things (see Eph. 1:20-21; Phil. 2:9; and Acts 2:31-33). See also Genesis 37:2 note.

40:3 ward. Prison; literally, *guard*.

40:4 season. A time. A while.

40:8 interpretations belong to God. Read Daniel 2:20-22.

This *is* the interpretation thereof: The
three baskets *are* three days:
19 Yet within three days shall Pharaoh
lift up thy head from off thee, and shall
hang thee on a tree; and the birds shall
eat thy flesh from off thee.
¶ 20 And it came to pass the third day,
which was Pharaoh's birthday, that he
made a feast unto all his servants: and
he lifted up the head of the chief butler
and of the chief baker among his servants.
21 And he restored the chief butler
unto his butlership again; and he gave
the cup into Pharaoh's hand:
22 But he hanged the chief baker: as
Joseph had interpreted to them.
23 Yet did not the chief butler remember Joseph, but forgat him.

Pharaoh's dream

41 And it came to pass at the end
of two full years, that Pharaoh
dreamed: and, behold, he stood by the
river.
2 And, behold, there came up out of
the river seven well favoured kine and
fatfleshed; and they fed in a meadow.
3 And, behold, seven other kine
came up after them out of the river, ill
favoured and leanfleshed; and stood by
the *other* kine upon the brink of the
river.
4 And the ill favoured and leanfleshed
kine did eat up the seven well favoured
and fat kine. So Pharaoh awoke.
5 And he slept and dreamed the second
time: and, behold, seven ears of corn
came up upon one stalk, rank and good.
6 And, behold, seven thin ears and
blasted with the east wind sprung up
after them.
7 And the seven thin ears devoured
the seven rank and full ears. And
Pharaoh awoke, and, behold, *it was* a
dream.
8 And it came to pass in the morning
that his spirit was troubled; and he sent
and called for all the magicians of Egypt,
and all the wise men thereof: and Pharaoh told them his dream; but *there was*
none that could interpret them unto
Pharaoh.
¶ 9 Then spake the chief butler unto
Pharaoh, saying, I do remember my
faults this day:
10 Pharaoh was wroth with his servants, and put me in ward in the captain
of the guard's house, *both* me and the
chief baker:
11 And we dreamed a dream in one
night, I and he; we dreamed each man
according to the interpretation of his
dream.
12 And *there was* there with us a young
man, an Hebrew, servant to the captain
of the guard; and we told him, and he
interpreted to us our dreams; to each
man according to his dream he did interpret.
13 And it came to pass, as he interpreted to us, so it was; me he restored
unto mine office, and him he hanged.

Joseph exalted in Egypt

¶ 14 Then Pharaoh sent and called Joseph, and they brought him hastily out
of the dungeon: and he shaved *himself*,
and changed his raiment, and came in
unto Pharaoh.
15 And Pharaoh said unto Joseph, I
have dreamed a dream, and *there is*
none that can interpret it: and I have
heard say of thee, *that* thou canst understand a dream to interpret it.
16 And Joseph answered Pharaoh,
saying, *It is* not in me: God shall give
Pharaoh an answer of peace.
17 And Pharaoh said unto Joseph, In
my dream, behold, I stood upon the
bank of the river:
18 And, behold, there came up out of

41:2 kine. Cow.
41:3 ill favoured. Ill-looking.
41:5 rank. Full.
41:6 blasted. Affected.

the river seven kine, fatfleshed and well
favoured; and they fed in a meadow:
19 And, behold, seven other kine came
up after them, poor and very ill favoured
and leanfleshed, such as I never saw in
all the land of Egypt for badness:
20 And the lean and the ill favoured
kine did eat up the first seven fat kine:
21 And when they had eaten them up,
it could not be known that they had
eaten them; but they *were* still ill favoured, as at the beginning. So I awoke.
22 And I saw in my dream, and, behold,
seven ears came up in one stalk, full and
good:
23 And, behold, seven ears, withered,
thin, *and* blasted with the east wind,
sprung up after them:
24 And the thin ears devoured the
seven good ears: and I told *this* unto the
magicians; but *there was* none that could
declare *it* to me.
¶25 And Joseph said unto Pharaoh,
The dream of Pharaoh *is* one: God
hath shewed Pharaoh what he *is* about
to do.
26 The seven good kine *are* seven
years; and the seven good ears *are*
seven years: the dream *is* one.
27 And the seven thin and ill favoured
kine that came up after them *are* seven
years; and the seven empty ears
blasted with the east wind shall be
seven years of famine.
28 This *is* the thing which I have spoken unto Pharaoh: What God *is* about
to do he sheweth unto Pharaoh.
29 Behold, there come seven years of
great plenty throughout all the land of
Egypt:
30 And there shall arise after them
seven years of famine; and all the
plenty shall be forgotten in the land of
Egypt; and the famine shall consume
the land;
31 And the plenty shall not be known
in the land by reason of that famine following; for it *shall be* very grievous.
32 And for that the dream was doubled
unto Pharaoh twice; *it is* because the
thing *is* established by God, and God
will shortly bring it to pass.
33 Now therefore let Pharaoh look out
a man discreet and wise, and set him
over the land of Egypt.
34 Let Pharaoh do *this,* and let him
appoint officers over the land, and take
up the fifth part of the land of Egypt in
the seven plenteous years.
35 And let them gather all the food of
those good years that come, and lay up
corn under the hand of Pharaoh, and let
them keep food in the cities.
36 And that food shall be for store to
the land against the seven years of famine, which shall be in the land
of Egypt; that the land perish not
through the famine.
¶37 And the thing was good in the
eyes of Pharaoh, and in the eyes of all
his servants.
38 And Pharaoh said unto his servants, Can we find *such a one* as this *is,*
a man in whom the Spirit of God *is?*
39 And Pharaoh said unto Joseph, Forasmuch as God hath shewed thee all
this, *there is* none so discreet and wise
as thou *art:*
40 Thou shalt be over my house, and
according unto thy word shall all my
people be ruled: only in the throne will
I be greater than thou.
41 And Pharaoh said unto Joseph, See,
I have set thee over all the land of
Egypt.
42 And Pharaoh took off his ring from
his hand, and put it upon Joseph's hand,
and arrayed him in vestures of fine
linen, and put a gold chain about his
neck;
43 And he made him to ride in the second chariot which he had; and they
cried before him, Bow the knee: and he
made him *ruler* over all the land of
Egypt.
44 And Pharaoh said unto Joseph, I *am*

41:24 declare. To make clear or manifest.

Pharaoh, and without thee shall no man
lift up his hand or foot in all the land of
Egypt.

Joseph's Gentile bride

¶45And Pharaoh called Joseph's name
Zaphnath-paaneah; and he gave him to
wife Asenath the daughter of Potipherah priest of On. And Joseph went out
over *all* the land of Egypt.
46And Joseph *was* thirty years old
when he stood before Pharaoh king of
Egypt. And Joseph went out from the
presence of Pharaoh, and went throughout all the land of Egypt.
47And in the seven plenteous years
the earth brought forth by handfuls.
48And he gathered up all the food of
the seven years, which were in the land
of Egypt, and laid up the food in the cities: the food of the field, which *was*
round about every city, laid he up in the
same.
49And Joseph gathered corn as the
sand of the sea, very much, until he left
numbering; for *it was* without number.
50And unto Joseph were born two
sons before the years of famine came,
which Asenath the daughter of Potipherah priest of On bare unto him.
51And Joseph called the name of the
firstborn Manasseh: For God, *said he,*
hath made me forget all my toil, and all
my father's house.
52And the name of the second called
he Ephraim: For God hath caused me
to be fruitful in the land of my affliction.
¶53And the seven years of plenteousness, that was in the land of Egypt,
were ended.
54And the seven years of dearth began to come, according as Joseph had
said: and the dearth was in all lands; but
in all the land of Egypt there was bread.
55And when all the land of Egypt was
famished, the people cried to Pharaoh
for bread: and Pharaoh said unto all the
Egyptians, Go unto Joseph; what he
saith to you, do.
56And the famine was over all the face
of the earth: and Joseph opened all the
storehouses, and sold unto the Egyptians; and the famine waxed sore in the
land of Egypt.
57And all countries came into Egypt
to Joseph for to buy *corn;* because that
the famine was *so* sore in all lands.

Joseph saves his brothers' lives

42 Now when Jacob saw that
there was corn in Egypt, Jacob
said unto his sons, Why do ye look one
upon another?
2And he said, Behold, I have heard
that there is corn in Egypt: get you
down thither, and buy for us from
thence; that we may live, and not die.
¶3And Joseph's ten brethren went
down to buy corn in Egypt.
4But Benjamin, Joseph's brother, Jacob sent not with his brethren; for he
said, Lest peradventure mischief befall
him.
5And the sons of Israel came to buy
corn among those that came: for the
*famine was in the land of Canaan.
6And Joseph *was* the governor over
the land, *and* he *it was* that sold to all
the people of the land: and Joseph's
brethren came, and bowed down themselves before him *with* their faces to the
earth.
7And Joseph saw his brethren, and he
knew them, but made himself strange
unto them, and spake roughly unto

41:45 Zaphnath-paaneah. Joseph's new name means *revealer of secret things.* It is in the Coptic language.
41:51 Manasseh. This name means *forgetting.*
41:52 Ephraim. This name means *fruitful.*
42:6 Joseph's brethren came, and bowed. Read what the brothers had said in Genesis 37:8.
42:7 strange. Foreign.

them; and he said unto them, Whence come ye? And they said, From the land of Canaan to buy food.

8 And Joseph knew his brethren, but they knew not him.

9 And Joseph remembered the dreams which he dreamed of them, and said unto them, Ye *are* spies; to see the nakedness of the land ye are come.

10 And they said unto him, Nay, my lord, but to buy food are thy servants come.

11 We *are* all one man's sons; we *are* true *men,* thy servants are no spies.

12 And he said unto them, Nay, but to see the nakedness of the land ye are come.

13 And they said, Thy servants *are* twelve brethren, the sons of one man in the land of Canaan; and, behold, the youngest *is* this day with our father, and one *is* not.

14 And Joseph said unto them, That *is it* that I spake unto you, saying, Ye *are* spies:

15 Hereby ye shall be proved: By the life of Pharaoh ye shall not go forth hence, except your youngest brother come hither.

16 Send one of you, and let him fetch your brother, and ye shall be kept in prison, that your words may be proved, whether *there be any* truth in you: or else by the life of Pharaoh surely ye *are* spies.

17 And he put them all together into ward three days.

18 And Joseph said unto them the third day, This do, and live; *for* I fear God:

19 If ye *be* true *men,* let one of your brethren be bound in the house of your prison: go ye, carry corn for the famine of your houses:

20 But bring your youngest brother unto me; so shall your words be verified, and ye shall not die. And they did so.

¶21 And they said one to another, We *are* verily guilty concerning our brother, in that we saw the anguish of his soul, when he besought us, and we would not hear; therefore is this distress come upon us.

22 And Reuben answered them, saying, Spake I not unto you, saying, Do not sin against the child; and ye would not hear? therefore, behold, also his blood is required.

23 And they knew not that Joseph understood *them;* for he spake unto them by an interpreter.

24 And he turned himself about from them, and wept; and returned to them again, and communed with them, and took from them Simeon, and bound him before their eyes.

¶25 Then Joseph commanded to fill their sacks with corn, and to restore every man's money into his sack, and to give them provision for the way: and thus did he unto them.

26 And they laded their asses with the corn, and departed thence.

27 And as one of them opened his sack to give his ass provender in the inn, he espied his money; for, behold, it *was* in his sack's mouth.

28 And he said unto his brethren, My money is restored; and, lo, *it is* even in my sack: and their heart failed *them,* and they were afraid, saying one to another, What *is* this *that* God hath done unto us?

¶29 And they came unto Jacob their father unto the land of Canaan, and told him all that befell unto them; saying,

30 The man, *who is* the lord of the land, spake roughly to us, and took us for spies of the country.

31 And we said unto him, We *are* true *men;* we are no spies:

32 We *be* twelve brethren, sons of our father; one *is* not, and the youngest *is* this day with our father in the land of Canaan.

33 And the man, the lord of the country, said unto us, Hereby shall I know that ye *are* true *men;* leave one of your brethren *here* with me, and take *food for* the famine of your households, and be gone:

[34]And bring your youngest brother
unto me: then shall I know that ye *are*
no spies, but *that* ye *are* true *men: so*
will I deliver you your brother, and ye
shall traffick in the land.

¶[35]And it came to pass as they emptied their sacks, that, behold, every
man's bundle of money *was* in his
sack: and when *both* they and their father saw the bundles of money, they
were afraid.

[36]And Jacob their father said unto
them, Me have ye bereaved *of my children:* Joseph *is* not, and Simeon *is* not,
and ye will take Benjamin *away:* all
these things are against me.

[37]And Reuben spake unto his father,
saying, Slay my two sons, if I bring him
not to thee: deliver him into my hand,
and I will bring him to thee again.

[38]And he said, My son shall not go
down with you; for his brother is dead,
and he is left alone: if mischief befall
him by the way in the which ye go, then
shall ye bring down my gray hairs with
sorrow to the grave.

43 And the *famine *was* sore in
the land.

[2]And it came to pass, when they had
eaten up the corn which they had
brought out of Egypt, their father said
unto them, Go again, buy us a little food.

[3]And Judah spake unto him, saying,
The man did solemnly protest unto us,
saying, Ye shall not see my face, except
your brother *be* with you.

[4]If thou wilt send our brother with us,
we will go down and buy thee food:

[5]But if thou wilt not send *him,* we will
not go down: for the man said unto us,
Ye shall not see my face, except your
brother *be* with you.

[6]And Israel said, Wherefore dealt ye
so ill with me, *as* to tell the man whether ye had yet a brother?

[7]And they said, The man asked us
straitly of our state, and of our kindred,
saying, *Is* your father yet alive? have ye
another brother? and we told him according to the tenor of these words:
could we certainly know that he would
say, Bring your brother down?

[8]And Judah said unto Israel his father,
Send the lad with me, and we will arise
and go; that we may live, and not die,
both we, and thou, *and* also our little
ones.

[9]I will be surety for him; of my hand
shalt thou require him: if I bring him not
unto thee, and set him before thee, then
let me bear the blame for ever:

[10]For except we had lingered, surely
now we had returned this second time.

[11]And their father Israel said unto
them, If *it must be* so now, do this; take
of the best fruits in the land in your
vessels, and carry down the man a present, a little balm, and a little honey,
spices, and myrrh, nuts, and almonds:

[12]And take double money in your
hand; and the money that was brought
again in the mouth of your sacks, carry
it again in your hand; peradventure it
was an oversight:

[13]Take also your brother, and arise, go
again unto the man:

[14]And God Almighty give you mercy
before the man, that he may send away
your other brother, and Benjamin. If I
be bereaved *of my children,* I am bereaved.

[15]And the men took that present, and
they took double money in their hand,
and Benjamin; and rose up, and went
down to Egypt, and stood before Joseph.

¶[16]And when Joseph saw Benjamin
with them, he said to the ruler of his
house, Bring *these* men home, and slay,
and make ready; for *these* men shall dine
with me at noon.

[17]And the man did as Joseph bade;
and the man brought the men into
Joseph's house.

[18]And the men were afraid, because
they were brought into Joseph's house;
and they said, Because of the money
that was returned in our sacks at the

43:7 straitly. Strictly, closely.

first time are we brought in; that he may
seek occasion against us, and fall upon
us, and take us for bondmen, and our
asses.
19And they came near to the steward
of Joseph's house, and they communed
with him at the door of the house,
20And said, O sir, we came indeed
down at the first time to buy food:
21And it came to pass, when we came
to the inn, that we opened our sacks,
and, behold, *every* man's money *was*
in the mouth of his sack, our money in
full weight: and we have brought it
again in our hand.

43:21 The Inn
An inn was originally only a plot of ground near a spring or well, sometimes secured by a wall or fence, allotted as a camping ground for the use of travelers. This was the "inn" of the Old Testament (Gen. 43:21, etc.). In later times, some wealthy benefactor would raise the wall, build a few arches, unite them to the wall by a roof, close them with doors, and separate them by partitions, thus providing a separate room for each party. The cattle were put in the central open space, or in sheds abutting on the outside wall, or in natural caves around it. This is the modern khan or caravansary in the East, and such, it is thought, was "the inn" at Bethlehem; though the word translated "inn" may simply mean "guest chamber," and is so rendered in Mark 14:14 and Luke 22:11.

22And other money have we brought
down in our hands to buy food: we
cannot tell who put our money in our
sacks.
23And he said, Peace *be* to you, fear
not: your God, and the God of your father, hath given you treasure in your
sacks: I had your money. And he
brought Simeon out unto them.
24And the man brought the men into
Joseph's house, and gave *them* water,
and they washed their feet; and he gave
their asses provender.
25And they made ready the present
against Joseph came at noon: for they
heard that they should eat bread there.
¶26And when Joseph came home,
they brought him the present which
was in their hand into the house, and
bowed themselves to him to the earth.
27And he asked them of *their* welfare,
and said, *Is* your father well, the old
man of whom ye spake? *Is* he yet alive?
28And they answered, Thy servant
our father *is* in good health, he *is* yet
alive. And they bowed down their
heads, and made obeisance.
29And he lifted up his eyes, and saw
his brother Benjamin, his mother's son,
and said, *Is* this your younger brother,
of whom ye spake unto me? And he said,
God be gracious unto thee, my son.
30And Joseph made haste; for his
bowels did yearn upon his brother:
and he sought *where* to weep; and he
entered into *his* chamber, and wept
there.
31And he washed his face, and went
out, and refrained himself, and said, Set
on bread.
32And they set on for him by himself,
and for them by themselves, and for the
Egyptians, which did eat with him, by
themselves: because the Egyptians
might not eat bread with the Hebrews;
for that *is* an abomination unto the
Egyptians.
33And they sat before him, the firstborn according to his birthright, and the
youngest according to his youth: and
the men marvelled one at another.
34And he took *and sent* messes unto
them from before him: but Benjamin's
mess was five times so much as any of

43:18 bondmen. Slaves.
43:24 provender. Dry feed.
43:30 his bowels did yearn. Today we would say that his heart yearned.
43:30 yearn. To long for earnestly or anxiously, to be moved with tenderness, grief, or pity.
43:34 mess. A dish of food.

theirs. And they drank, and were merry
with him.

44 And he commanded the steward of his house, saying, Fill the
men's sacks *with* food, as much as they
can carry, and put every man's money
in his sack's mouth.
2And put my cup, the silver cup, in
the sack's mouth of the youngest, and
his corn money. And he did according
to the word that Joseph had spoken.
3As soon as the morning was light,
the men were sent away, they and their
asses.
4*And* when they were gone out of the
city, *and* not *yet* far off, Joseph said unto
his steward, Up, follow after the men;
and when thou dost overtake them, say
unto them, Wherefore have ye rewarded evil for good?
5*Is* not this *it* in which my lord
drinketh, and whereby indeed he
divineth? ye have done evil in so doing.
¶6And he overtook them, and he
spake unto them these same words.
7And they said unto him, Wherefore
saith my lord these words? God forbid
that thy servants should do according
to this thing:
8Behold, the money, which we found
in our sacks' mouths, we brought again
unto thee out of the land of Canaan: how
then should we steal out of thy lord's
house silver or gold?
9With whomsoever of thy servants it
be found, both let him die, and we also
will be my lord's bondmen.
10And he said, Now also *let* it *be* according unto your words; he with whom
it is found shall be my servant; and ye
shall be blameless.
11Then they speedily took down
every man his sack to the ground, and
opened every man his sack.
12And he searched, *and* began at the
eldest, and left at the youngest: and the
cup was found in Benjamin's sack.
13Then they rent their clothes, and
laded every man his ass, and returned
to the city.
¶14And Judah and his brethren came
to Joseph's house; for he *was* yet
there: and they fell before him on the
ground.
15And Joseph said unto them, What
deed *is* this that ye have done? wot ye
not that such a man as I can certainly
divine?
16And Judah said, What shall we say
unto my lord? what shall we speak? or
how shall we clear ourselves? God hath
found out the iniquity of thy servants:
behold, we *are* my lord's servants, both
we, and *he* also with whom the cup is
found.
17And he said, God forbid that I
should do so: *but* the man in whose
hand the cup is found, he shall be my
servant; and as for you, get you up in
peace unto your father.
¶18Then Judah came near unto him,
and said, Oh my lord, let thy servant, I
pray thee, speak a word in my lord's
ears, and let not thine anger burn
against thy servant: for thou *art* even as
Pharaoh.
19My lord asked his servants, saying,
Have ye a father, or a brother?
20And we said unto my lord, We have
a father, an old man, and a child of his
old age, a little one; and his brother is
dead, and he alone is left of his mother,
and his father loveth him.
21And thou saidst unto thy servants,
Bring him down unto me, that I may set
mine eyes upon him.
22And we said unto my lord, The
lad cannot leave his father: for *if* he
should leave his father, *his father* would
die.
23And thou saidst unto thy servants,
Except your youngest brother come
down with you, ye shall see my face no
more.
24And it came to pass when we came
up unto thy servant my father, we told
him the words of my lord.
25And our father said, Go again, *and*
buy us a little food.
26And we said, We cannot go down: if
our youngest brother be with us, then
will we go down: for we may not see the

man's face, except our youngest brother *be* with us.

[27]And thy servant my father said unto us, Ye know that my wife bare me two *sons:*

[28]And the one went out from me, and I said, Surely he is torn in pieces; and I saw him not since:

[29]And if ye take this also from me, and mischief befall him, ye shall bring down my gray hairs with sorrow to the grave.

[30]Now therefore when I come to thy servant my father, and the lad *be* not with us; seeing that his life is bound up in the lad's life;

[31]It shall come to pass, when he seeth that the lad *is* not *with us,* that he will die: and thy servants shall bring down the gray hairs of thy servant our father with sorrow to the grave.

[32]For thy servant became surety for the lad unto my father, saying, If I bring him not unto thee, then I shall bear the blame to my father for ever.

[33]Now therefore, I pray thee, let thy servant abide instead of the lad a bondman to my lord; and let the lad go up with his brethren.

[34]For how shall I go up to my father, and the lad *be* not with me? lest peradventure I see the evil that shall come on my father.

Joseph is revealed to his brothers

45 Then Joseph could not refrain himself before all them that stood by him; and he cried, Cause every man to go out from me. And there stood no man with him, while Joseph made himself known unto his brethren.

[2]And he wept aloud: and the Egyptians and the house of Pharaoh heard.

[3]And Joseph said unto his brethren, I *am* Joseph; doth my father yet live? And his brethren could not answer him; for they were troubled at his presence.

[4]And Joseph said unto his brethren, Come near to me, I pray you. And they came near. And he said, I *am* Joseph your brother, whom ye sold into Egypt.

[5]Now therefore be not grieved, nor angry with yourselves, that ye sold me hither: for God did send me before you to preserve life.

[6]For these two years *hath* the famine *been* in the land: and yet *there are* five years, in the which *there shall* neither *be* earing nor harvest.

[7]And God sent me before you to preserve you a posterity in the earth, and to save your lives by a great deliverance.

[8]So now *it was* not you *that* sent me hither, but God: and he hath made me a father to Pharaoh, and lord of all his house, and a ruler throughout all the land of Egypt.

[9]Haste ye, and go up to my father, and say unto him, Thus saith thy son Joseph, God hath made me lord of all Egypt: come down unto me, tarry not:

[10]And thou shalt dwell in the land of Goshen, and thou shalt be near unto me, thou, and thy children, and thy children's children, and thy flocks, and thy herds, and all that thou hast:

[11]And there will I nourish thee; for yet *there are* five years of famine; lest thou, and thy household, and all that thou hast, come to poverty.

[12]And, behold, your eyes see, and the eyes of my brother Benjamin, that *it is* my mouth that speaketh unto you.

[13]And ye shall tell my father of all my glory in Egypt, and of all that ye have seen; and ye shall haste and bring down my father hither.

[14]And he fell upon his brother Benjamin's neck, and wept; and Benjamin wept upon his neck.

44:30 and. Here the word means *if.*
44:33 let they servant abide instead. Judah's change of heart is truly proved at last.
45:3 troubled. This word means *terrified.*
45:6 earing. Plowing.

15 Moreover he kissed all his brethren, and wept upon them: and after that his brethren talked with him.

¶ 16 And the fame thereof was heard in Pharaoh's house, saying, Joseph's brethren are come: and it pleased Pharaoh well, and his servants.

17 And Pharaoh said unto Joseph, Say unto thy brethren, This do ye; lade your beasts, and go, get you unto the land of Canaan;

18 And take your father and your households, and come unto me: and I will give you the good of the land of Egypt, and ye shall eat the fat of the land.

19 Now thou art commanded, this do ye; take you wagons out of the land of Egypt for your little ones, and for your wives, and bring your father, and come.

20 Also regard not your stuff; for the good of all the land of Egypt *is* yours.

21 And the children of Israel did so: and Joseph gave them wagons, according to the commandment of Pharaoh, and gave them provision for the way.

22 To all of them he gave each man changes of raiment; but to Benjamin he gave three hundred *pieces* of silver, and five changes of raiment.

23 And to his father he sent after this *manner;* ten asses laden with the good things of Egypt, and ten she asses laden with corn and bread and meat for his father by the way.

24 So he sent his brethren away, and they departed: and he said unto them, See that ye fall not out by the way.

¶ 25 And they went up out of Egypt, and came into the land of Canaan unto Jacob their father,

26 And told him, saying, Joseph *is* yet alive, and he *is* governor over all the land of Egypt. And Jacob's heart fainted, for he believed them not.

27 And they told him all the words of Joseph, which he had said unto them: and when he saw the wagons which Joseph had sent to carry him, the spirit of Jacob their father revived:

28 And Israel said, *It is* enough; Joseph my son *is* yet alive: I will go and see him before I die.

Jacob goes to Egypt

46 And Israel took his journey with all that he had, and came to Beer-sheba, and offered sacrifices unto the God of his father Isaac.

2 And God spake unto Israel in the visions of the night, and said, Jacob, Jacob. And he said, Here *am* I.

3 And he said, I *am* God, the God of thy father: fear not to go down into Egypt; for I will there make of thee a great nation:

46:3 Following God's Lead
God sometimes allows His children to do something which they want very much to do, although He has not led them to do that thing. But almost always, if a child goes ahead of God's leading, trouble comes to him. God knows that the trouble will come but allows His child to learn in that way, often making good come out of it, as only God can. God would not say "No" to the old man who longed to see his son again, but trouble came in this case for Israel, for the whole nation were soon made slaves in Egypt, and were cruelly treated. The whole nation of Israel were descendants of Jacob and his twelve sons.

4 I will go down with thee into Egypt; and I will also surely bring thee up *again:* and Joseph shall put his hand upon thine eyes.

5 And Jacob rose up from Beer-sheba: and the sons of Israel carried Jacob their father, and their little ones, and their wives, in the wagons which Pharaoh had sent to carry him.

6 And they took their cattle, and their goods, which they had gotten in the land of Canaan, and came into Egypt, Jacob, and all his seed with him:

7 His sons, and his sons' sons with him, his daughters, and his sons' daughters, and all his seed brought he with him into Egypt.

¶ 8 And these *are* the names of the children of Israel, which came into

Egypt, Jacob and his sons: Reuben, Jacob's firstborn.

9 And the sons of Reuben; Hanoch, and Phallu, and Hezron, and Carmi.

¶ 10 And the sons of Simeon; Jemuel, and Jamin, and Ohad, and Jachin, and Zohar, and Shaul the son of a Canaanitish woman.

¶ 11 And the sons of Levi; Gershon, Kohath, and Merari.

¶ 12 And the sons of Judah; Er, and Onan, and Shelah, and Pharez, and Zarah: but Er and Onan died in the land of Canaan. And the sons of Pharez were Hezron and Hamul.

¶ 13 And the sons of Issachar; Tola, and Phuvah, and Job, and Shimron.

¶ 14 And the sons of Zebulun; Sered, and Elon, and Jahleel.

15 These *be* the sons of Leah, which she bare unto Jacob in Padan-aram, with his daughter Dinah: all the souls of his sons and his daughters *were* thirty and three.

¶ 16 And the sons of Gad; Ziphion, and Haggi, Shuni, and Ezbon, Eri, and Arodi, and Areli.

¶ 17 And the sons of Asher; Jimnah, and Ishuah, and Isui, and Beriah, and Serah their sister: and the sons of Beriah; Heber, and Malchiel.

18 These *are* the sons of Zilpah, whom Laban gave to Leah his daughter, and these she bare unto Jacob, *even* sixteen souls.

19 The sons of Rachel Jacob's wife; Joseph, and Benjamin.

¶ 20 And unto Joseph in the land of Egypt were born Manasseh and Ephraim, which Asenath the daughter of Potipherah priest of On bare unto him.

¶ 21 And the sons of Benjamin *were* Belah, and Becher, and Ashbel, Gera, and Naaman, Ehi, and Rosh, Muppim, and Huppim, and Ard.

22 These *are* the sons of Rachel, which were born to Jacob: all the souls *were* fourteen.

¶ 23 And the sons of Dan; Hushim.

¶ 24 And the sons of Naphtali; Jahzeel, and Guni, and Jezer, and Shillem.

25 These *are* the sons of Bilhah, which Laban gave unto Rachel his daughter, and she bare these unto Jacob: all the souls *were* seven.

26 All the souls that came with Jacob into Egypt, which came out of his loins, besides Jacob's sons' wives, all the souls *were* threescore and six;

27 And the sons of Joseph, which were born him in Egypt, *were* two souls: all the souls of the house of Jacob, which came into Egypt, *were* threescore and ten.

¶ 28 And he sent Judah before him unto Joseph, to direct his face unto Goshen; and they came into the land of Goshen.

29 And Joseph made ready his chariot, and went up to meet Israel his father, to Goshen, and presented himself unto him; and he fell on his neck, and wept on his neck a good while.

30 And Israel said unto Joseph, Now let me die, since I have seen thy face, because thou *art* yet alive.

31 And Joseph said unto his brethren, and unto his father's house, I will go up, and shew Pharaoh, and say unto him, My brethren, and my father's house, which *were* in the land of Canaan, are come unto me;

32 And the men *are* shepherds, for their trade hath been to feed cattle; and they have brought their flocks, and their herds, and all that they have.

33 And it shall come to pass, when Pharaoh shall call you, and shall say, What *is* your occupation?

34 That ye shall say, Thy servants' trade hath been about cattle from our youth even until now, both we, *and* also

---

46:27 threescore and ten. This is seventy, although verse 26 says threescore and six, that is, sixty-six. This is not a mistake. The other four were Jacob himself and Joseph and his two sons who were already in Egypt. All together they made up the "house of Jacob."

our fathers: that ye may dwell in the
land of Goshen; for every shepherd *is*
an abomination unto the Egyptians.

Joseph and his family exalted

47 Then Joseph came and told
Pharaoh, and said, My father
and my brethren, and their flocks, and
their herds, and all that they have, are
come out of the land of Canaan; and,
behold, they *are* in the land of Goshen.
2 And he took some of his brethren,
even five men, and presented them unto
Pharaoh.
3 And Pharaoh said unto his brethren,
What *is* your occupation? And they
said unto Pharaoh, Thy servants *are*
shepherds, both we, *and* also our fathers.
4 They said moreover unto Pharaoh,
For to sojourn in the land are we come;
for thy servants have no pasture for
their flocks; for the famine *is* sore in the
land of Canaan: now therefore, we pray
thee, let thy servants dwell in the land
of Goshen.
5 And Pharaoh spake unto Joseph,
saying, Thy father and thy brethren are
come unto thee:
6 The land of Egypt *is* before thee; in
the best of the land make thy father and
brethren to dwell; in the land of Goshen
let them dwell: and if thou knowest *any*
men of activity among them, then make
them rulers over my cattle.
7 And Joseph brought in Jacob his father, and set him before Pharaoh: and
Jacob blessed Pharaoh.
8 And Pharaoh said unto Jacob, How
old *art* thou?
9 And Jacob said unto Pharaoh, The
days of the years of my pilgrimage
are an hundred and thirty years: few
and evil have the days of the years
of my life been, and have not attained
unto the days of the years of the life
of my fathers in the days of their pilgrimage.
10 And Jacob blessed Pharaoh, and
went out from before Pharaoh.
¶ 11 And Joseph placed his father and
his brethren, and gave them a possession in the land of Egypt, in the best of
the land, in the land of Rameses, as
Pharaoh had commanded.
12 And Joseph nourished his father,
and his brethren, and all his father's
household, with bread, according to
their families.
¶ 13 And *there was* no bread in all the
land; for the famine *was* very sore, so
that the land of Egypt and *all* the land
of Canaan fainted by reason of the famine.
14 And Joseph gathered up all the
money that was found in the land of
Egypt, and in the land of Canaan, for the
corn which they bought: and Joseph
brought the money into Pharaoh's
house.
15 And when money failed in the land
of Egypt, and in the land of Canaan, all
the Egyptians came unto Joseph, and
said, Give us bread: for why should we
die in thy presence? for the money
faileth.
16 And Joseph said, Give your cattle;
and I will give you for your cattle, if
money fail.
17 And they brought their cattle unto
Joseph: and Joseph gave them bread *in
exchange* for horses, and for the flocks,
and for the cattle of the herds, and for
the asses: and he fed them with bread
for all their cattle for that year.
18 When that year was ended, they
came unto him the second year, and said
unto him, We will not hide *it* from my
lord, how that our money is spent; my
lord also hath our herds of cattle; there
is not ought left in the sight of my lord,
but our bodies, and our lands:
19 Wherefore shall we die before thine
eyes, both we and our land? buy us and
our land for bread, and we and our land
will be servants unto Pharaoh: and give

47:8 How old art thou? In all Eastern countries, a very old man was greatly respected. Even kings bowed down in the presence of old age.

us seed, that we may live, and not die,
that the land be not desolate.
20 And Joseph bought all the land of
Egypt for Pharaoh; for the Egyptians
sold every man his field, because the
famine prevailed over them: so the land
became Pharaoh's.
21 And as for the people, he removed
them to cities from *one* end of the borders of Egypt even to the *other* end
thereof.
22 Only the land of the priests bought
he not; for the priests had a portion
assigned them of Pharaoh, and did eat
their portion which Pharaoh gave them:
wherefore they sold not their lands.
23 Then Joseph said unto the people,
Behold, I have bought you this day and
your land for Pharaoh: lo, *here is* seed
for you, and ye shall sow the land.
24 And it shall come to pass in the increase, that ye shall give the fifth *part*
unto Pharaoh, and four parts shall
be your own, for seed of the field, and
for your food, and for them of your
households, and for food for your little
ones.
25 And they said, Thou hast saved
our lives: let us find grace in the sight
of my lord, and we will be Pharaoh's
servants.
26 And Joseph made it a law over the
land of Egypt unto this day, *that* Pharaoh
should have the fifth *part;* except the
land of the priests only, *which* became
not Pharaoh's.
¶27 And Israel dwelt in the land of
Egypt, in the country of Goshen; and
they had possessions therein, and grew,
and multiplied exceedingly.
28 And Jacob lived in the land of Egypt
seventeen years: so the whole age of
Jacob was an hundred forty and seven
years.
29 And the time drew nigh that Israel
must die: and he called his son Joseph,
and said unto him, If now I have found
grace in thy sight, put, I pray thee, thy
hand under my thigh, and deal kindly
and truly with me; bury me not, I pray
thee, in Egypt:
30 But I will lie with my fathers, and
thou shalt carry me out of Egypt, and
bury me in their buryingplace. And he
said, I will do as thou hast said.
31 And he said, Swear unto me. And
he sware unto him. And Israel bowed
himself upon the bed's head.
48 And it came to pass after these
things, that *one* told Joseph,
Behold, thy father *is* sick: and he took
with him his two sons, Manasseh and
Ephraim.
2 And *one* told Jacob, and said, Behold,
thy son Joseph cometh unto thee: and
Israel strengthened himself, and sat
upon the bed.
3 And Jacob said unto Joseph, God
Almighty appeared unto me at Luz in
the land of Canaan, and blessed me,
4 And said unto me, Behold, I will
make thee fruitful, and multiply thee,
and I will make of thee a multitude of
people; and will give this land to thy
seed after thee *for* an everlasting possession.
¶5 And now thy two sons, Ephraim
and Manasseh, which were born unto
thee in the land of Egypt before I came
unto thee into Egypt, *are* mine; as Reuben and Simeon, they shall be mine.
6 And thy issue, which thou begettest
after them, shall be thine, *and* shall be
called after the name of their brethren
in their inheritance.
7 And as for me, when I came from
Padan, Rachel died by me in the land of
Canaan in the way, when yet *there was*
but a little way to come unto Ephrath:
and I buried her there in the way of
Ephrath; the same *is* Beth-lehem.
8 And Israel beheld Joseph's sons, and
said, Who *are* these?
9 And Joseph said unto his father,
They *are* my sons, whom God hath
given me in this *place.* And he said,

47:29 put, I pray thee, thy hand. This was the sign of making a very sure promise.
48:5 shall be mine. That is, they should have a share in the Promised Land.

Bring them, I pray thee, unto me, and I
will bless them.
10 Now the eyes of Israel were dim for
age, *so that* he could not see. And he
brought them near unto him; and he
kissed them, and embraced them.
11 And Israel said unto Joseph, I had
not thought to see thy face: and, lo, God
hath shewed me also thy seed.
12 And Joseph brought them out from
between his knees, and he bowed himself with his face to the earth.
13 And Joseph took them both, Ephraim in his right hand toward Israel's left
hand, and Manasseh in his left hand
toward Israel's right hand, and brought
them near unto him.
14 And Israel stretched out his right
hand, and laid *it* upon Ephraim's head,
who *was* the younger, and his left hand
upon Manasseh's head, guiding his
hands wittingly; for Manasseh *was* the
firstborn.
¶15 And he blessed Joseph, and said,
God, before whom my fathers Abraham
and Isaac did walk, the God which fed
me all my life long unto this day,
16 The Angel which redeemed me
from all evil, bless the lads; and let my
name be named on them, and the name
of my fathers Abraham and Isaac; and
let them grow into a multitude in the
midst of the earth.
17 And when Joseph saw that his father laid his right hand upon the head
of Ephraim, it displeased him: and he
held up his father's hand, to remove it
from Ephraim's head unto Manasseh's
head.
18 And Joseph said unto his father, Not
so, my father: for this *is* the firstborn;
put thy right hand upon his head.
19 And his father refused, and said,
I know *it,* my son, I know *it:* he also
shall become a people, and he also
shall be great: but truly his younger
brother shall be greater than he, and
his seed shall become a multitude of
nations.
20 And he blessed them that day, saying, In thee shall Israel bless, saying,
God make thee as Ephraim and as Manasseh: and he set Ephraim before
Manasseh.
21 And Israel said unto Joseph, Behold, I die: but God shall be with you,
and bring you again unto the land of
your fathers.
22 Moreover I have given to thee one
portion above thy brethren, which I
took out of the hand of the Amorite with
my sword and with my bow.

Jacob's dying blessing

49 And Jacob called unto his sons,
and said, Gather yourselves together, that I may tell you *that* which
shall befall you in the last days.
2 Gather yourselves together, and
hear, ye sons of Jacob; and hearken unto
Israel your father.
¶3 Reuben, thou *art* my firstborn, my
might, and the beginning of my strength,
the excellency of dignity, and the excellency of power:
4 Unstable as water, thou shalt not
excel; because thou wentest up to thy
father's bed; then defiledst thou *it:* he
went up to my couch.
¶5 Simeon and Levi *are* brethren; instruments of cruelty *are in* their habitations.
6 O my soul, come not thou into their
secret; unto their assembly, mine honour,

48:14 wittingly. Intentionally, knowingly.

49:1 Jacob called unto his sons. Here Jacob tells the future of each tribe that is to descend from his sons. The prophecies sound like riddles, but that was according to the custom of "wise men" in those days. It was the Holy Spirit who told Jacob what to say.

49:4 thou shalt not excel. That is, thou shalt not have the birthright. (Read the Gen. 25:31 note). The earthly material rights went to Joseph's sons, and the right to be in the line of Messiah went to Judah. Read 1 Chronicles 5:1-2.

be not thou united: for in their anger
they slew a man, and in their selfwill
they digged down a wall.
7 Cursed *be* their anger, for *it was*
fierce; and their wrath, for it was cruel:
I will divide them in Jacob, and scatter
them in Israel.
¶ 8 Judah, thou *art he* whom thy brethren shall praise: thy hand *shall be* in the
neck of thine enemies; thy father's children shall bow down before thee.
9 Judah *is* a lion's whelp: from the
prey, my son, thou art gone up: he
stooped down, he couched as a lion, and
as an old lion; who shall rouse him up?
10 The sceptre shall not depart from
Judah, nor a lawgiver from between his
feet, until Shiloh come; and unto him
shall the gathering of the people *be.*

49:10 The Promise of Christ
All the prophecies are interesting to study, but Judah's is the most important; it was of his tribe that King David, and all the rightful Jewish kings, and *the* King, the Lord Jesus Christ, were born. Shiloh, meaning *Peace-bringer,* refers to the Lord Jesus Christ. He is the One who will gather the Jewish people together out of all the countries of the earth, and His rule will bring peace to all the peoples of the earth. Verse 11 looks forward to His ride into Jerusalem when He offered Himself to Israel as their King. Wine pictures His own blood that was to stain His garments when He was crucified for *all* mankind, not just the Jews.

11 Binding his foal unto the vine, and
his ass's colt unto the choice vine; he
washed his garments in wine, and his
clothes in the blood of grapes:
12 His eyes *shall be* red with wine, and
his teeth white with milk.
¶ 13 Zebulun shall dwell at the haven
of the sea; and he *shall be* for an haven
of ships; and his border *shall be* unto
Zidon.
¶ 14 Issachar *is* a strong ass couching
down between two burdens:
15 And he saw that rest *was* good, and
the land that *it was* pleasant; and bowed
his shoulder to bear, and became a servant unto tribute.
¶ 16 Dan shall judge his people, as one
of the tribes of Israel.
17 Dan shall be a serpent by the way,
an adder in the path, that biteth the
horse heels, so that his rider shall fall
backward.
18 I have waited for thy salvation,
O LORD.
¶ 19 Gad, a troop shall overcome him:
but he shall overcome at the last.
¶ 20 Out of Asher his bread *shall be* fat,
and he shall yield royal dainties.
¶ 21 Naphtali *is* a hind let loose: he
giveth goodly words.
¶ 22 Joseph *is* a fruitful bough, *even* a
fruitful bough by a well; *whose* branches
run over the wall:
23 The archers have sorely grieved
him, and shot *at him,* and hated him:
24 But his bow abode in strength, and
the arms of his hands were made strong
by the hands of the mighty *God* of Jacob; (from thence *is* the shepherd, the
stone of Israel:)
25 *Even* by the God of thy father, who
shall help thee; and by the Almighty,
who shall bless thee with blessings of
heaven above, blessings of the deep
that lieth under, blessings of the
breasts, and of the womb:
26 The blessings of thy father have
prevailed above the blessings of my
progenitors unto the utmost bound of
the everlasting hills: they shall be on
the head of Joseph, and on the crown
of the head of him that was separate
from his brethren.
¶ 27 Benjamin shall ravin *as* a wolf: in
the morning he shall devour the prey,
and at night he shall divide the spoil.

49:24 from thence. "From thence" refers not to Joseph but to the God of Jacob. "The shepherd, the stone of Israel" is, of course, the Lord Jesus. Jacob is saying here that the Messiah will be the Son of the God who made Joseph strong.
49:27 ravin. To seize upon prey.

¶ 28 All these *are* the twelve tribes of Israel: and this *is it* that their father spake unto them, and blessed them; every one according to his blessing he blessed them.

29 And he charged them, and said unto them, I am to be gathered unto my people: bury me with my fathers in the cave that *is* in the field of Ephron the Hittite,

30 In the cave that *is* in the field of Machpelah, which *is* before Mamre, in the land of Canaan, which Abraham bought with the field of Ephron the Hittite for a possession of a buryingplace.

31 There they buried Abraham and Sarah his wife; there they buried Isaac and Rebekah his wife; and there I buried Leah.

32 The purchase of the field and of the cave that *is* therein *was* from the children of Heth.

Jacob dies

33 And when Jacob had made an end of commanding his sons, he gathered up his feet into the bed, and yielded up the ghost, and was gathered unto his people.

50 And Joseph fell upon his father's face, and wept upon him, and kissed him.

2 And Joseph commanded his servants the physicians to embalm his father: and the physicians embalmed Israel.

3 And forty days were fulfilled for him; for so are fulfilled the days of those which are embalmed: and the Egyptians mourned for him threescore and ten days.

4 And when the days of his mourning were past, Joseph spake unto the house of Pharaoh, saying, If now I have found grace in your eyes, speak, I pray you, in the ears of Pharaoh, saying,

5 My father made me swear, saying, Lo, I die: in my grave which I have digged for me in the land of Canaan, there shalt thou bury me. Now therefore let me go up, I pray thee, and bury my father, and I will come again.

6 And Pharaoh said, Go up, and bury thy father, according as he made thee swear.

¶ 7 And Joseph went up to bury his father: and with him went up all the servants of Pharaoh, the elders of his house, and all the elders of the land of Egypt,

8 And all the house of Joseph, and his brethren, and his father's house: only their little ones, and their flocks, and their herds, they left in the land of Goshen.

9 And there went up with him both chariots and horsemen: and it was a very great company.

10 And they came to the threshingfloor of Atad, which *is* beyond Jordan, and there they mourned with a great and very sore lamentation: and he made a mourning for his father seven days.

11 And when the inhabitants of the land, the Canaanites, saw the mourning in the floor of Atad, they said, This *is* a grievous mourning to the Egyptians: wherefore the name of it was called Abel-mizraim, which *is* beyond Jordan.

12 And his sons did unto him according as he commanded them:

13 For his sons carried him into the land of Canaan, and buried him in the cave of the field of Machpelah, which Abraham bought with the field for a possession of a buryingplace of Ephron the Hittite, before Mamre.

¶ 14 And Joseph returned into Egypt, he, and his brethren, and all that went up with him to bury his father, after he had buried his father.

¶ 15 And when Joseph's brethren saw that their father was dead, they said, Joseph will peradventure hate us, and will certainly requite us all the evil which we did unto him.

16 And they sent a messenger unto Joseph, saying, Thy father did command before he died, saying,

17 So shall ye say unto Joseph, Forgive,

I pray thee now, the trespass of thy
brethren, and their sin; for they did unto
thee evil: and now, we pray thee, forgive
the trespass of the servants of the God
of thy father. And Joseph wept when
they spake unto him.
18And his brethren also went and fell
down before his face; and they said,
Behold, we *be* thy servants.
19And Joseph said unto them, Fear
not: for *am* I in the place of God?
20But as for you, ye thought evil
against me; *but* God meant it unto good,
to bring to pass, as *it is* this day, to save
much people alive.
21Now therefore fear ye not: I will
nourish you, and your little ones. And
he comforted them, and spake kindly
unto them.
¶22And Joseph dwelt in Egypt, he,
and his father's house: and Joseph lived
an hundred and ten years.
23And Joseph saw Ephraim's children
of the third *generation:* the children also
of Machir the son Manasseh were
brought up upon Joseph's knees.
24And Joseph said unto his brethren,
I die: and God will surely visit you, and
bring you out of this land unto the land
which he sware to Abraham, to Isaac,
and to Jacob.
25And Joseph took an oath of the children of Israel, saying, God will surely
visit you, and ye shall carry up my
bones from hence.

Joseph dies

26So Joseph died, *being* an hundred
and ten years old: and they embalmed
him, and he was put in a coffin in Egypt.

50:17 Joseph wept. Likewise, the Lord Jesus Christ is grieved when we do not understand how kind and gracious and forgiving He is.

50:26 a coffin in Egypt. The whole failure of man to measure up to the righteousness of God shows very clearly when we read the first words of this book along with the last. It begins, "In the beginning God," and ends, "in a coffin in Egypt."

The Second Book of Moses, called

EXODUS

THEME

The name Exodus means *going out.* The book is about the *going out* of the children of Israel from Egypt, where they had come in Joseph's time, to Canaan, the land God had promised to give to the descendants of Abraham. It tells of their escape from being slaves in Egypt, and of their being formed into a nation with its own government and laws.

THE LESSON IN EXODUS

Exodus is important not only for the history of the Jews, but because of the spiritual lessons it teaches, for "all these things happened unto them for ensamples" (1 Corinthians 10:11). The great lesson God wants us to learn from Exodus is the lesson of redemption, or how God can save sinners and free them from the power of sin and Satan. We learn this lesson from the *types or pictures.

The three main types are:

1. Egypt and Pharaoh. They are pictures of the world and of Satan who is often called the Prince of this world (look this up in John 12:31; 14:30; 16:11). Just as the Israelites were slaves in Egypt, so everybody today is, by nature, the slave of sin and under the power of Satan (Romans 6:16-18).

2. The Passover. Here is a picture of the only way we can be saved from the power of sin, by the death of the Lord Jesus Christ on the cross for us (1 Corinthians 5:7), for the Passover lamb was a type of Him.

3. The tabernacle and the priesthood. These both illustrate the Christian life. The tabernacle speaks of approach to God through the Lord Jesus Christ and the priesthood speaks of the Christian's privilege of worship and praise (Hebrews 9:11 and 1 Peter 2:9).

THE WRITER

Moses wrote the material for the first five books of the Bible. See Exodus 24:4 and 34:27. The book of Exodus was evidently in existence at the time of Joshua (Joshua 1:7,8). The Lord Jesus quoted from it in Mark 12:26 and Luke 20:37.

PASSAGES TO NOTE

The Passover is found in chapter 12.
The Ten Commandments are found in chapter 20.

OUTLINE OF EXODUS

I.	Deliverance from Egypt	Exodus 1:1—15:27
II.	The Wilderness Journey	Exodus 16:1—18:27
III.	Israel at Sinai	Exodus 19:1—40:38

I. Deliverance from Egypt (1:1—15:27)

1 Now these *are* the names of the
children of *Israel, which came
into *Egypt; every man and his household came with *Jacob.
2 Reuben, Simeon, Levi, and Judah,
3 Issachar, Zebulun, and Benjamin,
4 Dan, and Naphtali, Gad, and Asher.
5 And all the souls that came out of the
loins of Jacob were seventy souls: for
*Joseph was in Egypt *already*.
6 And Joseph died, and all his brethren, and all that generation.
7 And the children of Israel were fruitful, and increased abundantly, and multiplied, and waxed exceeding mighty;
and the land was filled with them.
¶ 8 Now there arose up a new king
over Egypt, which knew not Joseph.
9 And he said unto his people, Behold,
the people of the children of Israel *are*
more and mightier than we:
10 Come on, let us deal wisely with
them; lest they multiply, and it come to
pass, that, when there falleth out any
war, they join also unto our enemies,
and fight against us, and *so* get them up
out of the land.
11 Therefore they did set over them
taskmasters to afflict them with their
burdens. And they built for *Pharaoh
treasure cities, Pithom and Raamses.
12 But the more they afflicted them,
the more they multiplied and grew. And
they were grieved because of the children of Israel.
13 And the Egyptians made the children of Israel to serve with rigour:

1:13 Slavery in Egypt
The phrase "to serve with rigour" means that the Egyptians treated the Israelites harshly and made them work hard. The process of making the Israelites slaves must have taken many years and lasted through the reigns of many kings. In the end, the Israelites had lost their lands and money and had even lost their courage and were contented to be slaves.

14 And they made their lives bitter
with hard bondage, in morter, and in
brick, and in all manner of service in the
field: all their service, wherein they
made them serve, *was* with rigour.
¶ 15 And the king of Egypt spake to the
Hebrew midwives, of which the name

1:8 A NEW KING IN EGYPT

It is thought that about sixty years after the death of Joseph, a revolution took place in Egypt and a new family of rulers came to the throne. The new king did not know of the service Joseph had rendered to the state, and he changed the policy of being friendly to the Israelites. He was suspicious of them for quite natural reasons:

1. they were foreigners;
2. they were shepherds as were the wild border tribes surrounding Egypt;
3. they lived in the land of Goshen on the northeast frontier of Egypt, where they could easily unite with the enemies of Egypt;
4. they were of a different religion and sacrificed animals such as bulls, which the Egyptians regarded as sacred or holy (Exod. 8:26).

1:7 increased. Seventy people and a large number of household slaves had come to Egypt. By the time of the Exodus, the Israelites numbered about 600,000. This increase was in fulfillment of the promise of God in Genesis 46:3-4.

1:11 Pharaoh. See Genesis 12:15 note.

of the one *was* Shiphrah, and the name of the other Puah:

16 And he said, When ye do the office of a midwife to the Hebrew women, and see *them* upon the stools; if it *be* a son, then ye shall kill him: but if it *be* a daughter, then she shall live.

17 But the midwives *feared *God, and did not as the king of Egypt commanded them, but saved the men children alive.

18 And the king of Egypt called for the midwives, and said unto them, Why have ye done this thing, and have saved the men children alive?

19 And the midwives said unto Pharaoh, Because the Hebrew women *are* not as the Egyptian women; for they *are* lively, and are delivered ere the midwives come in unto them.

20 Therefore God dealt well with the midwives: and the people multiplied, and waxed very mighty.

21 And it came to pass, because the midwives feared God, that he made them houses.

22 And Pharaoh charged all his people, saying, Every son that is born ye shall cast into the river, and every daughter ye shall save alive.

Moses, the deliverer

2 And there went a man of the house of Levi, and took *to wife* a daughter of Levi.

2 And the woman conceived, and bare a son: and when she saw him that he *was a* goodly **child*, she hid him three months.

3 And when she could not longer hide him, she took for him an ark of bulrushes, and daubed it with slime and with pitch, and put the child therein; and she laid *it* in the flags by the river's brink.

4 And his sister stood afar off, to wit what would be done to him.

¶5 And the daughter of Pharaoh came down to wash *herself* at the river; and her maidens walked along by the river's side; and when she saw the ark among the flags, she sent her maid to fetch it.

6 And when she had opened *it,* she saw the child: and, behold, the babe wept. And she had compassion on him, and said, This *is one* of the Hebrews' children.

7 Then said his sister to Pharaoh's daughter, Shall I go and call to thee a nurse of the Hebrew women, that she may nurse the child for thee?

8 And Pharaoh's daughter said to her, Go. And the maid went and called the child's mother.

9 And Pharaoh's daughter said unto her, Take this child away, and nurse it for me, and I will give *thee* thy wages. And the woman took the child, and nursed it.

10 And the child grew, and she brought him unto Pharaoh's daughter, and he became her son. And she called his name *Moses: and she said, Because I drew him out of the water.

The exile of Moses

¶11 And it came to pass in those days, when Moses was grown, that he went out unto his brethren, and looked on their burdens: and he spied an Egyptian smiting an Hebrew, one of his brethren.

12 And he looked this way and that way, and when he saw that *there was* no man, he slew the Egyptian, and hid him in the sand.

13 And when he went out the second

1:17 feared God. Read the Psalm19:9 note.
2:1 daughter of Levi. See Numbers 26:59 note.
2:2 hid. Look up Acts 7:20-38 and Hebrews 11:23-29.
2:10 Moses. The name "Moses" means to *draw out of the water.* People often name children after important events. See verse 22 where Moses followed the same custom for his son.
2:11 grown. He was forty years old.

day, behold, two men of the Hebrews
strove together: and he said to him that
did the wrong, Wherefore smitest thou
thy fellow?
14And he said, Who made thee a
prince and a judge over us? intendest
thou to kill me, as thou killedst the
Egyptian? And Moses feared, and said,
Surely this thing is known.
15Now when Pharaoh heard this
thing, he sought to slay Moses. But
Moses fled from the face of Pharaoh,
and dwelt in the land of *Midian: and he
sat down by a well.

2:15 The Land of Midian
Midian was the country located on the eastern gulf of the Red Sea. It was inhabited by shepherds who were descendants of Keturah, one of the wives of Abraham. They still worshipped the true God, and their chief, Reuel (also called Jethro), was also the priest. (See Gen. 25:2; Exod. 18:1; Num. 10:29; Judg. 1:16.)

16Now the priest of Midian had seven
daughters: and they came and drew
water, and filled the troughs to water
their father's flock.
17And the shepherds came and drove
them away: but Moses stood up and
helped them, and watered their flock.
18And when they came to Reuel their
father, he said, How *is it that* ye are
come so soon to day?
19And they said, An Egyptian delivered us out of the hand of the shepherds, and also drew *water* enough for
us, and watered the flock.
20And he said unto his daughters,
And where *is* he? why *is* it *that* ye have
left the man? call him, that he may eat
bread.
21And Moses was content to dwell
with the man: and he gave Moses Zipporah his daughter.
22And she bare *him* a son, and he
called his name Gershom: for he said, I
have been a stranger in a strange land.
¶23And it came to pass in process of
time, that the king of Egypt died: and
the children of Israel sighed by reason
of the bondage, and they cried, and their
cry came up unto God by reason of the
bondage.
24And God heard their groaning, and
God remembered his *covenant with
*Abraham, with *Isaac, and with Jacob.
25And God looked upon the children
of Israel, and God had respect unto
them.

God's call to Moses

3 Now Moses kept the flock of Jethro
his father in law, the priest of
Midian: and he led the flock to the backside of the desert, and came to the
mountain of God, *even* to *Horeb.
2And the *angel of the LORD appeared unto him in a flame of *fire out
of the midst of a bush: and he looked,
and, behold, the bush burned with fire,
and the bush *was* not consumed.
3And Moses said, I will now turn
aside, and see this great sight, why the
bush is not burnt.
4And when the LORD saw that he
turned aside to see, God called unto
him out of the midst of the bush, and
said, Moses, Moses. And he said, Here
am I.
5And he said, Draw not nigh hither:
put off thy shoes from off thy feet, for
the place whereon thou standest *is*
*holy ground.
6Moreover he said, I *am* the God of
thy father, the God of Abraham, the God

2:18 Reuel. "Reuel" is called "Raguel" in Numbers 10:29 and "Jethro" in several other places (Exod. 3:1; 4:18; 18:1-2,5-6,9-10,12).
3:1 backside. The back part or rear.
3:1 mountain. This was Mount Sinai, the place where God gave the Law to Israel (chap. 19). Horeb was probably the range of mountains which included Sinai.
3:2 angel of the LORD. God Himself was present in the bush in the form of a flame of fire. See Hebrews 1:4 note, "Angels."

3:5-6 In God's Presence
As a sinful man, Moses had to be told not to draw near to God. He realized his unfitness even to look (vs. 6). Taking off one's shoes was a sign of respect in the East and showed Moses' reverence for the presence of God. Although when we are saved we can know God and approach Him without fear, we must still remember the reverence due to Him in our worship and our service.

of Isaac, and the God of Jacob. And
Moses hid his face; for he was afraid to
look upon God.
¶7And the LORD said, I have surely
seen the affliction of my people which
are in Egypt, and have heard their cry
by reason of their taskmasters; for I
know their sorrows;
8And I am come down to deliver
them out of the hand of the Egyptians,
and to bring them up out of that land
unto a good land and a large, unto a land
flowing with milk and honey; unto the
place of the Canaanites, and the Hittites, and the Amorites, and the Perizzites, and the Hivites, and the
Jebusites.
9Now therefore, behold, the cry of
the children of Israel is come unto me:
and I have also seen the oppression
wherewith the Egyptians oppress
them.
10Come now therefore, and I will
send thee unto Pharaoh, that thou
mayest bring forth my people the children of Israel out of Egypt.
11And Moses said unto God, Who *am*
I, that I should go unto Pharaoh, and
that I should bring forth the children of
Israel out of Egypt?
12And he said, Certainly I will be with
thee; and this *shall be* a token unto thee,
that I have sent thee: When thou hast
brought forth the people out of Egypt,
ye shall serve God upon this mountain.
¶13And Moses said unto God, Behold,
when I come unto the children of Israel,
and shall say unto them, The God of
your fathers hath sent me unto you; and
they shall say to me, What *is* his name?
what shall I say unto them?
14And God said unto Moses, I AM
THAT I AM: and he said, Thus shalt
thou say unto the children of Israel, I
AM hath sent me unto you.
15And God said moreover unto Moses, Thus shalt thou say unto the children of Israel, The LORD God of your
fathers, the God of Abraham, the God
of Isaac, and the God of Jacob, hath sent
me unto you: this *is* my name for ever,
and this *is* my memorial unto all generations.
16Go, and gather the elders of Israel
together, and say unto them, The LORD
God of your fathers, the God of Abraham, of Isaac, and of Jacob, appeared
unto me, saying, I have surely visited
you, and *seen* that which is done to you
in Egypt:
17And I have said, I will bring you up
out of the affliction of Egypt unto the
land of the Canaanites, and the Hittites,
and the Amorites, and the Perizzites,
and the Hivites, and the Jebusites, unto
a land flowing with milk and honey.
18And they shall hearken to thy voice:
and thou shalt come, thou and the elders of Israel, unto the king of Egypt,
and ye shall say unto him, The LORD
God of the Hebrews hath met with us:
and now let us go, we beseech thee,
three days' journey into the wilderness,
that we may *sacrifice to the LORD our
God.

3:8 flowing. The richness and fertility of the land of Canaan are described in this picturesque way. (See Exod. 33:3.)
3:14 I AM. God meant that He was the same unchanging God who had made the promises to Abraham and that He would fulfill all He had said. See *names of God.
3:18 elders of Israel. See Ruth 4:2 note, "The Elders of the City."
3:18 three days' journey. A way of expressing distance; a day's journey might be as much as twenty-four miles.

¶ 19 And I am sure that the king of Egypt will not let you go, no, not by a mighty hand.

20 And I will stretch out my hand, and smite Egypt with all my wonders which I will do in the midst thereof: and after that he will let you go.

21 And I will give this people favour in the sight of the Egyptians: and it shall come to pass, that, when ye go, ye shall not go empty:

22 But every woman shall borrow of her neighbour, and of her that sojourneth in her house, jewels of silver, and jewels of gold, and raiment: and ye shall put *them* upon your sons, and upon your daughters; and ye shall spoil the Egyptians.

Moses' objections

4 And Moses answered and said, But, behold, they will not believe me, nor hearken unto my voice: for they will say, The LORD hath not appeared unto thee.

2 And the LORD said unto him, What *is* that in thine hand? And he said, A rod.

3 And he said, Cast it on the ground. And he cast it on the ground, and it became a serpent; and Moses fled from before it.

4 And the LORD said unto Moses, Put forth thine hand, and take it by the tail. And he put forth his hand, and caught it, and it became a rod in his hand:

5 That they may believe that the LORD God of their fathers, the God of Abraham, the God of Isaac, and the God of Jacob, hath appeared unto thee.

¶ 6 And the LORD said furthermore unto him, Put now thine hand into thy bosom. And he put his hand into his bosom: and when he took it out, behold, his hand *was* *leprous as snow.

7 And he said, Put thine hand into thy bosom again. And he put his hand into his bosom again; and plucked it out of his bosom, and, behold, it was turned again as his *other* flesh.

8 And it shall come to pass, if they will not believe thee, neither hearken to the voice of the first sign, that they will believe the voice of the latter sign.

9 And it shall come to pass, if they will not believe also these two signs, neither hearken unto thy voice, that thou shalt take of the water of the river, and pour *it* upon the dry *land:* and the water which thou takest out of the river shall become blood upon the dry *land.*

¶ 10 And Moses said unto the LORD, O my Lord, I *am* not eloquent, neither heretofore, nor since thou hast spoken unto thy servant: but I *am* slow of speech, and of a slow tongue.

11 And the LORD said unto him, Who hath made man's mouth? or who maketh the dumb, or deaf, or the seeing, or the blind? have not I the LORD?

12 Now therefore go, and I will be with thy mouth, and teach thee what thou shalt say.

13 And he said, O my Lord, send, I pray thee, by the hand *of him whom* thou wilt send.

Aaron's help promised

14 And the anger of the LORD was kindled against Moses, and he said, *Is* not *Aaron the Levite thy brother? I know that he can speak well. And also, behold, he cometh forth to meet thee: and when he seeth thee, he will be glad in his heart.

15 And thou shalt speak unto him, and

3:22 borrow. The Hebrew word means simply *ask.* The Egyptians had oppressed the Israelites for years and made them work for very low wages. This was just to get back what was really due to them, so it was not dishonest.

4:13 send. Moses' answer implied "choose a better man to send" and seemed to doubt the power of God. Contrast this with the answer of Isaiah (Isa. 6:8).

4:14 Aaron. See Exodus 28:1 and Leviticus 8:2 .

4:15 with thy mouth. See *inspiration.

put words in his mouth: and I will be
with thy mouth, and with his mouth,
and will teach you what ye shall do.
16 And he shall be thy spokesman
unto the people: and he shall be, *even*
he shall be to thee instead of a mouth,
and thou shalt be to him instead of God.
17 And thou shalt take this rod in thine
hand, wherewith thou shalt do signs.
¶ 18 And Moses went and returned to
Jethro his father in law, and said unto
him, Let me go, I pray thee, and return
unto my brethren which *are* in Egypt,
and see whether they be yet alive. And
Jethro said to Moses, Go in *peace.

The return to Egypt

19 And the LORD said unto Moses
in Midian, Go, return into Egypt: for
all the men are dead which sought thy
life.
20 And Moses took his wife and his
sons, and set them upon an ass, and he
returned to the land of Egypt: and Moses took the rod of God in his hand.
21 And the LORD said unto Moses,
When thou goest to return into Egypt,
see that thou do all those wonders before Pharaoh, which I have put in thine
hand: but I will harden his heart, that he
shall not let the people go.
22 And thou shalt say unto Pharaoh,
Thus saith the LORD, Israel *is* my son,
even my firstborn:
23 And I say unto thee, Let my son go,
that he may serve me: and if thou refuse to let him go, behold, I will slay thy
son, *even* thy firstborn.
¶ 24 And it came to pass by the way in
the inn, that the LORD met him, and
sought to kill him.
25 Then Zipporah took a sharp stone,
and cut off the foreskin of her son, and
cast *it* at his feet, and said, Surely a
bloody husband *art* thou to me.
26 So he let him go: then she said, A
bloody husband *thou art,* because of the
*circumcision.
¶ 27 And the LORD said to Aaron, Go
into the wilderness to meet Moses. And
he went, and met him in the mount of
God, and kissed him.
28 And Moses told Aaron all the words
of the LORD who had sent him, and all
the signs which he had commanded
him.

The message to the people

¶ 29 And Moses and Aaron went and
gathered together all the elders of the
children of Israel:
30 And Aaron spake all the words
which the LORD had spoken unto Moses, and did the signs in the sight of the
people.
31 And the people believed: and
when they heard that the LORD had
visited the children of Israel, and that
he had looked upon their affliction,
then they bowed their heads and worshipped.

The first interview with Pharaoh

5 And afterward Moses and Aaron
went in, and told Pharaoh, Thus
saith the LORD God of Israel, Let my
people go, that they may hold a feast
unto me in the wilderness.

4:21 PHARAOH'S HARDENED HEART

The expression "to harden the heart" means *to become stubborn or obstinate.* When God said that He would harden Pharaoh's heart, He meant that He would allow Pharaoh to be stubborn in refusing the demands of the Israelites. Pharaoh's question in 5:2 ("Who is the LORD, that I should obey his voice to let Israel go?") was sufficiently answered by the miracles and plagues, but, even so, he persisted in his obstinate decision to go against God. He made up his mind of his own free will, and God let him go his own wicked way. The expression occurs eighteen times in the next chapters. (See Isa. 6:9-10.)

4:24 sought to kill him. Moses had been disobedient to the LORD, who had to give him a stern reminder that he must obey God.

2 And Pharaoh said, Who *is* the LORD, that I should obey his voice to let Israel go? I know not the LORD, neither will I let Israel go.

3 And they said, The God of the Hebrews hath met with us: let us go, we pray thee, three days' journey into the desert, and sacrifice unto the LORD our God; lest he fall upon us with pestilence, or with the sword.

4 And the king of Egypt said unto them, Wherefore do ye, Moses and Aaron, let the people from their works? get you unto your burdens.

5 And Pharaoh said, Behold, the people of the land now *are* many, and ye make them rest from their burdens.

6 And Pharaoh commanded the same day the taskmasters of the people, and their officers, saying,

7 Ye shall no more give the people straw to make brick, as heretofore: let them go and gather straw for themselves.

8 And the tale of the bricks, which they did make heretofore, ye shall lay upon them; ye shall not diminish *ought* thereof: for they *be* idle; therefore they cry, saying, Let us go *and* sacrifice to our God.

9 Let there more work be laid upon the men, that they may labour therein; and let them not regard vain words.

Increased burdens

¶ 10 And the taskmasters of the people went out, and their officers, and they spake to the people, saying, Thus saith Pharaoh, I will not give you straw.

11 Go ye, get you straw where ye can find it: yet not ought of your work shall be diminished.

12 So the people were scattered abroad throughout all the land of Egypt to gather stubble instead of straw.

13 And the taskmasters hasted *them,* saying, Fulfil your works, *your* daily tasks, as when there was straw.

14 And the officers of the children of Israel, which Pharaoh's taskmasters had set over them, were beaten, *and* demanded, Wherefore have ye not fulfilled your task in making brick both yesterday and to day, as heretofore?

¶ 15 Then the officers of the children of Israel came and cried unto Pharaoh, saying, Wherefore dealest thou thus with thy servants?

16 There is no straw given unto thy servants, and they say to us, Make brick: and, behold, thy servants *are* beaten; but the fault *is* in thine own people.

17 But he said, Ye *are* idle, *ye are* idle: therefore ye say, Let us go *and* do sacrifice to the LORD.

18 Go therefore now, *and* work; for there shall no straw be given you, yet shall ye deliver the tale of bricks.

19 And the officers of the children of Israel did see *that* they *were* in evil *case,* after it was said, Ye shall not minish *ought* from your bricks of your daily task.

¶ 20 And they met Moses and Aaron, who stood in the way, as they came forth from Pharaoh:

21 And they said unto them, The LORD look upon you, and judge; because ye have made our savour to be abhorred in the eyes of Pharaoh, and in the eyes of his servants, to put a sword in their hand to slay us.

22 And Moses returned unto the LORD, and said, Lord, wherefore hast thou *so* evil entreated this people? why *is* it *that* thou hast sent me?

23 For since I came to Pharaoh to speak in thy name, he hath done evil to this people; neither hast thou delivered thy people at all.

5:2 Who is the LORD? See Exodus 4:21 note, and look up Exodus 7:17; 8:22; 9:14; 14:4,18.
5:4 let. An old word meaning *prevent.*
5:8 tale. An old word meaning *number* or *quantity.*
5:19 minish. To diminish or lessen.

God's encouragement to Moses

6 Then the LORD said unto Moses,
Now shalt thou see what I will do
to Pharaoh: for with a strong hand shall
he let them go, and with a strong hand
shall he drive them out of his land.
2 And God spake unto Moses, and said
unto him, I *am* the LORD:
3 And I appeared unto Abraham,
unto Isaac, and unto Jacob, by *the name
of* God Almighty, but by my name
JEHOVAH was I not known to them.
4 And I have also established my covenant with them, to give them the land
of Canaan, the land of their pilgrimage,
wherein they were strangers.
5 And I have also heard the groaning
of the children of Israel, whom the
Egyptians keep in bondage; and I have
remembered my covenant.
6 Wherefore say unto the children of
Israel, I *am* the LORD, and I will bring
you out from under the burdens of the
Egyptians, and I will rid you out of their
bondage, and I will redeem you with a
stretched out arm, and with great judgments:

6:6 God's Promise to Redeem
To "redeem" means to *buy back.* The Israelites had been free, but they were now slaves of Pharaoh, and God "bought them back" to liberty. This is the meaning of *redemption. We were born slaves to sin and needed to be redeemed by Christ, whose death on the cross was the price of our freedom. God made man in His own image; man sinned and lost companionship with his Creator. God thus redeemed him–bought him back–by the shedding of Christ's most precious blood at Calvary. (Read John 3:16.)

7 And I will take you to me for a people, and I will be to you a God: and ye
shall know that I *am* the LORD your
God, which bringeth you out from under the burdens of the Egyptians.
8 And I will bring you in unto the land,
concerning the which I did swear to
give it to Abraham, to Isaac, and to Jacob; and I will give it you for an heritage: I *am* the LORD.
¶ 9 And Moses spake so unto the children of Israel: but they hearkened not
unto Moses for anguish of spirit, and for
cruel bondage.
10 And the LORD spake unto Moses,
saying,
11 Go in, speak unto Pharaoh king of
Egypt, that he let the children of Israel
go out of his land.
12 And Moses spake before the LORD,
saying, Behold, the children of Israel
have not hearkened unto me; how then
shall Pharaoh hear me, who *am* of *uncircumcised lips?
13 And the LORD spake unto Moses
and unto Aaron, and gave them a charge
unto the children of Israel, and unto
Pharaoh king of Egypt, to bring the
children of Israel out of the land of
Egypt.

The families of Israel

¶ 14 These *be* the heads of their fathers'
houses: The sons of Reuben the firstborn of Israel; Hanoch, and Pallu, Hezron, and Carmi: these *be* the families of
Reuben.
15 And the sons of Simeon; Jemuel,
and Jamin, and Ohad, and *Jachin, and
Zohar, and Shaul the son of a Canaanitish woman: these *are* the families of
Simeon.
¶ 16 And these *are* the names of the
sons of Levi according to their generations; Gershon, and Kohath, and Merari: and the years of the life of Levi
were an hundred thirty and seven
years.
17 The sons of Gershon; Libni, and
Shimi, according to their families.
18 And the sons of Kohath; Amram,

6:3 JEHOVAH. The name "Jehovah" means *the LORD,* but the Israelites did not understand all that the name implied. See *names of God and the Genesis 2:4 note.
6:4 covenant. A "covenant" is a promise and an agreement. Read Genesis 15:18.
6:8 I did swear to give it. Read verse 4 and Genesis 15:18.

and Izhar, and Hebron, and Uzziel: and
the years of the life of Kohath *were* an
hundred thirty and three years.
19 And the sons of Merari; Mahali and
Mushi: these *are* the families of Levi
according to their generations.
20 And Amram took him Jochebed his
father's sister to wife; and she bare him
Aaron and Moses: and the years of the
life of Amram *were* an hundred and
thirty and seven years.
¶21 And the sons of Izhar; *Korah, and
Nepheg, and Zichri.
22 And the sons of Uzziel; Mishael,
and Elzaphan, and Zithri.
23 And Aaron took him Elisheba,
daughter of Amminadab, sister of Na-
ashon, to wife; and she bare him Nadab,
and Abihu, Eleazar, and Ithamar.
24 And the sons of Korah; Assir, and
Elkanah, and Abiasaph: these *are* the
families of the Korhites.
25 And Eleazar Aaron's son took him
one of the daughters of Putiel to wife;
and she bare him *Phinehas: these *are*
the heads of the fathers of the Levites
according to their families.
26 These *are* that Aaron and Moses, to
whom the LORD said, Bring out the
children of Israel from the land of Egypt
according to their armies.
27 These *are* they which spake to Pharaoh king of Egypt, to bring out the
children of Israel from Egypt: these *are*
that Moses and Aaron.
¶28 And it came to pass on the day
when the LORD spake unto Moses in the
land of Egypt,
29 That the LORD spake unto Moses,
saying, I *am* the LORD: speak thou unto
Pharaoh king of Egypt all that I say unto
thee.
30 And Moses said before the LORD,
Behold, I *am* of uncircumcised lips, and
how shall Pharaoh hearken unto me?

The nine plagues

7 And the LORD said unto Moses,
See, I have made thee a god to
*Pharaoh: and Aaron thy brother shall
be thy prophet.
2 Thou shalt speak all that I command
thee: and Aaron thy brother shall speak
unto Pharaoh, that he send the children
of *Israel out of his land.
3 And I will *harden Pharaoh's heart,
and multiply my signs and my wonders
in the land of *Egypt.
4 But Pharaoh shall not hearken unto
you, that I may lay my hand upon Egypt,
and bring forth mine armies, *and* my
people the children of Israel, out of the
land of Egypt by great judgments.
5 And the Egyptians shall know that I
am the LORD, when I stretch forth mine
hand upon Egypt, and bring out the
children of Israel from among them.
6 And Moses and Aaron did as the
LORD commanded them, so did they.
7 And Moses *was* fourscore years old,
and Aaron fourscore and three years
old, when they spake unto Pharaoh.
¶8 And the LORD spake unto Moses
and unto Aaron, saying,
9 When Pharaoh shall speak unto you,
saying, Shew a *miracle for you: then
thou shalt say unto Aaron, Take thy rod,
and cast *it* before Pharaoh, *and* it shall
become a serpent.

The second interview with Pharaoh

10 And Moses and Aaron went in unto
Pharaoh, and they did so as the LORD
had commanded: and Aaron cast down
his rod before Pharaoh, and before his
servants, and it became a serpent.
11 Then Pharaoh also called the wise
men and the sorcerers: now the magicians of Egypt, they also did in like
manner with their enchantments.
12 For they cast down every man his

7:10 serpent. See Exodus 4:2-4.

7:11 like manner. The names of the sorcerers, Jannes and Jambres, are given in 2 Timothy 3:8. They were heathen priests who wielded certain satanic powers. They could do miracles, but these were far inferior to those performed by Moses and Aaron. See verses 22 and 8:7,18.

rod, and they became serpents: but
Aaron's rod swallowed up their rods.
13And he hardened Pharaoh's heart,
that he hearkened not unto them; as the
LORD had said.

The third interview with Pharaoh

¶14And the LORD said unto Moses,
Pharaoh's heart *is* hardened, he refuseth
to let the people go.
15Get thee unto Pharaoh in the morning; lo, he goeth out unto the water; and
thou shalt stand by the river's brink
against he come; and the rod which was
turned to a serpent shalt thou take in
thine hand.
16And thou shalt say unto him, The
LORD God of the Hebrews hath sent
me unto thee, saying, Let my people
go, that they may serve me in the wilderness: and, behold, hitherto thou
wouldest not hear.
17Thus saith the LORD, In this thou
shalt know that I *am* the LORD: behold,
I will smite with the rod that *is* in mine
hand upon the waters which *are* in the
river, and they shall be turned to blood.
18And the fish that *is* in the river shall
die, and the river shall stink; and the
Egyptians shall lothe to drink of the
water of the river.
¶19And the LORD spake unto Moses,
Say unto Aaron, Take thy rod, and
stretch out thine hand upon the waters
of Egypt, upon their streams, upon their
rivers, and upon their ponds, and upon
all their pools of water, that they may
become blood; and *that* there may be
blood throughout all the land of Egypt,
both in *vessels of* wood, and in *vessels of*
stone.

The first plague

20And Moses and Aaron did so, as the
LORD commanded; and he lifted up the rod,
and smote the waters that *were* in the river,
in the sight of Pharaoh, and in the sight
of his servants; and all the waters that
were in the river were turned to blood.
21And the fish that *was* in the river
died; and the river stank, and the Egyptians could not drink of the water of the
river; and there was blood throughout
all the land of Egypt.
22And the magicians of Egypt did so
with their enchantments: and Pharaoh's
heart was hardened, neither did he hearken unto them; as the LORD had said.
23And Pharaoh turned and went into
his house, neither did he set his heart
to this also.
24And all the Egyptians digged round
about the river for water to drink; for
they could not drink of the water of the
river.
25And seven days were fulfilled, after
that the LORD had smitten the river.

The fourth interview with Pharaoh

8 And the LORD spake unto *Moses,
Go unto Pharaoh, and say unto him,
Thus saith the LORD, Let my people go,
that they may serve me.
2And if thou refuse to let *them* go,
behold, I will smite all thy borders with
frogs:
3And the river shall bring forth frogs
abundantly, which shall go up and come
into thine house, and into thy bedchamber, and upon thy bed, and into the
house of thy servants, and upon thy
people, and into thine ovens, and into
thy kneadingtroughs:
4And the frogs shall come up both on
thee, and upon thy people, and upon all
thy servants.

The second plague

¶5And the LORD spake unto Moses,
Say unto Aaron, Stretch forth thine
hand with thy rod over the streams,
over the rivers, and over the ponds, and
cause frogs to come up upon the land
of Egypt.
6And Aaron stretched out his hand
over the waters of Egypt; and the frogs
came up, and covered the land of Egypt.
7And the magicians did so with their

7:22 did so. See verse 11 and 4:21 notes.

enchantments, and brought up frogs
upon the land of Egypt.
¶ 8 Then Pharaoh called for Moses and
Aaron, and said, Intreat the LORD, that
he may take away the frogs from me,
and from my people; and I will let the
people go, that they may do sacrifice
unto the LORD.
9 And Moses said unto Pharaoh, Glory
over me: when shall I intreat for thee,
and for thy servants, and for thy people, to destroy the frogs from thee and
thy houses, *that* they may remain in the
river only?
10 And he said, To morrow. And he
said, *Be it* according to thy word: that
thou mayest know that *there is* none like
unto the LORD our God.
11 And the frogs shall depart from
thee, and from thy houses, and from thy
servants, and from thy people; they
shall remain in the river only.
12 And Moses and Aaron went out
from Pharaoh: and Moses cried unto
the LORD because of the frogs which he
had brought against Pharaoh.
13 And the LORD did according to the
word of Moses; and the frogs died out
of the houses, out of the villages, and
out of the fields.
14 And they gathered them together
upon heaps: and the land stank.
15 But when Pharaoh saw that there
was respite, he hardened his heart, and
hearkened not unto them; as the LORD
had said.

The third plague

¶ 16 And the LORD said unto Moses,
Say unto Aaron, Stretch out thy rod, and
smite the dust of the land, that it may
become lice throughout all the land of
Egypt.
17 And they did so; for Aaron
stretched out his hand with his rod, and
smote the dust of the earth, and it became lice in man, and in beast; all the
dust of the land became lice throughout
all the land of Egypt.
18 And the magicians did so with their
enchantments to bring forth lice, but
they could not: so there were lice upon
man, and upon beast.
19 Then the magicians said unto Pharaoh, This *is* the finger of God: and
Pharaoh's heart was hardened, and he
hearkened not unto them; as the LORD
had said.

The fifth interview with Pharaoh

¶ 20 And the LORD said unto Moses,
Rise up early in the morning, and stand
before Pharaoh; lo, he cometh forth to
the water; and say unto him, Thus saith
the LORD, Let my people go, that they
may serve me.
21 Else, if thou wilt not let my people
go, behold, I will send swarms *of flies*
upon thee, and upon thy servants, and
upon thy people, and into thy houses:
and the houses of the Egyptians shall
be full of swarms *of flies,* and also the
ground whereon they *are.*
22 And I will sever in that day the
land of Goshen, in which my people
dwell, that no swarms *of flies* shall be
there; to the end thou mayest know
that I *am* the LORD in the midst of the
earth.
23 And I will put a division between
my people and thy people: to morrow
shall this sign be.

The fourth plague

24 And the LORD did so; and there
came a grievous swarm *of flies* into the
house of Pharaoh, and *into* his servants'
houses, and into all the land of Egypt:
the land was corrupted by reason of the
swarm *of flies.*

8:16 lice. These first three plagues were over all the land, and they affected both Israelites and Egyptians. The next six plagues were on the Egyptians only—not over the land of Goshen where the children of Israel lived. See 9:27 note, "The Ten Plagues."

8:18 they could not. It was not within the sorcerers' power to create life. God alone has that power.

The sixth interview with Pharaoh

¶25 And Pharaoh called for Moses and
for Aaron, and said, Go ye, sacrifice to
your God in the land.

8:25 Pharaoh's Compromises
Pharaoh wanted to keep his hold over the Israelites by letting them have part of what they asked. He suggested four compromises (8:25,28; 10:11,24) to keep them in or near Egypt. This shows just what Satan tries to do with people even after they have been saved. If he cannot prevent them from becoming Christians, then he tries to spoil their Christian life by enticing them to live for worldly things and not for the Lord Jesus Christ. See James 4:4 for the Christians' answer to this temptation.

26 And Moses said, It is not meet so
to do; for we shall sacrifice the *abomination of the Egyptians to the LORD our
God: lo, shall we sacrifice the abomination of the Egyptians before their eyes,
and will they not stone us?
27 We will go three days' journey
into the wilderness, and sacrifice to
the LORD our God, as he shall command
us.
28 And Pharaoh said, I will let you go,
that ye may sacrifice to the LORD your
God in the wilderness; only ye shall not
go very far away: intreat for me.
29 And Moses said, Behold, I go out
from thee, and I will intreat the LORD
that the swarms *of flies* may depart from
Pharaoh, from his servants, and from
his people, to morrow: but let not Pharaoh deal deceitfully any more in not
letting the people go to sacrifice to the
LORD.
30 And Moses went out from Pharaoh,
and intreated the LORD.
31 And the LORD did according to the
word of Moses; and he removed the
swarms *of flies* from Pharaoh, from his
servants, and from his people; there
remained not one.
32 And Pharaoh hardened his heart at
this time also, neither would he let the
people go.

The seventh interview with Pharaoh

9 Then the LORD said unto Moses,
Go in unto Pharaoh, and tell him,
Thus saith the LORD God of the Hebrews, Let my people go, that they may
serve me.
2 For if thou refuse to let *them* go, and
wilt hold them still,
3 Behold, the hand of the LORD is
upon thy cattle which *is* in the field,
upon the horses, upon the asses, upon
the camels, upon the oxen, and upon
the sheep: *there shall be* a very grievous
murrain.
4 And the LORD shall sever between
the cattle of Israel and the cattle of
Egypt: and there shall nothing die of all
that is the children's of Israel.
5 And the LORD appointed a set time,
saying, To morrow the LORD shall do
this thing in the land.

The fifth plague

6 And the LORD did that thing on the
morrow, and all the cattle of Egypt died:
but of the cattle of the children of Israel
died not one.
7 And Pharaoh sent, and, behold,
there was not one of the cattle of the
Israelites dead. And the heart of Pharaoh was hardened, and he did not let
the people go.

The sixth plague

¶8 And the LORD said unto Moses and
unto Aaron, Take to you handfuls of
ashes of the furnace, and let Moses
sprinkle it toward the heaven in the
sight of Pharaoh.

8:26 the abomination of the Egyptians. The cow was the animal which the Egyptians worshipped (see Gen. 46:34). If the Israelites had sacrificed one of these animals, the Egyptians would have been furious.
9:3 murrain. A cattle disease.

9 And it shall become small dust in all
the land of Egypt, and shall be a boil
breaking forth *with* blains upon man,
and upon beast, throughout all the land
of Egypt.
10 And they took ashes of the furnace,
and stood before Pharaoh; and Moses
sprinkled it up toward heaven; and it
became a boil breaking forth *with* blains
upon man, and upon beast.
11 And the magicians could not stand
before Moses because of the boils; for
the boil was upon the magicians, and
upon all the Egyptians.
12 And the LORD hardened the heart
of Pharaoh, and he hearkened not unto
them; as the LORD had spoken unto
Moses.

The eight interview with Pharaoh

¶ 13 And the LORD said unto Moses,
Rise up early in the morning, and stand
before Pharaoh, and say unto him, Thus
saith the LORD God of the Hebrews, Let
my people go, that they may serve me.
14 For I will at this time send all my
plagues upon thine heart, and upon thy
servants, and upon thy people; that
thou mayest know that *there is* none like
me in all the earth.
15 For now I will stretch out my hand,
that I may smite thee and thy people
with pestilence; and thou shalt be cut
off from the earth.
16 And in very deed for this *cause* have
I raised thee up, for to shew *in* thee my
power; and that my name may be declared throughout all the earth.
17 As yet exaltest thou thyself against
my people, that thou wilt not let them
go?
18 Behold, to morrow about this time
I will cause it to rain a very grievous
hail, such as hath not been in Egypt
since the foundation thereof even until
now.
19 Send therefore now, *and* gather thy
cattle, and all that thou hast in the field;
for upon every man and beast which
shall be found in the field, and shall not
be brought home, the hail shall come
down upon them, and they shall die.
20 He that feared the word of the LORD
among the servants of Pharaoh made
his servants and his cattle flee into the
houses:
21 And he that regarded not the word
of the LORD left his servants and his
cattle in the field.

The seventh plague

¶ 22 And the LORD said unto Moses,
Stretch forth thine hand toward heaven,
that there may be hail in all the land of
Egypt, upon man, and upon beast, and
upon every herb of the field, throughout
the land of Egypt.
23 And Moses stretched forth his rod
toward heaven: and the LORD sent
thunder and hail, and the *fire ran along
upon the ground; and the LORD rained
hail upon the land of Egypt.
24 So there was hail, and fire mingled
with the hail, very grievous, such as
there was none like it in all the land of
Egypt since it became a nation.
25 And the hail smote throughout all
the land of Egypt all that *was* in the
field, both man and beast; and the hail
smote every herb of the field, and brake
every tree of the field.
26 Only in the land of Goshen, where
the children of Israel *were*, was there no
hail.
¶ 27 And Pharaoh sent, and called for
Moses and Aaron, and said unto them,
I have sinned this time: the LORD *is*
righteous, and I and my people *are*
wicked.
28 Intreat the LORD (for *it is* enough)
that there be no *more* mighty thunderings and hail; and I will let you go,
and ye shall stay no longer.
29 And Moses said unto him, As soon

9:9 blains. These were ulcers that made the priests unclean. The priests could not perform their duties in public if there was anything the matter with them. They had to be thoroughly clean.

as I am gone out of the city, I will spread
abroad my hands unto the LORD; *and*
the thunder shall cease, neither shall
there be any more hail; that thou
mayest know how that the earth *is* the
LORD'S.
30 But as for thee and thy servants, I
know that ye will not yet *fear the LORD
God.
31 And the flax and the barley was
smitten: for the barley *was* in the ear,
and the flax *was* bolled.
32 But the wheat and the rie were not
smitten: for they *were* not grown up.
33 And Moses went out of the city
from Pharaoh, and spread abroad his
hands unto the LORD: and the thunders
and hail ceased, and the rain was not
poured upon the earth.
34 And when Pharaoh saw that
the rain and the hail and the thunders
were ceased, he sinned yet more, and
hardened his heart, he and his servants.
35 And the heart of Pharaoh was hardened, neither would he let the children
of Israel go; as the LORD had spoken by
Moses.

The ninth interview with Pharaoh

10 And the LORD said unto Moses,
Go in unto Pharaoh: for I have
hardened his heart, and the heart of his
servants, that I might shew these my
signs before him:
2 And that thou mayest tell in the ears
of thy son, and of thy son's son, what
things I have wrought in Egypt, and my
signs which I have done among them;
that ye may know how that I *am* the
LORD.
3 And Moses and *Aaron came in unto
Pharaoh, and said unto him, Thus saith
the LORD God of the Hebrews, How
long wilt thou refuse to humble thyself

9:27 THE TEN PLAGUES

Water turned to blood	Exodus 7:14-25	Fish died. Main water source not usable.
Frogs cover the land	Exodus 8:1-15	Millions of frogs infested every area. When they died their decaying bodies reeked.
Lice or gnats	Exodus 8:16-19	Although the insect type is uncertain, it would have caused extreme discomfort for all living creatures.
Swarms of flies	Exodus 8:20-32	The buzzing and biting of flies bring both discomfort and disease.
Diseased livestock	Exodus 9:1-7	The exact nature of this plague is not known; however, there is no mention that it was ever withdrawn.
Boils	Exodus 9:8-12	Painful boils afflicted humans and cattle. This is the first plague to directly affect humans. No mention is made that it was withdrawn.
Hail and fire	Exodus 9:13-35	Hail, a rare phenomena in Egypt, destroyed the flax, the barley and the trees, and killed humans and animals.
Locusts	Exodus 10:1-20	Any vegetation remaining from the hail storm was now eaten by the locusts.
Darkness	Exodus 10:21-29	This intense and terrifying darkness lasted three days.
Death of firstborn	Exodus 11:1–12:36	The cause of this selective killing of the firstborn humans and animals is because the blood of the Passover lamb was not applied to their door.

9:31 bolled. Bearing pods or round seed vessels.
9:35 heart of Pharaoh was hardened. See 4:21 note.

before me? let my people go, that they may serve me.

4 Else, if thou refuse to let my people go, behold, to morrow will I bring the locusts into thy coast:

5 And they shall cover the face of the earth, that one cannot be able to see the earth: and they shall eat the residue of that which is escaped, which remaineth unto you from the hail, and shall eat every tree which groweth for you out of the field:

6 And they shall fill thy houses, and the houses of all thy servants, and the houses of all the Egyptians; which neither thy fathers, nor thy fathers' fathers have seen, since the day that they were upon the earth unto this day. And he turned himself, and went out from Pharaoh.

7 And Pharaoh's servants said unto him, How long shall this man be a snare unto us? let the men go, that they may serve the LORD their God: knowest thou not yet that Egypt is destroyed?

The third compromise refused

8 And Moses and Aaron were brought again unto Pharaoh: and he said unto them, Go, serve the LORD your God: *but* who *are* they that shall go?

9 And Moses said, We will go with our young and with our old, with our sons and with our daughters, with our flocks and with our herds will we go; for we *must hold* a feast unto the LORD.

10 And he said unto them, Let the LORD be so with you, as I will let you go, and your little ones: look *to it;* for evil *is* before you.

11 Not so: go now ye *that are* men, and serve the LORD; for that ye did desire. And they were driven out from Pharaoh's presence.

The eighth plague

¶ 12 And the LORD said unto Moses, Stretch out thine hand over the land of Egypt for the locusts, that they may come up upon the land of Egypt, and eat every herb of the land, *even* all that the hail hath left.

13 And Moses stretched forth his rod over the land of Egypt, and the LORD brought an east wind upon the land all that day, and all *that* night; *and* when it was morning, the east wind brought the locusts.

14 And the locusts went up over all the land of Egypt, and rested in all the coasts of Egypt: very grievous *were they;* before them there were no such locusts as they, neither after them shall be such.

15 For they covered the face of the whole earth, so that the land was darkened; and they did eat every herb of the land, and all the fruit of the trees which the hail had left: and there remained not any green thing in the trees, or in the herbs of the field, through all the land of Egypt.

¶ 16 Then Pharaoh called for Moses and Aaron in haste; and he said, I have sinned against the LORD your God, and against you.

17 Now therefore forgive, I pray thee, my *sin only this once, and intreat the LORD your God, that he may take away from me this *death only.

18 And he went out from Pharaoh, and intreated the LORD.

19 And the LORD turned a mighty strong west wind, which took away the locusts, and cast them into the Red sea; there remained not one locust in all the coasts of Egypt.

20 But the LORD hardened Pharaoh's heart, so that he would not let the children of Israel go.

The ninth plague

¶ 21 And the LORD said unto Moses, Stretch out thine hand toward heaven, that there may be darkness over the land of Egypt, even darkness *which* may be felt.

10:5 residue. The rest, the remainder.
10:11 go now ye that are men. See 8:25 note, "Pharaoh's Compromises."

22 And Moses stretched forth his hand
toward heaven; and there was a thick
darkness in all the land of Egypt three
days:
23 They saw not one another, neither
rose any from his place for three days:
but all the children of Israel had light in
their dwellings.

The last interview with Pharaoh

¶24 And Pharaoh called unto Moses,
and said, Go ye, serve the LORD; only
let your flocks and your herds be
stayed: let your little ones also go with
you.
25 And Moses said, Thou must give us
also sacrifices and burnt-offerings, that
we may *sacrifice unto the LORD our
God.

The fourth compromise refused

26 Our cattle also shall go with us;
there shall not an hoof be left behind;
for thereof must we take to serve the
LORD our God; and we know not with
what we must serve the LORD, until we
come thither.
¶27 But the LORD hardened Pharaoh's
heart, and he would not let them go.
28 And Pharaoh said unto him, Get
thee from me, take heed to thyself, see
my face no more; for in *that* day thou
seest my face thou shalt die.
29 And Moses said, Thou hast spoken
well, I will see thy face again no more.

Judgment foretold

11 And the LORD said unto Moses,
Yet will I bring one plague *more*
upon Pharaoh, and upon Egypt; afterwards he will let you go hence: when he
shall let *you* go, he shall surely thrust
you out hence altogether.
2 Speak now in the ears of the people,
and let every man *borrow of his neighbour, and every woman of her neighbour, jewels of silver, and jewels of
gold.
3 And the LORD gave the people
favour in the sight of the Egyptians.
Moreover the man Moses *was* very
great in the land of Egypt, in the sight
of Pharaoh's servants, and in the sight
of the people.
4 And Moses said, Thus saith the
LORD, About midnight will I go out into
the midst of Egypt:
5 And all the firstborn in the land of
Egypt shall die, from the firstborn of
Pharaoh that sitteth upon his throne,
even unto the firstborn of the maidservant that *is* behind the mill; and all the
firstborn of beasts.

11:5 Mill
A mill was not a building, but a pair of millstones made of granite or basalt, placed one upon the other. The lower stone was larger and stationary, and the upper one was loose, with a hole through its center into which the grain was put. This upper stone was turned briskly around by a wooden handle, fixed in its surface near the circumference. The grinding was always done by women, generally by two at a time (Matt. 24:41), seated on the ground opposite each other, each holding the handle and alternately pushing and pulling the stone in its revolution. The Mosaic Law mercifully prohibited the seizure of millstones for debt (Deut. 24:6).

6 And there shall be a great cry
throughout all the land of Egypt, such
as there was none like it, nor shall be
like it any more.
7 But against any of the children of
Israel shall not a dog move his tongue,
against man or beast: that ye may know
how that the LORD doth put a difference
between the Egyptians and Israel.
8 And all these thy servants shall
come down unto me, and bow down

10:24 flocks. See 8:25 note, "Pharaoh's Compromises." Just as Moses rightly demanded a complete separation from Egypt, so the Christian must be completely separated from the world, and all its interests. See Deuteronomy 22:9-11 note, "A Separate People."

11:6 great cry. When a death occurred, a loud wailing was made by the relatives.

themselves unto me, saying, Get thee
out, and all the people that follow thee:
and after that I will go out. And he went
out from Pharaoh in a great anger.
9 And the LORD said unto Moses, Pharaoh shall not hearken unto you; that
my wonders may be multiplied in the
land of Egypt.
10 And Moses and Aaron did all these
wonders before Pharaoh: and the LORD
hardened Pharaoh's heart, so that he
would not let the children of Israel go
out of his land.

Passover: Instructions given

12 And the LORD spake unto Moses and Aaron in the land of
Egypt, saying,
2 This *month *shall be* unto you the
beginning of *months: it *shall be* the
first month of the year to you.
¶3 Speak ye unto all the congregation
of Israel, saying, In the tenth *day* of this
month they shall take to them every
man a lamb, according to the house of
their fathers, a lamb for an house:
4 And if the household be too little for
the lamb, let him and his neighbour
next unto his house take *it* according to
the number of the souls; every man
according to his eating shall make your
count for the lamb.
5 Your lamb shall be without blemish,
a male of the first year: ye shall take *it*
out from the sheep, or from the goats:
6 And ye shall keep it up until the fourteenth day of the same month: and the
whole assembly of the congregation of
Israel shall kill it in the evening.
7 And they shall take of the *blood,
and strike *it* on the two side posts and
on the upper door post of the houses,
wherein they shall eat it.
8 And they shall eat the flesh in that
night, roast with fire, and *unleavened
bread; *and* with bitter *herbs* they shall
eat it.
9 Eat not of it raw, nor sodden at all
with water, but roast *with* fire; his head
with his legs, and with the purtenance
thereof.
10 And ye shall let nothing of it remain
until the morning; and that which remaineth of it until the morning ye shall
burn with fire.
11 And thus shall ye eat it; *with* your

12:3 THE MEANING OF PASSOVER

This chapter on the Passover is a very important chapter for the following reasons:

1. It begins the history of the children of Israel as a nation. At last the time of slavery ended and they escaped to Canaan where they finally set up their kingdom. They always remembered their escape in the yearly feast of the Passover (see Lev. 23:5 note).
2. It is a picture of the Lord Jesus Christ as our Saviour. The "lamb . . . without blemish" (vs. 5) speaks of the Lord Jesus and His perfect life and character (read John 1:29 to see by what name John the Baptist identified Him). "In the evening" (vs. 6) means, in the Hebrew, between noon and sunset, the very time at which our Lord was crucified. "The blood sprinkled on the door posts" (see vss. 7,12-13) speaks of the blood of our Saviour shed for us on the cross. When the blood was sprinkled on the doorposts, it was a sign that the punishment had already been carried out on the innocent lamb, and therefore God could pass over the house and spare the firstborn. The Egyptians could have been saved in this way too, for they were told of it (see 11:4-7). "The eating of the lamb" (see vs. 8) teaches us that just as our bodies need food, so our Christian life needs to be nourished by feeding on Christ as the Bread of Life. We do this by reading about Him in the Bible and learning all we can of His life and death. "Unleavened bread" (vs. 8) is bread made without yeast. This speaks of the absence of sin in Christ. See *leaven.

12:2 first month. The first month of the Hebrew calendar is about the time that we call April. See Genesis 7:11 note, "The Hebrew Calendar."
12:4 count. A summing up or account.

loins girded, your shoes on your feet, and your staff in your hand; and ye shall eat it in haste: it *is* the LORD'S *passover.

Judgment on the firstborn

¶12For I will pass through the land of Egypt this night, and will smite all the firstborn in the land of Egypt, both man and beast; and against all the gods of Egypt I will execute *judgment: I *am* the LORD.

12:12 The Gods and Goddesses of Egypt
Ancient Egyptian religion was very complex. There were dozens of local and regional gods and goddesses, each having a different function. Egyptians needed numerous gods to support their belief that everything that occurred was the act of some god.

Osiris	god of the underworld/afterlife
Isis	wife of Osiris
Horus	son of Isis and Osiris
Hapi	god of the Nile River
Ra	sun god
Ptah	patron of craftsmen
Bes	god of amusements and games
Min	god of virility and fertility
Thoth	god of wisdom and letters
Hathor	goddess of love
Hegit	goddess of fertility
Amon	sun god

13And the blood shall be to you for a token upon the houses where ye *are:* and when I see the blood, I will pass over you, and the plague shall not be upon you to destroy *you,* when I smite the land of Egypt.

14And this day shall be unto you for a memorial; and ye shall keep it a feast to the LORD throughout your generations; ye shall keep it a feast by an ordinance for ever.

15Seven days shall ye eat unleavened bread; even the first day ye shall put away *leaven out of your houses: for whosoever eateth *leavened bread from the first day until the seventh day, that soul shall be cut off from Israel.

16And in the first day *there shall be* an *holy *convocation, and in the seventh day there shall be an holy convocation to you; no manner of work shall be done in them, save *that* which every man must eat, that only may be done of you.

17And ye shall observe *the feast of* unleavened bread; for in this selfsame day have I brought your armies out of the land of Egypt: therefore shall ye observe this day in your generations by an ordinance for ever.

¶18In the first *month,* on the fourteenth day of the month at even, ye shall eat unleavened bread, until the one and twentieth day of the month at even.

19Seven days shall there be no leaven found in your houses: for whosoever eateth that which is leavened, even that soul shall be cut off from the congregation of Israel, whether he be a stranger, or born in the land.

20Ye shall eat nothing leavened; in all your habitations shall ye eat unleavened bread.

¶21Then Moses called for all the *elders of Israel, and said unto them, Draw out and take you a lamb according to your families, and kill the passover.

22And ye shall take a bunch of hyssop, and dip *it* in the blood that *is* in the bason, and strike the lintel and the two side posts with the blood that *is* in the bason; and none of you shall go out at the door of his house until the morning.

23For the LORD will pass through to smite the Egyptians; and when he seeth the blood upon the lintel, and on the two

---

12:11 the LORD's passover. See verse 3 note.
12:14 for ever. This feast of the Passover is still observed by many Jews today.
12:15 Seven days. See Leviticus 23:4 note.
12:15 unleavened bread. See verse 3 note.
12:16 convocation. A gathering or a meeting.
12:22 hyssop. This is a small plant with white blossoms (1 Kings 4:33), suitable to use to sprinkle blood. It is also a symbol of humble service.

side posts, the LORD will pass over the
door, and will not suffer the destroyer to
come in unto your houses to smite *you.*
24And ye shall observe this thing for
an ordinance to thee and to thy sons for
ever.
25And it shall come to pass, when ye
be come to the land which the LORD will
give you, according as he hath promised, that ye shall keep this service.
26And it shall come to pass, when
your children shall say unto you, What
mean ye by this service?
27That ye shall say, It *is* the sacrifice
of the LORD'S passover, who passed
over the houses of the children of Israel
in Egypt, when he smote the Egyptians,
and delivered our houses. And the people bowed the head and worshipped.
28And the children of Israel went
away, and did as the LORD had commanded Moses and Aaron, so did they.
¶29And it came to pass, that at midnight the LORD smote all the firstborn
in the land of Egypt, from the firstborn
of Pharaoh that sat on his throne unto
the firstborn of the captive that *was* in
the dungeon; and all the firstborn of
cattle.
30And Pharaoh rose up in the night,
he, and all his servants, and all the
Egyptians; and there was a great cry in
Egypt; for *there was* not a house where
there was not one dead.
¶31And he called for Moses and
Aaron by night, and said, Rise up, *and*
get you forth from among my people,
both ye and the children of Israel; and
go, serve the LORD, as ye have said.
32Also take your flocks and your
herds, as ye have said, and be gone; and
bless me also.
33And the Egyptians were urgent
upon the people, that they might send
them out of the land in haste; for they
said, We *be* all dead *men.*
34And the people took their dough
before it was leavened, their kneadingtroughs being bound up in their
clothes upon their shoulders.
35And the children of Israel did according to the word of Moses; and they
*borrowed of the Egyptians jewels of
silver, and jewels of gold, and raiment:
36And the LORD gave the people
favour in the sight of the Egyptians, so
that they lent unto them *such things as*
they required. And they spoiled the
Egyptians.

The departure from Egypt

¶37And the children of Israel journeyed from Rameses to Succoth, about
six hundred thousand on foot *that were*
men, beside children.
38And a mixed multitude went up also
with them; and flocks, and herds, *even*
very much cattle.
39And they baked unleavened cakes
of the dough which they brought forth
out of Egypt, for it was not leavened;
because they were thrust out of Egypt,
and could not tarry, neither had they
prepared for themselves any victual.
¶40Now the sojourning of the children of Israel, who dwelt in Egypt, *was*
four hundred and thirty years.
41And it came to pass at the end of the
four hundred and thirty years, even the
selfsame day it came to pass, that all
the hosts of the LORD went out from the
land of Egypt.
42It *is* a night to be much observed
unto the LORD for bringing them out
from the land of Egypt: this *is* that night
of the LORD to be observed of all the
children of Israel in their generations.
¶43And the LORD said unto Moses
and Aaron, This *is* the ordinance of the
passover: There shall no stranger eat
thereof:
44But every man's servant that is

12:28 did as the LORD had commanded. The people had faith to believe the promises of the LORD. See *faith.

12:36 lent. The word means *gave.*

12:38 mixed. See Numbers 11:4 note.

bought for money, when thou hast circumcised him, then shall he eat thereof.
45A foreigner and an hired servant
shall not eat thereof.
46In one house shall it be eaten; thou
shalt not carry forth ought of the flesh
abroad out of the house; neither shall
ye break a bone thereof.
47All the congregation of Israel shall
keep it.
48And when a stranger shall sojourn
with thee, and will keep the passover
to the LORD, let all his males be circumcised, and then let him come near and
keep it; and he shall be as one that is
born in the land: for no *uncircumcised
person shall eat thereof.
49One *law shall be to him that is
homeborn, and unto the stranger that
sojourneth among you.
50Thus did all the children of Israel;
as the LORD commanded Moses and
Aaron, so did they.
51And it came to pass the selfsame
day, *that* the LORD did bring the children
of Israel out of the land of Egypt by their
armies.

Firstborn to be set apart

13 And the LORD spake unto Moses, saying,
2Sanctify unto me all the firstborn,
whatsoever openeth the womb among
the children of *Israel, *both* of man and
of beast: it *is* mine.
¶3And Moses said unto the people,
Remember this day, in which ye came
out from *Egypt, out of the house of
bondage; for by strength of hand the
LORD brought you out from this *place:*
there shall no leavened bread be eaten.
4This day came ye out in the month
Abib.
5And it shall be when the LORD shall
bring thee into the land of the Canaanites, and the Hittites, and the Amorites,
and the Hivites, and the Jebusites,
which he sware unto thy fathers to give
thee, a land *flowing with milk and honey, that thou shalt keep this service in
this month.
6Seven days thou shalt eat unleavened bread, and in the seventh day *shall*
be a feast to the LORD.
7Unleavened bread shall be eaten
seven days; and there shall no leavened
bread be seen with thee, neither shall
there be leaven seen with thee in all thy
quarters.
¶8And thou shalt shew thy son in that
day, saying, *This is done* because of that
which the LORD did unto me when I
came forth out of Egypt.
9And it shall be for a sign unto thee
upon thine hand, and for a memorial
between thine eyes, that the LORD'S
law may be in thy mouth: for with a
strong hand hath the LORD brought
thee out of Egypt.
10Thou shalt therefore keep this ordinance in his season from year to year.
¶11And it shall be when the LORD
shall bring thee into the land of the Canaanites, as he sware unto thee and to
thy fathers, and shall give it thee,
12That thou shalt set apart unto the
LORD all that openeth the matrix, and
every firstling that cometh of a beast
which thou hast; the males *shall be* the
LORD'S.
13And every firstling of an ass thou
shalt *redeem with a lamb; and if thou
wilt not redeem it, then thou shalt break
his neck: and all the firstborn of man

13:2 The Meaning of Sanctification
To "sanctify" something means to *set it apart for God,* as, for example, a soldier is recruited for an army. Because God had specifically saved the Israelites' firstborn from judgment and death, He had a claim on them. So in the New Testament, Christians are called "sanctified" because they have been saved from the judgment of their sin and are set apart for God. See Genesis 2:3 note; see also Hebrews 10:10-14.

13:3 leavened. See *leaven.

among thy children shalt thou redeem.

¶ 14 And it shall be when thy son asketh thee in time to come, saying, What *is* this? that thou shalt say unto him, By strength of hand the LORD brought us out from Egypt, from the house of bondage:

15 And it came to pass, when *Pharaoh would hardly let us go, that the LORD slew all the firstborn in the land of Egypt, both the firstborn of man, and the firstborn of beast: therefore I sacrifice to the LORD all that openeth the matrix, being males; but all the firstborn of my children I redeem.

16 And it shall be for a token upon thine hand, and for *frontlets between thine eyes: for by strength of hand the LORD brought us forth out of Egypt.

The first part of the journey

¶ 17 And it came to pass, when Pharaoh had let the people go, that *God led them not *through* the way of the land of the *Philistines, although that *was* near; for God said, Lest peradventure the people repent when they see war, and they return to Egypt:

18 But God led the people about, *through* the way of the wilderness of the Red sea: and the children of Israel went up harnessed out of the land of Egypt.

19 And Moses took the bones of *Joseph with him: for he had straitly sworn the children of Israel, saying, God will surely visit you; and ye shall carry up my bones away hence with you.

20 And they took their journey from Succoth, and encamped in Etham, in the edge of the wilderness.

¶ 21 And the LORD went before them by day in a pillar of a cloud, to lead them the way; and by night in a pillar of fire, to give them light; to go by day and night:

22 He took not away the pillar of the cloud by day, nor the pillar of fire by night, *from* before the people.

The Red Sea

14 And the LORD spake unto *Moses, saying,

2 Speak unto the children of Israel, that they turn and encamp before Pi-hahiroth, between Migdol and the sea, over against *Baal-zephon: before it shall ye encamp by the sea.

3 For Pharaoh will say of the children of Israel, They *are* entangled in the land, the wilderness hath shut them in.

4 And I will *harden Pharaoh's heart, that he shall follow after them; and I will be honoured upon Pharaoh, and upon all his host; that the Egyptians may know that I *am* the LORD. And they did so.

¶ 5 And it was told the king of Egypt that the people fled: and the heart of Pharaoh and of his servants was turned against the people, and they said, Why have we done this, that we have let Israel go from serving us?

6 And he made ready his chariot, and took his people with him:

7 And he took six hundred chosen chariots, and all the chariots of Egypt, and captains over every one of them.

8 And the LORD hardened the heart of Pharaoh king of Egypt, and he pursued after the children of Israel: and the children of Israel went out with an high hand.

9 But the Egyptians pursued after

13:16 frontlets. These are explained in Deuteronomy 6:8.

13:17 repent. See Zechariah 8:14 note, "Repentance."

13:18 harnessed. This means equipped for a long journey. See 12:11 for fuller instructions. Their long flowing garments were tied around their waists, and strong leather sandals were worn.

13:19 the bones of Joseph. Read Genesis 50:24-25.

13:21 cloud . . . fire. These were the outward signs of God's presence with them. See Genesis 3:24 note, "flaming sword."

14:2 turn. The Israelites journeyed for three days and camped at Pi-hahiroth between the mountains and the Red Sea.

them, all the horses *and* chariots of Pharaoh, and his horsemen, and his army, and overtook them encamping by the sea, beside Pi-hahiroth, before Baal-zephon.

¶ 10 And when Pharaoh drew nigh, the children of Israel lifted up their eyes, and, behold, the Egyptians marched after them; and they were sore afraid: and the children of Israel cried out unto the LORD.

11 And they said unto Moses, Because *there were* no graves in Egypt, hast thou taken us away to die in the wilderness? wherefore hast thou dealt thus with us, to carry us forth out of Egypt?

12 *Is* not this the word that we did tell thee in Egypt, saying, Let us alone, that we may serve the Egyptians? For *it had been* better for us to serve the Egyptians, than that we should die in the wilderness.

¶ 13 And Moses said unto the people, Fear ye not, stand still, and see the *salvation of the LORD, which he will shew to you to day: for the Egyptians whom ye have seen to day, ye shall see them again no more for ever.

14 The LORD shall fight for you, and ye shall hold your peace.

¶ 15 And the LORD said unto Moses, Wherefore criest thou unto me? speak unto the children of Israel, that they go forward:

16 But lift thou up thy rod, and stretch out thine hand over the sea, and divide it: and the children of Israel shall go on dry *ground* through the midst of the sea.

17 And I, behold, I will harden the hearts of the Egyptians, and they shall follow them: and I will get me honour upon Pharaoh, and upon all his host, upon his chariots, and upon his horsemen.

18 And the Egyptians shall know that I *am* the LORD, when I have gotten me honour upon Pharaoh, upon his chariots, and upon his horsemen.

¶ 19 And the *angel of God, which went before the camp of Israel, removed and went behind them; and the pillar of the cloud went from before their face, and stood behind them:

20 And it came between the camp of the Egyptians and the camp of Israel; and it was a cloud and darkness *to them,* but it gave light by night *to these:* so that the one came not near the other all the night.

21 And Moses stretched out his hand over the sea; and the LORD caused the sea to go *back* by a strong east wind all that night, and made the sea dry *land,* and the waters were divided.

22 And the children of Israel went into the midst of the sea upon the dry *ground:* and the waters *were* a wall unto them on their right hand, and on their left.

¶ 23 And the Egyptians pursued, and went in after them to the midst of the sea, *even* all Pharaoh's horses, his chariots, and his horsemen.

24 And it came to pass, that in the morning watch the LORD looked unto the host of the Egyptians through the pillar of fire and of the cloud, and troubled the host of the Egyptians,

25 And took off their chariot wheels,

14:11 graves in Egypt. This was said in sarcasm, for Egypt was famous for its wonderful tombs, the Pyramids.

14:17 honour. The LORD knew that His name would be glorified when the Egyptians were conquered, for the defeated Egyptians would know that only the power of God had triumphed against their wrongdoing (vs. 25).

14:19 angel of God. This means the presence of God as described in the 13:21 note. See also *angels.

14:22 the children of Israel went. The Israelites had faith to believe that God would keep them from drowning. See *faith.

14:24 morning watch. The night was divided into three parts or watches. The early morning was the third watch.

that they drave them heavily: so that
the Egyptians said, Let us flee from the
face of Israel; for the LORD fighteth for
them against the Egyptians.
¶ 26 And the LORD said unto Moses,
Stretch out thine hand over the sea,
that the waters may come again upon
the Egyptians, upon their chariots, and
upon their horsemen.
27 And Moses stretched forth his hand
over the sea, and the sea returned to his
strength when the morning appeared;
and the Egyptians fled against it; and
the LORD overthrew the Egyptians in
the midst of the sea.
28 And the waters returned, and covered the chariots, and the horsemen,
and all the host of Pharaoh that came
into the sea after them; there remained
not so much as one of them.
29 But the children of Israel walked
upon dry *land* in the midst of the sea;
and the waters *were* a wall unto them
on their right hand, and on their left.
30 Thus the LORD saved Israel that
day out of the hand of the Egyptians;
and Israel saw the Egyptians dead upon
the sea shore.
31 And Israel saw that great work
which the LORD did upon the Egyptians: and the people feared the LORD,
and believed the LORD, and his servant
Moses.

The song of the redeemed Israelites

15 Then sang Moses and the children of Israel this song unto the
LORD, and spake, saying, I will sing unto
the LORD, for he hath triumphed gloriously: the horse and his rider hath he
thrown into the sea.
2 The LORD *is* my strength and song,
and he is become my salvation: he *is* my
God, and I will prepare him an habitation;
my father's God, and I will exalt him.
3 The LORD *is* a man of war: the LORD
is his name.
4 Pharaoh's chariots and his host hath
he cast into the sea: his chosen captains
also are drowned in the Red sea.
5 The depths have covered them: they
sank into the bottom as a stone.
6 Thy right hand, O LORD, is become
glorious in power: thy right hand,
O LORD, hath dashed in pieces the enemy.

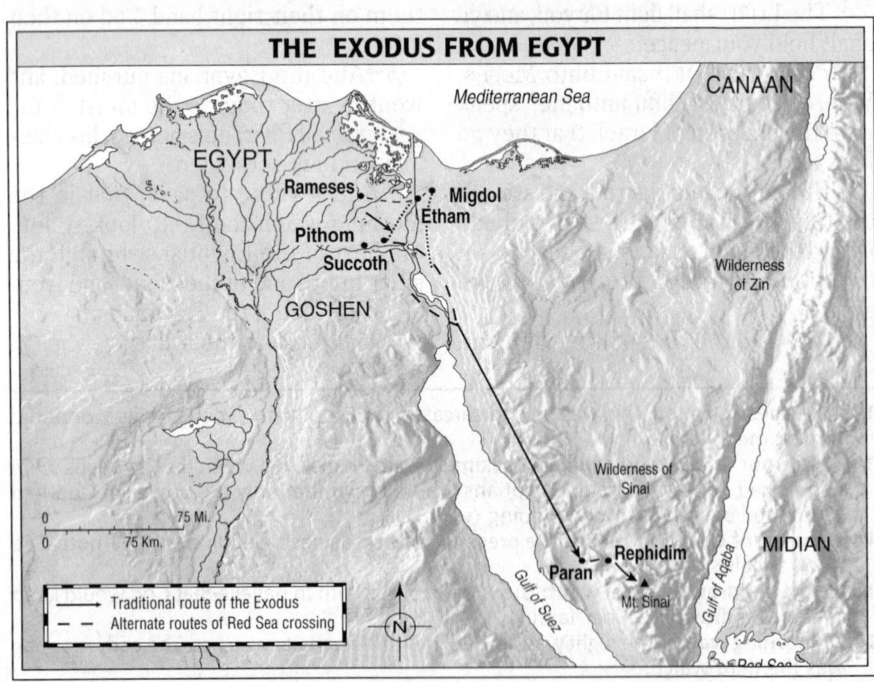

7 And in the greatness of thine excellency thou hast overthrown them that
rose up against thee: thou sentest forth
thy wrath, *which* consumed them as
stubble.
8 And with the blast of thy nostrils
the waters were gathered together, the
floods stood upright as an heap, *and* the
depths were congealed in the heart of
the sea.
9 The enemy said, I will pursue, I will
overtake, I will divide the spoil; my
lust shall be satisfied upon them; I will
draw my sword, my hand shall destroy
them.
10 Thou didst blow with thy wind, the
sea covered them: they sank as lead in
the mighty waters.
11 Who *is* like unto thee, O LORD,
among the gods? who *is* like thee, glorious in holiness, fearful *in* praises,
doing wonders?
12 Thou stretchedst out thy right
hand, the earth swallowed them.
13 Thou in thy *mercy hast led forth
the people *which* thou hast *redeemed:
thou hast guided *them* in thy strength
unto thy holy habitation.
14 The people shall hear, *and* be afraid:
sorrow shall take hold on the inhabitants of Palestina.
15 Then the dukes of *Edom shall be
amazed; the mighty men of *Moab, trembling shall take hold upon them; all the
inhabitants of Canaan shall melt away.
16 *Fear and dread shall fall upon
them; by the greatness of thine arm
they shall be *as* still as a stone; till thy
people pass over, O LORD, till the people
pass over, *which* thou hast purchased.
17 Thou shalt bring them in, and plant
them in the *mountain of thine inheritance, *in* the place, O LORD, *which* thou
hast made for thee to dwell in, *in* the
*Sanctuary, O Lord, *which* thy hands
have established.
18 The LORD shall reign for ever and
ever.
19 For the horse of Pharaoh went in
with his chariots and with his horsemen
into the sea, and the LORD brought
again the waters of the sea upon them;
but the children of Israel went on dry
land in the midst of the sea.
¶ 20 And *Miriam the prophetess, the
sister of Aaron, took a timbrel in her
hand; and all the women went out after
her with timbrels and with dances.
21 And Miriam answered them, Sing
ye to the LORD, for he hath triumphed
gloriously; the horse and his rider hath
he thrown into the sea.

Wilderness troubles

¶ 22 So Moses brought Israel from the
Red sea, and they went out into the

15:22 THE JOURNEY THROUGH THE WILDERNESS

The journey of the Israelites through the wilderness is a picture of the life of a Christian passing though this world. The Passover and the escape from Egypt show how we are saved by the death of our Lord from the penalty of sin. But when we are saved, we do not go immediately to heaven. We still have to live our lives in this world and face temptations and difficulties. The history of the Israelites in the wilderness teaches us how to face any difficulties and overcome them. This is shown in the next verses. The waters of Marah (Marah means *bitter*) speak of sorrow and trouble. They were made sweet or easy to bear after the tree had been thrown into them. The tree is a picture of the cross of the Lord Jesus. When we think of how patiently He bore the cross, and what He did for us, we should be able to bear any trouble that may come to us, but we do not even have to bear the burden of it, for He invites us to cast our cares and our troubles upon Him (1 Pet. 5:7; see also Heb. 4:15-16).

15:9 lust. To desire, wish, pleasure.
15:20 Miriam. Moses' sister, who had helped to watch over him in the ark of bulrushes (see 2:4-8; Num. 12).
15:20 timbrel. A musical instrument something like a tambourine.

wilderness of Shur; and they went
three days in the wilderness, and found
no water.
23And when they came to Marah,
they could not drink of the waters of
Marah, for they *were* bitter: therefore
the name of it was called Marah.
24And the people murmured against
Moses, saying, What shall we drink?
25And he cried unto the LORD; and
the LORD shewed him a tree, *which*
when he had cast into the waters, the
waters were made sweet: there he
made for them a statute and an ordinance, and there he proved them,
26And said, If thou wilt diligently
hearken to the voice of the LORD thy
God, and wilt do that which is right in
his sight, and wilt give ear to his commandments, and keep all his statutes,
I will put none of these diseases upon
thee, which I have brought upon the
Egyptians: for I *am* the LORD that
healeth thee.
¶27And they came to Elim, where
were twelve wells of water, and threescore and ten palm trees: and they encamped there by the waters.

II. Wilderness Journey (16:1—18:27)

16 And they took their journey
from Elim, and all the congregation of the children of Israel came unto
the wilderness of Sin, which *is* between
Elim and *Sinai, on the fifteenth day of
the second month after their departing
out of the land of Egypt.
2And the whole congregation of the
children of Israel murmured against
Moses and *Aaron in the wilderness:
3And the children of Israel said unto
them, Would to God we had died by the
hand of the LORD in the land of Egypt,
when we sat by the flesh pots, *and*
when we did eat bread to the full; for ye
have brought us forth into this wilderness, to kill this whole assembly with
hunger.
¶4Then said the LORD unto Moses,
Behold, I will rain bread from heaven
for you; and the people shall go out and
gather a certain rate every day, that I
may *prove them, whether they will
walk in my law, or no.
5And it shall come to pass, that on the
sixth day they shall prepare *that* which
they bring in; and it shall be twice as
much as they gather daily.
6And Moses and Aaron said unto all
the children of Israel, At even, then ye
shall know that the LORD hath brought
you out from the land of Egypt:
7And in the morning, then ye shall
see the glory of the LORD; for that he
heareth your murmurings against the
LORD: and what *are* we, that ye murmur
against us?
8And Moses said, *This shall be,* when
the LORD shall give you in the evening
flesh to eat, and in the morning bread
to the full; for that the LORD heareth
your murmurings which ye murmur
against him: and what *are* we? your
murmurings *are* not against us, but
against the LORD.
¶9And Moses spake unto Aaron, Say
unto all the congregation of the children
of Israel, Come near before the LORD:
for he hath heard your murmurings.
10And it came to pass, as Aaron spake
unto the whole congregation of the children of Israel, that they looked toward
the wilderness, and, behold, the glory
of the LORD appeared in the cloud.
11And the LORD spake unto Moses,
saying,
12I have heard the murmurings of the
children of Israel: speak unto them,
saying, At even ye shall eat flesh, and
in the morning ye shall be filled with
bread; and ye shall know that I *am* the
LORD your God.

15:26 the LORD that healeth thee. Another of these wonderful names for God. For the whole list and more about these names, see *names of God.
15:27 Elim. The name means *trees.*
16:7 glory of the LORD. See13:21 note.

God's provision

13And it came to pass, that at even
the quails came up, and covered the
camp: and in the morning the dew lay
round about the host.
¶14And when the dew that lay was
gone up, behold, upon the face of the
wilderness *there lay* a small round thing,
as small as the hoar frost on the ground.
15And when the children of Israel saw
it, they said one to another, It *is* *manna: for they *wist not what it *was.* And
Moses said unto them, This *is* the bread
which the LORD hath given you to eat.
16This *is* the thing which the LORD
hath commanded, Gather of it every
man according to his eating, an omer for
every man, *according to* the number of
your persons; take ye every man for
them which *are* in his tents.
17And the children of Israel did so,
and gathered, some more, some less.
18And when they did mete *it* with an
omer, he that gathered much had nothing over, and he that gathered little had
no lack; they gathered every man according to his eating.
19And Moses said, Let no man leave
of it till the morning.
20Notwithstanding they hearkened
not unto Moses; but some of them left
of it until the morning, and it bred
worms, and stank: and Moses was
wroth with them.
21And they gathered it every morning, every man according to his eating:
and when the sun waxed hot, it melted.
¶22And it came to pass, *that* on the
sixth day they gathered twice as much
bread, two omers for one *man:* and all
the rulers of the congregation came and
told Moses.

Sabbath given to Israel

23And he said unto them, This *is that*
which the LORD hath said, To morrow
is the rest of the holy *sabbath unto the
LORD: bake *that* which ye will bake *to
day,* and seethe that ye will seethe; and
that which remaineth over lay up for
you to be kept until the morning.
24And they laid it up till the morning,
as Moses bade: and it did not stink,
neither was there any worm therein.
25And Moses said, Eat that to day; for
to day *is* a sabbath unto the LORD: to day
ye shall not find it in the field.
26Six days ye shall gather it; but on
the seventh day, *which is* the sabbath,
in it there shall be none.
¶27And it came to pass, *that* there
went out *some* of the people on the seventh day for to gather, and they found
none.
28And the LORD said unto Moses,
How long refuse ye to keep my commandments and my *laws?
29See, for that the LORD hath given
you the sabbath, therefore he giveth
you on the sixth day the bread of two

16:15 MANNA FROM HEAVEN

The word "manna" comes from the Hebrew word meaning *What is it?* It was a food which God specially provided. It is described in verses 14 and 31, and Numbers 11:7. It was like hoarfrost (frost), the gray-white frost that covers the ground in the autumn, and like coriander seeds which were a gray-white. It is a picture of Christ as the Living Bread who came down from heaven to be the food for our souls. We become Christians when we believe in the Lord Jesus Christ who died upon the cross to take the punishment that we deserve, and as Christians we must learn about Him by reading His Word; we must think of Him and pray to Him. This is the feeding on Christ that makes us strong Christians.

16:13 quails. See Numbers 11:31 where a similar incident occurred.
16:16 omer. This is about two quarts.
16:18 mete. Measure.
16:23 sabbath. See *Sabbath.
16:23 seethe. To boil.

days; abide ye every man in his place,
let no man go out of his place on the
seventh day.

30 So the people rested on the seventh
day.

31 And the house of Israel called the
name thereof Manna: and it *was* like
coriander seed, white; and the taste of
it *was* like wafers *made* with honey.

¶32 And Moses said, This *is* the thing
which the LORD commandeth, Fill an
omer of it to be kept for your generations; that they may see the bread
wherewith I have fed you in the wilderness, when I brought you forth from the
land of Egypt.

33 And Moses said unto Aaron, Take
a pot, and put an omer full of manna
therein, and lay it up before the LORD,
to be kept for your generations.

34 As the LORD commanded Moses,
so Aaron laid it up before the Testimony, to be kept.

35 And the children of Israel did eat
manna forty years, until they came to a
land inhabited; they did eat manna, until they came unto the borders of the
land of Canaan.

36 Now an omer *is* the tenth *part* of an
*ephah.

17 And all the congregation of the
children of Israel journeyed
from the wilderness of Sin, after their
journeys, according to the commandment of the LORD, and pitched in Rephidim: and *there was* no water for the
people to drink.

2 Wherefore the people did chide with
Moses, and said, Give us water that we
may drink. And Moses said unto them,
Why chide ye with me? wherefore do ye
*tempt the LORD?

3 And the people thirsted there for
water; and the people murmured
against Moses, and said, Wherefore *is*
this *that* thou hast brought us up out of
Egypt, to kill us and our children and our
cattle with thirst?

4 And Moses cried unto the LORD,
saying, What shall I do unto this people? they be almost ready to stone me.

Water from the rock

5 And the LORD said unto Moses, Go
on before the people, and take with thee
of the elders of Israel; and thy rod,
wherewith thou smotest the river, take
in thine hand, and go.

6 Behold, I will stand before thee
there upon the *rock in *Horeb; and
thou shalt smite the rock, and there
shall come water out of it, that the people may drink. And Moses did so in the
sight of the elders of Israel.

7 And he called the name of the place
Massah, and Meribah, because of the
chiding of the children of Israel, and
because they *tempted the LORD, saying, Is the LORD among us, or not?

The 1st battle: Amalekites

¶8 Then came *Amalek, and fought
with Israel in Rephidim.

17:8 The Amalekites
The Amalekites were descended from Amalek, the grandson of Esau. They were always the enemies of the children of Israel. The Amalekites are a picture of the flesh, which is what Paul calls the old sinful nature which still remains in Christians even after their sins are forgiven. It is the flesh that sometimes hinders Christians from living good and holy lives. It can only be defeated by prayer and dependence on the Holy Spirit. See Galatians 5:17-26.

16:36 ephah. About three-fifths of a bushel; thus an omer is about two quarts.
17:2 tempt. See Mark 1:13 note, "The Temptation of Jesus."
17:3 murmured. The continual unbelief of the people is in strong contrast to the patience of Moses. See 14:11; 15:24.
17:7 Massah. Massah means *temptation*, and Meribah means *strife*.
17:9 Joshua. This is the first mention of the man who was to be the leader of the people after the death of Moses. See Exodus 24:9,13-15; 33:11; Numbers 13:8,16; 14:6,30; and the book of Joshua.

9 And Moses said unto *Joshua, Choose us out men, and go out, fight with Amalek: to morrow I will stand on the top of the hill with the rod of God in mine hand.

10 So Joshua did as Moses had said to him, and fought with Amalek: and Moses, Aaron, and Hur went up to the top of the hill.

11 And it came to pass, when Moses held up his hand, that Israel prevailed: and when he let down his hand, Amalek prevailed.

12 But Moses' hands *were* heavy; and they took a stone, and put *it* under him, and he sat thereon; and Aaron and Hur stayed up his hands, the one on the one side, and the other on the other side; and his hands were steady until the going down of the sun.

13 And Joshua discomfited Amalek and his people with the edge of the sword.

14 And the LORD said unto Moses, Write this *for* a memorial in a book, and rehearse *it* in the ears of Joshua: for I will utterly put out the remembrance of Amalek from under heaven.

15 And Moses built an *altar, and called the name of it Jehovah-nissi:

16 For he said, Because the LORD hath sworn *that* the LORD *will have* war with Amalek from generation to generation.

The visit of Jethro

18 When Jethro, the priest of *Midian, Moses' father in law, heard of all that God had done for Moses, and for Israel his people, *and* that the LORD had brought Israel out of Egypt;

2 Then Jethro, Moses' father in law, took Zipporah, Moses' wife, after he had sent her back,

3 And her two sons; of which the name of the one *was* Gershom; for he said, I have been an alien in a strange land:

4 And the name of the other *was* Eliezer; for the God of my father, *said he, was* mine help, and delivered me from the sword of Pharaoh:

5 And Jethro, Moses' father in law, came with his sons and his wife unto Moses into the wilderness, where he encamped at the mount of God:

6 And he said unto Moses, I thy father in law Jethro am come unto thee, and thy wife, and her two sons with her.

¶ 7 And Moses went out to meet his father in law, and did obeisance, and kissed him; and they asked each other of *their* welfare; and they came into the tent.

8 And Moses told his father in law all that the LORD had done unto Pharaoh and to the Egyptians for Israel's sake, *and* all the travail that had come upon them by the way, and *how* the LORD delivered them.

9 And Jethro rejoiced for all the goodness which the LORD had done to Israel, whom he had delivered out of the hand of the Egyptians.

10 And Jethro said, Blessed *be* the LORD, who hath delivered you out of the hand of the Egyptians, and out of the hand of Pharaoh, who hath delivered the people from under the hand of the Egyptians.

17:10 Hur. Hur is thought to be the husband of Miriam. See also 31:2.
17:14 Write this. See *inspiration.
17:14 put out. See how this was fulfilled in 1 Samuel 15.
17:15 altar. To see why people built altars, read Genesis 8:20.
17:15 Jehovah-nissi. "The LORD is my Banner," or Jehovah-Nissi, is another name for God. See *names of God for the whole list.
18:1 Jethro. He is sometimes called "Reul" or "Raguel." See Exodus 2:18 note.
18:5 mount of God. Sinai; see Exodus 3:1 note. Sinai is mentioned thirty-one times in the first five books of the Bible.
18:7 did obeisance. Moses treated his father-in-law very respectfully. He probably bowed low before him.
18:8 travail. Trouble.

11 Now I know that the LORD *is* greater than all gods: for in the thing wherein they dealt proudly *he was* above them.

12 And Jethro, Moses' father in law, took a burnt-offering and sacrifices for God: and Aaron came, and all the *elders of Israel, to eat bread with Moses' father in law before God.

¶ 13 And it came to pass on the morrow, that Moses sat to judge the people: and the people stood by Moses from the morning unto the evening.

14 And when Moses' father in law saw all that he did to the people, he said, What *is* this thing that thou doest to the people? why sittest thou thyself alone, and all the people stand by thee from morning unto even?

15 And Moses said unto his father in law, Because the people come unto me to enquire of God:

16 When they have a matter, they come unto me; and I judge between one and another, and I do make *them* know the statutes of God, and his laws.

17 And Moses' father in law said unto him, The thing that thou doest *is* not good.

18 Thou wilt surely wear away, both thou, and this people that *is* with thee: for this thing *is* too heavy for thee; thou art not able to perform it thyself alone.

19 Hearken now unto my voice, I will give thee counsel, and God shall be with thee: Be thou for the people to Godward, that thou mayest bring the causes unto God:

20 And thou shalt teach them ordinances and laws, and shalt shew them the way wherein they must walk, and the work that they must do.

21 Moreover thou shalt provide out of all the people able men, such as fear God, men of truth, hating covetousness; and place *such* over them, *to be* rulers of thousands, *and* rulers of hundreds, rulers of fifties, and rulers of tens:

22 And let them judge the people at all seasons: and it shall be, *that* every great matter they shall bring unto thee, but every small matter they shall judge: so shall it be easier for thyself, and they shall bear *the burden* with thee.

23 If thou shalt do this thing, and God command thee *so,* then thou shalt be able to endure, and all this people shall also go to their place in peace.

¶ 24 So Moses hearkened to the voice of his father in law, and did all that he had said.

25 And Moses chose able men out of all Israel, and made them heads over the people, rulers of thousands, rulers of hundreds, rulers of fifties, and rulers of tens.

26 And they judged the people at all seasons: the hard causes they brought unto Moses, but every small matter they judged themselves.

¶ 27 And Moses let his father in law depart; and he went his way into his own land.

III. Israel at Sinai (19:1—40:38)

19 In the third *month, when the children of *Israel were gone forth out of the land of *Egypt, the same day came they *into* the wilderness of Sinai.

2 For they were departed from Rephidim, and were come *to* the desert of Sinai, and had pitched in the wilderness; and there Israel camped before the mount.

Fifth Dispensation: Law
(Ex. 19:3—Matt. 27:35)

3 And Moses went up unto *God, and the LORD called unto him out of the mountain, saying, Thus shalt thou say

---

18:12 burnt-offering. See Leviticus 1:4 note.

19:1 third month. According to the Hebrew calendar, June would be the third month. See Genesis 7:11 note, "The Hebrew Calendar." The children of Israel had left on April 15, 1446 B.C., and had now been on their journey two months.

to the house of *Jacob, and tell the children of Israel;
4Ye have seen what I did unto the
Egyptians, and *how* I bare you on eagles' wings, and brought you unto myself.
5Now therefore, if ye will obey my
voice indeed, and keep my *covenant,
then ye shall be a *peculiar treasure
unto me above all people: for all the
earth *is* mine:
6And ye shall be unto me a kingdom
of priests, and an *holy nation. These
are the words which thou shalt speak
unto the children of Israel.
7And Moses came and called for the
elders of the people, and laid before
their faces all these words which the
LORD commanded him.
8And all the people answered together, and said, All that the LORD
hath spoken we will do. And Moses
returned the words of the people unto
the LORD.
¶9And the LORD said unto Moses, Lo,
I come unto thee in a thick cloud, that
the people may hear when I speak with
thee, and believe thee for ever. And
Moses told the words of the people unto
the LORD.
10And the LORD said unto Moses, Go
unto the people, and sanctify them to
day and to morrow, and let them wash
their clothes,
11And be ready against the third day:
for the third day the LORD will come
down in the sight of all the people upon
mount Sinai.
12And thou shalt set bounds unto the
people round about, saying, Take heed
to yourselves, *that ye* go *not* up into
the mount, or touch the border of it:
whosoever toucheth the mount shall be
surely put to death:
13There shall not an hand touch it, but
he shall surely be stoned, or shot
through; whether *it be* beast or man, it
shall not live: when the trumpet
soundeth long, they shall come up to
the mount.
¶14And Moses went down from the
mount unto the people, and sanctified
the people; and they washed their
clothes.
15And he said unto the people, Be

19:8 The Purpose of the Law
The people unanimously agreed to do all that God commanded. Yet they failed! God knew that they would fail, and He gave the Law to show them their need of the Saviour. Paul explained this in the New Testament in Galatians 3:24. God gave the Law to show people that they are sinners. The Law, however, does not cleanse. The Law is like a mirror; in the mirror you see that your face is dirty, but the mirror does not make your face clean. So, when people see by the Law that they are sinners, they must seek what will cleanse them. It is the blood of the Redeemer, our Lord Jesus Christ, which cleanses us from sin (Gal. 3:24; 1 John 1:7). See *Law.

19:3-5 THE FIFTH DISPENSATION: THE AGE OF LAW

This marks a very important stage in the history both of Israel and of mankind: It started the dispensation of law. This was the fifth of the dispensations, or periods of time, in the history of God's relationship with man. In this dispensation, God chose a special people, Israel, and gave them very careful instructions on how to live right. In spite of every advantage, and though their great men—prophets and judges and patriarchs—spoke God's words to them, they still failed to reach God's standard or to please Him. By failing to reach God's standard, they proved that man cannot save himself and that he needs a Saviour. The dispensation thus ended with the coming of this Saviour, who is Christ the Lord. See *dispensations.

19:6 kingdom of priests. The children of Israel as a whole failed to be this kingdom of priests, this holy nation, because of sin. Only when we are saved from sin by the blood of Christ do we become His priests and holy in His sight (1 Pet. 2:9).
19:6 These are the words. See *inspiration.

ready against the third day: come not at
your wives.
16 And it came to pass on the third day
in the morning, that there were thunders and lightnings, and a thick cloud
upon the mount, and the voice of the
trumpet exceeding loud; so that all
the people that *was* in the camp trembled.
17 And Moses brought forth the people out of the camp to meet with God;
and they stood at the nether part of the
mount.
18 And mount Sinai was altogether on
a smoke, because the LORD descended
upon it in *fire: and the smoke thereof
ascended as the smoke of a furnace, and
the whole mount quaked greatly.
19 And when the voice of the trumpet
sounded long, and waxed louder and
louder, Moses spake, and God answered him by a voice.
¶20 And the LORD came down upon
mount Sinai, on the top of the mount:
and the LORD called Moses *up* to the top
of the mount; and Moses went up.
21 And the LORD said unto Moses, Go
down, charge the people, lest they
break through unto the LORD to gaze,
and many of them perish.
22 And let the priests also, which
come near to the LORD, sanctify themselves, lest the LORD break forth upon
them.
23 And Moses said unto the LORD, The
people cannot come up to mount Sinai:
for thou chargedst us, saying, Set
bounds about the mount, and sanctify it.
24 And the LORD said unto him, Away,
get thee down, and thou shalt come up,
thou, and Aaron with thee: but let not
the priests and the people break
through to come up unto the LORD, lest
he break forth upon them.
25 So Moses went down unto the people, and spake unto them.

Fifth Covenant: Mosaic—The Law

20 And God spake all these words,
saying,
2 I *am* the LORD thy God, which have
brought thee out of the land of Egypt,
out of the house of bondage.
3 Thou shalt have no other gods before me.
4 Thou shalt not make unto thee any

20:1 THE MOSAIC COVENANT

The Mosaic Covenant put Israel into a new relationship with God. He was to be their King and they were to be His people, chosen especially out of all the nations to keep His law and live for Him and witness to the nations around them that He was *the* God. Within this nation, the Messiah, known to us as the Lord Jesus Christ, was to be born of a woman. The basis of this relationship was the covenant with Moses. A covenant is an agreement between two or more parties–this one between God and Moses, who represented the Israelites. It was conditional: If the Israelites would keep the Law which God would give them, God would keep His promises of blessing to them. The next few chapters give the terms or rules of the Mosaic *covenant. It is in three parts:

1. The Ten Commandments (20:1-26).
2. The Judgments (21:1–24:11).
3. The Ordinances (24:12–31:18).

All three parts form the Law, and are what is meant whenever the Law is mentioned. See *Law.

19:17 nether. Lower.

19:25 Moses . . . spake. There are three parts in the giving of the Law:

1. God spoke to Moses, who told the people (chaps. 20–24).
2. Moses went up into Mount Sinai for forty days and received the two tables of stone, and the instructions for the tabernacle and priests (chaps. 25–32).
3. Moses made the second tables of stone, after he had broken the first tables when the people sinned, and God again wrote on them (chap. 34).

20:2 I am. The Ten Commandments which follow (vss. 2-17) can be divided into two parts. The first four give our duty to God; the next six, our duty to our fellowmen. No one ever kept them perfectly except the Lord Jesus Christ. See Matthew 22:35-40.

*graven image, or any likeness *of any*
thing that *is* in heaven above, or that *is*
in the earth beneath, or that *is* in the
water under the earth:
5Thou shalt not bow down thyself to
them, nor serve them: for I the LORD
thy God *am* a *jealous God, visiting the
iniquity of the fathers upon the children
unto the third and fourth *generation* of
them that hate me;
6And shewing mercy unto thousands
of them that love me, and keep my commandments.
7Thou shalt not take the name of the
LORD thy God in vain; for the LORD will
not hold him guiltless that taketh his
name in vain.
8Remember the sabbath day, to keep
it holy.
9Six days shalt thou labour, and do all
thy work:
10But the seventh day *is* the sabbath
of the LORD thy God: *in it* thou shalt not
do any work, thou, nor thy son, nor
thy daughter, thy manservant, nor thy
maidservant, nor thy cattle, nor thy
stranger that *is* within thy gates:
11For *in* six days the LORD made
heaven and earth, the sea, and all that
in them *is,* and rested the seventh day:
wherefore the LORD blessed the sabbath day, and hallowed it.
¶12Honour thy father and thy mother: that thy days may be long upon the
land which the LORD thy God giveth
thee.
13Thou shalt not kill.
14Thou shalt not commit adultery.
15Thou shalt not steal.
16Thou shalt not bear false witness
against thy neighbour.
17Thou shalt not covet thy neighbour's house, thou shalt not covet thy
neighbour's wife, nor his manservant,
nor his maidservant, nor his ox, nor his
ass, nor any thing that *is* thy neighbour's.
¶18And all the people saw the thunderings, and the lightnings, and the
noise of the trumpet, and the mountain
smoking: and when the people saw *it,*
they removed, and stood afar off.
19And they said unto *Moses, Speak
thou with us, and we will hear: but let
not God speak with us, lest we die.
20And Moses said unto the people,
Fear not: for God is come to *prove you,
and that his fear may be before your
faces, that ye sin not.
21And the people stood afar off, and
Moses drew near unto the thick darkness where God *was.*
¶22And the LORD said unto Moses,
Thus thou shalt say unto the children

20:5 THE EFFECT OF SIN

When people do wrong, they must realize that their sin will affect not only themselves but others too. God has given His word in language that everyone can understand, and we and our descendants must pay for disobedience. Some people say, "God is not fair. If I do wrong, let me be punished. Why should God punish my children?" The answer is that God is not punishing their children any more than a doctor punishes a patient who refuses to obey his orders and suffers the consequences. Suppose a father gives his son land for a garden and flower seeds to plant in it. If the child is foolish enough to plant weed seeds instead of the flower seeds, weeds will come up. That is not a punishment from the father for not obeying him; that is the son's own fault. Read Galatians 6:7.

20:5 a jealous God. God is the only One who can be rightfully jealous, for there is no other who is higher or more wonderful than He in any way. His is the "power and the glory for ever," and He must demand the honor that belongs to Him.

20:7 hold. To consider.

20:12 Honour. See Matthew 15:4; 19:19; Mark 7:10. For other times that the Lord Jesus spoke of the Law, read Matthew 5:21,27; Luke 18:20; Mark 10:19.

20:21 afar off. Today we do not have to stay "afar off" from the presence of God. Read Hebrews 10:19-22.

of Israel, Ye have seen that I have talked with you from heaven.

23 Ye shall not make with me gods of *silver, neither shall ye make unto you gods of gold.

¶ 24 An altar of earth thou shalt make unto me, and shalt *sacrifice thereon thy burnt-offerings, and thy *peace-offerings, thy sheep, and thine oxen: in all places where I record my name I will come unto thee, and I will bless thee.

25 And if thou wilt make me an altar of stone, thou shalt not build it of hewn stone: for if thou lift up thy tool upon it, thou hast polluted it.

26 Neither shalt thou go up by steps unto mine altar, that thy nakedness be not discovered thereon.

The Law: judgments
Master and servants

21 Now these *are* the judgments which thou shalt set before them.

2 If thou buy an Hebrew servant, six years he shall serve: and in the seventh he shall go out free for nothing.

3 If he came in by himself, he shall go out by himself: if he were married, then his wife shall go out with him.

4 If his master have given him a wife, and she have born him sons or daughters; the wife and her children shall be her master's, and he shall go out by himself.

5 And if the servant shall plainly say, I love my master, my wife, and my children; I will not go out free:

6 Then his master shall bring him unto the judges; he shall also bring him to the door, or unto the door post; and his master shall bore his ear through with an aul; and he shall serve him for ever.

¶ 7 And if a man sell his daughter to be a maidservant, she shall not go out as the menservants do.

8 If she please not her master, who hath betrothed her to himself, then shall he let her be redeemed: to sell her unto a strange nation he shall have no power, seeing he hath dealt deceitfully with her.

9 And if he have betrothed her unto his son, he shall deal with her after the manner of daughters.

10 If he take him another *wife;* her food, her raiment, and her duty of marriage, shall he not diminish.

11 And if he do not these three unto her, then shall she go out free without money.

Injuries to people

¶ 12 He that smiteth a man, so that he die, shall be surely put to death.

13 And if a man lie not in wait, but God deliver *him* into his hand; then I will appoint thee a place whither he shall flee.

14 But if a man come presumptuously upon his neighbour, to slay him with guile; thou shalt take him from mine altar, that he may die.

¶ 15 And he that smiteth his father, or his mother, shall be surely put to death.

¶ 16 And he that stealeth a man, and selleth him, or if he be found in his hand, he shall surely be put to death.

¶ 17 And he that curseth his father, or his mother, shall surely be put to death.

¶ 18 And if men strive together, and one smite another with a stone, or with *his* fist, and he die not, but keepeth *his* bed:

19 If he rise again, and walk abroad upon his staff, then shall he that smote *him* be quit: only he shall pay *for* the loss of his time, and shall cause *him* to be thoroughly healed.

¶ 20 And if a man smite his servant, or his maid, with a rod, and he die under his hand; he shall be surely punished.

21:12 death. See Genesis 9:6.
21:13 place. See Numbers 35:11.
21:14 take him from mine altar. Read about the death of Joab in 1 Kings 2:29.

21 Notwithstanding, if he continue a day or two, he shall not be punished: for he *is* his money.

¶ 22 If men strive, and hurt a woman with child, so that her fruit depart *from her,* and yet no mischief follow: he shall be surely punished, according as the woman's husband will lay upon him; and he shall pay as the judges *determine.*

23 And if *any* mischief follow, then thou shalt give life for life,

24 Eye for eye, tooth for tooth, hand for hand, foot for foot,

25 Burning for burning, wound for wound, stripe for stripe.

¶ 26 And if a man smite the eye of his servant, or the eye of his maid, that it perish; he shall let him go free for his eye's sake.

27 And if he smite out his manservant's tooth, or his maidservant's tooth; he shall let him go free for his tooth's sake.

¶ 28 If an ox gore a man or a woman, that they die: then the ox shall be surely stoned, and his flesh shall not be eaten; but the owner of the ox *shall be* quit.

29 But if the ox were wont to push with his horn in time past, and it hath been testified to his owner, and he hath not kept him in, but that he hath killed a man or a woman; the ox shall be stoned, and his owner also shall be put to death.

30 If there be laid on him a sum of money, then he shall give for the *ransom of his life whatsoever is laid upon him.

31 Whether he have gored a son, or have gored a daughter, according to this judgment shall it be done unto him.

32 If the ox shall push a manservant or a maidservant; he shall give unto their master thirty shekels of silver, and the ox shall be stoned.

¶ 33 And if a man shall open a pit, or if a man shall dig a pit, and not cover it, and an ox or an ass fall therein;

34 The owner of the pit shall make *it* good, *and* give money unto the owner of them; and the dead *beast* shall be his.

¶ 35 And if one man's ox hurt another's, that he die; then they shall sell the live ox, and divide the money of it; and the dead *ox* also they shall divide.

36 Or if it be known that the ox hath used to push in time past, and his owner hath not kept him in; he shall surely pay ox for ox; and the dead shall be his own.

Injury to property

22 If a man shall steal an ox, or a sheep, and kill it, or sell it; he shall restore five oxen for an ox, and four sheep for a sheep.

¶ 2 If a thief be found breaking up, and be smitten that he die, *there shall* no blood *be shed* for him.

3 If the sun be risen upon him, *there shall be* blood *shed* for him; *for* he should make full restitution; if he have nothing, then he shall be sold for his theft.

4 If the theft be certainly found in his hand alive, whether it be ox, or ass, or sheep; he shall restore double.

¶ 5 If a man shall cause a field or vineyard to be eaten, and shall put in his beast, and shall feed in another man's field; of the best of his own field, and of the best of his own vineyard, shall he make restitution.

¶ 6 If fire break out, and catch in thorns, so that the stacks of corn, or the standing corn, or the field, be consumed *therewith;* he that kindled the fire shall surely make restitution.

¶ 7 If a man shall deliver unto his neighbour money or stuff to keep, and it be stolen out of the man's house; if the thief be found, let him pay double.

8 If the thief be not found, then the master of the house shall be brought unto the judges, *to see* whether he have put his hand unto his neighbour's goods.

21:32 shekels. A shekel is a weight equal to two-fifths of an ounce.

9 For all manner of *trespass, *whether it be* for ox, for ass, for sheep, for raiment, *or* for any manner of lost thing, which *another* challengeth to be his, the cause of both parties shall come before the judges; *and* whom the judges shall condemn, he shall pay double unto his neighbour.

10 If a man deliver unto his neighbour an ass, or an ox, or a sheep, or any beast, to keep; and it die, or be hurt, or driven away, no man seeing *it:*

11 *Then* shall an oath of the LORD be between them both, that he hath not put his hand unto his neighbour's goods; and the owner of it shall accept *thereof,* and he shall not make *it* good.

12 And if it be stolen from him, he shall make restitution unto the owner thereof.

13 If it be torn in pieces, *then* let him bring it *for* witness, *and* he shall not make good that which was torn.

¶ 14 And if a man *borrow *ought* of his neighbour, and it be hurt, or die, the owner thereof *being* not with it, he shall surely make *it* good.

15 *But* if the owner thereof *be* with it, he shall not make *it* good: if it *be* an hired *thing,* it came for his hire.

Moral injuries

¶ 16 And if a man entice a maid that is not betrothed, and lie with her, he shall surely endow her to be his wife.

17 If her father utterly refuse to give her unto him, he shall pay money according to the dowry of virgins.

¶ 18 Thou shalt not suffer a *witch to live.

¶ 19 Whosoever lieth with a beast shall surely be put to death.

¶ 20 He that sacrificeth unto *any* god, save unto the LORD only, he shall be utterly destroyed.

¶ 21 Thou shalt neither vex a stranger, nor oppress him: for ye were strangers in the land of Egypt.

¶ 22 Ye shall not afflict any widow, or fatherless child.

23 If thou afflict them in any wise, and they cry at all unto me, I will surely hear their cry;

24 And my wrath shall wax hot, and I will kill you with the sword; and your wives shall be widows, and your children fatherless.

¶ 25 If thou lend money to *any of* my people *that is* poor by thee, thou shalt not be to him as an usurer, neither shalt thou lay upon him *usury.

26 If thou at all take thy neighbour's raiment to pledge, thou shalt deliver it unto him by that the sun goeth down:

27 For that *is* his covering only, it *is* his raiment for his skin: wherein shall he sleep? and it shall come to pass, when he crieth unto me, that I will hear; for I *am* gracious.

¶ 28 Thou shalt not revile the gods, nor curse the ruler of thy people.

¶ 29 Thou shalt not delay *to offer* the first of thy ripe fruits, and of thy liquors: the firstborn of thy sons shalt thou give unto me.

30 Likewise shalt thou do with thine oxen, *and* with thy sheep: seven days it shall be with his dam; on the eighth day thou shalt give it me.

¶ 31 And ye shall be holy men unto me: neither shall ye eat *any* flesh *that is* torn of beasts in the field; ye shall cast it to the dogs.

23 Thou shalt not raise a false report: put not thine hand with the wicked to be an unrighteous witness.

¶ 2 Thou shalt not follow a multitude to *do* evil; neither shalt thou speak in a

---

22:9 challengeth. Claims.
22:18 a witch. A witch was one who foretold the future by the power of Satan.
22:25 an usurer. A usurer was one who lent money to others but made the lenders pay usury or too much interest upon that money. It was all right to charge some interest, but it was wrong to charge over the fair amount.
22:28 curse the ruler. Paul quoted this in Acts 23:5.
22:29 firstborn. Read chapter 13.

cause to decline after many to wrest
judgment:
¶3 Neither shalt thou countenance a
poor man in his cause.
¶4 If thou meet thine enemy's ox or
his ass going astray, thou shalt surely
bring it back to him again.
5 If thou see the ass of him that hateth
thee lying under his burden, and
wouldest forbear to help him, thou shalt
surely help with him.
6 Thou shalt not wrest the judgment
of thy poor in his cause.
7 Keep thee far from a false matter;
and the innocent and righteous slay
thou not: for I will not justify the
wicked.
¶8 And thou shalt take no gift: for the
gift blindeth the wise, and perverteth
the words of the righteous.
¶9 Also thou shalt not oppress a
stranger: for ye know the heart of a
stranger, seeing ye were strangers in
the land of Egypt.
¶10 And six years thou shalt sow thy
land, and shalt gather in the fruits
thereof:
11 But the seventh *year* thou shalt let
it rest and lie still; that the poor of thy
people may eat: and what they leave the
beasts of the field shall eat. In like manner thou shalt deal with thy vineyard,
and with thy oliveyard.
12 Six days thou shalt do thy work, and
on the seventh day thou shalt rest: that
thine ox and thine ass may rest, and the
son of thy handmaid, and the stranger,
may be refreshed.
13 And in all *things* that I have said
unto you be circumspect: and make no
mention of the name of other gods, neither let it be heard out of thy mouth.
¶14 Three times thou shalt keep a
feast unto me in the year.
15 Thou shalt keep the feast of *unleavened bread: (thou shalt eat unleavened bread seven days, as I commanded
thee, in the time appointed of the month
Abib; for in it thou camest out from
Egypt: and none shall appear before me
empty:)
16 And the feast of harvest, the firstfruits of thy labours, which thou hast
sown in the field: and the feast of ingathering, *which is* in the end of the
year, when thou hast gathered in thy
labours out of the field.
17 Three times in the year all thy

23:16 THE FEAST OF WEEKS

The Feast of Weeks (Exod. 34:22) or the Feast of Harvest (Exod. 23:16), or of Pentecost (Acts 2:1, from the Greek word for the "fiftieth day"), was kept at the end of seven complete weeks from the sixteenth of Nisan. The passages about it are in Exodus 23:16; Leviticus 23:15-21; Numbers 28:26-31.

1. The festival lasted only one day.
2. Its chief feature was the offering of two leavened loaves, made from the new grain of the now-completed harvest, which together with two lambs as a thank offering were waved before the Lord.
3. It was preeminently an expression of gratitude for the harvest, which began with the first ripe sheaf of barley at the Passover and ended with that of the two loaves of the newly ripened wheat.
4. In its festive joy the servants and strangers, the fatherless and the widow, were to share with the freeborn Israelite (Deut. 16:11).

23:2 decline. To turn aside.
23:2 wrest. To pervert.
23:3 poor. People were to be absolutely fair—just as honest with a rich man as with a poor man and just as good to a poor man as to a rich man. See also verse 8.
23:10 six years. These brief instructions were for the children of Israel to observe in the wilderness. Later, Leviticus gave fuller instructions for the feasts (see vs. 14) to be observed when the Israelites got to the Promised Land (Lev. 23–25).

males shall appear before the Lord GOD.

18 Thou shalt not offer the blood of my sacrifice with *leavened bread; neither shall the fat of my sacrifice remain until the morning.

19 The first of the firstfruits of thy land thou shalt bring into the house of the LORD thy God. Thou shalt not seethe a kid in his mother's milk.

Instructions for conquest

¶20 Behold, I send an *Angel before thee, to keep thee in the way, and to bring thee into the place which I have prepared.

21 Beware of him, and obey his voice, provoke him not; for he will not pardon your transgressions: for my name *is* in him.

22 But if thou shalt indeed obey his voice, and do all that I speak; then I will be an enemy unto thine enemies, and an adversary unto thine adversaries.

23 For mine Angel shall go before thee, and bring thee in unto the Amorites, and the Hittites, and the Perizzites, and the Canaanites, and the Hivites, and the Jebusites: and I will cut them off.

24 Thou shalt not bow down to their gods, nor serve them, nor do after their works: but thou shalt utterly overthrow them, and quite break down their images.

25 And ye shall serve the LORD your God, and he shall bless thy bread, and thy water; and I will take sickness away from the midst of thee.

26 There shall nothing cast their young, nor be barren, in thy land: the number of thy days I will fulfil.

27 I will send my *fear before thee, and will destroy all the people to whom thou shalt come, and I will make all thine enemies turn their backs unto thee.

28 And I will send hornets before thee, which shall drive out the Hivite, the Canaanite, and the Hittite, from before thee.

29 I will not drive them out from before thee in one year; lest the land become desolate, and the beast of the field multiply against thee.

30 By little and little I will drive them out from before thee, until thou be increased, and inherit the land.

31 And I will set thy bounds from the Red sea even unto the sea of the *Philistines, and from the desert unto the river: for I will deliver the inhabitants of the land into your hand; and thou shalt drive them out before thee.

32 Thou shalt make no covenant with them, nor with their gods.

33 They shall not dwell in thy land, lest they make thee *sin against me: for if thou serve their gods, it will surely be a snare unto thee.

Covenant accepted by the people

24 And he said unto Moses, Come up unto the LORD, thou, and *Aaron, Nadab, and Abihu, and seventy of the *elders of Israel; and worship ye afar off.

2 And Moses alone shall come near the LORD: but they shall not come nigh; neither shall the people go up with him.

¶3 And Moses came and told the people all the words of the LORD, and all the judgments: and all the people answered with one voice, and said, All the words which the LORD hath said will we do.

4 And Moses wrote all the words of the LORD, and rose up early in the morning, and builded an *altar under

---

23:31 sea of the Philistines. The Mediterranean; "from the desert unto the river" meant from the desert south of Palestine to the Euphrates River.

24:1 Nadab, and Abihu. See Leviticus 8:1-2 and 10:1.

24:3 all. See Exodus 19:8 note.

24:3 the words. See *inspiration.

24:4 builded an altar. Until the larger tabernacle was built, an altar with twelve pillars was called the tabernacle. See why people built altars (Gen. 8:20 note).

the hill, and twelve pillars, according to
the twelve tribes of Israel.
5And he sent young men of the children of Israel, which offered burnt-
offerings, and sacrificed peace-offerings
of oxen unto the LORD.
6And Moses took half of the blood,
and put *it* in basons; and half of the
blood he sprinkled on the altar.
7And he took the book of the covenant, and read in the audience of the
people: and they said, All that the
LORD hath said will we do, and be
obedient.
8And Moses took the blood, and
sprinkled *it* on the people, and said,
Behold the blood of the covenant, which
the LORD hath made with you concerning all these words.
¶9Then went up Moses, and Aaron,
Nadab, and Abihu, and seventy of the
elders of Israel:
10And they saw the God of Israel: and
there was under his feet as it were a
paved work of a sapphire stone, and as
it were the body of heaven in *his* clear-
ness.
11And upon the nobles of the children
of Israel he laid not his hand: also they
saw God, and did eat and drink.

The Law: ordinances

¶12And the LORD said unto Moses,
Come up to me into the mount, and be
there: and I will give thee tables of
stone, and a *law, and commandments
which I have written; that thou mayest
teach them.
13And Moses rose up, and his minister *Joshua: and Moses went up into
the mount of God.
14And he said unto the elders, Tarry
ye here for us, until we come again unto
you: and, behold, Aaron and *Hur *are*
with you: if any man have any matters
to do, let him come unto them.
15And Moses went up into the mount,
and a cloud covered the mount.
16And the glory of the LORD abode
upon mount *Sinai, and the cloud covered it six days: and the seventh day he
called unto Moses out of the midst of
the cloud.
17And the sight of the glory of the
LORD *was* like devouring fire on the top
of the mount in the eyes of the children
of Israel.
18And Moses went into the midst of
the cloud, and gat him up into the
mount: and Moses was in the mount
forty days and forty nights.

The tabernacle: materials

25 And the LORD spake unto Moses, saying,
2Speak unto the children of *Israel,
that they bring me an *offering: of
every man that giveth it willingly with
his heart ye shall take my offering.
3And this *is* the offering which ye
shall take of them; gold, and silver, and
brass,
4And *blue, and purple, and scarlet,
and fine *linen, and goats' *hair,*
5And rams' skins dyed red, and badgers' skins, and shittim wood,
6*Oil for the light, spices for anointing oil, and for sweet *incense,
7Onyx stones, and stones to be set in
the ephod, and in the breastplate.
8And let them make me a *sanctuary;
that I may dwell among them.
9According to all that I shew thee,
after the pattern of the *tabernacle, and

24:8 blood. See Hebrews 9:20.
24:10 saw the God of Israel. No one has ever seen God the Father (Deut. 4:15; John 1:18), but these men could probably see some outward sign of His presence, probably as a bright cloud or as a great blaze of light, whose brilliance could only be described as being like sapphires.
24:11 eat and drink. They feasted on the meat of the offerings.
25:5 shittim wood. This was acacia wood. Many acacia trees grow on Sinai. They are about as tall as mulberry trees, and their wood is very hard and lasts for a long time.
25:7 ephod. This was part of the clothing of the high priest.

> **25:9 The Tabernacle**
> The word "tabernacle" means a *dwelling place*. The tabernacle was a very beautiful tent in which the Israelites could worship God as they journeyed from place to place. God gave very careful instructions for the making of it, showing us that—both then and now—in the worship of God we must follow His Word and not just our own ideas. The finished tabernacle was a wonderful picture or *type of the Lord Jesus Christ.

the pattern of all the instruments thereof, even so shall ye make *it*.

Tabernacle: the ark

¶ 10 And they shall make an *ark *of* shittim wood: two *cubits and a half *shall be* the length thereof, and a cubit and a half the breadth thereof, and a cubit and a half the height thereof.

> **25:10 The Ark of the Covenant**
> The ark is the first thing mentioned because it was the most sacred part of the tabernacle. It was a chest of shittim or acacia wood (see vs. 5 note) covered with gold. The wood was just the hard, strong desert wood which grew in the dry, sandy soil. It reminds us of the humanity of our Lord (Isa. 53:2), while the gold, which always speaks of God, reminds us that the Lord Jesus Christ is also God.

11 And thou shalt overlay it with pure gold, within and without shalt thou overlay it, and shalt make upon it a crown of gold round about.

12 And thou shalt cast four rings of gold for it, and put *them* in the four corners thereof; and two rings *shall be* in the one side of it, and two rings in the other side of it.

13 And thou shalt make staves *of* shittim wood, and overlay them with gold.

14 And thou shalt put the staves into the rings by the sides of the ark, that the ark may be borne with them.

15 The staves shall be in the rings of the ark: they shall not be taken from it.

16 And thou shalt put into the ark the testimony which I shall give thee.

17 And thou shalt make a mercy seat *of* pure gold: two cubits and a half *shall be* the length thereof, and a cubit and a half the breadth thereof.

> **25:17 The Mercy Seat**
> The mercy seat was a lid for the chest. It had the same measurements as the ark. The word means a *covering*; the mercy seat covered the ark. See note on *propitiation.

18 And thou shalt make two cherubims *of* gold, *of* beaten work shalt thou make them, in the two ends of the mercy seat.

19 And make one cherub on the one end, and the other cherub on the other end: *even* of the mercy seat shall ye make the cherubims on the two ends thereof.

20 And the cherubim shall stretch forth *their* wings on high, covering the mercy seat with their wings, and their faces *shall look* one to another; toward the mercy seat shall the faces of the cherubims be.

21 And thou shalt put the mercy seat above upon the ark; and in the ark thou shalt put the testimony that I shall give thee.

22 And there I will meet with thee, and I will commune with thee from above the mercy seat, from between the two cherubims which *are* upon the ark of the testimony, of all *things* which I will give thee in commandment unto the children of Israel.

25:10 cubits. One cubit is eighteen inches.
25:11 crown of gold. A rim of gold along the edge of the table.
25:16 testimony. The tables of stone which God later gave to Moses with the Law written on them were the "testimony."
25:18 cherubims. These were two gold figures representing angels. The cherubims always speak of or stand for the holiness of God. See Ezekiel 1:5 note. "Cherubim" or "cherubims" are the plurals of "cherub" (vs. 19).

Tabernacle: table of shewbread

¶ 23 Thou shalt also make a table *of*
shittim wood: two cubits *shall be* the
length thereof, and a cubit the breadth
thereof, and a cubit and a half the height
thereof.
24 And thou shalt overlay it with pure
gold, and make thereto a crown of gold
round about.
25 And thou shalt make unto it a border of an hand breadth round about, and
thou shalt make a golden crown to the
border thereof round about.
26 And thou shalt make for it four
rings of gold, and put the rings in the
four corners that *are* on the four feet
thereof.
27 Over against the border shall the
rings be for places of the staves to bear
the table.
28 And thou shalt make the staves *of*
shittim wood, and overlay them with
gold, that the table may be borne with
them.
29 And thou shalt make the dishes
thereof, and spoons thereof, and covers
thereof, and bowls thereof, to cover
withal: *of* pure gold shalt thou make
them.
30 And thou shalt set upon the table
*shewbread before me alway.

Tabernacle: golden candlestick

¶ 31 And thou shalt make a *candlestick *of* pure gold: *of* beaten work shall
the candlestick be made: his shaft, and
his branches, his bowls, his knops, and
his flowers, shall be of the same.
32 And six branches shall come out of
the sides of it; three branches of the
candlestick out of the one side, and
three branches of the candlestick out of
the other side:
33 Three bowls made like unto almonds, *with* a knop and a flower in one
branch; and three bowls made like almonds in the other branch, *with* a knop
and a flower: so in the six branches that
come out of the candlestick.
34 And in the candlestick *shall be* four
bowls made like unto almonds, *with*
their knops and their flowers.
35 And *there shall be* a knop under two
branches of the same, and a knop under two branches of the same, and a
knop under two branches of the same,
according to the six branches that proceed out of the candlestick.
36 Their knops and their branches
shall be of the same: all it *shall be* one
beaten work *of* pure gold.
37 And thou shalt make the seven
lamps thereof: and they shall light the
lamps thereof, that they may give light
over against it.
38 And the tongs thereof, and the
snuffdishes thereof, *shall be of* pure
gold.
39 *Of* a talent of pure gold shall he
make it, with all these vessels.
40 And look that thou make *them* after
their pattern, which was shewed thee
in the mount.

Tabernacle: curtains

26 Moreover thou shalt make the
tabernacle *with* ten curtains *of*

26:1 The Tabernacle Curtains
Fine linen in the Bible refers to righteousness. Almost everything in the tabernacle reveals the Lord Jesus, and these ten curtains of fine linen make us think of His perfect and sinless life, which was righteous in every detail. The colors also have a meaning: Blue speaks of His coming from heaven, purple of His royalty as the descendant of King David, and scarlet of His blood shed on the cross.

25:30 shewbread. The word means *presence bread*, because the twelve loaves were always on the table in God's presence. "Shew" is the old spelling for "show."

25:31 knops. An old spelling for "knobs," flower buds; in this case, carved imitations of buds.

25:39 talent of pure gold. A talent was a weight equal to seventy-five pounds.

fine twined linen, and blue, and purple, and scarlet: *with* cherubims of *cunning work shalt thou make them.

2 The length of one curtain *shall be* eight and twenty cubits, and the breadth of one curtain four cubits: and every one of the curtains shall have one measure.

3 The five curtains shall be coupled together one to another; and *other* five curtains *shall be* coupled one to another.

4 And thou shalt make loops of blue upon the edge of the one curtain from the selvedge in the coupling; and likewise shalt thou make in the uttermost edge of *another* curtain, in the coupling of the second.

5 Fifty loops shalt thou make in the one curtain, and fifty loops shalt thou make in the edge of the curtain that *is* in the coupling of the second; that the loops may take hold one of another.

6 And thou shalt make fifty taches of gold, and couple the curtains together with the taches: and it shall be one tabernacle.

¶ 7 And thou shalt make curtains *of* goats' *hair* to be a covering upon the tabernacle: eleven curtains shalt thou make.

8 The length of one curtain *shall be* thirty cubits, and the breadth of one curtain four cubits: and the eleven curtains *shall be all* of one measure.

9 And thou shalt couple five curtains by themselves, and six curtains by themselves, and shalt double the sixth curtain in the forefront of the tabernacle.

10 And thou shalt make fifty loops on the edge of the one curtain *that is* outmost in the coupling, and fifty loops in the edge of the curtain which coupleth the second.

11 And thou shalt make fifty taches of brass, and put the taches into the loops, and couple the tent together, that it may be one.

12 And the remnant that remaineth of the curtains of the tent, the half curtain that remaineth, shall hang over the backside of the tabernacle.

13 And a cubit on the one side, and a cubit on the other side of that which remaineth in the length of the curtains of the tent, it shall hang over the sides of the tabernacle on this side and on that side, to cover it.

14 And thou shalt make a covering for the tent *of* rams' skins dyed red, and a covering above *of* badgers' skins.

Tabernacle: boards

¶ 15 And thou shalt make boards for the tabernacle *of* shittim wood standing up.

16 Ten cubits *shall be* the length of a board, and a cubit and a half *shall be* the breadth of one board.

17 Two tenons *shall there be* in one board, set in order one against another: thus shalt thou make for all the boards of the tabernacle.

18 And thou shalt make the boards for the tabernacle, twenty boards on the south side southward.

19 And thou shalt make forty sockets of silver under the twenty boards; two sockets under one board for his two tenons, and two sockets under another board for his two tenons.

20 And for the second side of the tabernacle on the north side *there shall be* twenty boards:

21 And their forty sockets *of* silver; two sockets under one board, and two sockets under another board.

22 And for the sides of the tabernacle westward thou shalt make six boards.

26:6 taches. Clasps like large hooks and eyes.

26:7 goats' hair. The curtains made a coarse outer covering of plain leather one yard longer than the other curtains.

26:14 rams' skins. The skins were used to make a red leather rug to go over the top of the other curtains.

26:17 tenons. These were projections to form sockets.

23 And two boards shalt thou make for the corners of the tabernacle in the two sides.

24 And they shall be coupled together beneath, and they shall be coupled together above the head of it unto one ring: thus shall it be for them both; they shall be for the two corners.

25 And they shall be eight boards, and their sockets *of* silver, sixteen sockets; two sockets under one board, and two sockets under another board.

¶26 And thou shalt make bars *of* shittim wood; five for the boards of the one side of the tabernacle,

27 And five bars for the boards of the other side of the tabernacle, and five bars for the boards of the side of the tabernacle, for the two sides westward.

28 And the middle bar in the midst of the boards shall reach from end to end.

29 And thou shalt overlay the boards with gold, and make their rings *of* gold *for* places for the bars: and thou shalt overlay the bars with gold.

30 And thou shalt rear up the tabernacle according to the fashion thereof which was shewed thee in the mount.

Tabernacle: inner veil

¶31 And thou shalt make a vail *of* blue, and purple, and scarlet, and fine twined linen of cunning work: with cherubims shall it be made:

32 And thou shalt hang it upon four pillars of shittim *wood* overlaid with gold: their hooks *shall be of* gold, upon the four sockets of silver.

33 And thou shalt hang up the vail under the taches, that thou mayest bring in thither within the vail the ark of the testimony: and the vail shall divide unto you between the holy *place* and the most holy.

34 And thou shalt put the mercy seat upon the ark of the testimony in the most holy *place*.

26:34 The Holy of Holies
The Holy of Holies is also called the "Holiest of All" and the "Most Holy Place." Located in the *tabernacle, the Holy of Holies was the section of the Holy Place which could be entered only by the high priest, and then only once a year (Heb. 9:7). The *ark of the covenant, covered by the *mercy seat and the *cherubim, was located here. It was a perfect cube, ten *cubits each way. Later, the temple in Jerusalem also had a section called the Holy of Holies.

35 And thou shalt set the table without the vail, and the candlestick over against the table on the side of the tabernacle toward the south: and thou shalt put the table on the north side.

¶36 And thou shalt make an hanging for the door of the tent, *of* blue, and purple, and scarlet, and fine twined linen, wrought with needlework.

37 And thou shalt make for the hanging five pillars *of* shittim *wood,* and overlay them with gold, *and* their hooks *shall be of* gold: and thou shalt cast five sockets of brass for them.

Tabernacle: brass altar

27 And thou shalt make an altar *of* shittim wood, five cubits long, and five cubits broad; the altar shall be foursquare: and the height thereof *shall be* three cubits.

27:1 The Altar
The altar was at the door of the tabernacle. On it all of the sacrifices were offered. See Leviticus 1–8 for details of the sacrifices. The altar was a hollow box, three yards square and one-and-a-half yards high, with hornlike projections at each corner to which the sacrificial animals were tied. It was covered with brass (vs. 2) because brass always stands for judgment. Every time an animal was killed on this brass altar, it was a reminder that God had to judge sin.

26:31 vail. The vail was a curtain hanging between the Holy Place and the Most Holy Place where the ark was. Its meaning is fully explained in Hebrews 10:20. See also Exodus 26:1 note; 34:33; and 2 Corinthians 3:13-16.

2 And thou shalt make the *horns of it upon the four corners thereof: his horns shall be of the same: and thou shalt overlay it with brass.

3 And thou shalt make his pans to receive his ashes, and his shovels, and his basons, and his fleshhooks, and his firepans: all the vessels thereof thou shalt make *of* brass.

4 And thou shalt make for it a grate of network *of* brass; and upon the net shalt thou make four brasen rings in the four corners thereof.

5 And thou shalt put it under the compass of the altar beneath, that the net may be even to the midst of the altar.

6 And thou shalt make staves for the altar, staves *of* shittim wood, and overlay them with brass.

7 And the staves shall be put into the rings, and the staves shall be upon the two sides of the altar, to bear it.

8 Hollow with boards shalt thou make it: as it was shewed thee in the mount, so shall they make *it*.

Tabernacle: court

¶9 And thou shalt make the court of the tabernacle: for the south side southward *there shall be* hangings for the court *of* fine twined linen of an hundred cubits long for one side:

10 And the twenty pillars thereof and their twenty sockets *shall be of* brass; the hooks of the pillars and their fillets *shall be of* silver.

11 And likewise for the north side in length *there shall be* hangings of an hundred *cubits* long, and his twenty pillars and their twenty sockets *of* brass; the hooks of the pillars and their fillets *of* silver.

12 And *for* the breadth of the court on the west side *shall be* hangings of fifty cubits: their pillars ten, and their sockets ten.

13 And the breadth of the court on the east side eastward *shall be* fifty cubits.

14 The hangings of one side *of the gate shall be* fifteen cubits: their

THE TABERNACLE AND ITS FURNISHINGS

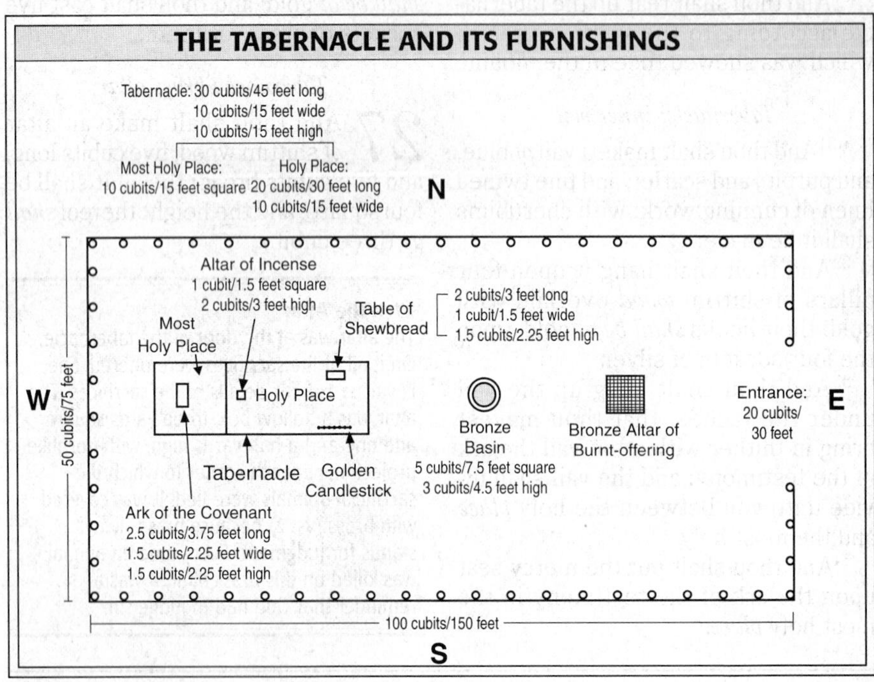

27:9 fine twined linen. See Exodus 26:1 note.
27:10 fillets. Bands or threads.

pillars three, and their sockets three.
15 And on the other side *shall be* hangings fifteen *cubits:* their pillars three,
and their sockets three.
¶16 And for the gate of the court *shall*
be an hanging of twenty cubits, *of* blue,
and purple, and scarlet, and fine twined
linen, wrought with needlework: *and*
their pillars *shall be* four, and their sockets four.
17 All the pillars round about the court
shall be filleted with silver; their hooks
shall be of silver, and their sockets of
brass.
18 The length of the court *shall be* an
hundred cubits, and the breadth fifty
every where, and the height five cubits
of fine twined linen, and their sockets
of brass.
19 All the vessels of the tabernacle in
all the service thereof, and all the pins
thereof, and all the pins of the court,
shall be of brass.

Tabernacle: oil for light

¶20 And thou shalt command the children of Israel, that they bring thee pure
oil olive beaten for the light, to cause
the lamp to burn always.
21 In the tabernacle of the congregation without the vail, which *is* before the
testimony, Aaron and his sons shall order it from evening to morning before
the LORD: *it shall be* a statute for ever
unto their generations on the behalf of
the children of Israel.

28 And take thou unto thee Aaron
thy brother, and his sons with
him, from among the children of Israel,
that he may minister unto me in the
priest's office, *even* Aaron, *Nadab and
Abihu, Eleazar and Ithamar, Aaron's
sons.
2 And thou shalt make *holy *garments for Aaron thy brother for glory
and for beauty.
3 And thou shalt speak unto all *that are*

28:2 THE PRIESTS' HOLY GARMENTS

The Hebrew word for "holy" is the same as the word for "*sanctify" in 13:2 and as "consecrate" in verse 3. It does not mean that the actual clothes were holy but that they were put to holy use.

The high priest wore:

1. the coat (28:39), a robe of fine linen worn next to the skin;
2. the embroidered coat or robe of the ephod (28:4,39), a long seamless garment trimmed around the hem with tassels in the form of pomegranates, and also trimmed with little bells;
3. the ephod (28:6-12), a short linen coat reaching from the shoulders to the knees, beautifully embroidered in gold, purple, and scarlet;
4. the breastplate (28:15-29), a pouch of linen to which was attached a gold framework containing twelve jewels engraved with the names of the twelve tribes. In the pouch were the Urim and the Thummim;
5. the Urim and the Thummim (28:30). The words mean *light* and *perfections*, and some people think that they refer to the twelve stones already described in verses 17-21. Others think that they were two special stones which were used in drawing lots, a method used when consulting the Lord on national problems. They are mentioned seven times: Exodus 28:30; Leviticus 8:8; Numbers 27:21; Deuteronomy 33:8; 1 Samuel 28:6; Ezra 2:63; Nehemiah 7:65;
6. the mitre (28:36-38), a turban for the head. It was adorned with a gold engraved band.

27:16 gate. The gate is a picture of the Lord Jesus Christ who later would say, "I am the door" (John 10:9). See also the Exodus 26:1 note, which includes the meanings of the colors.

27:20 oil olive. Oil is a *type of the Holy Spirit. Just as the oil was needed in the lamps of the tabernacle to make them burn, the Holy Spirit in the believer makes his light shine before men (Matt. 5:16). See *Trinity.

28:3 spirit of wisdom. The Holy Spirit is spoken of here. See *Trinity.

28:3 consecrate. The same word is often translated "sanctify."

wise hearted, whom I have filled with the spirit of wisdom, that they may make Aaron's garments to *consecrate him, that he may minister unto me in the priest's office.

High priest's garments

4 And these *are* the garments which they shall make; a breastplate, and an ephod, and a robe, and a broidered coat, a mitre, and a girdle: and they shall make holy garments for Aaron thy brother, and his sons, that he may minister unto me in the priest's office.

5 And they shall take gold, and blue, and purple, and scarlet, and fine linen.

¶ 6 And they shall make the ephod *of* gold, *of* blue, and *of* purple, *of* scarlet, and fine twined linen, with cunning work.

7 It shall have the two shoulderpieces thereof joined at the two edges thereof; and *so* it shall be joined together.

8 And the curious girdle of the ephod, which *is* upon it, shall be of the same, according to the work thereof; *even of* gold, *of* blue, and purple, and scarlet, and fine twined linen.

9 And thou shalt take two onyx stones, and grave on them the names of the children of Israel:

10 Six of their names on one stone, and *the other* six names of the rest on the other stone, according to their birth.

11 With the work of an engraver in stone, *like* the engravings of a signet, shalt thou engrave the two stones with the names of the children of Israel: thou shalt make them to be set in ouches of gold.

12 And thou shalt put the two stones upon the shoulders of the ephod *for* stones of memorial unto the children of Israel: and Aaron shall bear their names before the LORD upon his two shoulders for a memorial.

13 And thou shalt make ouches *of* gold;

14 And two chains *of* pure gold at the ends; *of* wreathen work shalt thou make them, and fasten the wreathen chains to the ouches.

¶ 15 And thou shalt make the breastplate of judgment with cunning work; after the work of the ephod thou shalt make it; *of* gold, *of* blue, and *of* purple, and *of* scarlet, and *of* fine twined linen, shalt thou make it.

16 Foursquare it shall be *being* doubled; a span *shall be* the length thereof, and a span *shall be* the breadth thereof.

17 And thou shalt set in it settings of stones, *even* four rows of stones: *the first* row *shall be* a sardius, a topaz, and a carbuncle: *this shall be* the first row.

18 And the second row *shall be* an emerald, a sapphire, and a diamond.

19 And the third row a ligure, an agate, and an amethyst.

20 And the fourth row a beryl, and an onyx, and a jasper: they shall be set in gold in their inclosings.

21 And the stones shall be with the names of the children of Israel, twelve, according to their names, *like* the engravings of a signet; every one with his name shall they be according to the twelve tribes.

¶ 22 And thou shalt make upon the breastplate chains at the ends *of* wreathen work *of* pure gold.

23 And thou shalt make upon the breastplate two rings of gold, and shalt put the two rings on the two ends of the breastplate.

24 And thou shalt put the two wreathen *chains* of gold in the two rings

---

28:8 curious girdle. "Curious" means that it was *beautifully made*.
28:11 ouches. These were settings for jewels, what we might call sockets today.
28:14 wreathen. Twisted; used in connection with "work."
28:15 cunning. Careful and beautiful.
28:16 a span. Nearly nine inches.
28:19 ligure. An unknown precious stone, probably the yellow jargoon, also called a zircon.

which are on the ends of the breastplate.
25And *the other* two ends of the two
wreathen *chains* thou shalt fasten in the
two ouches, and put *them* on the
shoulderpieces of the ephod before it.
¶26And thou shalt make two rings of
gold, and thou shalt put them upon the
two ends of the breastplate in the border thereof, which *is* in the side of the
ephod inward.
27And two *other* rings of gold thou
shalt make, and shalt put them on the
two sides of the ephod underneath, toward the forepart thereof, over against
the *other* coupling thereof, above the
curious girdle of the ephod.
28And they shall bind the breastplate
by the rings thereof unto the rings of
the ephod with a lace of blue, that *it* may
be above the curious girdle of the
ephod, and that the breastplate be not
loosed from the ephod.
29And Aaron shall bear the names of
the children of Israel in the breastplate
of judgment upon his heart, when he
goeth in unto the holy *place,* for a memorial before the LORD continually.
¶30And thou shalt put in the breastplate of judgment the Urim and the
Thummim; and they shall be upon
Aaron's heart, when he goeth in before
the LORD: and Aaron shall bear the
judgment of the children of Israel upon
his heart before the LORD continually.
¶31And thou shalt make the robe of
the ephod all *of* blue.
32And there shall be an hole in the top
of it, in the midst thereof: it shall have
a binding of woven work round about
the hole of it, as it were the hole of an
habergeon, that it be not rent.
¶33And *beneath* upon the hem of it
thou shalt make pomegranates *of* blue,
and *of* purple, and *of* scarlet, round
about the hem thereof; and bells of gold
between them round about:
34A golden bell and a pomegranate, a
golden bell and a pomegranate, upon
the hem of the robe round about.
35And it shall be upon Aaron to minister: and his sound shall be heard when
he goeth in unto the holy *place* before
the LORD, and when he cometh out,
that he die not.
¶36And thou shalt make a plate *of*
pure gold, and grave upon it, *like* the engravings of a signet, HOLINESS TO
THE LORD.
37And thou shalt put it on a blue lace,
that it may be upon the mitre; upon the
forefront of the mitre it shall be.
38And it shall be upon Aaron's forehead, that Aaron may bear the iniquity
of the holy things, which the children
of Israel shall hallow in all their holy
gifts; and it shall be always upon his
forehead, that they may be accepted
before the LORD.
¶39And thou shalt embroider the coat
of fine linen, and thou shalt make the
mitre *of* fine linen, and thou shalt make
the girdle *of* needlework.

Garments for the priest

¶40And for Aaron's sons thou shalt
make coats, and thou shalt make for
them girdles, and bonnets shalt thou
make for them, for glory and for beauty.
41And thou shalt put them upon
Aaron thy brother, and his sons with
him; and shalt *anoint them, and consecrate them, and *sanctify them, that
they may minister unto me in the
priest's office.
42And thou shalt make them linen
breeches to cover their nakedness;
from the loins even unto the thighs they
shall reach:
43And they shall be upon Aaron, and
upon his sons, when they come in unto
the tabernacle of the congregation, or
when they come near unto the altar to

28:30 the Urim and the Thummim. See verse 2 note.
28:38 bear the iniquity. Aaron was to be responsible for any neglect of holy things by the children of Israel.
28:40 bonnets. Turbans.

minister in the holy *place;* that they
bear not iniquity, and die: *it shall be* a
statute for ever unto him and his seed
after him.

Consecration of the priests

29 And this *is* the thing that thou
shalt do unto them to hallow
them, to minister unto me in the priest's
office: Take one young bullock, and two
rams without blemish,
2 And *unleavened bread, and cakes
unleavened tempered with oil, and wafers unleavened anointed with oil: *of*
wheaten flour shalt thou make them.
3 And thou shalt put them into one
basket, and bring them in the basket,
with the bullock and the two rams.
4 And Aaron and his sons thou shalt
bring unto the door of the tabernacle of
the congregation, and shalt wash them
with water.
5 And thou shalt take the garments,
and put upon Aaron the coat, and the
robe of the ephod, and the ephod, and
the breastplate, and gird him with the
curious girdle of the ephod:
6 And thou shalt put the mitre upon
his head, and put the holy crown upon
the mitre.
7 Then shalt thou take the anointing
oil, and pour *it* upon his head, and anoint
him.
8 And thou shalt bring his sons, and
put coats upon them.
9 And thou shalt gird them with
girdles, Aaron and his sons, and put the
bonnets on them: and the priest's office
shall be theirs for a perpetual statute:
and thou shalt consecrate Aaron and his
sons.

The offerings (Lev. 1:1—6:7)

10 And thou shalt cause a bullock to be
brought before the tabernacle of the
congregation: and Aaron and his sons
shall put their hands upon the head of
the bullock.
11 And thou shalt kill the bullock before the LORD, *by* the door of the tabernacle of the congregation.
12 And thou shalt take of the *blood of
the bullock, and put *it* upon the horns
of the altar with thy finger, and pour
all the blood beside the bottom of the
altar.
13 And thou shalt take all the fat that
covereth the inwards, and the caul *that*
is above the liver, and the two kidneys,
and the fat that *is* upon them, and burn
them upon the altar.
14 But the flesh of the bullock, and his
skin, and his *dung, shalt thou burn
with *fire without the camp: it *is* a *sin-
offering.
¶ 15 Thou shalt also take one ram; and
Aaron and his sons shall put their hands
upon the head of the ram.
16 And thou shalt slay the ram, and
thou shalt take his blood, and sprinkle
it round about upon the altar.
17 And thou shalt cut the ram in
pieces, and wash the inwards of him,
and his legs, and put *them* unto his
pieces, and unto his head.
18 And thou shalt burn the whole ram
upon the altar: it *is* a burnt-offering unto
the LORD: it *is* a sweet savour, an offering made by fire unto the LORD.
¶ 19 And thou shalt take the other ram;
and Aaron and his sons shall put their
hands upon the head of the ram.
20 Then shalt thou kill the ram, and
take of his blood, and put *it* upon the tip
of the right ear of Aaron, and upon the
tip of the right ear of his sons, and upon
the thumb of their right hand, and upon
the great toe of their right foot, and
sprinkle the blood upon the altar round
about.
21 And thou shalt take of the blood that
is upon the altar, and of the anointing oil,

29:1 do unto them. These instructions for consecrating the priests are full of meaning. They are more fully explained in Leviticus 8 and 9 notes.
29:2 tempered. Mixed or compounded.
29:14 without the camp. See Leviticus 4:12 note.

and sprinkle *it* upon Aaron, and upon his
garments, and upon his sons, and upon
the garments of his sons with him: and
he shall be hallowed, and his garments,
and his sons, and his sons' garments
with him.
22 Also thou shalt take of the ram the
fat and the rump, and the fat that
covereth the inwards, and the caul
above the liver, and the two kidneys, and
the fat that *is* upon them, and the right
shoulder; for it *is* a ram of consecration:
23 And one loaf of bread, and one cake
of oiled bread, and one wafer out of the
basket of the unleavened bread that *is*
before the LORD:
24 And thou shalt put all in the hands
of Aaron, and in the hands of his sons;
and shalt wave them *for* a wave-
offering before the LORD.
25 And thou shalt receive them of
their hands, and burn *them* upon the
altar for a burnt-offering, for a sweet
savour before the LORD: it *is* an offering made by fire unto the LORD.
26 And thou shalt take the breast of
the ram of Aaron's consecration, and
wave it *for* a wave-offering before the
LORD: and it shall be thy part.
27 And thou shalt sanctify the breast
of the wave-offering, and the shoulder
of the heave-offering, which is waved,
and which is heaved up, of the ram of
the consecration, *even* of *that* which *is*
for Aaron, and of *that* which is for his
sons:
28 And it shall be Aaron's and his sons'
by a statute for ever from the children
of Israel: for it *is* an heave-offering: and
it shall be an heave-offering from the
children of Israel of the *sacrifice of
their *peace-offerings, *even* their
heave-offering unto the LORD.
¶29 And the holy garments of Aaron
shall be his sons' after him, to be
anointed therein, and to be consecrated in them.
30 *And* that son that is priest in his
stead shall put them on seven days,
when he cometh into the tabernacle of
the congregation to minister in the holy
place.
¶31 And thou shalt take the ram of the
consecration, and seethe his flesh in the
holy place.
32 And Aaron and his sons shall eat
the flesh of the ram, and the bread that
is in the basket, *by* the door of the tabernacle of the congregation.
33 And they shall eat those things
wherewith the *atonement was made,
to consecrate *and* to sanctify them: but
a stranger shall not eat *thereof,* because
they *are* holy.

29:33 Atonement
The Hebrew word means *to cover*. It means that each sacrifice covered the sin of the man or woman who offered it and secured God's forgiveness. The punishment was placed upon the victim, and the offerer was able to go free. We know from Hebrews 10:11 that the blood of animals could not really take away the sins of anyone, but each sacrifice prophesied of the great sacrifice of the Lord Jesus Christ on the cross. God looked on and forward to that, and so He was able to pass over the sins that had been covered in this *dispensation. See Romans 3:24 note.

34 And if ought of the flesh of the consecrations, or of the bread, remain unto
the morning, then thou shalt burn the
remainder with fire: it shall not be eat-
en, because it *is* holy.
35 And thus shalt thou do unto Aaron,
and to his sons, according to all *things*
which I have commanded thee: seven
days shalt thou consecrate them.
36 And thou shalt offer every day a
bullock *for* a sin-offering for atonement:
and thou shalt cleanse the altar, when
thou hast made an atonement for it, and
thou shalt anoint it, to sanctify it.

29:27 heave-offering. Before the priests ate of the offerings, they raised them in their arms and waved them back and forth. This was to say that the food was really God's. It was like a thanksgiving.

37 Seven days thou shalt make an atonement for the altar, and sanctify it; and it shall be an altar most holy: whatsoever toucheth the altar shall be holy.

Morning and evening sacrifices

¶38 Now this *is that* which thou shalt offer upon the altar; two lambs of the first year day by day continually.

39 The one lamb thou shalt offer in the morning; and the other lamb thou shalt offer at even:

40 And with the one lamb a tenth deal of flour mingled with the fourth part of an hin of beaten oil; and the fourth part of an hin of *wine *for* a *drink-offering.

41 And the other lamb thou shalt offer at even, and shalt do thereto according to the meat-offering of the morning, and according to the drink-offering thereof, for a sweet savour, an offering made by fire unto the LORD.

42 *This shall be* a continual burnt-offering throughout your generations *at* the door of the tabernacle of the congregation before the LORD: where I will meet you, to speak there unto thee.

43 And there I will meet with the children of Israel, and *the tabernacle* shall be sanctified by my glory.

44 And I will sanctify the tabernacle of the congregation, and the altar: I will sanctify also both Aaron and his sons, to minister to me in the priest's office.

¶45 And I will dwell among the children of Israel, and will be their *God.

46 And they shall know that I *am* the LORD their God, that brought them forth out of the land of *Egypt, that I may dwell among them: I *am* the LORD their God.

Altar of incense

30 And thou shalt make an *altar to burn incense upon: *of* *shittim wood shalt thou make it.

2 A cubit *shall be* the length thereof, and a cubit the breadth thereof; foursquare shall it be: and two cubits *shall be* the height thereof: the horns thereof *shall be* of the same.

3 And thou shalt overlay it with pure gold, the top thereof, and the sides thereof round about, and the horns thereof; and thou shalt make unto it a crown of gold round about.

4 And two golden rings shalt thou make to it under the crown of it, by the two corners thereof, upon the two sides of it shalt thou make *it;* and they shall be for places for the staves to bear it withal.

5 And thou shalt make the staves *of* shittim wood, and overlay them with gold.

6 And thou shalt put it before the vail that *is* by the ark of the testimony, before the *mercy seat that *is* over the testimony, where I will meet with thee.

7 And *Aaron shall burn thereon sweet incense every morning: when he dresseth the lamps, he shall burn incense upon it.

8 And when Aaron lighteth the lamps at even, he shall burn incense upon it, a perpetual incense before the LORD throughout your generations.

9 Ye shall offer no strange incense thereon, nor burnt-sacrifice, nor meat-offering; neither shall ye pour drink-offering thereon.

10 And Aaron shall make an atonement upon the horns of it once in a year with the blood of the sin-offering of atonements: once in the year shall he

30:1 Incense
This is always a *type of prayer and praise offered to God. It was a sweet-smelling powder that gave off a perfume while burning. The altar on which it was offered is a type of our Lord in whose name we are told to pray. See Hebrews 13:15 and Revelation 8:3-4.

29:40 a tenth deal. This means a tenth *part.*
29:40 hin. A hin is about four quarts.
29:41 meat-offering. Meal-offering. See Leviticus 2:1 note.

make atonement upon it throughout your generations: it *is* most holy unto the LORD.

Ransom money

¶11 And the LORD spake unto *Moses, saying,

12 When thou takest the sum of the children of Israel after their number, then shall they give every man a *ransom for his soul unto the LORD, when thou numberest them; that there be no plague among them, when *thou* numberest them.

13 This they shall give, every one that passeth among them that are numbered, half a shekel after the shekel of the sanctuary: (a shekel *is* twenty gerahs:) an half shekel *shall be* the offering of the LORD.

14 Every one that passeth among them that are numbered, from twenty years old and above, shall give an offering unto the LORD.

15 The rich shall not give more, and the poor shall not give less than half a shekel, when *they* give an offering unto the LORD, to make an atonement for your souls.

16 And thou shalt take the atonement *money of the children of Israel, and shalt appoint it for the service of the tabernacle of the congregation; that it may be a memorial unto the children of Israel before the LORD, to make an atonement for your souls.

The cleansing

¶17 And the LORD spake unto Moses, saying,

18 Thou shalt also make a laver *of* brass, and his foot *also of* brass, to wash *withal:* and thou shalt put it between the tabernacle of the congregation and the altar, and thou shalt put water therein.

19 For Aaron and his sons shall wash their hands and their feet thereat:

20 When they go into the tabernacle of the congregation, they shall wash with water, that they die not; or when they come near to the altar to minister, to burn offering made by fire unto the LORD:

21 So they shall wash their hands and their feet, that they die not: and it shall be a statute for ever to them, *even* to him and to his seed throughout their generations.

¶22 Moreover the LORD spake unto Moses, saying,

23 Take thou also unto thee principal spices, of pure myrrh five hundred *shekels,* and of sweet cinnamon half so much, *even* two hundred and fifty *shekels,* and of sweet calamus two hundred and fifty *shekels,*

24 And of cassia five hundred *shekels,* after the shekel of the sanctuary, and of oil olive an hin:

25 And thou shalt make it an oil of holy ointment, an ointment compound after the art of the apothecary: it shall be an holy anointing oil.

26 And thou shalt anoint the tabernacle of the congregation therewith, and the ark of the testimony,

27 And the table and all his vessels, and the candlestick and his vessels, and the altar of incense,

28 And the altar of burnt-offering with all his vessels, and the laver and his foot.

29 And thou shalt sanctify them, that they may be most holy: whatsoever toucheth them shall be holy.

30 And thou shalt anoint Aaron and his

30:13 a shekel. The Israelites had to pay a small amount of silver to remind them that they owed their lives to God because He had redeemed them out of Egypt. Silver always refers to *redemption. A silver shekel was a piece of silver weighing two-fifths of an ounce. Perhaps Peter was thinking of this in 1 Peter 1:18.

30:13 gerahs. One gerah weighs 8.8 grains. It is the smallest unit of weight.

30:18 laver. The laver was a large bowl in which the priests washed their hands and feet. See John 13:3-10 note for the spiritual meaning of this.

30:23 calamus. A sweet Arabian reed.

sons, and consecrate them, that *they*
may minister unto me in the priest's
office.
31 And thou shalt speak unto the children of Israel, saying, This shall be an
holy anointing oil unto me throughout
your generations.
32 Upon man's flesh shall it not be
poured, neither shall ye make *any other*
like it, after the composition of it: it *is*
holy, *and* it shall be holy unto you.
33 Whosoever compoundeth *any* like
it, or whosoever putteth *any* of it upon
a stranger, shall even be cut off from his
people.
¶ 34 And the LORD said unto Moses,
Take unto thee sweet spices, stacte,
and onycha, and galbanum; *these* sweet
spices with pure frankincense: of each
shall there be a like *weight:*
35 And thou shalt make it a perfume,
a confection after the art of the apothecary, tempered together, pure *and*
holy:
36 And thou shalt beat *some* of it very
small, and put of it before the testimony in the tabernacle of the congregation, where I will meet with thee: it
shall be unto you most holy.
37 And *as for* the perfume which thou
shalt make, ye shall not make to yourselves according to the composition
thereof: it shall be unto thee holy for
the LORD.
38 Whosoever shall make like unto
that, to smell thereto, shall even be cut
off from his people.

Workmen for the tabernacle

31 And the LORD spake unto Moses, saying,
2 See, I have called by name Bezaleel
the son of Uri, the son of *Hur, of the
tribe of *Judah:
3 And I have filled him with the spirit
of God, in wisdom, and in understanding, and in knowledge, and in all manner of workmanship,
4 To devise cunning works, to work in
gold, and in silver, and in brass,
5 And in cutting of stones, to set *them,*
and in carving of timber, to work in all
manner of workmanship.
6 And I, behold, I have given with him
Aholiab, the son of Ahisamach, of the
tribe of Dan: and in the hearts of all that
are wise hearted I have put wisdom,
that they may make all that I have commanded thee;
7 The *tabernacle of the congregation, and the *ark of the testimony, and
the *mercy seat that *is* thereupon, and
all the furniture of the tabernacle,
8 And the table and his furniture, and
the pure *candlestick with all his furniture, and the altar of *incense,
9 And the altar of burnt-offering with
all his furniture, and the laver and his
foot,
10 And the cloths of service, and the
*holy garments for Aaron the priest,
and the garments of his sons, to minister in the priest's office,
11 And the anointing *oil, and sweet
incense for the holy *place:* according to
all that I have commanded thee shall
they do.

The sign of the sabbath

¶ 12 And the LORD spake unto Moses,
saying,
13 Speak thou also unto the children
of *Israel, saying, Verily my sabbaths ye
shall keep: for it *is* a sign between me
and you throughout your generations;
that *ye* may know that I *am* the LORD
that doth sanctify you.
14 Ye shall keep the *sabbath therefore; for it *is* holy unto you: every one
that defileth it shall surely be put to
death: for whosoever doeth *any* work
therein, that soul shall be cut off from
among his people.
15 Six days may work be done; but in
the seventh *is* the sabbath of rest, holy
to the LORD: whosoever doeth *any*

30:35 confection. A compound made of various spices.
31:13 my sabbaths. See Genesis 2:3; Exodus 20:8-11.

work in the sabbath day, he shall surely be put to death.

16 Wherefore the children of Israel shall keep the sabbath, to observe the sabbath throughout their generations, *for* a perpetual *covenant.

17 It *is* a sign between me and the children of Israel for ever: for *in* six days the LORD made *heaven and earth, and on the seventh day he rested, and was refreshed.

¶ 18 And he gave unto Moses, when he had made an end of communing with him upon mount *Sinai, two tables of testimony, tables of stone, written with the finger of God.

The sin of the people

32 And when the people saw that Moses delayed to come down out of the mount, the people gathered themselves together unto Aaron, and said unto him, Up, make us gods, which shall go before us; for *as for* this Moses, the man that brought us up out of the land of Egypt, we wot not what is become of him.

2 And Aaron said unto them, Break off the golden earrings, which *are* in the ears of your wives, of your sons, and of your daughters, and bring *them* unto me.

3 And all the people brake off the golden earrings which *were* in their ears, and brought *them* unto Aaron.

4 And he received *them* at their hand, and fashioned it with a graving tool, after he had made it a molten calf: and they said, These *be* thy gods, O Israel, which brought thee up out of the land of Egypt.

5 And when Aaron saw *it,* he built an altar before it; and Aaron made proclamation, and said, To morrow *is* a feast to the LORD.

6 And they rose up early on the morrow, and offered burnt-offerings, and brought peace-offerings: and the people sat down to eat and to drink, and rose up to play.

¶ 7 And the LORD said unto Moses, Go, get thee down; for thy people, which thou broughtest out of the land of Egypt, have corrupted *themselves:*

8 They have turned aside quickly out of the way which I commanded them: they have made them a molten calf, and have worshipped it, and have sacrificed thereunto, and said, These *be* thy gods, O Israel, which have brought thee up out of the land of Egypt.

9 And the LORD said unto Moses, I have seen this people, and, behold, it *is* a stiffnecked people:

10 Now therefore let me alone, that my wrath may wax hot against them, and that I may consume them: and I will make of thee a great nation.

11 And Moses besought the LORD his God, and said, LORD, why doth thy wrath wax hot against thy people, which thou hast brought forth out of the land of Egypt with great power, and with a mighty hand?

12 Wherefore should the Egyptians speak, and say, For mischief did he bring them out, to slay them in the mountains, and to consume them from the face of the earth? Turn from thy fierce wrath, and repent of this evil against thy people.

31:18 tables of stone. See Exodus 19:25 note.

31:18 the finger of God. See *inspiration.

32:1 And when. Moses was up in the mountain for forty days (24:18). This is what happened in the camp while he was absent. It shows a terrible lack of faith and trust in God, that the Israelites would go back to worshipping idols so soon after hearing the Law. Although they had promised to do all that God had told them (24:7), it wasn't long before they were ready to break the second commandment (20:4).

32:4 calf. The cow was the animal which the Egyptians worshipped (see Exod. 8:26 note).

32:11 thy people. Compare this verse with verse 7. God laid upon Moses a responsibility for leading the people, and Moses pleaded that the people were also in the hands of God.

13Remember *Abraham, *Isaac, and
Israel, thy servants, to whom thou
swarest by thine own self, and saidst
unto them, I will multiply your seed as
the stars of heaven, and all this land that
I have spoken of will I give unto your
seed, and they shall inherit *it* for ever.
14And the LORD repented of the evil
which he thought to do unto his people.

The return of Moses

¶15And Moses turned, and went
down from the mount, and the two tables of the testimony *were* in his hand:
the tables *were* written on both their
sides; on the one side and on the other
were they written.
16And the tables *were* the work of
God, and the writing *was* the writing of
God, graven upon the tables.
17And when *Joshua heard the noise
of the people as they shouted, he said
unto Moses, *There is* a noise of war in
the camp.
18And he said, *It is* not the voice of
them that shout for mastery, neither *is*
it the voice of *them that* cry for being
overcome: *but* the noise of *them that*
sing do I hear.
¶19And it came to pass, as soon as he
came nigh unto the camp, that he saw
the calf, and the dancing: and Moses'
anger waxed hot, and he cast the tables
out of his hands, and brake them beneath the mount.
20And he took the calf which they had
made, and burnt *it* in the fire, and
ground *it* to powder, and strawed *it* upon
the water, and made the children of Israel drink *of it*.
21And Moses said unto Aaron, What
did this people unto thee, that thou hast
brought so great a sin upon them?
22And Aaron said, Let not the anger
of my lord wax hot: thou knowest the
people, that they *are set* on mischief.
23For they said unto me, Make us
gods, which shall go before us: for *as for*
this Moses, the man that brought us up
out of the land of Egypt, we wot not
what is become of him.
24And I said unto them, Whosoever
hath any gold, let them break *it* off. So
they gave *it* me: then I cast it into the
fire, and there came out this calf.
¶25And when Moses saw that the
people *were* naked; (for Aaron had made
them naked unto *their* shame among
their enemies:)

Judgment on the people

26Then Moses stood in the gate of the
camp, and said, Who *is* on the LORD'S
side? *let him come* unto me. And all the
sons of Levi gathered themselves together unto him.
27And he said unto them, Thus saith
the LORD God of Israel, Put every man
his sword by his side, *and* go in and out
from gate to gate throughout the camp,
and slay every man his brother, and
every man his companion, and every
man his neighbour.
28And the children of Levi did according to the word of Moses: and there fell
of the people that day about three thousand men.
29For Moses had said, *Consecrate
yourselves to day to the LORD, even
every man upon his son, and upon his
brother; that he may bestow upon you
a blessing this day.

Confession of Moses

¶30And it came to pass on the morrow, that Moses said unto the people,
Ye have sinned a great sin: and now I
will go up unto the LORD; peradventure
I shall make an atonement for your sin.
31And Moses returned unto the
LORD, and said, Oh, this people have
sinned a great sin, and have made them
gods of gold.
32Yet now, if thou wilt forgive their
sin—; and if not, blot me, I pray thee,
out of thy book which thou hast written.
33And the LORD said unto Moses,

32:16 the writing of God. See *inspiration.

Whosoever hath sinned against me, him will I blot out of my book.

34 Therefore now go, lead the people unto *the place* of which I have spoken unto thee: behold, mine *Angel shall go before thee: nevertheless in the day when I visit I will visit their sin upon them.

35 And the LORD plagued the people, because they made the calf, which Aaron made.

The people repent

33 And the LORD said unto Moses, Depart, *and* go up hence, thou and the people which thou hast brought up out of the land of Egypt, unto the land which I sware unto Abraham, to Isaac, and to *Jacob, saying, Unto thy seed will I give it:

2 And I will send an angel before thee; and I will drive out the Canaanite, the *Amorite, and the Hittite, and the Perizzite, the Hivite, and the Jebusite:

3 Unto a land *flowing with milk and honey: for I will not go up in the midst of thee; for thou *art* a stiffnecked people: lest I consume thee in the way.

¶4 And when the people heard these evil tidings, they mourned: and no man did put on him his ornaments.

5 For the LORD had said unto Moses, Say unto the children of Israel, Ye *are* a stiffnecked people: I will come up into the midst of thee in a moment, and consume thee: therefore now put off thy ornaments from thee, that I may know what to do unto thee.

6 And the children of Israel stripped themselves of their ornaments by the mount *Horeb.

7 And Moses took the tabernacle, and pitched it without the camp, afar off from the camp, and called it the Tabernacle of the congregation. And it came to pass, *that* every one which sought the LORD went out unto the tabernacle of the congregation, which *was* without the camp.

8 And it came to pass, when Moses went out unto the tabernacle, *that* all the people rose up, and stood every man *at* his tent door, and looked after Moses, until he was gone into the tabernacle.

9 And it came to pass, as Moses entered into the tabernacle, the cloudy *pillar descended, and stood *at* the door of the tabernacle, and *the LORD* talked with Moses.

10 And all the people saw the cloudy pillar stand *at* the tabernacle door: and all the people rose up and worshipped, every man *in* his tent door.

11 And the LORD spake unto Moses face to face, as a man speaketh unto his friend. And he turned again into the camp: but his servant Joshua, the son of Nun, a young man, departed not out of the tabernacle.

Moses' prayer

¶12 And Moses said unto the LORD, See, thou sayest unto me, Bring up this people: and thou hast not let me know whom thou wilt send with me. Yet thou hast said, I know thee by name, and thou hast also found grace in my sight.

13 Now therefore, I pray thee, if I have found grace in thy sight, shew me now thy way, that I may know thee, that I may find grace in thy sight: and consider that this nation *is* thy people.

14 And he said, My presence shall go *with thee,* and I will give thee rest.

15 And he said unto him, If thy presence go not *with me,* carry us not up hence.

16 For wherein shall it be known here that I and thy people have found grace

---

33:4 these evil tidings. That is, the news that God Himself would not go with them on their journey (vs. 3).

33:7 tabernacle. This does not mean the tabernacle of God, because that was not yet built. This was probably an altar like that in Exodus 24:4 (see its note).

33:9 cloudy pillar. See Exodus 13:21 note.

in thy sight? *is it* not in that thou goest
with us? so shall we be separated, I and
thy people, from all the people that *are*
upon the face of the earth.
17 And the LORD said unto Moses, I
will do this thing also that thou hast
spoken: for thou hast found grace in my
sight, and I know thee by name.

Moses' vision

18 And he said, I beseech thee, shew
me thy glory.
19 And he said, I will make all my
goodness pass before thee, and I will
proclaim the name of the LORD before
thee; and will be gracious to whom I will
be gracious, and will shew mercy on
whom I will shew mercy.
20 And he said, Thou canst not see my
face: for there shall no man see me, and
live.
21 And the LORD said, Behold, *there is*
a place by me, and thou shalt stand upon
a *rock:
22 And it shall come to pass, while my
glory passeth by, that I will put thee in
a clift of the rock, and will cover thee
with my hand while I pass by:
23 And I will take away mine hand, and
thou shalt see my back parts: but my
face shall not be seen.

Second tables of Law

34 And the LORD said unto Moses,
Hew thee two tables of stone
like unto the first: and I will write upon
these tables the words that were in the
first tables, which thou brakest.
2 And be ready in the morning, and
come up in the morning unto mount
Sinai, and present thyself there to me
in the top of the mount.
3 And no man shall come up with thee,
neither let any man be seen throughout
all the mount; neither let the flocks nor
herds feed before that mount.
4 And he hewed two tables of stone
like unto the first; and Moses rose up
early in the morning, and went up unto
mount Sinai, as the LORD had commanded him, and took in his hand the
two tables of stone.
¶5 And the LORD descended in the
cloud, and stood with him there, and
proclaimed the name of the LORD.
6 And the LORD passed by before him,
and proclaimed, The LORD, The LORD
God, merciful and gracious, longsuffering, and abundant in goodness and
truth,
7 Keeping mercy for thousands, forgiving iniquity and transgression and
sin, and that will by no means clear *the*
guilty; visiting the iniquity of the fathers
upon the children, and upon the
children's children, unto the third and
to the fourth *generation.*
8 And Moses made haste, and bowed
his head toward the earth, and worshipped.
9 And he said, If now I have found
grace in thy sight, O Lord, let my Lord,
I pray thee, go among us; for it *is* a
stiffnecked people; and pardon our iniquity and our sin, and take us for thine
inheritance.

The renewed promise

¶10 And he said, Behold, I make a covenant: before all thy people I will do
marvels, such as have not been done in
all the earth, nor in any nation: and all
the people among which thou *art* shall
see the work of the LORD: for it *is* a
terrible thing that I will do with thee.
11 Observe thou that which I command thee this day: behold, I drive out
before thee the Amorite, and the Canaanite, and the Hittite, and the Perizzite, and the Hivite, and the Jebusite.
12 Take heed to thyself, lest thou
make a covenant with the inhabitants of
the land whither thou goest, lest it be
for a snare in the midst of thee:

33:20 see my face. See Exodus 24:10 note.
34:1 I will write. See *inspiration.
34:10 covenant. An agreement.

13 But ye shall destroy their altars,
break their images, and cut down their
groves:
14 For thou shalt worship no other
god: for the LORD, whose name *is* Jealous, *is* a *jealous God:
15 Lest thou make a covenant with the
inhabitants of the land, and they go a
whoring after their gods, and do sacrifice unto their gods, and *one* call thee,
and thou eat of his sacrifice;
16 And thou take of their daughters
unto thy sons, and their daughters go a
whoring after their gods, and make thy
sons go a whoring after their gods.
17 Thou shalt make thee no molten
gods.

Repeated instructions

¶ 18 The feast of unleavened bread
shalt thou keep. Seven days thou shalt
eat unleavened bread, as I commanded
thee, in the time of the *month Abib:
for in the month Abib thou camest out
from Egypt.
19 All that openeth the matrix *is* mine;
and every firstling among thy cattle,
whether ox or sheep, *that is male.*
20 But the firstling of an ass thou shalt
redeem with a lamb: and if thou redeem
him not, then shalt thou break his neck.
All the firstborn of thy sons thou shalt
redeem. And none shall appear before
me empty.
¶ 21 Six days thou shalt work, but on
the seventh day thou shalt rest: in earing
time and in harvest thou shalt rest.
¶ 22 And thou shalt observe the feast
of weeks, of the firstfruits of wheat harvest, and the feast of ingathering at the
year's end.
¶ 23 Thrice in the year shall all your
men children appear before the Lord
GOD, the God of Israel.
24 For I will cast out the nations before
thee, and enlarge thy borders: neither
shall any man desire thy land, when
thou shalt go up to appear before the
LORD thy God thrice in the year.
25 Thou shalt not offer the blood of my
sacrifice with *leaven; neither shall the
sacrifice of the feast of the *passover be
left unto the morning.
26 The first of the firstfruits of thy land
thou shalt bring unto the house of the
LORD thy God. Thou shalt not seethe a
kid in his mother's milk.
27 And the LORD said unto Moses,
Write thou these words: for after the
tenor of these words I have made a covenant with thee and with Israel.
28 And he was there with the LORD
forty days and forty nights; he did neither eat bread, nor drink water. And he
wrote upon the tables the words of the
covenant, the *ten commandments.
¶ 29 And it came to pass, when Moses
came down from mount Sinai with the
two tables of testimony in Moses' hand,
when he came down from the mount,
that Moses wist not that the skin of his
face shone while he talked with him.
30 And when Aaron and all the children of Israel saw Moses, behold, the
skin of his face shone; and they were
afraid to come nigh him.
31 And Moses called unto them; and
Aaron and all the rulers of the congregation returned unto him: and Moses
talked with them.
32 And afterward all the children of
Israel came nigh: and he gave them in
commandment all that the LORD had
spoken with him in mount Sinai.
33 And *till* Moses had done speaking
with them, he put a vail on his face.
34 But when Moses went in before the
LORD to speak with him, he took the
vail off, until he came out. And he came
out, and spake unto the children of

34:13 groves. See Deuteronomy 16:21 and Judges 3:7 notes.
34:21 in earing time. Plowing time.
34:27 covenant. See *covenant.
34:29 wist. Knew.
34:33 vail. See 2 Corinthians 3:13-16 note.

Israel *that* which he was commanded.
35 And the children of Israel saw the
face of Moses, that the skin of Moses'
face shone: and Moses put the vail upon
his face again, until he went in to speak
with him.

The building of the tabernacle

35 And Moses gathered all the
congregation of the children of
Israel together, and said unto them,
These *are* the words which the LORD
hath commanded, that *ye* should do
them.
2 Six days shall work be done, but on
the seventh day there shall be to you an
*holy day, a sabbath of rest to the LORD:
whosoever doeth work therein shall be
put to death.
3 Ye shall kindle no fire throughout
your habitations upon the sabbath day.
¶ 4 And Moses spake unto all the congregation of the children of Israel, saying, This *is* the thing which the LORD
commanded, saying,
5 Take ye from among you an offering
unto the LORD: whosoever *is* of a willing heart, let him bring it, an offering
of the LORD; gold, and *silver, and
brass,
6 And *blue, and purple, and scarlet,
and fine *linen, and goats' *hair,*
7 And rams' skins dyed red, and badgers' skins, and *shittim wood,
8 And oil for the light, and spices for
anointing oil, and for the sweet incense,
9 And onyx stones, and stones to be
set for the *ephod, and for the breastplate.
10 And every wise hearted among you
shall come, and make all that the LORD
hath commanded;
11 The tabernacle, his tent, and his
covering, his *taches, and his boards,
his bars, his pillars, and his sockets,
12 The ark, and the staves thereof,
with the *mercy seat, and the vail of the
covering,
13 The table, and his staves, and all his
vessels, and the *shewbread,
14 The candlestick also for the light,
and his furniture, and his lamps, with
the oil for the light,
15 And the incense altar, and his staves,
and the anointing oil, and the sweet incense, and the hanging for the door at
the entering in of the tabernacle,
16 The altar of burnt-offering, with his
brasen grate, his staves, and all his vessels, the *laver and his foot,
17 The hangings of the court, his pillars, and their sockets, and the hanging
for the door of the court,
18 The pins of the tabernacle, and the
pins of the court, and their cords,
19 The cloths of service, to do service
in the holy *place,* the *holy *garments
for Aaron the priest, and the garments
of his sons, to minister in the priest's
office.
¶ 20 And all the congregation of the
children of Israel departed from the
presence of Moses.
21 And they came, every one whose
heart stirred him up, and every one
whom his spirit made willing, *and* they
brought the LORD'S offering to the work
of the tabernacle of the congregation,
and for all his service, and for the holy
garments.
22 And they came, both men and wom-
en, as many as were willing hearted,
and brought bracelets, and earrings, and
rings, and tablets, all jewels of gold: and
every man that offered *offered* an offering of gold unto the LORD.
23 And every man, with whom was
found blue, and purple, and scarlet, and
fine linen, and goats' *hair,* and red skins
of rams, and badgers' skins, brought
them.
24 Every one that did offer an offering
of silver and brass brought the LORD'S
offering: and every man, with whom
was found shittim wood for any work of
the service, brought *it.*

35:2 six days. See Exodus 20:9-10.
35:22 tablets. Ornaments for a necklace.

25 And all the women that were wise hearted did spin with their hands, and brought that which they had spun, *both* of blue, and of purple, *and* of scarlet, and of fine linen.

26 And all the women whose heart stirred them up in wisdom spun goats' *hair.*

27 And the rulers brought onyx stones, and stones to be set, for the ephod, and for the breastplate;

28 And spice, and oil for the light, and for the anointing oil, and for the sweet incense.

29 The children of Israel brought a willing offering unto the LORD, every man and woman, whose heart made them willing to bring for all manner of work, which the LORD had commanded to be made by the hand of Moses.

¶ 30 And Moses said unto the children of Israel, See, the LORD hath called by name Bezaleel the son of Uri, the son of *Hur, of the tribe of Judah;

31 And he hath filled him with the spirit of *God, in wisdom, in understanding, and in knowledge, and in all manner of workmanship;

32 And to devise curious works, to work in gold, and in silver, and in brass,

33 And in the cutting of stones, to set *them,* and in carving of wood, to make any manner of *cunning work.

34 And he hath put in his heart that he may teach, *both* he, and Aholiab, the son of Ahisamach, of the tribe of Dan.

35 Them hath he filled with wisdom of heart, to work all manner of work, of the engraver, and of the cunning workman, and of the embroiderer, in blue, and in purple, in scarlet, and in fine linen, and of the weaver, *even* of them that do any work, and of those that devise cunning work.

36 Then wrought Bezaleel and Aholiab, and every wise hearted man, in whom the LORD put wisdom and understanding to know how to work all manner of work for the service of the *sanctuary, according to all that the LORD had commanded.

2 And *Moses called Bezaleel and Aholiab, and every wise hearted man, in whose heart the LORD had put wisdom, *even* every one whose heart stirred him up to come unto the work to do it:

3 And they received of Moses all the offering, which the children of Israel had brought for the work of the service of the sanctuary, to make it *withal.* And they brought yet unto him free *offerings every morning.

¶ 4 And all the wise men, that wrought all the work of the sanctuary, came every man from his work which they made;

5 And they spake unto Moses, saying, The people bring much more than enough for the service of the work, which the LORD commanded to make.

6 And Moses gave commandment, and they caused it to be proclaimed throughout the camp, saying, Let neither man nor woman make any more work for the offering of the sanctuary.

35:22 BRACELETS

Bracelets for the arms and anklets for the legs were commonly worn by Eastern married women of all ranks and were regarded as an excellent way of investing money, since they could not be taken for the debts of the husband. They were usually cablelike rings, with an opening through which the wrist could be slipped; but the higher classes wore bracelets formed like broad bands, richly ornamented, jointed and closed by a pin passing through sockets. The anklets were similar in form but frequently adorned with little bells. Both are still common in the East, with scarcely any variation in the patterns. They are made of gold, silver, brass, and colored glass, the last being extensively manufactured at Hebron. Those worn by the Hebrews were never jeweled, and some men seem to have used bracelets as well as women (Gen. 38:18; 2 Sam. 1:10).

36:3 free offerings. Freewill or voluntary offerings. See Leviticus 1:3 note.

So the people were restrained from
bringing.

7For the stuff they had was sufficient
for all the work to make it, and too
much.

¶8And every wise hearted man
among them that wrought the work of
the tabernacle made ten curtains *of* fine
twined linen, and blue, and purple, and
scarlet: *with* cherubims of cunning
work made he them.

9The length of one curtain *was* twenty and eight *cubits, and the breadth of
one curtain four cubits: the curtains
were all of one size.

10And he coupled the five curtains
one unto another: and *the other* five curtains he coupled one unto another.

11And he made loops of blue on the
edge of one curtain from the selvedge
in the coupling: likewise he made in the
uttermost side of *another* curtain, in the
coupling of the second.

12Fifty loops made he in one curtain,
and fifty loops made he in the edge of
the curtain which *was* in the coupling
of the second: the loops held one *curtain* to another.

13And he made fifty taches of gold,
and coupled the curtains one unto another with the taches: so it became one
tabernacle.

¶14And he made curtains *of* goats'
hair for the tent over the tabernacle:
eleven curtains he made them.

15The length of one curtain *was* thirty
cubits, and four cubits *was* the breadth
of one curtain: the eleven curtains *were*
of one size.

16And he coupled five curtains by
themselves, and six curtains by themselves.

17And he made fifty loops upon the
uttermost edge of the curtain in the
coupling, and fifty loops made he upon
the edge of the curtain which coupleth
the second.

18And he made fifty taches *of* brass to
couple the tent together, that it might
be one.

19And he made a covering for the tent
of rams' skins dyed red, and a covering
of badgers' skins above *that.*

¶20And he made boards for the tabernacle *of* shittim wood, standing up.

21The length of a board *was* ten cubits, and the breadth of a board one cubit and a half.

22One board had two *tenons, equally distant one from another: thus did
he make for all the boards of the tabernacle.

23And he made boards for the tabernacle; twenty boards for the south side
southward:

24And forty sockets of silver he made
under the twenty boards; two sockets
under one board for his two tenons, and
two sockets under another board for his
two tenons.

25And for the other side of the tabernacle, *which is* toward the north corner,
he made twenty boards,

26And their forty sockets of silver;
two sockets under one board, and two
sockets under another board.

27And for the sides of the tabernacle
westward he made six boards.

28And two boards made he for the corners of the tabernacle in the two sides.

29And they were coupled beneath,
and coupled together at the head
thereof, to one ring: thus he did to both
of them in both the corners.

30And there were eight boards; and
their sockets *were* sixteen sockets of
silver, under every board two sockets.

¶31And he made bars of shittim wood;
five for the boards of the one side of the
tabernacle,

32And five bars for the boards of the
other side of the tabernacle, and five
bars for the boards of the tabernacle for
the sides westward.

33And he made the middle bar to
shoot through the boards from the one
end to the other.

34And he overlaid the boards with
gold, and made their rings *of* gold *to be*
places for the bars, and overlaid the
bars with gold.

¶35And he made a vail *of* blue, and

purple, and scarlet, and fine twined
linen: *with* cherubims made he it of
cunning work.
36 And he made thereunto four pillars
of shittim *wood,* and overlaid them with
gold: their hooks *were of* gold; and he
cast for them four sockets of silver.
¶ 37 And he made an hanging for the
tabernacle door *of* blue, and purple, and
scarlet, and fine twined linen, of needlework;
38 And the five pillars of it with their
hooks: and he overlaid their *chapiters
and their *fillets with gold: but their
five sockets *were of* brass.

37 And Bezaleel made the *ark *of*
shittim wood: two cubits and a
half *was* the length of it, and a cubit and
a half the breadth of it, and a cubit and
a half the height of it:
2 And he overlaid it with pure gold
within and without, and made a crown
of gold to it round about.
3 And he cast for it four rings of gold,
to be set by the four corners of it; even
two rings upon the one side of it, and
two rings upon the other side of it.
4 And he made staves *of* shittim wood,
and overlaid them with gold.
5 And he put the staves into the rings
by the sides of the ark, to bear the ark.
¶ 6 And he made the *mercy seat *of*
pure gold: two cubits and a half *was* the
length thereof, and one cubit and a half
the breadth thereof.
7 And he made two cherubims *of* gold,
beaten out of one piece made he them,
on the two ends of the mercy seat;
8 One cherub on the end on this side,
and another cherub on the *other* end on
that side: out of the mercy seat made
he the cherubims on the two ends
thereof.
9 And the cherubims spread out *their*
wings on high, *and* covered with their
wings over the mercy seat, with
their faces one to another; *even* to the
mercy seatward were the faces of the
cherubims.
¶ 10 And he made the table *of* shittim
wood: two cubits *was* the length
thereof, and a cubit the breadth thereof,
and a cubit and a half the height thereof:
11 And he overlaid it with pure gold,
and made thereunto a crown of gold
round about.
12 Also he made thereunto a border of
an handbreadth round about; and made
a crown of gold for the border thereof
round about.
13 And he cast for it four rings of gold,
and put the rings upon the four corners
that *were* in the four feet thereof.
14 Over against the border were the
rings, the places for the staves to bear
the table.
15 And he made the staves *of* shittim
wood, and overlaid them with gold, to
bear the table.
16 And he made the vessels which
were upon the table, his dishes, and his
spoons, and his bowls, and his covers
to cover withal, *of* pure gold.
¶ 17 And he made the *candlestick *of*
pure gold: *of* beaten work made he the
candlestick; his shaft, and his branch,
his bowls, his *knops, and his flowers,
were of the same:
18 And six branches going out of the
sides thereof; three branches of the
candlestick out of the one side thereof,
and three branches of the candlestick
out of the other side thereof:
19 Three bowls made after the fashion
of almonds in one branch, a knop and
a flower; and three bowls made like almonds in another branch, a knop and a
flower: so throughout the six branches
going out of the candlestick.
20 And in the candlestick *were* four
bowls made like almonds, his knops,
and his flowers:
21 And a knop under two branches of
the same, and a knop under two
branches of the same, and a knop under two branches of the same, according to the six branches going out of it.
22 Their knops and their branches

36:38 chapiters. The capitals or tops of pillars or columns.

were of the same: all of it *was* one beat-
en work *of* pure gold.
23 And he made his seven lamps, and
his *snuffers, and his snuffdishes, *of*
pure gold.
24 *Of* a talent of pure gold made he it,
and all the vessels thereof.
¶25 And he made the *incense *altar
of shittim wood: the length of *it was* a
cubit, and the breadth of it a cubit; it *was*
foursquare; and two cubits *was* the
height of it; the *horns thereof were of
the same.
26 And he overlaid it with pure gold,
both the top of it, and the sides thereof
round about, and the horns of it: also he
made unto it a crown of gold round
about.
27 And he made two rings of gold for
it under the crown thereof, by the two
corners of it, upon the two sides
thereof, to be places for the staves to
bear it withal.
28 And he made the staves *of* shittim
wood, and overlaid them with gold.
¶29 And he made the holy anointing
*oil, and the pure incense of sweet
spices, according to the work of the
apothecary.

38 And he made the altar of burnt-
offering *of* *shittim wood: five
cubits *was* the length thereof, and five
cubits the breadth thereof; *it was* foursquare; and three cubits the height
thereof.
2 And he made the horns thereof on
the four corners of it; the horns thereof
were of the same: and he overlaid it
with brass.
3 And he made all the vessels of the
altar, the pots, and the shovels, and
the basons, *and* the fleshhooks, and the
firepans: all the vessels thereof made
he *of* brass.
4 And he made for the altar a brasen
grate of network under the compass
thereof beneath unto the midst of it.
5 And he cast four rings for the four
ends of the grate of brass, *to be* places
for the staves.
6 And he made the staves *of* shittim
wood, and overlaid them with brass.
7 And he put the staves into the rings
on the sides of the altar, to bear it
withal; he made the altar hollow with
boards.
¶8 And he made the *laver *of* brass,
and the foot of it *of* brass, of the looking-
glasses of *the women* assembling, which
assembled *at* the door of the *tabernacle of the congregation.
¶9 And he made the court: on the
south side southward the hangings of
the court *were of* fine twined linen, an
hundred cubits:
10 Their pillars *were* twenty, and their
brasen sockets twenty; the hooks of the
pillars and their fillets *were of* silver.
11 And for the north side *the hangings*
were an hundred cubits, their pillars
were twenty, and their sockets of brass
twenty; the hooks of the pillars and
their fillets *of* silver.
12 And for the west side *were* hangings
of fifty cubits, their pillars ten, and their
sockets ten; the hooks of the pillars and
their fillets *of* silver.
13 And for the east side eastward fifty
cubits.
14 The hangings of the one side *of the*
gate were fifteen cubits; their pillars
three, and their sockets three.
15 And for the other side of the court
gate, on this hand and that hand, *were*
hangings of fifteen cubits; their pillars
three, and their sockets three.
16 All the hangings of the court round
about *were* of fine twined linen.
17 And the sockets for the pillars *were*
of brass; the hooks of the pillars and
their fillets *of* silver; and the overlaying
of their chapiters *of* silver; and all the
pillars of the court *were* filleted with
silver.
18 And the hanging for the gate of the
court *was* needlework, *of* blue, and purple, and scarlet, and fine twined linen:
and twenty cubits *was* the length, and
the height in the breadth *was* five cubits, answerable to the hangings of the
court.
19 And their pillars *were* four, and their

sockets *of* brass four; their hooks *of*
silver, and the overlaying of their
chapiters and their fillets *of* silver.
20 And all the pins of the tabernacle,
and of the court round about, *were of*
brass.

Cost of the tabernacle

¶21 This is the sum of the tabernacle,
even of the tabernacle of testimony, as
it was counted, according to the commandment of Moses, *for* the service of
the Levites, by the hand of Ithamar, son
to *Aaron the priest.
22 And Bezaleel the son of Uri, the son
of *Hur, of the tribe of *Judah, made all
that the LORD commanded Moses.
23 And with him *was* Aholiab, son of
Ahisamach, of the tribe of Dan, an engraver, and a cunning workman, and an
embroiderer in blue, and in purple, and
in scarlet, and fine linen.
24 All the gold that was occupied for
the work in all the work of the holy
place, even the gold of the offering, was
twenty and nine talents, and seven hundred and thirty shekels, after the shekel
of the sanctuary.
25 And the silver of them that were
numbered of the congregation *was* an
hundred talents, and a thousand seven
hundred and threescore and fifteen
shekels, after the shekel of the sanctuary:
26 A bekah for every man, *that is,*
half a shekel, after the shekel of the
sanctuary, for every one that went to be
numbered, from twenty years old and
upward, for six hundred thousand
and three thousand and five hundred
and fifty *men.*
27 And of the hundred talents of silver
were cast the sockets of the sanctuary,
and the sockets of the vail; an hundred
sockets of the hundred talents, a talent
for a socket.
28 And of the thousand seven hundred
seventy and five *shekels* he made hooks
for the pillars, and overlaid their
chapiters, and filleted them.
29 And the brass of the offering *was*
seventy talents, and two thousand and
four hundred shekels.
30 And therewith he made the sockets
to the door of the tabernacle of the congregation, and the brasen altar, and the
brasen grate for it, and all the vessels
of the altar,
31 And the sockets of the court round
about, and the sockets of the court gate,
and all the pins of the tabernacle, and
all the pins of the court round about.

Aaron's holy garments (31:10)

39 And of the blue, and purple, and
scarlet, they made cloths of service, to do service in the holy *place,* and
made the *holy garments for Aaron; as
the LORD commanded Moses.
2 And he made the ephod *of* gold, blue,
and purple, and scarlet, and fine twined
linen.
3 And they did beat the gold into thin
plates, and cut *it into* wires, to work *it*
in the blue, and in the purple, and in the
scarlet, and in the fine linen, *with* *cunning work.
4 They made shoulderpieces for it, to
couple *it* together: by the two edges
was it coupled together.
5 And the *curious girdle of his ephod,
that *was* upon it, *was* of the same, according to the work thereof; *of* gold,
blue, and purple, and scarlet, and fine
twined linen; as the LORD commanded
Moses.
¶6 And they wrought onyx stones inclosed in *ouches of gold, graven, as
signets are graven, with the names of
the children of *Israel.
7 And he put them on the shoulders
of the ephod, *that they should be* stones
for a memorial to the children of Israel;
as the LORD commanded Moses.
¶8 And he made the breastplate *of* cunning work, like the work of the ephod;

38:26 bekah. A bekah was a weight equal to about one-fourth of an ounce.
39:1 blue. See Exodus 26:1 note.

of gold, blue, and purple, and scarlet, and fine twined linen.

9 It was foursquare; they made the breastplate double: a *span *was* the length thereof, and a span the breadth thereof, *being* doubled.

10 And they set in it four rows of stones: *the first* row *was* a sardius, a topaz, and a carbuncle: this *was* the first row.

11 And the second row, an emerald, a sapphire, and a diamond.

12 And the third row, a ligure, an agate, and an amethyst.

13 And the fourth row, a beryl, an onyx, and a jasper: *they were* inclosed in ouches of gold in their inclosings.

14 And the stones *were* according to the names of the children of Israel, twelve, according to their names, *like* the engravings of a signet, every one with his name, according to the twelve tribes.

15 And they made upon the breastplate chains at the ends, *of* wreathen work *of* pure gold.

16 And they made two ouches *of* gold, and two gold rings; and put the two rings in the two ends of the breastplate.

17 And they put the two wreathen chains of gold in the two rings on the ends of the breastplate.

18 And the two ends of the two wreathen chains they fastened in the two ouches, and put them on the shoulderpieces of the ephod, before it.

19 And they made two rings of gold, and put *them* on the two ends of the breastplate, upon the border of it, which *was* on the side of the ephod inward.

20 And they made two *other* golden rings, and put them on the two sides of the ephod underneath, toward the forepart of it, over against the *other* coupling thereof, above the curious girdle of the ephod.

21 And they did bind the breastplate by his rings unto the rings of the ephod with a lace of blue, that it might be above the curious girdle of the ephod, and that the breastplate might not be loosed from the ephod; as the LORD commanded Moses.

¶22 And he made the robe of the ephod *of* woven work, all *of* blue.

23 And *there was* an hole in the midst of the robe, as the hole of an habergeon, *with* a band round about the hole, that it should not rend.

24 And they made upon the hems of the robe pomegranates *of* blue, and purple, and scarlet, *and* twined *linen.*

25 And they made bells *of* pure gold, and put the bells between the pomegranates upon the hem of the robe, round about between the pomegranates;

26 A bell and a pomegranate, a bell and a pomegranate, round about the hem of the robe to minister *in;* as the LORD commanded Moses.

¶27 And they made coats *of* fine linen *of* woven work for Aaron, and for his sons,

28 And a mitre *of* fine linen, and goodly bonnets *of* fine linen, and linen breeches *of* fine twined linen,

29 And a girdle *of* fine twined linen, and blue, and purple, and scarlet, *of* needlework; as the LORD commanded Moses.

¶30 And they made the plate of the holy crown *of* pure gold, and wrote upon it a writing, *like to* the engravings of a signet, HOLINESS TO THE LORD.

31 And they tied unto it a lace of blue, to fasten *it* on high upon the mitre; as the LORD commanded Moses.

The work completed

¶32 Thus was all the work of the tabernacle of the tent of the congregation finished: and the children of Israel did according to all that the LORD commanded Moses, so did they.

39:23 habergeon. This was a coat of mail, like armor, for covering the body from the neck to the waist. It had a small, round neck hole. The "robe of the ephod" was the same shape as a habergeon. See Exodus 28:2 note.

¶33 And they brought the tabernacle
unto Moses, the tent, and all his furniture, his *taches, his boards, his bars,
and his pillars, and his sockets,
34 And the covering of rams' skins
dyed red, and the covering of badgers'
skins, and the vail of the covering,
35 The ark of the testimony, and the
staves thereof, and the *mercy seat,
36 The table, *and* all the vessels
thereof, and the *shewbread,
37 The pure candlestick, *with* the
lamps thereof, *even with* the lamps to be
set in order, and all the vessels thereof,
and the oil for light,
38 And the golden altar, and the
anointing oil, and the sweet incense,
and the hanging for the tabernacle door,
39 The brasen altar, and his grate of
brass, his staves, and all his vessels, the
laver and his foot,
40 The hangings of the court, his pillars, and his sockets, and the hanging
for the court gate, his cords, and his
pins, and all the vessels of the service
of the tabernacle, for the tent of the
congregation,
41 The cloths of service to do service
in the *holy place,* and the holy garments
for Aaron the priest, and his sons' garments, to minister in the priest's office.
42 According to all that the LORD commanded Moses, so the children of Israel
made all the work.
43 And Moses did look upon all the
work, and, behold, they have done it as
the LORD had commanded, even so had
they done it: and Moses blessed them.

The Tabernacle set up

40 And the LORD spake unto Moses, saying,
2 On the first day of the first month
shalt thou set up the tabernacle of the
tent of the congregation.
3 And thou shalt put therein the ark of
the testimony, and cover the ark with
the vail.
4 And thou shalt bring in the table, and
set in order the things that are to be set
in order upon it; and thou shalt bring in
the candlestick, and light the lamps
thereof.
5 And thou shalt set the altar of gold
for the incense before the ark of the
testimony, and put the hanging of the
door to the tabernacle.
6 And thou shalt set the altar of the
burnt-offering before the door of the
tabernacle of the tent of the congregation.
7 And thou shalt set the laver between
the tent of the congregation and the
altar, and shalt put water therein.
8 And thou shalt set up the court
round about, and hang up the hanging
at the court gate.
9 And thou shalt take the anointing oil,
and anoint the tabernacle, and all that
is therein, and shalt hallow it, and all the
vessels thereof: and it shall be holy.
10 And thou shalt anoint the altar of
the burnt-offering, and all his vessels,
and sanctify the altar: and it shall be an
altar most holy.
11 And thou shalt anoint the laver and
his foot, and sanctify it.
12 And thou shalt bring Aaron and his
sons unto the door of the tabernacle of
the congregation, and wash them with
water.
13 And thou shalt put upon Aaron the
holy garments, and anoint him, and
sanctify him; that he may minister unto
me in the priest's office.
14 And thou shalt bring his sons, and
clothe them with coats:
15 And thou shalt anoint them, as thou
didst anoint their father, that they may
minister unto me in the priest's office:
for their anointing shall surely be an
everlasting priesthood throughout their
generations.
16 Thus did Moses: according to all
that the LORD commanded him, so
did he.
¶17 And it came to pass in the first
month in the second year, on the first
day of the month, *that* the tabernacle
was reared up.
18 And Moses reared up the tabernacle, and fastened his sockets, and set up

the boards thereof, and put in the bars
thereof, and reared up his pillars.
19 And he spread abroad the tent over
the tabernacle, and put the covering of
the tent above upon it; as the LORD
commanded Moses.
¶ 20 And he took and put the testimony into the ark, and set the staves on
the ark, and put the mercy seat above
upon the ark:
21 And he brought the ark into the tabernacle, and set up the vail of the covering, and covered the ark of the
testimony; as the LORD commanded
Moses.
¶ 22 And he put the table in the tent of
the congregation, upon the side of the
tabernacle northward, without the vail.
23 And he set the bread in order upon
it before the LORD; as the LORD had
commanded Moses.
¶ 24 And he put the candlestick in the
tent of the congregation, over against
the table, on the side of the tabernacle
southward.
25 And he lighted the lamps before the
LORD; as the LORD commanded Moses.
¶ 26 And he put the golden altar in the
tent of the congregation before the vail:
27 And he burnt sweet incense thereon;
as the LORD commanded Moses.
¶ 28 And he set up the hanging *at* the
door of the tabernacle.
29 And he put the altar of burnt-
offering *by* the door of the tabernacle of
the tent of the congregation, and offered
upon it the burnt-offering and the meat-
offering; as the LORD commanded
Moses.
¶ 30 And he set the laver between the
tent of the congregation and the altar,
and put water there, to wash *withal.*
31 And Moses and Aaron and his sons
washed their hands and their feet
thereat:
32 When they went into the tent of the
congregation, and when they came near
unto the altar, they washed; as the
LORD commanded Moses.
33 And he reared up the court round
about the tabernacle and the altar, and
set up the hanging of the court gate. So
Moses finished the work.
¶ 34 Then a cloud covered the tent of
the congregation, and the glory of the
LORD filled the tabernacle.
35 And Moses was not able to enter
into the tent of the congregation, because the cloud abode thereon, and
the glory of the LORD filled the tabernacle.
36 And when the cloud was taken up
from over the tabernacle, the children
of Israel went onward in all their journeys:
37 But if the cloud were not taken up,
then they journeyed not till the day that
it was taken up.
38 For the cloud of the LORD *was* upon
the tabernacle by day, and fire was on
it by night, in the sight of all the house
of Israel, throughout all their journeys.

40:34 cloud. See Leviticus 16:2; 1 Kings 8:10-11.

The Third Book of Moses, called

LEVITICUS

THEME

The third book of Moses, called Leviticus after the Levites or priests, gave the children of Israel instructions for the worship of God and for a daily life suitable to God's people. Exodus told how they were redeemed from the power of Pharaoh and the bondage of Egypt and called to be a special people for God, with the tabernacle set up in their midst as a dwelling place for God (Exodus 25:8). Leviticus took them a step farther and showed them how to carry on the worship of God correctly, how to approach Him through sacrifice, and how to live holy lives pleasing to Him.

THINGS TO NOTE

The key word in Leviticus is "holiness" (see Leviticus 19:2). The New Testament has nearly ninety references to Leviticus. The Lord Jesus Christ was of course familiar with it, and Matthew 8:4; 12:4; and 15:3-6 are all references to its rules.

THE MEANING

Leviticus has a wonderful meaning for Christians today, for they too have been rescued from the bondage of sin and know redemption through the blood of Jesus Christ, of which the book of Exodus is a picture (see Exodus 12:3 note). All the various offerings speak of the work of Christ. The consecrated priests are a picture of how God would have us approach Him, and the instructions for holy living remind us that Christian people should be holy in every detail of their lives.

OUTLINE OF LEVITICUS

- I. The Offerings — Leviticus 1:7—6:7
  - A. The Burnt-Offering
  - B. Meat-Offering
  - C. Peace-Offering
  - D. Sin-Offering
  - E. Trespass-Offering
- II. The Laws of the Offerings — Leviticus 6:8—7:38
- III. The Law of the Priests — Leviticus 8–10
- IV. The Law of Purity — Leviticus 11–15
  - A. Food
  - B. Motherhood
  - C. Leprosy

V.	The Law of the Day of Atonement	Leviticus 16
VI.	The Law of Sacrifice	Leviticus 17
VII.	The Law of Human Relationships	Leviticus 18–22
VIII.	The Law of the Feasts of the LORD	Leviticus 23; 24
IX.	The Law of the Land	Leviticus 25; 26
X.	The Law of Vows	Leviticus 27

I. The Offerings (1:1—6:7)
A. The Burnt-Offering (Lev. 6:8-13)

1 And the LORD called unto *Moses,
and spake unto him out of the tabernacle of the congregation, saying,
2 Speak unto the children of *Israel,
and say unto them, If any man of you
bring an *offering unto the LORD, ye
shall bring your offering of the cattle,
even of the herd, and of the flock.
3 If his offering *be* a burnt-sacrifice of
the herd, let him offer a male without
blemish: he shall offer it of his own voluntary will at the door of the tabernacle of the congregation before the
LORD.
4 And he shall put his hand upon the
head of the burnt-offering; and it shall
be accepted for him to make *atonement for him.

1:2 THE FIVE DIFFERENT OFFERINGS

There were five kinds of offerings that people might bring to the LORD:

1. the Burnt-Offering (1; 6:8-13);
2. the Meat-Offering (2; 6:14-23);
3. the Peace-Offering (3; 7:11-38);
4. the Sin-Offering (4; 6:24-30);
5. the Trespass-Offering (5:1–6:7; 7:1-7).

The work of the Lord Jesus Christ for us is very wonderful. He lived a perfect life and died a perfect death, but we are so weak and imperfect that we cannot understand it all. So God has given us accounts of these different offerings that we may learn in detail what Christ has done for us. Each offering illustrates a different aspect of His life and death.

1:4 THE BURNT-OFFERING

1. The sacrifice was an animal without blemish. This speaks of the Lord Jesus who was absolutely perfect and always did God's will when He was on earth (Luke 3:22; 22:42).
2. The one making the offering put his hand on the animal (vs. 4) to say; "My sins are to cause this animal's death." When it died, it was a substitute for the sinner (vs. 4). So Jesus was our substitute; that is, He died in our place (Rom. 4:25; 6:3-4).
3. Five animals could be used as offerings:
   a) Bullock, or ox (vs. 5)
   b) Sheep, or lamb (vs. 10)
   c) Goat (vs. 10)
   d) Pigeon, and turtledove (vs. 14)

A rich man brought a bullock, and a poor man, a pigeon. Each animal, however, speaks of Christ as our sacrifice.

1:1 Moses. Look up Hebrews 11:23-29 for God's estimate of Moses' greatness.

1:1 tabernacle. The wonderful tent which God had instructed Moses to make for His dwelling place among the. Israelites (Exod. 25–38).

1:3 his own voluntary will. God does not bless or want a gift that is not given to Him willingly. The Lord Jesus Christ gave himself willingly on the cross (John 10:14-18).

5 And he shall kill the bullock before the LORD: and the priests, *Aaron's sons, shall bring the *blood, and sprinkle the blood round about upon the *altar that *is by* the door of the tabernacle of the congregation.

6 And he shall flay the burnt-offering, and cut it into his pieces.

7 And the sons of Aaron the priest shall put *fire upon the altar, and lay the wood in order upon the fire:

8 And the priests, Aaron's sons, shall lay the parts, the head, and the fat, in order upon the wood that *is* on the fire which *is* upon the altar:

9 But his inwards and his legs shall he wash in water: and the priest shall burn all on the altar, *to be* a burnt-sacrifice, an offering made by fire, of a sweet savour unto the LORD.

¶10 And if his offering *be* of the flocks, *namely,* of the sheep, or of the goats, for a burnt-sacrifice; he shall bring it a male without blemish.

11 And he shall kill it on the side of the altar northward before the LORD: and the priests, Aaron's sons, shall sprinkle his blood round about upon the altar.

12 And he shall cut it into his pieces, with his head and his fat: and the priest shall lay them in order on the wood that *is* on the fire which *is* upon the altar:

13 But he shall wash the inwards and the legs with water: and the priest shall bring *it* all, and burn *it* upon the altar: it *is* a burnt-sacrifice, an offering made by fire, of a sweet savour unto the LORD.

¶14 And if the burnt-sacrifice for his offering to the LORD *be* of fowls, then he shall bring his offering of turtledoves, or of young pigeons.

15 And the priest shall bring it unto the altar, and wring off his head, and burn *it* on the altar; and the blood thereof shall be wrung out at the side of the altar:

16 And he shall pluck away his crop with his feathers, and cast it beside the altar on the east part, by the place of the ashes:

17 And he shall cleave it with the wings thereof, *but* shall not divide *it* asunder: and the priest shall burn it upon the altar, upon the wood that *is* upon the fire: it *is* a burnt-sacrifice, an offering made by fire, of a sweet savour unto the LORD.

B. Meat-Offering (Lev. 6:14-23)

2 And when any will offer a meat-offering unto the LORD, his offering shall be *of* fine flour; and he shall pour *oil upon it, and put frankincense thereon:

2 And he shall bring it to Aaron's sons the priests: and he shall take thereout his handful of the flour thereof, and of

---

1:5 the blood. Over and over again in the sacrifices, it was impressed upon the people that if sins were to be forgiven, they must be paid for in blood (Heb. 9:22). The blood was the outpouring of life that, of course, always looked forward to the sacrifice of our Lord, to whom all these symbols pointed.

1:8 fire. Fire stands for the holiness of God. Because of this, it also stands for:

1. judgment, since God in holiness must judge sin;
2. the manner in which God sometimes revealed Himself (read about the burning bush in Exod. 3:2-6);
3. purifying by burning away that which is impure (1 Cor. 3:12-14). As the fire was to be kept burning on the altar (6:12), never to go out, so God's holiness is unchanging, as is His love and faithfulness.

1:9 a sweet savour. A source of satisfaction, this and the next two offerings, in Leviticus 2 and 3, are pictures of Christ's giving God pleasure and satisfaction such as we could never give because of our sin. The last two offerings, in Leviticus 4 and 5, show the Lord Jesus bearing the penalty of our sin. In the first three, we see Christ symbolically making good our failure to please God by pleasing Him perfectly. In the last two, we see a picture of Jesus taking the punishment of the sins that really belonged to us.

the oil thereof, with all the frankincense
thereof; and the priest shall burn the
memorial of it upon the altar, *to be* an
offering made by fire, of a sweet savour
unto the LORD:
3 And the remnant of the meat-offerings *shall be* Aaron's and his sons': *it is*
a thing most *holy of the offerings of
the LORD made by fire.
¶ 4 And if thou bring an oblation of a
meat-offering baken in the oven, *it shall*
be unleavened cakes of fine flour mingled with oil, or unleavened wafers
anointed with oil.
¶ 5 And if thy oblation *be* a meat-
offering *baken* in a pan, it shall be *of* fine
flour unleavened, mingled with oil.
6 Thou shalt part it in pieces, and pour
oil thereon: it *is* a meat-offering.
¶ 7 And if thy oblation *be* a meat-
offering *baken* in the fryingpan, it shall
be made *of* fine flour with oil.
8 And thou shalt bring the meat-
offering that is made of these things unto
the LORD: and when it is presented unto
the priest, he shall bring it unto the altar.
9 And the priest shall take from the
meat-offering a memorial thereof, and
shall burn *it* upon the altar: *it is* an offering made by fire, of a sweet savour
unto the LORD.
10 And that which is left of the meat-
offering *shall be* Aaron's and his sons':
it is a thing most holy of the offerings
of the LORD made by fire.
11 No meat-offering, which ye shall
bring unto the LORD, shall be made with
*leaven: for ye shall burn no leaven, nor
any honey, in any offering of the LORD
made by fire.
¶ 12 As for the oblation of the firstfruits, ye shall offer them unto the
LORD: but they shall not be burnt on the
altar for a sweet savour.
13 And every oblation of thy meat-
offering shalt thou season with *salt;
neither shalt thou suffer the salt of the
*covenant of thy *God to be lacking
from thy meat-offering: with all thine
offerings thou shalt offer salt.
14 And if thou offer a meat-offering
of thy firstfruits unto the LORD, thou
shalt offer for the meat-offering of thy
firstfruits green ears of corn dried by
the fire, *even* corn beaten out of full
ears.
15 And thou shalt put oil upon it, and
lay frankincense thereon: it *is* a meat-
offering.
16 And the priest shall burn the memorial of it, *part* of the beaten corn
thereof, and *part* of the oil thereof, with

2:1 THE MEAT-OFFERING

This is really the meal-offering (flour), as indicated in later translations of the Bible. See *How We Got Our English Bible,* page xxiii. The meal-offering was closely connected with the burnt-offering, and the Israelites probably offered both together. Both offerings speak of Christ. The burnt-offering shows His perfect death, while the meal-offering shows His perfect life and humanity as seen in the Gospel of Luke, which should be read in connection with this. Note also:

1. "Fine flour" speaks of the purity of His life and character. He was called "that holy thing" (Luke 1:35).
2. "Oil" speaks of the Holy Spirit (Luke 1:35; 3:22).
3. "Frankincense" was a fragrant powder which gave off a sweet smell when burnt and speaks of the joy Christ's perfection gave to God His Father (Luke 3:22).
4. "Salt" (vs. 13) preserves and is a picture of divine wisdom (Mark 9:49-50; Col. 4:6).
5. "Leaven" was forbidden since it speaks of evil and corruption, and Christ was completely sinless (2 Cor. 5:21; 1 Pet. 2:22; see *leaven).

2:4 oblation. Offering or sacrifice.

2:11 honey. Honey was not used in the offering because it was likely to become sour; thus it is a poor symbol of the grace of our Lord Jesus Christ. See verse 1 note, "The Meat-Offering."

2:13 salt. See verse 1 note, number 4.

all the frankincense thereof: *it is* an offering made by fire unto the LORD.

C. Peace-Offering (Lev. 7:11-38)

3 And if his oblation *be* a sacrifice of
*peace-offering, if he offer *it* of the
herd; whether *it be* a male or female, he
shall offer it without blemish before the
LORD.

> **3:1 The Peace-Offering**
> When we become Christians, we do not only have our sins forgiven, but we come to know God as our Father (John 1:12). We can speak to Him and worship Him without fear. This is because the Lord Jesus has made "peace through the blood of his cross" (Col. 1:20), and God now looks on us just as He looks on His beloved Son. The peace-offering was a picture or *type of this work of our Saviour for us. Look up Romans 5:1; 1 Corinthians 1:3; and Philippians 4:7.

2 And he shall lay his hand upon the
head of his offering, and kill it *at* the
door of the tabernacle of the congregation: and Aaron's sons the priests shall
sprinkle the blood upon the altar round
about.
3 And he shall offer of the sacrifice of
the peace-offering an offering made by
fire unto the LORD; the fat that covereth
the inwards, and all the fat that *is* upon
the inwards,
4 And the two kidneys, and the fat that
is on them, which *is by* the flanks, and
the caul above the liver, with the kidneys, it shall he take away.
5 And Aaron's sons shall burn it on the
altar upon the burnt-sacrifice, which *is*
upon the wood that *is* on the fire: *it is*
an offering made by fire, of a sweet
savour unto the LORD.
¶ 6 And if his offering for a sacrifice of
peace-offering unto the LORD *be* of the
flock; male or female, he shall offer it
without blemish.
7 If he offer a lamb for his offering,
then shall he offer it before the LORD.
8 And he shall lay his hand upon the
head of his offering, and kill it before the
tabernacle of the congregation: and
Aaron's sons shall sprinkle the blood
thereof round about upon the altar.
9 And he shall offer of the sacrifice of
the peace-offering an offering made by
fire unto the LORD; the fat thereof, *and*
the whole rump, it shall he take off hard
by the backbone; and the fat that
covereth the inwards, and all the fat that
is upon the inwards,
10 And the two kidneys, and the fat
that *is* upon them, which *is* by the
flanks, and the caul above the liver, with
the kidneys, it shall he take away.
11 And the priest shall burn it upon
the altar: *it is* the food of the offering
made by fire unto the LORD.
¶ 12 And if his offering *be* a goat, then
he shall offer it before the LORD.
13 And he shall lay his hand upon the
head of it, and kill it before the tabernacle of the congregation: and the sons
of Aaron shall sprinkle the blood
thereof upon the altar round about.
14 And he shall offer thereof his offering, *even* an offering made by fire unto
the LORD; the fat that covereth the inwards, and all the fat that *is* upon the
inwards,
15 And the two kidneys, and the fat
that *is* upon them, which *is* by the
flanks, and the caul above the liver, with
the kidneys, it shall he take away.
16 And the priest shall burn them
upon the altar: *it is* the food of the offering made by fire for a sweet savour:
all the fat *is* the LORD'S.
17 *It shall be* a perpetual statute for
your generations throughout all your
dwellings, that ye eat neither fat nor
blood.

D. Sin-Offering (Lev. 6:24-30)

4 And the LORD spake unto Moses,
saying,
2 Speak unto the children of Israel,
saying, If a soul shall *sin through ignorance against any of the commandments of the LORD *concerning things*
which ought not to be done, and shall
do against any of them:
3 If the priest that is anointed do sin

4:1 The Sin-Offering
This offering and the next, the trespass-offering (chap. 5) are different from the previous three (see 1:2 note). Here the illustration is of Christ as our Sin-Bearer, who took the punishment of our sin on the cross. Look up Isaiah 53; 1 Peter 2:24; and 3:18 for the meaning of this. God can never overlook sin. He must punish it. The Israelites offered the sin-offering and were forgiven because God looked forward to the time when Christ would die on the cross and be the real sacrifice for sin, when He became sin for us (2 Cor. 5:21). See John 1:29; and Romans 3:25 note.

according to the sin of the people; then let him bring for his sin, which he hath sinned, a young bullock without blemish unto the LORD for a *sin-offering.

4 And he shall bring the bullock unto the door of the tabernacle of the congregation before the LORD; and shall lay his hand upon the bullock's head, and kill the bullock before the LORD.

5 And the priest that is anointed shall take of the bullock's blood, and bring it to the tabernacle of the congregation:

6 And the priest shall dip his finger in the blood, and sprinkle of the blood seven times before the LORD, before the vail of the *sanctuary.

7 And the priest shall put *some* of the blood upon the *horns of the altar of sweet *incense before the LORD, which *is* in the tabernacle of the congregation; and shall pour all the blood of the bullock at the bottom of the altar of the burnt-offering, which *is at* the door of the tabernacle of the congregation.

8 And he shall take off from it all the fat of the bullock for the sin-offering; the fat that covereth the inwards, and all the fat that *is* upon the inwards,

9 And the two kidneys, and the fat that *is* upon them, which *is* by the flanks, and the caul above the liver, with the kidneys, it shall he take away,

10 As it was taken off from the bullock of the sacrifice of peace-offerings: and the priest shall burn them upon the altar of the burnt-offering.

11 And the skin of the bullock, and all his flesh, with his head, and with his legs, and his inwards, and his *dung,

12 Even the whole bullock shall he carry forth without the camp unto a *clean place, where the ashes are poured out, and burn him on the wood with fire: where the ashes are poured out shall he be burnt.

¶13 And if the whole congregation of Israel sin through ignorance, and the thing be hid from the eyes of the assembly, and they have done *somewhat against* any of the commandments of the LORD *concerning things* which should not be done, and are guilty;

14 When the sin, which they have sinned against it, is known, then the congregation shall offer a young bullock for the sin, and bring him before the tabernacle of the congregation.

15 And the *elders of the congregation shall lay their hands upon the head of the bullock before the LORD: and the bullock shall be killed before the LORD.

16 And the priest that is anointed shall bring of the bullock's blood to the tabernacle of the congregation:

17 And the priest shall dip his finger *in some* of the blood, and sprinkle *it* seven times before the LORD, *even* before the vail.

18 And he shall put *some* of the blood upon the horns of the altar which *is* before the LORD, that *is* in the tabernacle of the congregation, and shall pour out all the blood at the bottom of the altar of the burnt-offering, which *is at* the door of the tabernacle of the congregation.

4:12 without the camp. The sin-offering was a holy offering to the LORD; therefore, it could not be burned in the midst of the sinful, unholy people. Just so, Jesus "suffered without the gate" (Heb. 13:12-13). We should leave the old sins and habits when we go to Him in faith for our salvation.

19 And he shall take all his fat from
him, and burn *it* upon the altar.
20 And he shall do with the bullock as
he did with the bullock for a sin-offering, so shall he do with this: and the
priest shall make an atonement for
them, and it shall be *forgiven them.
21 And he shall carry forth the bullock
without the camp, and burn him as
he burned the first bullock: it *is* a sin-
offering for the congregation.
¶22 When a ruler hath sinned, and
done *somewhat* through ignorance
against any of the commandments of
the LORD his God *concerning things*
which should not be done, and is guilty;
23 Or if his sin, wherein he hath
sinned, come to his knowledge; he shall
bring his offering, a kid of the goats, a
male without blemish:
24 And he shall lay his hand upon the
head of the goat, and kill it in the place
where they kill the burnt-offering before the LORD: it *is* a sin-offering.
25 And the priest shall take of the
blood of the sin-offering with his finger,
and put *it* upon the horns of the altar of
burnt-offering, and shall pour out his
blood at the bottom of the altar of burnt-
offering.
26 And he shall burn all his fat upon
the altar, as the fat of the sacrifice of
peace-offerings: and the priest shall
make an atonement for him as concerning his sin, and it shall be forgiven him.
¶27 And if any one of the common people sin through ignorance, while he
doeth *somewhat against* any of the commandments of the LORD *concerning*
things which ought not to be done, and
be guilty;
28 Or if his sin, which he hath sinned,
come to his knowledge: then he shall
bring his offering, a kid of the goats, a
female without blemish, for his sin
which he hath sinned.
29 And he shall lay his hand upon the
head of the sin-offering, and slay the
sin-offering in the place of the burnt-
offering.
30 And the priest shall take of the
blood thereof with his finger, and put
it upon the horns of the altar of burnt-
offering, and shall pour out all the blood
thereof at the bottom of the altar.
31 And he shall take away all the fat
thereof, as the fat is taken away from off
the sacrifice of peace-offerings; and the
priest shall burn *it* upon the altar for a
sweet savour unto the LORD; and the
priest shall make an atonement for him,
and it shall be forgiven him.
32 And if he bring a lamb for a sin-offering, he shall bring it a female without blemish.
33 And he shall lay his hand upon the
head of the sin-offering, and slay it for
a sin-offering in the place where they
kill the burnt-offering.
34 And the priest shall take of the
blood of the sin-offering with his finger,
and put *it* upon the horns of the altar of
burnt-offering, and shall pour out all the
blood thereof at the bottom of the altar:
35 And he shall take away all the fat
thereof, as the fat of the lamb is taken
away from the sacrifice of the peace-
offerings; and the priest shall burn
them upon the altar, according to the
offerings made by fire unto the LORD:
and the priest shall make an atonement
for his sin that he hath committed, and
it shall be forgiven him.

E. Trespass-Offering (Lev. 7:1-7)

5 And if a soul sin, and hear the
voice of swearing, and *is* a witness,
whether he hath seen or known *of it;* if
he do not utter *it,* then he shall bear his
iniquity.
2 Or if a soul touch any *unclean thing,
whether *it be* a carcase of an unclean
beast, or a carcase of unclean cattle, or
the carcase of unclean creeping things,
and *if* it be hidden from him; he also
shall be unclean, and guilty.

4:20 forgiven. See Acts 10:43 note, on remission of sins.
5:1 utter. To disclose, make known.

3 Or if he touch the uncleanness of
man, whatsoever uncleanness *it be* that
a man shall be defiled withal, and it be
hid from him; when he knoweth *of it,*
then he shall be guilty.
4 Or if a soul swear, pronouncing with
his lips to do evil, or to do good, whatsoever *it be* that a man shall pronounce
with an oath, and it be hid from him;
when he knoweth *of it,* then he shall be
guilty in one of these.
5 And it shall be, when he shall be
guilty in one of these *things,* that he
shall *confess that he hath sinned in
that *thing:*
6 And he shall bring his trespass-
offering unto the LORD for his sin which
he hath sinned, a female from the flock,
a lamb or a kid of the goats, for a sin-
offering; and the priest shall make an
atonement for him concerning his sin.

5:6 The Trespass-Offering
The trespass-offering is very similar to the sin-offering because both speak of the Lord Jesus Christ as our Sin-Bearer, but this offering reminds us of sins, first against God and then also against our fellowmen, for which the wages must be paid (Rom. 6:23). See 6:5 note.

7 And if he be not able to bring a lamb,
then he shall bring for his trespass,
which he hath committed, two turtledoves, or two young pigeons, unto the
LORD; one for a sin-offering, and the
other for a burnt-offering.
8 And he shall bring them unto the
priest, who shall offer *that* which *is* for
the sin-offering first, and wring off his
head from his neck, but shall not divide
it asunder:
9 And he shall sprinkle of the blood of
the sin-offering upon the side of the
altar; and the rest of the blood shall be
wrung out at the bottom of the altar: it
is a sin-offering.
10 And he shall offer the second *for* a
burnt-offering, according to the manner: and the priest shall make an atonement for him for his sin which he hath
sinned, and it shall be forgiven him.
¶11 But if he be not able to bring two
turtledoves, or two young pigeons, then
he that sinned shall bring for his offering the tenth part of an *ephah of fine
flour for a sin-offering; he shall put no
oil upon it, neither shall he put *any*
frankincense thereon: for it *is* a sin-
offering.
12 Then shall he bring it to the priest,
and the priest shall take his handful of
it, *even* a memorial thereof, and burn *it*
on the altar, according to the offerings
made by fire unto the LORD: it *is* a sin-
offering.
13 And the priest shall make an atonement for him as touching his sin that he
hath sinned in one of these, and it shall
be forgiven him: and *the remnant* shall
be the priest's, as a meat-offering.
¶14 And the LORD spake unto Moses,
saying,
15 If a soul commit a trespass, and sin
through ignorance, in the holy things of
the LORD; then he shall bring for his
trespass unto the LORD a ram without
blemish out of the flocks, with thy estimation by shekels of *silver, after the
shekel of the sanctuary, for a trespass-
offering:
16 And he shall make amends for the
harm that he hath done in the holy
thing, and shall add the fifth part thereto, and give it unto the priest: and the
priest shall make an atonement for him
with the ram of the trespass-offering,
and it shall be forgiven him.
¶17 And if a soul sin, and commit any
of these things which are forbidden to
be done by the commandments of the
LORD; though he wist *it* not, yet is he
guilty, and shall bear his iniquity.
18 And he shall bring a ram without
blemish out of the flock, with thy estimation, for a trespass-offering, unto the
priest: and the priest shall make an
atonement for him concerning his igno-

5:5 confess. See 1 John 1:9.

rance wherein he erred and wist *it* not,
and it shall be forgiven him.
19 It *is* a trespass-offering: he hath
certainly trespassed against the LORD.
6 And the LORD spake unto Moses,
saying,
2 If a soul sin, and commit a trespass
against the LORD, and lie unto his
neighbour in that which was delivered
him to keep, or in fellowship, or in a
thing taken away by violence, or hath
deceived his neighbour;
3 Or have found that which was lost,
and lieth concerning it, and sweareth
falsely; in any of all these that a man
doeth, sinning therein:
4 Then it shall be, because he hath
sinned, and is guilty, that he shall restore that which he took violently away,
or the thing which he hath deceitfully
gotten, or that which was delivered him
to keep, or the lost thing which he
found,
5 Or all that about which he hath
sworn falsely; he shall even restore it
in the principal, and shall add the fifth
part more thereto, *and* give it unto him
to whom it appertaineth, in the day of
his trespass-offering.

6:5 Undoing Wrong
When a man sinned, he not only displeased God, but he injured his neighbor. His trespass-offering could take away his guilt in the sight of God (5:6), but he had to show that he was sorry by making good or paying back the loss or injury to the man whom he had wronged. This reminds us of the teaching of faith and works in Romans 4:2 and James 2:21. We trust in the work of the Lord Jesus on the cross for God's forgiveness, but we must live good lives after we are born again or people will not believe in our conversion (James 2:26), and our lives will not speak of our Saviour to those who do not know Him.

6 And he shall bring his trespass-
offering unto the LORD, a ram without
blemish out of the flock, with thy estimation, for a trespass-offering, unto the
priest:
7 And the priest shall make an atonement for him before the LORD: and it
shall be forgiven him for any thing of all
that he hath done in trespassing
therein.

II. Laws of the Offerings (6:8—7:38)

¶8 And the LORD spake unto Moses,
saying,
9 Command Aaron and his sons, saying, This *is* the *law of the burnt-offering: It *is* the burnt-offering, because of
the burning upon the altar all night unto
the morning, and the fire of the altar
shall be burning in it.
10 And the priest shall put on his *lin-
en garment, and his linen breeches
shall he put upon his flesh, and take up
the ashes which the fire hath consumed
with the burnt-offering on the altar, and
he shall put them beside the altar.
11 And he shall put off his *garments,
and put on other garments, and carry
forth the ashes without the camp unto
a clean place.
12 And the fire upon the altar shall be
burning in it; it shall not be put out: and
the priest shall burn wood on it every
morning, and lay the burnt-offering in
order upon it; and he shall burn thereon
the fat of the peace-offerings.
13 The fire shall ever be burning upon
the altar; it shall never go out.
¶14 And this *is* the law of the meat-
offering: the sons of Aaron shall offer it
before the LORD, before the altar.
15 And he shall take of it his handful,
of the flour of the meat-offering, and of
the oil thereof, and all the frankincense
which *is* upon the meat-offering, and
shall burn *it* upon the altar *for* a sweet
savour, *even* the memorial of it, unto the
LORD.
16 And the remainder thereof shall
Aaron and his sons eat: with *unleavened bread shall it be eaten in the holy

6:9 This is the law. The next few chapters give many details about the offerings, to make sure that everything was carried out according to the will of God.

place; in the court of the tabernacle of
the congregation they shall eat it.
17 It shall not be baken with *leaven.
I have given it *unto them for* their portion of my offerings made by fire; it *is*
most holy, as *is* the sin-offering, and as
the trespass-offering.
18 All the males among the children of
Aaron shall eat of it. *It shall be* a statute
for ever in your generations concerning the offerings of the LORD made by
fire: every one that toucheth them shall
be holy.
¶ 19 And the LORD spake unto Moses,
saying,
20 This *is* the offering of Aaron and of
his sons, which they shall offer unto the
LORD in the day when he is anointed;
the tenth part of an ephah of fine flour
for a meat-offering perpetual, half of it
in the morning, and half thereof at
night.
21 In a pan it shall be made with oil;
and when it is baken, thou shalt bring it
in: *and* the baken pieces of the meat-
offering shalt thou offer *for* a sweet
savour unto the LORD.
22 And the priest of his sons that is
anointed in his stead shall offer it: *it is*
a statute for ever unto the LORD; it shall
be wholly burnt.
23 For every meat-offering for the
priest shall be wholly burnt: it shall not
be eaten.
¶ 24 And the LORD spake unto Moses,
saying,
25 Speak unto Aaron and to his sons,
saying, This *is* the law of the sin-offering: In the place where the burnt-offering is killed shall the sin-offering be
killed before the LORD: it *is* most holy.
26 The priest that offereth it for sin
shall eat it: in the holy place shall it be
eaten, in the court of the tabernacle of
the congregation.
27 Whatsoever shall touch the flesh
thereof shall be holy: and when there is
sprinkled of the blood thereof upon any
garment, thou shalt wash that whereon
it was sprinkled in the holy place.
28 But the earthen vessel wherein it
is sodden shall be broken: and if it be
sodden in a brasen pot, it shall be both
scoured, and rinsed in water.
29 All the males among the priests
shall eat thereof: it *is* most holy.
30 And no sin-offering, whereof *any*
of the blood is brought into the tabernacle of the congregation to *reconcile
withal in the holy *place,* shall be eaten:
it shall be burnt in the fire.

7 Likewise this *is* the law of the
trespass-offering: it *is* most holy.
2 In the place where they kill the
burnt-offering shall they kill the trespass-offering: and the *blood thereof
shall he sprinkle round about upon the
*altar.
3 And he shall offer of it all the fat
thereof; the rump, and the fat that
covereth the inwards,
4 And the two kidneys, and the fat that
is on them, which *is* by the flanks, and
the caul *that is* above the liver, with the
kidneys, it shall he take away:
5 And the priest shall burn them upon
the altar *for* an offering made by *fire
unto the LORD: it *is* a trespass-offering.
6 Every male among the priests shall
eat thereof: it shall be eaten in the holy
place: it *is* most holy.
7 As the sin-offering *is,* so *is* the trespass-offering: *there is* one law for them:
the priest that maketh *atonement
therewith shall have *it.*
8 And the priest that offereth any
man's burnt-offering, *even* the priest
shall have to himself the skin of the
burnt-offering which he hath offered.
9 And all the meat-offering that is
baken in the oven, and all that is
dressed in the fryingpan, and in the pan,
shall be the priest's that offereth it.
10 And every meat-offering, mingled

6:28 sodden. Boiled.

6:30 reconcile. This is translated from the same Hebrew word that means *to cover* or *to atone,* so recalling atonement. See Exodus 29:33 note.

with oil, and dry, shall all the sons of *Aaron have, one *as much* as another.

11 And this *is* the law of the *sacrifice of peace-offerings, which he shall offer unto the LORD.

12 If he offer it for a thanksgiving, then he shall offer with the sacrifice of thanksgiving unleavened cakes mingled with oil, and unleavened wafers anointed with oil, and cakes mingled with oil, of fine flour, fried.

13 Besides the cakes, he shall offer *for* his offering *leavened bread with the sacrifice of thanksgiving of his peace-offerings.

7:13 Leavened Bread
Leaven was forbidden in the meal-offering (2:11), but it was allowed here. This was because in the sacrifice of the meal-offering, which was a picture of the perfect Lord Jesus Christ, no evil could be suggested. In this offering, however, which foreshadows the Christians' worship of God, leaven was permitted. This was to show that although our sins are forgiven, there is still the old, sinful nature in us, and it will be there until we are fully perfected in Christ in heaven (compare Matt. 13:33; 1 Cor. 5:6-7).

14 And of it he shall offer one out of the whole *oblation *for* an *heave-offering unto the LORD, *and* it shall be the priest's that sprinkleth the blood of the peace-offerings.

15 And the flesh of the sacrifice of his peace-offerings for thanksgiving shall be eaten the same day that it is offered; he shall not leave any of it until the morning.

16 But if the sacrifice of his offering *be* a vow, or a voluntary offering, it shall be eaten the same day that he offereth his sacrifice: and on the morrow also the remainder of it shall be eaten:

17 But the remainder of the flesh of the sacrifice on the third day shall be burnt with fire.

18 And if *any* of the flesh of the sacrifice of his peace-offerings be eaten at all on the third day, it shall not be accepted, neither shall it be imputed unto him that offereth it: it shall be an *abomination, and the soul that eateth of it shall bear his iniquity.

19 And the flesh that toucheth any unclean *thing* shall not be eaten; it shall be burnt with fire: and as for the flesh, all that be clean shall eat thereof.

20 But the soul that eateth *of* the flesh of the sacrifice of peace-offerings, that *pertain* unto the LORD, having his uncleanness upon him, even that soul shall be cut off from his people.

21 Moreover the soul that shall touch any unclean *thing, as* the uncleanness of man, or *any* unclean beast, or any abominable unclean *thing,* and eat of the flesh of the sacrifice of peace-offerings, which *pertain* unto the LORD, even that soul shall be cut off from his people.

¶22 And the LORD spake unto *Moses, saying,

23 Speak unto the children of *Israel, saying, Ye shall eat no manner of fat, of ox, or of sheep, or of goat.

24 And the fat of the beast that dieth of itself, and the fat of that which is torn with beasts, may be used in any other use: but ye shall in no wise eat of it.

25 For whosoever eateth the fat of the beast, of which men offer an offering made by fire unto the LORD, even the soul that eateth *it* shall be cut off from his people.

26 Moreover ye shall eat no manner of blood, *whether it be* of fowl or of beast, in any of your dwellings.

27 Whatsoever soul *it be* that eateth

7:18 neither shall it be imputed unto him. To "impute" means to *put to another's account, to attribute to another*. The peace-offering would not make peace if the flesh was eaten on the third day.

7:18 an abomination. A sacrifice offered to God that was not in accordance with His laws would be hated by Him. It would be better to offer no sacrifice at all than to offer one in sinful disobedience.

any manner of blood, even that soul shall be cut off from his people.

¶ 28 And the LORD spake unto Moses, saying,

29 Speak unto the children of Israel, saying, He that offereth the sacrifice of his peace-offerings unto the LORD shall bring his oblation unto the LORD of the sacrifice of his peace-offerings.

30 His own hands shall bring the offerings of the LORD made by fire, the fat with the breast, it shall he bring, that the breast may be waved *for* a wave-offering before the LORD.

31 And the priest shall burn the fat upon the altar: but the breast shall be Aaron's and his sons'.

32 And the right shoulder shall ye give unto the priest *for* an heave offering of the sacrifices of your peace-offerings.

33 He among the sons of Aaron, that offereth the blood of the peace-offerings, and the fat, shall have the right shoulder for *his* part.

34 For the wave breast and the heave shoulder have I taken of the children of Israel from off the sacrifices of their peace-offerings, and have given them unto Aaron the priest and unto his sons by a statute for ever from among the children of Israel.

¶ 35 This *is the portion* of the anointing of Aaron, and of the anointing of his sons, out of the offerings of the LORD made by fire, in the day *when* he presented them to minister unto the LORD in the priest's office;

36 Which the LORD commanded to be given them of the children of Israel, in the day that he anointed them, *by* a statute for ever throughout their generations.

37 This *is* the law of the burnt-offering, of the meat-offering, and of the sin-offering, and of the trespass-offering, and of the consecrations, and of the sacrifice of the peace-offerings;

38 Which the LORD commanded Moses in mount *Sinai, in the day that he commanded the children of Israel to offer their oblations unto the LORD, in the wilderness of Sinai.

III. The Law of the Priests (8–10)

8 And the LORD spake unto Moses, saying,

2 Take Aaron and his sons with him, and the garments, and the anointing *oil, and a bullock for the sin-offering, and two rams, and a basket of unleavened bread;

3 And gather thou all the congregation

8:2-4 LESSONS OF THE PRIESTHOOD

This portion (chap. 8) describes how Moses carried out the instructions for the priesthood already given in Exodus 28 and 29. From it we may learn two lessons:

1. The present work of the Lord Jesus Christ. The offerings illustrated His work on the cross as the perfect sacrifice, bearing the punishment of our sins. The priesthood goes a step further and shows what Christ does for us after we have become Christians, how He leads us and cares for us and helps us to worship God correctly. Hebrews 7:23-28 teaches us that the Old Testament high priest is a *type of Christ, who continually lives in the presence of God as our representative. That means that He is there to speak for us. See also Hebrews 9:11-12,24.
2. All Christians are priests. Just as Aaron's sons were associated with him in the priesthood, when we are saved from our sins we too are called priests. Our great joy and also our duty is to approach God and to worship Him. We are not to be afraid of Him but to live close to Him. The sacrifice we offer is "the sacrifice of praise . . . giving thanks to his name" (Heb. 13:15). Every believer is a priest because he can approach God directly through the Lord Jesus Christ and does not need any other priest to bring him into God's presence. See 1 Peter 2:5 note.

7:30 wave-offering. See Exodus 29:27 note on the heave-offering.

8:2 Take Aaron and his sons. Moses was acting under God's instructions here. The priests were not to consecrate themselves. They presented themselves to God, as the believers in the Lord Jesus Christ are told to do in Romans 12:1.

together unto the door of the *tabernacle of the congregation.
4 And Moses did as the LORD commanded him; and the assembly was
gathered together unto the door of the
tabernacle of the congregation.
5 And Moses said unto the congregation, This *is* the thing which the LORD
commanded to be done.
6 And Moses brought Aaron and his
sons, and washed them with water.
7 And he put upon him the coat, and
girded him with the girdle, and clothed
him with the robe, and put the *ephod
upon him, and he girded him with the
*curious girdle of the ephod, and bound
it unto him therewith.
8 And he put the breastplate upon
him: also he put in the breastplate the
Urim and the Thummim.
9 And he put the mitre upon his head;
also upon the mitre, *even* upon his forefront, did he put the golden plate, the
*holy crown; as the LORD commanded
Moses.
10 And Moses took the anointing oil,
and anointed the tabernacle and all that
was therein, and sanctified them.
11 And he sprinkled thereof upon the
altar seven times, and anointed the altar and all his vessels, both the *laver
and his foot, to sanctify them.
12 And he poured of the anointing oil
upon Aaron's head, and anointed him,
to sanctify him.
13 And Moses brought Aaron's sons,
and put coats upon them, and girded
them with girdles, and put bonnets
upon them; as the LORD commanded
Moses.
14 And he brought the bullock for the
sin-offering: and Aaron and his sons laid
their hands upon the head of the bullock
for the sin-offering.
15 And he slew *it;* and Moses took the
blood, and put *it* upon the horns of the
altar round about with his finger, and
purified the altar, and poured the blood
at the bottom of the altar, and sanctified
it, to make *reconciliation upon it.
16 And he took all the fat that *was*
upon the inwards, and caul *above* the
liver, and the two kidneys, and their fat,
and Moses burned *it* upon the altar.
17 But the bullock, and his hide, his
flesh, and his *dung, he burnt with fire
without the camp; as the LORD commanded Moses.
¶18 And he brought the ram for the
burnt-offering: and Aaron and his sons
laid their hands upon the head of the
ram.
19 And he killed *it;* and Moses sprinkled the blood upon the altar round
about.
20 And he cut the ram into pieces; and
Moses burnt the head, and the pieces,
and the fat.
21 And he washed the inwards and the
legs in water; and Moses burnt the
whole ram upon the altar: it *was* a
burnt-sacrifice for a sweet savour, *and*
an offering made by fire unto the LORD;
as the LORD commanded Moses.
¶22 And he brought the other ram, the
ram of consecration: and Aaron and his
sons laid their hands upon the head of
the ram.
23 And he slew *it;* and Moses took of
the blood of it, and put *it* upon the tip of
Aaron's right ear, and upon the thumb
of his right hand, and upon the great toe
of his right foot.
24 And he brought Aaron's sons, and
Moses put of the blood upon the tip of
their right ear, and upon the thumbs
of their right hands, and upon the great
toes of their right feet: and Moses
sprinkled the blood upon the altar round
about.

8:6 washed them with water. See John 13:3-10.
8:7 And he put upon him. See Exodus 28:2 note, "The Priests' Holy Garments."
8:22 the other ram. Read Exodus 29:1,19,31.
8:23 Moses took of the blood. The touching of the ear, thumb, and toe with the blood of the ram teaches us that in everything we hear and do and everywhere we go, we are to remember that we are bought with the precious blood of Christ.

25 And he took the fat, and the rump,
and all the fat that *was* upon the inwards, and the caul *above* the liver, and
the two kidneys, and their fat, and the
right shoulder:
26 And out of the basket of unleavened
bread, that *was* before the LORD, he took
one unleavened cake, and a cake of oiled
bread, and one wafer, and put *them* on
the fat, and upon the right shoulder:
27 And he put all upon Aaron's hands,
and upon his sons' hands, and waved
them *for* a wave-offering before the
LORD.
28 And Moses took them from off their
hands, and burnt *them* on the altar upon
the burnt-offering: they *were* consecrations for a sweet savour: it *is* an offering made by fire unto the LORD.
29 And Moses took the breast, and
waved it *for* a wave-offering before the
LORD: *for* of the ram of consecration it
was Moses' part; as the LORD commanded Moses.
30 And Moses took of the anointing oil,
and of the blood which *was* upon the altar, and sprinkled *it* upon Aaron, *and* upon
his garments, and upon his sons, and
upon his sons' garments with him;
and sanctified Aaron, *and* his garments,
and his sons, and his sons' garments
with him.
¶ 31 And Moses said unto Aaron and
to his sons, Boil the flesh *at* the door
of the tabernacle of the congregation:
and there eat it with the bread that *is*
in the basket of consecrations, as I commanded, saying, Aaron and his sons
shall eat it.
32 And that which remaineth of the
flesh and of the bread shall ye burn with
fire.
33 And ye shall not go out of the door
of the tabernacle of the congregation *in*
seven days, until the days of your consecration be at an end: for seven days
shall he *consecrate you.
34 As he hath done this day, *so* the
LORD hath commanded to do, to make
an atonement for you.
35 Therefore shall ye abide *at* the door
of the tabernacle of the congregation
day and night seven days, and keep the
charge of the LORD, that ye die not: for
so I am commanded.
36 So Aaron and his sons did all things
which the LORD commanded by the
hand of Moses.

The priests begin their ministry

9 And it came to pass on the eighth
day, *that* Moses called Aaron and
his sons, and the elders of Israel;
2 And he said unto Aaron, Take thee
a young calf for a sin-offering, and a ram
for a burnt-offering, without blemish,
and offer *them* before the LORD.
3 And unto the children of Israel thou
shalt speak, saying, Take ye a kid of the
goats for a sin-offering; and a calf and a
lamb, *both* of the first year, without
blemish, for a burnt-offering;
4 Also a bullock and a ram for *peace-
offerings, to sacrifice before the LORD;
and a *meat-offering mingled with
oil: for to day the LORD will appear unto
you.
¶ 5 And they brought *that* which Moses commanded before the tabernacle
of the congregation: and all the congregation drew near and stood before the
LORD.
6 And Moses said, This *is* the thing
which the LORD commanded that ye
should do: and the glory of the LORD
shall appear unto you.
7 And Moses said unto Aaron, Go unto
the altar, and offer thy sin-offering, and
thy burnt-offering, and make an atonement for thyself, and for the people: and
offer the offering of the people, and
make an atonement for them; as the
LORD commanded.
¶ 8 Aaron therefore went unto the altar, and slew the calf of the sin-offering,
which *was* for himself.
9 And the sons of Aaron brought the
blood unto him: and he dipped his finger
in the blood, and put *it* upon the horns
of the altar, and poured out the blood at
the bottom of the altar:
10 But the fat, and the kidneys, and the

caul above the liver of the sin-offering,
he burnt upon the altar; as the LORD
commanded Moses.
11 And the flesh and the hide he burnt
with fire without the camp.
12 And he slew the burnt-offering; and
Aaron's sons presented unto him the
blood, which he sprinkled round about
upon the altar.
13 And they presented the burnt-
offering unto him, with the pieces
thereof, and the head: and he burnt *them*
upon the altar.
14 And he did wash the inwards and
the legs, and burnt *them* upon the burnt-
offering on the altar.
¶ 15 And he brought the people's offering, and took the goat, which *was* the
sin-offering for the people, and slew it,
and offered it for sin, as the first.
16 And he brought the burnt-offering,
and offered it according to the manner.
17 And he brought the meat-offering,
and took an handful thereof, and burnt
it upon the altar, beside the burnt-
sacrifice of the morning.
18 He slew also the bullock and the
ram *for* a sacrifice of peace-offerings,
which *was* for the people: and Aaron's
sons presented unto him the blood,
which he sprinkled upon the altar round
about,
19 And the fat of the bullock and of the
ram, the rump, and that which covereth
the inwards, and the kidneys, and the
caul *above* the liver:
20 And they put the fat upon the
breasts, and he burnt the fat upon
the altar:
21 And the breasts and the right shoulder Aaron waved *for* a wave-offering
before the LORD; as Moses commanded.
22 And Aaron lifted up his hand toward the people, and blessed them,
and came down from offering of the
sin-offering, and the burnt-offering,
and peace-offerings.
23 And Moses and Aaron went into the
tabernacle of the congregation, and
came out, and blessed the people: and
the glory of the LORD appeared unto all
the people.
24 And there came a fire out from before the LORD, and consumed upon the
altar the burnt-offering and the fat:
which when all the people saw, they
shouted, and fell on their faces.

The story of Nadab and Abihu

10 And Nadab and Abihu, the
sons of Aaron, took either of
them his *censer, and put fire therein,
and put *incense thereon, and offered
strange fire before the LORD, which he
commanded them not.
2 And there went out fire from the
LORD, and devoured them, and they
died before the LORD.
3 Then Moses said unto Aaron, This
is it that the LORD spake, saying, I will
be sanctified in them that come nigh
me, and before all the people I will be
glorified. And Aaron held his peace.
4 And Moses called Mishael and Elzaphan, the sons of Uzziel the uncle of
Aaron, and said unto them, Come near,
carry your brethren from before the
*sanctuary out of the camp.

10:1-2 NADAB AND ABIHU

These were the two older sons of Aaron. Their sin was:

1. in offering incense at a time when God had not commanded it (Exod. 30:7-9);
2. in setting it alight with fire that they had kindled themselves, and not using the fire from the brazen altar which was always burning. See Leviticus 6:13.

God in His love and righteousness had to punish them severely in order to make it quite plain that reverence and care must be shown in His worship.

10:2 devoured them. God often dealt with people of the Old Testament in a severe way, especially when a sin first occurred, to show His displeasure and hatred of that sin. God's grace and love through Christ's blood spare us such punishment today.

5 So they went near, and carried them in their coats out of the camp; as Moses had said.

6 And Moses said unto Aaron, and unto Eleazar and unto Ithamar, his sons, Uncover not your heads, neither rend your clothes; lest ye die, and lest wrath come upon all the people: but let your brethren, the whole house of Israel, bewail the burning which the LORD hath kindled.

7 And ye shall not go out from the door of the tabernacle of the congregation, lest ye die: for the anointing oil of the LORD *is* upon you. And they did according to the word of Moses.

¶8 And the LORD spake unto Aaron, saying,

9 Do not drink *wine nor strong drink, thou, nor thy sons with thee, when ye go into the tabernacle of the congregation, lest ye die: *it shall be* a statute for ever throughout your generations:

10 And that ye may put difference between holy and unholy, and between unclean and *clean;

11 And that ye may teach the children of Israel all the statutes which the LORD hath spoken unto them by the hand of Moses.

¶12 And Moses spake unto Aaron, and unto Eleazar and unto Ithamar, his sons that were left, Take the meat-offering that remaineth of the offerings of the LORD made by fire, and eat it without *leaven beside the altar: for it *is* most holy:

13 And ye shall eat it in the holy place, because it *is* thy due, and thy sons' due, of the sacrifices of the LORD made by fire: for so I am commanded.

14 And the wave breast and heave shoulder shall ye eat in a clean place; thou, and thy sons, and thy daughters with thee: for *they be* thy due, and thy sons' due, *which* are given out of the sacrifices of peace-offerings of the children of Israel.

15 The heave shoulder and the wave breast shall they bring with the offerings made by fire of the fat, to wave *it for* a wave-offering before the LORD; and it shall be thine, and thy sons' with thee, by a statute for ever; as the LORD hath commanded.

¶16 And Moses diligently sought the goat of the *sin-offering, and, behold, it was burnt: and he was angry with Eleazar and Ithamar, the sons of Aaron *which were* left *alive,* saying,

17 Wherefore have ye not eaten the sin-offering in the holy place, seeing it *is* most holy, and **God* hath given it you to *bear the iniquity of the congregation, to make atonement for them before the LORD?

18 Behold, the blood of it was not brought in within the holy *place:* ye should indeed have eaten it in the holy *place,* as I commanded.

19 And Aaron said unto Moses, Behold, this day have they offered their sin-offering and their burnt-offering before the LORD; and such things have befallen me: and *if* I had eaten the sin-offering to day, should it have been accepted in the sight of the LORD?

20 And when Moses heard *that,* he was content.

IV. The Law of Purity (11–15)

A. Food

11 And the LORD spake unto Moses and to Aaron, saying unto them,

2 Speak unto the children of Israel, saying, These *are* the beasts which ye shall eat among all the beasts that *are* on the earth.

11:2 The Laws about Food

These laws about food were to keep the Israelites well.They show us the care that God always has for His people in every little detail of their lives. Obedience to these laws kept the Hebrews a very healthy race. Christians, however, are not under these particular laws today (see Col. 2:16-17), yet certainly we have rules of health made known to us instinctively according to the wisdom of God.

[3]Whatsoever parteth the hoof, and is
clovenfooted, *and* cheweth the cud,
among the beasts, that shall ye eat.
[4]Nevertheless these shall ye not eat
of them that chew the cud, or of them
that divide the hoof: *as* the camel, because he cheweth the cud, but divideth
not the hoof; he *is* *unclean unto you.
[5]And the coney, because he cheweth
the cud, but divideth not the hoof; he *is*
unclean unto you.
[6]And the hare, because he cheweth
the cud, but divideth not the hoof; he *is*
unclean unto you.
[7]And the swine, though he divide the
hoof, and be clovenfooted, yet he
cheweth not the cud; he *is* unclean to
you.
[8]Of their flesh shall ye not eat, and
their carcase shall ye not touch; they
are unclean to you.
¶[9]These shall ye eat of all that *are* in
the waters: whatsoever hath fins and
scales in the waters, in the seas, and in
the rivers, them shall ye eat.
[10]And all that have not fins and scales
in the seas, and in the rivers, of all that
move in the waters, and of any living
thing which *is* in the waters, they *shall
be* an abomination unto you:
[11]They shall be even an abomination
unto you; ye shall not eat of their flesh,
but ye shall have their carcases in
abomination.
[12]Whatsoever hath no fins nor scales
in the waters, that *shall be* an abomination unto you.
¶[13]And these *are they which* ye shall
have in abomination among the fowls;
they shall not be eaten, they *are* an
abomination: the eagle, and the ossifrage, and the ospray,
[14]And the vulture, and the kite after
his kind;
[15]Every raven after his kind;
[16]And the owl, and the night hawk,
and the cuckow, and the hawk after his
kind,
[17]And the little owl, and the cormorant, and the great owl,
[18]And the swan, and the pelican, and
the gier eagle,
[19]And the stork, the heron after her
kind, and the lapwing, and the bat.
[20]All fowls that creep, going upon *all*
four, *shall be* an abomination unto you.
[21]Yet these may ye eat of every flying creeping thing that goeth upon *all*
four, which have legs above their feet,
to leap withal upon the earth;
[22]*Even* these of them ye may eat; the
locust after his kind, and the bald locust
after his kind, and the beetle after his
kind, and the grasshopper after his
kind.
[23]But all *other* flying creeping things,
which have four feet, *shall be* an abomination unto you.
[24]And for these ye shall be unclean:
whosoever toucheth the carcase of
them shall be unclean until the even.
[25]And whosoever beareth *ought* of
the carcase of them shall wash his
clothes, and be unclean until the even.
[26]*The carcases* of every beast which
divideth the hoof, and *is* not clovenfooted, nor cheweth the cud, *are* unclean unto you: every one that toucheth
them shall be unclean.
[27]And whatsoever goeth upon his
paws, among all manner of beasts that
go on *all* four, those *are* unclean unto
you: whoso toucheth their carcase shall
be unclean until the even.
[28]And he that beareth the carcase of
them shall wash his clothes, and be
unclean until the even: they *are* unclean
unto you.
¶[29]These also *shall be* unclean unto
you among the creeping things that

11:5 coney. A rabbit.
11:6 hare. This is not the animal that we know by this name. We are not sure what animal is meant by the word *arnebeth,* here translated "hare."
11:7 swine. A pig.
11:13 ossifrage. A bearded vulture; literally, bone-breaker.

creep upon the earth; the weasel, and
the mouse, and the tortoise after his
kind,
30And the ferret, and the chameleon,
and the lizard, and the snail, and the
mole.
31These *are* unclean to you among all
that creep: whosoever doth touch them,
when they be dead, shall be unclean
until the even.
32And upon whatsoever *any* of them,
when they are dead, doth fall, it shall be
unclean; whether *it be* any vessel of
wood, or raiment, or skin, or sack, whatsoever vessel *it be,* wherein *any* work
is done, it must be put into water, and it
shall be unclean until the even; so it
shall be cleansed.
33And every earthen vessel, whereinto *any* of them falleth, whatsoever
is in it shall be unclean; and ye shall
break it.
34Of all meat which may be eaten,
that on which *such* water cometh shall
be unclean: and all drink that may be
drunk in every *such* vessel shall be
unclean.
35And every *thing* whereupon *any*
part of their carcase falleth shall be unclean; *whether it be* oven, or ranges for
pots, they shall be broken down: *for*
they *are* unclean, and shall be unclean
unto you.
36Nevertheless a fountain or pit,
wherein there is plenty of water, shall be
clean: but that which toucheth their
carcase shall be unclean.
37And if *any part* of their carcase fall
upon any sowing seed which is to be
sown, it *shall be* clean.
38But if *any* water be put upon the
seed, and *any part* of their carcase fall
thereon, it *shall be* unclean unto you.
39And if any beast, of which ye may
eat, die; he that toucheth the carcase
thereof shall be unclean until the even.
40And he that eateth of the carcase of
it shall wash his clothes, and be unclean
until the even: he also that beareth the
carcase of it shall wash his clothes, and
be unclean until the even.
41And every creeping thing that
creepeth upon the earth *shall be* an
abomination; it shall not be eaten.
42Whatsoever goeth upon the belly,
and whatsoever goeth upon *all* four, or
whatsoever hath more feet among all
creeping things that creep upon the
earth, them ye shall not eat; for they *are*
an abomination.
43Ye shall not make yourselves abominable with any creeping thing that
creepeth, neither shall ye make yourselves unclean with them, that ye
should be defiled thereby.

11:47 Clean and Unclean Animals
The general rule was that the Israelites could eat any land animal that had *both* divided hoofs *and* chewed the cud; or any water animal that had fins *and* scales. See the listings in Leviticus 11:1-47 and Deuteronomy 14:3-20.

Clean Creatures	Unclean Creatures
ox	camels
sheep	rock badgers
lambs	coneys
goats	swine
mountain sheep	lizards
wild goats	weasels
roebuck (gazelles)	eels
pygarg (antelopes)	shell fish
hart (deer)	catfish
fish	ossifrage
most birds	eagles
quail	vultures
doves	falcons
pigeons	kites
locusts	glede
crickets	ostriches
grasshoppers	owls
katydids	swan
beetles	cuckow (sea gulls)
chamois	hawks
	pelicans
	ospray
	cormorants
	storks
	herons
	lapwing (hoopoes)
	bats
	winged creatures
	snails

11:35 ranges. Chimney racks.

44 For I *am* the LORD your God: ye shall therefore sanctify yourselves, and ye shall be holy; for I *am* holy: neither shall ye defile yourselves with any manner of creeping thing that creepeth upon the earth.

45 For I *am* the LORD that bringeth you up out of the land of *Egypt, to be your God: ye shall therefore be holy, for I *am* holy.

46 This *is* the law of the beasts, and of the fowl, and of every living creature that moveth in the waters, and of every creature that creepeth upon the earth:

47 To make a difference between the *unclean and the clean, and between the beast that may be eaten and the beast that may not be eaten.

B. Motherhood

12 And the LORD spake unto Moses, saying,

2 Speak unto the children of Israel, saying, If a woman have conceived seed, and born a man child: then she shall be unclean seven days; according to the days of the separation for her infirmity shall she be unclean.

3 And in the eighth day the flesh of his foreskin shall be circumcised.

4 And she shall then continue in the blood of her purifying three and thirty days; she shall touch no hallowed thing, nor come into the sanctuary, until the days of her purifying be fulfilled.

5 But if she bear a maid child, then she shall be unclean two weeks, as in her separation: and she shall continue in the blood of her purifying threescore and six days.

6 And when the days of her purifying are fulfilled, for a son, or for a daughter, she shall bring a lamb of the first year for a burnt-offering, and a young pigeon, or a turtledove, for a sin-offering, unto the door of the tabernacle of the congregation, unto the priest:

7 Who shall offer it before the LORD, and make an atonement for her; and she shall be cleansed from the issue of her blood. This *is* the *law for her that hath born a male or a female.

8 And if she be not able to bring a lamb, then she shall bring two turtles, or two young pigeons; the one for the burnt-offering, and the other for a sin-offering: and the priest shall make an atonement for her, and she shall be clean.

C. Leprosy

13 And the LORD spake unto *Moses and *Aaron, saying,

2 When a man shall have in the skin of his flesh a rising, a scab, or bright spot, and it be in the skin of his flesh *like* the plague of *leprosy; then he shall be brought unto Aaron the priest, or unto one of his sons the priests:

3 And the priest shall look on the plague in the skin of the flesh: and *when* the hair in the plague is turned white, and the plague in sight *be* deeper than the skin of his flesh, it *is* a plague of leprosy: and the priest shall look on him, and pronounce him unclean.

13:2 A DISEASE CALLED LEPROSY

Leprosy was a loathsome and incurable disease and in the Bible is used as a *type of sin, because:

1. Just as it was a poison that got into the blood of a person, so people are born in sin (Ps. 51:5).
2. It showed itself first in small ways. People can pretend that they are not sinners; they can be outwardly good, but the sin and the poison are there just the same.
3. It was incurable by human means. Sin cannot be cleansed except by the blood of the Lord Jesus Christ (Acts 4:12; Heb. 9:22).
4. Just as lepers had to be sent away from the camp, so sin separates us from God (Isa. 59:2).

People in the Bible who had leprosy are to be found in Numbers 12; 2 Kings 5; Matthew 8:2; and Luke 17:12.

12:6 a young pigeon. See Luke 2:22-24.

4 If the bright spot *be* white in the skin
of his flesh, and in sight *be* not deeper
than the skin, and the hair thereof be
not turned white; then the priest shall
shut up *him that hath* the plague seven
days:
5 And the priest shall look on him the
seventh day: and, behold, *if* the plague
in his sight be at a stay, *and* the plague
spread not in the skin; then the priest
shall shut him up seven days more:
6 And the priest shall look on him
again the seventh day: and, behold, *if*
the plague *be* somewhat dark, *and* the
plague spread not in the skin, the priest
shall pronounce him clean: it *is but* a
scab: and he shall wash his clothes, and
be clean.
7 But if the scab spread much abroad
in the skin, after that he hath been seen
of the priest for his cleansing, he shall
be seen of the priest again:
8 And *if* the priest see that, behold,
the scab spreadeth in the skin, then the
priest shall pronounce him unclean: it
is a leprosy.
¶ 9 When the plague of leprosy is in a
man, then he shall be brought unto the
priest;
10 And the priest shall see *him:* and,
behold, *if* the rising *be* white in the skin,
and it have turned the hair white, and
there be quick raw flesh in the rising;
11 It *is* an old leprosy in the skin of his
flesh, and the priest shall pronounce
him unclean, and shall not shut him up:
for he *is* unclean.
12 And if a leprosy break out abroad in
the skin, and the leprosy cover all the
skin of *him that hath* the plague from his
head even to his foot, wheresoever the
priest looketh;
13 Then the priest shall consider: and,
behold, *if* the leprosy have covered all
his flesh, he shall pronounce *him* clean
that hath the plague: it is all turned
white: he *is* clean.
14 But when raw flesh appeareth in
him, he shall be unclean.
15 And the priest shall see the raw
flesh, and pronounce him to be unclean:
for the raw flesh *is* unclean: it *is* a leprosy.
16 Or if the raw flesh turn again, and
be changed unto white, he shall come
unto the priest;
17 And the priest shall see him: and,
behold, *if* the plague be turned into
white; then the priest shall pronounce
him clean *that hath* the plague: he *is*
clean.
¶ 18 The flesh also, in which, *even* in the
skin thereof, was a boil, and is healed,
19 And in the place of the boil there be
a white rising, or a bright spot, white,
and somewhat reddish, and it be
shewed to the priest;
20 And if, when the priest seeth it,
behold, it *be* in sight lower than the
skin, and the hair thereof be turned
white; the priest shall pronounce him
unclean: it *is* a plague of leprosy broken
out of the boil.
21 But if the priest look on it, and,
behold, *there be* no white hairs therein,
and *if* it *be* not lower than the skin, but
be somewhat dark; then the priest shall
shut him up seven days:
22 And if it spread much abroad in the
skin, then the priest shall pronounce
him unclean: it *is* a plague.
23 But if the bright spot stay in his
place, *and* spread not, it *is* a burning
boil; and the priest shall pronounce him
clean.
¶ 24 Or if there be *any* flesh, in the skin
whereof *there is* a hot burning, and the
quick *flesh* that burneth have a white
bright spot, somewhat reddish, or
white;
25 Then the priest shall look upon it:
and, behold, *if* the hair in the bright spot
be turned white, and it *be in* sight deeper than the skin; it *is* a leprosy broken
out of the burning: wherefore the priest
shall pronounce him unclean: it *is* the
plague of leprosy.
26 But if the priest look on it, and,
behold, *there be* no white hair in the
bright spot, and it *be* no lower than the
other skin, but *be* somewhat dark; then
the priest shall shut him up seven days:

27 And the priest shall look upon him
the seventh day: *and* if it be spread
much abroad in the skin, then the priest
shall pronounce him unclean: it *is* the
plague of leprosy.
28 And if the bright spot stay in his
place, *and* spread not in the skin, but it
be somewhat dark; it *is* a rising of the
burning, and the priest shall pronounce
him clean: for it *is* an inflammation of
the burning.
¶ 29 If a man or woman have a plague
upon the head or the beard;
30 Then the priest shall see the
plague: and, behold, if it *be* in sight
deeper than the skin; *and there be* in it
a yellow thin hair; then the priest shall
pronounce him unclean: it *is* a dry scall,
even a leprosy upon the head or beard.
31 And if the priest look on the plague
of the scall, and, behold, it *be* not in sight
deeper than the skin, and *that there is*
no black hair in it; then the priest shall
shut up *him that hath* the plague of the
scall seven days:
32 And in the seventh day the priest
shall look on the plague: and, behold, *if*
the scall spread not, and there be in it
no yellow hair, and the scall *be* not in
sight deeper than the skin;
33 He shall be shaven, but the scall
shall he not shave; and the priest shall
shut up *him that hath* the scall seven
days more:
34 And in the seventh day the priest
shall look on the scall: and, behold, *if*
the scall be not spread in the skin, nor
be in sight deeper than the skin; then
the priest shall pronounce him clean:
and he shall wash his clothes, and be
clean.
35 But if the scall spread much in the
skin after his cleansing;
36 Then the priest shall look on him:
and, behold, if the scall be spread in the
skin, the priest shall not seek for yellow hair; he *is* unclean.
37 But if the scall be in his sight at a
stay, and *that* there is black hair grown
up therein; the scall is healed, he *is*
clean: and the priest shall pronounce
him clean.
¶ 38 If a man also or a woman have in
the skin of their flesh bright spots, *even*
white bright spots;
39 Then the priest shall look: and,
behold, *if* the bright spots in the skin of
their flesh *be* darkish white; it *is* a freck-
led spot *that* groweth in the skin; he *is*
clean.
40 And the man whose hair is fallen off
his head, he *is* bald; *yet is* he clean.
41 And he that hath his hair fallen off
from the part of his head toward his
face, he *is* forehead bald: *yet is* he clean.
42 And if there be in the bald head, or
bald forehead, a white reddish sore; it
is a leprosy sprung up in his bald head,
or his bald forehead.
43 Then the priest shall look upon it:
and, behold, *if* the rising of the sore *be*
white reddish in his bald head, or in his
bald forehead, as the leprosy appeareth
in the skin of the flesh;
44 He is a *leprous man, he *is* unclean:
the priest shall pronounce him utterly
unclean; his plague *is* in his head.
45 And the leper in whom the plague
is, his clothes shall be rent, and his head
bare, and he shall put a covering upon
his upper lip, and shall cry, Unclean,
unclean.
46 All the days wherein the plague
shall be in him he shall be defiled; he *is*
unclean: he shall dwell alone; without
the camp *shall* his habitation *be.*
¶ 47 The garment also that the plague
of leprosy is in, *whether it be* a woollen
garment, or a *linen garment;
48 Whether *it be* in the warp, or woof;
of linen, or of woollen; whether in a
skin, or in any thing made of skin;
49 And if the plague be greenish or
reddish in the garment, or in the skin,
either in the warp, or in the woof, or
in any thing of skin; it *is* a plague of

13:30,33 scall. An open wound or sore on the head or face.
13:45 rent. Torn.

leprosy, and shall be shewed unto the
priest:
50 And the priest shall look upon
the plague, and shut up *it that hath* the
plague seven days:
51 And he shall look on the plague on
the seventh day: if the plague be spread
in the garment, either in the warp, or
in the woof, or in a skin, *or* in any work
that is made of skin; the plague *is* a fretting leprosy; it *is* unclean.
52 He shall therefore burn that garment, whether warp or woof, in woollen
or in linen, or any thing of skin, wherein
the plague is: for it *is* a fretting leprosy; it shall be burnt in the fire.
53 And if the priest shall look, and,
behold, the plague be not spread in the
garment, either in the warp, or in the
woof, or in any thing of skin;
54 Then the priest shall command that
they wash *the thing* wherein the plague
is, and he shall shut it up seven days
more:
55 And the priest shall look on the
plague, after that it is washed: and, behold, *if* the plague have not changed his
colour, and the plague be not spread; it
is unclean; thou shalt burn it in the fire;
it *is* fret inward, *whether* it *be* bare within
or without.
56 And if the priest look, and, behold,
the plague *be* somewhat dark after the
washing of it; then he shall rend it out
of the garment, or out of the skin, or out
of the warp, or out of the woof:
57 And if it appear still in the garment,
either in the warp, or in the woof, or in
any thing of skin; it *is* a spreading
plague: thou shalt burn that wherein the
plague *is* with fire.
58 And the garment, either warp, or
woof, or whatsoever thing of skin *it*
be, which thou shalt wash, if the plague
be departed from them, then it shall be
washed the second time, and shall be
clean.
59 This *is* the law of the plague of leprosy in a garment of woollen or linen,
either in the warp, or woof, or any thing
of skins, to pronounce it clean, or to
pronounce it unclean.

The cleansing of the leper

14 And the LORD spake unto Moses, saying,
2 This shall be the law of the leper in
the day of his cleansing: He shall be
brought unto the priest:

14:2 The Method of Cleansing
No leper was ever cured by medicines, but God by a miracle sometimes healed, as in the case of Naaman (2 Kings 5). The rules to be observed in such a case are an interesting *type of our cleansing from sin. Two birds were taken—one was killed and the other was dipped in the blood of the slain bird and released. As the living bird rose into the air with his wings and body splattered with blood, it would look to the leper as if the slain bird were raised from the dead. It was a picture of what Christ would do someday for all of us, who are sinners. He was crucified for our sins but raised from the dead and ascended into heaven, showing that the work of saving us was finished. See Romans 4:25.

3 And the priest shall go forth out of
the camp; and the priest shall look, and,
behold, *if* the plague of leprosy be
healed in the leper;
4 Then shall the priest command to
take for him that is to be cleansed two
*birds alive *and* clean, and cedar wood,
and scarlet, and *hyssop:
5 And the priest shall command that
one of the birds be killed in an earthen
vessel over running water:
6 As for the living bird, he shall take
it, and the cedar wood, and the scarlet,
and the hyssop, and shall dip them and
the living bird in the *blood of the bird
that was killed over the running water:
7 And he shall sprinkle upon him that
is to be cleansed from the leprosy seven
times, and shall pronounce him clean,
and shall let the living bird loose into
the open field.

13:51-52 fretting. To "fret" is to corrode or to eat away, as an ulcer does.

8 And he that is to be cleansed shall
wash his clothes, and shave off all his
hair, and wash himself in water, that he
may be clean: and after that he shall
come into the camp, and shall tarry
abroad out of his tent seven days.
9 But it shall be on the seventh day,
that he shall shave all his hair off his
head and his beard and his eyebrows,
even all his hair he shall shave off: and
he shall wash his clothes, also he shall
wash his flesh in water, and he shall be
clean.
10 And on the eighth day he shall take
two he lambs without blemish, and one
ewe lamb of the first year without blemish, and three tenth deals of fine flour
for a meat-offering, mingled with *oil,
and one log of oil.
11 And the priest that maketh *him*
clean shall present the man that is to be
made clean, and those things, before
the LORD, *at* the door of the *tabernacle of the congregation:
12 And the priest shall take one he
lamb, and offer him for a *trespass-
offering, and the log of oil, and wave
them *for* a wave-offering before the
LORD:
13 And he shall slay the lamb in the
place where he shall kill the sin-offering
and the burnt-offering, in the holy
place: for as the sin-offering *is* the
priest's, *so is* the trespass-offering: it *is*
most holy:
14 And the priest shall take *some* of
the blood of the trespass-offering, and
the priest shall put *it* upon the tip of the
right ear of him that is to be cleansed,
and upon the thumb of his right hand,
and upon the great toe of his right foot:
15 And the priest shall take *some* of the
log of oil, and pour *it* into the palm of
his own left hand:
16 And the priest shall dip his right
finger in the oil that *is* in his left hand,
and shall sprinkle of the oil with his finger seven times before the LORD:
17 And of the rest of the oil that *is* in
his hand shall the priest put upon the
tip of the right ear of him that is to be
cleansed, and upon the thumb of his
right hand, and upon the great toe of
his right foot, upon the blood of the
trespass-offering:
18 And the remnant of the oil that *is*
in the priest's hand he shall pour upon
the head of him that is to be cleansed:
and the priest shall make an *atonement for him before the LORD.
19 And the priest shall offer the sin-
offering, and make an atonement for
him that is to be cleansed from his uncleanness; and afterward he shall kill
the burnt-offering:
20 And the priest shall offer the burnt-
offering and the meat-offering upon the
*altar: and the priest shall make an
atonement for him, and he shall be clean.
21 And if he *be* poor, and cannot get so
much; then he shall take one lamb *for* a
trespass-offering to be waved, to make
an atonement for him, and one *tenth
deal of fine flour mingled with oil for a
meat-offering, and a log of oil;
22 And two turtledoves, or two young
pigeons, such as he is able to get; and
the one shall be a sin-offering, and the
other a burnt-offering.
23 And he shall bring them on the
eighth day for his cleansing unto the
priest, unto the door of the tabernacle
of the congregation, before the LORD.
24 And the priest shall take the lamb
of the trespass-offering, and the log of
oil, and the priest shall wave them *for*
a wave-offering before the LORD:
25 And he shall kill the lamb of the
trespass-offering, and the priest shall
take *some* of the blood of the trespass-
offering, and put *it* upon the tip of the
right ear of him that is to be cleansed,
and upon the thumb of his right hand,
and upon the great toe of his right foot:
26 And the priest shall pour of the oil
into the palm of his own left hand:
27 And the priest shall sprinkle with
his right finger *some* of the oil that *is* in

14:10 one log. A log is about one-half pint.

his left hand seven times before the
LORD:
28 And the priest shall put of the oil
that *is* in his hand upon the tip of the
right ear of him that is to be cleansed,
and upon the thumb of his right hand,
and upon the great toe of his right foot,
upon the place of the blood of the trespass-offering:
29 And the rest of the oil that *is* in the
priest's hand he shall put upon the head
of him that is to be cleansed, to make
an atonement for him before the LORD.
30 And he shall offer the one of the
turtledoves, or of the young pigeons,
such as he can get;
31 *Even* such as he is able to get, the
one *for* a sin-offering, and the other
for a burnt-offering, with the meat-
offering: and the priest shall make an
atonement for him that is to be cleansed
before the LORD.
32 This *is* the law *of him* in whom *is*
the plague of leprosy, whose hand is not
able to get *that which pertaineth* to his
cleansing.
¶33 And the LORD spake unto Moses
and unto Aaron, saying,
34 When ye be come into the land of
Canaan, which I give to you for a possession, and I put the plague of leprosy
in a house of the land of your possession;
35 And he that owneth the house shall
come and tell the priest, saying, It
seemeth to me *there is* as it were a
plague in the house:
36 Then the priest shall command that
they empty the house, before the priest
go *into it* to see the plague, that all that
is in the house be not made unclean:
and afterward the priest shall go in to
see the house:
37 And he shall look on the plague,
and, behold, *if* the plague *be* in the walls
of the house with hollow strakes,
greenish or reddish, which in sight *are*
lower than the wall;
38 Then the priest shall go out of the
house to the door of the house, and shut
up the house seven days:
39 And the priest shall come again the
seventh day, and shall look: and, behold,
if the plague be spread in the walls of
the house;
40 Then the priest shall command that
they take away the stones in which the
plague *is*, and they shall cast them into
an unclean place without the city:
41 And he shall cause the house to be
scraped within round about, and they
shall pour out the dust that they scrape
off without the city into an unclean place:
42 And they shall take other stones,
and put *them* in the place of those
stones; and he shall take other morter,
and shall plaister the house.
43 And if the plague come again, and
break out in the house, after that he
hath taken away the stones, and after
he hath scraped the house, and after it
is plaistered;
44 Then the priest shall come and
look, and, behold, *if* the plague be
spread in the house, it *is* a fretting leprosy in the house: it *is* unclean.
45 And he shall break down the house,
the stones of it, and the timber thereof,
and all the morter of the house; and he
shall carry *them* forth out of the city into
an unclean place.
46 Moreover he that goeth into the
house all the while that it is shut up
shall be unclean until the even.
47 And he that lieth in the house shall
wash his clothes; and he that eateth in
the house shall wash his clothes.
48 And if the priest shall come in, and
look *upon it*, and, behold, the plague
hath not spread in the house, after the
house was plaistered: then the priest
shall pronounce the house clean, because the plague is healed.
49 And he shall take to cleanse the
house two birds, and cedar wood, and
scarlet, and hyssop:

14:34 the plague of leprosy in a house. See Leviticus 13:2; compare Numbers 5:2 and Zechariah 3:4 notes.

[50]And he shall kill the one of the
birds in an earthen vessel over running
water:
[51]And he shall take the cedar wood,
and the hyssop, and the scarlet, and the
living bird, and dip them in the blood of
the slain bird, and in the running water,
and sprinkle the house seven times:
[52]And he shall cleanse the house with
the blood of the bird, and with the running water, and with the living bird, and
with the cedar wood, and with the hyssop, and with the scarlet:
[53]But he shall let go the living bird
out of the city into the open fields, and
make an atonement for the house: and
it shall be clean.
[54]This *is* the law for all manner of
plague of leprosy, and scall,
[55]And for the leprosy of a garment,
and of a house,
[56]And for a rising, and for a scab, and
for a bright spot:
[57]To teach when *it is* unclean, and
when *it is* clean: this *is* the law of leprosy.

Law of cleanliness

15 And the LORD spake unto Moses and to Aaron, saying,
[2]Speak unto the children of *Israel,
and say unto them, When any man hath
a running issue out of his flesh, *because
of* his issue he *is* unclean.
[3]And this shall be his uncleanness in
his issue: whether his flesh run with his
issue, or his flesh be stopped from his
issue, it *is* his uncleanness.
[4]Every bed, whereon he lieth that
hath the issue, is unclean: and every
thing, whereon he sitteth, shall be unclean.
[5]And whosoever toucheth his bed
shall wash his clothes, and bathe *himself* in water, and be unclean until the
even.
[6]And he that sitteth on *any* thing
whereon he sat that hath the issue shall
wash his clothes, and bathe *himself* in
water, and be unclean until the even.
[7]And he that toucheth the flesh of
him that hath the issue shall wash his
clothes, and bathe *himself* in water, and
be unclean until the even.
[8]And if he that hath the issue spit
upon him that is clean; then he shall
wash his clothes, and bathe *himself* in
water, and be unclean until the even.
[9]And what saddle soever he rideth
upon that hath the issue shall be unclean.
[10]And whosoever toucheth any thing
that was under him shall be unclean
until the even: and he that beareth *any
of* those things shall wash his clothes,
and bathe *himself* in water, and be unclean until the even.
[11]And whomsoever he toucheth that
hath the issue, and hath not rinsed his
hands in water, he shall wash his
clothes, and bathe *himself* in water, and
be unclean until the even.
[12]And the vessel of earth, that he
toucheth which hath the issue, shall be
broken: and every vessel of wood shall
be rinsed in water.
[13]And when he that hath an issue is
cleansed of his issue; then he shall
number to himself seven days for his
cleansing, and wash his clothes, and
bathe his flesh in running water, and
shall be clean.
[14]And on the eighth day he shall take
to him two turtledoves, or two young
pigeons, and come before the LORD
unto the door of the tabernacle of the
congregation, and give them unto the
priest:
[15]And the priest shall offer them, the
one *for* a sin-offering, and the other *for*
a burnt-offering; and the priest shall
make an atonement for him before the
LORD for his issue.
[16]And if any man's seed of copulation

14:49 scarlet. A band of twice-dyed scarlet wool tied together the living bird, the hyssop (see Exod. 12:22), and the cedar after they were dipped into the blood. Scarlet is the color of redemption.

go out from him, then he shall wash all
his flesh in water, and be unclean until
the even.
17 And every garment, and every
skin, whereon is the seed of copulation,
shall be washed with water, and be unclean until the even.
18 The woman also with whom man
shall lie *with* seed of copulation, they
shall *both* bathe *themselves* in water, and
be unclean until the even.
¶ 19 And if a woman have an issue, *and*
her issue in her flesh be blood, she shall
be put apart seven days: and whosoever
toucheth her shall be unclean until the
even.
20 And every thing that she lieth upon
in her separation shall be unclean:
every thing also that she sitteth upon
shall be unclean.
21 And whosoever toucheth her bed
shall wash his clothes, and bathe *himself* in water, and be unclean until the
even.
22 And whosoever toucheth any thing
that she sat upon shall wash his clothes,
and bathe *himself* in water, and be unclean until the even.
23 And if it *be* on *her* bed, or on any
thing whereon she sitteth, when he
toucheth it, he shall be unclean until the
even.
24 And if any man lie with her at all,
and her flowers be upon him, he shall
be unclean seven days; and all the bed
whereon he lieth shall be unclean.
25 And if a woman have an issue of her
blood many days out of the time of her
separation, or if it run beyond the time
of her separation; all the days of the
issue of her uncleanness shall be as the
days of her separation: she *shall be* unclean.
26 Every bed whereon she lieth all the
days of her issue shall be unto her as
the bed of her separation: and whatsoever she sitteth upon shall be unclean,
as the uncleanness of her separation.
27 And whosoever toucheth those
things shall be unclean, and shall wash
his clothes, and bathe *himself* in water,
and be unclean until the even.
28 But if she be cleansed of her issue,
then she shall number to herself seven
days, and after that she shall be clean.
29 And on the eighth day she shall take
unto her two turtles, or two young pigeons, and bring them unto the priest,
to the door of the tabernacle of the congregation.
30 And the priest shall offer the one *for*
a sin-offering, and the other *for* a burnt-
offering; and the priest shall make an
atonement for her before the LORD for
the issue of her uncleanness.
31 Thus shall ye separate the children
of Israel from their uncleanness; that
they die not in their uncleanness, when
they defile my tabernacle that *is* among
them.
32 This *is* the law of him that hath an
issue, and *of him* whose seed goeth
from him, and is defiled therewith;
33 And of her that is sick of her flowers, and of him that hath an issue, of the
man, and of the woman, and of him that
lieth with her that is unclean.

V. The Law of the Day of Atonement (16)

16 And the LORD spake unto Moses after the *death of the two
sons of Aaron, when they offered before
the LORD, and died;
2 And the LORD said unto Moses,
Speak unto Aaron thy brother, that he
come not at all times into the holy *place*
within the vail before the *mercy seat,
which *is* upon the *ark; that he die not:
for I will appear in the cloud upon the
mercy seat.
3 Thus shall Aaron come into the holy
place: with a young bullock for a *sin-
offering, and a ram for a burnt-offering.
4 He shall put on the holy linen coat,
and he shall have the linen breeches
upon his flesh, and shall be girded with

16:1 the death of the two sons. See Leviticus 10:1-2.
16:4 attired. Covered (as on his head).

a linen girdle, and with the linen mitre
shall he be attired: these *are* holy *garments; therefore shall he wash his flesh
in water, and *so* put them on.
5And he shall take of the congregation of the children of Israel two kids of
the goats for a sin-offering, and one ram
for a burnt-offering.
6And Aaron shall offer his bullock of
the sin-offering, which *is* for himself,
and make an atonement for himself, and
for his house.
7And he shall take the two goats, and
present them before the LORD *at* the
door of the tabernacle of the congregation.
8And Aaron shall cast lots upon the
two goats; one lot for the LORD, and the
other lot for the scapegoat.
9And Aaron shall bring the goat upon
which the LORD'S lot fell, and offer him
for a sin-offering.
10But the goat, on which the lot fell
to be the scapegoat, shall be presented
alive before the LORD, to make an
atonement with him, *and* to let him go
for a scapegoat into the wilderness.
11And Aaron shall bring the bullock
of the sin-offering, which *is* for himself,
and shall make an atonement for himself, and for his house, and shall kill the
bullock of the sin-offering which *is* for
himself:
12And he shall take a *censer full of
burning coals of fire from off the altar
before the LORD, and his hands full of
sweet *incense beaten small, and bring
it within the vail:
13And he shall put the incense upon
the fire before the LORD, that the cloud
of the incense may cover the mercy
seat that *is* upon the testimony, that he
die not:
14And he shall take of the blood of the
bullock, and sprinkle *it* with his finger
upon the mercy seat eastward; and before the mercy seat shall he sprinkle of
the blood with his finger seven times.
¶15Then shall he kill the goat of the
sin-offering, that *is* for the people, and
bring his blood within the vail, and do
with that blood as he did with the blood
of the bullock, and sprinkle it upon the
mercy seat, and before the mercy seat:
16And he shall make an atonement for
the holy *place,* because of the uncleanness of the children of Israel, and because of their transgressions in all their
sins: and so shall he do for the tabernacle of the congregation, that remaineth
among them in the midst of their uncleanness.
17And there shall be no man in the
tabernacle of the congregation when he
goeth in to make an atonement in the
holy *place,* until he come out, and have
made an atonement for himself, and for
his household, and for all the congregation of Israel.
18And he shall go out unto the altar
that *is* before the LORD, and make an
atonement for it; and shall take of the
blood of the bullock, and of the blood of
the goat, and put *it* upon the *horns of
the altar round about.
19And he shall sprinkle of the blood
upon it with his finger seven times, and
cleanse it, and hallow it from the uncleanness of the children of Israel.
¶20And when he hath made an end of
reconciling the holy *place,* and the tabernacle of the congregation, and the
altar, he shall bring the live goat:
21And Aaron shall lay both his hands
upon the head of the live goat, and *confess over him all the iniquities of the
children of Israel, and all their transgressions in all their sins, putting them
upon the head of the goat, and shall
send *him* away by the hand of a fit man
into the wilderness:
22And the goat shall bear upon him all
their iniquities unto a land not inhabited: and he shall let go the goat in the
wilderness.
23And Aaron shall come into the tabernacle of the congregation, and shall
put off the linen garments, which he put

16:5 two kids of the goats. See verse 30 note.

on when he went into the holy *place,*
and shall leave them there:
24 And he shall wash his flesh with
water in the holy place, and put on his
garments, and come forth, and offer his
burnt-offering, and the burnt-offering of
the people, and make an atonement for
himself, and for the people.
25 And the fat of the sin-offering shall
he burn upon the altar.
26 And he that let go the goat for the
scapegoat shall wash his clothes, and
bathe his flesh in water, and afterward
come into the camp.
27 And the bullock *for* the sin-offering,
and the goat *for* the sin-offering, whose
blood was brought in to make atonement in the holy *place,* shall *one* carry
forth without the camp; and they shall
burn in the fire their skins, and their
flesh, and their *dung.
28 And he that burneth them shall
wash his clothes, and bathe his flesh in
water, and afterward he shall come into
the camp.
¶29 And *this* shall be a statute for ever
unto you: *that* in the seventh *month,
on the tenth *day* of the month, ye shall
afflict your souls, and do no work at all,
whether it be one of your own country,
or a stranger that sojourneth among
you:
30 For on that day shall *the priest* make
an atonement for you, to cleanse you,
that ye may be *clean from all your sins
before the LORD.
31 It *shall be* a *sabbath of rest unto
you, and ye shall afflict your souls, by a
statute for ever.
32 And the priest, whom he shall
*anoint, and whom he shall *consecrate
to minister in the priest's office in his
father's stead, shall make the atonement, and shall put on the linen clothes,
even the holy garments:
33 And he shall make an atonement for
the holy *sanctuary, and he shall make
an atonement for the tabernacle of the
congregation, and for the altar, and he
shall make an atonement for the
priests, and for all the people of the
congregation.
34 And this shall be an everlasting
statute unto you, to make an atonement
for the children of Israel for all their sins
once a year. And he did as the LORD
commanded Moses.

VI. The Law of Sacrifice (17)

17 And the LORD spake unto Moses, saying,
2 Speak unto Aaron, and unto his
sons, and unto all the children of Israel,
and say unto them; This *is* the thing
which the LORD hath commanded, saying,
3 What man soever *there be* of the
house of Israel, that killeth an ox, or
lamb, or goat, in the camp, or that
killeth *it* out of the camp,
4 And bringeth it not unto the door of
the tabernacle of the congregation, to
offer an offering unto the LORD before
the tabernacle of the LORD; blood shall
be imputed unto that man; he hath shed
blood; and that man shall be cut off from
among his people:
5 To the end that the children of Israel

16:30 THE DAY OF ATONEMENT

On the Day of Atonement, which was held once a year, the high priest offered a sacrifice for the sins of all the people. The meaning of this day is explained in Hebrews 9:11-28. From Hebrews, we learn that the Day of Atonement is a picture of the work of the Lord Jesus Christ in two ways:

1. As the High Priest. This is explained in the notes on Hebrews 9.
2. As the sacrifice of the two goats. One goat was killed as a sin-offering. The other, called the scapegoat, was set free and sent away to be lost in the desert after the sins of the people had been confessed over it. This teaches us that Christ not only died for our sins on the cross, but also that our sins are completely removed (Heb. 10:10,17). God says that He will remember them no more (Jer. 31:34).

may bring their sacrifices, which they
offer in the open field, even that they
may bring them unto the LORD, unto the
door of the tabernacle of the congregation, unto the priest, and offer them *for*
*peace-offerings unto the LORD.
6 And the priest shall sprinkle the
blood upon the altar of the LORD *at* the
door of the tabernacle of the congregation, and burn the fat for a sweet savour
unto the LORD.
7 And they shall no more offer their
sacrifices unto devils, after whom they
have gone a whoring. This shall be a
statute for ever unto them throughout
their generations.
¶ 8 And thou shalt say unto them,
Whatsoever man *there be* of the house
of Israel, or of the strangers which sojourn among you, that offereth a burnt-offering of *sacrifice,
9 And bringeth it not unto the door of
the tabernacle of the congregation, to
offer it unto the LORD; even that man
shall be cut off from among his people.
¶ 10 And whatsoever man *there be* of
the house of Israel, or of the strangers
that sojourn among you, that eateth any
manner of blood; I will even set my face
against that soul that eateth blood, and
will cut him off from among his people.
11 For the life of the flesh *is* in the
blood: and I have given it to you upon
the altar to make an atonement for your
souls: for it *is* the blood *that* maketh an
atonement for the soul.
12 Therefore I said unto the children
of Israel, No soul of you shall eat blood,
neither shall any stranger that
sojourneth among you eat blood.
13 And whatsoever man *there be* of the
children of Israel, or of the strangers
that sojourn among you, which hunteth
and catcheth any beast or fowl that may
be eaten; he shall even pour out the
blood thereof, and cover it with dust.
14 For *it is* the life of all flesh; the blood
of it *is* for the life thereof: therefore I
said unto the children of Israel, Ye shall
eat the blood of no manner of flesh: for
the life of all flesh *is* the blood thereof:
whosoever eateth it shall be cut off.
15 And every soul that eateth that
which died *of itself,* or that which was
torn *with beasts, whether it be* one of
your own country, or a stranger, he shall
both wash his clothes, and bathe *himself* in water, and be *unclean until the
even: then shall he be clean.
16 But if he wash *them* not, nor bathe
his flesh; then he shall bear his iniquity.

17:10 Forbidden Blood

Eating blood was forbidden because blood was to be used as an offering for atonement and to be sprinkled on the mercy seat. Serious consequences were prescribed by God for those who violated this command. When the blood of the animal was shed and put on the altar, it showed that the life had been given up for someone else. So when we speak of the blood of the Lord Jesus Christ, we mean that the blood showed that His life was given up on the cross for us.

VII. The Law of Human Relationships (18–22)

18 And the LORD spake unto Moses, saying,
2 Speak unto the children of Israel,
and say unto them, I am the LORD your
*God.
3 After the doings of the land of
*Egypt, wherein ye dwelt, shall ye not
do: and after the doings of the land of
Canaan, whither I bring you, shall ye
not do: neither shall ye walk in their
ordinances.
4 Ye shall do my judgments, and keep
mine ordinances, to walk therein: I *am*
the LORD your God.

17:11 it is the blood that maketh an atonement. This verse is just as important in the Old Testament as Hebrews 9:22 is in the New Testament. Both tell us that sin can be covered and forgiven only through shed blood; both testify to the death of our Lord on Calvary.

5Ye shall therefore keep my statutes,
and my judgments: which if a man do,
he shall live in them: I *am* the LORD.
¶6None of you shall approach to any
that is near of kin to him, to uncover
their nakedness: I *am* the LORD.
7The nakedness of thy father, or the
nakedness of thy mother, shalt thou not
uncover: she *is* thy mother; thou shalt
not uncover her nakedness.
8The nakedness of thy father's wife
shalt thou not uncover: it *is* thy father's
nakedness.
9The nakedness of thy sister, the
daughter of thy father, or daughter of
thy mother, *whether she be* born at
home, or born abroad, *even* their nakedness thou shalt not uncover.
10The nakedness of thy son's daughter, or of thy daughter's daughter, *even*
their nakedness thou shalt not uncover: for theirs *is* thine own nakedness.
11The nakedness of thy father's
wife's daughter, begotten of thy father,
she *is* thy sister, thou shalt not uncover her nakedness.
12Thou shalt not uncover the nakedness of thy father's sister: she *is* thy
father's near kinswoman.
13Thou shalt not uncover the nakedness of thy mother's sister: for she *is*
thy mother's near kinswoman.
14Thou shalt not uncover the nakedness of thy father's brother, thou shalt
not approach to his wife: she *is* thine
aunt.
15Thou shalt not uncover the nakedness of thy daughter in law: she *is* thy
son's wife; thou shalt not uncover her
nakedness.
16Thou shalt not uncover the nakedness of thy brother's wife: it *is* thy
brother's nakedness.
17Thou shalt not uncover the nakedness of a woman and her daughter, neither shalt thou take her son's daughter,
or her daughter's daughter, to uncover
her nakedness; *for* they *are* her near
kinswomen: it *is* wickedness.
18Neither shalt thou take a wife to her
sister, to vex *her,* to uncover her nakedness, beside the other in her life *time.*
19Also thou shalt not approach unto
a woman to uncover her nakedness, as
long as she is put apart for her uncleanness.
20Moreover thou shalt not lie carnally
with thy neighbour's wife, to defile thyself with her.
21And thou shalt not let any of thy
seed pass through *the fire* to *Molech,
neither shalt thou profane the name of
thy God: I *am* the LORD.
22Thou shalt not lie with mankind, as
with womankind: it *is* *abomination.
23Neither shalt thou lie with any
beast to defile thyself therewith: neither shall any woman stand before a
beast to lie down thereto: it *is* confusion.
24Defile not ye yourselves in any of
these things: for in all these the nations
are defiled which I cast out before you:
25And the land is defiled: therefore I
do visit the iniquity thereof upon it, and
the land itself vomiteth out her inhabitants.
26Ye shall therefore keep my statutes
and my judgments, and shall not commit *any* of these abominations; *neither*
any of your own nation, nor any stranger that sojourneth among you:
27(For all these abominations have
the men of the land done, which *were*
before you, and the land is defiled;)
28That the land spue not you out also,
when ye defile it, as it spued out the
nations that *were* before you.
29For whosoever shall commit any of
these abominations, even the souls that
commit *them* shall be cut off from
among their people.
30Therefore shall ye keep mine ordinance, that *ye* commit not *any one* of
these abominable customs, which were
committed before you, and that ye defile not yourselves therein: I *am* the
LORD your God.

19 And the LORD spake unto *Moses, saying,
2Speak unto all the congregation of
the children of Israel, and say unto

them, Ye shall be holy: for I the LORD
your God *am* holy.
¶3Ye shall *fear every man his mother, and his father, and keep my sabbaths:
I *am* the LORD your God.
¶4Turn ye not unto idols, nor make to
yourselves molten gods: I *am* the LORD
your God.
¶5And if ye offer a sacrifice of peace-
offerings unto the LORD, ye shall offer
it at your own will.
6It shall be eaten the same day ye
offer it, and on the morrow: and if ought
remain until the third day, it shall be
burnt in the *fire.
7And if it be eaten at all on the third
day, it *is* abominable; it shall not be accepted.
8Therefore *every one* that eateth it
shall bear his iniquity, because he hath
profaned the hallowed thing of the
LORD: and that soul shall be cut off from
among his people.
¶9And when ye reap the harvest of
your land, thou shalt not wholly reap the
corners of thy field, neither shalt thou
gather the gleanings of thy harvest.
10And thou shalt not glean thy *vineyard, neither shalt thou gather *every*
grape of thy vineyard; thou shalt leave
them for the poor and stranger: I *am* the
LORD your God.
¶11Ye shall not steal, neither deal
falsely, neither lie one to another.
¶12And ye shall not swear by my
name falsely, neither shalt thou profane
the name of thy God: I *am* the LORD.
¶13Thou shalt not defraud thy neighbour, neither rob *him:* the wages of him
that is hired shall not abide with thee
all night until the morning.
¶14Thou shalt not curse the deaf, nor
put a stumblingblock before the blind,
but shalt fear thy God: I *am* the LORD.
¶15Ye shall do no unrighteousness in
*judgment: thou shalt not respect the
person of the poor, nor honour the person of the mighty: *but* in *righteousness shalt thou judge thy neighbour.
¶16Thou shalt not go up and down *as*
a talebearer among thy people: neither
shalt thou stand against the blood of thy
neighbour: I *am* the LORD.
¶17Thou shalt not hate thy brother in
thine heart: thou shalt in any wise rebuke thy neighbour, and not suffer sin
upon him.
¶18Thou shalt not avenge, nor bear
any grudge against the children of thy
people, but thou shalt love thy neighbour as thyself: I *am* the LORD.
¶19Ye shall keep my statutes. Thou
shalt not let thy cattle gender with a
diverse kind: thou shalt not sow thy
field with mingled seed: neither shall a
garment mingled of *linen and woollen
come upon thee.
¶20And whosoever lieth carnally with
a woman, that *is* a bondmaid, betrothed
to an husband, and not at all *redeemed,
nor freedom given her; she shall be
scourged; they shall not be put to death,
because she was not free.
21And he shall bring his trespass-
offering unto the LORD, unto the door
of the tabernacle of the congregation,
even a ram for a trespass-offering.
22And the priest shall make an atonement for him with the ram of the trespass-offering before the LORD for his
sin which he hath done: and the sin
which he hath done shall be *forgiven
him.
¶23And when ye shall come into the
land, and shall have planted all manner
of trees for food, then ye shall count the
fruit thereof as *uncircumcised: three
years shall it be as uncircumcised unto
you: it shall not be eaten of.
24But in the fourth year all the fruit

19:2 I the LORD your God am holy. Mankind needs to recognize the holiness of God. Because of His perfect holiness, He hates sin and must judge it. But His love for the sinner is so great that He gave His only Son to be our Saviour (John 3:16; Rom. 5:8).
19:9 when ye reap the harvest. See Ruth 2:2.
19:17 in any wise. In any way or manner.

thereof shall be holy to praise the LORD
withal.
25And in the fifth year shall ye eat of
the fruit thereof, that it may yield unto
you the increase thereof: I *am* the LORD
your God.
¶26Ye shall not eat *any thing* with the
blood: neither shall ye use enchantment, nor observe times.
27Ye shall not round the corners of
your heads, neither shalt thou mar the
corners of thy beard.
28Ye shall not make any cuttings in
your flesh for the dead, nor print any
marks upon you: I *am* the LORD.
¶29Do not prostitute thy daughter, to
cause her to be a *whore; lest the land
fall to whoredom, and the land become
full of wickedness.
¶30Ye shall keep my sabbaths, and
reverence my sanctuary: I *am* the LORD.
¶31Regard not them that have *familiar spirits, neither seek after wizards,
to be defiled by them: I *am* the LORD
your God.
¶32Thou shalt rise up before the hoary
head, and honour the face of the old
man, and fear thy God: I *am* the LORD.
¶33And if a stranger sojourn with
thee in your land, ye shall not vex him.
34*But* the stranger that dwelleth with
you shall be unto you as one born
among you, and thou shalt love him as
thyself; for ye were strangers in the
land of Egypt: I *am* the LORD your God.
¶35Ye shall do no unrighteousness in
judgment, in meteyard, in weight, or in
measure.
36*Just balances, just *weights, a just
*ephah, and a just *hin, shall ye have: I
am the LORD your God, which brought
you out of the land of Egypt.
37Therefore shall ye observe all my
statutes, and all my judgments, and do
them: I *am* the LORD.

20 And the LORD spake unto Moses, saying,
2Again, thou shalt say to the children
of Israel, Whosoever *he be* of the children of Israel, or of the strangers that
sojourn in Israel, that giveth *any* of his
seed unto Molech; he shall surely be
put to death: the people of the land shall
stone him with stones.
3And I will set my face against that
man, and will cut him off from among
his people; because he hath given of his
seed unto Molech, to defile my sanctuary, and to profane my *holy name.
4And if the people of the land do any
ways hide their eyes from the man,
when he giveth of his seed unto Molech, and kill him not:
5Then I will set my face against that
man, and against his family, and will cut
him off, and all that go a whoring after
him, to commit whoredom with Molech, from among their people.
¶6And the soul that turneth after such
as have familiar spirits, and after wizards, to go a whoring after them, I will
even set my face against that soul, and
will cut him off from among his people.
¶7Sanctify yourselves therefore, and
be ye holy: for I *am* the LORD your God.
8And ye shall keep my statutes, and
do them: I *am* the LORD which sanctify
you.
¶9For every one that curseth his father or his mother shall be surely put
to death: he hath cursed his father or his
mother; his *blood *shall be* upon him.
¶10And the man that committeth
adultery with *another* man's wife, *even*
he that committeth adultery with his
neighbour's wife, the adulterer and the
adulteress shall surely be put to death.
11And the man that lieth with his
father's wife hath uncovered his father's
nakedness: both of them shall surely be
put to death; their blood *shall be* upon
them.
12And if a man lie with his daughter
in law, both of them shall surely be put

19:35 meteyard. A measuring rod.

20:2 Molech. Molech was an idol to whom the heathen people would sometimes sacrifice their babies.

to death: they have wrought confusion;
their blood *shall be* upon them.
13 If a man also lie with mankind, as
he lieth with a woman, both of them
have committed an abomination: they
shall surely be put to death; their blood
shall be upon them.
14 And if a man take a wife and her
mother, it *is* wickedness: they shall be
burnt with fire, both he and they; that
there be no wickedness among you.
15 And if a man lie with a beast, he
shall surely be put to death: and ye shall
slay the beast.
16 And if a woman approach unto any
beast, and lie down thereto, thou shalt
kill the woman, and the beast: they shall
surely be put to death; their blood *shall
be* upon them.
17 And if a man shall take his sister, his
father's daughter, or his mother's
daughter, and see her nakedness, and
she see his nakedness; it *is* a wicked
thing; and they shall be cut off in the
sight of their people: he hath uncovered
his sister's nakedness; he shall bear his
iniquity.
18 And if a man shall lie with a woman
having her sickness, and shall uncover
her nakedness; he hath discovered
her fountain, and she hath uncovered
the fountain of her blood: and both of
them shall be cut off from among their
people.
19 And thou shalt not uncover the nakedness of thy mother's sister, nor of
thy father's sister: for he uncovereth
his near kin: they shall bear their iniquity.
20 And if a man shall lie with his
uncle's wife, he hath uncovered his
uncle's nakedness: they shall bear their
sin; they shall die childless.
21 And if a man shall take his brother's
wife, it *is* an unclean thing: he hath uncovered his brother's nakedness; they
shall be childless.
¶22 Ye shall therefore keep all my statutes, and all my judgments, and do
them: that the land, whither I bring you
to dwell therein, spue you not out.
23 And ye shall not walk in the manners of the nation, which I cast out before you: for they committed all these
things, and therefore I abhorred them.
24 But I have said unto you, Ye shall
inherit their land, and I will give it unto
you to possess it, a land that *floweth
with milk and honey: I *am* the LORD
your God, which have separated you
from *other* people.
25 Ye shall therefore put difference
between clean beasts and unclean, and
between unclean fowls and clean: and
ye shall not make your souls abominable by beast, or by fowl, or by any manner of living thing that creepeth on the
ground, which I have separated from
you as unclean.
26 And ye shall be holy unto me: for I
the LORD *am* holy, and have severed
you from *other* people, that ye should be
mine.
¶27 A man also or woman that hath a
familiar spirit, or that is a wizard, shall
surely be put to death: they shall stone
them with stones: their blood *shall be*
upon them.

21 And the LORD said unto Moses, Speak unto the priests the
sons of *Aaron, and say unto them,
There shall none be defiled for the dead
among his people:
2 But for his kin, that is near unto him,
that is, for his mother, and for his father,
and for his son, and for his daughter, and
for his brother,
3 And for his sister a virgin, that is
nigh unto him, which hath had no husband; for her may he be defiled.
4 *But* he shall not defile himself, *being*
a chief man among his people, to profane himself.
5 They shall not make baldness upon
their head, neither shall they shave off
the corner of their beard, nor make any
cuttings in their flesh.
6 They shall be holy unto their God,
and not profane the name of their God:
for the offerings of the LORD made by
fire, *and* the bread of their God, they do
offer: therefore they shall be holy.

7They shall not take a wife *that is* a
whore, or profane; neither shall they
take a woman put away from her husband: for he *is* holy unto his God.
8Thou shalt sanctify him therefore;
for he offereth the bread of thy God: he
shall be holy unto thee: for I the LORD,
which sanctify you, *am* holy.
¶9And the daughter of any priest, if
she profane herself by playing the
whore, she profaneth her father: she
shall be burnt with fire.
10And *he that is* the high priest among
his brethren, upon whose head the
anointing *oil was poured, and that is
consecrated to put on the garments,
shall not uncover his head, nor rend his
clothes;
11Neither shall he go in to any dead
body, nor defile himself for his father, or
for his mother;
12Neither shall he go out of the sanctuary, nor profane the sanctuary of his
God; for the crown of the anointing oil
of his God *is* upon him: I *am* the LORD.
13And he shall take a wife in her virginity.
14A widow, or a divorced woman, or
profane, *or* an harlot, these shall he not
take: but he shall take a virgin of his
own people to wife.
15Neither shall he profane his seed
among his people: for I the LORD do
sanctify him.
¶16And the LORD spake unto Moses,
saying,
17Speak unto Aaron, saying, Whosoever *he be* of thy seed in their generations that hath *any* blemish, let
him not approach to offer the bread of
his God.
18For whatsoever man *he be* that hath
a blemish, he shall not approach: a blind
man, or a lame, or he that hath a flat
nose, or any thing superfluous,
19Or a man that is brokenfooted, or
brokenhanded,
20Or crookbackt, or a dwarf, or that
hath a blemish in his eye, or be scurvy,
or scabbed, or hath his stones broken;
21No man that hath a blemish of the
seed of Aaron the priest shall come
nigh to offer the offerings of the LORD
made by fire: he hath a blemish; he shall
not come nigh to offer the bread of his
God.
22He shall eat the bread of his God,
both of the most holy, and of the holy.
23Only he shall not go in unto the vail,
nor come nigh unto the *altar, because
he hath a blemish; that he profane not
my sanctuaries: for I the LORD do sanctify them.
24And Moses told *it* unto Aaron, and
to his sons, and unto all the children of
*Israel.

Separation of the priests

22 And the LORD spake unto Moses, saying,
2Speak unto Aaron and to his sons,
that they separate themselves from the
holy things of the children of Israel, and
that they profane not my holy name *in
those things* which they hallow unto me:
I *am* the LORD.
3Say unto them, Whosoever *he be* of
all your seed among your generations,
that goeth unto the holy things, which
the children of Israel hallow unto the
LORD, having his uncleanness upon
him, that soul shall be cut off from my
presence: I *am* the LORD.
4What man soever of the seed of
Aaron *is* a *leper, or hath a running
issue; he shall not eat of the holy
things, until he be *clean. And whoso
toucheth any thing *that is* unclean *by* the
dead, or a man whose seed goeth from
him;
5Or whosoever toucheth any creeping thing, whereby he may be made
unclean, or a man of whom he may take
uncleanness, whatsoever uncleanness
he hath;
6The soul which hath touched any

21:17 Whosoever . . . hath any blemish. The priests had to be as perfect as was humanly possible, for they were *types of the Lord Jesus Christ.

such shall be unclean until even, and
shall not eat of the holy things, unless
he wash his flesh with water.
7 And when the sun is down, he shall
be clean, and shall afterward eat of the
holy things; because it *is* his food.
8 That which dieth of itself, or is torn
with beasts, he shall not eat to defile
himself therewith: I *am* the LORD.
9 They shall therefore keep mine ordinance, lest they bear *sin for it, and
die therefore, if they profane it: I the
LORD do sanctify them.
10 There shall no stranger eat *of* the
holy thing: a sojourner of the priest, or
an hired servant, shall not eat *of* the
holy thing.
11 But if the priest buy *any* soul with
his *money, he shall eat of it, and he that
is born in his house: they shall eat of his
meat.
12 If the priest's daughter also be
married unto a stranger, she may not
eat of an *offering of the holy things.
13 But if the priest's daughter be a
widow, or divorced, and have no child,
and is returned unto her father's house,
as in her youth, she shall eat of her
father's meat: but there shall no stranger eat thereof.
¶14 And if a man eat *of* the holy thing
unwittingly, then he shall put the fifth
part thereof unto it, and shall give *it*
unto the priest with the holy thing.
15 And they shall not profane the holy
things of the children of Israel, which
they offer unto the LORD;
16 Or suffer them to *bear the iniquity of *trespass, when they eat their
holy things: for I the LORD do sanctify
them.

Sacrifices must be perfect types of the Lord Jesus Christ

¶17 And the LORD spake unto Moses,
saying,
18 Speak unto Aaron, and to his sons,
and unto all the children of Israel, and
say unto them, Whatsoever *he be* of the
house of Israel, or of the strangers in
Israel, that will offer his *oblation for all
his vows, and for all his freewill-offerings, which they will offer unto the
LORD for a burnt-offering;
19 *Ye shall offer* at your own will a male
without blemish, of the beeves, of the
sheep, or of the goats.
20 *But* whatsoever hath a blemish,
that shall ye not offer: for it shall not be
acceptable for you.
21 And whosoever offereth a sacrifice
of peace-offerings unto the LORD to
accomplish *his* vow, or a freewill-offering in beeves or sheep, it shall be *perfect to be accepted; there shall be no
blemish therein.
22 Blind, or broken, or maimed, or
having a wen, or scurvy, or scabbed, ye
shall not offer these unto the LORD, nor
make an offering by fire of them upon
the altar unto the LORD.
23 Either a bullock or a lamb that hath
any thing superfluous or lacking in his
parts, that mayest thou offer *for* a freewill offering; but for a vow it shall not
be accepted.
24 Ye shall not offer unto the LORD
that which is bruised, or crushed, or
broken, or cut; neither shall ye make
any offering thereof in your land.
25 Neither from a stranger's hand
shall ye offer the bread of your God of
any of these; because their corruption
is in them, *and* blemishes *be* in them:
they shall not be accepted for you.
¶26 And the LORD spake unto Moses,
saying,
27 When a bullock, or a sheep, or a
goat, is brought forth, then it shall be
seven days under the dam; and from the
eighth day and thenceforth it shall be
accepted for an offering made by fire
unto the LORD.
28 And *whether it be* cow or ewe, ye
shall not kill it and her young both in
one day.
29 And when ye will offer a sacrifice of
thanksgiving unto the LORD, offer *it* at
your own will.
30 On the same day it shall be eaten
up; ye shall leave none of it until the
morrow: I *am* the LORD.

31 Therefore shall ye keep my commandments, and do them: I *am* the
LORD.
32 Neither shall ye profane my holy
name; but I will be hallowed among the
children of Israel: I *am* the LORD which
hallow you,
33 That brought you out of the land of
Egypt, to be your God: I *am* the LORD.

VIII. Law of the Feasts of the LORD (23; 24)

23 And the LORD spake unto Moses, saying,
2 Speak unto the children of Israel,
and say unto them, *Concerning* the
*feasts of the LORD, which ye shall pro-
claim *to be* holy convocations, *even*
these *are* my feasts.
3 Six days shall work be done: but the
seventh day *is* the *sabbath of rest, an
holy *convocation; ye shall do no work
therein: it *is* the sabbath of the LORD in
all your dwellings.
¶ 4 These *are* the feasts of the LORD,
even holy convocations, which ye shall
proclaim in their seasons.
5 In the fourteenth *day* of the first
*month at even *is* the LORD'S *passover.
6 And on the fifteenth day of the same
month *is* the feast of *unleavened bread
unto the LORD: seven days ye must eat
unleavened bread.
7 In the first day ye shall have an holy
convocation: ye shall do no servile work
therein.
8 But ye shall offer an offering made
by fire unto the LORD seven days: in the
seventh day *is* an holy convocation: ye
shall do no servile work *therein.*
¶ 9 And the LORD spake unto Moses,
saying,
10 Speak unto the children of Israel,
and say unto them, When ye be come
into the land which I give unto you, and
shall reap the harvest thereof, then ye
shall bring a sheaf of the *firstfruits of
your harvest unto the priest:
11 And he shall wave the sheaf before
the LORD, to be accepted for you: on the
morrow after the sabbath the priest
shall wave it.
12 And ye shall offer that day when ye
wave the sheaf an he lamb without
blemish of the first year for a burnt-
offering unto the LORD.
13 And the *meat-offering thereof
shall be two tenth deals of fine flour
mingled with oil, an offering made by
fire unto the LORD *for* a sweet savour:
and the *drink-offering thereof *shall be*
of *wine, the fourth *part* of an *hin.
14 And ye shall eat neither bread, nor
parched corn, nor green ears, until the
selfsame day that ye have brought an
offering unto your God: *it shall be* a statute for ever throughout your generations in all your dwellings.
¶ 15 And ye shall count unto you from
the morrow after the sabbath, from the
day that ye brought the sheaf of the
wave-offering; seven sabbaths shall be
complete:
16 Even unto the morrow after the

23:2 convocations. Meetings.

23:4 the feasts of the LORD. There were seven great religious festivals that the Israelites were to hold every year. They are pictures of the blessings that the coming of the Lord Jesus Christ was to bring one day.

23:5 passover. This was a symbol of the death of Christ as the Lamb of God. See 1 Corinthians 5:7 and 1 Peter 1:19. It was kept in memory of the time that the angel of the LORD passed over the houses which had the blood-sprinkled doorways (see Exod. 12:3 note).

23:6 the feast of unleavened bread. This took place the day after the Passover (Exod. 12:14-20). It speaks of our remembrance of Christ's death. See 1 Corinthians 11:23-26. See also *leaven, Matthew 13:33.

23:10 firstfruits of your harvest. The Israelites collected the first sheaves of corn and offered them to God as a thanksgiving for the harvest. In 1 Corinthians 15:20 Christ is called "the firstfruits of them that slept" because He rose from the dead. This feast speaks to us of our joy in His resurrection.

seventh sabbath shall ye number fifty
days; and ye shall offer a new meat-
offering unto the LORD.

23:16 The Feast of Pentecost
Fifty days after the seventh Sabbath marked the time for the Feast of Pentecost (called the "Feast of Weeks" in Deut. 16:10). This feast took place fifty days after the Feast of Firstfruits. It was exactly fifty days from the resurrection of our Lord Jesus Christ to the Day of Pentecost described in Acts 2:1-4. So this feast speaks especially of the coming of the Holy Spirit.

17 Ye shall bring out of your habitations two wave loaves of two tenth
deals: they shall be of fine flour; they
shall be baken with *leaven; *they are* the
firstfruits unto the LORD.
18 And ye shall offer with the bread
seven lambs without blemish of the
first year, and one young bullock, and
two rams: they shall be *for* a burnt-
offering unto the LORD, with their
meat-offering, and their drink-offerings, *even* an offering made by fire, of
sweet savour unto the LORD.
19 Then ye shall *sacrifice one kid of
the goats for a *sin-offering, and two
lambs of the first year for a sacrifice of
*peace-offerings.
20 And the priest shall wave them
with the bread of the firstfruits *for* a
wave-offering before the LORD, with
the two lambs: they shall be holy to the
LORD for the priest.
21 And ye shall proclaim on the selfsame day, *that* it may be an holy convocation unto you: ye shall do no servile
work *therein: it shall be* a statute for
ever in all your dwellings throughout
your generations.
¶22 And when ye reap the harvest of
your land, thou shalt not make clean
riddance of the corners of thy field
when thou reapest, neither shalt thou
gather any gleaning of thy harvest: thou
shalt leave them unto the poor, and to
the stranger: I *am* the LORD your God.
¶23 And the LORD spake unto Moses,
saying,
24 Speak unto the children of Israel,
saying, In the seventh month, in the
first *day* of the month, shall ye have a
sabbath, a memorial of blowing of trumpets, an holy convocation.
25 Ye shall do no servile work *therein:*
but ye shall offer an offering made by
fire unto the LORD.
¶26 And the LORD spake unto Moses,
saying,
27 Also on the tenth *day* of this seventh month *there shall be* a day of
*atonement: it shall be an holy convo-
cation unto you; and ye shall afflict your
souls, and offer an offering made by fire
unto the LORD.
28 And ye shall do no work in that
same day: for it *is* a day of atonement,
to make an atonement for you before
the LORD your God.
29 For whatsoever soul *it be* that shall
not be afflicted in that same day, he shall
be cut off from among his people.
30 And whatsoever soul *it be* that
doeth any work in that same day, the
same soul will I destroy from among his
people.
31 Ye shall do no manner of work: *it
shall be* a statute for ever throughout

23:17 wave loaves. Fifty days after the wave sheaf was offered (vss. 10-11), the wave loaves were offered. This was another *type, because just fifty days after our Lord was raised from the dead, came *Pentecost, when the church was formed by the baptism of the *Holy Spirit. Notice that the wave sheaf had no *leaven in it, just as Christ had no evil in Him; but the wave loaves were baked with leaven, for in spite of the presence of the Holy Spirit and His guidance, and in spite of the presence and teaching of the Word, there is still evil in the church.

23:24 In the seventh month. This feast, the Feast of Trumpets, speaks prophetically of the still-future blessing of the Jews after the end of the *church age. See Isaiah 18:3,7; 27:12-13.

23:27 a day of atonement. This feast is more fully explained in the Leviticus 16:30 note.

your generations in all your dwellings.
[32]It *shall be* unto you a sabbath of rest,
and ye shall afflict your souls: in the
ninth *day* of the month at even, from
even unto even, shall ye celebrate your
sabbath.
¶[33]And the LORD spake unto Moses,
saying,
[34]Speak unto the children of Israel,
saying, The fifteenth day of this seventh month *shall be* the feast of tabernacles *for* seven days unto the LORD.

23:34 The Feast of Tabernacles
Tabernacles were tents or booths made of branches, in which the Israelites were to live during this feast. Each time they celebrated this feast, it reminded them of the years they had lived in tents on the way from Egypt to Canaan, and of God's care for them. Look up Ezra 3:4 and Nehemiah 8:14. The feast speaks of the final rejoicing of all God's people of every age and time when the kingdom of God is set up on earth. See Revelation 21:3.

[35]On the first day *shall be* an holy convocation: ye shall do no servile work
therein.
[36]Seven days ye shall offer an offering made by fire unto the LORD: on the
eighth day shall be an holy convocation
unto you; and ye shall offer an offering
made by fire unto the LORD: it *is* a solemn assembly; *and* ye shall do no servile work *therein.*
[37]These *are* the feasts of the LORD,
which ye shall proclaim *to be* holy convocations, to offer an offering made by
fire unto the LORD, a burnt-offering, and
a meat-offering, a sacrifice, and drink-
offerings, every thing upon his day:
[38]Beside the sabbaths of the LORD,
and beside your gifts, and beside all
your vows, and beside all your freewill-
offerings, which ye give unto the LORD.
[39]Also in the fifteenth day of the seventh month, when ye have gathered in
the fruit of the land, ye shall keep a feast
unto the LORD seven days: on the first
day *shall be* a sabbath, and on the eighth
day *shall be* a sabbath.
[40]And ye shall take you on the first
day the boughs of goodly trees,
branches of palm trees, and the boughs
of thick trees, and willows of the brook;
and ye shall rejoice before the LORD
your God seven days.
[41]And ye shall keep it a feast unto the
LORD seven days in the year. *It shall be*
a statute for ever in your generations:
ye shall celebrate it in the seventh
month.
[42]Ye shall dwell in booths seven days;
all that are Israelites born shall dwell in
booths:
[43]That your generations may know
that I made the children of Israel to
dwell in booths, when I brought them
out of the land of Egypt: I *am* the LORD
your God.
[44]And Moses declared unto the children of Israel the feasts of the LORD.

The oil for the holy place

24 And the LORD spake unto Moses, saying,
[2]Command the children of Israel, that
they bring unto thee pure oil olive beat-
en for the light, to cause the lamps to
burn continually.
[3]Without the vail of the testimony, in
the *tabernacle of the congregation,
shall Aaron order it from the evening
unto the morning before the LORD continually: *it shall be* a statute for ever in
your generations.
[4]He shall order the lamps upon the
pure *candlestick before the LORD continually.

The shewbread

¶[5]And thou shalt take fine flour, and
bake twelve cakes thereof: two tenth
deals shall be in one cake.
[6]And thou shalt set them in two rows,

24:3 the vail of the testimony. The great curtain which hung between the Holy Place and the Holy of Holies (Exod. 26:33).
24:5 deals. A "deal" means a *part*.

six on a row, upon the pure table before
the LORD.
7And thou shalt put pure frankincense upon *each* row, that it may be on
the bread for a memorial, *even* an offering made by fire unto the LORD.
8Every sabbath he shall set it in order before the LORD continually, *being*
taken from the children of Israel by an
everlasting *covenant.
9And it shall be Aaron's and his sons';
and they shall eat it in the holy place:
for it *is* most holy unto him of the offerings of the LORD made by fire by a
perpetual statute.

The penalty for blasphemy

¶10And the son of an Israelitish woman, whose father *was* an Egyptian, went
out among the children of Israel: and
this son of the Israelitish *woman* and a
man of Israel strove together in the
camp;
11And the Israelitish woman's son
blasphemed the name *of the LORD,* and
cursed. And they brought him unto
Moses: (and his mother's name *was*
Shelomith, the daughter of Dibri, of the
tribe of Dan:)
12And they put him in ward, that the
mind of the LORD might be shewed
them.
13And the LORD spake unto Moses,
saying,
14Bring forth him that hath cursed
without the camp; and let all that heard
him lay their hands upon his head, and
let all the congregation stone him.
15And thou shalt speak unto the children of Israel, saying, Whosoever
curseth his *God shall bear his sin.
16And he that blasphemeth the name
of the LORD, he shall surely be put to
*death, *and* all the congregation shall
certainly stone him: as well the stranger, as he that is born in the land, when
he blasphemeth the name *of the LORD,*
shall be put to death.
¶17And he that killeth any man shall
surely be put to death.
18And he that killeth a beast shall
make it good; beast for beast.
19And if a man cause a blemish in his
neighbour; as he hath done, so shall it
be done to him;
20Breach for breach, eye for eye,
tooth for tooth: as he hath caused a
blemish in a man, so shall it be done to
him *again.*
21And he that killeth a beast, he shall
restore it: and he that killeth a man, he
shall be put to death.
22Ye shall have one manner of *law,
as well for the stranger, as for one of
your own country: for I *am* the LORD
your God.
¶23And Moses spake to the children
of Israel, that they should bring forth
him that had cursed out of the camp,
and stone him with stones. And the
children of Israel did as the LORD commanded Moses.

IX. The Law of the Land (25; 26)

The sabbath year

25 And the LORD spake unto *Moses in mount *Sinai, saying,
2Speak unto the children of Israel,
and say unto them, When ye come
into the land which I give you, then
shall the land keep a sabbath unto the
LORD.
3Six years thou shalt sow thy field,
and six years thou shalt prune thy
*vineyard, and gather in the fruit
thereof;
4But in the seventh year shall be a
sabbath of rest unto the land, a sabbath

25:4 the seventh year. This was a year of rest for the people and the land. It was to remind the people of God's claims over them, for the land really was His, and He had placed them in it. The crops were so plentiful that they could easily have enough to last from the sixth to the eighth year. Just as there was a *Sabbath day, so also was there to be a Sabbath year. Every farmer knows that soil needs rest, just as people need it.

for the LORD: thou shalt neither sow thy
field, nor prune thy vineyard.
5 That which groweth of its own accord of thy harvest thou shalt not reap,
neither gather the grapes of thy vine
undressed: *for* it is a year of rest unto
the land.
6 And the sabbath of the land shall be
meat for you; for thee, and for thy servant, and for thy maid, and for thy hired
servant, and for thy stranger that
sojourneth with thee,
7 And for thy cattle, and for the beast
that *are* in thy land, shall all the increase
thereof be meat.

The year of jubilee

¶8 And thou shalt number seven sabbaths of years unto thee, seven times
seven years; and the space of the seven
sabbaths of years shall be unto thee
forty and nine years.
9 Then shalt thou cause the trumpet
of the *jubile to sound on the tenth *day*
of the seventh month, in the day of
atonement shall ye make the trumpet
sound throughout all your land.
10 And ye shall hallow the fiftieth year,
and proclaim liberty throughout *all* the
land unto all the inhabitants thereof: it
shall be a jubile unto you; and ye shall
return every man unto his possession,
and ye shall return every man unto his
family.
11 A jubile shall that fiftieth year be
unto you: ye shall not sow, neither reap
that which groweth of itself in it, nor
gather *the grapes* in it of thy vine undressed.
12 For it *is* the jubile; it shall be holy
unto you: ye shall eat the increase
thereof out of the field.
13 In the year of this jubile ye shall
return every man unto his possession.
14 And if thou sell ought unto thy
neighbour, or buyest *ought* of thy neighbour's hand, ye shall not oppress one
another:
15 According to the number of years
after the jubile thou shalt buy of thy
neighbour, *and* according unto the number of years of the fruits he shall sell
unto thee:
16 According to the multitude of years
thou shalt increase the price thereof,
and according to the fewness of years
thou shalt diminish the price of it: for
according to the number *of the years* of
the fruits doth he sell unto thee.
17 Ye shall not therefore oppress one
another; but thou shalt *fear thy God:
for I *am* the LORD your God.
¶18 Wherefore ye shall do my statutes,
and keep my judgments, and do them;
and ye shall dwell in the land in safety.
19 And the land shall yield her fruit,
and ye shall eat your fill, and dwell
therein in safety.
20 And if ye shall say, What shall we
eat the seventh year? behold, we shall
not sow, nor gather in our increase:
21 Then I will command my blessing
upon you in the sixth year, and it shall
bring forth fruit for three years.
22 And ye shall sow the eighth year,
and eat *yet* of old fruit until the ninth
year; until her fruits come in ye shall
eat *of* the old *store*.
¶23 The land shall not be sold for ever:
for the land *is* mine; for ye *are* strangers and sojourners with me.
24 And in all the land of your possession ye shall grant a *redemption for
the land.

25:4-5 THE YEAR OF JUBILEE

Every fiftieth year, the Israelites were to keep a year of rest in which slaves were set free, debts cancelled, and land given back. This has two meanings:

1. It pictures the "acceptable year of the Lord," which is what the Lord Jesus called His coming in Luke 4:19, for He brought rest and happiness and freedom from the yoke of sin for all who would believe on Him.
2. It is prophetic of the future day when the Jews will be restored to Palestine and be blessed again by God.

Law, treating the poor kindly

¶[25]If thy brother be waxen poor, and
hath sold away *some* of his possession,
and if any of his kin come to redeem it,
then shall he redeem that which his
brother sold.

[26]And if the man have none to
redeem it, and himself be able to redeem it;

[27]Then let him count the years of the
sale thereof, and restore the overplus
unto the man to whom he sold it; that
he may return unto his possession.

[28]But if he be not able to restore *it* to
him, then that which is sold shall remain in the hand of him that hath
bought it until the year of jubile: and in
the jubile it shall go out, and he shall
return unto his possession.

[29]And if a man sell a dwelling house
in a walled city, then he may redeem it
within a whole year after it is sold; *within* a full year may he redeem it.

[30]And if it be not redeemed within the
space of a full year, then the house that
is in the walled city shall be established
for ever to him that bought it throughout his generations: it shall not go out
in the jubile.

[31]But the houses of the villages
which have no wall round about them
shall be counted as the fields of the
country: they may be redeemed, and
they shall go out in the jubile.

[32]Notwithstanding the cities of the
Levites, *and* the houses of the cities of
their possession, may the Levites redeem at any time.

[33]And if a man purchase of the Levites, then the house that was sold, and
the city of his possession, shall go out
in *the year of* jubile: for the houses of the
cities of the Levites *are* their possession among the children of Israel.

[34]But the field of the suburbs of their
cities may not be sold; for it *is* their
perpetual possession.

¶[35]And if thy brother be waxen poor,
and fallen in decay with thee; then thou
shalt relieve him: *yea, though he be* a
stranger, or a sojourner; that he may
live with thee.

[36]Take thou no *usury of him, or increase: but fear thy God; that thy
brother may live with thee.

[37]Thou shalt not give him thy money upon usury, nor lend him thy victuals
for increase.

[38]I *am* the LORD your God, which
brought you forth out of the land of
*Egypt, to give you the land of Canaan,
and to be your God.

¶[39]And if thy brother *that dwelleth* by
thee be waxen poor, and be sold unto
thee; thou shalt not compel him to
serve as a bondservant:

[40]*But* as an hired servant, *and* as
a sojourner, he shall be with thee,
and shall serve thee unto the year of
jubile:

[41]And *then* shall he depart from thee,
both he and his children with him, and
shall return unto his own family, and
unto the possession of his fathers shall
he return.

[42]For they *are* my servants, which I
brought forth out of the land of Egypt:
they shall not be sold as bondmen.

[43]Thou shalt not rule over him with
rigour; but shalt fear thy God.

[44]Both thy bondmen, and thy bondmaids, which thou shalt have, *shall be*
of the heathen that are round about you;
of them shall ye buy bondmen and
bondmaids.

[45]Moreover of the children of the
strangers that do sojourn among you, of
them shall ye buy, and of their families
that *are* with you, which they begat in
your land: and they shall be your possession.

[46]And ye shall take them as an inheritance for your children after you, to
inherit *them for* a possession; they shall
be your bondmen for ever: but over
your brethren the children of Israel, ye
shall not rule one over another with
rigour.

25:44 heathen. Nations.

Law of redemption

¶47 And if a sojourner or stranger wax
rich by thee, and thy brother *that*
dwelleth by him wax poor, and sell himself unto the stranger *or* sojourner by
thee, or to the stock of the stranger's
family:
48 After that he is sold he may be redeemed again; one of his brethren may
redeem him:
49 Either his uncle, or his uncle's son,
may redeem him, or *any* that is nigh of
kin unto him of his family may redeem
him; or if he be able, he may redeem
himself.
50 And he shall reckon with him that
bought him from the year that he was
sold to him unto the year of jubile: and
the price of his sale shall be according
unto the number of years, according to
the time of an hired servant shall it be
with him.
51 If *there be* yet many years *behind,*
according unto them he shall give again
the price of his redemption out of the
money that he was bought for.
52 And if there remain but few years
unto the year of jubile, then he shall
count with him, *and* according unto his
years shall he give him again the price
of his redemption.
53 *And* as a yearly hired servant shall
he be with him: *and the other* shall not
rule with rigour over him in thy sight.
54 And if he be not redeemed in these
years, then he shall go out in the year
of jubile, *both* he, and his children with
him.
55 For unto me the children of Israel
are servants; they *are* my servants
whom I brought forth out of the land of
Egypt: I *am* the LORD your God.

Conditions of blessing

26 Ye shall make you no idols nor
*graven image, neither rear you
up a standing image, neither shall ye set
up *any* image of stone in your land, to
bow down unto it: for I *am* the LORD
your God.
¶2 Ye shall keep my sabbaths, and reverence my *sanctuary: I *am* the LORD.
¶3 If ye walk in my statutes, and keep
my commandments, and do them;
4 Then I will give you rain in due season, and the land shall yield her increase, and the trees of the field shall
yield their fruit.
5 And your threshing shall reach unto
the vintage, and the vintage shall reach
unto the sowing time: and ye shall eat
your bread to the full, and dwell in your
land safely.
6 And I will give peace in the land, and
ye shall lie down, and none shall make
you afraid: and I will rid evil beasts out
of the land, neither shall the sword go
through your land.
7 And ye shall chase your enemies,
and they shall fall before you by the
sword.
8 And five of you shall chase an hundred, and an hundred of you shall put
ten thousand to flight: and your enemies shall fall before you by the sword.
9 For I will have respect unto you, and
make you fruitful, and multiply you, and
establish my covenant with you.
10 And ye shall eat old store, and bring
forth the old because of the new.
11 And I will set my tabernacle among
you: and my soul shall not abhor you.
12 And I will walk among you, and
will be your God, and ye shall be my
people.
13 I *am* the LORD your God, which
brought you forth out of the land of
Egypt, that ye should not be their bondmen; and I have broken the bands of
your yoke, and made you go upright.
¶14 But if ye will not hearken unto me,
and will not do all these commandments;
15 And if ye shall despise my statutes,

25:49 any that is nigh of kin. Read Ruth 1:11 note, "Following the Law."

26:1 Ye shall make you no idols. This was the second commandment, and verse 2 was the fourth. See Exodus 20:4,8.

or if your soul abhor my judgments, so
that ye will not do all my commandments, *but* that ye break my covenant:
[16]I also will do this unto you; I will
even appoint over you terror, consumption, and the burning ague, that shall
consume the eyes, and cause sorrow of
heart: and ye shall sow your seed in
vain, for your enemies shall eat it.
[17]And I will set my face against you,
and ye shall be slain before your enemies: they that hate you shall reign
over you; and ye shall flee when none
pursueth you.
[18]And if ye will not yet for all this
hearken unto me, then I will punish you
seven times more for your sins.
[19]And I will break the pride of your
power; and I will make your heaven as
iron, and your earth as brass:
[20]And your strength shall be spent in
vain: for your land shall not yield her
increase, neither shall the trees of the
land yield their fruits.
¶[21]And if ye walk contrary unto me,
and will not hearken unto me; I will
bring seven times more plagues upon
you according to your sins.
[22]I will also send wild beasts among
you, which shall rob you of your children, and destroy your cattle, and make
you few in number; and your *high* ways
shall be desolate.
[23]And if ye will not be reformed by
me by these things, but will walk contrary unto me;
[24]Then will I also walk contrary unto
you, and will punish you yet seven
times for your sins.
[25]And I will bring a sword upon you,
that shall avenge the quarrel of *my* covenant: and when ye are gathered together within your cities, I will send the
pestilence among you; and ye shall be
delivered into the hand of the enemy.
[26]*And* when I have broken the staff of
your bread, ten women shall bake your
bread in one oven, and they shall deliver *you* your bread again by weight: and
ye shall eat, and not be satisfied.
[27]And if ye will not for all this hearken unto me, but walk contrary unto
me;
[28]Then I will walk contrary unto you
also in fury; and I, even I, will chastise
you seven times for your sins.
[29]And ye shall eat the flesh of your
sons, and the flesh of your daughters
shall ye eat.
[30]And I will destroy your *high
places, and cut down your images, and
cast your carcases upon the carcases of
your idols, and my soul shall abhor you.
[31]And I will make your cities waste,
and bring your sanctuaries unto desolation, and I will not smell the savour
of your sweet odours.
[32]And I will bring the land into desolation: and your enemies which dwell
therein shall be astonished at it.
[33]And I will scatter you among the
heathen, and will draw out a sword after you: and your land shall be desolate,
and your cities waste.
[34]Then shall the land enjoy her sabbaths, as long as it lieth desolate, and
ye *be* in your enemies' land; *even* then
shall the land rest, and enjoy her sabbaths.
[35]As long as it lieth desolate it shall
rest; because it did not rest in your sabbaths, when ye dwelt upon it.
[36]And upon them that are left *alive* of
you I will send a faintness into their
hearts in the lands of their enemies; and
the sound of a shaken leaf shall chase
them; and they shall flee, as fleeing
from a sword; and they shall fall when
none pursueth.
[37]And they shall fall one upon

26:30 high places. On these hills, idols were set up and worshipped.

26:33 And I will scatter you. All this was fulfilled hundreds of years later when the northern tribes were conquered and taken away by the Assyrians and the southern tribes by Babylon. See 2 Kings 17 to the end of the book and the book of Isaiah. The Jewish people are still scattered among the nations.

another, as it were before a sword,
when none pursueth: and ye shall have
no power to stand before your enemies.
38And ye shall perish among the heathen, and the land of your enemies shall
eat you up.
39And they that are left of you shall
pine away in their iniquity in your enemies' lands; and also in the iniquities of
their fathers shall they pine away with
them.
40If they shall *confess their iniquity, and the iniquity of their fathers, with
their trespass which they trespassed
against me, and that also they have
walked contrary unto me;
41And *that* I also have walked contrary unto them, and have brought
them into the land of their enemies; if
then their *uncircumcised hearts be
humbled, and they then accept of the
punishment of their iniquity:
42Then will I remember my covenant
with *Jacob, and also my covenant with
*Isaac, and also my covenant with
*Abraham will I remember; and I will
remember the land.
43The land also shall be left of them,
and shall enjoy her sabbaths, while she
lieth desolate without them: and they
shall accept of the punishment of their
iniquity: because, even because they
despised my judgments, and because
their soul abhorred my statutes.
44And yet for all that, when they be
in the land of their enemies, I will not
cast them away, neither will I abhor
them, to destroy them utterly, and to
break my covenant with them: for I *am*
the LORD their God.
45But I will for their sakes remember
the covenant of their ancestors, whom
I brought forth out of the land of Egypt
in the sight of the heathen, that I might
be their God: I *am* the LORD.
46These *are* the statutes and judgments and *laws, which the LORD made
between him and the children of Israel
in mount Sinai by the hand of Moses.

X. The Law of Vows (27)

27 And the LORD spake unto Moses, saying,
2Speak unto the children of Israel,
and say unto them, When a man shall
make a singular vow, the persons *shall*
be for the LORD by thy estimation.

27:2 Making a Vow
The vow was a voluntary undertaking on the part of any Israelite, to give himself and his possessions to God. Since all the people who made vows could not serve in the tabernacle, each of those who could not do so gave large gifts to God instead. The size of the gift was decided by the priest, according to the wealth or poverty of the man who offered the vow. We have no such order in the New Testament, but so great is the love of Christ that, when we are born again, we owe our whole lives and all our possessions to God—not just a part—to be used for Him (see Rom. 12:1-2; 1 Cor. 6:19-20).

3And thy estimation shall be of the
male from twenty years old even unto
sixty years old, even thy estimation
shall be fifty shekels of silver, after the
shekel of the sanctuary.
4And if it *be* a female, then thy estimation shall be thirty shekels.
5And if *it be* from five years old even
unto twenty years old, then thy estimation shall be of the male twenty shekels, and for the female ten shekels.
6And if *it be* from a month old even
unto five years old, then thy estimation
shall be of the male five shekels of silver, and for the female thy estimation
shall be three shekels of silver.
7And if *it be* from sixty years old and
above; if *it be* a male, then thy estimation shall be fifteen shekels, and for the
female ten shekels.
8But if he be poorer than thy estimation, then he shall present himself before the priest, and the priest shall
value him; according to his ability that
vowed shall the priest value him.
9And if *it be* a beast, whereof men
bring an offering unto the LORD, all that

26:40 If they shall confess. See 1 Kings 8:33-34; Nehemiah 9:2; and 1 John 1:9.

any man giveth of such unto the LORD shall be holy.

10 He shall not alter it, nor change it, a good for a bad, or a bad for a good: and if he shall at all change beast for beast, then it and the exchange thereof shall be holy.

11 And if *it be* any unclean beast, of which they do not offer a sacrifice unto the LORD, then he shall present the beast before the priest:

12 And the priest shall value it, whether it be good or bad: as thou valuest it, *who art* the priest, so shall it be.

13 But if he will at all redeem it, then he shall add a fifth *part* thereof unto thy estimation.

¶ 14 And when a man shall sanctify his house *to be* holy unto the LORD, then the priest shall estimate it, whether it be good or bad: as the priest shall estimate it, so shall it stand.

15 And if he that sanctified it will redeem his house, then he shall add the fifth *part* of the money of thy estimation unto it, and it shall be his.

16 And if a man shall sanctify unto the LORD *some part* of a field of his possession, then thy estimation shall be according to the seed thereof: an homer of barley seed *shall be valued* at fifty shekels of silver.

17 If he sanctify his field from the year of jubile, according to thy estimation it shall stand.

18 But if he sanctify his field after the jubile, then the priest shall reckon unto him the money according to the years that remain, even unto the year of the jubile, and it shall be abated from thy estimation.

19 And if he that sanctified the field will in any wise redeem it, then he shall add the fifth *part* of the money of thy estimation unto it, and it shall be assured to him.

20 And if he will not redeem the field, or if he have sold the field to another man, it shall not be redeemed any more.

21 But the field, when it goeth out in the jubile, shall be holy unto the LORD, as a field devoted; the possession thereof shall be the priest's.

22 And if *a man* sanctify unto the LORD a field which he hath bought, which *is* not of the fields of his possession;

23 Then the priest shall reckon unto him the worth of thy estimation, *even* unto the year of the jubile: and he shall give thine estimation in that day, *as* a holy thing unto the LORD.

24 In the year of the jubile the field shall return unto him of whom it was bought, *even* to him to whom the possession of the land *did belong*.

25 And all thy estimations shall be according to the shekel of the sanctuary: twenty gerahs shall be the shekel.

¶ 26 Only the firstling of the beasts, which should be the LORD'S firstling, no man shall sanctify it; whether *it be* ox, or sheep: it *is* the LORD'S.

27 And if *it be* of an unclean beast, then he shall redeem *it* according to thine estimation, and shall add a fifth *part* of it thereto: or if it be not redeemed, then it shall be sold according to thy estimation.

28 Notwithstanding no devoted thing, that a man shall devote unto the LORD of all that he hath, *both* of man and beast, and of the field of his possession, shall be sold or redeemed: every devoted thing *is* most holy unto the LORD.

29 None devoted, which shall be devoted of men, shall be redeemed; *but* shall surely be put to death.

30 And all the tithe of the land, *whether* of the seed of the land, *or* of the fruit of the tree, *is* the LORD'S: *it is* holy unto the LORD.

31 And if a man will at all redeem *ought*

27:16 homer. A homer is about six bushels.

27:30 tithe. A tenth part or ten percent. Christians are told to lay aside regularly, as the Lord prospers them, a sum to be used in the Lord's service. See 1 Corinthians 16:1-2; and 2 Corinthians 8:4-5,7-15.

of his tithes, he shall add thereto the
fifth *part* thereof.
32 And concerning the tithe of the
herd, or of the flock, *even* of whatsoever
passeth under the rod, the tenth shall
be holy unto the LORD.
33 He shall not search whether it be
good or bad, neither shall he change it:
and if he change it at all, then both it and
the change thereof shall be holy; it shall
not be redeemed.
34 These *are* the commandments,
which the LORD commanded Moses for
the children of Israel in mount Sinai.

27:32 whatsoever passeth under the rod. The animals were probably counted as they passed under the rod, or staff, of the shepherd.

The Fourth Book of Moses, called

NUMBERS

BACKGROUND

The name of the book of Numbers comes from the two *numberings* or countings of the people in chapters 1:19 and 26:4. The book gives the history of the Israelites from the point at which Exodus ended, when they were in the wilderness of Sinai in the second month of the second year after the departure from Egypt, to the end of the wilderness wanderings in the tenth month of the fortieth year, when they were in the plains of Moab, facing the Land of Canaan. Very little is said about the thirty-nine years of wandering in the wilderness, for it was a time of failure. If the children of Israel had had more faith and had entered the land when God meant them to do so, they would have been in Canaan within less than two years after they left Egypt. Because they would not trust God, even after all He had done for them, they needed to be punished by the thirty-nine years of waiting, until all the unbelievers had died, and a new generation was ready to enter the land.

THE WRITER

Moses prepared the material for the book of Numbers (33:2). The period covered is from 1490 to 1451 B.C.

THE MEANING

There are several meanings:

1. The book of Numbers gives a picture of the service and daily life of God's people.
2. It is a warning of failure as is explained in 1 Corinthians 10:1-5.
3. It contains one of the great prophetic messages of the Bible in the prophecies of Balaam (chapters 23; 24).

OUTLINE OF NUMBERS

I.	The Preparation for the Journey	Numbers 1:1—10:10
II.	The Journey Begun and the Failure to Enter the Land	Numbers 10:11—14:45
III.	The 39 Years of Wandering	Numbers 15:1—19:22
IV.	Events of the 40th Year	Numbers 20:1—21:35
V.	Events in the Plains of Moab, Facing the Land	Numbers 22:1—36:13

I. Preparation for the Journey (1:1—10:10)

Numbering the people

1 And the LORD spake unto *Moses in the wilderness of *Sinai, in the *tabernacle of the congregation, on the first *day* of the second *month, in the second year after they were come out of the land of *Egypt, saying,

2 Take ye the sum of all the congregation of the children of *Israel, after their families, by the house of their fathers, with the number of *their* names, every male by their polls;

3 From twenty years old and upward, all that are able to go forth to war in Israel: thou and *Aaron shall number them by their armies.

4 And with you there shall be a man of every tribe; every one head of the house of his fathers.

¶5 And these *are* the names of the men that shall stand with you: of *the tribe of* Reuben; Elizur the son of Shedeur.

6 Of Simeon; Shelumiel the son of Zurishaddai.

7 Of Judah; Nahshon the son of Amminadab.

8 Of Issachar; Nethaneel the son of Zuar.

9 Of Zebulun; Eliab the son of Helon.

10 Of the children of *Joseph: of *Ephraim; Elishama the son of Ammihud: of *Manasseh; Gamaliel the son of Pedahzur.

11 Of Benjamin; Abidan the son of Gideoni.

12 Of Dan; Ahiezer the son of Ammishaddai.

13 Of Asher; Pagiel the son of Ocran.

14 Of Gad; Eliasaph the son of Deuel.

15 Of Naphtali; Ahira the son of Enan.

16 These *were* the renowned of the congregation, princes of the tribes of their fathers, heads of thousands in Israel.

¶17 And Moses and Aaron took these men which are expressed by *their* names:

18 And they assembled all the congregation together on the first *day* of the second month, and they declared their pedigrees after their families, by the house of their fathers, according to the number of the names, from twenty years old and upward, by their polls.

19 As the LORD commanded Moses, so he numbered them in the wilderness of Sinai.

20 And the children of Reuben, Israel's eldest son, by their generations, after their families, by the house of their fathers, according to the number of the names, by their polls, every male from twenty years old and upward, all that were able to go forth to war;

21 Those that were numbered of them, *even* of the tribe of Reuben, *were* forty and six thousand and five hundred.

¶22 Of the children of Simeon, by their generations, after their families, by the house of their fathers, those that were numbered of them, according to the number of the names, by their polls, every male from twenty years old and upward, all that were able to go forth to war;

23 Those that were numbered of them, *even* of the tribe of Simeon, *were* fifty and nine thousand and three hundred.

¶24 Of the children of Gad, by their generations, after their families, by the house of their fathers, according to the number of the names, from twenty

---

1:1 second month. It was now one month after the erection of the tabernacle in Exodus 40:17.

1:2 Take ye the sum. Moses was told to count or *number the people. For the other numberings of the Israelites, see Exodus 38:25-26; Numbers 26:2; 2 Samuel 24:2; 1 Chronicles 21:2.

1:18 by their polls. "Poll" is another word for "head." The Jewish count was by the number of heads there were.

years old and upward, all that were able to go forth to war;

25 Those that were numbered of them, *even* of the tribe of Gad, *were* forty and five thousand six hundred and fifty.

¶ 26 Of the children of Judah, by their generations, after their families, by the house of their fathers, according to the number of the names, from twenty years old and upward, all that were able to go forth to war;

27 Those that were numbered of them, *even* of the tribe of Judah, *were* threescore and fourteen thousand and six hundred.

¶ 28 Of the children of Issachar, by their generations, after their families, by the house of their fathers, according to the number of the names, from twenty years old and upward, all that were able to go forth to war;

29 Those that were numbered of them, *even* of the tribe of Issachar, *were* fifty and four thousand and four hundred.

¶ 30 Of the children of Zebulun, by their generations, after their families, by the house of their fathers, according to the number of the names, from twenty years old and upward, all that were able to go forth to war;

31 Those that were numbered of them, *even* of the tribe of Zebulun, *were* fifty and seven thousand and four hundred.

¶ 32 Of the children of Joseph, *namely,* of the children of Ephraim, by their generations, after their families, by the house of their fathers, according to the number of the names, from twenty years old and upward, all that were able to go forth to war;

33 Those that were numbered of them, *even* of the tribe of Ephraim, *were* forty thousand and five hundred.

¶ 34 Of the children of Manasseh, by their generations, after their families, by the house of their fathers, according to the number of the names, from twenty years old and upward, all that were able to go forth to war;

35 Those that were numbered of them, *even* of the tribe of Manasseh, *were* thirty and two thousand and two hundred.

¶ 36 Of the children of Benjamin, by their generations, after their families, by the house of their fathers, according to the number of the names, from twenty years old and upward, all that were able to go forth to war;

37 Those that were numbered of them, *even* of the tribe of Benjamin, *were* thirty and five thousand and four hundred.

¶ 38 Of the children of Dan, by their generations, after their families, by the house of their fathers, according to the number of the names, from twenty years old and upward, all that were able to go forth to war;

39 Those that were numbered of them, *even* of the tribe of Dan, *were* threescore and two thousand and seven hundred.

¶ 40 Of the children of Asher, by their generations, after their families, by the house of their fathers, according to the number of the names, from twenty years old and upward, all that were able to go forth to war;

41 Those that were numbered of them, *even* of the tribe of Asher, *were* forty and one thousand and five hundred.

¶ 42 Of the children of Naphtali, throughout their generations, after their families, by the house of their fathers, according to the number of the names, from twenty years old and upward, all that were able to go forth to war;

43 Those that were numbered of them, *even* of the tribe of Naphtali, *were* fifty and three thousand and four hundred.

44 These *are* those that were numbered, which Moses and Aaron numbered, and the princes of Israel, *being* twelve men: each one was for the house of his fathers.

45 So were all those that were numbered of the children of Israel, by the house of their fathers, from twenty

years old and upward, all that were able
to go forth to war in Israel;
46Even all they that were numbered
were six hundred thousand and three
thousand and five hundred and fifty.
¶47But the Levites after the tribe of
their fathers were not numbered among
them.
48For the LORD had spoken unto
Moses, saying,
49Only thou shalt not number the
tribe of Levi, neither take the sum of
them among the children of Israel:
50But thou shalt appoint the Levites
over the tabernacle of testimony, and over
all the vessels thereof, and over all things
that *belong* to it: they shall bear the tabernacle, and all the vessels thereof; and
they shall minister unto it, and shall encamp round about the tabernacle.
51And when the tabernacle setteth
forward, the Levites shall take it down:
and when the tabernacle is to be
pitched, the Levites shall set it up: and
the stranger that cometh nigh shall be
put to *death.
52And the children of Israel shall
pitch their tents, every man by his own
camp, and every man by his own standard, throughout their hosts.
53But the Levites shall pitch round
about the tabernacle of testimony, that
there be no wrath upon the congregation of the children of Israel: and the
Levites shall keep the charge of the
tabernacle of testimony.
54And the children of Israel did according to all that the LORD commanded Moses, so did they.

Arrangement of the camp

2 And the LORD spake unto Moses
and unto Aaron, saying,
2Every man of the children of Israel
shall pitch by his own standard, with
the ensign of their father's house: far off
about the tabernacle of the congregation shall they pitch.
3And on the east side toward the rising of the sun shall they of the standard
of the camp of Judah pitch throughout
their armies: and Nahshon the son of
Amminadab *shall be* captain of the children of Judah.
4And his host, and those that were
numbered of them, *were* threescore and
fourteen thousand and six hundred.
5And those that do pitch next unto
him *shall be* the tribe of Issachar: and
Nethaneel the son of Zuar *shall be* captain of the children of Issachar.
6And his host, and those that were
numbered thereof, *were* fifty and four
thousand and four hundred.
7*Then* the tribe of Zebulun: and Eliab the son of Helon *shall be* captain of
the children of Zebulun.
8And his host, and those that were
numbered thereof, *were* fifty and seven
thousand and four hundred.
9All that were numbered in the
camp of Judah *were* an hundred thousand and fourscore thousand and six
thousand and four hundred, throughout their armies. These shall first set
forth.
¶10On the south side *shall be* the standard of the camp of Reuben according
to their armies: and the captain of the

2:2 THE TRIBES' STANDARDS

Tradition says that the flags, or standards, for the tribes of Dan, Judah, Reuben, and Ephraim, who were the leaders on the north, east, south, and west respectively, were:

1. Dan: the figure of an eagle
2. Judah: the figure of a lion
3. Reuben: the figure of a man's head
4. Ephraim: the figure of a calf

The colors of the flags may have corresponded to the color of the twelve stones in the breastplate of the high priest (Exod. 28:15-21).

children of Reuben *shall be* Elizur the
son of Shedeur.
11And his host, and those that were
numbered thereof, *were* forty and six
thousand and five hundred.
12And those which pitch by him *shall*
be the tribe of Simeon: and the captain
of the children of Simeon *shall be* Shelumiel the son of Zurishaddai.
13And his host, and those that were
numbered of them, *were* fifty and nine
thousand and three hundred.
14Then the tribe of Gad: and the captain of the sons of Gad *shall be* Eliasaph
the son of Reuel.
15And his host, and those that were
numbered of them, *were* forty and five
thousand and six hundred and fifty.
16All that were numbered in the camp
of Reuben *were* an hundred thousand
and fifty and one thousand and four
hundred and fifty, throughout their armies. And they shall set forth in the
second rank.
¶17Then the tabernacle of the congregation shall set forward with the
camp of the Levites in the midst of the
camp: as they encamp, so shall they set
forward, every man in his place by their
standards.
¶18On the west side *shall be* the standard of the camp of Ephraim according
to their armies: and the captain of the
sons of Ephraim *shall be* Elishama the
son of Ammihud.
19And his host, and those that were
numbered of them, *were* forty thousand
and five hundred.
20And by him *shall be* the tribe of
Manasseh: and the captain of the children of Manasseh *shall be* Gamaliel the
son of Pedahzur.
21And his host, and those that were
numbered of them, *were* thirty and two
thousand and two hundred.
22Then the tribe of Benjamin: and the
captain of the sons of Benjamin *shall be*
Abidan the son of Gideoni.
23And his host, and those that were
numbered of them, *were* thirty and five
thousand and four hundred.
24All that were numbered of the camp
of Ephraim *were* an hundred thousand
and eight thousand and an hundred,
throughout their armies. And they shall
go forward in the third rank.
¶25The standard of the camp of Dan
shall be on the north side by their armies: and the captain of the children of
Dan *shall be* Ahiezer the son of Ammishaddai.
26And his host, and those that were
numbered of them, *were* threescore and
two thousand and seven hundred.
27And those that encamp by him *shall*
be the tribe of Asher: and the captain of
the children of Asher *shall be* Pagiel the
son of Ocran.
28And his host, and those that were
numbered of them, *were* forty and one
thousand and five hundred.
¶29Then the tribe of Naphtali: and the
captain of the children of Naphtali *shall*
be Ahira the son of Enan.
30And his host, and those that were
numbered of them, *were* fifty and three
thousand and four hundred.
31All they that were numbered in the
camp of Dan *were* an hundred thousand
and fifty and seven thousand and six
hundred. They shall go hindmost with
their standards.
¶32These *are* those which were numbered of the children of Israel by the
house of their fathers: all those that
were numbered of the camps throughout their hosts *were* six hundred thousand and three thousand and five
hundred and fifty.
33But the Levites were not numbered among the children of Israel; as
the LORD commanded Moses.
34And the children of Israel did according to all that the LORD commanded Moses: so they pitched by their
standards, and so they set forward,
every one after their families, according to the house of their fathers.

Families of the priests

3 These also *are* the generations of
Aaron and Moses in the day *that*

the LORD spake with Moses in mount Sinai.

2 And these *are* the names of the sons of Aaron; Nadab the firstborn, and Abihu, Eleazar, and Ithamar.

3 These *are* the names of the sons of Aaron, the priests which were anointed, whom he consecrated to minister in the priest's office.

4 And *Nadab and Abihu died before the LORD, when they offered strange *fire before the LORD, in the wilderness of Sinai, and they had no children: and Eleazar and Ithamar ministered in the priest's office in the sight of Aaron their father.

¶5 And the LORD spake unto Moses, saying,

6 Bring the tribe of Levi near, and present them before Aaron the priest, that they may minister unto him.

7 And they shall keep his charge, and the charge of the whole congregation before the tabernacle of the congregation, to do the service of the tabernacle.

8 And they shall keep all the instruments of the tabernacle of the congregation, and the charge of the children of Israel, to do the service of the tabernacle.

9 And thou shalt give the Levites unto Aaron and to his sons: they *are* wholly given unto him out of the children of Israel.

10 And thou shalt appoint Aaron and his sons, and they shall wait on their priest's office: and the stranger that cometh nigh shall be put to death.

11 And the LORD spake unto Moses, saying,

12 And I, behold, I have taken the Levites from among the children of Israel instead of all the firstborn that openeth the matrix among the children of Israel: therefore the Levites shall be mine;

13 Because all the firstborn *are* mine; *for* on the day that I smote all the firstborn in the land of Egypt I hallowed unto me all the firstborn in Israel, both man and beast: mine shall they be: I *am* the LORD.

¶14 And the LORD spake unto Moses in the wilderness of Sinai, saying,

15 Number the children of Levi after the house of their fathers, by their families: every male from a month old and upward shalt thou number them.

16 And Moses numbered them according to the word of the LORD, as he was commanded.

17 And these were the sons of Levi by their names; Gershon, and Kohath, and Merari.

18 And these *are* the names of the sons of Gershon by their families; Libni, and Shimei.

19 And the sons of Kohath by their families; Amram, and Izehar, Hebron, and Uzziel.

20 And the sons of Merari by their families; Mahli, and Mushi. These *are* the families of the Levites according to the house of their fathers.

21 Of Gershon *was* the family of the Libnites, and the family of the Shimites: these *are* the families of the Gershonites.

22 Those that were numbered of them, according to the number of all the males, from a month old and upward, *even* those that were numbered of them *were* seven thousand and five hundred.

23 The families of the Gershonites shall pitch behind the tabernacle westward.

24 And the chief of the house of the father of the Gershonites *shall be* Eliasaph the son of Lael.

25 And the charge of the sons of Gershon in the tabernacle of the congregation *shall be* the tabernacle, and the tent, the covering thereof, and the hang-

---

3:4 died before the LORD. See the story of this in Leviticus 10.
3:7 charge. This speaks of a particular duty.
3:12 I have taken the Levites. See verse 40 note.

ing for the door of the tabernacle of the congregation,

26 And the hangings of the court, and the curtain for the door of the court, which *is* by the tabernacle, and by the *altar round about, and the cords of it for all the service thereof.

¶27 And of Kohath *was* the family of the Amramites, and the family of the Izeharites, and the family of the Hebronites, and the family of the Uzzielites: these *are* the families of the Kohathites.

28 In the number of all the males, from a month old and upward, *were* eight thousand and six hundred, keeping the charge of the *sanctuary.

29 The families of the sons of Kohath shall pitch on the side of the tabernacle southward.

30 And the chief of the house of the father of the families of the Kohathites *shall be* Elizaphan the son of Uzziel.

31 And their charge *shall be* the *ark, and the table, and the *candlestick, and the altars, and the vessels of the sanctuary wherewith they minister, and the hanging, and all the service thereof.

32 And Eleazar the son of Aaron the priest *shall be* chief over the chief of the Levites, *and have* the oversight of them that keep the charge of the sanctuary.

¶33 Of Merari *was* the family of the Mahlites, and the family of the Mushites: these *are* the families of Merari.

34 And those that were numbered of them, according to the number of all the males, from a month old and upward, *were* six thousand and two hundred.

35 And the chief of the house of the father of the families of Merari *was* Zuriel the son of Abihail: *these* shall pitch on the side of the tabernacle northward.

36 And *under* the custody and charge of the sons of Merari *shall be* the boards of the tabernacle, and the bars thereof, and the pillars thereof, and the sockets thereof, and all the vessels thereof, and all that serveth thereto,

37 And the pillars of the court round about, and their sockets, and their pins, and their cords.

¶38 But those that encamp before the tabernacle toward the east, *even* before the tabernacle of the congregation eastward, *shall be* Moses, and Aaron and his sons, keeping the charge of the sanctuary for the charge of the children of Israel; and the stranger that cometh nigh shall be put to death.

39 All that were numbered of the Levites, which Moses and Aaron numbered at the commandment of the LORD, throughout their families, all the males from a month old and upward, *were* twenty and two thousand.

Levites taken for firstborn

¶40 And the LORD said unto Moses, Number all the firstborn of the males of the children of Israel from a month old and upward, and take the number of their names.

41 And thou shalt take the Levites for me (I *am* the LORD) instead of all the

---

3:40 THE NUMBERING OF THE FIRSTBORN

1. God had claimed the firstborn in Exodus 13 (see Exod. 13:2 note, "The Meaning of Sanctification"). Now He said that He would take the tribe of Levi to serve Him instead of the firstborn (vs. 12).
2. Moses numbered the Levites (vs. 39) at 22,000.
3. He then numbered the firstborn (vs. 43) at 22,273.
4. This left 273 firstborn to be redeemed, for that many more had been claimed by the LORD.
5. From these 273, he took five shekels apiece.
6. The total of 1,365 shekels was handed over to Aaron to be used in the LORD's service.

3:41 I am the LORD. God paused here for a moment to remind His people that it is His right, because He is the LORD, to choose to take the Levites instead of the firstborn.

firstborn among the children of Israel;
and the cattle of the Levites instead of
all the firstlings among the cattle of the
children of Israel.
42 And Moses numbered, as the LORD
commanded him, all the firstborn
among the children of Israel.
43 And all the firstborn males by the
number of names, from a month old
and upward, of those that were numbered of them, were twenty and two
thousand two hundred and threescore
and thirteen.
¶44 And the LORD spake unto Moses,
saying,
45 Take the Levites instead of all the
firstborn among the children of Israel,
and the cattle of the Levites instead of
their cattle; and the Levites shall be
mine: I *am* the LORD.
46 And for those that are to be redeemed of the two hundred and threescore and thirteen of the firstborn of the
children of Israel, which are more than
the Levites;
47 Thou shalt even take five shekels
apiece by the poll, after the shekel of
the sanctuary shalt thou take *them:* (the
shekel *is* twenty *gerahs:)
48 And thou shalt give the *money,
wherewith the odd number of them is
to be redeemed, unto Aaron and to his
sons.
49 And Moses took the redemption
money of them that were over and
above them that were redeemed by
the Levites:
50 Of the firstborn of the children of
Israel took he the money; a thousand
three hundred and threescore and five
shekels, after the shekel of the sanctuary:
51 And Moses gave the money of
them that were redeemed unto Aaron
and to his sons, according to the word
of the LORD, as the LORD commanded
Moses.

Service of the Kohathites

4 And the LORD spake unto Moses
and unto Aaron, saying,
2 Take the sum of the sons of Kohath
from among the sons of Levi, after
their families, by the house of their
fathers,
3 From thirty years old and upward
even until fifty years old, all that enter
into the host, to do the work in the tabernacle of the congregation.
4 This *shall be* the service of the sons
of Kohath in the tabernacle of the congregation, *about* the most *holy things:
¶5 And when the camp setteth forward, Aaron shall come, and his sons,
and they shall take down the covering
vail, and cover the ark of testimony
with it:
6 And shall put thereon the covering
of badgers' skins, and shall spread over
it a cloth wholly of *blue, and shall put
in the staves thereof.
7 And upon the table of *shewbread
they shall spread a cloth of blue, and put
thereon the dishes, and the spoons, and
the bowls, and covers to cover withal:
and the continual bread shall be thereon:
8 And they shall spread upon them a
cloth of scarlet, and cover the same
with a covering of badgers' skins, and
shall put in the staves thereof.
9 And they shall take a cloth of
blue, and cover the candlestick of the
light, and his lamps, and his tongs,
and his snuffdishes, and all the *oil vessels thereof, wherewith they minister
unto it:

He chose Abraham to be the father of the Jewish race. He chose Isaac and Jacob to be the men through whom the line should be carried on, until in His sovereign will, He chose to send His Son into the world to die that those who believe in Him might never die (John 11:25,26).

4:5 covering vail. See Exodus 26:31.
4:5 ark of testimony. See Exodus 25:10-22.
4:7 shewbread. See Exodus 25:30.
4:9 candlestick. See Exodus 25:31-38.

10 And they shall put it and all the vessels thereof within a covering of badgers' skins, and shall put *it* upon a bar.
11 And upon the golden altar they
shall spread a cloth of blue, and cover
it with a covering of badgers' skins, and
shall put to the staves thereof:
12 And they shall take all the instruments of ministry, wherewith they minister in the sanctuary, and put *them* in a
cloth of blue, and cover them with a
covering of badgers' skins, and shall put
them on a bar:
13 And they shall take away the ashes
from the altar, and spread a purple cloth
thereon:
14 And they shall put upon it all the vessels thereof, wherewith they minister
about it, *even* the *censers, the fleshhooks, and the shovels, and the basons,
all the vessels of the altar; and they shall
spread upon it a covering of badgers'
skins, and put to the staves of it.
15 And when Aaron and his sons have
made an end of covering the sanctuary,
and all the vessels of the sanctuary, as
the camp is to set forward; after that,
the sons of Kohath shall come to bear
it: but they shall not touch *any* holy
thing, lest they die. These *things are*
the burden of the sons of Kohath in the
tabernacle of the congregation.

Eleazar's duties

¶16 And to the office of Eleazar the
son of Aaron the priest *pertaineth* the oil
for the light, and the sweet *incense,
and the daily *meat-offering, and the
anointing oil, *and* the oversight of all
the tabernacle, and of all that therein *is,*
in the sanctuary, and in the vessels
thereof.
¶17 And the LORD spake unto Moses
and unto Aaron, saying,
18 Cut ye not off the tribe of the families of the Kohathites from among the
Levites:
19 But thus do unto them, that they
may live, and not die, when they approach unto the most holy things:
Aaron and his sons shall go in, and appoint them every one to his service and
to his burden:
20 But they shall not go in to see when
the holy things are covered, lest they
die.

Service of the Gershonites

¶21 And the LORD spake unto Moses,
saying,
22 Take also the sum of the sons of
Gershon, throughout the houses of
their fathers, by their families;
23 From thirty years old and upward
until fifty years old shalt thou number
them; all that enter in to perform the
service, to do the work in the tabernacle of the congregation.
24 This *is* the service of the families
of the Gershonites, to serve, and for
burdens:
25 And they shall bear the curtains of
the tabernacle, and the tabernacle of the
congregation, his covering, and the covering of the badgers' skins that *is* above
upon it, and the hanging for the door of
the tabernacle of the congregation,
26 And the hangings of the court, and
the hanging for the door of the gate of
the court, which *is* by the tabernacle
and by the altar round about, and their
cords, and all the instruments of their
service, and all that is made for them:
so shall they serve.

4:15 Reverence to God
Severe punishments needed to be given for those who sinned against the holiness of God. Absolute reverence toward God, toward His place of worship, and toward the necessary articles used in His worship needed to be learned. He is the same God today, and although we may approach Him in boldness and love, through the Lord Jesus Christ, we must not forget His holiness and the reverence due Him.

4:11 golden altar. See Exodus 30:1-5.
4:16 oil . . . incense. See Exodus 30:23-25,34.

27 At the appointment of Aaron and
his sons shall be all the service of the
sons of the Gershonites, in all their
burdens, and in all their service: and ye
shall appoint unto them in charge all
their burdens.
28 This *is* the service of the families
of the sons of Gershon in the tabernacle
of the congregation: and their charge
shall be under the hand of Ithamar the
son of Aaron the priest.

Service of the Merarites

¶ 29 As for the sons of Merari, thou
shalt number them after their families,
by the house of their fathers;
30 From thirty years old and upward
even unto fifty years old shalt thou
number them, every one that entereth
into the service, to do the work of the
tabernacle of the congregation.
31 And this *is* the charge of their burden, according to all their service in the
tabernacle of the congregation; the
boards of the tabernacle, and the bars
thereof, and the pillars thereof, and
sockets thereof,
32 And the pillars of the court round
about, and their sockets, and their pins,
and their cords, with all their instruments, and with all their service: and by
name ye shall reckon the instruments
of the charge of their burden.
33 This *is* the service of the families
of the sons of Merari, according to all
their service, in the tabernacle of the
congregation, under the hand of Ithamar the son of Aaron the priest.
¶ 34 And Moses and Aaron and the
chief of the congregation numbered the
sons of the Kohathites after their families, and after the house of their fathers,
35 From thirty years old and upward
even unto fifty years old, every one that
entereth into the service, for the work
in the tabernacle of the congregation:
36 And those that were numbered of
them by their families were two thousand seven hundred and fifty.
37 These *were* they that were numbered of the families of the Kohathites,
all that might do service in the tabernacle of the congregation, which Moses
and Aaron did number according to the
commandment of the LORD by the hand
of Moses.
38 And those that were numbered of
the sons of Gershon, throughout their
families, and by the house of their fathers,
39 From thirty years old and upward
even unto fifty years old, every one
that entereth into the service, for the
work in the tabernacle of the congregation,
40 Even those that were numbered of
them, throughout their families, by the
house of their fathers, were two thousand and six hundred and thirty.
41 These *are* they that were numbered
of the families of the sons of Gershon,
of all that might do service in the tabernacle of the congregation, whom
Moses and Aaron did number according
to the commandment of the LORD.
¶ 42 And those that were numbered of
the families of the sons of Merari,
throughout their families, by the house
of their fathers,
43 From thirty years old and upward
even unto fifty years old, every one that
entereth into the service, for the work
in the tabernacle of the congregation,
44 Even those that were numbered of
them after their families, were three
thousand and two hundred.
45 These *be* those that were numbered of the families of the sons of
Merari, whom Moses and Aaron numbered according to the word of the
LORD by the hand of Moses.
46 All those that were numbered of
the Levites, whom Moses and Aaron
and the chief of Israel numbered, after
their families, and after the house of
their fathers,
47 From thirty years old and upward
even unto fifty years old, every one that
came to do the service of the ministry,
and the service of the burden in the tabernacle of the congregation,
48 Even those that were numbered of

them, were eight thousand and five
hundred and fourscore.
49 According to the commandment of
the LORD they were numbered by the
hand of Moses, every one according to
his service, and according to his burden: thus were they numbered of him,
as the LORD commanded Moses.

Cleanliness and health

5 And the LORD spake unto Moses,
saying,
2 Command the children of Israel, that
they put out of the camp every *leper,
and every one that hath an issue, and
whosoever is defiled by the dead:
3 Both male and female shall ye put
out, without the camp shall ye put
them; that they defile not their camps,
in the midst whereof I dwell.
4 And the children of Israel did so, and
put them out without the camp: as the
LORD spake unto Moses, so did the children of Israel.
¶5 And the LORD spake unto Moses,
saying,
6 Speak unto the children of Israel,
When a man or woman shall commit
any *sin that men commit, to do a *trespass against the LORD, and that person
be guilty;
7 Then they shall *confess their sin
which they have done: and he shall recompense his trespass with the principal thereof, and add unto it the fifth *part*
thereof, and give *it* unto *him* against
whom he hath trespassed.
8 But if the man have no kinsman to
recompense the trespass unto, let the
trespass be recompensed unto the
LORD, *even* to the priest; beside the ram
of the *atonement, whereby an atonement shall be made for him.
9 And every offering of all the holy
things of the children of Israel, which
they bring unto the priest, shall be his.
10 And every man's hallowed things
shall be his: whatsoever any man giveth
the priest, it shall be his.
¶11 And the LORD spake unto Moses,
saying,
12 Speak unto the children of Israel,
and say unto them, If any man's wife go
aside, and commit a trespass against
him,
13 And a man lie with her carnally, and
it be hid from the eyes of her husband,
and be kept close, and she be defiled,
and *there be* no witness against her, neither she be taken *with the manner;*
14 And the spirit of jealousy come
upon him, and he be jealous of his wife,
and she be defiled: or if the spirit of jealousy come upon him, and he be jealous
of his wife, and she be not defiled:
15 Then shall the man bring his wife
unto the priest, and he shall bring her
offering for her, the tenth *part* of an
*ephah of barley meal; he shall pour no
oil upon it, nor put frankincense
thereon; for it *is* an offering of jealousy,
an offering of memorial, bringing iniquity to remembrance.
16 And the priest shall bring her near,
and set her before the LORD:
17 And the priest shall take holy water in an earthen vessel; and of the dust
that is in the floor of the tabernacle the
priest shall take, and put *it* into the
water:
18 And the priest shall set the woman
before the LORD, and uncover the
woman's head, and put the offering of
memorial in her hands, which *is* the
jealousy offering: and the priest shall
have in his hand the bitter water that
causeth the curse:
19 And the priest shall charge her by
an oath, and say unto the woman, If no
man have lain with thee, and if thou hast
not gone aside to uncleanness *with another* instead of thy husband, be thou

---

5:2 Command the children of Israel. These laws were necessary for the cleanliness and health of the camp. It was like a quarantine.
5:8 kinsman. See Ruth 1:11 note. See also *redemption.
5:13 with the manner. Caught in the very act.

free from this bitter water that causeth
the curse:
20 But if thou hast gone aside *to an-*
other instead of thy husband, and if thou
be defiled, and some man have lain with
thee beside thine husband:
21 Then the priest shall charge the
woman with an oath of cursing, and
the priest shall say unto the woman,
The LORD make thee a curse and an
oath among thy people, when the LORD
doth make thy thigh to rot, and thy belly
to swell;
22 And this water that causeth the
curse shall go into thy bowels, to make
thy belly to swell, and *thy* thigh to rot:
And the woman shall say, *Amen, amen.
23 And the priest shall write these
curses in a book, and he shall blot *them*
out with the bitter water:
24 And he shall cause the woman to
drink the bitter water that causeth the
curse: and the water that causeth the
curse shall enter into her, *and become*
bitter.
25 Then the priest shall take the jealousy offering out of the woman's hand,
and shall wave the offering before the
LORD, and offer it upon the altar:
26 And the priest shall take an handful of the offering, even the memorial
thereof, and burn *it* upon the altar, and
afterward shall cause the woman to
drink the water.
27 And when he hath made her to
drink the water, then it shall come to
pass, *that,* if she be defiled, and have
done trespass against her husband, that
the water that causeth the curse shall
enter into her, *and become* bitter, and
her belly shall swell, and her thigh shall
rot: and the woman shall be a curse
among her people.
28 And if the woman be not defiled,
but be *clean; then she shall be free,
and shall conceive seed.
29 This *is* the *law of jealousies, when
a wife goeth aside *to another* instead of
her husband, and is defiled;
30 Or when the spirit of jealousy
cometh upon him, and he be jealous
over his wife, and shall set the woman
before the LORD, and the priest shall
execute upon her all this law.
31 Then shall the man be guiltless
from iniquity, and this woman shall bear
her iniquity.

The Nazarite's vow

6 And the LORD spake unto Moses,
saying,
2 Speak unto the children of Israel,
and say unto them, When either man or
woman shall separate *themselves* to vow
a vow of a *Nazarite, to separate *them-*
selves unto the LORD:
3 He shall separate *himself* from
*wine and strong drink, and shall drink
no vinegar of wine, or vinegar of strong
drink, neither shall he drink any liquor
of grapes, nor eat moist grapes, or
dried.

6:2 A NAZARITE

The word must clearly to be distinguished from a Nazarene (an inhabitant of Nazareth). It can also be spelled "Nazirite" and means *one who is separated.*

Sometimes people wanted to give themselves to work for the LORD in a very special way. They might have decided that they wanted to do this special work for one or two months, or for one or two years, or even longer. To show that they had taken this vow of the Nazarite, they promised also to keep certain signs:

1. They would drink no wine.
2. They would let their hair grow long (men and women both took this vow).
3. They would not touch anything that was dead.

What corresponds to this in the New Testament is that we are urged to present our bodies to God as living sacrifices (Rom. 12:1); and the Nazarite's three signs correspond to self-control, willingness to bear reproach for Christ's sake, and separation from sin. Well-known Nazarites were Samson (Judg. 13–16) and John the Baptist (Luke 1:15).

4 All the days of his separation shall he eat nothing that is made of the vine tree, from the kernels even to the husk.

5 All the days of the vow of his separation there shall no razor come upon his head: until the days be fulfilled, in the which he separateth *himself* unto the LORD, he shall be holy, *and* shall let the locks of the hair of his head grow.

6 All the days that he separateth *himself* unto the LORD he shall come at no dead body.

7 He shall not make himself *unclean for his father, or for his mother, for his brother, or for his sister, when they die: because the consecration of his *God *is* upon his head.

8 All the days of his separation he *is* holy unto the LORD.

9 And if any man die very suddenly by him, and he hath defiled the head of his consecration; then he shall shave his head in the day of his cleansing, on the seventh day shall he shave it.

10 And on the eighth day he shall bring two turtles, or two young pigeons, to the priest, to the door of the tabernacle of the congregation:

11 And the priest shall offer the one for a *sin-offering, and the other for a burnt-offering, and make an atonement for him, for that he sinned by the dead, and shall hallow his head that same day.

12 And he shall *consecrate unto the LORD the days of his separation, and shall bring a lamb of the first year for a *trespass-offering: but the days that were before shall be lost, because his separation was defiled.

¶13 And this *is* the law of the Nazarite, when the days of his separation are fulfilled: he shall be brought unto the door of the tabernacle of the congregation:

14 And he shall offer his offering unto the LORD, one he lamb of the first year without blemish for a burnt-offering, and one ewe lamb of the first year without blemish for a sin-offering, and one ram without blemish for *peace-offerings,

15 And a basket of *unleavened bread, cakes of fine flour mingled with oil, and wafers of unleavened bread anointed with oil, and their meat-offering, and their drink-offerings.

16 And the priest shall bring *them* before the LORD, and shall offer his sin-offering, and his burnt-offering:

17 And he shall offer the ram *for* a *sacrifice of peace-offerings unto the LORD, with the basket of unleavened bread: the priest shall offer also his meat-offering, and his *drink-offering.

18 And the Nazarite shall shave the head of his separation *at* the door of the tabernacle of the congregation, and shall take the hair of the head of his separation, and put *it* in the fire which *is* under the sacrifice of the peace-offerings.

19 And the priest shall take the sodden shoulder of the ram, and one unleavened cake out of the basket, and one unleavened wafer, and shall put *them* upon the hands of the Nazarite, after *the hair of* his separation is shaven:

20 And the priest shall wave them *for* a wave-offering before the LORD: this *is* holy for the priest, with the wave breast and heave shoulder: and after that the Nazarite may drink wine.

21 This *is* the law of the Nazarite who hath vowed, *and of* his offering unto the LORD for his separation, beside that *that* his hand shall get: according to the vow which he vowed, so he must do after the law of his separation.

¶22 And the LORD spake unto Moses, saying,

23 Speak unto Aaron and unto his sons, saying, On this wise ye shall bless the children of Israel, saying unto them,

24 The LORD bless thee, and keep thee:

6:10 two turtles. Turtledoves. All these offerings are described in Leviticus 1.
6:23 wise. Manner or way.
6:23 On this wise ye shall bless. This is called the "Aaronic Benediction" (vss. 24-26).

25 The LORD make his face shine upon
thee, and be gracious unto thee:
26 The LORD lift up his countenance
upon thee, and give thee peace.
27 And they shall put my name upon
the children of Israel; and I will bless
them.

Gifts of the princes

7 And it came to pass on the day
that *Moses had fully set up the
*tabernacle, and had anointed it, and
*sanctified it, and all the instruments
thereof, both the altar and all the vessels thereof, and had anointed them,
and sanctified them;
2 That the princes of *Israel, heads of
the house of their fathers, who *were* the
princes of the tribes, and were over
them that were numbered, offered:
3 And they brought their offering before the LORD, six covered wagons, and
twelve oxen; a wagon for two of the
princes, and for each one an ox: and they
brought them before the tabernacle.
4 And the LORD spake unto Moses,
saying,
5 Take *it* of them, that they may be to
do the service of the tabernacle of the
congregation; and thou shalt give them
unto the Levites, to every man according to his service.
6 And Moses took the wagons and the
oxen, and gave them unto the Levites.
7 Two wagons and four oxen he gave
unto the sons of Gershon, according to
their service:
8 And four wagons and eight oxen he
gave unto the sons of Merari, according unto their service, under the hand
of Ithamar the son of *Aaron the priest.
9 But unto the sons of Kohath he gave
none: because the service of the sanctuary belonging unto them *was that*
they should bear upon their shoulders.
¶ 10 And the princes offered for dedicating of the altar in the day that it was
anointed, even the princes offered their
offering before the altar.
11 And the LORD said unto Moses,
They shall offer their offering, each
prince on his day, for the dedicating of
the altar.

Sacarifices offered by princes

¶ 12 And he that offered his offering
the first day was Nahshon the son of
Amminadab, of the tribe of *Judah:
13 And his offering *was* one *silver
charger, the weight thereof *was* an hundred and thirty *shekels,* one silver bowl
of seventy shekels, after the shekel of
the sanctuary; both of them *were* full of
fine flour mingled with oil for a meat-
offering:
14 One spoon of ten *shekels* of gold, full
of incense:
15 One young bullock, one ram, one
lamb of the first year, for a burnt-
offering:
16 One kid of the goats for a sin-
offering:
17 And for a sacrifice of peace-offerings,
two oxen, five rams, five he goats, five
lambs of the first year: this *was* the offering of Nahshon the son of Amminadab.
¶ 18 On the second day Nethaneel the
son of Zuar, prince of Issachar, did offer:
19 He offered *for* his offering one silver charger, the weight whereof *was* an
hundred and thirty *shekels,* one silver
bowl of seventy shekels, after the shekel of the sanctuary; both of them full of
fine flour mingled with oil for a meat-
offering:
20 One spoon of gold of ten *shekels,* full
of incense:
21 One young bullock, one ram, one
lamb of the first year, for a burnt-
offering:
22 One kid of the goats for a sin-
offering:
23 And for a sacrifice of peace-offerings,
two oxen, five rams, five he goats, five
lambs of the first year: this *was* the offering of Nethaneel the son of Zuar.

7:1 anointed it. See Leviticus 8:10-11 for the rules for anointing the altar.

¶24 On the third day Eliab the son of Helon, prince of the children of Zebulun, *did offer:*

25 His offering *was* one silver charger, the weight whereof *was* an hundred and thirty *shekels,* one silver bowl of seventy shekels, after the shekel of the sanctuary; both of them full of fine flour mingled with oil for a meat-offering:

26 One golden spoon of ten *shekels,* full of incense:

27 One young bullock, one ram, one lamb of the first year, for a burnt-offering:

28 One kid of the goats for a sin-offering:

29 And for a sacrifice of peace-offerings, two oxen, five rams, five he goats, five lambs of the first year: this *was* the offering of Eliab the son of Helon.

¶30 On the fourth day Elizur the son of Shedeur, prince of the children of Reuben, *did offer:*

31 His offering *was* one silver charger of the weight of an hundred and thirty *shekels,* one silver bowl of seventy shekels, after the shekel of the sanctuary; both of them full of fine flour mingled with oil for a meat-offering:

32 One golden spoon of ten *shekels,* full of incense:

33 One young bullock, one ram, one lamb of the first year, for a burnt-offering:

34 One kid of the goats for a sin-offering:

35 And for a sacrifice of peace-offerings, two oxen, five rams, five he goats, five lambs of the first year: this *was* the offering of Elizur the son of Shedeur.

¶36 On the fifth day Shelumiel the son of Zurishaddai, prince of the children of Simeon, *did offer:*

37 His offering *was* one silver charger, the weight whereof *was* an hundred and thirty *shekels,* one silver bowl of seventy shekels, after the shekel of the sanctuary; both of them full of fine flour mingled with oil for a meat-offering:

38 One golden spoon of ten *shekels,* full of incense:

39 One young bullock, one ram, one lamb of the first year, for a burnt-offering:

40 One kid of the goats for a sin-offering:

41 And for a sacrifice of peace-offerings, two oxen, five rams, five he goats, five lambs of the first year: this *was* the offering of Shelumiel the son of Zurishaddai.

¶42 On the sixth day Eliasaph the son of Deuel, prince of the children of Gad, *offered:*

43 His offering *was* one silver charger of the weight of an hundred and thirty *shekels,* a silver bowl of seventy shekels, after the shekel of the sanctuary; both of them full of fine flour mingled with oil for a meat-offering:

44 One golden spoon of ten *shekels,* full of incense:

45 One young bullock, one ram, one lamb of the first year, for a burnt-offering:

46 One kid of the goats for a sin-offering:

47 And for a sacrifice of peace-offerings, two oxen, five rams, five he goats, five lambs of the first year: this *was* the offering of Eliasaph the son of Deuel.

¶48 On the seventh day Elishama the son of Ammihud, prince of the children of *Ephraim, *offered:*

49 His offering *was* one silver charger, the weight whereof *was* an hundred and thirty *shekels,* one silver bowl of seventy shekels, after the shekel of the sanctuary; both of them full of fine flour mingled with oil for a meat-offering:

50 One golden spoon of ten *shekels,* full of incense:

51 One young bullock, one ram, one lamb of the first year, for a burnt-offering:

52 one kid of the goats for a sin-offering:

53 And for a sacrifice of peace-offerings, two oxen, five rams, five he goats, five lambs of the first year: this *was* the offering of Elishama the son of Ammihud.

¶ 54 On the eighth day *offered* Gamaliel the son of Pedahzur, prince of the
children of *Manasseh:
55 His offering *was* one silver charger
of the weight of an hundred and thirty
shekels, one silver bowl of seventy
shekels, after the shekel of the sanctuary; both of them full of fine flour mingled with oil for a meat-offering:
56 One golden spoon of ten *shekels,* full
of incense:
57 One young bullock, one ram, one
lamb of the first year, for a burnt-
offering:
58 One kid of the goats for a sin-
offering:
59 And for a sacrifice of peace-offerings,
two oxen, five rams, five he goats, five
lambs of the first year: this *was* the offering of Gamaliel the son of Pedahzur.
¶ 60 On the ninth day Abidan the son
of Gideoni, prince of the children of
Benjamin, *offered:*
61 His offering *was* one silver charger,
the weight whereof *was* an hundred and
thirty *shekels,* one silver bowl of seventy shekels, after the shekel of the sanctuary; both of them full of fine flour
mingled with oil for a meat-offering:
62 One golden spoon of ten *shekels,* full
of incense:
63 One young bullock, one ram, one
lamb of the first year, for a burnt-
offering:
64 One kid of the goats for a sin-
offering:
65 And for a sacrifice of peace-offerings,
two oxen, five rams, five he goats, five
lambs of the first year: this *was* the offering of Abidan the son of Gideoni.
¶ 66 On the tenth day Ahiezer the son
of Ammishaddai, prince of the children
of Dan, *offered:*
67 His offering *was* one silver charger,
the weight whereof *was* an hundred and
thirty *shekels,* one silver bowl of seventy shekels, after the shekel of the sanctuary; both of them full of fine flour
mingled with oil for a meat-offering:
68 One golden spoon of ten *shekels,* full
of incense:
69 One young bullock, one ram, one
lamb of the first year, for a burnt-
offering:
70 One kid of the goats for a sin-
offering:
71 And for a sacrifice of peace-offerings,
two oxen, five rams, five he goats, five
lambs of the first year: this *was* the
offering of Ahiezer the son of Ammishaddai.
¶ 72 On the eleventh day Pagiel the
son of Ocran, prince of the children of
Asher, *offered:*
73 His offering *was* one silver charger,
the weight whereof *was* an hundred and
thirty *shekels,* one silver bowl of seventy shekels, after the shekel of the sanctuary; both of them full of fine flour
mingled with oil for a meat-offering:
74 One golden spoon of ten *shekels,* full
of incense:
75 One young bullock, one ram, one
lamb of the first year, for a burnt-
offering:
76 One kid of the goats for a sin-
offering:
77 And for a sacrifice of peace-offerings,
two oxen, five rams, five he goats, five
lambs of the first year: this *was* the offering of Pagiel the son of Ocran.
¶ 78 On the twelfth day Ahira the son
of Enan, prince of the children of Naphtali, *offered:*
79 His offering *was* one silver charger,
the weight whereof *was* an hundred and
thirty *shekels,* one silver bowl of seventy shekels, after the shekel of the sanctuary; both of them full of fine flour
mingled with oil for a meat-offering:
80 One golden spoon of ten *shekels,* full
of incense:
81 One young bullock, one ram, one
lamb of the first year, for a burnt-
offering:
82 One kid of the goats for a sin-
offering:
83 And for a sacrifice of peace-offerings,
two oxen, five rams, five he goats, five
lambs of the first year: this *was* the offering of Ahira the son of Enan.
84 This *was* the dedication of the altar,

in the day when it was anointed, by the
princes of Israel: twelve chargers of
silver, twelve silver bowls, twelve
spoons of gold:
85 Each charger of silver *weighing* an
hundred and thirty *shekels,* each bowl
seventy: all the silver vessels *weighed*
two thousand and four hundred *shekels,*
after the shekel of the sanctuary:
86 The golden spoons *were* twelve, full
of incense, *weighing* ten *shekels* apiece,
after the shekel of the sanctuary: all the
gold of the spoons *was* an hundred and
twenty *shekels.*
87 All the oxen for the burnt-offering
were twelve bullocks, the rams twelve,
the lambs of the first year twelve, with
their meat-offering: and the kids of the
goats for sin-offering twelve.
88 And all the oxen for the sacrifice of
the peace-offerings *were* twenty and
four bullocks, the rams sixty, the he
goats sixty, the lambs of the first year
sixty. This *was* the dedication of the altar, after that it was anointed.
89 And when Moses was gone into the
tabernacle of the congregation to speak
with him, then he heard the voice of one
speaking unto him from off the *mercy
seat that *was* upon the ark of testimony, from between the two cherubims:
and he spake unto him.

Lamps and candlestick

8 And the LORD spake unto Moses,
saying,
2 Speak unto Aaron, and say unto him,
When thou lightest the lamps, the
seven lamps shall give light over
against the candlestick.
3 And Aaron did so; he lighted the
lamps thereof over against the candlestick, as the LORD commanded Moses.
4 And this work of the candlestick *was*
of beaten gold, unto the shaft thereof,
unto the flowers thereof, *was* beaten
work: according unto the pattern which
the LORD had shewed Moses, so he
made the candlestick.

Cleansing of the Levites

¶5 And the LORD spake unto Moses,
saying,
6 Take the Levites from among the
children of Israel, and cleanse them.
7 And thus shalt thou do unto them,
to cleanse them: Sprinkle water of purifying upon them, and let them shave
all their flesh, and let them wash their
clothes, and *so* make themselves clean.
8 Then let them take a young bullock
with his meat-offering, *even* fine flour
mingled with oil, and another young
bullock shalt thou take for a sin-
offering.
9 And thou shalt bring the Levites
before the tabernacle of the congregation: and thou shalt gather the whole
assembly of the children of Israel together:
10 And thou shalt bring the Levites
before the LORD: and the children of
Israel shall put their hands upon the
Levites:
11 And Aaron shall offer the Levites
before the LORD *for* an offering of the
children of Israel, that they may execute the service of the LORD.
12 And the Levites shall lay their
hands upon the heads of the bullocks:
and thou shalt offer the one *for* a sin-
offering, and the other *for* a burnt-
offering, unto the LORD, to make an
atonement for the Levites.
13 And thou shalt set the Levites before Aaron, and before his sons, and
offer them *for* an offering unto the
LORD.
14 Thus shalt thou separate the Levites from among the children of Israel:
and the Levites shall be mine.
15 And after that shall the Levites go

7:89 to speak. The LORD had promised to speak with Moses from above the mercy seat (Exod. 25:22).

8:4 according unto the pattern. See Exodus 25:40. Moses followed God's instructions very carefully.

in to do the service of the tabernacle of the congregation: and thou shalt cleanse them, and offer them *for* an offering.

16 For they *are* wholly given unto me from among the children of Israel; instead of such as open every womb, *even instead of* the firstborn of all the children of Israel, have I taken them unto me.

17 For all the firstborn of the children of Israel *are* mine, *both* man and beast: on the day that I smote every firstborn in the land of *Egypt I sanctified them for myself.

18 And I have taken the Levites for all the firstborn of the children of Israel.

19 And I have given the Levites *as* a gift to Aaron and to his sons from among the children of Israel, to do the service of the children of Israel in the tabernacle of the congregation, and to make an atonement for the children of Israel: that there be no plague among the children of Israel, when the children of Israel come nigh unto the sanctuary.

20 And Moses, and Aaron, and all the congregation of the children of Israel, did to the Levites according unto all that the LORD commanded Moses concerning the Levites, so did the children of Israel unto them.

21 And the Levites were purified, and they washed their clothes; and Aaron offered them *as* an offering before the LORD; and Aaron made an atonement for them to cleanse them.

22 And after that went the Levites in to do their service in the tabernacle of the congregation before Aaron, and before his sons: as the LORD had commanded Moses concerning the Levites, so did they unto them.

¶23 And the LORD spake unto Moses, saying,

24 This *is it* that *belongeth* unto the Levites: from twenty and five years old and upward they shall go in to wait upon the service of the tabernacle of the congregation:

25 And from the age of fifty years they shall cease waiting upon the service *thereof,* and shall serve no more:

26 But shall minister with their brethren in the tabernacle of the congregation, to keep the charge, and shall do no service. Thus shalt thou do unto the Levites touching their charge.

The Passover

9 And the LORD spake unto Moses in the wilderness of *Sinai, in the first *month of the second year after they were come out of the land of Egypt, saying,

2 Let the children of Israel also keep the *passover at his appointed season.

3 In the fourteenth day of this month, at even, ye shall keep it in his appointed season: according to all the rites of it, and according to all the ceremonies thereof, shall ye keep it.

4 And Moses spake unto the children of Israel, that they should keep the passover.

5 And they kept the passover on the fourteenth day of the first month at even in the wilderness of Sinai: according to all that the LORD commanded Moses, so did the children of Israel.

¶6 And there were certain men, who were defiled by the dead body of a man, that they could not keep the passover on that day: and they came before Moses and before Aaron on that day:

7 And those men said unto him, We *are* defiled by the dead body of a man: wherefore are we kept back, that we may not offer an offering of the LORD in his appointed season among the children of Israel?

8 And Moses said unto them, Stand still, and I will hear what the LORD will command concerning you.

9:6 defiled by the dead body of a man. If someone touched a dead body, that person was unclean for seven days and could not take part in the worship, because he had to stay separate from everyone until he had been cleansed (see Num. 19).

¶9 And the LORD spake unto Moses,
saying,
10 Speak unto the children of Israel,
saying, If any man of you or of your
posterity shall be unclean by reason of
a dead body, or *be* in a journey afar off,
yet he shall keep the passover unto the
LORD.
11 The fourteenth day of the second
month at even they shall keep it, *and*
eat it with unleavened bread and bitter
herbs.
12 They shall leave none of it unto the
morning, nor break any bone of it: according to all the ordinances of the passover they shall keep it.
13 But the man that *is* clean, and is not
in a journey, and forbeareth to keep the
passover, even the same soul shall be
cut off from among his people: because
he brought not the offering of the LORD
in his appointed season, that man shall
bear his sin.
14 And if a stranger shall sojourn
among you, and will keep the passover
unto the LORD; according to the ordinance of the passover, and according to
the manner thereof, so shall he do: ye
shall have one ordinance, both for the
stranger, and for him that was born in
the land.

The guiding cloud

¶15 And on the day that the tabernacle was reared up the cloud covered the
tabernacle, *namely,* the tent of the testimony: and at even there was upon the
tabernacle as it were the appearance of
*fire, until the morning.
16 So it was alway: the cloud covered
it *by day,* and the appearance of fire by
night.
17 And when the cloud was taken up
from the tabernacle, then after that the
children of Israel journeyed: and in
the place where the cloud abode, there
the children of Israel pitched their tents.
18 At the commandment of the LORD
the children of Israel journeyed, and at
the commandment of the LORD they
pitched: as long as the cloud abode upon
the tabernacle they rested in their
tents.
19 And when the cloud tarried long
upon the tabernacle many days, then
the children of Israel kept the charge of
the LORD, and journeyed not.
20 And *so* it was, when the cloud was
a few days upon the tabernacle; according to the commandment of the LORD
they abode in their tents, and according
to the commandment of the LORD they
journeyed.
21 And *so* it was, when the cloud abode
from even unto the morning, and *that*
the cloud was taken up in the morning,
then they journeyed: whether *it was* by
day or by night that the cloud was tak-
en up, they journeyed.
22 Or *whether it were* two days, or a
month, or a year, that the cloud tarried
upon the tabernacle, remaining
thereon, the children of Israel abode in
their tents, and journeyed not: but
when it was taken up, they journeyed.
23 At the commandment of the LORD
they rested in the tents, and at the commandment of the LORD they journeyed:
they kept the charge of the LORD, at the
commandment of the LORD by the hand
of Moses.

The silver trumpets

10 And the LORD spake unto Moses, saying,
2 Make thee two trumpets of silver; of
a whole piece shalt thou make them:
that thou mayest use them for the

9:12 nor break any bone. The Lord Jesus Christ is our Passover Lamb (see Exod. 12:3 note, "The Meaning of Passover"). This was symbolic because not a bone of the Lord's body was broken when He died (John 19:36).

9:15 on the day that the tabernacle was reared up. This was the same occasion as Exodus 40:33-38.

9:15 the cloud. The sign of the presence of the LORD. See Exodus 13:21 note.

10:2 two trumpets of silver. Look up Joel 2:1.

calling of the assembly, and for the journeying of the camps.
3 And when they shall blow with
them, all the assembly shall assemble
themselves to thee at the door of the
tabernacle of the congregation.
4 And if they blow *but* with one *trumpet,* then the princes, *which are* heads
of the thousands of Israel, shall gather
themselves unto thee.
5 When ye blow an alarm, then the
camps that lie on the east parts shall go
forward.
6 When ye blow an alarm the second
time, then the camps that lie on the
south side shall take their journey: they
shall blow an alarm for their journeys.
7 But when the congregation is to be
gathered together, ye shall blow, but ye
shall not sound an alarm.
8 And the sons of Aaron, the priests,
shall blow with the trumpets; and they
shall be to you for an ordinance for ever
throughout your generations.
9 And if ye go to war in your land
against the enemy that oppresseth you,
then ye shall blow an alarm with the
trumpets; and ye shall be remembered
before the LORD your God, and ye shall
be saved from your enemies.
10 Also in the day of your gladness,
and in your solemn days, and in the
beginnings of your months, ye shall
blow with the trumpets over your
burnt-offerings, and over the sacrifices
of your peace-offerings; that they may
be to you for a memorial before your
God: I *am* the LORD your God.

II. The Journey Begun (10:11—14:45)

From Sinai to Paran

¶11 And it came to pass on the twentieth *day* of the second month, in the
second year, that the cloud was taken
up from off the tabernacle of the testimony.
12 And the children of Israel took their
journeys out of the wilderness of Sinai;

10:10 THE FEASTS AND FESTIVALS SUMMARIZED

1. The weekly festival was the Sabbath, commemorating God's rest from creation and the Israelites' deliverance from bondage in Egypt (Exod. 20:8-11).
2. The monthly festival was the day of the new moon, on which rest was not required, but the day was marked by additional services (Num. 10:10; 28:11).
3. The new moon of the seventh month, Tishri, or the Feast of Trumpets, began the civil year, and that of Abib the ecclesiastical year (Exod. 12:2; Num. 29:1). The seventh month was our October.
4. The great festivals were:
   a) Passover, on the eve of the fourteenth day of Abib, which lasted to the twenty-first day (Exod. 12).
   b) Pentecost (the fiftieth day after), or the Feast of Weeks, on the completion of the harvest (Exod. 23:16; Deut. 16:9-11).
   c) Tabernacles, from the fifteenth to the twenty-third of Tishri (October), commemorating the ingathering of all fruits (Exod. 34:22; Lev. 23:34-43). The people lived for a week in booths, to remind them of their desert wanderings. The last day was "the great day" (John 7:37). This feast was preceded by the Day of Atonement (Lev. 16).
5. Every seventh year was a sabbatical year, when the land had rest. Every fiftieth year was a Jubilee year, when slaves were freed, land sold reverted back to its original owner, and mortgages were cancelled.
6. To these festivals was added the Feast of Purim ("Lots"), on the fourteenth and fifteenth of Adar (March), in remembrance of the deliverance of the Jews by Esther (Esther 9:24-26).
7. Another festival added was the Feast of the Dedication (of the second temple), celebrated on the twenty-fifth of Kislev (December), (John 10:22).

10:5 on the east parts. Judah, Issachar, and Zebulun. See 2:2 note, "The Tribes' Standards."

10:6 on the south side. Reuben, Simeon, and Gad. See 2:2 note.

and the cloud rested in the wilderness of Paran.

13 And they first took their journey according to the commandment of the LORD by the hand of Moses.

¶14 In the first *place* went the standard of the camp of the children of Judah according to their armies: and over his host *was* Nahshon the son of Amminadab.

15 And over the host of the tribe of the children of Issachar *was* Nethaneel the son of Zuar.

16 And over the host of the tribe of the children of Zebulun *was* Eliab the son of Helon.

17 And the tabernacle was taken down; and the sons of Gershon and the sons of Merari set forward, bearing the tabernacle.

¶18 And the standard of the camp of Reuben set forward according to their armies: and over his host *was* Elizur the son of Shedeur.

19 And over the host of the tribe of the children of Simeon *was* Shelumiel the son of Zurishaddai.

20 And over the host of the tribe of the children of Gad *was* Eliasaph the son of Deuel.

21 And the Kohathites set forward, bearing the *sanctuary: and *the other* did set up the tabernacle against they came.

¶22 And the standard of the camp of the children of Ephraim set forward according to their armies: and over his host *was* Elishama the son of Ammihud.

23 And over the host of the tribe of the children of Manasseh *was* Gamaliel the son of Pedahzur.

24 And over the host of the tribe of the children of Benjamin *was* Abidan the son of Gideoni.

¶25 And the standard of the camp of the children of Dan set forward, *which was* the *rereward of all the camps throughout their hosts: and over his host *was* Ahiezer the son of Ammishaddai.

26 And over the host of the tribe of the children of Asher *was* Pagiel the son of Ocran.

27 And over the host of the tribe of the children of Naphtali *was* Ahira the son of Enan.

28 Thus *were* the journeyings of the children of Israel according to their armies, when they set forward.

¶29 And Moses said unto Hobab, the son of Raguel the Midianite, Moses' father in law, We are journeying unto the place of which the LORD said, I will give it you: come thou with us, and we will do thee good: for the LORD hath spoken good concerning Israel.

10:29 Hobab
Hobab was probably the son of Moses' father-in-law and therefore Moses' brother-in-law. Raguel is the same as Reuel or Jethro (Exod. 2:18; 18:1). Hobab's knowledge of the country and the people would be a great help to Moses. Hobab eventually settled in Canaan (Judg. 1:16).

30 And he said unto him, I will not go; but I will depart to mine own land, and to my kindred.

31 And he said, Leave us not, I pray thee; forasmuch as thou knowest how we are to encamp in the wilderness, and thou mayest be to us instead of eyes.

32 And it shall be, if thou go with us, yea, it shall be, that what goodness the LORD shall do unto us, the same will we do unto thee.

¶33 And they departed from the mount of the LORD three days' journey: and the *ark of the *covenant of the LORD went before them in the three days' journey, to search out a resting place for them.

34 And the cloud of the LORD *was* upon them by day, when they went out of the camp.

35 And it came to pass, when the ark set forward, that Moses said, Rise up, LORD, and let thine enemies be scattered; and let them that hate thee flee before thee.

36 And when it rested, he said, Return, O LORD, unto the many thousands of Israel.

The people complain

11 And *when* the people complained, it displeased the LORD:
and the LORD heard *it;* and his anger
was kindled; and the fire of the LORD
burnt among them, and consumed *them*
that were in the uttermost parts of the
camp.
2And the people cried unto Moses;
and when Moses prayed unto the LORD,
the fire was quenched.
3And he called the name of the place
Taberah: because the fire of the LORD
burnt among them.
¶4And the mixt multitude that *was*
among them fell a lusting: and the children of Israel also wept again, and said,
Who shall give us flesh to eat?
5We remember the fish, which we did
eat in Egypt freely; the cucumbers, and
the melons, and the leeks, and the on-
ions, and the garlick:
6But now our soul *is* dried away: *there*
is nothing at all, beside this *manna,
before our eyes.
7And the manna *was* as coriander
seed, and the colour thereof as the
colour of bdellium.
8*And* the people went about, and
gathered *it,* and ground *it* in mills, or
beat *it* in a mortar, and baked *it* in pans,
and made cakes of it: and the taste of it
was as the taste of fresh *oil.
9And when the dew fell upon
the camp in the night, the manna fell
upon it.

Moses' complaint to the LORD

¶10Then Moses heard the people
weep throughout their families, every
man in the door of his tent: and the anger of the LORD was kindled greatly;
Moses also was displeased.
11And Moses said unto the LORD,
Wherefore hast thou afflicted thy servant? and wherefore have I not found
favour in thy sight, that thou layest the
burden of all this people upon me?
12Have I conceived all this people?
have I begotten them, that thou
shouldest say unto me, Carry them in
thy bosom, as a nursing father beareth

11:4 ISRAEL'S COMPLAINTS

Shortly after being delivered from slavery in Egypt, the Israelites began to complain about one thing after the other. Through Moses' patience and God's understanding and love, their concerns were alleviated.

Complaint	God's remedy	Reference
Pharaoh's soldiers will kill us!	Red sea divided	Exodus 14:11-12
What shall we drink?	Water sweetened at Marah	Exodus 15:24
We will die of hunger!	Manna sent	Exodus 16:3
Will we die of thirst?	Water from a rock	Exodus 17:3
Who will give us meat?	Quails sent	Numbers 11:4
We'll never conquer the Promised Land!	God spares the people but they wander for 40 years	Numbers 14:3
Moses acts like a prince over us.	God kills the complainers	Numbers 16:3,13
There's no water!	Water from a rock	Numbers 20:5
There's no water or food. And we're sick of manna.	Snakes/bronze snake	Numbers 21:5

11:3 Taberah. Burning.
11:4 the mixt multitude. These were the people of mixed Israelite and Egyptian birth who had attached themselves to the Israelites during their escape from Egypt.
11:7 colour. Probably bdellium was a name for pearls. Coriander seeds were gray-white pods of the coriander plant which was used in Egypt for spicing food. (See Exod. 16:15 note, "Manna from Heaven.")

the sucking child, unto the land which
thou swarest unto their fathers?
13Whence should I have flesh to give
unto all this people? for they weep unto
me, saying, Give us flesh, that we
may eat.
14I am not able to bear all this people
alone, because *it is* too heavy for me.
15And if thou deal thus with me, kill
me, I pray thee, out of hand, if I have
found favour in thy sight; and let me not
see my wretchedness.

Appointment of 70 elders

¶16And the LORD said unto Moses,
Gather unto me seventy men of the
*elders of Israel, whom thou knowest
to be the elders of the people, and officers over them; and bring them unto
the tabernacle of the congregation, that
they may stand there with thee.
17And I will come down and talk with
thee there: and I will take of the spirit
which *is* upon thee, and will put *it* upon
them; and they shall bear the burden of
the people with thee, that thou bear *it*
not thyself alone.
18And say thou unto the people,
Sanctify yourselves against to morrow, and ye shall eat flesh: for ye have
wept in the ears of the LORD, saying,
Who shall give us flesh to eat? for *it*
was well with us in Egypt: therefore
the LORD will give you flesh, and ye
shall eat.
19Ye shall not eat one day, nor two
days, nor five days, neither ten days,
nor twenty days;
20*But* even a whole month, until it
come out at your nostrils, and it be
loathsome unto you: because that ye
have despised the LORD which *is* among
you, and have wept before him, saying,
Why came we forth out of Egypt?
21And Moses said, The people,
among whom I *am, are* six hundred
thousand footmen; and thou hast said,
I will give them flesh, that they may eat
a whole month.
22Shall the flocks and the herds be
slain for them, to suffice them? or shall
all the fish of the sea be gathered together for them, to suffice them?
23And the LORD said unto Moses, Is
the LORD'S hand waxed short? thou
shalt see now whether my word shall
come to pass unto thee or not.
¶24And Moses went out, and told the
people the words of the LORD, and gathered the seventy men of the elders of
the people, and set them round about
the tabernacle.
25And the LORD came down in a
cloud, and spake unto him, and took of
the spirit that *was* upon him, and gave
it unto the seventy elders: and it came
to pass, *that,* when the spirit rested
upon them, they prophesied, and did
not cease.

11:25 The Power of the Spirit
Moses had had enough power by the Holy Spirit to lead the people as God directed him. Now because he complained of the burden, God took of the Spirit in Moses and gave it to the seventy men. The power of the Spirit is always infinite, but it was now working in seventy-one men, counting Moses, instead of in Moses alone.

26But there remained two *of the* men
in the camp, the name of the one
was Eldad, and the name of the other
Medad: and the spirit rested upon
them; and they *were* of them that were
written, but went not out unto the
tabernacle: and they prophesied in the
camp.
27And there ran a young man, and
told Moses, and said, Eldad and Medad
do prophesy in the camp.
28And *Joshua the son of Nun, the
servant of Moses, *one* of his young men,
answered and said, My lord Moses, forbid them.
29And Moses said unto him, Enviest
thou for my sake? would God that all
the LORD'S people were *prophets, *and*

11:24 the words of the LORD. See *inspiration.

that the LORD would put his spirit upon
them!
[30]And Moses gat him into the camp,
he and the elders of Israel.

The quails followed by plague

¶[31]And there went forth a wind from
the LORD, and brought quails from the
sea, and let *them* fall by the camp, as it
were a day's journey on this side, and
as it were a day's journey on the other
side, round about the camp, and as it
were two *cubits *high* upon the face of
the earth.
[32]And the people stood up all that day,
and all *that* night, and all the next day,
and they gathered the quails: he that
gathered least gathered ten homers:
and they spread *them* all abroad for
themselves round about the camp.
[33]And while the flesh *was* yet between their teeth, ere it was chewed,
the wrath of the LORD was kindled
against the people, and the LORD smote
the people with a very great plague.
[34]And he called the name of that place
Kibroth-hattaavah: because there they
buried the people that lusted.

11:34 The Result of Sin
"Kibroth-hattaavah" means *graves of lust.* The people were punished for their sin of complaining of the LORD's provision for them. He had supplied their every need; He had cared for them; He had led them out of the terrible slavery of Egypt. Despite all that, now the people were looking back to that country and that slavery and saying that they wanted the food that they had had back there. God once again needed to show them how displeasing sin is to Him, and that He knew what was best for them in every way.

[35]*And* the people journeyed from
Kibroth-hattaavah unto Hazeroth; and
abode at Hazeroth.

Discontent of Miriam and Aaron

12 And *Miriam and Aaron spake
against Moses because of the
Ethiopian woman whom he had married: for he had married an Ethiopian
woman.

12:1 Miriam and Aaron
Miriam was the oldest of the children of Amram and Jochebed. She was at least twelve years older than Moses (Exod. 2:4-8). She was a prophetess (Exod. 15:20); that is, she sometimes received messages from God, either in dreams or in visions, to give to the people. Aaron was three years older than Moses and was honored by being the chosen high priest of God. The positions that Miriam and Aaron held probably led them to think that they were just as important as Moses. The Ethiopian woman of whom they were jealous may have been Zipporah (Exod. 2:21), or she may have been another wife whom Moses married after the death of Zipporah.

[2]And they said, Hath the LORD indeed spoken only by Moses? hath he
not spoken also by us? And the LORD
heard *it.*
[3](Now the man Moses *was* very
meek, above all the men which *were*
upon the face of the earth.)
[4]And the LORD spake suddenly unto
Moses, and unto Aaron, and unto Miriam, Come out ye three unto the tabernacle of the congregation. And they
three came out.
[5]And the LORD came down in the
*pillar of the cloud, and stood *in* the
door of the tabernacle, and called
Aaron and Miriam: and they both came
forth.
[6]And he said, Hear now my words: If
there be a *prophet among you, *I* the
LORD will make myself known unto him
in a vision, *and* will speak unto him in
a dream.

11:31 a day's journey. About twenty-four miles.
11:31 two cubits high. This means that the quails flew at about two feet, eleven inches off the ground. This made the birds easily accessible to the people, so that they could slay them.

7 My servant Moses *is* not so, who *is*
faithful in all mine house.
8 With him will I speak mouth to
mouth, even apparently, and not in dark
speeches; and the similitude of the
LORD shall he behold: wherefore then
were ye not afraid to speak against my
servant Moses?
9 And the anger of the LORD was kindled against them; and he departed.
10 And the cloud departed from off the
tabernacle; and, behold, Miriam *became*
*leprous, *white* as snow: and Aaron
looked upon Miriam, and, behold, *she*
was leprous.
11 And Aaron said unto Moses, Alas,
my lord, I beseech thee, lay not the *sin
upon us, wherein we have done foolishly, and wherein we have sinned.
12 Let her not be as one dead, of whom
the flesh is half consumed when he
cometh out of his mother's womb.
13 And Moses cried unto the LORD,
saying, Heal her now, O *God, I beseech thee.
¶14 And the LORD said unto Moses, If
her father had but spit in her face,
should she not be ashamed seven days?
let her be shut out from the camp seven
days, and after that let her be received
in *again.*
15 And Miriam was shut out from the
camp seven days: and the people journeyed not till Miriam was brought in
again.
16 And afterward the people removed
from Hazeroth, and pitched in the wilderness of Paran.

The spies and their report

13 And the LORD spake unto *Moses, saying,
2 Send thou men, that they may
search the land of Canaan, which I give
unto the children of *Israel: of every
tribe of their fathers shall ye send a
man, every one a ruler among them.
3 And Moses by the commandment of
the LORD sent them from the wilderness of Paran: all those men *were* heads
of the children of Israel.
4 And these *were* their names: of the
tribe of Reuben, Shammua the son of
Zaccur.
5 Of the tribe of Simeon, Shaphat the
son of Hori.
6 Of the tribe of Judah, *Caleb the son
of Jephunneh.
7 Of the tribe of Issachar, Igal the son
of *Joseph.
8 Of the tribe of *Ephraim, Oshea the
son of Nun.
9 Of the tribe of Benjamin, Palti the
son of Raphu.
10 Of the tribe of Zebulun, Gaddiel the
son of Sodi.
11 Of the tribe of Joseph, *namely,* of
the tribe of *Manasseh, Gaddi the son
of Susi.
12 Of the tribe of Dan, Ammiel the son
of Gemalli.
13 Of the tribe of Asher, Sethur the
son of Michael.
14 Of the tribe of Naphtali, Nahbi the
son of Vophsi.
15 Of the tribe of Gad, Geuel the son
of Machi.
16 These *are* the names of the men

13:16 Joshua
Jehoshua, or Joshua, means *Saviour* or *Deliverer.* This name is the Hebrew form of Jesus. It is thus a good name, for *Joshua was a *type of the Lord Jesus Christ as the Saviour of His people.

12:7 faithful in all mine house. See Hebrews 3:1-6. God pointed out that Moses was even closer to Him than a prophet, because a prophet only received messages, but Moses had spoken with God face-to-face and had been given a sight of God's glory.
12:8 apparently. Plainly, openly.
12:8 similitude of the LORD. Evidently meaning the vision that Moses had in Exodus 33:18-23.
13:2 Send thou men. Look up Moses' account of this in Deuteronomy 1:19-46.

which Moses sent to spy out the land.
And Moses called Oshea the son of Nun
Jehoshua.
¶17 And Moses sent them to spy out
the land of Canaan, and said unto them,
Get you up this *way* southward, and go
up into the *mountain:
18 And see the land, what it *is;* and the
people that dwelleth therein, whether
they *be* strong or weak, few or many;
19 And what the land *is* that they dwell
in, whether it *be* good or bad; and what
cities *they be* that they dwell in, whether in tents, or in strong holds;
20 And what the land *is,* whether it *be*
fat or lean, whether there be wood
therein, or not. And be ye of good courage, and bring of the fruit of the land.
Now the time *was* the time of the
firstripe grapes.
¶21 So they went up, and searched the
land from the wilderness of Zin unto
Rehob, as men come to Hamath.
22 And they ascended by the south,
and came unto Hebron; where Ahiman,
Sheshai, and Talmai, the children of
Anak, *were.* (Now Hebron was built
seven years before *Zoan in Egypt.)

13:22 Giants in the Land
The children of Anak were a giant race of men descended from Arba (Josh. 14:15) who were afterwards almost exterminated by Joshua (Josh. 11:21). The few who escaped fled to the land of the Philistines and appear again in David's time. Goliath of Gath was doubtless a descendant of the children of Anak (1 Sam. 17:4).

23 And they came unto the brook of
Eshcol, and cut down from thence a
branch with one cluster of grapes, and
they bare it between two upon a staff;
and *they brought* of the pomegranates,
and of the figs.
24 The place was called the brook
Eshcol, because of the cluster of grapes
which the children of Israel cut down
from thence.
25 And they returned from searching
of the land after forty days.
¶26 And they went and came to Moses, and to *Aaron, and to all the congregation of the children of Israel, unto
the wilderness of Paran, to Kadesh; and
brought back word unto them, and unto
all the congregation, and shewed them
the fruit of the land.
27 And they told him, and said, We
came unto the land whither thou
sentest us, and surely it *floweth with
milk and honey; and this *is* the fruit
of it.
28 Nevertheless the people *be* strong
that dwell in the land, and the cities *are*
walled, *and* very great: and moreover
we saw the children of Anak there.
29 The Amalekites dwell in the land of
the south: and the Hittites, and the Jebusites, and the Amorites, dwell in the
mountains: and the Canaanites dwell by
the sea, and by the coast of Jordan.
30 And Caleb stilled the people before
Moses, and said, Let us go up at once,
and possess it; for we are well able to
overcome it.
31 But the men that went up with
him said, We be not able to go up
against the people; for they *are* stronger than we.
32 And they brought up an evil report
of the land which they had searched
unto the children of Israel, saying, The
land, through which we have gone to
search it, *is* a land that eateth up the
inhabitants thereof; and all the people
that we saw in it *are* men of a great stature.
33 And there we saw the giants, the
sons of Anak, *which come* of the giants:
and we were in our own sight as grasshoppers, and so we were in their sight.

Failure through unbelief

14 And all the congregation lifted
up their voice, and cried; and
the people wept that night.
2 And all the children of Israel mur-

14:2 murmured. This is the usual complaint of the people.

mured against Moses and against
Aaron: and the whole congregation said
unto them, Would God that we had died
in the land of *Egypt! or would God we
had died in this wilderness!
[3]And wherefore hath the LORD
brought us unto this land, to fall by the
sword, that our wives and our children
should be a prey? were it not better for
us to return into Egypt?
[4]And they said one to another, Let us
make a captain, and let us return into
Egypt.
[5]Then Moses and Aaron fell on their
faces before all the assembly of the congregation of the children of Israel.
¶[6]And Joshua the son of Nun, and Caleb the son of Jephunneh, *which were* of
them that searched the land, rent their
clothes:
[7]And they spake unto all the company of the children of Israel, saying,
The land, which we passed through to
search it, *is* an exceeding good land.
[8]If the LORD delight in us, then he
will bring us into this land, and give it
us; a land which floweth with milk and
honey.
[9]Only rebel not ye against the LORD,
neither fear ye the people of the land;
for they *are* bread for us: their defence
is departed from them, and the LORD *is*
with us: fear them not.
[10]But all the congregation bade stone
them with stones. And the glory of the
LORD appeared in the *tabernacle of the
congregation before all the children of
Israel.
¶[11]And the LORD said unto Moses,
How long will this people provoke me?
and how long will it be ere they believe
me, for all the signs which I have
shewed among them?
[12]I will smite them with the pestilence, and disinherit them, and will
make of thee a greater nation and
mightier than they.
¶[13]And Moses said unto the LORD,
Then the Egyptians shall hear *it,* (for
thou broughtest up this people in thy
might from among them;)
[14]And they will tell *it* to the inhabitants of this land: *for* they have heard
that thou LORD *art* among this people,
that thou LORD art seen face to face,
and *that* thy cloud standeth over them,
and *that* thou goest before them, by
daytime in a pillar of a cloud, and in a
pillar of fire by night.
¶[15]Now *if* thou shalt kill *all* this people as one man, then the nations which
have heard the fame of thee will speak,
saying,
[16]Because the LORD was not able to
bring this people into the land which he
sware unto them, therefore he hath
slain them in the wilderness.
[17]And now, I beseech thee, let the
power of my Lord be great, according
as thou hast spoken, saying,
[18]The LORD *is* longsuffering, and
of great *mercy, forgiving iniquity and

14:12 MOSES' DEVOTION

God twice offered (here and in Exod. 32:10) to start a new nation with Moses. The faithful devotion of Moses to their cause is in strong contrast to the people's treatment of him. At ten different times (vs. 22) the Israelites complained and made Moses angry:

1. at the Red Sea with Pharaoh in pursuit (Exod. 14:11-12);
2. at Marah when the water was too bitter to drink (Exod. 15:23-24);
3. when they were hungry and yearned for the food of Egypt (Exod. 16:2-3);
4. when they gathered more manna than they needed (Exod. 16:20);
5. when they expected to find manna on the Sabbath (Exod. 16:27);
6. at Rephidim when there was no water (Exod. 17:1-3);
7. at Sinai when they worshipped a golden calf (Exod. 32:7-10);
8. at Taberah when they complained and God punished them with fire (Num. 11:1);
9. when they were tired of manna and wanted meat (Num. 11:4);
10. when they were afraid of the "giants" in the land and feared dying (Num. 14:2).

transgression, and by no means clearing *the guilty,* visiting the iniquity of the fathers upon the children unto the third and fourth *generation.*

19 Pardon, I beseech thee, the iniquity of this people according unto the greatness of thy mercy, and as thou hast *forgiven this people, from Egypt even until now.

20 And the LORD said, I have pardoned according to thy word:

21 But *as* truly *as* I live, all the earth shall be filled with the glory of the LORD.

22 Because all those men which have seen my glory, and my *miracles, which I did in Egypt and in the wilderness, and have tempted me now these ten times, and have not hearkened to my voice;

23 Surely they shall not see the land which I sware unto their fathers, neither shall any of them that provoked me see it:

24 But my servant Caleb, because he had another spirit with him, and hath followed me fully, him will I bring into the land whereinto he went; and his seed shall possess it.

25 (Now the Amalekites and the Canaanites dwelt in the valley.) To morrow turn you, and get you into the wilderness by the way of the Red sea.

¶26 And the LORD spake unto Moses and unto Aaron, saying,

27 How long *shall I bear with* this evil congregation, which murmur against me? I have heard the murmurings of the children of Israel, which they murmur against me.

28 Say unto them, *As truly as* I live, saith the LORD, as ye have spoken in mine ears, so will I do to you:

29 Your carcases shall fall in this wilderness; and all that were numbered of you, according to your whole number, from twenty years old and upward, which have murmured against me,

30 Doubtless ye shall not come into the land, *concerning* which I sware to make you dwell therein, save Caleb the son of Jephunneh, and Joshua the son of Nun.

31 But your little ones, which ye said should be a prey, them will I bring in, and they shall know the land which ye have despised.

32 But *as for* you, your carcases, they shall fall in this wilderness.

33 And your children shall wander in the wilderness forty years, and bear your whoredoms, until your carcases be wasted in the wilderness.

34 After the number of the days in which ye searched the land, *even* forty days, each day for a year, shall ye bear your iniquities, *even* forty years, and ye shall know my breach of promise.

35 I the LORD have said, I will surely do it unto all this evil congregation, that are gathered together against me: in this wilderness they shall be consumed, and there they shall die.

36 And the men, which Moses sent to search the land, who returned, and made all the congregation to murmur against him, by bringing up a slander upon the land,

37 Even those men that did bring up the evil report upon the land, died by the plague before the LORD.

38 But Joshua the son of Nun, and

14:24 But my servant Caleb. See 13:30 and 14:6-9 to see why Caleb and Joshua were allowed to enter the land when the rest of the people, because of their unbelief, were not allowed.

14:25 turn you. The children of Israel were right on the edge of the land that God had promised them, two years after they left Egypt, but because of their unbelief they were turned back into the wilderness.

14:30 Caleb . . . and Joshua. These were the only two grown-ups who lived through the forty years of wandering in the wilderness and entered the land. For references to Joshua see Exodus 17:9; and for Caleb, look up Numbers 13:6,30; 14:24; 26:65; 32:12; Joshua 14:6,13-14; 15:14; Judges 1:12.

Caleb the son of Jephunneh, *which were*
of the men that went to search the land,
lived *still.*
[39]And Moses told these sayings unto
all the children of Israel: and the people mourned greatly.
¶[40]And they rose up early in the
morning, and gat them up into the top
of the mountain, saying, Lo, we *be here,*
and will go up unto the place which the
LORD hath promised: for we have
sinned.
[41]And Moses said, Wherefore now do
ye transgress the commandment of the
LORD? but it shall not prosper.
[42]Go not up, for the LORD *is* not
among you; that ye be not smitten before your enemies.
[43]For the Amalekites and the Canaanites *are* there before you, and ye
shall fall by the sword: because ye are
turned away from the LORD, therefore
the LORD will not be with you.
[44]But they presumed to go up unto
the hill top: nevertheless the ark of the
covenant of the LORD, and Moses, departed not out of the camp.
[45]Then the Amalekites came down,
and the Canaanites which dwelt in that
hill, and smote them, and discomfited
them, *even* unto Hormah.

III. The 39 Years of Wandering (15:1—19:22)

15 And the LORD spake unto Moses, saying,
[2]Speak unto the children of Israel,
and say unto them, When ye be come
into the land of your habitations, which
I give unto you,
[3]And will make an *offering by *fire
unto the LORD, a burnt-offering, or a
*sacrifice in performing a vow, or in a
freewill-offering, or in your solemn
*feasts, to make a sweet savour unto
the LORD, of the herd, or of the flock:
[4]Then shall he that offereth his of-

15:2 The Years of Wandering
The years of wandering which followed were quite unnecessary, because the children of Israel could have entered and conquered Canaan as soon as the spies came back, had they only trusted God. The wilderness journey up to this time is a picture of the Christian's life in this world on his way to the heavenly country. These years of wandering, however, are not a *type, but a warning of the consequences of not believing God and trusting Him. See 1 Corinthians 10:1-5. Because the adults could never go into the land, they had to teach their children what to do when they "come into the land."

fering unto the LORD bring a *meat-
offering of a *tenth deal of flour mingled
with the fourth *part* of an *hin of oil.
[5]And the fourth *part* of an hin of
*wine for a *drink-offering shalt thou
prepare with the burnt-offering or sacrifice, for one lamb.
[6]Or for a ram, thou shalt prepare *for*
a meat-offering two tenth deals of flour
mingled with the third *part* of an hin of
oil.
[7]And for a drink-offering thou shalt
offer the third *part* of an hin of wine, *for*
a sweet savour unto the LORD.
[8]And when thou preparest a bullock
for a burnt-offering, or *for* a sacrifice in
performing a vow, or *peace-offerings
unto the LORD:
[9]Then shall he bring with a bullock a
meat-offering of three tenth deals of
flour mingled with half an hin of oil.
[10]And thou shalt bring for a drink-
offering half an hin of wine, *for* an offering made by fire, of a sweet savour unto
the LORD.
[11]Thus shall it be done for one bullock, or for one ram, or for a lamb, or a
kid.
[12]According to the number that ye
shall prepare, so shall ye do to every
one according to their number.

14:45 discomfited. Routed.
15:5 drink offering. See Genesis 35:14 note, "The Drink-Offering."
15:9 deals. Parts.

13 All that are born of the country shall
do these things after this manner, in
offering an offering made by fire, of a
sweet savour unto the LORD.
14 And if a stranger sojourn with you,
or whosoever *be* among you in your
generations, and will offer an offering
made by fire, of a sweet savour unto the
LORD; as ye do, so he shall do.
15 One ordinance *shall be both* for you
of the congregation, and also for the
stranger that sojourneth *with you,* an
ordinance for ever in your generations:
as ye *are,* so shall the stranger be before the LORD.
16 One *law and one manner shall be
for you, and for the stranger that
sojourneth with you.
¶17 And the LORD spake unto Moses,
saying,
18 Speak unto the children of Israel,
and say unto them, When ye come into
the land whither I bring you,
19 Then it shall be, that, when ye eat
of the bread of the land, ye shall offer
up an *heave-offering unto the LORD.
20 Ye shall offer up a cake of the first
of your dough *for* an heave-offering:
as *ye do* the heave-offering of the
threshingfloor, so shall ye heave it.
21 Of the first of your dough ye shall
give unto the LORD an heave-offering in
your generations.
¶22 And if ye have erred, and not observed all these commandments, which
the LORD hath spoken unto Moses,
23 *Even* all that the LORD hath commanded you by the hand of Moses, from
the day that the LORD commanded
Moses, and henceforward among your
generations;
24 Then it shall be, if *ought* be committed by ignorance without the knowledge of the congregation, that all the
congregation shall offer one young bullock for a burnt-offering, for a sweet
savour unto the LORD, with his meat-
offering, and his drink-offering, according to the manner, and one kid of the
goats for a *sin-offering.
25 And the priest shall make an
*atonement for all the congregation of
the children of Israel, and it shall be
forgiven them; for it *is* ignorance: and
they shall bring their offering, a sacrifice made by fire unto the LORD, and
their sin-offering before the LORD, for
their ignorance:
26 And it shall be forgiven all the congregation of the children of Israel, and the
stranger that sojourneth among them;
seeing all the people *were* in ignorance.

15:9 OFFERINGS FOR THE ALTAR

Offers for the altar were either animal or vegetable.

The animal offerings were:

1. burnt-offerings
2. peace-offerings
3. sin-offerings

The vegetable offerings were:

1. meal-offerings and drink-offerings for the great altar in the court
2. incense and meal-offerings for the altar in the Holy Place

Every burnt-offering and peace-offering was accompanied by a meal-offering and drink-offering (Num. 15:5,7,10) in proportion to the type of animal as follows:

Animal	Wine	Flour	Oil
With a bullock	½ hin	3/10th ephah	½ hin
With a ram	⅓ hin	2/10th ephah	⅓ hin
With a he-lamb or kid	¼ hin	1/10th ephah	¼ hin

15:19 heave-offering. Exodus 29:27 has a note on the heave- or wave-offering.

¶27 And if any soul sin through ignorance, then he shall bring a she goat of
the first year for a sin-offering.
28 And the priest shall make an atonement for the soul that sinneth ignorantly, when he sinneth by ignorance
before the LORD, to make an atonement
for him; and it shall be forgiven him.
29 Ye shall have one law for him that
sinneth through ignorance, *both for*
him that is born among the children of
Israel, and for the stranger that sojourneth among them.
¶30 But *the soul that doeth *ought*
presumptuously, *whether he be* born in
the land, or a stranger, the same reproacheth the LORD; and that soul shall
be cut off from among his people.

15:30 Willful Sinning
The phrase "the soul that doeth ought presumptuously" refers to anyone who acted in a way that he knew was sinful or forbidden in the law. (See Deut. 17:12-13; Ps. 19:13.) Notice the tragic consequences of willful, presumptuous sin. When Christ came in love and grace and died for the sinner, He rose again and dwells in the heart of the believer to empower him or her to live victoriously over temptation and sin.

31 Because he hath despised the word
of the LORD, and hath broken his commandment, that soul shall utterly be cut
off; his iniquity *shall be* upon him.

The man who broke the Sabbath

¶32 And while the children of Israel
were in the wilderness, they found a
man that gathered sticks upon the *sabbath day.
33 And they that found him gathering
sticks brought him unto Moses and
Aaron, and unto all the congregation.
34 And they put him in ward, because
it was not declared what should be done
to him.
35 And the LORD said unto Moses,
The man shall be surely put to death:
all the congregation shall stone him
with stones without the camp.
36 And all the congregation brought
him without the camp, and stoned him
with stones, and he died; as the LORD
commanded Moses.

The fringe of blue

¶37 And the LORD spake unto Moses,
saying,
38 Speak unto the children of Israel,
and bid them that they make them
fringes in the borders of their *garments throughout their generations,
and that they put upon the fringe of the
borders a ribband of blue:
39 And it shall be unto you for a fringe,
that ye may look upon it, and remember all the commandments of the
LORD, and do them; and that ye seek
not after your own heart and your own
eyes, after which ye use to go a whoring:
40 That ye may remember, and do all
my commandments, and be *holy unto
your God.
41 I *am* the LORD your God, which
brought you out of the land of Egypt,
to be your God: I *am* the LORD your
God.

The rebellion of Korah

16 Now *Korah, the son of Izhar,
the son of Kohath, the son of
Levi, and Dathan and Abiram, the sons
of Eliab, and On, the son of Peleth, sons
of Reuben, took *men:*
2 And they rose up before Moses,
with certain of the children of Israel,
two hundred and fifty princes of the
assembly, famous in the congregation,
men of renown:
3 And they gathered themselves together against Moses and against
Aaron, and said unto them, *Ye take* too

15:38 a ribband of blue. Blue, the heavenly color, was worn by the priests to show that they were to live heavenly lives. Now the ribbon of blue was to be worn by all the children of Israel (vss. 38-40).

16:1-3 Korah
Korah, a great-grandson of Levi and a cousin of Moses, led a very serious rebellion against the authority of Moses and Aaron. He was a Kohathite and had the most sacred duty of all the Levites to perform (4:34-35), but in spite of this he envied Aaron's family the priesthood. He was joined by some of the tribes of Reuben who were probably trying to regain the lost leadership of the tribes which had once been Reuben's as the eldest son of Jacob, but which had been lost because of sin (1 Chron. 5:1). These rebels were jealous of the priests, and they claimed that all Israelites had an equal right to carry on the services of the tabernacle.

much upon you, seeing all the congregation *are* holy, every one of them, and
the LORD *is* among them: wherefore
then lift ye up yourselves above the
congregation of the LORD?
4 And when Moses heard *it,* he fell
upon his face:
5 And he spake unto Korah and unto
all his company, saying, Even to morrow the LORD will shew who *are* his,
and *who is* holy; and will cause *him* to
come near unto him: even *him* whom
he hath chosen will he cause to come
near unto him.
6 This do; Take you censers, Korah,
and all his company;
7 And put fire therein, and put *incense in them before the LORD to morrow: and it shall be *that* the man whom
the LORD doth choose, he *shall be* holy:
ye take too much upon you, ye sons of
Levi.
8 And Moses said unto Korah, Hear, I
pray you, ye sons of Levi:
9 *Seemeth it but* a small thing unto you,
that the God of Israel hath separated
you from the congregation of Israel, to
bring you near to himself to do the service of the tabernacle of the LORD, and
to stand before the congregation to
minister unto them?
10 And he hath brought thee near *to
him,* and all thy brethren the sons of
Levi with thee: and seek ye the priesthood also?
11 For which cause *both* thou and all
thy company *are* gathered together
against the LORD: and what *is* Aaron,
that ye murmur against him?
¶ 12 And Moses sent to call Dathan and
Abiram, the sons of Eliab: which said,
We will not come up:
13 *Is it* a small thing that thou hast
brought us up out of a land that *floweth
with milk and honey, to kill us in the
wilderness, except thou make thyself
altogether a prince over us?
14 Moreover thou hast not brought
us into a land that floweth with milk
and honey, or given us inheritance of
fields and vineyards: wilt thou put out
the eyes of these men? we will not
come up.
15 And Moses was very wroth, and
said unto the LORD, Respect not thou
their offering: I have not taken one ass
from them, neither have I hurt one of
them.
16 And Moses said unto Korah, Be
thou and all thy company before the
LORD, thou, and they, and Aaron, to
morrow:
17 And take every man his *censer,
and put incense in them, and bring ye
before the LORD every man his censer,
two hundred and fifty censers; thou
also, and Aaron, each *of you* his censer.
18 And they took every man his censer, and put fire in them, and laid incense thereon, and stood in the door of
the tabernacle of the congregation with
Moses and Aaron.
19 And Korah gathered all the congre-

16:6 censers. These were metal pans for taking burning coals from the altar. The priests sprinkled incense on the coals.

16:13 Is it a small thing . . . ? Once again the Israelites looked back with longing to Egypt and blamed Moses because they had not gone into the Promised Land. It was their own faith that had failed (chaps. 13–14).

gation against them unto the door of the
tabernacle of the congregation: and
the glory of the LORD appeared unto all
the congregation.
20And the LORD spake unto Moses
and unto Aaron, saying,
21Separate yourselves from among
this congregation, that I may consume
them in a moment.
22And they fell upon their faces, and
said, O God, the God of the spirits of all
*flesh, shall one man sin, and wilt thou
be wroth with all the congregation?
¶23And the LORD spake unto Moses,
saying,
24Speak unto the congregation, saying, Get you up from about the tabernacle of Korah, Dathan, and Abiram.
25And Moses rose up and went unto
Dathan and Abiram; and the elders of
Israel followed him.
26And he spake unto the congregation, saying, Depart, I pray you, from
the tents of these wicked men, and
touch nothing of theirs, lest ye be consumed in all their sins.
27So they gat up from the tabernacle
of Korah, Dathan, and Abiram, on every
side: and Dathan and Abiram came out,
and stood in the door of their tents, and
their wives, and their sons, and their
little children.
28And Moses said, Hereby ye shall
know that the LORD hath sent me to do
all these works; for *I have* not *done them*
of mine own mind.
29If these men die the common death
of all men, or if they be visited after the
visitation of all men; *then* the LORD hath
not sent me.
30But if the LORD make a new thing,
and the earth open her mouth, and
swallow them up, with all that *appertain*
unto them, and they go down quick
into *the pit; then ye shall understand
that these men have provoked the
LORD.
¶31And it came to pass, as he had
made an end of speaking all these
words, that the ground clave asunder
that *was* under them:
32And the earth opened her mouth,
and swallowed them up, and their
houses, and all the men that *appertained*
unto Korah, and all *their* goods.
33They, and all that *appertained* to
them, went down alive into the pit, and
the earth closed upon them: and they
perished from among the congregation.
34And all Israel that *were* round about
them fled at the cry of them: for they
said, Lest the earth swallow us up *also*.
35And there came out a fire from the
LORD, and consumed the two hundred
and fifty men that offered incense.

16:31-35 Judgment of the Rebels
The severe judgment that fell on the rebels was because they had actually attacked the authority of God Himself, since He had appointed the order of the priests. The judgment fell as follows:
1. Korah and the Reubenites were swallowed up.
2. The 250 men who had taken the incense, thereby defying the priesthood, were killed by fire descending from God. Note that the sons of Korah did not join their father and were saved (see 26:11 note, "The Children of Korah").

¶36And the LORD spake unto Moses,
saying,
37Speak unto Eleazar the son of Aaron
the priest, that he take up the censers
out of the burning, and scatter thou the
fire yonder; for they are hallowed.
38The censers of these sinners
against their own souls, let them make
them broad plates *for* a covering of the
*altar: for they offered them before the
LORD, therefore they are hallowed: and
they shall be a sign unto the children of
Israel.
39And Eleazar the priest took the
brasen censers, wherewith they that
were burnt had offered; and they were
made broad *plates for* a covering of the
altar:

16:30 quick. An old word that means *alive*. See "alive" in verse 33.

40 *To be* a memorial unto the children of Israel, that no stranger, which is not of the seed of Aaron, come near to offer incense before the LORD; that he be not as Korah, and as his company: as the LORD said to him by the hand of Moses.

¶41 But on the morrow all the congregation of the children of Israel murmured against Moses and against Aaron, saying, Ye have killed the people of the LORD.

42 And it came to pass, when the congregation was gathered against Moses and against Aaron, that they looked toward the tabernacle of the congregation: and, behold, the cloud covered it, and the glory of the LORD appeared.

43 And Moses and Aaron came before the tabernacle of the congregation.

¶44 And the LORD spake unto Moses, saying,

45 Get you up from among this congregation, that I may consume them as in a moment. And they fell upon their faces.

¶46 And Moses said unto Aaron, Take a censer, and put fire therein from off the altar, and put on incense, and go quickly unto the congregation, and make an atonement for them: for there is wrath gone out from the LORD; the plague is begun.

47 And Aaron took as Moses commanded, and ran into the midst of the congregation; and, behold, the plague was begun among the people: and he put on incense, and made an atonement for the people.

48 And he stood between the dead and the living; and the plague was stayed.

49 Now they that died in the plague were fourteen thousand and seven hundred, beside them that died about the matter of Korah.

50 And Aaron returned unto Moses unto the door of the tabernacle of the congregation: and the plague was stayed.

Aaron's rod that budded

17 And the LORD spake unto Moses, saying,

2 Speak unto the children of Israel, and take of every one of them a rod according to the house of *their* fathers, of all their princes according to the house of their fathers twelve rods: write thou every man's name upon his rod.

> **17:2,8 Aaron's Rod Buds**
> This miracle of Aaron's rod budding was a sign to the Israelites that it was God who had chosen Aaron to be His high priest. It pictured the Lord Jesus Christ, God's anointed Son, who died but who rose again and lives.

3 And thou shalt write Aaron's name upon the rod of Levi: for one rod *shall be* for the head of the house of their fathers.

4 And thou shalt lay them up in the tabernacle of the congregation before the testimony, where I will meet with you.

5 And it shall come to pass, *that* the man's rod, whom I shall choose, shall blossom: and I will make to cease from me the murmurings of the children of Israel, whereby they murmur against you.

¶6 And Moses spake unto the children of Israel, and every one of their princes gave him a rod apiece, for each prince one, according to their fathers' houses, *even* twelve rods: and the rod of Aaron *was* among their rods.

7 And Moses laid up the rods before the LORD in the tabernacle of witness.

8 And it came to pass, that on the morrow Moses went into the tabernacle of witness; and, behold, the rod of Aaron for the house of Levi was budded, and brought forth buds, and bloomed blossoms, and yielded almonds.

9 And Moses brought out all the rods from before the LORD unto all the chil-

---

16:50 stayed. Stopped, held back.

dren of Israel: and they looked, and took every man his rod.

¶10 And the LORD said unto Moses, Bring Aaron's rod again before the testimony, to be kept for a token against the rebels; and thou shalt quite take away their murmurings from me, that they die not.

11 And Moses did *so:* as the LORD commanded him, so did he.

12 And the children of Israel spake unto Moses, saying, Behold, we die, we perish, we all perish.

13 Whosoever cometh any thing near unto the tabernacle of the LORD shall die: shall we be consumed with dying?

Duties of Aaron and Levites confirmed

18 And the LORD said unto Aaron, Thou and thy sons and thy father's house with thee shall *bear the iniquity of the *sanctuary: and thou and thy sons with thee shall bear the iniquity of your priesthood.

18:1 God's Reassurance
The people were so afraid after the terrible events of the rebellion that they asked the question at the end of chapter 17: "Shall we be consumed with dying?" This repetition of the instructions for the work of the priests was to reassure the people that as long as the priests continued to offer the sacrifices as God had ordained, no further judgment would fall upon them.

2 And thy brethren also of the tribe of Levi, the tribe of thy father, bring thou with thee, that they may be joined unto thee, and minister unto thee: but thou and thy sons with thee *shall minister* before the tabernacle of witness.

3 And they shall keep thy charge, and the charge of all the tabernacle: only they shall not come nigh the vessels of the sanctuary and the altar, that neither they, nor ye also, die.

4 And they shall be joined unto thee, and keep the charge of the tabernacle of the congregation, for all the service of the tabernacle: and a stranger shall not come nigh unto you.

5 And ye shall keep the charge of the sanctuary, and the charge of the altar: that there be no wrath any more upon the children of Israel.

6 And I, behold, I have taken your brethren the Levites from among the children of Israel: to you *they are* given *as* a gift for the LORD, to do the service of the tabernacle of the congregation.

7 Therefore thou and thy sons with thee shall keep your priest's office for every thing of the altar, and within the vail; and ye shall serve: I have given your priest's office *unto you as* a service of gift: and the stranger that cometh nigh shall be put to death.

¶8 And the LORD spake unto Aaron, Behold, I also have given thee the charge of mine heave-offerings of all the hallowed things of the children of Israel; unto thee have I given them by reason of the anointing, and to thy sons, by an ordinance for ever.

9 This shall be thine of the most holy things, *reserved* from the fire: every *oblation of theirs, every meat-offering of theirs, and every *sin-offering of theirs, and every *trespass-offering of theirs, which they shall *render unto me, *shall be* most holy for thee and for thy sons.

10 In the most holy *place* shalt thou eat it; every male shall eat it: it shall be holy unto thee.

11 And this *is* thine; the heave-offering of their gift, with all the wave-offerings of the children of Israel: I have given them unto thee, and to thy sons and to thy daughters with thee, by a statute for ever: every one that is *clean in thy house shall eat of it.

17:10 token. A sign.
18:11 heave-offering. See Exodus 29:27 note.

12 All the best of the *oil, and all the best of the wine, and of the wheat, the firstfruits of them which they shall offer unto the LORD, them have I given thee.

13 *And* whatsoever is first ripe in the land, which they shall bring unto the LORD, shall be thine; every one that is clean in thine house shall eat *of* it.

14 Every thing devoted in Israel shall be thine.

15 Every thing that openeth the matrix in all flesh, which they bring unto the LORD, *whether it be* of men or beasts, shall be thine: nevertheless the firstborn of man shalt thou surely redeem, and the firstling of *unclean beasts shalt thou redeem.

16 And those that are to be redeemed from a month old shalt thou redeem, according to thine estimation, for the *money of five shekels, after the shekel of the sanctuary, which *is* twenty gerahs.

17 But the firstling of a cow, or the firstling of a sheep, or the firstling of a goat, thou shalt not redeem; they *are* holy: thou shalt sprinkle their *blood upon the altar, and shalt burn their fat *for* an offering made by fire, for a sweet savour unto the LORD.

18 And the flesh of them shall be thine, as the wave breast and as the right shoulder are thine.

19 All the heave-offerings of the holy things, which the children of Israel offer unto the LORD, have I given thee, and thy sons and thy daughters with thee, by a statute for ever: it *is* a covenant of salt for ever before the LORD unto thee and to thy seed with thee.

¶20 And the LORD spake unto Aaron, Thou shalt have no inheritance in their land, neither shalt thou have any part among them: I *am* thy part and thine inheritance among the children of Israel.

21 And, behold, I have given the children of Levi all the tenth in Israel for an inheritance, for their service which they serve, *even* the service of the tabernacle of the congregation.

22 Neither must the children of Israel henceforth come nigh the tabernacle of the congregation, lest they bear sin, and die.

23 But the Levites shall do the service of the tabernacle of the congregation, and they shall bear their iniquity: *it shall be* a statute for ever throughout your generations, that among the children of Israel they have no inheritance.

24 But the tithes of the children of Israel, which they offer *as* an heave-offering unto the LORD, I have given to the Levites to inherit: therefore I have said unto them, Among the children of Israel they shall have no inheritance.

¶25 And the LORD spake unto Moses, saying,

26 Thus speak unto the Levites, and say unto them, When ye take of the children of Israel the tithes which I have given you from them for your inheritance, then ye shall offer up an heave-offering of it for the LORD, *even* a tenth *part* of the tithe.

27 And *this* your heave-offering shall be reckoned unto you, as though *it were* the corn of the threshingfloor, and as the fulness of the winepress.

28 Thus ye also shall offer an heave-offering unto the LORD of all your tithes, which ye receive of the children of Israel; and ye shall give thereof the LORD'S heave-offering to Aaron the priest.

29 Out of all your gifts ye shall offer every heave-offering of the LORD, of all the best thereof, *even* the hallowed part thereof out of it.

30 Therefore thou shalt say unto them, When ye have heaved the best

---

18:15 matrix. The womb.
18:19 a covenant of salt. See number 4 of the Leviticus 2:1 note, "The Meat-Offering."
18:24 the tithes. The tithe was the tenth or ten percent of what the people had. It was paid to the LORD and belonged to Him. See the Leviticus 27:30 note, "Making a Vow."

thereof from it, then it shall be counted unto the Levites as the increase of
the threshingfloor, and as the increase
of the winepress.
31 And ye shall eat it in every place,
ye and your households: for it *is* your
reward for your service in the tabernacle of the congregation.
32 And ye shall bear no sin by reason
of it, when ye have heaved from it the
best of it: neither shall ye pollute the
holy things of the children of Israel, lest
ye die.

The red heifer sacrifice

19 And the LORD spake unto *Moses and unto *Aaron, saying,
2 This *is* the ordinance of the law
which the LORD hath commanded, saying, Speak unto the children of *Israel,
that they bring thee a red heifer without spot, wherein *is* no blemish, *and*
upon which never came yoke:

19:2 The Red Heifer
All the sacrifices described in Leviticus spoke of and looked forward to the death of Christ, each in a different way. Here Christ's death is again declared. The sacrifice looks forward to Christians as they go through the world, sometimes falling into sin and needing forgiveness. If we confess the sin, we are forgiven, all because of the work of the Lord Jesus Christ on the cross. Look up 1 John 1:7,9.

3 And ye shall give her unto Eleazar
the priest, that he may bring her forth
without the camp, and *one* shall slay her
before his face:
4 And Eleazar the priest shall take of
her blood with his finger, and sprinkle
of her blood directly before the tabernacle of the congregation seven times:
5 And *one* shall burn the heifer in his
sight; her skin, and her flesh, and her
blood, with her *dung, shall he burn:
6 And the priest shall take cedar
wood, and *hyssop, and scarlet, and
cast *it* into the midst of the burning of
the heifer.
7 Then the priest shall wash his
clothes, and he shall bathe his flesh in
water, and afterward he shall come into
the camp, and the priest shall be unclean until the even.
8 And he that burneth her shall wash
his clothes in water, and bathe his flesh
in water, and shall be unclean until the
even.
9 And a man *that is* clean shall gather
up the ashes of the heifer, and lay *them*
up without the camp in a clean place,
and it shall be kept for the congregation
of the children of Israel for a water of
separation: it *is* a purification for sin.
10 And he that gathereth the ashes of
the heifer shall wash his clothes, and be
unclean until the even: and it shall be
unto the children of Israel, and unto the
stranger that sojourneth among them,
for a statute for ever.
¶ 11 He that toucheth the dead body of
any man shall be unclean seven days.
12 He shall purify himself with it on
the third day, and on the seventh day he
shall be clean: but if he purify not himself the third day, then the seventh day
he shall not be clean.
13 Whosoever toucheth the dead body
of any man that is dead, and purifieth
not himself, defileth the tabernacle of
the LORD; and that soul shall be cut off
from Israel: because the water of separation was not sprinkled upon him, he
shall be unclean; his uncleanness *is* yet
upon him.
14 This *is* the law, when a man dieth
in a tent: all that come into the tent, and
all that *is* in the tent, shall be unclean
seven days.

19:9 a man that is clean. This speaks of being clean in the sight of the LORD, because the man has kept himself free from anything that would make him unclean in God's sight. The wise rules God gave Moses are like the laws of health and cleanliness that we should obey in the present time.

19:9 a water of separation. See how this was used in Numbers 19:13,20-21; 31:23.

15 And every open vessel, which hath no covering bound upon it, *is* unclean.

16 And whosoever toucheth one that is slain with a sword in the open fields, or a dead body, or a bone of a man, or a grave, shall be unclean seven days.

17 And for an unclean *person* they shall take of the ashes of the burnt heifer of purification for sin, and running water shall be put thereto in a vessel:

18 And a clean person shall take hyssop, and dip *it* in the water, and sprinkle *it* upon the tent, and upon all the vessels, and upon the persons that were there, and upon him that touched a bone, or one slain, or one dead, or a grave:

19 And the clean *person* shall sprinkle upon the unclean on the third day, and on the seventh day: and on the seventh day he shall purify himself, and wash his clothes, and bathe himself in water, and shall be clean at even.

20 But the man that shall be unclean, and shall not purify himself, that soul shall be cut off from among the congregation, because he hath defiled the sanctuary of the LORD: the water of separation hath not been sprinkled upon him; he *is* unclean.

21 And it shall be a perpetual statute unto them, that he that sprinkleth the water of separation shall wash his clothes; and he that toucheth the water of separation shall be unclean until even.

22 And whatsoever the unclean *person* toucheth shall be unclean; and the soul that toucheth *it* shall be unclean until even.

IV. Events of the 40th Year (20:1—21:35)

Miriam dies

20 Then came the children of Israel, *even* the whole congregation, into the desert of Zin in the first month: and the people abode in Kadesh; and *Miriam died there, and was buried there.

20:1 The Lost Years

Thirty-eight years of wandering took place between the last verse of chapter 19 and the first verse of chapter 20. No mention is made of them except in chapter 33 where the camps are given. It was a time of idolatry when the rites of the Law were gravely neglected (Josh. 5:2-5; Ezek. 20:13; Amos 5:25-26; Acts 7:42-43), but God's goodness never failed (Deut. 2:7; 29:5). Some of these people who were gathered against Moses and Aaron had been the children who had left Egypt thirty-nine years before. Many others had been born in the wilderness. The older generation had died out, according to God's Word (Num. 14:31-35).

Thirst at Meribah-Kadesh

2 And there was no water for the congregation: and they gathered themselves together against Moses and against Aaron.

3 And the people chode with Moses, and spake, saying, Would *God that we had died when our brethren died before the LORD!

4 And why have ye brought up the congregation of the LORD into this wilderness, that we and our cattle should die there?

5 And wherefore have ye made us to come up out of *Egypt, to bring us in unto this evil place? it *is* no place of seed, or of figs, or of vines, or of pomegranates; neither *is* there any water to drink.

6 And Moses and Aaron went from the presence of the assembly unto the door of the *tabernacle of the congregation, and they fell upon their faces: and the glory of the LORD appeared unto them.

¶7 And the LORD spake unto Moses, saying,

8 Take the rod, and gather thou the assembly together, thou, and Aaron thy brother, and speak ye unto the rock before their eyes; and it shall give forth his water, and thou shalt bring forth to them water out of the rock: so thou

20:3 chode. Murmured or complained. See 14:12 note, "Moses' Devotion."

shalt give the congregation and their beasts drink.

9 And Moses took the rod from before the LORD, as he commanded him.

10 And Moses and Aaron gathered the congregation together before the rock, and he said unto them, Hear now, ye rebels; must we fetch you water out of this rock?

11 And Moses lifted up his hand, and with his rod he smote the rock twice: and the water came out abundantly, and the congregation drank, and their beasts *also*.

¶ 12 And the LORD spake unto Moses and Aaron, Because ye believed me not, to sanctify me in the eyes of the children of Israel, therefore ye shall not bring this congregation into the land which I have given them.

20:12 Moses' Disobedience
God told Moses to *speak* to the rock (vs. 8). Moses disobeyed this command, perhaps to exalt himself in the eyes of the people. Notice also that in verse 10 he said, "Must *we* fetch you water out of this rock?" He took the honor that belonged to God.

13 This *is* the water of Meribah; because the children of Israel strove with the LORD, and he was sanctified in them.

The sin of Edom

¶ 14 And Moses sent messengers from Kadesh unto the king of *Edom, Thus saith thy brother Israel, Thou knowest all the travail that hath befallen us:

15 How our fathers went down into Egypt, and we have dwelt in Egypt a long time; and the Egyptians vexed us, and our fathers:

16 And when we cried unto the LORD, he heard our voice, and sent an *angel, and hath brought us forth out of Egypt: and, behold, we *are* in Kadesh, a city in the uttermost of thy border:

17 Let us pass, I pray thee, through thy country: we will not pass through the fields, or through the vineyards, neither will we drink *of* the water of the wells: we will go by the king's *high* way, we will not turn to the right hand nor to the left, until we have passed thy borders.

18 And Edom said unto him, Thou shalt not pass by me, lest I come out against thee with the sword.

19 And the children of Israel said unto him, We will go by the high way: and if I and my cattle drink of thy water, then I will pay for it: I will only, without *doing* any thing *else,* go through on my feet.

20 And he said, Thou shalt not go through. And Edom came out against him with much people, and with a strong hand.

21 Thus Edom refused to give Israel passage through his border: wherefore Israel turned away from him.

¶ 22 And the children of Israel, *even* the whole congregation, journeyed from Kadesh, and came unto mount Hor.

The death of Aaron

23 And the LORD spake unto Moses and Aaron in mount Hor, by the coast of the land of Edom, saying,

24 Aaron shall be gathered unto his people: for he shall not enter into the land which I have given unto the children of Israel, because ye rebelled against my word at the water of Meribah.

25 Take Aaron and Eleazar his son, and bring them up unto mount Hor:

26 And strip Aaron of his garments, and put them upon Eleazar his son: and Aaron shall be gathered *unto his people,* and shall die there.

27 And Moses did as the LORD commanded: and they went up into mount Hor in the sight of all the congregation.

28 And Moses stripped Aaron of his

20:12 to sanctify me. To *set Me apart,* or to *give Me honor due Me,* is meant here.
20:14 the king of Edom. A descendant of Esau (Gen. 25:30).
20:14 travail. Sorrow and trouble.

garments, and put them upon Eleazar his son; and Aaron died there in the top of the mount: and Moses and Eleazar came down from the mount.

29 And when all the congregation saw that Aaron was dead, they mourned for Aaron thirty days, *even* all the house of Israel.

Victory over the Canaanites

21 And *when* king Arad the Canaanite, which dwelt in the south, heard tell that Israel came by the way of the spies; then he fought against Israel, and took *some* of them prisoners.

2 And Israel vowed a vow unto the LORD, and said, If thou wilt indeed deliver this people into my hand, then I will utterly destroy their cities.

3 And the LORD hearkened to the voice of Israel, and delivered up the Canaanites; and they utterly destroyed them and their cities: and he called the name of the place Hormah.

¶4 And they journeyed from mount Hor by the way of the Red sea, to compass the land of Edom: and the soul of the people was much discouraged because of the way.

The serpent of brass

5 And the people spake against God, and against Moses, Wherefore have ye brought us up out of Egypt to die in the wilderness? for *there is* no bread, neither *is there any* water; and our soul loatheth this light bread.

6 And the LORD sent fiery serpents among the people, and they bit the people; and much people of Israel died.

¶7 Therefore the people came to Moses, and said, We have sinned, for we have spoken against the LORD, and against thee; pray unto the LORD, that he take away the serpents from us. And Moses prayed for the people.

21:8 The Fiery Serpent
The serpent was a *type of sin, and brass (vs. 9) was a type of judgment, as in the case of the brazen (brass) altar, a type of the cross upon which Christ offered Himself (see Exod. 27:1-2; Heb. 9:13-14). A brass serpent was a picture of sin punished and judged. Whoever looked at the serpent was cured. It is a wonderful figure of the judgment of God against sin and of Christ who bore our sins. Now anyone who trusts Him–looks to Him–is saved. The Lord Jesus Christ Himself explains it in John 3:14-15. Also look up Romans 8:3 and 2 Corinthians 5:21.

8 And the LORD said unto Moses, Make thee a fiery serpent, and set it upon a pole: and it shall come to pass, that every one that is bitten, when he looketh upon it, shall live.

9 And Moses made a serpent of brass, and put it upon a pole, and it came to pass, that if a serpent had bitten any man, when he beheld the serpent of brass, he lived.

¶10 And the children of Israel set forward, and pitched in Oboth.

11 And they journeyed from Oboth, and pitched at Ije-abarim, in the wilderness which *is* before *Moab, toward the sunrising.

¶12 From thence they removed, and pitched in the valley of Zared.

13 From thence they removed, and pitched on the other side of Arnon, which *is* in the wilderness that cometh out of the coasts of the Amorites: for Arnon *is* the border of Moab, between Moab and the Amorites.

14 Wherefore it is said in the book of the wars of the LORD, What he did in the Red sea, and in the brooks of Arnon,

15 And at the stream of the brooks that goeth down to the dwelling of Ar, and lieth upon the border of Moab.

16 And from thence *they went* to Beer:

21:1 king Arad. This means that he was king of Arad.
21:3 Hormah. Hormah means *utter destruction.*
21:5 spake against. This was the twelfth time the children of Israel had murmured against God. See 20:3 and references in Numbers 14:12 note, "Moses' Devotion."

that *is* the well whereof the LORD spake unto Moses, Gather the people together, and I will give them water.

¶ 17 Then Israel sang this song, Spring up, O well; sing ye unto it:

18 The princes digged the well, the nobles of the people digged it, by *the direction of* the lawgiver, with their staves. And from the wilderness *they went* to Mattanah:

19 And from Mattanah to Nahaliel: and from Nahaliel to Bamoth:

20 And from Bamoth *in* the valley, that *is* in the country of Moab, to the top of Pisgah, which looketh toward Jeshimon.

Victory over Sihon and Og

¶ 21 And Israel sent messengers unto Sihon king of the Amorites, saying,

22 Let me pass through thy land: we will not turn into the fields, or into the vineyards; we will not drink *of* the waters of the well: *but* we will go along by the king's *high* way, until we be past thy borders.

23 And Sihon would not suffer Israel to pass through his border: but Sihon gathered all his people together, and went out against Israel into the wilderness: and he came to Jahaz, and fought against Israel.

24 And Israel smote him with the edge of the sword, and possessed his land from Arnon unto Jabbok, even unto the children of Ammon: for the border of the children of Ammon *was* strong.

25 And Israel took all these cities: and Israel dwelt in all the cities of the Amorites, in Heshbon, and in all the villages thereof.

26 For Heshbon *was* the city of Sihon the king of the Amorites, who had fought against the former king of Moab, and taken all his land out of his hand, even unto Arnon.

27 Wherefore they that speak in proverbs say, Come into Heshbon, let the city of Sihon be built and prepared:

28 For there is a *fire gone out of Heshbon, a flame from the city of Sihon: it hath consumed Ar of Moab, *and* the lords of the *high places of Arnon.

29 Woe to thee, Moab! thou art undone, O people of *Chemosh: he hath given his sons that escaped, and his daughters, into captivity unto Sihon king of the Amorites.

30 We have shot at them; Heshbon is perished even unto Dibon, and we have laid them waste even unto Nophah, which *reacheth* unto Medeba.

¶ 31 Thus Israel dwelt in the land of the Amorites.

32 And Moses sent to spy out Jaazer, and they took the villages thereof, and drove out the Amorites that *were* there.

¶ 33 And they turned and went up by the way of *Bashan: and Og the king of Bashan went out against them, he, and all his people, to the battle at Edrei.

34 And the LORD said unto Moses, Fear him not: for I have delivered him into thy hand, and all his people, and his land; and thou shalt do to him as thou didst unto Sihon king of the Amorites, which dwelt at Heshbon.

35 So they smote him, and his sons, and all his people, until there was none left him alive: and they possessed his land.

V. Events on Plains of Moab (22:1—36:13)

22 And the children of Israel set forward, and pitched in the plains of Moab on this side Jordan *by* Jericho.

Plot of Balak of Moab

¶ 2 And Balak the son of Zippor saw all that Israel had done to the Amorites.

3 And Moab was sore afraid of the people, because they *were* many: and Moab was distressed because of the children of Israel.

4 And Moab said unto the *elders of *Midian, Now shall this company lick

---

21:22 Let me pass through. See Judges 11:15-23.

22:3 The Moabites
The Moabites were descendants of Lot, the nephew of Abraham, and so were related to the Israelites. Midian (vs. 4) means the Midianites were also related by blood to the Israelites (see Exod. 2:15 note, "The Land of Midian"), but they did not join in the cursing. The idea of cursing an enemy (vs. 6) was quite normal or typical at this time; it was supposed to bring misfortune upon the enemy.

up all *that are* round about us, as the ox licketh up the grass of the field. And Balak the son of Zippor *was* king of the Moabites at that time.

The story of Balaam

5He sent messengers therefore unto *Balaam the son of Beor to Pethor, which *is* by the river of the land of the children of his people, to call him, saying, Behold, there is a people come out from Egypt: behold, they cover the face of the earth, and they abide over against me:
6Come now therefore, I pray thee, curse me this people; for they *are* too mighty for me: peradventure I shall prevail, *that* we may smite them, and *that* I may drive them out of the land: for I wot that he whom thou blessest *is* blessed, and he whom thou cursest is cursed.
7And the elders of Moab and the elders of Midian departed with the rewards of divination in their hand; and they came unto Balaam, and spake unto him the words of Balak.
8And he said unto them, Lodge here this night, and I will bring you word again, as the LORD shall speak unto me: and the princes of Moab abode with Balaam.
9And God came unto Balaam, and said, What men *are* these with thee?
10And Balaam said unto God, Balak the son of Zippor, king of Moab, hath sent unto me, *saying,*
11Behold, *there is* a people come out of Egypt, which covereth the face of the earth: come now, curse me them; peradventure I shall be able to overcome them, and drive them out.
12And God said unto Balaam, Thou shalt not go with them; thou shalt not curse the people: for they *are* blessed.
13And Balaam rose up in the morning, and said unto the princes of Balak, Get you into your land: for the LORD refuseth to give me leave to go with you.
14And the princes of Moab rose up, and they went unto Balak, and said, Balaam refuseth to come with us.
¶15And Balak sent yet again princes, more, and more honourable than they.
16And they came to Balaam, and said to him, Thus saith Balak the son of Zippor, Let nothing, I pray thee, hinder thee from coming unto me:

22:5 BALAAM

Balaam was evidently well-known as one who dealt in "divination" (vs. 7) and "enchantments" (24:1), which means that he had a knowledge of supernatural things and had certain supernatural powers, rather like the Egyptian sorcerers in Exodus 7:11. He had come to know of God, perhaps through hearing of His great deeds on behalf of the Israelites, and he tried to combine his evil sorcery with the worship of the true God. His greed, however, made him accept the tempting offer of Balak (vss. 15-17), in spite of God's warning (vs. 12). He was used by God, though he was so unworthy, to pronounce a remarkable prophecy about the Israelites. Having failed to curse Israel, and so having lost his reward (24:11), he tried to ruin the Israelites by getting them to mix with the idol-worshipping Moabites (25:1; 31:16). He was finally executed by the Israelites (31:8). He is quoted in the New Testament as a terrible example of one who tried to go against God for the sake of a reward (see 2 Pet. 2:15; Jude 11; Rev. 2:14).

22:6,11 peradventure. Perhaps.
22:6 I wot. I know.

17 For I will promote thee unto very great honour, and I will do whatsoever thou sayest unto me: come therefore, I pray thee, curse me this people.

18 And Balaam answered and said unto the servants of Balak, If Balak would give me his house full of *silver and gold, I cannot go beyond the word of the LORD my God, to do less or more.

19 Now therefore, I pray you, tarry ye also here this night, that I may know what the LORD will say unto me more.

20 And God came unto Balaam at night, and said unto him, If the men come to call thee, rise up, *and* go with them; but yet the word which I shall say unto thee, that shalt thou do.

21 And Balaam rose up in the morning, and saddled his ass, and went with the princes of Moab.

¶22 And God's anger was kindled because he went: and the angel of the LORD stood in the way for an adversary against him. Now he was riding upon his ass, and his two servants *were* with him.

23 And the ass saw the angel of the LORD standing in the way, and his sword drawn in his hand: and the ass turned aside out of the way, and went into the field: and Balaam smote the ass, to turn her into the way.

24 But the angel of the LORD stood in a path of the vineyards, a wall *being* on this side, and a wall on that side.

25 And when the ass saw the angel of the LORD, she thrust herself unto the wall, and crushed Balaam's foot against the wall: and he smote her again.

26 And the angel of the LORD went further, and stood in a narrow place, where *was* no way to turn either to the right hand or to the left.

27 And when the ass saw the angel of the LORD, she fell down under Balaam: and Balaam's anger was kindled, and he smote the ass with a staff.

28 And the LORD opened the mouth of the ass, and she said unto Balaam, What have I done unto thee, that thou hast smitten me these three times?

29 And Balaam said unto the ass, Because thou hast mocked me: I would there were a sword in mine hand, for now would I kill thee.

30 And the ass said unto Balaam, *Am* not I thine ass, upon which thou hast ridden ever since *I was* thine unto this day? was I ever wont to do so unto thee? And he said, Nay.

31 Then the LORD opened the eyes of Balaam, and he saw the angel of the LORD standing in the way, and his sword drawn in his hand: and he bowed down his head, and fell flat on his face.

32 And the angel of the LORD said unto him, Wherefore hast thou smitten thine ass these three times? behold, I went out to withstand thee, because *thy* way is perverse before me:

33 And the ass saw me, and turned from me these three times: unless she had turned from me, surely now also I had slain thee, and saved her alive.

34 And Balaam said unto the angel of the LORD, I have sinned; for I knew not that thou stoodest in the way against me: now therefore, if it displease thee, I will get me back again.

35 And the angel of the LORD said unto Balaam, Go with the men: but only the word that I shall speak unto thee, that thou shalt speak. So Balaam went with the princes of Balak.

¶36 And when Balak heard that Balaam was come, he went out to meet him unto a city of Moab, which *is* in the border of Arnon, which *is* in the utmost coast.

37 And Balak said unto Balaam, Did I not earnestly send unto thee to call thee? wherefore camest thou not unto me? am I not able indeed to promote thee to honour?

22:22 because he went. God had forbidden Balaam to go, yet when he insisted on going, God allowed it (vs. 20), but only to work out His own purposes. Balaam was warned on his journey that he was to speak only what God told him to say.

38 And Balaam said unto Balak, Lo, I
am come unto thee: have I now any
power at all to say any thing? the word
that God putteth in my mouth, that shall
I speak.
39 And Balaam went with Balak, and
they came unto Kirjath-huzoth.
40 And Balak offered oxen and sheep,
and sent to Balaam, and to the princes
that *were* with him.
41 And it came to pass on the morrow,
that Balak took Balaam, and brought
him up into the high places of *Baal,
that thence he might see the utmost
part of the people.

First prophecy: hill of Baal

23 And Balaam said unto Balak,
Build me here seven altars, and
prepare me here seven oxen and seven
rams.
2 And Balak did as Balaam had spoken; and Balak and Balaam offered on
every *altar a bullock and a ram.
3 And Balaam said unto Balak, Stand
by thy burnt-offering, and I will go:
peradventure the LORD will come to
meet me: and whatsoever he sheweth
me I will tell thee. And he went to an
high place.
4 And God met Balaam: and he said
unto him, I have prepared seven altars,
and I have offered upon *every* altar a
bullock and a ram.
5 And the LORD put a word in
Balaam's mouth, and said, Return unto
Balak, and thus thou shalt speak.
6 And he returned unto him, and, lo,
he stood by his burnt-sacrifice, he, and
all the princes of Moab.
7 And he took up his parable, and said,
Balak the king of Moab hath brought me
from Aram, out of the mountains of the
east, *saying,* Come, curse me *Jacob,
and come, defy Israel.
8 How shall I curse, whom God hath
not cursed? or how shall I defy, *whom*
the LORD hath not defied?
9 For from the top of the rocks I see
him, and from the hills I behold him: lo,
the people shall dwell alone, and shall
not be reckoned among the nations.
10 Who can count the dust of Jacob, and
the number of the fourth *part* of Israel?
Let me die the *death of the righteous,
and let my last end be like his!
11 And Balak said unto Balaam, What
hast thou done unto me? I took thee to
curse mine enemies, and, behold, thou
hast blessed *them* altogether.
12 And he answered and said, Must I
not take heed to speak that which the
LORD hath put in my mouth?

Second prophecy: Mt. Pisgah

13 And Balak said unto him, Come, I
pray thee, with me unto another place,
from whence thou mayest see them:
thou shalt see but the utmost part of
them, and shalt not see them all: and
curse me them from thence.
¶14 And he brought him into the field
of Zophim, to the top of Pisgah, and
built seven altars, and offered a bullock
and a ram on *every* altar.
15 And he said unto Balak, Stand here
by thy burnt-offering, while I meet *the*
LORD yonder.
16 And the LORD met Balaam, and put
a word in his mouth, and said, Go again
unto Balak, and say thus.
17 And when he came to him, behold,
he stood by his burnt-offering, and the
princes of Moab with him. And Balak
said unto him, What hath the LORD
spoken?

22:41 the utmost. This means the end of the camp. From the hill of Baal, he could see only one of the four sections of the encampment (see Num. 2:2 note, "The Tribes' Standards").

23:5 the LORD put a word. See *inspiration. Compare also 22:38.

23:13 thou shalt see but the utmost part. This really means "you can only see the fourth part of the encampment; you do not see all of the people." From Pisgah (vs. 14) Balaam had a better view.

18And he took up his parable, and
said, Rise up, Balak, and hear; hearken
unto me, thou son of Zippor:
19God *is* not a man, that he should lie;
neither the son of man, that he should
*repent: hath he said, and shall he not
do *it?* or hath he spoken, and shall he
not make it good?
20Behold, I have received *command-*
ment to bless: and he hath blessed; and
I cannot reverse it.
21He hath not beheld iniquity in Jacob, neither hath he seen perverseness
in Israel: the LORD his God *is* with him,
and the shout of a king *is* among them.

23:21 Proof of God's Love
One of the most wonderful proofs of God's love to the Israelites is seen here. In spite of all their sin and failure, He loved them and was going to bless them. When we are His through the Lord Jesus Christ, God looks upon us as having His own righteousness in Christ (2 Cor. 5:21). See also Ephesians 1:3-4.

22God brought them out of Egypt; he
hath as it were the strength of an unicorn.
23Surely *there is* no enchantment
against Jacob, neither *is there* any divination against Israel: according to this
time it shall be said of Jacob and of Israel, What hath God wrought!
24Behold, the people shall rise up as
a great lion, and lift up himself as a
young lion: he shall not lie down until
he eat *of* the prey, and drink the blood
of the slain.
¶25And Balak said unto Balaam, Neither curse them at all, nor bless them
at all.
26But Balaam answered and said unto
Balak, Told not I thee, saying, All that
the LORD speaketh, that I must do?

Third prophecy: hill of Peor

¶27And Balak said unto Balaam,
Come, I pray thee, I will bring thee unto
another place; peradventure it will
please God that thou mayest curse me
them from thence.
28And Balak brought Balaam unto the
top of Peor, that looketh toward Jeshimon.
29And Balaam said unto Balak, Build
me here seven altars, and prepare me
here seven bullocks and seven rams.
30And Balak did as Balaam had said,
and offered a bullock and a ram on *every*
altar.

24 And when Balaam saw that it
pleased the LORD to bless Israel, he went not, as at other times, to
seek for enchantments, but he set his
face toward the wilderness.
2And Balaam lifted up his eyes, and
he saw Israel abiding *in his tents* according to their tribes; and the spirit of God
came upon him.
3And he took up his parable, and said,
Balaam the son of Beor hath said, and
the man whose eyes are open hath said:
4He hath said, which heard the words
of God, which saw the vision of the Almighty, falling *into a trance,* but having
his eyes open:
5How goodly are thy tents, O Jacob,
and thy tabernacles, O Israel!
6As the valleys are they spread forth,
as gardens by the river's side, as the
trees of lign aloes which the LORD hath
planted, *and* as cedar trees beside the
waters.
7He shall pour the water out of his
buckets, and his seed *shall be* in many
waters, and his king shall be higher
than Agag, and his kingdom shall be
exalted.

23:22 unicorn. A name for a wild ox.
23:28 toward Jeshimon. This means looking toward the wilderness.
24:4 falling into a trance. Balaam had a sort of dream or vision during which he spoke the words of the LORD.
24:6 lign aloes. These were very precious trees.
24:7 Agag. This is the title of the kings of the Amalekites, who were very powerful at this time (see 1 Sam. 15:9).

[8]God brought him forth out of Egypt; he hath as it were the strength of an unicorn: he shall eat up the nations his enemies, and shall break their bones, and pierce *them* through with his arrows.

[9]He couched, he lay down as a lion, and as a great lion: who shall stir him up? Blessed *is* he that blesseth thee, and cursed *is* he that curseth thee.

¶[10]And Balak's anger was kindled against Balaam, and he smote his hands together: and Balak said unto Balaam, I called thee to curse mine enemies, and, behold, thou hast altogether blessed *them* these three times.

[11]Therefore now flee thou to thy place: I thought to promote thee unto great honour; but, lo, the LORD hath kept thee back from honour.

[12]And Balaam said unto Balak, Spake I not also to thy messengers which thou sentest unto me, saying,

[13]If Balak would give me his house full of silver and gold, I cannot go beyond the commandment of the LORD, to do *either* good or bad of mine own mind; *but* what the LORD saith, that will I speak?

[14]And now, behold, I go unto my people: come *therefore, and* I will advertise thee what this people shall do to thy people in the latter days.

¶[15]And he took up his parable, and said, Balaam the son of Beor hath said, and the man whose eyes are open hath said:

[16]He hath said, which heard the words of God, and knew the knowledge of the most High, *which* saw the vision of the Almighty, falling *into a trance,* but having his eyes open:

[17]I shall see him, but not now: I shall behold him, but not nigh: there shall come a Star out of Jacob, and a Sceptre shall rise out of Israel, and shall smite the corners of Moab, and destroy all the children of Sheth.

[18]And Edom shall be a possession, *Seir also shall be a possession for his enemies; and Israel shall do valiantly.

[19]Out of Jacob shall come he that shall have dominion, and shall destroy him that remaineth of the city.

¶[20]And when he looked on *Amalek, he took up his parable, and said, Amalek *was* the first of the nations; but his latter end *shall be* that he perish for ever.

[21]And he looked on the Kenites, and took up his parable, and said, Strong is thy dwellingplace, and thou puttest thy nest in a rock.

[22]Nevertheless the Kenite shall be wasted, until *Asshur shall carry thee away captive.

[23]And he took up his parable, and said, Alas, who shall live when God doeth this!

[24]And ships *shall come* from the coast of Chittim, and shall afflict Asshur, and shall afflict Eber, and he also shall perish for ever.

24:24 Chittim
This usually means the island of Cyprus, but here it is used in a general way to mean the coasts of Greece and Italy. It refers to the future rise of those empires and their conquest of the Eastern peoples of the country around the two rivers of the Tigris and Euphrates–these Eastern peoples are ascribed as Asshur and Eber.

24:9 Blessed. Compare this verse with God's promise to Abraham in Genesis 12:3 and 27:29.
24:14 advertise. To give notice or inform.
24:16 falling into a trance. It was Balaam who fell into the trance (see vs. 4).
24:17 there shall come. Balsam here prophesied the coming of the Lord Jesus Christ to set up His *kingdom.
24:20 the first of the nations. This means that Amalek was the first of the nations to fight against the Israelites (Exod. 17:8).
24:21 Kenites. These were the descendants of Hobab the son of Jethro, Moses' father-in-law. See Judges 1:16 note.

25 And Balaam rose up, and went and returned to his place: and Balak also went his way.

Israelites' sin: Baal worship

25 And *Israel abode in Shittim, and the people began to commit whoredom with the daughters of Moab.

2 And they called the people unto the sacrifices of their gods: and the people did eat, and bowed down to their gods.

25:2 Idol Worship
From Numbers 31:16, we gather that this idea of worshipping Baal was on the advice of Balaam. It was expressly forbidden in Exodus 34:14-16. The "doctrine of Balaam" (Rev. 2:14) seen today is the lowering of Christian behavior and standards to the level of the unchristian society. God does not want this; those who serve Him are always to be a separated people and lights in the world around them, set apart from the world and its darkness.

3 And Israel joined himself unto Baal-peor: and the anger of the LORD was kindled against Israel.

4 And the LORD said unto *Moses, Take all the heads of the people, and hang them up before the LORD against the sun, that the fierce anger of the LORD may be turned away from Israel.

5 And Moses said unto the judges of Israel, Slay ye every one his men that were joined unto Baal-peor.

¶6 And, behold, one of the children of Israel came and brought unto his brethren a Midianitish woman in the sight of Moses, and in the sight of all the congregation of the children of Israel, who *were* weeping *before* the door of the tabernacle of the congregation.

7 And when *Phinehas, the son of Eleazar, the son of *Aaron the priest, saw *it*, he rose up from among the congregation, and took a javelin in his hand;

8 And he went after the man of Israel into the tent, and thrust both of them through, the man of Israel, and the woman through her belly. So the plague was stayed from the children of Israel.

9 And those that died in the plague were twenty and four thousand.

¶10 And the LORD spake unto Moses, saying,

11 Phinehas, the son of Eleazar, the son of Aaron the priest, hath turned my wrath away from the children of Israel, while he was zealous for my sake among them, that I consumed not the children of Israel in my jealousy.

12 Wherefore say, Behold, I give unto him my *covenant of *peace:

13 And he shall have it, and his seed after him, *even* the covenant of an everlasting priesthood; because he was zealous for his God, and made an *atonement for the children of Israel.

14 Now the name of the Israelite that was slain, *even* that was slain with the Midianitish woman, *was* Zimri, the son of Salu, a prince of a chief house among the Simeonites.

15 And the name of the Midianitish woman that was slain *was* Cozbi, the daughter of Zur; he *was* head over a people, *and* of a chief house in Midian.

¶16 And the LORD spake unto Moses, saying,

17 Vex the *Midianites, and smite them:

18 For they vex you with their wiles, wherewith they have beguiled you in the matter of Peor, and in the matter of Cozbi, the daughter of a prince of Midian, their sister, which was slain in the day of the plague for Peor's sake.

25:3 Baal-Peor. This means the god Baal, who was worshipped at the city of Peor.
25:9 twenty and four thousand. First Corinthians 10:8 gives the number at 23,000. Probably 23,000 died in the plague and 1,000 were killed (vs. 5), making a total of 24,000.
25:18 vex. To harass or torment.
25:18 wiles. Trickery or deceit.

Counting the new generation

26 And it came to pass after the
plague, that the LORD spake
unto Moses and unto Eleazar the son of
Aaron the priest, saying,
2 Take the sum of all the congregation
of the children of Israel, from twenty
years old and upward, throughout their
fathers' house, all that are able to go to
war in Israel.
3 And Moses and Eleazar the priest
spake with them in the plains of Moab
by Jordan *near* Jericho, saying,
4 *Take the sum of the people,* from
twenty years old and upward; as the
LORD commanded Moses and the children of Israel, which went forth out of
the land of Egypt.
¶5 Reuben, the eldest son of Israel: the
children of Reuben; Hanoch, *of whom
cometh* the family of the Hanochites: of
Pallu, the family of the Palluites:
6 Of Hezron, the family of the Hezronites: of Carmi, the family of the Carmites.
7 These *are* the families of the Reubenites: and they that were numbered
of them were forty and three thousand
and seven hundred and thirty.
8 And the sons of Pallu; Eliab.
9 And the sons of Eliab; Nemuel, and
Dathan, and Abiram. This *is that* Dathan
and Abiram, *which were* famous in the
congregation, who strove against Moses and against Aaron in the company
of *Korah, when they strove against the
LORD:
10 And the earth opened her mouth,
and swallowed them up together with
Korah, when that company died, what
time the fire devoured two hundred and
fifty men: and they became a sign.
11 Notwithstanding the children of
Korah died not.
¶12 The sons of Simeon after their
families: of Nemuel, the family of the
Nemuelites: of Jamin, the family of
the Jaminites: of *Jachin, the family of
the Jachinites:

26:11 The Children of Korah
Evidently the sons of Korah did not join their father's rebellion, and they moved away when Moses told the congregation to depart from the tents of the rebels (16:23-29). For their history and duties as Levites, look up 1 Chronicles 9:19,33, where they were appointed as gatekeepers and temple guards; and in 2 Chronicles 31:14 as treasurers. Many of the psalms were written for them to sing. Look up Psalm 84 and others with the heading "For the sons of Korah."

13 Of Zerah, the family of the Zarhites:
of Shaul, the family of the Shaulites.
14 These *are* the families of the Simeonites, twenty and two thousand and
two hundred.
¶15 The children of Gad after their
families: of Zephon, the family of the
Zephonites: of Haggi, the family of
the Haggites: of Shuni, the family of the
Shunites:
16 Of Ozni, the family of the Oznites:
of Eri, the family of the Erites:
17 Of Arod, the family of the Arodites:
of Areli, the family of the Arelites.
18 These *are* the families of the children of Gad according to those that
were numbered of them, forty thousand
and five hundred.
¶19 The sons of Judah *were* Er and
Onan: and Er and Onan died in the land
of Canaan.
20 And the sons of Judah after their
families were; of Shelah, the family of
the Shelanites: of Pharez, the family
of the Pharzites: of Zerah, the family of
the Zarhites.
21 And the sons of Pharez were; of
Hezron, the family of the Hezronites:
of Hamul, the family of the Hamulites.
22 These *are* the families of Judah according to those that were numbered of
them, threescore and sixteen thousand
and five hundred.
¶23 *Of* the sons of Issachar after their
families: *of* Tola, the family of the

26:9 Dathan and Abiram. See the story in chapter 16.

Tolaites: of Pua, the family of the
Punites:
[24]Of Jashub, the family of the Jashub-
ites: of Shimron, the family of the Shim-
ronites.
[25]These *are* the families of Issachar
according to those that were numbered
of them, threescore and four thousand
and three hundred.
¶[26]*Of* the sons of Zebulun after their
families: of Sered, the family of the
Sardites: of Elon, the family of the Elo-
nites: of Jahleel, the family of the
Jahleelites.
[27]These *are* the families of the
Zebulunites according to those that
were numbered of them, threescore
thousand and five hundred.
¶[28]The sons of *Joseph after their
families *were* *Manasseh and *Ephraim.
[29]Of the sons of Manasseh: of Machir,
the family of the Machirites: and
Machir begat *Gilead: of Gilead *come*
the family of the Gileadites.
[30]These *are* the sons of Gilead: *of*
Jeezer, the family of the Jeezerites: of
Helek, the family of the Helekites:
[31]And *of* Asriel, the family of the
Asrielites: and *of* *Shechem, the family of the Shechemites:
[32]And *of* Shemida, the family of the
Shemidaites: and *of* Hepher, the family
of the Hepherites.
¶[33]And Zelophehad the son of Hepher had no sons, but daughters: and
the names of the daughters of Zelophehad *were* Mahlah, and Noah, Hoglah,
Milcah, and Tirzah.
[34]These *are* the families of Manasseh, and those that were numbered of
them, fifty and two thousand and seven
hundred.
¶[35]These *are* the sons of Ephraim after their families: of Shuthelah, the family of the Shuthalhites: of Becher, the
family of the Bachrites: of Tahan, the
family of the Tahanites.
[36]And these *are* the sons of Shuthelah: of Eran, the family of the Eranites.
[37]These *are* the families of the sons
of Ephraim according to those that
were numbered of them, thirty and
two thousand and five hundred. These
are the sons of Joseph after their families.
¶[38]The sons of Benjamin after their
families: of Bela, the family of the
Belaites: of Ashbel, the family of
the Ashbelites: of Ahiram, the family of
the Ahiramites:
[39]Of Shupham, the family of the Shu-
phamites: of Hupham, the family of the
Huphamites.
[40]And the sons of Bela were Ard and
Naaman: *of Ard,* the family of the
Ardites: *and* of Naaman, the family of
the Naamites.
[41]These *are* the sons of Benjamin after their families: and they that were
numbered of them *were* forty and five
thousand and six hundred.
¶[42]These *are* the sons of Dan after
their families: of Shuham, the family of
the Shuhamites. These *are* the families
of Dan after their families.
[43]All the families of the Shuhamites,
according to those that were numbered
of them, *were* threescore and four thousand and four hundred.
¶[44]*Of* the children of Asher after
their families: of Jimna, the family of the
Jimnites: of Jesui, the family of the Jesu-
ites: of Beriah, the family of the
Beriites.
[45]Of the sons of Beriah: of Heber, the
family of the Heberites: of Malchiel, the
family of the Malchielites.
[46]And the name of the daughter of
Asher *was* Sarah.
[47]These *are* the families of the sons
of Asher according to those that were
numbered of them; *who were* fifty and
three thousand and four hundred.
¶[48]*Of* the sons of Naphtali after their
families: of Jahzeel, the family of the Jah-
zeelites: of Guni, the family of the Gu-
nites:
[49]Of Jezer, the family of the Jezerites:

26:33 Zelophehad. See chapter 27.

of Shillem, the family of the Shillemites.

50 These *are* the families of Naphtali according to their families: and they that were numbered of them *were* forty and five thousand and four hundred.

51 These *were* the numbered of the children of Israel, six hundred thousand and a thousand seven hundred and thirty.

¶52 And the LORD spake unto Moses, saying,

53 Unto these the land shall be divided for an inheritance according to the number of names.

54 To many thou shalt give the more inheritance, and to few thou shalt give the less inheritance: to every one shall his inheritance be given according to those that were numbered of him.

55 Notwithstanding the land shall be divided by lot: according to the names of the tribes of their fathers they shall inherit.

56 According to the lot shall the possession thereof be divided between many and few.

¶57 And these *are* they that were numbered of the Levites after their families: of Gershon, the family of the Gershonites: of Kohath, the family of the Kohathites: of Merari, the family of the Merarites.

58 These *are* the families of the Levites: the family of the Libnites, the family of the Hebronites, the family of the Mahlites, the family of the Mushites, the family of the Korathites. And Kohath begat Amram.

59 And the name of Amram's wife *was* Jochebed, the daughter of Levi, whom *her mother* bare to Levi in Egypt: and she bare unto Amram Aaron and Moses, and *Miriam their sister.

60 And unto Aaron was born Nadab, and Abihu, Eleazar, and Ithamar.

61 And *Nadab and Abihu died, when they offered strange fire before the LORD.

62 And those that were numbered of them were twenty and three thousand, all males from a month old and upward: for they were not numbered among the children of Israel, because there was no inheritance given them among the children of Israel.

¶63 These *are* they that were numbered by Moses and Eleazar the priest, who numbered the children of Israel in the plains of Moab by Jordan *near* Jericho.

64 But among these there was not a man of them whom Moses and Aaron the priest numbered, when they numbered the children of Israel in the wilderness of *Sinai.

65 For the LORD had said of them, They shall surely die in the wilderness. And there was not left a man of them, save *Caleb the son of Jephunneh, and *Joshua the son of Nun.

The law of inheritance

27 Then came the daughters of Zelophehad, the son of Hepher, the son of Gilead, the son of Machir, the son of Manasseh, of the families of Manasseh the son of Joseph: and these *are* the names of his daughters; Mahlah, Noah, and Hoglah, and Milcah, and Tirzah.

2 And they stood before Moses, and before Eleazar the priest, and before the princes and all the congregation, *by* the door of the *tabernacle of the congregation, saying,

3 Our father died in the wilderness, and he was not in the company of them that gathered themselves together against

---

26:51 These were the numbered. In chapter 1 there had been 603,550, and now there were 601,730.

26:59 daughter of Levi. This means a "descendant" of Levi, since Jochebed, Moses' mother, was born about two hundred years after Levi.

26:61 died. See Leviticus 10.

26:65 save Caleb . . . and Joshua. See Numbers 14:30.

the LORD in the company of Korah; but
died in his own *sin, and had no sons.
4Why should the name of our father
be done away from among his family,
because he hath no son? Give unto us
therefore a possession among the brethren of our father.
5And Moses brought their cause before the LORD.
¶6And the LORD spake unto Moses,
saying,
7The daughters of Zelophehad speak
right: thou shalt surely give them a
possession of an inheritance among
their father's brethren; and thou shalt
cause the inheritance of their father to
pass unto them.
8And thou shalt speak unto the children of Israel, saying, If a man die, and
have no son, then ye shall cause his
inheritance to pass unto his daughter.
9And if he have no daughter, then ye
shall give his inheritance unto his
brethren.
10And if he have no brethren, then ye
shall give his inheritance unto his
father's brethren.
11And if his father have no brethren,
then ye shall give his inheritance unto
his *kinsman that is next to him of his
family, and he shall possess it: and it
shall be unto the children of Israel a
statute of *judgment, as the LORD commanded Moses.
¶12And the LORD said unto Moses,
Get thee up into this mount Abarim,
and see the land which I have given
unto the children of Israel.
13And when thou hast seen it, thou
also shalt be gathered unto thy people,
as Aaron thy brother was gathered.
14For ye rebelled against my commandment in the desert of Zin, in the
strife of the congregation, to sanctify
me at the water before their eyes: that
is the water of Meribah in Kadesh in the
wilderness of Zin.

27:13 Life after Death
Life does not end at the grave; it is eternal. Those who die in faith, believing in the Lord, go at once into His presence (Luke 23:39-43; John 3:16). Aaron had already died and had gone to be with the Lord and with his people who had died before him. Now Moses is to die, physically (see *death), and will go to *paradise to be with Aaron, with his people, and with his Lord.

Moses prepares for death

¶15And Moses spake unto the LORD,
saying,
16Let the LORD, the *God of the spirits of all flesh, set a man over the congregation,
17Which may go out before them, and
which may go in before them, and which
may lead them out, and which may
bring them in; that the congregation of
the LORD be not as sheep which have
no shepherd.
¶18And the LORD said unto Moses,
Take thee Joshua the son of Nun, a man
in whom *is* the spirit, and lay thine hand
upon him;
19And set him before Eleazar the
priest, and before all the congregation;
and give him a charge in their sight.
20And thou shalt put *some* of thine
honour upon him, that all the congregation of the children of Israel may be
obedient.
21And he shall stand before Eleazar
the priest, who shall ask *counsel* for him
after the judgment of Urim before the
LORD: at his word shall they go out, and
at his word they shall come in, *both* he,
and all the children of Israel with him,
even all the congregation.
22And Moses did as the LORD commanded him: and he took Joshua, and
set him before Eleazar the priest, and
before all the congregation:
23And he laid his hands upon him, and

27:14 ye rebelled. See Numbers 20:7-12.
27:18 Joshua. See references in Exodus 17:9 note.
27:23 a charge. Advice, instruction. See Deuteronomy 3:28; 31:8.

gave him a charge, as the LORD commanded by the hand of Moses.

The order of the offerings

28 And the LORD spake unto Moses, saying,

2 Command the children of Israel, and say unto them, My offering, *and* my bread for my sacrifices made by *fire, *for* a sweet savour unto me, shall ye observe to offer unto me in their due season.

3 And thou shalt say unto them, This *is* the offering made by fire which ye shall offer unto the LORD; two lambs of the first year without spot day by day, *for* a continual burnt-offering.

4 The one lamb shalt thou offer in the morning, and the other lamb shalt thou offer at even;

5 And a tenth *part* of an *ephah of flour for a *meat-offering, mingled with the fourth *part* of an *hin of beaten *oil.

6 *It is* a continual burnt-offering, which was ordained in mount Sinai for a sweet savour, a sacrifice made by fire unto the LORD.

7 And the *drink-offering thereof *shall be* the fourth *part* of an hin for the one lamb: in the *holy *place* shalt thou cause the strong *wine to be poured unto the LORD *for* a drink-offering.

8 And the other lamb shalt thou offer at even: as the meat-offering of the morning, and as the drink-offering thereof, thou shalt offer *it,* a sacrifice made by fire, of a sweet savour unto the LORD.

¶ 9 And on the *sabbath day two lambs of the first year without spot, and two tenth deals of flour *for* a meat-offering, mingled with oil, and the drink-offering thereof:

10 *This is* the burnt-offering of every sabbath, beside the continual burnt-offering, and his drink-offering.

¶ 11 And in the beginnings of your months ye shall offer a burnt-offering unto the LORD; two young bullocks, and one ram, seven lambs of the first year without spot;

12 And three tenth deals of flour *for* a meat-offering, mingled with oil, for one bullock; and two tenth deals of flour *for* a meat-offering, mingled with oil, for one ram;

13 And a several *tenth deal of flour mingled with oil *for* a meat-offering unto one lamb; *for* a burnt-offering of a sweet savour, a sacrifice made by fire unto the LORD.

14 And their drink-offerings shall be half an hin of wine unto a bullock, and the third *part* of an hin unto a ram, and a fourth *part* of an hin unto a lamb: this *is* the burnt-offering of every month throughout the months of the year.

15 And one kid of the goats for a *sin-offering unto the LORD shall be offered, beside the continual burnt-offering, and his drink-offering.

The Passover

16 And in the fourteenth day of the first month *is* the *passover of the LORD.

17 And in the fifteenth day of this month *is* the feast: seven days shall *unleavened bread be eaten.

18 In the first day *shall be* an holy convocation; ye shall do no manner of servile work *therein:*

19 But ye shall offer a sacrifice made by fire *for* a burnt-offering unto the LORD; two young bullocks, and one ram, and seven lambs of the first year: they shall be unto you without blemish:

20 And their meat-offering *shall be of* flour mingled with oil: three tenth deals shall ye offer for a bullock, and two tenth deals for a ram;

21 A several tenth deal shalt thou offer for every lamb, throughout the seven lambs:

22 And one goat *for* a sin-offering, to make an atonement for you.

23 Ye shall offer these beside the

28:18 convocation. Meeting or gathering.

burnt-offering in the morning, which *is* for a continual burnt-offering.

24After this manner ye shall offer daily, throughout the seven days, the meat of the sacrifice made by fire, of a sweet savour unto the LORD: it shall be offered beside the continual burnt-offering, and his drink-offering.

25And on the seventh day ye shall have an holy convocation; ye shall do no servile work.

The firstfruits

¶26Also in the day of the firstfruits, when ye bring a new meat-offering unto the LORD, after your weeks *be out*, ye shall have an holy convocation; ye shall do no servile work:

27But ye shall offer the burnt-offering for a sweet savour unto the LORD; two young bullocks, one ram, seven lambs of the first year;

28And their meat-offering of flour mingled with oil, three tenth deals unto one bullock, two tenth deals unto one ram,

29A several tenth deal unto one lamb, throughout the seven lambs;

30*And* one kid of the goats, to make an atonement for you.

31Ye shall offer *them* beside the continual burnt-offering, and his meat-offering, (they shall be unto you without blemish) and their drink-offerings.

Feast of trumpets

29 And in the seventh month, on the first *day* of the month, ye shall have an holy convocation; ye shall do no servile work: it is a day of blowing the trumpets unto you.

2And ye shall offer a burnt-offering for a sweet savour unto the LORD; one young bullock, one ram, *and* seven lambs of the first year without blemish:

3And their meat-offering *shall be of* flour mingled with oil, three tenth deals for a bullock, *and* two tenth deals for a ram,

4And one tenth deal for one lamb, throughout the seven lambs:

5And one kid of the goats *for* a sin-offering, to make an atonement for you:

6Beside the burnt-offering of the month, and his meat-offering, and the

29:7-11 THE DAY OF ATONEMENT

This fast was observed on the tenth of the month Tishri (October) as the great day of national humiliation and atonement of the sins both of the priests and the people. The ritual is prescribed in Leviticus 16:23,26-33; Numbers 29:7-11. On this day:

1. The high priest arrayed, not in his gorgeous robes, in the white linen garments common to himself and the rest of his order brought a bullock as a sin-offering and a ram as a burnt-offering for himself and the priests.
2. He then brought to the door of the tabernacle two he-goats as a sin-offering and a ram for a burnt-offering for the people.
3. Having presented them before the LORD, he cast two lots upon them, one inscribed "for Jehovah," the other "for azazel," Hebrew for "scapegoat" (or dismissal, Lev. 16:8).
4. Then he slaughtered the bullock at the brazen altar and, having put incense on the mercy seat of the ark in the Holy of Holies, sprinkled the blood seven times before it, and made atonement for himself and his own order.
5. He next slaughtered the goat on which the lot for Jehovah had fallen, and he sprinkled its blood as a sin-offering for the people as he had done with the blood of the bullock, and, as he returned, sprinkled the blood of both animals on the golden altar of incense.
6. Then coming forth, he laid both his hands on the goat upon which the lot for azazel had fallen ("the scapegoat"), and having solemnly confessed over it the sins of the people, sent it away "by the hand of a fit man" into the wilderness, "unto a land not inhabited," (Lev. 16:21-22) to be there let loose, laden with its burden of the sins of the people.

The key to the expressive imagery of this great day of expiation, or atonement is given in Hebrews 9:7-14.

daily burnt-offering, and his meat-
offering, and their drink-offerings, according unto their manner, for a sweet
savour, a *sacrifice made by fire unto
the LORD.

The day of atonement

¶7 And ye shall have on the tenth *day*
of this seventh month an holy convocation; and ye shall afflict your souls: ye
shall not do any work *therein:*
8 But ye shall offer a burnt-offering
unto the LORD *for* a sweet savour; one
young bullock, one ram, *and* seven
lambs of the first year; they shall be
unto you without blemish:
9 And their meat-offering *shall be of*
flour mingled with oil, three tenth deals
to a bullock, *and* two tenth deals to one
ram,
10 A several tenth deal for one lamb,
throughout the seven lambs:
11 One kid of the goats *for* a sin-
offering; beside the sin-offering of
atonement, and the continual burnt-
offering, and the meat-offering of it, and
their drink-offerings.

The feast of tabernacles

¶12 And on the fifteenth day of the
seventh month ye shall have an holy
convocation; ye shall do no servile
work, and ye shall keep a feast unto the
LORD seven days:
13 And ye shall offer a burnt-offering,
a sacrifice made by fire, of a sweet
savour unto the LORD; thirteen young
bullocks, two rams, *and* fourteen lambs
of the first year; they shall be without
blemish:
14 And their meat-offering *shall be of*
flour mingled with oil, three tenth deals
unto every bullock of the thirteen bullocks, two tenth deals to each ram of the
two rams,
15 And a several tenth deal to each
lamb of the fourteen lambs:
16 And one kid of the goats *for* a sin-
offering; beside the continual burnt-
offering, his meat-offering, and his
drink-offering.

¶17 And on the second day *ye shall offer* twelve young bullocks, two rams,
fourteen lambs of the first year without
spot:
18 And their meat-offering and their
drink-offerings for the bullocks, for the
rams, and for the lambs, *shall be* according to their number, after the manner:
19 And one kid of the goats *for* a sin-
offering; beside the continual burnt-
offering, and the meat-offering thereof,
and their drink-offerings.

¶20 And on the third day eleven bullocks, two rams, fourteen lambs of the
first year without blemish;
21 And their meat-offering and their
drink-offerings for the bullocks, for the
rams, and for the lambs, *shall be* according to their number, after the manner:
22 And one goat *for* a sin-offering;
beside the continual burnt-offering,
and his meat-offering, and his drink-
offering.

¶23 And on the fourth day ten bullocks, two rams, *and* fourteen lambs of
the first year without blemish:
24 Their meat-offering and their
drink-offerings for the bullocks, for the
rams, and for the lambs, *shall be* according to their number, after the manner:
25 And one kid of the goats *for* a sin-
offering; beside the continual burnt offering, his meat-offering, and his
drink-offering.

¶26 And on the fifth day nine bullocks,
two rams, *and* fourteen lambs of the
first year without spot:
27 And their meat-offering and their
drink-offerings for the bullocks, for the
rams, and for the lambs, *shall be* according to their number, after the manner:
28 And one goat *for* a sin-offering; beside
the continual burnt-offering, and his
meat-offering, and his drink-offering.

¶29 And on the sixth day eight bullocks, two rams, *and* fourteen lambs of
the first year without blemish:
30 And their meat-offering and their
drink-offerings for the bullocks, for the
rams, and for the lambs, *shall be* according to their number, after the manner:

31And one goat *for* a sin-offering; beside the continual burnt-offering, his
meat-offering, and his drink-offering.
¶32And on the seventh day seven bullocks, two rams, *and* fourteen lambs of
the first year without blemish:
33And their meat-offering and their
drink-offerings for the bullocks, for the
rams, and for the lambs, *shall be* according to their number, after the manner:
34And one goat *for* a sin-offering; beside the continual burnt-offering, his
meat-offering, and his drink-offering.
¶35On the eighth day ye shall have a
solemn assembly: ye shall do no servile
work *therein:*
36But ye shall offer a burnt-offering,
a sacrifice made by fire, of a sweet
savour unto the LORD: one bullock, one
ram, seven lambs of the first year without blemish:
37Their meat-offering and their
drink-offerings for the bullock, for the
ram, and for the lambs, *shall be* according to their number, after the manner:
38And one goat *for* a sin-offering;
beside the continual burnt-offering,
and his meat-offering, and his drink-
offering.
39These *things* ye shall do unto the
LORD in your set feasts, beside your
vows, and your freewill-offerings, for
your burnt-offerings, and for your
meat-offerings, and for your drink-
offerings, and for your peace-offerings.
40And Moses told the children of Israel according to all that the LORD commanded Moses.

The law for vows

30 And Moses spake unto the
heads of the tribes concerning
the children of Israel, saying, This *is*
the thing which the LORD hath commanded.
2If a man vow a vow unto the LORD,
or swear an oath to bind his soul with a
bond; he shall not break his word, he
shall do according to all that proceedeth
out of his mouth.
3If a woman also vow a vow unto the
LORD, and bind *herself* by a bond, *being*
in her father's house in her youth;
4And her father hear her vow, and her
bond wherewith she hath bound her
soul, and her father shall hold his peace
at her: then all her vows shall stand, and
every bond wherewith she hath bound
her soul shall stand.
5But if her father disallow her in the
day that he heareth; not any of her
vows, or of her bonds wherewith she
hath bound her soul, shall stand: and
the LORD shall forgive her, because her
father disallowed her.
6And if she had at all an husband,
when she vowed, or uttered ought out
of her lips, wherewith she bound her
soul;
7And her husband heard *it,* and held
his peace at her in the day that he heard
it: then her vows shall stand, and her
bonds wherewith she bound her soul
shall stand.
8But if her husband disallowed her on
the day that he heard *it;* then he shall
make her vow which she vowed, and

29:39 THE APPOINTED FEASTS

These were the feasts which the LORD had appointed (Lev. 23):

1. The Passover
2. The Feast of Unleavened Bread
3. The Feast of Firstfruits
4. The Feast of Pentecost (wave loaves)
5. The Feast of Trumpets
6. The Day of Atonement
7. The Feast of Tabernacles

The feasts were to be held at times set by God. Read the Leviticus 23 notes to see why they were to be held at these times.

that which she uttered with her lips, wherewith she bound her soul, of none effect: and the LORD shall forgive her.

9 But every vow of a widow, and of her that is divorced, wherewith they have bound their souls, shall stand against her.

10 And if she vowed in her husband's house, or bound her soul by a bond with an oath;

11 And her husband heard *it,* and held his peace at her, *and* disallowed her not: then all her vows shall stand, and every bond wherewith she bound her soul shall stand.

12 But if her husband hath utterly made them void on the day he heard *them; then* whatsoever proceeded out of her lips concerning her vows, or concerning the bond of her soul, shall not stand: her husband hath made them void; and the LORD shall forgive her.

13 Every vow, and every binding oath to afflict the soul, her husband may establish it, or her husband may make it void.

14 But if her husband altogether hold his peace at her from day to day; then he establisheth all her vows, or all her bonds, which *are* upon her: he confirmeth them, because he held his peace at her in the day that he heard *them.*

15 But if he shall any ways make them void after that he hath heard *them;* then he shall bear her iniquity.

16 These *are* the statutes, which the LORD commanded Moses, between a man and his wife, between the father and his daughter, *being yet* in her youth in her father's house.

War against the Midianites

31 And the LORD spake unto *Moses, saying,

2 Avenge the children of *Israel of the *Midianites: afterward shalt thou be gathered unto thy people.

3 And Moses spake unto the people, saying, Arm some of yourselves unto the war, and let them go against the Midianites, and avenge the LORD of *Midian.

4 Of every tribe a thousand, throughout all the tribes of Israel, shall ye send to the war.

5 So there were delivered out of the thousands of Israel, a thousand of *every* tribe, twelve thousand armed for war.

6 And Moses sent them to the war, a thousand of *every* tribe, them and *Phinehas the son of Eleazar the priest, to the war, with the holy instruments, and the trumpets to blow in his hand.

7 And they warred against the Midianites, as the LORD commanded Moses; and they slew all the males.

8 And they slew the kings of Midian, beside the rest of them that were slain; *namely,* Evi, and Rekem, and Zur, and *Hur, and Reba, five kings of Midian: *Balaam also the son of Beor they slew with the sword.

9 And the children of Israel took *all* the women of Midian captives, and their little ones, and took the spoil of all their cattle, and all their flocks, and all their goods.

10 And they burnt all their cities wherein they dwelt, and all their goodly castles, with fire.

11 And they took all the spoil, and all the prey, *both* of men and of beasts.

12 And they brought the captives, and the prey, and the spoil, unto Moses, and Eleazar the priest, and unto the congregation of the children of Israel, unto the camp at the plains of *Moab, which *are* by Jordan *near* Jericho.

¶ 13 And Moses, and Eleazar the priest,

31:2 Avenge. Moses had been given this command before (Num. 25:16-18).
31:2 afterward. The war against Midian was Moses' last task before his death.
31:2 gathered unto thy people. See Numbers 27:13.
31:6 trumpets. See Numbers 10:9.
31:10 castles. This means *encampments* or *camps.*

and all the princes of the congregation,
went forth to meet them without the
camp.
[14]And Moses was wroth with the officers of the host, *with* the captains over
thousands, and captains over hundreds,
which came from the battle.
[15]And Moses said unto them, Have
ye saved all the women alive?
[16]Behold, these caused the children
of Israel, through the counsel of Balaam, to commit *trespass against the
LORD in the matter of Peor, and there
was a plague among the congregation
of the LORD.
[17]Now therefore kill every male
among the little ones, and kill every
woman that hath known man by lying
with him.
[18]But all the women children, that
have not known a man by lying with
him, keep alive for yourselves.
[19]And do ye abide without the camp
seven days: whosoever hath killed any
person, and whosoever hath touched
any slain, purify *both* yourselves and
your captives on the third day, and on
the seventh day.
[20]And purify all *your* raiment, and all
that is made of skins, and all work of
goats' *hair,* and all things made of wood.
¶[21]And Eleazar the priest said unto
the men of war which went to the battle, This *is* the ordinance of the *law
which the LORD commanded Moses;
[22]Only the gold, and the *silver, the
brass, the iron, the tin, and the lead,
[23]Every thing that may abide the fire,
ye shall make *it* go through the fire, and
it shall be *clean: nevertheless it shall
be purified with the water of separation:
and all that abideth not the fire ye shall
make go through the water.
[24]And ye shall wash your clothes on
the seventh day, and ye shall be clean, and
afterward ye shall come into the camp.
¶[25]And the LORD spake unto Moses,
saying,
[26]Take the sum of the prey that was
taken, *both* of man and of beast, thou,
and Eleazar the priest, and the chief
fathers of the congregation:
[27]And divide the prey into two parts;
between them that took the war upon
them, who went out to battle, and between all the congregation:
[28]And levy a tribute unto the LORD of
the men of war which went out to battle: one soul of five hundred, *both* of the
persons, and of the beeves, and of the
asses, and of the sheep:
[29]Take *it* of their half, and give *it* unto
Eleazar the priest, *for* an *heave-offering of the LORD.
[30]And of the children of Israel's half,
thou shalt take one portion of fifty, of
the persons, of the beeves, of the asses,
and of the flocks, of all manner of
beasts, and give them unto the Levites,
which keep the charge of the tabernacle of the LORD.
[31]And Moses and Eleazar the priest
did as the LORD commanded Moses.
[32]And the booty, *being* the rest of the
prey which the men of war had caught,
was six hundred thousand and seventy
thousand and five thousand sheep,
[33]And threescore and twelve thousand beeves,
[34]And threescore and one thousand
asses,
[35]And thirty and two thousand persons in all, of women that had not
known man by lying with him.
[36]And the half, *which was* the portion
of them that went out to war, was in
number three hundred thousand and
seven and thirty thousand and five hundred sheep:
[37]And the LORD'S tribute of the sheep
was six hundred and threescore and fifteen.
[38]And the beeves *were* thirty and six
thousand; of which the LORD'S tribute
was threescore and twelve.
[39]And the asses *were* thirty thousand

31:26 the prey. Spoils of war, booty.
31:33 beeves. Oxen.

and five hundred; of which the LORD'S tribute *was* threescore and one.

40 And the persons *were* sixteen thousand; of which the LORD'S tribute *was* thirty and two persons.

41 And Moses gave the tribute, *which was* the LORD'S heave-offering, unto Eleazar the priest, as the LORD commanded Moses.

42 And of the children of Israel's half, which Moses divided from the men that warred,

43 (Now the half *that pertained unto* the congregation was three hundred thousand and thirty thousand *and* seven thousand and five hundred sheep,

44 And thirty and six thousand beeves,

45 And thirty thousand asses and five hundred,

46 And sixteen thousand persons;)

47 Even of the children of Israel's half, Moses took one portion of fifty, *both* of man and of beast, and gave them unto the Levites, which kept the charge of the tabernacle of the LORD; as the LORD commanded Moses.

¶48 And the officers which *were* over thousands of the host, the captains of thousands, and captains of hundreds, came near unto Moses:

49 And they said unto Moses, Thy servants have taken the sum of the men of war which *are* under our charge, and there lacketh not one man of us.

50 We have therefore brought an *oblation for the LORD, what every man hath gotten, of jewels of gold, chains, and bracelets, rings, earrings, and tablets, to make an *atonement for our souls before the LORD.

51 And Moses and Eleazar the priest took the gold of them, *even* all wrought jewels.

52 And all the gold of the offering that they offered up to the LORD, of the captains of thousands, and of the captains of hundreds, was sixteen thousand seven hundred and fifty shekels.

53 (For the men of war had taken spoil, every man for himself.)

54 And Moses and Eleazar the priest took the gold of the captains of thousands and of hundreds, and brought it into the tabernacle of the congregation, *for* a memorial for the children of Israel before the LORD.

Reuben, Gad, and half Manasseh settle

32 Now the children of Reuben and the children of Gad had a very great multitude of cattle: and when they saw the land of Jazer, and the land of *Gilead, that, behold, the place *was* a place for cattle;

32:1-5 The Tribes of Reuben and Gad
These children of Israel, who wanted to stay just outside the land that God had offered to them, are like Christians today who try to live half for the world and half for Christ. That kind of living can only bring trouble. It almost always leads to a denial of Christ and His power, as it did in this case, because many years later when our Lord was on the earth the Gadarenes, descendants of Gad, preferred earthly riches to Him (read Luke 8:26-37) and begged Him to leave their country.

2 The children of Gad and the children of Reuben came and spake unto Moses, and to Eleazar the priest, and unto the princes of the congregation, saying,

3 Ataroth, and Dibon, and Jazer, and Nimrah, and Heshbon, and Elealeh, and Shebam, and Nebo, and Beon,

4 *Even* the country which the LORD smote before the congregation of Israel, *is* a land for cattle, and thy servants have cattle:

5 Wherefore, said they, if we have found *grace in thy sight, let this land

31:50 tablets. Necklaces.
31:52 shekels. The gold shekel was a weight equal to about two-fifths of an ounce.
32:1 Jazer. See Numbers 21:32 for the account of the conquest of this bit of land.

be given unto thy servants for a possession, *and* bring us not over Jordan.
¶6 And Moses said unto the children
of Gad and to the children of Reuben,
Shall your brethren go to war, and shall
ye sit here?
7 And wherefore discourage ye the
heart of the children of Israel from going over into the land which the LORD
hath given them?
8 Thus did your fathers, when I sent
them from Kadesh-barnea to see the
land.
9 For when they went up unto the
valley of Eshcol, and saw the land, they
discouraged the heart of the children of
Israel, that they should not go into the
land which the LORD had given them.
10 And the LORD'S anger was kindled
the same time, and he sware, saying,
11 Surely none of the men that came
up out of *Egypt, from twenty years old
and upward, shall see the land which I
sware unto *Abraham, unto *Isaac, and
unto *Jacob; because they have not
wholly followed me:
12 Save *Caleb the son of Jephunneh
the Kenezite, and *Joshua the son of
Nun: for they have wholly followed the
LORD.
13 And the LORD'S anger was kindled
against Israel, and he made them wander in the wilderness forty years, until
all the generation, that had done evil in
the sight of the LORD, was consumed.
14 And, behold, ye are risen up in your
fathers' stead, an increase of sinful men,
to augment yet the fierce anger of the
LORD toward Israel.
15 For if ye turn away from after him,
he will yet again leave them in the wilderness; and ye shall destroy all this
people.
¶16 And they came near unto him,
and said, We will build sheepfolds
here for our cattle, and cities for our
little ones:
17 But we ourselves will go ready
armed before the children of Israel,
until we have brought them unto their
place: and our little ones shall dwell in
the fenced cities because of the inhabitants of the land.
18 We will not return unto our houses,
until the children of Israel have inherited every man his inheritance.
19 For we will not inherit with them
on yonder side Jordan, or forward; because our inheritance is fallen to us on
this side Jordan eastward.
¶20 And Moses said unto them, If ye
will do this thing, if ye will go armed
before the LORD to war,
21 And will go all of you armed over
Jordan before the LORD, until he hath
driven out his enemies from before
him,
22 And the land be subdued before the
LORD: then afterward ye shall return,
and be guiltless before the LORD, and
before Israel; and this land shall be your
possession before the LORD.
23 But if ye will not do so, behold, ye

32:23 Sin Can't Hide

The phrase "your sin will find you out" is just as true today as it was when it was written and as it was hundreds of years before that, when Cain killed his brother Abel (Gen. 4:8). The Holy Spirit speaking through James (1:15) says, "Sin, when it is finished, bringeth forth death." It may be possible to hide your sin from your closest friends and even from your family, but there are two from whom you cannot hide it–God and yourself. Your sin will always find you out, and there are no "little" sins in God's sight, for it was because of sin that the Lord Jesus Christ was put to death (Rom. 3:8-9). See what God says about sin in 1 John 1:9; 2:1-5.

32:8 Thus did your fathers. Moses referred to the sad events of Numbers 13:26-33.
32:14 to augment. To increase.
32:17 we ourselves will go. See Joshua 4:12-13 and 22:3-4 for the fulfillment of the promise. Their later history is indicated in Judges 5:16; 2 Kings 15:29; and 1 Chronicles 5:25-26.

have sinned against the LORD: and be
sure your sin will find you out.
24 Build you cities for your little ones,
and folds for your sheep; and do that
which hath proceeded out of your
mouth.
25 And the children of Gad and the
children of Reuben spake unto Moses,
saying, Thy servants will do as my lord
commandeth.
26 Our little ones, our wives, our
flocks, and all our cattle, shall be there
in the cities of Gilead:
27 But thy servants will pass over,
every man armed for war, before the
LORD to battle, as my lord saith.
28 So concerning them Moses commanded Eleazar the priest, and Joshua
the son of Nun, and the chief fathers of
the tribes of the children of Israel:
29 And Moses said unto them, If the
children of Gad and the children of Reuben will pass with you over Jordan,
every man armed to battle, before the
LORD, and the land shall be subdued
before you; then ye shall give them the
land of Gilead for a possession:
30 But if they will not pass over with
you armed, they shall have possessions
among you in the land of Canaan.
31 And the children of Gad and the
children of Reuben answered, saying,
As the LORD hath said unto thy servants, so will we do.
32 We will pass over armed before the
LORD into the land of Canaan, that the
possession of our inheritance on this
side Jordan *may be* ours.
33 And Moses gave unto them, *even* to
the children of Gad, and to the children
of Reuben, and unto half the tribe of
*Manasseh the son of *Joseph, the
kingdom of Sihon king of the Amorites,
and the kingdom of Og king of *Bashan,
the land, with the cities thereof in the
coasts, *even* the cities of the country
round about.
¶34 And the children of Gad built Dibon, and Ataroth, and Aroer,
35 And Atroth, Shophan, and Jaazer,
and Jogbehah,
36 And Beth-nimrah, and Beth-haran,
fenced cities: and folds for sheep.
37 And the children of Reuben built
Heshbon, and Elealeh, and Kirjathaim,
38 And Nebo, and *Baal-meon, (their
names being changed,) and Shibmah:
and gave other names unto the cities
which they builded.
39 And the children of Machir the son
of Manasseh went to Gilead, and took
it, and dispossessed the *Amorite
which *was* in it.
40 And Moses gave Gilead unto
Machir the son of Manasseh; and he
dwelt therein.
41 And Jair the son of Manasseh went
and took the small towns thereof, and
called them Havoth-jair.
42 And Nobah went and took Kenath,
and the villages thereof, and called it
Nobah, after his own name.

The journeys from Egypt to Jordan

33 These *are* the journeys of the
children of Israel, which went
forth out of the land of Egypt with their
armies under the hand of Moses and
*Aaron.
2 And Moses wrote their goings out
according to their journeys by the commandment of the LORD: and these
are their journeys according to their
goings out.
3 And they departed from Rameses in
the first *month, on the fifteenth day
of the first month; on the morrow after
the passover the children of Israel went
out with an high hand in the sight of all
the Egyptians.
4 For the Egyptians buried all *their*
firstborn, which the LORD had smitten
among them: upon their gods also the
LORD executed judgments.
5 And the children of Israel removed
from Rameses, and pitched in Succoth.
6 And they departed from Succoth,

33:3 the first month. Abib (April).

and pitched in Etham, which *is* in the
edge of the wilderness.
7And they removed from Etham, and
turned again unto Pi-hahiroth, which *is*
before Baal-zephon: and they pitched
before Migdol.
8And they departed from before Pi-
hahiroth, and passed through the midst
of the sea into the wilderness, and went
three days' journey in the wilderness of
Etham, and pitched in Marah.
9And they removed from Marah, and
came unto Elim: and in Elim *were*
twelve fountains of water, and threescore and ten palm trees; and they
pitched there.
10And they removed from Elim, and
encamped by the Red sea.
11And they removed from the Red sea,
and encamped in the wilderness of Sin.
12And they took their journey out of
the wilderness of Sin, and encamped in
Dophkah.
13And they departed from Dophkah,
and encamped in Alush.
14And they removed from Alush, and
encamped at Rephidim, where was no
water for the people to drink.
15And they departed from Rephidim,
and pitched in the wilderness of *Sinai.
16And they removed from the desert of
Sinai, and pitched at Kibroth-hattaavah.
17And they departed from Kibroth-
hattaavah, and encamped at Hazeroth.
18And they departed from Hazeroth,
and pitched in Rithmah.
19And they departed from Rithmah,
and pitched at Rimmon-parez.
20And they departed from Rimmon-
parez, and pitched in Libnah.
21And they removed from Libnah,
and pitched at Rissah.
22And they journeyed from Rissah,
and pitched in Kehelathah.
23And they went from Kehelathah,
and pitched in mount Shapher.
24And they removed from mount
Shapher, and encamped in Haradah.
25And they removed from Haradah,
and pitched in Makheloth.

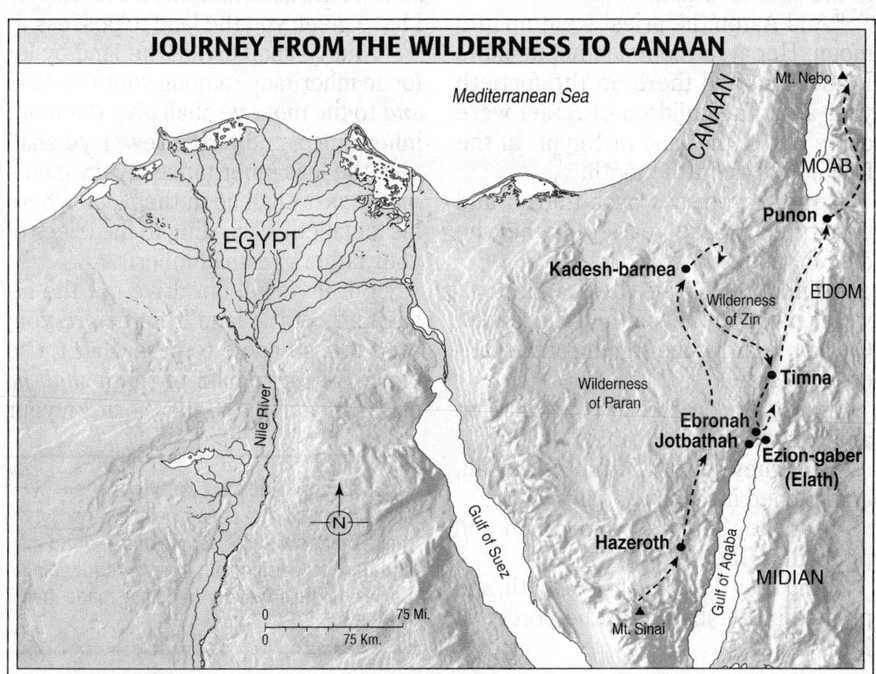

33:9 threescore and ten. Seventy. A score equals twenty.

26And they removed from Makheloth, and encamped at Tahath.
27And they departed from Tahath,
and pitched at Tarah.
28And they removed from Tarah, and
pitched in Mithcah.
29And they went from Mithcah, and
pitched in Hashmonah.
30And they departed from Hashmonah, and encamped at Moseroth.
31And they departed from Moseroth,
and pitched in Bene-jaakan.
32And they removed from Bene-jaakan, and encamped at Hor-hagidgad.
33And they went from Hor-hagidgad,
and pitched in Jotbathah.
34And they removed from Jotbathah,
and encamped at Ebronah.
35And they departed from Ebronah,
and encamped at Ezion-gaber.
36And they removed from Ezion-
gaber, and pitched in the wilderness of
Zin, which *is* Kadesh.
37And they removed from Kadesh,
and pitched in mount Hor, in the edge
of the land of *Edom.
38And Aaron the priest went up into
mount Hor at the commandment of the
LORD, and died there, in the fortieth
year after the children of Israel were
come out of the land of Egypt, in the
first *day* of the fifth month.
39And Aaron *was* an hundred and
twenty and three years old when he
died in mount Hor.
40And king Arad the Canaanite,
which dwelt in the south in the land of
Canaan, heard of the coming of the children of Israel.
41And they departed from mount Hor,
and pitched in Zalmonah.
42And they departed from Zalmonah,
and pitched in Punon.
43And they departed from Punon, and
pitched in Oboth.
44And they departed from Oboth, and
pitched in Ije-abarim, in the border of
Moab.
45And they departed from Iim, and
pitched in Dibon-gad.
46And they removed from Dibon-gad,
and encamped in Almon-diblathaim.
47And they removed from Almon-
diblathaim, and pitched in the mountains of Abarim, before Nebo.
48And they departed from the mountains of Abarim, and pitched in the
plains of Moab by Jordan *near* Jericho.
49And they pitched by Jordan, from
Beth-jesimoth *even* unto Abel-shittim
in the plains of Moab.
¶50And the LORD spake unto Moses
in the plains of Moab by Jordan *near* Jericho, saying,
51Speak unto the children of Israel,
and say unto them, When ye are passed
over Jordan into the land of Canaan;
52Then ye shall drive out all the inhabitants of the land from before you,
and destroy all their pictures, and destroy all their molten images, and quite
pluck down all their *high places:
53And ye shall dispossess *the inhabitants* of the land, and dwell therein: for
I have given you the land to possess it.
54And ye shall divide the land by lot
for an inheritance among your families:
and to the more ye shall give the more
inheritance, and to the fewer ye shall
give the less inheritance: every man's
inheritance shall be in the place where
his lot falleth; according to the tribes of
your fathers ye shall inherit.
55But if ye will not drive out the inhabitants of the land from before you;
then it shall come to pass, that those
which ye let remain of them *shall be*
pricks in your eyes, and thorns in your

33:55 Choose Friends Carefully
See Judges 2:3. The LORD's people cannot make friends with the people of the world and have fellowship with them without going the way of those whom they have made their friends.

33:52 quite pluck down. Demolish.
33:55 pricks. Barbs.

sides, and shall vex you in the land
wherein ye dwell.
56Moreover it shall come to pass, *that*
I shall do unto you, as I thought to do
unto them.

Boundaries

34 And the LORD spake unto Moses, saying,
2Command the children of Israel, and
say unto them, When ye come into the
land of Canaan; (this *is* the land that
shall fall unto you for an inheritance,
even the land of Canaan with the coasts
thereof:)
3Then your south quarter shall be
from the wilderness of Zin along by the
coast of Edom, and your south border
shall be the outmost coast of the salt
sea eastward:
4And your border shall turn from the
south to the ascent of Akrabbim, and
pass on to Zin: and the going forth
thereof shall be from the south to Kadesh-barnea, and shall go on to Hazar-
addar, and pass on to Azmon:
5And the border shall fetch a compass
from Azmon unto the river of Egypt, and
the goings out of it shall be at the sea.
6And *as for* the western border, ye
shall even have the great sea for a border: this shall be your west border.
7And this shall be your north border:
from the great sea ye shall point out for
you mount Hor:
8From mount Hor ye shall point out
your border unto the entrance of Hamath; and the goings forth of the border shall be to Zedad:
¶9And the border shall go on to Ziph-
ron, and the goings out of it shall be at
Hazar-enan: this shall be your north
border.
10And ye shall point out your east
border from Hazar-enan to Shepham:
11And the coast shall go down from
Shepham to Riblah, on the east side of
Ain; and the border shall descend, and
shall reach unto the side of the sea of
Chinnereth eastward:
12And the border shall go down to
Jordan, and the goings out of it shall be
at the salt sea: this shall be your land
with the coasts thereof round about.

The allotment of the land

13And Moses commanded the children of Israel, saying, This *is* the land
which ye shall inherit by lot, which the
LORD commanded to give unto the nine
tribes, and to the half tribe:
14For the tribe of the children of Reuben according to the house of their fathers, and the tribe of the children of
Gad according to the house of their fathers, have received *their inheritance;*
and half the tribe of Manasseh have
received their inheritance:
15The two tribes and the half tribe
have received their inheritance on this
side Jordan *near* Jericho eastward, toward the sunrising.
16And the LORD spake unto Moses,
saying,
17These *are* the names of the men
which shall divide the land unto you:
Eleazar the priest, and Joshua the son
of Nun.
18And ye shall take one prince of
every tribe, to divide the land by inheritance.
19And the names of the men *are*
these: Of the tribe of *Judah, Caleb the
son of Jephunneh.
20And of the tribe of the children of
Simeon, Shemuel the son of Ammihud.

34:2 Command the children. See Genesis 14:3 and Joshua 15:2 for more about the boundaries of the land.
34:5 fetch a compass. Go around.
34:5 the river of Egypt. The Nile.
34:6 the great sea. The Mediterranean.
34:11 sea of Chinnereth. The Gennesaret, also known as the Sea of Galilee, and the Lake (Sea) of Tiberias.
34:12 the salt sea. The Dead Sea.

21Of the tribe of Benjamin, Elidad the
son of Chislon.
22And the prince of the tribe of the
children of Dan, Bukki the son of Jogli.
23The prince of the children of
Joseph, for the tribe of the children
of Manasseh, Hanniel the son of
*Ephod.
24And the prince of the tribe of the
children of *Ephraim, Kemuel the son
of Shiphtan.
25And the prince of the tribe of the
children of Zebulun, Elizaphan the son
of Parnach.
26And the prince of the tribe of the
children of Issachar, Paltiel the son of
Azzan.
27And the prince of the tribe of the
children of Asher, Ahihud the son of
Shelomi.
28And the prince of the tribe of the
children of Naphtali, Pedahel the son of
Ammihud.
29These *are they* whom the LORD
commanded to divide the inheritance
unto the children of Israel in the land of
Canaan.

Cities of the Levites

35 And the LORD spake unto Moses in the plains of Moab by Jordan *near* Jericho, saying,
2Command the children of Israel, that
they give unto the Levites of the inheritance of their possession cities to dwell
in; and ye shall give *also* unto the Levites suburbs for the cities round about
them.
3And the cities shall they have to
dwell in; and the suburbs of them shall
be for their cattle, and for their goods,
and for all their beasts.
4And the suburbs of the cities, which
ye shall give unto the Levites, *shall
reach* from the wall of the city and outward a thousand *cubits round about.
5And ye shall measure from without
the city on the east side two thousand
cubits, and on the south side two thousand cubits, and on the west side two
thousand cubits, and on the north side
two thousand cubits; and the city *shall
be* in the midst: this shall be to them the
suburbs of the cities.
6And among the cities which ye shall
give unto the Levites *there shall be* six
cities for refuge, which ye shall appoint
for the manslayer, that he may flee
thither: and to them ye shall add forty
and two cities.

35:6 The Cities of Refuge
The cities of refuge were there to protect anyone who killed someone "unawares" (vs. 11), which means *by mistake*. If a man was killed, his nearest relation, called "the revenger (or *avenger) of blood" (vs. 19, etc.), had to avenge his relative by seeking out his murderer and killing him. If the murder was only an accident, the man who had done it could escape at once to a city of refuge (vss. 6, 11, etc.), and there the revenger of blood could not touch him. The cities of refuge are a picture of the safety that is ours when we trust Christ as our Saviour. We no longer have to pay the penalty of our sin—we are safe in Him. See Romans 8:1 and Hebrews 6:18.

7*So* all the cities which ye shall give
to the Levites *shall be* forty and eight
cities: them *shall ye give* with their suburbs.
8And the cities which ye shall give
shall be of the possession of the children
of Israel: from *them that have* many ye
shall give many; but from *them that have*
few ye shall give few: every one shall
give of his cities unto the Levites according to his inheritance which he
inheriteth.

Cities of refuge

¶9And the LORD spake unto Moses,
saying,
10Speak unto the children of Israel,
and say unto them, When ye be come
over Jordan into the land of Canaan;
11Then ye shall appoint you cities to
be *cities of refuge for you; that the

35:2 suburbs. Pastureland.

slayer may flee thither, which killeth
any person at unawares.
12 And they shall be unto you cities for
refuge from the avenger; that the
manslayer die not, until he stand before
the congregation in judgment.
13 And of these cities which ye shall
give six cities shall ye have for refuge.
14 Ye shall give three cities on this
side Jordan, and three cities shall ye
give in the land of Canaan, *which* shall
be cities of refuge.
15 These six cities shall be a refuge,
both for the children of Israel, and for
the stranger, and for the sojourner
among them: that every one that killeth
any person unawares may flee thither.
16 And if he smite him with an instrument of iron, so that he die, he *is* a
murderer: the murderer shall surely be
put to death.
17 And if he smite him with throwing
a stone, wherewith he may die, and he
die, he *is* a murderer: the murderer
shall surely be put to death.
18 Or *if* he smite him with an hand
weapon of wood, wherewith he may die,
and he die, he *is* a murderer: the murderer shall surely be put to death.
19 The revenger of *blood himself
shall slay the murderer: when he
meeteth him, he shall slay him.
20 But if he thrust him of hatred, or
hurl at him by laying of wait, that he die;
21 Or in enmity smite him with his
hand, that he die: he that smote *him* shall
surely be put to death; *for* he *is* a murderer: the revenger of blood shall slay
the murderer, when he meeteth him.
22 But if he thrust him suddenly without enmity, or have cast upon him any
thing without laying of wait,
23 Or with any stone, wherewith a
man may die, seeing *him* not, and cast
it upon him, that he die, and *was* not his
enemy, neither sought his harm:
24 Then the congregation shall judge
between the slayer and the revenger of
blood according to these judgments:
25 And the congregation shall deliver
the slayer out of the hand of the
revenger of blood, and the congregation
shall restore him to the city of his refuge, whither he was fled: and he shall
abide in it unto the death of the high
priest, which was anointed with the
holy *oil.
26 But if the slayer shall at any time
come without the border of the city of
his refuge, whither he was fled;
27 And the revenger of blood find him
without the borders of the city of his
refuge, and the revenger of blood kill
the slayer; he shall not be guilty of
blood:
28 Because he should have remained
in the city of his refuge until the death
of the high priest: but after the death of
the high priest the slayer shall return
into the land of his possession.
29 So these *things* shall be for a statute of judgment unto you throughout
your generations in all your dwellings.
30 Whoso killeth any person, the murderer shall be put to death by the mouth
of witnesses: but one witness shall not
testify against any person *to cause him*
to die.
31 Moreover ye shall take no satisfaction for the life of a murderer, which *is*
guilty of death: but he shall be surely
put to death.
32 And ye shall take no satisfaction for
him that is fled to the city of his refuge,
that he should come again to dwell in
the land, until the death of the priest.
33 So ye shall not pollute the land
wherein ye *are:* for blood it defileth the

35:30 by the mouth of witnesses. More than one person had to have seen the murder and testify to that fact.

35:32 satisfaction. The man who had committed the unintentional murder could not offer a sum of money to pay for it but had to stay in the city of refuge until the death of the high priest (vs. 25). If it were an intentional murder, he had to pay for it with his life.

land: and the land cannot be cleansed of
the blood that is shed therein, but by
the blood of him that shed it.
34 Defile not therefore the land which
ye shall inhabit, wherein I dwell: for I
the LORD dwell among the children of
Israel.

The law of inheritance

36 And the chief fathers of the families of the children of Gilead,
the son of Machir, the son of Manasseh,
of the families of the sons of Joseph,
came near, and spake before Moses, and
before the princes, the chief fathers of
the children of Israel:
2 And they said, The LORD commanded my lord to give the land for
an inheritance by lot to the children
of Israel: and my lord was commanded by the LORD to give the inheritance of Zelophehad our brother unto
his daughters.
3 And if they be married to any of the
sons of the *other* tribes of the children
of Israel, then shall their inheritance be
taken from the inheritance of our fathers, and shall be put to the inheritance of the tribe whereunto they are
received: so shall it be taken from the
lot of our inheritance.
4 And when the jubile of the children
of Israel shall be, then shall their inheritance be put unto the inheritance of the
tribe whereunto they are received: so
shall their inheritance be taken away
from the inheritance of the tribe of our
fathers.
5 And Moses commanded the children of Israel according to the word
of the LORD, saying, The tribe of the
sons of Joseph hath said well.
6 This *is* the thing which the LORD
doth command concerning the daughters of Zelophehad, saying, Let them
marry to whom they think best; only to
the family of the tribe of their father
shall they marry.
7 So shall not the inheritance of the
children of Israel remove from tribe to
tribe: for every one of the children of
Israel shall keep himself to the inheritance of the tribe of his fathers.
8 And every daughter, that possesseth
an inheritance in any tribe of the children of Israel, shall be wife unto one of
the family of the tribe of her father, that
the children of Israel may enjoy every
man the inheritance of his fathers.
9 Neither shall the inheritance remove from *one* tribe to another tribe;
but every one of the tribes of the children of Israel shall keep himself to his
own inheritance.
10 Even as the LORD commanded Moses, so did the daughters of Zelophehad:
11 For Mahlah, Tirzah, and Hoglah,
and Milcah, and Noah, the daughters of
Zelophehad, were married unto their
father's brothers' sons:
12 *And* they were married into the
families of the sons of Manasseh the
son of Joseph, and their inheritance
remained in the tribe of the family of
their father.
13 These *are* the commandments and
the judgments, which the LORD commanded by the hand of Moses unto the
children of Israel in the plains of Moab
by Jordan *near* Jericho.

35:33 blood of him that shed it. See Genesis 9:6.
36:4 jubile. See Leviticus 25:10.

The Fifth Book of Moses, called

DEUTERONOMY

BACKGROUND

The name Deuteronomy comes from two Greek words, *deuteros* meaning *second,* and *nomos* meaning *law.* It is not a *second* law nor merely a *repetition* of the Law, but is a summary of the chief points of the Law as it affected the people in general, and was given by Moses in three great speeches to the children of Israel, as they were in the plain of Moab just about to enter the Promised Land. Since all those who had come out of Egypt had died in the wilderness because of their disobedience (see Numbers 32), now Moses wished to emphasize to their children the importance of obeying God and the Law which had been given at Sinai (Exodus 19; 20).

THE MEANING

The key thought is "Thou shalt," and the key verses, 11:26-28. The lesson is that obedience to God brings happiness and blessing, and this applies to Christians today as well as to the Israelites of old. Deuteronomy gives some very important prophecies about the future of the Jews in chapters 28–30. Passages from this book were quoted by Christ in the temptation (see Matthew 4:4 note), and by Paul (Romans 10:6,19; 15:10).

THE WRITER

The materials for Deuteronomy, as in the case of the first four books of the Bible, were prepared by Moses (see Deuteronomy 31:24). It seems clear that the book must have been prepared in about the fortieth year of the wandering, 1491 B.C. The last chapter, since it contains an account of the death of Moses, was undoubtedly written by someone else—perhaps by Joshua.

OUTLINE OF DEUTERONOMY

I.	Moses' First Speech: the Wilderness Journey	Deuteronomy 1:1—4:40
II.	The Cities of Refuge	Deuteronomy 4:41-49; 19:1-13
III.	Moses' Second Speech: the Law	Deuteronomy 5:1—26:19
IV.	Moses' Third Speech: Blessing and Curse	Deuteronomy 27:1—28:68
V.	The Palestinian Covenant	Deuteronomy 29:1—30:20
VI.	Moses' Last Speech, Song, and Blessing	Deuteronomy 31:1—33:29
VII.	Moses' Death	Deuteronomy 34:1-12

I. Moses' First Speech (1:1—4:40)

1 These *be* the words which *Moses spake unto all *Israel on this side Jordan in the wilderness, in the plain over against the Red *sea,* between Paran, and Tophel, and Laban, and Hazeroth, and Dizahab.

2 (*There are* eleven days' *journey* from *Horeb by the way of mount *Seir unto Kadesh-barnea.)

> **1:2 A Long, Short Journey**
> Because of their unbelief, the children of Israel spent forty years traveling a distance that should have taken only eleven days!

3 And it came to pass in the fortieth year, in the eleventh *month, on the first *day* of the month, *that* Moses spake unto the children of Israel, according unto all that the LORD had given him in commandment unto them;

4 After he had slain Sihon the king of the Amorites, which dwelt in Heshbon, and Og the king of *Bashan, which dwelt at Astaroth in Edrei:

5 On this side Jordan, in the land of *Moab, began Moses to declare this *law, saying,

History from Horeb to Kadesh-Barnea

6 The LORD our *God spake unto us in Horeb, saying, Ye have dwelt long enough in this mount:

7 Turn you, and take your journey, and go to the mount of the Amorites, and unto all *the places* nigh thereunto, in the plain, in the hills, and in the vale, and in the south, and by the sea side, to the land of the Canaanites, and unto *Lebanon, unto the great river, the river Euphrates.

8 Behold, I have set the land before you: go in and possess the land which the LORD sware unto your fathers, *Abraham, *Isaac, and *Jacob, to give unto them and to their seed after them.

¶9 And I spake unto you at that time, saying, I am not able to bear you myself alone:

10 The LORD your God hath multiplied you, and, behold, ye *are* this day as the stars of heaven for multitude.

11 (The LORD God of your fathers make you a thousand times so many more as ye *are,* and bless you, as he hath promised you!)

12 How can I myself alone bear your cumbrance, and your *burden, and your strife?

13 Take you wise men, and understanding, and known among your tribes, and I will make them rulers over you.

14 And ye answered me, and said, The thing which thou hast spoken *is* good *for us* to do.

15 So I took the chief of your tribes, wise men, and known, and made them heads over you, captains over thousands, and captains over hundreds, and captains over fifties, and captains over tens, and officers among your tribes.

16 And I charged your judges at that time, saying, Hear *the causes* between your brethren, and judge righteously between *every* man and his brother, and the stranger *that is* with him.

17 Ye shall not respect persons in judgment; *but* ye shall hear the small as well as the great; ye shall not be afraid of the face of man; for the *judgment *is* God's: and the cause that is too hard for you, bring *it* unto me, and I will hear it.

18 And I commanded you at that time all the things which ye should do.

¶19 And when we departed from Horeb, we went through all that great and terrible wilderness, which ye saw by the way of the mountain of the Amorites, as the LORD our God commanded us; and we came to Kadesh-barnea.

20 And I said unto you, Ye are come unto the mountain of the Amorites, which the LORD our God doth give unto us.

1:4 Sihon. See the story in Numbers 21:24.
1:8 possess the land. Read the LORD's promises to Abraham in Genesis 12:1-7.

21Behold, the LORD thy God hath set
the land before thee: go up *and* possess
it, as the LORD God of thy fathers hath
said unto thee; fear not, neither be discouraged.
¶22And ye came near unto me every
one of you, and said, We will send men
before us, and they shall search us out
the land, and bring us word again by
what way we must go up, and into what
cities we shall come.
23And the saying pleased me well:
and I took twelve men of you, one of a
tribe:
24And they turned and went up into
the mountain, and came unto the valley
of Eshcol, and searched it out.
25And they took of the fruit of the
land in their hands, and brought *it* down
unto us, and brought us word again, and
said, *It is* a good land which the LORD
our God doth give us.

Failure to enter land (see Num. 13)

26Notwithstanding ye would not go
up, but rebelled against the commandment of the LORD your God:
27And ye murmured in your tents,
and said, Because the LORD hated us,
he hath brought us forth out of the land
of *Egypt, to deliver us into the hand
of the Amorites, to destroy us.
28Whither shall we go up? our brethren have discouraged our heart, saying,
The people *is* greater and taller than
we; the cities *are* great and walled up
to heaven; and moreover we have seen
the sons of *the Anakims there.
29Then I said unto you, Dread not,
neither be afraid of them.
30The LORD your God which goeth
before you, he shall fight for you, according to all that he did for you in
Egypt before your eyes;
31And in the wilderness, where thou
hast seen how that the LORD thy God
bare thee, as a man doth bear his son,
in all the way that ye went, until ye
came into this place.
32Yet in this thing ye did not believe
the LORD your God,
33Who went in the way before you, to
search you out a place to pitch your
tents *in,* in *fire by night, to shew you
by what way ye should go, and in a cloud
by day.
34And the LORD heard the voice of
your words, and was wroth, and sware,
saying,
35Surely there shall not one of these
men of this evil generation see that
good land, which I sware to give unto
your fathers,
36Save *Caleb the son of Jephunneh;
he shall see it, and to him will I give the
land that he hath trodden upon, and to
his children, because he hath wholly
followed the LORD.
37Also the LORD was angry with me
for your sakes, saying, Thou also shalt
not go in thither.
38*But* *Joshua the son of Nun, which
standeth before thee, he shall go in
thither: encourage him: for he shall
cause Israel to inherit it.
39Moreover your little ones, which ye
said should be a prey, and your children,
which in that day had no knowledge
between good and evil, they shall go in
thither, and unto them will I give it, and
they shall possess it.
40But *as for* you, turn you, and take
your journey into the wilderness by the
way of the Red sea.
41Then ye answered and said unto
me, We have sinned against the LORD,
we will go up and fight, according to all
that the LORD our God commanded us.
And when ye had girded on every man
his weapons of war, ye were ready to go
up into the hill.
42And the LORD said unto me, Say
unto them, Go not up, neither fight; for
I *am* not among you; lest ye be smitten
before your enemies.
43So I spake unto you; and ye would
not hear, but rebelled against the commandment of the LORD, and went presumptuously up into the hill.
44And the Amorites, which dwelt in
that mountain, came out against
you, and chased you, as bees do, and

destroyed you in Seir, *even* unto Hormah.
45And ye returned and wept before
the LORD; but the LORD would not hearken to your voice, nor give ear unto you.

> **1:45 Presumptuous Sin**
> The LORD does not hear those who come to Him in unbelief. The children of Israel sinned "presumptuously" (vs. 43). This refers to anyone who acted in a way that he knew was sinful or forbidden in the Law. (See Deut. 17:12-13; Ps. 19:13.) Notice the tragic consequences of willful, presumptuous sin. When Christ came in love and grace and died for the sinner, He rose again, and dwells in the heart of the believer to empower him or her to live victoriously over temptation and sin.

46So ye abode in Kadesh many days,
according unto the days that ye abode
there.

Wilderness wanderings and battles

2 Then we turned, and took our
journey into the wilderness by the
way of the Red sea, as the LORD spake
unto me: and we compassed mount Seir
many days.
2And the LORD spake unto me,
saying,
3Ye have compassed this mountain
long enough: turn you northward.
4And command thou the people, saying, Ye *are* to pass through the coast of
your brethren the children of *Esau,
which dwell in Seir; and they shall be
afraid of you: take ye good heed unto
yourselves therefore:
5Meddle not with them; for I will not
give you of their land, no, not so much
as a footbreadth; because I have given
mount Seir unto Esau *for* a possession.
6Ye shall buy meat of them for money,
that ye may eat; and ye shall also buy
water of them for money, that ye may
drink.
7For the LORD thy God hath blessed
thee in all the works of thy hand: he
knoweth thy walking through this great
wilderness: these forty years the LORD
thy God *hath been* with thee; thou hast
lacked nothing.
8And when we passed by from our
brethren the children of Esau, which
dwelt in Seir, through the way of the
plain from Elath, and from Ezion-gaber,
we turned and passed by the way of the
wilderness of Moab.
9And the LORD said unto me, Distress not the Moabites, neither contend
with them in battle: for I will not give
thee of their land *for* a possession; because I have given Ar unto the children
of *Lot *for* a possession.
10The Emims dwelt therein in times
past, a people great, and many, and tall,
as the Anakims;
11Which also were accounted giants,
as the Anakims; but the Moabites call
them Emims.
12The Horims also dwelt in Seir beforetime; but the children of Esau succeeded them, when they had destroyed
them from before them, and dwelt in
their stead; as Israel did unto the land
of his possession, which the LORD gave
unto them.
13Now rise up, *said I,* and get you
over the brook Zered. And we went
over the brook Zered.
14And the space in which we came
from Kadesh-barnea, until we were
come over the brook Zered, *was* thirty
and eight years; until all the generation
of the men of war were wasted out from
among the host, as the LORD sware
unto them.

2:4 your brethren. Esau, whose descendants were the Edomites, was the brother of Jacob, the ancestor of the children of Israel.
2:5 I have given. See the story in Genesis 36:6-8.
2:9 children of Lot. See Genesis 19:36-38 for the story of Lot. The people mentioned in the next few verses were the original inhabitants of Canaan and were giants. See Genesis 14:5-6.

15 For indeed the hand of the LORD
was against them, to destroy them from
among the host, until they were consumed.
¶16 So it came to pass, when all the
men of war were consumed and dead
from among the people,
17 That the LORD spake unto me,
saying,
18 Thou art to pass over through Ar,
the coast of Moab, this day:
19 And *when* thou comest nigh over
against the children of Ammon, distress
them not, nor meddle with them: for I
will not give thee of the land of the children of Ammon *any* possession; because I have given it unto the children
of Lot *for* a possession.
20 (That also was accounted a land of
giants: giants dwelt therein in old time;
and the Ammonites call them Zamzum-
mims;
21 A people great, and many, and tall,
as the Anakims; but the LORD destroyed them before them; and they
succeeded them, and dwelt in their
stead:
22 As he did to the children of Esau,
which dwelt in Seir, when he destroyed
the Horims from before them; and they
succeeded them, and dwelt in their
stead even unto this day:
23 And the Avims which dwelt in Ha-
zerim, *even* unto Azzah, the Caphto-
rims, which came forth out of Caphtor,
destroyed them, and dwelt in their
stead.)
¶24 Rise ye up, take your journey, and
pass over the river Arnon: behold, I
have given into thine hand Sihon the
*Amorite, king of Heshbon, and his
land: begin to possess *it,* and contend
with him in battle.
25 This day will I begin to put the
dread of thee and the fear of thee upon
the nations *that are* under the whole
heaven, who shall hear report of thee,
and shall tremble, and be in anguish
because of thee.
¶26 And I sent messengers out of the
wilderness of Kedemoth unto Sihon
king of Heshbon with words of peace,
saying,
27 Let me pass through thy land: I will
go along by the high way, I will neither
turn unto the right hand nor to the left.
28 Thou shalt sell me meat for money, that I may eat; and give me water for
money, that I may drink: only I will pass
through on my feet;
29 (As the children of Esau which
dwell in Seir, and the Moabites which
dwell in Ar, did unto me;) until I shall
pass over Jordan into the land which the
LORD our God giveth us.
30 But Sihon king of Heshbon would
not let us pass by him: for the LORD thy
God hardened his spirit, and made his
heart obstinate, that he might deliver
him into thy hand, as *appeareth* this day.
31 And the LORD said unto me, Behold, I have begun to give Sihon and his
land before thee: begin to possess, that
thou mayest inherit his land.
32 Then Sihon came out against us, he
and all his people, to fight at Jahaz.
33 And the LORD our God delivered
him before us; and we smote him, and
his sons, and all his people.

2:34 Total Destruction
This was in accordance with God's command. The danger was that the Israelites, with their precious vision of God's love and justice, would intermingle and intermarry with an idolatrous and sinful people, and that they themselves would worship idols. The eternal fate of the "little ones," those beneath the age of responsibility, was assured by God's plan of salvation fulfilled when Christ died on the cross.

34 And we took all his cities at that
time, and utterly destroyed the men,
and the women, and the little ones, of
every city, we left none to remain:
35 Only the cattle we took for a prey
unto ourselves, and the spoil of the cities which we took.
36 From Aroer, which *is* by the brink
of the river of Arnon, and *from* the city
that *is* by the river, even unto *Gilead,
there was not one city too strong for us:

the LORD our God delivered all unto us:

37 Only unto the land of the children of Ammon thou camest not, *nor* unto any place of the river Jabbok, nor unto the cities in the mountains, nor unto whatsoever the LORD our God forbad us.

Victory over Og (Num. 21:33-35)

3 Then we turned, and went up the way to Bashan: and Og the king of Bashan came out against us, he and all his people, to battle at Edrei.

2 And the LORD said unto me, Fear him not: for I will deliver him, and all his people, and his land, into thy hand; and thou shalt do unto him as thou didst unto Sihon king of the Amorites, which dwelt at Heshbon.

3 So the LORD our God delivered into our hands Og also, the king of Bashan, and all his people: and we smote him until none was left to him remaining.

4 And we took all his cities at that time, there was not a city which we took not from them, threescore cities, all the region of Argob, the kingdom of Og in Bashan.

5 All these cities *were* fenced with high walls, gates, and bars; beside unwalled towns a great many.

6 And we utterly destroyed them, as we did unto Sihon king of Heshbon, utterly destroying the men, women, and children, of every city.

7 But all the cattle, and the spoil of the cities, we took for a prey to ourselves.

8 And we took at that time out of the hand of the two kings of the Amorites the land that *was* on this side Jordan, from the river of Arnon unto mount Hermon;

9 (*Which* Hermon the Sidonians call Sirion; and the Amorites call it Shenir;)

10 All the cities of the plain, and all Gilead, and all Bashan, unto Salchah and Edrei, cities of the kingdom of Og in Bashan.

11 For only Og king of Bashan remained of the remnant of giants; behold, his bedstead *was* a bedstead of iron; *is* it not in Rabbath of the children of Ammon? nine *cubits *was* the length thereof, and four cubits the breadth of it, after the cubit of a man.

3:11 A Giant Bed
The bed was about thirteen feet long by six feet wide. Og evidently belonged to one of the giant tribes of eastern Palestine. See 2:9 note.

12 And this land, *which* we possessed at that time, from Aroer, which *is* by the river Arnon, and half mount Gilead, and the cities thereof, gave I unto the Reubenites and to the Gadites.

13 And the rest of Gilead, and all Bashan, *being* the kingdom of Og, gave I unto the half tribe of *Manasseh; all the region of Argob, with all Bashan, which was called the land of giants.

14 Jair the son of Manasseh took all the country of Argob unto the coasts of Geshuri and Maachathi; and called them after his own name, Bashan-havoth-jair, unto this day.

15 And I gave Gilead unto Machir.

16 And unto the Reubenites and unto the Gadites I gave from Gilead even unto the river Arnon half the valley, and the border even unto the river Jabbok, *which is* the border of the children of Ammon;

17 The plain also, and Jordan, and the coast *thereof,* from *Chinnereth even unto the *sea of the plain, *even* the salt sea, under Ashdoth-pisgah eastward.

¶ 18 And I commanded you at that time, saying, The LORD your God hath given you this land to possess it: ye shall pass over armed before your brethren the children of Israel, all *that are* meet for the war.

19 But your wives, and your little ones, and your cattle, (*for* I know that ye have much cattle,) shall abide in your cities which I have given you;

20 Until the LORD have given rest unto your brethren, as well as unto you,

3:18 meet for the war. Able to fight.

and *until* they also possess the land
which the LORD your God hath given
them beyond Jordan: and *then* shall ye
return every man unto his possession,
which I have given you.
¶21 And I commanded Joshua at that
time, saying, Thine eyes have seen all
that the LORD your God hath done unto
these two kings: so shall the LORD do
unto all the kingdoms whither thou
passest.
22 Ye shall not fear them: for the LORD
your God he shall fight for you.
23 And I besought the LORD at that
time, saying,
24 O Lord GOD, thou hast begun to shew
thy servant thy greatness, and thy mighty
hand: for what God *is there* in heaven or
in earth, that can do according to thy
works, and according to thy might?
25 I pray thee, let me go over, and see
the good land that *is* beyond Jordan, that
goodly mountain, and Lebanon.
26 But the LORD was wroth with me
for your sakes, and would not hear me:
and the LORD said unto me, Let it suffice thee; speak no more unto me of this
matter.
27 Get thee up into the top of Pisgah,
and lift up thine eyes westward, and
northward, and southward, and eastward, and behold *it* with thine eyes: for
thou shalt not go over this Jordan.
28 But charge Joshua, and encourage
him, and strengthen him: for he shall go
over before this people, and he shall
cause them to inherit the land which
thou shalt see.
29 So we abode in the valley over
against Beth-peor.

Moses advises new generation

4 Now therefore hearken, O Israel,
unto the statutes and unto the
judgments, which I teach you, for to do
them, that ye may live, and go in and
possess the land which the LORD God
of your fathers giveth you.
2 Ye shall not add unto the word which
I command you, neither shall ye diminish *ought* from it, that ye may keep the
commandments of the LORD your God
which I command you.
3 Your eyes have seen what the LORD
did because of *Baal-peor: for all the
men that followed Baal-peor, the LORD
thy God hath destroyed them from
among you.
4 But ye that did cleave unto the LORD
your God *are* alive every one of you
this day.
5 Behold, I have taught you statutes
and judgments, even as the LORD my
God commanded me, that ye should
do so in the land whither ye go to possess it.
6 Keep therefore and do *them;* for this
is your wisdom and your understanding
in the sight of the nations, which shall
hear all these statutes, and say, Surely
this great nation *is* a wise and understanding people.
7 For what nation *is there so* great, who
hath God so nigh unto them, as the
LORD our God *is* in all *things that* we call
upon him *for?*
8 And what nation *is there so* great,
that hath statutes and judgments *so*
righteous as all this law, which I set
before you this day?
9 Only take heed to thyself, and keep
thy soul diligently, lest thou forget the
things which thine eyes have seen, and
lest they depart from thy heart all the
days of thy life: but teach them thy
sons, and thy sons' sons;
10 *Specially* the day that thou stoodest
before the LORD thy God in *Horeb,

3:26 the LORD was wroth. Turn back to Numbers 20:12 and 27:14 to see why the LORD would not allow Moses to enter the Promised Land.
4:1 statutes. Laws.
4:2 word which I command. See *inspiration.
4:10 Horeb. Horeb and Sinai were part of the same mountain range. Read Exodus 19 to learn about the day when the people stood before the LORD.

when the LORD said unto me, Gather
me the people together, and I will make
them hear my words, that they may
learn to fear me all the days that they
shall live upon the earth, and *that* they
may teach their children.
11And ye came near and stood under
the mountain; and the mountain burned
with fire unto the midst of heaven, with
darkness, clouds, and thick darkness.
12And the LORD spake unto you out
of the midst of the fire: ye heard the
voice of the words, but saw no similitude; only *ye heard* a voice.
13And he declared unto you his *covenant, which he commanded you to
perform, *even* *ten commandments;
and he wrote them upon two tables of
stone.
¶14And the LORD commanded me at
that time to teach you statutes and judgments, that ye might do them in the
land whither ye go over to possess it.
15Take ye therefore good heed unto
yourselves; for ye saw no manner of
similitude on the day *that* the LORD
spake unto you in Horeb out of the
midst of the fire:
16Lest ye corrupt *yourselves,* and
make you a *graven image, the similitude of any figure, the likeness of male
or female,
17The likeness of any beast that *is* on
the earth, the likeness of any winged
fowl that flieth in the air,
18The likeness of any thing that
creepeth on the ground, the likeness of
any fish that *is* in the waters beneath
the earth:
19And lest thou lift up thine eyes unto
heaven, and when thou seest the sun,
and the moon, and the stars, *even* all the
host of heaven, shouldest be driven to
worship them, and serve them, which
the LORD thy God hath divided unto all
nations under the whole heaven.
20But the LORD hath taken you, and
brought you forth out of the iron furnace, *even* out of Egypt, to be unto him
a people of inheritance, as *ye are* this
day.
21Furthermore the LORD was angry
with me for your sakes, and sware that
I should not go over Jordan, and that I
should not go in unto that good land,
which the LORD thy God giveth thee *for*
an inheritance:
22But I must die in this land, I must
not go over Jordan: but ye shall go over,
and possess that good land.
23Take heed unto yourselves, lest ye
forget the covenant of the LORD your
God, which he made with you, and
make you a graven image, *or* the likeness of any *thing,* which the LORD thy
God hath forbidden thee.
24For the LORD thy God *is* a consuming fire, *even* a *jealous God.
¶25When thou shalt beget children,
and children's children, and ye shall
have remained long in the land, and
shall corrupt *yourselves,* and make a
graven image, *or* the likeness of any
thing, and shall do evil in the sight of the
LORD thy God, to provoke him to anger:
26I call heaven and earth to witness
against you this day, that ye shall soon
utterly perish from off the land whereunto ye go over Jordan to possess it; ye
shall not prolong *your* days upon it, but
shall utterly be destroyed.
27And the LORD shall scatter you
among the nations, and ye shall be left
few in number among the heathen,
whither the LORD shall lead you.
28And there ye shall serve gods, the

4:27 Moses' First Prophecy
This is Moses' first prophecy or foretelling of the future. It was fulfilled when the children of Israel were carried captive to Assyria and Babylon, for they did much "evil in the sight of the LORD" (vs. 25).

4:13 ten commandments. See verse 16 note.
4:16 Lest ye corrupt yourselves. Moses repeats here, and in the following verses, the thoughts of the first and second commandments (Exod. 20:3-6).

work of men's hands, wood and stone,
which neither see, nor hear, nor eat, nor
smell.
[29]But if from thence thou shalt seek
the LORD thy God, thou shalt find *him,*
if thou seek him with all thy heart and
with all thy soul.
[30]When thou art in tribulation, and all
these things are come upon thee, *even*
in the latter days, if thou turn to the
LORD thy God, and shalt be obedient
unto his voice;

4:30 A Great Tribulation
This means great *trouble.* The great trouble or tribulation that will cause the children of Israel to turn to the LORD and be "obedient unto His voice" (vs. 30) has not yet come (though, of course, we know that there have been many times of tribulation for them), but it will surely come in the latter days at the end of this age, a tribulation such as has never been known before (Matt. 24:21). Read Hosea 3:4-5 and see *Great Tribulation.

[31](For the LORD thy God *is* a merciful God;) he will not forsake thee, neither destroy thee, nor forget the
covenant of thy fathers which he sware
unto them.

4:31 God's Promise
This was the first time that this promise was given to God's people, but it was not the only time. Read Deuteronomy 31:6; Joshua 1:5; 1 Chronicles 28:20; Hebrews 13:5.

[32]For ask now of the days that are
past, which were before thee, since the
day that God *created man upon the
earth, and *ask* from the one side of
heaven unto the other, whether there
hath been *any such thing* as this great
thing *is,* or hath been heard like it?
[33]Did *ever* people hear the voice of
God speaking out of the midst of the
fire, as thou hast heard, and live?
[34]Or hath God assayed to go *and* take
him a nation from the midst of *another*
nation, by temptations, by signs, and by
wonders, and by war, and by a mighty
hand, and by a stretched out arm, and
by great terrors, according to all that
the LORD your God did for you in Egypt
before your eyes?
[35]Unto thee it was shewed, that thou
mightest know that the LORD he *is* God;
there is none else beside him.
[36]Out of heaven he made thee to hear
his voice, that he might instruct thee:
and upon earth he shewed thee his
great fire; and thou heardest his words
out of the midst of the fire.
[37]And because he loved thy fathers,
therefore he chose their seed after
them, and brought thee out in his sight
with his mighty power out of Egypt;
[38]To drive out nations from before
thee greater and mightier than thou *art,*
to bring thee in, to give thee their land
for an inheritance, as *it is* this day.
[39]Know therefore this day, and consider *it* in thine heart, that the LORD he
is God in heaven above, and upon the
earth beneath: *there is* none else.
[40]Thou shalt keep therefore his statutes, and his commandments, which I
command thee this day, that it may go
well with thee, and with thy children
after thee, and that thou mayest prolong *thy* days upon the earth, which the
LORD thy God giveth thee, for ever.

II. The Cities of Refuge (4:41-49; 19:1-13)

¶[41]Then Moses severed three cities
on this side Jordan toward the sunrising;
[42]That the slayer might flee thither,
which should kill his neighbour unawares, and hated him not in times past;

4:34 temptations. Trials.
4:37 their seed. Their descendants.
4:41 severed. Separated.
4:42 which should kill his neighbour unawares. The cities of refuge were for those who killed someone unintentionally, that is, by accident.

and that fleeing unto one of these cities he might live:
43 *Namely,* Bezer in the wilderness, in
the plain country, of the Reubenites;
and Ramoth in Gilead, of the Gadites;
and Golan in Bashan, of the Manassites.
¶ 44 And this *is* the law which Moses
set before the children of Israel:
45 These *are* the testimonies, and the
statutes, and the judgments, which
Moses spake unto the children of Israel,
after they came forth out of Egypt,
46 On this side Jordan, in the valley
over against Beth-peor, in the land of
Sihon king of the Amorites, who dwelt
at Heshbon, whom Moses and the children of Israel smote, after they were
come forth out of Egypt:
47 And they possessed his land, and
the land of Og king of Bashan, two kings
of the Amorites, which *were* on this side
Jordan toward the sunrising;
48 From Aroer, which *is* by the bank of
the river Arnon, even unto mount
*Sion, which *is* Hermon,
49 And all the plain on this side Jordan
eastward, even unto the sea of the plain,
under the springs of Pisgah.

III. Moses' Second Speech
(5:1—26:19)

5 And Moses called all Israel, and
said unto them, Hear, O Israel, the
statutes and judgments which I speak
in your ears this day, that ye may learn
them, and keep, and do them.
2 The LORD our God made a covenant
with us in Horeb.
3 The LORD made not this covenant
with our fathers, but with us, *even* us,
who *are* all of us here alive this day.
4 The LORD talked with you face to
face in the mount out of the midst of the
fire,
5 (I stood between the LORD and you
at that time, to shew you the word of
the LORD: for ye were afraid by reason
of the fire, and went not up into the
mount;) saying,
¶ 6 I *am* the LORD thy God, which
brought thee out of the land of Egypt,
from the house of bondage.
7 Thou shalt have none other gods
before me.
8 Thou shalt not make thee *any*
graven image, *or* any likeness *of any
thing* that *is* in heaven above, or that *is*
in the earth beneath, or that *is* in the
waters beneath the earth:
9 Thou shalt not bow down thyself
unto them, nor serve them: for I the
LORD thy God *am* a jealous God, visiting the iniquity of the fathers upon the
children unto the third and fourth *generation* of them that hate me,
10 And shewing *mercy unto thousands of them that love me and keep my
commandments.
11 Thou shalt not take the name of the
LORD thy God in vain: for the LORD will
not hold *him* guiltless that taketh his
name in vain.
12 Keep the *sabbath day to sanctify
it, as the LORD thy God hath commanded thee.
13 Six days thou shalt labour, and do all
thy work:
14 But the seventh day *is* the sabbath
of the LORD thy God: *in it* thou shalt not
do any work, thou, nor thy son, nor thy
daughter, nor thy manservant, nor thy
maidservant, nor thine ox, nor thine
ass, nor any of thy cattle, nor thy
stranger that *is* within thy gates; that
thy manservant and thy maidservant
may rest as well as thou.
15 And remember that thou wast a
servant in the land of Egypt, and *that*
the LORD thy God brought thee out
thence through a mighty hand and by a
stretched out arm: therefore the LORD
thy God commanded thee to keep the
sabbath day.
¶ 16 Honour thy father and thy moth-

4:49 the sea of the plain. The Dead Sea.
5:5 saying. This word continues the thought of verse 4.
5:6 I am the LORD. The Ten Commandments are repeated here. See Exodus 20:1-17.

er, as the LORD thy God hath commanded thee; that thy days may be prolonged, and that it may go well with thee, in the land which the LORD thy God giveth thee.

17 Thou shalt not kill.

18 Neither shalt thou commit adultery.

19 Neither shalt thou steal.

20 Neither shalt thou bear false witness against thy neighbour.

21 Neither shalt thou desire thy neighbour's wife, neither shalt thou covet thy neighbour's house, his field, or his manservant, or his maidservant, his ox, or his ass, or any *thing* that *is* thy neighbour's.

¶22 These words the LORD spake unto all your assembly in the mount out of the midst of the fire, of the cloud, and of the thick darkness, with a great voice: and he added no more. And he wrote them in two tables of stone, and delivered them unto me.

23 And it came to pass, when ye heard the voice out of the midst of the darkness, (for the mountain did burn with fire,) that ye came near unto me, *even* all the heads of your tribes, and your *elders;

24 And ye said, Behold, the LORD our God hath shewed us his glory and his greatness, and we have heard his voice out of the midst of the fire: we have seen this day that God doth talk with man, and he liveth.

25 Now therefore why should we die? for this great fire will consume us: if we hear the voice of the LORD our God any more, then we shall die.

26 For who *is there of* all flesh, that hath heard the voice of the living God speaking out of the midst of the fire, as we *have,* and lived?

27 Go thou near, and hear all that the LORD our God shall say: and speak thou unto us all that the LORD our God shall speak unto thee; and we will hear *it,* and do *it.*

28 And the LORD heard the voice of your words, when ye spake unto me; and the LORD said unto me, I have heard the voice of the words of this people, which they have spoken unto thee: they have well said all that they have spoken.

29 O that there were such an heart in them, that they would fear me, and keep all my commandments always, that it might be well with them, and with their children for ever!

30 Go say to them, Get you into your tents again.

31 But as for thee, stand thou here by me, and I will speak unto thee all the commandments, and the statutes, and the judgments, which thou shalt teach them, that they may do *them* in the land which I give them to possess it.

32 Ye shall observe to do therefore as the LORD your God hath commanded

5:12 THE SABBATH

Sabbath is the Hebrew word meaning *cessation,* and so it means *rest* in this context. It is clear that God gave instructions to the Israelites for the Sabbath observance (Exod. 16:23-26). This is verified by Nehemiah (Neh. 9:14-15). It is included as part of the Ten Commandments (Exod. 20:8-11), and God indicated it would be a special *sign* of a "perpetual covenant" between God and the nation (Exod. 31:13-17). The Sabbath was observed by our Lord and the apostles, though the minute and burdensome traditions of the Pharisees were rejected, and the spirit of the observance was reasserted by Jesus' saying, "The sabbath was made for man" in Mark 2:27.

The transition from the Jewish economy to the church shows a dramatic change in this observance. The church began to meet on the "first day of the week" as a time to come together for instruction and worship (Acts 20:7; 1 Cor. 16:2). This change came about to celebrate the resurrection of Christ who rose from the dead to conquer sin and death on "the first day of the week" (Mark 16:9; Matt. 28:1; John 20:1-9). Jesus appeared to the disciples on the "first day of the week" (John 20:19). Thus the New Testament church adopted worship on the "first day of the week" (our Sunday) in lieu of the Sabbath.

you: ye shall not turn aside to the right hand or to the left.

33 Ye shall walk in all the ways which the LORD your God hath commanded you, that ye may live, and *that it may be* well with you, and *that* ye may prolong *your* days in the land which ye shall possess.

Moses' summary of the Law

6 Now these *are* the commandments, the statutes, and the judgments, which the LORD your God commanded to teach you, that ye might do *them* in the land whither ye go to possess it:

2 That thou mightest fear the LORD thy God, to keep all his statutes and his commandments, which I command thee, thou, and thy son, and thy son's son, all the days of thy life; and that thy days may be prolonged.

¶ 3 Hear therefore, O Israel, and observe to do *it;* that it may be well with thee, and that ye may increase mightily, as the LORD God of thy fathers hath promised thee, in the land that floweth with milk and honey.

4 Hear, O Israel: The LORD our God *is* one LORD:

5 And thou shalt love the LORD thy God with all thine heart, and with all thy soul, and with all thy might.

6 And these words, which I command thee this day, shall be in thine heart:

7 And thou shalt teach them diligently unto thy children, and shalt talk of them when thou sittest in thine house, and when thou walkest by the way, and when thou liest down, and when thou risest up.

8 And thou shalt bind them for a sign upon thine hand, and they shall be as *frontlets between thine eyes.

9 And thou shalt write them upon the posts of thy house, and on thy gates.

10 And it shall be, when the LORD thy God shall have brought thee into the

6:8 A Constant Reminder
Frontlets were prayers or verses of Scripture written out and bound on the forehead. This was done that the people might constantly be reminded of the Law and its importance, and of the word of God. In Jesus' day, however, the *Pharisees, leaders of the Jewish people, made these phylacteries broad (Matt. 23:5) and bound them upon their foreheads in pride, as if they were saying, "See how good I am!" which, of course, could not please God. Phylacteries were sometimes bound to the arms also.

land which he sware unto thy fathers, to Abraham, to Isaac, and to Jacob, to give thee great and goodly cities, which thou buildedst not,

11 And houses full of all good *things,* which thou filledst not, and wells digged, which thou diggedst not, vineyards and olive trees, which thou plantedst not; when thou shalt have eaten and be full;

12 *Then* beware lest thou forget the LORD, which brought thee forth out of the land of Egypt, from the house of bondage.

13 Thou shalt fear the LORD thy God, and serve him, and shalt swear by his name.

14 Ye shall not go after other gods, of the gods of the people which *are* round about you;

15 (For the LORD thy God *is* a jealous God among you) lest the anger of the LORD thy God be kindled against thee, and destroy thee from off the face of the earth.

¶ 16 Ye shall not tempt the LORD your God, as ye tempted *him* in Massah.

17 Ye shall diligently keep the commandments of the LORD your God, and his testimonies, and his statutes, which he hath commanded thee.

18 And thou shalt do *that which is* right and good in the sight of the LORD: that it may be well with thee, and that thou mayest go in and possess the good land

6:5 thou shalt love the LORD thy God. The Lord Jesus called this the "Great Commandment" in Matthew 22:37-38. He also referred to it in Mark 12:30 and Luke 10:27.

which the LORD sware unto thy fathers,
19To cast out all thine enemies from
before thee, as the LORD hath spoken.
20*And* when thy son asketh thee in
time to come, saying, What *mean* the
testimonies, and the statutes, and the
judgments, which the LORD our God
hath commanded you?
21Then thou shalt say unto thy son,
We were *Pharaoh's bondmen in Egypt;
and the LORD brought us out of Egypt
with a mighty hand:
22And the LORD shewed signs and
wonders, great and sore, upon Egypt,
upon Pharaoh, and upon all his household, before our eyes:
23And he brought us out from thence,
that he might bring us in, to give us the
land which he sware unto our fathers.
24And the LORD commanded us to
do all these statutes, to fear the LORD
our God, for our good always, that
he might preserve us alive, as *it is* at
this day.
25And it shall be our *righteousness,
if we observe to do all these commandments before the LORD our God, as he
hath commanded us.

6:25 Our Righteousness
Read Romans 10:5. In Romans, the apostle Paul explained in-depth that our own righteousness, however good from man's standpoint, is not enough to meet God's standard of absolute holiness. Christ in our lives, and the righteousness of God in Him, is the only solution. See also Isaiah 64:6

Command for separation repeated

7 When the LORD thy *God shall
bring thee into the land whither
thou goest to possess it, and hath cast
out many nations before thee, the Hittites, and the Girgashites, and the
Amorites, and the Canaanites, and the
Perizzites, and the Hivites, and the Jebusites, seven nations greater and
mightier than thou;
2And when the LORD thy God shall
deliver them before thee; thou shalt
smite them, *and* utterly destroy them;
thou shalt make no covenant with them,
nor shew mercy unto them:
3Neither shalt thou make marriages
with them; thy daughter thou shalt not
give unto his son, nor his daughter shalt
thou take unto thy son.
4For they will turn away thy son from
following me, that they may serve other
gods: so will the anger of the LORD be
kindled against you, and destroy thee
suddenly.
5But thus shall ye deal with them; ye
shall destroy their altars, and break
down their images, and cut down their
groves, and burn their graven images
with *fire.
6For thou *art* an *holy people unto
the LORD thy God: the LORD thy God
hath chosen thee to be a special people
unto himself, above all people that *are*
upon the face of the earth.
7The LORD did not set his love upon
you, nor choose you, because ye were
more in number than any people; for ye
were the fewest of all people:
8But because the LORD loved you,
and because he would keep the oath
which he had sworn unto your fathers,
hath the LORD brought you out with a
mighty hand, and *redeemed you out of
the house of bondmen, from the hand
of Pharaoh king of *Egypt.
9Know therefore that the LORD thy
God, he *is* God, the faithful God, which
keepeth covenant and mercy with them
that love him and keep his commandments to a thousand generations;
10And repayeth them that hate him to
their face, to destroy them: he will not
be slack to him that hateth him, he will
repay him to his face.
11Thou shalt therefore keep the commandments, and the statutes, and the
judgments, which I command thee this
day, to do them.

6:21 We were Pharaoh's bondmen. Read Exodus 2:23-25.
7:2 thou shalt smite them. Verses 4-6 explain this.

Promise of victory through obedience

¶ 12 Wherefore it shall come to pass, if ye hearken to these judgments, and keep, and do them, that the LORD thy God shall keep unto thee the covenant and the mercy which he sware unto thy fathers:

13 And he will love thee, and bless thee, and multiply thee: he will also bless the fruit of thy womb, and the fruit of thy land, thy corn, and thy *wine, and thine *oil, the increase of thy kine, and the flocks of thy sheep, in the land which he sware unto thy fathers to give thee.

14 Thou shalt be blessed above all people: there shall not be male or female barren among you, or among your cattle.

15 And the LORD will take away from thee all sickness, and will put none of the evil diseases of Egypt, which thou knowest, upon thee; but will lay them upon all *them* that hate thee.

16 And thou shalt consume all the people which the LORD thy God shall deliver thee; thine eye shall have no pity upon them: neither shalt thou serve their gods; for that *will be* a snare unto thee.

17 If thou shalt say in thine heart, These nations *are* more than I; how can I dispossess them?

18 Thou shalt not be afraid of them: *but* shalt well remember what the LORD thy God did unto Pharaoh, and unto all Egypt;

19 The great temptations which thine eyes saw, and the signs, and the wonders, and the mighty hand, and the stretched out arm, whereby the LORD thy God brought thee out: so shall the LORD thy God do unto all the people of whom thou art afraid.

20 Moreover the LORD thy God will send the hornet among them, until they that are left, and hide themselves from thee, be destroyed.

21 Thou shalt not be affrighted at them: for the LORD thy God *is* among you, a mighty God and terrible.

22 And the LORD thy God will put out those nations before thee by little and little: thou mayest not consume them at once, lest the beasts of the field increase upon thee.

23 But the LORD thy God shall deliver them unto thee, and shall destroy them with a mighty destruction, until they be destroyed.

24 And he shall deliver their kings into thine hand, and thou shalt destroy their name from under heaven: there shall no man be able to stand before thee, until thou have destroyed them.

25 The graven images of their gods shall ye burn with fire: thou shalt not desire the *silver or gold *that is* on them, nor take *it* unto thee, lest thou be snared therein: for it *is* an *abomination to the LORD thy God.

26 Neither shalt thou bring an abomination into thine house, lest thou be a cursed thing like it: *but* thou shalt utterly detest it, and thou shalt utterly abhor it; for it *is* a cursed thing.

A reminder of God's care

8 All the commandments which I command thee this day shall ye observe to do, that ye may live, and multiply, and go in and possess the land which the LORD sware unto your fathers.

2 And thou shalt remember all the way which the LORD thy God led thee these forty years in the wilderness, to humble thee, *and* to prove thee, to know what *was* in thine heart, whether thou wouldest keep his commandments, or no.

3 And he humbled thee, and suffered thee to hunger, and fed thee with *manna, which thou knewest not, neither did thy fathers know; that he might make

---

7:16 snare. A temptation too strong for the people to resist.
7:25 snared. See verse 16 note.
8:2 to prove thee. To test or try the people for their own good.

thee know that man doth not live by
bread only, but by every *word* that
proceedeth out of the mouth of the
LORD doth man live.
4Thy raiment waxed not old upon
thee, neither did thy foot swell, these
forty years.

Blessing promised in the land

5Thou shalt also consider in thine
heart, that, as a man *chasteneth his
son, *so* the LORD thy God chasteneth
thee.

8:5 Staying on the Right Path
Sometimes a father or mother has to punish a child to show the child that he or she is doing wrong. This is the meaning of chastisement, the loving way of bringing the child back to the right path. Children are chastened for their own good. God the Father loves His children more than any earthly parent can, and He is more anxious than an earthly parent that His children stay on the right paths–the paths of His choosing. Read Hebrews 12:5-6 and Revelation 3:19.

6Therefore thou shalt keep the commandments of the LORD thy God, to
walk in his ways, and to *fear him.
7For the LORD thy God bringeth thee
into a good land, a land of brooks of
water, of fountains and depths that
spring out of valleys and hills;
8A land of wheat, and barley, and
vines, and fig trees, and pomegranates;
a land of oil olive, and honey;
9A land wherein thou shalt eat bread
without scarceness, thou shalt not lack
any *thing* in it; a land whose stones *are*
iron, and out of whose hills thou mayest
dig brass.
10When thou hast eaten and art full,
then thou shalt bless the LORD thy God
for the good land which he hath given
thee.

Warning against worshipping false gods

11Beware that thou forget not the
LORD thy God, in not keeping his commandments, and his judgments, and his
statutes, which I command thee this
day:
12Lest *when* thou hast eaten and art
full, and hast built goodly houses, and
dwelt *therein;*
13And *when* thy herds and thy flocks
multiply, and thy silver and thy gold is
multiplied, and all that thou hast is
multiplied;
14Then thine heart be lifted up, and
thou forget the LORD thy God, which
brought thee forth out of the land of
Egypt, from the house of bondage;
15Who led thee through that great
and terrible wilderness, *wherein were*
fiery serpents, and *scorpions, and
drought, where *there was* no water; who
brought thee forth water out of the rock
of flint;
16Who fed thee in the wilderness
with manna, which thy fathers knew
not, that he might humble thee, and that
he might prove thee, to do thee good at
thy latter end;
17And thou say in thine heart, My
power and the might of *mine* hand hath
gotten me this wealth.
18But thou shalt remember the LORD
thy God: for *it is* he that giveth thee
power to get wealth, that he may establish his covenant which he sware unto
thy fathers, as *it is* this day.
19And it shall be, if thou do at all forget the LORD thy God, and walk after
other gods, and serve them, and worship them, I testify against you this day
that ye shall surely perish.

8:3 by bread only. These words were used by our Lord in meeting His temptation. See Matthew 4.
8:9 stones are iron. This refers to the mineral wealth of Canaan. The word "brass" here means *copper*.
8:14 thine heart be lifted up. This refers to self-satisfaction or conceit, a dependence on themselves instead of on God. Those who prosper often believe that they deserve the credit instead of God (see vss. 17-18).

20 As the nations which the LORD
destroyeth before your face, so shall
ye perish; because ye would not be
obedient unto the voice of the LORD
your God.

Warning against self-righteousness

9 Hear, O *Israel: Thou *art* to pass
over Jordan this day, to go in to
possess nations greater and mightier
than thyself, cities great and fenced up
to heaven,

> **9:1 The Walls of the City**
> The children of Israel had become accustomed to camps in the wilderness. The high walls around the heathen cities frightened them, because the walls seemed too high and strong to climb over or break through. They forgot that their God was the One who went before them. (vs. 3).

2 A people great and tall, the children
of *the Anakims, whom thou knowest,
and *of whom* thou hast heard *say,* Who
can stand before the children of Anak!
3 Understand therefore this day, that
the LORD thy God *is* he which goeth
over before thee; *as* a consuming fire he
shall destroy them, and he shall bring
them down before thy face: so shalt
thou drive them out, and destroy them
quickly, as the LORD hath said unto
thee.
4 Speak not thou in thine heart, after
that the LORD thy God hath cast them
out from before thee, saying, For my
righteousness the LORD hath brought
me in to possess this land: but for the
wickedness of these nations the LORD
doth drive them out from before thee.
5 Not for thy righteousness, or for the
uprightness of thine heart, dost thou go
to possess their land: but for the wickedness of these nations the LORD thy
God doth drive them out from before
thee, and that he may perform the word
which the LORD sware unto thy fathers,
*Abraham, *Isaac, and *Jacob.
6 Understand therefore, that the
LORD thy God giveth thee not this good
land to possess it for thy righteousness;
for thou *art* a stiffnecked people.
¶ 7 Remember, *and* forget not, how
thou provokedst the LORD thy God to
wrath in the wilderness: from the day
that thou didst depart out of the land of
Egypt, until ye came unto this place, ye
have been rebellious against the LORD.
8 Also in *Horeb ye provoked the
LORD to wrath, so that the LORD was
angry with you to have destroyed you.
9 When I was gone up into the mount
to receive the tables of stone, *even* the
tables of the covenant which the LORD
made with you, then I abode in the
mount forty days and forty nights, I
neither did eat bread nor drink water:
10 And the LORD delivered unto me
two tables of stone written with the finger of God; and on them *was written*
according to all the words, which the
LORD spake with you in the mount out
of the midst of the fire in the day of the
assembly.
11 And it came to pass at the end of
forty days and forty nights, *that* the
LORD gave me the two tables of stone,
even the tables of the covenant.
12 And the LORD said unto me, Arise,
get thee down quickly from hence; for
thy people which thou hast brought
forth out of Egypt have corrupted *themselves;* they are quickly turned aside out
of the way which I commanded them;
they have made them a molten image.
13 Furthermore the LORD spake unto
me, saying, I have seen this people,
and, behold, it *is* a stiffnecked people:
14 Let me alone, that I may destroy
them, and blot out their name from
under heaven: and I will make of thee a
nation mightier and greater than they.
15 So I turned and came down from

9:6 a stiffnecked people. Stubborn and disobedient.
9:8 in Horeb ye provoked the LORD to wrath. Read Exodus 32, which tells of the golden calf, and see Exodus 32:1 note.

the mount, and the mount burned with
fire: and the two tables of the covenant
were in my two hands.
16 And I looked, and, behold, ye had
sinned against the LORD your God, *and*
had made you a molten calf: ye had
turned aside quickly out of the way
which the LORD had commanded you.
17 And I took the two tables, and cast
them out of my two hands, and brake
them before your eyes.
18 And I fell down before the LORD, as
at the first, forty days and forty nights:
I did neither eat bread, nor drink water,
because of all your sins which ye
sinned, in doing wickedly in the sight of
the LORD, to provoke him to anger.
19 For I was afraid of the anger and hot
displeasure, wherewith the LORD was
wroth against you to destroy you. But
the LORD hearkened unto me at that
time also.
20 And the LORD was very angry with
*Aaron to have destroyed him: and I
prayed for Aaron also the same time.
21 And I took your *sin, the calf which
ye had made, and burnt it with fire, and
stamped it, *and* ground *it* very small,
even until it was as small as dust: and I
cast the dust thereof into the brook that
descended out of the mount.
22 And at Taberah, and at Massah, and
at Kibroth-hattaavah, ye provoked the
LORD to wrath.

Sin of unbelief at Kadesh-Barnea

23 Likewise when the LORD sent you
from Kadesh-barnea, saying, Go up and
possess the land which I have given
you; then ye rebelled against the commandment of the LORD your God, and
ye believed him not, nor hearkened to
his voice.
24 Ye have been rebellious against the
LORD from the day that I knew you.
25 Thus I fell down before the LORD
forty days and forty nights, as I fell
down *at the first;* because the LORD had
said he would destroy you.
26 I prayed therefore unto the LORD,
and said, O Lord GOD, destroy not thy
people and thine inheritance, which
thou hast redeemed through thy greatness, which thou hast brought forth out
of Egypt with a mighty hand.
27 Remember thy servants, Abraham,
Isaac, and Jacob; look not unto the stubbornness of this people, nor to their
wickedness, nor to their sin:
28 Lest the land whence thou broughtest us out say, Because the LORD was
not able to bring them into the land
which he promised them, and because
he hated them, he hath brought them
out to slay them in the wilderness.
29 Yet they *are* thy people and thine
inheritance, which thou broughtest
out by thy mighty power and by thy
stretched out arm.

Preservation of new tables of Law

10 At that time the LORD said unto
me, Hew thee two tables of
stone like unto the first, and come up
unto me into the mount, and make thee
an *ark of wood.
2 And I will write on the tables the
words that were in the first tables
which thou brakest, and thou shalt put
them in the ark.
3 And I made an ark *of* *shittim wood,
and hewed two tables of stone like unto
the first, and went up into the mount,
having the two tables in mine hand.
4 And he wrote on the tables, according to the first writing, the *ten commandments, which the LORD spake
unto you in the mount out of the midst
of the fire in the day of the assembly:
and the LORD gave them unto me.
5 And I turned myself and came down
from the mount, and put the tables in
the ark which I had made; and there
they be, as the LORD commanded me.

Some of the journeys

¶ 6 And the children of Israel took
their journey from Beeroth of the children of Jaakan to Mosera: there Aaron
died, and there he was buried; and Eleazar his son ministered in the priest's
office in his stead.

7 From thence they journeyed unto Gudgodah; and from Gudgodah to Jotbath, a land of rivers of waters.

¶ 8 At that time the LORD separated the tribe of Levi, to bear the ark of the covenant of the LORD, to stand before the LORD to minister unto him, and to bless in his name, unto this day.

9 Wherefore Levi hath no part nor inheritance with his brethren; the LORD *is* his inheritance, according as the LORD thy God promised him.

10 And I stayed in the mount, according to the first time, forty days and forty nights; and the LORD hearkened unto me at that time also, *and* the LORD would not destroy thee.

11 And the LORD said unto me, Arise, take *thy* journey before the people, that they may go in and possess the land, which I sware unto their fathers to give unto them.

A reminder of duty to God

¶ 12 And now, Israel, what doth the LORD thy God require of thee, but to fear the LORD thy God, to walk in all his ways, and to love him, and to serve the LORD thy God with all thy heart and with all thy soul,

13 To keep the commandments of the LORD, and his statutes, which I command thee this day for thy good?

14 Behold, the heaven and the heaven of heavens *is* the LORD'S thy God, the earth *also,* with all that therein *is.*

15 Only the LORD had a delight in thy fathers to love them, and he chose their seed after them, *even* you above all people, as *it is* this day.

16 Circumcise therefore the foreskin of your heart, and be no more stiffnecked.

17 For the LORD your God *is* God of gods, and Lord of lords, a great God, a mighty, and a terrible, which regardeth not persons, nor taketh reward:

18 He doth execute the *judgment of the fatherless and widow, and loveth the stranger, in giving him food and raiment.

19 Love ye therefore the stranger: for ye were strangers in the land of Egypt.

20 Thou shalt fear the LORD thy God; him shalt thou serve, and to him shalt thou cleave, and swear by his name.

21 He *is* thy praise, and he *is* thy God, that hath done for thee these great and terrible things, which thine eyes have seen.

22 Thy fathers went down into Egypt with threescore and ten persons; and now the LORD thy God hath made thee as the stars of heaven for multitude.

God's past help (Exod. 12–15; Num. 16)

11 Therefore thou shalt love the LORD thy God, and keep his charge, and his statutes, and his judgments, and his commandments, alway.

2 And know ye this day: for *I speak* not with your children which have not known, and which have not seen the

11:2 Have Faith

Numbers 14, with the notes on that chapter, tells which of those who came out of Egypt (Exod. 12:33,37,41) were to be allowed to enter the Promised Land. The little children who came out of Egypt and were now grown up knew of the wonders of the LORD about which Moses spoke. However, their children had not actually seen what the LORD had done in leading this great people forth, so Moses is saying, "I am not talking to your children. I am talking to you. You have no excuse if you have no faith in God, because you have seen what He has constantly been doing for you."

10:16 Circumcise . . . your heart. The symbol of Israel's separation, circumcision of their bodies (see Gen. 17:10 note, "Circumcision") was to be applied in a spiritual way to their hearts. The people were to live before men as if they meant in their hearts that which was practiced upon their bodies under the command of the LORD.

11:2 chastisement. See 8:5 note.

chastisement of the LORD your God, his
greatness, his mighty hand, and his
stretched out arm,
3And his *miracles, and his acts,
which he did in the midst of Egypt unto
Pharaoh the king of Egypt, and unto all
his land;
4And what he did unto the army of
Egypt, unto their horses, and to their
chariots; how he made the water of the
Red sea to overflow them as they pursued after you, and *how* the LORD hath
destroyed them unto this day;
5And what he did unto you in the wilderness, until ye came into this place;
6And what he did unto *Dathan and
Abiram, the sons of Eliab, the son of
Reuben: how the earth opened her
mouth, and swallowed them up, and
their households, and their tents, and
all the substance that *was* in their possession, in the midst of all Israel:
7But your eyes have seen all the
great acts of the LORD which he did.
8Therefore shall ye keep all the commandments which I command you this
day, that ye may be strong, and go in and
possess the land, whither ye go to possess it;
9And that ye may prolong *your* days
in the land, which the LORD sware unto
your fathers to give unto them and to
their seed, a land that *floweth with
milk and honey.

The land described

¶10For the land, whither thou goest in
to possess it, *is* not as the land of Egypt,
from whence ye came out, where thou
sowedst thy seed, and wateredst *it* with
thy foot, as a garden of herbs:
11But the land, whither ye go to possess it, *is* a land of hills and valleys, *and*
drinketh water of the rain of heaven:
12A land which the LORD thy God
careth for: the eyes of the LORD thy
God *are* always upon it, from the beginning of the year even unto the end of
the year.
¶13And it shall come to pass, if ye
shall hearken diligently unto my commandments which I command you this
day, to love the LORD your God, and to
serve him with all your heart and with
all your soul,
14That I will give *you* the rain of your
land in his due season, the first rain
and the latter rain, that thou mayest
gather in thy corn, and thy wine, and
thine oil.
15And I will send grass in thy fields
for thy cattle, that thou mayest eat and
be full.
16Take heed to yourselves, that your
heart be not deceived, and ye turn
aside, and serve other gods, and worship them;
17And *then* the LORD'S wrath be kindled against you, and he shut up the
heaven, that there be no rain, and that
the land yield not her fruit; and *lest* ye
perish quickly from off the good land
which the LORD giveth you.

Israel's reward for obedience

¶18Therefore shall ye lay up these my
words in your heart and in your soul,
and bind them for a sign upon your
hand, that they may be as *frontlets
between your eyes.
19And ye shall teach them your children, speaking of them when thou
sittest in thine house, and when thou

11:10 A Better Land
Moses is here contrasting the rolling hills, valleys, and woods of Canaan, and its abundant rainfall with the flat, dry plains of Egypt, where the crops depended on the Nile, which overflowed for only one hundred days of the year. The water had to be stored in tanks and pools and pumped out through artificial channels. This is what Moses meant by "wateredst it with thy foot."

11:14 first rain and the latter rain. The early rains of autumn and the latter rains of spring are spoken of here. See verse 17 and the additional message to the people about the cutting off of the rain (Jer. 3:3), and the prophecy about its return (Joel 2:23).

walkest by the way, when thou liest
down, and when thou risest up.
20 And thou shalt write them upon the
door posts of thine house, and upon thy
gates:
21 That your days may be multiplied,
and the days of your children, in the
land which the LORD sware unto your
fathers to give them, as the days of
heaven upon the earth.
¶22 For if ye shall diligently keep all
these commandments which I command you, to do them, to love the LORD
your God, to walk in all his ways, and
to cleave unto him;
23 Then will the LORD drive out all
these nations from before you, and ye
shall possess greater nations and
mightier than yourselves.
24 Every place whereon the soles of
your feet shall tread shall be yours:
from the wilderness and *Lebanon,
from the river, the river Euphrates,
even unto the uttermost sea shall your
coast be.
25 There shall no man be able to stand
before you: *for* the LORD your God shall
lay the fear of you and the dread of you
upon all the land that ye shall tread
upon, as he hath said unto you.

Blessing and curse set before Israel

¶26 Behold, I set before you this day
a blessing and a curse;
27 A blessing, if ye obey the commandments of the LORD your God,
which I command you this day:
28 And a curse, if ye will not obey the
commandments of the LORD your God,
but turn aside out of the way which I
command you this day, to go after other
gods, which ye have not known.
29 And it shall come to pass, when the
LORD thy God hath brought thee in unto
the land whither thou goest to possess
it, that thou shalt put the blessing upon
mount Gerizim, and the curse upon
mount Ebal.
30 *Are* they not on the other side Jordan,
by the way where the sun goeth down,
in the land of the Canaanites, which
dwell in the champaign over against
Gilgal, beside the plains of Moreh?
31 For ye shall pass over Jordan to go
in to possess the land which the LORD
your God giveth you, and ye shall possess it, and dwell therein.
32 And ye shall observe to do all the
statutes and judgments which I set before you this day.

One place of worship: chosen by God

12 These *are* the statutes and judgments, which ye shall observe
to do in the land, which the LORD
God of thy fathers giveth thee to possess it, all the days that ye live upon the
earth.
2 Ye shall utterly destroy all the places,
wherein the nations which ye shall possess served their gods, upon the high
mountains, and upon the hills, and *under every green tree:
3 And ye shall overthrow their altars,
and break their pillars, and burn their
groves with fire; and ye shall hew down
the graven images of their gods, and
destroy the names of them out of that
place.
4 Ye shall not do so unto the LORD
your God.

12:3 The Idol Groves

The Hebrew word for "groves" is *Asherah* and really means a wooden image of the goddess Ashtoreth, the goddess of love of the Canaanites (corresponding to the goddess Ishtar of the Babylonians, Venus of the Romans, and Aphrodite of the Greeks). The image of the idol was often set up in a grove of trees to be worshipped. See Judges 2:13 note, as well as Judges 3:7.

11:24 the uttermost sea. The Mediterranean Sea.

11:29 put the blessing . . . and the curse. Read additional directions about this command in Deuteronomy 27:2-8,12-13.

11:30 champaign. Flat, open country or a plain.

[5]But unto the place which the LORD
your God shall choose out of all your
tribes to put his name there, *even* unto
his habitation shall ye seek, and thither
thou shalt come:
[6]And thither ye shall bring your
burnt-offerings, and your sacrifices, and
your *tithes, and heave-offerings of
your hand, and your vows, and your
freewill-offerings, and the firstlings of
your herds and of your flocks:
[7]And there ye shall eat before the
LORD your God, and ye shall rejoice in
all that ye put your hand unto, ye and
your households, wherein the LORD thy
God hath blessed thee.
[8]Ye shall not do after all *the things* that
we do here this day, every man whatsoever *is* right in his own eyes.
[9]For ye are not as yet come to the
rest and to the inheritance, which the
LORD your God giveth you.
[10]But *when* ye go over Jordan, and
dwell in the land which the LORD your
God giveth you to inherit, and *when*
he giveth you rest from all your enemies round about, so that ye dwell in
safety;
[11]Then there shall be a place which
the LORD your God shall choose to
cause his name to dwell there; thither
shall ye bring all that I command you;
your burnt-offerings, and your sacrifices, your tithes, and the *heave-offering of your hand, and all your choice
vows which ye vow unto the LORD:
[12]And ye shall rejoice before the
LORD your God, ye, and your sons, and
your daughters, and your menservants,
and your maidservants, and the Levite
that *is* within your gates; forasmuch
as he hath no part nor inheritance
with you.
[13]Take heed to thyself that thou offer
not thy burnt-offerings in every place
that thou seest:
[14]But in the place which the LORD
shall choose in one of thy tribes, there
thou shalt offer thy burnt-offerings, and
there thou shalt do all that I command
thee.
[15]Notwithstanding thou mayest kill
and eat flesh in all thy gates, whatsoever thy soul lusteth after, according to
the blessing of the LORD thy God which
he hath given thee: the unclean and the
clean may eat thereof, as of the roebuck, and as of the hart.
[16]Only ye shall not eat the *blood; ye
shall pour it upon the earth as water.
¶[17]Thou mayest not eat within thy
gates the tithe of thy corn, or of thy
wine, or of thy oil, or the firstlings of
thy herds or of thy flock, nor any of thy
vows which thou vowest, nor thy freewill-offerings, or heave-offering of
thine hand:
[18]But thou must eat them before the
LORD thy God in the place which the
LORD thy God shall choose, thou, and
thy son, and thy daughter, and thy manservant, and thy maidservant, and the
Levite that *is* within thy gates: and thou
shalt rejoice before the LORD thy God
in all that thou puttest thine hands unto.
[19]Take heed to thyself that thou forsake not the Levite as long as thou
livest upon the earth.
¶[20]When the LORD thy God shall enlarge thy border, as he hath promised
thee, and thou shalt say, I will eat flesh,
because thy soul longeth to eat flesh;
thou mayest eat flesh, whatsoever thy
soul lusteth after.
[21]If the place which the LORD thy God
hath chosen to put his name there be
too far from thee, then thou shalt kill
of thy herd and of thy flock, which the

12:6 freewill-offerings. See Leviticus 1:3 note.
12:15 eat flesh. See Deuteronomy 12:23 note.
12:15 lusteth after. Wishes for or desires.
12:15 the unclean and the clean. Read Numbers 19:9 note. See also Leviticus 11:47 note for names and descriptions of the animals that were clean or unclean to the Israelites.

LORD hath given thee, as I have commanded thee, and thou shalt eat in thy
gates whatsoever thy soul lusteth
after.
22 Even as the roebuck and the hart is
eaten, so thou shalt eat them: the unclean and the clean shall eat *of* them
alike.
23 Only be sure that thou eat not the
blood: for the blood *is* the life; and thou
mayest not eat the life with the flesh.

12:23 The Rule on Blood
Eating blood was forbidden because blood was to be used as an offering for atonement and was to be sprinkled on the mercy seat. Serious consequences were prescribed by God for those who violated this command. When we speak of the blood of the Lord Jesus Christ, we mean that the blood showed that His life was given up on the cross for us.

24 Thou shalt not eat it; thou shalt
pour it upon the earth as water.
25 Thou shalt not eat it; that it may go
well with thee, and with thy children
after thee, when thou shalt do *that*
which is right in the sight of the LORD.
26 Only thy holy things which thou
hast, and thy vows, thou shalt take, and
go unto the place which the LORD shall
choose:
27 And thou shalt offer thy burnt-
offerings, the flesh and the blood, upon
the *altar of the LORD thy God: and the
blood of thy sacrifices shall be poured
out upon the altar of the LORD thy God,
and thou shalt eat the flesh.
28 Observe and hear all these words
which I command thee, that it may go
well with thee, and with thy children
after thee for ever, when thou doest *that*
which is good and right in the sight of
the LORD thy God.
¶29 When the LORD thy God shall cut
off the nations from before thee,
whither thou goest to possess them,
and thou succeedest them, and dwellest
in their land;
30 Take heed to thyself that thou be
not snared by following them, after that
they be destroyed from before thee;
and that thou enquire not after their
gods, saying, How did these nations
serve their gods? even so will I do likewise.
31 Thou shalt not do so unto the LORD
thy God: for every abomination to the
LORD, which he hateth, have they done
unto their gods; for even their sons and
their daughters they have burnt in the
fire to their gods.
32 What thing soever I command you,
observe to do it: thou shalt not add
thereto, nor diminish from it.

False prophets

13 If there arise among you a
*prophet, or a dreamer of dreams,
and giveth thee a sign or a wonder,
2 And the sign or the wonder come to
pass, whereof he spake unto thee, saying, Let us go after other gods, which
thou hast not known, and let us serve
them;
3 Thou shalt not hearken unto the
words of that prophet, or that dreamer
of dreams: for the LORD your *God
*proveth you, to know whether ye love
the LORD your God with all your heart
and with all your soul.
4 Ye shall walk after the LORD your
God, and fear him, and keep his commandments, and obey his voice, and
ye shall serve him, and cleave unto
him.
5 And that prophet, or that dreamer
of dreams, shall be put to death; because he hath spoken to turn *you*
away from the LORD your God, which
brought you out of the land of *Egypt,
and *redeemed you out of the house
of bondage, to thrust thee out of the
way which the LORD thy God commanded thee to walk in. So shalt thou
put the evil away from the midst of
thee.
¶6 If thy brother, the son of thy mother, or thy son, or thy daughter, or the
wife of thy bosom, or thy friend, which
is as thine own soul, entice thee secretly, saying, Let us go and serve other

gods, which thou hast not known, thou,
nor thy fathers;
7 *Namely,* of the gods of the people
which *are* round about you, nigh unto
thee, or far off from thee, from the *one*
end of the earth even unto the *other* end
of the earth;
8 Thou shalt not consent unto him,
nor hearken unto him; neither shall
thine eye pity him, neither shalt thou
spare, neither shalt thou conceal him:
9 But thou shalt surely kill him; thine
hand shall be first upon him to put him
to death, and afterwards the hand of all
the people.
10 And thou shalt stone him with
stones, that he die; because he hath
sought to thrust thee away from the
LORD thy God, which brought thee out
of the land of Egypt, from the house of
bondage.
11 And all Israel shall hear, and fear,
and shall do no more any such wickedness as this is among you.
¶ 12 If thou shalt hear *say* in one of thy
cities, which the LORD thy God hath
given thee to dwell there, saying,
13 *Certain* men, the *children of Belial, are gone out from among you, and
have withdrawn the inhabitants of their
city, saying, Let us go and serve other
gods, which ye have not known;
14 Then shalt thou enquire, and make
search, and ask diligently; and, behold,
if it be truth, *and* the thing certain, *that*
such *abomination is wrought among
you;
15 Thou shalt surely smite the inhabitants of that city with the edge of the
sword, destroying it utterly, and all that
is therein, and the cattle thereof, with
the edge of the sword.
16 And thou shalt gather all the spoil
of it into the midst of the street thereof,
and shalt burn with fire the city, and
all the spoil thereof every whit, for
the LORD thy God: and it shall be an
heap for ever; it shall not be built
again.
17 And there shall cleave nought of the
cursed thing to thine hand: that the
LORD may turn from the fierceness of
his anger, and shew thee *mercy, and
have compassion upon thee, and multiply thee, as he hath sworn unto thy fathers;
18 When thou shalt hearken to the
voice of the LORD thy God, to keep all
his commandments which I command
thee this day, to do *that which is* right
in the eyes of the LORD thy God.

Food laws for Israel

14 Ye *are* the children of the LORD
your God: ye shall not cut yourselves, nor make any baldness between
your eyes for the dead.

14:1 A Forbidden Practice
Heathen priests often shaved their hair as a sign of sorrow or mourning. The Israelites were forbidden to copy this heathen custom.

2 For thou *art* an *holy people unto
the LORD thy God, and the LORD hath
chosen thee to be a *peculiar people unto himself, above all the nations that *are*
upon the earth.
¶ 3 Thou shalt not eat any abominable
thing.
4 These *are* the beasts which ye shall
eat: the ox, the sheep, and the goat,
5 The hart, and the roebuck, and the
fallow deer, and the wild goat, and
the pygarg, and the wild ox, and the
chamois.
6 And every beast that parteth the
hoof, and cleaveth the cleft into two

13:13 children of Belial. Belial means *worthless* or *wicked.* As used in the Bible, the phrase "of Belial" undoubtedly speaks of those who deliberately oppose the love of God and prefer to serve Satan.
14:2 peculiar. This word does not mean *strange.* It means *belonging in a special way to God.*
14:3 abominable thing. This means *unclean thing.*
14:5 pygarg. An antelope.

claws, *and* cheweth the cud among the
beasts, that ye shall eat.
7Nevertheless these ye shall not eat
of them that chew the cud, or of them
that divide the cloven hoof; *as* the
camel, and the *hare, and the coney:
for they chew the cud, but divide not
the hoof; *therefore* they *are* unclean unto
you.
8And the swine, because it divideth
the hoof, yet cheweth not the cud, it *is*
unclean unto you: ye shall not eat of
their flesh, nor touch their dead carcase.
¶9These ye shall eat of all that *are* in
the waters: all that have fins and scales
shall ye eat:
10And whatsoever hath not fins and
scales ye may not eat; it *is* unclean unto
you.
¶11*Of* all clean *birds ye shall eat.
12But these *are they* of which ye shall
not eat: the eagle, and ossifrage, and the
ospray,
13And the glede, and the kite, and the
vulture after his kind,
14And every raven after his kind,
15And the owl, and the night hawk,
and the cuckow, and the hawk after his
kind,
16The little owl, and the great owl,
and the swan,
17And the pelican, and the gier eagle,
and the cormorant,
18And the stork, and the heron after
her kind, and the lapwing, and the bat.
19And every creeping thing that flieth
is unclean unto you: they shall not be
eaten.
20*But of* all clean fowls ye may eat.
¶21Ye shall not eat *of* any thing that
dieth of itself: thou shalt give it unto the
stranger that *is* in thy gates, that he may
eat it; or thou mayest sell it unto an
alien: for thou *art* an holy people unto
the LORD thy God. Thou shalt not
seethe a kid in his mother's milk.

Tithe to be given to the LORD

22Thou shalt truly tithe all the increase of thy seed, that the field
bringeth forth year by year.
23And thou shalt eat before the LORD
thy God, in the place which he shall
choose to place his name there, the
tithe of thy corn, of thy wine, and of
thine oil, and the firstlings of thy herds
and of thy flocks; that thou mayest learn
to *fear the LORD thy God always.
24And if the way be too long for thee,
so that thou art not able to carry it; *or*
if the place be too far from thee, which
the LORD thy God shall choose to set
his name there, when the LORD thy God
hath blessed thee:
25Then shalt thou turn *it* into money,
and bind up the money in thine hand,
and shalt go unto the place which the
LORD thy God shall choose:
26And thou shalt bestow that money
for whatsoever thy soul lusteth after,
for oxen, or for sheep, or for wine, or for
strong drink, or for whatsoever thy soul
desireth: and thou shalt eat there before
the LORD thy God, and thou shalt rejoice, thou, and thine household,
27And the Levite that *is* within thy
gates; thou shalt not forsake him; for he
hath no part nor inheritance with thee.
¶28At the end of three years thou
shalt bring forth all the tithe of thine increase the same year, and shalt lay *it* up
within thy gates:
29And the Levite, (because he hath
no part nor inheritance with thee,) and
the stranger, and the fatherless, and the

14:12 ossifrage and the ospray. Both were kinds of hawks, as are the "glede" and the "kite" in verse 13.

14:13 vulture. Several different kinds of birds belong to the vulture group. These birds eat carrion—dead and decaying flesh. The "gier eagle" (vs. 17) is not an eagle but a kind of small vulture.

14:18 lapwing. This has been translated in later versions of the Bible (see **How We Got Our English Bible*, p. xxiii) as "hoopoe," which is a very beautiful but very filthy bird of Palestine.

widow, which *are* within thy gates, shall come, and shall eat and be satisfied; that the LORD thy God may bless thee in all the work of thine hand which thou doest.

Sabbatic or 7th year (Lev. 25)

15 At the end of *every* seven years thou shalt make a release.

Debts to be cancelled

2 And this *is* the manner of the release: Every creditor that lendeth *ought* unto his neighbour shall release *it;* he shall not exact *it* of his neighbour, or of his brother; because it is called the LORD'S release.

3 Of a foreigner thou mayest exact *it again:* but *that* which is thine with thy brother thine hand shall release;

4 Save when there shall be no poor among you; for the LORD shall greatly bless thee in the land which the LORD thy God giveth thee *for* an inheritance to possess it:

5 Only if thou carefully hearken unto the voice of the LORD thy God, to observe to do all these commandments which I command thee this day.

6 For the LORD thy God blesseth thee, as he promised thee: and thou shalt lend unto many nations, but thou shalt not borrow; and thou shalt reign over many nations,but they shall not reign over thee.

Poor to be cared for

¶ 7 If there be among you a poor man of one of thy brethren within any of thy gates in thy land which the LORD thy God giveth thee, thou shalt not *harden thine heart, nor shut thine hand from thy poor brother:

8 But thou shalt open thine hand wide unto him, and shalt surely lend him sufficient for his need, *in that* which he wanteth.

9 Beware that there be not a thought in thy wicked heart, saying, The seventh year, the year of release, is at hand; and thine eye be evil against thy poor brother, and thou givest him nought; and he cry unto the LORD against thee, and it be *sin unto thee.

10 Thou shalt surely give him, and thine heart shall not be grieved when thou givest unto him: because that for this thing the LORD thy God shall bless thee in all thy works, and in all that thou puttest thine hand unto.

11 For the poor shall never cease out of the land: therefore I command thee, saying, Thou shalt open thine hand wide unto thy brother, to thy poor, and to thy needy, in thy land.

Hebrew slaves to be released

¶ 12 *And* if thy brother, an Hebrew man, or an Hebrew woman, be sold unto thee, and serve thee six years; then in the seventh year thou shalt let him go free from thee.

13 And when thou sendest him out free from thee, thou shalt not let him go away empty:

14 Thou shalt furnish him liberally out of thy flock, and out of thy floor, and out of thy winepress: *of that* wherewith the LORD thy God hath blessed thee thou shalt give unto him.

15 And thou shalt remember that thou wast a bondman in the land of Egypt, and the LORD thy God redeemed thee: therefore I command thee this thing to day.

The permanent slave

16 And it shall be, if he say unto thee, I will not go away from thee; because he loveth thee and thine house, because he is well with thee;

17 Then thou shalt take an aul, and thrust *it* through his ear unto the door, and he shall be thy servant for ever. And also unto thy maidservant thou shalt do likewise.

18 It shall not seem hard unto thee, when thou sendest him away free from

---

15:11 the poor shall never cease. See what our Lord said about this in Matthew 26:11.

15:17 A Committed Servant
Because the servant promised to obey, his ear, with which he would hear his master's voice, was pierced with the awl, a sharp tool. He that hath an ear is supposed to hear (see Rev. 2:7,11,17,29; 3:6,13,22), because as Christians, we who have Jesus as Lord are His bondslaves (compare Rom. 1:1; 2 Pet. 1:1).

thee; for he hath been worth a double
hired servant *to thee,* in serving thee six
years: and the LORD thy God shall bless
thee in all that thou doest.

Firstlings to be dedicated to God

¶19All the firstling males that come
of thy herd and of thy flock thou shalt
sanctify unto the LORD thy God: thou
shalt do no work with the firstling of thy
bullock, nor shear the firstling of thy
sheep.
20Thou shalt eat *it* before the LORD
thy God year by year in the place which
the LORD shall choose, thou and thy
household.
21And if there be *any* blemish therein,
as if it be lame, or blind, *or have* any ill
blemish, thou shalt not *sacrifice it unto
the LORD thy God.
22Thou shalt eat it within thy gates: the
*unclean and the clean *person shall eat
it* alike, as the roebuck, and as the hart.
23Only thou shalt not eat the blood
thereof; thou shalt pour it upon the
ground as water.

Passover to be kept (Lev. 23)

16 Observe the month of Abib, and
keep the *passover unto the
LORD thy God: for in the month of Abib
the LORD thy God brought thee forth out
of Egypt by night.
2Thou shalt therefore sacrifice the
passover unto the LORD thy God, of the
flock and the herd, in the place which
the LORD shall choose to place his name
there.
3Thou shalt eat no *leavened bread
with it; seven days shalt thou eat *unleavened bread therewith, *even* the
bread of affliction; for thou camest forth
out of the land of Egypt in haste: that
thou mayest remember the day when
thou camest forth out of the land of
Egypt all the days of thy life.
4And there shall be no leavened
bread seen with thee in all thy coast
seven days; neither shall there *any
thing* of the flesh, which thou sacri-
ficedst the first day at even, remain all
night until the morning.
5Thou mayest not sacrifice the passover within any of thy gates, which the
LORD thy God giveth thee:
6But at the place which the LORD thy
God shall choose to place his name in,
there thou shalt sacrifice the passover
at even, at the going down of the sun,
at the season that thou camest forth out
of Egypt.
7And thou shalt roast and eat *it* in the
place which the LORD thy God shall
choose: and thou shalt turn in the morning, and go unto thy tents.
8Six days thou shalt eat unleavened
bread: and on the seventh day *shall be*
a solemn assembly to the LORD thy
God: thou shalt do no work *therein.*

Feast of weeks of Pentecost

¶9Seven weeks shalt thou number
unto thee: begin to number the seven
weeks from *such time as* thou beginnest
to put the sickle to the corn.
10And thou shalt keep the feast of
weeks unto the LORD thy God with a
tribute of a freewill-offering of thine
hand, which thou shalt give *unto the
LORD thy God,* according as the LORD
thy God hath blessed thee:

15:21 blemish. See Leviticus 1:4 note, "Burnt-Offering," to see why the sacrificed animal had to be perfect.

16:1 month of Abib. This was the first month of the Hebrew calendar, our April.

16:10 the feast of weeks. Note that Leviticus 23 gives seven feasts. This summary (vss. 1-15) mentions only three of these. The notes on Leviticus 23 give the meanings of the feasts. See Numbers 29:39 note for a list of all seven of them.

11 And thou shalt rejoice before the
LORD thy God, thou, and thy son, and
thy daughter, and thy manservant, and
thy maidservant, and the Levite that *is*
within thy gates, and the stranger, and
the fatherless, and the widow, that *are*
among you, in the place which the LORD
thy God hath chosen to place his name
there.
12 And thou shalt remember that thou
wast a bondman in Egypt: and thou
shalt observe and do these statutes.

The feast of tabernacles

¶ 13 Thou shalt observe the feast of
tabernacles seven days, after that thou
hast gathered in thy corn and thy wine:
14 And thou shalt rejoice in thy feast,
thou, and thy son, and thy daughter, and
thy manservant, and thy maidservant,
and the Levite, the stranger, and the
fatherless, and the widow, that *are* within thy gates.
15 Seven days shalt thou keep a solemn feast unto the LORD thy God in the
place which the LORD shall choose:
because the LORD thy God shall bless
thee in all thine increase, and in all the
works of thine hands, therefore thou
shalt surely rejoice.
¶ 16 Three times in a year shall all thy
males appear before the LORD thy God
in the place which he shall choose;
in the feast of unleavened bread, and in
the feast of weeks, and in the feast of
tabernacles: and they shall not appear
before the LORD empty:
17 Every man *shall give* as he is able,
according to the blessing of the LORD
thy God which he hath given thee.

Judges to judge fairly

¶ 18 Judges and officers shalt thou
make thee in all thy gates, which the
LORD thy God giveth thee, throughout
thy tribes: and they shall judge the people with *just judgment.
19 Thou shalt not wrest judgment;
thou shalt not respect persons, neither
take a gift: for a gift doth blind the eyes
of the wise, and pervert the words of
the righteous.
20 That which is altogether just shalt
thou follow, that thou mayest live, and
inherit the land which the LORD thy
God giveth thee.

Groves and images forbidden

¶ 21 Thou shalt not plant thee a grove
of any trees near unto the altar of the
LORD thy God, which thou shalt make
thee.
22 Neither shalt thou set thee up *any*
image; which the LORD thy God hateth.

Offerings must be perfect

17 Thou shalt not sacrifice unto
the LORD thy God *any* bullock,
or sheep, wherein is blemish, *or* any
evilfavouredness: for that *is* an abomination unto the LORD thy God.

Idolaters to be stoned

¶ 2 If there be found among you, within any of thy gates which the LORD thy
God giveth thee, man or woman, that
hath wrought wickedness in the sight
of the LORD thy God, in transgressing
his *covenant,
3 And hath gone and served other
gods, and worshipped them, either the
sun, or moon, or any of the host of heav-
en, which I have not commanded;
4 And it be told thee, and thou hast
heard *of it,* and enquired diligently, and,
behold, *it be* true, *and* the thing certain,
that such abomination is wrought in
*Israel:
5 Then shalt thou bring forth that man
or that woman, which have committed
that wicked thing, unto thy gates, *even*
that man or that woman, and shalt stone
them with stones, till they die.
6 At the mouth of two witnesses, or
three witnesses, shall he that is worthy
of death be put to death; *but* at the
mouth of one witness he shall not be
put to death.

17:1 evilfavouredness. Ugliness, deformity.

7 The hands of the witnesses shall be first upon him to put him to death, and afterward the hands of all the people. So thou shalt put the evil away from among you.

Obedience to the priests and Levites

¶8 If there arise a matter too hard for thee in judgment, between blood and blood, between plea and plea, and between stroke and stroke, *being* matters of controversy within thy gates: then shalt thou arise, and get thee up into the place which the LORD thy God shall choose;

9 And thou shalt come unto the priests the Levites, and unto the judge that shall be in those days, and enquire; and they shall shew thee the sentence of judgment:

10 And thou shalt do according to the sentence, which they of that place which the LORD shall choose shall shew thee; and thou shalt observe to do according to all that they inform thee:

11 According to the sentence of the *law which they shall teach thee, and according to the judgment which they shall tell thee, thou shalt do: thou shalt not decline from the sentence which they shall shew thee, *to* the right hand, nor *to* the left.

12 And the man that will do presumptuously, and will not hearken unto the priest that standeth to minister there before the LORD thy God, or unto the judge, even that man shall die: and thou shalt put away the evil from Israel.

13 And all the people shall hear, and fear, and do no more presumptuously.

Instructions for the future king

¶14 When thou art come unto the land which the LORD thy God giveth thee, and shalt possess it, and shalt dwell therein, and shalt say, I will set a king over me, like as all the nations that *are* about me;

15 Thou shalt in any wise set *him* king over thee, whom the LORD thy God shall choose: *one* from among thy brethren shalt thou set king over thee: thou mayest not set a stranger over thee, which *is* not thy brother.

16 But he shall not multiply horses to himself, nor cause the people to return to Egypt, to the end that he should multiply horses: forasmuch as the LORD hath said unto you, Ye shall henceforth return no more that way.

17 Neither shall he multiply wives to himself, that his heart turn not away: neither shall he greatly multiply to himself silver and gold.

18 And it shall be, when he sitteth upon the throne of his *kingdom, that he shall write him a copy of this law in a book out of *that which is* before the priests the Levites:

19 And it shall be with him, and he shall read therein all the days of his life: that he may learn to fear the LORD his God, to keep all the words of this law and these statutes, to do them:

20 That his heart be not lifted up above his brethren, and that he turn not aside from the commandment, *to* the right hand, or *to* the left: to the end that he may prolong *his* days in his kingdom, he, and his children, in the midst of Israel.

The portion of the priests and Levites

18 The priests the Levites, *and* all the tribe of Levi, shall have no part nor inheritance with Israel: they shall eat the *offerings of the LORD made by fire, and his inheritance.

17:8 between blood and blood. These all stood for arguments, legal controversies, or fights.
17:11 thou shalt not decline. Thou shalt not turn.
17:14 and shalt say. For the fulfillment of this, see 1 Samuel 8:5-7.
17:15 from among thy brethren. From their own people, the children of Israel.
17:16 he shall not multiply horses. This prohibition and that of verse 17 were both ignored and disobeyed by Solomon. See 1 Kings 10:28; 11:1-4.

2 Therefore shall they have no inheritance among their brethren: the LORD *is* their inheritance, as he hath said unto them.

¶3 And this shall be the priest's due from the people, from them that offer a sacrifice, whether *it be* ox or sheep; and they shall give unto the priest the shoulder, and the two cheeks, and the maw.

4 The firstfruit *also* of thy corn, of thy wine, and of thine oil, and the first of the fleece of thy sheep, shalt thou give him.

5 For the LORD thy God hath chosen him out of all thy tribes, to stand to minister in the name of the LORD, him and his sons for ever.

¶6 And if a Levite come from any of thy gates out of all Israel, where he sojourned, and come with all the desire of his mind unto the place which the LORD shall choose;

7 Then he shall minister in the name of the LORD his God, as all his brethren the Levites *do,* which stand there before the LORD.

8 They shall have like portions to eat, beside that which cometh of the sale of his patrimony.

Heathen practices forbidden

¶9 When thou art come into the land which the LORD thy God giveth thee, thou shalt not learn to do after the abominations of those nations.

10 There shall not be found among you *any one* that maketh his son or his daughter to pass through the fire, *or* that useth divination, *or* an observer of times, or an enchanter, or a *witch,

11 Or a charmer, or a consulter with *familiar spirits, or a wizard, or a necromancer.

12 For all that do these things *are* an abomination unto the LORD: and because of these abominations the LORD thy God doth drive them out from before thee.

13 Thou shalt be perfect with the LORD thy God.

14 For these nations, which thou shalt possess, hearkened unto observers of times, and unto diviners: but as for thee, the LORD thy God hath not suffered thee so *to do.*

The true Prophet foretold

¶15 The LORD thy God will raise up unto thee a Prophet from the midst of thee, of thy brethren, like unto me; unto him ye shall hearken;

18:15 The Prophet
The New Testament makes it clear that the Lord Jesus Christ is meant in verses 15-19. See John 1:21; Acts 3:22-23; 7:37.

16 According to all that thou desiredst of the LORD thy God in *Horeb in the day of the assembly, saying, Let me not hear again the voice of the LORD my God, neither let me see this great fire any more, that I die not.

17 And the LORD said unto me, They have well *spoken that* which they have spoken.

18 I will raise them up a Prophet from among their brethren, like unto thee, and will put my words in his mouth; and he shall speak unto them all that I shall command him.

19 And it shall come to pass, *that* whosoever will not hearken unto my

---

18:3 maw. The stomach of animals.
18:8 sale of his patrimony. That which has been given to him (see vss. 1-7).
18:10 pass through the fire. This speaks of the death by burning of their sons and daughters in the fire-worship of the god Molech. See Leviticus 20:2 note.
18:11 necromancer. One who pretends to call up the dead for purposes of divination (fortune-telling).
18:13 perfect. Righteous and sincere.
18:16 the day of the assembly. Read Exodus 19.

words which he shall speak in my name,
I will require *it* of him.

A test for false prophets

20But the prophet, which shall presume
to speak a word in my name, which I
have not commanded him to speak, or
that shall speak in the name of other
gods, even that prophet shall die.
21And if thou say in thine heart, How
shall we know the word which the LORD
hath not spoken?
22When a prophet speaketh in the
name of the LORD, if the thing follow
not, nor come to pass, that *is* the thing
which the LORD hath not spoken, *but*
the prophet hath spoken it presumptuously: thou shalt not be afraid of him.

The cities of refuge

19 When the LORD thy *God hath
cut off the nations, whose land
the LORD thy God giveth thee, and thou
succeedest them, and dwellest in their
cities, and in their houses;
2Thou shalt separate three cities for
thee in the midst of thy land, which the
LORD thy God giveth thee to possess it.
3Thou shalt prepare thee a way, and
divide the coasts of thy land, which the
LORD thy God giveth thee to inherit,
into three parts, that every slayer may
flee thither.
¶4And this *is* the case of the slayer,
which shall flee thither, that he may
live: Whoso killeth his neighbour ignorantly, whom he hated not in time past;
5As when a man goeth into the wood
with his neighbour to hew wood, and
his hand fetcheth a stroke with the
axe to cut down the tree, and the head
slippeth from the helve, and lighteth
upon his neighbour, that he die; he shall
flee unto one of those cities, and live:
6Lest the avenger of the blood pursue the slayer, while his heart is hot,
and overtake him, because the way is
long, and slay him; whereas he *was* not
worthy of death, inasmuch as he hated
him not in time past.
7Wherefore I command thee, saying,
Thou shalt separate three cities for
thee.
8And if the LORD thy God enlarge thy
coast, as he hath sworn unto thy fathers, and give thee all the land which
he promised to give unto thy fathers;
9If thou shalt keep all these commandments to do them, which I command thee this day, to love the LORD thy
God, and to walk ever in his ways; then
shalt thou add three cities more for
thee, beside these three:
10That innocent blood be not shed in
thy land, which the LORD thy God
giveth thee *for* an inheritance, and *so*
blood be upon thee.
¶11But if any man hate his neighbour,
and lie in wait for him, and rise up against
him, and smite him mortally that he die,
and fleeth into one of these cities:
12Then the *elders of his city shall
send and fetch him thence, and deliver
him into the hand of the *avenger of
blood, that he may die.
13Thine eye shall not pity him, but
thou shalt put away *the guilt of* innocent
blood from Israel, that it may go well
with thee.

Landmarks not to be removed

¶14Thou shalt not remove thy neighbour's *landmark, which they of old
time have set in thine inheritance,
which thou shalt inherit in the land that
the LORD thy God giveth thee to possess it.

Law of two witnesses
(17:6,7; Num. 35:30)

¶15One witness shall not rise up
against a man for any iniquity, or for any

18:19 I will require it of him. "I will hold him [the believer] responsible for his words," is meant here.
19:5 helve. Handle of an axe.
19:6 avenger of the blood. See *avenger of blood.

> **19:14 Landmarks**
> In biblical times, landmarks were usually a single block or small pile of stones laid on the ground. They are still that way today in Palestine. Since the stones might easily be shifted by a dishonest landowner, there was a severe curse upon their removal (Deut. 27:17). The land was allotted to the tribes and the ownership was marked by landmarks (Josh. 15–17). In Egypt, the land had to be remeasured and allotted after each inundation, or flooding, of the Nile River.

sin, in any sin that he sinneth: at the
mouth of two witnesses, or at the mouth
of three witnesses, shall the matter be
established.
¶16 If a false witness rise up against
any man to testify against him *that
which is* wrong;
17 Then both the men, between whom
the controversy *is,* shall stand before
the LORD, before the priests and the
judges, which shall be in those days;
18 And the judges shall make diligent
inquisition: and, behold, *if* the witness
be a false witness, *and* hath testified
falsely against his brother;
19 Then shall ye do unto him, as he
had thought to have done unto his
brother: so shalt thou put the evil away
from among you.
20 And those which remain shall hear,
and fear, and shall henceforth commit
no more any such evil among you.
21 And thine eye shall not pity; *but* life
shall go for life, eye for eye, tooth for
tooth, hand for hand, foot for foot.

Rules for warfare

20 When thou goest out to battle
against thine enemies, and
seest horses, and chariots, *and* a people more than thou, *be not afraid of
them: for the LORD thy God *is* with
thee, which brought thee up out of the
land of *Egypt.
2 And it shall be, when ye are come
nigh unto the battle, that the priest shall
approach and speak unto the people,
3 And shall say unto them, Hear, O
Israel, ye approach this day unto battle
against your enemies: let not your hearts
faint, fear not, and do not tremble, neither be ye terrified because of them;
4 For the LORD your God *is* he that
goeth with you, to fight for you against
your enemies, to save you.
¶5 And the officers shall speak unto
the people, saying, What man *is there*
that hath built a new house, and hath
not dedicated it? let him go and return
to his house, lest he die in the battle,
and another man dedicate it.
6 And what man *is he* that hath planted a vineyard, and hath not *yet* eaten of
it? let him *also* go and return unto his
house, lest he die in the battle, and another man eat of it.
7 And what man *is there* that hath betrothed a wife, and hath not taken her?
let him go and return unto his house,
lest he die in the battle, and another
man take her.
8 And the officers shall speak further
unto the people, and they shall say,
What man *is there that is* fearful and
fainthearted? let him go and return unto
his house, lest his brethren's heart faint
as well as his heart.
9 And it shall be, when the officers
have made an end of speaking unto the
people, that they shall make captains of
the armies to lead the people.
¶10 When thou comest nigh unto a
city to fight against it, then proclaim
*peace unto it.
11 And it shall be, if it make thee answer of peace, and open unto thee, then
it shall be, *that* all the people *that is*
found therein shall be tributaries unto
thee, and they shall serve thee.
12 And if it will make no peace with
thee, but will make war against thee,
then thou shalt besiege it:

19:18 inquisition. Search, examination.

13 And when the LORD thy God hath
delivered it into thine hands, thou shalt
smite every male thereof with the edge
of the sword:
14 But the women, and the little ones,
and the cattle, and all that is in the city,
even all the spoil thereof, shalt thou take
unto thyself; and thou shalt eat the spoil
of thine enemies, which the LORD thy
God hath given thee.
15 Thus shalt thou do unto all the cities *which are* very far off from thee,
which *are* not of the cities of these nations.
16 But of the cities of these people,
which the LORD thy God doth give thee
for an inheritance, thou shalt save alive
nothing that breatheth:
17 But thou shalt utterly destroy
them; *namely,* the Hittites, and the
Amorites, the Canaanites, and the Perizzites, the Hivites, and the Jebusites;
as the LORD thy God hath commanded
thee:
18 That they teach you not to do after
all their abominations, which they have
done unto their gods; so should ye sin
against the LORD your God.
¶ 19 When thou shalt besiege a city a
long time, in making war against it to
take it, thou shalt not destroy the trees
thereof by forcing an axe against them:
for thou mayest eat of them, and thou
shalt not cut them down (for the tree of
the field *is* man's *life*) to employ *them*
in the siege:
20 Only the trees which thou knowest
that they *be* not trees for meat, thou
shalt destroy and cut them down; and
thou shalt build bulwarks against the
city that maketh war with thee, until it
be subdued.

Rule for unsolved murder

21 If *one* be found slain in the land
which the LORD thy God giveth
thee to possess it, lying in the field, *and*
it be not known who hath slain him:
2 Then thy elders and thy judges shall
come forth, and they shall measure
unto the cities which *are* round about
him that is slain:
3 And it shall be, *that* the city *which is*
next unto the slain man, even the elders
of that city shall take an heifer, which
hath not been wrought with, *and* which
hath not drawn in the yoke;
4 And the elders of that city shall bring
down the heifer unto a rough valley,
which is neither eared nor sown, and
shall strike off the heifer's neck there
in the valley:
5 And the priests the sons of Levi
shall come near; for them the LORD thy
God hath chosen to minister unto him,
and to bless in the name of the LORD;
and by their word shall every controversy and every stroke be *tried:*
6 And all the elders of that city, *that are*
next unto the slain *man,* shall wash
their hands over the heifer that is beheaded in the valley:
7 And they shall answer and say, Our
hands have not shed this blood, neither
have our eyes seen *it.*
8 Be merciful, O LORD, unto thy people Israel, whom thou hast *redeemed,
and lay not innocent blood unto thy
people of Israel's charge. And the blood
shall be *forgiven them.
9 So shalt thou put away the *guilt of*
innocent blood from among you, when
thou shalt do *that which is* right in the
sight of the LORD.

Marriage of captive women

¶ 10 When thou goest forth to war
against thine enemies, and the LORD
thy God hath delivered them into thine
hands, and thou hast taken them captive,
11 And seest among the captives a

20:17 utterly destroy. See Deuteronomy 2:34 note.
20:20 bulwarks. Fortifications.
21:3 heifer. A young cow.
21:4 eared. To plow.

beautiful woman, and hast a desire unto her, that thou wouldest have her to thy wife;

12 Then thou shalt bring her home to thine house; and she shall shave her head, and pare her nails;

13 And she shall put the raiment of her captivity from off her, and shall remain in thine house, and bewail her father and her mother a full month: and after that thou shalt go in unto her, and be her husband, and she shall be thy wife.

14 And it shall be, if thou have no delight in her, then thou shalt let her go whither she will; but thou shalt not sell her at all for money, thou shalt not make merchandise of her, because thou hast humbled her.

¶ 15 If a man have *two wives, one beloved, and another hated, and they have born him children, *both* the beloved and the hated; and *if* the firstborn son be hers that was hated:

16 Then it shall be, when he maketh his sons to inherit *that* which he hath, *that* he may not make the son of the beloved firstborn before the son of the hated, *which is indeed* the firstborn:

17 But he shall acknowledge the son of the hated *for* the firstborn, by giving him a double portion of all that he hath: for he *is* the beginning of his strength; the right of the firstborn *is* his.

Treatment of disobedient son

¶ 18 If a man have a stubborn and rebellious son, which will not obey the voice of his father, or the voice of his mother, and *that,* when they have *chastened him, will not hearken unto them:

19 Then shall his father and his mother lay hold on him, and bring him out unto the elders of his city, and unto the gate of his place;

20 And they shall say unto the elders of his city, This our son *is* stubborn and rebellious, he will not obey our voice; *he is* a glutton, and a drunkard.

21 And all the men of his city shall stone him with stones, that he die: so shalt thou put evil away from among you; and all Israel shall hear, and fear.

¶ 22 And if a man have committed a *sin worthy of death, and he be to be put to death, and thou hang him on a tree:

23 His body shall not remain all night upon the tree, but thou shalt in any wise bury him that day; (for he that is hanged *is* accursed of God;) that thy land be not defiled, which the LORD thy God giveth thee *for* an inheritance.

Various laws

22 Thou shalt not see the brother's ox or his sheep go astray, and hide thyself from them: thou shalt in any case bring them again unto thy brother.

2 And if thy brother *be* not nigh unto thee, or if thou know him not, then thou shalt bring it unto thine own house, and it shall be with thee until thy brother seek after it, and thou shalt restore it to him again.

3 In like manner shalt thou do with his ass; and so shalt thou do with his raiment; and with all lost thing of thy brother's, which he hath lost, and thou hast found, shalt thou do likewise: thou mayest not hide thyself.

¶ 4 Thou shalt not see thy brother's ass or his ox fall down by the way, and hide thyself from them: thou shalt surely help him to lift *them* up again.

¶ 5 The woman shall not wear that which pertaineth unto a man, neither shall a man put on a woman's garment: for all that do so *are* *abomination unto the LORD thy God.

¶ 6 If a bird's nest chance to be before thee in the way in any tree, or on the ground, *whether they be* young ones, or

---

21:17 firstborn. See *birthright.

21:23 he that is hanged. This is part of the curse that the Lord Jesus Christ took upon Himself for us; He hung upon the cross for our sins. Read Galatians 3:13.

22:1 thy brother. One of their own people.

eggs, and the dam sitting upon the
young, or upon the eggs, thou shalt not
take the dam with the young:
7 *But* thou shalt in any wise let the
dam go, and take the young to thee; that
it may be well with thee, and *that* thou
mayest prolong *thy* days.
¶ 8 When thou buildest a new house,
then thou shalt make a battlement for
thy roof, that thou bring not blood upon
thine house, if any man fall from thence.
¶ 9 Thou shalt not sow thy vineyard
with divers seeds: lest the fruit of thy
seed which thou hast sown, and the
fruit of thy vineyard, be defiled.

22:9-11 A Separate People
In verses 9-11 God is impressing upon His people the idea of separation. These verses give pictures of unlike things being used together. It is as if God were saying, "Just as the different seeds being sowed together would cause defilement, just as the ox and ass would not work well together, just as one material would wear out more quickly than another and spoil the garment, so you, My people, are to have no fellowship with those who are not My people. You are to be a separate people." Read 2 Corinthians 6:14-18 for what He says to Christians today. See also 2 Corinthians 6:17 note, "Separation."

¶ 10 Thou shalt not plow with an ox
and an ass together.
¶ 11 Thou shalt not wear a garment of
divers sorts, *as* of woollen and *linen
together.
¶ 12 Thou shalt make thee fringes
upon the four quarters of thy vesture,
wherewith thou coverest *thyself.*
¶ 13 If any man take a wife, and go in
unto her, and hate her,
14 And give occasions of speech
against her, and bring up an evil name
upon her, and say, I took this woman,
and when I came to her, I found her not
a maid:
15 Then shall the father of the damsel,
and her mother, take and bring forth *the
tokens of* the damsel's virginity unto the
elders of the city in the gate:
16 And the damsel's father shall say
unto the elders, I gave my daughter
unto this man to wife, and he hateth
her;
17 And, lo, he hath given occasions of
speech *against her,* saying, I found not
thy daughter a maid; and yet these *are
the tokens of* my daughter's virginity.
And they shall spread the cloth before
the elders of the city.
18 And the elders of that city shall take
that man and chastise him;
19 And they shall amerce him in an
hundred *shekels* of silver, and give *them*
unto the father of the damsel, because
he hath brought up an evil name upon
a virgin of Israel: and she shall be his
wife; he may not put her away all his
days.
20 But if this thing be true, *and the
tokens of* virginity be not found for the
damsel:
21 Then they shall bring out the damsel to the door of her father's house,
and the men of her city shall stone her
with stones that she die: because she
hath wrought folly in Israel, to play the
*whore in her father's house: so shalt
thou put evil away from among you.
¶ 22 If a man be found lying with a
woman married to an husband, then
they shall both of them die, *both* the
man that lay with the woman, and the
woman: so shalt thou put away evil from
Israel.
¶ 23 If a damsel *that is* a virgin be betrothed unto an husband, and a man find
her in the city, and lie with her;
24 Then ye shall bring them both out
unto the gate of that city, and ye shall
stone them with stones that they die;
the damsel, because she cried not, *be-*

22:6 the dam. The mother bird.
22:12 fringes. Numbers 15:39 tells us that the fringes were to remind the Jewish people of "all the commandments of the LORD."
22:19 amerce. To punish by assessment or fine.

ing in the city; and the man, because
he hath humbled his neighbour's wife:
so thou shalt put away evil from among
you.
¶25But if a man find a betrothed damsel in the field, and the man force her,
and lie with her: then the man only that
lay with her shall die:
26But unto the damsel thou shalt do
nothing; *there is* in the damsel no sin
worthy of death: for as when a man
riseth against his neighbour, and
slayeth him, even so *is* this matter:
27For he found her in the field, *and*
the betrothed damsel cried, and *there*
was none to save her.
¶28If a man find a damsel *that is* a virgin, which is not betrothed, and lay hold
on her, and lie with her, and they be
found;
29Then the man that lay with her
shall give unto the damsel's father fifty
shekels of silver, and she shall be his
wife; because he hath humbled her, he
may not put her away all his days.
¶30A man shall not take his father's
wife, nor discover his father's skirt.

Various laws (continued)

23 He that is wounded in the
stones, or hath his privy mem-
ber cut off, shall not enter into the congregation of the LORD.
2A bastard shall not enter into the
congregation of the LORD; even to his
tenth generation shall he not enter into
the congregation of the LORD.
3An Ammonite or Moabite shall not
enter into the congregation of the
LORD; even to their tenth generation
shall they not enter into the congregation of the LORD for ever:
4Because they met you not with
bread and with water in the way, when
ye came forth out of Egypt; and because
they hired against thee *Balaam the son
of Beor of Pethor of Mesopotamia, to
curse thee.
5Nevertheless the LORD thy God
would not hearken unto Balaam; but the
LORD thy God turned the curse into a
blessing unto thee, because the LORD
thy God loved thee.
6Thou shalt not seek their peace nor
their prosperity all thy days for ever.
¶7Thou shalt not abhor an Edomite;
for he *is* thy brother: thou shalt not abhor an Egyptian; because thou wast a
stranger in his land.
8The children that are begotten of
them shall enter into the congregation
of the LORD in their third generation.
¶9When the host goeth forth against
thine enemies, then keep thee from
every wicked thing.
¶10If there be among you any man,
that is not *clean by reason of uncleanness that chanceth him by night, then
shall he go abroad out of the camp, he
shall not come within the camp:
11But it shall be, when evening
cometh on, he shall wash *himself* with
water: and when the sun is down, he
shall come into the camp *again*.
¶12Thou shalt have a place also without the camp, whither thou shalt go
forth abroad:
13And thou shalt have a paddle upon
thy weapon; and it shall be, when thou
wilt ease thyself abroad, thou shalt dig
therewith, and shalt turn back and cover that which cometh from thee:
14For the LORD thy God walketh in
the midst of thy camp, to deliver thee,
and to give up thine enemies before
thee; therefore shall thy camp be *holy:
that he see no *unclean thing in thee,
and turn away from thee.
¶15Thou shalt not deliver unto his
master the servant which is escaped
from his master unto thee:
16He shall dwell with thee, *even*
among you, in that place which he
shall choose in one of thy gates, where
it liketh him best: thou shalt not oppress him.

23:7 Edomite. A descendant of Esau.
23:16 liketh. To please.

¶17 There shall be no whore of the
daughters of *Israel, nor a sodomite of
the sons of Israel.
18 Thou shalt not bring the hire of a
whore, or the price of a dog, into the
house of the LORD thy God for any vow:
for even both these *are* abomination
unto the LORD thy God.
¶19 Thou shalt not lend upon *usury
to thy brother; usury of money, usury
of victuals, usury of any thing that is
lent upon usury:
20 Unto a stranger thou mayest lend
upon usury; but unto thy brother thou
shalt not lend upon usury: that the
LORD thy God may bless thee in all that
thou settest thine hand to in the land
whither thou goest to possess it.
¶21 When thou shalt vow a vow unto
the LORD thy God, thou shalt not slack
to pay it: for the LORD thy God will
surely require it of thee; and it would
be sin in thee.
22 But if thou shalt forbear to vow, it
shall be no sin in thee.
23 That which is gone out of thy lips
thou shalt keep and perform; *even* a
freewill-offering, according as thou
hast vowed unto the LORD thy God,
which thou hast promised with thy
mouth.
¶24 When thou comest into thy neighbour's vineyard, then thou mayest eat
grapes thy fill at thine own pleasure;
but thou shalt not put *any* in thy vessel.
25 When thou comest into the standing corn of thy neighbour, then thou
mayest pluck the ears with thine hand;
but thou shalt not move a sickle unto
thy neighbour's standing corn.

The law of divorce

24 When a man hath taken a wife,
and married her, and it come to
pass that she find no favour in his eyes,
because he hath found some uncleanness in her: then let him write her a bill
of divorcement, and give *it* in her hand,
and send her out of his house.
2 And when she is departed out of his
house, she may go and be another
man's *wife*.
3 And *if* the latter husband hate her,
and write her a bill of divorcement, and
giveth *it* in her hand, and sendeth her
out of his house; or if the latter husband
die, which took her *to be* his wife;
4 Her former husband, which sent her
away, may not take her again to be his
wife, after that she is defiled; for that
is abomination before the LORD: and
thou shalt not cause the land to sin,
which the LORD thy God giveth thee *for*
an inheritance.

Various laws

¶5 When a man hath taken a new wife,
he shall not go out to war, neither shall
he be charged with any business: *but* he
shall be free at home one year, and shall
cheer up his wife which he hath taken.
¶6 No man shall take the nether or the
upper millstone to pledge: for he taketh
a man's life to pledge.

24:6 The Millstone Rule
If one of the millstones were taken, the former owner could no longer run his mill to grind grain, and his means of making a living would be gone.

¶7 If a man be found stealing any of his
brethren of the children of Israel, and
maketh merchandise of him, or selleth
him; then that thief shall die; and thou
shalt put evil away from among you.
¶8 Take heed in the plague of *leprosy, that thou observe diligently, and do
according to all that the priests the
Levites shall teach you: as I commanded them, *so* ye shall observe to do.
9 Remember what the LORD thy God
did unto *Miriam by the way, after that
ye were come forth out of Egypt.

23:25 thou mayest pluck the ears. See Matthew 12:1-8; Mark 2:23-28; Luke 6:1-5.
24:1 a bill of divorcement. See Matthew 19:8 and 1 Corinthians 7:10-16 for Christ's explanation of this and for the Christian attitude toward divorce.

¶ 10 When thou dost lend thy brother
any thing, thou shalt not go into his
house to fetch his pledge.
11 Thou shalt stand abroad, and the
man to whom thou dost lend shall bring
out the pledge abroad unto thee.
12 And if the man *be* poor, thou shalt
not sleep with his pledge:
13 In any case thou shalt deliver him
the pledge again when the sun goeth
down, that he may sleep in his own raiment, and bless thee: and it shall be
*righteousness unto thee before the
LORD thy God.
¶ 14 Thou shalt not oppress an hired
servant *that is* poor and needy, *whether
he be* of thy brethren, or of thy strangers that *are* in thy land within thy
gates:
15 At his day thou shalt give *him* his
hire, neither shall the sun go down upon
it; for he *is* poor, and setteth his heart
upon it: lest he cry against thee unto
the LORD, and it be sin unto thee.
16 The fathers shall not be put to
death for the children, neither shall the
children be put to death for the fathers:
every man shall be put to death for his
own sin.
¶ 17 Thou shalt not pervert the judgment of the stranger, *nor* of the fatherless; nor take a widow's raiment to
pledge:
18 But thou shalt remember that thou
wast a bondman in Egypt, and the
LORD thy God *redeemed thee thence:
therefore I command thee to do this
thing.
¶ 19 When thou cuttest down thine
harvest in thy field, and hast forgot a
sheaf in the field, thou shalt not go again
to fetch it: it shall be for the stranger,
for the fatherless, and for the widow:
that the LORD thy God may bless thee
in all the work of thine hands.
20 When thou beatest thine olive tree,
thou shalt not go over the boughs again:
it shall be for the stranger, for the fatherless, and for the widow.
21 When thou gatherest the grapes of
thy vineyard, thou shalt not glean *it* afterward: it shall be for the stranger, for
the fatherless, and for the widow.
22 And thou shalt remember that thou
wast a bondman in the land of Egypt:
therefore I command thee to do this
thing.

Various laws (continued)

25 If there be a controversy between men, and they come unto
judgment, that *the judges* may judge
them; then they shall justify the righteous, and condemn the wicked.
2 And it shall be, if the wicked man *be*
worthy to be beaten, that the judge shall
cause him to lie down, and to be beat-
en before his face, according to his fault,
by a certain number.
3 Forty *stripes he may give him, *and*
not exceed: lest, *if* he should exceed,
and beat him above these with many
stripes, then thy brother should seem
vile unto thee.
¶ 4 Thou shalt not muzzle the ox when
he treadeth out *the corn.*
¶ 5 If brethren dwell together, and one
of them die, and have no child, the wife
of the dead shall not marry without unto
a stranger: her husband's brother shall
go in unto her, and take her to him to
wife, and perform the duty of an
husband's brother unto her.
6 And it shall be, *that* the firstborn
which she beareth shall succeed in the
name of his brother *which is* dead, that
his name be not put out of Israel.
7 And if the man like not to take his
brother's wife, then let his brother's
wife go up to the gate unto the *elders,
and say, My husband's brother refuseth
to raise up unto his brother a name in
Israel, he will not perform the duty of
my husband's brother.

24:19 When thou cuttest down thine harvest. See Ruth 2.
25:1 justify. To acquit or find innocent.
25:7 up to the gate. See Ruth 4:1.

8 Then the elders of his city shall call him, and speak unto him: and *if* he stand *to it,* and say, I like not to take her;

9 Then shall his brother's wife come unto him in the presence of the elders, and loose his shoe from off his foot, and spit in his face, and shall answer and say, So shall it be done unto that man that will not build up his brother's house.

10 And his name shall be called in Israel, The house of him that hath his shoe loosed.

¶ 11 When men strive together one with another, and the wife of the one draweth near for to deliver her husband out of the hand of him that smiteth him, and putteth forth her hand, and taketh him by the secrets:

12 Then thou shalt cut off her hand, thine eye shall not pity *her.*

¶ 13 Thou shalt not have in thy bag divers *weights, a great and a small.

14 Thou shalt not have in thine house divers measures, a great and a small.

15 *But* thou shalt have a *perfect and *just weight, a perfect and just measure shalt thou have: that thy days may be lengthened in the land which the LORD thy *God giveth thee.

16 For all that do such things, *and* all that do unrighteously, *are* an abomination unto the LORD thy God.

Amalek to be destroyed (1 Sam. 15:2,3)

¶ 17 Remember what *Amalek did unto thee by the way, when ye were come forth out of Egypt;

18 How he met thee by the way, and smote the hindmost of thee, *even* all *that were* feeble behind thee, when thou *wast* faint and weary; and he feared not God.

19 Therefore it shall be, when the LORD thy God hath given thee rest from all thine enemies round about, in the land which the LORD thy God giveth thee *for* an inheritance to possess it, *that* thou shalt blot out the remembrance of Amalek from under *heaven; thou shalt not forget *it.*

Firstfruits (Exod. 23:16-19)

26 And it shall be, when thou *art* come in unto the land which the LORD thy God giveth thee *for* an inheritance, and possessest it, and dwellest therein;

2 That thou shalt take of the first of all the fruit of the earth, which thou shalt bring of thy land that the LORD thy God giveth thee, and shalt put *it* in a basket, and shalt go unto the place which the LORD thy God shall choose to place his name there.

3 And thou shalt go unto the priest that shall be in those days, and say unto him, I profess this day unto the LORD thy God, that I am come unto the country which the LORD sware unto our fathers for to give us.

4 And the priest shall take the basket out of thine hand, and set it down before the *altar of the LORD thy God.

5 And thou shalt speak and say before the LORD thy God, A Syrian ready to perish *was* my father, and he went down into *Egypt, and sojourned there with a few, and became there a nation, great, mighty, and populous:

6 And the Egyptians evil entreated us, and afflicted us, and laid upon us hard bondage:

7 And when we cried unto the LORD God of our fathers, the LORD heard our voice, and looked on our affliction, and our labour, and our oppression:

8 And the LORD brought us forth out of Egypt with a mighty hand, and with an outstretched arm, and with great terribleness, and with signs, and with wonders:

9 And he hath brought us into this place, and hath given us this land, *even* a land that *floweth with milk and honey.

25:8 stand to. To agree to or abide by.

26:5 A Syrian. Jacob, the father or ancestor of the Israelites, fled into Syria to escape the anger of his brother Esau (Gen. 28:5; Hos.12:12).

10 And now, behold, I have brought
the firstfruits of the land, which thou,
O LORD, hast given me. And thou shalt
set it before the LORD thy God, and
worship before the LORD thy God:
11 And thou shalt rejoice in every
good *thing* which the LORD thy God
hath given unto thee, and unto thine
house, thou, and the Levite, and the
stranger that *is* among you.

The prayer

¶ 12 When thou hast made an end of
tithing all the *tithes of thine increase
the third year, *which is* the year of tithing, and hast given *it* unto the Levite,
the stranger, the fatherless, and the
widow, that they may eat within thy
gates, and be filled;
13 Then thou shalt say before the
LORD thy God, I have brought away the
hallowed things out of *mine* house, and
also have given them unto the Levite,
and unto the stranger, to the fatherless,
and to the widow, according to all thy
commandments which thou hast commanded me: I have not transgressed
thy commandments, neither have I forgotten *them:*
14 I have not eaten thereof in my
*mourning, neither have I taken away
ought thereof for *any* unclean *use,* nor
given *ought* thereof for the dead: *but* I
have hearkened to the voice of the
LORD my God, *and* have done according to all that thou hast commanded me.
15 Look down from thy holy habitation, from heaven, and bless thy people
Israel, and the land which thou hast
given us, as thou swarest unto our fathers, a land that floweth with milk and
honey.

The promise

¶ 16 This day the LORD thy God hath
commanded thee to do these statutes
and judgments: thou shalt therefore
keep and do them with all thine heart,
and with all thy soul.
17 Thou hast avouched the LORD
this day to be thy God, and to walk in
his ways, and to keep his statutes, and
his commandments, and his judgments,
and to hearken unto his voice:
18 And the LORD hath avouched thee
this day to be his *peculiar people, as
he hath promised thee, and that *thou*
shouldest keep all his commandments;
19 And to make thee high above all
nations which he hath made, in praise,
and in name, and in honour; and that
thou mayest be an holy people unto the
LORD thy God, as he hath spoken.

IV. Moses' Third Speech (27:1—28:68)

27 And *Moses with the elders of
Israel commanded the people,
saying, Keep all the commandments
which I command you this day.
2 And it shall be on the day when ye
shall pass over Jordan unto the land
which the LORD thy God giveth thee,
that thou shalt set thee up great stones,
and plaister them with plaister:
3 And thou shalt write upon them all
the words of this *law, when thou art
passed over, that thou mayest go in
unto the land which the LORD thy God
giveth thee, a land that floweth with
milk and honey; as the LORD God of thy
fathers hath promised thee.
4 Therefore it shall be when ye be
gone over Jordan, *that* ye shall set up
these stones, which I command you
this day, in mount Ebal, and thou shalt
plaister them with plaister.
5 And there shalt thou build an altar
unto the LORD thy God, an altar of
stones: thou shalt not lift up *any* iron
tool upon them.
6 Thou shalt build the altar of the
LORD thy God of whole stones: and thou

26:17 avouched. Declared.
27:2 thou shalt set thee up great stones. This was done in Joshua 8:31. See also Deuteronomy 11:29.
27:2 plaister. Plaster.

shalt offer burnt-offerings thereon unto
the LORD thy God:
7 And thou shalt offer *peace-offerings,
and shalt eat there, and rejoice before
the LORD thy God.
8 And thou shalt write upon the
stones all the words of this law very
plainly.

Blessings and curses

¶ 9 And Moses and the priests the Levites spake unto all Israel, saying, Take
heed, and hearken, O Israel; this day
thou art become the people of the LORD
thy God.
10 Thou shalt therefore obey the voice
of the LORD thy God, and do his commandments and his statutes, which I
command thee this day.
¶ 11 And Moses charged the people
the same day, saying,
12 These shall stand upon mount Gerizim to bless the people, when ye are
come over Jordan; Simeon, and Levi,
and *Judah, and Issachar, and *Joseph,
and Benjamin:
13 And these shall stand upon mount
Ebal to curse; Reuben, Gad, and Asher,
and Zebulun, Dan, and Naphtali.
¶ 14 And the Levites shall speak, and
say unto all the men of Israel with a loud
voice,
15 Cursed *be* the man that maketh *any*
graven or molten image, an abomination unto the LORD, the work of the
hands of the craftsman, and putteth *it*
in *a* secret *place.* And all the people shall
answer and say, Amen.
16 Cursed *be* he that setteth light by
his father or his mother. And all the
people shall say, Amen.
17 Cursed *be* he that removeth his
neighbour's *landmark. And all the
people shall say, Amen.
18 Cursed *be* he that maketh the blind
to wander out of the way. And all the
people shall say, Amen.
19 Cursed *be* he that perverteth the
judgment of the stranger, fatherless,
and widow. And all the people shall say,
Amen.
20 Cursed *be* he that lieth with his
father's wife; because he uncovereth
his father's skirt. And all the people
shall say, Amen.
21 Cursed *be* he that lieth with any
manner of beast. And all the people
shall say, Amen.
22 Cursed *be* he that lieth with his sister, the daughter of his father, or the
daughter of his mother. And all the people shall say, Amen.
23 Cursed *be* he that lieth with his
mother in law. And all the people shall
say, Amen.
24 Cursed *be* he that smiteth his
neighbour secretly. And all the people
shall say, Amen.
25 Cursed *be* he that taketh *reward to
slay an innocent person. And all the
people shall say, Amen.
26 Cursed *be* he that confirmeth not *all*
the words of this law to do them. And
all the people shall say, Amen.

Conditions of blessing

28 And it shall come to pass, if
thou shalt hearken diligently
unto the voice of the LORD thy God, to
observe *and* to do all his commandments which I command thee this day,
that the LORD thy God will set thee on
high above all nations of the earth:
2 And all these blessings shall come
on thee, and overtake thee, if thou shalt
hearken unto the voice of the LORD thy
God.
3 Blessed *shalt* thou *be* in the city, and
blessed *shalt* thou *be* in the field.
4 Blessed *shall be* the fruit of thy body,
and the fruit of thy ground, and the fruit
of thy cattle, the increase of thy kine,
and the flocks of thy sheep.
5 Blessed *shall be* thy basket and thy
store.
6 Blessed *shalt* thou *be* when thou
comest in, and blessed *shalt* thou *be*
when thou goest out.

27:15 Amen. So be it; it is true.

7 The LORD shall cause thine enemies
that rise up against thee to be smitten
before thy face: they shall come out
against thee one way, and flee before
thee seven ways.
8 The LORD shall command the blessing upon thee in thy storehouses, and
in all that thou settest thine hand unto;
and he shall bless thee in the land which
the LORD thy God giveth thee.
9 The LORD shall establish thee an
holy people unto himself, as he hath
sworn unto thee, if thou shalt keep the
commandments of the LORD thy God,
and walk in his ways.
10 And all people of the earth shall see
that thou art called by the name of the
LORD; and they shall be afraid of thee.
11 And the LORD shall make thee plenteous in goods, in the fruit of thy body,
and in the fruit of thy cattle, and in the
fruit of thy ground, in the land which the
LORD sware unto thy fathers to give thee.
12 The LORD shall open unto thee his
good treasure, the heaven to give the
rain unto thy land in his season, and to
bless all the work of thine hand: and
thou shalt lend unto many nations, and
thou shalt not borrow.
13 And the LORD shall make thee the
head, and not the tail; and thou shalt be
above only, and thou shalt not be beneath; if that thou hearken unto the
commandments of the LORD thy God,
which I command thee this day, to observe and to do *them:*
14 And thou shalt not go aside from
any of the words which I command thee
this day, *to* the right hand, or *to* the left,
to go after other gods to serve them.

Results of disobedience

¶ 15 But it shall come to pass, if thou
wilt not hearken unto the voice of the
LORD thy God, to observe to do all his
commandments and his statutes which
I command thee this day; that all these
curses shall come upon thee, and overtake thee:
16 Cursed *shalt* thou *be* in the city, and
cursed *shalt* thou *be* in the field.
17 Cursed *shall be* thy basket and thy
store.
18 Cursed *shall be* the fruit of thy body,
and the fruit of thy land, the increase of
thy kine, and the flocks of thy sheep.
19 Cursed *shalt* thou *be* when thou
comest in, and cursed *shalt* thou *be*
when thou goest out.
20 The LORD shall send upon thee
cursing, vexation, and rebuke, in all that
thou settest thine hand unto for to do,
until thou be destroyed, and until thou
perish quickly; because of the wickedness of thy doings, whereby thou hast
forsaken me.
21 The LORD shall make the pestilence cleave unto thee, until he have
consumed thee from off the land,
whither thou goest to possess it.
22 The LORD shall smite thee with a
consumption, and with a fever, and
with an inflammation, and with an
extreme burning, and with the sword,
and with blasting, and with mildew;
and they shall pursue thee until thou
perish.
23 And thy heaven that *is* over thy
head shall be brass, and the earth that
is under thee *shall be* iron.
24 The LORD shall make the rain of thy
land powder and dust: from heaven
shall it come down upon thee, until thou
be destroyed.
25 The LORD shall cause thee to be
smitten before thine enemies: thou
shalt go out one way against them, and
flee seven ways before them: and shalt

28:13 the head, and not the tail. Read Isaiah 9:14-15.
28:15 it shall come to pass. All these terrible disasters, some of them happening even to this day, did come to pass for the Israelites when they forgot God and worshipped idols.
28:22 blasting. Blight, deteriorate, or affect badly.
28:23 brass . . . iron. The sky and the earth would seem like this because the rain supply would be cut off, so that instead of rain they would have powder and dust (vs. 24).

be removed into all the kingdoms of the earth.

26 And thy carcase shall be meat unto all fowls of the air, and unto the beasts of the earth, and no man shall fray *them* away.

27 The LORD will smite thee with the botch of Egypt, and with the *emerods, and with the scab, and with the itch, whereof thou canst not be healed.

28 The LORD shall smite thee with madness, and blindness, and astonishment of heart:

29 And thou shalt grope at noonday, as the blind gropeth in darkness, and thou shalt not prosper in thy ways: and thou shalt be only oppressed and spoiled evermore, and no man shall save *thee.*

30 Thou shalt betroth a wife, and another man shall lie with her: thou shalt build an house, and thou shalt not dwell therein: thou shalt plant a vineyard, and shalt not gather the grapes thereof.

31 Thine ox *shall be* slain before thine eyes, and thou shalt not eat thereof: thine ass *shall be* violently taken away from before thy face, and shall not be restored to thee: thy sheep *shall be* given unto thine enemies, and thou shalt have none to rescue *them.*

32 Thy sons and thy daughters *shall be* given unto another people, and thine eyes shall look, and fail *with longing* for them all the day long: and *there shall be* no might in thine hand.

33 The fruit of thy land, and all thy labours, shall a nation which thou knowest not eat up; and thou shalt be only oppressed and crushed alway:

34 So that thou shalt be mad for the sight of thine eyes which thou shalt see.

35 The LORD shall smite thee in the knees, and in the legs, with a sore botch that cannot be healed, from the sole of thy foot unto the top of thy head.

36 The LORD shall bring thee, and thy king which thou shalt set over thee, unto a nation which neither thou nor thy fathers have known; and there shalt thou serve other gods, wood and stone.

37 And thou shalt become an astonishment, a proverb, and a byword, among all nations whither the LORD shall lead thee.

38 Thou shalt carry much seed out into the field, and shalt gather *but* little in; for the locust shall consume it.

39 Thou shalt plant vineyards, and dress *them,* but shalt neither drink *of* the wine, nor gather *the grapes;* for the worms shall eat them.

40 Thou shalt have olive trees throughout all thy coasts, but thou shalt not *anoint *thyself* with the *oil; for thine olive shall cast *his fruit.*

41 Thou shalt beget sons and daughters, but thou shalt not enjoy them; for they shall go into captivity.

42 All thy trees and fruit of thy land shall the locust consume.

43 The stranger that *is* within thee shall get up above thee very high; and thou shalt come down very low.

44 He shall lend to thee, and thou shalt not lend to him: he shall be the head, and thou shalt be the tail.

45 Moreover all these curses shall come upon thee, and shall pursue thee, and overtake thee, till thou be destroyed; because thou hearkenedst not unto the voice of the LORD thy God, to keep his commandments and his statutes which he commanded thee:

46 And they shall be upon thee for a sign and for a wonder, and upon thy seed for ever.

28:36 A Prophecy
This prophecy was fulfilled for the children of Israel, who lived in the northern part of Palestine, and were called Israel, when the king of Assyria carried the people and their king away to his country (2 Kings 17:3-8); and for Judah, who lived in the southern part of Palestine, when the king of Babylon made them his captives (2 Kings 24:11-16).

28:26 fray. To scare, frighten away.
28:27 botch. Eruption of the skin, a boil.

47 Because thou servedst not the
LORD thy God with joyfulness, and with
gladness of heart, for the abundance of
all *things;*
48 Therefore shalt thou serve thine
enemies which the LORD shall send
against thee, in hunger, and in thirst, and
in nakedness, and in want of all *things:*
and he shall put a yoke of iron upon thy
neck, until he have destroyed thee.
49 The LORD shall bring a nation
against thee from far, from the end of
the earth, *as swift* as the eagle flieth; a
nation whose tongue thou shalt not
understand;

28:49 Another Prophecy
It is thought that this refers to the Roman Empire, whose emblem was the eagle and whose language, Latin, the Jews did not know. They ruled Palestine from 63 B.C. and, after a rebellion, destroyed Jerusalem in A.D. 70.

50 A nation of fierce countenance,
which shall not regard the person of the
old, nor shew favour to the young:
51 And he shall eat the fruit of thy cattle, and the fruit of thy land, until thou
be destroyed: which *also* shall not leave
thee *either* corn, wine, or oil, *or* the increase of thy kine, or flocks of thy
sheep, until he have destroyed thee.
52 And he shall besiege thee in all thy
gates, until thy high and fenced walls
come down, wherein thou trustedst,
throughout all thy land: and he shall
besiege thee in all thy gates throughout all thy land, which the LORD thy
God hath given thee.
53 And thou shalt eat the fruit of thine
own body, the flesh of thy sons and of
thy daughters, which the LORD thy God
hath given thee, in the siege, and in the
straitness, wherewith thine enemies
shall distress thee:
54 *So that* the man *that is* tender
among you, and very delicate, his eye
shall be evil toward his brother, and toward the wife of his bosom, and toward
the remnant of his children which he
shall leave:
55 So that he will not give to any of
them of the flesh of his children whom
he shall eat: because he hath nothing
left him in the siege, and in the straitness, wherewith thine enemies shall
distress thee in all thy gates.
56 The tender and delicate woman
among you, which would not adventure
to set the sole of her foot upon the
ground for delicateness and tenderness, her eye shall be evil toward the
husband of her bosom, and toward her
son, and toward her daughter,
57 And toward her young one that
cometh out from between her feet, and
toward her children which she shall
bear: for she shall eat them for want of
all *things* secretly in the siege and
straitness, wherewith thine enemy
shall distress thee in thy gates.
58 If thou wilt not observe to do all the
words of this law that are written in this
book, that thou mayest *fear this glorious and fearful name, THE LORD
THY GOD;
59 Then the LORD will make thy
plagues wonderful, and the plagues of
thy seed, *even* great plagues, and of long
continuance, and sore sicknesses, and
of long continuance.
60 Moreover he will bring upon thee
all the diseases of Egypt, which thou
wast afraid of; and they shall cleave
unto thee.
61 Also every sickness, and every
plague, which *is* not written in the book
of this law, them will the LORD bring
upon thee, until thou be destroyed.
62 And ye shall be left few in number,
whereas ye were as the stars of heaven

28:51 kine. Cows.
28:52 And he shall besiege thee. Verses 52-57 describe some of the horrors of the siege.
28:53 straitness. Scarcity of food, severe famine.
28:56 adventure. To venture.

for multitude; because thou wouldest
not obey the voice of the LORD thy God.
63And it shall come to pass, *that* as
the LORD rejoiced over you to do you
good, and to multiply you; so the LORD
will rejoice over you to destroy you, and
to bring you to nought; and ye shall be
plucked from off the land whither thou
goest to possess it.
64And the LORD shall scatter thee
among all people, from the one end of
the earth even unto the other; and there
thou shalt serve other gods, which neither thou nor thy fathers have known,
even wood and stone.

28:64 A Final Prophecy
The final fulfillment of this prophecy was after the destruction of Jerusalem in A.D. 70 when the Jews were driven from their country. They have been scattered throughout the world ever since.

65And among these nations shalt
thou find no ease, neither shall the
sole of thy foot have rest: but the
LORD shall give thee there a trembling heart, and failing of eyes, and
sorrow of mind:
66And thy life shall hang in doubt before thee; and thou shalt fear day and
night, and shalt have none *assurance
of thy life:
67In the morning thou shalt say,
Would God it were even! and at even
thou shalt say, Would God it were
morning! for the fear of thine heart
wherewith thou shalt fear, and for
the sight of thine eyes which thou
shalt see.
68And the LORD shall bring thee
into Egypt again with ships, by the
way whereof I spake unto thee, Thou
shalt see it no more again: and there
ye shall be sold unto your enemies for
bondmen and bondwomen, and no
man shall buy *you*.

V. The Palestinan Covenant (29:1—30:20)
The Sixth Covenant

29 These *are* the *words of the
covenant, which the LORD commanded Moses to make with the children of *Israel in the land of *Moab,
beside the covenant which he made
with them in *Horeb.

29:1 The Palestinian Covenant
A *covenant is an agreement between two or more parties. Here God made a covenant with the Israelites about the terms on which they were to enter the land of Palestine. Their history shows how they broke the covenant and lost the land. The covenant also said that if they repented, they would be restored to the land and to prosperity. This is still to be fulfilled in the future.

An appeal to Israel

¶2And Moses called unto all Israel,
and said unto them, Ye have seen all that
the LORD did before your eyes in the
land of Egypt unto *Pharaoh, and unto
all his servants, and unto all his land;
3The great temptations which thine
eyes have seen, the signs, and those
great *miracles:
4Yet the LORD hath not given you an
heart to perceive, and eyes to see, and
ears to hear, unto this day.
5And I have led you forty years in the
wilderness: your clothes are not waxen
old upon you, and thy shoe is not waxen
old upon thy foot.
6Ye have not eaten bread, neither
have ye drunk wine or strong drink:
that ye might know that I *am* the LORD
your God.
7And when ye came unto this place,
Sihon the king of Heshbon, and Og the
king of *Bashan, came out against us
unto battle, and we smote them:
8And we took their land, and gave it
for an inheritance unto the Reubenites,
and to the Gadites, and to the half tribe
of *Manasseh.

28:68 into Egypt again. When Titus besieged Rome in A.D. 70, thousands of Israelites were sent down into Egypt as slaves.
29:4 the LORD hath not given you an heart. Read 2 Corinthians 3:14-16.

[9]Keep therefore the words of this
covenant, and do them, that ye may
prosper in all that ye do.
¶[10]Ye stand this day all of you before
the LORD your God; your captains of
your tribes, your elders, and your officers, *with* all the men of Israel,
[11]Your little ones, your wives, and thy
stranger that *is* in thy camp, from the
hewer of thy wood unto the drawer of
thy water:
[12]That thou shouldest enter into covenant with the LORD thy God, and into
his oath, which the LORD thy God
maketh with thee this day:
[13]That he may establish thee to day
for a people unto himself, and *that* he
may be unto thee a God, as he hath said
unto thee, and as he hath sworn unto
thy fathers, to *Abraham, to *Isaac, and
to *Jacob.
[14]Neither with you only do I make
this covenant and this oath;
[15]But with *him* that standeth here
with us this day before the LORD our
God, and also with *him* that *is* not here
with us this day:
[16](For ye know how we have dwelt in
the land of Egypt; and how we came
through the nations which ye passed
by;
[17]And ye have seen their abominations, and their idols, wood and stone,
*silver and gold, which *were* among
them:)

Warning against unbelief

[18]Lest there should be among you
man, or woman, or family, or tribe,
whose heart turneth away this day from
the LORD our God, to go *and* serve the
gods of these nations; lest there should
be among you a root that beareth gall
and wormwood;
[19]And it come to pass, when he
heareth the words of this curse, that he
bless himself in his heart, saying, I shall
have peace, though I walk in the imagination of mine heart, to add drunkenness to thirst:
[20]The LORD will not spare him, but
then the anger of the LORD and his jealousy shall smoke against that man, and
all the curses that are written in this
book shall lie upon him, and the LORD
shall blot out his name from under
heaven.
[21]And the LORD shall separate him
unto evil out of all the tribes of Israel,
according to all the curses of the covenant that are written in this book of
the law:
[22]So that the generation to come of
your children that shall rise up after
you, and the stranger that shall come
from a far land, shall say, when they
see the plagues of that land, and the
sicknesses which the LORD hath laid
upon it;
[23]*And that* the whole land thereof *is*
brimstone, and salt, *and* burning, *that*
it is not sown, nor beareth, nor any
grass groweth therein, like the overthrow of Sodom, and Gomorrah, Admah, and Zeboim, which the LORD
overthrew in his anger, and in his wrath:
[24]Even all nations shall say, Wherefore hath the LORD done thus unto this
land? what *meaneth* the heat of this
great anger?
[25]Then men shall say, Because they
have forsaken the covenant of the LORD
God of their fathers, which he made
with them when he brought them forth
out of the land of Egypt:
[26]For they went and served other
gods, and worshipped them, gods
whom they knew not, and *whom* he had
not given unto them:
[27]And the anger of the LORD was

29:18 gall and wormwood. These refer to poison: An idol worshipper in the tribe would be likely to turn many others aside from the worship of the true God, and so would be a poisonous root in the land. Read Hebrews 12:15.

29:23 Sodom, and Gomorrah. See the story in Genesis 19. The other two places, Admah and Zeboim, were cities nearby that were destroyed at the same time.

kindled against this land, to bring upon it all the curses that are written in this book:

28 And the LORD rooted them out of their land in anger, and in wrath, and in great indignation, and cast them into another land, as *it is* this day.

29 The secret *things belong* unto the LORD our God: but those *things which are* revealed *belong* unto us and to our children for ever, that *we* may do all the words of this law.

Terms of the covenant

30 And it shall come to pass, when all these things are come upon thee, the blessing and the curse, which I have set before thee, and thou shalt call *them* to mind among all the nations, whither the LORD thy God hath driven thee,

> **30:1-10 Terms of the Agreement**
> There are four points to note in this agreement:
> 1. If the children of Israel were disobedient, they would be scattered.
> 2. If they repented when scattered, God would hear them.
> 3. They would return to the land (vss. 3-8).
> 4. They would prosper (vss. 9-10).
>
> The future of the Jews is explained by Paul in Romans 10 and 11.

2 And shalt return unto the LORD thy God, and shalt obey his voice according to all that I command thee this day, thou and thy children, with all thine heart, and with all thy soul;

3 That then the LORD thy God will turn thy captivity, and have compassion upon thee, and will return and gather thee from all the nations, whither the LORD thy God hath scattered thee.

4 If *any* of thine be driven out unto the outmost *parts* of heaven, from thence will the LORD thy God gather thee, and from thence will he fetch thee:

5 And the LORD thy God will bring thee into the land which thy fathers possessed, and thou shalt possess it; and he will do thee good, and multiply thee above thy fathers.

6 And the LORD thy God will circumcise thine heart, and the heart of thy seed, to love the LORD thy God with all thine heart, and with all thy soul, that thou mayest live.

7 And the LORD thy God will put all these curses upon thine enemies, and on them that hate thee, which persecuted thee.

8 And thou shalt return and obey the voice of the LORD, and do all his commandments which I command thee this day.

9 And the LORD thy God will make thee plenteous in every work of thine hand, in the fruit of thy body, and in the fruit of thy cattle, and in the fruit of thy land, for good: for the LORD will again rejoice over thee for good, as he rejoiced over thy fathers:

10 If thou shalt hearken unto the voice of the LORD thy God, to keep his commandments and his statutes which are written in this book of the law, *and* if thou turn unto the LORD thy God with all thine heart, and with all thy soul.

Final warning and appeal

¶ 11 For this commandment which I command thee this day, it *is* not hidden from thee, neither *is* it far off.

12 It *is* not in heaven, that thou shouldest say, Who shall go up for us to heaven, and bring it unto us, that we may hear it, and do it?

13 Neither *is* it beyond the sea, that thou shouldest say, Who shall go over the sea for us, and bring it unto us, that we may hear it, and do it?

14 But the word *is* very nigh unto thee, in thy mouth, and in thy heart, that thou mayest do it.

¶ 15 See, I have set before thee this day life and good, and *death and evil;

16 In that I command thee this day to love the LORD thy God, to walk in his ways, and to keep his commandments and his statutes and his judgments, that thou mayest live and multiply: and the

LORD thy God shall bless thee in the
land whither thou goest to possess it.
17But if thine heart turn away, so that
thou wilt not hear, but shalt be drawn
away, and worship other gods, and
serve them;
18I denounce unto you this day, that
ye shall surely perish, *and that* ye shall
not prolong *your* days upon the land,
whither thou passest over Jordan to go
to possess it.
19I call heaven and earth to record
this day against you, *that* I have set
before you life and death, blessing and
cursing: therefore choose life, that both
thou and thy seed may live:
20That thou mayest love the LORD
thy God, *and* that thou mayest obey his
voice, and that thou mayest cleave unto
him: for he *is* thy life, and the length of
thy days: that thou mayest dwell in the
land which the LORD sware unto thy
fathers, to Abraham, to Isaac, and to
Jacob, to give them.

VI. Moses' Last Speech (31:1—33:29)

31 And Moses went and spake
these words unto all Israel.
2And he said unto them, I *am* an hundred and twenty years old this day; I can
no more go out and come in: also the
LORD hath said unto me, Thou shalt not
go over this Jordan.
3The LORD thy *God, he will go over
before thee, *and* he will destroy these
nations from before thee, and thou shalt
possess them: *and* *Joshua, he shall go
over before thee, as the LORD hath said.
4And the LORD shall do unto them as
he did to Sihon and to Og, kings of the
Amorites, and unto the land of them,
whom he destroyed.
5And the LORD shall give them up
before your face, that ye may do unto
them according unto all the commandments which I have commanded you.
6Be strong and of a good courage,
fear not, nor be afraid of them: for the
LORD thy God, he *it is* that doth go with
thee; he will not fail thee, nor forsake
thee.

To Joshua

¶7And Moses called unto Joshua, and
said unto him in the sight of all Israel,
Be strong and of a good courage: for
thou must go with this people unto the
land which the LORD hath sworn unto
their fathers to give them; and thou
shalt cause them to inherit it.
8And the LORD, he *it is* that doth go
before thee; he will be with thee, he will
not fail thee, neither forsake thee: fear
not, neither be dismayed.

To the priests

¶9And Moses wrote this law, and delivered it unto the priests the sons
of Levi, which bare the *ark of the
covenant of the LORD, and unto all the
*elders of Israel.
10And Moses commanded them, saying, At the end of *every* seven years, in
the solemnity of the year of release, in
the feast of tabernacles,
11When all Israel is come to appear
before the LORD thy God in the place
which he shall choose, thou shalt read
this law before all Israel in their hearing.
12Gather the people together, men,
and women, and children, and thy
stranger that *is* within thy gates, that
they may hear, and that they may learn,
and fear the LORD your God, and observe to do all the words of this law:
13And *that* their children, which have
not known *any thing,* may hear, and
learn to fear the LORD your God, as long
as ye live in the land whither ye go over
Jordan to possess it.

A last warning from God Himself

¶14And the LORD said unto Moses,
Behold, thy days approach that thou
must die: call Joshua, and present yourselves in the *tabernacle of the congregation, that I may give him a charge.
And Moses and Joshua went, and presented themselves in the tabernacle of
the congregation.
15And the LORD appeared in the tabernacle in a *pillar of a cloud: and the

pillar of the cloud stood over the door of the tabernacle.

¶16 And the LORD said unto Moses, Behold, thou shalt sleep with thy fathers; and this people will rise up, and go a whoring after the gods of the strangers of the land, whither they go *to be* among them, and will forsake me, and break my covenant which I have made with them.

17 Then my anger shall be kindled against them in that day, and I will forsake them, and I will hide my face from them, and they shall be devoured, and many evils and troubles shall befall them; so that they will say in that day, Are not these evils come upon us, because our God *is* not among us?

18 And I will surely hide my face in that day for all the evils which they shall have wrought, in that they are turned unto other gods.

19 Now therefore write ye this song for you, and teach it the children of Israel: put it in their mouths, that this song may be a witness for me against the children of Israel.

20 For when I shall have brought them into the land which I sware unto their fathers, that *floweth with milk and honey; and they shall have eaten and filled themselves, and waxen fat; then will they turn unto other gods, and serve them, and provoke me, and break my covenant.

21 And it shall come to pass, when many evils and troubles are befallen them, that this song shall testify against them as a witness; for it shall not be forgotten out of the mouths of their seed: for I know their imagination which they go about, even now, before I have brought them into the land which I sware.

To the Levites

¶22 Moses therefore wrote this song the same day, and taught it the children of Israel.

23 And he gave Joshua the son of Nun a charge, and said, Be strong and of a good courage: for thou shalt bring the children of Israel into the land which I sware unto them: and I will be with thee.

¶24 And it came to pass, when Moses had made an end of writing the words of this law in a book, until they were finished,

25 That Moses commanded the Levites, which bare the ark of the covenant of the LORD, saying,

26 Take this book of the law, and put it in the side of the ark of the covenant of the LORD your God, that it may be there for a witness against thee.

27 For I know thy rebellion, and thy stiff neck: behold, while I am yet alive with you this day, ye have been rebellious against the LORD; and how much more after my death?

¶28 Gather unto me all the elders of your tribes, and your officers, that I may speak these words in their ears, and call *heaven and earth to record against them.

29 For I know that after my death ye will utterly corrupt *yourselves,* and turn aside from the way which I have commanded you; and evil will befall you in the latter days; because ye will do evil in the sight of the LORD, to provoke him to anger through the work of your hands.

30 And Moses spake in the ears of all the congregation of Israel the words of this song, until they were ended.

The Song of Moses

32 Give ear, O ye heavens, and I will speak; and hear, O earth, the words of my mouth.

2 My *doctrine shall drop as the rain, my speech shall distil as the dew, as the small rain upon the tender herb, and as the showers upon the grass:

3 Because I will publish the name of the LORD: ascribe ye greatness unto our God.

31:20 covenant. See 29:1 note.
31:24 the words of this law. See *inspiration.

4*He is* the *Rock, his work *is* perfect:
for all his ways *are* *judgment: a God of
truth and without iniquity, *just and
right *is* he.
5They have corrupted themselves,
their spot *is* not *the spot* of his children:
they are a perverse and crooked generation.
6Do ye thus requite the LORD, O foolish people and unwise? *is* not he thy
father *that* hath bought thee? hath he
not made thee, and established thee?
¶7Remember the days of old, consider the years of many generations: ask
thy father, and he will shew thee; thy
elders, and they will tell thee.
8When the most High divided to the
nations their inheritance, when he separated the sons of *Adam, he set the
bounds of the people according to the
number of the children of Israel.
9For the LORD'S portion *is* his people;
Jacob *is* the lot of his inheritance.
10He found him in a desert land, and
in the waste howling wilderness; he led
him about, he instructed him, he kept
him as the *apple of his eye.
11As an eagle stirreth up her nest,
fluttereth over her young, spreadeth
abroad her wings, taketh them, beareth
them on her wings:
12*So* the LORD alone did lead him,
and *there was* no strange god with him.
13He made him ride on the high
places of the earth, that he might eat
the increase of the fields; and he made
him to suck honey out of the rock, and
oil out of the flinty rock;
14Butter of kine, and milk of sheep,
with fat of lambs, and rams of the breed
of Bashan, and goats, with the fat of kidneys of wheat; and thou didst drink the
pure blood of the grape.
¶15But *Jeshurun waxed fat, and
kicked: thou art waxen fat, thou art
grown thick, thou art covered *with fatness;* then he forsook God *which* made
him, and lightly esteemed the Rock of
his *salvation.
16They provoked him to jealousy
with strange *gods,* with abominations
provoked they him to anger.
17They sacrificed unto devils, not to
God; to gods whom they knew not, to
new *gods that* came newly up, whom
your fathers feared not.

32:11 The Eagle Comparison
This is a wonderful illustration of God's loving care for His people by comparing His loving, watchful eye with that of the eagle for her young (Exod. 19:4; Ruth 2:12). Read Psalms 17:8; 36:7; 57:1; 61:4; 63:7; 91:1,4; Matthew 23:37.

32:1 SONGS OF THE BIBLE

Who sang	Occasion	Reference
Moses and Miriam	after crossing the Red Sea	Exodus 15:1
Israelites	upon reaching the well at Beer	Numbers 21:17
Moses	to help remember Israel's history	Deuteronomy 32
Deborah and Barak	at the defeat of a Canaanite king	Judges 5
Hannah	upon presenting Samuel to the Lord	1 Samuel 2
David	at his deliverance from his enemies and Saul	2 Samuel 22
Mary	at her visit with Elisabeth	Luke 1:46-55
Zacharias	at the naming of his son, John	Luke 1:68-79
Angels	at the birth of Jesus	Luke 2:13
Simeon	at seeing the Christ child	Luke 2:29
Creatures and elders in heaven	at the opening of the scroll	Revelation 5:9; 19:1

32:10 the apple of his eye. See Zechariah 2:8 note. See also Psalm 17:8.
32:15 Jeshurun. This name means *the upright one;* it is used as a name for Israel.
32:17 devils. Demons.

18Of the Rock *that* begat thee thou art
unmindful, and hast forgotten God that
formed thee.
19And when the LORD saw *it,* he abhorred *them,* because of the provoking
of his sons, and of his daughters.
20And he said, I will hide my face from
them, I will see what their end *shall be:*
for they *are* a very *froward generation,
children in whom *is* no *faith.
21They have moved me to jealousy
with *that which is* not God; they have
provoked me to anger with their vanities: and I will move them to jealousy
with *those which are* not a people; I will
provoke them to anger with a foolish
nation.
22For a *fire is kindled in mine anger,
and shall burn unto the lowest *hell,
and shall consume the earth with her
increase, and set on fire the foundations
of the mountains.
23I will heap mischiefs upon them; I
will spend mine arrows upon them.
24*They shall be* burnt with hunger, and
devoured with burning heat, and with
bitter destruction: I will also send the
teeth of beasts upon them, with the
poison of serpents of the dust.
25The sword without, and terror
within, shall destroy both the young
man and the virgin, the suckling *also*
with the man of gray hairs.
26I said, I would *scatter them into
corners, I would make the remembrance of them to cease from among
men:
27Were it not that I feared the wrath
of the enemy, lest their adversaries
should behave themselves strangely,
and lest they should say, Our hand *is*
high, and the LORD hath not done all
this.
28For they *are* a nation void of counsel, neither *is there any* understanding
in them.
29O that they were wise, *that* they
understood this, *that* they would consider their latter end!
30How should one chase a thousand,
and two put ten thousand to flight, except their Rock had sold them, and the
LORD had shut them up?
31For their rock *is* not as our Rock,
even our enemies themselves *being*
judges.
32For their vine *is* of the vine of Sodom, and of the fields of Gomorrah: their
grapes *are* grapes of gall, their clusters
are bitter:
33Their wine *is* the poison of dragons,
and the cruel venom of asps.
34*Is* not this laid up in store with me,
and sealed up among my treasures?
35To me *belongeth* vengeance, and
recompence; their foot shall slide in *due*
time: for the day of their calamity *is* at
hand, and the things that shall come
upon them make haste.
36For the LORD shall judge his people, and repent himself for his servants, when he seeth that *their* power
is gone, and *there is* none shut up, or
left.
37And he shall say, Where *are* their
gods, *their* rock in whom they trusted,
38Which did eat the fat of their sacrifices, *and* drank the wine of their drink-
offerings? let them rise up and help you,
and be your protection.
39See now that I, *even* I, *am* he, and
there is no god with me: I kill, and I
make alive; I wound, and I heal: neither
is there any that can deliver out of my
hand.
40For I lift up my hand to heaven, and
say, I live for ever.
41If I whet my glittering sword, and
mine hand take hold on judgment; I will
*render vengeance to mine enemies,
and will reward them that hate me.
42I will make mine arrows drunk with
blood, and my sword shall devour flesh;
and that with the blood of the slain and
of the captives, from the beginning of
revenges upon the enemy.
43Rejoice, O ye nations, *with* his people: for he will avenge the blood of his

32:20 froward. Self-willed, stubborn, disobedient.

servants, and will render vengeance to
his adversaries, and will be merciful
unto his land, *and* to his people.
¶44 And Moses came and spake all the
words of this song in the ears of the
people, he, and Hoshea the son of Nun.
45 And Moses made an end of speaking all these words to all Israel:
46 And he said unto them, Set your
hearts unto all the words which I testify among you this day, which ye shall
command your children to observe to
do, all the words of this law.
47 For it *is* not a vain thing for you;
because it *is* your life: and through this
thing ye shall prolong *your* days in the
land, whither ye go over Jordan to possess it.
48 And the LORD spake unto Moses
that selfsame day, saying,
49 Get thee up into this mountain Abarim, *unto* mount Nebo, which *is* in the
land of Moab, that *is* over against Jericho; and behold the land of Canaan,
which I give unto the children of Israel
for a possession:
50 And die in the mount whither thou
goest up, and be gathered unto thy people; as *Aaron thy brother died in
mount Hor, and was gathered unto his
people:
51 Because ye trespassed against me
among the children of Israel at the
waters of Meribah-Kadesh, in the wilderness of Zin; because ye sanctified
me not in the midst of the children of
Israel.
52 Yet thou shalt see the land before
thee; but thou shalt not go thither unto the
land which I give the children of Israel.

33:1 Moses' Blessing of Israel
There is a difference between this blessing and the one given by Jacob in Genesis 49. It is thought that this one looks ahead to the still-future blessing of Israel, when they will once again return to their land and the Lord's *kingdom will be set up.

Moses blesses the tribes

33 And this *is* the blessing, wherewith *Moses the man of God
blessed the children of Israel before his
death.
2 And he said, The LORD came from
*Sinai, and rose up from *Seir unto
them; he shined forth from mount Paran, and he came with ten thousands of
*saints: from his right hand *went* a fiery
*law for them.
3 Yea, he loved the people; all his
saints *are* in thy hand: and they sat
down at thy feet; *every one* shall receive
of thy words.
4 Moses commanded us a law, *even*
the inheritance of the congregation of
Jacob.
5 And he was king in Jeshurun, when
the heads of the people *and* the tribes
of Israel were gathered together.
¶6 Let Reuben live, and not die; and
let *not* his men be few.
¶7 And this *is the blessing* of *Judah:
and he said, Hear, LORD, the voice of
Judah, and bring him unto his people: let
his hands be sufficient for him; and be
thou an help *to him* from his enemies.
¶8 And of Levi he said, *Let* thy Thummim and thy Urim *be* with thy *holy
one, whom thou didst *prove at Massah, *and with* whom thou didst strive at
the waters of Meribah;
9 Who said unto his father and to his
mother, I have not seen him; neither
did he acknowledge his brethren, nor
knew his own children: for they have
observed thy word, and kept thy covenant.

32:44 Hoshea. Joshua.
33:2 saints. This word is not used here as a title, such as the expression "Saint Paul," but of God's people as a whole. Read 1 Corinthians 1:2.
33:6 Let Reuben live. Beginning with this verse, Moses gives the blessing to each of the tribes, calling each by name.
33:8 Massah . . . Meribah. See Exodus 17:5-7.

33:8 Urim and Thummim
These words mean "Lights and Perfections." They were the sacred symbols (worn upon the breastplate of the high priest, "upon his heart"), by which God gave responses for the guidance of His people in temporal matters. What the Urim and Thummim were is unknown; they are introduced in Exodus 28:30 without explanation, as if they were familiar to the Israelites of that day. Some scholars suppose that they were the twelve stones of the breastplate; others that they were two additional stones concealed in its fold. Josephus adds to these the two sardonyx buttons, worn on the shoulders, which, he says, emitted luminous rays when the response was favorable. We do not need the Urim and Thummim today since we have God's perfect word to give us direction and doctrine (Ps. 119:133; Prov. 16:9).

10 They shall teach Jacob thy judgments, and Israel thy law: they shall put *incense before thee, and whole burnt-sacrifice upon thine *altar.

11 Bless, LORD, his substance, and accept the work of his hands: smite through the loins of them that rise against him, and of them that hate him, that they rise not again.

¶ 12 *And* of Benjamin he said, The beloved of the LORD shall dwell in safety by him; *and the LORD* shall cover him all the day long, and he shall dwell between his shoulders.

¶ 13 And of *Joseph he said, Blessed of the LORD *be* his land, for the precious things of heaven, for the dew, and for the deep that coucheth beneath,

14 And for the precious fruits *brought forth* by the sun, and for the precious things put forth by the moon,

15 And for the chief things of the ancient mountains, and for the precious things of the lasting hills,

16 And for the precious things of the earth and *fulness thereof, and *for* the good will of him that dwelt in the bush: let *the blessing* come upon the head of Joseph, and upon the top of the head of him *that was* separated from his brethren.

17 His glory *is like* the firstling of his bullock, and his *horns *are like* the horns of unicorns: with them he shall push the people together to the ends of the earth: and they *are* the ten thousands of *Ephraim, and they *are* the thousands of Manasseh.

¶ 18 And of Zebulun he said, Rejoice, Zebulun, in thy going out; and, Issachar, in thy tents.

19 They shall call the people unto the mountain; there they shall offer sacrifices of *righteousness: for they shall suck *of* the abundance of the seas, and *of* treasures hid in the sand.

¶ 20 And of Gad he said, Blessed *be* he that enlargeth Gad: he dwelleth as a lion, and teareth the arm with the crown of the head.

21 And he provided the first part for himself, because there, *in* a portion of the lawgiver, *was he* seated; and he came with the heads of the people, he executed the justice of the LORD, and his judgments with Israel.

¶ 22 And of Dan he said, Dan *is* a lion's whelp: he shall leap from Bashan.

¶ 23 And of Naphtali he said, O Naphtali, satisfied with favour, and full with the blessing of the LORD: possess thou the west and the south.

¶ 24 And of Asher he said, *Let* Asher *be* blessed with children; let him be acceptable to his brethren, and let him dip his foot in oil.

25 Thy shoes *shall be* iron and brass; and as thy days, *so shall* thy strength *be.*

¶ 26 *There is* none like unto the God of Jeshurun, *who* rideth upon the heaven in thy help, and in his excellency on the sky.

27 The eternal God *is thy* refuge, and underneath *are* the everlasting arms: and he shall thrust out the enemy from

33:13 coucheth. Lies flat.

before thee; and shall say, Destroy
them.
28 Israel then shall dwell in safety
alone: the fountain of Jacob *shall be*
upon a land of corn and wine; also his
heavens shall drop down dew.
29 Happy *art* thou, O Israel: who *is* like
unto thee, O people saved by the LORD,
the shield of thy help, and who *is* the
sword of thy excellency! and thine enemies shall be found liars unto thee;
and thou shalt tread upon their high
places.

VII. Moses' Death (34:1-12)

Moses views the land

34 And Moses went up from the
plains of Moab unto the mountain of Nebo, to the top of Pisgah, that
is over against Jericho. And the LORD
shewed him all the land of Gilead, unto
Dan,
2 And all Naphtali, and the land of
Ephraim, and Manasseh, and all the
land of Judah, unto the utmost sea,
3 And the south, and the plain of the
valley of Jericho, the city of palm trees,
unto Zoar.
4 And the LORD said unto him, This *is*
the land which I sware unto Abraham,
unto Isaac, and unto Jacob, saying, I will
give it unto thy seed: I have caused thee
to see *it* with thine eyes, but thou shalt
not go over thither.

Moses dies

¶5 So Moses the servant of the LORD
died there in the land of Moab, according to the word of the LORD.
6 And he buried him in a valley in the
land of Moab, over against Beth-peor:
but no man knoweth of his sepulchre
unto this day.
¶7 And Moses *was* an hundred and
twenty years old when he died: his eye
was not dim, nor his natural force
abated.
¶8 And the children of Israel wept for
Moses in the plains of Moab thirty days:
so the days of weeping *and* mourning
for Moses were ended.

Joshua follows Moses as leader

¶9 And Joshua the son of Nun was
full of the spirit of wisdom; for Moses
had laid his hands upon him: and the
children of Israel hearkened unto him,
and did as the LORD commanded
Moses.
¶10 And there arose not a prophet
since in Israel like unto Moses, whom
the LORD knew face to face,
11 In all the signs and the wonders,
which the LORD sent him to do in the
land of Egypt to Pharaoh, and to all his
servants, and to all his land,
12 And in all that mighty hand, and in
all the great terror which Moses
shewed in the sight of all Israel.

34:10 whom the LORD knew face to face. See Exodus 33:11 and Numbers 12:6-8.

The Book of

JOSHUA

THEME

The name "Joshua" means *Jehovah is Salvation,* or *Jehovah Savior* (see 1:1 note, "A New Leader"). After Moses' death, God addressed Joshua as He had spoken to Moses.

BACKGROUND

Joshua, the son of Nun, of the tribe of Ephraim (1 Chronicles 7:27), was born in Egypt at the time of Israel's slavery. He is first mentioned in Exodus 17:9, when Moses appointed him to take charge of the armies of Israel as they fought against Amalek. He was with Moses after the giving of the Law (Exodus 32:17), and was also in the tabernacle when God revealed Himself (Exodus 33:11). He was chosen to represent his tribe when the spies were sent into the land (Numbers 13:8), and he and Caleb were the only men who left Egypt who were allowed to enter the land (Numbers 14:30). Moses prayed for a successor, and was told to appoint Joshua (Numbers 27:15-23). Joshua was encouraged by Moses (Deuteronomy 31:7,8), who also laid hands on him for the service (Deuteronomy 34:9). He was about forty-four years old when he left Egypt. He spent forty years in the wilderness, and the events of the book of Joshua cover about twenty-six year, according to Ussher. He died at the age of one hundred and ten (Joshua 24:29).

OUTLINE OF JOSHUA

I.	The Conquest of Canaan	Joshua 1:1—12:24
II.	The Division of Canaan	Joshua 13:1—22:34
III.	The Farewell of Joshua	Joshua 23:1—24:33

I. The Conquest of Canaan (1:1—12:24)

God's command to Joshua

1 Now after the death of *Moses
the servant of the LORD it came to
pass, that the LORD spake unto *Joshua
the son of Nun, Moses' minister, saying,
2 Moses my servant is dead; now
therefore arise, go over this Jordan,
thou, and all this people, unto the land

1:1 death of Moses. See Deuteronomy 34:1-8.

1:2 Moses my servant is dead. Moses was not allowed to enter the Promised Land because of his sin, that is, his unbelief and rebellion (Num. 20:12; 27:12-14; Deut. 3:26-27). Moses was an illustration of the *Law with its demands of obedience and penalties

1:1 A New Leader
Joshua was the successor of Moses as leader of the people of Israel. He had been trained by Moses, and is called "his minister" (assistant) (Exod. 24:13). Joshua's name is written in several ways: "Oshea" (Num. 13:8); "Jehoshua" (Num. 13:16); "Hoshea" (Deut. 32:44). The name that is above every name, Jesus, is the Greek form of this Hebrew name (Acts 7:45; Heb. 4:8). Joshua is an important *type of Christ. See also the introduction to this book.

which I do give to them, *even* to the
children of *Israel.
3Every place that the sole of your
foot shall tread upon, that have I given
unto you, as I said unto Moses.
4From the wilderness and this *Lebanon even unto the great river, the river
Euphrates, all the land of the Hittites,
and unto the great sea toward the going down of the sun, shall be your coast.
5There shall not any man be able to
stand before thee all the days of thy life:
as I was with Moses, *so* I will be with
thee: I will not fail thee, nor forsake
thee.
6Be strong and of a good courage: for
unto this people shalt thou divide for an
inheritance the land, which I sware unto
their fathers to give them.
7Only be thou strong and very courageous, that thou mayest observe to
do according to all the *law, which Moses my servant commanded thee: turn
not from it *to* the right hand or *to* the
left, that thou mayest prosper whithersoever thou goest.
8This book of the law shall not depart
out of thy mouth; but thou shalt meditate therein day and night, that thou
mayest observe to do according to all
that is written therein: for then thou
shalt make thy way prosperous, and
then thou shalt have good success.
9Have not I commanded thee? Be
strong and of a good courage; be not
*afraid, neither be thou dismayed: for
the LORD thy *God *is* with thee
whithersoever thou goest.

Joshua commands the people

¶ 10Then Joshua commanded the officers of the people, saying,
11Pass through the host, and command the people, saying, Prepare you
victuals; for within three days ye shall
pass over this Jordan, to go in to possess

1:11 Possessing the Land
God gave the land to Israel in promise. It only became theirs in reality when they took possession of it. This is stated clearly in verse 3. It is the difference between "owning" a thing and "possessing" it. All things are stored up for us in Christ (Eph. 1:3), but it is only as they are accepted by faith that we can be said to have them as our own. Most of us "own" far more than we actually "possess."

---

for disobedience (Gal. 3:10). The Law was only "till the seed [Christ] should come" (Gal. 3:19) and was "our schoolmaster to bring us unto Christ" (Gal. 3:24). Moses (a *type of the Law) must die, that Joshua (a type of the Saviour) may succeed.

1:4 From the wilderness and this Lebanon. This wilderness was the Desert of Arabia, and formed the southern border of the Promised Land; it reached to Lebanon in the north. On the east and west, the boundaries were the Euphrates River and the Mediterranean Sea. The time of greatest expansion was in the days of David and Solomon, but the whole land has never yet been fully occupied by Israel—that is still to take place in the future.

1:6 unto this people . . . the land. The land had been promised to Abraham and his seed (Gen. 12:6-7; 13:14-15). Later the promise was confirmed by a solemn covenant between God and Abraham (Gen. 15:18-21). God reminded Moses of the Abrahamic covenant when He sent him to Egypt (Exod. 6:8), and the promise was now to be realized. It is a figure of the blessings that believers have in Christ Jesus.

1:11 ye shall pass over this Jordan. The course of the river Jordan is almost due north and south. Israel had traveled through the wilderness, and they had arrived on the

the land, which the LORD your God
giveth you to possess it.
¶ 12 And to the Reubenites, and to the
Gadites, and to half the tribe of *Manasseh, spake Joshua, saying,
13 Remember the word which Moses
the servant of the LORD commanded you,
saying, The LORD your God hath given
you rest, and hath given you this land.
14 Your wives, your little ones, and
your cattle, shall remain in the land
which Moses gave you on this side Jordan; but ye shall pass before your brethren armed, all the mighty men of valour,
and help them;
15 Until the LORD have given your
brethren rest, as *he hath given* you, and
they also have possessed the land
which the LORD your God giveth them:
then ye shall return unto the land of
your possession, and enjoy it, which
Moses the LORD'S servant gave you on
this side Jordan toward the sunrising.
¶ 16 And they answered Joshua, saying,
All that thou commandest us we will do,
and whithersoever thou sendest us, we
will go.
17 According as we hearkened unto
Moses in all things, so will we hearken
unto thee: only the LORD thy God be
with thee, as he was with Moses.
18 Whosoever *he be* that doth rebel
against thy commandment, and will not
hearken unto thy words in all that thou
commandest him, he shall be put to
death: only be strong and of a good
courage.

Rahab and the spies

2 And Joshua the son of Nun sent
out of Shittim two men to spy secretly, saying, Go view the land, even
Jericho. And they went, and came into
an harlot's house, named *Rahab, and
lodged there.
2 And it was told the king of Jericho,
saying, Behold, there came men in
hither to night of the children of Israel
to search out the country.
3 And the king of Jericho sent unto
Rahab, saying, Bring forth the men that
are come to thee, which are entered
into thine house: for they be come to
search out all the country.
4 And the woman took the two men,
and hid them, and said thus, There
came men unto me, but I *wist not
whence they *were:*
5 And it came to pass *about the time*
of shutting of the gate, when it was
dark, that the men went out: whither
the men went I wot not: pursue after
them quickly; for ye shall overtake
them.
6 But she had brought them up to the
roof of the house, and hid them with the
stalks of flax, which she had laid in order upon the roof.
7 And the men pursued after them the
way to Jordan unto the fords: and as

2:1 Rahab
Rahab does not appear to have been a good woman, but she was kind to the spies. This verse and Joshua 6:17,25 say Rahab was a harlot. She could have been an innkeeper and that would account for them seeking lodging with her. She had heard of how God had delivered Israel (2:9-11), and she believed God's word (Heb. 11:31). She became the mother of David's great-grandfather, Boaz, and was therefore an ancestress of the Lord Jesus Christ (Matt. 1:5).

eastern side of the river, where Reuben, Gad, and half the tribe of Manasseh had been given their inheritance (Num. 32).

2:5 shutting of the gate. Jericho was a fortified city with very massive walls for defense. The only way into or out of the city was through the gates, which were generally closed at dusk (Neh. 7:3; 13:19). They were guarded because of enemies (Neh. 11:19; 13:22).

2:6 the roof of the house. The roofs of Mideastern houses were flat, as they are in many places today. They were frequently made of branches and twigs laid on the rafters, and then covered with earth and lime to make a floor. They were used for a variety of purposes. Compare Mark 2:4.

soon as they which pursued after them were gone out, they shut the gate.

¶ 8 And before they were laid down, she came up unto them upon the roof;

9 And she said unto the men, I know that the LORD hath given you the land, and that your terror is fallen upon us, and that all the inhabitants of the land faint because of you.

10 For we have heard how the LORD dried up the water of the Red sea for you, when ye came out of *Egypt; and what ye did unto the two kings of the Amorites, that *were* on the other side Jordan, Sihon and Og, whom ye utterly destroyed.

11 And as soon as we had heard *these things,* our hearts did melt, neither did there remain any more courage in any man, because of you: for the LORD your God, he *is* God in *heaven above, and in earth beneath.

12 Now therefore, I pray you, swear unto me by the LORD, since I have shewed you kindness, that ye will also shew kindness unto my father's house, and give me a true token:

13 And *that* ye will save alive my father, and my mother, and my brethren, and my sisters, and all that they have, and deliver our lives from death.

14 And the men answered her, Our life for yours, if ye utter not this our business. And it shall be, when the LORD hath given us the land, that we will deal kindly and truly with thee.

15 Then she let them down by a cord through the window: for her house *was* upon the town wall, and she dwelt upon the wall.

16 And she said unto them, Get you to the mountain, lest the pursuers meet you; and hide yourselves there three days, until the pursuers be returned: and afterward may ye go your way.

17 And the men said unto her, We *will be* blameless of this thine oath which thou hast made us swear.

2:18 The Scarlet Thread
This scarlet thread is also called a cord (vs. 15), and a line (vs. 21), and it was a rope strong enough to hold a man (vs. 15). It is an illustration or *type of the gospel, because it had saved the spies and would save others who put their faith in it, as Rahab did when she hung it out. Scarlet is the color which speaks of salvation by sacrifice through blood (Exod. 12:13; Lev. 17:11), and reminds us of the "precious blood of Christ" (1 Pet. 1:18-19).

18 Behold, *when* we come into the land, thou shalt bind this line of scarlet thread in the window which thou didst let us down by: and thou shalt bring thy father, and thy mother, and thy brethren, and all thy father's household, home unto thee.

19 And it shall be, *that* whosoever shall go out of the doors of thy house into the street, his *blood *shall be* upon his head, and we *will be* guiltless: and whosoever shall be with thee in the house, his blood *shall be* on our head, if *any* hand be upon him.

20 And if thou utter this our business, then we will be quit of thine oath which thou hast made us to swear.

21 And she said, According unto your words, so *be* it. And she sent them away, and they departed: and she bound the scarlet line in the window.

22 And they went, and came unto the mountain, and abode there three days, until the pursuers were returned: and the pursuers sought *them* throughout all the way, but found *them* not.

¶ 23 So the two men returned, and descended from the mountain, and passed over, and came to Joshua the son of Nun, and told him all *things* that befell them:

24 And they said unto Joshua, Truly the LORD hath delivered into our hands all the land; for even all the inhabitants of the country do faint because of us.

2:10 Sihon and Og. The two kings of the Amorites (Josh. 9:10) were defeated by Israel when they refused to allow the Israelites to pass through their lands (Num. 21:21-35).

Crossing the Jordan

3 And Joshua rose early in the morning; and they removed from Shittim, and came to Jordan, he and all the children of Israel, and lodged there before they passed over.

2 And it came to pass after three days, that the officers went through the host;

3 And they commanded the people, saying, When ye see the *ark of the covenant of the LORD your God, and the priests the Levites bearing it, then ye shall remove from your place, and go after it.

4 Yet there shall be a space between you and it, about two thousand *cubits by measure: come not near unto it, that ye may know the way by which ye must go: for ye have not passed *this* way heretofore.

5 And Joshua said unto the people, Sanctify yourselves: for to morrow the LORD will do wonders among you.

6 And Joshua spake unto the priests, saying, Take up the ark of the covenant, and pass over before the people. And they took up the ark of the covenant, and went before the people.

¶7 And the LORD said unto Joshua, This day will I begin to magnify thee in the sight of all Israel, that they may know that, as I was with Moses, *so* I will be with thee.

8 And thou shalt command the priests that bear the ark of the covenant, saying, When ye are come to the brink of the water of Jordan, ye shall stand still in Jordan.

¶9 And Joshua said unto the children of Israel, Come hither, and hear the words of the LORD your God.

10 And Joshua said, Hereby ye shall know that the living God *is* among you, and *that* he will without fail drive out from before you the Canaanites, and the Hittites, and the Hivites, and the Perizzites, and the Girgashites, and the Amorites, and the Jebusites.

11 Behold, the ark of the covenant of the Lord of all the earth passeth over before you into Jordan.

12 Now therefore take you twelve men out of the tribes of Israel, out of every tribe a man.

13 And it shall come to pass, as soon as the soles of the feet of the priests that bear the ark of the LORD, the Lord of all the earth, shall rest in the waters of Jordan, *that* the waters of Jordan shall be cut off *from* the waters that come down from above; and they shall stand upon an heap.

¶14 And it came to pass, when the people removed from their tents, to pass over Jordan, and the priests bearing the ark of the covenant before the people;

15 And as they that bare the ark were come unto Jordan, and the feet of the priests that bare the ark were dipped in the brim of the water, (for Jordan overfloweth all his banks all the time of harvest,)

16 That the waters which came down from above stood *and* rose up upon an heap very far from the city *Adam, that *is* beside Zaretan: and those that came

---

3:1 Jordan. The river Jordan stood between Israel and the Land of Promise and had to be crossed if they would enter the land. It is a *type of the believer's spiritual death, because he can only cross into new life in Christ by dying with Him spiritually (Gal. 2:20; Col. 3:3). Canaan is not a type of heaven as the place where the Father is and where believers in Christ go when they die, but of the "heavenly places" into which the believer enters by faith in Christ (Eph. 1:3; 2:5-6) to fight in heavenly warfare (Eph. 6:11-12). Jordan speaks therefore of the place of death of the *old man and his deeds.

3:4 a space between you and it. This was a Sabbath day's journey (see Acts 1:12 note, "Journey on the Sabbath").

3:10 drive out from before you. God was long-suffering with the Canaanite nations and waited patiently before sending judgment upon them (Gen. 15:16). These nations had to be driven out because of their terrible sinfulness and cruelties, and Israel was warned against their idolatrous practices (Deut. 12:31; 18:9-14; 20:17-18).

down toward the *sea of the plain, *even* the salt sea, failed, *and* were cut off: and the people passed over right against Jericho.

17And the priests that bare the ark of the covenant of the LORD stood firm on dry ground in the midst of Jordan, and all the Israelites passed over on dry ground, until all the people were passed clean over Jordan.

3:17 Crossing the Jordan
God performed a miracle at the crossing of the Jordan, as He did at the crossing of the Red Sea (Exod. 14:21). Here also is a *type for believers, to help us understand salvation more fully: As the priests went down into the river, so Christ went down into the place of death and judgment to open the way to life and eternity with God for all believers.

A sign and a memorial

4 And it came to pass, when all the people were clean passed over Jordan, that the LORD spake unto Joshua, saying,

2Take you twelve men out of the people, out of every tribe a man,

3And command ye them, saying, Take you hence out of the midst of Jordan, out of the place where the priests' feet stood firm, twelve stones, and ye shall carry them over with you, and leave

4:2-3 Twelve Stones
Each man represented his tribe, and each tribe was represented by a stone for a sign (vss. 6-8) and a memorial (vss. 7,21-22) to Israel. Twelve stones were set up in Jordan where the priests' feet had stood (vss. 9-10). When the water flowed back over the stones, the stones were covered and then buried. Twelve other stones were taken out of the riverbed and set up in Gilgal (vs. 20), where they became a memorial. As the first group of stones speak of death, so the second speak of resurrection, and they thus illustrate the truth of the believer's death and resurrection with Christ (Rom. 6:4-6; compare 2 Cor. 5:17).

3:17 Miracles in Israel's Early History

Miracle	Reference
Crossing the Jordan River	Joshua 3:14-17
The fall of Jericho	Joshua 6:6-25
The sun and moon stand still	Joshua 10:12-14
Death of Uzzah	2 Samuel 6:7
Jeroboam's hand withered; altar destroyed	1 Kings 13:4-6

them in the lodging place, where ye shall lodge this night.

4Then Joshua called the twelve men, whom he had prepared of the children of Israel, out of every tribe a man:

5And Joshua said unto them, Pass over before the ark of the LORD your God into the midst of Jordan, and take you up every man of you a stone upon his shoulder, according unto the number of the tribes of the children of Israel:

6That this may be a sign among you, *that* when your children ask *their fathers* in time to come, saying, What *mean* ye by these stones?

7Then ye shall answer them, That the waters of Jordan were cut off before the ark of the covenant of the LORD; when it passed over Jordan, the waters of Jordan were cut off: and these stones shall be for a memorial unto the children of Israel for ever.

8And the children of Israel did so as Joshua commanded, and took up twelve stones out of the midst of Jordan, as the LORD spake unto Joshua, according to the number of the tribes of the children of Israel, and carried them over with them unto the place where they lodged, and laid them down there.

9And Joshua set up twelve stones in the midst of Jordan, in the place where the feet of the priests which bare the ark of the covenant stood: and they are there unto this day.

¶10For the priests which bare the ark stood in the midst of Jordan, until every thing was finished that the LORD

3:17 clean. Entirely, completely.

commanded Joshua to speak unto the
people, according to all that Moses
commanded Joshua: and the people
hasted and passed over.
11And it came to pass, when all the
people were clean passed over, that
the ark of the LORD passed over, and the
priests, in the presence of the people.
12And the children of Reuben, and the
children of Gad, and half the tribe of
Manasseh, passed over armed before
the children of Israel, as Moses spake
unto them:
13About forty thousand prepared for
war passed over before the LORD unto
battle, to the plains of Jericho.
¶14On that day the LORD magnified
Joshua in the sight of all Israel; and they
feared him, as they feared Moses, all
the days of his life.
15And the LORD spake unto Joshua,
saying,
16Command the priests that bear the
ark of the testimony, that they come up
out of Jordan.
17Joshua therefore commanded the
priests, saying, Come ye up out of
Jordan.
18And it came to pass, when the
priests that bare the ark of the covenant
of the LORD were come up out of the
midst of Jordan, *and* the soles of the
priests' feet were lifted up unto the dry
land, that the waters of Jordan returned
unto their place, and flowed over all his
banks, as *they did* before.
¶19And the people came up out of Jordan on the tenth *day* of the first *month,
and encamped in Gilgal, in the east border of Jericho.
20And those twelve stones, which
they took out of Jordan, did Joshua pitch
in Gilgal.
21And he spake unto the children of
Israel, saying, When your children shall
ask their fathers in time to come, saying, What *mean* these stones?
22Then ye shall let your children
know, saying, Israel came over this Jordan on dry land.
23For the LORD your God dried up the
waters of Jordan from before you, until
ye were passed over, as the LORD your
God did to the Red sea, which he dried
up from before us, until we were gone
over:
24That all the people of the earth
might know the hand of the LORD, that
it *is* mighty: that ye might *fear the
LORD your God for ever.

Reproach rolled away

5 And it came to pass, when all the
kings of the Amorites, which *were*
on the side of Jordan westward, and all
the kings of the Canaanites, which *were*
by the sea, heard that the LORD had
dried up the waters of Jordan from before the children of Israel, until we were
passed over, that their heart melted,
neither was there spirit in them any
more, because of the children of Israel.
¶2At that time the LORD said unto
Joshua, Make thee sharp knives, and
circumcise again the children of Israel
the second time.
3And Joshua made him sharp knives,
and circumcised the children of Israel
at the hill of the foreskins.
4And this *is* the cause why Joshua did
circumcise: All the people that came out
of Egypt, *that were* males, *even* all the
men of war, died in the wilderness by
the way, after they came out of Egypt.
5Now all the people that came out
were circumcised: but all the people
that were born in the wilderness by the
way as they came forth out of Egypt,
them they had not circumcised.
6For the children of Israel walked forty years in the wilderness, till all the
people *that were* men of war, which
came out of Egypt, were consumed,
because they obeyed not the voice of

5:2 circumcise again the children of Israel. Circumcision had not been observed for over forty years. "Gilgal" means *rolling away* and speaks of rolling away the disgrace of Egypt. See *circumcision.

the LORD: unto whom the LORD sware that he would not shew them the land, which the LORD sware unto their fathers that he would give us, a land that *floweth with milk and honey.

7 And their children, *whom* he raised up in their stead, them Joshua circumcised: for they were *uncircumcised, because they had not circumcised them by the way.

8 And it came to pass, when they had done circumcising all the people, that they abode in their places in the camp, till they were whole.

9 And the LORD said unto Joshua, This day have I rolled away the reproach of Egypt from off you. Wherefore the name of the place is called Gilgal unto this day.

¶ 10 And the children of Israel encamped in Gilgal, and kept the *passover on the fourteenth day of the month at even in the plains of Jericho.

11 And they did eat of the old corn of the land on the morrow after the passover, unleavened cakes, and parched *corn* in the selfsame day.

¶ 12 And the *manna ceased on the morrow after they had eaten of the old corn of the land; neither had the children of Israel manna any more; but they did eat of the fruit of the land of Canaan that year.

¶ 13 And it came to pass, when Joshua was by Jericho, that he lifted up his eyes and looked, and, behold, there stood a man over against him with his sword drawn in his hand: and Joshua went unto him, and said unto him, *Art* thou for us, or for our adversaries?

14 And he said, Nay; but *as* captain of the host of the LORD am I now come. And Joshua fell on his face to the earth, and did worship, and said unto him, What saith my lord unto his servant?

15 And the captain of the LORD'S host said unto Joshua, Loose thy shoe from off thy foot; for the place whereon thou standest *is* *holy. And Joshua did so.

5:13-15 The Heavenly Warrior
The man whom Joshua saw and who declared Himself to be the captain of the LORD's hosts was God Himself (Josh. 6:2), doubtless in the person of the Lord Jesus Christ (see *theophany). Joshua wisely accepted His leadership (compare Heb. 2:10).

The siege and fall of Jericho

6 Now Jericho was straitly shut up because of the children of Israel: none went out, and none came in.

2 And the LORD said unto Joshua, See, I have given into thine hand Jericho, and the king thereof, *and* the mighty men of valour.

3 And ye shall compass the city, all *ye* men of war, *and* go round about the city once. Thus shalt thou do six days.

4 And seven priests shall bear before the ark seven trumpets of rams' *horns: and the seventh day ye shall compass the city seven times, and the priests shall blow with the trumpets.

5 And it shall come to pass, that when they make a long *blast* with the ram's horn, *and* when ye hear the sound of the trumpet, all the people shall shout with a great shout; and the wall of the city shall fall down flat, and the people shall ascend up every man straight before him.

6:1 Jericho was straitly shut up. Jericho was a fortified city that stood in the way of Israel's entry into the land. It was called the "city of palm trees" (Deut. 34:3) and was apparently a city of some importance and wealth (Josh. 6:24).

6:4 seven trumpets of rams' horns. These were "trumpets of jubilee," for the entrance of Israel into Canaan was a time of jubilee. The trumpet of jubilee is mentioned in Leviticus 25:9 and was sounded on the tenth day of the seventh month in the fiftieth year, because this had to do with liberty and restoration. There may, therefore, be something of this thought in the sounding of the trumpets as Israel entered the land given to them by God; the priests were officiating with the emblems of festival instead of warfare.

6:4 The Number Seven
The number seven is found repeatedly in the Scriptures and has a special meaning. It is the number of divine perfection or completeness. There were seven priests to bear the ark, seven trumpets, and on the seventh day they were to go around the city seven times. God wanted to demonstrate His complete destruction of Jericho.

¶6And Joshua the son of Nun called
the priests, and said unto them, Take
up the ark of the covenant, and let
seven priests bear seven trumpets of
rams' horns before the ark of the
LORD.
7And he said unto the people, Pass
on, and compass the city, and let him
that is armed pass on before the ark of
the LORD.
¶8And it came to pass, when Joshua
had spoken unto the people, that the
seven priests bearing the seven trumpets of rams' horns passed on before
the LORD, and blew with the trumpets:
and the ark of the covenant of the LORD
followed them.
¶9And the armed men went before
the priests that blew with the trumpets,
and the *rereward came after the ark,
the priests going on, and blowing with
the trumpets.
10And Joshua had commanded the
people, saying, Ye shall not shout, nor
make any noise with your voice, neither
shall *any* word proceed out of your
mouth, until the day I bid you shout;
then shall ye shout.
11So the ark of the LORD compassed
the city, going about *it* once: and they
came into the camp, and lodged in the
camp.
¶12And Joshua rose early in the
morning, and the priests took up the
ark of the LORD.
13And seven priests bearing seven
trumpets of rams' horns before the ark
of the LORD went on continually, and
blew with the trumpets: and the armed
men went before them; but the rereward came after the ark of the LORD,
the priests going on, and blowing with the
trumpets.
14And the second day they compassed the city once, and returned into
the camp: so they did six days.
15And it came to pass on the seventh
day, that they rose early about the
dawning of the day, and compassed the
city after the same manner seven
times: only on that day they compassed
the city seven times.
16And it came to pass at the seventh
time, when the priests blew with the
trumpets, Joshua said unto the people,
Shout; for the LORD hath given you the
city.
¶17And the city shall be accursed,
even it, and all that *are* therein, to the
LORD: only *Rahab the harlot shall live,
she and all that *are* with her in the
house, because she hid the messengers
that we sent.
18And ye, in any wise keep *yourselves*
from the accursed thing, lest ye make
yourselves accursed, when ye take of the
accursed thing, and make the camp of
Israel a curse, and trouble it.
19But all the *silver, and gold, and
vessels of brass and iron, *are* consecrated unto the LORD: they shall come into
the treasury of the LORD.
20So the people shouted when *the
priests* blew with the trumpets: and it
came to pass, when the people heard the
sound of the trumpet, and the people
shouted with a great shout, that the wall
fell down flat, so that the people went

6:17 And the city shall be accursed. "Accursed" has the idea of "devoted." The same word is used in Leviticus 27:28: "Every devoted thing is most holy unto the LORD." This means that it belonged completely to the LORD. Jericho was the first city captured and was a firstfruits of judgment against evil in the Promised Land. In the case of Jericho, it was a *firstfruits of judgment vowed to the LORD.

up into the city, every man straight before him, and they took the city.

21 And they utterly destroyed all that *was* in the city, both man and woman, young and old, and ox, and sheep, and ass, with the edge of the sword.

22 But Joshua had said unto the two men that had spied out the country, Go into the harlot's house, and bring out thence the woman, and all that she hath, as ye sware unto her.

23 And the young men that were spies went in, and brought out Rahab, and her father, and her mother, and her brethren, and all that she had; and they brought out all her kindred, and left them without the camp of Israel.

24 And they burnt the city with *fire, and all that *was* therein: only the silver, and the gold, and the vessels of brass and of iron, they put into the treasury of the house of the LORD.

25 And Joshua saved Rahab the harlot alive, and her father's household, and all that she had; and she dwelleth in Israel *even* unto this day; because she hid the messengers, which Joshua sent to spy out Jericho.

6:25 Rahab's Deliverance
Rahab's deliverance is an illustration of the gospel: She was given a promise of deliverance (2:17-20); she believed the promise and acted accordingly (2:21); and then gathered her family with her in the shelter of her home for safety (6:23; compare Acts 16:31).

¶26 And Joshua adjured *them* at that time, saying, Cursed *be* the man before the LORD, that riseth up and buildeth this city Jericho: he shall lay the foundation thereof in his firstborn, and in his youngest *son* shall he set up the gates of it.

27 So the LORD was with Joshua; and his fame was *noised* throughout all the country.

The defeat of Israel

7 But the children of *Israel committed a *trespass in the accursed thing: for Achan, the son of Carmi, the son of Zabdi, the son of Zerah, of the tribe of *Judah, took of the accursed thing: and the anger of the LORD was kindled against the children of Israel.

7:1 A Nation's Sin
This verse indicates the unity of the nation in the sight of God. The trespass was committed by Achan, one man, but his sin involved the whole nation. The principle is stated in the New Testament in the words, "No man liveth unto himself" (see Rom. 14:7). There is a parallel between Achan and his sin, and that of Ananias and Sapphira, who "lie[d] to the Holy Ghost" (Acts 5:3; compare Josh. 7:11).

2 And *Joshua sent men from Jericho to Ai, which *is* beside *Beth-aven, on the east side of *Beth-el, and spake unto them, saying, Go up and view the country. And the men went up and viewed Ai.

3 And they returned to Joshua, and said unto him, Let not all the people go up; but let about two or three thousand men go up and smite Ai; *and* make not all the people to labour thither; for they *are but* few.

4 So there went up thither of the people about three thousand men: and they fled before the men of Ai.

5 And the men of Ai smote of them about thirty and six men: for they chased them *from* before the gate *even* unto Shebarim, and smote them in the going down: wherefore the hearts of the people melted, and became as water.

¶6 And Joshua rent his clothes, and fell to the earth upon his face before the ark of the LORD until the eventide, he and the *elders of Israel, and put dust upon their heads.

6:26 Cursed be . . . buildeth . . . Jericho. The fulfillment of this curse is recorded in 1 Kings 16:34.

7 And Joshua said, Alas, O Lord GOD, wherefore hast thou at all brought this people over Jordan, to deliver us into the hand of the Amorites, to destroy us? would to *God we had been content, and dwelt on the other side Jordan!

8 O Lord, what shall I say, when Israel turneth their backs before their enemies!

9 For the Canaanites and all the inhabitants of the land shall hear *of it,* and shall environ us round, and cut off our name from the earth: and what wilt thou do unto thy great name?

¶ 10 And the LORD said unto Joshua, Get thee up; wherefore liest thou thus upon thy face?

11 Israel hath sinned, and they have also transgressed my covenant which I commanded them: for they have even taken of the accursed thing, and have also stolen, and dissembled also, and they have put *it* even among their own stuff.

12 Therefore the children of Israel could not stand before their enemies, *but* turned *their* backs before their enemies, because they were accursed: neither will I be with you any more, except ye destroy the accursed from among you.

13 Up, sanctify the people, and say, Sanctify yourselves against to morrow: for thus saith the LORD God of Israel, *There is* an accursed thing in the midst of thee, O Israel: thou canst not stand before thine enemies, until ye take away the accursed thing from among you.

14 In the morning therefore ye shall be brought according to your tribes: and it shall be, *that* the tribe which the LORD taketh shall come according to the families *thereof;* and the family which the LORD shall take shall come by households; and the household which the LORD shall take shall come man by man.

15 And it shall be, *that* he that is taken with the accursed thing shall be burnt with fire, he and all that he hath: because he hath transgressed the covenant of the LORD, and because he hath wrought folly in Israel.

¶ 16 So Joshua rose up early in the morning, and brought Israel by their tribes; and the tribe of Judah was taken:

17 And he brought the family of Judah; and he took the family of the Zarhites: and he brought the family of the Zarhites man by man; and Zabdi was taken:

18 And he brought his household man by man; and Achan, the son of Carmi, the son of Zabdi, the son of Zerah, of the tribe of Judah, was taken.

19 And Joshua said unto Achan, My son, give, I pray thee, glory to the LORD God of Israel, and make confession unto him; and tell me now what thou hast done; hide *it* not from me.

20 And Achan answered Joshua, and said, Indeed I have sinned against the LORD God of Israel, and thus and thus have I done:

21 When I saw among the spoils a goodly Babylonish garment, and two hundred shekels of silver, and a wedge of gold of fifty shekels weight, then I coveted them, and took them; and, behold, they *are* hid in the earth in the midst of my tent, and the silver under it.

¶ 22 So Joshua sent messengers, and they ran unto the tent; and, behold, *it was* hid in his tent, and the silver under it.

7:7 Alas, O Lord GOD, wherefore . . . ? Joshua questioned God. This is the way of the human heart (compare Exod. 5:22; Num. 14:3; Ps. 78:17-20). The reason for failure is always in us, never in God (Matt. 17:17,20).

7:20 sinned against the LORD God. Compare Psalm 51:4. While Achan's sin had injured others, it was against God, who had given them His law. Achan recounted the steps leading to the sin: "I saw . . . I coveted . . . and took them . . . they are hid" (vs. 21).

[23]And they took them out of the
midst of the tent, and brought them
unto Joshua, and unto all the children
of Israel, and laid them out before the
LORD.
[24]And Joshua, and all Israel with him,
took Achan the son of Zerah, and the
silver, and the garment, and the wedge
of gold, and his sons, and his daughters,
and his oxen, and his asses, and his
sheep, and his tent, and all that he had:
and they brought them unto the valley
of Achor.
[25]And Joshua said, Why hast thou
troubled us? the LORD shall trouble thee
this day. And all Israel stoned him with
stones, and burned them with fire, after
they had stoned them with stones.

7:25 A Form of Punishment
Stoning was the mode of death inflicted for certain sins in Israel, including idolatry (Lev. 20:2) and blasphemy (1 Kings 21:10; compare Acts 7:54-60).

[26]And they raised over him a great
heap of stones unto this day. So the
LORD turned from the fierceness of his
anger. Wherefore the name of that place
was called, The valley of Achor, unto
this day.

The conquest of Ai

8 And the LORD said unto Joshua,
Fear not, neither be thou dismayed: take all the people of war with
thee, and arise, go up to Ai: see, I have
given into thy hand the king of Ai, and
his people, and his city, and his land:
[2]And thou shalt do to Ai and her king
as thou didst unto Jericho and her king:
only the spoil thereof, and the cattle
thereof, shall ye take for a prey unto
yourselves: lay thee an ambush for the
city behind it.
¶[3]So Joshua arose, and all the people
of war, to go up against Ai: and Joshua
chose out thirty thousand mighty men
of valour, and sent them away by night.
[4]And he commanded them, saying,
Behold, ye shall lie in wait against the
city, *even* behind the city: go not very
far from the city, but be ye all ready:
[5]And I, and all the people that *are*
with me, will approach unto the city:
and it shall come to pass, when they
come out against us, as at the first, that
we will flee before them,
[6](For they will come out after us) till
we have drawn them from the city; for
they will say, They flee before us, as at
the first: therefore we will flee before
them.
[7]Then ye shall rise up from the ambush, and seize upon the city: for the
LORD your God will deliver it into your
hand.
[8]And it shall be, when ye have taken
the city, *that* ye shall set the city on fire:

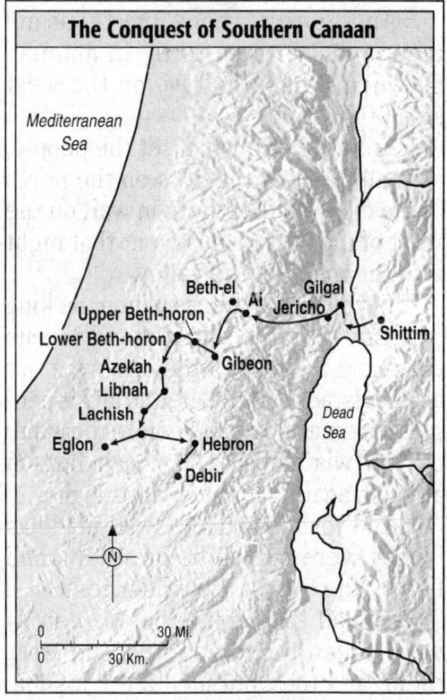

7:26 The valley of Achor. Achan is also called "Achar, the troubler of Israel" (1 Chron. 2:7). The Hebrew word for trouble is "Akar." The name of the valley and the man's name are both, therefore, a play on the word trouble. The Valley of Achor is equally well named the Valley of Trouble.

according to the commandment of the
LORD shall ye do. See, I have commanded you.
¶9 Joshua therefore sent them forth:
and they went to lie in ambush, and
abode between Beth-el and Ai, on the
west side of Ai: but Joshua lodged that
night among the people.
10 And Joshua rose up early in the
morning, and numbered the people, and
went up, he and the elders of Israel,
before the people to Ai.

8:10 Numbering the People
This was the numbering, perhaps better described as the mustering, of the men of war (vs. 11). It was not the numbering of the whole people.

11 And all the people, *even the people*
of war that *were* with him, went up, and
drew nigh, and came before the city, and
pitched on the north side of Ai: now
there was a valley between them and Ai.
12 And he took about five thousand
men, and set them to lie in ambush
between Beth-el and Ai, on the west
side of the city.
13 And when they had set the people,
even all the host that *was* on the north
of the city, and their liers in wait on the
west of the city, Joshua went that night
into the midst of the valley.
¶14 And it came to pass, when the king
of Ai saw *it*, that they hasted and rose up
early, and the men of the city went out
against Israel to battle, he and all his people, at a time appointed, before the plain;
but he *wist not that *there were* liers in
ambush against him behind the city.
15 And Joshua and all Israel made as
if they were beaten before them, and
fled by the way of the wilderness.
16 And all the people that *were* in Ai
were called together to pursue after
them: and they pursued after Joshua,
and were drawn away from the city.
17 And there was not a man left in Ai
or Beth-el, that went not out after Israel: and they left the city open, and
pursued after Israel.
18 And the LORD said unto Joshua,
Stretch out the spear that *is* in thy hand
toward Ai; for I will give it into thine
hand. And Joshua stretched out the
spear that *he had* in his hand toward the
city.
19 And the ambush arose quickly out
of their place, and they ran as soon as
he had stretched out his hand: and they
entered into the city, and took it, and
hasted and set the city on fire.
20 And when the men of Ai looked
behind them, they saw, and, behold, the
smoke of the city ascended up to heav-
en, and they had no power to flee this
way or that way: and the people that
fled to the wilderness turned back upon
the pursuers.
21 And when Joshua and all Israel saw
that the ambush had taken the city, and
that the smoke of the city ascended,
then they turned again, and slew the
men of Ai.
22 And the other issued out of the city
against them; so they were in the midst
of Israel, some on this side, and some on
that side: and they smote them, so that
they let none of them remain or escape.
23 And the king of Ai they took alive,
and brought him to Joshua.
24 And it came to pass, when Israel
had made an end of slaying all the inhabitants of Ai in the field, in the wilderness wherein they chased them, and
when they were all fallen on the edge
of the sword, until they were consumed, that all the Israelites returned
unto Ai, and smote it with the edge of
the sword.
25 And *so* it was, *that* all that fell that
day, both of men and women, *were*
twelve thousand, *even* all the men of Ai.
26 For Joshua drew not his hand back,

8:26 Joshua drew not his hand back. See verse 18. Like Moses before him, who held up his hands in prayer (Exod. 17:11-12), so Joshua held out his spear in obedience to the command of God, until victory was given.

wherewith he stretched out the spear, until he had utterly destroyed all the inhabitants of Ai.

27 Only the cattle and the spoil of that city Israel took for a prey unto themselves, according unto the word of the LORD which he commanded Joshua.

28 And Joshua burnt Ai, and made it an heap for ever, *even* a desolation unto this day.

29 And the king of Ai he hanged on a tree until eventide: and as soon as the sun was down, Joshua commanded that they should take his carcase down from the tree, and cast it at the entering of the gate of the city, and raise thereon a great heap of stones, *that remaineth* unto this day.

¶30 Then Joshua built an *altar unto the LORD God of Israel in mount Ebal,

31 As *Moses the servant of the LORD commanded the children of Israel, as it is written in the *book of the law of Moses, an altar of whole stones, over which no man hath lift up *any* iron: and they offered thereon burnt-offerings unto the LORD, and sacrificed *peace-offerings.

¶32 And he wrote there upon the stones a copy of the law of Moses, which he wrote in the presence of the children of Israel.

33 And all Israel, and their elders, and officers, and their judges, stood on this side the ark and on that side before the priests the Levites, which bare the ark of the covenant of the LORD, as well the stranger, as he that was born among them; half of them over against mount Gerizim, and half of them over against mount Ebal; as Moses the servant of the LORD had commanded before, that they should bless the people of Israel.

34 And afterward he read all the words of the law, the blessings and cursings, according to all that is written in the book of the law.

35 There was not a word of all that Moses commanded, which Joshua read not before all the congregation of Israel, with the women, and the little ones, and the strangers that were conversant among them.

Deceived by the Gibeonites

9 And it came to pass, when all the kings which *were* on this side Jordan, in the hills, and in the valleys, and in all the coasts of the great sea over against *Lebanon, the Hittite, and the *Amorite, the Canaanite, the Perizzite, the Hivite, and the Jebusite, heard *thereof;*

9:1 The Kings of Canaan
The Canaanite nations were seven in number. They are mentioned frequently in the Old Testament, but the full list is not always given: the Canaanites, Hittites, Hivites, Perizzites, Girgashites, Amorites, and Jebusites (Josh. 3:10; 24:11). They were of one mind in their opposition to the people of God. God commanded Israel to drive them out and destroy them because of their sin, but Israel failed to do so.

2 That they gathered themselves together, to fight with Joshua and with Israel, with one accord.

¶3 And when the inhabitants of Gibeon heard what Joshua had done unto Jericho and to Ai,

---

8:31 an altar of whole stones, over which no man hath lift up any iron. This was in accordance with God's command in Exodus 20:25. The altar was the place of worship and sacrifice, and nothing of man could be allowed there.

8:32 a copy of the law of Moses. See Deuteronomy 27:12-13: "These shall stand upon Mount Gerizim to bless the people . . . and . . . upon Mount Ebal to curse."

9:3 the inhabitants of Gibeon. They are called "Hivites" (vs. 7) and are stated to be descendants of Canaan, the son of Ham (Gen. 10:17,20; 1 Chron 1:8,15). They were a commercial and prosperous people, with much cattle (Gen. 34:10,23). The Gibeonites had four cities, of which Gibeon was the largest and most influential (Josh. 9:17; 10:2).

4 They did work wilily, and went and
made as if they had been ambassadors,
and took old sacks upon their asses,
and wine bottles, old, and rent, and
bound up;
5 And old shoes and clouted upon
their feet, and old *garments upon
them; and all the bread of their provision was dry *and* mouldy.
6 And they went to Joshua unto the
camp at Gilgal, and said unto him, and
to the men of Israel, We be come from
a far country: now therefore make ye a
league with us.
7 And the men of Israel said unto the
Hivites, Peradventure ye dwell among
us; and how shall we make a league
with you?
8 And they said unto Joshua, We *are*
thy servants. And Joshua said unto
them, Who *are* ye? and from whence
come ye?
9 And they said unto him, From a very
far country thy servants are come because of the name of the LORD thy God:
for we have heard the fame of him, and
all that he did in *Egypt,
10 And all that he did to the two kings
of the Amorites, that *were* beyond Jordan, to Sihon king of Heshbon, and to
Og king of *Bashan, which *was* at *Ashtaroth.
11 Wherefore our elders and all the
inhabitants of our country spake to us,
saying, Take victuals with you for the
journey, and go to meet them, and say
unto them, We *are* your servants: therefore now make ye a league with us.
12 This our bread we took hot *for* our
provision out of our houses on the day
we came forth to go unto you; but now,
behold, it is dry, and it is mouldy:
13 And these bottles of wine, which
we filled, *were* new; and, behold, they
be rent: and these our garments and our
shoes are become old by reason of the
very long journey.
14 And the men took of their victuals,
and asked not *counsel* at the mouth of
the LORD.
15 And Joshua made peace with them,
and made a league with them, to let
them live: and the princes of the congregation sware unto them.
¶ 16 And it came to pass at the end of
three days after they had made a league
with them, that they heard that they
were their neighbours, and *that* they
dwelt among them.
17 And the children of Israel journeyed, and came unto their cities on the
third day. Now their cities *were* Gibeon,
and Chephirah, and Beeroth, and
Kirjath-jearim.
18 And the children of Israel smote
them not, because the princes of the
congregation had sworn unto them by
the LORD God of Israel. And all the congregation murmured against the
princes.
19 But all the princes said unto all the
congregation, We have sworn unto them
by the LORD God of Israel: now therefore we may not touch them.
20 This we will do to them; we will
even let them live, lest wrath be upon
us, because of the oath which we sware
unto them.
21 And the princes said unto them, Let
them live; but let them be hewers of
wood and drawers of water unto all the
congregation; as the princes had promised them.
¶ 22 And Joshua called for them, and he

9:4 bottles, old, and rent. These wine bottles were made of the skins of animals—goats, oxen, or buffalo.

9:5 clouted. Patched.

9:15 Joshua made . . . a league with them. Israel had been especially warned against making a league with any of the nations of Canaan, so they wouldn't be led into their sins (Exod. 23:32-33; 34:12). Joshua's act was therefore in direct disobedience to God's command. The reason for the disobedience is given in verse 14.

9:20 because of the oath which we sware. The law was, "If a man . . . swear an oath . . . he shall not break his word" (Num. 30:2).

spake unto them, saying, Wherefore have ye beguiled us, saying, We *are* very far from you; when ye dwell among us?

23Now therefore ye *are* cursed, and there shall none of you be freed from being bondmen, and hewers of wood and drawers of water for the house of my God.

24And they answered Joshua, and said, Because it was certainly told thy servants, how that the LORD thy God commanded his servant Moses to give you all the land, and to destroy all the inhabitants of the land from before you, therefore we were sore afraid of our lives because of you, and have done this thing.

25And now, behold, we *are* in thine hand: as it seemeth good and right unto thee to do unto us, do.

26And so did he unto them, and delivered them out of the hand of the children of Israel, that they slew them not.

27And Joshua made them that day hewers of wood and drawers of water for the congregation, and for the altar of the LORD, even unto this day, in the place which he should choose.

Victory over the kings

10 Now it came to pass, when Adoni-zedek king of *Jerusalem had heard how Joshua had taken Ai, and had utterly destroyed it; as he had done to Jericho and her king, so he had done to Ai and her king; and how the inhabitants of Gibeon had made peace with Israel, and were among them;

2That they feared greatly, because Gibeon *was* a great city, as one of the royal cities, and because it *was* greater than Ai, and all the men thereof *were* mighty.

10:1 Jerusalem
This is the first mention of Jerusalem by this name in the Bible. It is mentioned as "Salem" (Gen. 14:18), was called "Jebusi" (Josh. 18:28), and "Jebus" (Judg. 19:10-11), and thus gave the name Jebusites to its inhabitants. The psalmist sang of this city as "the perfection of beauty" (Ps. 50:2); "beautiful for situation the joy of the whole earth" (Ps. 48:2). It is called "the city of God" (Ps. 46:4), and "the holy city" (Neh. 11:1). It has a long history and still has a great future in store. About the future restoration of Israel we read, "They shall dwell in the midst of Jerusalem: and they shall be my people, and I will be their God" (Zech. 8:8). The Bible closes with a wonderful description of new Jerusalem (see Rev. 21–22).

3Wherefore Adoni-zedek king of Jerusalem sent unto Hoham king of Hebron, and unto Piram king of Jarmuth, and unto Japhia king of *Lachish, and unto Debir king of Eglon, saying,

4Come up unto me, and help me, that we may smite Gibeon: for it hath made peace with Joshua and with the children of Israel.

5Therefore the five kings of the Amorites, the king of Jerusalem, the king of Hebron, the king of Jarmuth, the king of Lachish, the king of Eglon, gathered themselves together, and went up, they and all their hosts, and encamped before Gibeon, and made war against it.

¶6And the men of Gibeon sent unto Joshua to the camp to Gilgal, saying, Slack not thy hand from thy servants; come up to us quickly, and save us, and help us: for all the kings of the Amorites that dwell in the mountains are gathered together against us.

7So Joshua ascended from Gilgal, he, and all the people of war with him, and all the mighty men of valour.

9:27 hewers of wood and drawers of water. The Gibeonites were included in the words spoken about Canaan: "Cursed be Canaan; a servant of servants shall he be unto his brethren" (Gen. 9:25). They became bondmen of Israel, doing the menial tasks of the sanctuary (Josh. 9:23), and for the "congregation, and for the altar of God" (vs. 27).

10:6 come . . . save us. According to their covenant with Israel, the Gibeonites had a right to call for help and sent a message to Joshua right away. Israel was bound by the oath that had been sworn (9:15), and immediate help was given.

¶8And the LORD said unto Joshua, Fear them not: for I have delivered them into thine hand; there shall not a man of them stand before thee.

9Joshua therefore came unto them suddenly, *and* went up from Gilgal all night.

10And the LORD discomfited them before Israel, and slew them with a great slaughter at Gibeon, and chased them along the way that goeth up to Beth-horon, and smote them to Azekah, and unto Makkedah.

11And it came to pass, as they fled from before Israel, *and* were in the going down to Beth-horon, that the LORD cast down great stones from heaven upon them unto Azekah, and they died: *they were* more which died with hailstones than *they* whom the children of Israel slew with the sword.

¶12Then spake Joshua to the LORD in the day when the LORD delivered up the Amorites before the children of Israel, and he said in the sight of Israel, Sun, stand thou still upon Gibeon; and thou, Moon, in the valley of Ajalon.

13And the sun stood still, and the moon stayed, until the people had avenged themselves upon their enemies. *Is* not this written in the book of Jasher? So the sun stood still in the midst of heaven, and hasted not to go down about a whole day.

14And there was no day like that before it or after it, that the LORD hearkened unto the voice of a man: for the LORD fought for Israel.

¶15And Joshua returned, and all Israel with him, unto the camp to Gilgal.

16But these five kings fled, and hid themselves in a cave at Makkedah.

17And it was told Joshua, saying, The five kings are found hid in a cave at Makkedah.

18And Joshua said, Roll great stones upon the mouth of the cave, and set men by it for to keep them:

19And stay ye not, *but* pursue after your enemies, and smite the hindmost of them; suffer them not to enter into their cities: for the LORD your God hath delivered them into your hand.

20And it came to pass, when Joshua and the children of Israel had made an end of slaying them with a very great slaughter, till they were consumed, that the rest *which* remained of them entered into fenced cities.

21And all the people returned to the camp to Joshua at Makkedah in peace: none moved his tongue against any of the children of Israel.

22Then said Joshua, Open the mouth of the cave, and bring out those five kings unto me out of the cave.

23And they did so, and brought forth those five kings unto him out of the cave, the king of Jerusalem, the king of Hebron, the king of Jarmuth, the king of Lachish, *and* the king of Eglon.

24And it came to pass, when they brought out those kings unto Joshua, that Joshua called for all the men of Israel, and said unto the captains of the men of war which went with him, Come near, put your feet upon the necks of

10:13 Time Stops

The sun standing still was a miraculous intervention of the Creator of the universe. While the laws of nature may have been set aside, the One who set them aside was the God who made them. As the plagues of Egypt were directed against the gods of Egypt (Exod. 12:12), this miracle was directed against the worshippers of *Baal and *Ashtaroth (Jer. 8:2). It proved to Israel that God was with them, and to the people of the land that Israel's God was the true God.

10:11 hailstones. Hailstones in Palestine, as big as a man's two fists, are known to have killed men and animals.

10:13 the book of Jasher. This book is mentioned twice in the Bible (see 2 Sam. 1:18). Nothing is known of it, although it is thought to have been a collection of heroic or epic poems, sometimes called "The Book of the Upright."

10:24 A Symbolic Act
Putting a foot on the neck of a king was a symbolic act, not a deed of cruelty, because the leaders were giving a sign of their oneness with God in carrying out a just sentence. It was a symbol also of coming victories over the enemy (see vs. 25), and it foreshadows a still greater victory to come (Rom. 16:20).

these kings. And they came near, and
put their feet upon the necks of them.
25 And Joshua said unto them, Fear not,
nor be dismayed, be strong and of good
courage: for thus shall the LORD do to
all your enemies against whom ye fight.
26 And afterward Joshua smote them,
and slew them, and hanged them on five
trees: and they were hanging upon the
trees until the evening.
27 And it came to pass at the time of
the going down of the sun, *that* Joshua
commanded, and they took them down
off the trees, and cast them into the
cave wherein they had been hid, and
laid great stones in the cave's mouth,
which remain until this very day.
28 And that day Joshua took Makkedah, and smote it with the edge of the
sword, and the king thereof he utterly
destroyed, them, and all the souls that
were therein; he let none remain: and he
did to the king of Makkedah as he did
unto the king of Jericho.
¶ 29 Then Joshua passed from Makkedah, and all Israel with him, unto Libnah, and fought against Libnah:
30 And the LORD delivered it also, and
the king thereof, into the hand of Israel;
and he smote it with the edge of the
sword, and all the souls that *were*
therein; he let none remain in it; but did
unto the king thereof as he did unto the
king of Jericho.
¶ 31 And Joshua passed from Libnah,
and all Israel with him, unto Lachish,
and encamped against it, and fought
against it:
32 And the LORD delivered Lachish
into the hand of Israel, which took it on
the second day, and smote it with the
edge of the sword, and all the souls that
were therein, according to all that he had
done to Libnah.
¶ 33 Then Horam king of Gezer came
up to help Lachish; and Joshua smote
him and his people, until he had left him
none remaining.
¶ 34 And from Lachish Joshua passed
unto Eglon, and all Israel with him; and
they encamped against it, and fought
against it:
35 And they took it on that day, and
smote it with the edge of the sword, and
all the souls that *were* therein he utterly destroyed that day, according to all
that he had done to Lachish.
36 And Joshua went up from Eglon,
and all Israel with him, unto Hebron;
and they fought against it:
37 And they took it, and smote it
with the edge of the sword, and the
king thereof, and all the cities thereof,
and all the souls that *were* therein; he
left none remaining, according to all
that he had done to Eglon; but destroyed it utterly, and all the souls
that *were* therein.
¶ 38 And Joshua returned, and all Israel with him, to Debir; and fought
against it:
39 And he took it, and the king thereof,
and all the cities thereof; and they
smote them with the edge of the sword,
and utterly destroyed all the souls that
were therein; he left none remaining: as
he had done to Hebron, so he did to
Debir, and to the king thereof; as he had
done also to Libnah, and to her king.
¶ 40 So Joshua smote all the country of
the hills, and of the south, and of the
vale, and of the springs, and all their
kings: he left none remaining, but utterly destroyed all that breathed, as the
LORD God of Israel commanded.
41 And Joshua smote them from Kadesh-barnea even unto *Gaza, and all
the country of Goshen, even unto Gibeon.
42 And all these kings and their land
did Joshua take at one time, because the
LORD God of Israel fought for Israel.

43 And Joshua returned, and all Israel with him, unto the camp to Gilgal.

Final conquest of Canaan

11 And it came to pass, when Jabin king of Hazor had heard *those things,* that he sent to Jobab king of Madon, and to the king of Shimron, and to the king of Achshaph,

2 And to the kings that *were* on the north of the mountains, and of the plains south of Chinneroth, and in the valley, and in the borders of Dor on the west,

3 *And to* the Canaanite on the east and on the west, and *to* the Amorite, and the Hittite, and the Perizzite, and the Jebusite in the mountains, and *to* the Hivite under Hermon in the land of Mizpeh.

4 And they went out, they and all their hosts with them, much people, even as the sand that *is* upon the sea shore in multitude, with horses and chariots very many.

5 And when all these kings were met together, they came and pitched together at the waters of Merom, to fight against Israel.

¶ 6 And the LORD said unto Joshua, *Be not afraid because of them: for to morrow about this time will I deliver them up all slain before Israel: thou shalt *hough their horses, and burn their chariots with fire.

7 So Joshua came, and all the people of war with him, against them by the waters of Merom suddenly; and they fell upon them.

8 And the LORD delivered them into the hand of Israel, who smote them, and chased them unto great Zidon, and unto Misrephoth-maim, and unto the valley of Mizpeh eastward; and they smote them, until they left them none remaining.

9 And Joshua did unto them as the LORD bade him: he houghed their horses, and burnt their chariots with fire.

¶ 10 And Joshua at that time turned back, and took Hazor, and smote the king thereof with the sword: for Hazor beforetime was the head of all those kingdoms.

11 And they smote all the souls that *were* therein with the edge of the sword, utterly destroying *them:* there was not any left to breathe: and he burnt Hazor with fire.

12 And all the cities of those kings, and all the kings of them, did Joshua take, and smote them with the edge of the sword, *and* he utterly destroyed them, as Moses the servant of the LORD commanded.

13 But *as for* the cities that stood still in their strength, Israel burned none of them, save Hazor only; *that* did Joshua burn.

14 And all the spoil of these cities, and the cattle, the children of Israel took for a prey unto themselves; but every man they smote with the edge of the sword, until they had destroyed them, neither left they any to breathe.

15 As the LORD commanded Moses his servant, so did Moses command Joshua, and so did Joshua; he left nothing undone of all that the LORD commanded Moses.

¶ 16 So Joshua took all that land, the

11:1 Jabin. The name means *wise* or *intelligent;* it seems to have been an official title of the king of Hazor. There was another king of the same name or title in Judges 4:2.

11:6 hough. To cut the hamstrings or "hocks" of animals. This made the horses unfit for military purposes, but they could still be used for agriculture.

11:8 Zidon. Zidon was a very old city named after the first of the sons of Canaan (Gen. 10:15,19). It was the capital city of ancient Phoenicia. Later, Tyre became the greater of the two, and they are generally coupled together as "Tyre and Sidon" (Matt. 11:22; Mark 3:8).

11:12 Moses . . . commanded. God spoke directly to Moses, who kept a record of the messages given (Deut. 20:15-18).

hills, and all the south country, and all
the land of Goshen, and the valley, and
the plain, and the *mountain of Israel,
and the valley of the same;
17 *Even* from the mount Halak, that
goeth up to *Seir, even unto *Baal-gad
in the valley of Lebanon under mount
Hermon: and all their kings he took,
and smote them, and slew them.
18 Joshua made war a long time with
all those kings.

11:18 Joshua at War
The wars of Joshua took about five or six years. This can be reckoned by the age of Caleb, who was eighty-five when he received his inheritance (14:8-10). He was forty when he came out of Egypt, and he spent about forty years in the wilderness. He must therefore have been about eighty when the Israelites entered the land, which leaves five years for this period of fighting.

19 There was not a city that made
peace with the children of Israel, save
the Hivites the inhabitants of Gibeon:
all *other* they took in battle.
20 For it was of the LORD to *harden
their hearts, that they should come
against Israel in battle, that he might
destroy them utterly, *and* that they
might have no favour, but that he might
destroy them, as the LORD commanded Moses.
¶21 And at that time came Joshua, and
cut off the *Anakims from the mountains, from Hebron, from Debir, from
Anab, and from all the mountains of
Judah, and from all the mountains of
Israel: Joshua destroyed them utterly
with their cities.
22 There was none of the Anakims left
in the land of the children of Israel: only
in Gaza, in *Gath, and in Ashdod, there
remained.
23 So Joshua took the whole land, ac-

11:21 Giants in the Land
The Anakims were a race of giants, "the sons of Anak," who lived in Kirjath-Arba, or Hebron, as it was called later, and the surrounding country (Gen. 23:2; Num. 13:22,33). Israel was afraid of the Anakims, apparently because of their great size (Num. 13:33). Goliath of Gath, who was slain by David, was of the same race. Their size can be seen from the description of Goliath, who was almost nine feet tall (1 Sam. 17:4-7).

cording to all that the LORD said unto
Moses; and Joshua gave it for an inheritance unto Israel according to their divisions by their tribes. And the land
rested from war.

The kings of Canaan

12 Now these *are* the kings of the
land, which the children of Israel smote, and possessed their land on
the other side Jordan toward the rising
of the sun, from the river Arnon unto
mount Hermon, and all the plain on the
east:
2 Sihon king of the Amorites, who
dwelt in Heshbon, *and* ruled from Aroer, which *is* upon the bank of the river
Arnon, and from the middle of the river,
and from half *Gilead, even unto the
river Jabbok, *which is* the border of the
children of Ammon;
3 And from the plain to the sea of
Chinneroth on the east, and unto the
*sea of the plain, *even* the salt sea on the

12:3 The Sea of Chinneroth
Chinneroth (or "Chinnereth," 13:27) is one of the several names for this lake. It is also called the Lake of Gennesaret (Luke 5:1); the Lake of Tiberias (John 21:1) and the Sea of Galilee (John 6:1). The "sea of the plain" is the Dead Sea, although this name does not appear in the Bible.

11:23 the land rested from war. Under the leadership of Joshua, Israel had conquered the land. There still remained land to be possessed, however (Josh. 13:1), but that was to be accomplished by the individual tribes in the part of the land given to them (Judg. 1).

east, the way to Beth-jeshimoth; and
from the south, under Ashdoth-pisgah:
¶ 4 And the coast of Og king of Bashan,
which was of the remnant of the giants,
that dwelt at *Ashtaroth and at Edrei,
5 And reigned in mount Hermon, and
in Salcah, and in all Bashan, unto the
border of the Geshurites and the Maachathites, and half Gilead, the border
of Sihon king of Heshbon.
6 Them did Moses the servant of the
LORD and the children of Israel smite:
and Moses the servant of the LORD
gave it *for* a possession unto the Reubenites, and the Gadites, and the half
tribe of Manasseh.
¶ 7 And these *are* the kings of the
country which Joshua and the children
of Israel smote on this side Jordan on
the west, from Baal-gad in the valley of
Lebanon even unto the mount Halak,
that goeth up to Seir; which Joshua gave
unto the tribes of Israel *for* a possession
according to their divisions;
8 In the mountains, and in the valleys,
and in the plains, and in the springs, and
in the wilderness, and in the south
country; the Hittites, the Amorites, and
the Canaanites, the Perizzites, the Hivites, and the Jebusites:
¶ 9 The king of Jericho, one; the king
of Ai, which *is* beside Beth-el, one;
10 The king of Jerusalem, one; the
king of Hebron, one;
11 The king of Jarmuth, one; the king
of Lachish, one;
12 The king of Eglon, one; the king of
Gezer, one;
13 The king of Debir, one; the king of
Geder, one;
14 The king of Hormah, one; the king
of Arad, one;
15 The king of Libnah, one; the king
of Adullam, one;
16 The king of Makkedah, one; the
king of Beth-el, one;
17 The king of Tappuah, one; the king
of Hepher, one;
18 The king of Aphek, one; the king of
Lasharon, one;
19 The king of Madon, one; the king
of Hazor, one;
20 The king of Shimron-meron, one;
the king of Achshaph, one;
21 The king of Taanach, one; the king
of *Megiddo, one;
22 The king of Kedesh, one; the king
of Jokneam of *Carmel, one;
23 The king of Dor in the coast of Dor,
one; the king of the nations of Gilgal,
one;
24 The king of Tirzah, one: all the
kings thirty and one.

The Conquest of Northern Canaan

12:7 this side Jordan. This phrase, which is used frequently, means west of the Jordan River (Josh. 9:1). The whole land was divided among the twelve tribes, but Reuben, Gad, and half the tribe of Manasseh had their inheritance on the "other side [of] Jordan"–the east (Josh. 12:1).

12:7 Seir. This was one of the names given to the land that was settled by the descendants of Esau. It was also called "Edom" (Num. 20:14,21) and "Idumea" (Ezek. 35:15; Mark 3:8).

II. The Division of Canaan (13:1—22:34)
Instructions concerning the division

13 Now *Joshua was old *and*
stricken in years; and the LORD
said unto him, Thou art old *and* strick-
en in years, and there remaineth yet
very much land to be possessed.

13:1 Subduing the Land
The fact that there remained "very much land to be possessed" appears contrary to the statement in 11:23 that "Joshua took the whole land." Joshua 11:23 indicates that the resistance of the land as a whole had been broken through Joshua's victories; thus, that which was conquered had to be settled and subdued by each tribe as it took up its inheritance.

2 This *is* the land that yet remaineth:
all the borders of the *Philistines, and
all Geshuri,
3 From *Sihor, which *is* before
Egypt, even unto the borders of Ekron northward, *which* is counted to the
Canaanite: five lords of the Philistines;
the Gazathites, and the Ashdothites, the
Eshkalonites, the Gittites, and the
Ekronites; also the Avites:
4 From the south, all the land of the
Canaanites, and Mearah that *is* beside
the Sidonians, unto Aphek, to the borders of the Amorites:
5 And the land of the Giblites, and all
Lebanon, toward the sunrising, from
Baal-gad under mount Hermon unto
the entering into Hamath.
6 All the inhabitants of the hill country from Lebanon unto Misrephoth-
maim, *and* all the Sidonians, them will
I drive out from before the children of
*Israel: only divide thou it by lot unto
the Israelites for an inheritance, as I
have commanded thee.
7 Now therefore divide this land for an
inheritance unto the nine tribes, and
the half tribe of *Manasseh,
8 With whom the Reubenites and the
Gadites have received their inheritance, which Moses gave them, beyond
Jordan eastward, *even* as Moses the
servant of the LORD gave them;
9 From Aroer, that *is* upon the bank of
the river Arnon, and the city that *is* in
the midst of the river, and all the plain
of Medeba unto Dibon;
10 And all the cities of Sihon king of
the Amorites, which reigned in Heshbon, unto the border of the children of
Ammon;
11 And Gilead, and the border of the
Geshurites and Maachathites, and all
mount Hermon, and all Bashan unto
Salcah;
12 All the kingdom of Og in Bashan,
which reigned in Ashtaroth and in Edrei, who remained of the remnant of the
giants: for these did Moses smite, and
cast them out.
13 Nevertheless the children of Israel
expelled not the Geshurites, nor the
Maachathites: but the Geshurites and
the Maachathites dwell among the Israelites until this day.
14 Only unto the tribe of Levi he gave
none inheritance; the sacrifices of
the LORD *God of Israel made by *fire
are their inheritance, as he said unto
them.
¶ 15 And Moses gave unto the tribe of
the children of Reuben *inheritance* according to their families.
16 And their coast was from Aroer,
that *is* on the bank of the river Arnon,

13:3 five lords of the Philistines. Compare Judges 3:3 and 1 Samuel 6:16. These were the princes of the five cities of Gaza, Ashdod, Ashkelon, Gath, and Ekron.

13:6 divide thou it by lot. This was commanded by God (Num. 26:55-56), who directed the outcome (compare Prov. 16:33).

13:14 none inheritance. The LORD God of Israel was the Levites' inheritance (vs. 33; Num. 18:20; Deut. 10:9; 18:1-2). Levi, as the tribe of the priests of God, was to be supported by the sacrifices "made by fire." Their ministry was in the sanctuary (Num. 18:5-8), and they were supported by the sanctuary (Num. 18:9-24).

and the city that *is* in the midst of the
river, and all the plain by Medeba;
17Heshbon, and all her cities that *are*
in the plain; Dibon, and Bamoth-baal,
and Beth-baal-meon,
18And Jahazah, and Kedemoth, and
Mephaath,
19And Kirjathaim, and Sibmah, and
Zareth-shahar in the mount of the
valley,
20And Beth-peor, and Ashdoth-
pisgah, and Beth-jeshimoth,
21And all the cities of the plain, and
all the kingdom of Sihon king of the
Amorites, which reigned in Heshbon,
whom Moses smote with the princes of
*Midian, Evi, and Rekem, and Zur, and
*Hur, and Reba, *which were* dukes of
Sihon, dwelling in the country.
¶22*Balaam also the son of Beor, the
soothsayer, did the children of Israel
slay with the sword among them that
were slain by them.
23And the border of the children of
Reuben was Jordan, and the border
thereof. This *was* the inheritance of the
children of Reuben after their families,
the cities and the villages thereof.
24And Moses gave *inheritance* unto
the tribe of Gad, *even* unto the children
of Gad according to their families.
25And their coast was Jazer, and all
the cities of Gilead, and half the land of
the children of Ammon, unto Aroer that
is before Rabbah;
26And from Heshbon unto Ramath-
mizpeh, and Betonim; and from Mahanaim unto the border of Debir;
27And in the valley, Beth-aram, and
Beth-nimrah, and Succoth, and Zaphon,
the rest of the kingdom of Sihon king
of Heshbon, Jordan and *his* border,
even unto the edge of the sea of *Chinnereth on the other side Jordan eastward.
28This *is* the inheritance of the children of Gad after their families, the cities, and their villages.
¶29And Moses gave *inheritance* unto
the half tribe of Manasseh: and *this* was
the possession of the half tribe of the
children of Manasseh by their families.
30And their coast was from Mahanaim, all Bashan, all the kingdom of
Og king of Bashan, and all the towns
of Jair, which *are* in Bashan, threescore
cities:
31And half Gilead, and Ashtaroth, and
Edrei, cities of the kingdom of Og in
Bashan, *were pertaining* unto the children of Machir the son of Manasseh,
even to the one half of the children of
Machir by their families.
32These *are the countries* which Moses did distribute for inheritance in the
plains of *Moab, on the other side Jordan, by Jericho, eastward.
33But unto the tribe of Levi Moses
gave not *any* inheritance: the LORD God
of Israel *was* their inheritance, as he
said unto them.

Division of the land

14 And these *are the countries*
which the children of Israel inherited in the land of Canaan, which
Eleazar the priest, and Joshua the son
of Nun, and the heads of the fathers of
the tribes of the children of Israel, distributed for inheritance to them.
2By lot *was* their inheritance, as the
LORD commanded by the hand of
*Moses, for the nine tribes, and *for*
the half tribe.
3For Moses had given the inheritance
of two tribes and an half tribe on the
other side Jordan: but unto the Levites
he gave none inheritance among them.
4For the children of *Joseph were two
tribes, Manasseh and *Ephraim: therefore they gave no part unto the Levites
in the land, save cities to dwell *in,* with

14:4 the children of Joseph were two tribes. The two sons of Joseph, Manasseh and Ephraim, were regarded by Jacob as his own sons (Gen. 48:5,14-20). Levi was not given a share of the land, but because of the two sons of Joseph there were still twelve tribes and twelve divisions of the land.

their suburbs for their cattle and for
their substance.
5 As the LORD commanded Moses, so
the children of Israel did, and they divided the land.
¶ 6 Then the children of *Judah came
unto Joshua in Gilgal: and *Caleb the
son of Jephunneh the Kenezite said
unto him, Thou knowest the thing that
the LORD said unto Moses the man of
God concerning me and thee in Kadesh-barnea.

14:6 Caleb
Caleb and Joshua were the only men who left Egypt who were allowed to enter the land of Canaan (Num. 14:22-30). Caleb's testimony rings true (vs. 8), and Moses added his word when giving the promise of inheritance (vs. 9). Caleb's faithfulness was rewarded by his receiving the inheritance promised him, and upon which his feet had trodden by faith (vss. 9,13).

7 Forty years old *was* I when Moses
the servant of the LORD sent me from
Kadesh-barnea to espy out the land;
and I brought him word again as *it was*
in mine heart.
8 Nevertheless my brethren that went
up with me made the heart of the people melt: but I wholly followed the
LORD my God.
9 And Moses sware on that day, saying, Surely the land whereon thy feet
have trodden shall be thine inheritance,
and thy children's for ever, because
thou hast wholly followed the LORD my
God.
10 And now, behold, the LORD hath
kept me alive, as he said, these forty
and five years, even since the LORD
spake this word unto Moses, while *the*
children of Israel wandered in the wilderness: and now, lo, I *am* this day fourscore and five years old.
11 As yet I *am as* strong this day as *I*
was in the day that Moses sent me: as
my strength *was* then, even so *is* my
strength now, for war, both to go out,
and to come in.
12 Now therefore give me this mountain, whereof the LORD spake in that
day; for thou heardest in that day how
*the Anakims *were* there, and *that* the
cities *were* great *and* fenced: if so be the
LORD *will be* with me, then I shall be
able to drive them out, as the LORD
said.
13 And Joshua blessed him, and gave
unto Caleb the son of Jephunneh Hebron for an inheritance.
14 Hebron therefore became the inheritance of Caleb the son of Jephunneh
the Kenezite unto this day, because that
he wholly followed the LORD God of
Israel.
15 And the name of Hebron before *was*
Kirjath-arba; *which Arba was* a great
man among the Anakims. And the land
had rest from war.

Division of the land (continued)

15 *This* then was the lot of the
tribe of the children of Judah by
their families; *even* to the border of
*Edom the wilderness of Zin southward
was the uttermost part of the south
coast.
2 And their south border was from the
shore of the salt sea, from the bay that
looketh southward:
3 And it went out to the south side to
Maaleh-acrabbim, and passed along to
Zin, and ascended up on the south side
unto Kadesh-barnea, and passed along
to Hezron, and went up to Adar, and
fetched a compass to Karkaa:
4 *From thence* it passed toward Azmon, and went out unto the river of
*Egypt; and the goings out of that coast

14:13 Hebron. This city is first mentioned in Genesis 13:18. It is also called "Kirjath-arba," or "city of Arba" (Gen. 23:2). We are told that it was a very ancient city, built seven years before Zoan in Egypt (Num. 13:22). It had holy associations for the Jews. Abraham had lived and worshipped there (Gen. 13:18) and was buried there with Sarah (Gen. 23; 25:7-11). The name "Hebron" means *alliance* or *fellowship*.

were at the sea: this shall be your south coast.

5 And the east border *was* the salt sea, *even* unto the end of Jordan. And *their* border in the north quarter *was* from the bay of the sea at the uttermost part of Jordan:

6 And the border went up to Beth-hogla, and passed along by the north of Beth-arabah; and the border went up to the stone of Bohan the son of Reuben:

7 And the border went up toward Debir from the valley of Achor, and so northward, looking toward Gilgal, that *is* before the going up to Adummim, which *is* on the south side of the river: and the border passed toward the waters of En-shemesh, and the goings out thereof were at En-rogel:

8 And the border went up by the valley of the son of Hinnom unto the south side of the Jebusite; the same *is* Jerusalem: and the border went up to the top of the mountain that *lieth* before the valley of Hinnom westward, which *is* at the end of the valley of the giants northward:

9 And the border was drawn from the top of the hill unto the fountain of the water of Nephtoah, and went out to the cities of mount Ephron; and the border was drawn to Baalah, which *is* Kirjath-jearim:

10 And the border compassed from Baalah westward unto mount Seir, and passed along unto the side of mount Jearim, which *is* Chesalon, on the north side, and went down to Beth-shemesh, and passed on to Timnah:

11 And the border went out unto the side of Ekron northward: and the border was drawn to Shicron, and passed along to mount Baalah, and went out unto Jabneel; and the goings out of the border were at the sea.

12 And the west border *was* to the great sea, and the coast *thereof.* This *is* the coast of the children of Judah round about according to their families.

¶ 13 And unto Caleb the son of Jephunneh he gave a part among the children of Judah, according to the commandment of the LORD to Joshua, *even* the city of Arba the father of Anak, which *city is* Hebron.

14 And Caleb drove thence the three sons of Anak, Sheshai, and Ahiman, and Talmai, the children of Anak.

15 And he went up thence to the inhabitants of Debir: and the name of Debir before *was* Kirjath-sepher.

¶ 16 And Caleb said, He that smiteth Kirjath-sepher, and taketh it, to him will I give Achsah my daughter to wife.

17 And Othniel the son of Kenaz, the brother of Caleb, took it: and he gave him Achsah his daughter to wife.

18 And it came to pass, as she came *unto him,* that she moved him to ask of her father a field: and she lighted off *her* ass; and Caleb said unto her, What wouldest thou?

15:17-18 A Sign of Respect
This act of alighting from the animal upon which she was riding was Achsah's way of expressing respect for her father. Even today, in some parts of the Orient it is a sign of respect to dismount a horse when meeting one higher in rank.

19 Who answered, Give me a blessing; for thou hast given me a south land; give me also springs of water. And he gave her the upper springs, and the nether springs.

20 This *is* the inheritance of the tribe of the children of Judah according to their families.

21 And the uttermost cities of the tribe of the children of Judah toward the coast of Edom southward were Kabzeel, and Eder, and Jagur,

22 And Kinah, and Dimonah, and Adadah,

15:19 springs of water. In the hot climate of the East, land was valuable only if it had a supply of water.

[23]And Kedesh, and Hazor, and Ithnan,
[24]Ziph, and Telem, and Bealoth,
[25]And Hazor, Hadattah, and Kerioth,
and Hezron, which *is* Hazor,
[26]Amam, and Shema, and Moladah,
[27]And Hazar-gaddah, and Heshmon,
and Beth-palet,
[28]And Hazar-shual, and *Beer-sheba,
and Bizjothjah,
[29]Baalah, and Iim, and Azem,
[30]And Eltolad, and Chesil, and Hormah,
[31]And Ziklag, and Madmannah, and
Sansannah,
[32]And Lebaoth, and Shilhim, and Ain,
and Rimmon: all the cities *are* twenty
and nine, with their villages:
[33]*And* in the valley, Eshtaol, and
Zoreah, and Ashnah,
[34]And Zanoah, and En-gannim, Tappuah, and Enam,
[35]Jarmuth, and Adullam, Socoh, and
Azekah,
[36]And Sharaim, and Adithaim, and
Gederah, and Gederothaim; fourteen
cities with their villages:
[37]Zenan, and Hadashah, and Migdal-
gad,
[38]And Dilean, and Mizpeh, and Joktheel,
[39]*Lachish, and Bozkath, and Eglon,
[40]And Cabbon, and Lahmam, and
Kithlish,
[41]And Gederoth, Beth-dagon, and
Naamah, and Makkedah; sixteen cities
with their villages:
[42]Libnah, and Ether, and Ashan,
[43]And Jiphtah, and Ashnah, and Nezib,
[44]And Keilah, and Achzib, and Mareshah; nine cities with their villages:
[45]Ekron, with her towns and her villages:
[46]From Ekron even unto the sea, all
that *lay* near Ashdod, with their villages:
[47]Ashdod with her towns and her villages, *Gaza with her towns and her
villages, unto the river of Egypt, and the
great sea, and the border *thereof:*
¶[48]And in the mountains, Shamir, and
Jattir, and Socoh,
[49]And Dannah, and Kirjath-sannah,
which *is* Debir,
[50]And Anab, and Eshtemoh, and
Anim,
[51]And Goshen, and Holon, and Giloh;
eleven cities with their villages:
[52]Arab, and Dumah, and Eshean,
[53]And Janum, and Beth-tappuah, and
Aphekah,
[54]And Humtah, and Kirjath-arba,
which *is* Hebron, and Zior; nine cities
with their villages:
[55]Maon, *Carmel, and Ziph, and
Juttah,
[56]And Jezreel, and Jokdeam, and Zanoah,
[57]Cain, Gibeah, and Timnah; ten cities with their villages:
[58]Halhul, Beth-zur, and Gedor,
[59]And Maarath, and Beth-anoth, and
Eltekon; six cities with their villages:
[60]Kirjath-baal, which *is* Kirjath-
jearim, and Rabbah; two cities with
their villages:
[61]In the wilderness, Beth-arabah,
Middin, and Secacah,
[62]And Nibshan, and the city of Salt,
and En-gedi; six cities with their villages.
¶[63]As for the Jebusites the inhabitants of Jerusalem, the children of Judah could not drive them out: but the
Jebusites dwell with the children of Judah at Jerusalem unto this day.

Division of the land (continued)

16 And the lot of the children of
Joseph fell from Jordan by Jeri-
cho, unto the water of Jericho on the east,
to the wilderness that goeth up from
Jericho throughout mount *Beth-el,
[2]And goeth out from Beth-el to Luz,
and passeth along unto the borders of
Archi to Ataroth,
[3]And goeth down westward to the
coast of Japhleti, unto the coast of Beth-
horon the nether, and to Gezer: and the
goings out thereof are at the sea.
[4]So the children of Joseph, Manasseh
and Ephraim, took their inheritance.
¶[5]And the border of the children of

Ephraim according to their families was
thus: even the border of their inheritance on the east side was Ataroth-
addar, unto Beth-horon the upper;
6 And the border went out toward the
sea to Michmethah on the north side;
and the border went about eastward
unto Taanath-shiloh, and passed by it on
the east to Janohah;
7 And it went down from Janohah to
Ataroth, and to Naarath, and came to
Jericho, and went out at Jordan.
8 The border went out from Tappuah
westward unto the river Kanah; and the
goings out thereof were at the sea. This
is the inheritance of the tribe of the
children of Ephraim by their families.
9 And the separate cities for the children of Ephraim *were* among the inheritance of the children of Manasseh, all
the cities with their villages.
10 And they drave not out the Canaanites that dwelt in Gezer: but the Canaanites dwell among the Ephraimites
unto this day, and serve under tribute.

Division of the Land

Division of the land (continued)

17 There was also a lot for the
tribe of Manasseh; for he *was*
the firstborn of Joseph; *to wit,* for
Machir the firstborn of Manasseh, the
father of Gilead: because he was a man
of war, therefore he had Gilead and
*Bashan.
2 There was also *a lot* for the rest of
the children of Manasseh by their families; for the children of Abiezer, and for
the children of Helek, and for the children of Asriel, and for the children of
*Shechem, and for the children of He-
pher, and for the children of Shemida:
these *were* the male children of Manasseh the son of Joseph by their families.
¶3 But Zelophehad, the son of Hepher,
the son of Gilead, the son of Machir, the
son of Manasseh, had no sons, but
daughters: and these *are* the names of
his daughters, Mahlah, and Noah, Hoglah, Milcah, and Tirzah.
4 And they came near before Eleazar
the priest, and before Joshua the son of
Nun, and before the princes, saying, The
LORD commanded Moses to give us an
inheritance among our brethren. Therefore according to the commandment of
the LORD he gave them an inheritance
among the brethren of their father.
5 And there fell ten portions to Manasseh, beside the land of Gilead and
Bashan, which *were* on the other side
Jordan;
6 Because the daughters of Manasseh
had an inheritance among his sons: and
the rest of Manasseh's sons had the
land of Gilead.
¶7 And the coast of Manasseh was
from Asher to Michmethah, that *lieth*
before Shechem; and the border went
along on the right hand unto the inhabitants of En-tappuah.
8 *Now* Manasseh had the land of Tappuah: but Tappuah on the border of
Manasseh *belonged* to the children of
Ephraim;

17:4 The LORD commanded Moses to give us an inheritance. See Numbers 27:1-11 for the law of inheritance.

9 And the coast descended unto the
river Kanah, southward of the river:
these cities of Ephraim *are* among the
cities of Manasseh: the coast of Manasseh also *was* on the north side of the
river, and the outgoings of it were at the
sea:
10 Southward *it was* Ephraim's, and
northward *it was* Manasseh's, and the
sea is his border; and they met together in Asher on the north, and in Issachar on the east.
11 And Manasseh had in Issachar and
in Asher Beth-shean and her towns,
and Ibleam and her towns, and the inhabitants of Dor and her towns, and the
inhabitants of Endor and her towns, and
the inhabitants of Taanach and her
towns, and the inhabitants of *Megiddo and her towns, *even* three countries.
12 Yet the children of Manasseh could
not drive out *the inhabitants of* those
cities; but the Canaanites would dwell
in that land.
13 Yet it came to pass, when the children of Israel were waxen strong, that
they put the Canaanites to tribute; but
did not utterly drive them out.
14 And the children of Joseph spake
unto Joshua, saying, Why hast thou
given me *but* one lot and one portion to
inherit, seeing I *am* a great people, forasmuch as the LORD hath blessed me
hitherto?
15 And Joshua answered them, If thou
be a great people, *then* get thee up to the
wood *country,* and cut down for thyself
there in the land of the Perizzites and
of the giants, if mount Ephraim be too
narrow for thee.
16 And the children of Joseph said, The
hill is not enough for us: and all the Canaanites that dwell in the land of the
valley have chariots of iron, *both they*
who *are* of Beth-shean and her towns,
and *they* who *are* of the valley of Jezreel.
17 And Joshua spake unto the house of
Joseph, *even* to Ephraim and to Manasseh, saying, Thou *art* a great people,
and hast great power: thou shalt not
have one lot *only:*
18 But the mountain shall be thine; for
it *is* a wood, and thou shalt cut it down:
and the outgoings of it shall be thine: for
thou shalt drive out the Canaanites,
though they have iron chariots, *and*
though they *be* strong.

The Tabernacle in Shiloh

18 And the whole congregation of
the children of Israel assembled
together at Shiloh, and set up the *tabernacle of the congregation there. And
the land was subdued before them.

Division of the land (continued)

2 And there remained among the children of Israel seven tribes, which had
not yet received their inheritance.

17:14 A Great People
The tribes of Manasseh and Ephraim said they were a "great" people, meaning great in number (vs. 14). Joshua made a play on the word "great": "If thou be a great people" (vs. 15), and "Thou art a great people" (vs. 17). He gave them work to do that would show how great they were (compare Prov. 16:32).

18:1 Shiloh
The life of Israel revolved around the tabernacle that was set up in the center of the camp. The tabernacle was erected at Shiloh and remained there for some time (1 Sam. 1:3; 2:14). It was the place where God revealed Himself to Samuel (1 Sam. 3:21). When judgment was to be sent on Israel, God reminded them of what took place in "Shiloh, where I set my name at the first" (Jer. 7:12). The place of blessing would be the place of a curse (Jer. 26:6; compare Mal. 2:2).

17:9,18 outgoings. Utmost limits or boundaries.
17:12 the Canaanites would dwell in that land. The Canaanites are a *type of the *flesh in the believer, as set forth in Romans 7 (compare Rom. 8:7). The day is coming when there shall "be no more the Canaanite in the house of the LORD of hosts" (Zech. 14:21).

3 And Joshua said unto the children of
Israel, How long *are* ye slack to go to
possess the land, which the LORD God
of your fathers hath given you?
4 Give out from among you three men
for *each* tribe: and I will send them, and
they shall rise, and go through the land,
and describe it according to the inheritance of them; and they shall come
again to me.
5 And they shall divide it into seven
parts: Judah shall abide in their coast on
the south, and the house of Joseph shall
abide in their coasts on the north.
6 Ye shall therefore describe the land
into seven parts, and bring *the description* hither to me, that I may cast lots
for you here before the LORD our God.
7 But the Levites have no part among
you; for the priesthood of the LORD *is*
their inheritance: and Gad, and Reuben,
and half the tribe of Manasseh, have
received their inheritance beyond Jordan on the east, which Moses the servant of the LORD gave them.
¶8 And the men arose, and went away:
and Joshua charged them that went to
describe the land, saying, Go and walk
through the land, and describe it, and
come again to me, that I may here cast
lots for you before the LORD in Shiloh.
9 And the men went and passed
through the land, and described it by
cities into seven parts in a book, and
came *again* to Joshua to the host at
Shiloh.
¶10 And Joshua cast lots for them in
Shiloh before the LORD: and there
Joshua divided the land unto the children of Israel according to their divisions.
¶11 And the lot of the tribe of the children of Benjamin came up according to
their families: and the coast of their lot
came forth between the children of Judah and the children of Joseph.
12 And their border on the north side
was from Jordan; and the border went
up to the side of Jericho on the north
side, and went up through the mountains westward; and the goings out
thereof were at the wilderness of
*Beth-aven.
13 And the border went over from
thence toward Luz, to the side of Luz,
which *is* Beth-el, southward; and the
border descended to Ataroth-adar, near
the hill that *lieth* on the south side of the
nether Beth-horon.
14 And the border was drawn *thence,*
and compassed the corner of the sea
southward, from the hill that *lieth* before
Beth-horon southward; and the goings
out thereof were at Kirjath-baal, which
is Kirjath-jearim, a city of the children
of Judah: this *was* the west quarter.
15 And the south quarter *was* from the
end of Kirjath-jearim, and the border
went out on the west, and went out to
the well of waters of Nephtoah:
16 And the border came down to the
end of the mountain that *lieth* before the
valley of the son of Hinnom, *and* which
is in the valley of the giants on the
north, and descended to the valley of
Hinnom, to the side of Jebusi on the
south, and descended to En-rogel,
17 And was drawn from the north, and
went forth to En-shemesh, and went
forth toward Geliloth, which *is* over
against the going up of Adummim, and
descended to the stone of Bohan the
son of Reuben,
18 And passed along toward the side
over against Arabah northward, and
went down unto Arabah:
19 And the border passed along to the
side of Beth-hoglah northward: and
the outgoings of the border were at the
north bay of the salt sea at the south
end of Jordan: this *was* the south coast.
20 And Jordan was the border of it on
the east side. This *was* the inheritance
of the children of Benjamin, by the
coasts thereof round about, according to
their families.

18:4,6 describe. To mark out.
18:7 Levites have no part. See Joshua 13:14 note.

21 Now the cities of the tribe of the
children of Benjamin according to their
families were Jericho, and Beth-hoglah,
and the valley of Keziz,
22 And Beth-arabah, and Zemaraim,
and Beth-el,
23 And Avim, and Parah, and Ophrah,
24 And Chephar-haammonai, and
Ophni, and Gaba; twelve cities with
their villages:
25 Gibeon, and Ramah, and Beeroth,
26 And Mizpeh, and Chephirah, and
Mozah,
27 And Rekem, and Irpeel, and Taralah,
28 And Zelah, Eleph, and Jebusi, which
is *Jerusalem, Gibeath, *and* Kirjath;
fourteen cities with their villages. This
is the inheritance of the children of
Benjamin according to their families.

Division of the land (continued)

19 And the second lot came forth
to Simeon, *even* for the tribe of
the children of Simeon according to
their families: and their inheritance was
within the inheritance of the children of
Judah.
2 And they had in their inheritance
*Beer-sheba, or Sheba, and Moladah,
3 And Hazar-shual, and Balah, and
Azem,
4 And Eltolad, and Bethul, and Hormah,
5 And Ziklag, and Beth-marcaboth,
and Hazar-susah,
6 And Beth-lebaoth, and Sharuhen;
thirteen cities and their villages:
7 Ain, Remmon, and Ether, and
Ashan; four cities and their villages:
8 And all the villages that *were* round
about these cities to Baalath-beer, Ra-
math of the south. This *is* the inheritance of the tribe of the children of
Simeon according to their families.
9 Out of the portion of the children of
Judah *was* the inheritance of the children of Simeon: for the part of the children of Judah was too much for them:
therefore the children of Simeon had
their inheritance within the inheritance
of them.
¶ 10 And the third lot came up for the
children of Zebulun according to their
families: and the border of their inheritance was unto Sarid:
11 And their border went up toward
the sea, and Maralah, and reached to
Dabbasheth, and reached to the river
that *is* before Jokneam;
12 And turned from Sarid eastward
toward the sunrising unto the border of
Chisloth-tabor, and then goeth out to
Daberath, and goeth up to Japhia,
13 And from thence passeth on along
on the east to Gittah-hepher, to Ittah-
kazin, and goeth out to Remmon-
methoar to Neah;
14 And the border compasseth it on the
north side to Hannathon: and the outgoings thereof are in the valley of
Jiphthah-el:
15 And Kattath, and Nahallal, and
Shimron, and Idalah, and Beth-lehem:
twelve cities with their villages.
16 This *is* the inheritance of the children of Zebulun according to their families, these cities with their villages.
¶ 17 *And* the fourth lot came out to Issachar, for the children of Issachar according to their families.
18 And their border was toward Jezreel, and Chesulloth, and Shunem,
19 And Haphraim, and Shihon, and
Anaharath,
20 And Rabbith, and Kishion, and
Abez,
21 And Remeth, and En-gannim, and
En-haddah, and Beth-pazzez;
22 And the coast reacheth to Tabor,
and Shahazimah, and Beth-shemesh;
and the outgoings of their border were
at Jordan: sixteen cities with their villages.
23 This *is* the inheritance of the tribe
of the children of Issachar according to

19:9 Out of the portion . . . children of Simeon. Simeon had no definite portion, in fulfillment of Genesis 49:5,7.

their families, the cities and their villages.
¶24And the fifth lot came out for the
tribe of the children of Asher according
to their families.
25And their border was Helkath, and
Hali, and Beten, and Achshaph,
26And Alammelech, and Amad, and
Misheal; and reacheth to *Carmel
westward, and to Shihor-libnath;
27And turneth toward the sunrising
to Beth-dagon, and reacheth to Zebulun, and to the valley of Jiphthah-el toward the north side of Beth-emek, and
Neiel, and goeth out to Cabul on the left
hand,
28And Hebron, and Rehob, and Hammon, and Kanah, *even* unto great Zidon;
29And *then* the coast turneth to Ramah, and to the strong city *Tyre; and
the coast turneth to Hosah; and the
outgoings thereof are at the sea from
the coast to Achzib:
30Ummah also, and Aphek, and Rehob: twenty and two cities with their
villages.
31This *is* the inheritance of the tribe
of the children of Asher according to
their families, these cities with their
villages.
¶32The sixth lot came out to the
children of Naphtali, *even* for the children of Naphtali according to their families.
33And their coast was from Heleph,
from Allon to Zaanannim, and Adami,
Nekeb, and Jabneel, unto Lakum; and
the outgoings thereof were at Jordan:
34And *then* the coast turneth westward to Aznoth-tabor, and goeth out
from thence to Hukkok, and reacheth to
Zebulun on the south side, and reacheth
to Asher on the west side, and to Judah
upon Jordan toward the sunrising.
35And the fenced cities *are* Ziddim,
Zer, and Hammath, Rakkath, and *Chinnereth,
36And Adamah, and Ramah, and
Hazor,
37And Kedesh, and Edrei, and En-
hazor,
38And Iron, and Migdal-el, Horem,
and Beth-anath, and Beth-shemesh;
nineteen cities with their villages.
39This *is* the inheritance of the tribe
of the children of Naphtali according to
their families, the cities and their villages.
¶40*And* the seventh lot came out for
the tribe of the children of Dan according to their families.
41And the coast of their inheritance was Zorah, and Eshtaol, and Ir-
shemesh,
42And Shaalabbin, and Ajalon, and
Jethlah,
43And Elon, and Thimnathah, and
Ekron,
44And Eltekeh, and Gibbethon, and
Baalath,
45And Jehud, and Bene-berak, and
Gath-rimmon,
46And Me-jarkon, and Rakkon, with
the border before Japho.
47And the coast of the children of Dan
went out *too little* for them: therefore
the children of Dan went up to fight
against Leshem, and took it, and smote
it with the edge of the sword, and possessed it, and dwelt therein, and called
Leshem, Dan, after the name of Dan
their father.
48This *is* the inheritance of the tribe
of the children of Dan according to their
families, these cities with their villages.
¶49When they had made an end of dividing the land for inheritance by their
coasts, the children of *Israel gave an
inheritance to *Joshua the son of Nun
among them:

19:49 Joshua's Inheritance
This act of Joshua's in leaving himself to the last is a sidelight on his fine character. The portion he received was according to the "word of the LORD" (vs. 50) and would be similar to the portion given to Caleb (see Josh. 14:6-15; 15:13-19).

50According to the word of the LORD
they gave him the city which he asked,
even Timnath-serah in mount Ephraim:

and he built the city, and dwelt therein.
51 These *are* the inheritances, which
Eleazar the priest, and Joshua the son
of Nun, and the heads of the fathers
of the tribes of the children of Israel,
divided for an inheritance by lot in
Shiloh before the LORD, at the door
of the tabernacle of the congregation.
So they made an end of dividing the
country.

The cities of refuge

20 The LORD also spake unto
Joshua, saying,
2 Speak to the children of Israel, saying, Appoint out for you *cities of refuge, whereof I spake unto you by the
hand of *Moses:

> **20:2 The Cities of Refuge**
> The cities of refuge were six in number and were appointed as havens of refuge for anyone who had killed a person unintentionally (Num. 35:6,11). The Jordan divided the land, and three cities were located on each side of the river (Num. 35:14). The laws governing these cities and those who could flee to them for refuge are given in Numbers 35; Deuteronomy 19:1-13 and Joshua 20:1-6. They are a *type of Christ to whom the sinner may flee for refuge. It is thus "we might have a strong consolation, who have fled for refuge to lay hold upon the hope set before us" (Heb. 6:18).

3 That the slayer that killeth *any* person unawares *and* unwittingly may flee
thither: and they shall be your refuge
from the avenger of blood.
4 And when he that doth flee unto one
of those cities shall stand at the entering of the gate of the city, and shall declare his cause in the ears of the *elders
of that city, they shall take him into the
city unto them, and give him a place,
that he may dwell among them.
5 And if the avenger of blood pursue
after him, then they shall not deliver
the slayer up into his hand; because he
smote his neighbour unwittingly, and
hated him not beforetime.
6 And he shall dwell in that city, until
he stand before the congregation for
judgment, *and* until the death of
the high priest that shall be in those
days: then shall the slayer return, and
come unto his own city, and unto his
own house, unto the city from whence
he fled.
¶ 7 And they appointed Kedesh in Galilee in mount Naphtali, and Shechem in
mount *Ephraim, and Kirjath-arba,
which *is* Hebron, in the mountain of
*Judah.
8 And on the other side Jordan by
Jericho eastward, they assigned Bezer
in the wilderness upon the plain out
of the tribe of Reuben, and Ramoth
in *Gilead out of the tribe of Gad, and
Golan in Bashan out of the tribe of
*Manasseh.
9 These were the cities appointed
for all the children of Israel, and for
the stranger that sojourneth among
them, that whosoever killeth *any* person at unawares might flee thither,
and not die by the hand of the avenger of blood, until he stood before the
congregation.

19:51 Eleazar the priest, and Joshua. God through Moses appointed those who should divide the land (Num. 34:17). The names of the "heads of the fathers" are also given (Num. 34:19-29).

20:3 unwittingly. Unconsciously, unintentionally.

20:3 avenger of blood. The word "avenger" also has the idea of "one who gets revenge" (Num. 35:19,21,24-25,27). This person would seek out the "manslayer" (one who had killed another) and take revenge. If the manslayer fled to a city of refuge he was safe until he faced the congregation to determine his guilt. If it was determined he had killed without malice he could stay in the city of refuge until the death of the high priest. At that time he was free to return to his land of possession (home). See Numbers 35:6-29.

The Levites' inheritance

21 Then came near the heads of the fathers of the Levites unto Eleazar the priest, and unto Joshua the son of Nun, and unto the heads of the fathers of the tribes of the children of Israel;

2 And they spake unto them at Shiloh in the land of Canaan, saying, The LORD commanded by the hand of Moses to give us cities to dwell in, with the suburbs thereof for our cattle.

3 And the children of Israel gave unto the Levites out of their inheritance, at the commandment of the LORD, these cities and their suburbs.

21:3 The Levites' Inheritance
Compare 13:33. Israel had been commanded to give the Levites cities and their suburbs to dwell in. These were to be forty-eight in number (Josh. 21:41; Num. 35:1-7). Six of these were to be *cities of refuge (Num. 35:6). It pleased God to make the priests dependent on a people obedient to Him in their worship. When Israel's spiritual life declined, they gave the "polluted . . . the blind . . . the lame and sick" to God (Mal. 1:6-10) and even robbed God (Mal. 3:8-9).

4 And the lot came out for the families of the Kohathites: and the children of *Aaron the priest, *which were* of the Levites, had by lot out of the tribe of Judah, and out of the tribe of Simeon, and out of the tribe of Benjamin, thirteen cities.

5 And the rest of the children of Kohath *had* by lot out of the families of the tribe of Ephraim, and out of the tribe of Dan, and out of the half tribe of Manasseh, ten cities.

6 And the children of Gershon *had* by lot out of the families of the tribe of Issachar, and out of the tribe of Asher, and out of the tribe of Naphtali, and out of the half tribe of Manasseh in Bashan, thirteen cities.

7 The children of Merari by their families *had* out of the tribe of Reuben, and out of the tribe of Gad, and out of the tribe of Zebulun, twelve cities.

8 And the children of Israel gave by lot unto the Levites these cities with their suburbs, as the LORD commanded by the hand of Moses.

¶ 9 And they gave out of the tribe of the children of Judah, and out of the tribe of the children of Simeon, these cities which are *here* mentioned by name,

10 Which the children of Aaron, *being* of the families of the Kohathites, *who were* of the children of Levi, had: for theirs was the first lot.

11 And they gave them the city of Arba the father of Anak, which *city is* Hebron, in the hill *country* of Judah, with the suburbs thereof round about it.

12 But the fields of the city, and the villages thereof, gave they to *Caleb the son of Jephunneh for his possession.

¶ 13 Thus they gave to the children of Aaron the priest Hebron with her suburbs, *to be* a city of refuge for the slayer; and Libnah with her suburbs,

14 And Jattir with her suburbs, and Eshtemoa with her suburbs,

15 And Holon with her suburbs, and Debir with her suburbs,

16 And Ain with her suburbs, and Juttah with her suburbs, *and* Beth-shemesh with her suburbs; nine cities out of those two tribes.

17 And out of the tribe of Benjamin, Gibeon with her suburbs, Geba with her suburbs,

18 Anathoth with her suburbs, and Almon with her suburbs; four cities.

19 All the cities of the children of Aaron, the priests, *were* thirteen cities with their suburbs.

¶ 20 And the families of the children of Kohath, the Levites which remained of the children of Kohath, even they had the cities of their lot out of the tribe of Ephraim.

21 For they gave them Shechem with her suburbs in mount Ephraim, *to be* a city of refuge for the slayer; and Gezer with her suburbs,

22 And Kibzaim with her suburbs, and Beth-horon with her suburbs; four cities.

[23]And out of the tribe of Dan, Eltekeh
with her suburbs, Gibbethon with her
suburbs,
[24]Aijalon with her suburbs, Gath-
rimmon with her suburbs; four cities.
[25]And out of the half tribe of Manasseh, Tanach with her suburbs, and
Gath-rimmon with her suburbs; two
cities.
[26]All the cities *were* ten with their
suburbs for the families of the children
of Kohath that remained.
¶[27]And unto the children of Gershon,
of the families of the Levites, out of the
other half tribe of Manasseh *they gave*
Golan in Bashan with her suburbs, *to be*
a city of refuge for the slayer; and Beesh-
terah with her suburbs; two cities.
[28]And out of the tribe of Issachar,
Kishon with her suburbs, Dabareh with
her suburbs,
[29]Jarmuth with her suburbs, En-
gannim with her suburbs; four cities.
[30]And out of the tribe of Asher, Mi-
shal with her suburbs, Abdon with her
suburbs,
[31]Helkath with her suburbs, and Rehob with her suburbs; four cities.
[32]And out of the tribe of Naphtali,
Kedesh in Galilee with her suburbs, *to
be* a city of refuge for the slayer; and
Hammoth-dor with her suburbs, and
Kartan with her suburbs; three cities.
[33]All the cities of the Gershonites
according to their families *were* thirteen
cities with their suburbs.
¶[34]And unto the families of the children of Merari, the rest of the Levites,
out of the tribe of Zebulun, Jokneam
with her suburbs, and Kartah with her
suburbs,
[35]Dimnah with her suburbs, Nahalal
with her suburbs; four cities.
[36]And out of the tribe of Reuben,
Bezer with her suburbs, and Jahazah
with her suburbs,
[37]Kedemoth with her suburbs, and
Mephaath with her suburbs; four cities.
[38]And out of the tribe of Gad, Ramoth
in Gilead with her suburbs, *to be* a city
of refuge for the slayer; and Mahanaim
with her suburbs,
[39]Heshbon with her suburbs, Jazer
with her suburbs; four cities in all.
[40]So all the cities for the children of
Merari by their families, which were
remaining of the families of the Levites,
were *by* their lot twelve cities.
[41]All the cities of the Levites within
the possession of the children of Israel
were forty and eight cities with their
suburbs.
[42]These cities were every one with
their suburbs round about them: thus
were all these cities.
¶[43]And the LORD gave unto Israel all
the land which he sware to give unto
their fathers; and they possessed it, and
dwelt therein.
[44]And the LORD gave them rest round
about, according to all that he sware
unto their fathers: and there stood not
a man of all their enemies before them;
the LORD delivered all their enemies
into their hand.
[45]There failed not ought of any good
thing which the LORD had spoken unto
the house of Israel; all came to pass.

21:45 Promises Kept
God gave the promise of the land to Abraham (Gen. 13:15; 15:18), to Isaac (Gen. 26:3), and to Jacob (Gen. 28:13). There was a delay in Israel's occupation of the land because of their sin in the wilderness (Num. 14:32-35) and even in the land through the sin of Achan (Josh. 7), but God's purpose did not change. His purpose never changes (compare Heb. 13:8); He will complete what He has begun (compare 1 John 1:7-9; 2:1-2; with Phil. 1:6; Rom. 8:28-39).

The altar of the two and one-half tribes

22 Then Joshua called the Reubenites, and the Gadites, and
the half tribe of Manasseh,
[2]And said unto them, Ye have kept all
that Moses the servant of the LORD

22:2 Moses the servant of the LORD commanded you. The command of Moses is recorded in Numbers 32:28-30. The two-and-one-half tribes were to send their armed

commanded you, and have obeyed my voice in all that I commanded you:

3 Ye have not left your brethren these many days unto this day, but have kept the charge of the commandment of the LORD your *God.

4 And now the LORD your God hath given rest unto your brethren, as he promised them: therefore now return ye, and get you unto your tents, *and* unto the land of your possession, which Moses the servant of the LORD gave you on the other side Jordan.

5 But take diligent heed to do the commandment and the *law, which Moses the servant of the LORD charged you, to love the LORD your God, and to walk in all his ways, and to keep his commandments, and to cleave unto him, and to serve him with all your heart and with all your soul.

6 So Joshua blessed them, and sent them away: and they went unto their tents.

¶ 7 Now to the *one* half of the tribe of Manasseh Moses had given *possession* in Bashan: but unto the *other* half thereof gave Joshua among their brethren on this side Jordan westward. And when Joshua sent them away also unto their tents, then he blessed them,

8 And he spake unto them, saying, Return with much riches unto your tents, and with very much cattle, with silver, and with gold, and with brass, and with iron, and with very much raiment: divide the spoil of your enemies with your brethren.

¶ 9 And the children of Reuben and the children of Gad and the half tribe of Manasseh returned, and departed from the children of Israel out of *Shiloh, which *is* in the land of Canaan, to go unto the country of Gilead, to the land of their possession, whereof they were possessed, according to the word of the LORD by the hand of Moses.

¶ 10 And when they came unto the borders of Jordan, that *are* in the land of Canaan, the children of Reuben and the children of Gad and the half tribe of Manasseh built there an *altar by Jordan, a great altar to see to.

22:10 A Great Altar
The altar by the Jordan was great to behold and could be seen afar off. This altar built by the two-and-one-half tribes was not for sacrifice but was a reminder that even though the Jordan River cut them off from their brethren on the other side, they were still one nation (vss. 26-29).

¶ 11 And the children of Israel heard say, Behold, the children of Reuben and the children of Gad and the half tribe of Manasseh have built an altar over against the land of Canaan, in the borders of Jordan, at the passage of the children of Israel.

12 And when the children of Israel heard *of it,* the whole congregation of the children of Israel gathered themselves together at Shiloh, to go up to war against them.

13 And the children of Israel sent unto the children of Reuben, and to the children of Gad, and to the half tribe of Manasseh, into the land of Gilead, *Phinehas the son of Eleazar the priest,

14 And with him ten princes, of each chief house a prince throughout all the tribes of Israel; and each one *was* an head of the house of their fathers among the thousands of Israel.

¶ 15 And they came unto the children of Reuben, and to the children of Gad, and to the half tribe of Manasseh, unto the land of Gilead, and they spake with them, saying,

16 Thus saith the whole congregation

---

men with the main body of Israel until all the land was conquered. Only then could they return to their own possessions.

22:12 to war against them. See the reason for this in verses 17 and 19 and their notes.

22:13 Phinehas. He was very zealous for the honor of God. He had been given a special promise because of his quick action against sin (see Num. 25:7-12).

of the LORD, What *trespass *is* this that
ye have committed against the God of
Israel, to turn away this day from following the LORD, in that ye have
builded you an altar, that ye might rebel this day against the LORD?
17*Is* the iniquity of Peor too little for
us, from which we are not cleansed
until this day, although there was a
plague in the congregation of the LORD,
18But that ye must turn away this day
from following the LORD? and it will be,
seeing ye rebel to day against the LORD,
that to morrow he will be wroth with
the whole congregation of Israel.
19Notwithstanding, if the land of your
possession *be* *unclean, *then* pass ye
over unto the land of the possession of
the LORD, wherein the LORD'S tabernacle dwelleth, and take possession
among us: but rebel not against the
LORD, nor rebel against us, in building
you an altar beside the altar of the LORD
our God.

22:19 Only One Altar
The worship of God centered on the altar of sacrifice in the tabernacle. As there was one God, so there was one altar. There is only one place where a holy God meets sinful man—at the cross of Christ, where sin was judged and reconciliation made (Rom. 5:10-11; 2 Cor. 5:19-21). The altar was a *type of this. Israel needed no other altar than that provided by God. We need no other Saviour than the Lord Jesus to present us perfect before God (Acts 4:12).

20Did not Achan the son of Zerah
commit a trespass in the accursed
thing, and wrath fell on all the congregation of Israel? and that man perished
not alone in his iniquity.
¶21Then the children of Reuben and
the children of Gad and the half tribe of
Manasseh answered, and said unto the
heads of the thousands of Israel,
22The LORD God of gods, the LORD
God of gods, he knoweth, and Israel he
shall know; if *it be* in rebellion, or if in
transgression against the LORD, (save
us not this day,)
23That we have built us an altar to
turn from following the LORD, or if to offer thereon burnt-offering or *meat-
offering, or if to offer *peace-offerings
thereon, let the LORD himself require *it;*
24And if we have not *rather* done it
for fear of *this* thing, saying, In time
to come your children might speak unto
our children, saying, What have ye to do
with the LORD God of Israel?
25For the LORD hath made Jordan a
border between us and you, ye children
of Reuben and children of Gad; ye have
no part in the LORD: so shall your children make our children cease from
*fearing the LORD.
26Therefore we said, Let us now prepare to build us an altar, not for burnt-
offering, nor for *sacrifice:
27But *that* it *may be* a witness between us, and you, and our generations
after us, that we might do the service
of the LORD before him with our burnt-
offerings, and with our sacrifices, and
with our peace-offerings; that your
children may not say to our children
in time to come, Ye have no part in the
LORD.
28Therefore said we, that it shall be,
when they should *so* say to us or to our
generations in time to come, that we
may say *again,* Behold the pattern of
the altar of the LORD, which our fathers
made, not for burnt-offerings, nor for
sacrifices; but it *is* a witness between
us and you.
29God forbid that we should rebel
against the LORD, and turn this day
from following the LORD, to build an
altar for burnt-offerings, for meat-
offerings, or for sacrifices, beside the

22:17 the iniquity of Peor. This is a reference to the plague that followed Israel's sin in "the matter of Peor" (Num. 25:18). Israel feared that the two-and-one-half tribes had built an altar to rebel against the LORD (vss. 16,18) and that their sin would bring judgment on all (vs. 18). Achan is quoted as an illustration of this (vs. 20; compare 7:1,5).

altar of the LORD our God that *is* before his tabernacle.

¶30 And when Phinehas the priest, and the princes of the congregation and heads of the thousands of Israel which *were* with him, heard the words that the children of Reuben and the children of Gad and the children of Manasseh spake, it pleased them.

31 And Phinehas the son of Eleazar the priest said unto the children of Reuben, and to the children of Gad, and to the children of Manasseh, This day we perceive that the LORD *is* among us, because ye have not committed this trespass against the LORD: now ye have delivered the children of Israel out of the hand of the LORD.

¶32 And Phinehas the son of Eleazar the priest, and the princes, returned from the children of Reuben, and from the children of Gad, out of the land of Gilead, unto the land of Canaan, to the children of Israel, and brought them word again.

33 And the thing pleased the children of Israel; and the children of Israel blessed God, and did not intend to go up against them in battle, to destroy the land wherein the children of Reuben and Gad dwelt.

34 And the children of Reuben and the children of Gad called the altar *Ed:* for it *shall be* a witness between us that the LORD *is* God.

III. The Farewell of Joshua (23:1—24:33)

23 And it came to pass a long time after that the LORD had given rest unto Israel from all their enemies round about, that Joshua waxed old *and* stricken in age.

2 And Joshua called for all Israel, *and* for their elders, and for their heads, and for their judges, and for their officers, and said unto them, I am old *and* stricken in age:

3 And ye have seen all that the LORD your God hath done unto all these nations because of you; for the LORD your God *is* he that hath fought for you.

4 Behold, I have divided unto you by lot these nations that remain, to be an inheritance for your tribes, from Jordan, with all the nations that I have cut off, even unto the great sea westward.

5 And the LORD your God, he shall expel them from before you, and drive them from out of your sight; and ye shall possess their land, as the LORD your God hath promised unto you.

6 Be ye therefore very courageous to keep and to do all that is written in the *book of the law of Moses, that ye turn not aside therefrom *to* the right hand or *to* the left;

7 That ye come not among these nations, these that remain among you; neither make mention of the names of their gods, nor cause to swear *by them,* neither serve them, nor bow yourselves unto them:

8 But cleave unto the LORD your God, as ye have done unto this day.

23:7 A Separate People
God demands that His people be separate from fellowship with the unbelieving and idolatrous world. The heathen nations were driven out because of their idolatry and evil. Note the repeated warnings (Exod. 23:32-33; Deut. 7:3). Christians are warned against these same evils (Eph. 5:11; 2 Cor. 6:14-15).

22:34 a witness between us. The word "Ed" means *witness*. The building of such memorials was a common practice. Jacob and Laban made a heap of stones and called it Jegar-sahadutha, or heap of witness (Gen. 31:45-49). While "the thing pleased the children of Israel" (Josh. 22:33), the Scripture does not say that it pleased God.

23:6 all that is written in the book of the law of Moses. The five books of Moses, Genesis to Deuteronomy, were the only portion of the Bible they had at that time. Joshua urged the people to obey God's Word, as he himself had been commanded to do (Josh. 1:8).

9 For the LORD hath driven out from before you great nations and strong: but *as for* you, no man hath been able to stand before you unto this day.

10 One man of you shall chase a thousand: for the LORD your God, he *it is* that fighteth for you, as he hath promised you.

11 Take good heed therefore unto yourselves, that ye love the LORD your God.

12 Else if ye do in any wise go back, and cleave unto the remnant of these nations, *even* these that remain among you, and shall make marriages with them, and go in unto them, and they to you:

13 Know for a certainty that the LORD your God will no more drive out *any of* these nations from before you; but they shall be snares and traps unto you, and scourges in your sides, and thorns in your eyes, until ye perish from off this good land which the LORD your God hath given you.

14 And, behold, this day I *am* going the way of all the earth: and ye know in all your hearts and in all your souls, that not one thing hath failed of all the good things which the LORD your God spake concerning you; all are come to pass unto you, *and* not one thing hath failed thereof.

23:15 Blessing and Curses
God had promised a blessing on obedience and a curse on disobedience. One was as sure as the other, and history shows this to be true. Adam disobeyed God and plunged the world into sin. Christ obeyed God and redeemed the world from sin (Rom. 5:19). Disobedience brought death; obedience brought life from the dead.

15 Therefore it shall come to pass, *that* as all good things are come upon you, which the LORD your God promised you; so shall the LORD bring upon you all evil things, until he have destroyed you from off this good land which the LORD your God hath given you.

16 When ye have transgressed the *covenant of the LORD your God, which he commanded you, and have gone and served other gods, and bowed yourselves to them; then shall the anger of the LORD be kindled against you, and ye shall perish quickly from off the good land which he hath given unto you.

Joshua's last words

24 And Joshua gathered all the tribes of Israel to Shechem, and called for the elders of Israel, and for their heads, and for their judges, and for their officers; and they presented themselves before God.

2 And Joshua said unto all the people, Thus saith the LORD God of Israel, Your fathers dwelt on the other side of the flood in old time, *even* Terah, the father of Abraham, and the father of Nachor: and they served other gods.

3 And I took your father Abraham from the other side of the flood, and led him throughout all the land of Canaan, and multiplied his seed, and gave him Isaac.

4 And I gave unto Isaac Jacob and Esau: and I gave unto Esau mount Seir, to possess it; but Jacob and his children went down into Egypt.

5 I sent Moses also and Aaron, and I plagued Egypt, according to that which I did among them: and afterward I brought you out.

23:10 One man of you shall chase a thousand. This is part of the promise given by God to Israel, on the condition of obedience (Lev. 26:3-8; Deut. 32:30). The same order is used by Moses and Joshua: obedience to God's Word (Josh. 23:6), separation from evil (vs. 7), and victory over the enemy (vs. 10). This truth is also taught in Romans 6:11-14, ending with the promise of victory in verse 14.

23:13 they shall be snares and traps unto you. The Israelites could only be endangered in their relationship to God by association with the Canaanites. The latter are an illustration of the *flesh—the *old man in the believer—which must be crucified (Gal. 2:20) and put off (Col. 3:9-10).

6And I brought your fathers out of
Egypt: and ye came unto the sea; and
the Egyptians pursued after your fathers with chariots and horsemen unto
the Red sea.
7And when they cried unto the LORD,
he put darkness between you and the
Egyptians, and brought the sea upon
them, and covered them; and your eyes
have seen what I have done in Egypt: and
ye dwelt in the wilderness a long season.
8And I brought you into the land of
the Amorites, which dwelt on the other
side Jordan; and they fought with you:
and I gave them into your hand, that ye
might possess their land; and I destroyed them from before you.
9Then Balak the son of Zippor, king
of Moab, arose and warred against Israel, and sent and called Balaam the son
of Beor to curse you:
10But I would not hearken unto Balaam; therefore he blessed you still: so
I delivered you out of his hand.
11And ye went over Jordan, and came
unto Jericho: and the men of Jericho
fought against you, the Amorites, and
the Perizzites, and the Canaanites, and
the Hittites, and the Girgashites, the
Hivites, and the Jebusites; and I delivered them into your hand.
12And I sent the hornet before you,
which drave them out from before you,
even the two kings of the Amorites; *but*
not with thy sword, nor with thy bow.
13And I have given you a land for
which ye did not labour, and cities which
ye built not, and ye dwell in them; of the
vineyards and oliveyards which ye
planted not do ye eat.
¶14Now therefore fear the LORD, and
serve him in sincerity and in truth: and
put away the gods which your fathers
served on the other side of the flood,
and in Egypt; and serve ye the LORD.
15And if it seem evil unto you to
serve the LORD, choose you this day
whom ye will serve; whether the gods
which your fathers served that *were* on
the other side of the flood, or the gods
of the Amorites, in whose land ye dwell:
but as for me and my house, we will
serve the LORD.

24:14 Serve the LORD
The "other side of the flood" does not mean the flood of Noah since Terah and Nahor were alive then (vs. 2). God brought Abraham from "the other side of the flood" (vs. 3). This is a way of saying they lived in idolatry since Abraham, Terah, and Nahor were idolaters (vs. 2). Abraham turned from idolatry and Joshua exhorts them to "put away the gods their fathers served" (vs. 14). When God calls us to Himself, we turn away from sin and self and come to Him (1 Thess. 1:9).

16And the people answered and said,
God forbid that we should forsake the
LORD, to serve other gods;
17For the LORD our God, he *it is* that
brought us up and our fathers out of
the land of Egypt, from the house of
bondage, and which did those great
signs in our sight, and preserved us in
all the way wherein we went, and
among all the people through whom we
passed:
18And the LORD drave out from before us all the people, even the Amorites which dwelt in the land: *therefore*
will we also serve the LORD; for he *is*
our God.
19And Joshua said unto the people, Ye
cannot serve the LORD: for he *is* an holy
God; he *is* a jealous God; he will not
forgive your transgressions nor your
sins.

24:12 the hornet before you. This is to be taken literally, for God commands strange armies to do His will. It may also be taken figuratively of the fear and terror that came on the nations (Josh. 2:9). In the promise God says; "I will send my fear before thee . . . and I will send hornets before thee" (Exod. 23:27-28; Deut. 7:20). Discoveries of archaeologists indicate another possible explanation: "The hornet" was a national symbol of Egypt, and it seems to be a fact that Egyptian forces invaded Palestine before the Israelites arrived.

> **24:27 The Words of the LORD**
> Note that here and in verse 2 Joshua proved himself to be a prophet. He used the same words that other prophets used also in proclaiming the *inspiration of their words (compare Jer. 1:2; Hos. 1:1; Hag. 1:1; Mal. 1:1). Notice all that the stone heard, and that it was to be a witness to the words if necessary. Compare this with our Lord's words to the Pharisees (Luke 19:40).

[20]If ye forsake the LORD, and serve strange gods, then he will turn and do you hurt, and consume you, after that he hath done you good.

[21]And the people said unto Joshua, Nay; but we will serve the LORD.

[22]And Joshua said unto the people, Ye *are* witnesses against yourselves that ye have chosen you the LORD, to serve him. And they said, *We are* witnesses.

[23]Now therefore put away, *said he,* the strange gods which *are* among you, and incline your heart unto the LORD God of Israel.

[24]And the people said unto Joshua, The LORD our God will we serve, and his voice will we obey.

[25]So Joshua made a covenant with the people that day, and set them a statute and an ordinance in Shechem.

¶[26]And Joshua wrote these words in the book of the law of God, and took a great stone, and set it up there under an oak, that *was* by the sanctuary of the LORD.

[27]And Joshua said unto all the people, Behold, this stone shall be a witness unto us; for it hath heard all the words of the LORD which he spake unto us: it shall be therefore a witness unto you, lest ye deny your God.

[28]So Joshua let the people depart, every man unto his inheritance.

¶[29]And it came to pass after these things, that Joshua the son of Nun, the servant of the LORD, died, *being* an hundred and ten years old.

[30]And they buried him in the border of his inheritance in Timnath-serah, which *is* in mount Ephraim, on the north side of the hill of Gaash.

[31]And Israel served the LORD all the days of Joshua, and all the days of the elders that overlived Joshua, and which had known all the works of the LORD, that he had done for Israel.

¶[32]And the bones of Joseph, which the children of Israel brought up out of Egypt, buried they in Shechem, in a parcel of ground which Jacob bought of the sons of Hamor the father of Shechem for an hundred pieces of silver: and it became the inheritance of the children of Joseph.

[33]And Eleazar the son of Aaron died; and they buried him in a hill *that pertained to* Phinehas his son, which was given him in mount Ephraim.

24:22 ye have chosen you the LORD. The nation of Israel had been chosen by God and was called to be a "holy people unto the LORD" (Deut. 7:6-7).

24:31 Israel served the LORD. Joshua governed the people for fourteen years, and the elders seem to have lived after him for only about three years. Notice, therefore, how short a time it was that Israel served the LORD.

24:32 the bones of Joseph. See Genesis 50:25.

The Book of

JUDGES

THEME

The book of Judges gives the history of the Israelites for about 300 years after the death of Joshua. It is a book of failure. Not only did the Israelites fail to conquer the whole land, thus failing to possess it fully as they could have done in the strength of the LORD, but they often lost what they had won and were enslaved by the heathen nations around them. The reason for the failure is found in the key verse of the book: Judges 17:6 (also 21:25). The name of Judges comes from the twelve men and one woman whom God raised up to deliver and govern, or *judge* Israel. The book is a type of the history of the church, with its loss of early purity and simplicity, and its many divisions; yet it has had, too, its revivals under strong and faithful leaders. It is also a warning for each Christian of how they should "hold fast the profession of [their] faith without wavering" (Hebrews 10:23).

THE WRITER

It is very probable that either Samuel or his school of prophets (1 Samuel 19:20; 2 Kings 2:3) wrote the book of Judges.

OUTLINE OF JUDGES

I.	Incomplete Victory	Judges 1:1-36
II.	Summary of the Spiritual History of Israel during This Period	Judges 2:1-23
III.	The Servitudes and the Judges	Judges 3:1—16:31
	A. First Servitude: Mesopotamia	
	B. Second Servitude: Moab	
	C. Third Servitude: Canaan	
	D. Fourth Servitude: Midian	
	E. Fifth Servitude: Ammonites	
	F. Sixth Servitude: Philistines	
IV.	Ignorance and Evil of the Nation	Judges 17:1—21:25

I. Incomplete Victory
(1:1-36)

1 Now after the death of *Joshua
it came to pass, that the children of
*Israel asked the LORD, saying, Who
shall go up for us against the Canaanites first, to fight against them?
2 And the LORD said, *Judah shall go
up: behold, I have delivered the land
into his hand.

1:1 Canaanites. Here, this is a general name given to all the people in Palestine. In 4:2, the Canaanites are the tribe to the north of Palestine.

1:2 Judah. The largest and leading tribe of the Israelites. Judah was the fourth son of

3 And Judah said unto Simeon his
brother, Come up with me into my lot,
that we may fight against the Canaanites; and I likewise will go with thee
into thy lot. So Simeon went with him.
4 And Judah went up; and the LORD
delivered the Canaanites and the Perizzites into their hand: and they slew of
them in Bezek ten thousand men.
5 And they found Adoni-bezek in Bezek: and they fought against him, and
they slew the Canaanites and the Perizzites.

1:5 A Just Punishment
Adoni-bezek's name means *the lord of Bezek*. Judah was not just being cruel when he cut off the thumbs and the big toes of Adoni-bezek, for Adoni-bezek confessed that he had done the same thing to seventy kings. God had commanded his just punishment (Lev. 24:19-20). The Lord has given us a new and better way today (see Matt. 5:38-45).

6 But Adoni-bezek fled; and they pursued after him, and caught him, and cut
off his thumbs and his great toes.
7 And Adoni-bezek said, Threescore
and ten kings, having their thumbs and
their great toes cut off, gathered *their*
meat under my table: as I have done, so
*God hath requited me. And they
brought him to *Jerusalem, and there
he died.
8 Now the children of Judah had
fought against Jerusalem, and had tak-
en it, and smitten it with the edge of the
sword, and set the city on fire.
¶9 And afterward the children of Judah went down to fight against the Canaanites, that dwelt in the mountain,
and in the south, and in the valley.
10 And Judah went against the Canaanites that dwelt in Hebron: (now the
name of Hebron before *was* Kirjath-
arba:) and they slew Sheshai, and Ahiman, and Talmai.
11 And from thence he went against
the inhabitants of Debir: and the name
of Debir before *was* Kirjath-sepher:
12 And *Caleb said, He that smiteth
Kirjath-sepher, and taketh it, to him will
I give Achsah my daughter to wife.

1:12 Caleb
This man was an old and stalwart Israelite who had come all the way from Egypt to Canaan. He and Joshua were the only spies to bring back a good report of the land (Num. 13:30) and were rewarded by God's promise that they only–of all the Israelites who had left Egypt–should live to enter the Promised Land (Num. 14:24; 32:12). At the age of eighty-five, Caleb was still a strong fighter and won his inheritance (Josh. 14:6-15). His name means *wholehearted*. He is a fine example of a faithful and victorious servant of God.

13 And Othniel the son of Kenaz,
Caleb's younger brother, took it: and
he gave him Achsah his daughter to
wife.
14 And it came to pass, when she came
to him, that she moved him to ask of her
father a field: and she lighted from off
her ass; and Caleb said unto her, What
wilt thou?
15 And she said unto him, Give me a
blessing: for thou hast given me a south
land; give me also springs of water. And
Caleb gave her the upper springs and
the nether springs.
¶16 And the children of the *Kenite,
*Moses' father in law, went up out of

Jacob, and he received a special blessing in Genesis 49:8-10. David was of this tribe, and later Christ was born of it also.

1:3 Simeon his brother. The land of the tribe or descendants of Simeon, the second son of Jacob, now the smallest of the tribes, lived next to the tribe of Judah. This was why the leaders of Judah asked help from Simeon.

1:8 Now the children of Judah had fought. See Deuteronomy 2:34 note to see why this kind of warfare was necessary.

1:16 Moses' father in law. See Exodus 2:15-22 and Exodus 18 for the full story of these relatives of Moses. One brother-in-law came with the Israelites to the land and settled there (see Num. 10:29; Judg. 4:11,17).

the city of palm trees with the children of Judah into the wilderness of Judah, which *lieth* in the south of Arad; and they went and dwelt among the people.

17 And Judah went with Simeon his brother, and they slew the Canaanites that inhabited Zephath, and utterly destroyed it. And the name of the city was called Hormah.

18 Also Judah took *Gaza with the coast thereof, and Askelon with the coast thereof, and Ekron with the coast thereof.

19 And the LORD was with Judah; and he drave out *the inhabitants of* the mountain; but could not drive out the inhabitants of the valley, because they had chariots of iron.

1:19 Mightier Than Iron Chariots
It was not just because of the chariots of iron that Judah (the "he" refers to Judah in this verse) could not drive out the inhabitants in the valley; it was because he did not have faith in God, who is able to prevail against chariots of iron and every weapon of the enemy. Had Judah not sought Simeon's help (vs. 3), but instead had relied on God alone, nothing could have stopped him.

20 And they gave Hebron unto Caleb, as Moses said: and he expelled thence the three sons of Anak.

21 And the children of Benjamin did not drive out the Jebusites that inhabited Jerusalem; but the Jebusites dwell with the children of Benjamin in Jerusalem unto this day.

¶22 And the house of *Joseph, they also went up against *Beth-el: and the LORD *was* with them.

23 And the house of Joseph sent to descry Beth-el. (Now the name of the city before *was* Luz.)

24 And the spies saw a man come forth out of the city, and they said unto him, Shew us, we pray thee, the entrance into the city, and we will shew thee mercy.

25 And when he shewed them the entrance into the city, they smote the city with the edge of the sword; but they let go the man and all his family.

26 And the man went into the land of the Hittites, and built a city, and called the name thereof Luz: which *is* the name thereof unto this day.

¶27 Neither did *Manasseh drive out *the inhabitants of* Beth-shean and her towns, nor Taanach and her towns, nor the inhabitants of Dor and her towns, nor the inhabitants of Ibleam and her towns, nor the inhabitants of *Megiddo and her towns: but the Canaanites would dwell in that land.

28 And it came to pass, when Israel was strong, that they put the Canaanites to tribute, and did not utterly drive them out.

1:28 Tax Money
The Israelites supposed that they could compromise with worshippers of idols by taking tribute, or tax money, from them. It was as if they said, "We will get money from these people and become rich. We'll give some of the money to God. We'll help the poor with it." But that was not pleasing to God. He did not say, "Take tribute money from the people"; He said, "Thou shalt smite them, and utterly destroy them" (Deut. 7:1-6).

¶29 Neither did *Ephraim drive out the Canaanites that dwelt in Gezer; but the Canaanites dwelt in Gezer among them.

¶30 Neither did Zebulun drive out the inhabitants of Kitron, nor the inhabitants of Nahalol; but the Canaanites dwelt among them, and became tributaries.

¶31 Neither did Asher drive out the inhabitants of Accho, nor the inhabitants of Zidon, nor of Ahlab, nor of Achzib, nor of Helbah, nor of Aphik, nor of Rehob:

1:16 the city of palm trees. Jericho.
1:23 descry. To spy out.
1:26 Hittites. A powerful people with a large empire to the north of Palestine.

[32]But the Asherites dwelt among the
Canaanites, the inhabitants of the land:
for they did not drive them out.
¶[33]Neither did Naphtali drive out the
inhabitants of Beth-shemesh, nor the
inhabitants of Beth-anath; but he dwelt
among the Canaanites, the inhabitants
of the land: nevertheless the inhabitants of Beth-shemesh and of Beth-
anath became tributaries unto them.
[34]And the Amorites forced the children of Dan into the mountain: for they
would not suffer them to come down to
the valley:
[35]But the Amorites would dwell in
mount Heres in Aijalon, and in Shaalbim: yet the hand of the house of Joseph
prevailed, so that they became tributaries.
[36]And the coast of the Amorites *was*
from the going up to Akrabbim, from
the rock, and upward.

II. Spiritual History (2:1-23)

2 And an *angel of the LORD came
up from Gilgal to Bochim, and said,
I made you to go up out of *Egypt, and
have brought you unto the land which I
sware unto your fathers; and I said, I
will never break my *covenant with
you.
[2]And ye shall make no league with
the inhabitants of this land; ye shall
throw down their altars: but ye have not
obeyed my voice: why have ye done
this?
[3]Wherefore I also said, I will not drive
them out from before you; but they
shall be *as thorns* in your sides, and
their gods shall be a snare unto you.
[4]And it came to pass, when the angel
of the LORD spake these words unto all
the children of Israel, that the people
lifted up their voice, and wept.
[5]And they called the name of that
place Bochim: and they sacrificed there
unto the LORD.
¶[6]And when Joshua had let the people go, the children of Israel went every
man unto his inheritance to possess the
land.
[7]And the people served the LORD all
the days of Joshua, and all the days of
the *elders that outlived Joshua, who
had seen all the great works of the
LORD, that he did for Israel.
[8]And Joshua the son of Nun, the servant of the LORD, died, *being* an hundred and ten years old.
[9]And they buried him in the border
of his inheritance in Timnath-heres, in
the mount of Ephraim, on the north
side of the hill Gaash.
[10]And also all that generation were
gathered unto their fathers: and there
arose another generation after them,
which knew not the LORD, nor yet the
works which he had done for Israel.
¶[11]And the children of Israel did evil
in the sight of the LORD, and served
Baalim:
[12]And they forsook the LORD God of
their fathers, which brought them out
of the land of Egypt, and followed other
gods, of the gods of the people that *were*
round about them, and bowed themselves unto them, and provoked the
LORD to anger.
[13]And they forsook the LORD, and
served *Baal and Ashtaroth.
¶[14]And the anger of the LORD was hot
against Israel, and he delivered them
into the hands of spoilers that spoiled
them, and he sold them into the hands

1:33 tributaries. See verse 28.
1:34 the Amorites forced the children of Dan. This chapter begins with victory but ends with defeat and the loss of part of the land that had been won. So in the first chapter we get the keynote of the book, which is the failure of the Israelites.
2:1 Gilgal. This was the first place in Palestine that the Israelites reached. See Joshua 5.
2:5 Bochim. This name means *weeping*.
2:11 Baalim. Plural of Baal. It means *images of Baal,* the chief god of the Canaanite tribes.
2:13 Ashtaroth. Plural of the word "Ashtoreth." It means *images of Ashtoreth,* who was the female goddess of the Canaanites.

of their enemies round about, so that they could not any longer stand before their enemies.

15 Whithersoever they went out, the hand of the LORD was against them for evil, as the LORD had said, and as the LORD had sworn unto them: and they were greatly distressed.

The judges

¶ 16 Nevertheless the LORD raised up judges, which delivered them out of the hand of those that spoiled them.

17 And yet they would not hearken unto their judges, but they went a whoring after other gods, and bowed themselves unto them: they turned quickly out of the way which their fathers walked in, obeying the commandments of the LORD; *but* they did not so.

18 And when the LORD raised them up judges, then the LORD was with the judge, and delivered them out of the hand of their enemies all the days of the judge: for it repented the LORD because of their groanings by reason of them that oppressed them and vexed them.

> **2:18 The Judges**
> These were ordinary tribesmen of Israel. Most were men of humble birth and connections. There was no king in Israel, for God was their King, but He raised up these men to govern and reform Israel.

19 And it came to pass, when the judge was dead, *that* they returned, and corrupted *themselves* more than their fathers, in following other gods to serve them, and to bow down unto them; they ceased not from their own doings, nor from their stubborn way.

¶ 20 And the anger of the LORD was hot against Israel; and he said, Because that this people hath transgressed my covenant which I commanded their fathers, and have not hearkened unto my voice;

21 I also will not henceforth drive out any from before them of the nations which Joshua left when he died:

22 That through them I may *prove Israel, whether they will keep the way of the LORD to walk therein, as their fathers did keep *it,* or not.

23 Therefore the LORD left those nations, without driving them out hastily; neither delivered he them into the hand of Joshua.

III. The Servitudes and the Judges (3:1—16:31)

3 Now these *are* the nations which the LORD left, to prove Israel by them, *even* as many *of Israel* as had not known all the wars of Canaan;

2 Only that the generations of the children of Israel might know, to teach them war, at the least such as before knew nothing thereof;

3 *Namely,* five lords of the *Philistines, and all the Canaanites, and the Sidonians, and the Hivites that dwelt in mount *Lebanon, from mount Baal-hermon unto the entering in of Hamath.

4 And they were to prove Israel by them, to know whether they would hearken unto the commandments of the LORD, which he commanded their fathers by the hand of Moses.

A. First Servitude: Mesopotamia

¶ 5 And the children of Israel dwelt among the Canaanites, Hittites, and Amorites, and Perizzites, and Hivites, and Jebusites:

6 And they took their daughters to be their wives, and gave their daughters to their sons, and served their gods.

7 And the children of Israel did evil in the sight of the LORD, and forgat the LORD their God, and served Baalim and the groves.

¶ 8 Therefore the anger of the LORD was hot against Israel, and he sold them into the hand of Chushan-rishathaim king of Mesopotamia: and the children of Israel served Chushan-rishathaim eight years.

Othniel, the first judge

9 And when the children of Israel cried unto the LORD, the LORD raised

> **3:8 The King of Mesopotamia**
> Chushan-rishathaim means *double wickedness.* Mesopotamia means *the country between the rivers,* which is the land between the Tigris and the Euphrates. The land of Shinar, where the tower of Babel had been built was in Mesopotamia; later the kingdom of Babylon arose there. Abraham had been called by God to leave it (Gen. 12:1). In the Bible Babylon is always a *type of the Christ-rejecting world, opposed to and hating God. A real and great enemy for the Christian to meet is the world, with its godlessness. We are in the world, but not of it. See 1 John 2:15.

up a deliverer to the children of Israel, who delivered them, *even* Othniel the son of Kenaz, Caleb's younger brother.

10 And the *Spirit of the LORD came upon him, and he judged Israel, and went out to war: and the LORD delivered Chushan-rishathaim king of Mesopotamia into his hand; and his hand prevailed against Chushan-rishathaim.

11 And the land had rest forty years. And Othniel the son of Kenaz died.

B. Second Servitude: Moab

¶ 12 And the children of Israel did evil again in the sight of the LORD: and the LORD strengthened Eglon the king of *Moab against Israel, because they had done evil in the sight of the LORD.

13 And he gathered unto him the children of Ammon and *Amalek, and went and smote Israel, and possessed the city of palm trees.

14 So the children of Israel served Eglon the king of Moab eighteen years.

Ehud, the second judge

15 But when the children of Israel cried unto the LORD, the LORD raised them up a deliverer, Ehud the son of Gera, a Benjamite, a man lefthanded: and by him the children of Israel sent a present unto Eglon the king of Moab.

16 But Ehud made him a dagger which had two edges, of a cubit length; and he did gird it under his raiment upon his right thigh.

17 And he brought the present unto Eglon king of Moab: and Eglon *was* a very fat man.

18 And when he had made an end to offer the present, he sent away the people that bare the present.

19 But he himself turned again from the quarries that *were* by Gilgal, and said, I have a secret errand unto thee, O king: who said, Keep silence. And all that stood by him went out from him.

20 And Ehud came unto him; and he was sitting in a summer parlour, which he had for himself alone. And Ehud said, I have a message from God unto thee. And he arose out of *his* seat.

21 And Ehud put forth his left hand, and took the dagger from his right thigh, and thrust it into his belly:

22 And the haft also went in after the blade; and the fat closed upon the blade, so that he could not draw the dagger out of his belly; and the dirt came out.

23 Then Ehud went forth through the porch, and shut the doors of the parlour upon him, and locked them.

24 When he was gone out, his servants came; and when they saw that, behold, the doors of the parlour *were*

3:9 Othniel. This man has already been mentioned (Judg. 1:13). He was the nephew of Caleb, and like him, was a great fighter. His name means *lion of God.*

3:10 the Spirit of the LORD. See Judges 14:19 note, "The Spirit of the LORD."

3:12 Eglon the king of Moab. The Moabites were related to the Israelites by their descent from Lot, Abraham's nephew, but they had always been bitter enemies (see Deut. 23:3-4). They are a *type of the *flesh, the sinful, natural man who is opposed to God since he has not been born again. Eglon, the king of Moab, is a symbol of self-indulgence.

3:15 a present. Probably tribute money from the enslaved Israelites.

3:22 haft. The handle of a knife or dagger.

locked, they said, Surely he covereth
his feet in his summer chamber.
25 And they tarried till they were
ashamed: and, behold, he opened not
the doors of the parlour; therefore they
took a key, and opened *them:* and, behold, their lord *was* fallen down dead on
the earth.
26 And Ehud escaped while they tarried, and passed beyond the quarries,
and escaped unto Seirath.
27 And it came to pass, when he was
come, that he blew a trumpet in the
mountain of Ephraim, and the children
of Israel went down with him from the
mount, and he before them.
28 And he said unto them, Follow after me: for the LORD hath delivered
your enemies the Moabites into your
hand. And they went down after him,
and took the fords of Jordan toward
Moab, and suffered not a man to pass
over.
29 And they slew of Moab at that time
about ten thousand men, all lusty, and
all men of valour; and there escaped not
a man.
30 So Moab was subdued that day under the hand of Israel. And the land had
rest fourscore years.

Shamgar, the third judge

¶31 And after him was Shamgar the
son of Anath, which slew of the Philistines six hundred men with an ox goad:
and he also delivered Israel.

C. Third Servitude: Canaan

4 And the children of Israel again did
evil in the sight of the LORD, when
Ehud was dead.
2 And the LORD sold them into the
hand of Jabin king of Canaan, that
reigned in Hazor; the captain of whose
host *was* Sisera, which dwelt in Harosheth of the *Gentiles.
3 And the children of Israel cried unto
the LORD: for he had nine hundred chariots of iron; and twenty years he mightily oppressed the children of Israel.

4:2 Sisera
The leader of the Canaanites is a picture of the devil with all his oppressive power. His defeat is also a *type of the defeat of the devil by the seed of the woman (Gen. 3:15), because Sisera was defeated by two women, Deborah and Jael.

Deborah and Barak, fourth and fifth judges

¶4 And Deborah, a prophetess, the
wife of Lapidoth, she judged Israel at
that time.
5 And she dwelt under the palm tree
of Deborah between Ramah and Beth-
el in mount Ephraim: and the children
of Israel came up to her for judgment.
6 And she sent and called Barak the
son of Abinoam out of Kedesh-naphta-
li, and said unto him, Hath not the LORD
God of Israel commanded, *saying,* Go
and draw toward mount Tabor, and take
with thee ten thousand men of the children of Naphtali and of the children of
Zebulun?
7 And I will draw unto thee to the
river Kishon Sisera, the captain of
Jabin's army, with his chariots and his
multitude; and I will deliver him into
thine hand.
8 And Barak said unto her, If thou wilt
go with me, then I will go: but if thou
wilt not go with me, *then* I will not go.
9 And she said, I will surely go with
thee: notwithstanding the journey that
thou takest shall not be for thine
honour; for the LORD shall sell Sisera
into the hand of a woman. And Deborah arose, and went with Barak to Kedesh.
¶10 And Barak called Zebulun and
Naphtali to Kedesh; and he went up
with ten thousand men at his feet: and
Deborah went up with him.
11 Now Heber the *Kenite, *which was*

3:29 lusty. Vigorous, strong.
4:5 palm tree. Evidently this was a landmark, for palm trees were rare in Palestine.

of the children of Hobab the father in
law of Moses, had severed himself from
the *Kenites, and pitched his tent unto
the plain of Zaanaim, which *is* by Kedesh.
12 And they shewed Sisera that Barak the son of Abinoam was gone up to
mount Tabor.
13 And Sisera gathered together all his
chariots, *even* nine hundred chariots of
iron, and all the people that *were* with
him, from Harosheth of the Gentiles
unto the river of Kishon.
14 And Deborah said unto Barak, Up;
for this *is* the day in which the LORD
hath delivered Sisera into thine hand:
is not the LORD gone out before thee?
So Barak went down from mount Tabor,
and ten thousand men after him.
15 And the LORD discomfited Sisera,
and all *his* chariots, and all *his* host, with
the edge of the sword before Barak; so
that Sisera lighted down off *his* chariot, and fled away on his feet.
16 But Barak pursued after the chariots, and after the host, unto Harosheth
of the Gentiles: and all the host of Sisera fell upon the edge of the sword; *and*
there was not a man left.
17 Howbeit Sisera fled away on his
feet to the tent of Jael the wife of Heber the Kenite: for *there was* peace between Jabin the king of Hazor and the
house of Heber the Kenite.
¶18 And Jael went out to meet Sisera,
and said unto him, Turn in, my lord,
turn in to me; fear not. And when he
had turned in unto her into the tent, she
covered him with a mantle.
19 And he said unto her, Give me, I
pray thee, a little water to drink; for I
am thirsty. And she opened a bottle of
milk, and gave him drink, and covered
him.
20 Again he said unto her, Stand in the
door of the tent, and it shall be, when
any man doth come and enquire of thee,
and say, Is there any man here? that
thou shalt say, No.
21 Then Jael Heber's wife took a nail
of the tent, and took an hammer in her
hand, and went softly unto him, and
smote the nail into his temples, and fastened it into the ground: for he was fast
asleep and weary. So he died.

4:21 A Lethal Weapon
A large tent peg for holding down the tent is meant by "nail." The "hammer" was the mallet used for knocking the pegs into the ground. Although it was an act of treachery to kill a sleeping fugitive, Jael was doing her best to aid Israel, whom she knew to be God's people.

22 And, behold, as Barak pursued Sisera, Jael came out to meet him, and said
unto him, Come, and I will shew thee
the man whom thou seekest. And when
he came into her *tent,* behold, Sisera lay
dead, and the nail *was* in his temples.
23 So God subdued on that day Jabin
the king of Canaan before the children
of Israel.
24 And the hand of the children of Israel prospered, and prevailed against
Jabin the king of Canaan, until they had
destroyed Jabin king of Canaan.

A song of praise

5 Then sang Deborah and Barak the
son of Abinoam on that day, saying,
2 Praise ye the LORD for the avenging
of Israel, when the people willingly offered themselves.
3 Hear, O ye kings; give ear, O ye
princes; I, *even* I, will sing unto the
LORD; I will sing *praise* to the LORD God
of Israel.
4 LORD, when thou wentest out of
*Seir, when thou marchedst out of the
field of *Edom, the earth trembled, and

4:11 Heber the Kenite. See Judges 1:16 note. He was at peace with Jabin and with Israel (see vs. 17).
4:17 Howbeit. Nevertheless.
5:1 Then sang. Compare the song of Moses in Exodus 15:1-21.

the heavens dropped, the clouds also
dropped water.
[5]The mountains melted from before
the LORD, *even* that *Sinai from before
the LORD God of Israel.
[6]In the days of Shamgar the son of
Anath, in the days of Jael, the highways
were unoccupied, and the travellers
walked through byways.
[7]*The inhabitants of* the villages
ceased, they ceased in Israel, until that
I Deborah arose, that I arose a mother
in Israel.
[8]They chose new gods; then *was* war
in the gates: was there a shield or spear
seen among forty thousand in Israel?
[9]My heart *is* toward the governors of
Israel, that offered themselves willingly
among the people. Bless ye the LORD.
[10]Speak, ye that ride on white asses,
ye that sit in judgment, and walk by the
way.
[11]*They that are delivered* from the
noise of archers in the places of drawing water, there shall they rehearse the
righteous acts of the LORD, *even* the
righteous acts *toward the inhabitants*
of his villages in Israel: then shall the
people of the LORD go down to the
gates.
[12]Awake, awake, Deborah: awake,
awake, utter a song: arise, Barak, and
lead thy captivity captive, thou son of
Abinoam.
[13]Then he made him that remaineth
have dominion over the nobles among
the people: the LORD made me have
dominion over the mighty.
[14]Out of Ephraim *was there* a root of
them against Amalek; after thee, Benjamin, among thy people; out of Machir
came down governors, and out of Zebulun they that handle the pen of the
writer.
[15]And the princes of Issachar *were*
with Deborah; even Issachar, and also
Barak: he was sent on foot into the valley. For the divisions of Reuben *there
were* great thoughts of heart.
[16]Why abodest thou among the
sheepfolds, to hear the bleatings of the
flocks? For the divisions of Reuben
there were great searchings of heart.
[17]*Gilead abode beyond Jordan: and
why did Dan remain in ships? Asher
continued on the sea shore, and abode
in his breaches.
[18]Zebulun and Naphtali *were* a people
that jeoparded their lives unto the death
in the high places of the field.
[19]The kings came *and* fought, then
fought the kings of Canaan in Taanach
by the waters of *Megiddo; they took
no gain of money.
[20]They fought from heaven; the stars
in their courses fought against Sisera.
[21]The river of Kishon swept them
away, that ancient river, the river Kishon. O my soul, thou hast trodden
down strength.
[22]Then were the horsehoofs broken
by the means of the pransings, the
pransings of their mighty ones.
[23]Curse ye Meroz, said the angel of
the LORD, curse ye bitterly the inhabitants thereof; because they came not to
the help of the LORD, to the help of the
LORD against the mighty.
[24]Blessed above women shall Jael the
wife of Heber the Kenite be, blessed
shall she be above women in the tent.
[25]He asked water, *and* she gave *him*
milk; she brought forth butter in a
lordly dish.
[26]She put her hand to the nail, and
her right hand to the workmen's hammer; and with the hammer she smote
Sisera, she smote off his head, when

5:6 Shamgar. See Judges 3:31.
5:11 noise of archers. The Canaanites had even crept up close to the wells and shot down the Israelites when they came to get water.
5:17 Dan remain in ships. The land allotted to the tribe of Dan was west of Judah and ran down to the seacoast. They possessed Joppa, the people's only seaport.
5:17 breaches. Creeks, harbors.
5:18 jeoparded. To hazard or risk, to jeopardize.

5:25 Butter
The Hebrews were ignorant of the art of churning butter; but they made a kind of clotted cream by subjecting new milk to fermentation, which imparted to it a pleasant acid flavor somewhat resembling that of lemon cream. Even now, churned butter is never used by native Syrians, but this clotted cream, called "leben," continues to be universally consumed. This was probably the "butter in a lordly dish" which Jael brought to Sisera, when she had "opened a bottle of milk" (Judg. 4:19; 5:25).

she had pierced and stricken through
his temples.
27At her feet he bowed, he fell, he lay
down: at her feet he bowed, he fell:
where he bowed, there he fell down
dead.
28The mother of Sisera looked out at
a window, and cried through the lattice,
Why is his chariot *so* long in coming?
why tarry the wheels of his chariots?

5:28 Windows
Windows in a Mideastern house consist mainly of apertures for the admission of light and air. They are sometimes partially closed with latticework, wooden trelliswork, or curtains. The mother of Sisera is described (Judg. 5:28) as having "looked out at a window, and cried through the lattice" (compare Song 2:9; Eccles. 12:3).

29Her wise ladies answered her, yea,
she returned answer to herself,
30Have they not sped? have they *not*
divided the prey; to every man a damsel *or* two; to Sisera a prey of divers
colours, a prey of divers colours of needlework, of divers colours of needlework on both sides, *meet* for the necks
of *them that take* the spoil?
31So let all thine enemies perish,
O LORD: but *let* them that love him *be*
as the sun when he goeth forth in his
might. And the land had rest forty years.

D. Fourth Servitude: Midian

6 And the children of Israel did evil
in the sight of the LORD: and the
LORD delivered them into the hand of
Midian seven years.

6:1 Serving the Midianites
The Midianites were descendants of Keturah, one of Abraham's wives (Gen. 25:1-4 and Exod. 2:1 note). Although related to the Israelites by blood, they were usually enemies and had helped the Moabites against Israel (see Num. 22:4,7; 25:6,16-18). Just as earthly things such as strife, greed, worry, and selfishness creep into and spread throughout the church today, so the Midianites especially attacked the *food* of the Israelites, showing how earthly, material things prevent the Christians from spending time with the Bible, their spiritual food, so weakening their spiritual lives.

2And the hand of Midian prevailed
against Israel: *and* because of the *Midianites the children of Israel made them
the dens which *are* in the mountains,
and caves, and strong holds.
3And *so* it was, when Israel had sown,
that the Midianites came up, and the
Amalekites, and the children of the
east, even they came up against them;
4And they encamped against them,
and destroyed the increase of the earth,
till thou come unto *Gaza, and left no
sustenance for Israel, neither sheep,
nor ox, nor ass.
5For they came up with their cattle
and their tents, and they came as grasshoppers for multitude; *for* both they
and their camels were without number: and they entered into the land to
destroy it.
6And Israel was greatly impoverished
because of the Midianites; and the children of Israel cried unto the LORD.
¶7And it came to pass, when the children of Israel cried unto the LORD because of the Midianites,
8That the LORD sent a *prophet unto

5:30 sped. Succeeded.

the children of Israel, which said unto
them, Thus saith the LORD God of Israel, I brought you up from Egypt, and
brought you forth out of the house of
bondage;
9 And I delivered you out of the hand of
the Egyptians, and out of the hand of all
that oppressed you, and drave them out
from before you, and gave you their land;
10 And I said unto you, I *am* the LORD
your God; fear not the gods of the Amorites, in whose land ye dwell: but ye
have not obeyed my voice.

Gideon, the sixth judge

¶11 And there came an angel of the
LORD, and sat under an oak which *was*
in Ophrah, that *pertained* unto *Joash
the Abi-ezrite: and his son Gideon
threshed wheat by the winepress, to
hide *it* from the Midianites.
12 And the angel of the LORD appeared
unto him, and said unto him, The LORD
is with thee, thou mighty man of valour.
13 And Gideon said unto him, Oh my
Lord, if the LORD be with us, why then
is all this befallen us? and where *be* all
his *miracles which our fathers told us
of, saying, Did not the LORD bring us up
from Egypt? but now the LORD hath
forsaken us, and delivered us into the
hands of the Midianites.
14 And the LORD looked upon him, and
said, Go in this thy might, and thou
shalt save Israel from the hand of the
Midianites: have not I sent thee?
15 And he said unto him, Oh my Lord,
wherewith shall I save Israel? behold,
my family *is* poor in Manasseh, and I *am*
the least in my father's house.
16 And the LORD said unto him, Surely I will be with thee, and thou shalt
smite the Midianites as one man.
17 And he said unto him, If now I have
found grace in thy sight, then shew me
a sign that thou talkest with me.
18 Depart not hence, I pray thee, until I come unto thee, and bring forth my
present, and set *it* before thee. And he
said, I will tarry until thou come again.
¶19 And Gideon went in, and made
ready a kid, and unleavened cakes of an
*ephah of flour: the flesh he put in a
basket, and he put the broth in a pot,
and brought *it* out unto him under the
oak, and presented *it.*

6:15 Resisting God's Call

More often than not, when God called people into His service, they resisted by coming up with a lot of excuses. This practice of resistance was true even of the strongest and best leaders in the Bible.

Character	Resistance	Reference
Moses	"Who am I?"	Exodus 3:11
Moses	"I don't know who You are."	Exodus 3:13
Moses	"No one will believe me or listen to me."	Exodus 4:1
Moses	"I'm not a good speaker."	Exodus 4:10
Moses	"Send someone else."	Exodus 4:13
Gideon	"I'm a nobody."	Judges 6:15
Saul	Hid in the baggage	1 Samuel 10:22
Solomon	"I am a little child."	1 Kings 3:7
Jeremiah	"I don't know how to speak."	Jeremiah 1:6
Jeremiah	"I'm only a child."	Jeremiah 1:6
Jonah	Said nothing; ran away	Jonah 1:2
Jonah	When he complied he was angry	Jonah 4:1

In contrast note the responses of Isaiah and Mary. When Isaiah was called he replied, "Here am I, send me" (Isaiah 6:8). Mary said, "I am the Lord's maidservant. Let it be to me according to your word" (Luke 1:38).

6:12 thou mighty man of valour. Gideon does not seem brave to us, for he was hiding as he did his work because he was afraid of the Midianites. The angel of God spoke of Gideon, however, as he would be when he went in the strength of the LORD (vss. 16,34, and 7:20-22).

20And the angel of God said unto him,
Take the flesh and the unleavened
cakes, and lay *them* upon this rock, and
pour out the broth. And he did so.
¶21Then the angel of the LORD put
forth the end of the staff that *was* in his
hand, and touched the flesh and the
unleavened cakes; and there rose up
fire out of the rock, and consumed the
flesh and the unleavened cakes. Then
the angel of the LORD departed out of
his sight.
22And when Gideon perceived that
he *was* an angel of the LORD, Gideon
said, Alas, O Lord GOD! for because I
have seen an angel of the LORD face
to face.
23And the LORD said unto him,
Peace *be* unto thee; fear not: thou shalt
not die.
24Then Gideon built an *altar there
unto the LORD, and called it Jehovah-
shalom: unto this day it *is* yet in Ophrah of the Abi-ezrites.
¶25And it came to pass the same
night, that the LORD said unto him,
Take thy father's young bullock, even
the second bullock of seven years old,
and throw down the altar of Baal that
thy father hath, and cut down the grove
that *is* by it:
26And build an altar unto the LORD
thy God upon the top of this rock, in the
ordered place, and take the second bullock, and offer a burnt-sacrifice with the
wood of the grove which thou shalt cut
down.
27Then Gideon took ten men of his
servants, and did as the LORD had said
unto him: and *so* it was, because he
feared his father's household, and the
men of the city, that he could not do *it*
by day, that he did *it* by night.
¶28And when the men of the city
arose early in the morning, behold, the
altar of Baal was cast down, and the
grove was cut down that *was* by it, and
the second bullock was offered upon the
altar *that was* built.
29And they said one to another, Who
hath done this thing? And when they
enquired and asked, they said, Gideon the son of Joash hath done this
thing.
30Then the men of the city said unto
Joash, Bring out thy son, that he may
die: because he hath cast down the altar of Baal, and because he hath cut
down the grove that *was* by it.
31And Joash said unto all that stood
against him, Will ye plead for Baal? will
ye save him? he that will plead for him,
let him be put to death whilst *it is yet*
morning: if he *be* a god, let him plead for
himself, because *one* hath cast down his
altar.
32Therefore on that day he called him
Jerubbaal, saying, Let Baal plead
against him, because he hath thrown
down his altar.
¶33Then all the Midianites and the
Amalekites and the children of the east
were gathered together, and went over,
and pitched in the valley of Jezreel.
34But the Spirit of the LORD came
upon Gideon, and he blew a trumpet;
and Abi-ezer was gathered after him.
35And he sent messengers throughout all Manasseh; who also was gathered after him: and he sent messengers
unto Asher, and unto Zebulun, and unto
Naphtali; and they came up to meet
them.
¶36And Gideon said unto God, If thou
wilt save Israel by mine hand, as thou
hast said,
37Behold, I will put a fleece of wool
in the floor; *and* if the dew be on the
fleece only, and *it be* dry upon all the
earth *beside,* then shall I know that thou
wilt save Israel by mine hand, as thou
hast said.
38And it was so: for he rose up early
on the morrow, and thrust the fleece

6:24 Jehovah-shalom. This means *Jehovah (the LORD) is peace.*
6:32 Jerubbaal. *Let Baal plead* is the meaning of this name, and it is another name for Gideon. See Judges 9:1.

together, and wringed the dew out of the fleece, a bowl full of water.

39 And Gideon said unto God, Let not thine anger be hot against me, and I will speak but this once: let me *prove, I pray thee, but this once with the fleece; let it now be dry only upon the fleece, and upon all the ground let there be dew.

40 And God did so that night: for it was dry upon the fleece only, and there was dew on all the ground.

Preparation for battle

7 Then Jerubbaal, who *is* Gideon, and all the people that *were* with him, rose up early, and pitched beside the well of Harod: so that the host of the Midianites were on the north side of them, by the hill of Moreh, in the valley.

2 And the LORD said unto Gideon, The people that *are* with thee *are* too many for me to give the Midianites into their hands, lest *Israel vaunt themselves against me, saying, Mine own hand hath saved me.

3 Now therefore go to, proclaim in the ears of the people, saying, Whosoever *is* fearful and afraid, let him return and depart early from mount Gilead. And there returned of the people twenty and two thousand; and there remained ten thousand.

4 And the LORD said unto Gideon, The people *are* yet *too* many; bring them down unto the water, and I will try them for thee there: and it shall be, *that* of whom I say unto thee, This shall go with thee, the same shall go with thee; and of whomsoever I say unto thee, This shall not go with thee, the same shall not go.

5 So he brought down the people unto the water: and the LORD said unto Gideon, Every one that lappeth of the water with his tongue, as a dog lappeth, him shalt thou set by himself; likewise every one that boweth down upon his knees to drink.

6 And the number of them that lapped, *putting* their hand to their mouth, were three hundred men: but all the rest of the people bowed down upon their knees to drink water.

Three hundred chosen

7 And the LORD said unto Gideon, By the three hundred men that lapped will I save you, and deliver the Midianites into thine hand: and let all the *other* people go every man unto his place.

8 So the people took victuals in their hand, and their trumpets: and he sent all *the rest of* Israel every man unto his tent, and retained those three hundred men: and the host of Midian was beneath him in the valley.

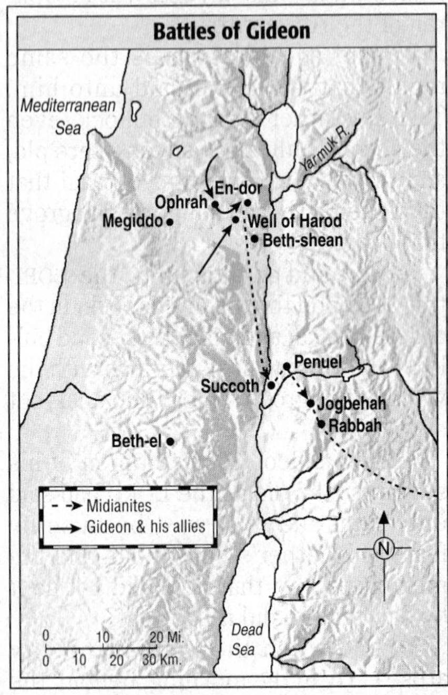

7:2 lest Israel vaunt themselves. The LORD had to teach the people once again that it was He alone who gave victories.

7:6 the number of them that lapped. By this simple test the LORD showed which men realized that they were on active service and drank out of their hands so that they could be ready to move on at an instant's notice.

¶[9]And it came to pass the same night,
that the LORD said unto him, Arise, get
thee down unto the host; for I have
delivered it into thine hand.
[10]But if thou fear to go down, go thou
with Phurah thy servant down to the
host:
[11]And thou shalt hear what they say;
and afterward shall thine hands be
strengthened to go down unto the host.
Then went he down with Phurah his
servant unto the outside of the armed
men that *were* in the host.
[12]And the Midianites and the Amalekites and all the children of the east
lay along in the valley like grasshoppers
for multitude; and their camels *were*
without number, as the sand by the sea
side for multitude.
[13]And when Gideon was come, behold, *there was* a man that told a dream
unto his fellow, and said, Behold, I
dreamed a dream, and, lo, a cake of barley bread tumbled into the host of Midian, and came unto a tent, and smote it
that it fell, and overturned it, that the
tent lay along.
[14]And his fellow answered and said,
This *is* nothing else save the sword of
Gideon the son of Joash, a man of Israel:
for into his hand hath *God delivered
Midian, and all the host.
¶[15]And it was *so,* when Gideon heard
the telling of the dream, and the interpretation thereof, that he worshipped,
and returned into the host of Israel, and
said, Arise; for the LORD hath delivered
into your hand the host of Midian.

Victory over Midianites

[16]And he divided the three hundred
men *into* three companies, and he put
a trumpet in every man's hand, with
empty pitchers, and lamps within the
pitchers.
[17]And he said unto them, Look on
me, and do likewise: and, behold, when
I come to the outside of the camp, it
shall be *that,* as I do, so shall ye do.
[18]When I blow with a trumpet, I and
all that *are* with me, then blow ye the
trumpets also on every side of all the
camp, and say, *The sword* of the LORD,
and of Gideon.
¶[19]So Gideon, and the hundred men
that *were* with him, came unto the outside of the camp in the beginning of the
middle watch; and they had but newly
set the watch: and they blew the trumpets, and brake the pitchers that *were*
in their hands.
[20]And the three companies blew the
trumpets, and brake the pitchers, and
held the lamps in their left hands, and
the trumpets in their right hands to
blow *withal:* and they cried, The sword
of the LORD, and of Gideon.
[21]And they stood every man in his
place round about the camp: and all the
host ran, and cried, and fled.
[22]And the three hundred blew the
trumpets, and the LORD set every
man's sword against his fellow, even
throughout all the host: and the host
fled to Beth-shittah in Zererath, *and* to
the border of Abel-meholah, unto Tabbath.
[23]And the men of Israel gathered
themselves together out of Naphtali,
and out of Asher, and out of all *Manasseh, and pursued after the Midianites.
¶[24]And Gideon sent messengers
throughout all mount *Ephraim, saying,
Come down against the Midianites,
and take before them the waters unto
Beth-barah and Jordan. Then all the
men of Ephraim gathered themselves
together, and took the waters unto
Beth-barah and Jordan.
[25]And they took two princes of the
Midianites, Oreb and Zeeb; and they
slew Oreb upon the rock Oreb, and
Zeeb they slew at the winepress of
Zeeb, and pursued Midian, and brought

7:16 Unusual Weapons
The empty pitchers and lamps were jugs of earthenware with torches inside. They represent human weakness illumined by God's light. Read 2 Corinthians 4:6-7, where Paul may have been thinking of this story.

the heads of Oreb and Zeeb to Gideon
on the other side Jordan.

Jealousy of tribe of Ephraim

8 And the men of Ephraim said unto
him, Why hast thou served us thus,
that thou calledst us not, when thou
wentest to fight with the Midianites?
And they did chide with him sharply.
2 And he said unto them, What have I
done now in comparison of you? *Is* not
the gleaning of the grapes of Ephraim
better than the vintage of Abi-ezer?
3 God hath delivered into your hands
the princes of Midian, Oreb and Zeeb:
and what was I able to do in comparison
of you? Then their anger was abated
toward him, when he had said that.

Final defeat of Midianites

¶ 4 And Gideon came to Jordan, *and*
passed over, he, and the three hundred
men that *were* with him, faint, yet pursuing *them.*
5 And he said unto the men of Succoth, Give, I pray you, loaves of bread
unto the people that follow me; for they
be faint, and I am pursuing after Zebah
and Zalmunna, kings of Midian.

8:5 Succoth
Succoth was a city on the main army route from Palestine to the East. Wandering tribes like the Midianites always came that way in their attacks on the Israelites: "the way of them that dwelt in tents" (vs. 11). The men of Succoth tried to remain neutral and not help either side, in case Gideon was defeated and the Midianites returned and took vengeance on them for them helping Gideon. The same applied to Penuel (vs. 8), whose men had even built a tower to protect them in the raids (vss. 9,17).

¶ 6 And the princes of Succoth said,
Are the hands of Zebah and Zalmunna
now in thine hand, that we should give
bread unto thine army?
7 And Gideon said, Therefore when
the LORD hath delivered Zebah and Zalmunna into mine hand, then I will tear
your flesh with the thorns of the wilderness and with briers.
¶ 8 And he went up thence to Penuel,
and spake unto them likewise: and the
men of Penuel answered him as the
men of Succoth had answered *him.*
9 And he spake also unto the men of
Penuel, saying, When I come again in
peace, I will break down this tower.
¶ 10 Now Zebah and Zalmunna *were* in
Karkor, and their hosts with them,
about fifteen thousand *men,* all that
were left of all the hosts of the children
of the east: for there fell an hundred and
twenty thousand men that drew sword.
¶ 11 And Gideon went up by the way
of them that dwelt in tents on the east
of Nobah and Jogbehah, and smote the
host: for the host was secure.
12 And when Zebah and Zalmunna
fled, he pursued after them, and took
the two kings of Midian, Zebah and Zalmunna, and discomfited all the host.
¶ 13 And Gideon the son of Joash
returned from battle before the sun
was up,
14 And caught a young man of the men
of Succoth, and enquired of him: and he
described unto him the princes of Succoth, and the *elders thereof, *even*
threescore and seventeen men.
15 And he came unto the men of Succoth, and said, Behold Zebah and Zalmunna, with whom ye did upbraid
me, saying, *Are* the hands of Zebah and
Zalmunna now in thine hand, that we

8:1 the men of Ephraim. In Genesis 48:14-22, Jacob had placed Ephraim before his elder brother Manasseh, and always after that, the descendants of Ephraim were proud and jealous of their rights. Because Gideon was of the tribe of Manasseh, the Ephraimites envied him. Read Judges 12:1 to see another instance of this. This really began the trouble and strife in Israel that ended in the division of the kingdom after the death of King Solomon (1 Kings 12). Our Lord dealt with such strife in a loving way (see Luke 22:24-27).
8:11 secure. Without worry.

should give bread unto thy men *that are*
weary?
16 And he took the elders of the city,
and thorns of the wilderness and briers,
and with them he taught the men of
Succoth.
17 And he beat down the tower of Penuel, and slew the men of the city.
¶ 18 Then said he unto Zebah and Zalmunna, What manner of men *were they*
whom ye slew at Tabor? And they answered, As thou *art,* so *were* they; each
one resembled the children of a king.
19 And he said, They *were* my brethren, *even* the sons of my mother: *as* the
LORD liveth, if ye had saved them alive,
I would not slay you.
20 And he said unto Jether his firstborn, Up, *and* slay them. But the youth
drew not his sword: for he feared, because he *was* yet a youth.
21 Then Zebah and Zalmunna said,
Rise thou, and fall upon us: for as the
man *is, so is* his strength. And Gideon
arose, and slew Zebah and Zalmunna,
and took away the ornaments that *were*
on their camels' necks.
¶ 22 Then the men of Israel said unto
Gideon, Rule thou over us, both thou,
and thy son, and thy son's son also: for
thou hast delivered us from the hand of
Midian.
23 And Gideon said unto them, I will
not rule over you, neither shall my son
rule over you: the LORD shall rule over
you.
¶ 24 And Gideon said unto them, I
would desire a request of you, that ye
would give me every man the earrings
of his prey. (For they had golden earrings, because they *were* Ishmaelites.)
25 And they answered, We will willingly give *them.* And they spread a garment, and did cast therein every man
the earrings of his prey.
26 And the weight of the golden earrings that he requested was a thousand
and seven hundred *shekels* of gold; beside ornaments, and collars, and purple
raiment that *was* on the kings of Midian, and beside the chains that *were*
about their camels' necks.
27 And Gideon made an ephod thereof,
and put it in his city, *even* in Ophrah: and
all Israel went thither a whoring after
it: which thing became a snare unto
Gideon, and to his house.
¶ 28 Thus was Midian subdued before
the children of Israel, so that they lifted up their heads no more. And the
country was in quietness forty years in
the days of Gideon.
¶ 29 And Jerubbaal the son of Joash
went and dwelt in his own house.
30 And Gideon had threescore and ten
sons of his body begotten: for he had
many wives.
31 And his concubine that *was* in
*Shechem, she also bare him a son,
whose name he called Abimelech.
32 And Gideon the son of Joash died in
a good old age, and was buried in the
sepulchre of Joash his father, in Ophrah
of the Abi-ezrites.

8:16 he taught the men. Gideon taught them that it was a dangerous thing not to give aid to the people of God.

8:21 Gideon arose, and slew Zebah and Zalmunna. The Israelites never forgot the victory of Gideon over the two kings and the two princes of Midian. Psalm 83:9-11 and Isaiah 9:4 and 10:26 refer to it. See also Hebrews 11:32.

8:22 Rule thou over us. The Israelites were always wanting a human leader, forgetting that God was their King. See 1 Samuel 8:7.

8:26 purple raiment. Purple was such an expensive dye that only kings could wear clothes of that color.

8:27 ephod. A shield or breastplate such as a magistrate or priest might wear. See Exodus 28:4.

8:27 a whoring. The Israelites made an idol of the ephod.

8:31 concubine. A member of a harem—not a wife but a woman at the beck and call of her master.

¶33 And it came to pass, as soon as
Gideon was dead, that the children of
Israel turned again, and went a whoring after Baalim, and made *Baal-berith
their god.
34 And the children of Israel remembered not the LORD their God, who had
delivered them out of the hands of all
their enemies on every side:
35 Neither shewed they kindness to
the house of Jerubbaal, *namely,* Gideon,
according to all the goodness which he
had shewed unto Israel.

Abimelech's conspiracy

9 And Abimelech the son of Jerubbaal went to Shechem unto his
mother's brethren, and communed with
them, and with all the family of the
house of his mother's father, saying,

9:1 Shechem
Shechem was a city of Ephraim. Abimelech, Gideon's son, was an Ephraimite through his mother, so he played upon the usual pride of the Ephraimites (see 8:1 note) to have himself made ruler instead of the other sons of Gideon, who were of Manasseh, their father's tribe. See 6:32 note about Jerubbaal.

2 Speak, I pray you, in the ears of all
the men of Shechem, Whether *is* better for you, either that all the sons of
*Jerubbaal, *which are* threescore and
ten persons, reign over you, or that one
reign over you? remember also that I
am your bone and your flesh.
3 And his mother's brethren spake of
him in the ears of all the men of Shechem all these words: and their hearts
inclined to follow Abimelech; for they
said, He *is* our brother.
4 And they gave him threescore and
ten *pieces* of silver out of the house of
Baal-berith, wherewith Abimelech
hired vain and light persons, which followed him.
5 And he went unto his father's house
at Ophrah, and slew his brethren the
sons of Jerubbaal, *being* threescore and
ten persons, upon one stone: notwithstanding yet Jotham the youngest son
of Jerubbaal was left; for he hid himself.
6 And all the men of Shechem gathered together, and all the house of *Millo, and went, and made Abimelech king,
by the plain of the pillar that *was* in
Shechem.
¶7 And when they told *it* to Jotham, he
went and stood in the top of mount
Gerizim, and lifted up his voice, and
cried, and said unto them, Hearken
unto me, ye men of Shechem, that God
may hearken unto you.
8 The trees went forth *on a time* to
*anoint a king over them; and they said
unto the olive tree, Reign thou over us.

9:8-15 A Parable
Verses 8 to 15 contain one of the Old Testament parables, or stories used to illustrate a truth in an interesting way. It is explained by Jotham in verses 16 to 20. The curse of Jotham was fulfilled (vs. 57). For the next parable, see 2 Samuel 12:1-4.

9 But the olive tree said unto them,
Should I leave my fatness, wherewith
by me they honour God and man, and
go to be promoted over the trees?
10 And the trees said to the fig *tree,
Come thou, *and* reign over us.
11 But the fig tree said unto them,
Should I forsake my sweetness, and my
good fruit, and go to be promoted over
the trees?
12 Then said the trees unto the vine,
Come thou, *and* reign over us.
13 And the vine said unto them,

8:33 Baal-berith. The name of this idol means *Baal in covenant,* as if the Israelites had made an agreement or covenant to worship Baal.
9:6 house of Millo. This was probably a tower, because verses 47 and 49 speak of the men of the tower of Shechem.
9:7 Gerizim. See Deuteronomy 11:29 and Joshua 8:33.

Should I leave my wine, which cheereth
God and man, and go to be promoted
over the trees?
14 Then said all the trees unto the
bramble, Come thou, *and* reign over us.
15 And the bramble said unto the
trees, If in truth ye anoint me king over
you, *then* come *and* put your trust in my
shadow: and if not, let fire come out of
the bramble, and devour the cedars of
*Lebanon.
16 Now therefore, if ye have done truly and sincerely, in that ye have made
Abimelech king, and if ye have dealt
well with Jerubbaal and his house, and
have done unto him according to the
deserving of his hands;
17 (For my father fought for you, and
adventured his life far, and delivered
you out of the hand of Midian:
18 And ye are risen up against my
father's house this day, and have slain
his sons, threescore and ten persons,
upon one stone, and have made Abimelech, the son of his maidservant, king
over the men of Shechem, because he
is your brother;)
19 If ye then have dealt truly and sincerely with Jerubbaal and with his
house this day, *then* rejoice ye in Abimelech, and let him also rejoice in you:
20 But if not, let fire come out from
Abimelech, and devour the men of Shechem, and the house of Millo; and let
fire come out from the men of Shechem, and from the house of Millo, and
devour Abimelech.
21 And Jotham ran away, and fled, and
went to Beer, and dwelt there, for fear
of Abimelech his brother.
¶22 When Abimelech had reigned
three years over Israel,
23 Then God sent an evil spirit between Abimelech and the men of Shechem; and the men of Shechem dealt
treacherously with Abimelech:
24 That the cruelty *done* to the threescore and ten sons of Jerubbaal might
come, and their *blood be laid upon
Abimelech their brother, which slew
them; and upon the men of Shechem,
which aided him in the killing of his
brethren.
25 And the men of Shechem set liers
in wait for him in the top of the mountains, and they robbed all that came
along that way by them: and it was told
Abimelech.
26 And Gaal the son of Ebed came
with his brethren, and went over to
Shechem: and the men of Shechem put
their confidence in him.

9:26 Gaal
Gaal was probably the captain of a group of men. Those of the Shechemites who did not want Abimelech to rule over them wanted Gaal to help them get rid of him. They were angry because Abimelech was the son of Gideon (Jerubbaal), who had pulled down the altar of Baal, their god at Shechem (see vs. 28, and 6:30,32).

27 And they went out into the fields,
and gathered their vineyards, and trode
the grapes, and made merry, and went
into the house of their god, and did eat
and drink, and cursed Abimelech.
28 And Gaal the son of Ebed said, Who
is Abimelech, and who *is* Shechem, that
we should serve him? *is* not *he* the son of
Jerubbaal? and Zebul his officer? serve
the men of Hamor the father of Shechem: for why should we serve him?
29 And would to God this people were
under my hand! then would I remove
Abimelech. And he said to Abimelech,
Increase thine army, and come out.

9:23 Then God sent an evil spirit. The explanation of this is in verse 24. It goes back to the same old law of "as he hath done, so shall it be done to him" (Lev. 24:19).

9:28 Zebul. Gaal was saying, "Who is Zebul the officer of Abimelech?" or, "Is Zebul strong simply because he is an officer? He is but one, and we are many."

9:28 men of Hamor. These were descendants of Hamor the Hivite, the founder of Shechem (Gen. 33:18; 34:2).

¶30And when Zebul the ruler of the
city heard the words of Gaal the son of
Ebed, his anger was kindled.
31And he sent messengers unto
Abimelech privily, saying, Behold, Gaal
the son of Ebed and his brethren be
come to Shechem; and, behold, they
fortify the city against thee.
32Now therefore up by night, thou
and the people that *is* with thee, and lie
in wait in the field:
33And it shall be, *that* in the morning,
as soon as the sun is up, thou shalt rise
early, and set upon the city: and, behold,
when he and the people that *is* with him
come out against thee, then mayest
thou do to them as thou shalt find occasion.
¶34And Abimelech rose up, and all
the people that *were* with him, by night,
and they laid wait against Shechem in
four companies.
35And Gaal the son of Ebed went out,
and stood in the entering of the gate of
the city: and Abimelech rose up, and the
people that *were* with him, from lying in
wait.
36And when Gaal saw the people, he
said to Zebul, Behold, there come people
down from the top of the mountains.
And Zebul said unto him, Thou seest
the shadow of the mountains as *if they*
were men.
37And Gaal spake again and said, See
there come people down by the middle
of the land, and another company come
along by the plain of Meonenim.
38Then said Zebul unto him, Where
is now thy mouth, wherewith thou
saidst, Who *is* Abimelech, that we
should serve him? *is* not this the people
that thou hast despised? go out, I
pray now, and fight with them.
39And Gaal went out before the men
of Shechem, and fought with Abimelech.
40And Abimelech chased him, and he
fled before him, and many were overthrown
and wounded, *even* unto the
entering of the gate.
41And Abimelech dwelt at Arumah: and
Zebul thrust out Gaal and his brethren,
that they should not dwell in Shechem.
42And it came to pass on the morrow,
that the people went out into the field;
and they told Abimelech.
43And he took the people, and divided
them into three companies, and laid
wait in the field, and looked, and, behold,
the people *were* come forth out of
the city; and he rose up against them,
and smote them.
44And Abimelech, and the company
that *was* with him, rushed forward, and
stood in the entering of the gate of the
city: and the two *other* companies ran
upon all *the people* that *were* in the fields,
and slew them.
45And Abimelech fought against the
city all that day; and he took the city, and
slew the people that *was* therein, and
beat down the city, and sowed it with
salt.
¶46And when all the men of the tower
of Shechem heard *that,* they entered
into an hold of the house of the god
Berith.
47And it was told Abimelech, that all
the men of the tower of Shechem were
gathered together.
48And Abimelech gat him up to
mount Zalmon, he and all the people
that *were* with him; and Abimelech took
an axe in his hand, and cut down a bough
from the trees, and took it, and laid *it*
on his shoulder, and said unto the people
that *were* with him, What ye have
seen me do, make haste, *and* do as I
have done.
49And all the people likewise cut
down every man his bough, and followed
Abimelech, and put *them* to the
hold, and set the hold on fire upon them;
so that all the men of the tower of Shechem
died also, about a thousand men
and women.

9:45 sowed it with salt. Nothing could grow in the land after this was done.
9:46 Berith. A covenant. See Judges 8:33 note.

¶50Then went Abimelech to Thebez,
and encamped against Thebez, and
took it.
51But there was a strong tower within the city, and thither fled all the men
and women, and all they of the city, and
shut *it* to them, and gat them up to the
top of the tower.
52And Abimelech came unto the tower, and fought against it, and went hard
unto the door of the tower to burn it
with fire.
53And a certain woman cast a piece
of a millstone upon Abimelech's head,
and all to brake his skull.
54Then he called hastily unto the
young man his armourbearer, and said
unto him, Draw thy sword, and slay me,
that men say not of me, A woman slew
him. And his young man thrust him
through, and he died.
55And when the men of Israel saw
that Abimelech was dead, they departed every man unto his place.
¶56Thus God rendered the wickedness of Abimelech, which he did unto his
father, in slaying his seventy brethren:
57And all the evil of the men of Shechem did God *render upon their heads:
and upon them came the curse of Jotham the son of Jerubbaal.

Tola, the seventh judge

10 And after Abimelech there
arose to defend Israel Tola the
son of Puah, the son of Dodo, a man of
Issachar; and he dwelt in Shamir in
mount Ephraim.
2And he judged Israel twenty and
three years, and died, and was buried in
Shamir.

Jair, the eighth judge

¶3And after him arose Jair, a Gileadite, and judged Israel twenty and two
years.

10:4 Riding on a Colt
Riding on a colt implies great wealth, for this was usually a sign of royalty. It was upon the colt of an ass, or donkey, that the Lord Jesus Christ rode into Jerusalem, He who was the true King, the Son of David (Matt. 21:1-11).

4And he had thirty sons that rode on
thirty ass colts, and they had thirty cities, which are called Havoth-jair unto
this day, which *are* in the land of Gilead.
5And Jair died, and was buried in
Camon.

E. Fifth Servitude: Ammonites

¶6And the children of Israel did evil
again in the sight of the LORD, and
served Baalim, and *Ashtaroth, and the
gods of Syria, and the gods of Zidon, and
the gods of *Moab, and the gods of the
children of Ammon, and the gods of the
*Philistines, and forsook the LORD, and
served not him.
7And the anger of the LORD was hot
against Israel, and he sold them into the
hands of the Philistines, and into the
hands of the children of Ammon.

10:7 Ammon
The Ammonites were descendants of Lot, Abraham's nephew, and thus were related to Israel. Ammon may be taken as a *type of worldly unbelief in the Bible and rejection of Christ as the truth of God (see Judg. 3:12 note). This unbelief can only be defeated by being open to the Word of God. Jephthah (the ninth judge) is a symbol of the open Word, for his name means *he opens*.

8And that year they vexed and oppressed the children of Israel: eighteen
years, all the children of Israel that *were*
on the other side Jordan in the land of
the Amorites, which *is* in Gilead.
9Moreover the children of Ammon
passed over Jordan to fight also against

9:53 all to brake. To break in pieces. Abimelech wasn't killed instantly—his head was not crushed by the millstone. See verse 54.
9:57 curse of Jotham. See verse 20.
10:8 vexed. Harassed or tormented.

Judah, and against Benjamin, and
against the house of Ephraim; so that
Israel was sore distressed.
¶ 10 And the children of Israel cried
unto the LORD, saying, We have sinned
against thee, both because we have forsaken our God, and also served Baalim.
11 And the LORD said unto the children of Israel, *Did* not *I deliver you* from
the Egyptians, and from the Amorites,
from the children of Ammon, and from
the Philistines?
12 The Zidonians also, and the Amalekites, and the Maonites, did oppress
you; and ye cried to me, and I delivered
you out of their hand.
13 Yet ye have forsaken me, and
served other gods: wherefore I will
deliver you no more.
14 Go and cry unto the gods which ye
have chosen; let them deliver you in the
time of your tribulation.
¶ 15 And the children of Israel said
unto the LORD, We have sinned: do
thou unto us whatsoever seemeth good
unto thee; deliver us only, we pray thee,
this day.
16 And they put away the strange gods
from among them, and served the
LORD: and his soul was grieved for the
misery of Israel.
17 Then the children of Ammon were
gathered together, and encamped in
Gilead. And the children of Israel assembled themselves together, and encamped in Mizpeh.
18 And the people *and* princes of Gilead said one to another, What man *is he*
that will begin to fight against the children of Ammon? he shall be head over
all the inhabitants of Gilead.

Jephthah, the ninth judge

11 Now Jephthah the Gileadite
was a mighty man of valour, and
he *was* the son of an harlot: and *Gilead begat Jephthah.
2 And Gilead's wife bare him sons; and
his wife's sons grew up, and they thrust
out Jephthah, and said unto him, Thou
shalt not inherit in our father's house;
for thou *art* the son of a strange woman.
3 Then Jephthah fled from his brethren, and dwelt in the land of Tob: and
there were gathered vain men to Jephthah, and went out with him.
¶ 4 And it came to pass in process of
time, that the children of Ammon made
war against Israel.
5 And it was so, that when the children of Ammon made war against Israel, the elders of Gilead went to fetch
Jephthah out of the land of Tob:
6 And they said unto Jephthah, Come,
and be our captain, that we may fight
with the children of Ammon.
7 And Jephthah said unto the elders of
Gilead, Did not ye hate me, and expel
me out of my father's house? and why
are ye come unto me now when ye are
in distress?
8 And the elders of Gilead said unto
Jephthah, Therefore we turn again to
thee now, that thou mayest go with us,
and fight against the children of Ammon, and be our head over all the inhabitants of Gilead.
9 And Jephthah said unto the elders of
Gilead, If ye bring me home again to
fight against the children of Ammon,
and the LORD deliver them before me,
shall I be your head?
10 And the elders of Gilead said unto
Jephthah, The LORD be witness between us, if we do not so according to
thy words.
11 Then Jephthah went with the elders of Gilead, and the people made him
head and captain over them: and Jephthah uttered all his words before the
LORD in Mizpeh.
¶ 12 And Jephthah sent messengers
unto the king of the children of Ammon,
saying, What hast thou to do with me,
that thou art come against me to fight
in my land?
13 And the king of the children of Ammon answered unto the messengers of

---

11:3 vain men. Idle, worthless men.

Jephthah, Because Israel took away my
land, when they came up out of *Egypt,
from Arnon even unto Jabbok, and unto
Jordan: now therefore restore those
lands again peaceably.
14 And Jephthah sent messengers
again unto the king of the children of
Ammon:
15 And said unto him, Thus saith
Jephthah, Israel took not away the land
of Moab, nor the land of the children of
Ammon:
16 But when Israel came up from
Egypt, and walked through the wilderness unto the Red sea, and came to
Kadesh;
17 Then Israel sent messengers unto
the king of *Edom, saying, Let me, I
pray thee, pass through thy land: but
the king of Edom would not hearken
thereto. And in like manner they sent
unto the king of Moab: but he would not
consent: and Israel abode in Kadesh.
18 Then they went along through the
wilderness, and compassed the land of
Edom, and the land of Moab, and came
by the east side of the land of Moab, and
pitched on the other side of Arnon, but
came not within the border of Moab: for
Arnon *was* the border of Moab.
19 And Israel sent messengers unto
Sihon king of the Amorites, the king of
Heshbon; and Israel said unto him, Let
us pass, we pray thee, through thy land
into my place.
20 But Sihon trusted not Israel to pass
through his coast: but Sihon gathered
all his people together, and pitched in
Jahaz, and fought against Israel.
21 And the LORD God of Israel delivered Sihon and all his people into the
hand of Israel, and they smote them: so
Israel possessed all the land of the Amorites, the inhabitants of that country.
22 And they possessed all the coasts
of the Amorites, from Arnon even unto
Jabbok, and from the wilderness even
unto Jordan.
23 So now the LORD God of Israel hath
dispossessed the Amorites from before
his people Israel, and shouldest thou
possess it?
24 Wilt not thou possess that which
*Chemosh thy god giveth thee to pos-
sess? So whomsoever the LORD our
God shall drive out from before us, them
will we possess.
25 And now *art* thou any thing better
than Balak the son of Zippor, king of
Moab? did he ever strive against Israel,
or did he ever fight against them,
26 While Israel dwelt in Heshbon and
her towns, and in Aroer and her towns,
and in all the cities that *be* along by the
coasts of Arnon, three hundred years?
why therefore did ye not recover *them*
within that time?
27 Wherefore I have not sinned
against thee, but thou doest me wrong
to war against me: the LORD the Judge
be judge this day between the children
of Israel and the children of Ammon.
28 Howbeit the king of the children of
Ammon hearkened not unto the words
of Jephthah which he sent him.
¶ 29 Then the Spirit of the LORD came
upon Jephthah, and he passed over Gilead, and Manasseh, and passed over
Mizpeh of Gilead, and from Mizpeh of
Gilead he passed over *unto* the children
of Ammon.
30 And Jephthah vowed a vow unto the
LORD, and said, If thou shalt without fail
deliver the children of Ammon into
mine hands,
31 Then it shall be, that whatsoever
cometh forth of the doors of my house
to meet me, when I return in peace
from the children of Ammon, shall surely be the LORD'S, and I will offer it up
for a burnt-offering.
¶ 32 So Jephthah passed over unto the

11:13 Because Israel took away my land. Numbers 21:21-25 describes how Israel conquered this territory but not from the Ammonites. Jephthah's reply (vss. 15-27) states the facts.

11:24 Chemosh. The war god of the Ammonites.

11:30-31 An Ancient Custom
Vowing a vow to the LORD was an ancient custom for generals at the beginning of a campaign. Many students of the Bible believe that verse 31 could read: "Whatsoever cometh forth . . . shall surely be the LORD's, *or* I will offer it," meaning that, if a person should come forth, he or she would be dedicated to the LORD's service; but if an animal should come forth, it would be offered as a sacrifice. It would seem as if, in the case of Jephthah's daughter, his vow required her to live a life of celibacy–that she could never marry (vss. 37-39). Whether she lived celibate or was offered as a sacrifice, the loyalty of Jephthah to his vow to Jehovah and the obedience of the daughter are exemplary. See what our Lord said about vows, however (Matt. 5:33-37).

children of Ammon to fight against
them; and the LORD delivered them into
his hands.
33And he smote them from Aroer,
even till thou come to Minnith, *even*
twenty cities, and unto the plain of the
vineyards, with a very great slaughter.
Thus the children of Ammon were subdued before the children of Israel.
¶34And Jephthah came to Mizpeh
unto his house, and, behold, his daughter came out to meet him with *timbrels and with dances: and she *was his*
only child; beside her he had neither
son nor daughter.
35And it came to pass, when he saw
her, that he rent his clothes, and said,
Alas, my daughter! thou hast brought
me very low, and thou art one of them
that trouble me: for I have opened my
mouth unto the LORD, and I cannot go
back.
36And she said unto him, My father,
if thou hast opened thy mouth unto the
LORD, do to me according to that which
hath proceeded out of thy mouth; forasmuch as the LORD hath taken vengeance for thee of thine enemies, *even*
of the children of Ammon.
37And she said unto her father, Let
this thing be done for me: let me alone
two months, that I may go up and down
upon the mountains, and bewail my virginity, I and my fellows.
38And he said, Go. And he sent her
away *for* two months: and she went with
her companions, and bewailed her virginity upon the mountains.
39And it came to pass at the end of two
months, that she returned unto her father, who did with her *according* to his
vow which he had vowed: and she knew
no man. And it was a custom in Israel,
40*That* the daughters of Israel went
yearly to lament the daughter of Jephthah the Gileadite four days in a year.

Men of Ephraim

12 And the men of Ephraim gathered themselves together, and
went northward, and said unto Jephthah,
Wherefore passedst thou over to fight
against the children of Ammon, and
didst not call us to go with thee? we will
burn thine house upon thee with fire.
2And Jephthah said unto them, I and
my people were at great strife with the
children of Ammon; and when I called
you, ye delivered me not out of their
hands.
3And when I saw that ye delivered *me*
not, I put my life in my hands, and
passed over against the children of
Ammon, and the LORD delivered them
into my hand: wherefore then are ye
come up unto me this day, to fight
against me?
4Then Jephthah gathered together all
the men of Gilead, and fought with
Ephraim: and the men of Gilead smote
Ephraim, because they said, Ye Gileadites *are* fugitives of Ephraim among the

11:35 I cannot go back. Jephthah could not break his vow to God. See the law about vows in Numbers 30:2.

11:37 bewail my virginity. She would now have to be dedicated to the LORD as a kind of priestess (see vss. 30-31 note, "An Ancient Custom") and could never take her place in Israel as a mother of a family.

Ephraimites, *and* among the Manassites.

[5]And the Gileadites took the passages of Jordan before the Ephraimites:
and it was *so,* that when those Ephraimites which were escaped said, Let me
go over; that the men of Gilead said
unto him, *Art* thou an Ephraimite? If he
said, Nay;

[6]Then said they unto him, Say now
Shibboleth: and he said Sibboleth: for
he could not frame to pronounce *it*
right. Then they took him, and slew
him at the passages of Jordan: and there
fell at that time of the Ephraimites forty and two thousand.

[7]And Jephthah judged Israel six
years. Then died Jephthah the Gileadite, and was buried in *one of* the cities
of Gilead.

Ibzan, the tenth judge

¶[8]And after him Ibzan of Beth-lehem
judged Israel.

[9]And he had thirty sons, and thirty
daughters, *whom* he sent abroad, and
took in thirty daughters from abroad for
his sons. And he judged Israel seven
years.

[10]Then died Ibzan, and was buried at
Beth-lehem.

Elon, the eleventh judge

¶[11]And after him Elon, a Zebulonite,
judged Israel; and he judged Israel ten
years.

[12]And Elon the Zebulonite died, and
was buried in Aijalon in the country of
Zebulun.

Abdon, the twelfth judge

¶[13]And after him Abdon the son of
Hillel, a Pirathonite, judged Israel.

[14]And he had forty sons and thirty
nephews, that rode on threescore and
ten ass colts: and he judged Israel eight
years.

[15]And Abdon the son of Hillel the
Pirathonite died, and was buried in Pir-
athon in the land of Ephraim, in the
mount of the Amalekites.

F. Sixth Servitude: Philistines

13 And the children of *Israel did
evil again in the sight of the
LORD; and the LORD delivered them
into the hand of the Philistines forty
years.

13:1 The Philistines
The Philistines oppressed Israel for the longest period of any of their enemies.They were the enemies of Israel until the time of King David. The Philistines had a religion full of ceremony, but they lacked knowledge and worship of the true God. The Philistines thus symbolize all the worldly religions that emphasize form and ritual to the exclusion of Christ's atoning work.

¶[2]And there was a certain man of Zorah, of the family of the Danites, whose
name *was* Manoah; and his wife *was*
barren, and bare not.

[3]And the *angel of the LORD appeared unto the woman, and said unto
her, Behold now, thou *art* barren, and
bearest not: but thou shalt conceive,
and bear a son.

[4]Now therefore beware, I pray thee,
and drink not wine nor strong drink,
and eat not any *unclean *thing:*

[5]For, lo, thou shalt conceive, and bear
a son; and no razor shall come on his
head: for the child shall be a *Nazarite
unto *God from the womb: and he shall
begin to deliver Israel out of the hand
of the Philistines.

¶[6]Then the woman came and told her

12:5 the Gileadites took the passages of Jordan. The men of Ephraim had crossed the river from the west into the land of Gilead, and now the Gileadites hurried back to the river's crossings first, so that the Ephraimites could not escape.
12:6 he could not frame. He could not pronounce the word correctly.
12:6 the passages. A ford, which was a shallow place to cross the river.
12:14 rode on threescore and ten ass colts. See Judges 10:4 note, "Riding on a Colt."

husband, saying, A man of God came unto me, and his countenance *was* like the countenance of an angel of God, very terrible: but I asked him not whence he *was,* neither told he me his name:

7 But he said unto me, Behold, thou shalt conceive, and bear a son; and now drink no wine nor strong drink, neither eat any unclean *thing:* for the child shall be a Nazarite to God from the womb to the day of his death.

¶8 Then Manoah intreated the LORD, and said, O my Lord, let the man of God which thou didst send come again unto us, and teach us what we shall do unto the child that shall be born.

9 And God hearkened to the voice of Manoah; and the angel of God came again unto the woman as she sat in the field: but Manoah her husband *was* not with her.

10 And the woman made haste, and ran, and shewed her husband, and said unto him, Behold, the man hath appeared unto me, that came unto me the *other* day.

11 And Manoah arose, and went after his wife, and came to the man, and said unto him, *Art* thou the man that spakest unto the woman? And he said, I *am.*

12 And Manoah said, Now let thy words come to pass. How shall we order the child, and *how* shall we do unto him?

13 And the angel of the LORD said unto Manoah, Of all that I said unto the woman let her beware.

14 She may not eat of any *thing* that cometh of the vine, neither let her drink wine or strong drink, nor eat any unclean *thing:* all that I commanded her let her observe.

¶15 And Manoah said unto the angel of the LORD, I pray thee, let us detain thee, until we shall have made ready a kid for thee.

16 And the angel of the LORD said unto Manoah, Though thou detain me, I will not eat of thy bread: and if thou wilt offer a burnt-offering, thou must offer it unto the LORD. For Manoah knew not that he *was* an angel of the LORD.

17 And Manoah said unto the angel of the LORD, What *is* thy name, that when thy sayings come to pass we may do thee honour?

18 And the angel of the LORD said unto him, Why askest thou thus after my name, seeing it *is* secret?

19 So Manoah took a kid with a *meat-offering, and offered *it* upon a rock unto the LORD: and *the angel* did wonderously; and Manoah and his wife looked on.

20 For it came to pass, when the flame went up toward heaven from off the *altar, that the angel of the LORD ascended in the flame of the altar. And Manoah and his wife looked on *it,* and fell on their faces to the ground.

21 But the angel of the LORD did no more appear to Manoah and to his wife. Then Manoah knew that he *was* an angel of the LORD.

22 And Manoah said unto his wife, We shall surely die, because we have seen God.

23 But his wife said unto him, If the LORD were pleased to kill us, he would not have received a burnt-offering and a meat-offering at our hands, neither would he have shewed us all these *things,* nor would as at this time have told us *such things* as these.

¶24 And the woman bare a son, and called his name Samson: and the child grew, and the LORD blessed him.

25 And the Spirit of the LORD began to move him at times in the camp of Dan between Zorah and Eshtaol.

14 And Samson went down to Timnath, and saw a woman in Timnath of the daughters of the Philistines.

2 And he came up, and told his father and his mother, and said, I have seen a

---

13:12 How shall we order the child . . . ? In effect, Manoah was saying, "How shall we train him (Samson)?"

woman in Timnath of the daughters of
the Philistines: now therefore get her
for me to wife.
3 Then his father and his mother said
unto him, *Is there* never a woman
among the daughters of thy brethren, or
among all my people, that thou goest to
take a wife of the *uncircumcised Philistines? And Samson said unto his father, Get her for me; for she pleaseth
me well.
4 But his father and his mother knew
not that it *was* of the LORD, that he
sought an occasion against the Philistines: for at that time the Philistines
had dominion over Israel.

Samson and the lion

¶5 Then went Samson down, and his
father and his mother, to Timnath, and
came to the vineyards of Timnath: and,
behold, a young lion roared against him.
6 And the Spirit of the LORD came
mightily upon him, and he rent him as
he would have rent a kid, and *he had*
nothing in his hand: but he told not his
father or his mother what he had done.
7 And he went down, and talked with
the woman; and she pleased Samson
well.

Samson's riddle

¶8 And after a time he returned to
take her, and he turned aside to see the
carcase of the lion: and, behold, *there*
was a swarm of bees and honey in the
carcase of the lion.
9 And he took thereof in his hands,
and went on eating, and came to his father and mother, and he gave them, and
they did eat: but he told not them that
he had taken the honey out of the carcase of the lion.
¶10 So his father went down unto the
woman: and Samson made there a feast;
for so used the young men to do.
11 And it came to pass, when they saw
him, that they brought thirty companions to be with him.
¶12 And Samson said unto them, I will
now put forth a riddle unto you: if ye can
certainly declare it me within the seven
days of the feast, and find *it* out, then I
will give you thirty sheets and thirty
change of *garments:
13 But if ye cannot declare *it* me, then
shall ye give me thirty sheets and thirty change of garments. And they said
unto him, Put forth thy riddle, that we
may hear it.
14 And he said unto them, Out of the
eater came forth meat, and out of the
strong came forth sweetness. And they
could not in three days expound the
riddle.
15 And it came to pass on the seventh
day, that they said unto Samson's wife,
Entice thy husband, that he may declare
unto us the riddle, lest we burn thee
and thy father's house with fire: have
ye called us to take that we have? *is it*
not *so?*
16 And Samson's wife wept before
him, and said, Thou dost but hate me,
and lovest me not: thou hast put forth
a riddle unto the children of my people, and hast not told *it* me. And he
said unto her, Behold, I have not told
it my father nor my mother, and shall
I tell *it* thee?
17 And she wept before him the seven
days, while their feast lasted: and it
came to pass on the seventh day, that
he told her, because she lay sore upon
him: and she told the riddle to the children of her people.
18 And the men of the city said unto
him on the seventh day before the sun
went down, What *is* sweeter than honey? and what *is* stronger than a lion?
And he said unto them, If ye had not
plowed with my heifer, ye had not found
out my riddle.

Samson's 1st attack on the Philistines

¶19 And the Spirit of the LORD came
upon him, and he went down to *Ashkelon, and slew thirty men of them, and

---

14:12 sheets. Linen garments, like shirts.

14:19 The Spirit of the LORD
In Old Testament times, the Holy Spirit came upon people for special work, but in New Testament times, He dwells within every Christian (read 1 Cor. 6:19).

took their spoil, and gave change of
garments unto them which expounded
the riddle. And his anger was kindled,
and he went up to his father's house.
20But Samson's wife was *given* to his
companion, whom he had used as his
friend.

15 But it came to pass within a
while after, in the time of wheat
harvest, that Samson visited his wife
with a kid; and he said, I will go in to my
wife into the chamber. But her father
would not suffer him to go in.
2And her father said, I verily thought
that thou hadst utterly hated her; therefore I gave her to thy companion: *is* not
her younger sister fairer than she? take
her, I pray thee, instead of her.

Samson's 2nd attack on the Philistines

¶3And Samson said concerning them,
Now shall I be more blameless than the
Philistines, though I do them a displeasure.
4And Samson went and caught three
hundred foxes, and took firebrands, and
turned tail to tail, and put a firebrand in
the midst between two tails.
5And when he had set the brands on
fire, he let *them* go into the standing
corn of the Philistines, and burnt up
both the shocks, and also the standing
corn, with the vineyards *and* olives.
¶6Then the Philistines said, Who
hath done this? And they answered,
Samson, the son in *law of the Timnite,
because he had taken his wife, and
given her to his companion. And the
Philistines came up, and burnt her and
her father with fire.
¶7And Samson said unto them,
Though ye have done this, yet will I be
avenged of you, and after that I will
cease.
8And he smote them hip and thigh
with a great slaughter: and he went
down and dwelt in the top of the rock
Etam.
¶9Then the Philistines went up, and
pitched in Judah, and spread themselves in Lehi.
10And the men of Judah said, Why are
ye come up against us? And they answered, To bind Samson are we come
up, to do to him as he hath done to us.
11Then three thousand men of Judah
went to the top of the rock Etam, and
said to Samson, Knowest thou not that
the Philistines *are* rulers over us? what
is this *that* thou hast done unto us? And
he said unto them, As they did unto me,
so have I done unto them.
12And they said unto him, We are
come down to bind thee, that we may
deliver thee into the hand of the Philistines. And Samson said unto them,
Swear unto me, that ye will not fall upon
me yourselves.
13And they spake unto him, saying,
No; but we will bind thee fast, and deliver thee into their hand: but surely we
will not kill thee. And they bound him
with two new cords, and brought him up
from the rock.

Samson's 3rd attack on the Philistines

¶14*And* when he came unto Lehi, the
Philistines shouted against him: and the
Spirit of the LORD came mightily upon
him, and the cords that *were* upon his
arms became as flax that was burnt with
fire, and his bands loosed from off his
hands.
15And he found a new jawbone of an
ass, and put forth his hand, and took it,
and slew a thousand men therewith.
16And Samson said, With the jawbone

15:4 foxes. Jackals.
15:16 With the jawbone of an ass, heaps upon heaps. This was a play on words in the original language: "With the jawbone of an ass have I made asses of them."

of an ass, heaps upon heaps, with the jaw of an ass have I slain a thousand men.

17 And it came to pass, when he had made an end of speaking, that he cast away the jawbone out of his hand, and called that place Ramath-lehi.

¶ 18 And he was sore athirst, and called on the LORD, and said, Thou hast given this great deliverance into the hand of thy servant: and now shall I die for thirst, and fall into the hand of the uncircumcised?

19 But God clave an hollow place that *was* in the jaw, and there came water thereout; and when he had drunk, his spirit came again, and he revived: wherefore he called the name thereof En-hakkore, which *is* in Lehi unto this day.

Samson, the thirteenth judge

20 And he judged Israel in the days of the Philistines twenty years.

Samson at Gaza

16 Then went Samson to *Gaza, and saw there an harlot, and went in unto her.

2 *And it was told* the Gazites, saying, Samson is come hither. And they compassed *him* in, and laid wait for him all night in the gate of the city, and were quiet all the night, saying, In the morning, when it is day, we shall kill him.

3 And Samson lay till midnight, and arose at midnight, and took the doors of the gate of the city, and the two posts, and went away with them, bar and all, and put *them* upon his shoulders, and carried them up to the top of an hill that *is* before Hebron.

Samson and Delilah

¶ 4 And it came to pass afterward, that he loved a woman in the valley of Sorek, whose name *was* Delilah.

5 And the lords of the *Philistines came up unto her, and said unto her, Entice him, and see wherein his great strength *lieth,* and by what *means* we may prevail against him, that we may bind him to afflict him: and we will give thee every one of us eleven hundred *pieces* of silver.

¶ 6 And Delilah said to Samson, Tell me, I pray thee, wherein thy great strength *lieth,* and wherewith thou mightest be bound to afflict thee.

7 And Samson said unto her, If they bind me with seven green withs that were never dried, then shall I be weak, and be as another man.

8 Then the lords of the Philistines brought up to her seven green withs which had not been dried, and she bound him with them.

9 Now *there were* men lying in wait, abiding with her in the chamber. And she said unto him, The Philistines *be* upon thee, Samson. And he brake the withs, as a thread of tow is broken when it toucheth the fire. So his strength was not known.

10 And Delilah said unto Samson, Behold, thou hast mocked me, and told me lies: now tell me, I pray thee, wherewith thou mightest be bound.

11 And he said unto her, If they bind me fast with new ropes that never were occupied, then shall I be weak, and be as another man.

12 Delilah therefore took new ropes, and bound him therewith, and said unto him, The Philistines *be* upon thee, Samson. And *there were* liers in wait abiding in the chamber. And he brake them from off his arms like a thread.

13 And Delilah said unto Samson, Hitherto thou hast mocked me, and told me lies: tell me wherewith thou mightest be bound. And he said unto her, If thou weavest the seven locks of my head with the web.

15:17 Ramath-lehi. The hill of the jawbone.
15:19 En-hakkore. This means *the well of him who cried.*
16:7 withs. Tough, flexible green hanging branches.
16:13 seven locks. This was Samson's hair plaited into seven braids.

14 And she fastened *it* with the pin,
and said unto him, The Philistines *be*
upon thee, Samson. And he awaked out
of his sleep, and went away with the pin
of the beam, and with the web.
¶15 And she said unto him, How canst
thou say, I love thee, when thine heart
is not with me? thou hast mocked me
these three times, and hast not told me
wherein thy great strength *lieth.*
16 And it came to pass, when she
pressed him daily with her words, and
urged him, *so* that his soul was vexed
unto death;
17 That he told her all his heart, and
said unto her. There hath not come a
razor upon mine head; for I *have been* a
*Nazarite unto God from my mother's
womb: if I be shaven, then my strength
will go from me, and I shall become
weak, and be like any *other* man.

16:17 Samson's Source of Strength
It was not the actual loss of his hair that took Samson's strength but the giving up of the sign of his being a Nazarite. He could no longer count on God's strength after he had sinned in this way.

18 And when Delilah saw that he had
told her all his heart, she sent and called
for the lords of the Philistines, saying,
Come up this once, for he hath shewed
me all his heart. Then the lords of the
Philistines came up unto her, and
brought *money in their hand.
19 And she made him sleep upon her
knees; and she called for a man, and she
caused him to shave off the seven locks
of his head; and she began to afflict him,
and his strength went from him.
20 And she said, The Philistines *be*
upon thee, Samson. And he awoke out
of his sleep, and said, I will go out as at
other times before, and shake myself.
And he wist not that the LORD was departed from him.
¶21 But the Philistines took him, and
put out his eyes, and brought him down
to Gaza, and bound him with fetters of
brass; and he did grind in the prison
house.
22 Howbeit the hair of his head began
to grow again after he was shaven.

The death of Samson

23 Then the lords of the Philistines
gathered them together for to offer a
great sacrifice unto Dagon their god,
and to rejoice: for they said, Our god
hath delivered Samson our enemy into
our hand.
24 And when the people saw him, they
praised their god: for they said, Our god
hath delivered into our hands our enemy, and the destroyer of our country,
which slew many of us.
25 And it came to pass, when their
hearts were merry, that they said, Call
for Samson, that he may make us sport.
And they called for Samson out of the
prison house; and he made them sport:
and they set him between the pillars.
26 And Samson said unto the lad that
held him by the hand, Suffer me that I
may feel the pillars whereupon the
house standeth, that I may lean upon
them.
27 Now the house was full of men and
women; and all the lords of the Philistines *were* there; and *there were* upon
the roof about three thousand men and
women, that beheld while Samson
made sport.
28 And Samson called unto the LORD,
and said, O Lord GOD, remember me, I
pray thee, and strengthen me, I pray
thee, only this once, O God, that I may
be at once avenged of the Philistines for
my two eyes.
29 And Samson took hold of the two
middle pillars upon which the house
stood, and on which it was borne up, of
the one with his right hand, and of the
other with his left.
30 And Samson said, Let me die with

16:20 wist not. Did not know.
16:21 grind. Samson ground meal between two stones, a task done by slaves.

the Philistines. And he bowed himself
with *all his* might; and the house fell
upon the lords, and upon all the people
that *were* therein. So the dead which he
slew at his death were more than *they*
which he slew in his life.
31 Then his brethren and all the house
of his father came down, and took him,
and brought *him* up, and buried him
between Zorah and Eshtaol in the
buryingplace of Manoah his father. And
he judged Israel twenty years.

16:31 Samson, a Man of Faith
Whatever his failures, Samson had been used wonderfully to deliver Israel, and he is mentioned in Hebrews 11:32 as a man of faith.

IV. Ignorance and Evil (17:1—21:25)

17 And there was a man of mount
*Ephraim, whose name *was*
Micah.

Religious ignorance leading to idolatry

2 And he said unto his mother, The
eleven hundred *shekels* of silver that
were taken from thee, about which thou
cursedst, and spakest of also in mine
ears, behold, the silver *is* with me; I
took it. And his mother said, Blessed *be
thou* of the LORD, my son.
3 And when he had restored the elev-
en hundred *shekels* of silver to his mother, his mother said, I had wholly
dedicated the silver unto the LORD from
my hand for my son, to make a *graven
image and a molten image: now therefore I will restore it unto thee.
4 Yet he restored the money unto his
mother; and his mother took two hundred *shekels* of silver, and gave them to
the founder, who made thereof a graven
image and a molten image: and they
were in the house of Micah.
5 And the man Micah had an house of
gods, and made an *ephod, and *teraphim, and consecrated one of his sons,
who became his priest.
6 In those days *there was* no king in
Israel, *but* every man did *that which was*
right in his own eyes.
¶ 7 And there was a young man out of
Beth-lehem-judah of the family of Judah, who *was* a Levite, and he sojourned there.
8 And the man departed out of the city
from Beth-lehem-judah to sojourn
where he could find *a place:* and he
came to mount Ephraim to the house
of Micah, as he journeyed.
9 And Micah said unto him, Whence
comest thou? And he said unto him, I
am a Levite of Beth-lehem-judah, and
I go to sojourn where I may find *a place.*
10 And Micah said unto him, Dwell
with me, and be unto me a father and a
priest, and I will give thee ten *shekels*
of silver by the year, and a suit of apparel, and thy victuals. So the Levite
went in.
11 And the Levite was content to

17:3 IDOLATRY

A graven image was made of wood, while a molten image was made of metal. Chapters 17 and 18 show the terrible ignorance and superstition of many of the people. In the story of the idolatry of Micah, note:

1. Micah disobeyed the second commandment (Exod. 20:4) by making an image of an idol. "Teraphim" (Judg. 17:5) were small images used as household gods.
2. Consecrating his son as priest (vs. 5) was contrary to the Law laid down in Numbers 3:10.
3. The Levite should not have been wandering about but should have been living in Bethlehem, the Levitical city that was his home (Josh. 21).

17:6 every man did that which was right in his own eyes. Remember that the book of Judges is a book of failure, and the reason for that failure is given in this verse, which is the key verse to the book and is repeated in 21:25. Read the introduction to this book again.

dwell with the man; and the young man was unto him as one of his sons.

12And Micah consecrated the Levite; and the young man became his priest, and was in the house of Micah.

13Then said Micah, Now know I that the LORD will do me good, seeing I have a Levite to *my* priest.

Extension of idolatry to tribe of Dan

18 In those days *there was* no king in Israel: and in those days the tribe of the Danites sought them an inheritance to dwell in; for unto that day *all their* inheritance had not fallen unto them among the tribes of Israel.

18:1 A Lost Inheritance
Through their own weakness and laziness, the Danites had lost part of their inheritance to the Amorites (Judg. 1:34), and part of it to the Philistines, who continually fought against them, since the Danites were the nearest Israelites to these tribes. The Danites were just as ignorant and superstitious as Micah, and they set up a regular system of idolatry (vs. 31), even though the ark of God was at Shiloh, which wasn't very far away, and they could have gone to it quite easily.

2And the children of Dan sent of their family five men from their coasts, men of valour, from Zorah, and from Eshtaol, to spy out the land, and to search it; and they said unto them, Go, search the land: who when they came to mount Ephraim, to the house of Micah, they lodged there.

3When they *were* by the house of Micah, they knew the voice of the young man the Levite: and they turned in thither, and said unto him, Who brought thee hither? and what makest thou in this *place?* and what hast thou here?

4And he said unto them, Thus and thus dealeth Micah with me, and hath hired me, and I am his priest.

5And they said unto him, Ask counsel, we pray thee, of God, that we may know whether our way which we go shall be prosperous.

6And the priest said unto them, Go in *peace: before the LORD *is* your way wherein ye go.

¶7Then the five men departed, and came to Laish, and saw the people that *were* therein, how they dwelt careless, after the manner of the Zidonians, quiet and secure; and *there was* no magistrate in the land, that might put *them* to shame in *any* thing; and they *were* far from the Zidonians, and had no business with *any* man.

8And they came unto their brethren to Zorah and Eshtaol: and their brethren said unto them, What *say* ye?

9And they said, Arise, that we may go up against them: for we have seen the land, and, behold, it *is* very good: and *are* ye still? be not slothful to go, *and* to enter to possess the land.

10When ye go, ye shall come unto a people secure, and to a large land: for God hath given it into your hands; a place where *there is* no want of any thing that *is* in the earth.

¶11And there went from thence of the family of the Danites, out of Zorah and out of Eshtaol, six hundred men appointed with weapons of war.

12And they went up, and pitched in Kirjath-jearim, in Judah: wherefore they called that place Mahaneh-dan

17:13 Now know I . . . The people had drifted so far from the teaching of the LORD and His Word that neither Micah nor his mother knew that the LORD would be displeased with them. Every man was doing "that which was right in his own eyes" (vs. 6). God must have complete obedience; Micah having a Levite for his priest was only partial obedience (see vs. 3 note, "Idolatry").

18:3 what makest thou in this place? The Danites were asking the Levite who lived with Micah, "What are you doing here?"

18:7 careless. Without care about possible danger.

18:11 appointed. Armed, equipped, or provided.

unto this day: behold, *it is* behind
Kirjath-jearim.
13 And they passed thence unto
mount Ephraim, and came unto the
house of Micah.
¶14 Then answered the five men that
went to spy out the country of Laish,
and said unto their brethren, Do ye
know that there is in these houses an
ephod, and teraphim, and a graven image, and a molten image? now therefore
consider what ye have to do.
15 And they turned thitherward, and
came to the house of the young man the
Levite, *even* unto the house of Micah,
and saluted him.
16 And the six hundred men appointed with their weapons of war, which
were of the children of Dan, stood by the
entering of the gate.
17 And the five men that went to spy
out the land went up, *and* came in
thither, *and* took the graven image, and
the ephod, and the teraphim, and the
molten image: and the priest stood in
the entering of the gate with the six
hundred men *that were* appointed with
weapons of war.
18 And these went into Micah's house,
and fetched the carved image, the
ephod, and the teraphim, and the molten image. Then said the priest unto
them, What do ye?
19 And they said unto him, Hold thy
peace, lay thine hand upon thy mouth,
and go with us, and be to us a father and
a priest: *is it* better for thee to be a
priest unto the house of one man, or
that thou be a priest unto a tribe and a
family in Israel?
20 And the priest's heart was glad, and
he took the ephod, and the teraphim,
and the graven image, and went in the
midst of the people.
21 So they turned and departed, and
put the little ones and the cattle and the
carriage before them.
¶22 *And* when they were a good way
from the house of Micah, the men that
were in the houses near to Micah's
house were gathered together, and
overtook the children of Dan.
23 And they cried unto the children of
Dan. And they turned their faces, and
said unto Micah, What aileth thee, that
thou comest with such a company?
24 And he said, Ye have taken away my
gods which I made, and the priest, and
ye are gone away: and what have I
more? and what *is* this *that* ye say unto
me, What aileth thee?
25 And the children of Dan said unto
him, Let not thy voice be heard among
us, lest angry fellows run upon thee,
and thou lose thy life, with the lives of
thy household.
26 And the children of Dan went their
way: and when Micah saw that they
were too strong for him, he turned and
went back unto his house.
27 And they took *the things* which Micah had made, and the priest which he
had, and came unto Laish, unto a people *that were* at quiet and secure: and
they smote them with the edge of the
sword, and burnt the city with fire.
28 And *there was* no deliverer, because
it *was* far from Zidon, and they had no
business with *any* man; and it was in the
valley that *lieth* by Beth-rehob. And
they built a city, and dwelt therein.
29 And they called the name of the city
Dan, after the name of Dan their father,
who was born unto Israel: howbeit the
name of the city *was* Laish at the first.
¶30 And the children of Dan set up the
graven image: and Jonathan, the son
of Gershom, the son of *Manasseh, he
and his sons were priests to the tribe
of Dan until the day of the captivity of
the land.
31 And they set them up Micah's graven
image, which he made, all the time that
the house of God was in *Shiloh.

Moral evil

19 And it came to pass in those
days, when *there was* no king in

18:14 teraphim. See 17:3 note, "Idolatry."

*Israel, that there was a certain Levite
sojourning on the side of mount Ephraim, who took to him a *concubine out
of Beth-lehem-judah.
2And his concubine played the
*whore against him, and went away
from him unto her father's house to
Beth-lehem-judah, and was there four
whole months.
3And her husband arose, and went
after her, to speak friendly unto her, *and*
to bring her again, having his servant
with him, and a couple of asses: and she
brought him into her father's house:
and when the father of the damsel saw
him, he rejoiced to meet him.
4And his father in law, the damsel's
father, retained him; and he abode with
him three days: so they did eat and
drink, and lodged there.
¶5And it came to pass on the fourth
day, when they arose early in the morning, that he rose up to depart: and the
damsel's father said unto his son in law,
Comfort thine heart with a morsel of
bread, and afterward go your way.
6And they sat down, and did eat and
drink both of them together: for the
damsel's father had said unto the man,
Be content, I pray thee, and tarry all
night, and let thine heart be merry.
7And when the man rose up to depart, his father in law urged him: therefore he lodged there again.
8And he arose early in the morning on
the fifth day to depart: and the damsel's
father said, Comfort thine heart, I pray
thee. And they tarried until afternoon,
and they did eat both of them.
9And when the man rose up to depart,
he, and his concubine, and his servant,
his father in law, the damsel's father, said
unto him, Behold, now the day draweth
toward evening, I pray you tarry all
night: behold, the day groweth to an
end, lodge here, that thine heart may be
merry; and to morrow get you early on
your way, that thou mayest go home.
10But the man would not tarry that
night, but he rose up and departed, and
came over against Jebus, which *is* *Jerusalem; and *there were* with him two
asses saddled, his concubine also *was*
with him.
11*And* when they *were* by Jebus, the
day was far spent; and the servant said
unto his master, Come, I pray thee, and
let us turn in into this city of the Jebusites, and lodge in it.
12And his master said unto him, We
will not turn aside hither into the city
of a stranger, that *is* not of the children
of Israel; we will pass over to Gibeah.
13And he said unto his servant,
Come, and let us draw near to one of
these places to lodge all night, in Gibeah, or in Ramah.
14And they passed on and went their
way; and the sun went down upon them
when they were by Gibeah, which
belongeth to Benjamin.
15And they turned aside thither, to go
in *and* to lodge in Gibeah: and when he
went in, he sat him down in a street of
the city: for *there was* no man that took
them into his house to lodging.
¶16And, behold, there came an old
man from his work out of the field at
even, which *was* also of mount Ephraim; and he sojourned in Gibeah: but the
men of the place *were* Benjamites.
17And when he had lifted up his eyes,
he saw a wayfaring man in the street of
the city: and the old man said, Whither
goest thou? and whence comest thou?
18And he said unto him, We *are* passing from Beth-lehem-judah toward the
side of mount Ephraim; from thence
am I: and I went to Beth-lehem-judah,
but I *am now* going to the house of
the LORD; and there *is* no man that receiveth me to house.
19Yet there is both straw and provender for our asses; and there is bread and
wine also for me, and for thy handmaid,
and for the young man *which is* with thy
servants: *there is* no want of any thing.
20And the old man said, Peace *be* with
thee; howsoever *let* all thy wants *lie*
upon me; only lodge not in the street.
21So he brought him into his house,
and gave provender unto the asses: and

they washed their feet, and did eat and drink.

¶22 *Now* as they were making their hearts merry, behold, the men of the city, certain sons of Belial, beset the house round about, *and* beat at the door, and spake to the master of the house, the old man, saying, Bring forth the man that came into thine house, that we may know him.

23 And the man, the master of the house, went out unto them, and said unto them, Nay, my brethren, *nay,* I pray you, do not *so* wickedly; seeing that this man is come into mine house, do not this folly.

24 Behold, *here is* my daughter a maiden, and his concubine; them I will bring out now, and humble ye them, and do with them what seemeth good unto you: but unto this man do not so vile a thing.

25 But the men would not hearken to him: so the man took his concubine, and brought her forth unto them; and they knew her, and abused her all the night until the morning: and when the day began to spring, they let her go.

26 Then came the woman in the dawning of the day, and fell down at the door of the man's house where her lord *was,* till it was light.

27 And her lord rose up in the morning, and opened the doors of the house, and went out to go his way: and, behold, the woman his concubine was fallen down *at* the door of the house, and her hands *were* upon the threshold.

28 And he said unto her, Up, and let us be going. But none answered. Then the man took her *up* upon an ass, and the man rose up, and gat him unto his place.

¶29 And when he was come into his house, he took a knife, and laid hold on his concubine, and divided her, *together* with her bones, into twelve pieces, and sent her into all the coasts of Israel.

30 And it was so, that all that saw it said, There was no such deed done nor seen from the day that the children of Israel came up out of the land of *Egypt unto this day: consider of it, take advice, and speak *your minds.*

Civil war

20

Then all the children of Israel went out, and the congregation was gathered together as one man, from Dan even to *Beer-sheba, with the land of *Gilead, unto the LORD in Mizpeh.

2 And the chief of all the people, *even* of all the tribes of Israel, presented themselves in the assembly of the people of *God, four hundred thousand footmen that drew sword.

3 (Now the children of Benjamin heard that the children of Israel were gone up to Mizpeh.) Then said the children of Israel, Tell *us,* how was this wickedness?

4 And the Levite, the husband of the woman that was slain, answered and said, I came into Gibeah that *belongeth* to Benjamin, I and my concubine, to lodge.

5 And the men of Gibeah rose against me, and beset the house round about upon me by night, *and* thought to have slain me: and my concubine have they forced, that she is dead.

6 And I took my concubine, and cut her in pieces, and sent her throughout all the country of the inheritance of Israel: for they have committed lewdness and folly in Israel.

7 Behold, ye *are* all children of Israel; give here your advice and counsel.

¶8 And all the people arose as one man, saying, We will not any *of us* go to his tent, neither will we any *of us* turn into his house.

9 But now this *shall be* the thing which we will do to Gibeah; *we will go up* by lot against it;

20:1 from Dan even to Beer-sheba. This phrase always refers to the most northern and most southern points of Israel. We read of the founding of Dan in Judges 18:29. Gilead was the land on the other side of the Jordan River.

10 And we will take ten men of an hundred throughout all the tribes of Israel,
and an hundred of a thousand, and a
thousand out of ten thousand, to fetch
victual for the people, that they may do,
when they come to Gibeah of Benjamin,
according to all the folly that they have
wrought in Israel.
11 So all the men of Israel were gathered against the city, knit together as
one man.
¶ 12 And the tribes of Israel sent men
through all the tribe of Benjamin, saying, What wickedness *is* this that is
done among you?
13 Now therefore deliver *us* the men,
the children of Belial, which *are* in Gibeah, that we may put them to death, and
put away evil from Israel. But the children of Benjamin would not hearken to
the voice of their brethren the children
of Israel:
14 But the children of Benjamin gathered themselves together out of the
cities unto Gibeah, to go out to battle
against the children of Israel.
15 And the children of Benjamin were
numbered at that time out of the cities
twenty and six thousand men that drew
sword, beside the inhabitants of Gibeah, which were numbered seven hundred chosen men.
16 Among all this people *there were*
seven hundred chosen men lefthanded;
every one could sling stones at an hair
breadth, and not miss.
17 And the men of Israel, beside Benjamin, were numbered four hundred
thousand men that drew sword: all
these *were* men of war.
¶ 18 And the children of Israel arose,
and went up to the house of God, and
asked counsel of God, and said, Which
of us shall go up first to the battle
against the children of Benjamin? And
the LORD said, Judah *shall go up* first.
19 And the children of Israel rose up
in the morning, and encamped against
Gibeah.
20 And the men of Israel went out to
battle against Benjamin; and the men of
Israel put themselves in array to fight
against them at Gibeah.
21 And the children of Benjamin came
forth out of Gibeah, and destroyed down
to the ground of the Israelites that day
twenty and two thousand men.
22 And the people the men of Israel
encouraged themselves, and set their
battle again in array in the place where
they put themselves in array the first
day.
23 (And the children of Israel went up
and wept before the LORD until even,
and asked counsel of the LORD, saying,
Shall I go up again to battle against the
children of Benjamin my brother? And
the LORD said, Go up against him.)
24 And the children of Israel came
near against the children of Benjamin
the second day.
25 And Benjamin went forth against
them out of Gibeah the second day, and
destroyed down to the ground of the
children of Israel again eighteen thousand men; all these drew the sword.
¶ 26 Then all the children of Israel, and
all the people, went up, and came unto
the house of God, and wept, and sat
there before the LORD, and fasted that
day until even, and offered burnt-offerings and peace-offerings before the
LORD.
27 And the children of Israel enquired
of the LORD, (for the *ark of the covenant of God *was* there in those days,
28 And *Phinehas, the son of Eleazar,
the son of *Aaron, stood before it in
those days,) saying, Shall I yet again go
out to battle against the children of
Benjamin my brother, or shall I cease?
And the LORD said, Go up; for to morrow I will deliver them into thine hand.
29 And Israel set liers in wait round
about Gibeah.

20:28 Phinehas
Aaron's grandson. He is mentioned in Numbers 25:7 and Joshua 24:33, so this incident must have occurred soon after the death of Joshua.

30 And the children of Israel went up
against the children of Benjamin on the
third day, and put themselves in array
against Gibeah, as at other times.
31 And the children of Benjamin went
out against the people, *and* were drawn
away from the city; and they began to
smite of the people, *and* kill, as at other
times, in the highways, of which one
goeth up to the house of God, and the
other to Gibeah in the field, about thirty men of Israel.
32 And the children of Benjamin said,
They *are* smitten down before us, as at
the first. But the children of Israel said,
Let us flee, and draw them from the city
unto the highways.
33 And all the men of Israel rose up
out of their place, and put themselves
in array at *Baal-tamar: and the liers in
wait of Israel came forth out of their
places, *even* out of the meadows of Gibeah.
34 And there came against Gibeah ten
thousand chosen men out of all Israel,
and the battle was sore: but they knew
not that evil *was* near them.
35 And the LORD smote Benjamin before Israel: and the children of Israel
destroyed of the Benjamites that day
twenty and five thousand and an hundred men: all these drew the sword.
36 So the children of Benjamin saw
that they were smitten: for the men
of Israel gave place to the Benjamites,
because they trusted unto the liers
in wait which they had set beside Gibeah.
37 And the liers in wait hasted, and
rushed upon Gibeah; and the liers in
wait drew *themselves* along, and smote
all the city with the edge of the sword.
38 Now there was an appointed sign
between the men of Israel and the
liers in wait, that they should make a
great flame with smoke rise up out of
the city.
39 And when the men of Israel retired
in the battle, Benjamin began to smite
and kill of the men of Israel about thirty persons: for they said, Surely they
are smitten down before us, as *in* the
first battle.
40 But when the flame began to arise
up out of the city with a pillar of smoke,
the Benjamites looked behind them,
and, behold, the flame of the city ascended up to heaven.
41 And when the men of Israel turned
again, the men of Benjamin were
amazed: for they saw that evil was
come upon them.
42 Therefore they turned *their backs*
before the men of Israel unto the way
of the wilderness; but the battle overtook them; and them which *came* out of
the cities they destroyed in the midst
of them.
43 *Thus* they inclosed the Benjamites
round about, *and* chased them, *and*
trode them down with ease over against
Gibeah toward the sunrising.
44 And there fell of Benjamin eighteen
thousand men; all these *were* men of
valour.
45 And they turned and fled toward
the wilderness unto the rock of Rimmon: and they gleaned of them in the
highways five thousand men; and pursued hard after them unto Gidom, and
slew two thousand men of them.
46 So that all which fell that day of
Benjamin were twenty and five thousand men that drew the sword; all these
were men of valour.
47 But six hundred men turned and
fled to the wilderness unto the rock
Rimmon, and abode in the rock Rimmon four months.
48 And the men of Israel turned again
upon the children of Benjamin, and
smote them with the edge of the sword,
as well the men of *every* city, as the beast,
and all that came to hand: also they set
on fire all the cities that they came to.

Results of the civil war

21 Now the men of Israel had
sworn in Mizpeh, saying, There
shall not any of us give his daughter
unto Benjamin to wife.
2 And the people came to the house of

21:2-3 Making Amends
The Israelites suddenly realized their rash and cruel violence in destroying almost the whole tribe of Benjamin, and they now tried to make amends with even more deeds of violence. The whole story gives a very sad picture of the sins into which they fell only a short time after the great events of the conquest of the land. Their history shows that even with every advantage and full instructions from God, people still have sinful hearts and will continue to sin—without the grace of God. The only hope for people is to put their trust in a Saviour who can cleanse and save them from sin and give them power to overcome evil, and this is what the Lord Jesus Christ came to do.

God, and abode there till even before God, and lifted up their voices, and wept sore;

3 And said, O LORD God of Israel, why is this come to pass in Israel, that there should be to day one tribe lacking in Israel?

4 And it came to pass on the morrow, that the people rose early, and built there an altar, and offered burnt-offerings and peace-offerings.

5 And the children of Israel said, Who *is there* among all the tribes of Israel that came not up with the congregation unto the LORD? For they had made a great oath concerning him that came not up to the LORD to Mizpeh, saying, He shall surely be put to death.

6 And the children of Israel repented them for Benjamin their brother, and said, There is one tribe cut off from Israel this day.

7 How shall we do for wives for them that remain, seeing we have sworn by the LORD that we will not give them of our daughters to wives?

¶8 And they said, What one *is there* of the tribes of Israel that came not up to Mizpeh to the LORD? And, behold, there came none to the camp from Jabesh-gilead to the assembly.

9 For the people were numbered, and, behold, *there were* none of the inhabitants of Jabesh-gilead there.

10 And the congregation sent thither twelve thousand men of the valiantest, and commanded them, saying, Go and smite the inhabitants of Jabesh-gilead with the edge of the sword, with the women and the children.

11 And this *is* the thing that ye shall do, Ye shall utterly destroy every male, and every woman that hath lain by man.

12 And they found among the inhabitants of Jabesh-gilead four hundred young virgins, that had known no man by lying with any male: and they brought them unto the camp to Shiloh, which *is* in the land of Canaan.

13 And the whole congregation sent *some* to speak to the children of Benjamin that *were* in the rock Rimmon, and to call peaceably unto them.

14 And Benjamin came again at that time; and they gave them wives which they had saved alive of the women of Jabesh-gilead: and yet so they sufficed them not.

15 And the people repented them for Benjamin, because that the LORD had made a breach in the tribes of Israel.

¶16 Then the elders of the congregation said, How shall we do for wives for them that remain, seeing the women are destroyed out of Benjamin?

17 And they said, *There must be* an inheritance for them that be escaped of Benjamin, that a tribe be not destroyed out of Israel.

18 Howbeit we may not give them wives of our daughters: for the children of Israel have sworn, saying, Cursed *be* he that giveth a wife to Benjamin.

19 Then they said, Behold, *there is* a feast of the LORD in Shiloh yearly *in a place* which *is* on the north side of Beth-el, on the east side of the highway that goeth up from Beth-el to Shechem, and on the south of Lebonah.

21:2 abode there till even. Stayed there until evening.

[20]Therefore they commanded the
children of Benjamin, saying, Go and lie
in wait in the vineyards;
[21]And see, and, behold, if the daughters of Shiloh come out to dance in
dances, then come ye out of the vineyards, and catch you every man his wife
of the daughters of Shiloh, and go to the
land of Benjamin.
[22]And it shall be, when their fathers
or their brethren come unto us to complain, that we will say unto them, Be
favourable unto them for our sakes:
because we reserved not to each man
his wife in the war: for ye did not give
unto them at this time, *that* ye should
be guilty.
[23]And the children of Benjamin did
so, and took *them* wives, according to
their number, of them that danced, whom
they caught: and they went and returned unto their inheritance, and repaired the cities, and dwelt in them.
[24]And the children of Israel departed
thence at that time, every man to his tribe
and to his family, and they went out from
thence every man to his inheritance.
[25]In those days *there was* no king in
Israel: every man did *that which was*
right in his own eyes.

The Book of

RUTH

BACKGROUND

The book of Ruth is the beautiful story of one of the ancestors of our Lord (Matthew 1:5). Naomi is the chief character as the book opens. She and her husband, Elimelch, and their sons, Mahlon and Chilion, lived in Beth-lehem-judah in the Land of Promise (Canaan or Palestine). They lived in the time of the judges, when many people "forsook the LORD and served Baal and Ashtaroth" (Judges 2:13). See the introduction to the book of Judges. Ruth, the Moabitess, later becomes the central figure of the book, and her marriage to Boaz is a lovely figure of the church's union with Christ.

THE LESSONS IN RUTH

There are several important lessons in this story for the Christian today:

1. A warning of the sorrow and misery which follow when God's children leave His place of blessing and disobey His revealed will for them (a Moabite was not even allowed to enter the congregation of the LORD. See Deuteronomy 23:3);

2. God's faithfulness in chastening, or child-training, His own when they are out of His will, and then in bringing them back to a place of blessing and fruitfulness (God sometimes has to punish His children in order to teach them lessons, just as fathers and mothers have to punish their children to train them);

3. As Boaz had the right by relationship to redeem the house of Elimelech (Ruth 1:11 note), so the Lord Jesus Christ has the right to redeem man out of the bondage of his sin, for Galatians 4:4,5 says: "When the fulness of the time was come, God sent forth His Son, made of a woman, made under the law, to redeem them that were under the law."

OUTLINE OF RUTH

I.	Testing	Ruth 1:1—2:2
II.	Chastening	Ruth 2:3-19
III.	Confession	Ruth 2:20-23
IV.	Blessing	Ruth 3:1—4:22

I. Testing (1:1—2:2)

1 Now it came to pass in the days when the *judges ruled, that there was a famine in the land. And a certain man of Beth-lehem-judah went to sojourn in the country of *Moab, he, and his wife, and his two sons.

2 And the name of the man *was* Elime-

1:1 Beth-lehem-judah. Names of places and people had meanings attached to them. Beth-lehem-judah means *house of bread* and *praise*.

1:1 The Country of Moab
Moab means *desire*. Moab was not far from Beth-lehem. The language was probably much like the Hebrew language that the Jewish people spoke, and the customs of the people were much like the customs of the Jewish people. However, there was one great difference. The people of Moab did not love and worship the one true God. They worshipped idols. God's people had no right to expect to be blessed in such a place.

lech, and the name of his wife Naomi,
and the name of his two sons Mahlon
and Chilion, Ephrathites of Beth-lehem-
judah. And they came into the country
of Moab, and continued there.

1:2 The Meaning of Names

1. Elimelech means *my God is King*.
2. Naomi means *pleasant*.
3. Mahlon means *sickly*.
4. Chilion means *pining* or *wasting away*.
5. Orpah means *hind* or *fawn*.
6. Ruth means *friendship*.
7. Mara means *bitter*.
8. Boaz means *quickness*.
9. Obed means *worshipper*.

3 And Elimelech Naomi's husband
died; and she was left, and her two sons.
4 And they took them wives of the
women of Moab; the name of the one *was*
Orpah, and the name of the other Ruth:
and they dwelled there about ten years.
5 And Mahlon and Chilion died also
both of them; and the woman was left
of her two sons and her husband.
¶ 6 Then she arose with her daughters
in law, that she might return from the
country of Moab: for she had heard in
the country of Moab how that the LORD
had visited his people in giving them
bread.
7 Wherefore she went forth out of the
place where she was, and her two
daughters in law with her; and they
went on the way to return unto the land
of Judah.
8 And Naomi said unto her two daughters in law, Go, return each to her
mother's house: the LORD deal kindly
with you, as ye have dealt with the
dead, and with me.
9 The LORD grant you that ye may find
rest, each *of you* in the house of her
husband. Then she kissed them; and
they lifted up their voice, and wept.
10 And they said unto her, Surely we
will return with thee unto thy people.
11 And Naomi said, Turn again, my
daughters: why will ye go with me? *are*
there yet *any more* sons in my womb,
that they may be your husbands?

1:11 Following the Law
It was the Jewish law that if a man died without having sons, his brother or the next of kin–the nearest male relative–must buy his possessions and marry his widow. If he was unable to because he was already married or could not afford to do so, then he publicly released all claim; and the next nearest male relative, the kinsman, took his place as redeemer (Deut. 25:5; Luke 20:28). See *redemption. Naomi knew that even if she were to marry again and have more sons born to her, Ruth and Orpah would not want to wait for those sons to grow up. Naomi thought it would be better for them to stay in Moab and marry again.

12 Turn again, my daughters, go *your*
way; for I am too old to have an husband. If I should say, I have hope, *if* I
should have an husband also to night,
and should also bear sons;
13 Would ye tarry for them till they
were grown? would ye stay for them
from having husbands? nay, my daughters; for it grieveth me much for your

1:2 Ephrathites. Ephrath is another name for Beth-lehem (Gen. 35:19; see also Ruth 4:11 note).

1:9 ye may find rest. Ruth and Orpah were still young women, and it was probable that they would marry again. In those days, a young woman needed the care and protection that she could get only in the home of her husband.

sakes that the hand of the LORD is gone
out against me.
14And they lifted up their voice, and
wept again: and Orpah kissed her mother in law; but Ruth clave unto her.
15And she said, Behold, thy sister in
law is gone back unto her people, and
unto her gods: return thou after thy sister in law.
16And Ruth said, Intreat me not to
leave thee, *or* to return from following
after thee: for whither thou goest, I will
go; and where thou lodgest, I will lodge:
thy people *shall be* my people, and thy
*God my God:
17Where thou diest, will I die, and
there will I be buried: the LORD do so
to me, and more also, *if ought* but
*death part thee and me.
18When she saw that she was
stedfastly minded to go with her, then
she left speaking unto her.
¶19So they two went until they came
to Beth-lehem. And it came to pass,
when they were come to Beth-lehem,
that all the city was moved about them,
and they said, *Is* this Naomi?
20And she said unto them, Call me
not Naomi, call me Mara: for the Almighty hath dealt very bitterly with me.
21I went out full, and the LORD hath
brought me home again empty: why
then call ye me Naomi, seeing the LORD
hath testified against me, and the Almighty hath afflicted me?
22So Naomi returned, and Ruth the
Moabitess, her daughter in law, with
her, which returned out of the country
of Moab: and they came to Beth-lehem
in the beginning of barley harvest.

2 And Naomi had a *kinsman of her
husband's, a mighty man of wealth,
of the family of Elimelech; and his name
was Boaz.
2And Ruth the Moabitess said unto
Naomi, Let me now go to the field, and
glean ears of corn after *him* in whose
sight I shall find grace. And she said
unto her, Go, my daughter.

II. Chastening (2:3-19)

3And she went, and came, and
gleaned in the field after the reapers:
and her hap was to light on a part of the
field *belonging* unto Boaz, who *was* of
the kindred of Elimelech.
¶4And behold, Boaz came from Beth-

2:3 God's Plan

It was not chance that directed Ruth to glean in the fields of this man of wealth. God was working in order to bless Ruth and Naomi. God, who directed Ruth to glean in these fields, also prepared the heart of Boaz to be kind to her.

1:16 Intreat me not to leave thee. Ruth was all that her name meant (see vs. 2 note, "The Meaning of Names"). She loved her mother-in-law enough to leave her own people and friends to go to a land and a people that she had never seen. She had also learned to love her husband's and Naomi's God.

1:19 Is this Naomi? Naomi was no longer the young, happy wife and mother whom the people of Bethlehem had known, and they did not recognize her after the years of sorrow.

1:20 Mara. Naomi did not believe that she looked *pleasant* as her name meant but that she looked *bitter,* as Mara meant. She did not blame anyone. She knew that God had permitted the sorrows that He might bring her back to Himself and to her own land of blessing.

1:22 in the beginning of barley harvest. This was probably in the month of April.

2:1 Boaz. He was a man of influence, power, and wealth in Beth-lehem. He was a relative of Ruth's father-in-law, Elimelech (3:2; 4:3).

2:2 Let me . . . glean. The LORD had told His people that when they were gathering their crops at harvesttime, they were to leave some grain or fruit for the poor of the land, or strangers, to glean or gather (read Lev. 19:9-10).

2:2 ears of corn. This was either wheat or barley. Corn in the Bible is a general name for grain. It never means the corn of America, which is maize.

lehem, and said unto the reapers, The
LORD *be* with you. And they answered
him, The LORD bless thee.
5 Then said Boaz unto his servant that
was set over the reapers, Whose damsel *is* this?
6 And the servant that was set over
the reapers answered and said, It *is* the
Moabitish damsel that came back with
Naomi out of the country of Moab:
7 And she said, I pray you, let me
glean and gather after the reapers
among the sheaves: so she came, and
hath continued even from the morning
until now, that she tarried a little in the
house.
8 Then said Boaz unto Ruth, Hearest
thou not, my daughter? Go not to glean
in another field, neither go from hence,
but abide here fast by my maidens:

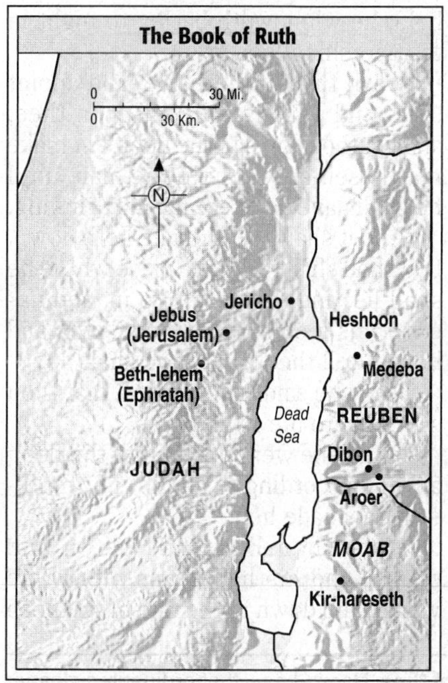

9 *Let* thine eyes *be* on the field that
they do reap, and go thou after them:
have I not charged the young men that
they shall not touch thee? and when
thou art athirst, go unto the vessels,
and drink of *that* which the young men
have drawn.
10 Then she fell on her face, and
bowed herself to the ground, and said
unto him, Why have I found grace in
thine eyes, that thou shouldest take
knowledge of me, seeing I *am* a
stranger?
11 And Boaz answered and said unto
her, It hath fully been shewed me, all
that thou hast done unto thy mother in
law since the death of thine husband:
and *how* thou hast left thy father and thy
mother, and the land of thy nativity, and
art come unto a people which thou
knewest not heretofore.
12 The LORD recompense thy work,
and a full reward be given thee of the
LORD God of *Israel, under whose wings
thou art come to trust.
13 Then she said, Let me find favour
in thy sight, my lord; for that thou hast
comforted me, and for that thou hast
spoken friendly unto thine handmaid,
though I be not like unto one of thine
handmaidens.
14 And Boaz said unto her, At meal-
time come thou hither, and eat of the
bread, and dip thy morsel in the vinegar. And she sat beside the reapers: and
he reached her parched *corn,* and she
did eat, and was sufficed, and left.
15 And when she was risen up to
glean, Boaz commanded his young
men, saying, Let her glean even among
the sheaves, and reproach her not:
16 And let fall also *some* of the handfuls of purpose for her, and leave *them,*

2:4 The LORD be with you. This was the usual form of greeting.
2:8 abide here fast. Stay close or nearby.
2:12 under whose wings. Read Psalms 17:8; 36:7; 57:1; 61:4; 63:7; 91:1,4; Matthew 23:37. This phrase is a wonderful illustration of God's loving care for His people by comparing His loving watch with that of the eagle for her young (Exod. 19:4; Deut. 32:11-12).
2:12 trust. Instead of saying "trust," which means to *take refuge,* the New Testament uses the words "faith" and "believe."

2:14 Sour Wine
Vinegar was a thin, sour wine that was much used by laborers in those days when the water was not safe to drink. The Hebrew term *homets* was applied to a beverage consisting usually of wine or strong drink turned sour. By itself it formed a nauseous draught (Ps. 69:21), and its acid taste passed into a proverb (Prov. 10:26). It was drunk by laborers as mentioned here. Similar to the *homets* of the Hebrews was the *acetum* of the Romans, which, under the name of "posca," was the ordinary drink of the Roman soldiers (Matt. 27:48; Mark 15:36; John 19:29-30).

that she may glean *them,* and rebuke
her not.
17So she gleaned in the field until
even, and beat out that she had gleaned:
and it was about an *ephah of barley.
¶18And she took *it* up, and went into
the city: and her mother in law saw
what she had gleaned: and she brought
forth, and gave to her that she had reserved after she was sufficed.
19And her mother in law said unto
her, Where hast thou gleaned to day?
and where wroughtest thou? blessed be
he that did take knowledge of thee. And
she shewed her mother in law with
whom she had wrought, and said, The
man's name with whom I wrought to
day *is* Boaz.

III. Confession (2:20-23)

20And Naomi said unto her daughter
in law, Blessed *be* he of the LORD, who
hath not left off his kindness to the living and to the dead. And Naomi said
unto her, The man *is* near of kin unto
us, one of our next kinsmen.
21And Ruth the Moabitess said, He
said unto me also, Thou shalt keep fast
by my young men, until they have ended all my harvest.
22And Naomi said unto Ruth her
daughter in law, *It is* good, my daughter, that thou go out with his maidens,
that they meet thee not in any other
field.
23So she kept fast by the maidens of
Boaz to glean unto the end of barley
harvest and of wheat harvest; and dwelt
with her mother in law.

IV. Blessing (3:1—4:22)

3 Then Naomi her mother in law
said unto her, My daughter, shall I
not seek rest for thee, that it may be
well with thee?
2And now *is* not Boaz of our kindred,
with whose maidens thou wast? Behold, he winnoweth barley to night in
the threshingfloor.
3Wash thyself therefore, and anoint
thee, and put thy raiment upon thee,
and get thee down to the floor: *but* make
not thyself known unto the man, until
he shall have done eating and drinking.
4And it shall be, when he lieth down,
that thou shalt mark the place where he
shall lie, and thou shalt go in, and uncover his feet, and lay thee down; and
he will tell thee what thou shalt do.
5And she said unto her, All that thou
sayest unto me I will do.
¶6And she went down unto the floor,
and did according to all that her mother in law bade her.
7And when Boaz had eaten and
drunk, and his heart was merry, he
went to lie down at the end of the heap

2:19 blessed be he that did take knowledge of thee. Naomi knew that ordinarily a gleaner would not have obtained nearly so much (vss. 15-16).
2:20 kinsmen. See Ruth 1:11 note, "Following the Law." Boaz was a *type of the Lord Jesus Christ, who *redeemed us, or bought us back, from the power of sin.
2:23 to glean unto the end. Wheat harvest came right after barley harvest.
3:1 rest for thee. See Ruth 1:9 note.
3:4 thou shalt go in. Naomi wanted Ruth to claim Boaz as the kinsman (see Ruth 1:11 note, "Following the Law") who should marry her and take care of her. There was a nearer relative whose duty it was to care for Ruth (vs. 12), but Ruth did not know about him.

of corn: and she came softly, and uncovered his feet, and laid her down.
¶8 And it came to pass at midnight,
that the man was afraid, and turned himself: and, behold, a woman lay at his feet.
9 And he said, Who *art* thou? And she
answered, I *am* Ruth thine handmaid:
spread therefore thy skirt over thine
handmaid; for thou *art* a near kinsman.
10 And he said, Blessed *be* thou of the
LORD, my daughter: *for* thou hast
shewed more kindness in the latter end
than at the beginning, inasmuch as thou
followedst not young men, whether
poor or rich.
11 And now, my daughter, fear not; I
will do to thee all that thou requirest:
for all the city of my people doth know
that thou *art* a virtuous woman.
12 And now it is true that I *am thy* near
kinsman: howbeit there is a kinsman
nearer than I.
13 Tarry this night, and it shall be in
the morning, *that* if he will perform
unto thee the part of a kinsman, well;
let him do the kinsman's part: but if he
will not do the part of a kinsman to thee,
then will I do the part of a kinsman to
thee, *as* the LORD liveth: lie down until
the morning.
¶14 And she lay at his feet until the
morning: and she rose up before one
could know another. And he said, Let it
not be known that a woman came into
the floor.
15 Also he said, Bring the vail that
thou hast upon thee, and hold it. And
when she held it, he measured six *measures* of barley, and laid *it* on her: and
she went into the city.
16 And when she came to her mother
in law, she said, Who *art* thou, my
daughter? And she told her all that the
man had done to her.
17 And she said, These six *measures*
of barley gave he me; for he said to me,
Go not empty unto thy mother in law.
18 Then said she, Sit still, my daughter, until thou know how the matter will
fall: for the man will not be in rest, until he have finished the thing this day.

4 Then went Boaz up to the gate,
and sat him down there: and, behold, the kinsman of whom Boaz spake
came by; unto whom he said, Ho, such
a one! turn aside, sit down here. And he
turned aside, and sat down.
2 And he took ten men of the elders
of the city, and said, Sit ye down here.
And they sat down.

4:2 The Elders of the City
Elders were the chief, or important, men in a city and were really the rulers of the land. They were old men, chosen for their positions because of their age, dignity, and wisdom. Read Exodus 4:29 and Judges 2:7. Even in New Testament times, the elders were chief men (Matt. 16:21). The word that the Arabs use for a chief man, "sheikh," means *old man* or *elder*.

3 And he said unto the kinsman, Naomi, that is come again out of the country of Moab, selleth a parcel of land,
which *was* our brother Elimelech's:
4 And I thought to advertise thee, saying, Buy *it* before the inhabitants, and
before the elders of my people. If thou
wilt redeem *it,* redeem *it:* but if thou
wilt not redeem *it, then* tell me, that I
may know: for *there is* none to redeem
it beside thee; and I *am* after thee. And
he said, I will redeem *it.*
5 Then said Boaz, What day thou
buyest the field of the hand of Naomi,
thou must buy *it* also of Ruth the Moabitess, the wife of the dead, to raise up the
name of the dead upon his inheritance.
¶6 And the kinsman said, I cannot redeem *it* for myself, lest I mar mine own

---

3:15 measures. A measure was probably about one bushel.
4:1 the kinsman of whom Boaz spake. See Ruth 3:12.
4:6 lest I mar mine own inheritance. This man probably already had children. If he married Ruth and children were born to them, his land would have to be divided among them all. That would "mar," or spoil, his inheritance by making it very small.

4:5 Naming the Firstborn
If a widow without children had sons after she had married the kinsman, the first son was given the name of her first husband, so that his name might not die out. Ruth's first child after Boaz married her would be counted as Mahlon's son. In that way, Mahlon's name would be remembered and would be handed down to other children. In the Far East, very often when there are no sons in a family, the father adopts a boy into the family to marry one of his daughters. When the boy is adopted, he is given his new father's family name. Even though the father may die, the children who are born to his adopted son and daughter "raise up the name of the dead," for that name will last as long as there are sons to carry it on (Deut. 25:5-10).

inheritance: redeem thou my right to
thyself; for I cannot redeem *it*.
7 Now this *was the manner* in former
time in Israel concerning redeeming
and concerning changing, for to confirm
all things; a man plucked off his shoe,
and gave *it* to his neighbour: and this
was a testimony in Israel.
8 Therefore the kinsman said unto
Boaz, Buy *it* for thee. So he drew off his
shoe.
¶ 9 And Boaz said unto the elders, and
unto all the people, Ye *are* witnesses
this day, that I have bought all that *was*
Elimelech's, and all that *was* Chilion's
and Mahlon's, of the hand of Naomi.
10 Moreover Ruth the Moabitess, the
wife of Mahlon, have I purchased to be
my wife, to raise up the name of the
dead upon his inheritance, that the
name of the dead be not cut off from
among his brethren, and from the gate
of his place: ye *are* witnesses this day.
11 And all the people that *were* in the
gate, and the elders, said, *We are* witnesses. The LORD make the woman
that is come into thine house like Rachel and like Leah, which two did build
the house of Israel: and do thou wor-
thily in Ephratah, and be famous in
Beth-lehem:
12 And let thy house be like the house
of Pharez, whom Tamar bare unto Judah, of the seed which the LORD shall
give thee of this young woman.
¶ 13 So Boaz took Ruth, and she was
his wife: and when he went in unto her,
the LORD gave her conception, and she
bare a son.
14 And the women said unto Naomi,
Blessed *be* the LORD, which hath not
left thee this day without a kinsman,
that his name may be famous in Israel.
15 And he shall be unto thee a restorer of *thy* life, and a nourisher of thine old
age: for thy daughter in law, which
loveth thee, which is better to thee than
seven sons, hath born him.
16 And Naomi took the child, and laid
it in her bosom, and became nurse
unto it.
17 And the women her neighbours
gave it a name, saying, There is a son
born to Naomi; and they called his name
Obed: he *is* the father of Jesse, the father of David.
¶ 18 Now these *are* the generations of
Pharez: Pharez begat Hezron,

4:17 Obed
The little son of Boaz and Ruth became the grandfather of the shepherd lad David, who slew Goliath and who was the great warrior who later became king of Israel. David was also the forefather of Mary and Joseph, the mother and foster father of the Lord Jesus Christ. Obed and Boaz and Ruth were thus the ancestors of the Lord Jesus (Matt. 1:5).

4:7 this was the manner in former time. See Deuteronomy 25:7-9.
4:11 like Rachel and like Leah. These were the wives of Jacob (see Gen. 29) who were the mothers of Jacob's (Israel's, Gen. 32:28) twelve sons (some through Leah's and Rachel's handmaids), who were the heads of the twelve tribes.
4:11 Ephratah. Another name for Bethlehem.
4:12 Pharez, whom Tamar bare. Pharez was the son of Judah (one of Jacob's twelve sons) and Tamar. He was the ancestor of a great family called Pharzites (Num. 26:20) and was a great-great-great-great grandfather of Boaz.

19 And Hezron begat Ram, and Ram
begat Amminadab,
20 And Amminadab begat Nahshon,
and Nahshon begat Salmon,
21 And Salmon begat Boaz, and Boaz
begat Obed,
22 And Obed begat Jesse, and Jesse
begat David.

The First Book of

SAMUEL

otherwise called, The First Book of the Kings

BACKGROUND

This book presents the personal history of Samuel, who was the last of the judges (see the introduction to the book of Judges), and gives an account of a change in the way of government of the Israelites. Samuel was also the first of another line of men called "prophets," whom God raised up, after the priests had become wicked and greedy (1 Samuel 2:12–17), to awaken the spiritual life of His people by writing and by preaching. During the days of Samuel, the people of Israel rejected God as their Ruler in rejecting His chosen leaders, and demanded a king such as the other nations had; so here began a new form of government for Israel. They had been ruled first by leaders whom God appointed: Moses and Joshua; then, next, they had been ruled by judges or by priests, such as Samuel and Eli; the line of kings began in the time of Samuel with Saul as the first king.

THE WRITER

It is very probable that Samuel wrote part of this book and that Nathan, the prophet, and Gad, the seer, added to his writings. Read 1 Chronicles 29:29.

THE TIME

The events recorded in 1 Samuel cover a period of 115 years from 1171 to 1056 B.C.

OUTLINE OF FIRST SAMUEL

I.	The Boy Samuel Serves in the Tabernacle	1 Samuel 1:1—3:18
II.	The Prophet Samuel Serves in the Nation	1 Samuel 3:19—8:22
III.	Saul, the King, Is Tested and Fails	1 Samuel 9:1—15:35
IV.	David, the New King, Is Exiled until Saul's Death	1 Samuel 16:1—31:13

I. The Boy Samuel Serves in the Tabernacle (1:1—3:18)

Hannah's sorrow

1 Now there was a certain man of
Ramathaim-zophim, of mount
*Ephraim, and his name *was* Elkanah,
the son of Jeroham, the son of Elihu, the
son of Tohu, the son of Zuph, an Ephrathite:
2And he had *two wives; the name of

1:1 an Ephrathite. This means that Samuel's father had come from the district of Ephrath, near Beth-lehem. Elkanah was a descendant of the sons of Korah, a Levite (1 Chron. 6:22-23).

the one *was* Hannah, and the name of
the other Peninnah: and Peninnah had
children, but Hannah had no children.
3And this man went up out of his city
yearly to worship and to *sacrifice unto
the LORD of hosts in *Shiloh. And the
two sons of Eli, Hophni and *Phinehas,
the priests of the LORD, *were* there.
¶4And when the time was that Elkanah offered, he gave to Peninnah his
wife, and to all her sons and her daughters, portions:
5But unto Hannah he gave a worthy
portion; for he loved Hannah: but the
LORD had shut up her womb.
6And her adversary also provoked
her sore, for to make her fret, because
the LORD had shut up her womb.
7And *as* he did so year by year, when
she went up to the house of the LORD,
so she provoked her; therefore she
wept, and did not eat.
8Then said Elkanah her husband to
her, Hannah, why weepest thou? and
why eatest thou not? and why is thy
heart grieved? *am* not I better to thee
than ten sons?
¶9So Hannah rose up after they had
eaten in Shiloh, and after they had
drunk. Now Eli the priest sat upon a
seat by a post of the temple of the
LORD.

1:9 The Temple of the LORD
This means the tabernacle, which the Israelites had carried all through the wilderness. The temple was not built until nearly 200 years later.

Hannah's prayer

10And she *was* in bitterness of soul,
and prayed unto the LORD, and wept
sore.
11And she vowed a vow, and said, O
LORD of hosts, if thou wilt indeed look
on the affliction of thine handmaid, and
remember me, and not forget thine
handmaid, but wilt give unto thine
handmaid a man child, then I will give
him unto the LORD all the days of his
life, and there shall no razor come upon
his head.
12And it came to pass, as she continued praying before the LORD, that Eli
marked her mouth.
13Now Hannah, she spake in her
heart; only her lips moved, but her
voice was not heard: therefore Eli
thought she had been drunken.

1:3 THE LORD OF HOSTS

This phrase is a translation from the Hebrew *Jehovah-Sabaoth. Sabaoth* means *hosts,* especially armies. It is a name that indicates that Jehovah has power to overcome all the enemies of His people, and so it is found in the Bible only in periods of Israel's great need for a deliverer:

1. in the time of establishing the kingdom (1 Sam. 17:45; Ps. 24);
2. in the time of national decay (1 Kings 18:15; Isa. 37:32; and eighty times by Jeremiah during the time of the captivity of Judah);
3. in the time of restoration from Babylonian captivity (Zech. 4:6);
4. in the promises of future blessing on Israel (Isa. 9:7; Jer. 31:35).

See also *names of God.

1:2 two wives. God does not approve of this. Although many of His people, following the custom of that day, had more than one wife, God's Word always shows that having more than one wife is the forerunner of unhappiness in the family life.

1:3 Shiloh. The place where the tabernacle was set up after Israel had conquered the Promised Land.

1:5 he gave a worthy portion. Certain sacrifices were used for food. After the blood had been offered to God, the worshippers cooked and ate the flesh of the animal (Lev. 7:15).

1:11 no razor. This was a *Nazarite vow of separation to God.

1:12 marked her mouth. Noticed that her mouth moved.

14 And Eli said unto her, How long wilt
thou be drunken? put away thy *wine
from thee.
15 And Hannah answered and said,
No, my lord, I *am* a woman of a sorrowful spirit: I have drunk neither wine nor
strong drink, but have poured out my
soul before the LORD.
16 Count not thine handmaid for a
daughter of Belial: for out of the abundance of my complaint and grief have I
spoken hitherto.
17 Then Eli answered and said, Go in
*peace: and the God of Israel grant
thee thy petition that thou hast asked of
him.
18 And she said, Let thine handmaid
find grace in thy sight. So the woman
went her way, and did eat, and her countenance was no more *sad*.
¶ 19 And they rose up in the morning
early, and worshipped before the LORD,
and returned, and came to their house
to Ramah: and Elkanah knew Hannah
his wife; and the LORD remembered
her.

The dedication of Samuel

20 Wherefore it came to pass, when
the time was come about after Hannah
had conceived, that she bare a son, and
called his name Samuel, *saying,* Because I have asked him of the LORD.
21 And the man Elkanah, and all his
house, went up to offer unto the LORD
the yearly sacrifice, and his vow.
22 But Hannah went not up; for she
said unto her husband, *I will not go up*
until the child be weaned, and *then* I will
bring him, that he may appear before
the LORD, and there abide for ever.
23 And Elkanah her husband said unto
her, Do what seemeth thee good; tarry
until thou have weaned him; only the
LORD establish his word. So the woman abode, and gave her son suck until
she weaned him.
¶ 24 And when she had weaned him,
she took him up with her, with three
bullocks, and one *ephah of flour, and a
bottle of wine, and brought him unto the
house of the LORD in Shiloh: and the
child *was* young.
25 And they slew a bullock, and
brought the child to Eli.

1:25 The Dedication Ceremony
Slaughtering a bullock was a part of the ceremony to dedicate the child to God. Three bullocks (vs. 24) made a large offering, so Elkanah must have been a rich man. See Leviticus 1:3 note.

26 And she said, Oh my lord, *as* thy
soul liveth, my lord, I *am* the woman
that stood by thee here, praying unto
the LORD.
27 For this child I prayed; and the
LORD hath given me my petition which
I asked of him:
28 Therefore also I have lent him to
the LORD; as long as he liveth he shall
be lent to the LORD. And he worshipped
the LORD there.

Hannah's praise and prophecy

2 And Hannah prayed, and said, My
heart rejoiceth in the LORD, mine
horn is exalted in the LORD: my mouth
is enlarged over mine enemies; because I rejoice in thy *salvation.
2 *There is* none holy as the LORD: for

1:20 Samuel. The name means *asked of God.* Hannah thus reminded herself that she had asked God for this son so that she could give him back to God to serve Him.

2:1 mine horn is exalted. This expression speaks of great power—just as a wild beast counted on its horns for power in a conflict. Compare this song with Mary's in Luke 1:46-55.

2:2 There is none holy as the LORD. An outstanding characteristic of Jehovah is His holiness. The gods of the heathen, who were often worshipped with degrading ceremonies, are sinful gods, but Jehovah is perfect in righteousness (Exod. 15:11).

2:2 rock like our God. A rock speaks of strength, a place of refuge that nothing can overthrow. The Lord Jesus Christ is said to be our *Rock, the rock of salvation (1 Cor. 10:4).

there is none beside thee: neither *is*
there any rock like our God.
3 Talk no more so exceeding proudly;
let *not* arrogancy come out of your
mouth: for the LORD *is* a God of knowledge, and by him actions are weighed.
4 The bows of the mighty men *are*
broken, and they that stumbled are
girded with strength.
5 *They that were* full have hired out
themselves for bread; and *they that were*
hungry ceased: so that the barren hath
born seven; and she that hath many
children is waxed feeble.
6 The LORD killeth, and maketh alive:
he bringeth down to the grave, and
bringeth up.
7 The LORD maketh poor, and maketh
rich: he bringeth low, and lifteth up.
8 He raiseth up the poor out of the
dust, *and* lifteth up the beggar from the
dunghill, to set *them* among princes,
and to make them inherit the throne of
glory: for the pillars of the earth *are* the
LORD'S, and he hath set the *world
upon them.
9 He will keep the feet of his *saints,
and the wicked shall be silent in darkness; for by strength shall no man prevail.

2:10 God's Judgment
Because Jehovah is holy, He abhors sin; therefore, the work of judgment in the Old Testament almost always refers to Him using the name Jehovah. Yet we must remember that He loves sinners and saves them, in spite of their sin, if they will put their trust in Him (Rom. 5:8; John 3:16).

10 The adversaries of the LORD shall
be broken to pieces; out of *heaven
shall he thunder upon them: the LORD
shall judge the ends of the earth; and
he shall give strength unto his king, and
exalt the horn of his anointed.

2:10 The Anointed One
The word for God's anointed is "Messiah" in the Old Testament and "Christ" in the New Testament. This is a reference to our Lord Jesus Christ when He returns to reign as King. Kings were anointed with oil when they were crowned, and this is why Christ is called the "Anointed."

Eli's sons

11 And Elkanah went to Ramah to his
house. And the child did minister unto
the LORD before Eli the priest.
¶ 12 Now the sons of Eli *were* sons of
Belial; they knew not the LORD.
13 And the priests' custom with the
people *was, that,* when any man offered
sacrifice, the priest's servant came,
while the flesh was in seething, with a
fleshhook of three teeth in his hand;
14 And he struck *it* into the pan, or
kettle, or caldron, or pot; all that the
fleshhook brought up the priest took for
himself. So they did in Shiloh unto all
the Israelites that came thither.
15 Also before they burnt the fat, the
priest's servant came, and said to the
man that sacrificed, Give flesh to roast
for the priest; for he will not have sodden flesh of thee, but raw.
16 And *if* any man said unto him, Let
them not fail to burn the fat presently,

2:8 the beggar from the dunghill. This is the absolute worst in wretchedness. When other men went to their homes for shelter, the beggar sought the city dump, where he laid down and covered himself with refuse and trash to protect himself from the cold night winds.

2:8 the pillars of the earth. This is evidently referring to the foundation of the world. Pillars are referred to by Job (Job 9:6) and the psalmist (Ps. 75:3). There is more to the creation than our finite minds can comprehend.

2:13 seething. Cooking. After offering certain sacrifices, the offerers were permitted by God to cook and eat the meat of the animal whose blood had been shed for their sins.

2:16 burn the fat. God had especially ordered that all the fat of every sacrifice must be burned (Lev. 3:9-11).

and *then* take *as much* as thy soul desireth; then he would answer him, *Nay;* but thou shalt give *it me* now: and if not, I will take *it* by force.

17 Wherefore the *sin of the young men was very great before the LORD: for men abhorred the offering of the LORD.

Samuel's childhood

¶ 18 But Samuel ministered before the LORD, *being* a child, girded with a linen *ephod.

19 Moreover his mother made him a little coat, and brought *it* to him from year to year, when she came up with her husband to offer the yearly sacrifice.

¶ 20 And Eli blessed Elkanah and his wife, and said, The LORD give thee seed of this woman for the loan which is lent to the LORD. And they went unto their own home.

21 And the LORD visited Hannah, so that she conceived, and bare three sons and two daughters. And the child Samuel grew before the LORD.

¶ 22 Now Eli was very old, and heard all that his sons did unto all Israel; and how they lay with the women that assembled *at* the door of the *tabernacle of the congregation.

23 And he said unto them, Why do ye such things? for I hear of your evil dealings by all this people.

24 Nay, my sons; for *it is* no good report that I hear: ye make the LORD'S people to transgress.

25 If one man sin against another, the judge shall judge him: but if a man sin against the LORD, who shall intreat for him? Notwithstanding they hearkened not unto the voice of their father, because the LORD would slay them.

26 And the child Samuel grew on, and was in favour both with the LORD, and also with men.

The warning to Eli

¶ 27 And there came a man of God unto Eli, and said unto him, Thus saith the LORD, Did I plainly appear unto the house of thy father, when they were in *Egypt in *Pharaoh's house?

28 And did I choose him out of all the tribes of Israel *to be* my priest, to offer upon mine *altar, to burn incense, to wear an ephod before me? and did I give unto the house of thy father all the *offerings made by fire of the children of Israel?

29 Wherefore kick ye at my sacrifice and at mine offering, which I have commanded *in my* habitation; and honourest thy sons above me, to make yourselves fat with the chiefest of all the offerings of Israel my people?

30 Wherefore the LORD God of Israel saith, I said indeed *that* thy house, and the house of thy father, should walk before me for ever: but now the LORD saith, Be it far from me; for them that honour me I will honour, and they that despise me shall be lightly esteemed.

31 Behold, the days come, that I will cut off thine arm, and the arm of thy father's house, that there shall not be an old man in thine house.

32 And thou shalt see an enemy *in my* habitation, in all *the wealth* which *God* shall give Israel: and there shall not be an old man in thine house for ever.

33 And the man of thine, *whom* I shall not cut off from mine altar, *shall be* to consume thine eyes, and to grieve thine heart: and all the increase of thine house shall die in the flower of their age.

2:17 abhorred the offering. Instead of rejoicing in the promise of forgiveness of sin, men hated to offer a sacrifice that would be stolen by the greedy priests; therefore, the people had stopped offering their sacrifices.

2:28 all the offerings. God provided that a certain portion of some of the sacrifices should be given to the priests for food (see Lev. 6:25-29; 7:6-7,32-36).

2:31 cut off thine arm. The last part of this verse explains the first part. The power of Eli's house would be taken away so that it would be just as if their arms were cut off.

2:31 there shall not be an old man. See 1 Samuel 4:11; 22:9,11,18-20.

34 And this *shall be* a sign unto thee, that shall come upon thy two sons, on Hophni and Phinehas; in one day they shall die both of them.

35 And I will raise me up a faithful priest, *that* shall do according to *that* which *is* in mine heart and in my mind: and I will build him a sure house; and he shall walk before mine anointed for ever.

2:35 A Faithful Priest
This phrase refers to Zadok, who replaced Abiathar the descendant of Eli (see 1 Kings 2:26-27,35), but it is even more a reference to the Lord Jesus Christ, a priest after the order of *Melchizedek. Christ replaced the priests of Aaron's line.

36 And it shall come to pass, *that* every one that is left in thine house shall come *and* crouch to him for a piece of *silver and a morsel of bread, and shall say, Put me, I pray thee, into one of the priests' offices, that I may eat a piece of bread.

The call of Samuel

3 And the child Samuel ministered unto the LORD before Eli. And the word of the LORD was precious in those days; *there was* no open vision.

2 And it came to pass at that time, when Eli *was* laid down in his place, and his eyes began to wax dim, *that* he could not see;

3 And ere the lamp of God went out in the temple of the LORD, where the *ark of God *was,* and Samuel was laid down *to sleep;*

4 That the LORD called Samuel: and he answered, Here *am* I.

5 And he ran unto Eli, and said, Here *am* I; for thou calledst me. And he said, I called not; lie down again. And he went and lay down.

6 And the LORD called yet again, Samuel. And Samuel arose and went to Eli, and said, Here *am* I; for thou didst call me. And he answered, I called not, my son; lie down again.

7 Now Samuel did not yet know the LORD, neither was the word of the LORD yet revealed unto him.

8 And the LORD called Samuel again the third time. And he arose and went to Eli, and said, Here *am* I; for thou didst call me. And Eli perceived that the LORD had called the child.

9 Therefore Eli said unto Samuel, Go,

3:3 THE TABERNACLE

The tabernacle was an oblong tent, with a wooden framework covered with cloth and skins, made by divine command as a movable place of worship in the wilderness. It was set up, taken down, and carried by the Levities. When stationary, the pillar of cloud rested on it. It consisted of a small inner compartment, the "Holy of Holies," entered only on the Day of Atonement by the high priest alone. This restricted area contained nothing but the ark with its mercy seat. A larger compartment, the "Holy Place, or sanctuary" (in which were the altar of incense, table of shewbread, and golden candlestick), was used for the daily service. These two sections were separated by a thick veil, and the whole was surrounded by the Court of the Tabernacle. When Joshua entered Canaan, he set up the tabernacle at Shiloh, where residences for the priests were added to it, and it assumed so permanent a character that it is even called "the temple" here in 1 Samuel.

3:1 the child Samuel. Notice the apparently hopeless contrast between the power and influence of the wicked priests, and the weakness of a little boy dedicated to God (read Zech. 4:6).

3:1 the word of the LORD was precious. Precious means *scarce*. Eli had fallen down on his responsibilities and was failing to teach the people God's word.

3:3 ere the lamp of God went out. Read Exodus 27:20-21. The lamp burned all night but grew dim or went out in the morning.

3:7 did not yet know the LORD. Samuel knew about Him, but he had never had any personal experience of surrendering or giving himself to God.

lie down: and it shall be, if he call thee, that thou shalt say, Speak, LORD; for thy servant heareth. So Samuel went and lay down in his place.

10 And the LORD came, and stood, and called as at other times, Samuel, Samuel. Then Samuel answered, Speak; for thy servant heareth.

¶ 11 And the LORD said to Samuel, Behold, I will do a thing in Israel, at which both the ears of every one that heareth it shall tingle.

12 In that day I will perform against Eli all *things* which I have spoken concerning his house: when I begin, I will also make an end.

13 For I have told him that I will judge his house for ever for the iniquity which he knoweth; because his sons made themselves vile, and he restrained them not.

14 And therefore I have sworn unto the house of Eli, that the iniquity of Eli's house shall not be purged with sacrifice nor offering for ever.

¶ 15 And Samuel lay until the morning, and opened the doors of the house of the LORD. And Samuel feared to shew Eli the vision.

16 Then Eli called Samuel, and said, Samuel, my son. And he answered, Here *am* I.

17 And he said, What *is* the thing that *the LORD* hath said unto thee? I pray thee hide *it* not from me: God do so to thee, and more also, if thou hide *any* thing from me of all the things that he said unto thee.

18 And Samuel told him every whit, and hid nothing from him. And he said, It *is* the LORD: let him do what seemeth him good.

II. The Prophet Samuel Serves in the Nation (3:19—8:22)

¶ 19 And Samuel grew, and the LORD was with him, and did let none of his words fall to the ground.

20 And all Israel from Dan even to *Beer-sheba knew that Samuel *was* established *to be* a *prophet of the LORD.

21 And the LORD appeared again in Shiloh: for the LORD revealed himself to Samuel in Shiloh by the word of the LORD.

Judgment on Israel and Eli's family

4 And the word of Samuel came to all Israel. Now Israel went out against the *Philistines to battle, and pitched beside Eben-ezer: and the Philistines pitched in Aphek.

2 And the Philistines put themselves in array against Israel: and when they joined battle, Israel was smitten before the Philistines: and they slew of the army in the field about four thousand men.

¶ 3 And when the people were come into the camp, the *elders of Israel said, Wherefore hath the LORD smitten us to day before the Philistines? Let us fetch the ark of the covenant of the LORD out of Shiloh unto us, that, when it cometh among us, it may save us out of the hand of our enemies.

4:3 Misplaced Trust
The elders had a superstitious trust in the ark, as though it were a charm with some magic power to help them. They trusted in the ark instead of trusting in the God of the ark.

4 So the people sent to Shiloh, that they might bring from thence the ark of the covenant of the LORD of hosts,

---

3:12 all things which I have spoken. See 1 Samuel 2:27-34.
3:15 opened the doors. At this period the tabernacle had been given a more permanent form by adding doors to the curtains at the entrance to the courtyard.
3:18 every whit. Wholly, everything.
3:19 fall to the ground. Samuel's words, including his prophecies, were not empty or wasted. The LORD blessed Samuel's words and he was careful to not allow any of God's words go unheeded.
3:21 the LORD appeared again in Shiloh. He again showed His grace and forgiveness because men again came to Shiloh to confess sins and offer sacrifices.

which dwelleth *between* the cherubims: and the two sons of Eli, Hophni and *Phinehas, *were* there with the ark of the covenant of God.

5 And when the ark of the covenant of the LORD came into the camp, all Israel shouted with a great shout, so that the earth rang again.

6 And when the Philistines heard the noise of the shout, they said, What *meaneth* the noise of this great shout in the camp of the Hebrews? And they understood that the ark of the LORD was come into the camp.

7 And the Philistines were afraid, for they said, God is come into the camp. And they said, Woe unto us! for there hath not been such a thing heretofore.

8 Woe unto us! who shall deliver us out of the hand of these mighty Gods? these *are* the Gods that smote the Egyptians with all the plagues in the wilderness.

9 Be strong, and quit yourselves like men, O ye Philistines, that ye be not servants unto the Hebrews, as they have been to you: quit yourselves like men, and fight.

¶ 10 And the Philistines fought, and Israel was smitten, and they fled every man into his tent: and there was a very great slaughter; for there fell of Israel thirty thousand footmen.

11 And the ark of God was taken; and the two sons of Eli, Hophni and Phinehas, were slain.

¶ 12 And there ran a man of Benjamin out of the army, and came to Shiloh the same day with his clothes rent, and with earth upon his head.

13 And when he came, lo, Eli sat upon a seat by the wayside watching: for his heart trembled for the ark of God. And when the man came into the city, and told *it,* all the city cried out.

14 And when Eli heard the noise of the crying, he said, What *meaneth* the noise of this tumult? And the man came in hastily, and told Eli.

15 Now Eli was ninety and eight years old; and his eyes were dim, that he could not see.

16 And the man said unto Eli, I *am* he that came out of the army, and I fled to day out of the army. And he said, What is there done, my son?

17 And the messenger answered and said, Israel is fled before the Philistines, and there hath been also a great slaughter among the people, and thy two sons also, Hophni and Phinehas, are dead, and the ark of God is taken.

18 And it came to pass, when he made mention of the ark of God, that he fell from off the seat backward by the side of the gate, and his neck brake, and he died: for he was an old man, and heavy. And he had judged Israel forty years.

¶ 19 And his daughter in law, Phinehas' wife, was with child, *near* to be delivered: and when she heard the tidings that the ark of God was taken, and that her father in law and her husband were dead, she bowed herself and travailed; for her pains came upon her.

20 And about the time of her death the women that stood by her said unto her, Fear not; for thou hast born a son. But she answered not, neither did she regard *it.*

21 And she named the child I-chabod, saying, The glory is departed from Israel: because the ark of God was taken, and because of her father in law and her husband.

22 And she said, The glory is departed from Israel: for the ark of God is taken.

4:4 dwelleth between the cherubims. Read Exodus 25:10-22.
4:8 plagues in the wilderness. This refers to the time God delivered Israel from Egypt and it is like a Philistine to mis-interpret what God and done.
4:10 footmen. Soldiers on foot.
4:11 two sons of Eli, Hophni and Phinehas, were slain. Read 1 Samuel 2:34.
4:12 clothes rent, and with earth upon his head. A sign of deep humiliation and grief.
4:21 I-chabod. The name means the *glory is departed.*

Judgment on the Philistines

5 And the Philistines took the ark of God, and brought it from Ebenezer unto Ashdod.

2 When the Philistines took the ark of God, they brought it into the house of Dagon, and set it by Dagon.

¶3 And when they of Ashdod arose early on the morrow, behold, Dagon *was* fallen upon his face to the earth before the ark of the LORD. And they took Dagon, and set him in his place again.

4 And when they arose early on the morrow morning, behold, Dagon *was* fallen upon his face to the ground before the ark of the LORD; and the head of Dagon and both the palms of his hands *were* cut off upon the threshold; only *the stump of* Dagon was left to him.

5 Therefore neither the priests of Dagon, nor any that come into Dagon's house, tread on the threshold of Dagon in Ashdod unto this day.

6 But the hand of the LORD was heavy upon them of Ashdod, and he destroyed them, and smote them with emerods, *even* Ashdod and the coasts thereof.

7 And when the men of Ashdod saw that *it was* so, they said, The ark of the God of Israel shall not abide with us: for his hand is sore upon us, and upon Dagon our god.

8 They sent therefore and gathered all the lords of the Philistines unto them, and said, What shall we do with the ark of the God of Israel? And they answered, Let the ark of the God of Israel be carried about unto *Gath. And they carried the ark of the God of Israel about *thither.*

9 And it was *so,* that, after they had carried it about, the hand of the LORD was against the city with a very great destruction: and he smote the men of the city, both small and great, and they had emerods in their secret parts.

¶10 Therefore they sent the ark of God to Ekron. And it came to pass, as the ark of God came to Ekron, that the Ekronites cried out, saying, They have brought about the ark of the God of Israel to us, to slay us and our people.

11 So they sent and gathered together all the lords of the Philistines, and said, Send away the ark of the God of Israel, and let it go again to his own place, that it slay us not, and our people: for there was a deadly destruction throughout all the city; the hand of God was very heavy there.

12 And the men that died not were smitten with the emerods: and the cry of the city went up to heaven.

The return of the ark

6 And the ark of the LORD was in the country of the Philistines seven *months.

2 And the Philistines called for the priests and the diviners, saying, What shall we do to the ark of the LORD? tell us wherewith we shall send it to his place.

3 And they said, If ye send away the ark of the God of Israel, send it not empty; but in any wise return him a trespass-offering: then ye shall be healed, and it shall be known to you why his hand is not removed from you.

4 Then said they, What *shall be* the trespass-offering which we shall return to him? They answered, Five golden

---

5:1 Ashdod. The Philistines had five chief cities, each ruled by a chief or lord: Gaza, Ashdod, Ashkelon, Gath, and Ekron (see 6:17).

5:2 Dagon. The special idol of the city of Ashdod. Dagon was the fish god. Its head, chest, and arms were made like a man, its tail, like a fish. It thus resembled imaginary mermen and mermaids.

5:6 emerods. An emerod was a sort of boil.

5:11 lords of the Philistines. See 5:1 note.

6:2 diviners. These were called "wise men," and they were supposed to know even the secrets of the gods. See note on "Divination, Magic, and Witchcraft," next page.

6:4 trespass-offering. Compare this with Leviticus 5:15-16.

emerods, and five golden mice, *according to* the number of the lords of the Philistines: for one plague *was* on you all, and on your lords.

5 Wherefore ye shall make images of your emerods, and images of your mice that mar the land; and ye shall give glory unto the God of Israel: peradventure he will lighten his hand from off you, and from off your gods, and from off your land.

6 Wherefore then do ye *harden your hearts, as the Egyptians and Pharaoh hardened their hearts? when he had wrought wonderfully among them, did they not let the people go, and they departed?

7 Now therefore make a new cart, and take two milch kine, on which there hath come no yoke, and tie the kine to the cart, and bring their calves home from them:

8 And take the ark of the LORD, and lay it upon the cart; and put the jewels of gold, which ye return him *for* a trespass-offering, in a coffer by the side

6:2 DIVINATION, MAGIC, AND WITCHCRAFT

From time immemorial, the Eastern nations have used "curious arts" (Acts 19:19) and have professed to hold communication with the spirit world through the medium of superstitious practices. Large numbers of magical formulae, lists of lucky and unlucky days, incantations, and similar things have been found inscribed upon Babylonian and Assyrian tablets, and there is evidence to show that to some extent similar practices prevailed in Egypt and Babylon (Pharaoh had his magicians, and Nebuchadnezzar had his astrologers). There are various Hebrew words by which these traffickers in superstitious rites were described. They may be classified as follows:

1. "Diviners" professed to see visions or to obtain information by gazing into a cup (Gen. 44:5), by means of arrows, by the inspection of livers of dead animals, and by teraphim, a kind of image (Ezek. 21:21). Compare the divination between the Midianites (Num. 22:7) and the Philistines (1 Sam. 6:2).
2. "Wizards," "witches," or "sorcerers," literally, *knowing ones,* were mind readers (Lev. 19:31; Deut. 18:11).
3. "Necromancers" (Deut. 18:11) were supposed to be possessed with familiar spirits, for example, the witch of En-dor (1 Sam. 28:7), who was professedly a "medium" between the living and the dead.
4. "Soothsayers," "monthly prognosticators," and "observers of times" were astrologers, who would draw horoscopes and foretell events by examining the placement—conjunction and oppositions—of the heavenly bodies (Isa 2:6; 47:13).
5. "Magicians" or "engravers" (Exod. 32:4) were perhaps originally a literary class. Compare the case of the magi or wise men who came from the East to worship Christ (Matt. 2:1-2,7-12).
6. "Enchanters" were serpent charmers, and another class were probably "conjurers," who were gifted with sleight of hand.

The Israelites were strictly forbidden to have anything to do with these various classes of superstition. Their practices were heathenish and idolatrous, and the use of these things diverted people's minds from God, the true source of knowledge and power. No witch was to live among the people (Exod. 22:18). Men were not to seek out wizards that "peep"ed and "mutter"ed but to seek the Law and the testimony of God (Isa. 8:19-21).

What the secrets of these practices were, or indeed of their later representatives in the Greek period (Acts 19:19), the Middle Ages, or more modern times (including the occult), none but the initiated could tell. Probably among their hidden arts there may be quickness of wit, the power of a strong will over a weak one, the possession of secret information, the strange gift called "clairvoyance," the modern hypnotism or "second sight," and the use of drugs and mechanical devices. God makes it clear in the Bible that believers are to have nothing to do with any of these practices but are to trust completely and only in the Lord and His Word.

6:4 mice. These golden mice were representatives from the Philistines of field mice that spoiled the crops.

6:7 two milch kine. Two milking cows, or cows that had young calves.

thereof; and send it away, that it may go.
9 And see, if it goeth up by the way of
his own coast to Beth-shemesh, *then* he
hath done us this great evil: but if not,
then we shall know that *it is* not his
hand *that* smote us; it *was* a chance *that*
happened to us.
¶10 And the men did so; and took two
milch kine, and tied them to the cart,
and shut up their calves at home:
11 And they laid the ark of the LORD
upon the cart, and the coffer with the
mice of gold and the images of their
emerods.
12 And the kine took the straight way
to the way of Beth-shemesh, *and* went
along the highway, lowing as they went,
and turned not aside *to* the right hand
or *to* the left; and the lords of the Philistines went after them unto the border of Beth-shemesh.

Judgment on Beth-shemesh

13 And *they of* Beth-shemesh *were*
reaping their wheat harvest in the valley: and they lifted up their eyes, and
saw the ark, and rejoiced to see *it*.
14 And the cart came into the field of
*Joshua, a Beth-shemite, and stood
there, where *there was* a great stone:
and they clave the wood of the cart, and
offered the kine a burnt-offering unto
the LORD.
15 And the Levites took down the ark
of the LORD, and the coffer that *was*
with it, wherein the jewels of gold *were*,
and put *them* on the great stone: and the
men of Beth-shemesh offered burnt-
offerings and sacrificed sacrifices the
same day unto the LORD.
16 And when the five lords of the Philistines had seen *it*, they returned to
Ekron the same day.
17 And these *are* the golden emerods
which the Philistines returned *for* a
trespass-offering unto the LORD; for
Ashdod one, for *Gaza one, for Askelon
one, for Gath one, for Ekron one;
18 And the golden mice, *according to*
the number of all the cities of the Philistines *belonging* to the five lords, *both*
of fenced cities, and of country villages,
even unto the great *stone of* *Abel,
whereon they set down the ark of the
LORD: *which stone remaineth* unto this
day in the field of Joshua, the Beth-
shemite.
¶19 And he smote the men of Beth-
shemesh, because they had looked into
the ark of the LORD, even he smote of
the people fifty thousand and threescore and ten men: and the people lamented, because the LORD had smitten
many of the people with a great slaughter.

> **6:19 Losing Respect**
> Read Numbers 4:20. Looking into the ark of the LORD was a grave sin. The LORD had commanded that no one look at the holy things. When men have lost all respect for the sacredness of holy things and break God's law, they must be punished.

20 And the men of Beth-shemesh said,
Who is able to stand before this holy
LORD God? and to whom shall he go up
from us?
¶21 And they sent messengers to the
inhabitants of Kirjath-jearim, saying,
The Philistines have brought again
the ark of the LORD; come ye down, *and*
fetch it up to you.

Revival in Israel

7 And the men of Kirjath-jearim
came, and fetched up the ark of the
LORD, and brought it into the house of

6:9 his own coast. The border of the land of Israel.
6:12 the kine took the straight way to the way of Beth-shemesh. The cows did the unnatural thing, turning away from their calves and leaving their own pastures for a strange country.
6:13 Beth-shemesh. A town belonging to Judah, on the border of Philistia.
6:21 Kirjath-jearim. This was a village of the Israelites, a few miles north of Beth-shemesh.

7:1 A New Location for the Ark
The tabernacle at Shiloh had been taken by the Philistines after the battle of Aphek (1 Sam. 4:10). Thus the ark was now located in the house of Abinadab in Kirjath-jearim and stayed there for twenty years (vs. 2). Tabernacle worship was not fully restored for about eighty years, until King David's time (see 2 Sam. 6).

Abinadab in the hill, and sanctified Eleazar his son to keep the ark of the LORD.

2 And it came to pass, while the ark abode in Kirjath-jearim, that the time was long; for it was twenty years: and all the house of *Israel lamented after the LORD.

¶3 And *Samuel spake unto all the house of Israel, saying, If ye do return unto the LORD with all your hearts, *then* put away the strange gods and *Ashtaroth from among you, and prepare your hearts unto the LORD, and serve him only: and he will deliver you out of the hand of the Philistines.

4 Then the children of Israel did put away Baalim and Ashtaroth, and served the LORD only.

5 And Samuel said, Gather all Israel to Mizpeh, and I will pray for you unto the LORD.

6 And they gathered together to Mizpeh, and drew water, and poured *it* out before the LORD, and fasted on that day, and said there, We have sinned against the LORD. And Samuel judged the children of Israel in Mizpeh.

7 And when the Philistines heard that the children of Israel were gathered together to Mizpeh, the lords of the Philistines went up against Israel. And when the children of Israel heard *it,* they were afraid of the Philistines.

8 And the children of Israel said to Samuel, Cease not to cry unto the LORD our *God for us, that he will save us out of the hand of the Philistines.

¶9 And Samuel took a sucking lamb, and offered *it for* a burnt-offering wholly unto the LORD: and Samuel cried unto the LORD for Israel; and the LORD heard him.

10 And as Samuel was offering up the burnt-offering, the Philistines drew near to battle against Israel: but the LORD thundered with a great thunder on that day upon the Philistines, and discomfited them; and they were smitten before Israel.

11 And the men of Israel went out of Mizpeh, and pursued the Philistines, and smote them, until *they came* under Beth-car.

12 Then Samuel took a stone, and set *it* between Mizpeh and Shen, and called the name of it Eben-ezer, saying, Hitherto hath the LORD helped us.

¶13 So the Philistines were subdued, and they came no more into the coast of Israel: and the hand of the LORD was against the Philistines all the days of Samuel.

14 And the cities which the Philistines had taken from Israel were restored to Israel, from Ekron even unto Gath; and the coasts thereof did Israel deliver out of the hands of the Philistines. And there was peace between Israel and the Amorites.

15 And Samuel judged Israel all the days of his life.

16 And he went from year to year in circuit to *Beth-el, and Gilgal, and Mizpeh, and judged Israel in all those places.

17 And his return *was* to Ramah; for there *was* his house; and there he judged Israel; and there he built an altar unto the LORD.

7:3 strange gods. Idols.
7:6 drew water, and poured it out. This drink-offering, a sign of repentance for sin, was associated with the *burnt-offering. It indicated that the very life of the offerer was ready to be poured out to do the will of God. Compare Numbers 15:5.
7:12 Eben-ezer. This means the *stone of help*.

7:17 An Altar for the LORD
During this time, when there was no tabernacle, the worship of God was carried on much as it had been in the days before the giving of the Law at Sinai. Wherever Samuel went, he built an altar on which he offered sacrifices, and God was pleased to accept such worship.

Israel rejects God as King

8 And it came to pass, when Samuel was old, that he made his sons
*judges over Israel.
2Now the name of his firstborn was
Joel; and the name of his second, Abiah:
they were judges in *Beer-sheba.
3And his sons walked not in his ways,
but turned aside after lucre, and took
bribes, and perverted *judgment.
4Then all the elders of Israel gathered themselves together, and came to
Samuel unto Ramah,
5And said unto him, Behold, thou art
old, and thy sons walk not in thy ways:
now make us a king to judge us like all
the nations.
¶6But the thing displeased Samuel,
when they said, Give us a king to judge
us. And Samuel prayed unto the LORD.
7And the LORD said unto Samuel,
Hearken unto the voice of the people in
all that they say unto thee: for they have
not rejected thee, but they have rejected me, that I should not reign over
them.
8According to all the works which
they have done since the day that I
brought them up out of *Egypt even
unto this day, wherewith they have forsaken me, and served other gods, so do
they also unto thee.
9Now therefore hearken unto their
voice: howbeit yet protest solemnly
unto them, and shew them the manner
of the king that shall reign over them.
¶10And Samuel told all the words of
the LORD unto the people that asked of
him a king.
11And he said, This will be the manner of the king that shall reign over you:
He will take your sons, and appoint
them for himself, for his chariots, and *to
be* his horsemen; and *some* shall run
before his chariots.
12And he will appoint him captains
over thousands, and captains over fifties; and *will set them* to ear his ground,
and to reap his harvest, and to make his
instruments of war, and instruments of
his chariots.
13And he will take your daughters *to
be* confectionaries, and *to be* cooks, and
to be bakers.
14And he will take your fields, and
your vineyards, and your oliveyards,
even the best *of them,* and give *them* to
his servants.
15And he will take the tenth of your
seed, and of your vineyards, and give to
his officers, and to his servants.
16And he will take your menservants,
and your maidservants, and your goodliest young men, and your asses, and
put *them* to his work.
17He will take the tenth of your
sheep: and ye shall be his servants.
18And ye shall cry out in that day because of your king which ye shall have
chosen you; and the LORD will not hear
you in that day.
¶19Nevertheless the people refused to
obey the voice of Samuel; and they said,
Nay; but we will have a king over us;
20That we also may be like all the
nations; and that our king may judge us,

8:1 he made his sons judges. This was not right. Only God had the right to appoint judges. Samuel should have sought God's will and appointed those whom He chose, whether they were Samuel's sons or not.

8:3 lucre. Money.

8:6 displeased Samuel. He had spent his life in teaching this nation that God was their King. Now, by asking for a king, they were rejecting God's plan for their government.

8:11 the manner of the king. The judges had never received any pay for their services for the people. The kings would demand service by force.

8:20 Like Everyone Else
It is disastrous for God's people to seek to be like the people who reject God, because He has called His people to come apart from the evil world. In demanding a king, the Israelites were denying the "glorious liberty of the children of God" (compare Rom. 8:21), for it is liberty to be subject to God rather than to man.

and go out before us, and fight our
battles.
21 And Samuel heard all the words of
the people, and he rehearsed them in
the ears of the LORD.
22 And the LORD said to Samuel, Hearken unto their voice, and make them a
king. And Samuel said unto the men of
Israel, Go ye every man unto his city.

III. Saul, the King, Is Tested and Fails
(9:1—15:35)
Saul chosen to be king

9 Now there was a man of Benjamin, whose name *was* Kish, the
son of Abiel, the son of Zeror, the son
of Bechorath, the son of Aphiah, a Benjamite, a mighty man of power.
2 And he had a son, whose name *was*
Saul, a choice young man, and a goodly:
and *there was* not among the children of
Israel a goodlier person than he: from
his shoulders and upward *he was* higher than any of the people.
3 And the asses of Kish Saul's father
were lost. And Kish said to Saul his son,
Take now one of the servants with thee,
and arise, go seek the asses.
4 And he passed through mount
*Ephraim, and passed through the land
of Shalisha, but they found *them* not:
then they passed through the land of
Shalim, and *there they were* not: and he
passed through the land of the Benjamites, but they found *them* not.
5 *And* when they were come to the
land of Zuph, Saul said to his servant
that *was* with him, Come, and let us
return; lest my father leave *caring* for
the asses, and take thought for us.
6 And he said unto him, Behold now,
there is in this city a man of God, and *he
is* an honourable man; all that he saith
cometh surely to pass: now let us go
thither; peradventure he can shew us
our way that we should go.
7 Then said Saul to his servant, But,
behold, *if* we go, what shall we bring the
man? for the bread is spent in our vessels, and *there is* not a present to bring
to the man of God: what have we?
8 And the servant answered Saul
again, and said, Behold, I have here at
hand the fourth part of a shekel of silver: *that* will I give to the man of God,
to tell us our way.
9 (Beforetime in Israel, when a man
went to enquire of God, thus he spake,
Come, and let us go to the seer: for *he
that is* now *called* a *Prophet was beforetime called a Seer.)
10 Then said Saul to his servant, Well
said; come, let us go. So they went unto
the city where the man of God *was*.
¶ 11 *And* as they went up the hill to the
city, they found young maidens going
out to draw water, and said unto them,
Is the seer here?
12 And they answered them, and said,
He is; behold, *he is* before you: make
haste now, for he came to day to the
city; for *there is* a *sacrifice of the people to day in the high place:
13 As soon as ye be come into the city,
ye shall *straightway find him, before
he go up to the high place to eat: for the
people will not eat until he come, because he doth bless the sacrifice; *and*
afterwards they eat that be bidden. Now
therefore get you up; for about this time
ye shall find him.
14 And they went up into the city: *and*
when they were come into the city, behold, Samuel came out against them, for
to go up to the high place.
¶ 15 Now the LORD had told Samuel in

9:12 sacrifice . . . in the high place. With the tabernacle destroyed, the people of Israel offered their sacrifices on altars built in every city and village, usually on a hill.

his ear a day before Saul came, saying,
16 To morrow about this time I will
send thee a man out of the land of Benjamin, and thou shalt anoint him *to be*
captain over my people Israel, that he
may save my people out of the hand of
the Philistines: for I have looked upon
my people, because their cry is come
unto me.
17 And when Samuel saw Saul, the
LORD said unto him, Behold the man
whom I spake to thee of! this same shall
reign over my people.
18 Then Saul drew near to Samuel in
the gate, and said, Tell me, I pray thee,
where the seer's house *is*.
19 And Samuel answered Saul, and
said, I *am* the seer: go up before me
unto the high place; for ye shall eat with
me to day, and to morrow I will let thee
go, and will tell thee all that *is* in thine
heart.
20 And as for thine asses that were
lost three days ago, set not thy mind on
them; for they are found. And on whom
is all the desire of Israel? *Is it* not on
thee, and on all thy father's house?
21 And Saul answered and said, *Am* not
I a Benjamite, of the smallest of the tribes
of Israel? and my family the least of all
the families of the tribe of Benjamin?
wherefore then speakest thou so to me?
22 And Samuel took Saul and his servant, and brought them into the parlour,
and made them sit in the chiefest place
among them that were bidden, which
were about thirty persons.
23 And Samuel said unto the cook,
Bring the portion which I gave thee, of
which I said unto thee, Set it by thee.
24 And the cook took up the shoulder,
and *that* which *was* upon it, and set *it*
before Saul. And *Samuel* said, Behold
that which is left! set *it* before thee,
and eat: for unto this time hath it been
kept for thee since I said, I have invited
the people. So Saul did eat with Samuel
that day.
¶25 And when they were come down
from the high place into the city, *Samuel* communed with Saul upon the top
of the house.
26 And they arose early: and it came
to pass about the spring of the day, that
Samuel called Saul to the top of the
house, saying, Up, that I may send thee
away. And Saul arose, and they went
out both of them, he and Samuel,
abroad.
27 *And* as they were going down to
the end of the city, Samuel said to Saul,
Bid the servant pass on before us, (and
he passed on,) but stand thou still a
while, that I may shew thee the word
of God.

Saul anointed and presented as king

10 Then Samuel took a vial of oil,
and poured *it* upon his head, and
kissed him, and said, *Is it* not because
the LORD hath anointed thee *to be* captain over his inheritance?
2 When thou art departed from me to
day, then thou shalt find two men by

9:16 a man out of the land of Benjamin. God chose the first king from the tribe of Benjamin, the smallest tribe (see Judg. 20; 21), yet Saul was larger in stature than the other Israelites (9:1-2).
9:16 anoint. See 2:10 note, "The Anointed One." See also 10:1 first note.
9:25 the top of the house. The flat roofs of the houses of that country were commonly used by the people as cool and quiet places for rest and conversation.
9:26 the spring of the day. Very early in the day.
10:1 oil, and poured it upon his head. This indicated that God, who had chosen this man for this office, would provide the wisdom and strength for Saul to perform his duties according to God's will.
10:1 kissed him. The sign of submission, a kiss, was given by the subject to the sovereign (see Ps. 2:12).
10:2 thou shalt find. Verses 2-7 contain three prophecies of unusual things that would happen to Saul on his way home, signs that would prove to him that Samuel spoke the truth when he said that God had chosen Saul to be king.

Rachel's sepulchre in the border of
Benjamin at Zelzah; and they will say
unto thee, The asses which thou
wentest to seek are found: and, lo, thy
father hath left the care of the asses,
and sorroweth for you, saying, What
shall I do for my son?
3Then shalt thou go on forward from
thence, and thou shalt come to the plain
of Tabor, and there shall meet thee
three men going up to God to Beth-el,
one carrying three kids, and another
carrying three loaves of bread, and another carrying a bottle of wine:
4And they will salute thee, and give
thee two *loaves* of bread; which thou
shalt receive of their hands.
5After that thou shalt come to the hill
of God, where *is* the garrison of the
*Philistines: and it shall come to pass,
when thou art come thither to the city,
that thou shalt meet a company of
prophets coming down from the high
place with a psaltery, and a tabret, and
a pipe, and a harp, before them; and
they shall prophesy:
6And the Spirit of the LORD will come
upon thee, and thou shalt prophesy with
them, and shalt be turned into another
man.
7And let it be, when these signs are
come unto thee, *that* thou do as occasion serve thee; for God *is* with thee.
8And thou shalt go down before me
to Gilgal; and, behold, I will come down
unto thee, to offer burnt-offerings, *and*
to sacrifice sacrifices of peace-offerings: seven days shalt thou tarry, till I
come to thee, and shew thee what thou
shalt do.
¶9And it was *so,* that when he had
turned his back to go from Samuel, God
gave him another heart: and all those
signs came to pass that day.
10And when they came thither to the
hill, behold, a company of prophets met
him; and the Spirit of God came upon
him, and he prophesied among them.

10:10 Saul's Prophecy
When men prophesied, they spoke God's message, controlled by the Holy Spirit. Usually they spoke in such exalted words and tones that those who listened knew that what they heard was more than the voice of man (see 1 Sam. 18:10 note).

11And it came to pass, when all that
knew him beforetime saw that, behold,
he prophesied among the prophets,
then the people said one to another,
What *is* this *that* is come unto the son
of Kish? *Is* Saul also among the prophets?
12And one of the same place answered and said, But who *is* their father? Therefore it became a proverb, *Is*
Saul also among the prophets?
13And when he had made an end of
prophesying, he came to the high place.
¶14And Saul's uncle said unto him
and to his servant, Whither went ye?
And he said, To seek the asses: and
when we saw that *they were* no where,
we came to Samuel.
15And Saul's uncle said, Tell me, I
pray thee, what Samuel said unto you.
16And Saul said unto his uncle, He
told us plainly that the asses were
found. But of the matter of the kingdom, whereof Samuel spake, he told
him not.

10:2 Rachel's sepulchre. This was near Beth-lehem (Gen. 35:19-20).
10:3 going up to God. Going up to worship God.
10:5 a company of prophets. Samuel had set up schools of prophets where he taught men the Law of God and the things of God. See 1 Samuel 19:19-20.
10:5 high place. See 1 Samuel 9:12 note.
10:5 psaltery. A stringed instrument, with ten or twelve strings, played by using the hand.
10:5 tabret. Tambourine.
10:8 seven days shalt thou tarry, till I come. Doubtless, Samuel explained to Saul that he was to obey these orders at some critical hour in the future. Saul's failure is recorded in 1 Samuel 13:8-10.

¶17 And Samuel called the people together unto the LORD to Mizpeh;
18 And said unto the children of Israel,
Thus saith the LORD God of Israel, I
brought up Israel out of Egypt, and delivered you out of the hand of the Egyptians, and out of the hand of all
kingdoms, *and* of them that oppressed
you:
19 And ye have this day rejected your
God, who himself saved you out of all
your adversities and your tribulations;
and ye have said unto him, *Nay,* but set
a king over us. Now therefore present
yourselves before the LORD by your
tribes, and by your thousands.
20 And when Samuel had caused all
the tribes of Israel to come near, the
tribe of Benjamin was taken.
21 When he had caused the tribe of
Benjamin to come near by their families, the family of Matri was taken, and
Saul the son of Kish was taken: and
when they sought him, he could not be
found.
22 Therefore they enquired of the
LORD further, if the man should yet
come thither. And the LORD answered,
Behold, he hath hid himself among the
stuff.
23 And they ran and fetched him
thence: and when he stood among the
people, he was higher than any of the
people from his shoulders and upward.
24 And Samuel said to all the people,
See ye him whom the LORD hath chosen, that *there is* none like him among
all the people? And all the people shouted, and said, God save the king.
25 Then Samuel told the people the
manner of the kingdom, and wrote *it* in
a book, and laid *it* up before the LORD.
And Samuel sent all the people away,
every man to his house.
¶26 And Saul also went home to Gibeah; and there went with him a band of
men, whose hearts God had touched.
27 But the children of *Belial said,
How shall this man save us? And they
despised him, and brought him no
presents. But he held his peace.

Saul's first victory

11 Then Nahash the Ammonite
came up, and encamped against
Jabesh-gilead: and all the men of
Jabesh said unto Nahash, Make a
covenant with us, and we will serve
thee.

11:1 Nahash the Ammonite
Nahash, whose name means *serpent,* was king of the Ammonites (see Gen. 19:37 note, and Judg. 10:7 note, "Ammon"), a wicked race whose origin was sinful and who constantly attacked God's people. Nahash subdued the people of God and brought disgrace upon them, but he was conquered by the man who was empowered by the Holy Spirit (vs. 6). Saul won this victory over his enemies because he first won a victory over his own pride (1 Sam. 10:16,21-22), his love of riches, and his desire for revenge (1 Sam. 10:27).

2 And Nahash the Ammonite answered them, On this *condition* will I
make *a covenant* with you, that I may
thrust out all your right eyes, and lay it
for a reproach upon all Israel.
3 And the *elders of Jabesh said unto
him, Give us seven days' respite, that
we may send messengers unto all the
coasts of Israel: and then, if *there be* no
man to save us, we will come out to
thee.

10:24 the LORD hath chosen. The LORD chose Saul because he was the people's ideal of what a king should be—humble and kindly, as well as big and handsome, but Saul was not the kind of king that the LORD would have chosen to please Himself (see 1 Sam. 13:14; 16:7).

11:1 a covenant. The men of Jabesh wanted an agreement with Nahash, such as, "If you will promise not to fight against us, we will serve you."

11:2 thrust out all your right eyes. It this were done to a man, he became unfit for warfare, because he then needed to expose his whole head to look from behind his shield.

¶ 4 Then came the messengers to Gibeah of Saul, and told the tidings in the
ears of the people: and all the people
lifted up their voices, and wept.
5 And, behold, Saul came after the
herd out of the field; and Saul said, What
aileth the people that they weep? And
they told him the tidings of the men of
Jabesh.
6 And the Spirit of God came upon
Saul when he heard those tidings, and
his anger was kindled greatly.
7 And he took a yoke of oxen, and
hewed them in pieces, and sent *them*
throughout all the coasts of Israel by
the hands of messengers, saying, Whosoever cometh not forth after Saul and
after Samuel, so shall it be done unto
his oxen. And the *fear of the LORD fell
on the people, and they came out with
one consent.
8 And when he numbered them in
Bezek, the children of Israel were three
hundred thousand, and the men of Judah thirty thousand.
9 And they said unto the messengers
that came, Thus shall ye say unto the
men of Jabesh-gilead, To morrow, by
that time the sun be hot, ye shall have
help. And the messengers came and
shewed *it* to the men of Jabesh; and
they were glad.
10 Therefore the men of Jabesh said,
To morrow we will come out unto you,
and ye shall do with us all that seemeth
good unto you.
11 And it was *so* on the morrow, that
Saul put the people in three companies;
and they came into the midst of the host
in the morning watch, and slew the
Ammonites until the heat of the day:
and it came to pass, that they which
remained were scattered, so that two of
them were not left together.
¶ 12 And the people said unto Samuel,
Who *is* he that said, Shall Saul reign
over us? bring the men, that we may
put them to death.
13 And Saul said, There shall not a
man be put to death this day: for to day
the LORD hath wrought *salvation in
Israel.
14 Then said Samuel to the people,
Come, and let us go to Gilgal, and renew the kingdom there.
15 And all the people went to Gilgal;
and there they made Saul king before
the LORD in Gilgal; and there they sacrificed sacrifices of peace-offerings
before the LORD; and there Saul and all
the men of Israel rejoiced greatly.

> **11:15 Gilgal**
> Gilgal was the place where God had rolled away the reproach of past failures when Israel first entered the land of Canaan (Josh. 5). Here they again agreed to start fresh with God.

Samuel warns the people

12 And Samuel said unto all Israel, Behold, I have hearkened
unto your voice in all that ye said unto
me, and have made a king over you.
2 And now, behold, the king walketh
before you: and I am old and grayheaded; and, behold, my sons *are* with
you: and I have walked before you from
my childhood unto this day.
3 Behold, here I *am:* witness against
me before the LORD, and before his
anointed: whose ox have I taken? or
whose ass have I taken? or whom have
I defrauded? whom have I oppressed?
or of whose hand have I received *any*
bribe to blind mine eyes therewith? and
I will restore it you.
4 And they said, Thou hast not defrauded us, nor oppressed us, neither
hast thou taken ought of any man's hand.

11:4 came the messengers to Gibeah. The tribe of Benjamin had married wives from Jabesh-gilead many years before (Judg. 21:14), so the two tribes were closely related. Naturally, the messengers came here first to find help.

11:13 There shall not a man be put to death this day. Contrast Saul's gracious spirit here with his pride and severity in 1 Samuel 14:43-44.

5And he said unto them, The LORD *is*
witness against you, and his anointed *is*
witness this day, that ye have not found
ought in my hand. And they answered,
He is witness.
¶6And Samuel said unto the people,
It is the LORD that advanced *Moses
and *Aaron, and that brought your fathers up out of the land of Egypt.
7Now therefore stand still, that I may
reason with you before the LORD of all
the righteous acts of the LORD, which
he did to you and to your fathers.
8When *Jacob was come into Egypt,
and your fathers cried unto the LORD,
then the LORD sent Moses and Aaron,
which brought forth your fathers out of
Egypt, and made them dwell in this
place.
9And when they forgat the LORD
their God, he sold them into the hand
of Sisera, captain of the host of Hazor,
and into the hand of the Philistines, and
into the hand of the king of *Moab, and
they fought against them.
10And they cried unto the LORD, and
said, We have sinned, because we have
forsaken the LORD, and have served
Baalim and *Ashtaroth: but now deliver us out of the hand of our enemies,
and we will serve thee.
11And the LORD sent *Jerubbaal,
and Bedan, and Jephthah, and Samuel,
and delivered you out of the hand of
your enemies on every side, and ye
dwelled safe.
12And when ye saw that Nahash the
king of the children of Ammon came
against you, ye said unto me, Nay; but
a king shall reign over us: when the
LORD your God *was* your king.
13Now therefore behold the king
whom ye have chosen, *and* whom ye
have desired! and, behold, the LORD
hath set a king over you.
14If ye will fear the LORD, and serve
him, and obey his voice, and not rebel
against the commandment of the LORD,
then shall both ye and also the king that
reigneth over you continue following
the LORD your God:
15But if ye will not obey the voice of
the LORD, but rebel against the commandment of the LORD, then shall the
hand of the LORD be against you, as *it
was* against your fathers.
¶16Now therefore stand and see this
great thing, which the LORD will do
before your eyes.
17*Is it* not wheat harvest to day? I will
call unto the LORD, and he shall send
thunder and rain; that ye may perceive
and see that your wickedness *is* great,
which ye have done in the sight of the
LORD, in asking you a king.

12:17 A Sign from God
The time of wheat harvest in June was the dry season, when it almost never rained. A thunderstorm at such a time was a real sign from God.

18So Samuel called unto the LORD;
and the LORD sent thunder and rain that
day: and all the people greatly feared
the LORD and Samuel.
19And all the people said unto Samuel, Pray for thy servants unto the
LORD thy God, that we die not: for we
have added unto all our sins *this* evil, to
ask us a king.
¶20And Samuel said unto the people,
Fear not: ye have done all this wickedness: yet turn not aside from following
the LORD, but serve the LORD with all
your heart;
21And turn ye not aside: for *then
should ye go* after vain *things,* which
cannot profit nor deliver; for they *are*
vain.
22For the LORD will not forsake his
people for his great name's sake: because it hath pleased the LORD to make
you his people.
23Moreover as for me, God forbid
that I should *sin against the LORD in
ceasing to pray for you: but I will teach
you the good and the right way:
24Only fear the LORD, and serve him
in truth with all your heart: for consider how great *things* he hath done
for you.

25 But if ye shall still do wickedly, ye shall be consumed, both ye and your king.

Saul's sin against the law of priesthood

13 Saul reigned one year; and when he had reigned two years over *Israel,

2 Saul chose him three thousand *men* of Israel; *whereof* two thousand were with Saul in Michmash and in mount *Beth-el, and a thousand were with Jonathan in Gibeah of Benjamin: and the rest of the people he sent every man to his tent.

3 And Jonathan smote the garrison of the Philistines that *was* in Geba, and the Philistines heard *of it.* And Saul blew the trumpet throughout all the land, saying, Let the Hebrews hear.

4 And all Israel heard say *that* Saul had smitten a garrison of the Philistines, and *that* Israel also was had in *abomination with the Philistines. And the people were called together after Saul to Gilgal.

¶5 And the Philistines gathered themselves together to fight with Israel, thirty thousand chariots, and six thousand horsemen, and people as the sand which *is* on the sea shore in multitude: and they came up, and pitched in Michmash, eastward from *Beth-aven.

6 When the men of Israel saw that they were in a strait, (for the people were distressed,) then the people did hide themselves in caves, and in thickets, and in rocks, and in high places, and in pits.

7 And *some of* the Hebrews went over Jordan to the land of Gad and Gilead. As for Saul, he *was* yet in Gilgal, and all the people followed him trembling.

¶8 And he tarried seven days, according to the set time that *Samuel *had appointed:* but Samuel came not to Gilgal; and the people were scattered from him.

9 And Saul said, Bring hither a burnt-offering to me, and *peace-offerings. And he offered the burnt-offering.

10 And it came to pass, that as soon as he had made an end of offering the burnt-offering, behold, Samuel came; and Saul went out to meet him, that he might salute him.

¶11 And Samuel said, What hast thou done? And Saul said, Because I saw that the people were scattered from me, and *that* thou camest not within the days appointed, and *that* the Philistines gathered themselves together at Michmash;

12 Therefore said I, The Philistines will come down now upon me to Gilgal, and I have not made supplication unto the LORD: I forced myself therefore, and offered a burnt-offering.

13 And Samuel said to Saul, Thou hast done foolishly: thou hast not kept the commandment of the LORD thy *God, which he commanded thee: for now would the LORD have established thy kingdom upon Israel for ever.

14 But now thy kingdom shall not continue: the LORD hath sought him a man after his own heart, and the LORD hath commanded him *to be* captain over his people, because thou hast not kept *that* which the LORD commanded thee.

The weakness of Israel

15 And Samuel arose, and gat him up from Gilgal unto Gibeah of Benjamin. And Saul numbered the people *that were* present with him, about six hundred men.

16 And Saul, and Jonathan his son, and the people *that were* present with them, abode in Gibeah of Benjamin: but the Philistines encamped in Michmash.

¶17 And the spoilers came out of the

13:13 thou hast not kept the commandment. According to the Law given Israel at Mount Sinai, only a priest had the right to offer a sacrifice to God. See Numbers 16:1-3 note, "Korah," and Numbers 16:31 note, "Judgment of the Rebels."

13:17 spoilers. Those who loot and rob.

camp of the Philistines in three companies: one company turned unto the way
that leadeth to Ophrah, unto the land of
Shual:
18 And another company turned the
way *to* Beth-horon: and another company turned *to* the way of the border that
looketh to the valley of Zeboim toward
the wilderness.
¶ 19 Now there was no smith found
throughout all the land of Israel: for the
Philistines said, Lest the Hebrews
make *them* swords or spears:
20 But all the Israelites went down to
the Philistines, to sharpen every man
his share, and his coulter, and his axe,
and his mattock.
21 Yet they had a file for the mattocks,
and for the coulters, and for the forks,
and for the axes, and to sharpen the
goads.
22 So it came to pass in the day of battle, that there was neither sword nor
spear found in the hand of any of the
people that *were* with Saul and Jonathan: but with Saul and with Jonathan
his son was there found.
23 And the garrison of the Philistines
went out to the passage of Michmash.

Saul's haughty pride

14 Now it came to pass upon a
day, that Jonathan the son of
Saul said unto the young man that bare
his armour, Come, and let us go over to
the Philistines' garrison, that *is* on the
other side. But he told not his father.
2 And Saul tarried in the uttermost
part of Gibeah under a pomegranate
tree which *is* in Migron: and the people
that *were* with him *were* about six hundred men;
3 And Ahiah, the son of Ahitub,
I-chabod's brother, the son of *Phinehas,
the son of Eli, the LORD'S priest in *Shiloh, wearing an *ephod. And the people knew not that Jonathan was gone.
¶ 4 And between the passages, by
which Jonathan sought to go over unto
the Philistines' garrison, *there was* a
sharp rock on the one side and a sharp
rock on the other side: and the name of
the one *was* Bozez, and the name of the
other Seneh.
5 The forefront of the one *was* situate
northward over against Michmash, and
the other southward over against
Gibeah.
6 And Jonathan said to the young man
that bare his armour, Come, and let us
go over unto the garrison of these *uncircumcised: it may be that the LORD
will work for us: for *there is* no restraint
to the LORD to save by many or by few.
7 And his armourbearer said unto him,
Do all that *is* in thine heart: turn thee;
behold, I *am* with thee according to thy
heart.
8 Then said Jonathan, Behold, we will
pass over unto *these* men, and we will
discover ourselves unto them.
9 If they say thus unto us, Tarry until we
come to you; then we will stand still in
our place, and will not go up unto them.
10 But if they say thus, Come up unto
us; then we will go up: for the LORD
hath delivered them into our hand: and
this *shall be* a sign unto us.
11 And both of them discovered themselves unto the garrison of the Philistines: and the Philistines said, Behold,
the Hebrews come forth out of the
holes where they had hid themselves.
12 And the men of the garrison answered Jonathan and his armourbearer,
and said, Come up to us, and we will
shew you a thing. And Jonathan said
unto his armourbearer, Come up after

13:20 share. The part of a plow that cuts the ground at the bottom of a furrow.
13:20 coulter. A knife or cutter attached to the plow to cut the ground in front of the share.
13:20 mattock. A digging tool.
13:21 goads. Pointed rods used to make the animals go forward.
14:6 uncircumcised. A term of contempt used by Israelites in referring to Gentiles.
14:8 discover ourselves. Show ourselves.
14:11 hid themselves. See 1 Samuel 13:6.

me: for the LORD hath delivered them
into the hand of Israel.
13And Jonathan climbed up upon his
hands and upon his feet, and his
armourbearer after him: and they fell
before Jonathan; and his armourbearer
slew after him.
14And that first slaughter, which Jonathan and his armourbearer made, was
about twenty men, within as it were an
half acre of land, *which* a yoke *of oxen*
might plow.
15And there was trembling in the
host, in the field, and among all the people: the garrison, and the spoilers, they
also trembled, and the earth quaked: so
it was a very great trembling.
16And the watchmen of Saul in Gibeah of Benjamin looked; and, behold, the
multitude melted away, and they went
on beating down *one another.*
17Then said Saul unto the people that
were with him, Number now, and see
who is gone from us. And when they
had numbered, behold, Jonathan and his
armourbearer *were* not *there.*
18And Saul said unto Ahiah, Bring
hither the *ark of God. For the ark of
God was at that time with the children
of Israel.
¶19And it came to pass, while Saul
talked unto the priest, that the noise
that *was* in the host of the Philistines
went on and increased: and Saul said
unto the priest, Withdraw thine hand.
20And Saul and all the people that
were with him assembled themselves,
and they came to the battle: and, behold, every man's sword was against
his fellow, *and there was* a very great
discomfiture.
21Moreover the Hebrews *that* were
with the Philistines before that time,
which went up with them into the camp
from the country round about, even they
also *turned* to be with the Israelites that
were with Saul and Jonathan.
22Likewise all the men of Israel
which had hid themselves in mount
Ephraim, *when* they heard that the Philistines fled, even they also followed
hard after them in the battle.
23So the LORD saved Israel that day:
and the battle passed over unto Beth-
aven.
¶24And the men of Israel were distressed that day: for Saul had adjured
the people, saying, Cursed *be* the man
that eateth *any* food until evening, that
I may be avenged on mine enemies. So
none of the people tasted *any* food.
25And all *they of* the land came to a
wood; and there was honey upon the
ground.
26And when the people were come
into the wood, behold, the honey
dropped; but no man put his hand to his
mouth: for the people feared the oath.
27But Jonathan heard not when his
father charged the people with the oath:
wherefore he put forth the end of the
rod that *was* in his hand, and dipped it
in an honeycomb, and put his hand to
his mouth; and his eyes were enlightened.
28Then answered one of the people,
and said, Thy father straitly charged the
people with an oath, saying, Cursed *be*
the man that eateth *any* food this day.
And the people were faint.
29Then said Jonathan, My father hath
troubled the land: see, I pray you, how

14:13 fell before Jonathan. See the promise in Leviticus 26:8.

14:18 Bring hither the ark. Saul was making the same mistake as Israel did (1 Sam. 4:10–6:1) by using the ark as a "good luck" charm to help win the battle. The ark was at Kirjath-jearim (see 1 Sam. 7:1 note, "A New Location for the Ark"), a long way from Gibeah, where Saul's camp was.

14:24 that I may be avenged. Saul, rejected by God (1 Sam. 13:14), declared a day of fasting in the hope that such an outward form of piety would persuade God to come to Saul's help against his enemies.

14:27 his eyes were enlightened. This means that he became stronger after he had satisfied his hunger, for the sweet honey renewed his energy. See Ephesians 1:18.

mine eyes have been enlightened, because I tasted a little of this honey.

30 How much more, if haply the people had eaten freely to day of the spoil of their enemies which they found? for had there not been now a much greater slaughter among the Philistines?

31 And they smote the Philistines that day from Michmash to Aijalon: and the people were very faint.

32 And the people flew upon the spoil, and took sheep, and oxen, and calves, and slew *them* on the ground: and the people did eat *them* with the blood.

¶ 33 Then they told Saul, saying, Behold, the people sin against the LORD, in that they eat with the blood. And he said, Ye have transgressed: roll a great stone unto me this day.

34 And Saul said, Disperse yourselves among the people, and say unto them, Bring me hither every man his ox, and every man his sheep, and slay *them* here, and eat; and sin not against the LORD in eating with the blood. And all the people brought every man his ox with him that night, and slew *them* there.

35 And Saul built an *altar unto the LORD: the same was the first altar that he built unto the LORD.

¶ 36 And Saul said, Let us go down after the Philistines by night, and spoil them until the morning light, and let us not leave a man of them. And they said, Do whatsoever seemeth good unto thee. Then said the priest, Let us draw near hither unto God.

37 And Saul asked counsel of God, Shall I go down after the Philistines? wilt thou deliver them into the hand of Israel? But he answered him not that day.

38 And Saul said, Draw ye near hither, all the chief of the people: and know and see wherein this sin hath been this day.

39 For, *as* the LORD liveth, which saveth Israel, though it be in Jonathan my son, he shall surely die. But *there* *was* not a man among all the people *that* answered him.

40 Then said he unto all Israel, Be ye on one side, and I and Jonathan my son will be on the other side. And the people said unto Saul, Do what seemeth good unto thee.

41 Therefore Saul said unto the LORD God of Israel, Give a perfect *lot.* And Saul and Jonathan were taken: but the people escaped.

42 And Saul said, Cast *lots* between me and Jonathan my son. And Jonathan was taken.

14:41-42 Casting Lots
It was common practice in Old Testament days to learn the will of God by casting lots (in some cases in the Old Testament, this was done with the *Urim and the Thummim). However, after the Holy Spirit came to dwell in Christians, the casting of lots was no longer needed and so it ceased, because the Holy Spirit is within believers to teach us the will of God, and we now have the full revelation of God in the Old and New Testaments.

43 Then Saul said to Jonathan, Tell me what thou hast done. And Jonathan told him, and said, I did but taste a little honey with the end of the rod that *was* in mine hand, *and,* lo, I must die.

44 And Saul answered, God do so and more also: for thou shalt surely die, Jonathan.

45 And the people said unto Saul, Shall Jonathan die, who hath wrought this great salvation in Israel? God forbid: *as* the LORD liveth, there shall not one hair of his head fall to the ground; for he hath wrought with God this day. So the people rescued Jonathan, that he died not.

46 Then Saul went up from following the Philistines: and the Philistines went to their own place.

¶ 47 So Saul took the kingdom over Israel, and fought against all his enemies on every side, against Moab, and against the children of Ammon, and

14:32 with the blood. This was a violation of God's word. Read Leviticus 17:10-14.

against *Edom, and against the kings of Zobah, and against the Philistines: and whithersoever he turned himself, he vexed *them.*

48And he gathered an host, and smote the Amalekites, and delivered Israel out of the hands of them that spoiled them.

49Now the sons of Saul were Jonathan, and Ishui, and Melchi-shua: and the names of his two daughters *were these;* the name of the firstborn Merab, and the name of the younger Michal:

50And the name of Saul's wife *was* Ahinoam, the daughter of Ahimaaz: and the name of the captain of his host *was* Abner, the son of Ner, Saul's uncle.

51And Kish *was* the father of Saul; and Ner the father of Abner *was* the son of Abiel.

52And there was sore war against the Philistines all the days of Saul: and when Saul saw any strong man, or any valiant man, he took him unto him.

Saul's disobedience and rejection

15 Samuel also said unto Saul, The LORD sent me to *anoint thee *to be* king over his people, over Israel: now therefore hearken thou unto the voice of the words of the LORD.

2Thus saith the LORD of hosts, I remember *that* which *Amalek did to Israel, how he laid *wait* for him in the way, when he came up from *Egypt.

3Now go and smite Amalek, and utterly destroy all that they have, and spare them not; but slay both man and woman, infant and suckling, ox and sheep, camel and ass.

4And Saul gathered the people together, and numbered them in Telaim, two hundred thousand footmen, and ten thousand men of Judah.

5And Saul came to a city of Amalek, and laid wait in the valley.

¶6And Saul said unto the *Kenites, Go, depart, get you down from among the Amalekites, lest I destroy you with them: for ye shewed kindness to all the children of Israel, when they came up out of Egypt. So the Kenites departed from among the Amalekites.

7And Saul smote the Amalekites from Havilah *until* thou comest to Shur, that *is* over against Egypt.

8And he took Agag the king of the Amalekites alive, and utterly destroyed all the people with the edge of the sword.

9But Saul and the people spared Agag, and the best of the sheep, and of the oxen, and of the fatlings, and the lambs, and all *that was* good, and would not utterly destroy them: but every thing *that was* vile and refuse, that they destroyed utterly.

¶10Then came the word of the LORD unto Samuel, saying,

11It repenteth me that I have set up Saul *to be* king: for he is turned back from following me, and hath not performed my commandments. And it grieved Samuel; and he cried unto the LORD all night.

12And when Samuel rose early to meet Saul in the morning, it was told Samuel, saying, Saul came to *Carmel, and, behold, he set him up a place, and is gone about, and passed on, and gone down to Gilgal.

13And Samuel came to Saul: and Saul said unto him, Blessed *be* thou of the LORD: I have performed the commandment of the LORD.

14And Samuel said, What *meaneth* then this bleating of the sheep in mine ears, and the lowing of the oxen which I hear?

15And Saul said, They have brought them from the Amalekites: for the people spared the best of the sheep and of the oxen, to *sacrifice unto the LORD thy God; and the rest we have utterly destroyed.

14:52 he took him. Read the warning of Samuel in 1 Samuel 8:11-16.

15:12 he set him up a place. Saul erected a memorial to himself to commemorate his victory.

15:14 Saul's Disobedience
Saul disobeyed God but pretended that he had obeyed. He destroyed all that was of no use, but he spared for himself the best of the sheep and oxen. Samuel, the LORD's messenger, heard the animals bleating and lowing. There are sometimes "bleating sheep" and "lowing oxen" in Christians' lives today. We put aside all that we do not want but spare, or hold onto, the worldly things that we like best. See what God says about this (vss. 22-23).

16Then Samuel said unto Saul, Stay, and I will tell thee what the LORD hath said to me this night. And he said unto him, Say on.
17And Samuel said, When thou *wast* little in thine own sight, *wast* thou not *made* the head of the tribes of Israel, and the LORD anointed thee king over Israel?
18And the LORD sent thee on a journey, and said, Go and utterly destroy the sinners the Amalekites, and fight against them until they be consumed.
19Wherefore then didst thou not obey the voice of the LORD, but didst fly upon the spoil, and didst evil in the sight of the LORD?
20And Saul said unto Samuel, Yea, I have obeyed the voice of the LORD, and have gone the way which the LORD sent me, and have brought Agag the king of Amalek, and have utterly destroyed the Amalekites.
21But the people took of the spoil, sheep and oxen, the chief of the things which should have been utterly destroyed, to sacrifice unto the LORD thy God in Gilgal.
22And Samuel said, Hath the LORD *as great* delight in burnt-offerings and sacrifices, as in obeying the voice of the LORD? Behold, to obey *is* better than sacrifice, *and* to hearken than the fat of rams.
23For rebellion *is as* the sin of witchcraft, and stubbornness *is as* iniquity and *idolatry. Because thou hast rejected the word of the LORD, he hath also rejected thee from *being* king.
¶24And Saul said unto Samuel, I have sinned: for I have transgressed the commandment of the LORD, and thy words: because I feared the people, and obeyed their voice.
25Now therefore, I pray thee, pardon my sin, and turn again with me, that I may worship the LORD.
26And Samuel said unto Saul, I will not return with thee: for thou hast rejected the word of the LORD, and the LORD hath rejected thee from being king over Israel.
27And as Samuel turned about to go away, he laid hold upon the skirt of his mantle, and it rent.
28And Samuel said unto him, The LORD hath rent the kingdom of Israel from thee this day, and hath given it to a neighbour of thine, *that is* better than thou.
29And also the Strength of Israel will not lie nor *repent: for he *is* not a man, that he should repent.
30Then he said, I have sinned: *yet* honour me now, I pray thee, before the elders of my people, and before Israel, and turn again with me, that I may worship the LORD thy God.
31So Samuel turned again after Saul; and Saul worshipped the LORD.
¶32Then said Samuel, Bring ye hither to me Agag the king of the Amalekites. And Agag came unto him delicately. And Agag said, Surely the bitterness of death is past.
33And Samuel said, As thy sword hath made women childless, so shall thy mother be childless among women. And Samuel hewed Agag in pieces before the LORD in Gilgal.
¶34Then Samuel went to Ramah; and Saul went up to his house to Gibeah of Saul.
35And Samuel came no more to see Saul until the day of his death: never-

15:32 delicately. Daintily, effeminately.

theless Samuel mourned for Saul: and the LORD repented that he had made Saul king over Israel.

IV. David, the New King, Is Exiled until Saul's Death (16:1—31:13)

God chooses a new king

16 And the LORD said unto Samuel, How long wilt thou mourn for Saul, seeing I have rejected him from reigning over Israel? fill thine horn with *oil, and go, I will send thee to Jesse the Bethlehemite: for I have provided me a king among his sons.

2 And Samuel said, How can I go? if Saul hear *it,* he will kill me. And the LORD said, Take an heifer with thee, and say, I am come to sacrifice to the LORD.

3 And call Jesse to the sacrifice, and I will shew thee what thou shalt do: and thou shalt anoint unto me *him* whom I name unto thee.

4 And Samuel did that which the LORD spake, and came to Beth-lehem. And the elders of the town trembled at his coming, and said, Comest thou peaceably?

5 And he said, Peaceably: I am come to sacrifice unto the LORD: sanctify yourselves, and come with me to the sacrifice. And he sanctified Jesse and his sons, and called them to the sacrifice.

¶6 And it came to pass, when they were come, that he looked on Eliab, and said, Surely the LORD'S anointed *is* before him.

7 But the LORD said unto Samuel, Look not on his countenance, or on the height of his stature; because I have refused him: for *the LORD seeth* not as man seeth; for man looketh on the outward appearance, but the LORD looketh on the heart.

8 Then Jesse called Abinadab, and made him pass before Samuel. And he said, Neither hath the LORD chosen this.

9 Then Jesse made Shammah to pass by. And he said, Neither hath the LORD chosen this.

10 Again, Jesse made seven of his sons to pass before Samuel. And Samuel said unto Jesse, The LORD hath not chosen these.

11 And Samuel said unto Jesse, Are here all *thy* children? And he said, There remaineth yet the youngest, and, behold, he keepeth the sheep. And Samuel said unto Jesse, Send and fetch him: for we will not sit down till he come hither.

12 And he sent, and brought him in. Now he *was* ruddy, *and* withal of a beautiful countenance, and goodly to look to. And the LORD said, Arise, anoint him: for this *is* he.

13 Then Samuel took the horn of oil, and anointed him in the midst of his brethren: and the Spirit of the LORD came upon *David from that day forward. So Samuel rose up, and went to Ramah.

David at the court of Saul

¶14 But the Spirit of the LORD departed from Saul, and an evil spirit from the LORD troubled him.

15 And Saul's servants said unto him, Behold now, an evil spirit from God troubleth thee.

16 Let our lord now command thy servants, *which are* before thee, to seek out a man, *who is* a cunning player on an harp: and it shall come to pass, when the evil spirit from God is upon thee,

---

16:5 I am come to sacrifice. Since the fall of Shiloh (1 Sam. 4), there had been no regular tabernacle service. Samuel, acting as priest, went from town to town, calling the people together for a time of confession and worship.

16:14 Spirit of the LORD departed. Read 1 Samuel 10:10 note, "Saul's Prophecy." It was because David saw the awful result in Saul's life when God's Spirit left him that he later feared the same things might happen to himself. David prayed in Psalm 51:11 that God would not allow that to happen to him, in spite of David's sin.

16:14 evil spirit from the LORD. The LORD permitted an evil spirit to come upon Saul to teach him the awful results of sin.

that he shall play with his hand, and
thou shalt be well.
[17]And Saul said unto his servants,
Provide me now a man that can play
well, and bring *him* to me.
[18]Then answered one of the servants,
and said, Behold, I have seen a son of
Jesse the Beth-lehemite, *that is* cunning in playing, and a mighty valiant
man, and a man of war, and prudent in
matters, and a comely person, and the
LORD *is* with him.
¶[19]Wherefore Saul sent messengers
unto Jesse, and said, Send me David thy
son, which *is* with the sheep.
[20]And Jesse took an ass *laden* with
bread, and a bottle of wine, and a kid,
and sent *them* by David his son unto
Saul.
[21]And David came to Saul, and stood
before him: and he loved him greatly;
and he became his armourbearer.
[22]And Saul sent to Jesse, saying, Let
David, I pray thee, stand before me; for
he hath found favour in my sight.
[23]And it came to pass, when the *evil*
spirit from God was upon Saul, that
David took an harp, and played with
his hand: so Saul was refreshed, and
was well, and the evil spirit departed
from him.

Saul's cowardice and David's courage

17 Now the *Philistines gathered
together their armies to battle,
and were gathered together at Shochoh,
which *belongeth* to *Judah, and pitched
between Shochoh and Azekah, in
Ephes-dammim.
[2]And Saul and the men of Israel were
gathered together, and pitched by the
valley of Elah, and set the battle in array against the Philistines.
[3]And the Philistines stood on a
mountain on the one side, and Israel
stood on a mountain on the other side:
and *there was* a valley between them.

Goliath's challenge

¶[4]And there went out a champion out
of the camp of the Philistines, named
Goliath, of *Gath, whose height *was* six
*cubits and a *span.
[5]And *he had* an helmet of brass upon
his head, and he *was* armed with a coat
of mail; and the weight of the coat *was*
five thousand shekels of brass.
[6]And *he had* greaves of brass upon his
legs, and a target of brass between his
shoulders.
[7]And the staff of his spear *was* like a
weaver's beam; and his spear's head
weighed six hundred shekels of iron: and
one bearing a shield went before him.
[8]And he stood and cried unto the armies of Israel, and said unto them, Why
are ye come out to set *your* battle in
array? *am* not I a Philistine, and ye servants to Saul? choose you a man for
you, and let him come down to me.
[9]If he be able to fight with me, and
to kill me, then will we be your servants: but if I prevail against him, and
kill him, then shall ye be our servants,
and serve us.
[10]And the Philistine said, I defy the
armies of Israel this day; give me a
man, that we may fight together.
[11]When Saul and all Israel heard
those words of the Philistine, they were
dismayed, and greatly afraid.
¶[12]Now David *was* the son of that

17:1 Goliath

Goliath, who was about nine feet, three inches tall, was one of the few remaining descendants of the giants who had once lived in Canaan. See Numbers 13:22 note, "Giants in the Land"; compare Deuteronomy 2:9 note.

17:5 five thousand shekels. Though the weight of the shekel varied in different countries, the coat of armor that Goliath wore probably weighed about 126 pounds.
17:6 greaves. Armor to protect the legs from the knee to the ankle.
17:6 target. A light shield.
17:7 six hundred shekels. Probably about fifteen pounds.

Ephrathite of Beth-lehem-judah, whose
name *was* Jesse; and he had eight sons:
and the man went among men *for* an old
man in the days of Saul.
13 And the three eldest sons of Jesse
went *and* followed Saul to the battle:
and the names of his three sons that
went to the battle *were* Eliab the firstborn, and next unto him Abinadab, and
the third Shammah.
14 And David *was* the youngest: and
the three eldest followed Saul.

David's errand to the army

15 But David went and returned from
Saul to feed his father's sheep at Beth-
lehem.
16 And the Philistine drew near morning and evening, and presented himself
forty days.
17 And Jesse said unto David his son,
Take now for thy brethren an *ephah of
this parched *corn,* and these ten loaves,
and run to the camp to thy brethren;
18 And carry these ten cheeses unto
the captain of *their* thousand, and look
how thy brethren fare, and take their
pledge.
19 Now Saul, and they, and all the men
of Israel, *were* in the valley of Elah,
fighting with the Philistines.
¶20 And David rose up early in the
morning, and left the sheep with a
keeper, and took, and went, as Jesse had
commanded him; and he came to the
trench, as the host was going forth to
the fight, and shouted for the battle.
21 For Israel and the Philistines had put
the battle in array, army against army.
22 And David left his carriage in the
hand of the keeper of the carriage, and
ran into the army, and came and saluted
his brethren.
23 And as he talked with them, behold,
there came up the champion, the Philistine of Gath, Goliath by name, out of
the armies of the Philistines, and spake
according to the same words: and David heard *them.*
24 And all the men of Israel, when
they saw the man, fled from him, and
were sore afraid.
25 And the men of Israel said, Have ye
seen this man that is come up? surely
to defy Israel is he come up: and it shall
be, *that* the man who killeth him, the
king will enrich him with great riches,
and will give him his daughter, and
make his father's house free in Israel.
26 And David spake to the men that
stood by him, saying, What shall be
done to the man that killeth this Philistine, and taketh away the reproach from
Israel? for who *is* this uncircumcised
Philistine, that he should defy the armies of the living God?
27 And the people answered him after
this manner, saying, So shall it be done
to the man that killeth him.
¶28 And Eliab his eldest brother heard
when he spake unto the men; and Eliab's anger was kindled against David,
and he said, Why camest thou down
hither? and with whom hast thou left
those few sheep in the wilderness? I
know thy pride, and the naughtiness of
thine heart; for thou art come down that
thou mightest see the battle.
29 And David said, What have I now
done? *Is there* not a cause?
¶30 And he turned from him toward
another, and spake after the same manner: and the people answered him again
after the former manner.

David's victory over Goliath

31 And when the words were heard
which David spake, they rehearsed

17:20 the trench. This was the circle of wagons around the encampment.

17:22 David left his carriage. This means that David left his baggage with the keeper who was looking after the wagons and the other baggage of the army.

17:29 What have I now done? Eliab had made fun of his younger brother in front of the soldiers (vs. 28), but David controlled his temper and answered quietly. This victory over himself was greater than his conquest of Goliath.

them before Saul: and he sent for him.

¶ 32 And David said to Saul, Let no man's heart fail because of him; thy servant will go and fight with this Philistine.

33 And Saul said to David, Thou art not able to go against this Philistine to fight with him: for thou *art but* a youth, and he a man of war from his youth.

34 And David said unto Saul, Thy servant kept his father's sheep, and there came a lion, and a bear, and took a lamb out of the flock:

35 And I went out after him, and smote him, and delivered *it* out of his mouth: and when he arose against me, I caught *him* by his beard, and smote him, and slew him.

36 Thy servant slew both the lion and the bear: and this uncircumcised Philistine shall be as one of them, seeing he hath defied the armies of the living God.

37 David said moreover, The LORD that delivered me out of the paw of the lion, and out of the paw of the bear, he will deliver me out of the hand of this Philistine. And Saul said unto David, Go, and the LORD be with thee.

¶ 38 And Saul armed David with his armour, and he put an helmet of brass upon his head; also he armed him with a coat of mail.

39 And David girded his sword upon his armour, and he assayed to go; for he had not proved *it.* And David said unto Saul, I cannot go with these; for I have not proved *them.* And David put them off him.

40 And he took his staff in his hand, and chose him five smooth stones out of the brook, and put them in a shepherd's bag which he had, even in a scrip; and his sling *was* in his hand: and he drew near to the Philistine.

41 And the Philistine came on and drew near unto David; and the man that bare the shield *went* before him.

42 And when the Philistine looked about, and saw David, he disdained him: for he was *but* a youth, and ruddy, and of a fair countenance.

43 And the Philistine said unto David, *Am* I a dog, that thou comest to me with staves? And the Philistine cursed David by his gods.

44 And the Philistine said to David, Come to me, and I will give thy flesh unto the fowls of the air, and to the beasts of the field.

45 Then said David to the Philistine, Thou comest to me with a sword, and with a spear, and with a shield: but I come to thee in the name of the LORD of hosts, the God of the armies of Israel, whom thou hast defied.

17:45 In the Name of the LORD
To do anything in the name of the LORD means to do it just for His honor and pleasure, with no selfish motive. David did not fight Goliath in order to get the rewards offered by Saul (vs. 25) but only to prove the reality and power of the living God whom the Philistines had despised.

46 This day will the LORD deliver thee into mine hand; and I will smite thee, and take thine head from thee; and I will give the carcases of the host of the Philistines this day unto the fowls of the air, and to the wild beasts of the earth; that all the earth may know that there is a God in Israel.

47 And all this assembly shall know that the LORD saveth not with sword and spear: for the battle *is* the LORD'S, and he will give you into our hands.

48 And it came to pass, when the Philistine arose, and came and drew nigh to meet David, that David hasted, and ran toward the army to meet the Philistine.

49 And David put his hand in his bag, and took thence a stone, and slang *it,* and smote the Philistine in his forehead, that the stone sunk into his forehead; and he fell upon his face to the earth.

17:40 a scrip. A small bag or wallet.

50 So David prevailed over the Philistine with a sling and with a stone, and smote the Philistine, and slew him; but *there was* no sword in the hand of David.

51 Therefore David ran, and stood upon the Philistine, and took his sword, and drew it out of the sheath thereof, and slew him, and cut off his head therewith. And when the Philistines saw their champion was dead, they fled.

52 And the men of Israel and of Judah arose, and shouted, and pursued the Philistines, until thou come to the valley, and to the gates of Ekron. And the wounded of the Philistines fell down by the way to Shaaraim, even unto Gath, and unto Ekron.

53 And the children of Israel returned from chasing after the Philistines, and they spoiled their tents.

54 And David took the head of the Philistine, and brought it to *Jerusalem; but he put his armour in his tent.

¶55 And when Saul saw David go forth against the Philistine, he said unto Abner, the captain of the host, Abner, whose son *is* this youth? And Abner said, *As* thy soul liveth, O king, I cannot tell.

17:55 Who Are You?
When Saul asked, "Whose son is this youth?" it does not mean that Saul had forgotten David, who had been with him before (see 1 Sam. 16:19-23). The king asked about the family from which had come such a courageous fighter as David. Saul was not particularly interested in the family tree of an armor-bearer or one who played the harp. But this young man might soon marry the king's daughter (vs. 25), and Saul wanted to know more about him now.

56 And the king said, Enquire thou whose son the stripling *is*.

57 And as David returned from the slaughter of the Philistine, Abner took him, and brought him before Saul with the head of the Philistine in his hand.

58 And Saul said to him, Whose son *art* thou, *thou* young man? And David answered, *I am* the son of thy servant Jesse the Bethlehemite.

The friendship of David and Jonathan

18 And it came to pass, when he had made an end of speaking unto Saul, that the soul of Jonathan was knit with the soul of David, and Jonathan loved him as his own soul.

2 And Saul took him that day, and would let him go no more home to his father's house.

3 Then Jonathan and David made a *covenant, because he loved him as his own soul.

4 And Jonathan stripped himself of the robe that *was* upon him, and gave it to David, and his garments, even to his sword, and to his bow, and to his girdle.

¶5 And David went out whithersoever Saul sent him, *and* behaved himself wisely: and Saul set him over the men of war, and he was accepted in the sight of all the people, and also in the sight of Saul's servants.

6 And it came to pass as they came, when David was returned from the slaughter of the Philistine, that the women came out of all cities of Israel, singing and dancing, to meet king Saul, with *tabrets, with joy, and with instruments of musick.

7 And the women answered *one another* as they played, and said, Saul hath slain his thousands, and David his ten thousands.

Saul's jealousy of David

8 And Saul was very wroth, and the saying displeased him; and he said, They have ascribed unto David ten thousands, and to me they have ascribed *but* thousands: and *what* can he have more but the kingdom?

17:56 stripling. A youth.
18:8 wroth. Angry.

9And Saul eyed David from that day
and forward.

¶10And it came to pass on the morrow, that the evil spirit from God came
upon Saul, and he prophesied in the
midst of the house: and David played
with his hand, as at other times: and
there was a javelin in Saul's hand.

11And Saul cast the javelin; for he
said, I will smite David even to the wall
with it. And David avoided out of his
presence twice.

¶12And Saul was afraid of David, because the LORD was with him, and was
departed from Saul.

13Therefore Saul removed him from
him, and made him his captain over a
thousand; and he went out and came in
before the people.

14And David behaved himself wisely
in all his ways; and the LORD *was* with
him.

15Wherefore when Saul saw that he
behaved himself very wisely, he was
afraid of him.

16But all Israel and Judah loved David, because he went out and came in
before them.

¶17And Saul said to David, Behold my
elder daughter Merab, her will I give
thee to wife: only be thou valiant for
me, and fight the LORD'S battles. For
Saul said, Let not mine hand be upon
him, but let the hand of the Philistines
be upon him.

18And David said unto Saul, Who *am*
I? and what *is* my life, *or* my father's
family in Israel, that I should be son in
law to the king?

19But it came to pass at the time
when Merab Saul's daughter should
have been given to David, that she was
given unto Adriel the Meholathite to
wife.

David's marriage to Saul's daughter

20And Michal Saul's daughter loved
David: and they told Saul, and the thing
pleased him.

21And Saul said, I will give him her,
that she may be a snare to him, and that
the hand of the Philistines may be
against him. Wherefore Saul said to
David, Thou shalt this day be my son
in law in *the one of* the twain.

¶22And Saul commanded his servants, *saying,* Commune with David
secretly, and say, Behold, the king hath
delight in thee, and all his servants
love thee: now therefore be the king's
son in law.

23And Saul's servants spake those
words in the ears of David. And David
said, Seemeth it to you *a* light *thing* to
be a king's son in law, seeing that I *am*
a poor man, and lightly esteemed?

24And the servants of Saul told him,
saying, On this manner spake David.

25And Saul said, Thus shall ye say to
David, The king desireth not any dowry,
but an hundred foreskins of the Philistines, to be avenged of the king's enemies. But Saul thought to make David
fall by the hand of the Philistines.

26And when his servants told David
these words, it pleased David well to be
the king's son in law: and the days were
not expired.

27Wherefore David arose and went,
he and his men, and slew of the Philistines two hundred men; and David
brought their foreskins, and they gave
them in full tale to the king, that he
might be the king's son in law. And Saul
gave him Michal his daughter to wife.

¶28And Saul saw and knew that the
LORD *was* with David, and *that* Michal
Saul's daughter loved him.

29And Saul was yet the more afraid of

18:9 eyed. Saul watched David suspiciously.

18:10 he prophesied. When the evil spirit came upon Saul, he was so controlled by a supernatural power that he spoke in the same unusual manner as those who were controlled by the Holy Spirit. (See 1 Sam. 10:10 note, "Saul's Prophecy").

18:10 played with his hand. Played music with his hand.

18:11 avoided. Escaped or withdrew.

David; and Saul became David's enemy
continually.
30Then the princes of the Philistines
went forth: and it came to pass, after
they went forth, *that* David behaved
himself more wisely than all the servants of Saul; so that his name was
much set by.

Jonathan protects David

19 And Saul spake to Jonathan his
son, and to all his servants, that
they should kill David.
2But Jonathan Saul's son delighted
much in David: and Jonathan told David, saying, Saul my father seeketh to
kill thee: now therefore, I pray thee,
take heed to thyself until the morning,
and abide in a secret *place,* and hide
thyself:
3And I will go out and stand beside
my father in the field where thou *art,*
and I will commune with my father of
thee; and what I see, that I will tell thee.
¶4And Jonathan spake good of David
unto Saul his father, and said unto him,
Let not the king *sin against his servant, against David; because he hath
not sinned against thee, and because his
works *have been* to thee-ward very
good:
5For he did put his life in his hand, and
slew the Philistine, and the LORD
wrought a great *salvation for all *Israel: thou sawest *it,* and didst rejoice:
wherefore then wilt thou sin against
innocent blood, to slay David without a
cause?
6And Saul hearkened unto the voice
of Jonathan: and Saul sware, *As* the
LORD liveth, he shall not be slain.
7And Jonathan called David, and Jonathan shewed him all those things. And
Jonathan brought David to Saul, and he
was in his presence, as in times past.
¶8And there was war again: and David went out, and fought with the Philistines, and slew them with a great
slaughter; and they fled from him.
9And the evil spirit from the LORD
was upon Saul, as he sat in his house
with his javelin in his hand: and David
played with *his* hand.
10And Saul sought to smite David
even to the wall with the javelin; but he
slipped away out of Saul's presence, and
he smote the javelin into the wall: and
David fled, and escaped that night.

Michal protects David

11Saul also sent messengers unto
David's house, to watch him, and to slay
him in the morning: and Michal David's
wife told him, saying, If thou save not
thy life to night, to morrow thou shalt
be slain.
¶12So Michal let David down through
a window: and he went, and fled, and
escaped.
13And Michal took an image, and laid
it in the bed, and put a pillow of goats'
hair for his bolster, and covered *it* with
a cloth.
14And when Saul sent messengers to
take David, she said, He *is* sick.
15And Saul sent the messengers
again to see David, saying, Bring him
up to me in the bed, that I may slay him.
16And when the messengers were
come in, behold, *there was* an image in
the bed, with a pillow of goats' *hair* for
his bolster.
17And Saul said unto Michal, Why
hast thou deceived me so, and sent
away mine enemy, that he is escaped?
And Michal answered Saul, He said
unto me, Let me go; why should I kill
thee?

The Holy Spirit protects David

¶18So David fled, and escaped, and
came to *Samuel to Ramah, and told
him all that Saul had done to him. And
he and Samuel went and dwelt in Naioth.
19And it was told Saul, saying, Behold, David *is* at Naioth in Ramah.
20And Saul sent messengers to take

18:30 that his name was much set by. David was highly regarded.

David: and when they saw the company of the *prophets prophesying, and
Samuel standing *as* appointed over
them, the Spirit of God was upon the
messengers of Saul, and they also
prophesied.
21 And when it was told Saul, he sent
other messengers, and they prophesied
likewise. And Saul sent messengers
again the third time, and they prophesied also.
22 Then went he also to Ramah, and
came to a great well that *is* in Sechu:
and he asked and said, Where *are* Samuel and David? And *one* said, Behold,
they be at Naioth in Ramah.
23 And he went thither to Naioth in
Ramah: and the Spirit of God was upon
him also, and he went on, and prophesied, until he came to Naioth in Ramah.
24 And he stripped off his clothes also,
and prophesied before Samuel in like
manner, and lay down naked all that day
and all that night. Wherefore they say,
Is Saul also among the prophets?

Jonathan again protects David

20 And David fled from Naioth in
Ramah, and came and said before Jonathan, What have I done? what
is mine iniquity? and what *is* my sin before thy father, that he seeketh my life?
2 And he said unto him, God forbid;
thou shalt not die: behold, my father
will do nothing either great or small, but
that he will shew it me: and why should
my father hide this thing from me? it *is*
not *so*.
3 And David sware moreover, and
said, Thy father certainly knoweth that
I have found grace in thine eyes; and he
saith, Let not Jonathan know this, lest
he be grieved: but truly *as* the LORD
liveth, and *as* thy soul liveth, *there is* but
a step between me and *death.
4 Then said Jonathan unto David,
Whatsoever thy soul desireth, I will
even do *it* for thee.
5 And David said unto Jonathan, Behold, to morrow *is* the new moon, and
I should not fail to sit with the king at
meat: but let me go, that I may hide
myself in the field unto the third *day* at
even.
6 If thy father at all miss me, then say,
David earnestly asked *leave* of me that
he might run to Beth-lehem his city: for
there is a yearly sacrifice there for all the
family.
7 If he say thus, *It is* well; thy servant
shall have *peace: but if he be very
wroth, *then* be sure that evil is determined by him.
8 Therefore thou shalt deal kindly

19:24 A PROPHET

The word "prophet" occurs 287 times in the Old Testament and means *one who speaks for God* with a message. Sometimes the word "seer" is used as one with a vision. The prophet was one who speaks forth a message communicated to him through divine inspiration. In biblical usage, the word retains its specific meaning. The power to foretell is more incidental to the prophetic gift than characteristic of it.

The essential qualities of the prophet are: inspiration and insight; and the power to speak. The second characteristic is borne out by the application of the word to:

1. the Old Testament prophets;
2. John the Baptist;
3. the Messiah; and
4. anyone who speaks in God's name and under His inspiration.

In Titus 1:12 the term "prophet" is applied to a Greek poet, since the poetic gift was considered a form of inspiration.

20:5 new moon. The first day of each month (determined by the new moon) was a special day of sacrifice, rest, and feasting (Num. 10:10; 28:11-15).

20:6 then say. This was not true, because David did not go to Beth-lehem. It seemed like a harmless lie, but it led to a series of falsehoods with disastrous results (1 Sam. 20:29; 21:2,10,13; 22:22). Satan is the father of lies (John 8:44).

with thy servant; for thou hast brought
thy servant into a covenant of the LORD
with thee: notwithstanding, if there be
in me iniquity, slay me thyself; for why
shouldest thou bring me to thy father?
9And Jonathan said, Far be it from
thee: for if I knew certainly that evil
were determined by my father to come
upon thee, then would not I tell it thee?
10Then said David to Jonathan, Who
shall tell me? or what *if* thy father answer thee roughly?
¶11And Jonathan said unto David,
Come, and let us go out into the field.
And they went out both of them into the
field.
12And Jonathan said unto David,
O LORD God of Israel, when I have
sounded my father about to morrow any
time, *or* the third *day,* and, behold, *if
there be* good toward David, and I then
send not unto thee, and shew it thee;
13The LORD do so and much more to
Jonathan: but if it please my father *to do*
thee evil, then I will shew it thee, and
send thee away, that thou mayest go in
peace: and the LORD be with thee, as he
hath been with my father.
14And thou shalt not only while yet I
live shew me the kindness of the LORD,
that I die not:
15But *also* thou shalt not cut off thy
kindness from my house for ever: no,
not when the LORD hath cut off the enemies of David every one from the face
of the earth.
16So Jonathan made *a covenant* with
the house of David, *saying,* Let the
LORD even require *it* at the hand of
David's enemies.
17And Jonathan caused David to
swear again, because he loved him: for
he loved him as he loved his own soul.
18Then Jonathan said to David, To
morrow *is* the new moon: and thou
shalt be missed, because thy seat will
be empty.
19And *when* thou hast stayed three
days, *then* thou shalt go down quickly,
and come to the place where thou didst
hide thyself when the business was *in
hand,* and shalt remain by the stone
Ezel.
20And I will shoot three arrows on the
side *thereof,* as though I shot at a mark.
21And, behold, I will send a lad, *saying,* Go, find out the arrows. If I expressly say unto the lad, Behold, the
arrows *are* on this side of thee, take
them; then come thou: for *there is* peace
to thee, and no hurt; *as* the LORD liveth.
22But if I say thus unto the young
man, Behold, the arrows *are* beyond
thee; go thy way: for the LORD hath
sent thee away.
23And *as touching* the matter which
thou and I have spoken of, behold, the
LORD *be* between thee and me for ever.
¶24So David hid himself in the field:
and when the new moon was come, the
king sat him down to eat meat.
25And the king sat upon his seat, as
at other times, *even* upon a seat by the
wall: and Jonathan arose, and Abner sat
by Saul's side, and David's place was
empty.
26Nevertheless Saul spake not any
thing that day: for he thought, Something hath befallen him, he is not clean;
surely he *is* not clean.
27And it came to pass on the morrow,
which was the second *day* of the month,
that David's place was empty: and Saul
said unto Jonathan his son, Wherefore
cometh not the son of Jesse to meat,
neither yesterday, nor to day?
28And Jonathan answered Saul, David
earnestly asked *leave* of me *to go* to
Beth-lehem:
29And he said, Let me go, I pray thee;

20:15 thy kindness from my house. See 2 Samuel 9 for David's fulfillment of this promise.

20:26 not clean. This means that Saul thought that David had touched something that made him unfit to worship God until he had gone through the ceremonial cleansing described in Leviticus 15.

for our family hath a sacrifice in the city;
and my brother, he hath commanded
me *to be there:* and now, if I have found
favour in thine eyes, let me get away,
I pray thee, and see my brethren.
Therefore he cometh not unto the
king's table.
30Then Saul's anger was kindled
against Jonathan, and he said unto him,
Thou son of the perverse rebellious
woman, do not I know that thou hast
chosen the son of Jesse to thine own
confusion, and unto the confusion of thy
mother's nakedness?
31For as long as the son of Jesse
liveth upon the ground, thou shalt not
be established, nor thy kingdom.
Wherefore now send and fetch him unto
me, for he shall surely die.
32And Jonathan answered Saul his
father, and said unto him, Wherefore
shall he be slain? what hath he done?
33And Saul cast a javelin at him to
smite him: whereby Jonathan knew that
it was determined of his father to slay
David.
34So Jonathan arose from the table in
fierce anger, and did eat no meat the
second day of the month: for he was
grieved for David, because his father
had done him shame.
¶35And it came to pass in the morning, that Jonathan went out into the field
at the time appointed with David, and a
little lad with him.
36And he said unto his lad, Run, find
out now the arrows which I shoot. *And*
as the lad ran, he shot an arrow beyond
him.
37And when the lad was come to the
place of the arrow which Jonathan had
shot, Jonathan cried after the lad, and
said, *Is* not the arrow beyond thee?
38And Jonathan cried after the lad,
Make speed, haste, stay not. And Jonathan's lad gathered up the arrows, and
came to his master.
39But the lad knew not any thing:
only Jonathan and David knew the
matter.
40And Jonathan gave his artillery
unto his lad, and said unto him, Go,
carry *them* to the city.
¶41*And* as soon as the lad was gone,
David arose out of *a place* toward the
south, and fell on his face to the ground,
and bowed himself three times: and
they kissed one another, and wept one
with another, until David exceeded.
42And Jonathan said to David, Go in
peace, forasmuch as we have sworn
both of us in the name of the LORD, saying, The LORD be between me and thee,
and between my seed and thy seed for
ever. And he arose and departed: and
Jonathan went into the city.

The priest protects David

21 Then came David to Nob to
Ahimelech the priest: and
Ahimelech was afraid at the meeting of
David, and said unto him, Why *art* thou
alone, and no man with thee?
2And David said unto Ahimelech the
priest, The king hath commanded me
a business, and hath said unto me, Let
no man know any thing of the business
whereabout I send thee, and what I
have commanded thee: and I have appointed *my* servants to such and such a
place.
3Now therefore what is under thine
hand? give *me* five *loaves of* bread in
mine hand, or what there is present.
4And the priest answered David, and
said, *There is* no common bread under
mine hand, but there is hallowed bread;
if the young men have kept themselves
at least from women.
5And David answered the priest, and

20:40 artillery. Bow and arrows.
21:1 Nob. This was a small town just north of Jerusalem, where the sacred vessels from the tabernacle had been kept by the priests.
21:2 Ahimelech. Another name for Ahiah (1 Sam. 14:3).
21:4 hallowed bread. This was the shewbread described in Exodus 25:30.

said unto him, Of a truth women *have*
been kept from us about these three
days, since I came out, and the vessels of
the young men are *holy, and *the bread*
is in a manner common, yea, though it
were sanctified this day in the vessel.
[6]So the priest gave him hallowed
bread: for there was no bread there but
the *shewbread, that was taken from
before the LORD, to put hot bread in the
day when it was taken away.

21:5-6 Eating the Shewbread
The Israelites were out of the will of God. Hallowed bread from disobedient children would bring no honor to Him. The shewbread was a *type of God, the wonderful provider. David, whose heart was right with God, was in need, and his need was met. See our Lord's reference to this incident in Matthew 12:1-8.

[7]Now a certain man of the servants
of Saul *was* there that day, detained
before the LORD; and his name *was*
Doeg, an Edomite, the chiefest of the
herdmen that *belonged* to Saul.
¶[8]And David said unto Ahimelech,
And is there not here under thine hand
spear or sword? for I have neither
brought my sword nor my weapons
with me, because the king's business
required haste.
[9]And the priest said, The sword of
Goliath the Philistine, whom thou
slewest in the valley of Elah, behold, it
is here wrapped in a cloth behind the
*ephod: if thou wilt take that, take *it:* for
there is no other save that here. And
David said, *There is* none like that; give
it me.
¶[10]And David arose, and fled that day
for fear of Saul, and went to Achish the
king of *Gath.
[11]And the servants of Achish said
unto him, *Is* not this David the king of
the land? did they not sing one to another of him in dances, saying, Saul
hath slain his thousands, and David his
ten thousands?
[12]And David laid up these words in
his heart, and was sore afraid of Achish
the king of Gath.
[13]And he changed his behaviour before them, and feigned himself mad in
their hands, and scrabbled on the doors
of the gate, and let his spittle fall down
upon his beard.
[14]Then said Achish unto his servants,
Lo, ye see the man is mad: wherefore
then have ye brought him to me?
[15]Have I need of mad men, that ye
have brought this *fellow* to play the mad
man in my presence? shall this *fellow*
come into my house?

David in exile at Adullam

22 *David therefore departed
thence, and escaped to the cave
Adullam: and when his brethren and all
his father's house heard *it,* they went
down thither to him.
[2]And every one *that was* in distress,
and every one that *was* in debt, and
every one *that was* discontented, gathered themselves unto him; and he became a captain over them: and there
were with him about four hundred men.
¶[3]And David went thence to Mizpeh
of *Moab: and he said unto the king of
Moab, Let my father and my mother, I
pray thee, come forth, *and be* with you,
till I know what God will do for me.
[4]And he brought them before the
king of Moab: and they dwelt with him
all the while that David was in the hold.
¶[5]And the *prophet Gad said unto
David, Abide not in the hold; depart,

21:9 behind the ephod. Goliath's sword was laid up with the sacred things of the priests, as a memorial to God's great power and victory over His enemies.
21:10 Achish the king of Gath. Achish was one of the five lords of the Philistines. Look up Psalms 34 and 56.
21:13 scrabbled on the doors. Scratched on the doors.
22:1 Adullam. A large cave in the hill country near the Dead Sea, six miles southeast of Beth-lehem.

and get thee into the land of Judah.
Then David departed, and came into the
forest of Hareth.

¶ 6 When Saul heard that David was
discovered, and the men that *were* with
him, (now Saul abode in Gibeah under
a tree in Ramah, having his spear in his
hand, and all his servants *were* standing
about him;)

7 Then Saul said unto his servants
that stood about him, Hear now, ye
Benjamites; will the son of Jesse give
every one of you fields and vineyards,
and make you all captains of thousands,
and captains of hundreds;

8 That all of you have conspired
against me, and *there is* none that
sheweth me that my son hath made a
league with the son of Jesse, and *there*
is none of you that is sorry for me, or
sheweth unto me that my son hath
stirred up my servant against me, to lie
in wait, as at this day?

¶ 9 Then answered Doeg the Edomite,
which was set over the servants of
Saul, and said, I saw the son of Jesse
coming to Nob, to Ahimelech the son of
Ahitub.

10 And he enquired of the LORD for
him, and gave him victuals, and gave
him the sword of Goliath the Philistine.

11 Then the king sent to call Ahimelech the priest, the son of Ahitub, and
all his father's house, the priests that
were in Nob: and they came all of them
to the king.

12 And Saul said, Hear now, thou son
of Ahitub. And he answered, Here I *am*,
my lord.

13 And Saul said unto him, Why have
ye conspired against me, thou and the
son of Jesse, in that thou hast given him
bread, and a sword, and hast enquired
of God for him, that he should rise
against me, to lie in wait, as at this day?

14 Then Ahimelech answered the
king, and said, And who *is so* faithful
among all thy servants as David, which
is the king's son in law, and goeth at thy
bidding, and is honourable in thine
house?

15 Did I then begin to enquire of God
for him? be it far from me: let not the
king impute *any* thing unto his servant,
nor to all the house of my father: for thy
servant knew nothing of all this, less or
more.

16 And the king said, Thou shalt surely die, Ahimelech, thou, and all thy
father's house.

¶ 17 And the king said unto the footmen that stood about him, Turn, and
slay the priests of the LORD; because
their hand also *is* with David, and because they knew when he fled, and did
not shew it to me. But the servants of
the king would not put forth their hand
to fall upon the priests of the LORD.

18 And the king said to Doeg, Turn
thou, and fall upon the priests. And
Doeg the Edomite turned, and he fell
upon the priests, and slew on that day
fourscore and five persons that did wear
a *linen ephod.

19 And Nob, the city of the priests,

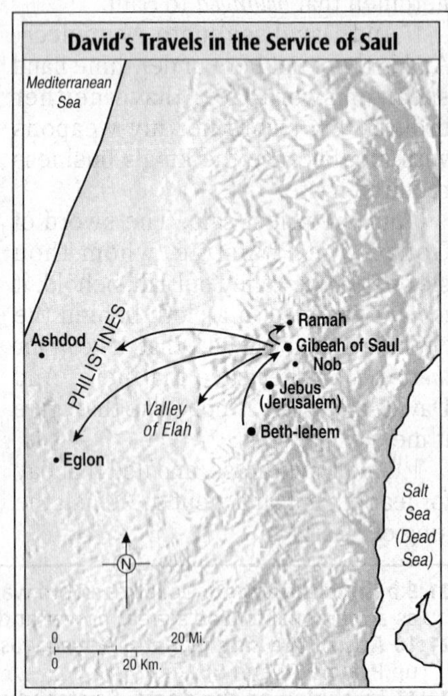

David's Travels in the Service of Saul

22:9 Doeg the Edomite. Read 1 Samuel 21:1-7.

smote he with the edge of the sword, both men and women, children and sucklings, and oxen, and asses, and sheep, with the edge of the sword.

¶ 20 And one of the sons of Ahimelech the son of Ahitub, named Abiathar, escaped, and fled after David.

21 And Abiathar shewed David that Saul had slain the LORD'S priests.

22 And David said unto Abiathar, I knew *it* that day, when Doeg the Edomite *was* there, that he would surely tell Saul: I have occasioned *the death* of all the persons of thy father's house.

23 Abide thou with me, fear not: for he that seeketh my life seeketh thy life: but with me thou *shalt be* in safeguard.

David protected by God

23 Then they told David, saying, Behold, the *Philistines fight against Keilah, and they rob the threshingfloors.

2 Therefore David enquired of the LORD, saying, Shall I go and smite these Philistines? And the LORD said unto David, Go, and smite the Philistines, and save Keilah.

3 And David's men said unto him, Behold, we be afraid here in *Judah: how much more then if we come to Keilah against the armies of the Philistines?

4 Then David enquired of the LORD yet again. And the LORD answered him and said, Arise, go down to Keilah; for I will deliver the Philistines into thine hand.

5 So David and his men went to Keilah, and fought with the Philistines, and brought away their cattle, and smote them with a great slaughter. So David saved the inhabitants of Keilah.

6 And it came to pass, when Abiathar the son of Ahimelech fled to David to Keilah, *that* he came down *with* an ephod in his hand.

¶ 7 And it was told Saul that David was come to Keilah. And Saul said, God hath delivered him into mine hand; for he is shut in, by entering into a town that hath gates and bars.

8 And Saul called all the people together to war, to go down to Keilah, to besiege David and his men.

¶ 9 And David knew that Saul secretly practised mischief against him; and he said to Abiathar the priest, Bring hither the ephod.

10 Then said David, O LORD God of Israel, thy servant hath certainly heard that Saul seeketh to come to Keilah, to destroy the city for my sake.

11 Will the men of Keilah deliver me up into his hand? will Saul come down, as thy servant hath heard? O LORD God of Israel, I beseech thee, tell thy servant. And the LORD said, He will come down.

12 Then said David, Will the men of Keilah deliver me and my men into the hand of Saul? And the LORD said, They will deliver *thee* up.

¶ 13 Then David and his men, *which were* about six hundred, arose and departed out of Keilah, and went whithersoever they could go. And it was told Saul that David was escaped from Keilah; and he forbare to go forth.

14 And David abode in the wilderness in strong holds, and remained in a *mountain in the wilderness of Ziph. And Saul sought him every day, but God delivered him not into his hand.

15 And David saw that Saul was come out to seek his life: and David *was* in the wilderness of Ziph in a wood.

¶ 16 And Jonathan Saul's son arose, and went to David into the wood, and strengthened his hand in God.

22:22 I have occasioned. This was the awful result that began with David's "little" lies (1 Sam. 20:6; 21:2).

23:9 Bring hither the ephod. This was the priestly garment that held the *Urim and Thummim, by which God showed His people His answers to their questions.

23:16 strengthened his hand in God. This is explained in the next two verses. Jonathan gave David words of encouragement and comfort in the LORD.

17 And he said unto him, Fear not: for the hand of Saul my father shall not find thee; and thou shalt be king over Israel, and I shall be next unto thee; and that also Saul my father knoweth.

18 And they two made a covenant before the LORD: and David abode in the wood, and Jonathan went to his house.

¶ 19 Then came up the Ziphites to Saul to Gibeah, saying, Doth not David hide himself with us in strong holds in the wood, in the hill of Hachilah, which *is* on the south of Jeshimon?

20 Now therefore, O king, come down according to all the desire of thy soul to come down; and our part *shall be* to deliver him into the king's hand.

21 And Saul said, Blessed *be* ye of the LORD; for ye have compassion on me.

22 Go, I pray you, prepare yet, and know and see his place where his haunt is, *and* who hath seen him there: for it is told me *that* he dealeth very subtilly.

23 See therefore, and take knowledge of all the lurking places where he hideth himself, and come ye again to me with the certainty, and I will go with you: and it shall come to pass, if he be in the land, that I will search him out throughout all the thousands of Judah.

24 And they arose, and went to Ziph before Saul: but David and his men *were* in the wilderness of Maon, in the plain on the south of Jeshimon.

25 Saul also and his men went to seek *him*. And they told David: wherefore he came down into a rock, and abode in the wilderness of Maon. And when Saul heard *that*, he pursued after David in the wilderness of Maon.

26 And Saul went on this side of the mountain, and David and his men on that side of the mountain: and David made haste to get away for fear of Saul; for Saul and his men compassed David and his men round about to take them.

¶ 27 But there came a messenger unto Saul, saying, Haste thee, and come; for the Philistines have invaded the land.

28 Wherefore Saul returned from pursuing after David, and went against the Philistines: therefore they called that place Sela-hammahlekoth.

¶ 29 And David went up from thence, and dwelt in strong holds at En-gedi.

David spares Saul's life

24 And it came to pass, when Saul was returned from following the Philistines, that it was told him, saying, Behold, David *is* in the wilderness of En-gedi.

2 Then Saul took three thousand chosen men out of all Israel, and went to seek David and his men upon the rocks of the wild goats.

3 And he came to the sheepcotes by the way, where *was* a cave; and Saul went in to cover his feet: and David and his men remained in the sides of the cave.

4 And the men of David said unto him, Behold the day of which the LORD said unto thee, Behold, I will deliver thine enemy into thine hand, that thou mayest do to him as it shall seem good unto thee. Then David arose, and cut off the skirt of Saul's robe privily.

5 And it came to pass afterward, that David's heart smote him, because he had cut off Saul's skirt.

6 And he said unto his men, The LORD forbid that I should do this thing unto my master, the LORD'S anointed, to stretch forth mine hand against him, seeing he *is* the anointed of the LORD.

23:28 Sela-hammahlekoth. The rock of divisions.

24:3 to cover his feet. This expression means *to take a nap*. It is customary in that hot climate to rest in a shaded place for a couple of hours in the middle of the day. Compare Judges 3:24.

24:6 the LORD's anointed. David reasoned that if God had appointed Saul to be king, God would remove him when He pleased (1 Sam. 26:9-11).

7 So David stayed his servants with these words, and suffered them not to rise against Saul. But Saul rose up out of the cave, and went on *his* way.

8 David also arose afterward, and went out of the cave, and cried after Saul, saying, My lord the king. And when Saul looked behind him, David stooped with his face to the earth, and bowed himself.

¶ 9 And David said to Saul, Wherefore hearest thou men's words, saying, Behold, David seeketh thy hurt?

10 Behold, this day thine eyes have seen how that the LORD had delivered thee to day into mine hand in the cave: and *some* bade *me* kill thee: but *mine eye* spared thee; and I said, I will not put forth mine hand against my lord; for he *is* the LORD'S anointed.

11 Moreover, my father, see, yea, see the skirt of thy robe in my hand: for in that I cut off the skirt of thy robe, and killed thee not, know thou and see that *there is* neither evil nor transgression in mine hand, and I have not sinned against thee; yet thou huntest my soul to take it.

12 The LORD judge between me and thee, and the LORD avenge me of thee: but mine hand shall not be upon thee.

13 As saith the proverb of the ancients, Wickedness proceedeth from the wicked: but mine hand shall not be upon thee.

14 After whom is the king of Israel come out? after whom dost thou pursue? after a dead dog, after a flea.

15 The LORD therefore be judge, and judge between me and thee, and see, and plead my cause, and deliver me out of thine hand.

¶ 16 And it came to pass, when David had made an end of speaking these words unto Saul, that Saul said, *Is* this thy voice, my son David? And Saul lifted up his voice, and wept.

17 And he said to David, Thou *art* more righteous than I: for thou hast rewarded me good, whereas I have rewarded thee evil.

18 And thou hast shewed this day how that thou hast dealt well with me: forasmuch as when the LORD had delivered me into thine hand, thou killedst me not.

19 For if a man find his enemy, will he let him go well away? wherefore the LORD reward thee good for that thou hast done unto me this day.

20 And now, behold, I know well that thou shalt surely be king, and that the kingdom of Israel shall be established in thine hand.

21 Swear now therefore unto me by the LORD, that thou wilt not cut off my seed after me, and that thou wilt not destroy my name out of my father's house.

22 And David sware unto Saul. And Saul went home; but David and his men gat them up unto the hold.

The death of Samuel

25 And *Samuel died; and all the Israelites were gathered together, and lamented him, and buried him in his house at Ramah. And David arose, and went down to the wilderness of Paran.

David kept from shedding blood

2 And *there was* a man in Maon, whose possessions *were* in Carmel; and the man *was* very great, and he had three thousand sheep, and a thousand goats: and he was shearing his sheep in Carmel.

3 Now the name of the man *was* Nabal; and the name of his wife Abigail: and *she was* a woman of good understanding, and of a beautiful countenance: but the man *was* churlish and evil in his doings; and he *was* of the house of *Caleb.

24:16 my son. David was Saul's son-in-law, for he had married Saul's daughter.

25:2 Carmel. Not Mount Carmel, near Galilee, but the sheep-raising district of southern Judaea.

¶ 4 And David heard in the wilderness
that Nabal did shear his sheep.
5 And David sent out ten young men,
and David said unto the young men, Get
you up to Carmel, and go to Nabal, and
greet him in my name:
6 And thus shall ye say to him that
liveth *in prosperity,* Peace *be* both to
thee, and peace *be* to thine house, and
peace *be* unto all that thou hast.
7 And now I have heard that thou hast
shearers: now thy shepherds which
were with us, we hurt them not, neither
was there ought missing unto them, all
the while they were in Carmel.
8 Ask thy young men, and they will
shew thee. Wherefore let the young
men find favour in thine eyes: for we
come in a good day: give, I pray thee,
whatsoever cometh to thine hand
unto thy servants, and to thy son David.
9 And when David's young men came,
they spake to Nabal according to all
those words in the name of David, and
ceased.
¶ 10 And Nabal answered David's servants, and said, Who *is* David? and who
is the son of Jesse? there be many servants now a days that break away every
man from his master.
11 Shall I then take my bread, and my
water, and my flesh that I have killed for
my shearers, and give *it* unto men,
whom I know not whence they *be?*
12 So David's young men turned their
way, and went again, and came and told
him all those sayings.
13 And David said unto his men, Gird
ye on every man his sword. And they
girded on every man his sword; and
David also girded on his sword: and
there went up after David about four
hundred men; and two hundred abode
by the stuff.
¶ 14 But one of the young men told Abigail, Nabal's wife, saying, Behold, David sent messengers out of the
wilderness to salute our master; and he
railed on them.
15 But the men *were* very good unto
us, and we were not hurt, neither
missed we any thing, as long as we
were conversant with them, when we
were in the fields:
16 They were a wall unto us both by
night and day, all the while we were
with them keeping the sheep.
17 Now therefore know and consider
what thou wilt do; for evil is determined
against our master, and against all his
household: for he *is such* a son of Belial, that *a man* cannot speak to him.
¶ 18 Then Abigail made haste, and took
two hundred loaves, and two *bottles of
wine, and five sheep ready dressed, and
five measures of parched *corn,* and an
hundred clusters of raisins, and two
hundred cakes of figs, and laid *them* on
asses.
19 And she said unto her servants, Go
on before me; behold, I come after you.
But she told not her husband Nabal.
20 And it was *so, as* she rode on the
ass, that she came down by the covert
of the hill, and, behold, David and his
men came down against her; and she
met them.
21 Now David had said, Surely in vain
have I kept all that this *fellow* hath in the
wilderness, so that nothing was missed
of all that *pertained* unto him: and he
hath requited me evil for good.
22 So and more also do *God unto the
enemies of David, if I leave of all that
pertain to him by the morning light any
that pisseth against the wall.
23 And when Abigail saw David, she
hasted, and lighted off the ass, and fell
before David on her face, and bowed
herself to the ground,
24 And fell at his feet, and said, Upon
me, my lord, *upon* me *let this* iniquity *be:*
and let thine handmaid, I pray thee,
speak in thine audience, and hear the
words of thine handmaid.

25:18 measures. A measure is about one bushel.
25:20 covert. Shelter, hiding place.

25 Let not my lord, I pray thee, regard
this man of Belial, *even* Nabal: for as his
name *is,* so *is* he; Nabal *is* his name, and
folly *is* with him: but I thine handmaid
saw not the young men of my lord,
whom thou didst send.
26 Now therefore, my lord, *as* the
LORD liveth, and *as* thy soul liveth, seeing the LORD hath withholden thee
from coming to *shed* *blood, and from
avenging thyself with thine own hand,
now let thine enemies, and they that
seek evil to my lord, be as Nabal.
27 And now this blessing which thine
handmaid hath brought unto my lord,
let it even be given unto the young men
that follow my lord.
28 I pray thee, forgive the *trespass of
thine handmaid: for the LORD will certainly make my lord a sure house; because my lord fighteth the battles of the
LORD, and evil hath not been found in
thee *all* thy days.
29 Yet a man is risen to pursue thee,
and to seek thy soul: but the soul of
my lord shall be bound in the bundle
of life with the LORD thy God; and the
souls of thine enemies, them shall he
sling out, *as out* of the middle of a
sling.

25:29 Life with the LORD
To "be bound in the bundle of life with the LORD" is still true today of those who are Christians. When we accept the Lord Jesus Christ as our Saviour, He gives us His own life to share with Him–He lives in us (John 14:20; Gal. 2:20; Col 3:3-4; also John 10:10).

30 And it shall come to pass, when the
LORD shall have done to my lord according to all the good that he hath spoken
concerning thee, and shall have appointed thee ruler over *Israel;
31 That this shall be no grief unto
thee, nor offence of heart unto my lord,
either that thou hast shed blood causeless, or that my lord hath avenged himself: but when the LORD shall have dealt
well with my lord, then remember thine
handmaid.
¶32 And David said to Abigail, Blessed
be the LORD God of Israel, which sent
thee this day to meet me:
33 And blessed *be* thy advice, and
blessed *be* thou, which hast kept me this
day from coming to *shed* blood, and from
avenging myself with mine own hand.
34 For in very deed, *as* the LORD God
of Israel liveth, which hath kept me
back from hurting thee, except thou
hadst hasted and come to meet me,
surely there had not been left unto
Nabal by the morning light any that
pisseth against the wall.
35 So David received of her hand *that*
which she had brought him, and said
unto her, Go up in peace to thine house;
see, I have hearkened to thy voice, and
have accepted thy person.
¶36 And Abigail came to Nabal; and,
behold, he held a feast in his house, like
the feast of a king; and Nabal's heart
was merry within him, for he *was* very
drunken: wherefore she told him nothing, less or more, until the morning
light.
37 But it came to pass in the morning,
when the wine was gone out of Nabal,
and his wife had told him these things,
that his heart died within him, and he
became *as* a stone.
38 And it came to pass about ten days
after, that the LORD smote Nabal, that
he died.

Abigail becomes David's wife

¶39 And when David heard that Nabal
was dead, he said, Blessed *be* the LORD,
that hath pleaded the cause of my reproach from the hand of Nabal, and hath
kept his servant from evil: for the LORD
hath returned the wickedness of Nabal
upon his own head. And David sent and
communed with Abigail, to take her to
him to wife.
40 And when the servants of David
were come to Abigail to Carmel, they

25:25 Nabal. The name means *fool.*

spake unto her, saying, David sent us
unto thee, to take thee to him to wife.
41And she arose, and bowed herself
on *her* face to the earth, and said, Behold, *let* thine handmaid *be* a servant to
wash the feet of the servants of my lord.
42And Abigail hasted, and arose, and
rode upon an ass, with five damsels of
hers that went after her; and she went
after the messengers of David, and became his wife.
43David also took Ahinoam of Jezreel; and they were also both of them his
wives.
¶44But Saul had given Michal his
daughter, David's wife, to Phalti the son
of Laish, which *was* of Gallim.

David again spares Saul's life

26 And the Ziphites came unto
Saul to Gibeah, saying, Doth not
David hide himself in the hill of Hachilah, *which is* before Jeshimon?
2Then Saul arose, and went down to
the wilderness of Ziph, having three
thousand chosen men of Israel with
him, to seek David in the wilderness of
Ziph.
3And Saul pitched in the hill of Hachilah, which *is* before Jeshimon, by the
way. But David abode in the wilderness,
and he saw that Saul came after him
into the wilderness.
4David therefore sent out spies, and
understood that Saul was come in very
deed.
¶5And David arose, and came to the
place where Saul had pitched: and David beheld the place where Saul lay, and
Abner the son of Ner, the captain of his
host: and Saul lay in the trench, and the
people pitched round about him.
6Then answered David and said to
Ahimelech the Hittite, and to Abishai
the son of Zeruiah, brother to Joab, saying, Who will go down with me to Saul
to the camp? And Abishai said, I will go
down with thee.
7So David and Abishai came to the
people by night: and, behold, Saul lay
sleeping within the trench, and his
spear stuck in the ground at his bolster:
but Abner and the people lay round
about him.
8Then said Abishai to David, God
hath delivered thine enemy into thine
hand this day: now therefore let me
smite him, I pray thee, with the spear
even to the earth at once, and I will not
smite him the second time.
9And David said to Abishai, Destroy
him not: for who can stretch forth his
hand against the LORD'S anointed, and
be guiltless?
10David said furthermore, *As* the
LORD liveth, the LORD shall smite him;
or his day shall come to die; or he shall
descend into battle, and perish.
11The LORD forbid that I should
stretch forth mine hand against the
LORD'S anointed: but, I pray thee, take
thou now the spear that *is* at his bolster,
and the cruse of water, and let us go.
12So David took the spear and the
cruse of water from Saul's bolster; and
they gat them away, and no man saw *it*,
nor knew *it*, neither awaked: for they
were all asleep; because a deep sleep
from the LORD was fallen upon them.
¶13Then David went over to the other
side, and stood on the top of an hill afar
off; a great space *being* between them:
14And David cried to the people, and
to Abner the son of Ner, saying,
Answerest thou not, Abner? Then Abner answered and said, *Who art* thou
that criest to the king?
15And David said to Abner, *Art* not
thou a *valiant* man? and who *is* like to
thee in Israel? wherefore then hast thou
not kept thy lord the king? for there
came one of the people in to destroy the
king thy lord.
16This thing *is* not good that thou hast
done. *As* the LORD liveth, ye *are* worthy to die, because ye have not kept
your master, the LORD'S anointed. And
now see where the king's spear *is*, and

25:43 his wives. See 1 Samuel 1:2 note.

the cruse of water that *was* at his bolster.

17 And Saul knew David's voice, and said, *Is* this thy voice, my son David? And David said, *It is* my voice, my lord, O king.

18 And he said, Wherefore doth my lord thus pursue after his servant? for what have I done? or what evil *is* in mine hand?

19 Now therefore, I pray thee, let my lord the king hear the words of his servant. If the LORD have stirred thee up against me, let him accept an *offering: but if *they be* the children of men, cursed *be* they before the LORD; for they have driven me out this day from *abiding in the inheritance of the LORD, saying, Go, serve other gods.

20 Now therefore, let not my blood fall to the earth before the face of the LORD: for the king of Israel is come out to seek a flea, as when one doth hunt a partridge in the mountains.

¶21 Then said Saul, I have sinned: return, my son David: for I will no more do thee harm, because my soul was precious in thine eyes this day: behold, I have played the *fool, and have erred exceedingly.

22 And David answered and said, Behold the king's spear! and let one of the young men come over and fetch it.

23 The LORD *render to every man his *righteousness and his faithfulness: for the LORD delivered thee into *my* hand to day, but I would not stretch forth mine hand against the LORD'S anointed.

24 And, behold, as thy life was much set by this day in mine eyes, so let my life be much set by in the eyes of the LORD, and let him deliver me out of all tribulation.

25 Then Saul said to David, Blessed *be* thou, my son David: thou shalt both do great *things,* and also shalt still prevail. So David went on his way, and Saul returned to his place.

David's faith fails

27 And David said in his heart, I shall now perish one day by the hand of Saul: *there is* nothing better for me than that I should speedily escape into the land of the Philistines; and Saul shall despair of me, to seek me any more in any coast of Israel: so shall I escape out of his hand.

2 And David arose, and he passed over with the six hundred men that *were* with him unto Achish, the son of Maoch, king of *Gath.

3 And David dwelt with Achish at Gath, he and his men, every man with his household, *even* David with his *two

26:25 THE ENCOUNTERS OF SAUL AND DAVID

Incident	Reference
David comes to calm Saul by playing the harp.	16:16,23
David becomes Saul's armorbearer.	16:21
David asks Saul to let him fight Goliath.	17:32-37
Saul's son, Jonathan, and David become close friends.	18:1; 20
Saul takes David into his own home.	18:2
Saul becomes jealous of David and tries to kill him.	18:6-12
Saul makes David captain in the army.	18:13
Saul's daughter, Michal, loves and marries David.	18:20-27
Saul tries to kill David.	18:25; 19; 20; 23
David encounters Saul in a cave.	24:3-4
David makes a promise to Saul.	24:21-22
David again spares Saul's life.	26:1-25

26:19 let him accept an offering. David meant, "If the LORD is afflicting me because I have sinned, I shall confess my sin. If He will tell me what it is, I shall bring an offering so that God may forgive me."

wives, Ahinoam the Jezreelitess, and
Abigail the Carmelitess, Nabal's wife.
4 And it was told Saul that David was
fled to Gath: and he sought no more
again for him.

David's falseness brings more trouble

¶5 And David said unto Achish, If I
have now found grace in thine eyes, let
them give me a place in some town in
the country, that I may dwell there: for
why should thy servant dwell in the
royal city with thee?
6 Then Achish gave him Ziklag that
day: wherefore Ziklag pertaineth unto
the kings of Judah unto this day.
7 And the time that David dwelt in the
country of the Philistines was a full year
and four months.
¶8 And David and his men went up,
and invaded the Geshurites, and the
Gezrites, and the Amalekites: for those
nations were of old the inhabitants of the
land, as thou goest to Shur, even unto
the land of *Egypt.
9 And David smote the land, and left
neither man nor woman alive, and took
away the sheep, and the oxen, and the
asses, and the camels, and the apparel,
and returned, and came to Achish.
10 And Achish said, Whither have ye
made a road to day? And David said,
Against the south of Judah, and against
the south of the Jerahmeelites, and
against the south of the *Kenites.
11 And David saved neither man nor
woman alive, to bring *tidings* to Gath,
saying, Lest they should tell on us, saying, So did David, and so *will be* his
manner all the while he dwelleth in the
country of the Philistines.
12 And Achish believed David, saying,
He hath made his people Israel utterly
to abhor him; therefore he shall be my
servant for ever.

28 And it came to pass in those
days, that the Philistines gathered their armies together for warfare,
to fight with Israel. And Achish said
unto *David, Know thou assuredly, that
thou shalt go out with me to battle, thou
and thy men.
2 And David said to Achish, Surely
thou shalt know what thy servant can
do. And Achish said to David, Therefore
will I make thee keeper of mine head
for ever.

The final downfall of Saul

¶3 Now Samuel was dead, and all Israel had lamented him, and buried him
in Ramah, even in his own city. And Saul
had put away those that had *familiar
spirits, and the wizards, out of the land.

28:3 Familiar Spirits
"Familiar spirits" refers to those who are dead with whom some people frequently held conversations, (these spirits were supposed to come and tell things to the person who had power over them). The people of Israel were forbidden to consult with such spirits or witches or wizards (Lev. 19:31; 20:6,27; Deut. 18:9-12). See also 1 Samuel 6:2 note, "Divination, Magic, and Witchcraft."

4 And the Philistines gathered themselves together, and came and pitched
in Shunem: and Saul gathered all Israel
together, and they pitched in Gilboa.
5 And when Saul saw the host of the
Philistines, he was afraid, and his heart
greatly trembled.
6 And when Saul enquired of the
LORD, the LORD answered him not,
neither by dreams, nor by Urim, nor by
*prophets.
¶7 Then said Saul unto his servants,
Seek me a woman that hath a familiar
spirit, that I may go to her, and enquire
of her. And his servants said to him,
Behold, *there is* a woman that hath a
familiar spirit at Endor.
8 And Saul disguised himself, and put
on other raiment, and he went, and two
men with him, and they came to the
woman by night: and he said, I pray

27:3 Nabal's wife. Nabal's widow.
27:10 a road. A raid.

thee, divine unto me by the familiar spirit, and bring me *him* up, whom I shall name unto thee.

9And the woman said unto him, Behold, thou knowest what Saul hath done, how he hath cut off those that have familiar spirits, and the wizards, out of the land: wherefore then layest thou a snare for my life, to cause me to die?

10And Saul sware to her by the LORD, saying, *As* the LORD liveth, there shall no punishment happen to thee for this thing.

11Then said the woman, Whom shall I bring up unto thee? And he said, Bring me up Samuel.

12And when the woman saw Samuel, she cried with a loud voice: and the woman spake to Saul, saying, Why hast thou deceived me? for thou *art* Saul.

13And the king said unto her, Be not afraid: for what sawest thou? And the woman said unto Saul, I saw gods ascending out of the earth.

14And he said unto her, What form *is* he of? And she said, An old man cometh up; and he *is* covered with a mantle. And Saul perceived that it *was* Samuel, and he stooped with *his* face to the ground, and bowed himself.

¶15And Samuel said to Saul, Why hast thou disquieted me, to bring me up? And Saul answered, I am sore distressed; for the Philistines make war against me, and God is departed from me, and answereth me no more, neither by prophets, nor by dreams: therefore I have called thee, that thou mayest make known unto me what I shall do.

16Then said Samuel, Wherefore then dost thou ask of me, seeing the LORD is departed from thee, and is become thine enemy?

17And the LORD hath done to him, as he spake by me: for the LORD hath rent the kingdom out of thine hand, and given it to thy neighbour, *even* to David:

18Because thou obeyedst not the voice of the LORD, nor executedst his fierce wrath upon *Amalek, therefore hath the LORD done this thing unto thee this day.

19Moreover the LORD will also deliver Israel with thee into the hand of the Philistines: and to morrow *shalt* thou and thy sons *be* with me: the LORD also shall deliver the host of Israel into the hand of the Philistines.

20Then Saul fell *straightway all along on the earth, and was sore afraid, because of the words of Samuel: and there was no strength in him; for he had eaten no bread all the day, nor all the night.

¶21And the woman came unto Saul, and saw that he was sore troubled, and said unto him, Behold, thine handmaid hath obeyed thy voice, and I have put my life in my hand, and have hearkened unto thy words which thou spakest unto me.

22Now therefore, I pray thee, hearken thou also unto the voice of thine handmaid, and let me set a morsel of bread before thee; and eat, that thou mayest have strength, when thou goest on thy way.

23But he refused, and said, I will not eat. But his servants, together with the woman, compelled him; and he hearkened unto their voice. So he arose from the earth, and sat upon the bed.

24And the woman had a fat calf in the house; and she hasted, and killed it, and took flour, and kneaded *it,* and did bake *unleavened bread thereof:

25And she brought *it* before Saul, and before his servants; and they did eat. Then they rose up, and went away that night.

God saves David from fighting against Israel

29 Now the *Philistines gathered together all their armies to Aphek: and the Israelites pitched by a fountain which *is* in Jezreel.

2And the lords of the Philistines passed on by hundreds, and by thousands: but David and his men passed on in the *rereward with Achish.

3Then said the princes of the Philistines, What *do* these Hebrews *here?*
And Achish said unto the princes of the
Philistines, *Is* not this David, the servant of Saul the king of Israel, which
hath been with me these days, or these
years, and I have found no fault in him
since he fell *unto me* unto this day?
4And the princes of the Philistines
were wroth with him; and the princes
of the Philistines said unto him, Make
this fellow return, that he may go again
to his place which thou hast appointed
him, and let him not go down with us
to battle, lest in the battle he be an adversary to us: for wherewith should he
reconcile himself unto his master?
should it not *be* with the heads of these
men?
5*Is* not this David, of whom they sang
one to another in dances, saying, Saul
slew his thousands, and David his ten
thousands?
¶6Then Achish called David, and said
unto him, Surely, *as* the LORD liveth,
thou hast been upright, and thy going
out and thy coming in with me in the
host *is* good in my sight: for I have not
found evil in thee since the day of thy
coming unto me unto this day: nevertheless the lords favour thee not.
7Wherefore now return, and go in
peace, that thou displease not the lords
of the Philistines.
¶8And David said unto Achish, But
what have I done? and what hast thou
found in thy servant so long as I have
been with thee unto this day, that I may
not go fight against the enemies of my
lord the king?
9And Achish answered and said to
David, I know that thou *art* good in my
sight, as an *angel of God: notwithstanding the princes of the Philistines
have said, He shall not go up with us to
the battle.
10Wherefore now rise up early in the
morning with thy master's servants
that are come with thee: and as soon as
ye be up early in the morning, and have
light, depart.
11So David and his men rose up early to depart in the morning, to return
into the land of the Philistines. And the
Philistines went up to Jezreel.

David avenges the destruction of Ziklag

30 And it came to pass, when David and his men were come to
Ziklag on the third day, that the Amalekites had invaded the south, and Ziklag, and smitten Ziklag, and burned it
with fire;
2And had taken the women captives,
that *were* therein: they slew not any,
either great or small, but carried *them*
away, and went on their way.
¶3So David and his men came to the
city, and, behold, *it was* burned with fire;
and their wives, and their sons, and
their daughters, were taken captives.
4Then David and the people that *were*
with him lifted up their voice and wept,
until they had no more power to weep.
5And David's *two wives were taken
captives, Ahinoam the Jezreelitess, and
Abigail the wife of Nabal the Carmelite.
6And David was greatly distressed;
for the people spake of stoning him,
because the soul of all the people was
grieved, every man for his sons and for
his daughters: but David encouraged
himself in the LORD his God.
7And David said to Abiathar the
priest, Ahimelech's son, I pray thee,
bring me hither the *ephod. And Abiathar brought thither the ephod to David.
8And David enquired at the LORD,
saying, Shall I pursue after this troop?
shall I overtake them? And he answered him, Pursue: for thou shalt
surely overtake *them,* and without fail
recover *all.*

29:8 the enemies of my lord the king. David did not really want to fight against Israel but offered his service, so that the Philistines would not kill him.
30:1 Ziklag. Read 1 Samuel 27:5-6.

[9]So David went, he and the six hundred men that *were* with him, and came to the brook Besor, where those that were left behind stayed.

[10]But David pursued, he and four hundred men: for two hundred abode behind, which were so faint that they could not go over the brook Besor.

¶[11]And they found an Egyptian in the field, and brought him to David, and gave him bread, and he did eat; and they made him drink water;

[12]And they gave him a piece of a cake of figs, and two clusters of raisins: and when he had eaten, his spirit came again to him: for he had eaten no bread, nor drunk *any* water, three days and three nights.

[13]And David said unto him, To whom *belongest* thou? and whence *art* thou? And he said, I *am* a young man of Egypt, servant to an Amalekite; and my master left me, because three days agone I fell sick.

[14]We made an invasion *upon* the south of the Cherethites, and upon *the coast* which *belongeth* to *Judah, and upon the south of Caleb; and we burned Ziklag with fire.

[15]And David said to him, Canst thou bring me down to this company? And he said, Swear unto me by God, that thou wilt neither kill me, nor deliver me into the hands of my master, and I will bring thee down to this company.

¶[16]And when he had brought him down, behold, *they were* spread abroad upon all the earth, eating and drinking, and dancing, because of all the great spoil that they had taken out of the land of the Philistines, and out of the land of Judah.

[17]And David smote them from the twilight even unto the evening of the next day: and there escaped not a man of them, save four hundred young men, which rode upon camels, and fled.

[18]And David recovered all that the Amalekites had carried away: and David rescued his two wives.

[19]And there was nothing lacking to them, neither small nor great, neither sons nor daughters, neither spoil, nor any *thing* that they had taken to them: David recovered all.

[20]And David took all the flocks and the herds, *which* they drave before those *other* cattle, and said, This *is* David's spoil.

¶[21]And David came to the two hundred men, which were so faint that they could not follow David, whom they had made also to abide at the brook Besor: and they went forth to meet David, and to meet the people that *were* with him: and when David came near to the people, he saluted them.

[22]Then answered all the wicked men and *men* of Belial, of those that went with David, and said, Because they went not with us, we will not give them *ought* of the spoil that we have recovered, save to every man his wife and his children, that they may lead *them* away, and depart.

[23]Then said David, Ye shall not do so, my brethren, with that which the LORD hath given us, who hath preserved us, and delivered the company that came against us into our hand.

[24]For who will hearken unto you in this matter? but as his part *is* that goeth down to the battle, so *shall* his part *be* that tarrieth by the stuff: they shall part alike.

[25]And it was *so* from that day forward, that he made it a statute and an ordinance for Israel unto this day.

¶[26]And when David came to Ziklag, he sent of the spoil unto the *elders of Judah, *even* to his friends, saying, Behold a present for you of the spoil of the enemies of the LORD;

[27]To *them* which *were* in *Beth-el, and to *them* which *were* in south Ramoth, and to *them* which *were* in Jattir,

---

30:13 agone. Ago.
30:24 stuff. The furniture or baggage of an army.

28 And to *them* which *were* in Aroer,
and to *them* which *were* in Siphmoth,
and to *them* which *were* in Eshtemoa,
29 And to *them* which *were* in Rachal,
and to *them* which *were* in the cities of
the Jerahmeelites, and to *them* which
were in the cities of the *Kenites,
30 And to *them* which *were* in Hormah,
and to *them* which *were* in Chor-ashan,
and to *them* which *were* in Athach,
31 And to *them* which *were* in Hebron,
and to all the places where David himself and his men were wont to haunt.

Saul's death

31 Now the Philistines fought
against Israel: and the men of
Israel fled from before the Philistines,
and fell down slain in mount Gilboa.
2 And the Philistines followed hard
upon Saul and upon his sons; and the
Philistines slew Jonathan, and Abinadab, and Melchi-shua, Saul's sons.
3 And the battle went sore against
Saul, and the archers hit him; and he
was sore wounded of the archers.
4 Then said Saul unto his armourbearer, Draw thy sword, and thrust me
through therewith; lest these uncircumcised come and thrust me through,
and abuse me. But his armourbearer
would not; for he was sore afraid.
Therefore Saul took a sword, and fell
upon it.
5 And when his armourbearer saw
that Saul was dead, he fell likewise upon
his sword, and died with him.
6 So Saul died, and his three sons, and
his armourbearer, and all his men, that
same day together.
¶7 And when the men of Israel that
were on the other side of the valley, and
they that *were* on the other side Jordan,
saw that the men of Israel fled, and that
Saul and his sons were dead, they forsook the cities, and fled; and the Philistines came and dwelt in them.
8 And it came to pass on the morrow,
when the Philistines came to strip the
slain, that they found Saul and his three
sons fallen in mount Gilboa.
9 And they cut off his head, and
stripped off his armour, and sent into
the land of the Philistines round about,
to publish *it in* the house of their idols,
and among the people.
10 And they put his armour in the
house of Ashtaroth: and they fastened
his body to the wall of Beth-shan.
¶11 And when the inhabitants of
Jabesh-gilead heard of that which the
Philistines had done to Saul;
12 All the valiant men arose, and went
all night, and took the body of Saul and
the bodies of his sons from the wall of
Beth-shan, and came to Jabesh, and
burnt them there.
13 And they took their bones, and buried *them* under a tree at Jabesh, and
fasted seven days.

31:5 Saul was dead. The armorbearer saw Saul was dead, and took his own life to die with the king.

31:10 the house of Ashtaroth. The Philistines thus claimed that their goddess, Ashtaroth, had defeated Jehovah, the God of Israel.

31:11 Jabesh-gilead. The inhabitants were relatives of the tribe of Benjamin (see 1 Sam. 11:4 note) and were indebted to Saul for saving them (1 Sam. 11:1-12).

The Second Book of

SAMUEL

otherwise called, The Second Book of the Kings

BACKGROUND

This book records the history of David's reign over Israel. It tells how Jerusalem became the political and religious center as David set up his throne there and built a new tabernacle for the ark of God on Mount Zion. It records the establishing of the kingdom of Israel in great power as David conquered the surrounding nations and put them under heavy tribute, thus preparing the way for the peace and prosperity of Solomon's reign.

THE TIME

The events recorded in 2 Samuel cover a period of about forty years.

OUTLINE OF 2 SAMUEL

I.	David Reigns over Judah in Hebron	2 Samuel 1:1—4:12
II.	David Is Established as King over All Israel	2 Samuel 5:1—10:19
III.	David's Sin Brings Trouble on His House	2 Samuel 11:1—14:33
IV.	David Is Threatened by Civil War	2 Samuel 15:1—20:26
V.	David's Faith and Strength Are Revived	2 Samuel 21:1—24:25

I. David Reigns over Judah (1:1-4:12)

1 Now it came to pass after the
death of Saul, when *David was
returned from the slaughter of the Amalekites, and David had abode two days
in Ziklag;
2 It came even to pass on the third day,
that, behold, a man came out of the
camp from Saul with his clothes rent,
and earth upon his head: and *so* it was,
when he came to David, that he fell to
the earth, and did obeisance.
3 And David said unto him, From
whence comest thou? And he said unto
him, Out of the camp of *Israel am I
escaped.
4 And David said unto him, How went
the matter? I pray thee, tell me. And he
answered, That the people are fled from
the battle, and many of the people also
are fallen and dead; and Saul and Jonathan his son are dead also.
5 And David said unto the young man
that told him, How knowest thou that
Saul and Jonathan his son be dead?
6 And the young man that told him
said, As I happened by chance upon
mount Gilboa, behold, Saul leaned upon

1:2 clothes rent, and earth upon his head. This was a sign of deep sorrow and mourning or of a real disaster (Gen. 37:29; 44:13; 1 Sam. 4:12).

his spear; and, lo, the chariots and
horsemen followed hard after him.
7And when he looked behind him, he
saw me, and called unto me. And I answered, Here *am* I.
8And he said unto me, Who *art* thou?
And I answered him, I *am* an Amalekite.
9And he said unto me again, Stand, I
pray thee, upon me, and slay me: for anguish is come upon me, because my life
is yet whole in me.
10So I stood upon him, and slew
him, because I was sure that he could
not live after that he was fallen: and I
took the crown that *was* upon his
head, and the bracelet that *was* on his
arm, and have brought them hither
unto my lord.

1:10 Saul's Death
Saul was mortally wounded by the Philistines. To escape further agony or torture by his foes, he fell upon his sword, and his armor-bearer thought that he was dead. Then Saul, yet alive, but in agony, raised himself on his spear and begged the Amalekite to kill him (compare 1 Sam. 31:4-5).

11Then David took hold on his
clothes, and rent them; and likewise all
the men that *were* with him:
12And they mourned, and wept, and
fasted until even, for Saul, and for
Jonathan his son, and for the people
of the LORD, and for the house of Israel; because they were fallen by the
sword.
¶13And David said unto the young
man that told him, Whence *art* thou?
And he answered, I *am* the son of a
stranger, an Amalekite.
14And David said unto him, How wast
thou not afraid to stretch forth thine
hand to destroy the LORD'S anointed?
15And David called one of the young
men, and said, Go near, *and* fall upon
him. And he smote him that he died.
16And David said unto him, Thy
*blood *be* upon thy head; for thy mouth
hath testified against thee, saying, I
have slain the LORD'S anointed.

David mourns for Saul and Jonathan

¶17And David lamented with this
lamentation over Saul and over Jonathan his son:
18(Also he bade them teach the
children of *Judah *the use of* the bow:
behold, *it is* written in the book of
*Jasher.)
19The beauty of Israel is slain upon
thy high places: how are the mighty fall-
en!
20Tell *it* not in *Gath, publish *it* not
in the streets of Askelon; lest the
daughters of the *Philistines rejoice,
lest the daughters of the *uncircumcised triumph.
21Ye mountains of Gilboa, *let there be*
no dew, neither *let there be* rain, upon
you, nor fields of *offerings: for there
the shield of the mighty is vilely cast
away, the shield of Saul, *as though he*
had not *been* anointed with *oil.
22From the blood of the slain, from
the fat of the mighty, the bow of Jonathan turned not back, and the sword of
Saul returned not empty.
23Saul and Jonathan *were* lovely and
pleasant in their lives, and in their
death they were not divided: they
were swifter than eagles, they were
stronger than lions.
24Ye daughters of Israel, weep over
Saul, who clothed you in scarlet, with
other delights, who put on ornaments of
gold upon your apparel.
25How are the mighty fallen in the
midst of the battle! O Jonathan, *thou*
wast slain in thine high places.
26I am distressed for thee, my brother Jonathan: very pleasant hast thou
been unto me: thy love to me was wonderful, passing the love of women.
27How are the mighty fallen, and the
weapons of war perished!

David received as king by the tribe of Judah

2 And it came to pass after this, that
David enquired of the LORD, saying, Shall I go up into any of the cities
of Judah? And the LORD said unto him,

Go up. And David said, Whither shall I
go up? And he said, Unto Hebron.
[2]So David went up thither, and his
*two wives also, Ahinoam the Jezreelit-
ess, and Abigail Nabal's wife the Carmelite.
[3]And his men that *were* with him did
David bring up, every man with his
household: and they dwelt in the cities
of Hebron.
[4]And the men of Judah came, and
there they anointed David king over the
house of Judah. And they told David,
saying, *That* the men of Jabesh-gilead
were they that buried Saul.
¶[5]And David sent messengers unto
the men of Jabesh-gilead, and said unto
them, Blessed *be* ye of the LORD, that
ye have shewed this kindness unto
your lord, *even* unto Saul, and have buried him.
[6]And now the LORD shew kindness
and truth unto you: and I also will requite you this kindness, because ye
have done this thing.
[7]Therefore now let your hands be
strengthened, and be ye valiant: for
your master Saul is dead, and also the
house of Judah have anointed me king
over them.

Saul's son made king of eleven tribes

¶[8]But Abner the son of Ner, captain
of Saul's host, took Ish-bosheth the son
of Saul, and brought him over to Mahanaim;

2:8 Mahanaim
Abner and Ish-bosheth established their headquarters at Mahanaim on the east side of the Jordan River so they would be a safe distance from David and his followers at Hebron and also because the Philistines had occupied most of the northern part of the land after they defeated the Israelites at Mount Gilboa (1 Sam. 31:7).

[9]And made him king over Gilead, and
over the Ashurites, and over Jezreel,
and over *Ephraim, and over Benjamin,
and over all Israel.
[10]Ish-bosheth Saul's son *was* forty
years old when he began to reign over
Israel, and reigned two years. But the
house of Judah followed David.
[11]And the time that David was king
in Hebron over the house of Judah was
seven years and six months.

Civil war between David and Ish-bosheth

¶[12]And Abner the son of Ner, and the
servants of Ish-bosheth the son of Saul,
went out from Mahanaim to Gibeon.
[13]And Joab the son of Zeruiah, and
the servants of David, went out, and
met together by the pool of Gibeon:
and they sat down, the one on the one
side of the pool, and the other on the
other side of the pool.
[14]And Abner said to Joab, Let the
young men now arise, and play before
us. And Joab said, Let them arise.
[15]Then there arose and went over by
number twelve of Benjamin, which *per-*
tained to Ish-bosheth the son of Saul,
and twelve of the servants of David.
[16]And they caught every one his fellow by the head, and *thrust* his sword
in his fellow's side; so they fell down
together: wherefore that place was
called Helkath-hazzurim, which *is* in
Gibeon.
[17]And there was a very sore battle
that day; and Abner was beaten, and the
men of Israel, before the servants of
David.
¶[18]And there were three sons of Zeruiah there, Joab, and Abishai, and Asahel: and Asahel *was as* light of foot as a
wild roe.
[19]And Asahel pursued after Abner;
and in going he turned not to the right
hand nor to the left from following Abner.

2:3 cities of Hebron. Every major city had under its rule all the smaller neighboring towns and villages that were associated with the main city.
2:14 play. To fence, fight with swords.
2:16 Helkath-hazzurim. The name means *field of the sword edges*.

[20]Then Abner looked behind him, and
said, *Art* thou Asahel? And he answered, I *am.*
[21]And Abner said to him, Turn thee
aside to thy right hand or to thy left, and
lay thee hold on one of the young men,
and take thee his armour. But Asahel
would not turn aside from following of
him.
[22]And Abner said again to Asahel,
Turn thee aside from following me:
wherefore should I smite thee to the
ground? how then should I hold up my
face to Joab thy brother?
[23]Howbeit he refused to turn aside:
wherefore Abner with the hinder end of
the spear smote him under the fifth *rib,*
that the spear came out behind him; and
he fell down there, and died in the same
place: and it came to pass, *that* as many
as came to the place where Asahel fell
down and died stood still.
[24]Joab also and Abishai pursued after
Abner: and the sun went down when
they were come to the hill of Ammah,
that *lieth* before Giah by the way of the
wilderness of Gibeon.
¶[25]And the children of Benjamin
gathered themselves together after
Abner, and became one troop, and stood
on the top of an hill.
[26]Then Abner called to Joab, and said,
Shall the sword devour for ever?
knowest thou not that it will be bitterness in the latter end? how long shall
it be then, ere thou bid the people return from following their brethren?
[27]And Joab said, *As* *God liveth, unless thou hadst spoken, surely then in
the morning the people had gone up
every one from following his brother.
[28]So Joab blew a trumpet, and all the
people stood still, and pursued after
Israel no more, neither fought they any
more.
[29]And Abner and his men walked all
that night through the plain, and passed
over Jordan, and went through all Bith-
ron, and they came to Mahanaim.
[30]And Joab returned from following
Abner: and when he had gathered all
the people together, there lacked of
David's servants nineteen men and
Asahel.
[31]But the servants of David had smitten of Benjamin, and of Abner's men, *so*
that three hundred and threescore men
died.
¶[32]And they took up Asahel, and buried him in the sepulchre of his father,
which *was in* Beth-lehem. And Joab and
his men went all night, and they came
to Hebron at break of day.

3 Now there was long war between
the house of Saul and the house of
David: but David waxed stronger and
stronger, and the house of Saul waxed
weaker and weaker.

David's family

¶[2]And unto David were sons born in
Hebron: and his firstborn was Amnon,
of Ahinoam the Jezreelitess;
[3]And his second, Chileab, of Abigail
the wife of Nabal the Carmelite; and the
third, Absalom the son of Maacah the
daughter of Talmai king of Geshur;
[4]And the fourth, Adonijah the son of
Haggith; and the fifth, Shephatiah the
son of Abital;
[5]And the sixth, Ithream, by Eglah
David's wife. These were born to David in Hebron.
¶[6]And it came to pass, while there
was war between the house of Saul and
the house of David, that Abner made
himself strong for the house of Saul.

Abner deserts to David

[7]And Saul had a *concubine, whose
name *was* Rizpah, the daughter of Aiah:
and *Ish-bosheth* said to Abner, Where-

2:22 how then should I hold up my face to Joab . . . ? When any man was slain by an enemy, his nearest kinsman became the *avenger of blood and considered it his solemn duty to clear the family name of all disgrace by putting to death the one who had slain his kinsman (compare 2 Sam. 3:30).

fore hast thou gone in unto my father's
concubine?
[8]Then was Abner very wroth for the
words of Ish-bosheth, and said, *Am* I a
dog's head, which against Judah do
shew kindness this day unto the house
of Saul thy father, to his brethren, and
to his friends, and have not delivered
thee into the hand of David, that thou
chargest me to day with a fault concerning this woman?
[9]So do God to Abner, and more also,
except, as the LORD hath sworn to David, even so I do to him;
[10]To translate the kingdom from the
house of Saul, and to set up the throne
of David over Israel and over Judah,
from Dan even to *Beer-sheba.
[11]And he could not answer Abner a
word again, because he feared him.
¶[12]And Abner sent messengers to
David on his behalf, saying, Whose *is*
the land? saying *also,* Make thy league
with me, and, behold, my hand *shall be*
with thee, to bring about all Israel unto
thee.
¶[13]And he said, Well; I will make a
league with thee: but one thing I require of thee, that is, Thou shalt not see
my face, except thou first bring Michal
Saul's daughter, when thou comest to
see my face.
[14]And David sent messengers to
Ish-bosheth Saul's son, saying, Deliver *me* my wife Michal, which I espoused
to me for an hundred foreskins of the
Philistines.
[15]And Ish-bosheth sent, and took her
from *her* husband, *even* from Phaltiel the
son of Laish.
[16]And her husband went with her
along weeping behind her to Bahurim.
Then said Abner unto him, Go, return.
And he returned.
¶[17]And Abner had communication
with the *elders of Israel, saying, Ye
sought for David in times past *to be* king
over you:
[18]Now then do *it:* for the LORD hath
spoken of David, saying, By the hand of
my servant David I will save my people Israel out of the hand of the Philistines, and out of the hand of all their
enemies.
[19]And Abner also spake in the ears of
Benjamin: and Abner went also to
speak in the ears of David in Hebron all
that seemed good to Israel, and that
seemed good to the whole house of
Benjamin.
[20]So Abner came to David to Hebron,
and twenty men with him. And David
made Abner and the men that *were* with
him a feast.

3:2 David's Family Tree

Jesse

Eliab
Abinadab
Shammah
Nethanel
Raddai
Ozem

David
(of Michal)
(of Ahinoam) Amnon
(of Abigail) Chileab
(of Maacah) Absalom
(of Haggith) Adonijah
(of Abital) Shephatiah
(of Eglah) Ithream
(of Bath-sheba) Shammuah
Shobab
Nathan
Solomon
(of ?) Ibhar, Elishua, Eliphelet
Nogah, Nepheg, Japhia,
Elishama, Eliada, Eliphelet

Zeruiah (daughter)
Abishai
Joab
Asahel

Abigail (daughter)

21 And Abner said unto David, I will arise and go, and will gather all Israel unto my lord the king, that they may make a league with thee, and that thou mayest reign over all that thine heart desireth. And David sent Abner away; and he went in *peace.

Joab kills Abner

¶22 And, Behold, the servants of David and Joab came from *pursuing* a troop, and brought in a great spoil with them: but Abner *was* not with David in Hebron; for he had sent him away, and he was gone in peace.

23 When Joab and all the host that *was* with him were come, they told Joab, saying, Abner the son of Ner came to the king, and he hath sent him away, and he is gone in peace.

24 Then Joab came to the king, and said, What hast thou done? behold, Abner came unto thee; why *is* it *that* thou hast sent him away, and he is quite gone?

25 Thou knowest Abner the son of Ner, that he came to deceive thee, and to know thy going out and thy coming in, and to know all that thou doest.

26 And when Joab was come out from David, he sent messengers after Abner, which brought him again from the well of Sirah: but David knew *it* not.

¶27 And when Abner was returned to Hebron, Joab took him aside in the gate to speak with him quietly, and smote him there under the fifth *rib,* that he died, for the blood of Asahel his brother.

28 And afterward when David heard *it,* he said, I and my kingdom *are* guiltless before the LORD for ever from the blood of Abner the son of Ner:

29 Let it rest on the head of Joab, and on all his father's house; and let there not fail from the house of Joab one that hath an issue, or that is a *leper, or that leaneth on a staff, or that falleth on the sword, or that lacketh bread.

30 So Joab and Abishai his brother slew Abner, because he had slain their brother Asahel at Gibeon in the battle.

¶31 And David said to Joab, and to all the people that *were* with him, Rend your clothes, and gird you with sackcloth, and mourn before Abner. And king David *himself* followed the bier.

32 And they buried Abner in Hebron: and the king lifted up his voice, and wept at the grave of Abner; and all the people wept.

33 And the king lamented over Abner, and said, Died Abner as a *fool dieth?

34 Thy hands *were* not bound, nor thy feet put into fetters: as a man falleth before wicked men, *so* fellest thou. And all the people wept again over him.

35 And when all the people came to cause David to eat meat while it was yet day, David sware, saying, So do God to me, and more also, if I taste bread, or ought else, till the sun be down.

36 And all the people took notice *of it,* and it pleased them: as whatsoever the king did pleased all the people.

37 For all the people and all Israel understood that day that it was not of the king to slay Abner the son of Ner.

38 And the king said unto his servants, Know ye not that there is a prince and a great man fallen this day in Israel?

39 And I *am* this day weak, though anointed king; and these men the sons of Zeruiah *be* too hard for me: the LORD shall reward the doer of evil according to his wickedness.

The murder of Ish-bosheth

4 And when Saul's son heard that Abner was dead in Hebron, his hands were feeble, and all the Israelites were troubled.

2 And Saul's son had two men *that were* captains of bands: the name of the one *was* Baanah, and the name of the other Rechab, the sons of Rimmon a Beerothite, of the children of Benjamin: (for Beeroth also was reckoned to Benjamin:

3 And the Beerothites fled to Gittaim, and were sojourners there until this day.)

4 And Jonathan, Saul's son, had a son

that was lame of *his* feet. He was five
years old when the tidings came of Saul
and Jonathan out of Jezreel, and his
nurse took him up, and fled: and it came
to pass, as she made haste to flee, that
he fell, and became lame. And his name
was *Mephibosheth.
5 And the sons of Rimmon the Beerothite, Rechab and Baanah, went, and
came about the heat of the day to the
house of Ish-bosheth, who lay on a bed
at noon.
6 And they came thither into the
midst of the house, *as though* they
would have fetched wheat; and they
smote him under the fifth *rib:* and
Rechab and Baanah his brother escaped.
7 For when they came into the house,
he lay on his bed in his *bedchamber,
and they smote him, and slew him, and
beheaded him, and took his head, and
gat them away through the plain all
night.
8 And they brought the head of Ish-
bosheth unto David to Hebron, and said
to the king, Behold the head of Ish-
bosheth the son of Saul thine enemy,
which sought thy life; and the LORD
hath avenged my lord the king this day
of Saul, and of his seed.
¶ 9 And David answered Rechab and
Baanah his brother, the sons of Rimmon
the Beerothite, and said unto them, *As*
the LORD liveth, who hath *redeemed
my soul out of all adversity,
10 When one told me, saying, Behold,
Saul is dead, thinking to have brought
good tidings, I took hold of him, and
slew him in Ziklag, who *thought* that I
would have given him a reward for his
tidings:
11 How much more, when wicked
men have slain a righteous person in
his own house upon his bed? shall I not
therefore now require his blood of your
hand, and take you away from the
earth?
12 And David commanded his young
men, and they slew them, and cut off
their hands and their feet, and hanged
them up over the pool in Hebron. But
they took the head of Ish-bosheth, and
buried *it* in the sepulchre of Abner in
Hebron.

II. David Is Established as King (5:1—10:19)

5 Then came all the tribes of Israel
to David unto Hebron, and spake,
saying, Behold, we *are* thy bone and thy
flesh.
2 Also in time past, when Saul was
king over us, thou wast he that leddest
out and broughtest in Israel: and the
LORD said to thee, Thou shalt feed my
people Israel, and thou shalt be a captain over Israel.
3 So all the elders of Israel came to the
king to Hebron; and king David made a
league with them in Hebron before the
LORD: and they anointed David king
over Israel.
¶ 4 David *was* thirty years old when he
began to reign, *and* he reigned forty
years.
5 In Hebron he reigned over Judah
seven years and six months: and in *Jerusalem he reigned thirty and three
years over all Israel and Judah.

David makes Jerusalem the capital of the kingdom

¶ 6 And the king and his men went to
Jerusalem unto the Jebusites, the inhabitants of the land: which spake unto
David, saying, Except thou take away
the blind and the lame, thou shalt not
come in hither: thinking, David cannot
come in hither.
7 Nevertheless David took the strong
hold of *Zion: the same *is* the city of
David.
8 And David said on that day, Whosoever getteth up to the gutter, and
smiteth the Jebusites, and the lame
and the blind, *that are* hated of David's
soul, *he shall be chief and captain.*
Wherefore they said, The blind and
the lame shall not come into the
house.
9 So David dwelt in the fort, and called

it the city of David. And David built
round about from Millo and inward.
10And David went on, and grew great,
and the LORD God of hosts *was* with
him.
¶11And Hiram king of *Tyre sent
messengers to David, and cedar trees,
and carpenters, and masons: and they
built David an house.
12And David perceived that the LORD
had established him king over Israel,
and that he had exalted his kingdom for
his people Israel's sake.
¶13And David took *him* more concubines and wives out of Jerusalem, after
he was come from Hebron: and there
were yet sons and daughters born to
David.
14And these *be* the names of those
that were born unto him in Jerusalem;
Shammuah, and Shobab, and Nathan,
and Solomon,
15Ibhar also, and Elishua, and Nepheg, and Japhia,
16And Elishama, and Eliada, and
Eliphalet.

War between David and the Philistines

¶17But when the Philistines heard
that they had anointed David king over
Israel, all the Philistines came up to
seek David; and David heard *of it,* and
went down to the hold.
18The Philistines also came and
spread themselves in the valley of
Rephaim.
19And David enquired of the LORD,
saying, Shall I go up to the Philistines?
wilt thou deliver them into mine hand?
And the LORD said unto David, Go up:
for I will doubtless deliver the Philistines into thine hand.
20And David came to *Baal-perazim,
and David smote them there, and said,
The LORD hath broken forth upon mine
enemies before me, as the breach of
waters. Therefore he called the name
of that place Baal-perazim.
21And there they left their images,
and David and his men burned them.
¶22And the Philistines came up yet
again, and spread themselves in the
valley of Rephaim.
23And when David enquired of the
LORD, he said, Thou shalt not go up; *but*
fetch a compass behind them, and come
upon them over against the mulberry
trees.
24And let it be, when thou hearest the
sound of a going in the tops of the mulberry trees, that then thou shalt bestir
thyself: for then shall the LORD go out
before thee, to smite the host of the
Philistines.
25And David did so, as the LORD had
commanded him; and smote the Philistines from Geba until thou come to
Gazer.

David decides to bring the ark of God to Jerusalem

6 Again, David gathered together all
the chosen *men* of Israel, thirty
thousand.

5:6 THE JEBUSITES' CHALLENGE

The Jebusites were saying to David, "You can not come into the city, because the blind and lame will turn you away." Thus the Jebusites, who had never been driven out of their strong fortress at Jerusalem when Joshua conquered the land, defied the God of Israel (Judg. 1:21), and declared that David could not capture their city, and that even blind men and cripples could protect it against all attack.

David's reply in verse 8 does not mean that he really hated all blind men and crippled people. David was referring to the boast that the Jebusites made and meant that he hated men who defied and ridiculed the power and authority of God.

5:9 Millo. The ancient fortress of the Jebusites on a hill guarding the northern approach to Jerusalem.

5:20 Baal-perazim. The name means *the master of breaking through* (1 Kings 18:26).

[2]And David arose, and went with all
the people that *were* with him from
Baale of Judah, to bring up from thence
the *ark of God, whose name is called
by the name of the LORD of hosts that
dwelleth *between* the cherubims.
[3]And they set the ark of God upon a
new cart, and brought it out of the
house of Abinadab that *was* in Gibeah:
and Uzzah and Ahio, the sons of Abinadab, drave the new cart.
[4]And they brought it out of the house
of Abinadab which *was* at Gibeah, accompanying the ark of God: and Ahio
went before the ark.
[5]And David and all the house of Israel
played before the LORD on all manner
of *instruments made of* fir wood, even
on harps, and on *psalteries, and on
*timbrels, and on cornets, and on cym-
bals.
¶[6]And when they came to Nachon's
threshingfloor, Uzzah put forth *his hand*
to the ark of God, and took hold of it;
for the oxen shook *it.*
[7]And the anger of the LORD was kindled against Uzzah; and God smote him
there for *his* error; and there he died by
the ark of God.
[8]And David was displeased, because
the LORD had made a breach upon Uzzah: and he called the name of the place
Perez-uzzah to this day.
[9]And David was afraid of the LORD
that day, and said, How shall the ark of
the LORD come to me?
[10]So David would not remove the ark
of the LORD unto him into the city of
David: but David carried it aside into
the house of Obed-edom the Gittite.
[11]And the ark of the LORD continued
in the house of Obed-edom the Gittite
three months: and the LORD blessed
Obed-edom, and all his household.

David brings the ark to Jerusalem in God's way

¶[12]And it was told king David, saying,
The LORD hath blessed the house of
Obed-edom, and all that *pertaineth* unto
him, because of the ark of God. So David went and brought up the ark of God
from the house of Obed-edom into the
city of David with gladness.
[13]And it was *so,* that when they that
bare the ark of the LORD had gone six
paces, he sacrificed oxen and fatlings.
[14]And David danced before the LORD
with all *his* might: and David *was* girded
with a *linen *ephod.
[15]So David and all the house of Israel
brought up the ark of the LORD with

6:3-7 MISHANDLING THE ARK OF GOD

Placing the ark on a cart was not according to God's Law. He had directed that the ark should be carried by poles that were thrust through the rings at its corners and were borne on the shoulders of the priests (Exod. 25:1-15; 1 Kings 8:7-8). To put the ark on a wagon, as David did here, was to copy the Philistines (1 Sam. 6). God expects His work to be done in His way.

It seemed like a severe judgment for God to kill Uzzah for touching the ark. But God had commanded that the ark should be kept covered and that no man should touch it. When men lose the sense of the sacredness of holy things and of the presence and holiness of God, it is better that one person be slain under the judgment of God than that thousands should drift into sin because of carelessness about holy things.

6:2 the ark of God. The ark of the covenant had been captured by the Philistines at the battle of Aphek (1 Sam. 4), and after seven months the Philistines had sent it back to Judah (1 Sam. 6). It had remained at Baale (the same place is also called "Kirjath-jearim" in 1 Chron.13:6) during the days of Samuel and Saul

6:13 when they that bare the ark. David had discarded the cart, and the ark was now being carried on the shoulders of the priests, as God had commanded. It was David's willingness to confess his sins and to make right whatever he had done wrong that made him a man after God's own heart.

shouting, and with the sound of the trumpet.

16 And as the ark of the LORD came into the city of David, Michal Saul's daughter looked through a window, and saw king David leaping and dancing before the LORD; and she despised him in her heart.

¶17 And they brought in the ark of the LORD, and set it in his place, in the midst of the *tabernacle that David had pitched for it: and David offered burnt-offerings and peace-offerings before the LORD.

18 And as soon as David had made an end of *offering burnt-offerings and peace-offerings, he blessed the people in the name of the LORD of hosts.

19 And he dealt among all the people, *even* among the whole multitude of Israel, as well to the women as men, to every one a cake of bread, and a good piece *of flesh,* and a flagon *of wine.* So all the people departed every one to his house.

¶20 Then David returned to bless his household. And Michal the daughter of Saul came out to meet David, and said, How glorious was the king of Israel to day, who uncovered himself to day in the eyes of the handmaids of his servants, as one of the vain fellows shamelessly uncovereth himself!

21 And David said unto Michal, *It was* before the LORD, which chose me before thy father, and before all his house, to appoint me ruler over the people of the LORD, over Israel: therefore will I play before the LORD.

22 And I will yet be more vile than thus, and will be base in mine own sight: and of the maidservants which thou hast spoken of, of them shall I be had in honour.

23 Therefore Michal the daughter of Saul had no child unto the day of her death.

David's desire to build a temple for God

7 And it came to pass, when the king sat in his house, and the LORD had given him rest round about from all his enemies;

2 That the king said unto Nathan the *prophet, See now, I dwell in an house of cedar, but the ark of God dwelleth within curtains.

3 And Nathan said to the king, Go, do all that *is* in thine heart; for the LORD *is* with thee.

Seventh covenant: Davidic

¶4 And it came to pass that night, that the word of the LORD came unto Nathan, saying,

5 Go and tell my servant *David, Thus saith the LORD, Shalt thou build me an house for me to dwell in?

6 Whereas I have not dwelt in *any* house since the time that I brought up the children of *Israel out of *Egypt, even to this day, but have walked in a tent and in a tabernacle.

7 In all *the places* wherein I have walked with all the children of Israel spake I a word with any of the tribes of Israel, whom I commanded to feed my people Israel, saying, Why build ye not me an house of cedar?

6:16 Michal . . . despised him. David had laid aside his long outer garments in order to join the crowd of people who were leaping in joy before the ark of the LORD, but Michal despised her husband for such a show of enthusiasm, feeling that by doing so he degraded himself to the level of the common people.

6:19 flagon of wine. A container of wine.

6:21 therefore will I play before the LORD. "Play" here means *to celebrate,* and David made it clear to Michal, who did not seem to want to worship God, that it was the LORD he was praising for the return of the ark. David made no apologies for his worship of his God, and neither should we. Michal's bitterness cost her dearly. According to verse 23, she was childless until her death. Christians who become bitter—for any reason—will pay a high price if we do not seek God's forgiveness and let nothing come between us and Him (see Heb. 12:15).

[8]Now therefore so shalt thou say
unto my servant David, Thus saith the
LORD of hosts, I took thee from the
sheepcote, from following the sheep, to
be ruler over my people, over Israel:
[9]And I was with thee whithersoever
thou wentest, and have cut off all thine
enemies out of thy sight, and have made
thee a great name, like unto the name
of the great *men* that *are* in the earth.
[10]Moreover I will appoint a place for
my people Israel, and will plant them,
that they may dwell in a place of their
own, and move no more; neither shall
the children of wickedness afflict them
any more, as beforetime,
[11]And as since the time that I commanded *judges *to be* over my people
Israel, and have caused thee to rest
from all thine enemies. Also the LORD
telleth thee that he will make thee an
house.
¶[12]And when thy days be fulfilled,
and thou shalt sleep with thy fathers, I
will set up thy seed after thee, which
shall proceed out of thy *bowels, and I
will establish his kingdom.
[13]He shall build an house for my
name, and I will stablish the throne of
his kingdom for ever.
[14]I will be his father, and he shall be
my son. If he commit iniquity, I will
*chasten him with the rod of men, and
with the *stripes of the children of men:
[15]But my *mercy shall not depart
away from him, as I took *it* from Saul,
whom I put away before thee.
[16]And thine house and thy kingdom
shall be established for ever before
thee: thy throne shall be established for
ever.
[17]According to all these words, and
according to all this vision, so did Nathan speak unto David.
¶[18]Then went king David in, and sat
before the LORD, and he said, Who *am*
I, O Lord GOD? and what *is* my house,
that thou hast brought me hitherto?
[19]And this was yet a small thing in thy
sight, O Lord GOD; but thou hast spoken also of thy servant's house for a
great while to come. And *is* this the
manner of man, O Lord GOD?
[20]And what can David say more unto
thee? for thou, Lord GOD, knowest thy
servant.
[21]For thy word's sake, and according
to thine own heart, hast thou done all
these great things, to make thy servant
know *them.*
[22]Wherefore thou art great, O LORD
God: for *there is* none like thee, neither
is there any God beside thee, according
to all that we have heard with our ears.
[23]And what one nation in the earth *is*
like thy people, *even* like Israel, whom
God went to *redeem for a people to
himself, and to make him a name, and

7:11 THE DAVIDIC COVENANT

Verses 12 to 16 describe what is known as the Davidic covenant or the covenant with David. Here, many centuries in advance, God promised:

1. to put David's family on the throne after him;
2. to establish the throne or authority forever in the hands of David's family;
3. to establish the kingdom forever so that it would never be overcome.

That God was wonderfully revealing the Lord Jesus Christ in these verses is evident:

1. Hebrews 1:5 declares that God spoke the opening words of 2 Samuel 7:14 to the Lord Jesus.
2. In Luke 1:31-33 the angel refers to this passage and declares that Jesus is the promised seed of David who is to sit forever on David's throne.

This covenant is unconditional, and God will surely keep it. Nothing in history prevents the fulfillment of this ages-old pledge, and it will be kept in God's appointed time when our Lord comes back into the world to establish a *kingdom that will never be cast down. See also *covenant.

7:13 stablish. To establish, confirm.

to do for you great things and terrible,
for thy land, before thy people, which
thou redeemedst to thee from Egypt,
from the nations and their gods?
24For thou hast confirmed to thyself
thy people Israel *to be* a people unto
thee for ever: and thou, LORD, art become their God.
25And now, O LORD God, the word
that thou hast spoken concerning thy
servant, and concerning his house, establish *it* for ever, and do as thou hast
said.
26And let thy name be magnified for
ever, saying, The LORD of hosts *is* the
God over Israel: and let the house of thy
servant David be established before
thee.
27For thou, O LORD of hosts, God of
Israel, hast revealed to thy servant,
saying, I will build thee an house: therefore hath thy servant found in his heart
to pray this *prayer unto thee.
28And now, O Lord GOD, thou *art* that
God, and thy words be true, and thou
hast promised this goodness unto thy
servant:
29Therefore now let it please thee to
bless the house of thy servant, that it
may continue for ever before thee: for
thou, O Lord GOD, hast spoken *it:* and
with thy blessing let the house of thy
servant be blessed for ever.

David conquers the surrounding nations

8 And after this it came to pass, that
David smote the *Philistines, and
subdued them: and David took Metheg-
ammah out of the hand of the Philistines.
2And he smote *Moab, and measured
them with a line, casting them down to
the ground; even with two lines measured he to put to death, and with one
full line to keep alive. And *so* the Moabites became David's servants, *and*
brought gifts.
¶3David smote also Hadadezer, the
son of Rehob, king of Zobah, as he went
to recover his border at the river Euphrates.
4And David took from him a thousand
chariots, and seven hundred horsemen,
and twenty thousand footmen: and David
*houghed all the chariot *horses,* but reserved of them *for* an hundred chariots.
5And when the Syrians of *Damascus
came to succour Hadadezer king of
Zobah, David slew of the Syrians two
and twenty thousand men.
6Then David put garrisons in Syria of
Damascus: and the Syrians became servants to David, *and* brought gifts. And
the LORD preserved David whithersoever he went.
7And David took the shields of gold
that were on the servants of Hadadezer,
and brought them to Jerusalem.
8And from Betah, and from Berothai,
cities of Hadadezer, king David took
exceeding much brass.
¶9When Toi king of Hamath heard
that David had smitten all the host of
Hadadezer,
10Then Toi sent Joram his son unto
king David, to salute him, and to bless
him, because he had fought against
Hadadezer, and smitten him: for Hadadezer had wars with Toi. And *Joram*
brought with him vessels of silver, and
vessels of gold, and vessels of brass:
11Which also king David did dedicate
unto the LORD, with the silver and gold
that he had dedicated of all nations
which he subdued;
12Of Syria, and of Moab, and of the
children of Ammon, and of the Philistines, and of *Amalek, and of the spoil
of Hadadezer, son of Rehob, king of
Zobah.

8:4 houghed. To cut the hamstrings of animals.

8:11 all nations which he subdued. These conquests of David's paved the way for the prosperity and peace of Solomon's reign. When Solomon came to the throne, all the surrounding nations were subject to the children of Israel and paid yearly tribute to King Solomon.

13And David gat *him* a name when he
returned from smiting of the Syrians in
the *valley of salt, *being* eighteen thousand *men.*
¶14And he put garrisons in Edom;
throughout all Edom put he garrisons,
and all they of Edom became David's
servants. And the LORD preserved David whithersoever he went.
15And David reigned over all Israel;
and David executed *judgment and justice unto all his people.
16And Joab the son of Zeruiah *was*
over the host; and Jehoshaphat the son
of Ahilud *was* recorder;
17And Zadok the son of Ahitub, and
Ahimelech the son of Abiathar, *were* the
priests; and Seraiah *was* the *scribe;
18And Benaiah the son of *Jehoiada
was over both the Cherethites and the
Pelethites; and David's sons were chief
rulers.

David's kindness to Mephibosheth

9 And David said, Is there yet any
that is left of the house of Saul, that
I may shew him kindness for Jonathan's
sake?
2And *there was* of the house of Saul a
servant whose name *was* Ziba. And
when they had called him unto David,
the king said unto him, *Art* thou Ziba?
And he said, Thy servant *is he.*
3And the king said, *Is* there not yet
any of the house of Saul, that I may
shew the kindness of *God unto him?
And Ziba said unto the king, Jonathan
hath yet a son, *which is* lame on *his* feet.
4And the king said unto him, Where
is he? And Ziba said unto the king, Behold, he *is* in the house of Machir, the
son of Ammiel, in Lo-debar.
¶5Then king David sent, and fetched
him out of the house of Machir, the son
of Ammiel, from Lo-debar.
6Now when Mephibosheth, the son

9:3 God's Kindness
According to the custom of those days, a king was expected to put to death all the relatives and friends of everyone who had opposed him before he came to the throne. Thus Mephibosheth, the grandson of Saul, expected death from the hand of David. But instead David forgave Mephibosheth, adopted him into the king's family, and seated him at the king's table as one of the king's own sons. This is a beautiful illustration of the kindness of God who forgave us when we were sinners for Christ's sake (Eph. 1:7), adopted us into His family (Eph. 1:5), and seated us with His own Son Christ Jesus (Eph. 2:6).

of Jonathan, the son of Saul, was come
unto David, he fell on his face, and did
reverence. And David said, Mephibosheth. And he answered, Behold thy
servant!
¶7And David said unto him, Fear not:
for I will surely shew thee kindness for
Jonathan thy father's sake, and will restore thee all the land of Saul thy father;
and thou shalt eat bread at my table
continually.
8And he bowed himself, and said,
What *is* thy servant, that thou shouldest
look upon such a dead dog as I *am?*
¶9Then the king called to Ziba, Saul's
servant, and said unto him, I have given
unto thy master's son all that pertained
to Saul and to all his house.
10Thou therefore, and thy sons, and
thy servants, shall till the land for him,
and thou shalt bring in *the fruits,* that
thy master's son may have food to eat:
but Mephibosheth thy master's son
shall eat bread alway at my table. Now
Ziba had fifteen sons and twenty servants.
11Then said Ziba unto the king, According to all that my lord the king hath
commanded his servant, so shall thy

8:18 Cherethites and the Pelethites. These were foreign soldiers who had attached themselves to David because they loved and admired him as a courageous captain, and they formed a royal bodyguard that stayed true to David through many of his deepest troubles.

servant do. As for Mephibosheth, *said*
the king, he shall eat at my table, as one
of the king's sons.
12 And Mephibosheth had a young
son, whose name *was* Micha. And all
that dwelt in the house of Ziba *were*
servants unto Mephibosheth.
13 So Mephibosheth dwelt in Jerusalem: for he did eat continually at the
king's table; and was lame on both his
feet.

David's kindness to Hanun; war against Syria

10 And it came to pass after this,
that the king of the children of
Ammon died, and Hanun his son
reigned in his stead.
2 Then said David, I will shew kindness unto Hanun the son of Nahash, as
his father shewed kindness unto me.
And David sent to comfort him by the
hand of his servants for his father. And
David's servants came into the land of
the children of Ammon.
3 And the princes of the children of
Ammon said unto Hanun their lord,
Thinkest thou that David doth honour
thy father, that he hath sent comforters unto thee? hath not David *rather*
sent his servants unto thee, to search
the city, and to spy it out, and to overthrow it?
4 Wherefore Hanun took David's servants, and shaved off the one half of
their beards, and cut off their garments
in the middle, *even* to their buttocks,
and sent them away.
5 When they told *it* unto David, he
sent to meet them, because the men
were greatly ashamed: and the king
said, Tarry at Jericho until your beards
be grown, and *then* return.
¶6 And when the children of Ammon
saw that they stank before David, the
children of Ammon sent and hired the
Syrians of Beth-rehob, and the Syrians
of Zoba, twenty thousand footmen, and
of king Maacah a thousand men, and of
Ish-tob twelve thousand men.
7 And when David heard of *it,* he sent
Joab, and all the host of the mighty men.
8 And the children of Ammon came
out, and put the battle in array at the
entering in of the gate: and the Syrians
of Zoba, and of Rehob, and Ish-tob, and
Maacah, *were* by themselves in the
field.
9 When Joab saw that the front of the
battle was against him before and behind, he chose of all the choice *men* of
Israel, and put *them* in array against the
Syrians:
10 And the rest of the people he delivered into the hand of Abishai his
brother, that he might put *them* in array
against the children of Ammon.
11 And he said, If the Syrians be too
strong for me, then thou shalt help me:
but if the children of Ammon be too

David's Conquests

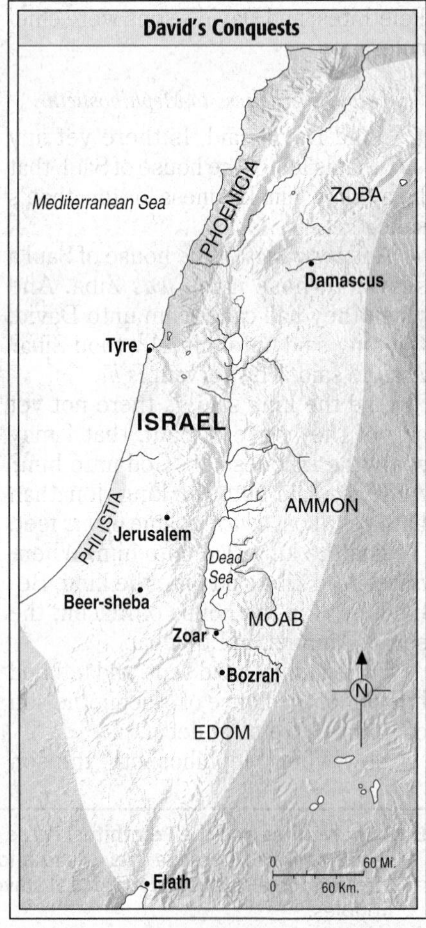

strong for thee, then I will come and
help thee.
12 Be of good courage, and let us play
the men for our people, and for the cities of our God: and the LORD do that
which seemeth him good.
13 And Joab drew nigh, and the people
that *were* with him, unto the battle
against the Syrians: and they fled before
him.
14 And when the children of Ammon
saw that the Syrians were fled, then fled
they also before Abishai, and entered
into the city. So Joab returned from the
children of Ammon, and came to Jerusalem.
¶15 And when the Syrians saw that
they were smitten before Israel, they
gathered themselves together.
16 And Hadarezer sent, and brought
out the Syrians that *were* beyond the
river: and they came to Helam; and
Shobach the captain of the host of
Hadarezer *went* before them.
17 And when it was told David, he
gathered all Israel together, and passed
over Jordan, and came to Helam. And
the Syrians set themselves in array
against David, and fought with him.
18 And the Syrians fled before Israel;
and David slew *the men of* seven hundred chariots of the Syrians, and forty
thousand horsemen, and smote Shobach
the captain of their host, who died there.
19 And when all the kings *that were*
servants to Hadarezer saw that they
were smitten before Israel, they made
peace with Israel, and served them. So
the Syrians feared to help the children
of Ammon any more.

III. David's Sin Brings Trouble (11:1—14:33)

11 And it came to pass, after the
year was expired, at the time
when kings go forth *to battle,* that David sent Joab, and his servants with
him, and all Israel; and they destroyed
the children of Ammon, and besieged
Rabbah. But David tarried still at *Jerusalem.
¶2 And it came to pass in an eveningtide, that David arose from off his bed,
and walked upon the roof of the king's
house: and from the roof he saw a woman washing herself; and the woman *was*
very beautiful to look upon.
3 And David sent and enquired after
the woman. And *one* said, *Is* not this
*Bath-sheba, the daughter of Eliam, the
wife of Uriah the Hittite?
4 And David sent messengers, and
took her; and she came in unto him, and
he lay with her; for she was purified
from her uncleanness: and she returned
unto her house.
5 And the woman conceived, and sent
and told David, and said, I *am* with child.
¶6 And David sent to Joab, *saying,*
Send me Uriah the Hittite. And Joab
sent Uriah to David.
7 And when Uriah was come unto
him, David demanded *of him* how Joab
did, and how the people did, and how
the war prospered.
8 And David said to Uriah, Go down to
thy house, and wash thy feet. And Uriah departed out of the king's house, and
there followed him a mess *of meat* from
the king.
9 But Uriah slept at the door of the
king's house with all the servants of his
lord, and went not down to his house.
10 And when they had told David, saying, Uriah went not down unto his
house, David said unto Uriah, Camest
thou not from *thy* journey? why *then*
didst thou not go down unto thine
house?
11 And Uriah said unto David, The
ark, and Israel, and *Judah, abide in
tents; and my lord Joab, and the servants of my lord, are encamped in the
open fields; shall I then go into mine
house, to eat and to drink, and to lie
with my wife? *as* thou livest, and *as* thy
soul liveth, I will not do this thing.
12 And David said to Uriah, Tarry here
to day also, and to morrow I will let thee
depart. So Uriah abode in Jerusalem
that day, and the morrow.
13 And when David had called him, he

did eat and drink before him; and he made him drunk: and at even he went out to lie on his bed with the servants of his lord, but went not down to his house.

¶ 14 And it came to pass in the morning, that David wrote a letter to Joab, and sent *it* by the hand of Uriah.

15 And he wrote in the letter, saying, Set ye Uriah in the forefront of the hottest battle, and retire ye from him, that he may be smitten, and die.

16 And it came to pass, when Joab observed the city, that he assigned Uriah unto a place where he knew that valiant men *were.*

17 And the men of the city went out, and fought with Joab: and there fell *some* of the people of the servants of David; and Uriah the Hittite died also.

¶ 18 Then Joab sent and told David all the things concerning the war;

19 And charged the messenger, saying, When thou hast made an end of telling the matters of the war unto the king,

20 And if so be that the king's wrath arise, and he say unto thee, Wherefore approached ye so nigh unto the city when ye did fight? knew ye not that they would shoot from the wall?

21 Who smote Abimelech the son of Jerubbesheth? did not a woman cast a piece of a millstone upon him from the wall, that he died in Thebez? why went ye nigh the wall? then say thou, Thy servant Uriah the Hittite is dead also.

¶ 22 So the messenger went, and came and shewed David all that Joab had sent him for.

23 And the messenger said unto David, Surely the men prevailed against us, and came out unto us into the field, and we were upon them even unto the entering of the gate.

24 And the shooters shot from off the wall upon thy servants; and *some* of the king's servants be dead, and thy servant Uriah the Hittite is dead also.

25 Then David said unto the messenger, Thus shalt thou say unto Joab, Let not this thing displease thee, for the sword devoureth one as well as another: make thy battle more strong against the city, and overthrow it: and encourage thou him.

¶ 26 And when the wife of Uriah heard that Uriah her husband was dead, she mourned for her husband.

27 And when the *mourning was past, David sent and fetched her to his house, and she became his wife, and bare him a son. But the thing that David had done displeased the LORD.

David's repentance

12 And the LORD sent Nathan unto David. And he came unto him, and said unto him, There were two men in one city; the one rich, and the other poor.

2 The rich *man* had exceeding many flocks and herds:

3 But the poor *man* had nothing, save one little ewe lamb, which he had bought and nourished up: and it grew up together with him, and with his children; it did eat of his own meat, and drank of his own cup, and lay in his bosom, and was unto him as a daughter.

4 And there came a traveller unto the rich man, and he spared to take of his own flock and of his own herd, to dress for the wayfaring man that was come unto him; but took the poor man's lamb, and dressed it for the man that was come to him.

5 And David's anger was greatly kindled against the man; and he said to Nathan, *As* the LORD liveth, the man that hath done this *thing* shall surely die:

6 And he shall restore the lamb four-

11:21 Who smote Abimelech . . . ? See Judges 9:50-55. In that section, Jerubbesheth is called Jerubbaal or Gideon (Judg. 8:35). Gideon was Abimelech's father.

12:4 wayfaring. Traveling on foot.

fold, because he did this thing, and because he had no pity.
¶7 And Nathan said to David, Thou *art*
the man. Thus saith the LORD God of
Israel, I anointed thee king over Israel,
and I delivered thee out of the hand of
Saul;
8 And I gave thee thy master's house,
and thy master's wives into thy bosom,
and gave thee the house of Israel and
of Judah; and if *that had been* too little, I
would moreover have given unto thee
such and such things.
9 Wherefore hast thou despised the
commandment of the LORD, to do evil
in his sight? thou hast killed Uriah the
Hittite with the sword, and hast taken
his wife *to be* thy wife, and hast slain
him with the sword of the children of
Ammon.
10 Now therefore the sword shall
never depart from thine house; because
thou hast despised me, and hast taken
the wife of Uriah the Hittite to be thy
wife.

12:10 There Will Be No Peace
Although David's sin was forgiven, he still reaped its harvest in his own family. From this time on, there were sin and jealousy and murder and revolt among his sons, so that his house never had peace. Sin always results in consequences, even though God is gracious and merciful to forgive us if we simply ask Him (Gal. 6:7-8).

11 Thus saith the LORD, Behold, I will
raise up evil against thee out of thine
own house, and I will take thy wives
before thine eyes, and give *them* unto
thy neighbour, and he shall lie with thy
wives in the sight of this sun.
12 For thou didst *it* secretly: but I will
do this thing before all Israel, and before the sun.
13 And David said unto Nathan, I have
sinned against the LORD. And Nathan
said unto David, The LORD also hath put
away thy *sin; thou shalt not die.
14 Howbeit, because by this deed thou
hast given great occasion to the enemies of the LORD to blaspheme, the
child also *that is* born unto thee shall
surely die.
¶15 And Nathan departed unto his
house. And the LORD struck the child
that Uriah's wife bare unto David, and
it was very sick.
16 David therefore besought God for
the child; and David fasted, and went in,
and lay all night upon the earth.
17 And the *elders of his house arose,
and went to him, to raise him up from
the earth: but he would not, neither did
he eat bread with them.
18 And it came to pass on the seventh
day, that the child died. And the servants of David feared to tell him that the
child was dead: for they said, Behold,
while the child was yet alive, we spake
unto him, and he would not hearken
unto our voice: how will he then vex
himself, if we tell him that the child is
dead?
19 But when David saw that his servants whispered, David perceived that
the child was dead: therefore David said
unto his servants, Is the child dead?
And they said, He is dead.
20 Then David arose from the earth,
and washed, and anointed *himself,* and
changed his apparel, and came into the
house of the LORD, and worshipped:
then he came to his own house; and
when he required, they set bread before
him, and he did eat.
21 Then said his servants unto him,
What thing *is* this that thou hast
done? thou didst fast and weep for the

12:7 Thou art the man. Nathan began by speaking a parable to David: "There were two men" (vs.1). This parable was to illustrate to David the gravity of his adultery with Bath-sheba and his murder of her husband, Uriah the Hittite, a loyal subject of David (2 Sam. 11). David was trying to cover up his sin, but God knows and sees all that is going on in our lives, even in our thoughts. See 1 Chronicles 20:1 note, "David in Jerusalem."

12:13 I have sinned. Read David's confession in Psalm 51. See also 2 Samuel 6:13 note.

child, *while it was* alive; but when the
child was dead, thou didst rise and eat
bread.
22 And he said, While the child was yet
alive, I fasted and wept: for I said, Who
can tell *whether* GOD will be gracious to
me, that the child may live?
23 But now he is dead, wherefore
should I fast? can I bring him back
again? I shall go to him, but he shall not
return to me.

The birth of Solomon

¶24 And David comforted Bath-sheba
his wife, and went in unto her, and lay
with her: and she bare a son, and he
called his name Solomon: and the LORD
loved him.
25 And he sent by the hand of Nathan
the prophet; and he called his name
Jedidiah, because of the LORD.

David subdues the Ammonites

¶26 And Joab fought against Rabbah of
the children of Ammon, and took the
royal city.
27 And Joab sent messengers to David, and said, I have fought against Rabbah, and have taken the city of waters.
28 Now therefore gather the rest of
the people together, and encamp
against the city, and take it: lest I take
the city, and it be called after my name.
29 And David gathered all the people
together, and went to Rabbah, and
fought against it, and took it.
30 And he took their king's crown
from off his head, the weight whereof
was a talent of gold with the precious
stones: and it was *set* on David's head.
And he brought forth the spoil of the
city in great abundance.
31 And he brought forth the people
that *were* therein, and put *them* under
saws, and under harrows of iron, and
under axes of iron, and made them pass
through the brick-kiln: and thus did he
unto all the cities of the children of
Ammon. So David and all the people
returned unto Jerusalem.

Amnon's sin

13 And it came to pass after this,
that Absalom the son of *David
had a fair sister, whose name *was* Tamar; and Amnon the son of David loved
her.
2 And Amnon was so vexed, that he
fell sick for his sister Tamar; for she *was*
a virgin; and Amnon thought it hard for
him to do any thing to her.
3 But Amnon had a friend, whose
name *was* Jonadab, the son of Shimeah
David's brother: and Jonadab *was* a very
subtil man.
4 And he said unto him, Why *art* thou,
being the king's son, lean from day to
day? wilt thou not tell me? And Amnon
said unto him, I love Tamar, my brother
Absalom's sister.
5 And Jonadab said unto him, Lay thee
down on thy bed, and make thyself sick:
and when thy father cometh to see
thee, say unto him, I pray thee, let my
sister Tamar come, and give me meat,
and dress the meat in my sight, that I
may see *it*, and eat *it* at her hand.
¶6 So Amnon lay down, and made
himself sick: and when the king was
come to see him, Amnon said unto the
king, I pray thee, let Tamar my sister
come, and make me a couple of cakes
in my sight, that I may eat at her hand.
7 Then David sent home to Tamar,
saying, Go now to thy brother Amnon's
house, and dress him meat.
8 So Tamar went to her brother
Amnon's house; and he was laid down.
And she took flour, and kneaded *it*, and
made cakes in his sight, and did bake
the cakes.
9 And she took a pan, and poured *them*
out before him; but he refused to eat.
And Amnon said, Have out all men from

12:25 Jedidiah. *The beloved of God* is the meaning of this name for Solomon.
12:31 put them under saws. This verse means that the Ammonites were made slaves and were put to work at various kinds of tasks.

me. And they went out every man from him.

10 And Amnon said unto Tamar, Bring the meat into the chamber, that I may eat of thine hand. And Tamar took the cakes which she had made, and brought *them* into the chamber to Amnon her brother.

11 And when she had brought *them* unto him to eat, he took hold of her, and said unto her, Come lie with me, my sister.

12 And she answered him, Nay, my brother, do not force me; for no such thing ought to be done in *Israel: do not thou this folly.

13 And I, whither shall I cause my shame to go? and as for thee, thou shalt be as one of the fools in Israel. Now therefore, I pray thee, speak unto the king; for he will not withhold me from thee.

14 Howbeit he would not hearken unto her voice: but, being stronger than she, forced her, and lay with her.

¶ 15 Then Amnon hated her exceedingly; so that the hatred wherewith he hated her *was* greater than the love wherewith he had loved her. And Amnon said unto her, Arise, be gone.

16 And she said unto him, *There is* no cause: this evil in sending me away *is* greater than the other that thou didst unto me. But he would not hearken unto her.

17 Then he called his servant that ministered unto him, and said, Put now this *woman* out from me, and bolt the door after her.

18 And *she had* a garment of divers colours upon her: for with such robes were the king's daughters *that were* virgins apparelled. Then his servant brought her out, and bolted the door after her.

¶ 19 And Tamar put ashes on her head, and rent her garment of divers colours that *was* on her, and laid her hand on her head, and went on crying.

20 And Absalom her brother said unto her, Hath Amnon thy brother been with thee? but hold now thy peace, my sister: he *is* thy brother; regard not this thing. So Tamar remained desolate in her brother Absalom's house.

¶ 21 But when king David heard of all these things, he was very wroth.

22 And Absalom spake unto his brother Amnon neither good nor bad: for Absalom hated Amnon, because he had forced his sister Tamar.

Absalom slays his brother

¶ 23 And it came to pass after two full years, that Absalom had sheepshearers in *Baal-hazor, which *is* beside *Ephraim: and Absalom invited all the king's sons.

24 And Absalom came to the king, and said, Behold now, thy servant hath sheepshearers; let the king, I beseech thee, and his servants go with thy servant.

25 And the king said to Absalom, Nay, my son, let us not all now go, lest we be chargeable unto thee. And he pressed him: howbeit he would not go, but blessed him.

26 Then said Absalom, If not, I pray thee, let my brother Amnon go with us. And the king said unto him, Why should he go with thee?

27 But Absalom pressed him, that he let Amnon and all the king's sons go with him.

¶ 28 Now Absalom had commanded his servants, saying, Mark ye now when Amnon's heart is merry with *wine, and when I say unto you, Smite Amnon; then kill him, fear not: have not I commanded you? be courageous and be valiant.

29 And the servants of Absalom did unto Amnon as Absalom had commanded. Then all the king's sons arose, and every man gat him up upon his mule, and fled.

¶ 30 And it came to pass, while they were in the way, that tidings came to

---

13:19 ashes. This was a sign of sorrow and mourning. See *sackcloth . . . ashes.

David, saying, Absalom hath slain all the king's sons, and there is not one of them left.

31 Then the king arose, and tare his garments, and lay on the earth; and all his servants stood by with their clothes rent.

32 And Jonadab, the son of Shimeah David's brother, answered and said, Let not my lord suppose *that* they have slain all the young men the king's sons; for Amnon only is dead: for by the appointment of Absalom this hath been determined from the day that he forced his sister Tamar.

33 Now therefore let not my lord the king take the thing to his heart, to think that all the king's sons are dead: for Amnon only is dead.

34 But Absalom fled. And the young man that kept the watch lifted up his eyes, and looked, and, behold, there came much people by the way of the hill side behind him.

35 And Jonadab said unto the king, Behold, the king's sons come: as thy servant said, so it is.

36 And it came to pass, as soon as he had made an end of speaking, that, behold, the king's sons came, and lifted up their voice and wept: and the king also and all his servants wept very sore.

Absalom's flight to Geshur

¶ 37 But Absalom fled, and went to Talmai, the son of Ammihud, king of Geshur. And *David* mourned for his son every day.

38 So Absalom fled, and went to Geshur, and was there three years.

39 And *the soul of* king David longed to go forth unto Absalom: for he was comforted concerning Amnon, seeing he was dead.

The recall of Absalom

14 Now Joab the son of Zeruiah perceived that the king's heart *was* toward Absalom.

2 And Joab sent to Tekoah, and fetched thence a wise woman, and said unto her, I pray thee, feign thyself to be a mourner, and put on now mourning apparel, and anoint not thyself with oil, but be as a woman that had a long time mourned for the dead:

3 And come to the king, and speak on this manner unto him. So Joab put the words in her mouth.

¶ 4 And when the woman of Tekoah spake to the king, she fell on her face to the ground, and did obeisance, and said, Help, O king.

5 And the king said unto her, What aileth thee? And she answered, I *am* indeed a widow woman, and mine husband is dead.

14:5 A Parable
This story told by the wise woman to King David is an Old Testament *parable. This parable is a comparison told in a story. A parable really is an object lesson to teach some spiritual or moral truth. It has been called "an earthly story with a heavenly meaning."

6 And thy handmaid had two sons, and they two strove together in the field, and *there was* none to part them, but the one smote the other, and slew him.

7 And, behold, the whole family is risen against thine handmaid, and they said, Deliver him that smote his brother, that we may kill him, for the life of his brother whom he slew; and we will destroy the heir also: and so they shall quench my coal which is left, and shall not leave to my husband *neither* name nor remainder upon the earth.

8 And the king said unto the woman, Go to thine house, and I will give charge concerning thee.

9 And the woman of Tekoah said unto the king, My lord, O king, the iniquity *be* on me, and on my father's house: and the king and his throne *be* guiltless.

10 And the king said, Whosoever saith

13:37 king of Geshur. Absalom's mother was the daughter of the king of Geshur (1 Chron. 3:2).

ought unto thee, bring him to me, and
he shall not touch thee any more.
11Then said she, I pray thee, let the
king remember the LORD thy God, that
thou wouldest not suffer the revengers
of blood to destroy any more, lest they
destroy my son. And he said, *As* the
LORD liveth, there shall not one hair of
thy son fall to the earth.

14:11 Getting Revenge
The "revengers of blood" here refer to the "avenger of blood" (Josh. 20:3). The word "avenger" is from the Hebrew root word that is frequently translated "redeem" (Lev. 25:25,48), and "redeemer" (Job 19:25; Prov. 23:11; Isa. 49:7). It is also translated "kinsman" and occurs twelve times in Ruth (chaps. 3 and 4). Both a redeemer and an avenger were "near kinsmen" (Ruth 3:9,12). It was a point of honor that the nearest relative of a person slain should avenge his death by destroying the slayer. This is called a "blood feud" and is still the custom in some places.

12Then the woman said, Let thine
handmaid, I pray thee, speak *one* word
unto my lord the king. And he said, Say
on.
13And the woman said, Wherefore
then hast thou thought such a thing
against the people of God? for the king
doth speak this thing as one which is
faulty, in that the king doth not fetch
home again his banished.
14For we must needs die, and *are* as
water spilt on the ground, which cannot
be gathered up again; neither doth God
respect *any* person: yet doth he devise
means, that his banished be not expelled from him.
15Now therefore that I am come to
speak of this thing unto my lord the
king, *it is* because the people have made
me afraid: and thy handmaid said, I will
now speak unto the king; it may be that
the king will perform the request of his
handmaid.
16For the king will hear, to deliver his
handmaid out of the hand of the man
that would destroy me and my son together out of the inheritance of God.
17Then thine handmaid said, The
word of my lord the king shall now be
comfortable: for as an *angel of God, so
is my lord the king to discern good and
bad: therefore the LORD thy God will be
with thee.
18Then the king answered and said
unto the woman, Hide not from me, I
pray thee, the thing that I shall ask thee.
And the woman said, Let my lord the
king now speak.
19And the king said, *Is not* the hand
of Joab with thee in all this? And the
woman answered and said, *As* thy soul
liveth, my lord the king, none can turn
to the right hand or to the left from
ought that my lord the king hath spoken: for thy servant Joab, he bade me,
and he put all these words in the mouth
of thine handmaid:
20To fetch about this form of speech
hath thy servant Joab done this thing:
and my lord *is* wise, according to the
wisdom of an angel of God, to know all
things that *are* in the earth.
¶21And the king said unto Joab, Behold now, I have done this thing: go
therefore, bring the young man Absalom again.
22And Joab fell to the ground on his
face, and bowed himself, and thanked
the king: and Joab said, To day thy servant knoweth that I have found grace in
thy sight, my lord, O king, in that the
king hath fulfilled the request of his
servant.
23So Joab arose and went to Geshur,
and brought Absalom to Jerusalem.

David's delayed forgiveness of Absalom sows seeds of bitterness

24And the king said, Let him turn to
his own house, and let him not see my

14:24 saw not the king's face. David's refusal to take Absalom back into the royal family was a great blow to Absalom's pride. David's stubbornness stirred up bitterness in Absalom's heart that led to civil war.

face. So Absalom returned to his own
house, and saw not the king's face.

¶25But in all Israel there was none to
be so much praised as Absalom for his
beauty: from the sole of his foot even
to the crown of his head there was no
blemish in him.

26And when he polled his head, (for
it was at every year's end that he polled
it: because *the hair* was heavy on him,
therefore he polled it:) he weighed the
hair of his head at two hundred shekels
after the king's weight.

27And unto Absalom there were born
three sons, and one daughter, whose
name *was* Tamar: she was a woman of
a fair countenance.

¶28So Absalom dwelt two full years in
Jerusalem, and saw not the king's face.

29Therefore Absalom sent for Joab, to
have sent him to the king; but he would
not come to him: and when he sent
again the second time, he would not
come.

30Therefore he said unto his servants, See, Joab's field is near mine, and
he hath barley there; go and set it on
fire. And Absalom's servants set the
field on fire.

31Then Joab arose, and came to Absalom unto *his* house, and said unto
him, Wherefore have thy servants set
my field on fire?

32And Absalom answered Joab, Behold, I sent unto thee, saying, Come
hither, that I may send thee to the king,
to say, Wherefore am I come from Geshur? *it had been* good for me *to have
been* there still: now therefore let me
see the king's face; and if there be *any*
iniquity in me, let him kill me.

33So Joab came to the king, and told
him: and when he had called for Absalom, he came to the king, and bowed
himself on his face to the ground before
the king: and the king kissed Absalom.

IV. David Threatened by Civil War (15:1—20:26)

Absalom's revolt

15 And it came to pass after this,
that Absalom prepared him
chariots and horses, and fifty men to
run before him.

2And Absalom rose up early, and
stood beside the way of the gate: and it
was *so,* that when any man that had a
controversy came to the king for judgment, then Absalom called unto him,
and said, Of what city *art* thou? And he
said, Thy servant *is* of one of the tribes
of Israel.

3And Absalom said unto him, See, thy
matters *are* good and right; but *there is*
no man *deputed* of the king to hear thee.

4Absalom said moreover, Oh that I
were made judge in the land, that every
man which hath any suit or cause might
come unto me, and I would do him justice!

5And it was *so,* that when any man
came nigh *to him* to do him obeisance,
he put forth his hand, and took him, and
kissed him.

6And on this manner did Absalom to
all Israel that came to the king for judgment: so Absalom stole the hearts of
the men of Israel.

The outbreak of Absalom's rebellion

¶7And it came to pass after forty
years, that Absalom said unto the king,
I pray thee, let me go and pay my vow,
which I have vowed unto the LORD, in
Hebron.

8For thy servant vowed a vow while
I abode at Geshur in Syria, saying, If
the LORD shall bring me again indeed
to Jerusalem, then I will serve the
LORD.

9And the king said unto him, Go in
peace. So he arose, and went to Hebron.

¶10But Absalom sent spies throughout all the tribes of Israel, saying, As

---

14:26 polled. Cut.

15:7 after forty years. This refers to forty years from the date of David's anointing to be king, not Absalom's age (1 Sam. 16:13).

soon as ye hear the sound of the trumpet, then ye shall say, Absalom reigneth
in Hebron.
11 And with Absalom went two hundred men out of Jerusalem, *that were*
called; and they went in their simplicity, and they knew not any thing.
12 And Absalom sent for Ahithophel
the Gilonite, David's counsellor, from
his city, *even* from Giloh, while he offered sacrifices. And the conspiracy was
strong; for the people increased continually with Absalom.

David's flight from Jerusalem

¶13 And there came a messenger to
David, saying, The hearts of the men of
Israel are after Absalom.
14 And David said unto all his servants
that *were* with him at Jerusalem, Arise,
and let us flee; for we shall not *else* escape from Absalom: make speed to depart, lest he overtake us suddenly, and
bring evil upon us, and smite the city
with the edge of the sword.
15 And the king's servants said unto
the king, Behold, thy servants *are ready*
to do whatsoever my lord the king shall
appoint.
16 And the king went forth, and all his
household after him. And the king left
ten women, *which were* concubines, to
keep the house.
17 And the king went forth, and all the
people after him, and tarried in a place
that was far off.
18 And all his servants passed on beside him; and all the Cherethites, and
all the Pelethites, and all the Gittites,
six hundred men which came after him
from *Gath, passed on before the king.
¶19 Then said the king to Ittai the Gittite, Wherefore goest thou also with us?
return to thy place, and abide with the
king: for thou *art* a stranger, and also an
exile.
20 Whereas thou camest *but* yesterday,
should I this day make thee go up and
down with us? seeing I go whither I may,
return thou, and take back thy brethren:
mercy and truth *be* with thee.
21 And Ittai answered the king, and
said, *As* the LORD liveth, and *as* my lord
the king liveth, surely in what place my
lord the king shall be, whether in
*death or life, even there also will thy
servant be.
22 And David said to Ittai, Go and pass
over. And Ittai the Gittite passed over,
and all his men, and all the little ones
that *were* with him.
23 And all the country wept with a
loud voice, and all the people passed
over: the king also himself passed over
the brook Kidron, and all the people
passed over, toward the way of the wilderness.
¶24 And lo Zadok also, and all the Levites *were* with him, bearing the *ark of
the covenant of *God: and they set
down the ark of God; and Abiathar went
up, until all the people had done passing out of the city.
25 And the king said unto Zadok,
Carry back the ark of God into the city:
if I shall find favour in the eyes of the
LORD, he will bring me again, and shew
me *both* it, and his habitation:
26 But if he thus say, I have no delight
in thee; behold, *here am* I, let him do to
me as seemeth good unto him.
27 The king said also unto Zadok the
priest, *Art not* thou a seer? return into
the city in peace, and your two sons
with you, Ahimaaz thy son, and Jonathan the son of Abiathar.
28 See, I will tarry in the plain of the
wilderness, until there come word from
you to certify me.
29 Zadok therefore and Abiathar carried the ark of God again to Jerusalem:
and they tarried there.
¶30 And David went up by the ascent
of *mount* Olivet, and wept as he went

15:23 the way of the wilderness. This was not the wilderness where Israel had wandered for forty years; it was the wilderness of Judaea, lying between Jerusalem and the Jordan Valley.

up, and had his head covered, and he
went barefoot: and all the people that
was with him covered every man his
head, and they went up, weeping as
they went up.
¶31 And *one* told David, saying, Ahithophel *is* among the conspirators with
Absalom. And David said, O LORD, I
pray thee, turn the counsel of Ahithophel into foolishness.
¶32 And it came to pass, that *when* David was come to the top *of the mount,*
where he worshipped God, behold, Hushai the Archite came to meet him with
his coat rent, and earth upon his head:
33 Unto whom David said, If thou
passest on with me, then thou shalt be
a burden unto me:
34 But if thou return to the city, and
say unto Absalom, I will be thy servant,
O king; *as* I *have been* thy father's servant hitherto, so *will* I now also *be* thy
servant: then mayest thou for me defeat the counsel of Ahithophel.
35 And *hast thou* not there with thee
Zadok and Abiathar the priests? therefore it shall be, *that* what thing soever
thou shalt hear out of the king's house,
thou shalt tell *it* to Zadok and Abiathar
the priests.
36 Behold, *they have* there with them
their two sons, Ahimaaz Zadok's *son,*
and Jonathan Abiathar's *son;* and by
them ye shall send unto me every thing
that ye can hear.
37 So Hushai David's friend came into
the city, and Absalom came into Jerusalem.

The false story of Ziba

16 And when David was a little
past the top *of the hill,* behold,
Ziba the servant of *Mephibosheth met
him, with a couple of asses saddled, and
upon them two hundred *loaves* of bread,
and an hundred bunches of raisins, and
an hundred of summer fruits, and a
bottle of wine.
2 And the king said unto Ziba, What
meanest thou by these? And Ziba said,
The asses *be* for the king's household
to ride on; and the bread and summer
fruit for the young men to eat; and the
wine, that such as be faint in the wilderness may drink.
3 And the king said, And where *is* thy
master's son? And Ziba said unto the
king, Behold, he abideth at Jerusalem:
for he said, To day shall the house of
Israel restore me the *kingdom of my
father.
4 Then said the king to Ziba, Behold,
thine *are* all that *pertained* unto Mephibosheth. And Ziba said, I humbly beseech thee *that* I may find grace in thy
sight, my lord, O king.

16:1 BOTTLE

In the Bible, the word "bottle" most often refers to a skin bottle.The larger bottles were made of the skin of a he-goat, the smaller of a kid's skin. When the animal was killed, its feet and its head were cut off, and it was drawn in this manner out of the skin, without cutting it open. The inside of the skin was afterward dressed with tannin, the openings at the legs and the tail were sewn up, and the skin was filled with a concoction of bark and water until it was saturated. When used for wine, the skins were hung up in the houses, and they became smoked and shriveled; hence the psalmist's simile, "like a bottle in the smoke" (Ps. 119:83). The bottles were mended by stitching on a patch and covering it over with pitch. They are still extensively manufactured at Hebron and are used by the vendors of water and wine at Jerusalem, who carry them strapped to their backs, and draw the liquid from a tap fixed in one of the hind legs.

16:1 Mephibosheth. See his story in 2 Samuel 9 and the 2 Samuel 9:3 note, "God's Kindness."

16:3 restore me the kingdom of my father. The apparent ingratitude of Mephibosheth only added to David's heartache at this time. It was not until months later that David learned that Ziba had lied about Mephibosheth (see 2 Sam. 19:24-30).

Shimei curses David

¶5And when king David came to Bahurim, behold, thence came out a man
of the family of the house of Saul, whose
name *was* Shimei, the son of Gera: he
came forth, and cursed still as he came.
6And he cast stones at David, and at
all the servants of king David: and all
the people and all the mighty men *were*
on his right hand and on his left.
7And thus said Shimei when he
cursed, Come out, come out, thou
bloody man, and thou man of Belial:
8The LORD hath returned upon thee
all the blood of the house of Saul, in
whose stead thou hast reigned; and the
LORD hath delivered the kingdom into
the hand of Absalom thy son: and, behold, thou *art taken* in thy mischief,
because thou *art* a bloody man.
¶9Then said Abishai the son of Zeruiah unto the king, Why should this dead
dog curse my lord the king? let me go
over, I pray thee, and take off his head.
10And the king said, What have I to
do with you, ye sons of Zeruiah? so let
him curse, because the LORD hath said
unto him, Curse David. Who shall then
say, Wherefore hast thou done so?
11And David said to Abishai, and to all
his servants, Behold, my son, which
came forth of my *bowels, seeketh my
life: how much more now *may this* Benjamite *do it?* let him alone, and let him
curse; for the LORD hath bidden him.
12It may be that the LORD will look on
mine affliction, and that the LORD will
requite me good for his cursing this day.
13And as David and his men went by
the way, Shimei went along on the hill's
side over against him, and cursed as he
went, and threw stones at him, and cast
dust.
14And the king, and all the people that
were with him, came weary, and refreshed themselves there.

Absalom enters Jerusalem

¶15And Absalom, and all the people
the men of Israel, came to Jerusalem,
and Ahithophel with him.
16And it came to pass, when Hushai
the Archite, David's friend, was come
unto Absalom, that Hushai said unto
Absalom, God save the king, God save
the king.
17And Absalom said to Hushai, *Is* this
thy kindness to thy friend? why
wentest thou not with thy friend?
18And Hushai said unto Absalom,
Nay; but whom the LORD, and this people, and all the men of Israel, choose,
his will I be, and with him will I abide.
19And again, whom should I serve?
should I not *serve* in the presence of his
son? as I have served in thy father's
presence, so will I be in thy presence.
¶20Then said Absalom to Ahithophel, Give counsel among you what
we shall do.
21And Ahithophel said unto Absalom,
Go in unto thy father's concubines,
which he hath left to keep the house;
and all Israel shall hear that thou art
abhorred of thy father: then shall the
hands of all that *are* with thee be strong.
22So they spread Absalom a tent upon
the top of the house; and Absalom went
in unto his father's concubines in the
sight of all Israel.
23And the counsel of Ahithophel,
which he counselled in those days, *was*
as if a man had enquired at the *oracle
of God: so *was* all the counsel of Ahithophel both with David and with Absalom.

The conflicting counsels of Ahithophel and Hushai

17 Moreover Ahithophel said unto
Absalom, Let me now choose
out twelve thousand men, and I will
arise and pursue after David this night:
2And I will come upon him while he
is weary and weak handed, and will
make him afraid: and all the people that
are with him shall flee; and I will smite
the king only:
3And I will bring back all the people
unto thee: the man whom thou seekest
is as if all returned: *so* all the people
shall be in peace.

4 And the saying pleased Absalom
well, and all the elders of Israel.
5 Then said Absalom, Call now Hushai
the Archite also, and let us hear likewise what he saith.
6 And when Hushai was come to Absalom, Absalom spake unto him, saying,
Ahithophel hath spoken after this manner: shall we do *after* his saying? if not;
speak thou.
7 And Hushai said unto Absalom, The
counsel that Ahithophel hath given *is*
not good at this time.
8 For, said Hushai, thou knowest thy
father and his men, that they *be* mighty
men, and they *be* chafed in their minds,
as a bear robbed of her whelps in the
field: and thy father *is* a man of war, and
will not lodge with the people.
9 Behold, he is hid now in some pit, or
in some *other* place: and it will come to
pass, when some of them be overthrown at the first, that whosoever
heareth it will say, There is a slaughter
among the people that follow Absalom.
10 And he also *that is* valiant, whose
heart *is* as the heart of a lion, shall utterly melt: for all Israel knoweth that
thy father *is* a mighty man, and *they*
which *be* with him *are* valiant men.
11 Therefore I counsel that all Israel
be generally gathered unto thee, from
Dan even to *Beer-sheba, as the sand
that *is* by the sea for multitude; and
that thou go to battle in thine own person.
12 So shall we come upon him in some
place where he shall be found, and we
will light upon him as the dew falleth on
the ground: and of him and of all the
men that *are* with him there shall not
be left so much as one.
13 Moreover, if he be gotten into a city,
then shall all Israel bring ropes to that
city, and we will draw it into the river,
until there be not one small stone found
there.
14 And Absalom and all the men of
Israel said, The counsel of Hushai the
Archite *is* better than the counsel of
Ahithophel. For the LORD had appointed to defeat the good counsel of Ahithophel, to the intent that the LORD might
bring evil upon Absalom.
¶15 Then said Hushai unto Zadok and
to Abiathar the priests, Thus and thus
did Ahithophel counsel Absalom and
the elders of Israel; and thus and thus
have I counselled.
16 Now therefore send quickly, and
tell David, saying, Lodge not this night
in the plains of the wilderness, but
speedily pass over; lest the king be
swallowed up, and all the people that
are with him.
17 Now Jonathan and Ahimaaz stayed
by En-rogel; for they might not be seen
to come into the city: and a wench went
and told them; and they went and told
king David.
18 Nevertheless a lad saw them, and
told Absalom: but they went both of
them away quickly, and came to a man's
house in Bahurim, which had a well in
his court; whither they went down.
19 And the woman took and spread a
covering over the well's mouth, and
spread ground corn thereon; and the
thing was not known.
20 And when Absalom's servants
came to the woman to the house, they
said, Where *is* Ahimaaz and Jonathan?
And the woman said unto them, They
be gone over the brook of water. And
when they had sought and could not find
them, they returned to *Jerusalem.
21 And it came to pass, after they were
departed, that they came up out of the
well, and went and told king David, and
said unto David, Arise, and pass quickly over the water: for thus hath Ahithophel counselled against you.
22 Then David arose, and all the people that *were* with him, and they passed
over Jordan: by the morning light there
lacked not one of them that was not
gone over Jordan.
¶23 And when Ahithophel saw that his

17:8 chafed. Heated, exasperated, angry.

counsel was not followed, he saddled *his* ass, and arose, and gat him home to his house, to his city, and put his household in order, and hanged himself, and died, and was buried in the sepulchre of his father.

Absalom pursues David into the land of Gilead

¶ 24 Then David came to Mahanaim. And Absalom passed over Jordan, he and all the men of Israel with him.

¶ 25 And Absalom made Amasa captain of the host instead of Joab: which Amasa *was* a man's son, whose name *was* Ithra an Israelite, that went in to Abigail the daughter of Nahash, sister to Zeruiah Joab's mother.

26 So Israel and Absalom pitched in the land of *Gilead.

¶ 27 And it came to pass, when David was come to Mahanaim, that Shobi the son of Nahash of Rabbah of the children of Ammon, and Machir the son of Ammiel of Lo-debar, and Barzillai the Gileadite of Rogelim,

28 Brought beds, and basons, and earthen vessels, and wheat, and barley, and flour, and parched *corn,* and beans, and lentiles, and parched *pulse,*

29 And honey, and butter, and sheep, and cheese of kine, for David, and for the people that *were* with him, to eat: for they said, The people *is* hungry, and weary, and thirsty, in the wilderness.

David's plea to spare Absalom

18 And David numbered the people that *were* with him, and set captains of thousands and captains of hundreds over them.

2 And David sent forth a third part of the people under the hand of Joab, and a third part under the hand of Abishai the son of Zeruiah, Joab's brother, and a third part under the hand of Ittai the Gittite. And the king said unto the people, I will surely go forth with you myself also.

3 But the people answered, Thou shalt not go forth: for if we flee away, they will not care for us; neither if half of us die, will they care for us: but now *thou art* worth ten thousand of us: therefore now *it is* better that thou succour us out of the city.

4 And the king said unto them, What seemeth you best I will do. And the king stood by the gate side, and all the people came out by hundreds and by thousands.

5 And the king commanded Joab and Abishai and Ittai, saying, *Deal* gently for my sake with the young man, *even* with Absalom. And all the people heard when the king gave all the captains charge concerning Absalom.

The slaying of Absalom

¶ 6 So the people went out into the field against Israel: and the battle was in the wood of Ephraim;

7 Where the people of Israel were slain before the servants of David, and there was there a great slaughter that day of twenty thousand *men.*

8 For the battle was there scattered over the face of all the country: and the wood devoured more people that day than the sword devoured.

¶ 9 And Absalom met the servants of David. And Absalom rode upon a mule, and the mule went under the thick boughs of a great oak, and his head caught hold of the oak, and he was taken up between the heaven and the earth; and the mule that *was* under him went away.

10 And a certain man saw *it,* and told Joab, and said, Behold, I saw Absalom hanged in an oak.

11 And Joab said unto the man that told him, And, behold, thou sawest *him,* and why didst thou not smite him there to the ground? and I would have given thee ten *shekels* of *silver, and a girdle.

12 And the man said unto Joab, Though I should receive a thousand *shekels* of silver in mine hand, *yet* would I not put forth mine hand against the king's son: for in our hearing the king charged thee and Abishai and Ittai,

saying, Beware that none *touch* the
young man Absalom.
13Otherwise I should have wrought
*falsehood against mine own life: for
there is no matter hid from the king,
and thou thyself wouldest have set thyself against *me.*
14Then said Joab, I may not tarry thus
with thee. And he took three darts in
his hand, and thrust them through the
heart of Absalom, while he *was* yet alive
in the midst of the oak.
15And ten young men that bare Joab's
armour compassed about and smote
Absalom, and slew him.
16And Joab blew the trumpet, and the
people returned from pursuing after
Israel: for Joab held back the people.
17And they took Absalom, and cast
him into a great pit in the wood, and
laid a very great heap of stones upon
him: and all Israel fled every one to his
tent.

David's grief over Absalom's death

¶18Now Absalom in his lifetime had
taken and reared up for himself a pillar,
which *is* in the king's dale: for he said,
I have no son to keep my name in remembrance: and he called the pillar after his own name: and it is called unto
this day, Absalom's place.
¶19Then said Ahimaaz the son of Zadok, Let me now run, and bear the king
tidings, how that the LORD hath avenged
him of his enemies.
20And Joab said unto him, Thou shalt
not bear tidings this day, but thou shalt
bear tidings another day: but this day
thou shalt bear no tidings, because the
king's son is dead.
21Then said Joab to Cushi, Go tell the
king what thou hast seen. And Cushi
bowed himself unto Joab, and ran.
22Then said Ahimaaz the son of Zadok yet again to Joab, But howsoever,
let me, I pray thee, also run after Cushi. And Joab said, Wherefore wilt thou
run, my son, seeing that thou hast no
tidings ready?
23But howsoever, *said he,* let me run.
And he said unto him, Run. Then Ahimaaz ran by the way of the plain, and
overran Cushi.
24And David sat between the two
gates: and the watchman went up to the
roof over the gate unto the wall, and lifted up his eyes, and looked, and behold
a man running alone.
25And the watchman cried, and told
the king. And the king said, If he *be*
alone, *there is* tidings in his mouth. And
he came apace, and drew near.
26And the watchman saw another
man running: and the watchman called
unto the porter, and said, Behold *another* man running alone. And the king
said, He also bringeth tidings.
27And the watchman said, Me
thinketh the running of the foremost is
like the running of Ahimaaz the son of
Zadok. And the king said, He *is* a good
man, and cometh with good tidings.
28And Ahimaaz called, and said unto
the king, All is well. And he fell down
to the earth upon his face before the
king, and said, Blessed *be* the LORD thy
God, which hath delivered up the men
that lifted up their hand against my lord
the king.
29And the king said, Is the young man
Absalom safe? And Ahimaaz answered,
When Joab sent the king's servant, and
me thy servant, I saw a great tumult, but
I knew not what *it was.*
30And the king said *unto him,* Turn
aside, *and* stand here. And he turned
aside, and stood still.
31And, behold, Cushi came; and Cushi said, Tidings, my lord the king: for
the LORD hath avenged thee this day of
all them that rose up against thee.
32And the king said unto Cushi, *Is* the
young man Absalom safe? And Cushi

18:18 I have no son. Compare this statement with 2 Samuel 14:27. It is believed that Absalom's sons had not been born when this pillar was erected, or that they had all died.

answered, The enemies of my lord the
king, and all that rise against thee to do
thee hurt, be as *that* young man *is*.
¶33And the king was much moved,
and went up to the chamber over the
gate, and wept: and as he went, thus he
said, O my son Absalom, my son, my
son Absalom! would God I had died for
thee, O Absalom, my son, my son!
19 And it was told Joab, Behold,
the king weepeth and mourneth
for Absalom.
2And the victory that day was *turned*
into *mourning unto all the people: for
the people heard say that day how the
king was grieved for his son.
3And the people gat them by stealth
that day into the city, as people being
ashamed steal away when they flee in
battle.
4But the king covered his face, and
the king cried with a loud voice, O my
son Absalom, O Absalom, my son, my
son!

Joab reproaches David

5And Joab came into the house to the
king, and said, Thou hast shamed this
day the faces of all thy servants, which
this day have saved thy life, and the
lives of thy sons and of thy daughters,
and the lives of thy wives, and the lives
of thy concubines;
6In that thou lovest thine enemies,
and hatest thy friends. For thou hast
declared this day, that thou regardest
neither princes nor servants: for this
day I perceive, that if Absalom had
lived, and all we had died this day, then
it had pleased thee well.
7Now therefore arise, go forth, and
speak comfortably unto thy servants:
for I swear by the LORD, if thou go not
forth, there will not tarry one with thee
this night: and that will be worse unto
thee than all the evil that befell thee
from thy youth until now.
¶8Then the king arose, and sat in the
gate. And they told unto all the people,
saying, Behold, the king doth sit in the
gate. And all the people came before the
king: for *Israel had fled every man to
his tent.

David returns to Jerusalem

¶9And all the people were at strife
throughout all the tribes of Israel,
saying, The king saved us out of the
hand of our enemies, and he delivered
us out of the hand of the *Philistines;
and now he is fled out of the land for
Absalom.
10And Absalom, whom we anointed
over us, is dead in battle. Now therefore
why speak ye not a word of bringing the
king back?
¶11And king *David sent to Zadok and
to Abiathar the priests, saying, Speak
unto the *elders of *Judah, saying, Why
are ye the last to bring the king back to
his house? seeing the speech of all Israel is come to the king, *even* to his
house.
12Ye *are* my brethren, ye *are* my
bones and my flesh: wherefore then are
ye the last to bring back the king?
13And say ye to Amasa, *Art* thou not
of my bone, and of my flesh? God do so
to me, and more also, if thou be not captain of the host before me continually
in the room of Joab.
14And he bowed the heart of all the
men of Judah, even as *the heart of* one
man; so that they sent *this word* unto
the king, Return thou, and all thy servants.
15So the king returned, and came to
Jordan. And Judah came to Gilgal, to go
to meet the king, to conduct the king
over Jordan.
¶16And Shimei the son of Gera, a
Benjamite, which *was* of Bahurim,
hasted and came down with the men of
Judah to meet king David.
17And *there were* a thousand men of
Benjamin with him, and Ziba the servant of the house of Saul, and his fifteen
sons and his twenty servants with him;
and they went over Jordan before the
king.
18And there went over a ferry boat to
carry over the king's household, and to

do what he thought good. And Shimei
the son of Gera fell down before the
king, as he was come over Jordan;
[19]And said unto the king, Let not my
lord impute iniquity unto me, neither do
thou remember that which thy servant
did perversely the day that my lord the
king went out of Jerusalem, that the
king should take it to his heart.
[20]For thy servant doth know that I
have sinned: therefore, behold, I am
come the first this day of all the house
of *Joseph to go down to meet my lord
the king.
[21]But Abishai the son of Zeruiah answered and said, Shall not Shimei be
put to death for this, because he cursed
the LORD'S anointed?
[22]And David said, What have I to do
with you, ye sons of Zeruiah, that ye
should this day be adversaries unto me?
shall there any man be put to death this
day in Israel? for do not I know that I
am this day king over Israel?
[23]Therefore the king said unto Shimei, Thou shalt not die. And the king
sware unto him.
¶[24]And *Mephibosheth the son of
Saul came down to meet the king, and
had neither dressed his feet, nor
trimmed his beard, nor washed his
clothes, from the day the king departed until the day he came *again* in peace.
[25]And it came to pass, when he was
come to Jerusalem to meet the king,
that the king said unto him, Wherefore
wentest not thou with me, Mephibosheth?
[26]And he answered, My lord, O king,
my servant deceived me: for thy servant said, I will saddle me an ass, that I
may ride thereon, and go to the king;
because thy servant *is* lame.
[27]And he hath slandered thy servant
unto my lord the king; but my lord the
king *is* as an angel of God: do therefore
what is good in thine eyes.
[28]For all *of* my father's house were
but dead men before my lord the king:
yet didst thou set thy servant among
them that did eat at thine own table.
What right therefore have I yet to cry
any more unto the king?
[29]And the king said unto him, Why
speakest thou any more of thy matters?
I have said, Thou and Ziba divide the
land.
[30]And Mephibosheth said unto the
king, Yea, let him take all, forasmuch as
my lord the king is come again in peace
unto his own house.
¶[31]And Barzillai the Gileadite came
down from Rogelim, and went over Jordan with the king, to conduct him over
Jordan.
[32]Now Barzillai was a very aged man,
even fourscore years old: and he had
provided the king of sustenance while
he lay at Mahanaim; for he *was* a very
great man.
[33]And the king said unto Barzillai,
Come thou over with me, and I will feed
thee with me in Jerusalem.
[34]And Barzillai said unto the king,
How long have I to live, that I should
go up with the king unto Jerusalem?
[35]I *am* this day fourscore years old:
and can I discern between good and
evil? can thy servant taste what I eat or
what I drink? can I hear any more the
voice of singing men and singing wom-
en? wherefore then should thy servant
be yet a burden unto my lord the king?
[36]Thy servant will go a little way over
Jordan with the king: and why should
the king recompense it me with such a
reward?
[37]Let thy servant, I pray thee, turn
back again, that I may die in mine own
city, *and be buried* by the grave of my
father and of my mother. But behold thy
servant Chimham; let him go over with
my lord the king; and do to him what
shall seem good unto thee.
[38]And the king answered, Chimham
shall go over with me, and I will do to
him that which shall seem good unto
thee: and whatsoever thou shalt require
of me, *that* will I do for thee.
[39]And all the people went over Jordan. And when the king was come over,
the king kissed Barzillai, and blessed

him; and he returned unto his own
place.
40 Then the king went on to Gilgal,
and Chimham went on with him: and all
the people of Judah conducted the king,
and also half the people of Israel.

Civil war begins again

¶41 And, behold, all the men of Israel
came to the king, and said unto the
king, Why have our brethren the men
of Judah stolen thee away, and have
brought the king, and his household,
and all David's men with him, over Jordan?
42 And all the men of Judah answered
the men of Israel, Because the king *is*
near of kin to us: wherefore then be ye
angry for this matter? have we eaten at
all of the king's *cost?* or hath he given
us any gift?
43 And the men of Israel answered the
men of Judah, and said, We have ten
parts in the king, and we have also more
right in David than ye: why then did ye
despise us, that our advice should not
be first had in bringing back our king?
And the words of the men of Judah were
fiercer than the words of the men of
Israel.
20 And there happened to be
there a man of Belial, whose
name *was* Sheba, the son of Bichri, a
Benjamite: and he blew a trumpet, and
said, We have no part in David, neither
have we inheritance in the son of Jesse: every man to his tents, O Israel.
2 So every man of Israel went up from
after David, *and* followed Sheba the son
of Bichri: but the men of Judah clave
unto their king, from Jordan even to
Jerusalem.
¶3 And David came to his house at Jerusalem; and the king took the ten
women *his* concubines, whom he had
left to keep the house, and put them in
ward, and fed them, but went not in
unto them. So they were shut up unto
the day of their death, living in widowhood.
¶4 Then said the king to Amasa, Assemble me the men of Judah within
three days, and be thou here present.
5 So Amasa went to assemble *the men*
of Judah: but he tarried longer than the
set time which he had appointed him.
6 And David said to Abishai, Now shall
Sheba the son of Bichri do us more
harm than *did* Absalom: take thou thy
lord's servants, and pursue after him,
lest he get him fenced cities, and escape
us.
7 And there went out after him Joab's
men, and the Cherethites, and the Pelethites, and all the mighty men: and
they went out of Jerusalem, to pursue
after Sheba the son of Bichri.
8 When they *were* at the great stone
which *is* in Gibeon, Amasa went before
them. And Joab's garment that he had
put on was girded unto him, and upon
it a girdle *with* a sword fastened upon
his loins in the sheath thereof; and as
he went forth it fell out.
9 And Joab said to Amasa, *Art* thou in
health, my brother? And Joab took
Amasa by the beard with the right hand
to kiss him.
10 But Amasa took no heed to the

20:10 Joab's Vengeance
Although Joab was loyal to David through all David's troubles, Joab was still full of vengeance against his own personal enemies. This was the third man whom David had promised to pardon who was killed by Joab because of personal enmity (2 Sam. 3:27; 18:14).

19:43 why then did ye despise us . . . ? This was another evidence of the jealousy that had broken out so often before between the tribes (Josh. 22; Judg. 8; 12; 20), a jealousy that would yet divide the nation in two (1 Kings 12:16).

20:8 went before them. Came to meet them.

20:8 a sword . . . fell out. This was doubtless to keep Amasa from suspecting any danger.

20:9 took Amasa by the beard with the right hand to kiss him. This was a mark of respect and affection.

sword that *was* in Joab's hand: so he smote him therewith in the fifth *rib,* and shed out his bowels to the ground, and struck him not again; and he died. So Joab and Abishai his brother pursued after Sheba the son of Bichri.

11 And one of Joab's men stood by him, and said, He that favoureth Joab, and he that *is* for David, *let him go* after Joab.

12 And Amasa wallowed in blood in the midst of the highway. And when the man saw that all the people stood still, he removed Amasa out of the highway into the field, and cast a cloth upon him, when he saw that every one that came by him stood still.

13 When he was removed out of the highway, all the people went on after Joab, to pursue after Sheba the son of Bichri.

¶ 14 And he went through all the tribes of Israel unto *Abel, and to Beth-maachah, and all the Berites: and they were gathered together, and went also after him.

15 And they came and besieged him in Abel of Beth-maachah, and they cast up a bank against the city, and it stood in the trench: and all the people that *were* with Joab battered the wall, to throw it down.

¶ 16 Then cried a wise woman out of the city, Hear, hear; say, I pray you, unto Joab, Come near hither, that I may speak with thee.

17 And when he was come near unto her, the woman said, *Art* thou Joab? And he answered, I *am he.* Then she said unto him, Hear the words of thine handmaid. And he answered, I do hear.

18 Then she spake, saying, They were wont to speak in old time, saying, They shall surely ask *counsel* at Abel: and so they ended *the matter.*

19 I *am one of them that are* peaceable *and* faithful in Israel: thou seekest to destroy a city and a mother in Israel: why wilt thou swallow up the inheritance of the LORD?

20 And Joab answered and said, Far be it, far be it from me, that I should swallow up or destroy.

21 The matter *is* not so: but a man of mount *Ephraim, Sheba the son of Bichri by name, hath lifted up his hand against the king, *even* against David: deliver him only, and I will depart from the city. And the woman said unto Joab, Behold, his head shall be thrown to thee over the wall.

22 Then the woman went unto all the people in her wisdom. And they cut off the head of Sheba the son of Bichri, and cast *it* out to Joab. And he blew a trumpet, and they retired from the city, every man to his tent. And Joab returned to Jerusalem unto the king.

¶ 23 Now Joab *was* over all the host of Israel: and Benaiah the son of *Jehoiada *was* over the Cherethites and over the Pelethites:

24 And Adoram *was* over the tribute: and Jehoshaphat the son of Ahilud *was* recorder:

25 And Sheva *was* *scribe: and Zadok and Abiathar *were* the priests:

26 And Ira also the Jairite was a chief ruler about David.

V. David's Faith Is Revived (21:1—24:25)

21 Then there was a famine in the days of David three years, year after year; and David enquired of the LORD. And the LORD answered, *It is* for Saul, and for *his* bloody house, because he slew the Gibeonites.

2 And the king called the Gibeonites, and said unto them; (now the Gibeonites *were* not of the children of Israel, but of the remnant of the Amorites; and the children of Israel had sworn unto them: and Saul sought to slay them in

---

20:15 bank. A mound for besieging a city.
20:19 a mother. A mother city—an important city.
21:2 Israel had sworn unto them. These were the people with whom Joshua had made an endless covenant of peace by eating their bread (Josh. 9).

his zeal to the children of Israel and Judah.)

3 Wherefore David said unto the Gibeonites, What shall I do for you? and wherewith shall I make the *atonement, that ye may bless the inheritance of the LORD?

4 And the Gibeonites said unto him, We will have no silver nor gold of Saul, nor of his house; neither for us shalt thou kill any man in Israel. And he said, What ye shall say, *that* will I do for you.

5 And they answered the king, The man that consumed us, and that devised against us *that* we should be destroyed from remaining in any of the coasts of Israel,

6 Let seven men of his sons be delivered unto us, and we will hang them up unto the LORD in Gibeah of Saul, *whom* the LORD did choose. And the king said, I will give *them.*

7 But the king spared Mephibosheth, the son of Jonathan the son of Saul, because of the LORD'S oath that *was* between them, between David and Jonathan the son of Saul.

8 But the king took the two sons of Rizpah the daughter of Aiah, whom she bare unto Saul, Armoni and Mephibosheth; and the five sons of Michal the daughter of Saul, whom she brought up for Adriel the son of Barzillai the Meholathite:

9 And he delivered them into the hands of the Gibeonites, and they hanged them in the hill before the LORD: and they fell *all* seven together, and were put to death in the days of harvest, in the first *days,* in the beginning of barley harvest.

¶ 10 And Rizpah the daughter of Aiah took sackcloth, and spread it for her upon the rock, from the beginning of harvest until water dropped upon them out of heaven, and suffered neither the birds of the air to rest on them by day, nor the beasts of the field by night.

11 And it was told David what Rizpah the daughter of Aiah, the *concubine of Saul, had done.

¶ 12 And David went and took the bones of Saul and the bones of Jonathan his son from the men of Jabesh-gilead, which had stolen them from the street of Beth-shan, where the Philistines had hanged them, when the Philistines had slain Saul in Gilboa:

13 And he brought up from thence the bones of Saul and the bones of Jonathan his son; and they gathered the bones of them that were hanged.

14 And the bones of Saul and Jonathan his son buried they in the country of Benjamin in Zelah, in the sepulchre of Kish his father: and they performed all that the king commanded. And after that *God was intreated for the land.

War again with the Philistines

¶ 15 Moreover the Philistines had yet war again with Israel; and David went down, and his servants with him, and fought against the Philistines: and David waxed faint.

16 And Ishbi-benob, which *was* of the sons of the giant, the weight of whose spear *weighed* three hundred *shekels* of brass in weight, he being girded with a new *sword,* thought to have slain David.

17 But Abishai the son of Zeruiah succoured him, and smote the Philistine, and killed him. Then the men of David sware unto him, saying, Thou shalt go no more out with us to battle, that thou quench not the light of Israel.

18 And it came to pass after this, that there was again a battle with the Philistines at Gob: then Sibbechai the Hushathite slew Saph, which *was* of the sons of the giant.

19 And there was again a battle in Gob with the Philistines, where Elhanan the son of Jaare-oregim, a Beth-lehemite, slew *the brother of* Goliath the Gittite, the staff of whose spear *was* like a weaver's beam.

21:7 oath . . . between David and Jonathan. See 1 Samuel 20:14-17 for the record of this.

20 And there was yet a battle in *Gath,
where was a man of *great* stature, that
had on every hand six fingers, and on
every foot six toes, four and twenty in
number; and he also was born to the
giant.
21 And when he defied Israel, Jonathan the son of Shimeah the brother of
David slew him.
22 These four were born to the giant
in Gath, and fell by the hand of David,
and by the hand of his servants.

David's praise for God's deliverance

22 And David spake unto the
LORD the words of this song in
the day *that* the LORD had delivered him
out of the hand of all his enemies, and
out of the hand of Saul:
2 And he said, The LORD *is* my rock,
and my fortress, and my deliverer;
3 The God of my rock; in him will I
*trust: *he is* my shield, and the horn of
my *salvation, my high tower, and my
refuge, my saviour; thou savest me
from violence.
4 I will call on the LORD, *who is* worthy to be praised: so shall I be saved
from mine enemies.
5 When the waves of death compassed
me, the floods of ungodly men made me
afraid;
6 The sorrows of *hell compassed me
about; the snares of death *prevented
me;

22:6 Hell
In the Old Testament, the Hebrew word *Sheol* is translated "hell." *Sheol* refers to the dark, mysterious abode of the dead. Some translations have "grave" or "pit," with the word *Sheol* in the margin, or they leave that word in the text. In the prophetic books, however, the word "hell" is retained. In the New Testament, the word "hell" is a translation of the Greek word *Hades,* the equivalent of the Hebrew *Sheol,* or of *Gehenna,* the place of torment.

7 In my distress I called upon the
LORD, and cried to my God: and he did
hear my voice out of his temple, and my
cry *did enter* into his ears.
8 Then the earth shook and trembled;
the foundations of heaven moved and
shook, because he was wroth.
9 There went up a smoke out of his
nostrils, and fire out of his mouth devoured: coals were kindled by it.

21:16 SHEKELS OF BRASS

This is an unusual expression, as we usually read of "shekels of silver." Insofar as we know, there were no brass or copper shekels until about the third century B.C.

The word "shekels" can refer to either weights or coinage. The system of weights employed by the Israelites was governed by grains, or beans. The smallest weight, the gerah, was equivalent to about eight grains.

8.8 grains	=	1 gerah
20 gerahs	=	1 shekel
50 shekels	=	1 maneh (1 pound)
60 manehs	=	1 talent

The silver shekel was a piece of silver weighing .40 ounces. For many centuries the value of things was determined by a standard set of weights since coins were not introduced until after the Israelites returned from exile. Only then did a reference to a shekel mean a coin.

It seems quite possible that, since Goliath's helmet was made of brass, the coat of mail was also constructed of brass. Its weight, five thousand shekels, was one hundred pounds. Possibly the translation should be: "and he was armed with a coat of mail of brass; and the weight of the coat was five thousand shekels."

Here in 2 Samuel 21:16 the word "shekels" was not in the original, and we cannot be sure what word should have been inserted.

22:1 the words of this song. See Psalm 18.

[10]He bowed the heavens also, and
came down; and darkness *was* under his
feet.
[11]And he rode upon a cherub, and did
fly: and he was seen upon the wings of
the wind.
[12]And he made darkness pavilions
round about him, dark waters, *and* thick
clouds of the skies.
[13]Through the brightness before him
were coals of fire kindled.
[14]The LORD thundered from heaven,
and the most High uttered his voice.
[15]And he sent out arrows, and scattered them; lightning, and discomfited
them.
[16]And the channels of the sea appeared, the foundations of the *world
were discovered, at the rebuking of the
LORD, at the blast of the breath of his
nostrils.
[17]He sent from above, he took me; he
drew me out of many waters;
[18]He delivered me from my strong
enemy, *and* from them that hated me:
for they were too strong for me.
[19]They prevented me in the day of
my calamity: but the LORD was my
stay.
[20]He brought me forth also into a
large place: he delivered me, because
he delighted in me.
[21]The LORD rewarded me according
to my *righteousness: according to the
cleanness of my hands hath he recompensed me.
[22]For I have kept the ways of the
LORD, and have not wickedly departed
from my God.
[23]For all his judgments *were* before
me: and *as for* his statutes, I did not
depart from them.
[24]I was also upright before him, and
have kept myself from mine iniquity.
[25]Therefore the LORD hath recompensed me according to my righteousness; according to my cleanness in his
eye sight.
[26]With the merciful thou wilt shew
thyself merciful, *and* with the upright
man thou wilt shew thyself upright.
[27]With the pure thou wilt shew thyself pure; and with the *froward thou
wilt shew thyself unsavoury.
[28]And the afflicted people thou wilt
save: but thine eyes *are* upon the
haughty, *that* thou mayest bring *them*
down.
[29]For thou *art* my lamp, O LORD: and
the LORD will lighten my darkness.
[30]For by thee I have run through a
troop: by my God have I leaped over a
wall.
[31]*As for* God, his way *is* perfect; the
word of the LORD *is* tried: he *is* a *buckler to all them that trust in him.
[32]For who *is* God, save the LORD? and
who *is* a rock, save our God?
[33]God *is* my strength *and* power: and
he maketh my way perfect.
[34]He maketh my feet like hinds' *feet:*
and setteth me upon my high places.
[35]He teacheth my hands to war; so
that a bow of steel is broken by mine
arms.
[36]Thou hast also given me the shield
of thy salvation: and thy gentleness
hath made me great.
[37]Thou hast enlarged my steps under
me; so that my feet did not slip.
[38]I have pursued mine enemies, and
destroyed them; and turned not again
until I had consumed them.
[39]And I have consumed them, and
wounded them, that they could not
arise: yea, they are fallen under my
feet.
[40]For thou hast girded me with
strength to battle: them that rose up
against me hast thou subdued under
me.
[41]Thou hast also given me the necks
of mine enemies, that I might destroy
them that hate me.
[42]They looked, but *there was* none to
save; *even* unto the LORD, but he answered them not.
[43]Then did I beat them as small as the

22:27 unsavoury. Without wisdom, foolish.

dust of the earth, I did stamp them as
the mire of the street, *and* did spread
them abroad.
44 Thou also hast delivered me from
the strivings of my people, thou hast
kept me *to be* head of the heathen: a
people *which* I knew not shall serve me.
45 Strangers shall submit themselves
unto me: as soon as they hear, they shall
be obedient unto me.
46 Strangers shall fade away, and they
shall be afraid out of their close places.
47 The LORD liveth; and blessed *be* my
rock; and exalted be the God of the rock
of my salvation.
48 It *is* God that avengeth me, and that
bringeth down the people under me,
49 And that bringeth me forth from
mine enemies: thou also hast lifted me
up on high above them that rose up
against me: thou hast delivered me
from the violent man.
50 Therefore I will give thanks unto
thee, O LORD, among the heathen, and
I will sing praises unto thy name.
51 *He is* the tower of salvation for his
king: and sheweth *mercy to his anointed, unto David, and to his seed for evermore.

The last words of David

23 Now these *be* the last words of
David. David the son of Jesse
said, and the man *who was* raised up on
high, the anointed of the God of *Jacob,
and the sweet psalmist of Israel, said,

> **23:1 David's Last Words**
> These were the last words that David spoke as the son of Jesse, the one who had been a shepherd boy and was now the great king of a great country. He was ready to proclaim, as in verse 2, that the Psalms were the words of the LORD, spoken by or through David.

2 The Spirit of the LORD spake by me,
and his word *was* in my tongue.
3 The God of Israel said, the Rock of
Israel spake to me, He that ruleth over
men *must be* *just, ruling in the *fear
of God.
4 And *he shall be* as the light of the
morning, *when* the sun riseth, *even* a
morning without clouds; *as* the tender
grass *springing* out of the earth by clear
shining after rain.
5 Although my house *be* not so with
God; yet he hath made with me an everlasting *covenant, ordered in all *things,*
and sure: for *this is* all my salvation, and
all *my* desire, although he make *it* not
to grow.
¶6 But *the sons* of Belial *shall be* all of
them as thorns thrust away, because
they cannot be taken with hands:
7 But the man *that* shall touch them
must be fenced with iron and the staff
of a spear; and they shall be utterly
burned with fire in the *same* place.

A review of David's mighty men

¶8 These *be* the names of the mighty
men whom David had: The Tachmonite
that sat in the seat, chief among the
captains; the same *was* Adino the
Eznite: *he lift up his spear* against eight
hundred, whom he slew at one time.
9 And after him *was* Eleazar the son
of Dodo the Ahohite, *one* of the three
mighty men with David, when they
defied the Philistines *that* were there
gathered together to battle, and the
men of Israel were gone away:
10 He arose, and smote the Philistines
until his hand was weary, and his hand
clave unto the sword: and the LORD
wrought a great victory that day; and
the people returned after him only to
spoil.
11 And after him *was* Shammah the
son of Agee the Hararite. And the Philistines were gathered together into a
troop, where was a piece of ground full
of lentiles: and the people fled from the
Philistines.
12 But he stood in the midst of the
ground, and defended it, and slew the
Philistines: and the LORD wrought a
great victory.
13 And three of the thirty chief went
down, and came to David in the harvest
time unto the cave of Adullam: and the

troop of the Philistines pitched in the valley of Rephaim.

14 And David *was* then in an hold, and the garrison of the Philistines *was* then *in* Beth-lehem.

15 And David longed, and said, Oh that one would give me drink of the water of the well of Beth-lehem, which *is* by the gate!

16 And the three mighty men brake through the host of the Philistines, and drew water out of the well of Beth-lehem, that *was* by the gate, and took *it,* and brought *it* to David: nevertheless he would not drink thereof, but poured it out unto the LORD.

17 And he said, Be it far from me, O LORD, that I should do this: *is not this* the blood of the men that went in jeopardy of their lives? therefore he would not drink it. These things did these three mighty men.

18 And Abishai, the brother of Joab, the son of Zeruiah, was chief among three. And he lifted up his spear against three hundred, *and* slew *them,* and had the name among three.

19 Was he not most honourable of three? therefore he was their captain: howbeit he attained not unto the *first* three.

20 And Benaiah the son of Jehoiada, the son of a valiant man, of Kabzeel, who had done many acts, he slew two lionlike men of *Moab: he went down also and slew a lion in the midst of a pit in time of snow:

21 And he slew an Egyptian, a goodly man: and the Egyptian had a spear in his hand; but he went down to him with a staff, and plucked the spear out of the Egyptian's hand, and slew him with his own spear.

22 These *things* did Benaiah the son of Jehoiada, and had the name among three mighty men.

23 He was more honourable than the thirty, but he attained not to the *first* three. And David set him over his guard.

24 Asahel the brother of Joab *was* one of the thirty; Elhanan the son of Dodo of Beth-lehem,

25 Shammah the Harodite, Elika the Harodite,

26 Helez the Paltite, Ira the son of Ikkesh the Tekoite,

27 Abiezer the Anethothite, Mebunnai the Hushathite,

28 Zalmon the Ahohite, Maharai the Netophathite,

29 Heleb the son of Baanah, a Netophathite, Ittai the son of Ribai out of Gibeah of the children of Benjamin,

30 Benaiah the Pirathonite, Hiddai of the brooks of Gaash,

31 Abi-albon the Arbathite, Azmaveth the Barhumite,

32 Eliahba the Shaalbonite, of the sons of Jashen, Jonathan,

33 Shammah the Hararite, Ahiam the son of Sharar the Hararite,

34 Eliphelet the son of Ahasbai, the son of the Maachathite, Eliam the son of Ahithophel the Gilonite,

35 Hezrai the Carmelite, Paarai the Arbite,

36 Igal the son of Nathan of Zobah, Bani the Gadite,

37 Zelek the Ammonite, Nahari the Beerothite, armourbearer to Joab the son of Zeruiah,

38 Ira an Ithrite, Gareb an Ithrite,

39 Uriah the Hittite: thirty and seven in all.

David's sin in numbering the people

24 And again the anger of the LORD was kindled against Israel, and he moved David against them to say, Go, number Israel and Judah.

23:17 is not this the blood . . . ? The water represented the lives that were risked to obtain it for their king. We have no right to use something that has cost the precious lives of others merely for our own satisfaction.

24:1 he moved David. 1 Chronicles 21:1 indicates Satan moved David to number Israel

2 For the king said to Joab the captain of the host, which *was* with him, Go now through all the tribes of Israel, from Dan even to Beer-sheba, and number ye the people, that I may know the number of the people.

> **24:2 The Wrong Motive**
> David's sin was in taking a count of the fighting men of Israel so that he would put his trust in his army instead of in God. David became afflicted with pride, and in numbering the people he acted as though they were his own property. They were not; they were a responsibility that God gave David to rule His people.

3 And Joab said unto the king, Now the LORD thy God add unto the people, how many soever they be, an hundredfold, and that the eyes of my lord the king may see *it:* but why doth my lord the king delight in this thing?

4 Notwithstanding the king's word prevailed against Joab, and against the captains of the host. And Joab and the captains of the host went out from the presence of the king, to number the people of Israel.

¶ 5 And they passed over Jordan, and pitched in Aroer, on the right side of the city that *lieth* in the midst of the river of Gad, and toward Jazer:

6 Then they came to Gilead, and to the land of Tahtim-hodshi; and they came to Dan-jaan, and about to Zidon,

7 And came to the strong hold of Tyre, and to all the cities of the Hivites, and of the Canaanites: and they went out to the south of Judah, *even* to Beer-sheba.

8 So when they had gone through all the land, they came to Jerusalem at the end of nine months and twenty days.

9 And Joab gave up the sum of the number of the people unto the king: and there were in Israel eight hundred thousand valiant men that drew the sword; and the men of Judah *were* five hundred thousand men.

David's choice of punishment

¶ 10 And David's heart smote him after that he had numbered the people. And David said unto the LORD, I have sinned greatly in that I have done: and now, I beseech thee, O LORD, take away the iniquity of thy servant; for I have done very foolishly.

11 For when David was up in the morning, the word of the LORD came unto the prophet Gad, David's seer, saying,

12 Go and say unto David, Thus saith the LORD, I offer thee three *things;* choose thee one of them, that I may *do it* unto thee.

13 So Gad came to David, and told him, and said unto him, Shall seven years of famine come unto thee in thy land? or wilt thou flee three months before thine enemies, while they pursue thee? or that there be three days' pestilence in thy land? now advise, and see what answer I shall return to him that sent me.

14 And David said unto Gad, I am in a great strait: let us fall now into the hand of the LORD; for his mercies *are* great: and let me not fall into the hand of man.

¶ 15 So the LORD sent a pestilence upon Israel from the morning even to the time appointed: and there died of

---

while here it indicates God moved David. This is similar to what happened to Job when Satan moved God against Job (compare Job 1:12; 2:3).

24:9 in Israel eight hundred thousand. The figures in this verse doubtless were the number of men who were trained to fight; the full military strength is given in 1 Chronicles 21:5.

24:10 David's heart smote him after that. For nine months and twenty days (vs. 8) the numbering had been going on. David saw his error. Sometimes sin is attractive before it is committed, but Satan cannot prevent us from seeing the ugliness of sin after it is committed, especially when the Spirit convicts our hearts.

24:13 seven years of famine. This refers to the famine's duration whereas the three years mentioned in 1 Chronicles 21:12 refers to the final three years.

the people from Dan even to Beer-sheba seventy thousand men.
[16]And when the angel stretched out
his hand upon Jerusalem to destroy it,
the LORD repented him of the evil, and
said to the angel that destroyed the
people, It is enough: stay now thine
hand. And the angel of the LORD was by
the threshingplace of Araunah the Jebusite.
[17]And David spake unto the LORD
when he saw the angel that smote the
people, and said, Lo, I have sinned, and
I have done wickedly: but these sheep,
what have they done? let thine hand, I
pray thee, be against me, and against
my father's house.

David buys Araunah's threshingfloor

¶[18]And Gad came that day to David,
and said unto him, Go up, rear an altar
unto the LORD in the threshingfloor of
Araunah the Jebusite.
[19]And David, according to the saying of Gad, went up as the LORD commanded.
[20]And Araunah looked, and saw the
king and his servants coming on toward
him: and Araunah went out, and bowed
himself before the king on his face upon
the ground.
[21]And Araunah said, Wherefore is my
lord the king come to his servant? And
David said, To buy the threshingfloor of
thee, to build an altar unto the LORD,
that the plague may be stayed from the
people.
[22]And Araunah said unto David, Let
my lord the king take and offer up what
seemeth good unto him: behold, *here be*
oxen for burnt-sacrifice, and threshing
instruments and *other* instruments of
the oxen for wood.
[23]All these *things* did Araunah, *as* a
king, give unto the king. And Araunah
said unto the king, The LORD thy God
accept thee.
[24]And the king said unto Araunah,
Nay; but I will surely buy *it* of thee at a
price: neither will I offer burnt-offerings unto the LORD my God of that
which doth cost me nothing. So David
bought the threshingfloor and the oxen
for fifty shekels of silver.

24:24 It Costs Nothing
David's refusal to offer a burnt-sacrifice that cost him nothing should be an encouragement to every one of us. How shameful that so many Christians would be ready to be yielded to God's will only if they could be sure it would cost them nothing, such as unpopularity or giving up their personal ambitions!

[25]And David built there an altar unto
the LORD, and offered burnt-offerings
and peace-offerings. So the LORD was
intreated for the land, and the plague
was stayed from Israel.

24:15 PLAGUES IN THE OLD TESTAMENT

Although the ten plagues on Egypt are the best known plagues of the Bible, other plagues were devastating to Israel.

Plague	Reason/Result	Reference
"the LORD plagued the people"	worshipped golden calf	Exodus 32:35
"a very great plague"	complained about no meat	Numbers 11:33
"the plague"	spies who brought a bad report	Numbers 14:37
"the plague"	people complained/14,700 died	Numbers 16:46-50
"the plague"	sexual immorality/24,000 died	Numbers 25:1-9
plague of tumors	Philistines stole the ark of the covenant	1 Samuel 5:9
3 day plague	David took a census/70,000 died	2 Samuel 24:15

24:24 fifty shekels. Compare 1 Chronicles 21:25. The passage here records the price paid just for the threshingfloor and the oxen, not for the piece of ground.
24:25 the plague was stayed. The plague was stopped.

The First Book of the

KINGS

commonly called, The Third Book of the Kings

BACKGROUND

The books of the Kings record the history of the kings of Israel and Judah from the reign of Solomon to the time when the Jewish people were carried into captivity. The books were written sometime during that captivity. They are more than history books, however, for they record the reigns of the kings in their relation to the true King of Kings, the LORD.

THE WRITER

According to Jewish tradition, the books were written by Jeremiah, and there is internal evidence and language evidence that this may be true.

SUMMARY

First Kings deals especially with the death of David; the attempted plot and failure of Adonijah; the reign of the wise and famous Solomon; the building and dedication of the temple; the death of Solomon; the division of the kingdom under Rehoboam and Jeroboam; and the history of the two kingdoms to the time of the reigns of Jehoram over Judah, and Ahaziah over Israel, in Samaria. First Kings also includes the miracles and ministry of Elijah.

OUTLINE OF 1 KINGS

I.	King David's Old Age and Death	1 Kings 1:1—2:11
II.	The Reign and Death of King Solomon	1 Kings 2:12—11:43
III.	The Division of the Kingdom	1 Kings 12:1—22:53

I. David's Old Age and Death
(1:1—2:11)

1 Now king *David was old *and*
stricken in years; and they covered
him with clothes, but he gat no heat.
2 Wherefore his servants said unto
him, Let there be sought for my lord the
king a young virgin: and let her stand
before the king, and let her cherish him,
and let her lie in thy bosom, that my
lord the king may get heat.
3 So they sought for a fair damsel
throughout all the coasts of *Israel, and
found Abishag a Shunammite, and
brought her to the king.
4 And the damsel *was* very fair, and
cherished the king, and ministered to
him: but the king knew her not.

1:3 Shunammite. A native of the city of Shunem, which was about five miles south of Mount Tabor.

Adonijah's plot to become king

¶ 5 Then Adonijah the son of Haggith exalted himself, saying, I will be king: and he prepared him chariots and horsemen, and fifty men to run before him.

1:5 Adonijah
Adonijah's name means *my LORD is Jehovah,* but he had a heart of pride and deceit. He was the oldest son of David, for Amnon had been slain by Absalom (2 Sam. 13:28), and Absalom by Joab (2 Sam. 18:14).

6 And his father had not displeased him at any time in saying, Why hast thou done so? and he also *was a* very goodly *man;* and *his mother* bare him after Absalom.

7 And he conferred with Joab the son of Zeruiah, and with Abiathar the priest: and they following Adonijah helped *him.*

8 But Zadok the priest, and Benaiah the son of *Jehoiada, and Nathan the *prophet, and Shimei, and Rei, and the mighty men which *belonged* to David, were not with Adonijah.

9 And Adonijah slew sheep and oxen and fat cattle by the stone of Zoheleth, which *is* by En-rogel, and called all his brethren the king's sons, and all the men of *Judah the king's servants:

The plot of Nathan and Bath-sheba

10 But Nathan the prophet, and Benaiah, and the mighty men, and Solomon his brother, he called not.

¶ 11 Wherefore Nathan spake unto Bath-sheba the mother of Solomon, saying, Hast thou not heard that Adonijah the son of Haggith doth reign, and David our lord knoweth *it* not?

12 Now therefore come, let me, I pray thee, give thee counsel, that thou mayest save thine own life, and the life of thy son Solomon.

13 Go and get thee in unto king David, and say unto him, Didst not thou, my lord, O king, swear unto thine handmaid, saying, Assuredly Solomon thy son shall reign after me, and he shall sit upon my throne? why then doth Adonijah reign?

14 Behold, while thou yet talkest there with the king, I also will come in after thee, and confirm thy words.

¶ 15 And Bath-sheba went in unto the king into the chamber: and the king was very old; and Abishag the Shunammite ministered unto the king.

16 And Bath-sheba bowed, and did obeisance unto the king. And the king said, What wouldest thou?

17 And she said unto him, My lord, thou swarest by the LORD thy *God unto thine handmaid, *saying,* Assuredly Solomon thy son shall reign after me, and he shall sit upon my throne.

18 And now, behold, Adonijah reigneth; and now, my lord the king, thou knowest *it* not:

19 And he hath slain oxen and fat cattle and sheep in abundance, and hath called all the sons of the king, and Abiathar the priest, and Joab the captain of the host: but Solomon thy servant hath he not called.

20 And thou, my lord, O king, the eyes of all Israel *are* upon thee, that thou shouldest tell them who shall sit on the throne of my lord the king after him.

21 Otherwise it shall come to pass, when my lord the king shall sleep with his fathers, that I and my son Solomon shall be counted offenders.

1:5 Haggith. One of David's wives. See 2 Samuel 3:4.

1:9 Adonijah slew sheep and oxen and fat cattle. These animals were slain by Adonijah to celebrate a feast, because he thought he was going to take the throne of his father David (vs. 25).

1:13 Solomon thy son shall reign. It was God's plan that Solomon should follow David as king. David had told Solomon of this while the boy was still very young (see 1 Chron. 22:5-6,10).

¶22 And, lo, while she yet talked with
the king, Nathan the prophet also
came in.
23 And they told the king, saying, Behold Nathan the prophet. And when he
was come in before the king, he bowed
himself before the king with his face to
the ground.
24 And Nathan said, My lord, O king,
hast thou said, Adonijah shall reign after
me, and he shall sit upon my throne?
25 For he is gone down this day, and
hath slain oxen and fat cattle and sheep
in abundance, and hath called all the
king's sons, and the captains of the
host, and Abiathar the priest; and, behold, they eat and drink before him, and
say, God save king Adonijah.
26 But me, *even* me thy servant, and
Zadok the priest, and Benaiah the son
of Jehoiada, and thy servant Solomon,
hath he not called.
27 Is this thing done by my lord the
king, and thou hast not shewed *it* unto
thy servant, who should sit on the
throne of my lord the king after him?
¶28 Then king David answered and
said, Call me Bath-sheba. And she came
into the king's presence, and stood before the king.
29 And the king sware, and said, *As* the
LORD liveth, that hath *redeemed my
soul out of all distress,
30 Even as I sware unto thee by the
LORD God of Israel, saying, Assuredly
Solomon thy son shall reign after me,
and he shall sit upon my throne in my
stead; even so will I certainly do this day.
31 Then Bath-sheba bowed with *her*
face to the earth, and did reverence to
the king, and said, Let my lord king
David live for ever.
¶32 And king David said, Call me Zadok the priest, and Nathan the prophet, and Benaiah the son of Jehoiada. And
they came before the king.
33 The king also said unto them, Take
with you the servants of your lord, and
cause Solomon my son to ride upon
mine own mule, and bring him down to
Gihon:
34 And let Zadok the priest and Nathan the prophet *anoint him there king
over Israel: and blow ye with the trumpet, and say, God save king Solomon.
35 Then ye shall come up after him,
that he may come and sit upon my
throne; for he shall be king in my stead:
and I have appointed him to be ruler
over Israel and over Judah.
36 And Benaiah the son of Jehoiada
answered the king, and said, *Amen:
the LORD God of my lord the king say
so *too*.
37 As the LORD hath been with my
lord the king, even so be he with Solomon, and make his throne greater than
the throne of my lord king David.
38 So Zadok the priest, and Nathan the
prophet, and Benaiah the son of Jehoiada, and the Cherethites, and the
Pelethites, went down, and caused Solomon to ride upon king David's mule,
and brought him to Gihon.

Solomon anointed king

39 And Zadok the priest took an horn
of *oil out of the *tabernacle, and

1:39 USES FOR OIL

Oil was used chiefly in times of joy and gladness (vs. 40). It is a *type of the Holy Spirit. It was made from the olive berry and was used for the following purposes:

1. for food (Exod. 29:2);
2. for cosmetics, or for anointing the body after the bath;
3. in connection with mourning for the dead (2 Sam. 14:2);
4. for medical treatments (Isa. 1:6; Mark 6:13);
5. for light (Matt. 25:3);
6. as an offering in the worship service (Lev. 2:1; 8:12); and
7. in the anointing of kings and priests (1 Sam. 16:13; Lev. 8:12).

anointed Solomon. And they blew the
trumpet; and all the people said, God
save king Solomon.
[40]And all the people came up after
him, and the people piped with pipes,
and rejoiced with great joy, so that the
earth rent with the sound of them.

Adonijah's fear and submission

¶[41]And Adonijah and all the guests
that *were* with him heard *it* as they had
made an end of eating. And when Joab
heard the sound of the trumpet, he said,
Wherefore *is this* noise of the city being in an uproar?
[42]And while he yet spake, behold,
Jonathan the son of Abiathar the priest
came: and Adonijah said unto him,
Come in; for thou *art* a valiant man, and
bringest good tidings.
[43]And Jonathan answered and said to
Adonijah, Verily our lord king David
hath made Solomon king.
[44]And the king hath sent with him
Zadok the priest, and Nathan the prophet, and Benaiah the son of Jehoiada, and
the Cherethites, and the Pelethites, and
they have caused him to ride upon the
king's mule:
[45]And Zadok the priest and Nathan
the prophet have anointed him king in
Gihon: and they are come up from
thence rejoicing, so that the city rang
again. This *is* the noise that ye have
heard.
[46]And also Solomon sitteth on the
throne of the kingdom.
[47]And moreover the king's servants
came to bless our lord king David, saying, God make the name of Solomon
better than thy name, and make his
throne greater than thy throne. And the
king bowed himself upon the bed.
[48]And also thus said the king,
Blessed *be* the LORD God of Israel,
which hath given *one* to sit on my throne
this day, mine eyes even seeing *it.*
[49]And all the guests that *were* with
Adonijah were afraid, and rose up, and
went every man his way.
¶[50]And Adonijah feared because of
Solomon, and arose, and went, and
caught hold on the horns of the altar.
[51]And it was told Solomon, saying,
Behold, Adonijah feareth king Solomon:
for, lo, he hath caught hold on the horns
of the altar, saying, Let king Solomon
swear unto me to day that he will not
slay his servant with the sword.
[52]And Solomon said, If he will shew
himself a worthy man, there shall not
an hair of him fall to the earth: but if
wickedness shall be found in him, he
shall die.
[53]So king Solomon sent, and they
brought him down from the altar. And
he came and bowed himself to king
Solomon: and Solomon said unto him,
Go to thine house.

David's last charge to Solomon

2 Now the days of David drew nigh
that he should die; and he charged
Solomon his son, saying,
[2]I go the way of all the earth: be thou
strong therefore, and shew thyself a
man;
[3]And keep the charge of the LORD thy
God, to walk in his ways, to keep his
statutes, and his commandments, and
his judgments, and his testimonies, as
it is written in the *law of Moses, that
thou mayest prosper in all that thou
doest, and whithersoever thou turnest
thyself:
[4]That the LORD may continue his
word which he spake concerning me,
saying, If thy children take heed to their
way, to walk before me in truth with all
their heart and with all their soul, there

1:42 Jonathan. The name means the *gift of the LORD*. There are at least sixteen different Jonathans listed in the Old Testament.

1:50 caught hold on the horns of the altar. The fear of death drove Adonijah to the altar. The horns were long pieces of wood at the four corners of the altar, and the one who clung to them meant to show that he was turning to God for protection and help.

shall not fail thee (said he) a man on the
throne of Israel.
[5]Moreover thou knowest also what Joab the son of Zeruiah did to me, *and* what he did to the two captains of the hosts of Israel, unto Abner the son of Ner, and unto Amasa the son of Jether, whom he slew, and shed the blood of war in peace, and put the blood of war upon his girdle that *was* about his loins, and in his shoes that *were* on his feet.
[6]Do therefore according to thy wisdom, and let not his hoar head go down to the grave in peace.
[7]But shew kindness unto the sons of Barzillai the Gileadite, and let them be of those that eat at thy table: for so they came to me when I fled because of Absalom thy brother.
[8]And, behold, *thou hast* with thee Shimei the son of Gera, a Benjamite of Bahurim, which cursed me with a grievous curse in the day when I went to Mahanaim: but he came down to meet me at Jordan, and I sware to him by the LORD, saying, I will not put thee to death with the sword.
[9]Now therefore hold him not guiltless: for thou *art* a wise man, and knowest what thou oughtest to do unto him; but his hoar head bring thou down to the grave with blood.

David's death

[10]So David slept with his fathers, and was buried in the city of David.
[11]And the days that David reigned over Israel *were* forty years: seven years reigned he in Hebron, and thirty and three years reigned he in *Jerusalem.

II. Reign and Death of Solomon (2:12—11:43)

¶[12]Then sat Solomon upon the throne of David his father; and his kingdom was established greatly.

The death of Adonijah

¶[13]And Adonijah the son of Haggith came to Bath-sheba the mother of Solomon. And she said, Comest thou peaceably? And he said, Peaceably.
[14]He said moreover, I have somewhat to say unto thee. And she said, Say on.
[15]And he said, Thou knowest that the

2:5 HINDERING GOD'S PLAN

God had instructed David that Solomon was to succeed him as king. Now all those who had attempted to spoil God's plan had to receive their punishment. These were:

1. Adonijah (1:5; compare 2:24-25);
2. Abiathar (1:7; compare 2:26-27);
3. Joab (1:7; compare 2:33-34);
4. Shimei (2 Sam. 16:5-13; 19:16-23; 1 Kings 2:8; compare 1 Kings 2:36-46).

Solomon acted in obedience to the wishes of his father David (1 Kings 2:5-9).

2:11 KING DAVID'S ACCOMPLISHMENTS

Organized the army	1 Chronicles 11; 12; 27
Set up a system of worship	1 Chronicles 23–26
Organized an administration for his kingdom	1 Chronicles 26:20-28
Built a palace	1 Chronicles 14:1-2
Gathered resources and made plans for the temple	1 Chronicles 22; 28; 29
Wrote psalms for use in worship	1 Chronicles 16:36; various Psalms
A loyal and dear friend to Jonathan	1 Samuel 18:20
Defeated the Philistines	1 Chronicles 14:8-17
Returned the ark of the covenant to Jerusalem	1 Chronicles 15
Conquered enemies in surrounding areas	1 Chronicles 18–20
A man after God's own heart	1 Samuel 13:14; Acts 13:22

kingdom was mine, and *that* all Israel
set their faces on me, that I should
reign: howbeit the kingdom is turned
about, and is become my brother's: for
it was his from the LORD.
16And now I ask one petition of thee,
deny me not. And she said unto him,
Say on.
17And he said, Speak, I pray thee,
unto Solomon the king, (for he will not
say thee nay,) that he give me Abishag
the Shunammite to wife.

2:17 Adonijah's Marriage
Adonijah's request was a scheme to take the kingdom from Solomon, his half brother. To marry a dead king's wife was, according to Eastern custom, claiming the rights of the king (2 Sam. 12:8; 16:21-22).

18And Bath-sheba said, Well; I will
speak for thee unto the king.
¶19Bath-sheba therefore went unto
king Solomon, to speak unto him for
Adonijah. And the king rose up to meet
her, and bowed himself unto her, and sat
down on his throne, and caused a seat
to be set for the king's mother; and she
sat on his right hand.
20Then she said, I desire one small
petition of thee; *I pray thee,* say me not
nay. And the king said unto her, Ask on,
my mother: for I will not say thee nay.
21And she said, Let Abishag the Shunammite be given to Adonijah thy
brother to wife.
22And king Solomon answered and
said unto his mother, And why dost
thou ask Abishag the Shunammite for
Adonijah? ask for him the kingdom also;
for he *is* mine elder brother; even for
him, and for Abiathar the priest, and for
Joab the son of Zeruiah.
23Then king Solomon sware by the
LORD, saying, God do so to me, and
more also, if Adonijah have not spoken
this word against his own life.
24Now therefore, *as* the LORD liveth,
which hath established me, and set me
on the throne of David my father, and
who hath made me an house, as he
promised, Adonijah shall be put to death
this day.
25And king Solomon sent by the hand
of Benaiah the son of Jehoiada; and he
fell upon him that he died.

Solomon removes Abiathar from the priesthood

¶26And unto Abiathar the priest said
the king, Get thee to Anathoth, unto
thine own fields; for thou *art* worthy of
death: but I will not at this time put thee
to death, because thou barest the *ark
of the Lord GOD before David my father,
and because thou hast been afflicted in
all wherein my father was afflicted.
27So Solomon thrust out Abiathar
from being priest unto the LORD; that
he might fulfil the word of the LORD,
which he spake concerning the house
of Eli in *Shiloh.

Joab's death

¶28Then tidings came to Joab: for Joab
had turned after Adonijah, though he
turned not after Absalom. And Joab fled
unto the tabernacle of the LORD, and
caught hold on the horns of the altar.
29And it was told king Solomon that
Joab was fled unto the tabernacle of the
LORD; and, behold, *he is* by the altar.
Then Solomon sent Benaiah the son of
Jehoiada, saying, Go, fall upon him.
30And Benaiah came to the tabernacle of the LORD, and said unto him,
Thus saith the king, Come forth. And
he said, Nay; but I will die here. And
Benaiah brought the king word again,
saying, Thus said Joab, and thus he answered me.
31And the king said unto him, Do as
he hath said, and fall upon him, and bury
him; that thou mayest take away the
innocent blood, which Joab shed, from
me, and from the house of my father.
32And the LORD shall return his blood
upon his own head, who fell upon two
men more righteous and better than he,
and slew them with the sword, my father David not knowing *thereof, to wit,*
Abner the son of Ner, captain of the host

of Israel, and Amasa the son of Jether,
captain of the host of Judah.
33 Their blood shall therefore return
upon the head of Joab, and upon the
head of his seed for ever: but upon David, and upon his seed, and upon his
house, and upon his throne, shall there
be peace for ever from the LORD.
34 So Benaiah the son of Jehoiada
went up, and fell upon him, and slew
him: and he was buried in his own
house in the wilderness.

Benaiah and Zadok promoted

¶35 And the king put Benaiah the son
of Jehoiada in his room over the host:
and Zadok the priest did the king put in
the room of Abiathar.

The death of Shimei

¶36 And the king sent and called for
Shimei, and said unto him, Build thee
an house in Jerusalem, and dwell there,
and go not forth thence any whither.
37 For it shall be, *that* on the day thou
goest out, and passest over the brook
Kidron, thou shalt know for certain that
thou shalt surely die: thy blood shall be
upon thine own head.
38 And Shimei said unto the king, The
saying *is* good: as my lord the king hath
said, so will thy servant do. And Shimei dwelt in Jerusalem many days.
39 And it came to pass at the end of
three years, that two of the servants
of Shimei ran away unto Achish son of
Maachah king of *Gath. And they told
Shimei, saying, Behold, thy servants *be*
in Gath.
40 And Shimei arose, and saddled his
ass, and went to Gath to Achish to seek
his servants: and Shimei went, and
brought his servants from Gath.
41 And it was told Solomon that Shimei
had gone from Jerusalem to Gath, and
was come again.
42 And the king sent and called for
Shimei, and said unto him, Did I not
make thee to swear by the LORD, and
protested unto thee, saying, Know for
a certain, on the day thou goest out, and
walkest abroad any whither, that thou
shalt surely die? and thou saidst unto
me, The word *that* I have heard *is* good.
43 Why then hast thou not kept the
oath of the LORD, and the commandment that I have charged thee with?
44 The king said moreover to Shimei,
Thou knowest all the wickedness which
thine heart is privy to, that thou didst
to David my father: therefore the LORD
shall return thy wickedness upon thine
own head;
45 And king Solomon *shall be* blessed,
and the throne of David shall be established before the LORD for ever.
46 So the king commanded Benaiah
the son of Jehoiada; which went out,
and fell upon him, that he died. And the
kingdom was established in the hand of
Solomon.

Solomon marries Pharaoh's daughter

3 And Solomon made affinity with
*Pharaoh king of *Egypt, and took
Pharaoh's daughter, and brought her
into the city of David, until he had made
an end of building his own house, and
the house of the LORD, and the wall of
Jerusalem round about.
2 Only the people sacrificed in *high
places, because there was no house
built unto the name of the LORD, until
those days.
3 And Solomon loved the LORD, walking in the statutes of David his father:
only he sacrificed and burnt *incense in
high places.

The great sacrifice at Gibeon

4 And the king went to Gibeon to
*sacrifice there; for that *was* the great

3:4 the great high place. Since God's house was not yet built and there was no central place of worship, the people still used high places here and there. Solomon followed this custom, but he chose the greatest and most important height, Mount Gibeon, where the tabernacle and altar of burnt-offering stood (2 Chron. 1:13).

high place: a thousand burnt-offerings
did Solomon offer upon that altar.

Solomon's vision of God

¶5 In Gibeon the LORD appeared to
Solomon in a dream by night: and God
said, Ask what I shall give thee.
6 And Solomon said, Thou hast
shewed unto thy servant David my father great *mercy, according as he
walked before thee in truth, and in
*righteousness, and in uprightness of
heart with thee; and thou hast kept for
him this great kindness, that thou hast
given him a son to sit on his throne, as
it is this day.
7 And now, O LORD my God, thou hast
made thy servant king instead of David
my father: and I *am but* a little child: I
know not *how* to go out or come in.

3:7 The Young Solomon
Early historians agree that Solomon was between twelve and fifteen years old when he was anointed, and that he became king when he was about twenty years old. In experience and practical wisdom, he was a very young king.

8 And thy servant *is* in the midst of thy
people which thou hast chosen, a great
people, that cannot be numbered nor
counted for multitude.
9 Give therefore thy servant an understanding heart to judge thy people,
that I may discern between good and
bad: for who is able to judge this thy so
great a people?
10 And the speech pleased the Lord,
that Solomon had asked this thing.
11 And God said unto him, Because
thou hast asked this thing, and hast not
asked for thyself long life; neither hast
asked riches for thyself, nor hast asked
the life of thine enemies; but hast asked
for thyself understanding to discern
judgment;
12 Behold, I have done according to
thy words: lo, I have given thee a wise
and an understanding heart; so that
there was none like thee before thee,
neither after thee shall any arise like
unto thee.
13 And I have also given thee that
which thou hast not asked, both riches,
and honour: so that there shall not be
any among the kings like unto thee all
thy days.
14 And if thou wilt walk in my ways,
to keep my statutes and my commandments, as thy father David did walk,
then I will lengthen thy days.

3:14 God's Promise
God's promise of long life to Solomon was conditional. Solomon did not fulfill the condition (he "forsook the LORD"; see 1 Kings 9:9), and he died when he was not quite sixty years old. Solomon is a *type of the believer today (Matt. 7:7; compare John 15:7). One "greater than Solomon" (Matt. 12:42) "hath abounded toward us in all wisdom and prudence" (Eph. 1:8).

15 And Solomon awoke; and, behold,
it was a dream. And he came to Jerusalem, and stood before the ark of the
covenant of the LORD, and offered up
burnt-offerings, and offered peace-
offerings, and made a feast to all his
servants.

Solomon uses his wisdom

¶16 Then came there two women, *that
were* harlots, unto the king, and stood
before him.
17 And the one woman said, O my
lord, I and this woman dwell in one
house; and I was delivered of a child
with her in the house.
18 And it came to pass the third day
after that I was delivered, that this
woman was delivered also: and we *were*
together; *there was* no stranger with us
in the house, save we two in the house.
19 And this woman's child died in the
night; because she overlaid it.
20 And she arose at midnight, and took
my son from beside me, while thine

3:18 save. Except.

handmaid slept, and laid it in her bosom, and laid her dead child in my bosom.

21 And when I rose in the morning to give my child suck, behold, it was dead: but when I had considered it in the morning, behold, it was not my son, which I did bear.

22 And the other woman said, Nay; but the living *is* my son, and the dead *is* thy son. And this said, No; but the dead *is* thy son, and the living *is* my son. Thus they spake before the king.

23 Then said the king, The one saith, This *is* my son that liveth, and thy son *is* the dead: and the other saith, Nay; but thy son *is* the dead, and my son *is* the living.

24 And the king said, Bring me a sword. And they brought a sword before the king.

25 And the king said, Divide the living child in two, and give half to the one, and half to the other.

26 Then spake the woman whose the living child *was* unto the king, for her *bowels yearned upon her son, and she said, O my lord, give her the living child, and in no wise slay it. But the other said, Let it be neither mine nor thine, *but* divide *it*.

27 Then the king answered and said, Give her the living child, and in no wise slay it: she *is* the mother thereof.

28 And all Israel heard of the judgment which the king had judged; and they feared the king: for they saw that the wisdom of God *was* in him, to do judgment.

The list of Solomon's princes and officers

4 So king Solomon was king over all Israel.

2 And these *were* the princes which he had; Azariah the son of Zadok the priest,

3 Elihoreph and Ahiah, the sons of Shisha, *scribes; Jehoshaphat the son of Ahilud, the recorder.

4 And Benaiah the son of Jehoiada *was* over the host: and Zadok and Abiathar *were* the priests:

5 And Azariah the son of Nathan *was* over the officers: and Zabud the son of Nathan *was* principal officer, *and* the king's friend:

6 And Ahishar *was* over the household: and Adoniram the son of Abda *was* over the tribute.

¶ 7 And Solomon had twelve officers over all Israel, which provided victuals for the king and his household: each man his month in a year made provision.

8 And these *are* their names: The son of *Hur, in mount *Ephraim:

9 The son of Dekar, in Makaz, and in Shaalbim, and Beth-shemesh, and Elon-beth-hanan:

10 The son of Hesed, in Aruboth; to him *pertained* Sochoh, and all the land of Hepher:

11 The son of Abinadab, in all the region of Dor; which had Taphath the daughter of Solomon to wife:

12 Baana the son of Ahilud; *to him pertained* Taanach and *Megiddo, and all Beth-shean, which *is* by Zartanah beneath Jezreel, from Beth-shean to Abel-meholah, *even* unto *the place that is* beyond Jokneam:

13 The son of Geber, in Ramoth-gilead; to him *pertained* the towns of Jair the son of *Manasseh, which *are* in *Gilead; to him *also pertained* the region of Argob, which *is* in *Bashan, threescore great cities with walls and brasen bars:

14 Ahinadab the son of Iddo *had* Mahanaim:

15 Ahimaaz *was* in Naphtali; he also took Basmath the daughter of Solomon to wife:

16 Baanah the son of Hushai *was* in Asher and in Aloth:

17 Jehoshaphat the son of Paruah, in Issachar:

3:26 yearned. To long for earnestly or anxiously, to be moved with tenderness, grief, or pity.

[18]Shimei the son of Elah, in Benjamin:
[19]Geber the son of Uri *was* in the
country of Gilead, in the country of Sihon king of the Amorites, and of Og
king of Bashan; and *he was* the only
officer which *was* in the land.

The riches of Solomon

¶[20]Judah and Israel *were* many, as the
sand which *is* by the sea in multitude,
eating and drinking, and making merry.
[21]And Solomon reigned over all kingdoms from the river unto the land of
the *Philistines, and unto the border of
Egypt: they brought presents, and
served Solomon all the days of his life.
¶[22]And Solomon's provision for one
day was thirty measures of fine flour,
and threescore measures of meal,
[23]Ten fat oxen, and twenty oxen out
of the pastures, and an hundred sheep,
beside harts, and roebucks, and
fallowdeer, and fatted fowl.
[24]For he had dominion over all *the
region* on this side the river, from Tiphsah even to Azzah, over all the kings on
this side the river: and he had peace on
all sides round about him.
[25]And Judah and Israel dwelt safely,
every man under his vine and under
his *fig tree, from Dan even to *Beer-
sheba, all the days of Solomon.
¶[26]And Solomon had forty thousand
stalls of horses for his chariots, and
twelve thousand horsemen.

4:26 Stalls for the Horses
Solomon's ownership of tens of thousands of horses was in disobedience to the law of Deuteronomy 17:16. Second Chronicles 9:5 speaks of four thousand stalls for horses and chariots. It should be remembered that Solomon bought horses to sell them again. The stalls that he is believed to have used have been uncovered by excavators at Megiddo.

[27]And those officers provided victual
for king Solomon, and for all that came
unto king Solomon's table, every man
in his month: they lacked nothing.
[28]Barley also and straw for the horses
and dromedaries brought they unto the
place where *the officers* were, every
man according to his charge.

Solomon's famed wisdom

¶[29]And God gave Solomon wisdom
and understanding exceeding much,
and largeness of heart, even as the sand
that *is* on the sea shore.
[30]And Solomon's wisdom excelled
the wisdom of all the children of the
east country, and all the wisdom of
Egypt.
[31]For he was wiser than all men; than
Ethan the Ezrahite, and *Heman, and
Chalcol, and Darda, the sons of Mahol:
and his fame was in all nations round
about.
[32]And he spake three thousand *proverbs: and his songs were a thousand
and five.
[33]And he spake of trees, from the
cedar tree that *is* in *Lebanon even
unto the *hyssop that springeth out of
the wall: he spake also of beasts, and
of fowl, and of creeping things, and of
fishes.
[34]And there came of all people to hear
the wisdom of Solomon, from all kings
of the earth, which had heard of his
wisdom.

Stone and timber for the temple

5 And Hiram king of *Tyre sent his
servants unto Solomon; for he had
heard that they had anointed him king
in the room of his father: for Hiram was
ever a lover of David.
[2]And Solomon sent to Hiram, saying,
[3]Thou knowest how that David my
father could not build an house unto the
name of the LORD his God for the wars

4:24 he had peace. Solomon's name means *peaceable* (see 1 Chron. 22:9).
5:1 Hiram king of Tyre. Hiram, a Gentile king, had supplied much of the material that David had laid aside for the temple.

which were about him on every side, until the LORD put them under the soles of his feet.

4But now the LORD my God hath given me rest on every side, *so that there is* neither adversary nor evil occurrent.

5And, behold, I purpose to build an house unto the name of the LORD my God, as the LORD spake unto David my father, saying, Thy son, whom I will set upon thy throne in thy room, he shall build an house unto my name.

6Now therefore command thou that they hew me cedar trees out of Lebanon; and my servants shall be with thy servants: and unto thee will I give hire for thy servants according to all that thou shalt appoint: for thou knowest that *there is* not among us any that can skill to hew timber like unto the Sidonians.

¶7And it came to pass, when Hiram heard the words of Solomon, that he rejoiced greatly, and said, Blessed *be* the LORD this day, which hath given unto David a wise son over this great people.

8And Hiram sent to Solomon, saying, I have considered the things which thou sentest to me for: *and* I will do all thy desire concerning timber of cedar, and concerning timber of fir.

9My servants shall bring *them* down from Lebanon unto the sea: and I will convey them by sea in floats unto the place that thou shalt appoint me, and will cause them to be discharged there, and thou shalt receive *them:* and thou shalt accomplish my desire, in giving food for my household.

10So Hiram gave Solomon cedar trees and fir trees *according to* all his desire.

11And Solomon gave Hiram twenty thousand measures of wheat *for* food to his household, and twenty measures of pure oil: thus gave Solomon to Hiram year by year.

12And the LORD gave Solomon wisdom, as he promised him: and there was peace between Hiram and Solomon; and they two made a league together.

¶13And king Solomon raised a levy out of all Israel; and the levy was thirty thousand men.

14And he sent them to Lebanon ten thousand a month by courses: a month they were in Lebanon, *and* two months at home: and Adoniram *was* over the levy.

15And Solomon had threescore and ten thousand that bare burdens, and fourscore thousand hewers in the mountains;

16Beside the chief of Solomon's officers which *were* over the work, three thousand and three hundred, which ruled over the people that wrought in the work.

17And the king commanded, and they brought great stones, costly stones, *and* hewed stones, to lay the foundation of the house.

18And Solomon's builders and Hiram's builders did hew *them,* and the stonesquarers: so they prepared timber and stones to build the house.

The description of the temple

6 And it came to pass in the four hundred and eightieth year after the children of Israel were come out of the land of Egypt, in the fourth year of Solomon's reign over Israel, in the month Zif, which *is* the second month, that he began to build the house of the LORD.

2And the house which king Solomon

5:4 occurrent. Chance, occurrence.

5:6 skill. To show skill in, to understand how to do something.

5:9 by sea in floats. Notice that the present-day method of floating logs from lumber camps is ages old.

5:11 twenty measures of pure oil. One liquid measure is about 86 gallons, so Solomon gave Hiram 1,720 gallons of pure oil each year ("year by year").

6:1 Solomon's Temple
The temple of Solomon shows what the house of God should always be:
1. a place of testimony with the Word of God as its center;
2. a sanctuary where God's name is hallowed and where He consecrates His children; and
3. a place where Christians are given rest from all worldly cares and worries, where they are at peace with each other, and where all are united in prayer to the praise and the glory of God's name. It is where God dwells in the midst of His people (2 Cor. 6:16; see also 1 Cor. 3:17).

built for the LORD, the length thereof
was threescore *cubits, and the breadth
thereof twenty *cubits,* and the height
thereof thirty cubits.
3 And the porch before the temple of
the house, twenty cubits *was* the length
thereof, according to the breadth of the
house; *and* ten cubits *was* the breadth
thereof before the house.
4 And for the house he made windows
of narrow lights.
¶5 And against the wall of the house
he built chambers round about, *against*
the walls of the house round about, *both*
of the temple and of the *oracle: and he
made chambers round about:
6 The nethermost chamber *was* five
cubits broad, and the middle *was* six cubits broad, and the third *was* seven cubits
broad: for without *in the wall* of the house
he made narrowed rests round about,
that *the beams* should not be fastened in
the walls of the house.
7 And the house, when it was in building, was built of stone made ready before it was brought thither: so that there
was neither hammer nor axe *nor* any
tool of iron heard in the house, while it
was in building.
8 The door for the middle chamber
was in the right side of the house: and
they went up with winding stairs into
the middle *chamber,* and out of the middle into the third.
9 So he built the house, and finished
it; and covered the house with beams
and boards of cedar.
10 And *then* he built chambers against
all the house, five cubits high: and they
rested on the house with timber of cedar.
¶11 And the word of the LORD came to
Solomon, saying,
12 *Concerning* this house which thou
art in building, if thou wilt walk in my
statutes, and execute my judgments,
and keep all my commandments to walk
in them; then will I perform my word
with thee, which I spake unto David thy
father:

6:12-13 Beyond a Building
Notice here the interruption in the account of the building of the temple. Solomon was in danger of becoming satisfied with himself because he was building a temple for the LORD. God, in verses 12 and 13, reminded Solomon that His favor was not won by giving Him costly gifts, but by obeying Him and His Word.

13 And I will dwell among the children
of Israel, and will not forsake my people Israel.
14 So Solomon built the house, and
finished it.
15 And he built the walls of the house
within with boards of cedar, both the
floor of the house, and the walls of the
cieling: *and* he covered *them* on the inside with wood, and covered the floor
of the house with planks of fir.
16 And he built twenty cubits on the
sides of the house, both the floor and
the walls with boards of cedar: he even
built *them* for it within, *even* for the oracle, *even* for the most *holy *place.*
17 And the house, that *is,* the temple
before it, was forty cubits *long.*
18 And the cedar of the house within
was carved with *knops and open flowers: all *was* cedar; there was no stone
seen.

6:6 nethermost. Lowest of all.

19 And the oracle he prepared in the house within, to set there the ark of the covenant of the LORD.

20 And the oracle in the forepart *was* twenty cubits in length, and twenty cubits in breadth, and twenty cubits in the height thereof: and he overlaid it with pure gold; and *so* covered the altar *which was of* cedar.

21 So Solomon overlaid the house within with pure gold: and he made a partition by the chains of gold before the oracle; and he overlaid it with gold.

22 And the whole house he overlaid with gold, until he had finished all the house: also the whole altar that *was* by the oracle he overlaid with gold.

¶ 23 And within the oracle he made two cherubims *of* olive tree, *each* ten cubits high.

24 And five cubits *was* the one wing of the cherub, and five cubits the other wing of the cherub: from the uttermost part of the one wing unto the uttermost part of the other *were* ten cubits.

25 And the other cherub *was* ten cubits: both the cherubims *were* of one measure and one size.

26 The height of the one cherub *was* ten cubits, and so *was it* of the other cherub.

27 And he set the cherubims within the inner house: and they stretched forth the wings of the cherubims, so that the wing of the one touched the *one* wall, and the wing of the other cherub touched the other wall; and their wings touched one another in the midst of the house.

28 And he overlaid the cherubims with gold.

29 And he carved all the walls of the house round about with carved figures of cherubims and palm trees and open flowers, within and without.

30 And the floor of the house he overlaid with gold, within and without.

¶ 31 And for the entering of the oracle he made doors *of* olive tree: the lintel *and* side posts *were* a fifth part *of the wall.*

32 The two doors also *were of* olive tree; and he carved upon them carvings of cherubims and palm trees and open flowers, and overlaid *them* with gold, and spread gold upon the cherubims, and upon the palm trees.

33 So also made he for the door of the temple posts *of* olive tree, a fourth part *of the wall.*

34 And the two doors *were of* fir tree: the two leaves of the one door *were* folding, and the two leaves of the other door *were* folding.

35 And he carved *thereon* cherubims and palm trees and open flowers: and covered *them* with gold fitted upon the carved work.

¶ 36 And he built the inner court with three rows of hewed stone, and a row of cedar beams.

¶ 37 In the fourth year was the foundation of the house of the LORD laid, in the month Zif:

38 And in the eleventh year, in the month Bul, which *is* the eighth month, was the house finished throughout all the parts thereof, and according to all the fashion of it. So was he seven years in building it.

Solomon's own house

7 But Solomon was building his own house thirteen years, and he finished all his house.

¶ 2 He built also the house of the forest of Lebanon; the length thereof *was* an hundred cubits, and the breadth thereof fifty cubits, and the height thereof thirty cubits, upon four rows of cedar pillars, with cedar beams upon the pillars.

3 And *it was* covered with cedar above upon the beams, that *lay* on forty five pillars, fifteen *in* a row.

4 And *there were* windows *in* three

7:2 the house of the forest of Lebanon. The palace was doubtless called this because it was built of cedar wood from the forests of Lebanon.

7:1 Solomon's Palace

Solomon's own house included all the buildings described in verses 1 to 12. The longer time spent on the building of Solomon's house, as compared with the seven-and-one-half years required to build the temple, can be accounted for as follows:

1. There were years of preparation for the temple, even before the death of David.
2. Only a few workmen were used for building the palace in comparison to the 180,000 workmen used in the construction of the temple.

rows, and light *was* against light *in* three ranks.

5 And all the doors and posts *were* square, with the windows: and light *was* against light *in* three ranks.

¶ 6 And he made a porch of pillars; the length thereof *was* fifty cubits, and the breadth thereof thirty cubits: and the porch *was* before them: and the *other* pillars and the thick beam *were* before them.

¶ 7 Then he made a porch for the throne where he might judge, *even* the porch of judgment: and *it was* covered with cedar from one side of the floor to the other.

¶ 8 And his house where he dwelt *had* another court within the porch, *which* was of the like work. Solomon made also an house for Pharaoh's daughter, whom he had taken *to wife,* like unto this porch.

9 All these *were of* costly stones, according to the measures of hewed stones, sawed with saws, within and without, even from the foundation unto the coping, and *so* on the outside toward the great court.

10 And the foundation *was of* costly stones, even great stones, stones of ten cubits, and stones of eight cubits.

11 And above *were* costly stones, after the measures of hewed stones, and cedars.

12 And the great court round about *was* with three rows of hewed stones, and a row of cedar beams, both for the inner court of the house of the LORD, and for the porch of the house.

¶ 13 And king Solomon sent and fetched Hiram out of Tyre.

14 He *was* a widow's son of the tribe of Naphtali, and his father *was* a man of Tyre, a worker in brass: and he was filled with wisdom, and understanding, and cunning to work all works in brass. And he came to king Solomon, and wrought all his work.

15 For he cast two pillars of brass, of eighteen cubits high apiece: and a line of twelve cubits did compass either of them about.

16 And he made two chapiters *of* molten brass, to set upon the tops of the pillars: the height of the one chapiter *was* five cubits, and the height of the other chapiter *was* five cubits:

17 *And* nets of checker work, and wreaths of chain work, for the chapiters which *were* upon the top of the pillars; seven for the one chapiter, and seven for the other chapiter.

18 And he made the pillars, and two rows round about upon the one network, to cover the chapiters that *were* upon the top, with pomegranates: and so did he for the other chapiter.

19 And the chapiters that *were* upon the top of the pillars *were* of lily work in the porch, four cubits.

20 And the chapiters upon the two pillars *had pomegranates* also above, over against the belly which *was* by the network: and the pomegranates *were* two hundred in rows round about upon the other chapiter.

7:13 Hiram out of Tyre. This was not King Hiram but a master workman who was highly esteemed by the king. This workman's father, who had died, was a Tyrian, and his mother, of the tribe of Dan, had later married a man of Naphtali (compare 2 Chron. 2:13-14, where he is called "Huram").

7:14 cunning. Skill, knowledge.

7:16 chapiters. The upper part or head of a pillar or column—a term used in modern architecture.

[21]And he set up the pillars in the
porch of the temple: and he set up the
right pillar, and called the name thereof
Jachin: and he set up the left pillar, and
he called the name thereof Boaz.
[22]And upon the top of the pillars *was*
lily work: so was the work of the pillars
finished.
¶[23]And he made a molten sea, ten cubits from the one brim to the other: *it
was* round all about, and his height *was*
five cubits: and a line of thirty cubits did
compass it round about.
[24]And under the brim of it round
about *there were* knops compassing it,
ten in a cubit, compassing the sea round
about: the knops *were* cast in two rows,
when it was cast.
[25]It stood upon twelve oxen, three
looking toward the north, and three looking toward the west, and three looking
toward the south, and three looking toward the east: and the sea *was set* above
upon them, and all their hinder parts *were*
inward.
[26]And it *was* an hand breadth thick,
and the brim thereof was wrought like
the brim of a cup, with flowers of lilies:
it contained two thousand baths.
¶[27]And he made ten bases of brass;
four cubits *was* the length of one base,
and four cubits the breadth thereof, and
three cubits the height of it.
[28]And the work of the bases *was* on
this *manner:* they had borders, and the
borders *were* between the ledges:
[29]And on the borders that *were* between the ledges *were* lions, oxen, and
cherubims: and upon the ledges *there
was* a base above: and beneath the lions
and oxen *were* certain additions made of
thin work.
[30]And every base had four brasen
wheels, and plates of brass: and the four
corners thereof had undersetters: under the *laver *were* undersetters molten, at the side of every addition.
[31]And the mouth of it within the
chapiter and above *was* a cubit: but
the mouth thereof *was* round *after* the
work of the base, a cubit and an half: and
also upon the mouth of it *were* gravings
with their borders, foursquare, not
round.
[32]And under the borders *were* four
wheels; and the axletrees of the wheels
were joined to the base: and the height
of a wheel *was* a cubit and a half a
cubit.
[33]And the work of the wheels *was*
like the work of a chariot wheel: their
axletrees, and their naves, and their
felloes, and their spokes, *were* all
molten.
[34]And *there were* four undersetters
to the four corners of one base: *and*
the undersetters *were* of the very base
itself.
[35]And in the top of the base *was there*
a round compass of half a cubit high: and
on the top of the base the ledges thereof
and the borders thereof *were* of the
same.
[36]For on the plates of the ledges
thereof, and on the borders thereof, he
graved cherubims, lions, and palm
trees, according to the proportion of
every one, and additions round about.
[37]After this *manner* he made the ten
bases: all of them had one casting, one
measure, *and* one size.
¶[38]Then made he ten lavers of brass:
one laver contained forty baths: *and*
every laver was four cubits: *and* upon
every one of the ten bases one laver.
[39]And he put five bases on the right
side of the house, and five on the left
side of the house: and he set the sea on

7:21 Jachin. This name means *he shall establish.*
7:21 Boaz. This name means *in it is strength.*
7:26 two thousand baths. This was probably the usual amount in the "molten sea" (vs. 23). Second Chronicles 4:5 gives the number as three thousand baths, probably the amount of water that the vessel would actually hold if it were filled to the top.
7:30, 34 undersetters. Pedestals, supports.
7:33 felloes. The pieces making up the rim of a wheel.

the right side of the house eastward
over against the south.
¶[40]And Hiram made the lavers, and
the shovels, and the basons. So Hiram
made an end of doing all the work that
he made king Solomon for the house of
the LORD:
[41]The two pillars, and the *two* bowls
of the chapiters that *were* on the top of
the two pillars; and the two networks,
to cover the two bowls of the chapiters
which *were* upon the top of the pillars;
[42]And four hundred pomegranates for
the two networks, *even* two rows of
pomegranates for one network, to cover the two bowls of the chapiters that
were upon the pillars;
[43]And the ten bases, and ten lavers
on the bases;
[44]And one sea, and twelve oxen under the sea;
[45]And the pots, and the shovels, and
the basons: and all these vessels, which
Hiram made to king Solomon for the
house of the LORD, *were of* bright brass.
[46]In the plain of Jordan did the king
cast them, in the clay ground between
Succoth and Zarthan.
[47]And Solomon left all the vessels
unweighed, because they were exceeding many: neither was the weight of the
brass found out.
[48]And Solomon made all the vessels
that *pertained* unto the house of the
LORD: the *altar of gold, and the table of
gold, whereupon the *shewbread *was,*
[49]And the *candlesticks of pure gold,
five on the right *side,* and five on the
left, before the oracle, with the flowers,
and the lamps, and the tongs *of* gold,
[50]And the bowls, and the *snuffers,
and the basons, and the spoons, and the
*censers *of* pure gold; and the hinges
of gold, *both* for the doors of the inner
house, the most holy *place, and* for
the doors of the house, *to wit,* of the
temple.
[51]So was ended all the work that king
Solomon made for the house of the
LORD. And Solomon brought in the
things which *David his father had dedicated; *even* the silver, and the gold, and
the vessels, did he put among the treasures of the house of the LORD.

The ark brought into the temple

8 Then Solomon assembled the elders of Israel, and all the heads of
the tribes, the chief of the fathers of the
children of Israel, unto king Solomon in
*Jerusalem, that they might bring up
the *ark of the covenant of the LORD
out of the city of David, which *is* *Zion.
[2]And all the men of Israel assembled
themselves unto king Solomon at the
feast in the month Ethanim, which *is*
the seventh month.
[3]And all the elders of Israel came, and
the priests took up the ark.
[4]And they brought up the ark of the
LORD, and the *tabernacle of the congregation, and all the holy vessels that
were in the tabernacle, even those did
the priests and the Levites bring up.
[5]And king Solomon, and all the congregation of Israel, that *were* assembled
unto him, were with him before the ark,
sacrificing sheep and oxen, that could
not be told nor numbered for multitude.
[6]And the priests brought in the ark of
the covenant of the LORD unto his
place, into the oracle of the house, to
the most holy *place, even* under the
wings of the cherubims.
[7]For the cherubims spread forth *their*
two wings over the place of the ark, and
the cherubims covered the ark and the
staves thereof above.
[8]And they drew out the staves, that
the ends of the staves were seen out in
the holy *place* before the oracle, and
they were not seen without: and there
they are unto this day.
[9]*There was* nothing in the ark save

8:1 Solomon assembled the elders. From one to three years passed between the time that the temple was built and the time of its dedication, which took place in the year of *Jubilee, during the *Feast of Tabernacles.

8:9 The Contents of the Ark
When we read in Hebrews 9:4 that the ark contained a golden pot of manna, Aaron's rod that budded, and the tables of stone, we must not be confused, since there is no contradiction between these two verses. Hebrews 9:4 refers to the ark in the tabernacle, not in the temple. Because Aaron's rod and the pot of manna were provisions for the wilderness, they would not have been in keeping with the reign of glory and peace, because now the people had come to a time of rest. When we are brought into glory, we will not need priestly intercession and help, or the manna, for we will have the Lord Jesus Christ. The Law contained in the Ten Commandments was included in the ark in the temple, for the Word of the Lord endures forever, and the whole foundation of that earthly kingdom over which our Lord will yet reign will be the law of righteousness.

the two tables of stone, which *Moses
put there at *Horeb, when the LORD
made *a covenant* with the children of
Israel, when they came out of the land
of Egypt.
10And it came to pass, when the
priests were come out of the holy *place,*
that the cloud filled the house of the
LORD,
11So that the priests could not stand
to minister because of the cloud: for the
glory of the LORD had filled the house
of the LORD.

Solomon's sermon of dedication

¶12Then spake Solomon, The LORD
said that he would dwell in thick darkness.
13I have surely built thee an house to
dwell in, a settled place for thee to abide
in for ever.
14And the king turned his face about,
and blessed all the congregation of Israel: (and all the congregation of Israel
stood;)
15And he said, Blessed *be* the LORD
*God of Israel, which spake with his
mouth unto David my father, and hath
with his hand fulfilled *it,* saying,
16Since the day that I brought forth
my people Israel out of Egypt, I chose
no city out of all the tribes of Israel to
build an house, that my name might be
therein; but I chose David to be over my
people Israel.
17And it was in the heart of David my
father to build an house for the name of
the LORD God of Israel.
18And the LORD said unto David my
father, Whereas it was in thine heart to
build an house unto my name, thou
didst well that it was in thine heart.
19Nevertheless thou shalt not build
the house; but thy son that shall come
forth out of thy loins, he shall build the
house unto my name.
20And the LORD hath performed his
word that he spake, and I am risen up
in the room of David my father, and sit
on the throne of Israel, as the LORD
promised, and have built an house for
the name of the LORD God of Israel.
21And I have set there a place for the
ark, wherein *is* the covenant of the
LORD, which he made with our fathers,
when he brought them out of the land
of Egypt.

Solomon's prayer of dedication

¶22And Solomon stood before the altar of the LORD in the presence of all the
congregation of Israel, and spread forth
his hands toward heaven:
23And he said, LORD God of Israel,
there is no God like thee, in heaven
above, or on earth beneath, who keepest

8:14 And the king turned his face about. When Solomon spoke the words in verses 12 and 13, his face was turned to the temple and he was speaking to the LORD, beholding the cloud that told him God was there. But now he turned toward the people who stood in reverence in the outer court.

8:22 Solomon stood before the altar of the LORD. When we notice the brief space given to the sermon as compared with the length of the prayer of Solomon, we must observe the importance of prayer in connection with all of our service.

covenant and mercy with thy servants
that walk before thee with all their
heart:
24 Who hast kept with thy servant
David my father that thou promisedst
him: thou spakest also with thy mouth,
and hast fulfilled *it* with thine hand, as
it is this day.
25 Therefore now, LORD God of Israel,
keep with thy servant David my father
that thou promisedst him, saying,
There shall not fail thee a man in my
sight to sit on the throne of Israel; so
that thy children take heed to their way,
that they walk before me as thou hast
walked before me.
26 And now, O God of Israel, let thy
word, I pray thee, be verified, which
thou spakest unto thy servant David my
father.
27 But will God indeed dwell on the
earth? behold, the heaven and heaven
of heavens cannot contain thee; how
much less this house that I have
builded?
28 Yet have thou respect unto the
*prayer of thy servant, and to his sup-
plication, O LORD my God, to hearken
unto the cry and to the prayer, which
thy servant prayeth before thee to day:
29 That thine eyes may be open toward this house night and day, *even* toward the place of which thou hast said,
My name shall be there: that thou
mayest hearken unto the prayer which
thy servant shall make toward this
place.
30 And hearken thou to the supplication of thy servant, and of thy people
Israel, when they shall pray toward this
place: and hear thou in heaven thy
dwelling place: and when thou hearest,
forgive.
¶31 If any man trespass against his
neighbour, and an oath be laid upon him
to cause him to swear, and the oath
come before thine altar in this house:
32 Then hear thou in heaven, and do,
and judge thy servants, condemning the
wicked, to bring his way upon his head;
and justifying the righteous, to give him
according to his righteousness.
¶33 When thy people Israel be smitten down before the enemy, because
they have sinned against thee, and shall
turn again to thee, and *confess thy
name, and pray, and make supplication
unto thee in this house:
34 Then hear thou in heaven, and forgive the *sin of thy people Israel, and
bring them again unto the land which
thou gavest unto their fathers.
¶35 When heaven is shut up, and there
is no rain, because they have sinned
against thee; if they pray toward this
place, and confess thy name, and turn
from their sin, when thou afflictest
them:
36 Then hear thou in heaven, and forgive the sin of thy servants, and of thy
people Israel, that thou teach them the
good way wherein they should walk,
and give rain upon thy land, which thou
hast given to thy people for an inheritance.
¶37 If there be in the land famine, if
there be pestilence, blasting, mildew,
locust, *or* if there be caterpiller; if their
enemy besiege them in the land of their
cities; whatsoever plague, whatsoever
sickness *there be;*
38 What prayer and supplication
soever be *made* by any man, *or* by all thy
people Israel, which shall know every
man the plague of his own heart, and
spread forth his hands toward this
house:
39 Then hear thou in heaven thy dwelling place, and forgive, and do, and give
to every man according to his ways,
whose heart thou knowest; (for thou,
even thou only, knowest the hearts of all
the children of men;)
40 That they may *fear thee all the

8:29 My name shall be there. Compare this with Deuteronomy 12:11.
8:31 trespass. To transgress, to sin.
8:31 an oath be laid upon him. This is literally, *he requires an oath of him.*

days that they live in the land which
thou gavest unto our fathers.
[41]Moreover concerning a stranger,
that *is* not of thy people Israel, but
cometh out of a far country for thy
name's sake;
[42](For they shall hear of thy great
name, and of thy strong hand, and of thy
stretched out arm;) when he shall come
and pray toward this house;
[43]Hear thou in heaven thy dwelling
place, and do according to all that the
stranger calleth to thee for: that all people of the earth may know thy name, to
fear thee, as *do* thy people Israel; and
that they may know that this house,
which I have builded, is called by thy
name.
¶[44]If thy people go out to battle
against their enemy, whithersoever
thou shalt send them, and shall pray
unto the LORD toward the city which
thou hast chosen, and *toward* the house
that I have built for thy name:
[45]Then hear thou in heaven their
prayer and their supplication, and maintain their cause.
[46]If they sin against thee, (for *there is*
no man that sinneth not,) and thou be
angry with them, and deliver them to
the enemy, so that they carry them
away captives unto the land of the enemy, far or near;
[47]*Yet* if they shall bethink themselves
in the land whither they were carried
captives, and *repent, and make supplication unto thee in the land of them that
carried them captives, saying, We have
sinned, and have done perversely, we
have committed wickedness;
[48]And *so* return unto thee with all
their heart, and with all their soul, in
the land of their enemies, which led
them away captive, and pray unto thee
toward their land, which thou gavest
unto their fathers, the city which thou
hast chosen, and the house which I have
built for thy name:
[49]Then hear thou their prayer and
their supplication in heaven thy dwelling place, and maintain their cause,
[50]And forgive thy people that have
sinned against thee and all their transgressions wherein they have transgressed against thee, and give them
compassion before them who carried
them captive, that they may have compassion on them:
[51]For they *be* thy people, and thine
inheritance, which thou broughtest
forth out of Egypt, from the midst of the
furnace of iron:
[52]That thine eyes may be open unto
the supplication of thy servant, and
unto the supplication of thy people Israel, to hearken unto them in all that
they call for unto thee.
[53]For thou didst separate them from
among all the people of the earth, *to be*
thine inheritance, as thou spakest by
the hand of Moses thy servant, when
thou broughtest our fathers out of
Egypt, O Lord GOD.

Solomon's blessing

[54]And it was *so,* that when Solomon
had made an end of praying all this
prayer and supplication unto the LORD,
he arose from before the altar of the
LORD, from kneeling on his knees with
his hands spread up to heaven.
[55]And he stood, and blessed all the
congregation of Israel with a loud voice,
saying,
[56]Blessed *be* the LORD, that hath
given rest unto his people Israel, according to all that he promised: there
hath not failed one word of all his good
promise, which he promised by the
hand of Moses his servant.
[57]The LORD our God be with us, as
he was with our fathers: let him not
leave us, nor forsake us:
[58]That he may incline our hearts unto
him, to walk in all his ways, and to keep
his commandments, and his statutes,

8:54 he arose . . . from kneeling. Note verse 22. As is so often done, Solomon first stood, then kneeled (see 2 Chron. 6:12-13).

and his judgments, which he commanded our fathers.
59 And let these my words, wherewith
I have made supplication before the
LORD, be nigh unto the LORD our God
day and night, that he maintain the
cause of his servant, and the cause of
his people Israel at all times, as the
matter shall require:
60 That all the people of the earth may
know that the LORD *is* God, *and that
there is* none else.
61 Let your heart therefore be *perfect with the LORD our God, to walk in
his statutes, and to keep his commandments, as at this day.

Sacrifice and rejoicing

¶62 And the king, and all Israel with
him, offered sacrifice before the LORD.
63 And Solomon offered a sacrifice of
*peace-offerings, which he offered unto
the LORD, two and twenty thousand
oxen, and an hundred and twenty thousand sheep. So the king and all the children of Israel dedicated the house of the
LORD.

8:63 The Peace-Offerings
The great number of animals used in this peace-offering was not extravagant. It was a picture, first of all, of the abundance that will be in Christ's future millennial *kingdom. Second, because of the great crowds who were in the city for that time of rejoicing, much food had to be provided. Leviticus 7:15 tells us that the peace-offering was to be eaten.

64 The same day did the king hallow
the middle of the court that *was* before
the house of the LORD: for there he offered burnt-offerings, and meat-offerings,
and the fat of the peace-offerings: because the brasen altar that *was* before
the LORD *was* too little to receive the
burnt-offerings, and meat-offerings, and
the fat of the peace-offerings.
65 And at that time Solomon held a
feast, and all Israel with him, a great
congregation, from the entering in of
Hamath unto the river of Egypt, before
the LORD our God, seven days and
seven days, *even* fourteen days.
66 On the eighth day he sent the people away: and they blessed the king, and
went unto their tents joyful and glad of
heart for all the goodness that the LORD
had done for David his servant, and for
Israel his people.

God again appears to Solomon

9 And it came to pass, when Solomon had finished the building of
the house of the LORD, and the king's
house, and all Solomon's desire which
he was pleased to do,
2 That the LORD appeared to Solomon
the second time, as he had appeared
unto him at Gibeon.
3 And the LORD said unto him, I have
heard thy prayer and thy supplication,
that thou hast made before me: I have
hallowed this house, which thou hast
built, to put my name there for ever;
and mine eyes and mine heart shall be
there perpetually.
4 And if thou wilt walk before me, as
David thy father walked, in integrity of
heart, and in uprightness, to do according to all that I have commanded thee,
and wilt keep my statutes and my judgments:
5 Then I will establish the throne of
thy *kingdom upon Israel for ever, as I
promised to David thy father, saying,
There shall not fail thee a man upon the
throne of Israel.
6 *But* if ye shall at all turn from following me, ye or your children, and will not
keep my commandments *and* my statutes which I have set before you, but go

---

8:65 a feast. *The* Feast of Tabernacles.
8:65 river of Egypt. Probably the Nile, though some suggest that it was a desert stream on the border of Egypt.
9:2 appeared unto him [Solomon] at Gibeon. See 1 Kings 3:5.

and serve other gods, and worship
them:
7 Then will I cut off Israel out of the
land which I have given them; and this
house, which I have hallowed for my
name, will I cast out of my sight; and
Israel shall be a proverb and a byword
among all people:
8 And at this house, *which* is high,
every one that passeth by it shall be
astonished, and shall hiss; and they
shall say, Why hath the LORD done thus
unto this land, and to this house?
9 And they shall answer, Because they
forsook the LORD their God, who
brought forth their fathers out of the
land of *Egypt, and have taken hold
upon other gods, and have worshipped
them, and served them: therefore hath
the LORD brought upon them all this
evil.

Solomon's gift to King Hiram

¶ 10 And it came to pass at the end of
twenty years, when Solomon had built
the two houses, the house of the LORD,
and the king's house,
11 (*Now* Hiram the king of Tyre had
furnished Solomon with cedar trees and
fir trees, and with gold, according to all
his desire,) that then king Solomon
gave Hiram twenty cities in the land of
Galilee.
12 And Hiram came out from Tyre to
see the cities which Solomon had given
him; and they pleased him not.
13 And he said, What cities *are* these
which thou hast given me, my brother?
And he called them the land of Cabul
unto this day.
14 And Hiram sent to the king sixscore talents of gold.

Solomon raises a tax

¶ 15 And this *is* the reason of the levy
which king Solomon raised; for to build
the house of the LORD, and his own
house, and *Millo, and the wall of Jerusalem, and Hazor, and *Megiddo, and
Gezer.
16 *For* *Pharaoh king of Egypt had
gone up, and taken Gezer, and burnt it
with fire, and slain the Canaanites that
dwelt in the city, and given it *for* a present unto his daughter, Solomon's wife.
17 And Solomon built Gezer, and
Beth-horon the nether,
18 and Baalath, and Tadmor in the wilderness, in the land,
19 And all the cities of store that Solomon had, and cities for his chariots,
and cities for his horsemen, and that
which Solomon desired to build in Jerusalem, and in Lebanon, and in all the
land of his dominion.
20 *And* all the people *that were* left of
the Amorites, Hittites, Perizzites, Hivites, and Jebusites, which *were* not of
the children of Israel,
21 Their children that were left after
them in the land, whom the children of
Israel also were not able utterly to destroy, upon those did Solomon levy a
tribute of bondservice unto this day.
22 But of the children of Israel did
Solomon make no bondmen: but they
were men of war, and his servants, and

9:13 The Land of Cabul
The meaning of this word is very interesting in view of the transaction between Solomon and King Hiram. Besides supplying Solomon with timber (1 Kings 5; 2 Chron. 2), Hiram also gave him five tons of gold (vss. 11,14), and Solomon gave the twenty cities in exchange for the gold. Hiram called the district that contained the twenty cities Solomon gave him by the name of one of them, Cabul, which probably means *displeasing, rubbish,* or *nothing;* and they were later returned to Solomon (2 Chron. 8:2).

9:16 his daughter, Solomon's wife. See 1 Kings 7:8.
9:18 Tadmor. This city, built at a fertile oasis in the desert between Palestine and Babylonia, later became the famous Palmyra. Both Tadmor, or Tamar, and Palmyra mean *the city of palms*.

his princes, and his captains, and rulers of his chariots, and his horsemen.

23 These *were* the chief of the officers that *were* over Solomon's work, five hundred and fifty, which bare rule over the people that wrought in the work.

¶24 But Pharaoh's daughter came up out of the city of David unto her house which *Solomon* had built for her: then did he build Millo.

¶25 And three times in a year did Solomon offer burnt-offerings and peace-offerings upon the altar which he built unto the LORD, and he burnt *incense upon the altar that *was* before the LORD. So he finished the house.

Solomon builds a navy

¶26 And king Solomon made a navy of ships in Ezion-geber, which *is* beside Eloth, on the shore of the Red sea, in the land of *Edom.

27 And Hiram sent in the navy his servants, shipmen that had knowledge of the sea, with the servants of Solomon.

28 And they came to *Ophir, and fetched from thence gold, four hundred and twenty talents, and brought *it* to king Solomon.

The Queen of Sheba visits Solomon

10 And when the queen of Sheba heard of the fame of Solomon concerning the name of the LORD, she came to *prove him with hard questions.

10:1 The Queen of Sheba
She was also called "queen of the south" (Matt. 12:42). Sheba was the center of a commercial nation. It was named after the grandson of Cush (1 Chron. 1:8-9), who settled in Abyssinia.

2 And she came to Jerusalem with a very great train, with camels that bare spices, and very much gold, and precious stones: and when she was come to Solomon, she communed with him of all that was in her heart.

3 And Solomon told her all her questions: there was not *any* thing hid from the king, which he told her not.

4 And when the queen of Sheba had seen all Solomon's wisdom, and the house that he had built,

5 And the meat of his table, and the sitting of his servants, and the attendance of his ministers, and their apparel, and his cupbearers, and his ascent by which he went up unto the house of the LORD; there was no more spirit in her.

6 And she said to the king, It was a true report that I heard in mine own land of thy acts and of thy wisdom.

7 Howbeit I believed not the words, until I came, and mine eyes had seen *it:* and, behold, the half was not told me: thy wisdom and prosperity exceedeth the fame which I heard.

8 Happy *are* thy men, happy *are* these thy servants, which stand continually before thee, *and* that hear thy wisdom.

9 Blessed be the LORD thy God, which delighted in thee, to set thee on the throne of Israel: because the LORD loved Israel for ever, therefore made he thee king, to do *judgment and justice.

10 And she gave the king an hundred and twenty talents of gold, and of spices very great store, and precious stones: there came no more such abundance of spices as these which the queen of Sheba gave to king Solomon.

11 And the navy also of Hiram, that brought gold from Ophir, brought in

10:11 The Almug Trees
These were also called algum trees (compare 2 Chron. 2:8; 9:10). The wood of this tree is believed to be the very precious sandalwood, which has been prized through all ages for its color, its fragrance, its durability, and its texture, which is close-grained and suitable for carving.

9:25 three times in a year. This refers to the Feasts of Passover, Pentecost, and Tabernacles.

from Ophir great plenty of *almug trees, and precious stones.

12 And the king made of the almug trees pillars for the house of the LORD, and for the king's house, harps also and *psalteries for singers: there came no such almug trees, nor were seen unto this day.

13 And king Solomon gave unto the queen of Sheba all her desire, whatsoever she asked, beside *that* which Solomon gave her of his royal bounty. So she turned and went to her own country, she and her servants.

Solomon's wealth and power

¶14 Now the weight of gold that came to Solomon in one year was six hundred threescore and six talents of gold.

15 Beside *that he had* of the merchantmen, and of the traffick of the spice merchants, and of all the kings of Arabia, and of the governors of the country.

¶16 And king Solomon made two hundred targets *of* beaten gold: six hundred *shekels* of gold went to one target.

17 And *he made* three hundred shields *of* beaten gold; three pound of gold went to one shield: and the king put them in the *house of the forest of Lebanon.

¶18 Moreover the king made a great throne of ivory, and overlaid it with the best gold.

19 The throne had six steps, and the top of the throne *was* round behind: and *there were* stays on either side on the place of the seat, and two lions stood beside the stays.

20 And twelve lions stood there on the one side and on the other upon the six steps: there was not the like made in any kingdom.

¶21 And all king Solomon's drinking vessels *were of* gold, and all the vessels of the house of the forest of Lebanon *were of* pure gold; none *were of* silver: it was nothing accounted of in the days of Solomon.

22 For the king had at sea a navy of Tharshish with the navy of Hiram: once in three years came the navy of Tharshish, bringing gold, and silver, ivory, and apes, and peacocks.

23 So king Solomon exceeded all the kings of the earth for riches and for wisdom.

¶24 And all the earth sought to Solomon, to hear his wisdom, which God had put in his heart.

25 And they brought every man his present, vessels of silver, and vessels of gold, and garments, and armour, and spices, horses, and mules, a rate year by year.

¶26 And Solomon gathered together chariots and horsemen: and he had a thousand and four hundred chariots, and twelve thousand horsemen, whom he bestowed in the cities for chariots, and with the king at Jerusalem.

27 And the king made silver *to be* in Jerusalem as stones, and cedars made he *to be* as the sycomore trees that *are* in the vale, for abundance.

¶28 And Solomon had horses brought out of Egypt, and *linen yarn: the king's merchants received the linen yarn at a price.

29 And a chariot came up and went out of Egypt for six hundred *shekels* of silver, and an horse for an hundred and fifty: and so for all the kings of the Hittites, and for the kings of Syria, did they bring *them* out by their means.

Solomon's foreign wives turn him from the LORD

11 But king Solomon loved many strange women, together with the daughter of Pharaoh, women of the Moabites, Ammonites, Edomites, Zidonians, *and* Hittites;

2 Of the nations *concerning* which the

11:1 Solomon loved many strange women. The LORD had prohibited mixed marriages with the nations of Canaan (Exod. 34:16; Deut. 7:3-4). This act of disobedience was the beginning of Solomon's downfall.

LORD said unto the children of Israel, Ye
shall not go in to them, neither shall
they come in unto you: *for* surely they
will turn away your heart after their gods:
Solomon clave unto these in love.
3 And he had seven hundred wives,
princesses, and three hundred concubines: and his wives turned away his
heart.
4 For it came to pass, when Solomon
was old, *that* his wives turned away his
heart after other gods: and his heart
was not *perfect with the LORD his
God, as *was* the heart of David his father.

5 For Solomon went after Ashtoreth
the goddess of the Zidonians, and after
Milcom the *abomination of the Ammonites.
6 And Solomon did evil in the sight of
the LORD, and went not fully after the
LORD, as *did* David his father.
7 Then did Solomon build an high
place for *Chemosh, the abomination of
*Moab, in the hill that *is* before Jerusalem, and for *Molech, the abomination
of the children of Ammon.
8 And likewise did he for all his
strange wives, which burnt incense and
sacrificed unto their gods.

God chastens Solomon

¶9 And the LORD was angry with Solomon, because his heart was turned
from the LORD God of Israel, which had
appeared unto him twice,

11:9 God's Anger
God's love for Solomon had not changed, but He did hate Solomon's sin. God's holiness demands that all sin must be punished (Gal. 6:7). The enemies of Solomon were roused against him by God, so that Solomon might know and confess what suffering there is in forsaking the fear of the LORD (Jer. 2:19).

10 And had commanded him concerning this thing, that he should not go
after other gods: but he kept not that
which the LORD commanded.
11 Wherefore the LORD said unto Solomon, Forasmuch as this is done of
thee, and thou hast not kept my *covenant and my statutes, which I have
commanded thee, I will surely rend the
kingdom from thee, and will give it to
thy servant.
12 Notwithstanding in thy days I will
not do it for David thy father's sake: *but*
I will rend it out of the hand of thy son.
13 Howbeit I will not rend away all the

11:7 the hill that is before Jerusalem. This hill, which was the sacred Mount of Olives, came to be called "the mount of corruption" in Solomon's days because of the idol worship that Solomon introduced there (2 Kings 23:13).

kingdom; *but* will give one tribe to thy son for David my servant's sake, and for Jerusalem's sake which I have chosen.

¶ 14 And the LORD stirred up an adversary unto Solomon, Hadad the Edomite: he *was* of the king's seed in Edom.

15 For it came to pass, when David was in Edom, and Joab the captain of the host was gone up to bury the slain, after he had smitten every male in Edom;

16 (For six months did Joab remain there with all Israel, until he had cut off every male in Edom:)

17 That Hadad fled, he and certain Edomites of his father's servants with him, to go into Egypt; Hadad *being* yet a little child.

18 And they arose out of *Midian, and came to Paran: and they took men with them out of Paran, and they came to Egypt, unto Pharaoh king of Egypt; which gave him an house, and appointed him victuals, and gave him land.

19 And Hadad found great favour in the sight of Pharaoh, so that he gave him to wife the sister of his own wife, the sister of Tahpenes the queen.

20 And the sister of Tahpenes bare him Genubath his son, whom Tahpenes weaned in Pharaoh's house: and Genubath was in Pharaoh's household among the sons of Pharaoh.

21 And when Hadad heard in Egypt that David slept with his fathers, and that Joab the captain of the host was dead, Hadad said to Pharaoh, Let me depart, that I may go to mine own country.

22 Then Pharaoh said unto him, But what hast thou lacked with me, that, behold, thou seekest to go to thine own country? And he answered, Nothing: howbeit let me go in any wise.

¶ 23 And God stirred him up *another* adversary, Rezon the son of Eliadah, which fled from his lord Hadadezer king of Zobah:

24 And he gathered men unto him, and became captain over a band, when David slew them *of Zobah:* and they went to *Damascus, and dwelt therein, and reigned in Damascus.

25 And he was an adversary to Israel all the days of Solomon, beside the mischief that Hadad *did:* and he abhorred Israel, and reigned over Syria.

Jeroboam rises

¶ 26 And Jeroboam the son of Nebat, an Ephrathite of Zereda, Solomon's servant, whose mother's name *was* Zeruah, a widow woman, even he lifted up *his* hand against the king.

27 And this *was* the cause that he lifted up *his* hand against the king: Solomon built Millo, *and* repaired the breaches of the city of David his father.

28 And the man Jeroboam *was* a mighty man of valour: and Solomon seeing the young man that he was industrious, he made him ruler over all the charge of the house of *Joseph.

The prophecy of Ahijah

29 And it came to pass at that time when Jeroboam went out of Jerusalem, that the *prophet Ahijah the Shilonite found him in the way; and he had clad himself with a new garment; and they two *were* alone in the field:

30 And Ahijah caught the new garment that *was* on him, and rent it *in* twelve pieces:

31 And he said to Jeroboam, Take thee ten pieces: for thus saith the LORD, the God of Israel, Behold, I will rend the kingdom out of the hand of Solomon, and will give ten tribes to thee:

32 (But he shall have one tribe for my servant David's sake, and for Jerusalem's sake, the city which I have chosen out of all the tribes of Israel:)

33 Because that they have forsaken me, and have worshipped Ashtoreth the

---

11:17 Hadad. Hadad joined Rezon (vs. 23) and later became king of Syria and forefather of the line of kings known as Ben-hadad. These kings brought great trouble to Israel.

11:26 an Ephrathite. Jeroboam was the first king of the northern tribes.

goddess of the Zidonians, Chemosh the
god of the Moabites, and Milcom the god
of the children of Ammon, and have not
walked in my ways, to do *that which is*
right in mine eyes, and *to keep* my statutes and my judgments, as *did* David his
father.
34 Howbeit I will not take the whole
kingdom out of his hand: but I will make
him prince all the days of his life for
David my servant's sake, whom I
chose, because he kept my commandments and my statutes:
35 But I will take the kingdom out of
his son's hand, and will give it unto
thee, *even* ten tribes.
36 And unto his son will I give one
tribe, that David my servant may have
a light alway before me in Jerusalem,
the city which I have chosen me to put
my name there.

11:36 The LORD's Promise
This chapter in the history of Israel is important because the kingdom was divided. Verse 36 shows us the integrity of the LORD in preserving one tribe for David's sake. Here we see a fulfillment of 2 Samuel 7:14-16. David's house remained a light "for ever," until the Son of David, Jesus Christ, came, who is "the true Light, which lighteth every man that cometh into the world" (John 1:9).

37 And I will take thee, and thou shalt
reign according to all that thy soul
desireth, and shalt be king over Israel.
38 And it shall be, if thou wilt hearken unto all that I command thee, and
wilt walk in my ways, and do *that is*
right in my sight, to keep my statutes
and my commandments, as David my
servant did; that I will be with thee,
and build thee a sure house, as I built
for David, and will give Israel unto
thee.
39 And I will for this afflict the seed of
David, but not for ever.
40 Solomon sought therefore to kill
Jeroboam. And Jeroboam arose, and fled
into Egypt, unto Shishak king of Egypt,
and was in Egypt until the death of Solomon.

Solomon's death and burial

¶41 And the rest of the acts of Solomon, and all that he did, and his wisdom, *are* they not written in the book
of the acts of Solomon?
42 And the time that Solomon reigned
in Jerusalem over all Israel *was* forty
years.
43 And Solomon slept with his fathers,
and was buried in the city of David his
father: and *Rehoboam his son reigned
in his stead.

11:42 ACCOMPLISHMENTS OF KING SOLOMON

Accomplishment	Reference
Nation was at peace	1 Chronicles 22:9
Built God's temple	1 Kings 6
Refined the centralized system of government	1 Kings 4:7-19
Built a magnificent palace and terraces	1 Kings 7:1-12
Built strategic cities:	
Megiddo, Hazor, Gezer, Lower Beth-horon, Baalath, Tadmor	1 Kings 9:15,17,18
Built up trade and trade routes	1 Kings 9:26-28; 10:22
Built fleet of ships	1 Kings 9:26
Renowned intellect: cataloged plant life,	
gathered information on birds, animals and insects	1 Kings 4:33
Wrote 3,000 proverbs and 1,500 songs	1 Kings 4:32
Author of books: Song of Solomon, Ecclesiastes, many Proverbs	see book introductions

11:37 I will take thee. Jeroboam did not wait for God to give him the kingdom; in his unbelief he tried to gain it in his own power (1 Kings 11:26).

11:38 if thou wilt . . . I will. Jeroboam never tried to fulfill the conditions under which God promised to bless him and be with him. Because of that, his family perished, and others became rulers over Israel.

III. The Division of the Kingdom (12:1—22:53)

12 And Rehoboam went to Shechem: for all Israel were come
to *Shechem to make him king.
2And it came to pass, when Jeroboam the son of Nebat, who was yet in
Egypt, heard *of it,* (for he was fled from
the presence of king Solomon, and Jeroboam dwelt in Egypt;)
3That they sent and called him. And
Jeroboam and all the congregation of
Israel came, and spake unto Rehoboam,
saying,
4Thy father made our yoke grievous:
now therefore make thou the grievous
service of thy father, and his heavy yoke
which he put upon us, lighter, and we
will serve thee.
5And he said unto them, Depart yet
for three days, then come again to me.
And the people departed.
¶6And king Rehoboam consulted
with the old men, that stood before Solomon his father while he yet lived, and
said, How do ye advise that I may answer this people?
7And they spake unto him, saying, If
thou wilt be a servant unto this people
this day, and wilt serve them, and answer them, and speak good words to
them, then they will be thy servants for
ever.
8But he forsook the counsel of the old
men, which they had given him, and
consulted with the young men that
were grown up with him, *and* which
stood before him:
9And he said unto them, What counsel give ye that we may answer this
people, who have spoken to me, saying,
Make the yoke which thy father did put
upon us lighter?
10And the young men that were
grown up with him spake unto him, saying, Thus shalt thou speak unto this
people that spake unto thee, saying,
Thy father made our yoke heavy, but
make thou *it* lighter unto us; thus shalt
thou say unto them, My little *finger*
shall be thicker than my father's loins.
11And now whereas my father did
lade you with a heavy yoke, I will add
to your yoke: my father hath chastised
you with whips, but I will chastise you
with scorpions.
¶12So Jeroboam and all the people
came to Rehoboam the third day, as the
king had appointed, saying, Come to me
again the third day.
13And the king answered the people
roughly, and forsook the old men's
counsel that they gave him;
14And spake to them after the counsel of the young men, saying, My father
made your yoke heavy, and I will add to
your yoke: my father *also* chastised you
with whips, but I will chastise you with
scorpions.
15Wherefore the king hearkened not
unto the people; for the cause was from
the LORD, that he might perform his
saying, which the LORD spake by Ahijah the Shilonite unto Jeroboam the son
of Nebat.

Ten tribes follow Jeroboam: he becomes king of Israel

¶16So when all Israel saw that the
king hearkened not unto them, the people answered the king, saying, What
portion have we in David? neither *have*

12:1 Rehoboam. Rehoboam's name means *enlarger of the people;* he is the only son of Solomon mentioned in the Scriptures.

12:1 Shechem. This is the same city as Sichem (Gen. 12:6). It was a place of great strength and importance, and later became a fortified dwelling place when Jeroboam took it over (see 1 Kings 12:25).

12:2 Jeroboam. See 1 Kings 11:26-40.

12:11 scorpions. Scourges were whips with bits of bones, etc., at the end of the parts of the whip and were more painful weapons than ordinary whips.

12:15 Ahijah. See 1 Kings 11:29-39. The LORD prophesied through Ahijah.

12:16 What portion have we in David? In 2 Samuel 5:1-2, these same people had come

we inheritance in the son of Jesse: to your tents, O Israel: now see to thine own house, David. So Israel departed unto their tents.

17 But *as for* the children of Israel which dwelt in the cities of *Judah, Rehoboam reigned over them.

18 Then king Rehoboam sent Adoram, who *was* over the tribute; and all Israel stoned him with stones, that he died. Therefore king Rehoboam made speed to get him up to his chariot, to flee to Jerusalem.

19 So Israel rebelled against the house of David unto this day.

20 And it came to pass, when all Israel heard that Jeroboam was come again, that they sent and called him unto the congregation, and made him king over all Israel: there was none that followed the house of David, but the tribe of Judah only.

> **12:20 The Southern Kingdom**
> The southern division of the kingdom was made up of two tribes, Judah and Benjamin. Since the tribe of Benjamin was very small, the name of the large tribe, Judah, was given to both tribes. The northern kingdom (the other ten tribes) was called Israel.

¶21 And when Rehoboam was come to Jerusalem, he assembled all the house of Judah, with the tribe of Benjamin, an hundred and fourscore thousand chosen men, which were warriors, to fight against the house of Israel, to bring the kingdom again to Rehoboam the son of Solomon.

22 But the word of God came unto Shemaiah the man of God, saying,

23 Speak unto Rehoboam, the son of Solomon, king of Judah, and unto all the house of Judah and Benjamin, and to the remnant of the people, saying,

24 Thus saith the LORD, Ye shall not go up, nor fight against your brethren the children of Israel: return every man to his house; for this thing is from me. They hearkened therefore to the word of the LORD, and returned to depart, according to the word of the LORD.

Jeroboam's wickedness destroys the nation's religious unity

¶25 Then Jeroboam built Shechem in mount Ephraim, and dwelt therein; and went out from thence, and built Penuel.

26 And Jeroboam said in his heart, Now shall the kingdom return to the house of David:

27 If this people go up to do *sacrifice in the house of the LORD at Jerusalem, then shall the heart of this people turn again unto their lord, *even* unto Rehoboam king of Judah, and they shall kill me, and go again to Rehoboam king of Judah.

28 Whereupon the king took counsel, and made two calves *of* gold, and said unto them, It is too much for you to go up to Jerusalem: behold thy gods, O Israel, which brought thee up out of the land of Egypt.

29 And he set the one in *Beth-el, and the other put he in Dan.

30 And this thing became a sin: for the people went *to worship* before the one, *even* unto Dan.

---

to David and said, in effect, "See, we are thy bone and thy flesh; thou hast led us; thou shalt be our king." Now they were saying, "We have no portion in David."

12:18 Adoram. This is the same name for Adoniram in 1 Kings 4:6; 5:14.

12:19 unto this day. This phrase would seem to refer to the time the writer of this particular book compiled and recorded his material.

12:23 the remnant of the people. These were probably some people who really belonged to the northern tribes, but because their homes were in the south, they cast their lot in with the southern tribes.

12:25 Jeroboam built Shechem. See 1 Kings 12:1 note, "Shechem."

12:25 Penuel. Penuel means *the face of God* (Judg. 8:8-9,17). It is also called "Peniel," the place where Jacob met the LORD face-to-face (Gen. 32:30).

12:28 A False Religion
The religion of Jeroboam, like every other false religion:
1. had its origin in the human heart (vs. 26);
2. was for selfish gain (vs. 27);
3. pretended to be to the advantage of the people (vs. 28);
4. was a sin against God (vs. 30; see Exod. 20:4); and
5. "the lowest of the people," who were not Levites and were probably the weakest spiritually, participated (vs. 31; 1 Kings 13:33).

31 And he made an house of *high
places, and made priests of the lowest
of the people, which were not of the
sons of Levi.
32 And Jeroboam ordained a feast in
the eighth *month, on the fifteenth day
of the month, like unto the feast that *is*
in Judah, and he offered upon the altar.
So did he in Beth-el, sacrificing unto the
calves that he had made: and he placed
in Beth-el the priests of the high places
which he had made.
33 So he offered upon the altar which
he had made in Beth-el the fifteenth day
of the eighth month, *even* in the month
which he had devised of his own heart;
and ordained a feast unto the children
of Israel: and he offered upon the altar,
and burnt incense.

Jeroboam's false altar and the man of God

13 And, behold, there came a man
of God out of Judah by the word
of the LORD unto Beth-el: and Jeroboam stood by the *altar to burn incense.
2 And he cried against the altar in the
word of the LORD, and said, O altar, altar, thus saith the LORD; Behold, a child
shall be born unto the house of *David,
*Josiah by name; and upon thee shall he
offer the priests of the high places that

13:2 A Promised Child
This remarkable prophecy was fulfilled about three hundred years later, almost one hundred years after the ten tribes had been carried away into captivity (see 2 Kings 23:15-18).

burn incense upon thee, and men's
bones shall be burnt upon thee.
3 And he gave a sign the same day,
saying, This *is* the sign which the LORD
hath spoken; Behold, the altar shall be
rent, and the ashes that *are* upon it shall
be poured out.
4 And it came to pass, when king Jeroboam heard the saying of the man of
God, which had cried against the altar
in Beth-el, that he put forth his hand
from the altar, saying, Lay hold on him.
And his hand, which he put forth against
him, dried up, so that he could not pull
it in again to him.
5 The altar also was rent, and the
ashes poured out from the altar, according to the sign which the man of God
had given by the word of the LORD.
6 And the king answered and said unto
the man of God, Intreat now the face of
the LORD thy God, and pray for me, that
my hand may be restored me again. And
the man of God besought the LORD,
and the king's hand was restored him
again, and became as *it was* before.
7 And the king said unto the man of
God, Come home with me, and refresh
thyself, and I will give thee a reward.
8 And the man of God said unto the
king, If thou wilt give me half thine
house, I will not go in with thee, neither
will I eat bread nor drink water in this
place:
9 For so was it charged me by the
word of the LORD, saying, Eat no bread,
nor drink water, nor turn again by the
same way that thou camest.

12:32-33 ordained. Appointed, ordered, or arranged.
13:1 a man of God. This "man of God" is nowhere named in the Bible (see also 2 Kings 23:17).
13:4 dried up. The hand became withered, numb, and lifeless.

Disobedience and death
of the man of God

10 So he went another way, and returned not by the way that he came to
Beth-el.
¶ 11 Now there dwelt an old prophet in
Beth-el; and his sons came and told him
all the works that the man of God had
done that day in Beth-el: the words
which he had spoken unto the king,
them they told also to their father.
12 And their father said unto them,
What way went he? For his sons had
seen what way the man of God went,
which came from Judah.
13 And he said unto his sons, Saddle
me the ass. So they saddled him the
ass: and he rode thereon,
14 And went after the man of God, and
found him sitting under an oak: and he
said unto him, *Art* thou the man of God
that camest from Judah? And he said,
I *am*.
15 Then he said unto him, Come home
with me, and eat bread.
16 And he said, I may not return with
thee, nor go in with thee: neither will I
eat bread nor drink water with thee in
this place:
17 For it was said to me by the word
of the LORD, Thou shalt eat no bread
nor drink water there, nor turn again to
go by the way that thou camest.
18 He said unto him, I *am* a prophet
also as thou *art;* and an *angel spake
unto me by the word of the LORD, saying, Bring him back with thee into thine
house, that he may eat bread and drink
water. *But* he lied unto him.

13:18 Knowing God's Will
This verse clearly illustrates the truth in Galatians 1:8-9: "Though . . . an angel from heaven, preach any other gospel . . . let him be accursed." No doubt the old prophet was sincere in asking the man of God to come and have fellowship with him, but this was not the will of God. We learn here that whenever the LORD makes known His will unto us, nothing–no afterthought, friend, or relative–should cause us to depart from it.

19 So he went back with him, and
did eat bread in his house, and drank
water.
¶ 20 And it came to pass, as they sat at
the table, that the word of the LORD
came unto the prophet that brought him
back:
21 And he cried unto the man of God
that came from Judah, saying, Thus
saith the LORD, Forasmuch as thou hast
disobeyed the mouth of the LORD, and
hast not kept the commandment which
the LORD thy God commanded thee,
22 But camest back, and hast eaten
bread and drunk water in the place, of
the which *the LORD* did say to thee, Eat
no bread, and drink no water; thy carcase shall not come unto the sepulchre
of thy fathers.
¶ 23 And it came to pass, after he had
eaten bread, and after he had drunk,
that he saddled for him the ass, *to wit,*
for the prophet whom he had brought
back.
24 And when he was gone, a lion met
him by the way, and slew him: and his
carcase was cast in the way, and the ass
stood by it, the lion also stood by the
carcase.
25 And, behold, men passed by, and
saw the carcase cast in the way, and the
lion standing by the carcase: and they
came and told *it* in the city where the
old prophet dwelt.
26 And when the prophet that brought
him back from the way heard *thereof,* he
said, It *is* the man of God, who was disobedient unto the word of the LORD:
therefore the LORD hath delivered him
unto the lion, which hath torn him, and
slain him, according to the word of the
LORD, which he spake unto him.
27 And he spake to his sons, saying,
Saddle me the ass. And they saddled
him.
28 And he went and found his carcase
cast in the way, and the ass and the lion
standing by the carcase: the lion had not
eaten the carcase, nor torn the ass.
29 And the prophet took up the carcase of the man of God, and laid it upon

the ass, and brought it back: and the old
prophet came to the city, to mourn and
to bury him.
30 And he laid his carcase in his own
grave; and they mourned over him, *saying,* Alas, my brother!
31 And it came to pass, after he had
buried him, that he spake to his sons,
saying, When I am dead, then bury me
in the sepulchre wherein the man of
God *is* buried; lay my bones beside his
bones:
32 For the saying which he cried by
the word of the LORD against the altar
in Beth-el, and against all the houses of
the high places which *are* in the cities
of *Samaria, shall surely come to pass.

Jeroboam's refusal to repent

¶33 After this thing Jeroboam returned not from his evil way, but made
again of the lowest of the people priests
of the high places: whosoever would, he
consecrated him, and he became *one* of
the priests of the high places.
34 And this thing became sin unto the
house of Jeroboam, even to cut *it* off,
and to destroy *it* from off the face of the
earth.

Death of Jeroboam's son

14 At that time Abijah the son of
Jeroboam fell sick.
2 And Jeroboam said to his wife, Arise,
I pray thee, and disguise thyself, that
thou be not known to be the wife of Jeroboam; and get thee to *Shiloh: behold,
there *is* Ahijah the prophet, which told
me that *I should be* king over this people.
3 And take with thee ten loaves, and
cracknels, and a cruse of honey, and go
to him: he shall tell thee what shall become of the child.
4 And Jeroboam's wife did so, and
arose, and went to Shiloh, and came to
the house of Ahijah. But Ahijah could
not see; for his eyes were set by reason of his age.
¶5 And the LORD said unto Ahijah, Behold, the wife of Jeroboam cometh to
ask a thing of thee for her son; for he *is*
sick: thus and thus shalt thou say unto
her: for it shall be, when she cometh in,
that she shall feign herself *to be* another
woman.
6 And it was *so,* when Ahijah heard the
sound of her feet as she came in at the
door, that he said, Come in, thou wife
of Jeroboam; why feignest thou thyself
to be another? for I *am* sent to thee *with*
heavy *tidings.*
7 Go, tell Jeroboam, Thus saith the
LORD *God of Israel, Forasmuch as I
exalted thee from among the people,
and made thee prince over my people
Israel,
8 And rent the kingdom away from the
house of David, and gave it thee: and *yet*
thou hast not been as my servant David, who kept my commandments, and
who followed me with all his heart, to
do *that* only *which was* right in mine
eyes;
9 But hast done evil above all that
were before thee: for thou hast gone
and made thee other gods, and molten
images, to provoke me to anger, and
hast cast me behind thy back:
10 Therefore, behold, I will bring evil
upon the house of Jeroboam, and will
cut off from Jeroboam him that pisseth

13:34 sin . . . to cut it off. Jeroboam's sin caused his house, the northern kingdom, to be "cut off" and destroyed from the "face of the earth."

14:1 Abijah the son of Jeroboam fell sick. This sickness and the death of the boy (1 Kings 14:1-18) was a partial fulfillment of the prophecy against Jeroboam (1 Kings 11:38).

14:3 cracknels. Small cakes or biscuits.

14:3 a cruse of honey. A small cup or vessel containing honey.

14:6 heavy. Sad.

14:10 Therefore, behold. Every man-child was to be destroyed so that the house of Jeroboam would be utterly wiped out.

against the wall, *and* him that is shut up
and left in Israel, and will take away the
remnant of the house of Jeroboam, as
a man taketh away dung, till it be all
gone.
11Him that dieth of Jeroboam in the
city shall the dogs eat; and him that
dieth in the field shall the fowls of the
air eat: for the LORD hath spoken *it*.
12Arise thou therefore, get thee to
thine own house: *and* when thy feet
enter into the city, the child shall die.
13And all Israel shall mourn for him,
and bury him: for he only of Jeroboam
shall come to the grave, because in him
there is found *some* good thing toward
the LORD God of Israel in the house of
Jeroboam.
14Moreover the LORD shall raise him
up a king over Israel, who shall cut off
the house of Jeroboam that day: but
what? even now.
15For the LORD shall smite Israel, as
a reed is shaken in the water, and he
shall root up Israel out of this good land,
which he gave to their fathers, and shall
*scatter them beyond the river, be-
cause they have made their groves,
provoking the LORD to anger.
16And he shall give Israel up because
of the sins of Jeroboam, who did *sin,
and who made Israel to sin.
¶17And Jeroboam's wife arose, and
departed, and came to Tirzah: *and* when
she came to the threshold of the door,
the child died;
18And they buried him; and all Israel
mourned for him, according to the
word of the LORD, which he spake by
the hand of his servant Ahijah the
prophet.

Death of Jeroboam

19And the rest of the acts of Jeroboam, how he warred, and how he reigned,
behold, they *are* written in the book of
the chronicles of the kings of Israel.
20And the days which Jeroboam
reigned *were* two and twenty years: and
he slept with his fathers, and Nadab his
son reigned in his stead.

Sin and death of Rehoboam

¶21And Rehoboam the son of Solomon
reigned in Judah. Rehoboam *was* forty
and one years old when he began to
reign, and he reigned seventeen years
in *Jerusalem, the city which the LORD
did choose out of all the tribes of Israel,
to put his name there. And his mother's
name *was* Naamah an Ammonitess.
22And Judah did evil in the sight of the
LORD, and they provoked him to jealousy with their sins which they had committed, above all that their fathers had
done.
23For they also built them high
places, and images, and groves, on
every high hill, and *under every green
tree.
24And there were also sodomites in
the land: *and* they did according to
all the abominations of the nations
which the LORD cast out before the children of Israel.
¶25And it came to pass in the fifth year
of king Rehoboam, *that* Shishak king of
Egypt came up against Jerusalem:

14:14 but what? even now. This prophecy had a *near* fulfillment in 1 Kings 15:29 and a *remote* fulfillment in 721 B.C. when the Assyrians took the northern kingdom of Israel captive. The idol instituted by Jeroboam was not overlooked by God.

14:17 Tirzah. An ancient Canaanite city. Do not confuse this with the youngest of the five daughters of Zelophehad (Num. 26:33).

14:21 And his mother's name. The "queen mother" in the Mideastern court was always an influential person. Her high position accounts for the frequent mention of the mother's name in the histories of the reigns of the various kings.

14:22 provoked him to jealousy. See *jealous God.

14:24 sodomites. These were especially wicked people who were noted for committing the same sins for which God had destroyed Sodom (Gen. 19). The sins were very often connected with evil idol worship.

26 And he took away the treasures of
the house of the LORD, and the treasures of the king's house; he even took
away all: and he took away all the
shields of gold which Solomon had
made.
27 And king Rehoboam made in their
stead brasen shields, and committed *them*
unto the hands of the chief of the guard,
which kept the door of the king's house.
28 And it was *so*, when the king went
into the house of the LORD, that the
guard bare them, and brought them
back into the guard chamber.
¶ 29 Now the rest of the acts of Rehoboam, and all that he did, *are* they not
written in the book of the chronicles of
the kings of Judah?
30 And there was war between Rehoboam and Jeroboam all *their* days.
31 And Rehoboam slept with his fathers, and was buried with his fathers
in the city of David. And his mother's
name *was* Naamah an Ammonitess.
And Abijam his son reigned in his stead.

Abijam's reign and death

15 Now in the eighteenth year of
king Jeroboam the son of Nebat
reigned Abijam over Judah.
2 Three years reigned he in Jerusalem. And his mother's name *was* Maachah, the daughter of Abishalom.
3 And he walked in all the sins of his
father, which he had done before him:
and his heart was not *perfect with the
LORD his God, as the heart of David his
father.
4 Nevertheless for David's sake did
the LORD his God give him a lamp in
Jerusalem, to set up his son after him,
and to establish Jerusalem:

15:1-4 Abijam's Reign
Abijam was also called "Abijah" (for example, see 2 Chron. 13), which means *my Father is Jehovah.* According to 2 Chronicles 11:20-21, Abijam was the oldest son of Rehoboam's second wife, Maachah, who was his favorite wife. It is believed that for this reason Rehoboam set Abijam above his brothers and made him his successor to the throne.

5 Because David did *that which was*
right in the eyes of the LORD, and
turned not aside from any *thing* that he
commanded him all the days of his life,
save only in the matter of Uriah the
Hittite.
6 And there was war between Rehoboam and Jeroboam all the days of his
life.
7 Now the rest of the acts of Abijam,
and all that he did, *are* they not written
in the book of the chronicles of the
kings of Judah? And there was war between Abijam and Jeroboam.
8 And Abijam slept with his fathers;
and they buried him in the city of David: and Asa his son reigned in his
stead.

Asa's reign and death

¶ 9 And in the twentieth year of Jeroboam king of Israel reigned Asa over
Judah.
10 And forty and one years reigned he
in Jerusalem. And his mother's name
was Maachah, the daughter of Abishalom.
11 And Asa did *that which was* right in
the eyes of the LORD, as *did* David his
father.
12 And he took away the sodomites

15:2 Maachah. Here she is called "the daughter of Abishalom," but in 2 Chronicles 11:20, she is called "the daughter of Absalom," and in 2 Chronicles 13:2, where she is called "Michaiah," her father is called Uriel. "Daughter" and "granddaughter" are often used interchangeably. It is probable that Abishalom is just another spelling of Absalom, who was Maachah's grandfather, and that her father, Uriel, was Absalom's son-in-law.

15:4 a lamp in Jerusalem. A light was kept burning night and day in every Eastern house. If the light went out for any reason, it was counted a great disaster. Having a son is like having a lamp in the house.

15:5 Uriah the Hittite. See 2 Samuel 11.

15:9 Asa Rules over Judah
If Abijam became king in the eighteenth year of Jeroboam (vs. 1), and Asa became king in the twentieth year, then Abijam did not reign a full three years (vs. 2). The incomplete years, as in other places, are calculated as though complete. In comparing verses 25 and 33, we note that verse 25 must mean only part of two years.

out of the land, and removed all the
idols that his fathers had made.
13And also Maachah his mother, even
her he removed from *being* queen, because she had made an idol in a grove;
and Asa destroyed her idol, and burnt
it by the brook Kidron.
14But the high places were not removed: nevertheless Asa's heart was
perfect with the LORD all his days.
15And he brought in the things which
his father had dedicated, and the things
which himself had dedicated, into the
house of the LORD, silver, and gold, and
vessels.
¶16And there was war between Asa
and Baasha king of Israel all their days.
17And Baasha king of Israel went up
against Judah, and built Ramah, that he
might not suffer any to go out or come
in to Asa king of Judah.
18Then Asa took all the silver and
the gold *that were* left in the treasures
of the house of the LORD, and the treasures of the king's house, and delivered
them into the hand of his servants: and
king Asa sent them to *Ben-hadad, the
son of Tabrimon, the son of Hezion,
king of Syria, that dwelt at Damascus,
saying,
19*There is* a league between me and
thee, *and* between my father and thy
father: behold, I have sent unto thee a
present of silver and gold; come and
break thy league with Baasha king of
Israel, that he may depart from me.
20So Ben-hadad hearkened unto king
Asa, and sent the captains of the hosts
which he had against the cities of Israel,
and smote Ijon, and Dan, and Abel-
beth-maachah, and all Cinneroth, with
all the land of Naphtali.
21And it came to pass, when Baasha
heard *thereof*, that he left off building of
Ramah, and dwelt in Tirzah.
22Then king Asa made a proclamation
throughout all Judah; none *was* ex-
empted: and they took away the stones
of Ramah, and the timber thereof,
wherewith Baasha had builded; and
king Asa built with them Geba of Benjamin, and Mizpah.
23The rest of all the acts of Asa, and
all his might, and all that he did, and the
cities which he built, *are* they not written in the book of the chronicles of the
kings of Judah? Nevertheless in the
time of his old age he was diseased in
his feet.
24And Asa slept with his fathers, and
was buried with his fathers in the city
of David his father: and Jehoshaphat his
son reigned in his stead.

15:18 Ben-hadad
Ben-hadad means *son of Hadad;* it is the name of three kings of Damascus (see 1 Kings 11:17 note):

1. Ben-hadad I, king of Damascus, who made an alliance with Asa and conquered a large portion of the north of Israel (vss. 18-20);
2. Ben-hadad II, son of Ben-hadad I and also a king of Damascus. He was murdered, probably by some of his own servants (2 Kings 8:7-15);
3. Ben-hadad III, son of Hazael, and also his successor to the throne of Syria.

Nadab's reign

¶25And Nadab the son of Jeroboam
began to reign over Israel in the second
year of Asa king of Judah, and reigned
over Israel two years.
26And he did evil in the sight of the
LORD, and walked in the way of his father, and in his sin wherewith he made
Israel to sin.

Nadab's death at the hands of Baasha

¶27And Baasha the son of Ahijah, of
the house of Issachar, conspired against
him; and Baasha smote him at Gibbethon,

which *belonged* to the *Philistines; for Nadab and all Israel laid siege to Gibbethon.

Baasha's reign

28 Even in the third year of Asa king of Judah did Baasha slay him, and reigned in his stead.

29 And it came to pass, when he reigned, *that* he smote all the house of Jeroboam; he left not to Jeroboam any that breathed, until he had destroyed him, according unto the saying of the LORD, which he spake by his servant Ahijah the Shilonite:

30 Because of the sins of Jeroboam which he sinned, and which he made Israel sin, by his provocation wherewith he provoked the LORD God of Israel to anger.

¶31 Now the rest of the acts of Nadab, and all that he did, *are* they not written in the book of the chronicles of the kings of Israel?

War between Asa (Judah) and Baasha (Israel)

32 And there was war between Asa and Baasha king of Israel all their days.

33 In the third year of Asa king of Judah began Baasha the son of Ahijah to reign over all Israel in Tirzah, twenty and four years.

34 And he did evil in the sight of the LORD, and walked in the way of Jeroboam, and in his sin wherewith he made Israel to sin.

Prophecy of Jehu against Baasha

16 Then the word of the LORD came to Jehu the son of Hanani against Baasha, saying,

2 Forasmuch as I exalted thee out of the dust, and made thee prince over my people Israel; and thou hast walked in the way of Jeroboam, and hast made my people Israel to sin, to provoke me to anger with their sins;

3 Behold, I will take away the posterity of Baasha, and the posterity of his house; and will make thy house like the house of Jeroboam the son of Nebat.

4 Him that dieth of Baasha in the city shall the dogs eat; and him that dieth of his in the fields shall the fowls of the air eat.

5 Now the rest of the acts of Baasha, and what he did, and his might, *are* they not written in the book of the chronicles of the kings of Israel?

6 So Baasha slept with his fathers, and was buried in Tirzah: and Elah his son reigned in his stead.

7 And also by the hand of the prophet Jehu the son of Hanani came the word of the LORD against Baasha, and against his house, even for all the evil that he did in the sight of the LORD, in provoking him to anger with the work of his hands, in being like the house of Jeroboam; and because he killed him.

Elah's reign and death

¶8 In the twenty and sixth year of Asa king of Judah began Elah the son of Baasha to reign over Israel in Tirzah, two years.

9 And his servant Zimri, captain of half *his* chariots, conspired against him, as he was in Tirzah, drinking himself drunk in the house of Arza steward of *his* house in Tirzah.

10 And Zimri went in and smote him, and killed him, in the twenty and seventh year of Asa king of Judah, and reigned in his stead.

¶11 And it came to pass, when he began to reign, as soon as he sat on his throne, *that* he slew all the house of Baasha: he left him not one that pisseth against a wall, neither of his kinsfolks, nor of his friends.

16:1 Then. Means *And.* This connects the closing sentence of the previous chapter with the material of this chapter. The chapter is not divided according to the beginning of the reign of King Baasha, but instead it begins with the prophecy that proclaimed the downfall of the kingdom.

[12]Thus did Zimri destroy all the
house of Baasha, according to the word
of the LORD, which he spake against
Baasha by Jehu the prophet,
[13]For all the sins of Baasha, and the
sins of Elah his son, by which they
sinned, and by which they made Israel
to sin, in provoking the LORD God of
Israel to anger with their vanities.
[14]Now the rest of the acts of Elah, and
all that he did, *are* they not written in
the book of the chronicles of the kings
of Israel?

Zimri, King of Israel

¶[15]In the twenty and seventh year of
Asa king of Judah did Zimri reign seven
days in Tirzah. And the people *were*
encamped against Gibbethon, which
belonged to the Philistines.
[16]And the people *that were* encamped
heard say, Zimri hath conspired, and
hath also slain the king: wherefore all
Israel made Omri, the captain of the host,
king over Israel that day in the camp.
[17]And Omri went up from Gibbethon,
and all Israel with him, and they besieged Tirzah.
[18]And it came to pass, when Zimri
saw that the city was taken, that he
went into the palace of the king's house,
and burnt the king's house over him
with fire, and died,
[19]For his sins which he sinned in doing evil in the sight of the LORD, in walking in the way of Jeroboam, and in his
sin which he did, to make Israel to sin.
[20]Now the rest of the acts of Zimri,
and his treason that he wrought, *are*
they not written in the book of the
chronicles of the kings of Israel?

Tibni and Omri: rival kings of Israel

¶[21]Then were the people of Israel divided into two parts: half of the people
followed Tibni the son of Ginath, to
make him king; and half followed Omri.

Death of Tibni

[22]But the people that followed Omri
prevailed against the people that followed Tibni the son of Ginath: so Tibni
died, and Omri reigned.

Omri, King of Israel

¶[23]In the thirty and first year of Asa
king of Judah began Omri to reign over
Israel, twelve years: six years reigned
he in Tirzah.

16:23 King Omri
King Omri is important and should be remembered because of two things:
1. He, who was more wicked than all the kings who had been before him (vs. 25), was the father of Ahab, the king who was even more wicked than Omri.
2. He founded the famous city of Samaria.

[24]And he bought the hill Samaria of
Shemer for two talents of silver, and
built on the hill, and called the name
of the city which he built, after the
name of Shemer, owner of the hill, Samaria.
¶[25]But Omri wrought evil in the eyes
of the LORD, and did worse than all that
were before him.
[26]For he walked in all the way of Jeroboam the son of Nebat, and in his sin
wherewith he made Israel to sin, to
provoke the LORD God of Israel to anger with their vanities.
[27]Now the rest of the acts of Omri
which he did, and his might that he
shewed, *are* they not written in the
book of the chronicles of the kings of
Israel?
[28]So Omri slept with his fathers, and
was buried in Samaria: and *Ahab his
son reigned in his stead.

Ahab, King of Israel

¶[29]And in the thirty and eighth year
of Asa king of Judah began Ahab the son
of Omri to reign over Israel: and Ahab
the son of Omri reigned over Israel in
Samaria twenty and two years.
[30]And Ahab the son of Omri did evil
in the sight of the LORD above all that
were before him.
[31]And it came to pass, as if it had been
a light thing for him to walk in the sins

16:29 King Ahab
The reign of Ahab was the climax of the wickedness and constant decline in the kingdom of Israel. It was Ahab who introduced Baal worship in Israel. This all resulted from his marriage to Jezebel, the daughter of Ethbaal, king of the Zidonians. Ahab also had a very wicked father (see vs. 23 note, "King Omri").

of Jeroboam the son of Nebat, that he
took to wife Jezebel the daughter of
Ethbaal king of the Zidonians, and
went and served *Baal, and worshipped
him.
32And he reared up an altar for Baal
in the house of Baal, which he had built
in Samaria.
33And Ahab made a grove; and Ahab
did more to provoke the LORD God of
Israel to anger than all the kings of Israel that were before him.
¶34In his days did Hiel the Beth-elite
build Jericho: he laid the foundation
thereof in Abiram his firstborn, and set
up the gates thereof in his youngest *son*

17:1 The Prophet Elijah
Elijah's name means *my God is Jehovah*. The word translated "inhabitants" was Tishbeh, so that it really means that he was from Tishbeh in Gilead. There is another Tishbe, or Thisbe in Naphtali. Elijah was not commissioned to reveal new truths, therefore, he was not among the prophets who told of future events. His was a preaching ministry intended to lead the people to see their sins and return to God. He was given power from the Holy Spirit to equip and enable him for his task.

Segub, according to the word of the
LORD, which he spake by *Joshua the
son of Nun.

Elijah predicts the three years' drought

17 And Elijah the Tishbite, *who
was* of the inhabitants of *Gilead, said unto Ahab, *As* the LORD God
of Israel liveth, before whom I stand,
there shall not be dew nor rain these
years, but according to my word.

Elijah fed by ravens at Cherith

2And the word of the LORD came unto
him, saying,
3Get thee hence, and turn thee eastward, and hide thyself by the brook
Cherith, that *is* before Jordan.
4And it shall be, *that* thou shalt drink
of the brook; and I have commanded the
ravens to feed thee there.
5So he went and did according unto
the word of the LORD: for he went and
dwelt by the brook Cherith, that *is* before Jordan.
6And the ravens brought him bread
and flesh in the morning, and bread and
flesh in the evening; and he drank of the
brook.
7And it came to pass after a while,
that the brook dried up, because there
had been no rain in the land.

Elijah fed by the poor woman at Zarephath

¶8And the word of the LORD came
unto him, saying,
9Arise, get thee to Zarephath, which

16:34 did Hiel the Beth-elite build Jericho. Five hundred years before this (Josh. 6:26), Joshua had prophesied against rebuilding the city and had said that it would result in the death of the children of the man who attempted it. Some archaeologists believe that Hiel, following cruel heathen custom, actually buried his little children in the walls.

17:3 hide thyself. No doubt Elijah's life would be in danger from the anger of King Ahab and his wicked wife Jezebel. They would probably blame Elijah for the drought (see 1 Kings 18:17). Both here and in 19:1-7, we see God's protection and care in behalf of the true servant who fearlessly gives God's message and does His work in His way. "Go ye therefore, and teach all nations . . . and, lo, I am with you always, even unto the end of the world" (Matt. 28:19-20).

17:9 Zarephath. Zarephath, which means *smelting place* or *refinement,* was in Phoenicia

belongeth to Zidon, and dwell there: behold, I have commanded a widow woman there to sustain thee.
10 So he arose and went to Zarephath.
And when he came to the gate of the
city, behold, the widow woman *was*
there gathering of sticks: and he called
to her, and said, Fetch me, I pray thee,
a little water in a vessel, that I may
drink.
11 And as she was going to fetch *it,* he
called to her, and said, Bring me, I
pray thee, a morsel of bread in thine
hand.
12 And she said, *As* the LORD thy God
liveth, I have not a cake, but an handful
of meal in a barrel, and a little *oil in
a cruse: and, behold, I *am* gathering two
sticks, that I may go in and dress it
for me and my son, that we may eat it,
and die.
13 And Elijah said unto her, Fear not;
go *and* do as thou hast said: but make
me thereof a little cake first, and bring
it unto me, and after make for thee and
for thy son.
14 For thus saith the LORD God of Israel, The barrel of meal shall not waste,
neither shall the cruse of oil fail, until
the day *that* the LORD sendeth rain upon
the earth.
15 And she went and did according to
the saying of Elijah: and she, and he,
and her house, did eat *many* days.
16 *And* the barrel of meal wasted not,
neither did the cruse of oil fail, according to the word of the LORD, which he
spake by Elijah.

Elijah raises the dead boy

¶17 And it came to pass after these
things, *that* the son of the woman, the
mistress of the house, fell sick; and his
sickness was so sore, that there was no
breath left in him.
18 And she said unto Elijah, What
have I to do with thee, O thou man of
God? art thou come unto me to call
my sin to remembrance, and to slay
my son?
19 And he said unto her, Give me thy
son. And he took him out of her bosom,
and carried him up into a loft, where
he abode, and laid him upon his own
bed.
20 And he cried unto the LORD, and
said, O LORD my God, hast thou also
brought evil upon the widow with
whom I sojourn, by slaying her son?
21 And he stretched himself upon the
child three times, and cried unto the
LORD, and said, O LORD my God, I pray
thee, let this child's soul come into him
again.
22 And the LORD heard the voice of
Elijah; and the soul of the child came
into him again, and he revived.
23 And Elijah took the child, and
brought him down out of the chamber
into the house, and delivered him unto
his mother: and Elijah said, See, thy son
liveth.
¶24 And the woman said to Elijah,
Now by this I know that thou *art* a man
of God, *and* that the word of the LORD
in thy mouth *is* truth.

Elijah meets Obadiah

18 And it came to pass *after* many
days, that the word of the LORD

17:17 Elijah's Power
Some have interpreted the phrase "no breath left in him" as meaning that the boy only seemed to be dead, but both the mother (vs. 18), who thought God had killed her son to punish her for her sins, and Elijah (vs. 20) speak of the "slaying" of the son. The secret of Elijah's power is seen in his constant pleading with God in prayer. The apostle James said: "Elias [Elijah] was a man subject to like passions as we are, and he prayed earnestly" (James 5:17).

just beyond the western border of Ahab's kingdom, near Sidon. The terrible drought extended as far as Phoenicia and continued there for a whole year. In the New Testament, Zarephath is called by the Greek name *Sarepta* (Luke 4:26).

came to Elijah in the third year, saying,
Go, shew thyself unto Ahab; and I will
send rain upon the earth.
[2]And Elijah went to shew himself
unto Ahab. And *there was* a sore famine
in Samaria.
[3]And Ahab called Obadiah, which *was*
the governor of *his* house. (Now Obadiah feared the LORD greatly:

18:3 Obadiah
Obadiah, whose name means *servant of the LORD,* was a high-ranking officer in the court of Ahab and must not be confused with the prophet who wrote the book called by his name. There are twelve different persons named "Obadiah" in the Old Testament.

[4]For it was *so,* when Jezebel cut off
the *prophets of the LORD, that Obadiah took an hundred prophets, and hid
them by fifty in a cave, and fed them
with bread and water.)
[5]And Ahab said unto Obadiah, Go into
the land, unto all fountains of water, and
unto all brooks: peradventure we may
find grass to save the horses and mules
alive, that we lose not all the beasts.
[6]So they divided the land between
them to pass throughout it: Ahab went
one way by himself, and Obadiah went
another way by himself.
¶[7]And as Obadiah was in the way, behold, Elijah met him: and he knew him,
and fell on his face, and said, *Art* thou
that my lord Elijah?
[8]And he answered him, I *am:* go, tell
thy lord, Behold, Elijah *is here.*
[9]And he said, What have I sinned,
that thou wouldest deliver thy servant
into the hand of Ahab, to slay me?
[10]*As* the LORD thy God liveth, there
is no nation or *kingdom, whither my
lord hath not sent to seek thee: and
when they said, *He is* not *there;* he took
an oath of the kingdom and nation, that
they found thee not.
[11]And now thou sayest, Go, tell thy
lord, Behold, Elijah *is here.*
[12]And it shall come to pass, *as soon
as* I am gone from thee, that the Spirit
of the LORD shall carry thee whither I
know not; and *so* when I come and tell
Ahab, and he cannot find thee, he shall
slay me: but I thy servant fear the LORD
from my youth.
[13]Was it not told my lord what I did
when Jezebel slew the prophets of the
LORD, how I hid an hundred men of the
LORD'S prophets by fifty in a cave, and
fed them with bread and water?
[14]And now thou sayest, Go, tell thy
lord, Behold, Elijah *is here:* and he shall
slay me.
[15]And Elijah said, *As* the LORD of

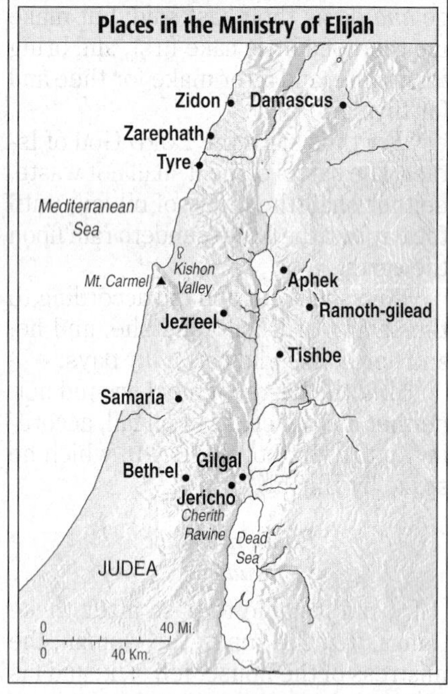

18:1 in the third year. See Luke 4:25 and James 5:17, which give "three years and six months" as the length of the drought.
18:6 Ahab went one way. Note that the famine and drought were so great that even the king was glad to go out to hunt for grass to save his animals.
18:12 the Spirit of the LORD shall carry thee. This expression is used in other places in the Scriptures: See Philip and the eunuch (Acts 8:39); see also 2 Kings 2:16.

hosts liveth, before whom I stand, I will
surely shew myself unto him to day.
16So Obadiah went to meet Ahab, and
told him: and Ahab went to meet Elijah.

Elijah meets and challenges Ahab

¶17And it came to pass, when Ahab
saw Elijah, that Ahab said unto him, *Art*
thou he that troubleth Israel?
18And he answered, I have not troubled Israel; but thou, and thy father's
house, in that ye have forsaken the
commandments of the LORD, and thou
hast followed Baalim.
19Now therefore send, *and* gather
to me all Israel unto mount *Carmel,
and the prophets of Baal four hundred
and fifty, and the prophets of the groves
four hundred, which eat at Jezebel's
table.
20So Ahab sent unto all the children
of Israel, and gathered the prophets
together unto mount Carmel.
21And Elijah came unto all the people, and said, How long halt ye between
two opinions? if the LORD *be* God, follow him: but if Baal, *then* follow him.
And the people answered him not a
word.
22Then said Elijah unto the people, I,
even I only, remain a *prophet of the
LORD; but Baal's prophets *are* four hundred and fifty men.
23Let them therefore give us two
bullocks; and let them choose one bullock for themselves, and cut it in pieces,
and lay *it* on wood, and put no fire *under:* and I will dress the other bullock,
and lay *it* on wood, and put no fire
under:
24And call ye on the name of your
gods, and I will call on the name of the
LORD: and the God that answereth by
fire, let him be God. And all the people
answered and said, It is well spoken.

The power of the LORD over other gods

25And Elijah said unto the prophets
of Baal, Choose you one bullock for
yourselves, and dress *it* first; for ye *are*
many; and call on the name of your
gods, but put no fire *under.*
26And they took the bullock which
was given them, and they dressed *it,* and
called on the name of Baal from morning even until noon, saying, O Baal, hear
us. But *there was* no voice, nor any that
answered. And they leaped upon the
altar which was made.

18:26 The Worship of Baal
The word "Baal" means *master, owner,* or *possessor*. Baalism was the worship of the powers of creation practiced by the Canaanite race. Their creed was that the heavenly bodies and the earth had sprung spontaneously out of a self-existent, chaotic deep and that the procreative power of the sun, acting upon the fertile womb of the earth, produced all visible matter. Thus it was significant that Ahab and his subjects abandoned God to the sole influence of this worship of nature, which resulted in the almost entire destruction of animal and vegetable life (see 18:5).

27And it came to pass at noon, that
Elijah mocked them, and said, Cry
aloud: for he *is* a god; either he is talking, or he is pursuing, or he is in a journey, *or* peradventure he sleepeth, and
must be awaked.
28And they cried aloud, and cut themselves after their manner with knives
and lancets, till the *blood gushed out
upon them.
29And it came to pass, when midday
was past, and they prophesied until the
time of the *offering of the *evening* *sacrifice, that *there was* neither voice, nor
any to answer, nor any that regarded.
30And Elijah said unto all the people,

18:22 I, even I only, remain. Elijah felt very lonely in his service and made this same complaint later (19:10,14), but notice how the LORD comforted him (19:18).

18:22 Baal's prophets. Note that the prophets of the groves (vs. 19) did not come. Since Baal was the god of fire, Elijah's test was a very fair one, and should have settled the question definitely.

Come near unto me. And all the people
came near unto him. And he repaired
the altar of the LORD *that was* broken
down.
31And Elijah took twelve stones, according to the number of the tribes of
the sons of *Jacob, unto whom the word
of the LORD came, saying, Israel shall
be thy name:
32And with the stones he built an altar in the name of the LORD: and he
made a trench about the altar, as great
as would contain two measures of
seed.
33And he put the wood in order, and
cut the bullock in pieces, and laid *him*
on the wood, and said, Fill four barrels
with water, and pour *it* on the burnt-
sacrifice, and on the wood.
34And he said, Do *it* the second time.
And they did *it* the second time. And he
said, Do *it* the third time. And they did
it the third time.
35And the water ran round about the
altar; and he filled the trench also with
water.
36And it came to pass at *the time of* the
offering of the *evening* sacrifice, that
Elijah the prophet came near, and said,
LORD God of *Abraham, *Isaac, and of
Israel, let it be known this day that thou
art God in Israel, and *that* I *am* thy servant, and *that* I have done all these
things at thy word.
37Hear me, O LORD, hear me, that
this people may know that thou *art* the
LORD God, and *that* thou hast turned
their heart back again.
38Then the fire of the LORD fell, and
consumed the burnt-sacrifice, and the
wood, and the stones, and the dust, and
licked up the water that *was* in the trench.
39And when all the people saw *it,*
they fell on their faces: and they said,
The LORD, he *is* the God; the LORD, he
is the God.
40And Elijah said unto them, Take the
prophets of Baal; let not one of them
escape. And they took them: and Elijah
brought them down to the brook Kishon, and slew them there.
¶41And Elijah said unto Ahab, Get
thee up, eat and drink; for *there is* a
sound of abundance of rain.

Elijah awaits God's answer on Mt. Carmel

42So Ahab went up to eat and to drink.
And Elijah went up to the top of Carmel; and he cast himself down upon the
earth, and put his face between his knees,
43And said to his servant, Go up now,
look toward the sea. And he went up,
and looked, and said, *There is* nothing.
And he said, Go again seven times.
44And it came to pass at the seventh
time, that he said, Behold, there ariseth
a little cloud out of the sea, like a man's
hand. And he said, Go up, say unto Ahab,
Prepare *thy chariot,* and get thee down,
that the rain stop thee not.
45And it came to pass in the mean
while, that the heaven was black with
clouds and wind, and there was a great
rain. And Ahab rode, and went to Jezreel.
46And the hand of the LORD was on
Elijah; and he girded up his loins, and
ran before Ahab to the entrance of Jezreel.

Elijah flees; he asks for death

19 And Ahab told Jezebel all that
Elijah had done, and withal how
he had slain all the prophets with the
sword.
2Then Jezebel sent a messenger unto
Elijah, saying, So let the gods do *to me,*
and more also, if I make not thy life as
the life of one of them by to morrow
about this time.
3And when he saw *that,* he arose, and
went for his life, and came to *Beer-
sheba, which *belongeth* to *Judah, and
left his servant there.
¶4But he himself went a day's jour-

19:1 withal. Besides, likewise.
19:3 his servant. Scripture does not tell us who the servant was, but tradition says that

ney into the wilderness, and came and
sat down under a juniper tree: and he
requested for himself that he might die;
and said, It is enough; now, O LORD,
take away my life; for I *am* not better
than my fathers.
5And as he lay and slept under a juniper tree, behold, then an *angel
touched him, and said unto him, Arise
and eat.
6And he looked, and, behold, *there
was* a cake baken on the coals, and a
cruse of water at his head. And he did
eat and drink, and laid him down again.
7And the angel of the LORD came
again the second time, and touched
him, and said, Arise *and* eat; because
the journey *is* too great for thee.

Elijah on Mt. Horeb

8And he arose, and did eat and drink,
and went in the strength of that meat
forty days and forty nights unto *Horeb
the mount of God.
¶9And he came thither unto a cave,
and lodged there; and, behold, the word
of the LORD *came* to him, and he said
unto him, What doest thou here, Elijah?
10And he said, I have been very jealous for the LORD God of hosts: for the
children of Israel have forsaken thy
*covenant, thrown down thine altars,
and slain thy prophets with the sword;
and I, *even* I only, am left; and they seek
my life, to take it away.
11And he said, Go forth, and stand
upon the mount before the LORD. And,
behold, the LORD passed by, and a great
and strong wind rent the *mountains,
and brake in pieces the rocks before the
LORD; *but* the LORD *was* not in the
wind: and after the wind an earthquake;
but the LORD *was* not in the earthquake:
12And after the earthquake a fire; *but*
the LORD *was* not in the fire: and after
the fire a still small voice.
13And it was *so,* when Elijah heard *it,*
that he wrapped his face in his mantle,
and went out, and stood in the entering
in of the cave. And, behold, *there came*
a voice unto him, and said, What doest
thou here, Elijah?
14And he said, I have been very jealous for the LORD God of hosts: because
the children of Israel have forsaken thy
covenant, thrown down thine altars, and
slain thy prophets with the sword; and
I, *even* I only, am left; and they seek my
life, to take it away.
15And the LORD said unto him, Go,
return on thy way to the wilderness of
*Damascus: and when thou comest,
*anoint Hazael *to be* king over Syria:

19:15 God's Instructions
When God told Elijah to go by way of the wilderness of Damascus, the LORD was sending him back by the same way that he came. After his communion with the LORD, the servant of the LORD went through the difficult paths from which he had fled with new courage, because he was assured of divine protection.

16And Jehu the son of Nimshi shalt
thou anoint *to be* king over Israel: and
*Elisha the son of Shaphat of Abel-
meholah shalt thou anoint *to be* prophet in thy room.
17And it shall come to pass, *that* him
that escapeth the sword of Hazael shall
Jehu slay: and him that escapeth from
the sword of Jehu shall Elisha slay.
18Yet I have left *me* seven thousand
in Israel, all the knees which have not
bowed unto Baal, and every mouth
which hath not kissed him.

---

he was the son of the widow of Zarephath (1 Kings 17:12-23). Elijah dismissed him before entering into communion with God, much like our Lord Jesus, who said to His disciples, "Sit ye here, while I go and pray yonder" (Matt. 26:36).

19:15 Hazael. Hazael was an officer of *Ben-hadad, king of Syria. His name means *God sees.* Note that Elijah (vss. 10,14) had spoken against the children of Israel, and God gave him a sad task to do. He was to anoint a man who would bring judgment against Elijah's own people.

19:18 kissed him. The act of kissing was one of religious greeting or homage. In Hosea

The call of Elisha

¶ 19 So he departed thence, and found
Elisha the son of Shaphat, who *was*
plowing *with* twelve yoke *of oxen* before
him, and he with the twelfth: and Elijah passed by him, and cast his mantle
upon him.

19:19 Appointing a Successor
Elijah did not say a word as he threw his mantle on Elisha, but his silent act was understood by Elisha, for this was the usual method of appointing a successor. The mantle was given to the one who was thought most fit to wear it, and as soon as that one received the holy mantle, he was given all the power of the one whom he was following.

---

20 And he left the oxen, and ran after
Elijah, and said, Let me, I pray thee,
kiss my father and my mother, and *then*
I will follow thee. And he said unto him,
Go back again: for what have I done to
thee?

21 And he returned back from him,
and took a yoke of oxen, and slew them,
and boiled their flesh with the instruments of the oxen, and gave unto the
people, and they did eat. Then he arose,
and went after Elijah, and ministered
unto him.

Ben-hadad attempts a siege against Samaria

20 And Ben-hadad the king of
Syria gathered all his host together: and *there were* thirty and two
kings with him, and horses, and chariots: and he went up and besieged *Samaria, and warred against it.

2 And he sent messengers to Ahab
king of *Israel into the city, and said
unto him, Thus saith Ben-hadad,

3 Thy silver and thy gold *is* mine; thy
wives also and thy children, *even* the
goodliest, *are* mine.

4 And the king of Israel answered and
said, My lord, O king, according to thy
saying, I *am* thine, and all that I have.

5 And the messengers came again,
and said, Thus speaketh Ben-hadad,
saying, Although I have sent unto thee,
saying, Thou shalt deliver me thy silver, and thy gold, and thy wives, and thy
children;

6 Yet I will send my servants unto
thee to morrow about this time, and
they shall search thine house, and the
houses of thy servants; and it shall be,
that whatsoever is pleasant in thine
eyes, they shall put *it* in their hand, and
take *it* away.

7 Then the king of Israel called all the
*elders of the land, and said, Mark, I
pray you, and see how this *man* seeketh
mischief: for he sent unto me for my
wives, and for my children, and for my
silver, and for my gold; and I denied him
not.

8 And all the elders and all the people
said unto him, Hearken not *unto him,*
nor consent.

9 Wherefore he said unto the messengers of Ben-hadad, Tell my lord the
king, All that thou didst send for to thy
servant at the first I will do: but this
thing I may not do. And the messengers
departed, and brought him word again.

10 And Ben-hadad sent unto him, and

13:2 it is shown to be a part of the worship of false gods (see also Ps. 2:12; 1 Cor. 16:20).

19:19 Elisha. Elisha's name means *God is salvation*. He is called "Eliseus" in Luke 4:27. He was one of the seven thousand of whom God spoke in verse 18.

19:21 took a yoke of oxen. The act of Elisha in the slaying of the oxen was one of sacrifice. It was an act of dedication in which he proclaimed to God and man that he was putting his hand to another plow, from which he would never turn back.

20:1 Ben-hadad the king of Syria gathered all his host. It is possible that this Ben-hadad was the same one who made the treaty with Asa (1 Kings 15:18), but it was more probable that this was a son or a grandson.

20:3 Thy silver and thy gold . . . thy wives also and thy children. The action of Ben-hadad was in keeping with the practice of that day.

said, The gods do so unto me, and more
also, if the dust of Samaria shall suffice
for handfuls for all the people that follow me.
11And the king of Israel answered and
said, Tell *him,* Let not him that girdeth
on *his harness* boast himself as he that
putteth it off.
12And it came to pass, when *Ben-hadad* heard this message, as he *was*
drinking, he and the kings in the
pavilions,that he said unto his servants,
Set *yourselves in array.* And they set
themselves in array against the city.

Ahab's instructions and promise of victory

¶13And, behold, there came a prophet unto Ahab king of Israel, saying,
Thus saith the LORD, Hast thou seen all
this great multitude? behold, I will deliver it into thine hand this day; and
thou shalt know that I *am* the LORD.
14And Ahab said, By whom? And he
said, Thus saith the LORD, *Even* by the
young men of the princes of the provinces. Then he said, Who shall order the
battle? And he answered, Thou.
15Then he numbered the young men
of the princes of the provinces, and they
were two hundred and thirty two: and
after them he numbered all the people,
even all the children of Israel, *being*
seven thousand.
16And they went out at noon. But
Ben-hadad *was* drinking himself drunk
in the pavilions, he and the kings, the
thirty and two kings that helped him.
17And the young men of the princes
of the provinces went out first; and
Ben-hadad sent out, and they told him,
saying, There are men come out of Samaria.
18And he said, Whether they be come
out for peace, take them alive; or
whether they be come out for war, take
them alive.
19So these young men of the princes
of the provinces came out of the city,
and the army which followed them.
20And they slew every one his man:
and the Syrians fled; and Israel pursued
them: and Ben-hadad the king of Syria
escaped on an horse with the horsemen.
21And the king of Israel went out, and
smote the horses and chariots, and slew
the Syrians with a great slaughter.

Further instructions lead to victory

¶22And the prophet came to the king
of Israel, and said unto him, Go,
strengthen thyself, and mark, and see
what thou doest: for at the return of the
year the king of Syria will come up
against thee.
23And the servants of the king of Syria said unto him, Their gods *are* gods of
the hills; therefore they were stronger
than we; but let us fight against them
in the plain, and surely we shall be
stronger than they.

20:23 Syrian Superstitions
The Syrians here were referring to God as a national or tribal god, speaking of Him just as they would of their own gods. The previous battle was fought in the hills, therefore, their superstitions and heathen ideas led them to believe that the God of Israel had no power in the valley. A false idea of God and of His power and ability is the source of ruin to many. "The people that do know their God shall be strong" (Dan. 11:32).

24And do this thing, Take the kings
away, every man out of his place, and
put captains in their rooms:
25And number thee an army, like the

20:10 The gods do so unto me. Ben-hadad used the same idolatrous oath as Jezebel had (1 Kings 19:2).

20:11 harness. Armor.

20:13 there came a prophet. The prophet was no doubt one of those whom Obadiah had hidden in a cave when Jezebel set out to slay all of the prophets (1 Kings 18:4).

20:22 for at the return of the year. This means *after the year was expired or over,* "at the time when kings go forth to battle" (2 Sam. 11:1).

army that thou hast lost, horse for
horse, and chariot for chariot: and we
will fight against them in the plain, *and*
surely we shall be stronger than they.
And he hearkened unto their voice, and
did so.
26And it came to pass at the return of
the year, that Ben-hadad numbered the
Syrians, and went up to Aphek, to fight
against Israel.
27And the children of Israel were
numbered, and were all present, and
went against them: and the children of
Israel pitched before them like two little flocks of kids; but the Syrians filled
the country.
¶28And there came a man of God, and
spake unto the king of Israel, and said,
Thus saith the LORD, Because the Syrians have said, The LORD *is* God of the
hills, but he *is* not God of the valleys,
therefore will I deliver all this great
multitude into thine hand, and ye shall
know that I *am* the LORD.
29And they pitched one over against
the other seven days. And *so* it was, that
in the seventh day the battle was joined:
and the children of Israel slew of the
Syrians an hundred thousand footmen
in one day.
30But the rest fled to Aphek, into the
city; and *there* a wall fell upon twenty
and seven thousand of the men *that*
were left. And Ben-hadad fled, and came
into the city, into an inner chamber.
¶31And his servants said unto him,
Behold now, we have heard that the
kings of the house of Israel *are* merciful kings: let us, I pray thee, put sackcloth on our loins, and ropes upon our
heads, and go out to the king of Israel:
peradventure he will save thy life.
32So they girded sackcloth on their
loins, and *put* ropes on their heads, and
came to the king of Israel, and said, Thy
servant Ben-hadad saith, I pray thee, let
me live. And he said, *Is* he yet alive? he
is my brother.
33Now the men did diligently observe
whether *any thing would come* from
him, and did hastily catch *it:* and they
said, Thy brother Ben-hadad. Then he
said, Go ye, bring him. Then Ben-hadad
came forth to him; and he caused him
to come up into the chariot.
34And *Ben-hadad* said unto him, The
cities, which my father took from thy
father, I will restore; and thou shalt
make streets for thee in Damascus, as
my father made in Samaria. Then *said*
Ahab, I will send thee away with this
covenant. So he made a covenant with
him, and sent him away.

Ahab's sin in sparing Ben-hadad

¶35And a certain man of the sons of
the prophets said unto his neighbour in
the word of the LORD, Smite me, I pray
thee. And the man refused to smite
him.
36Then said he unto him, Because
thou hast not obeyed the voice of the
LORD, behold, as soon as thou art departed from me, a lion shall slay thee.
And as soon as he was departed from
him, a lion found him, and slew him.
37Then he found another man, and
said, Smite me, I pray thee. And the
man smote him, so that in smiting he
wounded *him.*
38So the prophet departed, and waited for the king by the way, and disguised himself with ashes upon his face.
39And as the king passed by, he cried
unto the king: and he said, Thy servant
went out into the midst of the battle;
and, behold, a man turned aside, and
brought a man unto me, and said, Keep

20:31 ropes upon our heads. These ropes were intended to express their submissiveness to Ahab, and he could hang them if he so desired.

20:32 my brother. This does not mean that Ben-hadad and Ahab were really brothers. It is an expression that one king used to another of the same position and rank.

20:38 disguised himself with ashes upon his face. The prophet put his headband over his eyes.

this man: if by any means he be missing, then shall thy life be for his life, or else thou shalt pay a talent of silver.

40 And as thy servant was busy here and there, he was gone. And the king of Israel said unto him, So *shall* thy judgment *be;* thyself hast decided *it.*

41 And he hasted, and took the ashes away from his face; and the king of Israel discerned him that he *was* of the prophets.

42 And he said unto him, Thus saith the LORD, Because thou hast let go out of *thy* hand a man whom I appointed to utter destruction, therefore thy life shall go for his life, and thy people for his people.

43 And the king of Israel went to his house heavy and displeased, and came to Samaria.

Ahab, coveting Naboth's vineyard, slays him

21 And it came to pass after these things, *that* Naboth the Jezreelite had a *vineyard, which *was* in Jezreel, hard by the palace of Ahab king of Samaria.

2 And Ahab spake unto Naboth, saying, Give me thy vineyard, that I may have it for a garden of herbs, because it *is* near unto my house: and I will give thee for it a better vineyard than it; *or,* if it seem good to thee, I will give thee the worth of it in money.

3 And Naboth said to Ahab, The LORD forbid it me, that I should give the inheritance of my fathers unto thee.

21:3 Naboth
Naboth was a sincere and loyal worshipper of the LORD God. The fact that he held fast to his possessions showed a steadfastness to the Law of Moses, which taught that land was to stay in a family (vs. 3; compare Lev. 25:23-28; Num. 36:7-8).

4 And Ahab came into his house heavy and displeased because of the word which Naboth the Jezreelite had spoken to him: for he had said, I will not give thee the inheritance of my fathers. And he laid him down upon his bed, and turned away his face, and would eat no bread.

¶ 5 But Jezebel his wife came to him, and said unto him, Why is thy spirit so sad, that thou eatest no bread?

6 And he said unto her, Because I spake unto Naboth the Jezreelite, and said unto him, Give me thy vineyard for money; or else, if it please thee, I will give thee *another* vineyard for it: and he answered, I will not give thee my vineyard.

7 And Jezebel his wife said unto him, Dost thou now govern the kingdom of Israel? arise, *and* eat bread, and let thine heart be merry: I will give thee the vineyard of Naboth the Jezreelite.

8 So she wrote letters in Ahab's name, and sealed *them* with his seal, and sent the letters unto the elders and to the nobles that *were* in his city, dwelling with Naboth.

9 And she wrote in the letters, saying, Proclaim a fast, and set Naboth on high among the people:

10 And set two men, sons of Belial, before him, to bear witness against him, saying, Thou didst blaspheme God and the king. And *then* carry him out, and stone him, that he may die.

11 And the men of his city, *even* the elders and the nobles who were the inhabitants in his city, did as Jezebel had sent unto them, *and* as it *was* written in the letters which she had sent unto them.

12 They proclaimed a fast, and set Naboth on high among the people.

13 And there came in two men, children of *Belial, and sat before him: and the men of Belial witnessed against him, *even* against Naboth, in the presence of the people, saying, Naboth did blaspheme God and the king. Then they carried him forth out of the city, and stoned him with stones, that he died.

14 Then they sent to Jezebel, saying, Naboth is stoned, and is dead.

¶ 15 And it came to pass, when Jezebel

heard that Naboth was stoned, and was
dead, that Jezebel said to Ahab, Arise,
take possession of the vineyard of Naboth the Jezreelite, which he refused to
give thee for money: for Naboth is not
alive, but dead.
16 And it came to pass, when Ahab
heard that Naboth was dead, that Ahab
rose up to go down to the vineyard of
Naboth the Jezreelite, to take possession of it.

Elijah pronounces Ahab's doom

¶17 And the word of the LORD came to
Elijah the Tishbite, saying,
18 Arise, go down to meet Ahab king
of Israel, which *is* in Samaria: behold,
he is in the vineyard of Naboth, whither
he is gone down to possess it.
19 And thou shalt speak unto him, saying, Thus saith the LORD, Hast thou
killed, and also taken possession? And
thou shalt speak unto him, saying, Thus
saith the LORD, In the place where dogs
licked the blood of Naboth shall dogs
lick thy blood, even thine.
20 And Ahab said to Elijah, Hast thou
found me, O mine enemy? And he answered, I have found *thee:* because thou
hast sold thyself to work evil in the
sight of the LORD.
21 Behold, I will bring evil upon thee,
and will take away thy posterity, and
will cut off from Ahab him that pisseth
against the wall, and him that is shut up
and left in Israel,
22 And will make thine house like the
house of Jeroboam the son of Nebat,
and like the house of Baasha the son of
Ahijah, for the provocation wherewith
thou hast provoked *me* to anger, and
made Israel to *sin.
23 And of Jezebel also spake the LORD,
saying, The dogs shall eat Jezebel by
the wall of Jezreel.
24 Him that dieth of Ahab in the city
the dogs shall eat; and him that dieth in
the field shall the fowls of the air eat.
¶25 But there was none like unto
Ahab, which did sell himself to work
wickedness in the sight of the LORD,
whom Jezebel his wife stirred up.
26 And he did very abominably in following idols, according to all *things* as
did the Amorites, whom the LORD cast
out before the children of Israel.

Ahab's repentance is rewarded

27 And it came to pass, when Ahab
heard those words, that he rent his
clothes, and put sackcloth upon his
flesh, and fasted, and lay in sackcloth,
and went softly.
28 And the word of the LORD came to
Elijah the Tishbite, saying,
29 Seest thou how Ahab humbleth
himself before me? because he
humbleth himself before me, I will not
bring the evil in his days: *but* in his
son's days will I bring the evil upon his
house.

Three years' peace between Syria and Israel

22 And they continued three
years without war between Syria and Israel.

Jehoshaphat's alliance with Ahab

2 And it came to pass in the third year,
that Jehoshaphat the king of Judah came
down to the king of Israel.
3 And the king of Israel said unto his
servants, Know ye that Ramoth in Gilead
is ours, and we *be* still, *and* take it not
out of the hand of the king of Syria?
4 And he said unto Jehoshaphat, Wilt
thou go with me to battle to Ramoth-
gilead? And Jehoshaphat said to the king
of Israel, I *am* as thou *art,* my people as
thy people, my horses as thy horses.

The lying prophets of Ahab

5 And Jehoshaphat said unto the king
of Israel, Enquire, I pray thee, at the
word of the LORD to day.

21:19 In the place . . . shall dogs lick thy blood. Read the fulfillment of this judgment of Ahab in 1 Kings 22:38.

6 Then the king of Israel gathered the
prophets together, about four hundred
men, and said unto them, Shall I go
against Ramoth-gilead to battle, or shall
I forbear? And they said, Go up; for the
Lord shall deliver *it* into the hand of the
king.
7 And Jehoshaphat said, *Is there* not
here a prophet of the LORD besides, that
we might enquire of him?
8 And the king of Israel said unto Jehoshaphat, *There is* yet one man, Micaiah the son of Imlah, by whom we may
enquire of the LORD: but I hate him; for
he doth not prophesy good concerning
me, but evil. And Jehoshaphat said, Let
not the king say so.
9 Then the king of Israel called an officer, and said, Hasten *hither* Micaiah
the son of Imlah.
10 And the king of Israel and Jehoshaphat the king of Judah sat each on his
throne, having put on their robes, in a
void place in the entrance of the gate of
Samaria; and all the prophets prophesied before them.
11 And Zedekiah the son of Chenaanah
made him horns of iron: and he said,
Thus saith the LORD, With these shalt
thou push the Syrians, until thou have
consumed them.
12 And all the prophets prophesied so,
saying, Go up to Ramoth-gilead, and
prosper: for the LORD shall deliver *it*
into the king's hand.

Micaiah's true prophecy

13 And the messenger that was gone
to call Micaiah spake unto him, saying,
Behold now, the words of the prophets
declare good unto the king with one
mouth: let thy word, I pray thee, be like
the word of one of them, and speak *that
which is* good.
14 And Micaiah said, *As* the LORD
liveth, what the LORD saith unto me,
that will I speak.
¶15 So he came to the king. And the
king said unto him, Micaiah, shall we go
against Ramoth-gilead to battle, or shall
we forbear? And he answered him, Go,
and prosper: for the LORD shall deliver
it into the hand of the king.
16 And the king said unto him, How
many times shall I adjure thee that thou
tell me nothing but *that which is* true in
the name of the LORD?
17 And he said, I saw all Israel scattered upon the hills, as sheep that have
not a shepherd: and the LORD said,
These have no master: let them return
every man to his house in peace.
18 And the king of Israel said unto Jehoshaphat, Did I not tell thee that he
would prophesy no good concerning
me, but evil?
19 And he said, Hear thou therefore
the word of the LORD: I saw the LORD
sitting on his throne, and all the host of
heaven standing by him on his right
hand and on his left.
20 And the LORD said, Who shall persuade Ahab, that he may go up and fall at
Ramoth-gilead? And one said on this
manner, and another said on that manner.
21 And there came forth a spirit, and
stood before the LORD, and said, I will
persuade him.
22 And the LORD said unto him,
Wherewith? And he said, I will go forth,
and I will be a lying spirit in the mouth
of all his prophets. And he said, Thou
shalt persuade *him,* and prevail also: go
forth, and do so.
23 Now therefore, behold, the LORD
hath put a lying spirit in the mouth of
all these thy prophets, and the LORD
hath spoken evil concerning thee.
24 But Zedekiah the son of Chenaanah
went near, and smote Micaiah on the
cheek, and said, Which way went the
Spirit of the LORD from me to speak
unto thee?
25 And Micaiah said, Behold, thou
shalt see in that day, when thou shalt go
into an inner chamber to hide thyself.

22:8 Micaiah. The name means *who is like Jehovah*. He is the same as "Micah" in 2 Chronicles 34:20.

26 And the king of Israel said, Take Micaiah, and carry him back unto Amon the governor of the city, and to Joash the king's son;

27 And say, Thus saith the king, Put this *fellow* in the prison, and feed him with bread of affliction and with water of affliction, until I come in peace.

28 And Micaiah said, If thou return at all in peace, the LORD hath not spoken by me. And he said, Hearken, O people, every one of you.

Defeat and death of Ahab

29 So the king of Israel and Jehoshaphat the king of Judah went up to Ramoth-gilead.

30 And the king of Israel said unto Jehoshaphat, I will disguise myself, and enter into the battle; but put thou on thy robes. And the king of Israel disguised himself, and went into the battle.

31 But the king of Syria commanded his thirty and two captains that had rule over his chariots, saying, Fight neither with small nor great, save only with the king of Israel.

32 And it came to pass, when the captains of the chariots saw Jehoshaphat, that they said, Surely it *is* the king of Israel. And they turned aside to fight against him: and Jehoshaphat cried out.

33 And it came to pass, when the captains of the chariots perceived that it *was* not the king of Israel, that they turned back from pursuing him.

34 And a *certain* man drew a bow at a venture, and smote the king of Israel between the joints of the harness: wherefore he said unto the driver of his chariot, Turn thine hand, and carry me out of the host; for I am wounded.

35 And the battle increased that day: and the king was stayed up in his chariot against the Syrians, and died at even: and the blood ran out of the wound into the midst of the chariot.

36 And there went a proclamation throughout the host about the going down of the sun, saying, Every man to his city, and every man to his own country.

¶37 So the king died, and was brought to Samaria; and they buried the king in Samaria.

38 And *one* washed the chariot in the pool of Samaria; and the dogs licked up his blood; and they washed his armour; according unto the word of the LORD which he spake.

39 Now the rest of the acts of Ahab, and all that he did, and the ivory house which he made, and all the cities that he built, *are* they not written in the book of the chronicles of the kings of Israel?

Ahaziah, King of Israel

40 So Ahab slept with his fathers; and Ahaziah his son reigned in his stead.

Jehoshaphat, King of Judah

¶41 And Jehoshaphat the son of Asa began to reign over Judah in the fourth year of Ahab king of Israel.

42 Jehoshaphat *was* thirty and five years old when he began to reign; and he reigned twenty and five years in Jerusalem. And his mother's name *was* Azubah the daughter of Shilhi.

43 And he walked in all the ways of Asa his father; he turned not aside from it, doing *that which was* right in the eyes of the LORD: nevertheless the high places were not taken away; *for* the people offered and burnt incense yet in the high places.

44 And Jehoshaphat made peace with the king of Israel.

45 Now the rest of the acts of Jehoshaphat, and his might that he shewed, and how he warred, *are* they not written in the book of the chronicles of the kings of Judah?

46 And the remnant of the sodomites, which remained in the days of his father Asa, he took out of the land.

47 *There was* then no king in Edom: a deputy *was* king.

22:38 according unto the word of the LORD. See 1 Kings 21:19.

48Jehoshaphat made ships of Tharshish to go to Ophir for gold: but they
went not; for the ships were broken at
Ezion-geber.
49Then said Ahaziah the son of Ahab
unto Jehoshaphat, Let my servants go
with thy servants in the ships. But Jehoshaphat would not.

Jehoshaphat dies, Jehoram reigns over Judah

¶50And Jehoshaphat slept with his fathers, and was buried with his fathers
in the city of David his father: and Jehoram his son reigned in his stead.

Ahaziah's evil reign over Israel

¶51Ahaziah the son of Ahab began to
reign over Israel in Samaria the seventeenth year of Jehoshaphat king of
Judah, and reigned two years over Israel.
52And he did evil in the sight of the
LORD, and walked in the way of his father, and in the way of his mother, and
in the way of Jeroboam the son of Nebat, who made Israel to sin:
53For he served Baal, and worshipped
him, and provoked to anger the LORD
God of Israel, according to all that his
father had done.

22:48 Tharshish. Tarshish (2 Chron. 20:36; see Jon. 1:3 note).

The Second Book of the

KINGS

commonly called, The Fourth Book of the Kings

BACKGROUND

This book contains the history of the kingdoms of Israel and Judah from the time of King Ahab to the captivity—a period of about three hundred years. During this time Amos and Hosea prophesied in Israel; and Obadiah, Joel, Isaiah, Micah, Nahum, Habakkuk, Zephaniah, and Jeremiah in Judah.

SUMMARY

The first half of the book is occupied principally with the ministry of Elisha. The second half of the book deals with events leading to the fall of Samaria and the captivity of Israel, and to the fall of Jerusalem and the captivity of Judah.

OUTLINE OF 2 KINGS

I.	Two Kings Rule Israel: Ahaziah and Jehoram	2 Kings 1:1—8:15
II.	Two Kings Rule Judah: Jehoram and Ahaziah	2 Kings 8:16—9:37
III.	Jehu Rules Israel; Athaliah and Jehoash Rule Judah	2 Kings 10:1—12:21
IV.	Jehoahaz, Jehoash, Jeroboam II Rule Israel; Amaziah Rules Judah	2 Kings 13:1—14:29
V.	Azariah (Uzziah) and Jothan Rule Judah; Zachariah and Hoshea Rule Israel The Fall of Israel	2 Kings 15:1—17:41
VI.	Hezekiah Rules Judah	2 Kings 18:1—20:21
VII.	Manasseh, Amon, Josiah Rule Judah	2 Kings 21:1—23:30
VIII.	Jehoahaz, Jehoiakim, Jehoiachin, Zedekiah Rule Judah	2 Kings 23:31—25:7
IX.	Fall of Judah	2 Kings 25:8-30

I. Two Kings Rule Israel
(1:1—8:15)

1 Then *Moab rebelled against Israel after the death of *Ahab.
[2]And Ahaziah fell down through a lattice in his upper chamber that *was* in *Samaria, and was sick: and he sent messengers, and said unto them, Go, enquire of Baal-zebub the god of Ekron whether I shall recover of this disease.
[3]But the *angel of the LORD said to Elijah the Tishbite, Arise, go up to meet

1:2 Ahaziah. See 1 Kings 22:51. His name means *Jehovah possesses.*
1:2 lattice. Either a kind of fence running around the roof of the house, or, as is more probable, a latticed skylight in the roof.

1:1 The People of Moab
"Then Moab rebelled" are the words that continue the account given in 1 Kings and follow in thought the last words of the previous book. King David had brought the people of Moab under his power, and they paid tribute to him and to the kings who followed him on the throne (see 2 Kings 3:4; 2 Sam. 8:2). When David's kingdom became divided, the people of Moab were partly under the authority of the kingdom of Israel and partly under the authority of the kingdom of Judah. When King Ahab died, they rose up in rebellion and shook off this yoke.

the messengers of the king of Samaria,
and say unto them, *Is it* not because
there is not a God in Israel, *that* ye go
to enquire of Baal-zebub the god of
Ekron?
4 Now therefore thus saith the LORD,
Thou shalt not come down from that
bed on which thou art gone up, but shalt
surely die. And Elijah departed.

1:3-4 Elijah
Elijah's name, which means *God-Jehovah,* or *my God is Jehovah,* marks his great ministry—to bring the sinning people of Israel back to the place where they would realize that the LORD is God, and that the gods worshipped by the various heathen nations were worse than useless.

¶5 And when the messengers turned
back unto him, he said unto them, Why
are ye now turned back?
6 And they said unto him, There came
a man up to meet us, and said unto us,
Go, turn again unto the king that sent
you, and say unto him, Thus saith the
LORD, *Is it* not because *there is* not a
God in Israel, *that* thou sendest to enquire of Baal-zebub the god of Ekron?
therefore thou shalt not come down
from that bed on which thou art gone
up, but shalt surely die.
7 And he said unto them, What manner of man *was he* which came up to
meet you, and told you these words?
8 And they answered him, *He was* an
hairy man, and girt with a girdle of
leather about his loins. And he said, It
is Elijah the Tishbite.
9 Then the king sent unto him a captain of fifty with his fifty. And he went
up to him: and, behold, he sat on the top
of an hill. And he spake unto him, Thou
man of God, the king hath said, Come
down.
10 And Elijah answered and said to the
captain of fifty, If I *be* a man of God, then
let *fire come down from *heaven, and
consume thee and thy fifty. And there
came down fire from heaven, and consumed him and his fifty.

1:10 A Miracle of Fire
God used miracles, especially in times of crisis, to show His divine glory and to display His power in the judgment of sin and in the deliverance of His people. These particular times of crisis were:

1. the deliverance of Israel under Moses from Egyptian bondage;
2. the time of Joshua and the judges;
3. the period of apostasy in Judah and Israel described in 1 and 2 Kings; and
4. the coming of Jesus Christ as Messiah.

Other miracles recorded in 2 Kings are: 2:7-8, 14,21-22; 3:16-20; 4:2-7,16-17,32-37,38-41, 42-44; 5:10-14,27; 6:5-7,18-20; 13:21; 19:35; 20:9-11.

11 Again also he sent unto him another captain of fifty with his fifty. And
he answered and said unto him, O man
of God, thus hath the king said, Come
down quickly.
12 And Elijah answered and said unto
them, If I *be* a man of God, let fire come
down from heaven, and consume thee
and thy fifty. And the fire of God came
down from heaven, and consumed him
and his fifty.
¶13 And he sent again a captain of the

1:9 captain of fifty. The army was made up of divisions of one thousand, of one hundred, and of fifty. Each division had its own leader (see Num. 31:14,48; 1 Sam. 8:12).

third fifty with his fifty. And the third
captain of fifty went up, and came and
fell on his knees before Elijah, and besought him, and said unto him, O man
of God, I pray thee, let my life, and the
life of these fifty thy servants, be precious in thy sight.
14 Behold, there came fire down from
heaven, and burnt up the two captains
of the former fifties with their fifties:
therefore let my life now be precious in
thy sight.
15 And the angel of the LORD said unto
Elijah, Go down with him: be not *afraid
of him. And he arose, and went down
with him unto the king.
16 And he said unto him, Thus saith
the LORD, Forasmuch as thou hast sent
messengers to enquire of Baal-zebub
the god of Ekron, *is it* not because *there*
is no God in Israel to enquire of his
word? therefore thou shalt not come
down off that bed on which thou art
gone up, but shalt surely die.

Jehoram becomes king

¶17 So he died according to the word
of the LORD which Elijah had spoken.
And Jehoram reigned in his stead in the
second year of Jehoram the son of Jehoshaphat king of *Judah; because he
had no son.
18 Now the rest of the acts of Ahaziah
which he did, *are* they not written in the
book of the chronicles of the kings of
Israel?

Elijah is taken up into Heaven

2 And it came to pass, when the
LORD would take up Elijah into
heaven by a whirlwind, that Elijah went
with *Elisha from Gilgal.
2 And Elijah said unto Elisha, Tarry
here, I pray thee; for the LORD hath
sent me to *Beth-el. And Elisha said
unto him, As the LORD liveth, and *as* thy
soul liveth, I will not leave thee. So they
went down to Beth-el.
3 And the sons of the *prophets that
were at Beth-el came forth to Elisha,
and said unto him, Knowest thou that
the LORD will take away thy master
from thy head to day? And he said, Yea,
I know *it;* hold ye your peace.
4 And Elijah said unto him, Elisha,
tarry here, I pray thee; for the LORD
hath sent me to Jericho. And he said, *As*
the LORD liveth, and *as* thy soul liveth,
I will not leave thee. So they came to
Jericho.
5 And the sons of the prophets that
were at Jericho came to Elisha, and said
unto him, Knowest thou that the LORD
will take away thy master from thy head
to day? And he answered, Yea, I know
it; hold ye your peace.
6 And Elijah said unto him, Tarry, I
pray thee, here; for the LORD hath
sent me to Jordan. And he said, *As* the
LORD liveth, and *as* thy soul liveth, I
will not leave thee. And they two went
on.
7 And fifty men of the sons of the
prophets went, and stood to view afar
off: and they two stood by Jordan.
8 And Elijah took his mantle, and
wrapped *it* together, and smote the
waters, and they were divided hither
and thither, so that they two went over
on dry ground.
¶9 And it came to pass, when they
were gone over, that Elijah said unto
Elisha, Ask what I shall do for thee,
before I be taken away from thee. And

2:2 I will not leave thee. This reminds us of the steadfastness and faithfulness of Ruth (see Ruth 1:16-18).

2:3 from thy head. It was the ancient custom for scholars to sit at their master's feet (see Acts 22:3). In this sense, Elijah would be taken from his position as teacher of Elisha, who sat at his feet.

2:8 mantle. Elijah used his mantle as Moses used his rod (Exod. 7:20; 14:16). Observe Elisha's use of the mantle in verse 14.

2:9 double portion. This does not mean that Elisha received twice what Elijah had, but the share of a father's possessions left to the oldest son, which was double the

Elisha said, I pray thee, let a double
portion of thy spirit be upon me.
[10]And he said, Thou hast asked a hard
thing: *nevertheless,* if thou see me *when*
I am taken from thee, it shall be so unto
thee; but if not, it shall not be *so.*
[11]And it came to pass, as they still
went on, and talked, that, behold, *there*
appeared a chariot of fire, and horses of
fire, and parted them both asunder;
and Elijah went up by a whirlwind into
heaven.

2:11 A Preview of the Rapture
The catching away of Elijah and Enoch (see Gen. 5:24) so that they went to heaven without tasting death is a *type of the *Rapture of the Christians who will be alive when the Lord Jesus Christ comes again (see 1 Thess. 4:15-17).

¶[12]And Elisha saw *it,* and he cried,
My father, my father, the chariot of Israel, and the horsemen thereof. And he
saw him no more: and he took hold of
his own clothes, and rent them in two
pieces.

Elisha's first miracles

[13]He took up also the mantle of Elijah that fell from him, and went back,
and stood by the bank of Jordan;
[14]And he took the mantle of Elijah
that fell from him, and smote the waters, and said, Where *is* the LORD God
of Elijah? and when he also had smitten the waters, they parted hither and
thither: and Elisha went over.
¶[15]And when the sons of the prophets which *were* to view at Jericho saw
him, they said, The spirit of Elijah doth
rest on Elisha. And they came to meet
him, and bowed themselves to the
ground before him.
[16]And they said unto him, Behold now,
there be with thy servants fifty strong
men; let them go, we pray thee, and seek
thy master: lest peradventure the Spirit
of the LORD hath taken him up, and cast
him upon some mountain, or into some
valley. And he said, Ye shall not send.
[17]And when they urged him till he
was ashamed, he said, Send. They sent
therefore fifty men; and they sought
three days, but found him not.

2:8 GARMENTS OF CLOTHING

The garments of Syrian men in the present day only differ a little from those worn in the time of Moses. The main articles of clothing are a coarse linen shirt, linen drawers, loose pantaloons with a girdle to sustain them, an inner vest buttoned to the throat, a long, loose robe with a leather girdle, an embroidered cloth or velvet jacket, a kaffiyeh, or silk handkerchief for the head (secured by a cord), hose, and sandals. Besides these, there was a long, loose robe with short sleeves that was worn in full dress (instead of the jacket or girded robe), and the aba, a coarse cloak of goat's or camel's hair that was very large, so it could be used as a covering by night as well as by day. It was the former that Christ laid aside when He washed the disciples' feet (John 13:4), and the latter with which Elijah smote the waters of the Jordan (2 Kings 2:8).

Women's dress varied according to their position in life (e.g., maid, wife, or widow). It differed from the men's principally in the veil and cap, which fit close to the head and concealed the hair. It was profusely covered with gold and silver ornaments and with charms. The list of female clothing in Isaiah 3:18-23 is scarcely intelligible now. The "hem of the garment" referred to in the New Testament (Matt. 9:20) is the fringe that all Jews wore in obedience to the order given in Numbers 15:38. It is now represented by the tallith or cloth worn by the Jews at prayers.

portion left to any other son in accordance with the law of Deuteronomy 21:17. Elisha's double use of the title "father" in addressing his master in verse 12, suits this request perfectly.

2:10 Thou hast asked a hard thing. You have made a great request.

2:17 ashamed. This means that he was at a loss to know how to refuse their persistent request any longer.

18 And when they came again to him,
(for he tarried at Jericho,) he said unto
them, Did I not say unto you, Go not?
¶ 19 And the men of the city said unto
Elisha, Behold, I pray thee, the situation of this city *is* pleasant, as my lord
seeth: but the water *is* naught, and the
ground barren.
20 And he said, Bring me a new cruse,
and put salt therein. And they bring *it*
to him.
21 And he went forth unto the spring
of the waters, and cast the salt in there,
and said, Thus saith the LORD, I have
healed these waters; there shall not be
from thence any more death or barren
land.
22 So the waters were healed unto this
day, according to the saying of Elisha
which he spake.
¶ 23 And he went up from thence unto
Beth-el: and as he was going up by the
way, there came forth little children out
of the city, and mocked him, and said
unto him, Go up, thou bald head; go up,
thou bald head.
24 And he turned back, and looked on
them, and cursed them in the name of
the LORD. And there came forth two
she bears out of the wood, and tare forty and two children of them.
25 And he went from thence to mount
*Carmel, and from thence he returned
to Samaria.

Jehoram's expedition against the Moabites

3 Now Jehoram the son of Ahab began to reign over Israel in Samaria
the eighteenth year of Jehoshaphat king
of Judah, and reigned twelve years.
2 And he wrought evil in the sight of
the LORD; but not like his father, and
like his mother: for he put away the
image of *Baal that his father had made.
3 Nevertheless he cleaved unto the
sins of Jeroboam the son of Nebat,
which made Israel to *sin; he departed
not therefrom.
¶ 4 And Mesha king of Moab was a
sheepmaster, and rendered unto the
king of Israel an hundred thousand
lambs, and an hundred thousand rams,
with the wool.
5 But it came to pass, when Ahab was
dead, that the king of Moab rebelled
against the king of Israel.
¶ 6 And king Jehoram went out of Samaria the same time, and numbered all
Israel.
7 And he went and sent to Jehoshaphat the king of Judah, saying, The king
of Moab hath rebelled against me: wilt
thou go with me against Moab to battle? And he said, I will go up: I *am* as
thou *art*, my people as thy people, *and*
my horses as thy horses.

2:24 Elisha's Curse

When Elisha "cursed them in the name of the LORD," he pronounced a curse upon them. He did this as the servant of the LORD, and because the insult to him was a sign of their hatred of God. The children were, literally, *very little children,* beneath the age of personal responsibility, and thus not eternally lost through their deaths. The whole episode is symbolic. Elijah, meaning *God who is Jehovah,* had just gone to heaven, as Christ, the Son of God, ascended. Elisha, meaning *the salvation of God,* had just come upon the scene, as Christ will come again to reign, "without sin unto salvation" (Heb. 9:28). Christ will come in righteousness to establish a kingdom of peace, but He will come in judgment, nevertheless, to destroy His enemies. By the curse upon the children by Elisha, God illustrated a great truth without affecting the eternal destiny of those judged.

2:20 cruse. A small cup or vessel for holding liquids.
2:21 cast the salt in. Salt is the symbol of purification (Matt. 5:13).
3:3 the sins of Jeroboam. These words refer to Jeroboam's acts described in 1 Kings 12:28,31-32. To keep the kingdom of Israel distinct from the kingdom of Judah, Jehoram—and other kings of Israel, too—sponsored the calf worship established by Jeroboam at Beth-el.

[8]And he said, Which way shall we go
up? And he answered, The way through
the wilderness of *Edom.
[9]So the king of Israel went, and the
king of Judah, and the king of Edom: and
they fetched a compass of seven days'
journey: and there was no water for the
host, and for the cattle that followed
them.
[10]And the king of Israel said, Alas!
that the LORD hath called these three
kings together, to deliver them into the
hand of Moab!
[11]But Jehoshaphat said, *Is there* not
here a *prophet of the LORD, that we
may enquire of the LORD by him? And
one of the king of Israel's servants answered and said, Here *is* Elisha the son
of Shaphat, which poured water on the
hands of Elijah.
[12]And Jehoshaphat said, The word of
the LORD is with him. So the king of
Israel and Jehoshaphat and the king
of Edom went down to him.
[13]And Elisha said unto the king of
Israel, What have I to do with thee? get
thee to the prophets of thy father, and
to the prophets of thy mother. And the
king of Israel said unto him, Nay: for the
LORD hath called these three kings together, to deliver them into the hand of
Moab.
[14]And Elisha said, *As* the LORD of
hosts liveth, before whom I stand, surely, were it not that I regard the presence
of Jehoshaphat the king of Judah, I
would not look toward thee, nor see
thee.
[15]But now bring me a minstrel. And
it came to pass, when the minstrel
played, that the hand of the LORD came
upon him.
[16]And he said, Thus saith the LORD,
Make this valley full of ditches.

3:15 An Inspired Musician
A minstrel was one who played on the harp. This request was made so that Elisha might be calm and ready to hear the voice of God's Spirit. For a similar use of music, read 1 Samuel 10:5-6.

[17]For thus saith the LORD, Ye shall
not see wind, neither shall ye see rain;
yet that valley shall be filled with water, that ye may drink, both ye, and your
cattle, and your beasts.
[18]And this is *but* a light thing in the
sight of the LORD: he will deliver the
Moabites also into your hand.
[19]And ye shall smite every fenced
city, and every choice city, and shall fell
every good tree, and stop all wells of
water, and mar every good piece of land
with stones.
[20]And it came to pass in the morning,
when the *meat-offering was offered,
that, behold, there came water by the
way of Edom, and the country was filled
with water.
¶[21]And when all the Moabites heard
that the kings were come up to fight
against them, they gathered all that
were able to put on armour, and upward,
and stood in the border.
[22]And they rose up early in the morning, and the sun shone upon the water,
and the Moabites saw the water on the
other side *as* red as blood:
[23]And they said, This *is* blood: the
kings are surely slain, and they have
smitten one another: now therefore,
Moab, to the spoil.
[24]And when they came to the camp of
Israel, the Israelites rose up and smote
the Moabites, so that they fled before
them: but they went forward smiting the
Moabites, even in *their* country.

3:9 fetched a compass of seven days' journey. Made a seven-day circuit or trip.
3:11 which poured water on the hands of Elijah. He served Elijah constantly and intimately. He was therefore the most reliable prophet since the translation (that is, the taking up in a whirlwind; read 2:11 and its note, "A Preview of the Rapture") of Elijah.
3:15 hand of the LORD. This expression is used often in the Scriptures to refer to supernatural power (see Ezek. 1:3; 3:14,22; 8:1).

25 And they beat down the cities, and on every good piece of land cast every man his stone, and filled it; and they stopped all the wells of water, and felled all the good trees: only in Kir-haraseth left they the stones thereof; howbeit the slingers went about *it,* and smote it.

¶26 And when the king of Moab saw that the battle was too sore for him, he took with him seven hundred men that drew swords, to break through *even* unto the king of Edom: but they could not.

27 Then he took his eldest son that should have reigned in his stead, and offered him *for* a burnt-offering upon the wall. And there was great indignation against Israel: and they departed from him, and returned to *their own* land.

Elisha and the poor widow

4 Now there cried a certain woman of the wives of the sons of the prophets unto Elisha, saying, Thy servant my husband is dead; and thou knowest that thy servant did *fear the LORD: and the creditor is come to take unto him my two sons to be bondmen.

2 And Elisha said unto her, What shall I do for thee? tell me, what hast thou in the house? And she said, Thine handmaid hath not any thing in the house, save a pot of oil.

3 Then he said, Go, *borrow thee vessels abroad of all thy neighbours, *even* empty vessels; borrow not a few.

4 And when thou art come in, thou shalt shut the door upon thee and upon thy sons, and shalt pour out into all those vessels, and thou shalt set aside that which is full.

5 So she went from him, and shut the door upon her and upon her sons, who brought *the vessels* to her; and she poured out.

6 And it came to pass, when the vessels were full, that she said unto her son, Bring me yet a vessel. And he said unto her, *There is* not a vessel more. And the oil stayed.

7 Then she came and told the man of God. And he said, Go, sell the oil, and pay thy debt, and live thou and thy children of the rest.

Elisha and the Shunammite woman

¶8 And it fell on a day, that Elisha passed to Shunem, where *was* a great woman; and she constrained him to eat bread. And *so* it was, *that* as oft as he passed by, he turned in thither to eat bread.

9 And she said unto her husband, Behold now, I perceive that this *is* an *holy man of God, which passeth by us continually.

10 Let us make a little chamber, I pray thee, on the wall; and let us set for him there a bed, and a table, and a stool, and a *candlestick: and it shall be, when he cometh to us, that he shall turn in thither.

11 And it fell on a day, that he came thither, and he turned into the chamber, and lay there.

12 And he said to Gehazi his servant, Call this Shunammite. And when he had called her, she stood before him.

13 And he said unto him, Say now unto her, Behold, thou hast been careful for us with all this care; what *is* to be done for thee? wouldest thou be spoken for to the king, or to the captain of the host?

3:25 Kir-haraseth. This was the capital city of the Moabites and therefore the strongest.

3:27 great indignation against Israel. The king's sacrifice of his son was so awful in the eyes of Israel's allies that they were sorry that they had any share in a war that led to such a thing. For that reason, they drew back from pressing the king of Moab any further.

4:2 save a pot of oil. One of the uses of oil was the anointing of the dead. It is possible that this pot of oil had been kept by the poor widow for her burial (see Matt. 26:12).

4:10 on the wall. Probably a room on the roof. Notice that in verse 21 the woman "went up" to lay the dead child on the prophet's bed.

And she answered, I dwell among mine
own people.
14 And he said, What then *is* to be
done for her? And Gehazi answered,
Verily she hath no child, and her husband is old.
15 And he said, Call her. And when he
had called her, she stood in the door.
16 And he said, About this season, according to the time of life, thou shalt
embrace a son. And she said, Nay, my
lord, *thou* man of God, do not lie unto
thine handmaid.

4:16 Divine Favor
There is given to this woman the same token of divine favor as was given to Sarah in her old age (read Gen. 18:10-15). This was altogether by the grace of God. As a Gentile, the Shunammite was an alien from the commonwealth of Israel, a stranger from the covenants of promise (Eph. 2:12). Just as God bestowed upon her favor to which she had no claim, so He shows His grace to us who have forfeited by our sin any claim to His blessing (see Eph. 2:13).

17 And the woman conceived, and
bare a son at that season that Elisha had
said unto her, according to the time of
life.
¶18 And when the child was grown, it
fell on a day, that he went out to his father to the reapers.
19 And he said unto his father, My
head, my head. And he said to a lad,
Carry him to his mother.
20 And when he had taken him, and
brought him to his mother, he sat on her
knees till noon, and *then* died.
21 And she went up, and laid him on
the bed of the man of God, and shut *the
door* upon him, and went out.
22 And she called unto her husband,
and said, Send me, I pray thee, one of
the young men, and one of the asses,
that I may run to the man of God, and
come again.
23 And he said, Wherefore wilt thou go
to him to day? *it is* neither *new moon,
nor *sabbath. And she said, *It shall be*
well.
24 Then she saddled an ass, and said

4:16 BIRTHS DIVINELY ANNOUNCED

Reference	Mother	Child	Announcement
Genesis 16:11	Hagar	Ishmael	The angel of the LORD announces: "Behold thou art with child, and shalt bear a son."
Genesis 17:19	Sarah	Isaac	God said: "Sarah thy wife shall bear thee a son indeed; and thou shalt call his name Isaac."
Judges 13:5	Wife of Manoah	Samson	The angel of the LORD announces: "For lo, thou shalt conceive, and bear a son."
Luke 1:13	Elisabeth	John the Baptist	The angel of the Lord appeared to Zacharias and said, "Thy wife Elisabeth shall bear thee a son . . . ."
Luke 1:31	Mary	Jesus	The angel Gabriel said, "Thou shalt conceive in thy womb, and bring forth a son."

Several other births are accredited to divine intervention although not given an official announcement:

Reference	Mother	Child	Announcement
Genesis 29:31	Leah	Reuben	When the LORD saw that Leah was unloved, He opened her womb.
Genesis 30:22	Rachel	Joseph	God remembered Rachel, and God listened to her and opened her womb.
1 Samuel 1:19-20	Hannah	Samuel	. . . the LORD remembered Hannah. Hannah conceived and bore a son.
2 Kings 4:17	Shunammite woman		. . . the woman conceived, and bare a son . . . of which Elisha had told her.

to her servant, Drive, and go forward; slack not *thy* riding for me, except I bid thee.

[25]So she went and came unto the man of God to mount Carmel. And it came to pass, when the man of God saw her afar off, that he said to Gehazi his servant, Behold, *yonder is* that Shunammite:

[26]Run now, I pray thee, to meet her, and say unto her, *Is it* well with thee? *is it* well with thy husband? *is it* well with the child? And she answered, *It is* well.

[27]And when she came to the man of God to the hill, she caught him by the feet: but Gehazi came near to thrust her away. And the man of God said, Let her alone; for her soul *is* vexed within her: and the LORD hath hid *it* from me, and hath not told me.

[28]Then she said, Did I desire a son of my lord? did I not say, Do not deceive me?

[29]Then he said to Gehazi, Gird up thy loins, and take my staff in thine hand, and go thy way: if thou meet any man, salute him not; and if any salute thee, answer him not again: and lay my staff upon the face of the child.

[30]And the mother of the child said, *As* the LORD liveth, and as thy soul liveth, I will not leave thee. And he arose, and followed her.

[31]And Gehazi passed on before them, and laid the staff upon the face of the child; but *there was* neither voice, nor hearing. Wherefore he went again to meet him, and told him, saying, The child is not awaked.

[32]And when Elisha was come into the house, behold, the child was dead, *and* laid upon his bed.

[33]He went in therefore, and shut the door upon them twain, and prayed unto the LORD.

[34]And he went up, and lay upon the child, and put his mouth upon his mouth, and his eyes upon his eyes, and his hands upon his hands: and he stretched himself upon the child; and the flesh of the child waxed warm.

[35]Then he returned, and walked in the house to and fro; and went up, and stretched himself upon him: and the child sneezed seven times, and the child opened his eyes.

[36]And he called Gehazi, and said, Call this Shunammite. So he called her. And when she was come in unto him, he said, Take up thy son.

[37]Then she went in, and fell at his feet, and bowed herself to the ground, and took up her son, and went out.

Elisha and the prophets

¶[38]And Elisha came again to Gilgal: and *there was* a dearth in the land; and the sons of the prophets *were* sitting before him: and he said unto his servant, Set on the great pot, and seethe pottage for the sons of the prophets.

[39]And one went out into the field to gather herbs, and found a wild vine, and gathered thereof wild gourds his lap full, and came and shred *them* into the pot of pottage: for they knew *them* not.

[40]So they poured out for the men to eat. And it came to pass, as they were eating of the pottage, that they cried out, and said, O *thou* man of God, *there is* death in the pot. And they could not eat *thereof.*

[41]But he said, Then bring meal. And he cast *it* into the pot; and he said, Pour out for the people, that they may eat. And there was no harm in the pot.

¶[42]And there came a man from Baal-

4:26 It is well. The woman did not mean to deceive. This was the common greeting in the countries of the East, and meant *peace.*

4:29 salute him not. A command that speaks of great haste.

4:34 lay upon the child. Elisha followed the example of his master Elijah; see 1 Kings 17:21.

4:38 sitting before him. The "sons of the prophets" were sitting before Elisha as his scholars.

shalisha, and brought the man of God
bread of the firstfruits, twenty loaves of
barley, and full ears of corn in the husk
thereof. And he said, Give unto the people, that they may eat.
43And his servitor said, What, should
I set this before an hundred men? He
said again, Give the people, that they
may eat: for thus saith the LORD, They
shall eat, and shall leave *thereof.*
44So he set *it* before them, and they
did eat, and left *thereof,* according to the
word of the LORD.

4:44 Feeding a Crowd
Notice that it was God and not Elisha who fed so many with so little. This is a foreshadowing of Christ's greater miracles (Matt. 14:15-21; 15:32-38; John 6:5-14).

Elisha and Naaman

5 Now Naaman, captain of the host
of the king of Syria, was a great man
with his master, and honourable, because by him the LORD had given deliverance unto Syria: he was also a mighty
man in valour, *but he was* a *leper.
2And the Syrians had gone out by
companies, and had brought away captive out of the land of Israel a little maid;
and she waited on Naaman's wife.
3And she said unto her mistress,
Would God my lord *were* with the
prophet that *is* in Samaria! for he would
recover him of his *leprosy.
4And *one* went in, and told his lord,
saying, Thus and thus said the maid that
is of the land of Israel.
5And the king of Syria said, Go to, go,
and I will send a letter unto the king of
Israel. And he departed, and took with
him ten talents of silver, and six thousand *pieces* of gold, and ten changes of
raiment.
6And he brought the letter to the king
of Israel, saying, Now when this letter
is come unto thee, behold, I have *therewith* sent Naaman my servant to thee,
that thou mayest recover him of his leprosy.
7And it came to pass, when the king
of Israel had read the letter, that he rent
his clothes, and said, *Am* I God, to kill
and to make alive, that this man doth
send unto me to recover a man of his
leprosy? wherefore consider, I pray
you, and see how he seeketh a quarrel
against me.
¶8And it was *so,* when Elisha the man
of God had heard that the king of Israel
had rent his clothes, that he sent to the
king, saying, Wherefore hast thou rent
thy clothes? let him come now to me,
and he shall know that there is a prophet in Israel.
9So Naaman came with his horses
and with his chariot, and stood at the
door of the house of Elisha.
10And Elisha sent a messenger unto
him, saying, Go and wash in Jordan
seven times, and thy flesh shall come
again to thee, and thou shalt be
*clean.
11But Naaman was wroth, and went
away, and said, Behold, I thought, He
will surely come out to me, and stand,
and call on the name of the LORD his
God, and strike his hand over the place,
and recover the leper.
12*Are* not Abana and Pharpar, rivers
of *Damascus, better than all the waters of Israel? may I not wash in them,
and be clean? So he turned and went
away in a rage.
13And his servants came near, and
spake unto him, and said, My father, *if*
the prophet had bid thee *do some* great
thing, wouldest thou not have done *it?*

4:42 bread of the firstfruits. The bringing of the firstfruits to Elisha is an indication that this man judged Elisha to be a true man of God (see Deut. 18:4).
4:43 servitor. A servant or attendant.
5:5 six thousand pieces of gold. This was doubtless six thousand shekels of gold.
5:11 strike. To rub gently.
5:13 My father. An address of respect and affection.

how much rather then, when he saith to thee, Wash, and be clean?

14 Then went he down, and dipped himself seven times in Jordan, according to the saying of the man of God: and his flesh came again like unto the flesh of a little child, and he was clean.

¶ 15 And he returned to the man of God, he and all his company, and came, and stood before him: and he said, Behold, now I know that *there is* no God in all earth, but in Israel: now therefore, I pray thee, take a blessing of thy servant.

16 But he said, *As* the LORD liveth, before whom I stand, I will receive none. And he urged him to take *it;* but he refused.

17 And Naaman said, Shall there not then, I pray thee, be given to thy servant two mules' burden of earth? for thy servant will henceforth offer neither burnt-offering nor *sacrifice unto other gods, but unto the LORD.

18 In this thing the LORD pardon thy servant, *that* when my master goeth into the house of Rimmon to worship there, and he leaneth on my hand, and I bow myself in the house of Rimmon: when I bow down myself in the house of Rimmon, the LORD pardon thy servant in this thing.

19 And he said unto him, Go in peace. So he departed from him a little way.

Elisha and Gehazi

¶ 20 But Gehazi, the servant of Elisha the man of God, said, Behold, my master hath spared Naaman this Syrian, in not receiving at his hands that which he brought: but, *as* the LORD liveth, I will run after him, and take somewhat of him.

21 So Gehazi followed after Naaman. And when Naaman saw *him* running after him, he lighted down from the chariot to meet him, and said, *Is* all well?

22 And he said, All *is* well. My master hath sent me, saying, Behold, even now there be come to me from mount *Ephraim two young men of the sons of the prophets: give them, I pray thee, a talent of silver, and two changes of *garments.

23 And Naaman said, Be content, take two talents. And he urged him, and bound two talents of silver in two bags, with two changes of garments, and laid *them* upon two of his servants; and they bare *them* before him.

24 And when he came to the tower, he took *them* from their hand, and bestowed *them* in the house: and he let the men go, and they departed.

25 But he went in, and stood before his master. And Elisha said unto him, Whence *comest thou,* Gehazi? And he said, Thy servant went no whither.

26 And he said unto him, Went not mine heart *with thee,* when the man turned again from his chariot to meet thee? *Is it* a time to receive *money, and to receive garments, and oliveyards, and vineyards, and sheep, and oxen, and menservants, and maidservants?

27 The leprosy therefore of Naaman shall cleave unto thee, and unto thy seed for ever. And he went out from his presence a leper *as white* as snow.

Elisha and the lost axe

6 And the sons of the prophets said unto Elisha, Behold now, the place where we dwell with thee is too strait for us.

2 Let us go, we pray thee, unto Jordan, and take thence every man a beam, and let us make us a place there, where we may dwell. And he answered, Go ye.

5:15 a blessing. Blessing here means *gift,* as in Genesis 33:10-11.

5:17 two mules' burden of earth. This earth would be used to build an altar (see Exod. 20:24). It was Naaman's idea that God would be more pleased with an altar built with the soil of the land of Israel.

6:1 strait. Narrow or confined.

3And one said, Be content, I pray
thee, and go with thy servants. And he
answered, I will go.
4So he went with them. And when
they came to Jordan, they cut down
wood.
5But as one was felling a beam, the
axe head fell into the water: and he
cried, and said, Alas, master! for it was
borrowed.
6And the man of God said, Where fell
it? And he shewed him the place. And
he cut down a stick, and cast *it* in
thither; and the iron did swim.
7Therefore said he, Take *it* up to thee.
And he put out his hand, and took it.

Elisha and the Syrian invasion

¶8Then the king of Syria warred
against Israel, and took counsel with his
servants, saying, In such and such a
place *shall be* my camp.
9And the man of God sent unto the
king of Israel, saying, Beware that thou
pass not such a place; for thither the
Syrians are come down.
10And the king of Israel sent to the
place which the man of God told him
and warned him of, and saved himself
there, not once nor twice.
11Therefore the heart of the king of
Syria was sore troubled for this thing;
and he called his servants, and said unto
them, Will ye not shew me which of us
is for the king of Israel?
12And one of his servants said, None,
my lord, O king: but Elisha, the prophet that *is* in Israel, telleth the king of
Israel the words that thou speakest in
thy bedchamber.
¶13And he said, Go and spy where he
is, that I may send and fetch him. And
it was told him, saying, Behold, *he is* in
Dothan.
14Therefore sent he thither horses,
and chariots, and a great host: and they
came by night, and compassed the city
about.
15And when the servant of the man
of God was risen early, and gone forth,
behold, an host compassed the city both
with horses and chariots. And his servant said unto him, Alas, my master!
how shall we do?
16And he answered, Fear not: for they
that *be* with us *are* more than they that
be with them.
17And Elisha prayed, and said, LORD,
I pray thee, open his eyes, that he may
see. And the LORD opened the eyes of
the young man; and he saw: and, behold, the mountain *was* full of horses
and chariots of fire round about Elisha.
18And when they came down to him,
Elisha prayed unto the LORD, and said,
Smite this people, I pray thee, with
blindness. And he smote them with
blindness according to the word of Elisha.
¶19And Elisha said unto them, This
is not the way, neither *is* this the city:
follow me, and I will bring you to the
man whom ye seek. But he led them to
Samaria.
20And it came to pass, when they
were come into Samaria, that Elisha
said, LORD, open the eyes of these *men,*
that they may see. And the LORD
opened their eyes, and they saw; and,
behold, *they were* in the midst of Samaria.
21And the king of Israel said unto
Elisha, when he saw them, My father,
shall I smite *them?* shall I smite *them?*
22And he answered, Thou shalt not
smite *them:* wouldest thou smite those
whom thou hast taken captive with thy
sword and with thy bow? set bread and
water before them, that they may eat
and drink, and go to their master.
23And he prepared great provision for
them: and when they had eaten and

6:16 they that be with us are more than they that be with them. Read Romans 8:31 and 2 Chronicles 32:7.

6:17 horses and chariots of fire. Fire here is a symbol of Deity (Deut. 4:24). This phrase, therefore, denotes the visible help of God in the lives of those who trust Him.

drunk, he sent them away, and they
went to their master. So the bands of
Syria came no more into the land of Israel.
¶24 And it came to pass after this, that
*Ben-hadad king of Syria gathered all
his host, and went up, and besieged
Samaria.
25 And there was a great famine in
Samaria: and, behold, they besieged it,
until an ass's head was *sold* for fourscore *pieces* of silver, and the fourth part
of a cab of dove's dung for five *pieces* of
silver.
26 And as the king of Israel was passing by upon the wall, there cried a woman unto him, saying, Help, my lord, O
king.
27 And he said, If the LORD do not help
thee, whence shall I help thee? out of
the barnfloor, or out of the winepress?
28 And the king said unto her, What
aileth thee? And she answered, This
woman said unto me, Give thy son, that
we may eat him to day, and we will eat
my son to morrow.
29 So we boiled my son, and did eat
him: and I said unto her on the next day,
Give thy son, that we may eat him: and
she hath hid her son.
¶30 And it came to pass, when the
king heard the words of the woman, that
he rent his clothes; and he passed by
upon the wall, and the people looked,
and, behold, *he had* sackcloth within
upon his flesh.
31 Then he said, God do so and more
also to me, if the head of Elisha the son
of Shaphat shall stand on him this day.
32 But Elisha sat in his house, and the
*elders sat with him; and *the king* sent
a man from before him: but ere the
messenger came to him, he said to the
elders, See ye how this son of a murderer hath sent to take away mine
head? look, when the messenger
cometh, shut the door, and hold him fast
at the door: *is* not the sound of his
master's feet behind him?
33 And while he yet talked with them,
behold, the messenger came down unto
him: and he said, Behold, this evil *is* of
the LORD; what should I wait for the
LORD any longer?

6:33 Corrective Judgment

The LORD must always punish disobedience to Him, which is sin. In mercy Christ took upon Himself at Calvary the sin of the world, and that sacrifice in our place is available to all who will believe in Him. The principle of judgment within the family of God is given in 2 Samuel 7:14-15; 12:13-14. The judgment of God is corrective, rather than a penalty.

7 Then Elisha said, Hear ye the
word of the LORD; Thus saith the
LORD, To morrow about this time *shall*
a measure of fine flour *be sold* for a shekel, and two measures of barley for a
shekel, in the gate of Samaria.
2 Then a lord on whose hand the king

6:24 gathered all his host, and went up. The bands of marauders (vs. 23) came up no more. This, however, was the disciplined and trained army.

6:25 ass's head. The ass was regarded as unclean for eating, yet so terrible was the famine that an ass's head was expensive to buy.

6:25 cab. A measure of quantity equal to one quart. One-fourth of a cab would be about a half of a pint.

6:29 did eat him. This condition was foretold as the result of disobedience to God in Leviticus 26:29 and Deuteronomy 28:52-53.

6:32 son of a murderer. Jehoram was the son of Ahab and Jezebel. Ahab is called a murderer because of his treatment of Naboth (1 Kings 21).

6:32 hold him fast at the door. This means, "Do not let him in."

7:1 gate of Samaria. Food brought from the country was sold at the gates of the city.

7:2 on whose hand the king leaned. This lord was a knight or chariot warrior. Whenever the king walked on foot, he would be attended by his chief warrior, and the king would rest his hand on the arm of the knight. Such an attendant to the king of Syria was Naaman of whom we read in chapter 5.

leaned answered the man of God, and
said, Behold, *if* the LORD would make
windows in *heaven, might this thing
be? And he said, Behold, thou shalt see
it with thine eyes, but shalt not eat
thereof.
¶ 3 And there were four leprous men
at the entering in of the gate: and they
said one to another, Why sit we here
until we die?
4 If we say, We will enter into the city,
then the famine *is* in the city, and we
shall die there: and if we sit still here,
we die also. Now therefore come, and
let us fall unto the host of the Syrians:
if they save us alive, we shall live; and
if they kill us, we shall but die.
5 And they rose up in the twilight, to
go unto the camp of the Syrians: and
when they were come to the uttermost
part of the camp of Syria, behold, *there
was* no man there.
6 For the Lord had made the host of
the Syrians to hear a noise of chariots,
and a noise of horses, *even* the noise of
a great host: and they said one to another, Lo, the king of *Israel hath hired
against us the kings of the Hittites, and
the kings of the Egyptians, to come
upon us.
7 Wherefore they arose and fled in the
twilight, and left their tents, and their
horses, and their asses, even the camp
as it *was,* and fled for their life.
8 And when these lepers came to the
uttermost part of the camp, they went
into one tent, and did eat and drink, and
carried thence silver, and gold, and raiment, and went and hid *it;* and came
again, and entered into another tent,
and carried thence *also,* and went and
hid *it.*
9 Then they said one to another, We
do not well: this day *is* a day of good tidings, and we hold our peace: if we tarry
till the morning light, some mischief
will come upon us: now therefore come,
that we may go and tell the king's
household.
10 So they came and called unto the
porter of the city: and they told them,
saying, We came to the camp of the
Syrians, and, behold, *there was* no man
there, neither voice of man, but horses
tied, and asses tied, and the tents as
they *were.*
11 And he called the *porters; and
they told *it* to the king's house within.
¶ 12 And the king arose in the night,
and said unto his servants, I will now
shew you what the Syrians have done
to us. They know that we *be* hungry;
therefore are they gone out of the camp
to hide themselves in the field, saying,
When they come out of the city, we
shall catch them alive, and get into the
city.
13 And one of his servants answered
and said, Let *some* take, I pray thee, five
of the horses that remain, which are left
in the city, (behold, they *are* as all the
multitude of Israel that are left in it:
behold, *I say,* they *are* even as all the
multitude of the Israelites that are consumed:) and let us send and see.
14 They took therefore two chariot

7:2 if the LORD would make windows. This was said mockingly in unbelief. But God does open windows in heaven for those who trust and obey Him (see Mal. 3:10).

7:3 four leprous men. Because of their dreadful disease, lepers were not permitted within the city. The law concerning them is found in Leviticus 13:46 and Numbers 5:2. See *leprosy.

7:6 a noise of chariots. For similar instances see 2 Samuel 5:24 and 2 Kings 19:7.

7:7 fled for their life. Read Proverbs 28:1.

7:10 porter of the city. This porter was not a carrier of baggage as in our day but a guard at the city gate.

7:13 let us send and see. The suggestion was that five scouts be sent to the camp of the Syrians. If they perished, then their fate would be no worse than the fate the multitude of Israel was sure to face if no divine deliverance came.

7:14 two chariot horses. That is, horses for two chariots, or two pairs of horses.

horses; and the king sent after the host of the Syrians, saying, Go and see.

15 And they went after them unto Jordan: and, lo, all the way *was* full of garments and vessels, which the Syrians had cast away in their haste. And the messengers returned, and told the king.

16 And the people went out, and spoiled the tents of the Syrians. So a measure of fine flour was *sold* for a shekel, and two measures of barley for a shekel, according to the word of the LORD.

¶17 And the king appointed the lord on whose hand he leaned to have the charge of the gate: and the people trode upon him in the gate, and he died, as the man of God had said, who spake when the king came down to him.

18 And it came to pass as the man of God had spoken to the king, saying, Two measures of barley for a shekel, and a measure of fine flour for a shekel, shall be to morrow about this time in the gate of Samaria:

19 And that lord answered the man of God, and said, Now, behold, *if* the LORD should make windows in heaven, might such a thing be? And he said, Behold, thou shalt see it with thine eyes, but shalt not eat thereof.

20 And so it fell out unto him: for the people trode upon him in the gate, and he died.

Elisha's authority with the king

8 Then spake *Elisha unto the woman, whose son he had restored to life, saying, Arise, and go thou and thine household, and sojourn wheresoever thou canst sojourn: for the LORD hath called for a famine; and it shall also come upon the land seven years.

2 And the woman arose, and did after the saying of the man of God: and she went with her household, and sojourned in the land of the *Philistines seven years.

3 And it came to pass at the seven years' end, that the woman returned out of the land of the Philistines: and she went forth to cry unto the king for her house and for her land.

4 And the king talked with Gehazi the servant of the man of God, saying, Tell me, I pray thee, all the great things that Elisha hath done.

5 And it came to pass, as he was telling the king how he had restored a dead body to life, that, behold, the woman, whose son he had restored to life, cried to the king for her house and for her land. And Gehazi said, My lord, O king, this *is* the woman, and this *is* her son, whom Elisha restored to life.

6 And when the king asked the woman, she told him. So the king appointed unto her a certain officer, saying, Restore all that *was* hers, and all the fruits of the field since the day that she left the land, even until now.

¶7 And Elisha came to Damascus; and Ben-hadad the king of Syria was sick; and it was told him, saying, The man of God is come hither.

8 And the king said unto *Hazael, Take a present in thine hand, and go, meet the man of God, and enquire of the

---

7:16 spoiled. Looted or plundered.

7:16 according to the word of the LORD. So plentiful was the booty that food was sold at unbelievably low prices, just as Elisha had foretold in verse 1.

7:17 have the charge of the gate. To keep order in the buying and selling. His death was the fulfillment of verse 2.

7:18 And it came to pass. This, along with verse 19, is a repetition of verses 1 and 2 to call to mind the exact fulfillment of Elisha's words.

8:1 Then spake Elisha. *Now Elisha had spoken*. This takes us back to the incident in chapter 4.

8:4 the king talked with Gehazi. This would seem to have been before Gehazi was stricken with leprosy (5:27).

8:8 enquire of the LORD. Ben-hadad, king of Syria, inquired of the LORD; Ahaziah, king of Israel, inquired of *Baal-zebub (1 Kings 1:2).

LORD by him, saying, Shall I recover of
this disease?
[9]So Hazael went to meet him, and
took a present with him, even of every
good thing of Damascus, forty camels'
burden, and came and stood before him,
and said, Thy son Ben-hadad king of
Syria hath sent me to thee, saying, Shall
I recover of this disease?
[10]And Elisha said unto him, Go, say
unto him, Thou mayest certainly recover:
howbeit the LORD hath shewed me
that he shall surely die.

8:11 A Direct Confrontation
Elisha looked Hazael straight in the eye, and Hazael was ashamed because he knew that his plan to seize Ben-hadad's throne was known to Elisha (see vss. 12-13,15).

[11]And he settled his countenance
stedfastly, until he was ashamed: and
the man of God wept.
[12]And Hazael said, Why weepeth my
lord? And he answered, Because I know
the evil that thou wilt do unto the children
of Israel: their strong holds wilt
thou set on fire, and their young men
wilt thou slay with the sword, and wilt
dash their children, and rip up their
women with child.
[13]And Hazael said, But what, *is* thy
servant a dog, that he should do this
great thing? And Elisha answered, The
LORD hath shewed me that thou *shalt*
be king over Syria.
[14]So he departed from Elisha, and
came to his master; who said to him,
What said Elisha to thee? And he answered,
He told me *that* thou shouldest
surely recover.
[15]And it came to pass on the morrow,
that he took a thick cloth, and dipped *it*
in water, and spread *it* on his face, so
that he died: and Hazael reigned in his
stead.

8:15 The Cause of Death
The king suffocated beneath the thick cloth. This was cleverly done, because a wet cloth upon the face was used to help reduce fever. Men would not suspect Hazael of having murdered the king.

II. Two Kings Rule Judah
(8:16—9:37)

¶[16]And in the fifth year of Joram the
son of *Ahab king of Israel, Jehoshaphat
being then king of *Judah, Jehoram the
son of Jehoshaphat king of Judah began
to reign.
[17]Thirty and two years old was he
when he began to reign; and he reigned
eight years in *Jerusalem.
[18]And he walked in the way of the
kings of Israel, as did the house of
Ahab: for the daughter of Ahab was his
wife: and he did evil in the sight of the
LORD.
[19]Yet the LORD would not destroy
Judah for *David his servant's sake, as
he promised him to give him alway a
light, *and* to his children.

Edom revolts
(2 Chron. 21:8-10)

¶[20]In his days Edom revolted from
under the hand of Judah, and made a
king over themselves.
[21]So Joram went over to Zair, and all
the chariots with him: and he rose by
night, and smote the Edomites which
compassed him about, and the captains
of the chariots: and the people fled into
their tents.

8:9 forty camels' burden. One camel's burden is about six hundred pounds, but it was customary to give only a small burden to each camel in order that the presentation might be more imposing and express greater respect.
8:16 Jehoram. Called "Joram" in verses 21,23-24.
8:19 the LORD would not destroy Judah. God is true to His promises. See what God had promised David (2 Sam. 7:12-13). See also 1 Kings 11:36; 2 Chronicles 21:7; Psalm 132:11.

Libnah revolts
(2 Chron. 21:10)

22Yet Edom revolted from under the
hand of Judah unto this day. Then Libnah revolted at the same time.
23And the rest of the acts of Joram,
and all that he did, *are* they not written
in the book of the chronicles of the
kings of Judah?
24And Joram slept with his fathers,
and was buried with his fathers in the
city of David: and Ahaziah his son
reigned in his stead.

Ahaziah's reign
(2 Chron. 22:1-4)

¶25In the twelfth year of Joram the
son of Ahab king of Israel did Ahaziah
the son of Jehoram king of Judah begin
to reign.
26Two and twenty years old *was* Ahaziah when he began to reign; and he
reigned one year in Jerusalem. And his
mother's name *was* Athaliah, the
daughter of Omri king of Israel.
27And he walked in the way of the
house of Ahab, and did evil in the sight
of the LORD, as *did* the house of Ahab:
for he *was* the son in law of the house
of Ahab.

Alliance with King of Israel
(2 Chron. 22:5-6)

¶28And he went with Joram the son
of Ahab to the war against Hazael king
of Syria in Ramoth-gilead; and the Syrians wounded Joram.
29And king Joram went back to be
healed in Jezreel of the wounds which
the Syrians had given him at Ramah,
when he fought against Hazael king of
Syria. And Ahaziah the son of Jehoram
king of Judah went down to see Joram
the son of Ahab in Jezreel, because he
was sick.

Jehu bocomes King of Israel
Judgment on the house of Ahab

9 And Elisha the *prophet called
one of the children of the prophets,
and said unto him, Gird up thy loins, and
take this box of oil in thine hand, and go
to Ramoth-gilead:
2And when thou comest thither, look
out there Jehu the son of Jehoshaphat
the son of Nimshi, and go in, and make
him arise up from among his brethren,
and carry him to an inner chamber;

> **9:2 Jehu**
> This name means *God is*. Jehu was probably given command of the Israelite army at Ramoth-gilead when Joram was wounded (8:29). Verse 5 shows that Jehu was a captain.

3Then take the box of oil, and pour *it*
on his head, and say, Thus saith the
LORD, I have anointed thee king over
Israel. Then open the door, and flee, and
tarry not.
¶4So the young man, *even* the young
man the prophet, went to Ramoth-
gilead.
5And when he came, behold, the captains of the host *were* sitting; and he
said, I have an errand to thee, O captain.
And Jehu said, Unto which of all us?
And he said, To thee, O captain.
6And he arose, and went into the
house; and he poured the oil on his
head, and said unto him, Thus saith the
LORD God of Israel, I have anointed
thee king over the people of the LORD,
even over Israel.
7And thou shalt smite the house of
Ahab thy master, that I may avenge the

8:22 Edom revolted. This fulfills the prophecy made in Genesis 27:40.
9:1 box of oil. A vial or bottle of oil.
9:1 Ramoth-gilead. A very strong and important city, affording a defense for Judah and Israel against the Syrians.
9:3 I have anointed thee. This anointing of Jehu was a duty that Elijah passed on to Elisha (read 1 Kings 19:16).
9:7 Jezebel. Jezebel killed the prophets (1 Kings 18:4) and other godly men (1 Kings 21:15).

blood of my servants the prophets, and
the blood of all the servants of the
LORD, at the hand of Jezebel.
8 For the whole house of Ahab shall
perish: and I will cut off from Ahab him
that pisseth against the wall, and him
that is shut up and left in Israel:
9 And I will make the house of Ahab
like the house of Jeroboam the son of
Nebat, and like the house of Baasha the
son of Ahijah:
10 And the dogs shall eat Jezebel in
the portion of Jezreel, and *there shall be*
none to bury *her.* And he opened the
door, and fled.
¶ 11 Then Jehu came forth to the servants of his lord: and *one* said unto him,
Is all well? wherefore came this mad
fellow to thee? And he said unto them,
Ye know the man, and his communication.
12 And they said, *It is* false; tell us now.
And he said, Thus and thus spake he to
me, saying, Thus saith the LORD, I have
anointed thee king over Israel.
13 Then they hasted, and took every
man his garment, and put *it* under him
on the top of the stairs, and blew with
trumpets, saying, Jehu is king.

Jehu slays Jehoram

14 So Jehu the son of Jehoshaphat the
son of Nimshi conspired against Joram.
(Now Joram had kept Ramoth-gilead,
he and all Israel, because of Hazael king
of Syria.
15 But king Joram was returned to be
healed in Jezreel of the wounds which
the Syrians had given him, when he
fought with Hazael king of Syria.) And
Jehu said, If it be your minds, *then* let
none go forth *nor* escape out of the city
to go to tell *it* in Jezreel.
16 So Jehu rode in a chariot, and went
to Jezreel; for Joram lay there. And
Ahaziah king of Judah was come down
to see Joram.
17 And there stood a watchman on the
tower in Jezreel, and he spied the company of Jehu as he came, and said, I see
a company. And Joram said, Take an
horseman, and send to meet them, and
let him say, *Is it* peace?
18 So there went one on horseback to
meet him, and said, Thus saith the king,
Is it peace? And Jehu said, What hast
thou to do with peace? turn thee behind
me. And the watchman told, saying,
The messenger came to them, but he
cometh not again.
19 Then he sent out a second on
horseback, which came to them, and
said, Thus saith the king, *Is it* peace?
And Jehu answered, What hast thou to
do with peace? turn thee behind me.
20 And the watchman told, saying, He
came even unto them, and cometh not
again: and the driving *is* like the driving of Jehu the son of Nimshi; for he
driveth furiously.
21 And Joram said, Make ready. And
his chariot was made ready. And Joram
king of Israel and Ahaziah king of Judah
went out, each in his chariot, and they
went out against Jehu, and met him in
the portion of Naboth the Jezreelite.
22 And it came to pass, when Joram
saw Jehu, that he said, *Is it* peace, Jehu?
And he answered, What peace, so long
as the whoredoms of thy mother Jezebel and her witchcrafts *are so* many?
23 And Joram turned his hands, and
fled, and said to Ahaziah, *There is*
treachery, O Ahaziah.
24 And Jehu drew a bow with his full
strength, and smote Jehoram between

9:10 the dogs shall eat Jezebel. For the fulfillment of this, see verses 35-36.
9:10 in the portion of Jezreel. Formerly Naboth's vineyard (1 Kings 21:15,23).
9:11 Ye know the man, and his communication. Jehu probably thought that his companions had arranged the prophet's coming to annoy him, and that that was why they denied any knowledge of what the prophet had said (vs. 12).
9:13 put it under him. This was a sign of their homage. Remember how this was done for Christ on His official entrance into Jerusalem (Matt. 21:8).

his arms, and the arrow went out at his heart, and he sunk down in his chariot.

25 Then said *Jehu* to Bidkar his captain, Take up, *and* cast him in the portion of the field of Naboth the Jezreelite: for remember how that, when I and thou rode together after Ahab his father, the LORD laid this burden upon him;

26 Surely I have seen yesterday the blood of Naboth, and the blood of his sons, saith the LORD; and I will requite thee in this plat, saith the LORD. Now therefore take *and* cast him into the plat *of ground,* according to the word of the LORD.

Jehu slays Ahaziah (2 Chron. 22:9)

¶27 But when Ahaziah the king of Judah saw *this,* he fled by the way of the garden house. And Jehu followed after him, and said, Smite him also in the chariot. *And they did so* at the going up to Gur, which *is* by Ibleam. And he fled to *Megiddo, and died there.

28 And his servants carried him in a chariot to Jerusalem, and buried him in his sepulchre with his fathers in the city of David.

29 And in the eleventh year of Joram the son of Ahab began Ahaziah to reign over Judah.

The slaying of Jezebel

¶30 And when Jehu was come to Jezreel, Jezebel heard *of it;* and she painted her face, and tired her head, and looked out at a window.

31 And as Jehu entered in at the gate, she said, *Had* Zimri peace, who slew his master?

32 And he lifted up his face to the window, and said, Who *is* on my side? who? And there looked out to him two *or* three eunuchs.

33 And he said, Throw her down. So they threw her down: and *some* of her blood was sprinkled on the wall, and on the horses: and he trode her under foot.

34 And when he was come in, he did eat and drink, and said, Go, see now this cursed *woman,* and bury her: for she *is* a king's daughter.

35 And they went to bury her: but they found no more of her than the skull, and the feet, and the palms of *her* hands.

36 Wherefore they came again, and told him. And he said, This *is* the word of the LORD, which he spake by his servant Elijah the Tishbite, saying, In the portion of Jezreel shall dogs eat the flesh of Jezebel:

37 And the carcase of Jezebel shall be as dung upon the face of the field in the portion of Jezreel; *so* that they shall not say, This *is* Jezebel.

III. Jehu Rules Israel (10:1—12:21)

Jehu brings judgment on the house of Ahab

10 And Ahab had seventy sons in Samaria. And Jehu wrote letters, and sent to Samaria, unto the rulers of Jezreel, to the elders, and to them that brought up Ahab's *children,* saying,

2 Now as soon as this letter cometh to you, seeing your master's sons *are* with you, and *there are* with you chariots and horses, a fenced city also, and armour;

3 Look even out the best and meetest of your master's sons, and set *him* on

---

9:25 burden. A name commonly given to a divine sentence against a person or a place. For examples, read Isaiah 13:1; 15:1; 17:1; see also 1 Kings 21:29.

9:26 plat. A small patch of ground, a plot.

9:27 garden house. A summerhouse.

9:30 tired her head. This means that she put on head ornaments or that she put on her crown. This was done on purpose to awe Jehu with her majesty as queen.

9:31 Zimri. Jezebel was warning Jehu that a fate like Zimri's might befall him (see 1 Kings 16:10-18).

9:36 word of the LORD. This was prophesied in 1 Kings 21:23.

10:1 sons. The word "sons" in the Old Testament often means *descendants* and would include grandsons as well.

his father's throne, and fight for your
master's house.
4But they were exceedingly afraid,
and said, Behold, two kings stood not
before him: how then shall we stand?
5And he that *was* over the house, and
he that *was* over the city, the elders
also, and the bringers up *of the children,*
sent to Jehu, saying, We *are* thy servants, and will do all that thou shalt bid
us; we will not make any king: do thou
that which is good in thine eyes.
6Then he wrote a letter the second
time to them, saying, If ye *be* mine, and
if ye will hearken unto my voice, take
ye the heads of the men your master's
sons, and come to me to Jezreel by to
morrow this time. Now the king's sons,
being seventy persons, *were* with the
great men of the city, which brought
them up.
7And it came to pass, when the letter came to them, that they took the
king's sons, and slew seventy persons,
and put their heads in baskets, and sent
him *them* to Jezreel.
¶8And there came a messenger, and
told him, saying, They have brought the
heads of the king's sons. And he said,
Lay ye them in two heaps at the entering in of the gate until the morning.
9And it came to pass in the morning,
that he went out, and stood, and said to
all the people, Ye *be* righteous: behold,
I conspired against my master, and slew
him: but who slew all these?
10Know now that there shall fall unto
the earth nothing of the word of the
LORD, which the LORD spake concerning the house of Ahab: for the LORD
hath done *that* which he spake by his
servant Elijah.
11So Jehu slew all that remained of
the house of Ahab in Jezreel, and all his
great men, and his kinsfolks, and his
priests, until he left him none remaining.

Jehu slays the princes of Judah
(2 Chron. 22:8)

¶12And he arose and departed, and
came to Samaria. *And* as he *was* at the
shearing house in the way,
13Jehu met with the brethren of Ahaziah king of Judah, and said, Who *are* ye?
And they answered, We *are* the brethren of Ahaziah; and we go down to salute the children of the king and the
children of the queen.
14And he said, Take them alive. And
they took them alive, and slew them at
the pit of the shearing house, *even* two
and forty men; neither left he any of
them.
¶15And when he was departed
thence, he lighted on Jehonadab the son
of Rechab *coming* to meet him: and he
saluted him, and said to him, Is thine
heart right, as my heart *is* with thy
heart? And Jehonadab answered, It is.
If it be, give *me* thine hand. And he gave
him his hand; and he took him up to him
into the chariot.
16And he said, Come with me, and
see my zeal for the LORD. So they made
him ride in his chariot.
17And when he came to Samaria, he
slew all that remained unto Ahab in
Samaria, till he had destroyed him, according to the saying of the LORD,
which he spake to Elijah.
¶18And Jehu gathered all the people
together, and said unto them, Ahab
served *Baal a little; *but* Jehu shall
serve him much.

Jehu exterminates Baal worship in Israel

19Now therefore call unto me all the
prophets of Baal, all his servants, and
all his priests; let none be wanting: for

10:7 slew seventy persons. See the prophecy in 1 Kings 21:21.
10:9 I conspired. See 2 Kings 9:14,24.
10:10 the word of the LORD, which the LORD spake. Read 1 Kings 21:19-24.
10:15 Jehonadab. This man is called "Jonadab" in Jeremiah 35:6,8,10,14,16,18-19.
10:17 LORD, which he spake to Elijah. Read 1 Kings 21:21.

I have a great sacrifice *to do* to Baal;
whosoever shall be wanting, he shall
not live. But Jehu did *it* in subtilty, to the
intent that he might destroy the worshippers of Baal.
20 And Jehu said, Proclaim a solemn
assembly for Baal. And they proclaimed *it.*
21 And Jehu sent through all Israel:
and all the worshippers of Baal came,
so that there was not a man left that
came not. And they came into the house
of Baal; and the house of Baal was full
from one end to another.
22 And he said unto him that *was* over
the vestry, Bring forth vestments for all
the worshippers of Baal. And he
brought them forth vestments.

10:22 The Vestment
It was and still is customary for every Jew when entering the synagogue for religious worship, to put on the tallith or scarf of white lamb's wool with blue stripes and fringes at each end. This was worn over the shoulders, except during prayers, when it covered the head. It marked the worshipper as being a true Israelite. It was perhaps some similar vestment which Jehu ordered "him that was over the vestry" to supply to each worshipper of Baal, the acceptance of which was proof that they were a true Baalite.

23 And Jehu went, and Jehonadab the
son of Rechab, into the house of Baal,
and said unto the worshippers of Baal,
Search, and look that there be here with
you none of the servants of the LORD,
but the worshippers of Baal only.
24 And when they went in to offer sacrifices and burnt-offerings, Jehu appointed fourscore men without, and
said, *If* any of the men whom I have
brought into your hands escape, *he that*
letteth him go, his life *shall be* for the life
of him.
25 And it came to pass, as soon as he
had made an end of offering the burnt-
offering, that Jehu said to the guard and
to the captains, Go in, *and* slay them;
let none come forth. And they smote
them with the edge of the sword; and
the guard and the captains cast *them*
out, and went to the city of the house
of Baal.
26 And they brought forth the images
out of the house of Baal, and burned
them.
27 And they brake down the image of
Baal, and brake down the house of Baal,
and made it a draught house unto this
day.
28 Thus Jehu destroyed Baal out of
Israel.

End of Jehu's reign

¶29 Howbeit *from* the sins of Jeroboam the son of Nebat, who made Israel
to *sin, Jehu departed not from after
them, *to wit,* the golden calves that *were*
in *Beth-el, and that *were* in Dan.
30 And the LORD said unto Jehu, Because thou hast done well in executing
that which is right in mine eyes, *and*
hast done unto the house of Ahab according to all that *was* in mine heart, thy
children of the fourth *generation* shall
sit on the throne of Israel.
31 But Jehu took no heed to walk in the
law of the LORD God of Israel with all his
heart: for he departed not from the sins
of Jeroboam, which made Israel to sin.
¶32 In those days the LORD began to
cut Israel short: and Hazael smote them
in all the coasts of Israel;
33 From Jordan eastward, all the land
of *Gilead, the Gadites, and the Reu-

10:27 brake down the house of Baal. See Daniel 3:29.
10:27 draught house. A dunghill or common sewer of the city. This was done so that the remembrance of the house of Baal might be made detestable forever.
10:29 golden calves. Read 1 Kings 12:28-29.
10:30 thy children. See 2 Kings 10:35; 13:1,10; 14:23; 15:8,12.
10:32 to cut Israel short. Diminished power always results from sin.
10:33 Gadites. A tribe of people descending from Gad, the seventh son of Jacob (Gen. 30:11).

benites, and the Manassites, from Aroer, which *is* by the river Arnon, even
Gilead and *Bashan.
34Now the rest of the acts of Jehu, and
all that he did, and all his might, *are* they
not written in the book of the chronicles of the kings of Israel?
35And Jehu slept with his fathers: and
they buried him in Samaria. And Jehoahaz his son reigned in his stead.
36And the time that Jehu reigned over
Israel in Samaria *was* twenty and eight
years.

Reign of Queen Athaliah in Judah
Athaliah attempts to end the royal line
(2 Chron. 22:10-12)

11 And when Athaliah the mother of Ahaziah saw that her son
was dead, she arose and destroyed all
the seed royal.
2But Jehosheba, the daughter of king
Joram, sister of Ahaziah, took Joash the
son of Ahaziah and stole him from
among the king's sons *which were* slain;
and they hid him, *even* him and his
nurse, in the bedchamber from Athaliah, so that he was not slain.

> **11:2 A Place to Hide**
> A "bedchamber" was not a sleeping room; if it were, Joash and his nurse might easily have been discovered. Rather, it was the storeroom in which the bedding was kept. No one would have been suspected of occupying that room. The storeroom would be only a temporary hiding place. Joash was therefore removed to one of the rooms in the temple (vs. 3).

3And he was with her hid in the house
of the LORD six years. And Athaliah did
reign over the land.

Joash made king
(2 Chron. 23:1-11)

¶4And the seventh year *Jehoiada
sent and fetched the rulers over hundreds, with the captains and the guard,
and brought them to him into the house
of the LORD, and made a covenant with
them, and took an oath of them in the
house of the LORD, and shewed them
the king's son.
5And he commanded them, saying,
This *is* the thing that ye shall do; A third
part of you that enter in on the *sabbath
shall even be keepers of the watch of
the king's house;
6And a third part *shall be* at the gate
of Sur; and a third part at the gate behind the guard: so shall ye keep the
watch of the house, that it be not broken down.
7And two parts of all you that go forth
on the sabbath, even they shall keep the
watch of the house of the LORD about
the king.
8And ye shall compass the king round
about, every man with his weapons in
his hand: and he that cometh within the
ranges, let him be slain: and be ye with
the king as he goeth out and as he
cometh in.
9And the captains over the hundreds
did according to all *things* that Jehoiada
the priest commanded: and they took
every man his men that were to come
in on the sabbath, with them that should
go out on the sabbath, and came to Jehoiada the priest.
10And to the captains over hundreds
did the priest give king David's spears
and shields, that *were* in the temple of
the LORD.
11And the guard stood, every man

10:33 Reubenites. Descendants of Reuben, the oldest son of Jacob and Leah (Gen. 29:32).
10:33 Manassites. Descendants of Manasseh, the elder of Joseph's two sons born in Egypt (Gen. 41:51).
11:2 Joash. This name means *strong is Jehovah.* He is also called "Jehoash" (vs. 21; 2 Kings 12:1-2, etc.).
11:4 Jehoiada. We know from verse 9 that Jehoiada was the high priest of the temple.
11:5 the king's house. This refers to that part of the temple that Joash occupied.
11:8 ranges. Ranks of soldiers.

with his weapons in his hand, round
about the king, from the right corner of
the temple to the left corner of the temple, *along* by the *altar and the temple.
12And he brought forth the king's
son, and put the crown upon him, and
gave him the testimony; and they made
him king, and anointed him; and they
clapped their hands, and said, God save
the king.

11:12 A Special Presentation
The people presented Joash with the Book of the Law (Exod. 25:21; 16:34) as the rule of his personal conduct and as the basis of his governmental rule. The custom of presenting a copy of the Bible to English kings at the coronation ceremony in Westminster Abbey is taken from this passage, as is the phrase used in the British Empire: "God save the king."

Athaliah is killed
(2 Chron. 23:12-15)

¶13And when Athaliah heard the
noise of the guard *and* of the people,
she came to the people into the temple
of the LORD.
14And when she looked, behold, the
king stood by a pillar, as the manner
was, and the princes and the trumpeters by the king, and all the people of the
land rejoiced, and blew with trumpets:
and Athaliah rent her clothes, and cried,
Treason, Treason.
15But Jehoiada the priest commanded the captains of the hundreds, the
officers of the host, and said unto them,
Have her forth without the ranges: and
him that followeth her kill with the
sword. For the priest had said, Let her
not be slain in the house of the LORD.
16And they laid hands on her; and she
went by the way by the which the
horses came into the king's house: and
there was she slain.

The revival led by Jehoiada
(2 Chron. 23:16-21)

¶17And Jehoiada made a covenant between the LORD and the king and the
people that they should be the LORD'S
people; between the king also and the
people.
18And all the people of the land went
into the house of Baal, and brake it
down; his altars and his images brake
they in pieces thoroughly, and slew
Mattan the priest of Baal before the altars. And the priest appointed officers
over the house of the LORD.
19And he took the rulers over hundreds, and the captains, and the guard,
and all the people of the land; and they
brought down the king from the house
of the LORD, and came by the way of the
gate of the guard to the king's house.
And he sat on the throne of the kings.
20And all the people of the land rejoiced, and the city was in quiet: and
they slew Athaliah with the sword *be-*
side the king's house.
21Seven years old *was* Jehoash when
he began to reign.

Reign of Joash
(2 Chron. 24)

12 In the seventh year of Jehu Jehoash began to reign; and forty
years reigned he in Jerusalem. And his
mother's name *was* Zibiah of *Beer-
sheba.
2And Jehoash did *that which was* right
in the sight of the LORD all his days
wherein Jehoiada the priest instructed
him.

11:14 pillar. This was probably one of the two pillars of the temple mentioned in 1 Kings 7:21, and called Jachin and Boaz (see the notes on that verse). These pillars could doubtless be seen by all in the court of the temple (read 2 Kings 23:3).
11:16 they laid hands on her. This may mean that the soldiers protected Athaliah from the anger of the people. She was put to death justly.
11:20 slew Athaliah. The wicked house of Ahab came to an end with the death of Athaliah. The royal line of David was once again established upon the throne with the accession of Joash.

3 But the *high places were not taken away: the people still sacrificed and burnt *incense in the high places.

The temple repaired
(2 Chron. 24: 4-14)

¶4 And Jehoash said to the priests, All the money of the dedicated things that is brought into the house of the LORD, *even* the money of every one that passeth *the account,* the money that every man is set at, *and* all the money that cometh into any man's heart to bring into the house of the LORD,

5 Let the priests take *it* to them, every man of his acquaintance: and let them repair the breaches of the house, wheresoever any breach shall be found.

6 But it was *so, that* in the three and twentieth year of king Jehoash the priests had not repaired the breaches of the house.

7 Then king Jehoash called for Jehoiada the priest, and the *other* priests, and said unto them, Why repair ye not the breaches of the house? now therefore receive no *more* money of your acquaintance, but deliver it for the breaches of the house.

8 And the priests consented to receive no *more* money of the people, neither to repair the breaches of the house.

9 But Jehoiada the priest took a chest, and bored a hole in the lid of it, and set it beside the altar, on the right side as one cometh into the house of the LORD: and the priests that kept the door put therein all the money *that was* brought into the house of the LORD.

10 And it was *so,* when they saw that *there was* much money in the chest, that the king's *scribe and the high priest came up, and they put up in bags, and told the money that was found in the house of the LORD.

11 And they gave the money, being told, into the hands of them that did the work, that had the oversight of the house of the LORD: and they laid it out to the carpenters and builders, that wrought upon the house of the LORD,

12 And to masons, and hewers of stone, and to buy timber and hewed stone to repair the breaches of the house of the LORD, and for all that was laid out for the house to repair *it.*

13 Howbeit there were not made for the house of the LORD bowls of *silver, snuffers, basons, trumpets, any vessels of gold, or vessels of silver, of the money *that* was brought into the house of the LORD:

14 But they gave that to the workmen, and repaired therewith the house of the LORD.

15 Moreover they reckoned not with the men, into whose hand they delivered the money to be bestowed on workmen: for they dealt faithfully.

16 The trespass money and sin money was not brought into the house of the LORD: it was the priests'.

The temple treasures given to the King of Syria

¶17 Then *Hazael king of Syria went up, and fought against *Gath, and took it: and Hazael set his face to go up to Jerusalem.

18 And Jehoash king of Judah took all the hallowed things that Jehoshaphat, and Jehoram, and Ahaziah, his fathers,

---

12:4 the money that every man is set at. This refers to the redemption price of a person who had devoted himself or his property to the LORD and wished to redeem himself or his property (see Lev. 27:1-8).
12:10 told. Means *counted;* also in verse 11.
12:13 snuffers. These were instruments used in putting out the flames of candles and lamps.
12:15 reckoned not. The honesty of these men made it unnecessary to keep an account of the money given them to pay the workmen.
12:16 trespass money and sin money. See Leviticus 5:15,18 for the explanation of this.
12:16 it was the priests'. Leviticus 7:7 and Numbers 18:19 give the law concerning this.

12:17 Gath
Gath was the city in which Goliath the giant lived (1 Sam. 17:4). According to the book of 2 Chronicles, Hazael's coming against Jerusalem was a punishment from the LORD for Joash's unfaithfulness to Him and his cruelty to the prophet Zechariah (read 2 Chron. 24:23-24).

kings of Judah, had dedicated, and his
own hallowed things, and all the gold
that was found in the treasures of the
house of the LORD, and in the king's
house, and sent *it* to Hazael king of Syria: and he went away from Jerusalem.

Joash is slain
(2 Chron. 24:25-27)

¶19 And the rest of the acts of Joash,
and all that he did, *are* they not written
in the book of the chronicles of the
kings of Judah?
20 And his servants arose, and made
a conspiracy, and slew Joash in the
house of *Millo, which goeth down to
Silla.
21 For Jozachar the son of Shimeath,
and Jehozabad the son of Shomer, his
servants, smote him, and he died; and
they buried him with his fathers in the
city of David: and Amaziah his son
reigned in his stead.

IV. Other Kings of Israel and Judah
(13:1—14:29)

13 In the three and twentieth year
of Joash the son of Ahaziah king
of Judah Jehoahaz the son of Jehu began to reign over *Israel in Samaria,
and reigned seventeen years.
2 And he did *that which was* evil in the
sight of the LORD, and followed the sins
of Jeroboam the son of Nebat, which
made Israel to sin; he departed not
therefrom.
¶3 And the anger of the LORD was kindled against Israel, and he delivered
them into the hand of Hazael king of
Syria, and into the hand of *Ben-hadad
the son of Hazael, all *their* days.

13:3 The LORD's Anger
God loves the sinner, but because He is holy, He must forever hate sin. The anger of the LORD is His hatred of sin. The anger of the LORD is sometimes shown in this life, as in this case (see also Judg. 2:14). But a more terrible judgment awaits the unrepentant, who do not turn from their sin, in the world to come (Matt. 3:7; Rom. 2:5; 5:9; Rev. 6:17). That is why Christ, our Saviour, went to the cross to bear the punishment of sin. He invites us to come and put our trust in Him for forgiveness and salvation (John 3:16; 6:37; 2 Cor. 5:21).

4 And Jehoahaz besought the LORD,
and the LORD hearkened unto him: for
he saw the oppression of Israel, because the king of Syria oppressed them.
5 (And the LORD gave Israel a saviour,
so that they went out from under the
hand of the Syrians: and the children of
Israel dwelt in their tents, as beforetime.
6 Nevertheless they departed not
from the sins of the house of Jeroboam,
who made Israel sin, *but* walked
therein: and there remained the grove
also in Samaria.)
7 Neither did he leave of the people to
Jehoahaz but fifty horsemen, and ten

12:21 Jozachar. He is called "Zabad" in 2 Chronicles 24:26.
13:1 to reign over Israel. Until now, 2 Kings has been concerned largely with the history of Judah. Now the record turns primarily to the history of Israel.
13:2 Jeroboam. Jeroboam had the distinction of being the founder of the kingdom of Israel and the man who made Israel sin.
13:5 saviour. The word "saviour" means *deliverer*. When spelled with a small "s," it refers to a human deliverer. When spelled with a capital "S," it refers to the Lord Jesus Christ, our Saviour from sin.
13:6 Samaria. A name sometimes applied to the kingdom of Israel; also, the capital city of the kingdom of Israel; as well as the middle province of Palestine between Galilee and Judaea.

chariots, and ten thousand footmen; for
the king of Syria had destroyed them,
and had made them like the dust by
threshing.

¶[8]Now the rest of the acts of Jehoahaz, and all that he did, and his might,
are they not written in the book of the
chronicles of the kings of Israel?

[9]And Jehoahaz slept with his fathers;
and they buried him in Samaria: and
Joash his son reigned in his stead.

> **13:9 Two Kings Named Joash**
> There are two Joashes in 2 Kings, and it is not always easy to distinguish between them. There is Joash, the king of Judah (chapters 11–12; 13:10), and there is Joash, the king of Israel, mentioned here.

Reign of Jehoash

¶[10]In the thirty and seventh year of
Joash king of Judah began Jehoash the
son of Jehoahaz to reign over Israel in
Samaria, *and reigned* sixteen years.

[11]And he did *that which was* evil in
the sight of the LORD; he departed not
from all the sins of Jeroboam the son of
Nebat, who made Israel sin: *but* he
walked therein.

[12]And the rest of the acts of Joash,
and all that he did, and his might wherewith he fought against Amaziah king of
Judah, *are* they not written in the book
of the chronicles of the kings of Israel?

[13]And Joash slept with his fathers;
and Jeroboam sat upon his throne: and
Joash was buried in Samaria with the
kings of Israel.

¶[14]Now Elisha was fallen sick of his
sickness whereof he died. And Joash
the king of Israel came down unto him,
and wept over his face, and said, O my
father, my father, the chariot of Israel,
and the horsemen thereof.

[15]And Elisha said unto him, Take bow
and arrows. And he took unto him bow
and arrows.

[16]And he said to the king of Israel,
Put thine hand upon the bow. And he
put his hand *upon it:* and Elisha put his
hands upon the king's hands.

[17]And he said, Open the window eastward. And he opened *it.* Then Elisha
said, Shoot. And he shot. And he said,
The arrow of the LORD'S deliverance,
and the arrow of deliverance from Syria: for thou shalt smite the Syrians in
Aphek, till thou have consumed *them.*

> **13:17 A Declaration of War**
> In Elisha's day, war was declared by the shooting of an arrow into the enemy's country. The arrow was shot eastward because the Syrians had settled themselves to the east of Samaria. Elisha put his hands on the bow (vs. 16) to indicate that supernatural power would attend the deeds of the king of Israel.

[18]And he said, Take the arrows. And
he took *them.* And he said unto the king
of Israel, Smite upon the ground. And
he smote thrice, and stayed.

[19]And the man of *God was wroth
with him, and said, Thou shouldest
have smitten five or six times; then
hadst thou smitten Syria till thou hadst
consumed *it:* whereas now thou shalt
smite Syria *but* thrice.

Death of Elisha: the miracle at his tomb

¶[20]And Elisha died, and they buried
him. And the bands of the Moabites

13:10 Jehoash. This is the Joash who is king of Israel.

13:14 Joash the king of Israel came down unto him. Joash's visit took place, of course, between that which is recorded in verses 9 and 12. After giving a brief outline of the history of Israel from the reign of Jehoahaz to Jeroboam, we are taken back to some of the details in the reign of Joash.

13:14 chariot of Israel. This implies that the man of God had been the secret of Israel's strength and conquests by his counsel and prayers.

13:18 Smite upon the ground. This stood for the conquering of the enemy.

13:19 wroth. Elisha was exasperated at Joash's small faith and lack of persistence.

13:19 but thrice. See verse 25.

invaded the land at the coming in of the
year.
21And it came to pass, as they were
burying a man, that, behold, they spied
a band *of men;* and they cast the man
into the sepulchre of Elisha: and when
the man was let down, and touched the
bones of Elisha, he revived, and stood
up on his feet.
¶22But Hazael king of Syria oppressed Israel all the days of Jehoahaz.
23And the LORD was gracious unto
them, and had compassion on them, and
had respect unto them, because of his
covenant with *Abraham, *Isaac, and
*Jacob, and would not destroy them,
neither cast he them from his presence
as yet.
24So Hazael king of Syria died; and
Ben-hadad his son reigned in his stead.
25And Jehoash the son of Jehoahaz
took again out of the hand of Ben-hadad
the son of Hazael the cities, which he
had taken out of the hand of Jehoahaz
his father by war. Three times did Joash beat him, and recovered the cities
of Israel.

Reign of Amaziah over Judah
(2 Chron. 25)

14 In the second year of Joash
son of Jehoahaz king of Israel
reigned Amaziah the son of Joash king
of *Judah.
2He was twenty and five years old
when he began to reign, and reigned
twenty and nine years in *Jerusalem.
And his mother's name *was* Jehoaddan
of Jerusalem.
3And he did *that which was* right in
the sight of the LORD, yet not like *David his father: he did according to all
things as Joash his father did.
4Howbeit the high places were not tak-
en away: as yet the people did *sacrifice
and burnt incense on the high places.
¶5And it came to pass, as soon as the
kingdom was confirmed in his hand,
that he slew his servants which had
slain the king his father.
6But the children of the murderers he
slew not: according unto that which is
written in the *book of the law of Moses, wherein the LORD commanded,
saying, The fathers shall not be put to
death for the children, nor the children
be put to death for the fathers; but
every man shall be put to death for his
own sin.
7He slew of *Edom in the *valley of
salt ten thousand, and took Selah by
war, and called the name of it Joktheel
unto this day.
¶8Then Amaziah sent messengers to
Jehoash, the son of Jehoahaz son of
Jehu, king of Israel, saying, Come, let
us look one another in the face.

Israel and Judah at war

9And Jehoash the king of Israel sent
to Amaziah king of Judah, saying, The
thistle that *was* in *Lebanon sent to the
cedar that *was* in Lebanon, saying, Give
thy daughter to my son to wife: and

13:23 his covenant with Abraham. See Genesis 12:1-3; Exodus 32:13.

13:23 as yet. These are very solemn words that are a warning of what is to come.

14:3 not like David. See 2 Chronicles 25:2 ("not with a perfect heart"). Amaziah gave outward obedience to the law of God but lacked the inner devotion of the heart.

14:5 slew his servants. It was a Mosaic Law that a son should avenge his father's murder. Notice the New Testament teaching (Matt. 5:38-39; Rom. 12:19).

14:6 slew not. The Law showed the responsibility of each individual for his own sin (see Deut. 24:16).

14:7 took Selah. This is a place known today as Petra, still visited by travelers because of its rock formation and famous ruins.

14:7 Joktheel. This means *given by God.*

14:8 look one another in the face. To meet in battle (see also in vs. 11).

14:9 The thistle that was in Lebanon. This is an Old Testament *parable. Jehoash represents Amaziah as a mean thistle and himself as a glorious cedar. The army of Israel is pictured as a wild beast.

there passed by a wild beast that *was* in Lebanon, and trode down the thistle.

10 Thou hast indeed smitten Edom, and thine heart hath lifted thee up: glory *of this,* and tarry at home: for why shouldest thou meddle to *thy* hurt, that thou shouldest fall, *even* thou, and Judah with thee?

11 But Amaziah would not hear. Therefore Jehoash king of Israel went up; and he and Amaziah king of Judah looked one another in the face at Beth-shemesh, which *belongeth* to Judah.

12 And Judah was put to the worse before Israel; and they fled every man to their tents.

13 And Jehoash king of Israel took Amaziah king of Judah, the son of Jehoash the son of Ahaziah, at Beth-shemesh, and came to Jerusalem, and brake down the wall of Jerusalem from the gate of Ephraim unto the corner gate, four hundred *cubits.

14 And he took all the gold and silver, and all the vessels that were found in the house of the LORD, and in the treasures of the king's house, and hostages, and returned to Samaria.

¶15 Now the rest of the acts of Jehoash which he did, and his might, and how he fought with Amaziah king of Judah, *are* they not written in the book of the chronicles of the kings of Israel?

Jeroboam becomes King of Israel

16 And Jehoash slept with his fathers, and was buried in Samaria with the kings of Israel; and Jeroboam his son reigned in his stead.

Death of Amaziah
(2 Chron. 25:26-28)

¶17 And Amaziah the son of Joash king of Judah lived after the death of Jehoash son of Jehoahaz king of Israel fifteen years.

18 And the rest of the acts of Amaziah, *are* they not written in the book of the chronicles of the kings of Judah?

19 Now they made a conspiracy against him in Jerusalem: and he fled to Lachish; but they sent after him to Lachish, and slew him there.

20 And they brought him on horses: and he was buried at Jerusalem with his fathers in the city of David.

Azariah becomes King of Judah

¶21 And all the people of Judah took Azariah, which *was* sixteen years old, and made him king instead of his father Amaziah.

22 He built Elath, and restored it to Judah, after that the king slept with his fathers.

Reign of Jeroboam II over Israel

¶23 In the fifteenth year of Amaziah the son of Joash king of Judah Jeroboam the son of Joash king of Israel began to reign in Samaria, *and reigned* forty and one years.

24 And he did *that which was* evil in the sight of the LORD: he departed not from all the sins of Jeroboam the son of Nebat, who made Israel to sin.

25 He restored the coast of Israel from the entering of Hamath unto the *sea of the plain, according to the word of the LORD God of Israel, which he spake by the hand of his servant Jonah, the son of Amittai, the prophet, which *was* of Gath-hepher.

26 For the LORD saw the affliction of Israel, *that it was* very bitter: for *there was* not any shut up, nor any left, nor any helper for Israel.

27 And the LORD said not that he

14:19 Lachish. The name means *invincible*. It was a royal city of the Amorites, captured by Joshua and made a part of Judah (Josh. 10:32; 15:39).

14:21 Azariah. He is called "Uzziah" in 2 Chronicles 26:1 and Isaiah 1:1.

14:22 Elath. A valuable seaport (see 1 Kings 9:26).

14:25 Hamath. This means *fortress*. It was a city of Syria often mentioned as the northern boundary of Palestine.

would blot out the name of Israel from
under *heaven: but he saved them
by the hand of Jeroboam the son of
Joash.
¶ 28 Now the rest of the acts of Jeroboam, and all that he did, and his might,
how he warred, and how he recovered
*Damascus, and Hamath, *which be-
longed* to Judah, for Israel, *are* they not
written in the book of the chronicles of
the kings of Israel?
29 And Jeroboam slept with his fathers, *even* with the kings of Israel; and
Zachariah his son reigned in his stead.

V. The Fall of Israel (15:1—17:41)
Reign of Azariah over Judah
(2 Chron. 26:1-3)

15 In the twenty and seventh year
of Jeroboam king of Israel began
Azariah son of Amaziah king of Judah to
reign.
2 Sixteen years old was he when he
began to reign, and he reigned two and
fifty years in Jerusalem. And his
mother's name *was* Jecholiah of Jerusalem.
3 And he did *that which was* right in
the sight of the LORD, according to all
that his father Amaziah had done;
4 Save that the high places were not
removed: the people sacrificed and
burnt incense still on the high places.
¶ 5 And the LORD smote the king, so
that he was a *leper unto the day of
his death, and dwelt in a several house.
And Jotham the king's son *was* over
the house, judging the people of the
land.
6 And the rest of the acts of Azariah,
and all that he did, *are* they not written
in the book of the chronicles of the
kings of Judah?
7 So Azariah slept with his fathers;
and they buried him with his fathers in
the city of David: and Jotham his son
reigned in his stead.

Reign of Zachariah over Israel

¶ 8 In the thirty and eighth year of Azariah king of Judah did Zachariah the
son of Jeroboam reign over Israel in Samaria six months.
9 And he did *that which was* evil in the
sight of the LORD, as his fathers had
done: he departed not from the sins of
Jeroboam the son of Nebat, who made
Israel to sin.
10 And Shallum the son of Jabesh conspired against him, and smote him before the people, and slew him, and
reigned in his stead.
11 And the rest of the acts of
Zachariah, behold, they *are* written in
the book of the chronicles of the kings
of Israel.
12 This *was* the word of the LORD
which he spake unto Jehu, saying, Thy
sons shall sit on the throne of Israel
unto the fourth *generation.* And so it
came to pass.

Reign of Shallum over Israel

¶ 13 Shallum the son of Jabesh began
to reign in the nine and thirtieth year
of Uzziah king of Judah; and he reigned
a full month in Samaria.
14 For Menahem the son of Gadi went
up from Tirzah, and came to Samaria,
and smote Shallum the son of Jabesh in

15:5 the LORD smote the king. In 2 Chronicles 26:16-21 the reason for God's smiting Azariah with leprosy is more fully given and should be read.

15:5 a several house. That is, a *separate* house. According to the Law (Lev. 13:46), lepers were required to live apart from other people so others would not be infected since leprosy was contagious.

15:10 smote him before the people. The prophet Amos had foretold this (Amos 7:9).

15:12 Thy sons . . . unto the fourth generation. These words were spoken to Jehu in 2 Kings 10:30.

15:13 Uzziah. Uzziah is another form of Azariah (vs. 1).

15:14 Tirzah. This name means *delight.* It was the capital of the kingdom of Israel from the time of Jeroboam until the reign of Omri.

Samaria, and slew him, and reigned in
his stead.
15 And the rest of the acts of Shallum,
and his conspiracy which he made, behold, they *are* written in the book of the
chronicles of the kings of Israel.

Reign of Menahem over Israel

¶16 Then Menahem smote Tiphsah,
and all that *were* therein, and the coasts
thereof from Tirzah: because they
opened not *to him,* therefore he smote
it; and all the women therein that were
with child he ripped up.
17 In the nine and thirtieth year of
Azariah king of Judah began Menahem
the son of Gadi to reign over Israel, *and*
reigned ten years in Samaria.
18 And he did *that which was* evil in
the sight of the LORD: he departed not
all his days from the sins of Jeroboam
the son of Nebat, who made Israel to
sin.
19 *And* Pul the king of Assyria came
against the land: and Menahem gave
Pul a thousand talents of silver, that his
hand might be with him to confirm the
kingdom in his hand.
20 And Menahem exacted the money
of Israel, *even* of all the mighty men of
wealth, of each man fifty shekels of silver, to give to the king of Assyria. So
the king of Assyria turned back, and
stayed not there in the land.
¶21 And the rest of the acts of Menahem, and all that he did, *are* they not
written in the book of the chronicles of
the kings of Israel?

Reign of Pekahiah over Israel

22 And Menahem slept with his fathers; and Pekahiah his son reigned in
his stead.
¶23 In the fiftieth year of Azariah king
of Judah Pekahiah the son of Menahem
began to reign over Israel in Samaria,
and reigned two years.
24 And he did *that which was* evil in
the sight of the LORD: he departed not
from the sins of Jeroboam the son of
Nebat, who made Israel to sin.
25 But Pekah the son of Remaliah, a
captain of his, conspired against him,
and smote him in Samaria, in the palace of the king's house, with Argob
and Arieh, and with him fifty men of the
Gileadites: and he killed him, and
reigned in his room.
26 And the rest of the acts of Pekahiah, and all that he did, behold, they *are*
written in the book of the chronicles of
the kings of Israel.

Reign of Pekah over Israel

¶27 In the two and fiftieth year of Azariah king of Judah Pekah the son of
Remaliah began to reign over Israel in
Samaria, *and reigned* twenty years.
28 And he did *that which was* evil in
the sight of the LORD: he departed not
from the sins of Jeroboam the son of
Nebat, who made Israel to sin.
29 In the days of Pekah king of Israel
came Tiglath-pileser king of Assyria,
and took Ijon, and Abel-beth-maachah,
and Janoah, and Kedesh, and Hazor, and
Gilead, and Galilee, all the land of
Naphtali, and carried them captive to
Assyria.
30 And Hoshea the son of Elah made
a conspiracy against Pekah the son of
Remaliah, and smote him, and slew
him, and reigned in his stead, in the
twentieth year of Jotham the son of
Uzziah.
31 And the rest of the acts of Pekah,

15:25 Gileadites. A family of the Israelites, descended from the grandson of Manasseh.
15:25 in his room. In his place.
15:29 Tiglath-pileser. Pul (2 Kings 15:19) and Tiglath-pileser are different names for the same king. He was probably Tiglath-pileser III, one of the greatest of the Assyrian kings.
15:29 Kedesh. One of the *cities of refuge. See Joshua 20:7.
15:29 Galilee. The most northern of the three divisions of Palestine.
15:30 Hoshea. This name means *help*. Hoshea was the last king of Israel.
15:30 smote him, and slew him. See Hosea 10:3,7,15.

and all that he did, behold, they *are* written in the book of the chronicles of the kings of Israel.

Reign of Jotham over Judah
(2 Chron. 26:23; 27)

¶ 32 In the second year of Pekah the son of Remaliah king of Israel began Jotham the son of Uzziah king of Judah to reign.

33 Five and twenty years old was he when he began to reign, and he reigned sixteen years in Jerusalem. And his mother's name *was* Jerusha, the daughter of Zadok.

34 And he did *that which was* right in the sight of the LORD: he did according to all that his father Uzziah had done.

¶ 35 Howbeit the high places were not removed: the people sacrificed and burned incense still in the high places. He built the higher gate of the house of the LORD.

¶ 36 Now the rest of the acts of Jotham, and all that he did, *are* they not written in the book of the chronicles of the kings of Judah?

37 In those days the LORD began to send against Judah *Rezin the king of Syria, and Pekah the son of Remaliah.

38 And Jotham slept with his fathers, and was buried with his fathers in the city of David his father: and Ahaz his son reigned in his stead.

Reign of Ahaz over Judah
(2 Chron. 28)

16 In the seventeenth year of Pekah the son of Remaliah Ahaz the son of Jotham king of Judah began to reign.

2 Twenty years old *was* Ahaz when he began to reign, and reigned sixteen years in Jerusalem, and did not *that which was* right in the sight of the LORD his God, like David his father.

3 But he walked in the way of the kings of Israel, yea, and made his son to pass through the fire, according to the abominations of the heathen, whom the LORD cast out from before the children of Israel.

16:3 The Worship of Molech
This was one of the features of the worship of *Molech. It may mean either that his son passed between two fires as an act of dedication to the pagan god, or that his son actually passed through the flame of a fire as a human sacrifice to the pagan god. This ceremony was forbidden to the children of Israel (Lev. 18:21; 20:1-5).

4 And he sacrificed and burnt incense in the high places, and on the hills, and under every green tree.

Invasion of Judah by Syria and Israel
(2 Chron. 28:5-8)

¶ 5 Then Rezin king of Syria and Pekah son of Remaliah king of Israel came up to Jerusalem to war: and they besieged Ahaz, but could not overcome *him*.

6 At that time Rezin king of Syria recovered Elath to Syria, and drave the Jews from Elath: and the Syrians came to Elath, and dwelt there unto this day.

The Assyrians aid Judah
(2 Chron. 28:16-21)

7 So Ahaz sent messengers to Tiglath-pileser king of Assyria, saying, I *am* thy servant and thy son: come up, and save me out of the hand of the king of Syria, and out of the hand of the king of Israel, which rise up against me.

8 And Ahaz took the silver and gold

15:35 the higher gate. The northern side of the temple was the highest side, because the temple was built on a slope. The gate on this northern side is meant here.

16:3 according to the abominations of the heathen. Read Deuteronomy 12:31.

16:4 under every green tree. This is one of the things expressly mentioned as among the wrongdoings of the heathen (Deut. 12:2).

16:7 Ahaz sent messengers. Ahaz sought help from the king of Assyria in the face of the most urgent warnings from the prophet Isaiah and assurances of divine help (Isa. 8:4).

that was found in the house of the LORD, and in the treasures of the king's house, and sent *it for* a present to the king of Assyria.

9 And the king of Assyria hearkened unto him: for the king of Assyria went up against Damascus, and took it, and carried *the people of* it captive to Kir, and slew Rezin.

¶ 10 And king Ahaz went to Damascus to meet Tiglath-pileser king of Assyria, and saw an altar that *was* at Damascus: and king Ahaz sent to Urijah the priest the fashion of the altar, and the pattern of it, according to all the workmanship thereof.

16:10 A Heathen Altar
This heathen altar was to replace the altar that had been designed according to the explicit direction of God (see vs. 15). It is to the shame of Urijah, the priest, that he raised no protest.

11 And Urijah the priest built an altar according to all that king Ahaz had sent from Damascus: so Urijah the priest made *it* against king Ahaz came from Damascus.

12 And when the king was come from Damascus, the king saw the altar: and the king approached to the altar, and offered thereon.

13 and he burnt his burnt-offering and his meat-offering, and poured his drink-offering, and sprinkled the *blood of his peace-offerings, upon the altar.

14 And he brought also the brasen altar, which *was* before the LORD, from the forefront of the house, from between the altar and the house of the LORD, and put it on the north side of the altar.

15 And king Ahaz commanded Urijah the priest, saying, Upon the great altar burn the morning burnt-offering, and the evening meat-offering, and the king's burnt-sacrifice, and his meat-offering, with the burnt-offering of all the people of the land, and their meat-offering, and their drink-offerings; and sprinkle upon it all the blood of the burnt-offering, and all the blood of the sacrifice: and the brasen altar shall be for me to enquire *by*.

16 Thus did Urijah the priest, according to all that king Ahaz commanded.

¶ 17 And king Ahaz cut off the borders of the bases, and removed the *laver from off them; and took down the sea from off the brasen oxen that *were* under it, and put it upon a pavement of stones.

18 And the covert for the sabbath that they had built in the house, and the king's entry without, turned he from the house of the LORD for the king of Assyria.

End of the reign of Ahaz

¶ 19 Now the rest of the acts of Ahaz which he did, *are* they not written in the book of the chronicles of the kings of Judah?

20 And Ahaz slept with his fathers, and was buried with his fathers in the city of David: and Hezekiah his son reigned in his stead.

Reign of Hoshea over Israel

17 In the twelfth year of Ahaz king of Judah began Hoshea the son

16:11 against king Ahaz came. This means made it *before* King Ahaz came.
16:15 for me to enquire by. This would seem to mean Ahaz wanted to enquire of the LORD. But the context of verses 9-15 indicates Ahaz was copying the altar of the Assyrians (v. 10). He was not interested in pleasing God, but wanted to "enquire" of the gods of Assyria since he turned "from the house of the LORD" (v. 18).
16:18 covert. This refers to a covered place used on the Sabbath by the king and his attendants.
16:20 Hezekiah. This name means *a strong support is Jehovah*. In accordance with his name, Hezekiah rid the nation of idolatry, restored the true worship of God, and declared his kingdom independent of Assyria.

of Elah to reign in Samaria over Israel
nine years.
2 And he did *that which was* evil in the
sight of the LORD, but not as the kings
of Israel that were before him.

Israel becomes tributary to Assyria

¶3 Against him came up Shalmaneser
king of Assyria; and Hoshea became his
servant, and gave him presents.

Israel carried captive into Assyria

4 And the king of Assyria found conspiracy in Hoshea: for he had sent messengers to So king of *Egypt, and
brought no present to the king of Assyria, as *he had done* year by year:
therefore the king of Assyria shut him
up, and bound him in prison.
¶5 Then the king of Assyria came up
throughout all the land, and went up to
Samaria, and besieged it three years.
¶6 In the ninth year of Hoshea the king
of Assyria took Samaria, and carried Israel away into Assyria, and placed them
in Halah and in Habor *by* the river of
Gozan, and in the cities of the Medes.

Sins of Israel which led to captivity

7 For *so* it was, that the children of
Israel had sinned against the LORD their
God, which had brought them up out of
the land of Egypt, from under the hand
of *Pharaoh king of Egypt, and had
feared other gods,
8 And walked in the statutes of the
heathen, whom the LORD cast out from
before the children of Israel, and of the
kings of Israel, which they had made.
9 And the children of Israel did secretly *those* things that *were* not right
against the LORD their God, and they
built them high places in all their cities,
from the tower of the watchmen to the
fenced city.
10 And they set them up images and
groves in every high hill, and under
every green tree:
11 And there they burnt incense in all
the high places, as *did* the heathen
whom the LORD carried away before
them; and wrought wicked things to
provoke the LORD to anger:
12 For they served idols, whereof the
LORD had said unto them, Ye shall not
do this thing.
13 Yet the LORD testified against Israel, and against Judah, by all the prophets, *and by* all the seers, saying, Turn
ye from your evil ways, and keep my
commandments *and* my statutes, according to all the law which I commanded your fathers, and which I sent to you
by my servants the prophets.
14 Notwithstanding they would not
hear, but hardened their necks, like to
the neck of their fathers, that did not
believe in the LORD their God.
15 And they rejected his statutes, and
his *covenant that he made with their
fathers, and his testimonies which he
testified against them; and they followed *vanity, and became vain, and
went after the heathen that *were* round
about them, *concerning* whom the LORD
had charged them, that they should not
do like them.

17:7 Israel's Sin
Read Deuteronomy 28:15-68. The ten tribes have never been restored to Palestine from this captivity. A small part of Judah returned under Zerubbabel, Ezra, and Nehemiah, and individuals out of the ten tribes went back, but the nation as a whole has never been restored to its land. This will be done in a day to come (Deut. 30:1-9; 2 Sam. 7:8-17).

17:3 Shalmaneser. The successor to Tiglath-pileser (2 Kings 15:29).
17:6 Halah. This was a district of the Assyrian empire in Mesopotamia.
17:9 from the tower of the watchmen to the fenced city. This is a way of saying that idolatry was universal among these people. The expression includes every place, from the large city to the small villages.
17:13 prophets. Read Jeremiah 18:11; 25:5; 35:15.
17:14 hardened their necks. A common expression to indicate unbelief.

16 And they left all the commandments of the LORD their God, and made
them molten images, *even* two calves,
and made a grove, and worshipped all
the host of heaven, and served *Baal.
17 And they caused their sons and
their daughters to pass through the fire,
and used divination and enchantments,
and sold themselves to do evil in the
sight of the LORD, to provoke him to
anger.
18 Therefore the LORD was very angry with Israel, and removed them out
of his sight: there was none left but the
tribe of Judah only.

17:18 Israel's Punishment
The Israelites were banished from the land that God had given them, and also from the temple. Thus the kingdom of Israel came to a shameful end. These people had failed in two ways:

1. They had revolted from the tribes of Judah and Benjamin and thus destroyed the unity of God's chosen nation.
2. They had abandoned the worship of God and had substituted idolatry–thus destroying their testimony, the sacred distinction to which God called them.

19 Also Judah kept not the commandments of the LORD their God, but
walked in the statutes of Israel which
they made.
20 And the LORD rejected all the seed
of Israel, and afflicted them, and delivered them into the hand of spoilers,
until he had cast them out of his sight.
21 For he rent Israel from the house
of David; and they made Jeroboam the
son of Nebat king: and Jeroboam drave
Israel from following the LORD, and
made them *sin a great sin.
22 For the children of Israel walked in
all the sins of Jeroboam which he did;
they departed not from them;
23 Until the LORD removed Israel out
of his sight, as he had said by all his
servants the prophets. So was Israel
carried away out of their own land to
Assyria unto this day.

Cities of Israel are repeopled

¶24 And the king of Assyria brought
men from *Babylon, and from Cuthah,
and from Ava, and from Hamath, and
from Sepharvaim, and placed *them*
in the cities of Samaria instead of
the children of Israel: and they possessed Samaria, and dwelt in the cities
thereof.
25 And *so* it was at the beginning of
their dwelling there, *that* they feared
not the LORD: therefore the LORD sent
lions among them, which slew *some* of
them.
26 Wherefore they spake to the king
of Assyria, saying, The nations which
thou hast removed, and placed in the
cities of Samaria, know not the manner
of the God of the land: therefore he hath
sent lions among them, and, behold,
they slay them, because they know not
the manner of the God of the land.
27 Then the king of Assyria commanded, saying, Carry thither one of the
priests whom ye brought from thence;
and let them go and dwell there, and let
him teach them the manner of the God
of the land.
28 Then one of the priests whom they
had carried away from Samaria came
and dwelt in *Beth-el, and taught them
how they should *fear the LORD.
29 Howbeit every nation made gods of
their own, and put *them* in the houses
of the high places which the *Samaritans had made, every nation in their
cities wherein they dwelt.
30 And the men of Babylon made
Succoth-benoth, and the men of Cuth

17:16 worshipped all the host of heaven. The idolatrous worship of the sun, moon, and stars, similar to astrology.

17:17 sold themselves to do evil. This speaks of complete surrender to evil.

17:30 Succoth-benoth. This means *booths of the daughters.* These were tents where evil practices were observed as religious ceremonies.

made Nergal, and the men of Hamath
made Ashima,
31And the Avites made Nibhaz and
Tartak, and the Sepharvites burnt their
children in fire to Adrammelech and
Anammelech, the gods of Sepharvaim.
32So they feared the LORD, and made
unto themselves of the lowest of them
priests of the high places, which sacrificed
for them in the houses of the high places.
33They feared the LORD, and served
their own gods, after the manner of the
nations whom they carried away from
thence.
34Unto this day they do after the former manners: they fear not the LORD,
neither do they after their statutes, or
after their ordinances, or after the law
and commandment which the LORD
commanded the children of Jacob, whom
he named Israel;
35With whom the LORD had made a
covenant, and charged them saying, Ye
shall not fear other gods, nor bow yourselves to them, nor serve them, nor
sacrifice to them:
36But the LORD, who brought you up
out of the land of Egypt with great power and a stretched out arm, him shall ye
fear, and him shall ye worship, and to
him shall ye do sacrifice.
37And the statutes, and the ordinances, and the law, and the commandment, which he wrote for you, ye shall
observe to do for evermore; and ye
shall not fear other gods.
38And the covenant that I have made
with you ye shall not forget; neither
shall ye fear other gods.
39But the LORD your God ye shall
fear; and he shall deliver you out of the
hand of all your enemies.
40Howbeit they did not hearken, but
they did after their former manner.
41So these nations feared the LORD,
and served their graven images, both
their children, and their children's children: as did their fathers, so do they
unto this day.

VI. Hezekiah Rules Judah
(18:1—20:21) (compare 2 Chron. 29)

18 Now it came to pass in the
third year of Hoshea son of Elah
king of Israel, *that* Hezekiah the son of
Ahaz king of Judah began to reign.
2Twenty and five years old was he
when he began to reign; and he reigned
twenty and nine years in Jerusalem. His
mother's name also *was* Abi, the daughter of Zachariah.
3And he did *that which was* right in
the sight of the LORD, according to all
that David his father did.

Revival under Hezekiah
(2 Chron. 29:3—31:21)

¶4He removed the *high places, and
brake the images, and cut down the
groves, and brake in pieces the brasen
serpent that Moses had made: for unto
those days the children of Israel did
burn *incense to it: and he called it
Nehushtan.

17:30 Nergal. The pagan god of war.
17:30 Ashima. A goat idol.
17:31 Nibhaz. An idol thought to be in the form of a dog.
17:31 Tartak. An idol thought to be in the form of a donkey.
17:31 Adrammelech. This corresponded to Molech, the Assyrian sun god.
17:31 Anammelech. An idol in the form of a rabbit.
17:33 They feared the LORD, and served their own gods. This mingled worship could only be an abomination in the sight of the LORD.
18:4 He removed the high places. A fuller account of Hezekiah's sweeping reformation is given in 2 Chronicles 29.
18:4 Nehushtan. This means *a thing of brass.* Read the story of the brazen serpent in Numbers 21:5-9. It was now nearly eight hundred fifty years old.
18:5 trusted. This is the characteristic Old Testament word for "faith" and "believe" as used in the New Testament.

[5]He trusted in the LORD God of Israel; so that after him was none like him among all the kings of Judah, nor *any* that were before him.

[6]For he clave to the LORD, *and* departed not from following him, but kept his commandments, which the LORD commanded Moses.

[7]And the LORD was with him; *and* he prospered whithersoever he went forth: and he rebelled against the king of Assyria, and served him not.

Hezekiah smites the Philistines

[8]He smote the *Philistines, *even* unto *Gaza, and the borders thereof, from the tower of the watchmen to the fenced city.

¶[9]And it came to pass in the fourth year of king Hezekiah, which *was* the seventh year of Hoshea son of Elah king of Israel, *that* Shalmaneser king of Assyria came up against Samaria, and besieged it.

[10]And at the end of three years they took it: *even* in the sixth year of Hezekiah, that *is* the ninth year of Hoshea king of Israel, Samaria was taken.

[11]And the king of Assyria did carry away Israel unto Assyria, and put them in Halah and in Habor *by* the river of Gozan, and in the cities of the Medes:

[12]Because they obeyed not the voice of the LORD their God, but transgressed his covenant, *and* all that Moses the servant of the LORD commanded, and would not hear *them,* nor do *them.*

Sennacherib invades Judah

¶[13]Now in the fourteenth year of king Hezekiah did Sennacherib king of Assyria come up against all the fenced cities of Judah, and took them.

[14]And Hezekiah king of Judah sent to the king of Assyria to *Lachish, saying, I have offended; return from me: that which thou puttest on me will I bear. And the king of Assyria appointed unto Hezekiah king of Judah three hundred talents of silver and thirty talents of gold.

[15]And Hezekiah gave *him* all the silver that was found in the house of the LORD, and in the treasures of the king's house.

[16]At that time did Hezekiah cut off *the gold from* the doors of the temple of the LORD, and *from* the pillars which Hezekiah king of Judah had overlaid, and gave it to the king of Assyria.

¶[17]And the king of Assyria sent Tartan and Rabsaris and Rab-shakeh from Lachish to king Hezekiah with a great host against Jerusalem. And they went up and came to Jerusalem. And when they were come up, they came and stood by the conduit of the upper pool, which *is* in the highway of the fuller's field.

[18]And when they had called to the king, there came out to them Eliakim the son of Hilkiah, which *was* over the household, and Shebna the *scribe, and Joah the son of *Asaph the recorder.

[19]And Rab-shakeh said unto them, Speak ye now to Hezekiah, Thus saith the great king, the king of Assyria, What confidence *is* this wherein thou trustest?

[20]Thou sayest, (but *they are but* vain words,) *I have* counsel and strength for the war. Now on whom dost thou trust, that thou rebellest against me?

[21]Now, behold, thou trustest upon the staff of this bruised reed, *even* upon

---

18:9 in the fourth year of king Hezekiah. Notice the contrast here. At the very same time that Hezekiah, the godly king, was restoring Judah to the true worship of God, the kingdom of Israel, under a wicked and ungodly king, was falling into ruins (read Prov. 14:34).

18:15 Hezekiah gave him. Compare 2 Kings 16:8.

18:17 Tartan. This man was the commander in chief of the Assyrian army.

18:17 the conduit of the upper pool. This was the aqueduct that brought water from the upper reservoir into the city.

18:17 the fuller's field. The place where the men stretched out their clothes to dry.

Egypt, on which if a man lean, it will go
into his hand, and pierce it: so *is* Pharaoh
king of Egypt unto all that trust on him.
22But if ye say unto me, We trust in
the LORD our God: *is* not that he, whose
high places and whose altars Hezekiah
hath taken away, and hath said to Judah
and Jerusalem, Ye shall worship before
this *altar in Jerusalem?
23Now therefore, I pray thee, give
pledges to my lord the king of Assyria,
and I will deliver thee two thousand
horses, if thou be able on thy part to set
riders upon them.
24How then wilt thou turn away the
face of one captain of the least of my
master's servants, and put thy trust on
Egypt for chariots and for horsemen?
25Am I now come up without the
LORD against this place to destroy it?
The LORD said to me, Go up against this
land, and destroy it.
26Then said Eliakim the son of Hilkiah, and Shebna, and Joah, unto Rab-
shakeh, Speak, I pray thee, to thy
servants in the Syrian language; for we
understand *it:* and talk not with us in
the Jews' language in the ears of the
people that *are* on the wall.
27But Rab-shakeh said unto them,
Hath my master sent me to thy master,
and to thee, to speak these words? *hath
he* not *sent me* to the men which sit
on the wall, that they may eat their
own *dung, and drink their own piss
with you.
28Then Rab-shakeh stood and cried
with a loud voice in the Jews' language,
and spake, saying, Hear the word of the
great king, the king of Assyria:
29Thus saith the king, Let not Hezekiah deceive you: for he shall not be
able to deliver you out of his hand:
30Neither let Hezekiah make you
trust in the LORD, saying, The LORD
will surely deliver us, and this city shall
not be delivered into the hand of the
king of Assyria.
31Hearken not to Hezekiah: for thus
saith the king of Assyria, Make *an
agreement* with me by a present, and
come out to me, and *then* eat ye every
man of his own vine, and every one of
his fig *tree, and drink ye every one the
waters of his cistern:
32Until I come and take you away to
a land like your own land, a land of corn
and wine, a land of bread and vineyards, a land of *oil olive and of honey,
that ye may live, and not die: and hearken not unto Hezekiah, when he
persuadeth you, saying, The LORD will
deliver us.
33Hath any of the gods of the nations
delivered at all his land out of the hand
of the king of Assyria?
34Where *are* the gods of Hamath,
and of Arpad? where *are* the gods of
Sepharvaim, Hena, and Ivah? have
they delivered Samaria out of mine
hand?
35Who *are* they among all the gods of
the countries, that have delivered their
country out of mine hand, that the LORD
should deliver Jerusalem out of mine
hand?
36But the people held their peace,
and answered him not a word: for the
king's commandment was, saying, Answer him not.
37Then came Eliakim the son of
Hilkiah, which *was* over the household,
and Shebna the scribe, and Joah the son
of Asaph the recorder, to Hezekiah with
their clothes rent, and told him the
words of Rab-shakeh.

Hezekiah's request of Isaiah

19 And it came to pass, when king
Hezekiah heard *it,* that he rent
his clothes, and covered himself with
sackcloth, and went into the house of
the LORD.
2And he sent Eliakim, which *was*
over the household, and Shebna the
scribe, and the *elders of the priests,

18:32 persuadeth. That is, deceiveth.
19:1 went into the house of the LORD. Read Isaiah 37:1.

covered with sackcloth, to Isaiah the
prophet the son of Amoz.
3And they said unto him, Thus saith
Hezekiah, This day *is* a day of trouble,
and of rebuke, and blasphemy: for the
children are come to the birth, and *there*
is not strength to bring forth.
4It may be the LORD thy *God will
hear all the words of Rab-shakeh, whom
the king of Assyria his master hath sent
to reproach the living God; and will
reprove the words which the LORD
thy God hath heard: wherefore lift
up *thy* *prayer for the *remnant that
are left.
5So the servants of king Hezekiah
came to Isaiah.

Isaiah's answer

¶6And Isaiah said unto them, Thus
shall ye say to your master, Thus saith
the LORD, *Be not afraid of the words
which thou hast heard, with which the
servants of the king of Assyria have
blasphemed me.
7Behold, I will send a blast upon him,
and he shall hear a rumour, and shall
return to his own land; and I will cause
him to fall by the sword in his own land.

Sennacherib defies God

¶8So Rab-shakeh returned, and found
the king of Assyria warring against Libnah: for he had heard that he was departed from Lachish.
9And when he heard say of Tirhakah
king of Ethiopia, Behold, he is come out
to fight against thee: he sent messengers again unto Hezekiah, saying,
10Thus shall ye speak to Hezekiah
king of Judah, saying, Let not thy God
in whom thou trustest deceive thee,
saying, Jerusalem shall not be delivered into the hand of the king of Assyria.
11Behold, thou hast heard what the
kings of Assyria have done to all lands,
by destroying them utterly: and shalt
thou be delivered?
12Have the gods of the nations delivered them which my fathers have
destroyed; *as* Gozan, and Haran, and
Rezeph, and the children of *Eden
which *were* in Thelasar?
13Where *is* the king of Hamath, and
the king of Arpad, and the king of the
city of Sepharvaim, of Hena, and Ivah?

Hezekiah's prayer

¶14And Hezekiah received the letter
of the hand of the messengers, and read
it: and Hezekiah went up into the house
of the LORD, and spread it before the
LORD.
15And Hezekiah prayed before the
LORD, and said, O LORD God of *Israel,
which dwellest *between* the cherubims,
thou art the God, *even* thou alone, of all
the kingdoms of the earth; thou hast
made heaven and earth.
16LORD, bow down thine ear, and
hear: open, LORD, thine eyes, and see:
and hear the words of Sennacherib,
which hath sent him to reproach the living God.
17Of a truth, LORD, the kings of Assyria have destroyed the nations and
their lands,
18And have cast their gods into the
fire: for they *were* no gods, but the work
of men's hands, wood and stone: therefore they have destroyed them.
19Now therefore, O LORD our God,
I beseech thee, save thou us out of his
hand, that all the kingdoms of the earth
may know that thou *art* the LORD God,
even thou only.

Jehovah's answer

¶20Then Isaiah the son of Amoz sent
to Hezekiah, saying, Thus saith the
LORD God of Israel, *That* which thou
hast prayed to me against Sennacherib
king of Assyria I have heard.

19:2 Isaiah the prophet. His name means *Jehovah has saved.* This is his first appearance in the Scriptures.
19:7 blast. See verses 35-37.

21 This *is* the word that the LORD hath
spoken concerning him; The virgin the
daughter of *Zion hath despised thee,
and laughed thee to scorn; the daughter of Jerusalem hath shaken her head
at thee.
22 Whom hast thou reproached and
blasphemed? and against whom hast
thou exalted *thy* voice, and lifted up
thine eyes on high? *even* against the
*Holy *One* of Israel.
23 By the messengers thou hast reproached the Lord, and hast said, With
the multitude of my chariots I am come
up to the height of the mountains, to the
sides of Lebanon, and will cut down the
tall cedar trees thereof, *and* the choice
fir trees thereof: and I will enter into
the lodgings of his borders, *and into* the
forest of his *Carmel.
24 I have digged and drunk strange
waters, and with the sole of my feet
have I dried up all the rivers of besieged
places.
25 Hast thou not heard long ago *how*
I have done it, *and* of ancient times that
I have formed it? now have I brought
it to pass, that thou shouldest be to
lay waste fenced cities *into* ruinous
heaps.
26 Therefore their inhabitants were of
small power, they were dismayed and
confounded; they were *as* the grass of
the field, and *as* the green herb, *as* the
grass on the house tops, and *as corn*
blasted before it be grown up.
27 But I know thy abode, and thy going out, and thy coming in, and thy rage
against me.
28 Because thy rage against me and
thy tumult is come up into mine ears,
therefore I will put my hook in thy nose,
and my bridle in thy lips, and I will turn
thee back by the way by which thou
camest.
29 And this *shall be* a sign unto thee,
Ye shall eat this year such things as
grow of themselves, and in the second
year that which springeth of the same;
and in the third year sow ye, and reap,
and plant vineyards, and eat the fruits
thereof.
30 And the remnant that is escaped of
the house of Judah shall yet again take
root downward, and bear fruit upward.
31 For out of Jerusalem shall go forth
a remnant, and they that escape out of
mount Zion: the zeal of the LORD *of
hosts* shall do this.
32 Therefore thus saith the LORD concerning the king of Assyria, He shall
not come into this city, nor shoot an
arrow there, nor come before it with
shield, nor cast a bank against it.
33 By the way that he came, by the
same shall he return, and shall not
come into this city, saith the LORD.
34 For I will defend this city, to save it,
for mine own sake, and for my servant
David's sake.

Assyrian army destroyed
(2 Chron. 32:21-22)

¶35 And it came to pass that night, that
the *angel of the LORD went out, and
smote in the camp of the Assyrians an
hundred fourscore and five thousand:
and when they arose early in the morning, behold, they *were* all dead corpses.
36 So Sennacherib king of Assyria departed, and went and returned, and
dwelt at Nineveh.
37 And it came to pass, as he was worshipping in the house of Nisroch his
god, that Adrammelech and Sharezer
his sons smote him with the sword: and

19:21 The virgin the daughter of Zion. Even the young women of Jerusalem, with the help of the LORD, would be able to destroy the enemy's power and cause them to return in shameful defeat to their own country.
19:25 Hast thou not heard long ago how I have done it? See Isaiah 10:5,24-27. The verses in Isaiah were written about thirty years earlier than when this was said.
19:29 a sign unto thee. This is addressed to Hezekiah.
19:32 bank. An embankment thrown up for the siege of a city.
19:35 when they arose. When the men of Jerusalem arose.

they escaped into the land of Armenia.
And Esar-haddon his son reigned in his
stead.

Hezekiah's illness and recovery

20 In those days was Hezekiah
sick unto *death. And the
prophet Isaiah the son of Amoz came to
him, and said unto him, Thus saith the
LORD, Set thine house in order; for thou
shalt die, and not live.
2 Then he turned his face to the wall,
and prayed unto the LORD, saying,
3 I beseech thee, O LORD, remember
now how I have walked before thee in
truth and with a perfect heart, and have
done *that which is* good in thy sight. And
Hezekiah wept sore.
4 And it came to pass, afore Isaiah was
gone out into the middle court, that the
word of the LORD came to him, saying,
5 Turn again, and tell Hezekiah the
captain of my people, Thus saith the
LORD, the God of *David thy father, I
have heard thy prayer, I have seen thy
tears: behold, I will heal thee: on the
third day thou shalt go up unto the
house of the LORD.
6 And I will add unto thy days fifteen
years; and I will deliver thee and this city
out of the hand of the king of Assyria;
and I will defend this city for mine own
sake, and for my servant David's sake.
7 And Isaiah said, Take a lump of figs.
And they took and laid *it* on the boil, and
he recovered.
¶8 And Hezekiah said unto Isaiah,
What *shall be* the sign that the LORD will
heal me, and that I shall go up into the
house of the LORD the third day?
9 And Isaiah said, This sign shalt thou
have of the LORD, that the LORD will do
the thing that he hath spoken: shall the
shadow go forward ten degrees, or go
back ten degrees?
10 And Hezekiah answered, It is a
light thing for the shadow to go down
ten degrees: nay, but let the shadow
return backward ten degrees.
11 And Isaiah the prophet cried unto
the LORD: and he brought the shadow
ten degrees backward, by which it had
gone down in the dial of Ahaz.

Hezekiah's folly
(2 Chron. 32:27-31)

¶12 At that time Berodach-baladan,
the son of Baladan, king of Babylon,
sent letters and a present unto Hezekiah: for he had heard that Hezekiah
had been sick.
13 And Hezekiah hearkened unto
them, and shewed them all the house
of his precious things, the silver, and
the gold, and the spices, and the precious ointment, and *all* the house of
his armour, and all that was found in his
treasures: there was nothing in his
house, nor in all his dominion, that
Hezekiah shewed them not.
¶14 Then came Isaiah the prophet
unto king Hezekiah, and said unto him,
What said these men? and from whence
came they unto thee? And Hezekiah
said, They are come from a far country,
even from Babylon.
15 And he said, What have they seen
in thine house? And Hezekiah answered, All *the things* that *are* in mine
house have they seen: there is nothing
among my treasures that I have not
shewed them.
16 And Isaiah said unto Hezekiah,
Hear the word of the LORD.
17 Behold, the days come, that all that
is in thine house, and that which thy fathers have laid up in store unto this day,
shall be carried into Babylon: nothing
shall be left, saith the LORD.
18 And of thy sons that shall issue

20:3 perfect heart. This refers to single-mindedness, sincerity, and dedication; Hezekiah did not claim to be sinless.

20:17 all . . . shall be carried into Babylon. The prophecy of verses 17 and 18 was very remarkable, for at that time Babylon was a very weak kingdom. Even so, the prophecy was literally fulfilled.

from thee, which thou shalt beget, shall
they take away; and they shall be eunuchs in the palace of the king of Babylon.
19Then said Hezekiah unto Isaiah,
Good *is* the word of the LORD which
thou hast spoken. And he said, *Is it* not
good, if peace and truth be in my days?

Death of Hezekiah
(2 Chron. 32:32-33)

¶20And the rest of the acts of Hezekiah, and all his might, and how he made
a pool, and a conduit, and brought water into the city, *are* they not written in
the book of the chronicles of the kings
of *Judah?
21And Hezekiah slept with his fathers: and Manasseh his son reigned in
his stead.

VII. Manasseh, Amon, and Josiah
(21:1—23:30)

21 Manasseh *was* twelve years
old when he began to reign, and
reigned fifty and five years in *Jerusalem. And his mother's name *was*
Hephzi-bah.
2And he did *that which was* evil in the
sight of the LORD, after the abominations of the heathen, whom the LORD
cast out before the children of Israel.
3For he built up again the high places
which Hezekiah his father had destroyed; and he reared up altars for
Baal, and made a grove, as did *Ahab
king of Israel; and worshipped all the
host of heaven, and served them.
4And he built altars in the house of
the LORD, of which the LORD said, In
Jerusalem will I put my name.
5And he built altars for all the host of
heaven in the two courts of the house
of the LORD.
6And he made his son pass through
the fire, and observed times, and used
enchantments, and dealt with familiar
spirits and wizards: he wrought much
wickedness in the sight of the LORD, to
provoke *him* to anger.

21:6 Observing the Signs
Manasseh watched for certain signs instead of seeking God's will: perhaps the flying of birds, perhaps thunder and lightning, or, as was often done, perhaps he marked arrows, then shook them up and drew one and let that be the answer as to what he was to do. Manasseh was more interested in practicing magic and consulting witches instead of serving the LORD.

7And he set a *graven image of the
grove that he had made in the house, of
which the LORD said to David, and to
Solomon his son, In this house, and in
Jerusalem, which I have chosen out of
all tribes of Israel, will I put my name
for ever:
8Neither will I make the feet of Israel
move any more out of the land which I
gave their fathers; only if they will observe to do according to all that I have
commanded them, and according to all
the *law that my servant *Moses commanded them.
9But they hearkened not: and Manasseh seduced them to do more evil than
did the nations whom the LORD destroyed before the children of Israel.
¶10And the LORD spake by his servants the prophets, saying,
11Because Manasseh king of Judah
hath done these abominations, *and* hath
done wickedly above all that the Amorites did, which *were* before him, and
hath made Judah also to sin with his
idols:
12Therefore thus saith the LORD God

20:21 Manasseh. This name means *making to forget.* He was the worst king of Judah; Hezekiah was the best.
21:1 Hephzi-bah. This name means *my delight is in her.* The name is given to the restored Zion by the prophet Isaiah (Isa. 62:4).
21:6 familiar spirits. Demon spirits.
21:7 which the LORD said to David. See 2 Samuel 7:13. For the words to Solomon, read 1 Kings 8:20.

of Israel, Behold, I *am* bringing *such* evil
upon Jerusalem and Judah, that whosoever heareth of it, both his ears shall
tingle.
13 And I will stretch over Jerusalem
the line of Samaria, and the plummet of
the house of Ahab: and I will wipe Jerusalem as *a man* wipeth a dish, wip-
ing *it,* and turning *it* upside down.
14 And I will forsake the remnant of
mine inheritance, and deliver them into
the hand of their enemies; and they
shall become a prey and a spoil to all
their enemies;
15 Because they have done *that which*
was evil in my sight,and have provoked
me to anger, since the day their fathers came forth out of Egypt, even
unto this day.
16 Moreover Manasseh shed innocent
blood very much, till he had filled Jerusalem from one end to another; beside
his sin wherewith he made Judah to sin,
in doing *that which was* evil in the sight
of the LORD.
¶ 17 Now the rest of the acts of Manasseh, and all that he did, and his sin that
he sinned, *are* they not written in the
book of the chronicles of the kings of
Judah?
18 And Manasseh slept with his fathers, and was buried in the garden of
his own house, in the garden of Uzza:
and Amon his son reigned in his stead.

Reign of Amon
(2 Chron. 33:20-25)

¶ 19 Amon *was* twenty and two years
old when he began to reign, and he
reigned two years in Jerusalem. And his
mother's name *was* Meshullemeth, the
daughter of Haruz of Jotbah.
20 And he did *that which was* evil in
the sight of the LORD, as his father
Manasseh did.
21 And he walked in all the way that
his father walked in, and served the
idols that his father served, and worshipped them:
22 And he forsook the LORD God of his
fathers, and walked not in the way of the
LORD.
¶ 23 And the servants of Amon conspired against him, and slew the king in
his own house.
24 And the people of the land slew all
them that had conspired against king
Amon; and the people of the land made
*Josiah his son king in his stead.

21:24 King Josiah
Josiah means *Jehovah heals.* In accordance with his name, it was during Josiah's reign that blessing was restored to Judah. Josiah was a good king who wiped out every vestige of idolatry. His death ended the prosperity of Judah. More than three hundred years before Josiah was born, his birth was prophesied and even his name foretold (see 1 Kings 13:2).

25 Now the rest of the acts of Amon
which he did, *are* they not written in the
book of the chronicles of the kings of
Judah?
26 And he was buried in his sepulchre
in the garden of Uzza: and Josiah his son
reigned in his stead.

Reign of Josiah
(2 Chron. 34; 35)

22 Josiah *was* eight years old
when he began to reign, and he
reigned thirty and one years in Jerusalem. And his mother's name *was* Jedi-
dah, the daughter of Adaiah of Boscath.
2 And he did *that which was* right in
the sight of the LORD, and walked in all
the way of David his father, and turned
not aside to the right hand or to the left.

Repairing of the temple

¶ 3 And it came to pass in the eighteenth year of king Josiah, *that* the king
sent Shaphan the son of Azaliah, the

21:13 the line of Samaria, and the plummet of the house of Ahab. This means that Jerusalem was to be measured by the same exact standard of divine justice that had measured Samaria and the wicked house of Ahab.

son of Meshullam, the scribe, to the
house of the LORD, saying,
4 Go up to Hilkiah the high priest, that
he may sum the silver which is brought
into the house of the LORD, which the
keepers of the door have gathered of
the people:
5 And let them deliver it into the hand
of the doers of the work, that have the
oversight of the house of the LORD: and
let them give it to the doers of the work
which *is* in the house of the LORD, to
repair the breaches of the house,
6 Unto carpenters, and builders, and
masons, and to buy timber and hewn
stone to repair the house.
7 Howbeit there was no reckoning
made with them of the money that was
delivered into their hand, because they
dealt faithfully.

The Law of Moses discovered

¶8 And Hilkiah the high priest said
unto Shaphan the scribe, I have found
the book of the law in the house of the
LORD. And Hilkiah gave the book to
Shaphan, and he read it.
9 And Shaphan the scribe came to the
king, and brought the king word again,
and said, Thy servants have gathered
the money that was found in the house,
and have delivered it into the hand of
them that do the work, that have the
oversight of the house of the LORD.
10 And Shaphan the scribe shewed the
king, saying, Hilkiah the priest hath
delivered me a book. And Shaphan read
it before the king.
11 And it came to pass, when the king
had heard the words of the book of the
law, that he rent his clothes.
12 And the king commanded Hilkiah
the priest, and Ahikam the son of Shaphan, and Achbor the son of Michaiah,
and Shaphan the scribe, and Asahiah a
servant of the king's, saying,
13 Go ye, enquire of the LORD for me,
and for the people, and for all Judah,
concerning the words of this book that
is found: for great *is* the wrath of the
LORD that is kindled against us, because
our fathers have not hearkened unto
the words of this book, to do according
unto all that which is written concerning us.
14 So Hilkiah the priest, and Ahikam,
and Achbor, and Shaphan, and Asahiah,
went unto *Huldah the prophetess, the
wife of Shallum the son of Tikvah, the
son of Harhas, keeper of the wardrobe;
(now she dwelt in Jerusalem in the college;) and they communed with her.

The words of Huldah the prophetess

¶15 And she said unto them, Thus
saith the LORD God of Israel, Tell the
man that sent you to me,
16 Thus saith the LORD, Behold, I will
bring evil upon this place, and upon the
inhabitants thereof, *even* all the words
of the book which the king of Judah hath
read:
17 Because they have forsaken me,
and have burned incense unto other
gods, that they might provoke me to
anger with all the works of their hands;
therefore my wrath shall be kindled
against this place, and shall not be
quenched.
18 But to the king of Judah which sent
you to enquire of the LORD, thus shall
ye say to him, Thus saith the LORD God
of Israel, *As touching* the words which
thou hast heard;

22:7 no reckoning. There is a similar account in 2 Kings 12:15; see its note. Two hundred fifty years had passed since the repair of the temple described there.
22:13 the wrath of the LORD. See 2 Kings 13:3 note, "The LORD's Anger."
22:14 Huldah the prophetess. Other women with the prophetic gifts were Miriam, the sister of Moses (Exod. 15:20), and Deborah (Judg. 4:4).
22:14 keeper of the wardrobe. The person in charge of the robes worn by the priests.
22:14 the college. This is a name that was given to a suburban part of the city.
22:14 communed. This means they spoke to her and consulted with her.
22:16 all the words. In 2 Chronicles 34:24 these words are seen as "curses."

19Because thine heart was tender,
and thou hast humbled thyself before
the LORD, when thou heardest what I
spake against this place, and against the
inhabitants thereof, that they should
become a desolation and a curse, and
hast rent thy clothes, and wept before
me; I also have heard *thee,* saith the
LORD.
20Behold therefore, I will gather thee
unto thy fathers, and thou shalt be gathered into thy grave in peace; and thine
eyes shall not see all the evil which I
will bring upon this place. And they
brought the king word again.

The Law read to the people

23 And the king sent, and they
gathered unto him all the elders
of Judah and of Jerusalem.
2And the king went up into the house
of the LORD, and all the men of Judah
and all the inhabitants of Jerusalem
with him, and the priests, and the
*prophets, and all the people, both
small and great: and he read in their
ears all the words of the book of the
*covenant which was found in the
house of the LORD.

The king's covenant

¶3And the king stood by a *pillar, and
made a covenant before the LORD, to
walk after the LORD, and to keep his
commandments and his testimonies
and his statutes with all *their* heart and
all *their* soul, to perform the words of
this covenant that were written in this
book. And all the people stood to the
covenant.

Josiah's further reforms

4And the king commanded Hilkiah
the high priest, and the priests of the
second order, and the keepers of the
door, to bring forth out of the temple of
the LORD all the vessels that were
made for *Baal, and for the grove, and
for all the host of heaven: and he burned
them without Jerusalem in the fields of
Kidron, and carried the ashes of them
unto Beth-el.
5And he put down the idolatrous
priests, whom the kings of Judah had
ordained to burn incense in the high
places in the cities of Judah, and in the
places round about Jerusalem; them
also that burned incense unto Baal, to
the sun, and to the moon, and to the
planets, and to all the host of heaven.
6And he brought out the grove from
the house of the LORD, without Jerusalem, unto the brook Kidron, and burned
it at the brook Kidron, and stamped *it*
small to powder, and cast the powder
thereof upon the graves of the children
of the people.
7And he brake down the houses of
the sodomites, that *were* by the house
of the LORD, where the women wove
hangings for the grove.
8And he brought all the priests out of
the cities of Judah, and defiled the high
places where the priests had burned
incense, from Geba to *Beer-sheba,
and brake down the high places of the

22:20 into thy grave in peace. Though Josiah died while he was at war (23:29-30), he was at peace with God, for God had postponed pouring out His wrath upon the people of Judah.

23:4 priests of the second order. This refers to those who were next in rank to the high priest.

23:4 the keepers of the door. These were probably Levites.

23:4 burned them. All this is in accordance with divine commands (Deut. 7:25; 12:3).

23:4 unto Beth-el. The ashes of the articles that had been used in the worship of idols were thrown upon the place where the first step was taken that led to the practice of idolatry among the LORD's people.

23:8 the high places. Altars had been erected around the gates of the city.

23:8 from Geba to Beer-sheba. A common way of saying "throughout all the land of Judah," just as "from Dan to Beer-sheba" was a popular way of speaking of the whole land of Canaan.

gates that *were* in the entering in of the
gate of *Joshua the governor of the city,
which *were* on a man's left hand at the
gate of the city.
9 Nevertheless the priests of the high
places came not up to the altar of the
LORD in Jerusalem, but they did eat of
the *unleavened bread among their
brethren.
10 And he defiled Topheth, which *is* in
the valley of the children of Hinnom,
that no man might make his son or his
daughter to pass through the fire to
*Molech.
11 And he took away the horses that
the kings of Judah had given to the
sun, at the entering in of the house of
the LORD, by the chamber of Nathan-
melech the chamberlain, which *was* in
the suburbs, and burned the chariots of
the sun with fire.
12 And the altars that *were* on the top
of the upper chamber of Ahaz, which
the kings of Judah had made, and the
altars which Manasseh had made in the
two courts of the house of the LORD, did
the king beat down, and brake *them*
down from thence, and cast the dust of
them into the brook Kidron.
13 And the high places that *were* before Jerusalem, which *were* on the right
hand of the mount of corruption, which
Solomon the king of Israel had builded
for Ashtoreth the *abomination of the
Zidonians, and for *Chemosh the abomination of the Moabites, and for Milcom
the abomination of the children of Ammon, did the king defile.
14 And he brake in pieces the images,
and cut down the groves, and filled their
places with the bones of men.
¶ 15 Moreover the altar that *was* at
Beth-el, *and* the high place which Jeroboam the son of Nebat, who made Israel to *sin, had made, both that altar
and the high place he brake down, and
burned the high place, *and* stamped *it*
small to powder, and burned the grove.
16 And as Josiah turned himself, he
spied the sepulchres that *were* there in
the mount, and sent, and took the bones
out of the sepulchres, and burned *them*
upon the altar, and polluted it, according to the word of the LORD which the
man of God proclaimed, who proclaimed these words.
17 Then he said, What title *is* that that
I see? And the men of the city told him,
It is the sepulchre of the man of God,
which came from Judah, and proclaimed
these things that thou hast done against
the altar of Beth-el.
18 And he said, Let him alone; let no
man move his bones. So they let his
bones alone, with the bones of the
prophet that came out of Samaria.
19 And all the houses also of the high
places that *were* in the cities of Samaria, which the kings of Israel had made
to provoke *the LORD* to anger, Josiah

23:9 the priests of the high places. They might no longer officiate in the sacrifices of the temple, although they were still supported by the offerings.

23:10 Topheth. This place had been associated with the worship of Molech. Because of the evil things done there, it became the dumping place for all that was foul and offensive. See *Tophet.

23:11 given to the sun. Given for the worship of the sun.

23:11 suburbs. The word here means *precincts* or *districts*.

23:12 on the top of the upper chamber. This means *on the roof*. These altars were erected to the sun, moon, and stars (see Zeph. 1:5; Jer. 19:13; 32:29).

23:13 mount of corruption. This was a name given to the Mount of Olives because of the heathen temples there.

23:14 bones of men. The Jews regarded contact with the dead as defiling. Therefore, these places would never again be used for any religious purpose.

23:15 altar that was at Beth-el. This had been established by Jeroboam at the time that the ten tribes revolted from Rehoboam. Read 1 Kings 12:28-29.

23:16 according to the word of the LORD. Read 1 Kings 13:2.

took away, and did to them according to
all the acts that he had done in Beth-el.
20 And he slew all the priests of the
high places that *were* there upon the
altars, and burned men's bones upon
them, and returned to Jerusalem.
¶21 And the king commanded all the
people, saying, Keep the *passover
unto the LORD your God, as *it is* written in the book of this covenant.
22 Surely there was not holden such a
passover from the days of the *judges
that judged Israel, nor in all the days of
the kings of Israel, nor of the kings of
Judah;
23 But in the eighteenth year of king
Josiah, *wherein* this passover was
holden to the LORD in Jerusalem.
¶24 Moreover the *workers with* *familiar spirits, and the wizards, and the
images, and the idols, and all the abominations that were spied in the land of
Judah and in Jerusalem, did Josiah put
away, that he might perform the words
of the law which were written in the
book that Hilkiah the priest found in the
house of the LORD.
25 And like unto him was there no
king before him, that turned to the
LORD with all his heart, and with all
his soul, and with all his might, according to all the law of Moses; neither after him arose there *any* like him.
¶26 Notwithstanding the LORD turned
not from the fierceness of his great
wrath, wherewith his anger was kindled
against Judah, because of all the provocations that Manasseh had provoked
him withal.
27 And the LORD said, I will remove
Judah also out of my sight, as I have
removed Israel, and will cast off this
city Jerusalem which I have chosen, and
the house of which I said, My name
shall be there.

Josiah's death

28 Now the rest of the acts of Josiah,
and all that he did, *are* they not written
in the book of the chronicles of the
kings of Judah?
¶29 In his days Pharaoh-nechoh king
of *Egypt went up against the king of
Assyria to the river Euphrates: and
king Josiah went against him; and he
slew him at Megiddo, when he had seen
him.
30 And his servants carried him in a
chariot dead from Megiddo, and brought
him to Jerusalem, and buried him in his
own sepulchre. And the people of the
land took Jehoahaz the son of Josiah,
and anointed him, and made him king
in his father's stead.

23:22 PASSOVER OBSERVANCES IN THE BIBLE

The Passover was to be observed every year; however, the Bible only records the following occurrences.

Occasion	Reference
The first Passover observed in Egypt	Exodus 12:14
First Passover in the Promised Land	Joshua 5:10
King Hezekiah observes Passover	2 Chronicles 30:1-20
King Josiah observes Passover	2 Kings 23:21-23
First Passover observance after captivity	Ezra 6:19-21
Christ and His disciples observe Passover	Matthew 26:17

23:22 such a passover. These words refer to the manner and the spirit in which the Passover was observed.
23:24 perform the words of the law. The laws for putting down those who had familiar spirits, and other similar laws, are found in Leviticus 19:31; 20:6,27.
23:27 My name shall be there. See 1 Kings 8:29.
23:29 Megiddo. This was a place of great military importance because it controlled the pass through the mountains between the plain of Sharon and the plain of Esdraelon. This place is also called *Armageddon.

VIII. Other Kings Rule Judah
(23:31—25:7)
Dethronement of Jehoahaz

¶ 31 Jehoahaz *was* twenty and three
years old when he began to reign; and
he reigned three months in Jerusalem.
And his mother's name *was* Hamutal,
the daughter of Jeremiah of Libnah.
32 And he did *that which was* evil in
the sight of the LORD, according to all
that his fathers had done.
33 And Pharaoh-nechoh put him in
bands at Riblah in the land of Hamath, that
he might not reign in Jerusalem; and put
the land to a tribute of an hundred talents of silver, and a talent of gold.

Reign of Jehoiakim
(2 Chron. 36:4-8)

34 And Pharaoh-nechoh made Eliakim
the son of Josiah king in the room of
Josiah his father, and turned his name
to Jehoiakim, and took Jehoahaz away:
and he came to Egypt, and died there.
35 And Jehoiakim gave the silver and
the gold to *Pharaoh; but he taxed the
land to give the money according to the
commandment of Pharaoh: he exacted
the silver and the gold of the people
of the land, of every one according to
his taxation, to give *it* unto Pharaoh-
nechoh.
¶ 36 Jehoiakim *was* twenty and five
years old when he began to reign; and
he reigned eleven years in Jerusalem.
And his mother's name *was* Zebudah,
the daughter of Pedaiah of Rumah.
37 And he did *that which was* evil in
the sight of the LORD, according to all
that his fathers had done.

24 In his days Nebuchadnezzar
king of *Babylon came up, and
Jehoiakim became his servant three
years: then he turned and rebelled
against him.
2 And the LORD sent against him
bands of the Chaldees, and bands of the
Syrians, and bands of the Moabites, and
bands of the children of Ammon, and
sent them against Judah to destroy it,
according to the word of the LORD,
which he spake by his servants the
prophets.
3 Surely at the commandment of the
LORD came *this* upon Judah, to remove
them out of his sight, for the sins of
Manasseh, according to all that he did;
4 And also for the innocent *blood that
he shed: for he filled Jerusalem with
innocent blood; which the LORD would
not pardon.
¶ 5 Now the rest of the acts of Jehoiakim, and all that he did, *are* they not
written in the book of the chronicles of
the kings of Judah?

Reign of Jehoiachin
(2 Chron. 36:8-9)

6 So Jehoiakim slept with his fathers:
and Jehoiachin his son reigned in his
stead.
7 And the king of Egypt came not
again any more out of his land: for the
king of Babylon had taken from the
river of Egypt unto the river Euphrates all that pertained to the king of
Egypt.
¶ 8 Jehoiachin *was* eighteen years old
when he began to reign, and he reigned
in Jerusalem three months. And his

23:35 according to his taxation. This means that everyone was compelled to pay in proportion to his wealth.

24:1 became his servant. Judah, under Jehoiakim, had been subject to the king of Egypt (23:34-35). Now Judah becomes subject to the king of Babylon for three years.

24:2 according to the word of the LORD. God's Word is sure. Read 2 Kings 20:17; 21:12-14. Read also Jeremiah 14, 15, and 16.

24:3 at the commandment of the LORD. Read 2 Kings 13:3 note, "The LORD's Anger"; see also 22:13.

24:6 Jehoiakim slept with his fathers. Note that the usual clause "and was buried" was not added here. Jeremiah had prophesied what was to happen to Jehoiakim's body (Jer. 22:18-19).

mother's name *was* Nehushta, the
daughter of Elnathan of Jerusalem.
9And he did *that which was* evil in the
sight of the LORD, according to all that
his father had done.
¶10At that time the servants of Nebuchadnezzar king of Babylon came up
against Jerusalem, and the city was
besieged.
11And Nebuchadnezzar king of Babylon came against the city, and his servants did besiege it.
12And Jehoiachin the king of Judah
went out to the king of Babylon, he, and
his mother, and his servants, and his
princes, and his officers: and the king
of Babylon took him in the eighth year
of his reign.
13And he carried out thence all the
treasures of the house of the LORD, and
the treasures of the king's house, and
cut in pieces all the vessels of gold
which Solomon king of Israel had made
in the temple of the LORD, as the LORD
had said.
14And he carried away all Jerusalem,
and all the princes, and all the mighty
men of valour, *even* ten thousand captives, and all the craftsmen and smiths:
none remained, save the poorest sort of
the people of the land.
15And he carried away Jehoiachin to
Babylon, and the king's mother, and the
king's wives, and his officers, and the
mighty of the land, *those* carried he into
captivity from Jerusalem to Babylon.
16And all the men of might, *even*
seven thousand, and craftsmen and
smiths a thousand, all *that were* strong
and apt for war, even them the king of
Babylon brought captive to Babylon.

Reign of Zedekiah
(2 Chron. 36:11-21)

¶17And the king of Babylon made Mattaniah his father's brother king in his
stead, and changed his name to Zedekiah.

24:17 A Sign of Authority
A person of great power, to show his authority, frequently changed the name of the one whom he put into office. For examples of the use of this power, we have the reference in 23:34 where Eliakim's name was changed to Jehoiakim; see also the changes in Daniel 1:7, and in Genesis 41:45, where Joseph's name was changed to Zaphnath-paaneah.

18Zedekiah *was* twenty and one years
old when he began to reign, and he
reigned eleven years in Jerusalem. And
his mother's name *was* Hamutal, the
daughter of Jeremiah of Libnah.
19And he did *that which was* evil in
the sight of the LORD, according to all
that Jehoiakim had done.
20For through the anger of the LORD
it came to pass in Jerusalem and Judah,
until he had cast them out from his
presence, that Zedekiah rebelled
against the king of Babylon.
25 And it came to pass in the ninth
year of his reign, in the tenth
month, in the tenth *day* of the month,
that Nebuchadnezzar king of Babylon
came, he, and all his host, against Jerusalem, and pitched against it; and they
built forts against it round about.
2And the city was besieged unto the
eleventh year of king Zedekiah.
3And on the ninth *day* of the *fourth*
month the famine prevailed in the city,
and there was no bread for the people
of the land.
¶4And the city was broken up, and all
the men of war *fled* by night by the way
of the gate between two walls, which *is*
by the king's garden: (now the Chaldees
were against the city round about:) and
the king went the way toward the plain.
5And the army of the Chaldees pursued after the king, and overtook him
in the plains of Jericho: and all his army
were scattered from him.

24:13 vessels of gold. We come across these vessels again in Daniel 5:2-3.
24:14 smiths. Workers in silver and gold—silversmiths, goldsmiths.
25:3 the famine prevailed. Read Jeremiah 52.

6So they took the king, and brought
him up to the king of Babylon to Riblah; and they gave judgment upon him.
7And they slew the sons of Zedekiah
before his eyes, and put out the eyes of
Zedekiah, and bound him with fetters of
brass, and carried him to Babylon.

IX. Fall of Judah (25:8-30)

¶8And in the fifth month, on the seventh *day* of the month, which *is* the
nineteenth year of king Nebuchadnezzar king of Babylon, came Nebuzar-
adan, captain of the guard, a servant of
the king of Babylon, unto Jerusalem:
9And he burnt the house of the LORD,
and the king's house, and all the houses
of Jerusalem, and every great *man's*
house burnt he with fire.
10And all the army of the Chaldees,
that *were with* the captain of the guard,
brake down the walls of Jerusalem
round about.
11Now the rest of the people *that were*
left in the city, and the fugitives that fell
away to the king of Babylon, with the
remnant of the multitude, did Nebuzar-
adan the captain of the guard carry
away.
12But the captain of the guard left of
the poor of the land *to be* vinedressers
and husbandmen.
13And the pillars of brass that *were* in
the house of the LORD, and the bases,
and the brasen sea that *was* in the house
of the LORD, did the Chaldees break in
pieces, and carried the brass of them to
Babylon.
14And the pots, and the shovels, and
the snuffers, and the spoons, and all the
vessels of brass wherewith they ministered, took they away.
15And the firepans, and the bowls,
and such things as *were* of gold, *in* gold,
and of silver, *in* silver, the captain of the
guard took away.
16The two pillars, one sea, and the
bases which Solomon had made for the
house of the LORD; the brass of all these
vessels was without weight.
17The height of the one pillar *was*
eighteen cubits, and the chapiter upon
it *was* brass: and the height of the
chapiter three cubits; and the wreathen
work, and pomegranates upon the
chapiter round about, all of brass: and
like unto these had the second pillar
with wreathen work.

25:13 The Meaning behind the Facts
Verses 13 to 17 are full of sorrowful meaning. The precious vessels mentioned here had been designed as *types of the coming glories of the King, the Lord Jesus Christ. Now that they were broken, the glory and beauty were gone from them, and they were carried away.

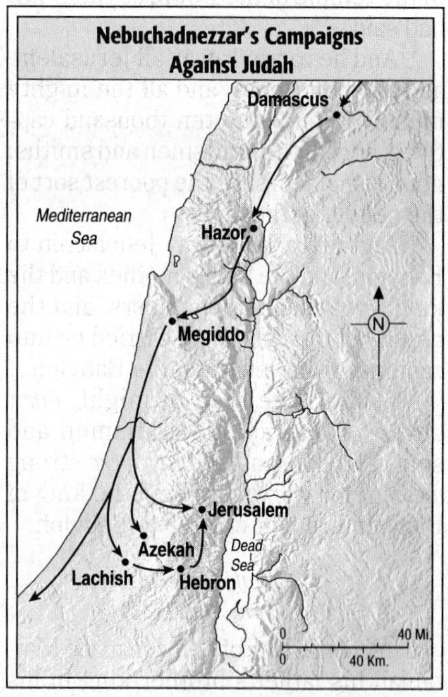

25:7 put out the eyes of Zedekiah. See what Jeremiah said in Jeremiah 32:4; 34:3.
25:16 one sea. The brazen sea (vs. 13).
25:16 without weight. This means the weight was unknown because they had not been weighed (see 1 Kings 7:47).

¶ 18 And the captain of the guard took
Seraiah the chief priest, and Zephaniah
the second priest, and the three keepers of the door:
19 And out of the city he took an officer that was set over the men of war,
and five men of them that were in the
king's presence, which were found in
the city, and the principal scribe of the
host, which mustered the people of the
land, and threescore men of the people
of the land *that were* found in the city:
20 And Nebuzar-adan captain of the
guard took these, and brought them to
the king of Babylon to Riblah:
21 And the king of Babylon smote
them, and slew them at Riblah in the
land of Hamath. So Judah was carried
away out of their land.

Gedaliah made governor of Palestine

¶ 22 And *as for* the people that remained
in the land of Judah, whom Nebuchadnezzar king of Babylon had left, even
over them he made Gedaliah the son of
Ahikam, the son of Shaphan, ruler.
23 And when all the captains of the
armies, they and their men, heard that
the king of Babylon had made Gedaliah
governor, there came to Gedaliah to
Mizpah, even Ishmael the son of Nethaniah, and Johanan the son of Careah,
and Seraiah the son of Tanhumeth the
Netophathite, and Jaazaniah the son of
a Maachathite, they and their men.
24 And Gedaliah sware to them, and to
their men, and said unto them, Fear not
to be the servants of the Chaldees: dwell
in the land, and serve the king of Babylon; and it shall be well with you.

Murder of Gedaliah: flight of the people to Egypt

25 But it came to pass in the seventh
month, that Ishmael the son of Nethaniah, the son of Elishama, of the seed
royal, came, and ten men with him, and
smote Gedaliah, that he died, and the
Jews and the Chaldees that were with
him at Mizpah.
26 And all the people, both small and
great, and the captains of the armies,
arose, and came to Egypt: for they were
afraid of the Chaldees.

25:26 Off to Egypt
Escaping to Egypt was in disobedience to the word of the LORD. As Jeremiah foretold, because they went into Egypt instead of remaining in their own land, they died in exile. Nebuchadnezzar invaded Egypt and killed the Pharaoh to whom Judah had gone for protection (see Jer. 42; 43; 44).

Jehoiachin released

¶ 27 And it came to pass in the seven
and thirtieth year of the captivity of
Jehoiachin king of Judah, in the twelfth
month, on the seven and twentieth *day*
of the month, *that* Evil-merodach king
of Babylon in the year that he began to
reign did lift up the head of Jehoiachin
king of Judah out of prison;
28 And he spake kindly to him, and set
his throne above the throne of the kings
that *were* with him in Babylon;
29 And changed his prison garments:
and he did eat bread continually before
him all the days of his life.
30 And his allowance *was* a continual
allowance given him of the king, a daily
rate for every day, all the days of his life.

25:21 So Judah was carried away. This marks the end of the southern kingdom (see Jer. 20:4).

25:27 lift up the head. This expression means *to show favor toward,* and is also found in Genesis 40:13,20.

25:29 changed his prison garments. He took these off and put on the clothing of a free man. But notice that although he was released from prison, Jehoiachin still remained subject to the king of Babylon.

The First Book of the

CHRONICLES

BACKGROUND

The two books of the Chronicles were originally one book in the Jewish Canon (see *How We Got Our English Bible*, p. xiii). They were divided for the sake of convenience at the time of the translation of the Old Testament books into Greek (the Septuagint version), during the third century before Christ. In the Hebrew Scriptures, Chronicles was placed at the end of the Old Testament. Thus the genealogies of Chronicles would lead up to those of Matthew 1.

The original name was "Acts of Days" (given in the Septuagint as "Things Omitted"), indicating that Chronicles is a book of records, or a sort of diary, compiled to give a record of the important genealogies and events which would be of help to the Jews in returning from captivity to Palestine.

Chronicles differs from the books of the Kings in that it gives a fuller account of the kingdom of Judah. It is thought by some that Kings gives the history from the human viewpoint and Chronicles from the divine viewpoint.

THE WRITER

Many think that the compiler was Ezra, which would place the date of the book around 450 B.C. We know (1 Chronicles 6:15) that it was written after Judah and Jerusalem were taken captive. The Hebrew language is mixed with Aramaic words and expressions, for the pure Hebrew was corrupted by the Chaldean language which the captives learned in Babylon. Since much is said about the Levitic priesthood and the singers in the temple, many believe that the author must have been a Levite who had a part in the services of worship. He refers to books which are now unknown: see 1 Chronicles 29:29; 2 Chronicles 9:29; 12:15; 13:22; 16:11; 20:34; 24:27; 26:22; 27:7; 32:32; 33:18. See 29:29 note, "Literature of the Hebrew People."

OUTLINE OF 1 CHRONICLES

I.	Official Genealogies	1 Chronicles 1:1—9:44
II.	Saul's Death and the Accession of David to the Throne	1 Chronicles 10:1—12:40
III.	Triumphs of David's Reign	1 Chronicles 13:1—21:30
IV.	David's Preparation for the Building of the Temple before His Death	1 Chronicles 22:1—29:30

I. Official Genealogies (1:1—9:44)
Adam to Noah

1 *Adam, Sheth, Enosh,
2Kenan, Mahalaleel, Jered,
3Henoch, Methuselah, Lamech,
4Noah, Shem, Ham, and Japheth.

1:1 The Genealogies
We must not consider these genealogies uninteresting and unimportant. They were very important to the Jews returning from captivity because they settled family relationships and the divisions of the land. To us they are important because through them we can trace the ancestry of Christ, who, according to prophecy, was the Son of David, the Son of Judah, the Son of Abraham, and the Son of Adam. Compare these genealogies with those in Matthew 1 and Luke 3.

Japheth's sons

¶5The sons of Japheth; Gomer, and
Magog, and Madai, and Javan, and Tubal, and Meshech, and Tiras.
6And the sons of Gomer; Ashchenaz,
and Riphath, and *Togarmah.
7And the sons of Javan; Elishah, and
Tarshish, Kittim, and Dodanim.

Ham's sons

¶8The sons of Ham; Cush, and Mizraim, Put, and Canaan.
9And the sons of Cush; Seba, and
Havilah, and Sabta, and Raamah, and Sabtecha. And the sons of Raamah; Sheba, and Dedan.
10And Cush begat Nimrod: he began
to be mighty upon the earth.
11And Mizraim begat Ludim, and
Anamim, and Lehabim, and Naphtuhim,
12And Pathrusim, and Casluhim, (of
whom came the *Philistines,) and Caphthorim.
13And Canaan begat Zidon his firstborn, and Heth,
14The Jebusite also, and the *Amorite, and the Girgashite,
15And the Hivite, and the Arkite, and
the Sinite,
16And the Arvadite, and the Zemarite, and the Hamathite.

Shem's sons

¶17The sons of Shem; Elam, and *Asshur, and Arphaxad, and Lud, and Aram, and Uz, and Hul, and Gether, and Meshech.
18And Arphaxad begat Shelah, and
Shelah begat Eber.
19And unto Eber were born two sons:
the name of the one *was* Peleg; because in his days the earth was divided: and his brother's name *was* Joktan.
20And Joktan begat Almodad, and
Sheleph, and Hazarmaveth, and Jerah,
21Hadoram also, and Uzal, and
Diklah,
22And Ebal, and Abimael, and Sheba,
23And Ophir, and Havilah, and Jobab.
All these *were* the sons of Joktan.
¶24Shem, Arphaxad, Shelah,

Shem to Abraham

25Eber, Peleg, Reu,
26Serug, Nahor, Terah,
27Abram; the same *is* *Abraham.

Ishmael's sons

28The sons of Abraham; *Isaac, and
Ishmael.
¶29These *are* their generations: The
firstborn of Ishmael, Nebaioth; then *Kedar, and Adbeel, and Mibsam,
30Mishma and Dumah, Massa, Ha-
dad, and Tema,
31Jetur, Naphish, and Kedemah.
These are the sons of Ishmael.

1:5 Gomer. These names in verse 5 have a place in prophecy. Read Ezekiel 38 and 39.
1:19 Peleg. The name means *division*.
1:27 Abram; the same is Abraham. See Genesis 17:5 for the record of the change in name from Abram to Abraham.
1:31 sons of Ishmael. The twelve sons of Ishmael are here named to show that God's promise to Abraham (Gen. 17:20) was fulfilled.

Sons of Keturah

¶32 Now the sons of Keturah, Abraham's *concubine: she bare Zimran, and Jokshan, and Medan, and *Midian, and Ishbak, and Shuah. And the sons of Jokshan; Sheba, and Dedan.

33 And the sons of Midian; *Ephah, and Epher, and Henoch, and Abida, and Eldaah. All these *are* the sons of Keturah.

Sons of Abraham and Isaac

¶34 And Abraham begat Isaac. The sons of Isaac; *Esau and *Israel.

Esau's sons (cf. Gen. 36:1-43)

¶35 The sons of Esau; Eliphaz, Reuel, and Jeush, and Jaalam, and *Korah.

36 The sons of Eliphaz; Teman, and Omar, Zephi, and Gatam, Kenaz, and Timna, and *Amalek.

37 The sons of Reuel; Nahath, Zerah, Shammah, and Mizzah.

38 And the sons of *Seir; Lotan, and Shobal, and Zibeon, and Anah, and Dishon, and Ezer, and Dishan.

39 And the sons of Lotan; Hori, and Homam: and Timna *was* Lotan's sister.

40 The sons of Shobal; Alian, and Manahath, and Ebal, Shephi, and Onam. And the sons of Zibeon; Aiah, and Anah.

41 The sons of Anah; Dishon. And the sons of Dishon; Amram, and Eshban, and Ithran, and Cheran.

42 The sons of Ezer; Bilhan, and Zavan, *and* Jakan. The sons of Dishan; Uz, and Aran.

Edom's early kings

¶43 Now these *are* the kings that reigned in the land of *Edom before *any* king reigned over the children of Israel; Bela the son of Beor: and the name of his city *was* Dinhabah.

44 And when Bela was dead, Jobab the son of Zerah of Bozrah reigned in his stead.

45 And when Jobab was dead, Husham of the land of the Temanites reigned in his stead.

46 And when Husham was dead, Hadad the son of Bedad, which smote Midian in the field of *Moab, reigned in his stead: and the name of his city *was* Avith.

47 And when Hadad was dead, Samlah of Masrekah reigned in his stead.

48 And when Samlah was dead, Shaul of Rehoboth by the river reigned in his stead.

49 And when Shaul was dead, Baal-hanan the son of Achbor reigned in his stead.

50 And when Baal-hanan was dead, Hadad reigned in his stead: and the name of his city *was* Pai; and his wife's name *was* Mehetabel, the daughter of Matred, the daughter of Mezahab.

The dukes of Edom

¶51 Hadad died also. And the dukes of Edom were; duke Timnah, duke Aliah, duke Jetheth,

52 Duke Aholibamah, duke Elah, duke Pinon,

53 Duke Kenaz, duke Teman, duke Mibzar,

54 Duke Magdiel, duke Iram. These *are* the dukes of Edom.

Jacob's (Israel's) sons

2 These *are* the sons of Israel; Reuben, Simeon, Levi, and *Judah, Issachar, and Zebulun,

2 Dan, *Joseph, and Benjamin, Naphtali, Gad, and Asher.

Judah's sons

¶3 The sons of Judah; Er, and Onan, and Shelah: *which* three were born unto

---

1:44 Jobab. King Jobab is probably Job (see also Gen. 36:32-33).

1:51 dukes of Edom. These were chiefs in the land. Possibly these dukes succeeded the kings.

2:1 sons of Israel. Israel is Jacob. See Genesis 32:24-28 for the change in his name (see also Gen. 32:25 note, "God's Touch on Jacob").

2:3 The Sons of Judah
Judah is listed first because the birthright was taken from Reuben on account of his sin (Gen. 35:22; 49:4 and its note). The advantages of the birthright were divided between Joseph and Judah. Joseph had the double portion, for the two tribes, Ephraim and Manasseh, descended from him; and to Judah was granted the dominion, and from him came the chief ruler, David and the Messiah, Christ (see 1 Chron. 5:1-2; Gen. 48:13-22; 49:1-12). Note that the birthright did not pass from the firstborn to the second-born in natural order. The choice illustrates God's sovereign will and grace.

him of the daughter of Shua the Canaan-
itess. And Er, the firstborn of Judah,
was evil in the sight of the LORD; and
he slew him.
4And Tamar his daughter in law bare
him Pharez and Zerah. All the sons of
Judah *were* five.
5The sons of Pharez; Hezron, and
Hamul.
6And the sons of Zerah; Zimri, and
Ethan, and *Heman, and Calcol, and
Dara: five of them in all.
7And the sons of Carmi; Achar, the
troubler of Israel, who transgressed in
the thing accursed.
8And the sons of Ethan; Azariah.
9The sons also of Hezron, that were
born unto him; Jerahmeel, and Ram,
and Chelubai.
¶10And Ram begat Amminadab; and
Amminadab begat Nahshon, prince of
the children of Judah;
11And Nahshon begat Salma, and Salma begat *Boaz,
12And Boaz begat Obed, and Obed
begat Jesse,

Jesse's children

¶13And Jesse begat his firstborn Eliab, and Abinadab the second, and
Shimma the third,
14Nethaneel the fourth, Raddai the
fifth,
15Ozem the sixth, David the seventh:
16Whose sisters *were* Zeruiah, and
Abigail. And the sons of Zeruiah; Abishai, and Joab, and Asahel, three.
17And Abigail bare Amasa: and the
father of Amasa *was* Jether the
Ishmeelite.

Hezron's children

¶18And *Caleb the son of Hezron
begat *children* of Azubah *his* wife, and
of Jerioth: her sons *are* these; Jesher,
and Shobab, and Ardon.
19And when Azubah was dead, Caleb
took unto him Ephrath, which bare him
*Hur.
20And Hur begat Uri, and Uri begat
Bezaleel.
¶21And afterward Hezron went in to
the daughter of Machir the father of
*Gilead, whom he married when he
was threescore years old; and she bare
him Segub.
22And Segub begat Jair, who had
three and twenty cities in the land of
Gilead.
23And he took Geshur, and Aram,
with the towns of Jair, from them,
with Kenath, and the towns thereof,
even threescore cities. All these *belonged to* the sons of Machir the father
of Gilead.
24And after that Hezron was dead
in Caleb-ephratah, then Abiah Hezron's
wife bare him Ashur the father of Tekoa.

2:7 Achar. This is Achan of Joshua 7. See Joshua 7:1 note , "A Nation's Sin"; see also Joshua 7:20 and 7:26 notes.
2:9 Ram. This is the Aram of Matthew 1:3.
2:9 Chelubai. Chelubai, or Caleb, the son of Hezron (see vs. 18), is the ancestor of Caleb, the son of Jephunneh (1 Chron. 4:15).
2:15 David the seventh. Compare 1 Samuel 17:12-14, where Jesse is said to have had eight sons. There is no mistake; doubtless one son died and left no children. It was proper to mention the eight in history, but it is not necessary in genealogy.

Jerahmeel's sons

¶ 25 And the sons of Jerahmeel the firstborn of Hezron were, Ram the firstborn, and Bunah, and Oren, and Ozem, *and* Ahijah.

26 Jerahmeel had also another wife, whose name *was* Atarah; she *was* the mother of Onam.

27 And the sons of Ram the firstborn of Jerahmeel were, Maaz, and Jamin, and Eker.

28 And the sons of Onam were, Shammai, and Jada. And the sons of Shammai; Nadab, and Abishur.

29 And the name of the wife of Abishur *was* Abihail, and she bare him Ahban, and Molid.

30 And the sons of Nadab; Seled, and Appaim: but Seled died without children.

31 And the sons of Appaim; Ishi. And the sons of Ishi; Sheshan. And the children of Sheshan; Ahlai.

32 And the sons of Jada the brother of Shammai; Jether, and Jonathan: and Jether died without children.

33 And the sons of Jonathan; Peleth, and Zaza. These were the sons of Jerahmeel.

Sheshan's children

¶ 34 Now Sheshan had no sons, but daughters. And Sheshan had a servant, an Egyptian, whose name *was* Jarha.

35 And Sheshan gave his daughter to Jarha his servant to wife; and she bare him Attai.

36 And Attai begat Nathan, and Nathan begat Zabad,

37 And Zabad begat Ephlal, and Ephlal begat Obed,

38 And Obed begat Jehu, and Jehu begat Azariah,

39 And Azariah begat Helez, and Helez begat Eleasah,

40 And Eleasah begat Sisamai, and Sisamai begat Shallum,

41 And Shallum begat Jekamiah, and Jekamiah begat Elishama.

Caleb's children
(see vss. 18-20)

¶ 42 Now the sons of Caleb the brother of Jerahmeel *were,* Mesha his firstborn, which *was* the father of Ziph; and the sons of Mareshah the father of Hebron.

43 And the sons of Hebron; Korah, and Tappuah, and Rekem, and Shema.

44 And Shema begat Raham, the father of Jorkoam: and Rekem begat Shammai.

45 And the son of Shammai *was* Maon: and Maon *was* the father of Beth-zur.

46 And Ephah, Caleb's concubine, bare Haran, and Moza, and Gazez: and Haran begat Gazez.

47 And the sons of Jahdai; Regem, and Jotham, and Geshan, and Pelet, and Ephah, and Shaaph.

48 Maachah, Caleb's concubine, bare Sheber, and Tirhanah.

49 She bare also Shaaph the father of Madmannah, Sheva the father of Machbenah, and the father of Gibea: and the daughter of Caleb *was* Achsah.

The sons of Caleb, Hur's son

¶ 50 These were the sons of Caleb the son of Hur, the firstborn of Ephratah; Shobal the father of Kirjath-jearim,

51 Salma the father of Beth-lehem, Hareph the father of Beth-gader.

52 And Shobal the father of Kirjath-jearim had sons; Haroeh, *and* half of the Manahethites.

53 And the families of Kirjath-jearim; the Ithrites, and the Puhites, and the Shumathites, and the Mishraites; of them came the Zareathites, and the Eshtaulites.

54 The sons of Salma; Beth-lehem, and the Netophathites, Ataroth, the house of Joab, and half of the Manahethites, the Zorites.

55 And the families of the *scribes

2:55 Kenites. The descendants of Jethro, the father-in-law of Moses (Judg. 1:16).

which dwelt at Jabez; the Tirathites,
the Shimeathites, *and* Suchathites.
These *are* the *Kenites that came of
Hemath, the father of the house of
Rechab.

David's family born in Hebron

3 Now these were the sons of David, which were born unto him in
Hebron; the firstborn Amnon, of Ahinoam the Jezreelitess; the second Daniel, of Abigail the Carmelitess:
2The third, Absalom the son of Maachah the daughter of Talmai king of
Geshur: the fourth, Adonijah the son of
Haggith:
3The fifth, Shephatiah of Abital: the
sixth, Ithream by Eglah his wife.
4*These* six were born unto him in
Hebron; and there he reigned seven
years and six months: and in *Jerusalem he reigned thirty and three years.

David's family born in Jerusalem

5And these were born unto him in
Jerusalem; Shimea, and Shobab, and
Nathan, and Solomon, four, of Bath-
shua the daughter of Ammiel:
6Ibhar also, and Elishama, and Eliphelet,
7And Nogah, and Nepheg, and Japhia,
8And Elishama, and Eliada, and
Eliphelet, nine.
9*These were* all the sons of David,
beside the sons of the concubines, and
Tamar their sister.

Solomon to Zedekiah

¶10And Solomon's son *was* *Rehoboam, Abia his son, Asa his son, Jehoshaphat his son,
11Joram his son, Ahaziah his son, *Joash his son,
12Amaziah his son, Azariah his son,
Jotham his son,
13Ahaz his son, *Hezekiah his son,
*Manasseh his son,
14Amon his son, *Josiah his son.
15And the sons of Josiah *were,* the
firstborn Johanan, the second Jehoiakim, the third Zedekiah, the fourth
Shallum.
16And the sons of Jehoiakim: Jeconiah his son, Zedekiah his son.

Jeconiah to Anani

¶17And the sons of Jeconiah; Assir,
Salathiel his son,
18Malchiram also, and Pedaiah, and
Shenazar, Jecamiah, Hoshama, and
Nedabiah.
19And the sons of Pedaiah *were,* *Zerubbabel, and Shimei: and the sons of
Zerubbabel; Meshullam, and Hananiah,
and Shelomith their sister:
20And Hashubah, and Ohel, and Berechiah, and Hasadiah, Jushab-hesed,
five.
21And the sons of Hananiah; Pelatiah,
and Jesaiah: the sons of Rephaiah, the
sons of Arnan, the sons of Obadiah, the
sons of Shechaniah.
22And the sons of Shechaniah; Shemaiah; and the sons of Shemaiah;
Hattush, and Igeal, and Bariah, and
Neariah, and Shaphat, six.
23And the sons of Neariah; Elioenai,
and Hezekiah, and Azrikam, three.
24And the sons of Elioenai *were,*
Hodaiah, and Eliashib, and Pelaiah, and
Akkub, and Johanan, and Dalaiah, and
Anani, seven.

2:55 house of Rechab. See Jeremiah 35 for the story of their obedience and God's favor.
3:5 Nathan. The genealogy of Christ is traced back to David through David's son Nathan (Luke 3:31). Joseph, the husband of Mary, Jesus' mother, was a descendant of David through Solomon (Matt. 1:6,16).
3:5 Bath-shua. That is, Bath-sheba (2 Sam. 11:3).
3:8 Elishama. Since this name occurs also in verse 6, one is probably Elishua (2 Sam. 5:15).
3:17 Assir. This word means *the captive*. It refers to Jeconiah, the captive.
3:17 Salathiel. The son of Salathiel was Zerubbabel (Matt. 1:12; Ezra 3:2; 5:2; Hag. 1:1,12).

Judah's descendants

4 The sons of Judah; Pharez, Hezron, and Carmi, and Hur, and Shobal.

2 And Reaiah the son of Shobal begat Jahath; and Jahath begat Ahumai and Lahad. These *are* the families of the Zorathites.

3 And these *were of* the father of Etam; Jezreel, and Ishma, and Idbash: and the name of their sister *was* Hazelelponi:

4 And Penuel the father of Gedor, and Ezer the father of Hushah. These *are* the sons of Hur, the firstborn of Ephratah, the father of Beth-lehem.

Ashur's descendants

¶5 And Ashur the father of Tekoa had *two wives, Helah and Naarah.

6 And Naarah bare him Ahuzam, and Hepher, and Temeni, and Haahashtari. These *were* the sons of Naarah.

7 And the sons of Helah *were,* Zereth, and Jezoar, and Ethnan.

8 And Coz begat Anub, and Zobebah, and the families of Aharhel the son of Harum.

The prayer of Jabez

¶9 And Jabez was more honourable than his brethren: and his mother called his name Jabez, saying, Because I bare him with sorrow.

10 And Jabez called on the *God of Israel, saying, Oh that thou wouldest bless me indeed, and enlarge my coast, and that thine hand might be with me, and that thou wouldest keep *me* from evil, that it may not grieve me! And God granted him that which he requested.

4:9-10 A Simple Prayer

The list of names is interrupted to record the prayer of Jabez, whose father's name is not even mentioned. Jabez was honorable because he prayed, and he prayed because he was honorable. He exalted God, and God, therefore, exalted him. This prayer illustrates Proverbs 3:5-6 (see Prov. 3:6 note, "The LORD's Guidance"); 1 Samuel 2:30; and John 12:26.

Chelub's descendants

¶11 And Chelub the brother of Shuah begat Mehir, which *was* the father of Eshton.

12 And Eshton begat Beth-rapha, and Paseah, and Tehinnah the father of Irnahash. These *are* the men of Rechah.

13 And the sons of Kenaz; Othniel, and Seraiah: and the sons of Othniel; Hathath.

14 And Meonothai begat Ophrah: and Seraiah begat Joab, the father of the valley of Charashim; for they were craftsmen.

15 And the sons of Caleb the son of Jephunneh; Iru, Elah, and Naam: and the sons of Elah, even Kenaz.

16 And the sons of Jehaleleel; Ziph, and Ziphah, Tiria, and Asareel.

17 And the sons of Ezra *were,* Jether, and Mered, and Epher, and Jalon: and she bare *Miriam, and Shammai, and Ishbah the father of Eshtemoa.

18 And his wife Jehudijah bare Jered the father of Gedor, and Heber the father of Socho, and Jekuthiel the father of Zanoah. And these *are* the sons of Bithiah the daughter of *Pharaoh, which Mered took.

19 And the sons of *his* wife Hodiah the sister of Naham, the father of Keilah the Garmite, and Eshtemoa the Maachathite.

20 And the sons of Shimon *were,* Amnon, and Rinnah, Ben-hanan, and Tilon. And the sons of Ishi *were,* Zoheth, and Ben-zoheth.

Shelah's descendants

¶21 The sons of Shelah the son of Judah *were,* Er the father of Lecah, and

---

4:1 Hur, and Shobal. These were sons of Caleb, the son of Hezron (see 1 Chron. 2:18-19).

4:14 valley of Charashim. The valley of the craftsmen.

Laadah the father of Mareshah, and the families of the house of them that wrought fine *linen, of the house of Ashbea,
[22]And Jokim, and the men of Chozeba, and Joash, and Saraph, who had the dominion in Moab, and Jashubi-lehem. And *these are* ancient things.
[23]These *were* the potters, and those that dwelt among *plants and hedges: there they dwelt with the king for his work.

Simeon's descendants and their homes

¶[24]The sons of Simeon *were*, Nemuel, and Jamin, Jarib, Zerah, *and* Shaul:
[25]Shallum his son, Mibsam his son, Mishma his son.
[26]And the sons of Mishma; Hamuel his son, Zacchur his son, Shimei his son.
[27]And Shimei had sixteen sons and six daughters; but his brethren had not many children, neither did all their family multiply, like to the children of Judah.
[28]And they dwelt at *Beer-sheba, and Moladah, and Hazar-shual,
[29]And at Bilhah, and at Ezem, and at Tolad,
[30]And at Bethuel, and at Hormah, and at Ziklag,
[31]And at Beth-marcaboth, and Hazar-susim, and at Beth-birei, and at Shaaraim. These *were* their cities unto the reign of David.
[32]And their villages *were*, Etam, and Ain, Rimmon, and Tochen, and Ashan, five cities:
[33]And all their villages that *were* round about the same cities, unto *Baal. These *were* their habitations, and their genealogy.
[34]And Meshobab, and Jamlech, and Joshah the son of Amaziah,
[35]And Joel, and Jehu the son of Josibiah, the son of Seraiah, the son of Asiel,
[36]And Elioenai, and Jaakobah, and Jeshohaiah, and Asaiah, and Adiel, and Jesimiel, and Benaiah,
[37]And Ziza the son of Shiphi, the son of Allon, the son of Jedaiah, the son of Shimri, the son of Shemaiah;
[38]These mentioned by *their* names *were* princes in their families: and the house of their fathers increased greatly.

Gedor and the Amalekites conquered

¶[39]And they went to the entrance of Gedor, *even* unto the east side of the valley, to seek pasture for their flocks.
[40]And they found fat pasture and good, and the land *was* wide, and quiet, and peaceable; for *they* of Ham had dwelt there of old.
[41]And these written by name came in the days of Hezekiah king of Judah, and smote their tents, and the habitations that were found there, and destroyed them utterly unto this day, and dwelt in their rooms: because *there was* pasture there for their flocks.
[42]And *some* of them, *even* of the sons of Simeon, five hundred men, went to mount Seir, having for their captains Pelatiah, and Neariah, and Rephaiah, and Uzziel, the sons of Ishi.
[43]And they smote the rest of the Amalekites that were escaped, and dwelt there unto this day.

The Reubenites and their homes

5 Now the sons of Reuben the firstborn of Israel, (for he *was* the firstborn; but, forasmuch as he defiled his father's bed, his *birthright was given unto the sons of Joseph the son of Israel: and the genealogy is not to be reckoned after the birthright.
[2]For Judah prevailed above his

4:43 rest of the Amalekites. These Amalekites remained after Saul and David had killed many in their respective battles (1 Sam. 15:8; 30:17; 2 Sam. 8:12). Saul was instructed to kill all of them (see 1 Sam. 15:3).

5:1 Reuben the firstborn. See 1 Chronicles 2:3 note, "The Sons of Judah."

brethren, and of him *came* the chief
ruler; but the birthright *was* Joseph's:)
3The sons, *I say,* of Reuben the firstborn of Israel *were,* Hanoch, and Pallu,
Hezron, and Carmi.
4The sons of Joel; Shemaiah his son,
Gog his son, Shimei his son,
5Micah his son, Reaia his son, Baal
his son,
6Beerah his son, whom Tilgath-
pilneser king of Assyria carried away
captive: he *was* prince of the Reubenites.
7And his brethren by their families,
when the genealogy of their generations was reckoned, *were* the chief, Jeiel, and Zechariah,
8And Bela the son of Azaz, the son of
Shema, the son of Joel, who dwelt in
Aroer, even unto Nebo and Baal-meon:
9And eastward he inhabited unto
the entering in of the wilderness from
the river Euphrates: because their
cattle were multiplied in the land of
Gilead.
10And in the days of Saul they made
war with the Hagarites, who fell by
their hand: and they dwelt in their tents
throughout all the east *land* of Gilead.

The Gadites and their homes

¶11And the children of Gad dwelt
over against them, in the land of *Bashan unto Salchah:
12Joel the chief, and Shapham the
next, and Jaanai, and Shaphat in Bashan.
13And their brethren of the house of
their fathers *were,* Michael, and Meshullam, and Sheba, and Jorai, and
Jachan, and Zia, and Heber, seven.
14These *are* the children of Abihail the
son of Huri, the son of Jaroah, the son
of Gilead, the son of Michael, the son
of Jeshishai, the son of Jahdo, the son of
Buz;
15Ahi the son of Abdiel, the son of
Guni, chief of the house of their fathers.
16And they dwelt in Gilead in Bashan,
and in her towns, and in all the suburbs
of *Sharon, upon their borders.
17All these were reckoned by *genealogies in the days of Jotham king of
Judah, and in the days of Jeroboam king
of Israel.

Conquests of Reuben, Gad, and half Manasseh

¶18The sons of Reuben, and the Gadites, and half the tribe of Manasseh, of
valiant men, men able to bear *buckler
and sword, and to shoot with bow, and
skilful in war, *were* four and forty thousand seven hundred and threescore,
that went out to the war.
19And they made war with the
Hagarites, with Jetur, and Nephish, and
Nodab.
20And they were helped against
them, and the Hagarites were delivered
into their hand, and all that *were* with
them: for they cried to God in the battle, and he was intreated of them; because they put their *trust in him.
21And they took away their cattle; of
their camels fifty thousand, and of
sheep two hundred and fifty thousand,
and of asses two thousand, and of men
an hundred thousand.
22For there fell down many slain, because the war *was* of God. And they
dwelt in their steads until the captivity.

The half tribe of Manasseh

¶23And the children of the half tribe
of Manasseh dwelt in the land: they
increased from Bashan unto Baal-
hermon and Senir, and unto mount
Hermon.
24And these *were* the heads of the
house of their fathers, even Epher, and
Ishi, and Eliel, and Azriel, and Jeremiah,
and Hodaviah, and Jahdiel, mighty men
of valour, famous men, *and* heads of the
house of their fathers.

5:10 Hagarites. The descendants of Ishmael, the son of Hagar and Abraham (Gen. 25:12; see also Ps. 83:6 and its note, "Past Generations").

The captivity of Reuben, Gad, and half Manasseh

¶[25]And they transgressed against the
God of their fathers, and went a whoring after the gods of the people of the
land, whom God destroyed before
them.
[26]And the God of Israel stirred up the
spirit of Pul king of Assyria, and the
spirit of Tilgath-pilneser king of Assyria,
and he carried them away, even the
Reubenites, and the Gadites, and the
half tribe of Manasseh, and brought
them unto Halah, and Habor, and Hara,
and to the river Gozan, unto this day.

Levi and the priestly line

6 The sons of Levi; Gershon, Kohath, and Merari.
[2]And the sons of Kohath; Amram,
Izhar, and Hebron, and Uzziel.
[3]And the children of Amram; *Aaron,
and *Moses, and Miriam. The sons also
of Aaron; Nadab, and Abihu, Eleazar,
and Ithamar.
¶[4]Eleazar begat *Phinehas, Phinehas
begat Abishua,
[5]And Abishua begat Bukki, and Bukki begat Uzzi,
[6]And Uzzi begat Zerahiah, and Zerahiah begat Meraioth,
[7]Meraioth begat Amariah, and Amariah begat Ahitub,
[8]And Ahitub begat Zadok, and Zadok
begat Ahimaaz,
[9]And Ahimaaz begat Azariah, and
Azariah begat Johanan,
[10]And Johanan begat Azariah, (he *it
is* that executed the priest's office in
the temple that Solomon built in Jerusalem:)
[11]And Azariah begat Amariah, and
Amariah begat Ahitub,
[12]And Ahitub begat Zadok, and Zadok
begat Shallum,
[13]And Shallum begat Hilkiah, and
Hilkiah begat Azariah,
[14]And Azariah begat Seraiah, and
Seraiah begat Jehozadak,
[15]And Jehozadak went *into captivity,*
when the LORD carried away Judah
and Jerusalem by the hand of Nebuchadnezzar.
¶[16]The sons of Levi; Gershom, Kohath, and Merari.
[17]And these *be* the names of the sons
of Gershom; Libni, and Shimei.
[18]And the sons of Kohath *were,* Amram, and Izhar, and Hebron, and Uzziel.
[19]The sons of Merari; Mahli, and
Mushi. And these *are* the families of the
Levites according to their fathers.
[20]Of Gershom; Libni his son, Jahath
his son, Zimmah his son,
[21]Joah his son, Iddo his son, Zerah his
son, Jeaterai his son.
[22]The sons of Kohath; Amminadab
his son, *Korah his son, Assir his son,
[23]Elkanah his son, and Ebiasaph his
son, and Assir his son,
[24]Tahath his son, Uriel his son, Uzziah his son, and Shaul his son.
[25]And the sons of Elkanah; Amasai,
and Ahimoth.
[26]*As for* Elkanah: the sons of Elkanah;
Zophai his son, and Nahath his son,
[27]Eliab his son, Jeroham his son, Elkanah his son.
[28]And the sons of *Samuel; the firstborn Vashni, and Abiah.
[29]The sons of Merari; Mahli, Libni
his son, Shimei his son, Uzza his son,

5:25 transgressed against the God of their fathers. The reason for the captivity of these tribes is given here. A fuller account is given in 2 Kings 17:7-23 (see also notes for these verses).

5:26 Tilgath-pilneser. This king of Assyria is possibly the same as Pul, king of Assyria, mentioned in verse 26 and in 2 Kings 15:19. His name is also spelled Tiglath-pileser (2 Kings 5:29).

6:1 sons of Levi. The priestly tribe. We have here the line of high priests from Levi to the time of the Exile.

6:15 Jehozadak. Also called Jozadak and Josedech. His son, Joshua, or Jeshua the high priest, returned from Babylon (Ezra 3:2; 5:2; Neh. 12:26; Hag. 1:1,12; Zech. 6:11).

30Shimea his son, Haggiah his son,
Asaiah his son.
31And these *are they* whom David set
over the service of song in the house
of the LORD, after that the ark had rest.
32And they ministered before the
dwelling place of the *tabernacle of
the congregation with singing, until
Solomon had built the house of the
LORD in Jerusalem: and *then* they
waited on their office according to
their order.
33And these *are* they that waited with
their children. Of the sons of the Kohathites: Heman a singer, the son of
Joel, the son of Shemuel,
34The son of Elkanah, the son of Jeroham, the son of Eliel, the son of Toah,
35The son of Zuph, the son of Elkanah, the son of Mahath, the son of
Amasai,
36The son of Elkanah, the son of Joel,
the son of Azariah, the son of Zephaniah,
37The son of Tahath, the son of Assir,
the son of Ebiasaph, the son of Korah,
38The son of Izhar, the son of Kohath,
the son of Levi, the son of Israel.
39And his brother Asaph, who stood
on his right hand, *even* Asaph the son
of Berachiah, the son of Shimea,
40The son of Michael, the son of Ba-
aseiah, the son of Malchiah,
41The son of Ethni, the son of Zerah,
the son of Adaiah,
42The son of Ethan, the son of Zimmah, the son of Shimei,
43The son of Jahath, the son of Gershom, the son of Levi.
44And their brethren the sons of
Merari *stood* on the left hand: Ethan the
son of Kishi, the son of Abdi, the son of
Malluch,
45The son of Hashabiah, the son of
Amaziah, the son of Hilkiah,
46The son of Amzi, the son of Bani,
the son of Shamer,
47The son of Mahli, the son of Mushi,
the son of Merari, the son of Levi.
48Their brethren also the Levites *were*
appointed unto all manner of service of
the tabernacle of the house of God.

The office of Aaron and
his line to Ahimaz

¶49But Aaron and his sons offered
upon the *altar of the burnt-offering,
and on the altar of *incense, *and were*
appointed for all the work of the *place*
most *holy, and to make an *atonement
for Israel, according to all that Moses
the servant of God had commanded.
50And these *are* the sons of Aaron;
Eleazar his son, Phinehas his son,
Abishua his son,
51Bukki his son, Uzzi his son, Zerahiah his son,
52Meraioth his son, Amariah his son,
Ahitub his son,
53Zadok his son, Ahimaaz his son.

The homes of the priests and Levites

¶54Now these *are* their dwelling
places throughout their castles in their
coasts, of the sons of Aaron, of the families of the Kohathites: for theirs was
the lot.
55And they gave them Hebron in the
land of Judah, and the suburbs thereof
round about it.
56But the fields of the city, and the
villages thereof, they gave to Caleb the
son of Jephunneh.
57And to the sons of Aaron they gave
the cities of Judah, *namely,* Hebron, *the*
city of refuge, and Libnah with her sub-

6:31 ark had rest. That is, when David brought the ark from the house of Obed-edom to Jerusalem (see 1 Chron.15:25-29 and 15:28 note, "The Ark").
6:33 Heman. Samuel's grandson, Heman, who wrote Psalm 88.
6:39 Asaph. This singer and seer (2 Chron. 29:30) is known to us as the author of many Psalms (see Pss. 50; 73–83). His sons were also singers in the temple (1 Chron. 25:1-2 and vs. 1 note, "The Ministry of Music"; Ezra 2:41).
6:44 Ethan. Ethan, or Jeduthun, is the author of Psalm 89.
6:57 city of refuge. See *cities of refuge.

urbs, and Jattir, and Eshtemoa, with
their suburbs,
58And Hilen with her suburbs, Debir
with her suburbs,
59And Ashan with her suburbs, and
Beth-shemesh with her suburbs:
60And out of the tribe of Benjamin;
Geba with her suburbs, and Alemeth
with her suburbs, and Anathoth with
her suburbs. All their cities throughout
their families *were* thirteen cities.
61And unto the sons of Kohath, *which
were* left of the family of that tribe, *were
cities given* out of the half tribe, *namely,
out of* the half *tribe* of Manasseh, by lot,
ten cities.
62And to the sons of Gershom
throughout their families out of the
tribe of Issachar, and out of the tribe of
Asher, and out of the tribe of Naphtali,
and out of the tribe of Manasseh in Bashan, thirteen cities.
63Unto the sons of Merari *were given*
by lot, throughout their families, out of
the tribe of Reuben, and out of the tribe
of Gad, and out of the tribe of Zebulun,
twelve cities.
64And the children of Israel gave to the
Levites *these* cities with their suburbs.
65And they gave by lot out of the tribe
of the children of Judah, and out of the
tribe of the children of Simeon, and out
of the tribe of the children of Benjamin,
these cities, which are called by *their*
names.
66And *the residue* of the families of the
sons of Kohath had cities of their coasts
out of the tribe of *Ephraim.
67And they gave unto them, *of* the
cities of refuge, *Shechem in mount
Ephraim with her suburbs; *they gave*
also Gezer with her suburbs,
68And Jokmeam with her suburbs,
and Beth-horon with her suburbs,
69And Aijalon with her suburbs, and
Gath-rimmon with her suburbs:
70And out of the half tribe of Manasseh; Aner with her suburbs, and Bileam with her suburbs, for the family of
the remnant of the sons of Kohath.
71Unto the sons of Gershom *were
given* out of the family of the half tribe
of Manasseh, Golan in Bashan with her
suburbs, and *Ashtaroth with her suburbs:
72And out of the tribe of Issachar;
Kedesh with her suburbs, Daberath
with her suburbs,
73And Ramoth with her suburbs, and
Anem with her suburbs:
74And out of the tribe of Asher; Mashal with her suburbs, and Abdon with
her suburbs,
75And Hukok with her suburbs, and
Rehob with her suburbs:
76And out of the tribe of Naphtali;
Kedesh in Galilee with her suburbs, and
Hammon with her suburbs, and Kirjathaim with her suburbs.
77Unto the rest of the children of Merari *were given* out of the tribe of Zebulun, Rimmon with her suburbs, Tabor
with her suburbs:
78And on the other side Jordan by
Jericho, on the east side of Jordan, *were
given them* out of the tribe of Reuben,
Bezer in the wilderness with her suburbs, and Jahzah with her suburbs,
79Kedemoth also with her suburbs,
and Mephaath with her suburbs:
80And out of the tribe of Gad; Ramoth
in Gilead with her suburbs, and Mahanaim with her suburbs,
81And Heshbon with her suburbs,
and Jazer with her suburbs.

Issachar's descendants

7 Now the sons of Issachar *were,*
Tola, and Puah, Jashub, and Shimron, four.
2And the sons of Tola; Uzzi, and Rephaiah, and Jeriel, and Jahmai, and
Jibsam, and Shemuel, heads of their
father's house, *to wit,* of Tola: *they were*
valiant men of might in their generations; whose number *was* in the days of
David two and twenty thousand and six
hundred.
3And the sons of Uzzi; Izrahiah: and
the sons of Izrahiah; Michael, and Obadiah, and Joel, Ishiah, five: all of them
chief men.

4 And with them, by their generations, after the house of their fathers,
were bands of soldiers for war, six and
thirty thousand *men:* for they had many
wives and sons.
5 And their brethren among all the
families of Issachar *were* valiant men of
might, reckoned in all by their genealogies fourscore and seven thousand.

Benjamin's descendants

¶6 *The sons* of Benjamin; Bela, and
Becher, and Jediael, three.

7:6 The Sons of Benjamin
In Genesis 46:21, we find all the names of Benjamin's ten sons; three are mentioned here, but five are given in 1 Chronicles 8:1-2. It is believed that the other five were killed in the awful slaughter of Judges 20. These genealogies are imperfect, however. Ruin had fallen upon Israel and it is, of course, reflected in the records that were kept. There were some who kept their lists carefully in Babylon; others were careless and were not mindful of the promises of God to His people. They lost the proof that they were really of His chosen family. Those who kept the records looked forward in faith to the time when they would return to their land.

7 And the sons of Bela; Ezbon, and
Uzzi, and Uzziel, and Jerimoth, and Iri,
five; heads of the house of *their* fathers,
mighty men of valour; and were reckoned by their genealogies twenty and
two thousand and thirty and four.
8 And the sons of Becher; Zemira,
and Joash, and Eliezer, and Elioenai, and
Omri, and Jerimoth, and Abiah, and
Anathoth, and Alameth. All these *are*
the sons of Becher.
9 And the number of them, after their
genealogy by their generations, heads
of the house of their fathers, mighty
men of valour, *was* twenty thousand and
two hundred.
10 The sons also of Jediael; Bilhan:
and the sons of Bilhan; Jeush, and Benjamin, and Ehud, and Chenaanah, and
Zethan, and Tharshish, and Ahishahar.
11 All these the sons of Jediael, by the
heads of their fathers, mighty men of
valour, *were* seventeen thousand and
two hundred *soldiers,* fit to go out for
war *and* battle.
12 Shuppim also, and Huppim, the
children of Ir, *and* Hushim, the sons of
Aher.

Naphtali's descendants

¶13 The sons of Naphtali; Jahziel, and
Guni, and Jezer, and Shallum, the sons
of Bilhah.

Manasseh's descendants

¶14 The sons of Manasseh; Ashriel,
whom she bare: (*but* his *concubine the
Aramitess bare Machir the father of
Gilead:
15 And Machir took to wife *the sister*
of Huppim and Shuppim, whose sister's
name *was* Maachah;) and the name of
the second *was* Zelophehad: and Zelophehad had daughters.
16 And Maachah the wife of Machir
bare a son, and she called his name
Peresh; and the name of his brother *was*
Sheresh; and his sons *were* Ulam and
Rakem.
17 And the sons of Ulam; Bedan.
These *were* the sons of Gilead, the son
of Machir, the son of Manasseh.
18 And his sister Hammoleketh bare
Ishod, and Abiezer, and Mahalah.
19 And the sons of Shemidah were,
Ahian, and Shechem, and Likhi, and
Aniam.

The Ephraimites and their homes

¶20 And the sons of Ephraim; Shuthelah, and Bered his son, and Tahath his
son, and Eladah his son, and Tahath his
son,
¶21 And Zabad his son, and Shuthelah
his son, and Ezer, and Elead, whom the
men of *Gath *that were* born in *that* land
slew, because they came down to take
away their cattle.
22 And Ephraim their father mourned
many days, and his brethren came to
comfort him.
¶23 And when he went in to his wife,

she conceived, and bare a son, and he
called his name Beriah, because it went
evil with his house.
[24](And his daughter *was* Sherah, who
built Beth-horon the nether, and the
upper, and Uzzen-sherah.)
[25]And Rephah *was* his son, also Re-
sheph, and Telah his son, and Tahan
his son,
[26]Laadan his son, Ammihud his son,
Elishama his son,
[27]Non his son, *Jehoshua his son.
¶[28]And their possessions and habitations *were,* *Beth-el and the towns
thereof, and eastward Naaran, and westward Gezer, with the towns thereof;
Shechem also and the towns thereof,
unto *Gaza and the towns thereof:
[29]And by the borders of the children
of Manasseh, Beth-shean and her
towns, Taanach and her towns, *Megiddo and her towns, Dor and her towns.
In these dwelt the children of Joseph
the son of *Israel.

Asher's descendants

¶[30]The sons of Asher; Imnah, and
Isuah, and Ishuai, and Beriah, and Serah their sister.
[31]And the sons of Beriah; Heber,
and Malchiel, who *is* the father of Birza-
vith.
[32]And Heber begat Japhlet, and Shomer, and Hotham, and Shua their sister.
[33]And the sons of Japhlet; Pasach, and
Bimhal, and Ashvath. These *are* the
children of Japhlet.
[34]And the sons of Shamer; Ahi, and
Rohgah, Jehubbah, and Aram.
[35]And the sons of his brother Helem;
Zophah, and Imna, and Shelesh, and
Amal.
[36]The sons of Zophah; Suah, and Har-
nepher, and Shual, and Beri, and Imrah,
[37]Bezer, and Hod, and Shamma, and
Shilshah, and Ithran, and Beera.
[38]And the sons of Jether; Jephunneh,
and Pispah, and Ara.
[39]And the sons of Ulla; Arah, and
Haniel, and Rezia.
[40]All these *were* the children of Asher,
heads of *their* father's house, choice *and*
mighty men of valour, chief of the
princes. And the number throughout
the genealogy of them that were apt
to the war *and* to battle *was* twenty and
six thousand men.

The chief Benjamites

8 Now Benjamin begat Bela his
firstborn, Ashbel the second, and
Aharah the third,
[2]Nohah the fourth, and Rapha the
fifth.
[3]And the sons of Bela were, Addar,
and Gera, and Abihud,
[4]And Abishua, and Naaman, and
Ahoah,
[5]And Gera, and Shephuphan, and
Huram.
[6]And these *are* the sons of Ehud:
these are the heads of the fathers of the
inhabitants of Geba, and they removed
them to Manahath:
[7]And Naaman, and Ahiah, and Gera,
he removed them, and begat Uzza, and
Ahihud.
[8]And Shaharaim begat *children* in the
country of *Moab, after he had sent
them away; Hushim and Baara *were* his
wives.
[9]And he begat of Hodesh his wife,
Jobab, and Zibia, and Mesha, and Malcham,
[10]And Jeuz, and Shachia, and Mirma.
These *were* his sons, heads of the fathers.
[11]And of Hushim he begat Abitub,
and Elpaal.
[12]The sons of Elpaal; Eber, and Mi-
sham, and Shamed, who built Ono, and
Lod, with the towns thereof:
[13]Beriah also, and Shema, who *were*
heads of the fathers of the inhabitants
of Aijalon, who drove away the inhabitants of Gath:
[14]And Ahio, Shashak, and Jeremoth,
[15]And Zebadiah, and Arad, and Ader,
[16]And Michael, and Ispah, and Joha,
the sons of Beriah;
[17]And Zebadiah, and Meshullam, and
Hezeki, and Heber,

18Ishmerai also, and Jezliah, and Jobab, the sons of Elpaal;
19And Jakim, and Zichri, and Zabdi,
20And Elienai, and Zilthai, and Eliel,
21And Adaiah, and Beraiah, and Shim-
rath, the sons of Shimhi;
22And Ishpan, and Heber, and Eliel,
23And Abdon, and Zichri, and Hanan,
24And Hananiah, and Elam, and Anto-
thijah,
25And Iphedeiah, and Penuel, the
sons of Shashak;
26And Shamsherai, and Shehariah,
and Athaliah,
27And Jaresiah, and Eliah, and Zichri,
the sons of Jeroham.
28These *were* heads of the fathers, by
their generations, chief *men*. These
dwelt in Jerusalem.
29And at Gibeon dwelt the father of
Gibeon; whose wife's name *was* Maachah:
30And his firstborn son Abdon,
and Zur, and Kish, and Baal, and Nadab,
31And Gedor, and Ahio, and Zacher.
32And Mikloth begat Shimeah. And
these also dwelt with their brethren in
Jerusalem, over against them.
¶33And Ner begat Kish, and Kish
begat Saul, and Saul begat Jonathan, and
Malchi-shua, and Abinadab, and Esh-
baal.
34And the son of Jonathan *was* Merib-
baal; and Merib-baal begat Micah.
35And the sons of Micah *were*, Pithon,
and Melech, and Tarea, and Ahaz.
36And Ahaz begat Jehoadah; and
Jehoadah begat Alemeth, and Azmaveth, and Zimri; and Zimri begat Moza,
37And Moza begat Binea: Rapha *was*
his son, Eleasah his son, Azel his son:
38And Azel had six sons, whose
names *are* these, Azrikam, Bocheru,
and Ishmael, and Sheariah, and Obadiah, and Hanan. All these *were* the sons
of Azel.
39And the sons of Eshek his brother
were, Ulam his firstborn, Jehush the
second, and Eliphelet the third.
40And the sons of Ulam were mighty
men of valour, archers, and had many
sons, and sons' sons, an hundred and
fifty. All these *are* of the sons of Benjamin.

The book of the kings

9 So all Israel were reckoned by genealogies; and, behold, they *were*
written in the book of the kings of Israel and *Judah, *who* were carried away
to *Babylon for their transgression.

9:1 The Public Records
This chapter indicates that one of the purposes of these records was to direct the Jews returning from captivity in Babylon with whom to become united and where to live. From the beginning of the nation, public records were kept. The complete list was kept in "the book of the kings of Israel and Judah." This is not the books of the Kings that we have in our Bibles. The genealogies of chapters 1 to 8 were taken from the long registers. The names in this chapter are those who lived in Jerusalem after the Exile.

The Israelites and their numbers

¶2Now the first inhabitants that *dwelt*
in their possessions in their cities *were*,
the Israelites, the priests, Levites, and
the *Nethinims.
3And in *Jerusalem dwelt of the children of Judah, and of the children of

8:33 Kish begat Saul. Saul's overthrow and death (1 Chron. 10:1-13; see vs. 13 note, "King Saul's Death") mark the beginning of the real historical records of the Chronicles.

8:34 Merib-baal. Another name for Mephibosheth (2 Sam. 9), whose favored place under King David is a delightful picture of God's grace (see 2 Sam. 9:3 note, "God's Kindness").

9:2 first inhabitants. These returning Jews were made up of four classes: 1) the people, or laymen, here called by the general name, Israelites, for while the northern kingdom of Israel did not return from captivity, it is likely that a few scattered families of that kingdom returned with Judah; 2) priests; 3) Levites; and 4) the *Nethinims.

Benjamin, and of the children of Ephraim, and *Manasseh;
4 Uthai the son of Ammihud, the son
of Omri, the son of Imri, the son of Bani,
of the children of Pharez the son of
Judah.
5 And of the Shilonites; Asaiah the
firstborn, and his sons.
6 And of the sons of Zerah; Jeuel, and
their brethren, six hundred and ninety.
7 And of the sons of Benjamin; Sallu
the son of Meshullam, the son of Hodaviah, the son of Hasenuah,
8 And Ibneiah the son of Jeroham, and
Elah the son of Uzzi, the son of Michri,
and Meshullam the son of Shephathiah,
the son of Reuel, the son of Ibnijah;
9 And their brethren, according to
their generations, nine hundred and fifty and six. All these men *were* chief of
the fathers in the house of their fathers.

The priests and their numbers

¶10 And of the priests; Jedaiah, and Jehoiarib, and *Jachin,
11 And Azariah the son of Hilkiah, the
son of Meshullam, the son of Zadok,
the son of Meraioth, the son of Ahitub,
the ruler of the house of God;
12 And Adaiah the son of Jeroham, the
son of Pashur, the son of Malchijah, and
Maasiai the son of Adiel, the son of Jah-
zerah, the son of Meshullam, the son of
Meshillemith, the son of Immer;
13 And their brethren, heads of the
house of their fathers, a thousand and
seven hundred and threescore; very
able men for the work of the service of
the house of God.

The Levites and certain of their duties

14 And of the Levites; Shemaiah the
son of Hasshub, the son of Azrikam, the
son of Hashabiah, of the sons of Merari;
15 And Bakbakkar, Heresh, and Galal,
and Mattaniah the son of Micah, the son
of Zichri, the son of *Asaph;
16 And Obadiah the son of Shemaiah,
the son of Galal, the son of *Jeduthun,
and Berechiah the son of Asa, the son
of Elkanah, that dwelt in the villages of
the Netophathites.
17 And the *porters *were,* Shallum,
and Akkub, and Talmon, and Ahiman,
and their brethren: Shallum *was* the
chief;
18 Who hitherto *waited* in the king's
gate eastward: they *were* porters in the
companies of the children of Levi.
19 And Shallum the son of Kore, the
son of Ebiasaph, the son of *Korah, and
his brethren, of the house of his father,
the Korahites, *were* over the work of the
service, keepers of the gates of the tabernacle: and their fathers, *being* over
the host of the LORD, *were* keepers of
the entry.
20 And *Phinehas the son of Eleazar
was the ruler over them in time past,
and the LORD *was* with him.
21 *And* Zechariah the son of Meshelemiah *was* porter of the door of the tabernacle of the congregation.
22 All these *which were* chosen to be
porters in the gates *were* two hundred
and twelve. These were reckoned by
their genealogy in their villages, whom
*David and Samuel the seer did ordain
in their set office.
23 So they and their children *had* the
oversight of the gates of the *house of
the LORD, *namely,* the house of the tabernacle, by wards.
24 In four quarters were the porters,
toward the east, west, north, and south.
25 And their brethren, *which were* in
their villages, *were* to come after seven
days from time to time with them.
26 For these Levites, the four chief
porters, were in *their* set office, and
were over the chambers and treasuries
of the house of God.
¶27 And they lodged round about the
house of God, because the charge *was*
upon them, and the opening thereof
every morning *pertained* to them.
28 And *certain* of them had the charge
of the ministering vessels, that they
should bring them in and out by tale.
29 *Some* of them also *were* appointed
to oversee the vessels, and all the

instruments of the *sanctuary, and the fine flour, and the *wine, and the *oil, and the frankincense, and the spices.

30 And _some_ of the sons of the priests made the ointment of the spices.

31 And Mattithiah, _one_ of the Levites, who _was_ the firstborn of Shallum the Korahite, had the set office over the things that were made in the pans.

32 And _other_ of their brethren, of the sons of the Kohathites, _were_ over the *shewbread, to prepare _it_ every *sabbath.

33 And these _are_ the singers, chief of the fathers of the Levites, _who remaining_ in the chambers _were_ free: for they were employed in _that_ work day and night.

34 These chief fathers of the Levites _were_ chief throughout their generations; these dwelt at Jerusalem.

The ancestry and descendants of King Saul

¶35 And in Gibeon dwelt the father of Gibeon, Jehiel, whose wife's name _was_ Maachah:

36 And his firstborn son Abdon, then Zur, and Kish, and Baal, and Ner, and Nadab,

37 And Gedor, and Ahio, and Zechariah, and Mikloth.

38 And Mikloth begat Shimeam. And they also dwelt with their brethren at Jerusalem, over against their brethren.

39 And Ner begat Kish; and Kish begat Saul; and Saul begat Jonathan, and Malchi-shua, and Abinadab, and Esh-baal.

40 And the son of Jonathan _was_ Merib-baal: and Merib-baal begat Micah.

41 And the sons of Micah _were_, Pithon, and Melech, and Tahrea, _and Ahaz._

42 And Ahaz begat Jarah; and Jarah begat Alemeth, and Azmaveth, and Zimri; and Zimri begat Moza;

43 And Moza begat Binea; and Rephaiah his son, Eleasah his son, Azel his son.

44 And Azel had six sons, whose names _are_ these, Azrikam, Bocheru, and Ishmael, and Sheariah, and Obadiah, and Hanan: these _were_ the sons of Azel.

II. Saul's Death and the Accession of David to the Throne (10:1—12:40)

The *death of King Saul (1 Sam. 31)

10 Now the *Philistines fought against Israel; and the men of Israel fled from before the Philistines, and fell down slain in mount Gilboa.

2 And the Philistines followed hard after Saul, and after his sons; and the Philistines slew Jonathan, and Abinadab, and Malchi-shua, the sons of Saul.

3 And the battle went sore against Saul, and the archers hit him, and he was wounded of the archers.

4 Then said Saul to his armourbearer, Draw thy sword, and thrust me through therewith; lest these *uncircumcised come and abuse me. But his armourbearer would not; for he was sore afraid. So Saul took a sword, and fell upon it.

5 And when his armourbearer saw that Saul was dead, he fell likewise on the sword, and died.

6 So Saul died, and his three sons, and all his house died together.

7 And when all the men of Israel that _were_ in the valley saw that they fled, and that Saul and his sons were dead, then they forsook their cities, and fled: and the Philistines came and dwelt in them.

¶8 And it came to pass on the morrow, when the Philistines came to strip the slain, that they found Saul and his sons fallen in mount Gilboa.

9 And when they had stripped him, they took his head, and his armour, and sent into the land of the Philistines round about, to carry tidings unto their idols, and to the people.

9:35 And in Gibeon. Verses 35 to 44 are a repetition of 8:29-38. The section in chapter 8 belongs in the genealogies of the tribe of Benjamin, and this repeated record in chapter 9 introduces Saul, whose death is next to be recorded.

10 And they put his armour in the house of their gods, and fastened his head in the temple of Dagon.

¶11 And when all Jabesh-gilead heard all that the Philistines had done to Saul,

12 They arose, all the valiant men, and took away the body of Saul, and the bodies of his sons, and brought them to Jabesh, and buried their bones under the oak in Jabesh, and fasted seven days.

The reason for Saul's death

¶13 So Saul died for his transgression which he committed against the LORD, *even* against the word of the LORD, which he kept not, and also for asking *counsel* of *one that had* a familiar spirit, to enquire *of it;*

> **10:13 King Saul's Death**
> It is definitely stated that Saul died because of his sin, for "the wages of sin is death" (Rom. 6:23). We too deserve death because of sin, but by God's grace we can say, "Christ died for my sins" and receive His gift of salvation. But the warning of 2 Thessalonians 1:7-9 is clear to all who do not obey the gospel. They, like Saul, will die for their sin.

14 And enquired not of the LORD: therefore he slew him, and turned the kingdom unto David the son of Jesse.

David anointed King over Israel
(2 Sam. 5:1-3)

11 Then all Israel gathered themselves to David unto Hebron, saying, Behold, we *are* thy bone and thy flesh.

2 And moreover in time past, even when Saul was king, thou *wast* he that leddest out and broughtest in Israel: and the LORD thy *God said unto thee, Thou shalt feed my people Israel, and thou shalt be ruler over my people Israel.

3 Therefore came all the *elders of Israel to the king to Hebron; and David made a *covenant with them in Hebron before the LORD; and they anointed David king over Israel, according to the word of the LORD by Samuel.

Jerusalem made the capital of the united kingdom (2 Sam. 5:6-12)

¶4 And David and all Israel went to Jerusalem, which *is* Jebus; where the Jebusites *were,* the inhabitants of the land.

5 And the inhabitants of Jebus said to David, Thou shalt not come hither. Nevertheless David took the castle of *Zion, which *is* the city of David.

> **11:5 A Place Called Zion**
> This Hebrew word means *fortified place*. Zion occupies the southwest part of what is now Jerusalem and is associated with the kingship of David both in history and prophecy (1 Chron. 11:7; Ps. 2:6; Isa. 2:3). Sometimes Zion refers to the entire city of Jerusalem, considered as the City of God (Ps. 48:2-3 and vs. 2 note, "Mount Zion"; Isa. 1:27; 2:3; 4:1-6; Rom. 11:26).

6 And David said, Whosoever smiteth the Jebusites first shall be chief and captain. So Joab the son of Zeruiah went first up, and was chief.

7 And David dwelt in the castle; therefore they called it the city of David.

8 And he built the city round about, even from *Millo round about: and Joab repaired the rest of the city.

9 So David waxed greater and greater: for the LORD of hosts *was* with him.

David's mighty men (2 Sam. 23:8-39)

¶10 These also *are* the chief of the mighty men whom David had, who

---

10:13 asking counsel of one that had a familiar spirit. See 1 Samuel 28:7-20 (and 28:3 note, "Familiar Spirits") for a detailed account of Saul's sin. See also 1 Samuel 13:13-14 and 15:22-26 for Saul's previous sin.

11:1 Hebron. David had already been king of Judah for seven-and-one-half years, with his capital at Hebron (2 Sam. 2:1-4). After he became king of Israel, he moved his capital to Jerusalem, where he reigned thirty-three years.

strengthened themselves with him in his kingdom, *and* with all Israel, to make him king, according to the word of the LORD concerning Israel.

11 And this *is* the number of the mighty men whom David had; Jashobeam, and Hachmonite, the chief of the captains: he lifted up his spear against three hundred slain *by him* at one time.

12 And after him *was* Eleazar the son of Dodo, the Ahohite, who *was one* of the three mighties.

13 He was with David at Pas-dammim, and there the Philistines were gathered together to battle, where was a parcel of ground full of barley; and the people fled from before the Philistines.

14 And they set themselves in the midst of *that* parcel, and delivered it, and slew the Philistines; and the LORD saved *them* by a great deliverance.

¶ 15 Now three of the thirty captains went down to the rock to David, into the cave of Adullam; and the host of the Philistines encamped in the valley of Rephaim.

16 And David *was* then in the hold, and the Philistines' garrison *was* then at Beth-lehem.

17 And David longed, and said, Oh that one would give me drink of the water of the well of Beth-lehem, that *is* at the gate!

18 And the three brake through the host of the Philistines, and drew water out of the well of Beth-lehem, that *was* by the gate, and took *it,* and brought *it* to David: but David would not drink *of* it, but poured it out to the LORD,

19 And said, My God forbid it me, that I should do this thing: shall I drink the blood of these men that have put their lives in jeopardy? for with *the jeopardy of* their lives they brought it. Therefore he would not drink it. These things did these three mightiest.

¶ 20 And Abishai the brother of Joab, he was chief of the three: for lifting up his spear against three hundred, he slew *them,* and had a name among the three.

21 Of the three, he was more honourable than the two; for he was their captain: howbeit he attained not to the *first* three.

22 Benaiah the son of *Jehoiada, the son of a valiant man of Kabzeel, who had done many acts; he slew two lionlike men of Moab: also he went down and slew a lion in a pit in a snowy day.

23 And he slew an Egyptian, a man of *great* stature, five *cubits high; and in the Egyptian's hand *was* a spear like a weaver's beam; and he went down to him with a staff, and plucked the spear out of the Egyptian's hand, and slew him with his own spear.

24 These *things* did Benaiah the son of Jehoiada, and had the name among the three mighties.

25 Behold, he was honourable among the thirty, but attained not to the *first* three: and David set him over his guard.

¶ 26 Also the valiant men of the armies *were,* Asahel the brother of Joab, Elhanan the son of Dodo of Beth-lehem,

27 Shammoth the Harorite, Helez the Pelonite,

28 Ira the son of Ikkesh the Tekoite, Abi-ezer the Antothite,

29 Sibbecai the Hushathite, Ilai the Ahohite,

30 Maharai the Netophathite, Heled the son of Baanah the Netophathite,

31 Ithai the son of Ribai of Gibeah, *that pertained* to the children of Benjamin, Benaiah the Pirathonite,

32 Hurai of the brooks of Gaash, Abiel the Arbathite,

33 Azmaveth the Baharumite, Eliahba the Shaalbonite,

34 The sons of Hashem the Gizonite, Jonathan the son of Shage the Hararite,

---

11:18 David . . . poured it out. David here showed his greatness, proof that he was a "man after mine [God's] own heart" (Acts 13:22): 1) he was humble; 2) he valued human life; and 3) he showed self-control in not quenching his thirst.

35 Ahiam the son of Sacar the Hararite, Eliphal the son of Ur,
36 Hepher the Mecherathite, Ahijah
the Pelonite,
37 Hezro the Carmelite, Naarai the
son of Ezbai,
38 Joel the brother of Nathan, Mibhar
the son of Haggeri,
39 Zelek the Ammonite, Naharai the
Berothite, the armourbearer of Joab the
son of Zeruiah,
40 Ira the Ithrite, Gareb the Ithrite,
41 Uriah the Hittite, Zabad the son of
Ahlai,
42 Adina the son of Shiza the Reuben-
ite, a captain of the Reubenites, and
thirty with him,
43 Hanan the son of Maachah, and
Joshaphat the Mithnite,
44 Uzzia the Ashterathite, Shama and
Jehiel the sons of Hothan the Aroerite,
45 Jediael the son of Shimri, and Joha
his brother, the Tizite,
46 Eliel the Mahavite, and Jeribai, and
Joshaviah, the sons of Elnaam, and Ith-
mah the Moabite,
47 Eliel, and Obed, and Jasiel the
Mesobaite.

David's mighty men (continued)

12 Now these *are* they that came
to David to Ziklag, while he yet
kept himself close because of Saul the
son of Kish: and they *were* among the
mighty men, helpers of the war.
2 *They were* armed with bows, and
could use both the right hand and the
left in *hurling* stones and *shooting* arrows out of a bow, *even* of Saul's brethren of Benjamin.
3 The chief *was* Ahiezer, then *Joash,
the sons of Shemaah the Gibeathite; and
Jeziel, and Pelet, the sons of Azmaveth;
and Berachah, and Jehu the Antothite,
4 And Ismaiah the Gibeonite, a mighty
man among the thirty, and over the thirty; and Jeremiah, and Jahaziel, and Johanan, and Josabad the Gederathite,
5 Eluzai, and Jerimoth, and Bealiah,
and Shemariah, and Shephatiah the
Haruphite,
6 Elkanah, and Jesiah, and Azareel,
and Joezer, and Jashobeam, the
Korhites,
7 And Joelah, and Zebadiah, the sons
of Jeroham of Gedor.

(1 Chron. 12:8-15 follows the events of 2 Sam. 5:17 and 1 Chron. 14:8)

8 And of the Gadites there separated
themselves unto David into the hold to
the wilderness men of might, *and* men
of war *fit* for the battle, that could handle shield and *buckler, whose faces
were like the faces of lions, and *were* as
swift as the roes upon the mountains;
9 Ezer the first, Obadiah the second,
Eliab the third,
10 Mishmannah the fourth, Jeremiah
the fifth,
11 Attai the sixth, Eliel the seventh,
12 Johanan the eighth, Elzabad the
ninth,
13 Jeremiah the tenth, Machbanai the
eleventh.
14 These *were* of the sons of Gad, captains of the host: one of the least *was*
over an hundred, and the greatest over
a thousand.
15 These *are* they that went over Jordan in the first *month, when it had
overflown all his banks; and they put to
flight all *them* of the valleys, *both* toward
the east, and toward the west.
16 And there came of the children of
Benjamin and Judah to the hold unto
David.
17 And David went out to meet them,
and answered and said unto them, If ye
be come peaceably unto me to help me,
mine heart shall be knit unto you: but
if *ye be come* to betray me to mine enemies, seeing *there is* no wrong in mine
hands, the God of our fathers look
thereon, and rebuke *it.*
18 Then the spirit came upon Amasai,

12:8 the hold. This was the cave of Adullam where David hid from Saul (1 Sam. 22:1,5).
12:18 Amasai. The Amasa of 2 Samuel 17:25.

who was chief of the captains, *and he said,* Thine *are we,* David, and on thy side, thou son of Jesse: *peace, peace *be* unto thee, and peace *be* to thine helpers; for thy God helpeth thee. Then David received them, and made them captains of the band.
19And there fell *some* of Manasseh to
David, when he came with the Philistines against Saul to battle: but they helped them not: for the lords of the Philistines upon advisement sent him away, saying, He will fall to his master Saul to *the jeopardy of* our heads.
20As he went to Ziklag, there fell to
him of Manasseh, Adnah, and Jozabad, and Jediael, and Michael, and Jozabad, and Elihu, and Zilthai, captains of the thousands that *were* of Manasseh.
21And they helped David against the
band *of the rovers:* for they *were* all mighty men of valour, and were captains in the host.

12:22 A Gathering of People
We must remember that these verses refer to the period when David, not yet king, was rejected by most of the people. It is typical of the Lord Jesus Christ, who, though now rejected by most of the world, is gathering to Himself a great host of people from all nations to be His followers (Acts 15:14).

22For at *that* time day by day there
came to David to help him, until *it was* a great host, like the host of God.

The men who made David king

¶23And these *are* the numbers of the
bands *that were* ready armed to the war, *and* came to David to Hebron, to turn the kingdom of Saul to him, according to the word of the LORD.
24The children of Judah that bare
shield and spear *were* six thousand and eight hundred, ready armed to the war.
25Of the children of Simeon, mighty
men of valour for the war, seven thousand and one hundred.
26Of the children of Levi four thou-
sand and six hundred.
27And Jehoiada *was* the leader of the
Aaronites, and with him *were* three thousand and seven hundred;
28And Zadok, a young man mighty of
valour, and of his father's house twenty and two captains.
29And of the children of Benjamin,
the kindred of Saul, three thousand: for hitherto the greatest part of them had kept the ward of the house of Saul.
30And of the children of *Ephraim
twenty thousand and eight hundred, mighty men of valour, famous throughout the house of their fathers.
31And of the half tribe of Manasseh
eighteen thousand, which were expressed by name, to come and make David king.
32And of the children of Issachar,
which were men that had understanding of the times, to know what Israel ought to do; the heads of them *were* two hundred; and all their brethren *were* at their commandment.
33Of Zebulun, such as went forth to
battle, expert in war, with all instruments of war, fifty thousand, which could keep rank: *they were* not of double heart.
34And of Naphtali a thousand cap-
tains, and with them with shield and spear thirty and seven thousand.
35And of the Danites expert in war
twenty and eight thousand and six hundred.
36And of Asher, such as went forth to
battle, expert in war, forty thousand.
37And on the other side of Jordan, of
the Reubenites, and the Gadites, and of the half tribe of Manasseh, with all manner of instruments of war for the battle, an hundred and twenty thousand.
38All these men of war, that could

12:38 All these men of war. There were 339,600 men (1 Chron. 12:23-27,29-31,33,37), besides the 1,224 chiefs and leaders (1 Chron. 12:27: "Jehoiada . . . and with him"; vs. 28: "Zadok . . . and twenty and two captains"; and vs. 32).

keep rank, came with a *perfect heart
to Hebron, to make David king over all
Israel: and all the rest also of Israel *were*
of one heart to make David king.
39And there they were with David
three days, eating and drinking: for
their brethren had prepared for them.
40Moreover they that were nigh
them, *even* unto Issachar and Zebulun
and Naphtali, brought bread on asses,
and on camels, and on mules, and on
oxen, *and* meat, meal, cakes of figs, and
bunches of raisins, and wine, and oil,
and oxen, and sheep abundantly: for
there was joy in Israel.

12:40 Joy in Israel
Joy in Israel followed David's ascending the throne of Israel (vs. 38). This foreshadows the joy that will be Israel's when the greater David, our Lord Himself, ascends the throne in Jerusalem at His second coming. See *kingdom.

III. Triumphs of David's Reign
(13:1—21:30)
*David sends for the *ark*
(2 Sam. 6:1-11)

13 And David consulted with the
captains of thousands and hundreds, *and* with every leader.
2And David said unto all the congregation of *Israel, If *it seem* good unto
you, and *that it be* of the LORD our God,
let us send abroad unto our brethren
every where, *that are* left in all the land
of Israel, and with them *also* to the
priests and Levites *which are* in their
cities *and* suburbs, that they may gather themselves unto us:
3And let us bring again the ark of our
God to us: for we enquired not at it in
the days of Saul.
4And all the congregation said that
they would do so: for the thing was
right in the eyes of all the people.
5So David gathered all Israel together, from Shihor of *Egypt even unto the
entering of Hemath, to bring the ark of
God from Kirjath-jearim.
6And David went up, and all Israel, to
Baalah, *that is*, to Kirjath-jearim, which
belonged to Judah, to bring up thence
the ark of God the LORD, that dwelleth
between the cherubims, whose name is
called *on it*.

13:7 The Importance of Obedience
The instructions for carrying the ark are found in Exodus 25:14; Numbers 4:15 (see its note, "Reverence to God"); 7:9; 10:21. David did not obey these instructions, so his good intentions and pious ceremonies were not acceptable to God (see 2 Sam. 6:3-7 note, "Mishandling the Ark of God"). Obedience to God's command is more important than formal religious rites. God can see our hearts and knows our minds, and He is not deceived by outward show. Our hearts must be right if our service is to be acceptable to Him (1 Sam. 15:22).

God's laws not followed

7And they carried the ark of God in a
new cart out of the house of Abinadab:
and Uzza and Ahio drave the cart.
8And David and all Israel played before God with all *their* might, and with
singing, and with harps, and with *psalteries, and with *timbrels, and with
cymbals, and with trumpets.

The consequence of disobedience

¶9And when they came unto the
threshingfloor of Chidon, Uzza put forth
his hand to hold the ark; for the oxen
stumbled.
10And the anger of the LORD was kindled against Uzza, and he smote him,
because he put his hand to the ark: and
there he died before God.
11And David was displeased, because
the LORD had made a breach upon Uzza:
wherefore that place is called Perez-
uzza to this day.
12And David was afraid of God that
day, saying, How shall I bring the ark of
God *home* to me?
13So David brought not the ark *home*
to himself to the city of David, but carried it aside into the house of Obed-
edom the Gittite.
14And the ark of God remained with

the family of Obed-edom in his house
three months. And the LORD blessed
the house of Obed-edom, and all that
he had.

David's power and reputation
(2 Sam. 5:11-25)

14 Now Hiram king of *Tyre sent
messengers to David, and timber of cedars, with masons and carpenters, to build him an house.
2 And David perceived that the LORD
had confirmed him king over Israel, for
his kingdom was lifted up on high, because of his people Israel.
¶3 And David took more wives at Jerusalem: and David begat more sons
and daughters.
4 Now these *are* the names of *his* children which he had in Jerusalem; Shammua, and Shobab, Nathan, and Solomon,
5 And Ibhar, and Elishua, and Elpalet,
6 And Nogah, and Nepheg, and Japhia,
7 And Elishama, and Beeliada, and
Eliphalet.
¶8 And when the Philistines heard
that David was anointed king over all Israel, all the Philistines went up to seek
David. And David heard *of it,* and went
out against them.
9 And the Philistines came and spread
themselves in the valley of Rephaim.
10 And David enquired of God, saying,
Shall I go up against the Philistines?
and wilt thou deliver them into mine
hand? And the LORD said unto him, Go
up; for I will deliver them into thine
hand.
11 So they came up to Baal-perazim;
and David smote them there. Then
David said, God hath broken in upon
mine enemies by mine hand like the
breaking forth of waters: therefore they
called the name of that place Baal-
perazim.
12 And when they had left their gods
there, David gave a commandment, and
they were burned with *fire.
13 And the Philistines yet again spread
themselves abroad in the valley.
14 Therefore David enquired again of
God; and God said unto him, Go not up
after them; turn away from them, and
come upon them over against the mulberry trees.
15 And it shall be, when thou shalt
hear a sound of going in the tops of the
mulberry trees, *that* then thou shalt go
out to battle: for God is gone forth before thee to smite the host of the Philistines.
16 David therefore did as God commanded him: and they smote the host
of the Philistines from Gibeon even to
Gazer.
17 And the fame of David went out into
all lands; and the LORD brought the fear
of him upon all nations.

14:10 A MAN AFTER GOD'S OWN HEART

This chapter shows us why David is called "a man after [God's] own heart" (Acts 13:22):

1. He acknowledged that God had made him king (vs. 2); he knew that he was only an instrument of God's grace.
2. He inquired of God in the time of trouble and did not trust his own wisdom (vs. 10).
3. He gave God the glory for his victory (vs. 11).
4. He destroyed the heathen idols in obedience to God's command (vs. 12).
5. He waited for God's signal to go again into battle (vs. 14).
6. He obeyed without questioning and thereby won the victory (vs. 16).

David was human and therefore a sinner, but the qualities of his life as illustrated in this chapter show him to be an admirable character and devoted to God.

14:17 the fame of David. David's exaltation and fame in the world came after his obedience to the will of God. In Philippians 2:5-11 we read that the Lord Jesus Christ, the greater David, was exalted by God because of His obedience, which even led Him to die on the cross. Read Christ's words in Luke 14:11; see also John 6:38; 8:29.

David obeys God in bringing the ark
(2 Sam. 6:12-23)

15 And *David made him houses in
the city of David, and prepared
a place for the ark of God, and pitched
for it a tent.
2 Then David said, None ought to carry the ark of God but the Levites: for
them hath the LORD chosen to carry the
ark of God, and to minister unto him for
ever.
3 And David gathered all Israel together to *Jerusalem, to bring up the
ark of the LORD unto his place, which
he had prepared for it.
4 And David assembled the children of
*Aaron, and the Levites:
5 Of the sons of Kohath; Uriel the
chief, and his brethren an hundred and
twenty:
6 Of the sons of Merari; Asaiah the
chief, and his brethren two hundred and
twenty:
7 Of the sons of Gershom; Joel the
chief, and his brethren an hundred and
thirty:
8 Of the sons of Elizaphan; Shemaiah the chief, and his brethren two hundred:
9 Of the sons of Hebron; Eliel the
chief, and his brethren fourscore:
10 Of the sons of Uzziel; Amminadab
the chief, and his brethren an hundred
and twelve.
11 And David called for Zadok and
Abiathar the priests, and for the Levites, for Uriel, Asaiah, and Joel, Shemaiah, and Eliel, and Amminadab,
12 And said unto them, Ye *are* the chief
of the fathers of the Levites: sanctify
yourselves, *both* ye and your brethren,
that ye may bring up the ark of the
LORD God of Israel unto *the place that* I
have prepared for it.
13 For because ye *did it* not at the first,
the LORD our God made a breach upon
us, for that we sought him not after the
due order.
14 So the priests and the Levites sanctified themselves to bring up the ark of
the LORD God of Israel.
15 And the children of the Levites
bare the ark of God upon their shoulders with the staves thereon, as *Moses commanded according to the word
of the LORD.
16 And David spake to the chief of the
Levites to appoint their brethren *to be*
the singers with instruments of musick, psalteries and harps and cymbals,
sounding, by lifting up the voice with
joy.
17 So the Levites appointed *Heman
the son of Joel; and of his brethren,
*Asaph the son of Berechiah; and of the
sons of Merari their brethren, Ethan
the son of Kushaiah;
18 And with them their brethren of the
second *degree,* Zechariah, Ben, and Jaa-
ziel, and Shemiramoth, and Jehiel, and
Unni, Eliab, and Benaiah, and Maaseiah, and Mattithiah, and Elipheleh, and
Mikneiah, and Obed-edom, and Jeiel,
the *porters.
19 So the singers, Heman, Asaph, and
Ethan, *were appointed* to sound with
cymbals of brass;
20 And Zechariah, and Aziel, and Shemiramoth, and Jehiel, and Unni, and
Eliab, and Maaseiah, and Benaiah, with
psalteries on Alamoth;
21 And Mattithiah, and Elipheleh, and
Mikneiah, and Obed-edom, and Jeiel,
and Azaziah, with harps on the *Sheminith to excel.
22 And Chenaniah, chief of the Levites, *was* for song: he instructed about
the song, because he *was* skilful.
23 And Berechiah and Elkanah *were*
doorkeepers for the ark.
24 And Shebaniah, and Jehoshaphat, and
Nethaneel, and Amasai, and Zechariah,

15:20 Alamoth. This is believed by some to have been a choir of virgins, for the word means *virgins*. See the inscription for Psalm 46 (see also Ps. 68:25). Others believe that this is one of the words used to indicate the range of the music—in this case, soprano.

and Benaiah, and Eliezer, the priests, did
blow with the trumpets before the ark
of God: and Obed-edom and Jehiah *were*
doorkeepers for the ark.

David's joy

¶25So David, and the elders of Israel,
and the captains over thousands, went
to bring up the ark of the covenant of
the LORD out of the house of Obed-
edom with joy.
26And it came to pass, when God
helped the Levites that bare the ark
of the covenant of the LORD, that they
offered seven bullocks and seven
rams.
27And David *was* clothed with a robe
of fine *linen, and all the Levites that
bare the ark, and the singers, and
Chenaniah the master of the song with
the singers: David also *had* upon him an
*ephod of linen.
28Thus all Israel brought up the ark
of the covenant of the LORD with shouting, and with sound of the cornet, and
with trumpets, and with cymbals, making a noise with psalteries and harps.

Michal's scorn
(2 Sam. 6:20-23)

¶29And it came to pass, *as* the ark of
the covenant of the LORD came to the
city of David, that Michal the daughter
of Saul looking out at a window saw king
David dancing and playing: and she despised him in her heart.

A holy celebration

16 So they brought the ark of God,
and set it in the midst of the tent
that David had pitched for it: and they
offered burnt-sacrifices and *peace-
offerings before God.
2And when David had made an end of
*offering the burnt-offerings and the
peace-offerings, he blessed the people
in the name of the LORD.
3And he dealt to every one of Israel,
both man and woman, to every one a
loaf of bread, and a good piece of flesh,
and a flagon *of *wine*.

Music for the praise of God

¶4And he appointed *certain* of the Levites to minister before the ark of the
LORD, and to record, and to thank and
praise the LORD God of Israel:
5Asaph the chief, and next to him
Zechariah, Jeiel, and Shemiramoth, and
Jehiel, and Mattithiah, and Eliab, and
Benaiah, and Obed-edom: and Jeiel
with *psalteries and with harps; but
Asaph made a sound with cymbals;
6Benaiah also and Jahaziel the priests
with trumpets continually before the
ark of the covenant of God.

15:28 THE ARK

The word means *a covered chest or box*. Three important arks are mentioned:

1. Noah's ark;
2. that in which the infant Moses was hidden by his mother; and
3. the ark of the covenant. This sacred object was a chest made of acacia wood overlaid with gold, the lid of which made up the "mercy seat" (Exod. 25:17 and note, "The Mercy Seat"), or place of propitiation, over which two cherubim extended their wings.

By divine command the following items were placed within the ark: the two tables of stone on which the Ten Commandments were engraved; an omer of manna; and Aaron's rod, which budded. The ark was 2½ cubits long, 1½ cubits wide, and 1½ cubits deep. Around its upper edge was a cornice of gold. The Levites carried the ark by means of two poles of shittim wood covered with gold, which were passed through two rings on each side of the ark. The ark was placed in front of the people on their march to the Promised Land.

The ark of the covenant had a glorious significance. The tabernacle, in which the ark was placed, was designed by God (Heb. 8:5) and was patterned after the true one in heaven (Heb. 8:2; 9:23). The ark of the covenant was covered by the mercy seat. This was placed in the Holy of Holies and it was over the ark that the glory cloud of God's presence rested (Lev. 16:2).

A psalm of thanksgiving

¶7Then on that day David delivered
first *this psalm* to thank the LORD into
the hand of Asaph and his brethren.
8Give thanks unto the LORD, call
upon his name, make known his deeds
among the people.
9Sing unto him, sing psalms unto
him, talk ye of all his wondrous works.
10Glory ye in his *holy name: let the
heart of them rejoice that seek the
LORD.
11Seek the LORD and his strength,
seek his face continually.
12Remember his marvellous works
that he hath done, his wonders, and the
judgments of his mouth;
13O ye seed of Israel his servant, ye
children of *Jacob, his chosen ones.
14He *is* the LORD our God; his judgments *are* in all the earth.
15Be ye mindful always of his covenant; the word *which* he commanded
to a thousand generations;
16*Even of the covenant* which he made
with *Abraham, and of his oath unto
*Isaac;
17And hath confirmed the same to
Jacob for a *law, *and* to Israel *for* an
everlasting covenant,
18Saying, Unto thee will I give the
land of Canaan, the lot of your inheritance;
19When ye were but few, even a few,
and strangers in it.
20And *when* they went from nation to
nation, and from *one* kingdom to another people;
21He suffered no man to do them
wrong: yea, he reproved kings for their
sakes,
22*Saying,* Touch not mine anointed,
and do my *prophets no harm.
23Sing unto the LORD, all the earth;
shew forth from day to day his *salvation.
24Declare his glory among the heathen; his marvellous works among all
nations.
25For great *is* the LORD, and greatly
to be praised: he also *is* to be feared
above all gods.
26For all the gods of the people *are*
idols: but the LORD made the heavens.
27Glory and honour *are* in his presence; strength and gladness *are* in his
place.
28Give unto the LORD, ye kindreds of
the people, give unto the LORD glory
and strength.
29Give unto the LORD the glory *due*
unto his name: bring an offering, and
come before him: worship the LORD in
the beauty of holiness.
30Fear before him, all the earth: the
*world also shall be stable, that it be not
moved.
31Let the heavens be glad, and let the
earth rejoice: and let *men* say among
the nations, The LORD reigneth.
32Let the sea roar, and the fulness
thereof: let the fields rejoice, and all
that *is* therein.
33Then shall the trees of the wood
sing out at the presence of the LORD,
because he cometh to judge the earth.
34O give thanks unto the LORD; for *he
is* good; for his *mercy *endureth* for
ever.
35And say ye, Save us, O God of our
salvation, and gather us together, and
deliver us from the heathen, that we
may give thanks to thy holy name, *and*
glory in thy praise.
36Blessed *be* the LORD God of Israel
for ever and ever. And all the people
said, *Amen, and praised the LORD.

The Levites who ministered before the ark

¶37So he left there before the ark of
the covenant of the LORD Asaph and
his brethren, to minister before the
ark continually, as every day's work
required:

16:7 first this psalm. To celebrate the bringing of the ark to Jerusalem, David composed a song of thanksgiving, which he gave to the chief musicians to be used in public worship. This song is found in Psalms 96; 105:1-15; 106:47-48.

16:37 Divided Worship
The ancient tabernacle of the wilderness was now divided: The ark was in Jerusalem, while the brazen altar, at least, and probably the vessels of the Holy Place (Exod. 25:23-40; 37:10-25; 40:22-27) were being used for worship at Gibeon. Asaph and the singers were with the ark at Jerusalem, and Zadok and the other priests ministered "before the tabernacle" at Gibeon (1 Chron. 16:39-42). This divided condition remained until the new temple was built under King Solomon.

38And Obed-edom with their brethren, threescore and eight; Obed-edom
also the son of *Jeduthun and Hosah *to
be* porters:
39And Zadok the priest, and his
brethren the priests, before the *tabernacle of the LORD in the high place that
was at Gibeon,
40To offer burnt-offerings unto the
LORD upon the *altar of the *burnt-
offering continually morning and evening, and *to do* according to all that is
written in the law of the LORD, which
he commanded Israel;
41And with them Heman and Jeduthun, and the rest that were chosen,
who were expressed by name, to give
thanks to the LORD, because his mercy
endureth for ever;
42And with them Heman and Jeduthun with trumpets and cymbals for
those that should make a sound, and
with musical instruments of God. And
the sons of Jeduthun *were* porters.
43And all the people departed every
man to his house: and David returned
to bless his house.

David and the LORD's house (2 Sam. 7)

17 Now it came to pass, as David
sat in his house, that David said
to Nathan the *prophet, Lo, I dwell in
an house of cedars, but the ark of the
covenant of the LORD *remaineth* under
curtains.
2Then Nathan said unto David, Do all
that *is* in thine heart; for *God *is* with
thee.

The LORD speaks through Nathan

¶3And it came to pass the same night,
that the word of God came to Nathan,
saying,
4Go and tell David my servant, Thus
saith the LORD, Thou shalt not build me
an house to dwell in:
5For I have not dwelt in an house
since the day that I brought up Israel
unto this day; but have gone from tent
to tent, and from *one* tabernacle *to another.*
6Wheresoever I have walked with all
Israel, spake I a word to any of the
*judges of Israel, whom I commanded
to feed my people, saying, Why have ye
not built me an house of cedars?

The covenant with David
(2 Sam. 7:4-17)

7Now therefore thus shalt thou say
unto my servant David, Thus saith
the LORD of hosts, I took thee from the
sheepcote, *even* from following the
sheep, that thou shouldest be ruler over
my people Israel:
8And I have been with thee whithersoever thou hast walked, and have cut
off all thine enemies from before thee,
and have made thee a name like the
name of the great men that *are* in the
earth.
9Also I will ordain a place for my people Israel, and will plant them, and they
shall dwell in their place, and shall be
moved no more; neither shall the chil-

17:2 Nathan said. Nathan's mistake was in passing judgment upon a spiritual matter without inquiring whether it was the Lord's will. David's plan and purpose were fine, but God had other plans that brought far greater honor to David than that of building a temple (17:4,10-14)

17:7 unto my servant David. This repeats the *covenant with David of 2 Samuel 7:4-17. See especially 2 Samuel 7:11 note, "The Davidic Covenant."

dren of wickedness waste them any
more, as at the beginning,
10 And since the time that I commanded judges *to be* over my people Israel.
Moreover I will subdue all thine enemies. Furthermore I tell thee that the
LORD will build thee an house.
¶ 11 And it shall come to pass, when thy
days be expired that thou must go *to be*
with thy fathers, that I will raise up thy
seed after thee, which shall be of thy
sons; and I will establish his kingdom.
12 He shall build me an house, and I
will stablish his throne for ever.
13 I will be his father, and he shall be
my son: and I will not take my mercy
away from him, as I took *it* from *him*
that was before thee:
14 But I will settle him in mine house
and in my kingdom for ever: and his
throne shall be established for evermore.
15 According to all these words, and
according to all this vision, so did Nathan speak unto David.

David's prayer

¶ 16 And David the king came and sat
before the LORD, and said, Who *am* I,
O LORD God, and what *is* mine house,
that thou hast brought me hitherto?
17 And *yet* this was a small thing in
thine eyes, O God; for thou hast *also*
spoken of thy servant's house for a
great while to come, and hast regarded
me according to the estate of a man of
high degree, O LORD God.
18 What can David *speak* more to thee
for the honour of thy servant? for thou
knowest thy servant.
19 O LORD, for thy servant's sake, and
according to thine own heart, hast thou
done all this greatness, in making
known all *these* great things.
20 O LORD, *there is* none like thee,
neither *is there any* God beside thee,
according to all that we have heard with
our ears.
21 And what one nation in the earth *is*
like thy people Israel, whom God went
to redeem *to be* his own people, to make
thee a name of greatness and terribleness, by driving out nations from before
thy people, whom thou hast *redeemed
out of Egypt?
22 For thy people Israel didst thou
make thine own people for ever; and
thou, LORD, becamest their God.
23 Therefore now, LORD, let the thing
that thou hast spoken concerning thy
servant and concerning his house be
established for ever, and do as thou hast
said.
24 Let it even be established, that thy
name may be magnified for ever, saying, The LORD of hosts *is* the God of
Israel, *even* a God to Israel: and *let* the
house of David thy servant *be* established before thee.
25 For thou, O my God, hast told thy
servant that thou wilt build him an
house: therefore thy servant hath found
in his heart to pray before thee.
26 And now, LORD, thou art God, and
hast promised this goodness unto thy
servant:
27 Now therefore let it please thee to
bless the house of thy servant, that it
may be before thee for ever: for thou
blessest, O LORD, and *it shall be* blessed
for ever.

The extension of David's power and reputation (2 Sam. 8:1-18)

18 Now after this it came to pass,
that David smote the *Philistines, and subdued them, and took

17:12 He shall build me an house. That is, Solomon. See 2 Chronicles 2:1-7:22. Read also Psalm 89:3-4,20-37; 1 Chronicles 22:10; 28:20.

17:14 established for evermore. The primary reference is to David's son, Solomon, but the covenant will finally and completely be fulfilled in Christ (Luke 1:32-33; Acts 15:14-16).

17:16 sat before the LORD. This beautiful picture suggests the communion between God and David. David's humility brought him close to God and prepared the way for his courageous triumphs as recorded in 1 Chronicles 18.

*Gath and her towns out of the hand of the Philistines.

2And he smote *Moab; and the Moabites became David's servants, *and* brought gifts.

¶3And David smote Hadarezer king of Zobah unto Hamath, as he went to stablish his dominion by the river Euphrates.

4And David took from him a thousand chariots, and seven thousand horsemen, and twenty thousand footmen: David also *houghed all the chariot *horses,* but reserved of them an hundred chariots.

5And when the Syrians of *Damascus came to help Hadarezer king of Zobah, David slew of the Syrians two and twenty thousand men.

6Then David put *garrisons* in Syriadamascus; and the Syrians became David's servants, *and* brought gifts. Thus the LORD preserved David whithersoever he went.

7And David took the shields of gold that were on the servants of Hadarezer, and brought them to Jerusalem.

8Likewise from Tibhath, and from Chun, cities of Hadarezer, brought David very much brass, wherewith Solomon made the brasen sea, and the pillars, and the vessels of brass.

¶9Now when Tou king of Hamath heard how David had smitten all the host of Hadarezer king of Zobah;

10He sent Hadoram his son to king David, to enquire of his welfare, and to congratulate him, because he had fought against Hadarezer, and smitten him; (for Hadarezer had war with Tou;) and *with him* all manner of vessels of gold and silver and brass.

¶11Them also king David dedicated unto the LORD, with the silver and the gold that he brought from all *these* nations; from *Edom, and from Moab, and from the children of Ammon, and from the Philistines, and from *Amalek.

12Moreover Abishai the son of Zeruiah slew of the Edomites in the valley of salt eighteen thousand.

¶13And he put garrisons in Edom; and all the Edomites became David's servants. Thus the LORD preserved David whithersoever he went.

¶14So David reigned over all Israel, and executed judgment and justice among all his people.

15And Joab the son Zeruiah *was* over the host; and Jehoshaphat the son of Ahilud, recorder.

16And Zadok the son of Ahitub, and Abimelech the son of Abiathar, *were* the priests; and Shavsha was *scribe;

17And Benaiah the son of *Jehoiada *was* over the *Cherethites and the Pelethites; and the sons of David *were* chief about the king.

The Ammonites invite war
(2 Sam. 10:1-19)

19 Now it came to pass after this, that Nahash the king of the children of Ammon died, and his son reigned in his stead.

2And David said, I will shew kindness unto Hanun the son of Nahash, because his father shewed kindness to me. And David sent messengers to comfort him concerning his father. So the servants of David came into the land of the children of Ammon to Hanun, to comfort him.

3But the princes of the children of Ammon said to Hanun, Thinkest thou that David doth honour thy father, that he hath sent comforters unto thee? are not his servants come unto thee for to search, and to overthrow, and to spy out the land?

18:4 seven thousand horsemen. 2 Samuel 8:4 has seven hundred horsemen.

18:12 Abishai. David's nephew and one of his chief generals (2 Sam. 23:18; 1 Chron. 11:20).

18:12 valley of salt. Probably one of the three valleys that unite at Beersheba. These make a natural frontier to Canaan.

4Wherefore Hanun took David's servants, and shaved them, and cut off
their *garments in the midst hard by
their buttocks, and sent them away.
5Then there went *certain,* and told
David how the men were served. And
he sent to meet them: for the men were
greatly ashamed. And the king said,
Tarry at Jericho until your beards be
grown, and *then* return.

The Ammonites hire Syrian help

¶6And when the children of Ammon
saw that they had made themselves
odious to David, Hanun and the children of Ammon sent a thousand talents
of silver to hire them chariots and
horsemen out of Mesopotamia, and out
of Syria-maachah, and out of Zobah.
7So they hired thirty and two thousand chariots, and the king of Maachah
and his people; who came and pitched
before Medeba. And the children of
Ammon gathered themselves together from their cities, and came to battle.

Joab leads the first campaign

8And when David heard *of it,* he sent
Joab, and all the host of the mighty men.
9And the children of Ammon came
out, and put the battle in array before
the gate of the city: and the kings that
were come *were* by themselves in the
field.
10Now when Joab saw that the battle
was set against him before and behind,
he chose out of all the choice of *Israel,
and put *them* in array against the Syrians.
11And the rest of the people he delivered unto the hand of Abishai his
brother, and they set *themselves* in array against the children of Ammon.
12And he said, If the Syrians be too
strong for me, then thou shalt help me:
but if the children of Ammon be too
strong for thee, then I will help thee.
13Be of good courage, and let us behave ourselves valiantly for our people, and for the cities of our God: and
let the LORD do *that which is* good in
his sight.
14So Joab and the people that *were*
with him drew nigh before the Syrians
unto the battle; and they fled before
him.
15And when the children of Ammon
saw that the Syrians were fled, they
likewise fled before Abishai his brother,
and entered into the city. Then Joab
came to Jerusalem.
¶16And when the Syrians saw that
they were put to the worse before Israel, they sent messengers, and drew
forth the Syrians that *were* beyond the
river: and Shophach the captain of the
host of Hadarezer *went* before them.

David leads the second campaign

17And it was told David; and he gathered all Israel, and passed over Jordan,
and came upon them, and set *the battle*
in array against them. So when David
had put the battle in array against the
Syrians, they fought with him.
18But the Syrians fled before Israel;
and David slew of the Syrians seven
thousand *men which fought in* chariots,
and forty thousand footmen, and killed
Shophach the captain of the host.
19And when the servants of Hadarezer saw that they were put to the
worse before Israel, they made peace
with David, and became his servants:
neither would the Syrians help the children of Ammon any more.

The Ammonite's chief city falls
(2 Sam. 12:26-31)

20 And it came to pass, that after
the year was expired, at the
time that kings go out *to battle,* Joab

20:1 David in Jerusalem
Second Samuel 11:2–12:25 with Psalm 51 explains David's stay at Jerusalem. David's fall into sin is not included in the account in Chronicles because God's grace is the outstanding distinction of this record, and grace had covered David's sin.

led forth the power of the army, and
wasted the country of the children of
Ammon, and came and besieged Rabbah. But David tarried at Jerusalem.
And Joab smote Rabbah, and destroyed it.
[2]And David took the crown of their
king from off his head, and found it to
weigh a talent of gold, and *there were*
precious stones in it; and it was set
upon David's head: and he brought
also exceeding much spoil out of the
city.
[3]And he brought out the people that
were in it, and cut *them* with saws, and
with harrows of iron, and with axes.
Even so dealt David with all the cities
of the children of Ammon. And David
and all the people returned to Jerusalem.

War with the Philistines

¶[4]And it came to pass after this, that
there arose war at Gezer with the Philistines; at which time Sibbechai the
Hushathite slew Sippai, *that was* of the
children of the giant: and they were
subdued.
[5]And there was war again with the
Philistines; and Elhanan the son of Jair
slew Lahmi the brother of Goliath the
Gittite, whose spear staff *was* like a
weaver's beam.
[6]And yet again there was war at Gath,
where was a man of *great* stature,
whose fingers and toes *were* four and
twenty, six *on each hand,* and six *on each
foot:* and he also was the son of the
giant.
[7]But when he defied Israel, Jonathan
the son of Shimea David's brother slew
him.
[8]These were born unto the giant in
Gath; and they fell by the hand of David, and by the hand of his servants.

David's sinful pride (2 Sam. 24:1-9)

21 And Satan stood up against Israel, and provoked *David to
number Israel.
[2]And David said to Joab and to the
rulers of the people, Go, number Israel
from *Beer-sheba even to Dan; and
bring the number of them to me, that I
may know *it.*

Joab protests

[3]And Joab answered, The LORD make
his people an hundred times so many
more as they *be:* but, my lord the king,
are they not all my lord's servants? why
then doth my lord require this thing? why
will he be a cause of *trespass to Israel?

Joab carries out the king's command

[4]Nevertheless the king's word prevailed against Joab. Wherefore Joab
departed, and went throughout all Israel, and came to *Jerusalem.
¶[5]And Joab gave the sum of the number of the people unto David. And all
they of Israel were a thousand thousand
and an hundred thousand men that
drew sword: and *Judah *was* four hundred threescore and ten thousand men
that drew sword.
[6]But Levi and Benjamin counted he
not among them: for the king's word
was abominable to Joab.
[7]And God was displeased with this
thing; therefore he smote Israel.
[8]And David said unto God, I have
sinned greatly, because I have done this
thing: but now, I beseech thee, do away
the iniquity of thy servant; for I have
done very foolishly.

21:1 Satan stood up against Israel. Satan fell through pride (Isa. 14:12-14; see vs. 12 note, "Lucifer"). He appealed to David's pride, the only reason for the census, or numbering. David was not satisfied with God's promise to make them a "great nation" (see 2 Sam. 24:2 note, "The Wrong Motive").

21:4 Joab departed, and went throughout all Israel. Joab, so reluctant to carry out the king's command, took nine months and twenty days to make the census (see 2 Sam. 24:4-9).

21:5 all they of Israel. See 2 Samuel 24:9 note.

The LORD speaks to David through Gad
(2 Sam. 24:10-17)

¶9 And the LORD spake unto Gad, David's seer, saying,

10 Go and tell David, saying, Thus saith the LORD, I offer thee three *things:* choose thee one of them, that I may do *it* unto thee.

11 So Gad came to David, and said unto him, Thus saith the LORD, Choose thee

12 Either three years' famine; or three months to be destroyed before thy foes, while that the sword of thine enemies overtaketh *thee;* or else three days the sword of the LORD, even the pestilence, in the land, and the *angel of the LORD destroying throughout all the coasts of Israel. Now therefore advise thyself what word I shall bring again to him that sent me.

13 And David said unto Gad, I am in a great strait: let me fall now into the hand of the LORD; for very great *are* his mercies: but let me not fall into the hand of man.

The LORD's judgment

¶14 So the LORD sent pestilence upon Israel: and there fell of Israel seventy thousand men.

21:13-14 David's Choice
David was wise in preferring to fall into God's hands rather than men's, for God's judgment is always tempered with mercy; but David learned that the punishment for his sin involved others who had not been directly guilty with him in his sin. The consequences of sin very frequently involve others.

15 And God sent an angel unto Jerusalem to destroy it: and as he was destroying, the LORD beheld, and he *repented him of the evil, and said to the angel that destroyed, It is enough, stay now thine hand. And the angel of the LORD stood by the threshingfloor of Ornan the Jebusite.

16 And David lifted up his eyes, and saw the angel of the LORD stand between the earth and the *heaven, having a drawn sword in his hand stretched out over Jerusalem. Then David and the *elders *of Israel, who were* clothed in sackcloth, fell upon their faces.

17 And David said unto God, *Is it* not I *that* commanded the people to be numbered? even I it is that have sinned and done evil indeed; but *as for* these sheep, what have they done? let thine hand, I pray thee, O LORD my God, be on me, and on my father's house; but not on thy people, that they should be plagued.

An altar unto the LORD
(2 Sam. 24:18-25)

¶18 Then the angel of the LORD commanded Gad to say to David, that David should go up, and set up an altar unto the LORD in the threshingfloor of Ornan the Jebusite.

19 And David went up at the saying of Gad, which he spake in the name of the LORD.

20 And Ornan turned back, and saw the angel; and his four sons with him hid themselves. Now Ornan was threshing wheat.

21 And as David came to Ornan, Ornan looked and saw David, and went out of the threshingfloor, and bowed himself to David with *his* face to the ground.

22 Then David said to Ornan, Grant me the place of *this* threshingfloor, that I may build an altar therein unto the LORD: thou shalt grant it me for the full price: that the plague may be stayed from the people.

23 And Ornan said unto David, Take *it* to thee, and let my lord the king do *that which is* good in his eyes: lo, I give *thee* the oxen *also* for burnt-offerings, and the threshing instruments for wood, and the wheat for the *meat-offering; I give it all.

24 And king David said to Ornan, Nay; but I will verily buy it for the full price: for I will not take *that* which *is* thine for

21:15 Ornan. He is also called Araunah (2 Sam. 24:16).

the LORD, nor offer burnt-offerings without cost.

25 So David gave to Ornan for the place six hundred shekels of gold by weight.

26 And David built there an altar unto the LORD, and offered burnt-offerings and peace-offerings, and called upon the LORD; and he answered him from heaven by *fire upon the altar of burnt-offering.

27 And the LORD commanded the angel; and he put up his sword again into the sheath thereof.

¶28 At that time when David saw that the LORD had answered him in the threshingfloor of Ornan the Jebusite, then he sacrificed there.

29 For the tabernacle of the LORD, which *Moses made in the wilderness, and the altar of the burnt-offering, *were* at that season in the high place at Gibeon.

30 But David could not go before it to enquire of God: for he was afraid because of the sword of the angel of the LORD.

IV. David's Preparation for Building the Temple before His Death (22:1—29:30)

22 Then David said, This *is* the house of the LORD God, and this *is* the *altar of the burnt-offering for Israel.

2 And David commanded to gather together the strangers that *were* in the land of Israel; and he set masons to hew wrought stones to build the house of God.

3 And David prepared iron in abundance for the nails for the doors of the gates, and for the joinings; and brass in abundance without weight;

4 Also cedar trees in abundance: for the Zidonians and they of *Tyre brought much cedar wood to David.

5 And David said, Solomon my son *is* young and tender, and the house *that is* to be builded for the LORD *must be* exceeding magnifical, of fame and of glory throughout all countries: I will *therefore* now make preparation for it. So David prepared abundantly before his *death.

David charges Solomon with the building of the temple

¶6 Then he called for Solomon his son, and charged him to build an house for the LORD God of Israel.

7 And David said to Solomon, My son, as for me, it was in my mind to build an house unto the name of the LORD my God:

8 But the word of the LORD came to me, saying, Thou hast shed *blood abundantly, and hast made great wars: thou shalt not build an house unto my name, because thou hast shed much blood upon the earth in my sight.

9 Behold, a son shall be born to thee, who shall be a man of rest; and I will give him rest from all his enemies round about: for his name shall be Solomon, and I will give peace and quietness unto Israel in his days.

10 He shall build an house for my name; and he shall be my son, and I *will be* his father; and I will establish the throne of his *kingdom over Israel for ever.

11 Now, my son, the LORD be with thee; and prosper thou, and build the house of the LORD thy God, as he hath said of thee.

12 Only the LORD give thee wisdom and understanding, and give thee charge

---

21:25 six hundred shekels. There is no real disagreement between this account and 2 Samuel 24:24. The account in 2 Samuel records the price paid for the threshing floor and oxen, fifty shekels; and 1 Chronicles 21:25 mentions the price paid for the whole place, where the temple was later built (2 Chron. 3:1).

22:1 This is the house of the LORD God. Chapters 22–29, concerning the preparation for the building of the temple, help fill the gap between 2 Samuel 24:25 and 1 Kings 1:1.

22:2 strangers that were in the land. Descendants of the Canaanites.

22:5 young and tender. See 1 Kings 3:7 note, "The Young Solomon."

concerning Israel, that thou mayest
keep the *law of the LORD thy God.
13 Then shalt thou prosper, if thou
takest heed to fulfil the statutes and
judgments which the LORD charged
Moses with concerning Israel: be
strong, and of good courage; dread not,
nor be dismayed.
14 Now, behold, in my trouble I have
prepared for the house of the LORD an
hundred thousand talents of gold, and
a thousand thousand talents of silver;
and of brass and iron without weight;
for it is in abundance: timber also and
stone have I prepared; and thou mayest
add thereto.
15 Moreover *there are* workmen with
thee in abundance, hewers and workers
of stone and timber, and all manner of
cunning men for every manner of work.
16 Of the gold, the silver, and the
brass, and the iron, *there is* no number.
Arise *therefore,* and be doing, and the
LORD be with thee.

David commands the princes to help Solomon

¶ 17 David also commanded all the
princes of Israel to help Solomon his
son, *saying,*
18 *Is* not the LORD your God with you?
and hath he *not* given you rest on every
side? for he hath given the inhabitants
of the land into mine hand; and the land
is subdued before the LORD, and before
his people.
19 Now set your heart and your soul
to seek the LORD your God; arise therefore, and build ye the *sanctuary of the
LORD God, to bring the *ark of the covenant of the LORD, and the *holy vessels of God, into the house that is to be
built to the name of the LORD.

David appoints Solomon king

23 So when David was old and full
of days, he made Solomon his
son king over Israel.

The numbers of the Levites

2 And he gathered together all the
princes of Israel, with the priests and
the Levites.
¶ 3 Now the Levites were numbered
from the age of thirty years and upward:
and their number by their polls, man by
man, was thirty and eight thousand.

23:3 The Age of the Levites
According to the *Law of Moses, the Levites entered their service at the age of thirty (Num. 4:1-4), with a training period beginning at the age of twenty-five (Num. 8:24). David, by his "last words," lowered the age limit to twenty (1 Chron. 23:27).

4 Of which, twenty and four thousand
were to set forward the work of the
house of the LORD; and six thousand
were officers and judges:
5 Moreover four thousand *were* *porters; and four thousand praised the
LORD with the instruments which I
made, *said David,* to praise *therewith.*

The divisions of the sons of Levi

6 And David divided them into courses
among the sons of Levi, *namely,* Gershon, Kohath, and Merari.
¶ 7 Of the Gershonites *were,* Laadan,
and Shimei.
8 The sons of Laadan; the chief *was*
Jehiel, and Zetham, and Joel, three.
9 The sons of Shimei; Shelomith, and
Haziel, and Haran, three. These *were*
the chief of the fathers of Laadan.
10 And the sons of Shimei *were,* Jahath, Zina, and Jeush, and Beriah.
These four *were* the sons of Shimei.
11 And Jahath was the chief, and Zizah
the second: but Jeush and Beriah had
not many sons; therefore they were in
one reckoning, according to *their* father's house.
¶ 12 The sons of Kohath; Amram, Izhar, Hebron, and Uzziel, four.
13 The sons of Amram; *Aaron and

23:1 made Solomon his son king. For Solomon's accession to the throne, see 1 Kings 1:33-40 and 1 Chronicles 28:4-5; 29:22-25.

Moses: and Aaron was separated, that
he should sanctify the most holy
things, he and his sons for ever, to burn
*incense before the LORD, to minister
unto him, and to bless in his name for
ever.
14 Now *concerning* Moses the man of
*God, his sons were named of the tribe
of Levi.
15 The sons of Moses *were,* Gershom,
and Eliezer.
16 Of the sons of Gershom, Shebuel
was the chief.
17 And the sons of Eliezer *were,* Rehabiah the chief. And Eliezer had none
other sons; but the sons of Rehabiah
were very many.
18 Of the sons of Izhar; Shelomith the
chief.
19 Of the sons of Hebron; Jeriah the
first, Amariah the second, Jahaziel the
third, and Jekameam the fourth.
20 Of the sons of Uzziel; *Michah the
first, and Jesiah the second.
¶21 The sons of Merari; Mahli, and
Mushi. The sons of Mahli; Eleazar, and
Kish.
22 And Eleazar died, and had no sons,
but daughters: and their brethren the
sons of Kish took them.
23 The sons of Mushi; Mahli, and
Eder, and Jeremoth, three.

New duties of the Levites

¶24 These *were* the sons of Levi after
the house of their fathers; *even* the chief
of the fathers, as they were counted by
number of names by their polls, that did
the work for the service of the house
of the LORD, from the age of twenty
years and upward.
25 For David said, The LORD God of
Israel hath given rest unto his people,
that they may dwell in Jerusalem for
ever:
26 And also unto the Levites; they
shall no *more* carry the *tabernacle, nor
any vessels of it for the service thereof.
27 For by the last words of David the
Levites *were* numbered from twenty
years old and above:
28 Because their office *was* to wait on
the sons of Aaron for the service of the
house of the LORD, in the courts, and
in the chambers, and in the purifying of
all holy things, and the work of the service of the house of God;

23:28 New Responsibilities for the Levites
The ark was now at rest in Jerusalem, and with the new temple to be built, all tabernacle worship would be centered there. Thus the Levites would no longer have to carry the tabernacle from place to place (vss. 25-26) but were given new duties in connection with temple worship.

29 Both for the *shewbread, and for
the fine flour for meat-offering, and for
the unleavened cakes, and for *that
which is baked in* the pan, and for that
which is fried, and for all manner of
measure and size;
30 And to stand every morning to
thank and praise the LORD, and likewise
at even;
31 And to offer all burnt-sacrifices
unto the LORD in the sabbaths, in the
*new moons, and on the *set feasts, by
number, according to the order commanded unto them, continually before
the LORD:
32 And that they should keep the
charge of the tabernacle of the congregation, and the charge of the holy *place,*
and the charge of the sons of Aaron
their brethren, in the service of the
house of the LORD.

Divisions of the sons of Aaron

24 Now *these are* the divisions of
the sons of Aaron. The sons of
Aaron; Nadab, and Abihu, Eleazar, and
Ithamar.
2 But *Nadab and Abihu died before
their father, and had no children: therefore Eleazar and Ithamar executed the
priest's office.

23:27 twenty years. See verse 3 note, "The Age of the Levites."

3And David distributed them, both Zadok of the sons of Eleazar, and Ahimelech of the sons of Ithamar, according to their offices in their service.

4And there were more chief men found of the sons of Eleazar than of the sons of Ithamar; and *thus* were they divided. Among the sons of Eleazar *there were* sixteen chief men of the house of *their* fathers, and eight among the sons of Ithamar according to the house of their fathers.

5Thus were they divided by lot, one sort with another; for the governors of the sanctuary, and governors *of the house* of God, were of the sons of Eleazar, and of the sons of Ithamar.

6And Shemaiah the son of Nethaneel the *scribe, *one* of the Levites, wrote them before the king, and the princes, and Zadok the priest, and Ahimelech the son of Abiathar, and *before* the chief of the fathers of the priests and Levites: one principal household being taken for Eleazar, and *one* taken for Ithamar.

7Now the first lot came forth to Jehoiarib, the second to Jedaiah,

8The third to Harim, the fourth to Seorim,

9The fifth to Malchijah, the sixth to Mijamin,

10The seventh to Hakkoz, the eighth to Abijah,

24:10 The Periods of Service
The divisions in 1 Chronicles 24 regulate the distribution of work among the priests and were followed by the Jews upon their return from captivity. There were twenty-four courses, or periods, of service. The course of Abijah (or Abia) was the eighth period. It is especially interesting because it is mentioned in Luke 1:5 as the one in which Zacharias, the father of John the Baptist, performed his service.

11The ninth to Jeshua, the tenth to Shecaniah,

12The eleventh to Eliashib, the twelfth to Jakim,

13The thirteenth to Huppah, the fourteenth to Jeshebeab,

14The fifteenth to Bilgah, the sixteenth to Immer,

15The seventeenth to Hezir, the eighteenth to Aphses,

16The nineteenth to Pethahiah, the twentieth to Jehezekel,

17The one and twentieth to *Jachin, the two and twentieth to Gamul,

18The three and twentieth to Delaiah, the four and twentieth to Maaziah.

19These *were* the orderings of them in their service to come into the house of the LORD, according to their manner, under Aaron their father, as the LORD God of Israel had commanded him.

Divisions of the Kohathites

¶20And the rest of the sons of Levi *were these:* Of the sons of Amram; Shubael: of the sons of Shubael; Jehdeiah.

21Concerning Rehabiah: of the sons of Rehabiah, the first *was* Isshiah.

22Of the Izharites; Shelomoth: of the sons of Shelomoth; Jahath.

23And the sons *of Hebron;* Jeriah *the first,* Amariah the second, Jahaziel the third, Jekameam the fourth.

24*Of* the sons of Uzziel; Michah: of the sons of Michah; Shamir.

25The brother of Michah *was* Isshiah: of the sons of Isshiah; Zechariah.

The sons of Merari

¶26The sons of Merari *were* Mahli and Mushi: the sons of Jaaziah; Beno.

27The sons of Merari by Jaaziah; Beno, and Shoham, and Zaccur, and Ibri.

28Of Mahli *came* Eleazar, who had no sons.

29Concerning Kish: the son of Kish *was* Jerahmeel.

30The sons also of Mushi; Mahli, and Eder, and Jerimoth. These *were* the sons of the Levites after the house of their fathers.

31These likewise cast lots over against their brethren the sons of Aaron in the presence of David the king, and Zadok, and Ahimelech, and the chief of the fathers of the priests and Levites,

even the principal fathers over against their younger brethren.

The musicians appointed and counted

25 Moreover David and the captains of the host separated to the service of the sons of *Asaph, and of *Heman, and of *Jeduthun, who should prophesy with harps, with *psalteries, and with cymbals: and the number of the workmen according to their service was:

25:1 The Ministry of Music
It is interesting to note that singing the praises of God is here called "prophesying." Many of the psalms, or songs, were composed by prophets and were prophetic in character, as were some of David's. The singing of songs was intended to strengthen the people in the LORD, as well as bring glory to God (see 1 Sam. 10:5).

2Of the sons of Asaph; Zaccur, and *Joseph, and Nethaniah, and Asarelah, the sons of Asaph under the hands of Asaph, which prophesied according to the order of the king.
3Of Jeduthun: the sons of Jeduthun; Gedaliah, and Zeri, and Jeshaiah, Hashabiah, and Mattithiah, six, under the hands of their father Jeduthun, who prophesied with a harp, to give thanks and to praise the LORD.
4Of Heman: the sons of Heman; Bukkiah, Mattaniah, Uzziel, Shebuel, and Jerimoth, Hananiah, Hanani, Eliathah, Giddalti, and Romamti-ezer, Joshbekashah, Mallothi, Hothir, *and* Mahazioth:
5All these *were* the sons of Heman the king's seer in the words of God, to lift up the *horn. And God gave to Heman fourteen sons and three daughters.
6All these *were* under the hands of their father for song *in* the house of the LORD, with cymbals, psalteries, and harps, for the service of the house of God, according to the king's order to Asaph, Jeduthun, and Heman.
7So the number of them, with their brethren that were instructed in the songs of the LORD, *even* all that were cunning, was two hundred fourscore and eight.

Divisions of the musicians

¶8And they cast lots, ward against *ward,* as well the small as the great, the teacher as the scholar.
9Now the first lot came forth for Asaph to Joseph: the second to Gedaliah, who with his brethren and sons *were* twelve:
10The third to Zaccur, *he,* his sons, and his brethren, *were* twelve:
11The fourth to Izri, *he,* his sons, and his brethren, *were* twelve:
12The fifth to Nethaniah, *he,* his sons, and his brethren, *were* twelve:
13The sixth to Bukkiah, *he,* his sons, and his brethren, *were* twelve:
14The seventh to Jesharelah, *he,* his sons, and his brethren, *were* twelve:
15The eighth to Jeshaiah, *he,* his sons, and his brethren, *were* twelve:
16The ninth to Mattaniah, *he,* his sons, and his brethren, *were* twelve:
17The tenth to Shimei, *he,* his sons, and his brethren, *were* twelve:
18The eleventh to Azareel, *he,* his sons, and his brethren, *were* twelve:
19The twelfth to Hashabiah, *he,* his sons, and his brethren, *were* twelve:
20The thirteenth to Shubael, *he,* his sons, and his brethren, *were* twelve:
21The fourteenth to Mattithiah, *he,* his sons, and his brethren, *were* twelve:
22The fifteenth to Jeremoth, *he,* his sons, and his brethren, *were* twelve:
23The sixteenth to Hananiah, *he,* his sons, and his brethren, *were* twelve:

25:4 Giddalti. This name and the five that follow it form a sentence in the Hebrew: "I have magnified and I have raised up help; sitting in trouble, I have spoken oracles plentiful." God gave Heman these sons (vs. 5), and the pious servant of the LORD gave his boys these names so that this meaning and message would be produced. He believed that God would so bless him that the sentence would be completed.

24The seventeenth to Joshbekashah,
he, his sons, and his brethren, *were*
twelve:
25The eighteenth to Hanani, *he,* his
sons, and his brethren, *were* twelve:
26The nineteenth to Mallothi, *he,* his
sons, and his brethren, *were* twelve:
27The twentieth to Eliathah, *he,* his
sons, and his brethren, *were* twelve:
28The one and twentieth to Hothir,
he, his sons, and his brethren, *were*
twelve:
29The two and twentieth to Giddalti,
he, his sons, and his brethren, *were*
twelve:
30The three and twentieth to Mahazioth, *he,* his sons, and his brethren,
were twelve:
31The four and twentieth to Romamti-ezer, *he,* his sons, and his brethren,
were twelve.

Divisions of the porters

26 Concerning the divisions of the
porters: Of the Korhites *was*
Meshelemiah the son of Kore, of the
sons of Asaph.
2And the sons of Meshelemiah *were,*
Zechariah the firstborn, Jediael the second, Zebadiah the third, Jathniel the
fourth,
3Elam the fifth, Jehohanan the sixth,
Elioenai the seventh.
4Moreover the sons of Obed-edom
were, Shemaiah the firstborn, Jehozabad the second, Joah the third, and Sacar the fourth, and Nethaneel the fifth,
5Ammiel the sixth, Issachar the seventh, Peulthai the eighth: for God
blessed him.
6Also unto Shemaiah his son were
sons born, that ruled throughout the
house of their father: for they *were*
mighty men of valour.
7The sons of Shemaiah; Othni, and
Rephael, and Obed, Elzabad, whose
brethren *were* strong men, Elihu, and
Semachiah.
8All these of the sons of Obed-edom:
they and their sons and their brethren,
able men for strength for the service,
were threescore and two of Obed-edom.
9And Meshelemiah had sons and
brethren, strong men, eighteen.
10Also Hosah, of the children of Merari, had sons; Simri the chief, (for
though he was not the firstborn, yet his
father made him the chief;)
11Hilkiah the second, Tebaliah the
third, Zechariah the fourth: all the sons
and brethren of Hosah *were* thirteen.
12Among these *were* the divisions of
the porters, *even* among the chief men,
having wards one against another, to
minister in the house of the LORD.

The gates of the porters chosen by lot

¶13And they cast lots, as well the
small as the great, according to the
house of their fathers, for every gate.
14And the lot eastward fell to Shelemiah. Then for Zechariah his son, a
wise counsellor, they cast lots; and his
lot came out northward.
15To Obed-edom southward; and to
his sons the house of Asuppim.
16To Shuppim and Hosah *the lot came*
forth westward, with the gate
Shallecheth, by the causeway of the
going up, ward against ward.
17Eastward *were* six Levites, northward four a day, southward four a day,
and toward Asuppim two *and* two.
18At Parbar westward, four at the
causeway, *and* two at Parbar.
19These *are* the divisions of the porters among the sons of Kore, and among
the sons of Merari.

26:1 porters. There were four thousand porters (1 Chron. 23:5) whose duties were to open and close all the gates, act as guards against intrusion, and assist and encourage worshippers.

26:1 of the Korhites . . . Asaph. This is Ebiasaph (9:19); *Asaph was a Gershonite (Num. 3:24).

26:5 God blessed him. God blessed Obed-edom because he had sheltered the ark (1 Chron. 13:14).

The charge of the treasures

¶20 And of the Levites, Ahijah *was*
over the treasures of the house of God,
and over the treasures of the dedicated things.
21 *As concerning* the sons of Laadan;
the sons of the Gershonite Laadan,
chief fathers, *even* of Laadan the Gershonite, *were* Jehieli.
22 The sons of Jehieli; Zetham, and
Joel his brother, *which were* over the
treasures of the house of the LORD.
23 Of the Amramites, *and* the Izharites, the Hebronites, *and* the Uzzielites:
24 And Shebuel the son of Gershom,
the son of Moses, *was* ruler of the treasures.
25 And his brethren by Eliezer; Rehabiah his son, and Jeshaiah his son, and
Joram his son, and Zichri his son, and
Shelomith his son.
26 Which Shelomith and his brethren
were over all the treasures of the dedicated things, which David the king, and
the chief fathers, the captains over
thousands and hundreds, and the captains of the host, had dedicated.
27 Out of the spoils won in battles did
they dedicate to maintain the house of
the LORD.
28 And all that *Samuel the seer, and
Saul the son of Kish, and Abner the son
of Ner, and Joab the son of Zeruiah, had
dedicated; *and* whosoever had dedicated *any thing, it was* under the hand of
Shelomith, and of his brethren.

Officers and judges

¶29 Of the Izharites, Chenaniah and
his sons *were* for the outward business
over *Israel, for officers and judges.
30 *And* of the Hebronites, Hashabiah
and his brethren, men of valour, a thousand and seven hundred, *were* officers
among them of Israel on this side Jordan westward in all the business of the
LORD, and in the service of the king.

26:29 Israel's Officers and Judges
These secretaries and magistrates took care of civil and religious affairs in the cities and towns outside of Jerusalem. It is said to be "outward business," the "business of the LORD and the service of the king" (vs. 30). As *Levites, they knew the Law well and were able to promote the administration of justice.

31 Among the Hebronites *was* Jerijah
the chief, *even* among the Hebronites,
according to the generations of his fathers. In the fortieth year of the reign
of David they were sought for, and there
were found among them mighty men of
valour at Jazer of *Gilead.
32 And his brethren, men of valour,
were two thousand and seven hundred
chief fathers, whom king David made
rulers over the Reubenites, the Gadites, and the half tribe of *Manasseh, for
every matter pertaining to God, and
affairs of the king.

Chief fathers and captains

27 Now the children of Israel after their number, *to wit,* the
chief fathers and captains of thousands
and hundreds, and their officers that
served the king in any matter of the
courses, which came in and went out
month by month throughout all the
*months of the year, of every course
were twenty and four thousand.
2 Over the first course for the first
month *was* Jashobeam the son of Zabdiel: and in his course *were* twenty and
four thousand.
3 Of the children of Perez *was* the
chief of all the captains of the host for
the first month.
4 And over the course of the second
month *was* Dodai an Ahohite, and of his
course *was* Mikloth also the ruler: in
his course likewise *were* twenty and
four thousand.
5 The third captain of the host for the
third month *was* Benaiah the son of *Je-

27:1 served the king. David had an army of 288,000 men, divided into twelve divisions (or corps), each division of 24,000 men serving a month in its turn.

hoiada, a chief priest: and in his course
were twenty and four thousand.
6This *is that* Benaiah, *who was* mighty
among the thirty, and above the thirty:
and in his course *was* Ammizabad his
son.
7The fourth *captain* for the fourth
month *was* Asahel the brother of Joab,
and Zebadiah his son after him: and in
his course *were* twenty and four thousand.
8The fifth captain for the fifth month
was Shamhuth the Izrahite: and in his
course *were* twenty and four thousand.
9The sixth *captain* for the sixth
month *was* Ira the son of Ikkesh the
Tekoite: and in his course *were* twenty
and four thousand.
10The seventh *captain* for the seventh month *was* Helez the Pelonite, of
the children of *Ephraim: and in his
course *were* twenty and four thousand.
11The eighth *captain* for the eighth
month *was* Sibbecai the Hushathite, of
the Zarhites: and in his course *were*
twenty and four thousand.
12The ninth *captain* for the ninth
month *was* Abi-ezer the Anetothite, of
the Benjamites: and in his course *were*
twenty and four thousand.
13The tenth *captain* for the tenth
month *was* Maharai the Netophathite,
of the Zarhites: and in his course *were*
twenty and four thousand.
14The eleventh *captain* for the eleventh month *was* Benaiah the Pirathonite, of the children of Ephraim: and in
his course *were* twenty and four thousand.
15The twelfth *captain* for the twelfth
month *was* Heldai the Netophathite, of
Othniel: and in his course *were* twenty
and four thousand.

Princes of the tribes

¶16Furthermore over the tribes of Israel: the ruler of the Reubenites *was*
Eliezer the son of Zichri: of the Simeonites, Shephatiah the son of Maachah:
17Of the Levites, Hashabiah the son
of Kemuel: of the Aaronites, Zadok:
18Of *Judah, Elihu, *one* of the brethren of *David: of Issachar, Omri the son
of Michael:
19Of Zebulun, Ishmaiah the son of
Obadiah: of Naphtali, Jerimoth the son
of Azriel:
20Of the children of Ephraim, Hoshea
the son of Azaziah: of the half tribe of
Manasseh, Joel the son of Pedaiah:
21Of the half *tribe* of Manasseh in Gilead, Iddo the son of Zechariah: of Benjamin, Jaasiel the son of Abner:
22Of Dan, Azareel the son of Jeroham.
These *were* the princes of the tribes of
Israel.

The numbering stopped

¶23But David took not the number of
them from twenty years old and under:
because the LORD had said he would
increase Israel like to the stars of the
heavens.
24Joab the son of Zeruiah began to
number, but he finished not, because
there fell wrath for it against Israel;
neither was the number put in the account of the chronicles of king David.

Overseers and officers

¶25And over the king's treasures *was*
Azmaveth the son of Adiel: and over the
storehouses in the fields, in the cities,
and in the villages, and in the castles,
was Jehonathan the son of Uzziah:
26And over them that did the work of
the field for tillage of the ground *was*
Ezri the son of Chelub:
27And over the vineyards was Shimei the Ramathite: over the increase of
the vineyards for the wine cellars *was*
Zabdi the Shiphmite:
28And over the olive trees and the
sycomore trees that *were* in the low
plains *was* Baal-hanan the Gederite:
and over the cellars of *oil *was* *Joash:
29And over the herds that fed in
*Sharon *was* Shitrai the Sharonite: and
over the herds *that were* in the valleys
was Shaphat the son of Adlai:
30Over the camels also *was* Obil the

Ishmaelite: and over the asses *was* Jehdeiah the Meronothite:
31 And over the flocks *was* Jaziz the
Hagerite. All these *were* the rulers of
the substance which *was* king David's.
32 Also Jonathan David's uncle was a
counsellor, a wise man, and a scribe:
and Jehiel the son of Hachmoni *was*
with the king's sons:
33 And Ahithophel *was* the king's
counsellor: and Hushai the Archite *was*
the king's companion:
34 And after Ahithophel *was* Jehoiada
the son of Benaiah, and Abiathar: and
the general of the king's army *was* Joab.

David charges the people
(compare 23:1)

28 And David assembled all the
princes of Israel, the princes of
the tribes, and the captains of the companies that ministered to the king by
course, and the captains over the thousands, and captains over the hundreds,
and the stewards over all the substance
and possession of the king, and of his
sons, with the officers, and with the
mighty men, and with all the valiant
men, unto *Jerusalem.
2 Then David the king stood up upon
his feet, and said, Hear me, my brethren, and my people: *As for me,* I *had* in
mine heart to build an house of rest for
the *ark of the covenant of the LORD,
and for the footstool of our God, and had
made ready for the building:
3 But God said unto me, Thou shalt
not build an house for my name, because thou *hast been* a man of war, and
hast shed *blood.
4 Howbeit the LORD God of Israel
chose me before all the house of my
father to be king over Israel for ever:
for he hath chosen Judah *to be* the ruler;
and of the house of Judah, the house of
my father; and among the sons of my
father he liked me to make *me* king over
all Israel:
5 And of all my sons, (for the LORD
hath given me many sons,) he hath chosen Solomon my son to sit upon the
throne of the *kingdom of the LORD
over Israel.
6 And he said unto me, Solomon thy
son, he shall build my house and my
courts: for I have chosen him *to be* my
son, and I will be his father.
7 Moreover I will establish his kingdom for ever, if he be constant to do my
commandments and my judgments, as
at this day.
8 Now therefore in the sight of all Israel the congregation of the LORD, and
in the audience of our God, keep and
seek for all the commandments of the
LORD your God: that ye may possess
this good land, and leave *it* for an inheritance for your children after you for
ever.

David charges Solomon to serve the LORD

¶9 And thou, Solomon my son, know
thou the God of thy father, and serve
him with a *perfect heart and with a
willing mind: for the LORD searcheth all
hearts, and understandeth all the imaginations of the thoughts: if thou seek
him, he will be found of thee; but if thou
forsake him, he will cast thee off for
ever.
10 Take heed now; for the LORD hath
chosen thee to build an house for the
*sanctuary: be strong, and do *it.*

Patterns and materials for the temple

¶11 Then David gave to Solomon his
son the pattern of the porch, and of the
houses thereof, and of the treasuries
thereof, and of the upper chambers
thereof, and of the inner parlours thereof, and of the place of the *mercy seat,
12 And the pattern of all that he had by

28:12 by the spirit. The Holy Spirit. Read also verse 19. The Spirit of the LORD revealed to David the details of the building of the temple, and worship therein, because the temple was to be a *type of Christ, and God alone was able to give instruction for its building.

the spirit, of the courts of the house of
the LORD, and of all the chambers round
about, of the treasuries of the house of
God, and of the treasuries of the dedicated things:
13 Also for the courses of the priests
and the Levites, and for all the work of
the service of the house of the LORD,
and for all the vessels of service in the
house of the LORD.
14 *He gave* of gold by weight for *things*
of gold, for all instruments of all manner of service; **silver also* for all instruments of silver by weight, for all
instruments of every kind of service:
15 Even the weight for the *candlesticks of gold, and for their lamps of
gold, by weight for every *candlestick,
and for the lamps thereof: and for the
candlesticks of silver by weight, *both* for
the candlestick, and *also* for the lamps
thereof, according to the use of every
candlestick.
16 And by weight *he gave* gold for the
tables of *shewbread, for every table;
and *likewise* silver for the tables of
silver:
17 Also pure gold for the fleshhooks,
and the bowls, and the cups: and for the
golden basons *he gave gold* by weight for
every bason; and *likewise silver* by
weight for every bason of silver:
18 And for the *altar of incense refined
gold by weight; and gold for the pattern
of the chariot of the cherubims, that
spread out *their wings,* and covered the
ark of the covenant of the LORD.
19 All *this, said David,* the LORD made
me understand in writing by *his* hand
upon me, *even* all the works of this
pattern.

David encourages his son in the LORD

20 And David said to Solomon his son,
Be strong and of good courage, and do
it: *fear not, nor be dismayed: for the
LORD God, *even* my God, *will be* with
thee; he will not fail thee, nor forsake
thee, until thou hast finished all the
work for the service of the house of the
LORD.
21 And, behold, the courses of the
priests and the Levites, *even they shall
be with thee* for all the service of the
house of God: and *there shall be* with
thee for all manner of workmanship
every willing skilful man, for any manner of service: also the princes and all
the people *will be* wholly at thy commandment.

David asks for consecrated gifts and service

29 Furthermore David the king
said unto all the congregation,
Solomon my son, whom alone God hath
chosen, *is yet* young and tender, and the
work *is* great: for the palace *is* not for
man, but for the LORD God.
2 Now I have prepared with all my
might for the house of my God the gold
for *things to be made* of gold, and the
silver for *things* of silver, and the brass
for *things* of brass, the iron for *things* of
iron, and wood for *things* of wood; onyx
stones, and *stones* to be set, glistering
stones, and of divers colours, and all
manner of precious stones, and marble
stones in abundance.
3 Moreover, because I have set my
affection to the house of my God, I have
of mine own proper good, of gold and
silver, *which* I have given to the house
of my God, over and above all that I
have prepared for the holy house,
4 *Even* three thousand talents of gold,
of the gold of Ophir, and seven thousand
talents of refined silver, to overlay the
walls of the houses *withal:*
5 The gold for *things* of gold, and the
silver for *things* of silver, and for all
manner of work *to be made* by the hands
of artificers. And who *then* is willing to
consecrate his service this day unto the
LORD?

The people's willing offerings

¶6 Then the chief of the fathers and
princes of the tribes of Israel, and the
captains of thousands and of hundreds,
with the rulers of the king's work, offered willingly,

29:5 Giving Willingly
This phrase "to consecrate his service . . . unto the LORD" means literally *to have the hands full for the LORD*. David's appeal was backed up by his own voluntary personal gifts (vss. 3-5). He led his people in giving because he himself had first given of his own wealth. The king and his people gave of their substance with sincerity and singleness of heart—they gave willingly, not of necessity. This also corresponds to the New Testament teaching (2 Cor. 9:7). Consecration and joy are close companions.

7 And gave for the service of the house of God of gold five thousand talents and ten thousand drams, and of silver ten thousand talents, and of brass eighteen thousand talents, and one hundred thousand talents of iron.

8 And they with whom *precious* stones were found gave *them* to the treasure of the house of the LORD, by the hand of Jehiel the Gershonite.

9 Then the people rejoiced, for that they offered willingly, because with perfect heart they offered willingly to the LORD: and David the king also rejoiced with great joy.

David's prayer of praise

¶ 10 Wherefore David blessed the LORD before all the congregation: and David said, Blessed *be* thou, LORD God of Israel our father, for ever and ever.

11 Thine, O LORD, *is* the greatness, and the power, and the glory, and the victory, and the majesty: for all *that is* in the heaven and in the earth *is thine;* thine *is* the kingdom, O LORD, and thou art exalted as head above all.

12 Both riches and honour *come* of thee, and thou reignest over all; and in thine hand *is* power and might; and in thine hand *it is* to make great, and to give strength unto all.

13 Now therefore, our God, we thank thee, and praise thy glorious name.

14 But who *am* I, and what *is* my people, that we should be able to offer so willingly after this sort? for all things *come* of thee, and of thine own have we given thee.

15 For we *are* strangers before thee, and sojourners, as *were* all our fathers: our days on the earth *are* as a shadow, and *there is* none abiding.

16 O LORD our God, all this store that we have prepared to build thee an house for thine holy name *cometh* of thine hand, and *is* all thine own.

17 I know also, my God, that thou triest the heart, and hast pleasure in uprightness. As for me, in the uprightness of mine heart I have willingly offered all these things: and now have I seen with joy thy people, which are present here, to offer willingly unto thee.

18 O LORD God of Abraham, Isaac, and of Israel, our fathers, keep this for ever in the imagination of the thoughts of the heart of thy people, and prepare their heart unto thee:

19 And give unto Solomon my son a perfect heart, to keep thy commandments, thy testimonies, and thy statutes, and to do all *these things,* and to build the palace, for the which I have made provision.

The worship and sacrifice of the people

¶ 20 And David said to all the congregation, Now bless the LORD your God. And all the congregation blessed the LORD God of their fathers, and bowed down their heads, and worshipped the LORD, and the king.

21 And they sacrificed sacrifices unto the LORD, and offered burnt-offerings unto the LORD, on the morrow after that day, *even* a thousand bullocks, a thousand rams, *and* a thou-

---

29:10 blessed the LORD. Note the order of this divine service: 1) giving willingly (vss. 3-8); 2) joy (vs. 9); 3) blessing (vs. 10); 4) prayer (vss. 11-19); and 5) worship (vs. 20).

sand lambs, with their drink-offerings, and sacrifices in abundance for
all Israel:
22And did eat and drink before the
LORD on that day with great gladness.
And they made Solomon the son of
David king the second time, and anointed *him* unto the LORD *to be* the chief
governor, and Zadok *to be* priest.

Solomon becomes king

23Then Solomon sat on the throne of
the LORD as king instead of David his
father, and prospered; and all Israel
obeyed him.
24And all the princes, and the mighty
men, and all the sons likewise of king
David, submitted themselves unto Solomon the king.
25And the LORD magnified Solomon
exceedingly in the sight of all Israel, and
bestowed upon him *such* royal majesty
as had not been on any king before him
in Israel.

David's reign ends in death
(1 Kings 2:10-12)

¶26Thus David the son of Jesse
reigned over all Israel.
27And the time that he reigned over
Israel *was* forty years; seven years
reigned he in Hebron, and thirty and
three *years* reigned he in Jerusalem.
28And he died in a good old age, full
of days, riches, and honour: and Solomon his son reigned in his stead.
29Now the acts of David the king, first
and last, behold, they *are* written in the
book of Samuel the seer, and in the book
of Nathan the prophet, and in the book
of Gad the seer,
30With all his reign and his might, and
the times that went over him, and over
Israel, and over all the kingdoms of the
countries.

29:29 Literature of the Hebrew People

The Old Testament points to a very extensive literature among the Hebrew people which has not been preserved. Among the uninspired books are the two mentioned here:

The Book of Nathan the Prophet (also in 2 Chron. 9:29), and *The Book of Gad the Seer.*

Among others are:

The Book of Jashar (Josh. 10:13; 2 Sam. 1:18);

The Book of the Acts of Solomon (1 Kings 11:41);

The Prophecy of Ahijah the Shilonite, and *The Visions of Iddo the Seer* (2 Chron. 9:29; compare 12:15; 13:22);

The Book of Shemaiah the Prophet (2 Chron. 12:15);

Isaiah's *The Acts of Uzziah* (2 Chron. 26:22);

and *The Sayings of the Seers* (2 Chron. 33:19).

Some of the facts recorded in these now lost books appear, under the guidance of the Holy Spirit, in the historical records of the Old Testament. The discoveries at and near Qumran included portions of over 200 non-canonical books.

29:22 they made Solomon . . . king the second time. The first occasion, done in haste at the time of Adonijah's rebellion, is recorded in 1 Kings 1:32-35. The second occasion is more fitting and in accord with the divine character of the kingship.

29:29 book of Nathan. The books of Nathan and Gad no longer exist (see introduction).

The Second Book of the

CHRONICLES

BACKGROUND

Second Chronicles continues the history begun in 1 Chronicles, and covers the same period of the history as the books of the Kings. It begins with the reign of Solomon, and continues through the reigns of the kings of Judah until the final captivity, covering a period of 427 years (Ussher). The people of Judah, led by their kings and princes, are pictured as sinking steadily into apostasy, with occasional spiritual revivals under Asa, Jehoshaphat, Joash, Hezekiah, and Josiah. The spiritual condition of the people is described by the prophets of the period, especially Isaiah, and their writings should be read in connection with the reading of 2 Chronicles. See also the introduction to 1 Chronicles.

OUTLINE OF 2 CHRONICLES

I.	Solomon Divinely Established on the Throne	2 Chronicles 1:1—9:31
II.	Rehoboam Becomes King	2 Chronicles 10:1-19
III.	Kings of Judah from Rehoboam to Zedekiah	2 Chronicles 11:1—36:23

I. Solomon Divinely Established on the Throne (1:1—9:31)

1 And Solomon the son of *David
was strengthened in his *kingdom,
and the LORD his *God *was* with him,
and magnified him exceedingly.

Solomon worships at Gibeon (1 Kings 3:4)

2 Then Solomon spake unto all *Israel, to the captains of thousands and of
hundreds, and to the judges, and to
every governor in all Israel, the chief
of the fathers.
3 So Solomon, and all the congregation with him, went to the high place
that *was* at Gibeon; for there was the
tabernacle of the congregation of God,
which *Moses the servant of the LORD
had made in the wilderness.
4 But the *ark of God had David
brought up from Kirjath-jearim to *the
place which* David had prepared for it:
for he had pitched a tent for it at *Jerusalem.
5 Moreover the brasen *altar, that
Bezaleel the son of Uri, the son of *Hur,

1:3 high place that was at Gibeon. See 1 Kings 3:4 note.
1:3 tabernacle of the congregation. The tabernacle was in Gibeon and the ark in Jerusalem (see 1 Chron. 16:37 note, "Divided Worship").
1:4 ark of God had David brought up. See 2 Samuel 6:2-17 and 1 Chronicles 15:25-16:2 for the record of this. (See also 2 Sam. 6:3-7 note, "Mishandling the Ark of God.")
1:5 brasen altar. See Exodus 27:1-2.

had made, he put before the tabernacle
of the LORD: and Solomon and the congregation sought unto it.
6And Solomon went up thither to the
brasen altar before the LORD, which
was at the tabernacle of the congregation, and offered a thousand burnt-
offerings upon it.

Solomon's prayer for wisdom
(1 Kings 3:5-15)

¶7In that night did God appear unto
Solomon, and said unto him, Ask what
I shall give thee.
8And Solomon said unto God, Thou
hast shewed great *mercy unto David
my father, and hast made me to reign
in his stead.
9Now, O LORD God, let thy promise
unto David my father be established:
for thou hast made me king over a people like the dust of the earth in multitude.
10Give me now wisdom and knowledge, that I may go out and come in
before this people: for who can judge
this thy people, *that is so* great?

1:10 Wisdom from God
Note that this wisdom was a God-given gift to Solomon, and that without it he would not have been able to properly use his riches, honor, and position. The Hebrew word for knowledge here, *madda,* is a rare one (used only here in vss. 10-12; and Dan. 1:17), which means *insight* or *inner consciousness.* Consequently, it means more than acquired knowledge. Wisdom is the power to apply rightly the knowledge that we have.

11And God said to Solomon, Because
this was in thine heart, and thou hast
not asked riches, wealth, or honour, nor
the life of thine enemies, neither yet
hast asked long life; but hast asked wisdom and knowledge for thyself, that
thou mayest judge my people, over
whom I have made thee king:
12Wisdom and knowledge *is* granted
unto thee; and I will give thee riches,
and wealth, and honour, such as none of
the kings have had that *have been* before
thee, neither shall there any after thee
have the like.

Solomon's strength and wealth

¶13Then Solomon came *from his journey* to the high place that *was* at Gibeon
to Jerusalem, from before the tabernacle of the congregation, and reigned
over Israel.
14And Solomon gathered chariots and
horsemen: and he had a thousand and
four hundred chariots, and twelve thousand horsemen, which he placed in the
chariot cities, and with the king at Jerusalem.
15And the king made silver and gold
at Jerusalem *as plenteous* as stones, and
cedar trees made he as the sycomore
trees that *are* in the vale for abundance.
16And Solomon had horses brought
out of *Egypt, and *linen yarn: the
king's merchants received the linen
yarn at a price.
17And they fetched up, and brought
forth out of Egypt a chariot for six hundred *shekels* of silver, and an horse for
an hundred and fifty: and so brought
they out *horses* for all the kings of the
Hittites, and for the kings of Syria, by
their means.

Preparations for building the temple
(1 Kings 5:1-18)

2 And Solomon determined to build
an house for the name of the LORD,
and an house for his kingdom.
2And Solomon told out threescore
and ten thousand men to bear burdens,
and fourscore thousand to hew in the
mountain, and three thousand and six
hundred to oversee them.
¶3And Solomon sent to Huram the
king of *Tyre, saying, As thou didst deal
with David my father, and didst send
him cedars to build him an house to
dwell therein, *even so deal with me.*
4Behold, I build an house to the name

2:3 Huram the king. *Hiram, king of Tyre.

of the LORD my God, to dedicate *it* to him, *and* to burn before him sweet *incense, and for the continual *shewbread, and for the burnt-offerings morning and evening, on the sabbaths, and on the *new moons, and on the solemn *feasts of the LORD our God. This *is an ordinance* for ever to Israel.

5 And the house which I build *is* great: for great *is* our God above all gods.

6 But who is able to build him an house, seeing the *heaven and heaven of heavens cannot contain him? who *am* I then, that I should build him an house, save only to burn *sacrifice before him?

7 Send me now therefore a man cunning to work in gold, and in silver, and in brass, and in iron, and in purple, and crimson, and *blue, and that can skill to grave with the cunning men that *are* with me in *Judah and in Jerusalem, whom David my father did provide.

8 Send me also cedar trees, fir trees, and algum trees, out of *Lebanon: for I know that thy servants can skill to cut timber in Lebanon; and, behold, my servants *shall be* with thy servants,

9 Even to prepare me timber in abundance: for the house which I am about to build *shall be* wonderful great.

10 And, behold, I will give to thy servants, the hewers that cut timber, twenty thousand measures of beaten wheat, and twenty thousand measures of barley, and twenty thousand *baths of *wine, and twenty thousand baths of *oil.

¶ 11 Then Huram the king of Tyre answered in writing, which he sent to Solomon, Because the LORD hath loved his people, he hath made thee king over them.

12 Huram said moreover, Blessed *be* the LORD God of Israel, that made heaven and earth, who hath given to David the king a wise son, endued with prudence and understanding, that might build an house for the LORD, and an house for his kingdom.

13 And now I have sent a cunning man, endued with understanding, of Huram my father's,

14 The son of a woman of the daughters of Dan, and his father *was* a man of Tyre, skilful to work in gold, and in silver, in brass, in iron, in stone, and in timber, in purple, in blue, and in fine linen, and in crimson; also to grave any manner of graving, and to find out every device which shall be put to him, with thy cunning men, and with the cunning men of my lord David thy father.

15 Now therefore the wheat, and the barley, the oil, and the wine, which my lord hath spoken of, let him send unto his servants:

16 And we will cut wood out of Lebanon, as much as thou shalt need: and we will bring it to thee in floats by sea to Joppa; and thou shalt carry it up to Jerusalem.

¶ 17 And Solomon numbered all the strangers that *were* in the land of Israel, after the *numbering wherewith David his father had numbered them; and they were found an hundred and fifty thousand and three thousand and six hundred.

18 And he set threescore and ten thousand of them *to be* bearers of burdens, and fourscore thousand *to be* hewers in the mountain, and three thousand and six hundred overseers to set the people a work.

Solomon builds the temple
(1 Kings 6:2—7:51)

3 Then Solomon began to build the house of the LORD at Jerusalem in mount Moriah, where *the LORD* appeared unto David his father, in the place that David had prepared in the

---

2:8 algum trees. See almug trees and 1 Kings 10:11 note, "The Almug Trees."

3:1 mount Moriah. This is the place where Abraham offered Isaac as a sacrifice (Gen. 22:2). See also 1 Chronicles 21:18-24.

threshingfloor of Ornan the Jebusite.
[2]And he began to build in the second
day of the second *month, in the fourth
year of his reign.

Measure and materials of the temple
(1 Kings 6:2—7:51)

¶[3]Now these *are the things wherein*
Solomon was instructed for the building of the house of God. The length by *cubits after the first measure *was* threescore cubits, and the breadth twenty cubits.
[4]And the porch that *was* in the front *of the house,* the length *of it was* according to the breadth of the house, twenty cubits, and the height *was* an hundred and twenty: and he overlaid it within with pure gold.
[5]And the greater house he *cieled with fir tree, which he overlaid with fine gold, and set thereon palm trees and chains.
[6]And he garnished the house with precious stones for beauty: and the gold *was* gold of Parvaim.
[7]He overlaid also the house, the beams, the posts, and the walls thereof, and the doors thereof, with gold; and graved cherubims on the walls.
[8]And he made the most holy house, the length whereof *was* according to the breadth of the house, twenty cubits, and the breadth thereof twenty cubits: and he overlaid it with fine gold, *amounting* to six hundred talents.
[9]And the weight of the nails *was* fifty shekels of gold. And he overlaid the upper chambers with gold.
[10]And in the most holy house he made two cherubims of image work, and overlaid them with gold.
¶[11]And the wings of the cherubims *were* twenty cubits long: one wing *of the one cherub was* five cubits, reaching to the wall of the house: and the other wing *was likewise* five cubits, reaching to the wing of the other cherub.
[12]And *one* wing of the other cherub *was* five cubits, reaching to the wall of the house: and the other wing *was* five cubits *also,* joining to the wing of the other cherub.
[13]The wings of these cherubims spread themselves forth twenty cubits: and they stood on their feet, and their faces *were* inward.
¶[14]And he made the vail *of* blue, and purple, and crimson, and fine linen, and wrought cherubims thereon.
[15]Also he made before the house two pillars of thirty and five cubits high, and the *chapiter that *was* on the top of each of them *was* five cubits.
[16]And he made chains, *as* in the oracle, and put *them* on the heads of the pillars; and made an hundred pomegranates, and put *them* on the chains.
[17]And he reared up the pillars before the temple, one on the right hand, and the other on the left; and called the name of that on the right hand*Jachin, and the name of that on the left *Boaz.

Building the temple (continued)

4 Moreover he made an altar of brass, twenty cubits the length thereof, and twenty cubits the breadth thereof, and ten cubits the height thereof.
¶[2]Also he made a molten sea of ten cubits from brim to brim, round in compass, and five cubits the height thereof; and a line of thirty cubits did compass it round about.
[3]And under it *was* the similitude of oxen, which did compass it round about: ten in a cubit, compassing the sea round about. Two rows of oxen *were* cast, when it was cast.

3:4 the height was an hundred and twenty. These measurements are also stated in 1 Kings 6:3, but this verse includes the height of the porch.
3:7 graved cherubims on the walls. These were not the *cherubim on the ark; they were engraved or carved figures Solomon had made (1 Kings 6:32,35).
4:1 altar of brass. Compare this with the *altar of shittim wood.

4 It stood upon twelve oxen, three looking toward the north, and three looking toward the west, and three looking toward the south, and three looking toward the east: and the sea *was set* above upon them, and all their hinder parts *were* inward.

5 And the thickness of it *was* an handbreadth, and the brim of it like the work of the brim of a cup, with flowers of lilies; *and* it received and held three thousand baths.

¶6 He made also ten lavers, and put five on the right hand, and five on the left, to wash in them: such things as they offered for the burnt-offering they washed in them; but the sea *was* for the priests to wash in.

7 And he made ten *candlesticks of gold according to their form, and set *them* in the temple, five on the right hand, and five on the left.

8 He made also ten tables, and placed *them* in the temple, five on the right side, and five on the left. And he made an hundred basons of gold.

¶9 Furthermore he made the court of the priests, and the great court, and doors for the court, and overlaid the doors of them with brass.

10 And he set the sea on the right side of the east end, over against the south.

11 And Huram made the pots, and the shovels, and the basons. And Huram finished the work that he was to make for king Solomon for the house of God;

12 *To wit,* the two pillars, and the pommels, and the *chapiters *which were* on the top of the two pillars, and the two wreaths to cover the two pommels of the chapiters which *were* on the top of the pillars;

13 And four hundred pomegranates on the two wreaths; two rows of pomegranates on each wreath, to cover the two pommels of the chapiters which *were* upon the pillars.

14 He made also bases, and lavers made he upon the bases;

15 One sea, and twelve oxen under it.

16 The pots also, and the shovels, and the fleshhooks, and all their instruments, did Huram his father make to king Solomon for the house of the LORD of bright brass.

17 In the plain of Jordan did the king cast them, in the clay ground between Succoth and Zeredathah.

18 Thus Solomon made all these vessels in great abundance: for the weight of the brass could not be found out.

¶19 And Solomon made all the vessels that *were for* the house of God, the golden altar also, and the tables whereon the shewbread *was set;*

20 Moreover the candlesticks with their lamps, that they should burn after the manner before the oracle, of pure gold;

21 And the flowers, and the lamps, and the tongs, *made he of* gold, *and* that perfect gold;

22 And the *snuffers, and the basons, and the spoons, and the *censers, *of* pure gold: and the entry of the house, the inner doors thereof for the most holy *place,* and the doors of the house of the temple, *were of* gold.

Solomon's temple finished
(1 Kings 8:1-11)

5 Thus all the work that Solomon made for the house of the LORD was finished: and Solomon brought in *all* the things that David his father had dedicated; and the silver, and the gold, and all the instruments, put he among the treasures of the house of God.

¶2 Then Solomon assembled the *el-

4:5 three thousand baths. See 1 Kings 7:26 note.

4:11 Huram made the pots. This was *Hiram, a workman from Tyre, not King Hiram (1 Kings 7:13-14).

4:12 pommels. The ball-like tops on the pillars. In 1 Kings 7:41, they are called "bowls."

4:20 oracle. The Most Holy Place where the divine utterances or oracles were given (see 2 Sam. 16:23; 1 Kings 6:16).

ders of Israel, and all the heads of the tribes, the chief of the fathers of the children of Israel, unto Jerusalem, to bring up the ark of the *covenant of the LORD out of the city of David, which *is* *Zion.

3 Wherefore all the men of Israel assembled themselves unto the king in the feast which *was* in the seventh month.

4 And all the elders of Israel came; and the Levites took up the ark.

5 And they brought up the ark, and the tabernacle of the congregation, and all the holy vessels that *were* in the tabernacle, these did the priests *and* the Levites bring up.

6 Also king Solomon, and all the congregation of Israel that were assembled unto him before the ark, sacrificed sheep and oxen, which could not be told nor numbered for multitude.

The ark placed in the holy of holies

7 And the priests brought in the ark of the covenant of the LORD unto his place, to the oracle of the house, into the most holy *place, even* under the wings of the cherubims:

8 For the cherubims spread forth *their* wings over the place of the ark, and the cherubims covered the ark and the staves thereof above.

9 And they drew out the staves *of the ark,* that the ends of the staves were seen from the ark before the oracle; but they were not seen without. And there it is unto this day.

10 *There was* nothing in the ark save the two tables which Moses put *therein* at *Horeb, when the LORD made *a covenant* with the children of Israel, when they came out of Egypt.

The glory of the LORD fills the temple

¶ 11 And it came to pass, when the priests were come out of the holy *place:* (for all the priests *that were* present were sanctified, *and* did not *then* wait by course:

12 Also the Levites *which were* the singers, all of them of *Asaph, of *Heman, of *Jeduthun, with their sons and their brethren, *being* arrayed in white linen, having cymbals and psalteries and harps, stood at the east end of the altar, and with them an hundred and twenty priests sounding with trumpets:)

13 It came even to pass, as the trumpeters and singers *were* as one, to make one sound to be heard in praising and thanking the LORD; and when they lifted up *their* voice with the trumpets and cymbals and instruments of musick, and praised the LORD, *saying,* For *he is* good; for his mercy *endureth* for ever: that *then* the house was filled with a cloud, *even* the house of the LORD;

14 So that the priests could not stand to minister by reason of the cloud: for the glory of the LORD had filled the house of God.

Solomon's sermon
(1 Kings 8:12-21)

6 Then said Solomon, The LORD hath said that he would dwell in the thick darkness.

2 But I have built an house of habitation for thee, and a place for thy dwelling for ever.

3 And the king turned his face, and blessed the whole congregation of Israel: and all the congregation of Israel stood.

4 And he said, Blessed *be* the LORD God of Israel, who hath with his hands fulfilled *that* which he spake with his mouth to my father David, saying,

5 Since the day that I brought forth my people out of the land of Egypt I chose no city among all the tribes of Israel to

---

5:3 feast which was in the seventh month. The *Feast of Tabernacles (see Lev. 23:34 note, "The Feast of Tabernacles").
5:12 psalteries. Stringed instruments, with ten or twelve strings, played by hand.
6:1 thick darkness. See Exodus 20:21.

build an house in, that my name might
be there; neither chose I any man to be
a ruler over my people Israel:
6 But I have chosen Jerusalem, that
my name might be there; and have chosen David to be over my people Israel.
7 Now it was in the heart of David my
father to build an house for the name of
the LORD God of Israel.
8 But the LORD said to David my father, Forasmuch as it was in thine
heart to build an house for my name,
thou didst well in that it was in thine
heart:
9 Notwithstanding thou shalt not build
the house; but thy son which shall come
forth out of thy loins, he shall build the
house for my name.
10 The LORD therefore hath performed his word that he hath spoken:
for I am risen up in the room of David
my father, and am set on the throne of
Israel, as the LORD promised, and have
built the house for the name of the
LORD God of Israel.
11 And in it have I put the ark, wherein
is the covenant of the LORD, that he
made with the children of Israel.

Solomon's prayer of dedication
(1 Kings 8:22-53)

¶12 And he stood before the altar of
the LORD in the presence of all the congregation of Israel, and spread forth his
hands:
13 For Solomon had made a brasen
scaffold, of five cubits long, and five
cubits broad, and three cubits high, and
had set it in the midst of the court: and
upon it he stood, and kneeled down
upon his knees before all the congregation of Israel, and spread forth his hands
toward heaven,
14 And said, O LORD God of Israel,
there is no God like thee in the heaven,
nor in the earth; which keepest covenant, and *shewest* mercy unto thy servants, that walk before thee with all
their hearts:
15 Thou which hast kept with thy servant David my father that which thou
hast promised him; and spakest with
thy mouth, and hast fulfilled *it* with
thine hand, as *it is* this day.
16 Now therefore, O LORD God of Israel, keep with thy servant David my
father that which thou hast promised
him, saying, There shall not fail thee a
man in my sight to sit upon the throne
of Israel; yet so that thy children take
heed to their way to walk in my *law,
as thou hast walked before me.
17 Now then, O LORD God of Israel, let
thy word be verified, which thou hast
spoken unto thy servant David.
18 But will God in very deed dwell
with men on the earth? behold, heaven
and the heaven of heavens cannot contain thee; how much less this house
which I have built!
19 Have respect therefore to the
*prayer of thy servant, and to his sup-
plication, O LORD my God, to hearken
unto the cry and the prayer which thy
servant prayeth before thee:
20 That thine eyes may be open upon
this house day and night, upon the place
whereof thou hast said that thou
wouldest put thy name there; to hearken unto the prayer which thy servant
prayeth toward this place.
21 Hearken therefore unto the supplications of thy servant, and of thy people Israel, which they shall make

6:12 The Altar

An altar was erected using stones or a single stone. Sometimes it was made of metal. Certain animals or parts of animals were burnt, and their blood was sprinkled on the altar. The first altar mentioned was the one built by Noah (Gen. 8:20). God commanded that the Hebrew altars be made of earth or of unhewn stones, without steps. The worshippers of Baal built their altars on hilltops, therefore, they were referred to as "altars on high places" (see Num. 22:41) and were an abomination to the LORD. In the temple at Jerusalem the brazen altar of burnt sacrifice was outside the Holy Place, in the court in front of it. The golden altar of incense stood inside the Holy Place.

toward this place: hear thou from thy
dwelling place, *even* from heaven; and
when thou hearest, forgive.
¶22 If a man *sin against his neighbour, and an oath be laid upon him to
make him swear, and the oath come
before thine altar in this house;
23 Then hear thou from heaven, and
do, and judge thy servants, by requit-
ing the wicked, by recompensing his
way upon his own head; and by justifying the righteous, by giving him according to his *righteousness.
¶24 And if thy people Israel be put to
the worse before the enemy, because
they have sinned against thee; and shall
return and *confess thy name, and pray
and make supplication before thee in
this house;
25 Then hear thou from the heavens,
and forgive the sin of thy people Israel,
and bring them again unto the land which
thou gavest to them and to their fathers.
¶26 When the heaven is shut up, and
there is no rain, because they have
sinned against thee; *yet* if they pray toward this place, and confess thy name,
and turn from their sin, when thou dost
afflict them;
27 Then hear thou from heaven, and
forgive the sin of thy servants, and of
thy people Israel, when thou hast
taught them the good way, wherein
they should walk; and send rain upon
thy land, which thou hast given unto thy
people for an inheritance.
¶28 If there be dearth in the land, if
there be pestilence, if there be blasting,
or mildew, locusts, or caterpillers; if
their enemies besiege them in the cities of their land; whatsoever sore or
whatsoever sickness *there be:*
29 *Then* what prayer *or* what supplication soever shall be made of any man,
or of all thy people Israel, when every
one shall know his own sore and his
own grief, and shall spread forth his
hands in this house:
30 Then hear thou from heaven thy
dwelling place, and forgive, and *render
unto every man according unto all his
ways, whose heart thou knowest; (for
thou only knowest the hearts of the
children of men:)
31 That they may *fear thee, to walk
in thy ways, so long as they live in the
land which thou gavest unto our fathers.
¶32 Moreover concerning the stranger, which is not of thy people Israel, but
is come from a far country for thy great
name's sake, and thy mighty hand, and
thy stretched out arm; if they come and
pray in this house;
33 Then hear thou from the heavens,
even from thy dwelling place, and do
according to all that the stranger calleth
to thee for; that all people of the earth
may know thy name, and fear thee, as
doth thy people Israel, and may know
that this house which I have built is
called by thy name.
34 If thy people go out to war against
their enemies by the way that thou
shalt send them, and they pray unto
thee toward this city which thou hast
chosen, and the house which I have
built for thy name;
35 Then hear thou from the heavens
their prayer and their supplication, and
maintain their cause.
36 If they sin against thee, (for *there is*
no man which sinneth not,) and thou be
angry with them, and deliver them over
before *their* enemies, and they carry
them away captives unto a land far off
or near;
37 Yet *if* they bethink themselves in
the land whither they are carried captive, and turn and pray unto thee in the
land of their captivity, saying, We have
sinned, we have done amiss, and have
dealt wickedly;
38 If they return to thee with all their
heart and with all their soul in the land
of their captivity, whither they have

6:38 pray toward . . . the city. Note that Daniel prayed toward Jerusalem when he was in captivity (Dan. 6:10).

carried them captives, and pray toward
their land, which thou gavest unto their
fathers, and *toward* the city which thou
hast chosen, and toward the house
which I have built for thy name:
39 Then hear thou from the heavens,
even from thy dwelling place, their
prayer and their supplications, and
maintain their cause, and forgive thy
people which have sinned against thee.
40 Now, my God, let, I beseech thee,
thine eyes be open, and *let* thine ears
be attent unto the prayer *that is made*
in this place.
41 Now therefore arise, O LORD God,
into thy resting place, thou, and the ark
of thy strength: let thy priests, O LORD
God, be clothed with *salvation, and let
thy *saints rejoice in goodness.
42 O LORD God, turn not away the face
of thine anointed: remember the mercies of David thy servant.

The LORD answers by sending fire from heaven

7 Now when Solomon had made an
end of praying, the *fire came
down from heaven, and consumed the
burnt-offering and the sacrifices; and
the glory of the LORD filled the house.

> **7:1 Fire from Heaven**
> God signified His acceptance of Solomon's prayer by sending fire to consume the sacrifices, just as the cloud filled the house with the "glory of the LORD" (2 Chron. 5:13-14) to signify His satisfaction with the new temple. For other cases of divine favor shown by fire from heaven, see, in the case of:
> 1. Moses (Lev. 9:24);
> 2. Gideon (Judg. 6:21);
> 3. David (1 Chron. 21:26); and
> 4. Elijah (1 Kings 18:38).

2 And the priests could not enter into
the house of the LORD, because the
glory of the LORD had filled the LORD'S
house.
3 And when all the children of *Israel
saw how the fire came down, and the
glory of the LORD upon the house, they
bowed themselves with their faces to
the ground upon the pavement, and
worshipped, and praised the LORD, *saying,* For *he is* good; for his *mercy
endureth for ever.

All Israel sacrifices and rejoices before the LORD (1 Kings 8:62-66)

¶ 4 Then the king and all the people offered sacrifices before the LORD.
5 And king Solomon offered a sacrifice
of twenty and two thousand oxen, and
an hundred and twenty thousand sheep:
so the king and all the people dedicated the house of *God.
6 And the priests waited on their offices: the Levites also with instruments
of musick of the LORD, which *David
the king had made to praise the LORD,
because his mercy *endureth* for ever,
when David praised by their ministry;
and the priests sounded trumpets before them, and all Israel stood.
7 Moreover Solomon hallowed the
middle of the court that *was* before the
house of the LORD: for there he offered
burnt-offerings, and the fat of the
*peace-offerings, because the brasen
*altar which Solomon had made was not
able to receive the burnt-offerings, and
the meat-offerings, and the fat.
¶ 8 Also at the same time Solomon
kept the feast seven days, and all Israel
with him, a very great congregation,
from the entering in of Hamath unto the
river of *Egypt.
9 And in the eighth day they made a
solemn assembly: for they kept the
dedication of the altar seven days, and
the feast seven days.
10 And on the three and twentieth day
of the seventh month he sent the people away into their tents, glad and merry in heart for the goodness that the
LORD had shewed unto David, and to
Solomon, and to Israel his people.

7:5 Solomon offered a sacrifice. See 1 Kings 8:63 note, "The Peace-Offerings."
7:8 the feast. The *Feast of Tabernacles.

[11]Thus Solomon finished the house
of the LORD, and the king's house: and
all that came into Solomon's heart to
make in the house of the LORD, and in
his own house, he prosperously effected.

The LORD speaks to Solomon
(1 Kings 9:1-9)

¶[12]And the LORD appeared to Solomon by night, and said unto him, I have
heard thy prayer, and have chosen this
place to myself for an house of sacrifice.
[13]If I shut up heaven that there be no
rain, or if I command the locusts to devour the land, or if I send pestilence
among my people;
[14]If my people, which are called by
my name, shall humble themselves,
and pray, and seek my face, and turn
from their wicked ways; then will I hear
from heaven, and will forgive their sin,
and will heal their land.

7:14 Receiving the LORD's Blessing
Four steps are mentioned here as necessary for the LORD to bless His people: humility, prayer, devotion, and repentance. In the following history of Israel and Judah, God did bless the people when they sought Him and turned from their wicked ways; but finally they became so involved in sin and idolatry that God sent judgment rather than blessing.

[15]Now mine eyes shall be open, and
mine ears attent unto the prayer *that is*
made in this place.
[16]For now have I chosen and sanctified this house, that my name may be
there for ever: and mine eyes and mine
heart shall be there perpetually.
[17]And as for thee, if thou wilt walk
before me, as David thy father walked,
and do according to all that I have commanded thee, and shalt observe my
statutes and my judgments;
[18]Then will I stablish the throne of
thy *kingdom, according as I have covenanted with David thy father, saying,
There shall not fail thee a man *to be*
ruler in Israel.
[19]But if ye turn away, and forsake my
statutes and my commandments, which
I have set before you, and shall go and
serve other gods, and worship them;
[20]Then will I pluck them up by the
roots out of my land which I have given
them; and this house, which I have
sanctified for my name, will I cast out
of my sight, and will make it *to be* a proverb and a byword among all nations.
[21]And this house, which is high, shall
be an astonishment to every one that
passeth by it; so that he shall say, Why
hath the LORD done thus unto this land,
and unto this house?
[22]And it shall be answered, Because
they forsook the LORD God of their fathers, which brought them forth out of
the land of Egypt, and laid hold on other
gods, and worshipped them, and served
them: therefore hath he brought all this
evil upon them.

The work of Solomon in his kingdom
(1 Kings 9:10-28)

8 And it came to pass at the end of
twenty years, wherein Solomon
had built the house of the LORD, and his
own house,
[2]That the cities which Huram had
restored to Solomon, Solomon built
them, and caused the children of Israel
to dwell there.
[3]And Solomon went to Hamath-
zobah, and prevailed against it.
[4]And he built Tadmor in the wilderness, and all the store cities, which he
built in Hamath.
[5]Also he built Beth-horon the upper,
and Beth-horon the nether, fenced cities, with walls, gates, and bars;

7:18 according as I have covenanted. This *covenant is found in 2 Samuel 7:12-16 (see 2 Sam. 7:11 note, "The Davidic Covenant").
8:2 cities which Huram had restored. Read 1 Kings 9:1-14; see especially verse 13 note, "The Land of Cabul."

6And Baalath, and all the store cities
that Solomon had, and all the chariot
cities, and the cities of the horsemen,
and all that Solomon desired to build in
*Jerusalem, and in *Lebanon, and
throughout all the land of his dominion.
¶7*As for* all the people *that were* left
of the Hittites, and the Amorites, and
the Perizzites, and the Hivites, and the
Jebusites, which *were* not of Israel,
8*But* of their children, who were left
after them in the land, whom the children of Israel consumed not, them
did Solomon make to pay tribute until
this day.
9But of the children of Israel did Solomon make no servants for his work;
but they *were* men of war, and chief of
his captains, and captains of his chariots and horsemen.
10And these *were* the chief of king
Solomon's officers, *even* two hundred
and fifty, that bare rule over the people.
¶11And Solomon brought up the
daughter of *Pharaoh out of the city of
David unto the house that he had built
for her: for he said, My wife shall not
dwell in the house of David king of Israel, because *the places are* holy, whereunto the *ark of the LORD hath come.

Sacrifices and feasts established

¶12Then Solomon offered burnt-
offerings unto the LORD on the altar of
the LORD, which he had built before
the porch,
13Even after a certain rate every day,
offering according to the commandment of *Moses, on the sabbaths, and
on the *new moons, and on the solemn
*feasts, three times in the year, *even* in
the feast of *unleavened bread, and in
the feast of weeks, and in the feast of
tabernacles.
¶14And he appointed, according to the
order of David his father, the courses of
the priests to their service, and the
Levites to their charges, to praise and
minister before the priests, as the duty
of every day required: the *porters also
by their courses at every gate: for so
had David the man of God commanded.
15And they departed not from the
commandment of the king unto the
priests and Levites concerning any
matter, or concerning the treasures.
16Now all the work of Solomon was
prepared unto the day of the foundation
of the house of the LORD, and until it
was finished. *So* the house of the LORD
was perfected.
¶17Then went Solomon to Ezion-geber, and to Eloth, at the sea side in the
land of *Edom.
18And Huram sent him by the hands
of his servants ships, and servants that
had knowledge of the sea; and they
went with the servants of Solomon to
*Ophir, and took thence four hundred
and fifty talents of gold, and brought
them to king Solomon.

8:18 Things More Valuable Than Gold
Gold was one thing of which Solomon had plenty, but there are some things said to be more valuable than gold:
1. the blood of Christ (1 Pet. 1:18-19)
2. the Word of God (Ps. 119:72,127)
3. the trial of your faith (1 Pet. 1:7)
4. the ornament of a meek and quiet spirit (1 Pet. 3:4; see also vs. 4 note, "The Inner Person")

Queen of Sheba visits Solomon
(1 Kings 10:1-13)

9 And when the *queen of Sheba
heard of the fame of Solomon, she
came to *prove Solomon with hard
questions at Jerusalem, with a very
great company, and camels that bare
spices, and gold in abundance, and precious stones: and when she was come

8:13 according to the commandment. See Numbers 29.
8:13 three times in the year. See 1 Kings 9:25 note.
8:17 Ezion-geber. A port on the upper arm of the Red Sea.
9:14 chapmen. Those who went about as traders or merchants.

to Solomon, she communed with him of
all that was in her heart.
2And Solomon told her all her questions: and there was nothing hid from
Solomon which he told her not.
3And when the queen of Sheba had
seen the wisdom of Solomon, and the
house that he had built,
4And the meat of his table, and the
sitting of his servants, and the attendance of his ministers, and their apparel; his cupbearers also, and their
apparel; and his ascent by which he
went up into the house of the LORD;
there was no more spirit in her.
5And she said to the king, *It was* a
true report which I heard in mine own
land of thine acts, and of thy wisdom:
6Howbeit I believed not their words,
until I came, and mine eyes had seen *it:*
and, behold, the one half of the greatness of thy wisdom was not told me: *for*
thou exceedest the fame that I heard.
7Happy *are* thy men, and happy *are*
these thy servants, which stand continually before thee, and hear thy wisdom.
8Blessed be the LORD thy God, which
delighted in thee to set thee on his
throne, *to be* king for the LORD thy God:
because thy God loved Israel, to establish them for ever, therefore made he
thee king over them, to do judgment
and justice.
9And she gave the king an hundred
and twenty talents of gold, and of spices
great abundance, and precious stones:
neither was there any such spice as the
queen of Sheba gave king Solomon.
10And the servants also of Huram,
and the servants of Solomon, which
brought gold from Ophir, brought algum
trees and precious stones.
11And the king made *of* the algum
trees terraces to the house of the LORD,
and to the king's palace, and harps and
*psalteries for singers: and there were
none such seen before in the land of
*Judah.
12And king Solomon gave to the
queen of Sheba all her desire, whatsoever she asked, beside *that* which she
had brought unto the king. So she
turned, and went away to her own land,
she and her servants.

Solomon's income and splendor
(1 Kings 10:14-29)

¶13Now the weight of gold that came
to Solomon in one year was six hundred
and threescore and six talents of gold;
14Beside *that which* chapmen and
merchants brought. And all the kings of
Arabia and governors of the country
brought gold and silver to Solomon.
¶15And king Solomon made two hundred targets *of* beaten gold: six hundred
shekels of beaten gold went to one
target.
16And three hundred shields *made he*
of beaten gold: three hundred *shekels* of
gold went to one shield. And the king
put them in the *house of the forest of
Lebanon.
17Moreover the king made a great
throne of ivory, and overlaid it with
pure gold.
18And *there were* six steps to the
throne, with a footstool of gold, *which*
were fastened to the throne, and stays
on each side of the sitting place, and two
lions standing by the stays:
19And twelve lions stood there on the
one side and on the other upon the six
steps. There was not the like made in
any kingdom.
¶20And all the drinking vessels of
king Solomon *were of* gold, and all the
vessels of the house of the forest of
Lebanon *were of* pure gold: none *were*
of silver; it was *not* any thing accounted of in the days of Solomon.
21For the king's ships went to *Tarshish with the servants of Huram:
every three years once came the ships
of Tarshish bringing gold, and silver,
ivory, and apes, and peacocks.
22And king Solomon passed all the
kings of the earth in riches and wisdom.
¶23And all the kings of the earth
sought the presence of Solomon, to
hear his wisdom, that God had put in his
heart.

9:22 Solomon as a Type of Christ
King Solomon, who sat upon the throne of his father David, ruled in peace and honor, and he received the homage of the rulers of the earth. In this way he is a *type of the Lord Jesus Christ who shall rule over the millennial *kingdom in peace and righteousness from His throne in Jerusalem (Isa. 2:3-4; 9:7; 11:1-5,10; Jer. 16:19; 23:5-6; 33:14-17).

24 And they brought every man his
present, vessels of silver, and vessels
of gold, and raiment, harness, and
spices, horses, and mules, a rate year
by year.
¶25 And Solomon had four thousand
stalls for horses and chariots, and
twelve thousand horsemen; whom he
bestowed in the chariot cities, and with
the king at Jerusalem.
¶26 And he reigned over all the kings
from the river even unto the land of
the *Philistines, and to the border of
Egypt.
27 And the king made silver in Jerusalem as stones, and cedar trees made
he as the sycomore trees that *are* in the
low plains in abundance.
28 And they brought unto Solomon
horses out of Egypt, and out of all
lands.

The death of Solomon
(1 Kings 11:41-43)

¶29 Now the rest of the acts of Solomon, first and last, *are* they not written in the *book of Nathan the
*prophet, and in the *prophecy of Ahi-
jah the Shilonite, and in the visions of
Iddo the seer against Jeroboam the son
of Nebat?
30 And Solomon reigned in Jerusalem
over all Israel forty years.
31 And Solomon slept with his fathers,
and he was buried in the city of David
his father: and *Rehoboam his son
reigned in his stead.

II. Rehoboam Becomes King (10:1-19)
(compare 1 Kings 12:1)

10 And Rehoboam went to Shechem: for to *Shechem were all
Israel come to make him king.

Rise of Jeroboam
(1 Kings 12:2-11)

2 And it came to pass, when Jeroboam the son of Nebat, who *was* in Egypt,
whither he had fled from the presence
of Solomon the king, heard *it,* that Jeroboam returned out of Egypt.
3 And they sent and called him. So
Jeroboam and all Israel came and spake
to Rehoboam, saying,
4 Thy father made our yoke grievous:
now therefore ease thou somewhat the
grievous servitude of thy father, and his
heavy yoke that he put upon us, and we
will serve thee.
5 And he said unto them, Come again
unto me after three days. And the people departed.
¶6 And king Rehoboam took counsel
with the old men that had stood before
Solomon his father while he yet lived,
saying, What counsel give ye *me* to return answer to this people?
7 And they spake unto him, saying, If
thou be kind to this people, and please
them, and speak good words to them,
they will be thy servants for ever.
8 But he forsook the counsel which
the old men gave him, and took counsel with the young men that were
brought up with him, that stood before
him.
9 And he said unto them, What advice
give ye that we may return answer to
this people, which have spoken to me,
saying, Ease somewhat the yoke that
thy father did put upon us?
10 And the young men that were
brought up with him spake unto him,
saying, Thus shalt thou answer the people that spake unto thee, saying, Thy

---

9:25 four thousand stalls. See 1 Kings 4:26 note, "Stalls for the Horses."
9:26 from the river. This is the Euphrates River. The promise found in Genesis 15:18, which sets the bounds of the land, is yet to be fulfilled.

father made our yoke heavy, but make
thou *it* somewhat lighter for us; thus
shalt thou say unto them, My little *fin-*
ger shall be thicker than my father's
loins.
11 For whereas my father put a heavy
yoke upon you, I will put more to your
yoke: my father chastised you with
whips, but I *will chastise you* with *scorpions.

The kingdom divided
(1 Kings 12:12-24)

12 So Jeroboam and all the people
came to Rehoboam on the third day, as
the king bade, saying, Come again to
me on the third day.
13 And the king answered them
roughly; and king Rehoboam forsook
the counsel of the old men,
14 And answered them after the advice of the young men, saying, My father made your yoke heavy, but I will
add thereto: my father chastised you
with whips, but I *will chastise you* with
scorpions.
15 So the king hearkened not unto the
people: for the cause was of God, that
the LORD might perform his word,
which he spake by the hand of Ahijah
the Shilonite to Jeroboam the son of
Nebat.
¶16 And when all Israel *saw* that the
king would not hearken unto them, the
people answered the king, saying, What
portion have we in David? and *we have*
*none inheritance in the son of Jesse:
every man to your tents, O Israel: *and*
now, David, see to thine own house. So
all Israel went to their tents.
17 But *as for* the children of Israel that
dwelt in the cities of Judah, Rehoboam
reigned over them.
18 Then king Rehoboam sent Hadoram that *was* over the tribute; and the
children of Israel stoned him with
stones, that he died. But king Rehoboam made speed to get him up to *his*
chariot, to flee to Jerusalem.
19 And Israel rebelled against the
house of David unto this day.

10:16 The Kingdom Divides
The reference to "all Israel" refers to the northern kingdom, often called Israel; the southern kingdom is known as Judah. This begins the divisions of the kingdom, resulting in strife and discord. Each kingdom was taken into captivity, but they shall be reunited in the land in the future *kingdom under Christ (Isa. 11:1-13; Jer. 23:5-6; Ezek. 37:15-28).

III. Kings from Rehoboam to Zedekiah
(11:1—36:23)
Rehoboam fortifies Judah

11 And when Rehoboam was
come to Jerusalem, he gathered
of the house of Judah and Benjamin an
hundred and fourscore thousand chosen *men,* which were warriors, to fight
against Israel, that he might bring the
kingdom again to Rehoboam.
2 But the word of the LORD came to
Shemaiah the man of God, saying,
3 Speak unto Rehoboam the son of
Solomon, king of Judah, and to all Israel
in Judah and Benjamin, saying,
4 Thus saith the LORD, Ye shall not go
up, nor fight against your brethren: return every man to his house: for this
thing is done of me. And they obeyed
the words of the LORD, and returned
from going against Jeroboam.
¶5 And Rehoboam dwelt in Jerusalem,
and built cities for defence in Judah.
6 He built even Bethlehem, and Etam,
and Tekoa,
7 And Beth-zur, and Shoco, and Adullam,
8 And *Gath, and Mareshah, and Ziph,
9 And Adoraim, and *Lachish, and
Azekah,
10 And Zorah, and Aijalon, and Hebron, which *are* in Judah and in Benjamin fenced cities.
11 And he fortified the strong holds,

10:18 over the tribute. These were forced laborers who were compelled to carry out the various public works.

and put captains in them, and store of
victual, and of *oil and *wine.
12And in every several city *he put*
shields and spears, and made them exceeding strong, having Judah and Benjamin on his side.

Godly Israelites come to Judah because of Jeroboam's apostasy

¶13And the priests and the Levites
that *were* in all Israel resorted to him
out of all their coasts.
14For the Levites left their suburbs
and their possession, and came to Judah and Jerusalem: for Jeroboam and
his sons had cast them off from executing the priest's office unto the LORD:
15And he ordained him priests for the
*high places, and for the devils, and for
the calves which he had made.
16And after them out of all the tribes
of Israel such as set their hearts to seek
the LORD God of Israel came to Jerusalem, to *sacrifice unto the LORD God of
their fathers.
17So they strengthened the kingdom
of Judah, and made Rehoboam the son
of Solomon strong, three years: for
three years they walked in the way of
David and Solomon.

Rehoboam's family

¶18And Rehoboam took him Mahalath the daughter of Jerimoth the son of
David to wife, *and* Abihail the daughter
of Eliab the son of Jesse;
19Which bare him children; Jeush,
and Shamariah, and Zaham.
20And after her he took Maachah the
daughter of Absalom; which bare him
Abijah, and Attai, and Ziza, and Shelomith.
21And Rehoboam loved Maachah the
daughter of Absalom above all his wives
and his concubines: (for he took eighteen wives, and threescore concubines;
and begat twenty and eight sons, and
threescore daughters.)
22And Rehoboam made Abijah the
son of Maachah the chief, *to be* ruler
among his brethren: for *he thought* to
make him king.
23And he dealt wisely, and dispersed
of all his children throughout all the
countries of Judah and Benjamin, unto
every fenced city: and he gave them
victual in abundance. And he desired
many wives.

Rehoboam forsakes the LORD

12 And it came to pass, when Rehoboam had established the
kingdom, and had strengthened himself, he forsook the *law of the LORD,
and all Israel with him.

12:1 Forgetting the Law
The first step in apostasy is to turn from the word of the LORD, a sin that comes as a result of pride in one's self and one's accomplishments, as in the case of Rehoboam. Note that disobeying God is followed by punishment in this historical account (for example, vs. 2). Note, too, the mercy of God promised in 2 Chronicles 7:14 and fulfilled in 2 Chronicles 12:7.

King of Egypt invades Judah (1 Kings 14:25-28)

2And it came to pass, *that* in the fifth
year of king Rehoboam Shishak king of
Egypt came up against Jerusalem, because they had transgressed against the
LORD,

11:15 he ordained. Jeroboam ordained the idolatrous priests.
11:15 for the devils. The word "devils" here means *hairy ones* or *goats.* In Egypt the worship of the sacred goat was an extremely evil ceremony, but Jeroboam patterned his religious rites after those of the Egyptians. The calves of this verse were also patterned and worshipped as were the golden calves of Egypt.
11:23 dispersed of all his children. This was a wise thing to do because Rehoboam's sons were made governors or rulers of the various provinces. This not only gave them places of importance; it prevented their conspiring against him.
11:23 he desired many wives. These wives were desired for his sons.

3 With twelve hundred chariots, and threescore thousand horsemen: and the people *were* without number that came with him out of Egypt; the Lubims, the Sukkiims, and the Ethiopians.

4 And he took the fenced cities which *pertained* to Judah, and came to Jerusalem.

¶ 5 Then came Shemaiah the prophet to Rehoboam, and *to* the princes of Judah, that were gathered together to Jerusalem because of Shishak, and said unto them, Thus saith the LORD, Ye have forsaken me, and therefore have I also left you in the hand of Shishak.

6 Whereupon the princes of Israel and the king humbled themselves; and they said, The LORD *is* righteous.

7 And when the LORD saw that they humbled themselves, the word of the LORD came to Shemaiah, saying, They have humbled themselves; *therefore* I will not destroy them, but I will grant them some deliverance; and my wrath shall not be poured out upon Jerusalem by the hand of Shishak.

8 Nevertheless they shall be his servants; that they may know my service, and the service of the kingdoms of the countries.

9 So Shishak king of Egypt came up against Jerusalem, and took away the treasures of the house of the LORD, and the treasures of the king's house; he took all: he carried away also the shields of gold which Solomon had made.

10 Instead of which king Rehoboam made shields of brass, and committed *them* to the hands of the chief of the guard, that kept the entrance of the king's house.

11 And when the king entered into the house of the LORD, the guard came and fetched them, and brought them again into the guard chamber.

12 And when he humbled himself, the wrath of the LORD turned from him, that he would not destroy *him* altogether: and also in Judah things went well.

The death of Rehoboam
(1 Kings 14:31)

¶ 13 So king Rehoboam strengthened himself in Jerusalem, and reigned: for Rehoboam *was* one and forty years old when he began to reign, and he reigned seventeen years in Jerusalem, the city which the LORD had chosen out of all the tribes of Israel, to put his name there. And his mother's name *was* Naamah an Ammonitess.

14 And he did evil, because he prepared not his heart to seek the LORD.

15 Now the acts of Rehoboam, first and last, *are* they not written in the book of Shemaiah the prophet, and of Iddo the seer concerning *genealogies? And *there were* wars between Rehoboam and Jeroboam continually.

16 And Rehoboam slept with his fathers, and was buried in the city of David: and Abijah his son reigned in his stead.

Abijah becomes king of Judah
(1 Kings 15:1-2)

13 Now in the eighteenth year of king Jeroboam began Abijah to reign over Judah.

2 He reigned three years in Jerusalem. His mother's name also *was* Michaiah the daughter of Uriel of Gibeah. And there was war between Abijah and Jeroboam.

War between Judah and Israel
(1 Kings 15:7)

3 And Abijah set the battle in array with an army of valiant men of war, *even* four hundred thousand chosen men:

12:3 Lubims. Libyans.
12:3 Sukkiims. Desert tribes.
12:15 book of Shemaiah. No longer in existence (see introduction to 1 Chronicles).
12:16 Abijah his son. See I Kings 15:1-4 note, "Abijam's Reign."
13:2 Michaiah. See 1 Kings 15:2 note.

Jeroboam also set the battle in array
against him with eight hundred thousand chosen men, *being* mighty men of
valour.
¶4And Abijah stood up upon mount
Zemaraim, which *is* in mount *Ephraim, and said, Hear me, thou Jeroboam,
and all *Israel;
5Ought ye not to know that the LORD
*God of Israel gave the *kingdom over
Israel to *David for ever, *even* to him
and to his sons by a *covenant of salt?

13:5 A Covenant of Salt
It was Mideastern custom, as well as Mosaic Law, to eat salt when a covenant was made, as a pledge of perpetual friendship, since salt is a preservative. Therefore, a lasting covenant is called a "covenant of salt" (see Lev. 2:13; Num. 18:19). The covenant of salt could not be broken.

6Yet Jeroboam the son of Nebat, the
servant of Solomon the son of David, is
risen up, and hath rebelled against his
lord.
7And there are gathered unto him
vain men, the *children of Belial,
and have strengthened themselves
against Rehoboam the son of Solomon,
when Rehoboam was young and ten-
derhearted, and could not withstand
them.
8And now ye think to withstand the
kingdom of the LORD in the hand of the
sons of David; and ye *be* a great multitude, and *there are* with you golden
calves, which Jeroboam made you for
gods.
9Have ye not cast out the priests of
the LORD, the sons of *Aaron, and the
Levites, and have made you priests
after the manner of the nations of *other*
lands? so that whosoever cometh to
*consecrate himself with a young bull-
ock and seven rams, *the same* may be a
priest of *them that are* no gods.
10But as for us, the LORD *is* our God,
and we have not forsaken him; and the
priests, which minister unto the LORD,
are the sons of Aaron, and the Levites
wait upon *their* business:
11And they burn unto the LORD every
morning and every evening burnt-
sacrifices and sweet *incense: the
*shewbread also *set they in order* upon
the pure table; and the *candlestick of
gold with the lamps thereof, to burn
every evening: for we keep the charge
of the LORD our God; but ye have forsaken him.
12And, behold, God himself *is* with us
for *our* captain, and his priests with
sounding trumpets to cry alarm against
you. O children of Israel, fight ye not
against the LORD God of your fathers;
for ye shall not prosper.
¶13But Jeroboam caused an ambushment to come about behind them: so
they were before Judah, and the
ambushment *was* behind them.
14And when Judah looked back, behold, the battle *was* before and behind:
and they cried unto the LORD, and the
priests sounded with the trumpets.

God gives victory to Judah

15Then the men of Judah gave a
shout: and as the men of Judah shouted, it came to pass, that God smote Jeroboam and all Israel before Abijah and
Judah.
16And the children of Israel fled before Judah: and God delivered them into
their hand.
17And Abijah and his people slew
them with a great slaughter: so there
fell down slain of Israel five hundred
thousand chosen men.
18Thus the children of Israel were

13:12 priests with sounding trumpets. In this connection, read Numbers 10.9.
13:12 fight ye not against the LORD. Fighting against God's people means fighting against God, which cannot prosper. Saul of Tarsus discovered this truth on the road to Damascus (Acts 9:5; compare Acts 5:39).
13:13 ambushment. An ambush, men lying in wait.

brought under at that time, and the children of Judah prevailed, because they
relied upon the LORD God of their fathers.
19And Abijah pursued after Jeroboam,
and took cities from him, *Beth-el with
the towns thereof, and Jeshanah with
the towns thereof, and Ephrain with the
towns thereof.
20Neither did Jeroboam recover
strength again in the days of Abijah: and
the LORD struck him, and he died.
¶21But Abijah waxed mighty, and married fourteen wives, and begat twenty
and two sons, and sixteen daughters.
22And the rest of the acts of Abijah,
and his ways, and his sayings, *are* written in the story of the prophet Iddo.

Asa becomes king of Judah
(1 Kings 15:8-10)

14 So Abijah slept with his fathers, and they buried him in
the city of David: and Asa his son
reigned in his stead. In his days the land
was quiet ten years.
2And Asa did *that which was* good and
right in the eyes of the LORD his God:
3For he took away the altars of the
strange *gods,* and the high places, and
brake down the images, and cut down
the groves:
4And commanded Judah to seek the
LORD God of their fathers, and to do the
law and the commandment.
5Also he took away out of all the cities of Judah the high places and the
images: and the kingdom was quiet
before him.
¶6And he built fenced cities in Judah:
for the land had rest, and he had no war
in those years; because the LORD had
given him rest.
7Therefore he said unto Judah, Let us
build these cities, and make about *them*
walls, and towers, gates, and bars, *while*
the land *is* yet before us; because we
have sought the LORD our God, we have
sought *him,* and he hath given us rest on
every side. So they built and prospered.

War with Ethiopians

8And Asa had an army *of men* that
bare targets and spears, out of Judah
three hundred thousand; and out of
Benjamin, that bare shields and drew
bows, two hundred and fourscore thousand: all these *were* mighty men of
valour.
¶9And there came out against them
Zerah the Ethiopian with an host of a
thousand thousand, and three hundred
chariots; and came unto Mareshah.
10Then Asa went out against him, and
they set the battle in array in the valley of Zephathah at Mareshah.
11And Asa cried unto the LORD his
God, and said, LORD, *it is* nothing with
thee to help, whether with many, or
with them that have no power: help us,
O LORD our God; for we rest on thee,
and in thy name we go against this
multitude. O LORD, thou *art* our God;
let not man prevail against thee.
12So the LORD smote the Ethiopians
before Asa and before Judah; and the
Ethiopians fled.
13And Asa and the people that *were*
with him pursued them unto Gerar: and
the Ethiopians were overthrown, that
they could not recover themselves; for
they were destroyed before the LORD,
and before his host; and they carried
away very much spoil.
14And they smote all the cities round
about Gerar; for the *fear of the LORD
came upon them: and they spoiled all
the cities; for there was exceeding
much spoil in them.
15They smote also the tents of cattle,
and carried away sheep and camels in
abundance, and returned to *Jerusalem.

13:22 the story of the prophet Iddo. One of the books which are now unknown (see introduction to 1 Chronicles).

14:1 Asa his son. See 1 Kings 15:9 note, "Asa Rules over Judah."

14:14 fear of the LORD came. This was a great terror sent by God.

The prophet Azariah's warning leads to reform under Asa

15 And the Spirit of God came upon Azariah the son of Oded:

2 And he went out to meet Asa, and said unto him, Hear ye me, Asa, and all *Judah and Benjamin; The LORD *is* with you, while ye be with him; and if ye seek him, he will be found of you; but if ye forsake him, he will forsake you.

3 Now for a long season Israel *hath been* without the true God, and without a teaching priest, and without law.

4 But when they in their trouble did turn unto the LORD God of Israel, and sought him, he was found of them.

5 And in those times *there was* no *peace to him that went out, nor to him that came in, but great vexations *were* upon all the inhabitants of the countries.

6 And nation was destroyed of nation, and city of city: for God did vex them with all adversity.

7 Be ye strong therefore, and let not your hands be weak: for your work shall be rewarded.

8 And when Asa heard these words, and the *prophecy of Oded the *prophet, he took courage, and put away the abominable idols out of all the land of Judah and Benjamin, and out of the cities which he had taken from mount Ephraim, and renewed the *altar of the LORD, that *was* before the porch of the LORD.

9 And he gathered all Judah and Benjamin, and the strangers with them out of Ephraim and *Manasseh, and out of Simeon: for they fell to him out of Israel in abundance, when they saw that the LORD his God *was* with him.

10 So they gathered themselves together at Jerusalem in the third *month, in the fifteenth year of the reign of Asa.

11 And they offered unto the LORD the same time, of the spoil *which* they had brought, seven hundred oxen and seven thousand sheep.

12 And they entered into a covenant to seek the LORD God of their fathers with all their heart and with all their soul;

13 That whosoever would not seek the LORD God of Israel should be put to *death, whether small or great, whether man or woman.

14 And they sware unto the LORD with a loud voice, and with shouting, and with trumpets, and with cornets.

15 And all Judah rejoiced at the oath: for they had sworn with all their heart, and sought him with their whole desire; and he was found of them: and the LORD gave them rest round about.

¶16 And also *concerning* Maachah the mother of Asa the king, he removed her from *being* queen, because she had made an idol in a grove: and Asa cut down her idol, and stamped *it,* and burnt *it* at the brook Kidron.

17 But the high places were not taken away out of Israel: nevertheless the heart of Asa was *perfect all his days.

¶18 And he brought into the house of God the things that his father had dedicated, and that he himself had dedicated, silver, and gold, and vessels.

19 And there was no *more* war unto the five and thirtieth year of the reign of Asa.

War between Judah and Israel (1 Kings 15:16-22)

16 In the six and thirtieth year of the reign of Asa Baasha king of Israel came up against Judah, and built Ramah, to the intent that he might let none go out or come in to Asa king of Judah.

2 Then Asa brought out silver and gold out of the treasures of the house

---

15:9 out of Israel. They came because they could not worship the one true God in their kingdom of Israel (vss. 3-4).

16:1 sixth and thirtieth year of the reign. It is understood that it was the thirty-sixth year of the kingdom and the sixteenth year of Asa's reign (compare15:19).

of the LORD and of the king's house, and
sent to *Ben-hadad king of Syria, that
dwelt at *Damascus, saying,
3 *There is* a league between me and
thee, as *there was* between my father
and thy father: behold, I have sent thee
silver and gold; go, break thy league
with Baasha king of Israel, that he may
depart from me.
4 And Ben-hadad hearkened unto king
Asa, and sent the captains of his armies
against the cities of Israel; and they
smote *Ijon, and Dan, and Abel-maim,
and all the store cities of Naphtali.
5 And it came to pass, when Baasha
heard *it,* that he left off building of Ramah, and let his work cease.
6 Then Asa the king took all Judah;
and they carried away the stones of
Ramah, and the timber thereof, wherewith Baasha was building; and he built
therewith Geba and Mizpah.

Hanani rebukes Asa and is imprisoned

¶ 7 And at that time Hanani the seer
came to Asa king of Judah, and said unto
him, Because thou hast relied on the
king of Syria, and not relied on the
LORD thy God, therefore is the host of
the king of Syria escaped out of thine
hand.
8 Were not the Ethiopians and the
*Lubims a huge host, with very many
chariots and horsemen? yet, because
thou didst rely on the LORD, he delivered them into thine hand.
9 For the eyes of the LORD run to and
fro throughout the whole earth, to shew
himself strong in the behalf of *them*
whose heart *is* perfect toward him.
Herein thou hast done foolishly: therefore from henceforth thou shalt have
wars.
10 Then Asa was wroth with the seer,
and put him in a prison house; for *he*
was in a rage with him because of this
thing. And Asa oppressed *some* of the
people the same time.
¶ 11 And, behold, the acts of Asa, first
and last, lo, they *are* written in the book
of the kings of Judah and Israel.

Death of Asa (1 Kings 15:23-24)

12 And Asa in the thirty and ninth year
of his reign was diseased in his feet,
until his disease *was* exceeding *great:*
yet in his disease he sought not to the
LORD, but to the physicians.
¶ 13 And Asa slept with his fathers, and
died in the one and fortieth year of his
reign.
14 And they buried him in his own
sepulchres, which he had made for himself in the city of David, and laid him in
the bed which was filled with sweet
odours and divers kinds *of spices* prepared by the apothecaries' art: and they
made a very great burning for him.

Jehoshaphat becomes king of Judah
(1 Kings 15:24)

17 And Jehoshaphat his son
reigned in his stead, and
strengthened himself against Israel.
2 And he placed forces in all the fenced
cities of Judah, and set garrisons in the
land of Judah, and in the cities of Ephraim, which Asa his father had taken.
3 And the LORD was with Jehoshaphat, because he walked in the first
ways of his father David, and sought not
unto Baalim;
4 But sought to the *LORD* God of his
father, and walked in his commandments, and not after the doings of Israel.
5 Therefore the LORD stablished the
kingdom in his hand; and all Judah
brought to Jehoshaphat presents; and
he had riches and honour in abundance.

16:11 book of the kings of Judah and Israel. No longer in existence (see introduction to 1 Chronicles).
16:12 the physicians. These were not physicians in the modern sense but superstitious priests who used various charms in their effort to cure the sick king.
16:14 great burning. Spices were burned around or near the dead king.

Revival in Judah

6 And his heart was lifted up in the
ways of the LORD: moreover he took
away the *high places and groves out
of Judah.
¶ 7 Also in the third year of his reign
he sent to his princes, *even* to Ben-hail,
and to Obadiah, and to Zechariah, and
to Nethaneel, and to Michaiah, to teach
in the cities of Judah.
8 And with them *he sent* Levites, *even*
Shemaiah, and Nethaniah, and Zebadiah, and Asahel, and Shemiramoth, and
Jehonathan, and Adonijah, and Tobijah,
and Tob-adonijah, Levites; and with
them Elishama and Jehoram, priests.
9 And they taught in Judah, and *had*
the book of the law of the LORD with
them, and went about throughout all the
cities of Judah, and taught the people.

Jehoshaphat's power and fame

¶ 10 And the fear of the LORD fell upon
all the kingdoms of the lands that *were*
round about Judah, so that they made
no war against Jehoshaphat.
11 Also *some* of the *Philistines
brought Jehoshaphat presents, and tribute silver; and the Arabians brought
him flocks, seven thousand and seven
hundred rams, and seven thousand and
seven hundred he goats.
¶ 12 And Jehoshaphat waxed great exceedingly; and he built in Judah castles,
and cities of store.
13 And he had much business in the
cities of Judah: and the men of war,
mighty men of valour, *were* in Jerusalem.
14 And these *are* the numbers of them
according to the house of their fathers:
Of Judah, the captains of thousands;
Adnah the chief, and with him mighty
men of valour three hundred thousand.
15 And next to him *was* Jehohanan the
captain, and with him two hundred and
fourscore thousand.
16 And next him *was* Amasiah the son
of Zichri, who willingly offered himself
unto the LORD; and with him two hundred thousand mighty men of valour.
17 And of Benjamin; Eliada a mighty
man of valour, and with him armed men
with bow and shield two hundred thousand.
18 And next him *was* Jehozabad, and
with him an hundred and fourscore
thousand ready prepared for the war.
19 These waited on the king, beside
those whom the king put in the fenced
cities throughout all Judah.

Jehoshaphat's alliance with Ahab, king of Israel (1 Kings 22:2-4)

18 Now Jehoshaphat had riches
and honour in abundance, and
joined affinity with *Ahab.

> **18:1 Three Alliances**
> Jehoshaphat was a good king of Judah (2 Chron. 17:4-5), but he made three alliances with *Israel that proved disastrous for Judah under Jehoshaphat's son Jehoram—alliances of:
> 1. marriage (2 Chron. 21:6);
> 2. war (2 Chron. 18:2-34); and
> 3. commerce (2 Chron. 20:35-37).

2 And after *certain* years he went
down to Ahab to *Samaria. And Ahab
killed sheep and oxen for him in abundance, and for the people that *he had*
with him, and persuaded him to go up
with him to Ramoth-gilead.
3 And Ahab king of Israel said unto
Jehoshaphat king of Judah, Wilt thou go
with me to Ramoth-gilead? And he answered him, I *am* as thou *art*, and my
people as thy people; and *we will be* with
thee in the war.

Ahab's false prophets (1 Kings 22:5-12)

¶ 4 And Jehoshaphat said unto the king
of Israel, Enquire, I pray thee, at the
word of the LORD to day.
5 Therefore the king of Israel gathered together of *prophets four hundred men, and said unto them, Shall we
go to Ramoth-gilead to battle, or shall
I forbear? And they said, Go up; for God
will deliver *it* into the king's hand.
6 But Jehoshaphat said, *Is there* not

here a prophet of the LORD besides, that
we might enquire of him?
7 And the king of Israel said unto Jehoshaphat, *There is* yet one man, by
whom we may enquire of the LORD: but
I hate him; for he never prophesied
good unto me, but always evil: the same
is Micaiah the son of Imla. And Jehoshaphat said, Let not the king say so.
8 And the king of Israel called for one
of his officers, and said, Fetch quickly
Micaiah the son of Imla.
9 And the king of Israel and Jehoshaphat king of Judah sat either of them on
his throne, clothed in *their* robes, and
they sat in a void place at the entering
in of the gate of Samaria; and all the
prophets prophesied before them.
10 And Zedekiah the son of Chenaanah
had made him *horns of iron, and said,
Thus saith the LORD, With these thou
shalt push Syria until they be consumed.
11 And all the prophets prophesied so,
saying, Go up to Ramoth-gilead, and
prosper: for the LORD shall deliver *it*
into the hand of the king.

Micaiah's true prophecy
(1 Kings 22:13-28)

12 And the messenger that went to
call Micaiah spake to him, saying, Behold, the words of the prophets *declare*
good to the king with one assent; let thy
word therefore, I pray thee, be like one
of theirs, and speak thou good.
13 And Micaiah said, *As* the LORD
liveth, even what my God saith, that
will I speak.
14 And when he was come to the king,
the king said unto him, Micaiah, shall
we go to Ramoth-gilead to battle, or
shall I forbear? And he said, Go ye up,
and prosper, and they shall be delivered
into your hand.
15 And the king said to him, How
many times shall I adjure thee that thou
say nothing but the truth to me in the
name of the LORD?
16 Then he said, I did see all Israel
scattered upon the mountains, as sheep
that have no shepherd: and the LORD
said, These have no master; let them
return *therefore* every man to his house
in peace.
17 And the king of Israel said to Jehoshaphat, Did I not tell thee *that* he
would not prophesy good unto me, but
evil?
18 Again he said, Therefore hear the
word of the LORD; I saw the LORD sitting upon his throne, and all the host of
*heaven standing on his right hand and
on his left.
19 And the LORD said, Who shall entice Ahab king of Israel, that he may go
up and fall at Ramoth-gilead? And one
spake saying after this manner, and another saying after that manner.
20 Then there came out a spirit, and
stood before the LORD, and said, I will
entice him. And the LORD said unto
him, Wherewith?
21 And he said, I will go out, and be a
lying spirit in the mouth of all his prophets. And *the LORD* said, Thou shalt entice *him*, and thou shalt also prevail: go
out, and do *even* so.
22 Now therefore, behold, the LORD
hath put a lying spirit in the mouth of
these thy prophets, and the LORD hath
spoken evil against thee.
23 Then Zedekiah the son of Chenaanah came near, and smote Micaiah
upon the cheek, and said, Which way
went the Spirit of the LORD from me to
speak unto thee?
24 And Micaiah said, Behold, thou
shalt see on that day when thou shalt go
into an inner chamber to hide thyself.
25 Then the king of Israel said, Take
ye Micaiah, and carry him back to
Amon the governor of the city, and to
*Joash the king's son;
26 And say, Thus saith the king, Put
this *fellow* in the prison, and feed him
with bread of affliction and with water
of affliction, until I return in peace.
27 And Micaiah said, If thou certainly
return in peace, *then* hath not the LORD
spoken by me. And he said, Hearken,
all ye people.

Battle of Ramoth-gilead; death of Ahab, king of Israel (1 Kings 22:29-40)

28 So the king of Israel and Jehoshaphat the king of Judah went up to Ramoth-gilead.

29 And the king of Israel said unto Jehoshaphat, I will disguise myself, and will go to the battle; but put thou on thy robes. So the king of Israel disguised himself; and they went to the battle.

30 Now the king of Syria had commanded the captains of the chariots that *were* with him, saying, Fight ye not with small or great, save only with the king of Israel.

31 And it came to pass, when the captains of the chariots saw Jehoshaphat, that they said, It *is* the king of Israel. Therefore they compassed about him to fight: but Jehoshaphat cried out, and the LORD helped him; and God moved them *to depart* from him.

32 For it came to pass, that, when the captains of the chariots perceived that it was not the king of Israel, they turned back again from pursuing him.

33 And a *certain* man drew a bow at a venture, and smote the king of Israel between the joints of the harness: therefore he said to his chariot man, Turn thine hand, that thou mayest carry me out of the host; for I am wounded.

34 And the battle increased that day: howbeit the king of Israel stayed *himself* up in *his* chariot against the Syrians until the even: and about the time of the sun going down he died.

Jehu rebukes the king for alliance with Ahab

19 And Jehoshaphat the king of Judah returned to his house in peace to Jerusalem.

2 And Jehu the son of Hanani the seer went out to meet him, and said to king Jehoshaphat, Shouldest thou help the ungodly, and love them that hate the LORD? therefore *is* wrath upon thee from before the LORD.

3 Nevertheless there are good things found in thee, in that thou hast taken away the groves out of the land, and hast prepared thine heart to seek *God.

Jehoshaphat leads in revival; Judges placed in cities of Judah

4 And Jehoshaphat dwelt at Jerusalem: and he went out again through the people from *Beer-sheba to mount *Ephraim, and brought them back unto the LORD God of their fathers.

¶ 5 And he set judges in the land throughout all the fenced cities of Judah, city by city,

6 And said to the judges, Take heed what ye do: for ye judge not for man, but for the LORD, who *is* with you in the judgment.

7 Wherefore now let the fear of the LORD be upon you; take heed and do *it:* for *there is* no iniquity with the LORD our God, nor respect of persons, nor taking of gifts.

¶ 8 Moreover in Jerusalem did Jehoshaphat set of the Levites, and *of* the priests, and of the chief of the fathers of *Israel, for the judgment of the LORD, and for controversies, when they returned to Jerusalem.

9 And he charged them, saying, Thus shall ye do in the fear of the LORD, faithfully, and with a *perfect heart.

10 And what cause soever shall come to you of your brethren that dwell in their cities, between blood and blood, between *law and commandment, statutes and judgments, ye shall even warn them that they *trespass not against the LORD, and *so* wrath come upon you, and upon your brethren: this do, and ye shall not trespass.

11 And, behold, Amariah the chief priest *is* over you in all matters of the LORD; and Zebadiah the son of Ishmael, the ruler of the house of Judah, for all the king's matters: also the Levites

---

19:7 fear of the LORD. Dread of God's displeasure, in this case.

shall be officers before you. Deal courageously, and the LORD shall be with the good.

Moabites invade Judah

20 It came to pass after this also,
that the children of *Moab, and
the children of Ammon, and with them
other beside the Ammonites, came
against Jehoshaphat to battle.
2Then there came some that told Jehoshaphat, saying, There cometh a
great multitude against thee from beyond the sea on this side Syria; and,
behold, they *be* in Hazazon-tamar,
which *is* En-gedi.

The king's prayer for divine help

3And Jehoshaphat feared, and set
himself to seek the LORD, and proclaimed a fast throughout all Judah.
4And Judah gathered themselves together, to ask *help* of the LORD: even out
of all the cities of Judah they came to
seek the LORD.
¶5And Jehoshaphat stood in the congregation of Judah and *Jerusalem, in
the house of the LORD, before the new
court,
6And said, O LORD God of our fathers,
art not thou God in heaven? and rulest
not thou over all the kingdoms of the
heathen? and in thine hand *is there not*
power and might, so that none is able
to withstand thee?
7*Art* not thou our God, *who* didst
drive out the inhabitants of this land
before thy people Israel, and gavest it
to the seed of *Abraham thy friend for
ever?
8And they dwelt therein, and have
built thee a *sanctuary therein for thy
name, saying,
9If, *when* evil cometh upon us, *as* the
sword, judgment, or pestilence, or famine, we stand before this house, and in
thy presence, (for thy name *is* in this
house,) and cry unto thee in our affliction, then thou wilt hear and help.
10And now, behold, the children of
Ammon and Moab and mount *Seir,
whom thou wouldest not let Israel invade, when they came out of the land
of *Egypt, but they turned from them,
and destroyed them not;
11Behold, *I say, how* they reward us,
to come to cast us out of thy possession,
which thou hast given us to inherit.
12O our God, wilt thou not judge
them? for we have no might against this
great company that cometh against us;
neither know we what to do: but our
eyes *are* upon thee.
13And all Judah stood before the
LORD, with their little ones, their
wives, and their children.

The LORD's answer

¶14Then upon Jahaziel the son of
Zechariah, the son of Benaiah, the son
of Jeiel, the son of Mattaniah, a Levite
of the sons of *Asaph, came the Spirit of
the LORD in the midst of the congregation;
15And he said, Hearken ye, all Judah,
and ye inhabitants of Jerusalem, and
thou king Jehoshaphat, Thus saith the
LORD unto you, *Be not afraid nor dismayed by reason of this great multitude; for the battle *is* not yours, but
God's.
16To morrow go ye down against
them: behold, they come up by the cliff
of Ziz; and ye shall find them at the end
of the brook, before the wilderness of
Jeruel.
17Ye shall not *need* to fight in this *battle:* set yourselves, stand ye *still,* and see
the *salvation of the LORD with you, O
Judah and Jerusalem: *fear not, nor be
dismayed; to morrow go out against
them: for the LORD *will be* with you.
18And Jehoshaphat bowed his head
with *his* face to the ground: and all Judah and the inhabitants of Jerusalem fell
before the LORD, worshipping the LORD.
19And the Levites, of the children of
the Kohathites, and of the children of the

20:7 Abraham thy friend. See Isaiah 41:8; James 2:23.

Korhites, stood up to praise the LORD
God of Israel with a loud voice on high.

The invading army destroyed

¶20 And they rose early in the morning, and went forth into the wilderness
of Tekoa: and as they went forth, Jehoshaphat stood and said, Hear me, O
Judah, and ye inhabitants of Jerusalem;
Believe in the LORD your God, so shall
ye be established; believe his prophets,
so shall ye prosper.
21 And when he had consulted with
the people, he appointed singers unto
the LORD, and that should praise the
beauty of holiness, as they went out
before the army, and to say, Praise the
LORD; for his *mercy *endureth* for ever.
¶22 And when they began to sing and
to praise, the LORD set ambushments
against the children of Ammon, Moab,
and mount Seir, which were come
against Judah; and they were smitten.
23 For the children of Ammon and
Moab stood up against the inhabitants
of mount Seir, utterly to slay and destroy *them:* and when they had made an
end of the inhabitants of Seir, every one
helped to destroy another.
24 And when Judah came toward the
watch tower in the wilderness, they
looked unto the multitude, and, behold,
they *were* dead bodies fallen to the
earth, and none escaped.
25 And when Jehoshaphat and his people came to take away the spoil of them,
they found among them in abundance
both riches with the dead bodies, and
precious jewels, which they stripped off
for themselves, more than they could
carry away: and they were three days
in gathering of the spoil, it was so much.

Jehoshaphat returns to Jerusalem
to reign in peace

¶26 And on the fourth day they assembled themselves in the valley of Berachah; for there they blessed the
LORD: therefore the name of the same
place was called, The valley of Berachah, unto this day.
27 Then they returned, every man of
Judah and Jerusalem, and Jehoshaphat
in the forefront of them, to go again to
Jerusalem with joy; for the LORD had
made them to rejoice over their enemies.
28 And they came to Jerusalem with
*psalteries and harps and trumpets
unto the house of the LORD.
29 And the fear of God was on all the
kingdoms of *those* countries, when they
had heard that the LORD fought against
the enemies of Israel.
30 So the realm of Jehoshaphat was
quiet: for his God gave him rest round
about.
¶31 And Jehoshaphat reigned over Judah: *he was* thirty and five years old
when he began to reign, and he reigned
twenty and five years in Jerusalem. And
his mother's name *was* Azubah the
daughter of Shilhi.
32 And he walked in the way of Asa his
father, and departed not from it, doing
that which was right in the sight of the
LORD.
33 Howbeit the high places were not
taken away: for as yet the people had
not prepared their hearts unto the God
of their fathers.
34 Now the rest of the acts of Jehoshaphat, first and last, behold, they *are*
written in the book of Jehu the son of
Hanani, who *is* mentioned in the book
of the kings of Israel.

Judah's commercial alliance with Israel
(1 Kings 22:47-49)

¶35 And after this did Jehoshaphat
king of Judah join himself with Ahaziah
king of Israel, who did very wickedly:
36 And he joined himself with him to
make ships to go to *Tarshish: and they
made the ships in Ezion-gaber.

20:21 beauty of holiness. Literally, *holy array* or *holy garments.*
20:26 Berachah. The name means *blessing.*
20:34 book of Jehu. No longer in existence (see introduction to 1 Chronicles).

37Then Eliezer the son of Dodavah of
Mareshah prophesied against Jehoshaphat, saying, Because thou hast joined
thyself with Ahaziah, the LORD hath
broken thy works. And the ships were
broken, that they were not able to go to
Tarshish.

Jehoram's evil reign over Judah
(2 Kings 8:16-24)

21 Now Jehoshaphat slept with
his fathers, and was buried with
his fathers in the city of *David. And
Jehoram his son reigned in his stead.
2And he had brethren the sons of Jehoshaphat, Azariah, and Jehiel, and
Zechariah, and Azariah, and Michael,
and Shephatiah: all these *were* the sons
of Jehoshaphat king of Israel.
3And their father gave them great
gifts of silver, and of gold, and of precious things, with fenced cities in *Judah: but the kingdom gave he to
Jehoram; because he *was* the firstborn.
4Now when Jehoram was risen up to
the kingdom of his father, he strengthened himself, and slew all his brethren
with the sword, and *divers* also of the
princes of Israel.
¶5Jehoram *was* thirty and two years
old when he began to reign, and he
reigned eight years in Jerusalem.
6And he walked in the way of the
kings of Israel, like as did the house of
Ahab: for he had the daughter of Ahab
to wife: and he wrought *that which was*
evil in the eyes of the LORD.
7Howbeit the LORD would not destroy the house of David, because of the
*covenant that he had made with David,
and as he promised to give a light to him
and to his sons for ever.

Revolt of Edom and Libnah
(2 Kings 8:20-22)

¶8In his days the Edomites revolted
from under the dominion of Judah, and
made themselves a king.
9Then Jehoram went forth with his
princes, and all his chariots with him:
and he rose up by night, and smote the
Edomites which compassed him in, and
the captains of the chariots.
10So the Edomites revolted from under the hand of Judah unto this day. The
same time *also* did Libnah revolt from
under his hand; because he had forsak-
en the LORD God of his fathers.
11Moreover he made high places in
the mountains of Judah, and caused the
inhabitants of Jerusalem to commit fornication, and compelled Judah *thereto*.

Elijah predicts a plague

¶12And there came a writing to him
from Elijah the *prophet, saying, Thus
saith the LORD God of David thy father,
Because thou hast not walked in the
ways of Jehoshaphat thy father, nor in
the ways of Asa king of Judah,
13But hast walked in the way of the
kings of Israel, and hast made Judah and
the inhabitants of Jerusalem to go a
whoring, like to the whoredoms of the
house of Ahab, and also hast slain thy
brethren of thy father's house, *which
were* better than thyself:
14Behold, with a great plague will the
LORD smite thy people, and thy children, and thy wives, and all thy goods:
15And thou *shalt have* great sickness
by disease of thy bowels, until thy bowels fall out by reason of the sickness day
by day.

Philistines and Arabians invade Judah

¶16Moreover the LORD stirred up
against Jehoram the spirit of the Philistines, and of the Arabians, that *were*
near the Ethiopians:
17And they came up into Judah, and
brake into it, and carried away all the
substance that was found in the king's
house, and his sons also, and his wives;
so that there was never a son left him,
save Jehoahaz, the youngest of his sons.

21:1 Jehoram. Jehoram reigned for a time with his father (2 Kings 8:16).
21:12 a writing to him. A prophecy that came to Jehoram after Elijah's death.

Jehoram's death

¶[18]And after all this the LORD smote
him in his bowels with an incurable disease.

[19]And it came to pass, that in process
of time, after the end of two years, his
bowels fell out by reason of his sickness: so he died of sore diseases. And
his people made no burning for him,
like the burning of his fathers.

[20]Thirty and two years old was he
when he began to reign, and he reigned
in Jerusalem eight years, and departed
without being desired. Howbeit they
buried him in the city of David, but not
in the sepulchres of the kings.

Ahaziah becomes king of Judah
(2 Kings 8:24-26)

22 And the inhabitants of Jerusalem made Ahaziah his youngest
son king in his stead: for the band of
men that came with the Arabians to the
camp had slain all the eldest. So Ahaziah the son of Jehoram king of Judah
reigned.

[2]Forty and two years old *was* Ahaziah when he began to reign, and he
reigned one year in Jerusalem. His
mother's name also *was* Athaliah the
daughter of Omri.

[3]He also walked in the ways of the
house of Ahab: for his mother was his
counsellor to do wickedly.

[4]Wherefore he did evil in the sight of
the LORD like the house of Ahab: for
they were his counsellors after the
*death of his father to his destruction.

Ahaziah allied with Israel
(2 Kings 8:28,29)

¶[5]He walked also after their counsel,
and went with Jehoram the son of Ahab
king of Israel to war against *Hazael
king of Syria at Ramoth-gilead: and the
Syrians smote Joram.

[6]And he returned to be healed in Jezreel because of the wounds which were
given him at Ramah, when he fought
with Hazael king of Syria. And Azariah
the son of Jehoram king of Judah went
down to see Jehoram the son of Ahab
at Jezreel, because he was sick.

[7]And the destruction of Ahaziah was
of God by coming to Joram: for when he
was come, he went out with Jehoram
against Jehu the son of Nimshi, whom
the LORD had anointed to cut off the
house of Ahab.

Ahaziah slain
(2 Kings 9:27-28)

[8]And it came to pass, that, when Jehu
was executing judgment upon the
house of Ahab, and found the princes of
Judah, and the sons of the brethren of
Ahaziah, that ministered to Ahaziah, he
slew them.

[9]And he sought Ahaziah: and they
caught him, (for he was hid in Samaria,) and brought him to Jehu: and when
they had slain him, they buried him:
Because, said they, he *is* the son of Jehoshaphat, who sought the LORD with
all his heart. So the house of Ahaziah
had no power to keep still the kingdom.

Royal seed of Judah, except Joash, slain
(2 Kings 11:1-3)

¶[10]But when Athaliah the mother of
Ahaziah saw that her son was dead, she
arose and destroyed all the seed royal
of the house of Judah.

22:10 God's Grace
This murderous act of Athaliah was an attempt by Satan to cut off the royal line of the Messiah (Gen. 49:10); but by the grace of God, one child, one-year-old Joash, was saved to perpetuate the royal line of Judah and David (2 Sam. 7:12; 1 Kings 2:4; 9:5; 2 Chron. 6:16).

21:19 no burning for him. See 2 Chronicles 16:14 note for the usual custom.
21:20 desired. Regretted.
22:1 Ahaziah. He is also called "Jehoahaz" and "Azariah," but the three names mean the same thing: *upheld by the LORD.*

11 But Jehoshabeath, the daughter of
the king, took Joash the son of Ahaziah, and stole him from among the
king's sons that were slain, and put
him and his nurse in a *bedchamber.
So Jehoshabeath, the daughter of king
Jehoram, the wife of *Jehoiada the
priest, (for she was the sister of Ahaziah,) hid him from Athaliah, so that she
slew him not.

Athaliah reigns over Judah

12 And he was with them hid in the
house of God six years: and Athaliah
reigned over the land.

Joash proclaimed king of Judah
(2 Kings 11:4-12)

23 And in the seventh year Jehoiada strengthened himself, and
took the captains of hundreds, Azariah
the son of Jeroham, and Ishmael the son
of Jehohanan, and Azariah the son of
Obed, and Maaseiah the son of Adaiah,
and Elishaphat the son of Zichri, into
covenant with him.
2 And they went about in Judah, and
gathered the Levites out of all the cities of Judah, and the chief of the fathers
of Israel, and they came to Jerusalem.
3 And all the congregation made a covenant with the king in the house of God.
And he said unto them, Behold, the
king's son shall reign, as the LORD hath
said of the sons of David.
4 This *is* the thing that ye shall do; A
third part of you entering on the *sabbath, of the priests and of the Levites,
shall be *porters of the doors;
5 And a third part *shall be* at the king's
house; and a third part at the gate of the
foundation: and all the people *shall be*
in the courts of the house of the LORD.
6 But let none come into the house of
the LORD, save the priests, and they
that minister of the Levites; they shall
go in, for they *are* *holy: but all the
people shall keep the watch of the
LORD.
7 And the Levites shall compass the
king round about, every man with his
weapons in his hand; and whosoever
else cometh into the house, he shall
be put to death: but be ye with the
king when he cometh in, and when he
goeth out.
8 So the Levites and all Judah did according to all things that Jehoiada the
priest had commanded, and took every
man his men that were to come in on
the sabbath, with them that were to go
out on the sabbath: for Jehoiada the
priest dismissed not the courses.
9 Moreover Jehoiada the priest delivered to the captains of hundreds spears,
and bucklers, and shields, that *had been*
king David's, which *were* in the house
of God.
10 And he set all the people, every
man having his weapon in his hand,
from the right side of the temple to the
left side of the temple, along by the
*altar and the temple, by the king round
about.
11 Then they brought out the king's
son, and put upon him the crown, and
gave him the testimony, and made him
king. And Jehoiada and his sons anointed him, and said, God save the king.

Athaliah slain
(2 Kings 11:13-16)

¶ 12 Now when Athaliah heard the
noise of the people running and praising the king, she came to the people
into the house of the LORD:
13 And she looked, and, behold, the
king stood at his *pillar at the entering
in, and the princes and the trumpets by
the king: and all the people of the land
rejoiced, and sounded with trumpets,
also the singers with instruments of
musick, and such as taught to sing
praise. Then Athaliah rent her clothes,
and said, Treason, Treason.
14 Then Jehoiada the priest brought
out the captains of hundreds that were
set over the host, and said unto them,
Have her forth of the ranges: and whoso
followeth her, let him be slain with the
sword. For the priest said, Slay her not
in the house of the LORD.

15 So they laid hands on her; and when she was come to the entering of the horse gate by the king's house, they slew her there.

Revival through Jehoiada, the priest (2 Kings 11:17-20)

¶16 And Jehoiada made a covenant between him, and between all the people, and between the king, that they should be the LORD'S people.

17 Then all the people went to the house of *Baal, and brake it down, and brake his altars and his images in pieces, and slew Mattan the priest of Baal before the altars.

18 Also Jehoiada appointed the offices of the house of the LORD by the hand of the priests the Levites, whom David had distributed in the house of the LORD, to offer the burnt-offerings of the LORD, as _it is_ written in the law of *Moses, with rejoicing and with singing, _as it was ordained_ by David.

19 And he set the porters at the gates of the house of the LORD, that none _which was_ *unclean in any thing should enter in.

20 And he took the captains of hundreds, and the nobles, and the governors of the people, and all the people of the land, and brought down the king from the house of the LORD: and they came through the high gate into the king's house, and set the king upon the throne of the kingdom.

21 And all the people of the land rejoiced: and the city was quiet, after that they had slain Athaliah with the sword.

Reign of Joash (2 Kings 12:1-3)

24 *Joash _was_ seven years old when he began to reign, and he reigned forty years in Jerusalem. His mother's name also _was_ Zibiah of *Beer-sheba.

2 And Joash did _that which was_ right in the sight of the LORD all the days of Jehoiada the priest.

3 And Jehoiada took for him *two wives; and he begat sons and daughters.

The temple repaired (2 Kings 12:4-16)

¶4 And it came to pass after this, _that_ Joash was minded to repair the house of the LORD.

5 And he gathered together the priests and the Levites, and said to them, Go out unto the cities of Judah, and gather of all Israel money to repair the house of your God from year to year, and see that ye hasten the matter. Howbeit the Levites hastened _it_ not.

6 And the king called for Jehoiada the chief, and said unto him, Why hast thou not required of the Levites to bring in out of Judah and out of Jerusalem the collection, _according to the commandment_ of Moses the servant of the LORD, and of the congregation of Israel, for the *tabernacle of witness?

7 For the sons of Athaliah, that wicked woman, had broken up the house of God; and also all the dedicated things of the house of the LORD did they bestow upon Baalim.

8 And at the king's commandment they made a chest, and set it without at the gate of the house of the LORD.

9 And they made a proclamation through Judah and Jerusalem, to bring in to the LORD the collection _that_ Moses the servant of God _laid_ upon Israel in the wilderness.

10 And all the princes and all the people rejoiced, and brought in, and cast into the chest, until they had made an end.

11 Now it came to pass, that at what time the chest was brought unto the king's office by the hand of the Levites, and when they saw that _there was_ much money, the king's *scribe and the high priest's officer came and emptied the chest, and took it, and carried it to his place again. Thus they did day by day, and gathered money in abundance.

24:6 according to the commandment of Moses. See Exodus 30:11-16.

[12]And the king and Jehoiada gave it
to such as did the work of the service
of the house of the LORD, and hired
masons and carpenters to repair the
house of the LORD, and also such as
wrought iron and brass to mend the
house of the LORD.
[13]So the workmen wrought, and the
work was perfected by them, and they
set the house of God in his state, and
strengthened it.
[14]And when they had finished *it,* they
brought the rest of the money before
the king and Jehoiada, whereof were
made vessels for the house of the
LORD, *even* vessels to minister, and to
offer *withal,* and spoons, and vessels
of gold and silver. And they offered
burnt-offerings in the house of the
LORD continually all the days of Jehoiada.

Death of Jehoiada the priest

¶[15]But Jehoiada waxed old, and was
full of days when he died; an hundred
and thirty years old *was he* when he
died.
[16]And they buried him in the city of
David among the kings, because he had
done good in Israel, both toward God,
and toward his house.

Apostasy in Judah

[17]Now after the death of Jehoiada
came the princes of Judah, and made
obeisance to the king. Then the king
hearkened unto them.
[18]And they left the house of the LORD
God of their fathers, and served groves
and idols: and wrath came upon Judah
and Jerusalem for this their trespass.
[19]Yet he sent *prophets to them, to
bring them again unto the LORD; and
they testified against them: but they
would not give ear.

Zechariah stoned

[20]And the Spirit of God came upon
Zechariah the son of Jehoiada the
priest, which stood above the people,
and said unto them, Thus saith God,
Why transgress ye the commandments
of the LORD, that ye cannot prosper?
because ye have forsaken the LORD, he
hath also forsaken you.
[21]And they conspired against him,
and stoned him with stones at the commandment of the king in the court of
the house of the LORD.
[22]Thus Joash the king remembered
not the kindness which Jehoiada his
father had done to him, but slew his
son. And when he died, he said, The
LORD look upon *it,* and require *it.*

Judah defeated by Syrian army

¶[23]And it came to pass at the end of
the year, *that* the host of Syria came up
against him: and they came to Judah and
Jerusalem, and destroyed all the
princes of the people from among the
people, and sent all the spoil of them
unto the king of *Damascus.
[24]For the army of the Syrians came
with a small company of men, and the
LORD delivered a very great host into
their hand, because they had forsaken
the LORD God of their fathers. So they
executed judgment against Joash.

Death of Joash
(2 Kings 12:19-21)

[25]And when they were departed from
him, (for they left him in great diseases,) his own servants conspired
against him for the blood of the sons of
Jehoiada the priest, and slew him on his
bed, and he died: and they buried him
in the city of David, but they buried him
not in the sepulchres of the kings.
[26]And these are they that conspired
against him; Zabad the son of Shimeath
an Ammonitess, and Jehozabad the son
of Shimrith a Moabitess.
¶[27]Now *concerning* his sons, and the
greatness of the burdens *laid* upon him,
and the repairing of the house of God,
behold, they *are* written in the story of

24:26 Zabad. He is called "Jozachar" in 2 Kings 12:21.

the book of the kings. And Amaziah his
son reigned in his stead.

Amaziah becomes king of Judah
(2 Kings 14:1-2)

25 Amaziah *was* twenty and five
years old *when* he began to
reign, and he reigned twenty and nine
years in Jerusalem. And his mother's
name *was* Jehoaddan of Jerusalem.
2 And he did *that which was* right in
the sight of the LORD, but not with a
*perfect heart.
¶3 Now it came to pass, when the
kingdom was established to him, that
he slew his servants that had killed the
king his father.
4 But he slew not their children, but
did as *it is* written in the *law in the
*book of Moses, where the LORD com-
manded, saying, The fathers shall not
die for the children, neither shall the
children die for the fathers, but every
man shall die for his own *sin.

Campaign against Edomites

¶5 Moreover Amaziah gathered Judah
together, and made them captains over
thousands, and captains over hundreds,
according to the houses of *their* fathers,
throughout all Judah and Benjamin: and
he numbered them from twenty years
old and above, and found them three
hundred thousand choice *men, able* to
go forth to war, that could handle spear
and shield.
6 He hired also an hundred thousand
mighty men of valour out of *Israel for
an hundred talents of silver.
7 But there came a man of *God to
him, saying, O king, let not the army of
Israel go with thee; for the LORD *is* not
with Israel, *to wit, with* all the children
of *Ephraim.

25:1 HEATHEN GODS WORSHIPPED IN ISRAEL AND JUDAH

From the first time they worshipped the golden calf in the wilderness (Exod. 32) the Israelites constantly strayed from God's command to love and serve only Him. They bowed down to the heathen idols of other nations.

God	Description	Reference
Adrammelech	god of the Sepharvites; required child sacrifice	2 Kings 17:31
Anammelech	god of the Sepharvites; required child sacrifice	2 Kings 17:31
Asherah (groves)	god of the Canaanites; associated with a pole	1 Kings 14:15; 2 Chronicles 24:18
Ashtoreth	god of the Sidonians	1 Samuel 12:10; 1 Kings 11:5
Baal	god of the Canaanites; god of rain and fertility; required prostitution	Judges 2:13; 1 Kings 16:31-32
Baal-berith	god of the Canaanites	Judges 8:33; 9:4
Baal-zebub	god of the Philistines of the city of Ekron	2 Kings 1:3
Chemosh	god of the Moabites	1 Kings 11:7,33
Dagon	god of the Philistines; god of farming	Judges 16:23; 1 Samuel 5:2-4
Molech	god of the Ammonites; required child sacrifice Also referred to as: Milcom, Malcam, Moloch	1 Kings 11:5,7 Zephaniah 1:5
Nergal	god of Cuth	2 Kings 17:30
Nibhaz	god of the Avites	2 Kings 17:31
Tartak	god of the Avites	2 Kings 17:31
Succoth-benoth	god of the Babylonians	2 Kings 17:30

24:27 the book of the kings. No longer in existence (see introduction to 1 Chronicles).
25:4 The fathers shall not die. See Deuteronomy 24:16.
25:7 Ephraim. Another name used to designate the ten-tribe kingdom of the north, Israel.

8 But if thou wilt go, do *it,* be strong
for the battle: God shall make thee fall
before the enemy: for God hath power
to help, and to cast down.
9 And Amaziah said to the man of God,
But what shall we do for the hundred
talents which I have given to the army
of Israel? And the man of God answered, The LORD is able to give thee
much more than this.
10 Then Amaziah separated them, *to
wit,* the army that was come to him out
of Ephraim, to go home again: wherefore their anger was greatly kindled
against Judah, and they returned home
in great anger.
¶ 11 And Amaziah strengthened himself, and led forth his people, and went
to the *valley of salt, and smote of the
children of Seir ten thousand.
12 And *other* ten thousand *left* alive did
the children of Judah carry away captive, and brought them unto the top of
the rock, and cast them down from the
top of the rock, that they all were broken in pieces.
¶ 13 But the soldiers of the army which
Amaziah sent back, that they should not
go with him to battle, fell upon the cities of Judah, from *Samaria even unto
Beth-horon, and smote three thousand
of them, and took much spoil.

Amaziah's lapse into idolatry

¶ 14 Now it came to pass, after that
Amaziah was come from the slaughter
of the Edomites, that he brought the
gods of the children of Seir, and set
them up *to be* his gods, and bowed down
himself before them, and burned *incense unto them.
15 Wherefore the anger of the LORD
was kindled against Amaziah, and he
sent unto him a prophet, which said
unto him, Why hast thou sought after
the gods of the people, which could not
deliver their own people out of thine
hand?
16 And it came to pass, as he talked
with him, that *the king* said unto him,
Art thou made of the king's counsel?
forbear; why shouldest thou be smitten? Then the prophet forbare, and said,
I know that God hath determined to
destroy thee, because thou hast done
this, and hast not hearkened unto my
counsel.

Judah defeated by Israel
(2 Kings 14:8-14)

¶ 17 Then Amaziah king of Judah took
advice, and sent to Joash, the son of
Jehoahaz, the son of Jehu, king of Israel,
saying, Come, let us see one another in
the face.
18 And Joash king of Israel sent to
Amaziah king of Judah, saying, The
thistle that *was* in *Lebanon sent to the
cedar that *was* in Lebanon, saying, Give
thy daughter to my son to wife: and
there passed by a wild beast that *was*
in Lebanon, and trode down the thistle.
19 Thou sayest, Lo, thou hast smitten
the Edomites; and thine heart lifteth
thee up to boast: abide now at home;
why shouldest thou meddle to *thine*
hurt, that thou shouldest fall, *even* thou,
and Judah with thee?
20 But Amaziah would not hear; for it
came of God, that he might deliver them
into the hand *of their enemies,* because
they sought after the gods of *Edom.
21 So Joash the king of Israel went up;
and they saw one another in the face,
both he and Amaziah king of Judah, at
Beth-shemesh, which *belongeth* to Judah.
22 And Judah was put to the worse
before Israel, and they fled every man
to his tent.
23 And Joash the king of Israel took
Amaziah king of Judah, the son of Joash,
the son of Jehoahaz, at Beth-shemesh,
and brought him to Jerusalem, and
brake down the wall of Jerusalem from
the gate of Ephraim to the corner gate,
four hundred *cubits.
24 And *he took* all the gold and the silver, and all the vessels that were found
in the house of God with Obed-edom,
and the treasures of the king's house,

the hostages also, and returned to Samaria.
¶ 25 And Amaziah the son of Joash king
of Judah lived after the death of Joash
son of Jehoahaz king of Israel fifteen
years.

Death of Amaziah

26 Now the rest of the acts of Amaziah, first and last, behold, *are* they not
written in the book of the kings of Judah and Israel?
¶ 27 Now after the time that Amaziah
did turn away from following the LORD
they made a conspiracy against him in
Jerusalem; and he fled to *Lachish: but
they sent to Lachish after him, and slew
him there.
28 And they brought him upon horses,
and buried him with his fathers in the
city of Judah.

Uzziah becomes king of Judah
(2 Kings 14:21)

26 Then all the people of Judah
took Uzziah, who *was* sixteen
years old, and made him king in the
room of his father Amaziah.
2 He built Eloth, and restored it to
Judah, after that the king slept with his
fathers.
3 Sixteen years old *was* Uzziah when
he began to reign, and he reigned fifty
and two years in *Jerusalem. His
mother's name also *was* Jecoliah of Jerusalem.
4 And he did *that which was* right in
the sight of the LORD, according to all
that his father Amaziah did.
5 And he sought God in the days of
Zechariah, who had understanding in
the visions of God: and as long as he
sought the LORD, God made him to
prosper.

Uzziah's successful reign

6 And he went forth and warred
against the *Philistines, and brake
down the wall of *Gath, and the wall of
Jabneh, and the wall of Ashdod, and
built cities about Ashdod, and among
the Philistines.
7 And God helped him against the
Philistines, and against the Arabians
that dwelt in Gur-baal, and the Me-
hunims.
8 And the Ammonites gave gifts to
Uzziah: and his name spread abroad
even to the entering in of *Egypt; for he
strengthened *himself* exceedingly.
9 Moreover Uzziah built towers in
Jerusalem at the corner gate, and at the
valley gate, and at the turning *of the
wall,* and fortified them.
10 Also he built towers in the desert,
and digged many wells: for he had much
cattle, both in the low country, and in
the plains: *husbandmen *also,* and vine
dressers in the mountains, and in *Carmel: for he loved husbandry.
11 Moreover Uzziah had an host of
fighting men, that went out to war by
bands, according to the number of their
account by the hand of Jeiel the scribe
and Maaseiah the ruler, under the hand
of Hananiah, *one* of the king's captains.
12 The whole number of the chief of
the fathers of the mighty men of valour
were two thousand and six hundred.
13 And under their hand *was* an army,
three hundred thousand and seven
thousand and five hundred, that made
war with mighty power, to help the king
against the enemy.
14 And Uzziah prepared for them
throughout all the host shields, and
spears, and helmets, and habergeons,
and bows, and slings *to cast* stones.
15 And he made in Jerusalem engines,
invented by cunning men, to be on the
towers and upon the bulwarks, to shoot
arrows and great stones withal. And his
name spread far abroad; for he was
marvellously helped, till he was strong.

Uzziah a leper because of disobedience

¶ 16 But when he was strong, his heart
was lifted up to *his* destruction: for he

26:1 Uzziah. See 2 Kings 14:21 note.

transgressed against the LORD his God,
and went into the temple of the LORD to
burn incense upon the altar of incense.
17 And Azariah the priest went in after him, and with him fourscore priests
of the LORD, *that were* valiant men:
18 And they withstood Uzziah the king,
and said unto him, *It appertaineth* not
unto thee, Uzziah, to burn incense unto
the LORD, but to the priests the sons of
*Aaron, that are consecrated to burn
incense: go out of the *sanctuary; for
thou hast trespassed; neither *shall it be*
for thine honour from the LORD God.
19 Then Uzziah was wroth, and *had* a
*censer in his hand to burn incense: and
while he was wroth with the priests, the
*leprosy even rose up in his forehead
before the priests in the house of the
LORD, from beside the incense altar.
20 And Azariah the chief priest, and all
the priests, looked upon him, and, behold, he *was* leprous in his forehead,
and they thrust him out from thence;
yea, himself hasted also to go out, because the LORD had smitten him.
21 And Uzziah the king was a leper
unto the day of his death, and dwelt in
a several house, *being* a leper; for he
was cut off from the house of the LORD:
and Jotham his son *was* over the king's
house, judging the people of the land.

Death of Uzziah

¶ 22 Now the rest of the acts of Uzziah, first and last, did Isaiah the prophet, the son of Amoz, write.
23 So Uzziah slept with his fathers,
and they buried him with his fathers in
the field of the burial which *belonged* to
the kings; for they said, He *is* a leper:
and Jotham his son reigned in his stead.

Jotham becomes king of Judah
(2 Kings 15:32-37)

27 Jotham *was* twenty and five
years old when he began to
reign, and he reigned sixteen years in
Jerusalem. His mother's name also *was*
Jerushah, the daughter of Zadok.
2 And he did *that which was* right in
the sight of the LORD, according to
all that his father Uzziah did: howbeit
he entered not into the temple of the
LORD. And the people did yet corruptly.
3 He built the high gate of the house
of the LORD, and on the wall of Ophel
he built much.
4 Moreover he built cities in the
mountains of *Judah, and in the forests
he built castles and towers.
¶ 5 He fought also with the king of the
Ammonites, and prevailed against
them. And the children of Ammon gave
him the same year an hundred talents
of *silver, and ten thousand measures
of wheat, and ten thousand of barley. So
much did the children of Ammon pay
unto him, both the second year, and the
third.
6 So Jotham became mighty, because
he prepared his ways before the LORD
his God.

Death of Jotham
(2 Kings 15:38)

¶ 7 Now the rest of the acts of Jotham,
and all his wars, and his ways, lo, they
are written in the book of the Kings of
Israel and Judah.
8 He was five and twenty years old
when he began to reign, and reigned
sixteen years in Jerusalem.
¶ 9 And Jotham slept with his fathers,
and they buried him in the city of

26:16 went into the temple. Uzziah took upon himself the priest's office in defiance of the commandment of God (vs. 18).
26:21 a several house. A separate house, apart from others.
26:22 did Isaiah. See Isaiah 1:1.
27:3 the high gate. See 2 Kings 15:35 note.
27:5 an hundred talents. See 2 Chronicles 25:9. The LORD was able to return the one hundred talents with wheat and barley as extras.
27:7 book of the Kings of Israel and Judah. No longer in existence (see introduction to 1 Chronicles).

*David: and Ahaz his son reigned in his
stead.

Reign of Ahaz over Judah
(2 Kings 16:1)

28 Ahaz *was* twenty years old
when he began to reign, and he
reigned sixteen years in Jerusalem:
but he did not *that which was* right in
the sight of the LORD, like David his
father:
2 For he walked in the ways of the
kings of Israel, and made also molten
images for Baalim.
3 Moreover he burnt incense in the
valley of the son of Hinnom, and burnt
his children in the fire, after the abominations of the heathen whom the LORD
had cast out before the children of Israel.
4 He sacrificed also and burnt incense
in the *high places, and on the hills, and
*under every green tree.

Israel and Syria defeat Judah
(2 Kings 16:5-6)

5 Wherefore the LORD his God delivered him into the hand of the king of
Syria; and they smote him, and carried
away a great multitude of them captives, and brought *them* to Damascus.
And he was also delivered into the hand
of the king of Israel, who smote him
with a great slaughter.
¶6 For Pekah the son of Remaliah
slew in Judah an hundred and twenty
thousand in one day, *which were* all valiant men; because they had forsaken
the LORD God of their fathers.
7 And Zichri, a mighty man of Ephraim, slew Maaseiah the king's son, and
Azrikam the governor of the house, and
Elkanah *that was* next to the king.
8 And the children of Israel carried
away captive of their brethren two hundred thousand, women, sons, and
daughters, and took also away much
spoil from them, and brought the spoil
to Samaria.

Oded, the prophet, intercedes

9 But a *prophet of the LORD was
there, whose name *was* Oded: and he
went out before the host that came to
Samaria, and said unto them, Behold,
because the LORD God of your fathers
was wroth with Judah, he hath delivered
them into your hand, and ye have slain
them in a rage *that* reacheth up unto
*heaven.
10 And now ye purpose to keep under
the children of Judah and Jerusalem
for bondmen and bondwomen unto
you: *but are there* not with you, even
with you, sins against the LORD your
God?
11 Now hear me therefore, and deliver the captives again, which ye have
taken captive of your brethren: for the
fierce wrath of the LORD *is* upon you.
12 Then certain of the heads of the
children of Ephraim, Azariah the son of
Johanan, Berechiah the son of Meshillemoth, and Jehizkiah the son of Shallum, and Amasa the son of Hadlai,
stood up against them that came from
the war,
13 And said unto them, Ye shall not
bring in the captives hither: for whereas
we have offended against the LORD *already,* ye intend to add *more* to our sins
and to our *trespass: for our trespass
is great, and *there is* fierce wrath against
Israel.
14 So the armed men left the captives
and the spoil before the princes and all
the congregation.

Edomites and Philistines invade Judah

15 And the men which were expressed
by name rose up, and took the captives,
and with the spoil clothed all that were
naked among them, and arrayed them,
and shod them, and gave them to eat
and to drink, and anointed them, and
carried all the feeble of them upon
asses, and brought them to Jericho, the
*city of palm trees, to their brethren:
then they returned to Samaria.

28:1 Ahaz. See Isaiah 7:1 for additional history of Ahaz's reign.

¶16 At that time did king Ahaz send unto the kings of Assyria to help him.

17 For again the Edomites had come and smitten Judah, and carried away captives.

18 The Philistines also had invaded the cities of the low country, and of the south of Judah, and had taken Beth-shemesh, and Ajalon, and Gederoth, and Shocho with the villages thereof, and Timnah with the villages thereof, Gimzo also and the villages thereof: and they dwelt there.

19 For the LORD brought Judah low because of Ahaz king of Israel; for he made Judah naked, and transgressed sore against the LORD.

20 And Tilgath-pilneser king of Assyria came unto him, and distressed him, but strengthened him not.

21 For Ahaz took away a portion *out* of the house of the LORD, and *out* of the house of the king, and of the princes, and gave *it* unto the king of Assyria: but he helped him not.

Ahaz falls into idolatry

¶22 And in the time of his distress did he trespass yet more against the LORD: this *is that* king Ahaz.

23 For he sacrificed unto the gods of Damascus, which smote him: and he said, Because the gods of the kings of Syria help them, *therefore* will I *sacrifice to them, that they may help me. But they were the ruin of him, and of all Israel.

24 And Ahaz gathered together the vessels of the house of God, and cut in pieces the vessels of the house of God, and shut up the doors of the house of the LORD, and he made him altars in every corner of Jerusalem.

25 And in every several city of Judah he made high places to burn incense unto other gods, and provoked to anger the LORD God of his fathers.

Death of Ahaz

¶26 Now the rest of his acts and of all his ways, first and last, behold, they *are* written in the book of the kings of Judah and Israel.

27 And Ahaz slept with his fathers, and they buried him in the city, *even* in Jerusalem: but they brought him not into the sepulchres of the kings of Israel: and *Hezekiah his son reigned in his stead.

Hezekiah becomes king of Judah
(2 Kings 18:1)

29 Hezekiah began to reign *when he was* five and twenty years old, and he reigned nine and twenty years in Jerusalem. And his mother's name *was* Abijah, the daughter of Zechariah.

2 And he did *that which was* right in the sight of the LORD, according to all that David his father had done.

Revival under Hezekiah
(2 Kings 18:4-7)

¶3 He in the first year of his reign, in the first *month, opened the doors of the house of the LORD, and repaired them.

4 And he brought in the priests and the Levites, and gathered them together into the east street,

5 And said unto them, Hear me, ye Levites, sanctify now yourselves, and sanctify the house of the LORD God of your fathers, and carry forth the filthiness out of the *holy *place.*

6 For our fathers have trespassed, and done *that which was* evil in the eyes of the LORD our God, and have forsaken him, and have turned away their faces from the habitation of the LORD, and turned *their* backs.

7 Also they have shut up the doors of the porch, and put out the lamps, and have not burned incense nor offered

---

28:23 the gods of Damascus, which smote him. These gods did not really smite Ahaz, but he believed that they did.

29:4 the east street. The open space opposite to the entrance of the temple.

burnt-offerings in the holy *place* unto
the God of Israel.
8 Wherefore the wrath of the LORD
was upon Judah and Jerusalem, and he
hath delivered them to trouble, to astonishment, and to hissing, as ye see
with your eyes.
9 For, lo, our fathers have fallen by the
sword, and our sons and our daughters
and our wives *are* in captivity for this.
10 Now *it is* in mine heart to make a
*covenant with the LORD God of Israel,
that his fierce wrath may turn away
from us.
11 My sons, be not now negligent: for
the LORD hath chosen you to stand before him, to serve him, and that ye
should minister unto him, and burn incense.
¶12 Then the Levites arose, Mahath
the son of Amasai, and Joel the son of
Azariah, of the sons of the Kohathites:
and of the sons of Merari, Kish the son
of Abdi, and Azariah the son of
Jehalelel: and of the Gershonites; Joah
the son of Zimmah, and *Eden the son
of Joah:
13 And of the sons of Elizaphan; Shimri, and Jeiel: and of the sons of *Asaph;
Zechariah, and Mattaniah:
14 And of the sons of *Heman; Jehiel,
and Shimei: and of the sons of *Jeduthun; Shemaiah, and Uzziel.
15 And they gathered their brethren,
and sanctified themselves, and came,
according to the commandment of the
king, by the words of the LORD, to
cleanse the house of the LORD.
16 And the priests went into the inner
part of the house of the LORD, to
cleanse *it,* and brought out all the uncleanness that they found in the temple of the LORD into the court of the
house of the LORD. And the Levites
took *it,* to carry *it* out abroad into the
brook Kidron.
17 Now they began on the first *day* of
the first month to sanctify, and on the
eighth day of the month came they to
the porch of the LORD: so they sanctified the house of the LORD in eight
days; and in the sixteenth day of the
first month they made an end.
18 Then they went in to Hezekiah the
king, and said, We have cleansed all the
house of the LORD, and the *altar of
burnt-offering, with all the vessels
thereof, and the *shewbread table, with
all the vessels thereof.
19 Moreover all the vessels, which
king Ahaz in his reign did cast away in
his transgression, have we prepared
and sanctified, and, behold, they *are*
before the altar of the LORD.

Temple worship restored

¶20 Then Hezekiah the king rose early, and gathered the rulers of the city,
and went up to the house of the LORD.
21 And they brought seven bullocks,
and seven rams, and seven lambs, and
seven he goats, for a *sin-offering for
the kingdom, and for the sanctuary, and
for Judah. And he commanded the
priests the sons of Aaron to offer *them*
on the altar of the LORD.
22 So they killed the bullocks, and the
priests received the *blood, and sprinkled *it* on the altar: likewise, when they
had killed the rams, they sprinkled the
blood upon the altar: they killed also the
lambs, and they sprinkled the blood
upon the altar.
23 And they brought forth the he goats
for the sin-offering before the king and
the congregation; and they laid their
hands upon them:
24 And the priests killed them, and
they made *reconciliation with their
blood upon the altar, to make an *atonement for all Israel: for the king commanded *that* the burnt-offering and the
sin-offering *should be made* for all Israel.
25 And he set the Levites in the house
of the LORD with cymbals, with *psalteries, and with harps, according to the
commandment of David, and of Gad the
king's seer, and Nathan the prophet: for

29:24 reconciliation. An offering.

so was the commandment of the LORD
by his prophets.
26And the Levites stood with the instruments of David, and the priests
with the trumpets.
27And Hezekiah commanded to offer
the burnt-offering upon the altar. And
when the burnt-offering began, the
song of the LORD began *also* with the
trumpets, and with the instruments *ordained* by David king of Israel.
28And all the congregation worshipped, and the singers sang, and the
trumpeters sounded: *and* all *this continued* until the burnt-offering was finished.
29And when they had made an end of
offering, the king and all that were present with him bowed themselves, and
worshipped.
30Moreover Hezekiah the king and
the princes commanded the Levites to
sing praise unto the LORD with the
words of David, and of Asaph the seer.
And they sang praises with gladness,
and they bowed their heads and worshipped.
31Then Hezekiah answered and said,
Now ye have consecrated yourselves
unto the LORD, come near and bring
sacrifices and thank offerings into the
house of the LORD. And the congregation brought in sacrifices and thank offerings; and as many as were of a free
heart burnt-offerings.
32And the number of the burnt-
offerings, which the congregation
brought, was threescore and ten bullocks, an hundred rams, *and* two hundred lambs: all these *were* for a
burnt-offering to the LORD.
33And the consecrated things *were* six
hundred oxen and three thousand
sheep.
34But the priests were too few, so
that they could not flay all the burnt-
offerings: wherefore their brethren the
Levites did help them, till the work was
ended, and until the *other* priests had
sanctified themselves: for the Levites
were more upright in heart to sanctify
themselves than the priests.
35And also the burnt-offerings *were* in
abundance,with the fat of the *peace-
offerings, and the drink-offerings for
every burnt-offering. So the service of
the house of the LORD was set in order.
36And Hezekiah rejoiced, and all the
people, that God had prepared the people: for the thing was *done* suddenly.

The Passover kept

30 And Hezekiah sent to all Israel
and Judah, and wrote letters
also to Ephraim and Manasseh, that
they should come to the house of the
LORD at Jerusalem, to keep the *passover unto the LORD God of Israel.
2For the king had taken counsel, and
his princes, and all the congregation in
Jerusalem, to keep the passover in the
second month.
3For they could not keep it at that
time, because the priests had not sanctified themselves sufficiently, neither
had the people gathered themselves
together to Jerusalem.
4And the thing pleased the king and
all the congregation.
5So they established a decree to
make proclamation throughout all Israel, from *Beer-sheba even to Dan,
that they should come to keep the passover unto the LORD God of Israel at
Jerusalem: for they had not done *it* of a
long *time in such sort* as it was written.
6So the posts went with the letters
from the king and his princes throughout all Israel and Judah, and according
to the commandment of the king, saying, Ye children of Israel, turn again unto
the LORD God of *Abraham, *Isaac, and

30:1 Ephraim and Manasseh. Hezekiah made an appeal to the tribes of the northern kingdom to renew their spiritual allegiance to the God of their fathers. This was not a political alliance. The result of the appeal is given in verses 10 and 11.
30:6 posts. A messenger, letter carrier.

Israel, and he will return to the *remnant of you, that are escaped out of the
hand of the kings of Assyria.
7 And be not ye like your fathers, and
like your brethren, which trespassed
against the LORD God of their fathers,
who therefore gave them up to desolation, as ye see.
8 Now be ye not stiffnecked, as your
fathers *were, but* yield yourselves unto
the LORD, and enter into his sanctuary,
which he hath sanctified for ever: and
serve the LORD your God, that the
fierceness of his wrath may turn away
from you.
9 For if ye turn again unto the LORD,
your brethren and your children *shall
find* compassion before them that lead
them captive, so that they shall come
again into this land: for the LORD your
God *is* gracious and merciful, and will
not turn away *his* face from you, if ye
return unto him.
10 So the posts passed from city to city
through the country of Ephraim and
Manasseh even unto Zebulun: but they
laughed them to scorn, and mocked
them.
11 Nevertheless divers of Asher and
Manasseh and of Zebulun humbled
themselves, and came to Jerusalem.
12 Also in Judah the hand of God was
to give them one heart to do the commandment of the king and of the
princes, by the word of the LORD.
¶ 13 And there assembled at Jerusalem
much people to keep the feast of *unleavened bread in the second month, a
very great congregation.
14 And they arose and took away the
altars that *were* in Jerusalem, and all the
altars for incense took they away, and
cast *them* into the brook Kidron.
15 Then they killed the passover on
the fourteenth *day* of the second month:
and the priests and the Levites were
ashamed, and sanctified themselves,
and brought in the burnt-offerings into
the house of the LORD.
16 And they stood in their place after
their manner, according to the law of
*Moses the man of God: the priests
sprinkled the blood, *which they received*
of the hand of the Levites.
17 For *there were* many in the congregation that were not sanctified: therefore the Levites had the charge of the
killing of the passovers for every one
that was not *clean, to sanctify *them*
unto the LORD.
18 For a multitude of the people, *even*
many of Ephraim, and Manasseh, Issachar, and Zebulun, had not cleansed
themselves, yet did they eat the pass-

30:1-20 PASSOVER

The Passover was a great historical festival. Year after year it recalled, as in a living drama, the great facts of the national deliverance from Egyptian bondage. The directions for its yearly celebration are given in Exodus 23:15; Leviticus 23:5-8; Numbers 28:16-25. It lasted from the fourteenth to the twenty-first day of the month of Nisan or Abib (April). The celebration was as follows:

1. On the tenth of that month each paschal company, which could not exceed twenty or be less than ten, was to select a lamb or kid, a male of the first year, and keep it until the fourteenth day.
2. On the fourteenth day, if the priest declared the animal free from blemish, it was to be slain between the evenings in the court of the tabernacle, and its blood poured around the altar of burnt-offering.
3. After the skin was removed, the animal was taken to the house where the paschal company intended to assemble, and there it was roasted with fire and eaten with unleavened bread and bitter herbs. No bone of the lamb was allowed to be broken.

Passover was the nation's annual birthday feast, the festival of redemption, its chief features being:

1. the offering of a single animal (also called "victim") for each paschal company;
2. the paschal meal, with which the festival began; and
3. the eating of unleavened bread during the whole festival.

over otherwise than it was written. But Hezekiah prayed for them, saying, The good LORD pardon every one

19 *That* prepareth his heart to seek God, the LORD God of his fathers, though *he be* not *cleansed* according to the purification of the sanctuary.

20 And the LORD hearkened to Hezekiah, and healed the people.

21 And the children of Israel that were present at Jerusalem kept the feast of unleavened bread seven days with great gladness: and the Levites and the priests praised the LORD day by day, *singing* with loud instruments unto the LORD.

22 And Hezekiah spake comfortably unto all the Levites that taught the good knowledge of the LORD: and they did eat throughout the feast seven days, offering peace-offerings, and making confession to the LORD God of their fathers.

23 And the whole assembly took counsel to keep other seven days: and they kept *other* seven days with gladness.

24 For Hezekiah king of Judah did give to the congregation a thousand bullocks and seven thousand sheep; and the princes gave to the congregation a thousand bullocks and ten thousand sheep: and a great number of priests sanctified themselves.

25 And all the congregation of Judah, with the priests and the Levites, and all the congregation that came out of Israel, and the strangers that came out of the land of Israel, and that dwelt in Judah, rejoiced.

26 So there was great joy in Jerusalem: for since the time of Solomon the *son of David king of Israel *there was* not the like in Jerusalem.

¶27 Then the priests the Levites arose and blessed the people: and their voice was heard, and their *prayer came *up* to his holy dwelling place, *even* unto heaven.

Idols destroyed in Judah

31 Now when all this was finished, all *Israel that were present went out to the cities of Judah, and brake the images in pieces, and cut down the groves, and threw down the high places and the altars out of all Judah and Benjamin, in *Ephraim also and Manasseh, until they had utterly destroyed them all. Then all the children of Israel returned, every man to his possession, into their own cities.

Hezekiah's religious reformation

¶2 And Hezekiah appointed the courses of the priests and the Levites after their courses, every man according to his service, the priests and Levites for burnt-offerings and for peace-offerings, to minister, and to give thanks, and to praise in the gates of the tents of the LORD.

3 *He appointed* also the king's portion of his substance for the burnt-offerings, *to wit,* for the morning and evening burnt-offerings, and the burnt-offerings for the sabbaths, and for the *new moons, and for the *set feasts, as *it is* written in the *law of the LORD.

4 Moreover he commanded the people that dwelt in Jerusalem to give the portion of the priests and the Levites, that they might be encouraged in the law of the LORD.

¶5 And as soon as the commandment came abroad, the children of Israel brought in abundance the firstfruits of corn, *wine, and *oil, and honey, and of all the increase of the field; and the tithe of all *things* brought they in abundantly.

6 And *concerning* the children of Israel and Judah, that dwelt in the cities of Judah, they also brought in the tithe of oxen and sheep, and the tithe of holy things which were consecrated unto the LORD their *God, and laid *them* by heaps.

31:2 courses of the priests. See 1 Chronicles 23:6; 24:1.
31:4 portion of the priests. See Numbers 18:8; Nehemiah 13:10.

7 In the third month they began to lay
the foundation of the heaps, and finished *them* in the seventh month.
8 And when Hezekiah and the princes
came and saw the heaps, they blessed
the LORD, and his people Israel.
9 Then Hezekiah questioned with the
priests and the Levites concerning the
heaps.
10 And Azariah the chief priest of the
house of Zadok answered him, and said,
Since *the people* began to bring the offerings into the house of the LORD, we
have had enough to eat, and have left
plenty: for the LORD hath blessed his
people; and that which is left *is* this
great store.
¶ 11 Then Hezekiah commanded to
prepare chambers in the house of the
LORD; and they prepared *them,*
12 And brought in the offerings and
the *tithes and the dedicated *things*
faithfully: over which Cononiah the
Levite *was* ruler, and Shimei his
brother *was* the next.
13 And Jehiel, and Azaziah, and Nahath, and Asahel, and Jerimoth, and
Jozabad, and Eliel, and Ismachiah, and
Mahath, and Benaiah, *were* overseers
under the hand of Cononiah and Shimei his brother, at the commandment of
Hezekiah the king, and Azariah the
ruler of the house of God.
14 And Kore the son of Imnah the Levite, the porter toward the east, *was*
over the freewill-offerings of God, to
distribute the oblations of the LORD,
and the most holy things.
15 And next him *were* Eden, and Min-

31:14 Porters

The porters were the doorkeepers and the police of the temple (1 Chron. 9:17-24). They lived on the adjoining Mount Ophel and were divided into companies under the command of the captain of the temple. One division was always on duty, keeping guard day and night. The historian Josephus says that it took twenty porters to shut the great brazen gates (Acts 21:30).

31:10 THE TEMPLE

The temple was the name given to the whole sacred area on Mount Moriah, including the sanctuary and the various courts. The sanctuary was planned according to the general design of the original Holy of Holies. In the Holy Place there were ten tables of shewbread and ten golden candlesticks (five of each on either side). The great brazen laver stood on twelve brazen oxen, with their faces pointing outwards. The altar of burnt offering was much larger than the original one. The accounts in Kings and Chronicles should be compared throughout.

In Herod's time there was a far greater elaboration of courts within the temple, and at one stage there was a trellised fence, and notices on stone tablets prohibiting the uncircumcised from passing within the sacred enclosures on pain of death.

The parts of the temple referred to in the New Testament are:

1. The Hieron, or sacred place as a whole, including the courts and precincts, from which Christ drove out those selling animals for sacrifice.
2. The Naos, or Holy Place. Christ was referring to this area when he said, "Destroy this temple, and in three days I will raise it up" (John 2:19).
3. Solomon's Porch, where Christ walked in wintertime and Peter preached to the multitude after healing the lame man. It was part of the colonnade or cloisters that ran around the outer court.
4. The treasury, where there were alms boxes with trumpet-shaped openings into which the rich and poor placed their offerings (Mark 12:41); these were in the women's court.
5. The Beautiful Gate, supposed to have stood facing east, where the Golden Gate stands now.
6. The doors or gates that were shut when Paul was excluded (Acts 21:30); these were the large folding doors at the entrance, and they were so heavy that it took twenty men to close them.
7. The middle wall or partition beyond which the Gentiles were not allowed to go.
8. The veil that was torn in two from top to bottom at Christ's death. This is usually thought to be the veil that separated the Holy of Holies from the Most Holy Place, but others think it was the first veil.

iamin, and Jeshua, and Shemaiah, Amariah, and Shecaniah, in the cities of the
priests, in *their* set office, to give to
their brethren by courses, as well to the
great as to the small:
16 Beside their genealogy of males,
from three years old and upward, *even*
unto every one that entereth into the
house of the LORD, his daily portion for
their service in their charges according
to their courses;
17 Both to the genealogy of the priests
by the house of their fathers, and the
Levites from twenty years old and upward, in their charges by their courses;
18 And to the genealogy of all their little ones, their wives, and their sons,
and their daughters, through all the
congregation: for in their set office they
sanctified themselves in holiness:
19 Also of the sons of Aaron the
priests, *which were* in the fields of the
suburbs of their cities, in every several city, the men that were expressed by
name, to give portions to all the males
among the priests, and to all that were
reckoned by *genealogies among the
Levites.

¶20 And thus did Hezekiah throughout all Judah, and wrought *that which
was* good and right and truth before the
LORD his God.
21 And in every work that he began in
the service of the house of God, and in
the law, and in the commandments, to
seek his God, he did *it* with all his heart,
and prospered.

*Sennacherib, king of Assyria, invades
Judah (2 Kings 18:13—19:37; Isa. 36:1-22)*

32 After these things, and the establishment thereof, Sennacherib king of Assyria came, and entered
into Judah, and encamped against the
fenced cities, and thought to win them
for himself.
2 And when Hezekiah saw that Sennacherib was come, and that he was
purposed to fight against *Jerusalem,
3 He took counsel with his princes and
his mighty men to stop the waters of
the fountains which *were* without the
city: and they did help him.
4 So there was gathered much people
together, who stopped all the fountains,
and the brook that ran through the

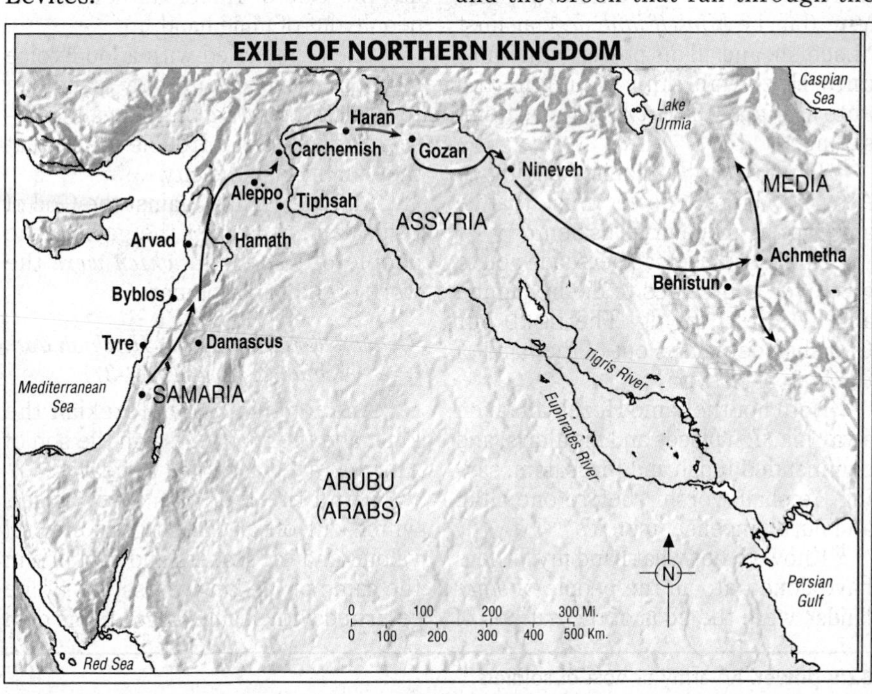

midst of the land, saying, Why should the kings of Assyria come, and find much water?

5 Also he strengthened himself, and built up all the wall that was broken, and raised *it* up to the towers, and another wall without, and repaired *Millo *in* the city of David, and made darts and shields in abundance.

6 And he set captains of war over the people, and gathered them together to him in the street of the gate of the city, and spake comfortably to them, saying,

7 Be strong and courageous, *be not afraid nor dismayed for the king of Assyria, nor for all the multitude that *is* with him: for *there be* more with us than with him:

8 With him *is* an arm of *flesh; but with us is the LORD our God to help us, and to fight our battles. And the people rested themselves upon the words of Hezekiah king of Judah.

Sennacherib seeks to terrify the people of Jerusalem

¶9 After this did Sennacherib king of Assyria send his servants to Jerusalem, (but he *himself laid siege* against *Lachish, and all his power with him,) unto Hezekiah king of Judah, and unto all Judah that *were* at Jerusalem, saying,

10 Thus saith Sennacherib king of Assyria, Whereon do ye *trust, that ye abide in the siege in Jerusalem?

11 Doth not Hezekiah persuade you to give over yourselves to die by famine and by thirst, saying, The LORD our God shall deliver us out of the hand of the king of Assyria?

12 Hath not the same Hezekiah taken away his high places and his altars, and commanded Judah and Jerusalem, saying, Ye shall worship before one altar, and burn *incense upon it?

13 Know ye not what I and my fathers have done unto all the people of *other* lands? were the gods of the nations of those lands any ways able to deliver their lands out of mine hand?

14 Who *was there* among all the gods of those nations that my fathers utterly destroyed, that could deliver his people out of mine hand, that your God should be able to deliver you out of mine hand?

15 Now therefore let not Hezekiah deceive you, nor persuade you on this manner, neither yet believe him: for no god of any nation or kingdom was able to deliver his people out of mine hand, and out of the hand of my fathers: how much less shall your God deliver you out of mine hand?

16 And his servants spake yet *more* against the LORD God, and against his servant Hezekiah.

Sennacherib defies the LORD Jehovah (2 Kings 19:8-13)

17 He wrote also letters to rail on the LORD God of Israel, and to speak against him, saying, As the gods of the nations of *other* lands have not delivered their people out of mine hand, so shall not the God of Hezekiah deliver his people out of mine hand.

18 Then they cried with a loud voice in the Jews' speech unto the people of Jerusalem that *were* on the wall, to affright them, and to trouble them; that they might take the city.

19 And they spake against the God of Jerusalem, as against the gods of the people of the earth, *which were* the work of the hands of man.

God answers the prayer of Hezekiah and Isaiah (2 Kings 19:14-37)

20 And for this *cause* Hezekiah the king, and the prophet Isaiah the son of Amoz, prayed and cried to heaven.

¶21 And the LORD sent an *angel, which cut off all the mighty men of valour, and the leaders and captains in the camp of the king of Assyria. So he returned with shame of face to his own

---

32:9 power. An army or host of soldiers.

land. And when he was come into the
house of his god, they that came forth
of his own bowels slew him there with
the sword.

Hezekiah prospers

22 Thus the LORD saved Hezekiah and
the inhabitants of Jerusalem from the
hand of Sennacherib the king of Assyria, and from the hand of all *other,* and
guided them on every side.
23 And many brought gifts unto the
LORD to Jerusalem, and presents to
Hezekiah king of Judah: so that he was
magnified in the sight of all nations from
thenceforth.

Hezekiah's illness and recovery
(2 Kings 20:1-11)

¶ 24 In those days Hezekiah was sick
to the *death, and prayed unto the
LORD: and he spake unto him, and he
gave him a sign.
25 But Hezekiah rendered not again
according to the benefit *done* unto him;
for his heart was lifted up: therefore
there was wrath upon him, and upon
Judah and Jerusalem.
26 Notwithstanding Hezekiah humbled himself for the pride of his heart,
both he and the inhabitants of Jerusalem,
so that the wrath of the LORD came not
upon them in the days of Hezekiah.

Hezekiah's wealth

¶ 27 And Hezekiah had exceeding
much riches and honour: and he made
himself treasuries for silver, and for
gold, and for precious stones, and for
spices, and for shields, and for all manner of pleasant jewels;
28 Storehouses also for the increase of
corn, and wine, and oil; and stalls for all
manner of beasts, and cotes for flocks.
29 Moreover he provided him cities,
and possessions of flocks and herds in
abundance: for God had given him substance very much.
30 This same Hezekiah also stopped
the upper watercourse of Gihon, and
brought it straight down to the west
side of the city of David. And Hezekiah
prospered in all his works.
¶ 31 Howbeit in *the business of* the ambassadors of the princes of *Babylon,
who sent unto him to enquire of the
wonder that was *done* in the land, God
left him, to try him, that he might know
all *that was* in his heart.

Death of Hezekiah
(2 Kings 20:20-21)

¶ 32 Now the rest of the acts of Hezekiah, and his goodness, behold, they *are*
written in the vision of Isaiah the prophet, the son of Amoz, *and* in the book of
the kings of Judah and Israel.
33 And Hezekiah slept with his fathers, and they buried him in the
chiefest of the sepulchres of the sons of
David: and all Judah and the inhabitants
of Jerusalem did him honour at his
death. And Manasseh his son reigned in
his stead.

Manasseh becomes king of Judah
(2 Kings 21:1-9)

33 Manasseh *was* twelve years
old when he began to reign, and
he reigned fifty and five years in Jerusalem:
2 But did *that which was* evil in the
sight of the LORD, like unto the abominations of the heathen, whom the LORD
had cast out before the children of Israel.
¶ 3 For he built again the high places
which Hezekiah his father had broken
down, and he reared up altars for
Baalim, and made groves, and worshipped all the host of heaven, and
served them.
4 Also he built altars in the house of
the LORD, whereof the LORD had said,
In Jerusalem shall my name be for ever.
5 And he built altars for all the host of
heaven in the two courts of the house
of the LORD.

32:28 cotes. Huts or sheds for sheep.

6 And he caused his children to pass through the fire in the valley of the son of Hinnom: also he *observed times, and used enchantments, and used witchcraft, and dealt with a familiar spirit, and with wizards: he wrought much evil in the sight of the LORD, to provoke him to anger.

7 And he set a carved image, the idol which he had made, in the house of God, of which God had said to *David and to Solomon his son, In this house, and in Jerusalem, which I have chosen before all the tribes of Israel, will I put my name for ever:

8 Neither will I any more remove the foot of Israel from out of the land which I have appointed for your fathers; so that they will take heed to do all that I have commanded them, according to the whole law and the statutes and the ordinances by the hand of Moses.

9 So Manasseh made *Judah and the inhabitants of Jerusalem to *err, *and* to do worse than the heathen, whom the LORD had destroyed before the children of Israel.

10 And the LORD spake to Manasseh, and to his people: but they would not hearken.

Manasseh's captivity and restoration

¶ 11 Wherefore the LORD brought upon them the captains of the host of the king of Assyria, which took Manasseh among the thorns, and bound him with fetters, and carried him to Babylon.

12 And when he was in affliction, he besought the LORD his God, and humbled himself greatly before the God of his fathers,

13 And prayed unto him: and he was intreated of him, and heard his supplication, and brought him again to Jerusalem into his kingdom. Then Manasseh knew that the LORD he *was* God.

End of Manasseh's reign
(2 Kings 21:17-18)

14 Now after this he built a wall without the city of David, on the west side of Gihon, in the valley, even to the entering in at the fish gate, and compassed about Ophel, and raised it up a very great height, and put captains of war in all the fenced cities of Judah.

15 And he took away the strange gods, and the idol out of the house of the LORD, and all the altars that he had built in the mount of the house of the LORD, and in Jerusalem, and cast *them* out of the city.

16 And he repaired the altar of the LORD, and sacrificed thereon peace-offerings and thank-offerings, and commanded Judah to serve the LORD God of Israel.

17 Nevertheless the people did sacrifice still in the high places, *yet* unto the LORD their God only.

¶ 18 Now the rest of the acts of Manasseh, and his prayer unto his God, and the words of the seers that spake to him in the name of the LORD God of Israel, behold, they *are written* in the book of the kings of Israel.

19 His prayer also, and *how God* was intreated of him, and all his *sin, and his trespass, and the places wherein he built high places, and set up groves and graven images, before he was humbled: behold, they *are* written among the sayings of the seers.

¶ 20 So Manasseh slept with his fathers, and they buried him in his own house: and Amon his son reigned in his stead.

Reign of Amon over Judah
(2 Kings 21:19-26)

¶ 21 Amon *was* two and twenty years old when he began to reign, and reigned two years in Jerusalem.

22 But he did *that which was* evil in the sight of the LORD, as did Manasseh his father: for Amon sacrificed unto all the

---

33:7 to David and to Solomon. See 2 Samuel 7:13 and 1 Kings 8:20.
33:18 book of the kings of Israel. No longer in existence (see introduction to 1 Chronicles).

carved images which Manasseh his father had made, and served them;
23 And humbled not himself before
the LORD, as Manasseh his father had
humbled himself; but Amon trespassed
more and more.
24 And his servants conspired against
him, and slew him in his own house.
¶25 But the people of the land slew all
them that had conspired against king
Amon; and the people of the land made
*Josiah his son king in his stead.

Josiah becomes king of Judah
(2 Kings 22:1-2)

34 Josiah *was* eight years old
when he began to reign, and he
reigned in Jerusalem one and thirty
years.
2 And he did *that which was* right in
the sight of the LORD, and walked in the
ways of David his father, and declined
neither to the right hand, nor to the left.

His early reformations

¶3 For in the eighth year of his reign,
while he was yet young, he began to
seek after the God of David his father:
and in the twelfth year he began to
purge Judah and Jerusalem from the
*high places, and the groves, and the
carved images, and the molten images.
4 And they brake down the altars of
Baalim in his presence; and the images,
that *were* on high above them, he cut
down; and the groves, and the carved
images, and the molten images, he
brake in pieces, and made dust *of them,*
and strowed *it* upon the graves of them
that had sacrificed unto them.
5 And he burnt the bones of the priests
upon their altars, and cleansed Judah
and Jerusalem.
6 And *so did he* in the cities of Manasseh, and Ephraim, and Simeon, even
unto Naphtali, with their mattocks
round about.
7 And when he had broken down the
altars and the groves, and had beaten
the graven images into powder, and
cut down all the idols throughout all
the land of Israel, he returned to Jerusalem.

The temple repaired
(2 Kings 22:3-7)

¶8 Now in the eighteenth year of his
reign, when he had purged the land, and
the house, he sent Shaphan the son of
Azaliah, and Maaseiah the governor of
the city, and Joah the son of Joahaz the
recorder, to repair the house of the
LORD his God.
9 And when they came to Hilkiah the
high priest, they delivered the money
that was brought into the house of God,
which the Levites that kept the doors
had gathered of the hand of Manasseh
and Ephraim, and of all the remnant of
Israel, and of all Judah and Benjamin;
and they returned to Jerusalem.
10 And they put *it* in the hand of the
workmen that had the oversight of the
house of the LORD, and they gave it to
the workmen that wrought in the house
of the LORD, to repair and amend the
house:
11 Even to the artificers and builders
gave they *it,* to buy hewn stone, and
timber for couplings, and to floor the
houses which the kings of Judah had
destroyed.
12 And the men did the work faithfully:
and the overseers of them *were* Jahath
and Obadiah, the Levites, of the sons of
Merari; and Zechariah and Meshullam, of
the sons of the Kohathites, to set *it* forward; and *other of* the Levites, all that
could skill of instruments of musick.
13 Also *they were* over the bearers of
burdens, and *were* overseers of all that
wrought the work in any manner of service: and of the Levites *there were*
*scribes, and officers, and *porters.

The Law of Moses found and read
(2 Kings 22:8-13)

¶14 And when they brought out the
money that was brought into the house
of the LORD, Hilkiah the priest found a
book of the law of the LORD *given* by
Moses.

15 And Hilkiah answered and said to Shaphan the *scribe, I have found the book of the law in the house of the LORD. And Hilkiah delivered the book to Shaphan.

16 And Shaphan carried the book to the king, and brought the king word back again, saying, All that was committed to thy servants, they do *it*.

17 And they have gathered together the money that was found in the house of the LORD, and have delivered it into the hand of the overseers, and to the hand of the workmen.

18 Then Shaphan the scribe told the king, saying, Hilkiah the priest hath given me a book. And Shaphan read it before the king.

19 And it came to pass, when the king had heard the words of the law, that he rent his clothes.

20 And the king commanded Hilkiah, and Ahikam the son of Shaphan, and Abdon the son of Micah, and Shaphan the scribe, and Asaiah a servant of the king's, saying,

21 Go, enquire of the LORD for me, and for them that are left in Israel and in Judah, concerning the words of the book that is found: for great *is* the wrath of the LORD that is poured out upon us, because our fathers have not kept the word of the LORD, to do after all that is written in this book.

Words of Huldah the prophetess (2 Kings 22:14-20)

22 And Hilkiah, and *they* that the king *had appointed,* went to *Huldah the prophetess, the wife of Shallum the son of Tikvath, the son of Hasrah, keeper of the wardrobe; (now she dwelt in Jerusalem in the college:) and they spake to her to that *effect*.

¶23 And she answered them, Thus saith the LORD God of Israel, Tell ye the man that sent you to me,

24 Thus saith the LORD, Behold, I will bring evil upon this place, and upon the inhabitants thereof, *even* all the curses that are written in the book which they have read before the king of Judah:

25 Because they have forsaken me, and have burned incense unto other gods, that they might provoke me to anger with all the works of their hands; therefore my wrath shall be poured out upon this place, and shall not be quenched.

26 And as for the king of Judah, who sent you to enquire of the LORD, so shall ye say unto him, Thus saith the LORD God of Israel *concerning* the words which thou hast heard;

27 Because thine heart was tender, and thou didst humble thyself before God, when thou heardest his words against this place, and against the inhabitants thereof, and humbledst thyself before me, and didst rend thy clothes, and weep before me; I have even heard *thee* also, saith the LORD.

28 Behold, I will gather thee to thy fathers, and thou shalt be gathered to thy grave in peace, neither shall thine eyes see all the evil that I will bring upon this place, and upon the inhabitants of the same. So they brought the king word again.

The king reads the Law and makes a covenant before the LORD (2 Kings 23:1-3)

¶29 Then the king sent and gathered together all the *elders of Judah and Jerusalem.

30 And the king went up into the house of the LORD, and all the men of Judah, and the inhabitants of Jerusalem, and the priests, and the Levites, and all the people, great and small: and he read in their ears all the words of the book of the covenant that was found in the house of the LORD.

31 And the king stood in his place, and

34:15 the book of the law. The importance of the Word of God in the revivals under Josiah is significant, because it reveals the great value God attaches to His Word. Its loss and neglect under preceding kings explain their apostasy and idolatry.

made a covenant before the LORD, to
walk after the LORD, and to keep his
commandments, and his testimonies,
and his statutes, with all his heart, and
with all his soul, to perform the words
of the covenant which are written in
this book.
32And he caused all that were present in Jerusalem and Benjamin to stand
to it. And the inhabitants of Jerusalem
did according to the covenant of God,
the God of their fathers.

Josiah's further reforms
(2 Kings 23:4-24)

33And Josiah took away all the abominations out of all the countries that
pertained to the children of Israel, and
made all that were present in Israel to
serve, *even* to serve the LORD their
God. *And* all his days they departed not
from following the LORD, the God of
their fathers.

The Passover observed
(2 Kings 23:21-23)

35 Moreover Josiah kept a passover unto the LORD in Jerusa-
lem: and they killed the passover on the
fourteenth *day* of the first *month.
2And he set the priests in their
charges, and encouraged them to the
service of the house of the LORD,
3And said unto the Levites that
taught all Israel, which were *holy unto
the LORD, Put the holy *ark in the
house which Solomon the son of David
king of Israel did build; *it shall* not *be* a
burden upon *your* shoulders: serve now
the LORD your God, and his people Israel,
4And prepare *yourselves* by the
houses of your fathers, after your
courses, according to the writing of
David king of Israel, and according to
the writing of Solomon his son.
5And stand in the holy *place* according to the divisions of the families of the
fathers of your brethren the people, and
after the division of the families of the
Levites.
6So kill the passover, and sanctify
yourselves, and prepare your brethren,
that *they* may do according to the word
of the LORD by the hand of Moses.
7And Josiah gave to the people, of the
flock, lambs and kids, all for the passover *offerings, for all that were present, to the number of thirty thousand,
and three thousand bullocks: these *were*
of the king's substance.
8And his princes gave willingly unto
the people, to the priests, and to the
Levites: Hilkiah and Zechariah and Jehiel, rulers of the house of God, gave
unto the priests for the passover offerings two thousand and six hundred
small cattle, and three hundred oxen.
9Conaniah also, and Shemaiah and
Nethaneel, his brethren, and Hashabiah and Jeiel and Jozabad, chief of the
Levites, gave unto the Levites for passover offerings five thousand *small cattle,* and five hundred oxen.
10So the service was prepared, and
the priests stood in their place, and the
Levites in their courses, according to
the king's commandment.
11And they killed the passover, and
the priests sprinkled *the *blood* from
their hands, and the Levites flayed
them.
12And they removed the burnt-offerings, that they might give according to
the divisions of the families of the people, to offer unto the LORD, as *it is* written in the *book of Moses. And so *did
they* with the oxen.
13And they roasted the passover with
fire according to the ordinance: but the
other holy *offerings* sod they in pots, and
in caldrons, and in pans, and divided
them speedily among all the people.
14And afterward they made ready for
themselves, and for the priests: because
the priests the sons of *Aaron *were
busied* in *offering of burnt-offerings
and the fat until night; therefore the

35:12 written in the book of Moses. See Leviticus 3:3.

Levites prepared for themselves, and
for the priests the sons of Aaron.
15 And the singers the sons of *Asaph
were in their place, according to the
commandment of David, and Asaph,
and *Heman, and *Jeduthun the king's
seer; and the porters *waited* at every
gate; they might not depart from their
service; for their brethren the Levites
prepared for them.
16 So all the service of the LORD was
prepared the same day, to keep the
passover, and to offer burnt-offerings
upon the *altar of the LORD, according
to the commandment of king Josiah.
17 And the children of Israel that were
present kept the passover at that time,
and the feast of unleavened bread seven
days.
18 And there was no passover like to
that kept in Israel from the days of
*Samuel the *prophet; neither did all
the kings of Israel keep such a passover
as Josiah kept, and the priests, and the
Levites, and all Judah and Israel that
were present, and the inhabitants of
Jerusalem.
19 In the eighteenth year of the reign
of Josiah was this passover kept.

Death of Josiah, the good king
(2 Kings 23:28-30)

¶20 After all this, when Josiah had prepared the temple, Necho king of *Egypt
came up to fight against Carchemish by
Euphrates: and Josiah went out against
him.
21 But he sent ambassadors to him,
saying, What have I to do with thee,
thou king of Judah? *I come* not against
thee this day, but against the house
wherewith I have war: for God commanded me to make haste: forbear thee
from *meddling with* God, who *is* with
me, that he destroy thee not.
22 Nevertheless Josiah would not turn
his face from him, but disguised himself, that he might fight with him, and
hearkened not unto the words of Necho
from the mouth of God, and came to
fight in the valley of *Megiddo.
23 And the archers shot at king Josiah; and the king said to his servants,
Have me away; for I am sore wounded.
24 His servants therefore took him
out of that chariot, and put him in the
second chariot that he had; and they
brought him to Jerusalem, and he died,
and was buried in *one of* the sepulchres
of his fathers. And all Judah and Jerusalem mourned for Josiah.
¶25 And Jeremiah lamented for Josiah:
and all the singing men and the singing
women spake of Josiah in their lamentations to this day, and made them an
ordinance in Israel: and, behold, they
are written in the lamentations.
26 Now the rest of the acts of Josiah, and
his goodness, according to *that which*
was written in the law of the LORD,
27 And his deeds, first and last, behold,
they *are* written in the book of the
Kings of Israel and Judah.

Jehoahaz becomes king of Judah
(2 Kings 23:31-32)

36 Then the people of the land
took Jehoahaz the son of Josiah,
and made him king in his father's stead
in Jerusalem.
2 Jehoahaz *was* twenty and three
years old when he began to reign, and
he reigned three months in Jerusalem.

Dethroned by king of Egypt
(2 Kings 23:33)

3 And the king of Egypt put him down
at Jerusalem, and condemned the land
in an hundred talents of silver and a
talent of gold.

35:18 no passover like to that. Note that this was also said of Hezekiah's Passover feast, but this Passover under Josiah—which followed Hezekiah's Passover observance—was even greater. See 2 Kings 23:22 note.

35:25 Jeremiah lamented for Josiah. Read Jeremiah's words in Lamentations 4:19-20; Jeremiah 22:10-18; and see also Zechariah 12:10-14.

Jehoiakim becomes king of Judah
(2 Kings 23:34-37)

¶4And the king of Egypt made Eliakim his brother king over Judah and Jerusalem, and turned his name to
Jehoiakim. And Necho took Jehoahaz
his brother, and carried him to Egypt.
5Jehoiakim *was* twenty and five years
old when he began to reign, and he
reigned eleven years in Jerusalem: and
he did *that which was* evil in the sight
of the LORD his God.

Jehoiakim taken captive to Babylon
(2 Kings 24:1-5)

6Against him came up Nebuchadnezzar king of Babylon, and bound him in
fetters, to carry him to Babylon.
7Nebuchadnezzar also carried of the
vessels of the house of the LORD to
Babylon, and put them in his temple at
Babylon.
8Now the rest of the acts of Jehoiakim, and his abominations which he did,
and that which was found in him, behold, they *are* written in the book of the
kings of Israel and Judah: and Jehoiachin his son reigned in his stead.

Reign of Jehoiachin over Judah
(2 Kings 24:6-10)

9Jehoiachin *was* eight years old when
he began to reign, and he reigned three
months and ten days in Jerusalem: and
he did *that which was* evil in the sight
of the LORD.
10And when the year was expired,
king Nebuchadnezzar sent, and brought
him to Babylon, with the goodly vessels
of the house of the LORD, and made
Zedekiah his brother king over Judah
and Jerusalem.

Zedekiah made king of Judah
(2 Kings 24:17-18)

¶11Zedekiah *was* one and twenty
years old when he began to reign, and
reigned eleven years in Jerusalem.
12And he did *that which was* evil
in the sight of the LORD his God, *and*

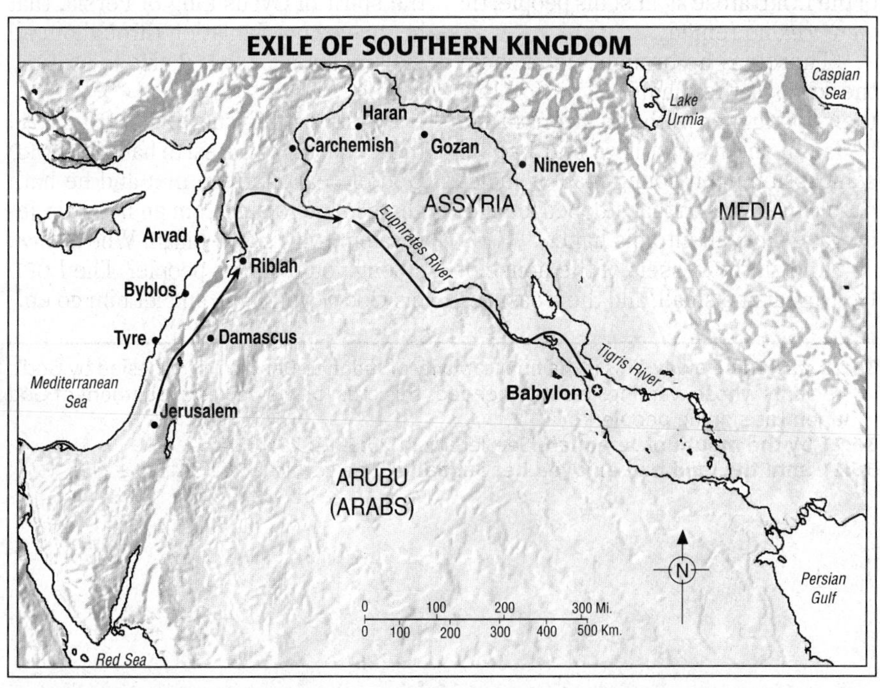

36:4 turned his name. Means *changed.* See 2 Kings 24:17 note, "A Sign of Authority."
36:10 brother. This is a word for a relative. Zedekiah was Jehoiachin's uncle.

humbled not himself before Jeremiah the prophet *speaking* from the mouth of the LORD.

13 And he also rebelled against king Nebuchadnezzar, who had made him swear by God: but he stiffened his neck, and hardened his heart from turning unto the LORD God of Israel.

¶ 14 Moreover all the chief of the priests, and the people, transgressed very much after all the abominations of the heathen; and polluted the house of the LORD which he had hallowed in Jerusalem.

Judah carried away captive to Babylon (2 Kings 25:1-21)

15 And the LORD God of their fathers sent to them by his messengers, rising up betimes, and sending; because he had compassion on his people, and on his dwelling place:

16 But they mocked the messengers of God, and despised his words, and misused his prophets, until the wrath of the LORD arose against his people, till *there was* no remedy.

17 Therefore he brought upon them the king of the Chaldees, who slew their young men with the sword in the house of their sanctuary, and had no compassion upon young man or maiden, old man, or him that stooped for age: he gave *them* all into his hand.

18 And all the vessels of the house of God, great and small, and the treasures of the house of the LORD, and the treasures of the king, and of his princes; all *these* he brought to Babylon.

19 And they burnt the house of God, and brake down the wall of Jerusalem, and burnt all the palaces thereof with fire, and destroyed all the goodly vessels thereof.

20 And them that had escaped from the sword carried he away to Babylon; where they were servants to him and his sons until the reign of the kingdom of Persia:

21 To fulfil the word of the LORD by the mouth of Jeremiah, until the land had enjoyed her sabbaths: *for* as long as she lay desolate she kept sabbath, to fulfil threescore and ten years.

Decree of Cyrus, king of Persia, for rebuilding the temple

¶ 22 Now in the first year of Cyrus king of Persia, that the word of the LORD *spoken* by the mouth of Jeremiah might be accomplished, the LORD stirred up the spirit of Cyrus king of Persia, that he made a proclamation throughout all his kingdom, and *put it* also in writing, saying,

23 Thus saith Cyrus king of Persia, All the kingdoms of the earth hath the LORD God of heaven given me; and he hath charged me to build him an house in Jerusalem, which *is* in Judah. Who *is there* among you of all his people? The LORD his God *be* with him, and let him go up.

36:20 carried he away. This is the final captivity of Judah to Babylon, prophesied by God's servants whose warnings went unheeded. This must be viewed as a judgment of God upon His sinning people.

36:21 by the mouth of Jeremiah. See Jeremiah 25:9-12; 29:10.

36:21 until the land had enjoyed her sabbaths. See Leviticus 26:33-43.

EZRA

BACKGROUND

The book of Ezra belongs to a group of books dealing with the history of the Jewish people who lived in Babylon, and with some of them who returned to Palestine. The other books in this post-captivity group are Nehemiah, Esther, Haggai, Zechariah, and Malachi.

In 588 B.C., some years before the events recorded in the book of Ezra occurred, a great foreign king, called Nebuchadnezzar, had swept through Palestine. He killed many people and carried back as captive to his own land the wise and wealthy of the children of Israel. Because His people had disobeyed Him and rejected Him, the LORD had allowed this severe punishment to come upon them—families were torn apart, homes were burned, and there was great sorrow. But the greatest tragedy was the destruction of the beautiful temple in Jerusalem. Now after seventy years of exile some of the Jews, by a decree of Cyrus the Great, were allowed to return and, after many delays and trials, the temple was rebuilt. Later Ezra and his group of people came back to the land and still later Nehemiah returned.

MEANING

The building of the temple by the people who returned to Jerusalem is a picture of what the LORD expects of all true believers today—as the temple was a testimony to the glory of God, so Christians are expected to bear testimony in their lives which will glorify the Lord Jesus Christ. The people who returned are a picture of those Christians who are willing to stand with the Lord, whatever the cost. The work of the enemies is a clear picture of the way in which Satan works. The way in which victory was won, through prayer and separation, pictures the victory that belongs to every Christian through the Lord Jesus Christ.

THE TIME

The events recorded in Ezra cover a period of about eighty years, 536–457 B.C.

OUTLINE OF EZRA

I.	Return of the First Group under Zerubbabel and Jeshua	Ezra 1:1—6:22
II.	Return of the Second Group under Ezra: Seventy-Eight Years Later	Ezra 7:1—10:44

I. Return of First Group
(1:1—6:22)

1 Now in the first year of Cyrus
king of Persia, that the word of the
LORD by the mouth of Jeremiah might
be fulfilled, the LORD stirred up the spirit
of Cyrus king of Persia, that he made a
proclamation throughout all his kingdom, and *put it* also in writing, saying,
2 Thus saith Cyrus king of Persia, The
LORD *God of heaven hath given me all
the kingdoms of the earth; and he hath
charged me to build him an house at
*Jerusalem, which *is* in *Judah.
3 Who *is there* among you of all his
people? his God be with him, and let
him go up to Jerusalem, which *is* in Judah, and build the house of the LORD
God of *Israel, (he *is* the God,) which
is in Jerusalem.
4 And whosoever remaineth in any
place where he sojourneth, let the men
of his place help him with silver, and
with gold, and with goods, and with
beasts, beside the *freewill-offering for
the house of God that *is* in Jerusalem.
¶5 Then rose up the chief of the fathers of Judah and Benjamin, and the
priests, and the Levites, with all *them*
whose spirit God had raised, to go up
to build the house of the LORD which *is*
in Jerusalem.
6 And all they that *were* about them
strengthened their hands with vessels
of silver, with gold, with goods, and with
beasts, and with precious things, beside
all *that* was willingly offered.
¶7 Also Cyrus the king brought forth
the vessels of the house of the LORD,
which Nebuchadnezzar had brought
forth out of Jerusalem, and had put
them in the house of his gods;
8 Even those did Cyrus king of Persia
bring forth by the hand of Mithredath
the treasurer, and numbered them unto
Sheshbazzar, the prince of Judah.

1:1 THE KINGS OF PERSIA

The kings of Persia were:

Cyrus the Great, 559–529 B.C. (2 Chron. 36:22-23; Ezra 1:1; Isa. 44:28);
Ahasuerus, or **Cambyses** son of Cyrus, 529–521 B.C. (Ezra 4:6);
Artaxerxes, 521 B.C., who pretended to be the younger son of Cyrus and only reigned for eight months (Ezra 4:7);
Darius the Great, 521–486 B.C. (Ezra 4:24; Dan. 9:1). Darius the Great must not be confused with Darius the Mede, who ruled (or was viceroy) for Cyrus over Babylon (Dan. 5:31; 6:1-28);
Ahasuerus, or as he is known in history, Xerxes, 486–465 B.C., is mentioned by Daniel (11:2) as the invader of Greece and is the king who married Esther (see the book of Esther); and
Artaxerxes Longimanus, 465–424 B.C., who was the son of Xerxes (Neh. 2:1; Ezra 7:1).
Several of these are titles, not names: Ahasuerus, Artaxerxes, and Darius mean the venerable king or the great emperor, as does Pharaoh.
Cyrus was mentioned by name in Isaiah 44:28 and 45:1-4, about two hundred years before he actually lived, and God promised that Cyrus would allow the Jews to rebuild the temple. (See Isa. 44:28 note, "A Great Prediction"; 45:1 note; and 45:4 note, "Eight Names Known before Birth.")

1:3 Who is there among you . . . ? All through the ages there have been some people who truly believe in and worship God and have not worshipped false gods. These special people are called a "*remnant," as we read in Ezra 9:8. These special people are usually few compared to the many who will not obey God, and those who returned to Jerusalem were few in comparison to those who remained in Persia.

1:6 strengthened their hands. Helped them.

1:7 vessels of the house of the LORD. Nebuchadnezzar had taken these vessels from the temple when he captured Jerusalem, and he had shamelessly placed them in the temple of his heathen gods, in open defiance of the living God (Dan. 1:2).

1:8 Sheshbazzar. The crown prince was also called "Zerubbabel" (Hag. 1:14; 2:2,21).

9 And this *is* the number of them: thirty chargers of gold, a thousand chargers of silver, nine and twenty knives,
10 Thirty basons of gold, silver basons
of a second *sort* four hundred and ten,
and other vessels a thousand.
11 All the vessels of gold and of silver
were five thousand and four hundred.
All *these* did Sheshbazzar bring up with
them of the captivity that were brought
up from *Babylon unto Jerusalem.

Those who returned under Zerubbabel and Jeshua

2 Now these *are* the children of the
province that went up out of the
captivity, of those which had been carried away, whom Nebuchadnezzar the
king of Babylon had carried away unto
Babylon, and came again unto Jerusalem and Judah, every one unto his
city;
2 Which came with *Zerubbabel:
Jeshua, Nehemiah, Seraiah, Reelaiah,
Mordecai, Bilshan, Mizpar, Bigvai, Rehum, Baanah. The number of the men
of the people of Israel:
3 The children of Parosh, two thousand an hundred seventy and two.
4 The children of Shephatiah, three
hundred seventy and two.
5 The children of Arah, seven hundred
seventy and five.
6 The children of Pahath-moab, of the
children of Jeshua *and* Joab, two thousand eight hundred and twelve.
7 The children of Elam, a thousand
two hundred fifty and four.
8 The children of Zattu, nine hundred
forty and five.
9 The children of Zaccai, seven hundred and threescore.
10 The children of Bani, six hundred
forty and two.
11 The children of Bebai, six hundred
twenty and three.
12 The children of Azgad, a thousand
two hundred twenty and two.
13 The children of Adonikam, six hundred sixty and six.
14 The children of Bigvai, two thousand fifty and six.
15 The children of Adin, four hundred
fifty and four.
16 The children of Ater of Hezekiah,
ninety and eight.
17 The children of Bezai, three hundred twenty and three.
18 The children of Jorah, an hundred
and twelve.
19 The children of Hashum, two hundred twenty and three.
20 The children of Gibbar, ninety and
five.
21 The children of Beth-lehem, an
hundred twenty and three.
22 The men of Netophah, fifty and
six.
23 The men of Anathoth, an hundred
twenty and eight.
24 The children of Azmaveth, forty
and two.
25 The children of Kirjath-arim, Chephirah, and Beeroth, seven hundred and
forty and three.
26 The children of Ramah and Gaba,
six hundred twenty and one.
27 The men of Michmas, an hundred
twenty and two.
28 The men of *Beth-el and Ai, two
hundred twenty and three.
29 The children of Nebo, fifty and two.
30 The children of Magbish, an hundred fifty and six.
31 The children of the other Elam, a
thousand two hundred fifty and four.
32 The children of Harim, three hundred and twenty.
33 The children of Lod, Hadid, and
Ono, seven hundred twenty and five.
34 The children of Jericho, three hundred forty and five.

1:9 chargers. Hollow plates for presenting offerings of fine flour and oil. See Numbers 7:79 and Matthew 14:8.

2:1 Now these are the children of the province that went up. The LORD took careful note of each person who took part in His work and of what each one did.

35The children of Senaah, three thousand and six hundred and thirty.
36The priests: the children of Jedaiah,
of the house of Jeshua, nine hundred
seventy and three.
37The children of Immer, a thousand
fifty and two.
38The children of Pashur, a thousand
two hundred forty and seven.
39The children of Harim, a thousand
and seventeen.
¶40The Levites: the children of Jeshua and Kadmiel, of the children of Hodaviah, seventy and four.
¶41The singers: the children of
*Asaph, an hundred twenty and eight.
¶42The children of the *porters: the
children of Shallum, the children of
Ater, the children of Talmon, the children of Akkub, the children of Hatita,
the children of Shobai, *in* all an hundred
thirty and nine.

2:43 The Nethinims
These were the temple servants–probably descendants of the Gibeonites whom Joshua made "hewers of wood and drawers of water" (Josh. 9:27; see also Neh. 3:26; 7:46). They accompanied the Jews to and from captivity and lived with the other servants of the temple on Mount Ophel, the southern continuation of Mount Moriah. See also Ezra 2:28,70.

¶43The Nethinims: the children of
Ziha, the children of Hasupha, the children of Tabbaoth,
44The children of Keros, the children
of Siaha, the children of Padon,
45The children of Lebanah, the children of Hagabah, the children of Akkub,
46The children of Hagab, the children
of Shalmai, the children of Hanan,
47The children of Giddel, the children
of Gahar, the children of Reaiah,
48The children of *Rezin, the children
of Nekoda, the children of Gazzam,
49The children of Uzza, the children
of Paseah, the children of Besai,
50The children of Asnah, the children of Mehunim, the children of Ne-
phusim,
51The children of Bakbuk, the children of Hakupha, the children of Harhur,
52The children of Bazluth, the children of Mehida, the children of Harsha,
53The children of Barkos, the children of Sisera, the children of Thamah,
54The children of Neziah, the children of Hatipha.
¶55The children of Solomon's servants: the children of Sotai, the children
of Sophereth, the children of Peruda,
56The children of Jaalah, the children
of Darkon, the children of Giddel,
57The children of Shephatiah, the children of Hattil, the children of Pochereth
of Zebaim, the children of Ami.
58All the Nethinims, and the children
of Solomon's servants, *were* three hundred ninety and two.
59And these *were* they which went up
from Tel-melah, Tel-harsa, Cherub,
Addan, *and* Immer: but they could not
shew their father's house, and their
seed, whether they *were* of Israel:
60The children of Delaiah, the children of Tobiah, the children of Nekoda,
six hundred fifty and two.
¶61And of the children of the priests:
the children of Habaiah, the children of
Koz, the children of Barzillai; which
took a wife of the daughters of Barzillai the Gileadite, and was called after
their name:
62These sought their register *among*
those that were reckoned by genealogy, but they were not found: therefore
were they, as polluted, put from the
priesthood.
63And the Tirshatha said unto them,
that they should not eat of the most
*holy things, till there stood up a priest
with Urim and with Thummim.
¶64The whole congregation together
was forty and two thousand three hundred *and* threescore,

2:63 Tirshatha. The Persian word for "governor"; it probably refers to Zerubbabel or Jeshua.

[65]Beside their servants and their
maids, of whom *there were* seven thousand three hundred thirty and seven:
and *there were* among them two hundred singing men and singing women.
[66]Their horses *were* seven hundred
thirty and six; their mules, two hundred
forty and five;
[67]Their camels, four hundred thirty
and five; *their* asses, six thousand seven
hundred and twenty.
¶[68]And *some* of the chief of the fathers, when they came to the house of
the LORD which *is* at Jerusalem, offered
freely for the house of God to set it up
in his place:
[69]They gave after their ability unto
the treasure of the work threescore and
one thousand drams of gold, and five
thousand pound of silver, and one hundred priests' *garments.
[70]So the priests, and the Levites, and
some of the people, and the singers, and
the porters, and the Nethinims, dwelt in
their cities, and all Israel in their cities.

Altar set up and foundations laid

3 And when the seventh *month was
come, and the children of Israel *were*
in the cities, the people gathered themselves together as one man to Jerusalem.
[2]Then stood up Jeshua the son of Jozadak, and his brethren the priests, and
Zerubbabel the son of Shealtiel, and his
brethren, and builded the *altar of the
God of Israel, to offer *burnt-offerings
thereon, as *it is* written in the *law of
*Moses the man of God.
[3]And they set the altar upon his bases; for fear *was* upon them because of
the people of those countries: and they
offered burnt-offerings thereon unto
the LORD, *even* burnt-offerings morning
and evening.
[4]They kept also the feast of tabernacles, as *it is* written, and *offered* the daily
burnt-offerings by number, according to
the custom, as the duty of every day
required;
[5]And afterward *offered* the continual
burnt-offering, both of the *new moons,

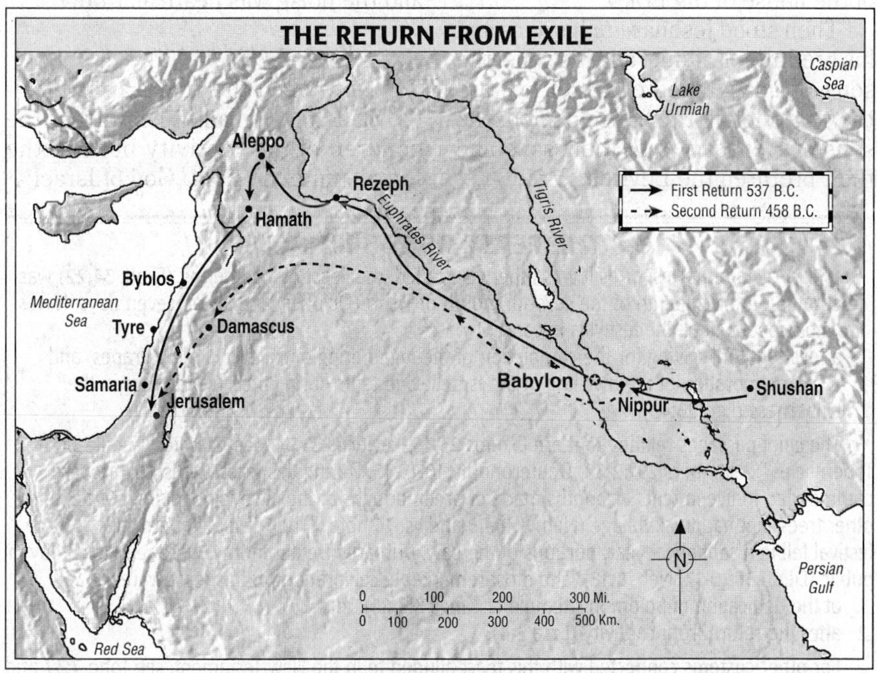

2:69 drams. The dram was a coin. This is the first mention of coined money in the Bible since coinage was not used in Palestine until after the exile.

and of all the *set feasts of the LORD
that were consecrated, and of every one
that willingly offered a freewill-offering
unto the LORD.
6 From the first day of the seventh
month began they to offer burnt-offerings
unto the LORD. But the foundation of the
temple of the LORD was not *yet* laid.
7 They gave money also unto the
masons, and to the carpenters; and
meat, and drink, and *oil, unto them of
Zidon, and to them of *Tyre, to bring
cedar trees from *Lebanon to the sea
of Joppa, according to the grant that
they had of Cyrus king of Persia.
¶8 Now in the second year of their
coming unto the house of God at Jerusalem, in the second month, began Zerubbabel the son of Shealtiel, and Jeshua
the son of Jozadak, and the *remnant of
their brethren the priests and the Levites, and all they that were come out
of the captivity unto Jerusalem; and appointed the Levites, from twenty years
old and upward, to set forward the work
of the house of the LORD.
9 Then stood Jeshua *with* his sons and
his brethren, Kadmiel and his sons, the
sons of Judah, together, to set forward
the workmen in the house of God: the
sons of Henadad, *with* their sons and
their brethren the Levites.
10 And when the builders laid the
foundation of the temple of the LORD,
they set the priests in their apparel with
trumpets, and the Levites the sons of
Asaph with cymbals, to praise the
LORD, after the ordinance of *David
king of Israel.
11 And they sang together by course
in praising and giving thanks unto the
LORD; because *he is* good, for his *mercy *endureth* for ever toward Israel. And
all the people shouted with a great
shout, when they praised the LORD,
because the foundation of the house of
the LORD was laid.
12 But many of the priests and Levites
and chief of the fathers, *who were* ancient men, that had seen the first house,
when the foundation of this house was
laid before their eyes, wept with a loud
voice; and many shouted aloud for joy:
13 So that the people could not discern
the noise of the shout of joy from the
noise of the weeping of the people: for
the people shouted with a loud shout,
and the noise was heard afar off.

Work stopped by adversaries

4 Now when the adversaries of Judah and Benjamin heard that the
children of the captivity builded the
temple unto the LORD God of Israel;

3:4 THE FEAST OF TABERNACLES

The Feast of Tabernacles, or as it was otherwise called, the Feast of Ingathering (Exod. 34:22) was celebrated on the fifteenth of the seventh month of Tishri (October) and lasted seven days. It was the most joyous of all the festivals because it was:

1. a feast of thanksgiving for the completion of the ingathering of fruits, including grapes, and
2. a commemoration of the dwelling of the Israelites in tents during their wanderings in the wilderness (Lev. 23:43).

The chief passages relating to it are Exodus 23:16; Leviticus 23:34 (see its note, "The Feast of Tabernacles"); Numbers 29:12-39; Deuteronomy 16:13-15. During this feast, the Israelites were commanded to live in tents or booths made of green boughs of the olive, pine, palm, myrtle, and other trees that had thick foliage (Neh. 8:14-15 and vs. 14 note, "The Feast of Tabernacles"). If the festival fell in a sabbatical year, portions of the Law, primarily Deuteronomy, were read each day in public (Deut. 31:10-12; Neh. 8:18). The most remarkable celebrations of this feast were:

1. at the dedication of Solomon's temple (1 Kings 8:2,65); and
2. after the return from captivity (Ezra 3:4).

For other customs connected with this feast alluded to in the New Testament, see John 7:37 and 8:12, which seems to allude to the lighting of the golden candelabra in the court of the women on the evenings of the festival.

4:1 The Enemies of the People
These adversaries were the people who now lived in the central part of Palestine called Samaria. The story of the king of Assyria bringing these adversaries, or enemies, to Samaria is told in 2 Kings 17. It is necessary to read this story before we can understand why the children of Israel were right in refusing to have any dealings with them. First, these enemies tried to unite with God's people in order to hinder them; second, they tried to interfere with the building; and third, they sent messages to the kings of Persia to try to have the work stopped. They did the same in Nehemiah's time (Neh. 4:1-6). They are an illustration of the people of the world who are never pleased to see God's work flourishing and who will do all in their power to hinder it. God tells us in 1 John 4:3-4 about our adversaries of today and how we may overcome them.

2 Then they came to Zerubbabel, and
to the chief of the fathers, and said unto
them, Let us build with you: for we
seek your God, as ye *do;* and we do
*sacrifice unto him since the days of
Esar-haddon king of Assur, which
brought us up hither.
3 But Zerubbabel, and Jeshua, and the
rest of the chief of the fathers of Israel,
said unto them, Ye have nothing to do
with us to build an house unto our God;
but we ourselves together will build
unto the LORD God of Israel, as king
Cyrus the king of Persia hath commanded us.
4 Then the people of the land weakened the hands of the people of Judah,
and troubled them in building,
5 And hired counsellors against them,
to frustrate their purpose, all the days
of Cyrus king of Persia, even until the
reign of Darius king of Persia.
¶6 And in the reign of Ahasuerus, in
the beginning of his reign, wrote they
unto him an accusation against the inhabitants of Judah and Jerusalem.
7 And in the days of *Artaxerxes
wrote Bishlam, Mithredath, Tabeel, and
the rest of their companions, unto Artaxerxes king of Persia; and the writing
of the letter *was* written in the Syrian
tongue, and interpreted in the Syrian
tongue.
8 Rehum the chancellor and Shimshai
the *scribe wrote a letter against Jerusalem to Artaxerxes the king in this
sort:
9 Then *wrote* Rehum the chancellor,
and Shimshai the scribe, and the rest of
their companions; the Dinaites, the
Apharsathchites, the Tarpelites, the
Apharsites, the Archevites, the Babylonians, the Susanchites, the Dehavites,
and the Elamites,
10 And the rest of the nations whom
the great and noble Asnapper brought
over, and set in the cities of *Samaria,
and the rest *that are* on this side the
river, and at such a time.
¶11 This *is* the copy of the letter that
they sent unto him, *even* unto Artaxerxes the king; Thy servants the men on
this side the river, and at such a time.
12 Be it known unto the king, that the
Jews which came up from thee to us are
come unto Jerusalem, building the rebellious and the bad city, and have set
up the walls *thereof,* and joined the foundations.

4:12 A False Statement
There is enough truth in this letter from Rehum the chancellor and Shimshai the scribe (vs. 8) to make it dangerous to those who were rebuilding, but this statement is false. The Israelites had done nothing but set up the altar and start work on the temple. There had been no permission given to "restore and to build Jerusalem" (Dan. 9:25), about which we are told in Nehemiah, and they had not built the walls or foundations.

4:5 Cyrus. See 1:1 note, "The Kings of Persia."
4:5 Darius. See 1:1 note.
4:6 Ahasuerus. See 1:1 note.
4:7 Artaxerxes. See 1:1 note.

13 Be it known now unto the king, that, if this city be builded, and the walls set up *again, then* will they not pay toll, tribute, and custom, and *so* thou shalt endamage the revenue of the kings.

14 Now because we have maintenance from *the king's* palace, and it was not meet for us to see the king's dishonour, therefore have we sent and certified the king;

15 That search may be made in the book of the records of thy fathers: so shalt thou find in the book of the records, and know that this city *is* a rebellious city, and hurtful unto kings and provinces, and that they have moved sedition within the same of old time: for which cause was this city destroyed.

16 We certify the king that, if this city be builded *again,* and the walls thereof set up, by this means thou shalt have no portion on this side the river.

¶17 *Then* sent the king an answer unto Rehum the chancellor, and *to* Shimshai the scribe, and *to* the rest of their companions that dwell in Samaria, and *unto* the rest beyond the river, Peace, and at such a time.

18 The letter which ye sent unto us hath been plainly read before me.

19 And I commanded, and search hath been made, and it is found that this city of old time hath made insurrection against kings, and *that* rebellion and sedition have been made therein.

20 There have been mighty kings also over Jerusalem, which have ruled over all *countries* beyond the river; and toll, tribute, and custom, was paid unto them.

21 Give ye now commandment to cause these men to cease, and that this city be not builded, until *another* commandment shall be given from me.

22 Take heed now that ye fail not to do this: why should damage grow to the hurt of the kings?

¶23 Now when the copy of king Artaxerxes' letter *was* read before Rehum, and Shimshai the scribe, and their companions, they went up in haste to Jerusalem unto the Jews, and made them to cease by force and power.

¶24 Then ceased the work of the house of God which *is* at Jerusalem. So it ceased unto the second year of the reign of Darius king of Persia.

Work continued

5 Then the *prophets, Haggai the prophet, and Zechariah the son of Iddo, prophesied unto the Jews that *were* in Judah and Jerusalem in the name of the God of Israel, *even* unto them.

2 Then rose up *Zerubbabel the son of Shealtiel, and Jeshua the son of Jozadak, and began to build the house of God which *is* at Jerusalem: and with them *were* the prophets of God helping them.

¶3 At the same time came to them Tatnai, governor on this side the river, and Shethar-boznai, and their companions, and said thus unto them, Who hath commanded you to build this house, and to make up this wall?

4 Then said we unto them after this manner, What are the names of the men that make this building?

5 But the eye of their God was upon the *elders of the Jews, that they could not cause them to cease, till the matter came to Darius: and then they returned answer by letter concerning this *matter.*

¶6 The copy of the letter that Tatnai, governor on this side the river, and Shethar-boznai, and his companions the Apharsachites, which *were* on this side the river, sent unto Darius the king:

7 They sent a letter unto him, wherein

5:1 Then the prophets, Haggai . . . and Zechariah. Even the Israelites' enemies could not have caused the work to cease if the hearts of the people of God had truly been ready to follow Him. As soon as the LORD stirred up the hearts of His children through the prophets, the work went on. See the books of Haggai and Zechariah.

was written thus; Unto Darius the king,
all peace.
8 Be it known unto the king, that we
went into the province of Judea, to the
house of the great God, which is builded
with great stones, and timber is laid in
the walls, and this work goeth fast on,
and prospereth in their hands.
9 Then asked we those elders, *and*
said unto them thus, Who commanded
you to build this house, and to make up
these walls?
10 We asked their names also, to certify thee, that we might write the
names of the men that *were* the chief of
them.
11 And thus they returned us answer,
saying, We are the servants of the God
of heaven and earth, and build the
house that was builded these many
years ago, which a great king of Israel
builded and set up.
12 But after that our fathers had provoked the God of heaven unto wrath, he
gave them into the hand of Nebuchadnezzar the king of Babylon, the Chaldean, who destroyed this house, and
carried the people away into Babylon.
13 But in the first year of Cyrus the
king of Babylon *the same* king Cyrus
made a decree to build this house of
God.
14 And the vessels also of gold and
silver of the house of God, which Nebuchadnezzar took out of the temple that
was in Jerusalem, and brought them
into the temple of Babylon, those did
Cyrus the king take out of the temple
of Babylon, and they were delivered
unto *one,* whose name *was* Sheshbazzar, whom he had made governor;
15 And said unto him, Take these vessels, go, carry them into the temple that
is in Jerusalem, and let the house of
God be builded in his place.
16 Then came the same Sheshbazzar,
and laid the foundation of the house of
God which *is* in Jerusalem: and since
that time even until now hath it been in
building, and *yet* it is not finished.
17 Now therefore, if *it seem* good to the
king, let there be search made in the
king's treasure house, which *is* there at
Babylon, whether it be *so,* that a decree
was made of Cyrus the king to build this
house of God at Jerusalem, and let the
king send his pleasure to us concerning this matter.

The temple finished

6 Then Darius the king made a decree, and search was made in the
house of the rolls, where the treasures
were laid up in Babylon.
2 And there was found at Achmetha,
in the palace that *is* in the province of
the Medes, a roll, and therein *was* a
record thus written:
3 In the first year of Cyrus the king *the*
same Cyrus the king made a decree
concerning the house of God at Jerusalem, Let the house be builded, the place
where they offered sacrifices, and let
the foundations thereof be strongly laid;
the height thereof threescore *cubits,
and the breadth thereof threescore cubits;
4 *With* three rows of great stones, and
a row of new timber: and let the
expences be given out of the king's
house:
5 And also let the golden and silver
vessels of the house of God, which
Nebuchadnezzar took forth out of the
temple which *is* at Jerusalem, and
brought unto Babylon, be restored, and
brought again unto the temple which *is*
at Jerusalem, *every one* to his place, and
place *them* in the house of God.
6 Now *therefore,* Tatnai, governor beyond the river, Shethar-boznai, and
your companions the Apharsachites,
which *are* beyond the river, be ye far
from thence:
7 Let the work of this house of God
alone; let the governor of the Jews and

5:11 many years ago. The temple was first built nearly five hundred years before.
5:11 a great king. Solomon.

the elders of the Jews build this house of God in his place.

8 Moreover I make a decree what ye shall do to the elders of these Jews for the building of this house of God: that of the king's goods, *even* of the tribute beyond the river, forthwith expences be given unto these men, that they be not hindered.

9 And that which they have need of, both young bullocks, and rams, and lambs, for the burnt-offerings of the God of heaven, wheat, salt, wine, and oil, according to the appointment of the priests which *are* at Jerusalem, let it be given them day by day without fail:

10 That they may offer sacrifices of sweet savours unto the God of heaven, and pray for the life of the king, and of his sons.

11 Also I have made a decree, that whosoever shall alter this word, let timber be pulled down from his house, and being set up, let him be hanged thereon; and let his house be made a dunghill for this.

12 And the God that hath caused his name to dwell there destroy all kings and people, that shall put to their hand to alter *and* to destroy this house of God which *is* at Jerusalem. I Darius have made a decree; let it be done with speed.

¶13 Then Tatnai, governor on this side the river, Shethar-boznai, and their companions, according to that which Darius the king had sent, so they did speedily.

14 And the elders of the Jews builded, and they prospered through the prophesying of Haggai the prophet and Zechariah the son of Iddo. And they builded, and finished *it,* according to the commandment of the God of Israel, and according to the commandment of Cyrus, and Darius, and Artaxerxes king of Persia.

15 And this house was finished on the third day of the month Adar, which was in the sixth year of the reign of Darius the king.

¶16 And the children of Israel, the priests, and the Levites, and the rest of the children of the captivity, kept the dedication of this house of God with joy,

17 And offered at the dedication of this house of God an hundred bullocks, two hundred rams, four hundred lambs; and for a *sin-offering for all Israel, twelve he goats, according to the number of the tribes of Israel.

18 And they set the priests in their divisions, and the Levites in their courses, for the service of God, which *is* at Jerusalem; as it is written in the *book of Moses.

19 And the children of the captivity kept the *passover upon the fourteenth *day* of the first month.

20 For the priests and the Levites were purified together, all of them *were* pure, and killed the passover for all the children of the captivity, and for their brethren the priests, and for themselves.

21 And the children of Israel, which were come again out of captivity, and all such as had separated themselves unto them from the filthiness of the heathen of the land, to seek the LORD God of Israel, did eat,

22 And kept the feast of *unleavened bread seven days with joy: for the LORD had made them joyful, and turned the heart of the king of Assyria unto them, to strengthen their hands in the work of the house of God, the God of Israel.

II. Return of Second Group (7:1—10:44)

7 Now after these things, in the reign of *Artaxerxes king of Persia, Ezra the son of Seraiah, the son of Azariah, the son of Hilkiah,

---

6:18 in their divisions . . . in their courses. See 1 Chronicles 23 and 24.

6:18 the book of Moses. The Pentateuch, composed of the first five books of the Old Testament.

2 The son of Shallum, the son of Zadok, the son of Ahitub,

3 The son of Amariah, the son of Azariah, the son of Meraioth,

4 The son of Zerahiah, the son of Uzzi, the son of Bukki,

5 The son of Abishua, the son of *Phinehas, the son of Eleazar, the son of *Aaron the chief priest:

6 This Ezra went up from *Babylon; and he *was* a ready scribe in the law of Moses, which the LORD God of *Israel had given: and the king granted him all his request, according to the hand of the LORD his God upon him.

7 And there went up *some* of the children of Israel, and of the priests, and the Levites, and the singers, and the porters, and the *Nethinims, unto *Jerusalem, in the seventh year of Artaxerxes the king.

8 And he came to Jerusalem in the fifth month, which *was* in the seventh year of the king.

9 For upon the first *day* of the first month began he to go up from Babylon, and on the first *day* of the fifth month came he to Jerusalem, according to the good hand of his God upon him.

10 For Ezra had prepared his heart to seek the law of the LORD, and to do *it,* and to teach in Israel statutes and judgments.

¶11 Now this *is* the copy of the letter that the king Artaxerxes gave unto Ezra the priest, the scribe, *even* a scribe of the words of the commandments of the LORD, and of his statutes to Israel.

12 Artaxerxes, king of kings, unto Ezra the priest, a scribe of the law of the God of *heaven, perfect *peace,* and at such a time.

13 I make a decree, that all they of the people of Israel, and *of* his priests and Levites, in my realm, which are minded of their own freewill to go up to Jerusalem, go with thee.

14 Forasmuch as thou art sent of the king, and of his seven counsellors, to enquire concerning *Judah and Jerusalem, according to the law of thy God which *is* in thine hand;

15 And to carry the silver and gold, which the king and his counsellors have freely offered unto the God of Israel, whose habitation *is* in Jerusalem,

16 And all the silver and gold that thou canst find in all the province of Babylon, with the *freewill-offering of the people, and of the priests, offering willingly for the house of their God which *is* in Jerusalem:

17 That thou mayest buy speedily with this money bullocks, rams, lambs, with their meat-offerings and their drink-offerings, and offer them upon the altar of the house of your God which *is* in Jerusalem.

18 And whatsoever shall seem good to thee, and to thy brethren, to do with the rest of the silver and the gold, that do after the will of your God.

19 The vessels also that are given thee for the service of the house of thy God, *those* deliver thou before the God of Jerusalem.

20 And whatsoever more shall be needful for the house of thy God, which thou shalt have occasion to bestow, bestow *it* out of the king's treasure house.

21 And I, *even* I Artaxerxes the king, do make a decree to all the treasurers which *are* beyond the river, that whatsoever Ezra the priest, the scribe of the law of the God of heaven, shall require of you, it be done speedily,

22 Unto an hundred talents of silver, and to an hundred measures of wheat, and to an hundred *baths of wine, and

---

7:7 And there went up some. From chapter 7 on to the end of the book is the story of a second company of believers who went to Jerusalem under the leadership of Ezra, whose name means *helper*. He was the best kind of leader, for God says in verse 10 of this chapter that he "had prepared his own heart to seek the law of the LORD" before he taught others.

to an hundred baths of oil, and salt without prescribing *how much.*

23 Whatsoever is commanded by the God of heaven, let it be diligently done for the house of the God of heaven: for why should there be wrath against the realm of the king and his sons?

24 Also we certify you, that touching any of the priests and Levites, singers, porters, Nethinims, or ministers of this house of God, it shall not be lawful to impose toll, tribute, or custom, upon them.

25 And thou, Ezra, after the wisdom of thy God, that *is* in thine hand, set magistrates and judges, which may judge all the people that *are* beyond the river, all such as know the *laws of thy God; and teach ye them that know *them* not.

26 And whosoever will not do the law of thy God, and the law of the king, let *judgment be executed speedily upon him, whether *it be* unto death, or to banishment, or to confiscation of goods, or to imprisonment.

¶ 27 Blessed *be* the LORD God of our fathers, which hath put *such a thing* as this in the king's heart, to beautify the house of the LORD which *is* in Jerusalem:

28 And hath extended mercy unto me before the king, and his counsellors, and before all the king's mighty princes. And I was strengthened as the hand of the LORD my God *was* upon me, and I gathered together out of Israel chief men to go up with me.

Those who returned with Ezra

8 These *are* now the chief of their fathers, and *this is* the genealogy of them that went up with me from Babylon, in the reign of Artaxerxes the king.

2 Of the sons of Phinehas; Gershom: of the sons of Ithamar; Daniel: of the sons of David; Hattush.

3 Of the sons of Shechaniah, of the sons of Pharosh; Zechariah: and with him were reckoned by genealogy of the males an hundred and fifty.

4 Of the sons of Pahath-moab; Elihoenai the son of Zerahiah, and with him two hundred males.

5 Of the sons of Shechaniah; the son of Jahaziel, and with him three hundred males.

6 Of the sons also of Adin; Ebed the son of Jonathan, and with him fifty males.

7 And of the sons of Elam; Jeshaiah the son of Athaliah, and with him seventy males.

8 And of the sons of Shephatiah; Zebadiah the son of Michael, and with him fourscore males.

9 Of the sons of Joab; Obadiah the son of Jehiel, and with him two hundred and eighteen males.

10 And of the sons of Shelomith; the son of Josiphiah, and with him an hundred and threescore males.

11 And of the sons of Bebai; Zechariah the son of Bebai, and with him twenty and eight males.

12 And of the sons of Azgad; Johanan the son of Hakkatan, and with him an hundred and ten males.

13 And of the last sons of Adonikam, whose names *are* these, Eliphelet, Jeiel, and Shemaiah, and with them threescore males.

14 Of the sons also of Bigvai; Uthai, and Zabbud, and with them seventy males.

¶ 15 And I gathered them together to the river than runneth to Ahava; and there abode we in tents three days: and I viewed the people, and the priests, and found there none of the sons of Levi.

16 Then sent I for Eliezer, for Ariel, for Shemaiah, and for Elnathan, and for Jarib, and for Elnathan, and for Nathan, and for Zechariah, and for Meshullam, chief men; also for Joiarib, and for Elnathan, men of understanding.

17 And I sent them with commandment unto Iddo the chief at the place Casiphia, and I told them what they should say unto Iddo, *and* to his brethren the Nethinims, at the place Casiph-

ia, that they should bring unto us ministers for the house of our God.
[18]And by the good hand of our God
upon us they brought us a man of understanding, of the sons of Mahli, the
son of Levi, the son of Israel; and Sherebiah, with his sons and his brethren,
eighteen;
[19]And Hashabiah, and with him Jeshaiah of the sons of Merari, his brethren and their sons, twenty;
[20]Also of the Nethinims, whom David and the princes had appointed for
the service of the Levites, two hundred
and twenty Nethinims: all of them were
expressed by name.
¶[21]Then I proclaimed a fast there, at
the river of Ahava, that we might afflict
ourselves before our God, to seek of
him a right way for us, and for our little
ones, and for all our substance.
[22]For I was ashamed to require of the
king a band of soldiers and horsemen to
help us against the enemy in the way:
because we had spoken unto the king,
saying, The hand of our God *is* upon all
them for good that seek him; but his
power and his wrath *is* against all them
that forsake him.
[23]So we fasted and besought our God
for this: and he was intreated of us.
¶[24]Then I separated twelve of the
chief of the priests, Sherebiah, Hashabiah, and ten of their brethren with them,
[25]And weighed unto them the silver,
and the gold, and the vessels, *even* the
offering of the house of our God, which
the king, and his counsellors, and his
lords, and all Israel *there* present, had
offered:
[26]I even weighed unto their hand six
hundred and fifty talents of silver, and
silver vessels an hundred talents, *and*
of gold an hundred talents;
[27]Also twenty basons of gold, of a
thousand *drams; and two vessels of
fine copper, precious as gold.
[28]And I said unto them, Ye *are* *holy
unto the LORD; the vessels *are* holy
also; and the silver and the gold *are* a
freewill-offering unto the LORD God of
your fathers.
[29]Watch ye, and keep *them,* until ye
weigh *them* before the chief of the
priests and the Levites, and chief of
the fathers of Israel, at Jerusalem, in
the chambers of the house of the LORD.
[30]So took the priests and the Levites
the weight of the silver, and the gold,
and the vessels, to bring *them* to Jerusalem unto the house of our God.
¶[31]Then we departed from the river
of Ahava on the twelfth *day* of the first
month, to go unto Jerusalem: and the
hand of our God was upon us, and he
delivered us from the hand of the enemy, and of such as lay in wait by the way.
[32]And we came to Jerusalem, and
abode there three days.

8:32 A Sign of Faith
This long journey from Babylon to Jerusalem with the many—perhaps six thousand—men, women, and children, as well as precious metals that were extremely valuable, was a remarkable example of Ezra's faith in the LORD God and in the heavenly Father's power to protect His own. This large group travelled over a road where there were many bandits and robbers ready to murder people for even a little money. Read in verse 22 Ezra's reason for travelling without the protection of soldiers.

¶[33]Now on the fourth day was the silver and the gold and the vessels
weighed in the house of our God by the
hand of Meremoth the son of Uriah
the priest; and with him *was* Eleazar
the son of Phinehas; and with them *was*
Jozabad the son of Jeshua, and Noadiah
the son of Binnui, Levites;
[34]By number *and* by weight of every
one: and all the weight was written at
that time.

8:22 For I was ashamed. Ezra knew what it meant to be a true witness for the LORD. He did not speak bravely for Him and then fail when time for action came. He trusted his God to care for him all the time and through anything. See verse 32 note.

35 *Also* the children of those that had been carried away, which were come out of the captivity, offered burnt-offerings unto the God of Israel, twelve bullocks for all Israel, ninety and six rams, seventy and seven lambs, twelve he goats *for* a sin-offering: all *this was* a burnt-offering unto the LORD.

¶36 And they delivered the king's commissions unto the king's lieutenants, and to the governors on this side the river: and they furthered the people, and the house of God.

The sinning, unseparated remnant

9 Now when these things were done, the princes came to me, saying, The people of Israel, and the priests, and the Levites, have not separated themselves from the people of the lands, *doing* according to their abominations, *even* of the Canaanites, the Hittites, the Perizzites, the Jebusites, the Ammonites, the Moabites, the Egyptians, and the Amorites.

2 For they have taken of their daughters for themselves, and for their sons: so that the holy seed have mingled themselves with the people of *those* lands: yea, the hand of the princes and rulers hath been chief in this *trespass.

3 And when I heard this thing, I rent my garment and my mantle, and plucked off the hair of my head and of my beard, and sat down astonied.

4 Then were assembled unto me every one that trembled at the words of the God of Israel, because of the transgression of those that had been carried away; and I sat astonied until the evening sacrifice.

¶5 And at the evening sacrifice I arose up from my heaviness; and having rent my garment and my mantle, I fell upon my knees, and spread out my hands unto the LORD my God.

6 And said, O my God, I am ashamed and blush to lift up my face to thee, my God: for our iniquities are increased over *our* head, and our trespass is grown up unto the heavens.

7 Since the days of our fathers *have* we *been* in a great trespass unto this day; and for our iniquities have we, our kings, *and* our priests, been delivered into the hand of the kings of the lands, to the sword, to captivity, and to a spoil, and to confusion of face, as *it is* this day.

8 And now for a little space *grace hath been *shewed* from the LORD our God, to leave us a *remnant to escape, and to give us a nail in his holy place, that our God may lighten our eyes, and give us a little reviving in our bondage.

9 For we *were* bondmen; yet our God hath not forsaken us in our bondage, but hath extended *mercy unto us in the sight of the kings of Persia, to give us a reviving, to set up the house of our God, and to repair the desolations thereof, and to give us a wall in Judah and in Jerusalem.

10 And now, O our God, what shall we say after this? for we have forsaken thy commandments,

11 Which thou hast commanded by thy servants the prophets, saying, The land, unto which ye go to possess it, is an *unclean land with the filthiness of the people of the lands, with their abominations, which have filled it from one end to another with their uncleanness.

12 Now therefore give not your daughters unto their sons, neither take their

---

9:1 The people . . . priests, and the Levites, have not separated themselves. When Ezra and his followers reached Jerusalem, they found that those who had come back earlier had fallen into sin by failing to keep themselves separate from the idol worshippers of the land. Before God's work could go on, there had to be a definite separation from fellowship with those who denied the one true God.

9:6 And said, O my God. For other wonderful biblical prayers, see Genesis 18:23-33; Exodus 32:11-12,31-32; Daniel 9:3-19.

9:7 confusion of face. A term that means *to be humbled in mind*. The Chinese have a similar expression, "to lose face," in contrast to "saving face."

daughters unto your sons, nor seek their peace or their wealth for ever: that ye may be strong, and eat the good of the land, and leave *it* for an inheritance to your children for ever.

13 And after all that is come upon us for our evil deeds, and for our great trespass, seeing that thou our God hast punished us less than our iniquities *deserve,* and hast given us *such* deliverance as this;

14 Should we again break thy commandments, and join in affinity with the people of these abominations? wouldest not thou be angry with us till thou hadst consumed *us,* so that *there should be* no remnant nor escaping?

15 O LORD God of Israel, thou *art* righteous: for we remain yet escaped, as *it is* this day: behold, we *are* before thee in our trespasses: for we cannot stand before thee because of this.

Sin forsaken

10 Now when Ezra had prayed, and when he had confessed, weeping and casting himself down before the house of God, there assembled unto him out of Israel a very great congregation of men and women and children: for the people wept very sore.

2 And Shechaniah the son of Jehiel, *one* of the sons of Elam, answered and said unto Ezra, We have trespassed against our God, and have taken strange wives of the people of the land: yet now there is hope in Israel concerning this thing.

3 Now therefore let us make a covenant with our God to put away all the wives, and such as are born of them, according to the counsel of my lord, and of those that tremble at the commandment of our God; and let it be done according to the law.

4 Arise; for *this* matter *belongeth* unto thee: we also *will be* with thee: be of good courage, and do *it.*

5 Then arose Ezra, and made the chief priests, the Levites, and all Israel, to swear that they should do according to this word. And they sware.

10:3 Unbelieving Wives
Not only had these Israelites deliberately disobeyed God in marrying unbelieving women (see Ezra 9:11-12), but they had actually taken part in the filthy practices of idol worship. If these men had led their wives to a heart belief in the true God and an understanding of His sacrifices, their wives could have become Israelites, accepted by the LORD, and not cast out. Today, in this *dispensation of grace, God deals differently with this matter. Although He gives His children strict instructions not to marry unbelievers (2 Cor. 6:14), He also gives special advice in 1 Corinthians 7:10-16 for those who are married to unbelievers.

¶ 6 Then Ezra rose up from before the house of God, and went into the chamber of Johanan the son of Eliashib: and *when* he came thither, he did eat no bread, nor drink water: for he mourned because of the transgression of them that had been carried away.

7 And they made proclamation throughout Judah and Jerusalem unto all the children of the captivity, that they should gather themselves together unto Jerusalem;

8 And that whosoever would not come within three days, according to the counsel of the princes and the elders, all his substance should be forfeited, and himself separated from the congregation of those that had been carried away.

¶ 9 Then all the men of Judah and Benjamin gathered themselves together unto Jerusalem within three days. It *was* the ninth month, on the twentieth *day* of the month; and all the people sat in the street of the house of God, trembling because of *this* matter, and for the great rain.

10 And Ezra the priest stood up, and said unto them, Ye have transgressed, and have taken strange wives, to increase the trespass of Israel.

11 Now therefore make confession unto the LORD God of your fathers, and do his pleasure: and separate yourselves

from the people of the land, and from the strange wives.

12 Then all the congregation answered and said with a loud voice, As thou hast said, so must we do.

13 But the people *are* many, and *it is* a time of much rain, and we are not able to stand without, neither *is this* a work of one day or two: for we are many that have transgressed in this thing.

14 Let now our rulers of all the congregation stand, and let all them which have taken strange wives in our cities come at appointed times, and with them the elders of every city, and the judges thereof, until the fierce wrath of our God for this matter be turned from us.

¶ 15 Only Jonathan the son of Asahel and Jahaziah the son of Tikvah were employed about this *matter:* and Meshullam and Shabbethai the Levite helped them.

16 And the children of the captivity did so. And Ezra the priest, *with* certain chief of the fathers, after the house of their fathers, and all of them by *their* names, were separated, and sat down in the first day of the tenth month to examine the matter.

17 And they made an end with all the men that had taken strange wives by the first day of the first month.

¶ 18 And among the sons of the priests there were found that had taken strange wives: *namely,* of the sons of Jeshua the son of Jozadak, and his brethren; Maaseiah, and Eliezer, and Jarib, and Gedaliah.

19 And they gave their hands that they would put away their wives; and *being* guilty, *they offered* a ram of the flock for their trespass.

20 And of the sons of Immer; Hanani, and Zebadiah.

21 And of the sons of Harim; Maaseiah, and Elijah, and Shemaiah, and Jehiel, and Uzziah.

22 And of the sons of Pashur; Elioenai, Maaseiah, Ishmael, Nethaneel, Jozabad, and Elasah.

23 Also of the Levites; Jozabad, and Shimei, and Kelaiah, (the same *is* Kelita,) Pethahiah, Judah, and Eliezer.

24 Of the singers also; Eliashib: and of the porters; Shallum, and Telem, and Uri.

25 Moreover of Israel: of the sons of Parosh; Ramiah, and Jeziah, and Malchiah, and Miamin, and Eleazar, and Malchijah, and Benaiah.

26 And of the sons of Elam; Mattaniah, Zechariah, and Jehiel, and Abdi, and Jeremoth, and Eliah.

27 And of the sons of Zattu; Elioenai, Eliashib, Mattaniah, and Jeremoth, and Zabad, and Aziza.

28 Of the sons also of Bebai; Jehohanan, Hananiah, Zabbai, *and* Athlai.

29 And of the sons of Bani; Meshullam, Malluch, and Adaiah, Jashub, and Sheal, and Ramoth.

30 And of the sons of Pahath-moab; Adna, and Chelal, Benaiah, Maaseiah, Mattaniah, Bezaleel, and Binnui, and Manasseh.

31 And *of* the sons of Harim; Eliezer, Ishijah, Malchiah, Shemaiah, Shimeon,

32 Benjamin, Malluch, *and* Shemariah.

33 Of the sons of Hashum; Mattenai, Mattathah, Zabad, Eliphelet, Jeremai, Manasseh, *and* Shimei.

34 Of the sons of Bani; Maadai, Amram, and Uel,

35 Benaiah, Bedeiah, Chelluh,

36 Vaniah, Meremoth, Eliashib,

37 Mattaniah, Mattenai, and Jaasau,

38 And Bani, and Binnui, Shimei,

39 And Shelemiah, and Nathan, and Adaiah,

40 Machnadebai, Shashai, Sharai,

41 Azareel, and Shelemiah, Shemariah,

42 Shallum, Amariah, *and* Joseph.

43 Of the sons of Nebo; Jeiel, Mattithiah, Zabad, Zebina, Jadau, and Joel, Benaiah.

44 All these had taken strange wives: and *some* of them had wives by whom they had children.

10:19 guilty, they offered a ram. See Leviticus 6:4-6.

The Book of

NEHEMIAH

BACKGROUND

The book tells of Nehemiah who in 444 B.C. led a party of Babylonian Jews to Jerusalem where they rebuilt the walls of the city and set up a government.

Fourteen years earlier Ezra had gone to Jerusalem to restore the temple worship (Ezra 7:6), but the walls were still broken down. The decree permitting him to go was the third issued which concerned Jerusalem and was important because it helps to make clear the Seventy Weeks prophecy of Daniel 9. The decree to build the walls marks the time when that prophecy began to be fulfilled. See Daniel 9:25.

Cyrus, in 536 B.C., had passed the first decree for the return of a party to rebuild the temple (Ezra 1:5). Attempts to stop the work were made in the reigns of his two successors, Ahasuerus and Artaxerxes, and were successful in the latter's reign (Ezra 4:6,7). Darius, in 519 B.C., issued the second decree allowing the work to go on again, and in 457 B.C. Ezra went up and the temple was dedicated (Ezra 6:16). Later Artaxerxes, in 444 B.C., issued the third decree permitting the walls to be built.

THEME

Nehemiah's name means *Comfort*, and he is a picture of any Christian today who seeks to stand loyal to God and the Scriptures in spite of opposition of all kinds. He was marked by prayer and dependence on God. Note the number of times he prayed: 1:4; 2:4; 4:4,9, and his phrase "the good hand of my God upon me" (2:8,18).

THE TIME

The events recorded here covered a period of about eleven years.

OUTLINE OF NEHEMIAH

I.	Nehemiah's Return	Nehemiah 1:1—2:20
II.	The Building of the Wall	Nehemiah 3:1-32
III.	The Opposition	Nehemiah 4:1—6:19
IV.	The Revival	Nehemiah 7:1—11:36
V.	Dedication of the Wall	Nehemiah 12:1-47
VI.	Restoration of Worship	Nehemiah 13:1-31

I. Nehemiah's Return (1:1—2:20)
*Nehemiah learns of the ruined state of *Jerusalem*

1 The words of Nehemiah the son of Hachaliah. And it came to pass in the month Chisleu, in the twentieth year, as I was in *Shushan the palace,

2 That Hanani, one of my brethren, came, he and *certain* men of *Judah; and I asked them concerning the Jews that had escaped, which were left of the captivity, and concerning *Jerusalem.

3 And they said unto me, The *remnant that are left of the captivity there in the province *are* in great affliction and reproach: the wall of Jerusalem also *is* broken down, and the gates thereof are burned with *fire.

¶ 4 And it came to pass, when I heard these words, that I sat down and wept, and mourned *certain* days, and fasted, and prayed before the God of *heaven,

5 And said, I beseech thee, O LORD God of heaven, the great and terrible God, that keepeth *covenant and *mercy for them that love him and observe his commandments:

6 Let thine ear now be attentive, and thine eyes open, that thou mayest hear the *prayer of thy servant, which I pray before thee now, day and night, for the children of *Israel thy servants, and *confess the sins of the children of Israel, which we have sinned against thee: both I and my father's house have sinned.

7 We have dealt very corruptly against thee, and have not kept the commandments, nor the statutes, nor the judgments, which thou commandedst thy servant *Moses.

Nehemiah's prayer

8 Remember, I beseech thee, the word that thou commandedst thy servant Moses, saying, *If* ye transgress, I will scatter you abroad among the nations:

9 But *if* ye turn unto me, and keep my commandments, and do them; though there were of you cast out unto the uttermost part of the heaven, *yet* will I gather them from thence, and will bring them unto the place that I have chosen to set my name there.

10 Now these *are* thy servants and thy people, whom thou hast *redeemed by thy great power, and by thy strong hand.

11 O Lord, I beseech thee, let now thine ear be attentive to the prayer of thy servant, and to the prayer of thy servants, who desire to *fear thy name: and prosper, I pray thee, thy servant this day, and grant him mercy in the sight of this man. For I was the king's cupbearer.

Artaxerxes passes the decree for the building of the wall of Jerusalem

2 And it came to pass in the month Nisan, in the twentieth year of Artaxerxes the king, *that* *wine *was* before him: and I took up the wine, and gave *it* unto the king. Now I had not been *beforetime* sad in his presence.

2 Wherefore the king said unto me, Why *is* thy countenance sad, seeing

---

1:4 prayed. Compare the prayer of Daniel for his people (Dan. 9:13-19).

1:8 Remember. Nehemiah knew the Scriptures and was quoting from Deuteronomy 28:63-67 and 30:1-5.

1:10 redeemed. When God brought the Israelites out of Egypt, He redeemed them with the blood of the Passover lamb. See Exodus 12:3 note, "The Meaning of Passover."

1:11 cupbearer. Nehemiah, a prince, was an official in the royal household. He held one of the highest positions in the imperial court.

2:1 Nisan. This was in April, four months after Nehemiah had heard the news of the state of Jerusalem. He had evidently spent the time in prayer and waiting upon God.

2:1 Artaxerxes. See Ezra 1:1 note, "The Kings of Persia." Artaxerxes was the son of Xerxes (the Ahasuerus of Esther) and was a pleasant, amiable king who took an interest in his servants. See also the introduction to this book.

thou *art* not sick? this *is* nothing *else* but
sorrow of heart. Then I was very sore
afraid,
3 And said unto the king, Let the king
live for ever: why should not my countenance be sad, when the city, the place
of my fathers' sepulchres, *lieth* waste,
and the gates thereof are consumed
with fire?
4 Then the king said unto me, For
what dost thou make request? So I
prayed to the God of heaven.
5 And I said unto the king, If it please
the king, and if thy servant have found
favour in thy sight, that thou wouldest
send me unto Judah, unto the city of my
fathers' sepulchres, that I may build it.
6 And the king said unto me, (the
queen also sitting by him,) For how long
shall thy journey be? and when wilt
thou return? So it pleased the king to
send me; and I set him a time.
7 Moreover I said unto the king, If it
please the king, let letters be given me
to the governors beyond the river, that
they may convey me over till I come
into Judah;
8 And a letter unto *Asaph the keeper of the king's forest, that he may give
me timber to make beams for the gates
of the palace which *appertained* to the
house, and for the wall of the city, and
for the house that I shall enter into. And
the king granted me, according to the
good hand of my God upon me.
¶ 9 Then I came to the governors beyond the river, and gave them the king's
letters. Now the king had sent captains
of the army and horsemen with me.
10 When Sanballat the Horonite, and
Tobiah the servant, the Ammonite,
heard *of it*, it grieved them exceedingly that there was come a man to seek
the welfare of the children of Israel.

Nehemiah's arrival in Jerusalem

11 So I came to Jerusalem, and was
there three days.
¶ 12 And I arose in the night, I and
some few men with me; neither told I
any man what my God had put in my
heart to do at Jerusalem: neither *was*
there any beast with me, save the beast
that I rode upon.
13 And I went out by night by the gate
of the valley, even before the dragon
well, and to the dung port, and viewed
the walls of Jerusalem, which were broken down, and the gates thereof were
consumed with fire.
14 Then I went on to the gate of the
fountain, and to the king's pool: but
there was no place for the beast *that was*
under me to pass.
15 Then went I up in the night by the
brook, and viewed the wall, and turned
back, and entered by the gate of the
valley, and *so* returned.
16 And the rulers knew not whither I
went, or what I did; neither had I as yet

2:6 time. Nehemiah was governor of Jerusalem for twelve years and then returned to Persia for a short time, but he got permission to return to Jerusalem again (see Neh. 13:6).

2:10 Sanballat . . . Tobiah. These were Samaritans who had opposed the building of the temple. See 6:1 note, "The Samaritan Leaders" and Ezra 4:1 note, "The Enemies of the People."

2:13 gate of the valley. This opened into the Valley of the Son of Hinnom. See also Nehemiah 3:13.

2:13 dragon well. A well or spring that once existed in the Valley of the Son of Hinnom. It was also called the "Jackal's Well" because of the animals that prowled around it.

2:13 port. A gate.

2:13 dung port. Outside the Dung Gate (see 3:14) was the dump or refuse heap of the city.

2:14 gate of the fountain. Water from the Pool of Siloam probably flowed out through this gate (see 3:15).

2:14 king's pool. Probably the Pool of Siloam, for it was near the king's garden (3:15).

2:15 brook. Kidron.

told *it* to the Jews, nor to the priests, nor to the nobles, nor to the rulers, nor to the rest that did the work.

¶17Then said I unto them, Ye see the distress that we *are* in, how Jerusalem *lieth* waste, and the gates thereof are burned with fire: come, and let us build up the wall of Jerusalem, that we be no more a reproach.

18Then I told them of the hand of my God which was good upon me; as also the king's words that he had spoken unto me. And they said, Let us rise up and build. So they strengthened their hands for *this* good *work*.

19But when Sanballat the Horonite, and Tobiah the servant, the Ammonite, and Geshem the Arabian, heard *it*, they laughed us to scorn, and despised us, and said, What *is* this thing that ye do? will ye rebel against the king?

20Then answered I them, and said unto them, The God of heaven, he will prosper us; therefore we his servants will arise and build: but ye have no portion, nor right, nor memorial, in Jerusalem.

II. The Building of the Wall (3:1-32)
The builders of the wall

3 Then Eliashib the high priest rose up with his brethren the priests, and they builded the sheep gate; they sanctified it, and set up the doors of it; even unto the tower of Meah they sanctified it, unto the tower of Hananeel.

2And next unto him builded the men of Jericho. And next to them builded Zaccur the son of Imri.

3But the fish gate did the sons of Hassenaah build, who *also* laid the beams thereof, and set up the doors thereof, the locks thereof, and the bars thereof.

4And next unto them repaired Meremoth the son of Urijah, the son of Koz. And next unto them repaired Meshullam the son of Berechiah, the son of Meshezabeel. And next unto them repaired Zadok the son of Baana.

5And next unto them the Tekoites repaired; but their nobles put not their necks to the work of their Lord.

6Moreover the old gate repaired *Jehoiada the son of Paseah, and Meshullam the son of Besodeiah; they laid the beams thereof, and set up the doors thereof, and the locks thereof, and the bars thereof.

7And next unto them repaired Melatiah the Gibeonite, and Jadon the Meronothite, the men of Gibeon, and of Mizpah, unto the throne of the governor on this side the river.

8Next unto him repaired Uzziel the son of Harhaiah, of the goldsmiths. Next unto him also repaired Hananiah

3:2 Different Kinds of Builders
The account of the builders is very interesting because of all the different kinds of people who helped and the ways in which they worked. Look at the priests (vs. 1), the lazy nobles (vs. 5), the goldsmiths and the apothecaries (vs. 8), the ruler who was not too proud to work himself (vs. 9), the daughters who helped (vs. 12), important rulers (vss. 15-19), the earnest worker (vs. 20), a lodger who had only one room (vs. 30), and many others. It is a picture of all the different kinds of people who are needed to carry on the work of God today.

3:1 Eliashib. The high priest was energetic in building the walls but was weak in allowing alliances with the Samaritans (see 13:4,7,28).

3:1 sheep gate. The Sheep Gate was the one by which the sheep for the sacrifices came in. Notice that the chapter begins and ends with references to the Sheep Gate.

3:1 tower of Meah . . . Hananeel. These towers were probably on each side of the Sheep Gate.

3:3 fish gate. Here the men of Tyre sold their fish (13:16). It is probably the "middle gate" of Jeremiah 39:3.

3:6 old gate. This may be translated "The gate of the old." It means, perhaps, that it was the gate of the old *city*, or old *wall*.

the son of *one of* the apothecaries, and
they fortified Jerusalem unto the broad
wall.
9And next unto them repaired Rephaiah the son of *Hur, the ruler of the half
part of Jerusalem.
10And next unto them repaired Jedaiah the son of Harumaph, even over
against his house. And next unto him
repaired Hattush the son of Hashabniah.
11Malchijah the son of Harim, and
Hashub the son of Pahath-moab, repaired the other piece, and the tower of
the furnaces.
12And next unto him repaired Shallum the son of Halohesh, the ruler of
the half part of Jerusalem, he and his
daughters.
13The valley gate repaired Hanun,
and the inhabitants of Zanoah; they built
it, and set up the doors thereof, the
locks thereof, and the bars thereof, and
a thousand *cubits on the wall unto the
dung gate.
14But the dung gate repaired
Malchiah the son of Rechab, the ruler
of part of Beth-haccerem; he build it,
and set up the doors thereof, the locks
thereof, and the bars thereof.
15But the gate of the fountain repaired Shallun the son of Col-hozeh, the
ruler of part of Mizpah; he built it, and
covered it, and set up the doors thereof,
the locks thereof, and the bars thereof,
and the wall of the pool of Siloah by the
king's garden, and unto the stairs that
go down from the city of *David.
16After him repaired Nehemiah the
son of Azbuk, the ruler of the half part
of Beth-zur, unto *the place* over against
the sepulchres of David, and to the pool
that was made, and unto the house of
the mighty.
17After him repaired the Levites,
Rehum the son of Bani. Next unto him
repaired Hashabiah, the ruler of the half
part of Keilah, in his part.
18After him repaired their brethren,
Bavai the son of Henadad, the ruler of
the half part of Keilah.
19And next to him repaired Ezer the
son of Jeshua, the ruler of Mizpah, another piece over against the going up to
the armoury at the turning *of the wall.*
20After him Baruch the son of Zabbai
earnestly repaired the other piece, from
the turning *of the wall* unto the door of
the house of Eliashib the high priest.
21After him repaired Meremoth the
son of Urijah the son of Koz another
piece, from the door of the house of
Eliashib even to the end of the house
of Eliashib.
22And after him repaired the priests,
the men of the plain.
23After him repaired Benjamin and
Hashub over against their house. After
him repaired Azariah the son of Maaseiah the son of Ananiah by his house.
24After him repaired Binnui the son
of Henadad another piece, from the
house of Azariah unto the turning *of the
wall,* even unto the corner.
25Palal the son of Uzai, over against
the turning *of the wall,* and the tower
which lieth out from the king's high
house, that *was* by the court of the
prison. After him Pedaiah the son of
Parosh.
26Moreover the *Nethinims dwelt in
Ophel, unto *the place* over against the
water gate toward the east, and the
tower that lieth out.
27After them the Tekoites repaired
another piece, over against the great
tower that lieth out, even unto the wall
of Ophel.
28From above the horse gate repaired
the priests, every one over against his
house.
29After them repaired Zadok the son
of Immer over against his house. After
him repaired also Shemaiah the son of
Shechaniah, the keeper of the east gate.
30After him repaired Hananiah the

3:11 tower of the furnaces. Ovens.
3:28 horse gate. This was close to the king's house.

son of Shelemiah, and Hanun the sixth
son of Zalaph, another piece. After him
repaired Meshullam the son of Berechiah over against his chamber.
31 After him repaired Malchiah the
goldsmith's son unto the place of the
Nethinims, and of the merchants, over
against the gate Miphkad, and to the
going up of the corner.
32 And between the going up of
the corner unto the sheep gate repaired
the goldsmiths and the merchants.

III. The Opposition (4:1—6:19)

Opposition by ridicule

4 But it came to pass, that when
Sanballat heard that we builded the
wall, he was wroth, and took great indignation, and mocked the Jews.
2 And he spake before his brethren
and the army of *Samaria, and said,
What do these feeble Jews? will they
fortify themselves? will they *sacrifice?
will they make an end in a day? will they
revive the stones out of the heaps of the
rubbish which are burned?
3 Now Tobiah the Ammonite *was* by
him, and he said, Even that which they
build, if a fox go up, he shall even break
down their stone wall.

The reply of prayer

4 Hear, O our God; for we are despised: and turn their reproach upon
their own head, and give them for a prey
in the land of captivity:
5 And cover not their iniquity, and let
not their *sin be blotted out from before
thee: for they have provoked *thee* to
anger before the builders.
6 So built we the wall; and all the wall
was joined together unto the half
thereof: for the people had a mind to
work.

Opposition by anger, answered again by prayer

¶7 But it came to pass, *that* when Sanballat, and Tobiah, and the Arabians, and
the Ammonites, and the Ashdodites,
heard that the walls of Jerusalem were
made up, *and* that the breaches began
to be stopped, then they were very
wroth,
8 And conspired all of them together
to come *and* to fight against Jerusalem,
and to hinder it.
9 Nevertheless we made our prayer
unto our God, and set a watch against
them day and night, because of them.

Opposition by discouraged Jews, met by faith and watching

10 And Judah said, The strength of the
bearers of burdens is decayed, and *there
is* much rubbish; so that we are not able
to build the wall.
11 And our adversaries said, They
shall not know, neither see, till we come
in the midst among them, and slay
them, and cause the work to cease.
12 And it came to pass, that when the
Jews which dwelt by them came, they
said unto us ten times, From all places
whence ye shall return unto us *they will
be upon you.*
¶13 Therefore set I in the lower places
behind the wall, *and* on the higher
places, I even set the people after their
families with their swords, their spears,
and their bows.
14 And I looked, and rose up, and said
unto the nobles, and to the rulers, and
to the rest of the people, Be not ye
afraid of them: remember the Lord,
which is great and terrible, and fight for
your brethren, your sons, and your
daughters, your wives, and your houses.
15 And it came to pass, when our en-

3:31 Miphkad. Hammiphkad. Probably near the northeast corner of the temple area.

4:10 Judah. Judah was made up of the Jews who lived in Jerusalem and who became discouraged by all the rubbish that had to be cleared away before building could continue. They were also afraid of surprise attacks.

4:12 the Jews which dwelt by them. These were the country Jews who lived in the districts near the Samaritans; these Jews had heard rumors about the intentions of the enemies.

emies heard that it was known unto us,
and God had brought their counsel to
nought, that we returned all of us to the
wall, every one unto his work.
16 And it came to pass from that time
forth, *that* the half of my servants
wrought in the work, and the other half
of them held both the spears, the
shields, and the bows, and the habergeons; and the rulers *were* behind all
the house of Judah.
17 They which builded on the wall, and
they that bare burdens, with those that
laded, *every one* with one of his hands
wrought in the work, and with the other
hand held a weapon.
18 For the builders, every one had his
sword girded by his side, and *so* builded.
And he that sounded the trumpet *was*
by me.
¶ 19 And I said unto the nobles, and to
the rulers, and to the rest of the people, The work *is* great and large, and we
are separated upon the wall, one far
from another.
20 In what place *therefore* ye hear the
sound of the trumpet, resort ye thither
unto us: our God shall fight for us.
21 So we laboured in the work: and
half of them held the spears from the
rising of the morning till the stars appeared.
22 Likewise at the same time said I
unto the people, Let every one with his
servant lodge within Jerusalem, that in
the night they may be a guard to us, and
labour on the day.
23 So neither I, nor my brethren, nor
my servants, nor the men of the guard
which followed me, none of us put off
our clothes, *saving that* every one put
them off for washing.

Opposition from within

5 And there was a great cry of the
people and of their wives against
their brethren the Jews.
2 For there were that said, We, our
sons, and our daughters, *are* many:
therefore we take up corn *for them,* that
we may eat, and live.

5:1-11 Injustice Reversed
The poor people were complaining of their poverty and hardships that had driven them to borrow money at high rates of interest (usury) and to even sell their children as slaves to the wealthy Jews in order to get food. Nehemiah reproved the greedy Jews severely for their actions and ordered them to give back the slaves and the interest and cancel the debts.

3 *Some* also there were that said, We
have mortgaged our lands, vineyards,
and houses, that we might buy corn,
because of the dearth.
4 There were also that said, We have
borrowed money for the king's tribute,
and that upon our lands and vineyards.
5 Yet now our flesh *is* as the flesh of
our brethren, our children as their children: and, lo, we bring into bondage our
sons and our daughters to be servants,
and *some* of our daughters are brought
unto bondage *already:* neither *is it* in
our power *to *redeem them;* for other
men have our lands and vineyards.
¶ 6 And I was very angry when I heard
their cry and these words.
7 Then I consulted with myself, and I
rebuked the nobles, and the rulers, and
said unto them, Ye exact *usury, every
one of his brother. And I set a great assembly against them.
8 And I said unto them, We after our
ability have redeemed our brethren the
Jews, which were sold unto the heathen; and will ye even sell your brethren? or shall they be sold unto us? Then
held they their peace, and found nothing *to answer.*
9 Also I said, It *is* not good that ye do:
ought ye not to walk in the fear of our
God because of the reproach of the heathen our enemies?
10 I likewise, *and* my brethren, and
my servants, might exact of them money and corn: I pray you, let us leave off
this usury.
11 Restore, I pray you, to them, even
this day, their lands, their vineyards,

their oliveyards, and their houses, also
the hundredth *part* of the money, and
of the corn, the wine, and the *oil, that
ye exact of them.
12 Then said they, We will restore
them, and will require nothing of them;
so will we do as thou sayest. Then I
called the priests, and took an oath of
them, that they should do according to
this promise.
13 Also I shook my lap, and said, So
God shake out every man from his
house, and from his labour, that
performeth not this promise, even thus
be he shaken out, and emptied. And all
the congregation said, *Amen, and
praised the LORD. And the people did
according to this promise.
¶ 14 Moreover from the time that I was
appointed to be their governor in the
land of Judah, from the twentieth year
even unto the two and thirtieth year of
*Artaxerxes the king, *that is,* twelve
years, I and my brethren have not eat-
en the bread of the governor.
15 But the former governors that *had
been* before me were chargeable unto
the people, and had taken of them bread
and wine, beside forty shekels of silver;
yea, even their servants bare rule over
the people: but so did not I, because of
the fear of God.
16 Yea, also I continued in the work of
this wall, neither bought we any land:
and all my servants *were* gathered
thither unto the work.
17 Moreover *there were* at my table an
hundred and fifty of the Jews and rulers,
beside those that came unto us from
among the heathen that *are* about us.
18 Now *that* which was prepared *for
me* daily *was* one ox *and* six choice
sheep; also fowls were prepared for me,
and once in ten days store of all sorts
of wine: yet for all this required not I the
bread of the governor, because the
bondage was heavy upon this people.
19 Think upon me, my God, for good,
according to all that I have done for this
people.

*Opposition by cunning, defeated
by refusal to stop the work*

6 Now it came to pass, when Sanballat, and Tobiah, and Geshem the
Arabian, and the rest of our enemies,
heard that I had builded the wall, and
that there was no breach left therein;
(though at that time I had not set up the
doors upon the gates;)

Treachery

2 That Sanballat and Geshem sent
unto me, saying, Come, let us meet
together in *some one of* the villages in
the plain of Ono. But they thought to do
me mischief.
3 And I sent messengers unto them,
saying, I *am* doing a great work, so that
I cannot come down: why should the
work cease, whilst I leave it, and come
down to you?
4 Yet they sent unto me four times
after this sort; and I answered them
after the same manner.
5 Then sent Sanballat his servant unto
me in like manner the fifth time with an
open letter in his hand;

6:1 THE SAMARITAN LEADERS

Sanballat, Tobiah, and Geshem were the leaders of the Samaritans. Sanballat was a Moabite (Horonite means of the city of Horonaim in Moab) and Tobiah was an Ammonite. This is significant, for both these races were ancient enemies of the Jews. Though related to them in a way through descent from Lot, the nephew of Abraham, these races had made a great deal of trouble for the Jews on their journey from Egypt to the Promised Land (see Deut. 23:3-6). Both Sanballat and Tobiah were related by marriage to leading Jews (6:17-19; 13:28), but they were jealous of the work of Nehemiah and did not want to see Jerusalem strong again. They are like many people today who pretend to be "religious" and who are even members of the church but who are not born again and who oppose all real Christian work and witness. Nehemiah shows how to deal with these hypocrites by refusing to compromise with them or to stop the work of God.

6 Wherein *was* written, It is reported
among the heathen, and Gashmu saith
it, that thou and the Jews think to rebel:
for which cause thou buildest the wall,
that thou mayest be their king, according to these words.

Compromise

7 And thou hast also appointed *prophets to preach of thee at Jerusalem, saying, *There is* a king in Judah: and now
shall it be reported to the king according to these words. Come now therefore, and let us take counsel together.
8 Then I sent unto him, saying, There
are no such things done as thou sayest,
but thou feignest them out of thine own
heart.
9 For they all made us afraid, saying,
Their hands shall be weakened from the
work, that it be not done. Now therefore, *O God,* strengthen my hands.

Religious falsehood

10 Afterward I came unto the house of
Shemaiah the son of Delaiah the son of
Mehetabeel, who *was* shut up; and he
said, Let us meet together in the house
of God, within the temple, and let us
shut the doors of the temple: for they
will come to slay thee; yea, in the night
will they come to slay thee.
11 And I said, Should such a man as
I flee? and who *is there,* that, *being* as I
am, would go into the temple to save
his life? I will not go in.
12 And, lo, I perceived that God had
not sent him; but that he pronounced
this *prophecy against me: for Tobiah
and Sanballat had hired him.
13 Therefore *was* he hired, that I
should be afraid, and do so, and sin, and
that they might have *matter* for an evil
report, that they might reproach me.
14 My God, think thou upon Tobiah
and Sanballat according to these their
works, and on the prophetess Noadiah,
and the rest of the prophets, that would
have put me in fear.
¶15 So the wall was finished in the
twenty and fifth *day* of *the month* Elul,
in fifty and two days.
16 And it came to pass, that when all
our enemies heard *thereof,* and all the
heathen that *were* about us saw *these
things,* they were much cast down in
their own eyes: for they perceived that
this work was wrought of our God.
¶17 Moreover in those days the nobles of Judah sent many letters unto
Tobiah, and *the letters* of Tobiah came
unto them.
18 For *there were* many in Judah sworn
unto him, because he *was* the son in law
of Shechaniah the son of Arah; and his
son Johanan had taken the daughter of
Meshullam the son of Berechiah.
19 Also they reported his good deeds
before me, and uttered my words to
him. *And* Tobiah sent letters to put me
in fear.

IV. The Revival (7:1—11:36)
Watch kept in the city

7 Now it came to pass, when the
wall was built, and I had set up the
doors, and the *porters and the singers
and the Levites were appointed,
2 That I gave my brother Hanani, and
Hananiah the ruler of the palace, charge
over *Jerusalem: for he *was* a faithful
man, and *feared God above many.
3 And I said unto them, Let not the
gates of Jerusalem be opened until the
sun be hot; and while they stand by, let
them shut the doors, and bar *them:* and
appoint watches of the inhabitants of
Jerusalem, every one in his watch, and
every one *to be* over against his house.
4 Now the city *was* large and great: but
the people *were* few therein, and the
houses *were* not builded.

Register of the people

¶5 And my God put into mine heart to
gather together the nobles, and the rulers, and the people, that they might be
reckoned by genealogy. And I found a

6:6 Gashmu. This is the Geshem of verse 1.

register of the genealogy of them which came up at the first, and found written therein,

6 These *are* the children of the province, that went up out of the captivity, of those that had been carried away, whom Nebuchadnezzar the king of *Babylon had carried away, and came again to Jerusalem and to *Judah, every one unto his city;

7 Who came with *Zerubbabel, Jeshua, Nehemiah, Azariah, Raamiah, Nahamani, Mordecai, Bilshan, Mispereth, Bigvai, Nehum, Baanah. The number, *I say,* of the men of the people of *Israel *was this;*

8 The children of Parosh, two thousand an hundred seventy and two.

9 The children of Shephatiah, three hundred seventy and two.

10 The children of Arah, six hundred fifty and two.

11 The children of Pahath-moab, of the children of Jeshua and Joab, two thousand and eight hundred *and* eighteen.

12 The children of Elam, a thousand two hundred fifty and four.

13 The children of Zattu, eight hundred forty and five.

14 The children of Zaccai, seven hundred and threescore.

15 The children of Binnui, six hundred forty and eight.

16 The children of Bebai, six hundred twenty and eight.

17 The children of Azgad, two thousand three hundred twenty and two.

18 The children of Adonikam, six hundred threescore and seven.

19 The children of Bigvai, two thousand threescore and seven.

20 The children of Adin, six hundred fifty and five.

21 The children of Ater of *Hezekiah, ninety and eight.

22 The children of Hashum, three hundred twenty and eight.

23 The children of Bezai, three hundred twenty and four.

24 The children of Hariph, an hundred and twelve.

25 The children of Gibeon, ninety and five.

26 The men of Beth-lehem and Netophah, an hundred fourscore and eight.

27 The men of Anathoth, an hundred twenty and eight.

28 The men of Beth-azmaveth, forty and two.

29 The men of Kirjath-jearim, Chephirah, and Beeroth, seven hundred forty and three.

30 The men of Ramah and Geba, six hundred twenty and one.

31 The men of Michmas, an hundred and twenty and two.

32 The men of *Beth-el and Ai, an hundred twenty and three.

33 The men of the other Nebo, fifty and two.

34 The children of the other Elam, a thousand two hundred fifty and four.

35 The children of Harim, three hundred and twenty.

36 The children of Jericho, three hundred forty and five.

37 The children of Lod, Hadid, and Ono, seven hundred twenty and one.

38 The children of Senaah, three thousand nine hundred and thirty.

¶ 39 The priests: the children of Jedaiah, of the house of Jeshua, nine hundred seventy and three.

40 The children of Immer, a thousand fifty and two.

41 The children of Pashur, a thousand two hundred forty and seven.

42 The children of Harim, a thousand and seventeen.

¶ 43 The Levites: the children of Jeshua, of Kadmiel, *and* of the children of Hodevah, seventy and four.

¶ 44 The singers: the children of *Asaph, an hundred forty and eight.

¶ 45 The porters: the children of Shallum, the children of Ater, the children of Talmon, the children of Akkub, the children of Hatita, the children of Shobai, an hundred thirty and eight.

¶ 46 The *Nethinims: the children of Ziha, the children of Hashupha, the children of Tabbaoth,

[47]The children of Keros, the children
of Sia, the children of Padon,
[48]The children of Lebana, the children of Hagaba, the children of Shalmai,
[49]The children of Hanan, the children
of Giddel, the children of Gahar,
[50]The children of Reaiah, the children
of *Rezin, the children of Nekoda,
[51]The children of Gazzam, the children of Uzza, the children of Phaseah,
[52]The children of Besai, the children
of Meunim, the children of Nephish-
esim,
[53]The children of Bakbuk, the children of Hakupha, the children of Harhur,
[54]The children of Bazlith, the children of Mehida, the children of Harsha,
[55]The children of Barkos, the children of Sisera, the children of Tamah,
[56]The children of Neziah, the children of Hatipha.
¶[57]The children of Solomon's servants: the children of Sotai, the children
of Sophereth, the children of Perida,
[58]The children of Jaala, the children
of Darkon, the children of Giddel,
[59]The children of Shephatiah, the
children of Hattil, the children of
Pochereth of Zebaim, the children of
Amon.
[60]All the Nethinims, and the children
of Solomon's servants, *were* three hundred ninety and two.
[61]And these *were* they which went up
also from Tel-melah, Tel-haresha, Cherub, Addon, and Immer: but they could
not shew their father's house, nor their
seed, whether they *were* of Israel.
[62]The children of Delaiah, the children of Tobiah, the children of Nekoda,
six hundred forty and two.
¶[63]And of the priests: the children of
Habaiah, the children of Koz, the children of Barzillai, which took *one* of the
daughters of Barzillai the Gileadite to
wife, and was called after their name.
[64]These sought their register *among*
those that were reckoned by genealogy, but it was not found: therefore were
they, as polluted, put from the priesthood.
[65]And the *Tirshatha said unto them,
that they should not eat of the most
*holy things, till there stood *up* a priest
with *Urim and Thummim.
¶[66]The whole congregation together
was forty and two thousand three hundred and threescore,
[67]Beside their manservants and their
maidservants, of whom *there were*
seven thousand three hundred thirty
and seven: and they had two hundred
forty and five singing men and singing
women.
[68]Their horses, seven hundred thirty and six: their mules, two hundred
forty and five:
[69]*Their* camels, four hundred thirty
and five: six thousand seven hundred
and twenty asses.
¶[70]And some of the chief of the fathers gave unto the work. The Tirshatha gave to the treasure a thousand
*drams of gold, fifty basons, five hun-
dred and thirty priests' *garments.
[71]And *some* of the chief of the fathers gave to the treasure of the work
twenty thousand drams of gold, and two
thousand and two hundred pounds of
silver.
[72]And *that* which the rest of the people gave *was* twenty thousand drams of
gold, and two thousand pound of silver,
and threescore and seven priests' garments.
[73]So the priests, and the Levites, and
the porters, and the singers, and *some*
of the people, and the Nethinims, and
all Israel, dwelt in their cities; and when
the seventh *month came, the children
of Israel *were* in their cities.

The Law read and explained

8 And all the people gathered themselves together as one man into
the street that *was* before the water
gate; and they spake unto Ezra the

8:1 Ezra the scribe. The same man who led the expedition of Ezra 7:7.

8:1 Public Readings of the Book of the Law

Occasion	Reference
Moses speaks to the people	Exodus 24:3
Moses repeats the law	Deuteronomy 5
Joshua reads the law	Joshua 8:34
Joshua renews the covenant	Joshua 24:25–26
Josiah reads the law	2 Kings 23:2; 2 Chronicles 34:29-30
Jehoshaphat teaches the law	2 Chronicles 17:9; 19:8
Ezra reads the law	Nehemiah 8; 13:1

*scribe to bring the *book of the law of *Moses, which the LORD had commanded to Israel.

2 And Ezra the priest brought the law before the congregation both of men and women, and all that could hear with understanding, upon the first day of the seventh month.

3 And he read therein before the street that *was* before the water gate from the morning until midday, before the men and the women, and those that could understand; and the ears of all the people *were attentive* unto the book of the law.

4 And Ezra the scribe stood upon a pulpit of wood, which they had made for the purpose; and beside him stood Mattithiah, and Shema, and Anaiah, and Urijah, and Hilkiah, and Maaseiah, on his right hand; and on his left hand, Pedaiah, and Mishael, and Malchiah, and Hashum, and Hashbadana, Zechariah, *and* Meshullam.

5 And Ezra opened the book in the sight of all the people; (for he was above all the people;) and when he opened it, all the people stood up:

6 And Ezra blessed the LORD, the great God. And all the people answered, Amen, Amen, with lifting up their hands: and they bowed their heads, and worshipped the LORD with *their* faces to the ground.

7 Also Jeshua, and Bani, and Sherebiah, Jamin, Akkub, Shabbethai, Hodijah, Maaseiah, Kelita, Azariah, Jozabad, Hanan, Pelaiah, and the Levites, caused the people to understand the law: and the people *stood* in their place.

8 So they read in the book in the law of God distinctly, and gave the sense, and caused *them* to understand the reading.

¶ 9 And Nehemiah, which *is* the Tirshatha, and Ezra the priest the scribe, and the Levites that taught the people, said unto all the people, This day *is* holy unto the LORD your God; mourn not, nor weep. For all the people wept, when they heard the words of the law.

10 Then he said unto them, Go your way, eat the fat, and drink the sweet, and send portions unto them for whom nothing is prepared: for *this* day *is* holy unto our Lord: neither be ye sorry; for the joy of the LORD is your strength.

11 So the Levites stilled all the people, saying, Hold your peace, for the day *is* holy; neither be ye grieved.

12 And all the people went their way to eat, and to drink, and to send portions, and to make great mirth, because they had understood the words that were declared unto them.

¶ 13 And on the second day were gathered together the chief of the fathers of all the people, the priests, and the Levites, unto Ezra the scribe, even to understand the words of the law.

14 And they found written in the law which the LORD had commanded by Moses, that the children of Israel should dwell in booths in the feast of the seventh month:

8:8 caused them to understand. The Hebrew language in which the Books of the Law were written (the first five books of the Bible) had become less used among the Jews. When they were in captivity they had used Aramaic, the Syrian language used by the Babylonians and Persians.

8:14 booths. Little shelters made of branches twined together.

8:14 The Feast of Tabernacles
The Feast of Tabernacles, described in Leviticus 23:34-44 (see also Lev. 23:34 note, "The Feast of Tabernacles"), was meant to remind the Jews of their journey to the Promised Land when they had lived in tents, but this part of the feast had not been observed at all since Joshua's time (Neh. 8:17).

15 And that they should publish and
proclaim in all their cities, and in Jerusalem, saying, Go forth unto the mount, and fetch olive branches, and pine branches, and myrtle branches, and palm branches, and branches of thick trees, to make booths, as *it is* written.
¶16 So the people went forth, and
brought *them,* and made themselves booths, every one upon the roof of his house, and in their courts, and in the courts of the house of God, and in the street of the water gate, and in the street of the gate of *Ephraim.
17 And all the congregation of them
that were come again out of the captivity made booths, and sat under the booths: for since the days of Jeshua the son of Nun unto that day had not the children of Israel done so. And there was very great gladness.
18 Also day by day, from the first day
unto the last day, he read in the book of the law of God. And they kept the feast seven days; and on the eighth day *was* a solemn assembly, according unto the manner.

Repentance and confession of sin

9 Now in the twenty and fourth day of this month the children of Israel were assembled with fasting, and with sackclothes, and earth upon them.
2 And the seed of Israel separated
themselves from all strangers, and stood and confessed their sins, and the iniquities of their fathers.
3 And they stood up in their place, and
read in the book of the law of the LORD their God *one* fourth part of the day; and *another* fourth part they confessed, and worshipped the LORD their God.
¶4 Then stood up upon the stairs, of
the Levites, Jeshua, and Bani, Kadmiel, Shebaniah, Bunni, Sherebiah, Bani, *and* Chenani, and cried with a loud voice unto the LORD their God.
5 Then the Levites, Jeshua, and Kad-
miel, Bani, Hashabniah, Sherebiah, Hodijah, Shebaniah, *and* Pethahiah, said, Stand up *and* bless the LORD your God for ever and ever: and blessed be thy glorious name, which is exalted above all blessing and praise.
6 Thou, *even* thou, *art* LORD alone;
thou hast made heaven, the heaven of heavens, with all their host, the earth, and all *things* that *are* therein, the seas, and all that *is* therein, and thou preservest them all; and the host of heaven worshippeth thee.
7 Thou *art* the LORD the God, who
didst choose Abram, and broughtest him forth out of Ur of the Chaldees, and gavest him the name of *Abraham;
8 And foundest his heart faithful be-
fore thee, and madest a *covenant with him to give the land of the Canaanites, the Hittites, the Amorites, and the Perizzites, and the Jebusites, and the Girgashites, to give *it, I say,* to his seed, and hast performed thy words; for thou *art* righteous:
9 And didst see the affliction of our
fathers in *Egypt, and heardest their cry by the Red sea;
10 And shewedst signs and wonders
upon *Pharaoh, and on all his servants, and on all the people of his land: for thou

---

9:2 separated. It was stated in the *Law that the Jews were not to mix with or marry people of the other nations surrounding them. They had forgotten this, and the reading of the Law brought it home to them. Look up Exodus 23:23-33 and Deuteronomy 7:1-6.

9:3 confessed. God is always willing to forgive when true confession is made, indicating repentance and faith in Him. Look up the promise in 1 John 1:9.

knewest that they dealt proudly against
them. So didst thou get thee a name, as
it is this day.
11 And thou didst divide the sea before
them, so that they went through the
midst of the sea on the dry land; and
their persecutors thou threwest into
the deeps, as a stone into the mighty
waters.
12 Moreover thou leddest them in the
day by a *cloudy pillar; and in the night
by a pillar of *fire, to give them light in
the way wherein they should go.
13 Thou camest down also upon
mount *Sinai, and spakest with them
from heaven, and gavest them right
judgments, and true *laws, good statutes and commandments:
14 And madest known unto them thy
holy *sabbath, and commandedst them
precepts, statutes, and laws, by the
hand of Moses thy servant:
15 And gavest them bread from heav-
en for their hunger, and broughtest
forth water for them out of the rock for
their thirst, and promisedst them that
they should go in to possess the land
which thou hadst sworn to give them.
16 But they and our fathers dealt
proudly, and *hardened their necks, and
hearkened not to thy commandments,
17 And refused to obey, neither were
mindful of thy wonders that thou didst
among them; but hardened their necks,
and in their rebellion appointed a captain to return to their bondage: but thou
art a God ready to pardon, gracious and
merciful, slow to anger, and of great
kindness, and forsookest them not.
18 Yea, when they had made them a
molten calf, and said, This *is* thy God
that brought thee up out of Egypt, and
had wrought great provocations;
19 Yet thou in thy manifold mercies
forsookest them not in the wilderness:
the pillar of the cloud departed not from
them by day, to lead them in the way;
neither the pillar of fire by night, to
shew them light, and the way wherein
they should go.
20 Thou gavest also thy good spirit to
instruct them, and withheldest not thy
*manna from their mouth, and gavest
them water for their thirst.
21 Yea, forty years didst thou sustain
them in the wilderness, so *that* they
lacked nothing; their clothes waxed not
old, and their feet swelled not.
22 Moreover thou gavest them kingdoms and nations, and didst divide them
into corners: so they possessed the
land of Sihon, and the land of the king
of Heshbon, and the land of Og king of
*Bashan.
23 Their children also multipliedst
thou as the stars of heaven, and
broughtest them into the land, concerning which thou hadst promised to their
fathers, that they should go in to possess *it*.
24 So the children went in and possessed the land, and thou subduedst
before them the inhabitants of the land,
the Canaanites, and gavest them into
their hands, with their kings, and the
people of the land, that they might do
with them as they would.
25 And they took strong cities, and a
fat land, and possessed houses full of all
goods, wells digged, vineyards, and
oliveyards, and fruit trees in abundance:
so they did eat, and were filled, and
became fat, and delighted themselves
in thy great goodness.
26 Nevertheless they were disobedient, and rebelled against thee, and cast
thy law behind their backs, and slew thy
prophets which testified against them
to turn them to thee, and they wrought
great provocations.
27 Therefore thou deliveredst them
into the hand of their enemies, who
vexed them: and in the time of their
trouble, when they cried unto thee,
thou heardest *them* from heaven; and
according to thy manifold mercies thou
gavest them saviours, who saved them
out of the hand of their enemies.
28 But after they had rest, they did evil
again before thee: therefore leftest thou
them in the hand of their enemies, so
that they had the dominion over them:

yet when they returned, and cried unto
thee, thou heardest *them* from heaven;
and many times didst thou deliver them
according to thy mercies;
29 And testifiedst against them, that
thou mightest bring them again unto
thy law: yet they dealt proudly, and
hearkened not unto thy commandments, but sinned against thy judgments, (which if a man do, he shall live
in them;) and withdrew the shoulder,
and *hardened their neck, and would
not hear.
30 Yet many years didst thou forbear
them, and testifiedst against them
by thy spirit in thy prophets: yet would
they not give ear: therefore gavest thou
them into the hand of the people of the
lands.
31 Nevertheless for thy great mercies'
sake thou didst not utterly consume
them, nor forsake them; for thou *art* a
gracious and merciful God.
32 Now therefore, our God, the great,
the mighty, and the terrible God, who
keepest covenant and *mercy, let not all
the trouble seem little before thee, that
hath come upon us, on our kings, on our
princes, and on our priests, and on our
prophets, and on our fathers, and on all
thy people, since the time of the kings
of Assyria unto this day.
33 Howbeit thou *art* *just in all that is
brought upon us; for thou hast done
right, but we have done wickedly:
34 Neither have our kings, our princes,
our priests, nor our fathers, kept thy law,
nor hearkened unto thy commandments
and thy testimonies, wherewith thou
didst testify against them.
35 For they have not served thee in
their kingdom, and in thy great goodness that thou gavest them, and in the
large and fat land which thou gavest
before them, neither turned they from
their wicked works.
36 Behold, we *are* servants this day,
and *for* the land that thou gavest unto
our fathers to eat the fruit thereof and
the good thereof, behold, we *are* servants in it:
37 And it yieldeth much increase unto
the kings whom thou hast set over us
because of our sins: also they have dominion over our bodies, and over our
cattle, at their pleasure, and we *are* in
great distress.
38 And because of all this we make
a sure *covenant,* and write *it;* and
our princes, Levites, *and* priests, seal
unto it.

The covenant signed

10 Now those that sealed *were,*
Nehemiah, the *Tirshatha, the
son of Hachaliah, and Zidkijah,
2 Seraiah, Azariah, Jeremiah,
3 Pashur, Amariah, Malchijah,
4 Hattush, Shebaniah, Malluch,
5 Harim, Meremoth, Obadiah,
6 Daniel, Ginnethon, Baruch,
7 Meshullam, Abijah, Mijamin,
8 Maaziah, Bilgai, Shemaiah: these
were the priests.
9 And the Levites: both Jeshua the
son of Azaniah, Binnui of the sons of
Henadad, Kadmiel;
10 And their brethren, Shebaniah,
Hodijah, Kelita, Pelaiah, Hanan,
11 Micha, Rehob, Hashabiah,
12 Zaccur, Sherebiah, Shebaniah,
13 Hodijah, Bani, Beninu.
14 The chief of the people; Parosh,
Pahath-moab, Elam, Zatthu, Bani,
15 Bunni, Azgad, Bebai,
16 Adonijah, Bigvai, Adin,
17 Ater, Hizkijah, Azzur,
18 Hodijah, Hashum, Bezai,
19 Hariph, Anathoth, Nebai,
20 Magpiash, Meshullam, Hezir,
21 Meshezabeel, Zadok, Jaddua,
22 Pelatiah, Hanan, Anaiah,
23 Hoshea, Hananiah, Hashub,
24 Hallohesh, Pileha, Shobek,
25 Rehum, Hashabnah, Maaseiah,
26 And Ahijah, Hanan, Anan,
27 Malluch, Harim, Baanah.
¶28 And the rest of the people, the
priests, the Levites, the porters, the
singers, the *Nethinims, and all they
that had separated themselves from the
people of the lands unto the law of God,

their wives, their sons, and their daughters, every one having knowledge, and
having understanding;
29 They clave to their brethren, their
nobles, and entered into a curse, and
into an oath, to walk in God's law, which
was given by Moses the servant of God,
and to observe and do all the commandments of the LORD our Lord, and his
judgments and his statutes;
30 And that we would not give our
daughters unto the people of the land,
nor take their daughters for our sons:
31 And *if* the people of the land bring
ware or any victuals on the sabbath day
to sell, *that* we would not buy it of them
on the sabbath, or on the holy day: and
that we would leave the seventh year,
and the exaction of every debt.
32 Also we made ordinances for us, to
charge ourselves yearly with the third
part of a shekel for the service of the
house of our God;
33 For the *shewbread, and for the
continual *meat-offering, and for the
continual burnt-offering, of the sabbaths, of the *new moons, for the *set
feasts, and for the holy *things,* and for
the *sin-offerings to make an *atonement for Israel, and *for* all the work of
the house of our God.
34 And we cast the lots among the
priests, the Levites, and the people, for
the wood-offering, to bring *it* into the
house of our God, after the houses of
our fathers, at times appointed year by
year, to burn upon the *altar of the
LORD our God, as *it is* written in the
law:
35 And to bring the firstfruits of our
ground, and the firstfruits of all fruit of
all trees, year by year, unto the house
of the LORD:
36 Also the firstborn of our sons, and
of our cattle, as *it is* written in the law,
and the firstlings of our herds and of our
flocks, to bring to the house of our God,
unto the priests that minister in the
house of our God:
37 And *that* we should bring the firstfruits of our dough, and our offerings,
and the fruit of all manner of trees, of
wine and of oil, unto the priests, to the
chambers of the house of our God; and
the *tithes of our ground unto the Levites, that the same Levites might have
the tithes in all the cities of our tillage.
38 And the priest the son of *Aaron
shall be with the Levites, when the
Levites take tithes: and the Levites
shall bring up the tithe of the tithes unto
the house of our God, to the chambers,
into the treasure house.
39 For the children of Israel and the
children of Levi shall bring the offering
of the corn, of the new wine, and the oil,
unto the chambers, where *are* the vessels of the *sanctuary, and the priests
that minister, and the porters, and the
singers: and we will not forsake the
house of our God.

The people of the country

11 And the rulers of the people
dwelt at Jerusalem: the rest of
the people also cast lots, to bring one
of ten to dwell in Jerusalem the *holy
city, and nine parts *to dwell* in *other* cities.
2 And the people blessed all the men,
that willingly offered themselves to
dwell at Jerusalem.
¶3 Now these *are* the chief of the
province that dwelt in Jerusalem: but in
the cities of Judah dwelt every one in
his possession in their cities, *to wit,* Israel, the priests, and the Levites, and
the Nethinims, and the children of Solomon's servants.
4 And at Jerusalem dwelt *certain* of

10:33 new moons. See Numbers 28:11-15.
11:1 one of ten. Now that the walls had been built, the area of the city was large, but the population was still very small, so volunteers, chosen by lot, came from the country to live in the city and defend it.
11:1 the holy city. This is the first time in the Bible that Jerusalem is called this.

the children of Judah, and of the children of Benjamin. Of the children of
Judah; Athaiah the son of Uzziah, the
son of Zechariah, the son of Amariah,
the son of Shephatiah, the son of
Mahalaleel, of the children of Perez;
5And Maaseiah the son of Baruch, the
son of Col-hozeh, the son of Hazaiah,
the son of Adaiah, the son of Joiarib, the
son of Zechariah, the son of Shiloni.
6All the sons of Perez that dwelt at
Jerusalem *were* four hundred threescore and eight valiant men.
7And these *are* the sons of Benjamin;
Sallu the son of Meshullam, the son of
Joed, the son of Pedaiah, the son of
Kolaiah, the son of Maaseiah, the son
of Ithiel, the son of Jesaiah.
8And after him Gabbai, Sallai, nine
hundred twenty and eight.
9And Joel the son of Zichri *was* their
overseer: and Judah the son of Senuah
was second over the city.
10Of the priests: Jedaiah the son of
Joiarib, *Jachin.
11Seraiah the son of Hilkiah, the son
of Meshullam, the son of Zadok, the son
of Meraioth, the son of Ahitub, *was* the
ruler of the house of God.
12And their brethren that did the
work of the house *were* eight hundred
twenty and two: and Adaiah the son of
Jeroham, the son of Pelaliah, the son
of Amzi, the son of Zechariah, the son
of Pashur, the son of Malchiah,
13And his brethren, chief of the fathers, two hundred forty and two: and
Amashai the son of Azareel, the son of
Ahasai, the son of Meshillemoth, the
son of Immer,
14And their brethren, mighty men of
valour, an hundred twenty and eight:
and their overseer *was* Zabdiel, the son
of *one of* the great men.
15Also of the Levites: Shemaiah the
son of Hashub, the son of Azrikam, the
son of Hashabiah, the son of Bunni;
16And Shabbethai and Jozabad, of the
chief of the Levites, *had* the oversight
of the outward business of the house
of God.
17And Mattaniah the son of Micha,
the son of Zabdi, the son of *Asaph, *was*
the principal to begin the thanksgiving
in *prayer: and Bakbukiah the second
among his brethren, and Abda the son
of Shammua, the son of Galal, the son
of *Jeduthun.
18All the Levites in the holy city *were*
two hundred fourscore and four.
19Moreover the porters, Akkub, Talmon, and their brethren that kept the
gates, *were* an hundred seventy and
two.
¶20And the residue of Israel, of the
priests, *and* the Levites, *were* in all the
cities of Judah, every one in his inheritance.
21But the Nethinims dwelt in Ophel:
and Ziha and Gispa *were* over the Nethinims.
22The overseer also of the Levites at
Jerusalem *was* Uzzi the son of Bani, the
son of Hashabiah, the son of Mattaniah, the son of Micha. Of the sons of
Asaph, the singers *were* over the business of the house of God.
23For *it was* the king's commandment
concerning them, that a certain portion
should be for the singers, due for every
day.
24And Pethahiah the son of Meshezabeel, of the children of Zerah the son
of Judah, *was* at the king's hand in all
matters concerning the people.
25And for the villages, with their
fields, *some* of the children of Judah
dwelt at Kirjath-arba, and *in* the villages
thereof, and at Dibon, and *in* the villages thereof, and at Jekabzeel, and *in*
the villages thereof,
26And at Jeshua, and at Moladah, and
at Beth-phelet,
27And at Hazar-shual, and at *Beer-
sheba, and *in* the villages thereof,
28And at Ziklag, and at Mekonah, and
in the villages thereof,
29And at En-rimmon, and at Zareah,
and at Jarmuth,
30Zanoah, Adullam, and *in* their villages, at *Lachish, and the fields thereof,
at Azekah, and *in* the villages thereof.

And they dwelt from Beer-sheba unto
the valley of Hinnom.
31The children also of Benjamin from
Geba *dwelt* at Michmash, and Aija, and
Beth-el, and *in* their villages,
32*And* at Anathoth, Nob, Ananiah,
33Hazor, Ramah, Gittaim,
34Hadid, Zeboim, Neballat,
35Lod, and Ono, the valley of craftsmen.
36And of the Levites *were* divisions *in*
Judah, *and* in Benjamin.

V. Dedication of the Wall (12:1-47)

12 Now these *are* the priests and
the Levites that went up with
*Zerubbabel the son of Shealtiel, and
Jeshua: Seraiah, Jeremiah, Ezra,
2Amariah, Malluch, Hattush,
3Shechaniah, Rehum, Meremoth,
4Iddo, Ginnetho, Abijah,
5Miamin, Maadiah, Bilgah,
6Shemaiah, and Joiarib, Jedaiah,
7Sallu, Amok, Hilkiah, Jedaiah. These
were the chief of the priests and of their
brethren in the days of Jeshua.
8Moreover the Levites: Jeshua, Binnui, Kadmiel, Sherebiah, Judah, *and*
Mattaniah, *which was* over the thanksgiving, he and his brethren.
9Also Bakbukiah and Unni, their
brethren, *were* over against them in the
watches.
¶10And Jeshua begat Joiakim, Joiakim
also begat Eliashib, and Eliashib begat
Joiada,
11And Joiada begat Jonathan, and Jonathan begat Jaddua.
12And in the days of Joiakim were
priests, the chief of the fathers: of Seraiah, Meraiah; of Jeremiah, Hananiah;
13Of Ezra, Meshullam; of Amariah,
Jehohanan;
14Of Melicu, Jonathan; of Shebaniah,
*Joseph;
15Of Harim, Adna; of Meraioth, Hel-
kai;
16Of Iddo, Zechariah; of Ginnethon,
Meshullam;
17Of Abijah, Zichri; of Miniamin, of
Moadiah, Piltai;
18Of Bilgah, Shammua; of Shemaiah,
Jehonathan;
19And of Joiarib, Mattenai; of Jedaiah,
Uzzi;
20Of Sallai, Kallai; of Amok, Eber;
21Of Hilkiah, Hashabiah; of Jedaiah,
Nethaneel.
¶22The Levites in the days of Eliashib, Joiada, and Johanan, and Jaddua,
were recorded chief of the fathers: also
the priests, to the reign of *Darius the
Persian.
23The sons of Levi, the chief of the
fathers, *were* written in the book of the
chronicles, even until the days of Johanan the son of Eliashib.
24And the chief of the Levites: Hashabiah, Sherebiah, and Jeshua the son of
Kadmiel, with their brethren over
against them, to praise *and* to give
thanks, according to the commandment
of *David the man of God, ward over
against ward.
25Mattaniah, and Bakbukiah, Obadiah, Meshullam, Talmon, Akkub, *were*
porters keeping the ward at the thresholds of the gates.
26These *were* in the days of Joiakim
the son of Jeshua, the son of Jozadak,
and in the days of Nehemiah the governor, and of Ezra the priest, the scribe.

The dedication

¶27And at the dedication of the wall
of Jerusalem they sought the Levites
out of all their places, to bring them to
Jerusalem, to keep the dedication with
gladness, both with thanksgivings, and
with singing, *with* cymbals, *psalteries,
and with harps.

12:1 went up with Zerubbabel. The first expedition to return under the decree of Cyrus, described in Ezra 1 and 2.
12:23 written in the book of the chronicles. See 1 Chronicles 9:14-22.
12:24 the commandment of David. See 1 Chronicles 23–25.

28 And the sons of the singers gathered themselves together, both out
of the plain country round about Jerusalem, and from the villages of Neto-
phathi;
29 Also from the house of Gilgal, and
out of the fields of Geba and Azmaveth:
for the singers had builded them villages round about Jerusalem.
30 And the priests and the Levites
purified themselves, and purified the
people, and the gates, and the wall.
31 Then I brought up the princes of
Judah upon the wall, and appointed two
great *companies of them that gave*
thanks, *whereof one* went on the right
hand upon the wall toward the *dung
gate:
32 And after them went Hoshaiah, and
half of the princes of Judah,
33 And Azariah, Ezra, and Meshullam,
34 Judah, and Benjamin, and Shemaiah, and Jeremiah,
35 And *certain* of the priests' sons with
trumpets; *namely,* Zechariah the son of
Jonathan, the son of Shemaiah, the son
of Mattaniah, the son of Michaiah, the
son of Zaccur, the son of Asaph:
36 And his brethren, Shemaiah, and
Azarael, Milalai, Gilalai, Maai, Nethaneel, and Judah, Hanani, with the musical
instruments of David the man of God,
and Ezra the scribe before them.
37 And at the fountain gate, which was
over against them, they went up by the
stairs of the city of David, at the going
up of the wall, above the house of David, even unto the water gate eastward.
38 And the other *company of them that
gave* thanks went over against *them,* and
I after them, and the half of the people
upon the wall, from beyond the *tower
of the furnaces even unto the broad
wall;
39 And from above the gate of Ephraim, and above the old gate, and above
the fish gate, and the tower of Hananeel, and the tower of Meah, even
unto the *sheep gate: and they stood
still in the prison gate.
40 So stood the two *companies of them
that gave* thanks in the house of God,
and I, and the half of the rulers with me:
41 And the priests; Eliakim, Maaseiah,
Miniamin, Michaiah, Elioenai, Zechariah, *and* Hananiah, with trumpets;
42 And Maaseiah, and Shemaiah, and
Eleazar, and Uzzi, and Jehohanan, and
Malchijah, and Elam, and Ezer. And the
singers sang loud, with Jezrahiah *their*
overseer.
43 Also that day they offered great
sacrifices, and rejoiced: for God had
made them rejoice with great joy: the
wives also and the children rejoiced: so
that the joy of Jerusalem was heard
even afar off.
¶ 44 And at that time were some
appointed over the chambers for the
treasures, for the offerings, for the firstfruits, and for the tithes, to gather into
them out of the fields of the cities the
portions of the *law for the priests and
Levites: for Judah rejoiced for the
priests and for the Levites that waited.
45 And both the singers and the porters kept the ward of their God, and the
ward of the purification, according to
the commandment of David, *and* of
Solomon his son.
46 For in the days of David and Asaph
of old *there were* chief of the singers, and
songs of praise and thanksgiving unto
God.
47 And all Israel in the days of Zerubbabel, and in the days of Nehemiah,
gave the portions of the singers and the
porters, every day his portion: and they
sanctified *holy things* unto the Levites;
and the Levites sanctified *them* unto the
children of Aaron.

VI. Restoration of Worship (13:1-31)

13 On that day they read in the
book of Moses in the audience

12:36 instruments of David. See 1 Chronicles 23:5 and 2 Chronicles 29:25-27.
13:1 book of Moses. Deuteronomy 23:3-5 was the passage they read.

of the people; and therein was found written, that the Ammonite and the Moabite should not come into the congregation of God for ever;

2 Because they met not the children of Israel with bread and with water, but hired Balaam against them, that he should curse them: howbeit our God turned the curse into a blessing.

3 Now it came to pass, when they had heard the law, that they separated from Israel all the mixed multitude.

¶ 4 And before this, Eliashib the priest, having the oversight of the chamber of the house of our God, *was* allied unto Tobiah:

5 And he had prepared for him a great chamber, where aforetime they laid the meat-offerings, the frankincense, and the vessels, and the tithes of the corn, the new wine, and the oil, which was commanded *to be given* to the Levites, and the singers, and the porters; and the offerings of the priests.

6 But in all this *time* was not I at Jerusalem: for in the two and thirtieth year of Artaxerxes king of Babylon came I unto the king, and after certain days obtained I leave of the king:

Nehemiah's second visit

7 And I came to Jerusalem, and understood of the evil that Eliashib did for Tobiah, in preparing him a chamber in the courts of the house of God.

8 And it grieved me sore: therefore I cast forth all the household stuff of Tobiah out of the chamber.

9 Then I commanded, and they cleansed the chambers: and thither brought I again the vessels of the house of God, with the meat-offering and the frankincense.

¶ 10 And I perceived that the portions of the Levites had not been given *them:* for the Levites and the singers, that did the work, were fled every one to his field.

11 Then contended I with the rulers, and said, Why is the house of God forsaken? And I gathered them together, and set them in their place.

13:7 The Return to Jerusalem
Nehemiah had gone back to Persia after about twelve years according to his promise to Artaxerxes (see Neh. 2:6). On Nehemiah's return to Jerusalem, he found that the people had not kept their promise of chapter 10. The presence of Tobiah the Ammonite in the temple was in direct defiance of Deuteronomy 23:3-4, and the temple worship had ceased because the Levites who carried it out had gone back to their homes to earn their livings since the people had failed to send in the offerings which maintained the Levites. The Sabbath was ignored, and many had married heathen wives. Nehemiah took firm steps to put all this right. He looked to God for his reward and did not care that he might become unpopular. Notice his appeal to God in verses 14, 22, and 31.

12 Then brought all Judah the tithe of the corn and the new wine and the oil unto the treasuries.

13 And I made treasurers over the treasuries, Shelemiah the priest, and Zadok the scribe, and of the Levites, Pedaiah: and next to them *was* Hanan the son of Zaccur, the son of Mattaniah: for they were counted faithful, and their office *was* to distribute unto their brethren.

14 Remember me, O my God, concerning this, and wipe not out my good deeds that I have done for the house of my God, and for the offices thereof.

¶ 15 In those days saw I in Judah *some* treading wine presses on the sabbath, and bringing in sheaves, and lading asses; as also wine, grapes, and figs, and all *manner of* burdens, which they brought into Jerusalem on the sabbath day: and I testified *against them* in the day wherein they sold victuals.

16 There dwelt men of Tyre also therein, which brought fish, and all manner of ware, and sold on the sabbath unto the children of Judah, and in Jerusalem.

13:3 mixed multitude. All those who were not real Jews by birth or by religious practice.

17 Then I contended with the nobles
of Judah, and said unto them, What evil
thing *is* this that ye do, and profane the
sabbath day?
18 Did not your fathers thus, and did not
our God bring all this evil upon us, and
upon this city? yet ye bring more wrath
upon Israel by profaning the sabbath.
19 And it came to pass, that when the
gates of Jerusalem began to be dark
before the sabbath, I commanded that
the gates should be shut, and charged
that they should not be opened till after
the sabbath: and *some* of my servants
set I at the gates, *that* there should
no burden be brought in on the sabbath
day.
20 So the merchants and sellers of all
kind of ware lodged without Jerusalem
once or twice.
21 Then I testified against them, and
said unto them, Why lodge ye about the
wall? if ye do *so* again, I will lay hands
on you. From that time forth came they
no *more* on the sabbath.
22 And I commanded the Levites that
they should cleanse themselves, and
that they should come *and* keep the
gates, to sanctify the sabbath day. Remember me, O my God, *concerning* this
also, and spare me according to the
greatness of thy mercy.
¶23 In those days also saw I Jews *that*
had married wives of Ashdod, of Ammon, *and* of Moab:
24 And their children spake half in the
speech of Ashdod, and could not speak
in the Jews' language, but according to
the language of each people.
25 And I contended with them, and
cursed them, and smote certain of
them, and plucked off their hair, and
made them swear by God, *saying,* Ye
shall not give your daughters unto their
sons, nor take their daughters unto
your sons, or for yourselves.
26 Did not Solomon king of Israel sin
by these things? yet among many nations was there no king like him, who
was beloved of his God, and God made
him king over all Israel: nevertheless
even him did outlandish women cause
to sin.
27 Shall we then hearken unto you to
do all this great evil, to transgress
against our God in marrying strange
wives?
28 And *one* of the sons of Joiada, the
son of Eliashib the high priest, *was* son
in law to Sanballat the Horonite: therefore I chased him from me.
29 Remember them, O my God, because they have defiled the priesthood,
and the covenant of the priesthood, and
of the Levites.
30 Thus cleansed I them from all
strangers, and appointed the wards of
the priests and the Levites, every one
in his business;
31 And for the wood-offering, at times
appointed, and for the firstfruits. Remember me, O my God, for good.

13:26 Solomon. See 1 Kings 11:1-8.
13:26 outlandish. Foreign.

The Book of

ESTHER

BACKGROUND

The book of Esther gives us a very interesting glimpse of the exiled Jews under Babylonian and Persian rule. It describes Gentile ill-feeling toward the Jews, and the Jews' escape from a massacre about one hundred years after they had been taken away from their country. A small party of them had gone back to Jerusalem when Cyrus the Great decreed that they might return to their land, in 536 B.C., but the mass of the people had settled down in Babylon and were content to remain there. The events recorded in the book of Esther fit in between the 6th and 7th chapters of Ezra.

Not once in this book is the name of God mentioned, and this is the only book in the Bible of which this is true. God had hidden His face from His people because of evil which they had done (see Deuteronomy 31:18), but He still loved them and was watching over them. Thus He raised up Esther and Mordecai to save them from one of the greatest dangers of their history.

LESSONS IN ESTHER

We learn two lessons from this book: first, that God never stops loving His people even though they may sin against Him; second, that He controls the affairs of men to bring about His plan for His people.

OUTLINE OF ESTHER

I.	The Story of Vashti	Esther 1:1-22
II.	The Choice of Esther as Queen	Esther 2:1-23
III.	The Plot of Haman	Esther 3:1-15
IV.	The Deliverance through Mordecai and Esther	Esther 4:1—8:17
V.	The Jews' Defense of Themselves	Esther 9:1-32
VI.	The Fame of Mordecai	Esther 10:1-3

I. The Story of Vashti (1:1-22)

1 Now it came to pass in the days of
*Ahasuerus, (this *is* Ahasuerus
which reigned, from India even unto
Ethiopia, *over* an hundred and seven
and twenty provinces:)

2 *That* in those days, when the king
Ahasuerus sat on the throne of his
kingdom, which *was* in Shushan the
palace,

3 In the third year of his reign, he
made a feast unto all his princes and his

1:2 Shushan. This was Susa, the old capital of the Persian Empire. The emperors usually spent the winters in Babylon and the summers in Shushan. The wonderful palace described in verses 5-6 was built by Darius the Great, father of Xerxes.

1:1 Ahasuerus
This is thought to be Xerxes, who ruled over the Persian Empire from about 486 to 465 B.C. He made the great expedition against Greece prophesied by Daniel (Dan. 11:2) and was defeated. It probably took place in the four years that came between Vashti's disgrace and Esther's coronation (1:12 and 2:17). (See Ezra 1:1 note, "The Kings of Persia.") "Ahasuerus" is a title rather than a name, and means *majesty*. It is used in a similar way to the title "Pharaoh."

servants; the power of Persia and Media, the nobles and princes of the provinces, *being* before him:
4When he shewed the riches of his glorious kingdom and the honour of his excellent majesty many days, *even* an hundred and fourscore days.
5And when these days were expired, the king made a feast unto all the people that were present in Shushan the palace, both unto great and small, seven days, in the court of the garden of the king's palace;
6*Where were* white, green, and *blue, *hangings,* fastened with cords of fine *linen and purple to silver rings and pillars of marble: the beds *were of* gold and silver, upon a pavement of red, and blue, and white, and black, marble.
7And they gave *them* drink in vessels of gold, (the vessels being diverse one from another,) and royal wine in abundance, according to the state of the king.
8And the drinking *was* according to the *law; none did compel: for so the king had appointed to all the officers of his house, that they should do according to every man's pleasure.
9Also Vashti the queen made a feast for the women *in* the royal house which *belonged* to king Ahasuerus.
¶10On the seventh day, when the heart of the king was merry with wine, he commanded Mehuman, Biztha, Harbona, Bigtha, and Abagtha, Zethar, and Carcas, the seven chamberlains that served in the presence of Ahasuerus the king,
11To bring Vashti the queen before the king with the crown royal, to shew the people and the princes her beauty: for she *was* fair to look on.
12But the queen Vashti refused to come at the king's commandment by *his* chamberlains: therefore was the king very wroth, and his anger burned in him.
¶13Then the king said to the wise men, which knew the times, (for so *was* the king's manner toward all that knew law and judgment:
14And the next unto him *was* Carshena, Shethar, Admatha, *Tarshish, Meres, Marsena, *and* Memucan, the seven princes of Persia and Media, which saw the king's face, *and* which sat the first in the kingdom;)

1:14 A Place of Power
The parentheses in verses 13 and 14 mean that those who were wise and who knew the law were the ones whom Ahasuerus chose to be "next unto him," who "sat first in the kingdom." They had great authority and power, second only to the king. The fact that they "saw the king's face" meant they were able to go into the inner court where he was.

15What shall we do unto the queen Vashti according to law, because she hath not performed the commandment of the king Ahasuerus by the chamberlains?
16And Memucan answered before the king and the princes, Vashti the queen hath not done wrong to the king only, but also to all the princes, and to all the people that *are* in all the provinces of the king Ahasuerus.
17For *this* deed of the queen shall come abroad unto all women, so that they shall despise their husbands in their eyes, when it shall be reported,

1:12 the queen Vashti refused. It would have been unladylike for her to appear at a drunken revel.

The king Ahasuerus commanded Vashti the queen to be brought in before him, but she came not.

18 *Likewise* shall the ladies of Persia and Media say this day unto all the king's princes, which have heard of the deed of the queen. Thus *shall there arise* too much contempt and wrath.

19 If it please the king, let there go a royal commandment from him, and let it be written among the laws of the Persians and the Medes, that it be not altered, That Vashti come no more before king Ahasuerus; and let the king give her royal estate unto another that is better than she.

20 And when the king's decree which he shall make shall be published throughout all his empire, (for it is great,) all the wives shall give to their husbands honour, both to great and small.

21 And the saying pleased the king and the princes; and the king did according to the word of Memucan:

22 For he sent letters into all the king's provinces, into every province according to the writing thereof, and to every people after their language, that every man should bear rule in his own house, and that *it* should be published according to the language of every people.

II. The Choice of Esther as Queen (2:1-23)

2 After these things, when the wrath of king Ahasuerus was appeased, he remembered Vashti, and what she had done, and what was decreed against her.

2 Then said the king's servants that ministered unto him, Let there be fair young virgins sought for the king:

3 And let the king appoint officers in all the provinces of his kingdom, that they may gather together all the fair young virgins unto Shushan the palace, to the house of the women unto the custody of Hege the king's chamberlain, keeper of the women; and let their things for purification be given *them:*

4 And let the maiden which pleaseth the king be queen instead of Vashti. And the thing pleased the king; and he did so.

¶5 *Now* in Shushan the palace there was a certain Jew, whose name *was* Mordecai, the son of Jair, the son of Shimei, the son of Kish, a Benjamite;

6 Who had been carried away from *Jerusalem with the captivity which had been carried away with Jeconiah king of *Judah, whom Nebuchadnezzar the king of *Babylon had carried away.

7 And he brought up Hadassah, that *is,* Esther, his uncle's daughter: for she had neither father nor mother, and the maid *was* fair and beautiful; whom Mordecai, when her father and mother were dead, took for his own daughter.

¶8 So it came to pass, when the king's commandment and his decree was heard, and when many maidens were gathered together unto Shushan the palace, to the custody of Hegai, that Esther was brought also unto the king's house, to the custody of Hegai, keeper of the women.

9 And the maiden pleased him, and she obtained kindness of him; and he speedily gave her her things for purification, with such things as belonged to her, and seven maidens, *which were* meet to be given her, out of the king's house: and he preferred her and her maids unto the best *place* of the house of the women.

10 Esther had not shewed her people nor her kindred: for Mordecai had charged her that she should not shew *it.*

11 And Mordecai walked every day

2:6 Jeconiah. The same as Jehoiachin (2 Kings 24:6).
2:7 Hadassah. This was her Hebrew name and means *myrtle;* Esther, her Persian name, means *star.*
2:8 Hegai. The same as Hege (vs. 3).

before the court of the women's house,
to know how Esther did, and what
should become of her.

¶12Now when every maid's turn was
come to go in to king Ahasuerus, after
that she had been twelve months, according to the manner of the women,
(for so were the days of their purifica-
tions accomplished, *to wit,* six months
with *oil of myrrh, and six months with
sweet odours, and with *other* things for
the purifying of the women;)

13Then thus came *every* maiden unto
the king; whatsoever she desired was
given her to go with her out of the house
of the women unto the king's house.

14In the evening she went, and on the
morrow she returned into the second
house of the women, to the custody of
Shaashgaz, the king's chamberlain,
which kept the concubines: she came in
unto the king no more, except the king
delighted in her, and that she were
called by name.

¶15Now when the turn of Esther, the
daughter of Abihail the uncle of Mordecai, who had taken her for his daughter,
was come to go in unto the king, she
required nothing but what Hegai the
king's chamberlain, the keeper of the
women, appointed. And Esther obtained favour in the sight of all them
that looked upon her.

16So Esther was taken unto king
Ahasuerus into his house royal in the
tenth month, which *is* the month Te-
beth, in the seventh year of his reign.

17And the king loved Esther above all
the women, and she obtained grace and
favour in his sight more than all the virgins; so that he set the royal crown
upon her head, and made her queen
instead of Vashti.

18Then the king made a great feast
unto all his princes and his servants,
even Esther's feast; and he made a release to the provinces, and gave gifts,
according to the state of the king.

19And when the virgins were gathered together the second time, then
Mordecai sat in the king's gate.

20Esther had not *yet* shewed her kindred nor her people; as Mordecai had
charged her: for Esther did the commandment of Mordecai, like as when
she was brought up with him.

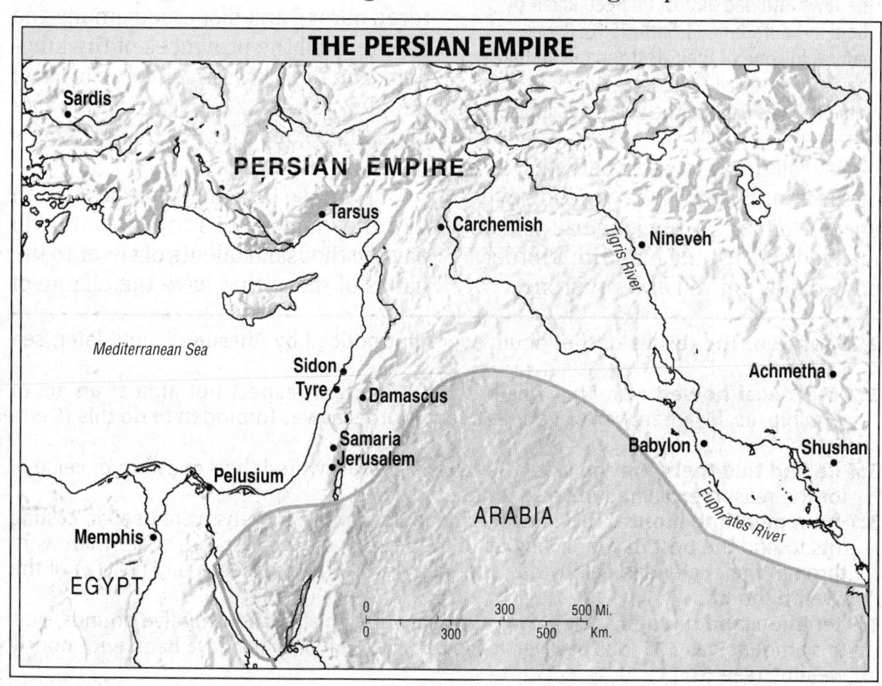

¶21 In those days, while Mordecai sat in the king's gate, two of the king's chamberlains, Bigthan and Teresh, of those which kept the door, were wroth, and sought to lay hand on the king Ahasuerus.

22 And the thing was known to Mordecai, who told *it* unto Esther the queen; and Esther certified the king *thereof* in Mordecai's name.

23 And when inquisition was made of the matter, it was found out; therefore they were both hanged on a tree: and it was written in the book of the chronicles before the king.

III. The Plot of Haman (3:1-15)

3 After these things did king Ahasuerus promote Haman the son of Hammedatha the Agagite, and advanced him, and set his seat above all the princes that *were* with him.

> **3:1 Haman**
> According to Jewish tradition, Agagite meant that he was descended from the royal house of the Amalekites (see Num. 24:7). The Amalekites had always been the enemies of the Jews and had almost all been killed by them in Saul's time (1 Sam. 15:8). It was natural for one of their descendants to hate the Jews, especially Mordecai, who was of the same tribe as Saul, for he was a Benjamite.

2 And all the king's servants, that *were* in the king's gate, bowed, and reverenced Haman: for the king had so commanded concerning him. But Mordecai bowed not, nor did *him* reverence.

3 Then the king's servants, which *were* in the king's gate, said unto Mordecai, Why transgressest thou the king's commandment?

4 Now it came to pass, when they spake daily unto him, and he hearkened not unto them, that they told Haman, to see whether Mordecai's matters would stand: for he had told them that he *was* a Jew.

5 And when Haman saw that Mordecai bowed not, nor did him reverence, then was Haman full of wrath.

6 And he thought scorn to lay hands on Mordecai alone; for they had shewed him the people of Mordecai: wherefore Haman sought to destroy all the Jews that *were* throughout the whole kingdom of Ahasuerus, *even* the people of Mordecai.

¶7 In the first month, that *is,* the month Nisan, in the twelfth year of king Ahasuerus, they cast Pur, that *is,* the lot, before Haman from day to day, and from month to month, *to* the twelfth *month,* that *is,* the month Adar.

¶8 And Haman said unto king Ahasuerus, There is a certain people scattered abroad and dispersed among the people in all the provinces of thy kingdom; and their laws *are* diverse from all people; neither keep they the king's laws: therefore it *is* not for the king's profit to suffer them.

9 If it please the king, let it be written that they may be destroyed: and I will pay ten thousand talents of silver to the hands of those that have the charge of

---

2:23 written. The results of the inquiry were not noticed by Ahasuerus until later; see Esther 6:1.

3:2 Mordecai bowed not. This was not just a mark of respect but almost an act of worship, as if Haman were a god; as a Jew, Mordecai was forbidden to do this (Deut. 6:13-14).

3:4 he had told them that he was a Jew. Mordecai answered their question of verse 3, for the reason explained in verse 2 note.

3:7 from month to month. This does not mean that twelve months were used in casting lots to find the best day for killing all of the Jews. It means that the "wise" men went through their calendar, day by day, until they chose the thirteenth day (vs. 12) of the twelfth month.

3:9 ten thousand talents. A talent was a weight equal to about seventy-five pounds, thus this amount was 375 tons of silver. It showed that Haman must have been enormously wealthy (see 5:11).

the business, to bring *it* into the king's treasuries.

10 And the king took his ring from his hand, and gave it unto Haman the son of Hammedatha the Agagite, the Jews' enemy.

11 And the king said unto Haman, The silver *is* given to thee, the people also, to do with them as it seemeth good to thee.

12 Then were the king's *scribes called on the thirteenth day of the first month, and there was written according to all that Haman had commanded unto the king's lieutenants, and to the governors that *were* over every province, and to the rulers of every people of every province according to the writing thereof, and *to* every people after their language; in the name of king Ahasuerus was it written, and sealed with the king's ring.

13 And the letters were sent by posts into all the king's provinces, to destroy, to kill, and to cause to perish, all Jews, both young and old, little children and women, in one day, *even* upon the thirteenth *day* of the twelfth month, which *is* the month Adar, and *to take* the spoil of them for a prey.

14 The copy of the writing for a commandment to be given in every province was published unto all people, that they should be ready against that day.

15 The posts went out, being hastened by the king's commandment, and the decree was given in Shushan the palace. And the king and Haman sat down to drink; but the city Shushan was perplexed.

IV. Deliverance through Mordecai and Esther (4:1—8:17)

4 When Mordecai perceived all that was done, Mordecai rent his clothes, and put on sackcloth with ashes, and went out into the midst of the city, and cried with a loud and a bitter cry;

2 And came even before the king's gate: for none *might* enter into the king's gate clothed with sackcloth.

3 And in every province, whithersoever the king's commandment and his decree came, *there was* great *mourning among the Jews, and fasting, and weeping, and wailing; and many lay in sackcloth and ashes.

¶4 So Esther's maids and her chamberlains came and told *it* her. Then was the queen exceedingly grieved; and she sent raiment to clothe Mordecai, and to take away his sackcloth from him: but he received *it* not.

5 Then called Esther for Hatach, *one* of the king's chamberlains, whom he had appointed to attend upon her, and gave him a commandment to Mordecai, to know what it *was*, and why it *was*.

6 So Hatach went forth to Mordecai unto the street of the city, which *was* before the king's gate.

7 And Mordecai told him of all that had happened unto him, and of the sum of the money that Haman had promised to pay to the king's treasuries for the Jews, to destroy them.

8 Also he gave him the copy of the writing of the decree that was given at *Shushan to destroy them, to shew *it* unto Esther, and to declare *it* unto her, and to charge her that she should go in unto the king, to make supplication unto him, and to make request before him for her people.

3:15 Special Messengers
Letters were carried by special messengers mounted on fast horses or camels. All over the vast empire were depots with supplies of horses for the use of royal messengers. At each depot a fresh messenger and a fresh horse took on the letter of dispatch. Even so, it took many months to reach the outer provinces, and this was why a date so long ahead as eleven months was chosen for the massacre.

3:13 Adar. From 9:24 we learn that Haman had picked this date by drawing lots.
4:7 the sum. See 3:9 note.

9 And Hatach came and told Esther
the words of Mordecai.

Esther's plan

¶ 10 Again Esther spake unto Hatach,
and gave him commandment unto Mordecai;
11 All the king's servants, and the
people of the king's provinces, do know,
that whosoever, whether man or woman, shall come unto the king into the
inner court, who is not called, *there is*
one law of his to put *him* to *death,
except such to whom the king shall hold
out the golden sceptre, that he may
live: but I have not been called to come
in unto the king these thirty days.
12 And they told to Mordecai Esther's
words.
13 Then Mordecai commanded to answer Esther, Think not with thyself that
thou shalt escape in the king's house,
more than all the Jews.
14 For if thou altogether holdest thy
peace at this time, *then* shall there enlargement and deliverance arise to the
Jews from another place; but thou and
thy father's house shall be destroyed: and
who knoweth whether thou art come to
the kingdom for *such* a time as this?
¶ 15 Then Esther bade *them* return
Mordecai *this answer,*
16 Go, gather together all the Jews
that are present in Shushan, and fast ye
for me, and neither eat nor drink three
days, night or day: I also and my maidens will fast likewise; and so will I go
in unto the king, which *is* not according
to the law: and if I perish, I perish.
17 So Mordecai went his way, and did
according to all that Esther had commanded him.

Esther's courage

5 Now it came to pass on the third
day, that Esther put on *her* royal
apparel, and stood in the inner court of
the king's house, over against the
king's house: and the king sat upon his
royal throne in the royal house, over
against the gate of the house.
2 And it was so, when the king saw Esther the queen standing in the court, *that*
she obtained favour in his sight: and the
king held out to Esther the golden sceptre
that *was* in his hand. So Esther drew
near, and touched the top of the sceptre.
3 Then said the king unto her, What
wilt thou, queen Esther? and what *is*
thy request? it shall be even given thee
to the half of the kingdom.
4 And Esther answered, If *it seem*
good unto the king, let the king and
Haman come this day unto the banquet
that I have prepared for him.
5 Then the king said, Cause Haman to
make haste, that he may do as Esther
hath said. So the king and Haman came
to the banquet that Esther had prepared.
¶ 6 And the king said unto Esther at
the banquet of wine, What *is* thy petition? and it shall be granted thee: and
what *is* thy request? even to the half of
the kingdom it shall be performed.
7 Then answered Esther, and said, My
petition and my request *is;*
8 If I have found favour in the sight of
the king, and if it please the king to
grant my petition, and to perform my
request, let the king and Haman come
to the banquet that I shall prepare for
them, and I will do to morrow as the
king hath said.
¶ 9 Then went Haman forth that day
joyful and with a glad heart: but when
Haman saw Mordecai in the king's gate,
that he stood not up, nor moved for
him, he was full of indignation against
Mordecai.
10 Nevertheless Haman refrained
himself: and when he came home, he
sent and called for his friends, and Zeresh his wife.
11 And Haman told them of the glory
of his riches, and the multitude of his
children, and all *the things* wherein the
king had promoted him, and how he had
advanced him above the princes and
servants of the king.
12 Haman said moreover, Yea, Esther
the queen did let no man come in with
the king unto the banquet that she had

prepared but myself; and to morrow am
I invited unto her also with the king.
13Yet all this availeth me nothing, so
long as I see Mordecai the Jew sitting
at the king's gate.
¶14Then said Zeresh his wife and all
his friends unto him, Let a gallows be
made of fifty *cubits high, and to morrow speak thou unto the king that Mordecai may be hanged thereon: then go
thou in merrily with the king unto the
banquet. And the thing pleased Haman;
and he caused the gallows to be made.

Mordecai honored

6 On that night could not the king
sleep, and he commanded to bring
the book of records of the chronicles;
and they were read before the king.
2And it was found written, that Mordecai had told of Bigthana and Teresh,
two of the king's chamberlains, the
keepers of the door, who sought to lay
hand on the king *Ahasuerus.
3And the king said, What honour and
dignity hath been done to Mordecai for
this? Then said the king's servants that
ministered unto him, There is nothing
done for him.
¶4And the king said, Who *is* in the
court? Now Haman was come into the outward court of the king's house, to speak
unto the king to hang Mordecai on the
gallows that he had prepared for him.
5And the king's servants said unto him,
Behold, Haman standeth in the court.
And the king said, Let him come in.
6So Haman came in. And the king
said unto him, What shall be done unto
the man whom the king delighteth to
honour? Now Haman thought in his
heart, To whom would the king delight
to do honour more than to myself?
7And Haman answered the king, For
the man whom the king delighteth to
honour,
8Let the royal apparel be brought
which the king *useth* to wear, and the
horse that the king rideth upon, and the
crown royal which is set upon his head:
9And let this apparel and horse be
delivered to the hand of one of the king's
most noble princes, that they may array
the man *withal* whom the king delighteth to honour, and bring him on
horseback through the street of the city,
and proclaim before him, Thus shall it
be done to the man whom the king
delighteth to honour.
10Then the king said to Haman, Make
haste, *and* take the apparel and the
horse, as thou hast said, and do even so
to Mordecai the Jew, that sitteth at the
king's gate: let nothing fail of all that
thou hast spoken.
11Then took Haman the apparel and
the horse, and arrayed Mordecai, and
brought him on horseback through the
street of the city, and proclaimed before
him, Thus shall it be done unto the man
whom the king delighteth to honour.
¶12And Mordecai came again to the
king's gate. But Haman hasted to his
house mourning, and having his head
covered.
13And Haman told Zeresh his wife
and all his friends every *thing* that had
befallen him. Then said his wise men
and Zeresh his wife unto him, If Mordecai *be* of the seed of the Jews, before
whom thou hast begun to fall, thou shalt
not prevail against him, but shalt surely fall before him.
14And while they *were* yet talking
with him, came the king's chamberlains, and hasted to bring Haman unto
the banquet that Esther had prepared.

Esther's banquet

7 So the king and Haman came to
banquet with Esther the queen.
2And the king said again unto Esther

6:1 chronicles. See 2:21-23.
6:8 crown royal. Probably the horse bore an emblem upon its head to show that it be-longed to the king; it is unlikely the king's crown was worn by another man.
7:1 banquet. In the Hebrew, it means *to drink.* The word "banquet" formerly meant only *dessert.*

on the second day at the banquet of wine, What *is* thy petition, queen Esther? and it shall be granted thee: and what *is* thy request? and it shall be performed, *even* to the half of the kingdom.

[3]Then Esther the queen answered and said, If I have found favour in thy sight, O king, and if it please the king, let my life be given me at my petition, and my people at my request:

[4]For we are sold, I and my people, to be destroyed, to be slain, and to perish. But if we had been sold for bondmen and bondwomen, I had held my tongue, although the enemy could not countervail the king's damage.

¶[5]Then the king Ahasuerus answered and said unto Esther the queen, Who is he, and where is he, that durst presume in his heart to do so?

[6]And Esther said, The adversary and enemy *is* this wicked Haman. Then Haman was afraid before the king and the queen.

¶[7]And the king arising from the banquet of wine in his wrath *went* into the palace garden: and Haman stood up to make request for his life to Esther the queen; for he saw that there was evil determined against him by the king.

[8]Then the king returned out of the palace garden into the place of the banquet of wine; and Haman was fallen upon the bed whereon Esther *was*. Then said the king, Will he force the queen also before me in the house? As the word went out of the king's mouth, they covered Haman's face.

[9]And Harbonah, one of the chamberlains, said before the king, Behold also, the gallows fifty cubits high, which Haman had made for Mordecai, who had spoken good for the king, standeth in the house of Haman. Then the king said, Hang him thereon.

[10]So they hanged Haman on the gallows that he had prepared for Mordecai. Then was the king's wrath pacified.

Protection for the Jews

8 On that day did the king Ahasuerus give the house of Haman the Jews' enemy unto Esther the queen. And Mordecai came before the king; for Esther had told what he *was* unto her.

[2]And the king took off his ring, which he had taken from Haman, and gave it unto Mordecai. And Esther set Mordecai over the house of Haman.

¶[3]And Esther spake yet again before the king, and fell down at his feet, and besought him with tears to put away the mischief of Haman the Agagite, and his device that he had devised against the Jews.

[4]Then the king held out the golden sceptre toward Esther. So Esther arose, and stood before the king,

[5]And said, If it please the king, and if I have found favour in his sight, and the thing *seem* right before the king, and I *be* pleasing in his eyes, let it be written to reverse the letters devised by Haman the son of Hammedatha the Agagite, which he wrote to destroy the Jews which *are* in all the king's provinces:

[6]For how can I endure to see the evil that shall come unto my people? or how can I endure to see the destruction of my kindred?

¶[7]Then the king Ahasuerus said unto Esther the queen and to Mordecai the Jew, Behold, I have given Esther the house of Haman, and him they have hanged upon the gallows, because he laid his hand upon the Jews.

[8]Write ye also for the Jews, as it liketh you, in the king's name, and seal *it* with the king's ring: for the writing which is

---

7:4 sold. For the price offered in 3:9.
7:4 countervail. To compensate for.
7:8 bed. At feasts the Persians reclined on ornamental couches such as 1:6 describes.
8:1 what he was unto her. It was safe now for Esther to confess that Mordecai the Jew was her cousin and guardian (2:7).

written in the king's name, and sealed
with the king's ring, may no man reverse.
9 Then were the king's scribes called
at that time in the third month, that *is,*
the month Sivan, on the three and twentieth *day* thereof; and it was written according to all that Mordecai commanded
unto the Jews, and to the lieutenants,
and the deputies and rulers of the provinces which *are* from India unto Ethiopia, an hundred twenty and seven
provinces, unto every province according to the writing thereof, and unto
every people after their language, and
to the Jews according to their writing,
and according to their language.
10 And he wrote in the king Ahasuerus' name, and sealed *it* with the king's
ring, and sent letters by posts on horseback, *and* riders on mules, camels, *and*
young dromedaries:
11 Wherein the king granted the Jews
which *were* in every city to gather
themselves together, and to stand for
their life, to destroy, to slay, and to
cause to perish, all the power of the
people and province that would assault
them, *both* little ones and women, and
to take the spoil of them for a prey,

8:11 Unchangeable Law
No law of the Medes and Persians was ever changed (see Dan. 6:8,12,15), so the king had to make another decree: that the Jewish people could defend themselves against the attack.

12 Upon one day in all the provinces
of king Ahasuerus, *namely,* upon the
thirteenth *day* of the twelfth month,
which *is* the month Adar.
13 The copy of the writing for a commandment to be given in every province *was* published unto all people, and
that the Jews should be ready against
that day to avenge themselves on their
enemies.
14 *So* the posts that rode upon mules
and camels went out, being hastened
and pressed on by the king's commandment. And the decree was given at
*Shushan the palace.
¶ 15 And Mordecai went out from the
presence of the king in royal apparel of
*blue and white, and with a great crown
of gold, and with a garment of fine *lin-
en and purple: and the city of Shushan
rejoiced and was glad.
16 The Jews had light, and gladness,
and joy, and honour.
17 And in every province, and in every
city, whithersoever the king's commandment and his decree came, the
Jews had joy and gladness, a feast and
a good day. And many of the people of
the land became Jews; for the fear of the
Jews fell upon them.

V. The Jews' Defense (9:1-32)

9 Now in the twelfth month, that *is,*
the month Adar, on the thirteenth
day of the same, when the king's commandment and his decree drew near to
be put in execution, in the day that the
enemies of the Jews hoped to have
power over them, (though it was turned
to the contrary, that the Jews had rule
over them that hated them;)
2 The Jews gathered themselves together in their cities throughout all the
provinces of the king *Ahasuerus, to
lay hand on such as sought their hurt:
and no man could withstand them; for
the fear of them fell upon all people.
3 And all the rulers of the provinces,
and the lieutenants, and the deputies,
and officers of the king, helped the
Jews; because the fear of Mordecai fell
upon them.
4 For Mordecai *was* great in the king's
house, and his fame went out throughout all the provinces: for this man Mordecai waxed greater and greater.
5 Thus the Jews smote all their enemies

9:5 all their enemies. It is thought that these were other captive peoples of the Persian Empire, as were the Jews, and not Persians, and so the emperor did not care if a number of them were killed.

with the stroke of the sword, and
slaughter, and destruction, and did what
they would unto those that hated them.
6And in Shushan the palace the Jews
slew and destroyed five hundred men.
7And Parshandatha, and Dalphon, and
Aspatha,
8And Poratha, and Adalia, and Arid-
atha,
9And Parmashta, and Arisai, and
Aridai, and Vajezatha,
10The ten sons of Haman the son of
Hammedatha, the enemy of the Jews,
slew they; but on the spoil laid they not
their hand.
11On that day the number of those
that were slain in Shushan the palace
was brought before the king.
¶12And the king said unto Esther the
queen, The Jews have slain and destroyed five hundred men in Shushan
the palace, and the ten sons of Haman;
what have they done in the rest of the
king's provinces? now what *is* thy petition? and it shall be granted thee: or
what *is* thy request further? and it shall
be done.
13Then said Esther, If it please the
king, let it be granted to the Jews which
are in Shushan to do to morrow also
according unto this day's decree, and let
Haman's ten sons be hanged upon the
gallows.
14And the king commanded it so to be
done: and the decree was given at
Shushan; and they hanged Haman's ten
sons.
15For the Jews that *were* in Shushan
gathered themselves together on the
fourteenth day also of the month Adar,
and slew three hundred men at
Shushan; but on the prey they laid not
their hand.
16But the other Jews that *were* in the
king's provinces gathered themselves
together, and stood for their lives, and
had rest from their enemies, and slew
of their foes seventy and five thousand,
but they laid not their hands on the prey,
17On the thirteenth day of the month
Adar; and on the fourteenth day of the
same rested they, and made it a day of
feasting and gladness.
18But the Jews that *were* at Shushan
assembled together on the thirteenth
day thereof, and on the fourteenth
thereof; and on the fifteenth *day* of the
same they rested, and made it a day of
feasting and gladness.
19Therefore the Jews of the villages,
that dwelt in the unwalled towns, made
the fourteenth day of the month Adar *a
day of* gladness and feasting, and a good
day, and of sending portions one to another.

Purim, the memorial feast

¶20And Mordecai wrote these things,
and sent letters unto all the Jews that
were in all the provinces of the king
Ahasuerus, *both* nigh and far,
21To stablish *this* among them, that
they should keep the fourteenth day of
the month Adar, and the fifteenth day
of the same, yearly,
22As the days wherein the Jews rested from their enemies, and the month
which was turned unto them from sorrow to joy, and from mourning into a
good day: that they should make them
days of feasting and joy, and of sending
portions one to another, and gifts to the
poor.
23And the Jews undertook to do as
they had begun, and as Mordecai had
written unto them;
24Because Haman the son of Hammedatha, the Agagite, the enemy of all
the Jews, had devised against the Jews
to destroy them, and had cast Pur, that
is, the lot, to consume them, and to
destroy them;

9:13 to do to morrow also. If the men in Shushan had not been destroyed, too, the Jews would have had no peace from terror. The ten sons of Haman were hanged. They too were the enemies of the Jews as was their father.

9:24 Pur. See 3:13 note.

9:24 The Feast of Purim
The Feast of Purim, or Lots, was instituted to commemorate the preservation of the Jews in Persia from the massacre with which they were threatened by the scheming of Haman (Esther 9:24-26). It began on the fourteenth day of the twelfth month, Adar (March), and lasted two days. It derived its name from the fact that Haman had cast lots to decide which day would be best for him to carry out the bloody decree that the king had issued at Haman's urgent request (9:24). After a preliminary fast on the thirteenth day of Adar, in memory of Esther's fast (4:16), the feast was celebrated with great rejoicing. The book of Esther was publicly read, and the name of Haman was cursed by young and old, along with noisy demonstrations of anger, contempt, and scorn.

25 But when *Esther* came before the king, he commanded by letters that his wicked device, which he devised against the Jews, should return upon his own head, and that he and his sons should be hanged on the gallows.

26 Wherefore they called these days Purim after the name of Pur. Therefore for all the words of this letter, and *of that* which they had seen concerning this matter, and which had come unto them,

27 The Jews ordained, and took upon them, and upon their seed, and upon all such as joined themselves unto them, so as it should not fail, that they would keep these two days according to their writing, and according to their *appointed* time every year;

28 And *that* these days *should be* remembered and kept throughout every generation, every family, every province, and every city; and *that* these days of Purim should not fail from among the Jews, nor the memorial of them perish from their seed.

29 Then Esther the queen, the daughter of Abihail, and Mordecai the Jew, wrote with all authority, to confirm this second letter of Purim.

30 And he sent the letters unto all the Jews, to the hundred twenty and seven provinces of the kingdom of Ahasuerus, *with* words of peace and truth,

31 To confirm these days of Purim in their times *appointed,* according as Mordecai the Jew and Esther the queen had enjoined them, and as they had decreed for themselves and for their seed, the matters of the fastings and their cry.

32 And the decree of Esther confirmed these matters of Purim; and it was written in the book.

VI. Mordecai's Fame (10:1-3)

10 And the king Ahasuerus laid a tribute upon the land, and *upon* the isles of the sea.

2 And all the acts of his power and of his might, and the declaration of the greatness of Mordecai, whereunto the king advanced him, *are* they not written in the book of the chronicles of the kings of Media and Persia?

3 For Mordecai the Jew *was* next unto king Ahasuerus, and great among the Jews, and accepted of the multitude of his brethren, seeking the wealth of his people, and speaking peace to all his seed.

9:31 fastings and their cry. This is described in 4:1,3.

The Book of

JOB

BACKGROUND

The book of Job is a drama or play in poetry about the things that happened in one year to a man named Job. We do not know who the author was, but the book was written in Hebrew, and is a literary masterpiece. The verses about animals and science are magnificent, and reveal the majesty and power of God in nature.

TIME

Job may well be the oldest book in the Bible, probably written before 1500 B.C. There is no mention, for example, of the laws which Exodus 19 and 20 tell that God gave Moses. Ezekiel refers to Job as a real person (Ezekiel 14:14–20), and James mentions his patience (James 5:11).

THEME

The problem of Job is, "Why do the righteous suffer and the wicked prosper?" Job was put to the test. His friends charged him with secret wickedness. He protested that he was innocent. All were silenced at last by God, who appeared as Judge and overwhelmed Job with a knowledge of his own nothingness and a sense of God's infinite power and wisdom.

OUTLINE OF JOB

I.	Introduction	Job 1:1—2:8
II.	Job Talks with His Wife	Job 2:9,10
III.	Job Talks with His Three Friends	Job 2:11—31:40
IV.	Job Talks with Elihu	Job 32:1—37:24
V.	God and Job	Job 38:1—41:34
VI.	Job's Last Answer	Job 42:1-6
VII.	Conclusion	Job 42:7-17

I. Introduction (1:1—2:8)

Job's character

1 There was a man in the land of Uz, whose name *was* Job; and that man was *perfect and upright, and one that *feared God, and eschewed evil.

Job's riches

2 And there were born unto him seven sons and three daughters.

3 His substance also was seven thousand sheep, and three thousand camels, and five hundred yoke of oxen, and five

1:1 Uz. A part of Edom and Idumea (Gen. 36:8; Lam. 4:21) south of the Dead Sea.

1:1 Job . . . was perfect and upright. Job's name means *one persecuted.* "Perfect" does not mean that he never sinned, because all human beings sin, but that he was in right relationship to God by fearing and trusting Him.

hundred she asses, and a very great
household; so that this man was the
greatest of all the men of the east.
4And his sons went and feasted *in
their* houses, every one his day; and
sent and called for their three sisters to
eat and to drink with them.

Job's devotion

5And it was so, when the days of *their*
feasting were gone about, that Job sent
and sanctified them, and rose up early
in the morning, and offered *burnt-
offerings *according* to the number of
them all: for Job said, It may be that
my sons have sinned, and cursed God
in their hearts. Thus did Job continually.

Satan's idea about the goodness of Job

¶6Now there was a day when the
sons of God came to present themselves before the LORD, and *Satan
came also among them.
7And the LORD said unto Satan,
Whence comest thou? Then Satan answered the LORD, and said, From going
to and fro in the earth, and from walking up and down in it.
8And the LORD said unto Satan, Hast
thou considered my servant Job, that
there is none like him in the earth, a
perfect and an upright man, one that
feareth God, and escheweth evil?
9Then Satan answered the LORD, and
said, Doth Job *fear God for nought?
10Hast not thou made an hedge
about him, and about his house, and
about all that he hath on every side?
thou hast blessed the work of his hands,
and his substance is increased in the
land.
11But put forth thine hand now, and
touch all that he hath, and he will curse
thee to thy face.

1:8 God's Control

"Hast thou considered my servant Job . . . ?" Job's troubles were not started by what Satan said but by the comment of God Himself. God knew that what Job needed was to really see himself. Satan was simply used by God to bring about His purpose. God left the means to Satan, and when Satan had used these up, proving nothing against Job (2:10), we hear no more of him in connection with Job. But God's purpose was not yet carried out–Job did not know his own heart. What Satan had failed to accomplish was brought about by the "sympathy" of Job's friends! Job was upright, but he began to focus on his own righteousness, proving that he had never truly and completely relied on God alone.

God allows Satan to test Job

12And the LORD said unto Satan, Behold, all that he hath *is* in thy power;
only upon himself put not forth thine
hand. So Satan went forth from the
presence of the LORD.
¶13And there was a day when his
sons and his daughters *were* eating and
drinking *wine in their eldest brother's
house:
14And there came a messenger unto
Job, and said, The oxen were plowing,
and the asses feeding beside them:
15And the Sabeans fell *upon them,* and
took them away; yea, they have slain
the servants with the edge of the
sword; and I only am escaped alone to
tell thee.
16While he *was* yet speaking, there
came also another, and said, The *fire
of God is fallen from *heaven, and hath
burned up the sheep, and the servants,
and consumed them; and I only am escaped alone to tell thee.
17While he *was* yet speaking, there
came also another, and said, The Chaldeans made out three bands, and fell

1:6 sons of God. *Angels.

1:14 there came a messenger. Satan has power over circumstances and over the elements if God allows it. This is a mystery of God. Satan used the common things of life to crush Job, such as the Sabeans (vs. 15), who were traveling traders; the lightning ("fire of God," vs. 16); the Chaldeans, roving robbers from the north (vs. 17); and a hurricane (vs. 19).

upon the camels, and have carried them
away, yea, and slain the servants with
the edge of the sword; and I only am
escaped alone to tell thee.
[18]While he *was* yet speaking, there
came also another, and said, Thy sons
and thy daughters *were* eating and drinking wine in their eldest brother's house:
[19]And, behold, there came a great
wind from the wilderness, and smote
the four corners of the house, and it
fell upon the young men, and they are
dead; and I only am escaped alone to tell
thee.
[20]Then Job arose, and rent his mantle, and shaved his head, and fell down
upon the ground, and worshipped,
[21]And said, Naked came I out of my
mother's womb, and naked shall I return thither: the LORD gave, and the
LORD hath taken away; blessed be the
name of the LORD.
[22]In all this Job sinned not, nor
charged God foolishly.

God allows Satan to test Job further

2 Again there was a day when the
sons of God came to present themselves before the LORD, and Satan came
also among them to present himself
before the LORD.
[2]And the LORD said unto Satan, From
whence comest thou? And Satan answered the LORD, and said, From going
to and fro in the earth, and from walking up and down in it.
[3]And the LORD said unto Satan, Hast
thou considered my servant Job, that
there is none like him in the earth, a
perfect and an upright man, one that
feareth God, and escheweth evil? and
still he holdeth fast his integrity, although thou movedst me against him,
to destroy him without cause.
[4]And Satan answered the LORD, and
said, Skin for skin, yea, all that a man
hath will he give for his life.
[5]But put forth thine hand now, and
touch his bone and his flesh, and he will
curse thee to thy face.
[6]And the LORD said unto Satan, Behold, he *is* in thine hand; but save his
life.
¶[7]So went Satan forth from the presence of the LORD, and smote Job with
sore boils from the sole of his foot unto
his crown.
[8]And he took him a potsherd to scrape
himself withal; and he sat down among
the ashes.

II. Job Talks with His Wife (2:9,10)

¶[9]Then said his wife unto him, Dost
thou still retain thine integrity? curse
God, and die.
[10]But he said unto her, Thou
speakest as one of the foolish women
speaketh. What? shall we receive good
at the hand of God, and shall we not
receive evil? In all this did not Job *sin
with his lips.

III. Job to His Friends (2:11—31:40)

¶[11]Now when Job's three friends
heard of all this evil that was come upon
him, they came every one from his own
place; Eliphaz the Temanite, and Bildad
the Shuhite, and Zophar the Naamathite: for they had made an appointment
together to come to mourn with him
and to comfort him.
[12]And when they lifted up their eyes
afar off, and knew him not, they lifted
up their voice, and wept; and they rent
every one his mantle, and sprinkled
dust upon their heads toward heaven.
[13]So they sat down with him upon the
ground seven days and seven nights,

1:20 rent his mantle. Job performed the customary mourning, and his prayer (vs. 21) shows his complete trust in God and admits God's right to take away his blessings according to His own purpose.
2:2 From going to and fro. Satan has the freedom to roam the whole universe.
2:8 potsherd. A piece of broken earthenware or pottery.
2:9 curse God, and die. Job's wife acted according to Satan's ideas, but Job did not.
2:10 evil. Disaster or illness (affliction).

and none spake a word unto him: for
they saw that *his* grief was very great.

Job's first speech

1) He wished never to have been born

3 After this opened Job his mouth,
and cursed his day.
[2]And Job spake, and said,
[3]Let the day perish wherein I was
born, and the night *in which* it was said,
There is a man child conceived.
[4]Let that day be darkness; let not
God regard it from above, neither let
the light shine upon it.
[5]Let darkness and the shadow of
*death stain it; let a cloud dwell upon it;
let the blackness of the day terrify it.
[6]*As for* that night, let darkness seize
upon it; let it not be joined unto the days
of the year, let it not come into the number of the months.
[7]Lo, let that night be solitary, let no
joyful voice come therein.
[8]Let them curse it that curse the day,
who are ready to raise up their *mourning.
[9]Let the stars of the twilight thereof be
dark; let it look for light, but *have* none;
neither let it see the dawning of the day:
[10]Because it shut not up the doors of
my *mother's* womb, nor hid sorrow from
mine eyes.

2) He wished to have died at birth

[11]Why died I not from the womb? *why*
did I *not* give up the ghost when I came
out of the belly?
[12]Why did the knees prevent me? or
why the breasts that I should suck?
[13]For now should I have lain still and
been quiet, I should have slept: then
had I been at rest,
[14]With kings and counsellors of the
earth, which built desolate places for
themselves;
[15]Or with princes that had gold, who
filled their houses with silver:
[16]Or as an hidden untimely birth I had
not been; as infants *which* never saw
light.
[17]There the wicked cease *from* troubling; and there the weary be at rest.
[18]*There* the prisoners rest together;
they hear not the voice of the oppressor.
[19]The small and great are there; and
the servant *is* free from his master.

3) He wondered why the sad had to live

[20]Wherefore is light given to him that
is in misery, and life unto the bitter *in*
soul;
[21]Which long for death, but it *cometh*
not; and dig for it more than for hid treasures;

2:11-13 JOB'S THREE FRIENDS

Job's friends were from different parts of Arabia: Eliphaz from Teman, in Edom; Bildad from Shuah, east of Palestine; and Zophar from Naamah, a small town in southwestern Judah.

Eliphaz first spoke in chapter 4. His hometown, Teman, was famous for the wisdom of its inhabitants, as we see from Obadiah 8-9 and Jeremiah 49:7. Eliphaz felt superior because of a mysterious vision, described in Job 4:12-16. Although many of the things Eliphaz said about the majesty and purity of God were true, he was hard and cold and arrogant, speaking only from his one remarkable experience, not from any real knowledge of God.

Bildad, who speaks first in chapter 8, was positive but not a good thinker, because his religion was based on what others had said. His arguments were true enough, but there was nothing new in them, and they were not at all helpful to Job's problem.

Zophar, first heard from in chapter 11, was a man of strong personal religious ideas who thought that he knew all about God and His ways. He was impatient and unreasonable with anyone who did not agree with him.

3:12 knees prevent me. This means knees *receive* me. In countries of the East, the father holds the newborn baby upon his knees as if to say, "This baby is mine and I shall care for him and protect him."

3:16 light. Life.

22 Which rejoice exceedingly, *and* are glad, when they can find the grave?

23 *Why is light given* to a man whose way is hid, and whom God hath hedged in?

24 For my sighing cometh before I eat, and my roarings are poured out like the waters.

25 For the thing which I greatly feared is come upon me, and that which I was afraid of is come unto me.

26 I was not in safety, neither had I rest, neither was I quiet; yet trouble came.

First speech of Eliphaz
1) Job, once a comforter, was now comfortless

4 Then Eliphaz the Temanite answered and said,

2 *If* we assay to commune with thee, wilt thou be grieved? but who can withhold himself from speaking?

3 Behold, thou hast instructed many, and thou hast strengthened the weak hands.

4 Thy words have upholden him that was falling, and thou hast strengthened the feeble knees.

5 But now it is come upon thee, and thou faintest; it toucheth thee, and thou art troubled.

6 *Is* not *this* thy fear, thy confidence, thy *hope, and the uprightness of thy ways?

7 Remember, I pray thee, who *ever* perished, being innocent? or where were the righteous cut off?

8 Even as I have seen, they that plow iniquity, and sow wickedness, reap the same.

9 By the blast of God they perish, and by the breath of his nostrils are they consumed.

10 The roaring of the lion, and the voice of the fierce lion, and the teeth of the young lions, are broken.

11 The old lion perisheth for lack of prey, and the stout lion's whelps are scattered abroad.

2) Eliphaz describes his vision

12 Now a thing was secretly brought to me, and mine ear received a little thereof.

13 In thoughts from the visions of the night, when deep sleep falleth on men,

14 Fear came upon me, and trembling, which made all my bones to shake.

15 Then a spirit passed before my face; the hair of my flesh stood up:

16 It stood still, but I could not discern the form thereof: an image *was* before mine eyes, *there was* silence, and I heard a voice, *saying,*

17 Shall mortal man be more *just than God? shall a man be more pure than his maker?

18 Behold, he put no *trust in his servants; and his *angels he charged with folly:

19 How much less *in* them that dwell in houses of clay, whose foundation *is* in the dust, *which* are crushed before the moth?

20 They are destroyed from morning to evening: they perish for ever without any regarding *it.*

21 Doth not their excellency *which is* in them go away? they die, even without wisdom.

3) Eliphaz continues his first speech

5 Call now, if there be any that will answer thee; and to which of the *saints wilt thou turn?

4:5 it is come upon thee. Disaster has come upon you (Job).
4:9 breath of his nostrils. God's breath is seen as a destroying wind also in Psalm 18:15; Isaiah 11:4; 30:33; 40:7.
4:10 The roaring of the lion. Eliphaz argued that wicked men, though they be as strong as lions, can be helpless before God's judgment and justice.
4:12 a little. A little sound, a whisper.
4:19 crushed before the moth. Crushed more easily or more quickly than a moth.
5:1 to which of the saints wilt thou turn? The argument is that it is absolutely useless to pray to holy people or to angels—they cannot answer or help. See Job 4:18.

[2]For wrath killeth the foolish man,
and envy slayeth the silly one.

4) Job should seek God

[3]I have seen the foolish taking root:
but suddenly I cursed his habitation.
[4]His children are far from safety, and
they are crushed in the gate, neither *is*
there any to deliver *them.*
[5]Whose harvest the hungry eateth
up, and taketh it even out of the thorns,
and the robber swalloweth up their substance.
[6]Although affliction cometh not forth
of the dust, neither doth trouble spring
out of the ground;
[7]Yet man is born unto trouble, as the
sparks fly upward.
[8]I would seek unto God, and unto
God would I commit my cause:
[9]Which doeth great things and unsearchable; marvellous things without
number:
[10]Who giveth rain upon the earth, and
sendeth waters upon the fields:
[11]To set up on high those that be low;
that those which mourn may be exalted to safety.
[12]He disappointeth the devices of the
crafty, so that their hands cannot perform *their* enterprise.
[13]He taketh the wise in their own
craftiness: and the counsel of the *froward is carried headlong.
[14]They meet with darkness in the
daytime, and grope in the noonday as in
the night.
[15]But he saveth the poor from the
sword, from their mouth, and from the
hand of the mighty.
[16]So the poor hath hope, and iniquity
stoppeth her mouth.
[17]Behold, happy *is* the man whom
God correcteth: therefore despise not
thou the chastening of the Almighty:
[18]For he maketh sore, and bindeth up:
he woundeth, and his hands make
whole.
[19]He shall deliver thee in six troubles: yea, in seven there shall no evil
touch thee.
[20]In famine he shall *redeem thee
from death: and in war from the power
of the sword.
[21]Thou shalt be hid from the scourge
of the tongue: neither shalt thou be
afraid of destruction when it cometh.
[22]At destruction and famine thou
shalt laugh: neither shalt thou be afraid
of the beasts of the earth.
[23]For thou shalt be in league with the
stones of the field: and the beasts of the
field shall be at *peace with thee.
[24]And thou shalt know that thy tabernacle *shall be* in peace; and thou
shalt visit thy habitation, and shalt
not sin.
[25]Thou shalt know also that thy seed
shall be great, and thine offspring as the
grass of the earth.
[26]Thou shalt come to *thy* grave in a
full age, like as a shock of corn cometh
in in his season.
[27]Lo this, we have searched it, so it
is; hear it, and know thou *it* for thy
good.

Job's answer to Eliphaz

1) He defended his bitterness

6 But Job answered and said,
[2]O that my grief were throughly
weighed, and my calamity laid in the
balances together!
[3]For now it would be heavier than the
sand of the sea: therefore my words are
swallowed up.

5:17 despise not thou the chastening of the Almighty. Other Scriptures with this thought are Proverbs 3:11-12 (see also its note, "The Chastening of the LORD"); Hebrews 12:5-11; Revelation 3:19.

5:18 he maketh sore, and bindeth up. Compare this verse with Deuteronomy 32:39 and Hosea 6:1.

5:19 in six troubles: yea, in seven. That is, in all successive troubles, no matter how many. Note the seven that are given in verses 20-23: famine, war, slander, destruction, pestilence, beasts of the earth, beasts of the field.

4 For the arrows of the Almighty *are*
within me, the poison whereof drinketh
up my spirit: the terrors of God do set
themselves in array against me.
5 Doth the wild ass bray when he hath
grass? or loweth the ox over his fodder?
6 Can that which is unsavoury be eat-
en without salt? or is there *any* taste in
the white of an egg?
7 The things *that* my soul refused to
touch *are* as my sorrowful meat.
8 Oh that I might have my request;
and that God would grant *me* the thing
that I long for!
9 Even that it would please God to
destroy me; that he would let loose his
hand, and cut me off!
10 Then should I yet have comfort;
yea, I would *harden myself in sorrow:
let him not spare; for I have not concealed the words of the *Holy One.
11 What *is* my strength, that I should
hope? and what *is* mine end, that I
should prolong my life?
12 *Is* my strength the strength of
stones? or *is* my flesh of brass?
13 *Is* not my help in me? and is wisdom
driven quite from me?

2) He was sorry for the attitudes of his friends

14 To him that is afflicted pity *should
be shewed* from his friend; but he
forsaketh the fear of the Almighty.
15 My brethren have dealt deceitfully
as a brook, *and* as the stream of brooks
they pass away;
16 Which are blackish by reason of the
ice, *and* wherein the snow is hid:
17 What time they wax warm, they
vanish: when it is hot, they are consumed out of their place.
18 The paths of their way are turned
aside; they go to nothing, and perish.
19 The troops of Tema looked, the
companies of Sheba waited for them.
20 They were confounded because
they had hoped; they came thither, and
were ashamed.
21 For now ye are nothing; ye see *my*
casting down, and are afraid.
22 Did I say, Bring unto me? or, Give
a reward for me of your substance?
23 Or, Deliver me from the enemy's
hand? or, Redeem me from the hand of
the mighty?
24 Teach me, and I will hold my
tongue: and cause me to understand
wherein I have erred.
25 How forcible are right words! but
what doth your arguing reprove?
26 Do ye imagine to reprove words,
and the speeches of one that is desperate, *which are* as wind?
27 Yea, ye overwhelm the fatherless,
and ye dig *a pit* for your friend.
28 Now therefore be content, look
upon me; for *it is* evident unto you if
I lie.
29 Return, I pray you, let it not be iniquity; yea, return again, my *righteousness *is* in it.
30 Is there iniquity in my tongue? cannot my taste discern perverse things?

3) Appeal against God's treatment of him

7 *Is there* not an appointed time to
man upon earth? *are not* his days
also like the days of an hireling?
2 As a servant earnestly desireth the
shadow, and as an hireling looketh for
the reward of his work:

6:15 A Comparison
Job likened his friends ("my brethren") to the little brooks that are rushing torrents in the winter but that dry up under the summer sun, cheating the hopes of travelers who look for water there and perish in the desert.

6:4 of the Almighty . . . of God. The afflictions themselves did not terrify Job as much as the fact that Job thought they came from God. Like Job, we may never know where the arrows come from, but we still must deal with them.

6:23 Redeem me from the hand of the mighty. That is, buy me back from the kidnapper, who holds his captives for ransom.

7:1 an appointed time. The length of a life.

3So am I made to possess months of
*vanity, and wearisome nights are ap-
pointed to me.
4When I lie down, I say, When shall I
arise, and the night be gone? and I am
full of tossings to and fro unto the dawning of the day.
5My flesh is clothed with worms and
clods of dust; my skin is broken, and
become loathsome.
6My days are swifter than a weaver's
shuttle, and are spent without hope.
7O remember that my life *is* wind:
mine eye shall no more see good.
8The eye of him that hath seen me
shall see me no *more:* thine eyes *are*
upon me, and I *am* not.
9*As* the cloud is consumed and vanisheth away: so he that goeth down to
the grave shall come up no *more.*
10He shall return no more to his
house, neither shall his place know him
any more.
11Therefore I will not refrain my
mouth; I will speak in the anguish of my
spirit; I will complain in the bitterness
of my soul.
12*Am* I a sea, or a whale, that thou
settest a watch over me?
13When I say, My bed shall comfort
me, my couch shall ease my complaint;
14Then thou scarest me with dreams,
and terrifiest me through visions:
15So that my soul chooseth stran-
gling, *and* death rather than my life.
16I loathe *it;* I would not live alway:
let me alone; for my days *are* vanity.
17What *is* man, that thou shouldest
magnify him? and that thou shouldest
set thine heart upon him?
18And *that* thou shouldest visit him
every morning, *and* try him every moment?
19How long wilt thou not depart from
me, nor let me alone till I swallow down
my spittle?
20I have sinned; what shall I do unto
thee, O thou preserver of men? why
hast thou set me as a mark against thee,
so that I am a burden to myself?
21And why dost thou not pardon my
transgression, and take away mine iniquity? for now shall I sleep in the dust;
and thou shalt seek me in the morning,
but I *shall* not *be.*

Bildad's first speech

*1) Job's need of *repentance*

8 Then answered Bildad the Shuhite, and said,
2How long wilt thou speak these
things? and *how long shall* the words of
thy mouth *be like* a strong wind?
3Doth *God pervert *judgment? or
doth the Almighty pervert justice?
4If thy children have sinned against
him, and he have cast them away for
their transgression;
5If thou wouldest seek unto God betimes, and make thy supplication to the
Almighty;
6If thou *wert* pure and upright; surely now he would awake for thee, and
make the habitation of thy righteousness prosperous.
7Though thy beginning was small,
yet thy latter end should greatly increase.

2) Appeal to the wisdom of the ancients

8For enquire, I pray thee, of the former age, and prepare thyself to the
search of their fathers:
9(For we *are but of* yesterday, and
know nothing, because our days upon
earth *are* a shadow:)
10Shall not they teach thee, *and* tell
thee, and utter words out of their heart?

7:3 vanity. Misery.
7:9 grave. Hades; see *hell.
7:9 shall come up no more. This does not speak of resurrection but means that a man who has died cannot come back to life to live and work as before.
7:19 till I swallow. This phrase was used as one would say today, "Just for a minute," or "Just let me take a breath."
7:21 sleep. Death. This would be a release and sign of God's grace, as Job says in 6:8-10.

8:11 Egyptian Sayings
"Can the rush . . . ? can the flag . . . ?" These were sayings, probably Egyptian, to illustrate that without a proper foundation things will not prosper in this world. The rush was probably the papyrus reed; the flag was the Nile reed–both plants of Egypt.

11Can the rush grow up without
mire? can the flag grow without water?
12Whilst it *is* yet in his greenness,
and not cut down, it withereth before
any *other* herb.
13So *are* the paths of all that forget
God; and the hypocrite's hope shall
perish:
14Whose hope shall be cut off, and
whose trust *shall be* a spider's web.
15He shall lean upon his house, but it
shall not stand: he shall hold it fast, but
it shall not endure.
16He *is* green before the sun, and his
branch shooteth forth in his garden.
17His roots are wrapped about the
heap, *and* seeth the place of stones.
18If he destroy him from his place,
then *it* shall deny him, *saying,* I have not
seen thee.
19Behold, this *is* the joy of his way,
and out of the earth shall others grow.

3) Prophecy of a happy future for Job

20Behold, God will not cast away a
*perfect *man,* neither will he help the
evil doers:
21Till he fill thy mouth with laughing,
and thy lips with rejoicing.
22They that hate thee shall be clothed
with shame; and the dwelling place of
the wicked shall come to nought.

Job's answer to Bildad
1) God's power kept man from proving his innocence

9 Then Job answered and said,
2I know *it is* so of a truth: but how
should man be just with God?
3If he will contend with him, he cannot answer him one of a thousand.
4*He is* wise in heart, and mighty in
strength: who hath hardened *himself*
against him, and hath prospered?
5Which removeth the mountains, and
they know not: which overturneth
them in his anger.
6Which shaketh the earth out of her
place, and the pillars thereof tremble.
7Which commandeth the sun, and it
riseth not; and sealeth up the stars.
8Which alone spreadeth out the heavens, and treadeth upon the waves of
the sea.
9Which maketh Arcturus, Orion, and
Pleiades, and the chambers of the south.
10Which doeth great things past
finding out; yea, and wonders without
number.
11Lo, he goeth by me, and I see *him*
not: he passeth on also, but I perceive
him not.
12Behold, he taketh away, who can
hinder him? who will say unto him,
What doest thou?
13*If* God will not withdraw his anger,
the proud helpers do stoop under him.
14How much less shall I answer

8:17 seeth the place of stones. That is, according to Bildad, Job's roots are in the stony surface soil.
8:18 I have not seen thee. The shoot makes no lasting impression. It disappears, and even the place in which it grew for a while knows nothing of it. So the wicked perish without a trace.
8:22 clothed with shame. See also Psalm 35:26.
9:2 just. As in Psalm 143:2 and Romans 3:20-28; 5:1, man cannot be justified before God, except through faith. Job was using words typical of a lawsuit, such as "contend" (vs. 3), "answer" (vs. 14), "judge" (vs. 15), etc.
9:9 chambers of the south. This speaks probably of the whole Southern Hemisphere of the heavens, containing the fixed places of certain brilliant stars or constellations, which become visible as one journeys south; for instance, the Southern Cross.
9:13 If God will not withdraw. Rather, *God will not withdraw.*

him, *and* choose out my words *to rea-*
son with him?
15 Whom, though I were righteous, *yet*
would I not answer, *but* I would make
supplication to my judge.
16 If I had called, and he had answered
me; *yet* would I not believe that he had
hearkened unto my voice.
17 For he breaketh me with a tempest,
and multiplieth my wounds without
cause.
18 He will not suffer me to take my
breath, but filleth me with bitterness.
19 If *I speak* of strength, lo, *he is*
strong: and if of judgment, who shall set
me a time *to plead?*
20 If I justify myself, mine own mouth
shall condemn me: *if I say,* I *am* perfect,
it shall also *prove me perverse.
21 *Though* I *were* perfect, *yet* would I not
know my soul: I would despise my life.
22 This *is* one *thing,* therefore I said
it, He destroyeth the perfect and the
wicked.
23 If the scourge slay suddenly, he will
laugh at the trial of the innocent.
24 The earth is given into the hand of
the wicked: he covereth the faces of the
judges thereof; if not, where, *and* who
is he?
25 Now my days are swifter than a
post: they flee away, they see no good.
26 They are passed away as the swift
ships: as the eagle that hasteth to the
prey.
27 If I say, I will forget my complaint,
I will leave off my heaviness, and comfort *myself:*
28 I am afraid of all my sorrows, I know
that thou wilt not hold me innocent.
29 *If* I be wicked, why then labour I in
vain?
30 If I wash myself with snow water,
and make my hands never so *clean;
31 Yet shalt thou plunge me in the
ditch, and mine own clothes shall abhor me.
32 For *he is* not a man, as I *am, that* I
should answer him, *and* we should
come together in judgment.
33 Neither is there any daysman betwixt us, *that* might lay his hand upon
us both.
34 Let him take his rod away from me,
and let not his fear terrify me:
35 *Then* would I speak, and not fear
him; but *it is* not so with me.

2) Job's attempt to find God's reason for his troubles

10 My soul is weary of my life; I
will leave my complaint upon
myself; I will speak in the bitterness of
my soul.
2 I will say unto God, Do not condemn
me; shew me wherefore thou contendest
with me.
3 *Is it* good unto thee that thou
shouldest oppress, that thou shouldest
despise the work of thine hands, and
shine upon the counsel of the wicked?
4 Hast thou eyes of *flesh? or seest
thou as man seeth?
5 *Are* thy days as the days of man? *are*
thy years as man's days,

9:26 Swift Ships
Rafts or ships of reed. These skiffs, made partly of wood and partly of reeds, are the vessels of bulrushes of Isaiah 18:2. They carried only one or two and, since they were light, were extremely fast. Job was saying that his days were passing as quickly as swift ships.

9:20 perfect. Here and in verse 22; see note on 1:1. Job meant, "I set my life as nothing."
9:23 scourge. Evidently an epidemic or plague. Any general calamity such as this was thought to be sent of God.
9:24 he covereth the faces of the judges. The judges were blind to what was right.
9:33 daysman. Literally, *the one who reproves,* or the one who stands between two contending parties and reconciles them. No one could stand thus between God and man until the Lord Jesus Christ came to be the Daysman or Mediator (1 Tim. 2:5).
10:4 seest thou as man seeth? The questions in verses 4 and 5 are answered in 1 Samuel 16:7 and Psalms 90 and 102:24-26.

6 That thou enquirest after mine iniquity, and searchest after my *sin?
7 Thou knowest that I am not wicked;
and *there is* none that can deliver out of
thine hand.
8 Thine hands have made me and
fashioned me together round about; yet
thou dost destroy me.
9 Remember, I beseech thee, that
thou hast made me as the clay; and wilt
thou bring me into dust again?
10 Hast thou not poured me out as
milk, and curdled me like cheese?
11 Thou hast clothed me with skin and
flesh, and hast fenced me with bones
and sinews.
12 Thou hast granted me life and
favour, and thy visitation hath preserved my spirit.
13 And these *things* hast thou hid in
thine heart: I know that this *is* with thee.
14 If I sin, then thou markest me, and
thou wilt not acquit me from mine iniquity.
15 If I be wicked, woe unto me; and *if*
I be righteous, *yet* will I not lift up my
head. *I am* full of confusion; therefore
see thou mine affliction;
16 For it increaseth. Thou huntest me
as a fierce lion: and again thou shewest
thyself marvellous upon me.
17 Thou renewest thy witnesses
against me, and increasest thine indignation upon me; changes and war *are*
against me.
18 Wherefore then hast thou brought
me forth out of the womb? Oh that I
had given up the ghost, and no eye had
seen me!
19 I should have been as though I had
not been; I should have been carried
from the womb to the grave.
20 *Are* not my days few? cease *then,*
and let me alone, that I may take comfort a little,

10:21 The Concept of Death
"The land of darkness" represents the thinking of Job's time about life after death, but Job had a hope of the Resurrection (Job 19:25-27; see vs. 25 note, "Job's Redeemer"). Contrast this verse with our present joyful hope (1 Thess. 4:16-17; 1 Cor. 15; see vs. 52 note, "A Final Resurrection").

21 Before I go *whence* I shall not return, *even* to the land of darkness and
the shadow of *death;
22 A land of darkness, as darkness *it-*
self; and of the shadow of death, without any order, and *where* the light *is* as
darkness.

Zophar's first speech
1) He wanted God to show Job His wisdom

11 Then answered Zophar the Naamathite, and said,
2 Should not the multitude of words
be answered? and should a man full of
talk be justified?
3 Should thy lies make men hold their
peace? and when thou mockest, shall no
man make thee ashamed?
4 For thou hast said, My *doctrine *is*
pure, and I am clean in thine eyes.
5 But oh that God would speak, and
open his lips against thee;
6 And that he would shew thee the
secrets of wisdom, that *they are* double
to that which is! Know therefore that
God exacteth of thee *less* than thine
iniquity *deserveth.*

2) God sends trouble upon men in punishment

7 Canst thou by searching find out
God? canst thou find out the Almighty
unto perfection?
8 *It is* as high as *heaven; what canst

11:6 double. Divine wisdom is different than human insight; there are two sides to it: an outward or superficial side that man can see; and an inner, hidden side, known only to God.
11:7 Canst thou . . . ? See Ecclesiastes 3:11 and Psalm 139.
11:8 It. This refers to the knowledge of God.

thou do? deeper than *hell; what canst
thou know?
[9]The measure thereof *is* longer than
the earth, and broader than the sea.
[10]If he cut off, and shut up, or gather
together, then who can hinder him?
[11]For he knoweth vain men: he seeth
wickedness also; will he not then consider *it?*
[12]For vain man would be wise, though
man be born *like* a wild ass's colt.

3) Zophar begged Job to stop sinning

[13]If thou prepare thine heart, and
stretch out thine hands toward him;
[14]If iniquity *be* in thine hand, put it far
away, and let not wickedness dwell in
thy tabernacles.
[15]For then shalt thou lift up thy face
without spot; yea, thou shalt be stedfast, and shalt not fear:
[16]Because thou shalt forget *thy* misery, *and* remember *it* as waters *that*
pass away:
[17]And *thine* age shall be clearer than
the noonday; thou shalt shine forth,
thou shalt be as the morning.
[18]And thou shalt be secure, because
there is *hope; yea, thou shalt dig
about thee, and thou shalt take thy rest
in safety.
[19]Also thou shalt lie down, and none
shall make *thee* afraid; yea, many shall
make suit unto thee.
[20]But the eyes of the wicked shall fail,
and they shall not escape, and their
hope *shall be as* the giving up of the
ghost.

Job answers his three friends
1) He disliked their attitudes of great wisdom

12 And Job answered and said,
[2]No doubt but ye *are* the people,
and wisdom shall die with you.
[3]But I have understanding as well as
you; I *am* not inferior to you: yea, who
knoweth not such things as these?
[4]I am *as* one mocked of his neighbour, who calleth upon God, and he
answereth him: the *just upright *man*
is laughed to scorn.
[5]He that is ready to slip with *his* feet
is as a lamp despised in the thought of
him that is at ease.
[6]The tabernacles of robbers prosper,
and they that provoke God are secure;
into whose hand God bringeth *abundantly.*
[7]But ask now the beasts, and they
shall teach thee; and the fowls of the air,
and they shall tell thee:
[8]Or speak to the earth, and it shall
teach thee: and the fishes of the sea
shall declare unto thee.
[9]Who knoweth not in all these that
the hand of the LORD hath wrought
this?
[10]In whose hand *is* the soul of every
living thing, and the breath of all mankind.
[11]Doth not the ear try words? and the
mouth taste his meat?
[12]With the ancient *is* wisdom; and in
length of days understanding.
[13]With him *is* wisdom and strength,
he hath counsel and understanding.
[14]Behold, he breaketh down, and it

11:17 age. Lifetime, as in Psalm 39:5.
11:17 noonday. As contrasted with dawn, noon is the time of fullest and steadiest light.
11:19 make suit unto thee. Literally, *stroke thy face;* that is, *flatter* or *entreat,* as in Proverbs 19:6.
11:20 the eyes of the wicked shall fail. The good fortune that the wicked think they are going to have will never really come.
11:20 giving up of the ghost. To breathe the last breath.
12:5 as a lamp despised. Those who thought they were safe spiritually felt no need for a lamp or a light for their way; those who were wise realized they needed God's light to help them along the way. See 1 Corinthians 10:12.
12:13 With him. That is, with God.

cannot be built again: he shutteth up a man, and there can be no opening.

15 Behold, he withholdeth the waters, and they dry up: also he sendeth them out, and they overturn the earth.

16 With him *is* strength and wisdom: the deceived and the deceiver *are* his.

17 He leadeth counsellors away spoiled, and maketh the judges *fools.

18 He looseth the bond of kings, and girdeth their loins with a girdle.

19 He leadeth princes away spoiled, and overthroweth the mighty.

20 He removeth away the speech of the trusty, and taketh away the understanding of the aged.

21 He poureth contempt upon princes, and weakeneth the strength of the mighty.

22 He discovereth deep things out of darkness, and bringeth out to light the shadow of death.

23 He increaseth the nations, and destroyeth them: he enlargeth the nations, and straiteneth them *again.*

24 He taketh away the heart of the chief of the people of the earth, and causeth them to wander in a wilderness *where there is* no way.

25 They grope in the dark without light, and he maketh them to stagger like *a* drunken *man.*

2) Job wanted to speak with God

13 Lo, mine eye hath seen all *this,* mine ear hath heard and understood it.

2 What ye know, *the same* do I know also: I *am* not inferior unto you.

3 Surely I would speak to the Almighty, and I desire to reason with God.

4 But ye *are* forgers of lies, ye *are* all physicians of no value.

5 Oh that ye would altogether hold your peace! and it should be your wisdom.

6 Hear now my reasoning, and hearken to the pleadings of my lips.

7 Will ye speak wickedly for God? and talk deceitfully for him?

8 Will ye accept his person? will ye contend for God?

9 Is it good that he should search you out? or as one man mocketh another, do ye *so* mock him?

10 He will surely reprove you, if ye do secretly accept persons.

11 Shall not his excellency make you afraid? and his dread fall upon you?

12 Your remembrances *are* like unto ashes, your bodies to bodies of clay.

13 Hold your peace, let me alone, that I may speak, and let come on me what *will.*

14 Wherefore do I take my flesh in my teeth, and put my life in mine hand?

15 Though he slay me, yet will I *trust in him: but I will maintain mine own ways before him.

16 He also *shall be* my *salvation: for an hypocrite shall not come before him.

17 Hear diligently my speech, and my declaration with your ears.

18 Behold now, I have ordered *my* cause; I know that I shall be justified.

19 Who *is* he *that* will plead with me? for now, if I hold my tongue, I shall give up the ghost.

12:17 spoiled. Plundered. The word is translated "stripped" in Micah 1:8, meaning deprived of outer garments and clothed as slaves and captives.

12:18 with a girdle. Job spoke here of kings being tied with ropes and led into captivity.

12:20 trusty. Eloquent.

12:20 aged. Elders, whose wisdom was their distinguishing characteristic.

12:21 weakeneth the strength of the mighty. Literally, *looseth the girdle of the strong.* The garments were tied up for active labor or battle, so to loose the girdle meant to make unfit to work or fight, as in Isaiah 5:27.

12:24 chief. Most important.

13:1 all this. This means all that Job had been speaking in 12:7-25. He repeated that changes in fortune are due to God.

13:15 Though he slay me. Job maintained his trust and hope in God. Compare with Psalm 23:4.

[20]Only do not two *things* unto me:
then will I not hide myself from thee.
[21]Withdraw thine hand far from me:
and let not thy dread make me afraid.
[22]Then call thou, and I will answer:
or let me speak, and answer thou me.

3) Job thought again of his sad condition

[23]How many *are* mine iniquities and
sins? make me to know my transgression and my sin.
[24]Wherefore hidest thou thy face, and
holdest me for thine enemy?
[25]Wilt thou break a leaf driven to
and fro? and wilt thou pursue the dry
stubble?
[26]For thou writest bitter things
against me, and makest me to possess
the iniquities of my youth.
[27]Thou puttest my feet also in the
stocks, and lookest narrowly unto all
my paths; thou settest a print upon the
heels of my feet.
[28]And he, as a rotten thing, consumeth, as a garment that is moth
eaten.

14 Man *that is* born of a woman *is*
of few days, and full of trouble.
[2]He cometh forth like a flower, and is
cut down: he fleeth also as a shadow,
and continueth not.
[3]And dost thou open thine eyes upon
such an one, and bringest me into
*judgment with thee?
[4]Who can bring a clean *thing* out of an
*unclean? not one.
[5]Seeing his days *are* determined, the
number of his months *are* with thee,
thou hast appointed his bounds that he
cannot pass;
[6]Turn from him, that he may rest, till
he shall accomplish, as an hireling, his
day.
[7]For there is hope of a tree, if it be cut
down, that it will sprout again, and that
the tender branch thereof will not
cease.
[8]Though the root thereof wax old in
the earth, and the stock thereof die in
the ground;
[9]*Yet* through the scent of water it will
bud, and bring forth boughs like a plant.
[10]But man dieth, and wasteth away:
yea, man giveth up the ghost, and
where *is* he?

14:10 Uncertain Hope
"Man giveth up the ghost, and where is he?" Job had no certain hope of a future life. He could not be sure what happened after death, but he had a wonderful faith that he would someday see God (Job 19:25-27). It was impossible for people to have a sure hope of resurrection until after the resurrection of the Lord Jesus Christ and the message of the gospel. See 1 Corinthians 15.

[11]*As* the waters fail from the sea, and
the flood decayeth and drieth up:
[12]So man lieth down, and riseth not:
till the heavens *be* no more, they shall
not awake, nor be raised out of their
sleep.
[13]Oh that thou wouldest hide me in
the grave, that thou wouldest keep me
secret, until thy wrath be past, that thou
wouldest appoint me a set time, and
remember me!

4) Job's hope of a resurrection

[14]If a man die, shall he live *again?* all
the days of my appointed time will I
wait, till my change come.
[15]Thou shalt call, and I will answer
thee: thou wilt have a desire to the
work of thine hands.
[16]For now thou numberest my steps:
dost thou not watch over my sin?
[17]My transgression *is* sealed up in a
bag, and thou sewest up mine iniquity.

13:27 stocks. Probably a sort of heavy wooden clog that the prisoner could drag around a little, not like the stocks that hold a person in a sitting position.
13:28 he. This refers to Job himself.
14:6 accomplish, as an hireling, his day. That is, satisfy the master by completing the day's work.

[18]And surely the mountain falling
cometh to nought, and the rock is removed out of his place.
[19]The waters wear the stones: thou
washest away the things which grow
out of the dust of the earth; and thou
destroyest the hope of man.
[20]Thou prevailest for ever against
him, and he passeth: thou changest his
countenance, and sendest him away.
[21]His sons come to honour, and he
knoweth *it* not; and they are brought
low, but he perceiveth *it* not of them.
[22]But his flesh upon him shall have
pain, and his soul within him shall
mourn.

Second speech of Eliphaz
1) He rebuked Job

15 Then answered Eliphaz the
Temanite, and said,
[2]Should a wise man utter vain knowledge, and fill his belly with the east
wind?
[3]Should he reason with unprofitable
talk? or with speeches wherewith he
can do no good?
[4]Yea, thou castest off *fear, and restrainest *prayer before God.
[5]For thy mouth uttereth thine iniquity, and thou choosest the tongue of the
crafty.
[6]Thine own mouth condemneth thee,
and not I: yea, thine own lips testify
against thee.
[7]*Art* thou the first man *that* was born?
or wast thou made before the hills?
[8]Hast thou heard the secret of God?
and dost thou restrain wisdom to thyself?
[9]What knowest thou, that we know
not? *what* understandest thou, which *is*
not in us?
[10]With us *are* both the grayheaded
and very aged men, much elder than
thy father.
[11]*Are* the consolations of God small
with thee? is there any secret thing
with thee?
[12]Why doth thine heart carry thee
away? and what do thy eyes wink at,
[13]That thou turnest thy spirit against
God, and lettest *such* words go out of
thy mouth?
[14]What *is* man, that he should be
*clean? and *he which is* born of a woman, that he should be righteous?
[15]Behold, he putteth no trust in his
*saints; yea, the heavens are not clean
in his sight.
[16]How much more abominable and
filthy *is* man, which drinketh iniquity
like water?

2) Eliphaz spoke of the conscience
and fate of the wicked

[17]I will shew thee, hear me; and that
which I have seen I will declare;
[18]Which wise men have told from
their fathers, and have not hid *it:*
[19]Unto whom alone the earth was
given, and no stranger passed among
them.
[20]The wicked man travaileth with
pain all *his* days, and the number of
years is hidden to the oppressor.
[21]A dreadful sound *is* in his ears: in
prosperity the destroyer shall come
upon him.
[22]He believeth not that he shall return out of darkness, and he is waited
for of the sword.
[23]He wandereth abroad for bread,
saying, Where *is it?* he knoweth that the
day of darkness is ready at his hand.
[24]Trouble and anguish shall make him
afraid; they shall prevail against him, as
a king ready to the battle.

14:22 flesh upon him shall have pain. This verse goes back to the thought of verse 1—the trouble and sorrow in the world.

15:4 fear, and restrainest prayer. Eliphaz accused Job falsely of arguing for his own righteousness instead of praying to God. Job 1:5 shows that Eliphaz was wrong about Job.

15:21 in prosperity the destroyer shall come. A wicked person is haunted by fear, even when he or she is perfectly safe.

15:22 waited for of the sword. That is, to be murdered.

25For he stretcheth out his hand
against God, and strengtheneth himself
against the Almighty.
26He runneth upon him, *even* on *his*
neck, upon the thick bosses of his bucklers:
27Because he covereth his face with
his fatness, and maketh collops of fat on
his flanks.
28And he dwelleth in desolate cities,
and in houses which no man inhabiteth,
which are ready to become heaps.
29He shall not be rich, neither shall
his substance continue, neither shall he
prolong the perfection thereof upon the
earth.
30He shall not depart out of darkness;
the flame shall dry up his branches, and
by the breath of his mouth shall he go
away.
31Let not him that is deceived trust
in *vanity: for vanity shall be his recompence.
32It shall be accomplished before his
time, and his branch shall not be green.
33He shall shake off his unripe grape
as the vine, and shall cast off his flower
as the olive.
34For the congregation of hypocrites
shall be desolate, and *fire shall consume the tabernacles of bribery.
35They conceive mischief, and bring
forth vanity, and their belly prepareth
deceit.

Job's fourth answer
1) He rejected the friends' useless speeches

16 Then Job answered and said,
2I have heard many such things:
miserable comforters *are* ye all.
3Shall vain words have an end? or what
emboldeneth thee that thou answerest?
4I also could speak as ye *do:* if your
soul were in my soul's stead, I could
heap up words against you, and shake
mine head at you.
5*But* I would strengthen you with my
mouth, and the moving of my lips
should asswage *your grief.*

2) He pictured his loneliness

6Though I speak, my grief is not asswaged: and *though* I forbear, what am
I eased?
7But now he hath made me weary:
thou hast made desolate all my company.
8And thou hast filled me with
wrinkles, *which* is a witness *against me:*
and my leanness rising up in me
beareth witness to my face.
9He teareth *me* in his wrath, who
hateth me: he gnasheth upon me with
his teeth; mine enemy sharpeneth his
eyes upon me.
10They have gaped upon me with
their mouth; they have smitten me
upon the cheek reproachfully; they
have gathered themselves together
against me.
11God hath delivered me to the ungodly, and turned me over into the
hands of the wicked.
12I was at ease, but he hath broken
me asunder: he hath also taken *me* by
my neck, and shaken me to pieces, and
set me up for his mark.
13His archers compass me round
about, he cleaveth my *reins asunder,
and doth not spare; he poureth out my
gall upon the ground.
14He breaketh me with breach upon
breach, he runneth upon me like a
giant.
15I have sewed sackcloth upon my

16:13 His archers. Job was saying that God had dashed him to the ground and then set him up for a target at which his three friends might shoot their arrows of words and arguments.

16:13 reins. The kidneys—spoken of as if they were the source of joy, pain, and other emotions.

16:15 sewed sackcloth upon my skin. This suggests that Job never stopped mourning. In a sense, his mourning clothes were sewed on, so that they never came off.

skin, and defiled my horn in the dust.
16 My face is foul with weeping, and
my eyelids *is* the shadow of *death;
17 Not for *any* injustice in mine hands:
also my prayer *is* pure.

3) Job knew that God would speak for him

18 O earth, cover not thou my blood,
and let my cry have no place.

16:18 A Cry for Punishment
Later, as recorded in the *Law, even the blood of wild animals caught for food had to be poured on the ground and covered with soil (see Lev. 17) since the blood was the life of man and beast, and, as such, forbidden for the Jews to consume. The covering up of the blood means that the wrong had been hidden. The uncovered blood cried for punishment (see Gen. 4:10).

19 Also now, behold, my witness *is* in
heaven, and my record *is* on high.
20 My friends scorn me: *but* mine eye
poureth out *tears* unto God.
21 Oh that one might plead for a man
with God, as a man *pleadeth* for his
neighbour!
22 When a few years are come, then I
shall go the way *whence* I shall not return.

17 My breath is corrupt, my days
are extinct, the graves *are ready*
for me.
2 *Are there* not mockers with me? and
doth not mine eye continue in their
provocation?
3 Lay down now, put me in a surety
with thee; who *is* he *that* will strike
hands with me?
4 For thou hast hid their heart from
understanding: therefore shalt thou not
exalt *them*.
5 He that speaketh flattery to *his*
friends, even the eyes of his children
shall fail.
6 He hath made me also a byword of
the people; and aforetime I was as a
*tabret.
7 Mine eye also is dim by reason of
sorrow, and all my members *are* as a
shadow.
8 Upright *men* shall be astonied at
this, and the innocent shall stir up himself against the hypocrite.
9 The righteous also shall hold on his
way, and he that hath clean hands shall
be stronger and stronger.

4) Job, without earthly hope, wished to die

10 But as for you all, do ye return, and
come now: for I cannot find *one* wise
man among you.
11 My days are past, my purposes are
broken off, *even* the thoughts of my
heart.
12 They change the night into day: the
light *is* short because of darkness.
13 If I wait, the grave *is* mine house: I
have made my bed in the darkness.
14 I have said to corruption, Thou *art*
my father: to the worm, *Thou art* my
mother, and my sister.
15 And where *is* now my *hope? as for
my hope, who shall see it?
16 They shall go down to the bars of
the *pit, when *our* rest together *is* in
the dust.

Bildad's second speech
1) The wicked must come to grief

18 Then answered Bildad the
Shuhite, and said,
2 How long *will it be ere* ye make an
end of words? mark, and afterwards we
will speak.
3 Wherefore are we counted as beasts,
and reputed vile in your sight?

16:15 horn. Just as the horn of an ox is its strength, so horn is often used to describe the strength and vigor of man.
16:21 Oh that one might plead. Job again begged for the *Daysman to speak for him before God.
17:16 the pit. Hades, the place of the departed spirits of the dead. See *hell.
18:3 reputed vile. Considered stupid.

[4]He teareth himself in his anger:
shall the earth be forsaken for thee? and
shall the rock be removed out of his
place?
[5]Yea, the light of the wicked shall be
put out, and the spark of his fire shall
not shine.
[6]The light shall be dark in his tabernacle, and his candle shall be put out
with him.
[7]The steps of his strength shall be
straitened, and his own counsel shall
cast him down.
[8]For he is cast into a net by his own
feet, and he walketh upon a snare.
[9]The gin shall take *him* by the heel,
and the robber shall prevail against
him.
[10]The snare *is* laid for him in the
ground, and a trap for him in the way.
[11]Terrors shall make him afraid on
every side, and shall drive him to his
feet.
[12]His strength shall be hungerbitten,
and destruction *shall be* ready at his
side.
[13]It shall devour the strength of his
skin: *even* the firstborn of death shall
devour his strength.
[14]His confidence shall be rooted out
of his tabernacle, and it shall bring him
to the king of terrors.
[15]It shall dwell in his tabernacle, because *it is* none of his: brimstone shall
be scattered upon his habitation.
[16]His roots shall be dried up beneath,
and above shall his branch be cut off.
[17]His remembrance shall perish from
the earth, and he shall have no name in
the street.
[18]He shall be driven from light into
darkness, and chased out of the *world.
[19]He shall neither have son nor nephew among his people, nor any remaining in his dwellings.
[20]They that come after *him* shall be
astonied at his day, as they that went
before were affrighted.
[21]Surely such *are* the dwellings of the
wicked, and this *is* the place *of him that*
knoweth not God.

Job's fifth answer
1) Job's impatience with his friends' words

19 Then Job answered and said,
[2]How long will ye vex my soul,
and break me in pieces with words?
[3]These ten times have ye reproached
me: ye are not ashamed *that* ye make
yourselves strange to me.
[4]And be it indeed *that* I have erred,
mine error remaineth with myself.
[5]If indeed ye will magnify *yourselves*
against me, and plead against me my
reproach:
[6]Know now that God hath overthrown me, and hath compassed me
with his net.

2) God—Job's Judge and Joy

[7]Behold, I cry out of wrong, but I am
not heard: I cry aloud, but *there is* no
judgment.
[8]He hath fenced up my way that I
cannot pass, and he hath set darkness
in my paths.
[9]He hath stripped me of my glory, and
taken the crown *from* my head.
[10]He hath destroyed me on every
side, and I am gone: and mine hope hath
he removed like a tree.
[11]He hath also kindled his wrath
against me, and he counteth me unto
him as *one of* his enemies.
[12]His troops come together, and raise

18:4 rock. The word is used here, as it is often in the Old Testament, to refer to God.
18:12 hungerbitten. Starved.
18:13 the firstborn of death. The most cruel kind of death is meant here.
18:14 his tabernacle. Bildad spoke of Job's body, which should be destroyed, and "it," meaning Job's soul, handed over to death, the "king of terrors."
19:3 ten times. Used as a number meaning *often*.
19:3 strange. Hard or wrong.

up their way against me, and encamp
round about my tabernacle.
13He hath put my brethren far from
me, and mine acquaintance are verily
estranged from me.
14My kinsfolk have failed, and my familiar friends have forgotten me.
15They that dwell in mine house, and
my maids, count me for a stranger: I am
an alien in their sight.
16I called my *servant, and he gave
me no answer; I intreated him with my
mouth.
17My breath is strange to my wife,
though I intreated for the children's
sake of mine own body.
18Yea, young children despised me; I
arose, and they spake against me.
19All my inward friends abhorred me:
and they whom I loved are turned
against me.
20My bone cleaveth to my skin and to
my flesh, and I am escaped with the
skin of my teeth.
21Have pity upon me, have pity upon
me, O ye my friends; for the hand of
God hath touched me.
22Why do ye persecute me as God,
and are not satisfied with my flesh?
23Oh that my words were now written! oh that they were printed in a
book!
24That they were graven with an iron
pen and lead in the rock for ever!
25For I know *that* my *redeemer
liveth, and *that* he shall stand at the latter *day* upon the earth:
26And *though* after my skin *worms*
destroy this *body,* yet in my flesh shall
I see God:
27Whom I shall see for myself, and
mine eyes shall behold, and not another; *though* my *reins be consumed
within me.

19:25 Job's Redeemer
The Hebrew word *goel* means the nearest relation, whose duty it was to avenge wrongs done to his kinsman (Num. 5:8) and to buy back his land if he lost it (Ruth 4). The same word came to be used for God, inasmuch as He was the deliverer of His people (Ps. 103:4; Isa. 19:20). It is a *type, too, of the Lord Jesus Christ, who bought back believers from the power of sin (1 Pet. 1:18-19). Job's faith was so strong that he counted on God as his deliverer and Redeemer, and Job knew that someday he would see God. See Job 14:10 note, "Uncertain Hope."

3) A threat to his friends

28But ye should say, Why persecute
we him, seeing the root of the matter
is found in me?
29Be ye afraid of the sword: for wrath
bringeth the punishments of the sword,
that ye may know *there is* a judgment.

Zophar's second speech

1) The shortness of the prosperity of the wicked

20 Then answered Zophar the Naamathite, and said,
2Therefore do my thoughts cause me
to answer, and for *this* I make haste.
3I have heard the check of my reproach, and the spirit of my understanding causeth me to answer.
4Knowest thou *not* this of old, since
man was placed upon earth,
5That the triumphing of the wicked *is*
short, and the joy of the hypocrite *but*
for a moment?
6Though his excellency mount up to
the heavens, and his head reach unto
the clouds;
7*Yet* he shall perish for ever like his
own *dung: they which have seen him
shall say, Where *is* he?
8He shall fly away as a dream, and

19:19 inward. Intimate, close.
19:24 rock. Writing on papyrus or skin (vs. 23), which are both perishable materials, was not enough. Job wanted his complaints cut deeply into a rock.
19:25 at the latter day. Literally, *the last,* as in Isaiah 48:12.
19:29 the sword. The sword of God in judgment.
20:3 check. Reproof, rebuke or scolding.

shall not be found: yea, he shall be
chased away as a vision of the night.
9 The eye also *which* saw him shall *see*
him no more; neither shall his place any
more behold him.
10 His children shall seek to please
the poor, and his hands shall restore
their goods.
11 His bones are full *of the* *sin of his
youth, which shall lie down with him in
the dust.
12 Though wickedness be sweet in his
mouth, *though* he hide it under his
tongue;
13 *Though* he spare it, and forsake it
not; but keep it still within his mouth:
14 *Yet* his meat in his bowels is turned,
it is the gall of asps within him.
15 He hath swallowed down riches,
and he shall vomit them up again: God
shall cast them out of his belly.
16 He shall suck the poison of asps:
the viper's tongue shall slay him.
17 He shall not see the rivers, the
floods, the brooks of honey and butter.
18 That which he laboured for shall he
restore, and shall not swallow *it* down:
according to *his* substance *shall* the restitution *be,* and he shall not rejoice
therein.
19 Because he hath oppressed *and*
hath forsaken the poor; *because* he hath
violently taken away an house which he
builded not;
20 Surely he shall not feel quietness in
his belly, he shall not save of that which
he desired.
21 There shall none of his meat be left;
therefore shall no man look for his
goods.
22 In the *fulness of his sufficiency he
shall be in straits: every hand of the
wicked shall come upon him.
23 *When* he is about to fill his belly,
God shall cast the fury of his wrath upon
him, and shall rain *it* upon him while he
is eating.
24 He shall flee from the iron weapon,
and the bow of steel shall strike him
through.
25 It is drawn, and cometh out of the
body; yea, the glittering sword cometh
out of his gall: terrors *are* upon him.
26 All darkness *shall be* hid in his secret places: a fire not blown shall consume him; it shall go ill with him that
is left in his tabernacle.
27 The heaven shall reveal his iniquity; and the earth shall rise up against
him.
28 The increase of his house shall depart, *and his goods* shall flow away in
the day of his wrath.
29 This *is* the portion of a wicked man
from God, and the heritage appointed
unto him by God.

Job's sixth answer
1) The mystery of the prosperity of the wicked

21 But Job answered and said,
2 Hear diligently my speech, and
let this be your consolations.
3 Suffer me that I may speak; and after that I have spoken, mock on.
4 As for me, *is* my complaint to man?
and if *it were so,* why should not my
spirit be troubled?
5 Mark me, and be astonished, and lay
your hand upon *your* mouth.
6 Even when I remember I am afraid,
and trembling taketh hold on my flesh.
7 Wherefore do the wicked live, become old, yea, are mighty in power?
8 Their seed is established in their
sight with them, and their offspring
before their eyes.
9 Their houses *are* safe from fear, neither *is* the rod of *God upon them.
10 Their bull gendereth, and faileth
not; their cow calveth, and casteth not
her calf.
11 They send forth their little ones
like a flock, and their children dance.
12 They take the timbrel and harp, and
rejoice at the sound of the organ.
13 They spend their days in wealth,
and in a moment go down to the grave.
14 Therefore they say unto God, Depart from us; for we desire not the
knowledge of thy ways.
15 What *is* the Almighty, that we

should serve him? and what profit
should we have, if we pray unto him?
16Lo, their good *is* not in their
hand: the counsel of the wicked is far
from me.
17How oft is the candle of the wicked put out! and *how oft* cometh their
destruction upon them! *God* distributeth sorrows in his anger.
18They are as stubble before the
wind, and as chaff that the storm
carrieth away.
19God layeth up his iniquity for his
children: he rewardeth him, and he shall
know *it*.
20His eyes shall see his destruction,
and he shall drink of the wrath of the
Almighty.
21For what pleasure *hath* he in his
house after him, when the number of
his months is cut off in the midst?
22Shall *any* teach God knowledge?
seeing he judgeth those that are high.
23One dieth in his full strength, being
wholly at ease and quiet.
24His breasts are full of milk, and his
bones are moistened with marrow.
25And another dieth in the bitterness
of his soul, and never eateth with pleasure.
26They shall lie down alike in the
dust, and the worms shall cover them.
27Behold, I know your thoughts, and
the devices *which* ye wrongfully imagine against me.
28For ye say, Where *is* the house of
the prince? and where *are* the dwelling
places of the wicked?
29Have ye not asked them that go
by the way? and do ye not know their
tokens,
30That the wicked is reserved to the
day of destruction? they shall be
brought forth to the day of wrath.
31Who shall declare his way to his
face? and who shall repay him *what* he
hath done?
32Yet shall he be brought to the grave,
and shall remain in the tomb.
33The clods of the valley shall be
sweet unto him, and every man shall
draw after him, as *there are* innumerable before him.
34How then comfort ye me in vain,
seeing in your answers there remaineth
*falsehood?

The third speech of Eliphaz
1) He told Job to ask forgiveness

22 Then Eliphaz the Temanite answered and said,
2Can a man be profitable unto God, as
he that is wise may be profitable unto
himself?
3*Is it* any pleasure to the Almighty,
that thou art righteous? or *is it* gain *to*
him that thou makest thy ways *perfect?
4Will he reprove thee for fear of
thee? will he enter with thee into *judgment?
5*Is* not thy wickedness great? and
thine iniquities infinite?
6For thou hast taken a pledge from
thy brother for nought, and stripped the
naked of their clothing.
7Thou hast not given water to the
weary to drink, and thou hast withholden bread from the hungry.
8But *as for* the mighty man, he had
the earth; and the honourable man
dwelt in it.

21:19 iniquity. This means *the punishment* of iniquity.
21:29 tokens. This word means *testimony.* The testimony of the travelers, those who "go by the way," is found in verses 30-33. It speaks of the life and death of the wicked.
21:30 day of destruction. Job knew that there would come a *Day of Judgment when the wicked would be judged.
21:33 clods of the valley. This refers to the earth that is heaped over the coffin of the wicked. Though he has a big funeral, he dies—just as all who have lived before him or who will live after him will until the time of the second coming of the Lord Jesus Christ.
22:6 naked. Slightly clothed.

9 Thou hast sent widows away empty, and the arms of the fatherless have
been broken.
10 Therefore snares *are* round about
thee, and sudden fear troubleth thee;
11 Or darkness, *that* thou canst not
see; and abundance of waters cover
thee.
12 *Is* not God in the height of heaven?
and behold the height of the stars, how
high they are!
13 And thou sayest, How doth God
know? can he judge through the dark
cloud?
14 Thick clouds *are* a covering to him,
that he seeth not; and he walketh in the
circuit of heaven.
15 Hast thou marked the old way
which wicked men have trodden?
16 Which were cut down out of time,
whose foundation was overflown with
a flood:
17 Which said unto God, Depart from
us: and what can the Almighty do for
them?
18 Yet he filled their houses with good
things: but the counsel of the wicked is
far from me.
19 The righteous see *it,* and are glad:
and the innocent laugh them to scorn.
20 Whereas our substance is not cut
down, but the remnant of them the fire
consumeth.
21 Acquaint now thyself with him, and
be at *peace: thereby good shall come
unto thee.
22 Receive, I pray thee, the law from
his mouth, and lay up his words in thine
heart.
23 If thou return to the Almighty, thou
shalt be built up, thou shalt put away
iniquity far from thy tabernacles.
24 Then shalt thou lay up gold as dust,
and the *gold* of Ophir as the stones of
the brooks.
25 Yea, the Almighty shall be thy defence, and thou shalt have plenty of
*silver.
26 For then shalt thou have thy delight
in the Almighty, and shalt lift up thy face
unto God.
27 Thou shalt make thy *prayer unto
him, and he shall hear thee, and thou
shalt pay thy vows.
28 Thou shalt also decree a thing, and
it shall be established unto thee: and
the light shall shine upon thy ways.
29 When *men* are cast down, then thou
shalt say, *There is* lifting up; and he shall
save the humble person.
30 He shall deliver the island of the
innocent: and it is delivered by the
pureness of thine hands.

Job's seventh answer
1) Job could not find God

23 Then Job answered and said,
2 Even to day *is* my complaint
bitter: my stroke is heavier than my
groaning.
3 Oh that I knew where I might find
him! *that* I might come *even* to his
seat!
4 I would order *my* cause before him,
and fill my mouth with arguments.
5 I would know the words *which* he
would answer me, and understand what
he would say unto me.
6 Will he plead against me with *his*
great power? No; but he would put
strength in me.
7 There the righteous might dispute
with him; so should I be delivered for
ever from my judge.
8 Behold, I go forward, but he *is* not
there; and backward, but I cannot perceive him:
9 On the left hand, where he doth
work, but I cannot behold *him:* he
hideth himself on the right hand, that I
cannot see *him:*
10 But he knoweth the way that I take:

22:16 flood. A reference to Genesis 7, the Flood that covered the earth.
22:24 Ophir. An important city, possibly in Arabia, where gold was obtained. See 1 Kings 9:28.

when he hath tried me, I shall come
forth as gold.
11 My foot hath held his steps, his way
have I kept, and not declined.
12 Neither have I gone back from the
commandment of his lips; I have esteemed the words of his mouth more
than my necessary *food.*
13 But he *is* in one *mind,* and who can
turn him? and *what* his soul desireth,
even *that* he doeth.
14 For he performeth *the thing that is*
appointed for me: and many such *things*
are with him.
15 Therefore am I troubled at his
presence: when I consider, I am afraid
of him.
16 For God maketh my heart soft, and
the Almighty troubleth me:
17 Because I was not cut off before the
darkness, *neither* hath he covered the
darkness from my face.

Job's seventh answer continued

24 Why, seeing times are not hidden from the Almighty, do they
that know him not see his days?
2 *Some* remove the landmarks; they
violently take away flocks, and feed
thereof.
3 They drive away the ass of the fatherless, they take the widow's ox for
a pledge.
4 They turn the needy out of the way:
the poor of the earth hide themselves
together.
5 Behold, *as* wild asses in the desert,
go they forth to their work; rising
betimes for a prey: the wilderness
yieldeth food for them *and* for *their*
children.
6 They reap *every one* his corn in the
field: and they gather the vintage of the
wicked.
7 They cause the naked to lodge without clothing, that *they have* no covering
in the cold.
8 They are wet with the showers of
the mountains, and embrace the rock
for want of a shelter.
9 They pluck the fatherless from the
breast, and take a pledge of the poor.
10 They cause *him* to go naked without clothing, and they take away the
sheaf *from* the hungry;
11 *Which* make oil within their walls,
and tread *their* winepresses, and suffer
thirst.
12 Men groan from out of the city, and
the soul of the wounded crieth out: yet
God layeth not folly *to them.*
13 They are of those that rebel against
the light; they know not the ways
thereof, nor abide in the paths thereof.
14 The murderer rising with the light
killeth the poor and needy, and in the
night is as a thief.
15 The eye also of the adulterer
waiteth for the twilight, saying, No
eye shall see me: and disguiseth *his*
face.
16 In the dark they dig through
houses, *which* they had marked for
themselves in the daytime: they know
not the light.
17 For the morning *is* to them even as
the shadow of *death: if *one* know *them,*
they are in the terrors of the shadow of
death.
18 He *is* swift as the waters; their portion is cursed in the earth: he beholdeth
not the way of the vineyards.

23:10 when he hath tried me. By faith Job sees his trial as from God—as a furnace from which, like gold, his life will come forth purified. See Psalm 66:10; James 1:12; and 1 Peter 1:7.

24:1 seeing times are not hidden. Job could not understand God's allowing the wicked to prosper. The fact that they did proved that his three friends were wrong in their statements that suffering is punishment for sin.

24:10 they take away the sheaf from the hungry. Even in harvesttime the laborers were famished.

24:11 tread their winepresses, and suffer thirst. The laborers were not allowed to drink even the grape juice that they pressed out.

19Drought and heat consume the snow waters: *so doth* the *grave *those which* have sinned.
20The womb shall forget him; the worm shall feed sweetly on him; he shall be no more remembered; and wickedness shall be broken as a tree.
21He evil entreateth the barren *that* beareth not: and doeth not good to the widow.
22He draweth also the mighty with his power: he riseth up, and no *man* is sure of life.
23*Though* it be given him *to be* in safety, whereon he resteth; yet his eyes *are* upon their ways.
24They are exalted for a little while, but are gone and brought low; they are taken out of the way as all *other,* and cut off as the tops of the ears of corn.
25And if *it be* not *so* now, who will make me a liar, and make my speech nothing worth?

Bildad's third speech
1) Man's sin in God's sight

25 Then answered Bildad the Shuhite, and said,
2Dominion and fear *are* with him, he maketh peace in his high places.
3Is there any number of his armies? and upon whom doth not his light arise?
4How then can man be justified with God? or how can he be *clean *that is* born of a woman?
5Behold even to the moon, and it shineth not; yea, the stars are not pure in his sight.
6How much less man, *that is* a worm? and the son of man, *which is* a worm?

Job's eighth answer
1) God's greatness

26 But Job answered and said,
2How hast thou helped *him that is* without power? *how* savest thou the arm *that hath* no strength?
3How hast thou counselled *him that hath* no wisdom? and *how* hast thou plentifully declared the thing as it is?
4To whom hast thou uttered words? and whose spirit came from thee?
5Dead *things* are formed from under the waters, and the inhabitants thereof.
6*Hell *is* naked before him, and destruction hath no covering.
7He stretcheth out the north over the empty place, *and* hangeth the earth upon nothing.
8He bindeth up the waters in his thick clouds; and the cloud is not rent under them.
9He holdeth back the face of his throne, *and* spreadeth his cloud upon it.
10He hath compassed the waters with bounds, until the day and night come to an end.

26:10 The Natural Law
Job demonstrated amazing knowledge of the waters. He realized that oceans, rivers, lakes, and clouds are made to cling around the earth by God's wisdom and authority expressed in natural law. His dominion over waters is told in Psalms 33:7; 104:9; Proverbs 8:29; Jeremiah 5:22.

11The pillars of heaven tremble and are astonished at his reproof.
12He divideth the sea with his power, and by his understanding he smiteth through the proud.
13By his spirit he hath garnished the heavens; his hand hath formed the crooked serpent.

24:24 they are taken out of the way as all other. The wicked die just as everyone else does.
25:4 How then can man be justified with God? This is the question of the ages, asked by Job in 4:17 and 9:2 (see note on 9:2).
26:7 hangeth the earth upon nothing. Job knew that the earth is suspended in space, held by the invisible force of gravity. This verse in the oldest book of the Bible contains that which scientists "discovered" centuries later.
26:8 bindeth. To imprison or confine closely.
26:13 the crooked serpent. See Isaiah 27:1; Revelation 12:9.

14Lo, these *are* parts of his ways: but
how little a portion is heard of him? but
the thunder of his power who can understand?

Job continues his eighth answer
2) His innocence

27 Moreover Job continued his
*parable, and said,
2*As* *God liveth, *who* hath taken away
my judgment; and the Almighty, *who*
hath vexed my soul;
3All the while my breath *is* in me, and
the spirit of God *is* in my nostrils;
4My lips shall not speak wickedness,
nor my tongue utter deceit.
5God forbid that I should justify you:
till I die I will not remove mine integrity from me.
6My *righteousness I hold fast, and
will not let it go: my heart shall not reproach *me* so long as I live.

3) The condition of the wicked

7Let mine enemy be as the wicked,
and he that riseth up against me as the
unrighteous.
8For what *is* the *hope of the hypocrite, though he hath gained, when God
taketh away his soul?
9Will God hear his cry when trouble
cometh upon him?
10Will he delight himself in the Almighty? will he always call upon God?
11I will teach you by the hand of God:
that which *is* with the Almighty will I
not conceal.
12Behold, all ye yourselves have seen
it; why then are ye thus altogether
vain?
13This *is* the portion of a wicked man
with God, and the heritage of oppressors, *which* they shall receive of the
Almighty.
14If his children be multiplied, *it is* for
the sword: and his offspring shall not be
satisfied with bread.
15Those that remain of him shall be
buried in death: and his widows shall
not weep.
16Though he heap up silver as the
dust, and prepare raiment as the clay;
17He may prepare *it,* but the *just
shall put *it* on, and the innocent shall
divide the silver.
18He buildeth his house as a moth,
and as a booth *that* the keeper maketh.
19The rich man shall lie down, but he
shall not be gathered: he openeth his
eyes, and he *is* not.
20Terrors take hold on him as waters,
a tempest stealeth him away in the night.
21The east wind carrieth him away,
and he departeth: and as a storm
hurleth him out of his place.
22For *God* shall cast upon him, and
not spare: he would fain flee out of his
hand.
23*Men* shall clap their hands at him,
and shall hiss him out of his place.

Job continues his eighth answer on wisdom
1) Wisdom is not found in a mine

28 Surely there is a vein for the
silver, and a place for gold *where*
they fine *it.*

26:14 how little a portion is heard of him. Job realized that all these wonders are like a whisper compared to the mighty thunder of God's glory and power.
27:2 vexed my soul. Made my soul bitter.
27:3 the spirit of God. The breath of God, which is the "breath of life" (Gen. 2:7).
27:8 gained. Compare the New Testament verse, Matthew 16:26.
27:15 his widows. This does not mean that a man had more than one wife. It refers to verse 13 and speaks of the widows of the oppressors.
27:18 booth. A flimsy hut, erected in vineyards or other gardens as a post for the watchman, who protected the fruit from theft or destruction by wild beasts.
27:19 The rich man . . . gathered. "Gathered" is the Old Testament word for death of the saints (Gen. 35:29; 49:33). The idea here is that the wicked rich man will not be like the believer. He will open his eyes and be in hell. Compare Luke 16:22-23.
28:1 vein. Mine.
28:1 fine. Refine.

[2]Iron is taken out of the earth, and
brass *is* molten *out of* the stone.
[3]He setteth an end to darkness,
and searcheth out all perfection: the
stones of darkness, and the shadow of
death.
[4]The flood breaketh out from the inhabitant; *even the waters* forgotten of the
foot: they are dried up, they are gone
away from men.
[5]*As for* the earth, out of it cometh
bread: and under it is turned up as it
were fire.
[6]The stones of it *are* the place of sapphires: and it hath dust of gold.
[7]*There is* a path which no fowl
knoweth, and which the vulture's eye
hath not seen:
[8]The lion's whelps have not trodden
it, nor the fierce lion passed by it.
[9]He putteth forth his hand upon the
rock; he overturneth the mountains by
the roots.
[10]He cutteth out rivers among the
rocks; and his eye seeth every precious
thing.
[11]He bindeth the floods from overflowing; and *the thing that is* hid
bringeth he forth to light.
[12]But where shall wisdom be found?
and where *is* the place of understanding?
[13]Man knoweth not the price thereof;
neither is it found in the land of the
living.
[14]The depth saith, It *is* not in me: and
the sea saith, *It is* not with me.

2) Wisdom cannot be bought

[15]It cannot be gotten for gold, neither
shall silver be weighed *for* the price
thereof.
[16]It cannot be valued with the gold of
*Ophir, with the precious onyx, or the
sapphire.
[17]The gold and the crystal cannot
equal it: and the exchange of it *shall not
be for* jewels of fine gold.
[18]No mention shall be made of coral,
or of pearls: for the price of wisdom *is*
above rubies.
[19]The topaz of Ethiopia shall not
equal it, neither shall it be valued with
pure gold.
[20]Whence then cometh wisdom? and
where *is* the place of understanding?
[21]Seeing it is hid from the eyes of all
living, and kept close from the fowls of
the air.
[22]Destruction and death say, We have
heard the fame thereof with our ears.

3) Wisdom is the fear of the Lord

[23]God understandeth the way thereof,
and he knoweth the place thereof.
[24]For he looketh to the ends of the
earth, *and* seeth under the whole
heaven;
[25]To make the weight for the winds;
and he weigheth the waters by measure.
[26]When he made a decree for the rain,
and a way for the lightning of the thunder:
[27]Then did he see it, and declare it;
he prepared it, yea, and searched it out.
[28]And unto man he said, Behold, the
*fear of the Lord, that *is* wisdom; and
to depart from evil *is* understanding.

4) Job remembered his past happiness

29 Moreover Job continued his
parable, and said,
[2]Oh that I were as *in* months past, as

28:3 He. God.
28:5 as it were fire. The earth is intensely hot toward the center. This is proven by geysers, volcanoes, and boiling springs.
28:12 where shall wisdom be found? Compare this and verse 20 with Proverbs 3:13-23 and 8:22-30. (See also Prov. 8:22 note, "Five Things about Wisdom.")
28:25 weight. A wonderful verse showing that it is God whose laws balance the clouds in the sky and govern the waters by weight.
28:28 the fear of the Lord, that is wisdom. The fear or reverence of the LORD is a main theme throughout Proverbs (see Prov. 1:7; 9:10).

in the days *when* God preserved me;
[3]When his candle shined upon my
head, *and when* by his light I walked
through darkness;
[4]As I was in the days of my youth,
when the secret of God *was* upon my
tabernacle;
[5]When the Almighty *was* yet with
me, *when* my children *were* about me;
[6]When I washed my steps with butter, and the rock poured me out rivers
of oil;
[7]When I went out to the gate through
the city, *when* I prepared my seat in the
street!
[8]The young men saw me, and hid
themselves: and the aged arose, *and*
stood up.
[9]The princes refrained talking, and
laid *their* hand on their mouth.
[10]The nobles held their peace, and
their tongue cleaved to the roof of their
mouth.
[11]When the ear heard *me,* then it
blessed me; and when the eye saw *me,*
it gave witness to me:
[12]Because I delivered the poor that
cried, and the fatherless, and *him that*
had none to help him.
[13]The blessing of him that was ready
to perish came upon me: and I caused
the widow's heart to sing for joy.
[14]I put on righteousness, and it
clothed me: my judgment *was* as a robe
and a diadem.
[15]I was eyes to the blind, and feet *was*
I to the lame.
[16]I *was* a father to the poor: and the
cause *which* I knew not I searched out.
[17]And I brake the jaws of the wicked,
and plucked the spoil out of his teeth.
[18]Then I said, I shall die in my nest,
and I shall multiply *my* days as the sand.
[19]My root *was* spread out by the waters, and the dew lay all night upon my
branch.
[20]My glory *was* fresh in me, and my
bow was renewed in my hand.
[21]Unto me *men* gave ear, and waited,
and kept silence at my counsel.
[22]After my words they spake not
again; and my speech dropped upon
them.
[23]And they waited for me as for the
rain; and they opened their mouth wide
as for the latter rain.
[24]*If* I laughed on them, they believed
it not; and the light of my countenance
they cast not down.
[25]I chose out their way, and sat chief,
and dwelt as a king in the army, as one
that comforteth the mourners.

5) Job compared his present condition with his past happiness

30 But now *they that are* younger
than I have me in derision,
whose fathers I would have disdained
to have set with the dogs of my flock.
[2]Yea, whereto *might* the strength of
their hands *profit* me, in whom old age
was perished?
[3]For want and famine *they were* solitary; fleeing into the wilderness in former time desolate and waste.
[4]Who cut up mallows by the bushes,
and juniper roots *for* their meat.
[5]They were driven forth from among
men, (they cried after them as *after* a
thief;)
[6]To dwell in the cliffs of the valleys,
in caves of the earth, and *in* the rocks.

29:4 the secret of God. See Psalm 25:14.
29:6 butter . . . oil. Symbols of overflowing abundance.
29:7 gate. The place where the leading citizens sat to judge cases and disputes.
29:11 blessed. Literally, *looked upon me as fortunate.*
29:14 my judgment. The just decisions rendered by Job were like a robe and a crown, which were both symbols of royalty and a type of Christ (Isa. 61:10).
29:24 If I laughed on them. People stood in such awe of Job that when he smiled graciously upon them, they could scarcely believe their good fortune.
30:1 set with the dogs of my flock. Job felt he'd been reduced to the equivalent of a simple shepherd.

7Among the bushes they brayed; under the nettles they were gathered together.
8*They were* children of *fools, yea,
children of base men: they were viler
than the earth.
9And now am I their song, yea, I am
their byword.
10They abhor me, they flee far from
me, and spare not to spit in my face.
11Because he hath loosed my cord,
and afflicted me, they have also let
loose the bridle before me.
12Upon *my* right *hand* rise the youth;
they push away my feet, and they raise
up against me the ways of their destruction.
13They mar my path, they set forward my calamity, they have no helper.
14They came *upon me* as a wide
breaking in *of waters:* in the desolation
they rolled themselves *upon me.*
15Terrors are turned upon me: they
pursue my soul as the wind: and my
welfare passeth away as a cloud.
16And now my soul is poured out
upon me; the days of affliction have
taken hold upon me.
17My bones are pierced in me in the
night season: and my sinews take no rest.
18By the great force *of my disease* is
my garment changed: it bindeth me
about as the collar of my coat.
19He hath cast me into the mire, and
I am become like dust and ashes.
20I cry unto thee, and thou dost not
hear me: I stand up, and thou regardest
me *not.*
21Thou art become cruel to me: with
thy strong hand thou opposest thyself
against me.
22Thou liftest me up to the wind;
thou causest me to ride *upon it,* and
dissolvest my substance.
23For I know *that* thou wilt bring me
to *death, and *to* the house appointed for
all living.
24Howbeit he will not stretch out *his*
hand to the *grave, though they cry in
his destruction.
25Did not I weep for him that was in
trouble? was *not* my soul grieved for the
poor?
26When I looked for good, then evil
came *unto me:* and when I waited for
light, there came darkness.
27My *bowels boiled, and rested not:
the days of affliction *prevented me.
28I went *mourning without the sun:
I stood up, *and* I cried in the congregation.
29I am a brother to dragons, and a
companion to owls.
30My skin is black upon me, and my
bones are burned with heat.
31My harp also is *turned* to mourning,
and my organ into the voice of them
that weep.

6) Job asked why he was punished

31 I made a *covenant with mine
eyes; why then should I think
upon a maid?
2For what portion of God *is there* from
above? and *what* inheritance of the Almighty from on high?
3*Is* not destruction to the wicked? and
a strange *punishment* to the workers of
iniquity?
4Doth not he see my ways, and count
all my steps?
5If I have walked with *vanity, or if
my foot hath hasted to deceit;
6Let me be weighed in an even
balance, that God may know mine integrity.
7If my step hath turned out of the
way, and mine heart walked after mine
eyes, and if any blot hath cleaved to
mine hands;

30:18 garment. The awful outward appearance of his disease.
30:29 a brother to dragons, and a companion to owls. Dragons are mentioned several times in the Bible (e.g., Rev. 12:9). The owl is an unclean bird (Lev. 11). Job sees himself as one in tribulation and a companion with evil.
30:31 harp . . . organ. These were usually instruments of joy.

8 *Then* let me sow, and let another eat; yea, let my offspring be rooted out.

9 If mine heart have been deceived by a woman, or *if* I have laid wait at my neighbour's door;

10 *Then* let my wife grind unto another, and let others bow down upon her.

11 For this *is* an heinous crime; yea, it *is* an iniquity *to be punished by* the judges.

12 For it *is* a fire *that* consumeth to destruction, and would root out all mine increase.

13 If I did despise the cause of my manservant or of my maidservant, when they contended with me;

14 What then shall I do when God riseth up? and when he visiteth, what shall I answer him?

15 Did not he that made me in the womb make him? and did not one fashion us in the womb?

16 If I have withheld the poor from *their* desire, or have caused the eyes of the widow to fail;

17 Or have eaten my morsel myself alone, and the fatherless hath not eaten thereof;

18 (For from my youth he was brought up with me, as *with* a father, and I have guided her from my mother's womb;)

19 If I have seen any perish for want of clothing, or any poor without covering;

20 If his loins have not blessed me, and *if* he were *not* warmed with the fleece of my sheep;

21 If I have lifted up my hand against the fatherless, when I saw my help in the gate:

22 *Then* let mine arm fall from my shoulder blade, and mine arm be broken from the bone.

23 For destruction *from* God *was* a terror to me, and by reason of his highness I could not endure.

24 If I have made gold my hope, or have said to the fine gold, *Thou art* my confidence;

25 If I rejoiced because my wealth *was* great, and because mine hand had gotten much;

26 If I beheld the sun when it shined, or the moon walking *in* brightness;

27 And my heart hath been secretly enticed, or my mouth hath kissed my hand:

28 This also *were* an iniquity *to be punished by* the judge: for I should have denied the God *that is* above.

29 If I rejoiced at the destruction of him that hated me, or lifted up myself when evil found him:

30 Neither have I suffered my mouth to *sin by wishing a curse to his soul.

31 If the men of my tabernacle said not, Oh that we had of his flesh! we cannot be satisfied.

32 The stranger did not lodge in the street: *but* I opened my doors to the traveller.

33 If I covered my transgressions as *Adam, by hiding mine iniquity in my bosom:

34 Did I fear a great multitude, or did the contempt of families terrify me, that I kept silence, *and* went not out of the door?

35 Oh that one would hear me! behold, my desire *is, that* the Almighty would answer me, and *that* mine adversary had written a book.

36 Surely I would take it upon my shoulder, *and* bind it *as* a crown to me.

37 I would declare unto him the number of my steps; as a prince would I go near unto him.

31:21 when I saw my help in the gate. When I knew that the judge would decide (unjustly) in my favor.

31:23 destruction from God. God's wrath was a terror to Job—he dared not do evil in the light of it.

31:26 the sun . . . the moon. In verses 26-28, Job spoke of the evil worship of the sun and the moon.

31:26 moon walking in brightness. The full moon.

[38]If my land cry against me, or that
the furrows likewise thereof complain;
[39]If I have eaten the fruits thereof
without money, or have caused the
owners thereof to lose their life:
[40]Let thistles grow instead of wheat,
and cockle instead of barley. The words
of Job are ended.

IV. Job Talks with Elihu (32:1—37:24)

32 So these three men ceased to
answer Job, because he *was*
righteous in his own eyes.

32:1 Job's Friends' Point of View
Eliphaz, Bildad, and Zophar agreed that prosperity is the reward of goodness. They decided that Job was really a bad man, even though he seemed good. Otherwise, according to their idea of God, Job's sufferings were unjust. Job, who was the sufferer, did not accuse God. The frequent prosperity of the wicked proved his friends wrong. Still claiming his innocence, Job could not explain his own sufferings. Before God he was helpless, and he could find no one to plead for him. His friends said much that is true, but they also showed a complete ignorance of the righteousness and ways of God and of man as a sinner. Although Job did not please God in his estimate of himself, he judged rightly in these other matters.

Elihu speaks

[2]Then was kindled the wrath of Elihu the son of Barachel the Buzite, of the
kindred of Ram: against Job was his

32:2 Elihu's Spiritual Viewpoint
Elihu stepped into the argument between Job and his friends with a more spiritual idea of the problem. He set forth the idea that God teaches people lessons through suffering. He urged Job to submit himself in loving confidence into God's hand, knowing that God's ways are right and perfect. Elihu's account of God was noble and true, but Elihu was too sure of himself and his own ideas. When God spoke, He did not mention one of the accusations that Elihu poured on Job.

wrath kindled, because he justified himself rather than God.
[3]Also against his three friends was
his wrath kindled, because they had
found no answer, and *yet* had condemned Job.
[4]Now Elihu had waited till Job
had spoken, because they *were* elder
than he.
[5]When Elihu saw that *there was* no
answer in the mouth of *these* three men,
then his wrath was kindled.
[6]And Elihu the son of Barachel the
Buzite answered and said, I *am* young,
and ye *are* very old; wherefore I was
afraid, and durst not shew you mine
opinion.
[7]I said, Days should speak, and multitude of years should teach wisdom.
[8]But *there is* a spirit in man: and the
inspiration of the Almighty giveth them
understanding.
[9]Great men are not *always* wise: neither do the aged understand judgment.
[10]Therefore I said, Hearken to me;
I also will shew mine opinion.
[11]Behold, I waited for your words;
I gave ear to your reasons, whilst ye
searched out what to say.
[12]Yea, I attended unto you, and, behold, *there was* none of you that convinced Job, *or* that answered his
words:
[13]Lest ye should say, We have found
out wisdom: God thrusteth him down,
not man.
[14]Now he hath not directed *his* words
against me: neither will I answer him
with your speeches.
[15]They were amazed, they answered
no more: they left off speaking.
[16]When I had waited, (for they spake
not, but stood still, *and* answered no
more;)
[17]*I said,* I will answer also my part, I
also will shew mine opinion.
[18]For I am full of matter, the spirit
within me constraineth me.
[19]Behold, my belly *is* as wine *which*

31:40 cockle. A weed found among corn.

hath no vent; it is ready to burst like
new *bottles.
[20]I will speak, that I may be refreshed: I will open my lips and answer.
[21]Let me not, I pray you, accept any
man's person, neither let me give flattering titles unto man.
[22]For I know not to give flattering
titles; *in so doing* my maker would soon
take me away.

Elihu addresses Job directly

1) An appeal for Job's attention

33 Wherefore, Job, I pray thee,
hear my speeches, and hearken
to all my words.
[2]Behold, now I have opened my
mouth, my tongue hath spoken in my
mouth.
[3]My words *shall be of* the uprightness
of my heart: and my lips shall utter
knowledge clearly.
[4]The Spirit of *God hath made me,
and the breath of the Almighty hath
given me life.
[5]If thou canst answer me, set *thy
words* in order before me, stand up.
[6]Behold, I *am* according to thy wish
in God's stead: I also am formed out of
the clay.
[7]Behold, my terror shall not make
thee afraid, neither shall my hand be
heavy upon thee.

2) God's ways are not like man's ways

[8]Surely thou hast spoken in mine
hearing, and I have heard the voice of
thy words, *saying,*
[9]I am *clean without transgression,
I *am* innocent; neither *is there* iniquity
in me.
[10]Behold, he findeth occasions
against me, he counteth me for his
enemy,
[11]He putteth my feet in the stocks, he
marketh all my paths.
[12]Behold, *in* this thou art not *just: I
will answer thee, that God is greater
than man.
[13]Why dost thou strive against him?
for he giveth not account of any of his
matters.

3) God speaks to man in many ways

[14]For God speaketh once, yea twice,
yet man perceiveth it not.
[15]In a dream, in a vision of the night,
when deep sleep falleth upon men, in
slumberings upon the bed;
[16]Then he openeth the ears of men,
and sealeth their instruction,
[17]That he may withdraw man *from his*
purpose, and hide pride from man.
[18]He keepeth back his soul from *the
pit, and his life from perishing by the
sword.
[19]He is *chastened also with pain
upon his bed, and the multitude of his
bones with strong *pain:*
[20]So that his life abhorreth bread, and
his soul dainty meat.
[21]His flesh is consumed away, that it
cannot be seen; and his bones *that* were
not seen stick out.
[22]Yea, his soul draweth near unto the
grave, and his life to the destroyers.
[23]If there be a messenger with him,
an interpreter, one among a thousand,
to shew unto man his uprightness:
[24]Then he is gracious unto him, and
saith, Deliver him from going down to
the pit: I have found a ransom.
[25]His flesh shall be fresher than a
child's: he shall return to the days of his
youth:
[26]He shall pray unto God, and he will
be favourable unto him: and he shall see
his face with joy: for he will *render
unto man his *righteousness.
[27]He looketh upon men, and *if any*
say, I have sinned, and perverted *that
which was* right, and it profited me
not;
[28]He will deliver his soul from going

33:24 ransom. A truly wonderful anticipation of the Lord Jesus Christ, who came to give His life as a ransom (Matt. 20:28), paying the price of sin; for "the wages of sin is death" (Rom. 6:23). See *atonement.

into the pit, and his life shall see the
light.

4) Elihu asks for Job's answer

29Lo, all these *things* worketh God
oftentimes with man,
30To bring back his soul from the pit,
to be enlightened with the light of the
living.
31Mark well, O Job, hearken unto me:
hold thy peace, and I will speak.
32If thou hast any thing to say, answer me: speak, for I desire to justify
thee.
33If not, hearken unto me: hold thy
peace, and I shall teach thee wisdom.

Elihu's second speech
1) The wise are to listen

34 Furthermore Elihu answered
and said,
2Hear my words, O ye wise *men;* and
give ear unto me, ye that have knowledge.
3For the ear trieth words, as the
mouth tasteth meat.
4Let us choose to us judgment: let us
know among ourselves what *is* good.

2) The charges against Job

5For Job hath said, I am righteous:
and God hath taken away my judgment.
6Should I lie against my right? my
wound *is* incurable without transgression.
7What man *is* like Job, *who* drinketh
up scorning like water?
8Which goeth in company with the
workers of iniquity, and walketh with
wicked men.
9For he hath said, It profiteth a man
nothing that he should delight himself
with God.

3) Foundation of government is justice

10Therefore hearken unto me, ye
men of understanding: far be it from
God, *that he should do* wickedness; and
from the Almighty, *that he should commit* iniquity.
11For the work of a man shall he render unto him, and cause every man to
find according to *his* ways.
12Yea, surely God will not do wickedly, neither will the Almighty pervert
judgment.
13Who hath given him a charge over
the earth? or who hath disposed the
whole *world?
14If he set his heart upon man, *if* he
gather unto himself his spirit and his
breath;
15All flesh shall perish together, and
man shall turn again unto dust.
16If now *thou hast* understanding,
hear this: hearken to the voice of my
words.
17Shall even he that hateth right govern? and wilt thou condemn him that is
most just?
18*Is it fit* to say to a king, *Thou art*
wicked? *and* to princes, *Ye are* ungodly?
19*How much less to him* that accepteth
not the persons of princes, nor regardeth the rich more than the poor? for
they all *are* the work of his hands.
20In a moment shall they die, and the
people shall be troubled at midnight,
and pass away: and the mighty shall be
taken away without hand.

*4) Justice is from God's knowledge
and goodness*

21For his eyes *are* upon the ways of
man, and he seeth all his goings.
22*There is* no darkness, nor shadow of
death, where the workers of iniquity
may hide themselves.
23For he will not lay upon man more
than right; that he should enter into
judgment with God.
24He shall break in pieces mighty
men without number, and set others in
their stead.
25Therefore he knoweth their works,

34:14 breath. Compare Psalm 104:29.
34:15 dust. Compare Genesis 3:19.

and he overturneth *them* in the night,
so that they are destroyed.
26He striketh them as wicked men in
the open sight of others;
27Because they turned back from
him, and would not consider any of his
ways:
28So that they cause the cry of the
poor to come unto him, and he heareth
the cry of the afflicted.

5) To murmur is to talk against God

29When he giveth quietness, who
then can make trouble? and when he
hideth *his* face, who then can behold
him? whether *it be done* against a nation, or against a man only:
30That the hypocrite reign not, lest
the people be ensnared.
31Surely it is meet to be said unto
God, I have borne *chastisement,* I will
not *offend *any more:*
32*That which* I see not teach thou me:
if I have done iniquity, I will do no more.
33*Should it be* according to thy mind?
he will recompense it, whether thou
refuse, or whether thou choose; and not
I: therefore speak what thou knowest.

6) Job was rebellious and without wisdom

34Let men of understanding tell me,
and let a wise man hearken unto me.
35Job hath spoken without knowledge, and his words *were* without wisdom.
36My desire *is that* Job may be tried
unto the end because of *his* answers for
wicked men.
37For he addeth rebellion unto his sin,
he clappeth *his hands* among us, and
multiplieth his words against God.

7) Job's complaint that godliness does not help a man

35 Elihu spake moreover, and
said,
2Thinkest thou this to be right, *that*
thou saidst, My righteousness *is* more
than God's?
3For thou saidst, What advantage will
it be unto thee? *and,* What profit shall I
have, *if I be cleansed* from my sin?
4I will answer thee, and thy companions with thee.

8) Righteousness and sin do not affect God

5Look unto the heavens, and see; and
behold the clouds *which* are higher than
thou.
6If thou sinnest, what doest thou
against him? or *if* thy transgressions be
multiplied, what doest thou unto him?
7If thou be righteous, what givest
thou him? or what receiveth he of thine
hand?
8Thy wickedness *may hurt* a man as
thou *art;* and thy righteousness *may
profit* the son of man.

9) Man's prayer is often like the instinctive cry of an animal

9By reason of the multitude of oppressions they make *the oppressed* to
cry: they cry out by reason of the arm
of the mighty.
10But none saith, Where *is* God my
maker, who giveth songs in the night;
11Who teacheth us more than the
beasts of the earth, and maketh us wiser than the fowls of heaven?
12There they cry, but none giveth
answer, because of the pride of evil
men.
13Surely God will not hear vanity,
neither will the Almighty regard it.
14Although thou sayest thou shalt not
see him, *yet* *judgment *is* before him;
therefore *trust thou in him.
15But now, because *it is* not *so,* he hath
visited in his anger; yet he knoweth *it*
not in great extremity:
16Therefore doth Job open his mouth
in vain; he multiplieth words without
knowledge.

10) God is great and just

36 Elihu also proceeded, and said,
2Suffer me a little, and I will
shew thee that *I have* yet to speak on
God's behalf.
3I will fetch my knowledge from afar,

and will ascribe righteousness to my
Maker.
4For truly my words *shall* not *be* false:
he that is perfect in knowledge *is* with
thee.
5Behold, God *is* mighty, and despiseth not *any: he is* mighty in strength
and wisdom.
6He preserveth not the life of the
wicked: but giveth right to the poor.
7He withdraweth not his eyes from
the righteous: but with kings *are they* on
the throne; yea, he doth establish them
for ever, and they are exalted.
8And if *they be* bound in fetters, *and*
be holden in cords of affliction;
9Then he sheweth them their work,
and their transgressions that they have
exceeded.
10He openeth also their ear to discipline, and commandeth that they return
from iniquity.
11If they obey and serve *him,* they
shall spend their days in prosperity, and
their years in pleasures.
12But if they obey not, they shall perish by the sword, and they shall die
without knowledge.
13But the hypocrites in heart heap up
wrath: they cry not when he bindeth
them.
14They die in youth, and their life *is*
among the *unclean.
15He delivereth the poor in his affliction, and openeth their ears in oppression.
16Even so would he have removed
thee out of the strait *into* a broad place,
where *there is* no straitness; and that
which should be set on thy table *should*
be full of fatness.
17But thou hast fulfilled the judgment
of the wicked: judgment and justice
take hold *on thee.*
18Because *there is* wrath, *beware* lest
he take thee away with *his* stroke: then
a great ransom cannot deliver thee.
19Will he esteem thy riches? *no,* not
gold, nor all the forces of strength.
20Desire not the night, when people
are cut off in their place.
21Take heed, regard not iniquity: for
this hast thou chosen rather than affliction.
22Behold, God exalteth by his power:
who teacheth like him?
23Who hath enjoined him his way? or
who can say, Thou hast wrought iniquity?

11) The wonders of God in nature

24Remember that thou magnify his
work, which men behold.
25Every man may see it; man may
behold *it* afar off.
26Behold, God *is* great, and we know
him not, neither can the number of his
years be searched out.
27For he maketh small the drops of
water: they pour down rain according to
the vapour thereof:
28Which the clouds do drop *and* distil upon man abundantly.
29Also can *any* understand the
spreadings of the clouds, *or* the noise of
his tabernacle?
30Behold, he spreadeth his light upon
it, and covereth the bottom of the sea.
31For by them judgeth he the people;
he giveth meat in abundance.
32With clouds he covereth the light;
and commandeth it *not to shine* by *the*
cloud that cometh betwixt.
33The noise thereof sheweth concerning it, the cattle also concerning
the vapour.

12) More about the wonders
of God in nature

37 At this also my heart trembleth, and is moved out of his
place.

36:21 this hast thou chosen. Compare this with Hebrews 11:25.
36:30 light. Lightning.
36:31 For by them. The storm is the agent both of judgment and, by fertilizing the earth, of plenty.

[2]Hear attentively the noise of his voice, and the sound *that* goeth out of his mouth.
[3]He directeth it under the whole heaven, and his lightning unto the ends of the earth.
[4]After it a voice roareth: he thundereth with the voice of his excellency; and he will not stay them when his voice is heard.
[5]God thundereth marvellously with his voice; great things doeth he, which we cannot comprehend.
[6]For he saith to the snow, Be thou *on* the earth; likewise to the small rain, and to the great rain of his strength.
[7]He sealeth up the hand of every man; that all men may know his work.
[8]Then the beasts go into dens, and remain in their places.
[9]Out of the south cometh the whirlwind: and cold out of the north.
[10]By the breath of God frost is given: and the breadth of the waters is straitened.
[11]Also by watering he wearieth the thick cloud: he scattereth his bright cloud:
[12]And it is turned round about by his counsels: that they may do whatsoever he commandeth them upon the face of the world in the earth.
[13]He causeth it to come, whether for correction, or for his land, or for *mercy.
[14]Hearken unto this, O Job: stand still, and consider the wondrous works of God.
[15]Dost thou know when God disposed them, and caused the light of his cloud to shine?
[16]Dost thou know the balancings of the clouds, the wondrous works of him which is perfect in knowledge?
[17]How thy garments *are* warm, when he quieteth the earth by the south *wind?*
[18]Hast thou with him spread out the sky, *which is* strong, *and* as a molten looking glass?
[19]Teach us what we shall say unto him; *for* we cannot order *our speech* by reason of darkness.
[20]Shall it be told him that I speak? if a man speak, surely he shall be swallowed up.
[21]And now *men* see not the bright light which *is* in the clouds: but the wind passeth, and cleanseth them.
[22]Fair weather cometh out of the north: with God *is* terrible majesty.
[23]*Touching* the Almighty, we cannot find him out: *he is* excellent in power, and in judgment, and in plenty of justice: he will not afflict.
[24]Men do therefore *fear him: he respecteth not any *that are* wise of heart.

V. God and Job (38:1—41:34)

1) A review of the wonders of nature

38 Then the LORD answered Job out of the whirlwind, and said,
[2]Who *is* this that darkeneth counsel by words without knowledge?
[3]Gird up now thy loins like a man; for I will demand of thee, and answer thou me.

37:3-4 lightning . . . thundereth. See Psalm 29:3-9 for a description of God's voice—the thunder.

37:6-7 snow . . . rain . . . sealeth up the hand of every man. Men are forced to stop work and seek refuge during a bad storm.

37:12 it is turned round about by his counsels. God causes it the sun to move in its circuit.

38:1 the LORD answered Job. Elihu had spoken. Job made no reply, and in the silence the voice of God was heard. Before this the discussions had been about God as if He were not there. Now Job was face-to-face with the LORD.

38:1 out of the whirlwind. In Old Testament times a great storm was the outward sign of God's presence. See Exodus 19:16; 1 Kings 19:11; Ezekiel 1:4; Nahum 1:3.

38:3 Gird up now thy loins. This means "Get ready for a contest." During work or battle, the lower garment was always tucked in so it didn't interfere with the freedom of movement.

4Where wast thou when I laid the
foundations of the earth? declare, if
thou hast understanding.
5Who hath laid the measures thereof,
if thou knowest? or who hath stretched
the line upon it?
6Whereupon are the foundations
thereof fastened? or who laid the corner stone thereof;
7When the morning stars sang together, and all the sons of God shouted
for joy?
8Or *who* shut up the sea with doors,
when it brake forth, *as if* it had issued
out of the womb?
9When I made the cloud the garment
thereof, and thick darkness a swad-
dlingband for it,
10And brake up for it my decreed
place, and set bars and doors,
11And said, Hitherto shalt thou come,
but no further: and here shall thy proud
waves be stayed?
12Hast thou commanded the morning
since thy days; *and* caused the dayspring to know his place;
13That it might take hold of the ends
of the earth, that the wicked might be
shaken out of it?
14It is turned as clay *to* the seal; and
they stand as a garment.
15And from the wicked their light is
withholden, and the high arm shall be
broken.
16Hast thou entered into the springs
of the sea? or hast thou walked in the
search of the depth?
17Have the gates of *death been
opened unto thee? or hast thou seen
the doors of the shadow of death?
18Hast thou perceived the breadth
of the earth? declare if thou knowest
it all.
19Where *is* the way *where* light
dwelleth? and *as for* darkness, where *is*
the place thereof,
20That thou shouldest take it to the
bound thereof, and that thou shouldest know the paths *to* the house
thereof?
21Knowest thou *it,* because thou wast
then born? or *because* the number of thy
days *is* great?
22Hast thou entered into the treasures of the snow? or hast thou seen
the treasures of the hail,
23Which I have reserved against the
time of trouble, against the day of battle and war?
24By what way is the light parted,
which scattereth the east wind upon the
earth?
25Who hath divided a watercourse for
the overflowing of waters, or a way for
the lightning of thunder;
26To cause it to rain on the earth,
where no man *is; on* the wilderness,
wherein *there is* no man;
27To satisfy the desolate and waste
ground; and to cause the bud of the tender herb to spring forth?
28Hath the rain a father? or who hath
begotten the drops of dew?
29Out of whose womb came the ice?
and the hoary frost of heaven, who hath
gendered it?
30The waters are hid as *with* a stone,
and the face of the deep is frozen.
31Canst thou bind the sweet influences of Pleiades, or loose the bands of
Orion?
32Canst thou bring forth Mazzaroth in
his season? or canst thou guide Arcturus with his sons?
33Knowest thou the ordinances of
heaven? canst thou set the dominion
thereof in the earth?
34Canst thou lift up thy voice to the

38:14 turned as clay to the seal. The reference is to the inscription on a clay seal that is written backward and, on being impressed on a soft object, is reversed and comes out in perfect order. So the sun changes the chaos of night into the order of day.

38:32 his sons. Offspring. It probably refers to the stars around Arcturus in the constellation Boötes, which has ten named stars.

38:33 ordinances. The reference to the LORD as the giver of the ordinances is found in Jeremiah 31:35.

clouds, that abundance of waters may
cover thee?
35Canst thou send lightnings, that
they may go, and say unto thee, Here
we *are?*
36Who hath put wisdom in the inward
parts? or who hath given understanding to the heart?
37Who can number the clouds in wisdom? or who can stay the bottles of
heaven,
38When the dust groweth into hardness, and the clods cleave fast together?

2) A review of the wonders of animal life

39Wilt thou hunt the prey for the lion?
or fill the appetite of the young lions,
40When they couch in *their* dens, *and*
abide in the covert to lie in wait?
41Who provideth for the raven his
food? when his young ones cry unto
God, they wander for lack of meat.

God and Job (continued)

39 Knowest thou the time when
the wild goats of the rock bring
forth? *or* canst thou mark when the
hinds do calve?
2Canst thou number the months *that*
they fulfil? or knowest thou the time
when they bring forth?
3They bow themselves, they bring
forth their young ones, they cast out
their sorrows.
4Their young ones are in good liking,
they grow up with corn; they go forth,
and return not unto them.
5Who hath sent out the wild ass free?
or who hath loosed the bands of the wild
ass?
6Whose house I have made the wilderness, and the barren land his dwellings.
7He scorneth the multitude of the
city, neither regardeth he the crying of
the driver.
8The range of the mountains *is* his
pasture, and he searcheth after every
green thing.
9Will the unicorn be willing to serve
thee, or abide by thy crib?
10Canst thou bind the unicorn with
his band in the furrow? or will he harrow the valleys after thee?
11Wilt thou trust him, because his
strength *is* great? or wilt thou leave thy
labour to him?

38:31-32 THE CONSTELLATIONS

The constellations mentioned in verses 31-32 are "the seven stars and Orion," referred to in Amos 5:8 (see also its note). "Sweet influences" means *twinkling.*

1. Orion stands for the storm and tempest. The bands (or belt) of Orion describe the combination of stars into a constellation, as though they are bound by invisible chains or bands.
2. The Pleiades form a beautiful little group of stars. Only six can be seen by most people, since one of the stars that was once clearly visible has become dimmer. With a telescope many hundreds of stars can be seen in the cluster. These have been photographed and look something like beautiful pearls on strings of light.
3. Mazzaroth is the Hebrew word for the twelve signs or constellations of the zodiac, although this verse is not in any way referring to or condoning astrology since the use of astrology was strictly forbidden by God, both then and now (see Deut. 18:10-14).
4. Arcturus is the fourth brightest star in the sky (twenty-four times brighter than our sun). It has been called "the Guardian of the Bear," referring to Ursa Major (the Great Bear), better known as the Big Dipper. Arcturus, which is part of the constellation Boötes and which circles the Big Dipper, can be found by tracing a path from the end of the handle of the Big Dipper to the bright star Arcturus. Shepherds used Arcturus for guidance at night but, of course, did not try to guide it.

39:7 crying of the driver. A description familiar to those who have traveled in the East and have heard the constant shouts of the drivers to their horses.

39:10 unicorn. A horned animal with great strength. See Numbers 23:22; Deuteronomy 33:17; Psalm 22:21.

12Wilt thou believe him, that he will bring home thy seed, and gather *it into* thy barn?

13*Gavest thou* the goodly wings unto the peacocks? or wings and feathers unto the ostrich?

14Which leaveth her eggs in the earth, and warmeth them in dust,

15And forgetteth that the foot may crush them, or that the wild beast may break them.

16She is hardened against her young ones, as though *they were* not hers: her labour is in vain without fear;

17Because *God hath deprived her of wisdom, neither hath he imparted to her understanding.

18What time she lifteth up herself on high, she scorneth the horse and his rider.

19Hast thou given the horse strength? hast thou clothed his neck with thunder?

20Canst thou make him afraid as a grasshopper? the glory of his nostrils *is* terrible.

21He paweth in the valley, and rejoiceth in *his* strength: he goeth on to meet the armed men.

22He mocketh at fear, and is not affrighted; neither turneth he back from the sword.

23The quiver rattleth against him, the glittering spear and the shield.

24He swalloweth the ground with fierceness and rage: neither believeth he that *it is* the sound of the trumpet.

25He saith among the trumpets, Ha, ha; and he smelleth the battle afar off, the thunder of the captains, and the shouting.

26Doth the hawk fly by thy wisdom, *and* stretch her wings toward the south?

27Doth the eagle mount up at thy command, and make her nest on high?

28She dwelleth and abideth on the rock, upon the crag of the rock, and the strong place.

29From thence she seeketh the prey, *and* her eyes behold afar off.

30Her young ones also suck up blood: and where the slain *are,* there *is* she.

God and Job (continued)

40 Moreover the LORD answered Job, and said,

2Shall he that contendeth with the Almighty instruct *him?* he that reproveth God, let him answer it.

The effect on Job

¶3Then Job answered the LORD, and said,

4Behold, I am vile; what shall I answer thee? I will lay mine hand upon my mouth.

5Once have I spoken; but I will not answer: yea, twice; but I will proceed no further.

The LORD's second answer to Job

¶6Then answered the LORD unto Job out of the whirlwind, and said,

40:6 The LORD's Response
The LORD's second answer to Job was, in effect, "Shall man charge God with unrighteousness in His rule of the world?" As Job had challenged God's rule of the world, he was ironically invited to clothe himself with the divine powers and take over ruling of the world, in which live such monsters as the behemoth and leviathan (40:6–41:34).

7Gird up thy loins now like a man: I will demand of thee, and declare thou unto me.

8Wilt thou also disannul my judgment? wilt thou condemn me, that thou mayest be righteous?

9Hast thou an arm like God? or canst thou thunder with a voice like him?

10Deck thyself now *with* majesty and excellency; and array thyself with glory and beauty.

11Cast abroad the rage of thy wrath: and behold every one *that is* proud, and abase him.

12Look on every one *that is* proud, *and* bring him low; and tread down the wicked in their place.

13 Hide them in the dust together; *and* bind their faces in secret.

14 Then will I also *confess unto thee that thine own right hand can save thee.

¶ 15 Behold now behemoth, which I made with thee; he eateth grass as an ox.

16 Lo now, his strength *is* in his loins, and his force *is* in the navel of his belly.

17 He moveth his tail like a cedar: the sinews of his stones are wrapped together.

18 His bones *are as* strong pieces of brass; his bones *are* like bars of iron.

19 He *is* the chief of the ways of God: he that made him can make his sword to approach *unto him.*

20 Surely the mountains bring him forth food, where all the beasts of the field play.

21 He lieth under the shady trees, in the covert of the reed, and fens.

22 The shady trees cover him *with* their shadow; the willows of the brook compass him about.

23 Behold, he drinketh up a river, *and* hasteth not: he trusteth that he can draw up Jordan into his mouth.

24 He taketh it with his eyes: *his* nose pierceth through snares.

God and Job (continued)

41 Canst thou draw out leviathan with an hook? or his tongue with a cord *which* thou lettest down?

2 Canst thou put an hook into his nose? or bore his jaw through with a thorn?

3 Will he make many supplications unto thee? will he speak soft *words* unto thee?

4 Will he make a *covenant with thee? wilt thou take him for a servant for ever?

5 Wilt thou play with him as *with* a bird? or wilt thou bind him for thy maidens?

6 Shall the companions make a banquet of him? shall they part him among the merchants?

7 Canst thou fill his skin with barbed irons? or his head with fish spears?

8 Lay thine hand upon him, remember the battle, do no more.

9 Behold, the *hope of him is in vain: shall not *one* be cast down even at the sight of him?

10 None *is so* fierce that dare stir him up: who then is able to stand before me?

11 Who hath *prevented me, that I should repay *him? whatsoever is* under the whole heaven is mine.

12 I will not conceal his parts, nor his power, nor his comely proportion.

13 Who can discover the face of his garment? *or* who can come *to him* with his double bridle?

14 Who can open the doors of his face? his teeth *are* terrible round about.

15 *His* scales *are his* pride, shut up together *as with* a close seal.

16 One is so near to another, that no air can come between them.

17 They are joined one to another, they stick together, that they cannot be sundered.

18 By his neesings a light doth shine, and his eyes *are* like the eyelids of the morning.

19 Out of his mouth go burning lamps, *and* sparks of fire leap out.

20 Out of his nostrils goeth smoke, as *out* of a seething pot or caldron.

21 His breath kindleth coals, and a flame goeth out of his mouth.

22 In his neck remaineth strength, and sorrow is turned into joy before him.

23 The flakes of his flesh are joined together: they are firm in themselves; they cannot be moved.

40:15 behemoth. A plural noun refering to a large land animal.
41:1 leviathan. This word is often used, as in Psalm 104:26, for any great beast of the waters.
41:17 sundered. Separated.
41:18 neesings. Sneezings.

24 His heart is as firm as a stone; yea, as hard as a piece of the nether *millstone.*

25 When he raiseth up himself, the mighty are afraid: by reason of breakings they purify themselves.

26 The sword of him that layeth at him cannot hold: the spear, the dart, nor the *habergeon.

27 He esteemeth iron as straw, *and* brass as rotten wood.

28 The arrow cannot make him flee: slingstones are turned with him into stubble.

29 Darts are counted as stubble: he laugheth at the shaking of a spear.

30 Sharp stones *are* under him: he spreadeth sharp pointed things upon the mire.

31 He maketh the deep to boil like a pot: he maketh the sea like a pot of ointment.

32 He maketh a path to shine after him; *one* would think the deep *to be* hoary.

33 Upon earth there is not his like, who is made without fear.

34 He beholdeth all high *things:* he *is* a king over all the children of pride.

VI. Job's Last Answer (42:1-6)

42 Then Job answered the LORD, and said,

2 I know that thou canst do every *thing,* and *that* no thought can be withholden from thee.

3 Who *is* he that hideth counsel without knowledge? therefore have I uttered that I understood not; things too wonderful for me, which I knew not.

4 Hear, I beseech thee, and I will speak: I will demand of thee, and declare thou unto me.

5 I have heard of thee by the hearing of the ear: but now mine eye seeth thee.

6 Wherefore I abhor *myself,* and repent in dust and ashes.

VII. Conclusion (42:7-17)

¶7 And it was *so,* that after the LORD had spoken these words unto Job, the LORD said to Eliphaz the Temanite, My wrath is kindled against thee, and against thy two friends: for ye have not spoken of me *the thing that is* right, as my servant Job *hath.*

8 Therefore take unto you now seven bullocks and seven rams, and go to my servant Job, and offer up for yourselves a burnt-offering; and my servant Job shall pray for you: for him will I accept: lest I deal with you *after your* folly, in that ye have not spoken of me *the thing which is* right, like my servant Job.

9 So Eliphaz the Temanite and Bildad the Shuhite *and* Zophar the Naamathite went, and did according as the LORD commanded them: the LORD also accepted Job.

10 And the LORD turned the captivity of Job, when he prayed for his friends:

41:26 layeth at . . . habergeon. Ordinary weapons are not effective against the beast.

41:30 Sharp stones are under him. Sharp stones refer to the leviathan's covering. Compare Ezekiel 28:13-16.

41:31 He maketh the deep to boil. The description in verses 31-32 is of the foam or waves on the water as the leviathan swims through it.

41:31 a pot of ointment. Like the medicine bowl in which steaming mixtures were prepared.

42:2 I know that thou canst do every thing, and that no thought can be withholden from thee. Job humbled himself before God. He realized that God could do even what seemed impossible to human eyes (Matt. 19:26). God knows the thoughts and intents of our hearts, and He will always accomplish His purposes in His time.

42:5 mine eye seeth thee. This does not mean that Job saw God with his physical eyes, since this would be contrary to John 1:18 (see vs. 18 note, "Seeing God"), but Job had understood Him and been in His presence. It was a spiritual sight to which he referred.

42:7 And it was so. Job was vindicated, honored, and blessed.

42:10 Job's Losses and Restoration

Losses	Restored
7 sons	7 sons
3 daughters	3 daughters
7,000 sheep	14,000 sheep
3,000 camels	6,000 camels
1,000 oxen	2,000 oxen
500 donkeys	1,000 donkeys
large household	lived 140 years
greatest man of the East	saw four generations of children

also the LORD gave Job twice as much
as he had before.
[11]Then came there unto him all his
brethren, and all his sisters, and all they
that had been of his acquaintance before, and did eat bread with him in his
house: and they bemoaned him, and
comforted him over all the evil that the
LORD had brought upon him: every man
also gave him a piece of money, and
every one an earring of gold.
[12]So the LORD blessed the latter end
of Job more than his beginning: for he
had fourteen thousand sheep, and six
thousand camels, and a thousand yoke
of oxen, and a thousand she asses.
[13]He had also seven sons and three
daughters.
[14]And he called the name of the first,
Jemima; and the name of the second,
Kezia; and the name of the third, Ker-
en-happuch.
[15]And in all the land were no women
found *so* fair as the daughters of Job:
and their father gave them inheritance
among their brethren.
[16]After this lived Job an hundred and
forty years, and saw his sons, and his
sons' sons, *even* four generations.
[17]So Job died, *being* old and full of
days.

42:6 THE PROBLEM SOLVED

The question, "Why do the righteous suffer?" is answered here, at least in part. One way the LORD uses suffering is to correct and purify the righteous—not to punish them for sins. Job was godly and possessed a wonderful faith that even his afflictions could not shake. But he was not humble enough and was inclined to be self-righteous. When brought into the presence of God, he realized his sinfulness and judged himself, and this opened the doors to restored happiness and greater fruitfulness. Christians often have the same problem, which is solved in the same way (Heb. 12:7-11; 1 Cor. 11:31-32; see also 1 Cor. 11:31 note). Sometimes the cause of suffering is not clear to us as humans. In these times, we must realize that we live in a fallen world, and suffering and pain are a part of this world (see Matt. 5:45). Even when we don't understand, we must cling to God and trust that, whatever His purpose in allowing suffering into our lives, He is with us. He will accomplish His purposes through whatever difficulties or suffering we are experiencing. Job realized this when he said, "Though he slay me, yet will I trust in him" (Job 13:15).

42:11 brethren, and all his sisters. This is an expression to indicate all Job's relatives. It was customary to present a gift to one who had recovered from an illness or escaped from danger.

42:12 more than his beginning. Job now had double the number of sheep, camels, oxen, and donkeys that he possessed in the beginning (see 1:3).

42:13 seven sons and three daughters. This, too, was a double measure, since the first ten would appear again, at the Resurrection, of which Job spoke in faith (19:25).

42:15 gave them inheritance. It was extremely unusual for daughters to receive an inheritance, except in cases where there were no sons.

42:16 an hundred and forty years. In this, too, Job was repaid twofold, having twice the usual life span, given in Psalm 90:10.

The Book of

PSALMS

BACKGROUND

The book of Psalms is a collection of songs or poems. It is the ancient Hebrew hymn book made available for mankind by translation. The word "psalm" is our rendering of the Hebrew *tehillim* which means *praises.*

TYPES OF PSALMS

Some of the psalms are individual psalms; that is, they were secret closet prayers, which were spoken to God Himself by different people to express their feelings, sufferings, and desires. Sometimes they were prayers of confession, and often they were cries for God's help in times of deep trouble.

Some of the individual psalms are called "Messianic psalms" because they are prophecies of our Lord's coming to earth, of His death, resurrection, second coming and final kingship. The most amazing of the Messianic psalms is Psalm 22, for it describes the crucifixion at a date when this unusual form of execution was unknown to the Jews. Though the psalms in which we can most clearly see a picture of the Lord Jesus Christ are given the title "Messianic," there are other prophetic psalms: the national psalms which foretell the future sufferings of the nation of Israel before their King and ours, the Lord Jesus Christ, as Messiah returns to the earth.

Other psalms, used especially for services in the temple, were called "temple psalms." A few of the psalms are called "imprecatory psalms." These are the cry of an oppressed people, calling upon God to defeat or curse their enemies.

The best-known psalm is the Twenty-third or Shepherd Psalm of David, which has been rendered into modern hymns.

THEME

The Hebrew Bible was divided into three parts: the Law, or Books of Moses; the Prophets; and the Writings. The Psalms had first place in the Writings (see Luke 24:44), and as a whole, appear as the keystone of Scripture, with Psalm 81:9,10—the exact center of the Bible—at the center of faith, stating what God expects of man, and what He does for those who obey Him.

STRUCTURE

The entire book of Psalms is divided into five books, each ending with a doxology or praise. Some have compared these five books of psalms to the five books of the Law, the Pentateuch.

WRITERS

A great many of the psalms were written by David; others were written by Asaph and the Sons of Korah; one was probably written by Moses (Psalm 90); and some believe that Solomon wrote two (Psalms 72; 127). Many of the writers are not known. Moses was the Lawgiver, David and his son, Solomon, were kings in Jerusalem, and a word may be said about the less known psalmists: David appointed three choirmasters for worship in the tabernacle (1 Chronicles 15:19); these musicians played the cymbals—so beating time. The first was Heman (Psalm 88) the second, Asaph (Psalms 50, 73–83; and the third, Ethan (Psalm 89).

OUTLINE OF PSALMS

I.	Book One	Psalms 1–41
II.	Book Two	Psalms 42–72
III.	Book Three	Psalms 73–89
IV.	Book Four	Psalms 90–106
V.	Book Five	Psalms 107–150

BOOK I

Psalm 1

1Blessed *is* the man that walketh not
in the counsel of the ungodly, nor
standeth in the way of sinners, nor sitteth in the seat of the scornful.

1:1 The Blessed Man
The blessed man spoken of here is the Lord Jesus Christ in *type (compare 2 Tim. 1:10). The word "blessed" could also have been translated "happy." The first three verses not only show forth the Lord, who is our example (1 Pet. 2:21); they show what the truly righteous man is–the example that Christians should show to others (1 Tim. 4:12).

2But his delight *is* in the *law of the
LORD; and in his law doth he meditate
day and night.
3And he shall be like a tree planted
by the rivers of water, that bringeth
forth his fruit in his season; his leaf also
shall not wither; and whatsoever he
doeth shall prosper.
4The ungodly *are* not so: but *are* like
the chaff which the wind driveth away.
5Therefore the ungodly shall not
stand in the *judgment, nor sinners in
the congregation of the righteous.
6For the LORD knoweth the way of
the righteous: but the way of the ungodly shall perish.

Psalm 2

Messianic

*The *Holy Spirit speaks*

1Why do the heathen rage, and the
people imagine a vain thing?
2The kings of the earth set themselves, and the rulers take counsel to-

1:3 tree planted by the rivers. Compare this thought with our Lord as the Vine (John 15:1-6). See also Matthew 21:18-22, where the fig tree was barren; and the fulfillment of the parable in Revelation 22:1-2.

1:3 whatsoever he doeth. This verse, with its picture of a tree, speaks of fruit bearing in service for God, which will prosper because it is for Him and of Him–in His power (see Phil. 4:13; Rom. 8:28).

Psalm 2. One of David's psalms (see Acts 4:25), though it is not given this title. It is a messianic psalm.

gether, against the LORD, and against
his anointed, *saying,*
3 Let us break their bands asunder,
and cast away their cords from us.
4 He that sitteth in the heavens shall
laugh: the Lord shall have them in derision.
5 Then shall he speak unto them in his
wrath, and vex them in his sore displeasure.

Jehovah speaks

6 Yet have I set my king upon my holy
hill of *Zion.

Christ speaks

7 I will declare the decree: the LORD
hath said unto me, Thou *art* my Son;
this day have I begotten thee.

> **2:7 The First Begotten**
> This does not refer to Jesus as a baby born in Bethlehem but to Christ raised from the dead by the Father's power (Acts 13:33), when He became the "firstborn" or first begotten of "many brethren" (Rom. 8:29)–that is, He was the first One who rose from the dead never to die again.

8 Ask of me, and I shall give *thee* the
heathen *for* thine inheritance, and
the uttermost parts of the earth *for* thy
possession.
9 Thou shalt break them with a rod of
iron; thou shalt dash them in pieces like
a potter's vessel.

The Holy Spirit speaks

10 Be wise now therefore, O ye kings:
be instructed, ye judges of the earth.
11 Serve the LORD with *fear, and rejoice with trembling.
12 Kiss the Son, lest he be angry, and
ye perish *from* the way, when his wrath
is kindled but a little. Blessed *are* all
they that put their *trust in him.

Psalm 3

The Morning Psalm

A Psalm of *David, when he fled from Absalom his son.

1 LORD, how are they increased that
trouble me! many *are* they that rise up
against me.
2 Many *there be* which say of my soul,
There is no help for him in *God. *Selah.
3 But thou, O LORD, *art* a shield for
me; my glory, and the lifter up of mine
head.
4 I cried unto the LORD with my voice,
and he heard me out of his holy hill.
Selah.
5 I laid me down and slept; I awaked;
for the LORD sustained me.
6 I will not be afraid of ten thousands
of people, that have set *themselves*
against me round about.
7 Arise, O LORD; save me, O my God:
for thou hast smitten all mine enemies
upon the cheek bone; thou hast broken
the teeth of the ungodly.
8 *Salvation *belongeth* unto the LORD:
thy blessing *is* upon thy people. Selah.

Psalm 4

To the chief Musician on Neginoth, A Psalm of David.

1 Hear me when I call, O God of my

2:2 his anointed. The Son of God, the Lord Jesus. This is a prophetic picture.
2:3 break their bands. The rejection of the Messiah's authority by those who would not submit to it (compare Luke 19:14).
2:6 my king. This is a prophecy of Christ's coming to Jerusalem to be rejected (Matt. 21:1-11), and returning to reign (Rev. 22:3).
2:7 Thou art my Son. This is explained in Acts 13:33; Hebrews 1:5; and 5:5.
2:9 break them. The Lord Jesus Christ will break the power of evildoers when He comes again. (See Rev. 2:27; 12:5; 19:15; compare 1 John 2:13-14.)
2:12 Kiss the Son. Receive Him as Saviour, worship Him, and love Him.
3:title. See 2 Samuel 15:13.
4:title. "Neginoth" means *smitings,* and speaks of smiting the strings of a harp with the hand.

*righteousness: thou hast enlarged me
when I was in distress; have *mercy
upon me, and hear my *prayer.
2 O ye sons of men, how long *will ye
turn* my glory into shame? *how long* will
ye love *vanity, *and* seek after leasing?
Selah.
3 But know that the LORD hath set
apart him that is godly for himself: the
LORD will hear when I call unto him.
4 Stand in awe, and *sin not: commune with your own heart upon your
bed, and be still. Selah.
5 Offer the sacrifices of righteousness, and put your trust in the LORD.
6 *There be* many that say, Who will
shew us *any* good? LORD, lift thou up
the light of thy countenance upon us.
7 Thou hast put gladness in my heart,
more than in the time *that* their corn
and their wine increased.
8 I will both lay me down in *peace,
and sleep: for thou, LORD, only makest
me dwell in safety.

Psalm 5

To the chief Musician upon Nehiloth,
A Psalm of David.

1 Give ear to my words, O LORD, consider my meditation.
2 Hearken unto the voice of my cry,
my King, and my God: for unto thee will
I pray.
3 My voice shalt thou hear in the
morning, O LORD; in the morning will
I direct *my prayer* unto thee, and will
look up.
4 For thou *art* not a God that hath pleasure in wickedness: neither shall evil
dwell with thee.
5 The foolish shall not stand in thy
sight: thou hatest all workers of iniquity.
6 Thou shalt destroy them that speak
leasing: the LORD will abhor the bloody
and deceitful man.
7 But as for me, I will come *into* thy
house in the multitude of thy mercy:
and in thy fear will I worship toward thy
holy temple.

5:7 The LORD's Mercy
We do not come to the LORD's house because we are worthy to come; we come even though we have a multitude of sins, for the LORD's mercy to those who believe in Him is even greater than all our sin.

8 Lead me, O LORD, in thy righteousness because of mine enemies; make
thy way straight before my face.
9 For *there is* no faithfulness in their
mouth; their inward part *is* very wickedness; their throat *is* an open sepulchre; they flatter with their tongue.
10 Destroy thou them, O God; let
them fall by their own counsels; cast
them out in the multitude of their transgressions; for they have rebelled
against thee.

5:10 Praying for Judgment
This psalm is one of the imprecatory prayers—humans praying for judgment on fellow humans. These prayers show that enforcement of righteousness is essential to society. They foreshadow the time when God will finally deal with those who refuse to accept and obey His love and salvation. Some of the other imprecatory psalms are 35, 58, 109.

11 But let all those that put their trust
in thee rejoice: let them ever shout for
joy, because thou defendest them: let
them also that love thy name be joyful
in thee.

4:1 enlarged. David was helpless and in trouble, but the LORD came to him and gave him strength and courage—a bigger man for bigger tasks.
4:2 leasing. Lies; all that is false and vain.
5:5 foolish. Those who foolishly choose not to serve the LORD but to serve Satan.
5:9 open sepulchre. In this life, we may stumble and fall. But those who believe the lies of the wicked will definitely stumble and fall into sin.

[12]For thou, LORD, wilt bless the righteous; with favour wilt thou compass him as *with* a shield.

Psalm 6

To the chief Musician on Neginoth upon Sheminith, A Psalm of David.

[1]O LORD, rebuke me not in thine anger, neither *chasten me in thy hot displeasure.
[2]Have mercy upon me, O LORD; for I *am* weak: O LORD, heal me; for my bones are vexed.
[3]My soul is also sore vexed: but thou, O LORD, how long?
[4]Return, O LORD, deliver my soul: oh save me for thy mercies' sake.
[5]For in *death *there is* no remembrance of thee: in the *grave who shall give thee thanks?
[6]I am weary with my groaning; all the night make I my bed to swim; I water my couch with my tears.
[7]Mine eye is consumed because of grief; it waxeth old because of all mine enemies.
[8]Depart from me, all ye workers of iniquity; for the LORD hath heard the voice of my weeping.
[9]The LORD hath heard my supplication; the LORD will receive my prayer.
[10]Let all mine enemies be ashamed and sore vexed: let them return *and* be ashamed suddenly.

Psalm 7

Shiggaion of David, which he sang unto the LORD, concerning the words of Cush the Benjamite.

[1]O LORD my God, in thee do I put my

TECHNICAL WORDS IN THE PSALMS

1. "Alamoth" (Ps. 46). This word means *set to maidens' voices*. It probably referred to the maidens' choir.
2. "Gittith" (Ps. 8). An instrument, or perhaps tune, invented in Gath.
3. "Higgaion" (Ps. 9:16). This word means *meditation*. Thus the verse is a matter for serious thought.
4. "Mahalath" (Ps. 88). This word may be the name of a musical instrument or it may possibly mean *dancing,* but the meaning is obscure.
5. "Maschil" (Ps. 32). This means *to give instruction*.
6. "Neginah" (Ps. 61). This means *with stringed instruments*.
7. "Neginoth" (Ps. 4). This word means *smiting* and speaks of smiting the strings of the harp with the hand.
8. "Nehiloth" (Ps. 5). This word means *a wood instrument,* perhaps the flute, and only occurs in the title of Psalm 5.
9. "Selah" (throughout the Psalms). A Hebrew musical word, meaning *a pause*. Wherever it occurred in the singing of the Psalms, the singers stopped and only the musical instruments were heard, while the people thought about the words that had gone before. In time it came to mean just the pause–a call to stop for a time of quiet thought on the wonderful words and works of the LORD.
10. "Sheminith" (Ps. 6). This means *upon the octave* or *the eighth* below the treble. It probably indicated the male choir.
11. "Shiggaion" (Ps. 7). This is a word derived from the verb "to err" or "to wonder"; it could mean *wild* or *ecstatic*. Therefore, this psalm was written to express intense emotion, as anguish or a lament.
12. "Michtam" (Ps. 16). This may mean *to cover,* as in covering one's mouth.

5:12 compass. Surround.
6:3 sore vexed. Literally, *greatly troubled.* In this penitential psalm, David is seeking God's forgiveness. See Psalm 38 note, "The Penitential Psalms."
6:8 Depart from me. Note Christ's use of these words in Matthew 7:23.
7:title. For more on the word "shiggaion," see Habakkuk 3:1 note.
7:title. the words of Cush the Benjamite. It is not known who Cush was, but he was

trust: save me from all them that persecute me, and deliver me:
2 Lest he tear my soul like a lion,
rending *it* in pieces, while *there is* none
to deliver.
3 O LORD my God, if I have done this;
if there be iniquity in my hands;
4 If I have rewarded evil unto him that
was at peace with me; (yea, I have delivered him that without cause is mine
enemy:)
5 Let the enemy persecute my soul,
and take *it;* yea, let him tread down my
life upon the earth, and lay mine honour
in the dust. Selah.
6 Arise, O LORD, in thine anger, lift up
thyself because of the rage of mine enemies: and awake for me *to* the *judgment *that* thou hast commanded.
7 So shall the congregation of the people compass thee about: for their sakes
therefore return thou on high.
8 The LORD shall judge the people:
judge me, O LORD, according to my
righteousness, and according to mine
integrity *that is* in me.
9 Oh let the wickedness of the wicked come to an end; but establish the
*just: for the righteous God trieth the
hearts and reins.
10 My defence *is* of God, which saveth
the upright in heart.
11 God judgeth the righteous, and God
is angry *with the wicked* every day.
12 If he turn not, he will whet his
sword; he hath bent his bow, and made
it ready.
13 He hath also prepared for him the
instruments of death; he ordaineth his
arrows against the persecutors.
14 Behold, he travaileth with iniquity, and hath conceived mischief, and
brought forth *falsehood.
15 He made a pit, and digged it, and is
fallen into the ditch *which* he made.
16 His mischief shall return upon his
own head, and his violent dealing shall
come down upon his own pate.
17 I will praise the LORD according to
his righteousness: and will sing praise
to the name of the LORD most high.

7:8 Standards of Righteousness

There are two standards of uprightness: first, as humans see their fellowmen; second, as humans are seen by God (Job 1:1; 42:5-6). David here refers to his own just reputation for fair-dealing (1 Sam. 24:1-13; 26:7-9), especially with Saul. Hence, he is a *type of Christ. But in the sight of God, this good king sinned (see Ps. 51 and notes).

---

probably one who joined with Saul in persecution of David. We do know that Cush was of the same tribe as Saul.

7:1 persecute. To pursue.

7:2 Lest he tear my soul. David referred to his most terrible enemy—perhaps Saul.

7:6 judgment that thou hast commanded. God has promised that He will punish rebels against His love, those who do evil to their fellowmen who are His servants (see Deut. 32:35,43).

7:9 trieth the hearts and reins. Tests the hearts and minds.

7:9 reins. Literally, *kidneys,* but in David's time, it referred to the place of our deepest thoughts and feelings, the source of emotions such as joy, pain, anger and compassion.

7:11 God judgeth the righteous. Judging is not always punishment (vss. 9-10). It may be acquittal when the defendant is innocent of the charge. David rejoices because God, not man, is the final Judge (Gen. 18:20-21,25), and in Christ as Redeemer, we are pardoned even when guilty (Rom. 8:31).

7:12 turn not. Persist in pursuing evil.

7:12 whet his sword. Literally, *sharpen his sword.* It again speaks of the judgment of God.

7:14 travaileth with iniquity. The wicked man is filled with evil thoughts and is not satisfied until he acts upon them.

7:17 LORD most high. See Genesis 14:18 second note.

Psalm 8. Here Christ is seen as the Son of Man (vs. 4). This is explained and quoted in Hebrews 1:1-4; 2:5-9.

Psalm 8

Messianic

To the chief Musician upon Gittith,
A Psalm of David.

[1]O LORD our Lord, how excellent *is*
thy name in all the earth! who hast set
thy glory above the heavens.
[2]Out of the mouth of babes and sucklings hast thou ordained strength because of thine enemies, that thou
mightest still the enemy and the
avenger.

8:2 God's Children
This is as though David has said "babies and even newborn babies" (see a fulfillment on Palm Sunday, Matt. 21:15-16). However, he did not mean little children only. He also meant those of all ages who, having for the first time put their trust in the Lord, have become by faith the children of God. The New Testament calls these "babes in Christ" (see 1 Cor. 3:1).

[3]When I consider thy heavens, the
work of thy fingers, the moon and the
stars, which thou hast ordained;
[4]What is man, that thou art mindful
of him? and the son of man, that thou
visitest him?
[5]For thou hast made him a little lower
than the *angels, and hast crowned him
with glory and honour.
[6]Thou madest him to have dominion
over the works of thy hands; thou hast
put all *things* under his feet:
[7]All sheep and oxen, yea, and the
beasts of the field;
[8]The fowl of the air, and the fish of the
sea, *and whatsoever* passeth through the
paths of the seas.
[9]O LORD our Lord, how excellent *is*
thy name in all the earth!

Psalm 9

To the chief Musician upon Muth-labben,
A Psalm of *David.

[1]I will praise *thee,* O LORD, with my
whole heart; I will shew forth all thy
marvellous works.
[2]I will be glad and rejoice in thee: I
will sing praise to thy name, O thou
most High.
[3]When mine enemies are turned
back, they shall fall and perish at thy
presence.
[4]For thou hast maintained my right
and my cause; thou satest in the throne
judging right.
[5]Thou hast rebuked the heathen,
thou hast destroyed the wicked, thou
hast put out their name for ever and
ever.
[6]O thou enemy, destructions are
come to a perpetual end: and thou hast
destroyed cities; their memorial is perished with them.
[7]But the LORD shall endure for ever:
he hath prepared his throne for judgment.
[8]And he shall judge the *world in
righteousness, he shall minister judgment to the people in uprightness.
[9]The LORD also will be a refuge for
the oppressed, a refuge in times of
trouble.
[10]And they that know thy name will

8:title. "Gittith" was an instrument, or perhaps a tune, invented in Gath. Possibly, since the name "Gath" means *winepress,* David may have brought one of the musical instruments from Gath (1 Sam. 21:10; 27:2) used during the grape harvest.

8:2 ordained strength. God uses the weak things of the world, if obedient, to confound the mighty, when rebellious (see 1 Cor. 1:26-31; and especially 2 Cor. 12:9-16; Phil. 4:13).

8:5 a little lower. Or "lower for a little while." See also Hebrews 2:6-9.

Psalm 9. Psalms 9 and 10 both give pictures of the coming times and *Jacob's Trouble.

9:title. "Muth-labben" means *death for the son*. It may refer to 2 Samuel 12:19.

9:6 perpetual end. Contrast with "endure for ever" (vs. 7). Man's destructions are temporary; God's throne is everlasting.

put their *trust in thee: for thou, LORD,
hast not forsaken them that seek thee.
11 Sing praises to the LORD, which
dwelleth in *Zion: declare among the
people his doings.
12 When he maketh inquisition for
*blood, he remembereth them: he
forgetteth not the cry of the humble.
13 Have mercy upon me, O LORD;
consider my trouble *which I suffer* of
them that hate me, thou that liftest me
up from the gates of death:
14 That I may shew forth all thy praise
in the gates of the daughter of Zion: I
will rejoice in thy *salvation.

9:14 The City Gates
The gates in the city were of great importance. There the elders and prominent men gathered to settle significant matters (Prov. 31:23). "Daughter of Zion" is a poetic phrase for "City of Zion" (see Isa. 52:2). Similarly, the *church is called the bride of Christ (John 3:29; Eph. 5:25-27).

15 The heathen are sunk down in the
*pit *that* they made: in the net which
they hid is their own foot taken.
16 The LORD is known *by* the judgment *which* he executeth: the wicked is
snared in the work of his own hands.
Higgaion. *Selah.
17 The wicked shall be turned into
*hell, *and* all the nations that forget
*God.
18 For the needy shall not alway be
forgotten: the expectation of the poor
shall *not* perish for ever.
19 Arise, O LORD; let not man prevail: let the heathen be judged in thy
sight.
20 Put them in *fear, O LORD: *that* the
nations may know themselves *to be but*
men. Selah.

Psalm 10

1 Why standest thou afar off, O LORD?
why hidest thou *thyself* in times of
trouble?
2 The wicked in *his* pride doth persecute the poor: let them be taken in
the devices that they have imagined.
3 For the wicked boasteth of his
heart's desire, and blesseth the covetous, *whom* the LORD abhorreth.
4 The wicked, through the pride of his
countenance, will not seek *after God:*
God *is* not in all his thoughts.
5 His ways are always grievous; thy
judgments *are* far above out of his sight:
as for all his enemies, he puffeth at
them.
6 He hath said in his heart, I shall not
be moved: for *I shall* never *be* in adversity.
7 His mouth is full of cursing and deceit and fraud: under his tongue *is* mischief and *vanity.
8 He sitteth in the lurking places of
the villages: in the secret places doth
he murder the innocent: his eyes are
privily set against the poor.
9 He lieth in wait secretly as a lion in
his den: he lieth in wait to catch the
poor: he doth catch the poor, when he
draweth him into his net.
10 He croucheth, *and* humbleth himself, that the poor may fall by his strong
ones.
11 He hath said in his heart, God hath
forgotten: he hideth his face; he will
never see *it*.
12 Arise, O LORD; O God, lift up thine
hand: forget not the humble.
13 Wherefore doth the wicked contemn God? he hath said in his heart,
Thou wilt not require *it*.
14 Thou hast seen *it;* for thou behold-

9:12 inquisition for blood. Vengeance.
9:13 gates of death. Compare Psalm 23:4.
9:16 Higgaion. See Psalm 6 note, "Technical Words in the Psalms."
10:10 humbleth himself. This does not refer to real humility here; it is false, pretended humility, and it is acted out—like a part in a play—to deceive people.
10:13 contemn. Despise, reject, renounce.

est mischief and spite, to requite *it* with
thy hand: the poor committeth himself
unto thee; thou art the helper of the
fatherless.
15Break thou the arm of the wicked
and the evil *man:* seek out his wickedness *till* thou find none.
16The LORD *is* King for ever and
ever: the heathen are perished out of
his land.
17LORD, thou hast heard the desire of
the humble: thou wilt prepare their
heart, thou wilt cause thine ear to hear:
18To judge the fatherless and the oppressed, that the man of the earth may
no more oppress.

Psalm 11

To the chief Musician, *A Psalm* of David.

1In the LORD put I my trust: How say
ye to my soul, Flee *as* a bird to your
*mountain?
2For, lo, the wicked bend *their* bow,
they make ready their arrow upon the
string, that they may privily shoot at the
upright in heart.
3If the foundations be destroyed,
what can the righteous do?
4The LORD *is* in his *holy temple, the
LORD'S throne *is* in *heaven: his eyes
behold, his eyelids try, the children of
men.
5The LORD trieth the righteous: but
the wicked and him that loveth violence
his soul hateth.
6Upon the wicked he shall rain
snares, *fire and brimstone, and an horrible tempest: *this shall be* the portion
of their cup.
7For the righteous LORD loveth *righteousness; his countenance doth behold
the upright.

11:6 A Hebrew Custom
It was an old Hebrew custom to give to every guest at a meal his own portion of the food in a large cup that was like a bowl. So God tells us, through David, that terrible judgment and His anger shall be the portion of the wicked in that day when they are judged for their sin.

Psalm 12

To the chief Musician upon *Sheminith,
A Psalm of David.

1Help, LORD; for the godly man
ceaseth; for the faithful fail from among
the children of men.
2They speak vanity every one with
his neighbour: *with* flattering lips *and*
with a double heart do they speak.
3The LORD shall cut off all flattering
lips, *and* the tongue that speaketh
proud things:
4Who have said, With our tongue will
we prevail; our lips *are* our own: who
is lord over us?
5For the oppression of the poor, for
the sighing of the needy, now will I
arise, saith the LORD; I will set *him* in
safety *from him that* puffeth at him.
6The words of the LORD *are* pure
words: *as* *silver tried in a furnace of
earth, purified seven times.

10:15 Break thou the arm. David is praying that God will take away the power of wicked men.
11:1 How say ye . . . ? When David wrote this psalm, he may have been having a difficult time in the court of Saul, who had become such a wicked king. Many times David wanted to run away, but here he reminds himself that his trust is in the LORD, and therefore he does not need to fear.
11:3 what can the righteous do? In this verse David asks a question; in the next verse he answers it, simply by remembering to trust the LORD, who is the answer to all our problems.
11:4 his eyelids try. Try means *test.* God watches us very closely and carefully and tests the motives of our hearts.
11:5 trieth. Tests, examines.
11:6 snares, fire and brimstone. God's judgment upon sin.
12:title. "Sheminith" is explained in the Psalm 6 note, "Technical Words in the Psalms."

7 Thou shalt keep them, O LORD, thou
shalt preserve them from this generation for ever.
8 The wicked walk on every side,
when the vilest men are exalted.

Psalm 13

To the chief Musician, A Psalm of David.

1 How long wilt thou forget me,
O LORD? for ever? how long wilt thou
hide thy face from me?
2 How long shall I take counsel in my
soul, *having* sorrow in my heart daily?
how long shall mine enemy be exalted
over me?
3 Consider *and* hear me, O LORD my
God: lighten mine eyes, lest I sleep the
sleep of *death;
4 Lest mine enemy say, I have prevailed against him; *and* those that trouble me rejoice when I am moved.
5 But I have trusted in thy *mercy;
my heart shall rejoice in thy salvation.
6 I will sing unto the LORD, because
he hath dealt bountifully with me.

Psalm 14

To the chief Musician,
A Psalm of David.

1 The *fool hath said in his heart,
There is no God. They are corrupt, they
have done abominable works, *there is*
none that doeth good.
2 The LORD looked down from heaven
upon the children of men, to see if there
were any that did understand, *and* seek
God.
3 They are all gone aside, they are *all*
together become filthy: *there is* none
that doeth good, no, not one.
4 Have all the workers of iniquity no
knowledge? who eat up my people *as*
they eat bread, and call not upon the
LORD.
5 There were they in great fear: for God
is in the generation of the righteous.
6 Ye have shamed the counsel of the
poor, because the LORD *is* his refuge.
7 Oh that the salvation of *Israel *were*
come out of Zion! when the LORD
bringeth back the captivity of his people, *Jacob shall rejoice, *and* Israel shall
be glad.

Psalm 15

A Psalm of *David.

1 LORD, who shall abide in thy *tabernacle? who shall dwell in thy holy hill?
2 He that walketh uprightly, and
worketh righteousness, and speaketh
the truth in his heart.
3 *He that* backbiteth not with his
tongue, nor doeth evil to his neighbour,
nor taketh up a reproach against his
neighbour.
4 In whose eyes a vile person is contemned; but he honoureth them that
*fear the LORD. *He that* sweareth to *his*
own hurt, and changeth not.
5 *He that* putteth not out his money to
usury, nor taketh reward against the

Psalm 14. Note that this psalm and Psalm 53 are almost exactly alike.
14:1 in his heart. Compare Jeremiah 17:9.
14:1 there is none. Compare this verse and verse 3 with Romans 3:10-12.
14:5 in great fear. There are times when the LORD's enemies are afraid of Him, because their consciences tell them that they have sinned against Him.
14:6 Ye have shamed. They have laughed at the poor, whose only refuge is in God's loving care.
15:4 contemned. Despised.
15:4 sweareth to his own hurt. Someone who tells the truth even when the truth will make things hard for him. Keeps a promise.
15:5 usury. A rate of interest on money lent that is much too high to be fair or just. See Exodus 22:25 note.
15:5 reward against the innocent. Bribes. For example, if a judge sends an innocent man to prison because he (the judge) has received money from the guilty man, whom he therefore sets free, that judge has taken a reward against an innocent man.

innocent. He that doeth these *things* shall never be moved.

Psalm 16

Messianic

Michtam of David.

[1]Preserve me, O *God: for in thee do
I put my *trust.
[2]*O my soul,* thou hast said unto the
LORD, Thou *art* my Lord: my goodness
extendeth not to thee;
[3]*But* to the saints that *are* in the
earth, and *to* the excellent, in whom *is*
all my delight.
[4]Their sorrows shall be multiplied
that hasten *after* another *god:* their
drink-offerings of blood will I not offer,
nor take up their names into my
lips.

16:4 The Worship of Other Gods
David referred to the gods of his day, Dagon, Baal, and the rest. These gods symbolized any object of worship in the heart that takes the place of God Himself, for instance, self and pleasure (2 Tim. 3:2,4). Whatever we love more than we love the Lord is our "god"–a false god that can only bring us sorrow.

[5]The LORD *is* the portion of mine inheritance and of my cup: thou maintainest my lot.
[6]The lines are fallen unto me in
pleasant *places;* yea, I have a goodly
heritage.
[7]I will bless the LORD, who hath
given me counsel: my *reins also instruct me in the night seasons.
[8]I have set the LORD always before
me: because *he is* at my right hand, I
shall not be moved.
[9]Therefore my heart is glad, and my
glory rejoiceth: my *flesh also shall rest
in *hope.

16:9 Man's Threefold Being
The threefold being of man consists of:
1. "Heart": the soul from which the actions and emotions spring.
2. "Glory": the spirit by which man can have fellowship with God.
3. "Flesh": the physical body.

All "dwell in safety" within God's care (Ps. 4:8).

[10]For thou wilt not leave my soul in
*hell; neither wilt thou suffer thine
Holy One to see corruption.
[11]Thou wilt shew me the path of life:
in thy presence *is* *fulness of joy; at thy
right hand *there are* pleasures for evermore.

Psalm 17

A *Prayer of David.

[1]Hear the right, O LORD, attend unto
my cry, give ear unto my prayer, *that
goeth* not out of feigned lips.

Psalm 16. This psalm is a messianic psalm because it points to the resurrection of Christ.
16:title. "Michtam" comes from a term that may mean *to cover,* so it could mean a covering of the lips, a silent prayer, or a prayer for covering and protection.
16:2 Thou art my Lord. Here the Messiah, the Lord Jesus Christ, was speaking through David. The Lord Jesus, when He came to earth, came as an obedient servant to do His Father's will; therefore He says as He speaks here to His Father, "Thou art my Lord."
16:2 goodness extendeth not. I have no good beyond You, Lord.
16:3 But to the saints . . . the excellent. As for the saints, they are excellent people, and we should follow the examples of godly people.
16:4 drink-offerings of blood. Gentiles offered the blood of animals as a sacrifice to their gods, sometimes drinking the blood.
16:5 maintainest my lot. God defends my cause or my appointed lot in life.
16:6 The lines . . . goodly heritage. In a parable, "lines" would be the cords by which each man's lot in life or his heritage was divided from his neighbor's. David knew that—through God—he had a wonderful inheritance.
16:10 not leave my soul in hell. Verses 9 and 10 are resurrection verses. David's assurance of eternal life foreshadowed the triumph of David's greater Son, our Lord, over the tomb. Peter quotes these great verses in his first sermon (Acts 2:25-31).
17:1 feigned lips. Dishonest, deceitful lips.

[2]Let my sentence come forth from
thy presence; let thine eyes behold the
things that are equal.
[3]Thou hast proved mine heart; thou
hast visited *me* in the night; thou hast
tried me, *and* shalt find nothing; I am
purposed *that* my mouth shall not transgress.
[4]Concerning the words of men, by
the word of thy lips I have kept *me from*
the paths of the destroyer.
[5]Hold up my goings in thy paths, *that*
my footsteps slip not.
[6]I have called upon thee, for thou wilt
hear me, O God: incline thine ear unto
me, *and hear* my speech.
[7]Shew thy marvellous lovingkindness, O thou that savest by thy right
hand them which put their trust *in thee*
from those that rise up *against them.*
[8]Keep me as the apple of the eye,
hide me under the shadow of thy wings,
[9]From the wicked that oppress me,
from my deadly enemies, *who* compass
me about.
[10]They are inclosed in their own fat:
with their mouth they speak proudly.
[11]They have now compassed us in
our steps: they have set their eyes bowing down to the earth;
[12]Like as a lion *that* is greedy of his
prey, and as it were a young lion lurking in secret places.
[13]Arise, O LORD, disappoint him,
cast him down: deliver my soul from
the wicked, *which is* thy sword:
[14]From men *which are* thy hand,
O LORD, from men of the *world, *which
have* their portion in *this* life, and
whose belly thou fillest with thy hid
treasure: they are full of children, and
leave the rest of their *substance* to
their babes.
[15]As for me, I will behold thy face in
*righteousness: I shall be satisfied,
when I awake, with thy likeness.

Psalm 18

To the chief Musician, *A Psalm* of David,
the servant of the LORD, who spake
unto the LORD the words of this song in
the day *that* the LORD delivered him from
the hand of all his enemies, and
from the hand of Saul: And he said,

[1]I will love thee, O LORD, my strength.
[2]The LORD *is* my *rock, and my fortress, and my deliverer; my God, my
strength, in whom I will trust; my buckler, and the *horn of my *salvation, *and*
my high tower.
[3]I will call upon the LORD, *who is
worthy* to be praised: so shall I be saved
from mine enemies.
[4]The sorrows of death compassed
me, and the floods of ungodly men
made me afraid.
[5]The sorrows of hell compassed me

17:2 equal. Fair, just, and right.
17:4 the destroyer. Satan.
17:10 inclosed in their own fat. "Fat" in this verse means *wealth* and *pride*.
17:11 bowing down to the earth. David's enemies watched him and pursued him like a bull that runs at his victim with a lowered head.
17:13 which is thy sword. By Thy sword.
17:14 men which are thy hand. Also can be translated: "Deliver my soul . . . from men by Thy hand, O LORD."
17:14 whose belly thou fillest. Even the enjoyments of those who forget God come from His bountiful goodness.
17:15 with thy likeness. It is indeed wonderful that David's assurance of immortality was enriched by the idea of likeness to a greater One than he (see 1 John 3:2).
18:2 buckler. Shield.
18:4 sorrows of death. Cords of death. David was surrounded by Saul's servants who tried repeatedly to kill him. In this, as in other respects, David is a *type of our Lord.
18:5 snares of death prevented me. Escape seemed impossible, because David was trapped by his enemies (1 Sam. 26:1-2).

about: the snares of death prevented me.
6 In my distress I called upon the
LORD, and cried unto my God: he heard
my voice out of his temple, and my cry
came before him, *even* into his ears.
7 Then the earth shook and trembled; the foundations also of the hills
moved and were shaken, because he
was wroth.

> **18:7 An Earthquake**
> David uses a marvelous picture of an earthquake and thunderstorm in the wild highlands of Palestine to describe his deliverance. See 1 Kings 19:11-12 for Elijah's similar experience. This also pictures for us the strange darkness and the shaking of the earth when the Lord Jesus Christ suffered and died upon the cross.

8 There went up a smoke out of his
nostrils, and *fire out of his mouth devoured: coals were kindled by it.
9 He bowed the heavens also, and
came down: and darkness *was* under his
feet.
10 And he rode upon a cherub, and did
fly: yea, he did fly upon the wings of the
wind.
11 He made darkness his secret place;
his pavilion round about him *were* dark
waters *and* thick clouds of the skies.
12 At the brightness *that was* before
him his thick clouds passed, hail *stones*
and coals of fire.
13 The LORD also thundered in the
heavens, and the Highest gave his
voice; hail *stones* and coals of fire.
14 Yea, he sent out his arrows, and
*scattered them; and he shot out light-
nings, and discomfited them.
15 Then the channels of waters were
seen, and the foundations of the world
were discovered at thy rebuke, O LORD,
at the blast of the breath of thy nostrils.
16 He sent from above, he took me, he
drew me out of many waters.
17 He delivered me from my strong
enemy, and from them which hated me:
for they were too strong for me.
18 They prevented me in the day of
my calamity: but the LORD was my stay.
19 He brought me forth also into a
large place; he delivered me, because
he delighted in me.
20 The LORD rewarded me according
to my righteousness; according to the
cleanness of my hands hath he recompensed me.
21 For I have kept the ways of the
LORD, and have not wickedly departed
from my God.
22 For all his judgments *were* before
me, and I did not put away his statutes
from me.
23 I was also upright before him, and
I kept myself from mine iniquity.
24 Therefore hath the LORD recompensed me according to my righteousness, according to the cleanness of my
hands in his eyesight.
25 With the merciful thou wilt shew
thyself merciful; with an upright man
thou wilt shew thyself upright;
26 With the pure thou wilt shew thyself pure; and with the *froward thou
wilt shew thyself froward.
27 For thou wilt save the afflicted people; but wilt bring down high looks.
28 For thou wilt light my candle: the
LORD my God will enlighten my darkness.
29 For by thee I have run through a
troop; and by my God have I leaped over
a wall.

18:18 prevented me. Confronted (see also vs. 5).
18:20 my righteousness. See 1 Samuel 24,26 for occasions when David, in dealing with Saul, returned good for evil. The verse does not mean that David was without sin in the sight of God (see Ps. 51; 2 Sam. 11; 24).
18:25 With the merciful. God does not change, but He must treat different men in different ways (see Rev. 22:11).
18:28 light my candle. Job 29:2-3 explains this phrase. See also Psalm 119:105.
18:29 run through a troop. Broken the ranks of his enemies.
18:29 leaped over a wall. Taken a walled fort or city.

30 *As for* God, his way *is* *perfect: the
word of the LORD is tried: he *is* a buckler to all those that trust in him.
31 For who *is* God save the LORD? or
who *is* a rock save our God?
32 *It is* God that girdeth me with
strength, and maketh my way perfect.
33 He maketh my feet like hinds' *feet,*
and setteth me upon my high places.
34 He teacheth my hands to war, so
that a bow of steel is broken by mine
arms.
35 Thou hast also given me the shield
of thy salvation: and thy right hand hath
holden me up, and thy gentleness hath
made me great.
36 Thou hast enlarged my steps under
me, that my feet did not slip.
37 I have pursued mine enemies, and
overtaken them: neither did I turn again
till they were consumed.
38 I have wounded them that they
were not able to rise: they are fallen
under my feet.
39 For thou hast girded me with
strength unto the battle: thou hast subdued under me those that rose up
against me.
40 Thou hast also given me the necks
of mine enemies; that I might destroy
them that hate me.
41 They cried, but *there was* none to
save *them: even* unto the LORD, but he
answered them not.
42 Then did I beat them small as the
dust before the wind: I did cast them out
as the dirt in the streets.
43 Thou hast delivered me from the
strivings of the people; *and* thou hast
made me the head of the heathen: a
people *whom* I have not known shall
serve me.
44 As soon as they hear of me, they
shall obey me: the strangers shall submit themselves unto me.
45 The strangers shall fade away, and
be afraid out of their close places.
46 The LORD liveth; and blessed *be* my
rock; and let the God of my salvation be
exalted.
47 *It is* God that avengeth me, and
subdueth the people under me.
48 He delivereth me from mine enemies: yea, thou liftest me up above
those that rise up against me: thou hast
delivered me from the violent man.
49 Therefore will I give thanks unto
thee, O LORD, among the heathen, and
sing praises unto thy name.
50 Great deliverance giveth he to his
king; and sheweth mercy to his anointed, to David, and to his seed for evermore.

Psalm 19

To the chief Musician, A Psalm of David.

1 The heavens declare the glory of
God; and the firmament sheweth his
handywork.
2 Day unto day uttereth speech, and
night unto night sheweth knowledge.
3 *There is* no speech nor language,
where their voice is not heard.
4 Their line is gone out through all the
earth, and their words to the end of the

18:30 tried. Proven.

18:36 enlarged my steps. Brought me from the narrow mountain paths into the open spaces.

18:41 They cried . . . unto the LORD. David's enemies (sinners) did not cry to the LORD in real faith in His power, for He always hears the prayer of faith. These evildoers defied the love of God and merely prayed for escape from consequences, without any true repentance or change of heart.

18:45 close places. Strongholds.

19:1 heavens. This wonderful psalm starts with a statement of the natural revelation of God (Rom. 1:20) and ends with God as "*my* strength, and *my* redeemer" (vs. 14)—from universal revelation to personal faith.

19:2 uttereth speech. Both day and night the heavens show God's power and tell of His glory.

19:4 Their line. The measure of their domain. The whole earth, David said, is included in

world. In them hath he set a tabernacle for the sun,
5 Which *is* as a bridegroom coming out
of his chamber, *and* rejoiceth as a strong
man to run a race.
6 His going forth *is* from the end of the
*heaven, and his circuit unto the ends
of it: and there is nothing hid from the
heat thereof.
7 The *law of the LORD *is* perfect, con-
verting the soul: the testimony of the
LORD *is* sure, making wise the simple.
8 The statutes of the LORD *are* right,
rejoicing the heart: the commandment
of the LORD *is* pure, enlightening the
eyes.
9 The fear of the LORD *is* *clean, enduring for ever: the judgments of
the LORD *are* true *and* righteous altogether.
10 More to be desired *are they* than
gold, yea, than much fine gold: sweeter also than honey and the honeycomb.
11 Moreover by them is thy servant
warned: *and* in keeping of them *there is*
great reward.
12 Who can understand *his* errors?
cleanse thou me from secret *faults.*
13 Keep back thy servant also from
presumptuous *sins;* let them not have
dominion over me: then shall I be upright, and I shall be innocent from the
great transgression.
14 Let the words of my mouth, and the
meditation of my heart, be acceptable
in thy sight, O LORD, my strength, and
my *redeemer.

Psalm 20

To the chief Musician, A Psalm of David.

1 The LORD hear thee in the day of
trouble; the name of the God of *Jacob
defend thee;
2 Send thee help from the *sanctuary,
and strengthen thee out of *Zion;
3 Remember all thy offerings, and accept thy burnt-sacrifice; *Selah.
4 Grant thee according to thine own
heart, and fulfil all thy counsel.
5 We will rejoice in thy salvation, and
in the name of our God we will set up
our banners: the LORD fulfil all thy petitions.
6 Now know I that the LORD saveth
his anointed; he will hear him from his
*holy heaven with the saving strength
of his right hand.
7 Some *trust* in chariots, and some in
horses: but we will remember the name
of the LORD our God.
8 They are brought down and fallen:
but we are risen, and stand upright.
9 Save, LORD: let the king hear us
when we call.

Psalm 21

Messianic

To the chief Musician, A Psalm of *David.

1 The king shall joy in thy strength,

---

the territory in which the LORD's power is made known by the heavens (see Rom. 1:19-20).

19:4 In them. In the heavens.

19:7 law of the LORD. Not merely the Ten Commandments, but the whole teaching of the Scriptures.

19:9 fear of the LORD. This means trust and faith in the LORD and His Word, and hatred for anything that is contrary to His will.

19:13 presumptuous sins. Rebellious, deliberate sins.

19:13 great transgression. Usually called "the unpardonable sin" (see Matt. 12:31 note, "The Unpardonable Sin").

20:2 sanctuary. The sacred or holy place of God.

20:6 his anointed. *Anointed* is the meaning of the words "Messiah" and "Christ." The verse foretells our Lord's victory over sin and death at the Cross—the empty tomb.

20:9 the king. The Lord Jesus Christ—the King, who would rule forever, whom God had promised to the Jews (see 2 Sam. 7:12-13).

Psalm 21. This psalm foretells Christ, the King of Kings.

21:1 joy. To rejoice.

O LORD; and in thy salvation how greatly shall he rejoice!

2 Thou hast given him his heart's desire, and hast not withholden the request of his lips. Selah.

3 For thou preventest him with the blessings of goodness: thou settest a crown of pure gold on his head.

4 He asked life of thee, *and* thou gavest *it* him, *even* length of days for ever and ever.

5 His glory *is* great in thy salvation: honour and majesty hast thou laid upon him.

6 For thou hast made him most blessed for ever: thou hast made him exceeding glad with thy countenance.

7 For the king trusteth in the LORD, and through the *mercy of the most High he shall not be moved.

8 Thine hand shall find out all thine enemies: thy right hand shall find out those that hate thee.

9 Thou shalt make them as a fiery oven in the time of thine anger: the LORD shall swallow them up in his wrath, and the fire shall devour them.

10 Their fruit shalt thou destroy from the earth, and their seed from among the children of men.

11 For they intended evil against thee: they imagined a mischievous device, *which* they are not able *to perform*.

12 Therefore shalt thou make them turn their back, *when* thou shalt make ready *thine arrows* upon thy strings against the face of them.

13 Be thou exalted, LORD, in thine own strength: *so* will we sing and praise thy power.

Psalm 22

Messianic

To the chief Musician upon Aijeleth Shahar, A Psalm of David.

1 My *God, my God, why hast thou forsaken me? *why art thou so* far from helping me, *and from* the words of my roaring?

2 O my God, I cry in the daytime, but thou hearest not; and in the night season, and am not silent.

22:2 No Answer
As the Lord Jesus hung on the cross, He cried out to His Father, and there was no answer. This was because our Saviour was taking the place of each lost, guilty sinner, and enduring God's punishment against all sin of all time (John 1:29).

3 But thou *art* holy, *O thou* that inhabitest the praises of *Israel.

4 Our fathers trusted in thee: they trusted, and thou didst deliver them.

5 They cried unto thee, and were delivered: they trusted in thee, and were not confounded.

6 But I *am* a worm, and no man; a reproach of men, and despised of the people.

7 All they that see me laugh me to scorn: they shoot out the lip, they shake the head *saying*,

8 He trusted on the LORD *that* he

21:2 his heart's desire. The salvation of sinners (see Isa. 53:11; Heb. 12:2).
21:3 preventest. See *prevent.
21:11 intended. Meditated, planned, or plotted.
21:12 thine arrows. A symbol of God's judgment against sin; it is a picture of the archer drawing the bow—making the bowstrings ready.
22:title. "Aijeleth Shahar" means *the hind of the morning dawn*. The hind (deer) stands for the lovely and innocent One who is driven to death; the morning dawn stands for joy that follows affliction. The psalm, therefore, represents the joy that springs forth after sorrow. The Messiah's deep sorrow (vss. 1 to 21) turns to joy (vss. 22-31).
22:1 why hast thou forsaken me? This was the awful cry of Christ on the cross when He who knew no sin (see Isa. 53:11) was made sin for us (Col. 2:13-14; Heb. 12:2).
22:1 roaring. Groaning or moaning.
22:6 a worm. The Lord of glory could have stooped no lower than this to save us!

would deliver him: let him deliver him,
seeing he delighted in him.
9But thou *art* he that took me out of
the womb: thou didst make me *hope
when I was upon my mother's breasts.
10I was cast upon thee from the
womb: thou *art* my God from my mother's belly.
11Be not far from me; for trouble *is*
near; for *there is* none to help.
12Many bulls have compassed me:
strong *bulls* of *Bashan have beset me
round.
13They gaped upon me *with* their
mouths, *as* a ravening and a roaring lion.
14I am poured out like water, and all
my bones are out of joint: my heart is
like wax; it is melted in the midst of my
*bowels.
15My strength is dried up like a potsherd; and my tongue cleaveth to my
jaws; and thou hast brought me into the
dust of *death.
16For dogs have compassed me: the
assembly of the wicked have inclosed
me: they pierced my hands and my feet.
17I may tell all my bones: they look
and stare upon me.
18They part my *garments among
them, and cast lots upon my vesture.
19But be not thou far from me, O LORD:
O my strength, haste thee to help me.
20Deliver my soul from the sword;
my darling from the power of the dog.
21Save me from the lion's mouth: for
thou hast heard me from the horns of
the unicorns.
22I will declare thy name unto my
brethren: in the midst of the congregation will I praise thee.
23Ye that *fear the LORD, praise him;
all ye the seed of Jacob, glorify him; and
fear him, all ye the seed of Israel.
24For he hath not despised nor abhorred the affliction of the afflicted;
neither hath he hid his face from him;
but when he cried unto him, he heard.
25My praise *shall be* of thee in the
great congregation: I will pay my vows
before them that fear him.
26The meek shall eat and be satisfied:
they shall praise the LORD that seek
him: your heart shall live for ever.
27All the ends of the world shall remember and turn unto the LORD: and
all the kindreds of the nations shall
worship before thee.
28For the *kingdom *is* the LORD'S:
and he *is* the governor among the nations.
29All *they that be* fat upon earth shall
eat and worship: all they that go down

22:12 Bashan. A well-watered country where the cattle were fat and strong.
22:14 bones are out of joint. The shaking that our Lord received as His cross was placed in the ground and the terrible, unnatural position in which He hung upon it caused His bones to be dislocated.
22:15 potsherd. A fragment of broken pottery.
22:16 dogs. The Hebrew way of referring to Gentiles (see Matt. 15:21-28), many of whom were in the crowd around the cross.
22:16 they pierced my hands and my feet. Another detail of the Crucifixion (John 20:24-29).
22:18 my garments. On the cross the Saviour was unclothed.
22:18 cast lots. See fulfillment in Matthew 27:35.
22:20 the sword. That is, destruction.
22:20 my darling. My soul, my life—what is most precious to a man.
22:20 the dog. Either Satan (Luke 4:13) or the evil in man that was revealed at the Cross.
22:21 the lion's mouth. Death is pictured here as a lion.
22:21 the horns of the unicorns. These symbolize all the dangers from which God had delivered His Son before the Crucifixion (see Matt. 2:16-18, for example).
22:25 the great congregation. The psalm here changes from the Crucifixion to the *Resurrection (compare Isa. 53:10).
22:25 pay my vows. Renew my promises to God and to my people.
22:29 they that be fat. The rich and great.
22:29 they that go down to the dust. The poor and lowly.

to the dust shall bow before him: and
none can keep alive his own soul.
30 A seed shall serve him; it shall be
accounted to the Lord for a generation.
31 They shall come, and shall declare
his righteousness unto a people that
shall be born, that he hath done *this*.

Psalm 23

The Shepherd Psalm
Messianic

A Psalm of David.

1 The LORD *is* my shepherd; I shall
not want.
2 He maketh me to lie down in green
pastures: he leadeth me beside the still
waters.
3 He restoreth my soul: he leadeth me
in the paths of *righteousness for his
name's sake.
4 Yea, though I walk through the valley of the shadow of death, I will fear no
evil: for thou *art* with me; thy rod and
thy staff they comfort me.
5 Thou preparest a table before me in
the presence of mine enemies: thou
anointest my head with *oil; my cup
runneth over.
6 Surely goodness and mercy shall
follow me all the days of my life: and I
will dwell in the house of the LORD for
ever.

Psalm 24

Messianic

A Psalm of David.

1 The earth *is* the LORD'S, and the fulness thereof; the *world, and they that
dwell therein.
2 For he hath founded it upon the seas,
and established it upon the floods.
3 Who shall ascend into the hill of the
LORD? or who shall stand in his holy
place?
4 He that hath clean hands, and a pure
heart; who hath not lifted up his soul
unto *vanity, nor sworn deceitfully.
5 He shall receive the blessing from
the LORD, and righteousness from the
God of his *salvation.
6 This *is* the generation of them that
seek him, that seek thy face, O Jacob.
Selah.

23:5 Anointing with Oil
Every good shepherd put soothing oil on his sheep when they were scratched by thorns or bruised by sharp stones. In a similar way, the Lord Jesus Christ soothes and comforts His people with His loving care.

22:30 A seed . . . a generation. The Lord Jesus Christ and all who by faith are born again into His family.

Psalm 23. This psalm foreshadows our Lord as the Good Shepherd (Luke 15:3-7; John 10; 21:15-17).

23:1 The LORD is my shepherd. As David watched over his sheep, so he knew that the Good Shepherd, the LORD, was watching over him.

23:2 green pastures . . . still waters. Glimpses of Christ as the Bread and the Water of Life for those who follow Him as Shepherd.

23:3 restoreth. The Shepherd as Saviour healing His sheep. When we follow Christ, He will help us and give us new strength—restore our souls.

23:4 thou. Notice how the third person "he" changes to the second person "thou" when perils assail the sheep. The Shepherd comes so close that we can speak to Him.

23:5 preparest. Read John 21:1-11 for a fulfillment of this verse.

23:6 all the days. Read how Paul as he aged (Philem. 9) was filled with God's goodness and mercy, in spite of infirmities and persecution (Phil. 4:10-13).

24:4 clean hands. The things that we do—our outward lives.

24:4 a pure heart. What we are—our inner lives and characters, even—or especially—when no one is around.

24:6 the generation. The race or family—all those who trust in the LORD and are members of His kingdom and of the family of God.

24:6 O Jacob. Or, "O God of Jacob." It is sometimes thought that God is so very close to His children that here He is called by the name of one of His servants.

7 Lift up your heads, O ye gates; and
be ye lift up, ye everlasting doors; and
the King of glory shall come in.
8 Who *is* this King of glory? The LORD
strong and mighty, the LORD mighty in
battle.
9 Lift up your heads, O ye gates; even
lift *them* up, ye everlasting doors; and
the King of glory shall come in.
10 Who is this King of glory? The
LORD of hosts, he *is* the King of glory.
Selah.

Psalm 25

A Psalm of David.

1 Unto thee, O LORD, do I lift up my
soul.
2 O my God, I *trust in thee: let me
not be ashamed, let not mine enemies
triumph over me.
3 Yea, let none that wait on thee be
ashamed: let them be ashamed which
transgress without cause.
4 Shew me thy ways, O LORD; teach
me thy paths.
5 Lead me in thy truth, and teach me:
for thou *art* the God of my salvation; on
thee do I wait all the day.
6 Remember, O LORD, thy tender
mercies and thy lovingkindnesses; for
they *have been* ever of old.
7 Remember not the sins of my youth,
nor my transgressions: according to thy
mercy remember thou me for thy goodness' sake, O LORD.
8 Good and upright *is* the LORD:
therefore will he teach sinners in the
way.
9 The meek will he guide in *judgment: and the meek will he teach his
way.
10 All the paths of the LORD *are* mercy
and truth unto such as keep his *covenant and his testimonies.
11 For thy name's sake, O LORD, pardon mine iniquity; for it *is* great.
12 What man *is* he that *feareth the
LORD? him shall he teach in the way
that he shall choose.
13 His soul shall dwell at ease; and his
seed shall inherit the earth.
14 The secret of the LORD *is* with
them that fear him; and he will shew
them his covenant.
15 Mine eyes *are* ever toward the
LORD; for he shall pluck my feet out of
the net.
16 Turn thee unto me, and have mercy upon me; for I *am* desolate and afflicted.
17 The troubles of my heart are enlarged: *O* bring thou me out of my distresses.
18 Look upon mine affliction and my
pain; and forgive all my sins.
19 Consider mine enemies; for they
are many; and they hate me with cruel
hatred.
20 O keep my soul, and deliver me: let

Psalm 25 Acrostic Poems

Psalm 25 is the first of the acrostic or alphabetical psalms. In an acrostic poem each verse begins with a letter of the Hebrew alphabet in order. There are a total of seven such poems in the Psalms:

Psalm 25	Psalm 34	Psalm 37
Psalm 111	Psalm 112	Psalm 119
Psalm 145		

24:7 ye gates. This recalls the return of the ark to Jerusalem (2 Sam. 6:1-15) and Christ's triumphant entry into Jerusalem on Palm Sunday (Matt. 21:1-11). Finally, it refers to the wonderful gates of the New Jerusalem (Rev. 21:12-13).

25:10 keep his covenant. A covenant is an agreement. God gives certain commandments, and in connection with those commandments He makes promises of blessing.

25:14 secret of the LORD. "Secret" is literally *friendship* here. The thoughts, desires, and longings of the LORD's heart; His intimate friendship and fellowship, which He longs to share with those of His children who reverence and love Him and seek Him with a whole heart. Truly knowing God as our Father and Friend cannot compare to any other relationship.

25:15 pluck my feet out of the net. David speaks of sin and temptation as a net.

me not be ashamed; for I put my trust
in thee.
21 Let integrity and uprightness preserve me; for I wait on thee.
22 *Redeem Israel, O God, out of all
his troubles.

Psalm 26

A Song of Integrity
A Psalm of David.

1 Judge me, O LORD; for I have walked
in mine integrity: I have trusted also in
the LORD; *therefore* I shall not slide.
2 Examine me, O LORD, and *prove
me; try my *reins and my heart.
3 For thy lovingkindness *is* before mine
eyes: and I have walked in thy truth.
4 I have not sat with vain persons,
neither will I go in with dissemblers.
5 I have hated the congregation of evil
doers; and will not sit with the wicked.
6 I will wash mine hands in innocency:
so will I compass thine *altar, O LORD:
7 That I may publish with the voice of
thanksgiving, and tell of all thy wondrous works.
8 LORD, I have loved the habitation of
thy house, and the place where thine
honour dwelleth.
9 Gather not my soul with sinners,
nor my life with bloody men:
10 In whose hands *is* mischief, and
their right hand is full of bribes.
11 But as for me, I will walk in mine
integrity: redeem me, and be merciful
unto me.
12 My foot standeth in an even place:
in the congregations will I bless the
LORD.

Psalm 27

A Song of Safety
A Psalm of *David.

1 The LORD *is* my light and my salvation; whom shall I fear? the LORD *is* the
strength of my life; of whom shall I be
afraid?
2 When the wicked, *even* mine enemies and my foes, came upon me to eat
up my flesh, they stumbled and fell.
3 Though an host should encamp
against me, my heart shall not fear:
though war should rise against me, in
this *will* I *be* confident.
4 One *thing* have I desired of the
LORD, that will I seek after; that I may
dwell in the house of the LORD all the
days of my life, to behold the beauty of
the LORD, and to enquire in his temple.
5 For in the time of trouble he shall
hide me in his pavilion: in the secret of
his *tabernacle shall he hide me; he
shall set me up upon a *rock.
6 And now shall mine head be lifted up
above mine enemies round about me:
therefore will I offer in his tabernacle
sacrifices of joy; I will sing, yea, I will
sing praises unto the LORD.
7 Hear, O LORD, *when* I cry with my
voice: have *mercy also upon me, and
answer me.
8 *When thou saidst,* Seek ye my face; my
heart said unto thee, Thy face, LORD,
will I seek.

Psalm 26. David seems to be very sure of himself and quite unaware of his moral danger (see 1 Cor. 10:12; Matt. 26:41). David's fall is described in 2 Samuel 11, and his repentance is expressed in Psalm 51.

26:6 compass thine altar. Come before or circle Your altar. Sometimes the priests walked around the altar as they made their sacrifices.

26:9 Gather not my soul with sinners. During his life, David sought the company of God's people; in his death he does not want to be with those who have rejected God.

Psalm 27. A song of safety and freedom from fear within God's care.

27:2 to eat up my flesh. To do all in their power to hurt me, to treat me cruelly, even to kill me (eat my flesh).

27:5 hide me in his pavilion: in the secret of his tabernacle. "Pavilion" is literally, *dwelling*; "secret," literally, *shelter.* In the center of the army, the king's pavilion or special tent was built, and there the soldiers would guard their king. God shelters us in His dwelling when we trust in Him.

9 Hide not thy face *far* from me; put not thy servant away in anger: thou hast been my help; leave me not, neither forsake me, O God of my salvation.

10 When my father and my mother forsake me, then the LORD will take me up.

11 Teach me thy way, O LORD, and lead me in a plain path, because of mine enemies.

12 Deliver me not over unto the will of mine enemies: for false witnesses are risen up against me, and such as breathe out cruelty.

13 *I had fainted,* unless I had believed to see the goodness of the LORD in the land of the living.

14 Wait on the LORD: be of good courage, and he shall strengthen thine heart: wait, I say, on the LORD.

Psalm 28

A Psalm of David.

1 Unto thee will I cry, O LORD my rock; be not silent to me: lest, *if* thou be silent to me, I become like them that go down into the *pit.

2 Hear the voice of my supplications, when I cry unto thee, when I lift up my hands toward thy *holy *oracle.

29:1 God's Glory and Majesty
Psalm 29 presents the glory and majesty of God and His great judgment by using the analogy of a great storm, and the psalm closes with the quiet and calm that mark the end of such a tornado (vs.11). This psalm is used in Jewish synagogues on the first day of the Feast of *Pentecost, which the Jewish people call *Shavnoth*.

3 Draw me not away with the wicked, and with the workers of iniquity, which speak peace to their neighbours, but mischief *is* in their hearts.

4 Give them according to their deeds, and according to the wickedness of their endeavours: give them after the work of their hands; render to them their desert.

5 Because they regard not the works of the LORD, nor the operation of his hands, he shall destroy them, and not build them up.

6 Blessed *be* the LORD, because he hath heard the voice of my supplications.

7 The LORD *is* my strength and my shield; my heart trusted in him, and I am helped: therefore my heart greatly rejoiceth; and with my song will I praise him.

8 The LORD *is* their strength, and he *is* the saving strength of his anointed.

9 Save thy people, and bless thine inheritance: feed them also, and lift them up for ever.

Psalm 29

The Thunderstorm Psalm

A Psalm of David.

1 Give unto the LORD, O ye mighty, give unto the LORD glory and strength.

2 Give unto the LORD the glory due unto his name; worship the LORD in the beauty of holiness.

3 The voice of the LORD *is* upon the waters: the *God of glory thundereth: the LORD *is* upon many waters.

4 The voice of the LORD *is* powerful;

27:14 Wait on the LORD. When we are going through difficulties or problems of any kind (e.g., illness, loss of a loved one, financial difficulties, etc.), sometimes God doesn't seem close, and we don't receive His help and strengthening as soon as we want it. But God does see our problems and is working all things for our good (Rom. 8:28) even when we can't see it. We must continue to trust and serve Him, knowing He is in control and will help us through the hard times (see Isa. 40:28-31).

28:1 like them that go down into the pit. Like the unsaved, who reject God's love and die in their sins.

28:3 Draw me not away with the wicked. The wicked will be bound as with chains and carried away to eternal punishment.

28:5 the operation. God's creation and works.

28:8 his anointed. "Anointed" means *set apart*.

the voice of the LORD *is* full of majesty.

5 The voice of the LORD breaketh the cedars; yea, the LORD breaketh the cedars of *Lebanon.

6 He maketh them also to skip like a calf; Lebanon and Sirion like a young *unicorn.

7 The voice of the LORD divideth the flames of *fire.

8 The voice of the LORD shaketh the wilderness; the LORD shaketh the wilderness of Kadesh.

9 The voice of the LORD maketh the hinds to calve, and discovereth the forests: and in his temple doth every one speak of *his* glory.

10 The LORD sitteth upon the flood; yea, the LORD sitteth King for ever.

11 The LORD will give strength unto his people; the LORD will bless his people with peace.

Psalm 30

A Psalm *and* Song *at* the dedication of the house of David.

1 I will extol thee, O LORD; for thou hast lifted me up, and hast not made my foes to rejoice over me.

Psalm 30 A Dedication
We do not know what house or temple was meant by this title, but Jewish people today use it in connection with their feast of Hanukkah, the Feast of the Dedication, which dates back to the time of the Maccabees (175–164 B.C.). It looks ahead to the time of the dedication of the future millennial temple. See *Millennium and Ezekiel 40–44.

2 O LORD my God, I cried unto thee, and thou hast healed me.

3 O LORD, thou hast brought up my soul from the *grave: thou hast kept me alive, that I should not go down to the pit.

4 Sing unto the LORD, O ye *saints of his, and give thanks at the remembrance of his holiness.

5 For his anger *endureth but* a moment; in his favour *is* life: weeping may endure for a night, but joy *cometh* in the morning.

6 And in my prosperity I said, I shall never be moved.

7 LORD, by thy favour thou hast made my *mountain to stand strong: thou didst hide thy face, *and* I was troubled.

8 I cried to thee, O LORD; and unto the LORD I made supplication.

9 What profit *is there* in my *blood, when I go down to the pit? Shall the dust praise thee? shall it declare thy truth?

10 Hear, O LORD, and have mercy upon me: LORD, be thou my helper.

11 Thou hast turned for me my *mourning into dancing: thou hast put off my sackcloth, and girded me with gladness;

12 To the end that *my* glory may sing praise to thee, and not be silent. O LORD my God, I will give thanks unto thee for ever.

Psalm 31

A Song of Trust in God

To the chief Musician, A Psalm of David.

1 In thee, O LORD, do I put my *trust; let me never be ashamed: deliver me in thy *righteousness.

2 Bow down thine ear to me; deliver me speedily: be thou my strong rock, for an house of defence to save me.

3 For thou *art* my rock and my fortress; therefore for thy name's sake lead me, and guide me.

4 Pull me out of the net that they have laid privily for me: for thou *art* my strength.

29:6 Sirion. A Sidonian name for Mount Hermon (Deut. 3:9), meaning breastplate, the shape of the mountain.

30:3 brought up my soul from the grave. Brought my soul from spiritual *death to life.

30:7 my mountain. David calls his happiness, his wealth, and health, a "mountain," because the LORD had been so good to him.

30:12 my glory. My tongue or my soul.

5Into thine hand I commit my spirit:
thou hast *redeemed me, O LORD God
of truth.
6I have hated them that regard lying
vanities: but I trust in the LORD.
7I will be glad and rejoice in thy mercy: for thou hast considered my trouble;
thou hast known my soul in adversities;
8And hast not shut me up into the
hand of the enemy: thou hast set my
feet in a large room.
9Have mercy upon me, O LORD, for I
am in trouble: mine eye is consumed
with grief, *yea,* my soul and my belly.
10For my life is spent with grief, and
my years with sighing: my strength
faileth because of mine iniquity, and my
bones are consumed.
11I was a reproach among all mine
enemies, but especially among my
neighbours, and a fear to mine acquaintance: they that did see me without fled
from me.
12I am forgotten as a dead man out of
mind: I am like a broken vessel.
13For I have heard the slander of
many: fear *was* on every side: while
they took counsel together against me,
they devised to take away my life.
14But I trusted in thee, O LORD: I
said, Thou *art* my God.
15My times *are* in thy hand: deliver
me from the hand of mine enemies, and
from them that persecute me.
16Make thy face to shine upon thy
servant: save me for thy mercies' sake.
17Let me not be ashamed, O LORD;
for I have called upon thee: let the wicked be ashamed, *and* let them be silent
in the grave.
18Let the lying lips be put to silence;
which speak grievous things proudly
and contemptuously against the righteous.
19*Oh* how great *is* thy goodness,
which thou hast laid up for them that
fear thee; *which* thou hast wrought for
them that trust in thee before the sons
of men!
20Thou shalt hide them in the secret
of thy presence from the pride of man:
thou shalt keep them secretly in a pavilion from the strife of tongues.
21Blessed *be* the LORD: for he hath
shewed me his marvellous kindness in
a strong city.
22For I said in my haste, I am cut off
from before thine eyes: nevertheless
thou heardest the voice of my supplications when I cried unto thee.
23O love the LORD, all ye his saints:
for the LORD preserveth the faithful, and
plentifully rewardeth the proud doer.
24Be of good courage, and he shall
strengthen your heart, all ye that *hope
in the LORD.

Psalm 32

A Song of Instruction

A Psalm of David, Maschil.

1Blessed *is he whose* transgression *is*
*forgiven, *whose* *sin *is* covered.
2Blessed *is* the man unto whom the
LORD imputeth not iniquity, and in
whose spirit *there is* no guile.

31:5 Into thine hand I commit my spirit. Our Lord said these words just before He died on the cross (Luke 23:46).
31:11 a fear to mine acquaintance. David's friends were afraid to be seen with him (compare Matt. 26:56,69-75).
31:11 without. In public, out-of-doors.
31:15 My times. My whole life.
31:23 the proud doer. God punishes the proud as his sin deserves—that is his reward.
Psalm 32. This is another penitential psalm in which David confessed his sin and rejoiced when the load of guilt was lifted (vs. 11). See also Psalm 38 note, "The Penitential Psalms."
32:title. The word "Maschil" means *giving instruction*.
32:2 imputeth not iniquity. See Philemon 18 note on the basic meaning of "imputation." See also Romans 4:6-8.
32:2 guile. Deceit, dishonesty.

[3]When I kept silence, my bones
waxed old through my roaring all the
day long.
[4]For day and night thy hand was
heavy upon me: my moisture is turned
into the drought of summer. *Selah.

32:4 Summer Drought
In Judaea, for a month every year in late summer, there was no rain, and all the land became dry, parched, and barren. Such was David's life until he confessed his sin (compare 1 John 1:8-9).

[5]I acknowledged my sin unto thee,
and mine iniquity have I not hid. I said,
I will *confess my transgressions unto
the LORD; and thou forgavest the iniquity of my sin. Selah.
[6]For this shall every one that is godly pray unto thee in a time when thou
mayest be found: surely in the floods of
great waters they shall not come nigh
unto him.
[7]Thou *art* my hiding place; thou shalt
preserve me from trouble; thou shalt
compass me about with songs of deliverance. Selah.
[8]I will instruct thee and teach thee in
the way which thou shalt go: I will guide
thee with mine eye.
[9]Be ye not as the horse, *or* as the
mule, *which* have no understanding:
whose mouth must be held in with bit
and bridle, lest they come near unto thee.
[10]Many sorrows *shall be* to the wicked: but he that trusteth in the LORD,
mercy shall compass him about.
[11]Be glad in the LORD, and rejoice, ye
righteous: and shout for joy, all *ye that
are* upright in heart.

Psalm 33

[1]Rejoice in the LORD, O ye righteous:
for praise is comely for the upright.
[2]Praise the LORD with harp: sing
unto him with the *psaltery *and* an instrument of ten strings.
[3]Sing unto him a new song; play skilfully with a loud noise.
[4]For the word of the LORD *is* right;
and all his works *are done* in truth.
[5]He loveth righteousness and *judgment: the earth is full of the goodness
of the LORD.
[6]By the word of the LORD were the
heavens made; and all the host of them
by the breath of his mouth.
[7]He gathereth the waters of the sea
together as an heap: he layeth up the
depth in storehouses.
[8]Let all the earth fear the LORD: let
all the inhabitants of the *world stand
in awe of him.
[9]For he spake, and it was *done;* he
commanded, and it stood fast.
[10]The LORD bringeth the counsel of
the heathen to nought: he maketh the
devices of the people of none effect.
[11]The counsel of the LORD standeth
for ever, the thoughts of his heart to all
generations.
[12]Blessed *is* the nation whose God *is*
the LORD: *and* the people *whom* he hath
chosen for his own inheritance.
[13]The LORD looketh from *heaven;
he beholdeth all the sons of men.

32:3 through my roaring. The roaring (groaning) of David's conscience made him sick and weak because of unconfessed sin.
32:4 thy hand was heavy upon me. The LORD was speaking constantly to David about his sin.
33:1 comely. Becoming, fitting.
33:7 gathereth the waters. God keeps the seas within their boundaries and keeps them from flooding the earth, though the sea is not flat but rounded like a "heap."
33:7 layeth up the depth in storehouses. The earth is full of incalculable wealth. The earth is also full of springs and wells so that we need not die of thirst.
33:10 devices. Plans, schemes, and falsehoods.
33:12 whom he hath chosen. This refers to Israel as the chosen people. Moreover, all who believe in the Lord have been chosen by Christ (John 15:16) to be His peculiar or special people (1 Pet. 2:9).

[14]From the place of his habitation he
looketh upon all the inhabitants of the
earth.
[15]He fashioneth their hearts alike; he
considereth all their works.
[16]There is no king saved by the multitude of an host: a mighty man is not
delivered by much strength.
[17]An horse *is* a vain thing for safety:
neither shall he deliver *any* by his great
strength.
[18]Behold, the eye of the LORD *is* upon
them that fear him, upon them that
hope in his *mercy;
[19]To deliver their soul from *death,
and to keep them alive in famine.
[20]Our soul waiteth for the LORD: he
is our help and our shield.
[21]For our heart shall rejoice in him,
because we have trusted in his holy
name.
[22]Let thy mercy, O LORD, be upon us,
according as we hope in thee.

Psalm 34

A Psalm of *David, when he changed his behaviour before Abimelech; who drove him away, and he departed.

[1]I will bless the LORD at all times: his
praise *shall* continually *be* in my mouth.
[2]My soul shall make her boast in the
LORD: the humble shall hear *thereof,* and
be glad.
[3]O magnify the LORD with me, and let
us exalt his name together.
[4]I sought the LORD, and he heard me,
and delivered me from all my fears.

Psalm 34 Title: Abimelech
See 1 Samuel 21:10-15. Abimelech was the title of every Philistine king, just as Pharaoh was the title of every Egyptian king. The Abimelech referred to here was Achish.

[5]They looked unto him, and were
lightened: and their faces were not
ashamed.
[6]This poor man cried, and the LORD
heard *him,* and saved him out of all his
troubles.
[7]The *angel of the LORD encampeth
round about them that fear him, and
delivereth them.
[8]O taste and see that the LORD *is*
good: blessed *is* the man *that* trusteth
in him.
[9]O fear the LORD, ye his saints: for
there is no want to them that fear him.
[10]The young lions do lack, and suffer
hunger: but they that seek the LORD
shall not want any good *thing.*
[11]Come, ye children, hearken unto
me: I will teach you the fear of the
LORD.
[12]What man *is he that* desireth life,
and loveth *many* days, that he may see
good?
[13]Keep thy tongue from evil, and thy
lips from speaking guile.
[14]Depart from evil, and do good; seek
*peace, and pursue it.
[15]The eyes of the LORD *are* upon the
righteous, and his ears *are open* unto
their cry.
[16]The face of the LORD *is* against
them that do evil, to cut off the remembrance of them from the earth.
[17]*The righteous* cry, and the LORD
heareth, and delivereth them out of all
their troubles.
[18]The LORD *is* nigh unto them that
are of a broken heart; and saveth such
as be of a contrite spirit.
[19]Many *are* the afflictions of the righteous: but the LORD delivereth him out
of them all.
[20]He keepeth all his bones: not one
of them is broken.

33:15 fashioneth. Creates.
Psalm 34. An acrostic psalm (see Ps. 25 note, "Acrostic Poems"). In this case one letter, *vau,* was omitted.
34:8 taste. Try the LORD; let Him prove how faithful, loving, and good He is to those who give their hearts and lives to Him.
34:9 no want. The LORD takes care of every need of His people (compare Ps. 23:1).

34:20 No Broken Bones
At the *Passover it was forbidden to break a bone of the slain lamb (Exod. 12:46; Num. 9:12). This was fulfilled in Christ's crucifixion. At Calvary they broke the legs of the two thieves, but since Jesus was already dead, they pierced His side, doing His body no other injury (John 19:31-37). The *church is Christ's body (Eph. 5:30) and "of his flesh, of his bones," and in Him not one of His own people can be "broken" (John 17:12).

21 Evil shall slay the wicked: and they
that hate the righteous shall be desolate.
22 The LORD *redeemeth the soul of
his servants: and none of them that
trust in him shall be desolate.

Psalm 35

A Song of Struggles
A Psalm of David.

1 Plead *my cause,* O LORD, with them
that strive with me: fight against them
that fight against me.
2 Take hold of shield and *buckler, and
stand up for mine help.
3 Draw out also the spear, and stop *the*
way against them that persecute me:
say unto my soul, I *am* thy *salvation.
4 Let them be confounded and put to
shame that seek after my soul: let them
be turned back and brought to confusion
that devise my hurt.
5 Let them be as chaff before the
wind: and let the angel of the LORD
chase *them.*
6 Let their way be dark and slippery:
and let the angel of the LORD persecute
them.
7 For without cause have they hid for
me their net *in* a pit, *which* without
cause they have digged for my soul.
8 Let destruction come upon him at
unawares; and let his net that he hath
hid catch himself: into that very destruction let him fall.
9 And my soul shall be joyful in the
LORD: it shall rejoice in his salvation.
10 All my bones shall say, LORD, who
is like unto thee, which deliverest the
poor from him that is too strong for him,
yea, the poor and the needy from him
that spoileth him?
11 False witnesses did rise up; they
laid to my charge *things* that I knew not.
12 They rewarded me evil for good *to*
the spoiling of my soul.
13 But as for me, when they were sick,
my clothing *was* sackcloth: I humbled
my soul with fasting; and my *prayer
returned into mine own bosom.
14 I behaved myself as though *he had*
been my friend *or* brother: I bowed
down heavily, as one that mourneth *for*
his mother.
15 But in mine adversity they rejoiced,
and gathered themselves together:
yea, the abjects gathered themselves
together against me, and I knew *it* not;
they did tear *me,* and ceased not:

34:21 Evil shall slay. Those who are lost are lost because of their own sin and rejection of God's love and gift of eternal life through Christ.
Psalm 35. This psalm was no doubt written when David was being persecuted by Saul. It's an imprecatory psalm (see Ps. 5:10 note, "Praying for Judgment").
35:1 Plead my cause. David used these words in 1 Samuel 24:15.
35:5 chaff. The empty shell that once covered a grain of wheat or corn and is blown away when the useless chaff is separated from the good grain. (See Jesus' analogy about the eternal destiny of believers and unbelievers in Matt. 3:12.)
35:10 All my bones. That is, all my being.
35:12 spoiling of my soul. David's enemies robbed his soul of its peace and made him troubled.
35:13 returned into mine own bosom. Brought blessing to David himself as well as to him for whom David had prayed.
35:15 the abjects. "Abjects" means attackers who were *low* and *mean.*
35:15 tear me. David speaks here of his good name and reputation being under attack by his enemies.

35:16 Entertainment
The hypocritical mockers referred to in this verse are the jesters or clowns who were paid to amuse the guests at a feast. They often did this by making fun of the enemies of the man who gave the feast.

16With hypocritical mockers in
*feasts, they gnashed upon me with
their teeth.
17Lord, how long wilt thou look on?
rescue my soul from their destructions,
my darling from the lions.
18I will give thee thanks in the great
congregation: I will praise thee among
much people.
19Let not them that are mine enemies wrongfully rejoice over me: *neither* let them wink with the eye that
hate me without a cause.
20For they speak not peace: but they
devise deceitful matters against *them
that are* quiet in the land.
21Yea, they opened their mouth wide
against me, *and* said, Aha, aha, our eye
hath seen *it*.
22*This* thou hast seen, O LORD: keep
not silence: O Lord, be not far from me.
23Stir up thyself, and awake to my
judgment, *even* unto my cause, my
*God and my Lord.
24Judge me, O LORD my God, according to thy righteousness; and let them
not rejoice over me.
25Let them not say in their hearts,
Ah, so would we have it: let them not
say, We have swallowed him up.
26Let them be ashamed and brought
to confusion together that rejoice at
mine hurt: let them be clothed with
shame and dishonour that magnify *themselves* against me.
27Let them shout for joy, and be glad,
that favour my righteous cause: yea, let
them say continually, Let the LORD be
magnified, which hath pleasure in the
prosperity of his servant.
28And my tongue shall speak of thy
righteousness *and* of thy praise all the
day long.

Psalm 36

To the chief Musician, *A Psalm* of David, the servant of the LORD.

1The transgression of the wicked
saith within my heart, *that there is* no
fear of God before his eyes.
2For he flattereth himself in his own
eyes, until his iniquity be found to be
hateful.
3The words of his mouth *are* iniquity
and deceit: he hath left off to be wise,
and to do good.
4He deviseth mischief upon his bed;
he setteth himself in a way *that is* not
good; he abhorreth not evil.
5Thy mercy, O LORD, *is* in the heavens; *and* thy faithfulness *reacheth* unto
the clouds.
6Thy righteousness *is* like the great
*mountains; thy judgments *are* a great
deep: O LORD, thou preservest man and
beast.
7How excellent *is* thy lovingkindness, O God! therefore the children of
men put their trust under the shadow
of thy wings.
8They shall be abundantly satisfied
with the fatness of thy house; and thou
shalt make them drink of the river of
thy pleasures.
9For with thee *is* the fountain of life:
in thy light shall we see light.
10O continue thy lovingkindness unto
them that know thee; and thy righteousness to the upright in heart.
11Let not the foot of pride come
against me, and let not the hand of the
wicked remove me.
12There are the workers of iniquity

35:16 gnashed upon me with their teeth. This same phrase occurs in Acts 7:54 when the Jews stoned Stephen. Compare Psalm 37:12.

35:19 wink with the eye. These sinful men winked at one another in unholy glee; they rejoiced when they were able to make David suffer.

36:7 the shadow of thy wings. See Ruth 2:12 note.

fallen: they are cast down, and shall not be able to rise.

Psalm 37

A Psalm of David.

1 Fret not thyself because of evildoers, neither be thou envious against the workers of iniquity.

2 For they shall soon be cut down like the grass, and wither as the green herb.

3 *Trust in the LORD, and do good; *so* shalt thou dwell in the land, and verily thou shalt be fed.

4 Delight thyself also in the LORD; and he shall give thee the desires of thine heart.

5 Commit thy way unto the LORD; trust also in him; and he shall bring *it* to pass.

6 And he shall bring forth thy *righteousness as the light, and thy judgment as the noonday.

7 Rest in the LORD, and wait patiently for him: fret not thyself because of him who prospereth in his way, because of the man who bringeth wicked devices to pass.

8 Cease from anger, and forsake wrath: fret not thyself in any wise to do evil.

9 For evildoers shall be cut off: but those that wait upon the LORD, they shall inherit the earth.

10 For yet a little while, and the wicked *shall* not *be:* yea, thou shalt diligently consider his place, and it *shall* not *be.*

11 But the meek shall inherit the earth; and shall delight themselves in the abundance of peace.

12 The wicked plotteth against the *just, and gnasheth upon him with his teeth.

13 The Lord shall laugh at him: for he seeth that his day is coming.

14 The wicked have drawn out the sword, and have bent their bow, to cast down the poor and needy, *and* to slay such as be of upright *conversation.

15 Their sword shall enter into their own heart, and their bows shall be broken.

16 A little that a righteous man hath *is* better than the riches of many wicked.

17 For the arms of the wicked shall be broken: but the LORD upholdeth the righteous.

18 The LORD knoweth the days of the upright: and their inheritance shall be for ever.

19 They shall not be ashamed in the evil time: and in the days of famine they shall be satisfied.

20 But the wicked shall perish, and the enemies of the LORD *shall be* as the fat of lambs: they shall consume; into smoke shall they consume away.

21 The wicked borroweth, and payeth not again: but the righteous sheweth mercy, and giveth.

22 For *such as be* blessed of him shall inherit the earth; and *they that be* cursed of him shall be cut off.

23 The steps of a *good* man are ordered by the LORD: and he delighteth in his way.

24 Though he fall, he shall not be utterly cast down: for the LORD upholdeth *him with* his hand.

25 I have been young, and *now* am old; yet have I not seen the righteous forsaken, nor his seed begging bread.

26 *He is* ever merciful, and lendeth; and his seed *is* blessed.

27 Depart from evil, and do good; and dwell for evermore.

Psalm 37. This is one of the great alphabetical or acrostic psalms (see Ps. 25 note, "Acrostic Poems"). In the Hebrew, there were twenty-two stanzas, each beginning with a letter of the Hebrew alphabet, in order.

37:1 envious against the workers of iniquity. Jealous of their wealth, their popularity, and their good fortune in this life.

37:11 the meek shall inherit the earth. See Christ's words in Matthew 5:5.

37:13 laugh at him. That is, the wicked man.

37:13 his day is coming. The day when the wicked man will be punished for his sin.

37:22 blessed . . . cursed of him. Of God.

28 For the LORD loveth judgment, and
forsaketh not his *saints; they are preserved for ever: but the seed of the
wicked shall be cut off.
29 The righteous shall inherit the
land, and dwell therein for ever.
30 The mouth of the righteous speaketh wisdom, and his tongue talketh of
judgment.
31 The *law of his God *is* in his heart;
none of his steps shall slide.
32 The wicked watcheth the righteous, and seeketh to slay him.
33 The LORD will not leave him in his
hand, nor condemn him when he is
judged.
34 Wait on the LORD, and keep his way,
and he shall exalt thee to inherit the
land: when the wicked are cut off, thou
shalt see *it.*
35 I have seen the wicked in great
power, and spreading himself like a
green bay tree.
36 Yet he passed away, and, lo, he *was*
not: yea, I sought him, but he could not
be found.
37 Mark the *perfect *man,* and behold
the upright: for the end of *that* man *is*
peace.
38 But the transgressors shall be destroyed together: the end of the wicked shall be cut off.

Psalm 38 The Penitential Psalms
Psalm 38 is one of the penitential psalms in which David repents of his sins. Disease had come upon him as the LORD laid His chastening hand upon David to bring him back to the ways of righteousness. This psalm shows us David's sufferings and sorrow. Some of the other penitential psalms are 6, 32, 51, and 130.

39 But the salvation of the righteous
is of the LORD: *he is* their strength in the
time of trouble.
40 And the LORD shall help them, and
deliver them: he shall deliver them
from the wicked, and save them, because they trust in him.

Psalm 38

A Penitential Psalm

A Psalm of David,
to bring to remembrance.

1 O LORD, rebuke me not in thy wrath:
neither *chasten me in thy hot displeasure.
2 For thine arrows stick fast in me,
and thy hand presseth me sore.
3 *There is* no soundness in my flesh
because of thine anger; neither *is there*
any rest in my bones because of my
*sin.
4 For mine iniquities are gone over
mine head: as an heavy burden they are
too heavy for me.
5 My wounds stink *and* are corrupt
because of my foolishness.
6 I am troubled; I am bowed down
greatly; I go *mourning all the day long.
7 For my loins are filled with a loathsome *disease:* and *there is* no soundness
in my flesh.
8 I am feeble and sore broken: I have
roared by reason of the disquietness of
my heart.
9 Lord, all my desire *is* before thee;
and my groaning is not hid from thee.
10 My heart panteth, my strength
faileth me: as for the light of mine eyes,
it also is gone from me.
11 My lovers and my friends stand
aloof from my sore; and my kinsmen
stand afar off.

37:33 in his hand. The LORD will not leave the righteous in the enemy's power, either human enemies or Satan.
37:33 when he is judged. When the enemy says untrue things against him (us), God will not condemn him (us).
37:35 green bay tree. A tree that is green all year. So, David thought, it seemed to be with the wicked: All year, year after year, the wicked seemed to make a show of all their wealth and power.
38:11 aloof. Afar off, at a distance.

12 They also that seek after my life lay snares *for me:* and they that seek my hurt speak mischievous things, and imagine deceits all the day long.

13 But I, as a deaf *man,* heard not; and *I was* as a dumb man *that* openeth not his mouth.

14 Thus I was as a man that heareth not, and in whose mouth *are* no reproofs.

15 For in thee, O LORD, do I *hope: thou wilt hear, O Lord my God.

16 For I said, *Hear me,* lest *otherwise* they should rejoice over me: when my foot slippeth, they magnify *themselves* against me.

17 For I *am* ready to halt, and my sorrow *is* continually before me.

18 For I will declare mine iniquity; I will be sorry for my sin.

19 But mine enemies *are* lively, *and* they are strong: and they that hate me wrongfully are multiplied.

20 They also that *render evil for good are mine adversaries; because I follow *the thing that* good *is.*

21 Forsake me not, O LORD: O my God, be not far from me.

22 Make haste to help me, O Lord my salvation.

Psalm 39

To the chief Musician, *even* to *Jeduthun,
A Psalm of David.

1 I said, I will take heed to my ways, that I sin not with my tongue: I will keep my mouth with a bridle, while the wicked is before me.

2 I was dumb with silence, I held my peace, *even* from good; and my sorrow was stirred.

3 My heart was hot within me, while I was musing the fire burned: *then* spake I with my tongue,

4 LORD, make me to know mine end, and the measure of my days, what it *is; that* I may know how frail I *am.*

5 Behold, thou hast made my days *as* an handbreadth; and mine age *is* as nothing before thee: verily every man at his best state *is* altogether *vanity. *Selah.

6 Surely every man walketh in a vain shew: surely they are disquieted in vain: he heapeth up *riches,* and knoweth not who shall gather them.

7 And now, Lord, what wait I for? my hope *is* in thee.

8 Deliver me from all my transgressions: make me not the reproach of the foolish.

9 I was dumb, I opened not my mouth; because thou didst *it.*

10 Remove thy stroke away from me: I am consumed by the blow of thine hand.

11 When thou with rebukes dost correct man for iniquity, thou makest his beauty to consume away like a moth: surely every man *is* vanity. Selah.

12 Hear my prayer, O LORD, and give ear unto my cry; hold not thy peace at my tears: for I *am* a stranger with thee, *and* a sojourner, as all my fathers *were.*

13 O spare me, that I may recover strength, before I go hence, and be no more.

38:17 halt. To limp, be lame; thus, to hesitate.

39:title. Jeduthun. One of the three musical directors or choirmasters appointed by David to serve in the temple. The others were Asaph and Heman (see introduction to Psalms).

39:1 I will keep my mouth with a bridle. This means, "I will keep a muzzle on my mouth."

39:2 even from good. In the presence of his enemies David did not speak at all, even to say things that were good, for fear he might start with good things and end by saying things that were bad.

39:3 My heart was hot. As David in his sorrow turned to thoughts of the LORD, his heart was warmed.

39:6 vain shew. Life, David says, passes quickly, like a shadow. See James 4:14.

39:12 sojourner. David did not look on this earth as his home—here he was a stranger, a visitor and a traveler for a time, but his eternal home was heaven.

40:1 Deliverance
David's faith and experience of deliverance from deep depression were personal, and also prophetic of the resurrection of the Lord Jesus Christ after Gethsemane and the cross. This has become the Christian's experience and praise when he or she is born again.

Psalm 40

Messianic

To the chief Musician,
A Psalm of *David.

[1]I waited patiently for the LORD; and
he inclined unto me, and heard my cry.
[2]He brought me up also out of an
horrible pit, out of the miry clay, and set
my feet upon a *rock, *and* established
my goings.
[3]And he hath put a new song in my
mouth, *even* praise unto our God: many
shall see *it,* and *fear, and shall trust in
the LORD.
[4]Blessed *is* that man that maketh the
LORD his trust, and respecteth not the
proud, nor such as turn aside to lies.
[5]Many, O LORD my God, *are* thy wonderful works *which* thou hast done, and
thy thoughts *which are* to us-ward: they
cannot be reckoned up in order unto
thee: *if* I would declare and speak *of
them,* they are more than can be numbered.
[6]*Sacrifice and *offering thou didst
not desire; mine ears hast thou opened:
burnt-offering and *sin-offering hast
thou not required.
[7]Then said I, Lo, I come: in the volume of the book *it is* written of me,
[8]I delight to do thy will, O my God:
yea, thy law *is* within my heart.
[9]I have preached righteousness in the
great congregation: lo, I have not refrained my lips, O LORD, thou knowest.
[10]I have not hid thy righteousness
within my heart; I have declared thy
faithfulness and thy salvation: I have
not concealed thy lovingkindness and
thy truth from the great congregation.
[11]Withhold not thou thy tender mercies from me, O LORD: let thy lovingkindness and thy truth continually
preserve me.
[12]For innumerable evils have compassed me about: mine iniquities have
taken hold upon me, so that I am not
able to look up; they are more than the
hairs of mine head: therefore my heart
faileth me.

40:12 Facing Anguish
Though David is speaking of his own experience when he was a fugitive during Absalom's rebellion (2 Sam. 15–17), the words are prophetic of Christ's deeper anguish when He hung on the cross to become sin for us (see Isa. 53:3-7).

[13]Be pleased, O LORD, to deliver me:
O LORD, make haste to help me.
[14]Let them be ashamed and confounded together that seek after my
soul to destroy it; let them be driven
backward and put to shame that wish
me evil.
[15]Let them be desolate for a reward
of their shame that say unto me, Aha,
aha.
[16]Let all those that seek thee rejoice
and be glad in thee: let such as love thy
salvation say continually, The LORD be
magnified.
[17]But I *am* poor and needy; *yet* the

Psalm 40. Foretells Christ.
40:6 Sacrifice and offering. Compare verses 6-8 with Numbers 15:30; 1 Samuel 15:22; Psalm 19:13; 51:15-16. Despite the deep meaning of Hebrew ritual as a *type of life in Christ, we find repeated warnings, as here, against the danger of substituting outward observances, however solemn, for inward obedience to God's will.
40:7 Lo, I come. When the Hebrew worship became too complicated and unreal (see Isa. 10:1-15), our Lord Himself came as the true sacrifice for sin. Read carefully Hebrews 10:1-10 where this psalm is quoted and explained.
40:7 in the volume of the book. In His eternal counsels. Compare with other "books" that God opens (Rev. 20:12).

Lord thinketh upon me: thou *art* my help and my deliverer; make no tarrying, O my God.

Psalm 41

Messianic

To the chief Musician, A Psalm of David.

1Blessed *is* he that considereth the poor: the LORD will deliver him in time of trouble.

2The LORD will preserve him, and keep him alive; *and* he shall be blessed upon the earth: and thou wilt not deliver him unto the will of his enemies.

3The LORD will strengthen him upon the bed of languishing: thou wilt make all his bed in his sickness.

4I said, LORD, be merciful unto me: heal my soul; for I have sinned against thee.

5Mine enemies speak evil of me, When shall he die, and his name perish?

6And if he come to see *me,* he speaketh vanity: his heart gathereth iniquity to itself; *when* he goeth abroad, he telleth *it.*

7All that hate me whisper together against me: against me do they devise my hurt.

8An evil disease, *say they,* cleaveth fast unto him: and *now* that he lieth he shall rise up no more.

9Yea, mine own familiar friend, in whom I trusted, which did eat of my bread, hath lifted up *his* heel against me.

10But thou, O LORD, be merciful unto me, and raise me up, that I may requite them.

11By this I know that thou favourest me, because mine enemy doth not triumph over me.

12And as for me, thou upholdest me in mine integrity, and settest me before thy face for ever.

13Blessed *be* the LORD *God of *Israel from everlasting, and to everlasting. *Amen, and Amen.

BOOK II

Psalm 42

A Song of Instruction

To the chief Musician, *Maschil, for the sons of Korah.

1As the hart panteth after the water brooks, so panteth my soul after thee, O God.

42:1 Remembering the Past
Psalm 42 opens the second section (Pss. 42–72). The psalms in this section compare with Israel's experiences in the wilderness (see Exod., etc.). Psalms 42 and 43 express the cry of an oppressed people, and belong together, for no title appears in Psalm 43, and the same refrain in 42:5,11, and 43:5 would indicate their originally being one psalm.

2My soul thirsteth for God, for the living God: when shall I come and appear before God?

3My tears have been my meat day and night, while they continually say unto me, Where *is* thy God?

4When I remember these *things,* I pour out my soul in me: for I had gone with the multitude, I went with them to the house of God, with the voice of joy and praise, with a multitude that kept holyday.

Psalm 41. This psalm continues the previous psalm and pictures the betrayal of the Lord by Judas.

41:9 familiar friend. In David's case, the allusion is to the traitor Ahithophel (2 Sam. 17:1-14). The Saviour applies the verse to Judas Iscariot (John 13:18-19).

42:title: sons of Korah. Temple singers. The psalms with this inscription may have belonged to a collection of psalms in the possession of the temple singers.

42:1 hart. Deer.

42:2 thirsteth. Compare Psalm 107:9; Isaiah 55:1; Jeremiah 29:13; Matthew 5:6; John 7:37; Revelation 7:16-17; 21:6; 22:1-2.

5Why art thou cast down, O my soul?
and *why* art thou disquieted in me? hope
thou in God: for I shall yet praise him
for the help of his countenance.
6O my God, my soul is cast down
within me: therefore will I remember
thee from the land of Jordan, and of the
Hermonites, from the hill Mizar.
7Deep calleth unto deep at the noise
of thy waterspouts: all thy waves and
thy billows are gone over me.
8*Yet* the LORD will command his
lovingkindness in the daytime, and in
the night his song *shall be* with me, *and*
my *prayer unto the God of my life.
9I will say unto God my rock, Why
hast thou forgotten me? why go I
mourning because of the oppression of
the enemy?
10*As* with a sword in my bones, mine
enemies reproach me; while they say
daily unto me, Where *is* thy God?
11Why art thou cast down, O my soul?
and why art thou disquieted within me?
hope thou in God: for I shall yet praise
him, *who is* the health of my countenance, and my God.

Psalm 43

1Judge me, O God, and plead my
cause against an ungodly nation: O deliver me from the deceitful and unjust
man.
2For thou *art* the God of my strength:
why dost thou cast me off? why go I
mourning because of the oppression of
the enemy?
3O send out thy light and thy truth:
let them lead me; let them bring me
unto thy *holy hill, and to thy tabernacles.
4Then will I go unto the *altar of
God, unto God my exceeding joy: yea,
upon the harp will I praise thee, O God
my God.
5Why art thou cast down, O my soul?
and why art thou disquieted within me?
hope in God: for I shall yet praise him,
who is the health of my countenance,
and my God.

Psalm 44

A Song of Remembrance and Prophecy

To the chief Musician for the sons of Korah, Maschil.

1We have heard with our ears, O God,
our fathers have told us, *what* work
thou didst in their days, in the times
of old.
2*How* thou didst drive out the heathen with thy hand, and plantedst them;
how thou didst afflict the people, and
cast them out.
3For they got not the land in possession by their own sword, neither did
their own arm save them: but thy right
hand, and thine arm, and the light of thy
countenance, because thou hadst a
favour unto them.
4Thou art my King, O God: command
deliverances for *Jacob.
5Through thee will we push down our
enemies: through thy name will we
tread them under that rise up against
us.
6For I will not *trust in my bow, neither shall my sword save me.
7But thou hast saved us from our
enemies, and hast put them to shame
that hated us.
8In God we boast all the day long, and
praise thy name for ever. Selah.
9But thou hast cast off, and put us to
shame; and goest not forth with our
armies.

42:7 all thy waves. So great was the psalmist's distress that it seemed as though the very depths of the sea had gone over him, yet in faith he could express the confidence of verse 8.

Psalm 44. This psalm tells of Israel's past struggles and tribulations to come, with a prayer for deliverance (vs. 4).

44:4 command deliverances. This entire psalm is prophetic of the condition in which Israel will find herself during the coming period of Great *Tribulation.

10 Thou makest us to turn back from
the enemy: and they which hate us spoil
for themselves.
11 Thou hast given us like sheep *appointed* for meat; and hast scattered us
among the heathen.
12 Thou sellest thy people for nought,
and dost not increase *thy wealth* by their
price.
13 Thou makest us a reproach to our
neighbours, a scorn and a derision to
them that are round about us.
14 Thou makest us a byword among
the heathen, a shaking of the head
among the people.
15 My confusion *is* continually before
me, and the shame of my face hath covered me,
16 For the voice of him that reproacheth and blasphemeth; by reason
of the enemy and avenger.
17 All this is come upon us; yet have
we not forgotten thee, neither have we
dealt falsely in thy *covenant.
18 Our heart is not turned back, neither have our steps declined from thy
way;
19 Though thou hast sore broken us in
the place of dragons, and covered us
with the shadow of *death.
20 If we have forgotten the name of
our God, or stretched out our hands to
a strange god;
21 Shall not God search this out? for
he knoweth the secrets of the heart.
22 Yea, for thy sake are we killed all
the day long; we are counted as sheep
for the slaughter.
23 Awake, why sleepest thou, O Lord?
arise, cast *us* not off for ever.
24 Wherefore hidest thou thy face, *and*
forgettest our affliction and our oppression?
25 For our soul is bowed down to the
dust: our belly cleaveth unto the earth.
26 Arise for our help, and *redeem us
for thy mercies' sake.

Psalm 45

Messianic

To the chief Musician upon Shoshannim,
for the *sons of Korah, *Maschil,
A Song of loves.

1 My heart is inditing a good matter:
I speak of the things which I have made
touching the king: my tongue *is* the pen
of a ready writer.
2 Thou art fairer than the children of
men: *grace is poured into thy lips: therefore God hath blessed thee for ever.
3 Gird thy sword upon *thy* thigh, O
most mighty, with thy glory and thy
majesty.
4 And in thy majesty ride prosperously because of truth and meekness
and *righteousness; and thy right hand
shall teach thee terrible things.
5 Thine arrows *are* sharp in the heart
of the king's enemies; *whereby* the people fall under thee.
6 Thy throne, O God, *is* for ever and

44:19 place of dragons. This may mean Jerusalem (see Jer. 9:11).

44:23 why sleepest thou . . . ? Compare Psalm 121:3-4 and Isaiah 54:7. The LORD did not sleep; because of the sins of the people, He just did not hear their cries.

Psalm 45. As a messianic psalm, this foreshadowes Christ as the bridegroom and Israel's Messiah.

45:title. "Shoshannim" means a song of lilies (see also Pss. 69; 80). The Song of Solomon refers to the "lily of the valley" (Song 2:1-2).

45:title. "A Song of loves" refers to a marriage song. It is the song of the bridegroom, Christ, as He claims His bride, the *church. The three psalms that follow (46; 47; 48) tell of the glorious results of His coming. See also *kingdom.

45:1 inditing. The Hebrew means *bubbling over with* or *overflowing*.

45:4 in thy majesty ride prosperously. For one brief day Christ did so by entering Jerusalem (see Luke 19:28-40), but this prophecy looks ahead to His second coming (Rev. 19:11-16).

45:6 Thy throne, O God, is for ever. See Hebrews 1:8-9 where the glory of the risen Lord is portrayed.

ever: the sceptre of thy *kingdom *is* a
right sceptre.
[7]Thou lovest righteousness, and
hatest wickedness: therefore God, thy
God, hath anointed thee with the *oil of
gladness above thy fellows.
[8]All thy *garments *smell* of myrrh,
and aloes, *and* cassia, out of the ivory
palaces, whereby they have made thee
glad.
[9]Kings' daughters *were* among thy
honourable women: upon thy right
hand did stand the queen in gold of
*Ophir.

45:9 An Allusion
Historically, this is doubtless an allusion to Solomon's political marriages (1 Kings 11:1) and to the visiting queen of Sheba (1 Kings 10:1), from whose territory in Ophir, Solomon is believed to have obtained gold (1 Kings 9:28). In *type, the queen is the *church. The king's daughters represent the various nations that will gather around Christ as King. See *kingdom and *Millennium.

[10]Hearken, O daughter, and consider,
and incline thine ear; forget also thine
own people, and thy father's house;
[11]So shall the king greatly desire thy
beauty: for he *is* thy Lord; and worship
thou him.
[12]And the daughter of *Tyre *shall be*
there with a gift; *even* the rich among the
people shall intreat thy favour.
[13]The king's daughter *is* all glorious
within: her clothing *is* of wrought gold.
[14]She shall be brought unto the king
in raiment of needlework: the virgins
her companions that follow her shall be
brought unto thee.
[15]With gladness and rejoicing shall
they be brought: they shall enter into
the king's palace.
[16]Instead of thy fathers shall be thy
children, whom thou mayest make
princes in all the earth.
[17]I will make thy name to be remembered in all generations: therefore
shall the people praise thee for ever and
ever.

Psalm 46

The Song of Fortitude
To the chief Musician for the
sons of Korah,
A Song upon *Alamoth.

[1]God *is* our refuge and strength, a
very present help in trouble.
[2]Therefore will not we fear, though
the earth be removed, and though the
mountains be carried into the midst of
the sea;
[3]*Though* the waters thereof roar *and*

45:7 above thy fellows. Here the *saints, the redeemed ones, are spoken of, for they have and will have glorious fellowship with their Lord. But His name stands alone.

45:8 myrrh, and aloes, and cassia. Myrrh and cassia were the chief ingredients of the holy anointing oil (Exod. 30); aloes were a chief spice. These expensive perfumes are appropriate for a king's wedding and also are symbolic of the perfect fragrance of Christ's life before God.

45:12 daughter of Tyre. Solomon had a special alliance with Tyre (1 Kings 5:1), which was noted for its great wealth. Thus assistance was given him in building the temple. Spiritually, this is an allusion to the nations that contribute of their wealth and effort to the *church and King of Kings.

45:13 The king's daughter. This is referring to the bride of Christ as the King's daughter. Verses 13-15 show the church's blessings as she unites with Him (see Rev. 19:7-8).

Psalm 46. This psalm is the basis of Martin Luther's hymn *Ein Feste Berg* (A Mighty Fortress).

46:title. "Alamoth" means *set to maidens' voices*. It expresses the heroism in this psalm of women's faith (Luke 23:27-31,55-56; Heb. 11:35; see also Ps. 6 note, "Technical Words in the Psalms").

46:1 God is our refuge. Psalms 46, 47, and 48 belong together. They had their origin in the great national deliverance when Judaea, under King Hezekiah, was delivered from Sennacherib (2 Kings 18–19). Prophetically, they look ahead to the result of the coming of the glorious King of Kings.

be troubled, *though* the mountains
shake with the swelling thereof. *Selah.
4*There is* a river, the streams whereof
shall make glad the city of God, the holy
place of the tabernacles of the most
High.
5God *is* in the midst of her; she shall
not be moved: God shall help her, *and*
that right early.
6The heathen raged, the kingdoms
were moved: he uttered his voice, the
earth melted.
7The LORD of hosts *is* with us; the
God of Jacob *is* our refuge. Selah.
8Come, behold the works of the
LORD, what desolations he hath made
in the earth.
9He maketh wars to cease unto the
end of the earth; he breaketh the bow,
and cutteth the spear in sunder; he
burneth the chariot in the fire.
10Be still, and know that I *am* God: I
will be exalted among the heathen, I
will be exalted in the earth.
11The LORD of hosts *is* with us; the
God of Jacob *is* our refuge. Selah.

Psalm 47

Messianic

To the chief Musician,
A Psalm for the sons of Korah.

1O clap your hands, all ye people;
shout unto *God with the voice of triumph.
2For the LORD most high *is* terrible;
he is a great King over all the earth.
3He shall subdue the people under
us, and the nations under our feet.
4He shall choose our inheritance for
us, the excellency of Jacob whom he
loved. Selah.
5God is gone up with a shout, the
LORD with the sound of a trumpet.
6Sing praises to God, sing praises:
sing praises unto our King, sing praises.
7For God *is* the King of all the earth:
sing ye praises with understanding.
8God reigneth over the heathen:
God sitteth upon the throne of his holiness.
9The princes of the people are gathered together, *even* the people of the
God of *Abraham: for the shields of the
earth *belong* unto God: he is greatly
exalted.

Psalm 48

A Song *and* Psalm for the
*sons of Korah.

1Great *is* the LORD, and greatly to be
praised in the city of our God, *in* the
*mountain of his holiness.
2Beautiful for situation, the joy of the
whole earth, *is* mount *Zion, *on* the
sides of the north, the city of the great
King.
3God is known in her palaces for a
refuge.

46:4 There is a river. The first hint of waters flowing abundantly through Jerusalem (see Ezek. 47:1 and its note, "The River of Blessings"; Zech. 14:8, with a spiritual significance suggested in John 4:13-14; Rev. 22:1-2).

46:5 God shall help her, and that right early. "Right early" means at the break of day. God will help us quickly. Compare Hebrews 4:16.

46:9 He maketh wars to cease. "Breaketh the bow," "cutteth the spear," "burneth the chariot" are expressions to prove that when Christ, the Prince of Peace, rules, all man-made implements of mechanized warfare will be eliminated. Compare Psalm 76:3; see also Isaiah 2:1-5; 11:1-9.

46:10 Be still. Contrast verses 3 and 6–"roar," "troubled," raged." Note one way Christ fulfilled this verse in Mark 4:33-41 and the great promise made through Paul to all who are in Christ (Phil. 4:7). Christians should take time each day to spend with God, giving Him the reverence and worship He deserves (see Ps. 100:3).

Psalm 47. This psalm depicts Christ's worldwide dominion. See verses 1-3,7-9: "all ye people," "all the earth," "the heathen."

47:5 gone up. Exalted.

48:1 city of our God. Jerusalem.

48:2 Mount Zion
The Jews' love and deep reverence for Jerusalem was not because of its beauty; it was rather because of their spiritual associations with it. Their zeal for God made it an especially holy place to them. Note that Melchizedek came to this mountain place–"Salem" (Gen. 14:18; see also its note, "Melchizekek"). Abraham sacrificed on this mountain–Mount Moriah (Gen. 22:2). The ark of the covenant was brought there (2 Sam. 6; see also Ps. 24:3). The temple was built there.

4For, lo, the kings were assembled,
they passed by together.
5They saw *it, and* so they marvelled;
they were troubled, *and* hasted away.
6Fear took hold upon them there, *and*
pain, as of a woman in travail.
7Thou breakest the ships of *Tarshish with an east wind.
8As we have heard, so have we seen
in the city of the LORD of hosts, in the
city of our God: God will establish it for
ever. Selah.
9We have thought of thy lovingkindness, O God, in the midst of thy temple.
10According to thy name, O God, so
is thy praise unto the ends of the earth:
thy right hand is full of righteousness.
11Let mount Zion rejoice, let the
daughters of *Judah be glad, because of
thy judgments.
12Walk about Zion, and go round
about her: tell the towers thereof.
13Mark ye well her bulwarks, consider her palaces; that ye may tell *it* to the
generation following.
14For this God *is* our God for ever and
ever: he will be our guide *even* unto
death.

Psalm 49

To the chief Musician,
A Psalm for the sons of Korah.

1Hear this, all *ye* people; give ear, all
ye inhabitants of the *world:
2Both low and high, rich and poor,
together.
3My mouth shall speak of wisdom;
and the meditation of my heart *shall be*
of understanding.
4I will incline mine ear to a *parable:
I will open my dark saying upon the
harp.
5Wherefore should I fear in the days
of evil, *when* the iniquity of my heels
shall compass me about?
6They that trust in their wealth, and
boast themselves in the multitude of
their riches;
7None *of them* can by any means redeem his brother, nor give to God a ransom for him:
8(For the *redemption of their soul *is*
precious, and it ceaseth for ever:)
9That he should still live for ever, *and*
not see corruption.
10For he seeth *that* wise men die,
likewise the *fool and the brutish
person perish, and leave their wealth to
others.
11Their inward thought *is, that* their
houses *shall continue* for ever, *and* their
dwelling places to all generations; they
call *their* lands after their own names.
12Nevertheless man *being* in honour
abideth not: he is like the beasts *that*
perish.
13This their way *is* their folly: yet
their posterity approve their sayings.
Selah.
14Like sheep they are laid in the
grave; death shall feed on them; and the
upright shall have dominion over them
in the morning; and their beauty shall
consume in the grave from their dwelling.
15But God will redeem my soul from
the power of the grave: for he shall receive me. Selah.
16Be not thou afraid when one is
made rich, when the glory of his house
is increased;
17For when he dieth he shall carry

49:4 open my dark saying. To explain a riddle or puzzling statement (Matt. 13:10-11; see Matt.13:11 note, "The Mysteries of the Kingdom").

nothing away: his glory shall not descend after him.

18 Though while he lived he blessed his soul: and *men* will praise thee, when thou doest well to thyself.

19 He shall go to the generation of his fathers; they shall never see light.

20 Man *that is* in honour, and understandeth not, is like the beasts *that* perish.

Psalm 50

A Psalm of Judgment by God

A Psalm of *Asaph.

1 The mighty God, *even* the LORD, hath spoken, and called the earth from the rising of the sun unto the going down thereof.

2 Out of Zion, the *perfection of beauty, God hath shined.

3 Our God shall come, and shall not keep silence: a fire shall devour before him, and it shall be very tempestuous round about him.

4 He shall call to the heavens from above, and to the earth, that he may judge his people.

5 Gather my *saints together unto me; those that have made a *covenant with me by *sacrifice.

6 And the heavens shall declare his righteousness: for God *is* judge himself. Selah.

7 Hear, O my people, and I will speak; O *Israel, and I will testify against thee: I *am* God, *even* thy God.

8 I will not reprove thee for thy sacrifices or thy burnt-offerings, *to have been* continually before me.

9 I will take no bullock out of thy house, *nor* he goats out of thy folds.

10 For every beast of the forest *is* mine, *and* the cattle upon a thousand hills.

11 I know all the fowls of the mountains: and the wild beasts of the field *are* mine.

12 If I were hungry, I would not tell thee: for the world *is* mine, and the fulness thereof.

13 Will I eat the flesh of bulls, or drink the blood of goats?

14 Offer unto God thanksgiving; and pay thy vows unto the most High:

15 And call upon me in the day of trouble: I will deliver thee, and thou shalt glorify me.

16 But unto the wicked God saith, What hast thou to do to declare my statutes, or *that* thou shouldest take my covenant in thy mouth?

17 Seeing thou hatest instruction, and castest my words behind thee.

18 When thou sawest a thief, then thou consentedst with him, and hast been partaker with adulterers.

19 Thou givest thy mouth to evil, and thy tongue frameth deceit.

20 Thou sittest *and* speakest against thy brother; thou slanderest thine own mother's son.

21 These *things* hast thou done, and I kept silence; thou thoughtest that I was altogether *such an one* as thyself: *but* I will reprove thee, and set *them* in order before thine eyes.

22 Now consider this, ye that forget God, lest I tear *you* in pieces, and *there be* none to deliver.

23 Whoso offereth praise glorifieth me: and to him that ordereth *his* *conversation *aright* will I shew the *salvation of God.

50:1 The mighty God, even the LORD, hath spoken. This psalm is a judgment psalm, for in it God is seen coming in righteousness to judge His people (see 1 Pet. 4:17).

50:5 Gather my saints. The allusion was to Israel with a covenant of sacrifice in the temple (compare Exod. 24). Because Christ is the sacrifice who superseded Jewish ritual, the passage is extended to His *church (see Rom. 4).

50:8 I will not reprove thee. The meaning seems to be that God accepts the sacrifices yet is above and beyond them in His majesty (vss. 9-13; see also Isa. 1:11-12; Jer. 7:22-23).

Psalm 51

A Song of Repentance

To the chief Musician, A Psalm of *David, when Nathan the *prophet came unto him, after he had gone in to Bath-sheba.

1Have *mercy upon me, O God, according to thy lovingkindness: according unto the multitude of thy tender mercies blot out my transgressions.
2Wash me throughly from mine iniquity, and cleanse me from my *sin.
3For I acknowledge my transgressions: and my sin *is* ever before me.

51:3 About Sin
There are a number of different words in the Bible that denote sin; in fact, there are at least ten Hebrew and eleven Greek words. Some are translated "sin," while others indicate "rebellion," "transgression," etc.–clearly from usage indicating sinfulness. Here are a few of the literal translations of some of these Hebrew and Greek words: "to miss the mark," "to turn from the right course," "to revolt against authority," "to distort the right," "to disobey," "to neglect," "to be guilty before God."

Sin may be defined, therefore, as that inborn and natural attitude of mind and consequent activity in all people that causes them to be less holy and righteous than the perfection of God. We all need to conform to God's perfect law, but we are impure and guilty before Him (Isa. 64:6; Rom. 3:25). Only faith in Christ's blood will make us acceptable in God's sight (Rom. 6:22-23).

4Against thee, thee only, have I sinned, and done *this* evil in thy sight: that thou mightest be justified when thou speakest, *and* be clear when thou judgest.
5Behold, I was shapen in iniquity; and in sin did my mother conceive me.
6Behold, thou desirest truth in the inward parts: and in the hidden *part* thou shalt make me to know wisdom.
7Purge me with *hyssop, and I shall be *clean: wash me, and I shall be whiter than snow.
8Make me to hear joy and gladness; *that* the bones *which* thou hast broken may rejoice.
9Hide thy face from my sins, and blot out all mine iniquities.
10Create in me a clean heart, O God; and renew a right spirit within me.
11Cast me not away from thy presence; and take not thy *holy spirit from me.
12Restore unto me the joy of thy salvation; and uphold me *with thy* free spirit.
13*Then* will I teach transgressors thy ways; and sinners shall be converted unto thee.
14Deliver me from bloodguiltiness, O God, thou God of my salvation: *and* my tongue shall sing aloud of thy *righteousness.
15O Lord, open thou my lips; and my mouth shall shew forth thy praise.
16For thou desirest not sacrifice; else would I give *it:* thou delightest not in burnt-offering.
17The sacrifices of God *are* a broken spirit: a broken and a contrite heart, O God, thou wilt not despise.
18Do good in thy good pleasure unto Zion: build thou the walls of *Jerusalem.
19Then shalt thou be pleased with the

51:title. after he had gone in to Bath-sheba. See 2 Samuel 11 and 12 for the story of David's fall into sin. This is the best-known penitential psalm (see Ps. 38 note, "The Penitential Psalms").

51:7 Purge me with hyssop . . . wash me. This speaks of the blood and water of purification of the Law (see Exod. 12:22; Lev. 14:1-7; Num. 19:1-19). Blood and water poured from our Saviour's side after He died on the cross (John 19:34).

51:11 take not thy holy spirit from me. David could remember the awfulness of King Saul's position after the *Holy Spirit was taken from him (1 Sam. 16:14).

51:17 contrite. Ground to powder; hence, repentant, humbled, and sorrowful.

51:18 build thou the walls. David was building Jerusalem at the time and wished to begin work on the temple (2 Sam. 7). See also Ezekiel's great vision of a future temple (Ezek. 40–44).

sacrifices of righteousness, with burnt-
offering and whole burnt-offering: then
shall they offer bullocks upon thine *altar.

Psalm 52

A Song of Instruction

To the chief Musician, *Maschil, *A Psalm* of David, when Doeg the Edomite came and told Saul, and said unto him, David is come to the house of Ahimelech.

1 Why boastest thou thyself in mischief, O mighty man? the goodness of
God *endureth* continually.
2 Thy tongue deviseth mischiefs; like
a sharp razor, working deceitfully.
3 Thou lovest evil more than good;
and lying rather than to speak righteousness. *Selah.
4 Thou lovest all devouring words,
O *thou* deceitful tongue.
5 God shall likewise destroy thee for
ever, he shall take thee away, and pluck
thee out of *thy* dwelling place, and root
thee out of the land of the living. Selah.
6 The righteous also shall see, and
*fear, and shall laugh at him:
7 Lo, *this is* the man *that* made not
God his strength; but trusted in the
abundance of his riches, *and* strengthened himself in his wickedness.
8 But I *am* like a green olive tree in
the house of God: I *trust in the mercy
of God for ever and ever.
9 I will praise thee for ever, because
thou hast done *it:* and I will wait on thy
name; for *it is* good before thy saints.

Psalm 53

A Song of Instruction

To the chief Musician upon Mahalath, Maschil, *A Psalm* of David.

1 The fool hath said in his heart, *There*
is no *God. Corrupt are they, and have
done abominable iniquity: *there is* none
that doeth good.
2 God looked down from *heaven
upon the children of men, to see if there
were *any* that did understand, that did
seek God.
3 Every one of them is gone back:
they are altogether become filthy; *there*
is none that doeth good, no, not one.
4 Have the workers of iniquity no
knowledge? who eat up my people *as*
they eat bread: they have not called
upon God.
5 There were they in great fear, *where*
no fear was: for God hath scattered the
bones of him that encampeth *against*
thee: thou hast put *them* to shame, because God hath despised them.
6 Oh that the salvation of Israel *were*
come out of Zion! When God bringeth
back the captivity of his people, *Jacob
shall rejoice, *and* Israel shall be glad.

Psalm 54

A Song of Instruction

To the chief Musician on *Neginoth, Maschil, *A Psalm* of David, when the Ziphims came and said to Saul, Doth not David hide himself with us?

1 Save me, O God, by thy name, and
judge me by thy strength.
2 Hear my *prayer, O God; give ear to
the words of my mouth.
3 For strangers are risen up against
me, and oppressors seek after my soul:
they have not set God before them.
Selah.
4 Behold, God *is* mine helper: the
Lord *is* with them that uphold my soul.
5 He shall reward evil unto mine enemies: cut them off in thy truth.
6 I will freely sacrifice unto thee: I

52:title. David is come to the house of Ahimelech. For when this incident took place, see 1 Samuel 21 and 22.

52:8 I trust in the mercy of God. David completely trusted the LORD despite Saul's continued pursuit of him and the treachery and murders of which Doeg the Edomite was guilty (see 1 Sam. 21:7; 22:9,18-19,22).

53:1 The fool hath said. See Psalm 14 and notes.

54:title. when the Ziphims came. Read about the Ziphites in 1 Samuel 23:19.

will praise thy name, O LORD; for *it is* good.

7 For he hath delivered me out of all trouble: and mine eye hath seen *his desire* upon mine enemies.

Psalm 55

Messianic

To the chief Musician on Neginoth, *Maschil, *A Psalm* of David.

1 Give ear to my prayer, O God; and hide not thyself from my supplication.

2 Attend unto me, and hear me: I mourn in my complaint, and make a noise;

3 Because of the voice of the enemy, because of the oppression of the wicked: for they cast iniquity upon me, and in wrath they hate me.

4 My heart is sore pained within me: and the terrors of *death are fallen upon me.

5 Fearfulness and trembling are come upon me, and horror hath overwhelmed me.

6 And I said, Oh that I had wings like a dove! *for then* would I fly away, and be at rest.

7 Lo, *then* would I wander far off, *and* remain in the wilderness. Selah.

8 I would hasten my escape from the windy storm *and* tempest.

9 Destroy, O Lord, *and* divide their tongues: for I have seen violence and strife in the city.

10 Day and night they go about it upon the walls thereof: mischief also and sorrow *are* in the midst of it.

11 Wickedness *is* in the midst thereof: deceit and guile depart not from her streets.

12 For *it was* not an enemy *that* reproached me; then I could have borne *it:* neither *was it* he that hated me *that* did magnify *himself* against me; then I would have hid myself from him:

13 But *it was* thou, a man mine equal, my guide, and mine acquaintance.

14 We took sweet counsel together, *and* walked unto the house of God in company.

15 Let death seize upon them, *and* let them go down *quick into *hell: for wickedness *is* in their dwellings, *and* among them.

16 As for me, I will call upon God; and the LORD shall save me.

17 Evening, and morning, and at noon, will I pray, and cry aloud: and he shall hear my voice.

18 He hath delivered my soul in *peace from the battle *that was* against me: for there were many with me.

19 God shall hear, and afflict them, even he that abideth of old. Selah. Because they have no changes, therefore they fear not God.

55:2 make a noise. Moan; mourn as does a dove (compare Isa. 38:14 and Ezek. 7:16); see also verse 6.

55:3 Because of the voice of the enemy. Though David was speaking here of the rebellion and treachery of Absalom and Ahithophel (see 2 Sam. 15–17), the psalm looks ahead to our Lord and His rejection by Israel and betrayal by Judas Iscariot (see vss. 12-14; compare Matt. 26:14-16,20-25).

55:9 divide their tongues. Confuse their counsel.

55:9 violence and strife in the city. Verses 9 to 11 give a prophetic picture of Jerusalem as it was to be, not only in the days of the Lord Jesus on earth, but even more, as it is to be during the reign of *Antichrist.

55:13 mine equal, my guide, and mine acquaintance. Judas was chosen of the Lord to be His disciple; he was a member of the tribe of Judah, as was the Lord; and he accompanied the Lord for three-and-a-half years.

55:15 Let death seize upon them. Verses 15,19-21, and 23 speak of the final end of those who rebel against the Lord and prefer such an end to the love and salvation He freely offers.

55:19 they have no changes. Those who will not believe do not change either their minds or their conduct (see Rev. 22:11).

55:20 A Broken Covenant
The *Beast out of the sea, the Roman prince, will make a covenant with the Jews who have returned to their land.They will be allowed to resume their temple worship. Everything will seem to be all right until, in the midst of the seven years of the *Tribulation, the Beast will break the covenant and will have himself set up as God (see Dan. 9:27; 2 Thess. 2:4; Rev. 13:4-8).

20 He hath put forth his hands against
such as be at peace with him: he hath
broken his covenant.
21 *The words* of his mouth were
smoother than butter, but war *was* in
his heart: his words were softer than
oil, yet *were* they drawn swords.
22 Cast thy burden upon the LORD,
and he shall sustain thee: he shall never
suffer the righteous to be moved.
23 But thou, O God, shalt bring them
down into *the pit of destruction: bloody
and deceitful men shall not live out half
their days; but I will trust in thee.

Psalm 56

A Golden Psalm

To the chief Musician upon Jonath-elem-rechokim, *Michtam of David, when the *Philistines took him in *Gath.

1 Be merciful unto me, O God: for
man would swallow me up; he fighting
daily oppresseth me.
2 Mine enemies would daily swallow
me up: for *they be* many that fight against
me, O thou most High.
3 What time I am afraid, I will trust in
thee.
4 In God I will praise his word, in God
I have put my trust; I will not fear what
*flesh can do unto me.
5 Every day they wrest my words: all
their thoughts *are* against me for evil.
6 They gather themselves together,
they hide themselves, they mark my
steps, when they wait for my soul.
7 Shall they escape by iniquity? in *thine*
anger cast down the people, O God.
8 Thou tellest my wanderings: put
thou my tears into thy bottle: *are they*
not in thy book?
9 When I cry *unto thee,* then shall mine
enemies turn back: this I know; for God
is for me.
10 In God will I praise *his* word: in the
LORD will I praise *his* word.
11 In God have I put my trust: I will
not be afraid what man can do unto me.
12 Thy vows *are* upon me, O God: I
will *render praises unto thee.
13 For thou hast delivered my soul
from death: *wilt* not *thou deliver* my feet
from falling, that I may walk before God
in the light of the living?

Psalm 57

A Golden Psalm

To the chief Musician, Al-taschith, Michtam of *David, when he fled from Saul in the cave.

1 Be merciful unto me, O God, be
merciful unto me: for my soul trusteth

56:title. "Jonath-elem-rechokim" means *the silent dove of the far ones* (of far-off lands or among strangers); or *the dove of the distant terebinths* (a kind of tree). In either case, it may have indicated the melody to which the psalm was to be sung. Compare Psalm 55:6-8.

56:title. when the Philistines took him in Gath. For the incident referred to here, see 1 Samuel 21:10-15.

56:8 tellest. Here the word "tell" means *to record*.

56:8 my tears into thy bottle. It was an Eastern custom for mourners of the dead to catch their tears in bottles and place them in the tombs with their dead loved ones. David is acknowledging here that he knows God cares about him and sees every single tear.

56:8 in thy book. Read about God's remembering love in Malachi 3:16 (see also its note, "The Book of Remembrance").

56:11 I will not be afraid. Compare Psalm 118:6 and also Hebrews 13:6.

57:title. "Al-taschith" means *do not destroy*.

in thee: yea, in the shadow of thy wings
will I make my refuge, until *these* calamities be overpast.
2I will cry unto God most high; unto
God that performeth *all things* for me.
3He shall send from heaven, and save
from the reproach of him that would
swallow me up. Selah. God shall send
forth his *mercy and his truth.
4My soul *is* among lions: *and* I lie *even*
among them that are set on fire, *even*
the sons of men, whose teeth *are* spears
and arrows, and their tongue a sharp
sword.
5Be thou exalted, O God, above the
heavens; *let* thy glory *be* above all the
earth.
6They have prepared a net for my
steps; my soul is bowed down: they
have digged a pit before me, into the
midst whereof they are fallen *them-*
selves. Selah.
7My heart is fixed, O God, my heart
is fixed: I will sing and give praise.
8Awake up, my glory; awake, *psaltery and harp: I *myself* will awake early.
9I will praise thee, O Lord, among
the people: I will sing unto thee among
the nations.
10For thy mercy *is* great unto the
heavens, and thy truth unto the clouds.
11Be thou exalted, O God, above the
heavens: *let* thy glory *be* above all the
earth.

Psalm 58

A Golden Psalm

To the chief Musician, Al-taschith,
Michtam of David.

1Do ye indeed speak *righteousness,
O congregation? do ye judge uprightly,
O ye sons of men?
2Yea, in heart ye work wickedness;
ye weigh the violence of your hands in
the earth.
3The wicked are estranged from the
womb: they go astray as soon as they
be born, speaking lies.
4Their poison *is* like the poison of a
serpent: *they are* like the deaf adder *that*
stoppeth her ear;
5Which will not hearken to the voice
of charmers, charming never so wisely.
6Break their teeth, O God, in their
mouth: break out the great teeth of the
young lions, O LORD.
7Let them melt away as waters *which*
run continually: *when* he bendeth *his*
bow to shoot his arrows, let them be as
cut in pieces.
8As a snail *which* melteth, let *every*
one of them pass away: *like* the untimely
birth of a woman, *that* they may not see
the sun.
9Before your pots can feel the thorns,
he shall take them away as with a whirlwind, both living, and in *his* wrath.
10The righteous shall rejoice when he
seeth the vengeance: he shall wash his
feet in the *blood of the wicked.
11So that a man shall say, Verily *there*
is a reward for the righteous: verily he
is a God that judgeth in the earth.

Psalm 59

A Golden Psalm

To the chief Musician, Al-taschith,
*Michtam of David; when Saul sent, and
they watched the house to kill him.

1Deliver me from mine enemies,

57:title. when he fled from Saul in the cave. Read about the incident referred to here in 1 Samuel 22:1-5.

Psalm 58. This is an imprecatory psalm (see Ps. 5:10 note, "Praying for Judgment").

58:4 adder that stoppeth her ear. The adder (cobra) is a poisonous serpent that will not heed the music of the snake charmer by which its evil instincts might be tamed and subdued. Thus do people sometimes close their ears to the gospel (Acts 7:54-57).

58:9 Before your pots can feel the thorns. This illustrates the suddenness of God's coming in judgment. The thought is, "Before the cooking pots can feel the heat from the lighted thorns, God shall take the people away."

59:title. they watched the house to kill him. Read about this incident in 1 Samuel 19:11-16.

O my *God: defend me from them that rise up against me.

2 Deliver me from the workers of iniquity, and save me from bloody men.

3 For, lo, they lie in wait for my soul: the mighty are gathered against me; not *for* my transgression, nor *for* my *sin, O LORD.

4 They run and prepare themselves without *my* fault: awake to help me, and behold.

5 Thou therefore, O LORD God of hosts, the God of *Israel, awake to visit all the heathen: be not merciful to any wicked transgressors. *Selah.

6 They return at evening: they make a noise like a dog, and go round about the city.

7 Behold, they belch out with their mouth: swords *are* in their lips: for who, *say they,* doth hear?

8 But thou, O LORD, shalt laugh at them; thou shalt have all the heathen in derision.

9 *Because of* his strength will I wait upon thee: for God *is* my defence.

10 The God of my mercy shall *prevent me: God shall let me see *my desire* upon mine enemies.

11 Slay them not, lest my people forget: *scatter them by thy power; and bring them down, O Lord our shield.

12 *For* the sin of their mouth *and* the words of their lips let them even be taken in their pride: and for cursing and lying *which* they speak.

13 Consume *them* in wrath, consume *them,* that they *may* not *be:* and let them know that God ruleth in *Jacob unto the ends of the earth. Selah.

14 And at evening let them return; *and* let them make a noise like a dog, and go round about the city.

15 Let them wander up and down for meat, and grudge if they be not satisfied.

16 But I will sing of thy power; yea, I will sing aloud of thy mercy in the morning: for thou hast been my defence and refuge in the day of my trouble.

17 Unto thee, O my strength, will I sing: for God *is* my defence, *and* the God of my mercy.

Psalm 60

A Golden Psalm

To the chief Musician upon Shushan-eduth, Michtam of David, to teach; when he strove with Aram-naharaim and with Aram-zobah, when Joab returned, and smote of *Edom in the *valley of salt twelve thousand.

1 O God, thou hast cast us off, thou hast scattered us, thou hast been displeased; O turn thyself to us again.

2 Thou hast made the earth to tremble; thou hast broken it: heal the breaches thereof; for it shaketh.

3 Thou hast shewed thy people hard things: thou hast made us to drink the *wine of astonishment.

4 Thou hast given a banner to them that *fear thee, that it may be displayed because of the truth. Selah.

5 That thy beloved may be delivered; save *with* thy right hand, and hear me.

6 God hath spoken in his holiness; I will rejoice, I will divide *Shechem, and mete out the valley of Succoth.

7 *Gilead *is* mine, and *Manasseh *is* mine; *Ephraim also *is* the strength of mine head; *Judah *is* my lawgiver;

8 Moab *is* my washpot; over Edom will I cast out my shoe: Philistia, triumph thou because of me.

59:15 grudge. To growl, grumble, or murmur.

60:title. "Shushan-eduth" means *the lily of testimony*.

60:title. when he strove . . . smote. This incident was with the Syrians and other peoples that David defeated (see 2 Sam. 8:1-14; Chron. 18:1-13).

60:5 That thy beloved. Verses 5-12 and Psalm 108:6-13 are alike in the Hebrew.

60:8 Moab is my washpot. This means that *Moab will be utterly humiliated.

60:8 over Edom will I cast out my shoe. Many Eastern kings would throw a shoe, thereby taking forcible possession of a territory. So Israel would possess *Edom.

60:8 Shoes
Shoes were only soles strapped under the foot. Frequently they were discarded, but an extra pair was taken along on a journey (Matt. 10:10). To unloose the clasp (or latchet) of the shoe, to bring the shoes to someone, or to carry them away was the responsibility of the lowest slave. "To pluck off the shoe" was and still is connected with certain kinds of contracts among the Jews (see Ruth 4:7). To kick, or cast off, one's shoe over a person was the symbol of his greatest humiliation, like stepping or walking on his neck (Ps. 60:8). Washing the feet of another was an act of a servant (Gen. 18:4 note; see also John 13:4-15; vs. 10 note, "The Washing of Feet"; and vs. 14 note). To shake off the dust from the shoe was an indication of placing a curse upon individuals or making a declaration of war against nations.

9Who will bring me *into* the strong
city? who will lead me into Edom?
10*Wilt* not thou, O God, *which* hadst
cast us off? and *thou*, O God, *which* didst
not go out with our armies?
11Give us help from trouble: for vain
is the help of man.
12Through God we shall do valiantly:
for he *it is that* shall tread down our
enemies.

Psalm 61

To the chief Musician upon Neginah,
A Psalm of David.

1Hear my cry, O God; attend unto my
*prayer.
2From the end of the earth will I cry
unto thee, when my heart is overwhelmed: lead me to the rock *that* is
higher than I.
3For thou hast been a shelter for me,
and a strong tower from the enemy.
4I will abide in thy *tabernacle for
ever: I will *trust in the covert of thy
wings. Selah.
5For thou, O God, hast heard my
vows: thou hast given *me* the heritage
of those that fear thy name.
6Thou wilt prolong the king's life:
and his years as many generations.
7He shall abide before God for ever:
O prepare mercy and truth, *which* may
preserve him.
8So will I sing praise unto thy name for
ever, that I may daily perform my vows.

Psalm 62

To the chief Musician, to *Jeduthun,
A Psalm of David.

1Truly my soul waiteth upon God:
from him *cometh* my *salvation.
2He only *is* my rock and my salvation;
he is my defence; I shall not be greatly
moved.
3How long will ye imagine mischief
against a man? ye shall be slain all of
you: as a bowing wall *shall ye be, and as*
a tottering fence.
4They only consult to cast *him* down
from his excellency: they delight in lies:
they bless with their mouth, but they
curse inwardly. Selah.
5My soul, wait thou only upon God;
for my expectation *is* from him.
6He only *is* my rock and my salvation:
he is my defence; I shall not be moved.
7In God *is* my salvation and my glory: the rock of my strength, *and* my
refuge, *is* in God.
8Trust in him at all times; ye people,
pour out your heart before him: God *is*
a refuge for us. Selah.
9Surely men of low degree *are* *vanity, *and* men of high degree *are* a lie: to
be laid in the balance, they *are* altogether *lighter* than vanity.

61:title. "Neginah" means *with stringed instruments*. See Psalm 6 note, "Technical Words in the Psalms."
61:2 rock that is higher than I. The Rock shelter is God Himself (see 62:2).
62:3 How long will ye imagine mischief . . . ? How long will you attack a man? David was addressing the enemies that were constant sources of peril to him. He was still speaking of them in verse 4.
62:9 men of low degree . . . men of high degree. Compare Luke 1:52 and James 2:1-9.

10 Trust not in oppression, and become not vain in robbery: if riches increase, set not your heart *upon them.*
11 God hath spoken once; twice have
I heard this; that power *belongeth* unto
God.
12 Also unto thee, O Lord, *belongeth*
mercy: for thou renderest to every man
according to his work.

Psalm 63

A Song of Loneliness

A Psalm of *David, when he was
in the wilderness of Judah.

1 O God, thou *art* my God; early will I
seek thee: my soul thirsteth for thee,
my *flesh longeth for thee in a dry and
thirsty land, where no water is;
2 To see thy power and thy glory, so
as I have seen thee in the *sanctuary.
3 Because thy lovingkindness *is* better than life, my lips shall praise thee.
4 Thus will I bless thee while I live: I
will lift up my hands in thy name.
5 My soul shall be satisfied as *with*
marrow and fatness; and my mouth
shall praise *thee* with joyful lips:
6 When I remember thee upon my
bed, *and* meditate on thee in the *night*
watches.
7 Because thou hast been my help,
therefore in the shadow of thy wings
will I rejoice.
8 My soul followeth hard after thee:
thy right hand upholdeth me.
9 But those *that* seek my soul, to destroy *it,* shall go into the lower parts of
the earth.
10 They shall fall by the sword: they
shall be a portion for foxes.
11 But the king shall rejoice in God;
every one that sweareth by him shall
glory: but the mouth of them that speak
lies shall be stopped.

Psalm 64

To the chief Musician, A Psalm of David.

1 Hear my voice, O God, in my prayer:
preserve my life from fear of the enemy.
2 Hide me from the secret counsel of
the wicked; from the insurrection of the
workers of iniquity:
3 Who whet their tongue like a sword,
and bend *their bows to shoot* their arrows, *even* bitter words:
4 That they may shoot in secret at the
perfect: suddenly do they shoot at him,
and fear not.
5 They encourage themselves *in* an
evil matter: they commune of laying
snares privily; they say, Who shall see
them?
6 They search out iniquities; they accomplish a diligent search: both the inward *thought* of every one *of them,* and
the heart, *is* deep.

Historical Connections of the Psalms

Psalm 7	1 Samuel 24:11,12	David hides from Saul.
Psalm 18	2 Samuel 22:1-51	David is delivered from his enemies.
Psalm 30	2 Samuel 24:25	David builds an altar.
Psalm 34	1 Samuel 21	David is delivered from his enemies.
Psalm 51	2 Samuel 11;12	David sins with Bath-sheba.
Psalm 52	1 Samuel 22:9	David is distressed over an informant.
Psalm 54	1 Samuel 23:19	David is distressed over an informant.
Psalm 56	1 Samuel 21:10-11	David is delivered from his enemies.
Psalm 57	1 Samuel 24:3-10	David hides from Saul.
Psalm 59	1 Samuel 19:11	Saul watches for David at his house.
Psalm 60	2 Samuel 8:13	David celebrates his victory.
Psalm 63	1 Samuel 23:14	David runs from Saul.
Psalm 142	1 Samuel 22:1; 24:3	David encounters Saul in a cave.

63:title. wilderness of Judah. For David's experience in the wilderness, see 1 Samuel 22–26.

7 But God shall shoot at them *with* an
arrow; suddenly shall they be wounded.
8 So they shall make their own tongue
to fall upon themselves: all that see
them shall flee away.
9 And all men shall fear, and shall declare the work of God; for they shall
wisely consider of his doing.
10 The righteous shall be glad in the
LORD, and shall trust in him; and all the
upright in heart shall glory.

Psalm 65

To the chief Musician,
A Psalm *and* Song of David.

1 Praise waiteth for thee, O *God, in
*Sion: and unto thee shall the vow be
performed.
2 O thou that hearest prayer, unto
thee shall all flesh come.
3 Iniquities prevail against me: *as for*
our transgressions, thou shalt purge
them away.
4 Blessed *is the man whom* thou
choosest, and causest to approach *unto*
thee, that he may dwell in thy courts: we
shall be satisfied with the goodness of
thy house, *even* of thy *holy temple.
5 *By* terrible things in *righteousness
wilt thou answer us, O God of our salvation; *who art* the confidence of all the
ends of the earth, and of them that are
afar off *upon* the sea:
6 Which by his strength setteth fast
the *mountains; *being* girded with
power:
7 Which stilleth the noise of the seas,
the noise of their waves, and the tumult
of the people.
8 They also that dwell in the uttermost parts are afraid at thy tokens: thou
makest the outgoings of the morning
and evening to rejoice.
9 Thou visitest the earth, and waterest
it: thou greatly enrichest it with the
river of God, *which* is full of water: thou
preparest them corn, when thou hast so
provided for it.
10 Thou waterest the ridges thereof
abundantly: thou settlest the furrows
thereof: thou makest it soft with showers: thou blessest the springing thereof.
11 Thou crownest the year with thy
goodness; and thy paths drop fatness.
12 They drop *upon* the pastures of the
wilderness: and the little hills rejoice on
every side.
13 The pastures are clothed with
flocks; the valleys also are covered over
with corn; they shout for joy, they also
sing.

Psalm 66

To the chief Musician, A Song *or* Psalm.

1 Make a joyful noise unto God, all ye
lands:
2 Sing forth the honour of his name:
make his praise glorious.
3 Say unto God, How terrible *art thou*
in thy works! through the greatness of
thy power shall thine enemies submit
themselves unto thee.
4 All the earth shall worship thee, and
shall sing unto thee; they shall sing *to*
thy name. *Selah.
5 Come and see the works of God: *he*
is terrible *in his* doing toward the children of men.
6 He turned the sea into dry *land:*
they went through the flood on foot:
there did we rejoice in him.
7 He ruleth by his power for ever; his
eyes behold the nations: let not the rebellious exalt themselves. Selah.
8 O bless our God, ye people, and
make the voice of his praise to be heard:
9 Which holdeth our soul in life, and
suffereth not our feet to be moved.
10 For thou, O God, hast proved us:
thou hast tried us, as *silver is tried.

65:1 Sion. This means the earthly *Zion, David's beloved city, Jerusalem.
65:8 outgoings. Utmost limits or boundaries.
66:6 He turned the sea. See Exodus 14:21.
66:6 they went through the flood on foot. See Joshua 3:13-17 and verse 17 note, "Crossing the Jordan."

[11]Thou broughtest us into the net; thou laidst affliction upon our loins.
[12]Thou hast caused men to ride over our heads; we went through *fire and through water: but thou broughtest us out into a wealthy *place.*
[13]I will go into thy house with burnt-offerings: I will pay thee my vows,
[14]Which my lips have uttered, and my mouth hath spoken, when I was in trouble.
[15]I will offer unto thee burnt-sacrifices of fatlings, with the *incense of rams; I will offer bullocks with goats. Selah.
[16]Come *and* hear, all ye that *fear God, and I will declare what he hath done for my soul.
[17]I cried unto him with my mouth, and he was extolled with my tongue.
[18]If I regard iniquity in my heart, the Lord will not hear *me:*
[19]*But* verily God hath heard *me;* he hath attended to the voice of my prayer.
[20]Blessed *be* God, which hath not turned away my prayer, nor his *mercy from me.

Psalm 67

To the chief Musician on *Neginoth, A Psalm *or* Song.

[1]God be merciful unto us, and bless us; *and* cause his face to shine upon us; Selah.
[2]That thy way may be known upon earth, thy saving health among all nations.
[3]Let the people praise thee, O God; let all the people praise thee.
[4]O let the nations be glad and sing for joy: for thou shalt judge the people righteously, and govern the nations upon earth. Selah.
[5]Let the people praise thee, O God; let all the people praise thee.
[6]*Then* shall the earth yield her increase; *and* God, *even* our own God, shall bless us.
[7]God shall bless us; and all the ends of the earth shall fear him.

Psalm 68

Messianic

To the chief Musician, A Psalm *or* Song of David.

[1]Let God arise, let his enemies be scattered: let them also that hate him flee before him.
[2]As smoke is driven away, *so* drive *them* away: as wax melteth before the fire, *so* let the wicked perish at the presence of God.
[3]But let the righteous be glad; let them rejoice before God: yea, let them exceedingly rejoice.
[4]Sing unto God, sing praises to his name: extol him that rideth upon the heavens by his name JAH, and rejoice before him.

68:4 God's Wonderful Names

"JAH" is a short, strong form of Jehovah. Since this psalm is filled with praise and honor to God, He is called by several of His wonderful names, so that we may see something of His majesty. Notice, "God," Elohim (vs. 1, etc.); "the Almighty," El Shaddai (vs. 14); "the LORD," Jehovah (vs. 16); "the Lord," Adonai (vs. 11); "the LORD God," Jehovah Elohim (vs. 18). For more names and their meanings, see *names of God.

[5]A father of the fatherless, and a judge of the widows, *is* God in his holy habitation.
[6]God setteth the solitary in families: he bringeth out those which are bound with chains: but the rebellious dwell in a dry *land.*
[7]O God, when thou wentest forth before thy people, when thou didst march through the wilderness; Selah:
[8]The earth shook, the heavens also

67:2 saving health. This means *salvation.*
68:1 Let God arise. These words were used when the ark was borne through the wilderness (Num. 10:35).

dropped at the presence of God: _even_
*Sinai itself _was moved_ at the presence
of God, the God of *Israel.
9Thou, O God, didst send a plentiful
rain, whereby thou didst confirm thine
inheritance, when it was weary.
10Thy congregation hath dwelt
therein: thou, O God, hast prepared of
thy goodness for the poor.
11The Lord gave the word: great _was_
the company of those that published _it._
12Kings of armies did flee apace: and
she that tarried at home divided the
spoil.
13Though ye have lien among the
pots, _yet shall ye be as_ the wings of a
dove covered with silver, and her feathers with yellow gold.
14When the Almighty scattered kings
in it, it was _white_ as snow in Salmon.
15The hill of God _is as_ the hill of *Bashan; an high hill _as_ the hill of Bashan.
16Why leap ye, ye high hills? _this is_
the hill _which_ God desireth to dwell in;
yea, the LORD will dwell _in it_ for ever.
17The chariots of God _are_ twenty
thousand, _even_ thousands of *angels:
the Lord _is_ among them, _as in_ Sinai, in
the holy _place._
18Thou hast ascended on high, thou
hast led captivity captive: thou hast received gifts for men; yea, _for_ the rebellious also, that the LORD God might
dwell _among them._
19Blessed _be_ the Lord, _who_ daily
loadeth us _with benefits, even_ the God of
our *salvation. Selah.
20_He that is_ our God _is_ the God of salvation; and unto God the Lord _belong_
the issues from *death.
21But God shall wound the head of his
enemies, _and_ the hairy scalp of such an
one as goeth on still in his trespasses.
22The Lord said, I will bring again
from Bashan, I will bring _my people_ again
from the depths of the sea:
23That thy foot may be dipped in the
blood of _thine_ enemies, _and_ the tongue
of thy dogs in the same.
24They have seen thy goings, O God;
even the goings of my God, my King, in
the sanctuary.
25The singers went before, the players on instruments _followed_ after;
among _them were_ the damsels playing
with *timbrels.
26Bless ye God in the congregations,
even the Lord, from the fountain of Israel.
27There _is_ little Benjamin _with_ their
ruler, the princes of *Judah _and_ their
council, the princes of Zebulun, _and_ the
princes of Naphtali.
28Thy God hath commanded thy
strength: strengthen, O God, that which
thou hast wrought for us.
29Because of thy temple at *Jerusalem
shall kings bring presents unto thee.

68:8 Sinai itself was moved. See Exodus 19:18 for Mount Sinai's quaking.

68:10 dwelt therein. Dwelt in the wilderness under God's loving care.

68:11 The Lord gave the word. The source of the word is the Lord (God's revelation). A large host has proclaimed it.

68:13 lien among the pots. This verse conveys the idea of: "Will ye lie among the sheepfolds, as the wings of a dove covered with silver and her pinions with yellow gold?" It is apparently a rebuke to those whose faith is negative. Not currently courageous, they will eventually be honored for a positive courage and testimony.

68:14 scattered kings in it. When God scattered the wicked kings in Canaan, they disappeared from in front of Him, the Sun of Righteousness, just as snow disappears when the sun shines on Mount Salmon.

68:14 Salmon. A hill near Shechem. Its gloomy and dark trees made snow seem especially white in contrast.

68:18 ascended on high. Quoted by Paul (Eph. 4:8; see notes).

68:20 issues from death. Deliverance from *death.

68:27 Benjamin . . . Naphtali. The twelve tribes are included here, though they are not all named. They ranged from Benjamin in the extreme south to Naphtali in the extreme north.

30 Rebuke the company of spearmen,
the multitude of the bulls, with the
calves of the people, *till every one* submit himself with pieces of silver: scatter thou the people *that* delight in war.
31 Princes shall come out of *Egypt;
Ethiopia shall soon stretch out her
hands unto God.
32 Sing unto God, ye kingdoms of the
earth; O sing praises unto the Lord;
Selah:
33 To him that rideth upon the heavens of heavens, *which were* of old; lo, he
doth send out his voice, *and that* a
mighty voice.
34 Ascribe ye strength unto God: his
excellency *is* over Israel, and his
strength *is* in the clouds.
35 O God, *thou art* terrible out of thy
holy places: the God of Israel *is* he that
giveth strength and power unto *his* people. Blessed *be* God.

Psalm 69

Messianic

To chief Musician upon *Shoshannim,
A Psalm of *David.

1 Save me, O God; for the waters are
come in unto *my* soul.
2 I sink in deep mire, where *there is* no
standing: I am come into deep waters,
where the floods overflow me.
3 I am weary of my crying: my throat
is dried: mine eyes fail while I wait for
my God.
4 They that hate me without a cause
are more than the hairs of mine head:
they that would destroy me, *being* mine
enemies wrongfully, are mighty: then
I restored *that* which I took not away.
5 O God, thou knowest my foolishness; and my sins are not hid from thee.
6 Let not them that wait on thee,
O Lord GOD of hosts, be ashamed for my
sake: let not those that seek thee be
confounded for my sake, O God of Israel.
7 Because for thy sake I have borne
reproach; shame hath covered my face.
8 I am become a stranger unto my
brethren, and an alien unto my mother's children.
9 For the zeal of thine house hath
eaten me up; and the reproaches of
them that reproached thee are fallen
upon me.
10 When I wept, *and *chastened* my
soul with fasting, that was to my reproach.
11 I made sackcloth also my garment;
and I became a proverb to them.
12 They that sit in the gate speak
against me; and I *was* the song of the
drunkards.
13 But as for me, my *prayer *is* unto
thee, O LORD, *in* an acceptable time:
O God, in the multitude of thy mercy
hear me, in the truth of thy salvation.
14 Deliver me out of the mire, and let
me not sink: let me be delivered from
them that hate me, and out of the deep
waters.
15 Let not the waterflood overflow
me, neither let the deep swallow me up,
and let not the *pit shut her mouth
upon me.
16 Hear me, O LORD; for thy lovingkindness *is* good: turn unto me according to the multitude of thy tender
mercies.

68:30 Rebuke the company of spearmen. The setting of this psalm is the end of the Tribulation. This verse, along with verses 31-32, describes the victory of God. The Millennium is in view in verse 29 (compare Isa. 2:2).

69:1 Save me, O God. Next to the Twenty-second Psalm, the Sixty-ninth Psalm is most frequently quoted from or referred to in the New Testament. Note especially the various references that are indicated in the other notes in this psalm.

69:4 They that hate me without a cause. Compare John 15:25.

69:8 I am become a stranger unto my brethren. Compare John 7:3-5.

69:9 the zeal of thine house. See John 2:17 and its note, "Zeal for the Temple."

69:9 the reproaches of them that reproached thee. See Romans 15:3.

69:12 They that sit in the gate. The rulers and elders of the land.

[17]And hide not thy face from thy servant; for I am in trouble: hear me
speedily.
[18]Draw nigh unto my soul, *and* *redeem it: deliver me because of mine
enemies.
[19]Thou hast known my reproach, and
my shame, and my dishonour: mine
adversaries *are* all before thee.
[20]Reproach hath broken my heart;
and I am full of heaviness: and I looked
for some to take pity, but *there was* none;
and for comforters, but I found none.
[21]They gave me also gall for my
meat; and in my thirst they gave me
vinegar to drink.
[22]Let their table become a snare before them: and *that which should have
been* for *their* welfare, *let it become* a trap.
[23]Let their eyes be darkened, that
they see not; and make their loins continually to shake.
[24]Pour out thine indignation upon
them, and let thy wrathful anger take
hold of them.
[25]Let their habitation be desolate;
and let none dwell in their tents.
[26]For they persecute *him* whom thou
hast smitten; and they talk to the grief
of those whom thou hast wounded.
[27]Add iniquity unto their iniquity:
and let them not come into thy righteousness.
[28]Let them be blotted out of the book
of the living, and not be written with the
righteous.
[29]But I *am* poor and sorrowful: let thy
salvation, O God, set me up on high.
[30]I will praise the name of God with
a song, and will magnify him with
thanksgiving.
[31]*This* also shall please the LORD
better than an ox *or* bullock that hath
horns and hoofs.
[32]The humble shall see *this, and* be

69:31 The Words of Samuel
This verse recalls the very words that Samuel had said to King Saul in David's youth (see 1 Sam. 15:22-23). When the author of the book of Hebrews was writing, over a thousand years after King David had died, the Holy Spirit brought these words to his memory, and we read of the perfect and only sacrifice for sin, the Lord Jesus Christ (Heb. 10:4-10).

glad: and your heart shall live that seek
God.
[33]For the LORD heareth the poor, and
despiseth not his prisoners.
[34]Let the *heaven and earth praise
him, the seas, and every thing that
moveth therein.
[35]For God will save *Zion, and will
build the cities of Judah: that they may
dwell there, and have it in possession.
[36]The seed also of his servants shall
inherit it: and they that love his name
shall dwell therein.

Psalm 70

To the chief Musician, *A Psalm* of David, to bring to remembrance.

[1]*Make haste,* O God, to deliver me;
make haste to help me, O LORD.
[2]Let them be ashamed and confounded that seek after my soul: let
them be turned backward, and put to
confusion, that desire my hurt.
[3]Let them be turned back for a reward of their shame that say, Aha, aha.
[4]Let all those that seek thee rejoice
and be glad in thee: and let such as love
thy salvation say continually, Let God
be magnified.
[5]But I *am* poor and needy: make
haste unto me, O God: thou *art* my help
and my deliverer; O LORD, make no
tarrying.

69:21 gall . . . and . . . vinegar. See Matthew 27:34 (and its note, "Vinegar"), 48; Mark 15:23,36; Luke 23:36; John 19:28-30.
69:22-23 table . . . trap . . . eyes be darkened. See Romans 11:9-10.
69:25 Let their habitation be desolate. See Matthew 23:38; Acts 1:20.
69:28 blotted out of the book of the living. See Exodus 32:33; Revelation 3:5.
Psalm 70. An almost exact repetition of Psalm 40:13-17.

Psalm 71

1In thee, O LORD, do I put my *trust: let me never be put to confusion.

2Deliver me in thy *righteousness, and cause me to escape: incline thine ear unto me, and save me.

3Be thou my strong habitation, whereunto I may continually resort: thou hast given commandment to save me; for thou _art_ my *rock and my fortress.

4Deliver me, O my *God, out of the hand of the wicked, out of the hand of the unrighteous and cruel man.

5For thou _art_ my *hope, O Lord GOD: _thou art_ my trust from my youth.

6By thee have I been holden up from the womb: thou art he that took me out of my mother's *bowels: my praise _shall be_ continually of thee.

7I am as a wonder unto many; but thou _art_ my strong refuge.

8Let my mouth be filled _with_ thy praise _and with_ thy honour all the day.

9Cast me not off in the time of old age; forsake me not when my strength faileth.

10For mine enemies speak against me; and they that lay wait for my soul take counsel together,

11Saying, God hath forsaken him: persecute and take him; for _there is_ none to deliver _him._

12O God, be not far from me: O my God, make haste for my help.

13Let them be confounded _and_ consumed that are adversaries to my soul; let them be covered _with_ reproach and dishonour that seek my hurt.

14But I will hope continually, and will yet praise thee more and more.

15My mouth shall shew forth thy righteousness _and_ thy salvation all the day; for I know not the numbers _thereof._

16I will go in the strength of the Lord GOD: I will make mention of thy righteousness, _even_ of thine only.

17O God, thou hast taught me from my youth: and hitherto have I declared thy wondrous works.

18Now also when I am old and greyheaded, O God, forsake me not; until I have shewed thy strength unto *_this_ generation, _and_ thy power to every one _that_ is to come.

19Thy righteousness also, O God, _is_ very high, who hast done great things: O God, who _is_ like unto thee!

20_Thou,_ which hast shewed me great and sore troubles, shalt *quicken me again, and shalt bring me up again from the depths of the earth.

21Thou shalt increase my greatness, and comfort me on every side.

22I will also praise thee with the *psaltery, _even_ thy truth, O my God: unto thee will I sing with the harp, O thou *Holy One of Israel.

23My lips shall greatly rejoice when I sing unto thee; and my soul, which thou hast *redeemed.

24My tongue also shall talk of thy righteousness all the day long: for they are confounded, for they are brought unto shame, that seek my hurt.

Psalm 72

Messianic

A Psalm for Solomon.

1Give the king thy judgments, O God, and thy righteousness unto the king's son.

2He shall judge thy people with righteousness, and thy poor with *judgment.

3The *mountains shall bring *peace

71:1 In thee, O LORD, do I put my trust. Notice the first three verses of Psalm 31. The thought is the same.

71:15 I know not the numbers. We cannot count the mercies of God (Ps. 5:7 and note, "The LORD's Mercy").

72:3 mountains . . . and the little hills. The word "mountain" in the Scriptures often speaks of political and governmental powers and kingdoms; hills are lesser powers, like small states (Isa. 40:4).

72:1 Solomon's Kingdom
This psalm was either written by Solomon, King David's son, or on his behalf. It describes his kingdom (see 1 Kings 4:21-28), but it looks ahead to David's greater Son, the Lord Jesus Christ and His *kingdom of righteousness. This wonderful time of peace and plenty can only happen when "all nations shall call him blessed" (Ps. 72:17).

to the people, and the little hills, by
righteousness.
4 He shall judge the poor of the people, he shall save the children of the
needy, and shall break in pieces the
oppressor.
5 They shall *fear thee as long as the
sun and moon endure, throughout all
generations.
6 He shall come down like rain upon
the mown grass: as showers *that* water
the earth.
7 In his days shall the righteous flourish; and abundance of peace so long as
the moon endureth.
8 He shall have dominion also from
sea to sea, and from the river unto the
ends of the earth.
9 They that dwell in the wilderness
shall bow before him; and his enemies
shall lick the dust.
10 The kings of *Tarshish and of the
*isles shall bring presents: the kings of
Sheba and Seba shall offer gifts.
11 Yea, all kings shall fall down before
him: all nations shall serve him.
12 For he shall deliver the needy when
he crieth; the poor also, and *him* that
hath no helper.
13 He shall spare the poor and needy,
and shall save the souls of the needy.
14 He shall redeem their soul from
deceit and violence: and precious shall
their blood be in his sight.
15 And he shall live, and to him shall
be given of the gold of Sheba: prayer
also shall be made for him continually;
and daily shall he be praised.
16 There shall be an handful of corn in
the earth upon the top of the mountains; the fruit thereof shall shake like
*Lebanon: and *they* of the city shall
flourish like grass of the earth.
17 His name shall endure for ever: his
name shall be continued as long as the
sun: and *men* shall be blessed in him:
all nations shall call him blessed.
18 Blessed *be* the LORD God, the God
of Israel, who only doeth wondrous
things.
19 And blessed *be* his glorious name
for ever: and let the whole earth be
filled *with* his glory; *Amen, and Amen.
20 The prayers of David the son of
Jesse are ended.

BOOK III

Psalm 73

A Psalm of *Asaph.

1 Truly God *is* good to Israel, *even* to
such as are of a *clean heart.
2 But as for me, my feet were almost
gone; my steps had well nigh slipped.
3 For I was envious at the foolish,
when I saw the prosperity of the wicked.
4 For *there are* no bands in their death:
but their strength *is* firm.
5 They *are* not in trouble *as other* men;
neither are they plagued like *other* men.
6 Therefore pride compasseth them

72:15 he shall live. This is a description of the "son of David," His Millennial reign, and the activities connected with it

72:20 prayers of David . . . are ended. This was a cry of worship and praise. The vision that the LORD had given David here answered and satisfied all his prayers—never would he have to pray for the vision of the kingdom. This was the last psalm in the second book of Psalms (see introduction).

73:4 there are no bands in their death. There are no pangs in their death. The wicked are proud and fearless in their defiance of God; criminals often face eternity with reckless indifference.

about as a chain; violence covereth
them *as* a garment.
7Their eyes stand out with fatness:
they have more than heart could wish.
8They are corrupt, and speak wickedly *concerning* oppression: they speak
loftily.
9They set their mouth against the
heavens, and their tongue walketh
through the earth.
10Therefore his people return hither:
and waters of a full *cup* are wrung out
to them.
11And they say, How doth God know?
and is there knowledge in the most
High?
12Behold, these *are* the ungodly, who
prosper in the *world; they increase *in*
riches.
13Verily I have cleansed my heart *in*
vain, and washed my hands in innocency.
14For all the day long have I been
plagued, and *chastened every morning.
15If I say, I will speak thus; behold, I
should offend *against* the generation of
thy children.
16When I thought to know this, it *was*
too painful for me;
17Until I went into the *sanctuary of
God; *then* understood I their end.
18Surely thou didst set them in slippery places: thou castedst them down
into destruction.
19How are they *brought* into desolation, as in a moment! they are utterly
consumed with terrors.
20As a dream when *one* awaketh; *so,*
O Lord, when thou awakest, thou shalt
despise their image.
21Thus my heart was grieved, and I
was pricked in my *reins.
22So foolish *was* I, and ignorant: I was
as a beast before thee.
23Nevertheless I *am* continually with
thee: thou hast holden *me* by my right
hand.
24Thou shalt guide me with thy counsel, and afterward receive me *to* glory.
25Whom have I in heaven *but thee?*
and *there is* none upon earth *that* I desire beside thee.
26My *flesh and my heart faileth: *but*
God *is* the strength of my heart, and my
portion for ever.
27For, lo, they that are far from thee
shall perish: thou hast destroyed all
them that go a whoring from thee.
28But *it is* good for me to draw near
to God: I have put my trust in the Lord
GOD, that I may declare all thy works.

Psalm 74

A Song of Instruction

*Maschil of Asaph.

1O God, why hast thou cast *us* off for
ever? *why* doth thine anger smoke
against the sheep of thy pasture?
2Remember thy congregation, *which*
thou hast purchased of old; the rod of
thine inheritance, *which* thou hast redeemed; this mount Zion, wherein thou
hast dwelt.
3Lift up thy feet unto the perpetual

73:10 his people return hither. God's people see the prosperity of the wicked and turn to their ways. They drink the waters of worldly pleasure and delight in them (compare Rev. 3:17-18).

73:13 I have cleansed my heart in vain. Asaph, as a man of God, is disturbed by the laxity of life around him (compare Elijah in 1 Kings 19:10).

73:15 If I say, I will speak. Here Asaph speaks. He cannot understand why the wicked prosper. He does not want to be faithless to the generations who lived before his time—those who served and loved the LORD, but he cannot understand why the wicked appear to be blessed while the godly suffer and are in need.

73:16 painful. Difficult.

73:17 the sanctuary of God. God Himself was the sanctuary to whom Asaph turned in his perplexity. Then he saw that this life is just like a dream. Someday the wicked will awake. The pleasures and riches will all be gone (vs. 27; compare Ps. 50:3-5).

74:2 purchased of old. Or redeemed. See Exodus 6:6 note.

74:3 The Point of Enemy Attack
Whenever enemy nations attacked the people of Israel, they made the temple a special point of attack, for they wanted to show their hatred of the God of these people. They did not know they could not destroy God by destroying His house. This is prophetic, too, of the final great profaning of the temple when the image of the *Beast will be set himself up to be worshipped (compare Dan. 9; Matt. 24:15).

desolations; *even* all *that* the enemy
hath done wickedly in the sanctuary.
4Thine enemies roar in the midst of
thy congregations; they set up their
ensigns *for* signs.
5*A man* was famous according as
he had lifted up axes upon the thick
trees.
6But now they break down the carved
work thereof at once with axes and
hammers.
7They have cast fire into thy sanctuary, they have defiled *by casting down*
the dwelling place of thy name to the
ground.
8They said in their hearts, Let us destroy them together: they have burned
up all the *synagogues of God in the
land.
9We see not our signs: *there is* no
more any *prophet: neither *is there*
among us any that knoweth how long.
10O God, how long shall the adversary reproach? shall the enemy blaspheme thy name for ever?
11Why withdrawest thou thy hand,
even thy right hand? pluck *it* out of thy
bosom.
12For God *is* my King of old, working
*salvation in the midst of the earth.
13Thou didst divide the sea by thy
strength: thou brakest the heads of the
dragons in the waters.
14Thou brakest the heads of *leviathan in pieces, *and* gavest him *to be*
meat to the people inhabiting the wilderness.
15Thou didst cleave the fountain
and the flood: thou driedst up mighty
rivers.
16The day *is* thine, the night also *is*
thine: thou hast prepared the light and
the sun.
17Thou hast set all the borders of the
earth: thou hast made summer and
winter.
18Remember this, *that* the enemy
hath reproached, O LORD, and *that* the
foolish people have blasphemed thy
name.
19O deliver not the soul of thy turtledove unto the multitude *of the wicked:*
forget not the congregation of thy poor
for ever.
20Have respect unto the *covenant:
for the dark places of the earth are full
of the habitations of cruelty.
21O let not the oppressed return
ashamed: let the poor and needy praise
thy name.
22Arise, O God, plead thine own
cause: remember how the foolish man
reproacheth thee daily.

74:4 they set up their ensigns. The enemy set up their signs as if they were signs from God Himself.

74:8 synagogues. This is the first time this word is used in the Bible. It is the Greek form for the Hebrew word which means "meeting place." The synagogue was a Jewish place of worship at a distance from the temple in Jerusalem, and when the temple was destroyed in A.D. 70, the synagogues continued throughout the world.

74:13 Thou didst divide the sea. See Exodus 14:21-22.

74:13 dragons in the waters. Compare Job 41 where dragons are identified.

74:15 Thou didst cleave the fountain. God gave the Israelites water to drink in a dry land (see Exod. 17:5-6; Num. 20:8-13).

74:15 thou driedst up mighty rivers. Read about this in Joshua 3:13-17 and see Joshua 3:17 note, "Crossing the Jordan."

74:16 day is thine. God's creative wisdom arranged our times (Gen. 1).

74:19 thy turtledove. This is a term of affection for Israel, just as are "sheep of thy pasture" (vs. 1) and "thy poor" (vs. 19).

23 Forget not the voice of thine enemies: the tumult of those that rise up
against thee increaseth continually.

Psalm 75

To the chief Musician, Al-taschith,
A Psalm *or* Song of Asaph.

1 Unto thee, O God, do we give thanks,
unto thee do we give thanks: for *that*
thy name is near thy wondrous works
declare.
2 When I shall receive the congregation I will judge uprightly.
3 The earth and all the inhabitants
thereof are dissolved: I bear up the pillars of it. *Selah.
4 I said unto the *fools, Deal not foolishly: and to the wicked, Lift not up the
horn:
5 Lift not up your horn on high: speak
not with a stiff neck.
6 For promotion *cometh* neither from
the east, nor from the west, nor from
the south.
7 But God *is* the judge: he putteth
down one, and setteth up another.
8 For in the hand of the LORD *there is*
a cup, and the wine is red; it is full of
mixture; and he poureth out of the
same: but the dregs thereof, all the
wicked of the earth shall wring *them*
out, *and* drink *them*.
9 But I will declare for ever; I will sing
praises to the God of *Jacob.
10 All the *horns of the wicked also
will I cut off; *but* the horns of the righteous shall be exalted.

Psalm 76

To the chief Musician on *Neginoth,
A Psalm *or* Song of *Asaph.

1 In *Judah *is* God known: his name *is*
great in *Israel.
2 In Salem also is his *tabernacle, and
his dwelling place in *Zion.
3 There brake he the arrows of the
bow, the shield, and the sword, and the
battle. Selah.
4 Thou *art* more glorious *and* excellent than the mountains of prey.
5 The stouthearted are spoiled, they
have slept their sleep: and none of the
men of might have found their hands.
6 At thy rebuke, O God of Jacob, both
the chariot and horse are cast into a
dead sleep.
7 Thou, *even* thou, *art* to be feared: and
who may stand in thy sight when once
thou art angry?
8 Thou didst cause judgment to be
heard from *heaven; the earth feared,
and was still,
9 When God arose to judgment, to
save all the meek of the earth. Selah.
10 Surely the wrath of man shall praise
thee: the remainder of wrath shalt thou
restrain.
11 Vow, and pay unto the LORD your

75:2 I shall receive the congregation. This speaks of the time in God's plan when He will surely arise in judgment.
75:6 promotion. Exaltation or help.
75:6 from the east, nor from the west, nor from the south. The north is not mentioned. Israel would not think of looking to the north for any help of any kind, because the enemy was going to descend upon them from the north.
75:8 in the hand of the LORD there is a cup. See *judgment. Here is the cup that our Lord (Matt. 26:39) was willing to drink on our behalf. Thus, this verse applies to those who rebel against His salvation and the great love for us for which He died.
76:4 mountains of prey. The great and powerful kingdoms of the earth.
76:5 they have slept their sleep. They fell asleep, or died in their sleep.
76:6 both the chariot and horse. Read the thrilling account in 2 Kings 18 and 19 (especially 19:35) when the Lord delivered His people.
76:10 wrath of man shall praise thee. Man's inhumanity to man demonstrates what man becomes when he rebels against the love of God. When someone gives his or her heart to God, however, the difference between the "old man" and the "new man" is an incredible contrast and change (see Eph. 4:22-24).

God: let all that be round about him
bring presents unto him that ought to
be feared.
12He shall cut off the spirit of princes:
he is terrible to the kings of the earth.

Psalm 77

To the chief Musician, to *Jeduthun,
A Psalm of Asaph.

1I cried unto *God with my voice,
even unto God with my voice; and he
gave ear unto me.
2In the day of my trouble I sought the
Lord: my sore ran in the night, and
ceased not: my soul refused to be comforted.
3I remembered God, and was troubled: I complained, and my spirit was
overwhelmed. Selah.
4Thou holdest mine eyes waking: I
am so troubled that I cannot speak.
5I have considered the days of old,
the years of ancient times.
6I call to remembrance my song in the
night: I commune with mine own heart:
and my spirit made diligent search.
7Will the Lord cast off for ever? and
will he be favourable no more?
8Is his *mercy clean gone for ever?
doth *his* promise fail for evermore?
9Hath God forgotten to be gracious?
hath he in anger shut up his tender
mercies? Selah.
10And I said, This *is* my infirmity: *but
I will remember* the years of the right
hand of the most High.
11I will remember the works of the
LORD: surely I will remember thy wonders of old.
12I will meditate also of all thy work,
and talk of thy doings.
13Thy way, O God, *is* in the sanctuary: who *is so* great a God as *our* God?
14Thou *art* the God that doest wonders: thou hast declared thy strength
among the people.
15Thou hast with *thine* arm *redeemed thy people, the sons of Jacob
and *Joseph. Selah.
16The waters saw thee, O God, the
waters saw thee; they were afraid:
the depths also were troubled.
17The clouds poured out water: the
skies sent out a sound: thine arrows
also went abroad.
18The voice of thy thunder *was* in the
heaven: the lightnings lightened the
world: the earth trembled and shook.
19Thy way *is* in the sea, and thy path
in the great waters, and thy footsteps
are not known.
20Thou leddest thy people like a flock
by the hand of *Moses and *Aaron.

Psalm 78

A Song of Instruction

*Maschil of Asaph.

1Give ear, O my people, *to* my *law:
incline your ears to the words of my
mouth.
2I will open my mouth in a *parable:
I will utter dark sayings of old:
3Which we have heard and known,
and our fathers have told us.
4We will not hide *them* from their
children, shewing to the generation to
come the praises of the LORD, and his
strength, and his wonderful works that
he hath done.
5For he established a testimony in
Jacob, and appointed a law in Israel,
which he commanded our fathers, that

77:3 I remembered God, and was troubled. The remembrance of God brought no comfort to Asaph, for it raised in his mind the questions of verses 7-9.

77:4 holdest mine eyes waking. "Thou holdest mine eyes open." The thoughts of the LORD so overwhelmed Asaph that he could not sleep.

77:10 the years of the right hand of the most High. Martin Luther understood this phrase to mean: "The right hand of the Most High can change everything."

77:20 Thou leddest thy people like a flock. God led the Israelites from Egypt to the Promised Land. The books of Exodus, Leviticus, Numbers, and Deuteronomy give a full account of this time of God's shepherding.

they should make them known to their
children:
6 That the generation to come might
know *them, even* the children *which*
should be born; *who* should arise and
declare *them* to their children:
7 That they might set their *hope in
God, and not forget the works of God,
but keep his commandments:
8 And might not be as their fathers, a
stubborn and rebellious generation; a
generation *that* set not their heart
aright, and whose spirit was not stedfast with God.
9 The children of *Ephraim, *being*
armed, *and* carrying bows, turned back
in the day of battle.
10 They kept not the covenant of God,
and refused to walk in his law;
11 And forgat his works, and his wonders that he had shewed them.
12 Marvellous things did he in the
sight of their fathers, in the land of
*Egypt, *in* the field of *Zoan.

78:12 God's Miracles
In this psalm, Asaph reviews the miracles that God had done for His people after He led them out of the land of Egypt. Then Asaph goes back to the time when they were still in Egypt, at the time of the plagues, and Asaph again tells how God brought them out of it and into their own Land of Canaan and to the time of King David.

13 He divided the sea, and caused
them to pass through; and he made the
waters to stand as an heap.
14 In the daytime also he led them
with a cloud, and all the night with a
light of fire.
15 He clave the rocks in the wilderness, and gave *them* drink as *out of* the
great depths.
16 He brought streams also out of the
rock, and caused waters to run down
like rivers.
17 And they sinned yet more against
him by provoking the most High in the
wilderness.
18 And they *tempted God in their
heart by asking meat for their lust.
19 Yea, they spake against God; they
said, Can God furnish a table in the wilderness?
20 Behold, he smote the rock, that the
waters gushed out, and the streams
overflowed; can he give bread also? can
he provide flesh for his people?
21 Therefore the LORD heard *this,* and
was wroth: so a fire was kindled against
Jacob, and anger also came up against
Israel;
22 Because they believed not in God,
and trusted not in his salvation:
23 Though he had commanded the
clouds from above, and opened the
doors of heaven,
24 And had rained down *manna upon
them to eat, and had given them of the
corn of heaven.
25 Man did eat *angels' food: he sent
them meat to the full.
26 He caused an east wind to blow in
the heaven: and by his power he
brought in the south wind.
27 He rained flesh also upon them as
dust, and feathered fowls like as the
sand of the sea:
28 And he let *it* fall in the midst of their
camp, round about their habitations.
29 So they did eat, and were well filled:
for he gave them their own desire;
30 They were not estranged from
their lust. But while their meat *was* yet
in their mouths,
31 The wrath of God came upon them,
and slew the fattest of them, and smote
down the chosen *men* of Israel.
32 For all this they sinned still, and
believed not for his wondrous works.
33 Therefore their days did he consume in *vanity, and their years in
trouble.
34 When he slew them, then they

78:9 The children of Ephraim. Here, as in many other places in the Bible, Ephraim stands for all the children of Israel, who "kept not the covenant of God, etc." (vs. 10 and following verses).

sought him: and they returned and enquired early after God.
[35]And they remembered that God
was their rock, and the high God their
*redeemer.
[36]Nevertheless they did flatter him
with their mouth, and they lied unto
him with their tongues.
[37]For their heart was not right with
him, neither were they stedfast in his
covenant.
[38]But he, *being* full of compassion,
forgave *their* iniquity, and destroyed
them not: yea, many a time turned he
his anger away, and did not stir up all his
wrath.
[39]For he remembered that they *were*
but flesh; a wind that passeth away, and
cometh not again.
[40]How oft did they provoke him in
the wilderness, *and* grieve him in the
desert!
[41]Yea, they turned back and tempted
God, and limited the *Holy One of
Israel.
[42]They remembered not his hand,
nor the day when he delivered them
from the enemy.
[43]How he had wrought his signs in
Egypt, and his wonders in the field of
Zoan:
[44]And had turned their rivers into
*blood; and their floods, that they could
not drink.
[45]He sent divers sorts of flies among
them, which devoured them; and frogs,
which destroyed them.
[46]He gave also their increase unto
the caterpiller, and their labour unto the
locust.
[47]He destroyed their vines with hail,
and their sycomore trees with frost.
[48]He gave up their cattle also to the
hail, and their flocks to hot thunderbolts.
[49]He cast upon them the fierceness
of his anger, wrath, and indignation, and
trouble, by sending evil angels *among*
them.
[50]He made a way to his anger; he
spared not their soul from *death, but
gave their life over to the pestilence;
[51]And smote all the firstborn in
Egypt; the chief of *their* strength in the
tabernacles of Ham:
[52]But made his own people to go
forth like sheep, and guided them in the
wilderness like a flock.
[53]And he led them on safely, so that
they feared not: but the sea overwhelmed
their enemies.
[54]And he brought them to the border
of his sanctuary, *even to* this *mountain,
which his right hand had purchased.
[55]He cast out the heathen also before
them, and divided them an inheritance
by line, and made the tribes of Israel to
dwell in their tents.
[56]Yet they tempted and provoked the
most high God, and kept not his testimonies:
[57]But turned back, and dealt unfaith-
fully like their fathers: they were
turned aside like a deceitful bow.
[58]For they provoked him to anger
with their *high places, and moved him
to jealousy with their graven images.
[59]When God heard *this,* he was
wroth, and greatly abhorred Israel:
[60]So that he forsook the tabernacle of
*Shiloh, the tent *which* he placed
among men;
[61]And delivered his strength into captivity, and his glory into the enemy's
hand.
[62]He gave his people over also unto
the sword; and was wroth with his inheritance.
[63]The fire consumed their young
men; and their maidens were not given
to marriage.
[64]Their priests fell by the sword; and
their widows made no lamentation.

78:39 he remembered that they were but flesh. See the beautiful verses 14-16 in Psalm 103.

78:61 delivered his strength into captivity. He gave His people into the hands of the enemy.

[65]Then the Lord awaked as one out of sleep, *and* like a mighty man that shouteth by reason of wine.
[66]And he smote his enemies in the hinder parts: he put them to a perpetual reproach.
[67]Moreover he refused the tabernacle of Joseph, and chose not the tribe of Ephraim:
[68]But chose the tribe of Judah, the mount Zion which he loved.
[69]And he built his sanctuary like high *palaces,* like the earth which he hath established for ever.
[70]He chose *David also his servant, and took him from the sheepfolds:
[71]From following the ewes great with young he brought him to feed Jacob his people, and Israel his inheritance.
[72]So he fed them according to the integrity of his heart; and guided them by the skilfulness of his hands.

Psalm 79

A Psalm of *Asaph.

[1]O God, the heathen are come into thine inheritance; thy holy temple have they defiled; they have laid *Jerusalem on heaps.
[2]The dead bodies of thy servants have they given *to be* meat unto the fowls of the heaven, the flesh of thy *saints unto the beasts of the earth.
[3]Their blood have they shed like water round about Jerusalem; and *there was* none to bury *them.*
[4]We are become a reproach to our neighbours, a scorn and derision to them that are round about us.
[5]How long, LORD? wilt thou be angry for ever? shall thy jealousy burn like fire?
[6]Pour out thy wrath upon the heathen that have not known thee, and upon the kingdoms that have not called upon thy name.
[7]For they have devoured Jacob, and laid waste his dwelling place.
[8]O remember not against us former iniquities: let thy tender mercies speedily *prevent us: for we are brought very low.
[9]Help us, O God of our salvation, for the glory of thy name: and deliver us, and purge away our sins, for thy name's sake.
[10]Wherefore should the heathen say, Where *is* their God? let him be known among the heathen in our sight *by* the revenging of the blood of thy servants *which is* shed.
[11]Let the sighing of the prisoner come before thee; according to the greatness of thy power preserve thou those that are appointed to die;
[12]And *render unto our neighbours sevenfold into their bosom their reproach, wherewith they have reproached thee, O Lord.
[13]So we thy people and sheep of thy pasture will give thee thanks for ever: we will shew forth thy praise to all generations.

Psalm 80

To the chief Musician upon Shoshannim-Eduth, A Psalm of Asaph.

[1]Give ear, O Shepherd of Israel, thou that leadest Joseph like a flock; thou that dwellest *between* the cherubims, shine forth.
[2]Before Ephraim and Benjamin and *Manasseh stir up thy strength, and come *and* save us.
[3]Turn us again, O God, and cause thy face to shine; and we shall be saved.

78:67 chose not the tribe of Ephraim. Here the tribe of Ephraim represents only the kingdom of the north in the divided kingdom. Judah (vs. 68), where Mount Zion and the tabernacle of the LORD were located, represented the southern kingdom.

80:title. "Shoshannim-Eduth" means *lilies of testimony,* as in Psalm 60.

80:2 Before Ephraim and Benjamin and Manasseh. These three tribes marched side by side through the wilderness (see Num. 2:17-24), directly behind the ark. Here the prayer is that God will again lead His people forth as in the days of old.

80:1 Shepherds in the Bible
Sheep were fundamental to human existence in Biblical times, providing meat, wool, hide and milk. It was a sign of wealth to own many sheep. Many Bible characters made their living as shepherds.

Abel	Genesis 4:2
Abraham	Genesis 13:7
Isaac	Genesis 26:20
Rachel	Genesis 29:9
Jacob	Genesis 30:36
Jacob's 12 sons	Genesis 37:22
Israelites in Egypt	Genesis 46:32-34; Exodus 9:5; 12:38
Zipporah	Exodus 2:16
Moses	Exodus 3:1
David	1 Samuel 16:11
Job	Job 42:12
Amos	Amos 1:1
Shepherds at Jesus' birth	Luke 2:8

4O LORD God of hosts, how long wilt
thou be angry against the *prayer of thy
people?
5Thou feedest them with the bread of
tears; and givest them tears to drink in
great measure.
6Thou makest us a strife unto our
neighbours: and our enemies laugh
among themselves.
7Turn us again, O God of hosts, and
cause thy face to shine; and we shall be
saved.
8Thou hast brought a vine out of
Egypt: thou hast cast out the heathen,
and planted it.
9Thou preparedst *room* before it, and
didst cause it to take deep root, and it
filled the land.
10The hills were covered with the
shadow of it, and the boughs thereof
were like the goodly cedars.
11She sent out her boughs unto the
sea, and her branches unto the river.
12Why hast thou *then* broken down
her hedges, so that all they which pass
by the way do pluck her?
13The boar out of the wood doth
waste it, and the wild beast of the field
doth devour it.
14Return, we beseech thee, O God of
hosts: look down from heaven, and behold, and visit this vine;
15And the *vineyard which thy right
hand hath planted, and the *branch *that*
thou madest strong for thyself.
16*It is* burned with *fire, *it is* cut
down: they perish at the rebuke of thy
countenance.
17Let thy hand be upon the man of thy
right hand, upon the son of man *whom*
thou madest strong for thyself.
18So will not we go back from thee:
*quicken us, and we will call upon thy
name.
19Turn us again, O LORD God of
hosts, cause thy face to shine; and we
shall be saved.

Psalm 81

To the chief Musician upon *Gittith,
A Psalm of Asaph.

1Sing aloud unto God our strength:
make a joyful noise unto the God of
*Jacob.
2Take a psalm, and bring hither the
timbrel, the pleasant harp with the
*psaltery.
3Blow up the trumpet in the *new
moon, in the time appointed, on our
solemn feast day.
4For this *was* a statute for Israel, *and*
a law of the God of Jacob.
5This he ordained in Joseph *for* a testimony, when he went out through the

---

80:8 a vine out of Egypt. Israel was the vine.
80:17 the son of man whom thou madest strong. See God's words in Exodus 4:22: "Israel is my son, even my firstborn."
81:3 new moon . . . solemn feast day. The *Passover feast of Exodus 12 is meant.
81:4 this was a statute. Read about this in Leviticus 23:24 (see its note, "The Feast of Tabernacles") and Numbers 10:10 (see note, "Feasts").
81:5 he went out through the land of Egypt. That is, at the original Passover (Exod. 12).

land of Egypt: *where* I heard a language *that* I understood not.

6 I removed his shoulder from the burden: his hands were delivered from the pots.

7 Thou calledst in trouble, and I delivered thee; I answered thee in the secret place of thunder: I proved thee at the waters of Meribah. *Selah.

> **81:7 Mount Sinai**
> Mount Sinai was referred to as "the secret place of thunder" (see Exod. 19:16). The word "Sinai" refers to both a mountain and the desert at it base, forming part of the peninsula between the gulfs of Suez and Aqaba. The district is close to the center of the triangular space formed by the two arms of the Red Sea.

8 Hear, O my people, and I will testify unto thee: O Israel, if thou wilt hearken unto me;

9 There shall no strange god be in thee; neither shalt thou worship any strange god.

10 I *am* the LORD thy God, which brought thee out of the land of Egypt: open thy mouth wide, and I will fill it.

11 But my people would not hearken to my voice; and Israel would none of me.

12 So I gave them up unto their own hearts' *lust: *and* they walked in their own counsels.

13 Oh that my people had hearkened unto me, *and* Israel had walked in my ways!

14 I should soon have subdued their enemies, and turned my hand against their adversaries.

15 The haters of the LORD should have submitted themselves unto him: but their time should have endured for ever.

16 He should have fed them also with the finest of the wheat: and with honey out of the rock should I have satisfied thee.

Psalm 82

A Psalm of *Asaph.

1 God standeth in the congregation of the mighty; he judgeth among the gods.

2 How long will ye judge unjustly, and accept the persons of the wicked? Selah.

3 Defend the poor and fatherless: do justice to the afflicted and needy.

4 Deliver the poor and needy: rid *them* out of the hand of the wicked.

5 They know not, neither will they understand; they walk on in darkness: all the foundations of the earth are out of course.

6 I have said, Ye *are* gods; and all of you *are* children of the most High.

7 But ye shall die like men, and fall like one of the princes.

8 Arise, O God, judge the earth: for thou shalt inherit all nations.

Psalm 83

A Song *or* Psalm of Asaph.

1 Keep not thou silence, O *God: hold not thy *peace, and be not still, O God.

2 For, lo, thine enemies make a tumult: and they that hate thee have lifted up the head.

3 They have taken crafty counsel against thy people, and consulted against thy hidden ones.

4 They have said, Come, and let us cut

81:7 the waters of Meribah. Read Exodus 17:5-7.

82:1 he judgeth among the gods. The "gods" were the rulers and judges of the people—those who were God's representatives as far as authority was concerned. See also verse 6, as well as what the Lord Jesus said many years later (John 10:34-36).

82:2 How long will ye judge unjustly . . . ? This was God's question to the rulers and judges among the people.

82:5 They know not. A description of the unfaithful rulers follows.

them off from *being* a nation; that the
name of *Israel may be no more in remembrance.
5For they have consulted together
with one consent: they are confederate
against thee:
6The tabernacles of *Edom, and the
Ishmaelites; of *Moab, and the Hagarenes;

83:6-8 Past Generations
Edom descended from Esau, Jacob's brother and rival (Gen. 25:24-34); the Ishmaelites descended from Abraham (Gen. 16); Moab and Ammon descended from Lot (Gen. 19:36-38); the Hagarenes were an Arab tribe with a name suggesting Hagar (Gen. 16); Amalek was a tribe founded by a grandson of Esau (Gen. 36:12). Assur (Ps. 83:8) means Assyria. The confederacy against Israel, made up of her neighbors, thus included some who were closely related by ancestry. Kinship through flesh and blood did not mean friendship.

7Gebal, and Ammon, and *Amalek;
the *Philistines with the inhabitants of
*Tyre;
8Assur also is joined with them: they
have holpen the children of *Lot. Selah.
9Do unto them as *unto* the *Midianites; as *to* Sisera, as *to* Jabin, at the
brook of Kison:
10*Which* perished at Endor: they became *as* *dung for the earth.
11Make their nobles like Oreb, and
like Zeeb: yea, all their princes as Zebah, and as Zalmunna:
12Who said, Let us take to ourselves
the houses of God in possession.
13O my God, make them like a wheel;
as the stubble before the wind.
14As the fire burneth a wood, and as
the flame setteth the mountains on
fire;
15So persecute them with thy tempest, and make them afraid with thy
storm.
16Fill their faces with shame; that
they may seek thy name, O LORD.
17Let them be confounded and troubled for ever; yea, let them be put to
shame, and perish:
18That *men* may know that thou,
whose name alone *is* JEHOVAH, *art* the
most high over all the earth.

Psalm 84

To the chief Musician upon *Gittith,
A Psalm for the *sons of Korah.

1How amiable *are* thy tabernacles,
O LORD of hosts!
2My soul longeth, yea, even fainteth
for the courts of the LORD: my heart and
my flesh crieth out for the living God.
3Yea, the sparrow hath found an
house, and the swallow a nest for herself, where she may lay her young, *even*
thine altars, O LORD of hosts, my King,
and my God.
4Blessed *are* they that dwell in thy
house: they will be still praising thee.
Selah.
5Blessed *is* the man whose strength
is in thee; in whose heart *are* the ways
of them.
6*Who* passing through the valley of
Baca make it a well; the rain also filleth
the pools.
7They go from strength to strength,
every one of them in *Zion appeareth
before God.
8O LORD God of hosts, hear my
prayer: give ear, O God of Jacob. Selah.
9Behold, O God our shield, and look
upon the face of thine anointed.

83:9 Do unto them as unto the Midianites. Asaph's glance at the past—Midianites (Judg. 6); Sisera and Jabin (Judg. 4); Oreb, Zeeb, Zebah, and Zalmunna (Judg. 7–8)—referred to events still fresh in the people's memories, when God helped them in their struggles.
83:13 a wheel. A rolling thing, rolling away to destruction.
84:1 amiable. Lovely.
84:6 the valley of Baca. This just means a place of sorrow or crying; it was not a real place.
84:9 thine anointed. This is "thy Messiah," and is a looking forward to our Lord Jesus Christ.

10 For a day in thy courts *is* better than
a thousand. I had rather be a doorkeeper in the house of my God, than to dwell
in the tents of wickedness.
11 For the LORD God *is* a sun and
shield: the LORD will give *grace and
glory: no good *thing* will he withhold
from them that walk uprightly.
12 O LORD of hosts, blessed *is* the man
that trusteth in thee.

Psalm 85

To the chief Musician,
A Psalm for the sons of Korah.

1 LORD, thou hast been favourable
unto thy land: thou hast brought back
the captivity of Jacob.
2 Thou hast *forgiven the iniquity of
thy people, thou hast covered all their
*sin. Selah.
3 Thou hast taken away all thy wrath:
thou hast turned *thyself* from the fierceness of thine anger.
4 Turn us, O God of our *salvation,
and cause thine anger toward us to
cease.
5 Wilt thou be angry with us for ever?
wilt thou draw out thine anger to all
generations?
6 Wilt thou not revive us again: that
thy people may rejoice in thee?
7 Shew us thy *mercy, O LORD, and
grant us thy salvation.
8 I will hear what God the LORD will
speak: for he will speak peace unto his
people, and to his *saints: but let them
not turn again to folly.
9 Surely his salvation *is* nigh them
that *fear him; that glory may dwell in
our land.
10 Mercy and truth are met together;
*righteousness and peace have kissed
each other.
11 Truth shall spring out of the earth;
and righteousness shall look down from
*heaven.
12 Yea, the LORD shall give *that which
is* good; and our land shall yield her increase.
13 Righteousness shall go before
him; and shall set *us* in the way of
his steps.

Psalm 86

A *Prayer of *David.

1 Bow down thine ear, O LORD, hear
me: for I *am* poor and needy.
2 Preserve my soul; for I *am* *holy:
O thou my God, save thy servant that
trusteth in thee.
3 Be merciful unto me, O Lord: for I
cry unto thee daily.
4 Rejoice the soul of thy servant: for
unto thee, O Lord, do I lift up my soul.
5 For thou, Lord, *art* good, and ready
to forgive; and plenteous in mercy unto
all them that call upon thee.
6 Give ear, O LORD, unto my prayer;
and attend to the voice of my supplications.
7 In the day of my trouble I will call
upon thee: for thou wilt answer me.
8 Among the gods *there is* none like
unto thee, O Lord; neither *are there any
works* like unto thy works.
9 All nations whom thou hast made
shall come and worship before thee,
O Lord; and shall glorify thy name.
10 For thou *art* great, and doest wondrous things: thou *art* God alone.
11 Teach me thy way, O LORD; I will
walk in thy truth: unite my heart to fear
thy name.
12 I will praise thee, O Lord my God,
with all my heart: and I will glorify thy
name for evermore.
13 For great *is* thy mercy toward me:
and thou hast delivered my soul from
the lowest *hell.
14 O God, the proud are risen against
me, and the assemblies of violent *men*
have sought after my soul; and have not
set thee before them.
15 But thou, O Lord, *art* a God full of
compassion, and gracious, longsuffering, and plenteous in mercy and truth.
16 O turn unto me, and have mercy
upon me; give thy strength unto thy
servant, and save the son of thine handmaid.

[17]Shew me a token for good; that they
which hate me may see *it,* and be
ashamed: because thou, LORD, hast
holpen me, and comforted me.

Psalm 87

A Psalm *or* Song for the *sons of Korah.

[1]His foundation *is* in the holy mountains.
[2]The LORD loveth the gates of Zion
more than all the dwellings of *Jacob.
[3]Glorious things are spoken of
thee, O city of God. *Selah.
[4]I will make mention of Rahab and
*Babylon to them that know me: behold
Philistia, and Tyre, with Ethiopia; this
man was born there.
[5]And of Zion it shall be said, This and
that man was born in her: and the highest himself shall establish her.
[6]The LORD shall count, when he
writeth up the people, *that* this *man* was
born there. Selah.
[7]As well the singers as the players on
instruments *shall be there:* all my
springs *are* in thee.

Psalm 88

Messianic

A Song *or* Psalm for the sons of Korah,
to the chief Musician upon
Mahalath Leannoth, *Maschil
of *Heman the Ezrahite.

[1]O LORD God of my salvation, I have
cried day *and* night before thee:
[2]Let my prayer come before thee:
incline thine ear unto my cry;
[3]For my soul is full of troubles: and
my life draweth nigh unto the *grave.
[4]I am counted with them that go
down into the *pit: I am as a man *that
hath* no strength:
[5]Free among the dead, like the slain
that lie in the grave, whom thou rememberest no more: and they are cut
off from thy hand.
[6]Thou hast laid me in the lowest pit,
in darkness, in the deeps.
[7]Thy wrath lieth hard upon me, and
thou hast afflicted *me* with all thy
waves. Selah.
[8]Thou hast put away mine acquaintance far from me; thou hast made me
an *abomination unto them: *I am* shut
up, and I cannot come forth.
[9]Mine eye mourneth by reason of affliction: LORD, I have called daily upon
thee, I have stretched out my hands
unto thee.
[10]Wilt thou shew wonders to the
dead? shall the dead arise *and* praise
thee? Selah.
[11]Shall thy lovingkindness be declared in the grave? *or* thy faithfulness
in destruction?
[12]Shall thy wonders be known in the
dark? and thy righteousness in the land
of forgetfulness?
[13]But unto thee have I cried, O LORD;
and in the morning shall my prayer
*prevent thee.
[14]LORD, why castest thou off my
soul? *why* hidest thou thy face from me?
[15]I *am* afflicted and ready to die from
my youth up: *while* I suffer thy terrors
I am distracted.
[16]Thy fierce wrath goeth over me;
thy terrors have cut me off.

87:1 His foundation. This is a psalm in praise of *Jerusalem.
87:4 make mention of Rahab. A name for Egypt (Ps. 89:10; Isa. 51:9).
87:4 this man was born there. In the day when Zion's King, the Lord Jesus Christ, comes to set up His *kingdom, nations will be born again as they turn to the "highest" (vs. 5) in adoration and worship (see Isa. 60:4-5; 66:8).
88:title. Obscure in meaning. "Mahalath" may be a musical instrument, and "Leannoth" (see vs. 7 where the word is used again) seems to signify affliction.
88:3 my soul is full of troubles. Think of the Lord Jesus Christ and His terrible death as you read this psalm.
88:5 Free among the dead. Cast off among the dead.
88:5 whom thou rememberest no more. Read the cry of our Lord in Matthew 27:46.

[17]They came round about me daily like water; they compassed me about together.

[18]Lover and friend hast thou put far from me, *and* mine acquaintance into darkness.

Psalm 89

Messianic

Maschil of Ethan the Ezrahite.

[1]I will sing of the mercies of the LORD for ever: with my mouth will I make known thy faithfulness to all generations.

[2]For I have said, Mercy shall be built up for ever: thy faithfulness shalt thou establish in the very heavens.

[3]I have made a *covenant with my chosen, I have sworn unto David my servant,

[4]Thy seed will I establish for ever, and build up thy throne to all generations. Selah.

[5]And the heavens shall praise thy wonders, O LORD: thy faithfulness also in the congregation of the saints.

[6]For who in the heaven can be compared unto the LORD? *who* among the sons of the mighty can be likened unto the LORD?

[7]*God is greatly to be feared in the assembly of the saints, and to be had in reverence of all *them that are* about him.

[8]O LORD God of hosts, who *is* a strong LORD like unto thee? or to thy faithfulness round about thee?

[9]Thou rulest the raging of the sea: when the waves thereof arise, thou stillest them.

[10]Thou hast broken Rahab in pieces, as one that is slain; thou hast scattered thine enemies with thy strong arm.

[11]The heavens *are* thine, the earth also *is* thine: *as for* the *world and the *fulness thereof, thou hast founded them.

[12]The north and the south thou hast *created them: Tabor and Hermon shall rejoice in thy name.

[13]Thou hast a mighty arm: strong is thy hand, *and* high is thy right hand.

[14]Justice and *judgment *are* the habitation of thy throne: mercy and truth shall go before thy face.

[15]Blessed *is* the people that know the joyful sound: they shall walk, O LORD, in the light of thy countenance.

[16]In thy name shall they rejoice all the day: and in thy righteousness shall they be exalted.

[17]For thou *art* the glory of their strength: and in thy favour our *horn shall be exalted.

[18]For the LORD *is* our defence; and the Holy One of *Israel *is* our king.

[19]Then thou spakest in vision to thy holy one, and saidst, I have laid help upon *one that is* mighty; I have exalted *one* chosen out of the people.

89:19 Looking toward Christ
Note that this psalm looks beyond David to the Lord Jesus Christ, the One about whom God spoke when He made His covenant with David. He is the "firstborn, higher than the kings of the earth" (vs. 27). God was speaking directly to and about David as well, however, as verses 30-32 show.

[20]I have found David my servant; with my holy *oil have I anointed him:

[21]With whom my hand shall be established: mine arm also shall strengthen him.

[22]The enemy shall not exact upon him; nor the son of wickedness afflict him.

[23]And I will beat down his foes before his face, and plague them that hate him.

[24]But my faithfulness and my mercy *shall be* with him: and in my name shall his horn be exalted.

[25]I will set his hand also in the sea, and his right hand in the rivers.

[26]He shall cry unto me, Thou *art* my

89:4 Thy seed will I establish. See 2 Samuel 7:5-17.
89:12 Tabor and Hermon. Mountains; see Joshua 19:22 and 12:1.

father, my God, and the *rock of my
salvation.
[27]Also I will make him *my* firstborn,
higher than the kings of the earth.
[28]My mercy will I keep for him for
evermore, and my covenant shall stand
fast with him.
[29]His seed also will I make *to endure*
for ever, and his throne as the days of
heaven.
[30]If his children forsake my *law, and
walk not in my judgments;
[31]If they break my statutes, and keep
not my commandments;
[32]Then will I visit their transgression
with the rod, and their iniquity with
*stripes.
[33]Nevertheless my lovingkindness
will I not utterly take from him, nor
suffer my faithfulness to fail.
[34]My covenant will I not break, nor
alter the thing that is gone out of my
lips.
[35]Once have I sworn by my holiness
that I will not lie unto David.
[36]His seed shall endure for ever, and
his throne as the sun before me.
[37]It shall be established for ever as
the moon, and *as* a faithful witness in
heaven. Selah.
[38]But thou hast cast off and abhorred,
thou hast been wroth with thine
anointed.
[39]Thou hast made void the covenant
of thy servant: thou hast profaned his
crown *by casting it* to the ground.

89:36-51 The Cry of the Remnant
Here, in verses 36 to the end, is the cry of the Jewish people, the *remnant, who are waiting for deliverance from the LORD. Note, moreover, that their hope is in the Messiah, the hope of the world, who bore in His bosom the sin and reproach of us all, Jew and Gentile alike (compare vs. 50 with Rom. 4:24-25). (This is the last psalm in the third book of Psalms—see introduction.)

[40]Thou hast broken down all his
hedges; thou hast brought his strong
holds to ruin.
[41]All that pass by the way spoil him:
he is a reproach to his neighbours.
[42]Thou hast set up the right hand of
his adversaries; thou hast made all his
enemies to rejoice.
[43]Thou hast also turned the edge of
his sword, and hast not made him to
stand in the battle.
[44]Thou hast made his glory to cease,
and cast his throne down to the ground.
[45]The days of his youth hast thou
shortened: thou hast covered him with
shame. Selah.
[46]How long, LORD? wilt thou hide
thyself for ever? shall thy wrath burn
like *fire?
[47]Remember how short my time is:
wherefore hast thou made all men in
vain?
[48]What man *is he that* liveth, and shall
not see *death? shall he deliver his soul
from the hand of the grave? Selah.
[49]Lord, where *are* thy former lovingkindnesses, *which* thou swarest unto
David in thy truth?
[50]Remember, Lord, the reproach of
thy servants; *how* I do bear in my
bosom *the reproach of* all the mighty
people;
[51]Wherewith thine enemies have reproached, O LORD; wherewith they
have reproached the footsteps of thine
anointed.
[52]Blessed *be* the LORD for evermore.
*Amen, and Amen.

BOOK IV

Psalm 90

A Prayer of *Moses the man of God.

[1]Lord, thou hast been our dwelling
place in all generations.
[2]Before the mountains were brought

90:1 Lord, thou hast been. This is probably the oldest of the psalms, perhaps written by Moses when he saw the people of God dying in the wilderness because of their unbelief, after they had been led out of the land of Egypt.

forth, or ever thou hadst formed the earth and the world, even from everlasting to everlasting, thou *art* God.

3 Thou turnest man to destruction; and sayest, Return, ye children of men.

4 For a *thousand years in thy sight *are but* as yesterday when it is past, and *as* a watch in the night.

5 Thou carriest them away as with a flood; they are *as* a sleep: in the morning *they are* like grass *which* groweth up.

6 In the morning it flourisheth, and groweth up; in the evening it is cut down, and withereth.

7 For we are consumed by thine anger, and by thy wrath are we troubled.

8 Thou hast set our iniquities before thee, our secret *sins* in the light of thy countenance.

9 For all our days are passed away in thy wrath: we spend our years as a tale *that is told.*

10 The days of our years *are* threescore years and ten; and if by reason of strength *they be* fourscore years, yet *is* their strength labour and sorrow; for it is soon cut off, and we fly away.

11 Who knoweth the power of thine anger? even according to thy fear, *so is* thy wrath.

12 So teach *us* to number our days, that we may apply *our* hearts unto wisdom.

13 Return, O LORD, how long? and let it repent thee concerning thy servants.

14 O satisfy us early with thy mercy; that we may rejoice and be glad all our days.

15 Make us glad according to the days *wherein* thou hast afflicted us, *and* the years *wherein* we have seen evil.

16 Let thy work appear unto thy servants, and thy glory unto their children.

17 And let the beauty of the LORD our God be upon us: and establish thou the work of our hands upon us; yea, the work of our hands establish thou it.

Psalm 91

1 He that dwelleth in the secret place of the most High shall abide under the shadow of the Almighty.

2 I will say of the LORD, *He is* my refuge and my fortress: my God; in him will I *trust.

3 Surely he shall deliver thee from the snare of the fowler, *and* from the noisome pestilence.

4 He shall cover thee with his feathers, and under his wings shalt thou trust: his truth *shall be thy* shield and *buckler.

5 Thou shalt not be afraid for the terror by night; *nor* for the arrow *that* flieth by day;

6 *Nor* for the pestilence *that* walketh in darkness; *nor* for the destruction *that* wasteth at noonday.

7 A thousand shall fall at thy side, and ten thousand at thy right hand; *but* it shall not come nigh thee.

8 Only with thine eyes shalt thou behold and see the reward of the wicked.

9 Because thou hast made the LORD, *which is* my refuge, *even* the most High, thy habitation;

10 There shall no evil befall thee, neither shall any plague come nigh thy dwelling.

11 For he shall give his *angels charge over thee, to keep thee in all thy ways.

12 They shall bear thee up in *their* hands, lest thou dash thy foot against a stone.

13 Thou shalt tread upon the lion and adder: the young lion and the dragon shalt thou trample under feet.

14 Because he hath set his love upon

90:3 Thou turnest man to destruction. "To dust" is the idea presented here. Man's body is destroyed and becomes dust when he dies. His soul is never destroyed.

90:5 they are like grass. Compare the beautiful verses in Psalm 103:14-16.

90:7 we are consumed. The reason for death on the earth is found in verse 8—iniquities and sin cause death (compare Gen. 2:17; 3:19; Rom. 6:23).

91:11 give his angels. The verse is misquoted by the devil when he tempted our Lord (Matt. 4:6).

me, therefore will I deliver him: I will set him on high, because he hath known my name.

15 He shall call upon me, and I will answer him: I *will be* with him in trouble; I will deliver him, and honour him.

16 With long life will I satisfy him, and shew him my *salvation.

Psalm 92

A Psalm *or* Song for the *sabbath day.

1 *It is a* good *thing* to give thanks unto the LORD, and to sing praises unto thy name, O most High:

2 To shew forth thy lovingkindness in the morning, and thy faithfulness every night,

3 Upon an instrument of ten strings, and upon the *psaltery; upon the harp with a solemn sound.

4 For thou, LORD, hast made me glad through thy work: I will triumph in the works of thy hands.

5 O LORD, how great are thy works! *and* thy thoughts are very deep.

6 A brutish man knoweth not; neither doth a *fool understand this.

7 When the wicked spring as the grass, and when all the workers of iniquity do flourish; *it is* that they shall be destroyed for ever:

8 But thou, LORD, *art most* high for evermore.

9 For, lo, thine enemies, O LORD, for, lo, thine enemies shall perish; all the workers of iniquity shall be scattered.

10 But my horn shalt thou exalt like *the horn of* an *unicorn: I shall be anointed with fresh oil.

11 Mine eye also shall see *my desire* on mine enemies, *and* mine ears shall hear *my desire* of the wicked that rise up against me.

12 The righteous shall flourish like the palm tree: he shall grow like a cedar in *Lebanon.

13 Those that be planted in the house of the LORD shall flourish in the courts of our God.

14 They shall still bring forth fruit in old age; they shall be fat and flourishing;

15 To shew that the LORD *is* upright: *he is* my rock, and *there is* no unrighteousness in him.

Psalm 93

1 The LORD reigneth, he is clothed with majesty; the LORD is clothed with strength, *wherewith* he hath girded himself: the world also is stablished, that it cannot be moved.

2 Thy throne *is* established of old: thou *art* from everlasting.

3 The floods have lifted up, O LORD, the floods have lifted up their voice; the floods lift up their waves.

4 The LORD on high *is* mightier than the noise of many waters, *yea, than* the mighty waves of the sea.

5 Thy testimonies are very sure: holiness becometh thine house, O LORD, for ever.

Psalm 94

1 O LORD God, to whom vengeance belongeth; O God, to whom vengeance belongeth, shew thyself.

2 Lift up thyself, thou judge of the earth: *render a reward to the proud.

3 LORD, how long shall the wicked, how long shall the wicked triumph?

4 *How long* shall they utter *and* speak hard things? *and* all the workers of iniquity boast themselves?

5 They break in pieces thy people, O LORD, and afflict thine heritage.

6 They slay the widow and the stranger, and murder the fatherless.

92:6 brutish man. One who acts senseless, like an animal.

93:3 floods lift up their waves. Floods, in the Bible often speak of rebellious uprisings against God or the people of God.

93:5 holiness becometh thine house. Compare Zechariah 14:20-21.

94:1 God, to whom vengeance belongeth. The Lord Jesus said, "Shall not God avenge his own elect?" (Luke 18:7).

7 Yet they say, The LORD shall not
see, neither shall the God of *Jacob
regard *it.*
8 Understand, ye brutish among the
people: and *ye* *fools, when will ye be
wise?
9 He that planted the ear, shall he not
hear? he that formed the eye, shall he
not see?
10 He that chastiseth the heathen,
shall not he correct? he that teacheth
man knowledge, *shall not he know?*
11 The LORD knoweth the thoughts of
man, that they *are* *vanity.
12 Blessed *is* the man whom thou
chastenest, O LORD, and teachest him
out of thy law;
13 That thou mayest give him rest
from the days of adversity, until *the pit
be digged for the wicked.
14 For the LORD will not cast off his
people, neither will he forsake his inheritance.
15 But judgment shall return unto
*righteousness: and all the upright in
heart shall follow it.
16 Who will rise up for me against the
evildoers? *or* who will stand up for me
against the workers of iniquity?
17 Unless the LORD *had been* my help,
my soul had almost dwelt in silence.
18 When I said, My foot slippeth; thy
*mercy, O LORD, held me up.
19 In the multitude of my thoughts
within me thy comforts delight my soul.
20 Shall the throne of iniquity have
fellowship with thee, which frameth
mischief by a law?
21 They gather themselves together
against the soul of the righteous, and
condemn the innocent *blood.
22 But the LORD is my defence; and
my God *is* the rock of my refuge.
23 And he shall bring upon them their
own iniquity, and shall cut them off in
their own wickedness; *yea,* the LORD
our God shall cut them off.

Psalm 95

1 O come, let us sing unto the LORD:
let us make a joyful noise to the *rock
of our salvation.
2 Let us come before his presence
with thanksgiving, and make a joyful
noise unto him with psalms.
3 For the LORD *is* a great *God, and a
great King above all gods.
4 In his hand *are* the deep places of
the earth: the strength of the hills *is*
his also.
5 The sea *is* his, and he made it: and
his hands formed the dry *land.*
6 O come, let us worship and bow
down: let us kneel before the LORD our
maker.
7 For he *is* our God; and we *are* the
people of his pasture, and the sheep of
his hand. To day if ye will hear his voice,
8 *Harden not your heart, as in the
provocation, *and* as *in* the day of *temptation in the wilderness:
9 When your fathers tempted me,
proved me, and saw my work.
10 Forty years long was I grieved with
**this* generation, and said, It *is* a peo-

94:13 pit be digged for the wicked. See for whom the pit was prepared (Matt. 25:41; Rev. 19:20; 20:10).

94:14 LORD will not cast off. Paul quoted this thought by asking a question and answering it (Rom. 11:1).

94:17 almost. Quickly or soon.

94:17 dwelt in silence. Died.

95:1 O come. This psalm is one of the many that is not signed, but like all of the psalms, signed or unsigned, its true author is the Holy Spirit. Compare verses 7-10 with Hebrews 3:7-9.

95:8 in the provocation. This is the scene refered to: "as at Meribah." See Exodus 17:7; Numbers 20:13; 27:14.

95:8 in the day of temptation. In the days of Massah in the wilderness (Exod. 17:7; Deut. 6:15).

ple that do *err in their heart, and they
have not known my ways:
11 Unto whom I sware in my wrath
that they should not enter into my rest.

Psalm 96

1 O sing unto the LORD a new song:
sing unto the LORD, all the earth.
2 Sing unto the LORD, bless his name;
shew forth his salvation from day to day.
3 Declare his glory among the heathen, his wonders among all people.
4 For the LORD *is* great, and greatly to
be praised: he *is* to be feared above all
gods.
5 For all the gods of the nations *are*
idols: but the LORD made the heavens.
6 Honour and majesty *are* before him:
strength and beauty *are* in his *sanctuary.
7 Give unto the LORD, O ye kindreds
of the people, give unto the LORD glory
and strength.
8 Give unto the LORD the glory *due
unto* his name: bring an *offering, and
come into his courts.
9 O worship the LORD in the beauty of
holiness: *fear before him, all the earth.
10 Say among the heathen *that* the
LORD reigneth: the *world also shall be
established that it shall not be moved:
he shall judge the people righteously.
11 Let the heavens rejoice, and let the
earth be glad; let the sea roar, and the
*fulness thereof.
12 Let the field be joyful, and all that
is therein: then shall all the trees of the
wood rejoice
13 Before the LORD: for he cometh, for
he cometh to judge the earth: he shall
judge the world with righteousness,
and the people with his truth.

Psalm 97

1 The LORD reigneth; let the earth
rejoice; let the multitude of *isles be
glad *thereof.*
2 Clouds and darkness *are* round about
him: righteousness and *judgment *are*
the habitation of his throne.
3 A *fire goeth before him, and
burneth up his enemies round about.
4 His lightnings enlightened the
world: the earth saw, and trembled.
5 The hills melted like wax at the
presence of the LORD, at the presence
of the Lord of the whole earth.
6 The heavens declare his righteousness, and all the people see his glory.
7 Confounded be all they that serve
graven images, that boast themselves
of idols: worship him, all *ye* gods.
8 *Zion heard, and was glad; and the
daughters of *Judah rejoiced because of
thy judgments, O LORD.
9 For thou, LORD, *art* high above all
the earth: thou art exalted far above
all gods.
10 Ye that love the LORD, hate evil: he
preserveth the souls of his *saints; he
delivereth them out of the hand of the
wicked.
11 Light is sown for the righteous, and
gladness for the upright in heart.
12 Rejoice in the LORD, ye righteous;
and give thanks at the remembrance of
his holiness.

Psalm 98

A Psalm.

1 O sing unto the LORD a new song;
for he hath done marvellous things: his
right hand, and his *holy arm, hath gotten him the victory.

96:1 O sing unto the LORD. Because Psalms 96 to 100 are full of joyful praise to the LORD, they are called "The Singing Psalms."

97:2 Clouds and darkness. The cloud is the cloud of glory that surrounds God. Note also that the Lord Jesus is to come again in the clouds of heaven (Matt. 26:64). Compare the "cloud and darkness" of Exodus 14:20.

97:7 worship him, all ye gods. In Hebrews 1:6 this verse is quoted, but there we read: "And let all the angels of God worship him." The thought is that the mighty ones, even though they be supernatural, must worship Him.

98:1 a new song. Verses 1-3 give the joyous theme of the new song.

2The LORD hath made known his
*salvation: his righteousness hath he
openly shewed in the sight of the heathen.
3He hath remembered his mercy and
his truth toward the house of *Israel:
all the ends of the earth have seen the
salvation of our God.
4Make a joyful noise unto the LORD,
all the earth: make a loud noise, and
rejoice, and sing praise.
5Sing unto the LORD with the harp;
with the harp, and the voice of a psalm.
6With trumpets and sound of cornet
make a joyful noise before the LORD,
the King.
7Let the sea roar, and the fulness
thereof; the world, and they that dwell
therein.
8Let the floods clap *their* hands: let
the hills be joyful together
9Before the LORD; for he cometh to
judge the earth: with righteousness
shall he judge the world, and the people with equity.

Psalm 99

1The LORD reigneth; let the people
tremble: he sitteth *between* the
cherubims; let the earth be moved.
2The LORD *is* great in Zion; and he *is*
high above all the people.
3Let them praise thy great and terrible name; *for* it *is* holy.
4The king's strength also loveth judgment; thou dost establish equity, thou
executest judgment and righteousness
in Jacob.
5Exalt ye the LORD our God, and
worship at his footstool; *for* he *is* holy.
6*Moses and *Aaron among his
priests, and *Samuel among them that
call upon his name; they called upon the
LORD, and he answered them.
7He spake unto them in the *cloudy
pillar: they kept his testimonies, and
the ordinance *that* he gave them.
8Thou answeredst them, O LORD our
God: thou wast a God that forgavest
them, though thou tookest vengeance
of their inventions.
9Exalt the LORD our God, and worship at his holy hill; for the LORD our
God *is* holy.

Psalm 100

A Psalm of praise.

1Make a joyful noise unto the LORD,
all ye lands.
2Serve the LORD with gladness:
come before his presence with singing.
3Know ye that the LORD he *is* God: *it*
is he *that* hath made us, and not we
ourselves; *we are* his people, and the
sheep of his pasture.
4Enter into his gates with thanksgiving, *and* into his courts with praise:
be thankful unto him, *and* bless his
name.
5For the LORD *is* good; his *mercy *is*
everlasting; and his truth *endureth* to all
generations.

Psalm 101

A Psalm of *David.

1I will sing of mercy and judgment:
unto thee, O LORD, will I sing.
2I will behave myself wisely in a
*perfect way. O when wilt thou come

98:7-8 Let the sea roar. . . . Let the floods clap their hands. Even nature shows forth the joy of the LORD. Compare Isaiah 55:1.
99:1 he sitteth between the cherubims. This was the LORD's place upon the throne of grace—grace for believers; judgment for those who refuse His grace.
99:7 He spake unto them in the cloudy pillar. Read Exodus 33:4-11.
99:8 vengeance of their inventions. Note the distinction between God's infinite love of the sinner and His hatred of the sin. The offender is forgiven; the offense or thought is condemned (see John 8:10-11).
100:1 Make a joyful noise. This is one of the great doxologies or praises to God in the Bible.

101:1 A Standard of Government
This psalm has been called "a mirror for kings and all those who are in authority." It sets a standard of good government for rulers which can only be obtained fully by absolute obedience to the mind and will of God in Christ Jesus. This psalm gives us an idea of our Lord's reign when He will be King.

unto me? I will walk within my house
with a perfect heart.
3I will set no wicked thing before
mine eyes: I hate the work of them that
turn aside; *it* shall not cleave to me.
4A *froward heart shall depart from
me: I will not know a wicked *person.*
5Whoso privily slandereth his neighbour, him will I cut off: him that hath an
high look and a proud heart will not I
suffer.
6Mine eyes *shall be* upon the faithful
of the land, that they may dwell with
me: he that walketh in a perfect way, he
shall serve me.
7He that worketh deceit shall not
dwell within my house: he that telleth
lies shall not tarry in my sight.
8I will early destroy all the wicked of
the land; that I may cut off all wicked
doers from the city of the LORD.

Psalm 102

Messianic

A *Prayer of the afflicted, when he is overwhelmed, and poureth out his complaint before the LORD.

1Hear my prayer, O LORD, and let my
cry come unto thee.
2Hide not thy face from me in the day
when I am in trouble; incline thine ear
unto me: in the day *when* I call answer
me speedily.
3For my days are consumed like
smoke, and my bones are burned as an
hearth.
4My heart is smitten, and withered
like grass; so that I forget to eat my
bread.
5By reason of the voice of my groaning my bones cleave to my skin.
6I am like a pelican of the wilderness:
I am like an owl of the desert.
7I watch, and am as a sparrow alone
upon the house top.
8Mine enemies reproach me all the
day; *and* they that are mad against me
are sworn against me.
9For I have eaten ashes like bread,
and mingled my drink with weeping,
10Because of thine indignation and
thy wrath: for thou hast lifted me up,
and cast me down.
11My days *are* like a shadow that
declineth; and I am withered like grass.
12But thou, O LORD, shalt endure for
ever; and thy remembrance unto all
generations.
13Thou shalt arise, *and* have mercy
upon Zion: for the time to favour her,
yea, the set time, is come.
14For thy servants take pleasure in
her stones, and favour the dust thereof.
15So the heathen shall *fear the name
of the LORD, and all the kings of the
earth thy glory.
16When the LORD shall build up Zion,
he shall appear in his glory.
17He will regard the prayer of the
destitute, and not despise their prayer.
18This shall be written for the generation to come: and the people which
shall be created shall praise the LORD.
19For he hath looked down from the
height of his *sanctuary; from *heaven
did the LORD behold the earth;
20To hear the groaning of the prisoner; to loose those that are appointed to
*death;
21To declare the name of the LORD in
Zion, and his praise in *Jerusalem;
22When the people are gathered together, and the kingdoms, to serve the
LORD.

101:2 when wilt thou come unto me? Compare Mark 13:32.
Psalm 102. Notice how this psalm shows two sides of the Lord's experience: His suffering as the Saviour and His glory as the King.

[23]He weakened my strength in the
way; he shortened my days.
[24]I said, O my *God, take me not
away in the midst of my days: thy years
are throughout all generations.
[25]Of old hast thou laid the foundation
of the earth: and the heavens *are* the
work of thy hands.
[26]They shall perish, but thou shalt
endure: yea, all of them shall wax old
like a garment; as a vesture shalt thou
change them, and they shall be
changed:
[27]But thou *art* the same, and thy
years shall have no end.
[28]The children of thy servants shall
continue, and their seed shall be established before thee.

Psalm 103

A Psalm of David.

[1]Bless the LORD, O my soul: and all
that is within me, *bless* his holy name.
[2]Bless the LORD, O my soul, and forget not all his benefits:
[3]Who forgiveth all thine iniquities;
who healeth all thy diseases;
[4]Who *redeemeth thy life from destruction; who crowneth thee with
lovingkindness and tender mercies;
[5]Who satisfieth thy mouth with good
things; so that thy youth is renewed like
the eagle's.
[6]The LORD executeth *righteousness and *judgment for all that are
oppressed.
[7]He made known his ways unto Moses, his acts unto the children of Israel.

103:3 A Promise from God
While sin, the sickness of the soul, is the first disease healed by the LORD, it is also sin that has caused bodily disease. In the days when Christ becomes King of Kings and Lord of Lords on earth, physical diseases will be healed, just as people were healed who came to Jesus when He was on earth. Today sin with its results is still on the earth, and as St. Augustine said: "Even when sin is forgiven thou still carriest about with thee an infirm body. Death is not yet swallowed up into victory; this corruptible has not yet put on incorruption; still the soul itself is shaken by passions and temptations."

[8]The LORD *is* merciful and gracious,
slow to anger, and plenteous in mercy.
[9]He will not always chide: neither
will he keep *his anger* for ever.
[10]He hath not dealt with us after our
sins; nor rewarded us according to our
iniquities.
[11]For as the heaven is high above the
earth, *so* great is his mercy toward them
that fear him.
[12]As far as the east is from the west,
so far hath he removed our transgressions from us.
[13]Like as a father pitieth *his* children,
so the LORD pitieth them that fear him.
[14]For he knoweth our frame; he
remembereth that we *are* dust.
[15]*As for* man, his days *are* as grass: as
a flower of the field, so he flourisheth.
[16]For the wind passeth over it, and it
is gone; and the place thereof shall
know it no more.
[17]But the mercy of the LORD *is* from

102:23 he shortened my days. The Lord Jesus Christ was only thirty-three when He was crucified.
102:24 thy years are throughout all generations. Note how this sentence and verses 25-28 answer verse 23 and the first part of verse 24. God thus answers His Son, the Lord Jesus Christ.
102:25 Of old hast thou laid the foundation of the earth. Proof that this psalm speaks of the Messiah is found in Hebrews 1:10-12.
102:27 thou art the same. Compare Hebrews 13:8.
103:1 Bless the LORD. This is still a great song of praise among Jewish worshippers.
103:5 renewed like the eagle's. Compare the promise of Isaiah 40:31.
103:7 He made known his ways unto Moses. Read Exodus 34:5-7.
103:12 As far as the east is from the west. This is a distance that can never be measured.

everlasting to everlasting upon them
that fear him, and his righteousness
unto children's children;
18To such as keep his *covenant, and
to those that remember his commandments to do them.
19The LORD hath prepared his throne
in the heavens; and his *kingdom
ruleth over all.
20Bless the LORD, ye his *angels, that
excel in strength, that do his commandments, hearkening unto the voice of his
word.
21Bless ye the LORD, all *ye* his hosts;
ye ministers of his, that do his pleasure.
22Bless the LORD, all his works in all
places of his dominion: bless the LORD,
O my soul.

Psalm 104

A Song of Creation

1Bless the LORD, O my soul. O LORD
my God, thou art very great; thou art
clothed with honour and majesty.
2Who coverest *thyself* with light as
with a garment: who stretchest out the
heavens like a curtain:
3Who layeth the beams of his chambers in the waters: who maketh the
clouds his chariot: who walketh upon
the wings of the wind:
4Who maketh his angels spirits; his
ministers a flaming *fire:
5*Who* laid the foundations of the
earth, *that* it should not be removed for
ever.
6Thou coveredst it with the deep as
with a garment: the waters stood above
the mountains.
7At thy rebuke they fled; at the voice
of thy thunder they hasted away.
8They go up by the mountains; they
go down by the valleys unto the place
which thou hast founded for them.
9Thou hast set a bound that they may
not pass over; that they turn not again
to cover the earth.
10He sendeth the springs into the
valleys, *which* run among the hills.
11They give drink to every beast of
the field: the wild asses quench their
thirst.
12By them shall the fowls of the
heaven have their habitation, *which*
sing among the branches.
13He watereth the hills from his
chambers: the earth is satisfied with the
fruit of thy works.
14He causeth the grass to grow for
the cattle, and herb for the service of
man: that he may bring forth food out
of the earth;
15And *wine *that* maketh glad the
heart of man, *and* *oil to make *his* face
to shine, and bread *which* strengtheneth
man's heart.
16The trees of the LORD are full *of
sap;* the cedars of *Lebanon, which he
hath planted;
17Where the birds make their nests:
as for the stork, the fir trees *are* her
house.
18The high hills *are* a refuge for
the wild goats; *and* the rocks for the
conies.
19He appointed the moon for seasons: the sun knoweth his going down.
20Thou makest darkness, and it is
night: wherein all the beasts of the forest do creep *forth.*
21The young lions roar after their
prey, and seek their meat from God.
22The sun ariseth, they gather themselves together, and lay them down in
their dens.

103:20 Bless the LORD. Compare the praises in verses 20-22 with the praises of Revelation 5:11-13.

Psalm 104. Psalm 104 sings praises to the Creator of heaven and earth as it tells of His marvelous works. It is perhaps the noblest description of nature ever expressed in words.

104:4 Who maketh his angels spirits. God makes His angels invisible yet effective (quoted in Heb. 1:7).

104:9 Thou hast set a bound. Read God's words to Noah in Genesis 9:11-17; see also Job 26:10.

23 Man goeth forth unto his work and
to his labour until the evening.
24 O LORD, how manifold are thy
works! in wisdom hast thou made them
all: the earth is full of thy riches.
25 *So is* this great and wide sea,
wherein *are* things creeping innumerable, both small and great beasts.
26 There go the ships: *there is* that *leviathan, *whom* thou hast made to play
therein.
27 These wait all upon thee; that thou
mayest give *them* their meat in due
season.
28 *That* thou givest them they gather:
thou openest thine hand, they are filled
with good.
29 Thou hidest thy face, they are troubled: thou takest away their breath,
they die, and return to their dust.
30 Thou sendest forth thy spirit, they
are created: and thou renewest the face
of the earth.
31 The glory of the LORD shall endure
for ever: the LORD shall rejoice in his
works.
32 He looketh on the earth, and it
trembleth: he toucheth the hills, and
they smoke.
33 I will sing unto the LORD as long as
I live: I will sing praise to my God while
I have my being.
34 My meditation of him shall be
sweet: I will be glad in the LORD.
35 Let the sinners be consumed out of
the earth, and let the wicked be no
more. Bless thou the LORD, O my soul.
Praise ye the LORD.

Psalm 105

A Song of History

1 O give thanks unto the LORD; call
upon his name: make known his deeds
among the people.
2 Sing unto him, sing psalms unto
him: talk ye of all his wondrous
works.
3 Glory ye in his *holy name: let the
heart of them rejoice that seek the
LORD.

105:1 God's Wonderful Works
This psalm was written by David and given by him to *Asaph and the other singers (1 Chron. 16:4-7). It was a song for the time of festival, the first fifteen verses of which were first recorded in 1 Chronicles 16:8-22. It is a history of much that happened to the children of Israel, but in addition to that it demonstrates God's wonderful works to His children.

4 Seek the LORD, and his strength:
seek his face evermore.
5 Remember his marvellous works
that he hath done; his wonders, and the
judgments of his mouth;
6 O ye seed of *Abraham his servant,
ye children of *Jacob his chosen.
7 He *is* the LORD our God: his judgments *are* in all the earth.
8 He hath remembered his covenant
for ever, the word *which* he commanded to a thousand generations.
9 Which *covenant* he made with Abraham, and his oath unto *Isaac;
10 And confirmed the same unto Jacob
for a *law, *and* to *Israel *for* an everlasting covenant:
11 Saying, Unto thee will I give the
land of Canaan, the lot of your inheritance:
12 When they were *but* a few men in
number; yea, very few, and strangers
in it.
13 When they went from one nation to
another, from *one* kingdom to another
people;
14 He suffered no man to do them
wrong: yea, he reproved kings for their
sakes;
15 *Saying,* Touch not mine anointed,
and do my *prophets no harm.
16 Moreover he called for a famine
upon the land: he brake the whole staff
of bread.
17 He sent a man before them, *even*
*Joseph, *who* was sold for a servant:
18 Whose feet they hurt with fetters:
he was laid in iron:
19 Until the time that his word came:
the word of the LORD tried him.

[20]The king sent and loosed him; *even*
the ruler of the people, and let him go
free.
[21]He made him lord of his house, and
ruler of all his substance:
[22]To bind his princes at his pleasure;
and teach his senators wisdom.
[23]Israel also came into *Egypt; and
Jacob sojourned in the land of Ham.
[24]And he increased his people greatly; and made them stronger than their
enemies.
[25]He turned their heart to hate his
people, to deal subtilly with his servants.
[26]He sent *Moses his servant; *and*
*Aaron whom he had chosen.
[27]They shewed his signs among
them, and wonders in the land of Ham.
[28]He sent darkness, and made it dark;
and they rebelled not against his word.
[29]He turned their waters into blood,
and slew their fish.
[30]Their land brought forth frogs in
abundance, in the chambers of their
kings.
[31]He spake, and there came divers
sorts of flies, *and* lice in all their coasts.
[32]He gave them hail for rain, *and*
flaming fire in their land.
[33]He smote their vines also and their
fig trees; and brake the trees of their
coasts.
[34]He spake, and the locusts came,
and caterpillers, and that without number,
[35]And did eat up all the herbs in their
land, and devoured the fruit of their
ground.
[36]He smote also all the firstborn in
their land, the chief of all their strength.
[37]He brought them forth also with
silver and gold: and *there was* not one
feeble *person* among their tribes.
[38]Egypt was glad when they departed: for the fear of them fell upon them.
[39]He spread a cloud for a covering;
and fire to give light in the night.
[40]*The people* asked, and he brought
quails, and satisfied them with the
bread of heaven.
[41]He opened the rock, and the waters
gushed out; they ran in the dry places
like a river.
[42]For he remembered his holy promise, *and* Abraham his servant.
[43]And he brought forth his people
with joy, *and* his chosen with gladness:
[44]And gave them the lands of the
heathen: and they inherited the labour
of the people;
[45]That they might observe his statutes, and keep his *laws. Praise ye the
LORD.

Psalm 106

[1]Praise ye the LORD. O give thanks
unto the LORD; for *he is* good: for his
*mercy *endureth* for ever.

106:1 The Hallelujah Psalms
This is the first great Hallelujah ("Praise ye the LORD") psalm. Note that it begins and ends with "Praise ye the LORD" (Hallelujah). See also Psalms 111; 112; 113; 117; 135; and 146–150. This psalm is also the last in the fourth book of Psalms (see introduction).

[2]Who can utter the mighty acts of the
LORD? *who* can shew forth all his
praise?
[3]Blessed *are* they that keep judgment, *and* he that doeth righteousness
at all times.
[4]Remember me, O LORD, with the
favour *that thou bearest unto* thy people:
O visit me with thy *salvation;
[5]That I may see the good of thy chosen, that I may rejoice in the gladness
of thy nation, that I may glory with thine
inheritance.
[6]We have sinned with our fathers, we
have committed iniquity, we have done
wickedly.
[7]Our fathers understood not thy wonders in Egypt; they remembered not the
multitude of thy mercies; but provoked
him at the sea, *even* at the Red sea.

106:7 provoked him . . . at the Red sea. Read Exodus 14:11.

8 Nevertheless he saved them for his name's sake, that he might make his mighty power to be known.

9 He rebuked the Red sea also, and it was dried up: so he led them through the depths, as through the wilderness.

10 And he saved them from the hand of him that hated *them,* and *redeemed them from the hand of the enemy.

11 And the waters covered their enemies: there was not one of them left.

12 Then believed they his words; they sang his praise.

13 They soon forgat his works; they waited not for his counsel:

14 But lusted exceedingly in the wilderness, and *tempted God in the desert.

15 And he gave them their request; but sent leanness into their soul.

16 They envied Moses also in the camp, *and* Aaron the saint of the LORD.

17 The earth opened and swallowed up Dathan, and covered the company of Abiram.

18 And a fire was kindled in their company; the flame burned up the wicked.

19 They made a calf in *Horeb, and worshipped the molten image.

20 Thus they changed their glory into the similitude of an ox that eateth grass.

21 They forgat God their saviour, which had done great things in Egypt;

22 Wondrous works in the land of Ham, *and* terrible things by the Red sea.

23 Therefore he said that he would destroy them, had not Moses his chosen stood before him in the breach, to turn away his wrath, lest he should destroy *them.*

24 Yea, they despised the pleasant land, they believed not his word:

25 But murmured in their tents, *and* hearkened not unto the voice of the LORD.

26 Therefore he lifted up his hand against them, to overthrow them in the wilderness:

27 To overthrow their seed also among the nations, and to *scatter them in the lands.

28 They joined themselves also unto Baal-peor, and ate the sacrifices of the dead.

29 Thus they provoked *him* to anger with their inventions: and the plague brake in upon them.

30 Then stood up *Phinehas, and executed judgment: and *so* the plague was stayed.

31 And that was counted unto him for righteousness unto all generations for evermore.

32 They angered *him* also at the waters of strife, so that it went ill with Moses for their sakes:

33 Because they provoked his spirit, so that he spake unadvisedly with his lips.

34 They did not destroy the nations, concerning whom the LORD commanded them:

35 But were mingled among the heathen, and learned their works.

36 And they served their idols: which were a snare unto them.

37 Yea, they sacrificed their sons and their daughters unto devils,

38 And shed innocent blood, *even* the blood of their sons and of their daughters, whom they sacrificed unto the idols of Canaan: and the land was polluted with blood.

39 Thus were they defiled with their own works, and went a whoring with their own inventions.

40 Therefore was the wrath of the LORD kindled against his people, insomuch that he abhorred his own inheritance.

41 And he gave them into the hand of the heathen; and they that hated them ruled over them.

42 Their enemies also oppressed them, and they were brought into subjection under their hand.

106:19 a calf in Horeb. Read Exodus 32.
106:32 the waters of strife. Read Numbers 20:7-13.

43 Many times did he deliver them;
but they provoked *him* with their counsel, and were brought low for their iniquity.
44 Nevertheless he regarded their
affliction, when he heard their cry:
45 And he remembered for them his
covenant, and repented according to the
multitude of his mercies.
46 He made them also to be pitied of
all those that carried them captives.
47 Save us, O LORD our God, and gather us from among the heathen, to give
thanks unto thy holy name, *and* to triumph in thy praise.
48 Blessed *be* the Lord God of Israel
from everlasting to everlasting: and let
all the people say, *Amen. Praise ye the
LORD.

BOOK V

Psalm 107

A Song of Gratitude

1 O give thanks unto the LORD, for *he
is* good: for his mercy *endureth* for ever.
2 Let the redeemed of the LORD say
so, whom he hath redeemed from the
hand of the enemy;
3 And gathered them out of the lands,
from the east, and from the west, from
the north, and from the south.
4 They wandered in the wilderness in
a solitary way; they found no city to
dwell in.
5 Hungry and thirsty, their soul fainted in them.
6 Then they cried unto the LORD in
their trouble, *and* he delivered them
out of their distresses.
7 And he led them forth by the right
way, that they might go to a city of habitation.
8 Oh that *men* would praise the LORD
for his goodness, and *for* his wonderful
works to the children of men!

107:4 A Picture of the Future
This is not a picture of the wilderness wanderings of the children of Israel just after they came out of the land of Egypt. It is a picture of the future, for it shows not only the Israelites' wanderings among the nations as prophesied by Moses (Deut. 28:64-65), but also their being regathered into their own land again (vss. 2-3: see also Isa. 43:5-6). It is also an anthem of all the redeemed, dealing with hardships (vs. 5), tyranny (vs. 10), seafaring (vss. 23-28), irrigation (vs. 33), and agriculture (vss. 36-37).

9 For he satisfieth the longing soul,
and filleth the hungry soul with goodness.
10 Such as sit in darkness and in the
shadow of death, *being* bound in *affliction and iron;
11 Because they rebelled against the
words of God, and contemned the counsel of the most High:
12 Therefore he brought down their
heart with labour; they fell down, and
there was none to help.
13 Then they cried unto the LORD in
their trouble, *and* he saved them out of
their distresses.
14 He brought them out of darkness
and the shadow of death, and brake
their bands in sunder.
15 Oh that *men* would praise the LORD
for his goodness, and *for* his wonderful
works to the children of men!
16 For he hath broken the gates of
brass, and cut the bars of iron in sunder.
17 *Fools because of their transgression, and because of their iniquities, are
afflicted.
18 Their soul abhorreth all manner of
meat; and they draw near unto the gates
of death.
19 Then they cry unto the LORD in
their trouble, *and* he saveth them out
of their distresses.
20 He sent his word, and healed them,

107:10 bound in affliction and iron. This is an illustration of unbelief and sin holding the children of Israel prisoner (see also Isa. 42:7; 49:9; Zech. 9:12).
107:14 brake their bands. Isaiah 45:2 and 61:1 proclaim the same wonderful truth.

and delivered *them* from their destructions.
[21]Oh that *men* would praise the LORD
for his goodness, and *for* his wonderful
works to the children of men!
[22]And let them *sacrifice the sacrifices of thanksgiving, and declare his
works with rejoicing.
[23]They that go down to the sea in
ships, that do business in great waters;
[24]These see the works of the LORD,
and his wonders in the deep.
[25]For he commandeth, and raiseth
the stormy wind, which lifteth up the
waves thereof.
[26]They mount up to the heaven, they
go down again to the depths: their soul
is melted because of trouble.
[27]They reel to and fro, and stagger
like a drunken man, and are at their
wits' end.
[28]Then they cry unto the LORD in
their trouble, and he bringeth them out
of their distresses.
[29]He maketh the storm a calm, so
that the waves thereof are still.
[30]Then are they glad because they be
quiet; so he bringeth them unto their
desired haven.
[31]Oh that *men* would praise the LORD
for his goodness, and *for* his wonderful
works to the children of men!
[32]Let them exalt him also in the congregation of the people, and praise him
in the assembly of the *elders.
[33]He turneth rivers into a wilderness, and the watersprings into dry
ground;
[34]A fruitful land into barrenness, for
the wickedness of them that dwell
therein.
[35]He turneth the wilderness into a
standing water, and dry ground into
watersprings.
[36]And there he maketh the hungry to
dwell, that they may prepare a city for
habitation;
[37]And sow the fields, and plant vineyards, which may yield fruits of increase.
[38]He blesseth them also, so that they
are multiplied greatly; and suffereth not
their cattle to decrease.
[39]Again, they are minished and
brought low through oppression, affliction, and sorrow.
[40]He poureth contempt upon princes,
and causeth them to wander in the wilderness, *where there is* no way.
[41]Yet setteth he the poor on high
from affliction, and maketh *him* families
like a flock.
[42]The righteous shall see *it,* and rejoice: and all iniquity shall stop her
mouth.
[43]Whoso *is* wise, and will observe
these *things,* even they shall understand the lovingkindness of the LORD.

Psalm 108

A Song *or* Psalm of *David.

[1]O *God, my heart is fixed; I will sing
and give praise, even with my glory.
[2]Awake, *psaltery and harp: I *myself*
will awake early.
[3]I will praise thee, O LORD, among
the people: and I will sing praises unto
thee among the nations.
[4]For thy mercy *is* great above the
heavens: and thy truth *reacheth* unto
the clouds.
[5]Be thou exalted, O God, above the
heavens: and thy glory above all the
earth;
[6]That thy *beloved may be delivered:
save *with* thy right hand, and answer me.
[7]God hath spoken in his holiness; I
will rejoice, I will divide *Shechem, and
mete out the valley of Succoth.
[8]*Gilead *is* mine; *Manasseh *is* mine;
*Ephraim also *is* the strength of mine
head; *Judah *is* my lawgiver;
[9]*Moab *is* my washpot; over *Edom

107:26 They mount up. Note that verses 26-27 continue the picture of the stormy sea.
Psalm 108. Note that verses 1-5 repeat Psalm 57:7-11 and that verses 6-13 repeat Psalm 60:5-11. See the notes on these psalms.

will I cast out my shoe; over Philistia
will I triumph.
10Who will bring me into the strong
city? who will lead me into Edom?
11*Wilt* not *thou,* O God, *who* hast cast
us off? and wilt not thou, O God, go
forth with our hosts?
12Give us help from trouble: for vain
is the help of man.
13Through God we shall do valiantly:
for he *it is that* shall tread down our
enemies.

Psalm 109

An Imprecatory Psalm

To the chief Musician, A Psalm of David.

1Hold not thy *peace, O God of my
praise;
2For the mouth of the wicked and the
mouth of the deceitful are opened
against me: they have spoken against
me with a lying tongue.
3They compassed me about also with
words of hatred; and fought against me
without a cause.
4For my love they are my adversaries: but I *give myself unto* *prayer.
5And they have rewarded me evil for
good, and hatred for my love.

109:1 A Cry for Justice
This is one of the imprecatory psalms (see Psalm 5:10 note, "Praying for Judgment"), directed this time against those who have spoken evil against David, the servant of the LORD. Remember that terrible wrongs had been inflicted, equal to any savagery of today. The anger of the LORD against such evil was also divinely unbounded (Matt. 18:6). Insofar as the injury is personal, the better way is forgiveness (Matt. 5:44), but here was tyranny over the helpless that exceeded any private grudge or grievance.

6Set thou a wicked man over him: and
let *Satan stand at his right hand.
7When he shall be judged, let him be
condemned: and let his prayer become
*sin.
8Let his days be few; *and* let another
take his office.
9Let his children be fatherless, and
his wife a widow.
10Let his children be continually
vagabonds, and beg: let them seek *their
bread* also out of their desolate places.
11Let the extortioner catch all that he
hath; and let the strangers spoil his
labour.
12Let there be none to extend mercy
unto him: neither let there be any to
favour his fatherless children.
13Let his posterity be cut off; *and* in
the generation following let their name
be blotted out.
14Let the iniquity of his fathers be
remembered with the LORD; and let not
the sin of his mother be blotted out.
15Let them be before the LORD continually, that he may cut off the memory of them from the earth.
16Because that he remembered not to
shew mercy, but persecuted the poor
and needy man, that he might even slay
the broken in heart.
17As he loved cursing, so let it come
unto him: as he delighted not in blessing, so let it be far from him.
18As he clothed himself with cursing
like as with his garment, so let it come
into his *bowels like water, and like oil
into his bones.
19Let it be unto him as the garment
which covereth him, and for a girdle
wherewith he is girded continually.
20*Let* this *be* the reward of mine adversaries from the LORD, and of them
that speak evil against my soul.
21But do thou for me, O GOD the

109:8 let another take his office. Notice that this is quoted about Judas Iscariot in Acts 1:20. Though the whole tone of this psalm is fearful in its wrath, it shows the dreadful hopelessness of those who are at odds with God or against Him. There can be nothing but eternal punishment for them unless they turn to Him in whom alone there is *salvation.

Lord, for thy name's sake: because thy
mercy *is* good, deliver thou me.
22For I *am* poor and needy, and my
heart is wounded within me.
23I am gone like the shadow when it
declineth: I am tossed up and down as
the locust.
24My knees are weak through fasting;
and my flesh faileth of fatness.
25I became also a reproach unto
them: *when* they looked upon me they
shaked their heads.
26Help me, O LORD my God: O save
me according to thy mercy:
27That they may know that this *is* thy
hand; *that* thou, LORD, hast done it.
28Let them curse, but bless thou:
when they arise, let them be ashamed;
but let thy servant rejoice.
29Let mine adversaries be clothed
with shame, and let them cover themselves with their own confusion, as with
a mantle.
30I will greatly praise the LORD with
my mouth; yea, I will praise him among
the multitude.
31For he shall stand at the right hand
of the poor, to save *him* from those that
condemn his soul.

Psalm 110

Messianic

A Psalm of David.

1The LORD said unto my Lord, Sit
thou at my right hand, until I make thine
enemies thy footstool.
2The LORD shall send the rod of thy
strength out of *Zion: rule thou in the
midst of thine enemies.
3Thy people *shall be* willing in the day
of thy power, in the beauties of holiness
from the womb of the morning: thou
hast the dew of thy youth.
4The LORD hath sworn, and will not
repent, Thou *art* a priest for ever after
the order of *Melchizedek.
5The Lord at thy right hand shall
strike through kings in the day of his
wrath.
6He shall judge among the heathen,
he shall fill *the places* with the dead bodies; he shall wound the heads over
many countries.
7He shall drink of the brook in the
way: therefore shall he lift up the
head.

Psalm 111

1Praise ye the LORD. I will praise the
LORD with *my* whole heart, in the assembly of the upright, and *in* the congregation.
2The works of the LORD *are* great,
sought out of all them that have pleasure therein.
3His work *is* honourable and glorious:
and his *righteousness endureth for
ever.
4He hath made his wonderful works
to be remembered: the LORD *is* gracious and full of compassion.
5He hath given meat unto them that
*fear him: he will ever be mindful of his
*covenant.
6He hath shewed his people the
power of his works, that he may give
them the heritage of the heathen.
7The works of his hands *are* verity
and *judgment; all his commandments
are sure.
8They stand fast for ever and ever,
and are done in truth and uprightness.

110:1 The LORD said unto my Lord. This is the psalm of Christ exalted as Lord and King. Note that Christ applied it to Himself (Matt. 22:41-46); Peter bore witness to it (Acts 2:32-36); as did the writer of Hebrews (10:12-13).

110:1 thine enemies thy footstool. See Luke 1:32 and 1 Corinthians 15:24-27.

110:5 day of his wrath. This looks forward to the Day of Judgment when the King must appear in His wrath. See also *Armageddon and *kingdom.

110:7 drink of the brook. This is the brook of humiliation, suffering, and death.

Psalm 111. An acrostic in the Hebrew (see Ps. 25 note, "Acrostic Poems").

[9]He sent *redemption unto his people: he hath commanded his covenant
for ever: *holy and reverend *is* his
name.
[10]The fear of the LORD *is* the beginning of wisdom: a good understanding
have all they that do *his commandments:* his praise endureth for ever.

Psalm 112

[1]Praise ye the LORD. Blessed *is* the
man *that* *feareth the LORD, *that*
delighteth greatly in his commandments.
[2]His seed shall be mighty upon earth:
the generation of the upright shall be
blessed.
[3]Wealth and riches *shall be* in his
house: and his righteousness endureth
for ever.
[4]Unto the upright there ariseth light
in the darkness: *he is* gracious, and full
of compassion, and righteous.
[5]A good man sheweth favour, and
lendeth: he will guide his affairs with
discretion.
[6]Surely he shall not be moved for
ever: the righteous shall be in everlasting remembrance.
[7]He shall not be afraid of evil tidings:
his heart is fixed, trusting in the LORD.
[8]His heart *is* established, he shall not
be afraid, until he see *his desire* upon his
enemies.
[9]He hath dispersed, he hath given to
the poor; his righteousness endureth for
ever; his horn shall be exalted with
honour.
[10]The wicked shall see *it,* and be
grieved; he shall gnash with his teeth,
and melt away: the desire of the wicked shall perish.

Psalms 113–118 The Great Hallel
Psalms 113 to 118 are called "The Great Hallel (praise) Psalms." They are six hymns of praise and were sung at three great feasts of the Jews: *Passover, *Pentecost, and the *Feast of Tabernacles. No doubt they were sung by Christ and His disciples in the Upper Room before His betrayal and arrest in Gethsemane (Matt. 26:30). At the Feast of the Passover, the Great Hallel was divided into two parts–Psalms 113 and 114 were sung before the feast, Psalms 115–118 after the meal. It was this second section that was sung by the Lord and His disciples.

Psalm 113

[1]Praise ye the LORD. Praise, O ye
servants of the LORD, praise the name
of the LORD.
[2]Blessed be the name of the LORD
from this time forth and for evermore.
[3]From the rising of the sun unto the
going down of the same the LORD'S
name *is* to be praised.
[4]The LORD *is* high above all nations,
and his glory above the heavens.
[5]Who *is* like unto the LORD our God,
who dwelleth on high,
[6]Who humbleth *himself* to behold
the things that are in *heaven, and in
the earth!
[7]He raiseth up the poor out of the
dust, *and* lifteth the needy out of the
dunghill;
[8]That he may set *him* with princes,
even with the princes of his people.
[9]He maketh the barren woman to
keep house, *and to be* a joyful mother
of children. Praise ye the LORD.

111:10 The fear of the LORD. Compare Proverbs 1:7 (see also its note, "The Fear of the LORD").
Psalm 112. An acrostic poem (see Ps. 25 note, "Acrostic Poems").
112:1 Blessed is the man. Compare Psalm 128:1.
112:3 Wealth. Prosperity.
113:4 high above all nations. Compare Isaiah 40:15,17, and 22.
113:9 He maketh the barren woman to keep house. Phrases from this psalm appear in Hannah's song of joy (1 Sam. 2:1-10); compare the Magnificat of our Lord's mother, Mary (Luke 1:46-54; see vs. 47 note, "Mary's Awareness").

Psalm 114

1When *Israel went out of *Egypt,
the house of *Jacob from a people of
strange language;
2*Judah was his *sanctuary, *and* Israel his dominion.
3The sea saw *it,* and fled: Jordan was
driven back.
4The *mountains skipped like rams,
and the little hills like lambs.
5What *ailed* thee, O thou sea, that
thou fleddest? thou Jordan, *that* thou
wast driven back?
6Ye mountains, *that* ye skipped like
rams; *and* ye little hills, like lambs?
7Tremble, thou earth, at the presence
of the Lord, at the presence of the *God
of Jacob;
8Which turned the rock *into* a standing water, the flint into a fountain of
waters.

Psalm 115

1Not unto us, O LORD, not unto us,
but unto thy name give glory, for thy
*mercy, *and* for thy truth's sake.
2Wherefore should the heathen say,
Where *is* now their God?
3But our God *is* in the heavens: he
hath done whatsoever he hath pleased.
4Their idols *are* silver and gold, the
work of men's hands.
5They have mouths, but they speak
not: eyes have they, but they see not:
6They have ears, but they hear
not: noses have they, but they smell not:
7They have hands, but they handle
not: feet have they, but they walk not:
neither speak they through their throat.
8They that make them are like unto
them; *so is* every one that trusteth in
them.
9O Israel, *trust thou in the LORD: he
is their help and their shield.
10O house of *Aaron, trust in the
LORD: he *is* their help and their shield.
11Ye that fear the LORD, trust in the
LORD: he *is* their help and their shield.
12The LORD hath been mindful of us:
he will bless *us;* he will bless the house
of Israel; he will bless the house of
Aaron.
13He will bless them that fear the
LORD, *both* small and great.
14The LORD shall increase you more
and more, you and your children.
15Ye *are* blessed of the LORD which
made heaven and earth.
16The heaven, *even* the heavens, *are*
the LORD'S: but the earth hath he given
to the children of men.
17The dead praise not the LORD, neither any that go down into silence.
18But we will bless the LORD from
this time forth and for evermore. Praise
the LORD.

Psalm 116

1I love the LORD, because he hath
heard my voice *and* my supplications.
2Because he hath inclined his ear
unto me, therefore will I call upon *him*
as long as I live.
3The sorrows of *death compassed
me, and the pains of *hell gat hold upon
me: I found trouble and sorrow.
4Then called I upon the name of the
LORD; O LORD, I beseech thee, deliver
my soul.
5Gracious *is* the LORD, and righteous;
yea, our God *is* merciful.
6The LORD preserveth the simple: I
was brought low, and he helped me.
7Return unto thy rest, O my soul; for

114:1 When Israel went out of Egypt. Read Exodus 12 and the chapters that follow it, in connection with Exodus 2:23-25.
114:2 Judah was his sanctuary. Read Exodus 19:6.
114:3 sea . . . fled: Jordan . . . driven back. The Red Sea (Exod. 14:21) and the Jordan River (Josh. 3:13-17; see also vs.17 note, "Crossing the Jordan").
114:8 rock into a standing water. See Exodus 17:6; compare Isaiah 35:6-7.
116:3 gat hold upon me. Found me.

the LORD hath dealt bountifully with
thee.
8 For thou hast delivered my soul
from death, mine eyes from tears, *and*
my feet from falling.
9 I will walk before the LORD in the
land of the living.
10 I believed, therefore have I spoken:
I was greatly afflicted:
11 I said in my haste, All men *are* liars.
12 What shall I *render unto the LORD
for all his benefits toward me?
13 I will take the cup of *salvation, and
call upon the name of the LORD.
14 I will pay my vows unto the LORD
now in the presence of all his people.
15 Precious in the sight of the LORD *is*
the death of his *saints.
16 O LORD, truly I *am* thy servant; I
am thy servant, *and* the son of thine
handmaid: thou hast loosed my bonds.
17 I will offer to thee the *sacrifice of
thanksgiving, and will call upon the
name of the LORD.
18 I will pay my vows unto the LORD
now in the presence of all his people,
19 In the courts of the LORD'S house,
in the midst of thee, O *Jerusalem.
Praise ye the LORD.

Psalm 117

1 O praise the LORD, all ye nations:
praise him, all ye people.
2 For his merciful kindness is great
toward us: and the truth of the LORD
endureth for ever. Praise ye the LORD.

Psalm 118

Messianic

1 O give thanks unto the LORD; for *he*
is good: because his mercy *endureth* for
ever.
2 Let Israel now say, that his mercy
endureth for ever.
3 Let the house of Aaron now say, that
his mercy *endureth* for ever.
4 Let them now that *fear the LORD
say, that his mercy *endureth* for ever.
5 I called upon the LORD in distress:
the LORD answered me, *and set me* in a
large place.
6 The LORD *is* on my side; I will not
fear: what can man do unto me?
7 The LORD taketh my part with them
that help me: therefore shall I see *my*
desire upon them that hate me.
8 *It is* better to trust in the LORD than
to put confidence in man.
9 *It is* better to trust in the LORD than
to put confidence in princes.
10 All nations compassed me about:
but in the name of the LORD will I destroy them.
11 They compassed me about; yea,
they compassed me about: but in the
name of the LORD I will destroy them.
12 They compassed me about like
bees; they are quenched as the *fire of
thorns: for in the name of the LORD I
will destroy them.
13 Thou hast thrust sore at me that I
might fall: but the LORD helped me.
14 The LORD *is* my strength and song,
and is become my salvation.
15 The voice of rejoicing and salvation
is in the tabernacles of the righteous:
the right hand of the LORD doeth valiantly.
16 The right hand of the LORD is exalted: the right hand of the LORD doeth
valiantly.
17 I shall not die, but live, and declare
the works of the LORD.
18 The LORD hath *chastened me
sore: but he hath not given me over
unto death.

116:10 I believed, therefore have I spoken. Quoted in 2 Corinthians 4:13.
Psalm 117. Part of this short psalm of praise was quoted by Paul (Rom. 15:11).
Psalm 118. We believe that this psalm was written after some of the children of Israel came back from their Babylonian exile and had completed their second temple (see Ezra 6:15-18; Neh. 8:13-18). The Feast of Tabernacles held at that time celebrated this event. It is, moreover, a prophecy of the Messiah (note especially vss. 22-27).
118:6 The LORD is on my side. Quoted in Hebrews 13:6.

19 Open to me the gates of *righteousness: I will go into them, *and* I will
praise the LORD:
20 This gate of the LORD, into which
the righteous shall enter.
21 I will praise thee: for thou hast
heard me, and art become my salvation.
22 The stone *which* the builders refused is become the head *stone* of the
corner.
23 This is the LORD'S doing; it *is* marvellous in our eyes.
24 This *is* the day *which* the LORD hath
made; we will rejoice and be glad in it.
25 Save now, I beseech thee, O LORD:
O LORD, I beseech thee, send now
prosperity.
26 Blessed *be* he that cometh in the
name of the LORD: we have blessed you
out of the house of the LORD.
27 God *is* the LORD, which hath
shewed us light: bind the sacrifice with
cords, *even* unto the *horns of the *altar.
28 Thou *art* my God, and I will praise
thee: *thou art* my God, I will exalt thee.
29 O give thanks unto the LORD; for *he*
is good: for his mercy *endureth* for ever.

Psalm 119

א ALEPH.

1 Blessed *are* the undefiled in the way,
who walk in the *law of the LORD.
2 Blessed *are* they that keep his testimonies, *and that* seek him with the
whole heart.
3 They also do no iniquity: they walk
in his ways.
4 Thou hast commanded *us* to keep
thy precepts diligently.
5 O that my ways were directed to
keep thy statutes!
6 Then shall I not be ashamed, when
I have respect unto all thy commandments.
7 I will praise thee with uprightness
of heart, when I shall have learned thy
righteous judgments.
8 I will keep thy statutes: O forsake
me not utterly.

ב BETH.

9 Wherewithal shall a young man
cleanse his way? by taking heed *thereto*
according to thy word.
10 With my whole heart have I sought
thee: O let me not wander from thy
commandments.
11 Thy word have I hid in mine heart,
that I might not *sin against thee.
12 Blessed *art* thou, O LORD: teach me
thy statutes.
13 With my lips have I declared all the
judgments of thy mouth.
14 I have rejoiced in the way of thy
testimonies, as *much as* in all riches.

PSALM 119 IN PRAISE OF THE LAW

Psalm 119 is an acrostic psalm (see Ps. 25 note, "Acrostic Poems"). The Hebrew alphabet of twenty-two letters divides this psalm into its sections of eight verses each. In the original Hebrew each of the verses in a section begins with the same letter—every verse in section Aleph, for example, begins with Aleph or A; every verse in section Beth begins with Beth, B.

This psalm is a great song of praise to the Law and the Word of God. Only three verses (90, 122, and 132) do not mention God's Word, which is called by ten different names in the psalm: "way," "law," "testimonies," "precepts," "statutes," "commandments," "judgments," "word," "words," and "righteousness."

118:19 gates of righteousness. The Lord Himself is the Way; He is the Door (John 10:9; 14:6).

118:22 refused. Rejected. Christ applied these words to Himself in Matthew 21:42.

118:25 Save now. This is the word "Hosanna," and with verse 26 is the cry of Matthew 21:9.

118:26 Blessed be he that cometh. Matthew 23:38 and 39 show both the tragic and glorious side of these words of praise.

[15]I will meditate in thy precepts, and
have respect unto thy ways.
[16]I will delight myself in thy statutes:
I will not forget thy word.

ג GIMEL.

[17]Deal bountifully with thy servant,
that I may live, and keep thy word.
[18]Open thou mine eyes, that I may
behold wondrous things out of thy law.
[19]I *am* a stranger in the earth: hide
not thy commandments from me.
[20]My soul breaketh for the longing
that it hath unto thy judgments at all
times.
[21]Thou hast rebuked the proud *that
are* cursed, which do *err from thy commandments.
[22]Remove from me reproach and contempt; for I have kept thy testimonies.
[23]Princes also did sit *and* speak
against me: *but* thy servant did meditate in thy statutes.
[24]Thy testimonies also *are* my delight
and my counsellors.

ד DALETH.

[25]My soul cleaveth unto the dust:
*quicken thou me according to thy
word.
[26]I have declared my ways, and thou
heardest me: teach me thy statutes.
[27]Make me to understand the way of
thy precepts: so shall I talk of thy wondrous works.
[28]My soul melteth for heaviness:
strengthen thou me according unto thy
word.
[29]Remove from me the way of lying:
and grant me thy law graciously.
[30]I have chosen the way of truth: thy
judgments have I laid *before me.*
[31]I have stuck unto thy testimonies:
O LORD, put me not to shame.
[32]I will run the way of thy commandments, when thou shalt enlarge my
heart.

ה HE.

[33]Teach me, O LORD, the way of
thy statutes; and I shall keep it *unto*
the end.
[34]Give me understanding, and I shall
keep thy law; yea, I shall observe it with
my whole heart.
[35]Make me to go in the path of thy
commandments; for therein do I delight.
[36]Incline my heart unto thy testimonies, and not to covetousness.
[37]Turn away mine eyes from beholding *vanity; *and* quicken thou me
in thy way.
[38]Stablish thy word unto thy servant,
who *is devoted* to thy fear.
[39]Turn away my reproach which I
fear: for thy judgments *are* good.
[40]Behold, I have longed after thy precepts: quicken me in thy righteousness.

ו VAU.

[41]Let thy mercies come also unto me,
O LORD, *even* thy salvation, according
to thy word.
[42]So shall I have wherewith to answer him that reproacheth me: for I
trust in thy word.
[43]And take not the word of truth utterly out of my mouth; for I have hoped
in thy judgments.
[44]So shall I keep thy law continually
for ever and ever.
[45]And I will walk at liberty: for I seek
thy precepts.
[46]I will speak of thy testimonies also
before kings, and will not be ashamed.
[47]And I will delight myself in thy
commandments, which I have loved.
[48]My hands also will I lift up unto thy
commandments, which I have loved;
and I will meditate in thy statutes.

ז ZAIN.

[49]Remember the word unto thy servant, upon which thou hast caused me
to *hope.

119:19 I am a stranger. The believer must always say this (compare Heb. 11:13).
119:32 enlarge my heart. When the affection or love of the heart is aroused for the Word, its commandments will be observed.

50 This *is* my comfort in my affliction:
for thy word hath quickened me.
51 The proud have had me greatly in
derision: *yet* have I not declined from
thy law.
52 I remembered thy judgments of old,
O LORD; and have comforted myself.
53 Horror hath taken hold upon me
because of the wicked that forsake thy
law.
54 Thy statutes have been my songs
in the house of my pilgrimage.
55 I have remembered thy name,
O LORD, in the night, and have kept thy
law.
56 This I had, because I kept thy precepts.

ח CHETH.

57 *Thou art* my portion, O LORD: I
have said that I would keep thy words.
58 I intreated thy favour with *my*
whole heart: be merciful unto me according to thy word.
59 I thought on my ways, and turned
my feet unto thy testimonies.
60 I made haste, and delayed not to
keep thy commandments.
61 The bands of the wicked have
robbed me: *but* I have not forgotten thy
law.
62 At midnight I will rise to give
thanks unto thee because of thy righteous judgments.
63 I *am* a companion of all *them* that
fear thee, and of them that keep thy
precepts.
64 The earth, O LORD, is full of thy
mercy: teach me thy statutes.

ט TETH.

65 Thou hast dealt well with thy servant, O LORD, according unto thy word.
66 Teach me good judgment and
knowledge: for I have believed thy
commandments.
67 Before I was afflicted I went astray:
but now have I kept thy word.
68 Thou *art* good, and doest good;
teach me thy statutes.
69 The proud have forged a lie against
me: *but* I will keep thy precepts with *my*
whole heart.
70 Their heart is as fat as grease; *but*
I delight in thy law.
71 *It is* good for me that I have been
afflicted; that I might learn thy statutes.
72 The law of thy mouth *is* better unto
me than thousands of gold and silver.

י JOD.

73 Thy hands have made me and fashioned me: give me understanding, that
I may learn thy commandments.
74 They that fear thee will be glad
when they see me; because I have
hoped in thy word.
75 I know, O LORD, that thy judgments
are right, and *that* thou in faithfulness
hast afflicted me.
76 Let, I pray thee, thy merciful kindness be for my comfort, according to
thy word unto thy servant.
77 Let thy tender mercies come unto
me, that I may live: for thy law *is* my
delight.
78 Let the proud be ashamed; for they
dealt perversely with me without a
cause: *but* I will meditate in thy precepts.
79 Let those that fear thee turn unto
me, and those that have known thy testimonies.
80 Let my heart be sound in thy statutes; that I be not ashamed.

כ CAPH.

81 My soul fainteth for thy salvation:
but I hope in thy word.
82 Mine eyes fail for thy word, saying,
When wilt thou comfort me?

119:61 have robbed me. Have wrapped around me.
119:70 fat as grease. Insensible, stupid.
119:73 heading. "Jod" is the smallest letter in the Hebrew alphabet. Note the Lord's reference to it in Matthew 5:18.

[83]For I am become like a bottle in the
smoke; *yet* do I not forget thy statutes.
[84]How many *are* the days of thy
servant? when wilt thou execute judgment on them that persecute me?
[85]The proud have digged pits for me,
which *are* not after thy law.
[86]All thy commandments *are* faithful:
they persecute me wrongfully; help
thou me.
[87]They had almost consumed me
upon earth; but I forsook not thy precepts.
[88]Quicken me after thy lovingkindness; so shall I keep the testimony of
thy mouth.

ל LAMED.

[89]For ever, O LORD, thy word is settled in *heaven.
[90]Thy faithfulness *is* unto all generations: thou hast established the earth,
and it abideth.
[91]They continue this day according to
thine ordinances: for all *are* thy servants.
[92]Unless thy law *had been* my delights, I should then have perished in
mine affliction.
[93]I will never forget thy precepts: for
with them thou hast quickened me.
[94]I *am* thine, save me; for I have
sought thy precepts.
[95]The wicked have waited for me to
destroy me: *but* I will consider thy testimonies.
[96]I have seen an end of all *perfection: *but* thy commandment *is* exceeding broad.

מ MEM.

[97]O how love I thy law! it *is* my meditation all the day.
[98]Thou through thy commandments
hast made me wiser than mine enemies: for they *are* ever with me.
[99]I have more understanding than all
my teachers: for thy testimonies *are* my
meditation.
[100]I understand more than the ancients, because I keep thy precepts.
[101]I have refrained my feet from every
evil way, that I might keep thy word.
[102]I have not departed from thy judgments: for thou hast taught me.
[103]How sweet are thy words unto my
taste! *yea, sweeter* than honey to my
mouth!
[104]Through thy precepts I get understanding: therefore I hate every false
way.

נ NUN.

[105]Thy word *is* a lamp unto my feet,
and a light unto my path.
[106]I have sworn, and I will perform *it,*
that I will keep thy righteous judgments.
[107]I am afflicted very much: quicken
me, O LORD, according unto thy word.
[108]Accept, I beseech thee, the *freewill-offerings of my mouth, O LORD, and
teach me thy judgments.
[109]My soul *is* continually in my hand:
yet do I not forget thy law.
[110]The wicked have laid a snare for
me: yet I erred not from thy precepts.
[111]Thy testimonies have I taken as an
heritage for ever: for they *are* the rejoicing of my heart.
[112]I have inclined mine heart to
perform thy statutes alway, *even unto*
the end.

ס SAMECH.

[113]I hate *vain* thoughts: but thy law
do I love.
[114]Thou *art* my hiding place and my
shield: I hope in thy word.
[115]Depart from me, ye evildoers:
for I will keep the commandments of
my God.

119:83 like a bottle in the smoke. Bottles were not made of glass but leather. These were hardened by being hung in smoke.
119:91 They continue. The heaven and the earth.
119:94 save me. Preserve me from evil.

116 Uphold me according unto thy
word, that I may live: and let me not be
ashamed of my hope.
117 Hold thou me up, and I shall be
safe: and I will have respect unto thy
statutes continually.
118 Thou hast trodden down all them
that err from thy statutes: for their deceit *is* *falsehood.
119 Thou puttest away all the wicked
of the earth *like* dross: therefore I love
thy testimonies.
120 My flesh trembleth for fear of
thee; and I am afraid of thy judgments.

ע AIN.

121 I have done judgment and justice:
leave me not to mine oppressors.
122 Be surety for thy servant for good:
let not the proud oppress me.
123 Mine eyes fail for thy salvation,
and for the word of thy righteousness.
124 Deal with thy servant according
unto thy mercy, and teach me thy statutes.
125 I *am* thy servant; give me understanding, that I may know thy testimonies.
126 *It is* time for *thee*, LORD, to work:
for they have made void thy law.
127 Therefore I love thy commandments above gold; yea, above fine gold.
128 Therefore I esteem all *thy* precepts
concerning all *things to be* right; *and* I
hate every false way.

פ PE.

129 Thy testimonies *are* wonderful:
therefore doth my soul keep them.
130 The entrance of thy words giveth
light; it giveth understanding unto the
simple.
131 I opened my mouth, and panted:
for I longed for thy commandments.
132 Look thou upon me, and be merciful unto me, as thou usest to do unto
those that love thy name.
133 Order my steps in thy word: and
let not any iniquity have dominion over
me.
134 Deliver me from the oppression of
man: so will I keep thy precepts.
135 Make thy face to shine upon thy
servant; and teach me thy statutes.
136 Rivers of waters run down mine
eyes, because they keep not thy law.

צ TZADDI.

137 Righteous *art* thou, O LORD, and
upright *are* thy judgments.
138 Thy testimonies *that* thou hast
commanded *are* righteous and very
faithful.
139 My zeal hath consumed me, because mine enemies have forgotten thy
words.
140 Thy word *is* very pure: therefore
thy servant loveth it.
141 I *am* small and despised: *yet* do not
I forget thy precepts.
142 Thy righteousness *is* an everlasting righteousness, and thy law *is* the
truth.
143 Trouble and anguish have taken
hold on me: *yet* thy commandments *are*
my delights.
144 The righteousness of thy testimonies *is* everlasting: give me understanding, and I shall live.

ק KOPH.

145 I cried with *my* whole heart; hear
me, O LORD: I will keep thy statutes.
146 I cried unto thee; save me, and I
shall keep thy testimonies.
147 I prevented the dawning of the
morning, and cried: I hoped in thy word.
148 Mine eyes *prevent the *night*
watches, that I might meditate in thy
word.

119:118 trodden down. Made nothing, set at nought.
119:122 Be surety for thy servant. A wonderful illustration of this is found in Genesis 43:9.
119:123 fail for. Long for or yearn after.

149Hear my voice according unto thy
lovingkindness: O LORD, quicken me
according to thy judgment.
150They draw nigh that follow after
mischief: they are far from thy law.
151Thou *art* near, O LORD; and all thy
commandments *are* truth.
152Concerning thy testimonies, I
have known of old that thou hast founded them for ever.

ר RESH.

153Consider mine affliction, and deliver me: for I do not forget thy law.
154Plead my cause, and deliver me:
quicken me according to thy word.
155Salvation *is* far from the wicked:
for they seek not thy statutes.
156Great *are* thy tender mercies,
O LORD: quicken me according to thy
judgments.
157Many *are* my persecutors and mine
enemies; *yet* do I not decline from thy
testimonies.
158I beheld the transgressors, and
was grieved; because they kept not thy
word.
159Consider how I love thy precepts:
quicken me, O LORD, according to thy
lovingkindness.
160Thy word *is* true *from* the beginning: and every one of thy righteous
judgments *endureth* for ever.

ש SCHIN.

161Princes have persecuted me without a cause: but my heart standeth in
awe of thy word.
162I rejoice at thy word, as one that
findeth great spoil.
163I hate and abhor lying: *but* thy law
do I love.
164Seven times a day do I praise thee
because of thy righteous judgments.

NUMBERS IN THE BIBLE

Numbers are used in the Bible with symbolic, as well as numeric, intent. The most prominent numerals that carry significant, or symbolic, meaning are three, four, seven, ten, and twelve, and sometimes multiples of these, for example, forty, and seventy multiplied by seven.

Number three, in addition to its numeric force, suggests the beginning, the middle, and the end, or "yesterday, and today, and forever." It is a divine and sacred number. There are three persons in the Godhead: the Father, the Son, and the Holy Spirit. Christ was in the grave "three days and three nights" (Matt. 12:40; compare 1 Cor. 15:4). God is addressed three times: "Holy, holy, holy" (Isa. 6:3). There are many triads in the Scriptures and in creation: three men and three measures of meal (Gen. 18:2,6); the three characteristics of the Thessalonian church (1 Thess. 1:3; see 1:3 note, "Three Principles"); the same triad of "faith, hope, and love" of 1 Corinthians 13. Note the sun, the moon, and the stars; or the air, the earth, and the waters also.

Number four, perhaps from the four points of the compass, has to do with completeness in another sense, a comprehensiveness of range or extent. Refer to the four empires of Daniel's prophecy (Dan. 2), the four Gospels, and the four living creatures around the throne of God (Rev. 4:6-8).

Number seven frequently signifies completeness also. There are seven days in the week. The messages to the seven churches in Asia (Rev. 2 and 3) suggest a complete message to the whole church; and the seven spirits of God signify the complete work of the Holy Spirit (Rev. 4:5; compare Rev. 1:4).

Number ten, in its multiples, often alludes to a time of waiting or of trial. Moses waited forty years in the desert (Acts 7:30), and our Lord lived here on earth, after His resurrection, for forty days (Acts 1:3). The Israelites wandered for forty years in the wilderness (Acts 7:36). Christ, at the time of His temptation, fasted forty days and forty nights (Matt. 4:1-2).

Number twelve seems especially to be connected with the nation Israel: twelve tribes, twelve stones in the breastplate of the high priest (Ex. 39:10-14), twelve loaves of shewbread (Lev. 24:5-6), twelve spies sent into Canaan (Num. 13:1-16), twelve stones placed in the Jordan as a memorial (Josh. 4:1-9), and the twelve disciples (Matt. 10:1-4).

119:164 Seven times a day. This was unceasing praise, for seven is the number of completion or perfection. See the note above, "Numbers in the Bible."

[165]Great *peace have they which love
thy law: and nothing shall *offend them.
[166]LORD, I have hoped for thy salvation, and done thy commandments.
[167]My soul hath kept thy testimonies;
and I love them exceedingly.
[168]I have kept thy precepts and thy
testimonies: for all my ways *are* before
thee.

ת TAU.

[169]Let my cry come near before thee,
O LORD: give me understanding according to thy word.
[170]Let my supplication come before
thee: deliver me according to thy word.
[171]My lips shall utter praise, when
thou hast taught me thy statutes.
[172]My tongue shall speak of thy word:
for all thy commandments *are* righteousness.
[173]Let thine hand help me; for I have
chosen thy precepts.
[174]I have longed for thy salvation,
O LORD; and thy law *is* my delight.
[175]Let my soul live, and it shall praise
thee; and let thy judgments help me.
[176]I have gone astray like a lost
sheep; seek thy servant; for I do not
forget thy commandments.

Psalm 120

A Song of degrees.

[1]In my distress I cried unto the LORD,
and he heard me.
[2]Deliver my soul, O LORD, from lying lips, *and* from a deceitful tongue.
[3]What shall be given unto thee? or
what shall be done unto thee, thou false
tongue?
[4]Sharp arrows of the mighty, with
coals of juniper.

Psalm 120: Pilgrim Songs
Note that Psalms 120 to 134 each have the same title: "A Song of degrees." They are also called "The Songs of Ascents." It is believed that they are pilgrim songs sung by the worshippers on their way to Jerusalem for the solemn feasts, three times each year (Lev. 23). Each psalm finds the worshippers nearer the city until they have entered the temple and worshipped God there. They are also spiritual "Songs of Ascent," for in them the heart is led higher and higher in its worship and praise of God.

[5]Woe is me, that I sojourn in Mesech,
that I dwell in the tents of *Kedar!
[6]My soul hath long dwelt with him
that hateth peace.
[7]I *am for* peace: but when I speak,
they *are* for war.

Psalm 121

A Song of degrees.

[1]I will lift up mine eyes unto the hills,
from whence cometh my help.
[2]My help *cometh* from the LORD,
which made heaven and earth.
[3]He will not suffer thy foot to be
moved: he that keepeth thee will not
slumber.
[4]Behold, he that keepeth *Israel shall
neither slumber nor sleep.
[5]The LORD *is* thy keeper: the LORD
is thy shade upon thy right hand.
[6]The sun shall not smite thee by day,
nor the moon by night.
[7]The LORD shall preserve thee from
all evil: he shall preserve thy soul.
[8]The LORD shall preserve thy going
out and thy coming in from this time
forth, and even for evermore.

119:176 like a lost sheep. Read Isaiah 53:6 and Luke 15:4.
120:4 Sharp arrows. Verse 4 answers the question of verse 3.
120:5 Mesech . . . Kedar. Meshech, one of Japheth's sons (Gen. 10:2) stands for the Gentiles. Kedar was one of the sons of Ishmael, who was the father of the Arabs (Gen. 25:13). The Israelites have not found peace with either group.
121:1 from whence cometh my help. Read this as a new sentence and a question. The answer comes then in verse 2. Man's help does not come from the hills; it comes only from the LORD (compare Ps. 123:1).

Psalm 122

A Song of degrees of *David.

[1]I was glad when they said unto me,
Let us go into the house of the LORD.
[2]Our feet shall stand within thy gates,
O *Jerusalem.
[3]Jerusalem is builded as a city that is
compact together:
[4]Whither the tribes go up, the tribes
of the LORD, unto the testimony of Israel, to give thanks unto the name of
the LORD.
[5]For there are set thrones of judgment, the thrones of the house of
David.
[6]Pray for the peace of Jerusalem:
they shall prosper that love thee.
[7]Peace be within thy walls, *and* prosperity within thy palaces.
[8]For my brethren and companions'
sakes, I will now say, Peace *be* within
thee.
[9]Because of the house of the LORD
our *God I will seek thy good.

Psalm 123

A *Song of degrees.

[1]Unto thee lift I up mine eyes, O thou
that dwellest in the heavens.
[2]Behold, as the eyes of servants
look unto the hand of their masters,
and as the eyes of a maiden unto the
hand of her mistress; so our eyes *wait*
upon the LORD our God, until that he
have *mercy upon us.
[3]Have mercy upon us, O LORD, have
mercy upon us: for we are exceedingly
filled with contempt.
[4]Our soul is exceedingly filled with
the scorning of those that are at ease,
and with the contempt of the proud.

Psalm 124

A Song of degrees of David.

[1]If *it had not been* the LORD who was
on our side, now may Israel say;
[2]If *it had not been* the LORD who was
on our side, when men rose up against us:
[3]Then they had swallowed us up
*quick, when their wrath was kindled
against us:
[4]Then the waters had overwhelmed
us, the stream had gone over our soul:
[5]Then the proud waters had gone
over our soul.
[6]Blessed *be* the LORD, who hath not
given us *as* a prey to their teeth.
[7]Our soul is escaped as a bird out of
the snare of the fowlers: the snare is
broken, and we are escaped.
[8]Our help *is* in the name of the LORD,
who made heaven and earth.

Psalm 125

A Song of degrees.

[1]They that *trust in the LORD *shall
be* as mount *Zion, *which* cannot be removed, *but* abideth for ever.
[2]As the *mountains *are* round about
Jerusalem, so the LORD *is* round about
his people from henceforth even for
ever.
[3]For the rod of the wicked shall not
rest upon the lot of the righteous; lest
the righteous put forth their hands unto
iniquity.
[4]Do good, O LORD, unto *those that be*
good, and to *them that are* upright in
their hearts.
[5]As for such as turn aside unto their
crooked ways, the LORD shall lead them
forth with the workers of iniquity: *but*
*peace *shall be* upon Israel.

122:3 compact. Firmly united, strongly built.
123:2 hand of their masters. In the East, servants watch their masters' hands for directions as to what they are to do.
125:3 rod of the wicked. Oppression will not always afflict the righteous. If it did, despair might drive them to sin.

Psalm 126

A *Song of degrees.

1When the LORD turned again the
captivity of Zion, we were like them
that dream.
2Then was our mouth filled with
laughter, and our tongue with singing:
then said they among the heathen,
The LORD hath done great things for
them.
3The LORD hath done great things for
us; *whereof* we are glad.
4Turn again our captivity, O LORD, as
the streams in the south.
5They that sow in tears shall reap
in joy.
6He that goeth forth and weepeth,
bearing precious seed, shall doubtless
come again with rejoicing, bringing his
sheaves *with him.*

Psalm 127

A Song of degrees for Solomon.

1Except the LORD build the house,
they labour in vain that build it: except
the LORD keep the city, the watchman
waketh *but* in vain.
2*It is* vain for you to rise up early, to
sit up late, to eat the bread of sorrows:
for so he giveth his beloved sleep.
3Lo, children *are* an heritage of the
LORD: *and* the fruit of the womb *is his*
reward.
4As arrows *are* in the hand of a mighty
man; so *are* children of the youth.
5Happy *is* the man that hath his
quiver full of them: they shall not be
ashamed, but they shall speak with the
enemies in the gate.

Psalm 128

A Song of degrees.

1Blessed *is* every one that *feareth
the LORD; that walketh in his ways.
2For thou shalt eat the labour of thine
hands: happy *shalt* thou *be,* and *it shall
be* well with thee.
3Thy wife *shall be* as a fruitful vine by
the sides of thine house: thy children
like olive plants round about thy table.
4Behold, that thus shall the man be
blessed that feareth the LORD.
5The LORD shall bless thee out of
Zion: and thou shalt see the good of
*Jerusalem all the days of thy life.
6Yea, thou shalt see thy children's
children, *and* peace upon *Israel.

Psalm 129

A *Song of degrees.

1Many a time have they afflicted me
from my youth, may Israel now say:
2Many a time have they afflicted me
from my youth: yet they have not prevailed against me.
3The plowers plowed upon my back:
they made long their furrows.
4The LORD *is* righteous: he hath cut
asunder the cords of the wicked.
5Let them all be confounded and
turned back that hate Zion.
6Let them be as the grass *upon* the
housetops, which withereth afore it
groweth up:

126:1 When the LORD turned again the captivity. This was written as a song of joy by someone who returned from the Babylonian captivity (see the introductions to Ezra and Nehemiah).

126:4 Turn again our captivity. This looks ahead to the complete restoration of the Jewish people when the Lord shall set up His *kingdom.

126:6 He that goeth forth. There is no greater joy than to see the fruit of the proclamation of the Word of God even though the going forth may cause anguish. See also Daniel 12:3 and Galatians 6:9.

127:2 giveth his beloved sleep. Even while we sleep, the LORD is supplying our every need. Therefore it is foolish to worry—to "eat the bread of sorrows."

129:6 grass upon the housetops. On flat roofs, grass springs up easily—perhaps from seed dropped by a bird or blown by the wind—but it does not have roots, for it has nothing to feed on.

7 Wherewith the mower filleth not his
hand; nor he that bindeth sheaves his
bosom.
8 Neither do they which go by say,
The blessing of the LORD *be* upon you:
we bless you in the name of the LORD.

Psalm 130

A Song of degrees.

1 Out of the depths have I cried unto
thee, O LORD.
2 Lord, hear my voice: let thine ears
be attentive to the voice of my supplications.
3 If thou, LORD, shouldest mark iniquities, O Lord, who shall stand?
4 But *there is* forgiveness with thee,
that thou mayest be feared.
5 I wait for the LORD, my soul doth
wait, and in his word do I *hope.
6 My soul *waiteth* for the Lord more
than they that watch for the morning: *I*
say, more than they that watch for the
morning.
7 Let Israel hope in the LORD: for with
the LORD *there is* *mercy, and with him
is plenteous redemption.
8 And he shall redeem Israel from all
his iniquities.

Psalm 131

A Song of degrees of *David.

1 LORD, my heart is not haughty, nor
mine eyes lofty: neither do I exercise
myself in great matters, or in things too
high for me.
2 Surely I have behaved and quieted
myself, as a *child that is weaned of his
mother: my soul *is* even as a weaned
child.
3 Let Israel hope in the LORD from
henceforth and for ever.

Psalm 132

A *Song of degrees.

1 LORD, remember David, *and* all his
afflictions:

132:1 Remember David
It is possible that this psalm was written by Solomon, David's son, at the time that the *ark of the covenant was taken from the tent-tabernacle to the temple (2 Chron. 5:1-14). See also the closing verses of Solomon's prayer of dedication of the temple (2 Chron. 6:41-42), and compare them with verses 8-10 of Psalm 132.

2 How he sware unto the LORD, *and*
vowed unto the mighty **God* of *Jacob;
3 Surely I will not come into the *tabernacle of my house, nor go up into my
bed;
4 I will not give sleep to mine eyes, *or*
slumber to mine eyelids,
5 Until I find out a place for the LORD,
an habitation for the mighty *God* of Jacob.
6 Lo, we heard of it at Ephratah: we
found it in the fields of the wood.
7 We will go into his tabernacles: we
will worship at his footstool.
8 Arise, O LORD, into thy rest; thou,
and the *ark of thy strength.
9 Let thy priests be clothed with
*righteousness; and let thy *saints
shout for joy.
10 For thy servant David's sake turn
not away the face of thine anointed.

129:8 The blessing of the LORD be upon you. This was a blessing that believing Israelites used (compare Ruth 2:4).

130:1 Out of the depths. Notice, as Martin Luther pointed out, that this psalm, along with Psalms 32, 51, and 143, teaches that the forgiveness of sins is given to those who have faith to believe in God—it is not by works (compare Eph. 2:8-10).

132:2 How he sware unto the LORD. Read David's words in 2 Samuel 7:1-3. Solomon carried out his father's wishes, as he was commanded to by the LORD (1 Chron. 17:3-6,11-15).

132:6 we heard of it at Ephratah: we found it. This speaks of the time that the ark of the covenant was taken away from the people of Israel, when the victors carried it to Kirjath-jearim and kept it for twenty years (1 Samuel 7).

11 The LORD hath sworn *in* truth unto David; he will not turn from it; Of the fruit of thy body will I set upon thy throne.

12 If thy children will keep my *covenant and my testimony that I shall teach them, their children shall also sit upon thy throne for evermore.

13 For the LORD hath chosen Zion; he hath desired *it* for his habitation.

14 This *is* my rest for ever: here will I dwell; for I have desired it.

15 I will abundantly bless her provision: I will satisfy her poor with bread.

16 I will also clothe her priests with *salvation: and her saints shall shout aloud for joy.

17 There will I make the horn of David to bud: I have ordained a lamp for mine anointed.

18 His enemies will I clothe with shame: but upon himself shall his crown flourish.

Psalm 133

A Song of degrees of David.

1 Behold, how good and how pleasant *it is* for brethren to dwell together in unity!

2 *It is* like the precious ointment upon the head, that ran down upon the beard, *even* *Aaron's beard: that went down to the skirts of his *garments;

3 As the dew of Hermon, *and as the dew* that descended upon the mountains of Zion: for there the LORD commanded the blessing, *even* life for evermore.

Psalm 134

A Song of degrees.

1 Behold, bless ye the LORD, all *ye* servants of the LORD, which by night stand in the house of the LORD.

2 Lift up your hands *in* the *sanctuary, and bless the LORD.

3 The LORD that made *heaven and earth bless thee out of Zion.

Psalm 135

1 Praise ye the LORD. Praise ye the name of the LORD; praise *him,* O ye servants of the LORD.

2 Ye that stand in the house of the LORD, in the courts of the house of our God,

3 Praise the LORD; for the LORD *is* good: sing praises unto his name; for *it is* pleasant.

4 For the LORD hath chosen Jacob unto himself, *and* *Israel for his *peculiar treasure.

5 For I know that the LORD *is* great, and *that* our Lord *is* above all gods.

6 Whatsoever the LORD pleased, *that* did he in heaven, and in earth, in the seas, and all deep places.

7 He causeth the vapours to ascend from the ends of the earth; he maketh lightnings for the rain; he bringeth the wind out of his treasuries.

8 Who smote the firstborn of *Egypt, both of man and beast.

9 *Who* sent tokens and wonders into the midst of thee, O Egypt, upon *Pharaoh, and upon all his servants.

132:11 The LORD hath sworn. Read 2 Samuel 7 and 1 Chronicles 17.

132:13 For the LORD hath chosen Zion. This and the verses that follow look ahead to the joyful time when the Lord will set up His *kingdom on this earth.

132:17 the horn of David to bud. Verses 17 and 18 speak especially of the Lord Jesus Christ.

133:2 precious ointment. Aaron's head was anointed with the precious oil when he became high priest (Lev. 8:12).

134:2 in the sanctuary. Notice that this is the final Song of Ascents, and the worshippers are in the temple.

135:8 Who smote the firstborn. Once again the psalmist looks back to the wonderful story of the deliverance of the Israelites, as he praises the LORD Jehovah (see Exod. 11–12).

[10]Who smote great nations, and slew mighty kings;
[11]Sihon king of the Amorites, and Og king of *Bashan, and all the kingdoms of Canaan:
[12]And gave their land *for* an heritage, an heritage unto Israel his people.
[13]Thy name, O LORD, *endureth* for ever; *and* thy memorial, O LORD, throughout all generations.
[14]For the LORD will judge his people, and he will repent himself concerning his servants.
[15]The idols of the heathen *are* silver and gold, the work of men's hands.
[16]They have mouths, but they speak not; eyes have they, but they see not;
[17]They have ears, but they hear not; neither is there *any* breath in their mouths.
[18]They that make them are like unto them: *so is* every one that trusteth in them.
[19]Bless the LORD, O house of Israel: bless the LORD, O house of Aaron:
[20]Bless the LORD, O house of Levi: ye that *fear the LORD, bless the LORD.
[21]Blessed be the LORD out of Zion, which dwelleth at *Jerusalem. Praise ye the LORD.

Psalm 136

[1]O give thanks unto the LORD; for *he is* good: for his *mercy *endureth* for ever.
[2]O give thanks unto the God of gods: for his mercy *endureth* for ever.
[3]O give thanks to the Lord of lords: for his mercy *endureth* for ever.
[4]To him who alone doeth great wonders: for his mercy *endureth* for ever.
[5]To him that by wisdom made the heavens: for his mercy *endureth* for ever.
[6]To him that stretched out the earth above the waters: for his mercy *endureth* for ever.
[7]To him that made great lights: for his mercy *endureth* for ever:
[8]The sun to rule by day: for his mercy *endureth* for ever:
[9]The moon and stars to rule by night: for his mercy *endureth* for ever.
[10]To him that smote Egypt in their firstborn: for his mercy *endureth* for ever:
[11]And brought out Israel from among them: for his mercy *endureth* for ever:
[12]With a strong hand, and with a stretched out arm: for his mercy *endureth* for ever.
[13]To him which divided the Red sea into parts: for his mercy *endureth* for ever:
[14]And made Israel to pass through the midst of it: for his mercy *endureth* for ever:
[15]But overthrew Pharaoh and his host in the Red sea: for his mercy *endureth* for ever.
[16]To him which led his people through the wilderness: for his mercy *endureth* for ever.
[17]To him which smote great kings: for his mercy *endureth* for ever:
[18]And slew famous kings: for his mercy *endureth* for ever:
[19]Sihon king of the Amorites: for his mercy *endureth* for ever:
[20]And Og the king of Bashan: for his mercy *endureth* for ever:
[21]And gave their land for an heritage: for his mercy *endureth* for ever:

135:14 the LORD will judge. Here and in verse 13 the psalmist looks to the future, for the deliverances of verses 8-12 were a *type of the future deliverance of God's people (read Jer. 16:14-15).

135:15 idols of the heathen. Here begins the famous exposure of idolatry, which was a menace to the Israelites' civilization then and is still a danger to God's people today, although in different forms. No thing or person should replace God as the highest priority in our lives.

136:1 his mercy endureth. God's kindness endures forever. It is seen in creation (vss. 5-9); in the wonderful history of the Israelites (vss. 10-22); and in His care and providence for His people even today (vss. 23-25).

[22]*Even* an heritage unto Israel his
servant: for his mercy *endureth* for ever.
[23]Who remembered us in our low
estate: for his mercy *endureth* for ever:
[24]And hath *redeemed us from our
enemies: for his mercy *endureth* for
ever.
[25]Who giveth food to all flesh: for his
mercy *endureth* for ever.
[26]O give thanks unto the God of
heaven: for his mercy *endureth* for ever.

Psalm 137 A Song from Exile
This sad hymn was written by one of the Israelites who had been exiled. Jerusalem was in ruins; the temple was destroyed. He may have been back in his own land by this time, viewing the terrible desolation, and remembering those who had caused it.

Psalm 137

[1]By the rivers of *Babylon, there we
sat down, yea, we wept, when we remembered Zion.
[2]We hanged our harps upon the willows in the midst thereof.
[3]For there they that carried us away
captive required of us a song; and they
that wasted us *required of us* mirth, *saying,* Sing us *one* of the songs of Zion.
[4]How shall we sing the LORD'S song
in a strange land?
[5]If I forget thee, O Jerusalem, let my
right hand forget *her cunning.*
[6]If I do not remember thee, let my
tongue cleave to the roof of my mouth;
if I prefer not Jerusalem above my chief
joy.
[7]Remember, O LORD, the children of
*Edom in the day of Jerusalem; who
said, Rase *it,* rase *it, even* to the foundation thereof.
[8]O daughter of Babylon, who art to be
destroyed; happy *shall he be,* that
rewardeth thee as thou hast served us.
[9]Happy *shall he be,* that taketh and
dasheth thy little ones against the
stones.

Psalm 138

A Psalm of *David.

[1]I will praise thee with my whole
heart: before the gods will I sing praise
unto thee.
[2]I will worship toward thy *holy temple, and praise thy name for thy lovingkindness and for thy truth: for thou hast
magnified thy word above all thy name.

138:2 God Revealed in Nature
Nature reveals God (see Rom. 1:20) so that man can say, "The heavens declare the glory of God; and the firmament sheweth his handiwork," but it is in the Scriptures–His Word–that the true character ("name") of God is revealed. These reveal the Lord Jesus Christ, who is the Word (John 1:1). In Him God's glory is seen in all its fullness (Col. 2:9; Heb. 1:3).

[3]In the day when I cried thou answeredst me, *and* strengthenedst me
with strength in my soul.
[4]All the kings of the earth shall praise
thee, O LORD, when they hear the
words of thy mouth.
[5]Yea, they shall sing in the ways of
the LORD: for great *is* the glory of the
LORD.
[6]Though the LORD *be* high, yet hath
he respect unto the lowly: but the proud
he knoweth afar off.
[7]Though I walk in the midst of trouble, thou wilt revive me: thou shalt
stretch forth thine hand against the

137:7 Rase it. Destroy it.
137:8 who art to be destroyed. Read Isaiah 13:1-6; 47; Jer. 25:12; 50:2.
137:9 Happy shall he be. An imprecatory verse that reveals what horrors had been inflicted on the Jews by their oppressors. Terrible as is the prayer, it is no more terrible than the wrongs that provoked a devout and godly Hebrew to respond in this way.
138:4 All the kings of the earth shall praise thee. Here David was a prophet. He spoke of the time when the Lord will set up His *kingdom and every knee will bow before Him (Phil. 2:10-11).

wrath of mine enemies, and thy right
hand shall save me.
8 The LORD will *perfect *that which*
concerneth me: thy mercy, O LORD,
endureth for ever: forsake not the works
of thine own hands.

Psalm 139

To the chief Musician,
A Psalm of David.

1 O LORD, thou hast searched me, and
known *me*.
2 Thou knowest my downsitting and
mine uprising, thou understandest my
thought afar off.
3 Thou compassest my path and my
lying down, and art acquainted *with* all
my ways.
4 For *there is* not a word in my tongue,
but, lo, O LORD, thou knowest it altogether.
5 Thou hast beset me behind and before, and laid thine hand upon me.
6 *Such* knowledge *is* too wonderful for
me; it is high, I cannot *attain* unto it.
7 Whither shall I go from thy spirit? or
whither shall I flee from thy presence?
8 If I ascend up into heaven, thou *art*
there: if I make my bed in *hell, behold,
thou *art there.*
9 *If* I take the wings of the morning,
and dwell in the uttermost parts of the
sea;
10 Even there shall thy hand lead me,
and thy right hand shall hold me.
11 If I say, Surely the darkness shall
cover me; even the night shall be light
about me.
12 Yea, the darkness hideth not from
thee; but the night shineth as the day:
the darkness and the light *are* both alike
to thee.
13 For thou hast possessed my *reins:
thou hast covered me in my mother's
womb.
14 I will praise thee; for I am fearfully
and wonderfully made: marvellous *are*
thy works; and *that* my soul knoweth
right well.
15 My substance was not hid from
thee, when I was made in secret, *and*
curiously wrought in the lowest parts
of the earth.
16 Thine eyes did see my substance,
yet being unperfect; and in thy book all
my members were written, *which* in continuance were fashioned, when *as yet*
there was none of them.

139:16 The Book of Life
Even before we were born, our names were written in the Book of Life, as we can tell by this passage. If we reject the Lord and His salvation, then our names are blotted out (see Exod. 32:32; Rev. 20:12,15; 21:27), and there is no more salvation for us.

17 How precious also are thy thoughts
unto me, O *God! how great is the sum
of them!
18 *If* I should count them, they are
more in number than the sand: when I
awake, I am still with thee.
19 Surely thou wilt slay the wicked,
O God: depart from me therefore, ye
bloody men.
20 For they speak against thee wickedly, *and* thine enemies take *thy name*
in vain.
21 Do not I hate them, O LORD, that
hate thee? and am not I grieved with
those that rise up against thee?

138:8 The LORD will perfect that which concerneth me. Read Philippians 1:6.
139:1 thou hast searched me, and known me. Verses 1-6 show us something of the omniscience of our God. He knows everything.
139:7 Whither shall I go. . . ? Verses 7-13 show us that God is omnipresent—He is everywhere. "Such knowledge is too wonderful" for us (vs. 6); we cannot understand it.
139:10 thy right hand shall hold me. Note the omniscient, omnipresent LORD's love and compassion for His own (vss. 3,5,10, etc.).
139:13 possessed . . . covered. Guided and guarded.
139:19 depart from me. David would have nothing to do with those who rejected his LORD (vss. 20-22).

[22]I hate them with perfect hatred: I
count them mine enemies.
[23]Search me, O God, and know my
heart: try me, and know my thoughts:
[24]And see if *there be any* wicked way
in me, and lead me in the way everlasting.

Psalm 140

To the chief Musician,
A Psalm of David.

[1]Deliver me, O LORD, from the evil
man: preserve me from the violent man;
[2]Which imagine mischiefs in *their*
heart; continually are they gathered
together *for* war.
[3]They have sharpened their tongues
like a serpent; adders' poison *is* under
their lips. *Selah.
[4]Keep me, O LORD, from the hands
of the wicked; preserve me from the
violent man; who have purposed to
overthrow my goings.
[5]The proud have hid a snare for me,
and cords; they have spread a net by the
wayside; they have set gins for me.
Selah.
[6]I said unto the LORD, Thou *art* my
God: hear the voice of my supplications,
O LORD.
[7]O GOD the Lord, the strength of my
*salvation, thou hast covered my head
in the day of battle.
[8]Grant not, O LORD, the desires of
the wicked: further not his wicked device; *lest* they exalt themselves. Selah.
[9]*As for* the head of those that compass me about, let the mischief of their
own lips cover them.
[10]Let burning coals fall upon them:
let them be cast into the fire; into deep
pits, that they rise not up again.
[11]Let not an evil speaker be established in the earth: evil shall hunt the
violent man to overthrow *him.*
[12]I know that the LORD will maintain
the cause of the afflicted, *and* the right
of the poor.
[13]Surely the righteous shall give
thanks unto thy name: the upright shall
dwell in thy presence.

Psalm 141

A Psalm of David.

[1]LORD, I cry unto thee: make haste
unto me; give ear unto my voice, when
I cry unto thee.
[2]Let my *prayer be set forth before
thee *as* *incense; *and* the lifting up of
my hands *as* the evening *sacrifice.
[3]Set a watch, O LORD, before my
mouth; keep the door of my lips.
[4]Incline not my heart to *any* evil
thing, to practise wicked works with
men that work iniquity: and let me not
eat of their dainties.
[5]Let the righteous smite me; *it shall
be* a kindness: and let him reprove me;
it shall be an excellent *oil, *which* shall
not break my head: for yet my prayer
also *shall be* in their calamities.
[6]When their judges are overthrown
in stony places, they shall hear my
words; for they are sweet.
[7]Our bones are scattered at the
grave's mouth, as when one cutteth and
cleaveth *wood* upon the earth.
[8]But mine eyes *are* unto thee, O GOD

140:5 gins. Traps.
141:2 prayer be set forth before thee as incense. Read more about prayers rising as incense in Revelation 8:3-4.
141:5 it shall be an excellent oil. For further instructions about accepting reproof, see Proverbs 10:17; 12:1; 13:18; 15:5; and 15:32.
141:5 my prayer also shall be in their calamities. "Even during their wickedness, I shall pray." David's dependence on God was not interrupted by public opinion around him.
141:6 When their judges are overthrown. David foresaw the time when the false and evil rulers would be overthrown. Then those who remained would remember his words about the things of the Lord.
141:7 Our bones are scattered. Read about the dry bones in Ezekiel 37 and its notes.

the Lord: in thee is my *trust; leave not
my soul destitute.
9 Keep me from the snares *which* they
have laid for me, and the gins of the
workers of iniquity.
10 Let the wicked fall into their own
nets, whilst that I withal escape.

Psalm 142

A Song of Instruction

*Maschil of David; A Prayer
when he was in the cave.

1 I cried unto the LORD with my voice;
with my voice unto the LORD did I make
my supplication.
2 I poured out my complaint before
him; I shewed before him my trouble.
3 When my spirit was overwhelmed
within me, then thou knewest my path.
In the way wherein I walked have they
privily laid a snare for me.
4 I looked on *my* right hand, and beheld, but *there was* no man that would
know me: refuge failed me; no man
cared for my soul.
5 I cried unto thee, O LORD: I said,
Thou *art* my refuge *and* my portion in
the land of the living.
6 Attend unto my cry; for I am brought
very low: deliver me from my persecutors; for they are stronger than I.
7 Bring my soul out of prison, that I
may praise thy name: the righteous
shall compass me about; for thou shalt
deal bountifully with me.

Psalm 143

A Psalm of David.

1 Hear my prayer, O LORD, give ear to
my supplications: in thy faithfulness
answer me, *and* in thy *righteousness.
2 And enter not into *judgment with
thy servant: for in thy sight shall no
man living be justified.
3 For the enemy hath persecuted my
soul; he hath smitten my life down to
the ground; he hath made me to dwell
in darkness, as those that have been
long dead.
4 Therefore is my spirit overwhelmed
within me; my heart within me is
desolate.
5 I remember the days of old; I meditate on all thy works; I muse on the
work of thy hands.
6 I stretch forth my hands unto thee:
my soul *thirsteth* after thee, as a thirsty
land. Selah.
7 Hear me speedily, O LORD: my spirit
faileth: hide not thy face from me, lest
I be like unto them that go down into
the *pit.
8 Cause me to hear thy lovingkindness in the morning; for in thee do I
trust: cause me to know the way
wherein I should walk; for I lift up my
soul unto thee.
9 Deliver me, O LORD, from mine enemies: I flee unto thee to hide me.
10 Teach me to do thy will; for thou *art*
my God: thy spirit *is* good; lead me into
the land of uprightness.
11 *Quicken me, O LORD, for thy
name's sake: for thy righteousness'
sake bring my soul out of trouble.
12 And of thy *mercy cut off mine enemies, and destroy all them that afflict
my soul: for I *am* thy servant.

Psalm 144

A Psalm of *David.

1 Blessed *be* the LORD my strength,
which teacheth my hands to war, *and*
my fingers to fight:
2 My goodness, and my fortress; my
high tower, and my deliverer; my
shield, and *he* in whom I trust; who
subdueth my people under me.
3 LORD, what *is* man, that thou takest
knowledge of him! *or* the son of man,
that thou makest account of him!

142:title. when he was in the cave. This psalm was written either at En-gedi (1 Sam. 24), or more probably at Adullam (1 Sam. 22).
143:1 in thy faithfulness . . . righteousness. Compare 1 John 1:9.

[4]Man is like to *vanity: his days *are* as a shadow that passeth away.

[5]Bow thy heavens, O LORD, and come down: touch the mountains, and they shall smoke.

[6]Cast forth lightning, and *scatter them: shoot out thine arrows, and destroy them.

[7]Send thine hand from above; rid me, and deliver me out of great waters, from the hand of strange children;

[8]Whose mouth speaketh vanity, and their right hand *is* a right hand of falsehood.

[9]I will sing a new song unto thee, O God: upon a *psaltery *and* an instrument of ten strings will I sing praises unto thee.

[10]*It is he* that giveth salvation unto kings: who delivereth David his servant from the hurtful sword.

[11]Rid me, and deliver me from the hand of strange children, whose mouth speaketh vanity, and their right hand *is* a right hand of falsehood:

[12]That our sons *may be* as plants grown up in their youth; *that* our daughters *may be* as corner stones, polished *after* the similitude of a palace:

[13]*That* our garners *may be* full, affording all manner of store: *that* our sheep may bring forth thousands and ten thousands in our streets:

[14]*That* our oxen *may be* strong to labour; *that there be* no breaking in, nor going out; that *there be* no complaining in our streets.

[15]Happy *is that* people, that is in such a case: *yea,* happy *is that* people, whose God *is* the LORD.

145:1 An Acrostic Psalm

Psalm 145 is an acrostic psalm (see Ps. 25 note, "Acrostic Poems"). One of the twenty-two letters, however, *N,* or *Nun,* has been omitted. Some interpret this as meaning that though it was a psalm of praise, it could not be perfect praise, because the Son of God had not yet died for the sins of the Old Testament saints (1 Cor. 15:3).

Psalm 145

David's *Psalm* of praise.

[1]I will extol thee, my *God, O king; and I will bless thy name for ever and ever.

[2]Every day will I bless thee; and I will praise thy name for ever and ever.

[3]Great *is* the LORD, and greatly to be praised; and his greatness *is* unsearchable.

[4]One generation shall praise thy works to another, and shall declare thy mighty acts.

[5]I will speak of the glorious honour of thy majesty, and of thy wondrous works.

[6]And *men* shall speak of the might of thy terrible acts: and I will declare thy greatness.

[7]They shall abundantly utter the memory of thy great goodness, and shall sing of thy righteousness.

[8]The LORD *is* gracious, and full of compassion; slow to anger, and of great mercy.

[9]The LORD *is* good to all: and his tender mercies *are* over all his works.

[10]All thy works shall praise thee, O LORD; and thy *saints shall bless thee.

[11]They shall speak of the glory of thy *kingdom, and talk of thy power;

[12]To make known to the sons of men his mighty acts, and the glorious majesty of his kingdom.

[13]Thy kingdom *is* an everlasting kingdom, and thy dominion *endureth* throughout all generations.

[14]The LORD upholdeth all that fall, and raiseth up all *those that be* bowed down.

[15]The eyes of all wait upon thee; and thou givest them their meat in due season.

[16]Thou openest thine hand, and satisfiest the desire of every living thing.

[17]The LORD *is* righteous in all his ways, and *holy in all his works.

[18]The LORD *is* nigh unto all them that call upon him, to all that call upon him in truth.

[19]He will fulfil the desire of them that
*fear him: he also will hear their cry,
and will save them.
[20]The LORD preserveth all them that
love him: but all the wicked will he destroy.
[21]My mouth shall speak the praise of
the LORD: and let all *flesh bless his
holy name for ever and ever.

Psalm 146

[1]Praise ye the LORD. Praise the
LORD, O my soul.
[2]While I live will I praise the LORD: I
will sing praises unto my God while I
have any being.
[3]Put not your trust in princes, *nor* in
the son of man, in whom *there is* no
help.
[4]His breath goeth forth, he returneth
to his earth; in that very day his
thoughts perish.
[5]Happy *is he* that *hath* the God of *Jacob for his help, whose *hope *is* in the
LORD his God:
[6]Which made *heaven, and earth, the
sea, and all that therein *is:* which
keepeth truth for ever:
[7]Which executeth judgment for the
oppressed: which giveth food to the
hungry. The LORD looseth the prisoners:
[8]The LORD openeth *the eyes of* the
blind: the LORD raiseth them that are
bowed down: the LORD loveth the righteous:
[9]The LORD preserveth the strangers;
he relieveth the fatherless and widow:
but the way of the wicked he turneth
upside down.
[10]The LORD shall reign for ever, *even*
thy God, O *Zion, unto all generations.
Praise ye the LORD.

Psalm 147

[1]Praise ye the LORD: for *it is* good to
sing praises unto our God; for *it is*
pleasant; *and* praise is comely.
[2]The LORD doth build up *Jerusalem:
he gathereth together the outcasts of
*Israel.
[3]He healeth the broken in heart, and
bindeth up their wounds.
[4]He telleth the number of the stars;
he calleth them all by *their* names.
[5]Great *is* our Lord, and of great power: his understanding *is* infinite.
[6]The LORD lifteth up the meek: he
casteth the wicked down to the ground.
[7]Sing unto the LORD with thanksgiving; sing praise upon the harp unto
our God:
[8]Who covereth the heaven with
clouds, who prepareth rain for the
earth, who maketh grass to grow upon
the mountains.
[9]He giveth to the beast his food, *and*
to the young ravens which cry.
[10]He delighteth not in the strength of
the horse: he taketh not pleasure in the
legs of a man.
[11]The LORD taketh pleasure in them
that fear him, in those that hope in his
mercy.
[12]Praise the LORD, O Jerusalem;
praise thy God, O Zion.
[13]For he hath strengthened the bars
of thy gates; he hath blessed thy children within thee.
[14]He maketh *peace *in* thy borders,
and filleth thee with the finest of the
wheat.
[15]He sendeth forth his commandment

146:1 Praise ye the LORD. Psalms 146–150 are all Hallelujah Psalms. Each begins and ends with praise to the LORD.

146:3 son of man, in whom there is no help. This does not speak of Christ, the Son of Man, but of any son of man. If Christ, however, had been only Son of Man and not the virgin-born Son of God, there would be no help (salvation) in Him. God gave His Son for our salvation (Isa. 9:6; compare Matt. 1:20-23).

147:4 He telleth the number of the stars. Compare this verse with the wonderful verse in Isaiah 40:26.

upon earth: his word runneth very
swiftly.
[16]He giveth snow like wool: he scattereth the hoarfrost like ashes.
[17]He casteth forth his ice like mor-
sels: who can stand before his cold?
[18]He sendeth out his word, and
melteth them: he causeth his wind to
blow, *and* the waters flow.
[19]He sheweth his word unto Jacob, his
statutes and his judgments unto Israel.
[20]He hath not dealt so with any nation: and *as for his* judgments, they have
not known them. Praise ye the LORD.

Psalm 148

[1]Praise ye the LORD. Praise ye the
LORD from the heavens: praise him in
the heights.
[2]Praise ye him, all his *angels: praise
ye him, all his hosts.
[3]Praise ye him, sun and moon: praise
him, all ye stars of light.
[4]Praise him, ye heavens of heavens,
and ye waters that *be* above the heavens.
[5]Let them praise the name of the
LORD: for he commanded, and they
were *created.
[6]He hath also stablished them for
ever and ever: he hath made a decree
which shall not pass.
[7]Praise the LORD from the earth, ye
dragons, and all deeps:
[8]*Fire, and hail; snow, and vapour;
stormy wind fulfilling his word:
[9]Mountains, and all hills; fruitful
trees, and all cedars:
[10]Beasts, and all cattle; creeping
things, and flying fowl:
[11]Kings of the earth, and all people;
princes, and all judges of the earth:
[12]Both young men, and maidens; old
men, and children:
[13]Let them praise the name of the
LORD: for his name alone is excellent;
his glory *is* above the earth and heaven.
[14]He also exalteth the horn of his
people, the praise of all his saints; *even*
of the children of Israel, a people near
unto him. Praise ye the LORD.

Psalm 149

[1]Praise ye the LORD. Sing unto the
LORD a new song, *and* his praise in the
congregation of saints.
[2]Let Israel rejoice in him that made
him: let the children of Zion be joyful in
their King.
[3]Let them praise his name in the
dance: let them sing praises unto him
with the timbrel and harp.
[4]For the LORD taketh pleasure in his
people: he will beautify the meek with
*salvation.
[5]Let the saints be joyful in glory: let
them sing aloud upon their beds.
[6]*Let* the high *praises* of God *be* in their
mouth, and a twoedged sword in their
hand;
[7]To execute vengeance upon the heathen, *and* punishments upon the people;
[8]To bind their kings with chains, and
their nobles with fetters of iron;
[9]To execute upon them the *judgment written: this honour have all his
saints. Praise ye the LORD.

Psalm 150

[1]Praise ye the LORD. Praise God in
his sanctuary: praise him in the firmament of his power.

148:7 dragons. Monsters of the deep.

149:2 Zion be joyful in their King. Compare Zechariah 9:9 with Matthew 21:5-15. Then read of the final fulfillment in Revelation 19 and 21.

149:6 a twoedged sword. See Hebrews 4:12; Revelation 1:16; 2:12; 19:15.

149:7 To execute vengeance. When the King comes in *judgment, He will use His restored people Israel in the execution of His judgments (read Isa. 54:14-17; 63:1-6; Mic. 4:11-13; 5:7-8).

150:1 Praise ye the LORD. Note that thirteen times in this psalm alone the psalmist instructs "every thing that hath breath" (vs. 6) to praise the LORD.

2 Praise him for his mighty acts:
praise him according to his excellent
greatness.
3 Praise him with the sound of the
trumpet: praise him with the psaltery
and harp.
4 Praise him with the timbrel and
dance: praise him with stringed instruments and organs.
5 Praise him upon the loud cymbals:
praise him upon the high sounding
cymbals.
6 Let every thing that hath breath
praise the LORD. Praise ye the LORD.

The PROVERBS

BACKGROUND

The book of Proverbs is one of the wisdom books of the Old Testament which represent the philosophy, or general beliefs, of the Hebrews. Proverbs deals primarily with the matter of the daily conduct of the children of God.

THE WRITER

Although Solomon is usually said to be the author, it would be better to say that Solomon collected the proverbs than to say that he wrote them. Some were copied by the men of Hezekiah's time (Proverbs 25:1); others are the words of Agur (Proverbs 30:1); and the last chapter represents the words of King Lemuel (Proverbs 31:1).

CHRIST'S REFERENCES TO PROVERBS

A comparison of the book of Proverbs with the Gospel record of the teaching ministry of the Lord Jesus Christ shows that the Lord made frequent use of the wisdom represented by this book. For example, compare

Proverbs 4:19 with John 12:35;
Proverbs 5:23 with John 8:24;
Proverbs 8:35 with John 6:47;
Proverbs 14:31 with Matthew 25:31-46;
Proverbs 18:21 with Matthew 12:37;
Proverbs 23:7 with Matthew 12:34; and so forth.

As we think of His use of the wisdom of Proverbs, we find that the Lord Jesus employed it in three ways:

1. He said positively what Proverbs says negatively; compare Proverbs 24:29 with Matthew 7:12.
2. He presented the truth of Proverbs much more briefly; compare Proverbs 2:1-5 with John 7:17.
3. He used parables, or stories, to express various truths; compare Proverbs 14:11 with Matthew 7:24-29.

OUTLINE OF PROVERBS

I.	Godliness Is Taught to Youth	Proverbs 1:1—7:27
II.	Godliness Is Made Possible through Wisdom	Proverbs 8:1—9:18
III.	Godliness Is Contrasted with Wickedness	Proverbs 10:1—31:31

I. Godliness Taught to Youth (1:1—7:27)

*1) True wisdom leads to *righteousness*

1 The proverbs of Solomon the *son of David, king of *Israel;

2 To know wisdom and instruction; to perceive the words of understanding;

3 To receive the instruction of wisdom, justice, and judgment, and equity;

4 To give subtilty to the simple, to the young man knowledge and discretion.

5 A wise *man* will hear, and will increase learning; and a man of understanding shall attain unto wise counsels:

6 To understand a proverb, and the interpretation; the words of the wise, and their dark sayings.

¶7 The *fear of the LORD *is* the beginning of knowledge: *but* *fools despise wisdom and instruction.

1:7 The Fear of the LORD

The fear of the LORD is the attitude of heart that the children of God should have toward their heavenly Father. While perfectly at home in His presence, and trusting Him reverently, they realize His greatness and stand in awe of Him. Such fear produces a hatred of evil as well as a love of God (Prov. 8:13). It leads to such conduct as will honor the LORD (Prov. 19:23; see also Prov. 14:27). It is the beginning or foundation of all of man's learning.

8 My son, hear the instruction of thy father, and forsake not the *law of thy mother:

9 For they *shall be* an ornament of grace unto thy head, and chains about thy neck.

¶10 My son, if sinners entice thee, consent thou not.

The temptings of thieves and murderers

11 If they say, Come with us, let us lay wait for *blood, let us lurk privily for the innocent without cause:

12 Let us swallow them up alive as the grave; and whole, as those that go down into the *pit:

13 We shall find all precious substance, we shall fill our houses with spoil:

14 Cast in thy lot among us; let us all have one purse:

15 My son, walk not thou in the way with them; refrain thy foot from their path:

16 For their feet run to evil, and make haste to shed blood.

17 Surely in vain the net is spread in the sight of any bird.

18 And they lay wait for their *own* blood; they lurk privily for their *own* lives.

19 So *are* the ways of every one that is greedy of gain; *which* taketh away the life of the owners thereof.

Wisdom's voice

¶20 Wisdom crieth without; she uttereth her voice in the streets:

21 She crieth in the chief place of concourse, in the openings of the gates: in the city she uttereth her words, *saying,*

22 How long, ye simple ones, will ye love simplicity? and the scorners delight in their scorning, and fools hate knowledge?

23 Turn you at my reproof: behold, I will pour out my spirit unto you, I will make known my words unto you.

¶24 Because I have called, and ye refused; I have stretched out my hand, and no man regarded;

25 But ye have set at nought all my

1:1 proverbs. Wise sayings. The book contains the wisdom of God presented for man's use.

1:4 discretion. Advice.

1:6 interpretation. The point or lesson of the proverb.

1:9 they. The instruction of the father and the law of the mother.

1:15 My son. A teacher calls his pupil "my son" in the East.

1:17 Surely in vain the net is spread. A bird would not fly into a net if he saw it spread in front of him, but evil men rush into death with their eyes open. They destroy themselves when they try to kill others (vss. 18-19).

1:22 The Downward Path
The three words "simple," "scorners," and "fools" mark the downward path of the one who refuses to listen to the words of wisdom. That is what happened with the Pharisees and rulers in our Lord's day. At first they allowed Him to read the Scriptures, but they did not listen to Him; they simply watched Him (Luke 14:1); then they murmured against Him; they were scorners (Luke 15:2); and they became fools who hated Him and wanted to crucify Him (Matt. 27:20; Luke 16:14).

counsel, and would none of my reproof:
26I also will laugh at your calamity; I
will mock when your fear cometh;
27When your fear cometh as desolation, and your destruction cometh as a
whirlwind; when distress and anguish
cometh upon you.
28Then shall they call upon me, but I
will not answer; they shall seek me
early, but they shall not find me:
29For that they hated knowledge, and
did not choose the fear of the LORD:
30They would none of my counsel:
they despised all my reproof.
31Therefore shall they eat of the fruit
of their own way, and be filled with their
own devices.
32For the turning away of the simple
shall slay them, and the prosperity of
fools shall destroy them.
33But whoso hearkeneth unto me
shall dwell safely, and shall be quiet
from fear of evil.

2) The knowledge of God

2 My son, if thou wilt receive my
words, and hide my commandments with thee;
2So that thou incline thine ear unto
wisdom, *and* apply thine heart to understanding;
3Yea, if thou criest after knowledge,
and liftest up thy voice for understanding;
4If thou seekest her as silver, and
searchest for her as *for* hid treasures;
5Then shalt thou understand the fear
of the LORD, and find the knowledge of
*God.

2:5 The Knowledge of God
It is not possible for any man to find God by searching for him (Job 11:7). God makes Himself known to all men who seek Him with sincere hearts. As you read verses 1-5 of this chapter again, you will see that the Lord Jesus presented the same truth when He said, "If any man will do his [God's] will, he shall know of the doctrine [teaching], whether it be of God" (John 7:17).

6For the LORD giveth wisdom: out of
his mouth *cometh* knowledge and understanding.
7He layeth up sound wisdom for the
righteous: *he is* a *buckler to them that
walk uprightly.
8He keepeth the paths of judgment,
and preserveth the way of his *saints.
9Then shalt thou understand *righteousness, and judgment, and equity;
yea, every good path.
¶10When wisdom entereth into thine
heart, and knowledge is pleasant unto
thy soul;
11Discretion shall preserve thee, understanding shall keep thee:
12To deliver thee from the way of the
evil *man,* from the man that speaketh
*froward things;
13Who leave the paths of uprightness,
to walk in the ways of darkness;
14Who rejoice to do evil, *and* delight
in the frowardness of the wicked;
15Whose ways *are* crooked, and *they*
froward in their paths:
16To deliver thee from the strange
woman, *even* from the stranger *which*
flattereth with her words;
17Which forsaketh the guide of her
youth, and forgetteth the *covenant of
her God.

2:1 hide. Lay or store up, as one would do with a treasure.
2:12 froward. Opposed to God.
2:16 strange. Evil.

18 For her house inclineth unto *death, and her paths unto the dead.

19 None that go unto her return again, neither take they hold of the paths of life.

20 That thou mayest walk in the way of good *men,* and keep the paths of the righteous.

21 For the upright shall dwell in the land, and the *perfect shall remain in it.

22 But the wicked shall be cut off from the earth, and the transgressors shall be rooted out of it.

3) The value of godliness

3 My son, forget not my law; but let thine heart keep my commandments:

2 For length of days, and long life, and *peace, shall they add to thee.

3 Let not mercy and truth forsake thee: bind them about thy neck; write them upon the table of thine heart:

4 So shalt thou find favour and good understanding in the sight of God and man.

¶5 *Trust in the LORD with all thine heart; and lean not unto thine own understanding.

6 In all thy ways acknowledge him, and he shall direct thy paths.

> **3:5-6 The LORD's Guidance**
> Our LORD promised to guide each of His children. The secret of this guidance is explained in Proverbs 3:5-6 with John 8:12. It consists of having faith, of surrendering our wills to God, and bringing our ways into submission to His will as revealed in the Word of God.

¶7 Be not wise in thine own eyes: fear the LORD, and depart from evil.

8 It shall be health to thy navel, and marrow to thy bones.

9 Honour the LORD with thy substance, and with the firstfruits of all thine increase:

10 So shall thy barns be filled with plenty, and thy presses shall burst out with new wine.

¶11 My son, despise not the chastening of the LORD; neither be weary of his correction:

> **3:11-12 The Chastening of the LORD**
> This is the LORD's way of training His children. The Word of God reveals three great principles that explain why Christians suffer:
> 1. to purify their characters (Heb. 12:10);
> 2. to make their service more fruitful (John 15:2); and
> 3. to permit them a share in the sufferings of Christ (1 Pet. 4:13).
>
> This verse gives a twofold warning to Christians who suffer. Read it again in this light.

12 For whom the LORD loveth he correcteth; even as a father the son *in whom* he delighteth.

¶13 Happy *is* the man *that* findeth wisdom, and the man *that* getteth understanding.

14 For the merchandise of it *is* better than the merchandise of silver, and the gain thereof than fine gold.

15 She *is* more precious than rubies: and all the things thou canst desire are not to be compared unto her.

16 Length of days *is* in her right hand; *and* in her left hand riches and honour.

17 Her ways *are* ways of pleasantness, and all her paths *are* peace.

18 She *is* a tree of life to them that lay hold upon her: and happy *is every one* that retaineth her.

19 The LORD by wisdom hath founded the earth; by understanding hath he established the heavens.

20 By his knowledge the depths are

3:3 thy neck; write them upon the table of thine heart. Mercy and truth bound around the neck can be seen by men; written on the heart, they are seen of God, and verse 4 is true in life.

3:8 It shall be health to thy navel. The fear of the LORD will bring spiritual blessing to man's whole being.

broken up, and the clouds drop down
the dew.
¶[21]My son, let not them depart from
thine eyes: keep sound wisdom and discretion:
[22]So shall they be life unto thy soul,
and grace to thy neck.
[23]Then shalt thou walk in thy way
safely, and thy foot shall not stumble.
[24]When thou liest down, thou shalt
not be afraid: yea, thou shalt lie down,
and thy sleep shall be sweet.
[25]*Be not afraid of sudden fear, neither of the desolation of the wicked,
when it cometh.
[26]For the LORD shall be thy confidence, and shall keep thy foot from being taken.
¶[27]Withhold not good from them to
whom it is due, when it is in the power
of thine hand to do *it*.
[28]Say not unto thy neighbour, Go, and
come again, and to morrow I will give;
when thou hast it by thee.
[29]Devise not evil against thy neighbour, seeing he dwelleth securely by
thee.
¶[30]Strive not with a man without
cause, if he have done thee no harm.
¶[31]Envy thou not the oppressor, and
choose none of his ways.
[32]For the froward *is* *abomination to
the LORD: but his secret *is* with the
righteous.
¶[33]The curse of the LORD *is* in the
house of the wicked: but he blesseth
the habitation of the *just.
[34]Surely he scorneth the scorners:
but he giveth grace unto the lowly.
[35]The wise shall inherit glory: but
shame shall be the promotion of fools.

4) Practical restraint exerted by wisdom

4 Hear, ye children, the instruction
of a father, and attend to know understanding.
[2]For I give you good *doctrine, forsake ye not my law.
[3]For I was my father's son, tender and
only *beloved* in the sight of my mother.
[4]He taught me also, and said unto me,
Let thine heart retain my words: keep
my commandments, and live.
[5]Get wisdom, get understanding: forget *it* not; neither decline from the
words of my mouth.
[6]Forsake her not, and she shall preserve thee: love her, and she shall keep
thee.
[7]Wisdom *is* the principal thing; *therefore* get wisdom: and with all thy getting
get understanding.

4:7 Wisdom
Wisdom, in Proverbs, is not merely an accumulation of knowledge–it is similar to the "Word" as used in the Gospel of John and refers to the Lord Jesus Christ, who is both the wisdom and power of God (1 Cor. 1:18-25). See Proverbs 8:22 note, "Five Things about Wisdom."

[8]Exalt her, and she shall promote
thee: she shall bring thee to honour,
when thou dost embrace her.
[9]She shall give to thine head an ornament of grace: a crown of glory shall
she deliver to thee.
[10]Hear, O my son, and receive my
sayings; and the years of thy life shall
be many.
[11]I have taught thee in the way of
wisdom; I have led thee in right paths.
[12]When thou goest, thy steps shall
not be straitened; and when thou runnest, thou shalt not stumble.
[13]Take fast hold of instruction; let *her*
not go: keep her; for she *is* thy life.
¶[14]Enter not into the path of the wicked, and go not in the way of evil *men*.
[15]Avoid it, pass not by it, turn from it,
and pass away.
[16]For they sleep not, except they
have done mischief; and their sleep is
taken away, unless they cause *some*
to fall.

4:12 thy steps shall not be straitened. The way will open up before you.
4:12 thou shalt not stumble. Compare Jude 24.

[17]For they eat the bread of wickedness, and drink the wine of violence.
[18]But the path of the just *is* as the
shining light, that shineth more and
more unto the perfect day.
[19]The way of the wicked *is* as darkness: they know not at what they stumble.
¶[20]My son, attend to my words; incline thine ear unto my sayings.
[21]Let them not depart from thine
eyes; keep them in the midst of thine
heart.
[22]For they *are* life unto those that find
them, and health to all their flesh.
¶[23]Keep thy heart with all diligence;
for out of it *are* the issues of life.

4:23 The Importance of the Heart
The importance of the heart is stressed throughout the Word of God. It is from the heart that the mouth speaks (Luke 6:45). The child of God is able to keep his heart with all diligence because the Holy Spirit lives within him (1 Cor. 6:19).

[24]Put away from thee a froward
mouth, and perverse lips put far from
thee.
[25]Let thine eyes look right on, and let
thine eyelids look straight before thee.
[26]Ponder the path of thy feet, and let
all thy ways be established.
[27]Turn not to the right hand nor to
the left: remove thy foot from evil.

5) The danger of sin

5 My son, attend unto my wisdom,
and bow thine ear to my understanding:
[2]That thou mayest regard discretion,
and *that* thy lips may keep knowledge.
¶[3]For the lips of a strange woman
drop *as* an honeycomb, and her mouth
is smoother than oil:
[4]But her end is bitter as *wormwood,
sharp as a twoedged sword.
[5]Her feet go down to death; her steps
take hold on *hell.
[6]Lest thou shouldest ponder the path
of life, her ways are moveable, *that* thou
canst not know *them.*
[7]Hear me now therefore, O ye children, and depart not from the words of
my mouth.
[8]Remove thy way far from her, and
come not nigh the door of her house:
[9]Lest thou give thine honour unto
others, and thy years unto the cruel:
[10]Lest strangers be filled with thy
wealth; and thy labours *be* in the house
of a stranger;
[11]And thou mourn at the last, when
thy flesh and thy body are consumed,
[12]And say, How have I hated instruction, and my heart despised reproof;
[13]And have not obeyed the voice of
my teachers, nor inclined mine ear to
them that instructed me!
[14]I was almost in all evil in the midst
of the congregation and assembly.
¶[15]Drink waters out of thine own cistern, and running waters out of thine
own well.
[16]Let thy fountains be dispersed
abroad, *and* rivers of waters in the
streets.
[17]Let them be only thine own, and
not strangers' with thee.
[18]Let thy fountain be blessed: and
rejoice with the wife of thy youth.
[19]*Let her be as* the loving hind and
pleasant roe; let her breasts satisfy thee
at all times; and be thou ravished always with her love.
[20]And why wilt thou, my son, be ravished with a strange woman, and embrace the bosom of a stranger?
[21]For the ways of man *are* before the
eyes of the LORD, and he pondereth all
his goings.
¶[22]His own iniquities shall take the
wicked himself, and he shall be holden
with the cords of his sins.
[23]He shall die without instruction;
and in the greatness of his folly he shall
go astray.

6) Godliness attended by obedience to the Word of God

6 My son, if thou be surety for thy
friend, *if* thou hast stricken thy
hand with a stranger,

2 Thou art snared with the words of
thy mouth, thou art taken with the
words of thy mouth.
3 Do this now, my son, and deliver
thyself, when thou art come into the
hand of thy friend; go, humble thyself,
and make sure thy friend.
4 Give not sleep to thine eyes, nor
slumber to thine eyelids.
5 Deliver thyself as a roe from the
hand *of the hunter,* and as a bird from the
hand of the fowler.
¶ 6 Go to the ant, thou sluggard; consider her ways, and be wise:
7 Which having no guide, overseer, or
ruler,
8 Provideth her meat in the summer,
and gathereth her food in the harvest.
9 How long wilt thou sleep, O sluggard? when wilt thou arise out of thy
sleep?
10 *Yet* a little sleep, a little slumber, a
little folding of the hands to sleep:
11 So shall thy poverty come as one
that travelleth, and thy want as an
armed man.
¶ 12 A naughty person, a wicked man,
walketh with a *froward mouth.
13 He winketh with his eyes, he
speaketh with his feet, he teacheth with
his fingers;
14 Frowardness *is* in his heart, he deviseth mischief continually; he soweth
discord.
15 Therefore shall his calamity come
suddenly; suddenly shall he be broken
without remedy.
¶ 16 These six *things* doth the LORD
hate: yea, seven *are* an abomination
unto him:
17 A proud look, a lying tongue, and
hands that shed innocent blood,
18 An heart that deviseth wicked
imaginations, feet that be swift in running to mischief,
19 A false witness *that* speaketh lies,
and he that soweth discord among
brethren.
¶ 20 My son, keep thy father's commandment, and forsake not the law of
thy mother:
21 Bind them continually upon thine
heart, *and* tie them about thy neck.
22 When thou goest, it shall lead thee;
when thou sleepest, it shall keep thee;
and *when* thou awakest, it shall talk with
thee.

6:22 A Picture of God's Work
In this verse we have a picture of the work of God the Father, who guides (Ps. 32:8); God the Son, who guards (Ps. 121:4); and God the Holy Spirit, who teaches (Luke 12:12). In verse 23 we see the same picture as we see the lamp, which guides; the light, which guards; and reproof, which teaches.

23 For the commandment *is* a lamp;
and the law *is* light; and reproofs of instruction *are* the way of life:
24 To keep thee from the evil woman,
from the flattery of the tongue of a
strange woman.
25 *Lust not after her beauty in thine
heart; neither let her take thee with her
eyelids.
26 For by means of a whorish woman
a man is brought to a piece of bread: and
the adulteress will hunt for the precious
life.
27 Can a man take fire in his bosom,
and his clothes not be burned?
28 Can one go upon hot coals, and his
feet not be burned?
29 So he that goeth in to his neighbour's wife; whosoever toucheth her
shall not be innocent.
30 *Men* do not despise a thief, if he
steal to satisfy his soul when he is
hungry;
31 But *if* he be found, he shall restore

6:2 Thou art. The "if"s of verse 1 should also appear before the two lines of verse 2.
6:12 A naughty person. A worthless person.
6:12 a froward mouth. A lying mouth.
6:13 winketh with his eyes. Winking is associated with sin in the Old Testament. It carries with it the thought of being proud and rebellious against God. See Job 15:12-13; Psalm 35:19; Proverbs 10:10.

sevenfold; he shall give all the substance of his house.
32 *But* whoso committeth adultery
with a woman lacketh understanding:
he *that* doeth it destroyeth his own soul.
33 A wound and dishonour shall he
get; and his reproach shall not be wiped
away.
34 For jealousy *is* the rage of a man:
therefore he will not spare in the day of
vengeance.
35 He will not regard any ransom; neither will he rest content, though thou
givest many gifts.

7) The wages of sin is death

7 My son, keep my words, and lay
up my commandments with thee.
2 Keep my commandments, and
live; and my *law as the apple of thine
eye.
3 Bind them upon thy fingers, write
them upon the table of thine heart.
4 Say unto wisdom, Thou *art* my sister; and call understanding *thy* kinswoman:
5 That they may keep thee from the
strange woman, from the stranger
which flattereth with her words.
¶6 For at the window of my house I
looked through my casement,
7 And beheld among the simple ones,
I discerned among the youths, a young
man void of understanding,
8 Passing through the street near her
corner; and he went the way to her
house,
9 In the twilight, in the evening, in the
black and dark night:
10 And, behold, there met him a woman *with* the attire of an harlot, and subtil
of heart.
11 (She *is* loud and stubborn; her feet
abide not in her house:
12 Now *is she* without, now in the
streets, and lieth in wait at every corner.)
13 So she caught him, and kissed him,
and with an impudent face said unto
him,
14 *I have* *peace-offerings with me;
this day have I payed my vows.
15 Therefore came I forth to meet
thee, diligently to seek thy face, and I
have found thee.
16 I have decked my bed with coverings of tapestry, with carved *works,* with
fine *linen of *Egypt.
17 I have perfumed my bed with
myrrh, aloes, and cinnamon.
18 Come, let us take our fill of love
until the morning: let us solace ourselves with loves.
19 For the goodman *is* not at home, he
is gone a long journey:

7:19 The Goodman

There is a symbolism here that should not be lost: The Master of the house is our Lord Jesus Christ. While He is absent, in body, from the earth, many people listen to the temptations of false religions. They turn aside from faithfulness and the worship of the one true God to go after attractive forms of religion.

20 He hath taken a bag of money with
him, *and* will come home at the day
appointed.
21 With her much fair speech she
caused him to yield, with the flattering
of her lips she forced him.
22 He goeth after her *straightway, as
an ox goeth to the slaughter, or as a
*fool to the correction of the stocks;
23 Till a dart strike through his liver;
as a bird hasteth to the snare, and
knoweth not that it *is* for his life.
¶24 Hearken unto me now therefore,
O ye children, and attend to the words
of my mouth.

7:2 apple of thine eye. "Apple" here means the *gate* through which the light enters the eye, and is the most important part of the eye, for it is the place of sight. It is treasured for that reason, and, as Christians, we should treasure God's commandments in the same way we protect our eyes. The LORD says that as one would protect that part of the eye, so He would protect His people.

7:22 straightway. Suddenly.

25 Let not thine heart decline to her
ways, go not astray in her paths.
26 For she hath cast down many
wounded: yea, many strong *men* have
been slain by her.
27 Her house *is* the way to hell, going
down to the chambers of death.

II. Godliness Made Possible through Wisdom (8:1—9:18)

*1) Jesus *Christ made unto us wisdom*

8 Doth not wisdom cry? and under
standing put forth her voice?

8:1 Wise People

Wisdom, a major theme of the book of Proverbs, is a highly regarded and cherished attribute in the Bible. Many Bible characters were credited as being wise.

Joseph	Genesis 41:39
Temple craftsmen	Exodus 31:6
The Israelites	Deuteronomy 4:5-6
Joshua	Deuteronomy 34:9
David	1 Samuel 18:14; 2 Samuel 14:20
Wise woman of Tekoah	2 Samuel 14:2
Wise woman of Abel-Beth-maachah	2 Samuel 20:15
Bath-sheba	1 Kings 1:17
Solomon	1 Kings 4:29
Hananiah, Mishael, Azariah	Daniel 1:17
Daniel	Daniel 2:14; 5:14
Wise men of Babylon	Daniel 2:14
Wise men from the East	Matthew 2:1
Jesus	Luke 2:52
Moses	Acts 7:22
Paul	2 Peter 3:15

2 She standeth in the top of *high
places, by the way in the places of the
paths.
3 She crieth at the gates, at the entry
of the city, at the coming in at the doors.
4 Unto you, O men, I call; and my voice
is to the sons of man.
5 O ye simple, understand wisdom:
and, ye *fools, be ye of an understanding heart.
6 Hear; for I will speak of excellent
things; and the opening of my lips *shall
be* right things.
7 For my mouth shall speak truth; and
wickedness *is* an abomination to my
lips.
8 All the words of my mouth *are* in
*righteousness; *there is* nothing froward or perverse in them.
9 They *are* all plain to him that understandeth, and right to them that find
knowledge.
10 Receive my instruction, and not
*silver; and knowledge rather than
choice gold.
11 For wisdom *is* better than rubies;
and all the things that may be desired
are not to be compared to it.
12 I wisdom dwell with prudence, and
find out knowledge of witty inventions.
13 The *fear of the LORD *is* to hate
evil: pride, and arrogancy, and the evil
way, and the froward mouth, do I hate.
14 Counsel *is* mine, and sound wisdom: I *am* understanding; I have
strength.
15 By me kings reign, and princes decree justice.
16 By me princes rule, and nobles,
even all the judges of the earth.
17 I love them that love me; and those
that seek me early shall find me.
18 Riches and honour *are* with me; *yea,*
durable riches and righteousness.
19 My fruit *is* better than gold, yea,
than fine gold; and my revenue than
choice silver.
20 I lead in the way of righteousness,
in the midst of the paths of *judgment:
21 That I may cause those that love
me to inherit substance; and I will fill
their treasures.
22 The LORD possessed me in the beginning of his way, before his works of
old.
23 I was set up from everlasting, from
the beginning, or ever the earth was.
24 When *there were* no depths, I was

8:4 Unto you, O men, I call. See verse 22 note, "Five Things about Wisdom."
8:5 fools. Dull or stupid.

brought forth; when *there were* no fountains abounding with water.
[25]Before the mountains were settled, before the hills was I brought
forth:
[26]While as yet he had not made the
earth, nor the fields, nor the highest
part of the dust of the *world.
[27]When he prepared the heavens, I
was there: when he set a compass upon
the face of the depth:
[28]When he established the clouds
above: when he strengthened the fountains of the deep:
[29]When he gave to the sea his decree,
that the waters should not pass his
commandment: when he appointed the
foundations of the earth:
[30]Then I was by him, *as* one brought
up *with him:* and I was daily *his* delight,
rejoicing always before him;
[31]Rejoicing in the habitable part of his
earth; and my delights *were* with the
sons of men.
[32]Now therefore hearken unto me, O
ye children: for blessed *are they that*
keep my ways.
[33]Hear instruction, and be wise, and
refuse it not.
[34]Blessed *is* the man that heareth me,
watching daily at my gates, waiting at
the posts of my doors.
[35]For whoso findeth me findeth life,
and shall obtain favour of the LORD.
[36]But he that sinneth against me
wrongeth his own soul: all they that
hate me love *death.

2) This wisdom delivers from sin

9 Wisdom hath builded her house,
she hath hewn out her seven pillars:
[2]She hath killed her beasts; she hath
mingled her *wine; she hath also furnished her table.
[3]She hath sent forth her maidens:
she crieth upon the highest places of
the city,
[4]Whoso *is* simple, let him turn in
hither: *as for* him that wanteth understanding, she saith to him,
[5]Come, eat of my bread, and drink of
the wine *which* I have mingled.
[6]Forsake the foolish, and live; and go
in the way of understanding.
[7]He that reproveth a scorner getteth
to himself shame: and he that rebuketh
a wicked *man getteth* himself a blot.
[8]Reprove not a scorner, lest he hate
thee: rebuke a wise man, and he will
love thee.
[9]Give *instruction* to a wise *man,* and
he will be yet wiser: teach a *just *man,*
and he will increase in learning.
[10]The fear of the LORD *is* the beginning of wisdom: and the knowledge of
the *holy *is* understanding.
[11]For by me thy days shall be multiplied, and the years of thy life shall be
increased.
[12]If thou be wise, thou shalt be wise
for thyself: but *if* thou scornest, thou
alone shalt bear *it.*
¶[13]A foolish woman *is* clamorous: *she*
is simple, and knoweth nothing.

8:22 FIVE THINGS ABOUT WISDOM

This passage says five things about wisdom:

1. Wisdom belongs to God eternally: "in the beginning of his way" (vs. 22).
2. Wisdom was before creation: "from the beginning, or ever the earth was" (vs. 23).
3. Wisdom existed eternally with God: "as one brought up with him" (vs. 30).
4. God found His pleasure in wisdom eternally: "I was daily his delight" (vs. 30).
5. It was the joy of wisdom to look forward to the creation of men and find pleasure in them: "my delights were with the sons of men" (vs. 31).

It is easy to see that this wisdom is more than knowledge. This wisdom is personal, and the five things said about it are true only of the Lord Jesus and His position in the Godhead (Col. 2:9) before He became "flesh and dwelt among us" (John 1:14). It is Christ Himself who is presented as wisdom in this chapter, just as He is presented as the Word in John 1:1-14 (see also John 1:1 note, "The Word").

14 For she sitteth at the door of her house, on a seat in the high places of the city,

15 To call passengers who go right on their ways:

16 Whoso *is* simple, let him turn in hither: and *as for* him that wanteth understanding, she saith to him,

17 Stolen waters are sweet, and bread *eaten* in secret is pleasant.

18 But he knoweth not that the dead *are* there; *and that* her guests *are* in the depths of hell.

III. Godliness Versus Wickedness (10:1—31:31)

10 The *proverbs of Solomon. A wise son maketh a glad father: but a foolish son *is* the heaviness of his mother.

2 Treasures of wickedness profit nothing: but righteousness delivereth from death.

3 The LORD will not suffer the soul of the righteous to famish: but he casteth away the substance of the wicked.

4 He becometh poor that dealeth *with* a slack hand: but the hand of the diligent maketh rich.

5 He that gathereth in summer *is* a wise son: *but* he that sleepeth in harvest *is* a son that causeth shame.

6 Blessings *are* upon the head of the just: but violence covereth the mouth of the wicked.

7 The memory of the just *is* blessed: but the name of the wicked shall rot.

8 The wise in heart will receive commandments: but a prating fool shall fall.

9 He that walketh uprightly walketh surely: but he that perverteth his ways shall be known.

10 He that winketh with the eye causeth sorrow: but a prating fool shall fall.

11 The mouth of a righteous *man is* a well of life: but violence covereth the mouth of the wicked.

12 Hatred stirreth up strifes: but love covereth all sins.

13 In the lips of him that hath understanding wisdom is found: but a rod *is* for the back of him that is void of understanding.

14 Wise *men* lay up knowledge: but the mouth of the foolish *is* near destruction.

15 The rich man's wealth *is* his strong city: the destruction of the poor *is* their poverty.

16 The labour of the righteous *tendeth* to life: the fruit of the wicked to *sin.

17 He *is in* the way of life that keepeth instruction: but he that refuseth reproof erreth.

18 He that hideth hatred *with* lying lips, and he that uttereth a slander, *is* a fool.

19 In the multitude of words there wanteth not sin: but he that refraineth his lips *is* wise.

20 The tongue of the just *is as* choice silver: the heart of the wicked *is* little worth.

21 The lips of the righteous feed many: but fools die for want of wisdom.

22 The blessing of the LORD, it maketh rich, and he addeth no sorrow with it.

23 *It is* as sport to a fool to do mischief: but a man of understanding hath wisdom.

24 The fear of the wicked, it shall come upon him: but the desire of the righteous shall be granted.

25 As the whirlwind passeth, so *is* the wicked no *more:* but the righteous *is* an everlasting foundation.

26 As vinegar to the teeth, and as smoke to the eyes, so *is* the sluggard to them that send him.

27 The fear of the LORD prolongeth

10:1 foolish. Self-willed.
10:9 surely. Securely.
10:9 known. Found out and punished.
10:25 an everlasting foundation. Compare Matthew 7:24-27.

days: but the years of the wicked shall
be shortened.
28 The *hope of the righteous *shall be*
gladness: but the expectation of the
wicked shall perish.
29 The way of the LORD *is* strength to
the upright: but destruction *shall be* to
the workers of iniquity.
30 The righteous shall never be removed: but the wicked shall not inhabit the earth.
31 The mouth of the just bringeth
forth wisdom: but the *froward tongue
shall be cut out.
32 The lips of the righteous know
what is acceptable: but the mouth of the
wicked *speaketh* frowardness.

Godliness and wickedness (continued)

11 A false balance *is* *abomination
to the LORD: but a just weight *is*
his delight.
2 *When* pride cometh, then cometh
shame: but with the lowly *is* wisdom.
3 The integrity of the upright shall
guide them: but the perverseness of
transgressors shall destroy them.
4 Riches profit not in the day of wrath:
but righteousness delivereth from
death.
5 The righteousness of the perfect
shall direct his way: but the wicked
shall fall by his own wickedness.
6 The righteousness of the upright
shall deliver them: but transgressors
shall be taken in *their own* naughtiness.
7 When a wicked man dieth, *his* expectation shall perish: and the hope of
unjust *men* perisheth.
8 The righteous is delivered out of
trouble, and the wicked cometh in his
stead.
9 An hypocrite with *his* mouth
destroyeth his neighbour: but through
knowledge shall the just be delivered.
10 When it goeth well with the righteous, the city rejoiceth: and when the
wicked perish, *there is* shouting.
11 By the blessing of the upright the
city is exalted: but it is overthrown by
the mouth of the wicked.
12 He that is void of wisdom despiseth
his neighbour: but a man of understanding holdeth his peace.
13 A talebearer revealeth secrets: but
he that is of a faithful spirit concealeth
the matter.
14 Where no counsel *is,* the people
fall: but in the multitude of counsellors
there is safety.
15 He that is surety for a stranger shall
smart *for it:* and he that hateth sure-
tiship is sure.
16 A gracious woman retaineth honour: and strong *men* retain riches.
17 The merciful man doeth good to his
own soul: but *he that is* cruel troubleth
his own flesh.
18 The wicked worketh a deceitful
work: but to him that soweth righteousness *shall be* a sure reward.
19 As righteousness *tendeth* to life: so
he that pursueth evil *pursueth it* to his
own death.
20 They that are of a froward heart *are*
abomination to the LORD: but *such as*
are upright in *their* way *are* his delight.
21 *Though* hand *join* in hand, the
wicked shall not be unpunished: but
the seed of the righteous shall be delivered.
22 *As* a jewel of gold in a swine's
snout, *so is* a fair woman which is without discretion.
23 The desire of the righteous *is* only
good: *but* the expectation of the wicked *is* wrath.
24 There is that scattereth, and yet

11:4 day of wrath. See *Day of the LORD.
11:12 wisdom. Compassion or sympathy in this verse.
11:12 despiseth. Reproaches.
11:24 scattereth . . . withholdeth. This speaks of a farmer sowing grain—a wise farmer scatters plenty of seed; a foolish farmer has a poor crop because he withholds the seed. In the same way, those who are wise and love the LORD will be happy to give to others—just as the farmer scatters and "yet increaseth." Those who are foolish and

increaseth; and *there is* that withholdeth
more than is meet, but *it tendeth* to
poverty.
25The liberal soul shall be made fat:
and he that watereth shall be watered
also himself.
26He that withholdeth corn, the
people shall curse him: but blessing
shall be upon the head of him that
selleth *it*.
27He that diligently seeketh good
procureth favour: but he that seeketh
mischief, it shall come unto him.
28He that trusteth in his riches shall
fall: but the righteous shall flourish as
a branch.
29He that troubleth his own house
shall inherit the wind: and the fool *shall*
be servant to the wise of heart.
30The fruit of the righteous *is* a *tree
of life; and he that winneth souls *is*
wise.
31Behold, the righteous shall be recompensed in the earth: much more the
wicked and the sinner.

Godliness and wickedness (continued)

12 Whoso loveth instruction loveth
knowledge: but he that hateth
reproof *is* brutish.
2A good *man* obtaineth favour of the
LORD: but a man of wicked devices will
he condemn.
3A man shall not be established by
wickedness: but the root of the righteous shall not be moved.
4A virtuous woman *is* a crown to her
husband: but she that maketh ashamed
is as rottenness in his bones.
5The thoughts of the righteous *are*
right: *but* the counsels of the wicked *are*
deceit.
6The words of the wicked *are* to lie
in wait for blood: but the mouth of the
upright shall deliver them.
7The wicked are overthrown, and *are*
not: but the house of the righteous shall
stand.
8A man shall be commended according to his wisdom: but he that is of a
perverse heart shall be despised.
9*He that is* despised, and hath a servant, *is* better than he that honoureth
himself, and lacketh bread.
10A righteous *man* regardeth the life
of his beast: but the tender mercies of
the wicked *are* cruel.
11He that tilleth his land shall be
satisfied with bread: but he that followeth vain *persons is* void of understanding.
12The wicked desireth the net of evil
men: but the root of the righteous
yieldeth *fruit*.
13The wicked is snared by the transgression of *his* lips: but the just shall
come out of trouble.
14A man shall be satisfied with good
by the fruit of *his* mouth: and the recompense of a man's hands shall be rendered unto him.
15The way of a fool *is* right in his own
eyes: but he that hearkeneth unto counsel *is* wise.
16A fool's wrath is presently known:
but a prudent *man* covereth shame.
17*He that* speaketh truth sheweth
forth righteousness: but a false witness
deceit.
18There is that speaketh like the
piercings of a sword: but the tongue of
the wise *is* health.
19The lip of truth shall be established
for ever: but a lying tongue *is* but for a
moment.
20Deceit *is* in the heart of them that

---

selfish hoard their money and possessions and that "tendeth to poverty." God loves a cheerful giver (2 Cor. 9:7). Paradoxically, the more we give, the more we get, whether it be financially or in other ways, though that should not be our motivation for giving.

12:9 He that is despised. This speaks of a man who is not noticed but who has worked faithfully so he is able to have a servant.

12:18 like the piercings of a sword. Bitter words cut like a sword; wise words bring comfort.

imagine evil: but to the counsellors of
peace *is* joy.
21There shall no evil happen to the
just: but the wicked shall be filled with
mischief.
22Lying lips *are* abomination to the
LORD: but they that deal truly *are* his
delight.
23A prudent man concealeth knowledge: but the heart of fools proclaimeth
foolishness.
24The hand of the diligent shall bear
rule: but the slothful shall be under
tribute.
25Heaviness in the heart of man maketh it stoop: but a good word maketh it
glad.
26The righteous *is* more excellent
than his neighbour: but the way of the
wicked seduceth them.
27The slothful *man* roasteth not that
which he took in hunting: but the substance of a diligent man *is* precious.
28In the way of righteousness *is* life;
and *in* the pathway *thereof there is* no
death.

Godliness and wickedness (continued)

13 A wise son *heareth* his father's
instruction: but a scorner heareth
not rebuke.
2A man shall eat good by the fruit of
his mouth: but the soul of the transgressors *shall eat* violence.
3He that keepeth his mouth keepeth
his life: *but* he that openeth wide his lips
shall have destruction.
4The soul of the sluggard desireth,
and *hath* nothing: but the soul of the
diligent shall be made fat.
5A righteous *man* hateth lying: but a
wicked *man* is loathsome, and cometh
to shame.
6Righteousness keepeth *him that is*
upright in the way: but wickedness
overthroweth the sinner.
7There is that maketh himself rich,
yet *hath* nothing: *there is* that maketh
himself poor, yet *hath* great riches.
8The ransom of a man's life *are* his
riches: but the poor heareth not rebuke.
9The light of the righteous rejoiceth:
but the lamp of the wicked shall be put
out.
10Only by pride cometh contention:
but with the well advised *is* wisdom.
11Wealth *gotten* by *vanity shall be
diminished: but he that gathereth by
labour shall increase.
12Hope deferred maketh the heart
sick: but *when* the desire cometh, *it is*
a tree of life.
13Whoso despiseth the word shall be
destroyed: but he that *feareth the
commandment shall be rewarded.
14The *law of the wise *is* a fountain
of life, to depart from the snares of
death.
15Good understanding giveth favour:
but the way of transgressors *is* hard.
16Every prudent *man* dealeth with
knowledge: but a *fool layeth open *his*
folly.
17A wicked messenger falleth into
mischief: but a faithful ambassador *is*
health.
18Poverty and shame *shall be to* him
that refuseth instruction: but he that
regardeth reproof shall be honoured.
19The desire accomplished is sweet

12:21 no evil. Nothing will happen to the just by accident; everything is in agreement with God's plan. Compare Romans 8:28.

12:22 abomination. A hateful thing such as an idol or object of worship. In this verse, it refers to lying, which God hates.

12:23 concealeth knowledge. The truly wise do not talk loudly of their learning. They are secure enough in their God-given abilities and God's blessing that they don't need to show off.

12:26 more excellent. The righteous are good examples to their neighbors, but the wicked try to lead their neighbors into sin.

13:9 lamp. Compare the thought of this verse with Matthew 25:1-13.

13:13 the word. The Word of God.

to the soul: but *it is* abomination to fools
to depart from evil.
20He that walketh with wise *men*
shall be wise: but a companion of fools
shall be destroyed.
21Evil pursueth sinners: but to the
righteous good shall be repayed.
22A good *man* leaveth an inheritance
to his children's children: and the wealth
of the sinner *is* laid up for the just.
23Much food *is in* the tillage of the
poor: but there is *that is* destroyed for
want of judgment.
24He that spareth his rod hateth his
son: but he that loveth him *chasteneth
him betimes.
25The righteous eateth to the satisfying of his soul: but the belly of the
wicked shall want.

Godliness and wickedness (continued)

14 Every wise woman buildeth
her house: but the foolish
plucketh it down with her hands.
2He that walketh in his uprightness
feareth the LORD: but *he that is* perverse in his ways despiseth him.
3In the mouth of the foolish *is* a rod
of pride: but the lips of the wise shall
preserve them.
4Where no oxen *are,* the crib *is* clean:
but much increase *is* by the strength of
the ox.
5A faithful witness will not lie: but a
false witness will utter lies.
6A scorner seeketh wisdom, and
findeth it not: but knowledge *is* easy
unto him that understandeth.
7Go from the presence of a foolish
man, when thou perceivest not *in him*
the lips of knowledge.
8The wisdom of the prudent *is* to
understand his way: but the folly of
*fools *is* deceit.
9Fools make a mock at sin: but among
the righteous *there is* favour.
10The heart knoweth his own bitterness; and a stranger doth not intermeddle with his joy.
11The house of the wicked shall be
overthrown: but the *tabernacle of the
upright shall flourish.
12There is a way which seemeth right
unto a man, but the end thereof *are* the
ways of *death.
13Even in laughter the heart is sorrowful; and the end of that mirth *is*
heaviness.
14The backslider in heart shall be
filled with his own ways: and a good
man *shall be satisfied* from himself.
15The simple believeth every word:
but the prudent *man* looketh well to his
going.
16A wise *man* feareth, and departeth
from evil: but the fool rageth, and is
confident.
17*He that is* soon angry dealeth foolishly: and a man of wicked devices is
hated.
18The simple inherit folly: but the
prudent are crowned with knowledge.
19The evil bow before the good; and
the wicked at the gates of the righteous.
20The poor is hated even of his own

13:22 an inheritance. This does not necessarily mean money. It may mean a good name, a fine reputation, and/or a legacy of godliness and service to the LORD, which is much more valuable than money.

13:24 chasteneth. See Proverbs 3:11 note, "The Chastening of the LORD."

14:10 a stranger. A stranger to God cannot understand the heart of a believer—either the believer's unhappiness and bitterness when there is unconfessed sin in his life, or his joy when he comes to God and confesses that sin and is restored to fellowship.

14:11 overthrown. Our Lord made use of the thought of this verse in the parable of the house built upon the sand and the house built upon the rock (Matt. 7:24-27). Only the life that is founded upon Christ will endure forever.

14:12 There is a way. False religions, not in accordance with the Word of God, are ways that may seem right, but they lead to death. Those who take part in such religions may even seem joyful, but their hearts are heavy (vs. 13). Only the Lord Jesus Christ can give full, true, and lasting joy, as well as eternal life.

neighbour: but the rich *hath* many
friends.
21 He that despiseth his neighbour
sinneth: but he that hath *mercy on the
poor, happy *is* he.
22 Do they not *err that devise evil?
but mercy and truth *shall be* to them
that devise good.
23 In all labour there is profit: but the
talk of the lips *tendeth* only to penury.
24 The crown of the wise *is* their
riches: *but* the foolishness of fools *is*
folly.
25 A true witness delivereth souls: but
a deceitful *witness* speaketh lies.
26 In the *fear of the LORD *is* strong
confidence: and his children shall have
a place of refuge.
27 The fear of the LORD *is* a fountain
of life, to depart from the snares of
death.
28 In the multitude of people *is* the
king's honour: but in the want of people *is* the destruction of the prince.
29 *He that is* slow to wrath *is* of great
understanding: but *he that is* hasty of
spirit exalteth folly.
30 A sound heart *is* the life of the flesh:
but envy the rottenness of the bones.
31 He that oppresseth the poor reproacheth his Maker: but he that honoureth him hath mercy on the poor.
32 The wicked is driven away in his
wickedness: but the righteous hath
hope in his death.
33 Wisdom resteth in the heart of him
that hath understanding: but *that which*
is in the midst of fools is made known.
34 *Righteousness exalteth a nation:
but sin *is* a reproach to any people.
35 The king's favour *is* toward a wise
servant: but his wrath is *against* him
that causeth shame.

Godliness and wickedness (continued)

15 A soft answer turneth away
wrath: but grievous words stir
up anger.
2 The tongue of the wise useth knowledge aright: but the mouth of fools
poureth out foolishness.
3 The eyes of the LORD *are* in every
place, beholding the evil and the good.
4 A wholesome tongue *is* a tree of life:
but perverseness therein *is* a breach in
the spirit.
5 A fool despiseth his father's instruction: but he that regardeth reproof is
prudent.
6 In the house of the righteous *is*
much treasure: but in the revenues of
the wicked is trouble.
7 The lips of the wise disperse knowledge: but the heart of the foolish *doeth*
not so.
8 The *sacrifice of the wicked *is* an
abomination to the LORD: but the
*prayer of the upright *is* his delight.
9 The way of the wicked *is* an abomination unto the LORD: but he loveth him
that followeth after righteousness.
10 Correction *is* grievous unto him
that forsaketh the way: *and* he that
hateth reproof shall die.
11 *Hell and destruction *are* before
the LORD: how much more then the
hearts of the children of men?
12 A scorner loveth not one that reproveth him: neither will he go unto the
wise.

14:31 his Maker. This verse presents the truth that Christ expressed in Matthew 25:31-46, "Inasmuch as ye have done it unto one of the least of these my brethren, ye have done it unto me" (vs. 40), for the Lord is our Maker.

15:1 soft answer . . . grievous words. There is a sharp contrast between what happens if we answer someone quietly and calmly rather than sharply and angrily. We can choose how to respond to conflict–the wise way is to prevent an argument by giving a "soft answer."

15:6 much treasure. All the unsearchable riches of Christ (see Eph. 1:3 and its note, "Heavenly Things"; 3:8).

15:11 before the LORD. The LORD sees all and knows all about the unseen world; how much more does He know the hearts of men!

13A merry heart maketh a cheerful
countenance: but by sorrow of the heart
the spirit is broken.
14The heart of him that hath understanding seeketh knowledge: but the
mouth of fools feedeth on foolishness.
15All the days of the afflicted *are* evil:
but he that is of a merry heart *hath* a
continual feast.
16Better *is* little with the fear of the
LORD than great treasure and trouble
therewith.
17Better *is* a dinner of herbs where
love is, than a stalled ox and hatred
therewith.
18A wrathful man stirreth up strife:
but *he that is* slow to anger appeaseth
strife.
19The way of the slothful *man is* as
an hedge of thorns: but the way of the
righteous *is* made plain.
20A wise son maketh a glad father:
but a foolish man despiseth his mother.
21Folly *is* joy to *him that is* destitute
of wisdom: but a man of understanding
walketh uprightly.
22Without counsel purposes are disappointed: but in the multitude of counsellors they are established.
23A man hath joy by the answer of his
mouth: and a word *spoken* in due season, how good *is it!*
24The way of life *is* above to the wise,
that he may depart from hell beneath.
25The LORD will destroy the house of
the proud: but he will establish the border of the widow.
26The thoughts of the wicked *are* an
abomination to the LORD: but *the words*
of the pure *are* pleasant words.
27He that is greedy of gain troubleth
his own house; but he that hateth gifts
shall live.
28The heart of the righteous studieth
to answer: but the mouth of the wicked poureth out evil things.
29The LORD *is* far from the wicked:
but he heareth the prayer of the righteous.
30The light of the eyes rejoiceth the
heart: *and* a good report maketh the
bones fat.
31The ear that heareth the reproof of
life abideth among the wise.
32He that refuseth instruction
despiseth his own soul: but he that
heareth reproof getteth understanding.
33The fear of the LORD *is* the instruction of wisdom; and before honour *is*
humility.

Godliness and wickedness (continued)

16 The preparations of the heart
in man, and the answer of the
tongue, *is* from the LORD.
2All the ways of a man *are* clean in his
own eyes; but the LORD weigheth the
spirits.
3Commit thy works unto the LORD,
and thy thoughts shall be established.

16:3 Controlling Our Thoughts
Many Christians lack strength and victory in their thoughts. They seem to have no control over them. This is so, even though we have received from God not "the spirit of fear; but of power, and of love, and of a sound mind" (2 Tim. 1:7). Paul teaches us that God has given Christians weapons that will enable them to bring "into captivity every thought to the obedience of Christ" (2 Cor. 10:5). Proverbs 16:3 teaches us how we can have this victory. If we allow God to take care of our works and commit everything to Him, He will also take care of our thoughts.

4The LORD hath made all *things* for
himself: yea, even the wicked for the
day of evil.
5Every one *that is* proud in heart *is*
an abomination to the LORD: *though*
hand *join* in hand, he shall not be unpunished.
6By mercy and truth iniquity is purged:

15:25 the border of the widow. The LORD will even take care of even the *boundaries* of the home of the widow.
15:26 pleasant words. Pleasing to God.

16:4 A Teaching Clarified
There is a great deal of false teaching based on this verse. It is even taught that God made some people wicked for Himself, but this is not true. To the contrary, Ecclesiastes 7:29 tells us that "God hath made man upright; but they have sought out many inventions." God does not cause evil (see James 1:13), although He can use even wicked people's actions to further His purposes (see Gen. 50:20). God made the *Day of Judgment that He Himself might be vindicated in all His holiness, and man, wicked by his own device, falls under the judgment of God.

and by the fear of the LORD *men* depart
from evil.
[7]When a man's ways please the
LORD, he maketh even his enemies to
be at peace with him.
[8]Better *is* a little with righteousness
than great revenues without right.
[9]A man's heart deviseth his way: but
the LORD directeth his steps.
[10]A divine sentence *is* in the lips of
the king: his mouth transgresseth not
in judgment.
[11]A *just weight and balance *are* the
LORD'S: all the *weights of the bag *are*
his work.
[12]*It is* an abomination to kings to
commit wickedness: for the throne is
established by righteousness.
[13]Righteous lips *are* the delight of
kings; and they love him that speaketh
right.
[14]The wrath of a king *is as* messengers of death: but a wise man will pacify it.
[15]In the light of the king's countenance *is* life; and his favour *is* as a cloud
of the latter rain.
[16]How much better *is it* to get wisdom than gold! and to get understanding rather to be chosen than silver!
[17]The highway of the upright *is* to
depart from evil: he that keepeth his
way preserveth his soul.
[18]Pride *goeth* before destruction, and
an haughty spirit before a fall.
[19]Better *it is to be* of an humble spirit
with the lowly, than to divide the spoil
with the proud.
[20]He that handleth a matter wisely
shall find good: and whoso trusteth in
the LORD, happy *is* he.
[21]The wise in heart shall be called
prudent: and the sweetness of the lips
increaseth learning.
[22]Understanding *is* a wellspring of
life unto him that hath it: but the instruction of fools *is* folly.
[23]The heart of the wise teacheth his
mouth, and addeth learning to his lips.
[24]Pleasant words *are as* an honeycomb, sweet to the soul, and health to
the bones.
[25]There is a way that seemeth right
unto a man, but the end thereof *are* the
ways of death.
[26]He that laboureth laboureth for
himself; for his mouth craveth it of him.
[27]An ungodly man diggeth up evil:
and in his lips *there is* as a burning fire.
[28]A *froward man soweth strife: and
a whisperer separateth chief friends.
[29]A violent man enticeth his neighbour, and leadeth him into the way *that*
is not good.
[30]He shutteth his eyes to devise
froward things: moving his lips he
bringeth evil to pass.
[31]The hoary head *is* a crown of glory,
if it be found in the way of righteousness.
[32]*He that is* slow to anger *is* better
than the mighty; and he that ruleth his
spirit than he that taketh a city.
[33]The lot is cast into the lap; but the
whole disposing thereof *is* of the LORD.

16:6 purged. Atoned for. At Calvary the Lord Jesus Christ, who is the Truth (John 14:6), in His mercy took the sin of the world upon Himself.
16:25 There is a way. See Proverbs 14:12. When the Holy Spirit repeats a truth, it is always done for additional emphasis.
16:33 The lot is cast into the lap. Though men may cast lots and make their own plans and schemes, God will carry out His plans.

Godliness and wickedness (continued)

17 Better *is* a dry morsel, and quietness therewith, than an house full of sacrifices *with* strife.

2 A wise servant shall have rule over a son that causeth shame, and shall have part of the inheritance among the brethren.

3 The *fining pot *is* for silver, and the furnace for gold: but the LORD trieth the hearts.

4 A wicked doer giveth heed to false lips; *and* a liar giveth ear to a naughty tongue.

5 Whoso mocketh the poor reproacheth his Maker: *and* he that is glad at calamities shall not be unpunished.

6 Children's children *are* the crown of old men; and the glory of children *are* their fathers.

7 Excellent speech becometh not a fool: much less do lying lips a prince.

8 A gift *is as* a precious stone in the eyes of him that hath it: whithersoever it turneth, it prospereth.

9 He that covereth a transgression seeketh love; but he that repeateth a matter separateth *very* friends.

10 A reproof entereth more into a wise man than an hundred stripes into a fool.

11 An evil *man* seeketh only rebellion: therefore a cruel messenger shall be sent against him.

12 Let a bear robbed of her whelps meet a man, rather than a fool in his folly.

13 Whoso rewardeth evil for good, evil shall not depart from his house.

14 The beginning of strife *is as* when one letteth out water: therefore leave off contention, before it be meddled with.

15 He that justifieth the wicked, and he that condemneth the just, even they both *are* *abomination to the LORD.

16 Wherefore *is there* a price in the hand of a fool to get wisdom, seeing *he hath* no heart *to it?*

17 A friend loveth at all times, and a brother is born for adversity.

18 A man void of understanding striketh hands, *and* becometh surety in the presence of his friend.

19 He loveth transgression that loveth strife: *and* he that exalteth his gate seeketh destruction.

20 He that hath a froward heart findeth no good: and he that hath a perverse tongue falleth into mischief.

21 He that begetteth a fool *doeth it* to his sorrow: and the father of a fool hath no joy.

22 A merry heart doeth good *like* a medicine: but a broken spirit drieth the bones.

23 A wicked *man* taketh a gift out of the bosom to pervert the ways of judgment.

24 Wisdom *is* before him that hath understanding; but the eyes of a fool *are* in the ends of the earth.

25 A foolish son *is* a grief to his father, and bitterness to her that bare him.

26 Also to punish the just *is* not good, *nor* to strike princes for equity.

27 He that hath knowledge spareth his words: *and* a man of understanding is of an excellent spirit.

28 Even a fool, when he holdeth his peace, is counted wise: *and* he that shutteth his lips *is esteemed* a man of understanding.

Godliness and wickedness (continued)

18 Through desire a man, having separated himself, seeketh *and* intermeddleth with all wisdom.

17:3 The fining pot. The refining pot. See 1 Peter 1:7.

17:10 stripes. Blows made by whips and the marks they leave.

17:19 exalteth his gate. In the East, a rich man has a high door; a poor man's is low. Therefore, one who exalts his gate is boasting to everyone that he has become wealthy.

17:23 a gift out of the bosom. In a fold of the robes, Easterners carry their money. This "gift" of the wicked would have been a bribe.

2 A fool hath no delight in understanding, but that his heart may discover
itself.
3 When the wicked cometh, *then*
cometh also contempt, and with ignominy reproach.
4 The words of a man's mouth *are as*
deep waters, *and* the wellspring of wisdom *as* a flowing brook.
5 *It is* not good to accept the person
of the wicked, to overthrow the righteous in judgment.
6 A fool's lips enter into contention,
and his mouth calleth for strokes.
7 A fool's mouth *is* his destruction,
and his lips *are* the snare of his soul.
8 The words of a talebearer *are* as
wounds, and they go down into the innermost parts of the belly.
9 He also that is slothful in his work
is brother to him that is a great waster.
10 The name of the LORD *is* a strong
tower: the righteous runneth into it,
and is safe.
11 The rich man's wealth *is* his strong
city, and as an high wall in his own conceit.
12 Before destruction the heart of
man is haughty, and before honour *is*
humility.
13 He that answereth a matter before he
heareth *it,* it *is* folly and shame unto him.
14 The spirit of a man will sustain his
infirmity; but a wounded spirit who can
bear?
15 The heart of the prudent getteth
knowledge; and the ear of the wise
seeketh knowledge.
16 A man's gift maketh room for him,
and bringeth him before great men.
17 *He that is* first in his own cause
seemeth just; but his neighbour cometh
and searcheth him.
18 The lot causeth contentions to
cease, and parteth between the mighty.
19 A brother offended *is harder to be*
won than a strong city: and *their* contentions *are* like the bars of a castle.
20 A man's belly shall be satisfied with
the fruit of his mouth; *and* with the increase of his lips shall he be filled.
21 Death and life *are* in the power of
the tongue: and they that love it shall
eat the fruit thereof.
22 *Whoso* findeth a wife findeth a good
thing, and obtaineth favour of the LORD.
23 The poor useth intreaties; but the
rich answereth roughly.
24 A man *that hath* friends must shew
himself friendly: and there is a friend
that sticketh closer than a brother.

Godliness and wickedness (continued)

19 Better *is* the poor that walketh
in his integrity, than *he that is*
perverse in his lips, and is a *fool.
2 Also, *that* the soul *be* without knowledge, *it is* not good; and he that hasteth
with *his* feet sinneth.
3 The foolishness of man perverteth
his way: and his heart fretteth against
the LORD.
4 Wealth maketh many friends; but
the poor is separated from his neighbour.
5 A false witness shall not be unpunished, and *he that* speaketh lies shall not
escape.
6 Many will intreat the favour of the
prince: and every man *is* a friend to him
that giveth gifts.
7 All the brethren of the poor do hate
him: how much more do his friends go
far from him? he pursueth *them with*
words, *yet* they *are* wanting *to him.*
8 He that getteth wisdom loveth his

18:10 The name of the LORD. Compare verses 10 and 11. The rich man trusts in his wealth in "his own conceit," but the righteous man is truly "safe" in the LORD's care.

18:21 it. The power of the tongue.

18:22 findeth a good thing, and obtaineth favour. God created marriage and pronounced it good (see Gen. 2:18,21-25). Strong marriages, those based on Christ, are important and needed in today's society. Jesus' first miracle was at a wedding (see John 2:1-11).

19:2 hasteth with his feet. Trying to become rich quickly leads to sin. Don't jump into anything hastily, financial or otherwise, without consulting the LORD.

own soul: he that keepeth understanding shall find good.
9 A false witness shall not be unpunished, and *he that* speaketh lies shall
perish.
10 Delight is not seemly for a fool;
much less for a servant to have rule
over princes.
11 The discretion of a man deferreth
his anger; and *it is* his glory to pass over
a transgression.
12 The king's wrath *is* as the roaring
of a lion; but his favour *is* as dew upon
the grass.
13 A foolish son *is* the calamity of his
father: and the contentions of a wife *are*
a continual dropping.
14 House and riches *are* the inheritance of fathers: and a prudent wife *is*
from the LORD.
15 Slothfulness casteth into a deep
sleep; and an idle soul shall suffer
hunger.
16 He that keepeth the commandment
keepeth his own soul; *but* he that
despiseth his ways shall die.
17 He that hath pity upon the poor
lendeth unto the LORD; and that which
he hath given will he pay him again.
18 *Chasten thy son while there is
hope, and let not thy soul spare for his
crying.
19 A man of great wrath shall suffer
punishment: for if thou deliver *him,* yet
thou must do it again.
20 Hear counsel, and receive instruction, that thou mayest be wise in thy
latter end.
21 *There are* many devices in a man's
heart; nevertheless the counsel of the
LORD, that shall stand.
22 The desire of a man *is* his kindness:
and a poor man *is* better than a liar.
23 The fear of the LORD *tendeth* to life:
and *he that hath it* shall abide satisfied;
he shall not be visited with evil.
24 A slothful *man* hideth his hand in
his bosom, and will not so much as bring
it to his mouth again.
25 Smite a scorner, and the simple will
beware: and reprove one that hath understanding, *and* he will understand
knowledge.
26 He that wasteth *his* father, *and*
chaseth away *his* mother, *is* a son that
causeth shame, and bringeth reproach.
27 Cease, my son, to hear the instruction *that causeth* to *err from the words
of knowledge.
28 An ungodly witness scorneth judgment: and the mouth of the wicked
devoureth iniquity.
29 Judgments are prepared for
scorners, and stripes for the back of
fools.

Godliness and wickedness (continued)

20 *Wine *is* a mocker, strong drink
is raging: and whosoever is deceived thereby is not wise.
2 The fear of a king *is* as the roaring
of a lion: *whoso* provoketh him to anger
sinneth *against* his own soul.
3 *It is* an honour for a man to cease
from strife: but every fool will be meddling.
4 The sluggard will not plow by reason of the cold; *therefore* shall he beg in
harvest, and *have* nothing.
5 Counsel in the heart of man *is like*
deep water; but a man of understanding will draw it out.
6 Most men will proclaim every one
his own goodness: but a faithful man
who can find?
7 The just *man* walketh in his integrity: his children *are* blessed after him.
8 A king that sitteth in the throne of

19:9 shall perish. The punishment of verse 5 is given here as the truth is emphasized.
19:16 the commandment. The Word of God.
19:19 thou must do it again. A man who has a bad temper must be helped again and again out of the troubles that he makes for himself.
19:24 A slothful man. A lazy man buries his hand in the dish and will not so much as bring it to his mouth again.

judgment scattereth away all evil with
his eyes.
[9]Who can say, I have made my heart
*clean, I am pure from my *sin?
[10]Divers *weights, *and* divers measures, both of them *are* alike abomination to the LORD.
[11]Even a child is known by his doings,
whether his work *be* pure, and whether *it be* right.
[12]The hearing ear, and the seeing
eye, the LORD hath made even both of
them.
[13]Love not sleep, lest thou come to
poverty; open thine eyes, *and* thou
shalt be satisfied with bread.
[14]*It is* naught, *it is* naught, saith the
buyer: but when he is gone his way,
then he boasteth.
[15]There is gold, and a multitude of
rubies: but the lips of knowledge *are* a
precious jewel.
[16]Take his garment that is surety *for*
a stranger: and take a pledge of him for
a strange woman.
[17]Bread of deceit *is* sweet to a man;
but afterwards his mouth shall be filled
with gravel.
[18]*Every* purpose is established by
counsel: and with good advice make
war.
[19]He that goeth about *as* a talebearer
revealeth secrets: therefore meddle not
with him that flattereth with his lips.
[20]Whoso curseth his father or his
mother, his lamp shall be put out in
obscure darkness.
[21]An inheritance *may be* gotten hastily at the beginning; but the end thereof
shall not be blessed.
[22]Say not thou, I will recompense
evil; *but* wait on the LORD, and he shall
save thee.
[23]Divers weights *are* an abomination
unto the LORD; and a false balance *is* not
good.
[24]Man's goings *are* of the LORD; how
can a man then understand his own
way?
[25]*It is* a snare to the man *who* devoureth *that which is* *holy, and after
vows to make enquiry.
[26]A wise king scattereth the wicked,
and bringeth the wheel over them.
[27]The spirit of man *is* the candle of
the LORD, searching all the inward parts
of the belly.

20:27 The Spirit of Man
Man differs from all animals because man can have fellowship with God. This is possible because man was created in the image of God (see Gen. 1:27 note, "In God's Image"). Sin has darkened men's minds, but the Holy Spirit enlightens men and brings them the knowledge of God (John 16:7-11).

[28]*Mercy and truth preserve the
king: and his throne is upholden by
mercy.
[29]The glory of young men *is* their
strength: and the beauty of old men *is*
the gray head.
[30]The blueness of a wound cleanseth
away evil: so *do* *stripes the inward
parts of the belly.

Godliness and wickedness (continued)

21 The king's heart *is* in the hand
of the LORD, *as* the rivers of

20:10 Divers weights, and divers measures. False weights and measures. This verse is repeated (vs. 23) to emphasize God's hatred of cheating.
20:17 Bread of deceit. Money or food earned by cheating or lying.
20:25 devoureth that which is holy. It is wrong for a man to say that a thing is holy and not make sure until after he has made his vows. We should not make vows to God hastily, without thinking and praying about it carefully. It is better to not make a vow than to make one and break it (Eccles. 5:4-5; see Eccles. 5:4 note).
20:27 the inward parts of the belly. The hidden thoughts of the heart.
21:1 as the rivers of water. In the East, rivers are redirected from their natural course to water or irrigate the land. Just as rivers can be redirected, so God can change or use anyone's heart, even that of kings, to accomplish His purposes.

water: he turneth it whithersoever
he will.
2 Every way of a man *is* right in his
own eyes: but the LORD pondereth the
hearts.
3 To do justice and judgment *is* more
acceptable to the LORD than *sacrifice.
4 An high look, and a proud heart, *and*
the plowing of the wicked, *is* sin.
5 The thoughts of the diligent *tend*
only to plenteousness; but of every one
that is hasty only to want.
6 The getting of treasures by a lying
tongue *is* a *vanity tossed to and fro of
them that seek *death.
7 The robbery of the wicked shall destroy them; because they refuse to do
judgment.
8 The way of man *is* *froward and
strange: but *as for* the pure, his work *is*
right.
9 *It is* better to dwell in a corner of the
housetop, than with a brawling woman
in a wide house.
10 The soul of the wicked desireth
evil: his neighbour findeth no favour in
his eyes.
11 When the scorner is punished,
the simple is made wise: and when the
wise is instructed, he receiveth knowledge.
12 The righteous *man* wisely considereth the house of the wicked: *but*
God overthroweth the wicked for *their*
wickedness.
13 Whoso stoppeth his ears at the cry
of the poor, he also shall cry himself, but
shall not be heard.
14 A gift in secret pacifieth anger: and
a reward in the bosom strong wrath.
15 *It is* joy to the just to do judgment:
but destruction *shall be* to the workers
of iniquity.
16 The man that wandereth out of the
way of understanding shall remain in
the congregation of the dead.
17 He that loveth pleasure *shall be* a
poor man: he that loveth wine and *oil
shall not be rich.
18 The wicked *shall be* a ransom for
the righteous, and the transgressor for
the upright.
19 *It is* better to dwell in the wilderness, than with a contentious and an
angry woman.
20 *There is* treasure to be desired and
oil in the dwelling of the wise; but a
foolish man spendeth it up.
21 He that followeth after *righteousness and mercy findeth life, righteousness, and honour.
22 A wise *man* scaleth the city of the
mighty, and casteth down the strength
of the confidence thereof.
23 Whoso keepeth his mouth and his
tongue keepeth his soul from troubles.
24 Proud *and* haughty scorner *is* his
name, who dealeth in proud wrath.
25 The desire of the slothful killeth
him; for his hands refuse to labour.
26 He coveteth greedily all the day
long: but the righteous giveth and
spareth not.
27 The sacrifice of the wicked *is* abomination: how much more, *when* he
bringeth it with a wicked mind?
28 A false witness shall perish: but the
man that heareth speaketh constantly.
29 A wicked man hardeneth his face:
but *as for* the upright, he directeth his
way.
30 *There is* no wisdom nor understanding nor counsel against the LORD.
31 The horse *is* prepared against the
day of battle: but safety *is* of the LORD.

Godliness and wickedness (continued)

22 A *good* name *is* rather to be chosen than great riches, *and* loving favour rather than silver and gold.
2 The rich and poor meet together:
the LORD *is* the maker of them all.

21:4 and the plowing of the wicked. Even the good things a lost person does are sinful.
21:8 The way of man is froward. The way of the guilty man is crooked.
21:27 mind. Purpose.
22:2 The rich and poor meet together. Before God, they are equal.

[3]A prudent *man* foreseeth the evil,
and hideth himself: but the simple pass
on, and are punished.
[4]By humility *and* the fear of the LORD
are riches, and honour, and life.
[5]Thorns *and* snares *are* in the way of
the froward: he that doth keep his soul
shall be far from them.
[6]Train up a child in the way he should
go: and when he is old, he will not depart from it.
[7]The rich ruleth over the poor, and
the borrower *is* servant to the lender.
[8]He that soweth iniquity shall reap
vanity: and the rod of his anger shall fail.
[9]He that hath a bountiful eye shall be
blessed; for he giveth of his bread to the
poor.
[10]Cast out the scorner, and contention shall go out; yea, strife and reproach shall cease.
[11]He that loveth pureness of heart,
for the grace of his lips the king *shall be*
his friend.

22:11 A Pure Heart
The Lord Jesus emphasized pureness of heart by saying, "Blessed are the pure in heart: for they shall see God" (Matt. 5:8). It is interesting to notice that in Matthew 5:8, "pure" means *cleansed*. Our hearts are made pure by the blood of Christ (Heb. 9:14).

[12]The eyes of the LORD preserve
knowledge, and he overthroweth the
words of the transgressor.
[13]The slothful *man* saith, *There is* a
lion without, I shall be slain in the
streets.
[14]The mouth of strange women *is* a
deep pit: he that is abhorred of the
LORD shall fall therein.
[15]Foolishness *is* bound in the heart of
a child; *but* the rod of correction shall
drive it far from him.
[16]He that oppresseth the poor to increase his *riches, and* he that giveth to
the rich, *shall* surely *come* to want.
[17]Bow down thine ear, and hear the
words of the wise, and apply thine heart
unto my knowledge.
[18]For *it is* a pleasant thing if thou keep
them within thee; they shall withal be
fitted in thy lips.
[19]That thy *trust may be in the LORD,
I have made known to thee this day,
even to thee.
[20]Have not I written to thee excellent
things in counsels and knowledge,
[21]That I might make thee know the
certainty of the words of truth; that
thou mightest answer the words of
truth to them that send unto thee?
[22]Rob not the poor, because he *is* poor:
neither oppress the afflicted in the gate:
[23]For the LORD will plead their cause,
and spoil the soul of those that spoiled
them.
[24]Make no friendship with an angry
man; and with a furious man thou shalt
not go:
[25]Lest thou learn his ways, and get a
snare to thy soul.
[26]Be not thou *one* of them that strike
hands, *or* of them that are sureties for
debts.
[27]If thou hast nothing to pay, why
should he take away thy bed from under thee?
[28]Remove not the ancient *landmark,
which thy fathers have set.
[29]Seest thou a man diligent in his
business? he shall stand before kings;
he shall not stand before mean *men.*

Godliness and wickedness (continued)

23 When thou sittest to eat with
a ruler, consider diligently what
is before thee:

22:13 There is a lion without. "Without" means *outside*. The lazy man does not care how foolish his excuse is for not working.
22:21 that thou mightest answer. Solomon had been taught excellent things (vs. 20) for a purpose. The queen of Sheba was one of the people who came to him for answers to her problems (1 Kings 10).
22:28 landmark. The boundary stone.
23:1 consider diligently what. Who, or, "him who is before thee."

[2]And put a knife to thy throat, if thou
be a man given to appetite.
[3]Be not desirous of his dainties: for
they *are* deceitful meat.
[4]Labour not to be rich: cease from
thine own wisdom.
[5]Wilt thou set thine eyes upon that
which is not? for *riches* certainly make
themselves wings; they fly away as an
eagle toward heaven.
[6]Eat thou not the bread of *him that*
hath an evil eye, neither desire thou his
dainty meats:
[7]For as he thinketh in his heart, so *is*
he: Eat and drink, saith he to thee; but
his heart *is* not with thee.
[8]The morsel *which* thou hast eaten
shalt thou vomit up, and lose thy sweet
words.
[9]Speak not in the ears of a fool: for he
will despise the wisdom of thy words.
[10]Remove not the old landmark; and
enter not into the fields of the fatherless:
[11]For their *redeemer *is* mighty; he
shall plead their cause with thee.
[12]Apply thine heart unto instruction,
and thine ears to the words of knowledge.
[13]Withhold not correction from the
child: for *if* thou beatest him with the
rod, he shall not die.
[14]Thou shalt beat him with the rod,
and shalt deliver his soul from *hell.
[15]My son, if thine heart be wise, my
heart shall rejoice, even mine.
[16]Yea, my *reins shall rejoice, when
thy lips speak right things.
[17]Let not thine heart envy sinners:
but *be thou* in the fear of the LORD all
the day long.
[18]For surely there is an end; and thine
expectation shall not be cut off.
[19]Hear thou, my son, and be wise,
and guide thine heart in the way.
[20]Be not among winebibbers; among
riotous eaters of flesh:
[21]For the drunkard and the glutton
shall come to poverty: and drowsiness
shall clothe *a man* with rags.
[22]Hearken unto thy father that begat
thee, and despise not thy mother when
she is old.
[23]Buy the truth, and sell *it* not; *also*
wisdom, and instruction, and understanding.
[24]The father of the righteous shall
greatly rejoice: and he that begetteth a
wise *child* shall have joy of him.
[25]Thy father and thy mother shall be
glad, and she that bare thee shall rejoice.
[26]My son, give me thine heart, and let
thine eyes observe my ways.
[27]For a *whore *is* a deep ditch; and a
strange woman *is* a narrow pit.
[28]She also lieth in wait as *for* a
prey, and increaseth the transgressors
among men.
[29]Who hath woe? who hath sorrow?
who hath contentions? who hath babbling? who hath wounds without cause?
who hath redness of eyes?
[30]They that tarry long at the wine;
they that go to seek mixed wine.
[31]Look not thou upon the wine when
it is red, when it giveth his colour in the
cup, *when* it moveth itself aright.
[32]At the last it biteth like a serpent,
and stingeth like an adder.
[33]Thine eyes shall behold strange
women, and thine heart shall utter perverse things.
[34]Yea, thou shalt be as he that lieth
down in the midst of the sea, or as he
that lieth upon the top of a mast.
[35]They have stricken me, *shalt thou*
say, and I was not sick; they have
beaten me, *and* I felt *it* not: when shall
I awake? I will seek it yet again.

23:2 And put a knife. You will ruin yourself.
23:18 an end; and thine expectation. A future and a hope—a life to come.
23:20 riotous. Gluttonous.
23:26 observe my ways. Delight in my ways.
23:27 whore . . . strange woman. An evil and adulterous woman.

Godliness and wickedness (continued)

24 Be not thou envious against
evil men, neither desire to be
with them.
2For their heart studieth destruction,
and their lips talk of mischief.
3Through wisdom is an house
builded; and by understanding it is established:
4And by knowledge shall the chambers be filled with all precious and
pleasant riches.
5A wise man *is* strong; yea, a man of
knowledge increaseth strength.
6For by wise counsel thou shalt make
thy war: and in multitude of counsellors
there is safety.
7Wisdom *is* too high for a fool: he
openeth not his mouth in the gate.
8He that deviseth to do evil shall be
called a mischievous person.
9The thought of foolishness *is* sin:
and the scorner *is* an *abomination to
men.
10*If* thou faint in the day of adversity,
thy strength *is* small.
11If thou forbear to deliver *them that
are* drawn unto death, and *those that are*
ready to be slain;
12If thou sayest, Behold, we knew it
not; doth not he that pondereth the
heart consider *it?* and he that keepeth
thy soul, doth *not* he know *it?* and shall
not he *render to *every* man according
to his works?
13My son, eat thou honey, because *it
is* good; and the honeycomb, *which is*
sweet to thy taste:
14So *shall* the knowledge of wisdom
be unto thy soul: when thou hast found
it, then there shall be a reward, and thy
expectation shall not be cut off.
15Lay not wait, O wicked *man,*
against the dwelling of the righteous;
spoil not his resting place:
16For a *just *man* falleth seven times,
and riseth up again: but the wicked shall
fall into mischief.
17Rejoice not when thine enemy
falleth, and let not thine heart be glad
when he stumbleth:
18Lest the LORD see *it,* and it displease him, and he turn away his wrath
from him.
19Fret not thyself because of evil
men, neither be thou envious at the
wicked;
20For there shall be no reward to the
evil *man;* the candle of the wicked shall
be put out.
21My son, fear thou the LORD and the
king: *and* meddle not with them that
are given to change:
22For their calamity shall rise suddenly; and who knoweth the ruin of
them both?
23These *things* also *belong* to the
wise. *It is* not good to have respect of
persons in judgment.
24He that saith unto the wicked, Thou
art righteous; him shall the people
curse, nations shall abhor him:
25But to them that rebuke *him* shall
be delight, and a good blessing shall
come upon them.
26*Every man* shall kiss *his* lips that
giveth a right answer.
27Prepare thy work without, and
make it fit for thyself in the field; and
afterwards build thine house.
28Be not a witness against thy neighbour without cause; and deceive *not*
with thy lips.
29Say not, I will do so to him as he
hath done to me: I will render to the
man according to his work.
30I went by the field of the slothful,

24:29 The Golden Rule
This verse presents the Golden Rule in negative form. We must not return evil for evil. When our Lord gave the Golden Rule He said, "Therefore all things whatsoever ye would that men should do to you, do ye even so to them" (Matt. 7:12).

24:6 safety. Victory.
24:26 kiss his lips. To honor.

and by the vineyard of the man void of
understanding;
31And, lo, it was all grown over with
thorns, *and* nettles had covered the face
thereof, and the stone wall thereof was
broken down.
32Then I saw, *and* considered *it* well:
I looked upon *it, and* received instruction.
33*Yet* a little sleep, a little slumber, a
little folding of the hands to sleep:
34So shall thy poverty come *as* one
that travelleth; and thy want as an
armed man.

Godliness and wickedness (continued)

25 These *are* also *proverbs of Solomon, which the men of *Hezekiah king of *Judah copied out.
2*It is* the glory of God to conceal a
thing: but the honour of kings *is* to
search out a matter.
3The heaven for height, and the earth
for depth, and the heart of kings *is* unsearchable.
4Take away the dross from the silver,
and there shall come forth a vessel for
the finer.
5Take away the wicked *from* before
the king, and his throne shall be established in righteousness.
6Put not forth thyself in the presence
of the king, and stand not in the place
of great *men:*
7For better *it is* that it be said unto
thee, Come up hither; than that thou
shouldest be put lower in the presence
of the prince whom thine eyes have
seen.
8Go not forth hastily to strive, lest
thou know not what to do in the end
thereof, when thy neighbour hath put
thee to shame.
9Debate thy cause with thy neighbour *himself;* and discover not a secret
to another:
10Lest he that heareth *it* put thee to
shame, and thine infamy turn not
away.
11A word fitly spoken *is like* apples of
gold in pictures of silver.
12*As* an earring of gold, and an ornament of fine gold, *so is* a wise reprover
upon an obedient ear.
13As the cold of snow in the time of
harvest, *so is* a faithful messenger to
them that send him: for he refresheth
the soul of his masters.
14Whoso boasteth himself of a false
gift *is like* clouds and wind without
rain.
15By long forbearing is a prince persuaded, and a soft tongue breaketh the
bone.
16Hast thou found honey? eat so
much as is sufficient for thee, lest thou
be filled therewith, and vomit it.
17Withdraw thy foot from thy
neighbour's house; lest he be weary of
thee, and *so* hate thee.
18A man that beareth false witness
against his neighbour *is* a maul, and a
sword, and a sharp arrow.
19Confidence in an unfaithful man in
time of trouble *is like* a broken tooth,
and a foot out of joint.
20*As* he that taketh away a garment
in cold weather, *and as* vinegar upon
nitre, so *is* he that singeth songs to an
heavy heart.
21If thine enemy be hungry, give him
bread to eat; and if he be thirsty, give
him water to drink:
22For thou shalt heap coals of fire
upon his head, and the LORD shall reward thee.
23The north wind driveth away rain:

25:11 pictures of silver. This literally means *baskets of silver.*

25:18 maul. A heavy hammer or a mallet. Lying or gossiping about someone is as vicious as if you hit him or her over the head with a club.

25:20 nitre. Carbonate of soda. One that "singeth songs to an heavy heart" is as inappropriate and wrong as mixing vinegar and soda or taking "away a garment in cold weather." Those who serve God are told to "rejoice with them that do rejoice, and weep with them that weep" (Rom. 12:15).

so *doth* an angry countenance a backbiting tongue.
24 *It is* better to dwell in the corner of
the housetop, than with a brawling
woman and in a wide house.
25 *As* cold waters to a thirsty soul, so
is good news from a far country.
26 A righteous man falling down before the wicked *is as* a troubled fountain, and a corrupt spring.
27 *It is* not good to eat much honey: so
for men to search their own glory *is not*
glory.
28 He that *hath* no rule over his own
spirit *is like* a city *that is* broken down,
and without walls.

Godliness and wickedness (continued)

26 As snow in summer, and as rain
in harvest, so honour is not
seemly for a *fool.
2 As the bird by wandering, as the
swallow by flying, so the curse causeless shall not come.
3 A whip for the horse, a bridle for the
ass, and a rod for the fool's back.
4 Answer not a fool according to his
folly, lest thou also be like unto him.
5 Answer a fool according to his folly,
lest he be wise in his own conceit.
6 He that sendeth a message by the
hand of a fool cutteth off the feet, *and*
drinketh damage.
7 The legs of the lame are not equal:
so *is* a *parable in the mouth of *fools.
8 As he that bindeth a stone in a sling,
so *is* he that giveth honour to a fool.
9 *As* a thorn goeth up into the hand of
a drunkard, so *is* a parable in the mouth
of fools.
10 The great *God* that formed all
things both rewardeth the fool, and
rewardeth transgressors.
11 As a dog returneth to his vomit, *so*
a fool returneth to his folly.
12 Seest thou a man wise in his own
conceit? *there is* more hope of a fool
than of him.
13 The slothful *man* saith, *There is* a
lion in the way; a lion *is* in the streets.
14 *As* the door turneth upon his hinges,
so *doth* the slothful upon his bed.
15 The slothful hideth his hand in *his*
bosom; it grieveth him to bring it again
to his mouth.
16 The sluggard *is* wiser in his own
conceit than seven men that can render
a reason.
17 He that passeth by, *and* meddleth
with strife *belonging* not to him, *is like*
one that taketh a dog by the ears.
18 As a mad *man* who casteth firebrands, arrows, and death,
19 So *is* the man *that* deceiveth his
neighbour, and saith, Am not I in sport?
20 Where no wood is, *there* the fire
goeth out: so where *there is* no talebearer, the strife ceaseth.
21 *As* coals *are* to burning coals, and
wood to fire; so *is* a contentious man to
kindle strife.
22 The words of a talebearer *are* as
wounds, and they go down into the innermost parts of the belly.
23 Burning lips and a wicked heart *are*
like a *potsherd covered with silver
dross.
24 He that hateth dissembleth with his
lips, and layeth up deceit within him;
25 When he speaketh fair, believe him

25:26 a troubled fountain. Just as a fountain or spring may be made impure, so the righteous who are not separated from the world are soon corrupted by the world.

26:4-5 Answer not a fool . . . Answer a fool. You cannot reason with a foolish man, because if you answer him so he will understand, you will become as foolish as he is; and if you answer him and he understands, he will think he is wise and be conceited. It is best to not even try to reason with a arrgoant fool.

26:8 As he that bindeth a stone. A stone tied up in a slingshot is useless, as is giving honor to someone who is not worthy of it.

26:9 a thorn . . . a parable. A thorn has a point as does a parable, but a drunkard cannot feel the thorn, and the fool does not understand the parable.

26:17 taketh a dog by the ears. This is a dangerous practice. Just as it is better not to bother a dog, it is best not to meddle with others' lives and problems.

not: for *there are* seven abominations in
his heart.
26 *Whose* hatred is covered by deceit,
his wickedness shall be shewed before
the *whole* congregation.
27 Whoso diggeth a pit shall fall
therein: and he that rolleth a stone, it
will return upon him.
28 A lying tongue hateth *those that are*
afflicted by it; and a flattering mouth
worketh ruin.

Godliness and wickedness (continued)

27 Boast not thyself of to morrow;
for thou knowest not what a day
may bring forth.
2 Let another man praise thee, and
not thine own mouth; a stranger, and
not thine own lips.
3 A stone *is* heavy, and the sand
weighty; but a fool's wrath *is* heavier
than them both.
4 Wrath *is* cruel, and anger *is* outrageous; but who *is* able to stand before
envy?
5 Open rebuke *is* better than secret
love.
6 Faithful *are* the wounds of a friend;
but the kisses of an enemy *are* deceitful.
7 The full soul loatheth an honeycomb; but to the hungry soul every bitter thing is sweet.
8 As a bird that wandereth from her
nest, so *is* a man that wandereth from
his place.
9 Ointment and perfume rejoice the
heart: so *doth* the sweetness of a man's
friend by hearty counsel.
10 Thine own friend, and thy father's
friend, forsake not; neither go into thy
brother's house in the day of thy calamity: *for* better *is* a neighbour *that is* near
than a brother far off.
11 My son, be wise, and make my
heart glad, that I may answer him that
reproacheth me.
12 A prudent *man* foreseeth the evil,
and hideth himself; *but* the simple pass
on, *and* are punished.
13 Take his garment that is surety for
a stranger, and take a pledge of him for
a strange woman.
14 He that blesseth his friend with a
loud voice, rising early in the morning,
it shall be counted a curse to him.
15 A continual dropping in a very rainy
day and a contentious woman are alike.
16 Whosoever hideth her hideth the
wind, and the ointment of his right
hand, *which* bewrayeth *itself.*
17 Iron sharpeneth iron; so a man
sharpeneth the countenance of his
friend.
18 Whoso keepeth the *fig tree shall
eat the fruit thereof: so he that waiteth
on his master shall be honoured.
19 As in water face *answereth* to face,
so the heart of man to man.
20 Hell and destruction are never full;
so the eyes of man are never satisfied.
21 *As* the *fining pot for silver, and the
furnace for gold; so *is* a man to his
praise.
22 Though thou shouldest bray a fool
in a mortar among wheat with a pes-
tle, *yet* will not his foolishness depart
from him.
23 Be thou diligent to know the state
of thy flocks, *and* look well to thy herds.
24 For riches *are* not for ever: and doth
the crown *endure* to every generation?
25 The hay appeareth, and the tender

27:1 Boast not thyself. Compare this with the story in Luke 12:16-20.
27:8 As a bird. A little bird that leaves the nest before it is strong enough to fly.
27:14 blesseth his friend with a loud voice. This is not true blessing–it is a blessing given that others may hear and give praise to the giver.
27:16 wind, and the ointment. It is as impossible to control a quarrelsome woman (see vs. 15) as it is to control the wind or the flow of oil by hand.
27:19 face answereth to face. As a face may be reflected in water, so man can see himself, or his heart, in other men.
27:21 so is a man to his praise. Praise tests a man as fire tests metals.
27:22 bray. To berate or belittle.

grass sheweth itself, and herbs of the
mountains are gathered.
26 The lambs *are* for thy clothing, and
the goats *are* the price of the field.
27 And *thou shalt have* goats' milk
enough for thy food, for the food of thy
household, and *for* the maintenance for
thy maidens.

Godliness and wickedness (continued)

28 The wicked flee when no man
pursueth: but the righteous are
bold as a lion.
2 For the transgression of a land many
are the princes thereof: but by a man of
understanding *and* knowledge the state
thereof shall be prolonged.
3 A poor man that oppresseth the poor
is like a sweeping rain which leaveth no
food.
4 They that forsake the *law praise
the wicked: but such as keep the law
contend with them.
5 Evil men understand not judgment:
but they that seek the LORD understand
all *things*.
6 Better *is* the poor that walketh in his
uprightness, than *he that is* perverse *in
his* ways, though he *be* rich.
7 Whoso keepeth the law *is* a wise
son: but he that is a companion of riotous *men* shameth his father.
8 He that by *usury and unjust gain
increaseth his substance, he shall gather it for him that will pity the poor.
9 He that turneth away his ear from
hearing the law, even his *prayer *shall
be* abomination.
10 Whoso causeth the righteous to
go astray in an evil way, he shall fall
himself into his own pit: but the upright shall have good *things* in possession.
11 The rich man *is* wise in his own
conceit; but the poor that hath understanding searcheth him out.
12 When righteous *men* do rejoice,
there is great glory: but when the wicked rise, a man is hidden.
13 He that covereth his sins shall not
prosper: but whoso confesseth and forsaketh *them* shall have mercy.
14 Happy *is* the man that feareth
alway: but he that hardeneth his heart
shall fall into mischief.
15 *As* a roaring lion, and a ranging
bear; *so is* a wicked ruler over the poor
people.
16 The prince that wanteth understanding *is* also a great oppressor: *but*
he that hateth covetousness shall prolong *his* days.
17 A man that doeth violence to the
blood of *any* person shall flee to *the
pit; let no man stay him.
18 Whoso walketh uprightly shall be
saved: but *he that is* perverse *in his*
ways shall fall at once.
19 He that tilleth his land shall have
plenty of bread: but he that followeth
after vain *persons* shall have poverty
enough.
20 A faithful man shall abound with
blessings: but he that maketh haste to
be rich shall not be innocent.
21 To have respect of persons *is* not
good: for for a piece of bread *that* man
will transgress.
22 He that hasteth to be rich *hath* an
evil eye, and considereth not that poverty shall come upon him.
23 He that rebuketh a man afterwards
shall find more favour than he that
flattereth with the tongue.
24 Whoso robbeth his father or his
mother, and saith, *It is* no transgression;
the same *is* the companion of a destroyer.
25 He that is of a proud heart stirreth

28:12 a man is hidden. Men hide themselves.
28:15 ranging bear. Charging bear—a "wicked ruler" is as concerned about the "poor people" as a "roaring lion" or a charging bear.
28:17 stay him. Help or support him.
28:18 he that is perverse in his ways. He that walks perversely or hypocritically in two ways.

up strife: but he that putteth his *trust
in the LORD shall be made fat.
26He that trusteth in his own heart is
a fool: but whoso walketh wisely, he
shall be delivered.
27He that giveth unto the poor shall
not lack: but he that hideth his eyes
shall have many a curse.
28When the wicked rise, men hide
themselves: but when they perish, the
righteous increase.

Godliness and wickedness (continued)

29 He, that being often reproved
hardeneth *his* neck, shall suddenly be destroyed, and that without
remedy.
2When the righteous are in authority, the people rejoice: but when the
wicked beareth rule, the people mourn.
3Whoso loveth wisdom rejoiceth his
father: but he that keepeth company
with harlots spendeth *his* substance.
4The king by judgment establisheth
the land: but he that receiveth gifts
overthroweth it.
5A man that flattereth his neighbour
spreadeth a net for his feet.
6In the transgression of an evil man
there is a snare: but the righteous doth
sing and rejoice.
7The righteous considereth the
cause of the poor: *but* the wicked
regardeth not to know *it.*
8Scornful men bring a city into a
snare: but wise *men* turn away wrath.
9*If* a wise man contendeth with a foolish man, whether he rage or laugh, *there*
is no rest.
10The bloodthirsty hate the upright:
but the just seek his soul.
11A fool uttereth all his mind: but a
wise *man* keepeth it in till afterwards.
12If a ruler hearken to lies, all his
servants *are* wicked.
13The poor and the deceitful man
meet together: the LORD lighteneth
both their eyes.
14The king that faithfully judgeth the
poor, his throne shall be established for
ever.
15The rod and reproof give wisdom:
but a child left *to himself* bringeth his
mother to shame.
16When the wicked are multiplied,
transgression increaseth: but the righteous shall see their fall.
17Correct thy son, and he shall give
thee rest; yea, he shall give delight unto
thy soul.
18Where *there is* no vision, the people perish: but he that keepeth the law,
happy *is* he.
19A servant will not be corrected by
words: for though he understand he will
not answer.
20Seest thou a man *that is* hasty in his
words? *there is* more hope of a fool than
of him.
21He that delicately bringeth up his
servant from a child shall have him become *his* son at the length.
22An angry man stirreth up strife, and
a furious man aboundeth in transgression.
23A man's pride shall bring him low:
but honour shall uphold the humble in
spirit.
24Whoso is partner with a thief hateth
his own soul: he heareth cursing, and
bewrayeth *it* not.
25The fear of man bringeth a snare:
but whoso putteth his trust in the LORD
shall be safe.
26Many seek the ruler's favour; but
every man's judgment *cometh* from the
LORD.
27An unjust man *is* an abomination to
the just: and *he that is* upright in the way
is abomination to the wicked.

28:27 he that hideth his eyes. He who closes his eyes to the trouble of the poor.
29:4 gifts. Bribes.
29:11 keepeth it in till afterwards. A wise man knows when to be quiet and when to speak.
29:18 the people perish. The people cast off restraint and live as if there is no God.
29:19 answer. Obey.

Godliness and wickedness (continued)

30 The words of Agur the son of
Jakeh, *even* the *prophecy: the
man spake unto Ithiel, even unto Ithiel
and Ucal,
2 Surely I *am* more brutish than *any*
man, and have not the understanding of
a man.
3 I neither learned wisdom, nor have
the knowledge of the *holy.
4 Who hath ascended up into *heav-
en, or descended? who hath gathered
the wind in his fists? who hath bound
the waters in a garment? who hath established all the ends of the earth? what
is his name, and what *is* his son's name,
if thou canst tell?

30:4 What Is His Son's Name?
Clearly the answer to the first four questions of this verse is God. Then we have the question: "What is his son's name?" There is no possible answer to this except Christ, whose name is Jesus (Matt. 1:21).

5 Every word of *God *is* pure: he *is* a
shield unto them that put their trust in
him.
6 Add thou not unto his words, lest he
reprove thee, and thou be found a liar.
7 Two *things* have I required of thee;
deny me *them* not before I die:
8 Remove far from me *vanity and
lies: give me neither poverty nor
riches; feed me with food convenient
for me:
9 Lest I be full, and deny *thee,* and say,
Who *is* the LORD? or lest I be poor, and
steal, and take the name of my God *in
vain.*
10 Accuse not a servant unto his master, lest he curse thee, and thou be
found guilty.
11 *There is* a generation *that* curseth
their father, and doth not bless their
mother.
12 *There is* a generation *that are* pure
in their own eyes, and *yet* is not washed
from their filthiness.
13 *There is* a generation, O how lofty
are their eyes! and their eyelids are lifted up.
14 *There is* a generation, whose teeth
are as swords, and their jaw teeth *as*
knives, to devour the poor from off
the earth, and the needy from *among*
men.
15 The horseleach hath two daughters, *crying,* Give, give. There are three
things that are never satisfied, *yea,* four
things say not, *It is* enough:
16 The *grave; and the barren womb;
the earth *that* is not filled with water;
and the fire *that* saith not, *It is* enough.
17 The eye *that* mocketh at *his* father,
and despiseth to obey *his* mother, the
ravens of the valley shall pick it out, and
the young eagles shall eat it.
18 There be three *things which* are too
wonderful for me, yea, four which I
know not:
19 The way of an eagle in the air; the
way of a serpent upon a rock; the way
of a ship in the midst of the sea; and the
way of a man with a maid.
20 Such *is* the way of an adulterous
woman; she eateth, and wipeth her
mouth, and saith, I have done no wickedness.
21 For three *things* the earth is disquieted, and for four *which* it cannot bear:
22 For a servant when he reigneth;
and a fool when he is filled with meat;
23 For an odious *woman* when she is
married; and an handmaid that is heir
to her mistress.
24 There be four *things which are* little upon the earth, but they *are* exceeding wise:
25 The ants *are* a people not strong,
yet they prepare their meat in the summer;
26 The conies *are but* a feeble folk, yet
make they their houses in the rocks;
27 The locusts have no king, yet go
they forth all of them by bands;
28 The spider taketh hold with her
hands, and is in kings' palaces.

30:6 Add thou not unto his words. Compare this with Revelation 22:18-19.

29 There be three *things* which go
well, yea, four are comely in going:
30 A lion *which is* strongest among
beasts, and turneth not away for any;
31 A greyhound; an he goat also;
and a king, against whom *there is* no rising up.
32 If thou hast done foolishly in lifting
up thyself, or if thou hast thought evil,
lay thine hand upon thy mouth.
33 Surely the churning of milk bringeth forth butter, and the wringing of the
nose bringeth forth blood: so the forcing of wrath bringeth forth strife.

Godliness and wickedness (continued)

31

The words of king Lemuel,
the prophecy that his mother
taught him.
2 What, my son? and what, the son of
my womb? and what, the son of my
vows?
3 Give not thy strength unto women,
nor thy ways to that which destroyeth
kings.
4 *It is* not for kings, O Lemuel, *it is* not
for kings to drink wine; nor for princes
strong drink:
5 Lest they drink, and forget the law,
and pervert the judgment of any of the
afflicted.
6 Give strong drink unto him that is
ready to perish, and wine unto those
that be of heavy hearts.
7 Let him drink, and forget his poverty, and remember his misery no more.
8 Open thy mouth for the dumb in the
cause of all such as are appointed to
destruction.
9 Open thy mouth, judge righteously,
and plead the cause of the poor and
needy.
¶ 10 Who can find a virtuous woman?
for her price *is* far above rubies.
11 The heart of her husband doth safely trust in her, so that he shall have no
need of spoil.
12 She will do him good and not evil
all the days of her life.
13 She seeketh wool, and flax, and
worketh willingly with her hands.

31:10 A Virtuous Woman
This superb poem is in the form of an acrostic, each verse beginning with a letter of the Hebrew alphabet in its proper order. It sums up the Hebrew ideal of honorable womanhood, secure in the home where God is obeyed. This is the kind of home in which the Lord Jesus grew up (Luke 2:39-40) and, as at Bethany, was a welcome guest (Luke 10:38-42; John 11:1-44; 12:1-9).

14 She is like the merchants' ships;
she bringeth her food from afar.
15 She riseth also while it is yet night,
and giveth meat to her household, and
a portion to her maidens.
16 She considereth a field, and buyeth
it: with the fruit of her hands she
planteth a vineyard.
17 She girdeth her loins with strength,
and strengtheneth her arms.
18 She perceiveth that her merchandise *is* good: her candle goeth not out
by night.
19 She layeth her hands to the spindle,
and her hands hold the distaff.
20 She stretcheth out her hand to the
poor; yea, she reacheth forth her hands
to the needy.
21 She is not afraid of the snow for her
household: for all her household *are*
clothed with scarlet.
22 She maketh herself coverings of
tapestry; her clothing *is* silk and purple.
23 Her husband is known in the gates,
when he sitteth among the elders of the
land.
24 She maketh fine linen, and selleth
it; and delivereth girdles unto the merchant.
25 Strength and honour *are* her clothing; and she shall rejoice in time to
come.
26 She openeth her mouth with wisdom; and in her tongue *is* the law of
kindness.
27 She looketh well to the ways of her
household, and eateth not the bread of
idleness.
28 Her children arise up, and call her

blessed; her husband *also,* and he
praiseth her.
29Many daughters have done virtuously, but thou excellest them all.
30Favour *is* deceitful, and beauty *is*
vain: *but* a woman *that* feareth the
LORD, she shall be praised.
31Give her of the fruit of her hands;
and let her own works praise her in the
gates.

ECCLESIASTES

or The Preacher

THEME

There are certain expressions which give the key thoughts of the book of Ecclesiastes. Solomon hunted unsuccessfully for heart satisfaction in "things under the sun," but all was "vanity" (worthlessness, nothingness). The expression "vanity" occurs 37 times; "under the sun," 29 times; "under the heavens," 3 times; "upon the earth," 7 times.

UNDERSTANDING ECCLESIASTES

We must distinguish carefully between *a true record* of Solomon's experiences (that is, *inspiration*), and *the truth* of God that is, *revelation*. In the Bible sometimes bad men, sometimes mistaken good men, and sometimes even the devil are quoted, but we are not to believe what they say. So in this book, by inspiration, God gives us an absolutely accurate account of what Solomon thought: the best reasonings of man possible apart from God's revelation. His ideas are not to be taken as God's answers to the problems, and no statement of this book should be considered the full truth of God unless it is confirmed by other Scripture.

The book is in the Bible, however, as a warning, or a red light to tell men to stop their foolish reasonings, and seek the truth from God and His Word only. Solomon comes to the point in his conclusion of this book, where after admitting the failure of human wisdom, he returns to God's "commandments" (God's Word) as the source of truth. As a result of these experiences, he wrote the book of Ecclesiastes to tell us what not to do, as he wrote the book of Proverbs to tell us what to do (Ecclesiastes 12:9-12).

THE WRITER

There is no doubt that Solomon is the author of the book, for he is the only "son of David" who was "king in Jerusalem" (Ecclesiastes 1:1). It is believed that he wrote the Song of Solomon when he was young and his heart was full of love to God, and that he wrote Ecclesiastes late in his life.

OUTLINE OF ECCLESIASTES

I.	Introduction: "All Is Vanity"	Ecclesiastes 1:1-3
II.	Why All Is Vanity	Ecclesiastes 1:4—6:12
III.	The Better Findings of Human Wisdom, or How to Make the Best Out of a Hopeless Situation	Ecclesiastes 7:1—10:20
IV.	The Old Man's Advice	Ecclesiastes 11:1—12:8
V.	The Only Satisfactory Solution to Life . . . and Death	Ecclesiastes 12:9-14

I. Introduction (1:1-3)
Title, and Writer of Book

1 The words of the Preacher, the
*son of *David, king in *Jerusalem.

Conclusion reached: All is vanity
(compare 12:8)

2*Vanity of vanities, saith the Preacher, vanity of vanities; all *is* vanity.
3What profit hath a man of all his
labour which he taketh under the sun?

1:2 All Is Vanity
Compare 12:8. That "all is vanity" is the conclusion that Solomon reaches after a study of "all things under the sun." He puts it here at the beginning of the book to show what he is writing to prove. It is the theme of the book.

II. Why All Is Vanity (1:4—6:12)
1) Nothing is permanent or complete

4*One* generation passeth away, and
another generation cometh: but the
earth abideth for ever.
5The sun also ariseth, and the sun
goeth down, and hasteth to his place
where he arose.
6The wind goeth toward the south,
and turneth about unto the north; it
whirleth about continually, and the wind
returneth again according to his cir-
cuits.
7All the rivers run into the sea; yet
the sea *is* not full; unto the place from
whence the rivers come, thither they
return again.

1:4 The Earth Endures
This is an example of the mistakes men make in their reasonings "under the sun," apart from God's revelation. So far as any man knows (from observation), the earth has always been here and will always remain, so this is a natural mistake to make. This statement is an inspired, and thus true account of what Solomon thought, but it is wrong because God reveals elsewhere (2 Pet. 3:10-13; Rev. 20:11) that the earth (in its present condition) will not abide forever. See the introduction to this book.

8All things *are* full of labour; man cannot utter *it:* the eye is not satisfied with
seeing, nor the ear filled with hearing.
9The thing that hath been, it *is that*
which shall be; and that which is done
is that which shall be done: and *there is*
no new *thing* under the sun.
10Is there *any* thing whereof it may
be said, See, this *is* new? it hath been
already of old time, which was before
us.
11*There is* no remembrance of former
things; neither shall there be *any* remembrance of *things* that are to come
with *those* that shall come after.

2) Nothing is satisfying
a. Wisdom cannot satisfy

¶12I the Preacher was king over *Israel in Jerusalem.
13And I gave my heart to seek and
search out by wisdom concerning all
things that are done under *heaven: this

1:1 the Preacher. The speaker for a congregation.
1:2 vanity. Vanity indicates emptiness, worthlessness, nothingness, uselessness, and utter meaninglessness.
1:4 One generation passeth away. This section shows the worthlessness and unsatisfying quality of the things of earth.
1:8 labour. Weariness.
1:11 things. Generations.
1:13 I gave my heart. Solomon set his mind to find out certain things. Nothing less than God and things eternal can satisfy the human heart. No experience or theory of life that omits this emphasis can possibly satisfy. The attempts of Solomon, and his failure, prove this.
1:13 by wisdom. Wisdom that does not bow humbly before God and make Him the very center, movement, and goal of one's universe is bound to bring heartache to the searcher.

sore travail hath *God given to the sons
of man to be exercised therewith.
[14]I have seen all the works that are
done under the sun; and, behold, all *is*
vanity and vexation of spirit.

1:14 Vexation of Spirit
Throughout the book this expression, "vexation of spirit," means *something futile and tiresome*. To know more of the misery of this world, without knowing the way out, will increase the mental anguish of any right-thinking person (vs. 18). Only when God is given His rightful place in our thinking can we obtain wisdom (Prov. 1:7). In Christ "are hid all the treasures of wisdom and knowledge" (Col. 2:3).

[15]*That which is* crooked cannot be
made straight: and that which is wanting cannot be numbered.
[16]I communed with mine own heart,
saying, Lo, I am come to great estate,
and have gotten more wisdom than all
they that have been before me in Jerusalem: yea, my heart had great experience of wisdom and knowledge.
[17]And I gave my heart to know wisdom, and to know madness and folly: I
perceived that this also is vexation of
spirit.
[18]For in much wisdom *is* much grief:
and he that increaseth knowledge increaseth sorrow.

b. Pleasure and riches cannot satisfy

2 I said in mine heart, *Go to now, I
will *prove thee with mirth, therefore enjoy pleasure: and, behold, this
also *is* vanity.
[2]I said of laughter, *It is* mad: and of
mirth, What doeth it?
[3]I sought in mine heart to give myself unto *wine, yet acquainting mine
heart with wisdom; and to lay hold on
folly, till I might see what *was* that good
for the sons of men, which they should

2:1 A Foolish Search
No one ever had as much money as Solomon (1 Kings 10:14,21,27), and no one ever had the liberty that Solomon had to use his money as he pleased. Since he was an absolute monarch, Solomon could indulge in any pleasure that he desired. If Solomon could not find satisfaction in his unlimited riches, how can anyone else succeed? Solomon's father, David, knew the way to true happiness (Ps. 16:11), and Solomon, after these foolish searchings, also returned to God's way (Eccles. 2:12-14 with Prov. 2:3-5; 3:15).

do under the heaven all the days of their
life.
[4]I made me great works; I builded me
houses; I planted me vineyards:
[5]I made me gardens and orchards,
and I planted trees in them of all *kind
of* fruits:
[6]I made me pools of water, to water
therewith the wood that bringeth forth
trees:
[7]I got *me* servants and maidens, and
had servants born in my house; also I
had great possessions of great and small
cattle above all that were in Jerusalem
before me:
[8]I gathered me also *silver and gold,
and the peculiar treasure of kings and
of the provinces: I gat me men singers
and women singers, and the delights of
the sons of men, *as* musical instruments, and that of all sorts.
[9]So I was great, and increased more
than all that were before me in Jerusalem: also my wisdom remained with
me.
[10]And whatsoever mine eyes desired
I kept not from them, I withheld not my
heart from any joy; for my heart rejoiced in all my labour: and this was my
portion of all my labour.
[11]Then I looked on all the works that
my hands had wrought, and on the

2:3 I sought in mine heart . . . with wisdom. I tried to cheer my flesh with wine, mine heart yet guiding me.
2:8 the peculiar treasure of kings. Jewels.

labour that I had laboured to do: and, behold, all *was* vanity and vexation of spirit, and *there was* no profit under the sun.

c. Materialism cannot satisfy

¶12And I turned myself to behold wisdom, and madness, and folly: for what
can the man *do* that cometh after the
king? *even* that which hath been already
done.
13Then I saw that wisdom excelleth
folly, as far as light excelleth darkness.
14The wise man's eyes *are* in his
head; but the *fool walketh in darkness:
and I myself perceived also that one
event happeneth to them all.
15Then said I in my heart, As it happeneth to the fool, so it happeneth even
to me; and why was I then more wise?
Then I said in my heart, that this also
is vanity.
16For *there is* no remembrance of the
wise more than of the fool for ever;
seeing that which now *is* in the days to
come shall all be forgotten. And how
dieth the wise *man?* as the fool.
17Therefore I hated life; because the
work that is wrought under the sun *is*
grievous unto me: for all *is* vanity and
vexation of spirit.
¶18Yea, I hated all my labour which I
had taken under the sun: because I
should leave it unto the man that shall
be after me.
19And who knoweth whether he shall
be a wise *man* or a fool? yet shall he
have rule over all my labour wherein I
have laboured, and wherein I have
shewed myself wise under the sun.
This *is* also vanity.
20Therefore I went about to cause my
heart to despair of all the labour which
I took under the sun.
21For there is a man whose labour *is* in
wisdom, and in knowledge, and in equity; yet to a man that hath not laboured
therein shall he leave it *for* his portion.
This also *is* vanity and a great evil.
22For what hath man of all his labour,
and of the vexation of his heart, wherein
he hath laboured under the sun?
23For all his days *are* sorrows, and his
travail grief; yea, his heart taketh not
rest in the night. This is also vanity.
¶24*There is* nothing better for a man,
than that he should eat and drink, and
that he should make his soul enjoy good
in his labour. This also I saw, that it *was*
from the hand of God.
25For who can eat, or who else can
hasten *hereunto,* more than I?
26For *God* giveth to a man that *is* good
in his sight wisdom, and knowledge,
and joy: but to the sinner he giveth travail, to gather and to heap up, that he
may give to *him that is* good before God.
This also *is* vanity and vexation of spirit.

d. Fatalism cannot satisfy

3 To every *thing there is* a season,
and a time to every purpose under
the heaven:

3:1 A False Theory
Fatalism is that false theory that says that all of life is planned for us by a chance fate, and we can do nothing to change it. It declares that we walk on to the stage of life to act a part, which is predestined or planned for us; and that we can no more think of changing it than the words of the character we play. The theory is proved false by the emphasis of the Word of God upon the value of the individual soul to God, and the constant appeals to decision; for each of us is personally responsible to God.

2:12 I turned myself. Materialism (a word that we often hear today) is that false theory of living that says that only the things that you can enjoy with your body are worthwhile. So "eat, drink, and be merry" is the outlook on life; for those who believe in this also believe that death ends all.
2:14 and I myself perceived. I began to understand.
2:16 more than. Even as.
2:21 in equity. With skill.
2:26 For God . . . in his sight. To the man that pleases Him, God gives all that he needs.

2 A time to be born, and a time to die;
a time to plant, and a time to pluck up
that which is planted;
3 A time to kill, and a time to heal;
a time to break down, and a time to
build up;
4 A time to weep, and a time to laugh;
a time to mourn, and a time to dance;
5 A time to cast away stones, and a
time to gather stones together; a time
to embrace, and a time to refrain from
embracing;
6 A time to get, and a time to lose; a
time to keep, and a time to cast away;
7 A time to rend, and a time to sew; a
time to keep silence, and a time to speak;
8 A time to love, and a time to hate; a
time of war, and a time of peace.
9 What profit hath he that worketh in
that wherein he laboureth?
10 I have seen the travail, which God
hath given to the sons of men to be
exercised in it.
11 He hath made every *thing* beautiful in his time: also he hath set the
*world in their heart, so that no man
can find out the work that God maketh
from the beginning to the end.
12 I know that *there is* no good in them,
but for *a man* to rejoice, and to do good
in his life.
13 And also that every man should eat
and drink, and enjoy the good of all his
labour, it *is* the gift of God.
14 I know that, whatsoever God doeth,
it shall be for ever: nothing can be put
to it, nor any thing taken from it: and
God doeth *it,* that *men* should *fear
before him.
15 That which hath been is now; and
that which is to be hath already been;
and God requireth that which is past.

e. Deism cannot satisfy

¶16 And moreover I saw under the sun
the place of judgment, *that* wickedness
was there; and the place of *righteousness, *that* iniquity *was* there.
17 I said in mine heart, God shall judge
the righteous and the wicked: for *there
is* a time there for every purpose and
for every work.
18 I said in mine heart concerning the
estate of the sons of men, that God
might manifest them, and that they
might see that they themselves are
beasts.
19 For that which befalleth the sons
of men befalleth beasts; even one
thing befalleth them: as the one dieth,
so dieth the other; yea, they have all
one breath; so that a man hath no preeminence above a beast: for all *is*
vanity.
20 All go unto one place; all are of the
dust, and all turn to dust again.
21 Who knoweth the spirit of man
that goeth upward, and the spirit of the
beast that goeth downward to the
earth?
22 Wherefore I perceive that *there is*
nothing better, than that a man should
rejoice in his own works; for that *is* his

3:16 Deism Denied

Deism is that false theory that says that if there is a personal God who created the world and us, no one can be sure of it and no one can know Him. In fact, God is not interested in mankind, this theory says, and has left the running of His world and its affairs to impersonal, unchangeable "laws of nature." Deism is proved to be false by the Scriptures' constant emphasis on God's love and concern for each individual (see 2 Pet. 3:9); and by the fact that God does rule and overrule in the affairs of individuals and nations, judging both in this life and in the life to come (Eccles. 12:13-14; Dan. 4:23-27; 5:24-28; Rom. 2:6,16).

3:11 set the world in their heart. Nothing in this passing world can satisfy; only things eternal, the things of God, satisfy the human heart.
3:12 no good in them, but for a man. The best that a man can do.
3:16 the place of judgment. The judgment was controlled by wickedness.
3:18 that they might see . . . are beasts. That they would see themselves as they are.
3:21 that goeth. Man and animals have different destinations.

portion: for who shall bring him to see
what shall be after him?

4 So I returned, and considered all
the oppressions that are done under the sun: and behold the tears of *such
as were* oppressed, and they had no
comforter; and on the side of their oppressors *there was* power; but they had
no comforter.

4:1 Oppression of the Poor
The French skeptic, Voltaire, after seeing the extreme wealth of the rich and poverty of the poor in the days just before the French Revolution, exclaimed, "The worst of all possible worlds is this. . . . And if there be a personal Creator, He must be a fiend. And as for me, I wish I had never been born." This is a typical reaction of a Deist (see Eccles. 3:16 note, "Deism Denied"). Voltaire failed to see that sin (the sin of men), and not God, has brought these woes to the human race; that even in this life those who oppress their fellowmen often reap a violent death (or, at least, hatred and loneliness); and that God will even the score in the final judgment.

2 Wherefore I praised the dead which
are already dead more than the living
which are yet alive.
3 Yea, better *is he* than both they,
which hath not yet been, who hath not
seen the evil work that is done under
the sun.
¶4 Again, I considered all travail, and
every right work, that for this a man is
envied of his neighbour. This *is* also
vanity and *vexation of spirit.
5 The fool foldeth his hands together,
and eateth his own flesh.
6 Better *is* an handful *with* quietness,
than both the hands full *with* travail and
vexation of spirit.
¶7 Then I returned, and I saw vanity
under the sun.
8 There is one *alone,* and *there is* not
a second; yea, he hath neither child nor
brother: yet *is there* no end of all his
labour; neither is his eye satisfied with
riches; neither *saith he,* For whom do I
labour, and bereave my soul of good?
This *is* also vanity, yea, it *is* a sore travail.
¶9 Two *are* better than one; because
they have a good reward for their
labour.
10 For if they fall, the one will lift up
his fellow: but woe to him *that is* alone
when he falleth; for *he hath* not another
to help him up.
11 Again, if two lie together, then they
have heat: but how can one be warm
alone?
12 And if one prevail against him, two
shall withstand him; and a threefold
cord is not quickly broken.
¶13 Better *is* a poor and a wise child
than an old and foolish king, who will no
more be admonished.
14 For out of prison he cometh to
reign; whereas also *he that is* born in his
kingdom becometh poor.
15 I considered all the living which
walk under the sun, with the second
child that shall stand up in his stead.
16 *There is* no end of all the people,
even of all that have been before them:
they also that come after shall not rejoice in him. Surely this also *is* vanity
and vexation of spirit.

f. Religion and religious practices cannot satisfy

5 Keep thy foot when thou goest to
the house of God, and be more
ready to hear, than to give the *sacrifice of *fools: for they consider not that
they do evil.
2 Be not rash with thy mouth, and let
not thine heart be hasty to utter *any*
thing before God: for God *is* in heaven,
and thou upon earth: therefore let thy
words be few.
3 For a dream cometh through the

3:22 bring him to see. Cause man to see his plight.
4:4 right. Skillful.
4:8 and there is not a second. This means that he has no one dependent upon him.
4:12 against him. There is strength in numbers.
5:2 let thy words be few. The longest public prayer recorded in the Bible (that of

5:1 Religion Alone Is Empty
Religion in itself, that is, the works of an unsaved heart done out of a sense of duty or self-preservation, cannot satisfy. However good these teachings that follow (5:1-9) may be in themselves, they will not bring the one who is not born again one inch nearer to God. One must first be saved and given a renewed heart before religious practices will be satisfactory and satisfying.

multitude of business; and a fool's voice
is known by multitude of words.
4When thou vowest a vow unto God,
defer not to pay it; for *he hath* no pleasure
in fools: pay that which thou hast vowed.
5Better *is it* that thou shouldest not
vow, than that thou shouldest vow and
not pay.
6Suffer not thy mouth to cause thy
flesh to *sin; neither say thou before
the *angel, that it *was* an error: wherefore should God be angry at thy voice,
and destroy the work of thine hands?
7For in the multitude of dreams and
many words *there are* also *divers* vanities: but fear thou God.
¶8If thou seest the oppression of the
poor, and violent perverting of judgment and justice in a province, marvel
not at the matter: for *he that is* higher
than the highest regardeth; and *there be*
higher than they.
¶9Moreover the profit of the earth is
for all: the king *himself* is served by the
field.

3) Disadvantages to riches
a. Man cannot eat them

10He that loveth silver shall not be
satisfied with silver; nor he that loveth
abundance with increase: this *is* also
vanity.
11When goods increase, they are increased that eat them: and what good
is there to the owners thereof, saving
the beholding *of them* with their eyes?

b. Man is not improved physically by them

12The sleep of a labouring man *is*
sweet, whether he eat little or much:
but the abundance of the rich will not
suffer him to sleep.

c. Man cannot take anything with him when he dies

13There is a sore evil *which* I have
seen under the sun, *namely,* riches kept
for the owners thereof to their hurt.
14But those riches perish by evil travail: and he begetteth a son, and *there*
is nothing in his hand.
15As he came forth of his mother's
womb, naked shall he return to go as he
came, and shall take nothing of his
labour, which he may carry away in his
hand.
16And this also *is* a sore evil, *that* in
all points as he came, so shall he go: and
what profit hath he that hath laboured
for the wind?
17All his days also he eateth in darkness, and *he hath* much sorrow and
wrath with his sickness.

d. Man should enjoy life while he can

¶18Behold *that* which I have seen: *it*
is good and comely *for one* to eat and to
drink, and to enjoy the good of all his
labour that he taketh under the sun all
the days of his life, which God giveth
him: for it *is* his portion.

Solomon at the dedication of the temple) requires but four minutes to repeat. One may well "pray long" in private prayer, but public prayer is quite different.

5:4 When thou vowest. Be careful what you promise God, for if the thing you promise is something right in itself, it will be a sin to you not to fulfill it. Mean what you say and say what you mean, and do not be a hypocrite or a liar.

5:8 for he that is higher than the highest. The one higher than the highest is the king. And "there be higher than they," that is, the LORD who is even higher than kings. He is higher regarding iniquity and will judge the offender, even if the king should fail to catch the slips of a minor official.

5:13 riches kept for. Riches bring harm to their owner.

5:18-20 An Empty Conclusion
Compare verses 18-20 with 6:11-12. This is the philosophical conclusion of all his searching, six avenues of which turned out to be blind alleys in 1:12–5:9. "Eat, drink and be merry (if you can); this is the best God has for you; this is the sum of life," was his conclusion. What a low estimate of the goal and privilege of life! How different from the conclusion that he reaches (12:13-14) when he returns to God's revelation.

19Every man also to whom God hath
given riches and wealth, and hath given
him power to eat thereof, and to take his
portion, and to rejoice in his labour; this
is the gift of God.
20For he shall not much remember
the days of his life; because God
answereth *him* in the joy of his heart.

e. Man must die and leave his riches

6 There is an evil which I have seen
under the sun, and it *is* common
among men:
2A man to whom God hath given
riches, wealth, and honour, so that he
wanteth nothing for his soul of all that he
desireth, yet God giveth him not power
to eat thereof, but a stranger eateth it:
this *is* vanity, and it *is* an evil disease.

4) There is no profit in life

¶3If a man beget an hundred *children,*
and live many years, so that the days of
his years be many, and his soul be not
filled with good, and also *that* he have
no burial; I say, *that* an untimely birth
is better than he.
4For he cometh in with vanity, and
departeth in darkness, and his name
shall be covered with darkness.
5Moreover he hath not seen the sun,
nor known *any thing:* this hath more
rest than the other.
¶6Yea, though he live a *thousand
years twice *told,* yet hath he seen no
good: do not all go to one place?
7All the labour of man *is* for his
mouth, and yet the appetite is not filled.
8For what hath the wise more than
the fool? what hath the poor, that knoweth to walk before the living?
¶9Better *is* the sight of the eyes than
the wandering of the desire: this *is* also
vanity and vexation of spirit.
10That which hath been is named already, and it is known that it *is* man:
neither may he contend with him that
is mightier than he.
¶11Seeing there be many things that
increase vanity, what *is* man the better?
12For who knoweth what *is* good for
man in *this* life, all the days of his vain
life which he spendeth as a shadow? for
who can tell a man what shall be after
him under the sun?

III. The Better Findings of Human Wisdom (7:1—10:20)

1) The seven better things

7 A good name *is* better than precious ointment; and the day of
*death than the day of one's birth.
¶2*It is* better to go to the house of
*mourning, than to go to the house of
feasting: for that *is* the end of all men;
and the living will lay *it* to his heart.
3Sorrow *is* better than laughter: for
by the sadness of the countenance the
heart is made better.
4The heart of the wise *is* in the house
of mourning; but the heart of fools *is* in
the house of mirth.
5*It is* better to hear the rebuke of the
wise, than for a man to hear the song
of fools.
6For as the crackling of thorns under
a pot, so *is* the laughter of the fool: this
also *is* *vanity.

6:1 common among men. Every man does evil.
6:8 what hath the wise . . . ? "What advantage does the wise have?"
6:11 what is man the better? See 5:18-20 note, "An Empty Conclusion."
6:12 who knoweth . . . who can tell . . . ? Only the Lord Jesus Christ can answer these questions, and He does (Mark 8:34-38; Luke 12:15; John 3:18,36).

¶7 Surely oppression maketh a wise
man mad; and a gift destroyeth the
heart.
8 Better *is* the end of a thing than
the beginning thereof: *and* the patient
in spirit *is* better than the proud in
spirit.
9 Be not hasty in thy spirit to be angry: for anger resteth in the bosom of
fools.
10 Say not thou, What is *the cause* that
the former days were better than these?
for thou dost not enquire wisely concerning this.

2) Advantages of being wise
a. Wisdom is good in itself

¶11 Wisdom *is* good with an inheritance: and *by it there is* profit to them
that see the sun.
12 For wisdom *is* a defence, *and* money *is* a defence: but the excellency of
knowledge *is, that* wisdom giveth life to
them that have it.

b. Wisdom gives insight to the problems of life

13 Consider the work of *God: for who
can make *that* straight, which he hath
made crooked?
14 In the day of prosperity be joyful,
but in the day of adversity consider:
God also hath set the one over against
the other, to the end that man should
find nothing after him.
15 All *things* have I seen in the days of
my vanity: there is a *just *man* that
perisheth in his righteousness, and
there is a wicked *man* that prolongeth
his life in his wickedness.
16 Be not righteous over much; neither make thyself over wise: why
shouldest thou destroy thyself?
17 Be not over much wicked, neither
be thou foolish: why shouldest thou die
before thy time?
18 *It is* good that thou shouldest take
hold of this; yea, also from this withdraw not thine hand: for he that
*feareth God shall come forth of them
all.
19 Wisdom strengtheneth the wise
more than ten mighty *men* which are in
the city.
20 For *there is* not a just man upon
earth, that doeth good, and sinneth not.
21 Also take no heed unto all words
that are spoken; lest thou hear thy servant curse thee:
22 For oftentimes also thine own heart
knoweth that thou thyself likewise hast
cursed others.

3) Things too puzzling for human wisdom

¶23 All this have I proved by wisdom:
I said, I will be wise; but it *was* far
from me.
24 That which is far off, and exceeding
deep, who can find it out?
25 I applied mine heart to know, and to
search, and to seek out wisdom, and the
reason *of things,* and to know the wickedness of folly, even of foolishness *and*
madness:
26 And I find more bitter than death
the woman, whose heart *is* snares and
nets, *and* her hands *as* bands: whoso
pleaseth God shall escape from her; but
the sinner shall be taken by her.
27 Behold, this have I found, saith the
preacher, *counting* one by one, to find
out the account:
28 Which yet my soul seeketh, but I
find not: one man among a thousand
have I found; but a woman among all
those have I not found.
29 Lo, this only have I found, that God

7:11 is good with. Even worldly wisdom has benefits (compare 6:5).

7:12 giveth life. Wisdom preserves life.

7:14 find nothing. Not find anything that shall be.

7:25 the wickedness of folly . . . and madness. Wickedness is folly, and foolishness is madness.

7:26 more bitter than death. Verses 26-28 contain a bitter reference to Solomon's thousand (heathen) wives, who treacherously led his heart from God (see 1 Kings 11:1-8).

hath made man upright; but they have
sought out many inventions.

4) The wisdom of obedience to kings

8 Who *is* as the wise *man?* and who
knoweth the interpretation of a
thing? a man's wisdom maketh his face
to shine, and the boldness of his face
shall be changed.
2 I *counsel thee* to keep the king's
commandment, and *that* in regard of the
oath of God.
3 Be not hasty to go out of his sight:
stand not in an evil thing; for he doeth
whatsoever pleaseth him.
4 Where the word of a king *is, there is*
power: and who may say unto him,
What doest thou?
5 Whoso keepeth the commandment
shall feel no evil thing: and a wise man's
heart discerneth both time and judgment.
¶6 Because to every purpose there is
time and judgment, therefore the misery of man *is* great upon him.
7 For he knoweth not that which
shall be: for who can tell him when it
shall be?
8 *There is* no man that hath power
over the spirit to retain the spirit; neither *hath he* power in the day of death:
and *there is* no discharge in *that* war;
neither shall wickedness deliver those
that are given to it.
9 All this have I seen, and applied my
heart unto every work that is done under the sun: *there is* a time wherein one
man ruleth over another to his own
hurt.
10 And so I saw the wicked buried,
who had come and gone from the place
of the holy, and they were forgotten in
the city where they had so done: this *is*
also vanity.
11 Because sentence against an evil
work is not executed speedily, therefore the heart of the sons of men is fully
set in them to do evil.
¶12 Though a sinner do evil an hundred times, and his *days* be prolonged,
yet surely I know that it shall be well
with them that fear God, which fear
before him:
13 But it shall not be well with the
wicked, neither shall he prolong *his*
days, *which are* as a shadow; because he
feareth not before God.
14 There is a vanity which is done
upon the earth; that there be just *men,*
unto whom it happeneth according to
the work of the wicked; again, there be
wicked *men,* to whom it happeneth according to the work of the righteous: I
said that this also *is* vanity.
15 Then I commended mirth, because
a man hath no better thing under the
sun, than to eat, and to drink, and to be
merry: for that shall abide with him of
his labour the days of his life, which God
giveth him under the sun.
¶16 When I applied mine heart to
know wisdom, and to see the business
that is done upon the earth: (for also
there is that neither day nor night seeth
sleep with his eyes:)
17 Then I beheld all the work of God,
that a man cannot find out the work that
is done under the sun: because though
a man labour to seek *it* out, yet he shall
not find *it;* yea further; though a wise
man think to know *it,* yet shall he not
be able to find *it.*

5) Death is certain, theefore, seek happiness in a quiet home life

9 For all this I considered in my
heart even to declare all this, that
the righteous, and the wise, and their

7:29 they have sought out many inventions. This speaks of the deceitfulness and perversity of the human heart. See Jeremiah 17:9.
8:1 boldness. Hardness or sternness.
8:3 stand. Persist.
8:10 who had come . . . had so done. This means *and they came to the grave;* and those who had done *right went away* from the Holy Place and were forgotten in the city.
9:1 to declare. To explore.

works, *are* in the hand of God: no man knoweth either love or hatred *by* all *that is* before them.

2 All *things come* alike to all: *there is* one event to the righteous, and to the wicked; to the good and to the *clean, and to the unclean; to him that sacrificeth, and to him that sacrificeth not: as *is* the good, so *is* the sinner; *and* he that sweareth, as *he* that feareth an oath.

3 This *is* an evil among all *things* that are done under the sun, that *there is* one event unto all: yea, also the heart of the sons of men is full of evil, and madness *is* in their heart while they live, and after that *they go* to the dead.

¶ 4 For to him that is joined to all the living there is *hope: for a living dog is better than a dead lion.

5 For the living know that they shall die: but the dead know not any thing, neither have they any more a reward; for the memory of them is forgotten.

6 Also their love, and their hatred, and their envy, is now perished; neither have they any more a portion for ever in any *thing* that is done under the sun.

¶ 7 Go thy way, eat thy bread with joy, and drink thy *wine with a merry heart; for God now accepteth thy works.

8 Let thy *garments be always white; and let thy head lack no ointment.

9 Live joyfully with the wife whom thou lovest all the days of the life of thy vanity, which he hath given thee under the sun, all the days of thy vanity: for that *is* thy portion in *this* life, and in thy labour which thou takest under the sun.

6) Do your best and leave the mysteries to God

10 Whatsoever thy hand findeth to do, do *it* with thy might; for *there is* no work, nor device, nor knowledge, nor wisdom, in the grave, whither thou goest.

¶ 11 I returned, and saw under the sun, that the race *is* not to the swift, nor the battle to the strong, neither yet bread to the wise, nor yet riches to men of understanding, nor yet favour to men of skill; but time and chance happeneth to them all.

12 For man also knoweth not his time: as the fishes that are taken in an evil net, and as the birds that are caught in the snare; so *are* the sons of men snared in an evil time, when it falleth suddenly upon them.

¶ 13 This wisdom have I seen also under the sun, and it *seemed* great unto me:

7) A parable of wisdom's value

14 *There was* a little city, and few men within it; and there came a great king against it, and besieged it, and built great bulwarks against it:

15 Now there was found in it a poor wise man, and he by his wisdom deliv-

9:10 The Grave
The word translated "grave" here is the Hebrew word *Sheol*, which does not mean the grave, but a place of departed spirits. This statement that there is no "knowledge" etc., in Sheol is the foolish and false reasoning of a man "under the sun" (1:13-14). This is corrected by our Lord Himself in the story He tells in Luke where there is plainly consciousness and memory in the case of the rich man who is in Sheol. (In Luke 16:23 the word "hell" is the Greek word *Hades,* which is the exact equal of the Hebrew word *Sheol.*)

9:15 A Poor Wise Man
Solomon pictures Christ who became poor for us (2 Cor. 8:9), and by His wisdom (the work of His death on the cross, 1 Cor. 1:18, 21-24) delivered (paid the price of redemption, Col. 1:20) the city (of mankind). But the world at large forgets and ignores what Christ has done for them ("yet no man remembered"). The great king of verse 14 refers to the devil, who comes against the city (of mankind) to destroy it (that is, the souls of men).

9:1 no man . . . is before them. Man does not know whether love or hatred is coming, for all is in the future.

ered the city; yet no man remembered
that same poor man.
16Then said I, Wisdom *is* better than
strength: nevertheless the poor man's
wisdom *is* despised, and his words are
not heard.
17The words of wise *men are* heard in
quiet more than the cry of him that
ruleth among fools.
18Wisdom *is* better than weapons of
war: but one sinner destroyeth much
good.

8) Beware of folly

10 Dead flies cause the ointment
of the apothecary to send forth
a stinking savour: *so doth* a little folly
him that is in reputation for wisdom *and*
honour.
2A wise man's heart *is* at his right
hand; but a *fool's heart at his left.
3Yea also, when he that is a fool
walketh by the way, his wisdom faileth
him, and he saith to every one *that* he
is a fool.
4If the spirit of the ruler rise up
against thee, leave not thy place; for
yielding pacifieth great offences.
5There is an evil *which* I have seen
under the sun, as an error *which* proceedeth from the ruler:
6Folly is set in great dignity, and the
rich sit in low place.
7I have seen servants upon horses,
and princes walking as servants upon
the earth.
8He that diggeth a pit shall fall into it;
and whoso breaketh an hedge, a serpent
shall bite him.
9Whoso removeth stones shall be
hurt therewith; *and* he that cleaveth
wood shall be endangered thereby.
10If the iron be blunt, and he do not
whet the edge, then must he put to
more strength: but wisdom *is* profitable
to direct.
11Surely the serpent will bite without
enchantment; and a babbler is no better.
12The words of a wise man's mouth
are gracious; but the lips of a fool will
swallow up himself.
13The beginning of the words of his
mouth *is* foolishness: and the end of his
talk *is* mischievous madness.
14A fool also is full of words: a man
cannot tell what shall be; and what shall
be after him, who can tell him?
15The labour of the foolish wearieth
every one of them, because he knoweth
not how to go to the city.
¶16Woe to thee, O land, when thy
king *is* a child, and thy princes eat in the
morning!
17Blessed *art* thou, O land, when thy
king *is* the son of nobles, and thy
princes eat in due season, for strength,
and not for drunkenness!
¶18By much slothfulness the building
decayeth; and through idleness of the
hands the house droppeth through.
¶19A feast is made for laughter, and
wine maketh merry: but money answereth all *things*.
¶20Curse not the king, no not in thy
thought; and curse not the rich in thy
*bedchamber: for a bird of the air shall
carry the voice, and that which hath
wings shall tell the matter.

IV. The Old Man's Advice (11:1—12:8)

1) Generosity is always repaid

11 Cast thy bread upon the waters: for thou shalt find it after
many days.

10:1 apothecary. One who makes perfume.

10:1 a little folly him . . . wisdom. The thought here is: "A little folly ruins the reputation." What a warning to believers to be careful of their testimony and avoid the very "appearance of evil" (Rom. 14:7,14,15,21; Eph. 5:4; 1 Thess. 5:22)!

10:11 the serpent will bite without enchantment. The serpent will bite when it is not charmed, and the slanderer is no better.

10:14 is full of words. A fool talks too much, and others cannot understand.

10:20 a bird of the air . . . shall tell. We get our expression "A little bird told me" from this passage.

> **11:1 Bread**
> Bread was principally in the form of thin cakes, baked on the hearth or in the oven. The bread eaten by the poor was made of barley meal, with oil instead of butter. They were leavened or unleavened, kneaded in a trough. Wheaten flour was common in Egypt but a luxury in Palestine, and it was one of the offerings in the sanctuary. The congregation was commanded to offer fine flour for twelve cakes (shewbread), to be placed every Sabbath in two rows on the table of shewbread. This bread was to be eaten by the priests in the sacred precincts (Exod. 25:30; Matt. 12:4).

2 Give a portion to seven, and also to
eight; for thou knowest not what evil
shall be upon the earth.
3 If the clouds be full of rain, they
empty *themselves* upon the earth: and if
the tree fall toward the south, or toward
the north, in the place where the tree
falleth, there it shall be.
4 He that observeth the wind shall not
sow; and he that regardeth the clouds
shall not reap.
5 As thou knowest not what *is* the way
of the spirit, *nor* how the bones *do grow*
in the womb of her that is with child:
even so thou knowest not the works of
God who maketh all.
6 In the morning sow thy seed, and in
the evening withhold not thine hand:
for thou knowest not whether shall
prosper, either this or that, or whether
they both *shall be* alike good.

2) Life is sweet-but even childhood and youth are vanity

¶ 7 Truly the light *is* sweet, and a
pleasant *thing it is* for the eyes to behold the sun:
8 But if a man live many years, *and*
rejoice in them all; yet let him remember the days of darkness; for they shall
be many. All that cometh *is* vanity.
¶ 9 Rejoice, O young man, in thy
youth; and let thy heart cheer thee in
the days of thy youth, and walk in the
ways of thine heart, and in the sight of
thine eyes: but know thou, that for all
these *things* God will bring thee into
*judgment.
10 Therefore remove sorrow from thy
heart, and put away evil from thy *flesh:
for childhood and youth *are* vanity.

3) In youth remember God, and death (A description of old age)

12 Remember now thy Creator in
the days of thy youth, while the
evil days come not, nor the years draw
nigh, when thou shalt say, I have no
pleasure in them;
2 While the sun, or the light, or the
moon, or the stars, be not darkened, nor
the clouds return after the rain:
3 In the day when the keepers of the
house shall tremble, and the strong
men shall bow themselves, and the
grinders cease because they are few,
and those that look out of the windows
be darkened,
4 And the doors shall be shut in the
streets, when the sound of the grinding
is low, and he shall rise up at the voice
of the bird, and all the daughters of
musick shall be brought low;
5 Also *when* they shall be afraid of *that
which is* high, and fears *shall be* in the
way, and the almond tree shall flourish,
and the grasshopper shall be a burden,
and desire shall fail: because man goeth
to his long home, and the mourners go
about the streets:
6 Or ever the silver cord be loosed, or
the golden bowl be broken, or the pitcher be broken at the fountain, or the
wheel broken at the cistern.
7 Then shall the dust return to the
earth as it was: and the spirit shall return unto God who gave it.

4) The conclusion of the search: Even death is vanity

¶ 8 Vanity of vanities, saith the preacher; all *is* vanity.

11:6 whether shall prosper. Which one shall prosper.

V. The Only Satisfactory Solution to Life . . . and Death (12:9-14)
1) Return to God's Word

9And moreover, because the preach-
er was wise, he still taught the people knowledge; yea, he gave good heed, and sought out, *and* set in order many proverbs.
10The preacher sought to find out ac-
ceptable words: and *that which was* written *was* upright, *even* words of truth.
11The words of the wise *are* as goads,
and as nails fastened *by* the masters of assemblies, *which* are given from one shepherd.
12And further, by these, my son, be
admonished: of making many books *there is* no end; and much study *is* a weariness of the flesh.

2) Final admonition: Trust and obey

¶13Let us hear the conclusion of the
whole matter: Fear God, and keep his commandments: for this *is* the whole *duty* of man.
14For God shall bring every work into
judgment, with every secret thing, whether *it be* good, or whether *it be* evil.

12:13 SOME GOOD ADVICE

This plainly teaches that God has revealed Himself in certain definite obligations, recorded permanently in written form–in other words, in His Word, the Bible. It proves also that Solomon forsook the uncharted sea of human ideas and returned to the safe harbor of God's Word, the Scriptures being the *only* authority in the moral and spiritual realm. Nothing less than trusting in God and obeying His Word will keep us happy and safe when we appear before Him in judgment (vs. 14).

In the New Testament language we would say, "Believe on the Lord Jesus Christ as your personal Saviour" (fear God), and "obey His Word" (keep His commandments), for (vs. 14) "we must all appear before the judgment seat of Christ" (2 Cor. 5:10) to be examined concerning "the things done in the body," not to see if we are saved, because John 5:24 says, "he that believeth . . . shall not come into condemnation," but to receive rewards and to purge away the worthless works (1 Cor. 4:5; 3:12-15).

12:8 Vanity of vanities. We have already seen that life without God (including youth and old age) is futile. Now we find that even death is powerless to deliver us from vanity.
12:9 set in order many proverbs. Many proverbs were written or compiled by Solomon to guard against the evils and vanity of life. He wants others to avoid his useless searches in human reasonings "under the sun" (vs. 12).
12:13 Let us hear the conclusion. Verse 13 has the idea of: "This is the end of the matter; all hath been heard. Fear God, and keep His commandments; for this is the duty of all men."

The SONG OF SOLOMON

THEME AND STRUCTURE

The Song of Songs, or the Song of Solomon, has for its key-thought the believer's fellowship with God, as pictured by the love of Solomon for the Shulamite, and her love for him. The book is made up of songs, or "canticles," some short and some long. These songs do not tell a consecutive story, but touch upon various incidents and conversations. The length and theme of each song and the record of who is speaking are indicated in the headings and notes. It is not make-believe, but real.

BACKGROUND AND SUMMARY

Solomon had a vineyard at Baal-harmon (evidently up north in the Lebanon country) which he rented out to keepers (Song of Solomon 8:11-12). One of these renting families was made up of some brothers and a sister, their father and mother having evidently died. Solomon visited the place, and, dressed as a shepherd, saw the young girl one day and was greatly charmed by her beauty, even though her brother had forced her to do much of the work so that she had become browned by the sun (Song 1:6).

She was pleased at the attentions of this stalwart stranger, mistaking him for one of the King's shepherds and never dreaming that he was the King. And so they fell in love. He kept his secret well (Song 1:7-8), but one day had to return to Jerusalem on state business. Before he left, he promised to return for her and marry her. This he did (Song 3:9-11), but one cannot wonder at her amazement (Song 3:6) in finding that her lover was the great King Solomon (Song 3:7).

She was very happy with him, but often felt out of place in the gorgeous court (Song 2:1; 6:13), and longed for her beloved Lebanon (Song 7:11–13). Sometimes she dreamed uneasily (Song 3:1; 5:2,7, etc.), but he constantly assured her that she was in her rightful place (Song 2:2; 6:8-9). And to please her (Song 7:11-13), Solomon returned with her (Song 8:5) on a visit to her old home where, after teasing her brothers over the way they had feared they would never be able to marry her off to anyone worthwhile (Song 8:8-10), she nevertheless requested and received of Solomon a generous share of the product of the farm for her brothers (Song 8:12).

MEANING

Thus Solomon becomes a *type of Christ, and the Shulamite (the feminine form of Solomon's name) becomes a type of the *Church (Ephesians

5:25,32). Christ wooed us as the humble Shepherd, who gave His life for us (John 10:11). He had gone away (Acts 1:9), but He promised to return and make us His own (John 14:2-3). When He returns, it will be in the glory of His Lordship and Kingship (John 17:24; Titus 2:13; Revelation 19:16), and we shall reign with Him (Revelation 1:5-6; 20:6; 1 Corinthians 6:2).

In this book, God puts His seal of approval upon the pure rapture of human love, and rebukes lust (unholy love). Much of the conversation takes place *after* the marriage of Solomon and the Shulamite. The Jews understood this, and called the book "The Holy of Holies," and godly men and women have always delighted to trace the love of Christ for them in the words of Solomon, and to respond to our Lord's love in the beautiful words of the Shulamite's love for Solomon.

OUTLINE OF SONG OF SOLOMON

I.	The Title	Song of Solomon 1:1
II.	Canticle 1	Song of Solomon 1:2-6
III.	Canticle 2	Song of Solomon 1:7-8
IV.	Canticle 3	Song of Solomon 1:9-17
V.	Canticle 4	Song of Solomon 2:1-7
VI.	Canticle 5	Song of Solomon 2:8-17
VII.	Canticle 6	Song of Solomon 3:1-5
VIII.	Canticle 7	Song of Solomon 3:6-11
IX.	Canticle 8	Song of Solomon 4:1-7
X.	Canticle 9	Song of Solomon 4:8—5:1
XI.	Canticle 10	Song of Solomon 5:2—6:3
XII.	Canticle 11	Song of Solomon 6:4—7:10
XIII.	Canticle 12	Song of Solomon 7:11—8:4
XIV.	Canticle 13	Song of Solomon 8:5-14

I. The Title (1:1)

1 The song of songs, which *is* Solomon's.

II. Canticle 1: A Song of Longing to Be Brought into the King's Presence (1:2-6)

(The bride speaks)

2 Let him kiss me with the kisses of his mouth:

(The ladies-in-waiting compliment the bride)

for thy love *is* better than *wine.

3 Because of the savour of thy good ointments thy name *is as* ointment poured forth, therefore do the virgins love thee.

(The bride commands)

4 Draw me,

(The ladies-in-waiting respond)

we will run after thee:

(The bride thinks out loud)

the king hath brought me into his chambers:

1:1 song of songs. This book is so called because it is the only one of Solomon's 1,005 songs (1 Kings 4:32) that God saw fit to inspire and preserve.

1:2 Canticle 1
A canticle is a short love poem.
Title: "A Song of Longing to Be Brought into the King's Presence"
Setting: the palace in Jerusalem
Time: before the marriage (see introduction to this book)
Occasion: The bride remembers a conversation that she had with her ladies-in-waiting while she was about to be carried into Solomon's presence, just before or during the lengthy wedding ceremony that accompanied Eastern weddings.

(The ladies-in-waiting reply)

we will be glad and rejoice in thee, we
will remember thy love more than
wine: the upright love thee.

(The embarrassed bride apologizes for her dark skin)

[5]I *am* black, but comely, O ye daughters of *Jerusalem, as the tents of *Kedar, as the curtains of Solomon.
[6]Look not upon me, because I *am*
black, because the sun hath looked
upon me: my mother's children were
angry with me; they made me the keeper of the vineyards; *but* mine own vineyard have I not kept.

III. Canticle 2: An Answer Which Did Not Answer (1:7-8)

(The Shulamite requests)

[7]Tell me, O thou whom my soul
loveth, where thou feedest, where thou
makest *thy flock* to rest at noon: for why
should I be as one that turneth aside by
the flocks of thy companions?

(Solomon replies)

¶[8]If thou know not, O thou fairest

1:7 Canticle 2
Title: "An Answer which Did Not Answer"
Setting: the bride's home in Lebanon
Time: before the marriage
Occasion: The Shulamite, who has fallen in love with a strange shepherd but does not know that he is Solomon, tries to find out who he is. The shepherd does not tell.

among women, go thy way forth by the
footsteps of the flock, and feed thy kids
beside the shepherds' tents.

IV. Canticle 3: Love's Admiration (1:9-17)

(The bridegroom speaks)

[9]I have compared thee, O my love, to
a company of horses in *Pharaoh's
chariots.

1:9 Canticle 3
Title: "Love's Admiration"
Setting: the palace in Jerusalem
Time: after the marriage, possibly at the wedding feast
Occasion: mutual admiration, with the ladies-in-waiting present, as was customary in those times

[10]Thy cheeks are comely with rows
of jewels, thy neck with chains *of gold.*

(The ladies-in-waiting promise the bride a beautiful garment)

[11]We will make thee borders of gold
with studs of silver.

(The bride speaks)

¶[12]While the king *sitteth* at his table,
my *spikenard sendeth forth the smell
thereof.
[13]A bundle of myrrh *is* my well-

1:5 I am black. Means: "I am swarthy because the sun scorched me" (vs. 6). She explains that her lazy brothers had kept her working so hard in the vineyard that she had no time left to care for her appearance: "mine own vineyard have I not kept" (vs. 6).

1:7 one that turneth aside by. "As one that wandereth beside the flocks"; that is, as one who is not known, not recognized.

1:9 my love. When "love" is used as a title of address, it is always the bride who is being addressed, for it is a feminine word. "Beloved" (as in vs. 16) always means that Solomon is being spoken to.

1:9 a company of horses. Horses were noted for their gracefulness and beauty.

beloved unto me; he shall lie all night
betwixt my breasts.
14 My beloved *is* unto me *as* a cluster
of camphire in the vineyards of
En-gedi.

(The bridegroom replies)

15 Behold, thou *art* fair, my love; behold, thou *art* fair; thou *hast* doves'
eyes.

(The bride answers him)

16 Behold, thou *art* fair, my beloved,
yea, pleasant: also our bed *is* green.
17 The beams of our house *are* cedar,
and our rafters of fir.

V. Canticle 4: A Song of (His) Perfect Love which Casts Out (Our) Fear (2:1-7)

(The timid bride speaks)

2 I *am* the rose of *Sharon, *and* the
lily of the valleys.

2:1 Canticle 4
Title: "A Song of (His) Perfect Love which Casts Out (Our) Fear" (compare 1 John 4:18)
Setting: the banquet room of the king's house
Time: after the marriage
Occasion: a little later on the same evening as Canticle 3 or soon afterward

(Solomon responds to her)

2 As the lily among thorns, so *is* my
love among the daughters.

(The bride says to the bridegroom)

3 As the apple tree among the trees of
the wood, so *is* my beloved among the
sons. I sat down under his shadow with
great delight, and his fruit *was* sweet to
my taste.
4 He brought me to the banqueting
house, and his banner over me *was*
love.

(The bride addresses her attendants)

5 Stay me with flagons, comfort me
with apples: for I *am* sick of love.
6 His left hand *is* under my head, and
his right hand doth embrace me.

(Solomon instructs the attendants)

7 I charge you, O ye daughters of
Jerusalem, by the roes, and by the hinds
of the field, that ye stir not up, nor
awake *my* love, till he please.

VI. Canticle 5: A Song of a Happy Visit and a Promised Return (2:8-17)

(The Shulamite recalls a visit)

1. She describes his approach

¶8 The voice of my beloved! behold,
he cometh leaping upon the mountains,
skipping upon the hills.
9 My beloved is like a roe or a young
hart: behold, he standeth behind our
wall, he looketh forth at the windows,
shewing himself through the lattice.

1:13 he shall lie. This refers to the custom of wearing some sweet-smelling spice, hanging from a chain around the neck.
1:16 beloved. See verse 9 note.
2:1 rose of Sharon. The Shulamite felt out of place in the court. She felt that she was more suited to the simple life of her Lebanon home, as symbolized by the flowers (crocus of Sharon) hidden in sheltered places among the rocks of the valley; nevertheless, it was a sweet, fragrant life (as the lily, or narcissus of the valleys). Contrary to the common interpretation, these words were not spoken by the bridegroom, but by the bride (see 2:2 note). Of course, our Lord is all that can be suggested by the beauty of the "lily of the valley" and more (5:16).
2:2 among thorns. The bridegroom compliments the bride by saying. "No, you are not out of place. It is true that you are different, but it is just that you are prettier, like a flower among thorns."
2:5 flagons. Raisin cakes.
2:5 sick of love. Lovesick or deeply in love.
2:7 till he please. He will come at *his* time.

2:8 Canticle 5
Title: "A Song of a Happy Visit and a Promised Return"
Setting: Lebanon
Time: during the courtship days
Occasion: a visit Solomon made to her vineyard home. Note that the Shulamite speaks the whole song, telling what she thought and what he said.

2. She tells what he said to her
(a) He asked her to come outside to walk with him

10My beloved spake, and said unto
me, Rise up, my love, my fair one, and
come away.
11For, lo, the winter is past, the rain
is over *and* gone;
12The flowers appear on the earth; the
time of the singing *of birds* is come, and
the voice of the turtle is heard in our land;
13The *fig tree putteth forth her green
figs, and the vines *with* the tender grape
give a *good* smell. Arise, my love, my fair
one, and come away.

(b) He longed to talk with her

¶14O my dove, *that art* in the clefts of
the rock, in the secret *places* of the
stairs, let me see thy countenance, let
me hear thy voice; for sweet *is* thy
voice, and thy countenance *is* comely.

(c) He called attention to needed repairs to the fence

15Take us the foxes, the little foxes,
that spoil the vines: for our vines *have*
tender grapes.

3. As he strode away after the walk, she watched him and said:

¶16My beloved *is* mine, and I *am* his:
he feedeth among the lilies.
17Until the day break, and the shadows flee away, turn, my beloved, and be
thou like a roe or a young hart upon the
mountains of Bether.

VII. Canticle 6: A Sad Song Which Ends Happily (3:1-5)

(The bride tells of a dream)

3 By night on my bed I sought him
whom my soul loveth: I sought
him, but I found him not.

3:1 Canticle 6
Title: "A Sad Song that Ends Happily"
Setting: the palace in Jerusalem
Time: after the marriage
Occasion: a dream (compare 5:2). Something of the uncertainty and loneliness of the days of separation at Lebanon creep into the bride's dream. She seeks her bridegroom, but not finding him, her dream becomes a nightmare. In her dream she remembers his love and drifts back to restful slumber (vs. 5).

2I will rise now, and go about the city
in the streets, and in the broad ways I
will seek him whom my soul loveth: I
sought him, but I found him not.
3The watchmen that go about the city
found me: *to whom I said,* Saw ye him
whom my soul loveth?
4*It was* but a little that I passed from
them, but I found him whom my soul
loveth: I held him, and would not let
him go, until I had brought him into my
mother's house, and into the chamber
of her that conceived me.

(Solomon's refrain)

5I charge you, O ye daughters of Jerusalem, by the roes, and by the hinds
of the field, that ye stir not up, nor
awake *my* love, till he please.

2:12 turtle. Turtledove.
2:15 the little foxes. These are a *type of the little sins that gnaw at the roots of the vine of our testimony before others, making us unfruitful.
2:16 he feedeth. Wherever this expression occurs, it indicates "He feedeth his flock."
2:17 Bether. Literally, *separation.*
3:7 bed. Palanquin (litter) or chariot.
3:7 threescore valiant men. Solomon's chosen bodyguard.

VIII. Canticle 7: A Song of an Amazing Marriage (3:6-11)

(The amazed Shulamite's question)

¶6Who *is* this that cometh out of the
wilderness like pillars of smoke, perfumed with myrrh and frankincense,
with all powders of the merchant?

3:6 Canticle 7
Title: "A Song of an Amazing Marriage"
Setting: Lebanon
Time: just before the marriage
Occasion: Solomon fulfills his promise and sends a gorgeous chariot to bring her to Jerusalem to marry him.

(An officer replies)

7Behold his bed, which *is* Solomon's;
threescore valiant men *are* about it, of
the valiant of *Israel.
8They all hold swords, *being* expert
in war: every man *hath* his sword upon
his thigh because of fear in the night.
9King Solomon made himself a chariot of the wood of *Lebanon.
10He made the pillars thereof *of* silver, the bottom thereof *of* gold, the covering of it *of* purple, the midst thereof
being paved *with* love, for the daughters
of Jerusalem.

(On arriving at Jerusalem, the maidens sing a wedding song)

11Go forth, O ye daughters of *Zion,
and behold king Solomon with the
crown wherewith his mother crowned
him in the day of his espousals, and in
the day of the gladness of his heart.

IX. Canticle 8: The Bridegroom's Solo of Delight (4:1-7)

4 Behold, thou *art* fair, my love; behold, thou *art* fair; thou *hast* doves'
eyes within thy locks: thy hair *is* as a
flock of goats, that appear from mount
*Gilead.

4:1 Canticle 8
Title: "The Bridegroom's Solo of Delight"
Setting: a private apartment in the palace in Jerusalem
Time: after the marriage
Occasion: The bride is brought into her beloved's presence by her attendants, who retire. Her joy is too deep for expression.

2Thy teeth *are* like a flock *of sheep that*
are even shorn, which came up from the
washing; whereof every one bear twins,
and none *is* barren among them.
3Thy lips *are* like a thread of scarlet,
and thy speech *is* comely: thy temples
are like a piece of a pomegranate within thy locks.
4Thy neck *is* like the tower of *David builded for an armoury, whereon
there hang a thousand bucklers, all
shields of mighty men.
5Thy two breasts *are* like two young
roes that are twins, which feed among
the lilies.
6Until the day break, and the shadows
flee away, I will get me to the mountain
of myrrh, and to the hill of frankincense.
7Thou *art* all fair, my love; *there is* no
spot in thee.

X. Canticle 9: The Song of His Eager Proposal and Her Glad Acceptance (4:8—5:1)

(Solomon's proposal)

¶8Come with me from Lebanon, *my*
spouse, with me from Lebanon: look
from the top of Amana, from the top of
Shenir and Hermon, from the lions'

4:8 Canticle 9
Title: "The Song of His Eager Proposal and Her Glad Acceptance"
Setting: Lebanon
Time: before their marriage
Occasion: when he proposes

4:7 all fair. This is typical, or a *type, of the way in which the Lord Jesus Christ sees us, for He sees us as we shall be when He has completed His work of grace in us (see Eph. 3:16-19).

dens, from the mountains of the leopards.

(Solomon's love-making)

9 Thou hast ravished my heart, my
sister, *my* spouse; thou hast ravished
my heart with one of thine eyes, with
one chain of thy neck.
10 How fair is thy love, my sister, *my*
spouse! how much better is thy love
than wine! and the smell of thine ointments than all spices!
11 Thy lips, O *my* spouse, drop *as* the
honeycomb: honey and milk *are* under
thy tongue; and the smell of thy garments *is* like the smell of Lebanon.
12 A garden inclosed *is* my sister, *my*
spouse; a spring shut up, a fountain
sealed.
13 Thy plants *are* an orchard of pomegranates, with pleasant fruits; camphire, with *spikenard,
14 Spikenard and saffron; calamus and
cinnamon, with all trees of frankincense; myrrh and aloes, with all the
chief spices:
15 A fountain of gardens, a well of living waters, and streams from Lebanon.
16 Awake, O north wind; and come,
thou south; blow upon my garden, *that*
the spices thereof may flow out.

(The Shulamite responds)

Let my beloved come into his garden,
and eat his pleasant fruits.

(Solomon replies)

5 I am come into my garden, my
sister, *my* spouse: I have gathered
my myrrh with my spice; I have eaten
my honeycomb with my honey; I have
drunk my wine with my milk: eat,
O friends;

(To which the Shulamite replies)

drink, yea, drink abundantly, O beloved.

XI. Canticle 10: The Song about the Altogether Lovely One (5:2—6:3)

(The Shulamite dreams of an urgent night visit)

¶2 I sleep, but my heart waketh: *it is*
the voice of my beloved that knocketh,
saying, Open to me, my sister, my love,
my dove, my undefiled: for my head is
filled with dew, *and* my locks with the
drops of the night.

5:2 Canticle 10
Title: "The Song about the Altogether Lovely One"
Setting: Jerusalem
Time: after the marriage
Occasion: another dream (see 3:1, Canticle 6, notes).

¶3 I have put off my coat; how shall I
put it on? I have washed my feet; how
shall I defile them?
4 My beloved put in his hand by the
hole *of the door,* and my *bowels were
moved for him.
5 I rose up to open to my beloved; and
my hands dropped *with* myrrh, and my
fingers *with* sweet smelling myrrh,
upon the handles of the lock.

(Her dream becomes a nightmare as she seeks him)

6 I opened to my beloved; but my beloved had withdrawn himself, *and* was
gone: my soul failed when he spake:
I sought him, but I could not find him;
I called him, but he gave me no answer.
7 The watchmen that went about the
city found me, they smote me, they
wounded me; the keepers of the walls
took away my veil from me.
8 I charge you, O daughters of Jerusalem, if ye find my beloved, that ye tell
him, that I *am* sick of love.

4:9 sister. A word indicating the purity of their love during courtship.
4:9 with one of thine eyes. With one look from your eyes.
5:4 bowels. Heart.
5:7 took away my veil. The shameful condition of an evil woman.
5:8 sick of love. See 2:5 note.

(The daughters of Jerusalem speak with irritation)

9What *is* thy beloved more than *another* beloved, O thou fairest among women? what *is* thy beloved more than *another* beloved, that thou dost so charge us?

(The bride's description of the altogether lovely bridegroom)

10My beloved *is* white and ruddy, the chiefest among ten thousand.
11His head *is as* the most fine gold, his locks *are* bushy, *and* black as a raven.
12His eyes *are* as *the eyes* of doves by the rivers of waters, washed with milk, *and* fitly set.
13His cheeks *are* as a bed of spices, *as* sweet flowers: his lips *like* lilies, dropping sweet smelling myrrh.
14His hands *are as* gold rings set with the beryl: his belly *is as* bright ivory overlaid *with* sapphires.
15His legs *are as* pillars of marble, set upon sockets of fine gold: his countenance *is* as Lebanon, excellent as the cedars.
16His mouth *is* most sweet: yea, he *is* altogether lovely. This *is* my beloved, and this *is* my friend, O daughters of Jerusalem.

(The daughters of Jerusalem desire to see the bridegroom)

6 Whither is thy beloved gone, O thou fairest among women? whither is thy beloved turned aside? that we may seek him with thee.

(The bride answers)

2My beloved is gone down into his garden, to the beds of spices, to feed in the gardens, and to gather lilies.
3I *am* my beloved's, and my beloved *is* mine: he feedeth among the lilies.

XII. Canticle 11: A Song of the Shulamite's Superiority (6:4—7:10)

(Solomon's praise of her breathtaking loveliness)

¶4Thou *art* beautiful, O my love, as Tirzah, comely as Jerusalem, terrible as *an army* with banners.

6:4 Canticle 11
Title: "A Song of the Shulamite's Superiority"
Setting: Jerusalem
Time: shortly after the marriage
Occasion: a time of communion (in the presence of others)

5Turn away thine eyes from me, for they have overcome me: thy hair *is* as a flock of goats that appear from Gilead.
6Thy teeth *are* as a flock of sheep which go up from the washing, whereof every one beareth twins, and *there is* not one barren among them.
7As a piece of a pomegranate *are* thy temples within thy locks.

(Solomon tells of her superior beauty)

8There are threescore queens, and fourscore concubines, and virgins without number.
9My dove, my undefiled is *but* one; she *is* the *only* one of her mother, she *is* the choice *one* of her that bare her.

(He quotes the other queen's warm praise of her)

The daughters saw her, and blessed her; *yea,* the queens and the concubines, and they praised her.

(The queen's praise)

¶10Who *is* she *that* looketh forth as the morning, fair as the moon, clear as

---

6:2 to feed. To feed his flock.
6:4 Tirzah. This was later to become the place of the palace of the kings of Israel (1 Kings 15:33) just as Jerusalem was the capital city of the kings of Judah.
6:4 terrible. Awesome, awe-inspiring.
6:7 within thy locks. Behind your veil (or locks).

the sun, *and* terrible as *an army* with
banners?

(The embarrassed Shulamite slips out into an adjoining garden)

11 I went down into the garden of nuts
to see the fruits of the valley, *and* to see
whether the vine flourished, *and* the
pomegranates budded.

(At Solomon's signal, courtiers lift her into a palanquin and carry her along)

12 Or ever I was aware, my soul made
me *like* the chariots of Amminadib.

(The women of the court cry out)

13 Return, return, O Shulamite; return,
return, that we may look upon thee.

(The amazed Shulamite replies)

What will ye see in the Shulamite?

(The women answer)

As it were the company of two armies.

(The palanquin halts at Solomon's command)

(The women of the court describe the Shulamite's beauty)

7 How beautiful are thy feet with
shoes, O prince's daughter! the
joints of thy thighs *are* like jewels, the
work of the hands of a cunning workman.
2 Thy navel *is like* a round goblet,
which wanteth not liquor: thy belly *is*
like an heap of wheat set about with
lilies.
3 Thy two breasts *are* like two young
roes *that are* twins.
4 Thy neck *is* as a tower of ivory; thine
eyes *like* the fishpools in Heshbon, by
the gate of Bath-rabbim: thy nose *is* as
the tower of Lebanon which looketh
toward *Damascus.
5 Thine head upon thee *is* like
*Carmel, and the hair of thine head
like purple; the king *is* held in the galleries.

(The bridegroom interrupts them with his own praise of her)

6 How fair and how pleasant art
thou, O love, for delights!
7 This thy stature is like to a palm
tree, and thy breasts to clusters *of*
grapes.
8 I said, I will go up to the palm tree, I
will take hold of the boughs thereof:
now also thy breasts shall be as clusters
of the vine, and the smell of thy nose
like apples;

6:12 chariots of Amminadib. Palanquin or litter (a kind of chariot carried by men) of the willing people. The bride was joyful over the fact that she was fully received by the people as their queen.

6:13 Return, return, O Shulamite. In the Hebrew Bible, chapter 7 begins with this verse. Chapter divisions were put in our Bible to help us to find the place. Sometimes the thought continues from one chapter to the next.

6:13 What will ye see . . . ? The thought is, "What can you see in me when the altogether lovely one is here?"

6:13 company of two armies. The dance of two companies, that is, "you are lovely like the beauty and grace of the dance of two companies (at the same time)."

7:1 prince's daughter. Although not a princess by birth, the Shulamite looked and acted like one.

7:1 the joints of thy thighs. "The Easterners still, as in ancient times, use the greatest plainness of speech throughout the Holy Land. At first, a Westerner's sense of delicacy is greatly shocked. Things, the very mention of which decency forbids amongst us, are there freely spoken of before women and children by people of the highest class and of the greatest respectability and refinement. . . . Seeing that the Bible claims to be an Eastern book, written in the East, and first and for long ages addressed to Easterners only, it could not possibly be genuine if these very matters which have given rise to such blasphemous statements by unbelievers were absent from its pages" (Neil: *Palestine Explored*).

7:5 held in the galleries. Held captive in the tresses.

9And the roof of thy mouth like the
best *wine

(The bride interrupts the bridegroom)

for my *beloved, that goeth *down*
sweetly, causing the lips of those that
are asleep to speak.
¶10I *am* my beloved's, and his desire
is toward me.

XIII. Canticle 12: The Song of a Homesick Bride (7:11—8:4)

(The Shulamite longs for Lebanon)

11Come, my beloved, let us go forth
into the field; let us lodge in the villages.

> **7:11 Canticle 12**
> *Title:* "The Song of a Homesick Bride"
> *Setting:* Jerusalem, and a village on the way to Lebanon
> *Time:* after the marriage
> *Occasion:* The bride, longing for the beautiful Lebanon country, suggests a trip home, and Solomon goes with her.

12Let us get up early to the vineyards; let us see if the vine flourish,
whether the tender grape appear, *and*
the pomegranates bud forth: there will
I give thee my loves.
13The mandrakes give a smell, and at
our gates *are* all manner of pleasant
fruits, new and old, *which* I have laid up
for thee, O my beloved.

(The bride becomes painfully aware of the great gap between her royal husband and her brothers)

8 O that thou *wert* as my brother,
that sucked the breasts of my
mother! *when* I should find thee without, I would kiss thee; yea, I should not
be despised.
2I would lead thee, *and* bring thee into
my mother's house, *who* would instruct
me: I would cause thee to drink of spiced
wine of the juice of my pomegranate.

(Reassured by his loving arms, she drifts off to sleep to his favorite chorus)

3His left hand *should be* under my
head, and his right hand should embrace me.
4I charge you, O daughters of Jerusalem, that ye stir not up, nor awake *my*
love, until he please.

> **8:5 Canticle 13**
> *Title:* "The Song of a Triumphant Homecoming"
> *Setting:* Lebanon
> *Time:* after their marriage
> *Occasion:* a kind of "second honeymoon" visit to the bride's former home

XIV. Canticle 13: The Song of a Triumphal Homecoming (8:5-14)

(The amazed brothers speak)

5Who *is* this that cometh up from
the wilderness, leaning upon her beloved?

(The bridegroom speaks)

I raised thee up under the apple tree:
there thy mother brought thee forth:
there she brought thee forth *that* bare
thee.
¶6Set me as a seal upon thine heart,
as a seal upon thine arm: for love *is*
strong as death; jealousy *is* cruel as the

8:2 who would instruct me. That you might instruct me.
8:4 until he please. See 2:7 note.
8:5 Who is this that cometh . . . ? The amazed inquiry of the startled brothers (and neighbors) at the unexpected appearance of a royal chariot in this out-of-the-way place.
8:5 I raised thee up. I awakened you. As they are driven up toward the bride's former home, Solomon points to an apple tree, where he once found her asleep and awakened her. It was on this spot that an earlier family home (or tent) stood, in which she was born.
8:6 Set me as a seal. Seeing some rather attractive young shepherds in the waiting group, for a moment Solomon fears that a former lover may arouse her attention, so he reminds her of the violent jealousy of his love (see Exod. 20:3,5).

grave: the coals thereof *are* coals of fire,
which hath a most vehement flame.

(The bride replies to Solomon)

¶7 Many waters cannot quench love,
neither can the floods drown it: if *a* man
would give all the substance of his
house for love, it would utterly be contemned.

(The Shulamite speaks to her brothers)

¶8 We have a little sister, and she hath
no breasts: what shall we do for our
sister in the day when she shall be spoken for?
9 If she *be* a wall, we will build upon
her a palace of silver: and if she *be* a
door, we will inclose her with boards of
cedar.
10 I *am* a wall, and my breasts like
towers: then was I in his eyes as one
that found favour.

(The Shulamite reminds Solomon of the terms of the contract for her family's vineyard)

11 Solomon had a vineyard at Baal-
hamon; he let out the vineyard unto
keepers; every one for the fruit thereof was to bring a thousand *pieces* of silver.

(She asks Solomon to give her brothers one-fifth of the products of the vineyard)

12 My vineyard, which *is* mine, *is* before me: thou, O Solomon, *must have* a
thousand, and those that keep the fruit
thereof two hundred.

(Her brothers respectfully accept these terms)

13 Thou that dwellest in the gardens,
the companions hearken to thy voice:

(Solomon, unconcerned over a few pieces of silver, teases her for her seriousness)

cause me to hear *it*.

(The Shulamite lovingly responds)

¶14 Make haste, my beloved, and be
thou like to a roe or to a young hart
upon the mountains of spices.

8:7 all the substance. The bride tells Solomon that he need have no fears, for she loves him for himself—not for his riches and position. She loved him before she knew who he was.

8:8 a little sister. The Shulamite's brothers had not been kind to her (1:6). Here she repeats a conversation they had had concerning her when she was much younger. They had despaired of ever marrying her off to any worthwhile husband (vss. 8-9). She good-naturedly reminds them of how wrong their estimate of her was. She has the great King Solomon for a husband (vs. 10).

8:13 it. "Thy voice." Solomon was saying, "Let us get away from this crowd, and live over again the happy days of our courtship here on these mountains."

8:14 Make haste. The bride likewise dismisses business with a wave of the hand and replies (vs. 14) with a favorite saying from the days of her courtship (2:17). And so they walk off together into the woods, hand in hand, to live over again the happy days of the past.

The Book of the Prophet

ISAIAH

THEME

The prophecy of Isaiah is, in a very real sense, the very heart of the Old Testament. Many of its themes come to their highest revelation in this book; for example: the person of Christ (Isaiah 7:14; 9:6,7); the sufferings of Christ (Isaiah 53); the reign of Christ (Isaiah 61); etc.

Isaiah is the prophet of the Evangel, for the gospel is written into its very fiber. It opens with an invitation to sinners to reason with the LORD that their sins may be made white as snow. It closes with the warning that eternal punishment awaits those who reject the LORD.

THE WRITER

Even among those who are agreed as to the *inspiration of this book, there are some who have declared that it is the work of two or more authors. Nevertheless, the fact remains that the entire book of Isaiah is the work of Isaiah, the son of Amos (see John 12:38-41, where Isaiah 53:1 and 6:10 are quoted as spoken by the one prophet). It is as unnecessary to say that Isaiah could not have foretold the acts of Cyrus (Isaiah 44:28; 45:1) before the life of Cyrus, as it would be to say that Isaiah could not foretell the virgin birth of Christ (Isaiah 7:14) and His vicarious death (Isaiah 53) before the death of Christ. *God* knows the end from the beginning. Prophecy is prewritten history. But it is more than foretelling. It is the forth-telling of God's Word.

THE TIME

The prophet Isaiah ministered during the reigns of Uzziah, Jotham, Ahaz, and Hezekiah, or from approximately 760–700 B.C., and at about the same time that Jonah, Amos, Hosea, and Micah were prophesying. This book, addressed in the first instance to Israel, has in it a message for all mankind.

OUTLINE OF ISAIAH

I.	The Security of Israel's Covenants	Isaiah 1:1—12:6
II.	The Judgment of Israel's Foes	Isaiah 13:1—23:18
III.	The Glory of Israel's Future Kingdom	Isaiah 24:1—27:13
IV.	A Warning against Israel's Sin	Isaiah 28:1—31:9
V.	The Kingdom of Israel's Christ	Isaiah 32:1—35:10
VI.	The Reward of Israel's Faith (under Hezekiah)	Isaiah 36:1—39:8
VII.	The Greatness of Israel's God	Isaiah 40:1—41:29
VIII.	The Ministry of Jehovah's Servant	Isaiah 42:1—53:12

IX.	The Invitation of Israel's Saviour	Isaiah 54:1—58:14
X.	The Establishment of Israel's Kingdom	Isaiah 59:1—63:19
XI.	The Eternal Destiny of Individual Souls	Isaiah 64:1—66:24

I. The Security of Israel's Covenants (1:1—12:6)

*Though *chastened, Israel will be restored*

1 The vision of Isaiah the son of Amoz, which he saw concerning *Judah and *Jerusalem in the days of Uzziah, Jotham, Ahaz, *and* *Hezekiah, kings of Judah.

2 Hear, O heavens, and give ear, O earth: for the LORD hath spoken, I have nourished and brought up children, and they have rebelled against me.

> **1:2 Isaiah's Call to Repent**
> The first call of the prophet Isaiah to Israel is a call to repentance. He told of many of the sins of Israel in these verses and reminded the people that their afflictions were judgments from God. Because of these, he called the people to repentance and promised that God Himself would cleanse them from their sin if they would return to the LORD (1:18).

3 The ox knoweth his owner, and the ass his master's crib: *but* *Israel doth not know, my people doth not consider.

4 Ah sinful nation, a people laden with iniquity, a seed of evildoers, children that are corrupters: they have forsaken the LORD, they have provoked the Holy One of Israel unto anger, they are gone away backward.

¶5 Why should ye be stricken any more? ye will revolt more and more: the whole head is sick, and the whole heart faint.

6 From the sole of the foot even unto the head *there is* no soundness in it; *but* wounds, and bruises, and putrifying sores: they have not been closed, neither bound up, neither mollified with ointment.

7 Your country *is* desolate, your cities *are* burned with *fire: your land, strangers devour it in your presence, and *it is* desolate, as overthrown by strangers.

8 And the daughter of *Zion is left as a cottage in a *vineyard, as a lodge in a garden of cucumbers, as a besieged city.

9 Except the LORD of hosts had left unto us a very small *remnant, we should have been as Sodom, *and* we should have been like unto Gomorrah.

¶10 Hear the word of the LORD, ye rulers of Sodom; give ear unto the *law of our *God, ye people of Gomorrah.

11 To what purpose *is* the multitude of your sacrifices unto me? saith the LORD: I am full of the burnt-offerings of rams, and the fat of fed beasts; and I delight not in the *blood of bullocks, or of lambs, or of he goats.

12 When ye come to appear before me, who hath required this at your hand, to tread my courts?

13 Bring no more vain oblations; *incense is an *abomination unto me; the *new moons and sabbaths, the calling of assemblies, I cannot away with; *it is* iniquity, even the solemn meeting.

14 Your new moons and your appointed *feasts my soul hateth: they are a trouble unto me; I am weary to bear *them*.

15 And when ye spread forth your hands, I will hide mine eyes from you: yea, when ye make many prayers, I will not hear: your hands are full of blood.

¶16 Wash you, make you *clean; put away the evil of your doings from before mine eyes; cease to do evil;

1:1 Isaiah. See introduction.
1:8 lodge. A hut.
1:13 away with. To put up with, to endure or tolerate.

17 Learn to do well; seek *judgment, relieve the oppressed, judge the fatherless, plead for the widow.

18 Come now, and let us reason together, saith the LORD: though your sins be as scarlet, they shall be as white as snow; though they be red like crimson, they shall be as wool.

19 If ye be willing and obedient, ye shall eat the good of the land:

20 But if ye refuse and rebel, ye shall be devoured with the sword: for the mouth of the LORD hath spoken *it.*

¶21 How is the faithful city become an harlot! it was full of judgment; *righteousness lodged in it; but now murderers.

22 Thy *silver is become dross, thy wine mixed with water:

23 Thy princes *are* rebellious, and companions of thieves: every one loveth gifts, and followeth after rewards: they judge not the fatherless, neither doth the cause of the widow come unto them.

24 Therefore saith the Lord, the LORD of hosts, the mighty One of Israel, Ah, I will ease me of mine adversaries, and avenge me of mine enemies:

¶25 And I will turn my hand upon thee, and purely purge away thy dross, and take away all thy tin:

1:26 A Future Government Revealed
The form of government during the reign of Christ on the earth is revealed in this verse. Israel was a theocracy under the judges (which means that its form of government was such that God was their King). The reign of Christ on earth will also be theocratic. According to Matthew 19:28, He will give His apostles the position of judges during His reign.

26 And I will restore thy *judges as at the first, and thy counsellors as at the beginning: afterward thou shalt be called, The city of righteousness, the faithful city.

27 Zion shall be *redeemed with judgment, and her converts with righteousness.

¶28 And the destruction of the transgressors and of the sinners *shall be* together, and they that forsake the LORD shall be consumed.

29 For they shall be ashamed of the oaks which ye have desired, and ye shall be confounded for the gardens that ye have chosen.

30 For ye shall be as an oak whose leaf fadeth, and as a garden that hath no water.

31 And the strong shall be as tow, and the maker of it as a spark, and they shall both burn together, and none shall quench *them.*

The kingdom of Christ will establish Israel and destroy idolatry

2 The word that Isaiah the son of Amoz saw concerning Judah and Jerusalem.

2 And it shall come to pass in the last days, *that* the *mountain of the LORD'S house shall be established in the top of the mountains, and shall be exalted above the hills; and all nations shall flow unto it.

3 And many people shall go and say, Come ye, and let us go up to the mountain of the LORD, to the house of the God of *Jacob; and he will teach us of his ways, and we will walk in his paths: for out of Zion shall go forth the law, and the word of the LORD from Jerusalem.

1:21 the faithful city. Jerusalem had become a "harlot," that is, a worshipper of idols.

1:29 the oaks which ye have desired. Verse 29 refers to the worship of idols and the places where such evil worship took place. Verses 30 and 31 refer to the effects of such worship.

2:3 out of Zion. Jerusalem will be the capital of the *kingdom of Christ when He returns to earth. From it will go the law that will govern the life of the people and the Word of the Lord that will guide their spiritual instruction. When He comes to reign, He will establish peace upon the earth (2:4).

[4]And he shall judge among the nations, and shall rebuke many people:
and they shall beat their swords into
plowshares, and their spears into
pruninghooks: nation shall not lift up
sword against nation, neither shall they
learn war any more.
[5]O house of Jacob, come ye, and let
us walk in the light of the LORD.
¶[6]Therefore thou hast forsaken thy
people the house of Jacob, because they
be replenished from the east, and *are*
soothsayers like the *Philistines, and
they please themselves in the children
of strangers.
[7]Their land also is full of silver and
gold, neither *is there any* end of their
treasures; their land is also full of
horses, neither *is there any* end of their
chariots:
[8]Their land also is full of idols; they
worship the work of their own hands,
that which their own fingers have
made:
[9]And the mean man boweth down,
and the great man humbleth himself:
therefore forgive them not.
¶[10]Enter into the rock, and hide thee
in the dust, for *fear of the LORD, and
for the glory of his majesty.
[11]The lofty looks of man shall be
humbled, and the haughtiness of men
shall be bowed down, and the LORD
alone shall be exalted in that day.
[12]For the day of the LORD of hosts
shall be upon every *one that is* proud and
lofty, and upon every *one that is* lifted
up; and he shall be brought low:
[13]And upon all the cedars of *Lebanon, *that are* high and lifted up, and
upon all the oaks of *Bashan,
[14]And upon all the high mountains,
and upon all the hills *that are* lifted up,
[15]And upon every high tower, and
upon every fenced wall,

2:12 The Day of the LORD
The "Day of the LORD" is the name given by the Scriptures to the time when Jesus Christ will return to the earth and rule over it as King of Kings. In one sense, the Day of the LORD is a day of judgment upon the unrighteous (2:12, 21). In another sense, the Day of the LORD is a day of gladness for His people. "The year of my redeemed is come" (63:4).

[16]And upon all the ships of *Tarshish,
and upon all pleasant pictures.
[17]And the loftiness of man shall be
bowed down, and the haughtiness of
men shall be made low: and the LORD
alone shall be exalted in that day.
[18]And the idols he shall utterly abolish.
[19]And they shall go into the holes of
the rocks, and into the caves of the
earth, for fear of the LORD, and for the
glory of his majesty, when he ariseth to
shake terribly the earth.
[20]In that day a man shall cast his idols
of silver, and his idols of gold, which
they made *each one* for himself to worship, to the moles and to the bats;
[21]To go into the clefts of the rocks,
and into the tops of the ragged rocks,
for fear of the LORD, and for the glory
of his majesty, when he ariseth to shake
terribly the earth.
[22]Cease ye from man, whose breath
is in his nostrils: for wherein is he to be
accounted of?

Israel must be punished because of her sin

3 For, behold, the Lord, the LORD of
hosts, doth take away from Jerusalem and from Judah the stay and the
staff, the whole stay of bread, and the
whole stay of water,
[2]The mighty man, and the man of

2:4 judge among the nations. Christ will decide the disputes of the nations.
2:6 replenished from the east. That is, with customs from the East.
2:6 they please themselves. The Israelites marry, or go into partnership with, the children of foreigners.
2:16 pleasant pictures. Stately pleasure vessels, beautiful crafts (ships).

3:1 A Double Future
Frequently in the prophetic Scriptures, the messages concern the immediate future of Israel, but also foretell the day of trouble, which is known as the *Great Tribulation. This is one of these Scriptures. For the immediate future it foretold the destruction of Jerusalem. It also describes the future suffering of Israel during the Great Tribulation, also called the time of *Jacob's Trouble.

war, the judge, and the *prophet, and
the prudent, and the ancient,
3The captain of fifty, and the honourable man, and the counsellor, and
the cunning artificer, and the eloquent
orator.
4And I will give children *to be* their
princes, and babes shall rule over them.
5And the people shall be oppressed,
every one by another, and every one by
his neighbour: the child shall behave
himself proudly against the ancient, and
the base against the honourable.
6When a man shall take hold of his
brother of the house of his father, *saying,* Thou hast clothing, be thou our
ruler, and *let* this ruin *be* under thy hand:
7In that day shall he swear, saying, I
will not be an healer; for in my house
is neither bread nor clothing: make me
not a ruler of the people.
8For Jerusalem is ruined, and Judah
is fallen: because their tongue and their
doings *are* against the LORD, to provoke
the eyes of his glory.
¶9The shew of their countenance
doth witness against them; and they declare their *sin as Sodom, they hide *it*
not. Woe unto their soul! for they have
rewarded evil unto themselves.
10Say ye to the righteous, that *it shall*
be well *with him:* for they shall eat the
fruit of their doings.
11Woe unto the wicked! *it shall be* ill
with him: for the reward of his hands
shall be given him.
¶12*As for* my people, children *are*
their oppressors, and women rule over
them. O my people, they which lead
thee cause *thee* to *err, and destroy the
way of thy paths.
13The LORD standeth up to plead, and
standeth to judge the people.
14The LORD will enter into judgment
with the ancients of his people, and the
princes thereof: for ye have eaten up
the vineyard; the spoil of the poor *is* in
your houses.
15What mean ye *that* ye beat my people to pieces, and grind the faces of the
poor? saith the Lord GOD of hosts.
¶16Moreover the LORD saith, Because
the daughters of Zion are haughty, and
walk with stretched forth necks and wanton eyes, walking and mincing *as* they
go, and making a tinkling with their feet:
17Therefore the Lord will smite with
a scab the crown of the head of the
daughters of Zion, and the LORD will
discover their secret parts.
18In that day the Lord will take away
the bravery of *their* tinkling ornaments
about their feet, and *their* cauls, and *their*
round tires like the moon,
19The chains, and the bracelets, and
the mufflers,
20The bonnets, and the ornaments of
the legs, and the headbands, and the
tablets, and the earrings,
21The rings, and nose jewels,
22The changeable suits of apparel,
and the mantles, and the wimples, and
the crisping pins,

3:6 let this ruin be under thy hand. The rich man is being asked to build up the ruined state of the city.
3:14 ancients. Elders.
3:16 mincing. Walking with very short steps.
3:18 bravery. Finery, showy dress.
3:18 cauls. Scarves on their heads.
3:19 mufflers. A covering or veil for the lower part of the face.
3:22 wimples. Veil or covering (cloak) for the throat or neck.
3:22 crisping pins. Purses.

23 The glasses, and the fine *linen,
and the hoods, and the vails.
24 And it shall come to pass, *that* instead of sweet smell there shall be
stink; and instead of a girdle a rent; and
instead of well set hair baldness; and
instead of a stomacher a girding of sackcloth; *and* burning instead of beauty.
25 Thy men shall fall by the sword, and
thy mighty in the war.
26 And her gates shall lament and
mourn; and she *being* desolate shall sit
upon the ground.

Israel will be holy during Christ's reign on earth

4 And in that day seven women
shall take hold of one man, saying,
We will eat our own bread, and wear our
own apparel: only let us be called by thy
name, to take away our reproach.
¶2 In that day shall the branch of the
LORD be beautiful and glorious, and the
fruit of the earth *shall be* excellent and
comely for them that are escaped of
Israel.
3 And it shall come to pass, *that he that*
is left in Zion, and *he that* remaineth in
Jerusalem, shall be called holy, *even*
every one that is written among the living in Jerusalem:
4 When the Lord shall have washed
away the filth of the daughters of Zion,
and shall have purged the blood of Jerusalem from the midst thereof by the
spirit of judgment, and by the spirit of
burning.
5 And the LORD will create upon every
dwelling place of mount Zion, and upon
her assemblies, a cloud and smoke by
day, and the shining of a flaming fire by
night: for upon all the glory *shall be* a
defence.
6 And there shall be a *tabernacle for
a shadow in the daytime from the heat,
and for a place of refuge, and for a covert from storm and from rain.

4:4 The Sin of Jerusalem
The sin of Jerusalem is the blood that has been spilt there—not only of the innocent prophets and righteous people, but it looks ahead to the death of the Lord Jesus Christ.

The sins of Israel

5 Now will I sing to my wellbeloved
a song of my *beloved touching his
vineyard. My wellbeloved hath a vineyard in a very fruitful hill:
2 And he fenced it, and gathered out
the stones thereof, and planted it with
the choicest vine, and built a tower
in the midst of it, and also made a winepress therein: and he looked that it
should bring forth grapes, and it brought
forth wild grapes.
3 And now, O inhabitants of Jerusalem, and men of Judah, judge, I pray
you, betwixt me and my vineyard.
4 What could have been done more to
my vineyard, that I have not done in it?
wherefore, when I looked that it should
bring forth grapes, brought it forth wild
grapes?
5 And now go to; I will tell you what I
will do to my vineyard: I will take away
the hedge thereof, and it shall be eaten

3:23 glasses. Mirrors.
3:24 a rent. A rope.
3:24 stomacher. Fine robe.
3:24 burning. The brand of a slave. This whole passage (vss. 16-24) speaks of the fates of God's people—their falling into slavery with its accompanying losses and degradation.
4:5 upon all the glory shall be a defence. Literally, *a covering* that shall be spread over all the glory. When the LORD sets up His *kingdom, the cloud of glory will not be only over the tabernacle as in former days (Exod. 40:34), but it will be spread over every dwelling place.
5:1 vineyard. In the Scriptures, Israel is pictured as a vineyard.
5:1 My wellbeloved. God's beloved is His only begotten Son, the Lord Jesus Christ (compare Luke 20:9-19).
5:2 looked. Expected.

up; *and* break down the wall thereof,
and it shall be trodden down:
6 And I will lay it waste: it shall not be
pruned, nor digged; but there shall
come up briers and thorns: I will also
command the clouds that they rain no
rain upon it.
7 For the vineyard of the LORD of
hosts *is* the house of Israel, and the men
of Judah his pleasant plant: and he
looked for judgment, but behold oppression; for righteousness, but behold
a cry.
¶8 Woe unto them that join house to
house, *that* lay field to field, till *there be*
no place, that they may be placed alone
in the midst of the earth!

5:8 Judgment on Five Sins
Judgment is pronounced against five sins in verses 8-22:
1. selfishness (vs. 8);
2. drunkenness (vss. 11 and 22);
3. stubbornness (vs. 18);
4. insincerity (vs. 20); and
5. pride (vs. 21).

9 In mine ears *said* the LORD of hosts,
Of a truth many houses shall be desolate,
even great and fair, without inhabitant.
10 Yea, ten acres of vineyard shall yield
one bath, and the seed of an *homer
shall yield an *ephah.
¶11 Woe unto them that rise up early
in the morning, *that* they may follow
strong drink; that continue until night,
till wine inflame them!
12 And the harp, and the viol, the
*tabret, and pipe, and wine, are in their
feasts: but they regard not the work of
the LORD, neither consider the operation of his hands.
¶13 Therefore my people are gone
into captivity, because *they have* no
knowledge: and their honourable men
are famished, and their multitude dried
up with thirst.
14 Therefore *hell hath enlarged herself, and opened her mouth without
measure: and their glory, and their
multitude, and their pomp, and he that
rejoiceth, shall descend into it.
15 And the mean man shall be brought
down, and the mighty man shall be
humbled, and the eyes of the lofty shall
be humbled:
16 But the LORD of hosts shall be exalted in judgment, and God that is holy
shall be sanctified in righteousness.
17 Then shall the lambs feed after
their manner, and the waste places of
the fat ones shall strangers eat.
18 Woe unto them that draw iniquity
with cords of *vanity, and sin as it were
with a cart rope:
19 That say, Let him make speed, *and*
hasten his work, that we may see *it:* and
let the counsel of the Holy One of Israel draw nigh and come, that we may
know *it!*
¶20 Woe unto them that call evil good,
and good evil; that put darkness for
light, and light for darkness; that put
bitter for sweet, and sweet for bitter!
21 Woe unto *them that are* wise in their
own eyes, and prudent in their own
sight!
22 Woe unto *them that are* mighty to
drink wine, and men of strength to mingle strong drink:
23 Which justify the wicked for reward, and take away the righteousness
of the righteous from him!
24 Therefore as the fire devoureth the
stubble, and the flame consumeth the
chaff, *so* their root shall be as rottenness, and their blossom shall go up as
dust: because they have cast away the
law of the LORD of hosts, and despised
the word of the Holy One of Israel.

5:7 cry. A cry for help.
5:10 bath. A bath is about six gallons.
5:14 hell hath enlarged herself. "The wages of sin is death" (Rom. 6:23). Isaiah describes the descent of man into death, saying that *hell, or death, hath enlarged herself to receive men.

25Therefore is the anger of the LORD
kindled against his people, and he hath
stretched forth his hand against them,
and hath smitten them: and the hills did
tremble, and their carcases *were* torn in
the midst of the streets. For all this his
anger is not turned away, but his hand
is stretched out still.
¶26And he will lift up an ensign to the
nations from far, and will hiss unto them
from the end of the earth: and, behold,
they shall come with speed swiftly:
27None shall be weary nor stumble
among them; none shall slumber nor
sleep; neither shall the girdle of their
loins be loosed, nor the latchet of their
shoes be broken:
28Whose arrows *are* sharp, and all
their bows bent, their horses' hoofs
shall be counted like flint, and their
wheels like a whirlwind:
29Their roaring *shall be* like a lion,
they shall roar like young lions: yea,
they shall roar, and lay hold of the prey,
and shall carry *it* away safe, and none
shall deliver *it*.
30And in that day they shall roar
against them like the roaring of the sea:
and if *one* look unto the land, behold
darkness *and* sorrow, and the light is
darkened in the heavens thereof.

The call of Isaiah

6 In the year that king Uzziah died
I saw also the Lord sitting upon a
throne, high and lifted up, and his train
filled the temple.
2Above it stood the seraphims: each
one had six wings; with twain he covered his face, and with twain he covered
his feet, and with twain he did fly.
3And one cried unto another, and
said, Holy, holy, holy, *is* the LORD of
hosts: the whole earth *is* full of his
glory.
4And the posts of the door moved at
the voice of him that cried, and the
house was filled with smoke.
¶5Then said I, Woe *is* me! for I am
undone; because I *am* a man of *unclean
lips, and I dwell in the midst of a people of unclean lips: for mine eyes have
seen the King, the LORD of hosts.
6Then flew one of the seraphims unto
me, having a live coal in his hand, *which*
he had taken with the tongs from off the
*altar:
7And he laid *it* upon my mouth, and
said, Lo, this hath touched thy lips; and

6:2 Seraphims
The seraphims are angelic beings. The word "seraphim," without the "s," is the plural of seraph, just as cherubim means more than one cherub. The Scripture reveals various orders of angels:
1. seraphim (6:2)
2. cherubim (Gen. 3:24)
3. holy angels (Mark 8:38)
4. fallen angels (Jude 6)
5. elect angels (1 Tim. 5:21)

Some angels are known by name: Gabriel (Luke 1:19,26-38) and Michael (Jude 9). The seraphim are revealed only in this passage of Isaiah. They appear here as the agents of cleansing by which God purifies people, just as the cherubim are agents of God's judgment.

6:1 king Uzziah died. See 2 Kings 15:5-7 to read of the death of the leprous King Uzziah (also called Azariah).

6:1 the Lord. The person whom Isaiah saw upon the throne was the Son of God (John 12:41). When this passage is studied together with Daniel 10:5-6 and Proverbs 8:22-30, we see the testimony of the Old Testament Scriptures to the preincarnate state of the Son of God (which means His life in heaven as God before He was born on earth as a man). The Lord Jesus claimed to bear this glory and asked that the Father would restore it to Him after His death and resurrection (John 17:5).

6:5 undone. This means that he was ruined and justly doomed to death.

6:5 mine eyes have seen the King. Compare John 1:18 note, "Seeing God."

6:6 live coal . . . from off the altar. The coal was from the *altar of burnt-offering and therefore stood not only for the fire of God's judgment upon sin and unclean lips, but also for the cleansing power of the blood of the Lord Jesus Christ.

thine iniquity is taken away, and thy sin
purged.
8 Also I heard the voice of the Lord,
saying, Whom shall I send, and who
will go for us? Then said I, Here *am* I;
send me.
¶ 9 And he said, Go, and tell this people, Hear ye indeed, but understand
not; and see ye indeed, but perceive not.
10 Make the heart of this people fat,
and make their ears heavy, and shut
their eyes; lest they see with their
eyes, and hear with their ears, and understand with their heart, and convert,
and be healed.
11 Then said I, Lord, how long? And
he answered, Until the cities be wasted without inhabitant, and the houses
without man, and the land be utterly
desolate,
12 And the LORD have removed men
far away, and *there be* a great forsaking
in the midst of the land.
¶ 13 But yet in it *shall be* a tenth, and *it*
shall return, and shall be eaten: as a teil
tree, and as an oak, whose substance *is*
in them, when they cast *their leaves: so*
the holy seed *shall be* the substance
thereof.

6:13 The Teil Tree
This is the terebinth tree, which grows all over the land of Palestine, and from which a kind of turpentine is obtained, so that it is sometimes called the turpentine tree. It loses its leaves in the autumn just as the oak tree does, but it has not died, and new leaves will come again in the spring. So, although the land of Israel has lost its people for a time, leaving it bare and empty, they, "the holy seed," will return.

The virgin-born Christ is Israel's hope

7 And it came to pass in the days of
Ahaz the son of Jotham, the son of
Uzziah, king of *Judah, *that* *Rezin the
king of Syria, and Pekah the son of
Remaliah, king of *Israel, went up toward *Jerusalem to war against it, but
could not prevail against it.
2 And it was told the house of *David,
saying, Syria is confederate with
*Ephraim. And his heart was moved,
and the heart of his people, as the trees
of the wood are moved with the wind.
3 Then said the LORD unto Isaiah, Go
forth now to meet Ahaz, thou, and
Shear-jashub thy son, at the end of the
conduit of the upper pool in the highway of the fuller's field;
4 And say unto him, Take heed, and be
quiet; fear not, neither be fainthearted
for the two tails of these smoking firebrands, for the fierce anger of Rezin
with Syria, and of the son of Remaliah.
5 Because Syria, Ephraim, and the son

6:9 understand not. Israel had rejected God, therefore, God was rejecting Israel (Hos. 4:6). The Lord Jesus Christ said (Matt. 13:13-15) that He spoke in parables to keep the unbelieving world from understanding the truth. He also said that the truth is easily seen by believing eyes (Matt. 13:11,16; see also 13:11 note, "The Mysteries of the Kingdom").

6:10 convert. To be converted.

6:13 a tenth, and it shall return. The *remnant of Judah, which was to return at the end of the seventy years of Babylonian captivity (see the introductions to the books of Ezra and Nehemiah).

7:1 Ahaz. He stands for the house of David (vs. 2), for Ahaz was David's direct descendant.

7:2 Ephraim. Israel, or the ten tribes who would not follow Rehoboam, Solomon's son, but went after Jeroboam to establish the northern kingdom (1 Kings 12), which later came to be called "Samaria." They had now gone into exile under Assyria (2 Kings 17:1-6) and have never returned to their land. The Samaritans were hated by the Jews because they were of mixed blood—part Jewish and part Gentile.

7:2 his heart was moved. The heart of Ahaz was moved with fear.

7:3 Shear-jashub. The name means *a *remnant shall return.*

7:4 tails of these smoking firebrands. The end of a torch which is held in the hand can do no harm.

of Remaliah, have taken evil counsel against thee, saying,

6 Let us go up against Judah, and vex it, and let us make a breach therein for us, and set a king in the midst of it, *even* the son of Tabeal:

7 Thus saith the Lord GOD, It shall not stand, neither shall it come to pass.

8 For the head of Syria *is* *Damascus, and the head of Damascus *is* Rezin; and within threescore and five years shall Ephraim be broken, that it be not a people.

9 And the head of Ephraim *is* *Samaria, and the head of Samaria *is* Remaliah's son. If ye will not believe, surely ye shall not be established.

¶ 10 Moreover the LORD spake again unto Ahaz, saying,

11 Ask thee a sign of the LORD thy *God; ask it either in the depth, or in the height above.

12 But Ahaz said, I will not ask, neither will I *tempt the LORD.

13 And he said, Hear ye now, O house of David; *Is it* a small thing for you to weary men, but will ye weary my God also?

14 Therefore the Lord himself shall give you a sign; Behold, a virgin shall conceive, and bear a son, and shall call his name *Immanuel.

15 Butter and honey shall he eat, that he may know to refuse the evil, and choose the good.

16 For before the child shall know to refuse the evil, and choose the good, the land that thou abhorrest shall be forsaken of both her kings.

¶ 17 The LORD shall bring upon thee, and upon thy people, and upon thy father's house, days that have not come, from the day that Ephraim departed from Judah; *even* the king of Assyria.

18 And it shall come to pass in that day, *that* the LORD shall hiss for the fly that *is* in the uttermost part of the rivers of *Egypt, and for the bee that *is* in the land of Assyria.

19 And they shall come, and shall rest all of them in the desolate valleys, and in the holes of the rocks, and upon all thorns, and upon all bushes.

20 In the same day shall the Lord shave with a razor that is hired, *namely,* by them beyond the river, by the king of Assyria, the head, and the hair of the feet: and it shall also consume the beard.

21 And it shall come to pass in that day, *that* a man shall nourish a young cow, and two sheep;

22 And it shall come to pass, for the abundance of milk *that* they shall give he shall eat butter: for butter and honey shall every one eat that is left in the land.

7:14 Immanuel

The name Immanuel means *God with us.* When Jesus Christ was born, God became "flesh, and dwelt among us" (John 1:14). Not only does the prophet predict the virgin birth of Christ, but he proclaims the deity of Christ in this wonderful Scripture.

7:14 virgin. The Hebrew word translated "virgin" occurs many times in the Old Testament and means *an unmarried woman.* Isaiah's prophecy of the virgin birth of the Messiah was literally fulfilled when Christ was born (Matt. 1:8-25; Luke 1:26-38).

7:15 Butter and honey. He will eat butter and honey when He knows to refuse evil and choose good.

7:16 the land. Northern Palestine and Syria.

7:17 The LORD shall bring upon thee. God was speaking through the prophet directly to Ahaz here, telling him of the miseries that were to come to him and to his people because of their sin.

7:20 a razor that is hired. This speaks of the king of Assyria.

7:20 the river. The Euphrates.

7:21 a young cow, and two sheep. The wealth of the land of Palestine had been in the cattle of the land. One cow and two sheep speaks of great poverty as do the butter and honey of verse 22.

23 And it shall come to pass in that day,
that every place shall be, where there
were a thousand vines at a thousand silverlings, it shall *even* be for briers and
thorns.
24 With arrows and with bows shall
men come thither; because all the land
shall become briers and thorns.
25 And *on* all hills that shall be digged
with the mattock, there shall not come
thither the fear of briers and thorns:
but it shall be for the sending forth of
oxen, and for the treading of lesser
cattle.

Assyrian invasion—a judgment from God

8 Moreover the LORD said unto me,
Take thee a great roll, and write in
it with a man's pen concerning Maher-
shalal-hash-baz.
2 And I took unto me faithful witnesses to record, Uriah the priest, and
Zechariah the son of Jeberechiah.
3 And I went unto the prophetess; and
she conceived, and bare a son. Then
said the LORD to me, Call his name
Maher-shalal-hash-baz.
4 For before the child shall have
knowledge to cry, My father, and my
mother, the riches of Damascus and the
spoil of Samaria shall be taken away
before the king of Assyria.
¶ 5 The LORD spake also unto me
again, saying,
6 Forasmuch as this people refuseth
the waters of Shiloah that go softly, and
rejoice in Rezin and Remaliah's son;
7 Now therefore, behold, the Lord
bringeth up upon them the waters of
the river, strong and many, *even* the king
of Assyria, and all his glory: and he shall
come up over all his channels, and go
over all his banks:
8 And he shall pass through Judah; he
shall overflow and go over, he shall
reach *even* to the neck; and the stretching out of his wings shall fill the breadth
of thy land, O Immanuel.
¶ 9 Associate yourselves, O ye people,
and ye shall be broken in pieces; and
give ear, all ye of far countries: gird
yourselves, and ye shall be broken in
pieces; gird yourselves, and ye shall be
broken in pieces.
10 Take counsel together, and it shall
come to nought; speak the word, and it
shall not stand: for God *is* with us.
¶ 11 For the LORD spake thus to me
with a strong hand, and instructed me
that I should not walk in the way of this
people, saying,
12 Say ye not, A confederacy, to all
them to whom this people shall say, A
confederacy; neither fear ye their fear,
nor be afraid.
13 Sanctify the LORD of hosts himself;
and *let* him *be* your fear, and *let* him *be*
your dread.
14 And he shall be for a *sanctuary;

8:14 Sanctuary
This was a holy place devoted to God. Sometimes the name was given to the entire *tabernacle or *temple; sometimes it was used for the Holy Place, and sometimes for the Holy of Holies. It was also sometimes used to refer to the furniture of the tabernacle. The earthly sanctuary is a *type of heaven, and God himself is called a "sanctuary" (in this verse and in Ezek. 11:16), for He is the only safe and sacred place for sinners and Christians alike who flee to Him in their need.

7:23 silverlings. A small silver coin, a shekel.
7:24 With arrows and with bows. Men will have to hunt for their food instead of raising it, because of the briars and thorns.
8:1 Maher-shalal-hashbaz. This name means *haste ye to the spoil.*
8:6 Rezin. The king of Syria (see Isa. 7:1).
8:6 Remaliah's son. Pekah, king of Israel (7:1). To speak of him in this way without calling him by name was a sign of contempt.
8:8 the neck. This probably stands for Jerusalem, which was the head of the land.
8:12 A confederacy. A plan to form an alliance with Egypt and Assyria.

but for a stone of stumbling and for a rock of offence to both the houses of Israel, for a gin and for a snare to the inhabitants of Jerusalem.

15 And many among them shall stumble, and fall, and be broken, and be snared, and be taken.

16 Bind up the testimony, seal the *law among my disciples.

17 And I will wait upon the LORD, that hideth his face from the house of *Jacob, and I will look for him.

18 Behold, I and the children whom the LORD hath given me *are* for signs and for wonders in Israel from the LORD of hosts, which dwelleth in mount *Zion.

¶ 19 And when they shall say unto you, Seek unto them that have *familiar spirits, and unto wizards that peep, and that mutter: should not a people seek unto their God? for the living to the dead?

20 To the law and to the testimony: if they speak not according to this word, *it is* because *there is* no light in them.

21 And they shall pass through it, hardly bestead and hungry: and it shall come to pass, that when they shall be hungry, they shall fret themselves, and curse their king and their God, and look upward.

22 And they shall look unto the earth; and behold trouble and darkness, dimness of anguish; and *they shall be* driven to darkness.

Christ will be Israel's King

9 Nevertheless the dimness *shall* not *be* such as *was* in her vexation, when at the first he lightly afflicted the land of Zebulun and the land of Naphtali, and afterward did more grievously afflict *her by* the way of the sea, beyond Jordan, in Galilee of the nations.

2 The people that walked in darkness have seen a great light: they that dwell in the land of the shadow of *death, upon them hath the light shined.

3 Thou hast multiplied the nation, *and* not increased the joy: they joy before thee according to the joy in harvest, *and* as *men* rejoice when they divide the spoil.

4 For thou hast broken the yoke of his burden, and the staff of his shoulder, the rod of his oppressor, as in the day of *Midian.

5 For every battle of the warrior *is* with confused noise, and garments rolled in blood; but *this* shall be with burning *and* fuel of fire.

6 For unto us a child is born, unto us a son is given: and the government shall be upon his shoulder: and his name shall be called Wonderful, Counsellor, The mighty God, The everlasting Father, The Prince of *Peace.

7 Of the increase of *his* government and peace *there shall be* no end, upon the throne of David, and upon his *kingdom, to order it, and to establish it with *judgment and with justice from henceforth even for ever. The zeal of the LORD of hosts will perform this.

¶ 8 The Lord sent a word into Jacob, and it hath lighted upon Israel.

9 And all the people shall know, *even* Ephraim and the inhabitant of Samaria, that say in the pride and stoutness of heart,

10 The bricks are fallen down, but we will build with hewn stones: the sycomores are cut down, but we will change *them into* cedars.

11 Therefore the LORD shall set up the adversaries of Rezin against him, and join his enemies together;

8:19 peep. To whisper, to utter low sounds.
8:20 To the law. The Bible, the Word of God, is the final test; the "law" and "testimony" mentioned here are God's Word.
8:21 hardly bestead. Greatly distressed.
9:2 great light. This great light is the Lord Jesus Christ. His first coming fulfilled this prophecy (Matt. 4:15-16; John 1:9).
9:3 not increased the joy. The translation should be that the LORD *has* increased the joy.
9:11 the adversaries of Rezin. The Assyrians.

12 The Syrians before, and the *Philistines behind; and they shall devour
Israel with open mouth. For all this his
anger is not turned away, but his hand
is stretched out still.
¶ 13 For the people turneth not unto
him that smiteth them, neither do they
seek the LORD of hosts.
14 Therefore the LORD will cut off
from Israel head and tail, branch and
rush, in one day.
15 The ancient and honourable, he *is*
the head; and the *prophet that
teacheth lies, he *is* the tail.
16 For the leaders of this people cause
them to *err; and *they that are* led of
them *are* destroyed.
17 Therefore the Lord shall have no
joy in their young men, neither shall
have *mercy on their fatherless and
widows: for every one *is* an hypocrite
and an evildoer, and every mouth
speaketh folly. For all this his anger is
not turned away, but his hand *is*
stretched out still.
¶ 18 For wickedness burneth as the
fire: it shall devour the briers and
thorns, and shall kindle in the thickets
of the forest, and they shall mount up
like the lifting up of smoke.
19 Through the wrath of the LORD of
hosts is the land darkened, and the people shall be as the fuel of the fire: no
man shall spare his brother.
20 And he shall snatch on the right
hand, and be hungry; and he shall eat
on the left hand, and they shall not be
satisfied: they shall eat every man the
flesh of his own arm:
21 *Manasseh, Ephraim; and Ephraim, Manasseh: *and* they together *shall
be* against Judah. For all this his anger
is not turned away, but his hand *is*
stretched out still.

God's judgment on Assyria

10 Woe unto them that decree unrighteous decrees, and that
write grievousness *which* they have
prescribed;
2 To turn aside the needy from judgment, and to take away the right from
the poor of my people, that widows may
be their prey, and *that* they may rob the
fatherless!
3 And what will ye do in the day of
visitation, and in the desolation *which*
shall come from far? to whom will ye
flee for help? and where will ye leave
your glory?
4 Without me they shall bow down
under the prisoners, and they shall fall
under the slain. For all this his anger is
not turned away, but his hand *is*
stretched out still.
¶ 5 O Assyrian, the rod of mine anger,
and the staff in their hand is mine indignation.
6 I will send him against an hypocritical nation, and against the people of my

---

9:6-7 THE SON OF GOD

The Holy Spirit reveals much about the person of the Lord Jesus Christ and His ministry through verses 6 and 7. As the son of Mary, "a child is born." As the Son of God, "a son is given." He is both Man and God. He bears upon His shoulder the responsibility of the government of the world. Among the names attributed to Him, we find "The everlasting Father," which might be translated, "The Father of the ages." It is He who planned the ages and fit them together to make all time accomplish the purposes of God. His government and peace will know no end. He will sit upon the throne of David when He comes to the earth the second time and establishes His kingdom upon it. "The zeal of the LORD of hosts" that brought Him to earth the first time will bring Him the second time and will accomplish all of the purposes of God enumerated in the Scriptures.

9:14 branch. The LORD will cut off their relationship (see John 15).
9:14 rush. Isaiah 9:15 identifies the "head and tail." The branch and rush have to do with the nation's relationship with God which will be cut off in one day (vs. 16). Compare John 15:1-6.
10:6 an hypocritical nation. Judah.

wrath will I give him a charge, to take
the spoil, and to take the prey, and to
tread them down like the mire of the
streets.
7Howbeit he meaneth not so, neither
doth his heart think so; but *it is* in his
heart to destroy and cut off nations not
a few.
8For he saith, *Are* not my princes altogether kings?
9*Is* not Calno as Carchemish? *is* not
Hamath as Arpad? *is* not Samaria as Damascus?
10As my hand hath found the kingdoms of the idols, and whose graven
images did excel them of Jerusalem and
of Samaria;
11Shall I not, as I have done unto Samaria and her idols, so do to Jerusalem
and her idols?
12Wherefore it shall come to pass,
that when the Lord hath performed his
whole work upon mount Zion and on
Jerusalem, I will punish the fruit of the
stout heart of the king of Assyria, and
the glory of his high looks.
13For he saith, By the strength of my
hand I have done *it,* and by my wisdom;
for I am prudent: and I have removed
the bounds of the people, and have
robbed their treasures, and I have put
down the inhabitants like a valiant *man:*
14And my hand hath found as a nest
the riches of the people: and as one
gathereth eggs *that are* left, have I gathered all the earth; and there was none
that moved the wing, or opened the
mouth, or peeped.
15Shall the axe boast itself against
him that heweth therewith? *or* shall the
saw magnify itself against him that
shaketh it? as if the rod should shake
itself against them that lift it up, *or* as if
the staff should lift up *itself, as if it were*
no wood.
16Therefore shall the Lord, the *Lord
of hosts, send among his fat ones leanness; and under his glory he shall kindle a burning like the burning of a fire.
17And the light of Israel shall be for a
fire, and his Holy One for a flame: and
it shall burn and devour his thorns and
his briers in one day;
18And shall consume the glory of his
forest, and of his fruitful field, both soul
and body: and they shall be as when a
standardbearer fainteth.
19And the rest of the trees of his forest shall be few, that a child may write
them.
¶20And it shall come to pass in that
day, *that* the *remnant of Israel, and
such as are escaped of the house of Jacob, shall no more again stay upon him
that smote them; but shall stay upon
the LORD, the Holy One of Israel, in
truth.

10:20 A Remnant of Israel
God has never failed to have a testimony in Israel. In her worst apostasy there has been a remnant that has been true to Him. That remnant is within the church today (Rom. 11:1). When the *church is caught up to be with the Lord (1 Thess. 4:16-17), a new remnant will be raised up in Israel that will be a witness to the world during the *Great Tribulation. This final remnant will welcome the Messiah when He comes to the earth to set up His *kingdom (Ezek. 20:33-44).

21The remnant shall return, *even* the
remnant of Jacob, unto the mighty God.
22For though thy people Israel be as
the sand of the sea, *yet* a remnant of

10:13 strength of my hand. God punishes the pride of nations. Assyria advanced its government by its conquests. God destroyed it. Nebuchadnezzar of Babylon boasted of his power, and God overthrew him until he recognized that God Himself rules in the kingdom of men.
10:17 the light of Israel. A name of the Lord Jesus Christ.
10:17 in one day. Read in 2 Kings 19:35 how this was fulfilled.
10:19 few, that a child may write. There were so few of the Assyrian soldiers left alive that even a small child could count them.
10:20 in that day. This phrase is often used to mean the *Day of the LORD.

them shall return: the consumption
decreed shall overflow with *righteousness.
[23]For the Lord GOD of hosts shall
make a consumption, even determined,
in the midst of all the land.
¶[24]Therefore thus saith the Lord GOD
of hosts, O my people that dwellest in
Zion, be not *afraid of the Assyrian: he
shall smite thee with a rod, and shall lift
up his staff against thee, after the manner of Egypt.
[25]For yet a very little while, and the
indignation shall cease, and mine anger
in their destruction.
[26]And the LORD of hosts shall stir up
a scourge for him according to the
slaughter of Midian at the rock of Oreb:
and *as* his rod *was* upon the sea, so shall
he lift it up after the manner of Egypt.
[27]And it shall come to pass in that day,
that his burden shall be taken away from
off thy shoulder, and his yoke from off
thy neck, and the yoke shall be destroyed because of the anointing.
[28]He is come to Aiath, he is passed
to Migron; at Michmash he hath laid up
his carriages:
[29]They are gone over the passage:
they have taken up their lodging at
Geba; Ramah is afraid; Gibeah of Saul
is fled.
[30]Lift up thy voice, O daughter of
Gallim: cause it to be heard unto Laish,
O poor Anathoth.
[31]Madmenah is removed; the inhabitants of Gebim gather themselves to
flee.
[32]As yet shall he remain at Nob that
day: he shall shake his hand *against* the
mount of the daughter of Zion, the hill
of Jerusalem.
[33]Behold, the Lord, the LORD of
hosts, shall lop the bough with terror:
and the high ones of stature *shall be*
hewn down, and the haughty shall be
humbled.
[34]And he shall cut down the thickets
of the forest with iron, and *Lebanon
shall fall by a mighty one.

Nature of Christ's kingdom in the Millennium

11 And there shall come forth a
rod out of the stem of Jesse, and
a *Branch shall grow out of his roots:
[2]And the spirit of the LORD shall rest
upon him, the spirit of wisdom and understanding, the spirit of counsel and
might, the spirit of knowledge and of
the fear of the LORD;
[3]And shall make him of quick understanding in the fear of the LORD: and he
shall not judge after the sight of his
eyes, neither reprove after the hearing
of his ears:
[4]But with righteousness shall he
judge the poor, and reprove with equity for the meek of the earth: and he
shall smite the earth with the rod of his
mouth, and with the breath of his lips
shall he slay the wicked.
[5]And righteousness shall be the
girdle of his loins, and faithfulness the
girdle of his reins.
[6]The wolf also shall dwell with the
lamb, and the leopard shall lie down
with the kid; and the calf and the young

10:22 the consumption decreed shall overflow with righteousness. "Consumption" is destruction; "overflow" is to overcome. Righteousness will overcome destruction.
10:24 after the manner of Egypt. As the Egyptians did in the time of Moses.
10:26 the slaughter of Midian. Just as Gideon was raised up to save the children of Israel from the Midianites (Judg. 7) so the Lord Jesus Christ will be the King who will finally save His people from their terrible oppressions (see Rev. 19:11-16).
10:27 the yoke shall be destroyed because of the anointing. Because of the coming of the Anointed One, the Lord Jesus Christ, to set up His kingdom, the yoke and burden of oppression will be removed.
10:28 He is come to Aiath. Verses 28-32, a description of the invasion of Palestine by Sennacherib, and a look at another attempted invasion, by the Roman prince, the *Beast, as he shall march against Jerusalem in a vain effort to rule the world.

lion and the fatling together; and a little child shall lead them.
7And the cow and the bear shall
feed; their young ones shall lie down
together: and the lion shall eat straw
like the ox.
8And the sucking child shall play on
the hole of the asp, and the weaned
child shall put his hand on the cockatrice' den.
9They shall not hurt nor destroy in all
my holy mountain: for the earth shall be
full of the knowledge of the LORD, as
the waters cover the sea.
10And in that day there shall be a root
of Jesse, which shall stand for an ensign
of the people; to it shall the *Gentiles
seek: and his rest shall be glorious.
¶11And it shall come to pass in that
day, *that* the Lord shall set his hand
again the second time to recover the
remnant of his people, which shall be
left, from Assyria, and from Egypt, and
from Pathros, and from Cush, and from
Elam, and from Shinar, and from Hamath, and from the islands of the sea.
12And he shall set up an ensign for
the nations, and shall assemble the outcasts of Israel, and gather together the
dispersed of Judah from the four corners of the earth.
13The envy also of Ephraim shall depart, and the adversaries of Judah shall
be cut off: Ephraim shall not envy Judah, and Judah shall not vex Ephraim.
14But they shall fly upon the shoulders of the Philistines toward the west;
they shall spoil them of the east together: they shall lay their hand upon
*Edom and *Moab; and the children of
Ammon shall obey them.
15And the LORD shall utterly destroy
the tongue of the Egyptian sea; and
with his mighty wind shall he shake his

11:1 THE BRANCH OF JESSE

This chapter presents Christ as the Messiah of Israel and describes His kingdom. The thought of the first verse is that Jesse is like a tree that has been blown over or cut down. From the stump of that tree comes a new shoot. That new shoot is Christ. As we study the chapter we find that the first verse tells us that the Messiah must be of the family of David (Jesse, David's father, 1 Sam. 17:12).

The second verse discloses that the entire ministry of the Messiah will be in the energy of the Holy Spirit.

From verses 3-5, we have a description of the reign of Christ upon the earth. Christ will rule in perfect righteousness when He comes to be King of Kings and Lord of Lords.

From verses 6-8, we discover that the curse now resting on nature will be removed when the Lord Jesus comes again. "Creation itself also shall be delivered from the bondage of corruption into the glorious liberty of the children of God" (Rom. 8:21).

In verse 9 we are told that the earth that has never known the LORD will know Him when He reigns over it.

Ignorance concerning the Lord will be unknown in the *Millennium. In the tenth verse, we see that the blessings of the Millennium will be worldwide in their extensiveness. Not only the people, Israel, but the Gentiles will be blessed at that time. Through the remainder of the chapter, we see that the LORD will restore His people in their land and will heal the breach between the two kingdoms of Israel so that He will reign over a united people.

In the twelth chapter, we have the hymn of Israel during the reign of Christ upon the earth. It is important for us to note at this time that the spiritual experience of believers in Christ in this *dispensation is in a sense a miniature of the millennial blessings of Israel. The Scriptures that describe the millennial blessings of Israel should be applied to Israel first of all, but we should not fail to find in them sources of great spiritual blessing for our need in this present hour. The Christian can also sing the hymn recorded in chapter 12 of this prophecy.

11:8 cockatrice. A poisonous snake.
11:15 the tongue of the Egyptian sea. The Gulf of Aqaba.

hand over the river, and shall smite it in the seven streams, and make *men* go over dryshod.

16 And there shall be an highway for the remnant of his people, which shall be left, from Assyria; like as it was to Israel in the day that he came up out of the land of Egypt.

Song of Israel during the Millennium

12 And in that day thou shalt say, O LORD, I will praise thee: though thou wast angry with me, thine anger is turned away, and thou comfortedst me.

2 Behold, God *is* my *salvation; I will *trust, and not be afraid: for the LORD JEHOVAH *is* my strength and *my* song; he also is become my salvation.

3 Therefore with joy shall ye draw water out of the wells of salvation.

4 And in that day shall ye say, Praise the LORD, call upon his name, declare his doings among the people, make mention that his name is exalted.

5 Sing unto the LORD; for he hath done excellent things: this *is* known in all the earth.

6 Cry out and shout, thou inhabitant of Zion: for great *is* the Holy One of Israel in the midst of thee.

II. The Judgment of Israel's Foes
(13:1—23:18)
*The burden of *Babylon*

13 The burden of Babylon, which Isaiah the son of Amoz did see.

2 Lift ye up a banner upon the high mountain, exalt the voice unto them, shake the hand, that they may go into the gates of the nobles.

3 I have commanded my sanctified ones, I have also called my mighty ones for mine anger, *even* them that rejoice in my highness.

4 The noise of a multitude in the mountains, like as of a great people; a tumultuous noise of the kingdoms of nations gathered together: the LORD of hosts mustereth the host of the battle.

5 They come from a far country, from the end of *heaven, *even* the LORD, and the weapons of his indignation, to destroy the whole land.

¶6 Howl ye; for the day of the LORD *is* at hand; it shall come as a destruction from the Almighty.

7 Therefore shall all hands be faint, and every man's heart shall melt:

8 And they shall be afraid: pangs and sorrows shall take hold of them; they shall be in pain as a woman that travaileth: they shall be amazed one at another; their faces *shall be as* flames.

9 Behold, the day of the LORD cometh, cruel both with wrath and fierce anger, to lay the land desolate: and he shall destroy the sinners thereof out of it.

10 For the stars of heaven and the constellations thereof shall not give their

13:9 God's Judgment
As is so frequently true in the prophetic Scriptures, the writing of a prophecy concerning an event of the immediate future becomes the opportunity for a prediction regarding the *Day of the LORD. Isaiah predicts the destruction of Babylon by the Medes. From verses 9-11, he looks ahead to the judgments of God that will be brought upon the world during the coming *Tribulation, which is the time that will elapse after the *church has been taken to be with the Lord and before He comes to earth to reign.

11:15 the river. The Euphrates.
13:1 burden. From chapter 13 through chapter 23 are recorded a series of prophecies against the nations that were neighbors to Israel. These prophecies are called a "burden" because they carry a heavy message of the wrath of God against these nations.
13:1 Babylon. Here the prophet is speaking of the whole confused world apart from the Lord. It refers to the Gentile world system with its failures and its oppression of the Jews.
13:5 the whole land. Chaldea.
13:9 cruel. Stern.

light: the sun shall be darkened in his
going forth, and the moon shall not
cause her light to shine.
11 And I will punish the *world for
their evil, and the wicked for their iniquity; and I will cause the arrogancy of
the proud to cease, and will lay low the
haughtiness of the terrible.
12 I will make a man more precious
than fine gold; even a man than the
golden wedge of *Ophir.
13 Therefore I will shake the heavens,
and the earth shall remove out of her
place, in the wrath of the LORD of hosts,
and in the day of his fierce anger.
14 And it shall be as the chased roe,
and as a sheep that no man taketh up:
they shall every man turn to his own
people, and flee every one into his own
land.
15 Every one that is found shall be
thrust through; and every one that is
joined *unto them* shall fall by the sword.
16 Their children also shall be dashed
to pieces before their eyes; their houses
shall be spoiled, and their wives ravished.
17 Behold, I will stir up the Medes
against them, which shall not regard
silver; and *as for* gold, they shall not
delight in it.
18 *Their* bows also shall dash the
young men to pieces; and they shall
have no pity on the fruit of the womb;
their eye shall not spare children.
¶19 And Babylon, the glory of kingdoms, the beauty of the Chaldees'
excellency, shall be as when *God overthrew Sodom and Gomorrah.
20 It shall never be inhabited, neither
shall it be dwelt in from generation to
generation: neither shall the Arabian
pitch tent there; neither shall the shepherds make their fold there.
21 But wild beasts of the desert shall
lie there; and their houses shall be full
of doleful creatures; and owls shall
dwell there, and satyrs shall dance
there.
22 And the wild beasts of the islands
shall cry in their desolate houses, and
dragons in *their* pleasant palaces: and
her time *is* near to come, and her days
shall not be prolonged.

Restoration of Israel

14 For the LORD will have mercy
on *Jacob, and will yet choose
*Israel, and set them in their own land:
and the strangers shall be joined with
them, and they shall cleave to the house
of Jacob.
2 And the people shall take them,
and bring them to their place: and the
house of Israel shall possess them in
the land of the LORD for servants and
handmaids: and they shall take them
captives, whose captives they were;
and they shall rule over their oppressors.
3 And it shall come to pass in the day
that the LORD shall give thee rest from
thy sorrow, and from thy *fear, and from
the hard bondage wherein thou wast
made to serve,
¶4 That thou shalt take up this proverb against the king of Babylon, and say,
How hath the oppressor ceased! the
golden city ceased!
5 The LORD hath broken the staff of

13:11 the world. Mankind.

13:12 more precious. More rare—harder to find. Those who have not fled will have been destroyed.

13:17 Behold, I will stir up the Medes against them. Here Isaiah turns to the real Babylon (see vs. 1 note) and prophesies its actual destruction, and that it will never be rebuilt (see also Jer. 51:61-64). This prophecy has been fulfilled in all of its details (Isa. 13:20-22).

14:1 will yet choose Israel. The unfaithfulness of Israel did not annul the *covenant that God made with Abraham. Israel has been sorely punished, but God will yet restore His people. This is confirmed in many passages of Scripture, such as Jeremiah 32:30-37; Romans 9; 10; 11.

the wicked, *and* the sceptre of the
rulers.
6 He who smote the people in wrath
with a continual stroke, he that ruled
the nations in anger, is persecuted, *and*
none hindereth.
7 The whole earth is at rest, *and* is
quiet: they break forth into singing.
8 Yea, the fir trees rejoice at thee, *and*
the cedars of Lebanon, *saying,* Since
thou art laid down, no feller is come up
against us.

Judgment of the Antichrist (Rev. 19:20)

9 *Hell from beneath is moved for
thee to meet *thee* at thy coming: it
stirreth up the dead for thee, *even* all
the chief ones of the earth; it hath
raised up from their thrones all the
kings of the nations.
10 All they shall speak and say unto
thee, Art thou also become weak as we?
art thou become like unto us?
11 Thy pomp is brought down to the
*grave, *and* the noise of thy viols:
the worm is spread under thee, and the
worms cover thee.

The sin and doom of Satan

¶12 How art thou fallen from heav-
en, O *Lucifer, son of the morning! *how*
art thou cut down to the ground, which
didst weaken the nations!
13 For thou hast said in thine heart, I
will ascend into heaven, I will exalt my
throne above the stars of God: I will sit
also upon the mount of the congregation, in the sides of the north:
14 I will ascend above the heights of
the clouds; I will be like the most High.
15 Yet thou shalt be brought down to
hell, to the sides of the *pit.
16 They that see thee shall narrowly
look upon thee, *and* consider thee, *saying, Is* this the man that made the earth
to tremble, that did shake kingdoms;
17 *That* made the world as a wilderness, and destroyed the cities thereof;
that opened not the house of his prisoners?

The destruction of Babylon

18 All the kings of the nations, *even* all
of them, lie in glory, every one in his
own house.
19 But thou art cast out of thy grave
like an abominable branch, *and as* the
raiment of those that are slain, thrust
through with a sword, that go down to
the stones of the pit; as a carcase trodden under feet.
20 Thou shalt not be joined with them
in burial, because thou hast destroyed
thy land, *and* slain thy people: the seed
of evildoers shall never be renowned.
21 Prepare slaughter for his children
for the iniquity of their fathers; that
they do not rise, nor possess the land,
nor fill the face of the world with cities.
22 For I will rise up against them, saith
the LORD of hosts, and cut off from Babylon the name, and remnant, and son,
and nephew, saith the LORD.
23 I will also make it a possession for
the bittern, and pools of water: and I
will sweep it with the besom of destruction, saith the LORD of hosts.
¶24 The LORD of hosts hath sworn,

14:12 Lucifer
Lucifer is one of the names given to Satan. As we read through the Word of God, we discover that Satan was created a cherub (Ezek. 28:16). He was of great wisdom and beauty and lived in "Eden the garden of God" (Ezek. 28:13) until he sinned. The sin of Satan was his plan to exalt himself above God (Isa. 14:13-14). This is his constant plan. It was the motive behind the temptation of Eve. It was his purpose in the temptation of Christ. It is his program throughout history. Nevertheless, he is doomed to be "brought down to hell" (vs. 15).

14:8 feller. A woodsman, one who cuts or fells trees.
14:22 Babylon. See 13:17 note.
14:23 besom. A broom.

saying, Surely as I have thought, so
shall it come to pass; and as I have purposed, *so* shall it stand:
25That I will break the Assyrian in my
land, and upon my mountains tread him
under foot: then shall his yoke depart
from off them, and his burden depart
from off their shoulders.
26This *is* the purpose that is purposed
upon the whole earth: and this *is* the
hand that is stretched out upon all the
nations.
27For the LORD of hosts hath purposed, and who shall disannul *it?* and his
hand *is* stretched out, and who shall
turn it back?

The burden of Palestine

¶28In the year that king Ahaz died
was this burden.
29Rejoice not thou, whole Palestina,
because the rod of him that smote thee
is broken: for out of the serpent's root
shall come forth a cockatrice, and his
fruit *shall be* a fiery flying serpent.
30And the firstborn of the poor shall
feed, and the needy shall lie down in
safety: and I will kill thy root with famine, and he shall slay thy remnant.
31Howl, O gate; cry, O city; thou,
whole Palestina, *art* dissolved: for there
shall come from the north a smoke, and
none *shall be* alone in his appointed
times.
32What shall *one* then answer the
messengers of the nation? That the
LORD hath founded *Zion, and the poor
of his people shall trust in it.

The burden of Moab

15 The *burden of Moab. Because
in the night Ar of Moab is laid
waste, *and* brought to silence; because
in the night Kir of Moab is laid waste,
and brought to silence;
2He is gone up to Bajith, and to Dibon, the high places, to weep: Moab
shall howl over Nebo, and over Medeba: on all their heads *shall be* baldness,
and every beard cut off.
3In their streets they shall gird
themselves with sackcloth: on the tops
of their houses, and in their streets,
every one shall howl, weeping abundantly.
4And Heshbon shall cry, and Elealeh:
their voice shall be heard *even* unto Jahaz: therefore the armed soldiers of
Moab shall cry out; his life shall be
grievous unto him.
5My heart shall cry out for Moab;
his fugitives *shall flee* unto Zoar, an
heifer of three years old: for by the
mounting up of Luhith with weeping
shall they go it up; for in the way of Horonaim they shall raise up a cry of destruction.
6For the waters of Nimrim shall be
desolate: for the hay is withered away,
the grass faileth, there is no green
thing.
7Therefore the abundance they have
gotten, and that which they have laid
up, shall they carry away to the brook
of the willows.
8For the cry is gone round about the
borders of Moab; the howling thereof
unto Eglaim, and the howling thereof
unto Beer-elim.
9For the waters of Dimon shall be full
of blood: for I will bring more upon Dimon, lions upon him that escapeth of
Moab, and upon the remnant of the
land.

14:29 him that smote thee. Shalmaneser V of Assyria.
14:30 firstborn of the poor. The extremely poor.
14:31 from the north a smoke. The Assyrian hosts in their marching would raise immense clouds of dust.
15:1 Moab. In 704 B.C., Sennacherib destroyed Moab. This portion of Scripture not only prophesied this, but it looks ahead to the final world battle of *Armageddon.
15:5 an heifer. Similar to Jeremiah 48:34. Judgment will come as a heifer used for sacrifice (compare Gen. 15:9).
15:9 Dimon. Dibon as in verse 2.

The burden of Moab (continued)

16 Send ye the lamb to the ruler of the land from Sela to the wilderness, unto the mount of the daughter of Zion.

2 For it shall be, *that,* as a wandering bird cast out of the nest, *so* the daughters of Moab shall be at the fords of Arnon.

3 Take counsel, execute *judgment; make thy shadow as the night in the midst of the noonday; hide the outcasts; bewray not him that wandereth.

4 Let mine outcasts dwell with thee, Moab; be thou a covert to them from the face of the spoiler: for the extortioner is at an end, the spoiler ceaseth, the oppressors are consumed out of the land.

5 And in *mercy shall the throne be established: and he shall sit upon it in truth in the *tabernacle of *David, judging, and seeking judgment, and hasting *righteousness.

¶ 6 We have heard of the pride of Moab; *he is* very proud: *even* of his haughtiness, and his pride, and his wrath: *but* his lies *shall* not *be* so.

7 Therefore shall Moab howl for Moab, every one shall howl: for the foundations of Kir-hareseth shall ye mourn; surely *they are* stricken.

8 For the fields of Heshbon languish, *and* the vine of Sibmah: the lords of the heathen have broken down the principal plants thereof, they are come *even* unto Jazer, they wandered *through* the wilderness: her branches are stretched out, they are gone over the sea.

¶ 9 Therefore I will bewail with the weeping of Jazer the vine of Sibmah: I will water thee with my tears, O Heshbon, and Elealeh: for the shouting for thy summer fruits and for thy harvest is fallen.

10 And gladness is taken away, and joy out of the plentiful field; and in the vineyards there shall be no singing, neither shall there be shouting: the treaders shall tread out no wine in *their* presses; I have made *their vintage* shouting to cease.

11 Wherefore my *bowels shall sound like an harp for Moab, and mine inward parts for Kir-haresh.

¶ 12 And it shall come to pass, when it is seen that Moab is weary on the high place, that he shall come to his *sanctuary to pray; but he shall not prevail.

13 This *is* the word that the LORD hath spoken concerning Moab since that time.

14 But now the LORD hath spoken, saying, Within three years, as the years of an hireling, and the glory of Moab shall be contemned, with all that great multitude; and the *remnant *shall be* very small *and* feeble.

The burden of Damascus

17 The burden of *Damascus. Behold, Damascus is taken away from *being* a city, and it shall be a ruinous heap.

2 The cities of Aroer *are* forsaken: they shall be for flocks, which shall lie down, and none shall make *them* afraid.

> **17:1 Damascus**
> Damascus is probably the oldest city in the world. It is first mentioned in Genesis 15:2 and is still inhabited. The Jews were trusting in the king of Damascus for their help; therefore, most of this chapter is written to the people of Damascus. It is a prophecy which is yet to be completely fulfilled.

3 The fortress also shall cease from *Ephraim, and the kingdom from Damascus, and the remnant of Syria: they

---

16:5 tabernacle of David. See Acts 15:16.
16:13 since that time. In times past.
16:14 Within three years. Isaiah predicted the fall of Moab, even dating it within three years of his prophecy. The prediction was literally fulfilled.

shall be as the glory of the children of
Israel, saith the LORD of hosts.
4 And in that day it shall come to pass,
that the glory of Jacob shall be made
thin, and the fatness of his flesh shall
wax lean.
5 And it shall be as when the harvestman gathereth the corn, and reapeth
the ears with his arm; and it shall be as
he that gathereth ears in the valley of
Rephaim.
¶ 6 Yet gleaning grapes shall be left in
it, as the shaking of an olive tree, two
or three berries in the top of the uppermost bough, four *or* five in the outmost
fruitful branches thereof, saith the
LORD God of Israel.
7 At that day shall a man look to his
Maker, and his eyes shall have respect
to the Holy One of Israel.
8 And he shall not look to the altars,
the work of his hands, neither shall respect *that* which his fingers have made,
either the groves, or the images.
¶ 9 In that day shall his strong cities be
as a forsaken bough, and an uppermost
branch, which they left because of the
children of Israel: and there shall be
desolation.
10 Because thou hast forgotten the
God of thy salvation, and hast not been
mindful of the *rock of thy strength,
therefore shalt thou plant pleasant
plants, and shalt set it with strange
slips:
11 In the day shalt thou make thy plant
to grow, and in the morning shalt thou
make thy seed to flourish: *but* the harvest *shall be* a heap in the day of grief
and of desperate sorrow.
¶ 12 Woe to the multitude of many people, *which* make a noise like the noise
of the seas; and to the rushing of nations, *that* make a rushing like the rushing of mighty waters!
13 The nations shall rush like the
rushing of many waters: but *God* shall
rebuke them, and they shall flee far off,
and shall be chased as the chaff of the
mountains before the wind, and like a
rolling thing before the whirlwind.
14 And behold at eveningtide trouble;
and before the morning he *is* not. This
is the portion of them that spoil us, and
the lot of them that rob us.

The burden of the land beyond Ethiopia

18 Woe to the land shadowing
with wings, which *is* beyond the
rivers of Ethiopia:
2 That sendeth ambassadors by the
sea, even in vessels of bulrushes upon
the waters, *saying,* Go, ye swift messengers, to a nation scattered and peeled,
to a people terrible from their beginning hitherto; a nation meted out and
trodden down, whose land the rivers
have spoiled!
3 All ye inhabitants of the world, and
dwellers on the earth, see ye, when
he lifteth up an ensign on the mountains; and when he bloweth a trumpet,
hear ye.
4 For so the LORD said unto me, I will
take my rest, and I will consider in my
dwelling place like a clear heat upon
herbs, *and* like a cloud of dew in the
heat of harvest.
5 For afore the harvest, when the bud
is perfect, and the sour grape is ripen-
ing in the flower, he shall both cut off
the sprigs with pruning hooks, and take
away *and* cut down the branches.
6 They shall be left together unto the
fowls of the mountains, and to the
beasts of the earth: and the fowls shall
summer upon them, and all the beasts
of the earth shall winter upon them.
¶ 7 In that time shall the present be
brought unto the LORD of hosts of a

17:3 the glory of. Here and in verse 4, this phrase refers to the wealth of corn and wine and cattle in which the people gloried.

18:2 That sendeth ambassadors. Probably an appeal came for an alliance with Egypt. God does not look with pleasure upon alliances between His people and unbelievers (2 Cor. 6:14-18; see also 6:17 note, "Separation").

18:7 the present. The present is the people of Israel, who have been scattered and stripped

people scattered and peeled, and from
a people terrible from their beginning
hitherto; a nation meted out and trodden under foot, whose land the rivers
have spoiled, to the place of the name
of the LORD of hosts, the mount Zion.

The burden of Egypt

19 The burden of *Egypt. Behold,
the LORD rideth upon a swift
cloud, and shall come into Egypt: and
the idols of Egypt shall be moved at his
presence, and the heart of Egypt shall
melt in the midst of it.
2 And I will set the Egyptians against
the Egyptians: and they shall fight
every one against his brother, and every
one against his neighbour; city against
city, *and* kingdom against kingdom.
3 And the spirit of Egypt shall fail in
the midst thereof; and I will destroy the
counsel thereof: and they shall seek to
the idols, and to the charmers, and to
them that have *familiar spirits, and
to the wizards.
4 And the Egyptians will I give over
into the hand of a cruel lord; and a fierce
king shall rule over them, saith the
Lord, the LORD of hosts.
5 And the waters shall fail from the
sea, and the river shall be wasted and
dried up.
6 And they shall turn the rivers far
away; *and* the brooks of defence shall
be emptied and dried up: the reeds and
flags shall wither.
7 The paper reeds by the brooks, by
the mouth of the brooks, and every
thing sown by the brooks, shall wither,
be driven away, and be no *more.*
8 The fishers also shall mourn, and all
they that cast angle into the brooks
shall lament, and they that spread nets
upon the waters shall languish.
9 Moreover they that work in fine flax,
and they that weave networks, shall be
confounded.
10 And they shall be broken in the
purposes thereof, all that make sluices
and ponds for fish.
¶ 11 Surely the princes of Zoan *are*
*fools, the counsel of the wise counsel-
lors of *Pharaoh is become brutish:
how say ye unto Pharaoh, I *am* the son
of the wise, the son of ancient kings?
12 Where *are* they? where *are* thy wise
men? and let them tell thee now, and let
them know what the LORD of hosts hath
purposed upon Egypt.
13 The princes of Zoan are become
fools, the princes of *Noph are deceived; they have also seduced Egypt,
even they that are the stay of the tribes
thereof.
14 The LORD hath mingled a perverse
spirit in the midst thereof: and they
have caused Egypt to *err in every
work thereof, as a drunken *man* stag-
gereth in his vomit.
15 Neither shall there be *any* work for
Egypt, which the head or tail, branch or
rush, may do.
16 In that day shall Egypt be like unto
women: and it shall be afraid and fear
because of the shaking of the hand of
the LORD of hosts, which he shaketh
over it.
17 And the land of *Judah shall be a
terror unto Egypt, every one that
maketh mention thereof shall be afraid
in himself, because of the counsel of the
LORD of hosts, which he hath determined against it.
¶ 18 In that day shall five cities in the
land of Egypt speak the language of
Canaan, and swear to the LORD of hosts;
one shall be called, The city of destruction.

---

of all their wealth but who will return in repentance and belief to the Lord Jesus Christ and own Him as King of Kings and Lord of Lords.

19:1 a swift cloud. Sargon, king of Assyria, was used by the LORD to carry out His will.

19:1 shall come into Egypt. The first seventeen verses have been fulfilled; the rest of the chapter is yet to be fulfilled.

19:8 angle. A fishing rod with a line and hook.

19:11 Zoan. The seat of the Egyptian court.

[19]In that day shall there be an *altar
to the LORD in the midst of the land of
Egypt, and a pillar at the border thereof
to the LORD.
[20]And it shall be for a sign and for a
witness unto the LORD of hosts in the
land of Egypt: for they shall cry unto the
LORD because of the oppressors, and he
shall send them a saviour, and a great
one, and he shall deliver them.
[21]And the LORD shall be known to
Egypt, and the Egyptians shall know
the LORD in that day, and shall do *sacrifice and *oblation; yea, they shall vow
a vow unto the LORD, and perform *it.*
[22]And the LORD shall smite Egypt: he
shall smite and heal *it:* and they shall
return *even* to the LORD, and he shall be
intreated of them, and shall heal them.
¶[23]In that day shall there be a highway out of Egypt to Assyria, and the Assyrian shall come into Egypt, and the
Egyptian into Assyria, and the Egyptians shall serve with the Assyrians.
[24]In that day shall Israel be the third
with Egypt and with Assyria, *even* a
blessing in the midst of the land:
[25]Whom the LORD of hosts shall
bless, saying, Blessed *be* Egypt my people, and Assyria the work of my hands,
and Israel mine inheritance.

Assyria's conquest of Egypt and Ethiopia

20 In the year that Tartan came
unto Ashdod, (when Sargon the
king of Assyria sent him,) and fought
against Ashdod, and took it;
[2]At the same time spake the LORD by
Isaiah the son of Amoz, saying, Go and
loose the sackcloth from off thy loins,
and put off thy shoe from thy foot. And
he did so, walking naked and barefoot.
[3]And the LORD said, Like as my servant Isaiah hath walked naked and barefoot three years *for* a sign and wonder
upon Egypt and upon Ethiopia;
[4]So shall the king of Assyria lead
away the Egyptians prisoners, and the
Ethiopians captives, young and old,
naked and barefoot, even with *their*
buttocks uncovered, to the shame of
Egypt.
[5]And they shall be afraid and
ashamed of Ethiopia their expectation,
and of Egypt their glory.
[6]And the inhabitant of this isle shall
say in that day, Behold, such *is* our
expectation, whither we flee for help to
be delivered from the king of Assyria:
and how shall we escape?

The burden of the desert

21 The *burden of the desert of
the sea. As whirlwinds in the
south pass through; *so* it cometh from
the desert, from a terrible land.
[2]A grievous vision is declared unto
me; the treacherous dealer dealeth
treacherously, and the spoiler spoileth.
Go up, O Elam: besiege, O Media; all
the sighing thereof have I made to
cease.
[3]Therefore are my loins filled with
pain: pangs have taken hold upon me,
as the pangs of a woman that travaileth:
I was bowed down at the hearing *of it;*
I was dismayed at the seeing *of it.*
[4]My heart panted, fearfulness
affrighted me: the night of my pleasure
hath he turned into fear unto me.
[5]Prepare the table, watch in the
watchtower, eat, drink: arise, ye
princes, *and* *anoint the shield.
[6]For thus hath the Lord said unto me,
Go, set a watchman, let him declare
what he seeth.

19:21 the Egyptians. From verses 21-25 the Holy Spirit declares that Egypt and Assyria will know the LORD when He comes to reign on earth. Israel will be established with them.

20:1 Tartan. See 2 Kings 18:17. Tartan means the one who was next to the Assyrian king in rank, or the commander in chief of the army.

20:2 walking naked and barefoot. As a slave.

21:1 the sea. The Euphrates is meant here.

21:4 the night of my pleasure. Belshazzar's feast (Dan. 5:1-31).

7And he saw a chariot *with* a couple
of horsemen, a chariot of asses, *and* a
chariot of camels; and he hearkened
diligently with much heed:
8And he cried, A lion: My lord, I stand
continually upon the watchtower in the
daytime, and I am set in my ward whole
nights:
9And, behold, here cometh a chariot
of men, *with* a couple of horsemen. And
he answered and said, *Babylon is fall-
en, is fallen; and all the graven images
of her gods he hath broken unto the
ground.

21:9 The Fall of Babylon
When we remember that this prophecy was uttered almost two hundred years before the fall of Babylon, it becomes very evident that this prophet spoke by the *inspiration of God. Babylon had not as yet even risen to its place of supremacy when Isaiah wrote this.

10O my threshing, and the corn of my
floor: that which I have heard of the
LORD of hosts, the *God of Israel, have
I declared unto you.

The burden of Dumah

¶11The burden of Dumah. He calleth
to me out of *Seir, Watchman, what of
the night? Watchman, what of the
night?
12The watchman said, The morning
cometh, and also the night: if ye will
enquire, enquire ye: return, come.

The burden of Arabia

¶13The burden upon Arabia. In the
forest in Arabia shall ye lodge, O ye
travelling companies of Dedanim.
14The inhabitants of the land of Tema
brought water to him that was thirsty,
they *prevented with their bread him
that fled.
15For they fled from the swords, from
the drawn sword, and from the bent
bow, and from the grievousness of war.
16For thus hath the Lord said unto
me, Within a year, according to the
years of an hireling, and all the glory of
*Kedar shall fail:
17And the residue of the number of
archers, the mighty men of the children
of Kedar, shall be diminished: for the
LORD God of Israel hath spoken *it*.

The burden of the valley of vision

22 The burden of the valley of vision. What aileth thee now, that
thou art wholly gone up to the housetops?
2Thou that art full of stirs, a tumultuous city, a joyous city: thy slain *men*
are not slain with the sword, nor dead
in battle.

Old Testament Prophets and Their Messages

Prophet	Message
Obadiah	Judgment on the nation of Edom
Joel	Plague of locusts
Jonah	Nineveh must repent
Amos	Judgment on Israel
Hosea	God's love is unceasing
Isaiah	The Messiah will come and save
Micah	Doom, destruction, deliverance
Nahum	Nineveh will be destroyed
Zephaniah	Judgment on Judah
Habakkuk	The Babylonian captivity
Jeremiah	Judgment for forgetting God
Ezekiel	God keeps His covenant promise
Daniel	God has a plan for the future
Haggai	The temple must be rebuilt
Zechariah	Hope in Christ's return
Malachi	God's complaint against Israel

21:11 Dumah. Idumea. The Edomites were descendants of Esau.
21:11 Seir. The principal mountain in Idumea.
21:13 Arabia. The Arabians are descendants of Ishmael, the son of Abraham and Hagar.
21:13 Dedanim. Descendants of Abraham.
21:14 Tema. Descendants of Abraham.
22:1 valley of vision. Jerusalem.
22:2 thy slain men are not slain with the sword. The men of Jerusalem were to experience spiritual death as well as physical death. See *death.

3 All thy rulers are fled together, they
are bound by the archers: all that are
found in thee are bound together, *which*
have fled from far.

4 Therefore said I, Look away from
me; I will weep bitterly, labour not to
comfort me, because of the spoiling of
the daughter of my people.

5 For *it is* a day of trouble, and of treading down, and of perplexity by the Lord
GOD of hosts in the valley of vision,
breaking down the walls, and of crying
to the mountains.

6 And Elam bare the quiver with chariots of men *and* horsemen, and Kir uncovered the shield.

7 And it shall come to pass, *that* thy
choicest valleys shall be full of chariots,
and the horsemen shall set themselves
in array at the gate.

¶8 And he discovered the covering of
Judah, and thou didst look in that day to
the armour of the house of the forest.

9 Ye have seen also the breaches of
the city of *David, that they are many:
and ye gathered together the waters of
the lower pool.

10 And ye have numbered the houses
of *Jerusalem, and the houses have ye
broken down to fortify the wall.

11 Ye made also a ditch between the
two walls for the water of the old pool:
but ye have not looked unto the maker
thereof, neither had respect unto him
that fashioned it long ago.

12 And in that day did the Lord GOD
of hosts call to weeping, and to *mourning, and to baldness, and to girding with
sackcloth:

13 And behold joy and gladness, slaying oxen, and killing sheep, eating flesh,
and drinking wine: let us eat and drink;
for to morrow we shall die.

14 And it was revealed in mine ears by
the LORD of hosts, Surely this iniquity
shall not be purged from you till ye die,
saith the Lord GOD of hosts.

¶15 Thus saith the Lord GOD of hosts,
Go, get thee unto this treasurer, *even*
unto Shebna, which *is* over the house,
and say,

16 What hast thou here? and whom
hast thou here, that thou hast hewed
thee out a sepulchre here, *as* he that
heweth him out a sepulchre on high,
and that graveth an habitation for himself in a rock?

17 Behold, the LORD will carry thee
away with a mighty captivity, and will
surely cover thee.

18 He will surely violently turn and
toss thee *like* a ball into a large country: there shalt thou die, and there the
chariots of thy glory *shall be* the shame
of thy lord's house.

19 And I will drive thee from thy sta-
tion, and from thy state shall he pull
thee down.

¶20 And it shall come to pass in that
day, that I will call my servant Eliakim
the son of Hilkiah:

21 And I will clothe him with thy robe,
and strengthen him with thy girdle, and
I will commit thy government into his
hand: and he shall be a father to the inhabitants of Jerusalem, and to the house
of Judah.

22 And the key of the house of David

22:8 he discovered the covering. This means *removed the protection*. King Hezekiah took the gold from the temple in Jerusalem to pay the Assyrians to stay away from his country. But his effort, because it lacked dependence upon God, was a failure.

22:8 the house of the forest. See 1 Kings 7:2. This was probably now used for an armory.

22:8 discovered. Uncovered, laid bare.

22:12 call to weeping. Notice verse 13. In spite of God's call for repentance and confession of sin, the people rejoiced and feasted, and the LORD had to pronounce the judgment of verse 14.

22:15 Shebna. Eliakim was later given Shebna's place as treasurer over the house. See verses 17-25 and 36:3; 37:2.

22:22 the key of the house of David. Although the immediate subject of this prophecy is Eliakim, the son of Hilkiah, we learn from Revelation 3:7 that Isaiah looked beyond

will I lay upon his shoulder; so he shall
open, and none shall shut; and he shall
shut, and none shall open.
23 And I will fasten him *as* a nail in a
sure place; and he shall be for a glorious throne to his father's house.
24 And they shall hang upon him all
the glory of his father's house, the offspring and the issue, all vessels of small
quantity, from the vessels of cups, even
to all the vessels of flagons.
¶25 In that day, saith the LORD of
hosts, shall the nail that is fastened in
the sure place be removed, and be cut
down, and fall; and the burden that *was*
upon it shall be cut off: for the LORD
hath spoken *it.*

The burden of Tyre

23 The burden of Tyre. Howl, ye
ships of *Tarshish; for it is laid
waste, so that there is no house, no
entering in: from the land of Chittim it
is revealed to them.
2 Be still, ye inhabitants of the isle;
thou whom the merchants of Zidon,
that pass over the sea, have replenished.
3 And by great waters the seed of
Sihor, the harvest of the river, *is* her
revenue; and she is a mart of nations.
4 Be thou ashamed, O Zidon: for the
sea hath spoken, *even* the strength of
the sea, saying, I travail not, nor bring
forth children, neither do I nourish up
young men, *nor* bring up virgins.
5 As at the report concerning Egypt,
so shall they be sorely pained at the
report of Tyre.
6 Pass ye over to Tarshish; howl, ye
inhabitants of the isle.
7 *Is* this your joyous *city,* whose antiquity *is* of ancient days? her own feet
shall carry her afar off to sojourn.
8 Who hath taken this counsel against
Tyre, the crowning *city,* whose merchants *are* princes, whose traffickers
are the honourable of the earth?
9 The LORD of hosts hath purposed it,
to stain the pride of all glory, *and* to
bring into contempt all the honourable
of the earth.
10 Pass through thy land as a river,
O daughter of Tarshish: *there is* no more
strength.
11 He stretched out his hand over the
sea, he shook the kingdoms: the LORD
hath given a commandment against the
merchant *city,* to destroy the strong
holds thereof.
12 And he said, Thou shalt no more
rejoice, O thou oppressed virgin,
daughter of Zidon: arise, pass over to
Chittim; there also shalt thou have no
rest.
13 Behold the land of the Chaldeans;
this people was not, *till* the Assyrian
founded it for them that dwell in the
wilderness: they set up the towers
thereof, they raised up the palaces
thereof; *and* he brought it to ruin.
14 Howl, ye ships of Tarshish: for your
strength is laid waste.
15 And it shall come to pass in that day,
that Tyre shall be forgotten seventy
years, according to the days of one king:
after the end of seventy years shall Tyre
sing as an harlot.

Eliakim and saw the Lord Jesus Christ. The vision of Christ is a revelation of His invincibility. Others may oppose Him but none can do so successfully.

22:25 shall the nail . . . be removed. Though the nail of verse 23 refers primarily to Eliakim and looks ahead to the Lord Jesus Christ, the nail of verse 25 refers to Shebna and his removal from his place of authority.

23:1 Tyre. The destruction of this island city took place about one hundred years later, when Nebuchadnezzar led an expedition against it.

23:1 Chittim. Cyprus.

23:3 great waters. The Mediterranean.

23:3 Sihor. Egypt.

23:3 river. The Nile.

23:7 her own feet. The "feet" of Tarshish were her ships.

23:15 The Fate of the Nations
While Babylonia was in power, Tyre remained in desolation, but when Persia conquered Babylonia, Tyre regained some of her former strength. Tyre was again destroyed, one hundred years later by Alexander the Great, nevertheless, as prophesied in Ezekiel 26 (see Ezek 26:2 note, "The Fall of a Great Nation") and has never been rebuilt. Verse 18, however, is a prophecy of her final conversion and restoration.

16 Take an harp, go about the city, thou
harlot that hast been forgotten; make
sweet melody, sing many songs, that
thou mayest be remembered.
¶ 17 And it shall come to pass after the
end of seventy years, that the LORD will
visit Tyre, and she shall turn to her hire,
and shall commit fornication with all the
kingdoms of the *world upon the face
of the earth.
18 And her merchandise and her hire
shall be holiness to the LORD: it shall
not be treasured nor laid up; for her
merchandise shall be for them that
dwell before the LORD, to eat sufficiently, and for durable clothing.

III. The Glory of Israel's Future Kingdom (24:1—27:13)

*Though punished, Israel will be established in her *kingdom*

24 Behold, the LORD maketh the
earth empty, and maketh it waste,
and turneth it upside down, and scattereth abroad the inhabitants thereof.
2 And it shall be, as with the people, so
with the priest; as with the servant, so
with his master; as with the maid,
so with her mistress; as with the buyer,
so with the seller; as with the lender, so
with the borrower; as with the taker of
*usury, so with the giver of usury to him.
3 The land shall be utterly emptied,
and utterly spoiled: for the LORD hath
spoken this word.
4 The earth mourneth *and* fadeth
away, the world languisheth *and* fadeth
away, the haughty people of the earth
do languish.
5 The earth also is defiled under the
inhabitants thereof; because they have
transgressed the *laws, changed the
ordinance, broken the everlasting *covenant.
6 Therefore hath the curse devoured
the earth, and they that dwell therein
are desolate: therefore the inhabitants
of the earth are burned, and few men
left.
7 The new wine mourneth, the vine
languisheth, all the merryhearted do
sigh.
8 The mirth of *tabrets ceaseth, the
noise of them that rejoice endeth, the
joy of the harp ceaseth.
9 They shall not drink wine with a
song; strong drink shall be bitter to
them that drink it.
10 The city of confusion is broken
down: every house is shut up, that no
man may come in.
11 *There is* a crying for wine in the
streets; all joy is darkened, the mirth of
the land is gone.
12 In the city is left desolation, and the
gate is smitten with destruction.
¶ 13 When thus it shall be in the midst
of the land among the people, *there shall
be* as the shaking of an olive tree, *and*

24:1-3 The Condition of the Earth
These verses describe the condition of the earth, and especially the land of Palestine, during the coming *Tribulation. It will be wasted by judgment until at the second coming of Christ, the nations of the earth will be broken (24:21 with Dan. 2:44-45). After this has come to pass, "the LORD of hosts shall reign in mount Zion, and in Jerusalem, and before his ancients gloriously" (Isa. 24:23). Notice the present tense used, as is frequently the case in the Bible, for the future, in order to express something that is absolutely certain to occur.

23:16 thou harlot that hast been forgotten. Tyre was a great center of idolatry.
24:10 city of confusion. Jerusalem in ruins.

as the gleaning grapes when the vintage
is done.
[14]They shall lift up their voice, they
shall sing for the majesty of the LORD,
they shall cry aloud from the sea.
[15]Wherefore glorify ye the LORD in
the fires, *even* the name of the LORD
God of Israel in the *isles of the sea.
[16]From the uttermost part of the
earth have we heard songs, *even* glory
to the righteous. But I said, My leanness, my leanness, woe unto me! the
treacherous dealers have dealt treacherously; yea, the treacherous dealers
have dealt very treacherously.
¶[17]Fear, and the *pit, and the snare,
are upon thee, O inhabitant of the earth.
[18]And it shall come to pass, *that* he
who fleeth from the noise of the fear
shall fall into the pit; and he that cometh
up out of the midst of the pit shall be
taken in the snare: for the windows
from on high are open, and the foundations of the earth do shake.
[19]The earth is utterly broken down,
the earth is clean dissolved, the earth
is moved exceedingly.
[20]The earth shall reel to and fro like
a drunkard, and shall be removed like a
cottage; and the transgression thereof
shall be heavy upon it; and it shall fall,
and not rise again.
¶[21]And it shall come to pass in that
day, *that* the LORD shall punish the host
of the high ones *that are* on high, and the
kings of the earth upon the earth.
[22]And they shall be gathered together, *as* prisoners are gathered in the pit,
and shall be shut up in the prison, and
after many days shall they be visited.
[23]Then the moon shall be confounded, and the sun ashamed, when
the LORD of hosts shall reign in mount
*Zion, and in Jerusalem, and before his
ancients gloriously.

Victories of Christ during His kingdom reign on earth

25 O LORD, thou *art* my God; I will
exalt thee, I will praise thy
name; for thou hast done wonderful
things; thy counsels of old *are* faithfulness *and* truth.
[2]For thou hast made of a city an heap;
of a defenced city a ruin: a palace of
strangers to be no city; it shall never be
built.
[3]Therefore shall the strong people
glorify thee, the city of the terrible nations shall fear thee.
[4]For thou hast been a strength to the
poor, a strength to the needy in his distress, a refuge from the storm, a shadow from the heat, when the blast of the
terrible ones *is* as a storm *against* the
wall.
[5]Thou shalt bring down the noise of
strangers, as the heat in a dry place;
even the heat with the shadow of a
cloud: the branch of the terrible ones
shall be brought low.
¶[6]And in this mountain shall the
LORD of hosts make unto all people a
feast of fat things, a feast of wines on
the lees, of fat things full of marrow, of
wines on the lees well refined.
[7]And he will destroy in this mountain
the face of the covering cast over all
people, and the vail that is spread over
all nations.
[8]He will swallow up *death in victory; and the Lord GOD will wipe away

25:8 Victory over Death
According to 1 Corinthians 15:54, Christ's victory over death will be brought about through the resurrection of His own blood-bought people. He conquered death at His own resurrection. That victory is the guarantee of our resurrection.

25:1 exalt thee. The song of this chapter, like the one in Isaiah 12, is often sung today, but more importantly it will be the song sung by Israel during the reign of Christ upon the earth—the time it particularly applies to. See *kingdom.

25:2 a city. Babylon is no doubt meant here.

25:6 mountain. Mount Zion. See also verses 7 and 10.

25:6 lees. Dregs or sediment.

tears from off all faces; and the rebuke of
his people shall he take away from off all
the earth: for the LORD hath spoken *it.*
¶9 And it shall be said in that day, Lo,
this *is* our God; we have waited for him,
and he will save us: this *is* the LORD; we
have waited for him, we will be glad and
rejoice in his *salvation.
10 For in this mountain shall the hand
of the LORD rest, and *Moab shall be
trodden down under him, even as straw
is trodden down for the dunghill.
11 And he shall spread forth his hands
in the midst of them, as he that
swimmeth spreadeth forth *his hands* to
swim: and he shall bring down their
pride together with the spoils of their
hands.
12 And the fortress of the high fort of
thy walls shall he bring down, lay low,
and bring to the ground, *even* to the
dust.

Worship of Israel during Christ's reign

26 In that day shall this song be
sung in the land of *Judah; We
have a strong city; salvation will *God*
appoint *for* walls and bulwarks.
2 Open ye the gates, that the righteous nation which keepeth the truth
may enter in.
3 Thou wilt keep *him* in perfect
*peace, *whose* mind *is* stayed *on thee:*
because he trusteth in thee.
4 *Trust ye in the LORD for ever: for
in the LORD JEHOVAH *is* everlasting
strength:
¶5 For he bringeth down them that
dwell on high; the lofty city, he layeth
it low; he layeth it low, *even* to the
ground; he bringeth it *even* to the dust.
6 The foot shall tread it down, *even* the
feet of the poor, *and* the steps of the
needy.
7 The way of the *just *is* uprightness:
thou, most upright, dost weigh the path
of the just.
8 Yea, in the way of thy judgments, O
LORD, have we waited for thee; the
desire of *our* soul *is* to thy name, and to
the remembrance of thee.
9 With my soul have I desired thee in
the night; yea, with my spirit within me
will I seek thee early: for when thy
judgments *are* in the earth, the inhabitants of the world will learn *righteousness.
10 Let favour be shewed to the wicked, *yet* will he not learn righteousness:
in the land of uprightness will he deal
unjustly, and will not behold the majesty
of the LORD.
11 LORD, *when* thy hand is lifted up,
they will not see: *but* they shall see, and
be ashamed for *their* envy at the people; yea, the fire of thine enemies shall
devour them.
¶12 LORD, thou wilt ordain peace for
us: for thou also hast wrought all our
works in us.
13 O LORD our God, *other* lords besides thee have had dominion over us:
but by thee only will we make mention
of thy name.
14 *They are* dead, they shall not live;
they are deceased, they shall not rise:
therefore hast thou visited and destroyed them, and made all their memory to perish.
15 Thou hast increased the nation,
O LORD, thou hast increased the nation:
thou art glorified: thou hadst removed
it far *unto* all the ends of the earth.
16 LORD, in trouble have they visited

25:12 thy walls. The walls of Babylon.
26:1 a strong city. Jerusalem.
26:2 the righteous nation. The faithful *remnant.
26:4 everlasting strength. In the Hebrew this is "the Rock of ages."
26:5 the lofty city. Babylon.
26:11 they shall see. Those who do not yield to God's grace must feel His wrath.
26:14 they shall not live. They do not have a part in the first resurrection (Rev. 20:6; see 20:5 note, " The First Resurrection") but in the second death (Rev. 20:14-15; see also 20:14 note).

thee, they poured out a *prayer *when*
thy chastening *was* upon them.
17 Like as a woman with child, *that*
draweth near the time of her delivery,
is in pain, *and* crieth out in her pangs;
so have we been in thy sight, O LORD.
18 We have been with child, we have
been in pain, we have as it were brought
forth wind; we have not wrought any
deliverance in the earth; neither have
the inhabitants of the world fallen.
19 Thy dead *men* shall live, *together*
with my dead body shall they arise.
Awake and sing, ye that dwell in dust:
for thy dew *is as* the dew of herbs, and
the earth shall cast out the dead.
¶ 20 Come, my people, enter thou into
thy chambers, and shut thy doors about
thee: hide thyself as it were for a little
moment, until the indignation be
overpast.
21 For, behold, the LORD cometh out
of his place to punish the inhabitants of
the earth for their iniquity: the earth
also shall disclose her blood, and shall
no more cover her slain.

Restoration of Israel during Christ's reign

27 In that day the LORD with his
sore and great and strong sword
shall punish *leviathan the piercing
serpent, even leviathan that crooked
serpent; and he shall slay the dragon
that *is* in the sea.
2 In that day sing ye unto her, A *vineyard of red wine.
3 I the LORD do keep it; I will water it
every moment: lest *any* hurt it, I will
keep it night and day.
4 Fury *is* not in me: who would set the
briers *and* thorns against me in battle?
I would go through them, I would burn
them together.
5 Or let him take hold of my strength,
that he may make peace with me; *and*
he shall make peace with me.
6 He shall cause them that come of
*Jacob to take root: *Israel shall blos-
som and bud, and fill the face of the
world with fruit.
¶ 7 Hath he smitten him, as he smote
those that smote him? *or* is he slain
according to the slaughter of them that
are slain by him?
8 In measure, when it shooteth forth,
thou wilt debate with it: he stayeth his
rough wind in the day of the east wind.
9 By this therefore shall the iniquity of
Jacob be purged; and this *is* all the fruit
to take away his *sin; when he maketh
all the stones of the *altar as chalk-
stones that are beaten in sunder, the
groves and images shall not stand up.
10 Yet the defenced city *shall be* desolate, *and* the habitation forsaken, and
left like a wilderness: there shall the
calf feed, and there shall he lie down,
and consume the branches thereof.
11 When the boughs thereof are withered, they shall be broken off: the wom-
en come, *and* set them on fire: for it *is*
a people of no understanding: therefore
he that made them will not have *mercy on them, and he that formed them
will shew them no favour.
¶ 12 And it shall come to pass in that
day, *that* the LORD shall beat off from the
channel of the river unto the stream of
*Egypt, and ye shall be gathered one by
one, O ye children of Israel.

26:19 Thy dead. Your dead shall live and my dead bodies shall arise. It is another prediction of the resurrection of the redeemed. It should be studied with Daniel 12:2; John 5:28-29; 1 Corinthians 15, etc.

26:20 indignation. This speaks of the *Day of the LORD.

26:21 the LORD cometh . . . to punish. This speaks of the Battle of *Armageddon.

27:1 leviathan the piercing serpent. This speaks of the foes of Israel and the *church, and especially of Satan, "the dragon, that old serpent, which is the Devil" (Rev. 20:2). For his slaying see Revelation 20:10.

27:2 In that day sing ye. They sing about the defeat of their enemies.

27:10 the defenced city. Jerusalem.

27:12 gathered one by one. The Bible repeats frequently God's promise to regather

[13]And it shall come to pass in that day, *that* the great trumpet shall be blown, and they shall come which were ready to perish in the land of Assyria, and the outcasts in the land of Egypt, and shall worship the LORD in the *holy mount at Jerusalem.

IV. Warning against Sin (28:1—31:9)

*The punishment of *Ephraim*

28 Woe to the crown of pride, to the drunkards of Ephraim, whose glorious beauty *is* a fading flower, which *are* on the head of the fat valleys of them that are overcome with wine!
[2]Behold, the Lord hath a mighty and strong one, *which* as a tempest of hail *and* a destroying storm, as a flood of mighty waters overflowing, shall cast down to the earth with the hand.
[3]The crown of pride, the drunkards of Ephraim, shall be trodden under feet:
[4]And the glorious beauty, which *is* on the head of the fat valley, shall be a fading flower, *and* as the hasty fruit before the summer; which *when* he that looketh upon it seeth, while it is yet in his hand he eateth it up.
¶[5]In that day shall the LORD of hosts be for a crown of glory, and for a diadem of beauty, unto the residue of his people,
[6]And for a spirit of *judgment to him that sitteth in judgment, and for strength to them that turn the battle to the gate.
¶[7]But they also have erred through wine, and through strong drink are out of the way; the priest and the *prophet have erred through strong drink, they are swallowed up of wine, they are out of the way through strong drink; they *err in vision, they stumble *in* judgment.
[8]For all tables are full of vomit *and* filthiness, *so that there is* no place *clean.*
¶[9]Whom shall he teach knowledge? and whom shall he make to understand *doctrine? *them that are* weaned from the milk, *and* drawn from the breasts.
[10]For precept *must be* upon precept, precept upon precept; line upon line, line upon line; here a little, *and* there a little:
[11]For with stammering lips and another tongue will he speak to this people.
[12]To whom he said, This *is* the rest *wherewith* ye may cause the weary to rest; and this *is* the refreshing: yet they would not hear.
[13]But the word of the LORD was unto them precept upon precept, precept upon precept; line upon line, line upon line; here a little, *and* there a little; that they might go, and fall backward, and be broken, and snared, and taken.
¶[14]Wherefore hear the word of the LORD, ye scornful men, that rule this people which *is* in *Jerusalem.
[15]Because ye have said, We have made a covenant with death, and with *hell are we at agreement; when the overflowing scourge shall pass through, it shall not come unto us: for we have made lies our refuge, and under *falsehood have we hid ourselves:
¶[16]Therefore thus saith the Lord GOD, Behold, I lay in Zion for a founda-

28:5 A Glorious Day
Again the prophet looks forward to the day when the Lord Jesus will be established upon the earth. The same prophet anticipating the coming of Christ in humiliation said that there was no beauty in Him (Isa. 53:2; see 53:1-5 note, "Christ's Suffering"). The glorious reign of Christ will present Him as a crown of glory and a diadem of beauty.

Israel. The LORD will gather Israel's children one by one. Although the promise is to Israel as a nation, its fulfillment will be to Israel individually.
28:1 crown of pride. Samaria was Ephraim's crown of pride.
28:4 hasty fruit. Figs ripen normally in August. Those which ripen before their time are picked and eaten at once, for they are unusual.

28:16 A Sure Foundation
The Lord Jesus is the stone which the builders rejected (1 Pet. 2:7). He is the only foundation that can be laid for eternal life (1 Cor. 3:11). He is presented by the prophet Isaiah in striking contrast to all others. Men may make a covenant with death and with hell, a refuge of lies and a hiding place of falsehood, but that will all be swept away. The only foundation that abides is Christ Himself.

tion a stone, a tried stone, a precious
corner *stone,* a sure foundation: he that
believeth shall not make haste.
17Judgment also will I lay to the line,
and righteousness to the *plummet:
and the hail shall sweep away the refuge of lies, and the waters shall overflow the hiding place.
¶18And your covenant with death
shall be disannulled, and your agreement with hell shall not stand; when the
overflowing scourge shall pass through,
then ye shall be trodden down by it.
19From the time that it goeth forth it
shall take you: for morning by morning
shall it pass over, by day and by night:
and it shall be a vexation only *to* understand the report.
20For the bed is shorter than that *a*
man can stretch himself *on it:* and the
covering narrower than that he can
wrap himself *in it.*
21For the LORD shall rise up as *in*
mount Perazim, he shall be wroth as *in*
the valley of Gibeon, that he may do his
work, his strange work; and bring to
pass his act, his strange act.
22Now therefore be ye not mockers,
lest your bands be made strong: for I
have heard from the Lord GOD of hosts
a consumption, even determined upon
the whole earth.
¶23Give ye ear, and hear my voice;
hearken, and hear my speech.
24Doth the plowman plow all day to
sow? doth he open and break the clods
of his ground?
25When he hath made plain the face
thereof, doth he not cast abroad the
fitches, and scatter the cummin, and
cast in the principal wheat and the appointed barley and rie in their place?

28:25 The Black Poppy
"Fitches" refer to the black poppy, the seed of which was called "poor man's pepper." God used this as an illustration of His judgments, along with cummin, another plant that has aromatic seeds, and bread corn (vss. 25-28). Some plants had to be beaten to make their fruit ready for use. Other plants needed only light tapping; and still others yielded their fruit all by themselves. The same is true with man–God knows when He may show mercy and when He must punish; but just as a farmer would not ruin his crop in the threshing, neither will God destroy His people that He is making fit for His use.

26For his *God doth instruct him to
discretion, *and* doth teach him.
27For the fitches are not threshed
with a threshing instrument, neither is
a cart wheel turned about upon the
cummin; but the fitches are beaten
out with a staff, and the cummin with
a rod.
28Bread *corn* is bruised; because he
will not ever be threshing it, nor break
it with the wheel of his cart, nor bruise
it *with* his horsemen.
29This also cometh forth from the
LORD of hosts, *which* is wonderful in
counsel, *and* excellent in working.

The reason for Israel's chastening

29 Woe to Ariel, to Ariel, the city
where *David dwelt! add ye year
to year; let them kill sacrifices.
2Yet I will distress Ariel, and there

28:21 Perazim. David, by God's help, conquered the Philistines at Baalperazim (2 Sam. 5:20; 1 Chron. 14:11).
28:21 Gibeon. See Joshua 10:1-27 for Joshua's great victory at Gibeon. David also won great battles there (2 Sam. 5:25; 1 Chron. 14:16).
29:1 Ariel. Lion of God, referring to the city of Jerusalem. The prophecy speaks first of the coming of Sennacherib and the destruction of his army by the LORD (2 Kings 19:33),

shall be heaviness and sorrow: and it shall be unto me as Ariel.

3 And I will camp against thee round about, and will lay siege against thee with a mount, and I will raise forts against thee.

4 And thou shalt be brought down, *and* shalt speak out of the ground, and thy speech shall be low out of the dust, and thy voice shall be, as of one that hath a familiar spirit, out of the ground, and thy speech shall whisper out of the dust.

¶ 5 Moreover the multitude of thy strangers shall be like small dust, and the multitude of the terrible ones *shall be* as chaff that passeth away: yea, it shall be at an instant suddenly.

6 Thou shalt be visited of the LORD of hosts with thunder, and with earthquake, and great noise, with storm and tempest, and the flame of devouring fire.

7 And the multitude of all the nations that fight against Ariel, even all that fight against her and her munition, and that distress her, shall be as a dream of a night vision.

8 It shall even be as when an hungry *man* dreameth, and, behold, he eateth; but he awaketh, and his soul is empty: or as when a thirsty man dreameth, and, behold, he drinketh; but he awaketh, and, behold, *he is* faint, and his soul hath appetite: so shall the multitude of all the nations be, that fight against mount Zion.

¶ 9 Stay yourselves, and wonder; cry ye out, and cry: they are drunken, but not with wine; they stagger, but not with strong drink.

10 For the LORD hath poured out upon you the spirit of deep sleep, and hath closed your eyes: the *prophets and your rulers, the seers hath he covered.

11 And the vision of all is become unto you as the words of a book that is sealed, which *men* deliver to one that is learned, saying, Read this, I pray thee: and he saith, I cannot; for it *is* sealed:

12 And the book is delivered to him that is not learned, saying, Read this, I pray thee: and he saith, I am not learned.

¶ 13 Wherefore the Lord said, Forasmuch as this people draw near *me* with their mouth, and with their lips do honour me, but have removed their heart far from me, and their fear toward me is taught by the precept of men:

14 Therefore, behold, I will proceed to do a marvellous work among this people, *even* a marvellous work and a wonder: for the wisdom of their wise *men* shall perish, and the understanding of their prudent *men* shall be hid.

15 Woe unto them that seek deep to hide their counsel from the LORD, and their works are in the dark, and they say, Who seeth us? and who knoweth us?

¶ 16 Surely your turning of things upside down shall be esteemed as the potter's clay: for shall the work say of him that made it, He made me not? or shall the thing framed say of him that framed it, He had no understanding?

17 *Is* it not yet a very little while, and *Lebanon shall be turned into a fruitful field, and the fruitful field shall be esteemed as a forest?

18 And in that day shall the deaf hear the words of the book, and the eyes of the blind shall see out of obscurity, and out of darkness.

19 The meek also shall increase *their* joy in the LORD, and the poor among men shall rejoice in the Holy One of Israel.

---

and second, it looks ahead to the *Great Tribulation when the times of the Gentiles has ended.

29:5 strangers. Enemies.

29:13 this people draw near me with their mouth. See Matthew 15:8-9 where the Lord Jesus quoted this verse.

20 For the terrible one is brought to
nought, and the scorner is consumed,
and all that watch for iniquity are cut off:
21 That make a man an offender for a
word, and lay a snare for him that
reproveth in the gate, and turn aside the
just for a thing of nought.
¶22 Therefore thus saith the LORD,
who *redeemed *Abraham, concerning
the house of Jacob, Jacob shall not now
be ashamed, neither shall his face now
wax pale.
23 But when he seeth his children, the
work of mine hands, in the midst of him,
they shall sanctify my name, and sanctify the Holy One of Jacob, and shall fear
the God of Israel.
¶24 They also that erred in spirit shall
come to understanding, and they that
murmured shall learn doctrine.

Egyptian alliance useless against Sennacherib

30 Woe to the rebellious children,
saith the LORD, that take counsel, but not of me; and that cover with
a covering, but not of my spirit, that
they may add sin to sin:
2 That walk to go down into Egypt,
and have not asked at my mouth; to
strengthen themselves in the strength
of *Pharaoh, and to trust in the shadow of Egypt!
3 Therefore shall the strength of Pharaoh be your shame, and the trust in the
shadow of Egypt *your* confusion.
4 For his princes were at *Zoan, and
his ambassadors came to Hanes.
5 They were all ashamed of a people
that could not profit them, nor be an
help nor profit, but a shame, and also a
reproach.
6 The burden of the beasts of the
south: into the land of trouble and anguish, from whence *come* the young and
old lion, the viper and fiery flying serpent, they will carry their riches upon
the shoulders of young asses, and their
treasures upon the bunches of camels,
to a people *that* shall not profit *them.*
7 For the Egyptians shall help in vain,
and to no purpose: therefore have I
cried concerning this, Their strength *is*
to sit still.
¶8 Now go, write it before them in a
table, and note it in a book, that it may
be for the time to come for ever and
ever:
9 That this *is* a rebellious people, lying children, children *that* will not hear
the *law of the LORD:
10 Which say to the seers, See not;
and to the prophets, Prophesy not unto
us right things, speak unto us smooth
things, prophesy deceits:
11 Get you out of the way, turn aside
out of the path, cause the Holy One of
Israel to cease from before us.
12 Wherefore thus saith the Holy One
of Israel, Because ye despise this word,
and trust in oppression and perverseness, and stay thereon:
13 Therefore this iniquity shall be to
you as a breach ready to fall, swelling
out in a high wall, whose breaking
cometh suddenly at an instant.
14 And he shall break it as the breaking of the potters' vessel that is broken
in pieces; he shall not spare: so that
there shall not be found in the bursting
of it a sherd to take fire from the hearth,
or to take water *withal* out of the *pit.
15 For thus saith the Lord GOD, the
Holy One of Israel; In returning and
rest shall ye be saved; in quietness and
in confidence shall be your strength:
and ye would not.
16 But ye said, No; for we will flee

30:1 rebellious children. Israel was planning an alliance with Egypt. God had forbidden this (Exod. 23:32).
30:6 bunches. Camels' humps.
30:8 write it . . . in a book. Another point of evidence of the *inspiration of the Bible.
30:8 a table. A tablet or card that everyone could read.
30:14 sherd. An old spelling of "shard," a piece or fragment of a thin, brittle material, as earthenware.

upon horses; therefore shall ye flee:
and, We will ride upon the swift; therefore shall they that pursue you be swift.
17 One thousand *shall flee* at the rebuke of one; at the rebuke of five shall
ye flee: till ye be left as a beacon upon
the top of a mountain, and as an ensign
on an hill.
¶ 18 And therefore will the LORD wait,
that he may be gracious unto you, and
therefore will he be exalted, that he
may have mercy upon you: for the LORD
is a God of judgment: blessed *are* all
they that wait for him.
19 For the people shall dwell in *Zion
at Jerusalem: thou shalt weep no more:
he will be very gracious unto thee at the
voice of thy cry; when he shall hear it,
he will answer thee.
20 And *though* the Lord give you the
bread of adversity, and the water of affliction, yet shall not thy teachers be
removed into a corner any more, but
thine eyes shall see thy teachers:
21 And thine ears shall hear a word
behind thee, saying, This *is* the way,
walk ye in it, when ye turn to the right
hand, and when ye turn to the left.
22 Ye shall defile also the covering of
thy graven images of silver, and the
ornament of thy molten images of gold:
thou shalt cast them away as a menstruous cloth; thou shalt say unto it, Get
thee hence.
23 Then shall he give the rain of thy
seed, that thou shalt sow the ground
withal; and bread of the increase of the
earth, and it shall be fat and plenteous:
in that day shall thy cattle feed in large
pastures.
24 The oxen likewise and the young
asses that ear the ground shall eat clean
provender, which hath been winnowed
with the shovel and with the fan.
25 And there shall be upon every high
mountain, and upon every high hill,
rivers *and* streams of waters in the day
of the great slaughter, when the towers
fall.
26 Moreover the light of the moon shall
be as the light of the sun, and the light
of the sun shall be sevenfold, as the light
of seven days, in the day that the LORD
bindeth up the breach of his people, and
healeth the stroke of their wound.
¶ 27 Behold, the name of the LORD
cometh from far, burning *with* his anger,
and the burden *thereof is* heavy: his lips
are full of indignation, and his tongue as
a devouring fire:
28 And his breath, as an overflowing
stream, shall reach to the midst of the
neck, to sift the nations with the sieve
of *vanity: and *there shall be* a bridle
in the jaws of the people, causing *them*
to err.
29 Ye shall have a song, as in the night
when a holy solemnity is kept; and gladness of heart, as when one goeth with
a pipe to come into the mountain of the
LORD, to the mighty One of Israel.
30 And the LORD shall cause his glorious voice to be heard, and shall shew
the lighting down of his arm, with the
indignation of *his* anger, and *with* the
flame of a devouring fire, *with* scattering, and tempest, and hailstones.
31 For through the voice of the LORD
shall the Assyrian be beaten down,
which smote with a rod.
32 And *in* every place where the
grounded staff shall pass, which the
LORD shall lay upon him, *it* shall be with
*tabrets and harps: and in battles of
shaking will he fight with it.
33 For *Tophet *is* ordained of old; yea,
for the king it is prepared; he hath
made *it* deep *and* large: the pile thereof
is fire and much wood; the breath of the
LORD, like a stream of brimstone, doth
kindle it.

Useless Egyptian alliance (continued)

31 Woe to them that go down to
Egypt for help; and stay on
horses, and trust in chariots, because
they are many; and in horsemen, because they are very strong; but they

30:17 as a beacon . . . an ensign. These are pictures of loneliness and desolation.

look not unto the Holy One of Israel,
neither seek the LORD!
2Yet he also *is* wise, and will bring
evil, and will not call back his words: but
will arise against the house of the evildoers, and against the help of them that
work iniquity.
3Now the Egyptians *are* men, and not
God; and their horses *flesh, and not
spirit. When the LORD shall stretch out
his hand, both he that helpeth shall fall,
and he that is holpen shall fall down, and
they all shall fail together.
¶4For thus hath the LORD spoken
unto me, Like as the lion and the young
lion roaring on his prey, when a multitude of shepherds is called forth against
him, *he* will not be afraid of their voice,
nor abase himself for the noise of them:
so shall the LORD of hosts come down
to fight for mount Zion, and for the hill
thereof.
5As birds flying, so will the LORD of
hosts defend Jerusalem; defending also
he will deliver *it; and* passing over he
will preserve *it.*
¶6Turn ye unto *him from* whom the
children of Israel have deeply revolted.
7For in that day every man shall cast
away his idols of silver, and his idols of
gold, which your own hands have made
unto you *for* a sin.
¶8Then shall the Assyrian fall with
the sword, not of a mighty man; and the
sword, not of a mean man, shall devour
him: but he shall flee from the sword,
and his young men shall be discomfited.
9And he shall pass over to his strong
hold for fear, and his princes shall be
afraid of the ensign, saith the LORD,
whose fire *is* in Zion, and his furnace in
Jerusalem.

V. The Kingdom of Christ (32:1—35:10)

The King shall be Israel's Protection

32 Behold, a king shall reign in
*righteousness, and princes
shall rule in judgment.
2And a man shall be as an hiding place
from the wind, and a covert from the
tempest; as rivers of water in a dry
place, as the shadow of a great *rock in
a weary land.
¶3And the eyes of them that see shall
not be dim, and the ears of them that
hear shall hearken.
4The heart also of the rash shall understand knowledge, and the tongue of
the stammerers shall be ready to speak
plainly.
5The vile person shall be no more
called liberal, nor the churl said *to be*
bountiful.
6For the vile person will speak
villany, and his heart will work iniquity, to practise hypocrisy, and to utter
error against the LORD, to make empty
the soul of the hungry, and he will cause
the drink of the thirsty to fail.
7The instruments also of the churl
are evil: he deviseth wicked devices to
destroy the poor with lying words, even
when the needy speaketh right.
8But the liberal deviseth liberal
things; and by liberal things shall he
stand.
¶9Rise up, ye women that are at ease;
hear my voice, ye careless daughters;
give ear unto my speech.
10Many days and years shall ye be
troubled, ye careless women: for the
vintage shall fail, the gathering shall not
come.
11Tremble, ye women that are at
ease; be troubled, ye careless ones:
strip you, and make you bare, and gird
sackcloth upon *your* loins.
12They shall lament for the teats,
for the pleasant fields, for the fruitful
vine.
13Upon the land of my people shall
come up thorns *and* briers; yea, upon
all the houses of joy *in* the joyous city:
14Because the palaces shall be forsaken; the multitude of the city shall be
left; the forts and towers shall be for

32:1 king. This king is Christ Himself. We have seen in chapter 11 that He will reign in righteousness; He, the Man, will be the protection of His people (32:2).

dens for ever, a joy of wild asses, a pasture of flocks;

¶[15]Until the spirit be poured upon us from on high, and the wilderness be a fruitful field, and the fruitful field be counted for a forest.

[16]Then judgment shall dwell in the wilderness, and righteousness remain in the fruitful field.

[17]And the work of righteousness shall be *peace; and the effect of righteousness quietness and *assurance for ever.

[18]And my people shall dwell in a peaceable habitation, and in sure dwellings, and in quiet resting places;

[19]When it shall hail, coming down on the forest; and the city shall be low in a low place.

¶[20]Blessed *are* ye that sow beside all waters, that send forth *thither* the feet of the ox and the ass.

The King will be an absolute Monarch (vs. 22)

33 Woe to thee that spoilest, and thou *wast* not spoiled; and dealest treacherously, and they dealt not treacherously with thee! when thou shalt cease to spoil, thou shalt be spoiled; *and* when thou shalt make an end to deal treacherously, they shall deal treacherously with thee.

[2]O LORD, be gracious unto us; we have waited for thee: be thou their arm every morning, our *salvation also in the time of trouble.

[3]At the noise of the tumult the people fled; at the lifting up of thyself the nations were scattered.

[4]And your spoil shall be gathered *like* the gathering of the caterpiller: as the running to and fro of locusts shall he run upon them.

[5]The LORD is exalted; for he dwelleth on high: he hath filled Zion with judgment and righteousness.

[6]And wisdom and knowledge shall be the stability of thy times, *and* strength of salvation: the fear of the LORD *is* his treasure.

[7]Behold, their valiant ones shall cry without: the ambassadors of peace shall weep bitterly.

[8]The highways lie waste, the wayfaring man ceaseth: he hath broken the covenant, he hath despised the cities, he regardeth no man.

[9]The earth mourneth *and* languisheth: Lebanon is ashamed *and* hewn down: Sharon is like a wilderness; and Bashan and Carmel shake off *their fruits.*

33:9 The Land of Sharon
Sharon was a rich and beautiful land between the central mountains and the Mediterranean. It stretched from Joppa northward to Mount Carmel. The rose of Sharon is undoubtedly the beautiful and sweet white narcissus, which grows in abundance on the plain. There are wonderful oak forests there in addition to fine pastureland.

[10]Now will I rise, saith the LORD; now will I be exalted; now will I lift up myself.

[11]Ye shall conceive chaff, ye shall bring forth stubble: your breath, *as* *fire, shall devour you.

[12]And the people shall be *as* the

33:1 thee that spoilest. This is addressed to Sennacherib, king of Assyria. He ceased to spoil (destroy and kill, as in war) because the LORD killed his soldiers (2 Kings 19:35), and he was dealt with treacherously when his own sons murdered him (2 Kings 19:37).

33:8 he hath broken the covenant. Hezekiah paid Sennacherib with gold that he stripped from the temple, in exchange for Sennacherib's promise not to harm or invade Palestine. Sennacherib broke the covenant and ruined the country as stated in verse 9.

33:9 Bashan. Even the name means *rich soil*. It was the tract of pastureland beyond the Jordan that was assigned to the half tribe of Manasseh.

33:9 Carmel. The name means *park* or *the vineyard of God*. It is a beautiful mountain, jutting out into the Mediterranean.

33:12 burnings of lime. Chopped thorns, the fuel for burning lime in a limekiln.

burnings of lime: *as* thorns cut up shall
they be burned in the fire.
13Hear, ye *that are* far off, what I have
done; and, ye *that are* near, acknowledge my might.
¶14The sinners in Zion are afraid;
fearfulness hath surprised the hypocrites. Who among us shall dwell with
the devouring fire? who among us shall
dwell with everlasting burnings?
15He that walketh righteously, and
speaketh uprightly; he that despiseth
the gain of oppressions, that shaketh
his hands from holding of bribes, that
stoppeth his ears from hearing of
blood, and shutteth his eyes from seeing evil;
16He shall dwell on high: his place of
defence *shall be* the munitions of rocks:
bread shall be given him; his waters
shall be sure.
¶17Thine eyes shall see the king in
his beauty: they shall behold the land
that is very far off.
18Thine heart shall meditate terror.
Where *is* the scribe? where *is* the receiver? where *is* he that counted the
towers?
19Thou shalt not see a fierce people,
a people of a deeper speech than thou
canst perceive; of a stammering tongue,
that thou canst not understand.
20Look upon Zion, the city of our solemnities: thine eyes shall see Jerusalem a quiet habitation, a *tabernacle
that shall not be taken down; not one of
the stakes thereof shall ever be removed, neither shall any of the cords
thereof be broken.
21But there the glorious LORD *will be*
unto us a place of broad rivers *and*
streams; wherein shall go no galley
with oars, neither shall gallant ship pass
thereby.
22For the LORD *is* our judge, the LORD
is our lawgiver, the LORD *is* our king;
he will save us.
23Thy tacklings are loosed; they
could not well strengthen their mast,
they could not spread the sail: then is
the prey of a great spoil divided; the
lame take the prey.
24And the inhabitant shall not say, I
am sick: the people that dwell therein
shall be *forgiven *their* iniquity.

33:22 A Perfect Government
When the Lord Jesus Christ establishes the kingdom of God upon the earth at His second coming, that kingdom will be an absolute monarchy. Every branch of government will be centered in Him—the judicial, legislative, and executive. Only then will perfect righteousness be assured during His reign. He will judge the people to insure the fulfillment of His law. He will create the law to insure righteous character of it. He will execute the law, assuring that the law of God will be done. This complete Ruler is also our Saviour.

The King will destroy Israel's enemies

34 Come near, ye nations, to hear;
and hearken, ye people: let the
earth hear, and all that is therein; the
*world, and all things that come forth
of it.
2For the indignation of the LORD *is*
upon all nations, and *his* fury upon all
their armies: he hath utterly destroyed
them, he hath delivered them to the
slaughter.
3Their slain also shall be cast out, and

33:17 shall see the king. When the Lord Jesus Christ sets up His *kingdom on earth, this prophecy will be fulfilled.
33:18 scribe . . . receiver . . . he that counted. These were three Assyrian officers. One wrote down the amount of the captured treasure—men or wealth; one weighed it; and one counted the "towers"—the captured chief men.
33:20 solemnities. Festivities.
33:21 gallant. Mighty or splendid.
33:23 Thy tacklings are loosed . . . the lame take the prey. The overthrow of the enemy is compared to a shipwreck—so complete that even crippled people could go off with treasures.

34:2 The Judgment of the Nations
This prediction anticipates the judgments of the future *Tribulation and second coming of Christ upon the nations of the world. They will all be gathered around Jerusalem to battle (Zech. 14:2). At the moment of their apparent triumph, Christ will return in glory and destroy them (Rev. 19:11-19). This is called the Battle of *Armageddon. At that time the heavens will open as the Son of God descends in glory (Isa. 34:4), and the wrath of God will fall upon the unbelieving world (34:8). It will be necessary for Christ to destroy the unrighteous rule of man in order to establish His righteous rule.

their stink shall come up out of their
carcases, and the mountains shall be
melted with their blood.
4And all the host of *heaven shall
be dissolved, and the heavens shall be
rolled together as a scroll: and all their
host shall fall down, as the leaf falleth
off from the vine, and as a falling *fig*
from the *fig tree.
5For my sword shall be bathed in
heaven: behold, it shall come down
upon Idumea, and upon the people of
my curse, to *judgment.
6The sword of the LORD is filled with
blood, it is made fat with fatness, *and*
with the blood of lambs and goats, with
the fat of the kidneys of rams: for the
LORD hath a sacrifice in Bozrah, and a
great slaughter in the land of Idumea.
7And the unicorns shall come down
with them, and the bullocks with the
bulls; and their land shall be soaked
with blood, and their dust made fat with
fatness.
8For *it is* the day of the LORD'S vengeance, *and* the year of recompences
for the controversy of Zion.
9And the streams thereof shall be
turned into pitch, and the dust thereof
into brimstone, and the land thereof
shall become burning pitch.
10It shall not be quenched night nor
day; the smoke thereof shall go up for
ever: from generation to generation it
shall lie waste; none shall pass through
it for ever and ever.
¶ 11But the cormorant and the bittern
shall possess it; the owl also and the
raven shall dwell in it: and he shall
stretch out upon it the line of confusion,
and the stones of emptiness.
12They shall call the nobles thereof to
the *kingdom, but none *shall be* there,
and all her princes shall be nothing.
13And thorns shall come up in her
palaces, nettles and brambles in the
fortresses thereof: and it shall be an
habitation of dragons, *and* a court for
owls.
14The wild beasts of the desert shall
also meet with the wild beasts of the
island, and the satyr shall cry to his fellow; the screech owl also shall rest
there, and find for herself a place of rest.
15There shall the great owl make her
nest, and lay, and hatch, and gather under her shadow: there shall the vultures
also be gathered, every one with her
mate.
¶ 16Seek ye out of the book of the
LORD, and read: no one of these shall
fail, none shall want her mate: for my
mouth it hath commanded, and his spirit it hath gathered them.
17And he hath cast the lot for them,
and his hand hath divided it unto them
by line: they shall possess it for ever,
from generation to generation shall
they dwell therein.

34:5 Idumea. Idumea or Edom, lying south of Judah, belonged to the descendants of Esau (Gen. 36:1). It stands for all that is against the people of God. Bozrah (vs. 6) was the ancient capital of Edom.
34:8 the day of the LORD's vengeance. See *Day of the LORD.
34:14 satyr. These were called "the wild beasts [evil spirits] of the desert." They were goats that were often worshipped with extremely evil ceremonies.
34:16 no one of these shall fail. Every prophecy God gave Isaiah would come to pass. Many prophecies are referred to in the New Testament. Compare Isaiah 7:14 with Matthew 1:21-23; Isaiah 53:4 with Matthew 8:17, for example.

The kingdom will be glorious

35 The wilderness and the solitary place shall be glad for
them; and the desert shall rejoice, and
blossom as the rose.
2It shall blossom abundantly, and rejoice even with joy and singing: the glory of *Lebanon shall be given unto it,
the excellency of Carmel and Sharon,
they shall see the glory of the LORD,
and the excellency of our *God.
¶3Strengthen ye the weak hands, and
confirm the feeble knees.
4Say to them *that are* of a fearful
heart, Be strong, fear not: behold, your
God will come *with* vengeance, *even*
God *with* a recompence; he will come
and save you.
5Then the eyes of the blind shall be
opened, and the ears of the deaf shall
be unstopped.
6Then shall the lame *man* leap as an
hart, and the tongue of the dumb sing:
for in the wilderness shall waters break
out, and streams in the desert.
7And the parched ground shall become a pool, and the thirsty land
springs of water: in the habitation of
dragons, where each lay, *shall be* grass
with reeds and rushes.
¶8And an highway shall be there, and
a way, and it shall be called The way of
holiness; the *unclean shall not pass
over it; but it *shall be* for those: the
wayfaring men, though *fools, shall not
*err *therein.*
9No lion shall be there, nor *any* ravenous beast shall go up thereon, it shall
not be found there; but the *redeemed
shall walk *there:*
10And the *ransomed of the LORD shall
return, and come to Zion with songs and
everlasting joy upon their heads: they
shall obtain joy and gladness, and sorrow and sighing shall flee away.

VI. Reward of Israel's Faith (36:1—39:8)

*Sennacherib invades *Judah and defies God*

36 Now it came to pass in the fourteenth year of king *Hezekiah,
that Sennacherib king of Assyria came
up against all the defenced cities of Judah, and took them.
2And the king of Assyria sent
Rabshakeh from *Lachish to *Jerusalem unto king Hezekiah with a great
army. And he stood by the conduit of
the upper pool in the highway of the
fuller's field.

36:2 Pools for Water
Being on top of a mountain, Jerusalem had an insufficient water supply. One spring that never failed to give water was located on Mount Moriah, which was nearby the city. This water was collected in the pool of Siloam, and its overflow went into the well of Joab. There were also two pools of Gihon on the west side of Jerusalem—that of Hezekiah by the Jaffa Gate; and that called Birket Israel near Saint Stephen's Gate, which was fed from a spring or reservoir under Pilate's house and the adjoining barracks. However, there is some uncertainty as to the position of these ancient pools. The houses of the wealthy had, and still have, extensive cisterns for storing rainwater. It is thought that the pool of Bethesda has recently been discovered 350 feet north of the Birket Israel.

3Then came forth unto him Eliakim,
Hilkiah's son, which was over the
house, and Shebna the scribe, and Joah,
*Asaph's son, the recorder.
¶4And Rabshakeh said unto them,
Say ye now to Hezekiah, Thus saith
the great king, the king of Assyria,
What confidence *is* this wherein thou
trustest?
5I say, *sayest thou,* (but *they are but*
vain words) *I have* counsel and strength

35:1 rejoice. The joy of the millennial reign of Christ is presented throughout this chapter. It will be a glad day for the world when He returns.
35:7 dragons. See Isaiah 27:1 and its note.
36:1 Sennacherib king of Assyria came up. See 2 Kings 18–19.

for war: now on whom dost thou *trust,
that thou rebellest against me?
6Lo, thou trustest in the staff of this
broken reed, on *Egypt; whereon if a
man lean, it will go into his hand, and
pierce it: so *is* *Pharaoh king of Egypt
to all that trust in him.
7But if thou say to me, We trust in the
LORD our God: *is it* not he, whose *high
places and whose altars Hezekiah hath
taken away, and said to Judah and to
Jerusalem, Ye shall worship before this
*altar?
8Now therefore give pledges, I pray
thee, to my master the king of Assyria,
and I will give thee two thousand
horses, if thou be able on thy part to set
riders upon them.
9How then wilt thou turn away the
face of one captain of the least of my
master's servants, and put thy trust on
Egypt for chariots and for horsemen?
10And am I now come up without the
LORD against this land to destroy it? the
LORD said unto me, Go up against this
land, and destroy it.
¶ 11Then said Eliakim and Shebna and
Joah unto Rabshakeh, Speak, I pray
thee, unto thy servants in the Syrian
language; for we understand *it:* and
speak not to us in the Jews' language,
in the ears of the people that *are* on the
wall.
¶ 12But Rabshakeh said, Hath my
master sent me to thy master and to
thee to speak these words? *hath he* not
sent me to the men that sit upon the
wall, that they may eat their own *dung,
and drink their own piss with you?
13Then Rabshakeh stood, and cried
with a loud voice in the Jews' language,
and said, Hear ye the words of the great
king, the king of Assyria.
14Thus saith the king, Let not Hezekiah deceive you: for he shall not be
able to deliver you.
15Neither let Hezekiah make you
trust in the LORD, saying, The LORD
will surely deliver us: this city shall not
be delivered into the hand of the king
of Assyria.
16Hearken not to Hezekiah: for thus
saith the king of Assyria, Make *an
agreement* with me *by* a present, and
come out to me: and eat ye every one
of his vine, and every one of his fig tree,

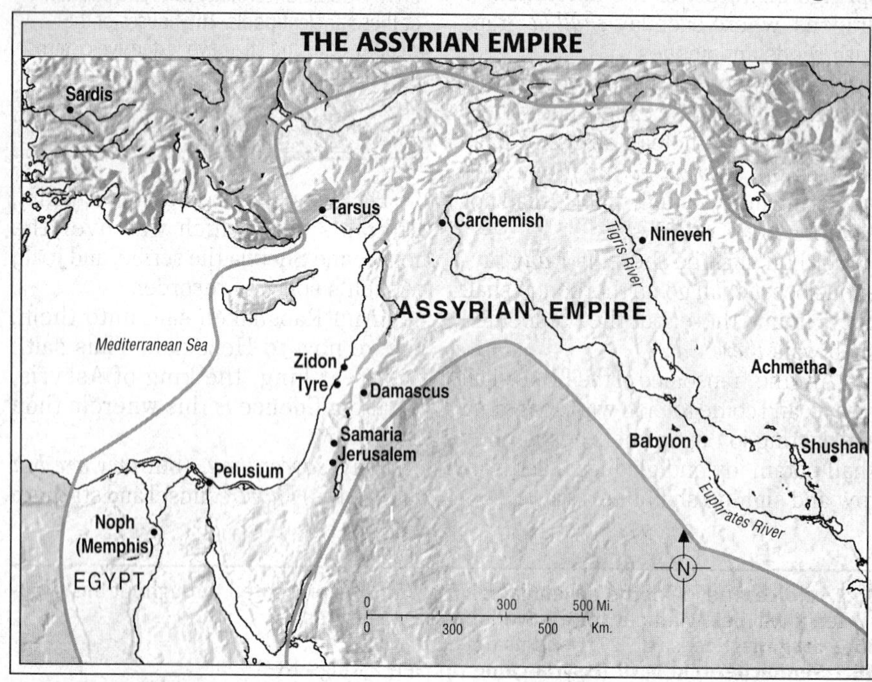

and drink ye every one the waters of his
own cistern;
17 Until I come and take you away to
a land like your own land, a land of corn
and wine, a land of bread and vineyards.
18 *Beware* lest Hezekiah persuade
you, saying, The LORD will deliver us.
Hath any of the gods of the nations delivered his land out of the hand of the
king of Assyria?
19 Where *are* the gods of Hamath and
Arphad? where *are* the gods of Sepharvaim? and have they delivered *Samaria out of my hand?
20 Who *are they* among all the gods of
these lands, that have delivered their
land out of my hand, that the LORD
should deliver Jerusalem out of my
hand?
21 But they held their peace, and answered him not a word: for the king's
commandment was, saying, Answer
him not.
¶22 Then came Eliakim, the son of
Hilkiah, that *was* over the household,
and Shebna the scribe, and Joah, the son
of Asaph, the recorder, to Hezekiah
with *their* clothes rent, and told him the
words of Rabshakeh.

Hezekiah trusts God and is delivered

37 And it came to pass, when king
Hezekiah heard *it,* that he rent
his clothes, and covered himself with
sackcloth, and went into the house of
the LORD.
2 And he sent Eliakim, who *was* over
the household, and Shebna the scribe,
and the *elders of the priests covered
with sackcloth, unto Isaiah the *prophet
the son of Amoz.
3 And they said unto him, Thus saith
Hezekiah, This day *is* a day of trouble,
and of rebuke, and of blasphemy: for the
children are come to the birth, and *there
is* not strength to bring forth.
4 It may be the LORD thy God will hear
the words of Rabshakeh, whom the king
of Assyria his master hath sent to reproach the living God, and will reprove
the words which the LORD thy God hath
heard: wherefore lift up *thy* *prayer for
the *remnant that is left.
5 So the servants of king Hezekiah
came to Isaiah.
¶6 And Isaiah said unto them, Thus
shall ye say unto your master, Thus
saith the LORD, *Be not afraid of the
words that thou hast heard, wherewith
the servants of the king of Assyria have
blasphemed me.
7 Behold, I will send a blast upon him,
and he shall hear a rumour, and return
to his own land; and I will cause him to
fall by the sword in his own land.
¶8 So Rabshakeh returned, and found
the king of Assyria warring against Libnah: for he had heard that he was departed from Lachish.
9 And he heard say concerning Tirhakah king of Ethiopia, He is come forth
to make war with thee. And when he
heard *it,* he sent messengers to Hezekiah, saying,
10 Thus shall ye speak to Hezekiah
king of Judah, saying, Let not thy God,
in whom thou trustest, deceive thee,
saying, Jerusalem shall not be given
into the hand of the king of Assyria.
11 Behold, thou hast heard what the
kings of Assyria have done to all lands
by destroying them utterly; and shalt
thou be delivered?
12 Have the gods of the nations delivered them which my fathers have destroyed, *as* Gozan, and Haran, and
Rezeph, and the children of *Eden
which *were* in Telassar?
13 Where *is* the king of Hamath, and
the king of Arphad, and the king of the
city of Sepharvaim, Hena, and Ivah?
¶14 And Hezekiah received the letter
from the hand of the messengers, and
read it: and Hezekiah went up unto the
house of the LORD, and spread it before
the LORD.
15 And Hezekiah prayed unto the
LORD, saying,
16 O LORD of hosts, God of *Israel,
that dwellest *between* the cherubims,
thou *art* the God, *even* thou alone, of all

the kingdoms of the earth: thou hast made heaven and earth.

17 Incline thine ear, O LORD, and hear; open thine eyes, O LORD, and see: and hear all the words of Sennacherib, which hath sent to reproach the living God.

18 Of a truth, LORD, the kings of Assyria have laid waste all the nations, and their countries,

19 And have cast their gods into the fire: for they *were* no gods, but the work of men's hands, wood and stone: therefore they have destroyed them.

20 Now therefore, O LORD our God, save us from his hand, that all the kingdoms of the earth may know that thou *art* the LORD, *even* thou only.

¶21 Then Isaiah the son of Amoz sent unto Hezekiah, saying, Thus saith the LORD God of Israel, Whereas thou hast prayed to me against Sennacherib king of Assyria:

22 This *is* the word which the LORD hath spoken concerning him; The virgin, the daughter of *Zion, hath despised thee, *and* laughed thee to scorn; the daughter of Jerusalem hath shaken her head at thee.

23 Whom hast thou reproached and blasphemed? and against whom hast thou exalted *thy* voice, and lifted up thine eyes on high? *even* against the *Holy One of Israel.

24 By thy servants hast thou reproached the Lord, and hast said, By the multitude of my chariots am I come up to the height of the mountains, to the sides of Lebanon; and I will cut down the tall cedars thereof, *and* the choice fir trees thereof: and I will enter into the height of his border, *and* the forest of his *Carmel.

25 I have digged, and drunk water; and with the sole of my feet have I dried up all the rivers of the besieged places.

26 Hast thou not heard long ago, *how* I have done it; *and* of ancient times, that I have formed it? now have I brought it to pass, that thou shouldest be to lay waste defenced cities *into* ruinous heaps.

27 Therefore their inhabitants *were* of small power, they were dismayed and confounded: they were *as* the grass of the field, and *as* the green herb, *as* the grass on the housetops, and *as corn* blasted before it be grown up.

28 But I know thy abode, and thy going out, and thy coming in, and thy rage against me.

29 Because thy rage against me, and thy tumult, is come up into mine ears, therefore will I put my hook in thy nose, and my bridle in thy lips, and I will turn thee back by the way by which thou camest.

30 And this *shall be* a sign unto thee, Ye shall eat *this* year such as groweth of itself; and the second year that which springeth of the same: and in the third year sow ye, and reap, and plant vineyards, and eat the fruit thereof.

31 And the remnant that is escaped of the house of Judah shall again take root downward, and bear fruit upward:

32 For out of Jerusalem shall go forth a remnant, and they that escape out of mount Zion: the zeal of the LORD of hosts shall do this.

33 Therefore thus saith the LORD concerning the king of Assyria, He shall not come into this city, nor shoot an arrow there nor come before it with shields, nor cast a bank against it.

34 By the way that he came, by the same shall he return, and shall not come into this city, saith the LORD.

35 For I will defend this city to save it for mine own sake, and for my servant *David's sake.

¶36 Then the *angel of the LORD went forth, and smote in the camp of the Assyrians a hundred and fourscore and five thousand: and when they arose early in the morning, behold, they *were* all dead corpses.

¶37 So Sennacherib king of Assyria

37:36 smote in the camp of the Assyrians. See Isaiah 10:12; 2 Kings 19:35.

departed, and went and returned, and
dwelt at Nineveh.
38 And it came to pass, as he was worshipping in the house of Nisroch his
god, that Adrammelech and Sharezer
his sons smote him with the sword; and
they escaped into the land of Armenia:
and Esar-haddon his son reigned in his
stead.

Hezekiah's sickness and recovery

38 In those days was Hezekiah
sick unto death. And Isaiah the
prophet the son of Amoz came unto
him, and said unto him, Thus saith the
LORD, Set thine house in order: for thou
shalt die, and not live.
2 Then Hezekiah turned his face toward the wall, and prayed unto the
LORD,
3 And said, Remember now, O LORD,
I beseech thee, how I have walked before thee in truth and with a *perfect
heart, and have done *that which is* good
in thy sight. And Hezekiah wept sore.
¶4 Then came the word of the LORD
to Isaiah, saying,
5 Go, and say to Hezekiah, Thus saith
the LORD, the God of David thy father,
I have heard thy prayer, I have seen thy
tears: behold, I will add unto thy days
fifteen years.
6 And I will deliver thee and this city
out of the hand of the king of Assyria:
and I will defend this city.
7 And this *shall be* a sign unto thee
from the LORD, that the LORD will do
this thing that he hath spoken;
8 Behold, I will bring again the shadow
of the degrees, which is gone down in
the sun dial of Ahaz, ten degrees backward. So the sun returned ten degrees,
by which degrees it was gone down.
¶9 The writing of Hezekiah king of Judah, when he had been sick, and was
recovered of his sickness:
10 I said in the cutting off of my days,

38:8 God's Miracle
This is one of the many miracles recorded in the Word of God. Science may say that it would destroy the world and be an utter impossibility to reverse the sun's rotation in order to make the shadow go backward on the sundial of Ahaz. Such assertions overlook the fact that if God were to remove His power, natural laws would collapse. God is superior to natural law. He made the world and its laws. Miracles are not impossible when one remembers the greatness of God.

I shall go to the gates of the grave: I am
deprived of the residue of my years.
11 I said, I shall not see the LORD, *even*
the LORD, in the land of the living: I
shall behold man no more with the inhabitants of the world.
12 Mine age is departed, and is removed from me as a shepherd's tent: I
have cut off like a weaver my life: he
will cut me off with pining sickness:
from day *even* to night wilt thou make
an end of me.
13 I reckoned till morning, *that,* as a
lion, so will he break all my bones: from
day *even* to night wilt thou make an end
of me.
14 Like a crane *or* a swallow, so did I
chatter: I did mourn as a dove: mine
eyes fail *with looking* upward: O LORD,
I am oppressed; undertake for me.
15 What shall I say? he hath both spoken unto me, and himself hath done *it:*
I shall go softly all my years in the bitterness of my soul.
16 O Lord, by these *things men* live,
and in all these *things is* the life of my
spirit: so wilt thou recover me, and
make me to live.
17 Behold, for *peace I had great bitterness: but thou hast in love to my soul
delivered it from the pit of corruption:
for thou hast cast all my sins behind thy
back.
18 For the grave cannot praise thee,

38:12 like a weaver. Hezekiah's thought was: "As a weaver cuts off his threads, my life is cut off."
38:18 the grave. In this verse the king does not assert that the dead in Christ are not

death can *not* celebrate thee: they that
go down into the pit cannot *hope for
thy truth.
19 The living, the living, he shall
praise thee, as I *do* this day: the father
to the children shall make known thy
truth.
20 The LORD *was ready* to save me:
therefore we will sing my songs to the
stringed instruments all the days of our
life in the house of the LORD.
21 For Isaiah had said, Let them take
a lump of figs, and lay *it* for a plaister
upon the boil, and he shall recover.
22 Hezekiah also had said, What *is* the
sign that I shall go up to the house of
the LORD?

Prophecy of the Babylonian captivity

39 At that time Merodach-baladan,
the son of Baladan, king of *Babylon, sent letters and a present to Hezekiah: for he had heard that he had been
sick, and was recovered.
2 And Hezekiah was glad of them, and
shewed them the house of his precious
things, the silver, and the gold, and the
spices, and the precious ointment, and
all the house of his armour, and all that
was found in his treasures: there was
nothing in his house, nor in all his dominion, that Hezekiah shewed them not.
¶3 Then came Isaiah the prophet unto
king Hezekiah, and said unto him, What
said these men? and from whence came
they unto thee? And Hezekiah said,
They are come from a far country unto
me, *even* from Babylon.
4 Then said he, What have they seen
in thine house? And Hezekiah answered, All that *is* in mine house have
they seen: there is nothing among my
treasures that I have not shewed them.
5 Then said Isaiah to Hezekiah, Hear
the word of the LORD of hosts:
6 Behold, the days come, that all that
is in thine house, and *that* which thy
fathers have laid up in store until this
day, shall be carried to Babylon: nothing shall be left, saith the LORD.
7 And of thy sons that shall issue from
thee, which thou shalt beget, shall they
take away; and they shall be eunuchs in
the palace of the king of Babylon.
8 Then said Hezekiah to Isaiah, Good
is the word of the LORD which thou hast
spoken. He said moreover, For there
shall be peace and truth in my days.

VII. Greatness of Israel's God (40:1—41:29)

God's greatness—the source of Israel's comfort

40 Comfort ye, comfort ye my people, saith your God.
2 Speak ye comfortably to Jerusalem,
and cry unto her, that her warfare is
accomplished, that her iniquity is pardoned: for she hath received of the
LORD'S hand double for all her sins.
¶3 The voice of him that crieth in the
wilderness, Prepare ye the way of the
LORD, make straight in the desert a
highway for our God.
4 Every valley shall be exalted, and
every mountain and hill shall be made
low: and the crooked shall be made
straight, and the rough places plain:
5 And the glory of the LORD shall be
revealed, and all *flesh shall see *it* together: for the mouth of the LORD hath
spoken *it*.
6 The voice said, Cry. And he said,
What shall I cry? All flesh *is* grass, and

---

praising Him in heaven. Rather, Hezekiah is saying that when one dies it is impossible for that person to continue to praise God on earth. The teachings about immortality were fully revealed by the Lord Jesus Christ (2 Tim. 1:10).

39:1 Merodach-baladan. See 2 Kings 20:12 for the parallel account of the foolish pride of Hezekiah. In that passage Merodach is called Berodach.

39:6 carried to Babylon. Thus Isaiah predicts the captivity of Judah in Babylon. The verse was literally fulfilled when Nebuchadnezzar conquered Jerusalem (2 Kings 25).

40:3 voice. This is a prediction of the ministry of John the Baptist. He came before Christ to prepare the way of the Lord (John 1:23).

40:1 Comfort to the People
The book of Isaiah divides itself into two great sections: the first, chapters 1–39; the second, chapters 40–66.

The messianic promises, which prophesy the coming of the Saviour, are prominent in both sections of the book, but chapters 40–66 bring a further note of comfort to God's people. They describe the person of the Messiah (42:1-4; see 42:1 note, "Christ as Servant"), the deity of the Messiah (44:6), the humiliation of the Messiah (53:2), the substitutionary death of the Messiah (53:5-6; see 53:1-5 note, "Christ's Suffering"), and the reign of the Messiah when He has established His *kingdom on the earth (59:20–60:3).

all the goodliness thereof *is* as the flower of the field:
7The grass withereth, the flower fadeth: because the spirit of the LORD bloweth upon it: surely the people *is* grass.
8The grass withereth, the flower fadeth: but the word of our God shall stand for ever.
¶9O Zion, that bringest good tidings, get thee up into the high mountain; O Jerusalem, that bringest good tidings, lift up thy voice with strength; lift *it* up, *be not afraid; say unto the cities of Judah, Behold your God!
10Behold, the Lord GOD will come with strong *hand*, and his arm shall rule for him: behold, his *reward *is* with him, and his work before him.
11He shall feed his flock like a shepherd: he shall gather the lambs with his arm, and carry *them* in his bosom, *and* shall gently lead those that are with young.
¶12Who hath measured the waters in the hollow of his hand, and meted out *heaven with the span, and comprehended the dust of the earth in a measure, and weighed the mountains in scales, and the hills in a balance?
13Who hath directed the Spirit of the LORD, or *being* his counsellor hath taught him?
14With whom took he counsel, and *who* instructed him, and taught him in the path of judgment, and taught him knowledge, and shewed to him the way of understanding?
15Behold, the nations *are* as a drop of a bucket, and are counted as the small dust of the balance: behold, he taketh up the *isles as a very little thing.
16And Lebanon *is* not sufficient to burn, nor the beasts thereof sufficient for a burnt-offering.
17All nations before him *are* as nothing; and they are counted to him less than nothing, and *vanity.
¶18To whom then will ye liken God? or what likeness will ye compare unto him?
19The workman melteth a *graven image, and the goldsmith spreadeth it over with gold, and casteth silver chains.
20He that *is* so impoverished that he hath no *oblation chooseth a tree *that* will not rot; he seeketh unto him a cunning workman to prepare a graven image, *that* shall not be moved.
21Have ye not known? have ye not heard? hath it not been told you from the beginning? have ye not understood from the foundations of the earth?
22*It is* he that sitteth upon the circle of the earth, and the inhabitants thereof

40:22 The Shape of the Earth
The word "circle" might be translated "globe." Many people think that the Bible teaches that the earth is flat. But it was ancient astronomy called science that made this assumption; for instance, the Ptolemaic Theory states that the sun moves around the earth. The Bible was written amid this scientific environment, but it never taught these errors.

40:6 All flesh is grass. Hundreds of years later, both James and Peter quoted these verses (James 1:10; 1 Pet. 1:24-25).
40:11 like a shepherd. Read John 10:1-16; Hebrews 13:20; 1 Peter 2:25; 5:4 to see how the Lord Jesus Christ fulfilled this prophecy.

are as grasshoppers; that stretcheth out the heavens as a curtain, and spreadeth them out as a tent to dwell in:

23 That bringeth the princes to nothing; he maketh the judges of the earth as vanity.

24 Yea, they shall not be planted; yea, they shall not be sown: yea, their stock shall not take root in the earth: and he shall also blow upon them, and they shall wither, and the whirlwind shall take them away as stubble.

25 To whom then will ye liken me, or shall I be equal? saith the Holy One.

26 Lift up your eyes on high, and behold who hath *created these *things,* that bringeth out their host by number: he calleth them all by names by the greatness of his might, for that *he is* strong in power; not one faileth.

27 Why sayest thou, O *Jacob, and speakest, O Israel, My way is hid from the LORD, and my judgment is passed over from my God?

¶28 Hast thou not known? hast thou not heard, *that* the everlasting God, the LORD, the Creator of the ends of the earth, fainteth not, neither is weary? *there is* no searching of his understanding.

29 He giveth power to the faint; and to *them that have* no might he increaseth strength.

30 Even the youths shall faint and be weary, and the young men shall utterly fall:

31 But they that wait upon the LORD shall renew *their* strength; they shall mount up with wings as eagles; they shall run, and not be weary; *and* they shall walk, and not faint.

God's greatness—the secret of Israel's restoration

41 Keep silence before me, O islands; and let the people renew *their* strength: let them come near; then let them speak: let us come near together to judgment.

2 Who raised up the righteous *man* from the east, called him to his foot, gave the nations before him, and made *him* rule over kings? he gave *them* as the dust to his sword, *and* as driven stubble to his bow.

3 He pursued them, *and* passed safely; *even* by the way *that* he had not gone with his feet.

4 Who hath wrought and done *it,* calling the generations from the beginning? I the LORD, the first, and with the last; I *am* he.

5 The isles saw *it,* and feared; the ends of the earth were afraid, drew near, and came.

¶6 They helped every one his neighbour; and *every one* said to his brother, Be of good courage.

7 So the carpenter encouraged the goldsmith, *and* he that smootheth *with* the hammer him that smote the anvil, saying, It *is* ready for the sodering: and he fastened it with nails, *that* it should not be moved.

¶8 But thou, Israel, *art* my servant, Jacob whom I have chosen, the seed of *Abraham my friend.

41:8 The Good Servant
Israel was not a good servant to God, and has not been yet, but the time will come when the nation will turn in faithfulness to her Master and King. David is also called the servant of God (Isa. 37:35), as is the Messiah the Lord Jesus Christ (42:1-12; 49:1-26). The Servant Messiah will be the One who will bring the servant Israel back to God (49:5-7; 50:4-6; 52:13-15; 53:1-12).

9 *Thou* whom I have taken from the ends of the earth, and called thee from the chief men thereof, and said unto

---

40:26 these things. The stars.

41:2 the righteous man. This is Abraham, who, coming from the east, was the father of the great nation, Israel.

41:7 the carpenter encouraged the goldsmith. The people, instead of putting their trust in God, ordered new idols to worship.

thee, Thou *art* my servant; I have chosen thee, and not cast thee away.
10*Fear thou not; for I *am* with thee:
be not dismayed; for I *am* thy *God: I
will strengthen thee; yea, I will help
thee; yea, I will uphold thee with the
right hand of my *righteousness.
11Behold, all they that were incensed
against thee shall be ashamed and confounded: they shall be as nothing; and
they that strive with thee shall perish.
12Thou shalt seek them, and shalt not
find them, *even* them that contended
with thee: they that war against thee
shall be as nothing, and as a thing of
nought.
13For I the LORD thy God will hold thy
right hand, saying unto thee, Fear not;
I will help thee.
14Fear not, thou worm Jacob, *and* ye
men of Israel; I will help thee, saith the
LORD, and thy *redeemer, the Holy One
of Israel.
15Behold, I will make thee a new
sharp threshing instrument having
teeth: thou shalt thresh the mountains,
and beat *them* small, and shalt make the
hills as chaff.
16Thou shalt fan them, and the wind
shall carry them away, and the whirlwind shall scatter them: and thou shalt
rejoice in the LORD, *and* shalt glory in
the Holy One of Israel.
17*When* the poor and needy seek water, and *there is* none, *and* their tongue
faileth for thirst, I the LORD will hear
them, *I* the God of Israel will not forsake them.
18I will open rivers in high places, and
fountains in the midst of the valleys: I
will make the wilderness a pool of water, and the dry land springs of water.
19I will plant in the wilderness the
cedar, the shittah tree, and the myrtle,
and the oil tree; I will set in the desert
the fir tree, *and* the pine, and the box
tree together:
20That they may see, and know, and
consider, and understand together, that
the hand of the LORD hath done this,
and the Holy One of Israel hath created it.
¶21Produce your cause, saith the
LORD; bring forth your strong *reasons,*
saith the King of Jacob.
22Let them bring *them* forth, and
shew us what shall happen: let them
shew the former things, what they *be,*
that we may consider them, and know
the latter end of them; or declare us
things for to come.
23Shew the things that are to come
hereafter, that we may know that ye
are gods: yea, do good, or do evil, that
we may be dismayed, and behold *it* together.
24Behold, ye *are* of nothing, and your
work of nought: an *abomination *is he
that* chooseth you.
25I have raised up *one* from the north,
and he shall come: from the rising of the
sun shall he call upon my name: and he
shall come upon princes as *upon*
morter, and as the potter treadeth clay.
26Who hath declared from the beginning, that we may know? and beforetime, that we may say, *He is* righteous?
yea, *there is* none that sheweth, yea,
there is none that declareth, yea, *there
is* none that heareth your words.
27The first *shall say* to Zion, Behold,
behold them: and I will give to Jerusalem one that bringeth good tidings.
28For I beheld, and *there was* no man;
even among them, and *there was* no
counsellor, that, when I asked of them,
could answer a word.
29Behold, they *are* all vanity; their

41:19 shittah tree. Acacia tree.
41:19 oil tree. This may be a small tree which grows on the Jordan plain. Its oil is used by the Arabs for healing wounds.
41:21 Produce your cause. State your arguments in favor of idolatry.
41:25 one from the north. Probably Cyrus, who was allowed by God to work His will upon the nations of the earth.
41:27 good tidings. See *gospel.

works *are* nothing: their molten images
are wind and confusion.

VIII. The Ministry of Jehovah's Servant (42:1—53:12)

Christ, the true Servant of Jehovah

42 Behold my servant, whom I
uphold; mine *elect, *in whom*
my soul delighteth; I have put my spirit
upon him: he shall bring forth judgment
to the *Gentiles.

> **42:1 Christ as Servant**
> This is a prediction about Christ Himself. In His whole life and ministry He was, above all, the Servant of the Lord. It is written of Him that He came to do the Father's will (Heb. 10:7). His gentleness is described in verse 2. His sufficiency to correct the discouragement of His children is beautifully pictured in verse 3. His own successful march to accomplish the Father's will is described in verse 4. In verse 6 we see that the Lord Jesus Christ brought a covenant to Israel and a light to the Gentiles. He offers salvation to Jew and Gentile alike.

2He shall not cry, nor lift up, nor
cause his voice to be heard in the street.
3A bruised reed shall he not break,
and the smoking flax shall he not
quench: he shall bring forth judgment
unto truth.
4He shall not fail nor be discouraged,
till he have set judgment in the earth:
and the isles shall wait for his *law.
¶5Thus saith God the LORD, he that
created the heavens, and stretched
them out; he that spread forth the earth,
and that which cometh out of it; he that
giveth breath unto the people upon it,
and spirit to them that walk therein:
6I the LORD have called thee in righteousness, and will hold thine hand, and
will keep thee, and give thee for a *covenant of the people, for a light of the
Gentiles;
7To open the blind eyes, to bring out
the prisoners from the prison, *and*
them that sit in darkness out of the prison house.
8I *am* the LORD: that *is* my name: and
my glory will I not give to another, neither my praise to graven images.
9Behold, the former things are come
to pass, and new things do I declare:
before they spring forth I tell you of
them.
10Sing unto the LORD a new song, *and*
his praise from the end of the earth, ye
that go down to the sea, and all that is
therein; the isles, and the inhabitants
thereof.
11Let the wilderness and the cities
thereof lift up *their voice,* the villages
that Kedar doth inhabit: let the inhabitants of the *rock sing, let them shout
from the top of the mountains.
12Let them give glory unto the LORD,
and declare his praise in the islands.
¶13The LORD shall go forth as a
mighty man, he shall stir up jealousy
like a man of war: he shall cry, yea, roar;
he shall prevail against his enemies.
14I have long time holden my peace;
I have been still, *and* refrained myself:
now will I cry like a travailing woman;
I will destroy and devour at once.
15I will make waste mountains and
hills, and dry up all their herbs; and I
will make the rivers islands, and I will
dry up the pools.
16And I will bring the blind by a way
that they knew not; I will lead them in
paths *that* they have not known: I will
make darkness light before them, and
crooked things straight. These things
will I do unto them, and not forsake
them.

42:1 I have put my spirit upon him. Notice the three persons of the Trinity here: I (God) have put my Spirit (the Holy Spirit) upon Him (the Lord Jesus Christ).
42:6 a light of the Gentiles. See verse 1 note, "Christ as Servant."
42:9 the former things are come to pass. Isaiah had prophesied that Sennacherib would invade Judaea. This had come to pass just as he had said (10:1-34; 37:1-38).
42:11 Kedar. Kedar was Ishmael's second son (Gen. 25:13). His descendants lived on the northwest side of Arabia and stand for the Arabians in general.

¶17 They shall be turned back, they shall be greatly ashamed, that *trust in graven images, that say to the molten images, Ye *are* our gods.

18 Hear, ye deaf; and look, ye blind, that ye may see.

¶19 Who *is* blind, but my servant? or deaf, as my messenger *that* I sent? who *is* blind as *he that is* perfect, and blind as the LORD'S servant?

20 Seeing many things, but thou observest not; opening the ears, but he heareth not.

21 The LORD is well pleased for his righteousness' sake; he will magnify the law, and make *it* honourable.

22 But this *is* a people robbed and spoiled; *they are* all of them snared in holes, and they are hid in prison houses: they are for a prey, and none delivereth; for a spoil, and none saith, Restore.

23 Who among you will give ear to this? *who* will hearken and hear for the time to come?

¶24 Who gave Jacob for a spoil, and Israel to the robbers? did not the LORD, he against whom we have sinned? for they would not walk in his ways, neither were they obedient unto his law.

25 Therefore he hath poured upon him the fury of his anger, and the strength of battle: and it hath set him on *fire round about, yet he knew not; and it burned him, yet he laid *it* not to heart.

Christ, the Saviour and King of Israel

43 But now thus saith the LORD that created thee, O Jacob, and he that formed thee, O *Israel, Fear not: for I have *redeemed thee, I have called *thee* by thy name; thou *art* mine.

2 When thou passest through the waters, I *will be* with thee; and through the rivers, they shall not overflow thee: when thou walkest through the fire, thou shalt not be burned; neither shall the flame kindle upon thee.

3 For I *am* the LORD thy God, the Holy One of Israel, thy Saviour: I gave *Egypt *for* thy *ransom, Ethiopia and Seba for thee.

4 Since thou wast precious in my sight, thou hast been honourable, and I have loved thee: therefore will I give men for thee, and people for thy life.

5 Fear not: for I *am* with thee: I will bring thy seed from the east, and gather thee from the west;

6 I will say to the north, Give up; and to the south, Keep not back: bring my sons from far, and my daughters from the ends of the earth;

7 *Even* every one that is called by my name: for I have created him for my glory, I have formed him; yea, I have made him.

¶8 Bring forth the blind people that have eyes, and the deaf that have ears.

9 Let all the nations be gathered together, and let the people be assembled: who among them can declare this, and shew us former things? let them bring forth their witnesses, that they may be justified: or let them hear, and say, *It is* truth.

10 Ye *are* my witnesses, saith the LORD, and my servant whom I have chosen: that ye may know and believe me, and understand that I *am* he: before me there was no God formed, neither shall there be after me.

11 I, *even* I, *am* the LORD; and beside me *there is* no saviour.

12 I have declared, and have saved, and I have shewed, when *there was* no strange *god* among you: therefore ye *are* my witnesses, saith the LORD, that I *am* God.

13 Yea, before the day *was* I *am* he; and *there is* none that can deliver out of my

---

43:2 when thou walkest through the fire. Note the LORD's protection of Shadrach, Meshach, and Abednego (Dan. 3:19-27).

43:3 Egypt . . . Ethiopia and Seba. God gave these countries to Cyrus as a ransom or reward for his allowing the Hebrew captives to go free.

hand: I will work, and who shall let it?
¶14Thus saith the LORD, your redeemer, the Holy One of Israel; For
your sake I have sent to Babylon, and
have brought down all their nobles, and
the Chaldeans, whose cry *is* in the
ships.
15I *am* the LORD, your Holy One, the
creator of Israel, your King.
16Thus saith the LORD, which maketh
a way in the sea, and a path in the
mighty waters;
17Which bringeth forth the chariot
and horse, the army and the power;
they shall lie down together, they shall
not rise: they are extinct, they are
quenched as tow.
¶18Remember ye not the former
things, neither consider the things of
old.
19Behold, I will do a new thing; now
it shall spring forth; shall ye not know
it? I will even make a way in the wilderness, *and* rivers in the desert.
20The beast of the field shall honour
me, the dragons and the owls: because
I give waters in the wilderness, *and* rivers in the desert, to give drink to my
people, my chosen.
21This people have I formed for myself; they shall shew forth my praise.
¶22But thou hast not called upon me,
O Jacob; but thou hast been weary of
me, O Israel.
23Thou hast not brought me the small
cattle of thy burnt-offerings; neither
hast thou honoured me with thy sacrifices. I have not caused thee to serve

43:21 God's Purposes
God created the Hebrew people for Himself. His purpose as revealed in the Scriptures was at least threefold:
1. to give the world the Messiah (Rom. 9:5);
2. to give the world the Scriptures (Rom. 3:2);
3. to give the world a testimony to God Himself (Isa. 44:8).

with an offering, nor wearied thee with
*incense.
24Thou hast bought me no sweet
cane with money, neither hast thou
filled me with the fat of thy sacrifices:
but thou hast made me to serve with
thy sins, thou hast wearied me with
thine iniquities.
25I, *even* I, *am* he that blotteth out thy
transgressions for mine own sake, and
will not remember thy sins.
26Put me in remembrance: let us
plead together: declare thou, that thou
mayest be justified.
27Thy first father hath sinned, and thy
teachers have transgressed against me.
28Therefore I have profaned the
princes of the *sanctuary, and have
given Jacob to the curse, and Israel to
reproaches.

Idolatry a poor substitute for the living God

44 Yet now hear, O Jacob my servant; and Israel, whom I have
chosen:
2Thus saith the LORD that made thee,
and formed thee from the womb, *which*

43:13 let. Hinder or prevent.
43:15 I am the LORD. The deity of the Saviour and Messiah is clearly taught by these verses (see also vs. 11). Jehovah, or the LORD, Himself is the King and the Saviour,
43:18 the former things. The destruction of Sennacherib's hosts (1 Kings 19).
43:18 the things of old. The destruction of Pharaoh and the Egyptians (Exod.14).
43:23 small cattle. One's personal possession of livestock.
43:24 sweet cane. This was calamus, which was used in making the precious ointment for the temple worship.
43:27 Thy first father. Jacob.
43:27 thy teachers. The priests.
44:1 Jacob my servant. Throughout this part of Isaiah, the nation Israel and the person of the Messiah are both called the servant. As one reads the text and context, he sees that at times the Messiah is spoken of (42:1), and at other times, the nation, as in this verse. See also 41:8 note, "The Good Servant."

will help thee; Fear not, O Jacob, my
servant; and thou, Jesurun, whom I
have chosen.
3For I will pour water upon him that
is thirsty, and floods upon the dry
ground: I will pour my spirit upon thy
seed, and my blessing upon thine offspring:
4And they shall spring up *as* among
the grass, as willows by the water
courses.
5One shall say, I *am* the LORD'S; and
another shall call *himself* by the name
of Jacob; and another shall subscribe
with his hand unto the LORD, and surname *himself* by the name of Israel.
6Thus saith the LORD the King of Israel, and his *redeemer the LORD of
hosts; I *am* the first, and I *am* the last;
and beside me *there is* no God.
7And who, as I, shall call, and shall
declare it, and set it in order for me,
since I appointed the ancient people?
and the things that are coming, and
shall come, let them shew unto them.
8Fear ye not, neither be afraid: have
not I told thee from that time, and have
declared *it?* ye *are* even my witnesses.
Is there a God beside me? yea, *there is*
no God; I know not *any.*
¶9They that make a *graven image
are all of them vanity; and their delec-
table things shall not profit; and they *are*
their own witnesses; they see not, nor
know; that they may be ashamed.
10Who hath formed a god, or molten
a graven image *that* is profitable for
nothing?
11Behold, all his fellows shall be
ashamed: and the workmen, they *are* of
men: let them all be gathered together,
let them stand up; *yet* they shall fear,
and they shall be ashamed together.
12The smith with the tongs both
worketh in the coals, and fashioneth it
with hammers, and worketh it with the
strength of his arms: yea, he is hungry,
and his strength faileth: he drinketh no
water, and is faint.
13The carpenter stretcheth out *his*
rule; he marketh it out with a line; he
fitteth it with planes, and he marketh it
out with the compass, and maketh it
after the figure of a man, according to
the beauty of a man; that it may remain
in the house.
14He heweth him down cedars, and
taketh the cypress and the oak, which
he strengtheneth for himself among the
trees of the forest: he planteth an ash,
and the rain doth nourish *it.*
15Then shall it be for a man to burn:
for he will take thereof, and warm himself; yea, he kindleth *it,* and baketh
bread; yea, he maketh a god, and
worshippeth *it;* he maketh it a graven
image, and falleth down thereto.
16He burneth part thereof in the fire;
with part thereof he eateth flesh; he
roasteth roast, and is satisfied: yea, he
warmeth *himself,* and saith, Aha, I am
warm, I have seen the fire:
17And the residue thereof he maketh
a god, *even* his graven image: he falleth
down unto it, and worshippeth *it,* and
prayeth unto it, and saith, Deliver me;
for thou *art* my god.
18They have not known nor understood: for he hath shut their eyes, that
they cannot see; *and* their hearts, that
they cannot understand.
19And none considereth in his heart,
neither *is there* knowledge nor understanding to say, I have burned part of it
in the fire; yea, also I have baked bread
upon the coals thereof; I have roasted
flesh, and eaten *it:* and shall I make the
residue thereof an abomination? shall I
fall down to the stock of a tree?
20He feedeth on ashes: a deceived

44:2 Jesurun. This name means *upright.* It stands for the nation of Israel and is a title of affection. See Deuteronomy 32:15; 33:5,26.
44:6 I am the first . . . last. The Lord Jesus Christ said this of Himself. It occurs three times in Isaiah and three times in Revelation: Isaiah 41:4; 44:6; 48:12; Revelation 1:8,17; 22:13.
44:19 abomination. An idol.

heart hath turned him aside, that he
cannot deliver his soul, nor say, *Is there*
not a lie in my right hand?
¶21Remember these, O Jacob and Israel; for thou *art* my servant: I have
formed thee; thou *art* my servant: O Israel, thou shalt not be forgotten of me.
22I have blotted out, as a thick cloud,
thy transgressions, and, as a cloud, thy
sins: return unto me; for I have redeemed thee.
23Sing, O ye heavens; for the LORD
hath done *it:* shout, ye lower parts of
the earth: break forth into singing, ye
mountains, O forest, and every tree
therein: for the LORD hath redeemed
Jacob, and glorified himself in Israel.
¶24Thus saith the LORD, thy redeemer, and he that formed thee from the
womb, I *am* the LORD that maketh all
things; that stretcheth forth the heavens alone; that spreadeth abroad the
earth by myself;
25That frustrateth the tokens of the
liars, and maketh diviners mad; that
turneth wise *men* backward, and
maketh their knowledge foolish;
26That confirmeth the word of his
servant, and performeth the counsel of
his messengers; that saith to *Jerusalem, Thou shalt be inhabited; and to the
cities of *Judah, Ye shall be built, and I
will raise up the decayed places thereof:
27That saith to the deep, Be dry, and
I will dry up thy rivers:
28That saith of *Cyrus, *He is* my
shepherd, and shall perform all my
pleasure: even saying to Jerusalem,
Thou shalt be built; and to the temple,
Thy foundation shall be laid.

The living God is the Saviour,
the Hope of His people

45 Thus saith the LORD to his
anointed, to Cyrus, whose right
hand I have holden, to subdue nations
before him; and I will loose the loins of
kings, to open before him the two
leaved gates; and the gates shall not be
shut;
2I will go before thee, and make the
crooked places straight: I will break in
pieces the gates of brass, and cut in
sunder the bars of iron:
3And I will give thee the treasures of
darkness, and hidden riches of secret
places, that thou mayest know that I,
the LORD, which call *thee* by thy name,
am the God of Israel.
4For Jacob my servant's sake, and
Israel mine *elect, I have even called
thee by thy name: I have surnamed
thee, though thou hast not known me.
¶5I *am* the LORD, and *there is* none
else, *there is* no God beside me: I girded

44:28 A Great Prediction
This verse is a central point of attack upon the historical trustworthiness of the claim that Isaiah wrote the entire book of Isaiah. In order to have written this chapter, it is necessary that Isaiah should have foretold the deliverance of the children of Israel from the Babylonian captivity, even predicting the name of the king, more than a hundred years before Cyrus was born. Such predictions are not believed possible by those who deny the supernatural element of Scripture. To the believing heart, however, it is perfectly possible for the Holy Spirit to foretell by name the person and ministry of any man. In fact, fulfillment of the many predictions of the Bible is one of the proofs that the Bible was truly given by the *inspiration of God.

45:1 anointed. Cyrus is the only Gentile to be called by the name "anointed." He is a Gentile *type of Christ; he is also called "my shepherd" (44:28). He fought for Israel and restored Jerusalem while he gave God the glory for his victories.

45:1 loose the loins. Make feeble.

45:1 the two leaved gates. The river Euphrates, which passed through Babylon, was walled on each side. Brass gates in these walls were the entrance to the city. On the night that Belshazaar was killed (Dan. 5:30), those gates had carelessly been left open. The Medes (Isa. 44:27) turned the course of the river and, marching along the dried riverbed, entered the city and finally conquered it.

45:4 Eight Names Known before Birth The person being addressed here was a conqueror whose first name was Agradates, but he has always been known by the name Cyrus, as foretold. Eight names were given by God before the births of those who were to bear them: Ishmael (Gen. 16:11); Isaac (Gen. 17:19); Solomon (1 Chron. 22:9); Josiah (1 Kings 13:2; see also its note, "A Promised Child"); Cyrus (Isa. 44:28); Immanuel (Isa. 7:14; see also its note, "Immanuel"); John the Baptist (Luke 1:13); Jesus (Matt. 1:21).

thee, though thou hast not known me:
6That they may know from the rising
of the sun, and from the west, that *there
is* none beside me. I *am* the LORD, and
there is none else.
7I form the light, and create darkness: I make *peace, and create evil: I
the LORD do all these *things*.
8Drop down, ye heavens, from above,
and let the skies pour down righteousness: let the earth open, and let them
bring forth *salvation, and let righteousness spring up together; I the
LORD have created it.
9Woe unto him that striveth with his
Maker! *Let* the potsherd *strive* with the
potsherds of the earth. Shall the clay
say to him that fashioneth it, What
makest thou? or thy work, He hath no
hands?
10Woe unto him that saith unto *his*
father, What begettest thou? or to the
woman, What hast thou brought forth?
¶11Thus saith the LORD, the Holy
One of Israel, and his Maker, Ask me of
things to come concerning my sons,
and concerning the work of my hands
command ye me.
12I have made the earth, and created
man upon it: I, *even* my hands, have
stretched out the heavens, and all their
host have I commanded.
13I have raised him up in righteousness, and I will direct all his ways: he
shall build my city, and he shall let go
my captives, not for price nor reward,
saith the LORD of hosts.
14Thus saith the LORD, The labour of
Egypt, and merchandise of Ethiopia and
of the Sabeans, men of stature, shall
come over unto thee, and they shall be
thine: they shall come after thee; in
chains they shall come over, and they
shall fall down unto thee, they shall
make supplication unto thee, *saying,*
Surely God *is* in thee; and *there is* none
else, *there is* no God.
¶15Verily thou *art* a God that hidest
thyself, O God of Israel, the Saviour.
16They shall be ashamed, and also
confounded, all of them: they shall go
to confusion together *that are* makers
of idols.
17*But* Israel shall be saved in the
LORD with an everlasting salvation: ye
shall not be ashamed nor confounded
*world without end.
18For thus saith the LORD that created the heavens; God himself that
formed the earth and made it; he hath
established it, he created it not in vain,
he formed it to be inhabited: I *am* the
LORD; and *there is* none else.
19I have not spoken in secret, in a
dark place of the earth: I said not unto
the seed of Jacob, Seek ye me in vain: I
the LORD speak righteousness, I declare things that are right.
¶20Assemble yourselves and come;
draw near together, ye *that are* escaped
of the nations: they have no knowledge
that set up the wood of their graven
image, and pray unto a god *that* cannot
save.

45:17 everlasting salvation. The promises of salvation and the possession of the land of Canaan as given to Abraham and his seed are eternal promises. The millennial reign of Christ on earth will be but a partial fulfillment of these promises. The blessings begun in the *Millennium will be continued forever.

45:18 in vain. To be empty.

45:19 I have not spoken in secret, in a dark place of the earth. It was in dark caves that heathen oracles were spoken.

21 Tell ye, and bring *them* near; yea, let them take counsel together: who hath declared this from ancient time? *who* hath told it from that time? *have* not I the LORD? and *there is* no God else beside me; a *just God and a Saviour; *there is* none beside me.

22 Look unto me, and be ye saved, all the ends of the earth: for I *am* God, and *there is* none else.

23 I have sworn by myself, the word is gone out of my mouth *in* righteousness, and shall not return, That unto me every knee shall bow, every tongue shall swear.

45:23 Universal Recognition of Christ
That "every knee shall bow" is quoted by Paul in Philippians 2:10. Although men may reject the Lord Jesus Christ to their own eternal loss, the time will come when they must confess that He is Lord to the glory of God the Father. This confession does not secure pardon for them, but it does secure universal recognition for Christ.

24 Surely, shall *one* say, in the LORD have I righteousness and strength: *even* to him shall *men* come; and all that are incensed against him shall be ashamed.

25 In the LORD shall all the seed of Israel be justified, and shall glory.

God is contrasted to idols

46 Bel boweth down, Nebo stoopeth, their idols were upon the beasts, and upon the cattle: your carriages *were* heavy loaden; *they are* a burden to the weary *beast*.

2 They stoop, they bow down together; they could not deliver the burden, but themselves are gone into captivity.

¶3 Hearken unto me, O house of *Jacob, and all the *remnant of the house of Israel, which are borne *by me* from the belly, which are carried from the womb:

4 And *even* to *your* old age I *am* he; and *even* to hoar hairs will I carry *you*: I have made, and I will bear; even I will carry, and will deliver *you*.

¶5 To whom will ye liken me, and make *me* equal, and compare me, that we may be like?

6 They lavish gold out of the bag, and weigh silver in the balance, *and* hire a goldsmith; and he maketh it a god: they fall down, yea, they worship.

7 They bear him upon the shoulder, they carry him, and set him in his place, and he standeth; from his place shall he not remove: yea, *one* shall cry unto him, yet can he not answer, nor save him out of his trouble.

8 Remember this, and shew yourselves men: bring *it* again to mind, O ye transgressors.

9 Remember the former things of old: for I *am* God, and *there is* none else; *I am* God, and *there is* none like me,

10 Declaring the end from the beginning, and from ancient times *the things* that are not *yet* done, saying, My counsel shall stand, and I will do all my pleasure:

46:10 Prewritten History
Prophecy is simply prewritten history. God, who is all wise, knows the future as well as the past. He has revealed much of that future through the prophetic portions of the Bible. Some prophecies have been fulfilled, while others await fulfillment, but all of them must eventually be brought to pass. Among the unfulfilled predictions of Scripture is the establishment of Israel in Zion as God's people (46:13).

46:1 Bel. This is a short form of *Baal. It stands for Merodach or Marduk, the chief of the Babylonian gods.
46:1 Nebo. The Babylonian god of literature and science. Here with Bel, he stands for Babylon itself. Nebuchadnezzar's name contained the god's name (Nebu).
46:1 they are a burden. When a nation was conquered, their gods were loaded on beasts of burden and carried into the country of the victor.
46:7 him. The "god" of verse 6.

11Calling a ravenous bird from the
east, the man that executeth my counsel from a far country: yea, I have spoken *it,* I will also bring it to pass; I have
purposed *it,* I will also do it.
¶12Hearken unto me, ye stouthearted, that *are* far from righteousness:
13I bring near my righteousness; it
shall not be far off, and my salvation
shall not tarry: and I will place salvation
in *Zion for Israel my glory.

Babylon judged because of her sin

47 Come down, and sit in the dust,
O virgin daughter of *Babylon,
sit on the ground: *there is* no throne,
O daughter of the Chaldeans: for thou
shalt no more be called tender and delicate.
2Take the millstones, and grind meal:
uncover thy locks, make bare the leg,
uncover the thigh, pass over the rivers.
3Thy nakedness shall be uncovered,
yea, thy shame shall be seen: I will take
vengeance, and I will not meet *thee as*
a man.
4*As for* our redeemer, the LORD of
hosts *is* his name, the Holy One of Israel.
5Sit thou silent, and get thee into
darkness, O daughter of the Chaldeans:
for thou shalt no more be called, The
lady of kingdoms.
¶6I was wroth with my people, I have
polluted mine inheritance, and given
them into thine hand: thou didst shew
them no *mercy; upon the ancient hast
thou very heavily laid thy yoke.
¶7And thou saidst, I shall be a lady for
ever: *so* that thou didst not lay these
things to thy heart, neither didst remember the latter end of it.
8Therefore hear now this, *thou that*
art given to pleasures, that dwellest
carelessly, that sayest in thine heart, I
am, and none else beside me; I shall not
sit *as* a widow, neither shall I know the
loss of children:
9But these two *things* shall come to
thee in a moment in one day, the loss
of children, and widowhood: they shall
come upon thee in their perfection for
the multitude of thy sorceries, *and* for
the great abundance of thine enchantments.
¶10For thou hast trusted in thy wickedness: thou hast said, None seeth me.
Thy wisdom and thy knowledge, it hath
perverted thee; and thou hast said
in thine heart, I *am,* and none else beside me.
¶11Therefore shall evil come upon
thee; thou shalt not know from whence
it riseth: and mischief shall fall upon
thee; thou shalt not be able to put if off:
and desolation shall come upon thee
suddenly, *which* thou shalt not know.
12Stand now with thine enchantments, and with the multitude of thy
sorceries, wherein thou hast laboured
from thy youth; if so be thou shalt be
able to profit, if so be thou mayest prevail.
13Thou art wearied in the multitude
of thy counsels. Let now the astrologers, the stargazers, the monthly prognosticators, stand up, and save thee
from *these things* that shall come upon
thee.
14Behold, they shall be as stubble;
the fire shall burn them; they shall not
deliver themselves from the power of
the flame: *there shall* not *be* a coal to
warm at, *nor* fire to sit before it.
15Thus shall they be unto thee with
whom thou hast laboured, *even* thy
merchants, from thy youth: they shall
wander every one to his quarter; none
shall save thee.

46:11 Calling a ravenous bird. This refers to Cyrus of Persia, whose standard was a golden eagle.

47:4 redeemer. The highest names of the Deity are ascribed to the Redeemer by the Bible. He is the LORD of Hosts who became our Redeemer. He became our Kinsman. He "was made flesh, and dwelt among us" (John 1:14). Then He paid our debt (1 Cor. 13:3-4) and delivers all who believe in Him from the bondage of sin (Rom. 3:25).

47:14 themselves. Their souls.

God will bring Israel through her sufferings into her kingdom

48 Hear ye this, O house of Jacob, which are called by the name of Israel, and are come forth out of the waters of Judah, which swear by the name of the LORD, and make mention of the *God of Israel, *but* not in truth, nor in *righteousness.

2 For they call themselves of the holy city, and stay themselves upon the God of Israel; The LORD of hosts *is* his name.

3 I have declared the former things from the beginning; and they went forth out of my mouth, and I shewed them; I did *them* suddenly, and they came to pass.

4 Because I knew that thou *art* obstinate, and thy neck *is* an iron sinew, and thy brow brass;

5 I have even from the beginning declared *it* to thee; before it came to pass I shewed *it* thee: lest thou shouldest say, Mine idol hath done them, and my *graven image, and my molten image, hath commanded them.

6 Thou hast heard, see all this; and will not ye declare *it?* I have shewed thee new things from this time, even hidden things, and thou didst not know them.

7 They are *created now, and not from the beginning; even before the day when thou heardest them not; lest thou shouldest say, Behold, I knew them.

8 Yea, thou heardest not; yea, thou knewest not; yea, from that time *that* thine ear was not opened: for I knew that thou wouldest deal very treacherously, and wast called a transgressor from the womb.

9 For my name's sake will I defer mine anger, and for my praise will I refrain for thee, that I cut thee not off.

10 Behold, I have refined thee, but not with silver; I have chosen thee in the furnace of affliction.

11 For mine own sake, *even* for mine own sake, will I do *it:* for how should *my name* be polluted? and I will not give my glory unto another.

¶ 12 Hearken unto me, O Jacob and Israel, my called; I *am* he; I *am* the first, I also *am* the last.

13 Mine hand also hath laid the foundation of the earth, and my right hand hath spanned the heavens: *when* I call unto them, they stand up together.

14 All ye, assemble yourselves, and hear; which among them hath declared these *things?* The LORD hath loved him: he will do his pleasure on Babylon, and his arm *shall be on* the Chaldeans.

15 I, *even* I, have spoken; yea, I have called him: I have brought him, and he shall make his way prosperous.

¶ 16 Come ye near unto me, hear ye this; I have not spoken in secret from the beginning; from the time that it was, there *am* I: and now the Lord GOD, and his Spirit, hath sent me.

17 Thus saith the LORD, thy Redeemer, the Holy One of Israel; I *am* the LORD thy God which teacheth thee to profit, which leadeth thee by the way *that* thou shouldest go.

18 O that thou hadst hearkened to my commandments! then had thy peace been as a river, and thy righteousness as the waves of the sea:

19 Thy seed also had been as the sand, and the offspring of thy *bowels like the gravel thereof; his name should not have been cut off nor destroyed from before me.

¶ 20 Go ye forth of Babylon, flee ye from the Chaldeans, with a voice of singing declare ye, tell this, utter it *even* to the end of the earth; say ye, The LORD hath redeemed his servant Jacob.

21 And they thirsted not *when* he led them through the deserts: he caused the waters to flow out of the rock for

---

48:6 new things. God graciously reveals new and hidden things to the prophets. This is equally true of both Testaments (compare Isa. 48:6 with John 16:13).

48:13 spanned. Stretched out.

them: he clave the rock also, and the
waters gushed out.
[22]*There is* no peace, saith the LORD,
unto the wicked.

Though rejected at His first coming,
Christ will restore Israel at His return

49 Listen, O *isles, unto me; and
hearken, ye people, from far;
The LORD hath called me from the
womb; from the bowels of my mother
hath he made mention of my name.
[2]And he hath made my mouth like a
sharp sword; in the shadow of his hand
hath he hid me, and made me a polished
shaft; in his quiver hath he hid me;
[3]And said unto me, Thou *art* my servant, O *Israel, in whom I will be glorified.
[4]Then I said, I have laboured in vain,
I have spent my strength for nought,
and in vain: *yet* surely my *judgment
is with the LORD, and my work with
my God.
¶[5]And now, saith the LORD that
formed me from the womb *to be* his
servant, to bring Jacob again to him,
Though Israel be not gathered, yet shall
I be glorious in the eyes of the LORD,
and my God shall be my strength.

49:5 A Wonderful Prophecy
This wonderful prophecy anticipated the fact that the first coming of the Messiah would not result in the conversion of Israel. In addition to this, Isaiah declared that although Israel would not be converted, the first coming of Christ would be concluded with His exaltation in the eyes of the LORD God.

[6]And he said, It is a light thing that
thou shouldest be my servant to raise
up the tribes of Jacob, and to restore the
preserved of Israel: I will also give thee
for a light to the *Gentiles, that thou
mayest be my salvation unto the end of
the earth.
[7]Thus saith the LORD, the Redeemer of Israel, *and* his *Holy One, to him
whom man despiseth, to him whom the
nation abhorreth, to a servant of rulers,
Kings shall see and arise, princes also
shall worship, because of the LORD that
is faithful, *and* the Holy One of Israel,
and he shall choose thee.
[8]Thus saith the LORD, In an acceptable time have I heard thee, and in a day
of salvation have I helped thee: and I
will preserve thee, and give thee for a
*covenant of the people, to establish
the earth, to cause to inherit the desolate heritages;
[9]That thou mayest say to the prisoners, Go forth; to them that *are* in darkness, Shew yourselves. They shall feed
in the ways, and their pastures *shall be*
in all high places.
[10]They shall not hunger nor thirst;
neither shall the heat nor sun smite
them: for he that hath mercy on them
shall lead them, even by the springs of
water shall he guide them.
[11]And I will make all my mountains
a way, and my highways shall be exalted.
[12]Behold, these shall come from far:
and, lo, these from the north and from
the west; and these from the land of
Sinim.
¶[13]Sing, O heavens; and be joyful,
O earth; and break forth into singing,
O mountains: for the LORD hath comforted his people, and will have mercy
upon his afflicted.
[14]But Zion said, The LORD hath forsaken me, and my Lord hath forgotten me.
[15]Can a woman forget her sucking
child, that she should not have compassion on the son of her womb? yea,

49:1 Listen, O isles. In verses 1-6, the Lord Jesus Christ, the Messiah, is speaking.
49:2 a polished shaft. An arrow.
49:7 Thus saith the LORD. Jehovah speaks in verses 7-12.
49:8 the people. The Hebrew nation.
49:9 in darkness. The Gentile nations.
49:12 Sinim. It is possible that this speaks of the invading forces.

they may forget, yet will I not forget
thee.
16Behold, I have graven thee upon
the palms of *my* hands; thy walls *are*
continually before me.
17Thy children shall make haste; thy
destroyers and they that made thee
waste shall go forth of thee.
¶18Lift up thine eyes round about,
and behold: all these gather themselves
together, *and* come to thee. *As* I live,
saith the LORD, thou shalt surely clothe
thee with them all, as with an ornament,
and bind them *on thee,* as a bride *doeth.*
19For thy waste and thy desolate
places, and the land of thy destruction,
shall even now be too narrow by reason
of the inhabitants, and they that swallowed thee up shall be far away.
20The children which thou shalt have,
after thou hast lost the other, shall say
again in thine ears, The place *is* too
strait for me: give place to me that I
may dwell.
21Then shalt thou say in thine heart,
Who hath begotten me these, seeing I
have lost my children, and am desolate,
a captive, and removing to and fro? and
who hath brought up these? Behold, I
was left alone; these, where *had* they
been?
22Thus saith the Lord GOD, Behold,
I will lift up mine hand to the Gentiles,
and set up my standard to the people:
and they shall bring thy sons in *their*
arms, and thy daughters shall be carried
upon *their* shoulders.
23And kings shall be thy nursing fathers, and their queens thy nursing
mothers: they shall bow down to thee
with *their* face toward the earth, and lick
up the dust of thy feet; and thou shalt
know that I *am* the LORD: for they shall
not be ashamed that wait for me.
¶24Shall the prey be taken from the
mighty, or the lawful captive delivered?
25But thus saith the LORD, Even the
captives of the mighty shall be taken
away, and the prey of the terrible shall
be delivered: for I will contend with him
that contendeth with thee, and I will
save thy children.
26And I will feed them that oppress
thee with their own flesh; and they shall
be drunken with their own blood, as
with sweet wine: and all flesh shall
know that I the LORD *am* thy Saviour
and thy Redeemer, the mighty One of
Jacob.

The humiliation of Christ, fulfilled at His first coming

50 Thus saith the LORD, Where *is*
the bill of your mother's divorcement, whom I have put away? or
which of my creditors *is it* to whom I
have sold you? Behold, for your iniquities
have ye sold yourselves, and for your
transgressions is your mother put away.
2Wherefore, when I came, *was there*
no man? when I called, *was there* none
to answer? Is my hand shortened at all,
that it cannot *redeem? or have I no
power to deliver? behold, at my rebuke
I dry up the sea, I make the rivers a
wilderness: their fish stinketh, because
there is no water, and dieth for thirst.
3I clothe the heavens with blackness,
and I make sackcloth their covering.
¶4The Lord GOD hath given me the
tongue of the learned, that I should
know how to speak a word in season to
him that is weary: he wakeneth morning by morning, he wakeneth mine ear
to hear as the learned.
5The Lord GOD hath opened mine
ear, and I was not rebellious, neither
turned away back.
6I gave my back to the smiters, and
my cheeks to them that plucked off the
hair: I hid not my face from shame and
spitting.

50:1 your mother's divorcement. Israel had been a faithless wife to her heavenly husband. He came (vs. 2) to win her back to Him, but she, with the Gentiles, put Him to death (vs. 6). Nevertheless, there was no bill of divorcement; God did not turn His own away: Israel herself turned away from Him.

50:6 Willing to Suffer
Our Lord suffered all of the indignities enumerated by this verse (Matt. 26:67; 27:26; John 18:22). We cannot fully understand the sufferings of Christ if we fail to see that they were willingly assumed. He gave His back to the smiters. Even His death was a voluntary offering up of Himself. He said, "No man taketh it [my life] from me, but I lay it down of myself" (John 10:18).

7For the Lord GOD will help me;
therefore shall I not be confounded:
therefore have I set my face like a flint,
and I know that I shall not be ashamed.
8*He is* near that justifieth me; who
will contend with me? let us stand together: who *is* mine adversary? let him
come near to me.
9Behold, the Lord GOD will help me;
who *is* he *that* shall condemn me? lo,
they all shall wax old as a garment; the
moth shall eat them up.
¶10Who *is* among you that *feareth
the LORD, that obeyeth the voice of his
servant, that walketh *in* darkness, and
hath no light? let him *trust in the name
of the LORD, and stay upon his God.
11Behold, all ye that kindle a fire, that
compass *yourselves* about with sparks:
walk in the light of your fire, and in the
sparks *that* ye have kindled. This shall
ye have of mine hand; ye shall lie down
in sorrow.

Israel will be delivered from her enemies

51 Hearken to me, ye that follow
after righteousness, ye that
seek the LORD: look unto the rock
whence ye are hewn, and to the hole of
the pit *whence* ye are digged.
2Look unto *Abraham your father,
and unto Sarah *that* bare you: for I called
him alone, and blessed him, and increased him.
3For the LORD shall comfort Zion: he
will comfort all her waste places; and he
will make her wilderness like *Eden,
and her desert like the garden of the
LORD; joy and gladness shall be found
therein, thanksgiving, and the voice of
melody.
¶4Hearken unto me, my people; and
give ear unto me, O my nation: for a
*law shall proceed from me, and I will
make my judgment to rest for a light of
the people.
5My righteousness *is* near; my *salvation is gone forth, and mine arms
shall judge the people; the isles shall
wait upon me, and on mine arm shall
they trust.
6Lift up your eyes to the heavens, and
look upon the earth beneath: for the
heavens shall vanish away like smoke,
and the earth shall wax old like a garment, and they that dwell therein shall
die in like manner: but my salvation
shall be for ever, and my righteousness
shall not be abolished.
¶7Hearken unto me, ye that know
righteousness, the people in whose
heart *is* my law; fear ye not the reproach of men, neither be ye afraid of
their revilings.
8For the moth shall eat them up like
a garment, and the worm shall eat them
like wool: but my righteousness shall
be for ever, and my salvation from generation to generation.
¶9Awake, awake, put on strength,
O arm of the LORD; awake, as in the
ancient days, in the generations of old.
Art thou not it that hath cut *Rahab, *and*
wounded the dragon?
10*Art* thou not it which hath dried the
sea, the waters of the great deep; that
hath made the depths of the sea a way
for the *ransomed to pass over?
11Therefore the *redeemed of the

50:9 they. The enemies of the Lord Jesus Christ.
51:2 Look unto Abraham. Compare the state of Israel (vs. 1) with Abraham (Deut. 26:5), for God chose them.
51:2 I called him alone. When Abraham was but one, I (God) called him.
51:9 Rahab. Egypt. The dragon is Satan, and the sea (vs. 10) is the Red Sea (see Exod. 14).

LORD shall return, and come with singing unto Zion; and everlasting joy *shall*
be upon their head: they shall obtain
gladness and joy; *and* sorrow and
*mourning shall flee away.
12I, *even* I, *am* he that comforteth you:
who *art* thou, that thou shouldest be
afraid of a man *that* shall die, and of the
son of man *which* shall be made *as*
grass;
13And forgettest the LORD thy maker,
that hath stretched forth the heavens,
and laid the foundations of the earth;
and hast feared continually every day
because of the fury of the oppressor, as
if he were ready to destroy? and where
is the fury of the oppressor?
14The captive exile hasteneth that he
may be loosed, and that he should not
die in the pit, nor that his bread should
fail.
15But I *am* the LORD thy God, that
divided the sea, whose waves roared:
The LORD of hosts *is* his name.
16And I have put my words in thy
mouth, and I have covered thee in the
shadow of mine hand, that I may plant
the heavens, and lay the foundations of
the earth, and say unto Zion, Thou *art*
my people.
¶17Awake, awake, stand up, O *Jerusalem, which hast drunk at the hand of
the LORD the cup of his fury; thou hast
drunken the dregs of the cup of trembling, *and* wrung *them* out.
18*There is* none to guide her among
all the sons *whom* she hath brought
forth; neither *is there any* that taketh
her by the hand of all the sons *that* she
hath brought up.
19These two *things* are come unto
thee; who shall be sorry for thee? desolation, and destruction, and the famine, and the sword: by whom shall I
comfort thee?
20Thy sons have fainted, they lie at
the head of all the streets, as a wild bull
in a net: they are full of the fury of the
LORD, the rebuke of thy God.
¶21Therefore hear now this, thou afflicted, and drunken, but not with wine:
22Thus saith thy Lord the LORD, and
thy God *that* pleadeth the cause of his
people, Behold, I have taken out of
thine hand the cup of trembling, *even*
the dregs of the cup of my fury; thou
shalt no more drink it again:
23But I will put it into the hand of
them that afflict thee; which have said
to thy soul, Bow down, that we may go
over: and thou hast laid thy body as the
ground, and as the street, to them that
went over.

Israel will become the holy city during Christ's reign

52 Awake, awake; put on thy
strength, O *Zion; put on thy
beautiful *garments, O Jerusalem, the
holy city: for henceforth there shall no
more come into thee the *uncircumcised and the *unclean.
2Shake thyself from the dust; arise,
and sit down, O Jerusalem: loose thyself from the bands of thy neck, O captive daughter of Zion.
3For thus saith the LORD, Ye have
sold yourselves for nought; and ye shall
be redeemed without money.
4For thus saith the Lord GOD, My
people went down aforetime into
*Egypt to sojourn there; and the Assyr-
ian oppressed them without cause.
5Now therefore, what have I here,
saith the LORD, that my people is tak-
en away for nought? they that rule over
them make them to howl, saith the
LORD; and my name continually every
day *is* blasphemed.
6Therefore my people shall know my
name: therefore *they shall know* in that
day that I *am* he that doth speak: behold, *it is* I.
¶7How beautiful upon the mountains

52:4 the Assyrian. The Pharaoh who oppressed the children of Israel (Exod. 1-14) was an Assyrian by race.

52:5 what have I here . . . ? What has happened?

are the feet of him that bringeth good
tidings, that publisheth *peace; that
bringeth good tidings of good, that
publisheth salvation; that saith unto
Zion, Thy God reigneth!
8Thy watchmen shall lift up the
voice; with the voice together shall
they sing: for they shall see eye to eye,
when the LORD shall bring again Zion.
¶9Break forth into joy, sing together,
ye waste places of Jerusalem: for the
LORD hath comforted his people, he
hath redeemed Jerusalem.
10The LORD hath made bare his holy
arm in the eyes of all the nations; and
all the ends of the earth shall see the
salvation of our God.
¶11Depart ye, depart ye, go ye out
from thence, touch no unclean *thing;* go
ye out of the midst of her; be ye clean,
that bear the vessels of the LORD.
12For ye shall not go out with haste,
nor go by flight: for the LORD will go
before you; and the God of Israel *will be*
your rereward.
¶13Behold, my servant shall deal pru-
dently, he shall be exalted and extolled,
and be very high.
14As many were astonied at thee; his
visage was so marred more than any
man, and his form more than the sons
of men:
15So shall he sprinkle many nations;
the kings shall shut their mouths at
him: for *that* which had not been told
them shall they see; and *that* which they
had not heard shall they consider.

The death of Christ as the Substitute for sinners—this is the crowning point of Christ's ministry as the Servant of God

53 Who hath believed our report?
and to whom is the arm of the
LORD revealed?
2For he shall grow up before him as a
tender plant, and as a root out of a dry
ground: he hath no form nor comeliness; and when we shall see him, *there*
is no beauty that we should desire him.
3He is despised and rejected of men;
a man of sorrows, and acquainted with
grief: and we hid as it were *our* faces

53:1-5 CHRIST'S SUFFERING

Selections from this chapter are quoted seven times in the New Testament by six different writers. In each case, the authors of the New Testament apply Isaiah 53 to the Lord Jesus Christ: Matthew 8:17; Mark 15:28; Luke 22:37; John 12:38; Acts 8:32-35; Romans 10:16; 1 Peter 2:22.

The vicariousness (vicarious means *substitutionary*, or that Christ suffered in our place) of the sufferings of Christ is declared at least eight times in this chapter. The gospel message does not only declare that Christ died. That of itself is a simple fact of history. The gospel is that "Christ died for our sins."

The following points outline this most important chapter:

1. The unbelief of Israel (vs. 1; see Rom. 10:16).
2. The humiliation of Christ (vss. 2-3). It seems strange to a Christian to read that there was no form or comeliness in Christ. Faith has opened the eyes of Christians to see the beauty of God in Him.
3. The vicarious ministry of Christ (vs. 4a).
4. The vicarious sufferings of Christ (vss. 4b-6). Christ was made sin for us "that we might be made the righteousness of God in him" (2 Cor. 5:21).
5. The silence of Christ (vss. 7-8).
6. The sufficiency of the sacrifice of Christ to put away sin (vss. 9-12).

52:7 him that bringeth good tidings. The Messiah. Paul quotes this verse in Romans 10:15.

52:12 rereward. Rear guard.

52:13 my servant. These verses (vss. 13-14) present a remarkable contrast. Verse 13 declares the exaltation of Christ. Verse 14 describes the results of the indescribable sufferings that He endured for us.

from him; he was despised, and we esteemed him not.
¶4Surely he hath borne our griefs,
and carried our sorrows: yet we did esteem him stricken, smitten of God, and
afflicted.
5But he *was* wounded for our transgressions, *he was* bruised for our iniquities: the chastisement of our peace
was upon him; and with his *stripes we
are healed.
6All we like sheep have gone astray;
we have turned every one to his own
way; and the LORD hath laid on him the
iniquity of us all.
7He was oppressed, and he was afflicted, yet he opened not his mouth: he
is brought as a lamb to the slaughter,
and as a sheep before her shearers is
dumb, so he openeth not his mouth.
8He was taken from prison and from
judgment: and who shall declare his
generation? for he was cut off out of the
land of the living: for the transgression
of my people was he stricken.
9And he made his grave with the
wicked, and with the rich in his *death;
because he had done no violence, neither *was any* deceit in his mouth.
¶10Yet it pleased the LORD to bruise
him; he hath put *him* to grief: when
thou shalt make his soul an *offering for
*sin, he shall see *his* seed, he shall prolong *his* days, and the pleasure of the
LORD shall prosper in his hand.
11He shall see of the travail of his soul,
and shall be satisfied: by his knowledge
shall my righteous servant justify
many; for he shall bear their iniquities.
12Therefore will I divide him *a portion*
with the great, and he shall divide the
spoil with the strong; because he hath
poured out his soul unto death: and he
was numbered with the transgressors;
and he bare the sin of many, and made
intercession for the transgressors.

IX. Invitation of Israel's Saviour (54:1—58:14)

Assurance that the LORD will restore Israel

54 Sing, O barren, thou *that* didst
not bear; break forth into singing, and cry aloud, thou *that* didst not
travail with child: for more *are* the children of the desolate than the children
of the married wife, saith the LORD.
2Enlarge the place of thy tent, and let
them stretch forth the curtains of thine
habitations: spare not, lengthen thy
cords, and strengthen thy stakes;
3For thou shalt break forth on the
right hand and on the left; and thy seed
shall inherit the Gentiles, and make the
desolate cities to be inhabited.
¶4Fear not; for thou shalt not be
ashamed: neither be thou confounded;
for thou shalt not be put to shame: for
thou shalt forget the shame of thy
youth, and shalt not remember the reproach of thy widowhood any more.
5For thy Maker *is* thine husband; the
LORD of hosts *is* his name; and thy *Redeemer the Holy One of Israel; The
*God of the whole earth shall he be
called.

54:5 The Wife of God
Israel is called the wife of God in several passages (Isa. 54:5; Jer. 31:32; and Hos. 2:1-23). Notice that it is always as an unfaithful wife that she is seen, and therefore God has had to disown her and put her away. This is not a divorce, however, as the world thinks of it today, for the husband will win His faithless wife back to Him and will forgive her for all her evil wanderings (vss. 5-10).

53:5 of our peace. He is our peace (Eph. 2:14).
53:9 with the rich in his death. Read about rich Joseph of Arimathaea in Matthew 27:57-60.
53:11 travail. Labor, pain, or trouble.
53:12 he was numbered with the transgressors. He was crucified between two thieves (Matt. 27:38).
53:12 he bare the sin of many. See 1 Peter 2:24.
53:12 made intercession for the transgressors. Read Luke 23:34.

6 For the LORD hath called thee as a
woman forsaken and grieved in spirit,
and a wife of youth, when thou wast
refused, saith thy God.
7 For a small moment have I forsaken
thee; but with great mercies will I
gather thee.
8 In a little wrath I hid my face from
thee for a moment; but with everlasting kindness will I have *mercy on
thee, saith the LORD thy Redeemer.
9 For this *is as* the waters of Noah
unto me: for *as* I have sworn that the
waters of Noah should no more go over
the earth; so have I sworn that I would
not be wroth with thee, nor rebuke
thee.
10 For the mountains shall depart, and
the hills be removed; but my kindness
shall not depart from thee, neither shall
the covenant of my peace be removed,
saith the LORD that hath mercy on thee.
¶11 O thou afflicted, tossed with tempest, *and* not comforted, behold, I will
lay thy stones with fair colors, and lay
thy foundations with sapphires.
12 And I will make thy windows of
agates, and thy gates of carbuncles, and
all thy borders of pleasant stones.
13 And all thy children *shall be* taught
of the LORD; and great *shall be* the peace
of thy children.
14 In *righteousness shalt thou be
established: thou shalt be far from oppression; for thou shalt not fear: and
from terror; for it shall not come near
thee.
15 Behold, they shall surely gather
together, *but* not by me: whosoever
shall gather together against thee shall
fall for thy sake.
16 Behold, I have *created the smith
that bloweth the coals in the fire, and
that bringeth forth an instrument for his
work; and I have created the waster to
destroy.
¶17 No weapon that is formed against
thee shall prosper; and every tongue
that shall rise against thee in judgment
thou shalt condemn. This *is* the heritage of the servants of the LORD, and
their righteousness *is* of me, saith the
LORD.

The Gospel invitation: salvation fully offered to all who turn to God

55 Ho, every one that thirsteth,
come ye to the waters, and he
that hath no money; come ye, buy, and
eat; yea, come, buy *wine and milk
without money and without price.
2 Wherefore do ye spend money for
that which is not bread? and your labour
for *that which* satisfieth not? hearken
diligently unto me, and eat ye *that which*
is good, and let your soul delight itself
in fatness.
3 Incline your ear, and come unto me:
hear, and your soul shall live; and I will
make an everlasting *covenant with
you, *even* the sure mercies of *David.
4 Behold, I have given him *for* a witness to the people, a leader and commander to the people.
5 Behold, thou shalt call a nation *that*
thou knowest not, and nations *that*
knew not thee shall run unto thee because of the LORD thy God, and for the
Holy One of *Israel; for he hath glorified thee.
¶6 Seek ye the LORD while he may be
found, call ye upon him while he is near:
7 Let the wicked forsake his way, and
the unrighteous man his thoughts: and
let him return unto the LORD, and he
will have mercy upon him; and to our
God, for he will abundantly pardon.
¶8 For my thoughts *are* not your
thoughts, neither *are* your ways my
ways, saith the LORD.
9 For *as* the heavens are higher than
the earth, so are my ways higher than

54:13 And all thy children shall be taught. See John 6:45 where the Lord Jesus Christ quotes this verse.

55:1 money. This speaks of merit—"Come to the LORD although you do not deserve to, and receive His bountiful and satisfying gifts."

55:3 David. The Son of David, the Lord Jesus Christ, is spoken of here (compare vs. 4).

your ways, and my thoughts than your
thoughts.
10For as the rain cometh down, and
the snow from heaven, and returneth
not thither, but watereth the earth, and
maketh it bring forth and bud, that it
may give seed to the sower, and bread
to the eater:
11So shall my word be that goeth
forth out of my mouth: it shall not return unto me void, but it shall accomplish that which I please, and it shall
prosper *in the thing* whereto I sent it.
12For ye shall go out with joy, and be
led forth with peace: the mountains and
the hills shall break forth before you
into singing, and all the trees of the field
shall clap *their* hands.
13Instead of the thorn shall come up
the fir tree, and instead of the brier
shall come up the myrtle tree: and it
shall be to the LORD for a name, for
an everlasting sign *that* shall not be
cut off.

A warning against sin

56 Thus saith the LORD, Keep ye
*judgment, and do justice: for
my salvation *is* near to come, and my
righteousness to be revealed.
2Blessed *is* the man *that* doeth this,
and the son of man *that* layeth hold on
it; that keepeth the *sabbath from polluting it, and keepeth his hand from
doing any evil.
¶3Neither let the son of the stranger,
that hath joined himself to the LORD,
speak, saying, The LORD hath utterly
separated me from his people: neither
let the eunuch say, Behold, I *am* a dry
tree.
4For thus saith the LORD unto the
eunuchs that keep my sabbaths, and
choose *the things* that please me, and
take hold of my covenant;
5Even unto them will I give in mine
house and within my walls a place and
a name better than of sons and of
daughters: I will give them an everlasting name, that shall not be cut off.
6Also the sons of the stranger, that
join themselves to the LORD, to serve
him, and to love the name of the LORD,
to be his servants, every one that
keepeth the sabbath from polluting it,
and taketh hold of my covenant;
7Even them will I bring to my holy
mountain, and make them joyful in my
house of *prayer: their burnt-offerings
and their sacrifices *shall be* accepted
upon mine *altar; for mine house shall
be called an house of prayer for all
people.
8The Lord GOD which gathereth the
outcasts of Israel saith, Yet will I gather *others* to him, beside those that are
gathered unto him.
¶9All ye beasts of the field, come to
devour, *yea,* all ye beasts in the forest.
10His watchmen *are* blind: they are all

Popular Readings from Isaiah

Isaiah 3:1-15	The plight of Judah and Jerusalem
Isaiah 6:1-13	God calls Isaiah
Isaiah 9:2-7	To us a child is born
Isaiah 11:1-10	A branch from Jesse
Isaiah 25	Praise to the LORD
Isaiah 34:1-4	Judgment of the nations
Isaiah 35:1-10	The joy of the redeemed
Isaiah 38:9-20	Hezekiah's prayer
Isaiah 40:1-11	Comfort for God's people
Isaiah 40:21-31	The power of God
Isaiah 42:1-9	The LORD's servant
Isaiah 43:1-13	Israel's Saviour
Isaiah 52:5-10	The salvation of God
Isaiah 53	The suffering servant
Isaiah 55	Water for the thirsty
Isaiah 60:1-9	The glory of Zion
Isaiah 65:17-25	A new heaven and new earth
Isaiah 66:12-16	Peace will come

56:7 my house of prayer. Read about the temple in Jerusalem (Matt. 21:12-13). There will be an actual temple in Jerusalem during the *Millennium.

56:8 others. Perhaps the LORD speaks here of the "other sheep" of John 10:16 (see John 10:16 note, "The Other Sheep").

56:10 watchmen. Shepherds, supposed to be guarding the flocks.

ignorant, they *are* all dumb dogs, they
cannot bark; sleeping, lying down, loving to slumber.
11 Yea, *they are* greedy dogs *which* can
never have enough, and they *are* shepherds *that* cannot understand: they all
look to their own way, every one for his
gain, from his quarter.
12 Come ye, *say they,* I will fetch wine,
and we will fill ourselves with strong
drink; and to morrow shall be as this
day, *and* much more abundant.

God's graciousness to those of a contrite spirit

57 The righteous perisheth, and
no man layeth *it* to heart: and
merciful men *are* taken away, none considering that the righteous is taken
away from the evil *to come.*
2 He shall enter into peace: they shall
rest in their beds, *each one* walking *in*
his uprightness.
¶3 But draw near hither, ye sons of the
sorceress, the seed of the adulterer and
the *whore.
4 Against whom do ye sport yourselves? against whom make ye a wide
mouth, *and* draw out the tongue? *are* ye
not children of transgression, a seed of
*falsehood,
5 Enflaming yourselves with idols
*under every green tree, slaying the
children in the valleys under the clifts
of the rocks?
6 Among the smooth *stones* of the
stream *is* thy portion; they, they *are* thy
lot: even to them hast thou poured a
*drink-offering, thou hast offered a
*meat-offering. Should I receive com-
fort in these?
7 Upon a lofty and high mountain hast
thou set thy bed: even thither wentest
thou up to offer *sacrifice.
8 Behind the doors also and the posts
hast thou set up thy remembrance: for
thou hast discovered *thyself to another*
than me, and art gone up; thou hast
enlarged thy bed, and made thee *a covenant* with them; thou lovedst their bed
where thou sawest *it.*
9 And thou wentest to the king with
ointment, and didst increase thy perfumes, and didst send thy messengers
far off, and didst debase *thyself even* unto
*hell.
¶10 Thou art wearied in the greatness
of thy way; *yet* saidst thou not, There is
no *hope: thou hast found the life of
thine hand; therefore thou wast not
grieved.
11 And of whom hast thou been afraid
or feared, that thou hast lied, and hast
not remembered me, nor laid *it* to thy
heart? have not I held my peace even
of old, and thou fearest me not?
12 I will declare thy righteousness, and
thy works; for they shall not profit thee.
13 When thou criest, let thy companies deliver thee; but the wind shall
carry them all away; *vanity shall take
them: but he that putteth his *trust in
me shall possess the land, and shall inherit my holy mountain;
14 And shall say, Cast ye up, cast ye
up, prepare the way, take up the stumblingblock out of the way of my people.
¶15 For thus saith the high and lofty
One that inhabiteth eternity, whose
name *is* Holy; I dwell in the high and
holy *place,* with him also *that is* of a contrite and humble spirit, to revive the
spirit of the humble, and to revive the
heart of the contrite ones.

57:4 Against whom. The idolatrous children of Israel mocked and made fun of those who were faithful to God and His law.

57:7 bed. Altar for worshipping idols.

57:8 set up thy remembrance. The Jewish people even brought the idols into their homes.

57:9 didst send thy messengers far off. Ambassadors were sent to bring idols from foreign countries to set up in God's holy temple.

57:15 the high and lofty One. An ancient Jewish writer has said, "Whenever the Scripture bears witness to the divine greatness, it brings out side by side with it the divine humility."

16 For I will not contend for ever, neither will I be always wroth: for the spirit
should fail before me, and the souls
which I have made.
17 For the iniquity of his covetousness
was I wroth, and smote him: I hid me,
and was wroth, and he went on fro-
wardly in the way of his heart.
18 I have seen his ways, and will
heal him: I will lead him also, and restore comforts unto him and to his
mourners.
¶ 19 I create the fruit of the lips; Peace,
peace to *him that is* far off, and to *him
that is* near, saith the LORD; and I will
heal him.
20 But the wicked *are* like the troubled
sea, when it cannot rest, whose waters
cast up mire and dirt.
21 *There is* no peace, saith my God, to
the wicked.

Blessings follow obedience to God

58 Cry aloud, spare not, lift up thy
voice like a trumpet, and shew
my people their transgression, and the
house of *Jacob their sins.
2 Yet they seek me daily, and delight
to know my ways, as a nation that did
righteousness, and forsook not the ordinance of their God: they ask of me the
ordinances of justice; they take delight
in approaching to God.
¶ 3 Wherefore have we fasted, *say they,*
and thou seest not? *wherefore* have we
afflicted our soul, and thou takest no
knowledge? Behold, in the day of your
fast ye find pleasure, and exact all your
labours.
4 Behold, ye fast for strife and debate,
and to smite with the fist of wickedness:
ye shall not fast as *ye do this* day, to
make your voice to be heard on high.
5 Is it such a fast that I have chosen?
a day for a man to afflict his soul? *is it*
to bow down his head as a bulrush, and
to spread sackcloth and ashes *under
him?* wilt thou call this a fast, and an
acceptable day to the LORD?
6 *Is* not this the fast that I have chosen? to loose the bands of wickedness,
to undo the heavy burdens, and to let
the oppressed go free, and that ye break
every yoke?
7 *Is it* not to deal thy bread to the hungry, and that thou bring the poor that
are cast out to thy house? when thou
seest the naked, that thou cover him;
and that thou hide not thyself from
thine own flesh?
¶ 8 Then shall thy light break forth as
the morning, and thine health shall
spring forth speedily: and thy righteousness shall go before thee; the glory
of the LORD shall be thy *rereward.
9 Then shalt thou call, and the LORD
shall answer; thou shalt cry, and he shall
say, Here I *am.* If thou take away from
the midst of thee the yoke, the putting
forth of the finger, and speaking vanity;
10 And *if* thou draw out thy soul to the
hungry, and satisfy the afflicted soul;
then shall thy light rise in obscurity, and
thy darkness *be* as the noonday:
11 And the LORD shall guide thee continually, and satisfy thy soul in drought,
and make fat thy bones: and thou shalt
be like a watered garden, and like a
spring of water, whose waters fail not.
12 And *they that shall be* of thee shall
build the old waste places: thou shalt
raise up the foundations of many generations; and thou shalt be called, The
repairer of the breach, The restorer of
paths to dwell in.
¶ 13 If thou turn away thy foot from the
sabbath, *from* doing thy pleasure on my
holy day; and call the sabbath a delight,
the holy of the LORD, honourable; and
shalt honour him, not doing thine own
ways, nor finding thine own pleasure,
nor speaking *thine own* words:
14 Then shalt thou delight thyself in
the LORD; and I will cause thee to ride

58:8 light. Illuminations.
58:9 yoke . . . finger . . . vanity. These words speak of slavery, bribery, and lying.
58:12 paths to dwell in. Paths that lead home.

upon the high places of the earth, and feed thee with the heritage of Jacob thy father: for the mouth of the LORD hath spoken *it.*

X. The Establishment of Israel's Kingdom (59:1—63:19)

*The *Redeemer will come to sinful Israel*

59 Behold, the LORD'S hand is not shortened, that it cannot save; neither his ear heavy, that it cannot hear:

2 But your iniquities have separated between you and your God, and your sins have hid *his* face from you, that he will not hear.

3 For your hands are defiled with blood, and your fingers with iniquity; your lips have spoken lies, your tongue hath muttered perverseness.

4 None calleth for justice, nor *any* pleadeth for truth: they trust in vanity, and speak lies; they conceive mischief, and bring forth iniquity.

5 They hatch cockatrice' eggs, and weave the spider's web: he that eateth of their eggs dieth, and that which is crushed breaketh out into a viper.

6 Their webs shall not become garments, neither shall they cover themselves with their works: their works *are* works of iniquity, and the act of violence *is* in their hands.

59:6 No Cover-up for Sin
Just as Adam and Eve could not cover their nakedness, and God needed to provide clothing (Gen. 3:7,21), so no amount of "good works" will cover sin. God alone can clothe us with the garment of His righteousness through the blood of His Son the Lord Jesus Christ.

7 Their feet run to evil, and they make haste to shed innocent blood: their thoughts *are* thoughts of iniquity; wasting and destruction *are* in their paths.

8 The way of *peace they know not; and *there is* no judgment in their goings: they have made them crooked paths: whosoever goeth therein shall not know peace.

¶ 9 Therefore is judgment far from us, neither doth justice overtake us: we wait for light, but behold obscurity; for brightness, *but* we walk in darkness.

10 We grope for the wall like the blind, and we grope as if *we had* no eyes: we stumble at noonday as in the night; *we are* in desolate places as dead *men.*

11 We roar all like bears, and mourn sore like doves: we look for judgment, but *there is* none; for *salvation, *but* it is far off from us.

12 For our transgressions are multiplied before thee, and our sins testify against us: for our transgressions *are* with us; and *as for* our iniquities, we know them;

13 In transgressing and lying against the LORD, and departing away from our God, speaking oppression and revolt, conceiving and uttering from the heart words of falsehood.

14 And judgment is turned away backward, and justice standeth afar off: for truth is fallen in the street, and equity cannot enter.

15 Yea, truth faileth; and he *that* departeth from evil maketh himself a prey: and the LORD saw *it,* and it displeased him that *there was* no judgment.

¶ 16 And he saw that *there was* no man, and wondered that *there was* no intercessor: therefore his arm brought salvation

58:14 the heritage of Jacob. The land of Palestine.
59:2 your iniquities. Verses 1-8 show that it is because of sin that people are separated from God.
59:7 Their feet run to evil. See this same picture of the sinful in Romans 3:15-17.
59:8 judgment. They have no fear of judgment.
59:12 our transgressions are with us. We know that we are sinners.
59:15 truth faileth. Truth is lacking.
59:15 a prey. The sinner invites persecution.

unto him; and his righteousness, it sustained him.

17 For he put on righteousness as a breastplate, and an helmet of salvation upon his head; and he put on the garments of vengeance *for* clothing, and was clad with zeal as a cloke.

18 According to *their* deeds, accordingly he will repay, fury to his adversaries, recompence to his enemies; to the islands he will repay recompence.

19 So shall they *fear the name of the LORD from the west, and his glory from the rising of the sun. When the enemy shall come in like a flood, the Spirit of the LORD shall lift up a standard against him.

¶20 And the Redeemer shall come to *Zion, and unto them that turn from transgression in Jacob, saith the LORD.

21 As for me, this *is* my covenant with them, saith the LORD; My spirit that *is* upon thee, and my words which I have put in thy mouth, shall not depart out of thy mouth, nor out of the mouth of thy seed, nor out of the mouth of thy seed's seed, saith the LORD, from henceforth and for ever.

The Glory of the LORD will arise on Israel

60 Arise, shine; for thy light is come, and the glory of the LORD is risen upon thee.

2 For, behold, the darkness shall cover the earth, and gross darkness the people: but the LORD shall arise upon thee, and his glory shall be seen upon thee.

3 And the *Gentiles shall come to thy light, and kings to the brightness of thy rising.

4 Lift up thine eyes round about, and see: all they gather themselves together, they come to thee: thy sons shall come from far, and thy daughters shall be nursed at *thy* side.

5 Then thou shalt see, and flow together, and thine heart shall fear, and be enlarged; because the abundance of the sea shall be converted unto thee, the forces of the Gentiles shall come unto thee.

6 The multitude of camels shall cover thee, the dromedaries of Midian and *Ephah; all they from Sheba shall come: they shall bring gold and *incense; and they shall shew forth the praises of the LORD.

7 All the flocks of *Kedar shall be gathered together unto thee, the rams of Nebaioth shall minister unto thee: they shall come up with acceptance on mine altar, and I will glorify the house of my glory.

8 Who *are* these *that* fly as a cloud, and as the doves to their windows?

¶9 Surely the *isles shall wait for me, and the ships of *Tarshish first, to bring thy sons from far, their silver and their gold with them, unto the name of the LORD thy *God, and to the Holy One of Israel, because he hath glorified thee.

10 And the sons of strangers shall build up thy walls, and their kings shall minister unto thee: for in my wrath I

59:17 righteousness as a breastplate. See *clothed with humility.

59:20 Redeemer shall come. When the LORD shall have fulfilled His purposes through the *church, the Redeemer will return to Zion (Rom. 11:25-26). He will both come to and come out of Zion. When He comes, the glory of the Lord will arise upon Israel (Isa. 60:1-3).

59:21 words which I have put in thy mouth. See *inspiration.

60:5 fear, and be enlarged. They will fear God and their devotion to Him will increase.

60:6 The multitude of camels. Verses 6-9 speak of the various methods and nations who will bring the exiled children of Israel home to their land, bringing with them silver and gold and incense.

60:6 Midian. A son of Abraham. He was Ephah's father (Gen. 25:4). His race lived close to the Ishmaelites, from whom the Arabians are descended. They had many camels on which they carried their merchandise.

60:7 Nebaioth. One of the Arabian pastoral tribes, descended from Ishmael's oldest son, just as Kedar was descended from his second son.

smote thee, but in my favour have I had
*mercy on thee.
11Therefore thy gates shall be open
continually; they shall not be shut day
nor night; that *men* may bring unto thee
the forces of the Gentiles, and *that* their
kings *may be* brought.
12For the nation and *kingdom that
will not serve thee shall perish; yea,
those nations shall be utterly wasted.
13The glory of *Lebanon shall come
unto thee, the fir tree, the pine tree, and
the box together, to beautify the place
of my *sanctuary; and I will make the
place of my feet glorious.
14The sons also of them that afflicted thee shall come bending unto thee;
and all they that despised thee shall
bow themselves down at the soles of
thy feet; and they shall call thee, The
city of the LORD, The Zion of the Holy
One of Israel.
¶15Whereas thou hast been forsaken
and hated, so that no man went through
thee, I will make thee an eternal excellency, a joy of many generations.
16Thou shalt also suck the milk of the
Gentiles, and shalt suck the breast of
kings: and thou shalt know that I the
LORD *am* thy Saviour and thy Redeemer, the mighty One of Jacob.
17For brass I will bring gold, and for
iron I will bring silver, and for wood
brass, and for stones iron: I will also
make thy officers peace, and thine exactors *righteousness.
18Violence shall no more be heard in
thy land, wasting nor destruction within
thy borders; but thou shalt call thy walls
Salvation, and thy gates Praise.
19The sun shall be no more thy light
by day; neither for brightness shall the
moon give light unto thee: but the LORD
shall be unto thee an everlasting light,
and thy God thy glory.

60:19 A Lasting Light
The prophet looks forward to the eternal day. His description of it is very similar to that which we find in Revelation 21 and 22. The LORD Himself will be the Light of that beautiful city. That city is reached only by faith in the Lord Jesus Christ.

20Thy sun shall no more go down;
neither shall thy moon withdraw itself:
for the LORD shall be thine everlasting
light, and the days of thy *mourning
shall be ended.
21Thy people also *shall be* all righteous: they shall inherit the land for
ever, the *branch of my planting, the
work of my hands, that I may be glorified.
22A little one shall become a thousand, and a small one a strong nation: I
the LORD will hasten it in his time.

Christ's two comings: 1. to proclaim the Gospel; 2. to establish the kingdom

61 The Spirit of the Lord GOD *is*
upon me; because the LORD
hath anointed me to preach good

61:1 The Advents of Christ
Both advents, or comings, of the Lord Jesus Christ appear in a single sentence in this remarkable chapter. When the Lord Jesus presented Himself as the Messiah in the synagogue in Nazareth, He read from these verses (Luke 4:18-21). He read only that portion of this sentence which proclaims the acceptable year of the LORD (vs. 2) and declared that this Scripture was then fulfilled. The rest of the prophecy, about the day of vengeance and the description of the establishment of Israel in the kingdom of Christ on the earth, will be literally fulfilled as was the first. The Crown must follow the Cross.

60:13 the place of my feet. It is with such Scriptures that the Bible teaches the literalness of the second coming of Christ. His feet will stand again on the Mount of Olives (Zech. 14:4; see also its note, "The Mount of Olives"). He will then establish His throne within the temple which will be built in Jerusalem. That will be "the place of the soles of my feet" (Ezek. 43:7). He will make that place glorious.

60:17 exactors. Tax collectors.

tidings unto the meek; he hath sent me to bind up the brokenhearted, to proclaim liberty to the captives, and the opening of the prison to *them that are* bound;

[2]To proclaim the acceptable year of the LORD, and the day of vengeance of our God; to comfort all that mourn;

[3]To appoint unto them that mourn in Zion, to give unto them beauty for ashes, the oil of joy for mourning, the garment of praise for the spirit of heaviness; that they might be called trees of righteousness, the planting of the LORD, that he might be glorified.

¶[4]And they shall build the old wastes, they shall raise up the former desolations, and they shall repair the waste cities, the desolations of many generations.

[5]And strangers shall stand and feed your flocks, and the sons of the alien *shall be* your plowmen and your vinedressers.

[6]But ye shall be named the Priests of the LORD: *men* shall call you the Ministers of our God: ye shall eat the riches of the Gentiles, and in their glory shall ye boast yourselves.

¶[7]For your shame *ye shall have* double; and *for* confusion they shall rejoice in their portion: therefore in their land they shall possess the double: everlasting joy shall be unto them.

[8]For I the LORD love judgment, I hate robbery for burnt-offering; and I will direct their work in truth, and I will make an everlasting *covenant with them.

[9]And their seed shall be known among the Gentiles, and their offspring among the people: all that see them shall acknowledge them, that they *are* the seed *which* the LORD hath blessed.

[10]I will greatly rejoice in the LORD, my soul shall be joyful in my God; for he hath clothed me with the garments of salvation, he hath covered me with the robe of righteousness, as a bridegroom decketh *himself* with ornaments, and as a bride adorneth *herself* with her jewels.

[11]For as the earth bringeth forth her bud, and as the garden causeth the things that are sown in it to spring forth; so the Lord GOD will cause righteousness and praise to spring forth before all the nations.

Jerusalem will be glorious during Christ's reign

62

For Zion's sake will I not hold my peace, and for *Jerusalem's sake I will not rest, until the righteousness thereof go forth as brightness, and the salvation thereof as a lamp *that* burneth.

[2]And the Gentiles shall see thy righteousness, and all kings thy glory: and thou shalt be called by a new name, which the mouth of the LORD shall name.

[3]Thou shalt also be a crown of glory in the hand of the LORD, and a royal diadem in the hand of thy God.

[4]Thou shalt no more be termed Forsaken; neither shall thy land any more be termed Desolate: but thou shalt be called Hephzi-bah, and thy land Beulah: for the LORD delighteth in thee, and thy land shall be married.

¶[5]For *as* a young man marrieth a virgin, *so* shall thy sons marry thee: and *as* the *bridegroom rejoiceth over the bride, *so* shall thy God rejoice over thee.

[6]I have set watchmen upon thy walls, O Jerusalem, *which* shall never hold their peace day nor night: ye that make

---

61:7 double. The thought is double honor.
62:2 a new name. See verses 4 and 12; Jeremiah 33:16; Revelation 2:17; 3:12.
62:3 a crown of glory. Israel will be exalted when the Lord Jesus returns to earth to reign. She will be a crown of glory in His hand. This whole chapter describes the future exaltation of Israel.
62:4 Hephzi-bah. This means *my delight is in her.*
62:4 Beulah. Married. See Isaiah 54:5 note, "The Wife of God."

mention of the LORD, keep not silence,
7 And give him no rest, till he establish, and till he make Jerusalem a praise
in the earth.
8 The LORD hath sworn by his right
hand, and by the arm of his strength,
Surely I will no more give thy corn *to be*
meat for thine enemies; and the sons of
the stranger shall not drink thy wine, for
the which thou hast laboured:
9 But they that have gathered it shall
eat it, and praise the LORD; and they
that have brought it together shall drink
it in the courts of my holiness.
¶ 10 Go through, go through the gates;
prepare ye the way of the people; cast
up, cast up the highways; gather out
the stones; lift up a standard for the
people.
11 Behold, the LORD hath proclaimed
unto the end of the *world, Say ye to
the daughter of Zion, Behold, thy salvation cometh; behold, his *reward *is*
with him, and his work before him.
12 And they shall call them, The *holy
people, The *redeemed of the LORD:
and thou shalt be called, Sought out, A
city not forsaken.

Christ will return as both Judge and Deliverer

63 Who *is* this that cometh from
*Edom, with dyed garments
from Bozrah? this *that is* glorious in his
apparel, travelling in the greatness of
his strength? I that speak in righteousness, mighty to save.
2 Wherefore *art thou* red in thine apparel, and thy garments like him that
treadeth in the winefat?
3 I have trodden the winepress
alone; and of the people *there was* none
with me: for I will tread them in mine
anger, and trample them in my fury; and
their blood shall be sprinkled upon my
garments, and I will stain all my raiment.
4 For the day of vengeance *is* in mine

63:1 Christ's Coming
The One who comes is the One who trod alone the winepress of the wrath of God (vs. 3). The Lord Jesus is the only One who has had this experience. He alone was able to say truly, "My God, my God, why hast thou forsaken me?" (Matt. 27:46). When He returns to earth, it will be to tread the unbelieving world as though it were cast into the winepress of God (see Rev. 19:11-16). His kingdom must be established. The day of His vengeance will be the year of His redeemed (vs. 4).

heart, and the year of my redeemed is
come.
5 And I looked, and *there was* none to
help; and I wondered that *there was*
none to uphold: therefore mine own
arm brought salvation unto me; and my
fury, it upheld me.
6 And I will tread down the people in
mine anger, and make them drunk in
my fury, and I will bring down their
strength to the earth.
¶ 7 I will mention the lovingkindnesses of the LORD, *and* the praises of
the LORD, according to all that the LORD
hath bestowed on us, and the great
goodness toward the house of *Israel,
which he hath bestowed on them according to his mercies, and according to
the multitude of his lovingkindnesses.
8 For he said, Surely they *are* my people, children *that* will not lie: so he was
their Saviour.
9 In all their affliction he was afflicted, and the *angel of his presence saved
them: in his love and in his pity he redeemed them; and he bare them, and
carried them all the days of old.
¶ 10 But they rebelled, and vexed his
*holy Spirit: therefore he was turned to
be their enemy, *and* he fought against
them.
11 Then he remembered the days of
old, *Moses, *and* his people, *saying*,
Where *is* he that brought them up out

63:1 dyed. Crimson.
63:10 vexed. Grieved.

of the sea with the shepherd of his flock? where *is* he that put his holy Spirit within him?

12 That led *them* by the right hand of Moses with his glorious arm, dividing the water before them, to make himself an everlasting name?

13 That led them through the deep, as an horse in the wilderness, *that* they should not stumble?

14 As a beast goeth down into the valley, the Spirit of the LORD caused him to rest: so didst thou lead thy people, to make thyself a glorious name.

¶ 15 Look down from *heaven, and behold from the habitation of thy holiness and of thy glory: where *is* thy zeal and thy strength, the sounding of thy *bowels and of thy mercies toward me? are they restrained?

16 Doubtless thou *art* our father, though *Abraham be ignorant of us, and Israel acknowledge us not: thou, O LORD, *art* our father, our *redeemer; thy name *is* from everlasting.

63:16 The Fatherhood of God

This revelation of the fatherhood of God is based upon the fact of redemption. Although the gospel revelation of the new birth (John 3:1-16; see 3:3 note, "Born Again" and 3:15 note, "Eternal Life") is not stated in the Old Testament, it was sufficiently implied there for Christ to rebuke Nicodemus for having failed to know it. Ezekiel 36:26 describes the new heart, and Isaiah 63:16 discloses the relationship of God to those who have been changed by faith in the Redeemer. This is prophetic.

¶ 17 O LORD, why hast thou made us to *err from thy ways, *and* hardened our heart from thy fear? Return for thy servants' sake, the tribes of thine inheritance.

18 The people of thy holiness have possessed *it* but a little while: our adversaries have trodden down thy sanctuary.

19 We are *thine:* thou never barest rule over them; they were not called by thy name.

XI. The Eternal Destiny of Individual Souls (64:1—66:24)

*The confession of Israel's *remnant*

64 Oh that thou wouldest rend the heavens, that thou wouldest come down, that the mountains might flow down at thy presence,

2 As *when* the melting *fire burneth, the fire causeth the waters to boil, to make thy name known to thine adversaries, *that* the nations may tremble at thy presence!

3 When thou didst terrible things *which* we looked not for, thou camest down, the mountains flowed down at thy presence.

4 For since the beginning of the world *men* have not heard, nor perceived by the ear, neither hath the eye seen, O God, beside thee, *what* he hath prepared for him that waiteth for him.

5 Thou meetest him that rejoiceth and worketh righteousness, *those that* remember thee in thy ways: behold, thou art wroth; for we have sinned: in those is continuance, and we shall be saved.

¶ 6 But we are all as an *unclean *thing,* and all our righteousnesses *are* as filthy rags; and we all do fade as a leaf; and our iniquities, like the wind, have taken us away.

7 And *there is* none that calleth upon thy name, that stirreth up himself to take hold of thee: for thou hast hid thy face from us, and hast consumed us, because of our iniquities.

¶ 8 But now, O LORD, thou *art* our fa-

63:11 shepherd. Shepherds, referring to Moses and Aaron.
63:17 made us to. Allowed us to.
64:4 men have not heard. Compare this with 1 Corinthians 2:9-10.
64:6 unclean thing. Like lepers—the filthy rags are those that lepers wrapped around their sores.
64:6 righteousnesses are as filthy rags. See *clothed with humility.
64:8 thou art our father. This speaks of God, the Creator of man, the One from whom all mankind came.

ther; we *are* the clay, and thou our potter; and we all *are* the work of thy hand.
9Be not wroth very sore, O LORD,
neither remember iniquity for ever:
behold, see, we beseech thee, we *are* all
thy people.
¶10Thy holy cities are a wilderness,
Zion is a wilderness, Jerusalem a desolation.
11Our holy and our beautiful house,
where our fathers praised thee, is
burned up with fire: and all our pleasant things are laid waste.
12Wilt thou refrain thyself for these
things, O LORD? wilt thou hold thy
peace, and afflict us very sore?

The salvation of God: eternal blessings for the redeemed

65 I am sought of *them that* asked
not *for me;* I am found of *them
that* sought me not: I said, Behold me,
behold me, unto a nation *that* was not
called by my name.
¶2I have spread out my hands all the
day unto a rebellious people, which
walketh in a way *that was* not good, after their own thoughts;
3A people that provoketh me to anger continually to my face; that
sacrificeth in gardens, and burneth incense upon altars of brick;
4Which remain among the graves,
and lodge in the monuments, which eat
swine's *flesh, and broth of abominable
things is in their vessels;
5Which say, Stand by thyself, come
not near to me; for I am holier than
thou. These *are* a smoke in my nose, a
fire that burneth all the day.
6Behold, *it is* written before me: I will
not keep silence, but will recompense,
even recompense into their bosom,
7Your iniquities, and the iniquities of
your fathers together, saith the LORD,
which have burned incense upon the
mountains, and blasphemed me upon
the hills: therefore will I measure their
former work into their bosom.
¶8Thus saith the LORD, As the new
wine is found in the cluster, and *one*
saith, Destroy it not; for a blessing *is* in
it: so will I do for my servants' sakes,
that I may not destroy them all.
9And I will bring forth a seed out of
*Jacob, and out of *Judah an inheritor
of my mountains: and mine *elect shall
inherit it, and my servants shall dwell
there.
10And *Sharon shall be a fold of
flocks, and the valley of Achor a place
for the herds to lie down in, for my people that have sought me.
¶11But ye *are* they that forsake the
LORD, that forget my holy mountain,
that prepare a table for that troop,
and that furnish the *drink-offering
unto that number.
12Therefore will I number you to the
sword, and ye shall all bow down to the
slaughter: because when I called, ye did
not answer; when I spake, ye did not
hear; but did evil before mine eyes, and
did choose *that* wherein I delighted not.

64:9 Be not wroth very sore. Do not continue to be angry.
64:11 our beautiful house. The temple at Jerusalem.
65:3 sacrificeth in gardens. Worshipping idols (vss. 3-7 speak of this). God's altars were of unhewn stone or gold, not brick (vs. 3).
65:4 eat swine's flesh. This was one of the unclean animals that Israel was forbidden to eat. See Leviticus 11 and 11:2 note, "The Laws about Food."
65:9 mine elect. This speaks of the Jews, God's chosen people, who would finally turn to Him in believing faith.
65:10 the valley of Achor. The name of the valley means *trouble*. Read about it in Joshua 7, especially verse 26; but it was to become peaceful and "a door of hope" (Hos. 2:15).
65:11 troop . . . number. These are said to mean *fortune* and *destiny*. Fortune (Gad) was a god of good luck as was Destiny (Meni). The table and drink-offering, or feast to bring good fortune, was held at about the time of the Passover Feast and was a heathen mockery of that sacred feast.

¶ 13Therefore thus saith the Lord
GOD, Behold, my servants shall eat, but
ye shall be hungry: behold, my servants
shall drink, but ye shall be thirsty: behold, my servants shall rejoice, but ye
shall be ashamed:
14Behold, my servants shall sing for
joy of heart, but ye shall cry for sorrow
of heart, and shall howl for *vexation of
spirit.
15And ye shall leave your name for a
curse unto my chosen: for the Lord
GOD shall slay thee, and call his servants by another name:
16That he who blesseth himself in the
earth shall bless himself in the God of
truth; and he that sweareth in the earth
shall swear by the God of truth; because
the former troubles are forgotten, and
because they are hid from mine eyes.
¶ 17For, behold, I create new heavens
and a new earth: and the former shall
not be remembered, nor come into
mind.
18But be ye glad and rejoice for ever
in that which I create: for, behold, I create Jerusalem a rejoicing, and her people a joy.
19And I will rejoice in Jerusalem, and
joy in my people: and the voice of weeping shall be no more heard in her, nor
the voice of crying.
20There shall be no more thence an
infant of days, nor an old man that hath
not filled his days: for the child shall die
an hundred years old; but the sinner
being an hundred years old shall be accursed.
21And they shall build houses, and
inhabit *them;* and they shall plant vineyards, and eat the fruit of them.
22They shall not build, and another
inhabit; they shall not plant, and another eat: for as the days of a tree *are*
the days of my people, and mine elect
shall long enjoy the work of their
hands.
23They shall not labour in vain, nor
bring forth for trouble; for they *are* the
seed of the blessed of the LORD, and
their offspring with them.
24And it shall come to pass, that before they call, I will answer; and while
they are yet speaking, I will hear.
¶ 25The wolf and the lamb shall feed
together, and the lion shall eat straw
like the bullock: and dust *shall be* the
serpent's meat. They shall not hurt nor
destroy in all my holy mountain, saith
the LORD.

Peace for the redeemed—eternal punishment for the transgressors

66 Thus saith the LORD, The heav-
en *is* my throne, and the earth
is my footstool: where *is* the house that
ye build unto me? and where *is* the
place of my rest?
2For all those *things* hath mine hand
made, and all those *things* have been,
saith the LORD: but to this *man* will I
look, *even* to *him that is* poor and of a
contrite spirit, and trembleth at my
word.
3He that killeth an ox *is as if* he slew
a man; he that sacrificeth a lamb, *as if*
he cut off a dog's neck; he that offereth
an oblation, as *if he offered* swine's blood;
he that burneth incense, *as if* he blessed
an idol. Yea, they have chosen their own
ways, and their soul delighteth in their
abominations.

65:17 new heavens and a new earth. This goes far beyond the millennial reign of Christ (see *Millennium). It is paralleled by the revelation of heaven given in Revelation 21:1. It must be understood that in order for anyone to participate in the new heaven and the new earth, he must first be a new creature in Christ (2 Cor. 5:17).
65:20 thence. From that time on.
65:20 accursed. Cut off because of sin.
65:25 dust shall be the serpent's meat. A mark of degradation or shame.
66:1 where is the house . . . ? The LORD is contrasting His home—the whole universe—with the temple at Jerusalem, which took forty-six years to build. Though the universe is His dwelling place, His true temple is in the heart of man (vs. 2; 1 Cor. 6:15,19).

[4]I also will choose their delusions, and will bring their fears upon them; because when I called, none did answer; when I spake, they did not hear: but they did evil before mine eyes, and chose *that* in which I delighted not.

¶[5]Hear the word of the LORD, ye that tremble at his word; Your brethren that hated you, that cast you out for my name's sake, said, Let the LORD be glorified: but he shall appear to your joy, and they shall be ashamed.

[6]A voice of noise from the city, a voice from the temple, a voice of the LORD that rendereth recompence to his enemies.

[7]Before she travailed, she brought forth; before her pain came, she was delivered of a man child.

[8]Who hath heard such a thing? who hath seen such things? Shall the earth be made to bring forth in one day? *or* shall a nation be born at once? for as soon as Zion travailed, she brought forth her children.

[9]Shall I bring to the birth, and not cause to bring forth? saith the LORD: shall I cause to bring forth, and shut *the womb?* saith thy God.

¶[10]Rejoice ye with Jerusalem, and be glad with her, all ye that love her: rejoice for joy with her, all ye that mourn for her:

[11]That ye may suck, and be satisfied with the breasts of her consolations; that ye may milk out, and be delighted with the abundance of her glory.

[12]For thus saith the LORD, Behold, I will extend peace to her like a river, and the glory of the Gentiles like a flowing stream: then shall ye suck, ye shall be borne upon *her* sides, and be dandled upon *her* knees.

[13]As one whom his mother comforteth, so will I comfort you; and ye shall be comforted in Jerusalem.

[14]And when ye see *this,* your heart shall rejoice, and your bones shall flourish like an herb: and the hand of the LORD shall be known toward his servants, and *his* indignation toward his enemies.

¶[15]For, behold, the LORD will come with fire, and with his chariots like a whirlwind, to render his anger with fury, and his rebuke with flames of fire.

[16]For by fire and by his sword will the LORD plead with all flesh: and the slain of the LORD shall be many.

[17]They that sanctify themselves, and purify themselves in the gardens behind one *tree* in the midst, eating swine's flesh, and the abomination, and the mouse, shall be consumed together, saith the LORD.

[18]For I *know* their works and their thoughts: it shall come, that I will gather all nations and tongues; and they shall come, and see my glory.

[19]And I will set a sign among them, and I will send those that escape of them unto the nations, *to* Tarshish, Pul, and Lud, that draw the bow, *to* Tubal, and Javan, *to* the isles afar off, that have not heard my fame, neither have seen my glory; and they shall declare my glory among the Gentiles.

[20]And they shall bring all your brethren *for* an offering unto the LORD out of all nations upon horses, and in chariots, and in litters, and upon mules, and upon swift beasts, to my holy mountain Jerusalem, saith the LORD, as the children of Israel bring an offering in a clean vessel into the house of the LORD.

¶[21]And I will also take of them for priests *and* for Levites, saith the LORD.

[22]For as the new heavens and the new earth, which I will make, shall remain before me, saith the LORD, so

---

66:15 the LORD will come with fire. This speaks of the *Day of the LORD.
66:16 by his sword. See *Armageddon.
66:20 for an offering unto the LORD. See 60:6 first note.
66:22 new heavens. See 65:17 note.

shall your seed and your name remain.
[23]And it shall come to pass, *that*
from one new moon to another, and
from one sabbath to another, shall all
flesh come to worship before me, saith
the LORD.
[24]And they shall go forth, and look
upon the carcases of the men that have
transgressed against me: for their
worm shall not die, neither shall their
fire be quenched; and they shall be an
abhorring unto all flesh.

66:24 Isaiah's Final Words
Isaiah brings his prophecy to a close with a graphic declaration of the fact of the eternal punishment of those who reject the LORD. This is his final word. It is of the utmost solemnity. He had invited men to come and reason with God. He had made known the Messiah and His vicarious death. He had proclaimed the glories of an eternal day. He closed his message with the solemn warning that the rejecters of God will be rejected by God eternally.

The Book of the Prophet

JEREMIAH

BACKGROUND

The book of Jeremiah was written by the prophet of that name. He lived in the Kingdom of Judah and was active from the reign of Josiah (2 Kings 22) until the captivity into Babylon (2 Kings 25). He was preaching in Jerusalem when that city was destroyed by Nebuchadnezzar, but he was not carried away into Babylon, being left in the land by the conquerors (Jeremiah 39:11-12). Against his own judgment he was taken to Egypt by the remnant of the Jews in Palestine, and in Egypt he died.

MESSAGE

Jeremiah's words are a wonderful revelation of the love of God for His unfaithful people. While setting forth the awful punishment which God would give to Israel because His people had broken His covenant, Jeremiah solemnly declared that God would be faithful to His unfaithful people. A new covenant would replace the old covenant that Israel broke, and Christ, the Messiah, would yet reign as her King.

The history of Jeremiah is a striking example of faithfulness to God on the part of the prophet. He wept as he declared the judgment of God upon His people, and earned the title of "the weeping prophet."

THE TIME

For almost fifty years, Jeremiah was the voice of God to Judah. The date of his ministry was from about 629 B.C. to about 580 B.C.

OUTLINE OF JEREMIAH

I.	The Call of Jeremiah	Jeremiah 1:1-19
II.	Sermons of Jeremiah	Jeremiah 2:1—12:17
III.	Object Lessons by Jeremiah	Jeremiah 13:1—19:15
IV.	Messages from Jeremiah	Jeremiah 20:1—29:32
V.	The Future of Israel	Jeremiah 30:1—33:26
VI.	Israel's Unfaithfulness	Jeremiah 34:1—36:32
VII.	Jeremiah's Personal History	Jeremiah 37:1—45:5
VIII.	Jeremiah's Prophecies against the Gentile Nations	Jeremiah 46:1—51:64
IX.	Conclusion: The Fall of Jerusalem	Jeremiah 52:1-34

I. The Call of Jeremiah (1:1-19)

1 The words of Jeremiah the son of
Hilkiah, of the priests that *were* in
Anathoth in the land of Benjamin:
2 To whom the word of the LORD came
in the days of *Josiah the son of Amon
king of *Judah, in the thirteenth year of
his reign.

1:2 the days of Josiah. See introduction.

[3]It came also in the days of Jehoiakim
the son of Josiah king of Judah, unto the
end of the eleventh year of Zedekiah
the son of Josiah king of Judah, unto the
carrying away of *Jerusalem captive in
the fifth *month.
[4]Then the word of the LORD came
unto me, saying,
[5]Before I formed thee in the belly I
knew thee; and before thou camest
forth out of the womb I sanctified thee,
and I ordained thee a *prophet unto the
nations.

1:5 God's Preparations
God prepared the men whom He later used as His prophets and the penmen of His Word. The Holy Spirit not only had a definite revelation to give from God, but He also had prepared men to do special work as the writers of Scripture. Jeremiah was chosen for his ministry and Paul likewise was chosen for his (Gal. 1:15). God molded these men, as He did all the writers of Scripture, so that their very natures would best serve to give His message to men in the Bible, the verbally inspired Word of God.

[6]Then said I, Ah, Lord GOD! behold,
I cannot speak: for I *am* a child.
¶[7]But the LORD said unto me, Say
not, I *am* a child: for thou shalt go to all
that I shall send thee, and whatsoever
I command thee thou shalt speak.
[8]*Be not afraid of their faces: for I *am*
with thee to deliver thee, saith the
LORD.
[9]Then the LORD put forth his hand,
and touched my mouth. And the LORD
said unto me, Behold, I have put my
words in thy mouth.
[10]See, I have this day set thee over
the nations and over the kingdoms, to
root out, and to pull down, and to destroy, and to throw down, to build, and
to plant.
¶[11]Moreover the word of the LORD
came unto me, saying, Jeremiah, what
seest thou? And I said, I see a rod of an
almond tree.

1:11 A Vision
The vision of the almond tree spoke of events that were going to happen soon. Just as the almond tree is the first tree of the East to blossom in the spring, so the events that Jeremiah spoke of were ready to spring upon the people. But it also looked ahead to another time. In Numbers 17, the rod of an almond tree became a *type of the resurrection of the Lord Jesus Christ. It is significant that Jeremiah's first vision would be the sign of the resurrection of Jesus Christ.

[12]Then said the LORD unto me, Thou
hast well seen: for I will hasten my
word to perform it.
[13]And the word of the LORD came
unto me the second time, saying, What
seest thou? And I said, I see a seething
pot; and the face thereof *is* toward the
north.
[14]Then the LORD said unto me, Out
of the north an evil shall break forth
upon all the inhabitants of the land.
[15]For, lo, I will call all the families of
the kingdoms of the north, saith the
LORD; and they shall come, and they
shall set every one his throne at the
entering of the gates of Jerusalem, and
against all the walls thereof round
about, and against all the cities of Judah.
[16]And I will utter my judgments
against them touching all their wickedness, who have forsaken me, and have
burned *incense unto other gods, and

1:9 I have put my words. God used Jeremiah's mouth to speak His words. See verse 5 note, "God's Preparations." Compare Isaiah 6:5-9.

1:10 I have this day set thee. The task that God gave to Jeremiah sounds like a summary of the eleventh chapter of Hebrews. The prophet bore the true characteristics of a man of faith.

1:13 a seething pot. The second vision that Jeremiah saw was of a boiling pot whose face was toward (tilting away from) the north. The prophecy was fulfilled when the armies of Babylon came from the north to destroy the city of Jerusalem.

1:13 toward. From.

worshipped the works of their own
hands.
¶17Thou therefore gird up thy loins,
and arise, and speak unto them all that
I command thee: be not dismayed at
their faces, lest I confound thee before
them.
18For, behold, I have made thee this
day a defenced city, and an iron pillar,
and brasen walls against the whole land,
against the kings of Judah, against the
princes thereof, against the priests
thereof, and against the people of the
land.
19And they shall fight against thee;
but they shall not prevail against thee;
for I *am* with thee, saith the LORD, to
deliver thee.

II. Sermons of Jeremiah (2:1—12:17)

*1) A call to *repentance*

2 Moreover the word of the LORD
came to me, saying,
2Go and cry in the ears of Jerusalem,

2:2 A Call to Repentance
The book of Jeremiah records several magnificent sermons that the prophet preached in Jerusalem. The first of these is found in Jeremiah 2:1–3:5. It is a call to repentance. The prophet reminded Israel of their zeal and holiness in the early days of their relationship to God. He asked the people to tell what sin they had found in God that they had forsaken Him (2:5). He rebuked the leaders of Israel (2:8). He reminded the people that a substitute for God Himself is a broken cistern that can hold no water (2:13). He uncovered their sin and declared that neither soap nor nitre (lye) could remove it (2:22). After making these accusations, the prophet protested against those who said, "There is no hope" (2:23) by telling them that God was calling the nation to return to Him (3:1).

saying, Thus saith the LORD; I remember thee, the kindness of thy youth, the
love of thine espousals, when thou
wentest after me in the wilderness, in
a land *that was* not sown.
3*Israel *was* holiness unto the LORD,
and the firstfruits of his increase: all
that devour him shall *offend; evil shall
come upon them, saith the LORD.
4Hear ye the word of the LORD,
O house of *Jacob, and all the families
of the house of Israel:
¶5Thus saith the LORD, What iniquity have your fathers found in me, that
they are gone far from me, and have
walked after *vanity, and are become
vain?
6Neither said they, Where *is* the LORD
that brought us up out of the land of
*Egypt, that led us through the wilder-
ness, through a land of deserts and of
pits, through a land of drought, and of
the shadow of *death, through a land
that no man passed through, and where
no man dwelt?
7And I brought you into a plentiful
country, to eat the fruit thereof and the
goodness thereof; but when ye entered,
ye defiled my land, and made mine heritage an *abomination.
8The priests said not, Where *is* the
LORD? and they that handle the *law
knew me not: the pastors also transgressed against me, and the *prophets
prophesied by *Baal, and walked after
things that do not profit.
¶9Wherefore I will yet plead with
you, saith the LORD, and with your
children's children will I plead.
10For pass over the *isles of Chittim,
and see; and send unto *Kedar, and consider diligently, and see if there be such
a thing.
11Hath a nation changed *their* gods,

1:17 confound. To put to confusion, to destroy.
1:18 a defenced city. Men could have no power to destroy Jeremiah because the LORD was his defense (vs. 19).
2:6 out of the land of Egypt. Read Exodus 12; 13; 14.
2:8 priests . . . pastors . . . prophets. This verse speaks of the leaders of the nation turning away from God to worship idols.
2:10 Chittim . . . Kedar. Chittim was west of Jerusalem; Kedar, east.

which *are* yet no gods? but my people
have changed their glory for *that which*
doth not profit.
12 Be astonished, O ye heavens, at
this, and be horribly afraid, be ye very
desolate, saith the LORD.
13 For my people have committed two
evils; they have forsaken me the fountain of living waters, *and* hewed them
out cisterns, broken cisterns, that can
hold no water.
¶14 *Is* Israel a servant? *is* he a homeborn *slave?* why is he spoiled?
15 The young lions roared upon him,
and yelled, and they made his land
waste: his cities are burned without
inhabitant.
16 Also the children of Noph and Tahapanes have broken the crown of thy
head.
17 Hast thou not procured this unto
thyself, in that thou hast forsaken the
LORD thy *God, when he led thee by
the way?
18 And now what hast thou to do in the
way of Egypt, to drink the waters of
Sihor? or what hast thou to do in the
way of Assyria, to drink the waters of
the river?
19 Thine own wickedness shall correct thee, and thy backslidings shall
reprove thee: know therefore and see
that *it is* an evil *thing* and bitter, that
thou hast forsaken the LORD thy God,
and that my *fear *is* not in thee, saith
the Lord GOD of hosts.
¶20 For of old time I have broken thy
yoke, *and* burst thy bands; and thou
saidst, I will not transgress; when upon
every high hill and *under every green
tree thou wanderest, playing the
harlot.
21 Yet I had planted thee a noble vine,
wholly a right seed: how then art thou
turned into the degenerate plant of a
strange vine unto me?
22 For though thou wash thee with
nitre, and take thee much sope, *yet*
thine iniquity is marked before me,
saith the Lord GOD.
23 How canst thou say, I am not polluted, I have not gone after Baalim? see
thy way in the valley, know what thou
hast done: *thou art* a swift dromedary
traversing her ways;
24 A wild ass used to the wilderness,
that snuffeth up the wind at her pleasure; in her occasion who can turn her
away? all they that seek her will not
weary themselves; in her month they
shall find her.
25 Withhold thy foot from being un-
shod, and thy throat from thirst: but
thou saidst, There is no *hope: no; for
I have loved strangers, and after them
will I go.
26 As the thief is ashamed when he is
found, so is the house of Israel ashamed;
they, their kings, their princes, and their
priests, and their prophets,
27 Saying to a stock, Thou *art* my father; and to a stone, Thou hast brought
me forth: for they have turned *their*
back unto me, and not *their* face: but in
the time of their trouble they will say,
Arise, and save us.
28 But where *are* thy gods that thou
hast made thee? let them arise, if they
can save thee in the time of thy trouble: for *according to* the number of thy
cities are thy gods, O Judah.
29 Wherefore will ye plead with me?
ye all have transgressed against me,
saith the LORD.
30 In vain have I smitten your children; they received no correction: your

---

2:16 Noph. Memphis in Egypt.
2:16 Tahapanes. A once powerful city in Egypt.
2:18 Sihor. The Nile.
2:18 the river. The Euphrates.
2:22 nitre. Lye or soda.
2:27 stock . . . stone. The stock of a tree was its trunk. Idols were made from this wood and from stone. The Israelites were praising idols instead of praying to God who could hear them and help them.

own sword hath devoured your prophets, like a destroying lion.
¶31O generation, see ye the word of
the LORD. Have I been a wilderness
unto Israel? a land of darkness? wherefore say my people, We are lords; we
will come no more unto thee?
32Can a maid forget her ornaments,
or a bride her attire? yet my people have
forgotten me days without number.
33Why trimmest thou thy way to seek
love? therefore hast thou also taught
the wicked ones thy ways.
34Also in thy skirts is found the blood
of the souls of the poor innocents: I
have not found it by secret search, but
upon all these.
35Yet thou sayest, Because I am innocent, surely his anger shall turn from
me. Behold, I will plead with thee, because thou sayest, I have not sinned.
36Why gaddest thou about so much
to change thy way? thou also shalt
be ashamed of Egypt, as thou wast
ashamed of Assyria.
37Yea, thou shalt go forth from him,
and thine hands upon thine head: for the
LORD hath rejected thy confidences,
and thou shalt not prosper in them.

Sermons of Jeremiah (continued)

3 They say, If a man put away his
wife, and she go from him, and become another man's, shall he return
unto her again? shall not that land be
greatly polluted? but thou hast played
the harlot with many lovers; yet return
again to me, saith the LORD.
2Lift up thine eyes unto the *high
places, and see where thou hast not been
lien with. In the ways hast thou sat for
them, as the Arabian in the wilderness;
and thou hast polluted the land with thy
whoredoms and with thy wickedness.
3Therefore the showers have been
withholden, and there hath been no latter rain; and thou hadst a whore's forehead, thou refusedst to be ashamed.
4Wilt thou not from this time cry unto
me, My father, thou *art* the guide of my
youth?
5Will he reserve *his anger* for ever?
will he keep *it* to the end? Behold, thou
hast spoken and done evil things as
thou couldest.

2) Another call to repentance

¶6The LORD said also unto me in the
days of Josiah the king, Hast thou seen
that which backsliding Israel hath done?
she is gone up upon every high mountain and under every green tree, and
there hath played the harlot.

3:6 A Second Sermon
Here begins Jeremiah's second sermon. It is another call to repentance, differing from the first message in that it looks forward to the day when the Lord Jesus Christ will reign in Jerusalem, and Israel will find her salvation in the LORD her God.

7And I said after she had done all
these *things,* Turn thou unto me. But
she returned not. And her treacherous
sister Judah saw *it.*
8And I saw, when for all the causes
whereby backsliding Israel committed
adultery I had put her away, and given
her a bill of divorce; yet her treacherous sister Judah feared not, but went
and played the harlot also.
9And it came to pass through the
lightness of her whoredom, that she
defiled the land, and committed adultery with stones and with stocks.
10And yet for all this her treacherous
sister Judah hath not turned unto me

2:37 thine hands upon thine head. This is a sign of misery.
3:2 high places. Idols were set up and worshipped on the high places. The Israelites turned to many idols and looked to them instead of loving and worshipping the one true God.
3:6 Israel. The northern kingdom. Judah (vs. 7) had seen what had happened to Israel because of her disobedience.
3:10 yet for all this. The sin of Judah was greater than the sin of the northern kingdom, Israel (see vs. 11), because Judah persisted in her idolatry when Israel had been led

with her whole heart, but feignedly,
saith the LORD.
11And the LORD said unto me, The
backsliding Israel hath justified herself
more than treacherous Judah.
¶12Go and proclaim these words toward the north, and say, Return, thou
backsliding Israel, saith the LORD; *and*
I will not cause mine anger to fall upon
you: for I *am* merciful, saith the LORD,
and I will not keep *anger* for ever.
13Only acknowledge thine iniquity,
that thou hast transgressed against the
LORD thy God, and hast scattered thy
ways to the strangers under every
green tree, and ye have not obeyed my
voice, saith the LORD.
14Turn, O backsliding children, saith
the LORD; for I am married unto you:
and I will take you one of a city, and two
of a family, and I will bring you to *Zion:

3:14 A Backslider

The unfaithfulness of the children of Israel in their relationship to God did not make God unfaithful in His relationship to them (2 Tim. 2:13). A backslider is a child of God who is out of fellowship with the Lord. God will restore such a one to Himself by discipline and by acts of wonderful grace. He is married to the backslider. See also Jeremiah 31:32.

15And I will give you pastors according to mine heart, which shall feed you
with knowledge and understanding.
16And it shall come to pass, when ye
be multiplied and increased in the land,
in those days, saith the LORD, they shall
say no more, The *ark of the covenant
of the LORD: neither shall it come to
mind: neither shall they remember it;
neither shall they visit *it;* neither shall
that be done any more.
17At that time they shall call Jerusalem the throne of the LORD; and all the
nations shall be gathered unto it, to the
name of the LORD, to Jerusalem: neither shall they walk any more after the
imagination of their evil heart.
18In those days the house of Judah
shall walk with the house of Israel, and
they shall come together out of the land
of the north to the land that I have given
for an inheritance unto your fathers.
19But I said, How shall I put thee
among the children, and give thee a
pleasant land, a goodly heritage of the
hosts of nations? and I said, Thou shalt
call me, My father; and shalt not turn
away from me.
¶20Surely *as* a wife treacherously departeth from her husband, so have ye
dealt treacherously with me, O house
of Israel, saith the LORD.
21A voice was heard upon the high
places, weeping *and* supplications of
the children of Israel: for they have
perverted their way, *and* they have forgotten the LORD their God.
22Return, ye backsliding children,
and I will heal your backslidings. Behold, we come unto thee; for thou *art*
the LORD our God.
23Truly in vain *is *salvation hoped for*
from the hills, *and from* the multitude
of mountains: truly in the LORD our God
is the salvation of Israel.

---

away into captivity. Judah just pretended to turn (she turned "feignedly") to God with her whole heart. Judgments that are poured out upon others constitute a call to repentance.

3:12 Go and proclaim. Verses 12-20 are spoken by the LORD; verse 21 by those of the children of Israel who are weeping because of their misery; the first half of verse 22 by the LORD; the rest of the chapter by the children of Israel returning from exile.

3:17 Jerusalem the throne of the LORD. Jerusalem will become the throne of the LORD when He returns to this earth to reign. His throne will be in the city of Jerusalem. From it He will rule the world.

3:18 they shall come together . . . to the land. A prophecy that looks forward, as does verse 17, to the time when the Jews as a separate nation will be back in Palestine. Although we never know when or precisely how God fulfills his prophecy, it is worthy noting that Israel did become an independently governed country in 1948 in the wake of World War II.

24 For shame hath devoured the labour of our fathers from our youth; their
flocks and their herds, their sons and
their daughters.
25 We lie down in our shame, and our
confusion covereth us: for we have
sinned against the LORD our God, we
and our fathers, from our youth even
unto this day, and have not obeyed the
voice of the LORD our God.

Sermons of Jeremiah (continued)

4 If thou wilt return, O Israel, saith
the LORD, return unto me: and if
thou wilt put away thine abominations
out of my sight, then shalt thou not remove.
2 And thou shalt swear, The LORD
liveth, in truth, in *judgment, and in
*righteousness; and the nations shall
bless themselves in him, and in him
shall they glory.
¶3 For thus saith the LORD to the men
of Judah and Jerusalem, Break up your
fallow ground, and sow not among
thorns.
4 Circumcise yourselves to the LORD,
and take away the foreskins of your
heart, ye men of Judah and inhabitants
of Jerusalem: lest my fury come forth
like *fire, and burn that none can
quench *it,* because of the evil of your
doings.
5 Declare ye in Judah, and publish in
Jerusalem; and say, Blow ye the trumpet in the land: cry, gather together, and
say, Assemble yourselves, and let us go
into the defenced cities.
6 Set up the standard toward Zion:
retire, stay not: for I will bring evil from
the north, and a great destruction.
7 The lion is come up from his thicket, and the destroyer of the *Gentiles
is on his way; he is gone forth from his
place to make thy land desolate; *and* thy
cities shall be laid waste, without an
inhabitant.
8 For this gird you with sackcloth, lament and howl: for the fierce anger of
the LORD is not turned back from us.
9 And it shall come to pass at that day,
saith the LORD, *that* the heart of the
king shall perish, and the heart of the
princes; and the priests shall be astonished, and the prophets shall wonder.
10 Then said I, Ah, Lord GOD! surely
thou hast greatly deceived this people
and Jerusalem, saying, Ye shall have
*peace; whereas the sword reacheth
unto the soul.
11 At that time shall it be said to this
people and to Jerusalem, A dry wind of
the high places in the wilderness toward the daughter of my people, not to
fan, nor to cleanse,
12 *Even* a full wind from those *places*
shall come unto me: now also will I give
sentence against them.
13 Behold, he shall come up as clouds,
and his chariots *shall be* as a whirlwind:
his horses are swifter than eagles. Woe
unto us! for we are spoiled.
14 O Jerusalem, wash thine heart from
wickedness, that thou mayest be saved.
How long shall thy vain thoughts lodge
within thee?
15 For a voice declareth from Dan, and
publisheth affliction from mount
*Ephraim.
16 Make ye mention to the nations;
behold, publish against Jerusalem, *that*
watchers come from a far country, and
give out their voice against the cities of
Judah.
17 As keepers of a field, are they
against her round about; because she
hath been rebellious against me, saith
the LORD.
18 Thy way and thy doings have procured these *things* unto thee; this *is* thy

---

4:3 fallow ground. Ground that has not been broken up or plowed. Man's heart must be broken and repentant before it is ready to receive the good seed of the Word.
4:7 The lion. Nebuchadnezzar, king of Babylon.
4:9 heart. Wisdom or courage.
4:12 a full wind. A hurricane wind.

wickedness, because it is bitter, because it reacheth unto thine heart.
¶[19]My *bowels, my bowels! I am pained at my very heart; my heart maketh a noise in me; I cannot hold my peace, because thou hast heard, O my soul, the sound of the trumpet, the alarm of war.
[20]Destruction upon destruction is cried; for the whole land is spoiled: suddenly are my tents spoiled, *and* my curtains in a moment.
[21]How long shall I see the standard, *and* hear the sound of the trumpet?
[22]For my people *is* foolish, they have not known me; they *are* sottish children, and they have none understanding: they *are* wise to do evil, but to do good they have no knowledge.
[23]I beheld the earth, and, lo, *it was* without form, and void; and the heavens, and they *had* no light.

4:23 The Earth's Condition
The words "without form, and void" are adopted from the first chapter of Genesis. There can be no doubt but that Jeremiah was familiar with the Law of Moses. As he anticipated the trouble that Israel would suffer again during the *Great Tribulation, he compared it to the condition of the earth described in Genesis 1:2.

[24]I beheld the mountains, and, lo, they trembled, and all the hills moved lightly.
[25]I beheld, and, lo, *there was* no man, and all the birds of the heavens were fled.
[26]I beheld, and, lo, the fruitful place *was* a wilderness, and all the cities thereof were broken down at the presence of the LORD, *and* by his fierce anger.
[27]For thus hath the LORD said, The whole land shall be desolate; yet will I not make a full end.
[28]For this shall the earth mourn, and the heavens above be black: because I have spoken *it,* I have purposed *it,* and will not *repent, neither will I turn back from it.
[29]The whole city shall flee for the noise of the horsemen and bowmen; they shall go into thickets, and climb up upon the rocks: every city *shall be* forsaken, and not a man dwell therein.
[30]And *when* thou *art* spoiled, what wilt thou do? Though thou clothest thyself with crimson, though thou deckest thee with ornaments of gold, though thou rentest thy face with painting, in vain shalt thou make thyself fair; *thy* lovers will despise thee, they will seek thy life.
[31]For I have heard a voice as of a woman in travail, *and* the anguish as of her that bringeth forth her first child, the voice of the daughter of Zion, *that* bewaileth herself, *that* spreadeth her hands, *saying,* Woe *is* me now! for my soul is wearied because of murderers.

Sermons of Jeremiah (continued)

5 Run ye to and fro through the streets of Jerusalem, and see now, and know, and seek in the broad places thereof, if ye can find a man, if there be *any* that executeth judgment, that seeketh the truth; and I will pardon it.
[2]And though they say, The LORD liveth; surely they swear falsely.

5:1 Jerusalem Compared to Sodom
Before God destroyed Sodom, He promised Abraham that He would spare the city if there were ten righteous men in it (Gen. 18:32). The prophet Jeremiah proclaimed in this sermon that if there was only one who executed judgment and sought the truth in Jerusalem, God would spare the city. Jeremiah quickly added, "They have refused to receive correction" (vs. 3).

4:19 I am pained. Jeremiah has been called "the weeping prophet" because he was so distressed at the judgment that his people were to suffer.
4:30 rentest thy face with painting. A more accurate translation is "enlargest (or shadest) thine eyes," as with makeup.
5:2 swear falsely. Worship insincerely.

3 O LORD, *are* not thine eyes upon the
truth? thou hast stricken them, but they
have not grieved; thou hast consumed
them, *but* they have refused to receive
correction: they have made their faces
harder than a rock; they have refused
to return.
4 Therefore I said, Surely these *are*
poor; they are foolish: for they know not
the way of the LORD, *nor* the judgment
of their God.
5 I will get me unto the great men, and
will speak unto them; for they have
known the way of the LORD, *and* the
judgment of their God: but these have
altogether broken the yoke, *and* burst
the bonds.
6 Wherefore a lion out of the forest
shall slay them, *and* a wolf of the evenings shall spoil them, a leopard shall
watch over their cities: every one
that goeth out thence shall be torn in
pieces: because their transgressions
are many, *and* their backslidings are
increased.
¶ 7 How shall I pardon thee for this?
thy children have forsaken me, and
sworn by *them that are* no gods: when I
had fed them to the full, they then committed adultery, and assembled themselves by troops in the harlots' houses.
8 They were *as* fed horses in the
morning: every one neighed after his
neighbour's wife.
9 Shall I not visit for these *things?*
saith the LORD: and shall not my soul
be avenged on such a nation as this?
¶ 10 Go ye up upon her walls, and destroy; but make not a full end: take away
her battlements; for they *are* not the
LORD'S.
11 For the house of Israel and the
house of Judah have dealt very treacherously against me, saith the LORD.
12 They have belied the LORD, and
said, *It is* not he; neither shall evil come
upon us; neither shall we see sword nor
famine:
13 And the prophets shall become
wind, and the word *is* not in them: thus
shall it be done unto them.
14 Wherefore thus saith the LORD God
of hosts, Because ye speak this word,
behold, I will make my words in thy
mouth fire, and this people wood, and
it shall devour them.
15 Lo, I will bring a nation upon you
from far, O house of Israel, saith the
LORD: it *is* a mighty nation, it *is* an ancient nation, a nation whose language
thou knowest not, neither understandest what they say.
16 Their quiver *is* as an open sepulchre, they *are* all mighty men.
17 And they shall eat up thine harvest,
and thy bread, *which* thy sons and thy
daughters should eat: they shall eat up
thy flocks and thine herds: they shall
eat up thy vines and thy fig trees: they
shall impoverish thy fenced cities,
wherein thou trustedst, with the sword.
18 Nevertheless in those days, saith
the LORD, I will not make a full end with
you.
¶ 19 And it shall come to pass, when ye
shall say, Wherefore doeth the LORD
our God all these *things* unto us? then
shalt thou answer them, Like as ye
have forsaken me, and served strange
gods in your land, so shall ye serve
strangers in a land *that is* not yours.
20 Declare this in the house of Jacob,
and publish it in Judah, saying,
21 Hear now this, O foolish people,
and without understanding; which have
eyes, and see not; which have ears, and
hear not:
22 Fear ye not me? saith the LORD:
will ye not tremble at my presence,
which have placed the sand *for* the
bound of the sea by a perpetual decree,
that it cannot pass it: and though the

5:5 broken the yoke, and burst the bonds. This speaks of the Scriptures and of the people's known duty toward God—a duty they had not been taking seriously.
5:6 lion . . . wolf . . . leopard. The Chaldeans or Babylonians.
5:9 visit. Punish.

waves thereof toss themselves, yet can
they not prevail; though they roar, yet
can they not pass over it?
[23]But this people hath a revolting and
a rebellious heart; they are revolted and
gone.
[24]Neither say they in their heart, Let
us now fear the LORD our God, that
giveth rain, both the former and the
latter, in his season: he reserveth unto
us the appointed weeks of the harvest.
¶[25]Your iniquities have turned away
these *things,* and your sins have withholden good *things* from you.
[26]For among my people are found
wicked *men:* they lay wait, as he that
setteth snares; they set a trap, they
catch men.
[27]As a cage is full of birds, so *are* their
houses full of deceit: therefore they are
become great, and waxen rich.
[28]They are waxen fat, they shine:
yea, they overpass the deeds of the
wicked: they judge not the cause, the
cause of the fatherless, yet they prosper; and the right of the needy do they
not judge.
[29]Shall I not visit for these *things?*
saith the LORD: shall not my soul be
avenged on such a nation as this?
¶[30]A wonderful and horrible thing is
committed in the land;
[31]The prophets prophesy falsely, and
the priests bear rule by their means;
and my people love *to have it* so: and
what will ye do in the end thereof?

Sermons of Jeremiah (continued)

6 O ye children of Benjamin, gather yourselves to flee out of the
midst of Jerusalem, and blow the trumpet in Tekoa, and set up a sign of fire in
Beth-haccerem: for evil appeareth out
of the north, and great destruction.
[2]I have likened the daughter of Zion
to a comely and delicate *woman.*
[3]The shepherds with their flocks
shall come unto her; they shall pitch
their tents against her round about; they
shall feed every one in his place.
[4]Prepare ye war against her; arise,
and let us go up at noon. Woe unto us!
for the day goeth away, for the shadows
of the evening are stretched out.
[5]Arise, and let us go by night, and let
us destroy her palaces.
¶[6]For thus hath the LORD of hosts
said, Hew ye down trees, and cast a
mount against Jerusalem: this *is* the
city to be visited; she *is* wholly oppression in the midst of her.
[7]As a fountain casteth out her waters,
so she casteth out her wickedness: violence and spoil is heard in her; before
me continually *is* grief and wounds.
[8]Be thou instructed, O Jerusalem,
lest my soul depart from thee; lest
I make thee desolate, a land not inhabited.
¶[9]Thus saith the LORD of hosts, They
shall throughly glean the *remnant of
Israel as a vine: turn back thine hand as
a grapegatherer into the baskets.
[10]To whom shall I speak, and give
warning, that they may hear? behold,
their ear *is* *uncircumcised, and they
cannot hearken: behold, the word of the
LORD is unto them a reproach; they
have no delight in it.
[11]Therefore I am full of the fury of the
LORD; I am weary with holding in: I will
pour it out upon the children abroad,
and upon the assembly of young men
together: for even the husband with the
wife shall be taken, the aged with *him*
that is full of days.
[12]And their houses shall be turned
unto others, *with their* fields and wives

5:30 wonderful. Astounding.
6:3 The shepherds with their flocks. The Babylonian generals with their soldiers.
6:9 They shall throughly glean. Nebuchadnezzar would return again and again to Jerusalem until he had taken away all of its people.
6:10 their ear is uncircumcised. Their ears were not dedicated to the LORD—they did not even listen to His words.
6:12 their houses. See Deuteronomy 28:30.

together: for I will stretch out my hand
upon the inhabitants of the land, saith
the LORD.
13For from the least of them even
unto the greatest of them every one *is*
given to covetousness; and from the
prophet even unto the priest every one
dealeth falsely.
14They have healed also the hurt *of
the daughter* of my people slightly, saying, Peace, peace; when *there is* no
peace.
15Were they ashamed when they had
committed abomination? nay, they were
not at all ashamed, neither could they
blush: therefore they shall fall among
them that fall: at the time *that* I visit
them they shall be cast down, saith the
LORD.
16Thus saith the LORD, Stand ye in
the ways, and see, and ask for the old
paths, where *is* the good way, and walk
therein, and ye shall find rest for your
souls. But they said, We will not walk
therein.
17Also I set watchmen over you,
saying, Hearken to the sound of the
trumpet. But they said, We will not
hearken.
¶18Therefore hear, ye nations, and
know, O congregation, what *is* among
them.
19Hear, O earth: behold, I will bring
evil upon this people, *even* the fruit of
their thoughts, because they have not
hearkened unto my words, nor to my
law, but rejected it.
20To what purpose cometh there to
me incense from Sheba, and the sweet
cane from a far country? your burnt-
offerings *are* not acceptable, nor your
sacrifices sweet unto me.
21Therefore thus saith the LORD,
Behold, I will lay stumblingblocks before this people, and the fathers and the
sons together shall fall upon them; the
neighbour and his friend shall perish.
22Thus saith the LORD, Behold, a
people cometh from the north country,
and a great nation shall be raised from
the sides of the earth.
23They shall lay hold on bow and
spear; they *are* cruel, and have no
*mercy; their voice roareth like the sea;
and they ride upon horses, set in array
as men for war against thee, O daughter of Zion.
24We have heard the fame thereof:
our hands wax feeble: anguish hath
taken hold of us, *and* pain, as of a
woman in travail.
25Go not forth into the field, nor walk
by the way; for the sword of the enemy
and fear *is* on every side.
¶26O daughter of my people, gird *thee*
with sackcloth, and wallow thyself in
ashes: make thee *mourning, *as for*
an only son, most bitter lamentation:
for the spoiler shall suddenly come
upon us.
27I have set thee *for* a tower *and* a
fortress among my people, that thou
mayest know and try their way.
28They *are* all grievous revolters,
walking with slanders: *they are* brass
and iron; they *are* all corrupters.
29The bellows are burned, the lead is
consumed of the fire; the founder
melteth in vain: for the wicked are not
plucked away.
30Reprobate *silver shall *men* call
them, because the LORD hath rejected
them.

Sermons of Jeremiah (continued)
3) Promise of security if Israel repents

7 The word that came to Jeremiah
from the LORD, saying,
2Stand in the gate of the LORD'S
house, and proclaim there this word,

6:20 your burnt-offerings are not acceptable. The LORD would not accept offerings that were given by disobedient, unclean people.
6:22 a great nation. The people of Babylon, the Chaldean nation.
6:26 sackcloth . . . ashes. Signs of mourning.
6:30 Reprobate silver. Old worn-out, rejected silver.

7:2 Another Sermon
Jeremiah stood within the gate of the temple and preached the sermon found in 7:1–10:25. His purpose in preaching was to tell Israel that the LORD said, "Amend your ways and your doings, and I will cause you to dwell in this place" (vs. 3). He exposed the folly of trusting in a mere form of godliness while denying the power thereof (vs. 4; see also 2 Tim. 3:5). The children of Israel had gone so far from God that they were offering human sacrifices in the Valley of Hinnom (vs. 31). Notwithstanding the awfulness of her sin, God, through the prophet, was still calling upon Judah to repent.

and say, Hear the word of the LORD, all
ye of *Judah, that enter in at these gates
to worship the LORD.
3Thus saith the LORD of hosts, the
God of Israel, Amend your ways and
your doings, and I will cause you to
dwell in this place.
4*Trust ye not in lying words, saying,
The temple of the LORD, The temple of
the LORD, The temple of the LORD, *are*
these.
5For if ye throughly amend your ways
and your doings; if ye throughly execute judgment between a man and his
neighbour;
6*If* ye oppress not the stranger, the
fatherless, and the widow, and shed not
innocent blood in this place, neither
walk after other gods to your hurt:
7Then will I cause you to dwell in this
place, in the land that I gave to your
fathers, for ever and ever.
¶8Behold, ye trust in lying words,
that cannot profit.
9Will ye steal, murder, and commit
adultery, and swear falsely, and burn
*incense unto Baal, and walk after
other gods whom ye know not;
10And come and stand before me in
this house, which is called by my name,
and say, We are delivered to do all these
abominations?
11Is this house, which is called by my
name, become a den of robbers in your
eyes? Behold, even I have seen *it,* saith
the LORD.
12But go ye now unto my place which
was in *Shiloh, where I set my name at
the first, and see what I did to it for the
wickedness of my people Israel.
13And now, because ye have done all
these works, saith the LORD, and I
spake unto you, rising up early and
speaking, but ye heard not; and I called
you, but ye answered not;
14Therefore will I do unto *this* house,
which is called by my name, wherein ye
trust, and unto the place which I gave
to you and to your fathers, as I have
done to Shiloh.
15And I will cast you out of my sight,
as I have cast out all your brethren, *even*
the whole seed of Ephraim.
16Therefore pray not thou for this
people, neither lift up cry nor *prayer
for them, neither make intercession to
me: for I will not hear thee.
¶17Seest thou not what they do in the
cities of Judah and in the streets of Jerusalem?
18The children gather wood, and the
fathers kindle the fire, and the women
knead *their* dough, to make cakes to the
queen of heaven, and to pour out drink-

7:11 a den of robbers. See Mark 11:17 (and its note, "Misuse of the Temple") where the Lord Jesus referred to this verse and to Isaiah 56:7.

7:12 my place which was in Shiloh. The tabernacle of the LORD was first set up at Shiloh (see Josh. 18:1 and its note, "Shiloh"). Because of the wickedness of the people, God allowed the ark of the covenant to be captured, and He Himself departed from Shiloh (1 Sam. 4:11; Ps. 78:60).

7:16 pray not thou for this people. It is very seldom that God tells His servants not to pray. In this case He told Jeremiah that not even prayer could lift the judgment that was pronounced upon Judah. It reminds us of 1 John 5:16.

7:18 the queen of heaven. The goddess *Ashtoreth, or Astarte. Ashtaroth is the plural form.

offerings unto other gods, that they
may provoke me to anger.
[19]Do they provoke me to anger? saith
the LORD: *do they* not *provoke* themselves to the confusion of their own
faces?
[20]Therefore thus saith the Lord GOD;
Behold, mine anger and my fury shall
be poured out upon this place, upon
man, and upon beast, and upon the trees
of the field, and upon the fruit of the
ground; and it shall burn, and shall not
be quenched.
¶[21]Thus saith the LORD of hosts, the
God of Israel; Put your burnt-offerings
unto your sacrifices, and eat flesh.
[22]For I spake not unto your fathers,
nor commanded them in the day that I
brought them out of the land of Egypt,
concerning burnt-offerings or sacrifices:
[23]But this thing commanded I them,
saying, Obey my voice, and I will be
your God, and ye shall be my people:
and walk ye in all the ways that I have
commanded you, that it may be well
unto you.
[24]But they hearkened not, nor inclined their ear, but walked in the counsels *and* in the imagination of their evil
heart, and went backward, and not forward.
[25]Since the day that your fathers
came forth out of the land of Egypt unto
this day I have even sent unto you all
my servants the prophets, daily rising
up early and sending *them:*
[26]Yet they hearkened not unto me,
nor inclined their ear, but *hardened
their neck: they did worse than their
fathers.
[27]Therefore thou shalt speak all
these words unto them; but they will
not hearken to thee: thou shalt also call
unto them; but they will not answer
thee.
[28]But thou shalt say unto them, This
is a nation that obeyeth not the voice of
the LORD their God, nor receiveth correction: truth is perished, and is cut off
from their mouth.
¶[29]Cut off thine hair, *O *Jerusalem,*
and cast *it* away, and take up a lamentation on high places; for the LORD hath
rejected and forsaken the generation of
his wrath.
[30]For the children of Judah have done
evil in my sight, saith the LORD: they
have set their abominations in the
house which is called by my name, to
pollute it.
[31]And they have built the high places
of *Tophet, which *is* in the valley of the
son of Hinnom, to burn their sons and
their daughters in the fire; which I commanded *them* not, neither came it into
my heart.
¶[32]Therefore, behold, the days come,
saith the LORD, that it shall no more be
called Tophet, nor the valley of the son
of Hinnom, but the valley of slaughter:
for they shall bury in Tophet, till there
be no place.
[33]And the carcases of this people
shall be meat for the fowls of the heav-
en, and for the beasts of the earth; and
none shall fray *them* away.
[34]Then will I cause to cease from the

7:21 eat flesh. The worshipper had not been allowed to eat the meat of the burnt-offering (Lev. 1), but it did not make any difference to God now, for He did not accept the offerings.

7:22 I spake not unto your fathers, nor commanded. Not until the children of Israel had broken the Ten Commandments (Exod. 20) did God give them the laws concerning burnt-offerings and sacrifices.

7:26 hardened their neck. It was as if their necks were stiffened so they could not or would not turn their heads to listen.

7:29 Cut off thine hair. This was a sign of mourning.

7:31 to burn their sons and their daughters. See verse 2 note, "Another Sermon."

7:33 And the carcases. This was partly fulfilled in the various destructions of Jerusalem, but it also looks forward to Revelation 19:17-21.

7:33 fray. Frighten.

cities of Judah, and from the streets of Jerusalem, the voice of mirth, and the voice of gladness, the voice of *the bridegroom, and the voice of the bride: for the land shall be desolate.

Sermons of Jeremiah (continued)

8 At that time, saith the LORD, they shall bring out the bones of the kings of Judah, and the bones of his princes, and the bones of the priests, and the bones of the prophets, and the bones of the inhabitants of Jerusalem, out of their graves:

2And they shall spread them before the sun, and the moon, and all the host of heaven, whom they have loved, and whom they have served, and after whom they have walked, and whom they have sought, and whom they have worshipped: they shall not be gathered, nor be buried; they shall be for *dung upon the face of the earth.

3And *death shall be chosen rather than life by all the residue of them that remain of this evil family, which remain in all the places whither I have driven them, saith the LORD of hosts.

¶4Moreover thou shalt say unto them, Thus saith the LORD; Shall they fall, and not arise? shall he turn away, and not return?

5Why *then* is this people of Jerusalem slidden back by a perpetual backsliding? they hold fast deceit, they refuse to return.

6I hearkened and heard, *but* they spake not aright: no man *repented him of his wickedness, saying, What have I done? every one turned to his course, as the horse rusheth into the battle.

7Yea, the stork in the heaven knoweth her appointed times; and the turtle and the crane and the swallow observe the time of their coming; but my people know not the judgment of the LORD.

8How do ye say, We *are* wise, and the *law of the LORD *is* with us? Lo, certainly in vain made he *it;* the pen of the *scribes *is* in vain.

9The wise *men* are ashamed, they are dismayed and taken: lo, they have rejected the word of the LORD; and what wisdom *is* in them?

10Therefore will I give their wives unto others, *and* their fields to them that shall inherit *them:* for every one from the least even unto the greatest is given to covetousness, from the *prophet even unto the priest every one dealeth falsely.

11For they have healed the hurt of the daughter of my people slightly, saying, Peace, peace; when *there is* no peace.

12Were they ashamed when they had committed *abomination? nay, they were not at all ashamed, neither could they blush: therefore shall they fall among them that fall: in the time of their visitation they shall be cast down, saith the LORD.

¶13I will surely consume them, saith the LORD: *there shall be* no grapes on the vine, nor figs on the fig tree, and the leaf shall fade; and *the things that* I have given them shall pass away from them.

14Why do we sit still? assemble yourselves, and let us enter into the defenced cities, and let us be silent there: for the LORD our *God hath put us to silence, and given us water of gall to drink, because we have sinned against the LORD.

15We looked for peace, but no good

8:1 At that time. When the Chaldeans took away everything of value from Jerusalem, they probably also robbed the tombs of their treasures.

8:2 dung. Refuse.

8:7 turtle. Turtledove.

8:12 visitation. Punishment.

8:13 fig tree. Israel in the Scriptures is often represented as a vine, a fig tree, or an olive tree.

8:14 water of gall. Water of bitterness.

came; and for a time of health, and behold trouble!
16The snorting of his horses was
heard from Dan: the whole land trembled at the sound of the neighing of his
strong ones; for they are come, and
have devoured the land, and all that is
in it; the city, and those that dwell
therein.
17For, behold, I will send serpents,
cockatrices, among you, which *will* not
be charmed, and they shall bite you,
saith the LORD.
¶ 18*When* I would comfort myself
against sorrow, my heart *is* faint in me.
19Behold the voice of the cry of the
daughter of my people because of them
that dwell in a far country: *Is* not the
LORD in Zion? *is* not her king in her?
Why have they provoked me to anger
with their graven images, *and* with
strange vanities?
20The harvest is past, the summer is
ended, and we are not saved.
21For the hurt of the daughter of my
people am I hurt; I am black; astonishment hath taken hold on me.
22*Is there* no balm in *Gilead; *is there*
no physician there? why then is not the
health of the daughter of my people
recovered?

8:22 The Balm of Gilead
This was the medicine brought from Gilead, which was famous for its balsam. Jeremiah speaks of the sin of Israel as if it were a sickness–a sickness that could not be cured by medicines or doctors. The people would not turn to the only One who could heal them.

Sermons of Jeremiah (continued)

9 Oh that my head were waters, and
mine eyes a fountain of tears, that
I might weep day and night for the slain
of the daughter of my people!
2Oh that I had in the wilderness a
lodging place of wayfaring men; that I
might leave my people, and go from
them! for they *be* all adulterers, an assembly of treacherous men.

9:2 A Lodging Place
In the East, a lodging place was a sort of free inn for travelers who had to provide their own food and bedding. They were filthy places, but the prophet would rather stay in a place like that than in the sinful city of Jerusalem.

3And they bend their tongues *like*
their bow *for* lies: but they are not valiant for the truth upon the earth; for
they proceed from evil to evil, and they
know not me, saith the LORD.
4Take ye heed every one of his neighbour, and trust ye not in any brother: for
every brother will utterly supplant, and
every neighbour will walk with slanders.
5And they will deceive every one his
neighbour, and will not speak the truth:
they have taught their tongue to speak
lies, *and* weary themselves to commit
iniquity.
6Thine habitation *is* in the midst of
deceit; through deceit they refuse to
know me, saith the LORD.
7Therefore thus saith the LORD of
hosts, Behold, I will melt them, and try
them; for how shall I do for the daughter of my people?
8Their tongue *is as* an arrow shot out;
it speaketh deceit: *one* speaketh peaceably to his neighbour with his mouth,
but in heart he layeth his wait.
¶9Shall I not visit them for these
things? saith the LORD: shall not my
soul be avenged on such a nation as
this?
10For the mountains will I take up a
weeping and wailing, and for the habitations of the wilderness a lamentation,
because they are burned up, so that

8:19 strange vanities. Foreign gods.
9:7 melt them, and try them. Like metal that is often melted and tested in order to be purified.
9:10 habitations. Dwelling places.

none can pass through *them;* neither
can *men* hear the voice of the cattle;
both the fowl of the heavens and the
beast are fled; they are gone.
11 And I will make Jerusalem heaps,
and a den of dragons; and I will make
the cities of Judah desolate, without an
inhabitant.
¶12 Who *is* the wise man, that may understand this? and *who is he* to whom
the mouth of the LORD hath spoken,
that he may declare it, for what the land
perisheth *and* is burned up like a wilderness, that none passeth through?
13 And the LORD saith, Because they
have forsaken my law which I set before them, and have not obeyed my
voice, neither walked therein;
14 But have walked after the imagination of their own heart, and after
Baalim, which their fathers taught
them:
15 Therefore thus saith the LORD of
hosts, the God of *Israel; Behold, I will
feed them, *even* this people, with
*wormwood, and give them water of gall
to drink.
16 I will *scatter them also among the
heathen, whom neither they nor their
fathers have known: and I will send a
sword after them, till I have consumed
them.
¶17 Thus saith the LORD of hosts,
Consider ye, and call for the mourning
women, that they may come; and send
for cunning *women,* that they may
come:
18 And let them make haste, and take
up a wailing for us, that our eyes may
run down with tears, and our eyelids
gush out with waters.
19 For a voice of wailing is heard out
of *Zion, How are we spoiled! we are
greatly confounded, because we have
forsaken the land, because our dwellings have cast *us* out.
20 Yet hear the word of the LORD, O ye
women, and let your ear receive the
word of his mouth, and teach your
daughters wailing, and every one her
neighbour lamentation.
21 For death is come up into our windows, *and* is entered into our palaces,
to cut off the children from without, *and*
the young men from the streets.
22 Speak, Thus saith the LORD, Even
the carcases of men shall fall as dung
upon the open field, and as the handful
after the harvestman, and none shall
gather *them.*
¶23 Thus saith the LORD, Let not the
wise *man* glory in his wisdom, neither
let the mighty *man* glory in his might,
let not the rich *man* glory in his riches:
24 But let him that glorieth glory in
this, that he understandeth and
knoweth me, that I *am* the LORD which
exercise lovingkindness, judgment, and
righteousness, in the earth: for in these
things I delight, saith the LORD.
¶25 Behold, the days come, saith the
LORD, that I will punish all *them which*
are circumcised with the uncircumcised;
26 *Egypt, and Judah, and *Edom, and
the children of Ammon, and *Moab, and
all *that are* in the utmost corners, that
dwell in the wilderness: for all *these*
nations *are* uncircumcised, and all the
house of Israel *are* uncircumcised in the
heart.

Sermons of Jeremiah (continued)

10 Hear ye the word which the
LORD speaketh unto you,
O house of Israel:
2 Thus saith the LORD, Learn not the
way of the heathen, and be not dismayed at the signs of heaven; for the
heathen are dismayed at them.
3 For the customs of the people *are*
vain: for *one* cutteth a tree out of the

10:2 signs of heaven. Those who did not know God and who did not trust in Him were afraid of thunder and lightning, eclipses and comets, or any unusual thing that they saw in the sky.

10:3 customs. Images. Verses 3-5 speak of the making of the images.

forest, the work of the hands of the
workman, with the axe.
4They deck it with silver and with
gold; they fasten it with nails and with
hammers, that it move not.
5They *are* upright as the palm tree,
but speak not: they must needs be
borne, because they cannot go. *Be not
afraid of them; for they cannot do evil,
neither also *is it* in them to do good.
6Forasmuch as *there is* none like unto
thee, O LORD; thou *art* great, and thy
name *is* great in might.
7Who would not *fear thee, O King
of nations? for to thee doth it appertain:
forasmuch as among all the wise *men*
of the nations, and in all their kingdoms,
there is none like unto thee.
8But they are altogether brutish and
foolish: the stock *is* a *doctrine of vanities.
9Silver spread into plates is brought
from *Tarshish, and gold from Uphaz,
the work of the workman, and of the
hands of the founder: *blue and purple
is their clothing: they *are* all the work
of cunning *men.*
10But the LORD *is* the true God, he *is*
the living God, and an everlasting king:
at his wrath the earth shall tremble, and
the nations shall not be able to abide his
indignation.
11Thus shall ye say unto them, The
gods that have not made the heavens
and the earth, *even* they shall perish
from the earth, and from under these
heavens.
12He hath made the earth by his power, he hath established the *world by his
wisdom, and hath stretched out the
heavens by his discretion.
13When he uttereth his voice, *there is*
a multitude of waters in the heavens,
and he causeth the vapours to ascend
from the ends of the earth; he maketh
lightnings with rain, and bringeth forth
the wind out of his treasures.
14Every man is brutish in *his* knowledge: every founder is confounded by
the *graven image: for his molten image *is* *falsehood, and *there is* no breath
in them.
15They *are* *vanity, *and* the work of
errors: in the time of their visitation
they shall perish.
16The portion of *Jacob *is* not like
them: for he *is* the former of all *things;*
and Israel *is* the rod of his inheritance:
The LORD of hosts *is* his name.
¶17Gather up thy wares out of the
land, O inhabitant of the fortress.
18For thus saith the LORD, Behold, I
will sling out the inhabitants of the land
at this once, and will distress them, that
they may find *it so.*
¶19Woe is me for my hurt! my wound
is grievous: but I said, Truly this *is* a
grief, and I must bear it.
20My *tabernacle is spoiled, and all
my cords are broken: my children are
gone forth of me, and they *are* not: *there*
is none to stretch forth my tent any
more, and to set up my curtains.
21For the pastors are become brutish,
and have not sought the LORD: therefore they shall not prosper, and all their
flocks shall be scattered.
22Behold, the noise of the bruit is
come, and a great commotion out of the
north country, to make the cities of Judah desolate, *and* a den of dragons.
¶23O LORD, I know that the way of

10:8 the stock is a doctrine of vanities. The teachings of idolatry are utterly false and worthless.

10:11 The gods. This verse was written in Chaldee, the language of the Babylonians, instead of in Hebrew. It told the Jewish exiles what to say in front of their captors.

10:16 former. The Maker, the One who formed all things.

10:21 pastors. This word means *shepherds*, but it speaks of the leaders of the Jewish people, King Jehoiakim, and the princes at this time.

10:22 bruit. Tidings or report.

10:23 the way of man is not in himself. Saint Augustine said: "Thou hast made us for Thyself, and the heart of man is restless until it finds its rest in Thee." The Bible shows

man *is* not in himself: *it is* not in man
that walketh to direct his steps.
24 O LORD, correct me, but with
*judgment; not in thine anger, lest thou
bring me to nothing.
25 Pour out thy fury upon the heathen
that know thee not, and upon the families that call not on thy name: for they
have eaten up Jacob, and devoured him,
and consumed him, and have made his
habitation desolate.

Sermons of Jeremiah (continued)
*4) Israel's broken *covenant*

11 The word that came to Jeremiah from the LORD, saying,
2 Hear ye the words of this covenant,
and speak unto the men of Judah, and
to the inhabitants of Jerusalem;

11:2 Jeremiah's Appeal
Here is another of Jeremiah's great appeals, ending at 12:17. In this message the prophet not only recounted the sins of Judah, but he brought the more serious charge that Judah had violated the covenant of God. "The house of Israel and the house of Judah have broken my covenant which I made with their fathers" (11:10). This message brought the wrath of the unbelievers of Israel upon the prophet. They wanted to kill him (11:21). Jeremiah declared that Judah would be punished severely because of their sin, but he added that God, in His faithfulness, would preserve Israel and finally return Israel to their heritage (12:15). The complete fulfillment of this great prophecy will be realized during the millennial reign of the Lord Jesus Christ.

3 And say thou unto them, Thus saith
the LORD God of Israel; Cursed *be* the
man that obeyeth not the words of this
covenant,
4 Which I commanded your fathers in
the day *that* I brought them forth out of
the land of Egypt, from the iron furnace,
saying, Obey my voice, and do them,
according to all which I command you:
so shall ye be my people, and I will be
your God:
5 That I may perform the oath which
I have sworn unto your fathers, to give
them a land *flowing with milk and honey, as *it is* this day. Then answered I, and
said, So be it, O LORD.
6 Then the LORD said unto me, Proclaim all these words in the cities of
Judah, and in the streets of Jerusalem,
saying, Hear ye the words of this covenant, and do them.
7 For I earnestly protested unto your
fathers in the day *that* I brought them
up out of the land of Egypt, *even* unto
this day, rising early and protesting,
saying, Obey my voice.
8 Yet they obeyed not, nor inclined
their ear, but walked every one in the
imagination of their evil heart: therefore I will bring upon them all the words
of this covenant, which I commanded
them to do; but they did *them* not.
9 And the LORD said unto me, A conspiracy is found among the men of Judah, and among the inhabitants of
Jerusalem.
10 They are turned back to the iniquities of their forefathers, which refused
to hear my words; and they went after
other gods to serve them: the house of
Israel and the house of Judah have broken my covenant which I made with
their fathers.
¶11 Therefore thus saith the LORD,
Behold, I will bring evil upon them,
which they shall not be able to escape;
and though they shall cry unto me, I will
not hearken unto them.

---

that man cannot find the way alone. Christ is the Way (John 14:6) who has promised to give the light of life to all who follow Him (John 8:12).

10:24 correct me. The prayer in verses 24 and 25 has been answered. The Babylonians have been destroyed, and though Israel is still being corrected, the nation has been saved from destruction.

11:2 this covenant. This was the Book of the Law that had been found during the reign of King Josiah, in the rubbish of the neglected temple (2 Kings 22:8–23:25).

11:5 So be it. This is a translation of the Hebrew word "Amen."

[12]Then shall the cities of Judah and
inhabitants of Jerusalem go, and cry
unto the gods unto whom they offer
incense: but they shall not save them
at all in the time of their trouble.
[13]For *according to* the number of thy
cities were thy gods, O Judah; and *according to* the number of the streets of
Jerusalem have ye set up altars to *that*
shameful thing, *even* altars to burn incense unto *Baal.
[14]Therefore pray not thou for this
people, neither lift up a cry or prayer
for them: for I will not hear *them* in the
time that they cry unto me for their
trouble.
[15]What hath my *beloved to do in
mine house, *seeing* she hath wrought
lewdness with many, and the holy flesh
is passed from thee? when thou doest
evil, then thou rejoicest.
[16]The LORD called thy name, A green
olive tree, fair, *and* of goodly fruit: with
the noise of a great tumult he hath kindled *fire upon it, and the branches of
it are broken.
[17]For the LORD of hosts, that planted
thee, hath pronounced evil against thee,
for the evil of the house of Israel and of
the house of Judah, which they have
done against themselves to provoke me
to anger in *offering incense unto Baal.
¶[18]And the LORD hath given me
knowledge *of it,* and I know *it:* then thou
shewedst me their doings.
[19]But I *was* like a lamb *or* an ox *that*
is brought to the slaughter; and I knew
not that they had devised devices
against me, *saying,* Let us destroy the
tree with the fruit thereof, and let us cut
him off from the land of the living, that
his name may be no more remembered.
[20]But, O LORD of hosts, that judgest
righteously, that triest the reins and the
heart, let me see thy vengeance on
them: for unto thee have I revealed my
cause.
[21]Therefore thus saith the LORD of
the men of Anathoth, that seek thy life,
saying, Prophesy not in the name of the
LORD, that thou die not by our hand:
[22]Therefore thus saith the LORD of
hosts, Behold, I will punish them: the
young men shall die by the sword; their
sons and their daughters shall die by
famine:
[23]And there shall be no remnant of
them: for I will bring evil upon the men
of Anathoth, *even* the year of their visitation.

Sermons of Jeremiah (continued)

12 Righteous *art* thou, O LORD,
when I plead with thee: yet let
me talk with thee of *thy* judgments:
Wherefore doth the way of the wicked
prosper? *wherefore* are all they happy
that deal very treacherously?
[2]Thou hast planted them, yea, they
have taken root: they grow, yea, they
bring forth fruit: thou *art* near in their
mouth, and far from their reins.
[3]But thou, O LORD, knowest me:
thou hast seen me, and tried mine heart
toward thee: pull them out like sheep
for the slaughter, and prepare them for
the day of slaughter.
[4]How long shall the land mourn, and
the herbs of every field wither, for the
wickedness of them that dwell therein?

11:15 the holy flesh. The meat of sacrifices would not be acceptable to God when the worshippers were wicked.
11:16 green olive tree. A symbol of Israel (compare Jer. 8:13 note).
11:19 the tree with the fruit. The tree here stood for the prophet; the fruit, for his message.
11:21 Anathoth. This was Jeremiah's hometown. It belonged to the priests, but because he prophesied to them in the name of the LORD, the priests joined with his family in a plot to kill him. Jeremiah is a *type of the Lord Jesus Christ, in that those of his own town tried to put him to death (compare Luke 4:16-29).
12:2 near . . . and far. The wicked priests spoke the words of the LORD, but their hearts and actions were far from Him.

12:4 A False Belief
The people did not want to believe Jeremiah when he prophesied their destruction. They believed their last end or their final outcome would be fine and prosperous, and they wanted to kill Jeremiah so that he might not see their prosperity or share in it.

the beasts are consumed, and the
*birds; because they said, He shall not
see our last end.
¶ 5 If thou hast run with the footmen,
and they have wearied thee, then how
canst thou contend with horses? and
if in the land of *peace, *wherein* thou
trustedst, *they wearied thee,* then how
wilt thou do in the swelling of Jordan?
6 For even thy brethren, and the
house of thy father, even they have
dealt treacherously with thee; yea, they
have called a multitude after thee: believe them not, though they speak fair
words unto thee.
¶ 7 I have forsaken mine house, I have
left mine heritage; I have given the
dearly beloved of my soul into the hand
of her enemies.
8 Mine heritage is unto me as a lion
in the forest; it crieth out against me:
therefore have I hated it.
9 Mine heritage *is* unto me *as* a speckled bird, the birds round about *are*
against her; come ye, assemble all the
beasts of the field, come to devour.
10 Many pastors have destroyed my
*vineyard, they have trodden my
portion under foot, they have made
my pleasant portion a desolate wilderness.
11 They have made it desolate, *and*
being desolate it mourneth unto me; the
whole land is made desolate, because
no man layeth *it* to heart.
12 The spoilers are come upon all high
places through the wilderness: for the
sword of the LORD shall devour from
the *one* end of the land even to the *other*
end of the land: no flesh shall have
peace.
13 They have sown wheat, but shall
reap thorns: they have put themselves
to pain, *but* shall not profit: and they
shall be ashamed of your revenues because of the fierce anger of the LORD.
¶ 14 Thus saith the LORD against all
mine evil neighbours, that touch the
inheritance which I have caused my
people Israel to inherit; Behold, I will
pluck them out of their land, and pluck
out the house of Judah from among
them.
15 And it shall come to pass, after that
I have plucked them out I will return,
and have compassion on them, and will
bring them again, every man to his heritage, and every man to his land.
16 And it shall come to pass, if they
will diligently learn the ways of my
people, to swear by my name, The
LORD liveth; as they taught my people
to swear by Baal; then shall they be
built in the midst of my people.
17 But if they will not obey, I will utterly pluck up and destroy that nation,
saith the LORD.

12:5 the footmen . . . with horses. The footmen were the men of Anathoth; the horses, the men of Jerusalem. The "land of peace" was Jeremiah's own city, the "swelling of Jordan" spoke of the anger he would have to face in Jerusalem. God was warning him of the terrible things that he would still have to endure.

12:7 mine house. Notice the wonderful love that the LORD had for His wandering children. Over and over again He uses the words "Me," "Mine," and "My."

12:8 hated it. God's heritage had become "odious" because of the evil described in verses 1-17.

12:10 pastors. Heathen princes are meant in this case.

12:12 the sword of the LORD. Here the LORD used the Chaldean army to accomplish His purpose.

12:14 evil neighbours. Egypt, Edom, Philistia, Ammon, Moab, and Syria. These nations will be restored and have spiritual blessing at some future time (vs. 15) on the conditions of verses 16 and 17.

III. Object Lessons (13:1—19:15)
*1) The *linen girdle*

13 Thus saith the LORD unto me,
Go and get thee a linen girdle,
and put it upon thy loins, and put it not
in water.

13:1 A Series of Object Lessons
From chapter 13 through chapter 19, Jeremiah presented a series of four signs by which he called the attention of the children of Israel to their wickedness and to the judgments that God had pronounced against them. The linen girdle was used as an illustration to show that Israel, whom God had worn as an ornament, would be carried captive to Babylon (vs. 4), where they would have to stay in the valley of the Euphrates. As the girdle was marred by the Euphrates, so God would mar the pride of Judah. The chapter teaches most clearly that "the wages of sin is death" (Rom. 6:23). (See also 14:1; 16:2; and 18:3 notes.)

2 So I got a girdle according to the
word of the LORD, and put *it* on my
loins.
3 And the word of the LORD came unto
me the second time, saying,
4 Take the girdle that thou hast got,
which *is* upon thy loins, and arise, go to
Euphrates, and hide it there in a hole
of the rock.
5 So I went, and hid it by Euphrates,
as the LORD commanded me.
6 And it came to pass after many days,
that the LORD said unto me, Arise, go
to Euphrates, and take the girdle from
thence, which I commanded thee to
hide there.
7 Then I went to Euphrates, and
digged, and took the girdle from the
place where I had hid it: and, behold, the
girdle was marred, it was profitable for
nothing.
8 Then the word of the LORD came
unto me, saying,
9 Thus saith the LORD, After this manner will I mar the pride of *Judah, and
the great pride of *Jerusalem.
10 This evil people, which refuse to
hear my words, which walk in the imagination of their heart, and walk after
other gods, to serve them, and to worship them, shall even be as this girdle,
which is good for nothing.
11 For as the girdle cleaveth to the
loins of a man, so have I caused to
cleave unto me the whole house of Israel and the whole house of Judah, saith
the LORD; that they might be unto me
for a people, and for a name, and for a
praise, and for a glory: but they would
not hear.
¶ 12 Therefore thou shalt speak unto
them this word; Thus saith the LORD
God of Israel, Every bottle shall be
filled with *wine: and they shall say
unto thee, Do we not certainly know
that every bottle shall be filled with
wine?
13 Then shalt thou say unto them,
Thus saith the LORD, Behold, I will fill
all the inhabitants of this land, even the
kings that sit upon *David's throne, and
the priests, and the prophets, and all the
inhabitants of Jerusalem, with drunkenness.
14 And I will dash them one against
another, even the fathers and the sons
together, saith the LORD: I will not pity,
nor spare, nor have *mercy, but destroy
them.
¶ 15 Hear ye, and give ear; be not
proud: for the LORD hath spoken.
16 Give glory to the LORD your God,
before he cause darkness, and before
your feet stumble upon the dark mountains, and, while ye look for light, he
turn it into the shadow of death, *and*
make *it* gross darkness.
17 But if ye will not hear it, my soul
shall weep in secret places for *your*

13:12 bottle shall be filled with wine. God is comparing Israel here to a wine jar. As a girdle adorns, wine refreshes. Israel was to adorn God to be His refreshment, but she refused to bring glory to His name, and He was forced to bring her to destruction (vs. 14).

pride; and mine eye shall weep sore,
and run down with tears, because the
LORD'S flock is carried away captive.
18 Say unto the king and to the queen,
Humble yourselves, sit down: for your
principalities shall come down, *even* the
crown of your glory.
19 The cities of the south shall be shut
up, and none shall open *them:* Judah
shall be carried away captive all of it, it
shall be wholly carried away captive.
20 Lift up your eyes, and behold them
that come from the north: where *is* the
flock *that* was given thee, thy beautiful
flock?
21 What wilt thou say when he shall
punish thee? for thou hast taught them
to be captains, *and* as chief over thee:
shall not sorrows take thee, as a woman in travail?
¶22 And if thou say in thine heart,
Wherefore come these things upon me?
For the greatness of thine iniquity are
thy skirts discovered, *and* thy heels
made bare.
23 Can the Ethiopian change his skin,
or the leopard his spots? *then* may ye
also do good, that are accustomed to do
evil.
24 Therefore will I *scatter them as
the stubble that passeth away by the
wind of the wilderness.
25 This *is* thy lot, the portion of thy
measures from me, saith the LORD;
because thou hast forgotten me, and
trusted in *falsehood.
26 Therefore will I discover thy skirts
upon thy face, that thy shame may appear.
27 I have seen thine adulteries, and thy
neighings, the lewdness of thy whoredom, *and* thine abominations on the hills
in the fields. Woe unto thee, O Jerusalem! wilt thou not be made *clean?
when *shall it* once *be?*

Object lessons (continued)
2) The drought

14 The word of the LORD that
came to Jeremiah concerning
the dearth.

14:1-4 The Second Object Lesson
God sent a great drought to the land at the time of Jeremiah's ministry. The prophet told Israel that the drought was a sign of the judgment that God would bring upon them to consume the false prophets (vs. 14) and to bring about the removal of Israel to all the kingdoms of the earth (15:4). The most striking statement in this sermon is that in 15:6, in which God says that He is "weary with repenting." He would no longer exercise patience toward Israel, although He promised that He would protect the faithful remnant within the nation, that little group that was true to Him (15:11).

2 Judah mourneth, and the gates
thereof languish; they are black unto
the ground; and the cry of Jerusalem is
gone up.
3 And their nobles have sent their little ones to the waters: they came to the
pits, *and* found no water; they returned
with their vessels empty; they were
ashamed and confounded, and covered
their heads.
4 Because the ground is chapt, for
there was no rain in the earth, the plowmen were ashamed, they covered their
heads.
5 Yea, the hind also calved in the field,
and forsook *it,* because there was no
grass.

13:18 the king and to the queen. The king was Jehoiachin; the queen, Nehushta, his mother.
13:21 he. King Nebuchadnezzar of Babylon.
13:22 thy heels made bare. Nakedness and bare feet were signs of slavery.
13:27 O Jerusalem! wilt thou not be made clean? Compare the lament of the Lord Jesus Christ (Matt. 23:37).
14:3 little ones. Servants.
14:3 pits. Cisterns.
14:4 chapt. Cracked, through heat and drought.

6And the wild asses did stand in the
high places, they snuffed up the wind
like dragons; their eyes did fail, because
there was no grass.
¶7O LORD, though our iniquities testify against us, do thou *it* for thy name's
sake: for our backslidings are many; we
have sinned against thee.
8O the *hope of Israel, the saviour
thereof in time of trouble, why
shouldest thou be as a stranger in the
land, and as a wayfaring man *that*
turneth aside to tarry for a night?
9Why shouldest thou be as a man
astonied, as a mighty man *that* cannot
save? yet thou, O LORD, *art* in the midst
of us, and we are called by thy name;
leave us not.
¶10Thus saith the LORD unto this
people, Thus have they loved to wander, they have not refrained their feet,
therefore the LORD doth not accept
them; he will now remember their iniquity, and visit their sins.
11Then said the LORD unto me, Pray
not for this people for *their* good.
12When they fast, I will not hear their
cry; and when they offer burnt-offering
and an *oblation, I will not accept them:
but I will consume them by the sword,
and by the famine, and by the pestilence.
¶13Then said I, Ah, Lord GOD! behold, the *prophets say unto them, Ye
shall not see the sword, neither shall ye
have famine; but I will give you assured
peace in this place.
14Then the LORD said unto me, The
prophets prophesy lies in my name: I
sent them not, neither have I commanded them, neither spake unto
them: they prophesy unto you a false
vision and divination, and a thing of
nought, and the deceit of their heart.
15Therefore thus saith the LORD concerning the prophets that prophesy in
my name, and I sent them not, yet they
say, Sword and famine shall not be in
this land; By sword and famine shall
those prophets be consumed.
16And the people to whom they
prophesy shall be cast out in the streets
of Jerusalem because of the famine
and the sword; and they shall have
none to bury them, them, their wives,
nor their sons, nor their daughters:
for I will pour their wickedness upon
them.
¶17Therefore thou shalt say this word
unto them; Let mine eyes run down
with tears night and day, and let them
not cease: for the virgin daughter of my
people is broken with a great breach,
with a very grievous blow.
18If I go forth into the field, then behold the slain with the sword! and if I
enter into the city, then behold them
that are sick with famine! yea, both the
prophet and the priest go about into a
land that they know not.

14:16 FAMINES IN THE BIBLE

Famine played a major role in changing people's lives and forcing them to move to other lands.

Event	Reference
Abram goes to Egypt to escape famine	Genesis 12:10
Famine forces Isaac to move to the land of the Philistines	Genesis 26
The seven-year, world-wide famine is managed by Joseph	Genesis 41:29-30,56
Jacob and his sons move to Egypt because of the famine	Genesis 45:9-11
Famine forces Naomi's family to move to Moab	Ruth 1:1
Three-year famine occurs during David's reign	2 Samuel 21:1
Famine strikes Samaria during Elijah's time	1 Kings 18:2
Famine occurs in Gilgal during Elisha's time	2 Kings 4:38
Famine in Samaria during Elisha's time	2 Kings 6:25
A seven-year famine occurs in Israel	2 Kings 8:1
Famine occurs in Jerusalem during siege	2 Kings 25:3; Jeremiah 52:6
Severe famine occurs throughout the Roman empire	Acts 11:28

19Hast thou utterly rejected Judah?
hath thy soul lothed Zion? why hast
thou smitten us, and *there is* no healing
for us? we looked for peace, and *there*
is no good; and for the time of healing,
and behold trouble!
20We acknowledge, O LORD, our
wickedness, *and* the iniquity of our fathers: for we have sinned against thee.
21Do not abhor *us,* for thy name's
sake, do not disgrace the throne of thy
glory: remember, break not thy covenant with us.
22Are there *any* among the vanities of
the *Gentiles that can cause rain? or
can the heavens give showers? *art* not
thou he, O LORD our *God? therefore
we will wait upon thee: for thou hast
made all these *things.*

Object lessons (continued)

15 Then said the LORD unto me,
Though *Moses and *Samuel
stood before me, *yet* my mind *could* not
be toward this people: cast *them* out of
my sight, and let them go forth.
2And it shall come to pass, if they say
unto thee, Whither shall we go forth?
then thou shalt tell them, Thus saith
the LORD; Such as *are* for *death, to
death; and such as *are* for the sword, to
the sword; and such as *are* for the famine, to the famine; and such as *are* for
the captivity, to the captivity.
3And I will appoint over them four
kinds, saith the LORD: the sword to slay,
and the dogs to tear, and the fowls of the
*heaven, and the beasts of the earth, to
devour and destroy.
4And I will cause them to be removed
into all kingdoms of the earth, because
of Manasseh the son of *Hezekiah king
of Judah, for *that* which he did in Jerusalem.
5For who shall have pity upon thee,
O Jerusalem? or who shall bemoan
thee? or who shall go aside to ask how
thou doest?
6Thou hast forsaken me, saith the
LORD, thou art gone backward: therefore will I stretch out my hand against
thee, and destroy thee; I am weary with
repenting.
7And I will fan them with a fan in the
gates of the land; I will bereave *them* of
children, I will destroy my people, *since*
they return not from their ways.
8Their widows are increased to me
above the sand of the seas: I have
brought upon them against the mother
of the young men a spoiler at noonday:
I have caused *him* to fall upon it suddenly, and terrors upon the city.
9She that hath borne seven languisheth: she hath given up the ghost;
her sun is gone down while *it was* yet
day: she hath been ashamed and confounded: and the residue of them will I
deliver to the sword before their enemies, saith the LORD.
¶10Woe is me, my mother, that thou
hast borne me a man of strife and a man
of contention to the whole earth! I have
neither lent on *usury, nor men have
lent to me on usury; *yet* every one of
them doth curse me.
11The LORD said, Verily it shall be
well with thy remnant; verily I will
cause the enemy to entreat thee *well*
in the time of evil and in the time of affliction.
12Shall iron break the northern iron
and the steel?
13Thy substance and thy treasures

14:22 vanities. Worthless idols.
15:4 Manasseh. Read about this wicked king in 2 Kings 20:21–21:18, and in 2 Chronicles 32:33–33:20. Though he repented before he died, the results of his sins and teachings remained.
15:9 She that hath borne seven. The destruction would be so very complete and terrible that even a mother who had had seven sons would not have one left.
15:11 remnant. See 14:1-4 note, "The Second Object Lesson."
15:12 iron. Judah.
15:12 northern iron and the steel. The Babylonians.

will I give to the spoil without price, and
that for all thy sins, even in all thy borders.
14And I will make *thee* to pass with
thine enemies into a land *which* thou
knowest not: for a fire is kindled in
mine anger, *which* shall burn upon you.
¶15O LORD, thou knowest: remember me, and visit me, and revenge me
of my persecutors; take me not away in
thy longsuffering: know that for thy
sake I have suffered rebuke.
16Thy words were found, and I did eat
them; and thy word was unto me the joy
and rejoicing of mine heart: for I am
called by thy name, O LORD God of
hosts.

15:16 The Law Found
The Book of the Law was found in the rubbish of the temple in the eighteenth year of King Josiah (2 Kings 22:3-10). There is a remarkable reference to Psalm 1 in these early chapters of Jeremiah. The prophet declared that he had not sat in the assembly of mockers but had declared himself in the law of the LORD. God rewarded Jeremiah by promising to deliver him out of the hands of the wicked (15:21). The other references to the first Psalm are found in Jeremiah 6:10 and 17:8. In 6:10, Israel is reproved because she did not delight herself in the law of the LORD, and in 17:8, the man who trusts in the LORD is likened to a tree planted by the waters.

17I sat not in the assembly of the
mockers, nor rejoiced; I sat alone because of thy hand: for thou hast filled
me with indignation.
18Why is my pain perpetual, and my
wound incurable, *which* refuseth to be
healed? wilt thou be altogether unto me
as a liar, *and as* waters *that* fail?
¶19Therefore thus saith the LORD, If
thou return, then will I bring thee again,
and thou shalt stand before me: and if
thou take forth the precious from the
vile, thou shalt be as my mouth: let
them return unto thee; but return not
thou unto them.
20And I will make thee unto this people a fenced brasen wall: and they shall
fight against thee, but they shall not
prevail against thee: for I *am* with thee
to save thee and to deliver thee, saith
the LORD.
21And I will deliver thee out of the
hand of the wicked, and I will *redeem
thee out of the hand of the terrible.

Object lessons (continued)
3) The unmarried prophet

16 The word of the LORD came also
unto me, saying,
2Thou shalt not take thee a wife, neither shalt thou have sons or daughters
in this place.

16:2 The Third Object Lesson
God frequently used the experiences of the prophets themselves as object lessons with which to teach the people. This is especially notable in the experience of Ezekiel (Ezek. 3:24-26; 5:1-4 and see 5:1 note, "An Object Lesson: Hair"; 12:11). Jeremiah served as a sign to Israel by not marrying. The purpose of the sign was to show the nation that their children would reap the harvest of their sin. See Exodus 20:5 note, "The Effect of Sin."

3For thus saith the LORD concerning
the sons and concerning the daughters
that are born in this place, and concerning their mothers that bare them, and
concerning their fathers that begat
them in this land;
4They shall die of grievous deaths;
they shall not be lamented; neither
shall they be buried; *but* they shall be
as *dung upon the face of the earth: and
they shall be consumed by the sword,
and by famine; and their carcases shall
be meat for the fowls of heaven, and for
the beasts of the earth.
5For thus saith the LORD, Enter not
into the house of *mourning, neither go
to lament nor bemoan them: for I have
taken away my peace from this people,
saith the LORD, *even* lovingkindness
and mercies.

16:4 grievous deaths. Deadly diseases.

6 Both the great and the small shall die in this land: they shall not be buried, neither shall *men* lament for them, nor cut themselves, nor make themselves bald for them:

7 Neither shall *men* tear *themselves* for them in mourning, to comfort them for the dead; neither shall *men* give them the cup of consolation to drink for their father or for their mother.

8 Thou shalt not also go into the house of feasting, to sit with them to eat and to drink.

9 For thus saith the LORD of hosts, the God of *Israel; Behold, I will cause to cease out of this place in your eyes, and in your days, the voice of mirth, and the voice of gladness, the voice of the *bridegroom, and the voice of the bride.

¶ 10 And it shall come to pass, when thou shalt shew this people all these words, and they shall say unto thee, Wherefore hath the LORD pronounced all this great evil against us? or what *is* our iniquity? or what *is* our *sin that we have committed against the LORD our God?

11 Then shalt thou say unto them, Because your fathers have forsaken me, saith the LORD, and have walked after other gods, and have served them, and have worshipped them, and have forsaken me, and have not kept my *law;

12 And ye have done worse than your fathers; for, behold, ye walk every one after the imagination of his evil heart, that they may not hearken unto me:

13 Therefore will I cast you out of this land into a land that ye know not, *neither* ye nor your fathers; and there shall ye serve other gods day and night; where I will not shew you favour.

¶ 14 Therefore, behold, the days come, saith the LORD, that it shall no more be said, The LORD liveth, that brought up the children of Israel out of the land of *Egypt;

15 But, The LORD liveth, that brought up the children of Israel from the land of the north, and from all the lands whither he had driven them: and I will bring them again into their land that I gave unto their fathers.

16:15 A Promise
Jehovah has always been known as the God who brought Israel out of Egypt. As the prophet anticipated the worldwide dispersion of the Jews and their regathering at the time of the reign of Christ, he declared that from then on Jehovah would be known as the God who had brought Israel back from the nations where they had been scattered.

¶ 16 Behold, I will send for many fishers, saith the LORD, and they shall fish them; and after will I send for many hunters, and they shall hunt them from every *mountain, and from every hill, and out of the holes of the rocks.

17 For mine eyes *are* upon all their ways: they are not hid from my face, neither is their iniquity hid from mine eyes.

18 And first I will recompense their iniquity and their sin double; because they have defiled my land, they have filled mine inheritance with the carcases of their detestable and abominable things.

19 O LORD, my strength, and my fortress, and my refuge in the day of affliction, the Gentiles shall come unto thee from the ends of the earth, and shall say, Surely our fathers have inherited lies, *vanity, and *things* wherein *there is* no profit.

20 Shall a man make gods unto himself, and they *are* no gods?

21 Therefore, behold, I will this once cause them to know, I will cause them to know mine hand and my might; and they shall know that my name *is* The LORD.

16:6 cut themselves, nor make themselves bald. These were signs of mourning as were those in verse 7.

16:21 my name is The LORD. Jehovah. See *names of God; *God—the Trinity.

Object lessons (continued)

17 The sin of Judah *is* written with
a pen of iron, *and* with the point
of a diamond: *it is* graven upon the table of their heart, and upon the *horns
of your altars;
2Whilst their children remember
their altars and their groves by the
green trees upon the high hills.
3O my mountain in the field, I will
give thy substance *and* all thy treasures
to the spoil, *and* thy high places for sin,
throughout all thy borders.
4And thou, even thyself, shalt discon-
tinue from thine heritage that I gave
thee; and I will cause thee to serve
thine enemies in the land which thou
knowest not: for ye have kindled a *fire
in mine anger, *which* shall burn for ever.
¶5Thus saith the LORD; Cursed *be* the
man that trusteth in man, and maketh
flesh his arm, and whose heart departeth from the LORD.
6For he shall be like the heath in the
desert, and shall not see when good
cometh; but shall inhabit the parched
places in the wilderness, *in* a salt land
and not inhabited.
7Blessed *is* the man that trusteth in
the LORD, and whose hope the LORD is.
8For he shall be as a tree planted by
the waters, and *that* spreadeth out her
roots by the river, and shall not see
when heat cometh, but her leaf shall be
green; and shall not be careful in the
year of drought, neither shall cease
from yielding fruit.
¶9The heart *is* deceitful above all
things, and desperately wicked: who can
know it?
10I the LORD search the heart, *I* try
the reins, even to give every man according to his ways, *and* according to
the fruit of his doings.
11*As* the partridge sitteth *on eggs,* and
hatcheth *them* not; *so* he that getteth
riches, and not by right, shall leave
them in the midst of his days, and at his
end shall be a *fool.
¶12A glorious high throne from the
beginning *is* the place of our *sanctuary.
13O LORD, the hope of Israel, all that
forsake thee shall be ashamed, *and* they
that depart from me shall be written in
the earth, because they have forsaken
the LORD, the fountain of living waters.
14Heal me, O LORD, and I shall be
healed; save me, and I shall be saved:
for thou *art* my praise.
¶15Behold, they say unto me, Where
is the word of the LORD? let it come
now.
16As for me, I have not hastened from
being a pastor to follow thee: neither
have I desired the woeful day; thou
knowest: that which came out of my
lips was *right* before thee.
17Be not a terror unto me: thou *art*
my hope in the day of evil.
18Let them be confounded that persecute me, but let not me be confounded: let them be dismayed, but let
not me be dismayed: bring upon them
the day of evil, and destroy them with
double destruction.
¶19Thus said the LORD unto me; Go
and stand in the gate of the children of
the people, whereby the kings of Judah
come in, and by the which they go out,
and in all the gates of Jerusalem;
20And say unto them, Hear ye the
word of the LORD, ye kings of Judah,
and all Judah, and all the inhabitants of
Jerusalem, that enter in by these gates:
21Thus saith the LORD; Take heed to
yourselves, and bear no burden on the
*sabbath day, nor bring *it* in by the gates
of Jerusalem;

17:3 my mountain in the field. Zion or Jerusalem in Judaea.
17:3 for sin. Because of sin.
17:6 heath. A tamarisk—a tree with feathery branches and tiny leaves.
17:8 For he shall be as a tree. Read Psalm 1.
17:9 desperately wicked. Incurably wicked.
17:13 written in the earth. Contrast this with "written in heaven" (Luke 10:20).

22Neither carry forth a burden out of
your houses on the sabbath day, neither
do ye any work, but hallow ye the sabbath day, as I commanded your fathers.
23But they obeyed not, neither inclined their ear, but made their neck
stiff, that they might not hear, nor receive instruction.
24And it shall come to pass, if ye diligently hearken unto me, saith the
LORD, to bring in no burden through the
gates of this city on the sabbath day, but
hallow the sabbath day, to do no work
therein;
25Then shall there enter into the
gates of this city kings and princes sitting upon the throne of David, riding in
chariots and on horses, they, and their
princes, the men of Judah, and the inhabitants of Jerusalem: and this city
shall remain for ever.
26And they shall come from the cities
of Judah, and from the places about Jerusalem, and from the land of Benjamin,
and from the plain, and from the mountains, and from the south, bringing
burnt-offerings, and sacrifices, and
meat-offerings, and *incense, and bringing sacrifices of praise, unto the house
of the LORD.
27But if ye will not hearken unto me
to hallow the sabbath day, and not to
bear a burden, even entering in at the
gates of Jerusalem on the sabbath day;
then will I kindle a fire in the gates
thereof, and it shall devour the palaces
of Jerusalem, and it shall not be
quenched.

Object lessons (continued)
4) The potter

18 The word which came to Jeremiah from the LORD, saying,
2Arise, and go down to the potter's
house, and there I will cause thee to
hear my words.
3Then I went down to the potter's
house, and, behold, he wrought a work
on the wheels.
4And the vessel that he made of clay
was marred in the hand of the potter:
so he made it again another vessel, as
seemed good to the potter to make *it.*
5Then the word of the LORD came to
me, saying,
6O house of Israel, cannot I do with
you as this potter? saith the LORD. Behold, as the clay *is* in the potter's hand,
so *are* ye in mine hand, O house of Israel.
7*At what* instant I shall speak concerning a nation, and concerning a kingdom, to pluck up, and to pull down, and
to destroy *it;*
8If that nation, against whom I have
pronounced, turn from their evil, I will
*repent of the evil that I thought to do
unto them.
9And *at what* instant I shall speak
concerning a nation, and concerning a
kingdom, to build and to plant *it;*
10If it do evil in my sight, that it obey
not my voice, then I will repent of the
good, wherewith I said I would benefit
them.
¶11Now therefore go to, speak to the
men of Judah, and to the inhabitants of
Jerusalem, saying, Thus saith the
LORD; Behold, I frame evil against you,
and devise a device against you: return
ye now every one from his evil way, and
make your ways and your doings good.
12And they said, There is no hope:
but we will walk after our own devices,
and we will every one do the imagination of his evil heart.

18:3 The Potter and the Clay
This is the fourth object lesson by which God spoke to Israel. It is a striking illustration of the power of God to mold, remake, and destroy. The vessel on the potter's wheel was marred, "so he made it again another vessel" (vs. 4). God reminded Israel that they were as clay in His hands (vs. 6). The vessel that He formed had been marred by sin, but God was able to remold that vessel. The people replied that it was useless (vs. 12) and sought to kill Jeremiah. When the nation had rejected the message, God sent the prophet to break the potter's vessel in the Valley of Hinnom and declare, "Even so will I break this people" (19:10-11).

13Therefore thus saith the LORD; Ask
ye now among the heathen, who hath
heard such things: the virgin of Israel
hath done a very horrible thing.
14Will *a man* leave the snow of *Lebanon *which cometh* from the rock of the
field? *or* shall the cold flowing waters
that come from another place be forsaken?
15Because my people hath forgotten
me, they have burned incense to vanity, and they have caused them to stumble in their ways *from* the ancient paths,
to walk in paths, *in* a way not cast up;
16To make their land desolate, *and* a
perpetual hissing; every one that
passeth thereby shall be astonished,
and wag his head.
17I will *scatter them as with an east
wind before the enemy; I will shew
them the back, and not the face, in the
day of their calamity.
¶18Then said they, Come, and let us
devise devices against Jeremiah; for the
law shall not perish from the priest, nor
counsel from the wise, nor the word
from the prophet. Come, and let us
smite him with the tongue, and let us
not give heed to any of his words.
19Give heed to me, O LORD, and hearken to the voice of them that contend
with me.
20Shall evil be recompensed for
good? for they have digged a pit for my
soul. Remember that I stood before
thee to speak good for them, *and* to
turn away thy wrath from them.
21Therefore deliver up their children
to the famine, and pour out their *blood*
by the force of the sword; and let their
wives be bereaved of their children, and
be widows; and let their men be put to
death; *let* their young men *be* slain by
the sword in battle.
22Let a cry be heard from their
houses, when thou shalt bring a troop
suddenly upon them: for they have
digged a pit to take me, and hid snares
for my feet.
23Yet, LORD, thou knowest all their
counsel against me to slay *me:* forgive
not their iniquity, neither blot out their
sin from thy sight, but let them be overthrown before thee; deal *thus* with them
in the time of thine anger.

Object lessons (continued)

19 Thus saith the LORD, Go and
get a potter's earthen bottle,
and *take* of the ancients of the people,
and of the ancients of the priests;
2And go forth unto the valley of the
son of Hinnom, which *is* by the entry
of the east gate, and proclaim there the
words that I shall tell thee,
3And say, Hear ye the word of the
LORD, O kings of *Judah, and inhabitants of *Jerusalem; Thus saith the
LORD of hosts, the God of Israel; Behold, I will bring evil upon this place,
the which whosoever heareth, his ears
shall tingle.
4Because they have forsaken me, and
have estranged this place, and have
burned incense in it unto other gods,
whom neither they nor their fathers
have known, nor the kings of Judah, and
have filled this place with the blood of
innocents;
5They have built also the *high
places of *Baal, to burn their sons with
fire *for* burnt-offerings unto Baal, which
I commanded not, nor spake *it,* neither
came *it* into my mind:
6Therefore, behold, the days come,
saith the LORD, that this place shall no
more be called *Tophet, nor The valley
of the son of Hinnom, but The valley of
slaughter.
7And I will make void the counsel of

19:2 valley of the son of Hinnom. See Joshua 15:8. There are still fields of clay like the kind potters use very near it.
19:2 east gate. Potter's gate.
19:7 the counsel of Judah and Jerusalem. They had planned to defeat Babylon by joining with Egypt.

19:6 A Place Called Tophet
Tophet, in the Valley of the Son of Hinnom (vs. 2), was once the place where the heathen god, Molech, was set up (2 Chron. 28:3; 33:6). King Josiah had done away with the evil practices (2 Kings 23:10), and the valley became a sort of dumping ground where fires were kept burning to destroy the refuse from the city of Jerusalem; therefore "Ge-Hinnom," as it was called, or gehenna (New Testament) became a *type of hell.

Judah and Jerusalem in this place; and
I will cause them to fall by the sword
before their enemies, and by the hands
of them that seek their lives: and their
carcases will I give to be meat for the
fowls of the heaven, and for the beasts
of the earth.
8 And I will make this city desolate,
and an hissing; every one that passeth
thereby shall be astonished and hiss
because of all the plagues thereof.
9 And I will cause them to eat the flesh
of their sons and the flesh of their
daughters, and they shall eat every one
the flesh of his friend in the siege and
straitness, wherewith their enemies,
and they that seek their lives, shall
straiten them.
10 Then shalt thou break the bottle in
the sight of the men that go with thee,
11 And shalt say unto them, Thus
saith the LORD of hosts; Even so will I
break this people and this city, as *one*
breaketh a potter's vessel, that cannot
be made whole again: and they shall
bury *them* in Tophet, till *there be* no
place to bury.
12 Thus will I do unto this place, saith
the LORD, and to the inhabitants
thereof, and *even* make this city as
Tophet:
13 And the houses of Jerusalem, and
the houses of the kings of Judah, shall
be defiled as the place of Tophet, because of all the houses upon whose
roofs they have burned incense unto all
the host of heaven, and have poured out
drink-offerings unto other gods.
14 Then came Jeremiah from Tophet,
whither the LORD had sent him to
prophesy; and he stood in the court of
the LORD'S house; and said to all the
people,
15 Thus saith the LORD of hosts, the
God of Israel; Behold, I will bring upon
this city and upon all her towns all the
evil that I have pronounced against it,
because they have *hardened their
necks, that they might not hear my
words.

IV. Messages from Jeremiah
(20:1—29:32)

1) The prophet's hesitation

20 Now Pashur the son of Immer
the priest, who *was* also chief
governor in the house of the LORD,
heard that Jeremiah prophesied these
things.
2 Then Pashur smote Jeremiah the
*prophet, and put him in the stocks that
were in the high gate of Benjamin,
which *was* by the house of the LORD.
3 And it came to pass on the morrow,
that Pashur brought forth Jeremiah out
of the stocks. Then said Jeremiah unto
him, The LORD hath not called thy
name Pashur, but Magor-missabib.
4 For thus saith the LORD, Behold, I
will make thee a terror to thyself, and
to all thy friends: and they shall fall by
the sword of their enemies, and thine
eyes shall behold *it:* and I will give all
Judah into the hand of the king of *Babylon, and he shall carry them captive
into Babylon, and shall slay them with
the sword.
5 Moreover I will deliver all the
strength of this city, and all the labours
thereof, and all the precious things

20:2 stocks. The head, hands, and feet were pushed through five holes in a beam of timber. The body had to be bent, of course, which caused great suffering.

20:3 Magor-missabib. Pashur meant *prosperity everywhere*; but Jeremiah prophesied that he should rather be Magor-missabib, which meant *terror everywhere*.

thereof, and all the treasures of the kings of Judah will I give into the hand of their enemies, which shall spoil them, and take them, and carry them to Babylon.

6 And thou, Pashur, and all that dwell in thine house shall go into captivity: and thou shalt come to Babylon, and there thou shalt die, and shalt be buried there, thou, and all thy friends, to whom thou hast prophesied lies.

¶ 7 O LORD, thou hast deceived me, and I was deceived: thou art stronger than I, and hast prevailed: I am in derision daily, every one mocketh me.

8 For since I spake, I cried out, I cried violence and spoil; because the word of the LORD was made a reproach unto me, and a derision, daily.

9 Then I said, I will not make mention of him, nor speak any more in his name. But *his word* was in mine heart as a burning fire shut up in my bones, and I was weary with forbearing, and I could not *stay.*

¶ 10 For I heard the defaming of many, fear on every side. Report, *say they,* and we will report it. All my familiars watched for my halting, *saying,* Peradventure he will be enticed, and we shall prevail against him, and we shall take our revenge on him.

11 But the LORD *is* with me as a mighty terrible one: therefore my persecutors shall stumble, and they shall not prevail: they shall be greatly ashamed; for they shall not prosper: *their* everlasting confusion shall never be forgotten.

12 But, O LORD of hosts, that triest the righteous, *and* seest the reins and the heart, let me see thy vengeance on them: for unto thee have I opened my cause.

13 Sing unto the LORD, praise ye the LORD: for he hath delivered the soul of the poor from the hand of evildoers.

¶ 14 Cursed *be* the day wherein I was born: let not the day wherein my mother bare me be blessed.

15 Cursed *be* the man who brought tidings to my father, saying, A man child is born unto thee; making him very glad.

16 And let that man be as the cities which the LORD overthrew, and *repented not: and let him hear the cry in the morning, and the shouting at noontide;

17 Because he slew me not from the womb; or that my mother might have been my grave, and her womb *to be* always great *with me.*

18 Wherefore came I forth out of the womb to see labour and sorrow, that my days should be consumed with shame?

Messages (continued)

2) The message of the King

21 The word which came unto Jeremiah from the LORD, when king Zedekiah sent unto him Pashur the son of Melchiah, and Zephaniah the son of Maaseiah the priest, saying,

21:1 A Message to the King
Through chapters 21 and 22 God directed a message to King Zedekiah of Judaea. God told the king that He set before him "the way of life, and the way of death" (21:8). The way of life was by obedience (22:3). It would have brought blessing. The way of death was by disobedience and ended in the rejection of Zedekiah and his descendants as heirs to the throne of David (22:24-30).

2 Enquire, I pray thee, of the LORD for us; for Nebuchadrezzar king of Babylon maketh war against us; if so be that the LORD will deal with us according to all his wondrous works, that he may go up from us.

20:7 deceived. Those who deceive are easily deceived.
20:8 because. Therefore.
20:10 All my familiars. "Familiars" mean *friends.* Those who knew Jeremiah watched to see whether he would do wrong, so that they could hold it against him.
21:1 Pashur. Pashur, the son of Melchiah, is to be distinguished from Pashur, the son of Immer in 20:1. About twenty years had passed.

¶ 3 Then said Jeremiah unto them, Thus shall ye say to Zedekiah:

4 Thus saith the LORD *God of Israel; Behold, I will turn back the weapons of war that *are* in your hands, wherewith ye fight against the king of Babylon, and *against* the Chaldeans, which besiege you without the walls, and I will assemble them into the midst of this city.

5 And I myself will fight against you with an outstretched hand and with a strong arm, even in anger, and in fury, and in great wrath.

6 And I will smite the inhabitants of this city, both man and beast: they shall die of a great pestilence.

7 And afterward, saith the LORD, I will deliver Zedekiah king of Judah, and his servants, and the people, and such as are left in this city from the pestilence, from the sword, and from the famine, into the hand of Nebuchadrezzar king of Babylon, and into the hand of their enemies, and into the hand of those that seek their life: and he shall smite them with the edge of the sword; he shall not spare them, neither have pity, nor have *mercy.

¶ 8 And unto this people thou shalt say, Thus saith the LORD; Behold, I set before you the way of life, and the way of *death.

9 He that abideth in this city shall die by the sword, and by the famine, and by the pestilence: but he that goeth out, and falleth to the Chaldeans that besiege you, he shall live, and his life shall be unto him for a prey.

10 For I have set my face against this city for evil, and not for good, saith the LORD: it shall be given into the hand of the king of Babylon, and he shall burn it with fire.

¶ 11 And touching the house of the king of Judah, *say,* Hear ye the word of the LORD;

12 O house of *David, thus saith the LORD; Execute *judgment in the morning, and deliver *him that is* spoiled out of the hand of the oppressor, lest my fury go out like fire, and burn that none can quench *it,* because of the evil of your doings.

13 Behold, I *am* against thee, O inhabitant of the valley, *and* rock of the plain, saith the LORD; which say, Who shall come down against us? or who shall enter into our habitations?

14 But I will punish you according to the fruit of your doings, saith the LORD: and I will kindle a fire in the forest thereof, and it shall devour all things round about it.

Messages (continued)

22 Thus saith the LORD; Go down to the house of the king of Judah, and speak there this word,

2 And say, Hear the word of the LORD, O king of Judah, that sittest upon the throne of David, thou, and thy servants, and thy people that enter in by these gates:

3 Thus saith the LORD; Execute ye judgment and *righteousness, and deliver the spoiled out of the hand of the oppressor: and do no wrong, do no violence to the stranger, the fatherless, nor the widow, neither shed innocent blood in this place.

4 For if ye do this thing indeed, then shall there enter in by the gates of this house kings sitting upon the throne of David, riding in chariots and on horses, he, and his servants, and his people.

5 But if ye will not hear these words, I swear by myself, saith the LORD, that this house shall become a desolation.

6 For thus saith the LORD unto the

21:9 unto him for a prey. Any Israelite who didn't truly serve God would have a life like that of one hunted.

21:12 in the morning. Without delay.

21:13 inhabitant of the valley, and rock. Jerusalem.

22:1 king of Judah. Jehoiakim. The events of chapter 22 happened about ten years before those of chapter 21.

king's house of Judah; Thou *art* *Gilead unto me, *and* the head of Lebanon: *yet* surely I will make thee a wilderness, *and* cities *which* are not inhabited.

7 And I will prepare destroyers against thee, every one with his weapons: and they shall cut down thy choice cedars, and cast *them* into the fire.

8 And many nations shall pass by this city, and they shall say every man to his neighbour, Wherefore hath the LORD done thus unto this great city?

9 Then they shall answer, Because they have forsaken the *covenant of the LORD their God, and worshipped other gods, and served them.

¶ 10 Weep ye not for the dead, neither bemoan him: *but* weep sore for him that goeth away: for he shall return no more, nor see his native country.

11 For thus saith the LORD touching Shallum the son of *Josiah king of Judah, which reigned instead of Josiah his father, which went forth out of this place; He shall not return thither any more:

12 But he shall die in the place whither they have led him captive, and shall see this land no more.

¶ 13 Woe unto him that buildeth his house by unrighteousness, and his chambers by wrong; *that* useth his neighbour's service without wages, and giveth him not for his work;

14 That saith, I will build me a wide house and large chambers, and cutteth him out windows; and *it is* cieled with cedar, and painted with vermilion.

15 Shalt thou reign, because thou closest *thyself* in cedar? did not thy father eat and drink, and do judgment and justice, *and* then *it was* well with him?

16 He judged the cause of the poor and needy; then *it was* well *with him: was* not this to know me? saith the LORD.

17 But thine eyes and thine heart *are* not but for thy covetousness, and for to shed innocent blood, and for oppression, and for violence, to do *it*.

18 Therefore thus saith the LORD concerning Jehoiakim the son of Josiah king of Judah; They shall not lament for him, *saying,* Ah my brother! or, Ah sister! they shall not lament for him, *saying,* Ah lord! or, Ah his glory!

19 He shall be buried with the burial of an ass, drawn and cast forth beyond the gates of Jerusalem.

¶ 20 Go up to Lebanon, and cry; and lift up thy voice in *Bashan, and cry from the passages: for all thy lovers are destroyed.

21 I spake unto thee in thy prosperity; *but* thou saidst, I will not hear. This *hath been* thy manner from thy youth, that thou obeyedst not my voice.

22 The wind shall eat up all thy pastors, and thy lovers shall go into captivity: surely then shalt thou be ashamed and confounded for all thy wickedness.

23 O inhabitant of Lebanon, that makest thy nest in the cedars, how gracious shalt thou be when pangs come upon thee, the pain as of a woman in travail!

24 *As* I live, saith the LORD, though Coniah the son of Jehoiakim king of Judah were the signet upon my right hand, yet would I pluck thee thence;

25 And I will give thee into the hand

22:6 Gilead. A region of rich pasturelands, fertile and beautiful.
22:10 the dead. King Josiah (2 Kings 22:20; 2 Chron. 35:24-25).
22:10 him that goeth away. King Jehoahaz (also called "Shallum") was the son of Josiah. Jehoahaz was taken captive to Egypt and died there.
22:14 cieled. Paneled, wainscoted.
22:15 thy father. Josiah.
22:23 O inhabitant of Lebanon. Jerusalem is meant here, for much of the city was built with the cedar of Lebanon.
22:24 Coniah. This was Jeconiah (1 Chron. 3:16). The first syllable of his name—"Je"—stood for his relationship to the LORD Jehovah. But the Holy Spirit led Jeremiah to drop the syllable, for God had cut Jeconiah off.

of them that seek thy life, and into the
hand *of them* whose face thou fearest,
even into the hand of Nebuchadrezzar
king of Babylon, and into the hand of the
Chaldeans.
26 And I will cast thee out, and thy
mother that bare thee, into another
country, where ye were not born; and
there shall ye die.
27 But to the land whereunto they
desire to return, thither shall they not
return.
28 *Is* this man Coniah a despised broken idol? *is he* a vessel wherein *is* no
pleasure? wherefore are they cast out,
he and his seed, and are cast into a land
which they know not?
29 O earth, earth, earth, hear the word
of the LORD.
30 Thus saith the LORD, Write ye this
man childless, a man *that* shall not prosper in his days: for no man of his seed
shall prosper, sitting upon the throne of
David, and ruling any more in Judah.

Messages (continued)
*3) The promise of the *Messiah*

23 Woe be unto the pastors that
destroy and scatter the sheep of
my pasture! saith the LORD.
2 Therefore thus saith the LORD God
of *Israel against the pastors that feed
my people; Ye have scattered my flock,
and driven them away, and have not
visited them: behold, I will visit upon
you the evil of your doings, saith the
LORD.
3 And I will gather the *remnant of my
flock out of all countries whither I have
driven them, and will bring them again
to their folds; and they shall be fruitful
and increase.
4 And I will set up shepherds over
them which shall feed them: and they
shall fear no more, nor be dismayed,
neither shall they be lacking, saith the
LORD.
¶5 Behold, the days come, saith the
LORD, that I will raise unto David a
righteous Branch, and a King shall
reign and prosper, and shall execute
judgment and justice in the earth.
6 In his days Judah shall be saved, and
Israel shall dwell safely: and this *is* his
name whereby he shall be called, THE
LORD OUR RIGHTEOUSNESS.
7 Therefore, behold, the days come,
saith the LORD, that they shall no more
say, The LORD liveth, which brought up
the children of Israel out of the land of
*Egypt;
8 But, The LORD liveth, which brought
up and which led the seed of the house
of Israel out of the north country, and
from all countries whither I had driven
them; and they shall dwell in their own
land.
¶9 Mine heart within me is broken because of the *prophets; all my bones
shake; I am like a drunken man, and like
a man whom *wine hath overcome,
because of the LORD, and because of the
words of his holiness.
10 For the land is full of adulterers; for
because of swearing the land mourneth;
the pleasant places of the wilderness
are dried up, and their course is evil,
and their force *is* not right.
11 For both prophet and priest are profane; yea, in my house have I found
their wickedness, saith the LORD.
12 Wherefore their way shall be unto
them as slippery *ways* in the darkness:
they shall be driven on, and fall therein:
for I will bring evil upon them, *even* the
year of their visitation, saith the LORD.
13 And I have seen folly in the prophets of *Samaria; they prophesied in
Baal, and caused my people Israel to
*err.

23:1 pastors. Leaders.
23:6 THE LORD OUR RIGHTEOUSNESS. *Jehovah-Tsidkenu.* See *names of God, *God—the Trinity.
23:8 from all countries. See 16:15 note, "A Promise."
23:10 adulterers. Idol worshippers.
23:10 swearing. Worshipping idols.

14 I have seen also in the prophets of Jerusalem an horrible thing: they commit adultery, and walk in lies: they strengthen also the hands of evildoers, that none doth return from his wickedness: they are all of them unto me as Sodom, and the inhabitants thereof as Gomorrah.

15 Therefore thus saith the LORD of hosts concerning the prophets; Behold, I will feed them with *wormwood, and make them drink the *water of gall: for from the prophets of Jerusalem is profaneness gone forth into all the land.

16 Thus saith the LORD of hosts, Hearken not unto the words of the prophets that prophesy unto you: they make you vain: they speak a vision of their own heart, *and* not out of the mouth of the LORD.

17 They say still unto them that despise me, The LORD hath said, Ye shall have *peace; and they say unto every one that walketh after the imagination of his own heart, No evil shall come upon you.

18 For who hath stood in the counsel of the LORD, and hath perceived and heard his word? who hath marked his word, and heard *it?*

19 Behold, a whirlwind of the LORD is gone forth in fury, even a grievous whirlwind: it shall fall grievously upon the head of the wicked.

20 The anger of the LORD shall not return, until he have executed, and till he have performed the thoughts of his heart: in the latter days ye shall consider it perfectly.

21 I have not sent these prophets, yet they ran: I have not spoken to them, yet they prophesied.

22 But if they had stood in my counsel, and had caused my people to hear my words, then they should have turned them from their evil way, and from the evil of their doings.

23 *Am* I a God at hand, saith the LORD, and not a God afar off?

24 Can any hide himself in secret places that I shall not see him? saith the LORD. Do not I fill *heaven and earth? saith the LORD.

25 I have heard what the prophets said, that prophesy lies in my name, saying, I have dreamed, I have dreamed.

26 How long shall *this* be in the heart of the prophets that prophesy lies? yea, *they are* prophets of the deceit of their own heart;

27 Which think to cause my people to forget my name by their dreams which they tell every man to his neighbour, as their fathers have forgotten my name for Baal.

28 The prophet that hath a dream, let him tell a dream; and he that hath my word, let him speak my word faithfully. What *is* the chaff to the wheat? saith the LORD.

29 *Is* not my word like as a *fire? saith the LORD; and like a hammer *that* breaketh the rock in pieces?

30 Therefore, behold, I *am* against the prophets, saith the LORD, that steal my words every one from his neighbour.

31 Behold, I *am* against the prophets, saith the LORD, that use their tongues, and say, He saith.

32 Behold, I *am* against them that prophesy false dreams, saith the LORD, and do tell them, and cause my people to err by their lies, and by their lightness;

23:16 make you vain. Give you false hope.

23:17 Ye shall have peace. They are mistaken who assume that God's love implies permission to live in indifference to His will. Unbelievers say, "God is a God of love; He would never send anyone to hell." See the answer in verses 19-31.

23:20 in the latter days. When the children of Israel had been carried away to exile in Babylon, they remembered the words of Jeremiah and knew that he had spoken the truth to them.

23:28 chaff to the wheat. The false prophet is the chaff while the true prophet is the wheat.

23:29 The Symbol of Fire
The Bible uses many symbols to express the ministry of the Word of God. That Word is like a fire and a hammer that breaks rocks (stony hearts) in pieces. It is also called the seed that brings forth eternal life (Luke 8:1). It is the mirror that reveals the glory of the LORD in contrast with our own sinfulness (2 Cor. 3:18; James 1:25). It is the water of life and of cleansing (Eph. 5:26; John 4:14). It is the sword of the Spirit that lays bare the thoughts of men's hearts (Heb. 4:12).

yet I sent them not, nor commanded
them: therefore they shall not profit
this people at all, saith the LORD.
¶33And when this people, or the
prophet, or a priest, shall ask thee, saying, What *is* the *burden of the LORD?
thou shalt then say unto them, What
burden? I will even forsake you, saith
the LORD.
34And *as for* the prophet, and the
priest, and the people, that shall say,
The burden of the LORD, I will even
punish that man and his house.
35Thus shall ye say every one to his
neighbour, and every one to his brother,
What hath the LORD answered? and,
What hath the LORD spoken?
36And the burden of the LORD shall ye
mention no more: for every man's word
shall be his burden; for ye have perverted the words of the living God, of the
LORD of hosts our God.
37Thus shalt thou say to the prophet, What hath the LORD answered thee?
and, What hath the LORD spoken?
38But since ye say, The burden of the
LORD; therefore thus saith the LORD;
Because ye say this word, The burden
of the LORD, and I have sent unto you,
saying, Ye shall not say, The burden of
the LORD;
39Therefore, behold, I, even I, will
utterly forget you, and I will forsake
you, and the city that I gave you and
your fathers, *and cast you* out of my
presence:
40And I will bring an everlasting reproach upon you, and a perpetual
shame, which shall not be forgotten.

Messages (continued)

4) Prediction of restoration of Israel

24 The LORD shewed me, and, behold, two baskets of figs *were*
set before the temple of the LORD, after that Nebuchadrezzar king of Babylon had carried away captive Jeconiah
the son of Jehoiakim king of Judah, and
the princes of Judah, with the carpenters and smiths, from Jerusalem, and
had brought them to Babylon.

24:1 God's Purpose
These baskets of figs disclose the purpose of God as rejecting the people of Judaea who were carried to Babylon, and those who went to Egypt. God promised to restore the land to those who went to Babylon (vss. 4-5), but no such promise was made to those who went to Egypt.

2One basket *had* very good figs, *even*
like the figs *that are* first ripe: and the
other basket *had* very naughty figs,
which could not be eaten, they were so
bad.
3Then said the LORD unto me, What
seest thou, Jeremiah? And I said, Figs;
the good figs, very good; and the evil,
very evil, that cannot be eaten, they are
so evil.
¶4Again the word of the LORD came
unto me, saying,
5Thus saith the LORD, the God of Israel; Like these good figs, so will I acknowledge them that are carried away
captive of Judah, whom I have sent out
of this place into the land of the Chaldeans for *their* good.

23:33 burden. In verses 33-40 the prophet is using the word burden in two ways: 1) a message from the LORD, 2) a heavy load.

24:3 the good figs. These were the captives like Daniel, Shadrach, Meshach, and Abednego (Dan. 1:7); and Nehemiah, Ezra, Ezekiel, and their friends.

[6]For I will set mine eyes upon them for good, and I will bring them again to this land: and I will build them, and not pull *them* down; and I will plant them, and not pluck *them* up.
[7]And I will give them an heart to know me, that I *am* the LORD: and they shall be my people, and I will be their God: for they shall return unto me with their whole heart.
¶[8]And as the evil figs, which cannot be eaten, they are so evil; surely thus saith the LORD, So will I give Zedekiah the king of Judah, and his princes, and the residue of Jerusalem, that remain in this land, and them that dwell in the land of Egypt:
[9]And I will deliver them to be removed into all the kingdoms of the earth for *their* hurt, *to be* a reproach and a proverb, a taunt and a curse, in all places whither I shall drive them.
[10]And I will send the sword, the famine, and the pestilence, among them, till they be consumed from off the land that I gave unto them and to their fathers.

Messages (continued)

25 The word that came to Jeremiah concerning all the people of *Judah in the fourth year of Jehoiakim the son of Josiah king of Judah, that *was* the first year of Nebuchadrezzar king of Babylon;
[2]The which Jeremiah the prophet spake unto all the people of Judah, and to all the inhabitants of *Jerusalem, saying,
[3]From the thirteenth year of Josiah the son of Amon king of Judah, even unto this day, that *is* the three and twentieth year, the word of the LORD hath come unto me, and I have spoken unto you, rising early and speaking; but ye have not hearkened.
[4]And the LORD hath sent unto you all his servants the prophets, rising early and sending *them;* but ye have not hearkened, nor inclined your ear to hear.
[5]They said, Turn ye again now every one from his evil way, and from the evil of your doings, and dwell in the land that the LORD hath given unto you and to your fathers for ever and ever:
[6]And go not after other gods to serve them, and to worship them, and provoke me not to anger with the works of your hands; and I will do you no hurt.
[7]Yet ye have not hearkened unto me, saith the LORD; that ye might provoke me to anger with the works of your hands to your own hurt.
¶[8]Therefore thus saith the LORD of hosts; Because ye have not heard my words,
[9]Behold, I will send and take all the families of the north, saith the LORD, and Nebuchadrezzar the king of Babylon, my servant, and will bring them against this land, and against the inhabitants thereof, and against all these nations round about, and will utterly destroy them, and make them an astonishment, and an hissing, and perpetual desolations.
[10]Moreover I will take from them the voice of mirth, and the voice of gladness, the voice of the *bridegroom, and the voice of the bride, the sound of the millstones, and the light of the candle.
[11]And this whole land shall be a desolation, *and* an astonishment; and these nations shall serve the king of Babylon seventy years.
¶[12]And it shall come to pass, when seventy years are accomplished, *that* I will punish the king of Babylon, and that nation, saith the LORD, for their iniquity, and the land of the Chaldeans, and will make it perpetual desolations.
[13]And I will bring upon that land all

25:3 the three and twentieth year. This was the twenty-third year of Jeremiah's ministry. Eighteen years were under Josiah, three months under Jehoahaz, and four years under Jehoiakim.

25:10 Moreover I will take from them. Compare Revelation 18:23.

> **25:11 An Improbable Prediction**
> God revealed that the captivity of the children of Israel in Babylon would last seventy years. He also declared that when the seventy years were over, Babylon would be punished and would become a perpetual desolation. Nothing seemed more improbable than this prediction at the time that Jeremiah spoke it. We are told in Daniel 9:2 that the prophet Daniel had read this declaration of Jeremiah. The message of Jeremiah was fulfilled. We know that when the seventy years were accomplished, Babylon fell and Cyrus, by his edict, permitted the return of those Jews who wished to restore the temple in Jerusalem (Ezra 1:1-3).

my words which I have pronounced
against it, *even* all that is written in this
book, which Jeremiah hath prophesied
against all the nations.
14 For many nations and great kings
shall serve themselves of them also:
and I will recompense them according
to their deeds, and according to the
works of their own hands.
¶15 For thus saith the LORD God of Israel unto me; Take the wine cup of this
fury at my hand, and cause all the nations, to whom I send thee, to drink it.
16 And they shall drink, and be moved,
and be mad, because of the sword that
I will send among them.
17 Then took I the cup at the LORD'S
hand, and made all the nations to drink,
unto whom the LORD had sent me:
18 *To wit,* Jerusalem, and the cities of
Judah, and the kings thereof, and the
princes thereof, to make them a desolation, an astonishment, an hissing, and
a curse; as *it is* this day;
19 *Pharaoh king of Egypt, and his
servants, and his princes, and all his
people;
20 And all the mingled people, and all
the kings of the land of Uz, and all the
kings of the land of the *Philistines, and
*Ashkelon, and Azzah, and Ekron, and
the remnant of Ashdod,
21 *Edom, and *Moab, and the children of Ammon,
22 And all the kings of Tyrus, and all
the kings of Zidon, and the kings of the
*isles which *are* beyond the sea,
23 Dedan, and Tema, and Buz, and all
that are in the utmost corners,
24 And all the kings of Arabia, and all
the kings of the mingled people that
dwell in the desert,
25 And all the kings of Zimri, and all
the kings of Elam, and all the kings of
the Medes,
26 And all the kings of the north, far
and near, one with another, and all the
kingdoms of the *world, which *are* upon
the face of the earth: and the king of
Sheshach shall drink after them.
27 Therefore thou shalt say unto
them, Thus saith the LORD of hosts, the
God of Israel; Drink ye, and be drunk-
en, and spue, and fall, and rise no more,
because of the sword which I will send
among you.
28 And it shall be, if they refuse to take
the cup at thine hand to drink, then
shalt thou say unto them, Thus saith
the LORD of hosts; Ye shall certainly
drink.
29 For, lo, I begin to bring evil on the
city which is called by my name, and
should ye be utterly unpunished? Ye
shall not be unpunished: for I will call
for a sword upon all the inhabitants of
the earth, saith the LORD of hosts.
30 Therefore prophesy thou against
them all these words, and say unto
them, The LORD shall roar from on

25:14 shall serve themselves of them. Shall make slaves of the Chaldeans.
25:17 the nations . . . unto whom the LORD had sent me. Judgment was to begin with Jerusalem (vs. 18) and end with Babylon–"Sheshach" (vs. 26).
25:26 Sheshach. Another name for Babylon.
25:29 the city. Jerusalem.
25:29 upon all the inhabitants of the earth. This prophecy is not just of the destruction to come upon the Jewish people, but it looks far ahead to the end of this age. See *dispensations.

high, and utter his voice from his *holy habitation; he shall mightily roar upon his habitation; he shall give a shout, as they that tread *the grapes,* against all the inhabitants of the earth.

25:30 A Great Judgment
This prophecy is very similar to that which is found in Revelation 14:14-20. When the iniquity of the world is full, it will be cast into the winepress of almighty God. Both prophecies look forward to the judgments that will accompany the second coming of Christ to earth. There was an anticipatory fulfillment of Jeremiah's prophecy in the invasion of Palestine by Nebuchadnezzar. This simply serves to illustrate the awfulness of the great judgments with which Christ will make ready His kingdom upon the earth.

31 A noise shall come *even* to the ends of the earth; for the LORD hath a controversy with the nations, he will plead with all flesh; he will give them *that are* wicked to the sword, saith the LORD.

32 Thus saith the LORD of hosts, Behold, evil shall go forth from nation to nation, and a great whirlwind shall be raised up from the coasts of the earth.

33 And the slain of the LORD shall be at that day from *one* end of the earth even unto the *other* end of the earth: they shall not be lamented, neither gathered, nor buried; they shall be *dung upon the ground.

¶34 Howl, ye shepherds, and cry; and wallow yourselves *in the ashes,* ye principal of the flock: for the days of your slaughter and of your dispersions are accomplished; and ye shall fall like a pleasant vessel.

35 And the shepherds shall have no way to flee, nor the principal of the flock to escape.

36 A voice of the cry of the shepherds, and an howling of the principal of the flock, *shall be heard:* for the LORD hath spoiled their pasture.

37 And the peaceable habitations are cut down because of the fierce anger of the LORD.

38 He hath forsaken his covert, as the lion: for their land is desolate because of the fierceness of the oppressor, and because of his fierce anger.

Messages (continued)

5) Message in the temple court

26 In the beginning of the reign of Jehoiakim the son of Josiah king of Judah came this word from the LORD, saying,

2 Thus saith the LORD; Stand in the court of the LORD'S house, and speak unto all the cities of Judah, which come to worship in the LORD'S house, all the words that I command thee to speak unto them; diminish not a word:

3 If so be they will hearken, and turn every man from his evil way, that I may *repent me of the evil, which I purpose to do unto them because of the evil of their doings.

4 And thou shalt say unto them, Thus saith the LORD; If ye will not hearken to me, to walk in my *law, which I have set before you,

5 To hearken to the words of my servants the prophets, whom I sent unto you, both rising up early, and sending *them,* but ye have not hearkened;

6 Then will I make this house like *Shiloh, and will make this city a curse to all the nations of the earth.

7 So the priests and the prophets and all the people heard Jeremiah speaking these words in the house of the LORD.

¶8 Now it came to pass, when Jeremiah had made an end of speaking all that the LORD had commanded *him* to speak unto all the people, that the priests and the prophets and all the

---

25:31 plead. Judge.
25:35 the shepherds shall have no way to flee. This is a prophecy of the attempt of King Zedekiah and his men of war to escape. They did not succeed. See 2 Kings 25:4-7.
26:6 a curse. A reminder of the wrath of God.

people took him, saying, Thou shalt surely die.

9 Why hast thou prophesied in the name of the LORD, saying, This house shall be like Shiloh, and this city shall be desolate without an inhabitant? And all the people were gathered against Jeremiah in the house of the LORD.

¶ 10 When the princes of Judah heard these things, then they came up from the king's house unto the house of the LORD, and sat down in the entry of the new gate of the LORD'S *house.*

11 Then spake the priests and the prophets unto the princes and to all the people, saying, This man *is* worthy to die; for he hath prophesied against this city, as ye have heard with your ears.

¶ 12 Then spake Jeremiah unto all the princes and to all the people, saying, The LORD sent me to prophesy against this house and against this city all the words that ye have heard.

13 Therefore now amend your ways and your doings, and obey the voice of the LORD your God; and the LORD will repent him of the evil that he hath pronounced against you.

14 As for me, behold, I *am* in your hand: do with me as seemeth good and meet unto you.

15 But know ye for certain, that if ye put me to death, ye shall surely bring innocent blood upon yourselves, and upon this city, and upon the inhabitants thereof: for of a truth the LORD hath sent me unto you to speak all these words in your ears.

¶ 16 Then said the princes and all the people unto the priests and to the prophets; This man *is* not worthy to die: for he hath spoken to us in the name of the LORD our God.

17 Then rose up certain of the *elders of the land, and spake to all the assembly of the people, saying,

18 Micah the Morasthite prophesied in the days of *Hezekiah king of Judah, and spake to all the people of Judah, saying, Thus saith the LORD of hosts; *Zion shall be plowed *like* a field, and Jerusalem shall become heaps, and the mountain of the house as the high places of a forest.

19 Did Hezekiah king of Judah and all Judah put him at all to death? did he not *fear the LORD, and besought the LORD, and the LORD *repented him of the evil which he had pronounced against them? Thus might we procure great evil against our souls.

20 And there was also a man that prophesied in the name of the LORD, Urijah the son of Shemaiah of Kirjath-jearim, who prophesied against this city and against this land according to all the words of Jeremiah:

26:20 Two Prophets
According to this chapter, there were two prophets who preached the same message in Jerusalem: Jeremiah and Urijah. Jehoiakim, the king, and his wicked counselors determined to put them to death. Jeremiah remained at his post of duty, and his life was spared (vss. 16,24). Urijah fled to Egypt, but the king sent men to bring Urijah back; then King Jehoiakim had him killed (vs. 23).

21 And when Jehoiakim the king, with all his mighty men, and all the princes, heard his words, the king sought to put him to death: but when Urijah heard it, he was afraid, and fled, and went into Egypt;

22 And Jehoiakim the king sent men into Egypt, *namely,* Elnathan the son of Achbor, and *certain* men with him into Egypt.

23 And they fetched forth Urijah out of Egypt, and brought him unto Jehoiakim the king; who slew him with the sword, and cast his dead body into the graves of the common people.

26:12 against. Concerning.

26:18 Zion shall be plowed like a field. See Micah 3:12. Jeremiah had every reason to be familiar with the prophecy of Micah, which was written over a hundred years earlier.

24Nevertheless the hand of Ahikam
the son of Shaphan was with Jeremiah,
that they should not give him into the
hand of the people to put him to death.

Messages (continued)
6) Appeal to Zedekiah to submit to Nebuchadnezzar

27 In the beginning of the reign of
Jehoiakim the son of Josiah king
of Judah came this word unto Jeremiah
from the LORD, saying,
2Thus saith the LORD to me; Make
thee bonds and yokes, and put them
upon thy neck,
3And send them to the king of Edom,
and to the king of Moab, and to the king
of the Ammonites, and to the king of
Tyrus, and to the king of Zidon, by the
hand of the messengers which come
to Jerusalem unto Zedekiah king of
Judah;
4And command them to say unto
their masters, Thus saith the LORD of
hosts, the *God of Israel; Thus shall ye
say unto your masters;
5I have made the earth, the man and
the beast that *are* upon the ground, by
my great power and by my outstretched
arm, and have given it unto whom it
seemed meet unto me.
6And now have I given all these lands
into the hand of Nebuchadnezzar the
king of *Babylon, my servant; and the
beasts of the field have I given him also
to serve him.
7And all nations shall serve him, and
his son, and his son's son, until the very
time of his land come: and then many
nations and great kings shall serve
themselves of him.
8And it shall come to pass, *that* the
nation and kingdom which will not
serve the same Nebuchadnezzar the
king of Babylon, and that will not put
their neck under the yoke of the king
of Babylon, that nation will I punish,
saith the LORD, with the sword, and
with the famine, and with the pestilence, until I have consumed them by
his hand.
9Therefore hearken not ye to your
prophets, nor to your diviners, nor to
your dreamers, nor to your enchanters,
nor to your sorcerers, which speak unto
you, saying, Ye shall not serve the king
of Babylon:
10For they prophesy a lie unto you, to
remove you far from your land; and that
I should drive you out, and ye should
perish.
11But the nations that bring their neck
under the yoke of the king of Babylon,
and serve him, those will I let remain
still in their own land, saith the LORD;
and they shall till it, and dwell therein.
¶12I spake also to Zedekiah king of
Judah according to all these words, saying, Bring your necks under the yoke
of the king of Babylon, and serve him
and his people, and live.
13Why will ye die, thou and thy people, by the sword, by the famine, and by
the pestilence, as the LORD hath spoken against the nation that will not
serve the king of Babylon?
14Therefore hearken not unto the
words of the prophets that speak unto
you, saying, Ye shall not serve the king

27:6 For God's Purpose
Nebuchadnezzar was used of God to carry out His purposes. The Jewish people had rejected God, who now turned them over to Gentile rule and dominion and commanded them to obey, for the *Times of the Gentiles (Luke 21:24) had begun. When these times are fulfilled, the time of Israel shall come with great glory to the Jews. Read Revelation 11 and notes.

26:24 Ahikam. A high official who was a good man. He was one of those who found the Scriptures in the temple (2 Kings 22:12).
27:1 the reign of Jehoiakim. God's message was given to Jeremiah in the time of Jehoiakim. Jeremiah announced it publicly thirteen years later, in the time of King Zedekiah (see vs. 12).
27:2 yokes. These were signs of slavery. The prophecy was literally fulfilled.

of Babylon: for they prophesy a lie unto
you.
15For I have not sent them, saith the
LORD, yet they prophesy a lie in my
name; that I might drive you out, and
that ye might perish, ye, and the prophets that prophesy unto you.
16Also I spake to the priests and to all
this people, saying, Thus saith the
LORD; Hearken not to the words of your
prophets that prophesy unto you, saying, Behold, the vessels of the LORD'S
house shall now shortly be brought
again from Babylon: for they prophesy
a lie unto you.
17Hearken not unto them; serve the
king of Babylon, and live: wherefore
should this city be laid waste?
18But if they *be* prophets, and if the
word of the LORD be with them, let
them now make intercession to the
LORD of hosts, that the vessels which
are left in the house of the LORD, and
in the house of the king of Judah, and
at Jerusalem, go not to Babylon.
¶19For thus saith the LORD of hosts
concerning the pillars, and concerning
the sea, and concerning the bases, and
concerning the residue of the vessels
that remain in this city,
20Which Nebuchadnezzar king of
Babylon took not, when he carried away
captive Jeconiah the son of Jehoiakim
king of Judah from Jerusalem to Babylon, and all the nobles of Judah and
Jerusalem;
21Yea, thus saith the LORD of hosts,
the God of Israel, concerning the vessels that remain *in* the house of the
LORD, and *in* the house of the king of
Judah and of Jerusalem;
22They shall be carried to Babylon,
and there shall they be until the day that
I visit them, saith the LORD; then will I
bring them up, and restore them to this
place.

Messages (continued)

28 And it came to pass the same
year, in the beginning of the
reign of Zedekiah king of Judah, in the
fourth year, *and* in the fifth *month, *that*
Hananiah the son of Azur the *prophet, which *was* of Gibeon, spake unto me
in the house of the LORD, in the presence of the priests and of all the people, saying,
2Thus speaketh the LORD of hosts,
the God of Israel, saying, I have broken
the yoke of the king of Babylon.
3Within two full years will I bring
again into this place all the vessels of
the LORD'S house, that Nebuchadnezzar king of Babylon took away from this
place, and carried them to Babylon:
4And I will bring again to this place Jeconiah the son of Jehoiakim king of Judah,
with all the captives of Judah, that went
into Babylon, saith the LORD: for I will
break the yoke of the king of Babylon.
¶5Then the prophet Jeremiah said
unto the prophet Hananiah in the presence of the priests, and in the presence
of all the people that stood in the house
of the LORD,
6Even the prophet Jeremiah said,
*Amen: the LORD do so: the LORD per-
form thy words which thou hast prophesied, to bring again the vessels of the
LORD'S house, and all that is carried
away captive, from Babylon into this
place.

27:16 the vessels. Here and in verses 19-22, the prophet spoke of the vessels of the LORD's house. These were carried to Babylon (2 Kings 24:13; 2 Chron. 36:5-7,18), restored by Cyrus (2 Chron. 36:22), and brought back to Jerusalem by Ezra (1:7-11).

28:3 Within two full years. Hananiah, the false prophet, prophesied deliverance for Israel in two years and could not see that he himself would be dead within two months (vss. 1,17).

28:6 Even the prophet Jeremiah. Jeremiah was humble and wanted what was best for the people. Though Jeremiah would be laughed at and counted as nothing if Hananiah's prophecy came true, even so, he was willing to say, "The LORD do so," for he loved Israel more than he loved his reputation.

[7]Nevertheless hear thou now this word that I speak in thine ears, and in the ears of all the people;

[8]The prophets that have been before me and before thee of old prophesied both against many countries, and against great kingdoms, of war, and of evil, and of pestilence.

[9]The prophet which prophesieth of peace, when the word of the prophet shall come to pass, *then* shall the prophet be known, that the LORD hath truly sent him.

¶[10]Then Hananiah the prophet took the yoke from off the prophet Jeremiah's neck, and brake it.

[11]And Hananiah spake in the presence of all the people, saying, Thus saith the LORD; Even so will I break the yoke of Nebuchadnezzar king of Babylon from the neck of all nations within the space of two full years. And the prophet Jeremiah went his way.

¶[12]Then the word of the LORD came unto Jeremiah *the prophet,* after that Hananiah the prophet had broken the yoke from off the neck of the prophet Jeremiah, saying,

[13]Go and tell Hananiah, saying, Thus saith the LORD; Thou hast broken the yokes of wood; but thou shalt make for them yokes of iron.

[14]For thus saith the LORD of hosts, the God of Israel; I have put a yoke of iron upon the neck of all these nations, that they may serve Nebuchadnezzar king of Babylon; and they shall serve him: and I have given him the beasts of the field also.

¶[15]Then said the prophet Jeremiah unto Hananiah the prophet, Hear now, Hananiah; The LORD hath not sent thee; but thou makest this people to *trust in a lie.

[16]Therefore thus saith the LORD; Behold, I will cast thee from off the face of the earth: this year thou shalt die, because thou hast taught rebellion against the LORD.

[17]So Hananiah the prophet died the same year in the seventh month.

Messages (continued)
*7) Message of *hope to the Jews in captivity*

29 Now these *are* the *words of the letter that Jeremiah the prophet sent from Jerusalem unto the residue of the elders which were carried away captives, and to the priests, and to the *prophets, and to all the people whom Nebuchadnezzar had carried away captive from Jerusalem to Babylon;

[2](After that Jeconiah the king, and the queen, and the eunuchs, the princes of Judah and Jerusalem, and the carpenters, and the smiths, were departed from Jerusalem;)

[3]By the hand of Elasah the son of Shaphan, and Gemariah the son of Hilkiah, (whom Zedekiah king of Judah sent unto Babylon to Nebuchadnezzar king of Babylon) saying,

[4]Thus saith the LORD of hosts, the God of *Israel, unto all that are carried away captives, whom I have caused to be carried away from Jerusalem unto Babylon;

[5]Build ye houses, and dwell *in them;* and plant gardens, and eat the fruit of them;

[6]Take ye wives, and beget sons and daughters; and take wives for your sons, and give your daughters to husbands, that they may bear sons and daughters; that ye may be increased there, and not diminished.

[7]And seek the *peace of the city whither I have caused you to be carried away captives, and pray unto the LORD for it: for in the peace thereof shall ye have peace.

29:1 captives. See 2 Kings 24:10-16. The rest of the people were carried away eleven years later. See 2 Kings 25:1-7.

29:3 Shaphan. Shaphan and Hilkiah, the fathers of the messengers, were the men who found the Scriptures in the temple (2 Kings 22:10).

¶8For thus saith the LORD of hosts,
the God of Israel; Let not your prophets and your diviners, that *be* in the
midst of you, deceive you, neither hearken to your dreams which ye cause to
be dreamed.
9For they prophesy falsely unto you
in my name: I have not sent them, saith
the LORD.
¶10For thus saith the LORD, That after seventy years be accomplished at
Babylon I will visit you, and perform my
good word toward you, in causing you
to return to this place.
11For I know the thoughts that I think
toward you, saith the LORD, thoughts of
peace, and not of evil, to give you an
expected end.
12Then shall ye call upon me, and ye
shall go and pray unto me, and I will
hearken unto you.
13And ye shall seek me, and find *me,*
when ye shall search for me with all
your heart.
14And I will be found of you, saith the
LORD: and I will turn away your captivity, and I will gather you from all the
nations, and from all the places whither
I have driven you, saith the LORD; and
I will bring you again into the place
whence I caused you to be carried away
captive.
¶15Because ye have said, The LORD
hath raised us up prophets in Babylon;
16*Know* that thus saith the LORD of
the king that sitteth upon the throne of
*David, and of all the people that
dwelleth in this city, *and* of your brethren that are not gone forth with you into
captivity;
17Thus saith the LORD of hosts; Behold, I will send upon them the sword,
the famine, and the pestilence, and will
make them like vile figs, that cannot be
eaten, they are so evil.
18And I will persecute them with the
sword, with the famine, and with the
pestilence, and will deliver them to be
removed to all the kingdoms of the
earth, to be a curse, and an astonishment, and an hissing, and a reproach,
among all the nations whither I have
driven them:
19Because they have not hearkened
to my words, saith the LORD, which I sent
unto them by my servants the prophets, rising up early and sending *them;*
but ye would not hear, saith the LORD.
¶20Hear ye therefore the word of the
LORD, all ye of the captivity, whom I
have sent from Jerusalem to Babylon:
21Thus saith the LORD of hosts, the
God of Israel, of *Ahab the son of Kolaiah, and of Zedekiah the son of Maaseiah, which prophesy a lie unto you in
my name; Behold, I will deliver them
into the hand of Nebuchadrezzar king of
Babylon; and he shall slay them before
your eyes;
22And of them shall be taken up a
curse by all the captivity of Judah which
are in Babylon, saying, The LORD make
thee like Zedekiah and like Ahab, whom
the king of Babylon roasted in the *fire;
23Because they have committed villany in Israel, and have committed adultery with their neighbours' wives, and
have spoken lying words in my name,
which I have not commanded them;
even I know, and *am* a witness, saith the
LORD.
¶24*Thus* shalt thou also speak to Shemaiah the Nehelamite, saying,
25Thus speaketh the LORD of hosts,
the God of Israel, saying, Because thou
hast sent letters in thy name unto all
the people that *are* at Jerusalem, and to
Zephaniah the son of Maaseiah the
priest, and to all the priests, saying,
26The LORD hath made thee priest in
the stead of *Jehoiada the priest, that
ye should be officers in the house of the

29:10 after seventy years. This verse contains the message that Jeremiah sent to the Jews who were in captivity in Babylon. It coincides with that other prophecy in Jeremiah 25:11. After the seventy years were accomplished, God made it possible for His people to return to their land.

LORD, for every man *that is* mad, and
maketh himself a prophet, that thou
shouldest put him in prison, and in the
stocks.
27 Now therefore why hast thou not
reproved Jeremiah of Anathoth, which
maketh himself a prophet to you?
28 For therefore he sent unto us *in*
Babylon, saying, This *captivity is* long:
build ye houses, and dwell *in them;* and
plant gardens, and eat the fruit of them.
29 And Zephaniah the priest read
this letter in the ears of Jeremiah the
prophet.
¶30 Then came the word of the LORD
unto Jeremiah, saying,
31 Send to all them of the captivity,
saying, Thus saith the LORD concerning Shemaiah the Nehelamite; Because
that Shemaiah hath prophesied unto
you, and I sent him not, and he caused
you to trust in a lie:
32 Therefore thus saith the LORD;
Behold, I will punish Shemaiah the
Nehelamite, and his seed: he shall not
have a man to dwell among this people;
neither shall he behold the good that I
will do for my people, saith the LORD;
because he hath taught rebellion
against the LORD.

V. Future of Israel (30:1—33:26)

1) Her time of trouble

30 The word that came to Jeremiah from the LORD, saying,
2 Thus speaketh the LORD God of Israel, saying, Write thee all the words
that I have spoken unto thee in a book.
3 For, lo, the days come, saith the
LORD, that I will bring again the captivity of my people Israel and Judah, saith
the LORD: and I will cause them to return to the land that I gave to their fathers, and they shall possess it.
¶4 And these *are* the words that the
LORD spake concerning Israel and concerning Judah.
5 For thus saith the LORD; We have

30:2 Great Writing
Several of the authors of Scripture declare their purpose to record in writing the messages of God (Deut. 17:18; Josh. 24:26; 1 Sam. 10:25; 2 Pet. 1:12-13; etc.). The findings of archaeology prove that men could and did write long before the days of Moses. See *inspiration. God knew that Jeremiah would not be carried away to Babylon, but that His people there would need His Word for instruction and help and comfort. Notice the help that Daniel received from his reading of Jeremiah (Dan. 9:2-4).

heard a voice of trembling, of fear, and
not of peace.
6 Ask ye now, and see whether a man
doth travail with child? wherefore do I
see every man with his hands on his
loins, as a woman in travail, and all faces
are turned into paleness?
7 Alas! for that day *is* great, so that
none *is* like it: it *is* even the time of
Jacob's trouble; but he shall be saved
out of it.
8 For it shall come to pass in that day,
saith the LORD of hosts, *that* I will break
his yoke from off thy neck, and will
burst thy bonds, and strangers shall no
more serve themselves of him:
9 But they shall serve the LORD their
God, and David their king, whom I will
raise up unto them.

30:7 Future Trouble
The children of Israel had suffered in varying degrees of intensity since their captivity in Babylon.The Scriptures reveal that the future will bring a time of trouble for Jacob–the Jewish people–that will be more severe than anything that that nation has known, worse, even, than what the nation suffered in the Holocaust or any time since. This time of intense suffering will be known as the *Great Tribulation. Nevertheless, God has promised to preserve the nation through its sufferings and to save it through the time of Jacob's Trouble.

30:6 travail. Labor, pain.
30:8 his yoke. The yoke of the *Antichrist.

¶10Therefore fear thou not, O my
servant Jacob, saith the LORD; neither
be dismayed, O Israel: for, lo, I will
save thee from afar, and thy seed from
the land of their captivity; and Jacob
shall return, and shall be in rest, and
be quiet, and none shall make *him*
afraid.
11For I *am* with thee, saith the LORD,
to save thee: though I make a full end
of all nations whither I have scattered
thee, yet will I not make a full end of
thee: but I will correct thee in measure,
and will not leave thee altogether unpunished.
12For thus saith the LORD, Thy bruise
is incurable, *and* thy wound *is* grievous.
13*There is* none to plead thy cause,
that thou mayest be bound up: thou hast
no healing medicines.
14All thy lovers have forgotten thee;
they seek thee not; for I have wounded thee with the wound of an enemy,
with the chastisement of a cruel one,
for the multitude of thine iniquity; *because* thy sins were increased.
15Why criest thou for thine affliction?
thy sorrow *is* incurable for the multitude of thine iniquity: *because* thy sins
were increased, I have done these
things unto thee.
16Therefore all they that devour thee
shall be devoured; and all thine adversaries, every one of them, shall go into
captivity; and they that spoil thee shall
be a spoil, and all that prey upon thee
will I give for a prey.
17For I will restore health unto thee,
and I will heal thee of thy wounds, saith
the LORD; because they called thee an
Outcast, *saying,* This *is* Zion, whom no
man seeketh after.
¶18Thus saith the LORD; Behold, I
will bring again the captivity of Jacob's tents, and have *mercy on his
dwellingplaces; and the city shall be
builded upon her own heap, and the
palace shall remain after the manner
thereof.
19And out of them shall proceed
thanksgiving and the voice of them that
make merry: and I will multiply them,
and they shall not be few; I will also
glorify them, and they shall not be
small.
20Their children also shall be as
aforetime, and their congregation shall

30:9 THE REIGN OF CHRIST

Chapters 30 through 33 of Jeremiah present one of the most complete revelations of the reign of Christ that is found anywhere in the Word of God. They have a definite relation to the experiences of Israel in the time of Jeremiah. They contain at least one reference to the first coming of Christ (Jer. 31:15; see its note, "A Prophecy of Weeping"). Nevertheless, the fact remains that the great message or burden of these chapters is about the kingdom of our Lord Jesus Christ as He will establish it upon His return to the earth.

The following details of the reign of Christ are found in these chapters:

1. The Messiah will be the King of Israel (30:9; 33:15-17).
2. Israel will be restored to the land of Palestine (30:10,18-20; 31:10-14,23-38; 32:15,32-37; 33:7).
3. Israel will be converted to the LORD (30:22; 31:11,31-34; 32:38-40; 33:7-8).
4. Israel will live in safety with the joy of the LORD as their portion (30:10; 33:11).
5. The millennial reign of Christ (see *Millennium) will mark the fulfillment of the promises made to Israel. These promises are established in the everlasting love of God and rest securely upon His faithfulness (31:1-3 and see also 31:1 note, "Israel's Future"; 33:14).

30:12 Thy bruise is incurable. There is no cure for sin as far as man is concerned: God alone has the healing power in the blood of the Lord Jesus Christ, which is necessary for the healing of all—Jew or Gentile (Isa. 53:5-6; 1 Pet. 2:24).

30:18 the palace. The temple, which will be rebuilt in Jerusalem.

30:21 their governor. Their Prince, the Lord Jesus Christ, who will be their Priest to stand before God for Israel.

be established before me, and I will punish all that oppress them.
[21]And their nobles shall be of themselves, and their governor shall proceed from the midst of them; and I will cause him to draw near, and he shall approach unto me: for who *is* this that engaged his heart to approach unto me? saith the LORD.
[22]And ye shall be my people, and I will be your God.
[23]Behold, the whirlwind of the LORD goeth forth with fury, a continuing whirlwind: it shall fall with pain upon the head of the wicked.
[24]The fierce anger of the LORD shall not return, until he have done *it*, and until he have performed the intents of his heart: in the latter days ye shall consider it.

Future of Israel (continued)
*2) Her future *covenant*

31 At the same time, saith the LORD, will I be the God of all the families of Israel, and they shall be my people.
[2]Thus saith the LORD, The people *which were* left of the sword found *grace in the wilderness; *even* Israel, when I went to cause him to rest.
[3]The LORD hath appeared of old unto me, *saying,* Yea, I have loved thee with an everlasting love: therefore with lovingkindness have I drawn thee.
[4]Again I will build thee, and thou shalt be built, O virgin of Israel: thou shalt again be adorned with thy *tabrets, and shalt go forth in the dances of them that make merry.
[5]Thou shalt yet plant vines upon the

31:1 ISRAEL'S FUTURE

Because Israel failed under the old *covenant made with the fathers when God brought them out of the land of Egypt through Moses, God promised through Jeremiah and other prophets that He would make a new *covenant with His people Israel. This proves very clearly that Israel's failure did not blot out the purposes of God for that people. The new covenant is revealed in Jeremiah 31:31-34 and Jeremiah 32:37-41. It is explained further in Hebrews 8:7-13 (see also Heb. 8:8 note, "The New Covenant") and Hebrews 10:15-18.

The terms of this covenant are as follows:

1. It takes the place of the old covenant that Israel had broken (Jer. 31:32; Heb. 8:7-8).
2. It is a covenant of *grace rather than of works (Jer. 31:31; Heb. 8:9).
3. The new covenant promises the new birth by which the law of God is written within the hearts of His people (Jer. 31:33; 32:39; Heb. 8:10; 10:16).
4. The new covenant promises the conversion of the nation Israel to God (Jer. 31:33-34; 32:38; Heb. 8:10).
5. The new covenant promises the forgiveness of sin (Jer. 31:34; Heb. 8:12; 10:17).
6. The new covenant promises to bring the blessings of God upon Israel (Jer. 32:39-40).
7. The new covenant is an everlasting covenant (Jer. 32:40).
8. Although the new covenant was made expressly with the children of Israel, the epistle to the Hebrews applies the benefits of grace that flow from the new covenant to the *church. The present ministry of our Lord is based upon His mediatorship of His better covenant (see Heb. 8:6). The privilege of the *saints during the present *dispensation to enter the holiest by the blood of Jesus is related to this new covenant (Heb. 10:14-22; see 10:22 note, "Assurance of Faith").
9. The communion service is based upon the new covenant (Luke 22:20). This does not mean the new covenant should be understood to declare that the millennial promises will not be kept to Israel. These promises will be literally kept. It does mean, however, that for the recent dispensation the natural branches have been broken out of the olive tree (Israel), and the wild branches, which represent the Gentile world, have been grafted in (see Rom. 11:17-24).

30:24 the latter days. The prophecies of this chapter have not been fulfilled. In the *latter days, they will be fully understood as they come to pass.
31:2 left of the sword. This speaks of Pharaoh's cruelty (Exod. 1–12).

mountains of *Samaria: the planters
shall plant, and shall eat *them* as common things.
[6]For there shall be a day, *that* the
watchmen upon the mount *Ephraim
shall cry, Arise ye, and let us go up to
Zion unto the LORD our God.
[7]For thus saith the LORD; Sing with
gladness for Jacob, and shout among the
chief of the nations: publish ye, praise
ye, and say, O LORD, save thy people,
the *remnant of Israel.
[8]Behold, I will bring them from the
north country, and gather them from
the coasts of the earth, *and* with them
the blind and the lame, the woman with
child and her that travaileth with child
together: a great company shall return
thither.
[9]They shall come with weeping, and
with supplications will I lead them: I
will cause them to walk by the rivers of
waters in a straight way, wherein they
shall not stumble: for I am a father to
Israel, and Ephraim *is* my firstborn.
¶[10]Hear the word of the LORD, O ye
nations, and declare *it* in the *isles afar
off, and say, He that scattered Israel will
gather him, and keep him, as a shepherd *doth* his flock.
[11]For the LORD hath *redeemed Jacob, and *ransomed him from the hand
of *him that was* stronger than he.
[12]Therefore they shall come and sing
in the height of Zion, and shall flow together to the goodness of the LORD, for
wheat, and for wine, and for *oil, and for
the young of the flock and of the herd:
and their soul shall be as a watered garden; and they shall not sorrow any more
at all.
[13]Then shall the virgin rejoice in the
dance, both young men and old together: for I will turn their *mourning into
joy, and will comfort them, and make
them rejoice from their sorrow.
[14]And I will satiate the soul of the
priests with fatness, and my people
shall be satisfied with my goodness,
saith the LORD.
¶[15]Thus saith the LORD; A voice was
heard in Ramah, lamentation, *and* bitter weeping; Rahel weeping for her
children refused to be comforted for her
children, because they *were* not.

31:15 A Prophecy of Weeping

Rachel, or "Rahel," was the mother of Joseph and Benjamin, from whose descendants came the kings of the northern and southern kingdoms: Israel and Judah. The name also stands for all Jewish mothers. The prophecy about her weeping was partially fulfilled when her children were carried away from their land, and was more completely fulfilled when the babies were killed by Herod (see Matt. 2:16-18). There will be weeping again, however, before the fulfillment of verses 16 and 17 comes to pass.

[16]Thus saith the LORD; Refrain thy
voice from weeping, and thine eyes
from tears: for thy work shall be rewarded, saith the LORD; and they shall
come again from the land of the enemy.
[17]And there is hope in thine end,
saith the LORD, that thy children shall
come again to their own border.
¶[18]I have surely heard Ephraim be-
moaning himself *thus;* Thou hast chastised me, and I was chastised, as a
bullock unaccustomed *to the yoke:* turn
thou me, and I shall be turned; for thou
art the LORD my God.
[19]Surely after that I was turned, I repented; and after that I was instructed,
I smote upon *my* thigh: I was ashamed,
yea, even confounded, because I did
bear the reproach of my youth.
[20]*Is* Ephraim my dear son? *is he* a
pleasant child? for since I spake against
him, I do earnestly remember him still:
therefore my *bowels are troubled for

31:7 the chief of the nations. Israel.
31:10 isles. The island nations.
31:15 Ramah. This means in the Hebrew *a high place,* and it probably speaks of a high place near Beth-lehem (Matt. 2:18).

him; I will surely have mercy upon him, saith the LORD.

21 Set thee up waymarks, make thee high heaps: set thine heart toward the highway, *even* the way *which* thou wentest: turn again, O virgin of Israel, turn again to these thy cities.

¶22 How long wilt thou go about, O thou backsliding daughter? for the LORD hath *created a new thing in the earth, A woman shall compass a man.

23 Thus saith the LORD of hosts, the God of Israel; As yet they shall use this speech in the land of *Judah and in the cities thereof, when I shall bring again their captivity; The LORD bless thee, O habitation of justice, *and* mountain of holiness.

24 And there shall dwell in Judah itself, and in all the cities thereof together, *husbandmen, and they *that* go forth with flocks.

25 For I have satiated the weary soul, and I have replenished every sorrowful soul.

26 Upon this I awaked, and beheld; and my sleep was sweet unto me.

¶27 Behold, the days come, saith the LORD, that I will sow the house of Israel and the house of Judah with the seed of man, and with the seed of beast.

28 And it shall come to pass, *that* like as I have watched over them, to pluck up, and to break down, and to throw down, and to destroy, and to afflict; so will I watch over them, to build, and to plant, saith the LORD.

29 In those days they shall say no more, The fathers have eaten a sour grape, and the children's teeth are set on edge.

30 But every one shall die for his own iniquity: every man that eateth the sour grape, his teeth shall be set on edge.

¶31 Behold, the days come, saith the LORD, that I will make a new covenant with the house of Israel, and with the house of Judah:

32 Not according to the covenant that I made with their fathers in the day *that* I took them by the hand to bring them out of the land of *Egypt; which my covenant they brake, although I was an husband unto them, saith the LORD:

33 But this *shall be* the covenant that I will make with the house of Israel; After those days, saith the LORD, I will put my law in their inward parts, and write it in their hearts; and will be their God, and they shall be my people.

34 And they shall teach no more every man his neighbour, and every man his brother, saying, Know the LORD: for they shall all know me, from the least of them unto the greatest of them, saith the LORD; for I will forgive their iniquity, and I will remember their *sin no more.

¶35 Thus saith the LORD, which giveth the sun for a light by day, *and* the ordinances of the moon and of the stars for a light by night, which divideth the sea when the waves thereof roar; The LORD of hosts *is* his name:

36 If those ordinances depart from before me, saith the LORD, *then* the seed of Israel also shall cease from being a nation before me for ever.

37 Thus saith the LORD; If heaven above can be measured, and the foundations of the earth searched out beneath, I will also cast off all the seed of Israel for all that they have done, saith the LORD.

¶38 Behold, the days come, saith the LORD, that the city shall be built to the LORD from the tower of Hananeel unto the gate of the corner.

39 And the measuring line shall yet go forth over against it upon the hill Gareb, and shall compass about to Goath.

40 And the whole valley of the dead bodies, and of the ashes, and all the fields unto the brook of Kidron, unto the corner of the horse gate toward the east, *shall be* *holy unto the LORD;

31:21 high heaps. Landmarks.
31:21 highway. The way that Israel took when they were led out of Egypt.

it shall not be plucked up, nor thrown
down any more for ever.

Future of Israel (continued)
3) Her security in the purposes of God

32 The word that came to Jeremiah from the LORD in the tenth
year of Zedekiah king of Judah, which
was the eighteenth year of Nebuchadrezzar.
2 For then the king of Babylon's army
besieged *Jerusalem: and Jeremiah the
prophet was shut up in the court of the
prison, which *was* in the king of Judah's
house.
3 For Zedekiah king of Judah had shut
him up, saying, Wherefore dost thou
prophesy, and say, Thus saith the LORD,
Behold, I will give this city into the hand
of the king of Babylon, and he shall
take it;
4 And Zedekiah king of Judah shall not
escape out of the hand of the Chaldeans, but shall surely be delivered into
the hand of the king of Babylon, and
shall speak with him mouth to mouth,
and his eyes shall behold his eyes;
5 And he shall lead Zedekiah to Babylon, and there shall he be until I visit
him, saith the LORD: though ye fight
with the Chaldeans, ye shall not prosper?
¶ 6 And Jeremiah said, The word of the
LORD came unto me, saying,
7 Behold, Hanameel the son of Shallum thine uncle shall come unto thee,
saying, Buy thee my field that *is* in
Anathoth: for the right of *redemption
is thine to buy *it.*
8 So Hanameel mine uncle's son came
to me in the court of the prison according to the word of the LORD, and said
unto me, Buy my field, I pray thee, that
is in Anathoth, which *is* in the country
of Benjamin: for the right of inheritance
is thine, and the redemption *is* thine;
buy *it* for thyself. Then I knew that this
was the word of the LORD.
9 And I bought the field of Hanameel
my uncle's son, that *was* in Anathoth,
and weighed him the *money, *even* seventeen shekels of silver.
10 And I subscribed the evidence, and
sealed *it,* and took witnesses, and
weighed *him* the money in the balances.
11 So I took the evidence of the purchase, *both* that which was sealed *according* to the *law and custom, and that
which was open:
12 And I gave the evidence of the purchase unto Baruch the son of Neriah,
the son of Maaseiah, in the sight of
Hanameel mine uncle's *son,* and in the
presence of the witnesses that subscribed the book of the purchase, before
all the Jews that sat in the court of the
prison.
¶ 13 And I charged Baruch before
them, saying,
14 Thus saith the LORD of hosts, the
God of Israel; Take these evidences, this
evidence of the purchase, both which is
sealed, and this evidence which is open;
and put them in an earthen vessel, that
they may continue many days.
15 For thus saith the LORD of hosts,
the God of Israel; Houses and fields and
vineyards shall be possessed again in
this land.

32:2 besieged. Came against.
32:5 until I visit him. Jeremiah 34:4-5 suggests that Zedekiah repented of his sins and turned to the LORD in faith before his death.
32:7 the right of redemption. See Leviticus 25:24-25,32; Ruth 4:4.
32:9 I bought the field. Though the field was then in the possession of the army of Babylon, Jeremiah had faith in God that the land of Judah would be restored. His buying the field would be a proof to Judah of the truth of his prophecies (see also vs. 15).
32:11 the evidence of the purchase. A copy was always made of a deed of purchase. The original, which contained the terms and conditions of the purchase, was sealed on the outside, but the copy, which just gave the fact of the purchase, was left open to read.

¶ 16 Now when I had delivered the evidence of the purchase unto Baruch the
son of Neriah, I prayed unto the LORD,
saying,
17 Ah Lord GOD! behold, thou hast
made the heaven and the earth by thy
great power and stretched out arm, *and*
there is nothing too hard for thee:
18 Thou shewest lovingkindness unto
thousands, and recompensest the iniquity of the fathers into the bosom of
their children after them: the Great, the
Mighty God, the LORD of hosts, *is* his
name,
19 Great in counsel, and mighty in
work: for thine eyes *are* open upon all
the ways of the sons of men: to give
every one according to his ways, and
according to the fruit of his doings:
20 Which hast set signs and wonders
in the land of Egypt, *even* unto this day,
and in Israel, and among *other* men; and
hast made thee a name, as at this day;
21 And hast brought forth thy people
Israel out of the land of Egypt with
signs, and with wonders, and with a
strong hand, and with a stretched out
arm, and with great terror;
22 And hast given them this land,
which thou didst swear to their fathers
to give them, a land *flowing with milk
and honey;
23 And they came in, and possessed it;
but they obeyed not thy voice, neither
walked in thy law; they have done nothing of all that thou commandedst them
to do: therefore thou hast caused all this
evil to come upon them:
24 Behold the mounts, they are come
unto the city to take it; and the city is
given into the hand of the Chaldeans,
that fight against it, because of the
sword, and of the famine, and of the pestilence: and what thou hast spoken is
come to pass; and, behold, thou seest *it*.
25 And thou hast said unto me, O Lord
GOD, Buy thee the field for money, and
take witnesses; for the city is given into
the hand of the Chaldeans.
¶ 26 Then came the word of the LORD
unto Jeremiah, saying,
27 Behold, I *am* the LORD, the God
of all flesh: is there any thing too hard
for me?
28 Therefore thus saith the LORD;
Behold, I will give this city into the hand
of the Chaldeans, and into the hand of
Nebuchadrezzar king of Babylon, and
he shall take it:
29 And the Chaldeans, that fight
against this city, shall come and set fire
on this city, and burn it with the houses,
upon whose roofs they have offered *incense unto *Baal, and poured out *drink-
offerings unto other gods, to provoke
me to anger.
30 For the children of Israel and the
children of Judah have only done evil
before me from their youth: for the children of Israel have only provoked me to
anger with the work of their hands,
saith the LORD.
31 For this city hath been to me *as* a
provocation of mine anger and of my
fury from the day that they built it even
unto this day; that I should remove it
from before my face,
32 Because of all the evil of the children of Israel and of the children of Judah, which they have done to provoke
me to anger, they, their kings, their
princes, their priests, and their prophets, and the men of Judah, and the inhabitants of Jerusalem.
33 And they have turned unto me the
back, and not the face: though I taught
them, rising up early and teaching *them*,
yet they have not hearkened to receive
instruction.
34 But they set their abominations in
the house, which is called by my name,
to defile it.

32:18 recompensest the iniquity. See Exod. 20:5 note.
32:24 the mounts. Mounds of earth raised high over the walls of the city by the enemy forces during a siege.
32:25 for. Though.

35 And they built the *high places of Baal, which *are* in the valley of the son of Hinnom, to cause their sons and their daughters to pass through *the fire* unto *Molech; which I commanded them not, neither came it into my mind, that they should do this *abomination, to cause Judah to sin.

¶36 And now therefore thus saith the LORD, the God of Israel, concerning this city, whereof ye say, It shall be delivered into the hand of the king of Babylon by the sword, and by the famine, and by the pestilence;

37 Behold, I will gather them out of all countries, whither I have driven them in mine anger, and in my fury, and in great wrath; and I will bring them again unto this place, and I will cause them to dwell safely:

38 And they shall be my people, and I will be their God:

39 And I will give them one heart, and one way, that they may *fear me for ever, for the good of them, and of their children after them:

40 And I will make an everlasting covenant with them, that I will not turn away from them, to do them good; but I will put my fear in their hearts, that they shall not depart from me.

41 Yea, I will rejoice over them to do them good, and I will plant them in this land assuredly with my whole heart and with my whole soul.

42 For thus saith the LORD; Like as I have brought all this great evil upon this people, so will I bring upon them all the good that I have promised them.

43 And fields shall be bought in this land, whereof ye say, *It is* desolate without man or beast; it is given into the hand of the Chaldeans.

44 Men shall buy fields for money, and subscribe evidences, and seal *them*, and take witnesses in the land of Benjamin, and in the places about Jerusalem, and in the cities of Judah, and in the cities of the mountains, and in the cities of the valley, and in the cities of the south: for I will cause their captivity to return, saith the LORD.

Future of Israel (continued)
4) Her future Kingdom (Messianic)

33

Moreover the word of the LORD came unto Jeremiah the second time, while he was yet shut up in the court of the prison, saying,

2 Thus saith the LORD the maker thereof, the LORD that formed it, to establish it; the LORD *is* his name;

3 Call unto me, and I will answer thee, and shew thee great and mighty things, which thou knowest not.

4 For thus saith the LORD, the *God of Israel, concerning the houses of this city, and concerning the houses of the kings of Judah, which are thrown down by the mounts, and by the sword;

5 They come to fight with the Chaldeans, but *it is* to fill them with the dead bodies of men, whom I have slain in mine anger and in my fury, and for all whose wickedness I have hid my face from this city.

6 Behold, I will bring it health and cure, and I will cure them, and will reveal unto them the abundance of peace and truth.

7 And I will cause the captivity of Judah and the captivity of Israel to return, and will build them, as at the first.

8 And I will cleanse them from all their iniquity, whereby they have sinned against me; and I will pardon all their iniquities, whereby they have sinned, and whereby they have transgressed against me.

¶9 And it shall be to me a name of joy, a praise and an honour before all the nations of the earth, which shall hear all the good that I do unto them: and they shall fear and tremble for all the good-

32:37 I will gather them out. The promises of verses 37-41 have not yet come to pass. See also Jeremiah 16:15; 23:8.

33:9 them. Jerusalem. "They" refers to the nations.

ness and for all the prosperity that I
procure unto it.
10 Thus saith the LORD; Again there
shall be heard in this place, which ye
say *shall be* desolate without man and
without beast, *even* in the cities of Judah, and in the streets of Jerusalem,
that are desolate, without man, and
without inhabitant, and without beast,
11 The voice of joy, and the voice of
gladness, the voice of the *bridegroom,
and the voice of the bride, the voice of
them that shall say, Praise the LORD of
hosts: for the LORD *is* good; for his
mercy *endureth* for ever: *and* of them
that shall bring the *sacrifice of praise
into the house of the LORD. For I will
cause to return the captivity of the land,
as at the first, saith the LORD.
12 Thus saith the LORD of hosts; Again
in this place, which is desolate without
man and without beast, and in all the
cities thereof, shall be an habitation of
shepherds causing *their* flocks to lie
down.
13 In the cities of the mountains, in the
cities of the vale, and in the cities of the
south, and in the land of Benjamin, and
in the places about Jerusalem, and in
the cities of Judah, shall the flocks pass
again under the hands of him that
telleth *them,* saith the LORD.
14 Behold, the days come, saith the
LORD, that I will perform that good
thing which I have promised unto the
house of Israel and to the house of Judah.
¶ 15 In those days, and at that time,
will I cause the *Branch of *righteousness to grow up unto David; and he
shall execute *judgment and righteousness in the land.
16 In those days shall Judah be
saved, and Jerusalem shall dwell safely: and this *is the name* wherewith she
shall be called, The LORD our righteousness.
¶ 17 For thus saith the LORD; David
shall never want a man to sit upon the
throne of the house of Israel;
18 Neither shall the priests the Levites want a man before me to offer
burnt-offerings, and to kindle meat-
offerings, and to do sacrifice continually.
¶ 19 And the word of the LORD came
unto Jeremiah, saying,
20 Thus saith the LORD; If ye can
break my covenant of the day, and my
covenant of the night, and that there
should not be day and night in their
season;
21 *Then* may also my covenant be broken with David my servant, that he
should not have a son to reign upon his
throne; and with the Levites the
priests, my ministers.
22 As the host of heaven cannot be
numbered, neither the sand of the sea
measured: so will I multiply the seed of
David my servant, and the Levites that
minister unto me.
23 Moreover the word of the LORD
came to Jeremiah, saying,
24 Considerest thou not what this people have spoken, saying, The two families which the LORD hath chosen, he
hath even cast them off? thus they have
despised my people, that they should be
no more a nation before them.
25 Thus saith the LORD; If my covenant *be* not with day and night, *and if*
I have not appointed the ordinances of
heaven and earth;
26 Then will I cast away the seed of
Jacob, and David my servant, *so* that I
will not take *any* of his seed *to be* rulers
over the seed of *Abraham, *Isaac, and
Jacob: for I will cause their captivity to
return, and have mercy on them.

33:13 telleth. Counts.
33:15 In those days. See *dispensations; see also the *covenant with David and *kingdom.
33:17 want. Lack.
33:20 If ye can break my covenant. This would be impossible to do.
33:22 host of heaven. Stars and planets.
33:24 this people. The doubters among the captives.

VI. Israel's Unfaithfulness (34:1—36:32)
1) Her false revival

34 The word which came unto
Jeremiah from the LORD, when
Nebuchadnezzar king of *Babylon, and
all his army, and all the kingdoms of the
earth of his dominion, and all the people, fought against Jerusalem, and
against all the cities thereof, saying,
2 Thus saith the LORD, the God of Israel; Go and speak to Zedekiah king of
Judah, and tell him, Thus saith the
LORD; Behold, I will give this city into
the hand of the king of Babylon, and he
shall burn it with fire:
3 And thou shalt not escape out of his
hand, but shalt surely be taken, and delivered into his hand; and thine eyes
shall behold the eyes of the king of Babylon, and he shall speak with thee mouth
to mouth, and thou shalt go to Babylon.
4 Yet hear the word of the LORD,
O Zedekiah king of Judah; Thus saith
the LORD of thee, Thou shalt not die by
the sword:
5 *But* thou shalt die in peace: and with
the burnings of thy fathers, the former
kings which were before thee, so shall
they burn *odours* for thee; and they will
lament thee, *saying,* Ah lord! for I have
pronounced the word, saith the LORD.
6 Then Jeremiah the *prophet spake
all these words unto Zedekiah king of
Judah in Jerusalem,
7 When the king of Babylon's army
fought against Jerusalem, and against
all the cities of Judah that were left,
against *Lachish, and against Azekah:
for these defenced cities remained of
the cities of Judah.
¶ 8 *This is* the word that came unto
Jeremiah from the LORD, after that the
king Zedekiah had made a covenant
with all the people which *were* at Jerusalem, to proclaim liberty unto them;
9 That every man should let his
manservant, and every man his maidservant, *being* an Hebrew or an He-
brewess, go free; that none should
serve himself of them, *to wit,* of a Jew
his brother.
10 Now when all the princes, and all
the people, which had entered into the
covenant, heard that every one should
let his manservant, and every one his
maidservant, go free, that none should
serve themselves of them any more,
then they obeyed, and let *them* go.
11 But afterward they turned, and
caused the servants and the handmaids,
whom they had let go free, to return,
and brought them into subjection for
servants and for handmaids.
¶ 12 Therefore the word of the LORD
came to Jeremiah from the LORD, saying,
13 Thus saith the LORD, the God of
Israel; I made a covenant with your fathers in the day that I brought them
forth out of the land of Egypt, out of the
house of bondmen, saying,
14 At the end of seven years let ye go
every man his brother an Hebrew,
which hath been sold unto thee; and
when he hath served thee six years,
thou shalt let him go free from thee: but
your fathers hearkened not unto me,
neither inclined their ear.
15 And ye were now turned, and had
done right in my sight, in proclaiming
liberty every man to his neighbour; and
ye had made a covenant before me in
the house which is called by my name:
16 But ye turned and polluted my
name, and caused every man his servant, and every man his handmaid,
whom ye had set at liberty at their pleasure, to return, and brought them into
subjection, to be unto you for servants
and for handmaids.

34:5 thou shalt die in peace. Zedekiah undoubtedly turned in faith to God, repenting of his evil way and disbelief before he died, a blind captive of Babylon.
34:13 I made a covenant. See Exodus 21:2; Deuteronomy 15:12.
34:16 at their pleasure. When the year of being set free came, it was the slave's right to choose whether he wished to go free or remain with his master (Exod. 21:5-6).

17 Therefore thus saith the LORD; Ye
have not hearkened unto me, in proclaiming liberty, every one to his
brother, and every man to his neighbour:
behold, I proclaim a liberty for you, saith
the LORD, to the sword, to the pestilence, and to the famine; and I will make
you to be removed into all the kingdoms
of the earth.
18 And I will give the men that have
transgressed my covenant, which have
not performed the words of the covenant which they had made before me,
when they cut the calf in twain, and
passed between the parts thereof,
19 The princes of Judah, and the
princes of Jerusalem, the eunuchs, and
the priests, and all the people of the
land, which passed between the parts
of the calf;
20 I will even give them into the hand
of their enemies, and into the hand of
them that seek their life: and their dead
bodies shall be for meat unto the fowls
of the heaven, and to the beasts of the
earth.
21 And Zedekiah king of Judah and his
princes will I give into the hand of their
enemies, and into the hand of them that
seek their life, and into the hand of the
king of Babylon's army, which are gone
up from you.
22 Behold, I will command, saith the
LORD, and cause them to return to this
city; and they shall fight against it, and
take it, and burn it with fire: and I will
make the cities of Judah a desolation
without an inhabitant.

Israel's unfaithfulness (continued)
2) By contrast, the loyalty of
the Rechabites

35 The word which came unto
Jeremiah from the LORD in the
days of Jehoiakim the son of *Josiah
king of Judah, saying,
2 Go unto the house of the Rechabites, and speak unto them, and bring
them into the house of the LORD, into
one of the chambers, and give them
wine to drink.
3 Then I took Jaazaniah the son of Jeremiah, the son of Habaziniah, and his
brethren, and all his sons, and the whole
house of the Rechabites;
4 And I brought them into the house
of the LORD, into the chamber of the
sons of Hanan, the son of Igdaliah, a
man of God, which *was* by the chamber
of the princes, which *was* above the
chamber of Maaseiah the son of Shallum, the keeper of the door:
5 And I set before the sons of the
house of the Rechabites pots full of
wine, and cups, and I said unto them,
Drink ye wine.
6 But they said, We will drink no wine:
for Jonadab the son of Rechab our father
commanded us, saying, Ye shall drink no
wine, *neither* ye, nor your sons for ever:
7 Neither shall ye build house, nor
sow seed, nor plant vineyard, nor have
any: but all your days ye shall dwell in
tents; that ye may live many days in the
land where ye *be* strangers.
8 Thus have we obeyed the voice of
Jonadab the son of Rechab our father in
all that he hath charged us, to drink no
wine all our days, we, our wives, our
sons, nor our daughters;
9 Nor to build houses for us to dwell
in: neither have we vineyard, nor field,
nor seed:
10 But we have dwelt in tents, and
have obeyed, and done according to all
that Jonadab our father commanded us.
11 But it came to pass, when Nebuchadrezzar king of Babylon came up

---

34:18 when they cut the calf in twain. See Genesis 15:1-18 note, "The Abrahamic Covenant" and Genesis 15:10,17. As the Israelites had passed between the parts of the calf cut in two pieces, they had solemnly promised to obey the Word of the LORD and had agreed that they would accept death if they did not keep their agreement.

35:2 Rechabites. See 2 Samuel 4:2. They were descendants of Hobab, Moses' brother in-law. Though they were Kenites, they were not idol worshippers but went with Israel to Canaan.

into the land, that we said, Come, and
let us go to Jerusalem for fear of the
army of the Chaldeans, and for fear of
the army of the Syrians: so we dwell at
Jerusalem.
¶ 12 Then came the word of the LORD
unto Jeremiah, saying,
13 Thus saith the LORD of hosts, the
God of *Israel; Go and tell the men of
Judah and the inhabitants of Jerusalem,
Will ye not receive instruction to hearken to my words? saith the LORD.
14 The words of Jonadab the son of
Rechab, that he commanded his sons
not to drink wine, are performed; for
unto this day they drink none, but obey
their father's commandment: notwithstanding I have spoken unto you, rising
early and speaking; but ye hearkened
not unto me.
15 I have sent also unto you all my
servants the *prophets, rising up early
and sending *them,* saying, Return ye
now every man from his evil way, and
amend your doings, and go not after
other gods to serve them, and ye shall
dwell in the land which I have given
to you and to your fathers: but ye have
not inclined your ear, nor hearkened
unto me.
16 Because the sons of Jonadab the
son of Rechab have performed the commandment of their father, which he
commanded them; but this people hath
not hearkened unto me:
17 Therefore thus saith the LORD God
of hosts, the God of Israel; Behold, I will
bring upon Judah and upon all the inhabitants of Jerusalem all the evil that I
have pronounced against them: because
I have spoken unto them, but they have
not heard; and I have called unto them,
but they have not answered.
¶ 18 And Jeremiah said unto the house
of the Rechabites, Thus saith the LORD
of hosts, the God of Israel; Because ye
have obeyed the commandment of Jonadab your father, and kept all his precepts, and done according unto all that
he hath commanded you:
19 Therefore thus saith the LORD of
hosts, the God of Israel; Jonadab the
son of Rechab shall not want a man to
stand before me for ever.

Israel's unfaithfulness (continued)
3) Her rejection of the Word of God

36 And it came to pass in the fourth
year of Jehoiakim the son of
Josiah king of Judah, *that* this word
came unto Jeremiah from the LORD,
saying,
2 Take thee a roll of a book, and write
therein all the words that I have spoken
unto thee against Israel, and against
Judah, and against all the nations, from
the day I spake unto thee, from the days
of Josiah, even into this day.

36:2 The Last Writings
This chapter records the writing of at least part of the book of Jeremiah. From Daniel 9:2 we know that the writings of Jeremiah reached the prophet Daniel before the latter prophet's death. The king of Israel attempted to destroy the Word of God (Jer. 36:23), but God preserved that Word for us (Jer. 36:28,32). See *inspiration–the words were God's words; the mouth was Jeremiah's; the pen was Baruch's (vs. 4).

3 It may be that the house of Judah will
hear all the evil which I purpose to do
unto them; that they may return every
man from his evil way; that I may forgive their iniquity and their sin.
4 Then Jeremiah called Baruch the
son of Neriah: and Baruch wrote from
the mouth of Jeremiah all the words of
the LORD, which he had spoken unto
him, upon a roll of a book.

35:14 notwithstanding I have spoken unto you. This chapter shows the contrast between the Rechabites, who obeyed their earthly father, and the Israelites, who refused to obey their heavenly Father.

36:2 from the days of Josiah. The prophecies of twenty-three years were contained in the roll.

5 And Jeremiah commanded Baruch,
saying, I *am* shut up; I cannot go into
the house of the LORD:
6 Therefore go thou, and read in the
roll, which thou hast written from my
mouth, the words of the LORD in the
ears of the people in the LORD'S house
upon the fasting day: and also thou shalt
read them in the ears of all Judah that
come out of their cities.
7 It may be they will present their
supplication before the LORD, and will
return every one from his evil way: for
great *is* the anger and the fury that
the LORD hath pronounced against this
people.
8 And Baruch the son of Neriah did
according to all that Jeremiah the
prophet commanded him, reading in
the book the words of the LORD in the
LORD'S house.
9 And it came to pass in the fifth year
of Jehoiakim the son of Josiah king of
Judah, in the ninth *month, *that* they
proclaimed a fast before the LORD to all
the people in Jerusalem, and to all the
people that came from the cities of Judah unto Jerusalem.
10 Then read Baruch in the book the
words of Jeremiah in the house of
the LORD, in the chamber of Gemariah
the son of Shaphan the *scribe, in the
higher court, at the entry of the new
gate of the LORD'S house, in the ears of
all the people.
¶ 11 When Michaiah the son of Gemariah, the son of Shaphan, had heard out
of the book all the words of the LORD,
12 Then he went down into the king's
house, into the scribe's chamber: and,
lo, all the princes sat there, *even* Elishama the scribe, and Delaiah the son of
Shemaiah, and Elnathan the son of
Achbor, and Gemariah the son of Shaphan, and Zedekiah the son of Hananiah, and all the princes.
13 Then Michaiah declared unto them
all the words that he had heard, when
Baruch read the book in the ears of the
people.
14 Therefore all the princes sent Jehudi the son of Nethaniah, the son of Shelemiah, the son of Cushi, unto Baruch,
saying, Take in thine hand the roll
wherein thou hast read in the ears of the
people, and come. So Baruch the son of
Neriah took the roll in his hand, and
came unto them.
15 And they said unto him, Sit down
now, and read it in our ears. So Baruch
read *it* in their ears.
16 Now it came to pass, when they had
heard all the words, they were afraid
both one and other, and said unto Baruch, We will surely tell the king of all
these words.
17 And they asked Baruch, saying, Tell
us now, How didst thou write all these
words at his mouth?
18 Then Baruch answered them, He
pronounced all these words unto me
with his mouth, and I wrote *them* with
ink in the book.
19 Then said the princes unto Baruch,
Go, hide thee, thou and Jeremiah; and
let no man know where ye be.
¶ 20 And they went in to the king into
the court, but they laid up the roll in the
chamber of Elishama the scribe, and
told all the words in the ears of the king.
21 So the king sent Jehudi to fetch the
roll: and he took it out of Elishama the
scribe's chamber. And Jehudi read it in
the ears of the king, and in the ears of
all the princes which stood beside the
king.
22 Now the king sat in the winterhouse
in the ninth month: and *there was a fire*
on the hearth burning before him.
23 And it came to pass, *that* when Jehudi had read three or four leaves, he
cut it with the penknife, and cast *it* into
the fire that *was* on the hearth, until all
the roll was consumed in the fire that
was on the hearth.
24 Yet they were not afraid, nor rent

36:5 I am shut up. Jeremiah was in prison (Jer. 33:1).
36:18 book. A scroll or roll; in those days they did not have books like ours. See verse 2.

their garments, *neither* the king, nor
any of his servants that heard all these
words.
25 Nevertheless Elnathan and Delaiah
and Gemariah had made intercession to
the king that he would not burn the roll:
but he would not hear them.
26 But the king commanded Jerahmeel the son of Hammelech, and Seraiah the son of Azriel, and Shelemiah the
son of Abdeel, to take Baruch the scribe
and Jeremiah the prophet: but the LORD
hid them.
¶ 27 Then the word of the LORD came
to Jeremiah, after that the king had
burned the roll, and the words which
Baruch wrote at the mouth of Jeremiah,
saying,
28 Take thee again another roll, and
write in it all the former words that
were in the first roll, which Jehoiakim
the king of Judah hath burned.
29 And thou shalt say to Jehoiakim the
king of Judah, Thus saith the LORD;
Thou hast burned this roll, saying, Why
hast thou written therein, saying, The
king of Babylon shall certainly come
and destroy this land, and shall cause to
cease from thence man and beast?
30 Therefore thus saith the LORD of
Jehoiakim king of Judah; He shall have
none to sit upon the throne of *David:
and his dead body shall be cast out in
the day to the heat, and in the night to
the frost.
31 And I will punish him and his seed
and his servants for their iniquity; and
I will bring upon them, and upon the
inhabitants of Jerusalem, and upon the
men of Judah, all the evil that I have
pronounced against them; but they
hearkened not.
¶ 32 Then took Jeremiah another roll,
and gave it to Baruch the scribe, the son
of Neriah; who wrote therein from the
mouth of Jeremiah all the words of the
book which Jehoiakim king of Judah had
burned in the fire: and there were added besides unto them many like words.

VII. Jeremiah's Personal History
(37:1—45:5)
1) His imprisonment

37 And king Zedekiah the son of
Josiah reigned instead of Coniah
the son of Jehoiakim, whom Nebuchadrezzar king of Babylon made king
in the land of *Judah.
2 But neither he, nor his servants, nor
the people of the land, did hearken unto
the words of the LORD, which he spake
by the prophet Jeremiah.
3 And Zedekiah the king sent Jehucal
the son of Shelemiah and Zephaniah the
son of Maaseiah the priest to the prophet Jeremiah, saying, Pray now unto the
LORD our God for us.
4 Now Jeremiah came in and went out
among the people: for they had not put
him into prison.
5 Then *Pharaoh's army was come
forth out of *Egypt: and when the Chaldeans that besieged Jerusalem heard
tidings of them, they departed from
Jerusalem.
¶ 6 Then came the word of the LORD
unto the prophet Jeremiah, saying,
7 Thus saith the LORD, the God of Israel; Thus shall ye say to the king of
Judah, that sent you unto me to enquire
of me; Behold, Pharaoh's army, which
is come forth to help you, shall return
to Egypt into their own land.
8 And the Chaldeans shall come again,
and fight against this city, and take it,
and burn it with fire.
9 Thus saith the LORD; Deceive not
yourselves, saying, The Chaldeans
shall surely depart from us: for they
shall not depart.
10 For though ye had smitten the
whole army of the Chaldeans that fight

37:1 And king Zedekiah . . . reigned. Compare this chapter with chapter 21, which chronologically belongs between chapters 37 and 38. Zedekiah gave Jeremiah two messages. The one in this chapter was given before that of chapter 21.
37:1 whom. This pronoun refers to Zedekiah.

against you, and there remained *but*
wounded men among them, *yet* should
they rise up every man in his tent, and
burn this city with fire.
¶11And it came to pass, that when the
army of the Chaldeans was broken up
from Jerusalem for fear of Pharaoh's
army,
12Then Jeremiah went forth out of
Jerusalem to go into the land of Benjamin, to separate himself thence in the
midst of the people.

37:12 Jeremiah's Prison Experiences
Jeremiah had five different kinds of prison experiences:
1. He was falsely arrested for treason and put into the dungeon (Jer. 37:11-16).
2. He was allowed to go out of the dungeon to stay in the court of the prison (Jer. 37:21).
3. He was put into the miry dungeon of Malchiah (Jer. 38:6).
4. Again he was released and kept in the court of the prison (Jer. 38:10-13).
5. He was carried away from the city in chains by Nebuzar-adan, captain of the guards, and at last released at Ramah (Jer. 40:1-4).

13And when he was in the gate of
Benjamin, a captain of the ward *was*
there, whose name *was* Irijah, the son
of Shelemiah, the son of Hananiah; and
he took Jeremiah the prophet, saying,
Thou fallest away to the Chaldeans.
14Then said Jeremiah, *It is* false; I fall
not away to the Chaldeans. But he hearkened not to him: so Irijah took Jeremiah, and brought him to the princes.
15Wherefore the princes were wroth
with Jeremiah, and smote him, and put
him in prison in the house of Jonathan
the scribe: for they had made that the
prison.
¶16When Jeremiah was entered into
the dungeon, and into the cabins, and
Jeremiah had remained there many
days;
17Then Zedekiah the king sent, and
took him out: and the king asked him
secretly in his house, and said, Is there
any word from the LORD? And Jeremiah
said, There is: for, said he, thou shalt be
delivered into the hand of the king of
Babylon.
18Moreover Jeremiah said unto king
Zedekiah, What have I offended against
thee, or against thy servants, or against
this people, that ye have put me in
prison?
19Where *are* now your prophets
which prophesied unto you, saying, The
king of Babylon shall not come against
you, nor against this land?
20Therefore hear now, I pray thee,
O my lord the king: let my supplication,
I pray thee, be accepted before thee;
that thou cause me not to return to the
house of Jonathan the scribe, lest I die
there.
21Then Zedekiah the king commanded that they should commit Jeremiah
into the court of the prison, and that
they should give him daily a piece of
bread out of the bakers' street, until all
the bread in the city were spent. Thus
Jeremiah remained in the court of the
prison.

Jeremiah's personal history (continued)

38 Then Shephatiah the son of
Mattan, and Gedaliah the son of
Pashur, and Jucal the son of Shelemiah,
and Pashur the son of Malchiah, heard
the words that Jeremiah had spoken
unto all the people, saying,
2Thus saith the LORD, He that remaineth in this city shall die by the
sword, by the famine, and by the pestilence: but he that goeth forth to the
Chaldeans shall live; for he shall have
his life for a prey, and shall live.
3Thus saith the LORD, This city shall
surely be given into the hand of the king
of Babylon's army, which shall take it.
4Therefore the princes said unto the

37:21 a piece of bread. This was a loaf of bread, or very possibly three small loaves of bread—the soldier's allowance for a day. See also Luke 11:5.

king, We beseech thee, let this man be put to *death: for thus he weakeneth the hands of the men of war that remain in this city, and the hands of all the people, in speaking such words unto them: for this man seeketh not the welfare of this people, but the hurt.

5 Then Zedekiah the king said, Behold, he *is* in your hand: for the king *is* not *he that* can do *any* thing against you.

6 Then took they Jeremiah, and cast him into the dungeon of Malchiah the son of Hammelech, that *was* in the court of the prison: and they let down Jeremiah with cords. And in the dungeon *there was* no water, but mire: so Jeremiah sunk in the mire.

¶ 7 Now when Ebed-melech the Ethiopian, one of the eunuchs which was in the king's house, heard that they had put Jeremiah in the dungeon; the king then sitting in the gate of Benjamin;

8 Ebed-melech went forth out of the king's house, and spake to the king, saying,
9 My lord the king, these men have done evil in all that they have done to Jeremiah the prophet, whom they have cast into the dungeon; and he is like to die for hunger in the place where he is: for *there is* no more bread in the city.

10 Then the king commanded Ebed-melech the Ethiopian, saying, Take from hence thirty men with thee, and take up Jeremiah the prophet out of the dungeon, before he die.

11 So Ebed-melech took the men with him, and went into the house of the king under *the treasury, and took thence old cast clouts and old rotten rags, and let them down by cords into the dungeon to Jeremiah.

12 And Ebed-melech the Ethiopian said unto Jeremiah, Put now *these* old cast clouts and rotten rags under thine armholes under the cords. And Jeremiah did so.

13 So they drew up Jeremiah with cords, and took him up out of the dungeon: and Jeremiah remained in the court of the prison.

¶ 14 Then Zedekiah the king sent, and took Jeremiah the prophet unto him into the third entry that *is* in the house of the LORD: and the king said unto Jeremiah, I will ask thee a thing; hide nothing from me.

15 Then Jeremiah said unto Zedekiah, If I declare *it* unto thee, wilt thou not surely put me to death? and if I give thee counsel, wilt thou not hearken unto me?

16 So Zedekiah the king sware secretly unto Jeremiah, saying, *As* the LORD liveth, that made us this soul, I will not put thee to death, neither will I give thee into the hand of these men that seek thy life.

17 Then said Jeremiah unto Zedekiah, Thus saith the LORD, the God of hosts, the God of Israel; If thou wilt assuredly go forth unto the king of Babylon's princes, then thy soul shall live, and this city shall not be burned with fire; and thou shalt live, and thine house:

18 But if thou wilt not go forth to the king of Babylon's princes, then shall this city be given into the hand of the Chaldeans, and they shall burn it with fire, and thou shalt not escape out of their hand.

19 And Zedekiah the king said unto Jeremiah, I am afraid of the Jews that are fallen to the Chaldeans, lest they deliver me into their hand, and they mock me.

20 But Jeremiah said, They shall not deliver *thee*. Obey, I beseech thee, the voice of the LORD, which I speak unto thee: so it shall be well unto thee, and thy soul shall live.

21 But if thou refuse to go forth, this

38:4 let this man be put to death. Compare this verse and the reason why the chief men wanted Jeremiah put to death with Jeremiah 26:11.

38:10 thirty men. Brave Ebed-melech rescued Jeremiah at such danger to himself from the mob that the thirty men were needed for his protection.

38:11 cast clouts. Old rags and patches of cloth or leather.

is the word that the LORD hath shewed
me:
22And, behold, all the women that are
left in the king of Judah's house *shall be*
brought forth to the king of Babylon's
princes, and those *women* shall say, Thy
friends have set thee on, and have prevailed against thee: thy feet are sunk in
the mire, *and* they are turned away back.
23So they shall bring out all thy wives
and thy children to the Chaldeans: and
thou shalt not escape out of their hand,
but shalt be taken by the hand of the
king of Babylon: and thou shalt cause
this city to be burned with fire.
¶24Then said Zedekiah unto Jeremiah, Let no man know of these words,
and thou shalt not die.
25But if the princes hear that I have
talked with thee, and they come unto
thee, and say unto thee, Declare unto
us now what thou hast said unto the
king, hide it not from us, and we will not
put thee to death; also what the king
said unto thee:
26Then thou shalt say unto them, I
presented my supplication before the
king, that he would not cause me to
return to Jonathan's house, to die there.
27Then came all the princes unto Jeremiah, and asked him: and he told them
according to all these words that the
king had commanded. So they left off
speaking with him; for the matter was
not perceived.
28So Jeremiah abode in the court of
the prison until the day that *Jerusalem
was taken: and he was *there* when Jerusalem was taken.

Jeremiah's personal history (continued)
2) His experience at the fall of Jerusalem

39 In the ninth year of Zedekiah
king of Judah, in the tenth month,
came Nebuchadrezzar king of Babylon
and all his army against Jerusalem, and
they besieged it.
2*And* in the eleventh year of Zedekiah, in the fourth month, the ninth *day*
of the month, the city was broken up.
3And all the princes of the king of
Babylon came in, and sat in the middle
gate, *even* Nergal-sharezer, Samgar-
nebo, Sarsechim, Rab-saris, Nergal-
sharezer, Rab-mag, with all the residue
of the princes of the king of Babylon.
¶4And it came to pass, *that* when Zedekiah the king of Judah saw them, and
all the men of war, then they fled, and
went forth out of the city by night, by
the way of the king's garden, by the
gate betwixt the two walls: and he went
out the way of the plain.
5But the Chaldeans' army pursued
after them, and overtook Zedekiah in
the plains of Jericho: and when they had
taken him, they brought him up to Nebuchadnezzar king of Babylon to Riblah
in the land of Hamath, where he gave
judgment upon him.
6Then the king of Babylon slew the
sons of Zedekiah in Riblah before his
eyes: also the king of Babylon slew all
the nobles of Judah.
7Moreover he put out Zedekiah's
eyes, and bound him with chains, to
carry him to Babylon.
¶8And the Chaldeans burned the
king's house, and the houses of the

38:24 Let no man know. The words of verses 24-26 are the last words recorded in the Bible as spoken by Zedekiah. His character to the last was weak because his dependence was upon man.

39:3 middle gate. The northern part of the city of Jerusalem was separated from the southern by a wall. In this was the middle gate.

39:3 Rab-saris . . . Rab-mag. These are not names but titles.

39:5 they brought him up to Nebuchadnezzar. With this final overthrow of Judah and the capture of its king, the *Times of the Gentiles began. See chapter 27:6 note, "For God's Purpose."

39:7 to carry him to Babylon. The prophecies of Ezekiel and Jeremiah, who both foretold that Zedekiah would see the king of Babylon but not the capital of Babylon, though he should die there, came true (Jer. 32:4; Ezek. 12:13).

39:7 Zedekiah's Judgment
Zedekiah had given an oath of allegiance to Nebuchadnezzar, which he had broken (2 Chron. 36:13). It was for this that Zedekiah received a terrible judgment:
1. the death of his sons (vs. 6);
2. the death of his nobles (vs. 6);
3. the loss of his eyes (vs. 7);
4. the loss of his freedom (vs. 7); and
5. his exile in Babylon (vs. 7).

people, with fire, and brake down the
walls of Jerusalem.
9Then Nebuzar-adan the captain of
the guard carried away captive into
Babylon the *remnant of the people
that remained in the city, and those that
fell away, that fell to him, with the rest
of the people that remained.
10But Nebuzar-adan the captain of
the guard left of the poor of the people,
which had nothing, in the land of Judah,
and gave them vineyards and fields at
the same time.
¶11Now Nebuchadrezzar king of Babylon gave charge concerning Jeremiah
to Nebuzar-adan the captain of the
guard, saying,
12Take him, and look well to him, and
do him no harm; but do unto him even
as he shall say unto thee.
13So Nebuzar-adan the captain of the
guard sent, and Nebushasban, Rab-
saris, and Nergal-sharezer, Rab-mag,
and all the king of Babylon's princes;
14Even they sent, and took Jeremiah
out of the court of the prison, and committed him unto Gedaliah the son of
Ahikam the son of Shaphan, that he
should carry him home: so he dwelt
among the people.
¶15Now the word of the LORD came
unto Jeremiah, while he was shut up in
the court of the prison, saying,
16Go and speak to Ebed-melech the
Ethiopian, saying, Thus saith the LORD
of hosts, the *God of Israel; Behold, I
will bring my words upon this city for
evil, and not for good; and they shall be
accomplished in that day before thee.
17But I will deliver thee in that day,
saith the LORD: and thou shalt not be
given into the hand of the men of whom
thou *art* afraid.
18For I will surely deliver thee, and
thou shalt not fall by the sword, but thy
life shall be for a prey unto thee: because thou hast put thy *trust in me,
saith the LORD.

Jeremiah's history (continued)
3) His ministry in Palestine after
Israel is carried away

40 The word that came to Jeremiah from the LORD, after that
Nebuzar-adan the captain of the guard
had let him go from Ramah, when he
had taken him being bound in chains
among all that were carried away captive of Jerusalem and Judah, which were
carried away captive unto *Babylon.
2And the captain of the guard took
Jeremiah, and said unto him, The LORD
thy God hath pronounced this evil upon
this place.
3Now the LORD hath brought *it,* and
done according as he hath said: because
ye have sinned against the LORD, and
have not obeyed his voice, therefore
this thing is come upon you.
4And now, behold, I loose thee this
day from the chains which *were* upon
thine hand. If it seem good unto thee to
come with me into Babylon, come; and
I will look well unto thee: but if it seem
ill unto thee to come with me into
Babylon, forbear: behold, all the land
is before thee: whither it seemeth
good and convenient for thee to go,
thither go.
5Now while he was not yet gone back,
he said, Go back also to Gedaliah the
son of Ahikam the son of Shaphan,
whom the king of Babylon hath made
governor over the cities of Judah, and
dwell with him among the people: or go
wheresoever it seemeth convenient
unto thee to go. So the captain of the
guard gave him victuals and a reward,
and let him go.
6Then went Jeremiah unto Gedaliah
the son of Ahikam to Mizpah; and dwelt

with him among the people that were
left in the land.
¶7Now when all the captains of the
forces which *were* in the fields, *even*
they and their men, heard that the king
of Babylon had made Gedaliah the son
of Ahikam governor in the land, and had
committed unto him men, and women,
and children, and of the poor of the land,
of them that were not carried away captive to Babylon;
8Then they came to Gedaliah to Mizpah, even Ishmael the son of Nethaniah, and Johanan and Jonathan the sons
of Kareah, and Seraiah the son of Tanhumeth, and the sons of Ephai the Netophathite, and Jezaniah the son of a
Maachathite, they and their men.
9And Gedaliah the son of Ahikam the
son of Shaphan sware unto them and to
their men, saying, Fear not to serve the
Chaldeans: dwell in the land, and serve
the king of Babylon, and it shall be well
with you.
10As for me, behold, I will dwell at
Mizpah to serve the Chaldeans, which
will come unto us: but ye, gather ye
*wine, and summer fruits, and *oil, and
put *them* in your vessels, and dwell in
your cities that ye have taken.
11Likewise when all the Jews that
were in *Moab, and among the Ammonites, and in *Edom, and that *were* in all
the countries, heard that the king of
Babylon had left a remnant of Judah, and
that he had set over them Gedaliah the
son of Ahikam the son of Shaphan;
12Even all the Jews returned out of all
places whither they were driven, and
came to the land of Judah, to Gedaliah,
unto Mizpah, and gathered wine and
summer fruits very much.
¶13Moreover Johanan the son of Kareah, and all the captains of the forces
that *were* in the fields, came to Gedaliah to Mizpah,
14And said unto him, Dost thou certainly know that Baalis the king of the
Ammonites hath sent Ishmael the son
of Nethaniah to slay thee? But Gedaliah the son of Ahikam believed them
not.
15Then Johanan the son of Kareah
spake to Gedaliah in Mizpah secretly,
saying, Let me go, I pray thee, and I will
slay Ishmael the son of Nethaniah, and
no man shall know *it:* wherefore should
he slay thee, that all the Jews which are
gathered unto thee should be scattered,
and the remnant in Judah perish?
16But Gedaliah the son of Ahikam
said unto Johanan the son of Kareah,
Thou shalt not do this thing: for thou
speakest falsely of Ishmael.

Jeremiah's history (continued)

41 Now it came to pass in the seventh month, *that* Ishmael the
son of Nethaniah the son of Elishama,
of the seed royal, and the princes of the
king, even ten men with him, came
unto Gedaliah the son of Ahikam to
Mizpah; and there they did eat bread
together in Mizpah.
2Then arose Ishmael the son of Nethaniah, and the ten men that were with
him, and smote Gedaliah the son of
Ahikam the son of Shaphan with the
sword, and slew him, whom the king of
Babylon had made governor over the
land.
3Ishmael also slew all the Jews that
were with him, *even* with Gedaliah, at
Mizpah, and the Chaldeans that were
found there, *and* the men of war.
4And it came to pass the second day
after he had slain Gedaliah, and no man
knew *it,*
5That there came certain from *Shechem, from *Shiloh, and from *Samaria, *even* fourscore men, having their
beards shaven, and their clothes rent,

41:1 Ishmael the son of Nethaniah. Since he was a member of the royal family, Ishmael was jealous of Gedaliah, who had been made governor over the land.

41:5 having their beards shaven. This, with the torn clothes and self-inflicted wounds, was a sign of the great sorrow of these eighty men, who came to worship in Jerusalem. Ishmael met them with the pretence of taking them to Gedaliah, but Ishmael

and having cut themselves, with *offerings and *incense in their hand, to bring *them* to the house of the LORD.

6 And Ishmael the son of Nethaniah went forth from Mizpah to meet them, weeping all along as he went: and it came to pass, as he met them, he said unto them, Come to Gedaliah the son of Ahikam.

7 And it was *so,* when they came into the midst of the city, that Ishmael the son of Nethaniah slew them, *and cast them* into the midst of the *pit, he, and the men that *were* with him.

8 But ten men were found among them that said unto Ishmael, Slay us not: for we have treasures in the field, of wheat, and of barley, and of oil, and of honey. So he forbare, and slew them not among their brethren.

9 Now the pit wherein Ishmael had cast all the dead bodies of the men, whom he had slain because of Gedaliah, *was* it which Asa the king had made for fear of Baasha king of *Israel: *and* Ishmael the son of Nethaniah filled it with *them that were* slain.

10 Then Ishmael carried away captive all the residue of the people that *were* in Mizpah, *even* the king's daughters, and all the people that remained in Mizpah, whom Nebuzar-adan the captain of the guard had committed to Gedaliah the son of Ahikam: and Ishmael the son of Nethaniah carried them away captive, and departed to go over to the Ammonites.

¶ 11 But when Johanan the son of Kareah, and all the captains of the forces that *were* with him, heard of all the evil that Ishmael the son of Nethaniah had done,

12 Then they took all the men, and went to fight with Ishmael the son of Nethaniah, and found him by the great waters that *are* in Gibeon.

13 Now it came to pass, *that* when all the people which *were* with Ishmael saw Johanan the son of Kareah, and all the captains of the forces that *were* with him, then they were glad.

14 So all the people that Ishmael had carried away captive from Mizpah cast about and returned, and went unto Johanan the son of Kareah.

15 But Ishmael the son of Nethaniah escaped from Johanan with eight men, and went to the Ammonites.

¶ 16 Then took Johanan the son of Kareah, and all the captains of the forces that *were* with him, all the remnant of the people whom he had recovered from Ishmael the son of Nethaniah, from Mizpah, after *that* he had slain Gedaliah the son of Ahikam, *even* mighty men of war, and the women, and the children, and the eunuchs, whom he had brought again from Gibeon:

17 And they departed, and dwelt in the habitation of Chimham, which is by Beth-lehem, to go to enter into Egypt,

18 Because of the Chaldeans: for they

41:17 An Interesting Link
Read about Chimham in 2 Samuel 19:37-40. This verse seems to be an interesting link. The homestead at Beth-lehem is first mentioned in Ruth as belonging to Boaz, the great-grandfather of David. As king, David showed kindness to the loyal Barzillai (2 Sam. 19:31-40), and Chimham was Barzillai's son. Here in 41:17, we have mention of property in Beth-lehem owned by Chimham, which seems to have come to him through the favor of David. This property is used by Jeremiah and his company as an inn where they stayed on their way to Egypt. It was at an inn in Beth-lehem that admission was sought for Mary at the birth of Jesus–also to be taken to Egypt. It is thus possible to ask whether Jesus was not excluded actually from the family home of the house of David, a thought that lends special meaning to Matthew 8:20.

---

and his men killed seventy of the men, probably for their clothes and food. Ten of the men bribed Ishmael not to kill them.

41:9 Asa . . . for fear of Baasha. Read about Asa and Baasha in 1 Kings 15:16-22 and 2 Chronicles 16:1-6.

were afraid of them, because Ishmael the son of Nethaniah had slain Gedaliah the son of Ahikam, whom the king of Babylon made governor in the land.

Jeremiah's history (continued)

42 Then all the captains of the forces, and Johanan the son of Kareah, and Jezaniah the son of Hoshaiah, and all the people from the least even unto the greatest, came near,

2 And said unto Jeremiah the *prophet, Let, we beseech thee, our supplication be accepted before thee, and pray for us unto the LORD thy God, *even* for all this remnant; (for we are left *but* a few of many, as thine eyes do behold us:)

3 That the LORD thy God may shew us the way wherein we may walk, and the thing that we may do.

4 Then Jeremiah the prophet said unto them, I have heard *you;* behold, I will pray unto the LORD your God according to your words; and it shall come to pass, *that* whatsoever thing the LORD shall answer you, I will declare *it* unto you; I will keep nothing back from you.

5 Then they said to Jeremiah, The LORD be a true and faithful witness between us, if we do not even according to all things for the which the LORD thy God shall send thee to us.

6 Whether *it be* good, or whether *it be* evil, we will obey the voice of the LORD our God, to whom we send thee; that it may be well with us, when we obey the voice of the LORD our God.

¶7 And it came to pass after ten days, that the word of the LORD came unto Jeremiah.

8 Then called he Johanan the son of Kareah, and all the captains of the forces which *were* with him, and all the people from the least even to the greatest,

9 And said unto them, Thus saith the LORD, the God of Israel, unto whom ye sent me to present your supplication before him;

10 If ye will still abide in this land, then will I build you, and not pull *you* down, and I will plant you, and not pluck *you* up: for I *repent me of the evil that I have done unto you.

11 *Be not afraid of the king of Babylon, of whom ye are afraid; be not afraid of him, saith the LORD: for I *am* with you to save you, and to deliver you from his hand.

12 And I will shew mercies unto you, that he may have *mercy upon you, and cause you to return to your own land.

¶13 But if ye say, We will not dwell in this land, neither obey the voice of the LORD your God,

14 Saying, No; but we will go into the land of Egypt, where we shall see no war, nor hear the sound of the trumpet, nor have hunger of bread; and there will we dwell:

15 And now therefore hear the word of the LORD, ye remnant of Judah; Thus saith the LORD of hosts, the God of Israel; If ye wholly set your faces to enter into Egypt, and go to sojourn there;

16 Then it shall come to pass, *that* the sword, which ye feared, shall overtake you there in the land of Egypt, and the famine, whereof ye were afraid, shall follow close after you there in Egypt; and there ye shall die.

17 So shall it be with all the men that set their faces to go into Egypt to sojourn there; they shall die by the sword, by the famine, and by the pestilence: and none of them shall remain or escape from the evil that I will bring upon them.

18 For thus saith the LORD of hosts, the God of Israel; As mine anger and my fury hath been poured forth upon the inhabitants of Jerusalem; so shall my fury be poured forth upon you, when ye shall enter into Egypt: and ye

---

42:1 Jezaniah. He was also called Azariah. See Jeremiah 43:2.

shall be an execration, and an astonishment, and a curse, and a reproach; and ye shall see this place no more.

¶[19]The LORD hath said concerning you, O ye remnant of Judah; Go ye not into Egypt: know certainly that I have admonished you this day.

[20]For ye dissembled in your hearts, when ye sent me unto the LORD your God, saying, Pray for us unto the LORD our God; and according unto all that the LORD our God shall say, so declare unto us, and we will do *it*.

[21]And *now* I have this day declared *it* to you; but ye have not obeyed the voice of the LORD your God, nor any *thing* for the which he hath sent me unto you.

[22]Now therefore know certainly that ye shall die by the sword, by the famine, and by the pestilence, in the place whither ye desire to go *and* to sojourn.

Jeremiah's history (continued)
4) He is taken to Egypt

43 And it came to pass, *that* when Jeremiah had made an end of speaking unto all the people all the words of the LORD their God, for which the LORD their God had sent him to them, *even* all these words,

[2]Then spake Azariah the son of Hoshaiah, and Johanan the son of Kareah, and all the proud men, saying unto Jeremiah, Thou speakest falsely: the LORD our God hath not sent thee to say, Go not into *Egypt to sojourn there:

[3]But Baruch the son of Neriah setteth thee on against us, for to deliver us into the hand of the Chaldeans, that they might put us to death, and carry us away captives into Babylon.

[4]So Johanan the son of Kareah, and all the captains of the forces, and all the people, obeyed not the voice of the LORD, to dwell in the land of *Judah.

[5]But Johanan the son of Kareah, and all the captains of the forces, took all the remnant of Judah, that were returned from all nations, whither they had been driven, to dwell in the land of Judah;

[6]*Even* men, and women, and children, and the king's daughters, and every person that Nebuzar-adan the captain of the guard had left with Gedaliah the son of Ahikam the son of Shaphan, and Jeremiah the prophet, and Baruch the son of Neriah.

43:6 Jeremiah in Egypt
Through these verses, we learn that when the *remnant of Israel that was left in the land by Nebuchadnezzar fled to Egypt, they took Jeremiah the prophet with them. Jeremiah concluded his ministry in Egypt and died there. His last predictions were concerning the nations that surrounded Israel. We find these in Jeremiah 46–52.

[7]So they came into the land of Egypt: for they obeyed not the voice of the LORD: thus came they *even* to Tahpanhes.

¶[8]Then came the word of the LORD unto Jeremiah in Tahpanhes, saying,

[9]Take great stones in thine hand, and hide them in the clay in the brickkiln, which *is* at the entry of *Pharaoh's house in Tahpanhes, in the sight of the men of Judah;

[10]And say unto them, Thus saith the LORD of hosts, the God of Israel; Behold, I will send and take Nebuchadrezzar the king of Babylon, my servant, and will set his throne upon these stones that I have hid; and he shall spread his royal pavilion over them.

43:5 all the remnant. Read 40:11-12.
43:7 Tahpanhes. A desert mound called Tell Defenneh represents this fortified city in Egypt today. A ruin was discovered here which was called "the palace of the daughters of Judah." It was probably built by Pharaoh for Zedekiah's daughters (41:10; 43:6). The name of the city is spelled in various ways. See Jeremiah 2:16 and Ezekiel 30:18.
43:9 brickkiln. Brick pavement.
43:10 he shall spread his royal pavilion. The great Jewish historian, Josephus, tells of Nebuchadnezzar's pitching his pavilion on the stones of the brick pavement.

[11]And when he cometh, he shall
smite the land of Egypt, *and deliver*
such *as are* for death to death; and such
as are for captivity to captivity; and such
as are for the sword to the sword.
[12]And I will kindle a *fire in the
houses of the gods of Egypt; and he
shall burn them, and carry them away
captives: and he shall array himself
with the land of Egypt, as a shepherd
putteth on his garment; and he shall go
forth from thence in *peace.
[13]He shall break also the images of
Beth-shemesh, that *is* in the land of
Egypt; and the houses of the gods of the
Egyptians shall he burn with fire.

43:13 Beth-shemesh
This means *house of the sun*, or temples dedicated to sun worship. There are at least four places of this name mentioned in the Bible:
1. on the border of the territory of Judah, near the land of the Philistines (Josh. 15:10);
2. in the eastern part of Issachar's territory (Josh. 19:22);
3. a city of Naphtali (Josh. 19:38); and
4. in the land of Egypt (Jer. 43:13). This was probably the city that was called "Heliopolis" by the Greeks and "On" by the Egyptians.

Jeremiah's history (continued)
5) His message to the Jews in Egypt

44 The word that came to Jeremiah concerning all the Jews
which dwell in the land of Egypt, which
dwell at Migdol, and at Tahpanhes, and
at *Noph, and in the country of Pathros,
saying,
[2]Thus saith the LORD of hosts, the
God of Israel; Ye have seen all the evil
that I have brought upon *Jerusalem,
and upon all the cities of Judah; and,
behold, this day they *are* a desolation,
and no man dwelleth therein,
[3]Because of their wickedness which
they have committed to provoke me to
anger, in that they went to burn incense, *and* to serve other gods, whom
they knew not, *neither* they, ye, nor
your fathers.
[4]Howbeit I sent unto you all my servants the *prophets, rising early and
sending *them*, saying, Oh, do not this
abominable thing that I hate.
[5]But they hearkened not, nor inclined
their ear to turn from their wickedness,
to burn no incense unto other gods.
[6]Wherefore my fury and mine anger
was poured forth, and was kindled in
the cities of Judah and in the streets of
Jerusalem; and they are wasted *and*
desolate, as at this day.
[7]Therefore now thus saith the LORD,
the God of hosts, the God of Israel;
Wherefore commit ye *this* great evil
against your souls, to cut off from you
man and woman, child and suckling, out
of Judah, to leave you none to remain;
[8]In that ye provoke me unto wrath
with the works of your hands, burning
incense unto other gods in the land of
Egypt, whither ye be gone to dwell, that
ye might cut yourselves off, and that ye
might be a curse and a reproach among
all the nations of the earth?
[9]Have ye forgotten the wickedness of
your fathers, and the wickedness of the
kings of Judah, and the wickedness of
their wives, and your own wickedness,
and the wickedness of your wives,
which they have committed in the land
of Judah, and in the streets of Jerusalem?
[10]They are not humbled *even* unto
this day, neither have they feared, nor
walked in my *law, nor in my statutes,
that I set before you and before your
fathers.
¶[11]Therefore thus saith the LORD of
hosts, the God of Israel; Behold, I will
set my face against you for evil, and to
cut off all Judah.

43:11 death to death. To death by the plague.
43:12 burn them, and carry them away. Burn the idols and carry away the worshippers.
44:1 The word . . . concerning all the Jews. Chapter 44 contains Jeremiah's last prophecy relating to Israel.

12 And I will take the remnant of Judah, that have set their faces to go into the land of Egypt to sojourn there, and they shall all be consumed, *and* fall in the land of Egypt; they shall *even* be consumed by the sword *and* by the famine: they shall die, from the least even unto the greatest, by the sword and by the famine: and they shall be an execration, *and* an astonishment, and a curse, and a reproach.

13 For I will punish them that dwell in the land of Egypt, as I have punished Jerusalem, by the sword, by the famine, and by the pestilence:

14 So that none of the remnant of Judah, which are gone into the land of Egypt to sojourn there, shall escape or remain, that they should return into the land of Judah, to the which they have a desire to return to dwell there: for none shall return but such as shall escape.

¶ 15 Then all the men which knew that their wives had burned incense unto other gods, and all the women that stood by, a great multitude, even all the people that dwelt in the land of Egypt, in Pathros, answered Jeremiah, saying,

16 *As for* the word that thou hast spoken unto us in the name of the LORD, we will not hearken unto thee.

17 But we will certainly do whatsoever thing goeth forth out of our own mouth, to burn incense unto the *queen of heaven, and to pour out drink-offerings unto her, as we have done, we, and our fathers, our kings, and our princes, in the cities of Judah, and in the streets of Jerusalem: for *then* had we plenty of victuals, and were well, and saw no evil.

18 But since we left off to burn incense to the queen of heaven, and to pour out drink-offerings unto her, we have wanted all *things,* and have been consumed by the sword and by the famine.

19 And when we burned incense to the queen of heaven, and poured out drink-offerings unto her, did we make her cakes to worship her, and pour out drink-offerings unto her, without our men?

¶ 20 Then Jeremiah said unto all the people, to the men, and to the women, and to all the people which had given him *that* answer, saying,

21 The incense that ye burned in the cities of Judah, and in the streets of Jerusalem, ye, and your fathers, your kings, and your princes, and the people of the land, did not the LORD remember them, and came it *not* into his mind?

22 So that the LORD could no longer bear, because of the evil of your doings, *and* because of the abominations which ye have committed; therefore is your land a desolation, and an astonishment, and a curse, without an inhabitant, as at this day.

23 Because ye have burned incense, and because ye have sinned against the LORD, and have not obeyed the voice of the LORD, nor walked in his law, nor in his statutes, nor in his testimonies; therefore this evil is happened unto you, as at this day.

24 Moreover Jeremiah said unto all the people, and to all the women, Hear the word of the LORD, all Judah that *are* in the land of Egypt:

25 Thus saith the LORD of hosts, the God of Israel, saying; Ye and your wives have both spoken with your mouths, and fulfilled with your hand, saying, We will surely perform our vows that we have vowed, to burn incense to the queen of heaven, and to pour out drink-offerings unto her: ye will surely accomplish your vows, and surely perform your vows.

26 Therefore hear ye the word of the LORD, all Judah that dwell in the land of Egypt; Behold, I have sworn by my

---

44:12 all. All idol worshippers.
44:14 such as shall escape. God has always had his faithful few. Read 1 Peter 3:20; Matthew 7:14; Revelation 3:4.
44:21 them . . . it. "Them" refers to the fathers; "it" to the incense that they burned.

great name, saith the LORD, that my
name shall no more be named in the
mouth of any man of Judah in all the
land of Egypt, saying, The Lord GOD
liveth.
27Behold, I will watch over them for
evil, and not for good: and all the men
of Judah that *are* in the land of Egypt
shall be consumed by the sword and by
the famine, until there be an end of
them.
28Yet a small number that escape the
sword shall return out of the land of
Egypt into the land of Judah, and all the
remnant of Judah, that are gone into the
land of Egypt to sojourn there, shall
know whose words shall stand, mine, or
theirs.
¶29And this *shall be* a sign unto you,
saith the LORD, that I will punish you
in this place, that ye may know that my
words shall surely stand against you for
evil:
30Thus saith the LORD; Behold, I will
give Pharaoh-hophra king of Egypt into
the hand of his enemies, and into the
hand of them that seek his life; as I gave
Zedekiah king of Judah into the hand of
Nebuchadrezzar king of Babylon, his
enemy, and that sought his life.

Jeremiah's history (continued)
6) His warning against false ambition

45 The word that Jeremiah the
prophet spake unto Baruch the
son of Neriah, when he had written
these words in a book at the mouth of
Jeremiah, in the fourth year of Jehoiakim the son of *Josiah king of Judah,
saying,
2Thus saith the LORD, the *God of
Israel, unto thee, O Baruch;
3Thou didst say, Woe is me now! for
the LORD hath added grief to my sorrow; I fainted in my sighing, and I find
no rest.
¶4Thus shalt thou say unto him, The
LORD saith thus; Behold, *that* which I
have built will I break down, and that
which I have planted I will pluck up,
even this whole land.
5And seekest thou great things for
thyself? seek *them* not: for, behold, I
will bring evil upon all flesh, saith the
LORD: but thy life will I give unto thee
for a prey in all places whither thou
goest.

45:1 Baruch
Baruch was the devoted friend of Jeremiah and became his secretary. Although he was of a noble family and might have risen to a high position, he was happy to stay with Jeremiah and share his troubles, and he was taken with his master into Egyptian captivity. According to Jewish tradition, a book called "Baruch" was written by Jeremiah's friend. This is untrue, however, for it is certain that the book was not written or compiled until hundreds of years after this Baruch had died.

VIII. Jeremiah's Prophecies against the Gentile Nations (46:1—51:64)
1) Against Egypt

46 The word of the LORD which
came to Jeremiah the prophet
against the *Gentiles;
2Against Egypt, against the army of
Pharaoh-necho king of Egypt, which
was by the river Euphrates in Carchemish, which Nebuchadrezzar king of
*Babylon smote in the fourth year
of Jehoiakim the son of Josiah king of
Judah.
3Order ye the *buckler and shield,
and draw near to battle.
4Harness the horses; and get up, ye
horsemen, and stand forth with *your*
helmets; furbish the spears, *and* put on
the brigandines.
5Wherefore have I seen them dismayed *and* turned away back? and their
mighty ones are beaten down, and are
fled apace, and look not back: *for* fear
was round about, saith the LORD.

46:1 against the Gentiles. Concerning the nations.
46:4 brigandines. Coats of mail, armor.

6 Let not the swift flee away, nor the
mighty man escape; they shall stumble,
and fall toward the north by the river
Euphrates.
7 Who *is* this *that* cometh up as a flood,
whose waters are moved as the rivers?
8 Egypt riseth up like a flood, and *his*
waters are moved like the rivers; and
he saith, I will go up, *and* will cover the
earth; I will destroy the city and the
inhabitants thereof.
9 Come up, ye horses; and rage, ye
chariots; and let the mighty men come
forth; the Ethiopians and the Libyans,
that handle the shield; and the Lydians,
that handle *and* bend the bow.
10 For this *is* the day of the Lord GOD
of hosts, a day of vengeance, that he
may avenge him of his adversaries: and
the sword shall devour, and it shall be
satiate and made drunk with their
blood: for the Lord GOD of hosts hath a
*sacrifice in the north country by the
river Euphrates.
11 Go up into *Gilead, and take balm,
O virgin, the daughter of Egypt: in vain
shalt thou use many medicines; *for* thou
shalt not be cured.
12 The nations have heard of thy
shame, and thy cry hath filled the land:
for the mighty man hath stumbled
against the mighty, *and* they are fallen
both together.
¶ 13 The word that the LORD spake to
Jeremiah the prophet, how Nebuchadrezzar king of Babylon should come *and*
smite the land of Egypt.
14 Declare ye in Egypt, and publish in
Migdol, and publish in Noph and in Tahpanhes: say ye, Stand fast, and prepare
thee; for the sword shall devour round
about thee.
15 Why are thy valiant *men* swept
away? they stood not, because the
LORD did drive them.
16 He made many to fall, yea, one fell
upon another: and they said, Arise, and
let us go again to our own people, and
to the land of our nativity, from the oppressing sword.
17 They did cry there, Pharaoh king of
Egypt *is but* a noise; he hath passed the
time appointed.
18 *As* I live, saith the King, whose
name *is* the LORD of hosts, Surely as
Tabor *is* among the mountains, and as
*Carmel by the sea, *so* shall he come.
19 O thou daughter dwelling in Egypt,
furnish thyself to go into captivity: for
Noph shall be waste and desolate without an inhabitant.
20 Egypt *is like* a very fair heifer, *but*
destruction cometh; it cometh out of
the north.
21 Also her hired men *are* in the midst
of her like fatted bullocks; for they also
are turned back, *and* are fled away together: they did not stand, because the
day of their calamity was come upon
them, *and* the time of their visitation.
22 The voice thereof shall go like a
serpent; for they shall march with an
army, and come against her with axes,
as hewers of wood.
23 They shall cut down her forest,
saith the LORD, though it cannot be
searched; because they are more than
the grasshoppers, and *are* innumerable.
24 The daughter of Egypt shall be confounded; she shall be delivered into the
hand of the people of the north.
25 The LORD of hosts, the God of Israel, saith; Behold, I will punish the
multitude of No, and Pharaoh, and
Egypt, with their gods, and their kings;
even Pharaoh, and *all* them that *trust
in him:
26 And I will deliver them into the
hand of those that seek their lives, and
into the hand of Nebuchadrezzar king of

46:16 to our own people. The Egyptians, who had been living in great luxury and who had therefore grown soft, had hired soldiers from the nations around them to fight for them against Babylon. In the destruction of Egypt, the hired soldiers desired to flee to their own countries.

46:22 they. The Babylonians. "Her" refers to the Egyptians.

Babylon, and into the hand of his servants: and afterward it shall be inhabited, as in the days of old, saith the LORD.
¶[27]But fear not thou, O my servant *Jacob, and be not dismayed, O Israel: for, behold, I will save thee from afar off, and thy seed from the land of their captivity; and Jacob shall return, and be in rest and at ease, and none shall make *him* afraid.
[28]Fear thou not, O Jacob my servant, saith the LORD: for I *am* with thee; for I will make a full end of all the nations whither I have driven thee: but I will not make a full end of thee, but correct thee in measure; yet will I not leave thee wholly unpunished.

Prophecies against nations (continued)
*2) Against Philistia and *Tyre*

47 The word of the LORD that came to Jeremiah the prophet against the *Philistines, before that Pharaoh smote *Gaza.
[2]Thus saith the LORD; Behold, waters rise up out of the north, and shall be an overflowing flood, and shall overflow the land, and all that is therein; the city, and them that dwell therein: then the men shall cry, and all the inhabitants of the land shall howl.
[3]At the noise of the stamping of the hoofs of his strong *horses,* at the rushing of his chariots, *and at* the rumbling of his wheels, the fathers shall not look back to *their* children for feebleness of hands;
[4]Because of the day that cometh to spoil all the Philistines, *and* to cut off from Tyrus and Zidon every helper that remaineth: for the LORD will spoil the Philistines, the *remnant of the country of Caphtor.
[5]Baldness is come upon Gaza; *Ashkelon is cut off *with* the remnant of their valley: how long wilt thou cut thyself?
[6]O thou sword of the LORD, how long *will it be* ere thou be quiet? put up thyself into thy scabbard, rest, and be still.
[7]How can it be quiet, seeing the LORD hath given it a charge against Ashkelon, and against the sea shore? there hath he appointed it.

Prophecies against nations (continued)
*3) Against *Moab*

48 Against Moab thus saith the LORD of hosts, the God of *Israel; Woe unto Nebo! for it is spoiled: Kiriathaim is confounded *and* taken: Misgab is confounded and dismayed.
[2]*There shall be* no more praise of Moab: in Heshbon they have devised evil against it; come, and let us cut it off from *being* a nation. Also thou shalt be cut down, O Madmen; the sword shall pursue thee.
[3]A voice of crying *shall be* from Horonaim, spoiling and great destruction.
[4]Moab is destroyed; her little ones have caused a cry to be heard.
[5]For in the going up of Luhith continual weeping shall go up; for in the going down of Horonaim the enemies have heard a cry of destruction.
[6]Flee, save your lives, and be like the *heath in the wilderness.
¶[7]For because thou hast trusted in thy works and in thy treasures, thou shalt also be taken: and *Chemosh shall go forth into captivity *with* his priests and his princes together.
[8]And the spoiler shall come upon every city, and no city shall escape: the valley also shall perish, and the plain

---

46:26 inhabited, as in the days of old. This prophecy has not yet been fulfilled.
46:27 fear not thou. The prophecies against the Gentile nations, contained in this chapter and in those that follow, have in many cases a double view. There was to be a swift and sudden destruction in the near future, and there is to be a final destruction at the time of the restoration of Israel. See Matthew 25:32 note, "The Judgment of the Nations."
47:2 waters. The Babylonians.
47:4 Caphtor. The original home of the Philistines.
48:5 Luhith . . . Horonaim. Luhith was on a hill, while Horonaim was in a valley.

shall be destroyed, as the LORD hath
spoken.
9Give wings unto Moab, that it may
flee and get away: for the cities thereof
shall be desolate, without any to dwell
therein.
10Cursed *be* he that doeth the work
of the LORD deceitfully, and cursed *be*
he that keepeth back his sword from
blood.
¶11Moab hath been at ease from his
youth, and he hath settled on his lees,
and hath not been emptied from vessel
to vessel, neither hath he gone into
captivity: therefore his taste remained
in him, and his scent is not changed.
12Therefore, behold, the days come,
saith the LORD, that I will send unto him
wanderers, that shall cause him to wander,
and shall empty his vessels, and
break their bottles.
13And Moab shall be ashamed of
Chemosh, as the house of Israel was
ashamed of *Beth-el their confidence.
¶14How say ye, We *are* mighty and
strong men for the war?
15Moab is spoiled, and gone up *out of*
her cities, and his chosen young men
are gone down to the slaughter, saith
the King, whose name *is* the LORD of
hosts.
16The calamity of Moab *is* near to
come, and his affliction hasteth fast.
17All ye that are about him, bemoan
him; and all ye that know his name, say,
How is the strong staff broken, *and* the
beautiful rod!
18Thou daughter that dost inhabit
Dibon, come down from *thy* glory, and
sit in thirst; for the spoiler of Moab shall
come upon thee, *and* he shall destroy
thy strong holds.
19O inhabitant of Aroer, stand by the
way, and espy; ask him that fleeth, and
her that escapeth, *and* say, What is done?
20Moab is confounded; for it is broken
down: howl and cry; and tell ye it in
Arnon, that Moab is spoiled,
21And *judgment is come upon the
plain country; upon Holon, and upon
Jahazah, and upon Mephaath,
22And upon Dibon, and upon Nebo,
and upon Beth-diblathaim,
23And upon Kiriathaim, and upon
Beth-gamul, and upon Beth-meon,
24And upon Kerioth, and upon Bozrah,
and upon all the cities of the land
of Moab, far or near.
25The horn of Moab is cut off, and his
arm is broken, saith the LORD.
¶26Make ye him drunken: for he magnified
himself against the LORD: Moab
also shall wallow in his vomit, and he
also shall be in derision.
27For was not Israel a derision unto
thee? was he found among thieves? for
since thou spakest of him, thou
skippedst for joy.
28O ye that dwell in Moab, leave the
cities, and dwell in the rock, and be like
the dove *that* maketh her nest in the
sides of the hole's mouth.
29We have heard the pride of Moab,
(he is exceeding proud) his loftiness,
and his arrogancy, and his pride, and the
haughtiness of his heart.
30I know his wrath, saith the LORD;
but *it shall* not *be* so; his lies shall not
so effect *it*.
31Therefore will I howl for Moab, and
I will cry out for all Moab; *mine heart*
shall mourn for the men of Kir-heres.
32O vine of Sibmah, I will weep for
thee with the weeping of Jazer: thy

48:11 settled on his lees. The lees are the dregs or sediment at the bottom of a bottle of wine.
48:13 ashamed of Beth-el. In Beth-el, Jeroboam, king of Israel, set up a golden calf for the people to worship.
48:19 Aroer. A city near Moab.
48:26 drunken. Not drunken with wine but with terrible sorrow because of his sin against the LORD.
48:32 Sibmah. A city in Moab that was famous for its grapevines.

plants are gone over the sea, they reach *even* to the sea of Jazer: the spoiler is fallen upon thy summer fruits and upon thy vintage.

33 And joy and gladness is taken from the plentiful field, and from the land of Moab; and I have caused *wine to fail from the winepresses: none shall tread with shouting; *their* shouting *shall be* no shouting.

34 From the cry of Heshbon *even* unto Elealeh, *and even* unto Jahaz, have they uttered their voice, from Zoar *even* unto Horonaim, *as* an heifer of three years old: for the waters also of Nimrim shall be desolate.

35 Moreover I will cause to cease in Moab, saith the LORD, him that offereth in the *high places, and him that burneth *incense to his gods.

36 Therefore mine heart shall sound for Moab like pipes, and mine heart shall sound like pipes for the men of Kir-heres: because the riches *that* he hath gotten are perished.

37 For every head *shall be* bald, and every beard clipped: upon all the hands *shall be* cuttings, and upon the loins sackcloth.

38 *There shall be* lamentation generally upon all the housetops of Moab, and in the streets thereof: for I have broken Moab like a vessel wherein *is* no pleasure, saith the LORD.

39 They shall howl, *saying,* How is it broken down! how hath Moab turned the back with shame! so shall Moab be a derision and a dismaying to all them about him.

40 For thus saith the LORD; Behold, he shall fly as an eagle, and shall spread his wings over Moab.

41 Kerioth is taken, and the strong holds are surprised, and the mighty men's hearts in Moab at that day shall be as the heart of a woman in her pangs.

42 And Moab shall be destroyed from *being* a people, because he hath magnified *himself* against the LORD.

43 Fear, and the *pit, and the snare, *shall be* upon thee, O inhabitant of Moab, saith the LORD.

44 He that fleeth from the fear shall fall into the pit; and he that getteth up out of the pit shall be taken in the snare: for I will bring upon it, *even* upon Moab, the year of their visitation, saith the LORD.

45 They that fled stood under the shadow of Heshbon because of the force: but a fire shall come forth out of Heshbon, and a flame from the midst of Sihon, and shall devour the corner of Moab, and the crown of the head of the tumultuous ones.

46 Woe be unto thee, O Moab! the people of Chemosh perisheth: for thy sons are taken captives, and thy daughters captives.

¶47 Yet will I bring again the captivity of Moab in the latter days, saith the LORD. Thus far *is* the judgment of Moab.

Prophecies against nations (continued)
4) Against various nations

49 Concerning the Ammonites, thus saith the LORD; Hath Israel no sons? hath he no heir? why *then* doth their king inherit Gad, and his people dwell in his cities?

2 Therefore, behold, the days come, saith the LORD, that I will cause an alarm of war to be heard in Rabbah of the Ammonites; and it shall be a desolate heap, and her daughters shall be burned with *fire: then shall Israel be heir unto them that were his heirs, saith the LORD.

3 Howl, O Heshbon, for Ai is spoiled: cry, ye daughters of Rabbah, gird you with sackcloth; lament, and run to and fro by the hedges; for their king shall go into captivity, *and* his priests and his princes together.

4 Wherefore gloriest thou in the valleys,

49:1 their king. The god of the Ammonites, Malcam or *Molech, was being worshipped in the territory which had belonged to Gad before the ten tribes were carried away into captivity. "His people" means Molech's people; "his cities" means the cities of Gad.

thy flowing valley, O backsliding daughter? that trusted in her treasures, *saying,* Who shall come unto me?
5 Behold, I will bring a fear upon thee,
saith the Lord GOD of hosts, from all
those that be about thee; and ye shall
be driven out every man right forth; and
none shall gather up him that wandereth.
6 And afterward I will bring again the
captivity of the children of Ammon,
saith the LORD.
¶7 Concerning *Edom, thus saith the
LORD of hosts; *Is* wisdom no more in
Teman? is counsel perished from the
prudent? is their wisdom vanished?
8 Flee ye, turn back, dwell deep,
O inhabitants of Dedan; for I will bring
the calamity of *Esau upon him, the
time *that* I will visit him.
9 If grapegatherers come to thee,
would they not leave *some* gleaning
grapes? if thieves by night, they will
destroy till they have enough.
10 But I have made Esau bare, I have
uncovered his secret places, and he
shall not be able to hide himself: his
seed is spoiled, and his brethren, and
his neighbours, and he *is* not.
11 Leave thy fatherless children, I will
preserve *them* alive; and let thy widows
trust in me.
12 For thus saith the LORD; Behold,
they whose judgment *was* not to drink
of the cup have assuredly drunken; and
art thou he *that* shall altogether go unpunished? thou shalt not go unpunished, but thou shalt surely drink *of it.*
13 For I have sworn by myself, saith
the LORD, that Bozrah shall become a
desolation, a reproach, a waste, and a
curse; and all the cities thereof shall be
perpetual wastes.
14 I have heard a rumour from the
LORD, and an ambassador is sent unto
the heathen, *saying,* Gather ye together, and come against her, and rise up to
the battle.
15 For, lo, I will make thee small
among the heathen, *and* despised
among men.
16 Thy terribleness hath deceived
thee, *and* the pride of thine heart,
O thou that dwellest in the clefts of the
rock, that holdest the height of the hill:
though thou shouldest make thy nest as
high as the eagle, I will bring thee down
from thence, saith the LORD.
17 Also Edom shall be a desolation:
every one that goeth by it shall be astonished, and shall hiss at all the
plagues thereof.
18 As in the overthrow of Sodom and
Gomorrah and the neighbour *cities*
thereof, saith the LORD, no man shall
abide there, neither shall a son of man
dwell in it.
19 Behold, he shall come up like a lion
from the swelling of Jordan against the
habitation of the strong: but I will suddenly make him run away from her: and
who *is* a chosen *man, that* I may appoint
over her? for who *is* like me? and who
will appoint me the time? and who *is*
that shepherd that will stand before
me?
20 Therefore hear the counsel of the

49:10 The Destruction of Edom
Though a "grapegatherer" leaves some grapes, and a thief leaves some treasures behind (vs. 9), the prophecy is that God will utterly destroy Edom because of its great sin. Esau, a descendant of Abraham, was the father of the nation Edom, as Jacob was the father of the nation of Israel. Esau had led his people into idolatry and terrible evil. He did not sin in ignorance of the consequences, but in full knowledge; therefore, the terrible judgment.

49:12 they whose judgment was not to drink. This speaks of Israel. God's children had to be punished for sin; how much more must those who are not His children! The second half of the verse applies to those who are not children—Edom, in this case.

49:19 he. The Babylonian general. "The strong" and "him" were the people of Edom. "Her" probably means Idumea, a section of Edom. The "shepherd" means the ruler.

LORD, that he hath taken against Edom; and his purposes, that he hath purposed against the inhabitants of Teman: Surely the least of the flock shall draw them out: surely he shall make their habitations desolate with them.
21The earth is moved at the noise of their fall, at the cry the noise thereof was heard in the Red sea.
22Behold, he shall come up and fly as the eagle, and spread his wings over Bozrah: and at that day shall the heart of the mighty men of Edom be as the heart of a woman in her pangs.
¶23Concerning Damascus. Hamath is confounded, and Arpad: for they have heard evil tidings: they are fainthearted; *there is* sorrow on the sea; it cannot be quiet.
24Damascus is waxed feeble, *and* turneth herself to flee, and fear hath seized on *her:* anguish and sorrows have taken her, as a woman in travail.
25How is the city of praise not left, the city of my joy!
26Therefore her young men shall fall in her streets, and all the men of war shall be cut off in that day, saith the LORD of hosts.
27And I will kindle a fire in the wall of Damascus, and it shall consume the palaces of *Ben-hadad.
¶28Concerning Kedar, and concerning the kingdoms of Hazor, which Nebuchadrezzar king of Babylon shall smite, thus saith the LORD; Arise ye, go up to Kedar, and spoil the men of the east.
29Their tents and their flocks shall they take away: they shall take to themselves their curtains, and all their vessels, and their camels; and they shall cry unto them, Fear *is* on every side.
¶30Flee, get you far off, dwell deep, O ye inhabitants of Hazor, saith the LORD; for Nebuchadrezzar king of Babylon hath taken counsel against you, and hath conceived a purpose against you.
31Arise, get you up unto the wealthy nation, that dwelleth without care, saith the LORD, which have neither gates nor bars, *which* dwell alone.
32And their camels shall be a booty, and the multitude of their cattle a spoil: and I will scatter into all winds them *that are* in the utmost corners; and I will bring their calamity from all sides thereof, saith the LORD.
33And Hazor shall be a dwelling for dragons, *and* a desolation for ever: there shall no man abide there, nor *any* son of man dwell in it.
¶34The word of the LORD that came to Jeremiah the *prophet against Elam in the beginning of the reign of Zedekiah king of *Judah, saying,
35Thus saith the LORD of hosts; Behold, I will break the bow of Elam, the chief of their might.
36And upon Elam will I bring the four winds from the four quarters of heaven, and will *scatter them toward all those winds; and there shall be no nation whither the outcasts of Elam shall not come.
37For I will cause Elam to be dismayed before their enemies, and before them that seek their life: and I will bring evil upon them *even* my fierce anger, saith the LORD; and I will send the sword after them, till I have consumed them:

49:22 he. The Babylonians.
49:23 Damascus. Since this was the capital of Syria, in this verse it stands for the whole country, just as today we often refer to Italy, for example, when we speak of its capital, Rome.
49:28 Kedar. The Arabians, descended from Ishmael.
49:28 Hazor. Neighbors of the Arabians.
49:34 Elam. Media was north, Persia was east, and Babylon was west of Elam. The Elamites were scattered because of the help they gave to Nebuchadnezzar when he fought against Judaea. See Acts 2:9 to read of the Elamites in Jerusalem about six hundred years later who heard the gospel in their own tongue.

38And I will set my throne in Elam, and will destroy from thence the king and the princes, saith the LORD.

¶39But it shall come to pass in the latter days, *that* I will bring again the captivity of Elam, saith the LORD.

Prophecies against nations (continued)
5) Against Babylon

50 The word that the LORD spake against Babylon *and* against the land of the Chaldeans by Jeremiah the prophet.

2Declare ye among the nations, and publish, and set up a standard; publish, *and* conceal not: say, Babylon is taken, Bel is confounded, Merodach is broken in pieces; her idols are confounded, her images are broken in pieces.

50:2 Six Prophecies for Babylon
It has been pointed out that chapters 50 and 51 contain six prophecies concerning Babylon. Each of these ends with a message of comfort for Israel. These messages of comfort are found in Jeremiah 50:7,20,34; 51:3,19,58. The LORD had given the government of the earth into the hands of Babylon after Israel's failure, but Babylon utterly failed and therefore had to be judged. See *Times of the Gentiles for the rule of the Gentile nations over the earth.

3For out of the north there cometh up a nation against her, which shall make her land desolate, and none shall dwell therein: they shall remove, they shall depart, both man and beast.

¶4In those days, and in that time, saith the LORD, the children of Israel shall come, they and the children of Judah together, going and weeping: they shall go, and seek the LORD their God.

5They shall ask the way to *Zion with their faces thitherward, *saying,* Come, and let us join ourselves to the LORD in a perpetual *covenant *that* shall not be forgotten.

6My people hath been lost sheep: their shepherds have caused them to go astray, they have turned them away *on* the mountains: they have gone from mountain to hill, they have forgotten their restingplace.

7All that found them have devoured them: and their adversaries said, We *offend not, because they have sinned against the LORD, the habitation of justice, even the LORD, the *hope of their fathers.

8Remove out of the midst of Babylon, and go forth out of the land of the Chaldeans, and be as the he goats before the flocks.

¶9For, lo, I will raise and cause to come up against Babylon an assembly of great nations from the north country: and they shall set themselves in array against her; from thence she shall be taken: their arrows *shall be* as of a mighty expert man; none shall return in vain.

10And Chaldea shall be a spoil: all that spoil her shall be satisfied, saith the LORD.

11Because ye were glad, because ye rejoiced, O ye destroyers of mine heritage, because ye are grown fat as the heifer at grass, and bellow as bulls;

12Your mother shall be sore confounded; she that bare you shall be ashamed: behold, the hindermost of the nations *shall be* a wilderness, a dry land, and a desert.

13Because of the wrath of the LORD it shall not be inhabited, but it shall be wholly desolate: every one that goeth

50:2 Bel . . . Merodach. The name of a Babylonian god.
50:3 out of the north. The country of the Medes. A future nation is also spoken of (see vss. 4-5).
50:6 shepherds. Rulers or leaders. The kings of Israel led the people in the setting up and worshipping of idols.
50:8 Remove out of the midst. This is addressed to the Israelites exiled in Babylon. The "he goats" were the leaders.
50:12 Your mother. Babylon. God is speaking to the "destroyers of mine heritage" (vs. 11).

by Babylon shall be astonished, and hiss
at all her plagues.
14Put yourselves in array against
Babylon round about: all ye that bend
the bow, shoot at her, spare no arrows:
for she hath sinned against the LORD.
15Shout against her round about: she
hath given her hand: her foundations
are fallen, her walls are thrown down:
for it *is* the vengeance of the LORD: take
vengeance upon her; as she hath done,
do unto her.
16Cut off the sower from Babylon,
and him that handleth the sickle in the
time of harvest: for fear of the oppressing sword they shall turn every one to
his people, and they shall flee every one
to his own land.
¶17Israel *is* a scattered sheep; the
lions have driven *him* away: first the
king of Assyria hath devoured him; and
last this Nebuchadrezzar king of Babylon hath broken his bones.
18Therefore thus saith the LORD of
hosts, the God of Israel; Behold, I will
punish the king of Babylon and his land,
as I have punished the king of Assyria.
19And I will bring Israel again to his
habitation, and he shall feed on *Carmel
and *Bashan, and his soul shall be
satisfied upon mount *Ephraim and
Gilead.
20In those days, and in that time, saith
the LORD, the iniquity of Israel shall be
sought for, and *there shall be* none; and
the sins of Judah, and they shall not be
found: for I will pardon them whom I
reserve.
¶21Go up against the land of Merathaim, *even* against it, and against the inhabitants of Pekod: waste and utterly
destroy after them, saith the LORD, and
do according to all that I have commanded thee.
22A sound of battle *is* in the land, and
of great destruction.
23How is the hammer of the whole
earth cut asunder and broken! how is
Babylon become a desolation among
the nations!
24I have laid a snare for thee, and thou
art also taken, O Babylon, and thou wast
not aware: thou art found, and also
caught, because thou hast striven
against the LORD.
25The LORD hath opened his armoury,
and hath brought forth the weapons of
his indignation: for this *is* the work of
the Lord GOD of hosts in the land of the
Chaldeans.
26Come against her from the utmost
border, open her storehouses: cast her
up as heaps, and destroy her utterly: let
nothing of her be left.
27Slay all her bullocks; let them go
down to the slaughter: woe unto them!
for their day is come, the time of their
visitation.
28The voice of them that flee and escape out of the land of Babylon, to declare in Zion the vengeance of the LORD
our God, the vengeance of his temple.
29Call together the archers against
Babylon: all ye that bend the bow, camp
against it round about; let none thereof
escape: recompense her according to
her work; according to all that she hath
done, do unto her: for she hath been

50:15 given her hand. Surrendered.
50:20 I will pardon them. God the Father here points to His Son, the Lord Jesus Christ, for in Him "the iniquity of Israel shall be sought for, and . . . shall not be found." See *names of God, *God—the Trinity for Christ as Saviour.
50:21 Merathaim. A name used for Babylon.
50:21 Pekod. A name used for the Chaldeans, the people of Babylon.
50:23 hammer of the whole earth. Babylon was God's hammer to break the nations, but the power of the hammer was taken away. See Daniel 5:17-23 to read the reason for this.
50:26 Come against her. This verse and verse 27 were addressed to the Medes, who with their allies were to capture Babylon (see Dan. 5:30-31).
50:28 vengeance of his temple. See Daniel 5:1-4 for the record of one Babylonian who sinned against God and His temple.

proud against the LORD, against the
Holy One of Israel.
30 Therefore shall her young men fall
in the streets, and all her men of war
shall be cut off in that day, saith the
LORD.
31 Behold, I *am* against thee, *O thou*
most proud, saith the Lord GOD of
hosts: for thy day is come, the time *that*
I will visit thee.
32 And the most proud shall stumble
and fall, and none shall raise him up: and
I will kindle a fire in his cities, and it
shall devour all round about him.
¶33 Thus saith the LORD of hosts; The
children of Israel and the children of
Judah *were* oppressed together: and all
that took them captives held them fast;
they refused to let them go.
34 Their *Redeemer *is* strong; the
LORD of hosts *is* his name: he shall
throughly plead their cause, that he
may give rest to the land, and disquiet
the inhabitants of Babylon.
¶35 A sword *is* upon the Chaldeans,
saith the LORD, and upon the inhabitants of Babylon, and upon her princes,
and upon her wise *men*.
36 A sword *is* upon the liars; and they
shall dote: a sword *is* upon her mighty
men; and they shall be dismayed.
37 A sword *is* upon their horses, and
upon their chariots, and upon all the
mingled people that *are* in the midst of
her; and they shall become as women:
a sword *is* upon her treasures; and they
shall be robbed.
38 A drought *is* upon her waters; and
they shall be dried up: for it *is* the land
of graven images, and they are mad
upon *their* idols.
39 Therefore the wild beasts of the
desert with the wild beasts of the islands shall dwell *there*, and the owls
shall dwell therein: and it shall be no
more inhabited for ever; neither shall
it be dwelt in from generation to generation.
40 As God overthrew Sodom and Gomorrah and the neighbour *cities*
thereof, saith the LORD; *so* shall no man
abide there, neither shall any son of
man dwell therein.
41 Behold, a people shall come from
the north, and a great nation, and many
kings shall be raised up from the coasts
of the earth.
42 They shall hold the bow and the
lance: they *are* cruel, and will not shew
mercy: their voice shall roar like the
sea, and they shall ride upon horses,
every one put in array, like a man to the
battle, against thee, O daughter of Babylon.
43 The king of Babylon hath heard the
report of them, and his hands waxed
feeble: anguish took hold of him, *and*
pangs as of a woman in travail.
44 Behold, he shall come up like a lion
from the swelling of Jordan unto the
habitation of the strong: but I will make
them suddenly run away from her: and
who *is* a chosen *man, that* I may appoint
over her? for who *is* like me? and who
will appoint me the time? and who *is*
that shepherd that will stand before
me?
45 Therefore hear ye the counsel of
the LORD, that he hath taken against
Babylon; and his purposes, that he hath
purposed against the land of the Chaldeans: Surely the least of the flock shall
draw them out: surely he shall make
their habitation desolate with them.
46 At the noise of the taking of Babylon the earth is moved, and the cry is
heard among the nations.

Prophecies against nations (continued)

51 Thus saith the LORD; Behold,
I will raise up against Babylon,
and against them that dwell in the midst
of them that rise up against me, a destroying wind;
2 And will send unto Babylon fanners,
that shall fan her, and shall empty her

50:36 dote. To act and talk foolishly.
50:44 lion. Cyrus, leader of the Medes and Persians, is indicated here.

land: for in the day of trouble they shall
be against her round about.
[3]Against *him that* bendeth let the archer bend his bow, and against *him that*
lifteth himself up in his brigandine: and
spare ye not her young men; destroy ye
utterly all her host.
[4]Thus the slain shall fall in the land
of the Chaldeans, and *they that are*
thrust through in her streets.
[5]For Israel *hath* not *been* forsaken,
nor Judah of his *God, of the LORD of
hosts; though their land was filled with
*sin against the Holy One of Israel.
[6]Flee out of the midst of Babylon, and
deliver every man his soul: be not cut
off in her iniquity; for this *is* the time
of the LORD'S vengeance; he will *render unto her a recompence.
[7]Babylon *hath been* a golden cup in the
LORD'S hand, that made all the earth
drunken: the nations have drunken of
her wine; therefore the nations are mad.
[8]Babylon is suddenly fallen and destroyed: howl for her; take balm for her
pain, if so she may be healed.
[9]We would have healed Babylon, but
she is not healed: forsake her, and let
us go every one into his own country:
for her judgment reacheth unto *heav-
en, and is lifted up *even* to the skies.
[10]The LORD hath brought forth our
*righteousness: come, and let us de-
clare in Zion the work of the LORD our
God.
[11]Make bright the arrows; gather the
shields: the LORD hath raised up the
spirit of the kings of the Medes: for his
device *is* against Babylon, to destroy it;
because it *is* the vengeance of the
LORD, the vengeance of his temple.
[12]Set up the standard upon the walls
of Babylon, make the watch strong, set
up the watchmen, prepare the am-
bushes: for the LORD hath both devised
and done that which he spake against
the inhabitants of Babylon.
[13]O thou that dwellest upon many
waters, abundant in treasures, thine
end is come, *and* the measure of thy
covetousness.
[14]The LORD of hosts hath sworn by
himself, *saying,* Surely I will fill thee
with men, as with caterpillers; and they
shall lift up a shout against thee.
[15]He hath made the earth by his power, he hath established the *world by his
wisdom, and hath stretched out the
heaven by his understanding.
[16]When he uttereth *his* voice, *there is*
a multitude of waters in the heavens;
and he causeth the vapours to ascend
from the ends of the earth: he maketh
lightnings with rain, and bringeth forth
the wind out of his treasures.
[17]Every man is brutish by *his* knowledge; every founder is confounded by
the *graven image: for his molten image *is* *falsehood, and *there is* no breath
in them.
[18]They *are* *vanity, the work of errors: in the time of their visitation they
shall perish.
[19]The portion of Jacob *is* not like
them; for he *is* the former of all things:
and *Israel is* the rod of his inheritance:
the LORD of hosts is his name.
[20]Thou *art* my battle axe *and* weapons of war: for with thee will I break in
pieces the nations, and with thee will I
destroy kingdoms;
[21]And with thee will I break in pieces
the horse and his rider; and with thee
will I break in pieces the chariot and his
rider;
[22]With thee also will I break in pieces
man and woman; and with thee will I
break in pieces old and young; and with
thee will I break in pieces the young
man and the maid;

51:7 a golden cup. Read Daniel 2:32,38 and Revelation 17:4.
51:13 many waters. The Euphrates.
51:13 measure. End or limit.
51:21 with thee. In these and the following verses, the charge is being given to Cyrus, the king of the Persians.

23 I will also break in pieces with thee the shepherd and his flock; and with thee will I break in pieces the husbandman and his yoke of oxen; and with thee will I break in pieces captains and rulers.

24 And I will render unto Babylon and to all the inhabitants of Chaldea all their evil that they have done in Zion in your sight, saith the LORD.

25 Behold, I *am* against thee, O destroying mountain, saith the LORD, which destroyest all the earth: and I will stretch out mine hand upon thee, and roll thee down from the rocks, and will make thee a burnt mountain.

26 And they shall not take of thee a stone for a corner, nor a stone for foundations; but thou shalt be desolate for ever, saith the LORD.

27 Set ye up a standard in the land, blow the trumpet among the nations, prepare the nations against her, call together against her the kingdoms of Ararat, Minni, and Ashchenaz; appoint a captain against her; cause the horses to come up as the rough caterpillers.

28 Prepare against her the nations with the kings of the Medes, the captains thereof, and all the rulers thereof, and all the land of his dominion.

29 And the land shall tremble and sorrow: for every purpose of the LORD shall be performed against Babylon, to make the land of Babylon a desolation without an inhabitant.

30 The mighty men of Babylon have forborn to fight, they have remained in *their* holds: their might hath failed; they became as women: they have burned her dwellingplaces; her bars are broken.

31 One post shall run to meet another, and one messenger to meet another, to shew the king of Babylon that his city is taken at *one* end,

32 And that the passages are stopped, and the reeds they have burned with fire, and the men of war are affrighted.

33 For thus saith the LORD of hosts, the God of Israel; The daughter of Babylon *is* like a threshingfloor, *it is* time to thresh her: yet a little while, and the time of her harvest shall come.

34 Nebuchadrezzar the king of Babylon hath devoured me, he hath crushed me, he hath made me an empty vessel, he hath swallowed me up like a dragon, he hath filled his belly with my delicates, he hath cast me out.

35 The violence done to me and to my flesh *be* upon Babylon, shall the inhabitant of Zion say; and my blood upon the inhabitants of Chaldea, shall *Jerusalem say.

36 Therefore thus saith the LORD; Behold, I will plead thy cause, and take vengeance for thee; and I will dry up her sea, and make her springs dry.

37 And Babylon shall become heaps, a dwellingplace for dragons, an astonishment, and an hissing, without an inhabitant.

38 They shall roar together like lions: they shall yell as lions' whelps.

39 In their heat I will make their *feasts, and I will make them drunken, that they may rejoice, and sleep a perpetual sleep, and not wake, saith the LORD.

40 I will bring them down like lambs to the slaughter, like rams with he goats.

41 How is Sheshach taken! and how is the praise of the whole earth surprised! how is Babylon become an astonishment among the nations!

42 The sea is come up upon Babylon:

51:25 destroying mountain. The term "mountain" in the Bible is often used in speaking of a great nation. Babylon is meant here.
51:31 at one end. On every quarter.
51:36 her sea. The Euphrates.
51:41 Sheshach. Babylon. It is called this because of their goddess, Shach. It was during one of the terrible five days' feasts to this goddess that Cyrus captured Babylon.
51:42 sea . . . waves. The army and soldiers of the Medes.

she is covered with the multitude of the
waves thereof.
[43]Her cities are a desolation, a dry
land, and a wilderness, a land wherein
no man dwelleth, neither doth *any* son
of man pass thereby.
[44]And I will punish Bel in Babylon,
and I will bring forth out of his mouth
that which he hath swallowed up: and
the nations shall not flow together any
more unto him: yea, the wall of Babylon
shall fall.
[45]My people, go ye out of the midst
of her, and deliver ye every man his soul
from the fierce anger of the LORD.
[46]And lest your heart faint, and ye
fear for the rumour that shall be heard
in the land; a rumour shall both come
one year, and after that in *another* year
shall come a rumour, and violence in the
land, ruler against ruler.
[47]Therefore, behold, the days come,
that I will do judgment upon the graven
images of Babylon: and her whole land
shall be confounded, and all her slain
shall fall in the midst of her.
[48]Then the heaven and the earth, and
all that *is* therein, shall sing for Babylon:
for the spoilers shall come unto her
from the north, saith the LORD.
[49]As Babylon *hath caused* the slain of
Israel to fall, so at Babylon shall fall the
slain of all the earth.
[50]Ye that have escaped the sword, go
away, stand not still: remember the
LORD afar off, and let Jerusalem come
into your mind.
[51]We are confounded, because we
have heard reproach: shame hath covered our faces: for strangers are come
into the sanctuaries of the LORD'S house.
[52]Wherefore, behold, the days come,
saith the LORD, that I will do judgment
upon her graven images: and through
all her land the wounded shall groan.
[53]Though Babylon should mount up
to heaven, and though she should fortify the height of her strength, *yet* from
me shall spoilers come unto her, saith
the LORD.
[54]A sound of a cry *cometh* from Babylon, and great destruction from the
land of the Chaldeans:
[55]Because the LORD hath spoiled
Babylon, and destroyed out of her the
great voice; when her waves do roar
like great waters, a noise of their voice
is uttered:
[56]Because the spoiler is come upon
her, *even* upon Babylon, and her mighty
men are taken, every one of their bows
is broken: for the LORD God of recompences shall surely requite.
[57]And I will make drunk her princes,
and her wise *men,* her captains, and her
rulers, and her mighty men: and they
shall sleep a perpetual sleep, and not
wake, saith the King, whose name *is* the
LORD of hosts.
[58]Thus saith the LORD of hosts; The
broad walls of Babylon shall be utterly
broken, and her high gates shall be
burned with fire; and the people shall
labour in vain, and the folk in the fire,
and they shall be weary.
¶[59]The word which Jeremiah the
prophet commanded Seraiah the son of
Neriah, the son of Maaseiah, when he
went with Zedekiah the king of Judah
into Babylon in the fourth year of his
reign. And *this* Seraiah *was* a quiet
prince.
[60]So Jeremiah wrote in a book all the
evil that should come upon Babylon,
even all these words that are written
against Babylon.
[61]And Jeremiah said to Seraiah,
When thou comest to Babylon, and
shalt see, and shalt read all these words;
[62]Then shalt thou say, O LORD, thou
hast spoken against this place, to cut it
off, that none shall remain in it, neither
man nor beast, but that it shall be desolate for ever.

51:44 the wall of Babylon. A wall three hundred feet high, ninety feet wide, and sixty miles long.

51:59 Seraiah. The high priest under King Zedekiah. See Jeremiah 52:24.

63 And it shall be, when thou hast
made an end of reading this book, *that*
thou shalt bind a stone to it, and cast it
into the midst of Euphrates:
64 And thou shalt say, Thus shall Babylon sink, and shall not rise from the
evil that I will bring upon her: and they
shall be weary. Thus far *are* the words
of Jeremiah.

IX. Conclusion: Fall of Jerusalem (52:1-34)

52 Zedekiah *was* one and twenty
years old when he began to
reign, and he reigned eleven years in
Jerusalem. And his mother's name *was*
Hamutal the daughter of Jeremiah of
Libnah.
2 And he did *that which was* evil in the
eyes of the LORD, according to all that
Jehoiakim had done.
3 For through the anger of the LORD
it came to pass in Jerusalem and Judah,
till he had cast them out from his presence, that Zedekiah rebelled against the
king of Babylon.
¶ 4 And it came to pass in the ninth
year of his reign, in the tenth month, in
the tenth *day* of the month, *that* Nebuchadrezzar king of Babylon came, he
and all his army, against Jerusalem, and
pitched against it, and built forts against
it round about.
5 So the city was besieged unto the
eleventh year of king Zedekiah.
6 And in the fourth month, in the ninth
day of the month, the famine was sore
in the city, so that there was no bread
for the people of the land.
7 Then the city was broken up, and all
the men of war fled, and went forth out
of the city by night by the way of the
gate between the two walls, which *was*
by the king's garden; (now the Chaldeans *were* by the city round about:) and
they went by the way of the plain.
¶ 8 But the army of the Chaldeans pursued after the king, and overtook Zedekiah in the plains of Jericho; and all his
army was scattered from him.
9 Then they took the king, and carried
him up unto the king of Babylon to Riblah in the land of Hamath; where he
gave judgment upon him.
10 And the king of Babylon slew the
sons of Zedekiah before his eyes: he
slew also all the princes of Judah in
Riblah.
11 Then he put out the eyes of Zedekiah; and the king of Babylon bound him
in chains, and carried him to Babylon,
and put him in prison till the day of his
death.
¶ 12 Now in the fifth month, in the
tenth *day* of the month, which *was* the
nineteenth year of Nebuchadrezzar
king of Babylon, came Nebuzar-adan,
captain of the guard, *which* served the
king of Babylon, into Jerusalem,
13 And burned the house of the LORD,
and the king's house; and all the houses
of Jerusalem, and all the houses of the
great *men*, burned he with fire:
14 And all the army of the Chaldeans,
that *were* with the captain of the guard,
brake down all the walls of Jerusalem
round about.
15 Then Nebuzar-adan the captain of
the guard carried away captive *certain*
of the poor of the people, and the residue of the people that remained in the
city, and those that fell away, that fell to
the king of Babylon, and the rest of the
multitude.
16 But Nebuzar-adan the captain of
the guard left *certain* of the poor of the
land for vinedressers and for husbandmen.

51:64 Thus shall Babylon sink. This refers to the destruction of Babylon and the fact that she will not rise again. Compare Jeremiah 25:12; 50:1.

52:1 Zedekiah was one and twenty years old. This chapter is a review of the history of the fall of Jerusalem.

52:4 tenth day. There is no disagreement here with the account as given in 2 Kings 25:8. We read in that verse that the Babylonians came "unto" Jerusalem on the seventh day. In this verse, we read that they came "against, "meaning *into* the city.

[17]Also the pillars of brass that *were* in
the house of the LORD, and the bases,
and the brasen sea that *was* in the house
of the LORD, the Chaldeans brake, and
carried all the brass of them to Babylon.
[18]The caldrons also, and the shovels,
and the snuffers, and the bowls, and the
spoons, and all the vessels of brass
wherewith they ministered, took they
away.
[19]And the basons, and the firepans,
and the bowls, and the caldrons, and the
candlesticks, and the spoons, and the
cups; *that* which *was* of gold *in* gold, and
that which *was* of silver *in* silver, took
the captain of the guard away.
[20]The two pillars, one sea, and twelve
brasen bulls that *were* under the bases,
which king Solomon had made in the
house of the LORD: the brass of all these
vessels was without weight.
[21]And *concerning* the pillars, the
height of one pillar *was* eighteen cubits;
and a fillet of twelve cubits did compass
it; and the thickness thereof *was* four
fingers: *it was* hollow.
[22]And a chapiter of brass *was* upon it;
and the height of one chapiter *was* five
cubits, with network and pomegranates
upon the chapiters round about, all *of*
brass. The second pillar also and the
pomegranates *were* like unto these.
[23]And there were ninety and six
pomegranates on a side; *and* all the
pomegranates upon the network *were*
an hundred round about.
¶[24]And the captain of the guard took
Seraiah the chief priest, and Zephaniah
the second priest, and the three keepers of the door:
[25]He took also out of the city an eunuch, which had the charge of the men
of war; and seven men of them that
were near the king's person, which
were found in the city; and the principal scribe of the host, who mustered the
people of the land; and threescore men
of the people of the land, that were
found in the midst of the city.
[26]So Nebuzar-adan the captain of the
guard took them, and brought them to
the king of Babylon to Riblah.
[27]And the king of Babylon smote
them, and put them to death in Riblah

52:17 TEMPLE PLUNDERERS

Name	Reference	What was done or taken
King Shishak of Egypt	1 Kings 14:25-27; 2 Chronicles 12:9	Took temple treasures and gold shields.
King Asa of Judah	1 Kings 15:16-19	Took silver and gold of the temple treasuries to bribe the King of Syria into an alliance.
Sons of Queen Athaliah of Judah	2 Chronicles 24:7	Broke into the temple, took the sacred objects and presented them to the Baalim.
King Jehoash of Judah	2 Kings 12:18	Took sacred objects and gold from the treasuries to bribe Hazael, king of Syria.
King Jehoash of Israel	2 Kings 14:14	Took all the gold and silver and all the sacred temple articles.
King Ahaz of Judah	2 Kings 16:8	Took all the silver and gold to pay tribute to the King of Assyria.
King Hezekiah of Judah	2 Kings 18:15-16	Took all the silver and stripped the gold from the temple doors and pillars to pay tribute to the King of Assyria.
Nebuchadnezzar of Babylon	2 Kings 24:13	Took all the temple treasures and all the gold articles.
Nebuzar-adan, captain of the guard of Nebuchadnezzar	Jeremiah 52:12-23; 2 Kings 25:9	Took all the bronze pillars and furnishings, all the utensils and articles made of solid gold or silver. Burned the temple.

in the land of Hamath. Thus Judah was
carried away captive out of his own
land.
28This *is* the people whom Nebuchadrezzar carried away captive: in the
seventh year three thousand Jews and
three and twenty:
29In the eighteenth year of Nebuchadrezzar he carried away captive
from Jerusalem eight hundred thirty
and two persons:
30In the three and twentieth year of
Nebuchadrezzar Nebuzar-adan the captain of the guard carried away captive
of the Jews seven hundred forty and
five persons: all the persons *were* four
thousand and six hundred.
¶31And it came to pass in the seven
and thirtieth year of the captivity of
Jehoiachin king of Judah, in the twelfth
month, in the five and twentieth *day*
of the month, *that* Evil-merodach king
of Babylon in the *first* year of his reign
lifted up the head of Jehoiachin king
of Judah, and brought him forth out of
prison,
32And spake kindly unto him, and set
his throne above the throne of the kings
that *were* with him in Babylon,
33And changed his prison garments:
and he did continually eat bread before
him all the days of his life.
34And *for* his diet, there was a continual diet given him of the king of Babylon, every day a portion until the day
of his death, all the days of his life.

The

LAMENTATIONS

of Jeremiah

BACKGROUND

The five elegies, or mournful poems, which make up this book were written by the prophet Jeremiah after the destruction of Jerusalem. In them the prophet, who spoke so unsparingly of the sins of his people in the book that bears his name, reveals his great sorrow over their destruction. He wept because he loved his people.

STRUCTURE

The first four elegies are acrostic in form; that is, each verse begins with a letter of the Hebrew alphabet, in most cases taking them in order. In the third chapter, there are sixty-six stanzas to the Hebrew poem that makes up the chapter, three times the twenty-two stanzas of the other chapters. In it the stanzas are in threes, each three beginning with the same letter of the Hebrew alphabet until the acrostic is completed with verses 64, 65 and 66.

THEME

The book of Lamentations is really an expression of the sorrow of the Messiah, the Lord Jesus Christ, who is burdened with the sin of His people and makes their grief His own.

OUTLINE OF LAMENTATIONS

I.	The First Elegy	Lamentations 1
II.	The Second Elegy	Lamentations 2
III.	The Third Elegy	Lamentations 3
IV.	The Fourth Elegy	Lamentations 4
V.	The Fifth Elegy	Lamentations 5

I. The First Elegy

1 How doth the city sit solitary, *that*
was full of people! *how* is she become as a widow! she *that was* great
among the nations, *and* princess among
the provinces, *how* is she become tributary!
[2]She weepeth sore in the night, and
her tears *are* on her cheeks: among
all her lovers she hath none to comfort
her: all her friends have dealt treacherously with her, they are become her enemies.
[3]Judah is gone into captivity because

1:2 lovers . . . friends. Those whom Jerusalem had trusted rather than God.

1:3 Judah is gone into captivity. This verse establishes the date of the writing of Lamentations. Jeremiah lived after the fall of Jerusalem and must have written these lamentations in his old age.

of affliction, and because of great
servitude: she dwelleth among the
heathen, she findeth no rest: all her
persecutors overtook her between the
straits.
4 The ways of Zion do mourn, because
none come to the solemn *feasts: all
her gates are desolate: her priests sigh,
her virgins are afflicted, and she *is* in
bitterness.
5 Her adversaries are the chief, her
enemies prosper; for the LORD hath afflicted her for the multitude of her
transgressions: her children are gone
into captivity before the enemy.

1:5 The Reason for Destruction
The cause of the destruction of Jerusalem and the captivity of Judah was sin. "Jerusalem hath grievously sinned; therefore she is removed" (vs. 8). The wages of sin is death (Rom. 6:23).

6 And from the daughter of Zion all
her beauty is departed: her princes are
become like harts *that* find no pasture,
and they are gone without strength
before the pursuer.
7 *Jerusalem remembered in the days
of her affliction and of her miseries all
her pleasant things that she had in the
days of old, when her people fell into
the hand of the enemy, and none did
help her: the adversaries saw her, *and*
did mock at her sabbaths.
8 Jerusalem hath grievously sinned;
therefore she is removed: all that
honoured her despise her, because they
have seen her nakedness: yea, she
sigheth, and turneth backward.
9 Her filthiness *is* in her skirts; she
remembereth not her last end; therefore she came down wonderfully: she
had no comforter. O LORD, behold my
affliction: for the enemy hath magnified
himself.
10 The adversary hath spread out his
hand upon all her pleasant things: for
she hath seen *that* the heathen entered
into her *sanctuary, whom thou didst
command *that* they should not enter
into thy congregation.
11 All her people sigh, they seek
bread; they have given their pleasant
things for meat to relieve the soul: see,
O LORD, and consider; for I am become
vile.
¶ 12 *Is it* nothing to you, all ye that pass
by? behold, and see if there be any sorrow like unto my sorrow, which is done
unto me, wherewith the LORD hath
afflicted *me* in the day of his fierce
anger.
13 From above hath he sent *fire into
my bones, and it prevaileth against
them: he hath spread a net for my feet,
he hath turned me back: he hath made
me desolate *and* faint all the day.
14 The yoke of my transgressions is
bound by his hand: they are wreathed,
and come up upon my neck: he hath
made my strength to fall, the Lord hath
delivered me into *their* hands, *from
whom* I am not able to rise up.
15 The Lord hath trodden under foot
all my mighty *men* in the midst of me:
he hath called an assembly against me
to crush my young men: the Lord hath
trodden the virgin, the daughter of Judah, *as* in a winepress.
16 For these *things* I weep; mine eye,
mine eye runneth down with water,
because the comforter that should relieve my soul is far from me: my children are desolate, because the enemy
prevailed.
17 Zion spreadeth forth her hands, *and
there is* none to comfort her: the LORD

1:4 ways of Zion. The roads leading up to Jerusalem to the temple, which had once been crowded with happy worshippers.

1:9 my affliction. Jeremiah's love for his people is beautifully revealed in the Lamentation. His love for Israel is equal to that of Moses (Exod. 32:31-32) and to that of Paul (Rom. 9:1-3).

1:11 I am become vile. Despised in the eyes of the other nations.

1:15 as in a winepress. The winepress is a symbol of the judgment of God (Isa. 63:3).

hath commanded concerning *Jacob,
that his adversaries *should be* round
about him: Jerusalem is as a menstruous woman among them.
¶ 18 The LORD is righteous; for I have
rebelled against his commandment:
hear, I pray you, all people, and behold
my sorrow: my virgins and my young
men are gone into captivity.
19 I called for my lovers, *but* they deceived me: my priests and mine *elders
gave up the ghost in the city, while they
sought their meat to relieve their souls.
20 Behold, O LORD; for I *am* in distress: my *bowels are troubled; mine
heart is turned within me; for I have
grievously rebelled: abroad the sword
bereaveth, at home *there is* as *death.
21 They have heard that I sigh: *there
is* none to comfort me: all mine enemies
have heard of my trouble; they are glad
that thou hast done *it:* thou wilt bring
the day *that* thou hast called, and they
shall be like unto me.
22 Let all their wickedness come before thee; and do unto them, as thou
hast done unto me for all my transgressions: for my sighs *are* many, and my
heart *is* faint.

II. The Second Elegy

2 How hath the Lord covered the
daughter of Zion with a cloud in his
anger, *and* cast down from *heaven
unto the earth the beauty of *Israel, and
remembered not his footstool in the day
of his anger!
2 The Lord hath swallowed up all the
habitations of Jacob, and hath not pitied:
he hath thrown down in his wrath the
strong holds of the daughter of Judah;
he hath brought *them* down to the
ground: he hath polluted the kingdom
and the princes thereof.
3 He hath cut off in *his* fierce anger all
the horn of Israel: he hath drawn back

2:2 God's Judgment
Persistence in sin always brings the judgment of God upon the sinner. The LORD had been very patient with His people, but when they abused His goodness He ceased to pity and acted in judgment (see Rom. 2:4-6). In this respect "the Lord was an enemy" (vs. 5) and "purposed to destroy the wall of the daughter of Zion" (vs. 8).

his right hand from before the enemy,
and he burned against Jacob like a flaming fire, *which* devoureth round about.
4 He hath bent his bow like an enemy:
he stood with his right hand as an adversary, and slew all *that were* pleasant
to the eye in the *tabernacle of the
daughter of Zion: he poured out his fury
like fire.
5 The Lord was as an enemy: he hath
swallowed up Israel, he hath swallowed
up all her palaces: he hath destroyed his
strong holds, and hath increased in the
daughter of Judah *mourning and lamentation.
6 And he hath violently taken away his
tabernacle, as *if it were of* a garden: he
hath destroyed his places of the assembly: the LORD hath caused the solemn
feasts and sabbaths to be forgotten in
Zion, and hath despised in the indignation of his anger the king and the priest.
7 The Lord hath cast off his *altar, he
hath abhorred his sanctuary, he hath
given up into the hand of the enemy the
walls of her palaces; they have made a
noise in the house of the LORD, as in the
day of a solemn feast.
8 The LORD hath purposed to destroy
the wall of the daughter of Zion: he hath
stretched out a line, he hath not withdrawn his hand from destroying: therefore he made the rampart and the wall
to lament; they languished together.
9 Her gates are sunk into the ground;
he hath destroyed and broken her bars:

1:21 the day that thou hast called. See Jeremiah 50 and 51 for the prophecies concerning Babylon.
2:1 footstool. The LORD was speaking of His temple here. See Isaiah 60:13.

her king and her princes *are* among the
*Gentiles: the law *is* no *more;* her
*prophets also find no vision from the
LORD.
10 The elders of the daughter of Zion
sit upon the ground, *and* keep silence:
they have cast up dust upon their heads;
they have girded themselves with sackcloth: the virgins of Jerusalem hang
down their heads to the ground.
11 Mine eyes do fail with tears, my
bowels are troubled, my liver is poured
upon the earth, for the destruction of
the daughter of my people; because the
children and the sucklings swoon in the
streets of the city.
12 They say to their mothers, Where
is corn and wine? when they swooned
as the wounded in the streets of the city,
when their soul was poured out into
their mothers' bosom.
13 What thing shall I take to witness
for thee? what thing shall I liken to
thee, O daughter of Jerusalem? what
shall I equal to thee, that I may comfort
thee, O virgin daughter of Zion? for thy
breach *is* great like the sea: who can
heal thee?
14 Thy prophets have seen vain and
foolish things for thee: and they have
not discovered thine iniquity, to turn
away thy captivity; but have seen for
thee false burdens and causes of banishment.
15 All that pass by clap *their* hands at
thee; they hiss and wag their head at
the daughter of Jerusalem, *saying, Is*
this the city that *men* call The perfection of beauty, The joy of the whole
earth?
16 All thine enemies have opened
their mouth against thee: they hiss and
gnash the teeth: they say, We have
swallowed *her* up: certainly this *is* the
day that we looked for; we have found,
we have seen *it.*
17 The LORD hath done *that* which he
had devised; he hath fulfilled his word
that he had commanded in the days of
old: he hath thrown down, and hath not
pitied: and he hath caused *thine* enemy
to rejoice over thee, he hath set up the
horn of thine adversaries.
18 Their heart cried unto the Lord,
O wall of the daughter of Zion, let tears
run down like a river day and night: give
thyself no rest; let not the apple of thine
eye cease.
19 Arise, cry out in the night: in the
beginning of the watches pour out
thine heart like water before the face
of the Lord: lift up thy hands toward
him for the life of thy young children,
that faint for hunger in the top of
every street.
¶20 Behold, O LORD, and consider to
whom thou hast done this. Shall the
women eat their fruit, *and* children of a
*span long? shall the priest and the
*prophet be slain in the sanctuary of the
Lord?
21 The young and the old lie on the
ground in the streets: my virgins and
my young men are fallen by the sword;
thou hast slain *them* in the day of thine
anger; thou hast killed, *and* not pitied.
22 Thou hast called as in a solemn day
my terrors round about, so that in the
day of the LORD'S anger none escaped
nor remained: those that I have
swaddled and brought up hath mine enemy consumed.

III. The Third Elegy

3 I *am* the man *that* hath seen affliction by the rod of his wrath.
2 He hath led me, and brought *me into*
darkness, but not *into* light.
3 Surely against me is he turned; he
turneth his hand *against me* all the day.
4 My *flesh and my skin hath he made
old; he hath broken my bones.
5 He hath builded against me, and
compassed *me* with gall and travail.

2:9 the law. Their Scriptures.
2:15 All that pass by. Compare 1 Kings 9:8; Jeremiah 18:16.
2:17 he hath fulfilled his word. See Leviticus 26:14-29; Deuteronomy 28:15-68.

[6]He hath set me in dark places, as
they that be dead of old.
[7]He hath hedged me about, that I cannot get out: he hath made my chain
heavy.
[8]Also when I cry and shout, he
shutteth out my *prayer.
[9]He hath inclosed my ways with
hewn stone, he hath made my paths
crooked.
[10]He *was* unto me *as* a bear lying in
wait, *and as* a lion in secret places.
[11]He hath turned aside my ways, and
pulled me in pieces: he hath made me
desolate.
[12]He hath bent his bow, and set me
as a mark for the arrow.
[13]He hath caused the arrows of his
quiver to enter into my *reins.
[14]I was a derision to all my people;
and their song all the day.
[15]He hath filled me with bitterness,
he hath made me drunken with *wormwood.
[16]He hath also broken my teeth with
gravel stones, he hath covered me with
ashes.
[17]And thou hast removed my soul far
off from *peace: I forgat prosperity.
[18]And I said, My strength and my
*hope is perished from the LORD:
[19]Remembering mine affliction and
my misery, the wormwood and the
gall.
[20]My soul hath *them* still in remembrance, and is humbled in me.
[21]This I recall to my mind, therefore
have I hope.
¶[22]*It is of* the LORD'S mercies that we
are not consumed, because his compassions fail not.
[23]*They are* new every morning: great
is thy faithfulness.
[24]The LORD *is* my portion, saith my
soul; therefore will I hope in him.
[25]The LORD *is* good unto them that
wait for him, to the soul *that* seeketh
him.
[26]*It is* good that *a man* should both
hope and quietly wait for the *salvation
of the LORD.
[27]*It is* good for a man that he bear the
yoke in his youth.
[28]He sitteth alone and keepeth silence, because he hath borne *it* upon
him.
[29]He putteth his mouth in the dust;
if so be there may be hope.
[30]He giveth *his* cheek to him that
smiteth him: he is filled full with reproach.
[31]For the Lord will not cast off for
ever:
[32]But though he cause grief, yet will
he have compassion according to the
multitude of his mercies.
[33]For he doth not afflict willingly nor
grieve the children of men.
[34]To crush under his feet all the prisoners of the earth,
[35]To turn aside the right of a man
before the face of the most High,
[36]To subvert a man in his cause, the
Lord approveth not.
¶[37]Who *is* he *that* saith, and it cometh
to pass, *when* the Lord commandeth *it*
not?
[38]Out of the mouth of the most High
proceedeth not evil and good?
[39]Wherefore doth a living man complain, a man for the punishment of his
sins?
[40]Let us search and try our ways, and
turn again to the LORD.
[41]Let us lift up our heart with *our*
hands unto *God in the heavens.
[42]We have transgressed and have rebelled: thou hast not pardoned.
[43]Thou hast covered with anger, and
persecuted us: thou hast slain, thou
hast not pitied.
[44]Thou hast covered thyself with a

3:14 their song. Their mocking song (see also vs. 63).
3:19 Remembering. Remember.
3:30 He giveth his cheek. The sorrow of the prophet points prophetically to the Man of Sorrows, the Lord Jesus Christ. Read Matthew 27:30; Mark 15:19.

cloud, that *our* prayer should not pass
through.
45Thou hast made us *as* the offscouring and refuse in the midst of the
people.
46All our enemies have opened their
mouths against us.
47Fear and a snare is come upon us,
desolation and destruction.
48Mine eye runneth down with rivers
of water for the destruction of the
daughter of my people.
49Mine eye trickleth down, and
ceaseth not, without any intermission,
50Till the LORD look down, and behold from heaven.
51Mine eye affecteth mine heart because of all the daughters of my city.
52Mine enemies chased me sore, like
a bird, without cause.
53They have cut off my life in the
dungeon, and cast a stone upon me.
54Waters flowed over mine head; *then*
I said, I am cut off.
¶55I called upon thy name, O LORD,
out of the low dungeon.
56Thou hast heard my voice: hide not
thine ear at my breathing, at my cry.
57Thou drewest near in the day *that*
I called upon thee: thou saidst, Fear not.
58O Lord, thou hast pleaded the
causes of my soul; thou hast *redeemed
my life.
59O LORD, thou hast seen my wrong:
judge thou my cause.
60Thou hast seen all their vengeance
and all their imaginations against me.
61Thou hast heard their reproach,
O LORD, *and* all their imaginations
against me;
62The lips of those that rose up
against me, and their device against me
all the day.
63Behold their sitting down, and their
rising up; I *am* their musick.
¶64*Render unto them a recompence, O LORD, according to the work
of their hands.
65Give them sorrow of heart, thy
curse unto them.
66Persecute and destroy them in anger from under the heavens of the
LORD.

IV. The Fourth Elegy

4 How is the gold become dim! *how*
is the most fine gold changed! the
stones of the sanctuary are poured out
in the top of every street.
2The precious sons of Zion, comparable to fine gold, how are they esteemed as earthen pitchers, the work
of the hands of the potter!
3Even the sea monsters draw out the
breast, they give suck to their young
ones: the daughter of my people *is become* cruel, like the ostriches in the
wilderness.
4The tongue of the sucking child
cleaveth to the roof of his mouth for
thirst: the young children ask bread,
and no man breaketh *it* unto them.
5They that did feed delicately are
desolate in the streets: they that were
brought up in scarlet embrace dung-
hills.
6For the punishment of the iniquity
of the daughter of my people is greater
than the punishment of the *sin of Sodom, that was overthrown as in a moment, and no hands stayed on her.

4:6 A Greater Punishment
Because Israel had more knowledge of God than Sodom had, and Israel sinned against that light, their punishment was more severe then the punishment of Sodom. This is an essential principle of justice and will be observed when God judges the world (Matt. 11:20-24; Rom. 2:12).

7Her Nazarites were purer than
snow, they were whiter than milk, they
were more ruddy in body than rubies,
their polishing *was* of sapphire:
8Their visage is blacker than a coal;
they are not known in the streets: their

4:6 no hands stayed on her. Her overthrow was from God Himself.
4:8 known. Recognized.

skin cleaveth to their bones; it is withered, it is become like a stick.
9*They that be* slain with the sword are
better than *they that be* slain with hunger: for these pine away, stricken through for *want of* the fruits of the field.
10The hands of the pitiful women
have sodden their own children: they were their meat in the destruction of the daughter of my people.
11The LORD hath accomplished his
fury; he hath poured out his fierce anger, and hath kindled a fire in Zion, and it hath devoured the foundations thereof.
12The kings of the earth, and all the
inhabitants of the *world, would not have believed that the adversary and the enemy should have entered into the gates of Jerusalem.
¶13For the sins of her prophets, *and*
the iniquities of her priests, that have shed the blood of the *just in the midst of her,
14They have wandered *as* blind *men*
in the streets, they have polluted themselves with blood, so that men could not touch their garments.
15They cried unto them, Depart ye;
it is *unclean; depart, depart, touch not: when they fled away and wandered, they said among the heathen, They shall no more sojourn *there.*
16The anger of the LORD hath divid-
ed them; he will no more regard them: they respected not the persons of the priests, they favoured not the elders.
17As for us, our eyes as yet failed for
our vain help: in our watching we have watched for a nation *that* could not save *us.*
18They hunt our steps, that we can-
not go in our streets: our end is near, our days are fulfilled; for our end is come.
19Our persecutors are swifter than
the eagles of the heaven: they pursued us upon the mountains, they laid wait for us in the wilderness.
20The breath of our nostrils, the
anointed of the LORD, was taken in their pits, of whom we said, Under his shadow we shall live among the heathen.
¶21Rejoice and be glad, O daughter of
*Edom, that dwellest in the land of Uz; the cup also shall pass through unto thee: thou shalt be drunken, and shalt make thyself naked.
¶22The punishment of thine iniquity
is accomplished, O daughter of Zion; he will no more carry thee away into captivity: he will visit thine iniquity, O daughter of Edom; he will discover thy sins.

V. The Fifth Elegy

5 Remember, O LORD, what is come
upon us: consider, and behold our reproach.
2Our inheritance is turned to strangers, our houses to aliens.
3We are orphans and fatherless, our
mothers *are* as widows.
4We have drunken our water for money; our wood is sold unto us.
5Our necks *are* under persecution:
we labour, *and* have no rest.
6We have given the hand *to* the

4:17 a nation that could not save. Egypt.
4:18 They. The Chaldeans.
4:21 Rejoice and be glad. This is in the spirit of Ecclesiastes 11:9. Laugh and have a good time with the pleasures of the world, if that is your aim in life, but the judgment of the LORD is coming just the same.
4:22 Zion . . . Edom. For Edom and Zion there will be judgment, but Zion will turn to her God, and her sins will be covered—not "discovered."
5:1 Remember, O LORD. Very fittingly, the final elegy (mournful poem) of Lamentations is a prayer, a prayer that recognizes the fierceness of God's wrath and at the same time looks to God as the hope of His people (vss.19-21).
5:6 given the hand. To surrender and become slaves.

Egyptians, *and to* the Assyrians, to be
satisfied with bread.
7Our fathers have sinned, *and are*
not; and we have borne their iniquities.
8Servants have ruled over us: *there is*
none that doth deliver *us* out of their
hand.
9We gat our bread with *the peril of* our
lives because of the sword of the wilderness.
10Our skin was black like an oven
because of the terrible famine.
11They ravished the women in Zion,
and the maids in the cities of Judah.
12Princes are hanged up by their
hand: the faces of elders were not honoured.
13They took the young men to grind,
and the children fell under the wood.
14The elders have ceased from the
gate, the young men from their musick.
15The joy of our heart is ceased; our
dance is turned into mourning.
16The crown is fallen *from* our head:
woe unto us, that we have sinned!
17For this our heart is faint; for these
things our eyes are dim.
18Because of the mountain of Zion,
which is desolate, the foxes walk
upon it.
19Thou, O LORD, remainest for ever;
thy throne from generation to generation.
20Wherefore dost thou forget us for
ever, *and* forsake us so long time?
21Turn thou us unto thee, O LORD,
and we shall be turned; renew our days
as of old.
22But thou hast utterly rejected us;
thou art very wroth against us.

The Book of the Prophet

EZEKIEL

BACKGROUND

The prophecy of Ezekiel was written by the prophet of that name, who had been carried to Babylon with one of the earlier groups of exiles of Judah. The prophet Ezekiel was a priest. His messages have to do in particular with the sin of Israel as the covenant people of God, and also with the re-establishment of the temple at the return of Christ to the earth. He presents a very complete picture of the millennial temple as it will be built in Jerusalem when Jesus Christ is King of Kings and Lord of Lords.

THE TIME

The time of Ezekiel's ministry was at the same time as that of Jeremiah and was also during the earlier years of the ministry of Daniel. Ezekiel preached to the Jews in their captivity while Jeremiah was preaching to the Jews in the land of Palestine.

THEME

Ezekiel disclosed the failure of Israel to keep the covenant of God. He then told of their chastisement in captivity because of that sin. Just in case anyone should think that Israel's failure had done away with the covenant of God with that people, Ezekiel declared that God will still fulfill the terms of that covenant and establish the children of Israel as His own special treasure upon the earth. The prophecy is filled with symbolisms. In each case the prophet gave the key to the meaning of the symbol employed. By their use he made his message to be most impressive.

OUTLINE OF EZEKIEL

I.	Ezekiel Is Prepared and Sent on His Prophetic Ministry	Ezekiel 1:1—3:9
II.	Ezekiel Is Sent as a Watchman	Ezekiel 3:10-21
III.	Ezekiel Sees the Glory of the LORD and His Ministry Is Exalted	Ezekiel 3:22—7:27
IV.	Ezekiel Speaks of the Sins of the People and God's Just Punishment of Them	Ezekiel 8:1—33:20
V.	The Future Kingdom of the Messiah	Ezekiel 33:21—36:38
VI.	Restoration of Israel and Judgment of the Nations	Ezekiel 37:1—39:29
VII.	Israel in the Kingdom Age	Ezekiel 40:1—48:35

I. Ezekiel Is Prepared and Sent (1:1—3:9)

A vision of the glory of God

1 Now it came to pass in the thirtieth year, in the fourth *month, in
the fifth *day* of the month, as I *was*
among the captives by the river of
Chebar, *that* the heavens were opened,
and I saw visions of *God.
2 In the fifth *day* of the month, which
was the fifth year of king Jehoiachin's
captivity,
3 The word of the LORD came expressly unto *Ezekiel the priest, the
son of Buzi, in the land of the Chaldeans by the river Chebar; and the hand
of the LORD was there upon him.
¶ 4 And I looked, and, behold, a whirlwind came out of the north, a great
cloud, and a *fire infolding itself, and a
brightness *was* about it, and out of the
midst thereof as the colour of amber,
out of the midst of the fire.
5 Also out of the midst thereof *came*
the likeness of four living creatures.
And this *was* their appearance; they had
the likeness of a man.
6 And every one had four faces, and
every one had four wings.
7 And their feet *were* straight feet; and
the sole of their feet *was* like the sole
of a calf's foot: and they sparkled like
the colour of burnished brass.
8 And *they had* the hands of a man
under their wings on their four sides;
and they four had their faces and their
wings.
9 Their wings *were* joined one to another; they turned not when they went;
they went every one straight forward.
10 As for the likeness of their faces,
they four had the face of a man, and the
face of a lion, on the right side: and they
four had the face of an ox on the left
side; they four also had the face of an
eagle.
11 Thus *were* their faces: and their
wings *were* stretched upward; two
wings of every one *were* joined one to
another, and two covered their bodies.
12 And they went every one straight
forward: whither the spirit was to go,
they went; *and* they turned not when
they went.
13 As for the likeness of the living
creatures, their appearance *was* like
burning coals of fire, *and* like the appearance of lamps: it went up and down
among the living creatures; and the fire
was bright, and out of the fire went
forth lightning.
14 And the living creatures ran and
returned as the appearance of a flash of
lightning.
¶ 15 Now as I beheld the living creatures, behold one wheel upon the earth
by the living creatures, with his four
faces.
16 The appearance of the wheels and
their work *was* like unto the colour of a
beryl: and they four had one likeness:
and their appearance and their work
was as it were a wheel in the middle of
a wheel.
17 When they went, they went upon
their four sides: *and* they turned not
when they went.
18 As for their rings, they were so high
that they were dreadful; and their rings
were full of eyes round about them four.
19 And when the living creatures went,
the wheels went by them: and when the
living creatures were lifted up from the
earth, the wheels were lifted up.
20 Whithersoever the spirit was to go,
they went, thither *was their* spirit to go;
and the wheels were lifted up over
against them: for the spirit of the living
creature *was* in the wheels.
21 When those went, *these* went; and
when those stood, *these* stood; and
when those were lifted up from the

1:1 the thirtieth year. Of the Babylonian kingdom, about 597 B.C.

1:3 in the land of the Chaldeans by the river Chebar. Ezekiel's ministry was in the land of Babylon. Many Jews were already there in captivity.

1:5 living creatures. The cherubim (see Ezek. 10:8 note, "Cherubim").

earth, the wheels were lifted up over
against them: for the spirit of the living
creature *was* in the wheels.

22And the likeness of the firmament
upon the heads of the living creature
was as the colour of the terrible crystal,

1:1 THE GLORY OF GOD

The first chapter of Ezekiel records a description of the glory of God as it was revealed to the prophet at the beginning of his ministry. On later occasions, we find this same vision referred to and partially described. Although it is impossible to visualize the representation of God that is contained in this chapter, there are certain elements of the vision that are used throughout Scripture in referring to the person and glory of God.

These details are as follows:

1. A whirlwind (vs. 4). When Elijah was taken up into heaven, it was by a whirlwind (2 Kings 2:1). This might well represent the almighty power of God.
2. A great cloud (vs. 4). When God revealed Himself to the children of Israel at Sinai, at the giving of the *Law, He came to them "in a thick cloud" (Exod. 19:9). The cloud was also conspicuous as it stood above the tabernacle during the wilderness journey of Israel and led the people toward the Promised Land (Exod. 40:36). This cloud speaks of the majesty of the presence of God.
3. A fire enfolding itself (vs. 4). We are told in Hebrews 12:29 that "our God is a consuming fire." This speaks of the perfect holiness of God.
4. The four living creatures (vs. 5). Four *cherubim. These angelic beings are revealed throughout the Scriptures as being in the presence of God (Gen. 3:22-24; Exod. 25:17-20). They are the ministers of the holiness of God. By the form of their faces, they present a revelation of the fourfold ministry of the Lord Jesus Christ. The face of a man indicates the humanity of our Lord, as set forth in the Gospel of Luke. The face of a lion speaks of His royalty, as presented by the Gospel of Matthew. The face of an ox speaks of His position as the Servant of Jehovah, the theme of the Gospel of Mark. The face of an eagle might well speak of His heavenly person or deity, as that subject is presented in the Gospel of John. These angelic beings act in perfect obedience to the will of God (1:20).
5. Coals of fire (vs. 13). According to Isaiah 6:6-7, the coals of fire speak of the cleansing power of God. They were applied to the lips of Isaiah in order that his lips might be purged from sin and become prepared to speak the message of the LORD.
6. The appearance of lamps (vs. 13). When God revealed Himself to Abram after the appearance of Melchizedek, it was as "a smoking furnace, and a burning lamp" (Gen. 15:17). This lamp may well represent the fact that God is light, and in Him is no darkness at all (James 1:17; 1 John 1:5).
7. The noise of great waters (vs. 24). On several occasions in Scripture, the voice of the LORD is presented as the sound of great waters (Rev. 1:15). Indeed, God is able to speak so clearly that a willing heart may hear Him. His Word creates the universe in which we live. His Word is authoritative because it is the Word of God.
8. The likeness as the appearance of a man (vs. 26). In the tenth chapter of Daniel, we find that the LORD was revealed in the appearance of a man. The description given of Him in Daniel 10 coincides perfectly with that given in Revelation 1. It is an unveiling of the eternal glory of the Son of God. The appearance like a man does not deny the spirituality of God (John 4:24). It brings Him, the majestic, all-powerful, infinite God into the place where we may know Him (Phil. 3:10).
9. The appearance of the bow (vs. 28). The rainbow, symbolic of God's *covenant with man, is associated with His throne in Revelation 4:3. It speaks of the faithfulness of God, who will keep every covenant that He has made with man. All of the details about the revelation of the glory of God overpower the prophet who saw it. Its significance to us is not intended to enable us to make an image of God through a painting or sculpture. Rather, it shows us that we do not worship at the altar of an unknown God but rather that we who believe in Christ have accepted the Word of the living God who has revealed Himself to men. The revelation gave strength to Ezekiel and enabled him to minister the word of God in the power of the Holy Spirit.

stretched forth over their heads above.
23 And under the firmament *were*
their wings straight, the one toward the
other: every one had two, which covered on this side, and every one had
two, which covered on that side, their
bodies.
24 And when they went, I heard the
noise of their wings, like the noise of
great waters, as the voice of the Almighty, the voice of speech, as the noise
of an host: when they stood, they let
down their wings.
25 And there was a voice from the firmament that *was* over their heads,
when they stood, *and* had let down their
wings.
¶ 26 And above the firmament that *was*
over their heads *was* the likeness of a
throne, as the appearance of a sapphire
stone: and upon the likeness of the
throne *was* the likeness as the appearance of a man above upon it.
27 And I saw as the colour of amber,
as the appearance of fire round about
within it, from the appearance of his
loins even upward, and from the appearance of his loins even downward, I
saw as it were the appearance of fire,
and it had brightness round about.
28 As the appearance of the bow that
is in the cloud in the day of rain, so *was*
the appearance of the brightness round
about. This *was* the appearance of the
likeness of the glory of the LORD. And
when I saw *it*, I fell upon my face, and I
heard a voice of one that spake.

Ezekiel's call to the prophetic ministry

2 And he said unto me, Son of man,
stand upon thy feet, and I will
speak unto thee.
2 And the spirit entered into me when
he spake unto me, and set me upon my
feet, that I heard him that spake unto me.
3 And he said unto me, Son of man, I
send thee to the children of *Israel, to
a rebellious nation that hath rebelled
against me: they and their fathers have
transgressed against me, *even* unto this
very day.
4 For *they are* impudent children and
stiffhearted. I do send thee unto them;
and thou shalt say unto them, Thus
saith the Lord GOD.
5 And they, whether they will hear, or
whether they will forbear, (for they *are*
a rebellious house,) yet shall know that
there hath been a *prophet among them.
¶ 6 And thou, son of man, be not
*afraid of them, neither be afraid of
their words, though briers and thorns
be with thee, and thou dost dwell among
*scorpions: be not afraid of their words,
nor be dismayed at their looks, though
they *be* a rebellious house.

2:1 EZEKIEL'S COMMISSION

Ezekiel's commission to his life's work is recorded in great detail in the second and third chapters of this book. It is noteworthy that the Holy Spirit gives Ezekiel the title that our Lord used of Himself, Son of Man. Ezekiel passed through much suffering, and in that way he was a *type of the Messiah, who took Israel's sin and shame upon Himself.

The following details make up the commission of Ezekiel:

1. His task was to be the messenger of the LORD to the children of Israel (2:3).
2. He was encouraged to fear no man as he presented the message from God (2:6).
3. In order to speak the word of God, it was necessary that he feed upon that word (3:1; see also John's experience in Rev. 10:9).
4. God required steadfastness. To this end He made Ezekiel's face "strong against their faces" (3:8).
5. The Holy Spirit gave Ezekiel the enabling from God that would make him effective in his ministry (3:12).
6. The commission given him brought with it a tremendous responsibility. He was placed as a watchman to the house of Israel (3:17).

This sixfold commission is typical of every commission that a child of God receives from his Lord.

[7]And thou shalt speak my words unto
them, whether they will hear, or whether they will forbear: for they *are* most
rebellious.
[8]But thou, son of man, hear what I
say unto thee; Be not thou rebellious
like that rebellious house: open thy
mouth, and eat that I give thee.
¶[9]And when I looked, behold, an hand
was sent unto me; and, lo, a roll of a
book *was* therein;
[10]And he spread it before me; and it
was written within and without: and
there was written therein lamentations,
and *mourning, and woe.

Ezekiel's responsibility as a prophet

3 Moreover he said unto me, Son of
man, eat that thou findest; eat this
roll, and go speak unto the house of Israel.
[2]So I opened my mouth, and he
caused me to eat that roll.
[3]And he said unto me, Son of man,
cause thy belly to eat, and fill thy *bowels with this roll that I give thee. Then
did I eat *it;* and it was in my mouth as
honey for sweetness.
¶[4]And he said unto me, Son of man,
go, get thee unto the house of Israel,
and speak with my words unto them.
[5]For thou *art* not sent to a people of
a strange speech and of an hard language, *but* to the house of Israel;
[6]Not to many people of a strange
speech and of an hard language, whose
words thou canst not understand. Surely, had I sent thee to them, they would
have hearkened unto thee.
[7]But the house of Israel will not hearken unto thee; for they will not hearken
unto me: for all the house of Israel *are*
impudent and hardhearted.
[8]Behold, I have made thy face strong
against their faces, and thy forehead
strong against their foreheads.
[9]As an adamant harder than flint have
I made thy forehead: fear them not,
neither be dismayed at their looks,
though they *be* a rebellious house.

II. Ezekiel Is Sent as a Watchman (3:10-21)

[10]Moreover he said unto me, Son of
man, all my words that I shall speak
unto thee receive in thine heart, and
hear with thine ears.
[11]And go, get thee to them of the captivity, unto the children of thy people,
and speak unto them, and tell them,
Thus saith the Lord GOD; whether they
will hear, or whether they will forbear.
[12]Then the spirit took me up, and I
heard behind me a voice of a great rushing, *saying,* Blessed *be* the glory of the
LORD from his place.
[13]*I heard* also the noise of the wings
of the living creatures that touched one
another, and the noise of the wheels
over against them, and a noise of a great
rushing.
[14]So the spirit lifted me up, and took
me away, and I went in bitterness, in the
heat of my spirit; but the hand of the
LORD was strong upon me.
¶[15]Then I came to them of the captivity at Tel-abib, that dwelt by the river
of Chebar, and I sat where they sat, and
remained there astonished among them
seven days.
[16]And it came to pass at the end of
seven days, that the word of the LORD
came unto me, saying,
[17]Son of man, I have made thee a
watchman unto the house of Israel:
therefore hear the word at my mouth,
and give them warning from me.
[18]When I say unto the wicked, Thou
shalt surely die; and thou givest him not
warning, nor speakest to warn the
wicked from his wicked way, to save his
life; the same wicked *man* shall die in
his iniquity; but his *blood will I require
at thine hand.
[19]Yet if thou warn the wicked, and he
turn not from his wickedness, nor from
his wicked way, he shall die in his iniquity; but thou hast delivered thy soul.
[20]Again, When a righteous *man* doth
turn from his *righteousness, and commit iniquity, and I lay a stumblingblock
before him, he shall die: because thou

hast not given him warning, he shall die
in his *sin, and his righteousness which
he hath done shall not be remembered;
but his blood will I require at thine
hand.
21 Nevertheless if thou warn the
righteous *man,* that the righteous sin
not, and he doth not sin, he shall surely live, because he is warned; also thou
hast delivered thy soul.

III. Ezekiel Sees the Glory of the LORD (3:22—7:27)

¶22 And the hand of the LORD was
there upon me; and he said unto me,
Arise, go forth into the plain, and I will
there talk with thee.
23 Then I arose, and went forth into
the plain: and, behold, the glory of the
LORD stood there, as the glory which I
saw by the river of Chebar: and I fell on
my face.
24 Then the spirit entered into me,
and set me upon my feet, and spake
with me, and said unto me, Go, shut
thyself within thine house.
25 But thou, O son of man, behold,
they shall put bands upon thee, and
shall bind thee with them, and thou
shalt not go out among them:
26 And I will make thy tongue cleave
to the roof of thy mouth, that thou shalt
be dumb, and shalt not be to them a reprover: for they *are* a rebellious house.
27 But when I speak with thee, I will
open thy mouth, and thou shalt say unto
them, Thus saith the Lord GOD; He that
heareth, let him hear; and he that forbeareth, let him forbear: for they *are* a
rebellious house.

Symbols that foretold the destruction of Jerusalem

4 Thou also, son of man, take thee
a tile, and lay it before thee, and

4:1 An Object Lesson: A Tile
The taking of a tile was an object lesson to the children of Israel. Upon the tile, which was two feet long and one foot wide, the prophet pictured the city. Hiding his face from that city with an iron pan, the prophet made the people to understand that God had hidden His face from the children of Israel because of their sin.

pourtray upon it the city, *even* *Jerusalem:
2 And lay siege against it, and build a
fort against it, and cast a mount against
it; set the camp also against it, and set
battering rams against it round about.
3 Moreover take thou unto thee an
iron pan, and set it *for* a wall of iron
between thee and the city: and set thy
face against it, and it shall be besieged,
and thou shalt lay siege against it. This
shall be a sign to the house of Israel.
4 Lie thou also upon thy left side, and
lay the iniquity of the house of Israel
upon it: *according* to the number of the
days that thou shalt lie upon it thou
shalt bear their iniquity.
5 For I have laid upon thee the years
of their iniquity, according to the number of the days, three hundred and ninety days: so shalt thou *bear the iniquity
of the house of Israel.
6 And when thou hast accomplished
them, lie again on thy right side, and
thou shalt bear the iniquity of the house
of *Judah forty days: I have appointed
thee each day for a year.
7 Therefore thou shalt set thy face
toward the siege of Jerusalem, and
thine arm *shall be* uncovered, and thou
shalt prophesy against it.
8 And, behold, I will lay bands upon
thee, and thou shalt not turn thee from
one side to another, till thou hast ended the days of thy siege.

3:25 bands upon thee. The Jews' unbelief and rebellion kept Ezekiel from speaking freely.

4:4 Lie thou also upon thy left side. Through lying perfectly still without eating, the prophet represented to Israel the siege of Jerusalem by the hosts of Babylon. It must be remembered that the siege of the destruction of Jerusalem was a judgment from God, because of the unfaithfulness of Israel to the LORD.

¶[9]Take thou also unto thee wheat,
and barley, and beans, and lentiles, and
millet, and fitches, and put them in one
vessel, and make thee bread thereof,
according to the number of the days that
thou shalt lie upon thy side, three hundred
and ninety days shalt thou eat thereof.
[10]And thy meat which thou shalt eat
shall be by weight, twenty shekels a
day: from time to time shalt thou eat it.
[11]Thou shalt drink also water by
measure, the sixth part of an *hin: from
time to time shalt thou drink.
[12]And thou shalt eat it *as* barley
cakes, and thou shalt bake it with *dung
that cometh out of man, in their sight.
[13]And the LORD said, Even thus shall
the children of Israel eat their defiled
bread among the *Gentiles, whither I
will drive them.
[14]Then said I, Ah Lord GOD! behold,
my soul hath not been polluted: for from
my youth up even till now have I not
eaten of that which dieth of itself, or is
torn in pieces; neither came there
abominable flesh into my mouth.
[15]Then he said unto me, Lo, I have
given thee cow's dung for man's dung,
and thou shalt prepare thy bread therewith.
[16]Moreover he said unto me, Son of
man, behold, I will break the staff of
bread in Jerusalem: and they shall eat
bread by weight, and with care; and
they shall drink water by measure, and
with astonishment:
[17]That they may want bread and water, and be astonied one with another,
and consume away for their iniquity.

Symbols (continued)

5 And thou, son of man, take thee a
sharp knife, take thee a barber's
razor, and cause *it* to pass upon thine
head and upon thy beard: then take thee
balances to weigh, and divide the *hair.*
[2]Thou shalt burn with fire a third part
in the midst of the city, when the days
of the siege are fulfilled: and thou shalt
take a third part, *and* smite about it with
a knife: and a third part thou shalt scatter in the wind; and I will draw out a
sword after them.
[3]Thou shalt also take thereof a few in
number, and bind them in thy skirts.
[4]Then take of them again, and cast
them into the midst of the fire, and burn
them in the fire; *for* thereof shall a fire
come forth into all the house of Israel.
¶[5]Thus saith the Lord GOD; This *is*
Jerusalem: I have set it in the midst of
the nations and countries *that are* round
about her.
[6]And she hath changed my judgments
into wickedness more than the nations,
and my statutes more than the countries that *are* round about her: for they
have refused my judgments and my
statutes, they have not walked in them.
[7]Therefore thus saith the Lord GOD;
Because ye multiplied more than the
nations that *are* round about you, *and*
have not walked in my statutes, neither
have kept my judgments, neither have
done according to the judgments of the
nations that *are* round about you;
[8]Therefore thus saith the Lord GOD;

5:1 An Object Lesson: Hair
This chapter records another object lesson by which the prophet showed Israel that a third of the city would be smitten, a third would die of the pestilence that occurred during the siege of Jerusalem, and a third would be scattered among the nations. The purpose of chapters 6 and 7 is to indicate that the iniquity of Israel had reached its climax and had to be judged.

4:9 make thee bread. Bread made of materials like these would be coarse and poor.
4:10 twenty shekels. Twenty shekels is eight ounces.
4:14 abominable. Spoiled, unclean.
4:15 therewith. Over it. The Arabs today, who have little wood, use camel dung for fuel. A Hebrew and a priest would become *unclean by using such animal matter.
5:7 the judgments of the nations. Israel had departed so far from the LORD that even the heathen nations around them had more effective laws than theirs.

Behold, I, even I, *am* against thee, and
will execute judgments in the midst of
thee in the sight of the nations.
[9]And I will do in thee that which I
have not done, and whereunto I will not
do any more the like, because of all
thine abominations.
[10]Therefore the fathers shall eat the
sons in the midst of thee, and the sons
shall eat their fathers; and I will execute
judgments in thee, and the whole *remnant of thee will I scatter into all the
winds.
[11]Wherefore, *as* I live, saith the Lord
GOD; Surely, because thou hast defiled
my *sanctuary with all thy detestable
things, and with all thine abominations,
therefore will I also diminish *thee;* neither shall mine eye spare, neither will
I have any pity.
¶[12]A third part of thee shall die with
the pestilence, and with famine shall
they be consumed in the midst of thee:
and a third part shall fall by the sword
round about thee; and I will scatter a
third part into all the winds, and I will
draw out a sword after them.
[13]Thus shall mine anger be accomplished, and I will cause my fury to rest
upon them, and I will be comforted: and
they shall know that I the LORD have
spoken *it* in my zeal, when I have accomplished my fury in them.
[14]Moreover I will make thee waste,
and a reproach among the nations that
are round about thee, in the sight of all
that pass by.
[15]So it shall be a reproach and a taunt,
an instruction and an astonishment
unto the nations that *are* round about
thee, when I shall execute judgments
in thee in anger and in fury and in furious rebukes. I the LORD have spoken *it.*
[16]When I shall send upon them the
evil arrows of famine, which shall be for
their destruction, *and* which I will send
to destroy you: and I will increase the
famine upon you, and will break your
staff of bread:
[17]So will I send upon you famine and
evil beasts, and they shall bereave thee;
and pestilence and blood shall pass
through thee; and I will bring the sword
upon thee. I the LORD have spoken *it.*

The preservation of a remnant in Israel

6 And the word of the LORD came
unto me, saying,
[2]Son of man, set thy face toward the
mountains of Israel, and prophesy
against them,
[3]And say, Ye mountains of Israel, hear
the word of the Lord GOD; Thus saith
the Lord GOD to the mountains, and
to the hills, to the rivers, and to the
valleys; Behold, I, *even* I, will bring a
sword upon you, and I will destroy your
*high places.
[4]And your altars shall be desolate,
and your images shall be broken: and I
will cast down your slain *men* before
your idols.
[5]And I will lay the dead carcases of
the children of Israel before their idols;
and I will scatter your bones round
about your altars.
[6]In all your dwellingplaces the cities
shall be laid waste, and the high places
shall be desolate; that your altars may
be laid waste and made desolate, and
your idols may be broken and cease, and
your images may be cut down, and your
works may be abolished.
[7]And the slain shall fall in the midst
of you, and ye shall know that I *am* the
LORD.
¶[8]Yet will I leave a remnant, that ye
may have *some* that shall escape the
sword among the nations, when ye shall
be scattered through the countries.

5:8 I, even I. This repetition is a solemn warning to Israel.
6:7 ye shall know that I am the LORD. This statement occurs twenty-one times in Ezekiel. It is as if God is saying: "You shall know that I am the living God (not a dead, useless idol). My promises and judgments are sure and will come to pass." "They shall know that I am the LORD" (vss. 10,14) also occurs many times in Ezekiel.

[9]And they that escape of you shall
remember me among the nations
whither they shall be carried captives,
because I am broken with their whorish
heart, which hath departed from me,
and with their eyes, which go a whoring after their idols: and they shall lothe
themselves for the evils which they
have committed in all their abominations.
[10]And they shall know that I *am* the
LORD, *and that* I have not said in vain
that I would do this evil unto them.
¶[11]Thus saith the Lord GOD; Smite
with thine hand, and stamp with thy
foot, and say, Alas for all the evil abominations of the house of Israel! for they
shall fall by the sword, by the famine,
and by the pestilence.
[12]He that is far off shall die of the
pestilence; and he that is near shall fall
by the sword; and he that remaineth and
is besieged shall die by the famine: thus
will I accomplish my fury upon them.
[13]Then shall ye know that I *am* the
LORD, when their slain *men* shall be
among their idols round about their altars, upon every high hill, in all the tops
of the mountains, and *under every
green tree, and under every thick oak,
the place where they did offer sweet
savour to all their idols.
[14]So will I stretch out my hand upon
them, and make the land desolate, yea,
more desolate than the wilderness toward Diblath, in all their habitations:
and they shall know that I *am* the LORD.

The judgment of God upon Israel

7 Moreover the word of the LORD
came unto me, saying,
[2]Also, thou son of man, thus saith the
Lord GOD unto the land of Israel; An
end, the end is come upon the four corners of the land.
[3]Now *is* the end *come* upon thee, and
I will send mine anger upon thee, and
will judge thee according to thy ways,
and will recompense upon thee all thine
abominations.
[4]And mine eye shall not spare thee,
neither will I have pity: but I will recompense thy ways upon thee, and thine
abominations shall be in the midst of thee:
and ye shall know that I *am* the LORD.
[5]Thus saith the Lord GOD; An evil, an
only evil, behold, is come.
[6]An end is come, the end is come: it
watcheth for thee; behold, it is come.
[7]The morning is come unto thee,
O thou that dwellest in the land: the time
is come, the day of trouble *is* near, and not
the sounding again of the mountains.
[8]Now will I shortly pour out my fury
upon thee, and accomplish mine anger
upon thee: and I will judge thee according to thy ways, and will recompense
thee for all thine abominations.
[9]And mine eye shall not spare, neither will I have pity: I will recompense
thee according to thy ways and thine
abominations *that* are in the midst of
thee; and ye shall know that I *am* the
LORD that smiteth.
[10]Behold the day, behold, it is come:
the morning is gone forth; the rod hath
blossomed, pride hath budded.
[11]Violence is risen up into a rod of wickedness: none of them *shall remain,* nor
of their multitude, nor of any of theirs:
neither *shall there be* wailing for them.
[12]The time is come, the day draweth
near: let not the buyer rejoice, nor the
seller mourn: for wrath *is* upon all the
multitude thereof.
[13]For the seller shall not return to

6:9 whorish heart. A heart that delighted in serving idols.
7:2 four corners. This speaks of the completeness of the judgment.
7:5 An evil, an only evil. A calamity, one sole calamity—the Babylonian invasion.
7:10 the day. The *day of wrath.
7:10 the rod hath blossomed. Israel's sin and pride, in budding, called for Nebuchadnezzar's ready rod of punishment. Nebuchadnezzar was the ruler of the Babylonians.
7:11 a rod of wickedness. A rod to punish wickedness.
7:13 seller shall not return. This verse and verse 12 refer to the Year of *Jubilee when

that which is sold, although they were
yet alive: for the vision *is* touching the
whole multitude thereof, *which* shall
not return; neither shall any strength-
en himself in the iniquity of his life.
14They have blown the trumpet, even
to make all ready; but none goeth to the
battle: for my wrath *is* upon all the
multitude thereof.
15The sword *is* without, and the pestilence and the famine within: he that
is in the field shall die with the sword;
and he that *is* in the city, famine and
pestilence shall devour him.
¶16But they that escape of them shall
escape, and shall be on the mountains
like doves of the valleys, all of them
mourning, every one for his iniquity.
17All hands shall be feeble, and all
knees shall be weak *as* water.
18They shall also gird *themselves* with
sackcloth, and horror shall cover them;
and shame *shall be* upon all faces, and
baldness upon all their heads.
19They shall cast their silver in the
streets, and their gold shall be removed: their silver and their gold shall
not be able to deliver them in the day
of the wrath of the LORD: they shall not
satisfy their souls, neither fill their
bowels: because it is the stumblingblock of their iniquity.
¶20As for the beauty of his ornament,
he set it in majesty: but they made the
images of their abominations *and* of
their detestable things therein: therefore have I set it far from them.
21And I will give it into the hands of
the strangers for a prey, and to the wicked of the earth for a spoil; and they shall
pollute it.
22My face will I turn also from them,
and they shall pollute my secret *place:*
for the robbers shall enter into it, and
defile it.
¶23Make a chain: for the land is full
of bloody crimes, and the city is full of
violence.
24Wherefore I will bring the worst of
the heathen, and they shall possess
their houses: I will also make the pomp
of the strong to cease; and their holy
places shall be defiled.
25Destruction cometh; and they shall
seek *peace, and *there shall be* none.
26Mischief shall come upon mischief,
and rumour shall be upon rumour; then
shall they seek a vision of the prophet;
but the *law shall perish from the
priest, and counsel from the ancients.
27The king shall mourn, and the
prince shall be clothed with desolation,
and the hands of the people of the land
shall be troubled: I will do unto them
after their way, and according to their
deserts will I judge them; and they shall
know that I *am* the LORD.

IV. Ezekiel Speaks of the Sins of the People (8:1—33:20)

The defilement of the temple by Israel

8 And it came to pass in the sixth
year, in the sixth **month,* in the
fifth *day* of the month, *as* I sat in mine
house, and the *elders of Judah sat before me, that the hand of the Lord GOD
fell there upon me.
2Then I beheld, and lo a likeness as
the appearance of *fire: from the appearance of his loins even downward,
fire; and from his loins even upward, as
the appearance of brightness, as the
colour of amber.
3And he put forth the form of an hand,
and took me by a lock of mine head; and
the spirit lifted me up between the

---

possessions went back to their original owners even though they had been sold. Ezekiel is warning the people that they will not live to see the Year of Jubilee.

7:16 doves of the valleys. Frightened doves fly to the mountains to escape the hunter.

7:20 his ornament . . . in majesty. This speaks of the temple.

7:23 Make a chain. This speaks of captivity and the people being enslaved.

8:1 elders of Judah sat before me. They were there to hear the preaching of Ezekiel.

8:3 by a lock of mine head. More than a year had passed since Ezekiel had shaved his head (5:1); his hair had had time to grow.

earth and the heaven, and brought me
in the visions of *God to Jerusalem, to
the door of the inner gate that looketh
toward the north; where *was* the seat
of the image of jealousy, which provoketh to jealousy.

4And, behold, the glory of the God of
*Israel *was* there, according to the vision that I saw in the plain.

¶5Then said he unto me, Son of man,
lift up thine eyes now the way toward
the north. So I lifted up mine eyes the
way toward the north, and behold
northward at the gate of the *altar this
image of jealousy in the entry.

6He said furthermore unto me, Son
of man, seest thou what they do? *even*
the great abominations that the house
of Israel committeth here, that I should
go far off from my sanctuary? but turn
thee yet again, *and* thou shalt see greater abominations.

¶7And he brought me to the door of
the court; and when I looked, behold a
hole in the wall.

8Then said he unto me, Son of man,
dig now in the wall: and when I had
digged in the wall, behold a door.

9And he said unto me, Go in, and behold the wicked abominations that they
do here.

10So I went in and saw; and behold
every form of creeping things, and
abominable beasts, and all the idols of
the house of Israel, pourtrayed upon
the wall round about.

11And there stood before them seventy men of the ancients of the house
of Israel, and in the midst of them stood
Jaazaniah the son of Shaphan, with
every man his *censer in his hand; and
a thick cloud of *incense went up.

12Then said he unto me, Son of man,
hast thou seen what the ancients of the
house of Israel do in the dark, every
man in the chambers of his imagery? for
they say, The LORD seeth us not; the
LORD hath forsaken the earth.

13He said also unto me, Turn thee yet
again, *and* thou shalt see greater abominations that they do.

14Then he brought me to the door of
the gate of the LORD'S house which *was*
toward the north; and, behold, there sat
women weeping for Tammuz.

¶15Then said he unto me, Hast thou
seen *this,* O son of man? turn thee yet
again, *and* thou shalt see greater abominations than these.

16And he brought me into the inner
court of the LORD'S house, and, behold,
at the door of the temple of the LORD,
between the porch and the altar, *were*
about five and twenty men, with their

8:4 GOD'S GLORY DEPARTS

Ezekiel records the departure of the glory of God from the temple in Jerusalem. In this verse, he records the fact that the glory of the God of Israel had filled the temple in fulfillment of the promises of God. In 9:3, the prophet pictures the ascension from the ark of the covenant of the glory of God. That Shekinah glory (*Shekinah* is a Hebrew word meaning *the glory of the LORD*) moved from the ark to the threshold of the house. In 10:4, the glory arose from the threshold of the house; and in 10:18, it departed from the threshold and stood over the cherubim.

In 11:23, we discover that the glory of God moved from the temple to the Mount of Olives, on the east of Jerusalem, then ascended to the Father. This is the exact route which was followed by Christ, who went from the temple to the cross, and in His resurrection body from Jerusalem to the mountain on the east, where He ascended to God.

The return of the glory of God to Israel is pictured in 43:2-5. It agrees exactly with what the Scriptures teach us about the return of Christ. The glory comes from the East as the Lord returns from the Mount of Olives (Zech. 14); it enters the house and fills the temple. This prophecy will be fulfilled when the Lord Jesus Christ returns to the earth to establish Himself as King and Lord.

8:11 Jaazaniah. Jaazaniah's father had a leading part in the reformation of Josiah (2 Kings 22).

8:14 Tammuz. The Babylonian god of spring and the husband or lover of the goddess Ishtar.

backs toward the temple of the LORD,
and their faces toward the east; and they
worshipped the sun toward the east.
¶17Then he said unto me, Hast thou
seen *this,* O son of man? Is it a light
thing to the house of Judah that they
commit the abominations which they
commit here? for they have filled the
land with violence, and have returned
to provoke me to anger: and, lo, they
put the branch to their nose.
18Therefore will I also deal in fury:
mine eye shall not spare, neither will I
have pity: and though they cry in mine
ears with a loud voice, *yet* will I not hear
them.

The departure of the Glory of God from the temple

9 He cried also in mine ears with a
loud voice, saying, Cause them that
have charge over the city to draw near,
even every man *with* his destroying
weapon in his hand.
2And, behold, six men came from
the way of the higher gate, which lieth
toward the north, and every man a
slaughter weapon in his hand; and one
man among them *was* clothed with
*linen, with a writer's inkhorn by his
side: and they went in, and stood beside
the brasen altar.
3And the glory of the God of Israel
was gone up from the cherub, whereupon he was, to the threshold of the
house. And he called to the man clothed
with linen, which *had* the writer's
inkhorn by his side;
4And the LORD said unto him, Go
through the midst of the city, through
the midst of Jerusalem, and set a mark
upon the foreheads of the men that sigh
and that cry for all the abominations
that be done in the midst thereof.
¶5And to the others he said in mine
hearing, Go ye after him through the
city, and smite: let not your eye spare,
neither have ye pity:
6Slay utterly old *and* young, both
maids, and little children, and women:
but come not near any man upon whom
is the mark; and begin at my sanctuary.
Then they began at the ancient men
which *were* before the house.
7And he said unto them, Defile the
house, and fill the courts with the slain:
go ye forth. And they went forth, and
slew in the city.
¶8And it came to pass, while they
were slaying them, and I was left, that
I fell upon my face, and cried, and said,
Ah Lord GOD! wilt thou destroy all the
residue of Israel in thy pouring out of
thy fury upon Jerusalem?
9Then said he unto me, The iniquity
of the house of Israel and Judah *is* exceeding great, and the land is full of
blood, and the city full of perverseness:
for they say, The LORD hath forsaken
the earth, and the LORD seeth not.
10And as for me also, mine eye shall
not spare, neither will I have pity, *but* I
will recompense their way upon their
head.
11And, behold, the man clothed with
linen, which *had* the inkhorn by his
side, reported the matter, saying, I have
done as thou hast commanded me.

The departure of the Glory (continued)

10 Then I looked, and, behold, in
the firmament that was above
the head of the cherubims there appeared over them as it were a sapphire
stone, as the appearance of the likeness
of a throne.
2And he spake unto the man clothed
with linen, and said, Go in between the
wheels, *even* under the cherub, and fill
thine hand with coals of fire from between the cherubims, and scatter *them*
over the city. And he went in in my sight.

10:2 coals of fire. The scattering of these coals over Jerusalem was a symbol of the judgment of God on that city. This is in contrast to the coal of fire in the life of Isaiah (Isa. 6). The LORD will cleanse all those who turn to Him in repentance and faith, but He will judge whoever rejects Him.

3 Now the cherubims stood on the
right side of the house, when the man
went in; and the cloud filled the inner
court.
4 Then the glory of the LORD went up
from the cherub, *and stood* over the
threshold of the house; and the house
was filled with the cloud, and the court
was full of the brightness of the LORD'S
glory.
5 And the sound of the cherubims'
wings was heard *even* to the outer
court, as the voice of the Almighty God
when he speaketh.
6 And it came to pass, *that* when he
had commanded the man clothed with
linen, saying, Take fire from between
the wheels, from between the
cherubims; then he went in, and stood
beside the wheels.
7 And *one* cherub stretched forth his
hand from between the cherubims unto
the fire that *was* between the cherubims, and took *thereof,* and put *it* into
the hands of *him that was* clothed with
linen: who took *it,* and went out.
¶8 And there appeared in the cherubims the form of a man's hand under
their wings.

10:8 Cherubim
The cherubim (or "cherubims") are angelic beings, the living creatures of 1:5. They are the ministers of God's righteousness, who guard the way of life (Gen. 3:24); they were placed on the mercy seat, which stood above the ark of the covenant in the tabernacle (Exod. 25:18-20). In the book of Ezekiel, they are seen in an active ministry of judgment upon sinful Israel.

9 And when I looked, behold the four
wheels by the cherubims, one wheel by
one cherub, and another wheel by another cherub: and the appearance of the
wheels *was* as the colour of a beryl stone.
10 And *as for* their appearances, they
four had one likeness, as if a wheel had
been in the midst of a wheel.
11 When they went, they went upon
their four sides; they turned not as they
went, but to the place whither the head
looked they followed it; they turned not
as they went.
12 And their whole body, and their
backs, and their hands, and their
wings, and the wheels, *were* full of eyes
round about, *even* the wheels that they
four had.
13 As for the wheels, it was cried unto
them in my hearing, O wheel.
14 And every one had four faces: the
first face *was* the face of a cherub, and
the second face *was* the face of a man,
and the third the face of a lion, and the
fourth the face of an eagle.
15 And the cherubims were lifted up.
This *is* the living creature that I saw by
the river of Chebar.
16 And when the cherubims went, the
wheels went by them: and when the
cherubims lifted up their wings to
mount up from the earth, the same
wheels also turned not from beside
them.
17 When they stood, *these* stood; and
when they were lifted up, *these* lifted up
themselves *also:* for the spirit of the living creature *was* in them.
18 Then the glory of the LORD departed from off the threshold of the house,
and stood over the cherubims.
19 And the cherubims lifted up their
wings, and mounted up from the earth
in my sight: when they went out, the
wheels also *were* beside them, and *every*
one stood at the door of the east gate of
the LORD'S house; and the glory of the
God of Israel *was* over them above.
20 This *is* the living creature that I saw
under the God of Israel by the river of
Chebar; and I knew that they *were* the
cherubims.
21 Every one had four faces apiece,
and every one four wings; and the likeness of the hands of a man *was* under
their wings.

10:13 O wheel. This was a command for the wheels to roll in order to carry out God's purposes.

22 And the likeness of their faces *was* the same faces which I saw by the river of Chebar, their appearances and themselves: they went every one straight forward.

Israel's preservation through her judgment

11 Moreover the spirit lifted me up, and brought me unto the east gate of the LORD'S house, which looketh eastward: and behold at the door of the gate five and twenty men; among whom I saw Jaazaniah the son of Azur, and Pelatiah the son of Benaiah, the princes of the people.

2 Then said he unto me, Son of man, these *are* the men that devise mischief, and give wicked counsel in this city:

3 Which say, *It is* not near; let us build houses: this *city is* the caldron, and we *be* the flesh.

¶ 4 Therefore prophesy against them, prophesy, O son of man.

5 And the Spirit of the LORD fell upon me, and said unto me, Speak; Thus saith the LORD; Thus have ye said, O house of Israel: for I know the things that come into your mind, *every one of* them.

6 Ye have multiplied your slain in this city, and ye have filled the streets thereof with the slain.

7 Therefore thus saith the Lord GOD; Your slain whom ye have laid in the midst of it, they *are* the flesh, and this *city is* the caldron: but I will bring you forth out of the midst of it.

8 Ye have feared the sword; and I will bring a sword upon you, saith the Lord GOD.

9 And I will bring you out of the midst thereof, and deliver you into the hands of strangers, and will execute judgments among you.

10 Ye shall fall by the sword; I will judge you in the border of Israel; and ye shall know that I *am* the LORD.

11 This *city* shall not be your caldron, neither shall ye be the flesh in the midst thereof; *but* I will judge you in the border of Israel:

12 And ye shall know that I *am* the LORD: for ye have not walked in my statutes, neither executed my judgments, but have done after the manners of the heathen that *are* round about you.

¶ 13 And it came to pass, when I prophesied, that Pelatiah the son of Benaiah died. Then fell I down upon my face, and cried with a loud voice, and said, Ah Lord GOD! wilt thou make a full end of the *remnant of Israel?

14 Again the word of the LORD came unto me, saying,

15 Son of man, thy brethren, *even* thy brethren, the men of thy kindred, and all the house of Israel wholly, *are* they unto whom the inhabitants of *Jerusalem have said, Get you far from the LORD: unto us is this land given in possession.

16 Therefore say, Thus saith the Lord GOD; Although I have cast them far off among the heathen, and although I have *scattered them among the countries, yet will I be to them as a little *sanctuary in the countries where they shall come.

17 Therefore say, Thus saith the Lord GOD; I will even gather you from the people, and assemble you out of the countries where ye have been scattered, and I will give you the land of Israel.

18 And they shall come thither, and they shall take away all the detestable things thereof and all the abominations thereof from thence.

19 And I will give them one heart, and I will put a new spirit within you; and I will take the stony heart out of their flesh, and will give them an heart of flesh:

20 That they may walk in my statutes, and keep mine ordinances, and do them: and they shall be my people, and I will be their God.

21 But *as for them* whose heart walketh after the heart of their detestable things and their abominations, I will recompense their way upon their own heads, saith the Lord GOD.

¶22Then did the cherubims lift up
their wings, and the wheels beside
them; and the glory of the God of Israel *was* over them above.
23And the glory of the LORD went up
from the midst of the city, and stood
upon the mountain which *is* on the east
side of the city.
¶24Afterwards the spirit took me up,
and brought me in a vision by the Spirit of God into Chaldea, to them of the
captivity. So the vision that I had seen
went up from me.
25Then I spake unto them of the captivity all the things that the LORD had
shewed me.

A prediction of the fall of Jerusalem

12 The word of the LORD also came
unto me, saying,
2Son of man, thou dwellest in the
midst of a rebellious house, which have
eyes to see, and see not; they have ears
to hear, and hear not: for they *are* a rebellious house.
3Therefore, thou son of man, prepare
thee stuff for removing, and remove by
day in their sight; and thou shalt remove from thy place to another place in
their sight: it may be they will consider, though they *be* a rebellious house.

12:3 Time to Move
Again the prophet is used as a symbol of the near-at-hand judgment of God upon Jerusalem. As Ezekiel prepared his things for moving, so God declared the days were at hand and that the inhabitants of Jerusalem and their king, Zedekiah (vs. 12), would move from their city. Though Zedekiah tried to escape, he was taken, blinded by the Babylonians, and died in their land, as prophesied in verse 13.

4Then shalt thou bring forth thy stuff
by day in their sight, as stuff for removing: and thou shalt go forth at even in
their sight, as they that go forth into
captivity.
5Dig thou through the wall in their
sight, and carry out thereby.
6In their sight shalt thou bear *it* upon
thy shoulders, *and* carry *it* forth in the
twilight: thou shalt cover thy face, that
thou see not the ground: for I have set
thee *for* a sign unto the house of Israel.
7And I did so as I was commanded:
I brought forth my stuff by day, as stuff
for captivity, and in the even I digged
through the wall with mine hand; I
brought *it* forth in the twilight, *and* I
bare *it* upon *my* shoulder in their sight.
¶8And in the morning came the word
of the LORD unto me, saying,
9Son of man, hath not the house of
Israel, the rebellious house, said unto
thee, What doest thou?
10Say thou unto them, Thus saith the
Lord GOD; This *burden *concerneth* the
prince in Jerusalem, and all the house
of Israel that *are* among them.
11Say, I *am* your sign: like as I have
done, so shall it be done unto them:
they shall remove *and* go into captivity.
12And the prince that *is* among them
shall bear upon *his* shoulder in the twilight, and shall go forth: they shall dig
through the wall to carry out thereby:
he shall cover his face, that he see not
the ground with *his* eyes.
13My net also will I spread upon him,
and he shall be taken in my snare: and
I will bring him to *Babylon *to* the land
of the Chaldeans; yet shall he not see
it, though he shall die there.
14And I will scatter toward every
wind all that *are* about him to help him,
and all his bands; and I will draw out the
sword after them.
15And they shall know that I *am* the
LORD, when I shall *scatter them
among the nations, and disperse them
in the countries.
16But I will leave a few men of them
from the sword, from the famine, and
from the pestilence; that they may declare all their abominations among the
heathen whither they come; and they
shall know that I *am* the LORD.
¶17Moreover the word of the LORD
came to me, saying,
18Son of man, eat thy bread with

quaking, and drink thy water with trembling and with carefulness;
19 And say unto the people of the land,
Thus saith the Lord GOD of the inhabitants of Jerusalem, *and* of the land of
Israel; They shall eat their bread with
carefulness, and drink their water with
astonishment, that her land may be
desolate from all that is therein, because of the violence of all them that
dwell therein.
20 And the cities that are inhabited
shall be laid waste, and the land shall be
desolate; and ye shall know that I *am*
the LORD.
¶21 And the word of the LORD came
unto me, saying,
22 Son of man, what *is* that proverb
that ye have in the land of Israel, saying, The days are prolonged, and every
vision faileth?
23 Tell them therefore, Thus saith the
Lord GOD; I will make this proverb to
cease, and they shall no more use it as
a proverb in Israel; but say unto them,
The days are at hand, and the effect of
every vision.
24 For there shall be no more any vain
vision nor flattering divination within
the house of Israel.
25 For I *am* the LORD: I will speak, and
the word that I shall speak shall come
to pass; it shall be no more prolonged:
for in your days, O rebellious house,
will I say the word, and will perform it,
saith the Lord GOD.
¶26 Again the word of the LORD came
to me, saying,
27 Son of man, behold, *they of* the
house of Israel say, The vision that he
seeth *is* for many days *to come,* and
he prophesieth of the times *that are*
far off.
28 Therefore say unto them, Thus
saith the Lord GOD; There shall none
of my words be prolonged any more, but
the word which I have spoken shall be
done, saith the Lord GOD.

God's word against false prophets

13 And the word of the LORD came
unto me, saying,
2 Son of man, prophesy against the
*prophets of Israel that prophesy, and
say thou unto them that prophesy out
of their own hearts, Hear ye the word
of the LORD;
3 Thus saith the Lord GOD; Woe unto
the foolish prophets, that follow their
own spirit, and have seen nothing!
4 O Israel, thy prophets are like the
foxes in the deserts.
5 Ye have not gone up into the gaps,
neither made up the hedge for the
house of Israel to stand in the battle in
the day of the LORD.
6 They have seen *vanity and lying
divination, saying, The LORD saith: and
the LORD hath not sent them: and they
have made *others* to *hope that they
would confirm the word.
7 Have ye not seen a vain vision, and
have ye not spoken a lying divination,
whereas ye say, The LORD saith *it;* albeit I have not spoken?
8 Therefore thus saith the Lord GOD;
Because ye have spoken vanity, and
seen lies, therefore, behold, I *am*
against you, saith the Lord GOD.
9 And mine hand shall be upon the
prophets that see vanity, and that divine
lies: they shall not be in the assembly
of my people, neither shall they be written in the writing of the house of Israel,
neither shall they enter into the land of
Israel; and ye shall know that I *am* the
Lord GOD.
¶10 Because, even because they have
seduced my people, saying, *Peace; and
there was no peace; and one built up a
wall, and, lo, others daubed it with
untempered *morter:*
11 Say unto them which daub *it* with
untempered *morter,* that it shall fall:
there shall be an overflowing shower;
and ye, O great hailstones, shall fall; and
a stormy wind shall rend *it.*

13:3 their own spirit. Not the Holy Spirit. They preached, not what the Word of God said, but what the people wanted to hear—that they would go back to Palestine quickly.

12Lo, when the wall is fallen, shall it
not be said unto you, Where *is* the daub-
ing wherewith ye have daubed *it?*
13Therefore thus saith the Lord GOD;
I will even rend *it* with a stormy wind
in my fury; and there shall be an overflowing shower in mine anger, and great
hailstones in *my* fury to consume *it.*
14So will I break down the wall that
ye have daubed with untempered
morter, and bring it down to the ground,
so that the foundation thereof shall be
discovered, and it shall fall, and ye shall
be consumed in the midst thereof: and
ye shall know that I *am* the LORD.
15Thus will I accomplish my wrath
upon the wall, and upon them that have
daubed it with untempered *morter,* and
will say unto you, The wall *is* no *more,*
neither they that daubed it;
16*To wit,* the prophets of Israel which
prophesy concerning Jerusalem, and
which see visions of peace for her, and
there is no peace, saith the Lord GOD.
¶17Likewise, thou son of man, set thy
face against the daughters of thy people, which prophesy out of their own
heart; and prophesy thou against them,
18And say, Thus saith the Lord GOD;
Woe to the *women* that sew pillows to
all armholes, and make kerchiefs upon
the head of every stature to hunt souls!
Will ye hunt the souls of my people, and
will ye save the souls alive *that come*
unto you?
19And will ye pollute me among my
people for handfuls of barley and for
pieces of bread, to slay the souls that
should not die, and to save the souls
alive that should not live, by your lying
to my people that hear *your* lies?
20Wherefore thus saith the Lord
GOD; Behold, I *am* against your pillows,
wherewith ye there hunt the souls to
make *them* fly, and I will tear them from
your arms, and will let the souls go,
even the souls that ye hunt to make
them fly.
21Your kerchiefs also will I tear, and
deliver my people out of your hand, and
they shall be no more in your hand to
be hunted; and ye shall know that I *am*
the LORD.
22Because with lies ye have made the
heart of the righteous sad, whom I have
not made sad; and strengthened the
hands of the wicked, that he should not
return from his wicked way, by promising him life:
23Therefore ye shall see no more
vanity, nor divine divinations: for I will
deliver my people out of your hand: and
ye shall know that I *am* the LORD.

God's word against the Elders of Israel

14 Then came certain of the elders
of *Israel unto me, and sat before me.
2And the word of the LORD came unto
me, saying,
3Son of man, these men have set up
their idols in their heart, and put the
stumblingblock of their iniquity before
their face: should I be enquired of at all
by them?
4Therefore speak unto them, and say
unto them, Thus saith the Lord GOD;
Every man of the house of Israel that
setteth up his idols in his heart, and
putteth the stumblingblock of his iniquity before his face, and cometh to the
*prophet; I the LORD will answer him
that cometh according to the multitude
of his idols;
5That I may take the house of Israel
in their own heart, because they are all
estranged from me through their idols.
¶6Therefore say unto the house of
Israel, Thus saith the Lord GOD; *Repent, and turn *yourselves* from your
idols; and turn away your faces from all
your abominations.
7For every one of the house of Israel,
or of the stranger that sojourneth in Israel, which separateth himself from me,
and setteth up his idols in his heart, and
putteth the stumblingblock of his iniquity before his face, and cometh to a

---

13:18 pillows to all armholes. Magic charms on their sleeves.

prophet to enquire of him concerning
me; I the LORD will answer him by
myself:
8And I will set my face against that
man, and will make him a sign and a
proverb, and I will cut him off from the
midst of my people; and ye shall know
that I *am* the LORD.
9And if the prophet be deceived when
he hath spoken a thing, I the LORD have
deceived that prophet, and I will stretch
out my hand upon him, and will destroy
him from the midst of my people Israel.
10And they shall bear the punishment
of their iniquity: the punishment of the
prophet shall be even as the punishment of him that seeketh *unto him;*
11That the house of Israel may go no
more astray from me, neither be polluted any more with all their transgressions; but that they may be my people,
and I may be their *God, saith the Lord
GOD.
¶12The word of the LORD came again
to me, saying,
13Son of man, when the land sinneth
against me by trespassing grievously,
then will I stretch out mine hand upon
it, and will break the staff of the bread
thereof, and will send famine upon it,
and will cut off man and beast from it:
14Though these three men, Noah,
Daniel, and Job, were in it, they should
deliver *but* their own souls by their
*righteousness, saith the Lord GOD.
¶15If I cause noisome beasts to pass
through the land, and they spoil it, so
that it be desolate, that no man may
pass through because of the beasts:
16*Though* these three men *were* in it,
as I live, saith the Lord GOD, they shall
deliver neither sons nor daughters;
they only shall be delivered, but the
land shall be desolate.
¶17Or *if* I bring a sword upon that
land, and say, Sword, go through the
land; so that I cut off man and beast
from it:
18Though these three men *were* in it,
as I live, saith the Lord GOD, they shall
deliver neither sons nor daughters, but
they only shall be delivered themselves.
¶19Or *if* I send a pestilence into that
land, and pour out my fury upon it in
blood, to cut off from it man and beast:
20Though Noah, Daniel, and Job, *were*
in it, *as* I live, saith the Lord GOD, they
shall deliver neither son nor daughter;
they shall *but* deliver their own souls by
their righteousness.
21For thus saith the Lord GOD; How
much more when I send my four sore
judgments upon Jerusalem, the sword,
and the famine, and the noisome beast,
and the pestilence, to cut off from it
man and beast?
¶22Yet, behold, therein shall be left a
remnant that shall be brought forth,
both sons and daughters: behold, they
shall come forth unto you, and ye shall
see their way and their doings: and ye
shall be comforted concerning the evil
that I have brought upon Jerusalem,
even concerning all that I have brought
upon it.
23And they shall comfort you, when
ye see their ways and their doings: and
ye shall know that I have not done without cause all that I have done in it, saith
the Lord GOD.

The uselessness of a disobedient people

15 And the word of the LORD came
unto me, saying,
2Son of man, What is the vine tree
more than any tree, *or than* *a branch

14:14 Men of Character
Daniel was still a young man when Ezekiel associated him with Noah and Job. It is a remarkable tribute to his character. Noah was upright (Gen. 6:9); Daniel, greatly beloved (Dan. 10:11); and Job, unequalled in the earth (Job 1:8). Daniel is one of the few men in the Bible who is not charged with being unfaithful.

14:19 blood. This stood for every kind of unnatural death.
15:2 the vine tree. Whenever the people of God are disobedient to the LORD, they lose

which is among the trees of the forest?
[3]Shall wood be taken thereof to do
any work? or will *men* take a pin of it to
hang any vessel thereon?
[4]Behold, it is cast into the *fire for
fuel; the fire devoureth both the ends
of it, and the midst of it is burned. Is it
meet for *any* work?
[5]Behold, when it was whole, it was
meet for no work: how much less shall
it be meet yet for *any* work, when the
fire hath devoured it, and it is burned?
¶[6]Therefore thus saith the Lord GOD;
As the vine tree among the trees of the
forest, which I have given to the fire for
fuel, so will I give the inhabitants of
Jerusalem.
[7]And I will set my face against them;
they shall go out from *one* fire, and *another* fire shall devour them; and ye
shall know that I *am* the LORD, when I
set my face against them.
[8]And I will make the land desolate,
because they have committed a *trespass, saith the Lord GOD.

The sin of Jerusalem

16 Again the word of the LORD
came unto me, saying,
[2]Son of man, cause Jerusalem to
know her abominations,
[3]And say, Thus saith the Lord GOD
unto Jerusalem; Thy birth and thy nativity *is* of the land of Canaan; thy father
was an *Amorite, and thy mother an
Hittite.
[4]And *as for* thy nativity, in the day
thou wast born thy navel was not cut,
neither wast thou washed in water to
supple *thee;* thou wast not salted at all,
nor swaddled at all.
[5]None eye pitied thee, to do any of
these unto thee, to have compassion
upon thee; but thou wast cast out in the
open field, to the lothing of thy person,
in the day that thou wast born.
¶[6]And when I passed by thee, and
saw thee polluted in thine own *blood,
I said unto thee *when thou wast* in thy
blood, Live; yea, I said unto thee *when
thou wast* in thy blood, Live.
[7]I have caused thee to multiply as the
bud of the field, and thou hast increased
and waxen great, and thou art come to
excellent ornaments: *thy* breasts are
fashioned, and thine hair is grown,
whereas thou *wast* naked and bare.
[8]Now when I passed by thee, and
looked upon thee, behold, thy time *was*
the time of love; and I spread my skirt
over thee, and covered thy nakedness:
yea, I sware unto thee, and entered into
a *covenant with thee, saith the Lord
GOD, and thou becamest mine.
[9]Then washed I thee with water; yea,
I throughly washed away thy blood from
thee, and I anointed thee with *oil.
[10]I clothed thee also with broidered
work, and shod thee with badgers' skin,
and I girded thee about with fine *lin-
en, and I covered thee with silk.
[11]I decked thee also with ornaments,
and I put bracelets upon thy hands, and
a chain on thy neck.
[12]And I put a jewel on thy forehead,
and earrings in thine ears, and a beautiful crown upon thine head.
[13]Thus wast thou decked with gold
and *silver; and thy raiment *was of* fine

16:2 Extreme Wickedness
The extreme wickedness of Jerusalem's sin is presented by the prophet in this chapter. He shows us that God had given Jerusalem unusual blessing and opportunity. The extreme wickedness of Jerusalem consisted in her having used the tokens of God's love as instruments of unrighteousness; therefore, the punishment of Jerusalem must be consistent with the enormity of her sin.

their usefulness. Israel is compared to a vine that was about to be consumed by fire, since nothing useful could be constructed from that vine.

15:4 the ends of it. The Assyrians burnt the northern end; the Egyptians the southern; and the Chaldeans were just in the midst of consuming the middle—Jerusalem.

15:6 so will I give the inhabitants of Jerusalem. Read how this prophecy was fulfilled in 2 Kings 25:9.

linen, and silk, and broidered work;
thou didst eat fine flour, and honey, and
oil: and thou wast exceeding beautiful,
and thou didst prosper into a kingdom.
14 And thy renown went forth among
the heathen for thy beauty: for it *was*
perfect through my comeliness, which
I had put upon thee, saith the Lord GOD.
¶ 15 But thou didst *trust in thine own
beauty, and playedst the harlot because
of thy renown, and pouredst out thy
fornications on every one that passed
by; his it was.
16 And of thy *garments thou didst
take, and deckedst thy *high places
with divers colours, and playedst the
harlot thereupon: *the like things* shall
not come, neither shall it be *so*.
17 Thou hast also taken thy fair jewels of my gold and of my silver, which I
had given thee, and madest to thyself
images of men, and didst commit
whoredom with them,
18 And tookest thy broidered garments, and coveredst them: and thou
hast set mine oil and mine *incense
before them.
19 My meat also which I gave thee,
fine flour, and oil, and honey, *wherewith*
I fed thee, thou hast even set it before
them for a sweet savour: and *thus* it
was, saith the Lord GOD.
20 Moreover thou hast taken thy sons
and thy daughters, whom thou hast
borne unto me, and these hast thou
sacrificed unto them to be devoured. *Is
this* of thy whoredoms a small matter,
21 That thou hast slain my children,
and delivered them to cause them to
pass through *the fire* for them?
22 And in all thine abominations and
thy whoredoms thou hast not remembered the days of thy youth, when thou
wast naked and bare, *and* wast polluted in thy blood.
23 And it came to pass after all thy
wickedness, (woe, woe unto thee! saith
the Lord GOD;)
24 *That* thou hast also built unto thee
an eminent place, and hast made thee
an high place in every street.
25 Thou hast built thy high place at
every head of the way, and hast made
thy beauty to be abhorred, and hast
opened thy feet to every one that passed
by, and multiplied thy whoredoms.
26 Thou hast also committed fornication with the Egyptians thy neighbours,
great of flesh; and hast increased thy
whoredoms, to provoke me to anger.
27 Behold, therefore I have stretched
out my hand over thee, and have diminished thine ordinary *food,* and delivered thee unto the will of them that
hate thee, the daughters of the *Philistines, which are ashamed of thy
lewd way.
28 Thou hast played the whore also
with the Assyrians, because thou wast
unsatiable; yea, thou hast played the
harlot with them, and yet couldest not
be satisfied.
29 Thou hast moreover multiplied thy
fornication in the land of Canaan unto
Chaldea; and yet thou wast not satisfied
herewith.
30 How weak is thine heart, saith the
Lord GOD, seeing thou doest all these
things, the work of an imperious
whorish woman;
31 In that thou buildest thine eminent
place in the head of every way, and
makest thine high place in every street;
and hast not been as an harlot, in that
thou scornest hire;
32 *But as* a wife that committeth adultery, *which* taketh strangers instead of
her husband!
33 They give gifts to all whores: but
thou givest thy gifts to all thy lovers,
and hirest them, that they may come
unto thee on every side for thy whoredom.
34 And the contrary is in thee from
other women in thy whoredoms, whereas none followeth thee to commit

---

16:15 playedst the harlot. Worshipped the idols of the nations around them.
16:20 these hast thou sacrificed. In the worship of *Molech.

whoredoms: and in that thou givest a
reward, and no reward is given unto
thee, therefore thou art contrary.
¶ 35 Wherefore, O harlot, hear the
word of the LORD:
36 Thus saith the Lord GOD; Because
thy filthiness was poured out, and thy
nakedness discovered through thy
whoredoms with thy lovers, and with all
the idols of thy abominations, and by
the blood of thy children, which thou
didst give unto them;
37 Behold, therefore I will gather all
thy lovers, with whom thou hast taken
pleasure, and all *them* that thou hast
loved, with all *them* that thou hast hated; I will even gather them round about
against thee, and will discover thy nakedness unto them, that they may see
all thy nakedness.
38 And I will judge thee, as women
that break wedlock and shed blood are
judged; and I will give thee blood in fury
and jealousy.
39 And I will also give thee into their
hand, and they shall throw down thine
eminent place, and shall break down thy
high places: they shall strip thee also of
thy clothes, and shall take thy fair jewels, and leave thee naked and bare.
40 They shall also bring up a company against thee, and they shall stone
thee with stones, and thrust thee
through with their swords.
41 And they shall burn thine houses
with fire, and execute judgments upon
thee in the sight of many women: and I
will cause thee to cease from playing
the harlot, and thou also shalt give no
hire any more.
42 So will I make my fury toward thee
to rest, and my jealousy shall depart
from thee, and I will be quiet, and will
be no more angry.
43 Because thou hast not remembered
the days of thy youth, but hast fretted
me in all these *things;* behold, therefore
I also will recompense thy way upon
thine head, saith the Lord GOD: and
thou shalt not commit this lewdness
above all thine abominations.
¶ 44 Behold, every one that useth
*proverbs shall use *this* proverb against
thee, saying, As *is* the mother, *so is* her
daughter.
45 Thou *art* thy mother's daughter,
that lotheth her husband and her children; and thou *art* the sister of thy sisters, which lothed their husbands and
their children: your mother *was* an Hittite, and your father an Amorite.
46 And thine elder sister *is* *Samaria,
she and her daughters that dwell at thy
left hand: and thy younger sister, that
dwelleth at thy right hand, *is* Sodom and
her daughters.
47 Yet hast thou not walked after their
ways, nor done after their abominations: but, as *if that were* a very little
thing, thou wast corrupted more than
they in all thy ways.
48 *As* I live, saith the Lord GOD, Sodom thy sister hath not done, she nor her
daughters, as thou hast done, thou and
thy daughters.
49 Behold, this was the iniquity of thy
sister Sodom, pride, fulness of bread,
and abundance of idleness was in her
and in her daughters, neither did she
strengthen the hand of the poor and
needy.
50 And they were haughty, and committed *abomination before me: therefore I took them away as I saw *good.*
51 Neither hath Samaria committed
half of thy sins; but thou hast multiplied
thine abominations more than they, and
hast justified thy sisters in all thine
abominations which thou hast done.
52 Thou also, which hast judged thy
sisters, bear thine own shame for thy
sins that thou hast committed more
abominable than they: they are more
righteous than thou: yea, be thou confounded also, and bear thy shame, in
that thou hast justified thy sisters.

16:37 thy lovers. Assyria and Chaldea, with whom Israel had made alliances.
16:37 them that thou hast hated. Moabites, Ammonites, and Philistines.

[53]When I shall bring again their captivity, the captivity of Sodom and her
daughters, and the captivity of Samar-
ia and her daughters, then *will I bring again* the captivity of thy captives in the
midst of them:
[54]That thou mayest bear thine own
shame, and mayest be confounded in all
that thou hast done, in that thou art a
comfort unto them.
[55]When thy sisters, Sodom and her
daughters, shall return to their former
estate, and Samaria and her daughters
shall return to their former estate, then
thou and thy daughters shall return to
your former estate.
[56]For thy sister Sodom was not mentioned by thy mouth in the day of thy
pride,
[57]Before thy wickedness was discovered, as at the time of *thy* reproach of
the daughters of Syria, and all *that are*
round about her, the daughters of the
Philistines, which despise thee round
about.
[58]Thou hast borne thy lewdness and
thine abominations, saith the LORD.
[59]For thus saith the Lord GOD; I will
even deal with thee as thou hast done,
which hast despised the oath in breaking the covenant.

God's faithfulness to His Covenant

¶[60]Nevertheless I will remember my
covenant with thee in the days of thy
youth, and I will establish unto thee an
everlasting covenant.
[61]Then thou shalt remember thy
ways, and be ashamed, when thou shalt
receive thy sisters, thine elder and thy
younger: and I will give them unto thee
for daughters, but not by thy covenant.
[62]And I will establish my covenant
with thee; and thou shalt know that I *am*
the LORD:
[63]That thou mayest remember, and
be confounded, and never open thy
mouth any more because of thy shame,
when I am pacified toward thee for all
that thou hast done, saith the Lord GOD.

The uselessness of Israel's conspiracy with Egypt against Babylon

17 And the word of the LORD came
unto me, saying,
[2]Son of man, put forth a riddle, and
speak a *parable unto the house of Israel;
[3]And say, Thus saith the Lord GOD; A
great eagle with great wings, long-
winged, full of feathers, which had
divers colours, came unto *Lebanon, and
took the highest branch of the cedar:
[4]He cropped off the top of his young
twigs, and carried it into a land of traffick; he set it in a city of merchants.
[5]He took also of the seed of the land,

17:3 The Symbolic Eagle
The symbolism of this chapter is explained in the chapter itself. This great eagle, which took the highest branch of the cedar of Lebanon, is Nebuchadnezzar, the king of Babylon, who came to Jerusalem (many of the houses in Jerusalem were built of cedars of Lebanon) and took away her king (see vs. 13). The second great eagle (vs. 7) is Pharaoh-Hophra, the king of Egypt, to whom the successor of the vanquished king of Jerusalem appealed for help; the prophet declared that Pharaoh would also carry away the successor of Israel's king and spoil the land. The spiritual message here is that we cannot escape the results of disobedience by turning to some human source of strength. God's people should repent when they are corrected by Him.

16:60 I will remember my covenant with thee. It is a great source of comfort for us to know that God abides faithful, even when His people are unfaithful to Him (2 Tim. 2:13). Were this not true, there would be no hope of salvation for anyone.
16:60 an everlasting covenant. Read Hebrews 8:8-12 and 8:8 note, "The New Covenant."
17:2 a parable. A story which compares one thing to another.
17:4 a land of traffick. Babylonia. The "city of merchants" was Babylon.
17:5 seed of the land. Zedekiah.

and planted it in a fruitful field; he placed *it* by great waters, *and* set it *as* a willow tree.

6And it grew, and became a spreading vine of low stature, whose branches turned toward him, and the roots thereof were under him: so it became a vine, and brought forth branches, and shot forth sprigs.

7There was also another great eagle with great wings and many feathers: and, behold, this vine did bend her roots toward him, and shot forth her branches toward him, that he might water it by the furrows of her plantation.

8It was planted in a good soil by great waters, that it might bring forth branches, and that it might bear fruit, that it might be a goodly vine.

9Say thou, Thus saith the Lord GOD; Shall it prosper? shall he not pull up the roots thereof, and cut off the fruit thereof, that it wither? it shall wither in all the leaves of her spring, even without great power or many people to pluck it up by the roots thereof.

10Yea, behold, *being* planted, shall it prosper? shall it not utterly wither, when the east wind toucheth it? it shall wither in the furrows where it grew.

¶11Moreover the word of the LORD came unto me, saying,

12Say now to the rebellious house, Know ye not what these *things mean?* tell *them,* Behold, the king of Babylon is come to *Jerusalem, and hath taken the king thereof, and the princes thereof, and led them with him to Babylon;

13And hath taken of the king's seed, and made a covenant with him, and hath taken an oath of him: he hath also taken the mighty of the land:

14That the kingdom might be base, that it might not lift itself up, *but* that by keeping of his covenant it might stand.

15But he rebelled against him in sending his ambassadors into *Egypt, that they might give him horses and much people. Shall he prosper? shall he escape that doeth such *things?* or shall he break the covenant, and be delivered?

16*As* I live, saith the Lord GOD, surely in the place *where* the king *dwelleth* that made him king, whose oath he despised, and whose covenant he brake, *even* with him in the midst of Babylon he shall die.

17Neither shall *Pharaoh with *his* mighty army and great company make for him in the war, by casting up mounts, and building forts, to cut off many persons:

18Seeing he despised the oath by breaking the covenant, when, lo, he had given his hand, and hath done all these *things,* he shall not escape.

19Therefore thus saith the Lord GOD; *As* I live, surely mine oath that he hath despised, and my covenant that he hath broken, even it will I recompense upon his own head.

20And I will spread my net upon him, and he shall be taken in my snare, and I will bring him to Babylon, and will plead with him there for his trespass that he hath trespassed against me.

21And all his fugitives with all his bands shall fall by the sword, and they that remain shall be scattered toward all winds: and ye shall know that I the LORD have spoken *it.*

¶22Thus saith the Lord GOD; I will also take of the highest branch of the high cedar, and will set *it;* I will crop off from the top of his young twigs a tender one, and will plant *it* upon an high *mountain and eminent:

17:5 a fruitful field. Palestine.
17:16 in the place. Babylon, where King Nebuchadnezzar lived, who made Zedekiah king.
17:18 he had given his hand. Zedekiah had made the covenant with Nebuchadnezzar.
17:20 my net . . . my snare. The Babylonian army.
17:22 of the highest branch. Here is a wonderful promise that the Messiah, our Lord Jesus Christ, would come from the royal family of David (see Matt. 1:1; Isa. 53:2).

23 In the mountain of the height of Israel will I plant it: and it shall bring forth boughs, and bear fruit, and be a goodly cedar: and under it shall dwell all fowl of every wing; in the shadow of the branches thereof shall they dwell.

24 And all the trees of the field shall know that I the LORD have brought down the high tree, have exalted the low tree, have dried up the green tree, and have made the dry tree to flourish: I the LORD have spoken and have done *it.*

Individual responsibility before God

18 The word of the LORD came unto me again, saying,

2 What mean ye, that ye use this proverb concerning the land of Israel, saying, The fathers have eaten sour grapes, and the children's teeth are set on edge?

3 *As* I live, saith the Lord GOD, ye shall not have *occasion* any more to use this proverb in Israel.

4 Behold, all souls are mine; as the soul of the father, so also the soul of the son is mine: the soul that sinneth, it shall die.

18:4 The Sinful Nature
Every person bears his or her own responsibility before God; it is not inherited by the children. The sinful nature is passed on to all the descendants of Adam, but every person bears his or her own responsibility before God (see also vs. 20).

¶5 But if a man be *just, and do that which is lawful and right,

6 *And* hath not eaten upon the mountains, neither hath lifted up his eyes to the idols of the house of Israel, neither hath defiled his neighbour's wife, neither hath come near to a menstruous woman,

7 And hath not oppressed any, *but* hath restored to the debtor his pledge, hath spoiled none by violence, hath given his bread to the hungry, and hath covered the naked with a garment;

8 He *that* hath not given forth upon *usury, neither hath taken any increase, *that* hath withdrawn his hand from iniquity, hath executed true *judgment between man and man,

9 Hath walked in my statutes, and hath kept my judgments, to deal truly; he *is* just, he shall surely live, saith the Lord GOD.

¶10 If he beget a son *that is* a robber, a shedder of blood, and *that* doeth the like to *any* one of these *things,*

11 And that doeth not any of those *duties,* but even hath eaten upon the mountains, and defiled his neighbour's wife,

12 Hath oppressed the poor and needy, hath spoiled by violence, hath not restored the pledge, and hath lifted up his eyes to the idols, hath committed abomination,

13 Hath given forth upon usury, and hath taken increase: shall he then live? he shall not live: he hath done all these abominations; he shall surely die; his blood shall be upon him.

¶14 Now, lo, *if* he beget a son, that seeth all his father's sins which he hath done, and considereth, and doeth not such like,

15 *That* hath not eaten upon the mountains, neither hath lifted up his eyes to the idols of the house of Israel, hath not defiled his neighbour's wife,

16 Neither hath oppressed any, hath not withholden the pledge, neither hath spoiled by violence, *but* hath given his bread to the hungry, and hath covered the naked with a garment,

17 *That* hath taken off his hand from the poor, *that* hath not received usury nor increase, hath executed my judgments, hath walked in my statutes; he

17:24 brought down the high . . . exalted the low. Note that Mary, the mother of our Lord Jesus Christ, repeated this prophecy in her song (Luke 1:52).
18:6 eaten upon the mountains. This speaks of the worship of idols upon the *high places.

shall not die for the iniquity of his father,
he shall surely live.
18 *As for* his father, because he cruelly oppressed, spoiled his brother by violence, and did *that* which *is* not good
among his people, lo, even he shall die
in his iniquity.
¶19 Yet say ye, Why? doth not the son
*bear the iniquity of the father? When
the son hath done that which is lawful
and right, *and* hath kept all my statutes,
and hath done them, he shall surely
live.
20 The soul that sinneth, it shall die.
The son shall not bear the iniquity of the
father, neither shall the father bear the
iniquity of the son: the righteousness
of the righteous shall be upon him, and
the wickedness of the wicked shall be
upon him.
21 But if the wicked will turn from all
his sins that he hath committed, and
keep all my statutes, and do that which
is lawful and right, he shall surely live,
he shall not die.
22 All his transgressions that he hath
committed, they shall not be mentioned
unto him: in his righteousness that he
hath done he shall live.
23 Have I any pleasure at all that the
wicked should die? saith the Lord GOD:
and not that he should return from his
ways, and live?
¶24 But when the righteous turneth
away from his righteousness, and committeth iniquity, *and* doeth according to
all the abominations that the wicked
man doeth, shall he live? All his righteousness that he hath done shall not
be mentioned: in his trespass that he
hath trespassed, and in his *sin that he
hath sinned, in them shall he die.
¶25 Yet ye say, The way of the Lord is
not equal. Hear now, O house of Israel;
Is not my way equal? are not your ways
unequal?
26 When a righteous *man* turneth
away from his righteousness, and
committeth iniquity, and dieth in them;
for his iniquity that he hath done shall
he die.
27 Again, when the wicked *man*
turneth away from his wickedness that
he hath committed, and doeth that
which is lawful and right, he shall save
his soul alive.
28 Because he considereth, and
turneth away from all his transgressions that he hath committed, he shall
surely live, he shall not die.
29 Yet saith the house of Israel, The
way of the Lord is not equal. O house
of Israel, are not my ways equal? are not
your ways unequal?
30 Therefore I will judge you, O house
of Israel, every one according to his
ways, saith the Lord GOD. Repent, and
turn *yourselves* from all your transgressions; so iniquity shall not be your ruin.
¶31 Cast away from you all your transgressions, whereby ye have transgressed; and make you a new heart
and a new spirit: for why will ye die, O
house of Israel?
32 For I have no pleasure in the *death
of him that dieth, saith the Lord GOD:
wherefore turn *yourselves,* and live ye.

God's word against the princes of Israel

19 Moreover take thou up a lamentation for the princes of
Israel,
2 And say, What *is* thy mother? A
lioness: she lay down among lions, she
nourished her whelps among young
lions.
3 And she brought up one of her
whelps: it became a young lion, and it

18:22 in his righteousness. Notice that this is not *by* his righteousness, but *in* the righteousness of God put over to the sinner's account (see Rom. 4:24-25).

18:31 a new heart and a new spirit. The entrance into the kingdom of God is always dependent upon the new birth, which is the consequence of true repentance (Acts 17:30; see also its note, "Repentance"), and receiving the Lord Jesus Christ as Saviour (John 1:12).

19:1 a lamentation. Verses 2-14 give us a *parable.

19:2 The Symbolic Lions
The symbolism of this chapter speaks of the punishment of God on the princes of Israel. The first young lion (vs. 3) was Jehoahaz, who was taken in chains to Egypt (2 Kings 23:33). The second lion (vs. 5) is Zedekiah, who later was taken captive and brought to Babylon (2 Chron. 36:6).

learned to catch the prey; it devoured
men.
4The nations also heard of him; he
was taken in their pit, and they brought
him with chains unto the land of Egypt.
5Now when she saw that she had
waited, *and* her *hope was lost, then
she took another of her whelps, *and*
made him a young lion.
6And he went up and down among the
lions, he became a young lion, and
learned to catch the prey, *and* devoured
men.
7And he knew their desolate palaces,
and he laid waste their cities; and the
land was desolate, and the *fulness
thereof, by the noise of his roaring.
8Then the nations set against him on
every side from the provinces, and
spread their net over him: he was taken
in their pit.
9And they put him in ward in chains,
and brought him to the king of *Babylon:
they brought him into holds, that
his voice should no more be heard upon
the mountains of Israel.
¶10Thy mother *is* like a vine in thy
blood, planted by the waters: she was
fruitful and full of branches by reason
of many waters.
11And she had strong rods for the
sceptres of them that bare rule, and
her stature was exalted among the
thick branches, and she appeared in her
height with the multitude of her
branches.
12But she was plucked up in fury, she
was cast down to the ground, and the
east wind dried up her fruit: her strong
rods were broken and withered; the fire
consumed them.
13And now she *is* planted in the wilderness,
in a dry and thirsty ground.
14And fire is gone out of a rod of her
branches, *which* hath devoured her
fruit, so that she hath no strong rod *to
be* a sceptre to rule. This *is* a lamentation,
and shall be for a lamentation.

God's word against Israel

20 And it came to pass in the seventh
year, in the fifth **month,*
the tenth *day* of the month, *that*
certain of the *elders of *Israel came to
enquire of the LORD, and sat before me.
2Then came the word of the LORD
unto me, saying,
3Son of man, speak unto the elders of
Israel, and say unto them, Thus saith
the Lord GOD; Are ye come to enquire
of me? *As* I live, saith the Lord GOD, I
will not be enquired of by you.
4Wilt thou judge them, son of man,
wilt thou judge *them?* cause them to
know the abominations of their fathers:
¶5And say unto them, Thus saith the
Lord GOD; In the day when I chose Israel,
and lifted up mine hand unto the
seed of the house of *Jacob, and made
myself known unto them in the land
of Egypt, when I lifted up mine hand
unto them, saying, I *am* the LORD your
*God;
6In the day *that* I lifted up mine hand
unto them, to bring them forth of the
land of Egypt into a land that I had espied
for them, *flowing with milk and
honey, which *is* the glory of all lands:
7Then said I unto them, Cast ye away
every man the abominations of his
eyes, and defile not yourselves with the

19:7 he knew. He plundered.
19:11 her stature was exalted. Israel had some prosperity while Babylon was ruling over the nation, but the prophet foretold Israel's bitter end when the city and temple would be destroyed by fire (vss. 12-14).
20:6 to bring them forth. See Exodus 3:8,17.

idols of Egypt: I *am* the LORD your God.

8 But they rebelled against me, and would not hearken unto me: they did not every man cast away the abominations of their eyes, neither did they forsake the idols of Egypt: then I said, I will pour out my fury upon them, to accomplish my anger against them in the midst of the land of Egypt.

9 But I wrought for my name's sake, that it should not be polluted before the heathen, among whom they *were,* in whose sight I made myself known unto them, in bringing them forth out of the land of Egypt.

¶10 Wherefore I caused them to go forth out of the land of Egypt, and brought them into the wilderness.

11 And I gave them my statutes, and shewed them my judgments, which *if* a man do, he shall even live in them.

12 Moreover also I gave them my sabbaths, to be a sign between me and them, that they might know that I *am* the LORD that *sanctify them.

13 But the house of Israel rebelled against me in the wilderness: they walked not in my statutes, and they despised my judgments, which *if* a man do, he shall even live in them; and my sabbaths they greatly polluted: then I said, I would pour out my fury upon them in the wilderness, to consume them.

14 But I wrought for my name's sake, that it should not be polluted before the heathen, in whose sight I brought them out.

15 Yet also I lifted up my hand unto them in the wilderness, that I would not bring them into the land which I had given *them,* flowing with milk and honey, which *is* the glory of all lands;

16 Because they despised my judgments, and walked not in my statutes, but polluted my sabbaths: for their heart went after their idols.

17 Nevertheless mine eye spared them from destroying them, neither did I make an end of them in the wilderness.

18 But I said unto their children in the wilderness, Walk ye not in the statutes of your fathers, neither observe their judgments, nor defile yourselves with their idols:

19 I *am* the LORD your God; walk in my statutes, and keep my judgments, and do them;

20 And hallow my sabbaths; and they shall be a sign between me and you, that ye may know that I *am* the LORD your God.

21 Notwithstanding the children rebelled against me: they walked not in my statutes, neither kept my judgments to do them, which *if* a man do, he shall even live in them; they polluted my sabbaths: then I said, I would pour out my fury upon them, to accomplish my anger against them in the wilderness.

22 Nevertheless I withdrew mine hand, and wrought for my name's sake, that it should not be polluted in the sight of the heathen, in whose sight I brought them forth.

23 I lifted up mine hand unto them also in the wilderness, that I would *scatter them among the heathen, and disperse them through the countries;

24 Because they had not executed my judgments, but had despised my statutes, and had polluted my sabbaths, and their eyes were after their fathers' idols.

25 Wherefore I gave them also statutes *that were* not good, and judgments whereby they should not live;

26 And I polluted them in their own gifts, in that they caused to pass through *the fire* all that openeth the womb, that I might make them desolate, to the end

---

20:12 the LORD that sanctify them. This phrase translates one of the *names of God—Jehovah-Mekaddishkem (see also Exod. 31:13; Lev. 20:8; Ezek. 37:28).

20:25 I gave them. I permitted them.

20:26 pass through the fire. See *Molech.

that they might know that I *am* the
LORD.
¶27 Therefore, son of man, speak unto
the house of Israel, and say unto them,
Thus saith the Lord GOD; Yet in this
your fathers have blasphemed me, in
that they have committed a trespass
against me.
28 *For* when I had brought them into
the land, *for* the which I lifted up mine
hand to give it to them, then they saw
every high hill, and all the thick trees,
and they offered there their sacrifices,
and there they presented the provocation of their *offering: there also they
made their sweet savour, and poured
out there their *drink-offerings.
29 Then I said unto them, What *is*
the high place whereunto ye go? And
the name thereof is called Bamah unto
this day.
30 Wherefore say unto the house of
Israel, Thus saith the Lord GOD; Are ye
polluted after the manner of your fathers? and commit ye whoredom after
their abominations?
31 For when ye offer your gifts, when
ye make your sons to pass through the
fire, ye pollute yourselves with all your
idols, even unto this day: and shall I be
enquired of by you, O house of Israel?
As I live, saith the Lord GOD, I will not
be enquired of by you.
32 And that which cometh into your
mind shall not be at all, that ye say, We
will be as the heathen, as the families
of the countries, to serve wood and
stone.

The judgment of regathered Israel at the Second Coming of Christ

¶33 *As* I live, saith the Lord GOD,
surely with a mighty hand, and with a
stretched out arm, and with fury poured
out, will I rule over you:
34 And I will bring you out from the
people, and will gather you out of
the countries wherein ye are scattered, with a mighty hand, and with a
stretched out arm, and with fury
poured out.
35 And I will bring you into the wilderness of the people, and there will I plead
with you face to face.
36 Like as I pleaded with your fathers
in the wilderness of the land of Egypt,
so will I plead with you, saith the Lord
GOD.
37 And I will cause you to pass under
the rod, and I will bring you into the
bond of the covenant:
38 And I will purge out from among
you the rebels, and them that transgress against me: I will bring them forth
out of the country where they sojourn,
and they shall not enter into the land of
Israel: and ye shall know that I *am* the
LORD.
39 As for you, O house of Israel, thus
saith the Lord GOD; Go ye, serve ye
every one his idols, and hereafter *also,*
if ye will not hearken unto me: but pollute ye my *holy name no more with
your gifts, and with your idols.
40 For in mine holy mountain, in the
mountain of the height of Israel, saith
the Lord GOD, there shall all the house
of Israel, all of them in the land, serve
me: there will I accept them, and there
will I require your offerings, and the
firstfruits of your oblations, with all
your holy things.
41 I will accept you with your sweet
savour, when I bring you out from the
people, and gather you out of the countries wherein ye have been scattered;
and I will be sanctified in you before the
heathen.
42 And ye shall know that I *am* the
LORD, when I shall bring you into the
land of Israel, into the country *for*
the which I lifted up mine hand to give
it to your fathers.
43 And there shall ye remember your

20:28 every high hill, and all the thick trees. Places of the wicked worship of idols and evil practices.
20:29 Bamah. The name means *high place*.

ways, and all your doings, wherein ye
have been defiled; and ye shall lothe
yourselves in your own sight for all
your evils that ye have committed.
44 And ye shall know that I *am* the
LORD, when I have wrought with you
for my name's sake, not according to
your wicked ways, nor according to
your corrupt doings, O ye house of Israel, saith the Lord GOD.
¶45 Moreover the word of the LORD
came unto me, saying,
46 Son of man, set thy face toward the
south, and drop *thy word* toward the
south, and prophesy against the forest
of the south field;
47 And say to the forest of the south,
Hear the word of the LORD; Thus saith
the Lord GOD; Behold, I will kindle a
fire in thee, and it shall devour every
green tree in thee, and every dry tree:
the flaming flame shall not be quenched,
and all faces from the south to the north
shall be burned therein.
48 And all flesh shall see that I the
LORD have kindled it: it shall not be
quenched.
49 Then said I, Ah Lord GOD! they say
of me, Doth he not speak *parables?

The setting aside of Israel until the return of Christ

21 And the word of the LORD came
unto me, saying,
2 Son of man, set thy face toward Jerusalem, and drop *thy word* toward the
holy places, and prophesy against the
land of Israel,
3 And say to the land of Israel, Thus
saith the LORD; Behold, I *am* against
thee, and will draw forth my sword out
of his sheath, and will cut off from thee
the righteous and the wicked.
4 Seeing then that I will cut off from
thee the righteous and the wicked,
therefore shall my sword go forth out
of his sheath against all flesh from the
south to the north:
5 That all flesh may know that I the
LORD have drawn forth my sword out
of his sheath: it shall not return any
more.
6 Sigh therefore, thou son of man,
with the breaking of *thy* loins; and with
bitterness sigh before their eyes.
7 And it shall be, when they say unto
thee, Wherefore sighest thou? that thou
shalt answer, For the tidings; because
it cometh: and every heart shall melt,
and all hands shall be feeble, and every
spirit shall faint, and all knees shall be
weak *as* water: behold, it cometh, and
shall be brought to pass, saith the Lord
GOD.
¶8 Again the word of the LORD came
unto me, saying,
9 Son of man, prophesy, and say, Thus
saith the LORD; Say, A sword, a sword
is sharpened, and also furbished:
10 It is sharpened to make a sore
slaughter; it is furbished that it may
glitter: should we then make mirth? it

20:35 FACE-TO-FACE JUDGMENT

Verses 33-38 teach us that when the Lord Jesus Christ comes to earth to establish His *kingdom, He will judge the nation Israel to determine who among them can enter the millennial reign of Christ. This judgment does not imply a special resurrection of the children of Israel. It speaks of the Israelites who will be on the earth at the time of the coming of the King. The rebels among them will be purged out, and the faithful *remnant will be established as the people of the King of Kings.

This judgment is a parallel to the judgment described in Matthew 25:31-46. Together, these Scriptures teach us that at His coming the Lord will determine who among the living are entitled to enter the millennial *kingdom. These judgments in no way affect the *church, which is the body of Christ. Before all these judgments, the Lord will have come for His own people and transported them to heaven (1 Thess. 4:13-18; see also 4:13 note, "Hope for the Dead").

21:10 it contemneth the rod. The sharp steel sword of the Babylonians would cut the wooden spears of the Israelites as if they were little twigs from the trees (see vs. 13).

contemneth the rod of my son, *as* every
tree.
[11]And he hath given it to be furbished, that it may be handled: this
sword is sharpened, and it is furbished,
to give it into the hand of the slayer.
[12]Cry and howl, son of man: for it
shall be upon my people, it *shall be* upon
all the princes of Israel: terrors by reason of the sword shall be upon my people: smite therefore upon *thy* thigh.
[13]Because *it is* a trial, and what if *the
sword* contemn even the rod? it shall be
no *more,* saith the Lord GOD.
[14]Thou therefore, son of man, prophesy, and smite *thine* hands together, and
let the sword be doubled the third time,
the sword of the slain: it *is* the sword
of the great *men that are* slain, which
entereth into their privy chambers.
[15]I have set the point of the sword
against all their gates, that *their* heart
may faint, and *their* ruins be multiplied:
ah! *it is* made bright, *it is* wrapped up
for the slaughter.
[16]Go thee one way or other, *either* on
the right hand, *or* on the left, whithersoever thy face *is* set.
[17]I will also smite mine hands together, and I will cause my fury to rest: I the
LORD have said *it.*
¶[18]The word of the LORD came unto
me again, saying,
[19]Also, thou son of man, appoint thee
two ways, that the sword of the king of
Babylon may come: both twain shall
come forth out of one land: and choose
thou a place, choose *it* at the head of the
way to the city.
[20]Appoint a way, that the sword may
come to Rabbath of the Ammonites, and
to *Judah in Jerusalem the defenced.
[21]For the king of Babylon stood at the
parting of the way, at the head of the two
ways, to use divination: he made *his*
arrows bright, he consulted with images, he looked in the liver.
[22]At his right hand was the divination
for Jerusalem, to appoint captains, to
open the mouth in the slaughter, to lift
up the voice with shouting, to appoint
battering rams against the gates, to cast
a mount, *and* to build a fort.
[23]And it shall be unto them as a false
divination in their sight, to them that
have sworn oaths: but he will call to
remembrance the iniquity, that they
may be taken.
[24]Therefore thus saith the Lord GOD;
Because ye have made your iniquity to
be remembered, in that your transgressions are discovered, so that in all your
doings your sins do appear; because, *I
say,* that ye are come to remembrance,
ye shall be taken with the hand.
¶[25]And thou, profane wicked prince
of Israel, whose day is come, when iniquity *shall have* an end,
[26]Thus saith the Lord GOD; Remove
the diadem, and take off the crown: this
shall not *be* the same: exalt *him that is*
low, and abase *him that is* high.
[27]I will overturn, overturn, overturn,
it: and it shall be no *more,* until he

21:15 wrapped up. Grasped.

21:21 the king of Babylon stood at the parting of the way. God determines the course of human history, and man's acts can be ruled and overruled by Him. When the king of Babylon was undecided as to which way he should go in his conquest, God knew which way he would turn, and through the king the judgment of God came upon disobedient Israel.

21:21 arrows . . . liver. Two arrows, one marked Ammon, one marked Jerusalem, were placed in a quiver. Whichever the king drew was accepted as a true sign. A liver of an animal or fowl, offered in sacrifice, was examined. If it were healthy, it meant that the expedition would prosper.

21:25 profane wicked prince of Israel. Zedekiah.

21:27 I will overturn, overturn, overturn, it. God declares that Israel will have no king until He comes "whose right it is" to reign. For 2,500 years this verse has had a literal fulfillment. Israel will continue to remain without a king until the Lord Jesus Christ returns as their King.

come whose right it is; and I will give
it *him*.
¶[28]And thou, son of man, prophesy
and say, Thus saith the Lord GOD concerning the Ammonites, and concerning their reproach; even say thou, The
sword, the sword *is* drawn: for the
slaughter *it is* furbished, to consume
because of the glittering:
[29]Whiles they see *vanity unto thee,
whiles they divine a lie unto thee, to
bring thee upon the necks of *them that
are* slain, of the wicked, whose day is
come, when their iniquity *shall have* an
end.
[30]Shall I cause *it* to return into his
sheath? I will judge thee in the place
where thou wast *created, in the land
of thy nativity.
[31]And I will pour out mine indignation
upon thee, I will blow against thee in
the *fire of my wrath, and deliver thee
into the hand of brutish men, *and* skilful to destroy.
[32]Thou shalt be for fuel to the fire; thy
blood shall be in the midst of the land;
thou shalt be no *more* remembered: for
I the LORD have spoken *it*.

The sins of Israel

22 Moreover the word of the LORD
came unto me, saying,
[2]Now, thou son of man, wilt thou
judge, wilt thou judge the bloody city?
yea, thou shalt shew her all her abominations.
[3]Then say thou, Thus saith the Lord
GOD, The city sheddeth blood in the
midst of it, that her time may come, and
maketh idols against herself to defile
herself.
[4]Thou art become guilty in thy blood
that thou hast shed; and hast defiled
thyself in thine idols which thou hast
made; and thou hast caused thy days to
draw near, and art come *even* unto thy
years: therefore have I made thee a
reproach unto the heathen, and a mocking to all countries.
[5]*Those that be* near, and *those that be*
far from thee, shall mock thee, *which
art* infamous *and* much vexed.
[6]Behold, the princes of Israel, every
one were in thee to their power to shed
blood.
[7]In thee have they set light by father
and mother: in the midst of thee have
they dealt by oppression with the
stranger: in thee have they vexed the
fatherless and the widow.
[8]Thou hast despised mine holy
things, and hast profaned my sabbaths.
[9]In thee are men that carry tales to
shed blood: and in thee they *eat upon
the mountains: in the midst of thee they
commit lewdness.
[10]In thee have they discovered their
fathers' nakedness: in thee have they

22:2 A SERIES OF TRANSGRESSIONS

The sins of Israel that are enumerated in this chapter are a series of transgressions of the Ten Commandments (Exod. 20:1-17; see also 20:2 note and 20:5 note, "The Effect of Sin").

1. Israel violated the first and second commandments by making idols (vss. 3-4).
2. Israel violated the fourth commandment by profaning the *Sabbath (vs. 8).
3. Israel violated the fifth commandment by disregarding the rights of parents (vs. 7).
4. Israel violated the sixth commandment by shedding blood (vs. 3)
5. Israel violated the seventh commandment by committing adultery (vs. 11).
6. Israel violated the tenth commandment by greedily taking gain of their neighbors (vs. 12).

As a punishment for Israel's sins, God decreed that He would scatter them among the heathen (vs. 15).

21:28 Ammonites, and concerning their reproach. The Ammonites rejoiced at the downfall of Jerusalem, but years later, they were utterly destroyed by the Chaldeans, and no longer exist. The people whom they reproached still exist and will be restored to their land.

22:2 the bloody city. Jerusalem.

humbled her that was set apart for pol-
lution.
11And one hath committed *abomination with his neighbour's wife; and another hath lewdly defiled his daughter
in *law; and another in thee hath humbled his sister, his father's daughter.
12In thee have they taken gifts to
shed blood; thou hast taken *usury and
increase, and thou hast greedily gained
of thy neighbours by extortion, and hast
forgotten me, saith the Lord GOD.
¶13Behold, therefore I have smitten
mine hand at thy dishonest gain which
thou hast made, and at thy blood which
hath been in the midst of thee.
14Can thine heart endure, or can
thine hands be strong, in the days that
I shall deal with thee? I the LORD have
spoken *it,* and will do *it.*
15And I will scatter thee among the
heathen, and disperse thee in the countries, and will consume thy filthiness
out of thee.
16And thou shalt take thine inheritance in thyself in the sight of the heathen, and thou shalt know that I *am* the
LORD.
17And the word of the LORD came
unto me, saying,
18Son of man, the house of Israel is
to me become dross: all they *are* brass,
and tin, and iron, and lead, in the midst
of the furnace; they are *even* the dross
of silver.
19Therefore thus saith the Lord GOD;
Because ye are all become dross, behold, therefore I will gather you into the
midst of Jerusalem.
20*As* they gather silver, and brass, and
iron, and lead, and tin, into the midst of
the furnace, to blow the fire upon it, to
melt *it;* so will I gather *you* in mine anger and in my fury, and I will leave *you
there,* and melt you.
21Yea, I will gather you, and blow
upon you in the fire of my wrath, and
ye shall be melted in the midst thereof.
22As silver is melted in the midst of
the furnace, so shall ye be melted in the
midst thereof; and ye shall know that I
the LORD have poured out my fury upon
you.
¶23And the word of the LORD came
unto me, saying,
24Son of man, say unto her, Thou *art*
the land that is not cleansed, nor rained
upon in the day of indignation.
25*There is* a conspiracy of her *prophets in the midst thereof, like a roaring
lion ravening the prey; they have devoured souls; they have taken the treasure and precious things; they have
made her many widows in the midst
thereof.
26Her priests have violated my law,
and have profaned mine holy things:
they have put no difference between
the holy and profane, neither have they
shewed *difference* between the *unclean and the *clean, and have hid their
eyes from my sabbaths, and I am profaned among them.
27Her princes in the midst thereof *are*
like wolves ravening the prey, to shed
blood, *and* to destroy souls, to get dishonest gain.
28And her prophets have daubed
them with untempered *morter,* seeing
vanity, and divining lies unto them, saying, Thus saith the Lord GOD, when the
LORD hath not spoken.
29The people of the land have used
oppression, and exercised robbery, and
have vexed the poor and needy: yea,
they have oppressed the stranger
wrongfully.
30And I sought for a man among
them, that should make up the hedge,
and stand in the gap before me for the

22:18 the dross of silver. In the refiner's fire, it should have been silver that was refined. In spite of the judgments upon them, however, Israel was only left that which was base and of no worth.

22:30 I sought for a man. Jeremiah was there, but he had been told that even his prayers were useless unless the people themselves would repent (Jer. 11:14).

land, that I should not destroy it: but I
found none.
31 Therefore have I poured out mine
indignation upon them; I have consumed them with the fire of my wrath:
their own way have I recompensed
upon their heads, saith the Lord GOD.

The larger responsibility of Jerusalem

23 The word of the LORD came
again unto me, saying,
2 Son of man, there were two women,
the daughters of one mother:
3 And they committed whoredoms in
*Egypt; they committed whoredoms in
their youth: there were their breasts
pressed, and there they bruised the
teats of their virginity.
4 And the names of them *were* Aholah
the elder, and Aholibah her sister: and
they were mine, and they bare sons
and daughters. Thus *were* their names;
*Samaria *is* Aholah, and *Jerusalem
Aholibah.

23:4 Unfaithful Women
God likened the kingdoms of Israel to two unfaithful women. The elder sister is thought of as the ten northern tribes, who because of their sin were delivered into the hand of the Assyrians. The younger sister is accused of greater wickedness than her older sister, because she did not repent when she saw the punishment of God come upon the northern kingdom. This younger sister represents the kingdom of Judah, which was taken into captivity by the Babylonians.

5 And Aholah played the harlot when
she was mine; and she doted on her
lovers, on the Assyrians *her* neighbours,
6 *Which were* clothed with *blue,
captains and rulers, all of them desirable young men, horsemen riding upon
horses.
7 Thus she committed her whoredoms with them, with all them *that were*
the chosen men of Assyria, and with all
on whom she doted: with all their idols
she defiled herself.
8 Neither left she her whoredoms
brought from Egypt: for in her youth
they lay with her, and they bruised the
breasts of her virginity, and poured their
whoredom upon her.
9 Wherefore I have delivered her
into the hand of her lovers, into the
hand of the Assyrians, upon whom she
doted.
10 These discovered her nakedness:
they took her sons and her daughters,
and slew her with the sword: and she
became famous among women; for they
had executed judgment upon her.
11 And when her sister Aholibah saw
this, she was more corrupt in her inordinate love than she, and in her whoredoms more than her sister in *her*
whoredoms.
12 She doted upon the Assyrians *her*
neighbours, captains and rulers clothed
most gorgeously, horsemen riding upon
horses, all of them desirable young
men.
13 Then I saw that she was defiled,
that they *took* both one way,
14 And *that* she increased her whoredoms: for when she saw men pourtrayed upon the wall, the images of
the Chaldeans pourtrayed with vermilion,
15 Girded with girdles upon their
loins, exceeding in dyed attire upon
their heads, all of them princes to look
to, after the manner of the Babylonians
of Chaldea, the land of their nativity:
16 And as soon as she saw them with
her eyes, she doted upon them, and sent
messengers unto them into Chaldea.
17 And the Babylonians came to her
into the bed of love, and they defiled her
with their whoredom, and she was polluted with them, and her mind was
alienated from them.
18 So she discovered her whoredoms,
and discovered her nakedness: then my
mind was alienated from her, like as my
mind was alienated from her sister.
19 Yet she multiplied her whoredoms,
in calling to remembrance the days of
her youth, wherein she had played the
harlot in the land of Egypt.

20For she doted upon their par-
amours, whose flesh *is as* the flesh of
asses, and whose issue *is like* the issue
of horses.
21Thus thou calledst to remembrance
the lewdness of thy youth, in bruising
thy teats by the Egyptians for the paps
of thy youth.
¶22Therefore, O Aholibah, thus saith
the Lord GOD; Behold, I will raise up
thy lovers against thee, from whom thy
mind is alienated, and I will bring them
against thee on every side;
23The Babylonians, and all the Chaldeans, Pekod, and Shoa, and Koa, *and*
all the Assyrians with them: all of them
desirable young men, captains and rulers, great lords and renowned, all of
them riding upon horses.
24And they shall come against thee
with chariots, wagons, and wheels, and
with an assembly of people, *which* shall
set against thee *buckler and shield
and helmet round about: and I will set
judgment before them, and they shall
judge thee according to their judgments.
25And I will set my jealousy against
thee, and they shall deal furiously with
thee: they shall take away thy nose and
thine ears; and thy *remnant shall fall
by the sword: they shall take thy sons
and thy daughters; and thy residue shall
be devoured by the fire.
26They shall also strip thee out of thy
clothes, and take away thy fair jewels.
27Thus will I make thy lewdness to
cease from thee, and thy whoredom
brought from the land of Egypt: so that
thou shalt not lift up thine eyes unto
them, nor remember Egypt any more.
28For thus saith the Lord GOD; Behold, I will deliver thee into the hand
of them whom thou hatest, into the
hand *of them* from whom thy mind is
alienated:
29And they shall deal with thee hate-
fully, and shall take away all thy labour,
and shall leave thee naked and bare: and
the nakedness of thy whoredoms shall
be discovered, both thy lewdness and
thy whoredoms.
30I will do these *things* unto thee,
because thou hast gone a whoring after
the heathen, *and* because thou art polluted with their idols.
31Thou hast walked in the way of thy
sister; therefore will I give her cup into
thine hand.
32Thus saith the Lord GOD; Thou
shalt drink of thy sister's cup deep and
large: thou shalt be laughed to scorn
and had in derision; it containeth much.
33Thou shalt be filled with drunkenness and sorrow, with the cup of astonishment and desolation, with the cup of
thy sister Samaria.
34Thou shalt even drink it and suck
it out, and thou shalt break the *sherds
thereof, and pluck off thine own breasts:
for I have spoken *it,* saith the Lord GOD.
35Therefore thus saith the Lord GOD;
Because thou hast forgotten me, and
cast me behind thy back, therefore bear
thou also thy lewdness and thy whoredoms.
¶36The LORD said moreover unto me;
Son of man, wilt thou judge Aholah and
Aholibah? yea, declare unto them their
abominations;
37That they have committed adultery, and blood *is* in their hands, and
with their idols have they committed
adultery, and have also caused their
sons, whom they bare unto me, to pass
for them through *the fire,* to devour
them.
38Moreover this they have done unto
me: they have defiled my *sanctuary in
the same day, and have profaned my
sabbaths.
39For when they had slain their children to their idols, then they came the
same day into my sanctuary to profane
it; and, lo, thus have they done in the
midst of mine house.
40And furthermore, that ye have sent
for men to come from far, unto whom a

23:23 Pekod, and Shoa, and Koa. Eastern nations.

messenger *was* sent; and, lo, they
came: for whom thou didst wash thyself, paintedst thy eyes, and deckedst
thyself with ornaments,
41And satest upon a stately bed, and
a table prepared before it, whereupon
thou hast set mine *incense and mine
*oil.
42And a voice of a multitude being at
ease *was* with her: and with the men of
the common sort *were* brought Sabeans
from the wilderness, which put bracelets upon their hands, and beautiful
crowns upon their heads.
43Then said I unto *her that was* old in
adulteries, Will they now commit
whoredoms with her, and she *with
them?*
44Yet they went in unto her, as they
go in unto a woman that playeth the
harlot: so went they in unto Aholah and
unto Aholibah, the lewd women.
¶45And the righteous men, they shall
judge them after the manner of adulteresses, and after the manner of women
that shed blood; because they *are* adulteresses, and blood *is* in their hands.
46For thus saith the Lord GOD; I will
bring up a company upon them, and will
give them to be removed and spoiled.
47And the company shall stone them
with stones, and dispatch them with
their swords; they shall slay their sons
and their daughters, and burn up their
houses with fire.
48Thus will I cause lewdness to cease
out of the land, that all women may be
taught not to do after your lewdness.
49And they shall recompense your
lewdness upon you, and ye shall bear
the sins of your idols: and ye shall know
that I *am* the Lord GOD.

Prediction of the destruction of Jerusalem

24 Again in the ninth year, in the
tenth month, in the tenth *day* of
the month, the word of the LORD came
unto me, saying,
2Son of man, write thee the name of
the day, *even* of this same day: the king
of Babylon set himself against Jerusalem this same day.
3And utter a *parable unto the rebellious house, and say unto them, Thus
saith the Lord GOD; Set on a pot, set *it*
on, and also pour water into it:
4Gather the pieces thereof into it,
even every good piece, the thigh, and
the shoulder; fill *it* with the choice
bones.
5Take the choice of the flock, and
burn also the bones under it, *and* make
it boil well, and let them seethe the
bones of it therein.
¶6Wherefore thus saith the Lord
GOD; Woe to the bloody city, to the pot
whose scum *is* therein, and whose
scum is not gone out of it! bring it out
piece by piece; let no lot fall upon it.
7For her blood is in the midst of her;
she set it upon the top of a rock; she
poured it not upon the ground, to cover it with dust;
8That it might cause fury to come up
to take vengeance; I have set her blood
upon the top of a rock, that it should not
be covered.
9Therefore thus saith the Lord GOD;
Woe to the bloody city! I will even make
the pile for fire great.
10Heap on wood, kindle the fire, consume the flesh, and spice it well, and let
the bones be burned.
11Then set it empty upon the coals
thereof, that the brass of it may be hot,

24:3 Set on a pot, set it on, and also pour water into it. The boiling pot represented the judgment of God that was soon to come upon Jerusalem. It is another of the object lessons found in the book of Ezekiel. See the people's boast (Ezek. 11:3) that they were as safe in Jerusalem as food is in a pot.

24:4-5 every good piece . . . also the bones. The princes and the people.

24:6 scum. Poison.

24:6 let no lot fall upon it. Literally, *without making any choice*. Prisoners were often selected for death or liberty by lot. There was to be no lot here. All were to be judged.

24:7 to cover it with dust. See Leviticus 17:13. Israel's guilt was not hidden.

and may burn, and *that* the filthiness of
it may be molten in it, *that* the scum of
it may be consumed.
12She hath wearied *herself* with lies,
and her great scum went not forth out
of her: her scum *shall be* in the fire.
13In thy filthiness *is* lewdness: because I have purged thee, and thou wast
not purged, thou shalt not be purged
from thy filthiness any more, till I have
caused my fury to rest upon thee.
14I the LORD have spoken *it:* it shall
come to pass, and I will do *it;* I will not
go back, neither will I spare, neither
will I repent; according to thy ways, and
according to thy doings, shall they judge
thee, saith the Lord GOD.
¶15Also the word of the LORD came
unto me, saying,
16Son of man, behold, I take away from
thee the desire of thine eyes with a
stroke: yet neither shalt thou mourn nor
weep, neither shall thy tears run down.
17Forbear to cry, make no *mourning
for the dead, bind the tire of thine head
upon thee, and put on thy shoes upon
thy feet, and cover not *thy* lips, and eat
not the bread of men.
18So I spake unto the people in the
morning: and at even my wife died;
and I did in the morning as I was commanded.
¶19And the people said unto me, Wilt
thou not tell us what these *things are* to
us, that thou doest *so?*

> **24:18 Another Object Lesson**
> The death of Ezekiel's wife became an object lesson to the children of Israel, inasmuch as the prophet was not allowed to mourn the loss of his wife. His lack of mourning became a symbol to the children of Israel of the fact that God Himself would neither pity nor spare that disobedient people.

20Then I answered them, The word
of the LORD came unto me, saying,
21Speak unto the house of Israel,
Thus saith the Lord GOD; Behold, I will
profane my sanctuary, the excellency of
your strength, the desire of your eyes,
and that which your soul pitieth; and
your sons and your daughters whom ye
have left shall fall by the sword.
22And ye shall do as I have done: ye
shall not cover *your* lips, nor eat the
bread of men.
23And your tires *shall be* upon your
heads, and your shoes upon your feet:
ye shall not mourn nor weep; but ye
shall pine away for your iniquities, and
mourn one toward another.
24Thus *Ezekiel is unto you a sign:
according to all that he hath done shall
ye do: and when this cometh, ye shall
know that I *am* the Lord GOD.
25Also, thou son of man, *shall it* not
be in the day when I take from them
their strength, the joy of their glory, the
desire of their eyes, and that whereupon they set their minds, their sons
and their daughters,
26*That* he that escapeth in that day
shall come unto thee, to cause *thee* to
hear *it* with *thine* ears?
27In that day shall thy mouth be
opened to him which is escaped, and
thou shalt speak, and be no more dumb:
and thou shalt be a sign unto them; and
they shall know that I *am* the LORD.

Prophecies of judgments upon Gentile nations

25 The word of the LORD came
again unto me, saying,
2Son of man, set thy face against the
Ammonites, and prophesy against
them;
3And say unto the Ammonites, Hear

24:17 make no mourning. This spoke of public mourning; they could mourn in secret (Ezek. 24:23).

24:17 bind the tire of thine head. The taking off of the turban was a sign of grief (Lev. 10:6; 13:45; 21:10). Covering the lips and taking off the shoes were public signs of mourning.

24:22 the bread of men. Food brought to the houses of the mourners by those who sympathized with them.

the word of the Lord GOD; Thus saith
the Lord GOD; Because thou saidst,
Aha, against my sanctuary, when it was
profaned; and against the land of Israel,
when it was desolate; and against the
house of Judah, when they went into
captivity;
4 Behold, therefore I will deliver thee
to the men of the east for a possession,
and they shall set their palaces in thee,
and make their dwellings in thee: they
shall eat thy fruit, and they shall drink
thy milk.
5 And I will make Rabbah a stable for
camels, and the Ammonites a couching
place for flocks: and ye shall know that
I *am* the LORD.
6 For thus saith the Lord GOD; Because thou hast clapped *thine* hands,
and stamped with the feet, and rejoiced
in heart with all thy despite against the
land of Israel;
7 Behold, therefore I will stretch out
mine hand upon thee, and will deliver
thee for a spoil to the heathen; and I will
cut thee off from the people, and I will
cause thee to perish out of the countries: I will destroy thee; and thou shalt
know that I *am* the LORD.
¶ 8 Thus saith the Lord GOD; Because
that Moab and *Seir do say, Behold, the
house of Judah *is* like unto all the heathen;
9 Therefore, behold, I will open the
side of Moab from the cities, from his
cities *which are* on his frontiers, the
glory of the country, Beth-jeshimoth,
Baal-meon, and Kiriathaim,
10 Unto the men of the east with the
Ammonites, and will give them in possession, that the Ammonites may not
be remembered among the nations.
11 And I will execute judgments upon
Moab; and they shall know that I *am* the
LORD.
¶ 12 Thus saith the Lord GOD; Because that Edom hath dealt against the
house of Judah by taking vengeance,
and hath greatly offended, and revenged
himself upon them;
13 Therefore thus saith the Lord GOD;
I will also stretch out mine hand upon
Edom, and will cut off man and beast
from it; and I will make it desolate from
Teman; and they of Dedan shall fall by
the sword.
14 And I will lay my vengeance upon
Edom by the hand of my people Israel:
and they shall do in Edom according to
mine anger and according to my fury;

25:2 JUDGMENT OF THE NATIONS

Chapters 25–32 of the prophecy of Ezekiel record the predicted wrath of God upon the nations that were neighbors of Israel. These nations had had the benefit of Israel's witness for God through the years. Yet they exulted in the destruction of Israel; they sinned against the LORD. Therefore the LORD announced, through the prophet, the destruction of these nations.

Throughout these prophecies, we must distinguish between what has already been fulfilled and what is still future. Much of what was foretold by Ezekiel has already taken place. However, when we read the prediction of the *Day of the LORD (e.g., 30:3), we recognize that portions of these prophecies are still to be fulfilled in the judgments that will immediately precede the second coming of the Lord Jesus Christ to the earth. The Ammonites lived to the east of the Dead Sea and to the north of the Moabites. Both of these nations were descendants of Lot (Gen. 19:33-38).

25:4 men of the east. Babylonians.

25:6 stamped with the feet. Danced for joy.

25:8 Moab. These descendants of Lot were known for their cruel hatred of the children of Israel. Their destruction was foretold by the prophet, and it has been literally fulfilled.

25:12 Edom. Edom is the name of a country lying south of the kingdom of Judah. The Edomites are descendants of Esau, the brother of Jacob. The long history of Edom is one of hatred to the children of Israel and the purposes of God through them. Edom has already suffered the judgment announced by Ezekiel.

and they shall know my vengeance,
saith the Lord GOD.
¶ 15 Thus saith the Lord GOD; Because the *Philistines have dealt by revenge, and have taken vengeance with
a despiteful heart, to destroy *it* for the
old hatred;

25:15 The Philistines Judged
Every Bible student is familiar with the story of the conflict between the Philistines, who inhabited the coastal areas of Palestine, and the children of Israel. The most famous event in that struggle was the battle between David and Goliath, the Philistine giant. The Philistines never learned to know the LORD. Therefore, their judgment was also announced by Ezekiel.

16 Therefore thus saith the Lord GOD;
Behold, I will stretch out mine hand
upon the Philistines, and I will cut off
the Cherethims, and destroy the remnant of the sea coast.
17 And I will execute great vengeance
upon them with furious rebukes; and
they shall know that I *am* the LORD,
when I shall lay my vengeance upon
them.

Prophecies of judgment against Tyre

26 And it came to pass in the eleventh year, in the first *day* of the
*month, *that* the word of the LORD
came unto me, saying,
2 Son of man, because that Tyrus hath
said against Jerusalem, Aha, she is broken *that was* the gates of the people:
she is turned unto me: I shall be replenished, *now* she is laid waste:
3 Therefore thus saith the Lord GOD;
Behold, I *am* against thee, O Tyrus, and
will cause many nations to come up
against thee, as the sea causeth his
waves to come up.
4 And they shall destroy the walls
of Tyrus, and break down her towers:
I will also scrape her dust from her,
and make her like the top of a rock.
5 It shall be *a place for* the spreading
of nets in the midst of the sea: for I have
spoken *it,* saith the Lord GOD: and it
shall become a spoil to the nations.
6 And her daughters which *are* in the
field shall be slain by the sword; and
they shall know that I *am* the LORD.
¶ 7 For thus saith the Lord GOD; Behold, I will bring upon Tyrus Nebuchadrezzar king of *Babylon, a king of kings,
from the north, with horses, and with
chariots, and with horsemen, and companies, and much people.
8 He shall slay with the sword thy
daughters in the field: and he shall
make a fort against thee, and cast a
mount against thee, and lift up the
*buckler against thee.
9 And he shall set engines of war
against thy walls, and with his axes he
shall break down thy towers.
10 By reason of the abundance of
his horses their dust shall cover thee:
thy walls shall shake at the noise of
the horsemen, and of the wheels, and
of the chariots, when he shall enter into
thy gates, as men enter into a city
wherein is made a breach.

26:2 The Fall of a Great Nation
The great nation of Tyre fell under the wrath of God because of its iniquity and pride. Its fate shows that without God people are brought to nothing. The prophecy has been literally fulfilled in all of its details, under Nebuchadnezzar (vs. 7) and Alexander (vs. 12).

There were two Tyres. The first was built on land which jutted out into the sea. This was captured by Nebuchadnezzar and demolished. Its ruins were thrown into the sea by Alexander the Great. Even the ground was scraped (vs. 4) to make a sort of causeway out to an island where the second Tyre had been built. This one was destroyed by Alexander.

26:1 the eleventh year. The eleventh year of Ezekiel's exile, one year before Jerusalem fell.
26:9 he . . . his. "Nebuchadrezzar" (vs. 7), usually spelled Nebuchadnezzar (Dan. 1:1).

11 With the hoofs of his horses shall
he tread down all thy streets: he shall
slay thy people by the sword, and thy
strong garrisons shall go down to the
ground.
12 And they shall make a spoil of thy
riches, and make a prey of thy merchandise: and they shall break down thy
walls, and destroy thy pleasant houses:
and they shall lay thy stones and thy
timber and thy dust in the midst of the
water.
13 And I will cause the noise of thy
songs to cease; and the sound of thy
harps shall be no more heard.
14 And I will make thee like the top of
a rock: thou shalt be *a place* to spread
nets upon; thou shalt be built no more:
for I the LORD have spoken *it,* saith the
Lord GOD.
¶15 Thus saith the Lord GOD to Tyrus;
Shall not the *isles shake at the sound
of thy fall, when the wounded cry, when
the slaughter is made in the midst of
thee?
16 Then all the princes of the sea shall
come down from their thrones, and lay
away their robes, and put off their broidered *garments: they shall clothe
themselves with trembling; they shall
sit upon the ground, and shall tremble
at *every* moment, and be astonished at
thee.
17 And they shall take up a lamentation for thee, and say to thee, How art
thou destroyed, *that wast* inhabited of
seafaring men, the renowned city,
which wast strong in the sea, she and
her inhabitants, which cause their terror *to be* on all that haunt it!
18 Now shall the isles tremble in the
day of thy fall; yea, the isles that *are* in
the sea shall be troubled at thy departure.
19 For thus saith the Lord GOD; When
I shall make thee a desolate city, like the
cities that are not inhabited; when I
shall bring up the deep upon thee, and
great waters shall cover thee;
20 When I shall bring thee down with
them that descend into the *pit, with
the people of old time, and shall set thee
in the low parts of the earth, in places
desolate of old, with them that go down
to the pit, that thou be not inhabited;
and I shall set glory in the land of the
living;
21 I will make thee a terror, and thou
shalt be no *more:* though thou be sought
for, yet shalt thou never be found again,
saith the Lord GOD.

God's judgment of Tyre

27 The word of the LORD came
again unto me, saying,
2 Now, thou son of man, take up a lamentation for Tyrus;
3 And say unto Tyrus, O thou that art
situate at the entry of the sea, *which art*
a merchant of the people for many isles,
Thus saith the Lord GOD; O Tyrus, thou
hast said, I *am* of perfect beauty.
4 Thy borders *are* in the midst of the
seas, thy builders have perfected thy
beauty.
5 They have made all thy *ship* boards
of fir trees of Senir: they have taken
cedars from *Lebanon to make masts
for thee.
6 *Of* the oaks of *Bashan have they
made thine oars; the company of the
Ashurites have made thy benches *of*
ivory, *brought* out of the isles of
Chittim.
7 Fine *linen with broidered work
from Egypt was that which thou
spreadest forth to be thy sail; blue and
purple from the isles of Elishah was
that which covered thee.
8 The inhabitants of Zidon and Arvad
were thy mariners: thy wise *men,* O
Tyrus, *that* were in thee, were thy pilots.
9 The ancients of Gebal and the wise

26:12 they. The soldiers of Alexander.
27:8 Zidon . . . Arvad . . . Tyrus. The common sailors came from Zidon and Arvad; the officers from Tyre.

men thereof were in thee thy calkers: all
the ships of the sea with their mariners
were in thee to occupy thy merchandise.
10They of Persia and of Lud and of
Phut were in thine army, thy men of
war: they hanged the shield and helmet
in thee; they set forth thy comeliness.
11The men of Arvad with thine army
were upon thy walls round about, and
the Gammadims were in thy towers:
they hanged their shields upon thy
walls round about; they have made thy
beauty perfect.
12*Tarshish *was* thy merchant by reason of the multitude of all *kind of* riches;
with silver, iron, tin, and lead, they traded in thy fairs.
13Javan, Tubal, and Meshech, they
were thy merchants: they traded the
persons of men and vessels of brass in
thy market.
14They of the house of Togarmah
traded in thy fairs with horses and
horsemen and mules.
15The men of Dedan *were* thy merchants; many isles *were* the merchandise of thine hand: they brought thee *for*
a present horns of ivory and ebony.
16Syria *was* thy merchant by reason
of the multitude of the wares of thy
making: they occupied in thy fairs with
emeralds, purple, and broidered work,
and fine linen, and coral, and agate.
17*Judah, and the land of *Israel, they
were thy merchants: they traded in thy
market wheat of Minnith, and Pannag,
and honey, and oil, and balm.
18*Damascus *was* thy merchant in
the multitude of the wares of thy making, for the multitude of all riches; in the
wine of Helbon, and white wool.
19Dan also and Javan going to and fro
occupied in thy fairs: bright iron, cassia, and calamus, were in thy market.
20Dedan *was* thy merchant in precious clothes for chariots.
21Arabia, and all the princes of *Kedar, they occupied with thee in lambs,
and rams, and goats: in these *were they*
thy merchants.
22The merchants of Sheba and Raamah, they *were* thy merchants: they
occupied in thy fairs with chief of all
spices, and with all precious stones, and
gold.
23Haran, and Canneh, and *Eden, the
merchants of Sheba, *Asshur, *and*
Chilmad, *were* thy merchants.
24These *were* thy merchants in all
sorts *of things,* in blue clothes, and
broidered work, and in chests of rich
apparel, bound with cords, and made of
cedar, among thy merchandise.
25The ships of Tarshish did sing of
thee in thy market: and thou wast replenished, and made very glorious in
the midst of the seas.
¶26Thy rowers have brought thee
into great waters: the east wind hath
broken thee in the midst of the seas.
27Thy riches, and thy fairs, thy merchandise, thy mariners, and thy pilots,
thy calkers, and the occupiers of thy
merchandise, and all thy men of war,
that *are* in thee, and in all thy company
which *is* in the midst of thee, shall fall
into the midst of the seas in the day of
thy ruin.
28The suburbs shall shake at the
sound of the cry of thy pilots.
29And all that handle the oar, the
mariners, *and* all the pilots of the sea,

27:9 occupy. Barter.
27:13 Javan, Tubal, and Meshech. The names of three of Noah's grandsons through Japheth (Gen. 10:2), probably referring here to Greece and Russia. It is thought by many that Tubal is the modern Tobolsk, and Mesheck, Moscow (see Ezek. 38:2 note). Except in Isaiah 66:19 and Psalm 120:5, Tubal and Meshech are always spoken of together.
27:14 Togarmah. Probably Armenia.
27:15 Dedan. This Dedan was in Syria, but the Dedan of verse 20 was in Arabia.
27:26 great waters. The eastern and western oceans.
27:26 the east wind hath broken thee. Note here the abrupt change from prosperity to ruin.

shall come down from their ships, they
shall stand upon the land;
30And shall cause their voice to be
heard against thee, and shall cry bitterly, and shall cast up dust upon their
heads, they shall wallow themselves in
the ashes:
31And they shall make themselves
utterly bald for thee, and gird them with
sackcloth, and they shall weep for
thee with bitterness of heart *and* bitter
wailing.
32And in their wailing they shall take
up a lamentation for thee, and lament
over thee, *saying,* What *city is* like
Tyrus, like the destroyed in the midst
of the sea?
33When thy wares went forth out of
the seas, thou filledst many people;
thou didst enrich the kings of the earth
with the multitude of thy riches and of
thy merchandise.
34In the time *when* thou shalt be broken by the seas in the depths of the
waters thy merchandise and all thy
company in the midst of thee shall fall.
35All the inhabitants of the isles shall
be astonished at thee, and their kings
shall be sore afraid, they shall be troubled in *their* countenance.
36The merchants among the people
shall hiss at thee; thou shalt be a terror, and never *shalt be* any more.

The King of Tyre and his judgment

28 The word of the LORD came
again unto me, saying,
2Son of man, say unto the prince of
Tyrus, Thus saith the Lord GOD; Because thine heart *is* lifted up, and thou
hast said, I *am* a *God, I sit *in* the seat
of God, in the midst of the seas; yet
thou *art* a man, and not God, though
thou set thine heart as the heart of God:
3Behold, thou *art* wiser than Daniel;
there is no secret that they can hide
from thee:
4With thy wisdom and with thine
understanding thou hast gotten thee
riches, and hast gotten gold and silver
into thy treasures:
5By thy great wisdom *and* by thy traffick hast thou increased thy riches, and
thine heart is lifted up because of thy
riches:
6Therefore thus saith the Lord GOD;
Because thou hast set thine heart as the
heart of God;
7Behold, therefore I will bring strangers upon thee, the terrible of the nations: and they shall draw their swords
against the beauty of thy wisdom, and
they shall defile thy brightness.
8They shall bring thee down to the
pit, and thou shalt die the deaths of
them that are slain in the midst of the
seas.
9Wilt thou yet say before him that
slayeth thee, I *am* God? but thou *shalt
be* a man, and no God, in the hand of him
that slayeth thee.
10Thou shalt die the deaths of the
*uncircumcised by the hand of strang-
ers: for I have spoken *it,* saith the Lord
GOD.
¶11Moreover the word of the LORD
came unto me, saying,
12Son of man, take up a lamentation
upon the king of Tyrus, and say unto
him, Thus saith the Lord GOD; Thou
sealest up the sum, full of wisdom, and
perfect in beauty.
13Thou hast been in Eden the garden
of God; every precious stone *was* thy
covering, the sardius, topaz, and the

28:2 The Coming Beast
The description of this ancient king, Ethbaal II, is such as to make him a *type of the coming *Beast. Comparing this verse with 2 Thessalonians 2:3-10 (see also 2:3 note, "Before the Lord Comes"), one is immediately impressed with the similarity in the sins of the two men. As the prince of Tyre was destroyed by the judgment of God in ancient days, so the coming world ruler, the *Beast, will be destroyed at the personal appearing of our Lord Jesus Christ.

28:12 Thou sealest up the sum. You are (Satan was) the perfection of wisdom and beauty.

28:12 A Type of Satan
Once more the ancient king of Tyrus is used as a symbol for a greater personality. From verses 12-17, the language is such as to be applicable only to Satan, the archenemy of God. Together with Isaiah 14:12 (see its note, "Lucifer"), describing the fall of Lucifer from heaven, it forms one of the most important revelations in Scripture regarding the origin and fall of Satan. God did not create a devil. He created a cherub (see *cherubim) and placed that cherub in a place of great importance in the kingdom of God. The description of this cherub is such as to indicate that he was the highest of all created beings, although in no sense the equal of God. When this high being sinned, he became Satan, the final example of the corrupting power of sin. The final doom of Satan is foretold in Revelation 20:10.

diamond, the beryl, the onyx, and the
jasper, the sapphire, the emerald, and
the carbuncle, and gold: the workmanship of thy *tabrets and of thy pipes was
prepared in thee in the day that thou
wast *created.
14 Thou *art* the anointed cherub that
covereth; and I have set thee *so:* thou
wast upon the *holy mountain of God;
thou hast walked up and down in the
midst of the stones of *fire.
15 Thou *wast* perfect in thy ways from
the day that thou wast created, till iniquity was found in thee.
16 By the multitude of thy merchandise they have filled the midst of thee
with violence, and thou hast sinned:
therefore I will cast thee as profane out
of the mountain of God: and I will destroy thee, O covering cherub, from the
midst of the stones of fire.
17 Thine heart was lifted up because
of thy beauty, thou hast corrupted thy
wisdom by reason of thy brightness: I
will cast thee to the ground, I will lay
thee before kings, that they may behold
thee.
18 Thou hast defiled thy sanctuaries
by the multitude of thine iniquities, by
the iniquity of thy traffick; therefore will
I bring forth a fire from the midst of
thee, it shall devour thee, and I will
bring thee to ashes upon the earth in
the sight of all them that behold thee.
19 All they that know thee among the
people shall be astonished at thee: thou
shalt be a terror, and never *shalt* thou
be any more.
¶20 Again the word of the LORD came
unto me, saying,
21 Son of man, set thy face against
Zidon, and prophesy against it,
22 And say, Thus saith the Lord GOD;
Behold, I *am* against thee, O Zidon; and
I will be glorified in the midst of thee:
and they shall know that I *am* the LORD,
when I shall have executed judgments
in her, and shall be sanctified in her.
23 For I will send into her pestilence,
and blood into her streets; and the
wounded shall be judged in the midst of
her by the sword upon her on every
side; and they shall know that I *am* the
LORD.
¶24 And there shall be no more a prick-
ing brier unto the house of Israel, nor
any grieving thorn of all *that are* round
about them, that despised them; and
they shall know that I *am* the Lord GOD.
25 Thus saith the Lord GOD; When I
shall have gathered the house of Israel
from the people among whom they are
scattered, and shall be sanctified in
them in the sight of the heathen, then
shall they dwell in their land that I have
given to my servant *Jacob.
26 And they shall dwell safely therein,
and shall build houses, and plant vineyards; yea, they shall dwell with confidence, when I have executed judgments

28:21 Zidon. This is a coastal nation, situated to the north of Tyre, on the eastern coast of the Mediterranean Sea.

28:25 gathered the house of Israel. In the midst of these pronouncements of restoration of Israel to its judgment against the Gentile nations of Israel's day, we find this promise of the future restoration of Israel to its place as God's anointed and chosen people.

upon all those that despise them round
about them; and they shall know that I
am the LORD their God.

Judgment against Egypt

29 In the tenth year, in the tenth
month, in the twelfth *day* of the
month, the word of the LORD came unto
me, saying,
2 Son of man, set thy face against
*Pharaoh king of *Egypt, and prophe-
sy against him, and against all Egypt:

29:2 Egypt's Judgment
Chapters 29–32 contain the predictions of judgment upon Egypt that were revealed to the prophet Ezekiel. Egypt loomed large in the history of Israel. It was in Egypt that Israel lay in bondage. It was from Egypt that they were delivered by God through the leadership of Moses, as we find recorded in the book of Exodus. When our Lord Jesus was a baby, He was taken to Egypt (Matt. 2:13-15). At the time of the pronouncement by Ezekiel, Egypt was one of the major nations of the world. The judgments foretold have been literally fulfilled. There is an aspect of them which is still future, as we see in Ezekiel 30:3. Egypt will play her part again in the alignment of the nations at the time of the second coming of Christ.

3 Speak, and say, Thus saith the Lord
GOD; Behold, I *am* against thee, Pharaoh king of Egypt, the great dragon
that lieth in the midst of his rivers,
which hath said, My river *is* mine own,
and I have made *it* for myself.
4 But I will put hooks in thy jaws, and
I will cause the fish of thy rivers to stick
unto thy scales, and I will bring thee up
out of the midst of thy rivers, and all the
fish of thy rivers shall stick unto thy
scales.
5 And I will leave thee *thrown* into the
wilderness, thee and all the fish of thy
rivers: thou shalt fall upon the open
fields; thou shalt not be brought together, nor gathered: I have given thee for
meat to the beasts of the field and to the
fowls of the heaven.
6 And all the inhabitants of Egypt shall
know that I *am* the LORD, because they
have been a staff of reed to the house
of Israel.
7 When they took hold of thee by thy
hand, thou didst break, and rend all
their shoulder: and when they leaned
upon thee, thou brakest, and madest all
their loins to be at a stand.
¶8 Therefore thus saith the Lord GOD;
Behold, I will bring a sword upon thee,
and cut off man and beast out of thee.
9 And the land of Egypt shall be desolate and waste; and they shall know
that I *am* the LORD: because he hath
said, The river *is* mine, and I have
made *it.*
10 Behold, therefore I *am* against
thee, and against thy rivers, and I will
make the land of Egypt utterly waste
and desolate, from the tower of Syene
even unto the border of Ethiopia.
11 No foot of man shall pass through
it, nor foot of beast shall pass through
it, neither shall it be inhabited forty
years.
12 And I will make the land of Egypt
desolate in the midst of the countries
that are desolate, and her cities among
the cities *that are* laid waste shall be
desolate forty years: and I will scatter
the Egyptians among the nations, and
will disperse them through the countries.
¶13 Yet thus saith the Lord GOD; At
the end of forty years will I gather the
Egyptians from the people whither they
were scattered:
14 And I will bring again the captivity
of Egypt, and will cause them to return
into the land of Pathros, into the land of
their habitation; and they shall be there
a base kingdom.
15 It shall be the basest of the kingdoms;
neither shall it exalt itself any more
above the nations: for I will diminish

29:3 dragon. Possibly the crocodile, the national emblem of Egypt.
29:14 a base kingdom. A subordinate kingdom ruled by another country.

them, that they shall no more rule over the nations.

16 And it shall be no more the confidence of the house of Israel, which bringeth *their* iniquity to remembrance, when they shall look after them: but they shall know that I *am* the Lord GOD.

¶17 And it came to pass in the seven and twentieth year, in the first *month,* in the first *day* of the month, the word of the LORD came unto me, saying,

18 Son of man, Nebuchadrezzar king of Babylon caused his army to serve a great service against Tyrus: every head *was* made bald, and every shoulder *was* peeled: yet had he no wages, nor his army, for Tyrus, for the service that he had served against it:

19 Therefore thus saith the Lord GOD; Behold, I will give the land of Egypt unto Nebuchadrezzar king of Babylon; and he shall take her multitude, and take her spoil, and take her prey; and it shall be the wages for his army.

20 I have given him the land of Egypt *for* his labour wherewith he served against it, because they wrought for me, saith the Lord GOD.

¶21 In that day will I cause the horn of the house of Israel to bud forth, and I will give thee the opening of the mouth in the midst of them; and they shall know that I *am* the LORD.

Judgment against Egypt (continued)

30 The word of the LORD came again unto me, saying,

2 Son of man, prophesy and say, Thus saith the Lord GOD; Howl ye, Woe worth the day!

3 For the day *is* near, even the day of the LORD *is* near, a cloudy day; it shall be the time of the heathen.

4 And the sword shall come upon Egypt, and great pain shall be in Ethiopia, when the slain shall fall in Egypt, and they shall take away her multitude, and her foundations shall be broken down.

5 Ethiopia, and Libya, and Lydia, and all the mingled people, and Chub, and the men of the land that is in league, shall fall with them by the sword.

6 Thus saith the LORD; They also that uphold Egypt shall fall; and the pride of her power shall come down: from the tower of Syene shall they fall in it by the sword, saith the Lord GOD.

7 And they shall be desolate in the midst of the countries *that are* desolate, and her cities shall be in the midst of the cities *that are* wasted.

8 And they shall know that I *am* the LORD, when I have set a fire in Egypt, and *when* all her helpers shall be destroyed.

9 In that day shall messengers go forth from me in ships to make the careless Ethiopians afraid, and great pain shall come upon them, as in the day of Egypt: for, lo, it cometh.

10 Thus saith the Lord GOD; I will also make the multitude of Egypt to cease by the hand of Nebuchadrezzar king of Babylon.

11 He and his people with him, the terrible of the nations, shall be brought to destroy the land: and they shall draw their swords against Egypt, and fill the land with the slain.

12 And I will make the rivers dry, and sell the land into the hand of the wicked: and I will make the land waste, and all that is therein, by the hand of strangers: I the LORD have spoken *it.*

13 Thus saith the Lord GOD; I will also destroy the idols, and I will cause *their* images to cease out of *Noph; and there shall be no more a prince of the land of Egypt: and I will put a *fear in the land of Egypt.

14 And I will make Pathros desolate,

29:20 they. The Babylonian soldiers.
30:6 from the tower of Syene. This meant from one end of Egypt to the other (see 29:10).
30:7 they shall be desolate. In the days of Ezekiel, Egypt was a great world power, but the prophecy was not fulfilled until more than one thousand years later.

and will set fire in *Zoan, and will execute judgments in No.
15And I will pour my fury upon Sin,
the strength of Egypt; and I will cut off
the multitude of No.
16And I will set fire in Egypt: Sin shall
have great pain, and No shall be rent
asunder, and Noph *shall have* distresses
daily.
17The young men of Aven and of Pi-
beseth shall fall by the sword: and these
cities shall go into captivity.
18At Tehaphnehes also the day shall
be darkened, when I shall break there
the yokes of Egypt: and the pomp of her
strength shall cease in her: as for her, a
cloud shall cover her, and her daughters
shall go into captivity.
19Thus will I execute judgments in
Egypt: and they shall know that I *am*
the LORD.
¶20And it came to pass in the eleventh year, in the first *month,* in the seventh *day* of the month, *that* the word of
the LORD came unto me, saying,
21Son of man, I have broken the arm
of Pharaoh king of Egypt; and, lo, it shall
not be bound up to be healed, to put a
roller to bind it, to make it strong to
hold the sword.
22Therefore thus saith the Lord GOD;
Behold, I *am* against Pharaoh king of
Egypt, and will break his arms, the
strong, and that which was broken; and
I will cause the sword to fall out of his
hand.
23And I will scatter the Egyptians
among the nations, and will disperse
them through the countries.
24And I will strengthen the arms of
the king of Babylon, and put my sword
in his hand: but I will break Pharaoh's
arms, and he shall groan before him with
the groanings of a deadly wounded *man.*
25But I will strengthen the arms of
the king of Babylon, and the arms of
Pharaoh shall fall down; and they shall
know that I *am* the LORD, when I shall
put my sword into the hand of the king
of Babylon, and he shall stretch it out
upon the land of Egypt.
26And I will scatter the Egyptians
among the nations, and disperse them
among the countries; and they shall
know that I *am* the LORD.

Judgment against Egypt (continued)

31 And it came to pass in the eleventh year, in the third *month,* in
the first *day* of the month, *that* the word
of the LORD came unto me, saying,
2Son of man, speak unto Pharaoh
king of Egypt, and to his multitude;
Whom art thou like in thy greatness?
¶3Behold, the Assyrian *was* a cedar
in Lebanon with fair branches, and with
a shadowing shroud, and of an high stature; and his top was among the thick
boughs.
4The waters made him great, the
deep set him up on high with her rivers running round about his plants, and
sent out her little rivers unto all the
trees of the field.
5Therefore his height was exalted
above all the trees of the field, and
his boughs were multiplied, and his
branches became long because of the
multitude of waters, when he shot forth.
6All the fowls of heaven made their
nests in his boughs, and under his
branches did all the beasts of the field
bring forth their young, and under his
shadow dwelt all great nations.
7Thus was he fair in his greatness, in
the length of his branches: for his root
was by great waters.
8The cedars in the garden of God
could not hide him: the fir trees were
not like his boughs, and the chesnut
trees were not like his branches; nor
any tree in the garden of God was like
unto him in his beauty.
9I have made him fair by the multitude of his branches: so that all the
trees of *Eden, that *were* in the garden
of God, envied him.
¶10Therefore thus saith the Lord
GOD; Because thou hast lifted up thyself in height, and he hath shot up his
top among the thick boughs, and his
heart is lifted up in his height;

11 I have therefore delivered him into the hand of the mighty one of the heathen; he shall surely deal with him: I have driven him out for his wickedness.

12 And strangers, the terrible of the nations, have cut him off, and have left him: upon the mountains and in all the valleys his branches are fallen, and his boughs are broken by all the rivers of the land; and all the people of the earth are gone down from his shadow, and have left him.

13 Upon his ruin shall all the fowls of the heaven remain, and all the beasts of the field shall be upon his branches:

14 To the end that none of all the trees by the waters exalt themselves for their height, neither shoot up their top among the thick boughs, neither their trees stand up in their height, all that drink water: for they are all delivered unto *death, to the nether parts of the earth, in the midst of the children of men, with them that go down to the pit.

15 Thus saith the Lord GOD; In the day when he went down to the *grave I caused a *mourning: I covered the deep for him, and I restrained the floods thereof, and the great waters were stayed: and I caused Lebanon to mourn for him, and all the trees of the field fainted for him.

16 I made the nations to shake at the sound of his fall, when I cast him down to *hell with them that descend into the pit: and all the trees of Eden, the choice and best of Lebanon, all that drink water, shall be comforted in the nether parts of the earth.

17 They also went down into hell with him unto *them that be* slain with the sword; and *they that were* his arm, *that* dwelt under his shadow in the midst of the heathen.

¶ 18 To whom art thou thus like in glory and in greatness among the trees of Eden? yet shalt thou be brought down with the trees of Eden unto the nether parts of the earth: thou shalt lie in the midst of the uncircumcised with *them that be* slain by the sword. This *is* Pharaoh and all his multitude, saith the Lord GOD.

Judgment against Egypt (continued)

32 And it came to pass in the twelfth year, in the twelfth *month, in the first *day* of the month, *that* the word of the LORD came unto me, saying,

2 Son of man, take up a lamentation for Pharaoh king of Egypt, and say unto him, Thou art like a young lion of the nations, and thou *art* as a whale in the seas: and thou camest forth with thy rivers, and troubledst the waters with thy feet, and fouledst their rivers.

3 Thus saith the Lord GOD; I will therefore spread out my net over thee with a company of many people; and they shall bring thee up in my net.

4 Then will I leave thee upon the land, I will cast thee forth upon the open field, and will cause all the fowls of the heaven to remain upon thee, and I will fill the beasts of the whole earth with thee.

5 And I will lay thy *flesh upon the mountains, and fill the valleys with thy height.

6 I will also water with thy blood the land wherein thou swimmest, *even* to the mountains; and the rivers shall be full of thee.

7 And when I shall put thee out, I will cover the heaven, and make the stars thereof dark; I will cover the sun with a cloud, and the moon shall not give her light.

31:11 the mighty one. Nebuchadnezzar.
32:2 the seas. Pharaoh passed from his own land and river into other nations disturbing them and injuring them.
32:3 my net. The Babylonians.
32:4 I leave thee upon the land. A sea animal upon the land is helpless and soon dies. This is the picture that God presented through Ezekiel.
32:5 height. Remains.

8 All the bright lights of heaven will I
make dark over thee, and set darkness
upon thy land, saith the Lord GOD.
9 I will also vex the hearts of many
people, when I shall bring thy destruction among the nations, into the countries which thou hast not known.
10 Yea, I will make many people
amazed at thee, and their kings shall be
horribly afraid for thee, when I shall
brandish my sword before them; and
they shall tremble at *every* moment,
every man for his own life, in the day
of thy fall.
¶11 For thus saith the Lord GOD; The
sword of the king of *Babylon shall
come upon thee.
12 By the swords of the mighty will I
cause thy multitude to fall, the terrible
of the nations, all of them: and they shall
spoil the pomp of Egypt, and all the
multitude thereof shall be destroyed.
13 I will destroy also all the beasts
thereof from beside the great waters;
neither shall the foot of man trouble
them any more, nor the hoofs of beasts
trouble them.
14 Then will I make their waters deep,
and cause their rivers to run like oil,
saith the Lord GOD.
15 When I shall make the land of Egypt
desolate, and the country shall be destitute of that whereof it was full, when
I shall smite all them that dwell therein,
then shall they know that I *am* the
LORD.
16 This *is* the lamentation wherewith
they shall lament her: the daughters of
the nations shall lament her: they shall
lament for her, *even* for Egypt, and for
all her multitude, saith the Lord GOD.
¶17 It came to pass also in the twelfth
year, in the fifteenth *day* of the month,
that the word of the LORD came unto
me, saying,
18 Son of man, wail for the multitude
of Egypt, and cast them down, *even* her,
and the daughters of the famous nations,
unto the nether parts of the earth, with
them that go down into *the pit.
19 Whom dost thou pass in beauty? go
down, and be thou laid with the uncircumcised.
20 They shall fall in the midst of *them*
that are slain by the sword: she is delivered to the sword: draw her and all
her multitudes.
21 The strong among the mighty shall
speak to him out of the midst of hell
with them that help him: they are gone
down, they lie uncircumcised, slain by
the sword.
22 *Asshur *is* there and all her company: his graves *are* about him: all of
them slain, fallen by the sword:
23 Whose graves are set in the sides
of the pit, and her company is round
about her grave: all of them slain, fall-
en by the sword, which caused terror in
the land of the living.
24 There *is* Elam and all her multitude
round about her grave, all of them slain,
fallen by the sword, which are gone
down uncircumcised into the nether
parts of the earth, which caused their
terror in the land of the living; yet have
they borne their shame with them that
go down to the pit.
25 They have set her a bed in the
midst of the slain with all her multitude:
her graves *are* round about him: all
of them uncircumcised, slain by the
sword: though their terror was caused
in the land of the living, yet have they
borne their shame with them that go
down to the pit: he is put in the midst
of *them that be* slain.
26 There *is* Meshech, Tubal, and all
her multitude: her graves *are* round
about him: all of them uncircumcised,
slain by the sword, though they caused
their terror in the land of the living.

32:17 month. It is still the twelfth month (see vs. 1).
32:18 nether parts. The depths.
32:22 him. Pharaoh.
32:25 They. Elam and Assyria. "Her" is spoken of Egypt, and "him" and "he" of Pharaoh.

27 And they shall not lie with the mighty *that are* fallen of the uncircumcised, which are gone down to hell with their weapons of war: and they have laid their swords under their heads, but their iniquities shall be upon their bones, though *they were* the terror of the mighty in the land of the living.

28 Yea, thou shalt be broken in the midst of the uncircumcised, and shalt lie with *them that are* slain with the sword.

29 There *is* *Edom, her kings, and all her princes, which with their might are laid by *them that were* slain by the sword: they shall lie with the uncircumcised, and with them that go down to the pit.

30 There *be* the princes of the north, all of them, and all the Zidonians, which are gone down with the slain; with their terror they are ashamed of their might; and they lie uncircumcised with *them that be* slain by the sword, and bear their shame with them that go down to the pit.

31 Pharaoh shall see them, and shall be comforted over all his multitude, *even* Pharaoh and all his army slain by the sword, saith the Lord GOD.

32 For I have caused my terror in the land of the living: and he shall be laid in the midst of the uncircumcised with *them that are* slain with the sword, *even* Pharaoh and all his multitude, saith the Lord GOD.

The responsibility of the Prophet for his ministry

33 Again the word of the LORD came unto me, saying,

2 Son of man, speak to the children of thy people, and say unto them, When I bring the sword upon a land, if the people of the land take a man of their coasts, and set him for their watchman:

3 If when he seeth the sword come upon the land, he blow the trumpet, and warn the people;

4 Then whosoever heareth the sound of the trumpet, and taketh not warning; if the sword come, and take him away, his blood shall be upon his own head.

5 He heard the sound of the trumpet, and took not warning; his blood shall be upon him. But he that taketh warning shall deliver his soul.

6 But if the watchman see the sword come, and blow not the trumpet, and the people be not warned; if the sword come, and take *any* person from among them, he is taken away in his iniquity; but his blood will I require at the watchman's hand.

¶7 So thou, O son of man, I have set thee a watchman unto the house of *Israel; therefore thou shalt hear the word at my mouth, and warn them from me.

8 When I say unto the wicked, O wicked *man,* thou shalt surely die; if thou dost not speak to warn the wicked from his way, that wicked *man* shall die in his iniquity; but his blood will I require at thine hand.

9 Nevertheless, if thou warn the wicked of his way to turn from it; if he do not turn from his way, he shall die in his iniquity; but thou hast delivered thy soul.

10 Therefore, O thou son of man, speak unto the house of Israel; Thus ye speak, saying, If our transgressions and our sins *be* upon us, and we pine away in them, how should we then live?

11 Say unto them, *As* I live, saith the Lord GOD, I have no pleasure in the death of the wicked; but that the wicked turn from his way and live: turn ye, turn ye from your evil ways; for why will ye die, O house of Israel?

12 Therefore, thou son of man, say unto the children of thy people, The *righteousness of the righteous shall

---

33:7 a watchman. The commission of Ezekiel as God's messenger to the children of Israel was declared in 3:17-21. It is repeated in this Scripture. In the repetition we find God defending His own righteousness and proclaiming that His ways are always right (see vs. 20).

not deliver him in the day of his transgression: as for the wickedness of the
wicked, he shall not fall thereby in the
day that he turneth from his wickedness; neither shall the righteous be able
to live for his *righteousness* in the day
that he sinneth.
13 When I shall say to the righteous,
that he shall surely live; if he *trust to
his own righteousness, and commit iniquity, all his righteousnesses shall not
be remembered; but for his iniquity that
he hath committed, he shall die for it.
14 Again, when I say unto the wicked,
Thou shalt surely die; if he turn from
his sin, and do that which is lawful and
right;
15 *If* the wicked restore the pledge,
give again that he had robbed, walk in
the statutes of life, without committing
iniquity; he shall surely live, he shall
not die.
16 None of his sins that he hath committed shall be mentioned unto him: he
hath done that which is lawful and right;
he shall surely live.
¶ 17 Yet the children of thy people say,
The way of the Lord is not equal: but
as for them, their way is not equal.
18 When the righteous turneth from
his righteousness, and committeth iniquity, he shall even die thereby.
19 But if the wicked turn from his
wickedness, and do that which is lawful and right, he shall live thereby.
¶ 20 Yet ye say, The way of the Lord is
not equal. O ye house of Israel, I will
judge you every one after his ways.

V. The Future Kingdom of the Messiah (33:21—36:38)

¶ 21 And it came to pass in the twelfth
year of our captivity, in the tenth *month,*
in the fifth *day* of the month, *that* one
that had escaped out of *Jerusalem came
unto me, saying, The city is smitten.
22 Now the hand of the LORD was
upon me in the evening, afore he that
was escaped came; and had opened my
mouth, until he came to me in the
morning; and my mouth was opened,
and I was no more dumb.
23 Then the word of the LORD came
unto me, saying,
24 Son of man, they that inhabit those
wastes of the land of Israel speak, saying, *Abraham was one, and he inherited the land: but we *are* many; the land
is given us for inheritance.
25 Wherefore say unto them, Thus
saith the Lord GOD; Ye eat with the
blood, and lift up your eyes toward your
idols, and shed blood: and shall ye possess the land?
26 Ye stand upon your sword, ye work
*abomination, and ye defile every one
his neighbour's wife: and shall ye possess the land?
27 Say thou thus unto them, Thus
saith the Lord GOD; *As* I live, surely
they that *are* in the wastes shall fall by
the sword, and him that *is* in the open
field will I give to the beasts to be devoured, and they that *be* in the forts and
in the caves shall die of the pestilence.
28 For I will lay the land most desolate,
and the pomp of her strength shall cease;
and the mountains of Israel shall be desolate, that none shall pass through.
29 Then shall they know that I *am* the
LORD, when I have laid the land most
desolate because of all their abominations which they have committed.
¶ 30 Also, thou son of man, the children
of thy people still are talking against
thee by the walls and in the doors of the
houses, and speak one to another, every
one to his brother, saying, Come, I pray
you, and hear what is the word that
cometh forth from the LORD.
31 And they come unto thee as the
people cometh, and they sit before thee
as my people, and they hear thy words,
but they will not do them: for with their
mouth they shew much love, *but* their
heart goeth after their covetousness.

33:25 Ye eat with the blood. See the command against this in Leviticus 19:26.
33:30 against thee. About you.

33:31 Israel's Refusal to Obey
The sin of Israel was not a sin of ignorance. It was their refusal to obey the Word of God, which was proclaimed unto them by the prophet. This stubborn disobedience accounts for the intense severity of the punishment that God has visited upon that nation.

32 And, lo, thou *art* unto them as a very
lovely song of one that hath a pleasant
voice, and can play well on an instrument: for they hear thy words, but they
do them not.
33 And when this cometh to pass, (lo,
it will come,) then shall they know that
a *prophet hath been among them.

God's word against unfaithful shepherds

34 And the word of the LORD came
unto me, saying,
2 Son of man, prophesy against the
shepherds of Israel, prophesy, and say
unto them, Thus saith the Lord GOD
unto the shepherds; Woe *be* to the shepherds of Israel that do feed themselves!
should not the shepherds feed the
flocks?
3 Ye eat the fat, and ye clothe you with
the wool, ye kill them that are fed: *but*
ye feed not the flock.
4 The diseased have ye not strengthened, neither have ye healed that which
was sick, neither have ye bound up *that*
which was broken, neither have ye
brought again that which was driven
away, neither have ye sought that which
was lost; but with force and with cruelty have ye ruled them.
5 And they were scattered, because
there is no shepherd: and they became
meat to all the beasts of the field, when
they were scattered.
6 My sheep wandered through all the
mountains, and upon every high hill:
yea, my flock was scattered upon all the
face of the earth, and none did search
or seek *after them.*
¶ 7 Therefore, ye shepherds, hear the
word of the LORD;
8 *As* I live, saith the Lord GOD, surely
because my flock became a prey, and
my flock became meat to every beast
of the field, because *there was* no shepherd, neither did my shepherds search
for my flock, but the shepherds fed
themselves, and fed not my flock;
9 Therefore, O ye shepherds, hear the
word of the LORD;
10 Thus saith the Lord GOD; Behold,
I *am* against the shepherds; and I will
require my flock at their hand, and
cause them to cease from feeding the
flock; neither shall the shepherds feed
themselves any more; for I will deliver
my flock from their mouth, that they
may not be meat for them.

God's promise to restore the Davidic Kingdom

¶ 11 For thus saith the Lord GOD; Behold, I, *even* I, will both search my
sheep, and seek them out.
12 As a shepherd seeketh out his flock
in the day that he is among his sheep
that are scattered; so will I seek out my
sheep, and will deliver them out of all
places where they have been scattered
in the cloudy and dark day.
13 And I will bring them out from the
people, and gather them from the countries, and will bring them to their own
land, and feed them upon the mountains
of Israel by the rivers, and in all the
inhabited places of the country.
14 I will feed them in a good pasture,

33:33 this. The judgment of verse 28.

34:2 Woe be to the shepherds of Israel. God did not fail to punish the false prophets of Israel. Their responsibility was great, because while pretending to represent God, they led the children of Israel away from Him.

34:11 I, will both search my sheep, and seek them out. The rest of this chapter is a promise by God that He will restore His people Israel to their land and to their fellowship with Him. This promise will be fulfilled when the Lord Jesus Christ comes to reign. See *kingdom and *remnant.

and upon the high mountains of Israel
shall their fold be: there shall they lie
in a good fold, and *in* a fat pasture shall
they feed upon the mountains of Israel.
15 I will feed my flock, and I will cause
them to lie down, saith the Lord GOD.
16 I will seek that which was lost, and
bring again that which was driven away,
and will bind up *that which was* broken,
and will strengthen that which was
sick: but I will destroy the fat and the
strong; I will feed them with *judgment.

34:17 A Division with Purpose
When the Lord Jesus Christ establishes the children of Israel as His people in His millennial reign, He will purge out from them all who refuse to be subject to Him (Ezek. 20:33-38). That judgment of Israel is very similar to the judgment of the nations at the time of the coming of our Lord (Matt. 25:31-46). The object of these judgments will be to determine who among the living peoples of the earth at the time of the return of Christ to earth, will be privileged to enter the millennial kingdom. See *kingdom and *Millennium.

17 And *as for* you, O my flock, thus
saith the Lord GOD; Behold, I judge
between cattle and cattle, between the
rams and the he goats.
18 *Seemeth it* a small thing unto you to
have eaten up the good pasture, but ye
must tread down with your feet the
residue of your pastures? and to have
drunk of the deep waters, but ye must
foul the residue with your feet?
19 And *as for* my flock, they eat that
which ye have trodden with your feet;
and they drink that which ye have
fouled with your feet.
¶20 Therefore thus saith the Lord
GOD unto them; Behold, I, *even* I, will
judge between the fat cattle and between the lean cattle.
21 Because ye have thrust with side
and with shoulder, and pushed all the
diseased with your horns, till ye have
*scattered them abroad;
22 Therefore will I save my flock, and
they shall no more be a prey; and I will
judge between cattle and cattle.
23 And I will set up one shepherd over
them, and he shall feed them, *even* my
servant *David; he shall feed them, and
he shall be their shepherd.
24 And I the LORD will be their *God,
and my servant David a prince among
them; I the LORD have spoken *it*.
25 And I will make with them a *covenant of *peace, and will cause the evil
beasts to cease out of the land: and they
shall dwell safely in the wilderness, and
sleep in the woods.
26 And I will make them and the
places round about my hill a blessing;
and I will cause the shower to come
down in his season; there shall be
showers of blessing.
27 And the tree of the field shall yield
her fruit, and the earth shall yield her
increase, and they shall be safe in their
land, and shall know that I *am* the LORD,
when I have broken the bands of their
yoke, and delivered them out of the
hand of those that served themselves
of them.
28 And they shall no more be a prey to
the heathen, neither shall the beast of
the land devour them; but they shall
dwell safely, and none shall make *them*
afraid.
29 And I will raise up for them a plant
of renown, and they shall be no more
consumed with hunger in the land, neither bear the shame of the heathen any
more.
30 Thus shall they know that I the
LORD their God *am* with them, and *that*
they, *even* the house of Israel, *are* my
people, saith the Lord GOD.
31 And ye my flock, the flock of my
pasture, *are* men, *and* I *am* your God,
saith the Lord GOD.

34:23 even my servant David. The Messiah is a Son of David (Matt. 1:1). In this Scripture the prophet sees the Messiah in the person of His earthly ancestor David. The "prince" (vs. 24), "shepherd," and "servant" is David's greater Son, our Lord Jesus Christ.

Judgment upon Mount Seir

35 Moreover the word of the LORD
came unto me, saying,
2Son of man, set thy face against
mount Seir, and prophesy against it,
3And say unto it, Thus saith the Lord
GOD; Behold, O mount Seir, I *am*
against thee, and I will stretch out mine
hand against thee, and I will make thee
most desolate.
4I will lay thy cities waste, and thou
shalt be desolate, and thou shalt know
that I *am* the LORD.
5Because thou hast had a perpetual
hatred, and hast shed *the blood of* the
children of Israel by the force of the
sword in the time of their calamity, in
the time *that their* iniquity *had* an end:
6Therefore, *as* I live, saith the Lord
GOD, I will prepare thee unto blood, and
blood shall pursue thee: sith thou hast
not hated blood, even blood shall pursue thee.
7Thus will I make mount Seir most
desolate, and cut off from it him that
passeth out and him that returneth.
8And I will fill his mountains with his
slain *men:* in thy hills, and in thy valleys, and in all thy rivers, shall they fall
that are slain with the sword.
9I will make thee perpetual desolations, and thy cities shall not return:
and ye shall know that I *am* the LORD.
10Because thou hast said, These two
nations and these two countries shall be
mine, and we will possess it; whereas
the LORD was there:
11Therefore, *as* I live, saith the Lord
GOD, I will even do according to thine
anger, and according to thine envy
which thou hast used out of thy hatred
against them; and I will make myself
known among them, when I have
judged thee.
12And thou shalt know that I *am* the
LORD, *and that* I have heard all thy blasphemies which thou hast spoken
against the mountains of Israel, saying,
They are laid desolate, they are given
us to consume.
13Thus with your mouth ye have
boasted against me, and have multiplied
your words against me: I have heard
them.
14Thus saith the Lord GOD; When the
whole earth rejoiceth, I will make thee
desolate.
15As thou didst rejoice at the inheritance of the house of Israel, because it
was desolate, so will I do unto thee:
thou shalt be desolate, O mount Seir,
and all Idumea, *even* all of it: and they
shall know that I *am* the LORD.

God's new covenant with Israel

36 Also, thou son of man, prophesy unto the mountains of Israel, and say, Ye mountains of Israel,
hear the word of the LORD:
2Thus saith the Lord GOD; Because
the enemy hath said against you, Aha,
even the ancient high places are ours
in possession:
3Therefore prophesy and say, Thus
saith the Lord GOD; Because they have
made *you* desolate, and swallowed you
up on every side, that ye might be a
possession unto the residue of the heathen, and ye are taken up in the lips of
talkers, and *are* an infamy of the people:
4Therefore, ye mountains of Israel,
hear the word of the Lord GOD; Thus
saith the Lord GOD to the mountains,
and to the hills, to the rivers, and to the
valleys, to the desolate wastes, and to
the cities that are forsaken, which became a prey and derision to the residue
of the heathen that *are* round about;

35:3 mount Seir. Another name for the Edomites (Deut. 2:4). Their constant hatred against the children of Israel was in reality a hatred for the LORD (see vs. 13). In a similar way, our Lord told Saul (Paul) that his persecution of the church was in reality a persecution of Himself (Acts 9:5).

35:6 sith. An old English word meaning *since*.

35:10 These two nations and these two countries. Samaria and Judah.

5 Therefore thus saith the Lord GOD;
Surely in the *fire of my jealousy have
I spoken against the residue of the heathen, and against all Idumea, which
have appointed my land into their possession with the joy of all *their* heart,
with despiteful minds, to cast it out for
a prey.
6 Prophesy therefore concerning the
land of Israel, and say unto the mountains, and to the hills, to the rivers, and
to the valleys, Thus saith the Lord GOD;
Behold, I have spoken in my jealousy
and in my fury, because ye have borne
the shame of the heathen:
7 Therefore thus saith the Lord GOD;
I have lifted up mine hand, Surely the
heathen that *are* about you, they shall
bear their shame.
¶ 8 But ye, O mountains of Israel, ye
shall shoot forth your branches, and
yield your fruit to my people of Israel;
for they are at hand to come.
9 For, behold, I *am* for you, and I will
turn unto you, and ye shall be tilled and
sown:
10 And I will multiply men upon you,
all the house of Israel, *even* all of it: and
the cities shall be inhabited, and the
wastes shall be builded:
11 And I will multiply upon you man
and beast; and they shall increase and
bring fruit: and I will settle you after
your old estates, and will do better *unto*
you than at your beginnings: and ye
shall know that I *am* the LORD.
12 Yea, I will cause men to walk upon
you, *even* my people Israel; and they
shall possess thee, and thou shalt be
their inheritance, and thou shalt no
more henceforth bereave them *of men*.
13 Thus saith the Lord GOD; Because
they say unto you, Thou *land* devourest
up men, and hast bereaved thy nations;
14 Therefore thou shalt devour men
no more, neither bereave thy nations
any more, saith the Lord GOD.
15 Neither will I cause *men* to hear in
thee the shame of the heathen any
more, neither shalt thou bear the reproach of the people any more, neither
shalt thou cause thy nations to fall any
more, saith the Lord GOD.
¶ 16 Moreover the word of the LORD
came unto me, saying,
17 Son of man, when the house of Israel dwelt in their own land, they defiled it by their own way and by their
doings: their way was before me as the
uncleanness of a removed woman.
18 Wherefore I poured my fury upon
them for the blood that they had shed
upon the land, and for their idols *where-*
with they had polluted it:
19 And I scattered them among the
heathen, and they were dispersed
through the countries: according to
their way and according to their doings
I judged them.
20 And when they entered unto the
heathen, whither they went, they profaned my *holy name, when they said
to them, These *are* the people of the
LORD, and are gone forth out of his land.
¶ 21 But I had pity for mine holy name,
which the house of Israel had profaned
among the heathen, whither they went.
22 Therefore say unto the house of
Israel, Thus saith the Lord GOD; I do
not *this* for your sakes, O house of Israel, but for mine holy name's sake,
which ye have profaned among the heathen, whither ye went.
23 And I will sanctify my great name,
which was profaned among the heathen, which ye have profaned in the

---

36:5 Idumea. Another name for *Edom.

36:6 the shame of the heathen. The evil reports and the evil ways of the heathen.

36:20 These are the people of the LORD. The heathen nations pointed at the Israelites in scorn as they compared the Israelites' behavior with what they professed to believe.

36:21 I had pity for mine holy name. God does not promise to restore Israel because of any faithfulness on the part of His people. His new covenant with them is based upon His own infinite grace and perfect holiness. He will keep the promises that He made to their fathers, because God is not willing to break His word (2 Tim. 2:13).

midst of them; and the heathen shall
know that I *am* the LORD, saith the Lord
GOD, when I shall be sanctified in you
before their eyes.
24 For I will take you from among the
heathen, and gather you out of all countries, and will bring you into your own
land.
¶25 Then will I sprinkle clean water
upon you, and ye shall be *clean: from
all your filthiness, and from all your
idols, will I cleanse you.
26 A new heart also will I give you, and
a new spirit will I put within you: and I
will take away the stony heart out of
your flesh, and I will give you an heart
of flesh.
27 And I will put my spirit within you,
and cause you to walk in my statutes,
and ye shall keep my judgments, and do
them.
28 And ye shall dwell in the land that
I gave to your fathers; and ye shall be
my people, and I will be your God.
29 I will also save you from all your
uncleannesses: and I will call for the
corn, and will increase it, and lay no
famine upon you.
30 And I will multiply the fruit of the
tree, and the increase of the field, that
ye shall receive no more reproach of
famine among the heathen.
31 Then shall ye remember your own
evil ways, and your doings that *were* not
good, and shall lothe yourselves in your
own sight for your iniquities and for
your abominations.
32 Not for your sakes do I *this,* saith
the Lord GOD, be it known unto you: be
ashamed and confounded for your own
ways, O house of Israel.
33 Thus saith the Lord GOD; In the day
that I shall have cleansed you from all
your iniquities I will also cause *you* to
dwell in the cities, and the wastes shall
be builded.
34 And the desolate land shall be
tilled, whereas it lay desolate in the
sight of all that passed by.
35 And they shall say, This land that
was desolate is become like the garden
of *Eden; and the waste and desolate
and ruined cities *are become* fenced, *and*
are inhabited.
36 Then the heathen that are left
round about you shall know that I the
LORD build the ruined *places, and* plant
that that was desolate: I the LORD have
spoken *it,* and I will do *it.*
37 Thus saith the Lord GOD; I will yet
for this be enquired of by the house of
Israel, to do *it* for them; I will increase
them with men like a flock.
38 As the holy flock, as the flock of
Jerusalem in her solemn *feasts; so
shall the waste cities be filled with
flocks of men: and they shall know that
I *am* the LORD.

36:24 THE TERMS OF THE NEW COVENANT

The remainder of this chapter presents the terms of the new covenant that God has made with His people Israel.

The promises of this covenant, as given in these verses, are:

1. Israel will be regathered from the nations, among whom the people have been scattered, and brought back to their own land (vs. 24);
2. Israel will be converted (vs. 25);
3. Israel will be reborn (vs. 26);
4. The Holy Spirit will be given to Israel (vs. 27);
5. Israel will hate themselves because of their sin. This is the fullest statement of Israel's repentance (vs. 31);
6. The land of Israel will become like the Garden of Eden (vs. 35); and
7. Israel will know that God is the LORD (vs. 38).

36:25 Then. See also verse 36. This word shows the time when these two prophecies are going to be fulfilled.

36:25 will I sprinkle. See Numbers 19 for an illustration of this cleansing,

VI. Restoration of Israel and Judgment of the Nations (37:1—39:29)

The re-establishment of Israel

37 The hand of the LORD was upon
me, and carried me out in the
spirit of the LORD, and set me down in
the midst of the valley which *was* full
of bones,

> **37:1 The Vision of the Bones**
> The vision of bones is fully explained in verses 11-14 of this chapter. The bones are the house of Israel scattered throughout the nations of the earth. They will be regathered in unbelief (vs. 8): "there was no breath in them." Then God will give them spiritual life when they recognize the Lord Jesus Christ as their Messiah (vs. 14). The purpose of the vision is to give us a picture of the regathering of the nation of Israel and the conversion of that nation when the Lord comes to reign.

2 And caused me to pass by them
round about: and, behold, *there were*
very many in the open valley; and, lo,
they were very dry.
3 And he said unto me, Son of man,
can these bones live? And I answered,
O Lord GOD, thou knowest.
4 Again he said unto me, Prophesy upon
these bones, and say unto them, O ye
dry bones, hear the word of the LORD.
5 Thus saith the Lord GOD unto these
bones; Behold, I will cause breath to
enter into you, and ye shall live:
6 And I will lay sinews upon you, and
will bring up flesh upon you, and cover
you with skin, and put breath in you,
and ye shall live; and ye shall know that
I *am* the LORD.
7 So I prophesied as I was commanded: and as I prophesied, there was a
noise, and behold a shaking, and the
bones came together, bone to his bone.
8 And when I beheld, lo, the sinews
and the flesh came up upon them, and
the skin covered them above: but *there*
was no breath in them.
9 Then said he unto me, Prophesy
unto the wind, prophesy, son of man,
and say to the wind, Thus saith the Lord
GOD; Come from the four winds, O
breath, and breathe upon these slain,
that they may live.
10 So I prophesied as he commanded
me, and the breath came into them, and
they lived, and stood up upon their feet,
an exceeding great army.
¶ 11 Then he said unto me, Son of man,
these bones are the whole house of Israel: behold, they say, Our bones are
dried, and our *hope is lost: we are cut
off for our parts.
12 Therefore prophesy and say unto
them, Thus saith the Lord GOD; Behold, O my people, I will open your
graves, and cause you to come up out
of your graves, and bring you into the
land of Israel.
13 And ye shall know that I *am* the
LORD, when I have opened your graves,
O my people, and brought you up out
of your graves,
14 And shall put my spirit in you, and
ye shall live, and I shall place you in
your own land: then shall ye know that
I the LORD have spoken *it,* and performed *it,* saith the LORD.
¶ 15 The word of the LORD came again
unto me, saying,
16 Moreover, thou son of man, take
thee one stick, and write upon it, For
*Judah, and for the children of Israel his
companions: then take another stick,
and write upon it, For *Joseph, the stick
of *Ephraim, and *for* all the house of
Israel his companions:
17 And join them one to another into

37:7 a noise, and behold a shaking. Thunder and an earthquake.

37:16 take thee one stick . . . then take another stick. The nation of Israel was divided into two kingdoms during the reign of Rehoboam. Through Ezekiel, God proclaimed that this breach within Israel will be perfectly healed when the Lord Jesus Christ comes to be their King (vs. 22). "David my servant [our Lord in the person of His father, David] shall be king over them, and they shall all have one shepherd" (vs. 24).

one stick; and they shall become one in
thine hand.
¶18 And when the children of thy people shall speak unto thee, saying, Wilt
thou not shew us what thou *meanest* by
these?
19 Say unto them, Thus saith the Lord
GOD; Behold, I will take the stick of Joseph, which *is* in the hand of Ephraim,
and the tribes of Israel his fellows, and
will put them with him, *even* with the
stick of Judah, and make them one stick,
and they shall be one in mine hand.
¶20 And the sticks whereon thou
writest shall be in thine hand before
their eyes.
21 And say unto them, Thus saith the
Lord GOD; Behold, I will take the children of Israel from among the heathen,
whither they be gone, and will gather
them on every side, and bring them into
their own land:
22 And I will make them one nation in
the land upon the *mountains of Israel;
and one king shall be king to them all:
and they shall be no more two nations,
neither shall they be divided into two
kingdoms any more at all:
23 Neither shall they defile themselves any more with their idols, nor
with their detestable things, nor with
any of their transgressions: but I will
save them out of all their dwellingplaces, wherein they have sinned, and
will cleanse them: so shall they be my
people, and I will be their God.
24 And David my servant *shall be* king
over them; and they all shall have one
shepherd: they shall also walk in my
judgments, and observe my statutes,
and do them.
25 And they shall dwell in the land that
I have given unto *Jacob my servant,
wherein your fathers have dwelt; and
they shall dwell therein, *even* they, and
their children, and their children's children for ever: and my servant David
shall be their prince for ever.
26 Moreover I will make a covenant of
peace with them; it shall be an everlasting covenant with them: and I will place
them, and multiply them, and will set
my *sanctuary in the midst of them for
evermore.
27 My *tabernacle also shall be with
them: yea, I will be their God, and they
shall be my people.
28 And the heathen shall know that I
the LORD do sanctify Israel, when my
sanctuary shall be in the midst of them
for evermore.

The prophecy against Gog and Magog

38 And the word of the LORD came
unto me, saying,
2 Son of man, set thy face against
*Gog, the land of Magog, the chief prince
of *Meshech and Tubal, and prophesy
against him,
3 And say, Thus saith the Lord GOD;
Behold I *am* against thee, O Gog, the
chief prince of Meshech and Tubal:
4 And I will turn thee back, and put
hooks into thy jaws, and I will bring
thee forth, and all thine army, horses
and horsemen, all of them clothed with
all sorts *of armour, even* a great company *with* bucklers and shields, all of them
handling swords:
5 Persia, Ethiopia, and Libya with
them; all of them with shield and helmet:
6 Gomer, and all his bands; the house
of *Togarmah of the north quarters, and
all his bands: *and* many people with
thee.
7 Be thou prepared, and prepare for
thyself, thou, and all thy company that
are assembled unto thee, and be thou a
guard unto them.
¶8 After many days thou shalt be visited: in the latter years thou shalt come
into the land *that is* brought back from
the sword, *and is* gathered out of many
people, against the mountains of Israel,
which have been always waste: but it is
brought forth out of the nations, and
they shall dwell safely all of them.

38:2 Meshech and Tubal. Russia. See Ezekiel 27:13 and 38:2 notes.

38:6 Gomer Defined
Gomer refers to one of the northern kingdoms, probably Germany. In the Talmud, Gomer is spoken of as Germani, or the Germans. The major portion of Germany was never connected with the old Roman Empire, and thus it seems likely that Germany will not be a part of the revived Roman Empire. The linking of Gomer with Rosh, Meshech, and Tubal confirms that a confederacy of nations will form during the *Great Tribulation, even though it may not have a part in the prophetic picture until after *Armageddon. See verse 2 note, "Gog and Magog."

9Thou shalt ascend and come like
a storm, thou shalt be like a cloud to
cover the land, thou, and all thy bands,
and many people with thee.
10Thus saith the Lord GOD; It shall
also come to pass, *that* at the same time
shall things come into thy mind, and
thou shalt think an evil thought:
11And thou shalt say, I will go up to
the land of unwalled villages; I will go
to them that are at rest, that dwell safely, all of them dwelling without walls,
and having neither bars nor gates,
12To take a spoil, and to take a prey;
to turn thine hand upon the desolate
places *that are now* inhabited, and upon
the people *that are* gathered out of the
nations, which have gotten cattle and
goods, that dwell in the midst of the
land.
13Sheba, and Dedan, and the merchants of *Tarshish, with all the young
lions thereof, shall say unto thee, Art
thou come to take a spoil? hast thou
gathered thy company to take a prey?
to carry away silver and gold, to take
away cattle and goods, to take a great
spoil?
¶14Therefore, son of man, prophesy
and say unto Gog, Thus saith the Lord
GOD; In that day when my people of
Israel dwelleth safely, shalt thou not
know *it?*
15And thou shalt come from thy place
out of the north parts, thou, and many
people with thee, all of them riding
upon horses, a great company, and a
mighty army:
16And thou shalt come up against my
people of Israel, as a cloud to cover the
land; it shall be in the latter days, and I

38:2 GOG AND MAGOG

There are various interpretations given of chapters 38 and 39 of this book, the prophecy against Gog. But the one that most completely agrees with the whole content of Scripture, it would seem, is that this is a prophecy of a coming federation of nations, including the countries listed in verses 5-6, that will attempt to destroy the nation of Israel and abolish the name of the Lord from the earth. Verse 3 could be translated, "O Gog, the prince of Rosh, Meshech, and Tubal." The Scythian Tauri in the Crimea was so called. The Araxes also were called Rhos. The names Moscow and Tobolsk may have been derived from the names Meshech and Tubal.

This invasion of Gog and Magog must be distinguished from the invasion predicted in Revelation 20:8-9. Revelation predicts an uprising of Gog and Magog at the end of the *Millennium, whereas Ezekiel's prophecy has to do with an attempted invasion of Palestine, which seems to take place at the very beginning of the millennial reign of Christ. There are some who believe that this activity on the part of Gog and Magog will be during the *Great Tribulation and will terminate at the Battle of *Armageddon. But that Gog and Magog do not fit into that picture seems to be clearly indicated in verses 8-12 of this chapter, for there we are told of a "land that is brought back from the sword . . . them that are at rest." Certainly that will not be the settled condition in Palestine during the Great Tribulation. Thus it would seem that Gog and Magog will attempt their invasion after Armageddon, and yet before there is a settled peace in Palestine.

38:13 Sheba, and Dedan. The Arabians.
38:13 Tarshish, with all the young lions. Perhaps the Western nations and their colonies.

will bring thee against my land, that the
heathen may know me, when I shall be
sanctified in thee, O Gog, before their
eyes.
17 Thus saith the Lord GOD; *Art* thou
he of whom I have spoken in old time
by my servants the *prophets of Israel,
which prophesied in those days *many*
years that I would bring thee against
them?
18 And it shall come to pass at the
same time when Gog shall come against
the land of Israel, saith the Lord GOD,
that my fury shall come up in my face.
19 For in my jealousy *and* in the fire
of my wrath have I spoken, Surely in
that day there shall be a great shaking
in the land of Israel;
20 So that the fishes of the sea, and the
fowls of the heaven, and the beasts of
the field, and all creeping things that
creep upon the earth, and all the men
that *are* upon the face of the earth, shall
shake at my presence, and the mountains shall be thrown down, and the
steep places shall fall, and every wall
shall fall to the ground.
21 And I will call for a sword against
him throughout all my mountains, saith
the Lord GOD: every man's sword shall
be against his brother.
22 And I will plead against him with
pestilence and with blood; and I will rain
upon him, and upon his bands, and upon
the many people that *are* with him, an
overflowing rain, and great hailstones,
fire, and brimstone.
23 Thus will I magnify myself, and
sanctify myself; and I will be known in
the eyes of many nations, and they shall
know that I *am* the LORD.

Prophecy against Gog and Magog
(continued)

39 Therefore, thou son of man,
prophesy against Gog, and say,
Thus saith the Lord GOD; Behold, I *am*
against thee, O Gog, the chief prince of
Meshech and Tubal:
2 And I will turn thee back, and leave
but the sixth part of thee, and will cause
thee to come up from the north parts,
and will bring thee upon the mountains
of *Israel:
3 And I will smite thy bow out of thy
left hand, and will cause thine arrows
to fall out of thy right hand.
4 Thou shalt fall upon the mountains
of Israel, thou, and all thy bands, and the
people that *is* with thee: I will give thee
unto the ravenous birds of every sort,
and *to* the beasts of the field to be devoured.
5 Thou shalt fall upon the open field:
for I have spoken *it,* saith the Lord GOD.
6 And I will send a fire on Magog, and
among them that dwell carelessly in the
*isles: and they shall know that I *am* the
LORD.
7 So will I make my holy name known
in the midst of my people Israel; and I
will not *let them* pollute my holy name
any more: and the heathen shall know
that I *am* the LORD, the Holy One in
Israel.
¶8 Behold, it is come, and it is done,
saith the Lord GOD; this *is* the day
whereof I have spoken.
9 And they that dwell in the cities of
Israel shall go forth, and shall set on fire
and burn the weapons, both the shields
and the bucklers, the bows and the arrows, and the handstaves, and the
spears, and they shall burn them with
fire seven years:
10 So that they shall take no wood
out of the field, neither cut down *any*
out of the forests; for they shall burn
the weapons with fire: and they shall
spoil those that spoiled them, and rob
those that robbed them, saith the Lord
GOD.
¶11 And it shall come to pass in that
day, *that* I will give unto Gog a place
there of graves in Israel, the valley of
the passengers on the east of the sea:
and it shall stop the *noses* of the passengers: and there shall they bury Gog and

---

39:6 Magog. See 38:2 note.

all his multitude: and they shall call *it*
The valley of Hamon-gog.
12And seven months shall the house
of Israel be burying of them, that they
may cleanse the land.
13Yea, all the people of the land shall
bury *them;* and it shall be to them a renown the day that I shall be glorified,
saith the Lord GOD.
14And they shall sever out men of
continual employment, passing through
the land to bury with the passengers
those that remain upon the face of the
earth, to cleanse it: after the end of
seven months shall they search.
15And the passengers *that* pass
through the land, when *any* seeth a
man's bone, then shall he set up a sign
by it, till the buriers have buried it in
the valley of Hamon-gog.
16And also the name of the city *shall
be* Hamonah. Thus shall they cleanse
the land.
¶17And, thou son of man, thus saith
the Lord GOD; Speak unto every feathered fowl, and to every beast of the
field, Assemble yourselves, and come;
gather yourselves on every side to my
*sacrifice that I do sacrifice for you,
even a great sacrifice upon the mountains of Israel, that ye may eat flesh, and
drink blood.
18Ye shall eat the flesh of the mighty,
and drink the blood of the princes of the
earth, of rams, of lambs, and of goats,
of bullocks, all of them fatlings of *Bashan.
19And ye shall eat fat till ye be full,
and drink blood till ye be drunken, of
my sacrifice which I have sacrificed for
you.
20Thus ye shall be filled at my table
with horses and chariots, with mighty
men, and with all men of war, saith the
Lord GOD.
21And I will set my glory among the
heathen, and all the heathen shall see
my judgment that I have executed, and
my hand that I have laid upon them.
22So the house of Israel shall know
that I *am* the LORD their God from that
day and forward.
¶23And the heathen shall know that
the house of Israel went into captivity
for their iniquity: because they trespassed against me, therefore hid I my
face from them, and gave them into the
hand of their enemies: so fell they all
by the sword.
24According to their uncleanness and
according to their transgressions have
I done unto them, and hid my face from
them.
25Therefore thus saith the Lord GOD;
Now will I bring again the captivity of
Jacob, and have *mercy upon the whole
house of Israel, and will be jealous for
my holy name;
26After that they have borne their
shame, and all their trespasses
whereby they have trespassed against
me, when they dwelt safely in their
land, and none made *them* afraid.
27When I have brought them again
from the people, and gathered them out
of their enemies' lands, and am sanctified in them in the sight of many nations;
28Then shall they know that I *am* the
LORD their God, which caused them to
be led into captivity among the heathen:
but I have gathered them unto their
own land, and have left none of them
any more there.
29Neither will I hide my face any
more from them: for I have poured out
my spirit upon the house of Israel, saith
the Lord GOD.

VII. Israel in the Kingdom Age (40:1—48:35)

Description of the millennial temple

40 In the five and twentieth year
of our captivity, in the beginning
of the year, in the tenth *day* of the
*month, in the fourteenth year after
that the city was smitten, in the selfsame day the hand of the LORD was
upon me, and brought me thither.

39:16 Hamonah. The multitude.

2 In the visions of *God brought he me into the land of Israel, and set me upon a very high mountain, by which *was* as the frame of a city on the south.

3 And he brought me thither, and, behold, *there was* a man, whose appearance *was* like the appearance of brass, with a line of flax in his hand, and a measuring reed; and he stood in the gate.

4 And the man said unto me, Son of man, behold with thine eyes, and hear with thine ears, and set thine heart upon all that I shall shew thee; for to the intent that I might shew *them* unto thee *art* thou brought hither: declare all that thou seest to the house of Israel.

5 And behold a wall on the outside of the house round about, and in the man's hand a measuring reed of six *cubits *long* by the cubit and an hand breadth: so he measured the breadth of the building, one reed; and the height, one reed.

40:5 The Future Temple
Chapters 40–42 describe in detail the construction of the temple that the children of Israel will have in Jerusalem during the millennial reign of Christ on earth. The description is so complete that a competent architect could draw a plan of the building from the instructions given in these chapters. This temple will be greater than the temple of Solomon (Hag. 2:9; see also its note, "The Temple at Christ's Return"). It will be the place from which our Lord will reign upon the earth (Ezek. 43:7).

¶ 6 Then came he unto the gate which looketh toward the east, and went up the stairs thereof, and measured the threshold of the gate, *which was* one reed broad; and the other threshold *of the gate, which was* one reed broad.

7 And *every* little chamber *was* one reed long, and one reed broad; and between the little chambers *were* five cubits; and the threshold of the gate by the porch of the gate within *was* one reed.

8 He measured also the porch of the gate within, one reed.

9 Then measured he the porch of the gate, eight cubits; and the posts thereof, two cubits; and the porch of the gate *was* inward.

10 And the little chambers of the gate eastward *were* three on this side, and three on that side; they three *were* of one measure: and the posts had one measure on this side and on that side.

11 And he measured the breadth of the entry of the gate, ten cubits; *and* the length of the gate, thirteen cubits.

12 The space also before the little chambers *was* one cubit *on this side,* and the space *was* one cubit on that side: and the little chambers *were* six cubits on this side, and six cubits on that side.

13 He measured then the gate from the roof of *one* little chamber to the roof of another: the breadth *was* five and twenty cubits, door against door.

14 He made also posts of threescore cubits, even unto the post of the court round about the gate.

15 And from the face of the gate of the entrance unto the face of the porch of the inner gate *were* fifty cubits.

16 And *there were* narrow windows to the little chambers, and to their posts within the gate round about, and likewise to the arches: and windows *were* round about inward: and upon *each* post *were* palm trees.

17 Then brought he me into the outward court, and, lo, *there were* chambers, and a pavement made for the court round about: thirty chambers *were* upon the pavement.

18 And the pavement by the side of the gates over against the length of the gates *was* the lower pavement.

19 Then he measured the breadth from the forefront of the lower gate unto the forefront of the inner court

40:3 a man. This was a *theophany.
40:3 measuring reed. A measuring rod.

without, an hundred cubits eastward and northward.

¶20 And the gate of the outward court that looked toward the north, he measured the length thereof, and the breadth thereof.

21 And the little chambers thereof *were* three on this side and three on that side; and the posts thereof and the arches thereof were after the measure of the first gate: the length thereof *was* fifty cubits, and the breadth five and twenty cubits.

22 And their windows, and their arches, and their palm trees, *were* after the measure of the gate that looketh toward the east; and they went up unto it by seven steps; and the arches thereof *were* before them.

23 And the gate of the inner court *was* over against the gate toward the north, and toward the east; and he measured from gate to gate an hundred cubits.

¶24 After that he brought me toward the south, and behold a gate toward the south: and he measured the posts thereof and the arches thereof according to these measures.

25 And *there were* windows in it and in the arches thereof round about, like those windows: the length *was* fifty cubits, and the breadth five and twenty cubits.

26 And *there were* seven steps to go up to it, and the arches thereof *were* before them: and it had palm trees, one on this side, and another on that side, upon the posts thereof.

27 And *there was* a gate in the inner court toward the south: and he measured from gate to gate toward the south an hundred cubits.

28 And he brought me to the inner court by the south gate: and he measured the south gate according to these measures;

29 And the little chambers thereof, and the posts thereof, and the arches thereof, according to these measures: and *there were* windows in it and in the arches thereof round about: *it was* fifty cubits long, and five and twenty cubits broad.

30 And the arches round about *were* five and twenty cubits long, and five cubits broad.

31 And the arches thereof *were* toward the utter court; and palm trees *were* upon the posts thereof: and the going up to it *had* eight steps.

¶32 And he brought me into the inner court toward the east: and he measured the gate according to these measures.

33 And the little chambers thereof, and the posts thereof, and the arches thereof, *were* according to these measures: and *there were* windows therein and in the arches thereof round about: *it was* fifty cubits long, and five and twenty cubits broad.

34 And the arches thereof *were* toward the outward court; and palm trees *were* upon the posts thereof, on this side, and on that side: and the going up to it *had* eight steps.

¶35 And he brought me to the north gate, and measured *it* according to these measures;

36 The little chambers thereof, the posts thereof, and the arches thereof, and the windows to it round about: the length *was* fifty cubits, and the breadth five and twenty cubits.

37 And the posts thereof *were* toward the utter court; and palm trees *were* upon the posts thereof, on this side, and on that side: and the going up to it *had* eight steps.

38 And the chambers and the entries thereof *were* by the posts of the gates, where they washed the burnt-offering.

¶39 And in the porch of the gate *were* two tables on this side, and two tables on that side, to slay thereon the burnt-offering and the *sin-offering and the *trespass-offering.

40 And at the side without, as one goeth up to the entry of the north gate,

---

40:40 as one goeth up to the entry. At the city.

were two tables; and on the other side,
which *was* at the porch of the gate, *were*
two tables.
41 Four tables *were* on this side, and
four tables on that side, by the side of
the gate; eight tables, whereupon they
slew *their sacrifices.*
42 And the four tables *were* of hewn
stone for the burnt-offering, of a cubit
and an half long, and a cubit and an half
broad, and one cubit high: whereupon
also they laid the instruments wherewith they slew the burnt-offering and
the sacrifice.
43 And within *were* hooks, an hand
broad, fastened round about: and upon
the tables *was* the flesh of the offering.
¶44 And without the inner gate *were*
the chambers of the singers in the inner court, which *was* at the side of the
north gate; and their prospect *was* toward the south: one at the side of the
east gate *having* the prospect toward
the north.
45 And he said unto me, This chamber,
whose prospect *is* toward the south, *is*
for the priests, the keepers of the
charge of the house.
46 And the chamber whose prospect *is*
toward the north *is* for the priests, the
keepers of the charge of the *altar:
these *are* the *sons of Zadok among the
sons of Levi, which come near to the
LORD to minister unto him.
47 So he measured the court, an hundred cubits long, and an hundred cubits
broad, foursquare; and the altar *that was*
before the house.
¶48 And he brought me to the porch of
the house, and measured *each* post of
the porch, five cubits on this side, and
five cubits on that side: and the breadth
of the gate *was* three cubits on this side,
and three cubits on that side.
49 The length of the porch *was* twenty cubits, and the breadth eleven cubits;
and *he brought me* by the steps whereby
they went up to it: and *there were* pillars
by the posts, one on this side, and another on that side.

Millennial temple (continued)

41 Afterward he brought me to
the temple, and measured the
posts, six cubits broad on the one side,
and six cubits broad on the other side,
which was the breadth of the tabernacle.
2 And the breadth of the door *was* ten
cubits; and the sides of the door *were*
five cubits on the one side, and five
cubits on the other side: and he measured the length thereof, forty cubits:
and the breadth, twenty cubits.
3 Then went he inward, and measured
the post of the door, two cubits; and the
door, six cubits; and the breadth of the
door, seven cubits.
4 So he measured the length thereof,
twenty cubits; and the breadth, twenty
cubits, before the temple: and he said
unto me, This *is* the most holy *place.*
5 After he measured the wall of the
house, six cubits; and the breadth of
every side chamber, four cubits, round
about the house on every side.
6 And the side chambers *were* three,
one over another, and thirty in order;
and they entered into the wall which
was of the house for the side chambers
round about, that they might have hold,
but they had not hold in the wall of the
house.
7 And *there was* an enlarging, and a
winding about still upward to the side
chambers: for the winding about of the
house went still upward round about
the house: therefore the breadth of the
house *was still* upward, and so increased *from* the lowest *chamber* to the
highest by the midst.
8 I saw also the height of the house
round about: the foundations of the side
chambers *were* a full reed of six great
cubits.
9 The thickness of the wall, which *was*

40:43 hooks. Instruments used in the temple for handling the sacrifices. Two pronged hooks were used for flaying animals.

for the side chamber without, *was* five
cubits: and *that* which *was* left *was* the
place of the side chambers that *were*
within.
10And between the chambers *was* the
wideness of twenty cubits round about
the house on every side.
11And the doors of the side chambers
were toward *the place that was* left, one
door toward the north, and another door
toward the south: and the breadth of the
place that was left *was* five cubits round
about.
12Now the building that *was* before
the separate place at the end toward the
west *was* seventy cubits broad;
and the wall of the building *was* five
cubits thick round about, and the length
thereof ninety cubits.
13So he measured the house, an hundred cubits long; and the separate place,
and the building, with the walls thereof,
an hundred cubits long;
14Also the breadth of the face of the
house, and of the separate place toward
the east, an hundred cubits.
15And he measured the length of the
building over against the separate place
which *was* behind it, and the galleries
thereof on the one side and on the other
side, an hundred cubits, with the inner
temple, and the porches of the court;
16The door posts, and the narrow
windows, and the galleries round about
on their three stories, over against the
door, cieled with wood round about, and
from the ground up to the windows, and
the windows *were* covered;
17To that above the door, even unto
the inner house, and without, and by all
the wall round about within and without, by measure.
18And *it was* made with cherubims
and palm trees, so that a palm tree *was*
between a cherub and a cherub; and
every cherub had two faces;
19So that the face of a man *was* toward
the palm tree on the one side, and the
face of a young lion toward the palm
tree on the other side: *it was* made
through all the house round about.
20From the ground unto above the
door *were* cherubims and palm trees
made, and *on* the wall of the temple.
21The posts of the temple *were*
squared, *and* the face of the sanctuary;
the appearance *of the one* as the appearance *of the other.*
22The altar of wood *was* three cubits
high, and the length thereof two cubits;
and the corners thereof, and the length
thereof, and the walls thereof, *were* of
wood: and he said unto me, This *is* the
table that *is* before the LORD.
23And the temple and the sanctuary
had two doors.
24And the doors had two leaves
apiece, two turning leaves; two *leaves*
for the one door, and two leaves for the
other *door.*
25And *there were* made on them, on
the doors of the temple, cherubims and
palm trees, like as *were* made upon the
walls; and *there were* thick planks upon
the face of the porch without.
26And *there were* narrow windows and
palm trees on the one side and on the
other side, on the sides of the porch,
and *upon* the side chambers of the
house, and thick planks.

Millennial temple (continued)

42 Then he brought me forth into
the utter court, the way toward
the north: and he brought me into the
chamber that *was* over against the separate place, and which *was* before the
building toward the north.
2Before the length of an hundred cubits *was* the north door, and the breadth
was fifty cubits.
3Over against the twenty *cubits*
which *were* for the inner court, and over
against the pavement which *was* for the
utter court, *was* gallery against gallery
in three *stories.*
4And before the chambers *was* a walk
of ten cubits breadth inward, a way of

41:16 cieled. Paneled.

one cubit; and their doors toward the north.

5 Now the upper chambers *were* shorter: for the galleries were higher than these, than the lower, and than the middlemost of the building.

6 For they *were* in three *stories,* but had not pillars as the pillars of the courts: therefore *the building* was straitened more than the lowest and the middlemost from the ground.

7 And the wall that *was* without over against the chambers, toward the utter court on the forepart of the chambers, the length thereof *was* fifty cubits.

8 For the length of the chambers that *were* in the utter court *was* fifty cubits: and, lo, before the temple *were* an hundred cubits.

9 And from under these chambers *was* the entry on the east side, as one goeth into them from the utter court.

10 The chambers *were* in the thickness of the wall of the court toward the east, over against the separate place, and over against the building.

11 And the way before them *was* like the appearance of the chambers which *were* toward the north, as long as they, *and* as broad as they: and all their goings out *were* both according to their fashions, and according to their doors.

12 And according to the doors of the chambers that *were* toward the south *was* a door in the head of the way, *even* the way directly before the wall toward the east, as one entereth into them.

¶ 13 Then said he unto me, The north chambers *and* the south chambers, which *are* before the separate place, they *be* *holy chambers, where the priests that approach unto the LORD shall eat the most holy things: there shall they lay the most holy things, and the *meat-offering, and the sin-offering, and the trespass-offering; for the place *is* holy.

14 When the priests enter therein, then shall they not go out of the holy *place* into the utter court, but there they shall lay their *garments wherein they minister; for they *are* holy; and shall put on other garments, and shall approach to *those things* which *are* for the people.

15 Now when he had made an end of measuring the inner house, he brought me forth toward the gate whose prospect *is* toward the east, and measured it round about.

16 He measured the east side with the measuring reed, five hundred reeds, with the measuring reed round about.

17 He measured the north side, five hundred reeds, with the measuring reed round about.

18 He measured the south side, five hundred reeds, with the measuring reed.

¶ 19 He turned about to the west side, *and* measured five hundred reeds with the measuring reed.

20 He measured it by the four sides: it had a wall round about, five hundred *reeds* long, and five hundred broad, to make a separation between the sanctuary and the profane place.

Millennial temple (continued)

43

Afterward he brought me to the gate, *even* the gate that looketh toward the east:

2 And, behold, the glory of the God of Israel came from the way of the east: and his voice *was* like a noise of many waters: and the earth shined with his glory.

3 And *it was* according to the appearance of the vision which I saw, *even* according to the vision that I saw when I came to destroy the city: and the vi-

43:2 God's Future Glory

This is a vision of the coming of the Lord in His glory to establish Himself as King of Israel and Lord of nations (see Ezek. 8:4 note, "God's Glory Departs"). The returning glory will come from heaven to the Mount of Olives (Zech. 14:4; see also its note, "The Mount of Olives"). From the Mount of Olives our Lord will enter Jerusalem and make His dwelling place in the new temple which Ezekiel describes (43:7).

sions *were* like the vision that I saw by
the river Chebar; and I fell upon my
face.
4And the glory of the LORD came into
the house by the way of the gate whose
prospect *is* toward the east.
5So the spirit took me up, and
brought me into the inner court; and,
behold, the glory of the LORD filled the
house.
6And I heard *him* speaking unto
me out of the house; and the man stood
by me.
¶7And he said unto me, Son of man,
the place of my throne, and the place of
the soles of my feet, where I will dwell
in the midst of the children of Israel for
ever, and my holy name, shall the house
of Israel no more defile, *neither* they,
nor their kings, by their whoredom, nor
by the carcases of their kings in their
*high places.
8In their setting of their threshold by
my thresholds, and their post by my
posts, and the wall between me and
them, they have even defiled my holy
name by their abominations that they
have committed: wherefore I have consumed them in mine anger.
9Now let them put away their whoredom, and the carcases of their kings, far
from me, and I will dwell in the midst
of them for ever.
¶10Thou son of man, shew the house
to the house of Israel, that they may be
ashamed of their iniquities: and let
them measure the pattern.
11And if they be ashamed of all that
they have done, shew them the form of
the house, and the fashion thereof, and
the goings out thereof, and the comings
in thereof, and all the forms thereof, and
all the ordinances thereof, and all the
forms thereof, and all the *laws thereof:
and write *it* in their sight, that they may
keep the whole form thereof, and all the
ordinances thereof, and do them.
12This *is* the law of the house; Upon
the top of the mountain the whole limit thereof round about *shall be* most holy.
Behold, this *is* the law of the house.
¶13And these *are* the measures of the
altar after the cubits: The cubit *is* a cubit and an hand breadth; even the bottom *shall be* a cubit, and the breadth a
cubit, and the border thereof by the
edge thereof round about *shall be* a
*span: and this *shall be* the higher place
of the altar.
14And from the bottom *upon* the
ground *even* to the lower settle *shall be*
two cubits, and the breadth one cubit;
and from the lesser settle *even* to the
greater settle *shall be* four cubits, and
the breadth *one* cubit.
15So the altar *shall be* four cubits; and
from the altar and upward *shall be* four
*horns.
16And the altar *shall be* twelve *cubits*
long, twelve broad, square in the four
squares thereof.
17And the settle *shall be* fourteen *cubits* long and fourteen broad in the four
squares thereof; and the border about
it *shall be* half a cubit; and the bottom
thereof *shall be* a cubit about; and his
stairs shall look toward the east.
¶18And he said unto me, Son of man,
thus saith the Lord GOD; These *are*
the ordinances of the altar in the day
when they shall make it, to offer burnt-
offerings thereon, and to sprinkle
*blood thereon.
19And thou shalt give to the priests

43:19 Future Sacrifices
This verse makes it sound like animal sacrifices will take place during the millennial reign of Christ, but it is more likely that this section of the chapter is referring to the time when the Israelites will return to Jerusalem from captivity and again offer sacrifices to God.

The verse can also look forward to the *Millennium—to contrast that because of the blood of the Lamb, no more animal sacrifices are needed (Heb. 10:4). We are now acceptable to God only through Christ's blood under the new covenant.

43:18 sprinkle blood. See Leviticus 1:5.

the Levites that be of the seed of Zadok,
which approach unto me, to minister
unto me, saith the Lord GOD, a young
bullock for a sin-offering.
20 And thou shalt take of the blood
thereof, and put *it* on the four horns of
it, and on the four corners of the settle, and upon the border round about:
thus shalt thou cleanse and purge it.
21 Thou shalt take the bullock also of
the sin-offering, and he shall burn it in
the appointed place of the house, without the *sanctuary.
22 And on the second day thou shalt
offer a kid of the goats without blemish
for a sin-offering; and they shall cleanse
the altar, as they did cleanse *it* with the
bullock.
23 When thou hast made an end of
cleansing *it,* thou shalt offer a young
bullock without blemish, and a ram out
of the flock without blemish.
24 And thou shalt offer them before
the LORD, and the priests shall cast salt
upon them, and they shall offer them up
for a burnt-offering unto the LORD.
25 Seven days shalt thou prepare
every day a goat *for* a sin-offering: they
shall also prepare a young bullock, and
a ram out of the flock, without blemish.
26 Seven days shall they purge the
altar and purify it; and they shall *consecrate themselves.
27 And when these days are expired,
it shall be, *that* upon the eighth day, and
so forward, the priests shall make your
burnt-offerings upon the altar, and your
*peace-offerings; and I will accept you,
saith the Lord GOD.

Millennial temple (continued)

44 Then he brought me back the
way of the gate of the outward
sanctuary which looketh toward the
east; and it *was* shut.
2 Then said the LORD unto me; This
gate shall be shut, it shall not be
opened, and no man shall enter in by it;
because the LORD, the God of Israel,
hath entered in by it, therefore it shall
be shut.
3 *It is* for the prince; the prince, he
shall sit in it to eat bread before the
LORD; he shall enter by the way of the
porch of *that* gate, and shall go out by
the way of the same.
¶4 Then brought he me the way of the
north gate before the house: and I
looked, and, behold, the glory of the
LORD filled the house of the LORD: and
I fell upon my face.
5 And the LORD said unto me, Son of
man, mark well, and behold with thine
eyes, and hear with thine ears all that I
say unto thee concerning all the ordinances of the house of the LORD, and all
the laws thereof; and mark well the
entering in of the house, with every
going forth of the sanctuary.
6 And thou shalt say to the rebellious,
even to the house of Israel, Thus saith
the Lord GOD; O ye house of Israel, let
it suffice you of all your abominations,
7 In that ye have brought *into my sanctuary* strangers, *uncircumcised in
heart, and uncircumcised in flesh, to be
in my sanctuary, to pollute it, *even* my
house, when ye offer my bread, the fat
and the blood, and they have broken my
*covenant because of all your abomina-
tions.
8 And ye have not kept the charge of
mine holy things: but ye have set keepers of my charge in my sanctuary for
yourselves.
¶9 Thus saith the Lord GOD; No
stranger, uncircumcised in heart, nor
uncircumcised in flesh, shall enter into
my sanctuary, of any stranger that *is*
among the children of Israel.
10 And the Levites that are gone away
far from me, when Israel went astray,
which went astray away from me after
their idols; they shall even bear their
iniquity.
11 Yet they shall be ministers in my
sanctuary, *having* charge at the gates
of the house, and ministering to the
house: they shall slay the burnt-
offering and the sacrifice for the people,
and they shall stand before them to
minister unto them.

12Because they ministered unto
them before their idols, and caused the
house of Israel to fall into iniquity;
therefore have I lifted up mine hand
against them, saith the Lord GOD, and
they shall bear their iniquity.
13And they shall not come near unto
me, to do the office of a priest unto me,
nor to come near to any of my holy
things, in the most holy *place:* but they
shall bear their shame, and their abominations which they have committed.
14But I will make them keepers of the
charge of the house, for all the service
thereof, and for all that shall be done
therein.
¶15But the priests the Levites, the
sons of Zadok, that kept the charge of
my sanctuary when the children of Israel went astray from me, they shall
come near to me to minister unto me,
and they shall stand before me to offer
unto me the fat and the blood, saith the
Lord GOD:
16They shall enter into my sanctuary,
and they shall come near to my table,
to minister unto me, and they shall
keep my charge.
¶17And it shall come to pass, *that*
when they enter in at the gates of the
inner court, they shall be clothed with
*linen garments; and no wool shall come
upon them, whiles they minister in the
gates of the inner court, and within.
18They shall have linen bonnets upon
their heads, and shall have linen
breeches upon their loins; they shall
not gird *themselves* with any thing that
causeth sweat.
19And when they go forth into the
utter court, *even* into the utter court to
the people, they shall put off their garments wherein they ministered, and lay
them in the holy chambers, and they
shall put on other garments; and they
shall not sanctify the people with their
garments.
20Neither shall they shave their
heads, nor suffer their locks to grow
long; they shall only poll their heads.
21Neither shall any priest drink
*wine, when they enter into the inner
court.
22Neither shall they take for their
wives a widow, nor her that is put away:
but they shall take maidens of the seed
of the house of Israel, or a widow that
had a priest before.
23And they shall teach my people *the
difference* between the holy and profane,
and cause them to discern between the
*unclean and the clean.
24And in controversy they shall stand
in *judgment; *and* they shall judge it
according to my judgments: and they
shall keep my laws and my statutes in
all mine assemblies; and they shall hallow my sabbaths.
25And they shall come at no dead
person to defile themselves: but for father, or for mother, or for son, or for
daughter, for brother, or for sister that
hath had no husband, they may defile
themselves.
26And after he is cleansed, they shall
reckon unto him seven days.
27And in the day that he goeth into
the sanctuary, unto the inner court, to
minister in the sanctuary, he shall offer
his sin-offering, saith the Lord GOD.
28And it shall be unto them for an inheritance: I *am* their inheritance: and
ye shall give them no possession in Israel: I *am* their possession.
29They shall eat the meat-offering,
and the sin-offering, and the trespass-
offering; and every dedicated thing in
Israel shall be theirs.

44:15 the sons of Zadok, that kept the charge of my sanctuary. When God announced the rejection of Eli and his sons from the priesthood because of their unfaithfulness, He predicted that He would raise up a faithful priest (1 Sam. 2:35; see also its note, "A Faithful Priest"). The faithfulness of Zadok to his priestly office will be rewarded by the selection of his sons to be the priests of the Lord in the millennial temple during the reign of Christ.

44:17 clothed. See *holy garments.

30 And the first of all the firstfruits of all *things,* and every *oblation of all, of every *sort* of your oblations, shall be the priest's: ye shall also give unto the priest the first of your dough, that he may cause the blessing to rest in thine house.

31 The priests shall not eat of any thing that is dead of itself, or torn, whether it be fowl or beast.

Divisions of the land during the Millennium

45 Moreover, when ye shall divide by lot the land for inheritance, ye shall offer an oblation unto the LORD, an holy portion of the land: the length *shall be* the length of five and twenty thousand *reeds,* and the breadth *shall be* ten thousand. This *shall be* holy in all the borders thereof round about.

2 Of this there shall be for the sanctuary five hundred *in length,* with five hundred *in breadth,* square round about; and fifty cubits round about for the suburbs thereof.

3 And of this measure shalt thou measure the length of five and twenty thousand, and the breadth of ten thousand: and in it shall be the sanctuary *and* the most holy *place.*

4 The holy *portion* of the land shall be for the priests the ministers of the sanctuary, which shall come near to minister unto the LORD: and it shall be a place for their houses, and an holy place for the sanctuary.

5 And the five and twenty thousand of length, and the ten thousand of breadth, shall also the Levites, the ministers of the house, have for themselves, for a possession for twenty chambers.

¶6 And ye shall appoint the possession of the city five thousand broad, and five and twenty thousand long, over against the oblation of the holy *portion:* it shall be for the whole house of *Israel.

¶7 And *a portion shall be* for the prince on the one side and on the other side of the oblation of the holy *portion,* and of the possession of the city, before the oblation of the holy *portion,* and before the possession of the city, from the west side westward, and from the east side eastward: and the length *shall be* over against one of the portions, from the west border unto the east border.

8 In the land shall be his possession in Israel: and my princes shall no more oppress my people; and *the rest of* the land shall they give to the house of Israel according to their tribes.

¶9 Thus saith the Lord GOD; Let it suffice you, O princes of Israel: remove violence and spoil, and execute judgment and justice, take away your exactions from my people, saith the Lord GOD.

10 Ye shall have *just balances, and a just *ephah, and a just *bath.

11 The ephah and the bath shall be of one measure, that the bath may contain the tenth part of an *homer, and the ephah the tenth part of an homer: the measure thereof shall be after the homer.

12 And the shekel *shall be* twenty *gerahs: twenty shekels, five and twenty shekels, fifteen shekels, shall be your maneh.

13 This *is* the oblation that ye shall offer; the sixth part of an ephah of an homer of wheat, and ye shall give the sixth part of an ephah of an homer of barley:

14 Concerning the ordinance of oil, the bath of oil, *ye shall offer* the tenth part of a bath out of the cor, *which is* an homer of ten baths; for ten baths *are* an homer:

15 And one lamb out of the flock, out of two hundred, out of the fat pastures of Israel; for a meat-offering, and for a burnt-offering, and for peace-offerings,

---

45:12 maneh. The maneh was a weight equal to about fifty or sixty pounds, less than a full talent.

45:14 cor. A cor is about sixty gallons.

to make *reconciliation for them, saith
the Lord GOD.
16All the people of the land shall give
this oblation for the prince in Israel.
17And it shall be the prince's part *to
give* burnt-offerings, and meat-offerings, and drink-offerings, in the *feasts,
and in the new moons, and in the sabbaths, in all solemnities of the house of
Israel: he shall prepare the sin-offering,
and the meat-offering, and the burnt-
offering, and the peace-offerings, to
make reconciliation for the house of
Israel.
18Thus saith the Lord GOD; In the
first *month,* in the first *day* of the month,
thou shalt take a young bullock without
blemish, and cleanse the sanctuary:
19And the priest shall take of the
blood of the sin-offering, and put *it* upon
the posts of the house, and upon the
four corners of the settle of the altar,
and upon the posts of the gate of the
inner court.
20And so thou shalt do the seventh
day of the month for every one that
erreth, and for *him that is* simple: so
shall ye *reconcile the house.
21In the first *month,* in the fourteenth
day of the month, ye shall have the
*passover, a feast of seven days; *un-
leavened bread shall be eaten.
22And upon that day shall the prince
prepare for himself and for all the
people of the land a bullock *for* a sin-
offering.
23And seven days of the feast he shall
prepare a burnt-offering to the LORD,
seven bullocks and seven rams without
blemish daily the seven days; and a kid
of the goats daily *for* a sin-offering.
24And he shall prepare a meat-
offering of an ephah for a bullock, and
an ephah for a ram, and an *hin of oil for
an ephah.
25In the seventh *month,* in the fifteenth day of the month, shall he do the
like in the feast of the seven days, according to the sin-offering, according to
the burnt-offering, and according to the
meat-offering, and according to the oil.

The worship of the prince and the people during the Millennium

46 Thus saith the Lord GOD; The
gate of the inner court that
looketh toward the east shall be shut
the six working days; but on the *sabbath it shall be opened, and in the day
of the *new moon it shall be opened.
2And the prince shall enter by the
way of the porch of *that* gate without,
and shall stand by the post of the gate,
and the priests shall prepare his burnt-
offering and his peace-offerings, and he
shall worship at the threshold of the
gate: then he shall go forth; but the gate
shall not be shut until the evening.
3Likewise the people of the land shall
worship at the door of this gate before
the LORD in the sabbaths and in the new
moons.
4And the burnt-offering that the
prince shall offer unto the LORD in the
sabbath day *shall be* six lambs without
blemish, and a ram without blemish.
5And the meat-offering *shall be* an
ephah for a ram, and the meat-offering
for the lambs as he shall be able to give,
and an hin of oil to an ephah.
6And in the day of the new moon *it
shall be* a young bullock without blemish, and six lambs, and a ram: they shall
be without blemish.
7And he shall prepare a meat-offering, an ephah for a bullock, and an ephah
for a ram, and for the lambs according
as his hand shall attain unto, and an hin
of oil to an ephah.
8And when the prince shall enter, he
shall go in by the way of the porch of
that gate, and he shall go forth by the
way thereof.
¶9But when the people of the land
shall come before the LORD in the solemn feasts, he that entereth in by the
way of the north gate to worship shall
go out by the way of the south gate; and
he that entereth by the way of the south
gate shall go forth by the way of the
north gate: he shall not return by the
way of the gate whereby he came in, but
shall go forth over against it.

10 And the prince in the midst of them, when they go in, shall go in; and when they go forth, shall go forth.

11 And in the feasts and in the solemnities the meat-offering shall be an ephah to a bullock, and ephah to a ram, and to the lambs as he is able to give, and an hin of oil to an ephah.

12 Now when the prince shall prepare a voluntary burnt-offering or peace-offerings voluntarily unto the LORD, *one* shall then open him the gate that looketh toward the east, and he shall prepare his burnt-offering and his peace-offerings, as he did on the sabbath day: then he shall go forth; and after his going forth *one* shall shut the gate.

13 Thou shalt daily prepare a burnt-offering unto the LORD *of* a lamb of the first year without blemish: thou shalt prepare it every morning.

14 And thou shalt prepare a meat-offering for it every morning, the sixth part of an ephah, and the third part of an hin of oil, to temper with the fine flour; a meat-offering continually by a perpetual ordinance unto the LORD.

15 Thus shall they prepare the lamb, and the meat-offering, and the oil, every morning *for* a continual burnt-offering.

¶ 16 Thus saith the Lord GOD; If the prince give a gift unto any of his sons, the inheritance thereof shall be his sons'; it *shall be* their possession by inheritance.

17 But if he give a gift of his inheritance to one of his servants, then it shall be his to the year of liberty; after it shall return to the prince: but his inheritance shall be his sons' for them.

18 Moreover the prince shall not take of the people's inheritance by oppression, to thrust them out of their possession; *but* he shall give his sons inheritance out of his own possession: that my people be not scattered every man from his possession.

¶ 19 After he brought me through the entry, which *was* at the side of the gate, into the holy chambers of the priests, which looked toward the north: and, behold, there *was* a place on the two sides westward.

20 Then said he unto me, This *is* the place where the priests shall boil the *trespass-offering and the *sin-offering, where they shall bake the meat-offering; that they bear *them* not out into the utter court, to sanctify the people.

21 Then he brought me forth into the utter court, and caused me to pass by the four corners of the court; and, behold, in every corner of the court *there was* a court.

22 In the four corners of the court *there were* courts joined of forty **cubits* long and thirty broad: these four corners *were* of one measure.

23 And *there was* a row *of building* round about in them, round about them four, and *it was* made with boiling places under the rows round about.

24 Then said he unto me, These *are* the places of them that boil, where the ministers of the house shall boil the *sacrifice of the people.

The river flowing from the temple during the Millennium

47 Afterward he brought me again unto the door of the house; and, behold, waters issued out from under the threshold of the house eastward: for the forefront of the house *stood toward* the east, and the waters came down from under from the right side of the house, at the south *side* of the *altar.

2 Then brought he me out of the way of the gate northward, and led me about the way without unto the utter gate by the way that looketh eastward; and, behold, there ran out waters on the right side.

3 And when the man that had the line in his hand went forth eastward, he

46:17 the year of liberty. See Leviticus 25:10.
47:3 the man that had the line. See Ezekiel 40:3.

measured a thousand cubits, and he
brought me through the waters; the
waters *were* to the ankles.
4 Again he measured a thousand, and
brought me through the waters; the
waters *were* to the knees. Again he
measured a thousand, and brought me
through; the waters *were* to the loins.
5 Afterward he measured a thousand;
and it was a river that I could not pass
over: for the waters were risen, waters
to swim in, a river that could not be
passed over.
¶6 And he said unto me, Son of man,
hast thou seen *this?* Then he brought
me, and caused me to return to the
brink of the river.
7 Now when I had returned, behold, at
the bank of the river *were* very many
trees on the one side and on the other.
8 Then said he unto me, These waters
issue out toward the east country, and
go down into the desert, and go into the
sea: *which being* brought forth into the
sea, the waters shall be healed.
9 And it shall come to pass, *that* every
thing that liveth, which moveth,
whithersoever the rivers shall come,
shall live: and there shall be a very great
multitude of fish, because these waters
shall come thither: for they shall be
healed; and every thing shall live
whither the river cometh.
10 And it shall come to pass, *that* the
fishers shall stand upon it from En-
gedi even unto En-eglaim; they shall
be a *place* to spread forth nets; their
fish shall be according to their kinds,
as the fish of the great sea, exceeding
many.
11 But the miry places thereof and the
marishes thereof shall not be healed;
they shall be given to salt.
12 And by the river upon the bank
thereof, on this side and on that side,
shall grow all trees for meat, whose leaf
shall not fade, neither shall the fruit
thereof be consumed: it shall bring forth
new fruit according to his months, because their waters they issued out of
the sanctuary: and the fruit thereof
shall be for meat, and the leaf thereof
for medicine.

The borders of the land during the millennial Kingdom

¶13 Thus saith the Lord GOD; This
shall be the border, whereby ye shall
inherit the land according to the twelve
tribes of Israel: *Joseph *shall have two*
portions.
14 And ye shall inherit it, one as well
as another: *concerning* the which I lifted up mine hand to give it unto your
fathers: and this land shall fall unto you
for inheritance.
15 And this *shall be* the border of the
land toward the north side, from the
great sea, the way of Hethlon, as men
go to Zedad;
16 Hamath, Berothah, Sibraim, which
is between the border of *Damascus

47:1-3 THE RIVER OF BLESSINGS

In Revelation 22:1, the blessings of eternal life are represented as a river in heaven proceeding from the "throne of God and of the Lamb." In Ezekiel 47, the blessings of eternal life, flowing from the glorified Lord, who will have returned to the earth to be its King, are set forth as the emerging of a mighty river. These blessings will flow to the entire world, which shall be "full of the knowledge of the LORD, as the waters cover the sea" (Isa. 11:9). Similar predictions are found in Joel 3:18 and Zechariah 14:8.

The increasing depth of the river ("to the ankles," vs. 3) may well symbolize two things. It might remind us that the further we go in the river of life with the Lord Jesus Christ, the deeper and more all-sufficient we find His blessings. That which is comparable to water up to the ankle becomes an overwhelming flood of grace as we get to know Him on a deeper level. The varying depths of the river may also remind us that there are portions of the Word of God which are simple and easy to understand, others which are profound, requiring a deeper search, and still other Scriptures of such infinite significance as to overwhelm us (Rom. 11:33).

and the border of Hamath; Hazar-hatticon, which *is* by the coast of Hauran.

17 And the border from the sea shall be Hazar-enan, the border of Damascus, and the north northward, and the border of Hamath. And *this is* the north side.

18 And the east side ye shall measure from Hauran, and from Damascus, and from *Gilead, and from the land of Israel *by* Jordan, from the border unto the east sea. And *this is* the east side.

19 And the south side southward, from Tamar *even* to the waters of strife *in* Kadesh, the river to the great sea. And *this is* the south side southward.

20 The west side also *shall be* the great sea from the border, till a man come over against Hamath. This *is* the west side.

21 So shall ye divide this land unto you according to the tribes of Israel.

¶22 And it shall come to pass, *that* ye shall divide it by lot for an inheritance unto you, and to the strangers that sojourn among you, which shall beget children among you: and they shall be unto you as born in the country among the children of Israel; they shall have inheritance with you among the tribes of Israel.

23 And it shall come to pass, *that* in what tribe the stranger sojourneth, there shall ye give *him* his inheritance, saith the Lord GOD.

The divisions of the land during the millennial Kingdom

48 Now these *are* the names of the tribes. From the north end to the coast of the way of Hethlon, as one goeth to Hamath, Hazar-enan, the border of Damascus northward, to the coast of Hamath; for these are his sides east *and* west; a *portion for* Dan.

2 And by the border of Dan, from the east side unto the west side, a *portion for* Asher.

3 And by the border of Asher, from the east side even unto the west side, a *portion for* Naphtali.

4 And by the border of Naphtali, from the east side unto the west side, a *portion for* Manasseh.

5 And by the border of Manasseh, from the east side unto the west side, a *portion for* Ephraim.

6 And by the border of Ephraim, from the east side even unto the west side, a *portion for* Reuben.

7 And by the border of Reuben, from the east side unto the west side, a *portion for* Judah.

¶8 And by the border of Judah, from the east side unto the west side, shall be the offering which ye shall offer of five and twenty thousand *reeds in* breadth, and *in* length as one of the *other* parts, from the east side unto the west side: and the sanctuary shall be in the midst of it.

9 The oblation that ye shall offer unto the LORD *shall be* of five and twenty thousand in length, and of ten thousand in breadth.

10 And for them, *even* for the priests, shall be *this* holy oblation; toward the north five and twenty thousand *in length,* and toward the west ten thousand in breadth, and toward the east ten thousand in breadth, and toward the south five and twenty thousand in length: and the sanctuary of the LORD shall be in the midst thereof.

11 *It shall be* for the priests that are sanctified of the sons of Zadok; which have kept my charge, which went not astray when the children of Israel went astray, as the Levites went astray.

12 And *this* oblation of the land that is

48:1 a portion for Dan. It is interesting to note that when God divides the land of Palestine among the tribes of Israel for the millennial reign of Christ, He will not make the division by lot, which was carried on under Joshua when the children of Israel entered the land. Israel's permanent inheritance in the land of Canaan will not be the result of chance.

offered shall be unto them a thing most
holy by the border of the Levites.
13 And over against the border of the
priests the Levites *shall have* five and
twenty thousand in length, and ten
thousand in breadth: all the length *shall*
be five and twenty thousand, and the
breadth ten thousand.
14 And they shall not sell of it, neither
exchange, nor alienate the firstfruits of
the land: for *it is* holy unto the LORD.
¶ 15 And the five thousand, that are left
in the breadth over against the five and
twenty thousand, shall be a profane
place for the city, for dwelling, and for
suburbs: and the city shall be in the
midst thereof.
16 And these *shall be* the measures
thereof; the north side four thousand
and five hundred, and the south side
four thousand and five hundred, and on
the east side four thousand and five
hundred, and the west side four thousand and five hundred.
17 And the suburbs of the city shall be
toward the north two hundred and fifty, and toward the south two hundred
and fifty, and toward the east two hundred and fifty, and toward the west two
hundred and fifty.
18 And the residue in length over
against the oblation of the holy *portion*
shall be ten thousand eastward, and
ten thousand westward: and it shall be
over against the oblation of the holy
portion; and the increase thereof shall
be for food unto them that serve the
city.
19 And they that serve the city shall
serve it out of all the tribes of Israel.
20 All the oblation *shall be* five and
twenty thousand by five and twenty
thousand: ye shall offer the holy oblation foursquare, with the possession of
the city.
¶ 21 And the residue *shall be* for the
prince, on the one side and on the other
of the holy oblation, and of the possession of the city, over against the five and
twenty thousand of the oblation toward
the east border, and westward over
against the five and twenty thousand
toward the west border, over against
the portions for the prince: and it shall
be the holy oblation; and the sanctuary
of the house *shall be* in the midst
thereof.
22 Moreover from the possession of
the Levites, and from the possession of
the city, *being* in the midst *of that* which
is the prince's, between the border of
Judah and the border of Benjamin, shall
be for the prince.
23 As for the rest of the tribes, from
the east side unto the west side, Benjamin *shall have* a *portion.*
24 And by the border of Benjamin,
from the east side unto the west side,
Simeon *shall have* a *portion.*
25 And by the border of Simeon, from
the east side unto the west side, Issachar a *portion.*
26 And by the border of Issachar, from
the east side unto the west side, Zebulun a *portion.*
27 And by the border of Zebulun, from
the east side unto the west side, Gad a
portion.
28 And by the border of Gad, at the
south side southward, the border shall
be even from Tamar *unto* the waters of
strife *in* Kadesh, *and* to the river toward the great sea.
29 This *is* the land which ye shall divide by lot unto the tribes of Israel for
inheritance, and these *are* their portions, saith the Lord GOD.
¶ 30 And these *are* the goings out of

48:35 God's Presence

This brief phrase, "The LORD is there" gathers into itself all of the blessings that God has promised to give to the earth and to His people Israel during the reign of Christ. Material prosperity, economic security, political deliverance from unjust rule would be empty things were it not for the presence of the LORD Himself. The glory of the *Millennium is the fact that the LORD is there. The book of Ezekiel opens with a vision of the glory of God and closes with His presence in the midst of His people.

the city on the north side, four thousand
and five hundred measures.
31 And the gates of the city *shall be*
after the names of the tribes of Israel:
three gates northward; one gate of Reuben, one gate of Judah, one gate of Levi.
32 And at the east side four thousand
and five hundred: and three gates; and
one gate of Joseph, one gate of Benjamin, one gate of Dan.
33 And at the south side four thousand
and five hundred measures: and three
gates; one gate of Simeon, one gate of
Issachar, one gate of Zebulun.
34 At the west side four thousand and
five hundred, *with* their three gates;
one gate of Gad, one gate of Asher, one
gate of Naphtali.
35 *It was* round about eighteen thousand *measures:* and the name of the city
from *that* day *shall be,* The LORD *is*
there.

The Book of

DANIEL

THEME

This important prophecy describes the future course of world rule from Daniel's time to the *Millennium, or the coming of Christ to reign. This period is called in the Bible the *Times of the Gentiles. Daniel describes the course and character of the Gentile rule, and then from chapter 7 on deals in detail with its effect on the Jews and Jerusalem.

THE WRITER

Daniel, who wrote the book, was a godly young Jew of royal birth and was among the captives taken to Babylon by Nebuchadnezzar. He lived during the years 606–534 B.C., at the same time, therefore, as Ezekiel, Ezra, and Jeremiah.

His life and faith have been of tremendous influence through many centuries. The nation of Israel had departed from God and become very sinful. After repeated warnings from the prophets, God allowed Israel to be conquered by Nebuchadnezzar and carried away to Babylon. Jerusalem was destroyed and never again became completely independent. It has remained under a mixture of Jewish and Gentile rule and will not be under complete Jewish rule until the return of Christ at the Millennium (Revelation 19:11).

OUTLINE OF DANIEL

I.	The Story of Daniel to the Second Year of Nebuchadnezzar	Daniel 1:1-21
II.	Nebuchadnezzar's Visions	Daniel 2:1—4:37
III.	The Story of Daniel under Belshazzar and Darius	Daniel 5:1—6:28
IV.	The Visions of Daniel	Daniel 7:1—12:13

I. The Story of Daniel to the Second Year of Nebuchadnezzar (1:1-21)

Daniel the youth

1 In the third year of the reign of Jehoiakim king of *Judah came Nebuchadnezzar king of *Babylon unto *Jerusalem, and besieged it.
2 And the Lord gave Jehoiakim king of
Judah into his hand, with part of the
vessels of the house of *God: which he

1:1 Jehoiakim. See the description of the fall of Jerusalem in 2 Kings 24:1-2; 2 Chronicles 36:5-7; Jeremiah 25:1; 52:12-20.

1:1 came Nebuchadnezzar. Nebuchadnezzar invaded Judah the year his father died, making him king. This was the third year of Jehoiakim's reign as king. Jeremiah records that Nebuchadnezzar became king in Jehoiakim's fourth year (Jer. 25:1).

1:2 vessels of the house. See 2 Kings 20:12-18; Daniel 5:1-3.

carried into the land of Shinar to the
house of his god; and he brought the vessels into the treasure house of his god.
¶3 And the king spake unto Ashpenaz
the master of his eunuchs, that he
should bring *certain* of the children of
*Israel, and of the king's seed, and of
the princes;
4 Children in whom *was* no blemish,
but well favoured, and skilful in all wisdom, and cunning in knowledge, and
understanding science, and such as *had*
ability in them to stand in the king's
palace, and whom they might teach
the learning and the tongue of the Chaldeans.
5 And the king appointed them a daily provision of the king's meat, and of
the *wine which he drank: so nourish-
ing them three years, that at the end
thereof they might stand before the
king.
6 Now among these were of the children of Judah, Daniel, Hananiah, Mishael, and Azariah:
7 Unto whom the prince of the eunuchs gave names: for he gave unto
Daniel *the name* of Belteshazzar; and to
Hananiah, of Shadrach; and to Mishael,
of Meshach; and to Azariah, of Abed-
nego.
¶8 But Daniel purposed in his heart
that he would not defile himself with
the portion of the king's meat, nor with
the wine which he drank: therefore he
requested of the prince of the eunuchs
that he might not defile himself.
9 Now God had brought Daniel into
favour and tender love with the prince
of the eunuchs.
10 And the prince of the eunuchs said
unto Daniel, I fear my lord the king,
who hath appointed your meat and your
drink: for why should he see your faces

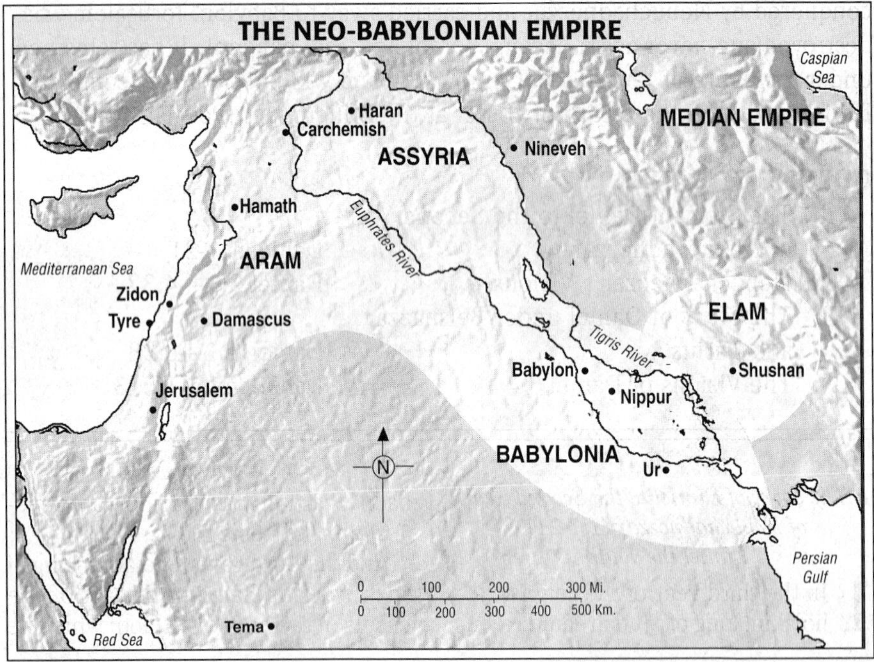

1:2 land of Shinar. The plain between the Tigris and the Euphrates on which Babylon was built.

1:8 purposed in his heart that he would not defile himself. The best food had been previously offered to idols, and therefore Daniel knew that it was wrong to eat it (compare Acts 15:29; 1 Cor. 8).

1:7 New Land, New Names
The Babylonian prince wanted these Jewish boys to forget their God. Each of them had been given a name by his parents that would remind him of the LORD. Their new names were to make them think of the Babylonian gods.

1. Daniel means *God is my judge*. Belteshazzar means *the prince of Bel* (a heathen god).
2. Hananiah means *God has been gracious*. Shadrach means *servant of Sin* (the moon god).
3. Mishael means *who is equal to God?* Meshach means *the shadow of the prince.*
4. Azariah means *God has helped*. Abednego means *servant of Ishtar* (a Babylonian goddess).

worse liking than the children which *are*
of your sort? then shall ye make *me*
endanger my head to the king.
11 Then said Daniel to Melzar, whom
the prince of the eunuchs had set over
Daniel, Hananiah, Mishael, and Azariah,
12 *Prove thy servants, I beseech thee,
ten days; and let them give us pulse to
eat, and water to drink.
13 Then let our countenances be
looked upon before thee, and the countenance of the children that eat of the
portion of the king's meat: and as thou
seest, deal with thy servants.
14 So he consented to them in this
matter, and proved them ten days.
15 And at the end of ten days their
countenances appeared fairer and fatter
in flesh than all the children which did
eat the portion of the king's meat.
16 Thus Melzar took away the portion
of their meat, and the wine that they
should drink; and gave them pulse.
¶ 17 As for these four children, God
gave them knowledge and skill in all
learning and wisdom: and Daniel had
understanding in all visions and
dreams.
18 Now at the end of the days that the
king had said he should bring them in,
then the prince of the eunuchs brought
them in before Nebuchadnezzar.
19 And the king communed with
them; and among them all was found
none like Daniel, Hananiah, Mishael,
and Azariah: therefore stood they before the king.
20 And in all matters of wisdom *and*
understanding, that the king enquired
of them, he found them ten times better than all the magicians *and* astrologers that *were* in all his realm.
21 And Daniel continued *even* unto the
first year of king *Cyrus.

II. Nebuchadnezzar's Visions
(2:1—4:37)

Nebuchadnezzar's dream

2 And in the second year of the
reign of Nebuchadnezzar Nebuchadnezzar dreamed dreams, wherewith his spirit was troubled, and his
sleep brake from him.

The wise men fail

2 Then the king commanded to call
the magicians, and the astrologers, and
the sorcerers, and the Chaldeans, for to
shew the king his dreams. So they came
and stood before the king.
3 And the king said unto them, I have
dreamed a dream, and my spirit was
troubled to know the dream.
4 Then spake the Chaldeans to the
king in Syriack, O king, live for ever:
tell thy servants the dream, and we will
shew the interpretation.

1:12 pulse. Herbs or vegetables grown from seed, therefore, a vegetable diet. See verse 8 note to find out why Daniel refused meat.

1:21 continued. Remained in office. Daniel served for sixty years in Babylon during the reigns of Nebuchadnezzar, Belshazzar, Darius, and Cyrus. (The kings who only reigned a short time are not mentioned. See Daniel 5:1 note, "Belshazzar.") Daniel lived for a few years longer than the first year of Cyrus's reign.

2:2 Chaldeans. The learned Chaldeans were supposed to be familiar with the wisdom of the ancients and the interpretation of dreams.

2:4 An Ancient Language
Syriack was the old Syrian language, also called Aramaic. Daniel used this language in 2:4–6:28 because the prophecies had to do with the Babylonians, and they understood this language. Thus the Babylonians were given the opportunity to learn of Daniel's God. After 6:28, he used Hebrew because his subject had to do with the fate of the Jews and Jerusalem. It was not necessary for the Babylonians to understand this.

5The king answered and said to the
Chaldeans, The thing is gone from me:
if ye will not make known unto me the
dream, with the interpretation thereof,
ye shall be cut in pieces, and your
houses shall be made a dunghill.
6But if ye shew the dream, and the
interpretation thereof, ye shall receive
of me gifts and rewards and great
honour: therefore shew me the dream,
and the interpretation thereof.
7They answered again and said, Let
the king tell his servants the dream,
and we will shew the interpretation
of it.
8The king answered and said, I
know of certainty that ye would gain
the time, because ye see the thing is
gone from me.
9But if ye will not make known unto
me the dream, *there is but* one decree
for you: for ye have prepared lying and
corrupt words to speak before me, till
the time be changed: therefore tell me
the dream, and I shall know that ye can
shew me the interpretation thereof.
¶10The Chaldeans answered before
the king, and said, There is not a man
upon the earth that can shew the king's
matter: therefore *there is* no king, lord,
nor ruler, *that* asked such things at any
magician, or astrologer, or Chaldean.
11And *it is* a rare thing that the king
requireth, and there is none other that
can shew it before the king, except the
gods, whose dwelling is not with flesh.
12For this cause the king was angry
and very furious, and commanded to
destroy all the wise *men* of Babylon.
13And the decree went forth that the
wise *men* should be slain; and they
sought Daniel and his fellows to be
slain.

The prayer meeting

¶14Then Daniel answered with counsel and wisdom to Arioch the captain of
the king's guard, which was gone forth
to slay the wise *men* of Babylon:
15He answered and said to Arioch the
king's captain, Why *is* the decree *so*
hasty from the king? Then Arioch made
the thing known to Daniel.
16Then Daniel went in, and desired of
the king that he would give him time,
and that he would shew the king the
interpretation.
17Then Daniel went to his house, and
made the thing known to Hananiah,
Mishael, and Azariah, his companions:
18That they would desire mercies of
the God of *heaven concerning this
secret; that Daniel and his fellows
should not perish with the rest of the
wise *men* of Babylon.

The dream revealed to Daniel

¶19Then was the secret revealed
unto Daniel in a night vision. Then
Daniel blessed the God of heaven.
20Daniel answered and said, Blessed
be the name of God for ever and ever:
for wisdom and might are his:
21And he changeth the times and the
seasons: he removeth kings, and
setteth up kings: he giveth wisdom
unto the wise, and knowledge to them
that know understanding:
22He revealeth the deep and secret
things: he knoweth what *is* in the darkness, and the light dwelleth with him.
23I thank thee, and praise thee, O
thou God of my fathers, who hast given
me wisdom and might, and hast made
known unto me now what we desired
of thee: for thou hast *now* made known
unto us the king's matter.
¶24Therefore Daniel went in unto Arioch, whom the king had ordained to
destroy the wise *men* of Babylon: he

went and said thus unto him; Destroy
not the wise *men* of Babylon: bring me
in before the king, and I will shew unto
the king the interpretation.
25 Then Arioch brought in Daniel before the king in haste and said thus unto
him, I have found a man of the captives
of Judah, that will make known unto the
king the interpretation.
26 The king answered and said to Daniel, whose name *was* Belteshazzar, Art
thou able to make known unto me the
dream which I have seen, and the interpretation thereof?
27 Daniel answered in the presence of
the king, and said, The secret which the
king hath demanded cannot the wise
men, the astrologers, the magicians, the
soothsayers, shew unto the king;
28 But there is a God in heaven that
revealeth secrets, and maketh known to
the king Nebuchadnezzar what shall be
in the latter days. Thy dream, and the
visions of thy head upon thy bed, are
these;
29 As for thee, O king, thy thoughts
came *into thy mind* upon thy bed, what
should come to pass hereafter: and he
that revealeth secrets maketh known to
thee what shall come to pass.
30 But as for me, this secret is not
revealed to me for *any* wisdom that I
have more than any living, but for *their*
sakes that shall make known the interpretation to the king, and that thou
mightest know the thoughts of thy
heart.
¶31 Thou, O king, sawest, and behold
a great image. This great image, whose
brightness *was* excellent, stood before
thee; and the form thereof *was* terrible.
32 This image's head *was* of fine gold,
his breast and his arms of silver, his
belly and his thighs of brass,
33 His legs of iron, his feet part of iron
and part of clay.
34 Thou sawest till that a stone was
cut out without hands, which smote the
image upon his feet *that were* of iron and
clay, and brake them to pieces.
35 Then was the iron, the clay, the
brass, the silver, and the gold, broken
to pieces together, and became like the
chaff of the summer threshingfloors;
and the wind carried them away, that no
place was found for them: and the stone
that smote the image became a great
mountain, and filled the whole earth.

The interpretation of the dream

¶36 This *is* the dream; and we will tell
the interpretation thereof before the
king.

*The world empires of Babylon,
Persia, Greece, and Rome*

37 Thou, O king, *art* a king of kings: for
the God of heaven hath given thee a

2:31 THE GREAT IMAGE

This image gives a very clear picture of the empires that would rule a great portion of the world from the time of Daniel to the coming of Christ's reign. They were first, Babylon, shown by the head (vss. 37-38); second, Media-Persia, shown in the two arms for the two parts of the empire (vs. 39); third, Greece, which was powerful at about the end of Old Testament times (vs. 39); fourth, Rome, which later divided into Eastern and Western Empires shown by the two legs. Although it has not yet occurred, it will divide later into ten different kingdoms, shown by the ten toes (vs. 41).

The metals of the image decrease in purity but increase in strength. This shows that each ruler declined in his own personal character but increased in the extent and strength of his empire. However, the Roman Empire as it will be in the future will lose even that great strength, since the strong iron will be mixed with brittle clay (vss. 40-43). The sudden destruction (vss. 34-35) of this coming world empire of the Gentiles will occur through the coming of the Lord Jesus Christ in person to overthrow the Gentiles (compare Rev. 16:14; 19:11-21), and to establish His *kingdom (compare Dan. 7:1-28; Rev. 20:1-6), which was rejected at His first advent (John 1:11).

2:34 stone. See 2:45 note.

kingdom, power, and strength, and
glory.
38And wheresoever the children of
men dwell, the beasts of the field and
the fowls of the heaven hath he given
into thine hand, and hath made thee
ruler over them all. Thou *art* this head
of gold.
39And after thee shall arise another
kingdom inferior to thee, and another
third kingdom of brass, which shall bear
rule over all the earth.
40And the fourth kingdom shall be
strong as iron: forasmuch as iron breaketh in pieces and subdueth all *things:*
and as iron that breaketh all these, shall
it break in pieces and bruise.
41And whereas thou sawest the feet
and toes, part of potters' clay, and part
of iron, the kingdom shall be divided;
but there shall be in it of the strength
of the iron, forasmuch as thou sawest
the iron mixed with miry clay.
42And *as* the toes of the feet *were* part
of iron, and part of clay, *so* the kingdom
shall be partly strong, and partly broken.
43And whereas thou sawest iron
mixed with miry clay, they shall mingle
themselves with the seed of men: but
they shall not cleave one to another,
even as iron is not mixed with clay.

The reign of Messiah

44And in the days of these kings shall
the God of heaven set up a kingdom,
which shall never be destroyed: and the
kingdom shall not be left to other people, *but* it shall break in pieces and consume all these kingdoms, and it shall
stand for ever.
45Forasmuch as thou sawest that the
stone was cut out of the mountain without hands, and that it brake in pieces the
iron, the brass, the clay, the silver, and
the gold; the great God hath made
known to the king what shall come to
pass hereafter: and the dream *is* certain, and the interpretation thereof
sure.

Daniel promoted

¶46Then the king Nebuchadnezzar
fell upon his face, and worshipped Daniel, and commanded that they should
offer an *oblation and sweet odours
unto him.
47The king answered unto Daniel,
and said, Of a truth *it is,* that your God
is a God of gods, and a Lord of kings, and
a revealer of secrets, seeing thou
couldst reveal this secret.
48Then the king made Daniel a
great man, and gave him many great
gifts, and made him ruler over the
whole province of Babylon, and chief of
the governors over all the wise *men* of
Babylon.
49Then Daniel requested of the king,
and he set Shadrach, Meshach, and
Abed-nego, over the affairs of the province of Babylon: but Daniel *sat* in the
gate of the king.

Idolatry enforced

3 Nebuchadnezzar the king made an
image of gold, whose height *was*
threescore *cubits, *and* the breadth

3:1 The Image of Gold
Nebuchadnezzar had many people of many religions under his rule. He thought that by uniting them in the worship of this image, he would bind them together and strengthen his position and kingdom. Despotism like this has been seen in the world more than once. This is what the False Prophet (the second beast) of Revelation 13:13-15 will do when he sets up the image of the Beast during the future *Tribulation, just before the Lord Jesus Christ comes in power to reign over the whole earth.

2:45 the stone. This means that a sudden stupendous event will end the Gentile rule. Christ is often spoken of as the stone (see 1 Pet. 2:4 notes), and this refers to the coming of Christ to set up His *kingdom.

2:49 sat in the gate of the king. Daniel became the prime minister.

thereof six cubits: he set it up in the
plain of Dura, in the province of Babylon.
2Then Nebuchadnezzar the king sent
to gather together the princes, the governors, and the captains, the judges, the
treasurers, the counsellors, the sheriffs, and all the rulers of the provinces,
to come to the dedication of the image
which Nebuchadnezzar the king had
set up.
3Then the princes, the governors,
and captains, the judges, the treasurers,
the counsellors, the sheriffs, and all the
rulers of the provinces, were gathered
together unto the dedication of the image that Nebuchadnezzar the king had
set up; and they stood before the image
that Nebuchadnezzar had set up.
4Then an herald cried aloud, To you
it is commanded, O people, nations, and
languages,
5*That* at what time ye hear the sound
of the cornet, flute, harp, sackbut,
*psaltery, dulcimer, and all kinds of
musick, ye fall down and worship the
golden image that Nebuchadnezzar the
king hath set up:
6And whoso falleth not down and
worshippeth shall the same hour be cast
into the midst of a burning fiery furnace.
7Therefore at that time, when all the
people heard the sound of the cornet,
flute, harp, sackbut, psaltery, and all
kinds of musick, all the people, the nations, and the languages, fell down *and*
worshipped the golden image that Nebuchadnezzar the king had set up.

The faithful few

¶8Wherefore at that time certain
Chaldeans came near, and accused the
Jews.
9They spake and said to the king
Nebuchadnezzar, O king, live for ever.
10Thou, O king, hast made a decree,
that every man that shall hear the
sound of the cornet, flute, harp, sackbut, psaltery, and dulcimer, and all kinds
of musick, shall fall down and worship
the golden image:
11And whoso falleth not down and
worshippeth, *that* he should be cast into
the midst of a burning fiery furnace.
12There are certain Jews whom thou
hast set over the affairs of the province
of Babylon, Shadrach, Meshach, and
Abed-nego; these men, O king, have
not regarded thee: they serve not thy
gods, nor worship the golden image
which thou hast set up.
¶13Then Nebuchadnezzar in *his* rage
and fury commanded to bring Shadrach,
Meshach, and Abed-nego. Then they
brought these men before the king.
14Nebuchadnezzar spake and said
unto them, *Is it* true, O Shadrach, Meshach, and Abed-nego, do not ye serve
my gods, nor worship the golden image
which I have set up?
15Now if ye be ready that at what time
ye hear the sound of the cornet, flute,
harp, sackbut, psaltery, and dulcimer,
and all kinds of musick, ye fall down and
worship the image which I have made;
well: but if ye worship not, ye shall be
cast the same hour into the midst of a
burning fiery furnace; and who *is* that
God that shall deliver you out of my
hands?
16Shadrach, Meshach, and Abed-
nego, answered and said to the king, O
Nebuchadnezzar, we *are* not careful to
answer thee in this matter.
17If it be *so,* our God whom we serve
is able to deliver us from the burning
fiery furnace, and he will deliver *us* out
of thine hand, O king.
18But if not, be it known unto thee,
O king, that we will not serve thy gods,
nor worship the golden image which
thou hast set up.

God's deliverance

¶19Then was Nebuchadnezzar full of
fury, and the form of his visage was
changed against Shadrach, Meshach,
and Abed-nego: *therefore* he spake, and
commanded that they should heat the
furnace one seven times more than it
was wont to be heated.
20And he commanded the most

mighty men that *were* in his army to bind Shadrach, Meshach, and Abed-nego, *and* to cast *them* into the burning fiery furnace.

21 Then these men were bound in their coats, their hosen, and their hats, and their *other* garments, and were cast into the midst of the burning fiery furnace.

22 Therefore because the king's commandment was urgent, and the furnace exceeding hot, the flame of the fire slew those men that took up Shadrach, Meshach, and Abed-nego.

23 And these three men, Shadrach, Meshach, and Abed-nego, fell down bound into the midst of the burning fiery furnace.

24 Then Nebuchadnezzar the king was astonied, and rose up in haste, *and* spake, and said unto his counsellors, Did not we cast three men bound into the midst of the fire? They answered and said unto the king, True, O king.

25 He answered and said, Lo, I see four men loose, walking in the midst of the fire, and they have no hurt; and the form of the fourth is like the Son of God.

The decree

¶26 Then Nebuchadnezzar came near to the mouth of the burning fiery furnace, *and* spake, and said, Shadrach, Meshach, and Abed-nego, ye servants of the most high God, come forth, and come *hither.* Then Shadrach, Meshach, and Abed-nego, came forth of the midst of the fire.

27 And the princes, governors, and captains, and the king's counsellors, being gathered together, saw these men, upon whose bodies the fire had no power, nor was an hair of their head singed, neither were their coats changed, nor the smell of fire had passed on them.

28 *Then* Nebuchadnezzar spake, and said, Blessed *be* the God of Shadrach, Meshach, and Abed-nego, who hath sent his *angel, and delivered his servants that trusted in him, and have changed the king's word, and yielded their bodies, that they might not serve nor worship any god, except their own God.

29 Therefore I make a decree, That every people, nation, and language, which speak any thing amiss against the God of Shadrach, Meshach, and Abed-nego, shall be cut in pieces, and their houses shall be made a dunghill: because there is no other God that can deliver after this sort.

30 Then the king promoted Shadrach, Meshach, and Abed-nego, in the province of Babylon.

The proclamation

4 Nebuchadnezzar the king, unto all people, nations, and languages, that dwell in all the earth; Peace be multiplied unto you.

2 I thought it good to shew the signs and wonders that the high God hath wrought toward me.

3 How great *are* his signs! and how mighty *are* his wonders! his kingdom *is* an everlasting kingdom, and his dominion *is* from generation to generation.

The vision

¶4 I Nebuchadnezzar was at rest in mine house, and flourishing in my palace:

5 I saw a dream which made me afraid, and the thoughts upon my bed and the visions of my head troubled me.

6 Therefore made I a decree to bring in all the wise *men* of Babylon before me, that they might make known unto me the interpretation of the dream.

7 Then came in the magicians, the

3:21 hosen. Trousers, pants.

3:25 like the Son of God. This was undoubtedly our Lord Jesus Christ Himself. See *theophany. How He cares for His own! It is an assurance to us today of His presence with us. See Matthew 18:20.

astrologers, the Chaldeans, and the
soothsayers: and I told the dream before them; but they did not make known
unto me the interpretation thereof.
¶8But at the last Daniel came in before me, whose name *was* Belteshazzar,
according to the name of my god, and
in whom *is* the spirit of the holy gods:
and before him I told the dream, *saying,*
9O Belteshazzar, master of the magicians, because I know that the spirit of
the holy gods *is* in thee, and no secret
troubleth thee, tell me the visions of my
dream that I have seen, and the interpretation thereof.
10Thus *were* the visions of mine head
in my bed; I saw, and behold a tree in
the midst of the earth, and the height
thereof *was* great.
11The tree grew, and was strong, and
the height thereof reached unto heav-
en, and the sight thereof to the end of
all the earth:
12The leaves thereof *were* fair, and the
fruit thereof much, and in it *was* meat
for all: the beasts of the field had shadow under it, and the fowls of the heav-
en dwelt in the boughs thereof, and all
flesh was fed of it.
13I saw in the visions of my head upon
my bed, and, behold, a watcher and an
holy one came down from heaven;
14He cried aloud, and said thus, Hew
down the tree, and cut off his branches,
shake off his leaves, and scatter his
fruit: let the beasts get away from under it, and the fowls from his branches:
15Nevertheless leave the stump of
his roots in the earth, even with a band
of iron and brass, in the tender grass of
the field; and let it be wet with the dew
of heaven, and *let* his portion *be* with the
beasts in the grass of the earth:
16Let his heart be changed from
man's, and let a beast's heart be given
unto him; and let seven times pass over
him.
17This matter *is* by the decree of the
watchers, and the demand by the word
of the holy ones: to the intent that the
living may know that the most High
ruleth in the kingdom of men, and
giveth it to whomsoever he will, and
setteth up over it the basest of men.
18This dream I king Nebuchadnezzar
have seen. Now thou, O Belteshazzar,
declare the interpretation thereof, forasmuch as all the wise *men* of my kingdom are not able to make known unto
me the interpretation: but thou *art* able;
for the spirit of the holy gods *is* in thee.

The interpretation

¶19Then Daniel, whose name *was*
Belteshazzar, was astonied for one hour,
and his thoughts troubled him. The king
spake, and said, Belteshazzar, let not
the dream, or the interpretation thereof, trouble thee. Belteshazzar answered
and said, My lord, the dream *be* to them
that hate thee, and the interpretation
thereof to thine enemies.
20The tree that thou sawest, which
grew, and was strong, whose height
reached unto the heaven, and the sight
thereof to all the earth;
21Whose leaves *were* fair, and the fruit
thereof much, and in it *was* meat for all;
under which the beasts of the field
dwelt, and upon whose branches the
fowls of the heaven had their habitation:
22It *is* thou, O king, that art grown and
become strong: for thy greatness is
grown, and reacheth unto heaven, and
thy dominion to the end of the earth.
23And whereas the king saw a watcher and an holy one coming down from
heaven, and saying, Hew the tree down,
and destroy it; yet leave the stump of
the roots thereof in the earth, even with

4:10 a tree. A symbol of greatness, either of a king or a nation (see vs. 22).
4:13 a watcher. Literally, *messenger*. Babylonians believed in spiritual beings they called "watchers," who watched over the universe. Christians would think of them as angels. See also verses 17 and 23.
4:16 seven times. Seven years.

a band of iron and brass, in the tender
grass of the field; and let it be wet with
the dew of heaven, and *let* his portion
be with the beasts of the field, till seven
times pass over him;
24 This *is* the interpretation, O king,
and this *is* the decree of the most High,
which is come upon my lord the king:
25 That they shall drive thee from
men, and thy dwelling shall be with the
beasts of the field, and they shall make
thee to eat grass as oxen, and they shall
wet thee with the dew of heaven, and
seven times shall pass over thee, till
thou know that the most High ruleth in
the kingdom of men, and giveth it to
whomsoever he will.
26 And whereas they commanded to
leave the stump of the tree roots; thy
kingdom shall be sure unto thee, after
that thou shalt have known that the
heavens do rule.
27 Wherefore, O king, let my counsel
be acceptable unto thee, and break off
thy sins by *righteousness, and thine
iniquities by shewing mercy to the
poor; if it may be a lengthening of thy
tranquility.

Nebuchadnezzar's humiliation and restoration

¶28 All this came upon the king Nebuchadnezzar.
29 At the end of twelve months he
walked in the palace of the kingdom of
Babylon.
30 The king spake, and said, Is not this
great Babylon, that I have built for the
house of the kingdom by the might of
my power, and for the honour of my
majesty?
31 While the word *was* in the king's
mouth, there fell a voice from heaven,
saying, O king Nebuchadnezzar, to thee
it is spoken; The kingdom is departed
from thee.
32 And they shall drive thee from
men, and thy dwelling *shall be* with the
beasts of the field: they shall make thee
to eat grass as oxen, and seven times
shall pass over thee, until thou know
that the most High ruleth in the kingdom of men, and giveth it to whomsoever he will.
33 The same hour was the thing fulfilled upon Nebuchadnezzar: and he was
driven from men, and did eat grass as
oxen, and his body was wet with the
dew of heaven, till his hairs were grown
like eagles' *feathers,* and his nails like
birds' *claws.*
34 And at the end of the days I Nebuchadnezzar lifted up mine eyes unto
heaven, and mine understanding returned unto me, and I blessed the most
High, and I praised and honoured him
that liveth for ever, whose dominion
is an everlasting dominion, and his
kingdom *is* from generation to generation:
35 And all the inhabitants of the earth
are reputed as nothing: and he doeth
according to his will in the army of
heaven, and *among* the inhabitants of
the earth: and none can stay his hand,
or say unto him, What doest thou?
36 At the same time my reason returned unto me; and for the glory of my
kingdom, mine honour and brightness
returned unto me; and my counsellors
and my lords sought unto me; and I was
established in my kingdom, and excellent majesty was added unto me.
37 Now I Nebuchadnezzar praise and
extol and honour the King of heaven, all
whose works *are* truth, and his ways
*judgment: and those that walk in pride
he is able to abase.

III. The Story of Daniel under Belshazzar and Darius (5:1—6:28)

Daniel under Belshazzar

5 Belshazzar the king made a great
feast to a thousand of his lords, and
drank wine before the thousand.
2 Belshazzar, whiles he tasted the
wine, commanded to bring the golden
and silver vessels which his father Nebuchadnezzar had taken out of the temple which *was* in Jerusalem; that the
king, and his princes, his wives, and his
concubines, might drink therein.

3 Then they brought the golden vessels that were taken out of the temple
of the house of God which *was* at Jerusalem; and the king, and his princes, his
wives, and his concubines, drank in
them.
4 They drank wine, and praised the
gods of gold, and of silver, of brass, of
iron, of wood, and of stone.

The handwriting on the wall

¶5 In the same hour came forth fingers of a man's hand, and wrote over
against the candlestick upon the
plaister of the wall of the king's palace:
and the king saw the part of the hand
that wrote.
6 Then the king's countenance was
changed, and his thoughts troubled him,
so that the joints of his loins were
loosed, and his knees smote one against
another.
7 The king cried aloud to bring in the
astrologers, the Chaldeans, and the
soothsayers. *And* the king spake, and
said to the wise *men* of Babylon, Whosoever shall read this writing, and shew
me the interpretation thereof, shall be
clothed with scarlet, and *have* a chain of
gold about his neck, and shall be the
third ruler in the kingdom.
8 Then came in all the king's wise
men: but they could not read the writing, nor make known to the king the
interpretation thereof.
9 Then was king Belshazzar greatly
troubled, and his countenance was
changed in him, and his lords were
astonied.
¶10 *Now* the queen, by reason of the
words of the king and his lords, came
into the banquet house: *and* the queen
spake and said, O king, live for ever: let
not thy thoughts trouble thee, nor let
thy countenance be changed:
11 There is a man in thy kingdom, in
whom *is* the spirit of the holy gods; and
in the days of thy father light and understanding and wisdom, like the wisdom of the gods, was found in him;
whom the king Nebuchadnezzar thy
father, the king, *I say,* thy father, made
master of the magicians, astrologers,
Chaldeans, *and* soothsayers;
12 Forasmuch as an excellent spirit,
and knowledge, and understanding, in-
terpreting of dreams, and shewing of
hard sentences, and dissolving of
doubts, were found in the same Daniel,
whom the king named Belteshazzar:
now let Daniel be called, and he will
shew the interpretation.
13 Then was Daniel brought in before
the king. *And* the king spake and said
unto Daniel, *Art* thou that Daniel, which
art of the children of the captivity of
Judah, whom the king my father
brought out of Jewry?
14 I have even heard of thee, that the
spirit of the gods *is* in thee, and *that*
light and understanding and excellent
wisdom is found in thee.
15 And now the wise *men,* the astrologers, have been brought in before me,

5:1 BELSHAZZAR

The grandson or descendant of Nebuchadnezzar (called in vs. 2, "his father"). The word "father" is often used in the Bible to indicate "ancestor." Nebuchadnezzar ruled from 604 to 561 B.C. Evil-Merodach (Awil-Marduk), his son, succeeded him and reigned only two years, from 561 to 560 B.C. Nebuchadnezzar's brother-in-law, Neriglissar, reigned then for four years, from 560 to 556 B.C. After a two-month reign by Labashi-Marduk in 556 B.C., the Babylonian Empire continued from 556 to 539 B.C. under the command of Nabonidus, Belshazzar's father. Belshazzar coreigned with his father from 553 to 539. While Nabonidus was away fighting the Persians, Belshazzar ruled as viceroy in Babylon. See Jeremiah 27:7: "All nations shall serve him [Nebuchadnezzar] and his son and his son's son until the very time of his land come." This means that Israel would continue under Babylonian rule until God's purpose for them was fulfilled.

5:3 vessels. See verse 23 and Daniel 1:2.

that they should read this writing, and make known unto me the interpretation thereof: but they could not shew the interpretation of the thing:

16 And I have heard of thee, that thou canst make interpretations, and dissolve doubts: now if thou canst read the writing, and make known to me the interpretation thereof, thou shalt be clothed with scarlet, and *have* a chain of gold about thy neck, and shalt be the third ruler in the kingdom.

¶ 17 Then Daniel answered and said before the king, Let thy gifts be to thyself, and give thy rewards to another; yet I will read the writing unto the king, and make known to him the interpretation.

18 O thou king, the most high God gave Nebuchadnezzar thy father a kingdom, and majesty, and glory, and honour:

19 And for the majesty that he gave him, all people, nations, and languages, trembled and feared before him: whom he would he slew; and whom he would he kept alive; and whom he would he set up; and whom he would he put down.

20 But when his heart was lifted up, and his mind hardened in pride, he was deposed from his kingly throne, and they took his glory from him:

21 And he was driven from the sons of men; and his heart was made like the beasts, and his dwelling *was* with the wild asses: they fed him with grass like oxen, and his body was wet with the dew of heaven; till he knew that the most high God ruled in the kingdom of men, and *that* he appointeth over it whomsoever he will.

22 And thou his son, O Belshazzar, hast not humbled thine heart, though thou knewest all this;

23 But hast lifted up thyself against the Lord of heaven; and they have brought the vessels of his house before thee, and thou, and thy lords, thy wives, and thy concubines, have drunk wine in them; and thou hast praised the gods of silver, and gold, of brass, iron, wood, and stone, which see not, nor hear, nor know: and the God in whose hand thy breath *is,* and whose *are* all thy ways, hast thou not glorified:

24 Then was the part of the hand sent from him; and this writing was written.

¶ 25 And this *is* the writing that was written, MENE, MENE, TEKEL, UPHARSIN.

26 This *is* the interpretation of the thing: MENE; God hath numbered thy kingdom, and finished it.

27 TEKEL; Thou art weighed in the balances, and art found wanting.

28 PERES; Thy kingdom is divided, and given to the *Medes and Persians.

5:28 The Medes and the Persians
The kingdom of Media had conquered Assyria and had united with the rising kingdom of Persia about 558 B.C. They defeated Nabonidus (see vs. 1 note, "Belshazzar") and besieged Babylon, which was thought to be absolutely safe. But by turning the river, which flowed through the city, from its course, they entered by the dry riverbed under the walls and, surprising the feasting Babylonians, took the city in 539 B.C.

29 Then commanded Belshazzar, and they clothed Daniel with scarlet, and *put* a chain of gold about his neck, and made a proclamation concerning him, that he should be the third ruler in the kingdom.

¶ 30 In that night was Belshazzar the king of the Chaldeans slain.

31 And *Darius the Median took the

5:16 third ruler. Belshazzar himself was the second ruler as viceroy for his father. See also verses 7 and 29.

5:31 Darius the Median. He was probably a general of the royal house of Media. Although Media was the older kingdom, Persia was the stronger, so Darius only ruled as viceroy over Babylon for Cyrus, the emperor of the whole Persian Empire.

kingdom, *being* about threescore and
two years old.

Daniel under Darius

6 It pleased Darius to set over the
kingdom an hundred and twenty
princes, which should be over the
whole kingdom;
[2]And over these three presidents; of
whom Daniel *was* first: that the princes
might give accounts unto them, and the
king should have no damage.
[3]Then this Daniel was preferred
above the presidents and princes, because an excellent spirit *was* in him;
and the king thought to set him over the
whole realm.

The plot against Daniel

¶[4]Then the presidents and princes
sought to find occasion against Daniel
concerning the kingdom; but they could
find none occasion nor fault; forasmuch
as he *was* faithful, neither was there any
error or fault found in him.
[5]Then said these men, We shall not
find any occasion against this Daniel,
except we find *it* against him concerning the *law of his God.
[6]Then these presidents and princes
assembled together to the king, and
said thus unto him, King Darius, live for
ever.
[7]All the presidents of the kingdom,
the governors, and the princes, the
counsellors, and the captains, have consulted together to establish a royal statute, and to make a firm decree, that
whosoever shall ask a petition of any
God or man for thirty days, save of thee,
O king, he shall be cast into the den of
lions.
[8]Now, O king, establish the decree,
and sign the writing, that it be not
changed, according to the law of the
Medes and Persians, which altereth not.
[9]Wherefore king Darius signed the
writing and the decree.
¶[10]Now when Daniel knew that the
writing was signed, he went into his
house; and his windows being open in
his chamber toward Jerusalem, he
kneeled upon his knees three times a
day, and prayed, and gave thanks before
his God, as he did aforetime.
[11]Then these men assembled, and
found Daniel praying and making supplication before his God.
[12]Then they came near, and spake
before the king concerning the king's
decree; Hast thou not signed a decree,
that every man that shall ask *a petition*
of any God or man within thirty days,
save of thee, O king, shall be cast into
the den of lions? The king answered
and said, The thing *is* true, according to
the law of the Medes and Persians,
which altereth not.
[13]Then answered they and said before the king, That Daniel, which *is* of
the children of the captivity of Judah,
regardeth not thee, O king, nor the decree that thou hast signed, but maketh
his petition three times a day.
[14]Then the king, when he heard *these*
words, was sore displeased with himself, and set *his* heart on Daniel to deliver him: and he laboured till the going
down of the sun to deliver him.
[15]Then these men assembled unto
the king, and said unto the king, Know,
O king, that the law of the Medes and
Persians *is*, That no decree nor statute
which the king establisheth may be
changed.

The lion's den

¶[16]Then the king commanded, and
they brought Daniel, and cast *him* into
the den of lions. *Now* the king spake and

6:8 the law of the Medes and Persians. See Esther 1:19. The rulers of this second empire did not have as much power as Nebuchadnezzar, but they were bound by the laws and influenced by the nobles. The laws of the Medes and Persians were never revoked or changed (see vs. 15).
6:10 toward Jerusalem. First Kings 8:29-50 and Psalm 5:7 explain this.

said unto Daniel, Thy God whom thou
servest continually, he will deliver thee.
17And a stone was brought, and laid
upon the mouth of the den; and the king
sealed it with his own signet, and with
the signet of his lords; that the purpose
might not be changed concerning
Daniel.

God delivers Daniel

¶18Then the king went to his palace,
and passed the night fasting: neither
were instruments of musick brought
before him: and his sleep went from
him.
19Then the king arose very early in
the morning, and went in haste unto the
den of lions.
20And when he came to the den, he
cried with a lamentable voice unto Daniel: *and* the king spake and said to Daniel, O Daniel, servant of the living God,
is thy God, whom thou servest continually, able to deliver thee from the lions?
21Then said Daniel unto the king, O
king, live for ever.
22My God hath sent his angel, and
hath shut the lions' mouths, that they
have not hurt me: forasmuch as before
him innocency was found in me; and
also before thee, O king, have I done no
hurt.
23Then was the king exceeding glad
for him, and commanded that they
should take Daniel up out of the den. So
Daniel was taken up out of the den, and
no manner of hurt was found upon him,
because he believed in his God.
¶24And the king commanded, and
they brought those men which had accused Daniel, and they cast *them* into
the den of lions, them, their children,
and their wives; and the lions had the
mastery of them, and brake all their
bones in pieces or ever they came at
the bottom of the den.

The king's decree

¶25Then king Darius wrote unto all
people, nations, and languages, that
dwell in all the earth; Peace be multiplied unto you.
26I make a decree, That in every dominion of my kingdom men tremble and
fear before the God of Daniel: for he *is*
the living God, and stedfast for ever, and
his kingdom *that* which shall not be
destroyed, and his dominion *shall be*
even unto the end.
27He delivereth and rescueth, and he
worketh signs and wonders in heaven
and in earth, who hath delivered Daniel from the power of the lions.
28So this Daniel prospered in the
reign of Darius, and in the reign of *Cyrus the Persian.

IV. The Visions of Daniel (7:1—12:13)

The four beasts

7 In the first year of Belshazzar king
of *Babylon Daniel had a dream
and visions of his head upon his bed:
then he wrote the dream, *and* told the
sum of the matters.
2Daniel spake and said, I saw in my
vision by night, and, behold, the four
winds of the heaven strove upon the
great sea.
3And four great beasts came up from
the sea, diverse one from another.

The empire of Babylon
(Dan. 2:37-38)

4The first *was* like a lion, and had
eagle's wings: I beheld till the wings
thereof were plucked, and it was lifted
up from the earth, and made stand upon
the feet as a man, and a man's heart was
given to it.

6:22 hath shut the lions' mouths. A wonderful experience and example of the power of God to overrule men's wrath and to keep His own people in times of trouble. Compare 2 Timothy 4:17. See also Luke 17:6.

7:3 the sea. A symbol in Scripture for the mass of mankind (the Gentile nations), which is restless and changing. See Revelation 17:15.

The empire of Media-Persia
(Dan. 2:39; 8:3-4; 11:2)

5And behold another beast, a second,
like to a bear, and it raised up itself on
one side, and *it had* three ribs in the
mouth of it between the teeth of it: and
they said thus unto it, Arise, devour
much flesh.

The empire of Greece under Alexander
(Dan. 2:39; 8:20-22; 11:3-4)

6After this I beheld, and lo another,
like a leopard, which had upon the back
of it four wings of a fowl; the beast had
also four heads; and dominion was
given to it.
7After this I saw in the night visions,
and behold a fourth *beast, dreadful and
terrible, and strong exceedingly; and it
had great iron teeth: it devoured and
brake in pieces, and stamped the residue with the feet of it: and it *was* diverse from all the beasts that *were*
before it; and it had ten horns.

The Roman empire
(Dan. 2:40-43; 7:23-24)

8I considered the horns, and, behold,
there came up among them another little horn, before whom there were three
of the first horns plucked up by the
roots: and, behold, in this horn *were*
eyes like the eyes of man, and a mouth
speaking great things.

The coming of the LORD to reign

¶9I beheld till the thrones were cast
down, and the Ancient of days did sit,
whose garment *was* white as snow, and
the hair of his head like the pure wool:
his throne *was like* the fiery flame, *and*
his wheels *as* burning fire.
10A fiery stream issued and came
forth from before him: thousand thousands ministered unto him, and ten
thousand times ten thousand stood before him: the judgment was set, and the
books were opened.
11I beheld then because of the voice
of the great words which the horn
spake: I beheld *even* till the beast was
slain, and his body destroyed, and given
to the burning flame.
12As concerning the rest of the
beasts, they had their dominion taken
away: yet their lives were prolonged for
a season and time.
¶13I saw in the night visions, and, behold, *one* like the Son of man came with
the clouds of heaven, and came to the
Ancient of days, and they brought him
near before him.

7:8 The Meaning of a Little Horn
A little horn represents someone very important in prophecy. He appears under different names in prophetic passages (see Dan. 9:26-27; 12:11; Matt. 24:15; 2 Thess. 2:4-8; Rev. 13:1,4-10). After the *church has been caught up to heaven (1 Thess. 4:16-17), a powerful ruler, who will arise among the ten kings of the Roman Empire, will subdue three of the ten kings. This will be the *Antichrist. He will be especially characterized by his blasphemy against God and his persecution of the Jews (see Dan. 7:23-26). A summary of his activities is given in notes on Revelation 13:1-10 (see all notes for those vss., including vs. 1, "A Beast from the Sea") and Daniel 9:24-27, "A Central Prophecy."

7:5 three ribs in the mouth of it. The Medo-Persian Empire conquered the countries of Babylonia, Egypt, and Lydia.
7:6 four heads. The Grecian Empire was divided into Greece, Thrace, Syria, and Egypt.
7:7 ten horns. A horn means a kingdom. The ten horns correspond to the ten toes of chapter 2 and are further described in Revelation 13:1 (see Rev. 13:1 note, "A Beast from the Sea," and Dan. 2:31 note, "The Great Image").
7:9 Ancient of days. This refers to the eternal character of Christ. See also Revelation 1:8,13-18.
7:11 the beast was slain. This beast is the little horn of verse 8, the *Antichrist. See Revelation 19:17-20, which tells of the final judgment by God of the Antichrist and his False Prophet (see also Rev. 19:20 note).

14And there was given him dominion,
and glory, and a kingdom, that all people, nations, and languages, should
serve him: his dominion *is* an everlasting dominion, which shall not pass
away, and his kingdom *that* which shall
not be destroyed.

The interpretation of the vision

¶15I Daniel was grieved in my spirit
in the midst of *my* body, and the visions
of my head troubled me.
16I came near unto one of them that
stood by, and asked him the truth of all
this. So he told me, and made me know
the interpretation of the things.
17These great beasts, which are four,
are four kings, *which* shall arise out of
the earth.
18But the *saints of the most High
shall take the kingdom, and possess the
kingdom for ever, even for ever and
ever.
19Then I would know the truth of the
fourth beast, which was diverse from all
the others, exceeding dreadful, whose
teeth *were of* iron, and his nails *of* brass;
which devoured, brake in pieces, and
stamped the residue with his feet;
20And of the ten horns that *were* in his
head, and *of* the other which came up,
and before whom three fell; even *of* that
horn that had eyes, and a mouth that
spake very great things, whose look
was more stout than his fellows.
21I beheld, and the same horn made
war with the saints, and prevailed
against them;
22Until the Ancient of days came, and
judgment was given to the saints of the
most High; and the time came that the
saints possessed the kingdom.
23Thus he said, The fourth beast shall
be the fourth kingdom upon earth,
which shall be diverse from all kingdoms, and shall devour the whole earth,
and shall tread it down, and break it in
pieces.
24And the ten horns out of this kingdom *are* ten kings *that* shall arise: and
another shall rise after them; and he
shall be diverse from the first, and he
shall subdue three kings.
25And he shall speak *great* words
against the most High, and shall wear
out the saints of the most High, and
think to change times and *laws: and
they shall be given into his hand until a time and times and the dividing of
time.
26But the judgment shall sit, and they
shall take away his dominion, to consume and to destroy *it* unto the end.
27And the kingdom and dominion,
and the greatness of the kingdom under the whole heaven, shall be given to
the people of the saints of the most
High, whose kingdom *is* an everlasting
kingdom, and all dominions shall serve
and obey him.
28Hitherto *is* the end of the matter.
As for me Daniel, my cogitations much
troubled me, and my countenance
changed in me: but I kept the matter in
my heart.

The vision of the ram and goat:
Media-Persia and Greece

8 In the third year of the reign of
king Belshazzar a vision appeared

7:14 there was given him dominion. Before the events of Daniel 2:34-35 take place, when the Lord Jesus Christ ends the world dominion of the Gentile powers, He is given His authority from God the Father. See also Revelation 5:1-7 and 11:15.

7:18 the saints of the most High shall take the kingdom. Not only Jewish people, but church saints as well, are meant—all who are God's people through faith, not simply those who have been designated "saints" by ecclesiastical bodies.

7:25 a time and times and the dividing of time. A time in prophecy means a year, so that this period means one year, two years, and half a year, or three and a half years. For the meaning of this, see the Revelation 13:5 and Revelation 13:14 notes, as well as the Daniel 9:24-27 note, "A Central Prophecy."

8:1 a vision. This vision that Daniel had just before the Babylonian Empire came to an

unto me, *even unto* me Daniel, after that
which appeared unto me at the first.
2And I saw in a vision; and it came to
pass, when I saw, that I *was* at *Shushan
in the palace, which *is* in the province
of Elam; and I saw in a vision, and I was
by the river of Ulai.
3Then I lifted up mine eyes, and saw,
and, behold, there stood before the
river a ram which had *two* horns: and
the *two* horns *were* high; but one *was*
higher than the other, and the higher
came up last.
4I saw the ram pushing westward,
and northward, and southward; so that
no beasts might stand before him, neither *was there any* that could deliver out
of his hand; but he did according to his
will, and became great.
5And as I was considering, behold, an
he goat came from the west on the face
of the whole earth, and touched not the
ground: and the goat *had* a notable horn
between his eyes.
6And he came to the ram that had *two*
horns, which I had seen standing before
the river, and ran unto him in the fury
of his power.
7And I saw him come close unto the
ram, and he was moved with choler
against him, and smote the ram, and
brake his two horns: and there was no
power in the ram to stand before him,
but he cast him down to the ground, and
stamped upon him: and there was none
that could deliver the ram out of his
hand.
8Therefore the he goat waxed very
great: and when he was strong, the
great horn was broken; and for it came
up four notable ones toward the four
winds of heaven.
9And out of one of them came forth a
little horn, which waxed exceeding
great, toward the south, and toward the
east, and toward the pleasant *land.*

8:9 Another Little Horn
This is a little difficult to understand, because the person referred to here as a "little horn" is probably not the same as the person in the vision of 7:8. That person arose from among the ten kings of the Roman Empire, while this one came from the four kingdoms of Alexander's generals. It is thought that this "little horn" in chapter 8 refers to a very powerful king of Syria called Antiochus Epiphanes, who ruled from 175 to 164 B.C. For a fuller account of his activities, read the 11:21 note. The name "little horn" is given to him because by his persecution of the Jews and his blasphemy against God, he is a *type of the little horn of chapter 7. As he behaved to the Jews in his reign, so would the future little horn behave in a time that is still future.

10And it waxed great, *even* to the host
of heaven; and it cast down *some* of the
host and of the stars to the ground, and
stamped upon them.

---

end—the third year of Belshazzar—gives greater details about the second and third empires of Media-Persia and Greece, previously described in chapters 2 and 7.

8:3 a ram which had two horns. The ram was the symbol of Persia and was on their banners and in their documents. The two horns are Media and Persia. "One was higher than the other, and the higher came up last" refers to the greater strength and later development of Persia (see vs. 20).

8:4 westward, and northward, and southward. Cyrus of Persia conquered as far as the Mediterranean, the Black Sea, and the Persian Gulf.

8:5 an he goat. The goat became the symbol of Greece. "Touched not the ground" refers to the speed of the conquests of Greece (see vs. 21). Since Greece was not considered a world power during Daniel's time, this was an amazing prophecy.

8:5 a notable horn. This stood for Alexander the Great of Macedonia, who established the Greek Empire. See verses 8, 21, and Daniel 11:3-4.

8:7 choler. Fierce temper, wrath.

8:8 four notable ones. Alexander died quite young, and his empire was divided among his four generals. The two who are important in this book are Ptolemy, who ruled Egypt, and Seleucus, who ruled Syria. See also references to them in verses 21-22 and in Daniel 11:4.

[11]Yea, he magnified *himself* even to
the prince of the host, and by him the
daily **sacrifice* was taken away, and the
place of his *sanctuary was cast down.
[12]And an host was given *him* against
the daily *sacrifice* by reason of transgression, and it cast down the truth to
the ground; and it practised, and prospered.
¶[13]Then I heard one saint speaking,
and another saint said unto that certain
saint which spake, How long *shall be* the
vision *concerning* the daily *sacrifice,* and
the transgression of desolation, to give
both the sanctuary and the host to be
trodden under foot?
[14]And he said unto me, Unto two
thousand and three hundred days; then
shall the sanctuary be cleansed.

Interpretation of the vision

¶[15]And it came to pass, when I, *even* I
Daniel, had seen the vision, and sought
for the meaning, then, behold, there stood
before me as the appearance of a man.
[16]And I heard a man's voice between
the banks of Ulai, which called, and said,
Gabriel, make this *man* to understand
the vision.
[17]So he came near where I stood: and
when he came, I was afraid, and fell
upon my face: but he said unto me,
Understand, O son of man: for at the
time of the end *shall be* the vision.
[18]Now as he was speaking with me, I
was in a deep sleep on my face toward
the ground: but he touched me, and set
me upright.
[19]And he said, Behold, I will make
thee know what shall be in the last end
of the indignation: for at the time appointed the end *shall be.*
[20]The ram which thou sawest having
two horns *are* the kings of Media and
Persia.
[21]And the rough goat *is* the king of
Grecia: and the great horn that *is* between his eyes *is* the first king.
[22]Now that being broken, whereas
four stood up for it, four kingdoms shall
stand up out of the nation, but not in his
power.
[23]And in the latter time of their
*kingdom, when the transgressors are
come to the full, a king of fierce countenance, and understanding dark sentences, shall stand up.
[24]And his power shall be mighty, but
not by his own power: and he shall destroy wonderfully, and shall prosper,
and practise, and shall destroy the
mighty and the holy people.
[25]And through his policy also he shall
cause craft to prosper in his hand; and
he shall magnify *himself* in his heart,
and by peace shall destroy many: he
shall also stand up against the Prince of
princes; but he shall be broken without
hand.
[26]And the vision of the evening and
the morning which was told *is* true:
wherefore shut thou up the vision; for
it *shall be* for many days.
[27]And I Daniel fainted, and was sick
certain days; afterward I rose up, and
did the king's business; and I was astonished at the vision, but none understood *it.*

The vision of the seventy weeks

9 In the first year of *Darius the son
of *Ahasuerus, of the seed of the
Medes, which was made king over the
realm of the Chaldeans;
[2]In the first year of his reign I Daniel
understood by books the number of the
years, whereof the word of the LORD
came to Jeremiah the *prophet, that he
would accomplish seventy years in the
desolations of *Jerusalem.

8:15 a man. This was a *theophany.
8:16 Gabriel. Gabriel and Michael are the only angels named in the Bible.
9:2 by books. Daniel must have looked up the prophecies in Jeremiah. See Jeremiah 25:11-12 (see the 25:11 note, "An Improbable Prediction") and 29:10. The books were not bound like our books today but were scrolls of parchment that could be rolled and unrolled.

Prayer and confession

¶ 3 And I set my face unto the Lord
*God, to seek by *prayer and supplica-
tions, with fasting, and sackcloth, and
ashes:
4 And I prayed unto the LORD my God,
and made my confession, and said, O
Lord, the great and dreadful God, keeping the *covenant and mercy to them
that love him, and to them that keep his
commandments;
5 We have sinned, and have committed iniquity, and have done wickedly,
and have rebelled, even by departing
from thy precepts and from thy judgments:
6 Neither have we hearkened unto thy
servants the *prophets, which spake in
thy name to our kings, our princes, and
our fathers, and to all the people of the
land.
7 O Lord, righteousness *belongeth*
unto thee, but unto us confusion of
faces, as at this day; to the men of *Judah, and to the inhabitants of Jerusalem,
and unto all *Israel, *that are* near, and
that are far off, through all the countries
whither thou hast driven them, because
of their *trespass that they have trespassed against thee.
8 O Lord, to us *belongeth* confusion of
face, to our kings, to our princes, and
to our fathers, because we have sinned
against thee.
9 To the Lord our God *belong* mercies
and forgivenesses, though we have rebelled against him;
10 Neither have we obeyed the voice
of the LORD our God, to walk in his
laws, which he set before us by his servants the prophets.
11 Yea, all Israel have transgressed thy
law, even by departing, that they might
not obey thy voice; therefore the curse
is poured upon us, and the oath that *is*
written in the law of *Moses the servant of God, because we have sinned
against him.
12 And he hath confirmed his words,
which he spake against us, and against
our judges that judged us, by bringing
upon us a great evil: for under the
whole heaven hath not been done as
hath been done upon Jerusalem.
13 As *it is* written in the law of Moses,
all this evil is come upon us: yet made
we not our prayer before the LORD our
God, that we might turn from our iniquities, and understand thy truth.
14 Therefore hath the LORD watched
upon the evil, and brought it upon us:
for the LORD our God *is* righteous in all
his works which he doeth: for we
obeyed not his voice.
15 And now, O Lord our God, that hast
brought thy people forth out of the
land of *Egypt with a mighty hand, and
hast gotten thee renown, as at this
day; we have sinned, we have done
wickedly.
¶ 16 O Lord, according to all thy righteousness, I beseech thee, let thine
anger and thy fury be turned away from
thy city Jerusalem, thy holy *mountain:
because for our sins, and for the iniquities of our fathers, Jerusalem and thy
people *are become* a reproach to all *that
are* about us.
17 Now therefore, O our God, hear the
prayer of thy servant, and his supplications, and cause thy face to shine upon
thy sanctuary that is desolate, for the
Lord's sake.
18 O my God, incline thine ear, and
hear; open thine eyes, and behold our
desolations, and the city which is called
by thy name: for we do not present our
supplications before thee for our
righteousnesses, but for thy great mercies.
19 O Lord, hear; O Lord, forgive; O
Lord, hearken and do; defer not, for
thine own sake, O my God: for thy city
and thy people are called by thy name.
¶ 20 And whiles I *was* speaking, and
praying, and confessing my *sin and the
sin of my people Israel, and presenting
my supplication before the LORD my
God for the holy mountain of my God;
21 Yea, whiles I *was* speaking in
prayer, even the man Gabriel, whom I
had seen in the vision at the beginning,

being caused to fly swiftly, touched me
about the time of the evening *oblation.
22And he informed *me,* and talked
with me, and said, O Daniel, I am now
come forth to give thee skill and understanding.
23At the beginning of thy supplications the commandment came forth,
and I am come to shew *thee;* for thou *art*
greatly beloved: therefore understand
the matter, and consider the vision.
24Seventy weeks are determined
upon thy people and upon thy *holy city,
to finish the transgression, and to make
an end of sins, and to make *reconciliation for iniquity, and to bring in everlasting righteousness, and to seal up the
vision and *prophecy, and to *anoint the
most Holy.
25Know therefore and understand,
that from the going forth of the commandment to restore and to build Jerusalem unto the *Messiah the Prince
shall be seven weeks, and threescore
and two weeks: the street shall be built
again, and the wall, even in troublous
times.
26And after threescore and two weeks
shall Messiah be cut off, but not for himself: and the people of the prince that
shall come shall destroy the city and the
sanctuary; and the end thereof *shall be*
with a flood, and unto the end of the war
desolations are determined.
27And he shall confirm the covenant
with many for one week: and in the
midst of the week he shall cause the
sacrifice and the oblation to cease, and
for the overspreading of abominations
he shall make *it* desolate, even until the
consummation, and that determined
shall be poured upon the desolate.

The vision of God's glory

10 In the third year of Cyrus *king
of Persia a thing was revealed

9:24-27 A CENTRAL PROPHECY

This is a very important prophecy, for it provides a framework into which we can fit many other prophecies of the Bible. It gives a quick outline of the important events in the future of the Jews from Daniel's time to the crucifixion of the Lord Jesus Christ, and then from the end of the church age to the coming of Christ to reign. The weeks are prophetic periods of seven years each, not seven days. The main points to remember are:

1. The calculation of the prophecy starts from the decree of Artaxerxes to rebuild Jerusalem, given to Nehemiah in 445 B.C. (see vs. 25; compare Neh. 2:1-8). Previous decrees had only given permission to rebuild the temple (see 2 Chron. 36:22-23; Ezra 1:1-3).
2. A period of seven weeks is mentioned in verse 25, which covers the forty-nine years of rebuilding and brings the date to about 406 B.C.
3. Then in the same verse (vs. 25) a period of sixty-two weeks, or 434 years, is mentioned until "Messiah the Prince," who was to be "cut off, but not for himself" (vs. 26). This must refer to the crucifixion of the Lord Jesus Christ, which took place about A.D. 30.
4. The destruction of Jerusalem by the Romans in A.D. 70 is foretold in verse 26.
5. At this point the prophecy is suspended. Sixty-nine weeks have been accounted for and one is left. We know that this age, the *dispensation of grace, when the gospel is being preached and the *church is being formed is not foretold in the Old Testament (see Matt. 13:10-11,17,34-35)–it is a parenthesis between the sixty-ninth and seventieth weeks. But when this interval ends with the removal of the church to heaven, the last week of the prophecy will be fulfilled.
6. The Seventieth Week tells of the history of the Jews under the *Antichrist of the revived Roman Empire, who is called here, "the prince that shall come" (vs. 26), who is the "little horn" of Daniel 7, and the *Beast of Revelation 13:1. He will make a treaty with the Jews for seven years (the last week) to allow them the free exercise of their religion in Jerusalem. In the middle of this period, he will break the treaty (vs. 27) and defile the temple by causing his own image to be worshipped there (see Dan. 12:11; 2 Thess. 2:3-4; see also 2 Thess. 2:3 note, "Before the Lord Comes"). This will be a sign to the Jews that the period known as the time of *Jacob's Trouble has begun.

unto Daniel, whose name was called
Belteshazzar; and the thing *was* true,
but the time appointed *was* long: and he
understood the thing, and had understanding of the vision.
2In those days I Daniel was *mourning three full weeks.
3I ate no pleasant bread, neither came
flesh nor wine in my mouth, neither did
I anoint myself at all, till three whole
weeks were fulfilled.
4And in the four and twentieth day of
the first *month, as I was by the side
of the great river, which *is* Hiddekel;
5Then I lifted up mine eyes, and
looked, and behold a certain man
clothed in *linen, whose loins *were*
girded with fine gold of Uphaz:
6His body also *was* like the beryl, and
his face as the appearance of lightning,
and his eyes as lamps of fire, and his
arms and his feet like in colour to polished brass, and the voice of his words
like the voice of a multitude.
7And I Daniel alone saw the vision:
for the men that were with me saw not
the vision; but a great quaking fell upon
them, so that they fled to hide themselves.
8Therefore I was left alone, and saw
this great vision, and there remained no
strength in me: for my comeliness was
turned in me into corruption, and I retained no strength.
9Yet heard I the voice of his words:
and when I heard the voice of his words,
then was I in a deep sleep on my face,
and my face toward the ground.
¶10And, behold, an hand touched me,
which set me upon my knees and *upon*
the palms of my hands.
11And he said unto me, O Daniel, a
man greatly beloved, understand the
words that I speak unto thee, and stand
upright: for unto thee am I now sent.
And when he had spoken this word unto
me, I stood trembling.
12Then said he unto me, Fear not,
Daniel: for from the first day that thou
didst set thine heart to understand, and
to *chasten thyself before thy God, thy
words were heard, and I am come for
thy words.
13But the prince of the kingdom of
Persia withstood me one and twenty
days: but, lo, Michael, one of the chief
princes, came to help me; and I remained there with the kings of Persia.
14Now I am come to make thee understand what shall befall thy people in
the latter days: for yet the vision *is* for
many days.
15And when he had spoken such
words unto me, I set my face toward the
ground, and I became dumb.
16And, behold, *one* like the similitude
of the sons of men touched my lips:
then I opened my mouth, and spake,
and said unto him that stood before me,
O my lord, by the vision my sorrows are
turned upon me, and I have retained no
strength.
17For how can the servant of this my
lord talk with this my lord? for as for me,
*straightway there remained no strength
in me, neither is there breath left in me.
18Then there came again and touched
me *one* like the appearance of a man,
and he strengthened me,
19And said, O man greatly beloved,
fear not: *peace *be* unto thee, be strong,
yea, be strong. And when he had spoken unto me, I was strengthened, and
said, Let my lord speak; for thou hast
strengthened me.
20Then said he, Knowest thou
wherefore I come unto thee? and now
will I return to fight with the prince of
Persia: and when I am gone forth, lo,
the prince of Grecia shall come.

10:4 Hiddekel. The Tigris River.
10:5 behold a certain man. This was a *theophany. Compare Revelation 1:13.
10:6 beryl. Chrysolite.
10:13 the prince of the kingdom of Persia. An evil being, who was directed by Satan and who tried to hinder God's purposes.
10:20 prince of Grecia. A similar being to the one spoken of in verse 13.

21But I will shew thee that which is
noted in the scripture of truth: and *there*
is none that holdeth with me in these
things, but Michael your prince.

The end of the Persian Empire

11 Also I in the first year of Darius the Mede, *even* I, stood to
confirm and to strengthen him.
2And now will I shew thee the truth.
Behold, there shall stand up yet three
kings in Persia; and the fourth shall be
far richer than *they* all: and by his
strength through his riches he shall stir
up all against the realm of Grecia.

The rise of the Grecian Empire

3And a mighty king shall stand up,
that shall rule with great dominion, and
do according to his will.
4And when he shall stand up, his
kingdom shall be broken, and shall be
divided toward the four winds of heav-
en; and not to his posterity, nor according to his dominion which he ruled: for
his kingdom shall be plucked up, even
for others beside those.
¶5And the king of the south shall be
strong, and *one* of his princes; and he
shall be strong above him, and have
dominion; his dominion *shall be* a great
dominion.
6And in the end of years they shall
join themselves together; for the king's
daughter of the south shall come to the
king of the north to make an agreement:
but she shall not retain the power of the
arm; neither shall he stand, nor his arm:
but she shall be given up, and they that
brought her, and he that begat her, and
he that strengthened her in *these* times.
7But out of *a branch of her roots
shall *one* stand up in his estate, which
shall come with an army, and shall enter into the fortress of the king of the
north, and shall deal against them, and
shall prevail:
8And shall also carry captives into
Egypt their gods, with their princes,
and with their precious vessels of silver and of gold; and he shall continue
more years than the king of the north.
9So the king of the south shall come
into *his* kingdom, and shall return into
his own land.
10But his sons shall be stirred up, and
shall assemble a multitude of great
forces: and *one* shall certainly come,
and overflow, and pass through: then
shall he return, and be stirred up, *even*
to his fortress.
11And the king of the south shall be

11:4 A Divided Empire
On the death of Alexander, his empire was divided among four generals. The kingdoms of two of them are mentioned here because they were the two that concerned the Jews. The "king of the south" (vs. 5) was Ptolemy of Egypt, and the "king of the north" (vs. 6) was Seleucus of Syria. From verses 5-20, certain historical details of the development of these two kingdoms are given.

10:21 Michael your prince. See also verse 13. Just as there were evil demons acting for Satan, so there were good spirits or *angels, carrying out God's purposes for Israel.
11:2 Behold. This prophecy gives even more details about the Persian and Greek Empires already described in chapters 2, 7, and 8.
11:2 three kings in Persia; and the fourth. These kings were Ahasuerus (Ezra 4:6); Artaxerxes (Ezra 4:7); Darius (Ezra 4:24); and Xerxes, who invaded Greece in 483 B.C.
11:3 a mighty king. Alexander the Great, who defeated the Persians and conquered as far as India. See Daniel 8:5 second note.
11:5 king of the south. South of Palestine was Egypt—see verse 4 note, "A Divided Empire."
11:5 he shall be strong. Seleucus, king of Syria in the north; see verse 4 note.
11:6 the king's daughter of the south. Berenice, daughter of Ptolemy II, married Antiochus II, who divorced his wife, Laodice, to marry Berenice. Laodice, however, killed Berenice and her son.
11:7 out of a branch of her roots. This means Berenice's brother, Ptolemy the Third.

moved with *choler, and shall come
forth and fight with him, *even* with the
king of the north: and he shall set forth
a great multitude; but the multitude
shall be given into his hand.
12*And* when he hath taken away the
multitude, his heart shall be lifted up;
and he shall cast down *many* ten thousands: but he shall not be strengthened
by it.
13For the king of the north shall return, and shall set forth a multitude
greater than the former, and shall certainly come after certain years with a
great army and with much riches.
14And in those times there shall
many stand up against the king of the
south: also the robbers of thy people
shall exalt themselves to establish the
vision; but they shall fall.
15So the king of the north shall come,
and cast up a mount, and take the most
fenced cities: and the arms of the south
shall not withstand, neither his chosen
people, neither *shall there be any*
strength to withstand.
16But he that cometh against him
shall do according to his own will, and
none shall stand before him: and he
shall stand in the glorious land, which
by his hand shall be consumed.
17He shall also set his face to enter
with the strength of his whole kingdom,
and upright ones with him; thus shall he
do: and he shall give him the daughter
of women, corrupting her: but she shall
not stand *on his side,* neither be for him.
18After this shall he turn his face unto
the *isles, and shall take many: but a
prince for his own behalf shall cause the
reproach offered by him to cease; without his own reproach he shall cause *it*
to turn upon him.
19Then he shall turn his face toward
the fort of his own land: but he shall
stumble and fall, and not be found.
20Then shall stand up in his estate a
raiser of taxes *in* the glory of the kingdom: but within few days he shall
be destroyed, neither in anger, nor in
battle.

The Little Horn

21And in his estate shall stand up a
vile person, to whom they shall not give
the honour of the kingdom: but he shall
come in peaceably, and obtain the kingdom by flatteries.
22And with the arms of a flood shall
they be overflown from before him, and
shall be broken; yea, also the prince of
the covenant.
23And after the league *made* with him
he shall work deceitfully: for he shall
come up, and shall become strong with
a small people.
24He shall enter peaceably even upon
the fattest places of the province; and
he shall do *that* which his fathers have
not done, nor his fathers' fathers; he
shall scatter among them the prey, and
spoil, and riches: *yea,* and he shall forecast his devices against the strong
holds, even for a time.
25And he shall stir up his power and
his courage against the king of the
south with a great army; and the king
of the south shall be stirred up to battle with a very great and mighty army;
but he shall not stand: for they shall
forecast devices against him.
26Yea, they that feed of the portion of
his meat shall destroy him, and his
army shall overflow: and many shall fall
down slain.
27And both these kings' hearts *shall
be* to do mischief, and they shall speak
lies at one table; but it shall not prosper: for yet the end *shall be* at the time
appointed.
28Then shall he return into his land
with great riches; and his heart *shall be*

11:21 a vile person. This refers to Antiochus Epiphanes, ruler of Syria. He is the little horn of chapter 8 (see 8:9 note, "Another Little Horn"). He persecuted the Jews fiercely and stopped the temple sacrifices. He himself went into the Holy of Holies and offered a sow upon the altar.

against the *holy covenant; and he shall
do *exploits,* and return to his own land.
29 At the time appointed he shall return, and come toward the south; but
it shall not be as the former, or as the
latter.
¶30 For the ships of Chittim shall
come against him: therefore he shall be
grieved, and return, and have indignation against the holy covenant: so shall
he do; he shall even return, and have
intelligence with them that forsake the
holy covenant.
31 And arms shall stand on his part,
and they shall pollute the sanctuary of
strength, and shall take away the daily
sacrifice, and they shall place the
*abomination that maketh desolate.
32 And such as do wickedly against the
covenant shall he corrupt by flatteries:
but the people that do know their God
shall be strong, and do *exploits.*
33 And they that understand among
the people shall instruct many: yet they
shall fall by the sword, and by flame, by
captivity, and by spoil, *many* days.
34 Now when they shall fall, they shall
be holpen with a little help: but many
shall cleave to them with flatteries.
35 And *some* of them of understanding
shall fall, to try them, and to purge, and
to make *them* white, *even* to the time of
the end: because *it is* yet for a time appointed.
36 And the king shall do according to
his will; and he shall exalt himself, and
magnify himself above every god, and
shall speak marvellous things against
the God of gods, and shall prosper till
the indignation be accomplished: for
that that is determined shall be done.
37 Neither shall he regard the God of
his fathers, nor the desire of women,
nor regard any god: for he shall magnify himself above all.
38 But in his estate shall he honour
the God of forces: and a god whom his
fathers knew not shall he honour with
gold, and silver, and with precious
stones, and pleasant things.
39 Thus shall he do in the most strong
holds with a strange god, whom he
shall acknowledge *and* increase with
glory: and he shall cause them to rule
over many, and shall divide the land for
gain.
40 And at the time of the end shall the
king of the south push at him: and the
king of the north shall come against him
like a whirlwind, with chariots, and with
horsemen, and with many ships; and he
shall enter into the countries, and shall
overflow and pass over.
41 He shall enter also into the glorious
land, and many *countries* shall be overthrown: but these shall escape out of his
hand, *even* *Edom, and *Moab, and the
chief of the children of Ammon.
42 He shall stretch forth his hand also
upon the countries: and the land of
Egypt shall not escape.

11:36 The False Prophet
This person is not the same as the little horn of chapters 7–8. See notes on chapters 7 and 8 and Revelation 13. There are many evidences from Daniel 7:36-38 that suggest that this is a Jew, for verse 37 speaks of "the God of his fathers"–Abraham, Isaac, and Jacob are always meant by the fathers in the Old Testament; "the desire of women"–every Jewish woman's great longing was to be the mother of the Messiah, and in verse 38 we read of his honoring a god "whom his fathers knew not." This person appears to be the False Prophet, the "beast out of the earth" of Revelation 13:11 (see its note, "The Beast from the Earth"). The False Prophet works for the Antichrist. He "doeth great wonders . . . and deceiveth them that dwell on earth by the means of those miracles which he had power to do in the sight of the beast [Antichrist]" (Rev. 13:13-14). Along with Satan and the Beast, the False Prophet completes the unholy trinity.

11:35 the time of the end. From now on the prophecy looks ahead to the period of the revived Roman Empire, after the *church has been caught up to heaven (1 Thess. 4:16-18).

43 But he shall have power over the treasures of gold and of silver, and over all the precious things of Egypt: and the Libyans and the Ethiopians *shall be* at his steps.

44 But tidings out of the east and out of the north shall trouble him: therefore he shall go forth with great fury to destroy, and utterly to make away many.

45 And he shall plant the tabernacles of his palace between the seas in the glorious holy mountain; yet he shall come to his end, and none shall help him.

The Great Tribulation

12 And at that time shall Michael stand up, the great prince which standeth for the children of thy people: and there shall be a time of trouble, such as never was since there was a nation *even* to that same time: and at that time thy people shall be delivered, every one that shall be found written in the book.

The Resurrection

2 And many of them that sleep in the dust of the earth shall awake, some to everlasting life, and some to shame *and* everlasting contempt.

Daniel's last vision

3 And they that be wise shall shine as the brightness of the firmament; and they that turn many to righteousness as the stars for ever and ever.

The time of the end

4 But thou, O Daniel, shut up the words, and seal the book, *even* to the time of the end: many shall run to and fro, and knowledge shall be increased.

¶5 Then I Daniel looked, and, behold, there stood other two, the one on this side of the bank of the river, and the other on that side of the bank of the river.

6 And *one* said to the man clothed in linen, which *was* upon the waters of the river, How long *shall it be to* the end of these wonders?

7 And I heard the man clothed in linen, which *was* upon the waters of the river, when he held up his right hand and his left hand unto heaven, and sware by him that liveth for ever that *it shall be* for a time, times, and an half; and when he shall have accomplished to scatter the power of the holy people, all these *things* shall be finished.

8 And I heard, but I understood not: then said I, O my Lord, what *shall be* the end of these *things?*

9 And he said, Go thy way, Daniel: for the words *are* closed up and sealed till the time of the end.

10 Many shall be purified, and made white, and tried; but the wicked shall do wickedly: and none of the wicked shall understand; but the wise shall understand.

11 And from the time *that* the daily *sacrifice* shall be taken away, and the abomination that maketh desolate set up, *there shall be* a thousand two hundred and ninety days.

12 Blessed *is* he that waiteth, and cometh to the thousand three hundred and five and thirty days.

13 But go thou thy way till the end *be:* for thou shalt rest, and stand in thy lot at the end of the days.

12:1 thy people. Daniel's people, the Jews.
12:1 a time of trouble. The *Great Tribulation (compare Matt. 24:15-26).
12:2 awake. See the *Resurrection.
12:7 a time, times, and an half. See 7:25 note.

HOSEA

BACKGROUND AND MEANING

God chose Israel to be His own nation, and showered love and blessing upon her. But she turned away from Him to other gods. Then He sent prophets to make her realize her sin.

Hosea was one of these prophets. He acted out his message by his life. At God's command he married a wife who was unfaithful to him. She loved other men and deliberately left him for all the pleasures and wealth she thought they could give her. Hosea was heart-broken and disowned her. But he still loved her, and finally bought her back and shut her away from everybody until she would realize her sin and turn back to him again.

His very trouble gave him a chance to speak God's message that Israel has treated her LORD in the same way. He has been like a loving husband to Israel, but because she turned away from Him, He will disown her. Nevertheless He loves her still, and when her heart turns to Him, He will take her back again.

OUTLINE OF HOSEA

The book of Hosea cannot be outlined any more than one could outline the sobbings of a heart-broken person.

---

1 The word of the LORD that came
unto Hosea, the son of Beeri, in the
days of Uzziah, Jotham, Ahaz, *and*
*Hezekiah, kings of Judah, and in the
days of Jeroboam the son of *Joash, king
of Israel.
2The beginning of the word of the
LORD by Hosea. And the LORD said to
Hosea, Go, take unto thee a wife of
whoredoms and children of whoredoms: for the land hath committed
great whoredom, *departing* from the
LORD.
3So he went and took Gomer the
daughter of Diblaim; which conceived,
and bare him a son.
4And the LORD said unto him, Call his
name Jezreel; for yet a little *while,* and
I will avenge the blood of Jezreel upon
the house of Jehu, and will cause to

1:1 The Divided Kingdom
The kingdom was divided after Solomon's death. The two tribes, Judah and little Benjamin, were called Judah, the ten tribes were called Israel (or Ephraim after the largest tribe).

1:2 whoredoms. Idolatry. Hosea's wife was an idol worshipper.

1:4 blood of Jezreel. God wanted to make the people see their sin, so the very name He told Hosea to give his son was to remind everyone who knew Jezreel of one of the worst crimes in Israel's history. It is recorded in 2 Kings 10:1-14.

cease the kingdom of the house of
Israel.
5 And it shall come to pass at that day,
that I will break the bow of Israel in the
valley of Jezreel.
¶6 And she conceived again, and bare
a daughter. And *God* said unto him,
Call her name Lo-ruhamah: for I will no
more have *mercy upon the house of
Israel; but I will utterly take them away.
7 But I will have mercy upon the
house of Judah, and will save them by
the LORD their God, and will not save
them by bow, nor by sword, nor by battle, by horses, nor by horsemen.
¶8 Now when she had weaned Lo-ruhamah, she conceived, and bare a son.
9 Then said *God,* Call his name Lo-
ammi: for ye *are* not my people, and I
will not be your *God.*
¶10 Yet the number of the children of
Israel shall be as the sand of the sea,
which cannot be measured nor numbered; and it shall come to pass, *that* in
the place where it was said unto them,
Ye *are* not my people, *there* it shall be
said unto them, *Ye are* the sons of the
living God.
11 Then shall the children of Judah and
the children of Israel be gathered together, and appoint themselves one
head, and they shall come up out of
the land: for great *shall be* the day of
Jezreel.

Israel to be restored

2 Say ye unto your brethren, Ammi;
and to your sisters, Ru-hamah.
2 Plead with your mother, plead: for
she *is* not my wife, neither *am* I her
husband: let her therefore put away
her whoredoms out of her sight, and her
adulteries from between her breasts;
3 Lest I strip her naked, and set her
as in the day that she was born, and
make her as a wilderness, and set her
like a dry land, and slay her with thirst.
4 And I will not have mercy upon her
children; for they *be* the children of
whoredoms.
5 For their mother hath played the
harlot: she that conceived them hath
done shamefully: for she said, I will go
after my lovers, that give *me* my bread
and my water, my wool and my flax,
mine *oil and my drink.
¶6 Therefore, behold, I will hedge up
thy way with thorns, and make a wall,
that she shall not find her paths.
7 And she shall follow after her lovers,
but she shall not overtake them; and
she shall seek them, but shall not find
them: then shall she say, I will go and
return to my first husband; for then *was*
it better with me than now.
8 For she did not know that I gave her
corn, and wine, and oil, and multiplied
her silver and gold, *which* they prepared
for *Baal.
9 Therefore will I return, and take
away my corn in the time thereof, and
my wine in the season thereof, and will
recover my wool and my flax *given* to
cover her nakedness.
10 And now will I discover her lewdness in the sight of her lovers, and none
shall deliver her out of mine hand.
11 I will also cause all her mirth to

1:6 Lo-ruhamah. Meaning *unpitied.*
1:9 Lo-ammi. This means *not my people.*
2:1 your brethren. The Israelites.
2:1 Ammi. Meaning *my people.*
2:1 Ru-hamah. Meaning *having obtained pity.*
2:2 she is not my wife. The nation of Israel was often called the wife of Jehovah because of His having chosen her for Himself. She was now disowned for a while. (See introduction to this book.)
2:5 their mother. Israel.
2:5 my lovers. Other gods, as Baal, etc.
2:6 I will hedge. The suffering of Jews through all the centuries is God's way of showing them that they can never find peace except in Him, in the Way (John 14:6) that He has provided.

cease, her feast days, her *new moons, and her sabbaths, and all her solemn *feasts.

12 And I will destroy her vines and her fig trees, whereof she hath said, These *are* my rewards that my lovers have given me: and I will make them a forest, and the beasts of the field shall eat them.

13 And I will visit upon her the days of Baalim, wherein she burned *incense to them, and she decked herself with her earrings and her jewels, and she went after her lovers, and forgat me, saith the LORD.

¶ 14 Therefore, behold, I will allure her, and bring her into the wilderness, and speak comfortably unto her.

15 And I will give her her vineyards from thence, and the valley of Achor for a door of hope: and she shall sing there, as in the days of her youth, and as in the day when she came up out of the land of *Egypt.

16 And it shall be at that day, saith the LORD, *that* thou shalt call me Ishi; and shalt call me no more Baali.

17 For I will take away the names of Baalim out of her mouth, and they shall no more be remembered by their name.

18 And in that day will I make a *covenant for them with the beasts of the field, and with the fowls of heaven, and *with* the creeping things of the ground: and I will break the bow and the sword and the battle out of the earth, and will make them to lie down safely.

19 And I will betroth thee unto me for ever; yea, I will betroth thee unto me in *righteousness, and in *judgment, and in lovingkindness, and in mercies.

20 I will even betroth thee unto me in faithfulness: and thou shalt know the LORD.

21 And it shall come to pass in that day, I will hear, saith the LORD, I will hear the heavens, and they shall hear the earth;

22 And the earth shall hear the corn, and the wine, and the oil; and they shall hear Jezreel.

23 And I will sow her unto me in the earth; and I will have mercy upon her that had not obtained mercy; and I will say to *them which were* not my people, Thou *art* my people; and they shall say, *Thou art* my God.

God's undying love for Israel

3 Then said the LORD unto me, Go yet, love a woman beloved of *her* friend, yet an adulteress, according to the love of the LORD toward the children of Israel, who look to other gods, and love flagons of wine.

2 So I bought her to me for fifteen *pieces* of silver, and *for* an *homer of barley, and an half homer of barley:

3 And I said unto her, Thou shalt abide

3:1 The Good of Suffering
God did not take from Hosea the heartbreaking love for the wife who had left him (see the introduction to this book). Sometimes our temporary sufferings teach us to glorify Him more than if our paths were made easy (2 Cor. 4:16-18).

2:12 destroy her vines. Palestine has been almost a wasteland for centuries.
2:15 valley of Achor. A place of trouble (see Josh. 7:26; Isa. 65:10) in Israel's history.
2:15 out of the land of Egypt. See Exodus 14–15.
2:16 Ishi. *My husband.*
2:16 Baali. *My Lord and Master*. This name was used by the Canaanites so much in the worship of their god that God hated it.
2:18 covenant for them with the beasts. See Isaiah 11:6-9.
2:22 Jezreel. This word means both *God scatters* (see prophecy of the punishment of Israel by scattering in Hos. 9:17) and *God sows*. God will sow or plant Israel again in their own land as surely as He has scattered them.
3:1 beloved of her friend. Loved by her husband, Hosea, despite her adultery. God wanted Israel to see His great love for them through Hosea's painful and difficult marriage.
3:2 bought. Wives were generally bought in the Eastern countries by paying a dowry of

for me many days; thou shalt not play the harlot, and thou shalt not be for *another* man: so *will* I also *be* for thee.

4 For the children of Israel shall abide many days without a king, and without a prince, and without a *sacrifice, and without an image, and without an *ephod, and *without* *teraphim:

5 Afterward shall the children of Israel return, and seek the LORD their God, and *David their king; and shall *fear the LORD and his goodness in the latter days.

God's charge against Israel

4 Hear the word of the LORD, ye children of Israel: for the LORD hath a controversy with the inhabitants of the land, because *there is* no truth, nor mercy, nor knowledge of God in the land.

2 By swearing, and lying, and killing, and stealing, and committing adultery, they break out, and blood toucheth blood.

3 Therefore shall the land mourn, and every one that dwelleth therein shall languish, with the beasts of the field, and with the fowls of heaven; yea, the fishes of the sea also shall be taken away.

4 Yet let no man strive, nor reprove another: for thy people *are* as they that strive with the priest.

5 Therefore shalt thou fall in the day, and the *prophet also shall fall with thee in the night, and I will destroy thy mother.

Israel's wilful ignorance

¶6 My people are destroyed for lack of knowledge: because thou hast rejected knowledge, I will also reject thee, that thou shalt be no priest to me: seeing thou hast forgotten the *law of thy God, I will also forget thy children.

7 As they were increased, so they sinned against me: *therefore* will I change their glory into shame.

8 They eat up the *sin of my people, and they set their heart on their iniquity.

9 And there shall be, like people, like priest: and I will punish them for their ways, and reward them their doings.

10 For they shall eat, and not have enough: they shall commit whoredom, and shall not increase: because they have left off to take heed to the LORD.

11 Whoredom and wine and new wine take away the heart.

Israel's idolatry

¶12 My people ask counsel at their stocks, and their staff declareth unto them: for the spirit of whoredoms hath caused *them* to *err, and they have gone a whoring from under their God.

13 They sacrifice upon the tops of the mountains, and burn incense upon the hills, under oaks and poplars and elms, because the shadow thereof *is* good: therefore your daughters shall commit whoredom, and your spouses shall commit adultery.

14 I will not punish your daughters when they commit whoredom, nor your spouses when they commit adultery: for themselves are separated with whores, and they sacrifice with harlots: therefore the people *that* doth not understand shall fall.

¶15 Though thou, Israel, play the harlot,

---

money or goods to the woman's father or brother. Hosea's wife had to be bought back (see *redemption), because she had left him and sold herself into slavery.

3:3 many days. Now already about 2,600 years.

3:5 David their king. This speaks of the coming of Christ, the Son of David (Matt. 1:1) to reign.

4:5 thy mother. Israel the nation—as if the individual Israelites were the nation's children.

4:6 priest. See Exodus 19:6.

4:13 They sacrifice. These were sacrifices to heathen gods whose temples were often groves of trees on some mountaintop. Many of the heathen sacrifices were carried on with immoral ceremonies.

yet let not Judah *offend; and come not
ye unto Gilgal, neither go ye up to Beth-
aven, nor swear, The LORD liveth.
16For Israel slideth back as a backsliding heifer: now the LORD will feed
them as a lamb in a large place.
17*Ephraim *is* joined to idols: let him
alone.
18Their drink is sour: they have committed whoredom continually: her rulers *with* shame do love, Give ye.
19The wind hath bound her up in her
wings, and they shall be ashamed because of their sacrifices.

4:19 The Symbol of the Spirit
As the wind or breath of air is sometimes a symbol of the Spirit of God, so here it is a symbol of the spirit of idol worship, therefore, the spirit of Satan.

5 Hear ye this, O priests; and hearken, ye house of Israel; and give ye
ear, O house of the king; for judgment
is toward you, because ye have been a
snare on Mizpah, and a net spread upon
Tabor.
2And the revolters are profound to
make slaughter, though I *have been* a
rebuker of them all.
3I know Ephraim, and Israel is not hid
from me: for now, O Ephraim, thou
committest whoredom, *and* Israel is
defiled.
4They will not frame their doings to
turn unto their God: for the spirit of
whoredoms *is* in the midst of them, and
they have not known the LORD.
5And the pride of Israel doth testify
to his face: therefore shall Israel and
Ephraim fall in their iniquity; Judah also
shall fall with them.
6They shall go with their flocks and
with their herds to seek the LORD; but
they shall not find *him;* he hath withdrawn himself from them.
7They have dealt treacherously
against the LORD: for they have begotten strange children: now shall a
month devour them with their portions.
8Blow ye the cornet in Gibeah, *and*
the trumpet in Ramah: cry aloud *at*
Beth-aven, after thee, O Benjamin.
9Ephraim shall be desolate in the day
of rebuke: among the tribes of Israel
have I made known that which shall
surely be.
10The princes of Judah were like
them that remove the bound: *therefore*
I will pour out my wrath upon them like
water.
11Ephraim *is* oppressed *and* broken
in judgment, because he willingly
walked after the commandment.
12Therefore *will* I *be* unto Ephraim as
a moth, and to the house of Judah as
rottenness.
13When Ephraim saw his sickness,
and Judah *saw* his wound, then went

4:15 Gilgal. This was once a holy city (Josh. 5:10; 1 Sam. 10:8; 15:21). It became a place of idols (Amos 4:4; 5:5).
4:15 Beth-aven. This means *house of vanity* or idols. It was once "Beth-el," *house of God.*
4:16 backsliding heifer. A balky calf that insists on sitting down when her master tries to lead her, just as Israel was doing with God by not obeying Him.
4:17 let him alone. See Matthew 15:14.
4:18 her rulers with shame do love. Her rulers are given up to shame.
5:6 shall not find him. God knows they are not yet seeking Him sincerely, and the Israelites or any of His people even today won't be able to find Him until they search for Him with all their hearts.
5:7 devour them with their portions. Destroy their property.
5:8 Blow ye. To warn of disaster.
5:8 after thee. Behind thee.
5:10 the bound. The boundary (see Deut. 19:14 and its note, "Landmarks").
5:11 the commandment. Not God's, but Jeroboam's who "made Israel to sin" (2 Kings 13:2). See also 1 Kings 12:28 and its note, "A False Religion."

Ephraim to the Assyrian, and sent to
king Jareb: yet could he not heal you,
nor cure you of your wound.
14For I *will be* unto Ephraim as a lion,
and as a young lion to the house of Judah: I, *even* I, will tear and go away; I
will take away, and none shall rescue
him.
¶15I will go *and* return to my place,
till they acknowledge their offence, and
seek my face: in their affliction they will
seek me early.

Israel will seek the LORD

6 Come, and let us return unto the
LORD: for he hath torn, and he will
heal us; he hath smitten, and he will
bind us up.
2After two days will he revive us: in
the third day he will raise us up, and we
shall live in his sight.

6:2 Repentance Comes Soon
If Psalm 90:4 and 2 Peter 3:8 apply here, then we may expect Israel's repentance soon, because they have been set aside by God for more than two thousand years now.

3Then shall we know, *if* we follow on
to know the LORD: his going forth is
prepared as the morning; and he shall
come unto us as the rain, as the latter
and former rain unto the earth.

¶4O Ephraim, what shall I do unto
thee? O Judah, what shall I do unto
thee? for your goodness *is* as a morning cloud, and as the early dew it goeth
away.
5Therefore have I hewed *them* by the
*prophets; I have slain them by the
words of my mouth: and thy judgments
are as the light *that* goeth forth.
6For I desired mercy, and not sacrifice; and the knowledge of God more
than burnt-offerings.
7But they like men have transgressed the covenant: there have they
dealt treacherously against me.
8*Gilead *is* a city of them that work
iniquity, *and is* polluted with blood.
9And as troops of robbers wait for a
man, *so* the company of priests murder
in the way by consent: for they commit
lewdness.
10I have seen an horrible thing in the
house of Israel: there *is* the whoredom
of Ephraim, Israel is defiled.
11Also, O Judah, he hath set an harvest for thee, when I returned the captivity of my people.
7 When I would have healed *Israel,
then the iniquity of Ephraim was
discovered, and the wickedness of *Samaria: for they commit *falsehood; and
the thief cometh in, *and* the troop of
robbers spoileth without.

5:13 to the Assyrian. Many times when Israel had sinned, God allowed some foreign army to invade the country. Then instead of turning to God, they would go to Assyria or to Egypt or to some other nation for help.
5:15 in their affliction. In the time of *Jacob's Trouble (Jer. 30:7; see also its note, "Future Trouble").
6:1 Come, and let us return to the LORD. This is what Israelites will say to each other when they do repent. Compare what the Prodigal Son said in Luke 15:18.
6:3 his going forth. The repentance of Israel is to be at the time when the Lord Jesus Christ comes from heaven and descends to earth (Ps. 110:3; Rom. 11:26).
6:3 prepared. God has set His own time for Christ to return to the earth (Mark 13:32).
6:3 latter and former rain. See Joel 2:23 note, "The Rainy Seasons."
6:9 priests murder. This does not speak of physical murder necessarily, but worse; the priests caused the people to lose eternal life by not leading them to the true God. Compare Genesis 3:4.
6:9 by consent. This happened in a *city of refuge, but the priests did not save men here; they murdered them by teaching them to worship idols. The priests consented through their silence.
6:11 he hath set. He hath *appointed* a harvest. The harvest of wrath will be fully manifested in the time of *Jacob's Trouble.

[2]And they consider not in their
hearts *that* I remember all their wickedness: now their own doings have
beset them about; they are before my
face.
[3]They make the king glad with their
wickedness, and the princes with their
lies.
[4]They *are* all adulterers, as an oven
heated by the baker, *who* ceaseth from
raising after he hath kneaded the
dough, until it be *leavened.
[5]In the day of our king the princes
have made *him* sick with *bottles of
wine; he stretched out his hand with
scorners.
[6]For they have made ready their
heart like an oven, whiles they lie in
wait: their baker sleepeth all the night;
in the morning it burneth as a flaming
fire.
[7]They are all hot as an oven, and have
devoured their judges; all their kings
are fallen: *there is* none among them
that calleth unto me.
[8]Ephraim, he hath mixed himself
among the people; Ephraim is a cake
not turned.
[9]Strangers have devoured his
strength, and he knoweth *it* not: yea,
gray hairs are here and there upon him,
yet he knoweth not.
[10]And the pride of Israel testifieth to
his face: and they do not return to the
LORD their *God, nor seek him for all
this.
¶[11]Ephraim also is like a silly dove
without heart: they call to Egypt, they
go to Assyria.
[12]When they shall go, I will spread
my net upon them; I will bring them
down as the fowls of the heaven; I will
chastise them, as their congregation
hath heard.
[13]Woe unto them! for they have fled
from me: destruction unto them! because they have transgressed against
me: though I have *redeemed them,
yet they have spoken lies against me.
[14]And they have not cried unto me
with their heart, when they howled
upon their beds: they assemble themselves for corn and wine, *and* they rebel against me.
[15]Though I have bound *and* strengthened their arms, yet do they imagine
mischief against me.
[16]They return, *but* not to the most
High: they are like a deceitful bow:
their princes shall fall by the sword for
the rage of their tongue: this *shall be*
their derision in the land of Egypt.

8 *Set* the trumpet to thy mouth. *He
shall come as an eagle against the
house of the LORD, because they have
transgressed my *covenant, and trespassed against my law.
[2]Israel shall cry unto me, My God, we
know thee.
[3]Israel hath cast off *the thing that is*
good: the enemy shall pursue him.
[4]They have set up kings, but not by
me: they have made princes, and I
knew *it* not: of their silver and their
gold have they made them idols, that
they may be cut off.
¶[5]Thy calf, O Samaria, hath cast *thee*
off; mine anger is kindled against them:
how long *will it be* ere they attain to
innocency?

7:4 as an oven. The inward wickedness of Israel became worse and worse, like an oven growing hotter and hotter.
7:8 Ephraim. Another name for the ten-tribe kingdom of Israel.
7:8 cake not turned. Their characters were weak and flabby, like a pancake baked only on one side.
7:11 call to Egypt. See 5:13 note.
8:1 Set the trumpet. Set it to your mouth to sound an alarm.
8:1 He shall come. The king of Assyria.
8:1 the house of the LORD. Israel.
8:2 we know thee. See Matthew 7:22-23.
8:5 Thy calf. One of Egypt's idols (see Exod. 32:4).

[6]For from Israel *was* it also: the workman made it; therefore it *is* not God: but
the calf of Samaria shall be broken in
pieces.
[7]For they have sown the wind, and
they shall reap the whirlwind: it hath no
stalk: the bud shall yield no meal: if so
be it yield, the strangers shall swallow
it up.
[8]Israel is swallowed up: now shall
they be among the *Gentiles as a vessel wherein *is* no pleasure.
[9]For they are gone up to Assyria, a
wild ass alone by himself: Ephraim hath
hired lovers.
[10]Yea, though they have hired among
the nations, now will I gather them, and
they shall sorrow a little for the burden
of the king of princes.
[11]Because Ephraim hath made many
altars to sin, altars shall be unto him to
sin.
[12]I have written to him the great
things of my law, *but* they were counted as a strange thing.
[13]They sacrifice flesh *for* the sacrifices of mine offerings, and eat *it; but*
the LORD accepteth them not; now
will he remember their iniquity, and
visit their sins: they shall return to
*Egypt.
[14]For Israel hath forgotten his Maker,
and buildeth temples; and *Judah hath
multiplied fenced cities: but I will send
a fire upon his cities, and it shall devour
the palaces thereof.

More about Israel's destruction

9 Rejoice not, O Israel, for joy, as
other people: for thou hast gone a
whoring from thy God, thou hast loved
a reward upon every cornfloor.
[2]The floor and the winepress shall
not feed them, and the new wine shall
fail in her.
[3]They shall not dwell in the LORD'S
land; but Ephraim shall return to Egypt,
and they shall eat *unclean *things* in
Assyria.
[4]They shall not offer wine *offerings* to
the LORD, neither shall they be pleasing unto him: their sacrifices *shall be*
unto them as the bread of mourners; all
that eat thereof shall be polluted: for
their bread for their soul shall not come
into the house of the LORD.
[5]What will ye do in the solemn day,
and in the day of the feast of the LORD?
[6]For, lo, they are gone because of
destruction: Egypt shall gather them
up, Memphis shall bury them: the
pleasant *places* for their silver, nettles
shall possess them: thorns *shall be* in
their tabernacles.
[7]The days of visitation are come, the
days of recompence are come; Israel
shall know *it:* the prophet *is* a *fool, the
spiritual man *is* mad, for the multitude
of thine iniquity, and the great hatred.
[8]The watchman of Ephraim *was* with
my God: *but* the prophet *is* a snare of a
fowler in all his ways, *and* hatred in the
house of his God.
[9]They have deeply corrupted *themselves,* as in the days of Gibeah: *therefore* he will remember their iniquity, he
will visit their sins.
[10]I found Israel like grapes in the
wilderness; I saw your fathers as the
firstripe in the *fig tree at her first time:

8:6 from Israel. That is, Israel made the calf so that they could worship it (see Exod. 32).
8:10 sorrow a little. Evidently this refers to the time of *Jacob's Trouble (see *Great Tribulation).
8:10 the burden. The "king of princes" is the Man of Sin, and the "burden" he shall put upon them is to worship his image at the holy altar in the temple in Jerusalem (see vs. 11 and Rev. 13:1 note, "A Beast from the Sea." See also Rev. 13:3,5,14 notes and 13:18 note, "The Number of the Beast").
9:7 prophet is a fool. Hosea would sound like a fool to people who did not believe God's Word.
9:10 grapes . . . the firstripe. Just as fruits in the desert places are refreshing and delicious to the traveler, so Israel had been to God in the midst of the heathen nations.

but they went to Baal-peor, and separated themselves unto *that* shame; and
their abominations were according as
they loved.
11 *As for* Ephraim, their glory shall fly
away like a bird, from the birth, and
from the womb, and from the conception.
12 Though they bring up their children, yet will I bereave them, *that there
shall* not *be* a man *left:* yea, woe also to
them when I depart from them!
13 Ephraim, as I saw Tyrus, *is* planted in a pleasant place: but Ephraim
shall bring forth his children to the
murderer.
14 Give them, O LORD: what wilt thou
give? give them a miscarrying womb
and dry breasts.
15 All their wickedness *is* in Gilgal: for
there I hated them: for the wickedness
of their doings I will drive them out of
mine house, I will love them no more:
all their princes *are* revolters.
16 Ephraim is smitten, their root is
dried up, they shall bear no fruit: yea,
though they bring forth, yet will I
slay *even* the beloved *fruit* of their
womb.
17 My God will cast them away, because they did not hearken unto him:
and they shall be wanderers among the
nations.

10

Israel *is* an empty vine, he
bringeth forth fruit unto himself: according to the multitude of his
fruit he hath increased the altars; according to the goodness of his land they
have made goodly images.
2 Their heart is divided; now shall
they be found faulty: he shall break
down their altars, he shall spoil their
images.
3 For now they shall say, We have no
king, because we feared not the LORD;
what then should a king do to us?
4 They have spoken words, swearing
falsely in making a covenant: thus
*judgment springeth up as hemlock in
the furrows of the field.
5 The inhabitants of Samaria shall fear
because of the calves of *Beth-aven: for
the people thereof shall mourn over it,
and the priests thereof *that* rejoiced on
it, for the glory thereof, because it is
departed from it.
6 It shall be also carried unto Assyria
for a present to king Jareb: *Ephraim
shall receive shame, and Israel shall be
ashamed of his own counsel.
7 *As for* Samaria, her king is cut off as
the foam upon the water.
8 The *high places also of Aven, the
*sin of Israel, shall be destroyed: the
thorn and the thistle shall come up on
their altars; and they shall say to the
mountains, Cover us; and to the hills,
Fall on us.
9 O Israel, thou hast sinned from the
days of Gibeah: there they stood: the
battle in Gibeah against the children of
iniquity did not overtake them.
10 *It is* in my desire that I should chastise them; and the people shall be gath-

---

9:11 from the birth. Everything Israel does will be blighted, like a baby that never has a chance to grow up.

9:14 Give them. This is Hosea's cry. The best he can ask for a people who are so sinful is that their children may never be born.

9:15 All their wickedness is in Gilgal. Gilgal was the place of "rolling away," but the Israelites' sins were not rolled away, for they loved sin and clung to it. See what they did at Gilgal (Josh. 5:2-9; 1 Sam. 8:7; 11:14-15; see also 1 Sam 11:15 note, "Gilgal"; 13:8-14).

10:1 according to the goodness. The richer the Israelites became, the more idols they made.

10:3 now they shall say. In self-will they demanded a king: God took their kings away as punishment. Like impudent children they say, "What good were our kings anyway!"

10:5 calves of Beth-aven. They worshipped a calf-god.

10:8 say to the mountains. The same event is prophesied in Revelation 6:15-17.

10:9 battle in Gibeah. See Judges 20.

ered against them, when they shall bind
themselves in their two furrows.
11 And Ephraim *is as* an heifer *that is*
taught, *and* loveth to tread out *the corn;*
but I passed over upon her fair neck: I
will make Ephraim to ride; Judah shall
plow, *and* *Jacob shall break his clods.
12 Sow to yourselves in *righteousness, reap in *mercy; break up your
fallow ground: for *it is* time to seek the
LORD, till he come and rain righteousness upon you.
13 Ye have plowed wickedness, ye have
reaped iniquity; ye have eaten the fruit of
lies: because thou didst *trust in thy
way, in the multitude of thy mighty men.
14 Therefore shall a tumult arise
among thy people, and all thy fortresses
shall be spoiled, as Shalman spoiled
Beth-arbel in the day of battle: the
mother was dashed in pieces upon *her*
children.
15 So shall *Beth-el do unto you because of your great wickedness: in a
morning shall the king of Israel utterly
be cut off.

11

When Israel *was* a child, then
I loved him, and called my son
out of Egypt.
2 *As* they called them, so they went
from them: they sacrificed unto Baalim,
and burned *incense to graven images.
3 I taught Ephraim also to go, taking
them by their arms; but they knew not
that I healed them.
4 I drew them with cords of a man,
with bands of love: and I was to them
as they that take off the yoke on their
jaws, and I laid meat unto them.
¶5 He shall not return into the land of
Egypt, but the Assyrian shall be his
king, because they refused to return.
6 And the sword shall abide on his cities, and shall consume his branches,
and devour *them,* because of their own
counsels.
7 And my people are bent to backsliding from me: though they called them
to the most High, none at all would
exalt *him.*
8 How shall I give thee up, Ephraim?
how shall I deliver thee, Israel? how
shall I make thee as Admah? *how* shall
I set thee as Zeboim? mine heart is
turned within me, my repentings are
kindled together.
9 I will not execute the fierceness of
mine anger, I will not return to destroy
Ephraim: for I *am* God, and not man;
the *Holy One in the midst of thee: and
I will not enter into the city.
10 They shall walk after the LORD: he
shall roar like a lion: when he shall roar,
then the children shall tremble from the
west.
11 They shall tremble as a bird out of
Egypt, and as a dove out of the land of
Assyria: and I will place them in their
houses, saith the LORD.
12 Ephraim compasseth me about
with lies, and the house of Israel with
deceit: but Judah yet ruleth with God,
and is faithful with the *saints.

11:1 Two Meanings of Israel
Hosea is referring here to Israel, the nation, but the Lord Jesus Christ identified Himself with Israel, so God says the same things sometimes about both Israel and His Son (see Matt. 2:15). That is the way that prophets used to speak and write. They often had at least two meanings to their words. The Holy Spirit used this custom to picture far-off events by speaking of those that were near at hand.

The phrase "called my son out of Egypt" refers to Jesus Christ, a fact confirmed in Matthew 2:15.

10:10 two furrows. Israel and Judah each would be taken captive and, like two oxen, made to plow in the place where each was.
11:2 they called them. Prophets called the people back to God (see vs. 7).
11:3 taught Ephraim also to go. God taught His people as a parent teaches a little child to walk.
11:8 Admah . . . Zeboim. These were companion cities to Sodom and Gomorrah and were also destroyed (Deut. 29:23).

12 Ephraim feedeth on wind, and followeth after the east wind: he daily increaseth lies and desolation; and they do make a covenant with the Assyrians, and oil is carried into Egypt.

2 The LORD hath also a controversy with Judah, and will punish Jacob according to his ways; according to his doings will he recompense him.

¶3 He took his brother by the heel in the womb, and by his strength he had power with God:

4 Yea, he had power over the *angel, and prevailed: he wept, and made supplication unto him: he found him in Beth-el, and there he spake with us;

5 Even the LORD God of hosts; the LORD *is* his memorial.

6 Therefore turn thou to thy God: keep mercy and judgment, and wait on thy God continually.

¶7 *He is* a merchant, the balances of deceit *are* in his hand: he loveth to oppress.

8 And Ephraim said, Yet I am become rich, I have found me out substance: *in* all my labours they shall find none iniquity in me that *were* sin.

9 And I *that am* the LORD thy God from the land of Egypt will yet make thee to dwell in tabernacles, as in the days of the solemn feast.

10 I have also spoken by the *prophets, and I have multiplied visions, and used similitudes, by the ministry of the prophets.

11 *Is there* iniquity *in* *Gilead? surely they are *vanity: they *sacrifice bullocks in Gilgal; yea, their altars *are* as heaps in the furrows of the fields.

12 And Jacob fled into the country of Syria, and Israel served for a wife, and for a wife he kept *sheep*.

13 And by a prophet the LORD brought Israel out of Egypt, and by a prophet was he preserved.

14 Ephraim provoked *him* to anger most bitterly: therefore shall he leave his *blood upon him, and his reproach shall his Lord return unto him.

13 When Ephraim spake trembling, he exalted himself in *Israel; but when he offended in *Baal, he died.

2 And now they sin more and more, and have made them molten images of their silver, *and* idols according to their own understanding, all of it the work of the craftsmen: they say of them, Let the men that sacrifice kiss the calves.

3 Therefore they shall be as the morning cloud, and as the early dew that passeth away, as the chaff *that* is driven with the whirlwind out of the floor, and as the smoke out of the chimney.

4 Yet I *am* the LORD thy *God from the land of Egypt, and thou shalt know no god but me: for *there is* no saviour beside me.

¶5 I did know thee in the wilderness, in the land of great drought.

6 According to their pasture, so were they filled; they were filled, and their heart was exalted; therefore have they forgotten me.

7 Therefore I will be unto them as a lion: as a leopard by the way will I observe *them:*

8 I will meet them as a bear *that is* bereaved *of her whelps,* and will rend the

---

12:2 Jacob. This speaks of the nation descended from Jacob, the Israelites.
12:3 took . . . had power. See Genesis 25:26 and 32:24-28.
12:7 He. Jacob and the nation descended from him.
12:9 tabernacles. Tents.
12:10 similitudes. *Types or illustrations.
12:12 Israel served for a wife. Read the story of Israel's (Jacob's) serving for Rachel in Genesis 29.
12:13 prophet. Moses, as the type of Christ.
13:1 spake trembling. When Israel were humble before God, they were blessed, but by Hosea's time, they had rebelled.
13:8 caul. Membrane cover or lining of the heart.

caul of their heart, and there will I devour them like a lion: the wild beast shall tear them.
¶9O Israel, thou hast destroyed thyself; but in me *is* thine help.
10I will be thy king: where *is any other* that may save thee in all thy cities? and thy judges of whom thou saidst, Give me a king and princes?
11I gave thee a king in mine anger, and took *him* away in my wrath.
12The iniquity of Ephraim *is* bound up; his sin *is* hid.
13The sorrows of a travailing woman shall come upon him: he *is* an unwise son; for he should not stay long in *the place of* the breaking forth of children.
14I will *ransom them from the power of the *grave; I will *redeem them from *death: O death, I will be thy plagues; O grave, I will be thy destruction: *repentance shall be hid from mine eyes.
¶15Though he be fruitful among *his* brethren, an east wind shall come, the wind of the LORD shall come up from the wilderness, and his spring shall become dry, and his fountain shall be dried up: he shall spoil the treasure of all pleasant vessels.
16*Samaria shall become desolate; for she hath rebelled against her God: they shall fall by the sword: their infants shall be dashed in pieces, and their women with child shall be ripped up.

14 O Israel, return unto the LORD thy God; for thou hast fallen by thine iniquity.

JERUSALEM DURING THE TIME OF THE PROPHETS

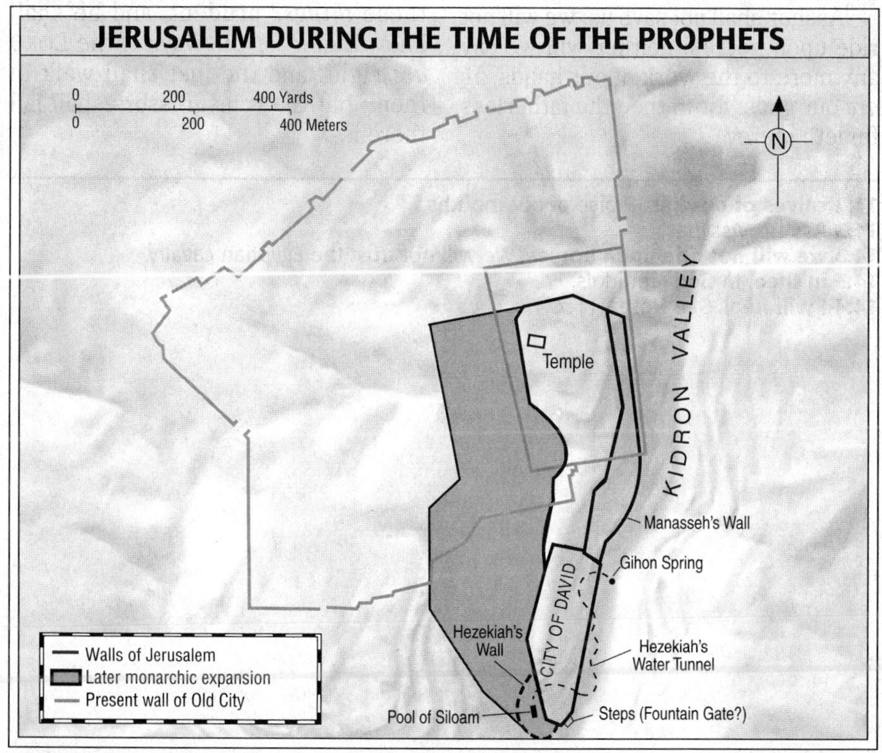

13:11 I gave thee a king. See 1 Samuel 8.
13:13 an unwise son. A man is foolish to stay in a place where the population is increasing very fast, for poverty is sure to come. Just so, Israel was sure to meet trouble.
13:14 repentance shall be hid. That is, God will not change His mind about destroying death. Hosea's words foreshadow Paul's great declaration about death and resurrection (1 Cor. 15:51-57).

13:16 Sin Causes Horrors
We must not suppose that God delights in the horrors mentioned here. It is sin and not God that causes such things. God sees sin, however, as we cannot. In the beginning, God ordained that sin would bring its own punishment. Therefore, we must put blame for the horrors of war, for instance, not on God, but on the existence of sin in the world, and on the fact that men love sin more than they love God. The babies, moreover, would be safe forever with the LORD, because they would not yet have reached the age when they would be held responsible to God for their sinful natures or for their wrongdoing.

2 Take with you words, and turn to the
LORD: say unto him, Take away all iniquity, and receive *us* graciously: so will we render the calves of our lips.
3 Asshur shall not save us; we will not
ride upon horses: neither will we say any more to the work of our hands, *Ye are* our gods: for in thee the fatherless findeth mercy.
¶4 I will heal their backsliding, I will
love them freely: for mine anger is turned away from him.
5 I will be as the dew unto Israel: he
shall grow as the lily, and cast forth his roots as Lebanon.
6 His branches shall spread, and his
beauty shall be as the olive tree, and his smell as Lebanon.
7 They that dwell under his shadow
shall return; they shall revive *as* the corn, and grow as the vine: the scent thereof *shall be* as the wine of Lebanon.
8 Ephraim *shall say,* What have I to do
any more with idols? I have heard *him,* and observed him: I *am* like a green fir tree. From me is thy fruit found.
9 Who *is* wise, and he shall understand
these *things?* prudent, and he shall know them? for the ways of the LORD *are* right, and the just shall walk in them: but the transgressors shall fall therein.

14:2 calves of our lips. Praise of our mouths.
14:3 Asshur. Assyria.
14:3 we will not ride upon horses. We will not trust the Egyptian cavalry.
14:3 in thee. In God, not idols.
14:4 I will heal. See Hosea 11:7.

JOEL

BACKGROUND

The prophet Joel lived in the 9th century B.C., when Elisha also was living. Joel was given a very clear vision of the state of the world at the time when the Lord Jesus Christ will return to earth to punish sin and set up His *kingdom. Joel and other prophets often referred to that future time as "the Day of the LORD," and the *Day of the LORD is the subject of his book. The prophet used an event of his own time, the great plague of locusts, to illustrate the great armies that will one day swarm over Palestine and lay waste the land. We should observe that whenever God prophesies of judgment, He always gives also a promise of blessing that will come to His people after the trouble has done its necessary work in them. This we shall see clearly in this prophecy.

OUTLINE OF JOEL

I.	The Day of the LORD	Joel 1:1—2:10
II.	The Jewish Remnant in the Day of the LORD	Joel 2:11—3:21

I. The Day of the LORD (1:1—2:10)

1) Desolation

1 The word of the LORD that came
to Joel the son of Pethuel.
2Hear this, ye old men, and give ear,
all ye inhabitants of the land. Hath this
been in your days, or even in the days
of your fathers?
3Tell ye your children of it, and *let*
your children *tell* their children, and
their children another generation.
4That which the palmerworm hath
left hath the locust eaten; and that
which the locust hath left hath the cankerworm eaten; and that which the cankerworm hath left hath the caterpiller
eaten.
5Awake, ye drunkards, and weep; and
howl, all ye drinkers of *wine, because
of the new wine; for it is cut off from
your mouth.
6For a nation is come up upon my
land, strong, and without number,
whose teeth *are* the teeth of a lion,
and he hath the cheek teeth of a great
lion.
7He hath laid my vine waste, and
barked my *fig tree: he hath made it
clean bare, and cast *it* away; the
branches thereof are made white.
¶8Lament like a virgin girded with
sackcloth for the husband of her youth.
9The *meat-offering and the *drink-
offering is cut off from the house of the
LORD; the priests, the LORD'S ministers, mourn.
10The field is wasted, the land
mourneth; for the corn is wasted: the

1:1 Joel. The prophet's name means *Jehovah is God*.
1:8 husband. In the East the man to whom a girl is engaged is called her husband.
1:9 cut off. The invading army of locust had ruined the crops.

new wine is dried up, the oil languisheth.
11Be ye ashamed, O ye *husbandmen; howl, O ye vinedressers, for the
wheat and for the barley; because the
harvest of the field is perished.
12The vine is dried up, and the fig
tree languisheth; the pomegranate tree,
the palm tree also, and the apple tree,
even all the trees of the field, are withered: because joy is withered away from
the sons of men.
13Gird yourselves, and lament, ye
priests: howl, ye ministers of the *altar: come, lie all night in sackcloth,
ye ministers of my *God: for the meat-
offering and the drink-offering is
withholden from the house of your God.
¶14Sanctify ye a fast, call a solemn
assembly, gather the *elders *and* all the
inhabitants of the land *into* the house of
the LORD your God, and cry unto the
LORD,

2) Destruction

15Alas for the day! for the day of the
LORD *is* at hand, and as a destruction
from the Almighty shall it come.
16Is not the meat cut off before our
eyes, *yea,* joy and gladness from the
house of our God?
17The seed is rotten under their
clods, the garners are laid desolate, the
barns are broken down; for the corn is
withered.
18How do the beasts groan! the herds
of cattle are perplexed, because they
have no pasture; yea, the flocks of
sheep are made desolate.
19O LORD, to thee will I cry: for the
*fire hath devoured the pastures of the
wilderness, and the flame hath burned
all the trees of the field.
20The beasts of the field cry also unto
thee: for the rivers of waters are dried
up, and the fire hath devoured the pastures of the wilderness.

3) Darkness

2 Blow ye the trumpet in *Zion, and
sound an alarm in my *holy mountain: let all the inhabitants of the land
tremble: for the day of the LORD
cometh, for *it is* nigh at hand;

The invading army

2A day of darkness and of gloominess,
a day of clouds and of thick darkness,
as the morning spread upon the mountains: a great people and a strong; there
hath not been ever the like, neither
shall be any more after it, *even* to the
years of many generations.
3A fire devoureth before them; and
behind them a flame burneth: the land
is as the garden of *Eden before them,
and behind them a desolate wilderness;
yea, and nothing shall escape them.
4The appearance of them *is* as the
appearance of horses; and as horsemen,
so shall they run.
5Like the noise of chariots on the tops
of mountains shall they leap, like the
noise of a flame of fire that devoureth
the stubble, as a strong people set in
battle array.
6Before their face the people shall be
much pained: all faces shall gather
blackness.
7They shall run like mighty men;
they shall climb the wall like men of
war; and they shall march every one on
his ways, and they shall not break their
ranks:
8Neither shall one thrust another;
they shall walk every one in his path:
and *when* they fall upon the sword, they
shall not be wounded.

1:15 day of the LORD. The end time of the present age when the Lord Jesus Christ is about to return in person.

2:1 the land. In the Day of the LORD, Israel will be judged as well as Gentile nations.

2:2 a great people. These armies will be of the Gentile nations, coming down from the north to take the land of Palestine, blossoming like Eden before the plague and destruction.

2:6 the people. Israel.

[9]They shall run to and fro in the city;
they shall run upon the wall, they shall
climb up upon the houses; they shall
enter in at the windows like a thief.

The Lord's return

[10]The earth shall quake before them;
the heavens shall tremble: the sun and
the moon shall be dark, and the stars
shall withdraw their shining:

2:10 A Great Earthquake
In Revelation 8:12 John describes the same event. Joel tells some of the details; John tells others.

II. The Jewish Remnant in the Day of the LORD (2:11—3:21)

*1) Their *repentance*

[11]And the LORD shall utter his voice
before his army: for his camp *is* very
great: for *he is* strong that executeth his
word: for the day of the LORD *is* great
and very terrible; and who can abide it?
¶[12]Therefore also now, saith the
LORD, turn ye *even* to me with all your
heart, and with fasting, and with
weeping, and with *mourning:
[13]And rend your heart, and not your
garments, and turn unto the LORD your
God: for he *is* gracious and merciful,
slow to anger, and of great kindness,
and repenteth him of the evil.
[14]Who knoweth *if* he will return and
repent, and leave a blessing behind him;
even a meat-offering and a drink-offering unto the LORD your God?
¶[15]Blow the trumpet in Zion, sanctify a fast, call a solemn assembly:
[16]Gather the people, sanctify the congregation, assemble the elders, gather
the children, and those that suck the
breasts: let the *bridegroom go forth of
his chamber, and the bride out of her
closet.
[17]Let the priests, the ministers of the
LORD, weep between the porch and the
altar, and let them say, Spare thy people, O LORD, and give not thine heritage
to reproach, that the heathen should
rule over them: wherefore should they
say among the people, Where *is* their
God?

2) Their rescue

¶[18]Then will the LORD be jealous for
his land, and pity his people.
[19]Yea, the LORD will answer and say
unto his people, Behold, I will send you
corn, and wine, and oil, and ye shall be
satisfied therewith: and I will no more
make you a reproach among the heathen:
[20]But I will remove far off from you
the northern *army,* and will drive him
into a land barren and desolate, with his
face toward the east sea, and his hinder
part toward the utmost sea, and his
stink shall come up, and his ill savour
shall come up, because he hath done
great things.
¶[21]Fear not, O land; be glad and rejoice: for the LORD will do great things.
[22]Be not *afraid, ye beasts of the
field: for the pastures of the wilderness
do spring, for the tree beareth her fruit,
the fig tree and the vine do yield their
strength.
[23]Be glad then, ye children of Zion,
and rejoice in the LORD your God: for
he hath given you the former rain mod-
erately, and he will cause to come down
for you the rain, the former rain, and
the latter rain in the first **month.*

2:9 the wall. Many cities in the East have walls that are wide enough to walk on.
2:11 his army. The hosts of saved ones, besides angels. Revelation 19 describes this scene, as does Zechariah 14.
2:11 abide. In this verse, abide means *to live safely through*.
2:12 now. Before the judgment falls.
2:17 thy people. Jews.
2:18 his land. Palestine.
2:20 the east sea. The Dead Sea.
2:20 the utmost sea. The Mediterranean.

2:23 The Rainy Seasons
There always used to be two rainy seasons in Palestine, one in the spring, the other in the fall. The second rain God withheld while Israel was scattered, but He promised here to send it again about the time when Israel was going to return. It is interesting to note that rain in the fall began again, lightly, about the beginning of the twentieth century, and has been increasing ever since. Compare Leviticus 26:4; Deuteronomy 11:14-17; 1 Kings 8:35-36.

24 And the floors shall be full of wheat, and the fats shall overflow with wine and oil.

3) Their restoration

25 And I will restore to you the years that the locust hath eaten, the cankerworm, and the caterpiller, and the palmerworm, my great army which I sent among you.

26 And ye shall eat in plenty, and be satisfied, and praise the name of the LORD your God, that hath dealt wondrously with you: and my people shall never be ashamed.

27 And ye shall know that I *am* in the midst of *Israel, and *that* I *am* the LORD your God, and none else: and my people shall never be ashamed.

2:32 A Remnant of Israel
The *remnant is believing Israelites. All through the history of the Jewish people, there have been those who remained true to the LORD in the midst of the national unbelief and rejection of Him. But there is also a wonderful promise of a remnant who, during the coming *Tribulation, will turn to the Lord Jesus Christ, their Messiah, and be His witnesses upon the earth after the *church has been removed and until He comes to set up His *kingdom.

4) Their regeneration

¶28 And it shall come to pass afterward, *that* I will pour out my spirit upon all flesh; and your sons and your daughters shall prophesy, your old men shall dream dreams, your young men shall see visions:

29 And also upon the servants and upon the handmaids in those days will I pour out my spirit.

Signs before Christ returns

30 And I will shew wonders in the heavens and in the earth, blood, and fire, and pillars of smoke.

31 The sun shall be turned into darkness, and the moon into blood, before the great and the terrible day of the LORD come.

32 And it shall come to pass, *that* whosoever shall call on the name of the LORD shall be delivered: for in mount Zion and in *Jerusalem shall be deliverance, as the LORD hath said, and in the *remnant whom the LORD shall call.

The last world battle

3 For, behold, in those days, and in that time, when I shall bring again the captivity of Judah and Jerusalem,

5) Recompense for their oppressors

2 I will also gather all nations, and will bring them down into the valley of Je-

3:2 The Final Struggle
The last battle of the last world war will not be between nations and nations, but between man and God! The struggle will be concerning the question of who shall rule the world—God or man. The answer is the Lord Jesus Christ, the only Man who is God (1 Tim. 3:16).

2:28 afterward. This is the same in Hebrew as the expression "the last days." More about this phrase is found in the note on Acts 2:16. Here Joel is speaking to Israel, and he evidently refers to the time right before the Lord Jesus Christ will come to rule in person on the earth.

3:1 bring again. The return of the Jews in great numbers to Palestine is a clear sign of the nearness of the Lord's return to earth.

3:2 valley of Jehoshaphat. The Plain of Armageddon.

hoshaphat, and will plead with them
there for my people and *for* my heritage
Israel, whom they have scattered
among the nations, and parted my
land.
[3]And they have cast lots for my people; and have given a boy for an harlot,
and sold a girl for wine, that they might
drink.
[4]Yea, and what have ye to do with me,
O Tyre, and Zidon, and all the coasts
of Palestine? will ye render me a recompence? and if ye recompense me,
swiftly *and* speedily will I return your
recompence upon your own head;
[5]Because ye have taken my silver
and my gold, and have carried into your
temples my goodly pleasant things:
[6]The children also of Judah and the
children of Jerusalem have ye sold unto
the Grecians, that ye might remove
them far from their border.
[7]Behold, I will raise them out of the
place whither ye have sold them, and
will return your recompence upon your
own head:
[8]And I will sell your sons and your
daughters into the hand of the children
of Judah, and they shall sell them to the
Sabeans, to a people far off: for the
LORD hath spoken *it*.
¶[9]Proclaim ye this among the Gentiles; Prepare war, wake up the mighty
men, let all the men of war draw near;
let them come up:
[10]Beat your plowshares into swords,
and your pruninghooks into spears: let
the weak say, I *am* strong.
[11]Assemble yourselves, and come,
all ye heathen, and gather yourselves

3:10 A Lasting Peace
Obviously the prophecy in Micah 4:3 can only take place after this prophecy is fulfilled, that is, after the last world war is over. Only when Christ, the Prince of Peace, reigns can there be lasting peace.

together round about: thither cause
thy mighty ones to come down, O
LORD.
[12]Let the heathen be wakened, and
come up to the valley of Jehoshaphat:
for there will I sit to judge all the heathen round about.
[13]Put ye in the sickle, for the harvest
is ripe: come, get you down; for the
press is full, the fats overflow; for their
wickedness *is* great.
[14]Multitudes, multitudes in the valley of decision: for the day of the LORD
is near in the valley of decision.
[15]The sun and the moon shall be
darkened, and the stars shall withdraw
their shining.
[16]The LORD also shall roar out of
Zion, and utter his voice from Jerusalem; and the heavens and the earth
shall shake: but the LORD *will be* the
hope of his people, and the strength of
the children of Israel.

6) Their rest

[17]So shall ye know that I *am* the
LORD your God dwelling in Zion, my
holy mountain: then shall Jerusalem be
holy, and there shall no strangers pass
through her any more.
¶[18]And it shall come to pass in that
day, *that* the mountains shall drop down

3:8 Sabeans. The people of Sheba.
3:9 Prepare war. This is the gathering of Joel 3:2, Zechariah 14:2, and Revelation 19:19 (see also Rev. 19:19 note, "The Battle of Armageddon").
3:11 thy mighty ones. The hosts of the LORD (see Joel 2:11 and its note).
3:13 sickle. This is an illustration. It is as if sinful people were vines in a field ready to be cut down. Compare Revelation 14:19.
3:14 valley of decision. Also known as, "valley of judgment." There the final decision will be shown as to who will rule the world, God's Man, Christ Jesus, or Satan's Man of Sin.
3:16 roar. Shout.
3:17 strangers. Gentiles to oppress Israel.

new wine, and the hills shall flow with
milk, and all the rivers of Judah shall
flow with waters, and a fountain shall
come forth of the house of the LORD,
and shall water the valley of Shittim.
[19]Egypt shall be a desolation, and
Edom shall be a desolate wilderness,
for the violence *against* the children of
Judah, because they have shed innocent
blood in their land.
[20]But Judah shall dwell for ever, and
Jerusalem from generation to generation.
[21]For I will cleanse their blood *that*
I have not cleansed: for the LORD
dwelleth in Zion.

3:18 the valley of Shittim. The Dead Sea Valley.
3:20 Judah. In this verse, Judah refers to anyone who has called on the Lord–Jew and Gentile alike. We will all dwell together in Christ's kingdom.
3:21 cleanse. Avenge.

AMOS

BACKGROUND AND SUMMARY

Amos was a native of the little town of Tekoa, six miles south of Beth-lehem in the kingdom of Judah. Jehovah took him while he was working as a shepherd, and sent him north to Beth-el, the center of idol worship and the residence of King Jeroboam II, who reigned (784–743 B.C.) over the kingdom of Israel. At the time Amos was there as God's prophet (about 760 B.C.), the Northern Kingdom, Israel, was at the height of its splendor, prosperity, and power, but, alas, idolatry, oppression, injustice, shameless immorality, and daring contempt of God were common sins. Though highly favored and loved by Jehovah, this sinful nation had to be punished. The mission of Amos was to expose these sins, and to inform the people that God "will punish you for all your iniquities" (Amos 3:2). Though Israel was especially threatened, the kingdom of Judah was also warned. The prophecy closes with a beautiful description of the future salvation of all Israel.

OUTLINE OF AMOS

I.	The Author and the Time of Prophecies: a Prelude	Amos 1:1—2:16
II.	The Sins of God's People, Israel Exposed, and the Judgment	Amos 3:1—6:14
III.	Five Vivid Visions	Amos 7:1—9:10
IV.	Promise of a Great Future Restoration of Israel	Amos 9:11-15

I. The Author and the Time of Prophecies: a Prelude (1:1—2:16)

1 The words of Amos, who was
among the herdmen of Tekoa,
which he saw concerning Israel in the
days of Uzziah king of *Judah, and in the
days of Jeroboam the son of *Joash king
of Israel, two years before the earthquake.
2And he said, The LORD will roar
from *Zion, and utter his voice from
Jerusalem; and the habitations of the
shepherds shall mourn, and the top of
*Carmel shall wither.

Judgments of God against the surrounding nations

3Thus saith the LORD; For three transgressions of *Damascus, and for four, I
will not turn away *the punishment* thereof; because they have threshed *Gilead
with threshing instruments of iron:
4But I will send a *fire into the house
of *Hazael, which shall devour the palaces of *Ben-hadad.
5I will break also the bar of Damascus, and cut off the inhabitant from the
plain of Aven, and him that holdeth the
sceptre from the house of *Eden: and

the people of Syria shall go into captivity unto Kir, saith the LORD.
¶6Thus saith the LORD; For three
transgressions of *Gaza, and for four, I
will not turn away *the punishment*
thereof; because they carried away captive the whole captivity, to deliver *them*
up to *Edom:
7But I will send a fire on the wall of
Gaza, which shall devour the palaces
thereof:
8And I will cut off the inhabitant from
Ashdod, and him that holdeth the
sceptre from *Ashkelon, and I will turn
mine hand against Ekron: and the remnant of the *Philistines shall perish,
saith the Lord GOD.
¶9Thus saith the LORD; For three
transgressions of Tyrus, and for four, I
will not turn away *the punishment*
thereof; because they delivered up the
whole captivity to Edom, and remembered not the brotherly *covenant:
10But I will send a fire on the wall of
Tyrus, which shall devour the palaces
thereof.
¶11Thus saith the LORD; For three
transgressions of Edom, and for four, I
will not turn away *the punishment*
thereof; because he did pursue his
brother with the sword, and did cast off
all pity, and his anger did tear perpetually, and he kept his wrath for ever:
12But I will send a fire upon Teman,
which shall devour the palaces of Bozrah.
¶13Thus saith the LORD; *For* three

1:13 Nations of Old
Ammon and Moab (2:1), nations taking their names and descent from the two sons of Lot, were old kingdoms on the east of the Jordan River. The purpose of Ammon's inhumane act described here was to leave Israel without defenders, hoping thus to secure more land.

transgressions of the children of Ammon, and for four, I will not turn away
the punishment thereof; because they
have ripped up the women with child of
Gilead, that they might enlarge their
border:
14But I will kindle a fire in the wall of
Rabbah, and it shall devour the palaces
thereof, with shouting in the day of battle, with a tempest in the day of the
whirlwind:
15And their king shall go into captivity, he and his princes together, saith
the LORD.

2 Thus saith the LORD; *For* three
transgressions of *Moab, and for
four, I will not turn away *the punishment*
thereof; because he burned the bones
of the king of Edom into lime:
2But I will send a fire upon Moab, and
it shall devour the palaces of Kirioth:
and Moab shall die with tumult, with
shouting, *and* with the sound of the
trumpet:
3And I will cut off the judge from
the midst thereof, and will slay all the
princes thereof with him, saith the
LORD.

1:5 Syria shall go into captivity. This preciction was fulfilled by Tiglath-Pileser when he captured Damascus, and carried the people away to Kir and slew Rezin (2 Kings 16:9).
1:7 fire . . . which shall devour. The prediction was fulfilled by Hezekiah (2 Kings 18:8).
1:8 Philistines shall perish. The Philistines, represented by these three main cities, were reduced still further by Psammeticus of Egypt and by Alexander the Great.
1:9 the brotherly covenant. This refers to the alliance made by King Hiram of Tyre with David and Solomon (2 Sam. 5:11; 1 Kings 5:1; 9:11-14).
1:10 fire on the wall of Tyrus. Tyre suffered fearfully at the hands of both Nebuchadnezzar and Alexander the Great.
1:12 Teman . . . Bozrah. These principal cities of Edom—Teman in the north and Bozrah in the south—represent the whole nation.
1:14 Rabbah. The only city of the Ammonites mentioned in Scripture.
2:1 burned the bones. The Moabites dug up the body of their enemy in order to burn the bones, which was a barbarous and cruel deed.
2:2 Kirioth. The chief city of Moab.

Judgment of God against Judah

¶4 Thus saith the LORD; For three
transgressions of Judah, and for four, I
will not turn away *the punishment*
thereof; because they have despised
the *law of the LORD, and have not kept
his commandments, and their lies
caused them to *err, after the which
their fathers have walked:
5 But I will send a fire upon Judah, and
it shall devour the palaces of Jerusalem.

Judgment of God against Israel

¶6 Thus saith the LORD; For three
transgressions of Israel, and for four, I will
not turn away *the punishment* thereof;
because they sold the righteous for silver, and the poor for a pair of shoes;
7 That pant after the dust of the earth
on the head of the poor, and turn aside
the way of the meek: and a man and his
father will go in unto the *same* maid, to
profane my *holy name:
8 And they lay *themselves* down upon
clothes laid to pledge by every *altar,
and they drink the wine of the condemned *in* the house of their god.
¶9 Yet destroyed I the *Amorite before them, whose height *was* like the
height of the cedars, and he *was* strong
as the oaks; yet I destroyed his fruit
from above, and his roots from beneath.
10 Also I brought you up from the land
of *Egypt, and led you forty years
through the wilderness, to possess the
land of the Amorite.
11 And I raised up of your sons for
*prophets, and of your young men for
Nazarites. *Is it* not even thus, O ye
children of Israel? saith the LORD.
12 But ye gave the Nazarites wine to
drink; and commanded the prophets,
saying, Prophesy not.
13 Behold, I am pressed under you, as
a cart is pressed *that is* full of sheaves.
14 Therefore the flight shall perish
from the swift, and the strong shall not
strengthen his force, neither shall the
mighty deliver himself:
15 Neither shall he stand that handleth
the bow; and *he that is* swift of foot shall
not deliver *himself:* neither shall he that
rideth the horse deliver himself.
16 And *he that is* courageous among

2:5 A BRIEF HISTORY OF JERUSALEM'S DESTRUCTION

The subsequent history of Jerusalem is as follows:

1. In 701 B.C. it was besieged by Sennacherib.
2. In 608 B.C. it was taken by Pharaoh Necoh.
3. In 586 B.C. it was plundered by Nebuchadnezzar.
4. About 516 B.C. the temple was rebuilt.
5. In 320 B.C. it was captured by Ptolemy Soter.
6. In 160 B.C. its walls were razed by Antiochus Epiphanes.
7. In 61 B.C. it was taken by Pompey.
8. On September 8, A.D. 70, it was destroyed by the Romans under Titus' rule.

2:8 clothes. The clothes were square pieces of cloth used by the poor as garments during the day and as blankets at night. Here the creditors were taking the garment the borrower was wearing as security for future payment. According to the law (Exod. 22:26), the garments were to be restored before the sun went down.

2:8 wine of the condemned. Literally, *the wine of the taxed or fined*. The money unjustly collected from the poor was spent on wine to be drunk at these immoral banquets.

2:9 the Amorite. Here, as in other passages (for example, Judg. 6:10), the Amorites represent all the inhabitants of Canaan. The great strength of those nations is indicated by the high cedars and the strong oaks of Palestine.

2:13 I am pressed. God was saying through Amos, "As a cart that is full of sheaves presses heavily, so I will press you into your place." Remember that Amos was a shepherd and a farmer. God uses men to present His Word, but He never expects them to speak as other than themselves. All through this book Amos shows his experience of agriculture.

the mighty shall flee away naked in that
day, saith the LORD.

II. The Sins of God's People (3:1—6:14)

3 Hear this word that the LORD hath
spoken against you, O children of
Israel, against the whole family which
I brought up from the land of Egypt,
saying,
2You only have I known of all the families of the earth: therefore I will punish you for all your iniquities.

> **3:2 God's Chosen People**
> This is the key verse in this prophecy. By an act of free choice and sovereign grace, God chose Israel to be His own "special" and "peculiar" people (Deut. 7:6-8; Exod. 19:5-6). God gave His beloved people the priesthood and the Law. They departed from God and His truth, yet looked for His favor. God sent Amos to these guilty people to tell them that He would visit them in judgment. God's love for His chosen people is everlasting, and His judgments against them, while true punishments, are also chastisements meant to bring them back to Him.

3Can two walk together, except they
be agreed?
4Will a lion roar in the forest, when
he hath no prey? will a young lion cry
out of his den, if he have taken nothing?
5Can a bird fall in a snare upon the
earth, where no gin *is* for him? shall *one*
take up a snare from the earth, and have
taken nothing at all?
6Shall a trumpet be blown in the city,
and the people not be afraid? shall there
be evil in a city, and the LORD hath not
done *it?*
7Surely the Lord GOD will do nothing,
but he revealeth his secret unto his
servants the prophets.
8The lion hath roared, who will not
*fear? the Lord GOD hath spoken, who
can but prophesy?

Surrounding nations to witness the guilt of Israel

¶9Publish in the palaces at Ashdod,
and in the palaces in the land of Egypt,
and say, Assemble yourselves upon the
mountains of *Samaria, and behold the
great tumults in the midst thereof, and
the oppressed in the midst thereof.
10For they know not to do right, saith
the LORD, who store up violence and
robbery in their palaces.
11Therefore thus saith the Lord GOD;
An adversary *there shall be* even round

3:1 the whole family. The message of Amos is chiefly meant for the ten northern tribes, known as Israel. But here and also in chapter 9, the two southern tribes, Judah and Benjamin, known as the kingdom of Judah, are included.

3:3 Can two walk together . . . ? The parable-like questions in verses 3-6 are asked to bring home to the hearts of the Israelites the fact that their sins have separated them from God, and that God is about to bring heavy judgment on them. Each contains a cause and an effect, leading to the great climax.

3:5 gin. A trap or snare.

3:6 evil. This evil is the trouble or calamity about to descend on apostate and guilty Israel because of its sins; this does not refer to *sin. The Hebrews, like the well-instructed Christians of today, knew that such events as wars, epidemics, and earthquakes were sent in the overruling love and plan of God.

3:7 his servants the prophets. This verse defines a prophet. The prophet is one to whom God reveals His will, and who comes forward to declare that will and purpose to man. Today we have the Bible, God's revelation to man, in which we learn the will of God and the purposes of God in His dealings with His creatures.

3:9 Ashdod . . . Egypt. Ashdod and Egypt represent unrighteous nations, regarded by Israel as godless heathen, but they were summoned to witness against Israel.

3:10 know not to do right. Israel had been sinning so long that they no longer knew how to do the right thing.

3:10 palaces. The frequent references to "palaces" imply that the wealthy people lived in luxury on the fruits of oppression.

3:11 An adversary. The Assyrians. See 2 Kings 17–18 for fulfillment of this prophecy.

about the land; and he shall bring down
thy strength from thee, and thy palaces
shall be spoiled.
[12]Thus saith the LORD; As the shepherd taketh out of the mouth of the lion
two legs, or a piece of an ear; so shall
the children of Israel be taken out that
dwell in Samaria in the corner of a bed,
and in Damascus *in* a couch.
[13]Hear ye, and testify in the house of
*Jacob, saith the Lord GOD, the God of
hosts,
[14]That in the day that I shall visit the
transgressions of Israel upon him I will
also visit the altars of *Beth-el: and the
*horns of the altar shall be cut off, and
fall to the ground.
[15]And I will smite the winter house
with the summer house; and the houses
of ivory shall perish, and the great
houses shall have an end, saith the LORD.

Captivity predicted

4 Hear this word, ye kine of *Bashan,
that *are* in the *mountain of Samaria, which oppress the poor, which crush
the needy, which say to their masters,
Bring, and let us drink.
[2]The Lord GOD hath sworn by his
holiness, that, lo, the days shall come
upon you, that he will take you away
with hooks, and your posterity with
fishhooks.

4:1 An Insult
The rulers and leaders in civil and social life are called "cows." Bashan, a region on the east of the Jordan, was renowned for its rich pastures and fine cattle. The bulls of Bashan were fierce in aspect (Ps. 22:12). The feminine word "kine," or cows, expressed the idea that the luxurious nobles of Israel were more like women than men.

[3]And ye shall go out at the breaches,
every *cow at that which is* before her;
and ye shall cast *them* into the palace,
saith the LORD.

Their false worship scorned

¶[4]Come to Beth-el, and transgress;
at Gilgal multiply transgression; and
bring your sacrifices every morning,
and your *tithes after three years:
[5]And offer a sacrifice of thanksgiving
with *leaven, and proclaim *and* publish
the free *offerings: for this liketh you,
O ye children of Israel, saith the Lord
GOD.

God's corrective measures

¶[6]And I also have given you cleanness of teeth in all your cities, and want
of bread in all your places: yet have ye
not returned unto me, saith the LORD.
[7]And also I have withholden the rain
from you, when *there were* yet three

3:12 As the shepherd taketh. Here is language and a figure taken from the daily life of Amos. He taught that nothing but the merest wrecks and fragments of the great and prosperous Israel would remain.

3:13 Hear ye. The surrounding nations are here addressed. They were about to witness Jehovah's punishment of Israel.

3:14 altars of Beth-el. Beth-el was a center of idol worship after Jeroboam the First had set up the golden calf there. In the day of God's visitation, the people and their idols would perish together.

4:2 posterity. Residue of the people.

4:3 breaches. Gaps in the city wall made by the enemy, through which the captive people would be led like cows.

4:3 cast them into the palace. They should be cast as slaves into the palace of Sennacherib.

4:4 Come to Beth-el, and transgress; at Gilgal. Beth-el (Gen. 12:8; 13) and Gilgal (Josh. 4:20-24; 5:10) were places of hallowed memories. Now both had become centers of idol worship. These words of Amos seem like a command, but really they are an extremely strong prohibition. He used bitter irony or sarcasm. See also verse 5.

4:6 cleanness of teeth. This is identical with want of bread. Famine was the first trouble in a list of chastisements intended to bring Israel back to Jehovah. Following famine came drought (vss. 7-8); "blasting," literally, *an exceeding scorching*, (vs. 9); pestilence (vs. 10); and fire (vs. 11).

months to the harvest: and I caused it
to rain upon one city, and caused it not
to rain upon another city: one piece was
rained upon, and the piece whereupon
it rained not withered.
8So two *or* three cities wandered unto
one city, to drink water; but they were
not satisfied: yet have ye not returned
unto me, saith the LORD.
9I have smitten you with blasting and
mildew: when your gardens and your
vineyards and your fig trees and your
olive trees increased, the palmerworm
devoured *them:* yet have ye not returned unto me, saith the LORD.
10I have sent among you the pestilence after the manner of Egypt: your
young men have I slain with the sword,
and have taken away your horses; and
I have made the stink of your camps to
come up unto your nostrils: yet have ye
not returned unto me, saith the LORD.
11I have overthrown *some* of you, as
God overthrew Sodom and Gomorrah,
and ye were as a firebrand plucked out
of the burning: yet have ye not returned
unto me, saith the LORD.

A solemn warning

12Therefore thus will I do unto thee,
O Israel: *and* because I will do this unto
thee, prepare to meet thy God, O Israel.
13For, lo, he that formeth the mountains, and createth the wind, and
declareth unto man what *is* his thought,
that maketh the morning darkness, and
treadeth upon the high places of the
earth, The LORD, The God of hosts, *is*
his name.

Lamentation for the fall of Israel

5 Hear ye this word which I take up
against you, *even* a lamentation, O
house of Israel.
2The virgin of Israel is fallen; she
shall no more rise: she is forsaken upon
her land; *there is* none to raise her up.
3For thus saith the Lord GOD; The
city that went out *by* a thousand shall
leave an hundred, and that which went
forth *by* an hundred shall leave ten, to
the house of Israel.

Seek the LORD, and live

¶4For thus saith the LORD unto the
house of Israel, Seek ye me, and ye
shall live:
5But seek not Beth-el, nor enter into
Gilgal, and pass not to *Beer-sheba: for
Gilgal shall surely go into captivity, and
Beth-el shall come to nought.
6Seek the LORD, and ye shall live; lest
he break out like fire in the house of
*Joseph, and devour *it,* and *there be*
none to quench *it* in Beth-el.
7Ye who turn judgment to wormwood, and leave off *righteousness in
the earth,
8*Seek him* that maketh the seven
stars and Orion, and turneth the shadow of *death into the morning, and
maketh the day dark with night: that
calleth for the waters of the sea, and
poureth them out upon the face of the
earth: The LORD *is* his name:
9That strengtheneth the spoiled
against the strong, so that the spoiled
shall come against the fortress.

4:12 prepare to meet thy God. Though all disciplinary measures had failed, God still loved His chosen people, and before He inflicted the last and worst judgment upon them, He solemnly warned them to prepare to meet Him.

5:1 against you. Amos was mourning the Israelites as if they had already been destroyed.

5:2 virgin. Israel had never before been subdued by foreigners.

5:7 wormwood. This is an herb with a bitter taste, and in this verse it is used to show that this was not true justice.

5:8 seven stars. This refers to the Pleiades, which is the most conspicuous star cluster that can be seen without a telescope. In this verse, the Pleiades and Orion, which is the brightest of the constellations, represent the heavenly bodies in general, for these show the power of God.

5:9 That strengtheneth the spoiled. Just as sudden destruction was to come against strong Israel, destruction would come upon the fortress.

[10]They hate him that rebuketh in the
gate, and they abhor him that speaketh
uprightly.
[11]Forasmuch therefore as your treading *is* upon the poor, and ye take from
him burdens of wheat: ye have built
houses of hewn stone, but ye shall not
dwell in them; ye have planted pleasant vineyards, but ye shall not drink
wine of them.
[12]For I know your manifold transgressions and your mighty sins: they
afflict the *just, they take a bribe, and
they turn aside the poor in the gate *from
their right.*
[13]Therefore the prudent shall keep
silence in that time; for it *is* an evil
time.
[14]Seek good, and not evil, that ye may
live: and so the LORD, the God of hosts,
shall be with you, as ye have spoken.
[15]Hate the evil, and love the good,
and establish judgment in the gate: it
may be that the LORD God of hosts will
be gracious unto the remnant of Joseph.

God's visitation

[16]Therefore the LORD, the God of
hosts, the Lord, saith thus; Wailing *shall
be* in all streets; and they shall say in all
the highways, Alas! alas! and they shall
call the husbandman to *mourning, and
such as are skilful of lamentation to
wailing.
[17]And in all vineyards *shall be* wailing:
for I will pass through thee, saith the
LORD.
[18]Woe unto you that desire the day of
the LORD! to what end *is* it for you? the
day of the LORD *is* darkness, and not
light.
[19]As if a man did flee from a lion, and
a bear met him; or went into the house,
and leaned his hand on the wall, and a
serpent bit him.
[20]*Shall* not the day of the LORD *be*
darkness, and not light? even very dark,
and no brightness in it?

God's hatred of mere forms of worship

¶[21]I hate, I despise your feast days,
and I will not smell in your solemn assemblies.
[22]Though ye offer me burnt-offerings
and your meat-offerings, I will not accept *them:* neither will I regard the
*peace-offerings of your fat beasts.
[23]Take thou away from me the noise
of thy songs; for I will not hear the
melody of thy viols.
[24]But let judgment run down as waters, and righteousness as a mighty
stream.

The idolatry of Israel

[25]Have ye offered unto me sacrifices
and offerings in the wilderness forty
years, O house of Israel?
[26]But ye have borne the *tabernacle
of your *Moloch and Chiun your images, the star of your god, which ye
made to yourselves.
[27]Therefore will I cause you to go into

5:13 the prudent shall keep silence. The prudent were those who feared God. Because of the wickedness, hatred, corruption, and selfish oppression of the leaders, the prudent men suffered in silence. They bowed before the righteous ways of God in judgment.

5:15 remnant of Joseph. Joseph is another name for the children of Israel.

5:16 skilful of lamentation. These were people who made it their profession to sing or chant mournful dirges at funerals. This is still done in some Eastern countries.

5:17 I will pass through thee. As in Egypt (Exod. 12:12-13), God would pass through, taking vengeance and causing the death wail.

5:21 I despise your feast days. Though the people of Israel maintained the form of the Mosaic worship, it was destitute of spiritual value, because Israel had turned from God to idols (compare Isa. 1:11).

5:26 ye have borne the tabernacle of . . . your images. Israel had been worshipping Moloch and Chiun. Chiun was the star god, associated with worshipping the planet Saturn. The Israelites were worshipping the creation rather than the Creator.

captivity beyond Damascus, saith the
LORD, whose name *is* The God of hosts.

Woe against the chief men who are at ease in their sins

6 Woe to them *that are* at ease in
Zion, and *trust in the mountain of
Samaria, *which are* named chief of the
nations, to whom the house of Israel
came!
2 Pass ye unto Calneh, and see; and
from thence go ye to Hamath the great:
then go down to *Gath of the Philistines: *be they* better than these kingdoms? or their border greater than your
border?
3 Ye that put far away the evil day,
and cause the seat of violence to come
near;
4 That lie upon beds of ivory, and
stretch themselves upon their couches,
and eat the lambs out of the flock, and
the calves out of the midst of the stall;
5 That chant to the sound of the viol,
and invent to themselves instruments
of musick, like *David;
6 That drink wine in bowls, and
*anoint themselves with the chief oint-
ments: but they are not grieved for the
affliction of Joseph.

Heavy punishment and awful judgments

¶7 Therefore now shall they go captive with the first that go captive, and
the banquet of them that stretched
themselves shall be removed.
8 The Lord GOD hath sworn by himself, saith the LORD the God of hosts, I
abhor the excellency of Jacob, and hate
his palaces: therefore will I deliver up
the city with all that is therein.
9 And it shall come to pass, if there
remain ten men in one house, that they
shall die.
10 And a man's uncle shall take him
up, and he that burneth him, to bring
out the bones out of the house, and shall
say unto him that *is* by the sides of the
house, *Is there* yet *any* with thee? and
he shall say, No. Then shall he say, Hold
thy tongue: for we may not make mention of the name of the LORD.
11 For, behold, the LORD commandeth,
and he will smite the great house with
breaches, and the little house with
clefts.

5:27 captivity beyond Damascus. The fulfillment of this prophecy is found in 2 Kings 17:6.

6:1 them that are at ease. The nobles and leaders of the Hebrews. The people came to these chief men of influence for justice and direction, but the rich were not interested in helping the poor and those in need. God is not pleased with this kind of selfishness, and He will judge it.

6:2 Calneh . . Hamath . . . Gath. Cities surrounding Israel and Judah that had been destroyed due to their pride. Israel was not immune to the same kind of judgment from God if they did not start obeying and worshipping Him.

6:2 these kingdoms. Israel and Judah.

6:3 the evil day. The approaching day of God's wrath.

6:6 Joseph. See 5:15 note.

6:7 banquet. Wine drinking (see vs. 6).

6:8 the excellency of Jacob. Pride and arrogance of the people.

6:10 uncle. The nearest relative, who at such times had the duty of burying the dead (Gen. 25:9; 35:29).

6:10 the bones. The dead body of one who died of the pestilence.

6:10 by the sides of the house . . . Hold thy tongue. In the innermost sections of the house. In times of great pestilence, the bodies of the dead were burned to avoid contagion. Such was the case here (vs. 9). Those who burned the bodies were afraid to even "mention" the "name of the LORD" for fear that additional judgment would fall on them.

6:11 the great house . . . the little house. It has been suggested that the "great house" refers to the ten northern tribes, Israel, and the "little house" to the two southern tribes, Judah.

¶[12]Shall horses run upon the rock? will *one* plow *there* with oxen? for ye have turned judgment into gall, and the fruit of righteousness into hemlock:
[13]Ye which rejoice in a thing of nought, which say, Have we not taken to us horns by our own strength?
[14]But, behold, I will raise up against you a nation, O house of Israel, saith the LORD the God of hosts; and they shall afflict you from the entering in of Hemath unto the river of the wilderness.

III. Five Vivid Visions (7:1—9:10)

7 Thus hath the Lord GOD shewed unto me; and, behold, he formed grasshoppers in the beginning of the shooting up of the latter growth; and, lo, *it was* the latter growth after the king's mowings.
[2]And it came to pass, *that* when they had made an end of eating the grass of the land, then I said, O Lord GOD, forgive, I beseech thee: by whom shall Jacob arise? for he *is* small.
[3]The LORD repented for this: It shall not be, saith the LORD.
¶[4]Thus hath the Lord GOD shewed unto me: and, behold, the Lord GOD called to contend by *fire, and it devoured the great deep, and did eat up a part.
[5]Then said I, O Lord GOD, cease, I beseech thee: by whom shall Jacob arise? for he *is* small.
[6]The LORD repented for this: This also shall not be, saith the Lord GOD.
¶[7]Thus he shewed me: and, behold, the Lord stood upon a wall *made* by a plumbline, with a plumbline in his hand.
[8]And the LORD said unto me, Amos, what seest thou? And I said, A plumbline. Then said the Lord, Behold, I will set a plumbline in the midst of my people *Israel: I will not again pass by them any more:
[9]And the high places of *Isaac shall be desolate, and the sanctuaries of Israel shall be laid waste; and I will rise against the house of Jeroboam with the sword.

Amos in danger as Amaziah tried to get rid of him

¶[10]Then Amaziah the priest of Bethel sent to Jeroboam king of Israel, saying, Amos hath conspired against thee in the midst of the house of Israel: the land is not able to bear all his words.
[11]For thus Amos saith, Jeroboam shall die by the sword, and Israel shall surely be led away captive out of their own land.
[12]Also Amaziah said unto Amos, O thou seer, go, flee thee away into the land of *Judah, and there eat bread, and prophesy there:
[13]But prophesy not again any more at Beth-el: for it *is* the king's chapel, and it *is* the king's court.

6:14 a nation. Assyria.
6:14 the entering in of Hemath unto the river of the wilderness. All Palestine from the north to the south.
7:1 grasshoppers. Locusts are often used as instruments of the wrath of God.
7:1 the king's mowings. The king's share, which was the portion of the early spring growth that was taken as tribute by the kings of Israel to feed their animals.
7:4 fire, and it devoured the great deep. The fire dried up the deep springs of water.
7:4 did eat up a part. Would have consumed or eaten up the land.
7:7 a plumbline. A plumb line is a perpendicular measuring line used not only when building but also when destroying houses. It symbolized God's searching investigation of Israel's condition.
7:8 pass by. Forgive.
7:9 house of Jeroboam. When Zachariah, the son of Jeroboam, was slain by Shallum (2 Kings 15:1-12), this prophecy was fulfilled.
7:12 eat bread. Amaziah suggested slyly that Amos preached for the money that he got out of it, but that was not true of Amos. It is never true of a sincere servant of God.

Amos pronounces doom upon Amaziah

¶ 14 Then answered Amos, and said to
Amaziah, I *was* no *prophet, neither
was I a prophet's son; but I *was* an
herdman, and a gatherer of sycomore
fruit:
15 And the LORD took me as I followed
the flock, and the LORD said unto me,
Go, prophesy unto my people Israel.
¶ 16 Now therefore hear thou the word
of the LORD: Thou sayest, Prophesy not
against Israel, and drop not *thy word*
against the house of Isaac.
17 Therefore thus saith the LORD; Thy
wife shall be an harlot in the city, and
thy sons and thy daughters shall fall by
the sword, and thy land shall be divided
by line; and thou shalt die in a polluted
land: and Israel shall surely go
into captivity forth of his land.

Fourth vision: the kingdom of Israel doomed

8 Thus hath the Lord GOD shewed
unto me: and behold a basket of
summer fruit.
2 And he said, Amos, what seest thou?
And I said, A basket of summer fruit.
Then said the LORD unto me, The end
is come upon my people of Israel; I will
not again pass by them any more.
3 And the songs of the temple shall be
howlings in that day, saith the Lord
GOD: *there shall be* many dead bodies in
every place; they shall cast *them* forth
with silence.

Further details of the sins and their judgments

¶ 4 Hear this, O ye that swallow up the
needy, even to make the poor of the
land to fail,
5 Saying, When will the *new moon
be gone, that we may sell corn? and the
*sabbath, that we may set forth wheat,
making the *ephah small, and the shekel
great, and falsifying the balances by
deceit?

8:5 Empty Worship
Though the people of Israel had departed from God and their worship was corrupt, they still kept an elaborate system of what they called "worship," and they reluctantly observed seasons that had been times of special holiness, or sacredness, such as the *new moon and the *Sabbath. Even on these days, they hated to stop their sinful ways of making money.

6 That we may buy the poor for *silver,
and the needy for a pair of shoes;
yea, and sell the refuse of the wheat?
7 The LORD hath sworn by the excellency
of Jacob, Surely I will never forget
any of their works.
8 Shall not the land tremble for this,
and every one mourn that dwelleth
therein? and it shall rise up wholly as a
flood; and it shall be cast out and
drowned, as *by* the flood of *Egypt.
9 And it shall come to pass in that
day, saith the Lord GOD, that I will
cause the sun to go down at noon, and

7:14 sycomore fruit. Small figs grew on the sycomore tree. Amos pricked or pinched these to make them ripen, as was necessary.

7:15 my people Israel. Not Judah, as Amaziah desired, but Israel.

7:17 a polluted land. Any land not his own, to the Hebrew, was polluted, or unclean.

8:1 basket of summer fruit. This symbolized the condition of Israel as now ready or ripe for its last punishment and the end of its national existence.

8:3 the songs. Their songs, whether the idlers' songs of 6:5 or the heartless songs of 5:23, were to be turned into lamentation, or "howlings," because of the many who would die—the "dead bodies."

8:5 making the ephah small, and the shekel great. Dishonest trading and selling.

8:7 the excellency of Jacob. In this verse, this expression has a different meaning than when read in 6:8. It means God Himself.

8:8 Shall not the land tremble . . . ? It may help to consider this as follows: "For this, shall not the land tremble as in an earthquake, and every dweller therein mourn when the whole land rises up as the Nile, and rolls to and fro, and then subsides like the river of Egypt after the mighty inundations?"

I will darken the earth in the clear day:

10And I will turn your feasts into mourning, and all your songs into lamentation; and I will bring up sackcloth upon all loins, and baldness upon every head; and I will make it as the mourning of an only *son,* and the end thereof as a bitter day.

¶11Behold, the days come, saith the Lord GOD, that I will send a famine in the land, not a famine of bread, nor a thirst for water, but of hearing the words of the LORD:

12And they shall wander from sea to sea, and from the north even to the east, they shall run to and fro to seek the word of the LORD, and shall not find *it.*

13In that day shall the fair virgins and young men faint for thirst.

14They that swear by the *sin of Samaria, and say, Thy god, O Dan, liveth; and, The manner of *Beer-sheba liveth; even they shall fall, and never rise up again.

Fifth vision: Jehovah stands beside the altar

9 I saw the LORD standing upon the altar: and he said, Smite the lintel of the door, that the posts may shake: and cut them in the head, all of them; and I will slay the last of them with the sword: he that fleeth of them shall not flee away, and he that escapeth of them shall not be delivered.

A small remnant saved in the destruction of the guilty nation

2Though they dig into hell, thence shall mine hand take them; though they climb up to heaven, thence will I bring them down:

3And though they hide themselves in the top of Carmel, I will search and take them out thence; and though they be hid from my sight in the bottom of the sea, thence will I command the serpent, and he shall bite them:

4And though they go into captivity before their enemies, thence will I command the sword, and it shall slay them: and I will set mine eyes upon them for evil, and not for good.

5And the Lord GOD of hosts *is* he that toucheth the land, and it shall melt, and all that dwell therein shall mourn: and it shall rise up wholly like a flood; and shall be drowned, as *by* the flood of Egypt.

6*It is* he that buildeth his stories in the heaven, and hath founded his troop in the earth; he that calleth for the waters of the sea, and poureth them out upon the face of the earth: The LORD *is* his name.

7*Are* ye not as children of the Ethiopians unto me, O children of Israel? saith the LORD. Have not I brought up Israel out of the land of Egypt? and the Philistines from Caphtor, and the Syrians from Kir?

8Behold, the eyes of the Lord GOD

8:9 darken. This is a common figure for great calamity.

8:11 famine . . . of hearing the words of the LORD. The people tried to drive Amos away from Beth-el. During times of prosperity they despised the Word of God. Therefore, in the time of their distress, God, acting in just punishment, would not speak to them by prophets or by dreams (1 Sam. 28:15).

8:14 swear by. Worship.

8:14 sin of Samaria . . . Thy god . . . manner of Beer-sheba. These three expressions refer to idol worship.

9:1 I saw the LORD. In this vision the people were assembled in the temple for protection from the judgment of God, but even there escape was impossible. Many were destroyed there by the falling temple, and the few who escaped that death fell by the sword. God sees into every hiding place (vss. 2-4).

9:5 the Lord GOD of hosts is he. Verses 5-6 are a description of the omnipotence or all-powerfulness of God.

9:6 troop. The visible sky which appears as a vault above the earth.

9:7 The Destiny of Nations
This verse teaches that just because the Israelites were God's chosen people that fact would not save them in the day of God's judgment. The fact that they were brought from Egypt to Canaan by the favor and power of God could not save them from being removed to Assyria. We also learn here the important part that God has in the destiny of nations.

are upon the sinful kingdom, and I will
destroy it from off the face of the earth;
saving that I will not utterly destroy the
house of Jacob, saith the LORD.
9For, lo, I will command, and I will sift
the house of Israel among all nations,
like as *corn* is sifted in a sieve, yet shall
not the least grain fall upon the earth.
10All the sinners of my people shall
die by the sword, which say, The evil
shall not overtake nor prevent us.

IV. Promise of a Great Future Restoration of Israel (9:11-15)

¶11In that day will I raise up the tabernacle of David that is fallen, and close
up the breaches thereof; and I will raise
up his ruins, and I will build it as in the
days of old:
12That they may possess the remnant
of Edom, and of all the heathen, which
are called by my name, saith the LORD
that doeth this.
13Behold, the days come, saith the
LORD, that the plowman shall overtake
the reaper, and the treader of grapes
him that soweth seed; and the mountains shall drop sweet wine, and all the
hills shall melt.
14And I will bring again the captivity
of my people of Israel, and they shall
build the waste cities, and inhabit *them;*
and they shall plant vineyards, and
drink the wine thereof; they shall also
make gardens, and eat the fruit of them.
15And I will plant them upon their
land, and they shall no more be pulled
up out of their land which I have given
them, saith the LORD thy God.

9:11 An Everlasting Kingdom
God's *covenant with David (2 Sam. 7) contained a promise that his descendants would have an everlasting *kingdom. That covenant and this prophecy find an adequate fulfillment in the Lord Jesus Christ, who as David's greater Son will be at the head of this everlasting kingdom. The apostle James, the half brother of Jesus, applied this passage to this present *dispensation (Acts 15:16-17), when believing Jews and Gentiles alike are sharers of the glories of the kingdom of God's Son.

9:13 National Peace and Prosperity
These sublime words of the prophet point to a future day when the Jews will be restored to their own land. That will be a time of national peace and prosperity (vs. 13) and a time of long and settled habitation (vs. 14). The glorious restoration of His chosen people will be effected by God's own power (vs. 15), and the reason will be the same that caused Him to choose them in the first place—because He loved them.

9:8 sinful kingdom. Israel. This kingdom collapsed in 722 B.C. (2 Kings 17:6).
9:8 not utterly destroy. A *remnant comprised of God-fearing believers would be spared.
9:9 Israel among all nations. This prophecy is now in the process of fulfillment. The house of Israel is being tossed about throughout all the nations, just as corn is shaken about in a sieve. Not a single grain (one of the godly elect) shall perish.
9:12 the remnant of Edom. Mankind is meant here—the remnant of Adam.
9:12 called by my name. This indicated God's possession or ownership.

Obadiah

BACKGROUND

To understand the book, we should know its historical background. Sela, later called Petra, was the capital of Edom. It was cut out of solid cliffs of rose-colored rock. Its majestic temples and palaces are, even in their ruins today, one of the wonders of the world. Since Sela could be reached only through a narrow ravine, which a handful of soldiers could guard against a great army, the Edomites felt impregnable against all enemies (verses 3,4), and were lifted up in pride (verse 3). History tells no clear story of how Sela was destroyed, but it stands here written that this was to be done, and the silent ruins have for centuries cried out to the truth of this prophecy. Obadiah made it plain that Sela's fall was to be accomplished through the treachery of allies (verses 5,7).

THE WRITER

Obadiah, the prophet whose name means *Servant of Jehovah,* wrote this book, which is the shortest book in the Old Testament. Obadiah prophesied shortly after the Babylonian invasion of Judah.

SUMMARY

The book deals, first, with the destruction of Edom (verse 9) because of its cruelty (verse 14) to the fleeing remnant of Judah during the Babylonian conquest of Palestine (verse 11); and second, with the millennial splendor of restored Judah after the Lord Jesus Christ returns and sets up His *kingdom (verses 17–21).

OUTLINE OF OBADIAH

I.	Title and Theme	Obadiah 1-4
II.	Edom's Defeat: the Method and Reason	Obadiah 5-14
III.	The Spiritual Law of Sowing and Harvesting	Obadiah 15-16
IV.	Millennial Blessing upon Israel	Obadiah 17-21

I. Title and Theme (vss. 1-4)

The vision of Obadiah. Thus saith the Lord GOD concerning Edom; We have heard a rumour from the LORD, and an ambassador is sent among the heathen, Arise ye, and let us rise up against her in battle.

2Behold, I have made thee small among the heathen: thou art greatly despised.

1 the Lord GOD. *Adonai Jehovah*, the covenant-keeping God, who is Master. See *names of God.

¶ 3 The pride of thine heart hath deceived thee, thou that dwellest in the clefts of the rock, whose habitation *is* high; that saith in his heart, Who shall bring me down to the ground?

4 Though thou exalt *thyself* as the eagle, and though thou set thy nest among the stars, thence will I bring thee down, saith the LORD.

II. Edom Defeated (vss. 5-14)

5 If thieves came to thee, if robbers by night, (how art thou cut off!) would they not have stolen till they had enough? if the grapegatherers came to thee, would they not leave *some* grapes?

6 How are *the things* of Esau searched out! *how* are his hidden things sought up!

7 All the men of thy confederacy have brought thee *even* to the border: the men that were at peace with thee have deceived thee, *and* prevailed against thee; *they that eat* thy bread have laid a wound under thee: *there is* none understanding in him.

8 Shall I not in that day, saith the LORD, even destroy the wise *men* out of Edom, and understanding out of the mount of Esau?

9 And thy mighty *men,* O Teman, shall be dismayed, to the end that every one of the mount of Esau may be cut off by slaughter.

Edom punished for cruelty to Judah

¶ 10 For *thy* violence against thy brother Jacob shame shall cover thee, and thou shalt be cut off for ever.

11 In the day that thou stoodest on the other side, in the day that the strangers carried away captive his forces, and foreigners entered into his gates, and cast lots upon Jerusalem, even thou *wast* as one of them.

12 But thou shouldest not have looked on the day of thy brother in the day that he became a stranger; neither shouldest thou have rejoiced over the children of Judah in the day of their destruction; neither shouldest thou have spoken proudly in the day of distress.

13 Thou shouldest not have entered into the gate of my people in the day of their calamity; yea, thou shouldest not have looked on their affliction in the day of their calamity, nor have laid *hands* on their substance in the day of their calamity;

14 Neither shouldest thou have stood in the crossway, to cut off those of his that did escape; neither shouldest thou have delivered up those of his that did remain in the day of distress.

III. Harvesting (vss. 15-16)

15 For the day of the LORD *is* near upon all the heathen: as thou hast done, it shall be done unto thee: thy reward shall return upon thine own head.

16 For as ye have drunk upon my holy mountain, *so* shall all the heathen drink continually, yea, they shall drink, and they shall swallow down, and they shall be as though they had not been.

---

3 dwellest in the clefts of the rock. This refers to Petra, the great cliff city (see the introduction to this book).

5,7 robbers by night . . . men of thy confederacy . . . have deceived thee. This refers to the fact that only treachery on the part of Edom's trusted allies made possible her capture, so impregnable were her natural defenses. (See vs. 7.)

5 have stolen. Steal.

5 grapes. Gleaning grapes.

6 Esau. The Edomites were the descendants of Esau, the brother of Jacob. The brothers were twins, but Esau hated his brother because it was prophesied that he must serve Jacob (Gen. 25:23,30). Esau's hatred of his brother Jacob (renamed "Israel"—Gen. 32:28) was inherited by the Edomites (Num. 20:14-22; 2 Chron. 21:8-17).

7 laid a wound. Laid a trap.

1:15 God's Day of Judgment
The Day of the LORD refers to that time when God openly judges, and it is unmistakably clear to all, through the pre-announcement of a prophet, that the judgment is from God (see Zeph. 1:14-18). All such days of the LORD are illustrations of and only a prelude to that greater final period of judgment, preeminently the *Day of the LORD. This day is described in Revelation 6–20: It begins with the pouring out of judgments on the earth and is climaxed by the personal return of Christ to destroy the enemies of God (Rev. 19:11-21) and set up His one-thousand year *kingdom reign (Rev. 20:1-6).

IV. Millennial Blessing (vss. 17-21)
(Esau's territory for Israel:
Num. 24:17-19)

¶17But upon mount Zion shall be deliverance, and there shall be holiness;
and the house of Jacob shall possess
their possessions.
18And the house of Jacob shall be a
fire, and the house of Joseph a flame,
and the house of Esau for stubble, and
they shall kindle in them, and devour
them; and there shall not be *any* remaining of the house of Esau; for the
LORD hath spoken *it*.
19And *they of* the south shall possess the mount of Esau; and *they of*
the plain the Philistines: and they
shall possess the fields of Ephraim,
and the fields of Samaria: and Benjamin *shall possess* Gilead.
20And the captivity of this host of the
children of Israel *shall possess* that of
the Canaanites, *even* unto Zarephath;
and the captivity of Jerusalem, which *is*
in Sepharad, shall possess the cities of
the south.
21And saviours shall come up on
mount Zion to judge the mount of
Esau; and the kingdom shall be the
LORD'S.

---

18 not be any remaining. Not an Edomite remains in the world today! At least, no one knows where any are. See Isaiah 34:5-17–Idumea is the land of Edom.
20 Sepharad. The Sephardic Jews. Some of them dwelt in Spain for centuries.
21 saviours. Judges, who will serve under the Lord Jesus Christ when He is worshipped as King of Kings and Lord of Lords.

JONAH

THE WRITER AND THE TIME

The book of Jonah was probably written by Jonah himself, and the experiences of which he tells happened in the eighth century before Christ was born.

THINGS TO NOTE

One of Jonah's prophecies is referred to in 2 Kings 14:25 as a definitely known utterance, and our Lord Jesus Christ was no less definite when He used Jonah's experience in the belly of the fish as a *type of His own death and resurrection (Matthew 12:38-41; 16:4; Luke 11:29,30). It is interesting to notice the one thing sent and the four things prepared by God to teach Jonah lessons (Jonah 1:4,17; 4:6,7,8).

THEME

This short book of forty-eight verses is a true and beautiful account, showing God's mercy toward one of His disobedient servants and toward a wicked city that repented.

OUTLINE OF JONAH

I. Jonah's Disobedience	Jonah 1
A. God's First Command to Jonah	
B. Jonah Disobeys	
C. God Preserves Jonah	
II. Jonah's Prayer	Jonah 2
A. Jonah in Trouble	
B. Jonah Delivered	
III. Jonah's Obedience	Jonah 3
A. God's Second Command to Jonah	
B. Jonah Obeys	
C. Nineveh Repents	
IV. Jonah's Discouragement	Jonah 4
A. Jonah Complains	
B. Object Lessons for Jonah	
C. The Mercy of God	

I. Jonah's Disobedience (1:1-17)

A. God's First Command to Jonah

1 Now the word of the LORD came
unto Jonah the son of Amittai, saying,
2 Arise, go to Nineveh, that great city,
and cry against it; for their wickedness
is come up before me.

B. Jonah Disobeys

3 But Jonah rose up to flee unto Tarshish from the presence of the LORD,
and went down to Joppa; and he found
a ship going to Tarshish: so he paid the
fare thereof, and went down into it, to
go with them unto Tarshish from the
presence of the LORD.
¶4 But the LORD sent out a great wind
into the sea, and there was a mighty
tempest in the sea, so that the ship was
like to be broken.
5 Then the mariners were afraid, and
cried every man unto his god, and cast
forth the wares that *were* in the ship into
the sea, to lighten *it* of them. But Jonah
was gone down into the sides of the
ship; and he lay, and was fast asleep.
6 So the shipmaster came to him, and
said unto him, What meanest thou, O
sleeper? arise, call upon thy God, if so
be that God will think upon us, that we
perish not.
7 And they said every one to his fellow, Come, and let us cast lots, that we
may know for whose cause this evil *is*
upon us. So they cast lots, and the lot
fell upon Jonah.

1:7 Casting Lots
It was the custom in Old Testament times to make choices by lot. Small stones, or little stone tablets on which something was written, were put into a container and shaken together; then one was taken out. The choice was made according to the stone that was chosen. Examples of casting lots may be found in the following passages: Leviticus 16:8; Joshua 18:6; 1 Samuel 14:42 (see also 14:21-42 note, "Casting Lots"); Nehemiah 10:34. The last record of its use in the Bible is in Acts 1:23-26, when the apostles chose a disciple to take the place of Judas. We do not need to cast lots now, because we have the Bible and the Spirit of God to guide us.

8 Then said they unto him, Tell us, we
pray thee, for whose cause this evil *is*
upon us; What *is* thine occupation? and
whence comest thou? what *is* thy country? and of what people *art* thou?
9 And he said unto them, I *am* an Hebrew; and I *fear the LORD, the God of

---

1:2 Nineveh. This was the capital of Assyria, far to the northeast of Palestine.
1:2 cry against it. This means that Jonah was to preach against the Ninevites' sins.
1:2 come up before me. Though God sees all that men do, expressions like this are sometimes used in Scripture to describe extreme wickedness (Gen. 6:13; 18:20-21; Ezra 9:6).
1:3 Tarshish. This city was probably in the south of Spain, near Gibraltar. It lay in the opposite direction from Nineveh, where God had told Jonah to go.
1:3 Joppa. This was one of the principal seaports of Palestine, called Jaffa today. Peter was at Joppa when he saw the vision of the great sheet lowered from heaven (Acts 10:5,9-16).
1:3 from the presence of the LORD. Jonah tried to flee from the LORD, but it is impossible to get away from Him (Ps. 139:7-12).
1:4 a great wind. This was the one thing that the LORD sent (see introduction).
1:4 like to be broken. The ship was in danger of being wrecked.
1:5 unto his god. The sailors, or mariners, prayed to heathen idols and gods.
1:5 the wares. This was the cargo that the ship was carrying.
1:5 into the sides. Jonah was below the decks, where there were probably small cabins.
1:6 shipmaster. The captain.
1:9 I fear the LORD. Two kinds of fear are spoken of in the Bible: 1) cowardly fear of men and things; and 2) the fear of the LORD, which is reverence, trust, and hatred of evil (see Ps. 19:9 note; Prov. 1:7 and its note, "The Fear of the LORD"; 8:13). The first kind of fear was shown by the sailors (vs. 10); the second kind of fear was within Jonah even though he did not always act as if he trusted the LORD.

*heaven, which hath made the sea and
the dry *land*.
10Then were the men exceedingly
afraid, and said unto him, Why hast thou
done this? For the men knew that he
fled from the presence of the LORD,
because he had told them.
¶11Then said they unto him, What
shall we do unto thee, that the sea may
be calm unto us? for the sea wrought,
and was tempestuous.
12And he said unto them, Take me up,
and cast me forth into the sea; so shall
the sea be calm unto you: for I know
that for my sake this great tempest *is*
upon you.
13Nevertheless the men rowed hard
to bring *it* to the land; but they could
not: for the sea wrought, and was tempestuous against them.
14Wherefore they cried unto the
LORD, and said, We beseech thee, O
LORD, we beseech thee, let us not perish for this man's life, and lay not upon
us innocent blood: for thou, O LORD,
hast done as it pleased thee.

1:17 God's Preparations
This was the first of the things prepared by God to save Jonah (see introduction). Here was a miracle. It is no more difficult to believe that this miracle actually happened than to believe the records of the many other miracles in the Bible. The Christian believes them because God's Word tells him that they occurred. The Lord Jesus Christ speaks of this miracle in Matthew 12:39-40, saying, "As Jonas was three days and three nights in the whale's belly . . ." The Greek word there translated "whale" is *ketos*, which can refer to any large sea creature.

C. God Preserves Jonah

15So they took up Jonah, and cast him
forth into the sea: and the sea ceased
from her raging.
16Then the men feared the LORD exceedingly, and offered a *sacrifice unto
the LORD, and made vows.
¶17Now the LORD had prepared a
great fish to swallow up Jonah. And Jonah was in the belly of the fish three
days and three nights.

II. Jonah's Prayer (2:1-10)

A. Jonah in Trouble

2 Then Jonah prayed unto the LORD
his God out of the fish's belly,
2And said, I cried by reason of mine
affliction unto the LORD, and he heard
me; out of the belly of *hell cried I, *and*
thou heardest my voice.
3For thou hadst cast me into the
deep, in the midst of the seas; and the
floods compassed me about: all thy billows and thy waves passed over me.
4Then I said, I am cast out of thy
sight; yet I will look again toward thy
holy temple.
5The waters compassed me about,
even to the soul: the depth closed me
round about, the weeds were wrapped
about my head.
6I went down to the bottoms of the
mountains; the earth with her bars *was*
about me for ever: yet hast thou
brought up my life from corruption, O
LORD my God.

B. Jonah Delivered

7When my soul fainted within me I
remembered the LORD: and my *prayer

1:11 the sea wrought. The sea was becoming increasingly rough and stormy.
1:12 for my sake. Jonah knew by this time that the trouble had come because of his disobedience (see vs. 4; see also Heb. 12:6,11).
1:14 lay not upon us innocent blood. The men were asking God not to blame them for Jonah's death if they threw him into the sea.
1:14 as it pleased thee. See Psalms 115:3; 135:6.
2:6 about me for ever. Jonah thought that he would be drowned.
2:7 I remembered the LORD. This is a turning point in Jonah's prayer and experience. God had prepared the great fish to save Jonah before he knew of it, but it was when he turned to the LORD in prayer that Jonah's discouragement disappeared and he began to be hopeful and thankful (Ps. 34:4-6; Isa. 65:24).

came in unto thee, into thine holy
temple.
8They that observe lying vanities forsake their own mercy.
9But I will sacrifice unto thee with the
voice of thanksgiving; I will pay *that* that
I have vowed. *Salvation *is* of the LORD.
¶10And the LORD spake unto the fish,
and it vomited out Jonah upon the dry
land.

III. Jonah's Obedience (3:1-10)

A. God's Second Command to Jonah

3 And the word of the LORD came
unto Jonah the second time, saying,
2Arise, go unto Nineveh, that great
city, and preach unto it the preaching
that I bid thee.

B. Jonah Obeys

3So Jonah arose, and went unto Nineveh, according to the word of the
LORD. Now Nineveh was an exceeding
great city of three days' journey.
4And Jonah began to enter into the
city a day's journey, and he cried, and
said, Yet forty days, and Nineveh shall
be overthrown.

C. Nineveh Repents

¶5So the people of Nineveh believed
God, and proclaimed a fast, and put on

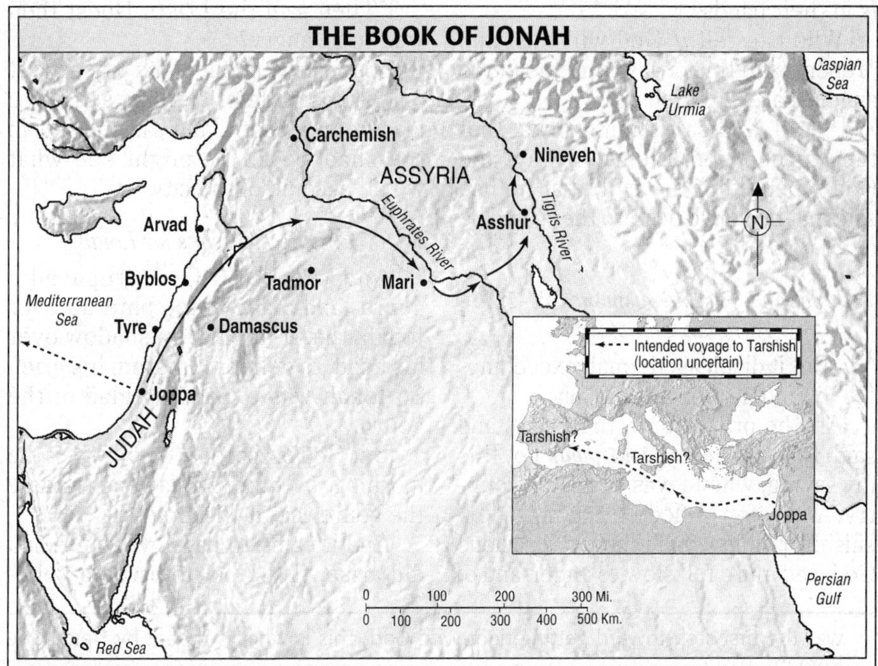

2:8 They that observe lying vanities. These are people who depend upon worthless idols, their own ideas, or the ideas of other men, without thinking and testing their thoughts according to God and His Word (Ps. 31:6; Acts 14:15).

2:8 forsake their own mercy. They turn away from the source of all mercy, which is God Himself (see Pss. 16:11; 34:8; 36:9; Isa. 55:7).

2:9 I will pay that that I have vowed. Jonah was ready from now on to keep his promises to God and to obey Him.

3:3 of three days' journey. It would have taken three days to walk through the whole city and the area around it. The Hebrew text makes no distinction between the actual city, the walls of which were only about eight miles in circumference (which accommodated about 175,000 people), and the administrative district of Nineveh, which was about thirty to sixty miles across, the reason it was three days' journey.

3:5 the people of Nineveh believed God. They believed His word spoken by Jonah. This

sackcloth, from the greatest of them
even to the least of them.
6For word came unto the king of Nineveh, and he arose from his throne, and
he laid his robe from him, and covered
him with sackcloth, and sat in ashes.
7And he caused *it* to be proclaimed
and published through Nineveh by the
decree of the king and his nobles, saying, Let neither man nor beast, herd nor
flock, taste any thing: let them not feed,
nor drink water:
8But let man and beast be covered
with sackcloth, and cry mightily unto
God: yea, let them turn every one from
his evil way, and from the violence that
is in their hands.
9Who can tell *if* God will turn and
*repent, and turn away from his fierce
anger, that we perish not?
¶10And God saw their works, that
they turned from their evil way; and
God repented of the evil, that he had
said that he would do unto them; and he
did *it* not.

IV. Jonah's Discouragement (4:1-11)

A. Jonah Complains

4 But it displeased Jonah exceedingly, and he was very angry.
2And he prayed unto the LORD, and
said, I pray thee, O LORD, *was* not this
my saying, when I was yet in my country? Therefore I fled before unto Tarshish: for I knew that thou *art* a gracious
God, and merciful, slow to anger, and of

4:1 Jonah's Displeasure
Jonah was not sorry that Nineveh was spared, because that showed the powerful effect of his preaching, but he knew that the Assyrians of Nineveh were enemies of his own people, Israel, and that if they continued powerful and prosperous, they would doubtlessly make future attacks on the Israelites. For that reason, Jonah would much rather have seen God destroy the Ninevites.

great kindness, and repentest thee of
the evil.
3Therefore now, O LORD, take, I beseech thee, my life from me; for *it is*
better for me to die than to live.
¶4Then said the LORD, Doest thou
well to be angry?
5So Jonah went out of the city, and sat
on the east side of the city, and there
made him a booth, and sat under it in
the shadow, till he might see what
would become of the city.

B. Object Lessons for Jonah

6And the LORD God prepared a
gourd, and made *it* to come up over
Jonah, that it might be a shadow over
his head, to deliver him from his grief.
So Jonah was exceeding glad of the
gourd.
7But God prepared a worm when the
morning rose the next day, and it smote
the gourd that it withered.
8And it came to pass, when the sun
did arise, that God prepared a vehe-

---

was the first step toward getting right with God. This is what is meant by *faith. See Romans 10:17.

3:5 a fast, and put on sackcloth. Going without food and wearing sackcloth were signs of sorrow and repentance. Sackcloth is a coarse cloth of a dark color, usually made of goat's hair (Rev. 6:12).

3:6 the king . . . sat in ashes. This was another sign of sorrow and repentance—by the king of Nineveh himself (Esther 4:1; Job 2:8).

3:8 turn every one from his evil way. Read Isaiah 55:7 and 1 Thessalonians 1:9.

4:5 a booth. A small shelter or hut, probably made of branches.

4:6 prepared a gourd. This was the second thing God prepared for Jonah (see introduction). The Hebrew word used here for gourd is from the Egyptian word for the *ricinus*, or castor oil plant, which grows quickly to a height of eight or ten feet. One large leaf grows on each branch. The plant fades rapidly when it is injured.

4:7 prepared a worm. The worm was the third thing prepared by God (see introduction). The worm destroyed the gourd under which Jonah found comfort and on which he took pity (vs. 10).

ment east wind; and the sun beat upon
the head of Jonah, that he fainted, and
wished in himself to die, and said, *It is*
better for me to die than to live.
[9]And God said to Jonah, Doest thou
well to be angry for the gourd? And he
said, I do well to be angry, *even* unto death.

C. The Mercy of God

[10]Then said the LORD, Thou hast had
pity on the gourd, for the which thou
hast not laboured, neither madest it
grow; which came up in a night, and
perished in a night:
[11]And should not I spare Nineveh,
that great city, wherein are more than
sixscore thousand persons that cannot
discern between their right hand and
their left hand; and *also* much cattle?

4:11 An Explanation
There were evidently more than 120,000 children in Nineveh so young that they did not know the difference between their right and left hands. Since there were that many young children, the total population of Nineveh, "the great city," must have been very large. God was trying to show Jonah (as God tries to show us) how much more important it is to care for souls than just for himself (or ourselves). God was very merciful when the Ninevites repented–just as He is today for those who repent.

4:8 east wind. The wind was the fourth thing prepared by God (see introduction). Since the gourd was gone, the east wind and the sun made Jonah hot and uncomfortable—even to the point that he wanted to die.

MICAH

THE WRITER

Micah was written by the prophet who bore that name. His name means *Who is like the LORD?* He was called the Morasthite because his home was in Moresheth-gath. He prophesied while Jothan, Ahaz, and Hezekiah were kings over Judah, and Pekahiah, Pekah, and Hoshea were kings over Israel. He lived in the time of Isaiah the prophet and his message was similar because the moral need of the people was the same. The great revival under Hezekiah was a result of the ministry of this prophet (compare Jeremiah 26:17-19).

STRUCTURE

The book is divided into three sections, each of which begins with a command to hear:

"Hear, all ye people"	Micah 1:2
"Hear, I pray you"	Micah 3:1
"Hear ye now what the LORD saith"	Micah 6:1

Each division of the book, as well as the book itself, begins with threatened judgment and ends with the promise of future mercy and blessing.

THE TIME

The events recorded in Micah cover a period of forty years, from 750 to 710 B.C (Ussher).

OUTLINE OF MICAH

I.	The Message to the Nations	Micah 1:1—2:13
II.	The Message to the Princes	Micah 3:1—5:15
III.	The Appeal to the People	Micah 6:1—7:20

I. The Message to the Nations (1:1—2:13)

*Judgment upon *Samaria and *Judah*

1 The word of the LORD that came
to Micah the Morasthite in the
days of Jotham, Ahaz, *and* *Hezekiah,
kings of Judah, which he saw concerning *Samaria and Jerusalem.

2 Hear, all ye people; hearken, O
earth, and all that therein is: and let the
Lord GOD be witness against you, the
Lord from his holy temple.

3 For, behold, the LORD cometh forth
out of his place, and will come down,
and tread upon the high places of the
earth.

1:3 cometh forth. This speaks of judgment that God will bring upon the people because of sin, which God will not allow to go unpunished.

1:2 God as a Witness
God knew the people's hearts, and if they were to let Him witness against them, it would be only to condemn themselves and to acknowledge that His judgments were righteous. Whenever His people sin, this is always the path of blessing. Compare 1 John 1:9.

4And the mountains shall be molten
under him, and the valleys shall be cleft,
as wax before the fire, *and* as the waters *that are* poured down a steep place.
5For the transgression of *Jacob *is* all
this, and for the sins of the house of *Israel. What *is* the transgression of Jacob?
is it not Samaria? and what *are* the high
places of Judah? *are they* not Jerusalem?
6Therefore I will make Samaria as an
heap of the field, *and* as plantings of a
vineyard: and I will pour down the
stones thereof into the valley, and I will
discover the foundations thereof.
7And all the graven images thereof
shall be beaten to pieces, and all the
hires thereof shall be burned with the
fire, and all the idols thereof will I lay
desolate: for she gathered *it* of the hire
of an harlot, and they shall return to the
hire of an harlot.
8Therefore I will wail and howl, I will
go stripped and naked: I will make a
wailing like the dragons, and *mourning as the owls.
9For her wound *is* incurable; for it is
come unto Judah; he is come unto the
gate of my people, *even* to Jerusalem.
¶10Declare ye *it* not at *Gath, weep
ye not at all: in the house of Aphrah roll
thyself in the dust.
11Pass ye away, thou inhabitant of
Saphir, having thy shame naked: the inhabitant of Zaanan came not forth in the
mourning of Beth-ezel; he shall receive
of you his standing.
12For the inhabitant of Maroth waited carefully for good: but evil came
down from the LORD unto the gate of
Jerusalem.
13O thou inhabitant of *Lachish, bind
the chariot to the swift beast: she *is* the
beginning of the *sin to the daughter of
*Zion: for the transgressions of Israel
were found in thee.
14Therefore shalt thou give presents
to Moresheth-gath: the houses of
Achzib *shall be* a lie to the kings of Israel.
15Yet will I bring an heir unto thee, O
inhabitant of Mareshah: he shall come
unto Adullam the glory of Israel.
16Make thee bald, and poll thee for
thy delicate children; enlarge thy baldness as the eagle; for they are gone into
captivity from thee.

1:10 A Call for Help
To "declare . . . it not at Gath" meant that the Philistines, the enemies of Israel, were not to be told of Israel's failure, sin, and judgment. The same expression is used with regard to Saul in 2 Samuel 1:20. The names of the various towns speak of the way in which they would call on each other for help. Jerusalem would plead with them, but they would not listen.

The causes of God's judgment

2 Woe to them that devise iniquity,
and work evil upon their beds!
when the morning is light, they practise

1:5 transgression of Jacob. Idol worship had been set up in Samaria. The *high places spoken of here are the altars set up for idols in Jerusalem.
1:6 Therefore I will make. In verses 6-16 the prophet has in view destruction through the actual invasion of Israel by the Assyrians, described in 2 Kings 17:1-18.
1:7 hires. Rewards for sin and costly vessels given to heathen temples.
1:15 the glory of Israel. The rich and noble of Israel would flee to the cave of Adullam for protection.
1:16 Make thee bald, and poll thee. "Poll thee" means *cut off your hair*. These were signs of mourning.
2:1 because it is in the power of their hand. It is not true that "might makes right."

it, because it is in the power of their hand.

2 And they covet fields, and take *them* by violence; and houses, and take *them* away: so they oppress a man and his house, even a man and his heritage.

3 Therefore thus saith the LORD; Behold, against this family do I devise an evil, from which ye shall not remove your necks; neither shall ye go haughtily: for this time *is* evil.

¶4 In that day shall *one* take up a *parable against you, and lament with a doleful lamentation, *and* say, We be utterly spoiled: he hath changed the portion of my people: how hath he removed *it* from me! turning away he hath divided our fields.

5 Therefore thou shalt have none that shall cast a cord by lot in the congregation of the LORD.

6 Prophesy ye not, *say they to them that* prophesy: they shall not prophesy to them, *that* they shall not take shame.

¶7 O *thou that art* named the house of Jacob, is the spirit of the LORD straitened? *are* these his doings? do not my words do good to him that walketh uprightly?

8 Even of late my people is risen up as an enemy: ye pull off the robe with the garment from them that pass by securely as men averse from war.

9 The women of my people have ye cast out from their pleasant houses; from their children have ye taken away my glory for ever.

10 Arise ye, and depart; for this *is* not *your* rest: because it is polluted, it shall destroy *you,* even with a sore destruction.

11 If a man walking in the spirit and *falsehood do lie, *saying,* I will prophesy unto thee of *wine and of strong drink; he shall even be the *prophet of this people.

A promise of restoration

¶12 I will surely assemble, O Jacob, all of thee; I will surely gather the *remnant of Israel; I will put them together as the sheep of Bozrah, as the flock in the midst of their fold: they shall make great noise by reason of *the multitude of* men.

2:12 The Shepherd's Task
The Good Shepherd would go ahead of the flock to clear the way and remove every obstacle. This was a promise to the faithful *remnant for a future day when the Lord Jesus shall come in power.

13 The breaker is come up before them: they have broken up, and have passed through the gate, and are gone out by it: and their king shall pass before them, and the LORD on the head of them.

II. The Message to the Princes (3:1—5:15)

*Sin and *judgment upon: 1) The rulers*

3 And I said, Hear, I pray you, O heads of Jacob, and ye princes of the house of Israel; *Is it* not for you to know judgment?

2 Who hate the good, and love the evil; who pluck off their skin from off them, and their flesh from off their bones;

3 Who also eat the flesh of my people, and flay their skin from off them; and they break their bones, and chop them in pieces, as for the pot, and as flesh within the caldron.

4 Then shall they cry unto the LORD,

2:3 I devise an evil. Compare with "devise iniquity" in verse 1. The punishment will correspond to the sin. Since man planned iniquity, God decreed the punishment of that sin. In this sense He devised evil against Israel. See Isaiah 45:7 note.

2:5 cast a cord. This means to *divide the land.*

2:7 my words do good. To the one who walks uprightly, God's words are pleasant. It is when His counsel is rejected that they become unpleasant.

2:11 If a man . . . do lie. If the people would not listen to the words of the Holy Spirit, they would have to listen to the unholy one, who the false prophets represented.

but he will not hear them: he will even hide his face from them at that time, as they have behaved themselves ill in their doings.

2) The prophets

¶5Thus saith the LORD concerning the *prophets that make my people *err, that bite with their teeth, and cry, *Peace; and he that putteth not into their mouths, they even prepare war against him.

6Therefore night *shall be* unto you, that ye shall not have a vision; and it shall be dark unto you, that ye shall not divine; and the sun shall go down over the prophets, and the day shall be dark over them.

7Then shall the seers be ashamed, and the diviners confounded: yea, they shall all cover their lips; for *there is* no answer of *God.

¶8But truly I am full of power by the spirit of the LORD, and of judgment, and of might, to declare unto Jacob his transgression, and to Israel his sin.

3) All ruling classes

9Hear this, I pray you, ye heads of the house of Jacob, and princes of the house of Israel, that abhor judgment, and pervert all equity.

10They build up Zion with blood, and Jerusalem with iniquity.

11The heads thereof judge for reward, and the priests thereof teach for hire, and the prophets thereof divine for money: yet will they lean upon the LORD, and say, *Is* not the LORD among us? none evil can come upon us.

12Therefore shall Zion for your sake be plowed *as* a field, and Jerusalem shall become heaps, and the mountain of the house as the high places of the forest.

The character of the coming kingdom

4 But in the last days it shall come to pass, *that* the mountain of the house of the LORD shall be established in the top of the mountains, and it shall be exalted above the hills; and people shall flow unto it.

2And many nations shall come, and say, Come, and let us go up to the mountain of the LORD, and to the house of the God of Jacob; and he will teach us of his ways, and we will walk in his paths: for the *law shall go forth of Zion, and the word of the LORD from Jerusalem.

¶3And he shall judge among many people, and rebuke strong nations afar off; and they shall beat their swords into plowshares, and their spears into pruninghooks: nation shall not lift up a sword against nation, neither shall they learn war any more.

4But they shall sit every man under his vine and under his *fig tree; and none shall make *them* afraid: for the

---

3:4 at that time. The time of the Assyrian invasion.

3:5 bite with their teeth. This stands for an abundance of food—the false prophets preached in order that they might receive money for their labors, not to feed the people with the Word of God.

3:8 But truly I am full of power. This verse is parenthetical. In contrast to the false prophets who cause the people to go astray, Micah declares himself to be a true prophet, full of the Spirit of the Lord.

3:11 judge for reward. Take bribes.

3:11 divine for money. Priests had been commanded to give their services. They were supported by *tithes.

3:12 the high places of the forest. Overgrown like a jungle. This was fulfilled when Jerusalem was destroyed by the Babylonians.

4:1 But in the last days. The prophet here repeats (vss. 1-3) the great predictions of Isaiah 2:2-4. We learn from Genesis 41:32 that when a thing is repeated, as here, it is "because the thing is established by God, and God will shortly bring it to pass." The Spirit of God inspired both Isaiah and Micah to write similar prophecies.

4:1 in the top of the mountains. At the head of the nations.

4:2 Symbolism of a Mountain
A mountain in Scripture stands for a great power; a hill for a smaller power. "The house of the LORD" in verse 1 is not any church building but the future temple in Jerusalem to which all nations will come to worship God, and from which the *Law shall go forth. The coming *kingdom will be supreme over all nations (vs. 1)–it will be worldwide in its extent and influence (vs. 2); the capital will be at Jerusalem (vs. 2; see also vs. 8); the kingdom will be established by judgment of the nations of the earth (vs. 3; compare Matt. 25:32-46); war will be done away with (vs. 3); problems having to do with money and riches will be solved (vs. 4); Israel will be regathered and restored to a place of authority (vs. 6); and the LORD will reign over them in Zion forever (vs. 7).

mouth of the LORD of hosts hath spoken *it*.
5For all people will walk every one in
the name of his god, and we will walk
in the name of the LORD our God for
ever and ever.

Israel to be regathered

6In that day, saith the LORD, will I
assemble her that halteth, and I will
gather her that is driven out, and her
that I have afflicted;
7And I will make her that halted a
remnant, and her that was cast far off a
strong nation: and the LORD shall reign
over them in mount Zion from henceforth, even for ever.
¶8And thou, O tower of the flock, the
strong hold of the daughter of Zion,
unto thee shall it come, even the first
dominion; the *kingdom shall come to
the daughter of Jerusalem.
9Now why dost thou cry out aloud?
is there no king in thee? is thy counsellor perished? for pangs have taken thee
as a woman in travail.
10Be in pain, and labour to bring forth,
O daughter of Zion, like a woman in travail: for now shalt thou go forth out of
the city, and thou shalt dwell in the field,
and thou shalt go *even* to *Babylon;
there shalt thou be delivered; there the
LORD shall *redeem thee from the hand
of thine enemies.

Final victory at Armageddon

¶11Now also many nations are gathered against thee, that say, Let her be
defiled, and let our eye look upon Zion.
12But they know not the thoughts of
the LORD, neither understand they his
counsel: for he shall gather them as the
sheaves into the floor.
13Arise and thresh, O daughter of
Zion: for I will make thine horn iron, and
I will make thy hoofs brass: and thou
shalt beat in pieces many people: and I
will *consecrate their gain unto the
LORD, and their substance unto the
Lord of the whole earth.

Messiah and His rejection

5 Now gather thyself in troops,
O daughter of troops: he hath laid
siege against us: they shall smite the
judge of Israel with a rod upon the
cheek.
2But thou, Beth-lehem Ephratah,
though thou be little among the thousands of Judah, *yet* out of thee shall he
come forth unto me *that is* to be ruler
in Israel; whose goings forth *have been*
from of old, from everlasting.
3Therefore will he give them up, until the time *that* she which travaileth
hath brought forth: then the remnant of

4:5 in the name of his god. The verse conveys the following: "All the peoples do now walk in the name of their god but shall walk in the name of the LORD our God forever."
4:8 tower of the flock. Jerusalem.
4:9 Now. Meanwhile. Also in verses 11 and 5:1.
5:1 they shall smite. Compare this with Isaiah 50:6; 53:4.
5:3 Therefore will he give them up. This refers to verse 1. Because of Israel's rejection of Christ the Judge, they would be given up until they passed through the *Great Tribulation.

his brethren shall return unto the children of Israel.

The Shepherd of Israel

¶4And he shall stand and feed in the
strength of the LORD, in the majesty of
the name of the LORD his God; and they
shall abide: for now shall he be great
unto the ends of the earth.
5And this *man* shall be the peace,
when the Assyrian shall come into our
land: and when he shall tread in our
palaces, then shall we raise against him
seven shepherds, and eight principal
men.
6And they shall waste the land of
Assyria with the sword, and the land of
Nimrod in the entrances thereof: thus
shall he deliver *us* from the Assyrian,
when he cometh into our land, and
when he treadeth within our borders.

The place of the remnant

7And the remnant of Jacob shall be in
the midst of many people as a dew from
the LORD, as the showers upon the
grass, that tarrieth not for man, nor
waiteth for the sons of men.
¶8And the remnant of Jacob shall be
among the *Gentiles in the midst of
many people as a lion among the beasts
of the forest, as a young lion among the
flocks of sheep: who, if he go through,

5:7 Israel's Future Character
When the *kingdom shall be reestablished with its center at Jerusalem and the Lord Jesus, the Messiah, reigning from there, the nation of Israel (the *remnant) will have a twofold character. As "dew" (vs. 7), they will be the channel of divine blessing in preaching the gospel of the kingdom. As a "lion" (vs. 8), they will be the instrument of God's anger upon those who disobey the gospel.

both treadeth down, and teareth in
pieces, and none can deliver.
9Thine hand shall be lifted up upon
thine adversaries, and all thine enemies
shall be cut off.

Deliverance from evil

10And it shall come to pass in that day,
saith the LORD, that I will cut off thy
horses out of the midst of thee, and I
will destroy thy chariots:
11And I will cut off the cities of thy
land, and throw down all thy strong
holds:
12And I will cut off witchcrafts out of
thine hand; and thou shalt have no *more*
soothsayers:
13Thy graven images also will I cut
off, and thy standing images out of the
midst of thee; and thou shalt no more
worship the work of thine hands.

5:2 A DESCRIPTION OF CHRIST

This verse is parenthetical, giving a description of the Judge of Israel who is smitten upon the cheek. It is a prophecy of the coming of the Lord Jesus Christ to live on earth. When the wise men from the East came to Herod asking the place of the birth of the Messiah, the Lord Jesus Christ, the scribes pointed to this verse as prophesying that it would be in Beth-lehem (Matt. 2:5-6). They knew the prophecy but, as far as we know, they did not give their hearts to the One of whom the prophets spoke.

There were two Beth-lehems, one in Judah and the other in Zebulon. The Spirit of God through the prophet, seven hundred years before the birth of the Lord Jesus Christ, told in which of these He would be born. To make sure that there would be no misunderstanding, both the Hebrew and the Aramaic names were given, Beth-lehem and Ephratah, both of which mean *house of bread*. Both the deity and humanity of Christ are clearly presented in this verse: As man, He was born as a baby in Beth-lehem; as God, He was "from of old, from everlasting" (compare Isa. 7:13-14; 9:6-7).

5:5 And this man shall be the peace. Christ made peace with God for us when He shed His blood on the cross (Eph. 2:15-16); He is our peace (Eph. 2:14); He brings peace to the heart at the new birth (Rom. 5:1; John 14:27), and to the world when He comes again (Isa. 9:7; Ps. 72:3,7).

14And I will pluck up thy groves out
of the midst of thee: so will I destroy thy
cities.
15And I will execute vengeance in
anger and fury upon the heathen, such
as they have not heard.

III. The Appeal (6:1—7:20)

6 Hear ye now what the LORD saith;
Arise, contend thou before the
mountains, and let the hills hear thy
voice.
2Hear ye, O mountains, the LORD'S
controversy, and ye strong foundations
of the earth: for the LORD hath a controversy with his people, and he will
plead with Israel.
3O my people, what have I done unto
thee? and wherein have I wearied thee?
testify against me.
4For I brought thee up out of the land
of *Egypt, and *redeemed thee out of
the house of servants; and I sent before
thee *Moses, *Aaron, and *Miriam.
5O my people, remember now what
Balak king of *Moab consulted, and
what *Balaam the son of Beor answered him from Shittim unto Gilgal;
that ye may know the *righteousness
of the LORD.
¶6Wherewith shall I come before the
LORD, *and* bow myself before the high
God? shall I come before him with
burnt-offerings, with calves of a year
old?
7Will the LORD be pleased with thousands of rams, *or* with ten thousands of
rivers of oil? shall I give my firstborn
for my transgression, the fruit of my
body *for* the sin of my soul?
8He hath shewed thee, O man, what
is good; and what doth the LORD require
of thee, but to do justly, and to love
*mercy, and to walk humbly with thy
God?

The certainty of judgment

9The LORD'S voice crieth unto the
city, and *the man of* wisdom shall see thy
name: hear ye the rod, and who hath
appointed it.
¶10Are there yet the treasures of wickedness in the house of the wicked, and
the scant measure *that is* abominable?
11Shall I count *them* pure with the
wicked balances, and with the bag of
deceitful *weights?
12For the rich men thereof are full of
violence, and the inhabitants thereof
have spoken lies, and their tongue *is*
deceitful in their mouth.
13Therefore also will I make *thee* sick
in smiting thee, in making *thee* desolate
because of thy sins.
14Thou shalt eat, but not be satisfied;
and thy casting down *shall be* in the
midst of thee; and thou shalt take hold,
but shalt not deliver; and *that* which
thou deliverest will I give up to the
sword.
15Thou shalt sow, but thou shalt not
reap; thou shalt tread the olives, but
thou shalt not *anoint thee with oil;
and sweet wine, but shalt not drink
wine.
¶16For the statutes of Omri are kept,
and all the works of the house of *Ahab,
and ye walk in their counsels; that I
should make thee a desolation, and the
inhabitants thereof an hissing: therefore ye shall bear the reproach of my
people.

The lament of the prophet

7 Woe is me! for I am as when they
have gathered the summer fruits,
as the grapegleanings of the vintage:
there is no cluster to eat: my soul desired the firstripe fruit.
2The good *man* is perished out of the
earth: and *there is* none upright among

6:4 I brought thee up. See Exodus 12:40-42.
6:5 Balak. See Numbers 22–24.
6:8 He hath shewed thee. See Deuteronomy 10:12.
6:9 the city. Jerusalem and its inhabitants.
6:9 hear ye the rod. Hear the punishment that is coming to you.
6:16 Omri . . . Ahab. See 1 Kings 16:23-34.

men: they all lie in wait for blood; they
hunt every man his brother with a net.
¶[3]That they may do evil with both
hands earnestly, the prince asketh, and
the judge *asketh* for a reward; and the
great *man*, he uttereth his mischievous
desire: so they wrap it up.
[4]The best of them *is* as a brier: the
most upright *is sharper* than a thorn
hedge: the day of thy watchmen *and* thy
visitation cometh; now shall be their
perplexity.
¶[5]Trust ye not in a friend, put ye not
confidence in a guide: keep the doors of
thy mouth from her that lieth in thy
bosom.
[6]For the son dishonoureth the father,
the daughter riseth up against her
mother, the daughter in law against her
mother in law; a man's enemies *are* the
men of his own house.

7:7 Speaking to the LORD
Micah 7:7-20 is, first of all, the confession and intercessory prayer of the prophet, who considered himself in the terrible state with Israel. He confesses the nation's sins as his own, accepts the wrath of God as rightly poured out on him, and looks forward with confidence to future deliverance. Intercession, or speaking to the LORD for the people, was the test of a true prophet. "But if they be prophets, and if the word of the LORD be with them, let them now make intercession to the LORD of hosts" (Jer. 27:18). It was here that Elijah failed, in that he made intercession against the people of Israel (Rom. 11:2-4) instead of on their behalf. He was removed from his office, and Elisha was put in his place. Micah also stands here for the sorrowing *remnant of Israel speaking during the coming *Tribulation.

The confession and intercession of the prophet

[7]Therefore I will look unto the LORD;
I will wait for the God of my salvation:
my God will hear me.
¶[8]Rejoice not against me, O mine enemy: when I fall, I shall arise; when I
sit in darkness, the LORD *shall be* a light
unto me.
[9]I will bear the indignation of the
LORD, because I have sinned against
him, until he plead my cause, and execute judgment for me: he will bring me
forth to the light, *and* I shall behold his
righteousness.
[10]Then *she that is* mine enemy shall
see *it*, and shame shall cover her which
said unto me, Where is the LORD thy
God? mine eyes shall behold her: now
shall she be trodden down as the mire
of the streets.
[11]*In* the day that thy walls are to be
built, *in* that day shall the decree be far
removed.
[12]*In* that day *also* he shall come even
to thee from Assyria, and *from* the fortified cities, and from the fortress even
to the river, and from sea to sea, and
from mountain to mountain.
[13]Notwithstanding the land shall be
desolate because of them that dwell
therein, for the fruit of their doings.
¶[14]Feed thy people with thy rod, the
flock of thine heritage, which dwell soli-
tarily *in* the wood, in the midst of Carmel: let them feed *in* Bashan and
Gilead, as in the days of old.
[15]According to the days of thy coming out of the land of Egypt will I shew
unto him marvellous *things*.
¶[16]The nations shall see and be confounded at all their might: they shall lay
their hand upon *their* mouth, their ears
shall be deaf.
[17]They shall lick the dust like a

7:4 the day of thy watchmen. A watchman is a prophet of God (compare Ezek. 33:7). The day of the judgments of which the prophets had spoken was surely coming.
7:8 I shall arise. See Proverbs 24:16. "When I fall" speaks of falling into affliction, difficult times, or trouble, not into sin.
7:12 the fortress. Egypt.
7:12 the river. The Euphrates.
7:15 According to the days. Verses 15-17 give God's answer to the prayer of verse 14.

serpent, they shall move out of their
holes like worms of the earth: they
shall be afraid of the LORD our God, and
shall fear because of thee.

The faith of the prophet

18Who *is* a God like unto thee, that
pardoneth iniquity, and passeth by the
transgression of the remnant of his
heritage? he retaineth not his anger
for ever, because he delighteth *in*
mercy.
19He will turn again, he will have
compassion upon us; he will subdue our
iniquities; and thou wilt cast all their
sins into the depths of the sea.
20Thou wilt perform the truth to Jacob, *and* the mercy to Abraham, which
thou hast sworn unto our fathers from
the days of old.

NAHUM

THE WRITER AND TIME

The prophet Nahum of Galilee (see Nahum 1:1, note) wrote the book called by his name. Nahum's name signified *Jehovah will avenge and comfort His people.* He prophesied during the latter part of Isaiah's ministry.

THEME

The theme of the book is God's judgment upon Assyria of which Nineveh was the capital:

1. in the time of her invasion of Judah (see notes on Nahum 1)
2. in the overthrow of Nineveh about one hundred years later (Nahum 2; 3).

The severity and finality of this judgment are explained by the fact that many years before, Jonah had come preaching that the city was even then ripe for judgment, which would fall upon it in forty days unless the people repented; but repentance delivered the city at that time (Jonah 3:4-5,10). Thus, having come to know the true God through Jonah's preaching, to return to idolatry was to apostatize. With their knowledge of the light their responsibility became even greater.

The Assyrian monarchs had already conquered and exiled the Northern (ten-tribe) Kingdom of Israel; had invaded Egypt and destroyed well-fortified No-Ammon (Nahum 3:8); and Sennacherib, having ravaged Judaea, was approaching Jerusalem as Nahum was uttering his message of consolation to Judah (Nahum 1:15) because of the immediate destruction of Sennacherib's army (Isaiah 37:33-37), and the eventual overthrow of the whole nation (Nahum 3:7,18-19).

Nahum's prophecy against Assyria seemed most unlikely, for she was at the height of her power, and Nineveh had a great wall upon which it is said that six chariots could ride abreast. Yet God destroyed Nineveh so utterly that skeptics denied that the city had ever existed, until Botta unearthed its remains in 1842.

OUTLINE OF NAHUM

I.	Title and Theme	Nahum 1:1-8
II.	The Verdict against Assyria	Nahum 1:9-14
III.	The Excited Messengers' Glad Report of Assyria's Downfall	Nahum 1:15
IV.	The Babylonians Will Overthrow Nineveh, Capital of Assyria	Nahum 2:1-12
V.	God's Judgment on Nineveh Vindicated	Nahum 2:13—3:7
VI.	The Dirge of Nineveh's Doom	Nahum 3:8-19

I. Title and Theme (1:1-8)

1 The *burden of Nineveh. The book
of the vision of Nahum the Elkoshite.

God avenges sin (2-6, 8), but is a stronghold to His own (7)

2 *God *is* jealous, and the LORD revengeth; the LORD revengeth, and *is*
furious; the LORD will take vengeance
on his adversaries, and he reserveth
wrath for his enemies.
3 The LORD *is* slow to anger, and great
in power, and will not at all acquit
the wicked: the LORD *hath* his way in the
whirlwind and in the storm, and the
clouds *are* the dust of his feet.
4 He rebuketh the sea, and maketh it
dry, and drieth up all the rivers: Bashan
languisheth, and Carmel, and the flower of Lebanon languisheth.
5 The mountains quake at him, and
the hills melt, and the earth is burned
at his presence, yea, the *world, and all
that dwell therein.
6 Who can stand before his indignation? and who can abide in the fierceness of his anger? his fury is poured out
like *fire, and the rocks are thrown
down by him.
7 The LORD *is* good, a strong hold in
the day of trouble; and he knoweth
them that *trust in him.
8 But with an overrunning flood he
will make an utter end of the place
thereof, and darkness shall pursue his
enemies.

II. The Verdict against Assyria (1:9-14)

9 What do ye imagine against the
LORD? he will make an utter end: affliction shall not rise up the second time.
10 For while *they be* folden together
as thorns, and while they are drunken
as drunkards, they shall be devoured as
stubble fully dry.
11 There is *one* come out of thee, that
imagineth evil against the LORD, a
wicked counsellor.
12 Thus saith the LORD: Though *they*
be quiet, and likewise many, yet thus
shall they be cut down, when he shall
pass through. Though I have afflicted
thee, I will afflict thee no more.
13 For now will I break his yoke from
off thee, and will burst thy bonds in sunder.
14 And the LORD hath given a commandment concerning thee, *that* no
more of thy name be sown: out of the
house of thy gods will I cut off the

1:1 Elkoshite. Elkosh was a village of Galilee; perhaps it was the town later known Capernaum, which means *village of Nahum*.
1:2 jealous. God has a jealous love for His people. It has been pointed out, for example, that of the thirty Roman emperors and governors who persecuted Christians, not one came to a peaceful end.
1:2 revengeth. Avenges.
1:3 will not at all acquit the wicked. Read the phrase: "But will by no means clear the guilty" (see Exod. 34:7). The majesty of God's holiness (vss. 4-6) is contrasted with His long-suffering (vs. 3a) and benevolence (vs. 7).
1:4 Bashan . . . Carmel . . . Lebanon. The most fertile regions in Palestine.
1:5 burned. Trembles, like an earthquake.
1:7 them that trust him. Hezekiah trusted God, and the Assyrian army was destroyed (Isa. 37:14-20,36-38).
1:9 imagine. Plan.
1:9 an utter end. Of Assyria and Nineveh.
1:10 while. Though.
1:11 one come out of thee. This one probably means Sennacherib (see Isa. 36).
1:12 quiet. In full strength; secure.
1:12 cut down. The Assyrian host will be "cut down" when "he [Jehovah] shall pass through" their camp (Isa. 37:36).
1:14 make thy grave. God solemnly warns them that He would personally make their grave.

graven image and the molten image: I will make thy grave; for thou art vile.

III. The Excited Messengers' Glad Report of Assyria's Downfall (1:15)

15Behold upon the mountains the feet
of him that bringeth good tidings, that
publisheth *peace! O *Judah, keep thy
solemn *feasts, perform thy vows: for
the wicked shall no more pass through
thee; he is utterly cut off.

1:15 A Future Peace
The good news for Judah and Jerusalem that they should have peace was fulfilled in relation to Nineveh with that city's destruction. The apostle Paul used this thought in relation to the glad tidings of peace with God through Christ (see Rom. 10:15). It is a sad thing for Israel that it will not be wholly true of her as a nation that "the wicked shall no more pass through thee; he is utterly cut off"; for this will not be fulfilled completely until Christ, the Prince of Peace, shall reign (see *kingdom).

IV. The Babylonians Will Overthrow Nineveh, Capital of Assyria (2:1-12)

2 He that dasheth in pieces is come
up before thy face: keep the munition, watch the way, make *thy* loins
strong, fortify *thy* power mightily.
2For the LORD hath turned away the
excellency of *Jacob, as the excellency
of *Israel: for the emptiers have emptied them out, and marred their vine
branches.

The night battle in Nineveh's streets

3The shield of his mighty men is made
red, the valiant men *are* in scarlet: the
chariots *shall be* with flaming torches in
the day of his preparation, and the fir
trees shall be terribly shaken.
4The chariots shall rage in the
streets, they shall justle one against
another in the broad ways: they shall
seem like torches, they shall run like
the lightnings.

2:4 A Night Battle
This clearly refers to a night battle in the streets of Nineveh, with chariots rushing here and there, colliding with one another in their haste. This took place about seven centuries before Christ.

The King of Nineveh tries to rally his forces

5He shall recount his worthies: they
shall stumble in their walk; they shall
make haste to the wall thereof, and the
defence shall be prepared.

Method of attack

6The gates of the rivers shall be
opened, and the palace shall be dissolved.

City spoiled and taken captive

7And Huzzab shall be led away captive, she shall be brought up, and her
maids shall lead *her* as with the voice of
doves, tabering upon their breasts.

2:1 He . . . is come up. This refers to Nabopolassar (the father of Nebuchadnezzar), who captured Nineveh about one hundred years after this prophecy.
2:1 face. Walls.
2:1 munition. Fortress, fortifications.
2:2 hath turned away. As Israel was "emptied" like a vine by Assyria's invasion, God will bring again such a destruction, only greater, upon Nineveh.
2:3 fir trees. Spears made from fir trees.
2:6 gates of the rivers. The city was protected by great moats (water barriers), but the foe made these a dry bed to march into the city by turning the waters into a different channel.
2:6 palace shall be dissolved. The palace shall become molten. King Sardanapalus, seeing the city lost, collected his wives and his treasures into the palace, which he then set on fire, and all perished in the flames.
2:7 Huzzab. Possibly another name for Nineveh.
2:7 tabering. Beating, as on a drum.

[8]But Nineveh *is* of old like a pool of
water: yet they shall flee away. Stand,
stand, *shall they cry;* but none shall look
back.
[9]Take ye the spoil of silver, take the
spoil of gold: for *there is* none end of the
store *and* glory out of all the pleasant
furniture.
[10]She is empty, and void, and waste:
and the heart melteth, and the knees
smite together, and much pain *is* in all
loins, and the faces of them all gather
blackness.
[11]Where *is* the dwelling of the lions,
and the feedingplace of the young
lions, where the lion, *even* the old lion,
walked, *and* the lion's whelp, and none
made *them* afraid?
[12]The lion did tear in pieces enough
for his whelps, and strangled for his li-
onesses, and filled his holes with prey,
and his dens with ravin.

V. God's Judgment upon Nineveh (2:13—3:7)

[13]Behold, I *am* against thee, saith the
LORD of hosts, and I will burn her chariots in the smoke, and the sword shall
devour thy young lions: and I will cut
off thy prey from the earth, and the
voice of thy messengers shall no more
be heard.

God will judge Nineveh because of:
1) Her cruel and bloody conquests

3 Woe to the bloody city! it *is* all full
of lies *and* robbery; the prey
departeth not;
[2]The noise of a whip, and the noise
of the rattling of the wheels, and of the
pransing horses, and of the jumping
chariots.
[3]The horseman lifteth up both the
bright sword and the glittering spear:
and *there is* a multitude of slain, and a
great number of carcases; and *there is*
none end of *their* corpses; they stumble upon their corpses:

2) Her loathsome idolatries

[4]Because of the multitude of the
whoredoms of the wellfavoured harlot,
the mistress of witchcrafts, that selleth
nations through her whoredoms, and
families through her witchcrafts.
[5]Behold, I *am* against thee, saith the
LORD of hosts; and I will discover thy
skirts upon thy face, and I will shew
the nations thy nakedness, and the
kingdoms thy shame.
[6]And I will cast abominable filth upon
thee, and make thee vile, and will set
thee as a gazingstock.
[7]And it shall come to pass, *that* all
they that look upon thee shall flee from
thee, and say, Nineveh is laid waste:
who will bemoan her? whence shall I
seek comforters for thee?

VI. The Dirge of Nineveh's Doom (3:8-19)

[8]Art thou better than populous No,
that was situate among the rivers, *that*
had the waters round about it, whose
rampart *was* the sea, *and* her wall *was*
from the sea?
[9]Ethiopia and Egypt *were* her
strength, and *it was* infinite; Put and
Lubim were thy helpers.
[10]Yet *was* she carried away, she went
into captivity: her young children also
were dashed in pieces at the top of all
the streets: and they cast lots for her
honourable men, and all her great men
were bound in chains.
[11]Thou also shalt be drunken: thou
shalt be hid, thou also shalt seek
strength because of the enemy.
[12]All thy strong holds *shall be like* fig

2:11 lions . . . young lions. The king and his household.
2:12 ravin. Torn flesh.
3:2 The noise of a whip. Verses 2-3 are a description of the Babylonian army advancing to the attack.
3:8 No. No-Ammon, or Thebes.
3:11 drunken. With the cup of God's wrath.
3:11 hid. Covered with the sands of the desert.

trees with the firstripe figs: if they be
shaken, they shall even fall into the
mouth of the eater.
13Behold, thy people in the midst of
thee *are* women: the gates of thy land
shall be set wide open unto thine enemies: the fire shall devour thy bars.
14Draw thee waters for the siege, fortify thy strong holds: go into clay, and
tread the morter, make strong the
brickkiln.
15There shall the fire devour thee;
the sword shall cut thee off, it shall eat
thee up like the cankerworm: make
thyself many as the cankerworm, make
thyself many as the locusts.
16Thou hast multiplied thy merchants
above the stars of heaven: the cankerworm spoileth, and flieth away.
17Thy crowned *are* as the locusts, and
thy captains as the great grasshoppers,
which camp in the hedges in the cold
day, *but* when the sun ariseth they flee
away, and their place is not known
where they *are*.
18Thy shepherds slumber, O king of
Assyria: thy nobles shall dwell *in the
dust:* thy people is scattered upon the
mountains, and no man gathereth
them.

Nineveh's doom forever: her enemies will rejoice

19*There is* no healing of thy bruise;
thy wound is grievous: all that hear the
bruit of thee shall clap the hands over
thee: for upon whom hath not thy wickedness passed continually?

3:18 shepherds. Generals.

HABAKKUK

THE WRITER

Habakkuk's name, in Hebrew, means *wrestler,* and by his words, he wrestled with God about the sin of the Israelites. Little is known about Habakkuk except that he prophesied toward the end of the reign of Josiah, King of Judah (637–608 B.C.).

THEME

In this prophecy Habakkuk is burdened by the question of why God allows evil. Some are anxious to get rid of evil because of the suffering that it brings, but Habakkuk wanted to get rid of it because he loved and worshipped God, and God is holy and hates evil. The prophet knew that suffering would come upon Israel if God judged evil, but he wanted God's will to be carried out even so.

OUTLINE OF HABAKKUK

I.	Habakkuk Speaks	Habakkuk 1:1-4
II.	God Answers	Habakkuk 1:5-11
III.	Habakkuk Speaks	Habakkuk 1:12-21
IV.	God Answers	Habakkuk 2:2-20
V.	Habakkuk Prays	Habakkuk 3:1-19

I. Habakkuk Speaks (1:1-4)

1 The *burden which Habakkuk the
*prophet did see.
2O LORD, how long shall I cry, and
thou wilt not hear! *even* cry out unto
thee *of* violence, and thou wilt not save!
3Why dost thou shew me iniquity, and
cause *me* to behold grievance? for spoiling and violence *are* before me: and
there are *that* raise up strife and contention.
4Therefore the *law is slacked, and
judgment doth never go forth: for the
wicked doth compass about the righteous; therefore wrong judgment
proceedeth.

II. God Answers (1:5-11)

¶5Behold ye among the heathen, and
regard, and wonder marvellously: for *I*
will work a work in your days, *which* ye
will not believe, though it be told *you.*
6For, lo, I raise up the Chaldeans, *that*
bitter and hasty nation, which shall

1:1 Habakkuk the prophet did see. See introduction.
1:4 slacked. Not enforced.
1:4 judgment. Justice.
1:5 among the heathen. During the time that Israel is scattered among the Gentile nations.
1:6 Chaldeans. Another name for the Babylonians.

> **1:5 Unbelievable Happenings**
> This "work" speaks not only of the coming Babylonian or Chaldean invasion, but it looks ahead to the work of our Lord on the cross. The apostle Paul quoted this verse hundreds of years later to the Jews who had gone to Antioch (Acts 13:41).

march through the breadth of the land,
to possess the dwellingplaces *that are*
not theirs.
7They *are* terrible and dreadful: their
judgment and their dignity shall proceed of themselves.
8Their horses also are swifter than
the leopards, and are more fierce than
the evening wolves: and their horsemen shall spread themselves, and
their horsemen shall come from far;
they shall fly as the eagle *that* hasteth
to eat.
9They shall come all for violence:
their faces shall sup up *as* the east wind,
and they shall gather the captivity as
the sand.
10And they shall scoff at the kings,
and the princes shall be a scorn unto
them: they shall deride every strong
hold; for they shall heap dust, and
take it.
11Then shall *his* mind change, and he
shall pass over, and offend, *imputing*
this his power unto his god.

III. Habakkuk Speaks (1:12—2:1)

¶12*Art* thou not from everlasting, O
LORD my God, mine Holy One? we
shall not die. O LORD, thou hast ordained them for judgment; and, O
mighty God, thou hast established
them for correction.
13*Thou art* of purer eyes than to behold evil, and canst not look on iniquity: wherefore lookest thou upon them
that deal treacherously, *and* holdest thy
tongue when the wicked devoureth *the
man that is* more righteous than he?
14And makest men as the fishes of
the sea, as the creeping things, *that
have* no ruler over them?
15They take up all of them with the
angle, they catch them in their net, and
gather them in their drag: therefore
they rejoice and are glad.
16Therefore they sacrifice unto their
net, and burn *incense unto their drag;
because by them their portion *is* fat, and
their meat plenteous.

> **1:11 For God's Purpose**
> The Bible teaches that rulers are ordained of God (Rom 13:1-7). Even the Roman emperors, cruel and wicked as many of them were, were so ordained to fulfill God's purpose in the world program. Our Lord clearly showed that the political leaders are to be rendered their dues (Matt. 22:15-22). Nebuchadnezzar was, in such a sense, God's servant (Jer. 27:6; see also its note, "For God's Purpose"), but as king of the Chaldeans he offended God by becoming proud of his power and commanding that an image of himself be worshipped (Dan. 3). He thus became a *type of the Beast out of the sea (Rev. 13:1-4; see also 13:1 note, "A Beast from the Sea").

1:7 judgment and their dignity shall proceed of themselves. They are a law unto themselves; they recognize no superiors.
1:9 their faces shall sup up. Just as the east wind destroys all green grass and growing plants in Palestine, so the Chaldeans would destroy Israel.
1:9 captivity. The captives of Israel.
1:10 heap dust. The Chaldeans would erect mounds of earth so that the walls of Jerusalem would be useless as a protection against them.
1:12 Art thou not from everlasting? Habakkuk thought of the holiness of God. He could not understand why God should choose the wicked Chaldeans to work His judgments (see also vs. 13).
1:12 we shall not die. An early text reads: "Thou shalt not die."
1:14 no ruler. No defender. The Chaldeans treated the Hebrews as if they were fish (see vs. 15).

17Shall they therefore empty their
net, and not spare continually to slay
the nations?

2 I will stand upon my watch, and
set me upon the tower, and will
watch to see what he will say unto me,
and what I shall answer when I am reproved.

IV. God Answers (2:2-20)

2And the LORD answered me, and
said, Write the vision, and make *it* plain
upon tables, that he may run that
readeth it.
3For the vision *is* yet for an appointed time, but at the end it shall speak,
and not lie: though it tarry, wait for it;
because it will surely come, it will not
tarry.
4Behold, his soul *which* is lifted up is
not upright in him: but the *just shall
live by his *faith.
¶5Yea also, because he transgresseth

2:4 God's Grace
"The just shall live by his faith" is an important doctrine of the grace of God, and it is quoted three times by New Testament writers, namely, in Romans 1:17 (see also Rom. 1:16-17 note, "Salvation by Faith"); Galatians 3:11; and Hebrews 10:38. It is through faith in God's Word and His provision that a guilty sinner becomes righteous and justified. Read Hebrews 11. These words about the just living by faith have had a tremendous influence in many lives, among them Martin Luther and John Wesley.

by *wine, *he is* a proud man, neither
keepeth at home, who enlargeth his
desire as *hell, and *is* as *death, and
cannot be satisfied, but gathereth unto
him all nations, and heapeth unto him
all people:
6Shall not all these take up a *parable against him, and a taunting proverb
against him, and say, Woe to him that
increaseth *that which is* not his! how
long? and to him that ladeth himself
with thick clay!
7Shall they not rise up suddenly that
shall bite thee, and awake that shall vex
thee, and thou shalt be for booties unto
them?
8Because thou hast spoiled many
nations, all the remnant of the people
shall spoil thee; because of men's
blood, and *for* the violence of the land,
of the city, and of all that dwell
therein.
¶9Woe to him that coveteth an evil
covetousness to his house, that he may
set his nest on high, that he may be
delivered from the power of evil!
10Thou hast consulted shame to thy
house by cutting off many people, and
hast sinned *against* thy soul.
11For the stone shall cry out of the
wall, and the beam out of the timber
shall answer it.
¶12Woe to him that buildeth a town
with blood, and stablisheth a city by
iniquity!
13Behold, *is it* not of the LORD of
hosts that the people shall labour in the

1:17 empty. The word means that the Chaldeans were constantly filling and emptying their nets—they did not cease in their slaying of the nations.
2:1 what I shall answer when I am reproved. This phrase means that Habakkuk would await the answer to his complaint. The answer follows immediately.
2:2 upon tables. Tablets that Habakkuk could write on.
2:2 may run. To tell others.
2:5 hell. This is a translation of the Hebrew word *Sheol* and refers, in the Old Testament, to the place to which the dead go. It corresponds to the Greek word *Hades*, translated "hell" in the New Testament (see Luke 16:23 note, "The Place Called Hell").
2:6 all these. The nations and people of verse 5 who will mock the power of the Chaldeans, whose day will be very short.
2:6 thick clay. This may speak of heavy rules inscribed on clay tablets, or even of great brick buildings.
2:11 the stone shall cry out. Compare Luke 19:40.
2:13 is it not. The LORD of hosts will bring this to pass.

very fire, and the people shall weary
themselves for very *vanity?
14For the earth shall be filled with the
knowledge of the glory of the LORD, as
the waters cover the sea.
¶15Woe unto him that giveth his neighbour drink, that puttest thy bottle to
him, and makest *him* drunken also, that
thou mayest look on their nakedness!
16Thou art filled with shame for glory: drink thou also, and let thy foreskin
be uncovered: the cup of the LORD'S
right hand shall be turned unto thee, and
shameful spewing *shall be* on thy glory.
17For the violence of *Lebanon shall
cover thee, and the spoil of beasts,
which made them afraid, because of
men's blood, and for the violence of the
land, of the city, and of all that dwell
therein.
¶18What profiteth the *graven image
that the maker thereof hath graven it;
the molten image, and a teacher of lies,
that the maker of his work trusteth
therein, to make dumb idols?
19Woe unto him that saith to the
wood, Awake; to the dumb stone, Arise,
it shall teach! Behold, it *is* laid over with
gold and silver, and *there is* no breath at
all in the midst of it.
20But the LORD *is* in his holy temple:
let all the earth keep silence before him.

2:20 God's Presence

This does not have direct reference to the fact that God meets His people in churches today, though He certainly does do that. It is a part of the vision Habakkuk saw of the time when the Lord Jesus Christ will enter the rebuilt temple at Jerusalem.

V. Habakkuk Prays (3:1-19)

3 A prayer of Habakkuk the prophet upon Shigionoth.
2O LORD, I have heard thy speech,
and was afraid: O LORD, revive thy
work in the midst of the years, in the
midst of the years make known; in
wrath remember mercy.
3God came from Teman, and the Holy
One from mount Paran. Selah. His glory covered the heavens, and the earth
was full of his praise.
4And *his* brightness was as the light;
he had horns *coming* out of his hand:
and there *was* the hiding of his power.
5Before him went the pestilence, and
burning coals went forth at his feet.
6He stood, and measured the earth:
he beheld, and drove asunder the

2:14 earth shall be filled. In the time of the reign of the Lord Jesus Christ on the earth. See *kingdom. This great prophecy is given five times: Numbers 14:21; Psalm 72:19; Isaiah 6:3; 11:9; Habakkuk 2:14.

2:16 the cup of the LORD's right hand. This speaks of the hand of power through which God's wrath will be accomplished.

2:16 unto thee. Unto Babylon.

2:17 violence of Lebanon. This speaks of the violence against Jerusalem and the temple, which was called Lebanon because it was built with cedar from the wonderful forest of Lebanon.

2:17 cover. Overwhelm.

2:17 the spoil of beasts. The nations, the Medes and Persians, would destroy the Chaldean kingdom.

2:19 that saith to the wood. In Revelation 13, it is predicted that the False Prophet will speak so to the image of the Beast.

3:1 Shigionoth. No one is sure what this means, although it has been thought to mean a sort of musical poem, perhaps of praise. It is the plural of the word "Shiggaion," found in the title of Psalm 7.

3:3 Teman . . . mount Paran. These were places that were visited by the children of Israel during their wilderness wanderings. God showed His glory there; He did not show Himself.

3:4 the hiding of his power. God's full power was hidden.

3:5 pestilence, and burning coals. Read about the plagues and the terrible lightning that manifested the power of the LORD to the Egyptians (Exod. 7–12).

3:6 measured. Made to tremble.

> **3:3 Selah**
> A Hebrew musical word, meaning a *pause*. Wherever it occurred in the singing of the Psalms, the singers stopped and only the musical instruments were heard while the people thought about the words that had gone before. In time it came to mean just the pause–a call to stop for a time of quiet thought on the wonderful words and works of the LORD.

nations; and the everlasting mountains
were scattered, the perpetual hills did
bow: his ways *are* everlasting.
7 I saw the tents of Cushan in affliction: *and* the curtains of the land of
Midian did tremble.
8 Was the LORD displeased against the
rivers? *was* thine anger against the rivers? *was* thy wrath against the sea, that
thou didst ride upon thine horses *and*
thy chariots of salvation?
9 Thy bow was made quite naked, *according* to the oaths of the tribes, *even
thy* word. Selah. Thou didst cleave the
earth with rivers.
10 The mountains saw thee, *and* they
trembled: the overflowing of the water
passed by: the deep uttered his voice,
and lifted up his hands on high.
11 The sun *and* moon stood still in
their habitation: at the light of thine
arrows they went, *and* at the shining of
thy glittering spear.
12 Thou didst march through the land
in indignation, thou didst thresh the
heathen in anger.
13 Thou wentest forth for the salvation of thy people, *even* for salvation
with thine anointed; thou woundedst
the head out of the house of the wicked, by discovering the foundation unto
the neck. Selah.
14 Thou didst strike through with his
staves the head of his villages: they
came out as a whirlwind to scatter me:
their rejoicing *was* as to devour the
poor secretly.
15 Thou didst walk through the sea
with thine horses, *through* the heap of
great waters.
16 When I heard, my belly trembled;
my lips quivered at the voice: rottenness entered into my bones, and I trembled in myself, that I might rest in the
day of trouble: when he cometh up unto

3:6 mountains were scattered. As in Revelation 16:20.
3:7 Cushan. Egypt. This speaks of the death of the firstborn (Exod. 12).
3:8 the rivers. The Nile, which was turned into blood by Moses at the command of God (Exod. 7:20-25).
3:8 the sea. The Red Sea when it was divided (Exod. 14:13-31). Pharaoh's men and horses perished; the people of the LORD and their chariots and all their belongings were saved.
3:9 bow was made quite naked. It was unsheathed and ready for use as in verse 11.
3:10 The mountains saw thee. See Exodus 19:16,18.
3:10 the deep . . . lifted up his hands. Read about the lifting of the waters in Exodus 14:22 and Joshua 3:16.
3:11 The sun and moon stood still. Read Joshua 10:13 and its note, "Time Stops."
3:11 at the light of thine arrows. Like light Your arrows flew; like lightning, Your glittering spear. This refers to the great victory that God gave to Joshua at Gibeon (see Josh. 10).
3:12 the land. Palestine.
3:13 the head. The head of the house of the wicked, their chief king.
3:13 discovering the foundation unto the neck. This means *laying him open from foot to neck*. That is how the wicked king was killed.
3:14 his staves. The spears of the wicked.
3:14 me. Israel.
3:15 the sea . . . the heap of great waters. The nations of Canaan.
3:16 When I heard. Habakkuk was terrified when he heard of the future triumph of the Chaldeans. The prophecy looks ahead, too, to the *Great Tribulation. Habakkuk's first thought in the verse ends with the word "myself." Start his new thought: "O that I might have rest when the Chaldeans come."

the people, he will invade them with his
troops.
¶ 17 Although the fig tree shall not
blossom, neither *shall* fruit *be* in the
vines; the labour of the olive shall fail,
and the fields shall yield no meat; the
flock shall be cut off from the fold, and
there shall be no herd in the stalls:
18 Yet I will rejoice in the LORD, I will
joy in the God of my salvation.
19 The LORD God *is* my strength, and
he will make my feet like hinds' *feet,* and
he will make me to walk upon mine
high places. To the chief singer on my
stringed instruments.

3:17 Rejoice in God
In spite of all the trouble to come, Habakkuk was determined to rejoice in God who saves (vs. 18). Even though He will come executing wrath and judgment upon the ungodly, He will come in mercy and for the salvation of the *remnant of Israel, who will be looking for Him in the last days.

3:19 hinds' feet. Surefooted as a deer. God's people can live with confidence and trust in God's promises to keep and strengthen us.
3:19 To the chief singer. The end of this prayer is a psalm to be sung to the accompaniment of stringed instruments.

ZEPHANIAH

BACKGROUND AND MEANING

Zephaniah lived during the reign of Josiah (2 Kings 22). He prophesied about the *Day of the LORD. While Josiah was king, there was a great revival, but this turning to the LORD in true repentance had not taken place when Zephaniah began his ministry. Probably his message encouraged the king and led the people to turn to the LORD. However, Zephaniah had to remind the people that their former sins were unjudged; and he prophesied that judgment was coming. It did come in Nebuchadnezzar's invasion and the captivity, but that, terrible as it was, was only a picture of the judgment that will come upon Israel as well as upon Gentiles who are on earth at the time of the severe *Tribulation in the Day of the LORD.

OUTLINE OF ZEPHANIAH

I.	Judgment to Come	Zephaniah 1:1-18
II.	Call for Repentance	Zephaniah 2:1—3:8
III.	Blessing to Come in the Kingdom Age	Zephaniah 3:9-20

I. Judgment to Come (1:1-18)

1 The word of the LORD which came
unto Zephaniah the son of Cushi,
the son of Gedaliah, the son of Amariah, the son of Hizkiah, in the days
of *Josiah the son of Amon, king of
*Judah.
2 I will utterly consume all *things* from
off the land, saith the LORD.
3 I will consume man and beast; I will
consume the fowls of the heaven, and the
fishes of the sea, and the stumblingblocks
with the wicked; and I will cut off man
from off the land, saith the LORD.
4 I will also stretch out mine hand
upon Judah, and upon all the inhabitants
of *Jerusalem; and I will cut off the
*remnant of *Baal from this place, *and*
the name of the Chemarims with the
priests;
5 And them that worship the host of
heaven upon the housetops; and them
that worship *and* that swear by the
LORD, and that swear by Malcham;

1:1 Hizkiah. Hezekiah. Zephaniah was probably a great-great-grandson of King Hezekiah.
1:2 from off the land. There is only one country that God speaks of as "the land," and that is Palestine.
1:3 stumblingblocks. Idols.
1:4 also. Even.
1:4 Chemarims. Baal's priests (compare 2 Kings 23:5).
1:5 host of heaven. See Genesis 11:4 note; 2 Kings 23:11-12: Jeremiah 19:13; Acts 7:42.
1:5 and. They pretended to worship both God and idols.
1:5 Malcham. *Molech, an Ammonite idol.

[6]And them that are turned back from
the LORD; and *those* that have not
sought the LORD, nor enquired for him.
[7]Hold thy peace at the presence of
the Lord GOD: for the day of the LORD
is at hand: for the LORD hath prepared
a *sacrifice, he hath bid his guests.
[8]And it shall come to pass in the day
of the LORD'S sacrifice, that I will punish the princes, and the king's children,
and all such as are clothed with strange
apparel.
[9]In the same day also will I punish all
those that leap on the threshold, which
fill their masters' houses with violence
and deceit.
[10]And it shall come to pass in that day,
saith the LORD, *that there shall be* the
noise of a cry from the fish gate, and an
howling from the second, and a great
crashing from the hills.
[11]Howl, ye inhabitants of Maktesh,
for all the merchant people are cut
down; all they that bear silver are cut
off.
[12]And it shall come to pass at that
time, *that* I will search Jerusalem with
candles, and punish the men that are
settled on their lees: that say in their
heart, The LORD will not do good, neither will he do evil.
[13]Therefore their goods shall become
a booty, and their houses a desolation:
they shall also build houses, but not
inhabit *them;* and they shall plant vineyards, but not drink the wine thereof.
[14]The great day of the LORD *is* near,
it is near, and hasteth greatly, *even* the
voice of the day of the LORD: the mighty
man shall cry there bitterly.

1:12 The Use of Candles
Here the concept of "with candles" means holding a light to all the dark corners. In most cases the word "candle" basically refers to a type of lamp (with the exception of Jer. 25:10). The Jews and most other ancient nations used earthenware lamps, shaped like a butter boat that was partially covered over and filled with oil for burning. The wick protruded through a lip or spout. It was set on a "candlestick," i.e., a lampstand. The woman seeking her lost piece of silver would have had this candlestick in one hand and a short hand broom in the other as she stooped and swept the house (Luke 15:8). The Jews frequently light their houses with seven-branched candelabra, or menorahs, in memory of the sacred lampstand within the sanctuary.

[15]That day *is* a day of wrath, a day of
trouble and distress, a day of wasteness
and desolation, a day of darkness and
gloominess, a day of clouds and thick
darkness,
[16]A day of the trumpet and alarm
against the fenced cities, and against
the high towers.
[17]And I will bring distress upon men,
that they shall walk like blind men, because they have sinned against the
LORD: and their blood shall be poured
out as dust, and their flesh as the
*dung.
[18]Neither their silver nor their gold
shall be able to deliver them in the day
of the LORD'S wrath; but the whole land
shall be devoured by the *fire of his jealousy: for he shall make even a speedy
riddance of all them that dwell in the
land.

1:7 at hand. The end times were often referred to as near or at hand, when they were still a couple of thousand years or more away (see Ps. 90:4).
1:7 guests. At the "supper of the great God" (Rev. 19:17).
1:8 strange apparel. Foreign. Wearing heathen clothing showed a desire for foreign (pagan) gods and ways.
1:9 leap on the threshold. "Leap on" means *avoid stepping on*. This was a pagan observance (see 1 Sam. 5:5) that God would judge.
1:10 second. Another gate.
1:11 Maktesh. A marketplace in Jerusalem.
1:14 it is near. At hand. See verse 7 note.
1:18 jealousy. God alone has a right to be *jealous when people worship other gods.

II. Call for Repentance (2:1—3:8)

2 Gather yourselves together, yea,
gather together, O nation not desired;
2 Before the decree bring forth, *before*
the day pass as the chaff, before the
fierce anger of the LORD come upon
you, before the day of the LORD'S anger
come upon you.
3 Seek ye the LORD, all ye meek of the
earth, which have wrought his *judgment; seek *righteousness, seek
meekness: it may be ye shall be hid in
the day of the LORD'S anger.
¶ 4 For *Gaza shall be forsaken, and
*Ashkelon a desolation: they shall drive
out Ashdod at the noon day, and Ekron
shall be rooted up.
5 Woe unto the inhabitants of the sea
coast, the nation of the Cherethites! the
word of the LORD *is* against you; O Canaan, the land of the *Philistines, I will
even destroy thee, that there shall be
no inhabitant.
6 And the sea coast shall be dwellings
and cottages for shepherds, and folds
for flocks.
7 And the coast shall be for the remnant of the house of Judah; they shall
feed thereupon: in the houses of Ashkelon shall they lie down in the evening: for the LORD their *God shall
visit them, and turn away their captivity.
¶ 8 I have heard the reproach of
*Moab, and the revilings of the children
of Ammon, whereby they have reproached my people, and magnified
themselves against their border.
9 Therefore *as* I live, saith the LORD
of hosts, the God of *Israel, Surely
Moab shall be as Sodom, and the children of Ammon as Gomorrah, *even* the
breeding of nettles, and saltpits, and
a perpetual desolation: the residue
of my people shall spoil them, and the
remnant of my people shall possess
them.
10 This shall they have for their pride,
because they have reproached and magnified *themselves* against the people of
the LORD of hosts.
11 The LORD *will be* terrible unto
them: for he will famish all the gods of
the earth; and *men* shall worship him,
every one from his place, *even* all the
*isles of the heathen.
¶ 12 Ye Ethiopians also, ye *shall be*
slain by my sword.
13 And he will stretch out his hand
against the north, and destroy Assyria;
and will make Nineveh a desolation,
and dry like a wilderness.
14 And flocks shall lie down in the
midst of her, all the beasts of the nations: both the cormorant and the bittern shall lodge in the upper lintels of
it; *their* voice shall sing in the windows;
desolation *shall be* in the thresholds: for
he shall uncover the cedar work.
15 This *is* the rejoicing city that dwelt
carelessly, that said in her heart, I *am*,
and *there is* none beside me: how is she
become a desolation, a place for beasts

2:1 nation not desired. Not desirable, or that hath no shame—Jerusalem.

2:2 Before the decree. This verse may be expressed in this way: "Before the judgment decree falls, bring forth works to show your repentance; before the fierce anger of the LORD comes upon you, for the day passes like chaff, and there is little time for repentance."

2:4 Gaza. There is a play on the names of the four cities. For instance, Gaza, which means *fortified* or *strength*, will be left desolate, while Ekron, which means *the firm rooted*, is to be uprooted.

2:11 famish all the gods. God was going to take away those who worshipped other gods.

2:12 my sword. Ethiopia controlled Egypt at this time. The Egyptians were "slain by [God's] sword" when the Assyrians invaded Egypt in 670 B.C.

2:13 he will stretch out. Nebuchadnezzar would stretch out his hand against the Assyria in 612 B.C.

2:14 cedar work. The wainscoting, the wooden linings of the rooms in the houses of Nineveh.

to lie down in! every one that passeth
by her shall hiss, *and* wag his hand.

3 Woe to her that is filthy and polluted, to the oppressing city!
[2]She obeyed not the voice; she re-
ceived not correction; she trusted
not in the LORD; she drew not near to
her God.
[3]Her princes within her *are* roaring
lions; her judges *are* evening wolves;
they gnaw not the bones till the morrow.
[4]Her prophets *are* light *and* treacherous persons: her priests have polluted
the sanctuary, they have done violence
to the law.
[5]The just LORD *is* in the midst thereof; he will not do iniquity: every morning doth he bring his judgment to light,
he faileth not; but the unjust knoweth
no shame.
[6]I have cut off the nations: their towers are desolate; I made their streets
waste, that none passeth by: their cities are destroyed, so that there is no
man, that there is none inhabitant.
[7]I said, Surely thou wilt fear me, thou
wilt receive instruction; so their dwelling should not be cut off, howsoever I
punished them: but they rose early, *and*
corrupted all their doings.
¶[8]Therefore wait ye upon me, saith
the LORD, until the day that I rise up
to the prey: for my determination *is*
to gather the nations, that I may assemble the kingdoms, to pour upon
them mine indignation, *even* all my
fierce anger: for all the earth shall
be devoured with the fire of my jealousy.

3:8 God's Purpose for Us
The ancient Jewish copyists made a note of the fact that all the letters of the Hebrew alphabet are found in this verse, and they took that to mean that the whole purpose of God for the earth is told in it. God's justice will prevail. The wicked will be punished, and the obedient will be blessed. (See Rev. 20:12 and its note, "The Dead.")

III. Blessing to Come in the Kingdom Age (3:9-20)

[9]For then will I turn to the people a
pure language, that they may all call
upon the name of the LORD, to serve
him with one consent.

3:9 One Language
At Babel, God changed the one language that all peoples spoke into many different languages (Gen. 11). This verse may mean that after the nations have been judged and the *kingdom is established, God will take away that curse and will cause all peoples to speak the same language again.

[10]From beyond the rivers of Ethiopia
my suppliants, *even* the daughter of my
dispersed, shall bring mine offering.
[11]In that day shalt thou not be
ashamed for all thy doings, wherein
thou hast transgressed against me: for
then I will take away out of the midst
of thee them that rejoice in thy pride,

3:1 her. Jerusalem.
3:3 gnaw not the bones. Literally this means, *They do not leave anything until the next day.*
3:4 polluted the sanctuary. The priests had profaned the sanctuary by introducing the worship of idols.
3:5 the unjust. The unrighteous judges of verse 3.
3:8 the day that I rise up to the prey. The day of God's wrath.
3:8 my jealousy. God's jealous love for His little flock.
3:9 the people. All God's people, Jews and Gentiles.
3:10 suppliants. Worshippers.
3:11 In that day. When God has judged and cleansed Israel.
3:11 them that rejoice in thy pride. "Them" refers to Jews who are proud and haughty because God chose Israel to be His people. God will remove the proud and save the humble.

and thou shalt no more be haughty because of my holy mountain.
12I will also leave in the midst of thee
an afflicted and poor people, and they
shall trust in the name of the LORD.
13The remnant of Israel shall not do
iniquity, nor speak lies; neither shall a
deceitful tongue be found in their
mouth: for they shall feed and lie down,
and none shall make *them* afraid.
¶14Sing, O daughter of Zion; shout, O
Israel; be glad and rejoice with all the
heart, O daughter of Jerusalem.
15The LORD hath taken away thy
judgments, he hath cast out thine enemy: the king of Israel, *even* the LORD,
is in the midst of thee: thou shalt not
see evil any more.
16In that day it shall be said to Jerusalem, Fear thou not: *and to* Zion, Let
not thine hands be slack.
17The LORD thy God in the midst of
thee *is* mighty; he will save, he will rejoice over thee with joy; he will rest
in his love, he will joy over thee with
singing.
18I will gather *them that are* sorrowful for the solemn assembly, *who* are of
thee, *to whom* the reproach of it *was* a
burden.
19Behold, at that time I will undo all
that afflict thee: and I will save her that
halteth, and gather her that was driven
out; and I will get them praise and fame
in every land where they have been put
to shame.
20At that time will I bring you *again*,
even in the time that I gather you: for I
will make you a name and a praise
among all people of the earth, when I
turn back your captivity before your
eyes, saith the LORD.

3:11 because of my holy mountain. In My holy name.
3:13 feed and lie down. Like sheep with a faithful shepherd. This certainly looks forward to the *Millennium when all Israel will know for sure the words written in Psalm 23: "The LORD is my shepherd." Those who are Christ's today know no want, for He is our Shepherd indeed.
3:14 daughter of Zion. "Daughter" seems to refer to the descendants of the Israelites, who will make up the nation Israel in the *Day of the LORD.
3:15 in the midst of thee. This cannot apply to the first coming of Christ, for they did see evil and affliction after that. This refers to the *Second Coming.
3:16 be slack. Grow weak.
3:17 he will rejoice . . . he will rest in his love. God will live among His people and rejoice over them. "Rest in" means *quiet you with*. God will comfort and give us peace through His great love for us.
3:18 sorrowful for the solemn assembly. Those whose worship was not sincere.
3:20 turn back your captivity. Restore you and bring you back to Palestine, out of captivity.

HAGGAI

BACKGROUND

A few thousand Israelites had returned to Palestine after the seventy years' Babylonian captivity (see Ezra and Nehemiah, and their introductions), and God sent Haggai, Zechariah, and Malachi to preach to them. This book contains Haggai's special message, which asked how they could expect blessing when the temple of the LORD was still lying in ruins.

STRUCTURE

Four messages were sent to the princes and people of Jerusalem by God through Haggai: each is introduced by the words: "came the Word of the LORD."

OUTLINE OF HAGGAI

I.	Introduction	Haggai 1:1-2
II.	God's First Message	Haggai 1:3-15
III.	God's Second Message	Haggai 2:1-9
IV.	God's Third Message	Haggai 2:10-19
V.	God's Fourth Message	Haggai 2:20-23

I. Introduction (1:1-2)

1 In the second year of *Darius the
king, in the sixth *month, in the
first day of the month, came the word
of the LORD by Haggai the *prophet
unto *Zerubbabel the son of Shealtiel,
governor of *Judah, and to *Joshua the
son of Josedech, the high priest, saying,
2 Thus speaketh the LORD of hosts,
saying, This people say, The time is not
come, the time that the LORD'S house
should be built.

II. God's First Message (1:3-15)

3 Then came the word of the LORD by
Haggai the prophet, saying,
4 *Is it* time for you, O ye, to dwell in
your *cieled houses, and this house *lie*
waste?
5 Now therefore thus saith the LORD
of hosts; Consider your ways.
6 Ye have sown much, and bring in
little; ye eat, but ye have not enough;
ye drink, but ye are not filled with
drink; ye clothe you, but there is none
warm; and he that earneth wages
earneth wages *to put it* into a bag with
holes.
¶7 Thus saith the LORD of hosts; Consider your ways.
8 Go up to the mountain, and bring
wood, and build the house; and I will

1:1 governor. By order of Persia, which ruled Palestine.
1:1 Joshua. Not the Joshua who led the children of Israel after Moses died. This is Joshua the high priest (see Zech. 3:1 second note).
1:4 this house. The temple of the LORD.

take pleasure in it, and I will be glorified, saith the LORD.
9Ye looked for much, and, lo, *it came*
to little; and when ye brought *it* home,
I did blow upon it. Why? saith the LORD
of hosts. Because of mine house that *is*
waste, and ye run every man unto his
own house.
10Therefore the heaven over you is
stayed from dew, and the earth is stayed
from her fruit.
11And I called for a drought upon the
land, and upon the mountains, and upon
the corn, and upon the new wine, and
upon the oil, and upon *that* which the
ground bringeth forth, and upon men,
and upon cattle, and upon all the labour
of the hands.
¶12Then Zerubbabel the son of Shealtiel, and Joshua the son of Josedech,
the high priest, with all the *remnant
of the people, obeyed the voice of the
LORD their *God, and the words of Haggai the prophet, as the LORD their God
had sent him, and the people did *fear
before the LORD.
13Then spake Haggai the LORD'S
messenger in the LORD'S message unto
the people, saying, I *am* with you, saith
the LORD.
14And the LORD stirred up the spirit
of Zerubbabel the son of Shealtiel, governor of Judah, and the spirit of Joshua
the son of Josedech, the high priest,
and the spirit of all the remnant of the
people; and they came and did work in
the house of the LORD of hosts, their
God,
15In the four and twentieth day of the
sixth month, in the second year of Darius the king.

III. God's Second Message (2:1-9)

2 In the seventh *month,* in the one
and twentieth *day* of the month,
came the word of the LORD by the
prophet Haggai, saying,
2Speak now to Zerubbabel the son of
Shealtiel, governor of Judah, and to
Joshua the son of Josedech, the high
priest, and to the residue of the people,
saying,
3Who *is* left among you that saw this
house in her first glory? and how do ye
see it now? *is it* not in your eyes in comparison of it as nothing?
4Yet now be strong, O Zerubbabel,
saith the LORD; and be strong, O Joshua,
son of Josedech, the high priest; and be
strong, all ye people of the land, saith
the LORD, and work: for I *am* with you,
saith the LORD of hosts:
5*According to* the word that I covenanted with you when ye came out of
Egypt, so my spirit remaineth among
you: fear ye not.
6For thus saith the LORD of hosts; Yet
once, it *is* a little while, and I will shake
the heavens, and the earth, and the sea,
and the dry *land;*
7And I will shake all nations, and the
desire of all nations shall come: and I

2:6 The Final Shaking
This shaking that the LORD speaks of has not happened yet. There have been many "shakings" of different countries, but no final shaking of both the sky and the earth. See Hebrews 12:26–it still had not happened when Hebrews was written. See also Revelation 10:7; 11:15-19; and 16:17-21, which describe the final shaking.

1:9 I did blow upon it. In other words, "Because of your sin I brought judgment upon your crops and activities, so that you did not thrive."
2:1 seventh month. October. This is the date when Haggai's message evidently took effect and the people began to build.
2:3 saw this house. Some of the very oldest people remembered seeing Solomon's temple before they were taken captive. They could easily see that this one they were building was not nearly as magnificent.
2:5 covenanted. See Exodus 25:22.
2:7 desire of all nations. This means that He alone who can satisfy, the Lord Jesus Christ, will come in person.

will fill this house with glory, saith the
LORD of hosts.
8 The silver *is* mine, and the gold *is*
mine, saith the LORD of hosts.
9 The glory of this latter house shall
be greater than of the former, saith the
LORD of hosts: and in this place will I
give peace, saith the LORD of hosts.

2:9 The Temple at Christ's Return
This does not refer to the temple that they were building (see vs. 3), nor the one that Herod built to please the Jews (Matt. 24:1-2), nor even the one that will be built during the coming *Tribulation (Matt. 24:15; 2 Thess. 2:3-4), but the one that will be built when the Lord Jesus Christ returns to earth (Ezek. 40–47).

IV. God's Third Message (2:10-19)

¶10 In the four and twentieth *day* of
the ninth *month,* in the second year of
Darius, came the word of the LORD by
Haggai the prophet, saying,
11 Thus saith the LORD of hosts;
Ask now the priests *concerning* the law,
saying,
12 If one bear holy flesh in the skirt of
his garment, and with his skirt do touch
bread, or pottage, or wine, or oil, or any
meat, shall it be holy? And the priests
answered and said, No.
13 Then said Haggai, If *one that is* unclean by a dead body touch any of these,
shall it be unclean? And the priests answered and said, It shall be unclean.
14 Then answered Haggai, and said,
So *is* this people, and so *is* this nation
before me, saith the LORD; and so *is*
every work of their hands; and that
which they offer there *is* unclean.
15 And now, I pray you, consider from
this day and upward, from before a
stone was laid upon a stone in the temple of the LORD:
16 Since those *days* were, when *one*
came to an heap of twenty *measures,*
there were *but* ten: when *one* came to
the pressfat for to draw out fifty *vessels*
out of the press, there were *but* twenty.
17 I smote you with blasting and with
mildew and with hail in all the labours
of your hands; yet ye *turned* not to me,
saith the LORD.
18 Consider now from this day and
upward, from the four and twentieth
day of the ninth *month, even* from the
day that the foundation of the LORD'S
temple was laid, consider *it.*
19 Is the seed yet in the barn? yea, as
yet the vine, and the fig tree, and the
pomegranate, and the olive tree, hath
not brought forth: from this day will I
bless *you.*

V. God's Fourth Message (2:20-23)

¶20 And again the word of the LORD
came unto Haggai in the four and twentieth *day* of the month, saying,
21 Speak to Zerubbabel, governor of
Judah, saying, I will shake the heavens
and the earth;
22 And I will overthrow the throne of
kingdoms, and I will destroy the
strength of the kingdoms of the heathen; and I will overthrow the chariots,
and those that ride in them; and the
horses and their riders shall come
down, every one by the sword of his
brother.
23 In that day, saith the LORD of hosts,
will I take thee, O Zerubbabel, my servant, the son of Shealtiel, saith the
LORD, and will make thee as a signet:
for I have chosen thee, saith the LORD
of hosts.

2:11 the law. Leviticus 22 tells about the laws mentioned in verses 12-13.
2:14 there. The altar of Ezra 3:2.
2:15 upward. Backward.
2:16 pressfat. The vat of a winepress.
2:18 upward. Forward.
2:23 Zerubbabel, my servant. Here Zerubbabel is a *type of the Lord Jesus Christ. The signet ring was the sign of royal power. The prophecy in verse 22 looks forward, of course, to the day when the Gentile world power will be overthrown.

ZECHARIAH

BACKGROUND

Zechariah and Haggai were prophets to the Jewish people, called the *Remnant, who had gone back to the land of Judah at the command of Cyrus, King of Persia, to rebuild their temple. (Read the introduction to the book of Ezra, and Ezra 1:1–5.) The two men prophesied in the same year (see Haggai 1:1 and Zechariah 1:1).

THE WRITER AND SUMMARY

Zechariah was a Jewish priest, brought up in the school of the prophets. Work on the rebuilding of the temple had been interrupted because of the opposition of enemies (Ezra 4:24), and so Zechariah encouraged his people to love God more so that they would continue the great task of rebuilding the temple in Jerusalem. Zechariah also prophesied of the coming of the Messiah (our Lord Jesus Christ) as the future Priest-King. Zechariah's prophecies looked beyond the day in which he lived to the time when Israel shall truly be made praiseworthy in the earth. He also spoke about Gentile nations because they lived in all the countries around Palestine.

The name *Judah*, often used in the book, refers not only to Judah, it seems, but often to Israel as a whole.

OUTLINE OF ZECHARIAH

I.	Symbols Teaching Jewish Hope in the Coming of the Messiah	Zechariah 1:1—6:15
II.	The Messengers from Babylon, Who Come to Hear the Word of God	Zechariah 7:1—8:23
III.	A Prophecy of the Rejection and the Later Coming in Power of the Messiah	Zechariah 9:1—14:21

I. Symbols Teaching Jewish Hope (1:1—6:15)

*Visions of *hope and blessing*

1 In the eighth *month, in the second year of *Darius, came the word
of the LORD unto Zechariah, the son of
Berechiah, the son of Iddo the *prophet, saying,
2The LORD hath been sore displeased
with your fathers.
3Therefore say thou unto them,
Thus saith the LORD of hosts; Turn ye

1:1 Darius. He was the Medo-Persian king.
1:1 LORD. Jehovah, who has great love even for His wayward children, is speaking. See *names of God.

1:1 Meanings of Names
1. Zechariah means *remembered of God.*
2. Berechiah means *blessed of God.*
3. Iddo means *the appointed time.*

These names contain the message of the book–God remembers His people and will bless them in His appointed time.

unto me, saith the LORD of hosts, and
I will turn unto you, saith the LORD of
hosts.
4Be ye not as your fathers, unto
whom the former *prophets have cried,
saying, Thus saith the LORD of hosts;
Turn ye now from your evil ways, and
from your evil doings: but they did not
hear, nor hearken unto me, saith the
LORD.
5Your fathers, where *are* they? and
the prophets, do they live for ever?
6But my words and my statutes,
which I commanded my servants the
prophets, did they not take hold of your
fathers? and they returned and said,
Like as the LORD of hosts thought to do

1:8 Understanding the Vision
The following verses are rather hard to understand unless we see that:
1. The man riding the red horse (vss. 8,10) and the Angel of the LORD (vss. 11-12) are one and the same. They are the One who is often spoken of as being the Angel of the LORD in the Old Testament, the Lord Jesus Christ in the glory that He had with the Father before He came to this earth as a baby.
2. The "angel that talked with me" (vss. 9,13) is an angel who explained Zechariah's visions to him.

unto us, according to our ways, and according to our doings, so hath he dealt
with us.

1st vision: the Rider among the myrtle trees

¶7Upon the four and twentieth day of
the eleventh month, which *is* the month
Sebat, in the second year of Darius,
came the word of the LORD unto Zechariah, the son of Berechiah, the son of
Iddo the prophet, saying,
8I saw by night, and behold a man
riding upon a red horse, and he stood
among the myrtle trees that *were* in the
bottom; and behind him *were there* red
horses, speckled, and white.

1:8 The Three Horses
The horses that Zechariah saw in his vision–upon which a heavenly host was riding to carry out the will of the LORD–stood for three things:
1. the red: The LORD will punish the Gentile nations who have been cruel to His people;
2. the speckled or mixed: He will show mercy with His judgment; and
3. the white: He will win the victory over all the nations of the world.

9Then said I, O my lord, what *are*
these? And the *angel that talked with
me said unto me, I will shew thee what
these *be*.
10And the man that stood among the
myrtle trees answered and said, These
are they whom the LORD hath sent to
walk to and fro through the earth.
11And they answered the angel of the
LORD that stood among the myrtle
trees, and said, We have walked to and

1:3 and I will. God cannot forgive us if we are not repentant or sorrowful before Him for our sins.

1:4 former prophets. Their main former prophets were Jeremiah and Isaiah. Read 2 Chronicles 24:19 to find out why God had to send prophets to His people so often.

1:4 they did not hear, nor hearken unto me. To ignore the prophets was to refuse to hear the LORD, because the prophets spoke His words.

1:8 red horse. Red stands for judgment or for blood. Israel is being oppressed by Gentile powers (see vs. 12). God will bring judgment, or punishment, upon the Gentiles.

1:8 myrtle trees that were in the bottom. These were a symbol of God's chosen people, Israel, who were buried in "a ravine" of sorrow (a translation of "in the bottom"), because of their Gentile enemies.

fro through the earth, and, behold, all
the earth sitteth still, and is at rest.

God's anger against the Gentile nations

¶ 12 Then the angel of the LORD answered and said, O LORD of hosts, how
long wilt thou not have *mercy on *Jerusalem and on the cities of *Judah,
against which thou hast had indignation
these threescore and ten years?
13 And the LORD answered the angel
that talked with me *with* good words
and comfortable words.
14 So the angel that communed with
me said unto me, Cry thou, saying,
Thus saith the LORD of hosts; I am jealous for Jerusalem and for *Zion with a
great jealousy.
15 And I am very sore displeased with
the heathen *that are* at ease: for I was
but a little displeased, and they helped
forward the affliction.

God's promise of blessing to Israel

16 Therefore thus saith the LORD; I
am returned to Jerusalem with mercies: my house shall be built in it, saith
the LORD of hosts, and a line shall be
stretched forth upon Jerusalem.
17 Cry yet, saying, Thus saith the
LORD of hosts; My cities through prosperity shall yet be spread abroad; and
the LORD shall yet comfort Zion, and
shall yet choose Jerusalem.

2nd vision: the four horns

¶ 18 Then lifted I up mine eyes, and
saw, and behold four horns.
19 And I said unto the angel that talked
with me, What *be* these? And he answered me, These *are* the horns which
have scattered Judah, *Israel, and Jerusalem.

3rd vision: the four smiths or workmen

20 And the LORD shewed me four carpenters.
21 Then said I, What come these to
do? And he spake, saying, These *are* the
horns which have scattered Judah, so
that no man did lift up his head: but
these are come to fray them, to cast out
the horns of the *Gentiles, which lifted up *their* horn over the land of Judah
to scatter it.

1:11 all the earth sitteth still. God's messengers see that most Gentiles do not try to help Israel in her trouble. They do not care.

1:12 threescore and ten years. The angel spoke of Jeremiah's prophecy (read Jer. 25:11-12 and vs. 11 note, "An Improbable Prediction"; 29:10) of the seventy years' captivity, which had now ended.

1:14 Cry thou. Zechariah was commanded of the LORD to make these things known.

1:14 jealous. The Lord God was moved with emotion for Israel because the Gentile nations added to Israel's sorrows.

1:16 my house shall be built in it. Nebuchadnezzar had destroyed the temple (586 B.C.).

1:16 line . . . upon Jerusalem. The LORD marked out the area and the plan of the new temple. It was completed four years after this (see Ezra 6:15).

1:17 Zion. This was a section of Jerusalem. It is the largest and highest of the four hills upon which the city of Jerusalem stood. Zion also stood for the city of Jerusalem itself.

1:18 horns. In the Bible, "horns" speak of power, often the power of a Gentile king (Ps. 75:10; Dan. 7:24; Amos 6:13; Rev. 17:12).

1:19 the horns which have scattered. The four powers which scattered the Jewish people were four world empires (Dan. 2; 7), Babylon, Medo-Persia, Greece, and Rome.

1:20 carpenters. These were craftsmen, perhaps carvers or smiths—workers in iron. These stood for the nations used to overthrow Israel's enemies. God wanted to make clear that He has an instrument to destroy every power that works against Him and His people.

1:21 fray. This is a translation of a Hebrew word meaning *to terrify*. The craftsmen were to crush the world powers that had scattered both Judah and Israel, and which were determined to wipe God's people out.

4th vision: man with measuring line

2 I lifted up mine eyes again, and
looked, and behold a man with a
measuring line in his hand.
2Then said I, Whither goest thou?
And he said unto me, To measure Jerusalem, to see what *is* the breadth
thereof, and what *is* the length thereof.
3And, behold, the angel that talked
with me went forth, and another angel
went out to meet him,

Jerusalem blessed in future

4And said unto him, Run, speak to
this young man, saying, Jerusalem shall
be inhabited *as* towns without walls for
the multitude of men and cattle therein:
5For I, saith the LORD, will be unto
her a wall of *fire round about, and will
be the glory in the midst of her.

2:8 The Glory Returns
"After the glory" speaks of the time when the *Shekinah* glory (see Gen. 3:24 second note) would again take up its dwelling place in the Holy of Holies in the temple (Exod. 40:34). Read of the departing of the glory from the temple and of its final return in Ezekiel 9:3; 10:4,18; 11:23; 43:2-5 (see also Ezek. 43:2 note, "God's Future Glory").

¶6Ho, ho, *come forth,* and flee from
the land of the north, saith the LORD:
for I have spread you abroad as the four
winds of the heaven, saith the LORD.
7Deliver thyself, O Zion, that dwellest *with* the daughter of *Babylon.
8For thus saith the LORD of hosts;
After the glory hath he sent me unto
the nations which spoiled you: for he
that toucheth you toucheth the apple of
his eye.
9For, behold, I will shake mine hand
upon them, and they shall be a spoil to
their servants: and ye shall know that
the LORD of hosts hath sent me.

The LORD's wonderful encouragements

¶10Sing and rejoice, O daughter of
Zion: for, lo, I come, and I will dwell in
the midst of thee, saith the LORD.
11And many nations shall be joined to
the LORD in that day, and shall be my
people: and I will dwell in the midst of
thee, and thou shalt know that the LORD
of hosts hath sent me unto thee.
12And the LORD shall inherit Judah
his portion in the *holy land, and shall
choose Jerusalem again.
13Be silent, O all flesh, before the
LORD: for he is raised up out of his holy
habitation.

2:1 a man. The same man seen in 1:8 is seen again by Zechariah.

2:1 measuring line. This speaks of the rebuilding of Jerusalem (see Ezek. 40:3,5; see also vs. 5 note, "The Future Temple").

2:4 Run, speak. Here the LORD told another angel to tell the young man with the measuring line that Jerusalem is to be larger than it had been in the past and that it is to have no wall around it.

2:4 towns without walls. Jerusalem will extend without limit way beyond its walls, and even so, the people will be safe, for the LORD will be the King and protector (vs. 5).

2:6 land of the north. Babylon is meant here, looking forward to the final Babylon (Rev. 17). This is all yet future. As the Jewish people who were in Babylon were told to come back to Jerusalem, so they will be called back from the north for the millennial reign of Christ.

2:8 the apple of his eye. In this verse, apple means *the pupil* through which light enters the eye. It is the most important part of the eye, because it is vital to our sight. It is treasured for that reason. The LORD says that as one would protect that part of the eye, so He would protect His people.

2:9 a spoil to their servants. The nations that have oppressed the Jewish people will be so completely overthrown that their slaves will be stronger than they and will be able to take from them any riches that they may have left.

2:12 inherit. This word means *to take as one's own possession.*

2:12 choose Jerusalem. Jerusalem was rejected by God because of Israel's sin. He now says, "I shall love her again."

5th vision: Joshua represents Israel

3 And he shewed me *Joshua the high priest standing before the angel of the LORD, and *Satan standing at his right hand to resist him.

2And the LORD said unto Satan, The LORD rebuke thee, O Satan; even the LORD that hath chosen Jerusalem rebuke thee: *is* not this a brand plucked out of the fire?

3Now Joshua was clothed with filthy garments, and stood before the angel.

4And he answered and spake unto those that stood before him, saying, Take away the filthy garments from him. And unto him he said, Behold, I have caused thine iniquity to pass from thee, and I will clothe thee with change of raiment.

5And I said, Let them set a fair mitre

3:8 THE PROPHECY OF THE BRANCH

Here is a definite prophecy, more than five hundred years before the coming of the Messiah. "My servant" is often used in the book of Isaiah for our Lord Jesus Christ as Messiah. So in Zechariah "the BRANCH" is also His name, as we read in 6:12, "whose name is The BRANCH." He is spoken of six times in the Scriptures as the Branch–(Isa. 4:2; 11:1 and its note, "The Branch of Jesse"; Zech. 3:8; 6:12; Jer. 23:5; 33:15), under four headings, and these four headings are presented in the four Gospels since they picture the Lord Jesus Christ:

1. "A righteous Branch, and a King" (Jer. 23:5; 33:15) in the Gospel of Matthew: "Behold, thy King" (Matt. 21:5).
2. "My servant the BRANCH" (Zech. 3:8) in the Gospel of Mark: "Behold, My Servant" (see Mark 10:44-45).
3. "The man whose name is The BRANCH" (Zech. 6:12) in the Gospel of Luke: "Behold, the Man" (see Luke 9:22).
4. "The branch of the LORD" (Isa. 4:2) in the Gospel of John: "Behold, your God" (see John 20:31).

3:1 he shewed me. The first three visions in chapters 1 and 2 are descriptive of outward deliverance, that is, deliverance from enemies, and the land was to be blessed. The visions in chapters 3 and 4 speak of inward spiritual blessings.

3:1 Joshua the high priest. He represented Jerusalem and its people as their mediator—he gave the people God's message and interceded with God for the people. There is only one perfect Mediator, the Lord Jesus Christ (1 Tim. 2:5).

3:1 angel of the LORD. The name LORD here is Jehovah. (See *names of God.) This angel was very probably our Lord Himself, as in Zechariah 1:12. Read verse 2 and note on *angels.

3:1 Satan . . . to resist him. Satan accused Joshua, that is, he spoke against Israel whom Joshua represented. See Job 1:6-7 and Revelation 12:10, where he is called the "accuser of our brethren."

3:2 The LORD rebuke thee. We are to resist the devil (James 4:7), but not even the angels dare rebuke him—that is for God to do (Jude 9), and He rebuked Satan now.

3:2 brand . . . fire. As the high priest, Joshua stood for, or represented, Israel. They had (and have) been so terribly troubled by their enemies that they had suffered almost as if they had been in a burning fire, but God in His grace will save them (see Lev. 26:44).

3:3 Joshua was clothed with filthy garments. Dirty garments are symbols of sinful lives. Joshua here represented sinful Israel (see Isa. 64:6).

3:4 he answered. The LORD is speaking here.

3:4 I have caused . . . change of raiment. The idea of clothing is kept before us (see vs. 3). We cannot be blessed of God if we live in sin. When the Lord causes iniquity to pass from us, He clothes us in the garment of the righteousness of God in Christ. See 1 Peter 5:5 note, "Clothed in Humility."

3:5 fair mitre. The priest's headdress, the mitre, had a plate of gold on the front of it engraved with the words: "HOLINESS TO THE LORD" (Exod. 28:36-38). The filthy clothes taken off, the changed clothes, and the mitre stand for cleansing, sanctification (read Gen. 2:3 and the note on sanctify), and holy service for the LORD.

upon his head. So they set a fair mitre
upon his head, and clothed him with
garments. And the angel of the LORD
stood by.
6 And the angel of the LORD protested unto Joshua, saying,
7 Thus saith the LORD of hosts; If thou
wilt walk in my ways, and if thou wilt
keep my charge, then thou shalt also
judge my house, and shalt also keep my
courts, and I will give thee places to
walk among these that stand by.

6th vision: My Servant the Branch

8 Hear now, O Joshua the high priest,
thou, and thy fellows that sit before
thee: for they *are* men wondered at: for,
behold, I will bring forth my servant the
*BRANCH.
9 For behold the stone that I have laid
before Joshua; upon one stone *shall be*
seven eyes: behold, I will engrave the
graving thereof, saith the LORD of
hosts, and I will remove the iniquity of
that land in one day.
10 In that day, saith the LORD of hosts,
shall ye call every man his neighbour
under the vine and under the *fig tree.

7th vision: the candlestick and the olive trees

4 And the angel that talked with me
came again, and waked me, as a
man that is wakened out of his sleep,
2 And said unto me, What seest thou?
And I said, I have looked, and behold a
candlestick all *of* gold, with a bowl upon
the top of it, and his seven lamps
thereon, and seven pipes to the seven
lamps, which *are* upon the top thereof:
3 And two olive trees by it, one upon
the right *side* of the bowl, and the other
upon the left *side* thereof.
4 So I answered and spake to the angel that talked with me, saying, What
are these, my lord?
5 Then the angel that talked with me
answered and said unto me, Knowest
thou not what these be? And I said, No,
my lord.
6 Then he answered and spake unto
me, saying, This *is* the word of the

3:7 my house. The tabernacle was the house of God. Many of these promises have never yet been fulfilled, but they surely will come to pass. They are as sure as God's Word.

3:8 thy fellows. These were Joshua's fellow priests.

3:9 stone that I have laid before Joshua. Our Lord Jesus Christ is the only stone upon which Israel can be built (see Isa. 28:16 and its note, "A Sure Foundation"); He is the stone on which the church is built. He said, "The stone which the builders rejected, the same is become the head of the corner" (Matt. 21:42; see also 1 Pet. 2:4-5).

3:9 seven eyes. In Revelation 5:6 these seven eyes are shown to be the seven Spirits of God (see Isa. 11:2).

3:9 I will engrave. The beauty and glory of the LORD that cannot be erased (scrubbed out) will be engraved or carved upon the stone.

3:9 remove the iniquity. God will one day remove all Israel's sin (see Rom. 11:25-26).

3:10 under the vine and under the fig tree. There will be rest and safety for the people of Israel in that day when the Lord sets up His kingdom on earth (Mic. 4:1-6). Read the note on the *kingdom.

4:1 waked me, as. Zechariah was not asleep. He was probably stunned by the great revelations given him in the visions. "Waked" means that his mind was made clear, so that he could understand these spiritual things.

4:2 bowl. The bowl was a sort of dish to hold oil, since the candlestick was really a lampstand.

4:2 pipes. Oil flowed through these to supply the lamps. Oil is a symbol of the Holy Spirit (see Exod. 27:20 note). The candlesticks, or lampstands, were pictures of Israel, who was chosen to bear light, or witness, to others for God.

4:3 two olive trees. These stood for God's two anointed ones (see vs. 14): Zerubbabel, a recognized leader of the exiles and the son of the governor of Judah (Hag. 1:1), who was told by the LORD to rebuild the temple, and Joshua the high priest. These two are *types of our LORD as King and High Priest (Matt. 2:2; Heb. 5:1-10).

4:6 Zerubbabel. See verse 3 note.

LORD unto *Zerubbabel, saying, Not by might, nor by power, but by my spirit, saith the LORD of hosts.

7 Who *art* thou, O great mountain? before Zerubbabel *thou shalt become* a plain: and he shall bring forth the head-stone *thereof with* shoutings, *crying,* *Grace, grace unto it.

8 Moreover the word of the LORD came unto me, saying,

9 The hands of Zerubbabel have laid the foundation of this house; his hands shall also finish it; and thou shalt know that the LORD of hosts hath sent me unto you.

10 For who hath despised the day of small things? for they shall rejoice, and shall see the plummet in the hand of Zerubbabel *with* those seven; they *are* the eyes of the LORD, which run to and fro through the whole earth.

¶11 Then answered I, and said unto him, What *are* these two olive trees upon the right *side* of the candlestick and upon the left *side* thereof?

12 And I answered again, and said unto him, What *be these* two olive branches which through the two golden pipes empty the golden *oil* out of themselves?

13 And he answered me and said, Knowest thou not what these *be?* And I said, No, my lord.

14 Then said he, These *are* the two anointed ones, that stand by the Lord of the whole earth.

4:10 The Day of Small Things
Israel had made many unfavorable comparisons between the glorious temple of Solomon and the structure then being built. They even designated the time of their rebuilding here as "the day of small things." Although the eyes of men looked with disdain upon the work at hand, the eyes of the LORD viewed with favor the building activity of Zerubbabel. They are the eyes of the LORD which run to and fro—Zechariah uses almost the same words of the prophet Hanani to Asa, "the eyes of the LORD run to and fro thoroughout the whole earth, to shew himself strong in behalf of them whose heart is perfect toward him" (2 Chron. 16:9). We must always keep in mind that God's "strength is made perfect in weakness" (2 Cor. 12:9).

8th vision: the great flying roll

5 Then I turned, and lifted up mine eyes, and looked, and behold a flying roll.

2 And he said unto me, What seest thou? And I answered, I see a flying roll; the length thereof *is* twenty *cubits, and the breadth thereof ten cubits.

4:6 Not by might . . . by my spirit. The temple was to be rebuilt in the power of God alone (see *Holy Spirit). Might stood for armies; power stood for what people might try to do in their own strength.

4:7 mountain. When Zerubbabel worked in the power of the Spirit, any difficulty would be removed.

4:7 headstone. This speaks again of our Lord Jesus Christ, the chief cornerstone (see Zech. 3:9 first note).

4:10 plummet. This is exactly the same as a plumb line. It is a light rope with a weight at one end, usually made of brass or lead. It is used as a test in building anything that has to be absolutely straight and upright—houses, walls, and so forth.

4:14 two anointed ones. Zerubbabel and Joshua (see explanation of vs. 3).

5:1 Then I turned. The first five visions in chapters 1–4 speak especially of God's forgiveness and Israel's restoration to their land and to God. The three visions in chapters 5 and 6 reveal especially that they must suffer judgment before they can come back to God.

5:1 a flying roll. A roll, literally, a *scroll*, in Scripture stands for a message from God, or of God's written Word (see Isa. 8:1; Jer. 36:2 and its note, "The Last Writings"; Ezek. 2:9; 3:1). In this vision it is God's Word that rebukes sin.

5:2 flying. Judgment will travel quickly and overtake the sinner.

5:2 length. The scroll is big, thirty feet long by fifteen feet wide, to show that the judgment that it reveals on Israel is also great.

3 Then said he unto me, This *is* the
curse that goeth forth over the face of
the whole earth: for every one that
stealeth shall be cut off *as* on this side
according to it; and every one that
sweareth shall be cut off *as* on that side
according to it.
4 I will bring it forth, saith the LORD
of hosts, and it shall enter into the
house of the thief, and into the house
of him that sweareth falsely by my
name: and it shall remain in the midst
of his house, and shall consume it with
the timber thereof and the stones
thereof.

9th vision: the ephah and the woman

¶5 Then the angel that talked with me
went forth, and said unto me, Lift up
now thine eyes, and see what *is* this
that goeth forth.
6 And I said, What *is* it? And he said,
This *is* an *ephah that goeth forth. He
said moreover, This *is* their resemblance through all the earth.
7 And, behold, there was lifted up a
talent of lead: and this *is* a woman that
sitteth in the midst of the ephah.
8 And he said, This *is* wickedness.
And he cast it into the midst of the
ephah; and he cast the weight of lead
upon the mouth thereof.
9 Then lifted I up mine eyes, and
looked, and, behold, there came out two
women, and the wind *was* in their
wings; for they had wings like the wings
of a stork: and they lifted up the ephah
between the earth and the heaven.
10 Then said I to the angel that talked
with me, Whither do these bear the
ephah?
11 And he said unto me, To build it an
house in the land of Shinar: and it shall
be established, and set there upon her
own base.

10th vision: the four chariots

6 And I turned, and lifted up mine
eyes, and looked, and, behold,
there came four chariots out from between two mountains; and the mountains *were* mountains of brass.

5:7 The Woman Described

The woman's name is "wickedness" (vs. 8). She is in the ephah with the cover of lead over her. As "ephah," "talent" (cover), and "lead" are measures used in business or commerce, so the woman in the ephah stands for wickedness in commerce. The vision here of the wicked woman sitting in the midst of commerce undoubtedly refers to the same development revealed through the apostle John in Revelation 18. It speaks of the overthrow and final judgment of wicked Babylon in the *Great Tribulation yet to come on earth, the destruction of the political-commercial, religionized world system.

5:4 it shall remain . . . and shall consume. God's curse is spoken of as "it." Both the crime and God's curse on it were written upon the roll. This is what the terrible disease leprosy does. Leprosy is a *type of sin. Sin hurts people's souls and ruins their lives, but our Lord Jesus Christ died for us, taking our sin upon Him so that we might be forgiven (see Lev.13:2 note, "A Disease Called Leprosy").

5:6 their resemblance. The symbol of all the sin of Israel is heaped together in one measure, so perfectly measured that all can see it.

5:7 a talent. The largest measure for weight the Jews had acted as a cover for the ephah (a basket).

5:8 cast it into the midst of the ephah. Wickedness was pushed back into the ephah, which the lead talent again closed up.

5:9 stork. The stork is an unclean bird (Lev. 11:13,19).

5:11 Shinar. God seemed to say, "Wickedness does not belong here in My land. Let her be carried to Shinar [Babylonia, see Dan. 1:2 second note], and there build her a temple." Only God could cause the land to be cleansed from wickedness.

6:1 four chariots. Horses and chariots often stand for God's power on the earth, or toward the earth (see Jer. 46:9-10; Joel 2:3-11; Nah. 3:1-7). We know that chariots of fire were round about Elisha (2 Kings 6:17).

6:1 mountains of brass. Locally, these were Mount Moriah and the Mount of Olives,

6:1 The Vision's Message
To understand this vision, we must compare it with the vision of the horses in chapter 1, which speaks of coming judgment on Gentile powers (nations). This vision has a twofold message. It not only shows judgment that was coming swiftly upon the Gentiles. It also looks ahead to God's wrath and final judgment of the Gentiles throughout the whole earth in the *Day of the LORD.

2In the first chariot *were* red horses;
and in the second chariot black horses;
3And in the third chariot white
horses; and in the fourth chariot grisled
and bay horses.
4Then I answered and said unto the
angel that talked with me, What *are*
these, my lord?
5And the angel answered and said
unto me, These *are* the four spirits of
the heavens, which go forth from standing before the Lord of all the earth.
6The black horses which *are* therein
go forth into the north country; and
the white go forth after them; and
the grisled go forth toward the south
country.
7And the bay went forth, and sought
to go that they might walk to and fro
through the earth: and he said, Get you
hence, walk to and fro through the
earth. So they walked to and fro through
the earth.
8Then cried he upon me, and spake
unto me, saying, Behold, these that go
toward the north country have quieted
my spirit in the north country.

6:5 The Four Chariots
The "four spirits" refers to the four chariots of verse 1. This looks beyond Israel and Babylon to the future day at the end of the *Great Tribulation period when God will judge the Gentile world powers. The stone of Daniel 2:34, the Lord Jesus Christ returning in power and glory (Rev. 19:11-21) to establish His millennial throne, is synonymous with these four chariots (compare Isa. 2:10-22).

Joshua's crowning and The Branch

¶9And the word of the LORD came
unto me, saying,
10Take of *them of* the captivity, *even* of
Heldai, of Tobijah, and of Jedaiah, which
are come from Babylon, and come thou
the same day, and go into the house of
*Josiah the son of Zephaniah;
11Then take silver and gold, and make
crowns, and set *them* upon the head of
Joshua the son of Josedech, the high
priest;
12And speak unto him, saying, Thus
speaketh the LORD of hosts, saying,
Behold the man whose name *is* The
*BRANCH; and he shall grow up out of
his place, and he shall build the temple
of the LORD:
13Even he shall build the temple of
the LORD; and he shall bear the glory,
and shall sit and rule upon his throne;
and he shall be a priest upon his
throne: and the counsel of peace shall
be between them both.
14And the crowns shall be to Helem,

through which Babylonian forces were to come. Prophetically, they speak of the power of God to judge righteously and show that His power will never change.

6:10 Take of them of the captivity. These were three Jewish exiles from Babylon. Read the introductions to this book and the book of Ezra.

6:11 make crowns. They also were to "make circlets for one crown," which was for Joshua, who represented Israel as their mediator (3:1). The crowning of Joshua teaches that after the Lord Jesus Christ has dealt with the nations in judgment, He will come to reign as King. He comes for judgment first before He can reign in righteousness (Ps. 2:5-6; Rev. 19:19-21; 20:4-6).

6:12 The BRANCH. This is Jesus Christ (see Zech. 3:8 note, "The Prophecy of the Branch"), whose real temple will be erected when He comes to reign.

6:13 his throne. The Lord Jesus shall reign (Rev. 3:21). See *kingdom.

6:13 he shall be a priest. He is to be Prophet, Priest, and King (Ps. 110; Heb. 7:1-3).

6:14 crowns . . . for a memorial in the temple. The crown was put in the temple as a

and to Tobijah, and to Jedaiah, and to
Hen the son of Zephaniah, for a memorial in the temple of the LORD.
[15]And they *that are* far off shall come
and build in the temple of the LORD, and
ye shall know that the LORD of hosts
hath sent me unto you. And *this* shall
come to pass, if ye will diligently obey
the voice of the LORD your *God.

II. The Messengers from Babylon (7:1—8:23)

A group comes to ask about fasts Zechariah begins a new method of prophesying

7 And it came to pass in the fourth
year of king *Darius, *that* the word
of the LORD came unto Zechariah in the
fourth *day* of the ninth *month, *even* in
Chisleu;
[2]When they had sent unto the house
of God Sherezer and Regem-melech,
and their men, to pray before the LORD,
[3]*And* to speak unto the priests which
were in the house of the LORD of hosts,
and to the *prophets, saying, Should I
weep in the fifth month, separating
myself, as I have done these so many
years?

God's answer

¶[4]Then came the word of the LORD
of hosts unto me, saying,
[5]Speak unto all the people of the land,
and to the priests, saying, When ye fasted and mourned in the fifth and seventh
month, even those seventy years, did
ye at all fast unto me, *even* to me?
[6]And when ye did eat, and when ye
did drink, did not ye eat *for yourselves,*
and drink *for yourselves?*
[7]*Should ye* not *hear* the words which
the LORD hath cried by the former
prophets, when *Jerusalem was inhabited and in prosperity, and the cities
thereof round about her, when *men*
inhabited the south and the plain?
¶[8]And the word of the LORD came
unto Zechariah, saying,
[9]Thus speaketh the LORD of hosts,
saying, Execute true judgment, and
shew mercy and compassions every
man to his brother:
[10]And oppress not the widow, nor the
fatherless, the stranger, nor the poor;
and let none of you imagine evil against
his brother in your heart.
[11]But they refused to hearken, and
pulled away the shoulder, and stopped
their ears, that they should not hear.
[12]Yea, they made their hearts *as* an
adamant stone, lest they should hear
the *law, and the words which the LORD
of hosts hath sent in his spirit by the
former prophets: therefore came a
great wrath from the LORD of hosts.

---

memorial to these three exiles, to show that the Lord Jesus Christ would certainly come to reign.

6:15 And this shall come to pass. Fulfillment of God's promises depends on obedience. The rejection of the Lord Jesus Christ by the Jewish people delayed the fulfillment of this blessing (see Matt. 23:39).

7:1 fourth year. This was two years after the visions were given (see Zech. 1:1).

7:2 Sherezer and Regem-melech. These were perhaps chief men who came to pray to the LORD and to consult the priests (prophets).

7:3 Should I weep. To weep on that day was their own idea, not God's, and it had become mere form and ritual. It had lost its reality.

7:3 fifth month. The ninth day of the fifth month was a time of weeping because of the destruction of the temple by Nebuchadnezzar in 586 B.C.

7:5 seventy years. This was since the beginning of the Captivity (see introductions to this book and the book of Ezra).

7:5 at all. Was it really for me?

7:6 when ye did eat, and when ye did drink. Their feasts were not worship.

7:7 not hear . . . former prophets. They did not listen to the former prophets when Jerusalem was prosperous. This was why their captivity and sorrow began.

7:12 adamant stone. Adamant stone (hard as flint) is an unusually hard stone like a diamond (see Ezek. 3:9).

13 Therefore it is come to pass, *that* as
he cried, and they would not hear; so
they cried, and I would not hear, saith
the LORD of hosts:
14 But I scattered them with a whirlwind among all the nations whom they
knew not. Thus the land was desolate
after them, that no man passed through
nor returned: for they laid the pleasant
land desolate.

God's promise of blessing to Israel

8 Again the word of the LORD of
hosts came *to me,* saying,
2 Thus saith the LORD of hosts; I was
jealous for *Zion with great jealousy,
and I was jealous for her with great
fury.

Millennial glory

3 Thus saith the LORD; I am returned
unto Zion, and will dwell in the midst
of Jerusalem: and Jerusalem shall be
called a city of truth; and the mountain
of the LORD of hosts the holy mountain.
4 Thus saith the LORD of hosts; There
shall yet old men and old women dwell
in the streets of Jerusalem, and every
man with his staff in his hand for very
age.
5 And the streets of the city shall be
full of boys and girls playing in the
streets thereof.
6 Thus saith the LORD of hosts; If it be
marvellous in the eyes of the *remnant
of this people in these days, should it
also be marvellous in mine eyes? saith
the LORD of hosts.

Further blessings promised

7 Thus saith the LORD of hosts; Behold, I will save my people from the east
country, and from the west country;
8 And I will bring them, and they shall
dwell in the midst of Jerusalem: and
they shall be my people, and I will be
their God, in truth and in *righteousness.
¶9 Thus saith the LORD of hosts; Let
your hands be strong, ye that hear in
these days these words by the mouth
of the prophets, which *were* in the day
that the foundation of the house of the
LORD of hosts was laid, that the temple
might be built.
10 For before these days there was no
hire for man, nor any hire for beast;

7:13 he cried. The LORD Himself pleaded with the people, but they would not hear; then, when it was too late, they cried unto Him (compare Matt. 25:1-13).

7:14 I scattered them. Although this was yet to happen, it was so certain that the LORD could say, "I scattered," rather than, "I will scatter them." For two thousand years, the Jews have been scattered among all the peoples of the earth (read Deut. 28:64 and its note, "Final Prophecy").

8:2 great jealousy . . . great fury. This refers to God's anger against the nations who oppressed the Jews in their captivity.

8:3 I am returned. The LORD had forsaken Israel because of their sin, but He will return.

8:3 will dwell. The Jewish people were scattered and the temple was destroyed. They will be brought back to their land, and the LORD will restore the temple worship.

8:3 city of truth. Because God who is the Truth will rule there (John 14:6), the city must have this name.

8:3 holy. *Set apart for God,* or *sanctified,* is what this word means.

8:3 mountain. Mount Zion.

8:4 old men . . . age. The Jews who will live in Jerusalem will live to old age because of God's care and goodness. (Isa. 65:20 is a good verse to read in connection with this.)

8:6 should it also be marvellous in mine eyes? This question means: "Because it seems too wonderful to the *remnant that I can do this, should it also seem too wonderful to Me?"

8:9 Let your hands be strong. This means *be brave* or *of good courage.*

8:9 the prophets. These are Haggai and Zechariah, who were then prophesying this blessing and were in Jerusalem when the foundation of the temple was laid (see Ezra 5:1-2).

neither *was there any* peace to him that
went out or came in because of the affliction: for I set all men every one
against his neighbour.
[11]But now I *will* not *be* unto the residue of this people as in the former days,
saith the LORD of hosts.
[12]For the seed *shall be* prosperous;
the vine shall give her fruit, and the
ground shall give her increase, and the
heavens shall give their dew; and I will
cause the remnant of this people to
possess all these *things.*
[13]And it shall come to pass, *that* as ye
were a curse among the heathen, O
house of *Judah, and house of *Israel;
so will I save you, and ye shall be a
blessing: fear not, *but* let your hands be
strong.
[14]For thus saith the LORD of hosts; As
I thought to punish you, when your fathers provoked me to wrath, saith the
LORD of hosts, and I repented not:
[15]So again have I thought in these
days to do well unto Jerusalem and to
the house of Judah: fear ye not.
¶[16]These *are* the things that ye shall
do; Speak ye every man the truth to his

8:14 Repentance
If one studies all the verses in the Old Testament which speak of repentance, he finds that it is used with the meaning that the person who has repented has changed his mind. However, God never changes His mind. He has always known what man is going to do and exactly what He Himself is going to do. Therefore, when the Bible speaks of God's repenting, it means that from man's viewpoint, God's action looks like a change of mind, but He is the One who changes not (Mal. 3:6; Heb. 13:8).

neighbour; execute the judgment of
truth and peace in your gates:
[17]And let none of you imagine evil in
your hearts against his neighbour; and
love no false oath: for all these *are*
things that I hate, saith the LORD.
¶[18]And the word of the LORD of hosts
came unto me, saying,
[19]Thus saith the LORD of hosts; The
fast of the fourth *month,* and the fast of
the fifth, and the fast of the seventh, and
the fast of the tenth, shall be to the
house of Judah joy and gladness, and
cheerful feasts; therefore love the truth
and peace.

Future worship to center in Jerusalem

[20]Thus saith the LORD of hosts; *It*
shall yet *come to pass,* that there shall
come people, and the inhabitants of
many cities:
[21]And the inhabitants of one *city* shall
go to another, saying, Let us go speedily to pray before the LORD, and to seek
the LORD of hosts: I will go also.
[22]Yea, many people and strong nations shall come to seek the LORD of
hosts in Jerusalem, and to pray before
the LORD.
[23]Thus saith the LORD of hosts; In
those days *it shall come to pass,* that ten
men shall take hold out of all languages
of the nations, even shall take hold of
the skirt of him that is a Jew, saying, We
will go with you: for we have heard *that*
God *is* with you.

III. A Prophecy of Messiah (9:1—14:21)

9 The burden of the word of the
LORD in the land of Hadrach, and
*Damascus *shall be* the rest thereof:

8:11 residue. See *remnant.
8:23 In those days. When Jerusalem is the world's religious center, the Jewish people will be missionaries to all the nations.
8:23 ten men. The word "ten" is often used in Scripture for an indefinite number (see Lev. 26:26; Num. 14:22; 1 Sam. 1:8).
9:1 burden. This word means *heavy* or *grievous;* these words of the LORD are a burden because they contain God's judgments or punishments.
9:1 land of Hadrach. This is no doubt in Syria, because it is here joined with Damascus, which is a city of Syria.

when the eyes of man, as of all the
tribes of Israel, *shall be* toward the
LORD.
[2]And Hamath also shall border
thereby; Tyrus, and Zidon, though it be
very wise.
[3]And Tyrus did build herself a strong
hold, and heaped up silver as the dust,
and fine gold as the mire of the streets.
[4]Behold, the Lord will cast her out,
and he will smite her power in the sea;
and she shall be devoured with *fire.
[5]*Ashkelon shall see *it,* and fear;
Gaza also *shall see it,* and be very sorrowful, and Ekron; for her expectation
shall be ashamed; and the king shall
perish from Gaza, and Ashkelon shall
not be inhabited.
[6]And a bastard shall dwell in Ashdod,
and I will cut off the pride of the *Philistines.
[7]And I will take away his blood
out of his mouth, and his abominations
from between his teeth: but he that remaineth, even he, *shall be* for our God,
and he shall be as a governor in Judah,
and Ekron as a Jebusite.
[8]And I will encamp about mine house
because of the army, because of him
that passeth by, and because of him that
returneth: and no oppressor shall pass
through them any more: for now have
I seen with mine eyes.

9:8 Jerusalem Protected
God will protect Jerusalem. Alexander the Great fought against and conquered the cities spoken of in verses 1-6, but he did not touch Jerusalem, for God protected it. This verse looks ahead, too, to the time when the LORD will set up His throne in Jerusalem, for then "no oppressor shall pass through them any more." (See *kingdom.)

Christ's triumphal entry

¶[9]Rejoice greatly, O daughter of Zion;
shout, O daughter of Jerusalem: behold,
thy King cometh unto thee: he *is* just,
and having *salvation; lowly, and riding
upon an ass, and upon a colt the foal of
an ass.

Christ's future world-kingdom, and Ephraim's deliverance

[10]And I will cut off the chariot from
*Ephraim, and the horse from Jerusa-

9:1 the rest thereof. Or resting place. This means that judgment will come (rest there) to Damascus.

9:2 Hamath. This was a city on the Sea of Galilee, while Tyre and Sidon were cities on the coast of Phoenicia.

9:2 though it be very wise. Tyre was proud because it was a great island stronghold.

9:4 smite her power . . . devoured with fire. God's judgment came. Alexander the Great of Greece defeated Tyre and completely destroyed the city.

9:5-6 Ashkelon . . . Gaza . . . Ekron . . . Ashdod. These were cities of the Philistines that were all overthrown (see Jer. 25).

9:6 bastard. Sometimes a child of mixed parentage—Jew and Gentile. In this verse, it can also mean *foreigners.*

9:7 take away his blood . . . abominations. It was God's commandment that no blood be eaten when the people ate meat (Lev. 19:26), for "the life of the flesh is in the blood" (see Lev. 17:11 note and 17:10 note, "Forbidden Blood"; and Lev. 17:12-14). First Samuel 14:32-33 tells of the people breaking this law.

9:7 he that remaineth. Even the *remnant will be sacred to God, "as a governor in Judah," while the people of Ekron, a city of the Philistines, will be like the Jebusites, whom Solomon, when he was king of Israel, made to be his slaves (1 Kings 9:20-21).

9:9 behold, thy King cometh. Our Lord Jesus Christ fulfilled this prophecy when He rode into Jerusalem (see Matt. 21:1-11).

9:9 just. Christ was just and righteous, and He bought our salvation by the cross (read Isa. 53; John 3:16 and 3:15-16 note, "Eternal Life").

9:9 riding upon an ass. In ancient days this was a sign of honor or dignity and peace. This was prophesied five hundred years before it came to pass. All of God's Word will be fulfilled, including the *Second Coming.

lem, and the battle bow shall be cut off: and he shall speak peace unto the heathen: and his dominion *shall be* from sea *even* to sea, and from river *even* to the ends of the earth.

11As for thee also, by the blood of thy covenant I have sent forth thy prisoners out of the pit wherein *is* no water.

¶12Turn you to the strong hold, ye prisoners of *hope: even to day do I declare *that* I will render double unto thee;

13When I have bent Judah for me, filled the bow with Ephraim, and raised up thy sons, O Zion, against thy sons, O Greece, and made thee as the sword of a mighty man.

14And the LORD shall be seen over them, and his arrow shall go forth as the lightning: and the Lord GOD shall blow the trumpet, and shall go with whirlwinds of the south.

15The LORD of hosts shall defend them; and they shall devour, and subdue with sling stones; and they shall drink, *and* make a noise as through *wine; and they shall be filled like bowls, *and* as the corners of the *altar.

16And the LORD their God shall save them in that day as the flock of his people: for *they shall be as* the stones of a crown, lifted up as an ensign upon his land.

17For how great *is* his goodness, and how great *is* his beauty! corn shall make the young men cheerful, and new wine the maids.

Ephraim and Judah to be blessed

10 Ask ye of the LORD rain in the time of the latter rain; *so* the LORD shall make bright clouds, and give them showers of rain, to every one grass in the field.

10:1 The Rains in Palestine
There are two rains in Palestine: the early and the latter rain. One is to aid the plow, and the other to make fruit to grow. Jeremiah 3:3 says that latter rain will be taken away because of sin, and it has been; here God promises that it will come again. But first and foremost this speaks of future blessing.

2For the idols have spoken *vanity, and the diviners have seen a lie, and have told false dreams; they comfort in vain: therefore they went their way as a flock, they were troubled, because *there was* no shepherd.

9:10 speak peace . . . and his dominion shall be from sea even to sea. This verse prophesies the glory of Christ's *kingdom on earth (see Ps. 72:7-8 and *Millennium).
9:11 blood of thy covenant. God confirmed the covenant between Him and His people and sealed it with blood (see Exod. 24:8 and its note on *covenant).
9:11 prisoners. The people of Israel were prisoners in the land of captivity and were to be delivered.
9:11 pit wherein is no water. It is believed that these dry pits were used as dungeons.
9:12 strong hold. The people were told to return to the land of Israel where the LORD would be their fortress and strength (stronghold). (See Joel 3:16.)
9:12 of hope. The Israelites' hope was in God's promises.
9:12 render double. Those who had been prisoners were to have twice what they had lost given to them (read Job 42:10).
9:13 Greece. Greece was defeated by Maccabean Jews (who lived in the time after the Old Testament was written and before Jesus Christ was born), but this verse undoubtedly refers also to Israel's future victory over all world powers.
9:14 And the LORD. This verse and the next give an illustration of the LORD leading Israel to victory.
9:16 they shall be as the stones of a crown. Israel will be like God's crown of glory.
9:16 as an ensign. As a shining banner or flag is raised high, so everyone will see Israel as God's people.
10:2 idols have spoken. The people foolishly consulted idols but, of course, the idols could give no help. Even today people make idols of many things, including money and power, but they are as useless to help and save us as a stone idol.

[3]Mine anger was kindled against the
shepherds, and I punished the goats: for
the LORD of hosts hath visited his flock
the house of Judah, and hath made them
as his goodly horse in the battle.
[4]Out of him came forth the corner, out
of him the nail, out of him the battle bow,
out of him every oppressor together.
¶[5]And they shall be as mighty *men,*
which tread down *their enemies* in the
mire of the streets in the battle: and
they shall fight, because the LORD *is*
with them, and the riders on horses
shall be confounded.
[6]And I will strengthen the house of
Judah, and I will save the house of *Joseph, and I will bring them again to
place them; for I have mercy upon
them: and they shall be as though I had
not cast them off: for I *am* the LORD
their God, and will hear them.
[7]And *they of* Ephraim shall be like a
mighty *man,* and their heart shall rejoice as through wine: yea, their children shall see *it,* and be glad; their heart
shall rejoice in the LORD.
[8]I will hiss for them, and gather them;
for I have *redeemed them: and they
shall increase as they have increased.

The dispersed regathered

[9]And I will sow them among the people: and they shall remember me in far
countries; and they shall live with their
children, and turn again.
[10]I will bring them again also out of
the land of *Egypt, and gather them out
of Assyria; and I will bring them into the
land of *Gilead and *Lebanon; and *place*
shall not be found for them.
[11]And he shall pass through the sea
with affliction, and shall smite the
waves in the sea, and all the deeps of
the river shall dry up: and the pride of
Assyria shall be brought down, and the
sceptre of Egypt shall depart away.
[12]And I will strengthen them in the
LORD; and they shall walk up and down
in his name, saith the LORD.

A dark prophecy

11 Open thy doors, O Lebanon, that the fire may devour thy cedars.

10:3 shepherds. The shepherds should be the religious leaders of the people, but these were false shepherds, who would not care for the flock.
10:3 goats. The goats stand for the unfaithful members of the shepherd's flock, in contrast to the sheep, who are faithful: The Eastern shepherd always divides the sheep from the goats (Matt. 25:33).
10:3 as his goodly horse. The LORD promises to change His poor leaderless sheep, the Jews, into proud warhorses doing the LORD's work.
10:3 in the battle. This speaks of the Battle of Armageddon. See the note on Revelation 16:16 note.
10:4 Out of him. This means *out of* Judah or *from* Judah.
10:4 came forth. This speaks of the past and prophesies of the future.
10:4 the corner. This is Christ, the cornerstone (Matt. 21:42; 1 Pet. 2:6).
10:4 nail. God says, "I will fasten him as a nail in a sure place" (Isa. 22:22-23), referring to our LORD as well as to restored Israel.
10:4 battle bow. The LORD here is the archer who uses the battle bow to shoot the arrows against the Enemy, Satan (see Ps. 45:5).
10:7 they of Ephraim. When Zechariah speaks of Joseph or of Ephraim, he speaks of the Jewish people who are still in captivity. Judah refers to those who have returned to the land.
10:8 hiss. A signal or a sound like a snake. The shepherd signals to his flock in this way (with a pipe).
10:8 increase as they have increased. They shall be as many as they once were.
10:10 I will bring them. The LORD will gather His people from the far countries and bring them to their own land.
11:1 Lebanon. Cedars of Lebanon were evergreen trees of different kinds. They stood for Israel's glory (Jer. 22:6-7).

2 Howl, fir tree; for the cedar is fall-
en; because the mighty are spoiled:
howl, O ye oaks of *Bashan; for the forest of the vintage is come down.
¶3 *There is* a voice of the howling of
the shepherds; for their glory is
spoiled: a voice of the roaring of young
lions; for the pride of Jordan is spoiled.
4 Thus saith the LORD my God; Feed
the flock of the slaughter;
5 Whose possessors slay them, and
hold themselves not guilty: and they
that sell them say, Blessed *be* the LORD;
for I am rich: and their own shepherds
pity them not.
6 For I will no more pity the inhabitants of the land, saith the LORD: but,
lo, I will deliver the men every one into
his neighbour's hand, and into the hand
of his king: and they shall smite the
land, and out of their hand I will not
deliver *them*.
7 And I will feed the flock of slaughter, *even* you, O poor of the flock. And I
took unto me two staves; the one I
called Beauty, and the other I called
Bands; and I fed the flock.
8 Three shepherds also I cut off in one
month; and my soul lothed them, and
their soul also abhorred me.
9 Then said I, I will not feed you: that
that dieth, let it die; and that that is to
be cut off, let it be cut off; and let the
rest eat every one the flesh of another.
¶10 And I took my staff, *even* Beauty,
and cut it asunder, that I might break my
covenant which I had made with all the
people.
11 And it was broken in that day: and
so the poor of the flock that waited upon
me knew that it *was* the word of the
LORD.
12 And I said unto them, If ye think
good, give *me* my price; and if not, forbear. So they weighed for my price
thirty *pieces* of silver.
13 And the LORD said unto me, Cast it

11:12 A Picture of Christ's Coming
Verses 12-14 give a picture of the first coming of the Lord Jesus to His people. He came in grace (John 1:17), or beauty, as the King to set up His kingdom (Matt. 4:17), which would, of course, be a kingdom of peace. The people would not have Him for their King (John 19:14-15), and He was sold for thirty pieces of silver (Matt. 26:15). This was the amount of money that was paid for a slave that had been injured (Exod. 21:32).

Graciousness had to be cut asunder—the LORD had to give them over to their punishment, and there could be no kingdom for the time (vs. 14). Read Matthew 27:3-10 to see what happened to the thirty pieces of silver that Judas was paid for betraying the Lord.

11:3 shepherds. These are bad leaders in this verse. The Good Shepherd (our Lord Jesus Christ, John 10:11) speaks in verse 4.
11:4 the flock of the slaughter. The sheep are led astray by bad shepherds. The LORD wants to feed (bless) them, but they will not listen to Him.
11:6 I will no more pity. Outside nations will oppress the land because they reject their Messiah, and the LORD, the true Shepherd, will not pity them.
11:6 they shall smite the land. God will not deliver His people. This was fulfilled by Titus in A.D. 70 when he took Jerusalem.
11:7 poor of the flock. The poor are the few who love the LORD—He will feed them.
11:7 staves. Two staves or staffs were used by shepherds: 1) to guide the sheep; 2) to protect them from any enemy.
11:7 Beauty. The name means *gracious favor of God*.
11:7 Bands. This means *union* or *God uniting* His people. An explanation of these two words, "Beauty" and "Bands," is found in verses 10-14.
11:8 Three shepherds. The three classes of leaders that Israel had called in the Old Testament, "priests . . . pastors . . . and prophets" (Jer. 2:8), and in the New Testament, "elders and chief priests and scribes" (Matt. 16:21). When the Lord came to earth, He pronounced woe and judgment upon them (Matt. 23); He cut them off.
11:10 Beauty, and cut it asunder. The LORD says, "I . . . break my covenant," that is, I will not be united with My people. The reason for this is given in verses 12-13.

unto the potter: a goodly price that I
was prised at of them. And I took the
thirty *pieces* of silver, and cast them to
the potter in the house of the LORD.
14Then I cut asunder mine other
staff, *even* Bands, that I might break the
brotherhood between Judah and Israel.
¶15And the LORD said unto me, Take
unto thee yet the instruments of a foolish shepherd.
16For, lo, I will raise up a shepherd in
the land, *which* shall not visit those that
be cut off, neither shall seek the young
one, nor heal that that is broken, nor
feed that that standeth still: but he shall
eat the flesh of the fat, and tear their
claws in pieces.
17Woe to the idol shepherd that
leaveth the flock! the sword *shall be*
upon his arm, and upon his right eye:
his arm shall be clean dried up, and his
right eye shall be utterly darkened.

*The Beast's armies besiege Jerusalem, and Israel is victorious (A future *prophecy)*

12 The burden of the word of the
LORD for Israel, saith the LORD,
which stretcheth forth the heavens, and
layeth the foundation of the earth, and
formeth the spirit of man within him.
2Behold, I will make Jerusalem a cup
of trembling unto all the people round
about, when they shall be in the siege
both against Judah *and* against Jerusalem.
¶3And in that day will I make Jerusalem a burdensome stone for all people:
all that burden themselves with it shall
be cut in pieces, though all the people
of the earth be gathered together
against it.

The LORD delivers Judah from siege

4In that day, saith the LORD, I will
smite every horse with astonishment,
and his rider with madness: and I will
open mine eyes upon the house of Judah, and will smite every horse of the
people with blindness.
5And the governors of Judah shall say
in their heart, The inhabitants of Jerusalem *shall be* my strength in the LORD
of hosts their *God.
¶6In that day will I make the governors
of Judah like an hearth of fire among the
wood, and like a torch of fire in a sheaf;
and they shall devour all the people
round about, on the right hand and on the
left: and Jerusalem shall be inhabited
again in her own place, *even* in Jerusalem.
7The LORD also shall save the tents
of Judah first, that the glory of the house
of *David and the glory of the inhabitants of Jerusalem do not magnify *themselves* against Judah.
8In that day shall the LORD defend the
inhabitants of Jerusalem; and he that is
feeble among them at that day shall be
as David; and the house of David *shall
be* as God, as the *angel of the LORD
before them.

11:13 I was prised at. Prized. This was the value that had been put on Jesus.
11:15 instruments of a foolish shepherd. These are the cruel staffs of the bad shepherd who wants to steal the sheep.
11:16 shepherd in the land. A wicked person will arise who will control and oppress the people of Palestine. He is the "little horn" (Dan. 7:8; see its note, "The Meaning of a Little Horn") and the "beast" (Rev. 13). See Revelation 19:20 note.
11:17 idol shepherd. The Beast (see vs. 16 note) is called by this name.
11:17 his arm, and upon his right eye. This is a description of God's punishment or judgment on the Beast at the time of his destruction. (See Rev. 19:20 note.)
12:1 burden. Here begins another heavy or sad message for Israel.
12:2 trembling. When the nations come to fight against Jerusalem, Judah and Jerusalem (the people) will be dizzy and reel because of their great suffering.
12:4 astonishment. This means *panic* or *great fear.*
12:6 governors. Just as fire burns wood, so the princes of Judah will be victorious.
12:8 In that day. This speaks of the future day when the wicked nations will try to kill all the people of Jerusalem. See *Day of the LORD.

¶[9]And it shall come to pass in that
day, *that* I will seek to destroy all the nations that come against Jerusalem.

The crucified Lord is revealed to His people

[10]And I will pour upon the house of
David, and upon the inhabitants of Jerusalem, the spirit of grace and of supplications: and they shall look upon me
whom they have pierced, and they shall
mourn for him, as one mourneth for *his*
only *son,* and shall be in bitterness for
him, as one that is in bitterness for *his*
firstborn.

12:10 Christ's Death

This prophecy speaks of Jesus Christ, for at His death this is quoted (John 19:37); but this occasion was not the fulfillment, for John omitted the words "that the scripture should be fulfilled" used in John 19:36 for a different prophecy from the Old Testament. There is yet a future time when this prophecy will be fulfilled, when the Lord returns in glory; and a believing *remnant of Israel will see Him and remember that it was the nation Israel that rejected Him and caused Him to be crucified and pierced with the sword (see Rev. 1:7).

[11]In that day shall there be a great
*mourning in Jerusalem, as the mourn-
ing of Hadadrimmon in the valley of
Megiddon.
[12]And the land shall mourn, every
family apart; the family of the house of
David apart, and their wives apart; the
family of the house of Nathan apart, and
their wives apart;
[13]The family of the house of Levi
apart, and their wives apart; the family
of Shimei apart, and their wives apart;
[14]All the families that remain, every
family apart, and their wives apart.

True repentance looks at the Cross

13 In that day there shall be a
fountain opened to the house of
David and to the inhabitants of *Jerusalem for *sin and for uncleanness.
¶[2]And it shall come to pass in that
day, saith the LORD of hosts, *that* I will
cut off the names of the idols out of the
land, and they shall no more be remembered: and also I will cause the prophets and the *unclean spirit to pass out
of the land.
[3]And it shall come to pass, *that* when
any shall yet prophesy, then his father
and his mother that begat him shall say
unto him, Thou shalt not live; for thou
speakest lies in the name of the LORD:
and his father and his mother that begat
him shall thrust him through when he
prophesieth.
[4]And it shall come to pass in that day,
that the prophets shall be ashamed
every one of his vision, when he hath
prophesied; neither shall they wear a
rough garment to deceive:
[5]But he shall say, I *am* no *prophet, I
am an husbandman; for man taught me
to keep cattle from my youth.
[6]And *one* shall say unto him, What *are*
these wounds in thine hands? Then he
shall answer, *Those* with which I was
wounded *in* the house of my friends.
¶[7]Awake, O sword, against my
shepherd, and against the man *that is*
my fellow, saith the LORD of hosts:

12:10 the spirit. The "spirit of grace" is the *Holy Spirit.

12:11 as the mourning of Hadadrimmon. Hadadrimmon was a city in the valley of Megiddo, in Palestine. Here the whole nation of Israel sorrowed when the good king, Josiah, died (see 2 Chron. 35:25).

13:1 fountain. A fountain is a place for cleansing. As water washes away impurity, so the blood of Christ cleanses us from all sin (see 1 John 1:9).

13:2 cut off the names of the idols. Even the names of idols will be forgotten.

13:2 prophets and the unclean spirit. All the false prophets will be gone.

13:3 thrust him through. God commanded that such should be done (Deut. 13:6-10).

13:4 prophets. False prophets are referred to in this verse. They wore a "rough garment" to deceive; for this garment was worn by true prophets (2 Kings 1:8; Matt. 3:4).

smite the shepherd, and the sheep shall
be scattered: and I will turn mine hand
upon the little ones.

The value of God's testing

8And it shall come to pass, *that* in all
the land, saith the LORD, two parts
therein shall be cut off *and* die; but the
third shall be left therein.
9And I will bring the third part through
the fire, and will refine them as silver is
refined, and will try them as gold is
tried: they shall call on my name, and I
will hear them: I will say, It *is* my people:
and they shall say, The LORD *is* my God.

The Lord's return in glory

14 Behold, the day of the LORD
cometh, and thy spoil shall be
divided in the midst of thee.

1) The nations gather against Jerusalem (see Armageddon).

2For I will gather all nations against
Jerusalem to battle; and the city shall
be taken, and the houses rifled, and the
women ravished; and half of the city
shall go forth into captivity, and the residue of the people shall not be cut off
from the city.
3Then shall the LORD go forth, and
fight against those nations, as when he
fought in the day of battle.

2) Physical changes in Palestine

¶4And his feet shall stand in that day
upon the mount of Olives, which *is* before Jerusalem on the east, and the
mount of Olives shall cleave in the
midst thereof toward the east and toward the west, *and there shall be* a very
great valley; and half of the mountain
shall remove toward the north, and half
of it toward the south.
5And ye shall flee *to* the valley of the
mountains; for the valley of the mountains shall reach unto Azal: yea, ye shall
flee, like as ye fled from before the
earthquake in the days of Uzziah king
of Judah: and the LORD my God shall
come, *and* all the saints with thee.
6And it shall come to pass in that day,
that the light shall not be clear, *nor* dark:
7But it shall be one day which shall
be known to the LORD, not day, nor
night: but it shall come to pass, *that* at
evening time it shall be light.

3) Living waters from Jerusalem

8And it shall be in that day, *that* living waters shall go out from Jerusa-

14:4 The Mount of Olives
When the Lord returns in glory, He will stand on the Mount of Olives, which will split in two. The valley that is formed will be an avenue of escape for Israel (vs. 5), and it will stand that way thereafter, as a testimony to the fulfillment of the Word of God. It was from the Mount of Olives that the Lord Jesus ascended into heaven (Luke 24:50–51; Acts 1:11–12). See also Isaiah 29:6; Nahum 1:5; Revelation 16:18–19.

14:6 A New Light
This light refers to the physical phenomenon which is spoken of again as attending the *Day of the LORD (see Amos 5:18; 8:9; Joel 2:31; Matt. 24:29). Finally, in the evening (vs. 7), darkness (the symbol of sin) will leave, and from that time there will probably be one everlasting day of light and glory.

13:7 smite the shepherd, and the sheep shall be scattered. Our Lord quotes this as referring to His betrayal and the fleeing of His disciples (read Matt. 26:31; Mark 14:50).

13:9 the third part. It seems clear that though Romans 11:26 says that "all Israel shall be saved," it must refer to all believing Israel there, for here Zechariah definitely affirms that one third, or the *remnant, will be saved.

14:5 the earthquake in the days of Uzziah. Read Amos 1:1.

14:5 all the saints. The *church, which will then be in heaven, will come with the Lord when He returns in glory. (See Rev. 19:11-14.)

14:8 living waters. This speaks of water that is fresh, not salty. A perfect description is given in Ezekiel 47:1-12; see 47:1-3 note, "A River of Blessing" (see Rev. 22:1-2).

lem; half of them toward the former
sea, and half of them toward the hinder sea: in summer and in winter shall
it be.

The Millennial returns of Christ

[9]And the LORD shall be king over all
the earth: in that day shall there be one
LORD, and his name one.
[10]All the land shall be turned as a
plain from Geba to Rimmon south of
Jerusalem: and it shall be lifted up, and
inhabited in her place, from Benjamin's
gate unto the place of the first gate,
unto the corner gate, and *from* the tower
of Hananeel unto the king's winepresses.
[11]And *men* shall dwell in it, and there
shall be no more utter destruction; but
Jerusalem shall be safely inhabited.
¶ [12]And this shall be the plague
wherewith the LORD will smite all the
people that have fought against Jerusalem; Their flesh shall consume away
while they stand upon their feet, and
their eyes shall consume away in their
holes, and their tongue shall consume
away in their mouth.
[13]And it shall come to pass in that day,
that a great tumult from the LORD shall
be among them; and they shall lay hold
every one on the hand of his neighbour,
and his hand shall rise up against the
hand of his neighbour.
[14]And Judah also shall fight at Jerusalem; and the wealth of all the heathen
round about shall be gathered together, gold, and silver, and apparel, in great
abundance.
[15]And so shall be the plague of the
horse, of the mule, of the camel, and of
the ass, and of all the beasts that shall
be in these tents, as this plague.

Jerusalem, the earth's religious center

¶ [16]And it shall come to pass, *that*
every one that is left of all the nations
which came against Jerusalem shall
even go up from year to year to worship
the King, the LORD of hosts, and to keep
the feast of tabernacles.

14:16 A New Purpose for the Feast of Tabernacles
Long before this, the people built little houses or booths of branches. They lived in these for a week each year to celebrate the time that they had been set free from Egypt (Lev. 23:40-42). Now it becomes a reminder of their everlasting deliverance from the world's nations.

[17]And it shall be, *that* whoso will not
come up of *all* the families of the earth
unto Jerusalem to worship the King,
the LORD of hosts, even upon them
shall be no rain.
[18]And if the family of Egypt go not up,
and come not, that *have* no *rain;* there
shall be the plague, wherewith the
LORD will smite the heathen that come
not up to keep the feast of tabernacles.
[19]This shall be the punishment of
Egypt, and the punishment of all na-

14:8 former sea. The Eastern sea, which is the Dead Sea, will no longer be the salty dead sea.
14:8 hinder sea. The Western sea. A stream of water that will never run dry will run from Jerusalem to the Mediterranean, the hinder sea.
14:9 the LORD shall be king. The *kingdom promised so often referred to in the Lord's Prayer (Matt. 6:9-13; see also its note, "The Lord's Prayer") will at last be established.
14:10 Geba. This is probably Geba in Samaria.
14:10 lifted up. Isaiah says that Jerusalem will be exalted (Isa. 2:2).
14:14 wealth . . . shall be gathered. The enemies will leave this great wealth behind when they are destroyed by the power of the LORD.
14:16 every one . . . shall . . . worship the King. All on earth must worship the Lord in Jerusalem. Isaiah says, "Every knee shall bow" (Isa. 45:23; see also its note, "Universal Recognition of Christ").
14:19 the punishment. God's purpose in this, as in every one of His punishments, was to make the people see their need of Him.

tions that come not up to keep the feast
of tabernacles.
¶[20]In that day shall there be upon the
bells of the horses, HOLINESS UNTO
THE LORD; and the pots in the LORD'S
house shall be like the bowls before the
altar.
[21]Yea, every pot in Jerusalem and in
Judah shall be holiness unto the LORD
of hosts: and all they that sacrifice shall
come and take of them, and seethe
therein: and in that day there shall be
no more the Canaanite in the house of
the LORD of hosts.

14:21 Canaanite. Used in this way, the word "Canaanite" means *a stranger*, an unclean, sinful person. All in God's house will be the LORD's holy people (Ezek. 43:7).

MALACHI

BACKGROUND

The city of Jerusalem was not built and the priests were offering their sacrifices in the second temple. Both Zechariah and Malachi prophesy the two advents of the Lord Jesus Christ, but Malachi also prophesies about the two who will come just before His first and second comings: John the Baptist (Malachi 3:1) and Elijah the prophet (Malachi 4:5-6)

THE WRITER

Malachi is the Hebrew for *my messenger.* The prophet is not mentioned elsewhere in the Old Testament, and the book that he wrote comes naturally at the end of the Old Testament, for it was the last portion of inspired Hebrew prophecy. It was written to the whole nation, but especially to the *remnant who returned after the seventy years' captivity in Babylon (see the introductions to Ezra and Nehemiah).

SUMMARY

The great message of Malachi is the LORD's word in Malachi 1:2: "I have loved you." The prophet tells the people of their corrupt priesthood and of their insincere worship, but he does not fail to commend those few who were faithful (see Malachi 3:16). He is the last inspired prophet for about four hundred years, that is, until the time of John the Baptist.

OUTLINE OF MALACHI

I.	God's Love for Israel	Malachi 1:1-5
II.	God Rebukes the Priests for Sin	Malachi 1:6—2:9
III.	God Rebukes the People	Malachi 2:10—3:18
IV.	Description of the Day of the LORD	Malachi 4:1-6

I. God's Love for Israel (1:1-5)

1 The *burden of the word of the
LORD to *Israel by Malachi.
2 I have loved you, saith the LORD. Yet
ye say, Wherein hast thou loved us?
Was not *Esau *Jacob's brother? saith
the LORD: yet I loved Jacob,
3 And I hated Esau, and laid his mountains and his heritage waste for the
dragons of the wilderness.

1:1 by Malachi. "By" means *by the hand of*. Malachi was only used to give God's message.
1:2 I have loved you. In spite of their sin, God still loved them (see Deut. 4:37; 7:8).
1:2 Wherein. This word is the key to the book. It is given seven times (1:2,6,7; 2:17; 3:7; 3:8; and 3:13, where "what" gives the same sense of "wherein"). The people had gone so far away from God that they asked Him to prove that He loved them.
1:2 I loved Jacob. God loved and chose Jacob though he did not deserve it. That He hated Esau (vs. 3) means in the Hebrew idiom that He did not choose him.
1:3 laid . . . his heritage waste. This land of Edom (that is, Esau's land) was very fertile;

[4]Whereas *Edom saith, We are impoverished, but we will return and build the desolate places; thus saith the LORD of hosts, They shall build, but I will throw down; and they shall call them, The border of wickedness, and, The people against whom the LORD hath indignation for ever.

[5]And your eyes shall see, and ye shall say, The LORD will be magnified from the border of Israel.

II. God Rebukes Priests (1:6—2:9)

¶[6]A son honoureth *his* father, and a servant his master: if then I *be* a father, where *is* mine honour? and if I *be* a master, where *is* my *fear? saith the LORD of hosts unto you, O priests, that despise my name. And ye say, Wherein have we despised thy name?

[7]Ye offer polluted bread upon mine *altar; and ye say, Wherein have we polluted thee? In that ye say, The table of the LORD *is* contemptible.

[8]And if ye offer the blind for *sacrifice, *is it* not evil? and if ye offer the lame and sick, *is it* not evil? offer it now unto thy governor; will he be pleased with thee, or accept thy person? saith the LORD of hosts.

[9]And now, I pray you, beseech *God that he will be gracious unto us: this hath been by your means: will he regard your persons? saith the LORD of hosts.

[10]Who *is there* even among you that would shut the doors *for nought?* neither do ye kindle *fire* on mine altar for nought. I have no pleasure in you, saith the LORD of hosts, neither will I accept an *offering at your hand.

[11]For from the rising of the sun even unto the going down of the same my name *shall be* great among the *Gentiles; and in every place *incense *shall be* offered unto my name, and a pure offering: for my name *shall be* great among the heathen, saith the LORD of hosts.

¶[12]But ye have profaned it, in that ye say, The table of the LORD *is* polluted; and the fruit thereof, *even* his meat, *is* contemptible.

[13]Ye said also, Behold, what a weariness *is it!* and ye have snuffed at it, saith the LORD of hosts; and ye brought *that which was* torn, and the lame, and the sick; thus ye brought an offering: should I accept this of your hand? saith the LORD.

[14]But cursed *be* the deceiver, which hath in his flock a male, and voweth, and sacrificeth unto the LORD a corrupt thing: for I *am* a great King, saith the LORD of hosts, and my name *is* dreadful among the heathen.

2 And now, O ye priests, this commandment *is* for you.

[2]If ye will not hear, and if ye will not lay *it* to heart, to give glory unto my name, saith the LORD of hosts, I will

---

today it is a desert. Verse 4 states that God will not allow it to be built up again by the Edomites.

1:4 The border of wickedness. The desolation of the country was used by the wickedness of its people.

1:6 I be a father. They were His nation. God was their national Father (see Isa. 63:16 note, "The Fatherhood of God").

1:7 polluted bread. The *shewbread in the temple was an offering to the LORD. It had to be changed every week. These priests offered moldy bread to the LORD (see Lev. 24:8). Bread here represents all the sacrifices.

1:7 table of the LORD is contemptible. They despised the brazen altar. They had shown their contempt by offering forbidden things for sacrifices (see vs. 8).

1:8 blind . . . lame and sick. These were forbidden for sacrifices (Lev. 22:22; Deut.15:21).

1:10 Who is there even among you . . . ? A good way to understand this verse is: "I would that one among you would shut the doors," that is, of the temple, "in order that such sacrifices would cease."

1:13 snuffed at it. Despised it—sniffed at it.

1:14 dreadful. To be feared or reverenced.

even send a curse upon you, and I will
curse your blessings: yea, I have cursed
them already, because ye do not lay *it*
to heart.
3 Behold, I will corrupt your seed, and
spread *dung upon your faces, *even* the
dung of your solemn feasts; and *one*
shall take you away with it.
4 And ye shall know that I have sent
this commandment unto you, that my
*covenant might be with Levi, saith the
LORD of hosts.
5 My covenant was with him of life
and *peace; and I gave them to him *for*
the fear wherewith he feared me, and
was afraid before my name.
6 The *law of truth was in his mouth,
and iniquity was not found in his lips:
he walked with me in peace and equity,
and did turn many away from iniquity.
7 For the priest's lips should keep
knowledge, and they should seek the
law at his mouth: for he *is* the messenger of the LORD of hosts.
8 But ye are departed out of the way;
ye have caused many to stumble at the
law; ye have corrupted the covenant of
Levi, saith the LORD of hosts.
9 Therefore have I also made you contemptible and base before all the people, according as ye have not kept my
ways, but have been partial in the law.

III. God Rebukes the People (2:10—3:18)

*1) *Sin against a brother*

10 Have we not all one father? hath not
one God *created us? why do we deal
treacherously every man against his
brother, by profaning the covenant of
our fathers?

2) Sin against a wife

¶ 11 Judah hath dealt treacherously,
and an *abomination is committed in
Israel and in *Jerusalem; for Judah hath
profaned the holiness of the LORD
which he loved, and hath married the
daughter of a strange god.
12 The LORD will cut off the man that
doeth this, the master and the scholar,
out of the tabernacles of Jacob, and him
that offereth an offering unto the LORD
of hosts.
13 And this have ye done again, covering the altar of the LORD with tears,
with weeping, and with crying out,
insomuch that he regardeth not the offering any more, or receiveth *it* with
good will at your hand.
¶ 14 Yet ye say, Wherefore? Because
the LORD hath been witness between
thee and the wife of thy youth, against
whom thou hast dealt treacherously:
yet *is* she thy companion, and the wife
of thy covenant.
15 And did not he make one? Yet had
he the residue of the spirit. And wherefore one? That he might seek a godly
seed. Therefore take heed to your
spirit, and let none deal treacherously
against the wife of his youth.
16 For the LORD, the God of Israel,
saith that he hateth putting away: for
one covereth violence with his garment,

2:2 I will curse your blessings. The blessings formerly promised will turn to curses (read Deut. 11 and 28).

2:3 corrupt. To rebuke or reject.

2:5 My covenant. God made His covenant with Levi. His tribe was chosen to be in charge of the tabernacle (Exod. 32:26-28; Num. 1:50).

2:9 partial in the law. They had favorites and had been unfair to others.

2:10 Have we not all one father? The prophet is speaking here and asks, "Is God not the Father of our nation?"

2:11 holiness of the LORD. Their separation to the LORD had been marred because they had married women belonging to idolatrous nations.

2:13 again. Repeatedly—again and again.

2:15 did not he make one? God unites husband and wife, and no one can really separate them (see Gen. 2:24). The question is, "Did not God make only one wife for Adam?"

2:16 covereth violence. Consider the following: "one wraps up his garment with violence," or takes away the protection due to a wife.

saith the LORD of hosts: therefore take heed to your spirit, that ye deal not treacherously.

3) Sin of insincerity

¶17Ye have wearied the LORD with your words. Yet ye say, Wherein have we wearied *him?* When ye say, Every one that doeth evil *is* good in the sight of the LORD, and he delighteth in them; or, Where *is* the God of *judgment?

Parenthesis: John the Baptist's message and the Coming of the LORD are foretold

3 Behold, I will send my messenger, and he shall prepare the way before me: and the Lord, whom ye seek, shall suddenly come to his temple, even the messenger of the covenant, whom ye delight in: behold, he shall come, saith the LORD of hosts.

2But who may abide the day of his coming? and who shall stand when he appeareth? for he *is* like a refiner's fire, and like fullers' sope:

3And he shall sit *as* a refiner and purifier of silver: and he shall purify the sons of Levi, and purge them as gold and silver, that they may offer unto the LORD an offering in *righteousness.

4Then shall the offering of Judah and Jerusalem be pleasant unto the LORD, as in the days of old, and as in former years.

5And I will come near to you to judgment; and I will be a swift witness against the sorcerers, and against the

2:15 THE HOLY SPIRIT

The Holy Spirit in the Old Testament is described in the following ways:

1. He is all-powerful—omnipotent (Gen. 1:2; Job 26:13; 33:4; Ps. 104:30).
2. He is everywhere—omnipresent (Ps. 139:7).
3. He turns men's hearts to the LORD (Gen. 6:3).
4. He gives men understanding (Job 32:8), skill (Exod. 28:3; 31:3), strength (Judg. 14:6,19; see 14:19 note, "The Spirit of the LORD"), and wisdom (Judg. 3:10; 6:34; 11:29; 13:25).
5. Through His power men receive revelations from God and are able to teach them to others (Num. 11:25; see also its note, "The Power of the Spirit"; 2 Sam. 23:2).
6. He gives power to God's servants (Ps. 51:12; Joel 2:28-29; Zech. 4:6).
7. He is called by many names: Holy (Ps. 51:11), good (Ps. 143:10), the Spirit of judgment and burning (Isa. 4:4; see also its note, "The Sin of Jerusalem"), of Jehovah, of wisdom, understanding, counsel, might, knowledge, the fear of the LORD (Isa. 11:2), and of grace and supplications (Zech. 12:10; see also its note, "Christ's Death").
8. He acts as He wills in the Old Testament—coming to men as He chooses and even employing a dumb animal (Num. 22:22-31). Not until New Testament times did the Holy Spirit come to dwell in every believing Christian.
9. When the Lord Jesus Christ comes to set up His kingdom, the Holy Spirit will be poured out upon all Israel (Ezek. 37:14; 39:29; Joel 2:28-29).

3:1 I will send. The Lord God speaks here.
3:1 my messenger. John the Baptist (see Matt. 11:10).
3:1 before me. This refers to our Lord Jesus Christ in His coming to earth in His first advent. He quotes this as referring to Himself (see Matt. 11:10; Mark 1:2; Luke 7:27).
3:1 suddenly come to his temple. A prophecy of the *second coming of the Lord Jesus Christ to earth.
3:1 messenger of the covenant. This is the "angel of the covenant," a title of the Lord Jesus Christ. The *covenant was made with Israel.
3:2 who may abide . . . ? This expression shows it to be a coming for judgment.
3:2 refiner's fire. A refiner uses his fire to remove all the impurities from silver; the LORD will do the same with Israel.
3:2 fullers' sope. This is a great cleanser and healer. A fuller is one who washes.
3:5 sorcerers. The sins of sorcery were very prevalent at the time of the prophet (see, for example, Zech. 10:2).

adulterers, and against false swearers,
and against those that oppress the hireling in *his* wages, the widow, and the
fatherless, and that turn aside the
stranger *from his right,* and fear not me,
saith the LORD of hosts.
6 For I *am* the LORD, I change not;
therefore ye sons of Jacob are not consumed.

III. Continued: People Who Rob God Rebuked

¶7 Even from the days of your fathers
ye are gone away from mine ordinances, and have not kept *them.* Return
unto me, and I will return unto you,
saith the LORD of hosts. But ye said,
Wherein shall we return?
¶8 Will a man rob God? Yet ye have
robbed me. But ye say, Wherein have
we robbed thee? In *tithes and *offerings.
9 Ye *are* cursed with a curse: for ye
have robbed me, *even* this whole nation.
10 Bring ye all the tithes into the
storehouse, that there may be meat in
mine house, and *prove me now herewith, saith the LORD of hosts, if I will
not open you the windows of *heav-
en, and pour you out a blessing, that
there shall not *be room* enough *to receive it.*
11 And I will rebuke the devourer for
your sakes, and he shall not destroy the
fruits of your ground; neither shall your
vine cast her fruit before the time in the
field, saith the LORD of hosts.
12 And all nations shall call you
blessed: for ye shall be a delightsome
land, saith the LORD of hosts.
¶13 Your words have been stout
against me, saith the LORD. Yet ye say,
What have we spoken *so much* against
thee?
14 Ye have said, It *is* vain to serve God:
and what profit *is it* that we have kept
his ordinance, and that we have walked
mournfully before the LORD of hosts?
15 And now we call the proud happy;
yea, they that work wickedness are set
up; yea, *they that* *tempt God are even
delivered.

The faithful remnant

¶16 Then they that feared the LORD
spake often one to another: and the
LORD hearkened, and heard *it,* and a
book of remembrance was written before him for them that feared the LORD,
and that thought upon his name.

3:16 The Book of Remembrance
God has a book in heaven in which is recorded all our faithfulness (see Ps. 56:8). Even kings of that day kept records of the acts of their citizens (see Esther 6:1-2).

17 And they shall be mine, saith the
LORD of hosts, in that day when I make
up my jewels; and I will spare them, as
a man spareth his own son that serveth
him.
18 Then shall ye return, and discern
between the righteous and the wicked,

3:18 The Nations Judged
This prophecy looks ahead to the time directly following the *Tribulation, when the Lord will come in power to establish His millennial *kingdom. When the nations are gathered before Him for judgment, the restored believing *remnant, saved during the coming *Tribulation and living at its conclusion, will be at His side as He judges. See *judgment.

3:10 storehouse. To Israel, this would be the temple.
3:12 delightsome. Delightful.
3:13 stout. Harsh.
3:16 they that feared the LORD. In spite of the unfaithful priests, the LORD had a faithful *remnant.
3:16 spake often one to another. They had fellowship together. They were real companions in the LORD.
3:17 jewels. Peculiar treasure—the LORD's faithful ones.

between him that serveth God and him
that serveth him not.

IV. The Day of the LORD (4:1-6)

4 For, behold, the day cometh, that
shall burn as an oven; and all the
proud, yea, and all that do wickedly,
shall be stubble: and the day that
cometh shall burn them up, saith the
LORD of hosts, that it shall leave them
neither root nor branch.
¶2 But unto you that fear my name
shall the Sun of righteousness arise
with healing in his wings; and ye shall
go forth, and grow up as calves of the
stall.
3 And ye shall tread down the wicked;
for they shall be ashes under the soles
of your feet in the day that I shall do *this,*
saith the LORD of hosts.
¶4 Remember ye the law of Moses my
servant, which I commanded unto him
in Horeb for all Israel, *with* the statutes
and judgments.

Elijah, the prophet, to appear before the worst judgments come

¶5 Behold, I will send you Elijah the
prophet before the coming of the great
and dreadful day of the LORD:
6 And he shall turn the heart of the
fathers to the children, and the heart of
the children to their fathers, lest I come
and smite the earth with a curse.

4:1 the day cometh. The *Day of the LORD.
4:1 burn as an oven. A terrible picture of judgment coming on sinners.
4:2 Sun of righteousness. A beautiful and meaningful title of our Lord Jesus Christ.
4:2 grow up. Skip or play happily.
4:6 he shall turn. One shall come in the spirit and power of Elijah, as did John the Baptist (Matt. 17:11-12), to turn the people of Israel to God and to unite them to one another.
4:6 curse. The Lord's coming will remove the earth's great curse. If we love the Lord Jesus Christ and believe that He died for our sins and rose again, the sorrows and judgments of this future Day of the LORD will not touch us.

BETWEEN THE OLD AND NEW TESTAMENTS

The books of Ezra and Nehemiah show the return of certain Jewish people to the land. The last book of the Old Testament, Malachi, tells of the condition of the remnant in the land under Persia. What happened between this time and the opening of the New Testament, about four centuries later, when Israel, much multiplied, is under Rome? We go to the historian Josephus, and to the author of the first book of the Maccabees, a reliable book of Jewish history, for the answer to this question.

The people had much independence, under mild Persia. When Greece conquered Medo-Persia, the Jewish high priests were made the political leaders. At this time, about 335 B.C., the high priest was the godly Jaddua. When he heard that Alexander the Great was about to march on Jerusalem, Jaddua, believing that the prophecies of Daniel were being fulfilled, went to meet Alexander.

Alexander, who had had a dream of such an event, fell on the ground before Jaddua, the representative of God, and promised to safeguard Jerusalem. However, he soon died. His generals divided the kingdom among themselves. Antigonus and Ptolemy Soter, the most prominent, became rivals. Soter besieged Jerusalem, killing many people and sending thousands to Egypt, where they lived in comfort, and were content to assume the Egyptian religion, speech, and customs.

In Palestine, many turned to the gods of the Greeks. However, there was the remnant of true believers (see Malachi 3:16-18).

Years went by. The first translation of the Scriptures was made in 277 B.C.—the Pentateuch was translated into Greek. Finally the Old Testament was complete and placed in the Imperial Library at Alexandria. This was the *Septuagint.

A new high priest, Onias, brought the Jews into great danger during the reign of Ptolemy Euergetes, around 247 B.C. The people were to pay a yearly tribute. Onias "forgot" to pay this tribute until Euergetes demanded the entire sum, giving as alternative the destruction of the Jewish state. Joseph, nephew of Onias, averted the calamity by purchasing the right to farm the taxes, thus becoming the first Jewish *publican.

King followed king. Syria and Egypt fought almost constantly, but no matter which side won, Palestine lost. Much of this time two parties had been striving for leadership. One group, the *Pharisees, held strictly to the *Law, but erred greatly by adding to it. The other group, the *Sadducees, wanted Greek culture, believing that Israel's only hope was in following the other nations. They even condoned the Greek religion.

Antiochus of Syria called himself "Epiphanes" (the Illustrious). This king, whose history was pre-written in Daniel 11:21-35, descended upon Jerusalem,

and slew forty thousand people in three days, and enslaved as many. He forced himself into the *Holy of Holies in the temple, setting up the "abomination of desolation" by erecting an idol-altar there. It was a time of horror for the godly Jews, and revived the ancient spirit in a remnant.

And old man, Mattathias, of the line of Asmoneus, arose. He dared to defy the cruel conquerors. Though he lived for not quite a year, he charged his five sons with cleansing the land and the temple. Judas, his third son, was called Maccabeus, the Hammer of God; the others came to be called the Maccabees, or Maccabeans. Again and again, the Jews in the strength of the Lord overcame the great armies of their enemies. They cleansed the temple and built a new altar.

Then Eleazar, brother of Judas Maccabeus, was killed. Judas, perhaps losing his confidence in God, made an alliance with Rome, now the dominant power of the West. When the Syrians again besieged them, Judas was conquered and slain. Jonathan, his brother, became leader. But murder and uprisings in high places were constant, and in 135 B.C., the last of the famous sons of the great Mattathias died.

John Hyrcanus, son of Simon Maccabeus, renewed the Roman league. His years were marked by trouble. In the time of Alexander Janneus, brother of John Hyrcanus, we find the first link with the New Testament: Alexander died in 79 B.C.; during his reign, then, Phanuel, the husband of Anna, died (see Luke 2:36-37—she had been a "widow of about fourscore and four years"). Through all the years Anna had waited for the consolation of Israel. Alexandra, Alexander's wife, succeeded him, appointing her weak son, Hyrcanus, high priest. Now an Idumean proselyte of Judaism, Antipater, governor of Idumea, came into power. Both he and his foes looked for aid to Pompey, a great Roman general. Pompey sent to Jerusalem for money. The Jewish soldiers manned their city for defense, but the Romans finally broke in, bringing the end of Jewish independence. Now Judaea was only a Roman province. This, then, was the bitter result of the act of Judas Maccabeus.

Julius Caesar came into full power. Antipater was made a free citizen of Rome and procurator of Judaea. He appointed his two sons, Phasael and Herod, governors of Galilee and Jerusalem, respectively. Then Julius Caesar was slain. Mark Antony, his friend, raised Phasael to tetrarch of Galilee, and Herod to tetrarch of Judaea. There was much opposition; Phasael committed suicide. Herod fled to Rome where Octavius Caesar named him King of Judaea and sent him back to Palestine. Eveyone hated him. Directly or indirectly he wiped out the whole Asmonean family.

Israel's hopes were quenched. But not through the seed of Mattathias was hope to come to Israel. Through the seed of David, not just Israel, but all the world was to be blessed. And the time had almost arrived. Now a mistake must be pointed out. Not until the sixth century of the Christian era did scholars decide to begin dating from the birth of our Lord. Then an error of four years was made, and strangely enough, Christ was born in 4 B.C.!

Herod had been so afraid of plots against him that he had even had his sons murdered. What wonder, then, that he saw in the questions of the Magi another scheme to seize his throne! He issued his terrible order that all the baby boys of Bethlehem be killed. But God's Word, living or written, cannot be destroyed. Herod himself died while the baby Jesus was hidden safely in Egypt.

Their Saviour King had come, but spiritual declension had blinded the eyes of the people: "He came unto his own, and his own received him not. But as many as received him, to them gave he power to become the sons of God, even to them that believe on his name" (John 1:11-12).

The New Testament

Concerning the New Testament

The New Testament, containing twenty-seven books, is that portion of Scripture which has come down to us (see *About the Bible and Its Author,* p. xix) since the earthly ministry, death, and resurrection of the Son of God, our Lord Jesus Christ. It records all that was done by and all that happened to our Lord, and the results of His passion and miraculous conquest over death and the grave; and His ascension, culminating in the gift of the Holy Spirit. Through the Spirit's power cowards became flaming heroes of evangelism, persecutors became staunch defenders of the faith, and uneducated and educated men became teachers of doctrine which has instructed, rebuked, encouraged, and exhorted the *church for nineteen centuries.

This testament is new in contrast to the old, for it is because of the work that our Lord Jesus Christ performed here that God the Father established a new covenant whereby our sins are washed away in the blood of His Son: "And He (the Lord Jesus Christ) took the cup . . . saying . . . This is my blood of the new testament, which is shed for many for the remission of sins (Matthew 26:27-28). Under the old covenant man was responsible to keep the Law, and failing, he offered the blood of the sacrifice which God accepted as a covering for the sin committed and confessed. The blood sacrifice was symbolic of the blood of Christ, the true Lamb of God, which was to be shed on the cross. Thus, under the old covenant man was saved, as it were, on credit, looking forward to Christ's death. The new covenant is better than the old, as God the Spirit has revealed through the writer of the Hebrews (see chapters 8 and 9).

The books of the New Testament may be divided into four classifications:

1. The Gospels, or The Books of Grace and Truth.
The Gospels contain inspired accounts of certain incidents in the life of Christ. Though they may be termed biographies, no one of the Gospels, nor even all of them combined, contains the full record of our Lord's life on earth. The first three Gospels (called the Synoptics) agree quite generally as to the events in the three years' service of the Servant Son, while the fourth Gospel, John's, is occupied more with the personal and intimate words of our Lord than with His deeds. More than a third of John deals with the last week of Christ's life. Each of the Gospel writers presents a particular phase of our Lord's person: Matthew, the King; Mark, the Servant; Luke, the Man; and John, God the Son. The Gospel records take us through the Cross, and so lead us from one *dispensation to another, from Law to grace. "The law was given by Moses, but grace and truth came by Jesus Christ" (John 1:17).

2. A Book of History.
The Acts of the Apostles introduces us to the advent of the Holy Spirit to dwell within the hearts of believers. It is through the power of the Spirit and not in their own strength, that the disciples of Christ witnessed in such wisdom and with such blessing and to such results during the Apostolic age and, in fact, ever since. This book gives us a history of the early *church from the time of our Lord's ascension until a few years prior to the destruction of Jerusalem by Titus in A.D. 70.

3. The Books of the Letters.
There are twenty-one epistles, or letters, in the New Testament, from Romans through Jude. These are divided into two groups, we might say, called The Pauline Epistles (Romans to Philemon), and the Jewish-Christian Epistles (Hebrews to Jude). The former give us church doctrine, while the latter carry us through the difficult transition from Law to grace, and show us that as we are all one in Christ, Jews and Gentiles alike, it is much better than in former days.

4. The Book of Prophecy—The Last Things.
The editors of these notes take the position that all that is written in the book of The Revelation, after the third chapter, is future. This book tells of the time of *Great Tribulation to come upon the earth, the overthrow of Satan and his vice-regents at Armageddon, the Millennial reign of the Son of David, Satan's final uprising and defeat, and looks through the beautiful gates of eternity. Revelation is the complement of Genesis. The Bible begins in a garden from which man is cast out because of sin. The Bible ends, as it were, in a garden wherein, cleansed from his sin, man rests beneath the leaves of the tree of healing power.

The Gospel according to Saint

MATTHEW

BACKGROUND

The word "gospel" means *Good News,* and this book is the good news concerning our Lord Jesus Christ, Israel's Messiah, the eternal Son of God. The Gospel according to Matthew is rightfully placed as the first book of the New Testament. The Old Testament closes with Malachi, who prophesies of the coming of Messiah. The New Testament opens with the immediate identification of Jesus Christ as the One who came in fulfillment of the prophecies of old, the son of David, the son of Abraham (see 2 Samuel 7:8-16; Genesis 12:1-3; Genesis 15:18).

THE WRITER AND TIME

The writer of this Gospel was Matthew, known also as Levi (Mark 2:14; Luke 5:27). The date of authorship was somewhere about A.D. 61 or 62.

SUMMARY

The Gospel according to Matthew presents Jesus as the King (see the introduction to the New Testament), and thus in His genealogy (see Matthew 1:1 note) He is traced back to David through Solomon. It is in this Gospel that the kingdom of heaven is announced so often: here only is the record of the visit of the wise men who came to visit the King; John the Baptist and our Lord Himself preached the message, "Repent ye, for the Kingdom of Heaven is at hand"; and in the Sermon on the Mount (Matthew 5–7) the constitution of the promised kingdom is set forth.

In this book the dispensational (see *dispensation) character of the Bible is very clearly evident, and it is in this Gospel particularly that the distinction between law and grace, etc., the purpose of Christ's coming to earth, the program for the church age, and the prophetic pattern prior to our Lord's return in power are set forth so clearly. Saint Augustine said: "Distinguish the ages, and the Scriptures are made plain," and it is the understanding of the dispensational teaching of this book which will clarify, more than anything else, the teaching of the whole New Testament.

OUTLINE OF MATTHEW

I. Jesus, the Son of David — Matthew 1:1—25:46
- A. The Genealogy, Birth, and Infancy of the King
- B. The King and Kingdom Presented and Rejected

C. The New Message of the King
D. The Mysteries of the Kingdom
E. The Ministry of the Rejected King
F. The King Will Return in Power and Glory

II. Jesus, the Son of Abraham. The Sacrifice of the Lamb — Matthew 26:1—27:66

III. Jesus, the Son of God — Matthew 28:1-20

A. The Resurrection of the Lord
B. "I Am with You Alway"

I. Jesus, the Son of David (1:1—25:46)

A. The Genealogy, Birth, and Infancy of the King

1 The book of the generation of Jesus
*Christ, the son of David, the son of
*Abraham.
2 Abraham begat *Isaac; and Isaac
begat *Jacob; and Jacob begat Judas and
his brethren;
3 And Judas begat Phares and Zara of
Thamar; and Phares begat Esrom; and
Esrom begat Aram;
4 And Aram begat Aminadab; and
Aminadab begat Naasson; and Naasson
begat Salmon;
5 And Salmon begat Booz of Rachab;
and Booz begat Obed of Ruth; and Obed
begat Jesse;
6 And Jesse begat David the king; and
David the king begat Solomon of her
that had been the wife of Urias;
7 And Solomon begat Roboam; and Roboam begat Abia; and Abia begat Asa;
8 And Asa begat Josaphat; and
Josaphat begat Joram; and Joram begat
Ozias;
9 And Ozias begat Joatham; and
Joatham begat Achaz; and Achaz begat
Ezekias;
10 And Ezekias begat Manasses; and
Manasses begat Amon; and Amon
begat Josias;
11 And Josias begat Jechonias and his
brethren, about the time they were carried away to *Babylon:
12 And after they were brought to
Babylon, Jechonias begat Salathiel; and
Salathiel begat Zorobabel;
13 And Zorobabel begat Abiud; and
Abiud begat Eliakim; and Eliakim begat
Azor;
14 And Azor begat Sadoc; and Sadoc
begat Achim; and Achim begat Eliud;
15 And Eliud begat Eleazar; and Eleazar begat Matthan; and Matthan begat
Jacob;
16 And Jacob begat *Joseph the hus-

1:1 generation of Jesus Christ. There are two genealogies of our Lord. Matthew traces His strictly regal ancestry through Joseph, His adopted father (Luke 4:22). This ancestry is through Solomon to David and Abraham. Luke traces his true hereditary descent through His mother, Mary, to Nathan, son of David, Abraham, and Adam. There is thus no discrepancy between the two pedigrees, each of which supplements the other (see also Luke 3:23 notes, including "Christ's Ancestry").

1:1 son of David, the son of Abraham. While Abraham lived about one thousand years before David, the Lord Jesus Christ is referred to first as the "son of David," because His first work was to present Himself as the King, David's Son. It was only after He was rejected by Israel, that rejection being fully manifested at Calvary, that He fulfilled His sacrificial ministry, the antitype of Isaac, Abraham's Son.

1:6 David the king. Observe that only David is mentioned as "king," not Solomon (vs. 7). This suggests that, in God's plan for our Lord's messiahship, Christ is the next King after David.

1:6 *that had been the wife.* See page xvii for the meaning of italics within the text.

band of Mary, of whom was born Jesus,
who is called Christ.

(1) The birth of Jesus
(Luke 1:26-35; 2:1-7; John 1:1-2,14)

17So all the generations from Abraham to David *are* fourteen generations;
and from David until the carrying away
into Babylon *are* fourteen generations;
and from the carrying away into Babylon unto Christ *are* fourteen generations.
¶18Now the birth of Jesus Christ was
on this wise: When as his mother Mary
was espoused to Joseph, before they
came together, she was found with child
of the Holy Ghost.
19Then Joseph her husband, being a
*just *man,* and not willing to make her
a publick example, was minded to put
her away privily.
20But while he thought on these
things, behold, the *angel of the Lord
appeared unto him in a dream, saying,
Joseph, thou son of David, fear not to
take unto thee Mary thy wife: for that
which is conceived in her is of the Holy
Ghost.
21And she shall bring forth a son, and
thou shalt call his name JESUS: for he
shall save his people from their sins.

O.T. prophecy fulfilled (1)

22Now all this was done, that it might
be fulfilled which was spoken of the
Lord by the *prophet, saying,
23Behold, a virgin shall be with child,
and shall bring forth a son, and they
shall call his name Emmanuel, which
being interpreted is, *God with us.
24Then Joseph being raised from
sleep did as the angel of the Lord had
bidden him, and took unto him his wife:
25And knew her not till she had
brought forth her firstborn son: and he
called his name JESUS.

(2) The visit of the wise men

2 Now when Jesus was born in Beth-
lehem of Judaea in the days of
*Herod the king, behold, there came
wise men from the east to *Jerusalem,

1:11 JECHONIAS

Jechonias, also known as Coniah, is mentioned in 1 Chronicles 3:16. In Jeremiah 22:28,30 a curse is pronounced on him; he was to be recorded as being childless, and it was promised that no man of his seed should prosper upon the throne of David. Thus Joseph could never have been written into the record of the kings nor could he have prospered upon the throne of David. Likewise, had Jesus been the natural son of Joseph the curse would have applied to Him also. But, because He was the adopted son, and not the seed, He had a right to the throne legally through Joseph and physically as the seed of David through Mary.

1:23 EMMANUEL OR JESUS

Emmanuel means, as the text indicates, *God with us.* The angel of the Lord told Joseph that he was to name the baby Jesus, and some have thought this contradictory. But the meaning of the names indicates that the babe, by either name, was the fulfillment of prophetic utterances, the Son of God and God the Son. Jesus (Hebrew "Joshua" from "Jehoshua") means, *Jehovah is the Saviour.* So then, both names clearly indicate that this One is God manifest in the flesh.

1:19 Joseph her husband. Eastern custom called espoused or engaged couples by the terms of husband and wife, since the betrothal was so sacred.

1:22 that it might be fulfilled. Matthew's Gospel, written particularly to present our Lord as the King of the Jews, again and again calls attention to the fact that events recorded were in fulfillment of Old Testament prophecy (see also 2:15; 2:17-18; 3:3; 4:14-16, etc.).

1:22 which was spoken. See Isaiah 7:14.

2:1 Herod the king. Herod the Great, the son of Antipater the Idumaean or Edomite king of Judaea, who built the temple in which our Lord taught later.

[2]Saying, Where is he that is born
King of the Jews? for we have seen his
star in the east, and are come to worship him.
[3]When Herod the king had heard
these things, he was troubled, and all
Jerusalem with him.
[4]And when he had gathered all the
chief priests and scribes of the people
together, he demanded of them where
Christ should be born.

2:4 The Scribes
These men not only made copies of the Law but were also its guardians, and they taught the Scriptures. The scribes were familiar with Old Testament Scriptures. While not all scribes were Pharisees, practically every Pharisee was a scribe. They certainly knew enough about the writing of the Old Testament to recognize that Messiah was to be born in Bethlehem of Judaea.

O.T. prophecy fulfilled (2)

[5]And they said unto him, In Bethlehem of Judaea: for thus it is written by
the prophet,
[6]And thou Bethlehem, *in* the land
of Juda, art not the least among the
princes of Juda: for out of thee shall
come a Governor, that shall rule my
people *Israel.
[7]Then Herod, when he had privily
called the wise men, enquired of them
diligently what time the star appeared.
[8]And he sent them to Bethlehem, and
said, Go and search diligently for the
young child; and when ye have found
him, bring me word again, that I may
come and worship him also.
[9]When they had heard the king, they
departed; and, lo, the star, which they
saw in the east, went before them, till
it came and stood over where the young
child was.
[10]When they saw the star, they rejoiced with exceeding great joy.
¶[11]And when they were come into
the house, they saw the young child
with Mary his mother, and fell down,
and worshipped him: and when they
had opened their treasures, they presented unto him gifts; gold, and frankincense, and myrrh.
[12]And being warned of God in a
dream that they should not return to
Herod, they departed into their own
country another way.

(3) The flight into Egypt

[13]And when they were departed, behold, the angel of the Lord appeareth to
Joseph in a dream, saying, Arise, and
take the young child and his mother, and
flee into *Egypt, and be thou there until I bring thee word: for Herod will seek
the young child to destroy him.
[14]When he arose, he took the young
child and his mother by night, and departed into Egypt:

O.T. prophecy fulfilled (3)

[15]And was there until the death of
Herod: that it might be fulfilled which was
spoken of the Lord by the prophet, saying, Out of Egypt have I called my son.

(4) Herod slaughters male children

¶[16]Then Herod, when he saw that he
was mocked of the wise men, was ex-

2:5 thus it is written. See Micah 5:2 and its note, "A Description of Christ."

2:11 with Mary his mother. Observe that the "young child" is mentioned before the mother, and that the wise men worshipped Him, not His mother Mary. It is to be noted, too, that they worshipped before they offered gifts.

2:11 gold, and frankincense, and myrrh. Gold is the symbol of deity; frankincense, of the fragrance and purity of our Lord's life; while myrrh was a burial spice speaking of His suffering. When our Lord comes again, gifts will be presented to Him (see Isa. 60:6); these gifts will be of two kinds: gold, and incense or frankincense. Myrrh will not be brought to Him when He comes again, for His suffering was only once. He died to die no more and to put an end to death.

2:15 that it might be fulfilled. See Hosea 11:1.

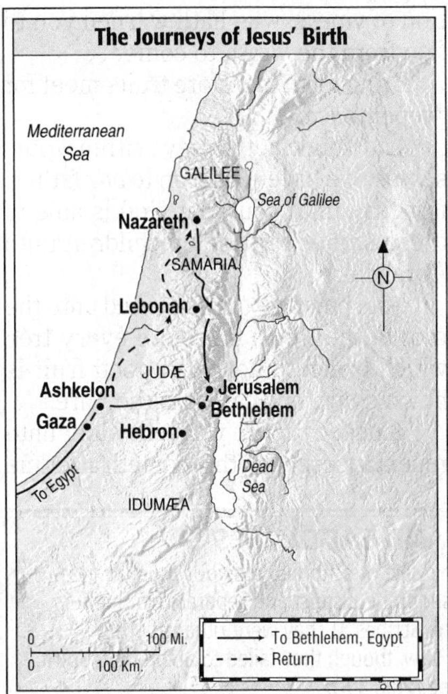

ceeding wroth, and sent forth, and slew
all the children that were in Bethlehem,
and in all the coasts thereof, from two
years old and under, according to the
time which he had diligently enquired
of the wise men.

O.T. prophecy fulfilled (4)

17 Then was fulfilled that which was
spoken by Jeremy the prophet, saying,
18 In Rama was there a voice heard,
lamentation, and weeping, and great
*mourning, Rachel weeping *for* her children, and would not be comforted, because they are not.

(5) The return to Nazareth
(Cf. Luke 2:39-40)

¶ 19 But when Herod was dead, behold, an angel of the Lord appeareth in
a dream to Joseph in Egypt,
20 Saying, Arise, and take the young
child and his mother, and go into the
land of Israel: for they are dead which
sought the young child's life.
21 And he arose, and took the young
child and his mother, and came into the
land of Israel.
22 But when he heard that Archelaus
did reign in Judaea in the room of his
father Herod, he was afraid to go
thither: notwithstanding, being warned
of God in a dream, he turned aside into
the parts of Galilee:

O.T. prophecy fulfilled (5)

23 And he came and dwelt in a city
called Nazareth: that it might be fulfilled which was spoken by the *prophets, He shall be called a Nazarene.

B. The King and Kingdom Presented
and Rejected

(1) The ministry of John the Baptist

3 In those days came John the Baptist, preaching in the wilderness of
Judaea,

O.T. prophecy fulfilled (6) (Mark 1:3-8;
Luke 3:2-17; John 1:6-8,19-28)

2 And saying, *Repent ye: for the kingdom of *heaven is at hand.
3 For this is he that was spoken of by
the prophet Esaias, saying, The voice

2:17 spoken by Jeremy the prophet. See Jeremiah 31:15 and its note, "A Prophecy of Weeping."
2:22 Archelaus. The son of Herod the Great.
2:22 room. In the place of.
2:23 spoken by the prophets. Possibly the allusion is to Isaiah 11:1, where our Lord is spoken of as a rod (*netzer*) out of the stem of Jesse (see also Isa. 11:1 note, "The Branch of Jesse").
3:2 kingdom of heaven. Literally, *the kingdom of the heavens,* promised long ago by God. It was the kingdom over which David's seed was to rule (2 Sam. 7:7-16 and 7:11 note, "The Davidic Covenant"; see also Ps. 89:3-4; Zech. 12:8). The King was now present among His people and ready to establish the kingdom. For more details and the new revelation concerning the mysteries of the kingdom of heaven, see Matthew 13:11 note, "The Mysteries of the Kingdom."
3:3 spoken of. See Isaiah 40:3.

of one crying in the wilderness, Prepare
ye the way of the Lord, make his paths
straight.
4And the same John had his raiment
of camel's hair, and a leathern girdle
about his loins; and his meat was locusts and wild honey.
5Then went out to him Jerusalem,
and all Judaea, and all the region round
about Jordan,
6And were baptized of him in Jordan,
confessing their sins.
¶ 7But when he saw many of the
Pharisees and Sadducees come to his
*baptism, he said unto them, O genera-
tion of vipers, who hath warned you to
flee from the wrath to come?
8Bring forth therefore fruits meet for
*repentance:
9And think not to say within yourselves, We have Abraham to *our* father:
for I say unto you, that God is able of
these stones to raise up children unto
Abraham.
10And now also the axe is laid unto the
root of the trees: therefore every tree
which bringeth not forth good fruit is
hewn down, and cast into the *fire.
11I indeed baptize you with water unto
repentance: but he that cometh after me

3:7 THE PHARISEES AND SADDUCEES

The name Pharisee means *separatist;* it is used by this sect or school of religious thought who believe that God's chosen people Israel were supposed to be distinct and separate from others. The Pharisees were usually scribes (see 2:4 note, "The Scribes"). They were ritualists who concerned themselves in abiding by the letter of the Law, though they failed to abide in its spirit, for the most part. Saul of Tarsus was a proud Pharisee (Phil. 3:5).

They were enemies to the Lord Jesus Christ from the very beginning of His ministry, and it was not long before they joined hands with their enemies, the *Sadducees, in order to destroy Jesus of Nazareth. Their common opposition to Christ developed through the fact that He was not a graduate of any of the rabbinical schools nor a member of the famed religious sects of the Israelites, and His words were spoken with all the authority of God Himself and often challenged not the Law, but the additions to the Law made by the Pharisees (compare Deut. 12:32). The honorable, direct, and incisive messages of John the Baptist and the Lord Jesus Christ frightened the Pharisees because these threatened to discredit their own teaching and self-opinionated piety.

The Sadducees were members of the religious school opposed to the *Pharisees. They were comparable to the rationalists of today. They believed in nothing supernatural. They discredited miracles and thus did not believe in resurrection. They denied the existence of angels and demons, etc. Strictly speaking, they were not a sect as were the Pharisees but comprised all the rationalists of that day.

3:11 VARIOUS BAPTISMS

In this verse John the Baptist was contrasting his own visible act of baptism with that of the baptism of the Lord. John's baptism was a symbol that acknowledged the need of cleansing and was submitted to by those who truly repented of their sins when they heard John's message. The baptism of the Lord was not an outward symbol; it was prophetic of the new birth and indwelling by the Holy Spirit that was to come upon those who believed in Jesus Christ as the Saviour from sin and received Him as their Saviour.

This second baptism signifies two events–the baptism with the Holy Ghost and the baptism with fire. The baptism with the Holy Ghost (Holy Spirit) came after Calvary on the Day of *Pentecost, and it comes on every believer when he is saved. The baptism with fire refers to judgment (for the fire is unquenchable; see Mark 9:43). This is the judgment which will come upon the nations that reject Christ at the time when He shall return to earth in power to reign.

3:4 his meat was locusts. This seems like a strange food to us. Nevertheless, even today the Arabs use the thorax, that is, the middle region of the body between the head and the abdomen, as food. The head, tail, legs, and wings are removed and allowed to dry. Sometimes dried locusts are stored away for lean seasons.

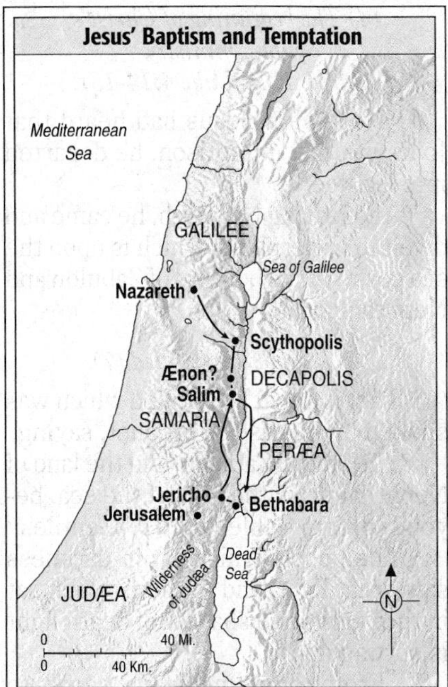

is mightier than I, whose shoes I am not
worthy to bear: he shall baptize you with
the Holy Ghost, and *with* fire:
12Whose fan *is* in his hand, and he will
throughly purge his floor, and gather his
wheat into the garner; but he will burn
up the chaff with unquenchable fire.

(2) The baptism of the Lord Jesus
(Mark 1:9-11; Luke 3:21-22;
cf. John 1:31-34)

¶13Then cometh Jesus from Galilee to
Jordan unto John, to be baptized of him.
14But John forbad him, saying, I have
need to be baptized of thee, and comest
thou to me?
15And Jesus answering said unto him,
Suffer *it to be so* now: for thus it becometh us to fulfil all *righteousness.
Then he suffered him.
16And Jesus, when he was baptized,
went up *straightway out of the water:
and, lo, the heavens were opened unto
him, and he saw the Spirit of God descending like a dove, and lighting upon
him:
17And lo a voice from heaven, saying,
This is my beloved Son, in whom I am
well pleased.

(3) The temptation of the Lord Jesus
(Mark 1:12-13; Luke 4:1-13;
cf. Gen. 3:6)

4 Then was Jesus led up of the
Spirit into the wilderness to be
*tempted of the *devil.
2And when he had fasted forty days

3:12 fan is in his hand. John's words clearly indicate that he, along with the other prophets (John the Baptist was the last of the Old Testament prophets), did not fully understand the two advents (or comings) of Christ: that our Lord was to come first in humiliation, and second in power. It is not at all surprising that the prophets did not understand this great truth, for Christ came first to present Himself as King, and Israel could have accepted Him. Here John the Baptist spoke first of the gift of the Holy Spirit ("he shall baptize you with the Holy Ghost"), who would attend Christ's ministry in His First Advent. Then John referred to Christ's Second Advent when he said that Christ would "purge his floor, and gather his wheat into the garner; but he will burn up the chaff with unquenchable fire."

3:15 Suffer it to be so now. John baptized those who repented of their sins. Why, then, should our Lord Jesus Christ, who was without sin (2 Cor. 5:21; Heb. 4:15), submit to John's baptism? Because, at the start of His ministry, He was, as a symbol of what He had come to earth to do, taking the sinner's place in death. In Old Testament times, before the high priest was anointed for service, he was washed (Exod. 29:4-7). So our Lord, before the beginning of His office as High Priest, was washed symbolically in baptism and anointed by the Spirit descending on Him like a dove (Matt. 3:16).

3:16 Spirit of God . . . lighting upon him. Here, for the first time in the New Testament, the Holy Trinity, Father, Son, and Holy Spirit (Holy Ghost) is manifested. The Son, the second person of the Trinity, comes out from the water; the Spirit, the third person, appears in the form of a dove; the Father, whose voice is heard coming out of heaven, expresses delight in His Son.

4:1 led up of the Spirit. In God's plan it was necessary for our Lord to be tempted by Satan so that He might take our place as One tempted in all things, yet without sin

and forty nights, he was afterward an
hungred.
3 And when the tempter came to him,
he said, If thou be the Son of God, command that these stones be made bread.
4 But he answered and said, It is written, Man shall not live by bread alone,
but by every word that proceedeth out
of the mouth of God.
5 Then the devil taketh him up into
the *holy city, and setteth him on a pinnacle of the temple,
6 And saith unto him, If thou be the
Son of God, cast thyself down: for it is
written, He shall give his *angels charge
concerning thee: and in *their* hands they
shall bear thee up, lest at any time thou
dash thy foot against a stone.
7 Jesus said unto him, It is written
again, Thou shalt not *tempt the Lord
thy God.
8 Again, the devil taketh him up into
an exceeding high mountain, and
sheweth him all the kingdoms of the
*world, and the glory of them;
9 And saith unto him, All these things
will I give thee, if thou wilt fall down and
worship me.
10 Then saith Jesus unto him, Get
thee hence, *Satan: for it is written,
Thou shalt worship the Lord thy God,
and him only shalt thou serve.
11 Then the devil leaveth him, and,
behold, angels came and ministered
unto him.

(4) The beginning of Christ's public ministry
(Mark 1:14; Luke 4:14-15)

¶ 12 Now when Jesus had heard that
John was cast into prison, he departed
into Galilee;
13 And leaving Nazareth, he came and
dwelt in Capernaum, which is upon the
sea coast, in the borders of Zabulon and
Nephthalim:

O.T. prophecy fulfilled (7)

14 That it might be fulfilled which was
spoken by Esaias the prophet, saying,
15 The land of Zabulon, and the land of
Nephthalim, *by* the way of the sea, beyond Jordan, Galilee of the *Gentiles;
16 The people which sat in darkness
saw great light; and to them which sat
in the region and shadow of death light
is sprung up.
¶ 17 From that time Jesus began to
preach, and to say, Repent: for the *kingdom of heaven is at hand.

(5) The call of Peter, Andrew, James, and John
(Mark 1:16-20; cf. Luke 5:2-11)

¶ 18 And Jesus, walking by the sea of
Galilee, saw two brethren, Simon
called *Peter, and Andrew his brother,
casting a net into the sea: for they were
fishers.
19 And he saith unto them, Follow me,
and I will make you fishers of men.

(Heb. 4:15). Observe that it was the Devil, Satan, who tempted Him and that the temptation lasted forty days (see Luke 4:2).

4:3 stones be made bread. Satan had no doubt as to who our Lord was. When Satan said, "If thou be the Son of God," he used the word "if" in the sense of "since," for Satan's whole purpose in tempting the Lord Jesus was that he might entice Him to act independent of the Father. The temptation of our Lord was very real. Jesus answered each temptation by quoting the Word of God in the Old Testament (see vss. 4,7,10).

4:4 It is written. See Deuteronomy 8:3.

4:5 the holy city. Jerusalem.

4:6 it is written. Observe that Satan also quotes Scripture (see Ps. 91:11-12) but not accurately, for he omitted the clause, "to keep thee in all thy ways" (Ps. 91:11).

4:7 It is written. See Deuteronomy 6:16.

4:9 All these things. Satan was within his province in offering these things to Christ, for he is a usurper and is called "the prince of this world" (see John 12:31; 14:30; 16:11).

4:10 it is written. See Deuteronomy 6:13; 10:20.

4:13 leaving Nazareth. For the reason of His departure, read Luke 4:16-30.

4:14 That it might be fulfilled. See Isaiah 9:1-2; 42:6-7.

20And they straightway left *their*
nets, and followed him.
21And going on from thence, he saw
other two brethren, James *the son* of
Zebedee, and John his brother, in a ship
with Zebedee their father, mending
their nets; and he called them.
22And they immediately left the ship
and their father, and followed him.
¶23And Jesus went about all Galilee,
teaching in their *synagogues, and
preaching the gospel of the kingdom,
and healing all manner of sickness
and all manner of disease among the
people.
24And his fame went throughout all
Syria: and they brought unto him all
sick people that were taken with divers
diseases and torments, and those which
were possessed with devils, and those
which were lunatick, and those that had
the palsy; and he healed them.
25And there followed him great multitudes of people from Galilee, and *from*
Decapolis, and *from* Jerusalem, and
from Judaea, and *from* beyond Jordan.

(6) The Sermon on the Mount
(Cf. Luke 6:20-49)
(a) The Beatitudes (cf. Luke 6:20-23)

5 And seeing the multitudes, he
went up into a mountain: and when
he was set, his disciples came unto him:
2And he opened his mouth, and
taught them, saying,
3Blessed *are* the poor in spirit: for
theirs is the kingdom of heaven.
4Blessed *are* they that mourn: for
they shall be comforted.
5Blessed *are* the meek: for they shall
inherit the earth.
6Blessed *are* they which do hunger
and thirst after righteousness: for they
shall be filled.

5:1 A SUPPOSED CONTRADICTION EXPLAINED

Destructive criticism has tried to discredit the accuracy of the Bible by drawing attention to the fact that here, before the pronouncement of the Beatitudes, our Lord went *up* into a mountain, while Luke's account (Luke 6:17) on the same occasion says, "He came *down* with them, and stood in the plain." Archaeological discoveries regarding the probable site of ancient Capernaum (now Tel Hum) have thrown some light on this apparent contradiction. Just northwest of Tel Hum is a mountain believed to be the site of the Sermon on the Mount. Halfway to its summit there is a break in the upward slope of the mountain, and this break is a large, flat plain. Here several thousand people could recline or rest comfortably. Unquestionably, our Lord took the Twelve up to the summit of the mountain, and just before delivering the Sermon on the Mount, He came down with them to this plain, and there delivered His message to the multitude. Both statements are absolutely accurate, as is the entire Bible. There appear to be contradictions only because we do not know all the facts.

5:3-16 THE SERMON ON THE MOUNT

Chapters 5, 6, and 7 contain Jesus' sermon called the "Sermon on the Mount," the most well-known sermon ever preached. It was delivered at the time in Christ's ministry when He was presenting the kingdom promised long ago (see Matt. 3:2 note and 13:11 note, "The Mysteries of the Kingdom"). It proclaims the constitution of that kingdom and applies in a particular sense to the government as it will be when Christ returns to reign. Christians, those who have been born again through faith in the Son of God, are heirs of the kingdom, and as such they should endeavor through Christ and His Spirit to live as closely as possible to the principles presented in this sermon.

The message of the Sermon on the Mount is not for the unsaved: there is no gospel in the Sermon on the Mount; the way of salvation is not declared within it.

4:23 gospel of the kingdom. See Matthew 3:2 note.
5:3 Blessed. Happy or joyous. Verses 3-12 contain what are known as the "Beatitudes." Those who are said to be happy are in that state, not through anything that they do, but because of who and what they are.

[7]Blessed *are* the merciful: for they
shall obtain *mercy.
[8]Blessed *are* the pure in heart: for
they shall see God.
[9]Blessed *are* the peacemakers: for
they shall be called the children of God.
[10]Blessed *are* they which are persecuted for righteousness' sake: for theirs
is the kingdom of heaven.
[11]Blessed are ye, when *men* shall revile you, and persecute *you,* and shall
say all manner of evil against you falsely, for my sake.
[12]Rejoice, and be exceeding glad: for
great *is* your *reward in heaven: for so
persecuted they the prophets which
were before you.

(b) The similitudes
(cf. Mark 4:21-23; Luke 8:16-18)

¶[13]Ye are the salt of the earth: but if
the salt have lost his savour, wherewith
shall it be salted? it is thenceforth good
for nothing, but to be cast out, and to be
trodden under foot of men.
[14]Ye are the light of the world. A city
that is set on an hill cannot be hid.
[15]Neither do men light a candle, and
put it under a bushel, but on a candlestick; and it giveth light unto all that are
in the house.
[16]Let your light so shine before men,
that they may see your good works, and
glorify your Father which is in heaven.

(c) Christ and the Law

¶[17]Think not that I am come to destroy the *law, or the prophets: I am not
come to destroy, but to fulfil.
[18]For verily I say unto you, Till heav-
en and earth pass, one jot or one tittle
shall in no wise pass from the law, till
all be fulfilled.
[19]Whosoever therefore shall break
one of these least commandments, and
shall teach men so, he shall be called
the least in the kingdom of heaven: but
whosoever shall do and teach *them,* the
same shall be called great in the kingdom of heaven.
[20]For I say unto you, That except
your righteousness shall exceed *the
righteousness* of the scribes and Pharisees, ye shall in no case enter into the
kingdom of heaven.
¶[21]Ye have heard that it was said by
them of old time, Thou shalt not kill;
and whosoever shall kill shall be in danger of the *judgment:
[22]But I say unto you, That whosoever
is angry with his brother without a
cause shall be in danger of the judgment: and whosoever shall say to his
brother, Raca, shall be in danger of the
council: but whosoever shall say, Thou
*fool, shall be in danger of *hell fire.
[23]Therefore if thou bring thy gift to
the *altar, and there rememberest that
thy brother hath ought against thee;

5:13 salt. The purpose of salt is to preserve from corruption as well as give flavor—or influence in the case of Christians in the world.

5:14 light. Whereas salt has one negative value, to preserve; light has a positive value, to shine. Light is needed where there is darkness.

5:17 I am not come to destroy. We have already observed in Matthew's Gospel that the Law and the Prophets were fulfilled again and again by the coming of Jesus Christ, who was made under the Law (Gal. 4:4); who lived perfectly and in obedience to the Law (John 8:46; 1 Pet. 2:21-22); who was the antitype, or fulfillment, of the Old Testament *type (Heb. 9:11-28; see also their notes, especially 9:11, "Christ as High Priest"; Gal. 3:13-14).

5:18 jot. This is the *yod,* the smallest letter of the Hebrew alphabet.

5:18 tittle. A small projection below the foot of some letters of the Hebrew alphabet.

5:22 Raca. Worthless one.

5:22 hell fire. The word translated "hell" is the Greek *Geena,* which means *Gehenna,* a place in the Valley of Hinnom where sacrifices were once offered. The word appears many times in the Gospels (only once elsewhere, James 3:6) and is used in every instance, except in James, by our Lord Himself. It is an expression which carries the same inference as "lake of fire."

[24]Leave there thy gift before the altar, and go thy way; first be *reconciled
to thy brother, and then come and offer
thy gift.
[25]Agree with thine adversary quickly, whiles thou art in the way with him;
lest at any time the adversary deliver
thee to the judge, and the judge deliver
thee to the officer, and thou be cast into
prison.
[26]Verily I say unto thee, Thou shalt
by no means come out thence, till thou
hast paid the uttermost farthing.
¶[27]Ye have heard that it was said by
them of old time, Thou shalt not commit adultery:
[28]But I say unto you, That whosoever
looketh on a woman to *lust after her
hath committed adultery with her already in his heart.
[29]And if thy right eye *offend thee,
pluck it out, and cast *it* from thee: for it
is profitable for thee that one of thy
members should perish, and not *that*
thy whole body should be cast into hell.
[30]And if thy right hand offend thee,
cut if off, and cast *it* from thee: for it is
profitable for thee that one of thy members should perish, and not *that* thy
whole body should be cast into hell.

(d) New laws
(cf. Matt. 19:3-11; Mark 10:2-12;
1 Cor. 7:10-15)

[31]It hath been said, Whosoever shall
put away his wife, let him give her a
writing of divorcement:
[32]But I say unto you, That whosoever
shall put away his wife, saving for the
cause of fornication, causeth her to
commit adultery: and whosoever shall
marry her that is divorced committeth
adultery.
¶[33]Again, ye have heard that it hath
been said by them of old time, Thou
shalt not forswear thyself, but shalt
perform unto the Lord thine oaths:
[34]But I say unto you, Swear not at all;
neither by heaven; for it is God's throne:
[35]Nor by the earth; for it is his footstool: neither by Jerusalem; for it is the
city of the great King.
[36]Neither shalt thou swear by thy
head, because thou canst not make one
hair white or black.
[37]But let your communication be,
Yea, yea; Nay, nay: for whatsoever is
more than these cometh of evil.
¶[38]Ye have heard that it hath been
said, An eye for an eye, and a tooth for a
tooth:
[39]But I say unto you, That ye resist
not evil: but whosoever shall smite thee
on thy right cheek, turn to him the
other also.
[40]And if any man will sue thee at the
law, and take away thy coat, let him
have *thy* cloke also.
[41]And whosoever shall compel thee
to go a mile, go with him twain.
[42]Give to him that asketh thee, and
from him that would *borrow of thee
turn not thou away.
¶[43]Ye have heard that it hath been
said, Thou shalt love thy neighbour, and
hate thine enemy.
[44]But I say unto you, Love your enemies, bless them that curse you, do
good to them that hate you, and pray for
them which despitefully use you, and
persecute you;
[45]That ye may be the children of your
Father which is in heaven: for he
maketh his sun to rise on the evil and
on the good, and sendeth rain on the
just and on the unjust.
[46]For if ye love them which love you,
what reward have ye? do not even the
*publicans the same?
[47]And if ye salute your brethren only,

5:29 offend thee. Causes you to sin.
5:33 Lord. Jehovah. See *names of God.
5:38 it hath been said. See Exodus 21:24; Leviticus 24:20; Deuteronomy 19:21.
5:43 it hath been said. See Leviticus 19:18; Deuteronomy 23:3-6.
5:44 bless. Pray for.

what do ye more *than others?* do not
even the publicans so?
48 Be ye therefore perfect, even as
your Father which is in heaven is
perfect.

(e) The motive of service and prayer

6 Take heed that ye do not your
alms before men, to be seen of
them: otherwise ye have no reward of
your Father which is in heaven.
2 Therefore when thou doest *thine*
alms, do not sound a trumpet before
thee, as the hypocrites do in the synagogues and in the streets, that they may
have glory of men. Verily I say unto
you, They have their reward.
3 But when thou doest alms, let not
thy left hand know what thy right hand
doeth:
4 That thine alms may be in secret:
and thy Father which seeth in secret
himself shall reward thee openly.
¶5 And when thou prayest, thou shalt
not be as the hypocrites *are:* for they
love to pray standing in the synagogues

6:9 THE LORD'S PRAYER

Verses 9-13 contain the well-known Lord's Prayer (which really should be referred to as the Disciple's Prayer). It is obvious that this prayer is not the Lord's personal prayer. He would never ask for forgiveness of sins, because He never sinned (2 Cor. 5:21). Christ's own prayer is found in John 17. The Lord's Prayer is a model prayer that our Lord taught to His disciples when they asked, "Lord, teach us to pray" (Luke 11:1). This is a *kingdom prayer–since the Sermon on the Mount contains the constitution of the kingdom; so in the kingdom, this prayer will be prayed.

In the church age in which we live, we are to pray to the Father in the name of Jesus Christ (John 14:13-14; 16:24) and on the basis of the blood shed on Calvary. Further, we know our sins are forgiven because Christ died for us, not because we forgive others. We were washed from our sins in Christ's own blood (Rev. 1:5). There is no thanksgiving in this prayer, but we are told to pray with thanksgiving (Phil. 4:6). Christians can certainly pray this prayer if they do so intelligently, if they realize what they are saying. No one but a Christian can call God his or her Father. No one but the Christian will honor or hold as holy God's name. The Christian longs for the time when the Lord shall come for His own (1 Thess. 4:13-18), but in praying for the Father's kingdom to come (see 1 Cor. 15:24 and its note, "The Kingdom"), which will be after Christ's earthly kingdom is set up–the millennial reign of the Son of David–we are certainly praying also for the *Rapture of the church.

Assuredly, the Christian would like to see the Father's will done on earth as it is in heaven. Certainly the Christian has a right to ask his or her heavenly Father for daily bread. And while it is absolutely true that the forgiveness of our debts or sins is by the blood of Christ and "without shedding of blood [there] is no remission" (Heb. 9:22), what Christian can come to the Father at the end of the day humbly confessing his personal sins, if in his heart he holds an unforgiving spirit toward a fellow believer (see vss. 14-15 of this chapter)? We are to forgive one another even as God for Christ's sake has forgiven us (Eph. 4:32). The Christian needs to be asking the Father constantly not to lead him into temptation and to deliver him from evil. This is the way of victory through the power of the Holy Ghost.

Proper prayer should begin with worship and should put the interests of God above our own interests. Prayer should acknowledge being happy in His will, ask for our daily needs, and seek the forgiveness of sins and victory over temptation. We should approach the Father on holy ground, that is, through the Lord Jesus Christ, recognizing that our standing is in Him and that we have no merit of our own. We should come to Him with thanksgiving upon our lips and in our hearts for His numerous blessings to us on this earth and in eternity to come.

5:48 perfect. Mature and fully developed. While we are on earth we retain the old nature; we are not *perfect as God the Father and Son are sinlessly perfect. But we can be mature insofar as we have progressed along the pathway toward heaven and Christ's presence. For example, an apple may not be due to ripen completely until October–but it may be ripe and ready to pick in September.

6:1 alms. Any righteous acts or good deeds.

and in the corners of the streets, that
they may be seen of men. Verily I say
unto you, They have their reward.
6 But thou, when thou prayest, enter
into thy closet, and when thou hast shut
thy door, pray to thy Father which is in
secret; and thy Father which seeth in
secret shall reward thee openly.
7 But when ye pray, use not vain repetitions, as the heathen *do:* for they
think that they shall be heard for their
much speaking.
8 Be not ye therefore like unto them:
for your Father knoweth what things ye
have need of, before ye ask him.

(f) The model of prayer
(Cf. Luke 11:1-13)

9 After this manner therefore pray ye:
Our Father which art in heaven, Hallowed be thy name.
10 Thy kingdom come. Thy will be
done in earth, as *it is* in heaven.
11 Give us this day our daily bread.
12 And forgive us our debts, as we forgive our debtors.
13 And lead us not into *temptation,
but deliver us from evil: For thine is the
kingdom, and the power, and the glory,
for ever. *Amen.
14 For if ye forgive men their trespasses, your heavenly Father will also
forgive you:
15 But if ye forgive not men their trespasses, neither will your Father forgive
your trespasses.

(g) More about motives of worship

¶16 Moreover when ye fast, be not, as
the hypocrites, of a sad countenance:
for they disfigure their faces, that they
may appear unto men to fast. Verily I
say unto you, They have their reward.
17 But thou, when thou fastest,
*anoint thine head, and wash thy face;
18 That thou appear not unto men to
fast, but unto thy Father which is in
secret: and thy Father, which seeth in
secret, shall reward thee openly.
¶19 Lay not up for yourselves treasures upon earth, where moth and rust
doth corrupt, and where thieves break
through and steal:
20 But lay up for yourselves treasures
in heaven, where neither moth nor rust
doth corrupt, and where thieves do not
break through nor steal:
21 For where your treasure is, there
will your heart be also.
22 The light of the body is the eye: if
therefore thine eye be single, thy whole
body shall be full of light.
23 But if thine eye be evil, thy whole
body shall be full of darkness. If therefore the light that is in thee be darkness,
how great *is* that darkness!
¶24 No man can serve two masters:
for either he will hate the one, and love
the other; or else he will hold to the
one, and despise the other. Ye cannot
serve God and mammon.
25 Therefore I say unto you, Take no
thought for your life, what ye shall eat,
or what ye shall drink; nor yet for your
body, what ye shall put on. Is not the life
more than meat, and the body than raiment?
26 Behold the fowls of the air: for they
sow not, neither do they reap, nor gather into barns; yet your heavenly Father
feedeth them. Are ye not much better
than they?
27 Which of you by taking thought can
add one cubit unto his stature?
28 And why take ye thought for raiment? Consider the lilies of the field,
how they grow; they toil not, neither do
they spin:

6:6 closet. An inner room.
6:7 much speaking. Many words. The use of the prayer wheels of the Buddhists in Tibet might be said to be "vain" repetition, for these wheels consist of single cylinders inscribed with certain prayers and revolving on spindles
6:9 After this manner. Notice that it does not say "in these words."
6:25 Take no thought. Do not worry or be anxious (see Phil. 4:6).

29And yet I say unto you, That even
Solomon in all his glory was not arrayed
like one of these.
30Wherefore, if God so clothe the
grass of the field, which to day is, and
to morrow is cast into the oven, *shall he*
not much more *clothe* you, O ye of little
*faith?
31Therefore take no thought, saying,
What shall we eat? or, What shall we
drink? or, Wherewithal shall we be
clothed?
32(For after all these things do the
Gentiles seek:) for your heavenly Father
knoweth that ye have need of all
these things.
33But seek ye first the *kingdom of
God, and his righteousness; and all
these things shall be added unto you.

6:33 The Kingdom of God
There is a distinction between the kingdom of heaven (Matt. 3:2 and note) and the kingdom of God used here. While the kingdom of heaven has to do with an earthly sphere and is organic and visible the kingdom of God reaches to all those in all the universe—angels, Old and New Testament saints now in glory, born-again believers living on the earth—all who voluntarily acknowledge Jesus Christ as the Son of God and as the rightful King of Kings and Lord of Lords. The kingdom of God, "not with observation," literally, *visibly* (Luke 17:20), is invisible. In the future, the kingdom of heaven will be blended into the kingdom of God, when our Lord, having put all His enemies under His feet, will deliver His kingdom to the Father (1 Cor. 15:24 and note, "The Kingdom").

34Take therefore no thought for the
morrow: for the morrow shall take
thought for the things of itself. Sufficient
unto the day *is* the evil thereof.
7 Judge not, that ye be not judged.
2For with what judgment ye judge,
ye shall be judged: and with what measure
ye mete, it shall be measured to
you again.
3And why beholdest thou the mote
that is in thy brother's eye, but considerest
not the beam that is in thine
own eye?
4Or how wilt thou say to thy brother,
Let me pull out the mote out of thine
eye; and, behold, a beam *is* in thine own
eye?
5Thou hypocrite, first cast out the
beam out of thine own eye; and then
shalt thou see clearly to cast out the
mote out of thy brother's eye.
¶6Give not that which is *holy unto the
dogs, neither cast ye your pearls before
swine, lest they trample them under
their feet, and turn again and rend you.
¶7Ask, and it shall be given you;
seek, and ye shall find; knock, and it
shall be opened unto you:
8For every one that asketh receiveth;
and he that seeketh findeth; and to him
that knocketh it shall be opened.
9Or what man is there of you, whom
if his son ask bread, will he give him a
stone?
10Or if he ask a fish, will he give him
a serpent?
11If ye then, being evil, know how to
give good gifts unto your children, how
much more shall your Father which is
in heaven give good things to them that
ask him?
12Therefore all things whatsoever ye
would that men should do to you, do ye
even so to them: for this is the law and
the prophets.
¶13Enter ye in at the strait gate: for
wide *is* the gate, and broad *is* the way,
that leadeth to destruction, and many
there be which go in thereat:
14Because strait *is* the gate, and narrow
is the way, which leadeth unto life,
and few there be that find it.

6:33 shall be added. Compare Colossians 3:1-3.
6:34 evil. Adversity, troubles.
7:1 Judge not. Do not condemn others. We should be examining our own hearts and motives instead of judging others. God is the Judge.
7:14 narrow is the way. See John 14:6.

(h) Warnings concerning false teachers and false profession

¶15 Beware of false prophets, which
come to you in sheep's clothing, but
inwardly they are ravening wolves.
16 Ye shall know them by their fruits.
Do men gather grapes of thorns, or figs
of thistles?
17 Even so every good tree bringeth
forth good fruit; but a corrupt tree
bringeth forth evil fruit.
18 A good tree cannot bring forth evil
fruit, neither *can* a corrupt tree bring
forth good fruit.
19 Every tree that bringeth not forth
good fruit is hewn down, and cast into
the fire.
20 Wherefore by their fruits ye shall
know them.
¶21 Not every one that saith unto me,
Lord, Lord, shall enter into the kingdom of heaven; but he that doeth the
will of my Father which is in heaven.
22 Many will say to me in that day,
Lord, Lord, have we not prophesied in
thy name? and in thy name have cast
out devils? and in thy name done many
wonderful works?
23 And then will I profess unto them,
I never knew you: depart from me, ye
that work iniquity.

(i) The parables begin—The parable of the house built upon the rock (1) (cf. Luke 6:47-49)

¶24 Therefore whosoever heareth
these sayings of mine, and doeth them,
I will liken him unto a wise man, which
built his house upon a rock:
25 And the rain descended, and the
floods came, and the winds blew, and
beat upon that house; and it fell not: for
it was founded upon a rock.
26 And every one that heareth these
sayings of mine, and doeth them not,
shall be likened unto a foolish man,
which built his house upon the sand:
27 And the rain descended, and the
floods came, and the winds blew, and
beat upon that house; and it fell: and
great was the fall of it.
28 And it came to pass, when Jesus
had ended these sayings, the people
were astonished at his *doctrine:
29 For he taught them as *one* having
authority, and not as the scribes.

(7) The miracles begin (1)—Christ heals a leper (Mark 1:40; Luke 5:12-14)

8 When he was come down from the
mountain, great multitudes followed him.
2 And, behold, there came a *leper
and worshipped him, saying, Lord, if
thou wilt, thou canst make me *clean.
3 And Jesus put forth *his* hand, and
touched him, saying, I will; be thou
clean. And immediately his *leprosy
was cleansed.
4 And Jesus saith unto him, See thou
tell no man; but go thy way, shew thyself to the priest, and offer the gift that
*Moses commanded, for a testimony
unto them.

(8) A miracle (2)—The centurion's servant healed (Luke 7:1-10)

¶5 And when Jesus was entered into
Capernaum, there came unto him a
centurion, beseeching him,
6 And saying, Lord, my servant lieth
at home sick of the palsy, grievously
tormented.
7 And Jesus saith unto him, I will
come and heal him.
8 The centurion answered and said,
Lord, I am not worthy that thou shouldest
come under my roof: but speak the word
only, and my servant shall be healed.
9 For I am a man under authority, having soldiers under me: and I say to this
man, Go, and he goeth; and to another,
Come, and he cometh; and to my servant, Do this, and he doeth *it.*

8:4 gift that Moses commanded. Leviticus 14:4-32.
8:5 centurion. An officer in the Roman army who commanded a company of a hundred.

[10]When Jesus heard *it*, he marvelled,
and said to them that followed, Verily I
say unto you, I have not found so great
faith, no, not in *Israel.
[11]And I say unto you, That many shall
come from the east and west, and shall
sit down with *Abraham, and *Isaac,
and *Jacob, in the kingdom of heaven.
[12]But the children of the kingdom
shall be cast out into outer darkness:
there shall be weeping and gnashing of
teeth.
[13]And Jesus said unto the centurion,
Go thy way; and as thou hast believed,
so be it done unto thee. And his servant
was healed in the selfsame hour.

(9) A miracle (3)—Peter's mother-in-law healed (Mark 1:29-34; Luke 4:38-41)

¶[14]And when Jesus was come into
Peter's house, he saw his wife's mother laid, and sick of a fever.
[15]And he touched her hand, and the
fever left her: and she arose, and ministered unto them.
¶[16]When the even was come, they
brought unto him many that were possessed with devils: and he cast out the
spirits with *his* word, and healed all that
were sick:

O.T. prophecy fulfilled (8)

[17]That it might be fulfilled which was
spoken by Esaias the *prophet, saying,
Himself took our infirmities, and bare
our sicknesses.
¶[18]Now when Jesus saw great multitudes about him, he gave commandment to depart unto the other side.

(10) The scribe's profession

[19]And a certain *scribe came, and
said unto him, Master, I will follow thee
whithersoever thou goest.
[20]And Jesus saith unto him, The foxes have holes, and the birds of the air
have nests; but the Son of man hath not
where to lay *his* head.
[21]And another of his disciples said
unto him, Lord, suffer me first to go and
bury my father.
[22]But Jesus said unto him, Follow me;
and let the dead bury their dead.

(11) A miracle (4)—The stilling of the storm (Mark 4:36-41; Luke 8:22-25)

¶[23]And when he was entered into a
ship, his disciples followed him.
[24]And, behold, there arose a great
tempest in the sea, insomuch that the

8:20 THE SON OF MAN

This is the first time that our Lord, whom we have heard of as the Son of David and the Son of God, refers to Himself as the Son of Man. As the Son of David, we think of His fulfilling that phase of His ministry that was Jewish in its character, whereas the Son of God is His divine title.

The expression "Son of man" is used by the Holy Spirit in addressing Ezekiel nearly a hundred times. In the New Testament it is the Lord who uses the title of Himself; while in Daniel 7:13-14, we find the same title used of our Lord Jesus Christ in a prophetic utterance of His coming in power to reign.

As a title, Son of Man belongs to our Lord both in His rejection and in His exaltation—He has always been the Son of God, though the world may sometimes doubt it. He was rejected as the Son of David, Israel's Messiah; as the Son of Man He came to earth, perfect God and perfect Man, having left heaven's glory and taken upon Himself the form of a servant (see Phil. 2:5-8 and the notes, especially 2:6, "The Form of God"). The first man (Adam) was of the earth; the second Man is the Lord from heaven (1 Cor. 15:47). When He comes again to reign, He will come in glory in the clouds of heaven to establish His kingdom—then He will be recognized as the Son of David and the Son of God.

8:17 That it might be fulfilled. See Isaiah 53:4 and 53:1-5 note, "Christ's Suffering."

ship was covered with the waves: but
he was asleep.
[25]And his disciples came to *him,* and
awoke him, saying, Lord, save us: we
perish.
[26]And he saith unto them, Why are ye
fearful, O ye of little faith? Then he
arose, and rebuked the winds and the
sea; and there was a great calm.
[27]But the men marvelled, saying,
What manner of man is this, that even
the winds and the sea obey him!

(12) A miracle (5)—Demons are subject to the Son of God (Mark 5:1-21; Luke 8:26-40)

¶[28]And when he was come to the
other side into the country of the
Gergesenes, there met him two possessed with devils, coming out of the
tombs, exceeding fierce, so that no man
might pass by that way.
[29]And, behold, they cried out, saying,
What have we to do with thee, Jesus,
thou Son of *God? art thou come hither
to torment us before the time?
[30]And there was a good way off from
them an herd of many swine feeding.
[31]So the devils besought him, saying,
If thou cast us out, suffer us to go away
into the herd of swine.
[32]And he said unto them, Go. And
when they were come out, they went
into the herd of swine: and, behold, the
whole herd of swine ran violently down
a steep place into the sea, and perished
in the waters.
[33]And they that kept them fled, and
went their ways into the city, and told
every thing, and what was befallen to
the possessed of the devils.
[34]And, behold, the whole city came
out to meet Jesus: and when they saw
him, they besought *him* that he would
depart out of their coasts.

(13) A miracle (6)—The healing of the palsied man (Mark 2:3-12; Luke 5:18-26)

9 And he entered into a ship, and
passed over, and came into his own
city.
[2]And, behold, they brought to him a
man sick of the palsy, lying on a bed: and
Jesus seeing their faith said unto the
sick of the palsy; Son, be of good cheer;
thy sins be *forgiven thee.
[3]And, behold, certain of the *scribes
said within themselves, This *man* blasphemeth.
[4]And Jesus knowing their thoughts
said, Wherefore think ye evil in your
hearts?
[5]For whether is easier, to say, *Thy*
sins be forgiven thee; or to say, Arise,
and walk?
[6]But that ye may know that the Son
of man hath power on earth to forgive
sins, (then saith he to the sick of the
palsy,) Arise, take up thy bed, and go
unto thine house.
[7]And he arose, and departed to his
house.
[8]But when the multitudes saw *it,*
they marvelled, and glorified God,
which had given such power unto men.

(14) The call of Matthew and the banquet in Matthew's house (cf. Mark 2:14-20)

¶[9]And as Jesus passed forth from
thence, he saw a man, named Matthew,
sitting at the *receipt of custom: and he
saith unto him, Follow me. And he
arose, and followed him.
¶[10]And it came to pass, as Jesus sat

8:28 the Gergesenes. The Gadarenes, near the town of Gadara, the capital of that region.
8:29 Jesus, thou Son of God. The demons as well as Satan (Matt. 4:3) recognized the deity of Christ.
8:29 before the time. The time for Satan and the demons to be tormented will be after the *Millennium, when they will be cast into the lake of fire prepared for them (Matt. 25:41). There they will be tormented day and night forever (Rev. 20:10).
9:9 Matthew. See introduction to this book.
9:9 receipt of custom. Toll or tax booth.

at meat in the house, behold, many publicans and sinners came and sat down
with him and his disciples.
11 And when the *Pharisees saw *it,*
they said unto his disciples, Why eateth
your Master with *publicans and sinners?
12 But when Jesus heard *that,* he said
unto them, They that be whole need not
a physician, but they that are sick.
13 But go ye and learn what *that*
meaneth, I will have mercy, and not
*sacrifice: for I am not come to call the
righteous, but sinners to *repentance.
¶ 14 Then came to him the disciples of
John, saying, Why do we and the Pharisees fast oft, but thy disciples fast not?
15 And Jesus said unto them, Can the
children of the bridechamber mourn, as
long as the *bridegroom is with them?
but the days will come, when the bridegroom shall be taken from them, and
then shall they fast.

(15) The parable of the garment and the skins (2) (Mark 2:21-22; Luke 5:36-39)

16 No man putteth a piece of new cloth
unto an old garment, for that which is
put in to fill it up taketh from the garment, and the rent is made worse.
17 Neither do men put new wine into
old *bottles: else the bottles break, and
the wine runneth out, and the bottles
perish: but they put new wine into new
bottles, and both are preserved.
¶ 18 While he spake these things unto
them, behold, there came a certain
ruler, and worshipped him, saying, My
daughter is even now dead: but come
and lay thy hand upon her, and she shall
live.
19 And Jesus arose, and followed him,
and *so did* his disciples.

(16) A miracle (7)—A sick woman cured (Mark 5:22-34; Luke 8:41-56)

¶ 20 And, behold, a woman, which was
diseased with an *issue of blood twelve
years, came behind *him,* and touched
the hem of his garment:
21 For she said within herself, If I may
but touch his garment, I shall be whole.
22 But Jesus turned him about, and
when he saw her, he said, Daughter, be
of good comfort; thy faith hath made
thee whole. And the woman was made
whole from that hour.

(17) A miracle (8)—Jarius' daughter raised from the dead— see also vss. 18,19 (cf. Mark 5:35-43; Luke 8:41-56)

23 And when Jesus came into the
ruler's house, and saw the minstrels
and the people making a noise,
24 He said unto them, Give place: for
the maid is not dead, but sleepeth. And
they laughed him to scorn.
25 But when the people were put forth,
he went in, and took her by the hand,
and the maid arose.
26 And the fame hereof went abroad
into all that land.

(18) A miracle (9)—Two blind men receive their sight

¶ 27 And when Jesus departed thence,
two blind men followed him, crying, and
saying, *Thou* *Son of *David, have
mercy on us.
28 And when he was come into the
house, the blind men came to him: and
Jesus saith unto them, Believe ye that

9:10 publicans. The publicans were tax collectors, Jews employed by the Roman government. They were not thought of highly by their employers, and they were despised by their own people, the Jews, because they were considered traitors. Many of these tax collectors were dishonest men who demanded extra funds from the people and kept the money for themselves.

9:13 I will have mercy. See Hosea 6:6.

9:23 minstrels and the people making a noise. Minstrels were flute players. Some of the people were hired mourners, employed to express grief they did not feel. This was a common practice in those times.

I am able to do this? They said unto him,
Yea, Lord.
[29]Then touched he their eyes, saying,
According to your faith be it unto you.
[30]And their eyes were opened; and
Jesus straitly charged them, saying, See
that no man know *it.*
[31]But they, when they were departed, spread abroad his fame in all that
country.

(19) A miracle (10)—
A demon cast out

¶[32]As they went out, behold, they
brought to him a dumb man possessed
with a devil.
[33]And when the devil was cast out,
the dumb spake: and the multitudes
marvelled, saying, It was never so seen
in Israel.
[34]But the Pharisees said, He casteth
out devils through the prince of the
devils.

(20) Further teaching and healing
(Mark 6:5-6)

[35]And Jesus went about all the cities
and villages, teaching in their *synagogues, and preaching the gospel of the
kingdom, and healing every sickness
and every disease among the people.
¶[36]But when he saw the multitudes,
he was moved with compassion on
them, because they fainted, and were
scattered abroad, as sheep having no
shepherd.
[37]Then saith he unto his disciples,
The harvest truly *is* plenteous, but the
labourers *are* few;
[38]Pray ye therefore the Lord of the
harvest, that he will send forth labourers into his harvest.

(21) The Twelve instructed and
sent forth to Israel
(Mark 6:7-13; Luke 9:1-6)

10 And when he had called unto
him his twelve disciples, he
gave them power *against* *unclean spirits, to cast them out, and to heal all
manner of sickness and all manner of
disease.

(22) The apostles named

[2]Now the names of the twelve *apostles are these; The first, Simon, who is
called *Peter, and Andrew his brother;
James *the son* of Zebedee, and John his
brother;
[3]Philip, and Bartholomew; Thomas,
and Matthew the *publican; James *the
son* of Alphaeus, and Lebbaeus, whose
surname was Thaddaeus;
[4]Simon the Canaanite, and *Judas
Iscariot, who also betrayed him.
[5]These twelve Jesus sent forth, and
commanded them, saying, Go not into
the way of the *Gentiles, and into *any*
city of the *Samaritans enter ye not:
[6]But go rather to the lost sheep of the
house of Israel.
[7]And as ye go, preach, saying, The
*kingdom of *heaven is at hand.
[8]Heal the sick, cleanse the *lepers,
raise the dead, cast out devils: freely ye
have received, freely give.
[9]Provide neither gold, nor silver, nor
brass in your purses,
[10]Nor *scrip for *your* journey, neither
two coats, neither shoes, nor yet
staves: for the workman is worthy of
his meat.
[11]And into whatsoever city or town
ye shall enter, enquire who in it is worthy; and there abide till ye go thence.

9:34 prince of the devils. Satan.

9:35 gospel of the kingdom. Gospel means *good news;* the gospel of the kingdom was the good news of the King present among them and the kingdom of heaven that He sought to establish in people's hearts and lives.

10:1 twelve disciples. One was chosen to represent each tribe of Israel. The Twelve had been "disciples," a word meaning *learner.* They now were appointed "apostles" (vs. 2), a term derived from the Greek and meaning the same as the Anglicized Latin word "missionaries," meaning *sent forth* (Matt. 28:19). First, they preached Christ to the Jews, then to the nearby Samaritans, and finally to all nations (Acts 1:8).

12And when ye come into an house,
salute it.
13And if the house be worthy, let your
*peace come upon it: but if it be not
worthy, let your peace return to you.
14And whosoever shall not receive
you, nor hear your words, when ye depart out of that house or city, shake off
the dust of your feet.
15Verily I say unto you, It shall be
more tolerable for the land of *Sodom
and Gomorrha in the day of judgment,
than for that city.
¶16Behold, I send you forth as sheep
in the midst of wolves: be ye therefore
wise as serpents, and harmless as
doves.
17But beware of men: for they will
deliver you up to the councils, and they
will scourge you in their synagogues;
18And ye shall be brought before governors and kings for my sake, for a testimony against them and the Gentiles.
19But when they deliver you up, take
no thought how or what ye shall speak:
for it shall be given you in that same
hour what ye shall speak.
20For it is not ye that speak, but the
Spirit of your Father which speaketh
in you.
21And the brother shall deliver up the
brother to death, and the father the
child: and the children shall rise up
against *their* parents, and cause them to
be put to death.
22And ye shall be hated of all *men* for
my name's sake: but he that endureth
to the end shall be saved.
23But when they persecute you in this
city, flee ye into another: for verily I say
unto you, Ye shall not have gone over
the cities of Israel, till the Son of man
be come.
24The disciple is not above *his* master, nor the servant above his lord.
25It is enough for the disciple that he
be as his master, and the servant as his
lord. If they have called the master of
the house *Beelzebub, how much more
shall they call them of his household?

10:25 Beelzebub
Beelzebub (or Baalzebub) was a title of a heathen deity–the guardian of the Ekronites (2 Kings 1:2). The word Beelzebub means *the lord of flies* and he was supposed to protect his worshippers from insects. The Jewish leaders in the New Testament times applied this title to Satan. As an expression of contempt, they blasphemously said that Christ was working in his power as He healed the masses. This is the best example of how much the scribes abhorred Jesus Christ (Matt. 12:24). Christians are told not to marvel if the world hates us (1 John 3:13) and if we live godly lives we will suffer persecution (2 Tim. 3:12). Thankfully, if we suffer, we will also reign with Him (2 Tim. 2:12) and even be joint-heirs (Rom. 8:17).

26Fear them not therefore: for there
is nothing covered, that shall not be
revealed; and hid, that shall not be
known.
27What I tell you in darkness, *that*
speak ye in light: and what ye hear in the
ear, *that* preach ye upon the housetops.
28And fear not them which kill the
body, but are not able to kill the soul:
but rather fear him which is able to destroy both soul and body in hell.
29Are not two sparrows sold for a farthing? and one of them shall not fall on
the ground without your Father.
30But the very hairs of your head are
all numbered.
31Fear ye not therefore, ye are of
more value than many sparrows.
32Whosoever therefore shall *confess
me before men, him will I confess also
before my Father which is in heaven.
33But whosoever shall deny me before men, him will I also deny before my
Father which is in heaven.

10:22 endureth to the end. See Matthew 24:13.
10:29 farthing. A copper coin worth about one-sixteenth of a denarius. A very small amount.
10:32 confess me before men. Compare Psalm 119:46; Luke 12:8; Revelation 3:8.
10:33 deny me before men. Compare Matthew 7:23; Luke 12:9.

[34]Think not that I am come to send
peace on earth: I came not to send
peace, but a sword.
[35]For I am come to set a man at variance against his father, and the daughter against her mother, and the daughter
in law against her mother in law.
[36]And a man's foes *shall be* they of his
own household.
[37]He that loveth father or mother
more than me is not worthy of me: and
he that loveth son or daughter more
than me is not worthy of me.
[38]And he that taketh not his cross,
and followeth after me, is not worthy
of me.
[39]He that findeth his life shall lose it:
and he that loseth his life for my sake
shall find it.
¶[40]He that receiveth you receiveth
me, and he that receiveth me receiveth
him that sent me.
[41]He that receiveth a prophet in the
name of a prophet shall receive a
prophet's reward; and he that receiveth
a righteous man in the name of a righteous man shall receive a righteous
man's reward.
[42]And whosoever shall give to drink
unto one of these little ones a cup of
cold *water* only in the name of a disciple, verily I say unto you, he shall in no
wise lose his reward.

(23) The question of John the Baptist (Luke 7:18-35)

11 And it came to pass, when Jesus
had made an end of command-
ing his twelve disciples, he departed
thence to teach and to preach in their
cities.
[2]Now when John had heard in the
prison the works of *Christ, he sent two
of his disciples,
[3]And said unto him, Art thou he that
should come, or do we look for another?

(24) Christ's answer to John's question

[4]Jesus answered and said unto them,
Go and shew John again those things
which ye do hear and see:
[5]The blind receive their sight, and
the lame walk, the lepers are cleansed,
and the deaf hear, the dead are raised
up, and the poor have the *gospel
preached to them.
[6]And blessed is *he,* whosoever shall
not be offended in me.
¶[7]And as they departed, Jesus began
to say unto the multitudes concerning
John, What went ye out into the wilderness to see? A reed shaken with the
wind?
[8]But what went ye out for to see? A
man clothed in soft raiment? behold,
they that wear soft *clothing* are in kings'
houses.

10:34 PEACE ON EARTH

"Peace on earth" here means peace among men. Peace of other kinds is also referred to in Scripture, such as peace with God, which has reference to the result of Christians having been given access before the throne of God by virtue of Christ's atoning sacrifice (see Rom. 5:1-2); and the peace of God, which can be the Christian's inner experience as a result of obedience (see John 16:33; Phil. 4:6-7; John 14:27).

Our Lord was indicating here that, although the angels' announcement of His birth in Bethlehem was made with the words, "On earth peace, good will toward men" (see Luke 2:14), and the messianic kingdom spoken of by the prophets (Isa. 9:6-7 and note, "The Son of God") and expected by the Israelites (Ps. 72:7) was to be one of peace, there would not be peace on the earth. Because of His rejection by His people Israel, peace would not come to earth until He should be accepted as King and should reign. The sword (division between people over who Christ was), rather than peace, would be the result of the gospel message.

10:35 to set a man at variance. See Micah 7:6.
11:5 The blind receive their sight. See Isaiah 35:5-7.

[9]But what went ye out for to see? A
prophet? yea, I say unto you, and more
than a prophet.

O.T. prophecy fulfilled (9)

[10]For this is *he,* of whom it is written,
Behold, I send my messenger before
thy face, which shall prepare thy way
before thee.
[11]Verily I say unto you, Among them
that are born of women there hath not
risen a greater than *John the Baptist:
notwithstanding he that is least in the
kingdom of heaven is greater than he.
[12]And from the days of John the Baptist until now the kingdom of heaven
suffereth violence, and the violent take
it by force.
[13]For all the *prophets and the *law
prophesied until John.
[14]And if ye will receive *it,* this is
*Elias, which was for to come.
[15]He that hath ears to hear, let him
hear.
¶[16]But whereunto shall I liken this
generation? It is like unto children sitting in the markets, and calling unto
their fellows,
[17]And saying, We have piped unto
you, and ye have not danced; we have
mourned unto you, and ye have not lamented.
[18]For John came neither eating nor
drinking, and they say, He hath a *devil.
[19]The Son of man came eating and
drinking, and they say, Behold a man
gluttonous, and a winebibber, a friend of
publicans and sinners. But wisdom is
justified of her children.

(25) Christ predicts judgment

¶[20]Then began he to upbraid the cities wherein most of his mighty works
were done, because they *repented not:
[21]Woe unto thee, Chorazin! woe unto
thee, Bethsaida! for if the mighty works,
which were done in you, had been done
in *Tyre and Sidon, they would have repented long ago in sackcloth and ashes.
[22]But I say unto you, It shall be more
tolerable for Tyre and Sidon at the day
of *judgment, than for you.
[23]And thou, Capernaum, which art
exalted unto heaven, shalt be brought
down to *hell: for if the mighty works,
which have been done in thee, had been

11:11 THE KINGDOM OF HEAVEN

John the Baptist received higher commendation from our Lord than any other man who ever lived. Nevertheless, John lived in the old dispensation, he was the last of the Old Testament prophets, and while he was the greatest of them all, his position in the sight of God was not comparable to that of any member of the body or bride of Christ. The Old Testament saints are saved through faith in God's Word, and by the blood, but they do not compose the church, which is a New Testament revelation.

We who make up the bride of Christ have a higher spiritual position through God's grace than any others, and it is to this our Lord was referring. The common application is generally that our Lord speaks here of the church age, and that the least in this present dispensation is greater than John in the old dispensation. We as Christian believers are higher in our standing than the Old Testament saints; however, we believe the primary meaning of the passage is not this.

What does our Lord mean by the kingdom of heaven as it is used here? It is not until the thirteenth chapter of this Gospel when the mystery parables are presented that the kingdom of heaven refers to this present age. At the time in which the events in chapter eleven took place, the earthly kingdom was still being offered by our Lord. Thus the least who is in the kingdom of heaven spoken of here, when it shall at last come, will be greater than John, who was the announcer of the coming kingdom. Our Lord's reference foreshadows the glories of the coming kingdom age, when the little one will be greater on earth in God's sight than John the Baptist could ever be here in the world.

11:10 of whom it is written. See Isaiah 40:3; Malachi 3:1.
11:14 Elias. Elijah; see Matthew 17:10-13.

done in Sodom, it would have remained
until this day.
24But I say unto you, That it shall be
more tolerable for the land of Sodom in
the day of judgment, than for thee.
¶25At that time Jesus answered and
said, I thank thee, O Father, Lord of
heaven and earth, because thou hast hid
these things from the wise and prudent,
and hast revealed them unto babes.
26Even so, Father: for so it seemed
good in thy sight.
27All things are delivered unto me of
my Father: and no man knoweth the Son,
but the Father; neither knoweth any
man the Father, save the Son, and *he* to
whomsoever the Son will reveal *him.*

C. The New Message of the King
(1) "Come unto Me"

¶28Come unto me, all *ye* that labour and
are heavy laden, and I will give you rest.
29Take my yoke upon you, and learn
of me; for I am meek and lowly in heart:
and ye shall find rest unto your souls.
30For my yoke *is* easy, and my burden
is light.

(2) The Son of Man Lord of the Sabbath
(Mark 2:23-28; Luke 6:1-5)

12 At that time Jesus went on the
sabbath day through the corn;
and his disciples were an hungred, and
began to pluck the ears of corn, and to
eat.
2But when the Pharisees saw *it,* they
said unto him, Behold, thy disciples do
that which is not lawful to do upon the
sabbath day.
3But he said unto them, Have ye not
read what David did, when he was an
hungred, and they that were with him;
4How he entered into the house of
God, and did eat the *shewbread, which

12:2 THE SABBATH DAY

"Sabbath" means *to rest.* The seventh day was the day on which God rested after Creation (Gen. 2:1-3), which He made known to Israel at Sinai (Neh. 9:14). The Sabbath was used as a sign for Israel, as was circumcision, to distinguish them as God's peculiar people—the first was a spiritual sign and the second a physical sign. The *Pharisees prided themselves for their observance of all the Mosaic commands and additional injunctions added by the elders.

Is the Christian required to keep the Sabbath? The Christian observes Sunday, the first day of the week as a day set aside for special worship, rejoicing, and fellowship with other Christians (Acts 20:7; 1 Cor. 16:2). The first day of the week, the day of the Resurrection, has been kept in memory of our Lord, who was raised from the dead and who is seated at the Father's right hand in heaven. Sunday is not the Sabbath; although it is often spoken of as the Sabbath day. There is no law for the Christian to keep Sunday as the Lord's Day; it is a liberty that Christians, who have been called to liberty, enjoy (Gal. 5:13). Israel was commanded to keep the Sabbath; Christians are privileged to enjoy the Lord's Day. As the Sabbath was a commemoration or a remembrance of a finished creation (and divine release, Deut. 5:15), so the Lord's Day, Sunday, commemorates a finished redemption.

11:25 wise and prudent. Those who were wise in their own eyes. See 1 Corinthians 1:26-29.

11:27 no man knoweth the Son, but the Father. See Matthew 16:16-18 and 16:18 note, "Peter."

11:27 save the Son. Except the Son. See John 14:6.

11:28 all ye that labour. This gracious invitation of our Lord reached out beyond Israel to the needy and sin-burdened of every nationality.

12:2 which is not lawful to do upon the sabbath day. The accusation is not against what the disciples were doing but rather against when they were doing it. It was permissible by Jewish Law for a man to pluck corn or fruit for his own immediate need from anyone's field (Deut. 23:24-25), but he was not permitted to move a sickle into his neighbor's corn; that is, he could not take more than his personal need. The accusation was against the disciples' plucking the corn on the Sabbath, for this would be considered labor and would be contrary to the Mosaic Law found in Exodus 20:10.

12:3 what David did. The record is found in 1 Samuel 21:1-6. David, God's anointed, was

was not lawful for him to eat, neither for
them which were with him, but only for
the priests?
5Or have ye not read in the law, how
that on the sabbath days the priests in
the temple profane the sabbath, and are
*blameless?
6But I say unto you, That in this place
is *one* greater than the temple.
7But if ye had known what *this*
meaneth, I will have *mercy, and not
sacrifice, ye would not have condemned
the guiltless.
8For the Son of man is Lord even of
the sabbath day.

(3) A miracle (11)—The man with the withered hand healed, and other miracles (Mark 3:1-6; Luke 6:6-11)

¶9And when he was departed thence,
he went into their *synagogue:
10And, behold, there was a man which
had *his* hand withered. And they asked
him, saying, Is it lawful to heal on the
sabbath days? that they might accuse
him.
11And he said unto them, What man
shall there be among you, that shall
have one sheep, and if it fall into a pit
on the sabbath day, will he not lay hold
on it, and lift *it* out?
12How much then is a man better
than a sheep? Wherefore it is lawful to
do well on the sabbath days.
13Then saith he to the man, Stretch
forth thine hand. And he stretched *it*
forth; and it was restored whole, like as
the other.
¶14Then the Pharisees went out, and
held a council against him, how they
might destroy him.
15But when Jesus knew *it,* he withdrew himself from thence: and great
multitudes followed him, and he healed
them all;
16And charged them that they should
not make him known:

O.T. prophecy fulfilled (10)

17That it might be fulfilled which was
spoken by Esaias the prophet, saying,
18Behold my servant, whom I have
chosen; my beloved, in whom my soul
is well pleased: I will put my spirit upon
him, and he shall shew judgment to the
Gentiles.
19He shall not strive, nor cry; neither
shall any man hear his voice in the
streets.
20A bruised reed shall he not break,
and smoking flax shall he not quench,
till he send forth judgment unto victory.
21And in his name shall the Gentiles
*trust.

(4) A miracle (12)—Another demon-possessed man is healed (Mark 3:22-30; Luke 11:14-23)

¶22Then was brought unto him one
possessed with a devil, blind, and dumb:
and he healed him, insomuch that the
blind and dumb both spake and saw.
23And all the people were amazed,

---

being persecuted by Saul. He was a fugitive and rejected by Israel. When he was hungry, he ate of the *shewbread, which was unlawful. In rejecting David, God's anointed, Israel was out of God's will and sinning against His Word. When this happens, holy ceremonies cease to be holy (1 Sam. 15:22), and thus the consecrated shewbread became common in God's sight (1 Sam. 21:5). Remember that this same observance by the priests was still going on in Jerusalem when our Lord spoke (see vs. 5).

12:5 profane. See Numbers 28:9-10. The priests and duties of the temple profaned the Sabbath.

12:6 greater than the temple. See 2 Chronicles 6:18; Isaiah 66:1-2.

12:7 I will have mercy, and not sacrifice. See 1 Samuel 15:22; Hosea 6:6.

12:17 That it might be fulfilled. See Isaiah 42:1-4. Esaias is the Greek form of Isaiah.

12:18 Gentiles. Here and in verse 21 is a clear indication that the ministry of Christ in all its fullness was to reach out beyond Israel to other nations.

12:23 Is not this the son of David? Obviously many people were ready to believe that

and said, Is not this the *son of David?
24But when the Pharisees heard *it,*
they said, This *fellow* doth not cast out
devils, but by Beelzebub the prince of
the devils.
25And Jesus knew their thoughts, and
said unto them, Every kingdom divided against itself is brought to desolation; and every city or house divided
against itself shall not stand:
26And if *Satan cast out Satan, he is
divided against himself; how shall then
his kingdom stand?
27And if I by Beelzebub cast out
devils, by whom do your children cast
them out? therefore they shall be your
judges.
28But if I cast out devils by the Spirit
of God, then the *kingdom of God is
come unto you.
29Or else how can one enter into a
strong man's house, and spoil his
goods, except he first bind the strong
man? and then he will spoil his house.
30He that is not with me is against
me; and he that gathereth not with me
scattereth abroad.

(5) The sin of blasphemy
(Mark 3:29-30)

¶31Wherefore I say unto you, All
manner of *sin and blasphemy shall be
forgiven unto men: but the blasphemy
against the *Holy* Ghost shall not be forgiven unto men.
32And whosoever speaketh a word
against the Son of man, it shall be forgiven him: but whosoever speaketh
against the Holy Ghost, it shall not be
forgiven him, neither in this *world,
neither in the *world* to come.
33Either make the tree good, and his
fruit good; or else make the tree corrupt, and his fruit corrupt: for the tree
is known by *his* fruit.
34O generation of vipers, how can ye,
being evil, speak good things? for out
of the abundance of the heart the mouth
speaketh.
35A good man out of the good treasure of the heart bringeth forth good
things: and an evil man out of the evil
treasure bringeth forth evil things.
36But I say unto you, That every idle
word that men shall speak, they shall
give account thereof in the day of judgment.
37For by thy words thou shalt be justified, and by thy words thou shalt be
condemned.

(6) The sign of Jonah
(Luke 11:29-44)

¶38Then certain of the scribes and of
the Pharisees answered, saying, Master, we would see a sign from thee.
39But he answered and said unto
them, An evil and adulterous generation seeketh after a sign; and there shall
no sign be given to it, but the sign of the
prophet Jonas:

12:31 The "Unpardonable Sin"
Verses 31 and 32 have troubled many Christians who have wondered whether they may have committed what they call "the unpardonable sin." What the Spirit of God describes here as unforgivable is to speak against the Holy Ghost (vs. 32). Since the blood of Christ shed on Calvary is able to cleanse us from every sin, there can be no one specific sin that cannot be forgiven except unbelief. The indication is that it is possible to initially reject God the Father, and yet come to know God through God the Son. It is also possible to initially reject the Lord Jesus Christ, and yet, convicted of sin by the Holy Spirit, be brought in the end to know Christ as Saviour. But if a man rejects God the Father and God the Son, and further closes his heart to the pleading of the Holy Spirit, then there is no way for him to be made righteous before God, for there can be no hope other than through the finished work of Christ and the convicting power of the Holy Spirit.

---

our Lord was the Messiah and waited for the religious leaders to guide them, but the latter were blind leaders of the blind (Matt. 15:14).
12:27 children. Compare Luke 9:49-50; 10:17.

40For as Jonas was three days and
three nights in the whale's belly; so
shall the Son of man be three days and
three nights in the heart of the earth.
41The men of Nineveh shall rise in
judgment with this generation, and
shall condemn it: because they repented at the preaching of Jonas; and, behold, a greater than Jonas *is* here.
42The queen of the south shall rise up
in the judgment with this generation,
and shall condemn it: for she came from
the uttermost parts of the earth to hear
the wisdom of Solomon; and, behold, a
greater than Solomon *is* here.

(7) The parable of the unclean spirit (3) (Luke 11:24-26)

43When the unclean spirit is gone
out of a man, he walketh through dry

12:36 THE SEVEN GREAT JUDGMENTS

When we read the word "judgment" in the Bible, or when we read about a judgment to come (even though the word itself may not be used), there are certain questions we should consider, since there are a number of "judgments" spoken of in God's Word.

The questions are these:

1. Where does the judgment take place?
2. When does the judgment take place?
3. Who or what is it that is to be judged?
4. Who is the judge?
5. What is the result of the judgment?

There are seven great judgments:

1. The judgment of believers' sins. This took place on the earth two thousand years ago when our Lord was made sin for us on the cross of Calvary. God the Father was there judging the sin of the world and the result is that "there is therefore now no condemnation [judgment] to them which are in Christ Jesus" (Rom. 8:1; see also John 5:24; Rom. 5:9; Gal. 3:13).

2. The believers' self-judgment. This is to take place while we are here on earth. We are to judge ourselves, with the result of a life more yielded to the Lord (1 Cor. 11:31; Heb. 12:7).

3. The judgment of believers' works. This will take place in the air when the church will be caught up at the *Rapture, when every child of God, raised at the Rapture shout, will have his work displayed before our Lord Jesus Christ—for reward or for loss (1 Cor. 3:11-15; 2 Cor. 5:10; Col. 3:24; 2 Tim. 4:8).

4. The judgment of nations. This will take place on the earth when our Lord returns in power to reign. Members of the Gentile nations will be judged by our Lord the King as to how they treated Israel. The sheep, those who have treated the nation of Israel righteously, will be put on His right hand to inherit kingdom blessing while the goats will be outside the kingdom in everlasting punishment (25:31-46).

5. The judgment of Israel. This is to take place under the eye of the Lord Jesus Christ, the Son of David, the true Messiah and King, to determine who of the nation of Israel will enter the land when His reign begins (Ps. 50:1-7; Ezek. 20: 33-44; Mal. 3:2-5; 4:1-2).

6. The judgment of angels. The judgment of Satan and his angels will take place after the *Millennium when Satan will have been loosed for a little while, and that judgment will result in him and his angels being cast into the lake of fire and brimstone prepared for them (Matt. 25:41; 2 Pet. 2:4; Jude 6; Rev. 20:10). Christians will have a part in this judgment.

7. The judgment of the Great White Throne. It will take place before God, when the thousand years have passed and Satan and his angels have been judged. Those who have died in unbelief will stand before the Great White Throne to be judged "according to their works . . . and whosoever was not found written in the book of life was cast into the lake of fire" (Rev. 20:11-15).

12:40 as Jonas was three days and three nights in the whale's belly. Our Lord here declared as fact what the Old Testament records about Jonah.
12:42 The queen of the south. The queen of Sheba (2 Chron. 9:1-12).
12:43 unclean spirit. A demon.

places, seeking rest, and findeth none.
44Then he saith, I will return into my
house from whence I came out; and
when he is come, he findeth *it* empty,
swept, and garnished.
45Then goeth he, and taketh with himself seven other spirits more wicked
than himself, and they enter in and dwell
there: and the last *state* of that man is
worse than the first. Even so shall it be
also unto this wicked generation.
¶46While he yet talked to the people,
behold, *his* mother and his brethren stood
without, desiring to speak with him.
47Then one said unto him, Behold,
thy mother and thy brethren stand
without, desiring to speak with thee.
48But he answered and said unto him
that told him, Who is my mother? and
who are my brethren?
49And he stretched forth his hand
toward his disciples, and said, Behold
my mother and my brethren!

(8) Christ defines relationship to Himself

50For whosoever shall do the will of
my Father which is in heaven, the same
is my brother, and sister, and mother.

D. The Mysteries of the Kingdom

13 The same day went Jesus out
of the house, and sat by the sea
side.
2And great multitudes were gathered
together unto him, so that he went into
a ship, and sat; and the whole multitude
stood on the shore.

(1) The parable of the sower (4) (Mark 4:1-20; Luke 8:4-15)

3And he spake many things unto
them in *parables, saying, Behold, a
sower went forth to sow;
4And when he sowed, some *seeds* fell
by the way side, and the fowls came and
devoured them up:
5Some fell upon stony places, where
they had not much earth: and forthwith
they sprung up, because they had no
deepness of earth:
6And when the sun was up, they were
scorched; and because they had no root,
they withered away.
7And some fell among thorns; and the
thorns sprung up, and choked them:
8But other fell into good ground, and
brought forth fruit, some an hundredfold, some sixtyfold, some thirtyfold.
9Who hath ears to hear, let him hear.
10And the disciples came, and said
unto him, Why speakest thou unto them
in parables?
11He answered and said unto them,
Because it is given unto you to know the
*mysteries of the kingdom of heaven,
but to them it is not given.
12For whosoever hath, to him shall be
given, and he shall have more abundance: but whosoever hath not, from
him shall be taken away even that he
hath.
13Therefore speak I to them in parables: because they seeing see not; and
hearing they hear not, neither do they
understand.

O.T. prophecy fulfilled (11)

14And in them is fulfilled the *prophecy of Esaias, which saith, By hearing
ye shall hear, and shall not understand;
and seeing ye shall see, and shall not
perceive:
15For this people's heart is waxed
gross, and *their* ears are dull of hearing,
and their eyes they have closed; lest at
any time they should see with *their* eyes,
and hear with *their* ears, and should understand with *their* heart, and should be
converted, and I should heal them.
16But blessed *are* your eyes, for they
see: and your ears, for they hear.
17For verily I say unto you, That
many prophets and righteous *men* have
desired to see *those things* which ye see,
and have not seen *them;* and to hear
those things which ye hear, and have not
heard *them.*

13:14 which saith. See Isaiah 6:9-10.

(2) The parable of the sower interpreted by Christ

¶18 Hear ye therefore the *parable of
the sower.
19 When any one heareth the word of
the kingdom, and understandeth *it* not,
then cometh the wicked *one,* and
catcheth away that which was sown in
his heart. This is he which received
seed by the way side.
20 But he that received the seed into
stony places, the same is he that heareth
the word, and anon with joy receiveth it;
21 Yet hath he not root in himself, but
dureth for a while: for when tribulation
or persecution ariseth because of the
word, by and by he is offended.
22 He also that received seed among
the thorns is he that heareth the word;
and the care of this world, and the deceitfulness of riches, choke the word,
and he becometh unfruitful.
23 But he that received seed into the
good ground is he that heareth the
word, and understandeth *it;* which also
beareth fruit, and bringeth forth, some
an hundredfold, some sixty, some thirty.

(3) The parable of the wheat and the tares (5) (vss. 24-30,36-43)

¶24 Another parable put he forth unto
them, saying, The kingdom of heaven
is likened unto a man which sowed good
seed in his field:
25 But while men slept, his enemy
came and sowed tares among the
wheat, and went his way.
26 But when the blade was sprung up,
and brought forth fruit, then appeared
the tares also.
27 So the servants of the householder
came and said unto him, Sir, didst not
thou sow good seed in thy field? from
whence then hath it tares?
28 He said unto them, An enemy hath

13:11 THE MYSTERIES OF THE KINGDOM

A mystery in the New Testament is not something mysterious, but a secret of divine truth that the Holy Spirit reveals to His believing servants and enables them to pass on to others.

The mysteries of the kingdom of heaven and the kingdom of heaven presented by John the Baptist and by our Lord in His early ministry have different meanings. The kingdom of heaven that was declared "at hand" (Matt. 3:2; 10:7) was the messianic earthly reign of the Son of David spoken of by the prophets, namely, Isaiah, Jeremiah, Ezekiel, Daniel, Hosea, etc. But the mysteries of the kingdom of heaven referred to in this chapter do not speak of the messianic earthly reign of Christ. Our Lord Himself taught this. See verse 17–certainly the prophets and righteous men were given to see and to hear of the messianic earthly reign of the Son of David. Refer to verses 34 and 35–assuredly, the messianic earthly reign of David's Son had not been kept "secret from the foundation of the world." Therefore, the mysteries of the kingdom of heaven must refer to something entirely new that was not known in ancient times.

Does the expression used here by our Lord, "the mysteries of the kingdom of heaven," mean, as some suggest, the *church? No–if by "church" one means the body of believers in Christ as the Saviour from sin. For according to our Lord's own interpretation of the second parable, that of the wheat and the tares (vss. 24-30 and 36-43), the tares indicate the children of Satan who will grow with the children of the kingdom until the end of the age. The kingdom of heaven referred to here cannot mean the church, then, for in the body of Christ there can never be children of Satan. All members of the church, in the strictest use of the word, are born-again believers in Christ, and as such are children of God, and not of Satan.

We can conclude that the revealing of the mysteries of the kingdom of heaven refers to a purely divine revelation for the disciples not previously revealed to the world at large. The purpose of the Lord's parables was to reveal and to conceal a matter–to those who cherished the truth, the mysteries would reveal something new and impressive. But to those who were insensitive to spiritual matters these mysteries would remain impenetrable (Matt. 13:13).

13:20 anon. Immediately.

done this. The servants said unto him,
Wilt thou then that we go and gather
them up?
29 But he said, Nay; lest while ye gather up the tares, ye root up also the wheat
with them.
30 Let both grow together until the
harvest: and in the time of harvest I will
say to the reapers, Gather ye together
first the tares, and bind them in bundles
to burn them: but gather the wheat into
my barn.

(4) The parable of the mustard seed (6)
(Mark 4:30-32)

¶31 Another parable put he forth unto
them, saying, The kingdom of heaven is
like to a grain of mustard seed, which a
man took, and sowed in his field:
32 Which indeed is the least of all
seeds: but when it is grown, it is the
greatest among herbs, and becometh a
tree, so that the birds of the air come
and lodge in the branches thereof.

(5) The parable of the leaven (7)
(Luke 13:20-21)

¶33 Another parable spake he unto
them; The kingdom of heaven is like
unto *leaven, which a woman took, and
hid in three measures of meal, till the
whole was *leavened.

(6) The reasons for the parables

34 All these things spake Jesus unto
the multitude in parables; and without a parable spake he not unto them:
35 That it might be fulfilled which was
spoken by the prophet, saying, I will
open my mouth in parables; I will utter
things which have been kept secret
from the foundation of the world.

(7) The parable of the wheat
and the tares
(vss. 24-30) interpreted

36 Then Jesus sent the multitude
away, and went into the house: and his
disciples came unto him, saying, Declare unto us the parable of the tares of
the field.
37 He answered and said unto them,
He that soweth the good seed is the
Son of man;
38 The field is the world; the good
seed are the children of the kingdom;
but the tares are the children of the
wicked *one;*
39 The enemy that sowed them is the
devil; the harvest is the end of the
world; and the reapers are the *angels.
40 As therefore the tares are gathered
and burned in the *fire; so shall it be in
the end of this world.
41 The Son of man shall send forth his
angels, and they shall gather out of his
kingdom all things that *offend, and
them which do iniquity;
42 And shall cast them into a furnace
of fire: there shall be wailing and gnashing of teeth.
43 Then shall the righteous shine forth

13:31 Another parable. To interpret any of these parables, we must begin by following our Lord's interpretation of the first two. If the field in the parable of the wheat and the tares is the world (vs. 38), then undoubtedly the field speaks of the world in every one of these parables in which it appears. Where we have expressions not directly interpreted by Christ in the first two parables, the only safe way of interpretation is to search other Scriptures for the meanings of the words or figures of speech.
13:32 birds of the air. Compare with "fowls" in verse 4 and Revelation 18:2.
13:33 leaven. Refer to Matthew 16:11-12; 1 Corinthians 5:6-7. See also *leaven.
13:33 woman. Some people believe that the *church is spoken of here, but the church is never referred to as a woman. It is rather the great ecumenical movement of the world—see the message to the church at Thyatira (Rev. 2:18-29).
13:33 meal. Meal (flour) comes from wheat and not from tares. For symbolism, compare Leviticus 2:1.
13:35 That it might be fulfilled. See Psalm 78:2.
13:35 world. Mankind.
13:39 end of the world. End of the age.

as the sun in the kingdom of their Father. Who hath ears to hear, let him hear.

(8) The parable of the hid treasure (8)

¶44 Again, the kingdom of heaven is
like unto treasure hid in a field; the which
when a man hath found, he hideth, and
for joy thereof goeth and selleth all that
he hath, and buyeth that field.

(9) The parable of the pearl of great price (9)

¶45 Again, the kingdom of heaven is
like unto a merchant man, seeking
goodly pearls:
46 Who, when he had found one pearl
of great price, went and sold all that he
had, and bought it.

(10) The parable of the dragnet (10)

¶47 Again, the kingdom of heaven is
like unto a net, that was cast into the
sea, and gathered of every kind:
48 Which, when it was full, they drew
to shore, and sat down, and gathered the
good into vessels, but cast the bad away.
49 So shall it be at the end of the
world: the angels shall come forth, and
sever the wicked from among the *just,
50 And shall cast them into the furnace
of fire: there shall be wailing and gnashing of teeth.

(11) The parable of the householder that bringeth forth treasure (11)

51 Jesus saith unto them, Have ye
understood all these things? They say
unto him, Yea, Lord.
52 Then said he unto them, Therefore
every scribe *which is* instructed unto
the kingdom of heaven is like unto a
man *that is* an householder, which
bringeth forth out of his treasure *things*
new and old.

(12) Unbelief in Nazareth (Mark 6:1-6; cf. Luke 4:16-32)

¶53 And it came to pass, *that* when
Jesus had finished these parables, he
departed thence.
54 And when he was come into his own
country, he taught them in their synagogue, insomuch that they were astonished, and said, Whence hath this *man*
this wisdom, and *these* mighty works?
55 Is not this the carpenter's son? is
not his mother called Mary? and his
brethren, James, and Joses, and Simon,
and Judas?
56 And his sisters, are they not all with
us? Whence then hath this *man* all
these things?
57 And they were offended in him. But
Jesus said unto them, A prophet is not
without honour, save in his own country, and in his own house.
58 And he did not many mighty works
there because of their unbelief.

E. The Ministry of the Rejected King

(1) Herod hears of Christ's mighty works

14 At that time *Herod the tetrarch
heard of the fame of Jesus,
2 And said unto his servants, This is
*John the Baptist; he is risen from the
dead; and therefore mighty works do
shew forth themselves in him.

(2) How John the Baptist was slain (Mark 6:14-29; Luke 9:7-9)

¶3 For Herod had laid hold on John,
and bound him, and put *him* in prison for

13:43 kingdom of their Father. See 1 Corinthians 15:24 and its note, "The Kingdom." This will be after the millennial reign of Christ is completed.
13:44 treasure. In one way, this can refer to Israel (see Exod. 19:5).
13:44 a man. The Son of Man, as in the second parable.
13:57 offended in him. See Matthew 11:6 and its note. The people of Jesus' hometown of Nazareth would not believe in Him. He could not do many miracles there because of their hardness of heart and unbelief (vs. 58).
14:1 Herod the tetrarch. Brother of Archelaus (see Matt. 2:22).
14:3 Herod had laid hold on John. Verses 3-12 are a parenthesis. This event occurred some months before those recorded in the rest of the chapter.

Herodias' sake, his brother Philip's wife.
[4]For John said unto him, It is not lawful for thee to have her.
[5]And when he would have put him to
death, he feared the multitude, because
they counted him as a *prophet.
[6]But when Herod's birthday was
kept, the daughter of Herodias danced
before them, and pleased Herod.
[7]Whereupon he promised with an
oath to give her whatsoever she would
ask.
[8]And she, being before instructed of
her mother, said, Give me here John
Baptist's head in a charger.
[9]And the king was sorry: nevertheless for the oath's sake, and them which
sat with him at meat, he commanded *it*
to be given *her.*
[10]And he sent, and beheaded John in
the prison.
[11]And his head was brought in a
charger, and given to the damsel: and
she brought *it* to her mother.
[12]And his disciples came, and took up
the body, and buried it, and went and
told Jesus.

(3) A miracle (13)—The feeding of the five thousand (Mark 6:30-44; Luke 9:10-17; John 6:1-14)

¶[13]When Jesus heard *of it,* he departed thence by ship into a desert place
apart: and when the people had heard
thereof, they followed him on foot out of
the cities.
[14]And Jesus went forth, and saw a
great multitude, and was moved with
compassion toward them, and he healed
their sick.
¶[15]And when it was evening, his disciples came to him, saying, This is a
desert place, and the time is now past;
send the multitude away, that they may
go into the villages, and buy themselves
victuals.
[16]But Jesus said unto them, They
need not depart; *give ye them to eat.
[17]And they say unto him, We have
here but five loaves, and two fishes.
[18]He said, Bring them hither to me.
[19]And he commanded the multitude
to sit down on the grass, and took the
five loaves, and the two fishes, and
looking up to heaven, he blessed, and
brake, and gave the loaves to *his* disciples, and the disciples to the multitude.
[20]And they did all eat, and were filled:
and they took up of the fragments that
remained twelve baskets full.
[21]And they that had eaten were about
five thousand men, beside women and
children.

(4) A miracle (14)—Our Lord walks on the water (Mark 6:45-56; John 6:15-21)

¶[22]And *straightway Jesus constrained his disciples to get into a ship,
and to go before him unto the other
side, while he sent the multitudes away.
[23]And when he had sent the multitudes away, he went up into a mountain
apart to pray: and when the evening was
come, he was there alone.
[24]But the ship was now in the midst
of the sea, tossed with waves: for the
wind was contrary.
[25]And in the fourth watch of the night
Jesus went unto them, walking on the
sea.
[26]And when the disciples saw him
walking on the sea, they were troubled,
saying, It is a spirit; and they cried out
for fear.
[27]But straightway Jesus spake unto
them, saying, Be of good cheer; it is I;
be not *afraid.
[28]And Peter answered him and said,
Lord, if it be thou, bid me come unto
thee on the water.
[29]And he said, Come. And when Peter was come down out of the ship, he
walked on the water, to go to Jesus.
[30]But when he saw the wind bois-
terous, he was afraid; and beginning

14:3 Herodias. The wife of Herod's half brother Philip.

to sink, he cried, saying, Lord, save me.
31And immediately Jesus stretched
forth *his* hand, and caught him, and said
unto him, O thou of little *faith, wherefore didst thou doubt?
32And when they were come into the
ship, the wind ceased.
33Then they that were in the ship
came and worshipped him, saying, Of a
truth thou art the Son of *God.
¶34And when they were gone over,
they came into the land of Gennesaret.
35And when the men of that place had
knowledge of him, they sent out into all
that country round about, and brought
unto him all that were diseased;
36And besought him that they might
only touch the hem of his garment: and
as many as touched were made perfectly whole.

(5) The scribes and Pharisees question Christ about his disciples

15 Then came to Jesus *scribes
and *Pharisees, which were of
*Jerusalem, saying,
2Why do thy disciples transgress the
*tradition of the *elders? for they wash
not their hands when they eat bread.

(6) The Lord Jesus answers and rebukes the scribes and Pharisees (Mark 7:1-23)

3But he answered and said unto
them, Why do ye also transgress the
commandment of God by your tradition?
4For God commanded, saying,
Honour thy father and mother: and, He
that curseth father or mother, let him
die the death.
5But ye say, Whosoever shall say to
his father or *his* mother, *It is* a gift, by
whatsoever thou mightest be profited
by me;
6And honour not his father or his
mother, *he shall be free.* Thus have ye
made the commandment of God of none
effect by your tradition.

O.T. prophecy fulfilled (12)

7*Ye* hypocrites, well did Esaias prophesy of you, saying,
8This people draweth nigh unto
me with their mouth, and honoureth
me with *their* lips; but their heart is far
from me.
9But in vain they do worship me,
teaching *for* doctrines the commandments of men.
¶10And he called the multitude, and
said unto them, Hear, and understand:

(7) The parable of man's defilement (12)

11Not that which goeth into the
mouth defileth a man; but that which
cometh out of the mouth, this defileth
a man.
12Then came his disciples, and said
unto him, Knowest thou that the Phar-

15:2 THE TRADITION OF THE ELDERS

The Jews of our Lord's time had two sets of laws:

1. the Mosaic Law, which is written in the Old Testament Scriptures;
2. the oral law passed down by word of mouth and at length written in the Talmud. This second set of laws was filled with ceremonial rites far more strict than the Mosaic ordinances, and it included additional teachings known as "the tradition of the elders." The *scribes and *Pharisees spent most of their time observing these various traditions and considered anyone unclean who failed to abide by these laws to the very letter. While they were strict in observing ceremony, in many cases their hearts were not right toward God.

14:33 Son of God. See Matthew 16:16; 27:54.
15:3 commandment of God. See Matthew 23:23; John 18:28.
15:4 God commanded, saying. See Exodus 20:12; Jeremiah 35:6,8,14,18-19.
15:5 a gift. See Mark 7:11 note.
15:7 well did Esaias prophecy of you, saying. See Isaiah 29:13.

isees were offended, after they heard
this saying?
[13]But he answered and said, Every
plant, which my heavenly Father hath
not planted, shall be rooted up.
[14]Let them alone: they be blind leaders of the blind. And if the blind lead the
blind, both shall fall into the ditch.

(8) Jesus explains the parable

[15]Then answered Peter and said unto
him, Declare unto us this parable.
[16]And Jesus said, Are ye also yet
without understanding?
[17]Do not ye yet understand, that
whatsoever entereth in at the mouth
goeth into the belly, and is cast out into
the draught?
[18]But those things which proceed out
of the mouth come forth from the heart;
and they defile the man.
[19]For out of the heart proceed evil
thoughts, murders, adulteries, fornications, thefts, false witness, blasphemies:
[20]These are *the things* which defile a
man: but to eat with unwashen hands
defileth not a man.
¶[21]Then Jesus went thence, and departed into the coasts of Tyre and Sidon.

(9) A miracle (15)—The healing of the daughter of the woman of Canaan (Mark 7:24-30)

[22]And, behold, a woman of Canaan
came out of the same coasts, and cried
unto him, saying, Have mercy on me,
O Lord, *thou* *Son of *David; my daughter is grievously vexed with a devil.
[23]But he answered her not a word.
And his disciples came and besought
him, saying, Send her away; for she
crieth after us.
[24]But he answered and said, I am
not sent but unto the lost sheep of the
house of *Israel.
[25]Then came she and worshipped
him, saying, Lord, help me.
[26]But he answered and said, It is not
meet to take the children's bread, and
to cast *it* to dogs.
[27]And she said, Truth, Lord: yet the
dogs eat of the crumbs which fall from
their masters' table.
[28]Then Jesus answered and said unto
her, O woman, great *is* thy faith: be it
unto thee even as thou wilt. And her
daughter was made whole from that
very hour.

(10) Further miracles of healing (cf. Mark 7:31-37)

[29]And Jesus departed from thence,
and came nigh unto the sea of Galilee;
and went up into a mountain, and sat
down there.
[30]And great multitudes came unto
him, having with them *those that were*
lame, blind, dumb, maimed, and many
others, and cast them down at Jesus'
feet; and he healed them:
[31]Insomuch that the multitude wondered, when they saw the dumb to
speak, the maimed to be whole, the
lame to walk, and the blind to see: and
they glorified the God of Israel.

(11) A miracle (16)—The feeding of the four thousand (Mark 8:1-9)

¶[32]Then Jesus called his disciples
unto him, and said, I have compassion
on the multitude, because they continue with me now three days, and have
nothing to eat: and I will not send them
away fasting, lest they faint in the way.
[33]And his disciples say unto him,
Whence should we have so much bread
in the wilderness, as to fill so great a
multitude?
[34]And Jesus saith unto them, How

15:19 out of the heart proceed. Compare with Galatians 5:19-21.

15:21 into the coasts of Tyre and Sidon. Jesus began to minister here among the Gentiles.

15:26 dogs. The Jews referred to the Gentiles as "dogs," but our Lord softened the term by using an affectionate variation—"little dogs."

many loaves have ye? And they said,
Seven, and a few little fishes.
35And he commanded the multitude
to sit down on the ground.
36And he took the seven loaves and
the fishes, and gave thanks, and brake
them, and gave to his disciples, and the
disciples to the multitude.
37And they did all eat, and were filled:
and they took up of the broken *meat* that
was left seven baskets full.
38And they that did eat were four thousand men, beside women and children.
39And he sent away the multitude,
and took ship, and came into the coasts
of Magdala.

(12) The Pharisees and Sadducees seek a sign from Heaven (Mark 8:10-12)

16 The Pharisees also with the
*Sadducees came, and *tempt-
ing desired him that he would shew
them a sign from *heaven.
2He answered and said unto them,
When it is evening, ye say, *It will be* fair
weather: for the sky is red.
3And in the morning, *It will be* foul
weather to day: for the sky is red and
lowring. O *ye* hypocrites, ye can discern
the face of the sky; but can ye not *discern* the signs of the times?
4A wicked and adulterous generation
seeketh after a sign; and there shall no
sign be given unto it, but the sign of the
prophet Jonas. And he left them, and
departed.
5And when his disciples were come
to the other side, they had forgotten to
take bread.

(13) What leaven stands for (Mark 8:13-21)

¶6Then Jesus said unto them, Take
heed and beware of the *leaven of the
Pharisees and of the Sadducees.
7And they reasoned among themselves, saying, *It is* because we have
taken no bread.
8*Which* when Jesus perceived, he
said unto them, O ye of little faith, why
reason ye among yourselves, because
ye have brought no bread?
9Do ye not yet understand, neither
remember the five loaves of the five
thousand, and how many baskets ye
took up?
10Neither the seven loaves of the four
thousand, and how many baskets ye
took up?
11How is it that ye do not understand
that I spake *it* not to you concerning
bread, that ye should beware of the
leaven of the Pharisees and of the
Sadducees?
12Then understood they how that he
bade *them* not beware of the leaven of
bread, but of the *doctrine of the Pharisees and of the Sadducees.

(14) Simon Peter's great profession of faith (cf. Mark 8:27-30; Luke 9:18-21; John 6:68-69)

¶13When Jesus came into the coasts
of Caesarea Philippi, he asked his disciples, saying, Whom do men say that I
the Son of man am?
14And they said, Some *say that thou
art* John the Baptist: some, *Elias;
and others, Jeremias, or one of the
prophets.
15He saith unto them, But whom say
ye that I am?
16And Simon *Peter answered and
said, Thou art the Christ, the Son of the
living God.
17And Jesus answered and said unto
him, Blessed art thou, Simon Bar-jona:
for flesh and *blood hath not revealed
it unto thee, but my Father which is in
heaven.

16:1 desired . . . a sign from heaven. See Matthew 12:38-41.
16:14 Jeremias. Jeremiah.
16:17 Bar-jona. Son of Jonas or John.
16:17 flesh. See John 6:63.

(15) The Church mentioned for the first time

[18]And I say also unto thee, That thou art Peter, and upon this *rock I will build my *church; and the gates of hell shall not prevail against it.

16:18 Peter
Peter comes from the Greek *petros* meaning *a piece of rock; movable stone.* The word "rock" in this verse is translated from another Greek word, *petra,* meaning *a mass of rock, an essential rock.* Our Lord was not stating here that His *church would be built upon Simon Peter, but upon this essential rock, that is, the fact of His deity, which Peter had just confessed. The use of the word "rock" was understood by the Jews to whom our Lord was speaking. When Moses struck the rock in the wilderness (Exod. 17:6), the rock was a symbol of the Son of God as recorded in 1 Corinthians 10:4. Had the Lord meant that the church was to be founded on Peter, certainly the latter would have understood this promise; yet in his first Epistle (1 Pet. 2:3-8) Simon Peter indicated no such thing.

(16) The keys of the kingdom promised to Peter

[19]And I will give unto thee the keys of the *kingdom of heaven: and whatsoever thou shalt bind on earth shall be bound in heaven: and whatsoever thou shalt loose on earth shall be loosed in heaven.
[20]Then charged he his disciples that they should tell no man that he was Jesus the Christ.

(17) Our Lord announces His coming death and resurrection (1)
(Mark 8:31-38; Luke 9:22-27)

¶[21]From that time forth began Jesus to shew unto his disciples, how that he must go unto Jerusalem, and suffer many things of the elders and chief priests and scribes, and be killed, and be raised again the third day.

(18) Peter rebukes Christ and in turn is strongly rebuked

[22]Then Peter took him, and began to rebuke him, saying, Be it far from thee, Lord: this shall not be unto thee.
[23]But he turned, and said unto Peter, Get thee behind me, Satan: thou art an offence unto me: for thou savourest not the things that be of God, but those that be of men.

(19) The cost of discipleship

¶[24]Then said Jesus unto his disciples, If any *man* will come after me, let him deny himself, and take up his cross, and follow me.
[25]For whosoever will save his life shall lose it: and whosoever will lose his life for my sake shall find it.
[26]For what is a man profited, if he shall gain the whole world, and lose his own soul? or what shall a man give in exchange for his soul?
[27]For the Son of man shall come in the glory of his Father with his angels; and then he shall *reward every man according to his works.

(20) The promise of the coming kingdom
(Mark 9:2-13; Luke 9:28-36)

[28]Verily I say unto you, There be some standing here, which shall not taste of *death, till they see the Son of man coming in his kingdom.

16:19 keys. These are the keys, not of heaven, but of the kingdom of heaven. The kingdom of heaven, as we have seen from the mystery parables of chapter 13, in this age is not an earthly sphere. The keys must refer to the ways of telling the world about Christ, and Peter made use of the keys to the Israelites on the Day of Pentecost (Acts 2:1-41) and to the Gentiles (Acts 10).

16:19 whatsoever thou shalt bind on earth. See Matthew 18:18 and notice that the same authority was given to the other apostles.

16:27 according to his works. See Ephesians 2:8-9; Revelation 20:12-13; see also 20:12 note, "The Dead."

16:28 see the Son of man coming in his kingdom. See 17:2 note, "The Transfiguration."

(21) A miracle (17)—The
transfiguration of Christ

17 And after six days Jesus taketh
Peter, James, and John his
brother, and bringeth them up into an
high mountain apart,
2 And was transfigured before them:
and his face did shine as the sun, and his
raiment was white as the light.
3 And, behold, there appeared unto
them *Moses and Elias talking with
him.
4 Then answered Peter, and said unto
Jesus, Lord, it is good for us to be here:
if thou wilt, let us make here *three
tabernacles; one for thee, and one for
Moses, and one for Elias.
5 While he yet spake, behold, a bright
cloud overshadowed them: and behold
a voice out of the cloud, which said,
This is my beloved Son, in whom I am
well pleased; hear ye him.
6 And when the disciples heard *it,*
they fell on their face, and were sore
afraid.
7 And Jesus came and touched them,
and said, Arise, and *be not afraid.
8 And when they had lifted up their
eyes, they saw no man, save Jesus only.
9 And as they came down from the
mountain, Jesus charged them, saying,
Tell the vision to no man, until the Son
of man be risen again from the dead.
10 And his disciples asked him, saying,
Why then say the scribes that Elias
must first come?
11 And Jesus answered and said unto
them, Elias truly shall first come, and
restore all things.
12 But I say unto you, That Elias is
come already, and they knew him not,
but have done unto him whatsoever
they listed. Likewise shall also the Son
of man suffer of them.
13 Then the disciples understood that
he spake unto them of *John the Baptist.

17:2 THE TRANSFIGURATION

The scene of the glorious transfiguration of our Lord has a great prophetic significance. In 16:28 the Lord Jesus had promised that some of the people standing there would not taste of death until they saw Him coming in His kingdom. All of those who stood there have long been in their graves, and our Lord has not yet come. What did He mean then? In verse 1 we find that Peter, James, and John, who had been standing there, were taken up into the mountain and there saw our Lord transfigured, and all that accompanied the transfiguration.

There are five foreshadowings of the coming of our Lord in power:

1. the Lord Jesus Christ appeared in the body of His glory;
2. Moses was there as a type of those whom Christ will bring with Him (Jude 14; Rev. 19:11-16), who have died in faith and whose graves are the special care of the Lord;
3. Elias (Elijah), who was taken up into heaven in a whirlwind (2 Kings 2:11 and its note, "A Preview of the Rapture"), was there as a type of all those whom Christ will bring with Him who never died, because they will have been taken in the Rapture (1 Thess. 4:13-17; see also 4:13 note, "Hope for the Dead");
4. Peter, James, and John, present at this scene, typify the *remnant of Israel who shall see Christ coming in power (Rev. 1:7); and
5. the multitude at the foot of the mountain (vs. 14) typify the nations on earth when the kingdom is established.

The presence of Moses, typical of the Law, and of Elijah, symbolic of the prophets, is evidence of the fact that the Law and the Prophets bear witness to the truth that Jesus is the Son of God and that He will come in power to reign.

17:5 a bright cloud. See Exodus 40:34; Mark 9:7; Acts 1:9, and *Shekinah.
17:5 This is my beloved Son. See Matthew 3:17.
17:8 saw no man, save Jesus only. "Save" means *except.* See Hebrews 12:2.
17:11 Elias truly shall first come. See Malachi 4:5. However, John the Baptist had already come in the power of Elijah (Matt. 17:12-13).

(22) The disciples unable to cure
(Mark 9:14-18; Luke 9:37-40)

¶14And when they were come to the
multitude, there came to him a *certain*
man, kneeling down to him, and saying,
15Lord, have mercy on my son: for he
is lunatick, and sore vexed: for ofttimes
he falleth into the fire, and oft into the
water.
16And I brought him to thy disciples,
and they could not cure him.

(23) A miracle (18)—The demon
cast out of the child
(cf. Mark 9:19-29; Luke 9:41-43)

17Then Jesus answered and said,
O faithless and perverse generation,
how long shall I be with you? how
long shall I suffer you? bring him hither
to me.
18And Jesus rebuked the *devil; and
he departed out of him: and the child
was cured from that very hour.
19Then came the disciples to Jesus
apart, and said, Why could not we cast
him out?
20And Jesus said unto them, Because
of your unbelief: for verily I say unto
you, If ye have faith as a grain of mustard seed, ye shall say unto this mountain, Remove hence to yonder place;
and it shall remove; and nothing shall
be impossible unto you.
21Howbeit this kind goeth not out but
by *prayer and fasting.

(24) Christ again announces His coming
death and resurrection (2)
(Mark 9:30-32; Luke 9:43-45)

¶22And while they abode in Galilee,
Jesus said unto them, The Son of man
shall be betrayed into the hands of
men:
23And they shall kill him, and the
third day he shall be raised again. And
they were exceeding sorry.

(25) A miracle (19)—Tribute money
from the mouth of a fish
(cf. Mark 12:13-17)

¶24And when they were come to Capernaum, they that received tribute
money came to Peter, and said, Doth not
your master pay tribute?

17:24 Tributes
There were two kinds of tribute:
1. the half-shekel, which every Jew, wherever he resided, was expected to contribute for the maintenance of the temple (Matt. 17:24); and
2. the tax, custom, dues, etc., taken from the Jews by their Roman rulers for the maintenance of the civil authorities (Matt. 22:17).

The former was, if possible (but not necessarily), paid in Jewish coin, the latter in Roman coin.

25He saith, Yes. And when he was
come into the house, Jesus prevented
him, saying, What thinkest thou, Simon? of whom do the kings of the earth
take custom or tribute? of their own
children, or of strangers?
26Peter saith unto him, Of strangers.
Jesus saith unto him, Then are the children free.
27Notwithstanding, lest we should
offend them, go thou to the sea, and cast
an hook, and take up the fish that first
cometh up; and when thou hast opened
his mouth, thou shalt find a piece of
money: that take, and give unto them
for me and thee.

(26) The greatest in the kingdom
of heaven
(Mark 9:33-37; Luke 9:46-48)

18 At the same time came the
disciples unto Jesus, saying,
Who is the greatest in the kingdom of
heaven?
2And Jesus called a little child unto
him, and set him in the midst of them,

17:25 prevented. Anticipated. Jesus anticipated Peter's question and spoke to him first.

3 And said, Verily I say unto you, Except ye be converted, and become as
little children, ye shall not enter into
the kingdom of heaven.
4 Whosoever therefore shall humble
himself as this little child, the same is
greatest in the kingdom of heaven.
5 And whoso shall receive one such
little child in my name receiveth me.
6 But whoso shall offend one of
these little ones which believe in me,
it were better for him that a millstone
were hanged about his neck, and *that*
he were drowned in the depth of the
sea.
¶ 7 Woe unto the *world because of
offences! for it must needs be that
offences come; but woe to that man by
whom the offence cometh!
8 Wherefore if thy hand or thy foot
offend thee, cut them off, and cast *them*
from thee: it is better for thee to enter
into life halt or maimed, rather than
having two hands or two feet to be cast
into everlasting fire.
9 And if thine eye offend thee, pluck
it out, and cast *it* from thee: it is better
for thee to enter into life with one eye,
rather than having two eyes to be cast
into *hell fire.
10 Take heed that ye despise not one
of these little ones; for I say unto you,
That in heaven their angels do always
behold the face of my Father which is
in heaven.

(27) The parable of the lost sheep (13) (cf. Luke 15:3-7)

11 For the Son of man is come to save
that which was lost.
12 How think ye? if a man have an hundred sheep, and one of them be gone
astray, doth he not leave the ninety and
nine, and goeth into the mountains, and
seeketh that which is gone astray?
13 And if so be that he find it, verily I
say unto you, he rejoiceth more of that
sheep, than of the ninety and nine which
went not astray.
14 Even so it is not the will of your
Father which is in heaven, that one of
these little ones should perish.

(28) A key for Church discipline

¶ 15 Moreover if thy brother shall
*trespass against thee, go and tell him
his fault between thee and him alone:
if he shall hear thee, thou hast gained
thy brother.
16 But if he will not hear *thee, then* take
with thee one or two more, that in the
mouth of two or three witnesses every
word may be established.
17 And if he shall neglect to hear
them, tell *it* unto the church: but if he
neglect to hear the church, let him be
unto thee as an heathen man and a
*publican.
18 Verily I say unto you, Whatsoever
ye shall bind on earth shall be bound in
heaven: and whatsoever ye shall loose
on earth shall be loosed in heaven.
19 Again I say unto you, That if two
of you shall agree on earth as touching
any thing that they shall ask, it shall be
done for them of my Father which is in
heaven.
20 For where two or three are gathered together in my name, there am I
in the midst of them.

18:6 millstone. One of a pair of circular stones, usually quite large, the upper of which turns upon the lower. These stones are used for grinding corn, etc. Jesus was warning that anyone who turned children away from faith in the Lord would receive severe punishment.

18:15 if thy brother shall trespass. Compare Galatians 6:1.

18:16 in the mouth of two or three witnesses. Compare Deuteronomy 17:6.

18:18 Whatsoever ye shall bind on earth. This same promise was given to Simon Peter (see Matt. 16:19 and its note). This appears to refer to church government, that is, discipline among members of the body of Christ, as the context (vss. 15-17,19) clearly shows. The disciples (see vs. 1) are here promised that their actions on earth in the matter of discipline among believers in Christ will be counted as correct in heaven.

(29) Parable of the forgiving king and the unforgiving servant (14)
(Luke 17:3-4)

¶21Then came Peter to him, and said,
Lord, how oft shall my brother *sin
against me, and I forgive him? till seven
times?
22Jesus saith unto him, I say not unto
thee, Until seven times: but, Until seventy times seven.
¶23Therefore is the kingdom of heav-
en likened unto a certain king, which
would take account of his servants.
24And when he had begun to reckon,
one was brought unto him, which owed
him ten thousand talents.
25But forasmuch as he had not to pay,
his lord commanded him to be sold, and
his wife, and children, and all that he
had, and payment to be made.
26The servant therefore fell down,
and worshipped him, saying, Lord,
have patience with me, and I will pay
thee all.
27Then the lord of that servant was
moved with compassion, and loosed
him, and forgave him the debt.
28But the same servant went out, and
found one of his fellowservants, which
owed him an hundred *pence: and he
laid hands on him, and took *him* by the
throat, saying, Pay me that thou owest.
29And his fellowservant fell down at
his feet, and besought him, saying,
Have patience with me, and I will pay
thee all.
30And he would not: but went and
cast him into prison, till he should pay
the debt.
31So when his fellowservants saw
what was done, they were very sorry,
and came and told unto their lord all that
was done.
32Then his lord, after that he had
called him, said unto him, O thou wicked servant, I forgave thee all that debt,
because thou desiredst me:
33Shouldest not thou also have had
compassion on thy fellowservant, even
as I had pity on thee?
34And his lord was wroth, and delivered him to the tormentors, till he
should pay all that was due unto him.
35So likewise shall my heavenly Father do also unto you, if ye from your
hearts forgive not every one his brother
their trespasses.

(30) Further healing, in Judaea

19 And it came to pass, *that* when
Jesus had finished these sayings, he departed from Galilee, and
came into the coasts of Judaea beyond
Jordan;
2And great multitudes followed him;
and he healed them there.

(31) The law of divorce
(cf. Matt. 5:31-32; Mark 10:1-12; Luke 16:18; 1 Cor. 7:10-15)

¶3The Pharisees also came unto him,
*tempting him, and saying unto him, Is
it lawful for a man to put away his wife
for every cause?
4And he answered and said unto
them, Have ye not read, that he which
made *them* at the beginning made them
male and female,
5And said, For this cause shall a man

18:21 till seven times? In the teachings of the rabbis, there are fourteen references to forgiveness that instruct men to forgive anywhere from one to three times but never any more than that.
18:23 take account of. Settle accounts with.
18:24 ten thousand talents. A talent was worth more than the amount someone could earn in fifteen years, so this debt was millions of dollars.
18:25 had not to pay. Was not able to repay.
18:28 an hundred pence. The plural of penny. This was a denarius equal to a full day's wage.
19:4 Have ye not read . . . ? See Genesis 1:27 and note, "In God's Image"; 2:23-24. Observe that our Lord confirms the Genesis narrative concerning the creation.

leave father and mother, and shall
cleave to his wife: and they twain shall
be one flesh?
6 Wherefore they are no more twain,
but one flesh. What therefore God hath
joined together, let not man put asunder.
7 They say unto him, Why did Moses
then command to give a writing of divorcement, and to put her away?
8 He saith unto them, Moses because
of the hardness of your hearts suffered
you to put away your wives: but from
the beginning it was not so.
9 And I say unto you, Whosoever shall
put away his wife, except *it be* for fornication, and shall marry another,
committeth adultery: and whoso
marrieth her which is put away doth
commit adultery.
¶ 10 His disciples say unto him, If the
case of the man be so with *his* wife, it
is not good to marry.
11 But he said unto them, All *men* cannot receive this saying, save *they* to
whom it is given.
12 For there are some eunuchs, which
were so born from *their* mother's
womb: and there are some eunuchs,
which were made eunuchs of men: and
there be eunuchs, which have made
themselves eunuchs for the kingdom of
heaven's sake. He that is able to receive
it, let him receive *it*.

(32) The Lord Jesus blesses little children (Mark 10:13-16; Luke 18:15-17)

¶ 13 Then were there brought unto
him little children, that he should put
his hands on them, and pray: and the
disciples rebuked them.
14 But Jesus said, Suffer little children,
and forbid them not, to come unto me:
for of such is the kingdom of heaven.
15 And he laid *his* hands on them, and
departed thence.

(33) Christ and a rich young ruler (Mark 10:17-30; Luke 18:18-30; cf. Luke 10:25-30)

¶ 16 And, behold, one came and said
unto him, *Good Master, what good
thing shall I do, that I may have *eternal life?
17 And he said unto him, Why callest
thou me good? *there is* none good but
one, *that is,* God: but if thou wilt enter
into life, keep the commandments.

19:17 Keep the Commandments
If it were possible for a man to keep the commandments perfectly, his reward would be eternal life. But the commandments show the perfect righteousness of God and, except for our Lord Himself, no man who ever lived could keep the Law, for "there is none righteous, no, not one" (Rom. 3:10), for "all have sinned, and come short of the glory of God" (Rom. 3:23). Our Lord was simply trying to show the young man who came to Him that while he might have thought he was keeping the commandments, he was not keeping them perfectly. It is evident that the Law was presented simply like a teacher, in order to bring us to Christ, so we can be justified by faith in Him (Gal. 3:24).

18 He saith unto him, Which? Jesus
said, Thou shalt do no murder, Thou
shalt not commit adultery, Thou shalt
not steal, Thou shalt not bear false witness,
19 Honour thy father and *thy* mother:
and, Thou shalt love thy neighbour as
thyself.
20 The young man saith unto him, All
these things have I kept from my youth
up: what lack I yet?
21 Jesus said unto him, If thou wilt be

19:7 Why did Moses then command . . . ? See Deuteronomy 24:1-4.
19:8 Moses . . . suffered you. In verses 7-8, the *Pharisees, as well as our Lord, confirmed the Mosaic authorship of Deuteronomy.
19:8 suffered. Allowed.
19:18-19. For these commandments, see Exodus 20:12-16.
19:19 love thy neighbour as thyself. See Leviticus 19:18.

*perfect, go *and* sell that thou hast, and
give to the poor, and thou shalt have
treasure in heaven: and come *and* follow me.
22But when the young man heard that
saying, he went away sorrowful: for he
had great possessions.
¶23Then said Jesus unto his disciples,
Verily I say unto you, That a rich man
shall hardly enter into the kingdom of
heaven.
24And again I say unto you, It is easier for a camel to go through the eye of
a needle, than for a rich man to enter
into the *kingdom of God.
25When his disciples heard *it,* they
were exceedingly amazed, saying, Who
then can be saved?
26But Jesus beheld *them,* and said
unto them, With men this is impossible; but with God all things are possible.

(34) The place of the apostles in the kingdom

¶27Then answered Peter and said
unto him, Behold, we have forsaken all,
and followed thee; what shall we have
therefore?
28And Jesus said unto them, Verily I
say unto you, That ye which have followed me, in the regeneration when the
Son of man shall sit in the throne of his
glory, ye also shall sit upon twelve
thrones, judging the twelve tribes of
Israel.
29And every one that hath forsaken
houses, or brethren, or sisters, or father, or mother, or wife, or children, or
lands, for my name's sake, shall receive
an hundredfold, and shall inherit everlasting life.
30But many *that are* first shall be last;
and the last *shall be* first.

(35) The parable of the labourers in the vineyard (15)

20 For the kingdom of heaven is
like unto a man *that is* an householder, which went out early in the
morning to hire labourers into his vineyard.
2And when he had agreed with the
labourers for a *penny a day, he sent
them into his vineyard.
3And he went out about the third
hour, and saw others standing idle in the
marketplace,
4And said unto them; Go ye also
into the vineyard, and whatsoever is
right I will give you. And they went
their way.
5Again he went out about the sixth
and ninth hour, and did likewise.
6And about the eleventh hour he
went out, and found others standing
idle, and saith unto them, Why stand ye
here all the day idle?
7They say unto him, Because no man
hath hired us. He saith unto them, Go
ye also into the vineyard; and whatsoever is right, *that* shall ye receive.
8So when even was come, the lord of
the vineyard saith unto his steward,
Call the labourers, and give them *their*
hire, beginning from the last unto the
first.
9And when they came that *were hired*
about the eleventh hour, they received
every man a penny.
10But when the first came, they supposed that they should have received
more; and they likewise received every
man a penny.
11And when they had received *it,*
they murmured against the goodman of
the house,
12Saying, These last have wrought
but one hour, and thou hast made them

19:25 Who then can be saved? See *salvation.
19:28 regeneration. Regeneration is a re-creation or renewing. Here it speaks of the new world and the renewed order of things on earth when Christ shall reign in the *Millennium.
19:28 judging. See Isaiah 1:26 and its note, "A Future Government Revealed."
20:1 vineyard. See Isaiah 5:7.

equal unto us, which have borne the
burden and heat of the day.
13But he answered one of them, and
said, Friend, I do thee no wrong: didst
not thou agree with me for a penny?
14 Take *that* thine *is,* and go thy way: I
will give unto this last, even as unto thee.
15 Is it not lawful for me to do what I
will with mine own? Is thine eye evil,
because I am good?
16 So the last shall be first, and the
first last: for many be called, but few
chosen.

(36) Christ again refers to His coming death and resurrection (3) (Mark 10:32-34; Luke 18:31-34; see Matt. 12:38-42; 16:21-28; 17:22-23)

¶17And Jesus going up to Jerusalem
took the twelve disciples apart in the
way, and said unto them,
18 Behold, we go up to Jerusalem; and
the Son of man shall be betrayed unto
the chief priests and unto the scribes,
and they shall condemn him to death,
19 And shall deliver him to the *Gentiles to mock, and to scourge, and to
crucify *him:* and the third day he shall
rise again.

(37) The request of James and John (Mark 10:35-45)

¶20Then came to him the mother of
Zebedee's children with her sons, worshipping *him,* and desiring a certain
thing of him.
21And he said unto her, What wilt
thou? She saith unto him, Grant that
these my two sons may sit, the one on
thy right hand, and the other on the left,
in thy kingdom.
22But Jesus answered and said, Ye
know not what ye ask. Are ye able to
drink of the cup that I shall drink of, and
to be baptized with the *baptism that I
am baptized with? They say unto him,
We are able.
23And he saith unto them, Ye shall
drink indeed of my cup, and be baptized
with the baptism that I am baptized
with: but to sit on my right hand, and
on my left, is not mine to give, but *it
shall be given to them* for whom it is prepared of my Father.
24And when the ten heard *it,* they
were moved with indignation against
the two brethren.
25But Jesus called them *unto him,* and
said, Ye know that the princes of the
Gentiles exercise dominion over them,
and they that are great exercise authority upon them.
26 But it shall not be so among you:
but whosoever will be great among you,
let him be your minister;
27 And whosoever will be chief among
you, let him be your servant:
28 Even as the Son of man came not
to be ministered unto, but to minister,
and to give his life a *ransom for many.

(38) A miracle (20)—Two blind men receive their sight (Mark 10:46-52; cf. Luke 18:35-43)

¶29And as they departed from Jericho, a great multitude followed him.
30And, behold, two blind men sitting by the way side, when they heard
that Jesus passed by, cried out, saying,
Have *mercy on us, O Lord, *thou* *Son
of David.
31And the multitude rebuked them,

20:15 Is it not lawful for me . . . ? See Romans 9:20-21.
20:16 last shall be first. See Matthew 19:30.
20:21 thy kingdom. When Christ shall reign during the *Millennium.
20:23 Ye shall drink indeed of my cup. James was one of the first martyrs (Acts 12:2), while John was exiled to the isle of Patmos "for the word of God, and for the testimony of Jesus Christ" (Rev. 1:9).
20:26 it shall not be so. See 1 Peter 5:3.
20:26 minister. Servant.
20:27 servant. Bondslave.
20:30 Son of David. See *Christ, Son of Man.

because they should hold their peace:
but they cried the more, saying, Have
mercy on us, O Lord, *thou* Son of David.
32 And Jesus stood still, and called
them, and said, What will ye that I shall
do unto you?
33 They say unto him, Lord, that our
eyes may be opened.
34 So Jesus had compassion *on them,*
and touched their eyes: and immediately their eyes received sight, and they
followed him.

(39) The King presents Himself to His people (Zech. 9:9; Mark 11:1-10; Luke 19:29-38)

21 And when they drew nigh unto
*Jerusalem, and were come to
*Bethphage, unto the *mount of Olives,
then sent Jesus two disciples,
2 Saying unto them, Go into the village
over against you, and *straightway ye
shall find an ass tied, and a colt with her:
loose *them,* and bring *them* unto me.
3 And if any *man* say ought unto you,
ye shall say, The Lord hath need of them;
and straightway he will send them.

O.T. prophecy fulfilled (13)

4 All this was done, that it might be
fulfilled which was spoken by the
*prophet, saying,
5 Tell ye the daughter of *Sion, Behold, thy King cometh unto thee, meek,
and sitting upon an ass, and a colt the
foal of an ass.
6 And the disciples went, and did as
Jesus commanded them,
7 And brought the ass, and the colt,
and put on them their clothes, and they
set *him* thereon.
8 And a very great multitude spread
their garments in the way; others cut
down branches from the trees, and
strawed *them* in the way.
9 And the multitudes that went before, and that followed, cried, saying,
*Hosanna to the Son of *David: Blessed
is he that cometh in the name of the
Lord; Hosanna in the highest.
10 And when he was come into Jerusalem, all the city was moved, saying,
Who is this?
11 And the multitude said, This is Jesus
the prophet of Nazareth of Galilee.

(40) Christ casts out from the temple the moneychangers (Mark 11:15-18; Luke 19:45-47; cf. John 2:13-16)

¶ 12 And Jesus went into the temple of
*God, and cast out all them that sold
and bought in the temple, and overthrew the tables of the moneychangers,
and the seats of them that sold doves,
13 And said unto them, It is written,
My house shall be called the house of
prayer; but ye have made it a *den of
thieves.
14 And the blind and the lame came to
him in the temple; and he healed them.
15 And when the chief priests and
*scribes saw the wonderful things that
he did, and the children crying in the
temple, and saying, Hosanna to the Son
of David; they were sore displeased,
16 And said unto him, Hearest thou
what these say? And Jesus saith unto
them, Yea; have ye never read, Out of
the mouth of babes and sucklings thou
hast *perfected praise?
17 And he left them, and went out of
the city into Bethany; and he lodged
there.

(41) A miracle (21)—The cursing and drying up of the fig tree (Mark 11:12-14,20-24)

¶ 18 Now in the morning as he returned into the city, he hungered.

21:4 that it might be fulfilled. Read Zechariah 9:9.
21:9 Hosanna . . . Blessed is he. The word "Hosanna" is taken from Psalm 118:25 (see its note) and means *salvation,* or *save now.* Something of this significance is shown in the phrase "God save the king." (See also Ps. 118:26 and its note; Mark 11:9.)
21:13 It is written. See Isaiah 56:7; Jeremiah 7:11.
21:16 have ye never read . . . ? See Psalm 8:2.

[19]And when he saw a *fig tree in the
way, he came to it, and found nothing
thereon, but leaves only, and said unto
it, Let no fruit grow on thee henceforward for ever. And presently the fig
tree withered away.
[20]And when the disciples saw *it,* they
marvelled, saying, How soon is the fig
tree withered away!
[21]Jesus answered and said unto them,
Verily I say unto you, If ye have *faith,
and doubt not, ye shall not only do this
which is done to the fig tree, but also if
ye shall say unto this mountain, Be thou
removed, and be thou cast into the sea;
it shall be done.
[22]And all things, whatsoever ye shall
ask in prayer, believing, ye shall receive.

(42) Christ's authority questioned (Mark 11:27-33; Luke 20:1-8)

¶[23]And when he was come into the
temple, the chief priests and the *elders of the people came unto him as he
was teaching, and said, By what authority doest thou these things? and who
gave thee this authority?
[24]And Jesus answered and said unto
them, I also will ask you one thing,
which if ye tell me, I in like wise will
tell you by what authority I do these
things.
[25]The baptism of John, whence was
it? from heaven, or of men? And they
reasoned with themselves, saying, If
we shall say, From heaven; he will say
unto us, Why did ye not then believe
him?
[26]But if we shall say, Of men; we
fear the people; for all hold John as a
prophet.
[27]And they answered Jesus, and said,
We cannot tell. And he said unto them,
Neither tell I you by what authority I do
these things.

(43) The parable of the two sons (16)

¶[28]But what think ye? A *certain* man
had two sons; and he came to the first,
and said, Son, go work to day in my
vineyard.
[29]He answered and said, I will not:
but afterward he *repented, and went.
[30]And he came to the second, and
said likewise. And he answered and
said, I *go,* sir: and went not.
[31]Whether of them twain did the will
of *his* father? They say unto him, The
first. Jesus saith unto them, Verily I say
unto you, That the *publicans and the
harlots go into the kingdom of God before you.
[32]For John came unto you in the way
of *righteousness, and ye believed him
not: but the publicans and the harlots
believed him: and ye, when ye had seen
it, repented not afterward, that ye might
believe him.

(44) The parable of the householder who demanded fruit (17) (Mark 12:1-9; Luke 20:9-19; cf. Isa. 5:1-7)

¶[33]Hear another *parable: There was
a certain householder, which planted a
vineyard, and hedged it round about,
and digged a winepress in it, and built
a tower, and let it out to *husbandmen,
and went into a far country:
[34]And when the time of the fruit drew
near, he sent his servants to the husbandmen, that they might receive the
fruits of it.
[35]And the husbandmen took his servants, and beat one, and killed another,
and stoned another.
[36]Again, he sent other servants more
than the first: and they did unto them
likewise.
[37]But last of all he sent unto them
his son, saying, They will reverence
my son.

21:19 leaves only. The fig tree in Palestine begins to show tender leaf buds toward the end of March, at the same time that tiny figs appear.
21:25 The baptism of John. The baptizing that John the Baptist performed.
21:37 my son. See John 3:16.

[38]But when the husbandmen saw the
son, they said among themselves, This
is the heir; come, let us kill him, and let
us seize on his inheritance.
[39]And they caught him, and cast *him*
out of the vineyard, and slew *him.*
[40]When the lord therefore of the
vineyard cometh, what will he do unto
those husbandmen?
[41]They say unto him, He will miserably destroy those wicked men, and will
let out *his* vineyard unto other husbandmen, which shall *render him the fruits
in their seasons.
[42]Jesus saith unto them, Did ye never
read in the scriptures, The stone which
the builders rejected, the same is become the head of the corner: this is the
Lord's doing, and it is marvellous in our
eyes?
[43]Therefore say I unto you, The kingdom of God shall be taken from you, and
given to a nation bringing forth the
fruits thereof.
[44]And whosoever shall fall on this
stone shall be broken: but on whomsoever it shall fall, it will grind him to
powder.
[45]And when the chief priests and
*Pharisees had heard his *parables,
they perceived that he spake of them.
[46]But when they sought to lay hands
on him, they feared the multitude, because they took him for a prophet.

(45) The parable of the marriage feast (18)
(Luke 14:16-24)

22 And Jesus answered and spake
unto them again by parables,
and said,
[2]The *kingdom of *heaven is like
unto a certain king, which made a marriage for his son,
[3]And sent forth his servants to call
them that were bidden to the wedding:
and they would not come.
[4]Again, he sent forth other servants,
saying, Tell them which are bidden,
Behold, I have prepared my dinner: my
oxen and *my* fatlings *are* killed, and all
things *are* ready: come unto the marriage.
[5]But they made light of *it,* and went
their ways, one to his farm, another to
his merchandise:
[6]And the *remnant took his servants,
and entreated *them* spitefully, and slew
them.
[7]But when the king heard *thereof,* he
was wroth: and he sent forth his armies,
and destroyed those murderers, and
burned up their city.
[8]Then saith he to his servants, The
wedding is ready, but they which were
bidden were not worthy.
[9]Go ye therefore into the highways,
and as many as ye shall find, bid to the
marriage.
[10]So those servants went out into the
highways, and gathered together all as
many as they found, both bad and good:
and the wedding was furnished with
guests.
¶[11]And when the king came in to see
the guests, he saw there a man which
had not on a wedding garment:
[12]And he saith unto him, Friend, how
camest thou in hither not having a wedding garment? And he was speechless.
[13]Then said the king to the servants,
Bind him hand and foot, and take him
away, and cast *him* into outer darkness;
there shall be weeping and gnashing of
teeth.
[14]For many are called, but few *are*
chosen.

(46) The Pharisees and Herodians attempt to trap Christ
(Mark 12:13-17; Luke 20:20-26)

¶[15]Then went the Pharisees, and
took counsel how they might entangle
him in *his* talk.
[16]And they sent out unto him their
disciples with the *Herodians, saying,

21:38 This is the heir. See Hebrews 1:2 and its note, "God's Son."
21:42 stone which the builders rejected. That is, Christ (Ps. 118:22-23; 1 Pet. 2:7).

Master, we know that thou art true, and
teachest the way of God in truth, neither carest thou for any *man:* for thou
regardest not the person of men.

22:16 The Herodians
The Herodians were not a religious sect like the Pharisees; they were a political party that supported the dynasty of the Herods. They feared Christ and His influence with many of the people would upset their political aims and ambitions.

17 Tell us therefore, What thinkest
thou? Is it lawful to give tribute unto
*Caesar, or not?

(47) Jesus answers His tempters

18 But Jesus perceived their wickedness, and said, Why *tempt ye me, *ye*
hypocrites?
19 Shew me the tribute money. And
they brought unto him a penny.
20 And he saith unto them, Whose *is*
this *image and *superscription?
21 They say unto him, Caesar's. Then
saith he unto them, Render therefore
unto Caesar the things which are
Caesar's; and unto God the things that
are God's.
22 When they had heard *these words,*
they marvelled, and left him, and went
their way.

(48) Jesus answers the Sadducees concerning the resurrection (Mark 12:18-27; Luke 20:27-38)

¶23 The same day came to him the
*Sadducees, which say that there is no
*resurrection, and asked him,
24 Saying, Master, Moses said, If a
man die, having no children, his brother
shall marry his wife, and raise up seed
unto his brother.
25 Now there were with us seven
brethren: and the first, when he had
married a wife, deceased, and, having
no issue, left his wife unto his brother:
26 Likewise the second also, and the
third, unto the seventh.
27 And last of all the woman died also.
28 Therefore in the resurrection
whose wife shall she be of the seven?
for they all had her.
29 Jesus answered and said unto them,
Ye do *err, not knowing the scriptures,
nor the power of God.
30 For in the resurrection they neither
marry, nor are given in marriage, but
are as the *angels of God in heaven.
31 But as touching the resurrection of
the dead, have ye not read that which
was spoken unto you by God, saying,
32 I am the God of *Abraham, and the
God of *Isaac, and the God of *Jacob?
God is not the God of the dead, but of
the living.
33 And when the multitude heard *this,*
they were astonished at his *doctrine.

(49) Jesus answers a lawyer and defines the greatest commandments (Mark 12:28-34; cf. Luke 19:25-28)

¶34 But when the Pharisees had heard
that he had put the Sadducees to silence, they were gathered together.
35 Then one of them, *which was* a lawyer, asked *him a question,* *tempting
him, and saying,
36 Master, which *is* the great commandment in the *law?

22:17 give tribute. Pay taxes.
22:17 Caesar. The Roman emperor.
22:24 Moses said. See Deuteronomy 25:5.
22:25 Now there were . . . seven brethren. This was not necessarily an actual case.
22:30 For in the resurrection. In these few words our Lord declares the fact of the Resurrection.
22:31 saying. See Exodus 3:6.
22:35 lawyer. Learned Jews were divided into three classes: 1) lawyers learned in the Mosaic Law; 2) scribes or grammarians who copied and interpreted the Scriptures; and 3) teachers or professors (Luke 2:46; Acts 22:3).

[37]Jesus said unto him, Thou shalt
love the Lord thy God with all thy heart,
and with all thy soul, and with all thy
mind.
[38]This is the first and great commandment.
[39]And the second *is* like unto it, Thou
shalt love thy neighbour as thyself.
[40]On these two commandments hang
all the law and the *prophets.

(50) The Lord confounds the Pharisees with questions about Christ (Mark 12:35-37; Luke 20:41-44)

¶[41]While the Pharisees were gathered together, Jesus asked them,
[42]Saying, What think ye of *Christ?
whose son is he? They say unto him,
The Son of David.
[43]He saith unto them, How then doth
David in spirit call him Lord, saying,
[44]The LORD said unto my Lord, Sit
thou on my right hand, till I make thine
enemies thy footstool?
[45]If David then call him Lord, how is
he his son?
[46]And no man was able to answer him
a word, neither durst any *man* from
that day forth ask him any more *questions.*

(51) Christ describes the Pharisees and pronounces woe upon them (Mark 12:38-40; Luke 20:45-47)

23 Then spake Jesus to the multitude, and to his disciples,
[2]Saying, The scribes and the Pharisees sit in *Moses' seat:
[3]All therefore whatsoever they bid
you observe, *that* observe and do; but
do not ye after their works: for they say,
and do not.
[4]For they bind heavy burdens and
grievous to be borne, and lay *them* on
men's shoulders; but they *themselves*
will not move them with one of their
fingers.
[5]But all their works they do for to be
seen of men: they make broad their
phylacteries, and enlarge the borders of
their garments,

23:5 Displays of Piety
A phylactery was a square or cube-shaped calfskin box bound to a person's forehead or left forearm near the elbow. It contained four specific texts of Scripture, namely: Exodus 13:2-10,11-16; Deuteronomy 6:4-9,13-23 (see Deut. 6:8 and its note, "A Constant Reminder").

The border of their garments, also called the hem or the fringe, was in accordance with Numbers 15:38. Because great importance was attached to this injunction, the Pharisees made sure that their own garments had very broad hems, mainly to be seen and perceived as pious by others.

[6]And love the uppermost rooms at
*feasts, and the chief seats in the *syn-
agogues,
[7]And greetings in the markets, and to
be called of men, Rabbi, Rabbi.
[8]But be not ye called Rabbi: for one
is your Master, *even* Christ; and all ye
are brethren.
[9]And call no *man* your father upon
the earth: for one is your Father, which
is in heaven.
[10]Neither be ye called masters: for
one is your Master, *even* Christ.
[11]But he that is greatest among you
shall be your servant.
[12]And whosoever shall exalt himself
shall be abased; and he that shall humble himself shall be exalted.
¶[13]But woe unto you, scribes and
Pharisees, hypocrites! for ye shut up
the kingdom of heaven against men:
for ye neither go in *yourselves,* neither
suffer ye them that are entering to
go in.

22:37 love the Lord thy God. See Deuteronomy 6:5.
22:39 love thy neighbour as thyself. See Leviticus 19:18.
22:43 saying. See Psalm 110:1.
23:2 sit in Moses' seat. Assume the place of Moses as the leaders of the people.

14 Woe unto you, scribes and Pharisees, hypocrites! for ye devour widows' houses, and for a pretence make long *prayer: therefore ye shall receive the greater *damnation.

15 Woe unto you, scribes and Pharisees, hypocrites! for ye compass sea and land to make one *proselyte, and when he is made, ye make him twofold more the *child of hell than yourselves.

16 Woe unto you, *ye* blind guides, which say, Whosoever shall swear by the temple, it is nothing; but whosoever shall swear by the gold of the temple, he is a debtor!

17 *Ye* *fools and blind: for whether is greater, the gold, or the temple that sanctifieth the gold?

18 And, Whosoever shall swear by the *altar, it is nothing; but whosoever sweareth by the gift that is upon it, he is guilty.

19 *Ye* fools and blind: for whether *is* greater, the gift, or the altar that sanctifieth the gift?

20 Whoso therefore shall swear by the altar, sweareth by it, and by all things thereon.

21 And whoso shall swear by the temple, sweareth by it, and by him that dwelleth therein.

22 And he that shall swear by heaven, sweareth by the throne of God, and by him that sitteth thereon.

23 Woe unto you, scribes and Pharisees, hypocrites! for ye pay tithe of mint and anise and cummin, and have omitted the weightier *matters* of the law, *judgment, mercy, and faith: these ought ye to have done, and not to leave the other undone.

24 *Ye* blind guides, which strain at a gnat, and swallow a camel.

25 Woe unto you, scribes and Pharisees, hypocrites! for ye make *clean the outside of the cup and of the platter, but within they are full of extortion and excess.

26 *Thou* blind *Pharisee, cleanse first that *which is* within the cup and platter, that the outside of them may be clean also.

27 Woe unto you, scribes and Pharisees, hypocrites! for ye are like unto whited sepulchres, which indeed appear beautiful outward, but are within full of dead *men's* bones, and of all uncleanness.

28 Even so ye also outwardly appear righteous unto men, but within ye are full of hypocrisy and iniquity.

29 Woe unto you, scribes and Pharisees, hypocrites! because ye build the tombs of the prophets, and garnish the sepulchres of the righteous,

30 And say, If we had been in the days of our fathers, we would not have been *partakers with them in the blood of the prophets.

31 Wherefore ye be witnesses unto yourselves, that ye are the children of them which killed the prophets.

32 Fill ye up then the measure of your fathers.

33 *Ye* serpents, *ye* generation of vipers, how can ye escape the damnation of hell?

¶34 Wherefore, behold, I send unto you prophets, and wise men, and scribes: and *some* of them ye shall kill and crucify; and *some* of them shall ye scourge in your synagogues, and persecute *them* from city to city:

23:16 debtor. Bound by an oath.

23:23 anise. A seed-bearing plant; either the anise or the dill, annuals bearing little flowers, and native of the Near East.

23:23 cummin. An annual of the parsley family, whose seeds are used in the East in making sauces or relishes.

23:27 whited sepulchres. Sepulchres were made of marble or clay; the latter were quite often whitewashed. Thus some of the graves appear whiter on the outside, but inside all of the graves there is nothing but decay.

23:31 ye are the children. See Acts 7:52.

35 That upon you may come all the
righteous blood shed upon the earth,
from the blood of righteous *Abel unto
the blood of Zacharias son of Barachias,
whom ye slew between the temple and
the altar.
36 Verily I say unto you, All these
things shall come upon this generation.

(52) The lament about Jerusalem and prophecy concerning the city (Luke 13:34-35)

37 O Jerusalem, Jerusalem, *thou* that
killest the prophets, and stonest them
which are sent unto thee, how often
would I have gathered thy children together, even as a hen gathereth her
chickens under *her* wings, and ye would
not!
38 Behold, your house is left unto you
desolate.
39 For I say unto you, Ye shall not see
me henceforth, till ye shall say, Blessed
is he that cometh in the name of the Lord.

F. The King Will Return in Power and Glory

(1) The Olivet discourse

24 And Jesus went out, and departed from the temple: and his disciples came to *him* for to shew him the buildings of the temple.

(a) Christ's prophecy (Mark 13:1-2; Luke 21:5-6)

2 And Jesus said unto them, See ye not all these things? verily I say unto you, There shall not be left here one stone upon another, that shall not be thrown down.

(b) The disciples' questions (Mark 13:3-4; Luke 21:7)

¶3 And as he sat upon the *mount of Olives, the disciples came unto him privately, saying, Tell us, when shall these things be? and what *shall be* the sign of thy coming, and of the end of the *world?

(c) Christ's answer—tribulation upon the earth (Mark 13:5-13; Luke 21:8-19)

4 And Jesus answered and said unto
them, Take heed that no man deceive
you.
5 For many shall come in my name,
saying, I am Christ; and shall deceive
many.
6 And ye shall hear of wars and
rumours of wars: see that ye be not
troubled: for all *these things* must come
to pass, but the end is not yet.
7 For nation shall rise against nation,
and kingdom against kingdom: and

24:3 CHRIST'S RETURN

The disciples knew nothing about the *Rapture (the coming of the Lord for His own), only about His coming in power to reign (see *kingdom). Nor were they familiar with the course of the *church age. They were interested in what would affect Israel; they were living in a Jewish age, toward the end of Daniel's sixty-ninth prophetic week (see Daniel 9:20-27 and 9:24-27 note, "A Central Prophecy").

It appears that our Lord's answer concerns the seventieth week of Daniel, an age when God will deal particularly with Israel, and a time just prior to His coming in power to set up the *Millennium. With that in mind, it would seem as though the first fourteen verses of this chapter concern the first half of Daniel's seventieth week, while verses 15-26 deal with the second half of the *Great Tribulation. Verses 27-31 speak directly of Christ's return in power. In the days in which we are living—still in the *church age—we see and hear things that seem to parallel certain prophecies in verses 4-14, indicating that that prophetic day of which these signs speak is very near.

23:35 righteous Abel. See Hebrews 12:24; Genesis 4:8-10.
23:35 Zacharias. See 2 Chronicles 24:20-22.
24:2 not be left here one stone upon another. This prophecy was fulfilled at the destruction of Jerusalem by Titus in the year A.D. 70.
24:5 many shall come. Compare verses 5-12 with Revelation 6:1-17.

there shall be famines, and pestilences,
and earthquakes, in divers places.
8All these *are* the beginning of sorrows.
9Then shall they deliver you up to be
afflicted, and shall kill you: and ye shall
be hated of all nations for my name's
sake.
10And then shall many be offended,
and shall betray one another, and shall
hate one another.
11And many false prophets shall rise,
and shall deceive many.
12And because iniquity shall abound,
the love of many shall wax cold.
13But he that shall endure unto the
end, the same shall be saved.
14And this *gospel of the kingdom
shall be preached in all the world for a
witness unto all nations; and then shall
the end come.
15When ye therefore shall see the
*abomination of desolation, spoken of
by Daniel the prophet, stand in the
*holy place, (whoso readeth, let him
understand:)
16Then let them which be in Judaea
flee into the mountains:
17Let him which is on the housetop
not come down to take any thing out of
his house:
18Neither let him which is in the field
return back to take his clothes.
19And woe unto them that are with
child, and to them that give suck in
those days!
20But pray ye that your flight be not
in the winter, neither on the *sabbath
day:
21For then shall be *great tribulation,
such as was not since the beginning
of the world to this time, no, nor ever
shall be.
22And except those days should be
shortened, there should no flesh be
saved: but for the *elect's sake those
days shall be shortened.
23Then if any man shall say unto
you, Lo, here *is* Christ, or there; believe
it not.
24For there shall arise false Christs,
and false prophets, and shall shew great
signs and wonders; insomuch that, if *it*
were possible, they shall deceive the
very elect.
25Behold, I have told you before.
26Wherefore if they shall say unto
you, Behold, he is in the desert; go not
forth: behold, *he is* in the secret chambers; believe *it* not.
27For as the lightning cometh out of
the east, and shineth even unto the
west; so shall also the coming of the
Son of man be.
28For wheresoever the carcase is,
there will the eagles be gathered together.

(d) The coming of the Son of Man in power
(Mark 13:24-37; Luke 21:25-28)

¶29Immediately after *the tribulation
of those days shall the sun be darkened,
and the moon shall not give her light,
and the stars shall fall from heaven, and
the powers of the heavens shall be
shaken:
30And then shall appear the sign of

24:12 iniquity. Lawlessness and sin. Read 2 Timothy 3:1-5.
24:15 by Daniel the prophet. See Daniel 9:27; 11:31; 12:11.
24:16 Then let them. The Jewish character of this passage is clearly indicated in the reference to Judaea, to the Sabbath day (vs. 20), and to the expression "the elect's sake" (vs. 22)—the elect (meaning *chosen*) referring first in the Gospels to Israel (as it does in the Old Testament; compare Isa. 45:4; 65:9,22), broadened later to refer to the *church, composed of Jews and Gentiles, as it refers to in the Epistles.
24:21 not since the beginning of the world. See Daniel 12:1.
24:22 for the elect's sake. See verse 16 note.
24:27 as the lightning. See Isaiah 30:30.
24:27 coming of the Son of man. See Revelation 19:11-16.
24:28 carcase is, there will the eagles be gathered together. See Revelation 19:17-21.

the Son of man in heaven: and then shall
all the tribes of the earth mourn, and
they shall see the Son of man coming
in the clouds of heaven with power and
great glory.
31 And he shall send his angels with a
great sound of a trumpet, and they shall
gather together his elect from the four
winds, from one end of heaven to the
other.

(e) The parable of the fig tree (19) (Mark 13:28-31; Luke 21:29-31)

32 Now learn a parable of the fig tree;
When his branch is yet tender, and
putteth forth leaves, ye know that summer *is* nigh:
33 So likewise ye, when ye shall see
all these things, know that it is near,
even at the doors.
34 Verily I say unto you, This generation shall not pass, till all these things
be fulfilled.
35 Heaven and earth shall pass away,
but my words shall not pass away.
¶36 But of that day and hour knoweth
no *man,* no, not the angels of heaven,
but my Father only.

(f) As it was in the days of Noah

37 But as the days of Noe *were,* so shall
also the coming of the Son of man be.
38 For as in the days that were before
the flood they were eating and drinking,
marrying and giving in marriage, until
the day that Noe entered into the *ark,
39 And knew not until the flood came,
and took them all away; so shall also the
coming of the Son of man be.
40 Then shall two be in the field; the
one shall be taken, and the other left.
41 Two *women shall be* grinding at the
mill; the one shall be taken, and the
other left.
¶42 Watch therefore: for ye know not
what hour your Lord doth come.
43 But know this, that if the goodman
of the house had known in what watch
the thief would come, he would have
watched, and would not have suffered
his house to be broken up.
44 Therefore be ye also ready: for in
such an hour as ye think not the Son of
man cometh.

(g) The parable of the faithful and wise servant (20)

45 Who then is a faithful and wise servant, whom his lord hath made ruler
over his household, to give them meat
in due season?
46 Blessed *is* that servant, whom his
lord when he cometh shall find so doing.
47 Verily I say unto you, That he shall
make him ruler over all his goods.

24:34 A GENERATION LIVES ON

The word "generation" is from the Greek word *genea,* the primary meaning of which is *race* or *tribe.* Since our Lord did not speak any untruth, and since these things did not all take place before those who heard His words passed on, we assume that one of the primary meanings of the word is meant here. So this verse means that the nation Israel will not pass away until all these things are fulfilled. How true this is! One of the great mysteries and miracles of the world is that this nation has survived without any home of its own throughout all these centuries–until 1948. This is in spite of the fact that in the natural course of events the Israelites would have been absorbed in the lands of their dwelling through intermarriage; etc., in a few generations. However, the nation is larger today than at any time in its history, and the Israelites are distinctively Israelites wherever they may be. It is a unique phenomenon.

24:30 they shall see the Son of man. See Revelation 1:7.
24:31 they shall gather together his elect. See Jeremiah 23:7-8.
24:32 fig tree. See Matthew 21:19 note.
24:36 of that day and hour. Compare with Acts 1:7.
24:37 Noe. Noah.

48 But and if that evil servant shall
say in his heart, My lord delayeth his
coming;
49 And shall begin to smite *his* fellowservants, and to eat and drink with
the drunken;
50 The lord of that servant shall
come in a day when he looketh not for
him, and in an hour that he is not aware
of,
51 And shall cut him asunder, and
appoint *him* his portion with the hypocrites: there shall be weeping and
gnashing of teeth.

(h) The parable of the ten virgins (21)

25 Then shall the kingdom of heav-
en be likened unto ten virgins,
which took their lamps, and went forth
to meet the *bridegroom.
2 And five of them were wise, and five
were foolish.
3 They that *were* foolish took their
lamps, and took no *oil with them:
4 But the wise took oil in their vessels
with their lamps.
5 While the bridegroom tarried, they
all slumbered and slept.
6 And at midnight there was a cry
made, Behold, the bridegroom cometh;
go ye out to meet him.
7 Then all those virgins arose, and
trimmed their lamps.
8 And the foolish said unto the wise,
Give us of your oil; for our lamps are
gone out.
9 But the wise answered, saying, *Not
so;* lest there be not enough for us and
you: but go ye rather to them that sell,
and buy for yourselves.
10 And while they went to buy, the
bridegroom came; and they that were
ready went in with him to the marriage:
and the door was shut.
11 Afterward came also the other virgins, saying, Lord, Lord, open to us.
12 But he answered and said, Verily I
say unto you, I know you not.
13 Watch therefore, for ye know neither the day nor the hour wherein the
Son of man cometh.

(i) The parable of the talents (22)

¶14 For *the kingdom of heaven is* as a
man travelling into a far country, *who*
called his own servants, and delivered
unto them his goods.
15 And unto one he gave five talents,
to another two, and to another one; to
every man according to his several
ability; and straightway took his journey.

25:1-3 MARRIAGE

The marriage ceremony was performed in the upper room of private houses. The betrothed couple stood under a canopy. The bride wore a veil, and both the bride and the bridegroom wore crowns, which were exchanged several times during the ceremony. The officiating minister was not a priest nor necessarily a rabbi, but an elder, who, standing under the canopy and holding a cup of blessing, invoked a benediction on the assembly. He gave a cup of wine to the betrothed, who pledged themselves to one another. The bridegroom then drained the cup, dashed it to the ground, and crushed it with his heel, a symbol, it is said, that their happiness could not be complete while Jerusalem was in the hands of the heathen.

The marriage contract was then read and attested by each person present by drinking a cup of wine. The friends next walked around the canopy, chanting psalms and showering rice on the couple. The ceremony was concluded by the elder invoking the seven blessings upon them, drinking the benedictory cup, and passing it around to the assembly.

After dark, the bridegroom led the bride to his home, attended by their friends. Others joined the procession, bearing lamps in token of respect. When everyone arrived at the bridegroom's house, all were invited to a feast, which the rich repeated for seven nights, or even longer.

24:51 hypocrites. See Matthew 23:13-15,23,27.
25:1 bridegroom. This might also refer to "the bridegroom and the bride."

[16]Then he that had received the five
talents went and traded with the same,
and made *them* other five talents.
[17]And likewise he that *had received*
two, he also gained other two.
[18]But he that had received one went
and digged in the earth, and hid his
lord's money.
[19]After a long time the lord of those
servants cometh, and reckoneth with
them.
[20]And so he that had received five
talents came and brought other five
talents, saying, Lord, thou deliveredst
unto me five talents: behold, I have
gained beside them five talents more.
[21]His lord said unto him, Well done,
thou good and faithful servant: thou hast
been faithful over a few things, I will
make thee ruler over many things: enter thou into the joy of thy lord.
[22]He also that had received two talents came and said, Lord, thou
deliveredst unto me two talents: behold, I have gained two other talents
beside them.
[23]His lord said unto him, Well done,
good and faithful servant; thou hast
been faithful over a few things, I will
make thee ruler over many things: enter thou into the joy of thy lord.
[24]Then he which had received the
one talent came and said, Lord, I knew
thee that thou art an hard man, reaping
where thou hast not sown, and gathering where thou hast not strawed:
[25]And I was afraid, and went and hid
thy talent in the earth: lo, *there* thou
hast *that is* thine.
[26]His lord answered and said unto
him, *Thou* wicked and slothful servant,
thou knewest that I reap where I sowed
not, and gather where I have not strawed:
[27]Thou oughtest therefore to have
put my money to the exchangers, and
then at my coming I should have received mine own with *usury.
[28]Take therefore the talent from
him, and give *it* unto him which hath ten
talents.
[29]For unto every one that hath shall
be given, and he shall have abundance:
but from him that hath not shall be
taken away even that which he hath.
[30]And cast ye the unprofitable servant into outer darkness: there shall be
weeping and gnashing of teeth.

(j) The judgment of the nations at Christ's return in power

¶[31]When the Son of man shall come
in his glory, and all the holy angels with
him, then shall he sit upon the throne
of his glory:
[32]And before him shall be gathered all
nations: and he shall separate them one
from another, as a shepherd divideth *his*
sheep from the goats:

25:32 The Judgment of the Nations
This verse is generally known as the judgment of the nations. See *judgment. He "shall set the sheep on the right hand, but the goats on the left" (vs. 33), does not mean that every member of one nation will be among the sheep and every member of another among the goats. The Lord will separate His true followers from hypocrites and unbelievers. See Joel 3:1-2,9-14; Revelation 21:24. What we really believe and who we are–and whether we've trusted in Christ for salvation–will be shown by the way we live. How we treat others is also important to God (Matt. 7:12).

[33]And he shall set the sheep on his
right hand, but the goats on the left.
[34]Then shall the King say unto them
on his right hand, Come, ye blessed of
my Father, inherit the kingdom prepared for you from the foundation of the
world:
[35]For I was an hungred, and ye gave me
meat: I was thirsty, and ye gave me drink:

25:19 reckoneth with them. See Romans 14:12.
25:29 unto every one that hath. See Matthew 13:12.
25:31 shall come in his glory. See Revelation 19:11-16.

I was a stranger, and ye took me in:
36 Naked, and ye clothed me: I was
sick, and ye visited me: I was in prison, and ye came unto me.
37 Then shall the righteous answer
him, saying, Lord, when saw we thee an
hungred, and fed *thee?* or thirsty, and
gave *thee* drink?
38 When saw we thee a stranger, and
took *thee* in? or naked, and clothed *thee?*
39 Or when saw we thee sick, or in
prison, and came unto thee?
40 And the King shall answer and say
unto them, Verily I say unto you, Inasmuch as ye have done *it* unto one of the
least of these my brethren, ye have
done *it* unto me.
41 Then shall he say also unto them on
the left hand, Depart from me, ye
cursed, into everlasting *fire, prepared
for the *devil and his angels:
42 For I was an hungred, and ye gave
me no meat: I was thirsty, and ye gave
me no drink:
43 I was a stranger, and ye took me not
in: naked, and ye clothed me not: sick,
and in prison, and ye visited me not.
44 Then shall they also answer him,
saying, Lord, when saw we thee an
hungred, or athirst, or a stranger, or
naked, or sick, or in prison, and did not
minister unto thee?
45 Then shall he answer them, saying,
Verily I say unto you, Inasmuch as ye
did *it* not to one of the least of these, ye
did *it* not to me.
46 And these shall go away into everlasting punishment: but the righteous
into life eternal.

II. Jesus, the Son of Abraham
(26:1—27:66).
The Sacrifice of the Lamb
(1) The consultation of the Jewish
authorities concerning Christ
(Mark 14:1-2; Luke 22:1-2)

26 And it came to pass, when
Jesus had finished all these sayings, he said unto his disciples,
2 Ye know that after two days is *the*
feast of the *passover, and the Son of
man is betrayed to be crucified.
3 Then assembled together the chief
priests, and the scribes, and the elders
of the people, unto the palace of the
high priest, who was called *Caiaphas,
4 And consulted that they might take
Jesus by subtilty, and kill *him.*
5 But they said, Not on the feast *day,*
lest there be an uproar among the
people.

(2) Mary of Bethany anoints the Lord
for burial
(Mark 14:3-9; John 12:1-8)

¶6 Now when Jesus was in Bethany, in
the house of Simon the *leper,
7 There came unto him a woman having an *alabaster box of very precious
ointment, and poured it on his head, as
he sat *at meat.*
8 But when his disciples saw *it,* they
had indignation, saying, To what purpose *is* this waste?
9 For this ointment might have been
sold for much, and given to the poor.
10 When Jesus understood *it,* he said
unto them, Why trouble ye the woman? for she hath wrought a good work
upon me.
11 For ye have the poor always with
you; but me ye have not always.
12 For in that she hath poured this
ointment on my body, she did *it* for my
burial.
13 Verily I say unto you, Wheresoever
this gospel shall be preached in the
whole world, *there* shall also this, that
this woman hath done, be told for a
memorial of her.

(3) Judas covenants to betray Christ
(Mark 14:10-11; Luke 22:3-6)

¶14 Then one of the twelve, called
*Judas Iscariot, went unto the chief
priests,
15 And said *unto them,* What will ye
give me, and I will deliver him unto you?

25:41 everlasting fire. See *hell.

And they covenanted with him for thirty
pieces of silver.

(4) The Passover
(Mark 14:12-21; Luke 22:7-20,24-30)

16 And from that time he sought opportunity to betray him.
¶17 Now the first *day* of the *feast of*
*unleavened bread the disciples came
to Jesus, saying unto him, Where wilt
thou that we prepare for thee to eat the
passover?
18 And he said, Go into the city to such
a man, and say unto him, The Master
saith, My time is at hand; I will keep the
passover at thy house with my disciples.
19 And the disciples did as Jesus had
appointed them; and they made ready
the passover.
20 Now when the even was come, he
sat down with the twelve.
21 And as they did eat, he said, Verily
I say unto you, that one of you shall
betray me.
22 And they were exceeding sorrowful, and began every one of them to say
unto him, Lord, is it I?
23 And he answered and said, He that
dippeth *his* hand with me in the dish,
the same shall betray me.
24 The Son of man goeth as it is written of him: but woe unto that man by
whom the Son of man is betrayed! it had
been good for that man if he had not
been born.
25 Then Judas, which betrayed him,
answered and said, Master, is it I? He
said unto him, Thou hast said.

(5) The institution of the Lord's Supper
(Mark 14:22-25; Luke 22:17-20;
1 Cor. 11:23-25)

¶26 And as they were eating, Jesus
took bread, and blessed *it*, and brake *it*,
and gave *it* to the disciples, and said,
Take, eat; this is my *body.
27 And he took the cup, and gave
thanks, and gave *it* to them, saying,
Drink ye all of it;
28 For this is my blood of the new
*testament, which is shed for many for
the *remission of sins.
29 But I say unto you, I will not drink
henceforth of this fruit of the vine, until that day when I drink it new with you
in my Father's kingdom.
30 And when they had sung an hymn,
they went out into the mount of Olives.

(6) The prophecy concerning Peter's
denial of Christ
(Mark 14:26-31; Luke 22:31-34;
John 13:36-38)

31 Then saith Jesus unto them, All ye
shall be offended because of me this
night: for it is written, I will smite the
shepherd, and the sheep of the flock
shall be scattered abroad.
32 But after I am risen again, I will go
before you into Galilee.
33 *Peter answered and said unto
him, Though all *men* shall be offended because of thee, *yet* will I never be
offended.
34 Jesus said unto him, Verily I say
unto thee, That this night, before the
cock crow, thou shalt deny me thrice.
35 Peter said unto him, Though I
should die with thee, yet will I not deny
thee. Likewise also said all the disciples.

(7) Gethsemane
(Mark 14:32-42; Luke 22:39-46;
John 18:1)

¶36 Then cometh Jesus with them
unto a place called *Gethsemane, and
saith unto the disciples, Sit ye here,
while I go and pray yonder.

26:26 Take, eat; this is my body. See 1 Corinthians 11:23-29 and 11:24 note, "The Symbolic Body."
26:28 testament. Covenant.
26:31 All ye shall be offended. See Matthew 26:56b.
26:31 it is written. See Zechariah 13:7.

[37]And he took with him Peter and the
two sons of Zebedee, and began to be
sorrowful and very heavy.
[38]Then saith he unto them, My soul is
exceeding sorrowful, even unto *death:
tarry ye here, and watch with me.
[39]And he went a little farther, and fell
on his face, and prayed, saying, O my
Father, if it be possible, let *this cup
pass from me: nevertheless not as I
will, but as thou *wilt.*
[40]And he cometh unto the disciples,
and findeth them asleep, and saith unto
Peter, What, could ye not watch with
me one hour?
[41]Watch and pray, that ye enter not
into *temptation: the spirit indeed *is*
willing, but the flesh *is* weak.
[42]He went away again the second
time, and prayed, saying, O my Father,
if this cup may not pass away from me,
except I drink it, thy will be done.
[43]And he came and found them
asleep again: for their eyes were heavy.
[44]And he left them, and went away
again, and prayed the third time, saying
the same words.
[45]Then cometh he to his disciples,
and saith unto them, Sleep on now, and
take *your* rest: behold, the hour is at
hand, and the Son of man is betrayed
into the hands of sinners.
[46]Rise, let us be going: behold, he is
at hand that doth betray me.

(8) Judas' betrayal and Christ's arrest
(Mark 14:43-50; Luke 22:47-53;
John 18:3-11)

¶[47]And while he yet spake, lo, Judas,
one of the twelve, came, and with him
a great multitude with swords and
staves, from the chief priests and elders
of the people.
[48]Now he that betrayed him gave
them a sign, saying, Whomsoever I
shall kiss, that same is he: hold him fast.
[49]And forthwith he came to Jesus,
and said, Hail, master; and kissed him.
[50]And Jesus said unto him, Friend,
wherefore art thou come? Then came
they, and laid hands on Jesus, and took
him.

(9) The amputation of the high
priest's servant's ear
(cf. Luke 22:51)

[51]And, behold, one of them which
were with Jesus stretched out *his* hand,
and drew his sword, and struck a servant of the high priest's, and smote off
his ear.
[52]Then said Jesus unto him, Put up
again thy sword into his place: for all
they that take the sword shall perish
with the sword.
[53]Thinkest thou that I cannot now
pray to my Father, and he shall presently give me more than twelve legions
of angels?
[54]But how then shall the scriptures
be fulfilled, that thus it must be?
[55]In that same hour said Jesus to the
multitudes, Are ye come out as against
a thief with swords and staves for to
take me? I sat daily with you teaching
in the temple, and ye laid no hold on me.

O.T. prophecy fulfilled (14)

[56]But all this was done, that the
scriptures of the prophets might be fulfilled. Then all the disciples forsook
him, and fled.

(10) Jesus before the high priest
(Mark 14:53-65; cf. John 18:12,19-24)

¶[57]And they that had laid hold on
Jesus led *him* away to Caiaphas the high
priest, where the scribes and the elders
were assembled.
[58]But Peter followed him afar off unto

26:37 two sons of Zebedee. James and John. See Mark 10:35.
26:50 Friend, wherefore art thou come? Why are you here? Jesus asked Judas this even though He knew the reason. Judas was supposed to be Christ's disciple and friend, but he became the Lord's betrayer.
26:51 one of them . . . drew his sword . . . smote off his ear. Simon Peter. See John 18:10.

the high priest's palace, and went in,
and sat with the servants, to see the
end.
59Now the chief priests, and elders,
and all the council, sought false witness
against Jesus, to put him to death;
60But found none: yea, though many
false witnesses came, *yet* found they
none. At the last came two false witnesses,
61And said, This *fellow* said, I am able
to destroy the temple of God, and to
build it in three days.
62And the high priest arose, and said
unto him, Answerest thou nothing?
what *is it which* these witness against
thee?
63But Jesus held his peace. And the
high priest answered and said unto him,
I adjure thee by the living God, that
thou tell us whether thou be the Christ,
the Son of God.
64Jesus saith unto him, Thou hast
said: nevertheless I say unto you, Hereafter shall ye see the Son of man sitting
on the right hand of power, and coming
in the clouds of heaven.
65Then the high priest rent his
clothes, saying, He hath spoken blasphemy; what further need have we of
witnesses? behold, now ye have heard
his blasphemy.
66What think ye? They answered and
said, He is guilty of death.
67Then did they spit in his face, and
buffeted him; and others smote *him*
with the palms of their hands,
68Saying, Prophesy unto us, thou
Christ, Who is he that smote thee?

(11) Peter denies the Lord
(Mark 14:66-72; Luke 22:55-62;
John 18:15-18,25-27)

¶69Now Peter sat without in the
palace: and a damsel came unto him,
saying, Thou also wast with Jesus of
Galilee.
70But he denied before *them* all, saying, I know not what thou sayest.
71And when he was gone out into the
porch, another *maid* saw him, and said
unto them that were there, This *fellow*
was also with Jesus of Nazareth.
72And again he denied with an oath, I
do not know the man.
73And after a while came unto *him*
they that stood by, and said to Peter,
Surely thou also art *one* of them; for thy
speech bewrayeth thee.
74Then began he to curse and to
swear, *saying,* I know not the man. And
immediately the cock crew.
75And Peter remembered the word of
Jesus, which said unto him, Before the

26:59 THE SANHEDRIN

Three groups made up the seventy-one members of the Sanhedrin:

1. the elders, who were the political and social "bigwigs";
2. the chief priests, usually twenty-four in number, including the high priest (and the high priest emeritus, if there was one), and the chief priests of the twenty-four temple orders or courses; and
3. the most famed group among the scribes, the scholars. They represented the nation politically, religiously, and in the realm of thought.

The Sanhedrin might be called the Israelites' Supreme Court, their only lawful civil court. Rome reserved the right to decide upon the death penalty.

26:59 false witness. See Psalm 35:11.
26:63 Jesus held his peace. See Isaiah 53:7.
26:64 coming in the clouds of heaven. See Revelation 19:11-16.
26:65 rent. Tore.
26:67 spit in his face. See Isaiah 50:6 and its note, "Willing to Suffer."
26:67 buffeted him. See Isaiah 52:14.
26:67 smote him. See Micah 5:1.
26:73 thy speech. Simon Peter, as a Galilean, spoke in that dialect. Note Acts 2:7.
26:73 bewrayeth. Betrayeth.
26:75 which said unto him. See Matthew 26:34.

cock crow, thou shalt deny me thrice.
And he went out, and wept bitterly.

(12) The Lord Jesus delivered to Pontius Pilate
(Mark 15:1; Luke 23:1; John 18:28)

27 When the morning was come,
all the chief priests and *elders
of the people took counsel against Jesus
to put him to death:
2 And when they had bound him, they
led *him* away, and delivered him to Pontius *Pilate the governor.

(13) Judas' death
(cf. Acts 1:16-19)

¶3 Then Judas, which had betrayed
him, when he saw that he was condemned, *repented himself, and
brought again the thirty pieces of silver
to the chief priests and elders,
4 Saying, I have sinned in that I have
betrayed the innocent blood. And
they said, What *is that* to us? see thou
to that.
5 And he cast down the pieces of silver in the temple, and departed, and
went and hanged himself.
6 And the chief priests took the silver
pieces, and said, It is not lawful for to
put them into the *treasury, because it
is the price of blood.
7 And they took counsel, and bought
with them the potter's field, to bury
strangers in.
8 Wherefore that field was called, The
field of blood, unto this day.

O.T. prophecy fulfilled (15)

9 Then was fulfilled that which was
spoken by Jeremy the *prophet, saying,
And they took the thirty pieces of silver, the price of him that was valued,
whom they of the children of *Israel did
value;
10 And gave them for the potter's
field, as the Lord appointed me.

(14) Jesus before Pilate
(Mark 15:2-15; Luke 23:2-7; John 18:29-38)

11 And Jesus stood before the governor: and the governor asked him, saying, Art thou the *King of the Jews?
And Jesus said unto him, Thou sayest.

O.T. prophecy fulfilled (16)

12 And when he was accused of the
chief priests and elders, he answered
nothing.
13 Then said Pilate unto him, Hearest
thou not how many things they witness
against thee?
14 And he answered him to never a
word; insomuch that the governor marvelled greatly.
15 Now at *that* feast the governor was
wont to release unto the people a prisoner, whom they would.
16 And they had then a notable prisoner, called Barabbas.
17 Therefore when they were gathered
together, Pilate said unto them, Whom
will ye that I release unto you? Barabbas, or Jesus which is called Christ?
18 For he knew that for envy they had
delivered him.
¶19 When he was set down on the
judgment seat, his wife sent unto him,
saying, Have thou nothing to do with
that *just man: for I have suffered
many things this day in a dream because of him.
20 But the chief priests and elders
persuaded the multitude that they
should ask Barabbas, and destroy Jesus.

27:6 because it is the price of blood. See Deuteronomy 23:18; Isaiah 61:8.
27:9 Then was fulfilled. The quotation is from Zechariah 11:12-13 (see also Zech. 11:12 note, "A Picture of Christ's Coming"). The words do not appear in the prophecy of Jeremiah, but in Old Testament times Jeremiah was considered the collector of some of the prophets' writings, which could be why his name is cited here.
27:12,14 nothing . . . never a word. See Isaiah 53:7.
27:15 wont. Accustomed.
27:16 Barabbas. Meaning *son of the father.*

21 The governor answered and said unto them, Whether of the twain will ye that I release unto you? They said, Barabbas.

22 Pilate saith unto them, What shall I do then with Jesus which is called Christ? *They* all say unto him, Let him be crucified.

23 And the governor said, Why, what evil hath he done? But they cried out the more, saying, Let him be crucified.

¶24 When Pilate saw that he could prevail nothing, but *that* rather a tumult was made, he took water, and washed *his* hands before the multitude, saying, I am innocent of the blood of this just person: see ye *to it.*

25 Then answered all the people, and said, His blood *be* on us, and on our children.

¶26 Then released he Barabbas unto them: and when he had scourged Jesus, he delivered *him* to be crucified.

(15) The King crowned with thorns (Mark 15:16-23; Luke 23:26-32; John 19:16-17)
O.T. prophecy fulfilled (17)

27 Then the soldiers of the governor took Jesus into the common hall, and gathered unto him the whole band *of soldiers.*

28 And they stripped him, and put on him a scarlet robe.

¶29 And when they had platted a crown of thorns, they put *it* upon his head, and a reed in his right hand: and they bowed the knee before him, and mocked him, saying, Hail, King of the Jews!

30 And they spit upon him, and took the reed, and smote him on the head.

31 And after that they had mocked him, they took the robe off from him, and put his own raiment on him, and led him away to crucify *him.*

32 And as they came out, they found a man of Cyrene, Simon by name: him they compelled to bear his cross.

(16) The Saviour is crucified (Mark 15:22-32; Luke 23:33-43; John 19:17-24)

33 And when they were come unto a place called Golgotha, that is to say, a place of a skull,

¶34 They gave him vinegar to drink mingled with gall: and when he had tasted *thereof,* he would not drink.

27:34 The Use of Vinegar
See Psalm 69:21. "Vinegar mingled with gall" could be translated "wine mingled with gall," a very bitter ingredient. Its aim was to stupefy the victim and cause him to lose consciousness. But our Lord preferred to remain completely conscious as He suffered for us.

Vinegar was practically always made from wine in the ancient world and is an acetic acid. Undiluted, it is undrinkable, of course. Thus to offer it to a thirsty man is nothing short of mockery.

O.T. prophecy fulfilled (18)

35 And they crucified him, and parted his garments, casting lots: that it might be fulfilled which was spoken by the prophet, They parted my garments among them, and upon my vesture did they cast lots.

36 And sitting down they watched him there;

37 And set up over his head his accusation written, THIS IS JESUS THE KING OF THE JEWS.

27:24 Pilate . . . washed his hands . . . saying. A Hebrew custom (Deut. 21:6) signifying the desire to escape from guilt for an act.

27:25 His blood be on us, and on our children. This would seem to be the reason for the suffering of the Jewish people during the last nineteen centuries.

27:27 into the common hall, and gathered unto him the whole band of soldiers. See Isaiah 53:8.

27:30 spit upon him . . . smote him. See Isaiah 50:6 (and its note, "Willing to Suffer"); Zechariah 13:7.

27:35 that it might be fulfilled. See Psalm 22:18.

O.T. prophecy fulfilled (19)

38Then were there two thieves crucified with him, one on the right hand,
and another on the left.
¶39And they that passed by reviled
him, wagging their heads,
40And saying, Thou that destroyest
the temple, and buildest *it* in three days,
save thyself. If thou be the Son of *God,
come down from the cross.
41Likewise also the chief priests
mocking *him,* with the *scribes and elders, said,
42He saved others; himself he cannot
save. If he be the King of Israel, let him
now come down from the cross, and we
will believe him.
43He trusted in God; let him deliver
him now, if he will have him: for he said,
I am the Son of God.
44The thieves also, which were crucified with him, cast the same in his
teeth.
45Now from the sixth hour there was
darkness over all the land unto the
ninth hour.
46And about the ninth hour Jesus
cried with a loud voice, saying, Eli,
Eli, lama sabachthani? that is to say,
My God, my God, why hast thou forsaken me?
47Some of them that stood there,
when they heard *that,* said, This *man*
calleth for *Elias.
48And *straightway one of them ran,
and took a spunge, and filled *it* with vinegar, and put *it* on a reed, and gave him
to drink.
49The rest said, Let be, let us see
whether Elias will come to save him.
¶50Jesus, when he had cried again
with a loud voice, yielded up the ghost.
51And, behold, the veil of the temple
was rent in twain from the top to the
bottom; and the earth did quake, and
the rocks rent;
52And the graves were opened; and
many bodies of the *saints which slept
arose,
53And came out of the graves after his
resurrection, and went into the *holy
city, and appeared unto many.
54Now when the *centurion, and they
that were with him, watching Jesus,
saw the earthquake, and those things
that were done, they feared greatly, saying, Truly this was the Son of God.
55And many women were there beholding afar off, which followed Jesus
from Galilee, ministering unto him:
56Among which was Mary Magdalene, and Mary the mother of James and
Joses, and the mother of Zebedee's children.

(17) The burial of the Lord Jesus
(Mark 15:42-47; Luke 23:50-56;
John 19:38-42)

57When the even was come, there
came a rich man of Arimathaea, named
*Joseph, who also himself was Jesus'
disciple:
58He went to Pilate, and begged the
body of Jesus. Then Pilate commanded
the body to be delivered.
59And when Joseph had taken the
body, he wrapped it in a clean *linen
cloth,

O.T. prophecy fulfilled (20)

60And laid it in his own new tomb,
which he had hewn out in the *rock: and
he rolled a great stone to the door of the
sepulchre, and departed.

27:38 two thieves crucified. See Isaiah 53:12.
27:45 ninth hour. Three o'clock in the afternoon.
27:46 saying. See Psalm 22:1.
27:50 ghost. Or, His *spirit.*
27:51 top to the bottom. The veil in the temple was not torn from the bottom up, by human hands, but from top to bottom, indicating that it was God who opened "a new and living way, which he hath consecrated for us, through the veil, that is to say, his flesh" (Heb. 10:20), into His presence.
27:60 his own new tomb. Joseph of Arimathaea offered his own tomb. See Isaiah 53:9.

61And there was Mary Magdalene,
and the other Mary, sitting over against
the sepulchre.
¶62Now the next day, that followed
the day of the preparation, the chief
priests and *Pharisees came together
unto Pilate,
63Saying, Sir, we remember that that
deceiver said, while he was yet alive,
After three days I will rise again.
64Command therefore that the sepulchre be made sure until the third day,
lest his disciples come by night, and
steal him away, and say unto the people, He is risen from the dead: so the
last error shall be worse than the first.
65Pilate said unto them, Ye have a
watch: go your way, make *it* as sure as
ye can.

(18) The sealing of the sepulchre

66So they went, and made the sepulchre sure, sealing the stone, and setting
a watch.

III. Jesus, the Son of God (28:1-20)
A. The Resurrection of the Lord
(Mark 16:1-14; Luke 24:1-49; John 20:1-23)

28 In the end of the sabbath, as it
began to dawn toward the first
day of the week, came Mary Magdalene
and the other Mary to see the sepulchre.
2And, behold, there was a great earthquake: for the angel of the Lord descended from heaven, and came and
rolled back the stone from the door, and
sat upon it.
3His countenance was like lightning,
and his raiment white as snow:
4And for fear of him the keepers did
shake, and became as dead *men.*
5And the angel answered and said
unto the women, Fear not ye: for I
know that ye seek Jesus, which was
crucified.
6He is not here: for he is risen, as he
said. Come, see the place where the
Lord lay.
7And go quickly, and tell his disciples
that he is risen from the dead; and, behold, he goeth before you into Galilee;
there shall ye see him: lo, I have told
you.
8And they departed quickly from the
sepulchre with fear and great joy; and
did run to bring his disciples word.

B. "I Am with You Alway"

¶9And as they went to tell his disciples, behold, Jesus met them, saying,
All hail. And they came and held him by
the feet, and worshipped him.

(1) The Lord appears in His resurrection body

10Then said Jesus unto them, Be not
afraid: go tell my brethren that they
go into Galilee, and there shall they
see me.

(2) The bribing of the Roman guards

¶11Now when they were going, behold, some of the watch came into the
city, and shewed unto the chief priests
all the things that were done.
12And when they were assembled
with the elders, and had taken counsel,
they gave large money unto the soldiers,
13Saying, Say ye, His disciples came
by night, and stole him *away* while we
slept.

27:64 be made sure. That is, to be sealed or made secure.

27:65 Ye have a watch. This expression indicates that Pilate gave them their request and let them have a watch or guard of soldiers. This precaution turned out to be definite evidence that our Lord's resurrection was not fraudulent.

28:6 as he said. See Matthew 16:21; 17:23; 20:19.

28:7 into Galilee. See Matthew 26:32.

28:9 All hail. Or, *Oh, joy!*

28:13 while we slept. For a Roman soldier to sleep while on watch was punishable by death.

[14]And if this come to the governor's
ears, we will persuade him, and secure
you.
[15]So they took the money, and did as
they were taught: and this saying is
commonly reported among the Jews
until this day.
¶[16]Then the eleven disciples went
away into Galilee, into a mountain where
Jesus had appointed them.
[17]And when they saw him, they worshipped him: but some doubted.

(3) The commission

[18]And Jesus came and spake unto
them, saying, All power is given unto
me in heaven and in earth.
¶[19]Go ye therefore, and teach all nations, baptizing them in the name of the
Father, and of the Son, and of the Holy
Ghost:
[20]Teaching them to observe all things
whatsoever I have commanded you:
and, lo, I am with you alway, *even* unto
the end of the world. Amen.

28:14 persuade. Satisfy.
28:20 world. Age. Through the Holy Spirit, even now Jesus continues to be with those who have trusted in Him for salvation, as He will be with us (and we with Him) forever.

The Gospel according to Saint

MARK

THE WRITER

The man whom God chose to write about the Lord Jesus in His active service among men was John, whose last name was Mark. His mother's name was Mary. It was this Mary who opened her house for prayer when Peter was in prison (Acts 12:12). Mark, although he was not an apostle, was a close friend of the apostles. We find his name in many places in the writings of Luke and Paul (Acts 12:12,25; 15:37,39; Colossians 4:10; 2 Timothy 4:11; Philemon 24). If God shows us his wisdom in the choice of Matthew, the hated tax collector under the Romans, to set forth Jesus as Messiah the King, how wonderful it is that Mark, the servant of the apostles, who failed in his service at one time (Acts 15:38; compare with 2 Timothy 4:11 to note Mark's later faithfulness), should speak about the tireless and faithful service of the blessed Lord.

THEME

Mark gives us a picture of Jesus as the faithful Servant of God. It is really the Gospel of the works of Christ (see Acts 10:38). Because it was written for the Romans whose watchword was "power," it brings before us the matchless power of the "mighty Miracle Worker," and the power of His love in the greatest of all miracles, His death and resurrection. This is the reason why Mark speaks more about the miracles of our Lord Jesus than he does about His parables.

Mark wrote his Gospel in the Greek language and he uses a word which is translated by three different English words; the word is *euthus* which is translated "immediately," "forthwith," "straightway." This is a word particularly applied to a servant, found about eighty times in the New Testament; it occurs in Mark alone about forty times.

THINGS TO NOTE

The key verse of Mark is 10:45.

This Gospel gives no genealogy of the Lord (no record of His birth), and no notice of His childhood or youth, for these things are not important in the account of a servant's life.

The date of writing was about A.D. 67.

OUTLINE OF MARK

I.	Introduction	Mark 1:1-13
II.	Christ's Ministry in Eastern Galilee	Mark 1:14—7:23
III.	Christ's Ministry in Northern Galilee	Mark 7:24—9:50

IV.	Christ's Ministry in Peraea	Mark 10:1-31
V.	Christ's Last Journey to Jerusalem and His Death	Mark 10:32—15:47
VI.	Christ's Resurrection and Ascension	Mark 16:1-20

I. Introduction (1:1-13)

1 The beginning of the *gospel of
Jesus *Christ, the Son of God;

*The *baptism and preaching of *John the Baptist (Matt. 3:1-11; Luke 3:1-16; John 1:6-8,19-28)*

2 As it is written in the *prophets,
Behold, I send my messenger before
thy face, which shall prepare thy way
before thee.
3 The voice of one crying in the wilderness, Prepare ye the way of the
Lord, make his paths straight.
4 John did baptize in the wilderness,
and preach the baptism of *repentance
for the *remission of sins.
5 And there went out unto him all the
land of Judaea, and they of Jerusalem,
and were all baptized of him in the river
of Jordan, confessing their sins.
6 And John was clothed with camel's
hair, and with a girdle of a skin about his
loins; and he did eat locusts and wild
honey;
7 And preached, saying, There cometh
one mightier than I after me, the latchet
of whose shoes I am not worthy to stoop
down and unloose.
8 I indeed have baptized you with
water: but he shall baptize you with the
Holy Ghost.

1:4 THE MESSAGE OF REPENTANCE

Verses 4-8 show how John went ahead of our Lord Jesus Christ to tell the people that our Lord had come and that He would soon show Himself to them. See also Matthew 3:1-11; Luke 3:1-16; John 1:6-8,19-28.

John told the Jewish people to "repent," that is, to change their minds and turn from their sins. We must remember that John was a prophet with a message like that of the Old Testament prophets–he was really the last of the Old Testament prophets. The New Testament times did not begin until the Lord Jesus Christ died on the cross at Calvary. John's message of repentance, therefore, is the same message that we find in the Old Testament books that the prophets wrote. It was God's desire that His earthly people, the Jews, should return to Him.

Frequently we find the words "return," "turn ye" in the Old Testament prophets. These mean the same as the word for "repent" that John uses here (read Isa. 55:7; Ezek. 33:11; Joel 2:12). The message was not for the Jews only. God speaks to our hearts in the same way. Each one of us has sinned against Him and needs to repent (see Acts 17:30-31).

1:1 gospel of Jesus Christ, the Son of God. The good news about His coming down to earth to be our Saviour. We may compare the different names of the gospel: "the gospel of the kingdom of God" (Mark 1:14); "the gospel of the grace of God" (Acts 20:24); "the gospel of God" (Rom. 1:1); "the gospel of Christ" (Rom. 1:16); and "the everlasting gospel" (Rev. 14:6).

1:1 Christ. Christ is the Greek form of the Hebrew word *Messiah,* meaning the *Anointed One.* "Jesus" brings before us His human nature; "Christ" speaks of His deity, that is, Jesus Christ is God. Never is the messiahship of our Lord separated from His deity.

1:2 in the prophets. This refers to what the prophets had to say about the ministry of John the Baptist (Mal. 3:1; Isa. 40:3).

1:7 latchet. The latchet was the thong or lace of the sandal that held it together. In the East only slaves loosened the thong when a guest entered the house. So mighty was Christ that John felt unworthy even to do this.

The baptism of the Lord Jesus
(Matt. 3:13-17; Luke 3:21-22)

¶9And it came to pass in those days,
that Jesus came from Nazareth of Galilee, and was baptized of John in Jordan.
10And *straightway coming up out of
the water, he saw the heavens opened, and the Spirit like a dove descending upon him:
11And there came a voice from *heaven, *saying,* Thou art my beloved Son, in whom I am well pleased.

The temptation of the Lord Jesus
(Matt. 4:1-11; Luke 4:1-13)

¶12And immediately the Spirit driveth him into the wilderness.
13And he was there in the wilderness
forty days, *tempted of *Satan; and was with the wild beasts; and the *angels ministered unto him.

II. Christ's Ministry in Eastern Galilee
(1:14—7:23)

¶14Now after that John was put in

1:9 THE BAPTISM OF JESUS

The baptism of Jesus showed that He was one with His people. John's baptism showed the people that they needed to repent and to confess their sins. Jesus was the only sinless, undefiled One. He did not need to repent, for His mind was always in perfect harmony with His Father. It was unnecessary for Him to confess, for He had no sin (1 John 3:5); He did no sin (1 Pet. 2:22); He knew no sin (2 Cor. 5:21).

In Matthew (see 3:13-17), we discover the reason for his baptism: "Thus it becometh us to fulfil all righteousness" (vs. 15). Our Lord Jesus Christ came into this world to die for our sins; He came to be the substitute, the One who takes the place of another, for sinners; in the very beginning of His public ministry, His sacrificial death for us was pictured in His baptism. Our Lord fulfilled all righteousness that we might be made the righteousness of God in Him (see also Luke 3:21-22). Just as the Father, Son, and Holy Spirit were in perfect unity regarding the creation of man (Gen. 1:26; see also 1:27 note, "In God's Image"), so here we find the Trinity in perfect harmony regarding the work of redemption that our Lord Jesus Christ had come to perform.

1:13 THE TEMPTATION OF JESUS

The word "tempted" is one that has caused a great deal of difficulty. Some people say that if Jesus possessed a sinless nature, that is, had no sin, how could He be tempted? This question is asked by people who do not understand what is meant by the word "tempted." One of the meanings is *to seduce* or *to lead astray.* This kind of temptation means that the person tempted has some evil in him that could make him yield and sin. This could never be true of our Lord Jesus Christ. He is holy in every part of His being. But the word "tempt" also means *to test.* To test means *to bring to trial and examination–to try, to prove.* It is in this sense that the word is used in connection with our Lord.

When Satan tested our Lord Jesus, he told Him that it was not necessary for Him to go to the cross. He could get the crown without this, if He would fall down and worship Satan. But our Lord did not fall into the temptation of Satan. It was His Father's will that Christ should die for us. Jesus came to do the Father's will (Heb. 10:7), and Satan tried to tempt Him not to do it.

1:10, 12 straightway . . . immediately. See the introduction to this book.

1:13 in the wilderness. While Mark does not give us the threefold temptation as recorded in Matthew and Luke (Matt. 4:1-11; Luke 4:1-13), he tells us something of real interest not found in the other two Gospels. The mention of the "wild beasts" is found only in Mark. The wilderness in which our Lord was tempted was the haunt at night of the wolf, the hyena, the jackal, and the leopard. This triumph in the wilderness at the beginning of His public ministry was a forecast of His victory over Satan by His death and resurrection.

1:14 Now after that. Between the Temptation recorded in verse 13 and the imprisonment of John the Baptist (vs. 14), a period of one year had passed. The events that took place during this time are not given to us in Mark, but are found in the Gospel according to John (1:19–4:54).

1:14 John was put in prison. The reason why Herod threw John into prison is given in Mark 6:17-18.

prison, Jesus came into Galilee, preaching the gospel of the *kingdom of God,
15 And saying, The time is fulfilled,
and the kingdom of God is at hand: *repent ye, and believe the gospel.

The call of four fishermen
(Matt. 4:18-22; Luke 5:10-11;
cf. John 1:35-42)

¶16 Now as he walked by the sea of
Galilee, he saw Simon and Andrew his
brother casting a net into the sea: for
they were fishers.
17 And Jesus said unto them, Come ye
after me, and I will make you to become
fishers of men.
18 And straightway they forsook their
nets, and followed him.
19 And when he had gone a little farther thence, he saw James the *son* of
Zebedee, and John his brother, who also
were in the ship mending their nets.
20 And straightway he called them:
and they left their father Zebedee in the
ship with the hired servants, and went
after him.

The man possessed of demons healed
(Luke 4:31-37)

¶21 And they went into Capernaum;
and straightway on the *sabbath day he
entered into the *synagogue, and taught.
22 And they were astonished at his
*doctrine: for he taught them as one that
had authority, and not as the *scribes.
23 And there was in their synagogue
a man with an *unclean spirit; and he
cried out,
24 Saying, Let *us* alone; what have we
to do with thee, thou Jesus of Nazareth?
art thou come to destroy us? I know
thee who thou art, the Holy One of God.
25 And Jesus rebuked him, saying,
Hold thy peace, and come out of him.
26 And when the unclean spirit had
torn him, and cried with a loud voice,
he came out of him.
27 And they were all amazed, insomuch that they questioned among
themselves, saying, What thing is this?
what new doctrine *is* this? for with authority commandeth he even the unclean spirits, and they do obey him.
28 And immediately his fame spread
abroad throughout all the region round
about Galilee.

The healing of Simon's wife's mother
(Matt. 8:14-15; Luke 4:38-39)

¶29 And forthwith, when they were
come out of the synagogue, they entered into the house of Simon and Andrew, with James and John.
30 But Simon's wife's mother lay sick
of a fever, and anon they tell him of her.
31 And he came and took her by the
hand, and lifted her up; and immediately the fever left her, and she ministered
unto them.

Casting out demons and healing
many diseased

¶32 And at even, when the sun did set,
they brought unto him all that were diseased, and them that were possessed
with devils.
33 And all the city was gathered together at the door.

1:17 Come ye after me. This was not the disciples' call to salvation. They had already believed in the Lord Jesus Christ. They had heard John's message (see John 1:29,37). This was a definite call to service, which comes after salvation (see also Matt. 4:18-22; Luke 5:10-11; John 1:35-42). Just as they had caught fish for a living, they were now to go and catch men for Jesus Christ (read also 1 Cor. 1:26-29).

1:22 he taught them as one that had authority. The scribes were the men who were supposed to explain the Scriptures to the people, but the authority they claimed was taken from oral teaching and writings called "the tradition of the elders" (Mark 7:5). The traditions were simply the words of man and were not a safe guide. Jesus is God, and when He spoke it was God who was speaking (see also Luke 4:31-37).

1:25 Hold thy peace. Our Lord uses the same word that He used when He calmed the storm (Mark 4:39). "Hold thy peace" really means *be quiet.*

34 And he healed many that were sick
of divers diseases, and cast out many
devils; and suffered not the devils to
speak, because they knew him.

The Lord Jesus plans a preaching tour in Galilee (Luke 4:42-44)

¶35 And in the morning, rising up a
great while before day, he went out, and
departed into a solitary place, and there
prayed.
36 And Simon and they that were with
him followed after him.
37 And when they had found him, they
said unto him, All *men* seek for thee.
38 And he said unto them, Let us go
into the next towns, that I may preach
there also: for therefore came I forth.
39 And he preached in their *synagogues
throughout all Galilee, and cast
out devils.

Healing a leper (Matt. 8:2-4; Luke 5:12-14)

¶40 And there came a *leper to him,
beseeching him, and kneeling down to
him, and saying unto him, If thou wilt,
thou canst make me *clean.
41 And Jesus, moved with compassion,
put forth *his* hand, and touched
him, and saith unto him, I will; be thou
clean.
42 And as soon as he had spoken, immediately
the *leprosy departed from
him, and he was cleansed.
43 And he straitly charged him, and
forthwith sent him away;
44 And saith unto him, See thou say
nothing to any man: but go thy way,
shew thyself to the priest, and offer for
thy cleansing those things which *Moses
commanded, for a testimony unto
them.
45 But he went out, and began to publish
it much, and to blaze abroad the
matter, insomuch that Jesus could no
more openly enter into the city, but was
without in desert places: and they came
to him from every quarter.

The man sick of the palsy healed (Matt. 9:1-8; Luke 5:18-26)

2 And again he entered into Capernaum,
after *some* days; and it
was noised that he was in the house.
2 And straightway many were gathered
together, insomuch that there was
no room to receive *them,* no, not so much
as about the door: and he preached the
word unto them.
3 And they come unto him, bringing
one sick of the palsy, which was borne
of four.
4 And when they could not come nigh
unto him for the press, they uncovered
the roof where he was: and when they
had broken *it* up, they let down the bed
wherein the sick of the palsy lay.
5 When Jesus saw their *faith, he said
unto the sick of the palsy, Son, thy sins
be *forgiven thee.
6 But there were certain of the scribes
sitting there, and reasoning in their
hearts,
7 Why doth this *man* thus speak
blasphemies? who can forgive sins but
God only?

1:34 divers diseases. The word "divers" comes from a Greek word which means *many-colored.* The diseases of these people were many (see also Matt. 8:16-17; Luke 4:40-41).

1:40 a leper. Read the law which had to do with the leper in Leviticus 13:44-46. He is a *type of a poor, lost sinner. See also Matthew 8:2-4; Luke 5:12-14.

1:44 shew thyself to the priest. Jesus always honored the *Law. Only the priest could pronounce the leper clean (see Lev. 14:2-20 and 14:2 note, "The Method of Cleansing").

2:4 uncovered the roof. They climbed the stairway that was on the outside of the house. The house had a flat roof, probably made of stone slabs, as did all houses in the East in those days.

2:7 who can forgive sins but God only? The scribes knew that the Lord Jesus was attributing to Himself the authority of God Himself.

[8]And immediately when Jesus perceived in his spirit that they so reasoned within themselves, he said unto
them, Why reason ye these things in
your hearts?
[9]Whether is it easier to say to the
sick of the palsy, *Thy* sins be forgiven
thee; or to say, Arise, and take up thy
bed, and walk?
[10]But that ye may know that the Son
of man hath power on earth to forgive
sins, (he saith to the sick of the palsy,)
[11]I say unto thee, Arise, and take up
thy bed, and go thy way into thine
house.
[12]And immediately he arose, took up
the bed, and went forth before them all;
insomuch that they were all amazed,
and glorified God, saying, We never saw
it on this fashion.

The call of Matthew (Levi)—
(Matt. 9:9-13; Luke 5:27-32)

¶[13]And he went forth again by the sea
side; and all the multitude resorted
unto him, and he taught them.
[14]And as he passed by, he saw Levi
the *son* of Alphaeus sitting at the receipt of custom, and said unto him, Follow me. And he arose and followed him.
¶[15]And it came to pass, that, as Jesus
sat at meat in his house, many *publicans and sinners sat also together with
Jesus and his disciples: for there were
many, and they followed him.
[16]And when the scribes and *Pharisees saw him eat with publicans and
sinners, they said unto his disciples,
How is it that he eateth and drinketh
with publicans and sinners?
[17]When Jesus heard *it,* he saith unto
them, They that are whole have no
need of the physician, but they that are
sick: I came not to call the righteous,
but sinners to repentance.
¶[18]And the disciples of John and of
the Pharisees used to fast: and they
come and say unto him, Why do the
disciples of John and of the Pharisees
fast, but thy disciples fast not?
[19]And Jesus said unto them, Can the
children of the bridechamber fast, while
the *bridegroom is with them? as long
as they have the bridegroom with them,
they cannot fast.
[20]But the days will come, when the
bridegroom shall be taken away from
them, and then shall they fast in those
days.

The parables of the cloth and the bottles
(cf. Matt. 9:16-17; Luke 5:36-39)

¶[21]No man also seweth a piece of new
cloth on an old garment: else the new
piece that filled it up taketh away from
the old, and the rent is made worse.

2:22 BOTTLES

The word means *wineskins.* The "bottles" in which the wine was kept were made of skins. Old skins were worn thin and stiff. They would not yield to new wine and its ferment. Our Lord taught by these parables that the *Law and *grace do not belong together (see also Matt. 9:16-17; Luke 5:36-39). We are not saved by doing anything; we are saved through the work that Christ has done. We are saved by God's grace from beginning to end. The meaning of verses 21 and 22 will be made clear if you compare them with Galatians 3:1-3 (see also Gal. 3:3 note, "Being Perfected"). The gospel of God's grace is the new wine; we must not put it into the old wineskins of the Law (see Rom. 3:20-31, especially vs. 20).

2:14 the receipt of custom. The place where taxes were paid. Matthew was employed as a tax collector for the Roman government (see also Matt. 9:9-12; Luke 5:27-32).

2:17 They that are whole. The Pharisees thought they were righteous and were not sick with sin, so the Lord had no message of salvation for them.

2:18 disciples of John . . . fast. John the Baptist had been thrown into prison, and so it was very natural that his followers were filled with sorrow.

2:19 the bridegroom. John the Baptist had spoken of Jesus as a bridegroom (see John 3:29).

[22]And no man putteth new wine into
old *bottles: else the new wine doth
burst the bottles, and the wine is spilled,
and the bottles will be marred: but new
wine must be put into new bottles.

Jesus Christ is Lord of the Sabbath
(Matt. 12:1-8; Luke 6:1-5)

¶[23]And it came to pass, that he went
through the corn fields on the sabbath
day; and his disciples began, as they
went, to pluck the ears of corn.
[24]And the Pharisees said unto him,
Behold, why do they on the sabbath day
that which is not lawful?
[25]And he said unto them, Have ye
never read what *David did, when he
had need, and was an hungred, he, and
they that were with him?
[26]How he went into the house of God
in the days of Abiathar the high priest,
and did eat the *shewbread, which is
not lawful to eat but for the priests, and
gave also to them which were with him?
[27]And he said unto them, The sabbath was made for man, and not man for
the sabbath:
[28]Therefore the Son of man is Lord
also of the sabbath.

Healing the man with the withered hand
(Matt. 12:10-14; Luke 6:6-11)

3 And he entered again into the
synagogue; and there was a man
there which had a withered hand.
[2]And they watched him, whether he
would heal him on the sabbath day; that
they might accuse him.
[3]And he saith unto the man which had
the withered hand, Stand forth.
[4]And he saith unto them, Is it lawful
to do good on the sabbath days, or to do
evil? to save life, or to kill? But they
held their peace.
[5]And when he had looked round about
on them with anger, being grieved for
the hardness of their hearts, he saith
unto the man, Stretch forth thine hand.
And he stretched *it* out: and his hand
was restored whole as the other.
¶[6]And the Pharisees went forth, and
straightway took counsel with the *Herodians against him, how they might
destroy him.

The multitudes healed

[7]But Jesus withdrew himself with his
disciples to the sea: and a great multitude from Galilee followed him, and
from Judaea,
[8]And from Jerusalem, and from Idu-
maea, and *from* beyond Jordan; and they
about *Tyre and Sidon, a great multitude, when they had heard what great
things he did, came unto him.
[9]And he spake to his disciples, that a
small ship should wait on him because
of the multitude, lest they should
throng him.
[10]For he had healed many; insomuch

2:24 why do they on the sabbath day that which is not lawful? The Law of Moses forbade reaping and threshing on the Sabbath because this meant work. Plucking the corn was interpreted by the Pharisees as reaping, and rubbing the hands as threshing—but it was not work. The Pharisees thus added to the Word of God, making it "of none effect" (read Matt. 15:6; Mark 7:8-9).

2:25 what David did. Read 1 Samuel 21:1-6.

2:27 The sabbath was made for man. It is God's gift to man. God in His matchless wisdom provided it to meet the needs of our souls and bodies.

3:6 Pharisees . . . Herodians. These groups were bitter enemies. The *Pharisees hated the *Herodians, but they hated the Lord Jesus Christ more. They showed their terrible bitterness when they became friendly with the Herodians for the sake of putting the Lord to death. Note the occasion when Pilate and Herod were made friends (Luke 23:12).

3:7 withdrew himself. Jesus knew that the Pharisees had made a plot to kill Him. Our Lord also knew that His hour was not yet come (John 7:30; 8:20; 13:1), so He went away to the seashore. Notice the other occasions of Jesus' withdrawing Himself in the Gospel of Mark (6:31; 6:46; 7:24,31; 10:1; 14:34).

that they pressed upon him for to touch
him, as many as had plagues.
11And unclean spirits, when they saw
him, fell down before him, and cried,
saying, Thou art the Son of God.
12And he straitly charged them that
they should not make him known.

The calling of the twelve apostles
(Matt. 10:1-4; Luke 6:12-16)

¶13And he goeth up into a mountain,
and calleth *unto him* whom he would:
and they came unto him.
14And he ordained twelve, that they
should be with him, and that he might
send them forth to preach,
15And to have power to heal sicknesses, and to cast out devils:
16And Simon he surnamed *Peter;
17And James the *son* of Zebedee, and
John the brother of James; and he surnamed them Boanerges, which is, The
sons of thunder:
18And Andrew, and Philip, and Bartholomew, and Matthew, and Thomas, and James the *son* of Alphaeus,
and Thaddaeus, and Simon the Canaanite,
19And *Judas Iscariot, which also betrayed him: and they went into an
house.
20And the multitude cometh together again, so that they could not so much
as eat bread.
21And when his friends heard *of it,*
they went out to lay hold on him: for
they said, He is beside himself.

The unpardonable sin
(Matt. 12:24-29; Luke 11:14-20)

¶22And the scribes which came down
from Jerusalem said, He hath Beelzebub, and by the prince of the devils
casteth he out devils.
23And he called them *unto him,* and
said unto them in *parables, How can
Satan cast out Satan?
24And if a kingdom be divided against
itself, that kingdom cannot stand.
25And if a house be divided against
itself, that house cannot stand.
26And if Satan rise up against himself,
and be divided, he cannot stand, but
hath an end.
27No man can enter into a strong
man's house, and spoil his goods, except he will first bind the strong man;
and then he will spoil his house.
28Verily I say unto you, All sins shall
be forgiven unto the sons of men, and
blasphemies wherewith soever they
shall blaspheme:
29But he that shall blaspheme
against the Holy Ghost hath never forgiveness, but is in danger of eternal
*damnation:
30Because they said, He hath an unclean spirit.

The new relationship
(Matt. 12:46-50; Luke 8:19-21)

¶31There came then his brethren and
his mother, and, standing without, sent
unto him, calling him.
32And the multitude sat about him,
and they said unto him, Behold, thy

3:14 he ordained twelve. See also Matthew 10:1-4; Luke 6:12-16. Their names are also given in Acts 1:13.

3:22 Beelzebub. This means *the god of flies,* an old god of the Philistines. The Jews called him the "god of filth," and they applied this name to Satan because they believed Satan to be the god of unclean spirits. (See also Matt. 10:25 note, "Beelzebub.")

3:27 the strong man. The strong man is Satan. The spoiler of the strong man, the One who will bind Satan, is our Lord Jesus Christ. His death and resurrection are proof that He will put all enemies under His feet (see 1 Cor. 15:25 and its note). The final triumph of our Lord over Satan is yet to be seen, but we can have victory over Satan now if we allow Jesus Christ to reign as Lord in our hearts.

3:29 blaspheme. See Matthew 12:31 note, "The Unpardonable Sin."

3:29 in danger of eternal damnation. He is bound by an eternal sin. There is no hope of salvation for someone who rejects the Holy Spirit.

mother and thy brethren without seek
for thee.
[33]And he answered them, saying,
Who is my mother, or my brethren?
[34]And he looked round about on them
which sat about him, and said, Behold
my mother and my brethren!
[35]For whosoever shall do the will of
God, the same is my brother, and my
sister, and mother.

The parable of the sower
(Matt. 13:1-23; Luke 8:4-15)

4 And he began again to teach by
the sea side: and there was gathered unto him a great multitude, so that
he entered into a ship, and sat in the
sea; and the whole multitude was by the
sea on the land.
[2]And he taught them many things by
parables, and said unto them in his doctrine,
[3]Hearken; Behold, there went out a
sower to sow:
[4]And it came to pass, as he sowed,
some fell by the way side, and the fowls
of the air came and devoured it up.
[5]And some fell on stony ground,
where it had not much earth; and immediately it sprang up, because it had
no depth of earth:
[6]But when the sun was up, it was
scorched; and because it had no root, it
withered away.
[7]And some fell among thorns, and the
thorns grew up, and choked it, and it
yielded no fruit.
[8]And other fell on good ground, and
did yield fruit that sprang up and increased; and brought forth, some thirty,
and some sixty, and some an hundred.
[9]And he said unto them, He that hath
ears to hear, let him hear.
[10]And when he was alone, they that
were about him with the twelve asked
of him the parable.
[11]And he said unto them, Unto you it
is given to know the *mystery of the kingdom of God: but unto them that are without, all *these* things are done in parables:
[12]That seeing they may see, and not
perceive; and hearing they may hear,
and not understand; lest at any time
they should be converted, and *their* sins
should be forgiven them.
¶[13]And he said unto them, Know ye
not this parable? and how then will ye
know all parables?
¶[14]The sower soweth the word.
[15]And these are they by the way side,
where the word is sown; but when they
have heard, Satan cometh immediately, and taketh away the word that was
sown in their hearts.
[16]And these are they likewise which
are sown on stony ground; who, when
they have heard the word, immediately receive it with gladness;
[17]And have no root in themselves,
and so endure but for a time: afterward,
when affliction or persecution ariseth
for the word's sake, immediately they
are offended.
[18]And these are they which are sown
among thorns, such as hear the word,
[19]And the cares of this *world, and
the deceitfulness of riches, and the
*lusts of other things entering in, choke

4:2 PARABLES

A parable really is an object lesson to teach some spiritual or moral truth. It has been called "an earthly story with a heavenly meaning."

In the Bible the word "parable" is used in several ways:

1. for pointed sayings or proverbs (Matt. 15:15; Mark 3:23; Luke 4:23);
2. for a figure or *type (Heb. 6:9; 11:19); and
3. for a comparison in the form of a story, as here.

3:35 the same is my brother. Those who do the will of God are brought into a relationship with Jesus that will last forever and ever (see also Matt. 12:46-50; Luke 8:19-21).

the word, and it becometh unfruitful.
20 And these are they which are sown
on good ground; such as hear the word,
and receive *it,* and bring forth fruit,
some thirtyfold, some sixty, and some
an hundred.

The parable of the burning lamp
(cf. Matt. 5:15-16; Luke 8:16; 11:33)

¶21 And he said unto them, Is a candle
brought to be put under a bushel, or under
a bed? and not to be set on a candlestick?
22 For there is nothing hid, which shall
not be manifested; neither was any
thing kept secret, but that it should
come abroad.
23 If any man have ears to hear, let him
hear.
24 And he said unto them, Take heed
what ye hear: with what measure ye
mete, it shall be measured to you: and
unto you that hear shall more be given.
25 For he that hath, to him shall be
given: and he that hath not, from him
shall be taken even that which he hath.

The seed growing secretly

¶26 And he said, So is the kingdom of
God, as if a man should cast seed into
the ground;
27 And should sleep, and rise night
and day, and the seed should spring and
grow up, he knoweth not how.
28 For the earth bringeth forth fruit of
herself; first the blade, then the ear,
after that the full corn in the ear.
29 But when the fruit is brought forth,
immediately he putteth in the sickle,
because the harvest is come.

The parable of the mustard seed
(Matt. 13:31-32; Luke 13:18-19)

¶30 And he said, Whereunto shall we
liken the kingdom of God? or with what
comparison shall we compare it?
31 *It is* like a grain of mustard seed,
which, when it is sown in the earth, is
less than all the seeds that be in the
earth:
32 But when it is sown, it groweth up,
and becometh greater than all herbs,
and shooteth out great branches; so that
the fowls of the air may lodge under the
shadow of it.
33 And with many such parables spake
he the word unto them, as they were
able to hear *it.*
34 But without a parable spake he not
unto them: and when they were alone,
he expounded all things to his disciples.

4:30 THE PARABLE OF THE MUSTARD SEED

If the kingdom of the heavens were, as many suppose, the *church, the *bride of Christ, then the *body of Christ should grow into a great tree, in which the sinners of all nations would find refuge. But comparing Scripture with Scripture, we cannot believe that our Lord taught that. The fowls of the parable of the sower are the Wicked One and his agents. The birds of Revelation 18:2 are unclean, hateful, and are connected with the Devil; therefore, it is indicated that the birds of the air of this parable are the children of Satan.

The teaching becomes clear when we see that the kingdom of the heavens is Christendom. The sower planted seed, the Word. This seed, deeply rooted in the field, (the world), has sprung up into an abnormal and monstrous growth (the mustard plant is a bush, not a tree)–the great ecclesiastical organizations of Romanism, Protestantism, and the world system. In the branches of this great organization, the Devil's agents lodge, the unconverted who possess only the outward form of Christianity but are not Christ's by true faith.

4:24 Take heed what ye hear. See Romans 10:17. If we hear anything that would lead us to reject the Lord Jesus Christ, we should not heed it (compare Luke 8:18).

4:26 seed into the ground. The life is in the seed, not in the soil. When the Word of God is planted in our hearts, we receive new life, for it is God who creates that life (see 1 Pet. 1:23-25). We cannot tell how it comes to pass, but we know when it shows itself. Just as we see growth in the natural life, so we observe growth in the spiritual life (see 1 John 2:12-14).

The tempest stilled
(Matt. 8:23-27; Luke 8:22-25)

¶35 And the same day, when the even
was come, he saith unto them, Let us
pass over unto the other side.
36 And when they had sent away the
multitude, they took him even as he
was in the ship. And there were also
with him other little ships.
37 And there arose a great storm of
wind, and the waves beat into the ship,
so that it was now full.
38 And he was in the hinder part of the
ship, asleep on a pillow: and they awake
him, and say unto him, Master, carest
thou not that we perish?
39 And he arose, and rebuked the
wind, and said unto the sea, Peace, be
still. And the wind ceased, and there
was a great calm.
40 And he said unto them, Why are ye
so fearful? how is it that ye have no faith?
41 And they feared exceedingly, and
said one to another, What manner of
man is this, that even the wind and the
sea obey him?

The demoniac cured
(Matt. 8:28-34; Luke 8:26-37)

5 And they came over unto the
other side of the sea, into the country of the Gadarenes.
2 And when he was come out of the
ship, immediately there met him out of
the tombs a man with an unclean spirit,
3 Who had *his* dwelling among the
tombs; and no man could bind him, no,
not with chains:
4 Because that he had been often
bound with fetters and chains, and the
chains had been plucked asunder by
him, and the fetters broken in pieces:
neither could any *man* tame him.

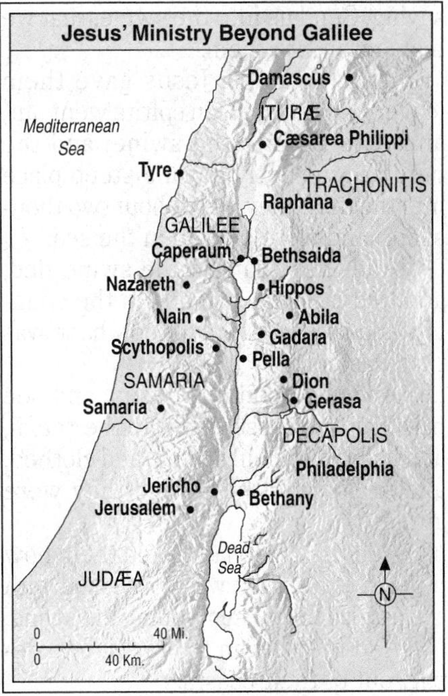

5 And always, night and day, he was in
the mountains, and in the tombs, crying, and cutting himself with stones.
6 But when he saw Jesus afar off, he
ran and worshipped him,
7 And cried with a loud voice, and said,
What have I to do with thee, Jesus, *thou*
Son of the most high God? I adjure thee
by God, that thou torment me not.
8 For he said unto him, Come out of
the man, *thou* unclean spirit.
9 And he asked him, What *is* thy
name? And he answered, saying, My
name *is* Legion: for we are many.
10 And he besought him much that he
would not send them away out of the
country.
11 Now there was there nigh unto the
mountains a great herd of swine feeding.
12 And all the devils besought him,

4:39 And he arose. Compare this with Psalm 107:25,29. The Lord Jesus Christ created the sea. Now He shows Himself Master of the sea.

5:2 a man with an unclean spirit. This man possessed of demons is one example of the power the Devil has over men who are his slaves (see also Matt. 8:28-34; Luke 8:26-37). The Lord Jesus came to destroy the works of the Devil (1 John 3:8).

5:9 My name is Legion. A Roman legion contained six thousand soldiers. The demons used the word to show how completely they possessed the man.

saying, Send us into the swine, that we
may enter into them.
13And forthwith Jesus gave them
leave. And the unclean spirits went out,
and entered into the swine: and the
herd ran violently down a steep place
into the sea, (they were about two thousand;) and were choked in the sea.
14And they that fed the swine fled,
and told *it* in the city, and in the country. And they went out to see what it was
that was done.
15And they come to Jesus, and see
him that was possessed with the *devil,
and had the legion, sitting, and clothed,
and in his right mind: and they were
afraid.
16And they that saw *it* told them how
it befell to him that was possessed with
the devil, and *also* concerning the swine.
17And they began to pray him to depart out of their coasts.
18And when he was come into the
ship, he that had been possessed with
the devil prayed him that he might be
with him.
19Howbeit Jesus suffered him not,
but saith unto him, Go home to thy
friends, and tell them how great things
the Lord hath done for thee, and hath
had compassion on thee.
20And he departed, and began to publish in Decapolis how great things Jesus
had done for him: and all *men* did
marvel.
¶21And when Jesus was passed over
again by ship unto the other side, much
people gathered unto him: and he was
nigh unto the sea.

The Lord Jesus heals a sick woman and raises Jairus' daughter
(Matt. 9:18-26; Luke 8:41-56)

22And, behold, there cometh one of
the rulers of the synagogue, Jairus by
name; and when he saw him, he fell at
his feet,
23And besought him greatly, saying,
My little daughter lieth at the point of
*death: *I pray thee,* come and lay thy
hands on her, that she may be healed;
and she shall live.
24And *Jesus* went with him; and much
people followed him, and thronged him.
25And a certain woman, which had an
issue of blood twelve years,
26And had suffered many things of
many physicians, and had spent all that
she had, and was nothing bettered, but
rather grew worse,
27When she had heard of Jesus, came
in the press behind, and touched his
garment.
28For she said, If I may touch but his
clothes, I shall be whole.
29And straightway the fountain of her
blood was dried up; and she felt in *her*
body that she was healed of that plague.
30And Jesus, immediately knowing in
himself that virtue had gone out of him,
turned him about in the press, and said,
Who touched my clothes?
31And his disciples said unto him,
Thou seest the multitude thronging
thee, and sayest thou, Who touched
me?
32And he looked round about to see
her that had done this thing.
33But the woman fearing and trem-

5:22 one of the rulers of the synagogue. Jairus was one of the elders of the Jewish congregation at Capernaum. He was not an enemy of Jesus as were the scribes and Pharisees of Jerusalem. Jairus shows real sincerity by falling at the feet of our Lord (vs. 22). He also revealed a genuine faith (vs. 23; see also Matt. 9:18-26; Luke 8:41-56).

5:25 an issue of blood. This poor woman's sickness caused her to be excluded from the services at the synagogue and separated her from her friends (Lev. 15:25-31). This disease is a true picture of what sin really does. It keeps us away from God and from fellowship with the children of God. But she still had access to the love of God in Christ.

5:31 Who touched me? Even though the crowd of people swarmed around Him, our Lord knew that someone had touched Him with a purpose. Our Lord could have allowed the woman to depart unnoticed, but she would have missed a great blessing. Our Saviour desires a confession of the mouth as well as belief of the heart (Rom. 10:10).

bling, knowing what was done in her,
came and fell down before him, and told
him all the truth.
34 And he said unto her, Daughter, thy
faith hath made thee whole; go in peace,
and be whole of thy plague.
¶35 While he yet spake, there came
from the ruler of the synagogue's *house*
certain which said, Thy daughter is
dead: why troublest thou the Master
any further?
36 As soon as Jesus heard the word
that was spoken, he saith unto the ruler
of the synagogue, Be not *afraid, only
believe.
37 And he suffered no man to follow
him, save Peter, and James, and John
the brother of James.
38 And he cometh to the house of the
ruler of the synagogue, and seeth the
tumult, and them that wept and wailed
greatly.
39 And when he was come in, he saith
unto them, Why make ye this ado, and
weep? the damsel is not dead, but
sleepeth.
40 And they laughed him to scorn. But
when he had put them all out, he taketh
the father and the mother of the damsel, and them that were with him, and
entereth in where the damsel was lying.
41 And he took the damsel by the
hand, and said unto her, Talitha cumi;
which is, being interpreted, Damsel, I
say unto thee, arise.
42 And straightway the damsel arose,
and walked; for she was *of the age* of
twelve years. And they were astonished with a great astonishment.
43 And he charged them straitly that
no man should know it; and commanded that something should be given her
to eat.

The Lord's rejection at Nazareth

6 And he went out from thence,
and came into his own country; and
his disciples follow him.
2 And when the sabbath day was come,
he began to teach in the synagogue: and
many hearing *him* were astonished, saying, From whence hath this *man* these
things? and what wisdom *is* this which
is given unto him, that even such mighty
works are wrought by his hands?
3 Is not this the carpenter, the son of
Mary, the brother of James, and Joses,
and of Juda, and Simon? and are not his
sisters here with us? And they were
offended at him.

6:3 An Insult Aimed at Jesus
The question, "Is not this the carpenter?" was really a sneer. Our Lord was not only rejected by people but despised by them (Isa. 53:3). Had they known Him, they would have realized that He did not come *from* such a humble place but that He came *to* it. He was God the Son, and as such had no beginning of days (see Isa. 9:6-7 and its note, "The Son of God"; Mic. 5:2 and its note, "A Description of Christ"; John 1:1-3 and 1:1 first note), but He humbled Himself and took upon Himself the form of a servant and was made in the likeness of men (Phil. 2:5-8).

4 But Jesus said unto them, A *prophet is not without honour, but in his own
country, and among his own kin, and in
his own house.
5 And he could there do no mighty
work, save that he laid his hands upon
a few sick folk, and healed *them*.

5:38 them that wept and wailed greatly. It was the custom in those days to have mourners who were paid to cry. They earned their money by wailing loudly.

5:39 sleepeth. Jesus spoke of sleep in this instance, not because Jairus' daughter had not suffered physical death, but because her soul was alive, and through Him, the Prince of Life, the soul was to take possession of the body once again. The child would awake as if she had been sleeping.

5:41 Talitha cumi. The words mean, *Little maid, arise,* or even more lovingly, *Little lamb, it is time to get up.*

6:3 offended at him. Instead of the Lord being a foundation stone for their faith, He was their stumbling stone. Compare this with Matthew 11:6; 1 Peter 2:7-8.

6And he marvelled because of their
unbelief. And he went round about the
villages, teaching.

The twelve apostles sent forth
(Matt. 10:1-42; Luke 9:1-6)

¶7And he called *unto him* the twelve,
and began to send them forth by two
and two; and gave them power over
unclean spirits;
8And commanded them that they
should take nothing for *their* journey,
save a staff only; no scrip, no bread, no
money in *their* purse:
9But *be* shod with sandals; and not put
on two coats.
10And he said unto them, In what
place soever ye enter into an house,
there abide till ye depart from that place.
11And whosoever shall not receive
you, nor hear you, when ye depart
thence, shake off the dust under your
feet for a testimony against them. Verily I say unto you, It shall be more
tolerable for *Sodom and Gomorrha
in the day of *judgment, than for that
city.
12And they went out, and preached
that men should repent.
13And they cast out many devils, and
anointed with *oil many that were sick,
and healed *them.*

John the Baptist slain
(cf. Matt. 14:1-14; Luke 9:7-9)

¶14And king *Herod heard *of him;*
(for his name was spread abroad:) and
he said, That *John the Baptist was ris-
en from the dead, and therefore mighty
works do shew forth themselves in
him.
15Others said, That it is *Elias. And
others said, That it is a prophet, or as
one of the prophets.
16But when Herod heard *thereof,* he
said, It is John, whom I beheaded: he is
risen from the dead.
17For Herod himself had sent forth
and laid hold upon John, and bound him
in prison for Herodias' sake, his brother
Philip's wife: for he had married her.
18For John had said unto Herod, It is
not lawful for thee to have thy brother's
wife.
19Therefore Herodias had a quarrel
against him, and would have killed him;
but she could not:

6:11 Handling Rejection
The apostles proclaimed a message that would bring a rich blessing to those who would receive it, but the responsibility for accepting it belonged to those who heard it. If the people rejected the testimony of our Lord's servants, His servants would leave them to the judgment of God and also depart from their towns. Paul did this same thing (Acts 13:51; 18:6).

6:7 two and two. The sending out of the Twelve is recorded in Matthew 10 and Luke 9:1-6. Only Mark tells us that they were sent out two by two. They had been chosen before this (Mark 1:16; 2:14; Luke 6:13), but now having been taught by the Lord Jesus Christ, they were sent out in His name.

6:8 commanded them. The instruction our Lord gave the Twelve on this occasion is given in greater length in Matthew 10:5-42 (see also Luke 9:1-6).

6:8 scrip. A wallet or small bag. It was for small articles or provisions. Pilgrims in Galilee always carried such bags when they went on journeys.

6:8 no money. Our Lord could meet their every need. It is interesting to note there is no record of Jesus' ever carrying money, and none was found in His garments when He died (see Matt. 22:19).

6:8 purse. Belt.

6:9 not put on two coats. This means that they were not to take a change of clothing with them.

6:13 anointed with oil. See James 5:14 (see also its second note).

6:14 king Herod. Herod Antipas, one of the four sons of Herod the Great. (See also Matt. 14:1-13; Luke 3:19-20; 9:7-9.)

6:15 Elias. Elijah.

[20]For Herod feared John, knowing
that he was a *just man and an holy, and
observed him; and when he heard him,
he did many things, and heard him
gladly.
[21]And when a convenient day was
come, that Herod on his birthday made
a supper to his lords, high captains, and
chief *estates* of Galilee;
[22]And when the daughter of the said
Herodias came in, and danced, and
pleased Herod and them that sat with
him, the king said unto the damsel, Ask
of me whatsoever thou wilt, and I will
give *it* thee.
[23]And he sware unto her, Whatsoever
thou shalt ask of me, I will give *it* thee,
unto the half of my kingdom.
[24]And she went forth, and said unto
her mother, What shall I ask? And she
said, The head of John the Baptist.
[25]And she came in straightway with
haste unto the king, and asked, saying,
I will that thou give me by and by in a
charger the head of John the Baptist.
[26]And the king was exceeding sorry;
yet for his oath's sake, and for their
sakes which sat with him, he would not
reject her.
[27]And immediately the king sent an
executioner, and commanded his head
to be brought: and he went and beheaded him in the prison,
[28]And brought his head in a charger,
and gave it to the damsel: and the damsel gave it to her mother.
[29]And when his disciples heard *of it,*
they came and took up his corpse, and
laid it in a tomb.

The return of the twelve and the feeding of the multitude (Matt. 14:13-21; Luke 9:10-17; John 6:5-13)

¶[30]And the *apostles gathered themselves together unto Jesus, and told
him all things, both what they had done,
and what they had taught.
[31]And he said unto them, Come ye
yourselves apart into a desert place,
and rest a while: for there were many
coming and going, and they had no leisure so much as to eat.
[32]And they departed into a desert
place by ship privately.
[33]And the people saw them departing, and many knew him, and ran afoot
thither out of all cities, and outwent
them, and came together unto him.
[34]And Jesus, when he came out, saw
much people, and was moved with compassion toward them, because they
were as sheep not having a shepherd:
and he began to teach them many
things.
[35]And when the day was now far
spent, his disciples came unto him, and
said, This is a desert place, and now the
time *is* far passed:
[36]Send them away, that they may go
into the country round about, and into
the villages, and buy themselves bread:
for they have nothing to eat.
[37]He answered and said unto them,
Give ye them to eat. And they say unto
him, Shall we go and buy two hundred
pennyworth of bread, and give them
to eat?
[38]He saith unto them, How many

6:20 observed him. Protected him.
6:25 by and by. Right away.
6:25 charger. A large dish or platter.
6:31 many coming and going. The time for celebrating the *Passover was very near (John 6:4).
6:34 as sheep not having a shepherd. Compare Isaiah 53:6. See also Luke 15:3-7; John 10:11,27-30.
6:36 Send them away. The disciples did not realize the omnipotence of the Lord.
6:37 Give ye them to eat. When our Lord gives a command, His power is behind that command (see also Matt. 14:13-21; Luke 9:10-17; John 6:5-13).
6:37 two hundred pennyworth. The word "penny" is the denarius, which was equal to a full day's wage.

loaves have ye? go and see. And when
they knew, they say, Five, and two
fishes.
39 And he commanded them to make
all sit down by companies upon the
green grass.
40 And they sat down in ranks, by hundreds, and by fifties.
41 And when he had taken the five
loaves and the two fishes, he looked up
to heaven, and blessed, and brake the
loaves, and gave *them* to his disciples to
set before them; and the two fishes divided he among them all.
42 And they did all eat, and were filled.
43 And they took up twelve baskets
full of the fragments, and of the fishes.
44 And they that did eat of the loaves
were about five thousand men.

The Lord walks on the water *(Matt. 14:22-32; John 6:15-21)*

45 And straightway he constrained his
disciples to get into the ship, and to go
to the other side before unto Bethsaida, while he sent away the people.
46 And when he had sent them away,
he departed into a mountain to pray.
47 And when even was come, the ship
was in the midst of the sea, and he alone
on the land.
48 And he saw them toiling in rowing;
for the wind was contrary unto them:
and about the fourth watch of the night
he cometh unto them, walking upon the
sea, and would have passed by them.
49 But when they saw him walking
upon the sea, they supposed it had been
a spirit, and cried out:
50 For they all saw him, and were troubled. And immediately he talked with
them, and saith unto them, Be of good
cheer: it is I; be not afraid.
51 And he went up unto them into the
ship; and the wind ceased: and they
were sore amazed in themselves beyond measure, and wondered.
52 For they considered not _the *mira-
cle_ of the loaves: for their heart was
hardened.

The Lord heals at Gennesaret *(Matt. 14:34-36)*

¶53 And when they had passed over,
they came into the land of Gennesaret,
and drew to the shore.
54 And when they were come out of
the ship, straightway they knew him,
55 And ran through that whole region
round about, and began to carry about
in beds those that were sick, where
they heard he was.
56 And whithersoever he entered, into
villages, or cities, or country, they laid
the sick in the streets, and besought
him that they might touch if it were
but the border of his garment: and as
many as touched him were made
whole.

Dispute about traditions *(Matt. 15:1-20)*

7 Then came together unto him the
Pharisees, and certain of the
*scribes, which came from *Jerusalem.
2 And when they saw some of his disciples eat bread with defiled, that is to
say, with unwashen, hands, they found
fault.
3 For the Pharisees, and all the Jews,
except they wash *their* hands oft, eat
not, holding the *tradition of the *elders.
4 And *when they come* from the market, except they wash, they eat not. And
many other things there be, which they
have received to hold, *as* the washing
of cups, and pots, brasen vessels, and
of tables.

6:44 five thousand men. The women and children were not counted.
6:48 fourth watch. Between three and six o'clock in the morning.
6:48 walking upon the sea. The Lord Jesus was Master of nature because He was the Creator (John 1:3; Col. 1:16; Heb. 1:2 and its note, "God's Son"; see also Matt. 14:22-32; John 6:15-21).
6:49 cried out. They screamed in terror.
6:52 considered. The word could be translated "understood."

7:3 The Tradition of the Elders
For many generations the *Law had been explained by certain teachers. These learned men elaborated the simple commands in the Old Testament, adding much to what God ordained. The Pharisees came to the place where they paid more attention to these additions, or the "tradition of the elders," than they did to the actual commandments of God (see vs. 13).

5 Then the Pharisees and scribes
asked him, Why walk not thy disciples
according to the tradition of the elders,
but eat bread with unwashen hands?
6 He answered and said unto them,
Well hath Esaias prophesied of you hypocrites, as it is written, This people
honoureth me with *their* lips, but their
heart is far from me.
7 Howbeit in vain do they worship me,
teaching *for* doctrines the commandments of men.
8 For laying aside the commandment
of *God, ye hold the tradition of men,
as the washing of pots and cups: and
many other such like things ye do.
9 And he said unto them, Full well ye
reject the commandment of God, that
ye may keep your own tradition.
10 For *Moses said, Honour thy father
and thy mother; and, Whoso curseth
father or mother, let him die the death:
11 But ye say, If a man shall say to his
father or mother, *It is* Corban, that is to
say, a gift, by whatsoever thou mightest be profited by me; *he shall be*
free.
12 And ye suffer him no more to do
ought for his father or his mother;
13 Making the word of God of none
effect through your tradition, which ye
have delivered: and many such like
things do ye.
¶ 14 And when he had called all the
people *unto him,* he said unto them,
Hearken unto me every one *of you,* and
understand:
15 There is nothing from without a
man, that entering into him can defile
him: but the things which come out of
him, those are they that defile the man.
16 If any man have ears to hear, let him
hear.
17 And when he was entered into the
house from the people, his disciples
asked him concerning the parable.
18 And he saith unto them, Are ye so
without understanding also? Do ye not
perceive, that whatsoever thing from
without entereth into the man, *it* cannot defile him;
19 Because it entereth not into his
heart, but into the belly, and goeth out
into the draught, purging all meats?
20 And he said, That which cometh out
of the man, that defileth the man.
21 For from within, out of the heart of
men, proceed evil thoughts, adulteries,
fornications, murders,

7:5 unwashen hands. When the Pharisees used these words about the disciples, we must not think that the disciples ate their food with dirty fingers. What is meant here is that the Pharisees found fault with the followers of our Lord because they did not wash according to the rules laid down in the traditions of the elders (see vs. 3 note).

7:6 Esaias prophesied. The words to which our Lord referred are found in Isaiah 29:13. Our Lord said that the outward acts do not mean a thing in the sight of God if the heart is not right (see 1 Sam. 15:22; 16:7).

7:10 Moses said. In order to prove that what our Lord said in verse 9 was true, He reminded these Pharisees that they did not obey the fifth commandment (Exod. 20:12; 21:17).

7:11 Corban. This means *a gift dedicated to God.* According to the tradition of the elders (vs. 3), if a person wanted to make his possession or property sacred, he would simply pronounce "Corban" over it, and then it was dedicated to the temple. In essence, people, especially the Pharisees, were neglecting their parents by giving their money to the temple. Jesus denounced them for using what seemed to others as a pious act to disobey God's command to honor their parents.

22 Thefts, covetousness, wickedness,
deceit, lasciviousness, an evil eye, blasphemy, pride, foolishness:
23 All these evil things come from
within, and defile the man.

III. Christ's Ministry in Northern Galilee (7:24—9:50)

¶24 And from thence he arose, and
went into the borders of Tyre and Sidon,
and entered into an house, and would
have no man know *it:* but he could not
be hid.

Our Lord and the Syrophenician woman (Matt. 15:21-28)

25 For a *certain* woman, whose young
daughter had an *unclean spirit, heard
of him, and came and fell at his feet:
26 The woman was a Greek, a Syrophenician by nation; and she besought
him that he would cast forth the devil
out of her daughter.
27 But Jesus said unto her, Let the
children first be filled: for it is not meet
to take the children's bread, and to cast
it unto the dogs.
28 And she answered and said unto
him, Yes, Lord: yet the dogs under the
table eat of the children's crumbs.
29 And he said unto her, For this saying go thy way; the devil is gone out of
thy daughter.
30 And when she was come to her
house, she found the devil gone out,
and her daughter laid upon the bed.

Our Lord heals the deaf and dumb man (Matt. 15:29-31)

¶31 And again, departing from the
coasts of Tyre and Sidon, he came unto
the sea of Galilee, through the midst of
the coasts of Decapolis.

7:25-30 The Woman from Canaan
Matthew tells us that this woman was from Canaan (Matt. 15:21-28). Her forefathers were the original inhabitants of that land; therefore, she belonged to the race of people whom the Jews hated. She was a Greek (vs. 26). Since her religion was that of a heathen, she had no claim upon Christ at all. But she was possessed of true humility (vss. 27-28). Our Lord referred to the Jewish nation when He spoke about the children (vs. 27). The word "dog" used by our Lord referred to little house dogs, not to the dogs that strayed about the streets. The woman took her place before our Lord as one who did not deserve His mercy. Her faith was honored by her daughter's healing (vss. 29-30).

32 And they bring unto him one that
was deaf, and had an impediment in his
speech; and they beseech him to put his
hand upon him.
33 And he took him aside from the multitude, and put his fingers into his ears,
and he spit, and touched his tongue;
34 And looking up to *heaven, he
sighed, and saith unto him, Ephphatha,
that is, Be opened.
35 And *straightway his ears were
opened, and the string of his tongue
was loosed, and he spake plain.
36 And he charged them that they
should tell no man: but the more he
charged them, so much the more a
great deal they published *it;*
37 And were beyond measure astonished, saying, He hath done all things
well: he maketh both the deaf to hear,
and the dumb to speak.

The feeding of the four thousand (Matt. 15:32-39)

8 In those days the multitude being very great, and having nothing

7:31 Decapolis. This means *ten cities* and refers to a group of cities that were allied against common foes; they were situated in the area between Damascus and the Arabian Desert and are generally listed as Scythopolis, Hippos, Gadara, Pella, Philadelphia, Gerasa, Dion, Canatha, Raphana, and Damascus.

7:34 Ephphatha. This means *be opened.* This word was from the Aramaic dialect, which was used as the ordinary speech of the people, though Greek was the official language. For another version of this story, see Matthew 15:29-31.

to eat, Jesus called his disciples *unto*
him, and saith unto them,
2 I have compassion on the multitude,
because they have now been with me
three days, and have nothing to eat:
3 And if I send them away fasting to
their own houses, they will faint by the
way: for divers of them came from far.
4 And his disciples answered him,
From whence can a man satisfy these
men with bread here in the wilderness?
5 And he asked them, How many
loaves have ye? And they said, Seven.
6 And he commanded the people to sit
down on the ground: and he took the
seven loaves, and gave thanks, and
brake, and gave to his disciples to set
before *them;* and they did set *them* before the people.
7 And they had a few small fishes: and
he blessed, and commanded to set them
also before *them.*
8 So they did eat, and were filled: and
they took up of the broken *meat* that
was left seven baskets.
9 And they that had eaten were about
four thousand: and he sent them away.

The Pharisees seek a sign
(Matt. 16:1-12)

¶10 And straightway he entered into
a ship with his disciples, and came into
the parts of Dalmanutha.
11 And the *Pharisees came forth, and
began to question with him, seeking of
him a sign from heaven, *tempting him.
12 And he sighed deeply in his spirit,
and saith, Why doth this generation
seek after a sign? verily I say unto you,
There shall no sign be given unto this
generation.

8:11 A Sign from Heaven

This was not the first time that the Pharisees tempted the Lord by asking for a sign from Him (read Matt. 12:38; John 2:18; 6:30). The Lord had performed wonderful miracles, but they wanted some signs from heaven such as the manna that came down to feed Israel in Moses' day, or the sun standing still for Joshua, or fire and rain that appeared when Elijah prayed. Even if the Lord had performed miracles like these, the Pharisees would still not have believed.

The leaven of the Pharisees and Herod

13 And he left them, and entering into
the ship again departed to the other
side.
¶14 Now *the disciples* had forgotten to
take bread, neither had they in the ship
with them more than one loaf.
15 And he charged them, saying, Take
heed, beware of the leaven of the Pharisees, and *of* the leaven of Herod.
16 And they reasoned among themselves, saying, *It is* because we have no
bread.
17 And when Jesus knew *it,* he saith
unto them, Why reason ye, because ye
have no bread? perceive ye not yet,
neither understand? have ye your heart
yet hardened?
18 Having eyes, see ye not? and having ears, hear ye not? and do ye not
remember?
19 When I brake the five loaves among
five thousand, how many baskets full of
fragments took ye up? They say unto
him, Twelve.
20 And when the seven among four
thousand, how many baskets full of
fragments took ye up? And they said,
Seven.

8:4 whence can a man . . . ? Unbelief always asks questions—faith always rests in the power of God to meet every need. God can furnish a table in the wilderness (see 2 Kings 7; Mark 6:37 and its first note). The miracle in Mark 6 was for the Jewish multitudes from Galilee; this was for a Gentile multitude from Decapolis.

8:15 leaven of the Pharisees, and of the leaven of Herod. In Matthew 16:6, our Lord said, "Beware of the leaven of the Pharisees and of the Sadducees." The leaven of the Pharisees means their self-righteous formality; they thought they were so good that they did not stand in need of the grace of God to save them. The leaven of the Sadducees (or of Herod, who was a Sadducee) means their unbelief.

[21]And he said unto them, How is it that ye do not understand?

The healing of the blind man at Bethsaida

¶[22]And he cometh to Bethsaida; and they bring a blind man unto him, and besought him to touch him.

[23]And he took the blind man by the hand, and led him out of the town; and when he had spit on his eyes, and put his hands upon him, he asked him if he saw ought.

[24]And he looked up, and said, I see men as trees, walking.

[25]After that he put *his* hands again upon his eyes, and made him look up: and he was restored, and saw every man clearly.

[26]And he sent him away to his house, saying, Neither go into the town, nor tell *it* to any in the town.

Peter's great confession of faith (cf. Matt. 16:31; Luke 9:18-20)

¶[27]And Jesus went out, and his disciples, into the towns of Caesarea Philippi: and by the way he asked his disciples, saying unto them, Whom do men say that I am?

[28]And they answered, John the Baptist: but some *say,* Elias; and others, One of the *prophets.

[29]And he saith unto them, But whom say ye that I am? And Peter answereth and saith unto him, Thou art the *Christ.

[30]And he charged them that they should tell no man of him.

¶[31]And he began to teach them, that the Son of man must suffer many things, and be rejected of the elders, and *of* the chief priests, and scribes, and be killed, and after three days rise again.

8:22-26 A MAN'S SIGHT RESTORED

Only Mark tells of this miracle. Our Lord restored the sight of other blind men, but this miracle is noted for the gradual way in which the man's sight was restored. All of Christ's miracles were performed in order to teach a deeper truth.

The parable that this miracle contains is very beautiful. We learn how our spiritual vision is renewed:

1. It is by the presence and power of the Lord Jesus Christ.
2. The moment we come to Jesus Christ and accept Him as our Saviour, we are no longer children of "darkness" but "children of light" (Eph. 5:8; Col. 1:13).
3. Though we do not see everything clearly when we are first saved, we are no longer blind (2 Cor. 4:4-6).

As we read the Word of God, and spend time in fellowship with the Lord Jesus, the Holy Spirit reveals things more clearly to us. Instead of seeing "men as trees" (Mark 8:24), we see "clearly" (vs. 25). Compare this passage with Philippians 1:6; 1 Peter 2:9; 1 John 2:27; Revelation 3:18.

8:23 led him out of the town. Read Matthew 11:20-27. Our Lord had pronounced the doom of Bethsaida because of the unbelief of its people. He knew the hardness of their hearts and that further testimony would be useless (see also Mark 8:26).

8:27 Whom do men say that I am? The Lord did not ask the disciples this question for the purpose of receiving information about Himself. He knew all things; it was for the sake of His followers that He asked the question. He was preparing them for fuller revelation of Himself.

8:29 Thou art the Christ. The record in Matthew (16:13-16; compare Luke 9:18-20) adds "the Son of the living God," but this is implied in Peter's answer here. The title "Christ" emphasizes messiahship; "Son of the living God" stresses Christ's deity. The messiahship and deity of our Lord Jesus should never be separated—Jesus is both Messiah and God (see John 1:40-41,49; 4:29,42; Acts 2:36; 5:31).

8:31 the Son of man must suffer. Our Lord knew the reason for His coming into the world. He knew that He had to suffer before entering His glory. He was to be rejected before He would come to reign (Isa. 53:3; see also 53:1-5 note, "Christ's Suffering"; 1 Pet. 1:11 and its note, "Christ's Suffering and Glory").

32 And he spake that saying openly.
And Peter took him, and began to rebuke him.
33 But when he had turned about and
looked on his disciples, he rebuked Peter, saying, Get thee behind me, *Satan:
for thou savourest not the things that
be of God, but the things that be of men.

The disciple's cross. The value of a soul
(Matt. 16:24-27; Luke 9:23-26)

¶34 And when he had called the people *unto him* with his disciples also, he
said unto them, Whosoever will come
after me, let him deny himself, and take
up his cross, and follow me.
35 For whosoever will save his life
shall lose it; but whosoever shall lose
his life for my sake and the *gospel's,
the same shall save it.
36 For what shall it profit a man, if he
shall gain the whole world, and lose his
own soul?
37 Or what shall a man give in exchange for his soul?
38 Whosoever therefore shall be
ashamed of me and of my words in this
adulterous and sinful generation; of him
also shall the Son of man be ashamed,
when he cometh in the glory of his Father with the holy *angels.

The transfiguration
(Matt. 16:28—17:8; Luke 9:27-36)

9 And he said unto them, Verily I
say unto you, That there be some
of them that stand here, which shall not
taste of death, till they have seen the
*kingdom of God come with power.
¶2 And after six days Jesus taketh
with him *Peter, and James, and John,
and leadeth them up into an high mountain apart by themselves: and he was
transfigured before them.
3 And his raiment became shining,
exceeding white as snow; so as no fuller
on earth can white them.
4 And there appeared unto them Elias
with Moses: and they were talking with
Jesus.

8:32 Peter took him, and began to rebuke him. To Peter the very idea of the Messiah being put to death was utterly impossible. At this time Peter did not discern the full meaning of Christ's first coming. The cross was absolutely necessary. The Lord's blood had to be shed that men might be redeemed.

8:33 Get thee behind me, Satan. Peter did not know that he was the instrument of Satan when he rebuked the Lord. This was not the only time Satan tried to turn our Saviour from the way to the cross. He tried it at the Temptation, before Christ's public ministry began, and again in Gethsemane.

8:34 let him deny himself, and take up his cross, and follow me. There is a cross for the follower of Christ as well as for Christ Himself. A cross always means death. For the Lord Jesus, the cross meant a cruel death as a sacrifice for our sins. Our cross is the denying of self, death to self, for Christ's sake (read Rom. 6:14-18; see also Rom. 6:16-17 note, "Salvation by Faith"; Phil. 3:7-10).

8:38 adulterous. Unfaithful to God.

9:1 shall not taste of death. See Matthew 17:2 note, "The Transfiguration."

9:2 after six days. Luke says eight days. The apparent contradiction merely means that Mark mentions the intervening days while Luke figures in the end days (Luke 9:28-36; compare Matt. 17:1-8).

9:2 transfigured. The Greek word here for "transfigured" is twice translated by other words in the New Testament. We find it in Romans 12:2 where it is translated "transformed," and in 2 Corinthians 3:18 where the word "changed" is used. God's grace transforms or changes us now, but when the Lord Jesus Christ comes again, we shall be like Him, for we shall see Him as He is (Rom. 8:29 and its note, "Predestination"; Phil 3:21; Col. 1:13; 3:4; 1 John 3:2).

9:3 fuller. One who cleans clothes, a launderer.

9:4 Elias with Moses. Elias refers to Elijah, who represented the Old Testament prophets; Moses represented the *Law; and the Lord Jesus Christ was the fulfillment of both the Law and the Prophets.

9:4 talking with Jesus. Luke tells us what they were talking about (9:31): the death,

5And Peter answered and said to
Jesus, Master, it is good for us to be
here: and let us make *three tabernacles; one for thee, and one for Moses,
and one for Elias.
6For he *wist not what to say; for
they were sore afraid.
7And there was a cloud that overshadowed them: and a voice came out
of the cloud, saying, This is my beloved
Son: hear him.
8And suddenly, when they had looked
round about, they saw no man any
more, save Jesus only with themselves.
¶9And as they came down from the
mountain, he charged them that they
should tell no man what things they had
seen, till the Son of man were risen
from the dead.
10And they kept that saying with
themselves, questioning one with another what the rising from the dead
should mean.
¶11And they asked him, saying, Why
say the scribes that Elias must first
come?
12And he answered and told them,
Elias verily cometh first, and restoreth
all things; and how it is written of the
Son of man, that he must suffer many
things, and be set at nought.
13But I say unto you, That Elias is
indeed come, and they have done unto
him whatsoever they listed, as it is
written of him.

The disciples' lack of faith.
Christ's power to heal
(Matt. 17:14-21; Luke 9:37-42)

¶14And when he came to *his* disciples,
he saw a great multitude about them,
and the scribes questioning with them.
15And straightway all the people,
when they beheld him, were greatly
amazed, and running to *him* saluted
him.
16And he asked the scribes, What
question ye with them?
17And one of the multitude answered
and said, Master, I have brought unto
thee my son, which hath a dumb spirit;
18And wheresoever he taketh him, he
teareth him: and he foameth, and
gnasheth with his teeth, and pineth
away: and I spake to thy disciples that
they should cast him out; and they
could not.
19He answereth him, and saith,
O faithless generation, how long shall
I be with you? how long shall I suffer
you? bring him unto me.
20And they brought him unto him:
and when he saw him, straightway the
spirit tare him; and he fell on the
ground, and wallowed foaming.
21And he asked his father, How long
is it ago since this came unto him? And
he said, Of a child.
22And ofttimes it hath cast him into
the *fire, and into the waters, to destroy
him: but if thou canst do any thing, have
compassion on us, and help us.
23Jesus said unto him, If thou canst
believe, all things *are* possible to him
that believeth.
24And straightway the father of the
child cried out, and said with tears,
Lord, I believe; help thou mine unbelief.
25When Jesus saw that the people
came running together, he rebuked the
foul spirit, saying unto him, *Thou* dumb
and deaf spirit, I charge thee, come out
of him, and enter no more into him.
26And *the spirit* cried, and rent him
sore, and came out of him: and he was

---

resurrection, and ascension of our Lord, which would be accomplished at Jerusalem. The Law and the Prophets, the sum and substance of the Old Testament, of which Moses and Elijah were representatives, had for ages declared by picture and prophecy that Jesus would come to die and be raised again.

9:5 three tabernacles. Three tents or shelters. Peter did not really know what the Transfiguration meant; later he learned its meaning (2 Pet. 1:16-18). By asking to build three tabernacles, he wrongly placed the Lord on the same level with Moses and Elijah.

as one dead; insomuch that many said,
He is dead.
27 But Jesus took him by the hand, and
lifted him up; and he arose.
28 And when he was come into the
house, his disciples asked him privately, Why could not we cast him out?
29 And he said unto them, This kind can
come forth by nothing, but by *prayer
and fasting.

9:29 Prayer and Fasting
Prayer means real heart communication with the Lord and utter dependence upon Him. Fasting does not simply mean going without food; there is a deeper meaning, that of denying self, losing sight of ourselves, and giving Christ His rightful place. It is only as we pray and fast that we can be useful in the Lord's hands.

The Lord Jesus again speaks of His death and resurrection (Matt. 17:22-23; Luke 9:43-45)

¶30 And they departed thence, and
passed through Galilee; and he would
not that any man should know *it*.
31 For he taught his disciples, and said
unto them, The Son of man is delivered
into the hands of men, and they shall kill
him; and after that he is killed, he shall
rise the third day.
32 But they understood not that saying, and were afraid to ask him.

True greatness in the Kingdom (Matt. 18:1-6; Luke 9:46-48)

¶33 And he came to Capernaum: and
being in the house he asked them, What
was it that ye disputed among yourselves by the way?
34 But they held their peace: for
by the way they had disputed among
themselves, who *should be* the greatest.
35 And he sat down, and called the
twelve, and saith unto them, If any man
desire to be first, *the same* shall be last
of all, and servant of all.
36 And he took a child, and set him in the
midst of them: and when he had taken
him in his arms, he said unto them,
37 Whosoever shall receive one of
such children in my name, receiveth
me: and whosoever shall receive me,
receiveth not me, but him that sent me.

The question of John (Luke 9:49-50)

¶38 And John answered him, saying,
Master, we saw one casting out devils
in thy name, and he followeth not
us: and we forbad him, because he followeth not us.
39 But Jesus said, Forbid him not: for
there is no man which shall do a *miracle in my name, that can lightly speak
evil of me.
40 For he that is not against us is on
our part.
41 For whosoever shall give you a cup
of water to drink in my name, because
ye belong to Christ, verily I say unto
you, he shall not lose his *reward.

A solemn warning about hell

42 And whosoever shall *offend one of
these little ones that believe in me, it is
better for him that a millstone were
hanged about his neck, and he were cast
into the sea.
43 And if thy hand offend thee, cut it
off: it is better for thee to enter into life
maimed, than having two hands to go
into hell, into the fire that never shall
be quenched:

9:31 delivered into the hands of men. By foretelling His death and resurrection, our Lord reminded His disciples that the glory, of which the Transfiguration was a picture, was to follow His sufferings (see also Matt. 17:22-23; Luke 9:43-45).

9:33 What was it that ye disputed among yourselves . . . ? The Lord not only always hears our words, He knows our very thoughts.

9:36 he took a child. Jesus took a child in His arms and used the child as a great object lesson. If you would be great, our Saviour implied, you must be simple, teachable, and trusting as a child (see Matt. 18:1-4).

9:43 hell. Gehenna. See Matthew 5:22, second note.

44Where their worm dieth not, and
the fire is not quenched.
45And if thy foot offend thee, cut it off:
it is better for thee to enter halt into life,
than having two feet to be cast into hell,
into the fire that never shall be
quenched:
46Where their worm dieth not, and
the fire is not quenched.
47And if thine eye offend thee, pluck
it out: it is better for thee to enter into
the kingdom of God with one eye, than
having two eyes to be cast into hell fire:
48Where their worm dieth not, and
the fire is not quenched.
49For every one shall be salted with
fire, and every *sacrifice shall be salted
with salt.
50Salt *is* good: but if the salt have lost
his saltness, wherewith will ye season
it? Have salt in yourselves, and have
peace one with another.

IV. Christ's Ministry in Peraea
(10:1-31)

10 And he arose from thence,
and cometh into the coasts of
Judaea by the farther side of Jordan: and
the people resort unto him again; and,
as he was wont, he taught them again.

Marriage and divorce
(cf. Matt. 5:31-32; 19:1-9; Luke 16:18)

¶2And the Pharisees came to him,
and asked him, Is it lawful for a man to
put away *his* wife? tempting him.
3And he answered and said unto
them, What did Moses command you?
4And they said, Moses suffered to
write a bill of divorcement, and to put
her away.
5And Jesus answered and said unto
them, For the hardness of your heart he
wrote you this precept.

9:44 A Description of Hell
Three times these same words are used (here, and in vss. 46 and 48). Christ was giving a description of the terrors of hell. He taught that punishment for the person who will not believe in Him and will not accept Him lasts forever. No pictures of hell are as terrible as those our Lord paints for us here (read Isa. 66:24 and its note, "Isaiah's Final Words").

6But from the beginning of the creation God made them male and female.
7For this cause shall a man leave his
father and mother, and cleave to his
wife;
8And they twain shall be one flesh: so
then they are no more twain, but one
flesh.
9What therefore God hath joined together, let not man put asunder.
10And in the house his disciples
asked him again of the same *matter.*
11And he saith unto them, Whosoever
shall put away his wife, and marry another, committeth adultery against her.
12And if a woman shall put away her
husband, and be married to another, she
committeth adultery.

The Lord Jesus blesses little children
(Matt. 19:13-15; Luke 18:15-17)

¶13And they brought young children
to him, that he should touch them: and
his disciples rebuked those that brought
them.
14But when Jesus saw *it,* he was
much displeased, and said unto them,
Suffer the little children to come unto
me, and forbid them not: for of such is
the kingdom of God.
15Verily I say unto you, Whosoever
shall not receive the kingdom of God as
a little child, he shall not enter therein.

10:4 Moses suffered to write a bill of divorcement. See Deuteronomy 24:1-4.
10:6 God made them male and female. See Genesis 2:21-25.
10:14 Suffer. Allow.
10:14 forbid them not. The Lord Jesus did not say that children make up the kingdom but that we must be childlike in our simple acceptance of Him in faith (vs. 15) if we are to enter the kingdom.

[16]And he took them up in his arms,
put *his* hands upon them, and blessed
them.

The rich young ruler
(Matt. 19:16-30; Luke 18:18-30;
cf. also Luke 10:25)

¶[17]And when he was gone forth into
the way, there came one running, and
kneeled to him, and asked him, Good
Master, what shall I do that I may inherit *eternal life?
[18]And Jesus said unto him, Why
callest thou me good? *there is* none good
but one, *that is,* God.
[19]Thou knowest the commandments,
Do not commit adultery, Do not kill, Do
not steal, Do not bear false witness,
Defraud not, Honour thy father and
mother.
[20]And he answered and said unto
him, Master, all these have I observed
from my youth.
[21]Then Jesus beholding him loved
him, and said unto him, One thing
thou lackest: go thy way, sell whatsoever thou hast, and give to the poor,
and thou shalt have treasure in heaven:
and come, take up the cross, and follow me.
[22]And he was sad at that saying, and
went away grieved: for he had great
possessions.
¶[23]And Jesus looked round about, and
saith unto his disciples, How hardly
shall they that have riches enter into
the kingdom of God!
[24]And the disciples were astonished
at his words. But Jesus answereth
again, and saith unto them, Children,
how hard is it for them that *trust in
riches to enter into the kingdom of
God!
[25]It is easier for a camel to go through
the eye of a needle, than for a rich man
to enter into the kingdom of God.
[26]And they were astonished out of
measure, saying among themselves,
Who then can be saved?
[27]And Jesus looking upon them saith,
With men *it is* impossible, but not with
God: for with God all things are possible.
¶[28]Then Peter began to say unto him,
Lo, we have left all, and have followed
thee.
[29]And Jesus answered and said,
Verily I say unto you, There is no man
that hath left house, or brethren, or
sisters, or father, or mother, or wife,
or children, or lands, for my sake, and
the gospel's,
[30]But he shall receive an hundredfold now in this time, houses, and brethren, and sisters, and mothers, and
children, and lands, with persecutions; and in the *world to come eternal life.
[31]But many *that are* first shall be last;
and the last first.

10:17 Good Master. The question of the young man showed that he was ignorant of God's way of salvation. When he asked, "What shall I do?" he implied that man must do something before he can be a possessor of eternal life. Eternal life is a gift; we do not earn it or work for it; we receive it as a gift from God (John 3:16 and 3:15-16 note, "Eternal Life"; 5:39-40; 10:28; Rom. 6:23).

10:17 Master. Teacher.

10:18 there is none good. There are only two ways to look at these words. If Jesus meant that He was not God, then He meant that He was not good. If Jesus meant that He was good, then He meant that He was God. He was telling the young man that he didn't realize to whom he was talking—that Christ is indeed God.

10:19 the commandments. See Exodus 20:12-16; Deuteronomy 5:16-20.

10:23 How hardly shall they that have riches enter. The Lord Jesus never taught that it was impossible for rich people to be saved. What He did teach was that people cannot be saved by trusting in their riches.

10:25 eye of a needle. Some people have thought that this was a little gate, but it was doubtless a real sewing needle that the Lord referred to.

10:30 in the world to come. In the future age, after this life.

V. Christ's Last Journey to Jerusalem and His Death (10:32—15:47)

*The Lord Jesus speaks again of His death and *resurrection (Matt. 20:17-19; Luke 18:31-33)*

¶32 And they were in the way going up to Jerusalem; and Jesus went before them: and they were amazed; and as they followed, they were afraid. And he took again the twelve, and began to tell them what things should happen unto him,

33 *Saying,* Behold, we go up to Jerusalem; and the Son of man shall be delivered unto the chief priests, and unto the scribes; and they shall condemn him to death, and shall deliver him to the *Gentiles:

34 And they shall mock him, and shall scourge him, and shall spit upon him, and shall kill him: and the third day he shall rise again.

The ambition of James and John (Matt. 20:20-28)

¶35 And James and John, the sons of Zebedee, come unto him, saying, Master, we would that thou shouldest do for us whatsoever we shall desire.

36 And he said unto them, What would ye that I should do for you?

37 They said unto him, Grant unto us that we may sit, one on thy right hand, and the other on thy left hand, in thy glory.

38 But Jesus said unto them, Ye know not what ye ask: can ye drink of the cup that I drink of? and be baptized with the *baptism that I am baptized with?

39 And they said unto him, We can. And Jesus said unto them, Ye shall indeed drink of the cup that I drink of; and with the baptism that I am baptized withal shall ye be baptized:

40 But to sit on my right hand and on my left hand is not mine to give; but *it shall be given to them* for whom it is prepared.

41 And when the ten heard *it,* they began to be much displeased with James and John.

42 But Jesus called them *to him,* and saith unto them, Ye know that they which are accounted to rule over the Gentiles exercise lordship over them; and their great ones exercise authority upon them.

43 But so shall it not be among you: but whosoever will be great among you, shall be your minister:

44 And whosoever of you will be the chiefest, shall be servant of all.

45 For even the Son of man came not to be ministered unto, but to minister, and to give his life a *ransom for many.

Blind Bartimaeus receives his sight (Matt. 20:29-34)

¶46 And they came to Jericho: and as he went out of Jericho with his disciples and a great number of people, blind Bartimaeus, the son of Timaeus, sat by the highway side begging.

47 And when he heard that it was Jesus of Nazareth, he began to cry out, and say, Jesus, *thou* *Son of David, have *mercy on me.

48 And many charged him that he should hold his peace: but he cried the more a great deal, *Thou* Son of David, have mercy on me.

49 And Jesus stood still, and commanded him to be called. And they call the blind man, saying unto him, Be of good comfort, rise; he calleth thee.

50 And he, casting away his garment, rose, and came to Jesus.

51 And Jesus answered and said unto him, What wilt thou that I should do unto

---

10:39 Ye shall indeed. James and John were to suffer martyrdom and exile, but they were not yet ready for this. Our Lord's "cup" was the cup of anguish that He would drink on the cross (read Matt. 26:39). The "baptism" refers to the flood of unspeakable suffering that He was to go through at Calvary.

10:46 Bartimaeus. "Bar" before a name means *son of.*

thee? The blind man said unto him,
Lord, that I might receive my sight.
52And Jesus said unto him, Go thy
way; thy *faith hath made thee whole.
And immediately he received his sight,
and followed Jesus in the way.

The Lord Jesus enters Jerusalem
(Matt. 21:1-9; Luke 19:29-38)

11 And when they came nigh to
Jerusalem, unto Bethphage and
Bethany, at the *mount of Olives, he
sendeth forth two of his disciples,
2And saith unto them, Go your way
into the village over against you: and as
soon as ye be entered into it, ye shall
find a colt tied, whereon never man sat;
loose him, and bring *him.*
3And if any man say unto you, Why
do ye this? say ye that the Lord hath
need of him; and straightway he will
send him hither.
4And they went their way, and found
the colt tied by the door without in a
place where two ways met; and they
loose him.
5And certain of them that stood there
said unto them, What do ye, loosing the
colt?
6And they said unto them even as
Jesus had commanded: and they let
them go.
7And they brought the colt to Jesus,
and cast their garments on him; and he
sat upon him.
8And many spread their garments in
the way: and others cut down branches
off the trees, and strawed *them* in the
way.

11:9 Hosanna
"Hosanna" means *Save now, I beseech Thee.* The Lord Jesus was presenting Himself as the King of Israel. Though He was the meek and lowly One riding on the colt of an ass, He was the rightful person to sit upon the throne of David, and so the people cried, "Blessed is he that cometh in the name of the Lord." The prophecy of Zechariah (9:9) was fulfilled when the Lord Jesus rode into Jerusalem. No one but the Lord Himself knew the real outcome of His royal visit. He knew that the same voices that heralded Him as King would soon be heard saying, "Crucify him." Though they said, "Save now," they refused His salvation and rejected Him as King (see also Matt. 21:1-9; Luke 19:29-38).

9And they that went before, and they
that followed, cried, saying, *Hosanna;
Blessed *is* he that cometh in the name
of the Lord:
10Blessed *be* the kingdom of our father David, that cometh in the name of
the Lord: Hosanna in the highest.
11And Jesus entered into Jerusalem,
and into the temple: and when he had
looked round about upon all things, and
now the eventide was come, he went
out unto Bethany with the twelve.

The barren fig tree
(Matt. 21:19-21)

¶12And on the morrow, when they
were come from Bethany, he was hungry:
13And seeing a fig tree afar off having leaves, he came, if haply he might
find any thing thereon: and when he
came to it, he found nothing but leaves;
for the time of figs was not *yet.*

10:52 thy faith hath made thee whole. The blind man could do nothing for himself, but his faith was that Christ could and would open his eyes. The blind man received his sight "immediately."
11:1 Bethphage. The name means *the house of unripe fruit.* It probably was given this name after the events of verses 12-14 and 20-24.
11:1 Bethany. The village of Martha, Mary, and Lazarus.
11:11 now the eventide was come. The Lord always went out of the city at evening (see vs. 19 note).
11:13 a fig tree. The fig tree speaks to us of the Jewish nation (see Jer. 24:1-6). The Jews were the Lord's own people; He came to His own, but when He came, He did not find the fruit of living faith and obedience (see John 1:11-12).
11:13 having leaves. Fig trees that have leaves on them usually have figs too. This tree

14 And Jesus answered and said unto it, No man eat fruit of thee hereafter for ever. And his disciples heard *it.*

The cleansing of the temple
(Matt. 21:12-16; Luke 19:45-47;
cf. also John 2:13-16)

¶15 And they come to Jerusalem: and Jesus went into the temple, and began to cast out them that sold and bought in the temple, and overthrew the tables of the moneychangers, and the seats of them that sold doves;

16 And would not suffer that any man should carry *any* vessel through the temple.

17 And he taught, saying unto them, Is it not written, My house shall be called of all nations the house of prayer? but ye have made it a den of thieves.

11:17 The Misuse of the Temple
The people had to purchase animals intended for sacrifice with temple money. Since most of them had only Roman coins, they had to first exchange those coins for the temple money. The moneychangers made unrighteous profit for themselves out of this transaction. They used reverence for God as a means of personal gain at the expense of the worshippers; in other words, they were using religion as a cloak to cover their wicked hearts (see Jer. 7:11; Matt. 21:12-16; Luke 19:45-47). Once before this Jesus had cleared the temple of moneychangers (John 2:13-19).

18 And the scribes and chief priests heard *it,* and sought how they might destroy him: for they feared him, because all the people was astonished at his *doctrine.

19 And when even was come, he went out of the city.

The Lord speaks of faith

¶20 And in the morning, as they passed by, they saw the fig tree dried up from the roots.

21 And Peter calling to remembrance saith unto him, Master, behold, the fig tree which thou cursedst is withered away.

22 And Jesus answering saith unto them, Have faith in God.

23 For verily I say unto you, That whosoever shall say unto this mountain, Be thou removed, and be thou cast into the sea; and shall not doubt in his heart, but shall believe that those things which he saith shall come to pass; he shall have whatsoever he saith.

24 Therefore I say unto you, What things soever ye desire, when ye pray, believe that ye receive *them,* and ye shall have *them.*

25 And when ye stand praying, forgive, if ye have ought against any: that your Father also which is in heaven may forgive you your trespasses.

26 But if ye do not forgive, neither will your Father which is in heaven forgive your trespasses.

The authority of the Lord Jesus
(Matt. 21:23-27; Luke 20:1-8)

¶27 And they come again to Jerusalem: and as he was walking in the temple, there come to him the chief priests, and the scribes, and the elders,

28 And say unto him, By what authority doest thou these things? and who gave thee this authority to do these things?

29 And Jesus answered and said unto them, I will also ask of you one question, and answer me, and I will tell you by what authority I do these things.

---

promised something by its leaves that it did not fulfill (see also Matt. 21:19-21). It is possible to have leaves of just an outward profession without bearing the fruit of true godliness (see 2 Tim. 3:5).

11:17 My house shall be called. See Isaiah 56:7.

11:19 when even was come. This implies "whenever evening came" or "every day when evening came," the Lord "went out of the city."

11:22 Have faith in God. The faith that God gives.

[30]The baptism of John, was *it* from
heaven, or of men? answer me.
[31]And they reasoned with themselves, saying, If we shall say, From
heaven; he will say, Why then did ye not
believe him?
[32]But if we shall say, Of men; they
feared the people: for all *men* counted
John, that he was a prophet indeed.
[33]And they answered and said unto
Jesus, We cannot tell. And Jesus answering saith unto them, Neither do I
tell you by what authority I do these
things.

The wicked husbandmen
(Matt. 21:33-46; Luke 20:9-19)

12 And he began to speak unto
them by *parables. A *certain*
man planted a vineyard, and set an hedge
about *it,* and digged *a place for* the winefat,
and built a tower, and let it out to husbandmen, and went into a far country.
[2] And at the season he sent to the
husbandmen a servant, that he might
receive from the husbandmen of the
fruit of the vineyard.
[3] And they caught *him,* and beat him,
and sent *him* away empty.
[4] And again he sent unto them another servant; and at him they cast
stones, and wounded *him* in the head,
and sent *him* away shamefully handled.

12:1 The Hedge of the Vineyard
God had purposely set a hedge around His vineyard (the people of Israel). This means that God had separated Israel from the other nations in order that they might be a chosen people to accomplish a distinct mission: to give the Saviour, the Lord Jesus Christ, to the world. The hedge also speaks of God's promise to protect Israel. Notice by the various symbols in this verse how God had made ample provision for Israel that they might bring forth fruit for Him.

[5] And again he sent another; and him
they killed, and many others; beating
some, and killing some.
[6] Having yet therefore one son, his
wellbeloved, he sent him also last
unto them, saying, They will reverence
my son.
[7] But those husbandmen said among
themselves, This is the heir; come, let
us kill him, and the inheritance shall be
ours.
[8] And they took him, and killed *him,*
and cast *him* out of the vineyard.
[9] What shall therefore the lord of the
vineyard do? he will come and destroy
the husbandmen, and will give the vineyard unto others.
[10] And have ye not read this scripture;
The stone which the builders rejected
is become the head of the corner:

12:1 vineyard. In the Old Testament, the vineyard is used to describe the Jewish nation. Read Isaiah 5:1-7; see also Psalm 80, particularly verse 15.
12:1 place for the winefat. This means the trough of the winepress, or the place that received the juice of the fruit.
12:1 tower. The watchtower where men sat to guard the fruit.
12:1 husbandmen. Tillers of the soil; farmers.
12:2 at the season. The season of harvest, when the fruit was ready to pick.
12:2-5 servant . . . beat him . . . wounded him . . . him they killed. God sent His servants, the prophets, to Israel, and our Lord tells in verses 3-5 how these messengers were treated by the husbandmen (the people of Israel). See how Elijah fled for his life (1 Kings 19:1-3); Micaiah was thrown into a dungeon (1 Kings 22:26-27); Jeremiah was also cast into prison (Jer. 37:15-16; see also 37:12 note, "Jeremiah's Prison Experiences"); Zechariah was stoned (2 Chron. 24:20-21); John the Baptist was beheaded (Mark 6:27); and many more suffered (Heb. 11:36-37).
12:6 one son, his wellbeloved. Here the Lord speaks about Himself. He was God's only Son (see Gal. 4:4). He clearly knew that the cross awaited Him.
12:10 this scripture. The Scriptures that tell us of the persecution of the prophets also tell of the rejection of Christ by Israel (Ps. 118:22-23; Isa. 53:3).
12:10 rejected. The stone is the Lord Jesus Christ, the Messiah of Israel; when He came

[11]This was the Lord's doing, and it is
marvellous in our eyes?
[12]And they sought to lay hold on him,
but feared the people: for they knew
that he had spoken the *parable against
them: and they left him, and went their
way.

The question of tribute
(Matt. 22:15-22; Luke 20:19-26)

¶[13]And they send unto him certain of
the Pharisees and of the *Herodians, to
catch him in *his* words.
[14]And when they were come, they say
unto him, Master, we know that thou art
true, and carest for no man: for thou
regardest not the person of men, but
teachest the way of God in truth: Is it
lawful to give tribute to *Caesar, or not?

12:14 Paying Taxes
The lawfulness of paying taxes to Rome was a question of dispute among the Jews. The Pharisees paid taxes but always under protest. The Herodians paid taxes more willingly than the Pharisees. It was a dangerous question to discuss. It is evident that they wanted the Lord to answer one of two words–yes or no. This was the trap. If Jesus answered yes, the Pharisees would have told the people that He could not be the Christ, their Messiah. But if Jesus answered no, the Herodians would have spread the news that He had spoken against Caesar.

[15]Shall we give, or shall we not give?
But he, knowing their hypocrisy, said
unto them, Why *tempt ye me? bring
me a penny, that I may see *it.*
[16]And they brought *it.* And he saith
unto them, Whose *is* this image and
*superscription? And they said unto
him, Caesar's.
[17]And Jesus answering said unto
them, Render to Caesar the things that
are Caesar's, and to God the things
that are God's. And they marvelled at
him.

The Sadducees and the resurrection
(Matt. 22:23-33; Luke 20:27-38)

¶[18]Then come unto him the *Sadducees, which say there is no resurrection; and they asked him, saying,
[19]Master, Moses wrote unto us, If a
man's brother die, and leave *his* wife
behind him, and leave no children, that
his brother should take his wife, and
raise up seed unto his brother.
[20]Now there were seven brethren:
and the first took a wife, and dying left
no seed.
[21]And the second took her, and died,
neither left he any seed: and the third
likewise.
[22]And the seven had her, and left no
seed: last of all the woman died also.
[23]In the resurrection therefore, when
they shall rise, whose wife shall she be

---

and presented Himself to Israel as their Messiah, they rejected Him. The rejected stone has become the head of the corner (Acts 4:11-12; Eph. 2:20; 1 Pet. 2:7).

12:13 catch him. The Pharisees and Herodians were trying to lay a trap of words in which to catch Jesus and trip Him up.

12:15 a penny. The most common coin of that day—a denarius (see Mark 6:37, second note).

12:16 image and superscription. The image of Tiberius Caesar, with the superscription, meaning *inscription,* around it, was stamped on the coin.

12:17 Render. Give.

12:17 to Caesar. If they traded with money that bore the image of Caesar, they acknowledged the authority of Caesar, and so they could not honestly refuse to pay tribute.

12:17 to God. Just as the image on the coin represented the authority of Caesar, so the image of God stamped upon man shows that man is responsible to God (see Gen. 1:27 and its note, "In God's Image"; 1 Cor. 11:7). Though a Christian's citizenship is in heaven, he must also remember that he is a citizen of the country where he lives (compare 1 Pet. 2:13-15). A good citizen should and will obey every law of the land if it is not contrary to the stated will of God.

12:19 Moses wrote. They probably referred to Deuteronomy 25:5-10.

of them? for the seven had her to wife.
24And Jesus answering said unto
them, Do ye not therefore *err, because
ye know not the scriptures, neither the
power of God?
25For when they shall rise from the
dead, they neither marry, nor are given
in marriage; but are as the angels which
are in heaven.
26And as touching the dead, that they
rise: have ye not read in the *book of
Moses, how in the bush God spake unto
him, saying, I *am* the God of *Abraham,
and the God of *Isaac, and the God of
*Jacob?
27He is not the God of the dead, but
the God of the living: ye therefore do
greatly err.

The scribe's question about the greatest commandment (Matt. 22:34-40; cf. Luke 10:25-37)

¶28And one of the scribes came, and
having heard them reasoning together,
and perceiving that he had answered
them well, asked him, Which is the first
commandment of all?
29And Jesus answered him, The first
of all the commandments *is,* Hear,
O *Israel; The Lord our God is one
Lord:
30And thou shalt love the Lord thy
God with all thy heart, and with all thy
soul, and with all thy mind, and with all
thy strength: this *is* the first commandment.
31And the second *is* like, *namely* this,
Thou shalt love thy neighbour as thyself. There is none other commandment greater than these.
32And the *scribe said unto him, Well,
Master, thou hast said the truth: for
there is one God; and there is none
other but he:
33And to love him with all the heart,
and with all the understanding, and with
all the soul, and with all the strength,
and to love *his* neighbour as himself, is
more than all whole burnt *offerings
and sacrifices.

12:28-29 THE GREATEST COMMANDMENT

When the scribe asked, "Which is the first commandment of all?" he meant, "Which is the first in importance?" The scribes divided the Law into 613 precepts—248 do's and 365 don'ts. Sabbath observance, circumcision, sacrifices, and fashion of religious robes were considered of the greatest importance.

In verses 29-31, Jesus passed over the external things. The summary of the *Law is to love God and to love others. Outward ceremonies and observances are useless if the heart is not right with God. Love is the most important quality we should have—to God and others—since "God is love" (1 John 4:8; see also 1 Cor. 13).

12:24 err. The word means *to wander astray;* it is from the same word that Jude used in connection with "wandering stars" (Jude 13).

12:24 know not the scriptures. The Sadducees, who didn't even believe in the resurrection of the dead, thought that they were intelligent about the Scriptures. Their deepest ignorance was that they were oblivious to their own ignorance. They were simply trying once again to trap or stump Jesus.

12:25 as the angels. Relationships that have to do with our mortal bodies will not exist when we have our resurrection bodies (see 1 Cor. 15:35-58; see also 15:35 note and 15:52 note, "A Final Resurrection").

12:26 in the bush God spake. See Exodus 3:6 and 3:5-6 note, "In God's Presence."

12:27 God of the living. He is still the God of Abraham, Isaac, and Jacob, though these patriarchs have long since ceased to dwell on the earth. By saying this to the Sadducees, our Lord proved to them that if they had read the *Law more carefully they would have discovered teaching concerning the fact of life after death.

12:29 The Lord our God. See Deuteronomy 6:4.

12:31 Thou shalt love thy neighbour. See Leviticus 19:18.

[34]And when Jesus saw that he answered discreetly, he said unto him, Thou art not far from the kingdom of God. And no man after that durst ask him *any question.*

David's Son and David's Lord (Matt. 22:41-46; Luke 20:41-44)

¶[35]And Jesus answered and said, while he taught in the temple, How say the scribes that Christ is the Son of David?
[36]For David himself said by the Holy Ghost, The LORD said to my Lord, Sit thou on my right hand, till I make thine enemies thy footstool.
[37]David therefore himself calleth him Lord; and whence is he *then* his son? And the common people heard him gladly.

The Lord denounces the scribes

¶[38]And he said unto them in his doctrine, Beware of the scribes, which love to go in long clothing, and *love* salutations in the marketplaces,
[39]And the chief seats in the *synagogues, and the uppermost rooms at *feasts:
[40]Which devour widows' houses, and for a pretence make long prayers: these shall receive greater *damnation.

The widow's mites (Luke 21:1-4)

¶[41]And Jesus sat over against the treasury, and beheld how the people cast money into the treasury: and many that were rich cast in much.
[42]And there came a certain poor widow, and she threw in two mites, which make a farthing.
[43]And he called *unto him* his disciples, and saith unto them, Verily I say unto you, That this poor widow hath cast more in, than all they which have cast into the treasury:

12:34 discreetly. Intelligently and wisely. This scribe understood that true obedience to God comes from the heart, which was why Jesus said to him, "Thou art not far from the kingdom of God." The scribe was touched by our Lord's answer. Understanding this was one thing, though; the repentance and faith needed to enter the kingdom seem to have been lacking for the scribe.

12:34 durst. Dared.

12:35 How say the scribes . . . ? Our Lord quoted Psalm 110:1. The scribes knew that David's Lord would become David's Son (or that He would be descended from David), but they were not willing to admit that "David's greater Son and David's Lord" stood before them. We believe that Christ is David's Lord because He is God; He is also David's Son because He is God incarnate (made flesh).

12:38 long clothing. Long robes were the dress of people who had places of dignity, such as kings and priests.

12:38 in the marketplaces. The scribes loved to be where people could see them and recognize their dignity and piety (or what the scribes supposed was piety).

12:39 chief seats. This means literally *the first seats*—the scribes loved to have the most important seats in the front row, not only so men could see them, but as a mark of special piety.

12:39 uppermost rooms. Compare Luke 14:7-15.

12:40 devour widows' houses. The Jewish leaders took away the homes of poor helpless widows. Since the teachers of the *Law received no pay, they depended on offerings from the people. In fact, they took advantage of their position, cheating the poor out of everything they had. The leaders were hypocritical, with no love or compassion in their hearts for their own people.

12:41 the treasury. There were about thirteen boxes made of brass into which people placed their offerings, which were then used to maintain the temple.

12:42 two mites. This was the smallest offering permitted. A mite was the smallest Jewish coin.

12:43 cast more in, than all. Christ introduced a new rule of finance that day. God judges our giving not so much by how much we give but by how much we have left after giving and in what spirit we give our tithes and offerings (see 2 Cor. 9:7).

[44]For all *they* did cast in of their abundance; but she of her want did cast in all that she had, *even* all her living.

The Olivet discourse
(cf. Matt. 24–25; Luke 21)

13 And as he went out of the temple, one of his disciples saith unto him, Master, see what manner of stones and what buildings *are* here!

[2]And Jesus answering said unto him, Seest thou these great buildings? there shall not be left one stone upon another, that shall not be thrown down.

[3]And as he sat upon the mount of Olives over against the temple, Peter and James and John and Andrew asked him privately,

[4]Tell us, when shall these things be? and what *shall be* the sign when all these things shall be fulfilled?

[5]And Jesus answering them began to say, Take heed lest any *man* deceive you:

The beginning of sorrows

[6]For many shall come in my name, saying, I am *Christ;* and shall deceive many.

[7]And when ye shall hear of wars and rumours of wars, be ye not troubled: for *such things* must needs be; but the end *shall* not *be* yet.

[8]For nation shall rise against nation, and kingdom against kingdom: and there shall be earthquakes in divers places, and there shall be famines and troubles: these *are* the beginnings of sorrows.

¶[9]But take heed to yourselves: for they shall deliver you up to councils; and in the synagogues ye shall be beaten: and ye shall be brought before rulers and kings for my sake, for a testimony against them.

[10]And the gospel must first be published among all nations.

[11]But when they shall lead *you,* and deliver you up, take no thought beforehand what ye shall speak, neither do ye premeditate: but whatsoever shall be given you in that hour, that speak ye: for it is not ye that speak, but the Holy Ghost.

[12]Now the brother shall betray the brother to *death, and the father the son; and children shall rise up against *their* parents, and shall cause them to be put to death.

13:1 what manner of stones. Josephus, the great Jewish historian, tells us that each of the massive foundation stones of the temple were 37½ feet long, 12 feet high, and 18 feet wide.

13:2 not be left one stone upon another. Though it seemed as if this structure would last forever, the temple was destroyed about forty years after our Lord uttered these words.

13:7 wars and rumours of wars. While it is true that these words found fulfillment in the period between the Crucifixion and the destruction of Jerusalem (A.D. 70), yet on a far larger scale they are being fulfilled today. This will be increasingly true as the day approaches for the *Great Tribulation to come upon the earth (see also Matt. 24–25).

13:8 beginnings of sorrows. The word "sorrows" only occurs in four places in the New Testament: Matthew 24:8; Acts 2:24; 1 Thessalonians 5:3, and here.

13:9 to councils. Some of the apostles who actually heard our Lord say these things found His words true within little more than fifty days after Christ's ascension (Acts 4:3-7; 5:27). Paul was brought before the same council (Acts 23:1).

13:9 ye shall be beaten. The apostle Paul had this experience (see 2 Cor. 11:24 and its note, "Severe Punishment"). The minister in a synagogue maintained order by beating offenders.

13:9 before rulers and kings. Paul stood before Felix (Acts 24:10-22), Festus (Acts 25:1-11), Agrippa (Acts 26:1-23), and Nero (see 2 Tim. 4:17 second note).

13:11 take no thought beforehand. Do not be anxious or worried beforehand. The Holy Spirit would be with them and is with every believer, no matter what difficult circumstance we may be going through.

[13]And ye shall be hated of all *men* for
my name's sake: but he that shall endure unto the end, the same shall be
saved.

13:13 The End
"The end" does not just refer to the death of the believer who trusts in Christ now (although that can be one meaning), but also to the end of the *Great Tribulation, which is in the future and will not come until after the believer is caught up to be with the Lord (1 Thess. 4:13-17), and his salvation completed. The Lord Jesus Christ was speaking especially to the Jews, who will, for the most part, become believers only after the *church has been caught up. They will then turn to Christ in belief and endure to the end. They will refuse the mark of the Beast (Rev. 20:4) and will suffer awful persecution, but their eternal salvation will be sure.

The Great Tribulation

¶[14]But when ye shall see the *abomination of desolation, spoken of by Daniel the *prophet, standing where it
ought not, (let him that readeth understand,) then let them that be in Judaea
flee to the mountains:
[15]And let him that is on the housetop
not go down into the house, neither
enter *therein*, to take any thing out of
his house:
[16]And let him that is in the field not
turn back again for to take up his garment.
[17]But woe to them that are with child,
and to them that give suck in those
days!
[18]And pray ye that your flight be not
in the winter.
[19]For *in* those days shall be affliction,
such as was not from the beginning of
the creation which *God created unto
this time, neither shall be.
[20]And except that the Lord had shortened those days, no flesh should be
saved: but for the *elect's sake, whom
he hath chosen, he hath shortened the
days.
[21]And then if any man shall say to
you, Lo, here *is* Christ; or, lo, *he is*
there; believe *him* not:
[22]For false Christs and false prophets
shall rise, and shall shew signs and
wonders, to seduce, if *it were* possible,
even the elect.
[23]But take ye heed: behold, I have
foretold you all things.

13:14 abomination of desolation. The Lord is referring to what is written in Daniel 9:27 (see Dan. 9:24-27 note, "A Central Prophecy") and 12:11. We learn from these passages that the *Beast, or Man of Sin (see 2 Thess. 2:3 and its note, "Before the Lord Comes"; Rev. 13) will fulfill this prophecy.

13:14 standing where it ought not. The *Antichrist will sit in the temple of God and be worshipped as God (2 Thess. 2:4).

13:14 flee to the mountains. While it is true that a similar thing happened when Jerusalem was destroyed by Titus in A.D. 70, the reference is also to a time in the future when the words will be completely fulfilled.

13:19 affliction. The term refers to the *Great Tribulation. The terrible things that happened in connection with the destruction of Jerusalem under Titus are described by the historian, Josephus. The horrors are beyond explanation. But an even worse thing is going to occur after the *church is taken away and the Man of Sin (see vs. 14 first note) is revealed.

13:20 except that the Lord had shortened those days. The Lord prophesied that this trouble would come upon Israel because of their rejection of their King and because of their disobedience. Yet in His mercy He will shorten those days, not only so Israel might be saved but also so His purpose might be fulfilled.

13:20 the elect's sake. The elect refers to the *remnant in Israel—to the Jews, not to the church. Notice the references to the elect in verses 22 and 27.

13:22 signs and wonders. Satan will work through the *Antichrist and the *False Prophet to perform certain signs and wonders, which will seem to show the power of God. The real fulfillment of these words is seen in Revelation 13:13-14.

The return of the Son of Man in glory

¶24 But in those days, after that tribulation, the sun shall be darkened, and
the moon shall not give her light,
25 And the stars of heaven shall fall,
and the powers that are in heaven shall
be shaken.
26 And then shall they see the Son of
man coming in the clouds with great
power and glory.
27 And then shall he send his angels,
and shall gather together his elect from
the four winds, from the uttermost part
of the earth to the uttermost part of
heaven.

The parable of the fig tree
(Matt. 24:32-35; Luke 21:29-31)

28 Now learn a parable of the fig tree;
When her branch is yet tender, and
putteth forth leaves, ye know that summer is near:
29 So ye in like manner, when ye shall
see these things come to pass, know
that it is nigh, *even* at the doors.
30 Verily I say unto you, that this generation shall not pass, till all these
things be done.
31 Heaven and earth shall pass away:
but my words shall not pass away.

The importance of watching for
the return of the Lord

¶32 But of that day and *that* hour
knoweth no man, no, not the angels
which are in heaven, neither the Son,
but the Father.
33 Take ye heed, watch and pray: for
ye know not when the time is.
34 *For the Son of man is* as a man taking a far journey, who left his house, and
gave authority to his servants, and to
every man his work, and commanded
the porter to watch.
35 Watch ye therefore: for ye know not
when the master of the house cometh,
at even, or at midnight, or at the cock-
crowing, or in the morning:
36 Lest coming suddenly he find you
sleeping.
37 And what I say unto you I say unto
all, Watch.

13:24 after that tribulation. Immediately after the time of *Tribulation, the physical signs in the heavens will be given. Our Lord is here confirming what was prophesied in the Old Testament (read Isa. 13:9-10 and see 13:9 note, "God's Judgment"; Ezek. 32:7-8; Joel 3:15).

13:26 Son of man coming. When Christ is spoken of as the "Son of Man" in relation to His second coming, it is safe to say that it refers to His coming after the Great Tribulation, as in Revelation 19:11-16 (see 19:11 note, "The Tribulation") and Matthew 24:29-30. The coming of the Lord Jesus Christ for His church will be before the coming *Tribulation, as in 1 Thessalonians 4:13-18 (see 4:13 note, "Hope for the Dead").

13:26 great power and glory. When Christ comes for His own (the church, those who have received Him as their personal Saviour), only they will see Him, but when He comes in great power and glory "every eye shall see him" (Rev. 1:7).

13:27 gather together his elect. This is not a reference to the *Rapture, the gathering up of the church (1 Thess. 4:13-18). This refers to the gathering of Israel from the four corners of the earth back to their own land. We find many references in the Old Testament to this event; see, for example, Isaiah 11:11-12; 27:13.

13:29 these things. The things our Lord has spoken about in verses 13-27.

13:30 this generation. This word does not refer to the people who were actually listening to the words of our Lord, but to the Jewish people as a race. The word "generation" comes from *genea,* the primary meaning of which is *tribe* or *race.* It is marvelous how God has kept the Jews as a separate race. In spite of the many attempts of Satan through wicked men to put an end to the Jews, they still survive and will survive because God has still His purpose to realize in them.

13:32 neither the Son. The Lord Jesus Christ, in His humanity, did not know the time of His return.

The chief priests and scribes plan to take Jesus
(Matt. 26:2-5; Luke 22:1-2)

14 After two days was *the feast of* the *passover, and of *unleavened bread: and the chief priests and the *scribes sought how they might take him by craft, and put *him* to death.

2 But they said, Not on the feast *day,* lest there be an uproar of the people.

The anointing at Bethany
(Matt. 26:6-13; John 12:1-8)

¶3 And being in Bethany in the house of Simon the *leper, as he sat at meat, there came a woman having an alabaster box of ointment of spikenard very precious; and she brake the box, and poured *it* on his head.

4 And there were some that had indignation within themselves, and said, Why was this waste of the ointment made?

5 For it might have been sold for more than three hundred *pence, and have been given to the poor. And they murmured against her.

6 And Jesus said, Let her alone; why trouble ye her? she hath wrought a good work on me.

7 For ye have the poor with you always, and whensoever ye will ye may do them good: but me ye have not always.

8 She hath done what she could: she is come aforehand to *anoint my body to the burying.

9 Verily I say unto you, Wheresoever this *gospel shall be preached throughout the whole world, *this* also that she hath done shall be spoken of for a memorial of her.

Judas plans to betray the Lord
(Matt. 26:14-16; Luke 22:3-6)

¶10 And *Judas Iscariot, one of the twelve, went unto the chief priests, to betray him unto them.

11 And when they heard *it,* they were glad, and promised to give him money. And he sought how he might conveniently betray him.

The Lord's last Passover and the first Lord's Supper
(Matt. 26:17-29; Luke 22:7-23; John 13:18-19)

¶12 And the first day of unleavened bread, when they killed the passover, his disciples said unto him, Where wilt thou that we go and prepare that thou mayest eat the passover?

14:1 by craft. This was the only way the Jewish leaders could take Him. If they had had the slightest evidence against our Lord, they certainly would not have planned to take Him slyly.

14:3 woman. We know that this woman was Mary of Bethany (John 12:3).

14:3 alabaster box. At Alabastron in Egypt there was a place where small vases were made for holding perfumes. The Greeks named these expensive vases after the city from which they came, calling them "Alabastrons."

14:3 spikenard. The most costly anointing oil then in existence. Mary of Bethany, the sister of Martha, and Lazarus, whom our Lord raised from the dead (John 11:1-44), broke the narrow neck of the small flask in order to pour the perfume on the head of her Lord.

14:4 Why was this waste . . . ? Mark gives no names here, but in John 12:4 we read that it was Judas Iscariot who began the murmuring. To know his reason for murmuring see John 12:6.

14:5 three hundred pence. Three hundred denarii would be more than the amount someone would earn in a year.

14:9 a memorial. The deed of Mary, after two thousand years, is still full of fragrance. The story of her love and devotion has spread everywhere.

14:11 money. Mark does not tell us how much Judas was given for this contemptible act; Matthew tells us it was thirty pieces of silver (Matt. 26:15); this was equal to 120 denarii. A denarius was equal to a full day's wage.

14:11 conveniently. Judas knew enough about the habits of our Lord to know when and how to betray Him without a crowd around (see Luke 22:6).

14:12 the first day of unleavened bread. See Exodus 12:8.

[13]And he sendeth forth two of his disciples, and saith unto them, Go ye into
the city, and there shall meet you a man
bearing a pitcher of water: follow him.
[14] And wheresoever he shall go in,
say ye to the goodman of the house,
The Master saith, Where is the guestchamber, where I shall eat the passover
with my disciples?
[15] And he will shew you a large upper
room furnished *and* prepared: there
make ready for us.
[16]And his disciples went forth, and
came into the city, and found as he had
said unto them: and they made ready
the passover.
¶[17]And in the evening he cometh
with the twelve.
[18]And as they sat and did eat, Jesus
said, Verily I say unto you, One of you
which eateth with me shall betray me.
[19]And they began to be sorrowful,
and to say unto him one by one, *Is* it I?
and another *said, Is* it I?
[20]And he answered and said unto
them, *It is* one of the twelve, that dippeth with me in the dish.
[21] The Son of man indeed goeth, as it
is written of him: but woe to that man
by whom the Son of man is betrayed!
good were it for that man if he had never
been born.
¶[22]And as they did eat, Jesus took
bread, and blessed, and brake *it,* and
gave to them, and said, Take, eat: this
is my *body.
[23]And he took the cup, and when he
had given thanks, he gave *it* to them:
and they all drank of it.
[24]And he said unto them, This is my
*blood of the new testament, which is
shed for many.
[25] Verily I say unto you, I will drink no
more of the fruit of the vine, until that day
that I drink it new in the kingdom of God.

Peter's denial foretold
(Matt. 26:31-35; Luke 22:31-34; John 13:36-38)

¶[26]And when they had sung an hymn,
they went out into the *mount of Olives.
[27]And Jesus saith unto them, All ye
shall be offended because of me this
night: for it is written, I will smite the
shepherd, and the sheep shall be scattered.
[28] But after that I am risen, I will go
before you into Galilee.

14:22-24 THE BODY AND BLOOD OF CHRIST

The body of our Lord was prepared for sacrifice (Heb. 10:5). In that body coursed the precious blood that was the price of our redemption. When that body was broken on the cross of Calvary, the Lord Jesus Christ actually became our substitute, bearing in His own body our sins (1 Pet. 2:24). Luke adds to these words, "which is given for you" (22:17-20; see also Matt. 26:26-29; 1 Cor. 11:23-26 and 11:24 note, "The Symbolic Body").

The bread and the wine were symbols of His literal body and blood. When believers today partake of the bread and wine as they sit at the "Lord's table" (1 Cor. 10:21), the symbols vividly bring before them the sufferings that Christ bore on our behalf.

14:13 two of his disciples. Peter and John (Luke 22:8; see also Matt. 26:17-19).
14:13 a man. Women generally performed the task of carrying water. The man would be conspicuous, therefore, by his task.
14:21 as it is written of him. See Psalm 22; Isaiah 53.
14:24 testament. *Covenant, promise.
14:24 shed for many. It is the blood that makes atonement; it is the blood that justifies; it is the blood that cleanses (see Heb. 9:12,14,22).
14:25 until that day. We partake of the Lord's Supper "till he come" (1 Cor. 11:24-26).
14:27 I will smite the shepherd. Here our Lord referred to Zechariah 13:7.
14:28 after that I am risen. These are not the words of a mere martyr facing death, but the words of One who is going to conquer death. He was giving up His life in order to take it again (compare John 10:18; Rev. 1:18).

29But Peter said unto him, Although
all shall be offended, yet *will* not I.
30And Jesus saith unto him, Verily I
say unto thee, That this day, *even* in this
night, before the cock crow twice, thou
shalt deny me thrice.
31But he spake the more vehemently, If I should die with thee, I will not
deny thee in any wise. Likewise also
said they all.

The agony in Gethsemane
(cf. Matt. 26:36-46; Luke 22:39-46;
John 18:1)

32And they came to a place which was
named Gethsemane: and he saith to
his disciples, Sit ye here, while I shall
pray.
33And he taketh with him Peter and
James and John, and began to be sore
amazed, and to be very heavy;
34And saith unto them, My soul is
exceeding sorrowful unto death: tarry
ye here, and watch.
35And he went forward a little, and
fell on the ground, and prayed that, if it
were possible, the hour might pass
from him.
36And he said, *Abba, Father, all
things *are* possible unto thee; take away
this *cup from me: nevertheless not
what I will, but what thou wilt.
37And he cometh, and findeth them
sleeping, and saith unto Peter, Simon,
sleepest thou? couldest not thou watch
one hour?
38Watch ye and pray, lest ye enter
into *temptation. The spirit truly *is*
ready, but the flesh *is* weak.
39And again he went away, and prayed,
and spake the same words.
40And when he returned, he found
them asleep again, (for their eyes were
heavy,) neither wist they what to answer him.
41And he cometh the third time, and
saith unto them, Sleep on now, and take
your rest: it is enough, the hour is come;
behold, the Son of man is betrayed into
the hands of sinners.
42Rise up, let us go; lo, he that betrayeth me is at hand.

The betrayal and desertion
(Matt. 26:47-56; Luke 22:47-53;
John 18:3-11)

¶43And immediately, while he yet
spake, cometh Judas, one of the twelve,
and with him a great multitude with
swords and staves, from the chief priest
and the scribes and the *elders.
44And he that betrayed him had given
them a token, saying, Whomsoever I
shall kiss, that same is he; take him, and
lead *him* away safely.
45And as soon as he was come, he
goeth *straightway to him, and saith,
Master, master; and kissed him.

14:36 The Symbolic Cup

Every ingredient in that cup was known to our Saviour and Lord, but it was His delight to do the Father's will. He knew that God would pour His wrath against sin into the cup, and He consented to drink it, and did so on the cross, because that is what He came to earth to do (John 12:27). The bitterest dreg was the separation when the Father turned His face from the Son, thus breaking the perfect communion of the eternal ages for the first and only time. But Christ was obedient to the Father's will, and now He holds in His pierced hand the cup of blessing that poor sinners may drink from abundantly.

14:32 Gethsemane. The word means *oil press.* Olives in the press yield their oil, which can be used for healing and light. Thus our Lord became the real "Man of Sorrows," as sorrow pressed hard upon His soul.

14:35 the hour. There was a crisis in the earthly history of our Lord characterized by Himself at "the hour." This hour was known to Him from all eternity; it was to endure the sufferings of this hour that He came into the world (see John 12:27).

14:44 a token. A common word used for a sign or signal.

14:45 Master, master. As far as we know, Judas Iscariot never called the Saviour by His title, Lord.

¶[46]And they laid their hands on him,
and took him.
[47]And one of them that stood by drew
a sword, and smote a servant of the high
priest, and cut off his ear.
[48]And Jesus answered and said unto
them, Are ye come out, as against a
thief, with swords and *with* staves to
take me?
[49]I was daily with you in the temple
teaching, and ye took me not: but the
scriptures must be fulfilled.
[50]And they all forsook him, and fled.
[51]And there followed him a certain
young man, having a linen cloth cast
about *his* naked *body;* and the young
men laid hold on him:
[52]And he left the linen cloth, and fled
from them naked.

Jesus before the Council
(Matt. 26:57-68; John 18:12-14,19-24)

¶[53]And they led Jesus away to the
high priest: and with him were assembled all the chief priests and the elders
and the scribes.
[54]And Peter followed him afar off,
even into the palace of the high priest:
and he sat with the servants, and
warmed himself at the fire.
[55]And the chief priests and all the
council sought for witness against Jesus
to put him to death; and found none.
[56]For many bare false witness against
him, but their witness agreed not together.
[57]And there arose certain, and bare
false witness against him, saying,
[58]We heard him say, I will destroy this
temple that is made with hands, and
within three days I will build another
made without hands.
[59]But neither so did their witness
agree together.
[60]And the high priest stood up in the
midst, and asked Jesus, saying, Answerest thou nothing? what *is it which*
these witness against thee?
[61]But he held his peace, and answered nothing. Again the high priest
asked him, and said unto him, Art thou
the *Christ, the Son of the Blessed?
[62]And Jesus said, I am: and ye shall
see the Son of man sitting on the right
hand of power, and coming in the clouds
of heaven.
[63]Then the high priest rent his clothes,
and saith, What need we any further
witnesses?
[64]Ye have heard the blasphemy: what
think ye? And they all condemned him
to be guilty of death.
[65]And some began to spit on him, and
to cover his face, and to buffet him, and

14:47 one of them. Peter (John 18:10).

14:49 the scriptures must be fulfilled. The Scriptures foretold that Christ was to be judged among the transgressors; however, the mob was ignorant of the fact that Scriptures were being fulfilled by their own actions.

14:50 all forsook him. See what the Lord had predicted (Mark 14:27).

14:53 the high priest. Caiaphas (John 18:13).

14:54 the palace. Within the outer court of the actual palace there appears to have been a large open square court; here Peter came.

14:58 I will destroy. These "witnesses" (false witnesses) knew only a partial truth (see Matt. 26:61; John 2:19,21).

14:61 he held his peace. See Isaiah 53:7.

14:62 Jesus said, I am. Jesus spoke up whenever His Father's honor and His oneness with the Father was in question. Christ could not deny the mission for which He had come to earth.

14:64 the blasphemy. They thought of Jesus as being only a man, but when Jesus announced that He would eventually sit "on the right hand of power" and come again "in the clouds of heaven," they understood this to mean that our Lord Jesus was placing Himself equal to God. Certainly this would have been blasphemy if Christ were not God (see John 1:18; 10:30; 14:9; Phil. 2:6; Col. 1:15; Heb. 1:3).

14:65 spit on him. This act was an expression of utter contempt (Num. 12:14; Deut. 25:9).

to say unto him, Prophesy: and the servants did strike him with the palms of
their hands.

The denial of our Lord by Peter
(Matt. 26:69-75; Luke 22:56-62;
John 18:16-18,25-27)

¶66 And as Peter was beneath in the
palace, there cometh one of the maids
of the high priest:
67 And when she saw Peter warming
himself, she looked upon him, and said,
And thou also wast with Jesus of Nazareth.
68 But he denied, saying, I know not,
neither understand I what thou sayest.
And he went out into the porch; and the
cock crew.
69 And a maid saw him again, and began to say to them that stood by, This
is *one* of them.
70 And he denied it again. And a little
after, they that stood by said again to
Peter, Surely thou art *one* of them: for
thou art a Galilaean, and thy speech
agreeth *thereto.*
71 But he began to curse and to swear,
saying, I know not this man of whom ye
speak.
72 And the second time the cock crew.
And Peter called to mind the word that
Jesus said unto him, Before the cock
crow twice, thou shalt deny me thrice.
And when he thought thereon, he wept.

The Lord before Pilate
(Matt. 27:1-2,11-26; Luke 23:1-7,13-18;
John 18:28—19:16)

15 And straightway in the morning the chief priests held a consultation with the elders and scribes
and the whole council, and bound Jesus,
and carried *him* away, and delivered *him*
to *Pilate.
2 And Pilate asked him, Art thou the
*King of the Jews? And he answering
said unto him, Thou sayest *it.*
3 And the chief priests accused him of
many things: but he answered nothing.
4 And Pilate asked him again, saying,
Answerest thou nothing? behold how
many things they witness against thee.
5 But Jesus yet answered nothing; so
that Pilate marvelled.
¶6 Now at *that* feast he released unto
them one prisoner, whomsoever they
desired.
7 And there was *one* named Barabbas, *which lay* bound with them that
had made insurrection with him, who
had committed murder in the insurrection.
8 And the multitude crying aloud began to desire *him to do* as he had ever
done unto them.
9 But Pilate answered them, saying,
Will ye that I release unto you the King
of the Jews?
10 For he knew that the chief priests
had delivered him for envy.
11 But the chief priests moved the
people, that he should rather release
Barabbas unto them.
12 And Pilate answered and said again
unto them, What will ye then that I shall
do *unto him* whom ye call the King of
the Jews?
13 And they cried out again, Crucify
him.
14 Then Pilate said unto them, Why,

This particular detail in the sufferings of our Lord was a fulfillment of Isaiah 50:6 (see also its note, "Willing to Suffer").

14:72 he wept. This weeping of Peter's was the first sign of what later proved to be true repentance (see also Matt. 26:69-75; Luke 22:56-62; John 18:16-18,25-27).

15:1 in the morning. The Jewish law did not allow the *Sanhedrin to try criminal cases at night. After daybreak, therefore, the council held a second meeting and confirmed their verdict.

15:2 Art thou the King of the Jews? The charge they brought against our Lord is not given in detail here. Luke (23:2) specifies three charges: 1) perverting the nation; 2) forbidding to give tribute to Caesar; and 3) saying that He Himself was Christ, a King.

15:6 Now at that feast. The *Passover.

what evil hath he done? And they cried
out the more exceedingly, Crucify him.
¶15And *so* Pilate, willing to content
the people, released Barabbas unto
them, and delivered Jesus, when he had
scourged *him,* to be crucified.

The mockery of the soldiers
(Matt. 27:27-31)

16And the soldiers led him away into
the hall, called Praetorium; and they
call together the whole band.
17And they clothed him with purple,
and platted a crown of thorns, and put
it about his *head,*

15:17 The Crown of Thorns
At certain times the Caesars wore laurel wreaths upon their heads; the crown of thorns, of course, was pure mockery. But the soldiers' act had deep significance, of which they were unaware. When sin entered the world, God cursed the ground (Gen. 3:17-18); since then thorns have became an emblem of the Curse. Not only did our blessed Lord voluntarily wear this crown, but He bore the curse of which the thorns were an emblem (see Gal. 3:13; see also its note and 3:10 note, "Curse or Blessing").

18And began to salute him, Hail, King
of the Jews!
19And they smote him on the head
with a reed, and did spit upon him, and
bowing *their* knees worshipped him.
20And when they had mocked him,
they took off the purple from him, and
put his own clothes on him, and led him
out to crucify him.
21And they compel one Simon a
Cyrenian, who passed by, coming out of
the country, the father of Alexander and
Rufus, to bear his cross.
22And they bring him unto the place
Golgotha, which is, being interpreted,
The place of a skull.
23And they gave him to drink *wine
mingled with myrrh: but he received *it*
not.

The Lord crucified
(Matt. 27:33-56; Luke 23:33-49;
John 19:17-37)

24And when they had crucified him,
they parted his garments, casting lots
upon them, what every man should
take.
25And it was the third hour, and they
crucified him.
26And the superscription of his accusation was written over, THE KING OF
THE JEWS.
27And with him they crucify two
thieves; the one on his right hand, and
the other on his left.

15:15 scourged him. This scourging was accompanied by terrible pain—some even died under it. Pieces of lead and sharp, pointed bones were often braided into the whips that were used, so that the flesh was literally torn from the back.
15:16 Praetorium. The common hall of the castle, which formed a kind of barracks or guard room.
15:17 clothed him with purple. Purple is known as the royal color. It may have been a general's cloak that they used, but it was a mockery of Christ's kingly claims.
15:23 wine mingled with myrrh. This was the customary drink given to deaden pain. Christ knew He was there as the bearer of sin, and so He remained conscious (vs. 37) until He realized the penalty had been borne and the work was fully completed.
15:24 parted his garments. See Psalm 22:18.
15:25 the third hour. Nine o'clock in the morning (compare John 19:14). John used the Roman method of telling time and Mark used the Hebrew method.
15:26 superscription. The cause of the execution was generally inscribed on a white tablet. It had been carried before Christ on the way to the place of crucifixion and was now hung above His head.
15:26 THE KING OF THE JEWS. Pilate had caused it to be written in three languages: the classic Hebrew of the people, the official Latin of the Romans, and the Greek of the foreign population (John 19:20). All classes of people were able to read it.
15:27 with him they crucify two thieves. The fulfillment of Isaiah 53:9,12.

[28]And the scripture was fulfilled,
which saith, And he was numbered with
the transgressors.
[29]And they that passed by railed on
him, wagging their heads, and saying,
Ah, thou that destroyest the temple,
and buildest *it* in three days,
[30]Save thyself, and come down from
the cross.
[31]Likewise also the chief priests
mocking said among themselves with
the scribes, He saved others; himself
he cannot save.
[32]Let Christ the King of Israel descend now from the cross, that we may
see and believe. And they that were
crucified with him reviled him.
[33]And when the sixth hour was come,
there was darkness over the whole land
until the ninth hour.
[34]And at the ninth hour Jesus cried
with a loud voice, saying, Eloi, Eloi,
lama sabachthani? which is, being interpreted, My God, my God, why hast thou
forsaken me?
[35]And some of them that stood by,
when they heard *it,* said, Behold, he
calleth *Elias.
[36]And one ran and filled a spunge full
of vinegar, and put *it* on a reed, and gave
him to drink, saying, Let alone; let us
see whether Elias will come to take him
down.
[37]And Jesus cried with a loud voice,
and gave up the ghost.
[38]And the veil of the temple was rent
in twain from the top to the bottom.
¶[39]And when the *centurion, which
stood over against him, saw that he so
cried out, and gave up the ghost, he said,
Truly this man was the Son of God.
[40]There were also women looking on
afar off: among whom was Mary Magdalene, and Mary the mother of James
the less and of Joses, and Salome;
[41](Who also, when he was in Galilee,
followed him, and ministered unto
him;) and many other women which
came up with him unto *Jerusalem.

The burial (Matt. 27:57-61; Luke 23:50-56; John 19:38-42)

¶[42]And now when the even was
come, because it was the preparation,
that is, the day before the *sabbath,
[43]Joseph of Arimathaea, an honourable counsellor, which also waited for
the *kingdom of God, came, and went
in boldly unto Pilate, and craved the
body of Jesus.

15:34 THE SEVEN CRIES FROM THE CROSS

1. "Father, forgive them, for they know not what they do." — Luke 23:34
2. "To day thou shalt be with me in paradise." — Luke 23:43
3. "Woman, behold thy son!" "Behold thy mother!" — John 19:26–27
4. "My God, My God, why hast thou forsaken me?" — Matthew 27:46; Mark 15:34
5. "I thirst." — John 19:28
6. "It is finished." — John 19:30
7. "Father, into thy hands I commend my spirit." — Luke 23:46

15:31 himself he cannot save. He came to accomplish the work necessary for our salvation; if He were to save us, He could not save Himself.
15:32 they that were crucified with him reviled. For the whole story see Matthew 27:44 and Luke 23:39-43.
15:33 sixth . . . until the ninth hour. From noon to three o'clock.
15:36 a spunage full of vinegar. This was a fulfillment of Psalm 69:21.
15:38 the veil of the temple. The veil separated the Holy Place from the Most Holy Place. Entrance into the very presence of God was now made possible for every believer (see Heb. 10:19-20). Observe that the veil "was rent in twain [in two] from the top to the bottom." This was not the work of man, but of God, because He had opened the way into the *Holy of Holies through His Son.
15:43 Joseph of Arimathaea. Joseph was a man of wealth (Matt. 27:57), a member of

44And Pilate marvelled if he were already dead: and calling *unto him* the centurion, he asked him whether he had been any while dead.
45And when he knew *it* of the centurion, he gave the body to Joseph.
46And he bought fine linen, and took him down, and wrapped him in the linen, and laid him in a sepulchre which was hewn out of a rock, and rolled a stone unto the door of the sepulchre.
47And Mary Magdalene and Mary *the mother* of Joses beheld where he was laid.

VI. Christ's Resurrection and Ascension (16:1-20)
(cf. Matt. 28; Luke 24; John 20)

16 And when the sabbath was past, Mary Magdalene, and Mary the *mother* of James, and Salome, had bought sweet spices, that they might come and anoint him.
2And very early in the morning the first *day* of the week, they came unto the sepulchre at the rising of the sun.
3And they said among themselves, Who shall roll us away the stone from the door of the sepulchre?
4And when they looked, they saw that the stone was rolled away: for it was very great.
5And entering into the sepulchre, they saw a young man sitting on the right side, clothed in a long white garment; and they were affrighted.
6And he saith unto them, Be not affrighted: Ye seek Jesus of Nazareth, which was crucified: he is risen; he is not here: behold the place where they laid him.
7But go your way, tell his disciples and Peter that he goeth before you into Galilee: there shall ye see him, as he said unto you.
8And they went out quickly, and fled from the sepulchre; for they trembled and were amazed: neither said they any thing to any *man;* for they were afraid.
¶9Now when *Jesus* was risen early the first *day* of the week, he appeared first to Mary Magdalene, out of whom he had cast seven devils.
10*And* she went and told them that had been with him, as they mourned and wept.

16:2 An Old Testament Picture of the Resurrection
The first day was our Sunday, the morning after the Sabbath. In the Old Testament there is a beautiful picture of the Resurrection. Christ is the firstfruits of those who slept (had died) (1 Cor. 15:20). In Leviticus 23 we have the record of the various feasts of the Lord. The Feast of Firstfruits presents the resurrection of our Lord; in Leviticus 23:11 we read that the priest was to wave the sheaf before the Lord in the morning after the Sabbath, and it was to be accepted by God for the people. When our Lord arose from the grave, what He had done on the cross–what He was in Himself (the firstfruits)–was accepted by God the Father for us. Therefore, we are accepted in the Beloved (Eph. 1:6).

---

the *Sanhedrin (Luke 23:50-51), and a secret disciple of Jesus (John 19:38). Now he was no longer a secret disciple.

15:46 laid him in a sepulchre. The fulfillment of Isaiah 53:9.

16:1 bought sweet spices. The women brought more spices to complete the embalming of His body. Why they came after the burial is explained in Luke 23:53-56.

16:4 the stone was rolled away. This was to allow the world to see that the tomb was empty. Our Lord, in His resurrection body, would not have been held back by the stone. He could enter a room even when the doors were shut (John 20:19). When He comes again, the dead in Christ shall arise: Tombstones, marble slabs, vaults, etc., will be no barrier.

16:5 a young man. Evidently an *angel.

16:7 and Peter. This strikes a very tender note. Our Lord knew that Peter would still be especially downcast because of his denial, so the angel made special mention of Peter's name.

16:9 The End of Mark
Verses 9-20 do not appear in the Vaticanus and Sinaiticus manuscripts. Consequently, some scholars have unwisely questioned the authenticity of these twelve verses. However, these verses are found in 618 of 620 Greek manuscripts that contain the 16th chapter of Mark (Burgon). The omission in the case of the Vatican and Sinaitic versions is mystifying; nevertheless, the second Gospel would certainly not conclude with the words "for they were afraid" in verse 8. The glorious gospel of Christ does not leave His disciples in an attitude of fear.

11 And they, when they had heard that
he was alive, and had been seen of her,
believed not.
¶ 12 After that he appeared in another
form unto two of them, as they walked,
and went into the country.
13 And they went and told *it* unto the
residue: neither believed they them.
¶ 14 Afterward he appeared unto the
eleven as they sat at meat, and upbraided them with their unbelief and
hardness of heart, because they believed not them which had seen him
after he was risen.
15 And he said unto them, Go ye into
all the world, and preach the gospel to
every creature.
16 He that believeth and is baptized
shall be saved; but he that believeth not
shall be damned.
17 And these signs shall follow them
that believe; In my name shall they cast
out devils; they shall speak with new
tongues;
18 They shall take up serpents; and if
they drink any deadly thing, it shall not
hurt them; they shall lay hands on the
sick, and they shall recover.
¶ 19 So then after the Lord had spoken
unto them, he was received up into
heaven, and sat on the right hand of God.
20 And they went forth, and preached
every where, the Lord working with
them, and confirming the word with
signs following. Amen.

16:16 damned. Judged.
16:17 these signs. The signs of verses 17 and 18 were given by the Lord when the early *church and Christianity were being established (see Acts 4:29-31; 5:12; 16:18; 2:4; 28:3-6; 9:32-35).
16:19 sat on the right hand of God. Christ is there as our Advocate and High Priest (see 1 John 2:1 and its note, "Our Advocate").
16:20 they went forth. An unfinished story. It was continued in the Acts of the Apostles, and it is going on today.
16:20 confirming the word with signs. See verse 17 note.

The Gospel according to Saint

LUKE

THE WRITER

The writer of this Gospel is believed to have been Luke, a medical doctor. He was a close associate of the Apostle Paul, who called him "the beloved physician" (Colossians 4:14). Luke accompanied Paul on two of his missionary journeys and was with him while that apostle was a prisoner of the Emperor Nero in Rome, where later Paul was put to death (2 Timothy 4:11). For other information about Luke see the introduction to the book of the Acts, since that book was also written by him.

BACKGROUND

Luke gives special medical details which only a doctor would write, for example, "full of leprosy"(Luke 5:12). It does not appear that he ever saw the Lord Jesus, but he collected the materials for this book from eye-witnesses of the life and ministry of Christ, including Mary, our Lord's mother, and carefully wrote the Gospel (Luke 1:2-3) about A.D. 61 under the direct guidance of the Holy Spirit.

THEME

Luke's message is that the Lord Jesus Christ, the "Son of Man," in His earthly ministry was perfect man even as He was perfect God.

OUTLINE OF LUKE

I.	Introduction—Why Luke Wrote	Luke 1:1-4
II.	The Birth and Childhood of John the Baptist and the Lord Jesus Christ	Luke 1:5—2:52
III.	Christ's Ministry Begins	Luke 3:1—4:13
IV.	Christ's Ministry in Galilee	Luke 4:14—9:50
V.	Christ's Ministry in Judaea and Peraea	Luke 9:51—19:27
VI.	The End of Christ's Public Ministry	Luke 19:28—21:38
VII.	Christ's Betrayal and Death	Luke 22:1—23:56
VIII.	Christ's Resurrection and Ascension	Luke 24:1-53

I. Introduction—
Why Luke Wrote (1:1-4)

1 Forasmuch as many have taken in hand to set forth in order a declaration of those things which are most surely believed among us,

2 Even as they delivered them unto us, which from the beginning were eye-witnesses, and ministers of the word;
3 It seemed good to me also, having had *perfect understanding of all things from the very first, to write unto

---

1:3 from the very first. This phrase has been translated from a Greek word which is also translated "from above." See John 3:31; 19:11; James 1:17; 3:15,17 for this

1:3 Theophilus
The name means *lover of God.* Theophilus, to whom Luke dedicated his Gospel and the Acts, was in all probability the author's personal friend, a Gentile. Some have suggested that this Gospel and the Acts were written to anyone who is a "lover of God."

thee in order, most excellent Theophilus,
4 That thou mightest know the certainty of those things, wherein thou
hast been instructed.

II. The Birth and Boyhood of John and Jesus (1:5—2:52)

John the Baptist's birth announced

¶5 There was in the days of Herod,
the king of Judaea, a certain priest
named Zacharias, of the course of Abia:
and his wife *was* of the daughters of
*Aaron, and her name *was* Elisabeth.
6 And they were both righteous before *God, walking in all the commandments and ordinances of the Lord
*blameless.
7 And they had no child, because that
Elisabeth was barren, and they both
were *now* well stricken in years.
8 And it came to pass, that while he
executed the priest's office before God
in the order of his course,
9 According to the custom of the
priest's office, his lot was to burn *incense when he went into the *temple
of the Lord.
10 And the whole multitude of the
people were praying without at the time
of incense.
11 And there appeared unto him an
*angel of the Lord standing on the right
side of the *altar of incense.
12 And when Zacharias saw *him,* he
was troubled, and fear fell upon him.
13 But the angel said unto him, Fear
not, Zacharias: for thy *prayer is heard;
and thy wife Elisabeth shall bear thee
a son, and thou shalt call his name John.
14 And thou shalt have joy and gladness; and many shall rejoice at his birth.
15 For he shall be great in the sight of
the Lord, and shall drink neither *wine
nor strong drink; and he shall be filled
with the Holy Ghost, even from his
mother's womb.
16 And many of the children of *Israel
shall he turn to the Lord their God.
17 And he shall go before him in the
spirit and power of *Elias, to turn the
hearts of the fathers to the children, and
the disobedient to the wisdom of the
*just; to make ready a people prepared
for the Lord.
18 And Zacharias said unto the angel,
Whereby shall I know this? for I am an
old man, and my wife well stricken in
years.
19 And the angel answering said unto
him, I am *Gabriel, that stand in the
presence of God; and am sent to speak
unto thee, and to shew thee these glad
tidings.
20 And, behold, thou shalt be dumb,
and not able to speak, until the day that
these things shall be performed, because thou believest not my words,
which shall be fulfilled in their season.
21 And the people waited for Zacharias, and marvelled that he tarried so
long in the temple.
22 And when he came out, he could

translation. Luke, however, uses the same Greek word in Acts 26:5, translated there, "from the beginning," and this is also the meaning here.

1:5 Herod. Herod the Great (see Matt. 2:1).

1:5 the course of Abia. See 1 Chronicles 24:10 note, "The Periods of Service."

1:6 righteous before God. Zacharias and Elisabeth kept the *Law as perfectly as it was humanly possible, of course; but the righteousness of God is only by faith (see Rom. 4:3,5).

1:17 spirit and power of Elias. That is, Elijah. See Matthew 17:10. See also Malachi 4:5.

1:20 thou shalt be dumb. Zacharias should have believed the message without asking for a sign.

not speak unto them: and they perceived that he had seen a vision in the
temple: for he beckoned unto them, and
remained speechless.
23And it came to pass, that, as soon as
the days of his ministration were accomplished, he departed to his own house.
24And after those days his wife
Elisabeth conceived, and hid herself
five months, saying,
25Thus hath the Lord dealt with me
in the days wherein he looked on *me,* to
take away my reproach among men.

The birth of the Lord announced

¶26And in the sixth month the angel
Gabriel was sent from God unto a city
of Galilee, named Nazareth,
27To a virgin espoused to a man
whose name was *Joseph, of the house
of *David; and the virgin's name *was*
Mary.
28And the angel came in unto her, and
said, Hail, *thou that art* highly favoured,
the Lord *is* with thee: blessed *art* thou
among women.
29And when she saw *him,* she was
troubled at his saying, and cast in her
mind what manner of salutation this
should be.
30And the angel said unto her, Fear
not, Mary: for thou hast found favour
with God.
31And, behold, thou shalt conceive in
thy womb, and bring forth a son, and
shalt call his name JESUS.
32He shall be great, and shall be
called the Son of the Highest: and the
Lord God shall give unto him the throne
of his father David:
33And he shall reign over the house
of Jacob for ever; and of his kingdom
there shall be no end.
34Then said Mary unto the angel,
How shall this be, seeing I know not a
man?
35And the angel answered and said
unto her, The Holy Ghost shall come
upon thee, and the power of the Highest shall overshadow thee: therefore
also that holy thing which shall be born
of thee shall be called the Son of God.
36And, behold, thy cousin Elisabeth,
she hath also conceived a son in her old
age: and this is the sixth month with
her, who was called barren.
37For with God nothing shall be impossible.
38And Mary said, Behold the handmaid of the Lord; be it unto me according to thy word. And the angel departed
from her.

Mary visits Elisabeth

39And Mary arose in those days, and
went into the hill country with haste,
into a city of Juda;
40And entered into the house of Zacharias, and saluted Elisabeth.
41And it came to pass, that, when
Elisabeth heard the salutation of Mary,
the babe leaped in her womb; and Elisabeth was filled with the Holy Ghost:
42And she spake out with a loud
voice, and said, Blessed *art* thou among
women, and blessed *is* the fruit of thy
womb.
43And whence *is* this to me, that the
mother of my Lord should come to me?
44For, lo, as soon as the voice of thy

1:30 found favour with God. Received grace from God (see also vs. 28).

1:32 his father David. Mary was a descendant of the great King David (see Luke 3:23-38 and 3:23 note, "Christ's Ancestry").

1:33 over the house of Jacob. The Lord Jesus Christ was the highest fulfillment of God's *covenant with David.

1:35 holy thing which shall be born. The beautiful story of the Lord Jesus' miraculous birth is part of the Christian faith. He was born supernaturally by the Holy Ghost. He had a body of flesh, but there was no sin in Him.

1:38 according to thy word. Sin came to man through Eve's disobedience (Gen. 3). The Saviour, who is able to save all the world from sin, came through Mary's faith and obedience to God's will.

salutation sounded in mine ears, the
babe leaped in my womb for joy.
45And blessed *is* she that believed:
for there shall be a performance of
those things which were told her from
the Lord.

Mary's hymn of praise: the Magnificat

46And Mary said, My soul doth magnify the Lord,
47And my spirit hath rejoiced in God
my Saviour.

1:47 Mary's Awareness
"My Saviour" is a very remarkable way for a mother to refer to her son. Because Mary was born in sin and shared the sin of the human race, she too needed a Saviour. When she heard that she was to be the mother of the Son of God, her soul rejoiced and she sang this beautiful song of wonder and praise called "The Magnificat," from the word "magnify" used in the opening line of this hymn of praise.

48For he hath regarded the low estate
of his handmaiden: for, behold, from
henceforth all generations shall call me
blessed.
49For he that is mighty hath done
to me great things; and holy *is* his
name.
50And his *mercy *is* on them that fear
him from generation to generation.
51He hath shewed strength with his
arm; he hath scattered the proud in the
imagination of their hearts.
52He hath put down the mighty from
their seats, and exalted them of low
degree.
53He hath filled the hungry with good
things; and the rich he hath sent empty away.
54He hath holpen his servant Israel,
in remembrance of *his* mercy;
55As he spake to our fathers, to *Abraham, and to his seed for ever.
56And Mary abode with her about
three months, and returned to her own
house.

The birth of John the Baptist

¶57Now Elisabeth's full time came
that she should be delivered; and she
brought forth a son.
58And her neighbours and her cous-
ins heard how the Lord had shewed
great mercy upon her; and they rejoiced
with her.
59And it came to pass, that on the
eighth day they came to circumcise the
child; and they called him Zacharias,
after the name of his father.
60And his mother answered and said,
Not *so;* but he shall be called John.
61And they said unto her, There is
none of thy kindred that is called by this
name.
62And they made signs to his father,
how he would have him called.
63And he asked for a writing table,
and wrote, saying, His name is John.
And they marvelled all.
64And his mouth was opened immediately, and his tongue *loosed,* and he
spake, and praised God.
65And fear came on all that dwelt
round about them: and all these sayings
were noised abroad throughout all the
hill country of Judaea.
66And all they that heard *them* laid
them up in their hearts, saying, What
manner of child shall this be! And the
hand of the Lord was with him.

Zacharias praises God

¶67And his father Zacharias was filled
with the Holy Ghost, and prophesied,
saying,
68Blessed *be* the Lord God of Israel;

1:54 holpen. Helped.
1:63 His name is John. Unbelief had closed the lips of Zacharias (vs. 20); now faithful obedience opened them.
1:68 the Lord . . . hath visited and redeemed his people. Notice that Zacharias used the past tense. Faith sees all God's promises as already fulfilled, since they are so certain.

for he hath visited and *redeemed his
people,
69And hath raised up an horn of salvation for us in the house of his servant
David;
70As he spake by the mouth of his
holy *prophets, which have been since
the *world began:
71That we should be saved from our
enemies, and from the hand of all that
hate us;
72To perform the mercy *promised* to
our fathers, and to remember his holy
*covenant;
73The oath which he sware to our father Abraham,
74That he would grant unto us, that
we being delivered out of the hand of
our enemies might serve him without
fear,
75In holiness and *righteousness before him, all the days of our life.
76And thou, child, shalt be called the
*prophet of the Highest: for thou shalt
go before the face of the Lord to prepare
his ways;
77To give knowledge of salvation unto
his people by the *remission of their sins,
78Through the tender mercy of our
God; whereby the dayspring from on
high hath visited us,
79To give light to them that sit in
darkness and *in* the shadow of *death,
to guide our feet into the way of *peace.
80And the child grew, and waxed
strong in spirit, and was in the deserts
till the day of his shewing unto Israel.

The birth of Jesus
(Matt. 1:18-25; 2:1; John 1:14)

2 And it came to pass in those days,
that there went out a decree from
*Caesar Augustus, that all the world
should be taxed.
2(*And* this taxing was first made
when Cyrenius was governor of Syria.)
3And all went to be taxed, every one
into his own city.
4And Joseph also went up from Galilee, out of the city of Nazareth, into
Judaea, unto the city of David, which is
called Bethlehem; (because he was of
the house and lineage of David:)
5To be taxed with Mary his espoused
wife, being great with child.
6And so it was, that, while they were
there, the days were accomplished that
she should be delivered.
7And she brought forth her firstborn
son, and wrapped him in swaddling
clothes, and laid him in a manger; because there was no room for them in
the inn.

The angels and the shepherds

¶8And there were in the same country shepherds *abiding in the field,
keeping watch over their flock by night.
9And, lo, the angel of the Lord came
upon them, and the *glory of the Lord
shone round about them: and they were
sore afraid.
10And the angel said unto them, Fear
not: for, behold, I bring you good tidings
of great joy, which shall be to all people.

1:69 horn of salvation. See 2 Samuel 22:3. The horn speaks of the wonderful power that God uses for His people. See *horn.

1:73 The oath which he sware. See Genesis 22:16-18.

2:1 Caesar Augustus. The first Roman emperor, who ruled from 27 B.C. to A.D. 14. The name Augustus was conferred on him by the senate. He was the great-nephew of Julius Caesar.

2:1 all the world. Romans regarded their great empire as the *orbis terrarum,* or "orb of the earth." All lands beyond its boundaries was considered outer barbarism.

2:1 taxed. Not taxation as we know the word, but a census, or numbering, of the people.

2:4 the city . . . called Bethlehem. Look up 1 Samuel 16:4 and Micah 5:2 (see also Mic. 5:2 note, "A Description of Christ"). The decree of Augustus was used by God to fulfill the Scripture which prophesied the birth of the Messiah at Bethlehem. His birth was also the fulfillment of the prophecy of Genesis 49:10 (see also its note, "The Promise of Christ").

[11]For unto you is born this day in the
city of David a Saviour, which is *Christ
the Lord.
[12]And this *shall be* a sign unto you; Ye
shall find the babe wrapped in swaddling clothes, lying in a manger.
[13]And suddenly there was with the
angel a multitude of the heavenly host
praising God, and saying,
[14]Glory to God in the highest, and on
earth peace, good will toward men.
¶[15]And it came to pass, as the *angels were gone away from them into
*heaven, the shepherds said one to
another, Let us now go even unto Bethlehem, and see this thing which is come
to pass, which the Lord hath made
known unto us.
[16]And they came with haste, and
found Mary, and Joseph, and the babe
lying in a manger.
[17]And when they had seen *it*, they
made known abroad the saying which
was told them concerning this child.
[18]And all they that heard *it* wondered
at those things which were told them by
the shepherds.
[19]But Mary kept all these things, and
pondered *them* in her heart.
[20]And the shepherds returned, glorifying and praising God for all the things
that they had heard and seen, as it was
told unto them.

The Lord Jesus is presented to His Father

¶[21]And when eight days were accomplished for the circumcising of the child,
his name was called JESUS, which was
so named of the angel before he was
conceived in the womb.
[22]And when the days of her purification according to the *law of Moses
were accomplished, they brought him
to *Jerusalem, to present *him* to the
Lord;
[23](As it is written in the law of the
Lord, Every male that openeth the
womb shall be called holy to the Lord;)
[24]And to offer a *sacrifice according
to that which is said in the law of the
Lord, A pair of turtledoves, or two
young pigeons.

Simeon's praise: The Nunc Dimittis and Benedictus

¶[25]And, behold, there was a man in
Jerusalem, whose name *was* Simeon;
and the same man *was* just and devout,
waiting for the consolation of Israel: and
the Holy Ghost was upon him.
[26]And it was revealed unto him by the
Holy Ghost, that he should not see
death, before he had seen the Lord's
Christ.
[27]And he came by the Spirit into the
temple: and when the parents brought
in the child Jesus, to do for him after the
custom of the law,
[28]Then took he him up in his arms,
and blessed God, and said,
[29]Lord, now lettest thou thy servant
depart in peace, according to thy word:
[30]For mine eyes have seen thy salvation,

2:11 a Saviour, which is Christ the Lord. The child did not *become* King and Saviour; He was born both King and Saviour. It was not a matter of opinion or argument. It was the prerogative and will of God.

2:21 when eight days were accomplished. This was in accordance with the Law in Leviticus 12:3. Our Lord was thus definitely a Jew.

2:21 his name was called JESUS. See Luke 1:31. His name means Saviour (see Matt. 1:21).

2:22 days of her purification. See Leviticus 12:1-6.

2:24 A pair of turtledoves. See Leviticus 12:8. Notice that Joseph and Mary were poor and could not afford a lamb for the sacrifice.

2:25 just and devout. See *righteousness, for this term explains Simeon's upright character.

2:25 consolation of Israel. A title of the Messiah.

2:25 Holy Ghost was upon him. Before *Pentecost, the Holy Ghost came *upon* people on special occasions. After Pentecost He came to dwell within believers.

2:28 Christ's Presentation
Every firstborn son was brought to the temple to be presented or given back to the Lord. Because Simeon, through the Holy Spirit, saw that the Christ child was different from all other babies ever presented, he took Him in his arms and praised God that the Promised One had come.

31Which thou hast prepared before
the face of all people;
32A light to lighten the Gentiles, and
the glory of thy people Israel.
33And Joseph and his mother marvelled at those things which were spoken of him.
34And Simeon blessed them, and said
unto Mary his mother, Behold, this
child is set for the fall and rising again
of many in Israel; and for a sign which
shall be spoken against;
35(Yea, a sword shall pierce through
thy own soul also,) that the thoughts of
many hearts may be revealed.

Anna's praise

¶36And there was one Anna, a prophetess, the daughter of Phanuel, of the
tribe of Aser: she was of a great age, and
had lived with an husband seven years
from her virginity;
37And she *was* a widow of about
fourscore and four years, which departed not from the temple, but served
God with fastings and prayers night and
day.
38And she coming in that instant gave
thanks likewise unto the Lord, and
spake of him to all them that looked for
*redemption in Jerusalem.

The return to Nazareth

¶39And when they had performed all
things according to the law of the Lord,
they returned into Galilee, to their own
city Nazareth.
40And the child grew, and waxed
strong in spirit, filled with wisdom: and
the *grace of God was upon him.

2:36 Anna, the Prophetess
Simeon, of Jerusalem in the southern kingdom, and Anna, of the tribe of Asher in the north, represented together all of the Jewish people–both Judah and Israel. Note that the shepherds, Simeon, and Anna all worshipped and adored the child but did not worship Mary. She also joins in the worship of her divine Son (see again Luke 1:47 and its note, "Mary's Awareness," and her sin-offering in 2:24).

2:32 A light to lighten the Gentiles. Salvation is of the Jews (John 4:22), and the gospel was addressed to them first (Rom. 1:16; Acts 13:46). Even so, it reaches out to the Gentiles too. Peter was shown this (Acts 10:35), and Paul points it out (Rom. 9:22-26).

2:32 the glory of thy people. Israel rejected the Messiah, and so were cast away for a time (Rom. 11:25), but when they do receive Him, as they surely will, He will be their glory (see *kingdom). Actually, though many of them do not recognize the fact, the Lord Jesus Christ has been their glory through the centuries. There has never been a name comparable with the name Jesus.

2:34 the fall and rising again of many. Some would stumble and fall because of their unbelief in Christ, but others would be raised through His salvation. He was "despised and rejected" (Isa. 53:3) by many, but He surely bore the griefs and carried the sorrows (Isa. 53:4-6) of all those who would allow Him to.

2:34-35 a sign which shall be spoken against . . . may be revealed. He was the sign to Israel, but they rejected Him. The sign is to all men today–some believe, while others reject Him. And just as a light reveals what is in a room, so He, the Light, reveals the sin that is in the resistant hearts of those who reject Christ.

2:35 a sword shall pierce through thy own soul. The hatred, rejection, and murder of her Son would bring great sorrow to the soul of Mary (see John 19:25).

2:40 the child grew. Jesus grew in body because of the tender care that He had in His godly home. He grew strong in spirit because of the instruction that He received at the

The Child Jesus at the Passover

¶41Now his parents went to Jerusalem every year at the feast of the *passover.
42And when he was twelve years old,
they went up to Jerusalem after the
custom of the feast.
43And when they had fulfilled the
days, as they returned, the child Jesus
tarried behind in Jerusalem; and Joseph
and his mother knew not *of it.*
44But they, supposing him to have
been in the company, went a day's journey; and they sought him among *their*
kinsfolk and acquaintance.
45And when they found him not, they
turned back again to Jerusalem, seeking him.
46And it came to pass, that after three
days they found him in the temple, sitting in the midst of the doctors, both
hearing them, and asking them questions.
47And all that heard him were astonished at his understanding and answers.
48And when they saw him, they were
amazed: and his mother said unto him,
Son, why hast thou thus dealt with us?
behold, thy father and I have sought
thee sorrowing.
49And he said unto them, How is it
that ye sought me? wist ye not that I
must be about my Father's business?
50And they understood not the saying which he spake unto them.
51And he went down with them, and
came to Nazareth, and was subject unto
them: but his mother kept all these sayings in her heart.
52And Jesus increased in wisdom and
stature, and in favour with God and
man.

2:49 A Father's Business
As the Son of God, Jesus was about His Father's business; as the son of Mary, He was obedient to her and returned home with her. Mary had spoken of Joseph as "thy father" (vs. 48), a term that would be used in the household. And Joseph *was* His legal father, by adoption.

III. Christ's Ministry Begins (3:1—4:13)

John the Baptist's message (Matt. 3:1-12; Mark 1:1-8; John 1:6-8,15-36)

3 Now in the fifteenth year of the
reign of Tiberius Caesar, Pontius
*Pilate being governor of Judaea, and
Herod being tetrarch of Galilee, and his
brother Philip tetrarch of Ituraea and of
the region of Trachonitis, and Lysanias
the tetrarch of Abilene,
2Annas and *Caiaphas being the high
priests, the word of God came unto John
the son of Zacharias in the wilderness.
3And he came into all the country
about Jordan, preaching the *baptism of
*repentance for the remission of sins;
4As it is written in the book of the
words of Esaias the prophet, saying,
The voice of one crying in the wilderness, Prepare ye the way of the Lord,
make his paths straight.
5Every valley shall be filled, and
every mountain and hill shall be brought
low; and the crooked shall be made
straight, and the rough ways *shall be*
made smooth;
6And all flesh shall see the salvation
of God.

---

synagogue, the place of worship. His soul was filled with wisdom because of His own personal understanding of the Scriptures.

2:49 wist ye not . . . ? Did you not know?

3:1 Tiberius Caesar. He succeeded Augustus (see 2:1 first note), reigning from A.D. 14 to 37.

3:1 Herod being tetrarch. Herod was the son of Herod the Great (Matt. 2:1). The Romans allowed him to rule over only part of his father's kingdom.

3:1 tetrarch. A ruler over one-fourth of a province or a kingdom.

3:4 The voice of one crying. See Isaiah 40:3-5.

7Then said he to the multitude that
came forth to be baptized of him, O generation of vipers, who hath warned you
to flee from the wrath to come?
8Bring forth therefore fruits worthy
of repentance, and begin not to say
within yourselves, We have Abraham to
our father: for I say unto you, That God
is able of these stones to raise up children unto Abraham.
9And now also the axe is laid unto the
root of the trees: every tree therefore
which bringeth not forth good fruit is
hewn down, and cast into the *fire.
10And the people asked him, saying,
What shall we do then?
11He answereth and saith unto them,
He that hath two coats, let him impart
to him that hath none; and he that hath
meat, let him do likewise.
12Then came also *publicans to be
baptized, and said unto him, Master,
what shall we do?
13And he said unto them, Exact no
more than that which is appointed you.
14And the soldiers likewise demanded of him, saying, And what shall we
do? And he said unto them, Do violence
to no man, neither accuse *any* falsely;
and be content with your wages.
15And as the people were in expectation, and all men mused in their
hearts of John, whether he were the
Christ, or not;
16John answered, saying unto *them*
all, I indeed baptize you with water; but
one mightier than I cometh, the latchet
of whose shoes I am not worthy to unloose: he shall baptize you with the
Holy Ghost and with fire:
17Whose fan *is* in his hand, and he will
throughly purge his floor, and will gather the wheat into his garner; but the
chaff he will burn with fire unquenchable.
18And many other things in his exhortation preached he unto the people.
19But Herod the tetrarch, being reproved by him for Herodias his brother
Philip's wife, and for all the evils which
Herod had done,
20Added yet this above all, that he
shut up John in prison.

The Lord's baptism
(Matt. 3:13-17; Mark 1:9-11)

¶21Now when all the people were
baptized, it came to pass, that Jesus also
being baptized, and praying, the heav-
en was opened,
22And the Holy Ghost descended in
a bodily shape like a dove upon him, and
a voice came from heaven, which said,
Thou art my beloved Son; in thee I am
well pleased.

Ancestry of Mary, the Lord's mother

¶23And Jesus himself began to be
about thirty years of age, being (as was
supposed) the son of Joseph, which was
the son of Heli,
24Which was *the son* of Matthat,
which was *the son* of Levi, which was *the*
son of Melchi, which was *the son* of
Janna, which was *the son* of Joseph,
25Which was *the son* of Mattathias,

3:7 generation of vipers. The Jewish leaders' teaching was poisonous.

3:8 fruits worthy of repentance. Compare this with the Lord's words in Luke 6:43-44; 13:5-9; John 15:1-8.

3:20 he shut up John in prison. This did not occur just at this time; it happened after John baptized the Lord. Luke puts it in here to conclude the story of John's ministry (see Matt. 14:1-2).

3:21 Jesus also being baptized. See Matthew 3:13-17; Mark 1:9-11 (see also Mark 1:9 note, "The Baptism of Jesus").

3:22 Thou art my beloved Son. Three things happened when the Lord Jesus Christ was baptized that did not happen when others were baptized: 1) The heavens were opened; 2) the Holy Spirit descended upon Him in the form of a dove; and 3) God's voice was heard. All three persons of the *Trinity were evident.

3:23 as was supposed. By legal adoption.

3:23 Christ's Ancestry
Joseph was Jacob's son by birth (Matt. 1:16) and Heli's son by marriage; so this is really the ancestry of Mary. In the next few verses are the names of all of Heli's ancestors back to Adam, which are, of course, the ancestors of Mary and of our Lord Jesus. They prove that Christ was not only the Son of God, but also the Son, or seed of the woman, promised to Eve thousands of years before (see Gen. 3:15 and its note, "The Promise of a Saviour").

which was *the son* of Amos, which was
the son of Naum, which was *the son* of
Esli, which was *the son* of Nagge,
26Which was *the son* of Maath, which
was *the son* of Mattathias, which was *the*
son of Semei, which was *the son* of Joseph, which was *the son* of Juda,
27Which was *the son* of Joanna, which
was *the son* of Rhesa, which was *the son*
of Zorobabel, which was *the son* of
Salathiel, which was *the son* of Neri,
28Which was *the son* of Melchi, which
was *the son* of Addi, which was *the son*
of Cosam, which was *the son* of Elmo-
dam, which was *the son* of Er,
29Which was *the son* of Jose, which
was *the son* of Eliezer, which was *the son*
of Jorim, which was *the son* of Matthat,
which was *the son* of Levi,
30Which was *the son* of Simeon, which
was *the son* of Juda, which was *the son*
of Joseph, which was *the son* of Jonan,
which was *the son* of Eliakim,
31Which was *the son* of Melea, which
was *the son* of Menan, which was *the son*
of Mattatha, which was *the son* of Nathan, which was *the son* of David,
32Which was *the son* of Jesse, which
was *the son* of Obed, which was *the son*
of Booz, which was *the son* of Salmon,
which was *the son* of Naasson,
33Which was *the son* of Aminadab,
which was *the son* of Aram, which was
the son of Esrom, which was *the son*
of Phares, which was *the son* of Juda,
34Which was *the son* of Jacob, which
was *the son* of *Isaac, which was *the son*
of Abraham, which was *the son* of Thara,
which was *the son* of Nachor,
35Which was *the son* of Saruch, which
was *the son* of Ragau, which was *the son*
of Phalec, which was *the son* of Heber,
which was *the son* of Sala,
36Which was *the son* of Cainan, which
was *the son* of Arphaxad, which was *the*
son of Sem, which was *the son* of Noe,
which was *the son* of Lamech,
37Which was *the son* of Mathusala,
which was *the son* of Enoch, which was
the son of Jared, which was *the son* of
Maleleel, which was *the son* of Cainan,
38Which was *the son* of Enos, which
was *the son* of Seth, which was *the son*
of *Adam, which was *the son* of God.

(Matt. 4:1-11; Mark 1:12-13)

4 And Jesus being full of the Holy
Ghost returned from Jordan, and
was led by the Spirit into the wilderness,
2Being forty days *tempted of the
*devil. And in those days he did eat
nothing: and when they were ended, he
afterward hungered.
3And the devil said unto him, If thou
be the Son of God, command this stone
that it be made bread.
4And Jesus answered him, saying,
It is written, That man shall not live
by bread alone, but by every word of
God.
5And the devil, taking him up into an
high mountain, shewed unto him all the
kingdoms of the world in a moment of
time.
6And the devil said unto him, All this
power will I give thee, and the glory of
them: for that is delivered unto me; and
to whomsoever I will I give it.
7If thou therefore wilt worship me, all
shall be thine.

4:4 man shall not live by bread alone. Our Lord quoted Deuteronomy 8:3.
4:6 that is delivered unto me. Satan will not be the prince of this world forever (see John 12:31).

8 And Jesus answered and said unto
him, Get thee behind me, *Satan: for
it is written, Thou shalt worship the
Lord thy God, and him only shalt thou
serve.
9 And he brought him to Jerusalem,
and set him on a pinnacle of the temple, and said unto him, If thou be the
Son of God, cast thyself down from
hence:
10 For it is written, He shall give his
angels charge over thee, to keep thee:

> **4:10 A Scripture Quoted**
> The Devil quoted Psalm 91:11-12, but he did not quote it correctly, for he left out "in all thy ways." The "way" of the Lord Jesus while He was on this earth was to be obedient to whatever His Father told Him to do. The Devil tried to tempt Him in two ways: 1) to act without consulting His Father; and 2) to escape the suffering and death on the cross. See Mark 1:13 note, "The Temptation of Jesus."

11 And in *their* hands they shall bear
thee up, lest at any time thou dash thy
foot against a stone.
12 And Jesus answering said unto him,
It is said, Thou shalt not tempt the Lord
thy God.
13 And when the devil had ended all
the *temptation, he departed from him
for a season.

IV. Christ's Ministry in Galilee
(4:14—9:50)

Jesus teaches in Galilee
(Matt. 4:12-16; Mark 1:14)

¶14 And Jesus returned in the power
of the Spirit into Galilee: and there
went out a fame of him through all the
region round about.
15 And he taught in their *synagogues, being glorified of all.

Jesus in the synagogue at Nazareth

¶16 And he came to Nazareth, where
he had been brought up: and, as his custom was, he went into the *synagogue
on the *sabbath day, and stood up for to
read.
17 And there was delivered unto him
the book of the prophet Esaias. And
when he had opened the book, he found
the place where it was written,
18 The Spirit of the Lord *is* upon me,
because he hath anointed me to preach
the *gospel to the poor; he hath sent
me to heal the brokenhearted, to preach
deliverance to the captives, and recov-
ering of sight to the blind, to set at liberty them that are bruised,
19 To preach the acceptable year of the
Lord.
20 And he closed the book, and he gave
it again to the minister, and sat down.
And the eyes of all them that were in
the synagogue were fastened on him.
21 And he began to say unto them,
This day is this scripture fulfilled in
your ears.
22 And all bare him witness, and wondered at the gracious words which proceeded out of his mouth. And they said,
Is not this Joseph's son?
23 And he said unto them, Ye will surely say unto me this proverb, Physician,
heal thyself: whatsoever we have heard
done in Capernaum, do also here in thy
country.
24 And he said, Verily I say unto you, No
prophet is accepted in his own country.
25 But I tell you of a truth, many widows were in Israel in the days of *Elias,

---

4:8 Thou shalt worship the Lord. See Deuteronomy 6:13 and 10:20.
4:12 Thou shalt not tempt the Lord thy God. See Deuteronomy 6:16.
4:18 The Spirit of the Lord is upon me. The Lord Jesus was reading from Isaiah 61:1-2 (see also Isa. 61:1 note, "The Advents of Christ"), but He stopped in the middle of verse 2, for His first coming was to bring good news, not judgment. Judgment will come with His second coming.
4:25 widows were in Israel in the days of Elias. That is, Elijah. The story is in 1 Kings 17:9-24 (see 17:17 note, "Elijah's Power").

when the heaven was shut up three
years and six months, when great famine was throughout all the land;
26 But unto none of them was Elias
sent, save unto Sarepta, *a city* of Sidon,
unto a woman *that was* a widow.
27 And many *lepers were in Israel in
the time of Eliseus the prophet; and
none of them was cleansed, saving Naaman the Syrian.
28 And all they in the synagogue,
when they heard these things, were
filled with wrath,
29 And rose up, and thrust him out of
the city, and led him unto the brow of
the hill whereon their city was built,
that they might cast him down headlong.
30 But he passing through the midst of
them went his way,

Jesus in the synagogue at Capernaum
(Mark 1:23-26)

31 And came down to Capernaum, a
city of Galilee, and taught them on the
sabbath days.
32 And they were astonished at his
*doctrine: for his word was with power.

The Lord casts out a demon

¶33 And in the synagogue there was a
man, which had a spirit of an *unclean
devil, and cried out with a loud voice,
34 Saying, Let *us* alone; what have we
to do with thee, *thou* Jesus of Nazareth?
art thou come to destroy us? I know
thee who thou art; the Holy One of God.
35 And Jesus rebuked him, saying,
Hold thy peace, and come out of him.
And when the devil had thrown him in
the midst, he came out of him, and hurt
him not.
36 And they were all amazed, and
spake among themselves, saying, What
a word *is* this! for with authority and
power he commandeth the unclean
spirits, and they come out.
37 And the fame of him went out into
every place of the country round about.

The healing of Simon's wife's mother
(Matt. 8:14-17; Mark 1:29-38)

¶38 And he arose out of the synagogue, and entered into Simon's house.
And Simon's wife's mother was taken
with a great fever; and they besought
him for her.
39 And he stood over her, and rebuked
the fever; and it left her: and immediately she arose and ministered unto
them.

Further ministry in Capernaum

¶40 Now when the sun was setting, all
they that had any sick with divers diseases brought them unto him; and he
laid his hands on every one of them, and
healed them.
41 And devils also came out of many,
crying out, and saying, Thou art Christ
the Son of God. And he rebuking *them*
suffered them not to speak: for they
knew that he was Christ.
42 And when it was day, he departed
and went into a desert place: and the
people sought him, and came unto him,
and stayed him, that he should not depart from them.
43 And he said unto them, I must
preach the *kingdom of God to other
cities also: for therefore am I sent.
44 And he preached in the synagogues
of Galilee.

Jesus teaches from a ship

5 And it came to pass, that, as the
people pressed upon him to hear
the word of God, he stood by the lake
of Gennesaret,
2 And saw two ships standing by the
lake: but the fishermen were gone out
of them, and were washing *their* nets.
3 And he entered into one of the ships,
which was Simon's, and prayed him that

4:27 cleansed, saving Naaman the Syrian. See 2 Kings 5:1-14.
4:41 suffered them not to speak. Our Lord did not need or want the witness of demons.
5:1 lake of Gennesaret. Also called the Sea of Galilee.

he would thrust out a little from the
land. And he sat down, and taught the
people out of the ship.

The miracle of the many fish

4Now when he had left speaking, he
said unto Simon, Launch out into the
deep, and let down your nets for a
draught.
5And Simon answering said unto him,
Master, we have toiled all the night, and
have taken nothing: nevertheless at thy
word I will let down the net.
6And when they had this done, they
inclosed a great multitude of fishes: and
their net brake.
7And they beckoned unto *their* part-
ners, which were in the other ship, that
they should come and help them. And
they came, and filled both the ships, so
that they began to sink.

Peter's fear and confession

8When Simon *Peter saw *it,* he fell
down at Jesus' knees, saying, Depart
from me; for I am a sinful man, O Lord.
9For he was astonished, and all that
were with him, at the draught of the
fishes which they had taken:

Fishers of men

10And so *was* also James, and John,
the sons of Zebedee, which were part-
ners with Simon. And Jesus said unto
Simon, Fear not; from henceforth thou
shalt catch men.
11And when they had brought their
ships to land, they forsook all, and followed him.

The man full of leprosy
(Matt. 8:2-4; Mark 1:40-44)

¶12And it came to pass, when he was
in a certain city, behold a man full of
*leprosy: who seeing Jesus fell on *his*
face, and besought him, saying, Lord, if
thou wilt, thou canst make me *clean.
13And he put forth *his* hand, and
touched him, saying, I will: be thou
clean. And immediately the leprosy
departed from him.
14And he charged him to tell no man:
but go, and shew thyself to the priest,
and offer for thy cleansing, according as
Moses commanded, for a testimony
unto them.
15But so much the more went there
a fame abroad of him: and great multitudes came together to hear, and to be
healed by him of their infirmities.

The Lord prays

¶16And he withdrew himself into the
wilderness, and prayed.

The paralyzed man forgiven and cured
(Matt. 9:2-8; Mark 2:1-12)

17And it came to pass on a certain day,
as he was teaching, that there were
*Pharisees and doctors of the law sit-
ting by, which were come out of every
town of Galilee, and Judaea, and Jerusalem: and the power of the Lord was
present to heal them.
¶18And, behold, men brought in a bed
a man which was taken with a palsy: and
they sought *means* to bring him in, and
to lay *him* before him.
19And when they could not find by
what *way* they might bring him in because of the multitude, they went upon
the housetop, and let him down through
the tiling with *his* couch into the midst
before Jesus.
20And when he saw their *faith, he
said unto him, Man, thy sins are *forgiven thee.
21And the *scribes and the Pharisees

5:11 they forsook all, and followed him. Simon Peter had already met the Lord (John 1:35-42), but he did not become a real follower or disciple until this meeting. "Catch men" (vs. 10) means that the Lord Jesus was going to make them great fishers of men, through whom thousands would be saved.

5:14 offer for thy cleansing, according as Moses commanded. See Leviticus 14:2-20 for this Law (see also 14:2 note, "The Method of Cleansing").

5:19 let him down through the tiling. See Mark 2:4 note.

began to reason, saying, Who is this
which speaketh blasphemies? Who can
forgive sins, but God alone?
22 But when Jesus perceived their
thoughts, he answering said unto them,
What reason ye in your hearts?
23 Whether is easier, to say, Thy sins
be forgiven thee; or to say, Rise up and
walk?
24 But that ye may know that the Son
of man hath power upon earth to forgive
sins, (he said unto the sick of the palsy,)
I say unto thee, Arise, and take up thy
couch, and go into thine house.
25 And immediately he rose up before
them, and took up that whereon he lay,
and departed to his own house, glorifying God.
26 And they were all amazed, and they
glorified God, and were filled with fear,
saying, We have seen strange things to
day.

The call of Matthew
(Matt. 9:9; Mark 2:13-14)

¶27 And after these things he went
forth, and saw a *publican, named Levi,
sitting at the *receipt of custom: and he
said unto him, Follow me.
28 And he left all, rose up, and followed him.

Matthew's feast
(Matt. 9:10-15; Luke 2:15-20)

29 And Levi made him a great feast in
his own house: and there was a great
company of publicans and of others that
sat down with them.
30 But their scribes and Pharisees
murmured against his disciples, saying,
Why do ye eat and drink with publicans
and sinners?
31 And Jesus answering said unto
them, They that are *whole need not a
physician; but they that are sick.
32 I came not to call the righteous, but
sinners to repentance.
¶33 And they said unto him, Why do
the disciples of John fast often, and
make prayers, and likewise *the disciples*
of the Pharisees; but thine eat and
drink?
34 And he said unto them, Can ye
make the children of the bridechamber
fast, while the *bridegroom is with
them?
35 But the days will come, when the
bridegroom shall be taken away from
them, and then shall they fast in those
days.

A parable: new garments and new wine
(Matt. 9:16-17; Mark 2:21-22)

¶36 And he spake also a *parable unto
them; No man putteth a piece of a new
garment upon an old; if otherwise, then
both the new maketh a rent, and the
piece that was *taken* out of the new
agreeth not with the old.
37 And no man putteth new wine into
old *bottles; else the new wine will
burst the bottles, and be spilled, and the
bottles shall perish.
38 But new wine must be put into new
bottles; and both are preserved.
39 No man also having drunk old *wine*
*straightway desireth new: for he saith,
The old is better.

The Lord of the Sabbath
(Matt. 12:1-8; Mark 2:23-28)

6 And it came to pass on the second sabbath after the first, that he
went through the corn fields; and his
disciples plucked the ears of corn, and
did eat, rubbing *them* in *their* hands.
2 And certain of the Pharisees said
unto them, Why do ye that which is not
lawful to do on the sabbath days?
3 And Jesus answering them said,
Have ye not read so much as this, what
David did, when himself was an
hungred, and they which were with him;
4 How he went into the house of God,
and did take and eat the *shewbread,
and gave also to them that were with
him; which it is not lawful to eat but for
the priests alone?

6:2 Why do ye . . . ? See Mark 2:24 note.

[5]And he said unto them, That the Son
of man is Lord also of the sabbath.
¶[6]And it came to pass also on another
sabbath, that he entered into the synagogue and taught: and there was a man
whose right hand was withered.
[7]And the scribes and Pharisees
watched him, whether he would heal on
the sabbath day; that they might find an
accusation against him.
[8]But he knew their thoughts, and said
to the man which had the withered
hand, Rise up, and stand forth in the
midst. And he arose and stood forth.
[9]Then said Jesus unto them, I will ask
you one thing; Is it lawful on the sabbath days to do good, or to do evil? to
save life, or to destroy *it?*
[10]And looking round about upon
them all, he said unto the man, Stretch
forth thy hand. And he did so: and his
hand was restored whole as the other.
[11]And they were filled with madness;
and communed one with another what
they might do to Jesus.

The twelve disciples chosen
(Matt. 10:2-4; Mark 3:13-19)

[12]And it came to pass in those days,
that he went out into a mountain to
pray, and continued all night in prayer
to God.
¶[13]And when it was day, he called *unto*
him his disciples: and of them he chose
twelve, whom also he named *apostles;
[14]Simon, (whom he also named Peter,) and Andrew his brother, James and
John, Philip and Bartholomew,
[15]Matthew and Thomas, James the
son of Alphaeus, and Simon called
Zelotes,
[16]And Judas *the brother* of James, and
*Judas Iscariot, which also was the
traitor.

Multitudes healed

¶[17]And he came down with them, and
stood in the plain, and the company of
his disciples, and a great multitude of
people out of all Judaea and Jerusalem,
and from the sea coast of *Tyre and Sidon, which came to hear him, and to be
healed of their diseases;
[18]And they that were vexed with unclean spirits: and they were healed.
[19]And the whole multitude sought to
touch him: for there went virtue out of
him, and healed *them* all.

A message to disciples
(Matt. 5:3-12)

¶[20]And he lifted up his eyes on his
disciples, and said, Blessed *be ye* poor:
for yours is the kingdom of God.
[21] Blessed *are ye* that hunger now: for
ye shall be filled. Blessed *are ye* that
weep now: for ye shall laugh.
[22] Blessed are ye, when men shall
hate you, and when they shall separate
you *from their company,* and shall reproach *you,* and cast out your name as
evil, for the Son of man's sake.
[23] Rejoice ye in that day, and leap for
joy: for, behold, your *reward *is* great
in heaven: for in the like manner did
their fathers unto the prophets.
[24] But woe unto you that are rich! for
ye have received your consolation.
[25] Woe unto you that are full! for ye
shall hunger. Woe unto you that laugh
now! for ye shall mourn and weep.
[26] Woe unto you, when all men shall
speak well of you! for so did their fathers to the false prophets.

6:13 apostles. The word in Greek means *sent ones.* It is the same word exactly as the anglicized word "missionary," from the Latin verb *mitto,* meaning *I send.* The Lord Jesus called them to be disciples or learners at first; then He chose twelve special men as His apostles to spread the good news that He had brought.

6:17 he came down with them, and stood in the plain. This is another account of the Sermon on the Mount (Matt. 5–7). The word "plain" used here signifies the great flat terrain partway up the mountain, clearly seen on the mount just northwest of Tel Hum (ancient Capernaum) and now considered by many to be the exact site of the Sermon on the Mount.

¶27 But I say unto you which hear,
Love your enemies, do good to them
which hate you,
28 Bless them that curse you, and pray
for them which despitefully use you.
29 And unto him that smiteth thee on
the *one* cheek offer also the other; and
him that taketh away thy cloke forbid
not *to take thy* coat also.
30 Give to every man that asketh of
thee; and of him that taketh away thy
goods ask *them* not again.
31 And as ye would that men should do
to you, do ye also to them likewise.
32 For if ye love them which love you,
what thank have ye? for sinners also
love those that love them.
33 And if ye do good to them which do
good to you, what thank have ye? for
sinners also do even the same.
34 And if ye lend *to them* of whom ye
hope to receive, what thank have ye?
for sinners also lend to sinners, to receive as much again.
35 But love ye your enemies, and do
good, and lend, hoping for nothing
again; and your reward shall be great,
and ye shall be the children of the Highest: for he is kind unto the unthankful
and *to* the evil.
36 Be ye therefore merciful, as your
Father also is merciful.
37 Judge not, and ye shall not be
judged: condemn not, and ye shall not
be condemned: forgive, and ye shall be
forgiven:
38 Give, and it shall be given unto you;
good measure, pressed down, and shak-
en together, and running over, shall
men give into your bosom. For with the
same measure that ye mete withal it
shall be measured to you again.

A parable: a blind leader

39 And he spake a parable unto them,
Can the blind lead the blind? shall they
not both fall into the ditch?
40 The disciple is not above his master: but every one that is *perfect shall
be as his master.
41 And why beholdest thou the mote
that is in thy brother's eye, but perceivest not the beam that is in thine
own eye?
42 Either how canst thou say to thy
brother, Brother, let me pull out the
mote that is in thine eye, when thou
thyself beholdest not the beam that is
in thine own eye? Thou hypocrite, cast
out first the beam out of thine own eye,
and then shalt thou see clearly to pull
out the mote that is in thy brother's
eye.
43 For a good tree bringeth not forth
corrupt fruit; neither doth a corrupt
tree bring forth good fruit.
44 For every tree is known by his own
fruit. For of thorns men do not gather
figs, nor of a bramble bush gather they
grapes.
45 A good man out of the good treasure of his heart bringeth forth that
which is good; and an evil man out of
the evil treasure of his heart bringeth
forth that which is evil: for of the abundance of the heart his mouth speaketh.
¶46 And why call ye me, Lord, Lord,
and do not the things which I say?

A parable: a house on a rock (Matt. 7:24-27)

47 Whosoever cometh to me, and
heareth my sayings, and doeth them, I
will shew you to whom he is like:
48 He is like a man which built an
house, and digged deep, and laid the
foundation on a rock: and when the
flood arose, the stream beat vehemently upon that house, and could not shake
it: for it was founded upon a rock.
49 But he that heareth, and doeth not,
is like a man that without a foundation
built an house upon the earth; against
which the stream did beat vehemently,

6:38 mete. Another word for measure.
6:39 the blind. False teachers—those who have not the light of God.
6:41 mote . . . beam. A mote is a small speck of dust; a beam is a large splinter.

and immediately it fell; and the ruin of that house was great.

The centurion's servant healed (Matt. 8:5-13)

7 Now when he had ended all his
sayings in the audience of the people, he entered into Capernaum.
2And a certain *centurion's servant,
who was dear unto him, was sick, and
ready to die.
3And when he heard of Jesus, he sent
unto him the *elders of the Jews, beseeching him that he would come and
heal his servant.
4And when they came to Jesus, they
besought him instantly, saying, That he
was worthy for whom he should do this:
5For he loveth our nation, and he hath
built us a synagogue.
6Then Jesus went with them. And
when he was now not far from the
house, the centurion sent friends to
him, saying unto him, Lord, trouble not
thyself: for I am not worthy that thou
shouldest enter under my roof:
7Wherefore neither thought I myself
worthy to come unto thee: but say in a
word, and my servant shall be healed.
8For I also am a man set under authority, having under me soldiers, and
I say unto one, Go, and he goeth; and to
another, Come, and he cometh; and to
my servant, Do this, and he doeth *it.*
9When Jesus heard these things, he
marvelled at him, and turned him about,
and said unto the people that followed
him, I say unto you, I have not found so
great faith, no, not in *Israel.
10And they that were sent, returning
to the house, found the servant whole
that had been sick.

The widow's son raised

¶11And it came to pass the day after,
that he went into a city called Nain; and
many of his disciples went with him,
and much people.
12Now when he came nigh to the gate
of the city, behold, there was a dead man
carried out, the only son of his mother,
and she was a widow: and much people
of the city was with her.
13And when the Lord saw her, he had
compassion on her, and said unto her,
Weep not.
14And he came and touched the bier:
and they that bare *him* stood still. And
he said, Young man, I say unto thee,
Arise.
15And he that was dead sat up, and
began to speak. And he delivered him
to his mother.
16And there came a fear on all: and
they glorified *God, saying, That a
great *prophet is risen up among us;
and, That God hath visited his people.
17And this rumour of him went forth
throughout all Judaea, and throughout
all the region round about.
18And the disciples of John shewed
him of all these things.

John's question and the answer (Matt. 11:2-15)

¶19And John calling *unto him* two of
his disciples sent *them* to Jesus, saying,
Art thou he that should come? or look
we for another?
20When the men were come unto
him, they said, John Baptist hath sent
us unto thee, saying, Art thou he that
should come? or look we for another?
21And in that same hour he cured
many of *their* infirmities and plagues,
and of evil spirits; and unto many *that
were* blind he gave sight.
22Then Jesus answering said unto
them, Go your way, and tell John what
things ye have seen and heard; how that
the blind see, the lame walk, the *lepers are cleansed, the deaf hear, the dead
are raised, to the poor the gospel is
preached.
23And blessed is *he,* whosoever shall
not be offended in me.

7:15 he that was dead sat up. See Matthew 11:5; Mark 5:41; John 11:1-46 for miracles of raising the dead.

John's honour

¶24And when the messengers of John
were departed, he began to speak unto
the people concerning John, What went
ye out into the wilderness for to see?
A reed shaken with the wind?
25 But what went ye out for to see? A
man clothed in soft raiment? Behold,
they which are gorgeously apparelled,
and live delicately, are in kings' courts.
26 But what went ye out for to see? A
prophet? Yea, I say unto you, and much
more than a prophet.
27 This is *he,* of whom it is written,
Behold, I send my messenger before
thy face, which shall prepare thy way
before thee.
28 For I say unto you, Among those
that are born of women there is not a
greater prophet than *John the Baptist:
but he that is least in the kingdom of
God is greater than he.
29And all the people that heard *him,*
and the *publicans, justified God, being
baptized with the *baptism of John.
30But the Pharisees and lawyers rejected the counsel of God against themselves, being not baptized of him.

The foolishness of unbelief
(Matt. 11:16-19)

¶31And the Lord said, Whereunto
then shall I liken the men of this generation? and to what are they like?
32 They are like unto children sitting
in the marketplace, and calling one to
another, and saying, We have piped unto
you, and ye have not danced; we have
mourned to you, and ye have not wept.
33 For John the Baptist came neither
eating bread nor drinking *wine; and ye
say, He hath a devil.
34 The Son of man is come eating and
drinking; and ye say, Behold a gluttonous man, and a winebibber, a friend of
publicans and sinners!
35 But wisdom is justified of all her
children.

7:35 Wisdom
To those who are not wise, wisdom may appear to be foolishness. If a man cannot read, he cannot receive help from a book even if he opens it. If the people who were compared to the children in the marketplace (vs. 32) had been children of wisdom, they would have mourned with John and repented of their sins, and they would have rejoiced with Christ when He brought them the good news of salvation.

Jesus anointed in the Pharisee's home

¶36And one of the Pharisees desired
him that he would eat with him. And he
went into the *Pharisee's house, and
sat down to meat.
37And, behold, a woman in the city,
which was a sinner, when she knew that
Jesus sat at meat in the Pharisee's
house, brought an *alabaster box of
ointment,
38And stood at his feet behind *him*
weeping, and began to wash his feet
with tears, and did wipe *them* with the
hairs of her head, and kissed his feet,
and anointed *them* with the ointment.
39Now when the Pharisee which had
bidden him saw *it,* he spake within himself, saying, This man, if he were a
prophet, would have known who and
what manner of woman *this is* that
toucheth him: for she is a sinner.
40And Jesus answering said unto him,
Simon, I have somewhat to say unto
thee. And he saith, Master, say on.
41 There was a certain creditor which

7:28 he that is least. There was no greater prophet than John the Baptist, yet the youngest believer who is in the kingdom of God is greater in the sight of God than John, because Jesus by His Holy Spirit dwells within the believer.
7:29 justified God. God said that they were sinners; by their repenting and being baptized, they acknowledged that what God said of them was true.
7:30 against. About themselves.
7:38 wash his feet. See Genesis 18:4 note.

had two debtors: the one owed five
hundred *pence, and the other fifty.
42And when they had nothing to pay,
he frankly forgave them both. Tell me
therefore, which of them will love him
most?
43Simon answered and said, I suppose that *he,* to whom he forgave most.
And he said unto him, Thou hast rightly judged.
44And he turned to the woman, and
said unto Simon, Seest thou this woman? I entered into thine house, thou
gavest me no water for my feet: but she
hath washed my feet with tears, and
wiped *them* with the hairs of her head.
45Thou gavest me no kiss: but this
woman since the time I came in hath
not ceased to kiss my feet.
46My head with oil thou didst not
*anoint: but this woman hath anointed
my feet with ointment.
47Wherefore I say unto thee, Her
sins, which are many, are forgiven; for
she loved much: but to whom little is
forgiven, *the same* loveth little.
48And he said unto her, Thy sins are
forgiven.
49And they that sat at meat with him
began to say within themselves, Who is
this that forgiveth sins also?
50And he said to the woman, Thy
faith hath saved thee; go in *peace.

The Lord's continued ministry in Galilee

8 And it came to pass afterward, that
he went throughout every city and
village, preaching and shewing the glad
tidings of the kingdom of God: and the
twelve *were* with him,
2And certain women, which had been
healed of evil spirits and infirmities,
Mary called Magdalene, out of whom
went seven devils,
3And Joanna the wife of Chuza
*Herod's steward, and Susanna, and
many others, which ministered unto
him of their substance.

A parable: the sower
(Matt. 13:1-23; Mark 4:1-20)

¶4And when much people were gathered together, and were come to him
out of every city, he spake by a parable:
5A sower went out to sow his seed:
and as he sowed, some fell by the way
side; and it was trodden down, and the
fowls of the air devoured it.
6And some fell upon a rock; and as
soon as it was sprung up, it withered
away, because it lacked moisture.
7And some fell among thorns; and the
thorns sprang up with it, and choked it.
8And other fell on good ground, and
sprang up, and bare fruit an hundredfold. And when he had said these
things, he cried, He that hath ears to
hear, let him hear.
9And his disciples asked him, saying,
What might this parable be?
10And he said, Unto you it is given to
know the *mysteries of the kingdom of
God: but to others in *parables; that
seeing they might not see, and hearing
they might not understand.
11Now the parable is this: The seed
is the word of God.
12Those by the way side are they that
hear; then cometh the devil, and taketh
away the word out of their hearts, lest
they should believe and be saved.
13They on the rock *are they,* which,
when they hear, receive the word with
joy; and these have no root, which for a
while believe, and in time of *temptation fall away.
14And that which fell among thorns
are they, which, when they have heard,
go forth, and are choked with cares and
riches and pleasures of *this* life, and
bring no fruit to *perfection.
15But that on the good ground are

7:47 for she loved much. Because her many sins were forgiven, she loved much.
7:50 Thy faith hath saved thee. It was not the ointment nor the tears nor even her love for Christ that saved the woman; it was her faith in the Lord, the only Saviour.
8:10 that seeing they might not see. See Isaiah 6:9 note.

they, which in an honest and good heart, having heard the word, keep *it,* and bring forth fruit with patience.

A parable: the candle
(Matt. 5:15-16; Mark 4:21-23; Luke 11:33)

¶16 No man, when he hath lighted a candle, covereth it with a vessel, or putteth *it* under a bed; but setteth *it* on a candlestick, that they which enter in may see the light.

17 For nothing is secret, that shall not be made manifest; neither *any thing* hid, that shall not be known and come abroad.

18 Take heed therefore how ye hear: for whosoever hath, to him shall be given; and whosoever hath not, from him shall be taken even that which he seemeth to have.

The Lord's mother and brethren
(Matt. 12:46-50; Mark 3:31-35)

¶19 Then came to him *his* mother and his brethren, and could not come at him for the press.

20 And it was told him *by certain* which said, Thy mother and thy brethren stand without, desiring to see thee.

21 And he answered and said unto them, My mother and my brethren are these which hear the word of God, and do it.

The calmed storm
(Matt. 8:23-27; Mark 4:36-41)

¶22 Now it came to pass on a certain day, that he went into a ship with his disciples: and he said unto them, Let us go over unto the other side of the lake. And they launched forth.

23 But as they sailed he fell asleep: and there came down a storm of wind on the lake; and they were filled *with water,* and were in jeopardy.

24 And they came to him, and awoke him, saying, Master, master, we perish. Then he arose, and rebuked the wind and the raging of the water: and they ceased, and there was a calm.

25 And he said unto them, Where is your faith? And they being afraid wondered, saying one to another, What manner of man is this! for he commandeth even the winds and water, and they obey him.

A demon-possessed man cured
(Matt. 8:28-34; Mark 5:1-17)

¶26 And they arrived at the country of the Gadarenes, which is over against Galilee.

27 And when he went forth to land, there met him out of the city a certain man, which had devils long time, and ware no clothes, neither abode in *any* house, but in the tombs.

28 When he saw Jesus, he cried out, and fell down before him, and with a loud voice said, What have I to do with thee, Jesus, *thou* Son of God most high? I beseech thee, torment me not.

29 (For he had commanded the unclean spirit to come out of the man. For oftentimes it had caught him: and he was kept bound with chains and in fetters; and he brake the bands, and was driven of the devil into the wilderness.)

30 And Jesus asked him, saying, What is thy name? And he said, Legion: because many devils were entered into him.

31 And they besought him that he would not command them to go out into the deep.

32 And there was there an herd of many swine feeding on the mountain: and they besought him that he would suffer them to enter into them. And he suffered them.

33 Then went the devils out of the man, and entered into the swine: and the herd ran violently down a steep

---

8:21 My mother and my brethren. Those who are saved by grace through faith are closer and dearer to Him than even His mother and brothers by natural birth.

8:30 Legion. See Mark 5:9 note.

place into the lake, and were choked.
34When they that fed *them* saw what
was done, they fled, and went and told
it in the city and in the country.
35Then they went out to see what
was done; and came to Jesus, and found
the man, out of whom the devils were
departed, sitting at the feet of Jesus,
clothed, and in his right mind: and they
were afraid.
36They also which saw *it* told them by
what means he that was possessed of
the devils was healed.
¶37Then the whole multitude of the
country of the Gadarenes round about
besought him to depart from them; for
they were taken with great fear: and he
went up into the ship, and returned
back again.
38Now the man out of whom the devils
were departed besought him that he
might be with him: but Jesus sent him
away, saying,
39 Return to thine own house, and
shew how great things God hath done
unto thee. And he went his way, and
published throughout the whole city
how great things Jesus had done unto
him.
40And it came to pass, that, when
Jesus was returned, the people *gladly*
received him: for they were all waiting
for him.

Jairus' sick child
(Matt. 9:18-26; Mark 5:22-43)

¶41And, behold, there came a man
named Jairus, and he was a *ruler of the
synagogue: and he fell down at Jesus'
feet, and besought him that he would
come into his house:
42For he had one only daughter, about
twelve years of age, and she lay a dying.
But as he went the people thronged
him.

A sick woman healed

¶43And a woman having *an issue of
blood twelve years, which had spent all
her living upon physicians, neither
could be healed of any,
44Came behind *him,* and touched the
border of his garment: and immediately
her issue of blood stanched.
45And Jesus said, Who *touched me?
When all denied, Peter and they that
were with him said, Master, the multitude
throng thee and press *thee,* and
sayest thou, Who touched me?
46And Jesus said, Somebody hath
touched me: for I perceive that virtue
is gone out of me.
47And when the woman saw that she
was not hid, she came trembling, and
falling down before him, she declared
unto him before all the people for what
cause she had touched him, and how
she was healed immediately.
48And he said unto her, Daughter, be
of good comfort: thy faith hath made
thee whole; go in peace.

The raising of Jairus' daughter

¶49While he yet spake, there cometh
one from the ruler of the synagogue's
house, saying to him, Thy daughter is
dead; trouble not the Master.
50But when Jesus heard *it,* he answered
him, saying, Fear not: believe
only, and she shall be made whole.
51And when he came into the house,
he suffered no man to go in, save Peter,
and James, and John, and the father
and the mother of the maiden.
52And all wept, and bewailed her: but
he said, Weep not; she is not dead, but
sleepeth.
53And they laughed him to scorn,
knowing that she was dead.
54And he put them all out, and took
her by the hand, and called, saying,
Maid, arise.
55And her spirit came again, and she
arose straightway: and he commanded
to give her meat.
56And her parents were astonished:
but he charged them that they should
tell no man what was done.

8:52 all wept, and bewailed. See Mark 5:38 note.

The disciples sent out in ministry
(Matt. 10:1-42; see Mark 6:7-13)

9 Then he called his twelve disciples together, and gave them power and authority over all devils, and to cure diseases.

2 And he sent them to preach the kingdom of God, and to heal the sick.

3 And he said unto them, Take nothing for *your* journey, neither staves, nor *scrip, neither bread, neither money; neither have two coats apiece.

4 And whatsoever house ye enter into, there abide, and thence depart.

5 And whosoever will not receive you, when ye go out of that city, shake off the very dust from your feet for a testimony against them.

6 And they departed, and went through the towns, preaching the gospel, and healing every where.

Herod's desire

¶ 7 Now Herod the *tetrarch heard of all that was done by him: and he was perplexed, because that it was said of some, that John was risen from the dead;

8 And of some, that *Elias had appeared; and of others, that one of the old *prophets was risen again.

9 And Herod said, John have I beheaded: but who is this, of whom I hear such things? And he desired to see him.

Feeding of the five thousand
(Matt. 14:13-21; Mark 6:30-44; John 6:1-14)

¶ 10 And the apostles, when they were returned, told him all that they had done. And he took them, and went aside privately into a desert place belonging to the city called Bethsaida.

11 And the people, when they knew *it,* followed him: and he received them, and spake unto them of the kingdom of God, and healed them that had need of healing.

12 And when the day began to wear away, then came the twelve, and said unto him, Send the multitude away, that they may go into the towns and country round about, and lodge, and get victuals: for we are here in a desert place.

13 But he said unto them, *Give ye them to eat. And they said, We have no more but five loaves and two fishes; except we should go and buy meat for all this people.

14 For they were about five thousand men. And he said to his disciples, Make them sit down by fifties in a company.

15 And they did so, and made them all sit down.

16 Then he took the five loaves and the two fishes, and looking up to *heaven, he blessed them, and brake, and gave to the disciples to set before the multitude.

17 And they did eat, and were all filled: and there was taken up of fragments that remained to them twelve baskets.

Peter's confession
(Matt. 16:13-20; Mark 8:27-30)

¶ 18 And it came to pass, as he was alone praying, his disciples were with him: and he asked them, saying, Whom say the people that I am?

19 They answering said, John the Baptist; but some *say,* Elias; and others *say,* that one of the old prophets is risen again.

20 He said unto them, But whom say ye that I am? Peter answering said, The *Christ of God.

21 And he straitly charged them, and commanded *them* to tell no man that thing;

9:2 he sent them to preach. Mark tells us that they went "two and two" (6:7). Matthew gives the longest account of the directions to the disciples (chap. 10). Note the changed directions in Luke 22:35-36.

9:9 John have I beheaded. Herod was afraid John the Baptist had risen from the dead. See Mark 6:16-29.

9:18 Whom say the people that I am? See Mark 8:27,29 notes.

The Lord speaks of things to come
(Matt. 16:21; Mark 8:31)

22Saying, The Son of man must suffer many things, and be rejected of the
elders and chief priests and scribes, and
be slain, and be raised the third day.
¶23And he said to *them* all, If any *man*
will come after me, let him deny himself, and take up his cross daily, and follow me.
24For whosoever will save his life
shall lose it: but whosoever will lose his
life for my sake, the same shall save it.
25For what is a man advantaged, if he
gain the whole *world, and lose himself,
or be cast away?
26For whosoever shall be ashamed of
me and of my words, of him shall the Son
of man be ashamed, when he shall come
in his own glory, and *in his* Father's, and
of the holy *angels.
27But I tell you of a truth, there be
some standing here, which shall not
taste of *death, till they see the kingdom of God.

The transfiguration
(Matt. 17:1-8; Mark 9:2-8)

¶28And it came to pass about an eight
days after these sayings, he took Peter
and John and James, and went up into a
mountain to pray.
29And as he prayed, the fashion of his
countenance was altered, and his raiment *was* white *and* glistering.
30And, behold, there talked with him
two men, which were *Moses and Elias:
31Who appeared in glory, and spake of
his decease which he should accomplish at *Jerusalem.
32But Peter and they that were with
him were heavy with sleep: and when
they were awake, they saw his glory,
and the two men that stood with him.
33And it came to pass, as they departed from him, Peter said unto Jesus,
Master, it is good for us to be here: and
let us make *three tabernacles; one for
thee, and one for Moses, and one for
Elias: not knowing what he said.
34While he thus spake, there came a
cloud, and overshadowed them: and
they feared as they entered into the
cloud.
35And there came a voice out of the
cloud, saying, This is my beloved Son:
hear him.
36And when the voice was past, Jesus
was found alone. And they kept *it* close,
and told no man in those days any of
those things which they had seen.

A sick child healed
(Matt. 17:14-21; Mark 9:14-29)

¶37And it came to pass, that on the
next day, when they were come down
from the hill, much people met him.
38And, behold, a man of the company
cried out, saying, Master, I beseech
thee, look upon my son: for he is mine
only child.
39And, lo, a spirit taketh him, and he
suddenly crieth out; and it teareth him
that he foameth again, and bruising him
hardly departeth from him.
40And I besought thy disciples to cast
him out; and they could not.
41And Jesus answering said, O faithless and perverse generation, how long
shall I be with you, and suffer you?
Bring thy son hither.
42And as he was yet a coming, the
devil threw him down, and tare *him*.
And Jesus rebuked the unclean spirit,

9:24 whosoever will save his life. This is a paradox, or truth expressed in apparent contradiction. Life that a man saves for himself is lost. It is saved if it is lost for Christ's sake. Following Jesus should be more important to us than even our own lives.

9:28 about an eight days. See Mark 9:2 note, "After six days."

9:29 his countenance was altered. The Lord Jesus had just told His disciples that He, the King, was to be rejected, slain, and raised again from the dead (vs. 22). Then He allowed Peter, James, and John to see Him as He will appear when He comes again to be King of Kings and Lord of Lords. See Matthew 17:2 note, "The Transfiguration."

9:30 Moses and Elias. See Mark 9:4 first note.

and healed the child, and delivered him
again to his father.

Jesus warns of His death
(Matt. 17:22-23; Mark 9:30-32)

¶43And they were all amazed at the
mighty power of God. But while they
wondered every one at all things which
Jesus did, he said unto his disciples,
44 Let these sayings sink down into
your ears: for the Son of man shall be
delivered into the hands of men.
45But they understood not this saying, and it was hid from them, that they
perceived it not: and they feared to ask
him of that saying.

The lesson of the child
(Matt. 18:1-5; Mark 9:33-37)

¶46Then there arose a reasoning
among them, which of them should be
greatest.
47And Jesus, perceiving the thought
of their heart, took a child, and set him
by him,
48And said unto them, Whosoever
shall receive this child in my name
receiveth me: and whosoever shall receive me receiveth him that sent me:
for he that is least among you all, the
same shall be great.

Service in the Lord's Name
(Mark 9:38-40)

¶49And John answered and said, Master, we saw one casting out devils in thy
name; and we forbad him, because he
followeth not with us.
50And Jesus said unto him, Forbid
him not: for he that is not against us is
for us.

V. Christ in Judaea and Peraea
(9:51—19:27)

¶51And it came to pass, when the
time was come that he should be received up, he stedfastly set his face to
go to Jerusalem,
52And sent messengers before his
face: and they went, and entered into a
village of the *Samaritans, to make
ready for him.
53And they did not receive him, because his face was as though he would
go to Jerusalem.
54And when his disciples James and
John saw *this*, they said, Lord, wilt thou
that we command *fire to come down
from heaven, and consume them, even
as Elias did?
55But he turned, and rebuked them,
and said, Ye know not what manner of
spirit ye are of.
56 For the Son of man is not come to
destroy men's lives, but to save *them*.
And they went to another village.

Tests for disciples
(Matt. 8:18-22)

¶57And it came to pass, that, as they
went in the way, a certain *man* said unto
him, Lord, I will follow thee whithersoever thou goest.
58And Jesus said unto him, Foxes
have holes, and birds of the air *have*
nests; but the Son of man hath not
where to lay *his* head.

9:58 A Homeless Man
The Lord Jesus had no home of His own. Sometimes He stayed with friends; other times He slept by the sea or in the mountains. He wanted the man to know that those who follow Him must be willing to suffer hardship in this world.

59And he said unto another, Follow
me. But he said, Lord, suffer me first
to go and bury my father.
60Jesus said unto him, Let the dead
bury their dead: but go thou and preach
the kingdom of God.

9:54 fire to come down from heaven. The story is found in 2 Kings 1:10,12 (see also 1:10 note, "A Miracle of Fire").

9:60 Let the dead bury their dead. Let the spiritually dead bury the physically dead. See *death.

61And another also said, Lord, I will
follow thee; but let me first go bid them
farewell, which are at home at my
house.
62And Jesus said unto him, No man,
having put his hand to the plough,
and looking back, is fit for the kingdom
of God.

The seventy sent out in ministry

10 After these things the Lord appointed other seventy also, and
sent them two and two before his face
into every city and place, whither he
himself would come.

10:1 The Seventy Ministers
Luke's Gospel is the only one that tells about the sending forth of the seventy. He wrote especially for the Gentiles. The seventy were sent into Samaria where the Twelve had been forbidden to go (Matt. 10:5). It was the time of the *Feast of Tabernacles; the Twelve had gone to the "lost sheep of the house of Israel" (Matt. 10:6) at the time of the *Passover, about six months earlier.

2Therefore said he unto them, The
harvest truly *is* great, but the labourers
are few: pray ye therefore the Lord of
the harvest, that he would send forth
labourers into his harvest.
3Go your ways: behold, I send you
forth as lambs among wolves.
4Carry neither purse, nor scrip, nor
shoes: and salute no man by the way.
5And into whatsoever house ye enter,
first say, Peace *be* to this house.
6And if the son of peace be there,
your peace shall rest upon it: if not, it
shall turn to you again.
7And in the same house remain, eating and drinking such things as they
give: for the labourer is worthy of his
hire. Go not from house to house.
8And into whatsoever city ye enter,
and they receive you, eat such things as
are set before you:
9And heal the sick that are therein,
and say unto them, The *kingdom of
God is come nigh unto you.
10But into whatsoever city ye enter,
and they receive you not, go your ways
out into the streets of the same, and say,
11Even the very dust of your city,
which cleaveth on us, we do wipe off
against you: notwithstanding be ye sure
of this, that the kingdom of God is come
nigh unto you.
12But I say unto you, that it shall be
more tolerable in that day for Sodom,
than for that city.

Judgment on the cities
(Matt. 11:20-24)

13Woe unto thee, Chorazin! woe unto
thee, Bethsaida! for if the mighty works
had been done in Tyre and Sidon, which
have been done in you, they had a great
while ago *repented, sitting in sackcloth and ashes.
14But it shall be more tolerable for
Tyre and Sidon at the *judgment, than
for you.
15And thou, Capernaum, which art
exalted to heaven, shalt be thrust down
to *hell.
16He that heareth you heareth me;
and he that despiseth you despiseth
me; and he that despiseth me despiseth
him that sent me.

9:62 No man . . . looking back. A good plowman keeps his eyes straight ahead on the furrow, because if he turns his head the row he's plowing to plant will be crooked.
10:3 lambs among wolves. The followers of Christ would have to bear much hardship and shame for the sake of their testimony, but they did not need to fear, because the Chief Shepherd was their protector.
10:4 Carry neither purse, nor scrip. See the directions to the Twelve in Luke 9:1-5; Matthew 10:1-42; and Mark 6:7-13.
10:4 salute no man. Greetings in the East were long and elaborate ceremony. The seventy were not supposed to waste their precious time on useless ceremonies.
10:6 if the son of peace be there. "There is no peace, saith my God, to the wicked" (Isa. 57:21).

¶[17]And the seventy returned again
with joy, saying, Lord, even the devils
are subject unto us through thy name.
[18]And he said unto them, I beheld
*Satan as lightning fall from heaven.
[19] Behold, I give unto you power to
tread on serpents and *scorpions, and
over all the power of the enemy: and
nothing shall by any means hurt you.
[20] Notwithstanding in this rejoice not,
that the spirits are subject unto you; but
rather rejoice, because your names are
written in heaven.

The Lord prays

¶[21]In that hour Jesus rejoiced in
spirit, and said, I thank thee, O Father,
Lord of heaven and earth, that thou hast
hid these things from the wise and prudent, and hast revealed them unto
babes: even so, Father; for so it seemed
good in thy sight.
[22] All things are delivered to me of my
Father: and no man knoweth who the
Son is, but the Father; and who the Father is, but the Son, and *he* to whom the
Son will reveal *him.*

The disciples' blessings

¶[23]And he turned him unto *his* disciples, and said privately, Blessed *are* the
eyes which see the things that ye see:
[24] For I tell you, that many prophets
and kings have desired to see those
things which ye see, and have not seen
them; and to hear those things which ye
hear, and have not heard *them.*

A lawyer questions the Lord
(See Matt. 22:34-40; Mark 12:28-34)

¶[25]And, behold, a certain lawyer
stood up, and *tempted him, saying,
Master, what shall I do to inherit *eternal life?
[26]He said unto him, What is written
in the *law? how readest thou?
[27]And he answering said, Thou shalt
love the Lord thy God with all thy heart,
and with all thy soul, and with all thy
strength, and with all thy mind; and thy
neighbour as thyself.

10:27 The Heart of the Law
See Deuteronomy 6:5 and Leviticus 19:18. The heart of the Law was love—not deeds or good work. If people love God with all of their heart, soul, strength, and mind, then their deeds toward God and their neighbors will be right, and there will be the obedience of faith to God, the One they love so much.

[28]And he said unto him, Thou hast
answered right: this do, and thou shalt
live.
[29]But he, willing to justify himself,
said unto Jesus, And who is my neighbour?

A parable: the good Samaritan

[30]And Jesus answering said, A certain *man* went down from Jerusalem to
Jericho, and fell among thieves, which
stripped him of his raiment, and wounded *him,* and departed, leaving *him* half
dead.
[31] And by chance there came down a
certain priest that way: and when he
saw him, he passed by on the other
side.
[32] And likewise a Levite, when he was
at the place, came and looked *on him,*
and passed by on the other side.
[33] But a certain *Samaritan, as he
journeyed, came where he was: and
when he saw him, he had compassion
on him,
[34] And went to *him,* and bound up his
wounds, pouring in oil and wine, and set
him on his own beast, and brought him
to an inn, and took care of him.
[35] And on the morrow when he departed, he took out two *pence, and
gave *them* to the host, and said unto
him, Take care of him; and whatsoever
thou spendest more, when I come
again, I will repay thee.
[36] Which now of these three, thinkest
thou, was neighbour unto him that fell
among the thieves?
[37]And he said, He that shewed *mercy on him. Then said Jesus unto him,
Go, and do thou likewise.

The Lord visits Martha and Mary

¶ 38 Now it came to pass, as they went,
that he entered into a certain village:
and a certain woman named Martha
received him into her house.
39 And she had a sister called Mary,
which also sat at Jesus' feet, and heard
his word.
40 But Martha was cumbered about
much serving, and came to him, and
said, Lord, dost thou not care that my
sister hath left me to serve alone? bid
her therefore that she help me.
41 And Jesus answered and said unto
her, Martha, Martha, thou art careful
and troubled about many things:
42 But one thing is needful: and Mary
hath chosen that good part, which shall
not be taken away from her.

A lesson on prayer

11 And it came to pass, that, as he
was praying in a certain place,
when he ceased, one of his disciples
said unto him, Lord, teach us to pray, as
John also taught his disciples.
2 And he said unto them, When ye
pray, say, *Our Father which art in
heaven, Hallowed be thy name. Thy
kingdom come. Thy will be done, as in
heaven, so in earth.
3 Give us day by day our daily bread.
4 And forgive us our sins; for we also
forgive every one that is indebted to us.
And lead us not into *temptation; but
deliver us from evil.
¶ 5 And he said unto them, Which of
you shall have a friend, and shall go unto
him at midnight, and say unto him,
Friend, lend me three loaves;
6 For a friend of mine in his journey
is come to me, and I have nothing to set
before him?
7 And he from within shall answer
and say, Trouble me not: the door is now
shut, and my children are with me in
bed; I cannot rise and give thee.
8 I say unto you, Though he will not rise
and give him, because he is his friend, yet
because of his importunity he will rise
and give him as many as he needeth.
9 And I say unto you, Ask, and it shall
be given you; seek, and ye shall find;
knock, and it shall be opened unto you.
10 For every one that asketh receiveth;
and he that seeketh findeth; and to him
that knocketh it shall be opened.
11 If a son shall ask bread of any of you
that is a father, will he give him a stone?
or if *he ask* a fish, will he for a fish give
him a serpent?
12 Or if he shall ask an egg, will he
offer him a scorpion?
13 If ye then, being evil, know how to
give good gifts unto your children: how
much more shall *your* heavenly Father
give the Holy Spirit to them that ask
him?

The mute man healed
(Matt. 12:22-37)

¶ 14 And he was casting out a *devil,
and it was dumb. And it came to pass,
when the devil was gone out, the dumb
spake; and the people wondered.

Unbelievers accuse the Lord of evil powers

15 But some of them said, He casteth
out devils through Beelzebub the chief
of the devils.
16 And others, *tempting *him,* sought
of him a sign from heaven.

11:8 because of his importunity. Persistence in prayers is proof of sincerity. There must be "continual coming" (Luke 18:5) in certain of our requests to our heavenly Father and Friend.

11:13 give the Holy Spirit. Apparently not one of the Lord's disciples asked for the gift of the Holy Spirit before the Lord Jesus left them. The Holy Spirit was given to them at *Pentecost (Acts 2) and now dwells in every believer in Christ.

11:15 Beelzebub the chief of the devils. See *Beelzebub and Matthew 10:25 note, "Beelzebub." Our Lord referred to Satan as Beelzebub, who was the chief of demons (vs. 18). He is the Devil.

17 But he, knowing their thoughts,
said unto them, Every kingdom divided against itself is brought to desolation; and a house *divided* against a
house falleth.
18 If Satan also be divided against himself, how shall his kingdom stand? because ye say that I cast out devils
through Beelzebub.
19 And if I by Beelzebub cast out devils, by whom do your sons cast *them*
out? therefore shall they be your
judges.
20 But if I with the finger of God cast
out devils, no doubt the kingdom of God
is come upon you.
21 When a strong man armed keepeth
his palace, his goods are in peace:
22 But when a stronger than he shall
come upon him, and overcome him, he
taketh from him all his armour wherein
he trusted, and divideth his spoils.
23 He that is not with me is against
me: and he that gathereth not with me
scattereth.
¶24 When the *unclean spirit is gone
out of a man, he walketh through dry
places, seeking rest; and finding none,
he saith, I will return unto my house
whence I came out.
25 And when he cometh, he findeth *it*
swept and garnished.
26 Then goeth he, and taketh *to him*
seven other spirits more wicked than
himself; and they enter in, and dwell
there: and the last *state* of that man is
worse than the first.

Blessing for believers

¶27 And it came to pass, as he spake
these things, a certain woman of the
company lifted up her voice, and said
unto him, Blessed *is* the womb that bare
thee, and the paps which thou hast
sucked.
28 But he said, Yea rather, blessed *are*
they that hear the word of God, and
keep it.

Signs from the Old Testament (Matt. 12:39-42)

¶29 And when the people were gathered thick together, he began to say,
This is an evil generation: they seek a
sign; and there shall no sign be given
it, but the sign of Jonas the prophet.
30 For as Jonas was a sign unto the
Ninevites, so shall also the Son of man
be to this generation.
31 The *queen of the south shall rise
up in the judgment with the men of this
generation, and condemn them: for
she came from the utmost parts of the
earth to hear the wisdom of Solomon;
and, behold, a greater than Solomon *is*
here.
32 The men of Nineve shall rise up in
the judgment with this generation, and
shall condemn it: for they repented at
the preaching of Jonas; and, behold, a
greater than Jonas *is* here.

A parable: the candlestick (Matt. 5:15-16; Mark 4:21-22)

33 No man, when he hath lighted a
candle, putteth *it* in a secret place, neither under a bushel, but on a candlestick, that they which come in may see
the light.
34 The light of the body is the eye:
therefore when thine eye is single, thy
whole body also is full of light; but when

11:21 a strong man armed. The strong man is the Devil, who holds men in his power and in the fear of death (Heb. 2:15). His palace is the soul of man which he keeps "in peace"-with no difficulty —until "a stronger than he," the Lord Jesus Christ, "overcome[s] him" (Luke 11:22). The Lord did this at the cross (Heb. 2:14).

11:24 return unto my house. This unclean demon called the soul of man his house. The man had perhaps decided to "turn over a new leaf" or clean up his life in his own strength. He had not given his soul to the keeping of Christ through His Holy Spirit, and he could not, therefore, prevent the return of the demon with his seven other demons.

11:26 worse than the first. See 2 Peter 2:20-21 and 2:20 note, "Of Wicked Men."

11:34 single. Good or healthy.

thine eye is evil, thy body also *is* full of
darkness.
35 Take heed therefore that the light
which is in thee be not darkness.
36 If thy whole body therefore *be* full
of light, having no part dark, the whole
shall be full of light, as when the bright
shining of a candle doth give thee
light.

Cleanness in God's sight

¶37 And as he spake, a certain *Pharisee besought him to dine with him: and
he went in, and sat down to meat.
38 And when the Pharisee saw *it,* he
marvelled that he had not first washed
before dinner.
39 And the Lord said unto him, Now
do ye *Pharisees make *clean the outside of the cup and the platter; but your
inward part is full of ravening and wickedness.
40 *Ye* *fools, did not he that made that
which is without make that which is
within also?
41 But rather give alms of such things
as ye have; and, behold, all things are
clean unto you.
42 But woe unto you, Pharisees! for ye
tithe mint and rue and all manner of
herbs, and pass over judgment and the
love of God: these ought ye to have
done, and not to leave the other undone.
43 Woe unto you, Pharisees! for ye
love the uppermost seats in the *synagogues, and greetings in the markets.
44 Woe unto you, *scribes and Pharisees, hypocrites! for ye are as graves
which appear not, and the men that
walk over *them* are not aware *of them.*
¶45 Then answered one of the lawyers, and said unto him, Master, thus
saying thou reproachest us also.
46 And he said, Woe unto you also, *ye*
lawyers! for ye lade men with burdens
grievous to be borne, and ye yourselves
touch not the burdens with one of your
fingers.
47 Woe unto you! for ye build the sepulchres of the prophets, and your fathers killed them.
48 Truly ye bear witness that ye allow
the deeds of your fathers: for they indeed killed them, and ye build their
sepulchres.
49 Therefore also said the wisdom of
God, I will send them prophets and
apostles, and *some* of them they shall
slay and persecute:
50 That the blood of all the prophets,
which was shed from the foundation of
the world, may be required of this generation;
51 From the blood of *Abel unto the
blood of Zacharias, which perished between the *altar and the temple: verily
I say unto you, It shall be required of
this generation.
52 Woe unto you, lawyers! for ye have
taken away the key of knowledge: ye
entered not in yourselves, and them
that were entering in ye hindered.

The scribes and Pharisees seek to trap the Lord

53 And as he said these things unto
them, the scribes and the Pharisees

11:34 evil. Diseased or bad, in this case.
11:38 he had not first washed. See Mark 7:5 note.
11:41 rather give alms. Give the things that are within, like our love and time, as alms. This speaks of the heart, the will, and the affections as yielded and given wholly to the Lord, that all actions may be truly acceptable to Him. Then "all things" will be clean.
11:44 as graves which appear not. In Matthew 23:27 the Lord compared the Pharisees to "whited sepulchres"–graves that are outwardly clean and obvious to the eye. Now He mentions concealed graves. Whether a person is outwardly religious or not makes no difference, those who reject Christ are alike inside—corrupted with sin.
11:45 reproachest. Insults.
11:49 the wisdom of God. This is Christ Himself (see 1 Cor. 1:24).
11:51 Abel . . . Zacharias. See Genesis 4:8 and 2 Chronicles 24:20-21.

11:52 Sins of the Lawyers
Note the sins of the lawyers that Christ presented here:
1. They made many burdensome and unnecessary laws;
2. They professed to have reverence for the former prophets, but they did not follow their teachings, and they had killed those who followed the prophets' teachings; and
3. They took away the key of knowledge–they did not truly know or present the *Law of Moses, which would have led them and their hearers to a knowledge of Christ (Rom. 10:4; Gal. 3:24; Heb. 10:1).

began to urge *him* vehemently, and to
provoke him to speak of many things:
54 Laying wait for him, and seeking to
catch something out of his mouth, that
they might accuse him.

Great crowds hear the Lord's message

12 In the mean time, when there
were gathered together an innumerable multitude of people, insomuch that they trode one upon another,
he began to say unto his disciples first
of all, Beware ye of the *leaven of the
Pharisees, which is hypocrisy.
2 For there is nothing covered, that
shall not be revealed; neither hid, that
shall not be known.
3 Therefore whatsoever ye have spoken in darkness shall be heard in the
light; and that which ye have spoken in
the ear in closets shall be proclaimed
upon the housetops.
4 And I say unto you my friends, Be
not *afraid of them that kill the body, and
after that have no more that they can do.
5 But I will forewarn you whom ye
shall fear: Fear him, which after he hath
killed hath power to cast into hell; yea,
I say unto you, Fear him.
6 Are not five sparrows sold for two
farthings, and not one of them is forgotten before God?
7 But even the very hairs of your head
are all numbered. Fear not therefore: ye
are of more value than many sparrows.

Confession and denial

8 Also I say unto you, Whosoever
shall *confess me before men, him shall
the Son of man also confess before the
angels of God:
9 But he that denieth me before men
shall be denied before the angels of
God.

Holiness and power of the Holy Ghost

10 And whosoever shall speak a word
against the Son of man, it shall be
*forgiven him: but unto him that blas-
phemeth against the Holy Ghost it shall
not be forgiven.
11 And when they bring you unto the
synagogues, and *unto* magistrates, and
powers, take ye no thought how or what
thing ye shall answer, or what ye shall
say:
12 For the Holy Ghost shall teach you
in the same hour what ye ought to say.

The Lord rebukes greediness

¶ 13 And one of the company said unto
him, Master, speak to my brother, that
he divide the inheritance with me.
14 And he said unto him, Man, who
made me a judge or a divider over you?

11:53 to provoke him to speak. This suggests an angry teacher who asks his student question after question in an attempt to trick him into giving the wrong answers, just as the scribes and Pharisees were trying to get Christ to do.
12:1 Beware ye of the leaven. See Mark 8:15 note.
12:5 Fear him, which . . . hath power to cast into hell. This is God Himself, the only One who has such power (see Rev. 20:10,12-15; see also 20:12 note, "The Dead" and Rev. 20:14 note).
12:6 two farthings. A farthing was a copper coin worth about one-sixteenth of a denarius–a very small amount.
12:14 who made me a judge . . . ? The Lord said, "My *kingdom is not of this world" (John 18:36), because the world had rejected Him (John 1:10-11; compare Isa. 53:3).

[15]And he said unto them, Take heed,
and beware of covetousness: for a
man's life consisteth not in the abundance of the things which he possesseth.

A parable: the foolish rich man

¶[16]And he spake a *parable unto
them, saying, The ground of a certain
rich man brought forth plentifully:
[17]And he thought within himself, saying, What shall I do, because I have no
room where to bestow my fruits?
[18]And he said, This will I do: I will
pull down my barns, and build greater;
and there will I bestow all my fruits and
my goods.
[19]And I will say to my soul, Soul, thou
hast much goods laid up for many
years; take thine ease, eat, drink, *and*
be merry.
[20]But God said unto him, *Thou* *fool,
this night thy soul shall be required of
thee: then whose shall those things be,
which thou hast provided?
[21]So *is* he that layeth up treasure for
himself, and is not rich toward God.

The Lord's care for His children

¶[22]And he said unto his disciples,
Therefore I say unto you, Take no thought
for your life, what ye shall eat; neither
for the body, what ye shall put on.
[23]The life is more than meat, and the
body *is more* than raiment.
[24]Consider the ravens: for they neither sow nor reap; which neither have
storehouse nor barn; and God feedeth
them: how much more are ye better
than the fowls?
[25]And which of you with taking
thought can add to his stature one
cubit?
[26]If ye then be not able to do that
thing which is least, why take ye
thought for the rest?
[27]Consider the lilies how they grow:
they toil not, they spin not; and yet I say
unto you, that Solomon in all his glory
was not arrayed like one of these.
[28]If then God so clothe the grass,
which is to day in the field, and to morrow is cast into the oven; how much
more *will he clothe* you, O ye of little
*faith?
[29]And seek not ye what ye shall eat,
or what ye shall drink, neither be ye of
doubtful mind.
[30]For all these things do the nations
of the world seek after: and your Father
knoweth that ye have need of these
things.
¶[31]But rather seek ye the kingdom of
God; and all these things shall be added
unto you.
[32]Fear not, little flock; for it is your
Father's good pleasure to give you the
kingdom.
[33]Sell that ye have, and give alms;
provide yourselves bags which wax not
old, a treasure in the heavens that
faileth not, where no thief approacheth,
neither moth corrupteth.
[34]For where your treasure is, there
will your heart be also.
[35]Let your loins be girded about, and
your lights burning;

A parable: servants watch for the master (Matt. 24:37—25:30)

[36]And ye yourselves like unto men
that wait for their lord, when he will
return from the wedding; that when he
cometh and knocketh, they may open
unto him immediately.
[37]Blessed *are* those servants, whom
the lord when he cometh shall find
watching: verily I say unto you, that he
shall gird himself, and make them to sit
down to meat, and will come forth and
serve them.

12:22 Take no thought for. Do not worry about.
12:35 loins be girded. The long, loose outer garments worn in Christ's day were usually fastened up before men traveled or worked. The Lord Jesus meant, therefore, "Be ready for action."

38 And if he shall come in the second watch, or come in the third watch, and find *them* so, blessed are those servants.
39 And this know, that if the goodman of the house had known what hour the thief would come, he would have watched, and not have suffered his house to be broken through.
40 Be ye therefore ready also: for the Son of man cometh at an hour when ye think not.

The Lord explains the parable further

¶41 Then *Peter said unto him, Lord, speakest thou this parable unto us, or even to all?
42 And the Lord said, Who then is that faithful and wise steward, whom *his* lord shall make ruler over his household, to give *them their* portion of meat in due season?
43 Blessed *is* that servant, whom his lord when he cometh shall find so doing.
44 Of a truth I say unto you, that he will make him ruler over all that he hath.
45 But and if that servant say in his heart, My lord delayeth his coming; and shall begin to beat the menservants and maidens, and to eat and drink, and to be drunken;
46 The lord of that servant will come in a day when he looketh not for *him,* and at an hour when he is not aware, and will cut him in sunder, and will appoint him his portion with the unbelievers.
47 And that servant, which knew his lord's will, and prepared not *himself,* neither did according to his will, shall be beaten with many *stripes.*
48 But he that knew not, and did commit things worthy of stripes, shall be beaten with few *stripes.* For unto whomsoever much is given, of him shall be much required: and to whom men have committed much, of him they will ask the more.

The Lord causes divisions

¶49 I am come to send fire on the earth; and what will I if it be already kindled?

12:49 Two Kinds of Fire
The Lord Jesus sent two kinds of fire to the earth: the fire of *Pentecost (Acts 2:3) and the fire of persecution and tribulation (John 15:20; 16:33; Matt. 10:34; see also 10:34 note, "Peace on Earth"). The rest of this chapter indicates that it is the fire of persecution of which He was speaking here. This was already kindled for Him.

50 But I have a baptism to be baptized with; and how am I straitened till it be accomplished!
51 Suppose ye that I am come to give peace on earth? I tell you, Nay; but rather division:
52 For from henceforth there shall be five in one house divided, three against two, and two against three.
53 The father shall be divided against the son, and the son against the father; the mother against the daughter, and the daughter against the mother; the mother in law against her daughter in law, and the daughter in law against her mother in law.

12:38 second watch. The Jews divided the night into three watches, during which guards were on duty. The second watch was from midnight until 3 A.M.

12:50 I have a baptism. Christ referred here to His death on the cross. See also Mark 10:39 note.

12:50 straitened. Distressed. The Lord always had with Him the conscious weight of His awful death, but His great love for us also continually pushed Him on to make the full atonement for sin for which He had come to earth.

12:52 one house divided. Light and darkness cannot live together (see John 7:43; 9:16; 10:19; 2 Cor. 6:14). Christ knew there would be tension and conflict in families when some would choose to follow Him while others would not.

The ignorance of unbelief

¶[54]And he said also to the people,
When ye see a cloud rise out of the west,
*straightway ye say, There cometh a
shower; and so it is.
55 And when *ye see* the south wind
blow, ye say, There will be heat; and it
cometh to pass.
56 *Ye* hypocrites, ye can discern the
face of the sky and of the earth; but how
is it that ye do not discern this time?
57 Yea, and why even of yourselves
judge ye not what is right?

A parable: be reconciled to God

¶58 When thou goest with thine adversary to the magistrate, *as thou art*
in the way, give diligence that thou
mayest be delivered from him; lest he
hale thee to the judge, and the judge
deliver thee to the officer, and the officer cast thee into prison.
59 I tell thee, thou shalt not depart
thence, till thou hast paid the very last
mite.

The folly of not repenting

13 There were present at that
season some that told him of
the Galilaeans, whose blood *Pilate had
mingled with their sacrifices.
2 And Jesus answering said unto
them, Suppose ye that these Galilaeans
were sinners above all the Galilaeans,
because they suffered such things?
3 I tell you, Nay: but, except ye *repent, ye shall all likewise perish.
4 Or those eighteen, upon whom the
tower in Siloam fell, and slew them,
think ye that they were sinners above
all men that dwelt in Jerusalem?
5 I tell you, Nay: but, except ye repent, ye shall all likewise perish.

A parable: the fruitless fig tree (see Isa. 5:1-7; Matt. 21:18-20)

¶6 He spake also this parable; A certain *man* had a fig tree planted in his
*vineyard; and he came and sought fruit
thereon, and found none.
7 Then said he unto the dresser of his
vineyard, Behold, these three years I
come seeking fruit on this fig tree, and
find none: cut it down; why cumbereth
it the ground?
8 And he answering said unto him,
Lord, let it alone this year also, till I
shall dig about it, and *dung *it:*
9 And if it bear fruit, *well:* and if not,
then after that thou shalt cut it down.

The Lord heals a woman on the Sabbath

¶10 And he was teaching in one of the
synagogues on the *sabbath.
11 And, behold, there was a woman
which had a spirit of infirmity eighteen
years, and was bowed together, and
could in no wise lift up *herself.*
12 And when Jesus saw her, he called
her to him, and said unto her, Woman,
thou art loosed from thine infirmity.
13 And he laid *his* hands on her: and
immediately she was made straight,
and glorified *God.
14 And the *ruler of the *synagogue
answered with indignation, because
that Jesus had healed on the sabbath
day, and said unto the people, There are
six days in which men ought to work:
in them therefore come and be healed,
and not on the sabbath day.
15 The Lord then answered him, and
said, *Thou* hypocrite, doth not each one
of you on the sabbath loose his ox or *his*
ass from the stall, and lead *him* away to
watering?
16 And ought not this woman, being a

13:6 a fig tree planted. The fig tree stands for Israel or the Jewish nation. Jesus had been with them for three years, teaching them the way of life, but the nation was like a barren tree, bearing no fruit for Him.

13:14 There are six days. The ruler of the synagogue quoted from the Ten Commandments. See Exodus 20:9. The ruler was indignant that Jesus healed on the Sabbath, but Jesus rebuked him for his lack of mercy and compassion in verses 15-16. Christ did this in such a way that "all his adversaries were ashamed," rightly so, while other people rejoiced in the "glorious things" Jesus was doing (vs. 17).

daughter of *Abraham, whom Satan hath
bound, lo, these eighteen years, be loosed
from this bond on the sabbath day?
17 And when he had said these things,
all his adversaries were ashamed: and
all the people rejoiced for all the glorious things that were done by him.

A parable: the mustard seed
(Matt. 13:31-32; Mark 4:30-32)

¶18 Then said he, Unto what is the
kingdom of God like? and whereunto
shall I resemble it?
19 It is like a grain of mustard seed,
which a man took, and cast into his garden; and it grew, and waxed a great tree;
and the fowls of the air lodged in the
branches of it.

A parable: leaven
(Matt. 13:33)

20 And again he said, Whereunto shall
I liken the kingdom of God?
21 It is like leaven, which a woman
took and hid in three measures of meal,
till the whole was *leavened.

The Lord journeys toward Jerusalem

¶22 And he went through the cities and
villages, teaching, and journeying toward Jerusalem.
23 Then said one unto him, Lord, are
there few that be saved? And he said
unto them,

The strait gate

¶24 Strive to enter in at the strait gate:
for many, I say unto you, will seek to
enter in, and shall not be able.
25 When once the master of the house
is risen up, and hath shut to the door,
and ye begin to stand without, and to
knock at the door, saying, Lord, Lord,

13:26-27 The Need to Believe
Dwelling with the people of God or having Christian friends does not save anyone. Simply listening to the words of the Lord without believing them to the point of salvation does not save anyone. Judas Iscariot had done all these things, yet he had never really known or believed in Jesus as his Saviour.

open unto us; and he shall answer and
say unto you, I know you not whence
ye are:
26 Then shall ye begin to say, We have
eaten and drunk in thy presence, and
thou hast taught in our streets.
27 But he shall say, I tell you, I know
you not whence ye are; depart from me,
all ye workers of iniquity.
28 There shall be weeping and gnashing of teeth, when ye shall see Abraham, and *Isaac, and *Jacob, and all the
prophets, in the kingdom of God, and
you *yourselves* thrust out.
29 And they shall come from the east,
and *from* the west, and from the north,
and *from* the south, and shall sit down
in the kingdom of God.
30 And, behold, there are last which
shall be first, and there are first which
shall be last.

The Pharisees warn of Herod's plans

¶31 The same day there came certain
of the Pharisees, saying unto him, Get
thee out, and depart hence: for Herod
will kill thee.
32 And he said unto them, Go ye, and
tell that fox, Behold, I cast out devils,
and I do cures to day and to morrow, and
the third *day* I shall be *perfected.
33 Nevertheless I must walk to day,
and to morrow, and the *day* following:

13:23 are there few that be saved? God is not willing to have anyone perish (see Rom. 11:32; 1 Tim. 2:3-4; 2 Pet. 3:9). But we cannot drift into salvation just because our parents or relatives are saved, for instance (compare Luke 13:24).
13:24 the strait gate. Narrow. This is the door of the Lord's mercy, which is still open. He is the Door and the Way (John 10:9; 14:6).
13:32 I shall be perfected. Jesus was saying, "I shall have finished the work that I came to do."
13:33 I must walk to day. Jesus had to go through Herod's country to Jerusalem.

for it cannot be that a *prophet perish
out of Jerusalem.

Lament over Jerusalem

34 O Jerusalem, Jerusalem, which
killest the prophets, and stonest them
that are sent unto thee; how often
would I have gathered thy children together, as a hen *doth gather* her brood
under *her* wings, and ye would not!
35 Behold, your house is left unto you
desolate: and verily I say unto you, Ye
shall not see me, until *the time* come
when ye shall say, Blessed *is* he that
cometh in the name of the Lord.

The Lord heals a man on the Sabbath

14 And it came to pass, as he
went into the house of one of
the chief Pharisees to eat bread on the
sabbath day, that they watched him.
2 And, behold, there was a certain
man before him which had the dropsy.
3 And Jesus answering spake unto the
lawyers and Pharisees, saying, Is it lawful to heal on the sabbath day?
4 And they held their peace. And he
took *him,* and healed him, and let him go;
5 And answered them, saying, Which
of you shall have an ass or an ox fallen
into a pit, and will not straightway pull
him out on the sabbath day?
6 And they could not answer him
again to these things.

A parable: the best choices

¶ 7 And he put forth a parable to those
which were bidden, when he marked
how they chose out the chief rooms;
saying unto them,
8 When thou art bidden of any *man* to
a wedding, sit not down in the highest
room; lest a more honourable man than
thou be bidden of him;
9 And he that bade thee and him come
and say to thee, Give this man place;
and thou begin with shame to take the
lowest room.
10 But when thou art bidden, go and
sit down in the lowest room; that when
he that bade thee cometh, he may say
unto thee, Friend, go up higher: then
shalt thou have worship in the presence
of them that sit at meat with thee.
11 For whosoever exalteth himself
shall be abased; and he that humbleth
himself shall be exalted.
¶ 12 Then said he also to him that bade
him, When thou makest a dinner or a
supper, call not thy friends, nor thy
brethren, neither thy kinsmen, nor *thy*
rich neighbours; lest they also bid thee
again, and a recompence be made thee.
13 But when thou makest a feast, call
the poor, the maimed, the lame, the
blind:
14 And thou shalt be blessed; for they
cannot recompense thee: for thou shalt
be recompensed at the *resurrection of
the *just.
¶ 15 And when one of them that sat at
meat with him heard these things, he
said unto him, Blessed *is* he that shall
eat bread in the kingdom of God.

A parable: the great supper
(See Matt. 22:1-14)

16 Then said he unto him, A certain
man made a great supper, and bade
many:

13:35 your house. The temple at Jerusalem.
13:35 until the time come. This time has not yet come. The Lord quoted Psalm 118:26. See Mark 11:9 note, "Hosanna."
14:7 chief rooms. That is, the best seats (compare vss. 8-9).
14:10 shalt thou have worship. You shall be honored.
14:12 call not thy friends. This does not mean that we are never to eat with friends. The Lord was simply forbidding invitations that are given for selfish purposes only.
14:14 resurrection of the just. The resurrection of the just is the first resurrection (see John 5:28-29; Rev. 20:6; see also Rev. 20:5-6 note, "The First Resurrection").
14:15 Blessed is he that shall eat. This was a pious interruption that our Lord used as a text to continue His instructions (vss. 16-24).

17 And sent his servant at supper time
to say to them that were bidden, Come;
for all things are now ready.
18 And they all with one *consent* began
to make excuse. The first said unto him,
I have bought a piece of ground, and I
must needs go and see it: I pray thee
have me excused.
19 And another said, I have bought five
yoke of oxen, and I go to *prove them:
I pray thee have me excused.
20 And another said, I have married a
wife, and therefore I cannot come.
21 So that servant came, and shewed
his lord these things. Then the master
of the house being angry said to his
servant, Go out quickly into the streets
and lanes of the city, and bring in hither
the poor, and the maimed, and the halt,
and the blind.
22 And the servant said, Lord, it is
done as thou hast commanded, and yet
there is room.
23 And the lord said unto the servant,
Go out into the highways and hedges,
and compel *them* to come in, that my
house may be filled.
24 For I say unto you, That none of
those men which were bidden shall
taste of my supper.

Another test for disciples
(See Matt. 10:37-39)

¶25 And there went great multitudes
with him: and he turned, and said unto
them,
26 If any *man* come to me, and hate
not his father, and mother, and wife, and
children, and brethren, and sisters, yea,
and his own life also, he cannot be my
disciple.
27 And whosoever doth not bear his
cross, and come after me, cannot be my
disciple.
28 For which of you, intending to build
a tower, sitteth not down first, and
counteth the cost, whether he have
sufficient to finish *it?*
29 Lest haply, after he hath laid the
foundation, and is not able to finish *it,*
all that behold *it* begin to mock him,
30 Saying, This man began to build,
and was not able to finish.
31 Or what king, going to make war
against another king, sitteth not down
first, and consulteth whether he be able with
ten thousand to meet him that cometh
against him with twenty thousand?
32 Or else, while the other is yet a
great way off, he sendeth an ambassage,
and desireth conditions of peace.
33 So likewise, whosoever he be of
you that forsaketh not all that he hath,
he cannot be my disciple.

A parable: salt
(See Matt. 5:13; Mark 9:50)

¶34 Salt *is* good: but if the salt have
lost his savour, wherewith shall it be
seasoned?
35 It is neither fit for the land, nor yet
for the dunghill; *but* men cast it out. He
that hath ears to hear, let him hear.

Jesus receives sinners

15 Then drew near unto him all
the *publicans and sinners for
to hear him.

14:18 began to make excuse. Note that the excuses were possessions (vs. 18), business (vs. 19), and pleasures (vs. 20).
14:23 compel them to come in. Outsiders were strongly urged to come to the feast that had not been originally prepared for them. See what Paul said in Acts 13:46 and 28:28.
14:26 If any . . . hate not. This does not mean to hate as we usually use the word. It means that we must not put love of anything or anyone before our love of God. To obey and please Him is our first duty as Christians.
14:27 bear his cross, and come after me. See Mark 8:34 note.
14:30 This man began to build. The parable of verses 16-24 invites men to come to the Lord. This parable (vss. 28-30) and the one that follows (vss. 31-33) invite them to count the cost and to continue as His disciples, to build upon the foundation that He has laid.

2 And the Pharisees and scribes murmured, saying, This man receiveth
sinners, and eateth with them.

A parable: the lost sheep
(See Matt. 18:12-14)

¶3 And he spake this parable unto
them, saying,
4 What man of you, having an hundred
sheep, if he lose one of them, doth not
leave the ninety and nine in the wilderness, and go after that which is lost,
until he find it?
5 And when he hath found *it,* he layeth
it on his shoulders, rejoicing.
6 And when he cometh home, he
calleth together *his* friends and neighbours, saying unto them, Rejoice with
me; for I have found my sheep which
was lost.
7 I say unto you, that likewise joy shall
be in *heaven over one sinner that repenteth, more than over ninety and
nine just persons, which need no *repentance.

A parable: the lost silver

¶8 Either what woman having ten
pieces of silver, if she lose one piece,
doth not light a candle, and sweep
the house, and seek diligently till she
find *it?*
9 And when she hath found *it,* she
calleth *her* friends and *her* neighbours
together, saying, Rejoice with me; for I
have found the piece which I had lost.
10 Likewise, I say unto you, there is
joy in the presence of the *angels of
God over one sinner that repenteth.

A parable: the prodigal son

¶11 And he said, A certain man had
two sons:
12 And the younger of them said to *his*
father, Father, give me the portion of
goods that falleth *to me.* And he divided unto them *his* living.
13 And not many days after the younger son gathered all together, and took
his journey into a far country, and there
wasted his substance with riotous
living.
14 And when he had spent all, there
arose a mighty famine in that land; and
he began to be in want.
15 And he went and joined himself to
a citizen of that country; and he sent
him into his fields to feed swine.
16 And he would fain have filled his
belly with the husks that the swine did
eat: and no man gave unto him.
17 And when he came to himself, he
said, How many hired servants of my
father's have bread enough and to
spare, and I perish with hunger!
18 I will arise and go to my father, and
will say unto him, Father, I have sinned
against heaven, and before thee,
19 And am no more worthy to be
called thy son: make me as one of thy
hired servants.
20 And he arose, and came to his father. But when he was yet a great way
off, his father saw him, and had compassion, and ran, and fell on his neck, and
kissed him.
21 And the son said unto him, Father,
I have sinned against heaven, and in thy
sight, and am no more worthy to be
called thy son.
22 But the father said to his servants,
Bring forth the best robe, and put *it* on
him; and put a ring on his hand, and
shoes on *his* feet:
23 And bring hither the fatted calf, and
kill *it;* and let us eat, and be merry:
24 For this my son was dead, and is
alive again; he was lost, and is found.
And they began to be merry.
25 Now his elder son was in the field:
and as he came and drew nigh to the
house, he heard musick and dancing.
26 And he called one of the servants,
and asked what these things meant.
27 And he said unto him, Thy brother
is come; and thy father hath killed the

15:15 to feed swine. Of all the occupations that a Jewish boy might be asked to do, feeding swine was probably the lowest and most despised.

fatted calf, because he hath received
him safe and sound.
28 And he was angry, and would not go
in: therefore came his father out, and
intreated him.
29 And he answering said to *his* father,
Lo, these many years do I serve thee,
neither transgressed I at any time thy
commandment: and yet thou never
gavest me a kid, that I might make
merry with my friends:
30 But as soon as this thy son was
come, which hath devoured thy living
with harlots, thou hast killed for him
the fatted calf.
31 And he said unto him, Son, thou art
ever with me, and all that I have is thine.
32 It was meet that we should make
merry, and be glad: for this thy brother
was dead, and is alive again; and was
lost, and is found.

A parable: the rich man and his steward

16 And he said also unto his disciples, There was a certain rich
man, which had a steward; and the same
was accused unto him that he had wasted his goods.
2 And he called him, and said unto
him, How is it that I hear this of thee?
give an account of thy stewardship; for
thou mayest be no longer steward.
3 Then the steward said within himself, What shall I do? for my lord taketh
away from me the stewardship: I cannot dig; to beg I am ashamed.
4 I am resolved what to do, that, when
I am put out of the stewardship, they
may receive me into their houses.
5 So he called every one of his lord's
debtors *unto him,* and said unto the
first, How much owest thou unto my
lord?
6 And he said, An hundred measures
of oil. And he said unto him, Take thy bill,
and sit down quickly, and write fifty.
7 Then said he to another, And how
much owest thou? And he said, An hundred measures of wheat. And he said
unto him, Take thy bill, and write fourscore.
8 And the lord commended the unjust
steward, because he had done wisely:
for the children of this *world are in
their generation wiser than the children
of light.
9 And I say unto you, Make to yourselves friends of the mammon of unrighteousness; that, when ye fail, they
may receive you into everlasting habitations.
10 He that is faithful in that which is
least is faithful also in much: and he that
is unjust in the least is unjust also in
much.
11 If therefore ye have not been faithful
in the unrighteous mammon, who will
commit to your *trust the true *riches?*
12 And if ye have not been faithful in
that which is another man's, who shall
give you that which is your own?
13 No servant can serve two masters:
for either he will hate the one, and love
the other; or else he will hold to the
one, and despise the other. Ye cannot
serve God and mammon.

The Lord rebukes the Pharisees

¶14 And the Pharisees also, who were
covetous, heard all these things: and
they derided him.
15 And he said unto them, Ye are they
which justify yourselves before men;
but God knoweth your hearts: for that
which is highly esteemed among men
is *abomination in the sight of God.

16:8 done wisely. The steward had done a right thing in a wrong way. He had shrewdly provided for his future life, which was right; but in doing so he robbed his master, which, of course, was wrong.

16:8 in their generation. In the sphere in which the "children of this world" moved, or among their worldly friends who would act in the same manner.

16:9 friends of the mammon of unrighteousness. God's own people may use earthly means to make eternal friends. "Mammon," money—or riches of any kind—may be used to do great good for God's kingdom.

[16] The *law and the *prophets *were*
until John: since that time the *kingdom of God is preached, and every man
presseth into it.
[17] And it is easier for heaven and
earth to pass, than one tittle of the law
to fail.

The Lord's teaching about divorce
(See Matt. 5:31-32; 19:3-11;
Mark 10:2-12; 1 Cor. 7:10-15)

¶[18] Whosoever putteth away his wife,
and marrieth another, committeth adultery: and whosoever marrieth her that
is put away from *her* husband committeth adultery.

The rich man and Lazarus

¶[19] There was a certain rich man,
which was clothed in purple and fine
*linen, and fared sumptuously every day:
[20] And there was a certain beggar
named Lazarus, which was laid at his
gate, full of sores,
[21] And desiring to be fed with the
crumbs which fell from the rich man's
table: moreover the dogs came and
licked his sores.
[22] And it came to pass, that the beggar died, and was carried by the angels
into Abraham's bosom: the rich man
also died, and was buried;
[23] And in *hell he lift up his eyes, being in torments, and seeth Abraham
afar off, and Lazarus in his bosom.
[24] And he cried and said, Father Abraham, have *mercy on me, and send
Lazarus, that he may dip the tip of his
finger in water, and cool my tongue; for
I am tormented in this flame.
[25] But Abraham said, Son, remember
that thou in thy lifetime receivedst thy
good things, and likewise Lazarus evil
things: but now he is comforted, and
thou art tormented.
[26] And beside all this, between us and
you there is a great gulf fixed: so that
they which would pass from hence to
you cannot; neither can they pass to us,
that *would come* from thence.
[27] Then he said, I pray thee therefore,
father, that thou wouldest send him to
my father's house:
[28] For I have five brethren; that he
may testify unto them, lest they also
come into this place of torment.
[29] Abraham saith unto him, They have
*Moses and the prophets; let them hear
them.
[30] And he said, Nay, father Abraham:
but if one went unto them from the
dead, they will repent.
[31] And he said unto him, If they hear
not Moses and the prophets, neither
will they be persuaded, though one rose
from the dead.

A warning

17 Then said he unto the disciples,
It is impossible but that offences will come: but woe *unto him,*
through whom they come!

16:23 THE PLACE CALLED HELL

Hell refers to *Hades,* which is the New Testament word corresponding to the Old Testament word *Sheol* (see Hab. 2:5 note). It is separated from paradise by an impassable gulf (vs. 26). In 2 Peter 2:4, the word "hell" speaks of a place where rebels against God are chained until the *Day of Judgment comes. It is the deep abyss or bottomless pit (Luke 8:31; Rev. 9:11). Hell, or Hades, is the place of judgment (Matt. 11:23; 16:18). Jesus Christ has its keys, and at the *Second Coming it will be cast into the lake of fire, the second death (Rev. 1:18; 20:13-14). The Lord warned men of the awful certainty of hell, and He Himself provided the means of escape from it when He took the sins of mankind and their punishment upon Himself on the cross of Calvary. Notice that hell is a real place of torment. People will still be able to think and feel there, as they will be able to do throughout eternity.

16:22 Abraham's bosom. This is referring to *paradise.
17:1 offences. Evil words or deeds that cause others to sin.

[2]It were better for him that a millstone were hanged about his neck,
and he cast into the sea, than that he
should *offend one of these little ones.

Forgiveness and faith
(See Matt. 18:15-35)

¶[3]Take heed to yourselves: If thy
brother *trespass against thee, rebuke
him; and if he repent, forgive him.
[4]And if he trespass against thee
seven times in a day, and seven times
in a day turn again to thee, saying, I
repent; thou shalt forgive him.
[5]And the *apostles said unto the
Lord, Increase our faith.
[6]And the Lord said, If ye had faith as
a grain of mustard seed, ye might say
unto this sycamine tree, Be thou plucked
up by the root, and be thou planted in
the sea; and it should obey you.

A servant's duty

¶[7]But which of you, having a servant
plowing or feeding cattle, will say unto
him by and by, when he is come from
the field, Go and sit down to meat?
[8]And will not rather say unto him,
Make ready wherewith I may sup, and
gird thyself, and serve me, till I have
eaten and drunken; and afterward thou
shalt eat and drink?
[9]Doth he thank that servant because
he did the things that were commanded him? I trow not.
[10]So likewise ye, when ye shall have
done all those things which are commanded you, say, We are unprofitable
servants: we have done that which was
our duty to do.

Ten lepers healed

¶[11]And it came to pass, as he went
to *Jerusalem, that he passed through
the midst of *Samaria and Galilee.
[12]And as he entered into a certain
village, there met him ten men that
were *lepers, which stood afar off:
[13]And they lifted up *their* voices, and
said, Jesus, Master, have mercy on us.
[14]And when he saw *them,* he said
unto them, Go shew yourselves unto
the priests. And it came to pass, that,
as they went, they were cleansed.
[15]And one of them, when he saw that
he was healed, turned back, and with a
loud voice glorified God,
[16]And fell down on *his* face at his feet,
giving him thanks: and he was a Samaritan.
[17]And Jesus answering said, Were
there not ten cleansed? but where *are*
the nine?
[18]There are not found that returned
to give glory to God, save this stranger.
[19]And he said unto him, Arise, go thy
way: thy faith hath made thee whole.

The Lord's coming to judge
(See Luke 19:11-12; Deut. 30:3)

¶[20]And when he was demanded of
the *Pharisees, when the kingdom of
God should come, he answered them
and said, The kingdom of God cometh
not with observation:
[21]Neither shall they say, Lo here! or,
lo there! for, behold, the kingdom of
God is within you.
¶[22]And he said unto the disciples,
The days will come, when ye shall desire to see one of the days of the Son of
man, and ye shall not see *it.*
[23]And they shall say to you, See here;
or, see there: go not after *them,* nor follow *them.*
[24]For as the lightning, that lighteneth
out of the one *part* under heaven,
shineth unto the other *part* under heav-

17:3 trespass. Sin.
17:14 shew yourselves unto the priests. According to the Law (Lev. 14), if a leper thought himself to be healed, he must show himself to the priest, who examined his flesh to see if the disease was still there. These men showed their faith by going to the priest at the command of Christ before they were healed. While they were in the act of obeying (on their way to the priest), they were healed.
17:21 within you. This means *in the midst.* Jesus Christ Himself is the King.

en; so shall also the Son of man be in
his day.
25 But first must he suffer many
things, and be rejected of this generation.
26 And as it was in the days of Noe, so
shall it be also in the days of the Son of
man.
27 They did eat, they drank, they married wives, they were given in marriage, until the day that Noe entered
into the *ark, and the flood came, and
destroyed them all.
28 Likewise also as it was in the days
of *Lot; they did eat, they drank, they
bought, they sold, they planted, they
builded;
29 But the same day that Lot went out
of Sodom it rained *fire and brimstone
from heaven, and destroyed *them* all.
30 Even thus shall it be in the day
when the Son of man is revealed.
31 In that day, he which shall be upon
the housetop, and his stuff in the house,
let him not come down to take it away:
and he that is in the field, let him likewise not return back.
32 Remember Lot's wife.
33 Whosoever shall seek to save his
life shall lose it; and whosoever shall
lose his life shall preserve it.
34 I tell you, in that night there shall
be two *men* in one bed; the one shall be
taken, and the other shall be left.
35 Two *women* shall be grinding together; the one shall be taken, and the
other left.
36 Two *men* shall be in the field; the
one shall be taken, and the other left.
37 **And they answered and said unto**
him, Where, Lord? And he said unto
them, Wheresoever the body *is*, thither
will the eagles be gathered together.

17:31 A Time of Judgment
A time is coming that is often spoken of as "that day," in the Old Testament as well as in the New, as "his day" (vs. 24), and as "the days of the Son of man" (vs. 26; compare vs. 30). The verses of this section clearly indicate that this will be a time of judgment. It will come with sudden unexpectedness (vs. 24); as in the days of Noah and the days of Lot (vss. 26,28) men will be overtaken with calamity without previous warning, as they are working or playing. Some will be delivered, as were Noah and Lot in their days (vs. 31), because it will be a time of separation (vss. 34-36). Many incorrectly believe that verses 34-36 refer to the *Rapture, since it describes one being taken and his or her companion being left behind.

A parable: the widow and the judge

18 And he spake a *parable unto
them *to this end,* that men ought
always to pray, and not to faint;
2 **Saying,** There was in a city a judge,
which feared not God, neither regarded man:
3 And there was a widow in that city;
and she came unto him, saying, Avenge
me of mine adversary.
4 And he would not for a while: but
afterward he said within himself,
Though I *fear not God, nor regard man;

17:26 in the days of Noe. Noah. See Genesis 6.
17:27 the flood came. See Genesis 7:11-12.
17:28 in the days of Lot. See Genesis 19.
17:32 Remember Lot's wife. See Genesis 19:26. She had her heart fixed on the evil city, Sodom, and was therefore destroyed with the city she loved more than God.
17:37 Wheresoever the body is. Wherever things are ready for judgment, there the judgment will fall. See also Revelation 19:17-19.
18:1 always to pray. Christ urged His people to pray or to be in an attitude of prayer on all occasions and in all circumstances.
18:1 not to faint. Not to lose heart or courage. Don't give up even if the Lord delays His answer.
18:3 came unto him. The widow kept coming to the judge until he answered her request.

5 Yet because this widow troubleth
me, I will avenge her, lest by her continual coming she weary me.
6 And the Lord said, Hear what the
unjust judge saith.
7 And shall not God avenge his own
*elect, which cry day and night unto
him, though he bear long with them?
8 I tell you that he will avenge them
speedily. Nevertheless when the Son of
man cometh, shall he find *faith on the
earth?

A parable: the Pharisee and the publican

¶9 And he spake this parable unto certain
which trusted in themselves that they
were righteous, and despised others:
10 Two men went up into the temple
to pray; the one a *Pharisee, and the
other a *publican.
11 The Pharisee stood and prayed thus
with himself, God, I thank thee, that I
am not as other men *are,* extortioners,
unjust, adulterers, or even as this
publican.
12 I fast twice in the week, I give *tithes
of all that I possess.
13 And the publican, standing afar off,
would not lift up so much as *his* eyes
unto heaven, but smote upon his breast,
saying, God be merciful to me a sinner.
14 I tell you, this man went down to
his house justified *rather* than the other:
for every one that exalteth himself shall
be abased; and he that humbleth himself shall be exalted.

The Lord blesses children
(Matt. 19:13-15; Mark 10:13-16)

¶15 And they brought unto him also
infants, that he would touch them: but
when *his* disciples saw *it,* they rebuked
them.
16 But Jesus called them *unto him,* and
said, Suffer little children to come unto
me, and forbid them not: for of such is
the kingdom of God.
17 Verily I say unto you, Whosoever
shall not receive the kingdom of God as
a little *child shall in no wise enter
therein.

The rich young ruler
(Matt. 19:16-30; Mark 10:17-31)

¶18 And a certain ruler asked him,
saying, *Good Master, what shall I do
to inherit *eternal life?
19 And Jesus said unto him, Why callest thou me good? none *is* good, save
one, *that is,* God.
20 Thou knowest the commandments,
Do not commit adultery, Do not kill,
Do not steal, Do not bear false witness,
Honour thy father and thy mother.
21 And he said, All these have I kept
from my youth up.
22 Now when Jesus heard these
things, he said unto him, Yet lackest
thou one thing: sell all that thou hast,
and distribute unto the poor, and thou
shalt have treasure in heaven: and
come, follow me.
23 And when he heard this, he was
very sorrowful: for he was very rich.
24 And when Jesus saw that he was
very sorrowful, he said, How hardly
shall they that have *riches enter into
the kingdom of God!
25 For it is easier for a camel to go
through a needle's eye, than for a
rich man to enter into the kingdom of
God.

18:7 avenge his own elect. See Revelation 6:10-11. The Lord will give judgment in their favor.
18:8 shall he find faith . . . ? Will He find this unceasing prayer of faith?
18:11 The Pharisee stood and prayed. Notice that he was talking with himself in his self-righteous pride. He was blind to his own sinfulness, and since he asked for nothing, he received nothing.
18:13 be merciful. Be Yourself my *propitiation.
18:13 a sinner. *The* sinner. The publican thought of himself as the only, or the worst sinner, in the world.
18:19 none is good, save one. See Mark 10:18 note.
18:25 a needle's eye. See Mark 10:25 note.

26 And they that heard *it* said, Who
then can be saved?
27 And he said, The things which
are impossible with men are possible
with God.

Reward for sacrifice

28 Then *Peter said, Lo, we have left
all, and followed thee.
29 And he said unto them, Verily I say
unto you, There is no man that hath left
house, or parents, or brethren, or wife, or
children, for the kingdom of God's sake,
30 Who shall not receive manifold
more in this present time, and in the
world to come life everlasting.

Jesus tells the twelve of His death and resurrection (Matt. 20:17-19; Mark 10:32-34)

¶31 Then he took *unto him* the twelve,
and said unto them, Behold, we go up
to Jerusalem, and all things that are
written by the prophets concerning the
Son of man shall be accomplished.
32 For he shall be delivered unto the
*Gentiles, and shall be mocked, and
spitefully entreated, and spitted on:
33 And they shall scourge *him,* and put
him to *death: and the third day he shall
rise again.
34 And they understood none of these
things: and this saying was hid from
them, neither knew they the things
which were spoken.

The blind man healed (See Matt. 20:29-34; Mark 10:46-52)

¶35 And it came to pass, that as he was
come nigh unto Jericho, a certain blind
man sat by the way side begging:
36 And hearing the multitude pass by,
he asked what it meant.
37 And they told him, that Jesus of
Nazareth passeth by.
38 And he cried, saying, Jesus, *thou*
*Son of David, have mercy on me.
39 And they which went before rebuked him, that he should hold his
peace: but he cried so much the more,
Thou Son of David, have mercy on me.
40 And Jesus stood, and commanded
him to be brought unto him: and when
he was come near, he asked him,
41 Saying, What wilt thou that I shall
do unto thee? And he said, Lord, that I
may receive my sight.
42 And Jesus said unto him, Receive
thy sight: thy faith hath saved thee.
43 And immediately he received his
sight, and followed him, glorifying God:
and all the people, when they saw *it,*
gave praise unto God.

Zacchaeus receives the Lord

19 And *Jesus* entered and passed
through Jericho.
2 And, behold, *there was* a man named
Zacchaeus, which was the chief among
the *publicans, and he was rich.
3 And he sought to see Jesus who he
was; and could not for the press, because he was little of stature.
4 And he ran before, and climbed up
into a sycomore tree to see him: for he
was to pass that *way.*
5 And when Jesus came to the place, he
looked up, and saw him, and said unto him,
Zacchaeus, make haste, and come down;
for to day I must abide at thy house.
6 And he made haste, and came down,
and received him joyfully.
7 And when they saw *it,* they all murmured, saying, That he was gone to be
guest with a man that is a sinner.
8 And Zacchaeus stood, and said unto
the Lord; Behold, Lord, the half of my
goods I give to the poor; and if I have
taken any thing from any man by false
accusation, I restore *him* fourfold.

18:30 manifold more. Many times more.
18:30 in the world to come. In the age to come.
19:8 I restore him fourfold. According to the Mosaic Law, five oxen had to be restored for one wrongly taken, and four sheep for one sheep (Exod. 22:1). Zacchaeus, as a tax collector for the Romans, was hated by the Jews, but he observed the Hebrew standard of making things right.

[9]And Jesus said unto him, This day is
*salvation come to this house, forso-
much as he also is a son of *Abraham.
[10]For the Son of man is come to seek
and to save that which was lost.

A parable: the ten pounds

¶[11]And as they heard these things, he
added and spake a parable, because he
was nigh to Jerusalem, and because
they thought that the kingdom of *God
should immediately appear.
[12]He said therefore, A certain nobleman went into a far country to receive
for himself a kingdom, and to return.

19:12 The Nobleman
Those who heard this story understood at least something of its meaning, for it was customary in those days for princes or noblemen to go to Rome to receive kingdoms from Caesar. They would then return to govern their kingdoms. Archelaus, the son of Herod, had done this. So the Lord pictured Himself as going to the far country, heaven, from where He will return.

[13]And he called his ten servants, and
delivered them ten pounds, and said
unto them, Occupy till I come.
[14]But his citizens hated him, and sent
a message after him, saying, We will not
have this *man* to reign over us.
[15]And it came to pass, that when he
was returned, having received the kingdom, then he commanded these servants to be called unto him, to whom he
had given the money, that he might
know how much every man had gained
by trading.
[16]Then came the first, saying, Lord,
thy pound hath gained ten pounds.
[17]And he said unto him, Well, thou
good servant: because thou hast been
faithful in a very little, have thou authority over ten cities.
[18]And the second came, saying, Lord,
thy pound hath gained five pounds.
[19]And he said likewise to him, Be
thou also over five cities.
[20]And another came, saying, Lord,
behold, *here is* thy pound, which I have
kept laid up in a napkin:
[21]For I feared thee, because thou art
an austere man: thou takest up that
thou layedst not down, and reapest that
thou didst not sow.
[22]And he saith unto him, Out of thine
own mouth will I judge thee, *thou* wicked servant. Thou knewest that I was
an austere man, taking up that I laid
not down, and reaping that I did not
sow:
[23]Wherefore then gavest not thou my
money into the bank, that at my coming I might have required mine own
with *usury?
[24]And he said unto them that stood
by, Take from him the pound, and give
it to him that hath ten pounds.
[25](And they said unto him, Lord, he
hath ten pounds.)
[26]For I say unto you, That unto every
one which hath shall be given; and from
him that hath not, even that he hath
shall be taken away from him.
[27]But those mine enemies, which
would not that I should reign over them,
bring hither, and slay *them* before me.

19:13 ten pounds. Ten pounds or minas was the amount someone earned in about thirty months.
19:13 Occupy till I come. Care faithfully for and do business with my possessions.
19:22 Out of thine own mouth. The servant lied to his master (vs. 21), and his words were used against him. It was as if the nobleman said, "You say that I am a hard and exacting master; therefore it will be to you as you say." Note that at the appearing of our Master every servant will share in His power in proportion to his activity for the Master while He was gone.
19:23 my money into the bank. The foolish servant didn't even put his master's money in the bank so it could at least gain interest. There are some Christians who cannot do active work for the Master. To them the Lord will say, "You could have prayed; you could have put the work into the hands of someone who could have supplied the need and cared for the work."

VI. The End of Christ's Public Ministry (19:28—21:38)—Hailed as king

¶[28]And when he had thus spoken, he
went before, ascending up to Jerusalem.
[29]And it came to pass, when he was
come nigh to *Bethphage and Bethany,
at the mount called *the *mount* of
Olives, he sent two of his disciples,
[30]Saying, Go ye into the village over
against *you;* in the which at your entering
ye shall find a colt tied, whereon yet never
man sat: loose him, and bring *him hither.*
[31] And if any man ask you, Why do ye
loose *him?* thus shall ye say unto him,
Because the Lord hath need of him.
[32]And they that were sent went their
way, and found even as he had said unto
them.
[33]And as they were loosing the colt,
the owners thereof said unto them,
Why loose ye the colt?
[34]And they said, The Lord hath need
of him.
[35]And they brought him to Jesus: and
they cast their garments upon the colt,
and they set Jesus thereon.
[36]And as he went, they spread their
clothes in the way.
[37]And when he was come nigh, even
now at the descent of the mount of Olives, the whole multitude of the disciples began to rejoice and praise God
with a loud voice for all the mighty
works that they had seen;
[38]Saying, Blessed *be* the King that
cometh in the name of the Lord: peace
in heaven, and glory in the highest.
[39]And some of the Pharisees from
among the multitude said unto him,
Master, rebuke thy disciples.
[40]And he answered and said unto
them, I tell you that, if these should
hold their peace, the stones would immediately cry out.

Sinning Jerusalem

¶[41]And when he was come near, he
beheld the city, and wept over it,
[42]Saying, If thou hadst known, even
thou, at least in this thy day, the things
which belong unto thy peace! but now
they are hid from thine eyes.
[43] For the days shall come upon thee,
that thine enemies shall cast a trench
about thee, and compass thee round,
and keep thee in on every side,
[44] And shall lay thee even with the
ground, and thy children within thee;
and they shall not leave in thee one
stone upon another; because thou
knewest not the time of thy visitation.
¶[45]And he went into the temple, and
began to cast out them that sold
therein, and them that bought;
[46]Saying unto them, It is written, My
house is the house of *prayer: but ye
have made it a *den of thieves.
[47]And he taught daily in the temple.
But the chief priests and the *scribes
and the chief of the people sought to
destroy him,
[48]And could not find what they might
do: for all the people were very attentive to hear him.

The Lord's enemies question Him (Matt. 21:23-27; Mark 11:27-33)

20 And it came to pass, *that* on
one of those days, as he taught
the people in the temple, and preached

19:38 Blessed be the King. See Mark 11:9 note, "Hosanna."
19:38 peace in heaven, and glory. See the words of the angels when the Lord Jesus Christ was born (Luke 2:14).
19:41-42 wept over it, Saying. As Man, Christ wept over the city that would not be saved (see John 1:11; Luke 13:34-35); as God, He spoke to it and warned of judgment to come.
19:42 now they are hid. When men know the truth and refuse it, righteous judgment blinds them and they perish (vss. 43-44).
19:43 thine enemies. Rome. This prophecy was fulfilled in A.D. 70.
19:44 the time of thy visitation. Christ had visited them in grace. Because of the Jews' refusal to have Him, God will visit them in wrath.
19:46 house of prayer. See Isaiah 56:7.

the *gospel, the chief priests and the
scribes came upon *him* with the *elders,
2And spake unto him, saying, Tell us,
by what authority doest thou these
things? or who is he that gave thee this
authority?
3And he answered and said unto
them, I will also ask you one thing; and
answer me:
4The baptism of John, was it from
heaven, or of men?
5And they reasoned with themselves,
saying, If we shall say, From heaven; he
will say, Why then believed ye him not?
6But and if we say, Of men; all the
people will stone us: for they be persuaded that John was a *prophet.
7And they answered, that they could
not tell whence *it was.*
8And Jesus said unto them, Neither
tell I you by what authority I do these
things.

A parable: the wicked husbandmen
(Matt. 21:33-46; Mark 12:1-12)

¶9Then began he to speak to the people this parable; A certain man planted
a vineyard, and let it forth to *husbandmen, and went into a far country for a
long time.
10And at the season he sent a servant
to the husbandmen, that they should
give him of the fruit of the vineyard: but
the husbandmen beat him, and sent *him*
away empty.
11And again he sent another servant:
and they beat him also, and entreated
him shamefully, and sent *him* away
empty.
12And again he sent a third: and they
wounded him also, and cast *him* out.
13Then said the lord of the vineyard,
What shall I do? I will send my beloved
son: it may be they will reverence *him*
when they see him.

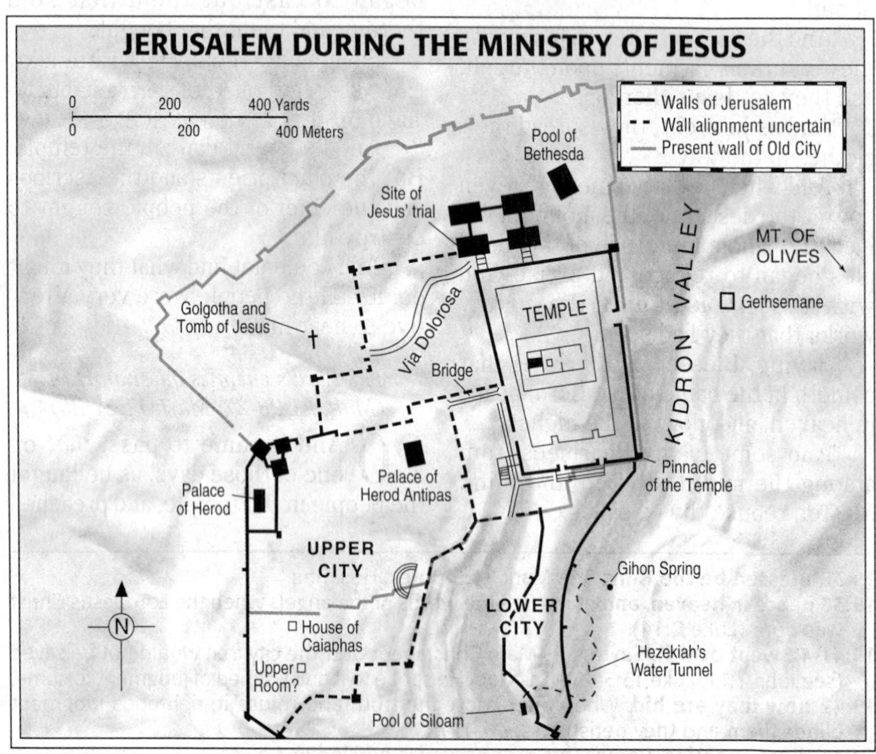

20:4 The baptism of John. John the Baptist (see Luke 3:1-18).
20:13 I will send my beloved son. See Mark 12:6 note.

14But when the husbandmen saw
him, they reasoned among themselves,
saying, This is the heir: come, let us kill
him, that the inheritance may be ours.
15So they cast him out of the vineyard, and killed *him.* What therefore
shall the lord of the vineyard do unto
them?
16He shall come and destroy these
husbandmen, and shall give the vineyard to others. And when they heard *it,*
they said, God forbid.
17And he beheld them, and said, What
is this then that is written, The stone
which the builders rejected, the same
is become the head of the corner?
18Whosoever shall fall upon that
stone shall be broken; but on whomsoever it shall fall, it will grind him to
powder.

Jesus questioned about tribute money
(Matt. 22:15-22; Mark 12:13-17)

¶19And the chief priests and the
scribes the same hour sought to lay
hands on him; and they feared the people: for they perceived that he had spoken this parable against them.
20And they watched *him,* and sent
forth spies, which should feign themselves *just men, that they might take
hold of his words, that so they might
deliver him unto the power and authority of the governor.
21And they asked him, saying, Master, we know that thou sayest and
teachest rightly, neither acceptest thou
the person *of any,* but teachest the way
of God truly:
22Is it lawful for us to give tribute
unto *Caesar, or no?
23But he perceived their craftiness,
and said unto them, Why *tempt ye me?
24Shew me a *penny. Whose *image
and superscription hath it? They answered and said, Caesar's.
25And he said unto them, *Render
therefore unto Caesar the things which
be Caesar's, and unto God the things
which be God's.
26And they could not take hold of his
words before the people: and they marvelled at his answer, and held their
*peace.

Jesus questioned about the resurrection
(Matt. 22:23-33; Mark 12:18-27)

¶27Then came to *him* certain of the
*Sadducees, which deny that there is
any *resurrection; and they asked him,
28Saying, Master, Moses wrote unto
us, If any man's brother die, having a
wife, and he die without children, that
his brother should take his wife, and
raise up seed unto his brother.
29There were therefore seven brethren: and the first took a wife, and died
without children.
30And the second took her to wife,
and he died childless.
31And the third took her; and in like
manner the seven also: and they left no
children, and died.
32Last of all the woman died also.
33Therefore in the resurrection
whose wife of them is she? for seven
had her to wife.
34And Jesus answering said unto
them, The children of this world marry,
and are given in marriage:
35But they which shall be accounted
worthy to obtain that world, and the
resurrection from the dead, neither
marry, nor are given in marriage:
36Neither can they die any more: for
they are equal unto the angels; and are
the children of God, being the children
of the resurrection.

20:17 The stone which the builders rejected. See Psalm 118:22-23.
20:25 unto Caesar . . . unto God. See Mark 12:17 notes.
20:28 Moses wrote unto us. See Deuteronomy 25:5-6.
20:35 accounted worthy to obtain that world. The Lord Jesus was now talking of heavenly relationships, because those relationships that have to do with our earthly bodies will not exist when we have our resurrection bodies (see 1 Cor. 15:35-58; see also vss. 35,42 notes and 15:52 note, "A Final Resurrection").

37Now that the dead are raised, even
Moses shewed at the bush, when he
calleth the Lord the God of Abraham, and
the God of *Isaac, and the God of *Jacob.
38For he is not a God of the dead, but
of the living: for all live unto him.

The scribes questioned and condemned (Matt. 22:41-46; Mark 12:35-40)

¶39Then certain of the scribes answering said, Master, thou hast well
said.
40And after that they durst not ask
him any *question at all.*
41And he said unto them, How say
they that *Christ is David's son?
42And David himself saith in the book
of Psalms, The LORD said unto my
Lord, Sit thou on my right hand,
43Till I make thine enemies thy footstool.
44David therefore calleth him Lord,
how is he then his son?
¶45Then in the audience of all the
people he said unto his disciples,
46Beware of the scribes, which desire
to walk in long robes, and love greetings in the markets, and the highest
seats in the *synagogues, and the chief
rooms at *feasts;
47Which devour widows' houses, and
for a shew make long prayers: the same
shall receive greater *damnation.

The widow's two mites (Mark 12:41-44)

21 And he looked up, and saw the
rich men casting their gifts into
the *treasury.
2And he saw also a certain poor widow casting in thither two mites.
3And he said, Of a truth I say unto
you, that this poor widow hath cast in
more than they all:
4For all these have of their abundance
cast in unto the *offerings of God: but
she of her penury hath cast in all the
living that she had.

Signs of the end times (See Matt. 24; 25; Mark 13)

¶5And as some spake of the temple,
how it was adorned with goodly stones
and gifts, he said,
6*As for* these things which ye behold,
the days will come, in the which there
shall not be left one stone upon another,
that shall not be thrown down.
7And they asked him, saying, Master,
but when shall these things be? and
what sign *will there be* when these
things shall come to pass?
8And he said, Take heed that ye be
not deceived: for many shall come in
my name, saying, I am *Christ;* and the
time draweth near: go ye not therefore
after them.
9But when ye shall hear of wars and
commotions, be not terrified: for these
things must first come to pass; but the
end *is* not by and by.
10Then said he unto them, Nation
shall rise against nation, and kingdom
against kingdom:
11And great earthquakes shall be in
divers places, and famines, and pestilences; and fearful sights and great
signs shall there be from *heaven.
12But before all these, they shall lay
their hands on you, and persecute
you, delivering *you* up to the synagogues, and into prisons, being brought
before kings and rulers for my name's
sake.
13And it shall turn to you for a testimony.
14Settle *it* therefore in your hearts,

20:37 Moses shewed at the bush. See Exodus 3:6 and 3:5-6 note, "In God's Presence."
20:38 he is . . . a God . . . of the living. See Mark 12:27 note.
20:41 How say they . . . ? See Mark 12:35 note.
20:46 long robes. See Mark 12:38-40 notes.
21:3 cast in more. Jesus admired and commended the widow for giving all that she had and used her giving as an example to His disciples. See Mark 12:42-43 note.
21:9 wars and commotions. See Mark 13:7 note.
21:12 delivering you up. See Mark 13:9 notes.

not to meditate before what ye shall
answer:
15For I will give you a mouth and wisdom, which all your adversaries shall
not be able to gainsay nor resist.
16And ye shall be betrayed both by
parents, and brethren, and kinsfolks,
and friends; and *some* of you shall they
cause to be put to death.
17And ye shall be hated of all *men* for
my name's sake.
18But there shall not an hair of your
head perish.
19In your patience possess ye your
souls.
20And when ye shall see Jerusalem
compassed with armies, then know that
the desolation thereof is nigh.
21Then let them which are in Judaea
flee to the mountains; and let them
which are in the midst of it depart out;
and let not them that are in the countries enter thereinto.
22For these be the days of vengeance,
that all things which are written may be
fulfilled.
23But woe unto them that are with
child, and to them that give suck, in
those days! for there shall be great distress in the land, and wrath upon this
people.
24And they shall fall by the edge of
the sword, and shall be led away captive
into all nations: and Jerusalem shall be
trodden down of the Gentiles, until the
*times of the Gentiles be fulfilled.

The Lord's return in glory
(See Matt. 24:29-31)

¶25And there shall be signs in the
sun, and in the moon, and in the stars;
and upon the earth distress of nations,
with perplexity; the sea and the waves
roaring;
26Men's hearts failing them for fear,
and for looking after those things which
are coming on the earth: for the powers of heaven shall be shaken.
27And then shall they see the Son of
man coming in a cloud with power and
great glory.
28And when these things begin to
come to pass, then look up, and lift up
your heads; for your *redemption
draweth nigh.

A parable: the budding fig tree
(Matt. 24:32-35; Mark 13:28-31)

¶29And he spake to them a parable;
Behold the *fig tree, and all the trees;
30When they now shoot forth, ye see
and know of your own selves that summer is now nigh at hand.
31So likewise ye, when ye see these
things come to pass, know ye that the
kingdom of God is nigh at hand.
32Verily I say unto you, This generation shall not pass away, till all be fulfilled.
33Heaven and earth shall pass away:
but my words shall not pass away.

Watchful prayer
(See Matt. 24:36-51; Mark 13:32-37)

¶34And take heed to yourselves, lest
at any time your hearts be overcharged

21:24 Times of the Gentiles
This period began when Judah was carried into captivity by Babylon under Nebuchadnezzar. It will end when the Gentile world power is destroyed by the coming of the Lord of glory (Dan. 2:34-35,44; Rev. 19:11,21; see Rev. 19:11 second note). Until then, Jerusalem will be "trodden down of the Gentiles"—subject to their political dominion.

21:14 not to meditate before. The disciples and followers of Christ were not to be anxious beforehand about what they would say. The Holy Spirit would guide them and give them the words when they needed them.

21:20 Jerusalem compassed with armies. Verses 20-24 refer to the siege of Jerusalem. This was literally fulfilled in A.D. 70 when the Romans, under Titus, overthrew the city. This terrible time was a foretaste of the awful time to come, which will end when the *times of the Gentiles are ended.

21:31 these things. The things about which Christ had been talking in verses 25-28.

with surfeiting, and drunkenness, and
cares of this life, and *so* that day come
upon you unawares.
35 For as a snare shall it come on all
them that dwell on the face of the whole
earth.
36 Watch ye therefore, and pray always, that ye may be accounted worthy
to escape all these things that shall
come to pass, and to stand before the
Son of man.
37 And in the day time he was teaching in the temple; and at night he went
out, and abode in the mount that is
called *the mount* of Olives.
38 And all the people came early in the
morning to him in the temple, for to
hear him.

VII. Christ's Betrayal and Death
(22:1—23:56)
(Matt. 26:2,14-15;
Mark 14:1-2,10-11)

22 Now the feast of unleavened
bread drew nigh, which is called
the *Passover.
2 And the chief priests and scribes
sought how they might kill him; for
they feared the people.
¶3 Then entered *Satan into Judas
surnamed Iscariot, being of the number
of the twelve.
4 And he went his way, and communed with the chief priests and captains, how he might betray him unto
them.
5 And they were glad, and covenanted to give him money.
6 And he promised, and sought opportunity to betray him unto them in the
absence of the multitude.

The Lord's Supper
(Matt. 26:17-20; Mark 14:12-25;
John 13)

¶7 Then came the day of unleavened
bread, when the passover must be killed.

22:7 The Passover Lamb
The fourteenth of Nisan began when the first three stars appeared on the thirteenth (Wednesday evening) and ended with the first three stars on the fourteenth (Thursday evening). The Passover lamb was killed between the two evenings. "In the time of Christ it was understood to refer to the interval between the commencement of the sun's decline and what was reckoned as the hour of its final disappearance (about 6 P.M.). The first three stars had become visible, and the threefold blast of silver trumpets from the Temple Mount rang it out to Jerusalem and far away that the Paschal had once more commenced" *(Edersheim).*

8 And he sent Peter and John, saying,
Go and prepare us the passover, that we
may eat.
9 And they said unto him, Where wilt
thou that we prepare?
10 And he said unto them, Behold,
when ye are entered into the city, there
shall a man meet you, bearing a pitcher of water; follow him into the house
where he entereth in.
11 And ye shall say unto the goodman
of the house, The Master saith unto
thee, Where is the guestchamber,
where I shall eat the passover with my
disciples?
12 And he shall shew you a large upper room furnished: there make ready.
13 And they went, and found as he had

22:1 feast of unleavened bread. The *Passover day was the fourteenth day of the month of Nisan (our April; see *month). The Feast of Unleavened Bread began on the fifteenth day and lasted for seven days (Lev. 23:5-6), This whole time, however, was called the Passover Feast. See Exodus 12:1-28 (see also Exod. 12:3 note, "The Meaning of Passover").

22:3 Then entered Satan. See also John 13:27. Satan entered twice into Judas—once to urge him to make the bargain with the chief priests and captains; then again after he received the sop, to urge him to finsh his work by actually betraying the Lord.

22:10 there shall a man meet you. See Mark 14:13 second note.

said unto them: and they made ready
the passover.
¶ 14 And when the hour was come, he
sat down, and the twelve apostles with
him.
15 And he said unto them, With desire
I have desired to eat this passover with
you before I suffer:

22:15 The Last Passover
The Passover Jesus celebrated with His disciples was the last true Passover. The Passover had celebrated God's deliverance of His people from the power and bondage of Egypt. Here the Lord gave a new memorial supper, the Lord's Supper, which was to be a remembrance of Him and a commemoration of His death until He comes again. This was a memorial of a more wonderful deliverance—the deliverance of the sinner from the bondage and power of sin and the Devil. Here, also, the Lord took His people out from under the old *covenant, or testament, into the new (vs. 20; see 1 Cor. 10:16).

16 For I say unto you, I will not any
more eat thereof, until it be fulfilled in
the *kingdom of God.
17 And he took the cup, and gave
thanks, and said, Take this, and divide
it among yourselves:
18 For I say unto you, I will not drink
of the fruit of the vine, until the kingdom of God shall come.
¶ 19 And he took bread, and gave
thanks, and brake *it,* and gave unto them,
saying, This is my *body which is given
for you: this do in remembrance of me.
20 Likewise also the cup after supper,
saying, This *cup *is* the new *testament
in my *blood, which is shed for you.

The Lord tells of His betrayal
(Matt. 26:21-25; Mark 14:18-21;
John 13:18-30)

¶ 21 But, behold, the hand of him that
betrayeth me *is* with me on the table.
22 And truly the Son of man goeth, as
it was determined: but woe unto that
man by whom he is betrayed!
23 And they began to enquire among
themselves, which of them it was that
should do this thing.

Greatness in disciples
(See Matt. 20:25-28; Mark 10:42-45)

¶ 24 And there was also a strife among
them, which of them should be accounted the greatest.
25 And he said unto them, The kings
of the Gentiles exercise lordship over
them; and they that exercise authority
upon them are called benefactors.
26 But ye *shall* not *be* so: but he that
is greatest among you, let him be as the
younger; and he that is chief, as he that
doth serve.
27 For whether *is* greater, he that
sitteth at meat, or he that serveth? *is*
not he that sitteth at meat? but I am
among you as he that serveth.
28 Ye are they which have continued
with me in my *temptations.
29 And I appoint unto you a kingdom,
as my Father hath appointed unto me;
30 That ye may eat and drink at my
table in my kingdom, and sit on thrones
judging the twelve tribes of *Israel.

A warning to Peter
(Matt. 26:33-35; Mark 14:29-31)

¶ 31 And the Lord said, Simon, Simon,
behold, Satan hath desired *to have* you,
that he may sift *you* as wheat:
32 But I have prayed for thee, that thy
faith fail not: and when thou art converted, strengthen thy brethren.
33 And he said unto him, Lord, I am
ready to go with thee, both into prison,
and to death.
34 And he said, I tell thee, Peter, the
cock shall not crow this day, before

22:20 This cup is the new testament. See Mark 14:24 notes, as well as Mark 14:22-24 note, "The Body and Blood of Christ."

22:28 Ye are they which have continued with me. Note the Lord's love and faith in these men in light of what He knew they were going to do very shortly (vss. 45-46,61-62; Matt. 26:56).

22:32 when thou art converted. This means *when you turn back to Me again,* because

that thou shalt thrice deny that thou knowest me.

The Lord warns of coming trial

¶35 And he said unto them, When I sent you without purse, and *scrip, and shoes, lacked ye any thing? And they said, Nothing.

36 Then said he unto them, But now, he that hath a purse, let him take *it,* and likewise *his* scrip: and he that hath no sword, let him sell his garment, and buy one.

37 For I say unto you, that this that is written must yet be accomplished in me, And he was reckoned among the transgressors: for the things concerning me have an end.

38 And they said, Lord, behold, here *are* two swords. And he said unto them, It is enough.

Jesus prays in the Garden of Gethsemane (Matt. 26:36-46; Mark 14:32-42; John 18:1)

¶39 And he came out, and went, as he was wont, to the *mount of Olives; and his disciples also followed him.

40 And when he was at the place, he said unto them, Pray that ye enter not into *temptation.

41 And he was withdrawn from them about a stone's cast, and kneeled down, and prayed,

42 Saying, Father, if thou be willing, remove this cup from me: nevertheless not my will, but thine, be done.

43 And there appeared an *angel unto him from heaven, strengthening him.

44 And being in an agony he prayed more earnestly: and his sweat was as it were great drops of blood falling down to the ground.

45 And when he rose up from prayer, and was come to his disciples, he found them sleeping for sorrow,

46 And said unto them, Why sleep ye? rise and pray, lest ye enter into temptation.

Judas betrays the Lord; and Jesus heals the high priest's servant (Matt. 26:47-56; Mark 14:43-50; John 18:3-11)

¶47 And while he yet spake, behold a multitude, and he that was called Judas, one of the twelve, went before them, and drew near unto Jesus to kiss him.

48 But Jesus said unto him, Judas, betrayest thou the Son of man with a kiss?

49 When they which were about him saw what would follow, they said unto him, Lord, shall we smite with the sword?

¶50 And one of them smote the servant of the high priest, and cut off his right ear.

51 And Jesus answered and said, Suffer ye thus far. And he touched his ear, and healed him.

52 Then Jesus said unto the chief priests, and captains of the temple, and the elders, which were come to him, Be ye come out, as against a thief, with swords and staves?

53 When I was daily with you in the temple, ye stretched forth no hands against me: but this is your hour, and the power of darkness.

---

the Lord knew that Satan was going to have his way with Simon Peter for a while, so that he would be weak and frightened (vss. 31,54-62), but that His prayer for Peter (vs. 32) would assuredly be answered, and he would be converted.

22:35 When I sent you. See Luke 9:3; 10:4.

22:36 he that hath no sword. The Lord was telling the disciples to prepare for spiritual warfare, though they did not understand and brought Him two swords (vs. 38). Had He meant actual swords, two would not have been enough. See also His words to Peter (Matt. 26:52), His words to Pilate (John 18:36), and Paul's words (2 Cor. 10:4).

22:37 And he was reckoned among. He was counted or numbered with. See Isaiah 53:12.

22:39 he . . . went . . . to the mount of Olives. The Garden of *Gethsemane was at the foot of the Mount of Olives.

Peter denies the Lord
(Matt. 26:57,69-75; Mark 14:53-54,66-72; John 18:12,15-18,25-27)

¶54Then took they him, and led *him*,
and brought him into the high priest's
house. And Peter followed afar off.
55And when they had kindled a fire in
the midst of the hall, and were set down
together, Peter sat down among them.
56But a certain maid beheld him as he
sat by the fire, and earnestly looked
upon him, and said, This man was also
with him.
57And he denied him, saying, Woman, I know him not.
58And after a little while another saw
him, and said, Thou art also of them.
And Peter said, Man, I am not.
59And about the space of one hour
after another confidently affirmed, saying, Of a truth this *fellow* also was with
him: for he is a Galilaean.
60And Peter said, Man, I know not
what thou sayest. And immediately,
while he yet spake, the cock crew.
61And the Lord turned, and looked
upon Peter. And Peter remembered the
word of the Lord, how he had said unto
him, Before the cock crow, thou shalt
deny me thrice.
62And Peter went out, and wept bitterly.

The cruel treatment of the Lord
(Matt. 26:67-68; Mark 14:65; John 18:22-23)

¶63And the men that held Jesus
mocked him, and smote *him*.
64And when they had blindfolded
him, they struck him on the face, and
asked him, saying, Prophesy, who is it
that smote thee?
65And many other things blasphemously spake they against him.

The Lord witnesses as to His Deity
(Matt. 26:59-68; Mark 14:55-65; John 18:19-24)

¶66And as soon as it was day, the elders of the people and the chief priests
and the scribes came together, and led
him into their council, saying,
67Art thou the Christ? tell us. And he
said unto them, If I tell you, ye will not
believe:
68And if I also ask *you*, ye will not
answer me, nor let *me* go.
69Hereafter shall the Son of man sit
on the right hand of the power of God.
70Then said they all, Art thou then
the Son of God? And he said unto them,
Ye say that I am.
71And they said, What need we any
further witness? for we ourselves have
heard of his own mouth.

Pilate questions the Lord
(Matt. 27:2,11-14; Mark 15:1-5; John 18:28-38)

23 And the whole multitude of
them arose, and led him unto
*Pilate.
2And they began to accuse him, saying, We found this *fellow* perverting the
nation, and forbidding to give tribute to
*Caesar, saying that he himself is
Christ a King.
3And Pilate asked him, saying, Art
thou the *King of the Jews? And he answered him and said, Thou sayest *it*.
4Then said Pilate to the chief priests
and *to* the people, I find no fault in this
man.
5And they were the more fierce,

22:54 high priest's house. The house of Caiaphas (John 18:13).
22:55 in the midst of the hall. See Mark 14:54 note.
22:55 among them. Peter stood with the enemies of Christ. See Psalm 1:1-3.
22:62 Peter went out, and wept bitterly. See Mark 14:72 note.
22:71 any further witness. The *Sanhedrin were not able to find any witnesses that agreed as to the charges against the Lord (Mark 14:55-59).
23:2 they began to accuse him. This is the only Gospel record that gives the charges that were brought against the Lord. There are three main charges (vs. 2); one was added in verse 5.

saying, He stirreth up the people,
teaching throughout all Jewry, beginning from Galilee to this place.
¶6When Pilate heard of Galilee, he
asked whether the man were a Galilaean.
7And as soon as he knew that he belonged unto *Herod's jurisdiction, he
sent him to Herod, who himself also
was at *Jerusalem at that time.

Herod questions the Lord

¶8And when Herod saw Jesus, he
was exceeding glad: for he was desirous to see him of a long *season,* because
he had heard many things of him; and
he hoped to have seen some *miracle
done by him.
9Then he questioned with him in
many words; but he answered him
nothing.
10And the chief priests and scribes
stood and vehemently accused him.

The Lord before Pilate again
(Matt. 27:15-26; Mark 15:6-15;
John 18:39-40)

11And Herod with his men of war set
him at nought, and mocked *him,* and
arrayed him in a gorgeous robe, and
sent him again to Pilate.

23:11 The Robe
This robe was no doubt a white robe, which was the Hebrew royal costume, for the Greek word is *lampran,* meaning *shining,* which is translated "white" in Revelation 15:6; 19:8. Later Jesus was dressed in a purple robe, the Roman imperial costume. He was worshipped, albeit in mockery, for what He was, the King of the Jews and the King of Kings, of all nations.

¶12And the same day Pilate and Herod were made friends together: for before they were at enmity between
themselves.
¶13And Pilate, when he had called together the chief priests and the rulers
and the people,
14Said unto them, Ye have brought
this man unto me, as one that perverteth the people: and, behold, I, having examined *him* before you, have
found no fault in this man touching
those things whereof ye accuse him:
15No, nor yet Herod: for I sent you to
him; and, lo, nothing worthy of death is
done unto him.
16I will therefore chastise him, and
release *him.*
17(For of necessity he must release
one unto them at the feast.)
18And they cried out all at once, saying, Away with this *man,* and release
unto us Barabbas:
19(Who for a certain sedition made in
the city, and for murder, was cast into
prison.)
20Pilate therefore, willing to release
Jesus, spake again to them.
21But they cried, saying, Crucify *him,*
crucify him.
22And he said unto them the third
time, Why, what evil hath he done? I
have found no cause of death in him:
I will therefore chastise him, and let
him go.

The Lord delivered to the Jews
(Matt. 27:33-38; Mark 15:22-28;
John 19:17-19)

23And they were instant with loud
voices, requiring that he might be crucified. And the voices of them and of the
chief priests prevailed.
24And Pilate gave sentence that it
should be as they required.
25And he released unto them him that
for sedition and murder was cast into
prison, whom they had desired; but he
delivered Jesus to their will.

23:7 he sent him to Herod. Only Luke gives the scene before Herod.
23:15 is done unto him. Has been done by Herod to Jesus.
23:17 at the feast. The *Passover Feast.
23:21 cried. Kept shouting.
23:22 I will therefore chastise him. Mark 15:15 (see its note) tells what the chastisement was—cruel scourging.

¶[26]And as they led him away, they
laid hold upon one Simon, a Cyrenian,
coming out of the country, and on him
they laid the cross, that he might bear
it after Jesus.
¶[27]And there followed him a great
company of people, and of women,
which also bewailed and lamented him.
[28]But Jesus turning unto them said,
Daughters of Jerusalem, weep not for
me, but weep for yourselves, and for
your children.
[29]For, behold, the days are coming, in
the which they shall say, Blessed *are*
the barren, and the wombs that never
bare, and the paps which never gave suck.
[30]Then shall they begin to say to the
mountains, Fall on us; and to the hills,
Cover us.
[31]For if they do these things in a green
tree, what shall be done in the dry?
[32]And there were also two others,
malefactors, led with him to be put to
death.
[33]And when they were come to the
place, which is called Calvary, there
they crucified him, and the malefactors,
one on the right hand, and the other on
the left.

The mockery of the rulers and soldiers

¶[34]Then said Jesus, Father, forgive
them; for they know not what they do.
And they parted his raiment, and cast
lots.
[35]And the people stood beholding.
And the rulers also with them derided
him, saying, He saved others; let him
save himself, if he be Christ, the chosen of God.
[36]And the soldiers also mocked him,
coming to him, and *offering him vinegar,
[37]And saying, If thou be the king of
the Jews, save thyself.
[38]And a *superscription also was
written over him in letters of Greek,
and Latin, and Hebrew, THIS IS THE
KING OF THE JEWS.

The saved thief
(See Matt. 27:44; Mark 15:32)

¶[39]And one of the malefactors which
were hanged railed on him, saying, If
thou be Christ, save thyself and us.
[40]But the other answering rebuked
him, saying, Dost not thou fear God,
seeing thou art in the same *condemnation?
[41]And we indeed justly; for we receive the due *reward of our deeds: but
this man hath done nothing amiss.
[42]And he said unto Jesus, Lord, remember me when thou comest into thy
kingdom.
[43]And Jesus said unto him, Verily I
say unto thee, To day shalt thou be with
me in paradise.

The death of Christ
(Matt. 27:50; Mark 15:37; John 19:30)

¶[44]And it was about the sixth hour,
and there was a darkness over all the
earth until the ninth hour.

23:29 the days are coming. See Luke 21:20 note.
23:30 say to the mountains, Fall on us. See Hosea 10:8.
23:31 a green tree. The "green tree" is the Lord who was led to His death like a rebel, though He had submitted to the Gentile authorities. The Jewish people who lived continually in a spirit of revolt are the "dry [wood]," who would, with good reason, bring down upon themselves the Roman sword.
23:32 two others, malefactors. See Isaiah 53:9,12, which this fulfilled.
23:33 Calvary. "Calvary" is the Latin name, and "Golgotha" is the Hebrew name of the hill on which crucifixions took place. The name means *the skull* and was probably given because of its appearance. See John 19:17.
23:34 parted his raiment. See Psalm 22:18.
23:35 let him save himself. See why He could not save Himself in Mark 15:31 note.
23:43 paradise. The abode of our Lord and of the saved, or blessed ones; the third heaven (see 2 Cor. 12:4 and 12:3-4 note, "Paradise"; Rev. 2:7).
23:44 about the sixth hour. See Mark 15:33 note.

[45]And the sun was darkened, and the veil of the temple was rent in the midst.

¶[46]And when Jesus had cried with a loud voice, he said, Father, into thy hands I commend my spirit: and having said thus, he gave up the ghost.

[47]Now when the *centurion saw what was done, he glorified God, saying, Certainly this was a righteous man.

[48]And all the people that came together to that sight, beholding the things which were done, smote their breasts, and returned.

[49]And all his acquaintance, and the women that followed him from Galilee, stood afar off, beholding these things.

The burial of the Lord
(Matt. 27:57-61; Mark 15:42-47; John 19:38-42)

¶[50]And, behold, *there was* a man named *Joseph, a counsellor; *and he was* a good man, and a just:

[51](The same had not consented to the counsel and deed of them;) *he was* of Arimathaea, a city of the Jews: who also himself waited for the kingdom of God.

[52]This *man* went unto Pilate, and begged the body of Jesus.

[53]And he took it down, and wrapped it in linen, and laid it in a sepulchre that was hewn in stone, wherein never man before was laid.

[54]And that day was the preparation, and the *sabbath drew on.

[55]And the women also, which came with him from Galilee, followed after, and beheld the sepulchre, and how his body was laid.

[56]And they returned, and prepared spices and ointments; and rested the sabbath day according to the commandment.

VIII. Christ's Resurrection and Ascension (24:1-53)
(Matt. 28:1-6; Mark 16:1-8; John 20:1-17)

24 Now upon the first *day* of the week, very early in the morning, they came unto the sepulchre, bringing the spices which they had prepared, and certain *others* with them.

[2]And they found the stone rolled away from the sepulchre.

[3]And they entered in, and found not the body of the Lord Jesus.

[4]And it came to pass, as they were much perplexed thereabout, behold, two men stood by them in shining garments:

[5]And as they were afraid, and bowed down *their* faces to the earth, they said unto them, Why seek ye the living among the dead?

[6]He is not here, but is risen: remember how he spake unto you when he was yet in Galilee,

---

23:46 cried with a loud voice. He cried the triumphant "It is finished" (see John 19:30 note).
23:46 gave up the ghost. See Matthew 27:50 note.
23:50 Joseph, a counsellor. See Mark 15:43 note.
23:53 laid it in a sepulchre. This fulfilled Isaiah 53:9.
23:54 that day was the preparation. See John 19:31 first note.
23:56 according to the commandment. See Exodus 20:10.
24:1 bringing the spices. See Mark 16:1 note.
24:1 certain others with them. Mary Magdalene, Mary, the mother of James and Joses, Salome (Matt. 28:1; Mark 16:1), Joanna (Luke 24:10; see Luke 8:3), and probably other women as well (vs. 10).
24:2 stone rolled away. See Mark 16:4 note.
24:3 Lord Jesus. This is the first time that the Lord's resurrection title is given to Him. He had been called Jesus and Lord, but never Lord Jesus. After this we find the title about forty times in the Epistles.
24:4 two men stood by them. Angels (see vs. 23).
24:5 the living. The Living One.
24:6 remember how he spake. See Matthew 12:40; 16:21; 17:22-23; 20:18-19; 26:2;

[7]Saying, The Son of man must be delivered into the hands of sinful men, and
be crucified, and the third day rise
again.
[8]And they remembered his words,
[9]And returned from the sepulchre,
and told all these things unto the elev-
en, and to all the rest.
[10]It was Mary Magdalene, and Joanna, and Mary *the mother* of James, and
other *women that were* with them, which
told these things unto the apostles.
[11]And their words seemed to them as
idle tales, and they believed them not.
[12]Then arose Peter, and ran unto the
sepulchre; and stooping down, he beheld the linen clothes laid by themselves, and departed, wondering in
himself at that which was come to pass.

The Lord reveals Himself on the Emmaus road

¶[13]And, behold, two of them went
that same day to a village called Emmaus, which was from Jerusalem *about*
threescore furlongs.
[14]And they talked together of all
these things which had happened.
[15]And it came to pass, that, while
they communed *together* and reasoned,
Jesus himself drew near, and went with
them.
[16]But their eyes were holden that
they should not know him.
[17]And he said unto them, What
manner of communications *are* these
that ye have one to another, as ye walk,
and are sad?
[18]And the one of them, whose name
was Cleopas, answering said unto him,
Art thou only a stranger in Jerusalem,
and hast not known the things which
are come to pass there in these days?
[19]And he said unto them, What
things? And they said unto him, Concerning Jesus of Nazareth, which was
a prophet mighty in deed and word before God and all the people:
[20]And how the chief priests and our
rulers delivered him to be condemned
to death, and have crucified him.
[21]But we trusted that it had been he
which should have redeemed Israel:
and beside all this, to day is the third
day since these things were done.
[22]Yea, and certain women also of our
company made us astonished, which
were early at the sepulchre;
[23]And when they found not his body,
they came, saying, that they had also
seen a vision of angels, which said that
he was alive.
[24]And certain of them which were
with us went to the sepulchre, and
found *it* even so as the women had said:
but him they saw not.
[25]Then he said unto them, O fools,
and slow of heart to believe all that the
prophets have spoken:
[26]Ought not Christ to have suffered
these things, and to enter into his glory?
[27]And beginning at Moses and all the
prophets, he expounded unto them in
all the scriptures the things concerning
himself.
[28]And they drew nigh unto the village, whither they went: and he made
as though he would have gone further.

John 2:19; etc. Notice also that His enemies remembered, sealed the tomb, and set soldiers to guard against His being carried out (Matt. 27:62-66).

24:7 must be delivered. These occurrences had to happen because they were predicted in the Scriptures.

24:13 two of them. Cleopas (vs. 18) and perhaps his wife Mary (John 19:25; compare Luke 24:29).

24:16 eyes were holden. The Lord would not reveal Himself to them until their souls were ready to receive and believe Him.

24:25 fools, and slow of heart. Men without understanding, dull-witted.

24:26 Ought not Christ to have suffered . . . ? It had to happen because it was predicted in the Scriptures.

24:28 he made as though he would have gone further. He was not simply pretending; had they not "constrained" or stopped Him (vs. 29), He would have gone on.

24:27 The Hebrew Bible
See verse 44. The Law of Moses, the Prophets, and the Psalms, or Writings, were the three divisions of the Hebrew Bible, our Old Testament. The protevangelium, or first announcement of the Saviour, was to Eve in the Garden of Eden (see Gen. 3:15 and its note, "The Promise of a Saviour").

29 But they constrained him, saying, Abide with us: for it is toward evening, and the day is far spent. And he went in to tarry with them.

30 And it came to pass, as he sat at meat with them, he took bread, and blessed *it,* and brake, and gave to them.

31 And their eyes were opened, and they knew him; and he vanished out of their sight.

32 And they said one to another, Did not our heart burn within us, while he talked with us by the way, and while he opened to us the scriptures?

33 And they rose up the same hour, and returned to Jerusalem, and found the eleven gathered together, and them that were with them,

34 Saying, The Lord is risen indeed, and hath appeared to Simon.

35 And they told what things *were done* in the way, and how he was known of them in breaking of bread.

The Lord appears to the disciples (See Matt. 28:16-17; Mark 16:14; John 20:19-23)

¶36 And as they thus spake, Jesus himself stood in the midst of them, and saith unto them, Peace *be* unto you.

37 But they were terrified and affrighted, and supposed that they had seen a spirit.

38 And he said unto them, Why are ye troubled? and why do thoughts arise in your hearts?

39 Behold my hands and my feet, that it is I myself: handle me, and see; for a spirit hath not flesh and bones, as ye see me have.

40 And when he had thus spoken, he shewed them *his* hands and *his* feet.

41 And while they yet believed not for joy, and wondered, he said unto them, Have ye here any meat?

42 And they gave him a piece of a broiled fish, and of an honeycomb.

43 And he took *it,* and did eat before them.

¶44 And he said unto them, These *are* the words which I spake unto you, while I was yet with you, that all things must be fulfilled, which were written in the law of Moses, and *in* the prophets, and *in* the psalms, concerning me.

45 Then opened he their understanding, that they might understand the scriptures,

46 And said unto them, Thus it is written, and thus it behoved Christ to suffer, and to rise from the dead the third day:

47 And that repentance and remission of sins should be preached in his name among all nations, beginning at Jerusalem.

48 And ye are witnesses of these things.

The promise of the Holy Spirit

¶49 And, behold, I send the promise of my Father upon you: but tarry ye in the city of Jerusalem, until ye be endued with power from on high.

24:30 took bread. At the table Jesus acted in the same manner as He had at the table of the Lord's Supper (22:19). He took the place of the master of the house, and the two saw that this was their risen Lord (compare vs. 31 with vs. 16).

24:34 appeared to Simon. See verse 12.

24:36 Peace be unto you. He had given His disciples and followers this peace (John 14:27).

24:37 they were terrified. In spite of the testimony of those who had seen the Lord Jesus, they were not yet convinced of the truth; they did not yet believe His promises to them.

24:49 the promise of my Father. Compare John 14:16-17 with Acts 1:8 and the fulfillment in Acts 2:4.

The Lord is carried up into heaven
(Mark 16:19-20; Acts 1:9-11)

¶[50]And he led them out as far as to
Bethany, and he lifted up his hands, and
blessed them.
[51]And it came to pass, while he
blessed them, he was parted from
them, and carried up into heaven.
[52]And they worshipped him, and returned to Jerusalem with great joy:
[53]And were continually in the temple,
praising and blessing God. Amen.

24:50 as far as to Bethany. Until they were opposite Bethany.
24:51 up into heaven. The third heaven. See *paradise.

The Gospel according to Saint

JOHN

THE WRITER AND TIME

The writer of this Gospel was the Apostle John, who also wrote the Epistles of John and the Revelation. His may have been the last of the Gospels to be written, probably about A.D. 90. John, a fisherman of Galilee, son of Zebedee and brother of James, was dearly loved by the Lord, for he sat next to Him at the Last Supper (John 13:23), and he calls himself one "whom Jesus loved" (John 20:2).

THEME

John gave his reason for writing in John 20:31—to show that the Lord Jesus Christ is the Son of God and the Savior of all who believe on Him. He did not attempt to give a *history* of the life of Christ, but chose some of the great signs and messages of our Lord. This is why John's Gospel is so very different from the other Gospels. The key word is "life."

OUTLINE OF JOHN

I.	Introduction: Jesus Christ as the Word of God	John 1:1-14
II.	The Witness of John the Baptist	John 1:15-34
III.	The Public Preaching of Christ	John 1:35—12:50
IV.	The Private Talks of Christ	John 13:1—17:26
V.	The Trial and Death of Christ	John 18:1—19:42
VI.	The Resurrection of Christ	John 20:1-31
VII.	The Days between the Resurrection and the Ascension	John 21:1-25

I. Introduction: Jesus Christ as the Word of God (1:1-14)

1 In the beginning was the Word, and the Word was with *God, and the Word was God.

2 The same was in the beginning with God.

3 All things were made by him; and without him was not any thing made that was made.

1:1 In the beginning. Three books have almost this same beginning: Genesis, John, and 1 John. We see the Lord Jesus Christ as the One who created and upholds all things, as the One who was made flesh and came to live on this earth, and as the One *who is eternal life. Each says, "He is God." "In the beginning" or "from the beginning" (1 John 1:1) means in eternity, for the Word has always been—the Word is God.

1:3 All things were made by him. Jesus Christ was one of the Trinity of Father, Son, and Holy Spirit who created the world (see Gen. 1 notes).

1:1 The Word
The Word is one of the most wonderful names used to describe the Lord Jesus Christ and His work. Words reveal thoughts and character; so the Lord Jesus expressed God's thoughts and showed us what God is like. God had partly revealed Himself before to the prophets and to the children of Israel, but they had not been able to approach Him, for they were sinful and God is holy. The Lord Jesus came to show God's love and that the Father wanted to save people from sin. He told His disciples, "He that hath seen me hath seen the Father" (John 14:9). The Bible is also called the Word of God because it is the written record of His thoughts and ways.

4In him was life; and the life was the
light of men.
5And the light shineth in darkness;
and the darkness comprehended it not.

Jesus Christ as the Light

¶6There was a man sent from God,
whose name *was* John.
7The same came for a witness, to
bear witness of the Light, that all *men*
through him might believe.
8He was not that Light, but *was sent*
to bear witness of that Light.
9*That* was the true Light, which lighteth
every man that cometh into the *world.
10He was in the world, and the world
was made by him, and the world knew
him not.
11He came unto his own, and his own
received him not.
12But as many as received him, to
them gave he power to become the
sons of God, *even* to them that believe
on his name:
13Which were born, not of blood, nor
of the will of the flesh, nor of the will of
man, but of God.
14And the Word was made flesh, and
dwelt among us, (and we beheld his
glory, the glory as of the only begotten
of the Father,) full of *grace and truth.

II. Witness of the Baptist (1:15-34)
(Matt. 3:1-17; Mark 1:1-11; Luke 3:1-18)

¶15John bare witness of him, and
cried, saying, This was he of whom I
spake, He that cometh after me is preferred before me: for he was before me.
16And of his *fulness have all we received, and grace for grace.
17For the *law was given by *Moses,
but grace and truth came by Jesus
*Christ.

1:17 The Law
The Law was given by God to Moses for the Jewish people to observe. It was just and right, and it demanded that all wrongdoing should be punished. It showed God's holiness and justice, but it could never save people, for they could not keep it perfectly (Gal. 3:11,19,23-24). While God has always been gracious, His grace was perfectly demonstrated through the death of His Son in the sinner's place. Thus grace "came by Jesus Christ."

1:5 light shineth in darkness. Jesus Christ came from heaven to light up this dark world of sin. He came to show people the way of salvation—He is the Way of salvation (John 14:6), but many would not "comprehend" or understand Him or His message.
1:6 a man sent from God, whose name was John. This was John the Baptist (see vss. 29-34).
1:11 his own. The first "his own" is neuter and speaks of Christ's own possessions, including the Jewish people. They, the second "his own," "received Him not," that is, through their leaders they officially rejected the Lord Jesus Christ as their King.
1:12 sons of God. Children of God.
1:13 born . . . of God. This is explained in John 3:3 note, "Born Again." See also 1 Peter 1:23.
1:14 Word was made flesh. Compare Romans 8:3; Philippians 2:8; Hebrews 2:14-18.
1:17 grace. "Grace" means *undeserved kindness.* This does not mean that God has changed, or that He just passes over or overlooks sin. But when Jesus Christ died on the cross, He bore the divine judgment for mankind's sins; therefore, God could deal with us in grace, forgiving us when we do not deserve forgiveness.

1:18 Seeing God
No man has seen God. No man can see God, because He is a Spirit and has no bodily form (John 4:24; Luke 24:39). When God wanted to speak to men in Old Testament times, He took a body or appeared in a flame of fire or in a bright cloud (Exod. 24:10). Men did not see Him, just the outward form. People could not even come near to God when He did reveal Himself like this, because they were sinful. But the Lord Jesus Christ took a human body and lived in this world, and through His perfect life, His love, and His goodness, people saw what God is like.

18 No man hath seen God at any time;
the only begotten Son, which is in the
bosom of the Father, he hath declared
him.
¶ 19 And this is the record of John, when
the Jews sent priests and Levites from
*Jerusalem to ask him, Who art thou?
20 And he confessed, and denied not;
but confessed, I am not the Christ.
21 And they asked him, What then?
Art thou *Elias? And he saith, I am not.
Art thou that *prophet? And he answered, No.
22 Then said they unto him, Who art
thou? that we may give an answer to
them that sent us. What sayest thou of
thyself?
23 He said, I *am* the voice of one crying in the wilderness, Make straight the
way of the Lord, as said the prophet
Esaias.
24 And they which were sent were of
the *Pharisees.
25 And they asked him, and said unto
him, Why baptizest thou then, if thou be
not that Christ, nor Elias, neither that
prophet?
26 John answered them, saying, I baptize with water: but there standeth one
among you, whom ye know not;
27 He it is, who coming after me is
preferred before me, whose shoe's
latchet I am not worthy to unloose.
28 These things were done in Betha-
bara beyond Jordan, where John was
baptizing.
¶ 29 The next day John seeth Jesus
coming unto him, and saith, Behold the
Lamb of God, which taketh away the
*sin of the world.
30 This is he of whom I said, After me
cometh a man which is preferred before
me: for he was before me.
31 And I knew him not: but that he
should be made manifest to *Israel, therefore am I come baptizing with water.
32 And John bare record, saying, I saw
the Spirit descending from *heaven like
a dove, and it abode upon him.
33 And I knew him not: but he that
sent me to baptize with water, the same
said unto me, Upon whom thou shalt
see the Spirit descending, and remaining on him, the same is he which
baptizeth with the Holy Ghost.
34 And I saw, and bare record that this
is the Son of God.

1:21 that prophet. Moses had prophesied this in Deuteronomy 18:15,18 (see Deut. 18:15 note, "The Prophet"). Elias was *Elijah, whose return had been prophesied by Malachi (see Mal. 4:5). John the Baptist denied that he was "that prophet" Moses wrote about; he also denied that he was Elijah or the Messiah.

1:23 Esaias. Isaiah. John was quoting from Isaiah 40:3. The priests and Levites (vs. 19) asked John, "Who art thou?" But John was more interested in telling them why he came—to prepare the way for the Messiah—rather than whom he was. The leaders were missing the point completely.

1:29 Lamb of God. All Jews knew of the Passover lamb, which had been killed on the night of the escape from Egypt to save the Israelites from the terrible judgment of God (see Exod. 12:3 and its note, "The Meaning of Passover"). Therefore they should have realized John's exclamation meant the Saviour—the true Lamb of God—had come.

1:30 he was before me. John the Baptist was about six months older than the Lord Jesus (Luke 1:36), but only as a man. Jesus as God was in the beginning—from all eternity (John 1:1).

III. Christ's Preaching (1:35—12:50)

¶35 Again the next day after John
stood, and two of his disciples;
36 And looking upon Jesus as he
walked, he saith, Behold the Lamb
of God!
37 And the two disciples heard him
speak, and they followed Jesus.
38 Then Jesus turned, and saw them
following, and saith unto them, What
seek ye? They said unto him, Rabbi,
(which is to say, being interpreted,
Master,) where dwellest thou?
39 He saith unto them, Come and see.
They came and saw where he dwelt,
and abode with him that day: for it was
about the tenth hour.
40 One of the two which heard John
speak, and followed him, was Andrew,
Simon *Peter's brother.
41 He first findeth his own brother
Simon, and saith unto him, We have
found the Messias, which is, being interpreted, the Christ.
42 And he brought him to Jesus. And
when Jesus beheld him, he said, Thou
art Simon the son of Jona: thou shalt be
called *Cephas, which is by interpretation, A stone.
¶43 The day following Jesus would go
forth into Galilee, and findeth Philip,
and saith unto him, Follow me.
44 Now Philip was of Bethsaida, the
city of Andrew and Peter.
45 Philip findeth Nathanael, and saith
unto him, We have found him, of whom
Moses in the law, and the *prophets, did
write, Jesus of Nazareth, the son of *Joseph.
46 And Nathanael said unto him, Can
there any good thing come out of Nazareth? Philip saith unto him, Come
and see.
47 Jesus saw Nathanael coming to
him, and saith of him, Behold an Israelite indeed, in whom is no guile!
48 Nathanael saith unto him, Whence
knowest thou me? Jesus answered and
said unto him, Before that Philip called
thee, when thou wast under the *fig
tree, I saw thee.
49 Nathanael answered and saith unto
him, Rabbi, thou art the Son of God;
thou art the King of Israel.
50 Jesus answered and said unto him,
Because I said unto thee, I saw thee
under the fig tree, believest thou? thou
shalt see greater things than these.
51 And he saith unto him, Verily, verily, I say unto you, Hereafter ye shall
see heaven open, and the *angels of
God ascending and descending upon
the Son of man.

The wedding: the first miracle

2 And the third day there was a
marriage in Cana of Galilee; and
the mother of Jesus was there:
2 And both Jesus was called, and his
disciples, to the marriage.
3 And when they wanted *wine, the
mother of Jesus saith unto him, They
have no wine.
4 Jesus saith unto her, Woman, what
have I to do with thee? mine hour is not
yet come.
5 His mother saith unto the servants,
Whatsoever he saith unto you, do *it.*
6 And there were set there six waterpots of stone, after the manner of the
purifying of the Jews, containing two or
three firkins apiece.

1:39 the tenth hour. Ten o'clock in the morning by Roman time.
1:45 Moses in the law. See Deuteronomy 18:15.
1:45 the son of Joseph. The legal or adopted son of Joseph (compare Matt. 1:18-25; Luke 1:26-35).
1:47 an Israelite indeed, in whom is no guile! Our Lord may have been referring to Psalm 32:1-2.
2:6 purifying of the Jews. Probably these jugs of water were originally intended to be used for washing their hands (see Matt. 15:2; see also its note, "The Tradition of the Elders").
2:6 firkins. One firkin is about nine gallons.

7Jesus saith unto them, Fill the
waterpots with water. And they filled
them up to the brim.
8And he saith unto them, Draw out
now, and bear unto the governor of the
feast. And they bare *it.*
9When the ruler of the feast had tasted the water that was made wine, and
knew not whence it was: (but the servants which drew the water knew;) the
governor of the feast called the bridegroom,
10And saith unto him, Every man at
the beginning doth set forth good wine;
and when men have well drunk, then
that which is worse: *but* thou hast kept
the good wine until now.
11This beginning of *miracles did
Jesus in Cana of Galilee, and manifested
forth his glory; and his disciples believed on him.
¶12After this he went down to Capernaum, he, and his mother, and his
brethren, and his disciples: and they
continued there not many days.

The first Temple purification

¶13And the Jews' *passover was at
hand, and Jesus went up to Jerusalem,
14And found in the temple those that
sold oxen and sheep and doves, and the
changers of money sitting:
15And when he had made a scourge
of small cords, he drove them all out of
the temple, and the sheep, and the
oxen; and poured out the changers'
money, and overthrew the tables;
16And said unto them that sold doves,
Take these things hence; make not my
Father's house an house of merchandise.
17And his disciples remembered that
it was written, The zeal of thine house
hath eaten me up.
¶18Then answered the Jews and said
unto him, What sign shewest thou unto
us, seeing that thou doest these things?

2:17 Zeal for the Temple
This is a quotation from Psalm 69:9. The outer courts of the temple were for the people of the Jewish religion who wanted to worship but who were not of pure Jewish birth. These courts had been made into a noisy market where doves and even sheep and oxen for sacrifices were sold, and Roman money, which was not allowed to be put into the temple coffers, was exchanged for Jewish coins. The Lord Jesus cleansed the temple twice: here, at the beginning of His preaching, and later, at the end of His earthly ministry (Matt. 21:12; Luke 19:45).

19Jesus answered and said unto them,
Destroy this temple, and in three days
I will raise it up.
20Then said the Jews, Forty and six
years was this temple in building, and
wilt thou rear it up in three days?
21But he spake of the temple of his
body.
22When therefore he was risen from
the dead, his disciples remembered that
he had said this unto them; and they
believed the scripture, and the word
which Jesus had said.
¶23Now when he was in Jerusalem at
the passover, in the feast *day,* many
believed in his name, when they saw
the miracles which he did.
24But Jesus did not commit himself
unto them, because he knew all *men,*
25And needed not that any should
testify of man: for he knew what was in
man.

The talk with Nicodemus

3 There was a man of the Pharisees, named Nicodemus, a ruler of
the Jews:
2The same came to Jesus by night,
and said unto him, Rabbi, we know that
thou art a teacher come from God: for
no man can do these miracles that thou
doest, except God be with him.

2:18 What sign shewest thou . . . ? Compare the Lord's answer in verse 19 with 8:28.
3:2 by night. Nicodemus, as a member of the Jewish Sanhedrin, or parliament, was a cautious politician. Later, as a believer in Christ, he showed more courage (John 19:39).

The teaching of the new birth

[3]Jesus answered and said unto him, Verily, verily, I say unto thee, Except a man be born again, he cannot see the *kingdom of God.

[4]Nicodemus saith unto him, How can a man be born when he is old? can he enter the second time into his mother's womb, and be born?

[5]Jesus answered, Verily, verily, I say unto thee, Except a man be born of water and *of* the Spirit, he cannot enter into the kingdom of God.

[6]That which is born of the flesh is flesh; and that which is born of the Spirit is spirit.

[7]Marvel not that I said unto thee, Ye must be born again.

[8]The wind bloweth where it listeth, and thou hearest the sound thereof, but canst not tell whence it cometh, and whither it goeth: so is every one that is born of the Spirit.

[9]Nicodemus answered and said unto him, How can these things be?

[10]Jesus answered and said unto him, Art thou a master of Israel, and knowest not these things?

[11]Verily, verily, I say unto thee, We speak that we do know, and testify that we have seen; and ye receive not our witness.

[12]If I have told you earthly things, and ye believe not, how shall ye believe, if I tell you *of* heavenly things?

[13]And no man hath ascended up to heaven, but he that came down from heaven, *even* the Son of man which is in heaven.

¶[14]And as Moses lifted up the serpent in the wilderness, even so must the Son of man be lifted up:

[15]That whosoever believeth in him should not perish, but have *eternal life.

¶[16]For God so loved the world, that he gave his only begotten Son, that whosoever believeth in him should not perish, but have everlasting life.

[17]For God sent not his Son into the

3:3 BORN AGAIN

We have all been born once and have human fathers. This first birth gave us a human life and a sinful human nature, handed down from Adam. Before we can be saved and know God, we must have what is similar to a second birth. God gives us a new nature–a new life that is like Him and wants to please Him. Only people who have this new life are really Christians, although many people try to be Christians by reforming themselves, and they think they are Christians because they live honestly or because they go to church.

We must be careful to distinguish between Christians and Gentiles. Many people speak of those who are not Jews as Christians. This is an incorrect use of the word. A Christian is one who believes in the Lord Jesus Christ as the Son of God and the only Saviour from sin. One who has such faith is born again by the Holy Spirit. The Lord Jesus made it clear that even those people who live most uprightly, like Nicodemus, who was a very religious Jew, must be born again. New birth comes when we take Jesus as our Saviour (John 3:16; see also 3:15-16 note, "Eternal Life"); how it comes is by water and the Spirit (vs. 5). The Holy Spirit leads us to believe the truths of the Bible and put our trust in the Lord Jesus Christ, our Sin-Bearer.

3:8 The wind bloweth. The Lord Jesus said that the work of the Holy Spirit in saving men is like the wind: 1) it is from heaven; 2) it cannot be seen; 3) its power and work can never be fully understood; 4) it can be heard; 5) it is very powerful, and what it does can be seen; and 6) it gives life–the breath of life made man a living soul.

3:14 serpent. Look up the story in Numbers 21:5-9 (see also Num. 21:8 note, "The Fiery Serpent").

3:15 perish. This means *to be utterly ruined* and or "lost" as in Matthew 18:11. It applies to all who do not believe on the Lord Jesus Christ as their Saviour and means that they are separated from God now and forever.

3:16 world. Mankind.

3:16 everlasting life. The same as *eternal life.

3:15-16 Eternal Life
When we are born into this world, we have physical life that lasts until we die. When we are *born again we receive eternal life, which is the life of God. It never ends, for when our bodies die at the end of our life, we go to heaven to be with God and go on living the eternal life that we start here and now. John's Gospel and Epistles have a great deal to tell us about this life (see John 5:26; 10:28; 14:6; 1 John 1:2). Eternal life is more than quantity, however; it is quality also–it is the life of Christ in the believer. "Christ liveth in me" (Gal. 2:20).

world to condemn the world; but that the world through him might be saved.

¶18 He that believeth on him is not condemned: but he that believeth not is condemned already, because he hath not believed in the name of the only begotten Son of God.

19 And this is the *condemnation, that light is come into the world, and men loved darkness rather than light, because their deeds were evil.

20 For every one that doeth evil hateth the light, neither cometh to the light, lest his deeds should be reproved.

21 But he that doeth truth cometh to the light, that his deeds may be made manifest, that they are wrought in God.

Last words of John the Baptist

¶22 After these things came Jesus and his disciples into the land of Judaea; and there he tarried with them, and baptized.

¶23 And John also was baptizing in Aenon near to Salim, because there was much water there: and they came, and were baptized.

24 For John was not yet cast into prison.

¶25 Then there arose a question between *some* of John's disciples and the Jews about purifying.

26 And they came unto John, and said unto him, Rabbi, he that was with thee beyond Jordan, to whom thou barest witness, behold, the same baptizeth, and all *men* come to him.

27 John answered and said, A man can receive nothing, except it be given him from heaven.

28 Ye yourselves bear me witness, that I said, I am not the Christ, but that I am sent before him.

29 He that hath the bride is the bridegroom: but the friend of the bridegroom, which standeth and heareth him, rejoiceth greatly because of the bridegroom's voice: this my joy therefore is fulfilled.

30 He must increase, but I *must* decrease.

Summary of the chapter

31 He that cometh from above is above all: he that is of the earth is earthly, and speaketh of the earth: he that cometh from heaven is above all.

32 And what he hath seen and heard, that he testifieth; and no man receiveth his testimony.

33 He that hath received his testimony hath set to his seal that God is true.

34 For he whom God hath sent speaketh the words of God: for God giveth not the Spirit by measure *unto him.*

35 The Father loveth the Son, and hath given all things into his hand.

36 He that believeth on the Son hath everlasting life: and he that believeth

---

3:24 John was not yet cast into prison. See Matthew 11:2; 14:3.

3:33 set to his seal. Certified. When people signed an agreement, a great seal was attached to show that it was agreed upon. So anyone who believes on the Lord Jesus and takes Him as Saviour has, as it were, put a seal upon God's offer of salvation and certified that salvation is real.

3:34 by measure. "By measure" means doled out in very small quantities. God has given everything freely to the Lord Jesus–there was not then nor is there now any limit to Christ's power.

not the Son shall not see life; but the wrath of God abideth on him.

The journey into Galilee

4 When therefore the Lord knew how the Pharisees had heard that Jesus made and baptized more disciples than John,

2 (Though Jesus himself baptized not, but his disciples,)

3 He left Judaea, and departed again into Galilee.

4 And he must needs go through *Samaria.

5 Then cometh he to a city of Samaria, which is called Sychar, near to the parcel of ground that *Jacob gave to his son Joseph.

6 Now Jacob's well was there. Jesus therefore, being wearied with *his* journey, sat thus on the well: *and* it was about the sixth hour.

7 There cometh a woman of Samaria to draw water: Jesus saith unto her, Give me to drink.

8 (For his disciples were gone away unto the city to buy meat.)

9 Then saith the woman of Samaria unto him, How is it that thou, being a Jew, askest drink of me, which am a woman of Samaria? for the Jews have no dealings with the *Samaritans.

10 Jesus answered and said unto her, If thou knewest the gift of God, and who it is that saith to thee, Give me to drink; thou wouldest have asked of him, and he would have given thee living water.

11 The woman saith unto him, Sir, thou hast nothing to draw with, and the well is deep: from whence then hast thou that living water?

12 Art thou greater than our father Jacob, which gave us the well, and drank thereof himself, and his children, and his cattle?

Jesus promises the Holy Spirit
(7:37-39)

13 Jesus answered and said unto her, Whosoever drinketh of this water shall thirst again:

14 But whosoever drinketh of the water that I shall give him shall never thirst; but the water that I shall give him shall be in him a well of water springing up into everlasting life.

15 The woman saith unto him, Sir, give me this water, that I thirst not, neither come hither to draw.

16 Jesus saith unto her, Go, call thy husband, and come hither.

17 The woman answered and said, I have no husband. Jesus said unto her, Thou hast well said, I have no husband:

18 For thou hast had five husbands; and he whom thou now hast is not thy husband: in that saidst thou truly.

19 The woman saith unto him, Sir, I perceive that thou art a prophet.

20 Our fathers worshipped in this mountain; and ye say, that in Jerusalem is the place where men ought to worship.

21 Jesus saith unto her, Woman, believe me, the hour cometh, when ye shall neither in this mountain, nor yet at Jerusalem, worship the Father.

22 Ye worship ye know not what: we

4:5 near to the parcel of ground. Plot of land. See Genesis 33:19.

4:6 wearied with his journey. Note that the Lord, though He was perfect God, was perfect Man also, and therefore grew tired (compare John 1:14).

4:6 the sixth hour. This was probably Roman time, six o'clock in the evening.

4:9 Samaritans. Look up 2 Kings 17:24-41 for the origin of these people, and you will realize why the Jews did not mix with them.

4:10 gift of God. Look up Romans 6:23 and Ephesians 2:8.

4:10 living water. Just as water satisfies thirst, so salvation satisfies the need of the sinner.

4:20 this mountain. Mount Gerizim, where the Samaritans had built a temple to rival the Jewish temple at Jerusalem.

4:22 Ye worship ye know not what. You worship, as it were, but you do not know God.

know what we worship: for *salvation
is of the Jews.
23 But the hour cometh, and now is,
when the true worshippers shall worship the Father in spirit and in truth: for
the Father seeketh such to worship him.
24 God *is* a Spirit: and they that worship him must worship *him* in spirit and
in truth.
25 The woman saith unto him, I know
that Messias cometh, which is called
Christ: when he is come, he will tell us
all things.
26 Jesus saith unto her, I that speak
unto thee am *he*.
¶ 27 And upon this came his disciples,
and marvelled that he talked with the
woman: yet no man said, What seekest
thou? or, Why talkest thou with her?
28 The woman then left her waterpot,
and went her way into the city, and saith
to the men,
29 Come, see a man, which told me all
things that ever I did: is not this the
Christ?
30 Then they went out of the city, and
came unto him.
¶ 31 In the mean while his disciples
prayed him, saying, Master, eat.
32 But he said unto them, I have meat
to eat that ye know not of.
33 Therefore said the disciples one to
another, Hath any man brought him
ought to eat?
34 Jesus saith unto them, My meat is
to do the will of him that sent me, and
to finish his work.
35 Say not ye, There are yet four
months, and *then* cometh harvest? behold, I say unto you, Lift up your eyes,
and look on the fields; for they are white
already to harvest.
36 And he that reapeth receiveth
wages, and gathereth fruit unto life
eternal: that both he that soweth and he
that reapeth may rejoice together.
37 And herein is that saying true, One
soweth, and another reapeth.
38 I sent you to reap that whereon ye
bestowed no labour: other men laboured,
and ye are entered into their labours.
¶ 39 And many of the Samaritans of
that city believed on him for the saying
of the woman, which testified, He told
me all that ever I did.
40 So when the Samaritans were come
unto him, they besought him that he
would tarry with them: and he abode
there two days.
41 And many more believed because
of his own word;
42 And said unto the woman, Now we
believe, not because of thy saying: for
we have heard *him* ourselves, and know
that this is indeed the Christ, the Saviour of the world.
¶ 43 Now after two days he departed
thence, and went into Galilee.
44 For Jesus himself testified, that a
prophet hath no honour in his own
country.
45 Then when he was come into Galilee, the Galilaeans received him, having seen all the things that he did at

---

4:22 of the Jews. Because the Lord Jesus, the Messiah, was born a Jew, and from the Jewish nation the message of salvation went out to all the world.

4:24 God is a Spirit. See John 1:18 note, "Seeing God."

4:24 worship him in spirit and in truth. This speaks of our spirits communing with God, who is a Spirit, in reality—not just pretending to worship because we think we should or participating in some ceremony in which we do not think about Him.

4:25 Messias cometh, which is called Christ. "Messiah" is the Hebrew word for the Greek word "Christ." They both mean *the Anointed One,* King, Priest, Lord, Saviour.

4:32 I have meat. Compare Job 23:12. Jesus Himself is spiritual food and nourishment. Communion with Him feeds and nurtures our souls.

4:35 white already to harvest. Notice that Philip found the Samaritans ready to believe when he went down to Samaria (Acts 8:5-8).

4:42 Saviour of the world. The Lord Jesus Christ died for all men. God loves them all and is willing to save all who come to Him through Christ (John 6:37); yet only those who believe are saved (Acts 16:31).

Jerusalem at the feast: for they also went unto the feast.

The healing of the nobleman's son

46So Jesus came again into Cana of Galilee, where he made the water wine. And there was a certain nobleman, whose son was sick at Capernaum.

47When he heard that Jesus was come out of Judaea into Galilee, he went unto him, and besought him that he would come down, and heal his son: for he was at the point of death.

48Then said Jesus unto him, Except ye see signs and wonders, ye will not believe.

49The nobleman saith unto him, Sir, come down ere my child die.

50Jesus saith unto him, Go thy way; thy son liveth. And the man believed the word that Jesus had spoken unto him, and he went his way.

51And as he was now going down, his servants met him, and told *him,* saying, Thy son liveth.

52Then enquired he of them the hour when he began to amend. And they said unto him, Yesterday at the seventh hour the fever left him.

53So the father knew that *it was* at the same hour, in the which Jesus said unto him, Thy son liveth: and himself believed, and his whole house.

54This *is* again the second *miracle *that* Jesus did, when he was come out of Judaea into Galilee.

The healing at the pool of Bethesda

5 After this there was a feast of the Jews; and Jesus went up to Jerusalem.

2Now there is at Jerusalem by the sheep *market* a pool, which is called in the Hebrew tongue Bethesda, having five porches.

3In these lay a great multitude of impotent folk, of blind, halt, withered, waiting for the moving of the water.

4For an *angel went down at a certain season into the pool, and troubled the water: whosoever then first after the troubling of the water stepped in was made whole of whatsoever disease he had.

5And a certain man was there, which had an infirmity thirty and eight years.

6When Jesus saw him lie, and knew that he had been now a long time *in that case,* he saith unto him, Wilt thou be made whole?

7The impotent man answered him, Sir, I have no man, when the water is troubled, to put me into the pool: but while I am coming, another steppeth down before me.

8Jesus saith unto him, Rise, take up thy bed, and walk.

9And immediately the man was made whole, and took up his bed, and walked: and on the same day was the *sabbath.

¶10The Jews therefore said unto him

4:45 the feast. This was the *Passover.
4:46 made the water wine. See John 2:1-11. This was Jesus' first miracle.
4:46 nobleman. He was a government official, probably an officer in Herod's service.
5:1 feast of the Jews. This may have been another *Passover Feast, a year after the one mentioned in 2:13 and 4:45.
5:2 sheep market. The Sheep Gate.
5:2 in the Hebrew tongue. Not in the classical Hebrew of the Old Testament, but in Aramaic, the language of those brought from Babylon, where the Jewish people had spent many years in captivity.
5:2 five porches. They were covered resting places, or pavilions, around the pool.
5:3 impotent folk . . . halt, withered. Sick people. "Halt" means *lame;* "withered" means *paralyzed.*
5:3 the moving of the water. This expression, and the "troubling of the water" noted in verses 4 and 7, may speak of the occasional bubbling of the spring, which made the people think an angel was "troubling the water," or there could have actually been an angel who did this.
5:10 The Jews. The Jewish leaders.

that was cured, It is the sabbath day: it is not lawful for thee to carry *thy* bed.

11 He answered them, He that made me whole, the same said unto me, Take up thy bed, and walk.

12 Then asked they him, What man is that which said unto thee, Take up thy bed, and walk?

13 And he that was healed *wist not who it was: for Jesus had conveyed himself away, a multitude being in *that* place.

14 Afterward Jesus findeth him in the temple, and said unto him, Behold, thou art made whole: sin no more, lest a worse thing come unto thee.

15 The man departed, and told the Jews that it was Jesus, which had made him whole.

16 And therefore did the Jews persecute Jesus, and sought to slay him, because he had done these things on the sabbath day.

Jesus claims to be the Son of God

¶17 But Jesus answered them, My Father worketh hitherto, and I work.

18 Therefore the Jews sought the more to kill him, because he not only had broken the sabbath, but said also that God was his Father, making himself equal with God.

19 Then answered Jesus and said unto them, Verily, verily, I say unto you, The Son can do nothing of himself, but what he seeth the Father do: for what things soever he doeth, these also doeth the Son likewise.

20 For the Father loveth the Son, and sheweth him all things that himself doeth: and he will shew him greater works than these, that ye may marvel.

21 For as the Father raiseth up the dead, and quickeneth *them;* even so the Son quickeneth whom he will.

22 For the Father judgeth no man, but hath committed all judgment unto the Son:

23 That all *men* should honour the Son, even as they honour the Father. He that honoureth not the Son honoureth not the Father which hath sent him.

24 Verily, verily, I say unto you, He that heareth my word, and believeth on him that sent me, hath everlasting life, and shall not come into condemnation; but is passed from death unto life.

25 Verily, verily, I say unto you, The hour is coming, and now is, when the dead shall hear the voice of the Son of God: and they that hear shall live.

26 For as the Father hath life in him-

5:18 Christ's Character

The Lord Jesus Christ is God. Note four things about Him in this chapter:

1. He has power to give life (vss. 21,25,28);
2. He will be the Judge of all (vss. 22,27);
3. He is to be honored as the Father is honored (vs. 23); and
4. He has life in Himself (vs. 26).

5:14 sin no more. An initial step in salvation is repentance—turning against the sins of the former sinful life.

5:14 a worse thing. To die in his sins would be the worst thing that could happen to the man.

5:19 nothing of himself. Jesus Christ is God and yet He is perfect Man. Note this verse and verse 30. Jesus is emphasizing here that He is equal with God, indeed, is as much God as God the Father, and therein lay His power.

5:21 quickeneth. This means *to give life;* here it refers to the giving of eternal life that comes with new birth. See *born again.

5:22 judgment. Jesus Christ will one day judge the whole earth and all the people who have ever lived. All who accept Him as Saviour will not come under this judgment, because their sins were judged and paid for when the Son of God shed His blood on the cross.

5:25 the dead. Those who are spiritually dead to God, as everyone is by nature. The physically dead are mentioned in verse 28. See Revelation 20:6,11-15 (see 20:12 note, "The Dead" and Rev. 20:14 note).

self; so hath he given to the Son to have
life in himself;
27 And hath given him authority to
execute judgment also, because he is
the Son of man.

The two resurrections

28 Marvel not at this: for the hour is
coming, in the which all that are in the
graves shall hear his voice,
29 And shall come forth; they that
have done good, unto the *resurrection
of life; and they that have done evil,
unto the resurrection of *damnation.
30 I can of mine own self do nothing: as
I hear, I judge: and my judgment is *just;
because I seek not mine own will, but the
will of the Father which hath sent me.
31 If I bear witness of myself, my witness is not true.
¶32 There is another that beareth witness of me; and I know that the witness
which he witnesseth of me is true.

5:31-33, 36-39 Four Witnesses
The Lord Jesus meant that the Jews would call the witness untrue, for the Law required that there be two witnesses before any evidence could be counted true (see Num. 35:30; Deut. 17:6). Christ, however, had four witnesses:
1. John the Baptist (vs. 33; 1:34);
2. the works which His Father gave Him (vs. 36);
3. the Father Himself (vss. 37-38; compare 1 John 5:10); and
4. the Scriptures (vs. 39).

The four witnesses to the Lord Jesus:
*1) *John the Baptist*

33 Ye sent unto John, and he bare witness unto the truth.
34 But I receive not testimony from
man: but these things I say, that ye
might be saved.
35 He was a burning and a shining
light: and ye were willing for a season
to rejoice in his light.

2) His works

¶36 But I have greater witness than
that of John: for the works which the Father hath given me to finish, the same
works that I do, bear witness of me, that
the Father hath sent me.

3) The Father (Matt. 3:17)

37 And the Father himself, which hath
sent me, hath borne witness of me. Ye
have neither heard his voice at any
time, nor seen his shape.
38 And ye have not his word *abiding
in you: for whom he hath sent, him ye
believe not.

4) The Scriptures (Luke 24:27,44-46)

¶39 Search the scriptures; for in them
ye think ye have eternal life: and they
are they which testify of me.
40 And ye will not come to me, that ye
might have life.
41 I receive not honour from men.
42 But I know you, that ye have not
the love of God in you.
43 I am come in my Father's name, and
ye receive me not: if another shall come
in his own name, him ye will receive.
44 How can ye believe, which receive
honour one of another, and seek not the
honour that *cometh* from God only?
45 Do not think that I will accuse you
to the Father: there is *one* that accuseth
you, *even* Moses, in whom ye *trust.
46 For had ye believed Moses, ye
would have believed me: for he wrote
of me.
47 But if ye believe not his writings,
how shall ye believe my words?

The Lord feeds five thousand
(Matt. 14:13-21; Mark 6:32-44;
Luke 9:10-17)

6 After these things Jesus went
over the sea of Galilee, which is *the*
sea of Tiberias.
2 And a great multitude followed him,

5:37 nor seen his shape. See John 1:18 note, "Seeing God."
5:46 Moses . . . wrote of me. Christ was the true servant of the Law, as He was of the prophets, for every ordinance of the Law, every sacrifice, pointed to Him (see vs. 39).

because they saw his *miracles which
he did on them that were diseased.
3And Jesus went up into a mountain,
and there he sat with his disciples.
4And the passover, a feast of the
Jews, was nigh.
¶5When Jesus then lifted up *his* eyes,
and saw a great company come unto
him, he saith unto Philip, Whence shall
we buy bread, that these may eat?
6And this he said to *prove him: for
he himself knew what he would do.
7Philip answered him, Two hundred
pennyworth of bread is not sufficient for
them, that every one of them may take
a little.
8One of his disciples, Andrew, Simon
Peter's brother, saith unto him,
9There is a lad here, which hath five
barley loaves, and two small fishes: but
what are they among so many?
10And Jesus said, Make the men sit
down. Now there was much grass in the
place. So the men sat down, in number
about five thousand.
11And Jesus took the loaves; and
when he had given thanks, he distributed to the disciples, and the disciples
to them that were set down; and likewise of the fishes as much as they
would.
12When they were filled, he said unto
his disciples, Gather up the fragments
that remain, that nothing be lost.
13Therefore they gathered *them* together, and filled twelve baskets with
the fragments of the five barley loaves,
which remained over and above unto
them that had eaten.
14Then those men, when they had
seen the miracle that Jesus did, said,
This is of a truth that prophet that
should come into the world.

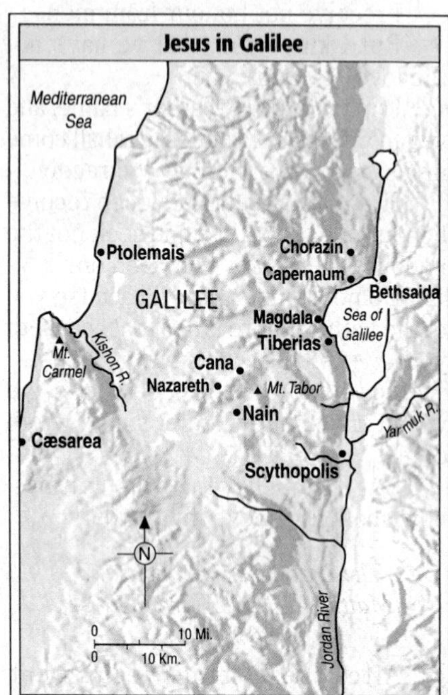

The Lord walks on the sea
(Matt. 14:22-36; Mark 6:45-56)

¶15When Jesus therefore perceived
that they would come and take him by
force, to make him a king, he departed
again into a mountain himself alone.
16And when even was *now* come, his
disciples went down unto the sea,
17And entered into a ship, and went
over the sea toward Capernaum. And it
was now dark, and Jesus was not come
to them.
18And the sea arose by reason of a
great wind that blew.
19So when they had rowed about five
and twenty or thirty *furlongs, they see
Jesus walking on the sea, and drawing
nigh unto the ship: and they were afraid.
20But he saith unto them, It is I; be
not *afraid.
21Then they willingly received him
into the ship: and immediately the ship
was at the land whither they went.

6:4 passover . . . was nigh. This is probably the third *Passover mentioned in the public life of the Lord Jesus.
6:7 pennyworth. The word "penny" is the denarius, which was equal to a full day's wage.
6:14 that prophet. See Deuteronomy 18:15,18 (see 18:15 note, "The Prophet").
6:15 to make him a king. Christ waited for His Father's time when He would be given

The Bread of Life

¶22 The day following, when the people which stood on the other side of the sea saw that there was none other boat there, save that one whereinto his disciples were entered, and that Jesus went not with his disciples into the boat, but *that* his disciples were gone away alone;

23 (Howbeit there came other boats from Tiberias nigh unto the place where they did eat bread, after that the Lord had given thanks:)

24 When the people therefore saw that Jesus was not there, neither his disciples, they also took shipping, and came to Capernaum, seeking for Jesus.

25 And when they had found him on the other side of the sea, they said unto him, Rabbi, when camest thou hither?

26 Jesus answered them and said, Verily, verily, I say unto you, Ye seek me, not because ye saw the miracles, but because ye did eat of the loaves, and were filled.

27 Labour not for the meat which perisheth, but for that meat which endureth unto everlasting life, which the Son of man shall give unto you: for him hath God the Father sealed.

28 Then said they unto him, What shall we do, that we might work the works of God?

29 Jesus answered and said unto them, This is the work of God, that ye believe on him whom he hath sent.

30 They said therefore unto him, What sign shewest thou then, that we may see, and believe thee? what dost thou work?

31 Our fathers did eat *manna in the desert; as it is written, He gave them bread from heaven to eat.

32 Then Jesus said unto them, Verily, verily, I say unto you, Moses gave you not that bread from heaven; but my Father giveth you the true bread from heaven.

33 For the bread of God is he which cometh down from heaven, and giveth life unto the world.

34 Then said they unto him, Lord, evermore give us this bread.

35 And Jesus said unto them, I am the bread of life: he that cometh to me shall never hunger; and he that believeth on me shall never thirst.

36 But I said unto you, That ye also have seen me, and believe not.

37 All that the Father giveth me shall come to me; and him that cometh to me I will in no wise cast out.

38 For I came down from heaven, not to do mine own will, but the will of him that sent me.

39 And this is the Father's will which hath sent me, that of all which he hath given me I should lose nothing, but should raise it up again at the last day.

40 And this is the will of him that sent me, that every one which seeth the Son, and believeth on him, may have everlasting life: and I will raise him up at the last day.

41 The Jews then murmured at him, because he said, I am the bread which came down from heaven.

42 And they said, Is not this Jesus, the son of Joseph, whose father and mother we know? how is it then that he saith, I came down from heaven?

43 Jesus therefore answered and said unto them, Murmur not among yourselves.

44 No man can come to me, except the Father which hath sent me draw him: and I will raise him up at the last day.

45 It is written in the prophets, And

---

the throne of David; He would take it without force. See *kingdom.

6:31 He gave them bread. See Nehemiah 9:15.

6:32 the true bread. The Lord Jesus Christ is the spiritual food for our daily lives (see also vss. 33,35,48). See also *manna.

6:37 All that the Father giveth me. Whoever will may come to Christ (3:16); those who do come will not be turned away.

6:40 I will raise him. This speaks of the *resurrection of believers in Christ.

they shall be all taught of God. Every
man therefore that hath heard, and hath
learned of the Father, cometh unto me.
46 Not that any man hath seen the
Father, save he which is of God, he hath
seen the Father.
47 Verily, verily, I say unto you, He
that believeth on me hath everlasting
life.
48 I am that bread of life.
49 Your fathers did eat manna in the
wilderness, and are dead.
50 This is the bread which cometh
down from heaven, that a man may eat
thereof, and not die.
51 I am the living bread which came
down from heaven: if any man eat of this
bread, he shall live for ever: and the
bread that I will give is my flesh, which
I will give for the life of the world.
52 The Jews therefore strove among
themselves, saying, How can this man
give us *his* flesh to eat?
53 Then Jesus said unto them, Verily,
verily, I say unto you, Except ye eat the
flesh of the Son of man, and drink his
blood, ye have no life in you.
54 Whoso eateth my flesh, and
drinketh my blood, hath *eternal life;
and I will raise him up at the last day.
55 For my flesh is meat indeed, and my
blood is drink indeed.
56 He that eateth my flesh, and
drinketh my blood, dwelleth in me, and
I in him.
57 As the living Father hath sent me,
and I live by the Father: so he that
eateth me, even he shall live by me.
58 This is that bread which came down
from heaven: not as your fathers did eat
manna, and are dead: he that eateth of
this bread shall live for ever.
59 These things said he in the *synagogue, as he taught in Capernaum.

The testing of the disciples
(Matt. 8:19-22; 10:36)

60 Many therefore of his disciples,
when they had heard *this*, said, This is
an hard saying; who can hear it?
61 When Jesus knew in himself that
his disciples murmured at it, he said
unto them, Doth this offend you?
62 *What* and if ye shall see the Son of
man ascend up where he was before?
63 It is the spirit that quickeneth; the
flesh profiteth nothing: the words that
I speak unto you, *they* are spirit, and *they*
are life.
64 But there are some of you that believe not. For Jesus knew from the beginning who they were that believed
not, and who should betray him.
65 And he said, Therefore said I unto

6:51 CHRIST'S FLESH

Verse 51 is the key verse to this great discourse. The Lord Jesus tells exactly how He was to be the Bread of Life. He, the living Son of God, was to give His body (His flesh) to be killed on the cross in order that all who trust in Him as Saviour (eating of that Bread) should have eternal life. St. Augustine said, "Believe, and thou hast eaten."

When He said, "whoso eateth my flesh" (vs. 54), the Lord was using the illustration of food to show the people what it is to take Him as their Saviour. Food and drink become part of us and sustain our lives; and so our Lord, dwelling in us, sustains our spiritual lives. It was the Passover time, when the people were thinking especially of the need to kill a lamb and eat its flesh. They were also reminded of the time in Egypt when they had sprinkled the blood of the lamb on their doors that their firstborn might not die. The Lord Jesus, the Lamb of God (John 1:29), knew that they could understand His references.

6:45 taught of God. A quotation from Isaiah 54:13.
6:46 seen the Father. Look up John 1:18 note, "Seeing God."
6:50 not die. This refers to the *second death.
6:62 ascend up. This was fulfilled in the Ascension (Mark 16:19).
6:63 flesh. In this verse flesh means our ordinary human nature, which cannot help us understand the things of God. See 2 Corinthians 5:16.

you, that no man can come unto me, except it were given unto him of my Father.
¶[66]From that *time* many of his disciples went back, and walked no more with him.

Peter's confession
(Matt. 16:13-20; Mark 8:27-30;
Luke 9:18-21)

[67]Then said Jesus unto the twelve,
Will ye also go away?
[68]Then Simon Peter answered him,
Lord, to whom shall we go? thou hast the words of eternal life.
[69]And we believe and are sure that
thou art that Christ, the Son of the living God.
[70]Jesus answered them, Have not I
chosen you twelve, and one of you is a *devil?
[71]He spake of *Judas Iscariot *the son*
of Simon: for he it was that should betray him, being one of the twelve.

The Lord and His brothers

7 After these things Jesus walked in Galilee: for he would not walk in Jewry, because the Jews sought to kill him.
[2]Now the Jews' feast of tabernacles
was at hand.
[3]His brethren therefore said unto
him, Depart hence, and go into Judaea, that thy disciples also may see the works that thou doest.
[4]For *there is* no man *that* doeth any
thing in secret, and he himself seeketh to be known openly. If thou do these things, shew thyself to the *world.
[5]For neither did his brethren believe
in him.
[6]Then Jesus said unto them, My time
is not yet come: but your time is alway ready.
[7]The world cannot hate you; but me
it hateth, because I testify of it, that the works thereof are evil.
[8]Go ye up unto this feast: I go not up
yet unto this feast; for my time is not yet full come.
[9]When he had said these words unto
them, he abode *still* in Galilee.

Jesus at the Feast of Tabernacles

¶[10]But when his brethren were gone
up, then went he also up unto the feast, not openly, but as it were in secret.
[11]Then the Jews sought him at the
feast, and said, Where is he?
[12]And there was much murmuring
among the people concerning him: for some said, He is a good man: others said, Nay; but he deceiveth the people.
[13]Howbeit no man spake openly of
him for fear of the Jews.
¶[14]Now about the midst of the feast
Jesus went up into the temple, and taught.
[15]And the Jews marvelled, saying,
How knoweth this man letters, having never learned?
[16]Jesus answered them, and said,
My *doctrine is not mine, but his that sent me.
[17]If any man will do his will, he shall
know of the doctrine, whether it be of *God, or *whether* I speak of myself.
[18]He that speaketh of himself seeketh
his own glory: but he that seeketh his glory that sent him, the same is true, and no unrighteousness is in him.
[19]Did not *Moses give you the *law,
and *yet* none of you keepeth the law? Why go ye about to kill me?
[20]The people answered and said,
Thou hast a devil: who goeth about to kill thee?
[21]Jesus answered and said unto
them, I have done one work, and ye all marvel.
[22]Moses therefore gave unto you
*circumcision; (not because it is of Moses, but of the fathers;) and ye on the sabbath day circumcise a man.

7:13 for fear of the Jews. The people were afraid to make the Jewish leaders angry.
7:15 having never learned. Jesus had not attended either of the great schools of theology in Jerusalem, that of Hillel or Shammai.

[23]If a man on the sabbath day receive
circumcision, that the law of Moses
should not be broken; are ye angry at
me, because I have made a man every
whit whole on the sabbath day?
[24]Judge not according to the appearance, but judge righteous judgment.
[25]Then said some of them of *Jerusalem, Is not this he, whom they seek
to kill?
[26]But, lo, he speaketh boldly, and they
say nothing unto him. Do the rulers
know indeed that this is the very
*Christ?
[27]Howbeit we know this man whence
he is: but when Christ cometh, no man
knoweth whence he is.
[28]Then cried Jesus in the temple as
he taught, saying, Ye both know me, and
ye know whence I am: and I am not
come of myself, but he that sent me is
true, whom ye know not.
[29]But I know him: for I am from him,
and he hath sent me.
[30]Then they sought to take him: but
no man laid hands on him, because his
hour was not yet come.
[31]And many of the people believed on
him, and said, When Christ cometh, will
he do more miracles than these which
this *man* hath done?
¶[32]The *Pharisees heard that the
people murmured such things concerning him; and the Pharisees and the chief
priests sent officers to take him.
[33]Then said Jesus unto them, Yet a
little while am I with you, and *then* I go
unto him that sent me.
[34]Ye shall seek me, and shall not find
me: and where I am, *thither* ye cannot
come.
[35]Then said the Jews among themselves, Whither will he go, that we shall
not find him? will he go unto the dispersed among the *Gentiles, and teach
the Gentiles?
[36]What *manner of* saying is this that
he said, Ye shall seek me, and shall not
find *me:* and where I am, *thither* ye cannot come?

The great prophecy about the Holy Spirit
(See 4:14)

[37]In the last day, that great *day* of the
feast, Jesus stood and cried, saying, If
any man thirst, let him come unto me,
and drink.
[38]He that believeth on me, as the
scripture hath said, out of his belly shall
flow rivers of living water.
[39](But this spake he of the Spirit,
which they that believe on him should

7:37 THE GREAT DAY OF THE FEAST

The great day was the eighth day (Lev. 23:36) or the last day of the Feast of Tabernacles that lasted seven days. This great day was a Sabbath of great rejoicing. Every day for the previous seven days the priest passed through the streets with water brought in a golden vessel from the Pool of Siloam. He poured this water on the altar while the people sang: "With joy shall ye draw water out of the wells of salvation" (Isa. 12:3).

The water stood for two things:

1. God had supplied the Israelites' need for water in the wilderness; and
2. God had promised that there would someday be rivers of water in the wilderness–a promise of spiritual blessing. On the last day, the eighth day, the priest did not carry the water.

This was also to show two things:

1. They were in the land and did not need the wilderness water; and
2. The spiritual blessings had not yet come. Therefore, when the Lord Jesus Christ called out, "If any man thirst, let him come unto me, and drink," the people who understood knew that they might have the spiritual blessings in Him and through Him (vs. 37).

7:27 whence he is. The people thought they knew that He was from Nazareth of Galilee.
7:35 dispersed among the Gentiles. See 1 Peter 1:1 and James 1:1.
7:38 out of his belly. Out of his heart.

receive: for the Holy Ghost was not yet
given; because that Jesus was not yet
glorified.)

The attitudes of the people and the rulers

¶40Many of the people therefore,
when they heard this saying, said, Of a
truth this is the Prophet.
41Others said, This is the Christ. But
some said, Shall Christ come out of
Galilee?
42Hath not the scripture said, That
Christ cometh of the seed of *David,
and out of the town of Bethlehem,
where David was?
43So there was a division among the
people because of him.
44And some of them would have tak-
en him; but no man laid hands on him.
¶45Then came the officers to the
chief priests and Pharisees; and they
said unto them, Why have ye not
brought him?
46The officers answered, Never man
spake like this man.
47Then answered them the Pharisees, Are ye also deceived?
48Have any of the rulers or of the
Pharisees believed on him?
49But this people who knoweth not
the law are cursed.
50Nicodemus saith unto them, (he
that came to Jesus by night, being one
of them,)
51Doth our law judge *any* man, before
it hear him, and know what he doeth?
52They answered and said unto
him, Art thou also of Galilee? Search,
and look: for out of Galilee ariseth no
prophet.
53And every man went unto his own
house.

The sinning woman

8 Jesus went unto the mount of
Olives.
2And early in the morning he came
again into the temple, and all the people came unto him; and he sat down,
and taught them.
3And the *scribes and Pharisees
brought unto him a woman taken in
adultery; and when they had set her in
the midst,
4They say unto him, Master, this
woman was taken in adultery, in the
very act.
5Now Moses in the law commanded
us, that such should be stoned: but what
sayest thou?
6This they said, *tempting him, that
they might have to accuse him. But
Jesus stooped down, and with *his* finger
wrote on the ground, *as though he heard
them not.*
7So when they continued asking him,
he lifted up himself, and said unto them,
He that is without *sin among you, let
him first cast a stone at her.
8And again he stooped down, and
wrote on the ground.
9And they which heard *it,* being convicted by *their own* conscience, went out
one by one, beginning at the eldest, *even*
unto the last: and Jesus was left alone,
and the woman standing in the midst.
10When Jesus had lifted up himself,
and saw none but the woman, he said
unto her, Woman, where are those thine
accusers? hath no man condemned
thee?

7:40 the Prophet. See Deuteronomy 18:15,18 and Deuteronomy 18:15 note, "The Prophet." Jesus was the fulfillment of Deuteronomy 18:15.
7:42 That Christ cometh of the seed of David. See 2 Samuel 7:12; Psalm 132:11.
7:42 out of the town of Bethlehem. See Micah 5:2 and its note, "A Description of Christ."
7:44 would have taken him. Some of the Jews would have arrested Him for claiming to be God.
7:50 Nicodemus. See John 3.
8:5 Moses in the law. See Leviticus 20:10. Both the adulteress and the adulterer should have been arrested—not just the woman. According to the Law, both would have been stoned. The leaders were again trying to trap Jesus.

11 She said, No man, Lord. And Jesus said unto her, Neither do I condemn thee: go, and sin no more.

The great talk on the Light of the World (1:9)

¶ 12 Then spake Jesus again unto them, saying, I am the light of the world: he that followeth me shall not walk in darkness, but shall have the light of life.

13 The Pharisees therefore said unto him, Thou bearest record of thyself; thy record is not true.

14 Jesus answered and said unto them, Though I bear record of myself, *yet* my record is true: for I know whence I came, and whither I go; but ye cannot tell whence I come, and whither I go.

15 Ye judge after the *flesh; I judge no man.

16 And yet if I judge, my judgment is true: for I am not alone, but I and the Father that sent me.

17 It is also written in your law, that the testimony of two men is true.

18 I am one that bear witness of myself, and the Father that sent me beareth witness of me.

19 Then said they unto him, Where is thy Father? Jesus answered, Ye neither know me, nor my Father: if ye had known me, ye should have known my Father also.

20 These words spake Jesus in the *treasury, as he taught in the temple: and no man laid hands on him; for his hour was not yet come.

21 Then said Jesus again unto them, I go my way, and ye shall seek me, and shall die in your sins: whither I go, ye cannot come.

22 Then said the Jews, Will he kill himself? because he saith, Whither I go, ye cannot come.

23 And he said unto them, Ye are from beneath; I am from above: ye are of this world; I am not of this world.

24 I said therefore unto you, that ye shall die in your sins: for if ye believe not that I am *he,* ye shall die in your sins.

25 Then said they unto him, Who art thou? And Jesus saith unto them, Even *the same* that I said unto you from the beginning.

26 I have many things to say and to judge of you: but he that sent me is true; and I speak to the world those things which I have heard of him.

27 They understood not that he spake to them of the Father.

28 Then said Jesus unto them, When ye have lifted up the Son of man, then shall ye know that I am *he,* and *that* I do nothing of myself; but as my Father hath taught me, I speak these things.

29 And he that sent me is with me: the Father hath not left me alone; for I do always those things that please him.

Jesus talks with believers and unbelievers

30 As he spake these words, many believed on him.

31 Then said Jesus to those Jews which believed on him, If ye continue in my word, *then* are ye my disciples indeed;

32 And ye shall know the truth, and the truth shall make you free.

¶ 33 They answered him, We be *Abraham's seed, and were never in bondage to any man: how sayest thou, Ye shall be made free?

8:12 the light of the world. During the Feast of Tabernacles, the great golden candelabra were lit at certain times in the treasury (vs. 20). Now the lights were out, and the Lord reminded them that He, the true Light, can never be dimmed.

8:15 I judge no man. The time was not yet come for this.

8:17 in your law. See Deuteronomy 19:15.

8:33 Abraham's seed. The descendants of Abraham, as all Jews were. See also verse 39. They were descendants of Abraham, but they were not his children in the sense of being his descendants in the faith (see Rom. 9:6-8). All people, whether Jews or Gentiles, who have true believing faith in God and His Word, are children of Abraham (see Gal. 3:7; compare Gal. 3:6-14).

[34]Jesus answered them, Verily, verily, I say unto you, Whosoever committeth sin is the servant of sin.
[35]And the servant abideth not in the house for ever: *but* the Son abideth ever.
[36]If the Son therefore shall make you free, ye shall be free indeed.
[37]I know that ye are Abraham's seed; but ye seek to kill me, because my word hath no place in you.
[38]I speak that which I have seen with my Father: and ye do that which ye have seen with your father.
[39]They answered and said unto him, Abraham is our father. Jesus saith unto them, If ye were Abraham's children, ye would do the works of Abraham.
[40]But now ye seek to kill me, a man that hath told you the truth, which I have heard of God: this did not Abraham.
[41]Ye do the deeds of your father. Then said they to him, We be not born of fornication; we have one Father, *even* God.
[42]Jesus said unto them, If God were your Father, ye would love me: for I proceeded forth and came from God; neither came I of myself, but he sent me.
[43]Why do ye not understand my speech? *even* because ye cannot hear my word.
[44]Ye are of *your* father the devil, and the *lusts of your father ye will do. He was a murderer from the beginning, and abode not in the truth, because there is no truth in him. When he speaketh a lie, he speaketh of his own: for he is a liar, and the father of it.
[45]And because I tell *you* the truth, ye believe me not.
[46]Which of you convinceth me of sin? And if I say the truth, why do ye not believe me?
[47]He that is of God heareth God's words: ye therefore hear *them* not, because ye are not of God.
[48]Then answered the Jews, and said unto him, Say we not well that thou art a *Samaritan, and hast a devil?
[49]Jesus answered, I have not a devil; but I honour my Father, and ye do dishonour me.
[50]And I seek not mine own glory: there is one that seeketh and judgeth.
[51]Verily, verily, I say unto you, If a man keep my saying, he shall never see death.
[52]Then said the Jews unto him, Now we know that thou hast a devil. Abraham is dead, and the *prophets; and thou sayest, If a man keep my saying, he shall never taste of death.
[53]Art thou greater than our father Abraham, which is dead? and the prophets are dead: whom makest thou thyself?
[54]Jesus answered, If I honour myself, my honour is nothing: it is my Father that honoureth me; of whom ye say, that he is your God:
[55]Yet ye have not known him; but I know him: and if I should say, I know him not, I shall be a liar like unto you: but I know him, and keep his saying.
[56]Your father Abraham rejoiced to see my day: and he saw *it,* and was glad.
[57]Then said the Jews unto him, Thou art not yet fifty years old, and hast thou seen Abraham?
[58]Jesus said unto them, Verily, verily,

8:51 THREE KINDS OF DEATH

There are three kinds of death:

1. spiritual death, which was the death Adam and Eve died when they sinned (Gen. 3:1-6; see also Gen. 3:6 note, "The Fall of Man"), and which meant they were dead toward God–Adam and Eve's perfect spiritual communion with God was broken. Since then everyone has been spiritually dead (Eph. 2:1) until he or she is accepted by God through faith in His Son;
2. physical death, the end of our life on earth; and
3. the *second death, the judgment of the unsaved at the Great White Throne (Rev. 20:14).

I say unto you, Before Abraham was,
I am.
[59]Then took they up stones to cast at
him: but Jesus hid himself, and went out
of the temple, going through the midst
of them, and so passed by.

The healing of the man born blind

9 And as *Jesus* passed by, he saw a
man which was blind from *his*
birth.
[2]And his disciples asked him, saying,
Master, who did sin, this man, or his
parents, that he was born blind?
[3]Jesus answered, Neither hath this
man sinned, nor his parents: but that
the works of God should be made manifest in him.
[4]I must work the works of him that
sent me, while it is day: the night
cometh, when no man can work.
[5]As long as I am in the world, I am the
light of the world.
[6]When he had thus spoken, he spat
on the ground, and made clay of the
spittle, and he anointed the eyes of the
blind man with the clay,
[7]And said unto him, Go, wash in the
pool of Siloam, (which is by interpretation, Sent.) He went his way therefore,
and washed, and came seeing.
¶[8]The neighbours therefore, and
they which before had seen him that he
was blind, said, Is not this he that sat
and begged?
[9]Some said, This is he: others *said,*
He is like him: *but* he said, I am *he.*
[10]Therefore said they unto him, How
were thine eyes opened?
[11]He answered and said, A man that
is called Jesus made clay, and anointed
mine eyes, and said unto me, Go to the
pool of Siloam, and wash: and I went and
washed, and I received sight.
[12]Then said they unto him, Where is
he? He said, I know not.
¶[13]They brought to the Pharisees
him that aforetime was blind.
[14]And it was the sabbath day when
Jesus made the clay, and opened his
eyes.
[15]Then again the Pharisees also
asked him how he had received his
sight. He said unto them, He put clay
upon mine eyes, and I washed, and do
see.
[16]Therefore said some of the Pharisees, This man is not of God, because
he keepeth not the sabbath day. Others
said, How can a man that is a sinner do
such *miracles? And there was a division among them.
[17]They say unto the blind man again,
What sayest thou of him, that he hath
opened thine eyes? He said, He is a
prophet.
[18]But the Jews did not believe concerning him, that he had been blind, and
received his sight, until they called the
parents of him that had received his
sight.
[19]And they asked them, saying, Is
this your son, who ye say was born
blind? how then doth he now see?
[20]His parents answered them and
said, We know that this is our son, and
that he was born blind:
[21]But by what means he now seeth,
we know not; or who hath opened his
eyes, we know not: he is of age; ask
him: he shall speak for himself.
[22]These *words* spake his parents,
because they feared the Jews: for the
Jews had agreed already, that if any man
did *confess that he was Christ, he
should be put out of the synagogue.
[23]Therefore said his parents, He is of
age; ask him.

8:58 I am. One of the *names of God (Exod. 3:14). The Jews thought that our Lord Jesus was committing a terrible sin, that He was blaspheming by claiming to be God. The punishment for blasphemy was death by stoning.

9:22 put out of the synagogue. To be cast out of the synagogue where the Jews met for worship meant that no one would have anything more to do with the person or people cast out, or excommunicated. The blind man's parents were afraid of being shunned by everyone.

24 Then again called they the man that
was blind, and said unto him, Give God
the praise: we know that this man is a
sinner.
25 He answered and said, Whether he
be a sinner *or no,* I know not: one thing
I know, that, whereas I was blind, now
I see.
26 Then said they to him again, What
did he to thee? how opened he thine
eyes?
27 He answered them, I have told you
already, and ye did not hear: wherefore
would ye hear *it* again? will ye also be
his disciples?
28 Then they reviled him, and said,
Thou art his disciple; but we are Moses' disciples.
29 We know that God spake unto Moses: *as for* this *fellow,* we know not from
whence he is.
30 The man answered and said unto
them, Why herein is a marvellous thing,
that ye know not from whence he is,
and *yet* he hath opened mine eyes.
31 Now we know that God heareth not
sinners: but if any man be a worshipper
of God, and doeth his will, him he
heareth.
32 Since the world began was it not
heard that any man opened the eyes of
one that was born blind.
33 If this man were not of God, he
could do nothing.
34 They answered and said unto him,
Thou wast altogether born in sins,
and dost thou teach us? And they cast
him out.
35 Jesus heard that they had cast him
out; and when he had found him, he said
unto him, Dost thou believe on the Son
of God?
36 He answered and said, Who is he,
Lord, that I might believe on him?
37 And Jesus said unto him, Thou hast
both seen him, and it is he that talketh
with thee.
38 And he said, Lord, I believe. And he
worshipped him.
¶39 And Jesus said, For judgment I
am come into this world, that they
which see not might see; and that they
which see might be made blind.
40 And *some* of the Pharisees which
were with him heard these words, and
said unto him, Are we blind also?
41 Jesus said unto them, If ye were
blind, ye should have no sin: but now ye
say, We see; therefore your sin
remaineth.

The great talk on the Good Shepherd

10 Verily, verily, I say unto you,
He that entereth not by the door
into the sheepfold, but climbeth up
some other way, the same is a thief and
a robber.
2 But he that entereth in by the door
is the shepherd of the sheep.
3 To him the porter openeth; and the
sheep hear his voice: and he calleth
his own sheep by name, and leadeth
them out.
4 And when he putteth forth his own
sheep, he goeth before them, and the
sheep follow him: for they know his
voice.
5 And a stranger will they not follow,
but will flee from him: for they know
not the voice of strangers.
6 This *parable spake Jesus unto
them: but they understood not what
things they were which he spake unto
them.

9:39 For judgment I am come. Compare John 8:15. He was not sent to judge (3:17), but because He had come, judgment followed, as people showed their faith or unbelief in Him.

9:39 they which see not . . . they which see. Those who have not understood the things of God, though they have minds like little children, may believe the revelation of the Lord Jesus Christ, and therefore see. Those who had been wise and had understood the Old Testament Law and covenant promises rested in what they knew. They did not want any further sight. Therefore, they could not go forward in knowledge, and they lost any true sight that they had. "Might be made blind" is "may become blind."

[7]Then said Jesus unto them again,
Verily, verily, I say unto you, I am the
door of the sheep.
[8]All that ever came before me are
thieves and robbers: but the sheep did
not hear them.
[9]I am the door: by me if any man enter in, he shall be saved, and shall go in
and out, and find pasture.
[10]The thief cometh not, but for to
steal, and to kill, and to destroy: I am
come that they might have life, and that
they might have *it* more abundantly.
[11]I am the good shepherd: the good
shepherd giveth his life for the sheep.
[12]But he that is an hireling, and not
the shepherd, whose own the sheep are
not, seeth the wolf coming, and leaveth
the sheep, and fleeth: and the wolf
catcheth them, and scattereth the
sheep.
[13]The hireling fleeth, because he is
an hireling, and careth not for the
sheep.
[14]I am the good shepherd, and know
my *sheep,* and am known of mine.
[15]As the Father knoweth me, even so
know I the Father: and I lay down my
life for the sheep.
[16]And other sheep I have, which are
not of this fold: them also I must
bring, and they shall hear my voice;

10:16 The Other Sheep
The Gentiles were referred to as the "other sheep" to whom the gospel was to be preached. The sheepfold was an enclosure with a high stone wall into which sheep could be driven at night for safety. The Jews, who refused to mix with any other nation, were like sheep inside the high wall of a fold. When the gospel began to be preached, both Jews and Gentiles were saved and came into the same fold–the *church of Christ.

and there shall be one fold, *and* one
shepherd.
[17]Therefore doth my Father love me,
because I lay down my life, that I might
take it again.
[18]No man taketh it from me, but I lay
it down of myself. I have power to lay
it down, and I have power to take it
again. This commandment have I received of my Father.
¶[19]There was a division therefore
again among the Jews for these sayings.
[20]And many of them said, He hath a
devil, and is mad; why hear ye him?
[21]Others said, These are not the
words of him that hath a devil. Can a
devil open the eyes of the blind?

Jesus questioned by the Jews

¶[22]And it was at Jerusalem the feast
of the dedication, and it was winter.

10:22 The Feast of Dedication
This feast was held on the twenty-fifth of the winter month Kislev, December, and lasted eight days. It was also known as the Feast of Lights. It was instituted to commemorate the cleansing of the temple after its defilement by Antiochus Epiphanes (Dan. 11:31). This feast was celebrated in almost the same manner as the Feast of Tabernacles–the offering of many sacrifices, the carrying of branches of trees, and other rejoicing. It is mentioned only once, here in John, in the canonical Scriptures.

[23]And Jesus walked in the temple in
Solomon's porch.
[24]Then came the Jews round about
him, and said unto him, How long dost
thou make us to doubt? If thou be the
Christ, tell us plainly.
[25]Jesus answered them, I told you,
and ye believed not: the works that I do

10:10 abundantly. This means full of joy and true happiness. When we are *born again we receive new life from Christ. This is happier, fuller, and much more satisfying than the ordinary human life.

10:18 No man taketh it from me. See Matthew 26:53 and John 18:11.

10:18 I have power. I have the right. Jesus could easily have stopped His trial and crucifixion if He had chosen to do so, but He came to do His Father's will and reconcile mankind to God.

in my Father's name, they bear witness
of me.
[26]But ye believe not, because ye are
not of my sheep, as I said unto you.
[27]My sheep hear my voice, and I
know them, and they follow me:
[28]And I give unto them *eternal life;
and they shall never perish, neither
shall any *man* pluck them out of my
hand.
[29]My Father, which gave *them* me, is
greater than all; and no *man* is able to
pluck *them* out of my Father's hand.
[30]I and *my* Father are one.
[31]Then the Jews took up stones again
to stone him.
[32]Jesus answered them, Many good
works have I shewed you from my Father;
for which of those works do ye
stone me?
[33]The Jews answered him, saying,
For a good work we stone thee not; but
for blasphemy; and because that thou,
being a man, makest thyself God.
[34]Jesus answered them, Is it not written
in your law, I said, Ye are gods?
[35]If he called them gods, unto whom
the word of God came, and the scripture
cannot be broken;
[36]Say ye of him, whom the Father
hath sanctified, and sent into the world,
Thou blasphemest; because I said, I am
the Son of God?
[37]If I do not the works of my Father,
believe me not.
[38]But if I do, though ye believe not
me, believe the works: that ye may
know, and believe, that the Father *is* in
me, and I in him.
[39]Therefore they sought again to take
him: but he escaped out of their hand,
[40]And went away again beyond Jordan
into the place where John at first
baptized; and there he abode.
[41]And many resorted unto him, and
said, John did no *miracle: but all things
that John spake of this man were true.
[42]And many believed on him there.

Lazarus raised from the dead

11 Now a certain *man* was sick,
named Lazarus, of Bethany, the
town of Mary and her sister Martha.
[2](It was *that* Mary which anointed
the Lord with ointment, and wiped his
feet with her hair, whose brother Lazarus
was sick.)
[3]Therefore his sisters sent unto him,
saying, Lord, behold, he whom thou
lovest is sick.
[4]When Jesus heard *that,* he said, This
sickness is not unto *death, but for the
glory of God, that the Son of God might
be glorified thereby.
[5]Now Jesus loved Martha, and her
sister, and Lazarus.
[6]When he had heard therefore that he
was sick, he abode two days still in the
same place where he was.
[7]Then after that saith he to *his* disciples,
Let us go into Judaea again.
[8]*His* disciples say unto him, Master,
the Jews of late sought to stone thee;
and goest thou thither again?
[9]Jesus answered, Are there not
twelve hours in the day? If any man
walk in the day, he stumbleth not, because
he seeth the light of this world.

10:30 I and my Father are one. Here the Lord answered again for the Jews their question of verse 24. He told them, "I and my Father in Our essence, Our real character, are one." Notice the Jews' unbelief, however (vs. 31). They did not really want to be told "plainly" (vs. 24), even though they had asked Christ for just that in verse 24.

10:34 Ye are gods. See Psalm 82:6. The Israelite judges were called gods because God used them as His instruments. He gave the Word through them (vs. 35). If those early Jewish leaders were called gods, Jesus was certainly not committing blasphemy by telling His people who He is—the Son of God.

11:2 that Mary. See John 12:3; Matthew 26:7; Mark 14:3.

11:9 twelve hours in the day. The Lord was telling them that just as a man may work in the daytime without fear of stumbling, so it was still work time for Him. He could safely continue His work, therefore, until the night—His hour—had come.

10But if a man walk in the night,
he stumbleth, because there is no light
in him.
11These things said he: and after that
he saith unto them, Our friend Lazarus
sleepeth; but I go, that I may awake him
out of sleep.
12Then said his disciples, Lord, if he
sleep, he shall do well.
13Howbeit Jesus spake of his death:
but they thought that he had spoken of
taking of rest in sleep.
14Then said Jesus unto them plainly,
Lazarus is dead.
15And I am glad for your sakes that I
was not there, to the intent ye may believe; nevertheless let us go unto him.
16Then said Thomas, which is called
Didymus, unto his fellow disciples, Let
us also go, that we may die with him.
17Then when Jesus came, he found
that he had *lain* in the grave four days
already.
18Now Bethany was nigh unto Jerusalem, about fifteen *furlongs off:
19And many of the Jews came to Martha and Mary, to comfort them concerning their brother.
20Then Martha, as soon as she heard
that Jesus was coming, went and met
him: but Mary sat *still* in the house.
21Then said Martha unto Jesus, Lord,
if thou hadst been here, my brother had
not died.
22But I know, that even now, whatsoever thou wilt ask of God, God will give
it thee.
23Jesus saith unto her, Thy brother
shall rise again.
24Martha saith unto him, I know that
he shall rise again in the *resurrection
at the last day.
25Jesus said unto her, I am the resurrection, and the life: he that believeth
in me, though he were dead, yet shall
he live:
26And whosoever liveth and believeth in me shall never die. Believest
thou this?
27She saith unto him, Yea, Lord: I
believe that thou art the Christ, the Son
of God, which should come into the
world.
28And when she had so said, she went
her way, and called Mary her sister secretly, saying, The Master is come, and
calleth for thee.
29As soon as she heard *that,* she arose
quickly, and came unto him.
30Now Jesus was not yet come into
the town, but was in that place where
Martha met him.
31The Jews then which were with her
in the house, and comforted her, when
they saw Mary, that she rose up hastily
and went out, followed her, saying, She
goeth unto the grave to weep there.
32Then when Mary was come where
Jesus was, and saw him, she fell down
at his feet, saying unto him, Lord, if
thou hadst been here, my brother had
not died.
33When Jesus therefore saw her
weeping, and the Jews also weeping
which came with her, he groaned in the
spirit, and was troubled,
34And said, Where have ye laid him?
They said unto him, Lord, come and
see.
35Jesus wept.
36Then said the Jews, Behold how he
loved him!
37And some of them said, Could not
this man, which opened the eyes of the

11:16 Didymus. Twin.

11:25 I am the resurrection. The Lord's salvation begins a new life, both now and after physical death, for He is the only salvation. With resurrection, true life begins (compare Gal. 2:20).

11:26 shall never die. This speaks of spiritual *death, not physical death.

11:27 thou art the Christ. Compare Martha's words here with Peter's confession in Matthew 16:16 and John 6:68-69.

11:28 The Master is come, and calleth for thee. Jesus wanted to speak to Mary privately as well. He loved Mary, Martha, and Lazarus very much.

11:35 Sharing Sorrow
Though Jesus knew that in a short time the tears of Mary and Martha would be forgotten, His love and sympathy were so very great that He wept with them. Though we have the promise that God will wipe away all tears from our eyes (Rev. 21:4), He still shares our sorrows with us because of His great love and compassion for us.

blind, have caused that even this man
should not have died?

Jesus at the grave of Lazarus

38Jesus therefore again groaning in
himself cometh to the grave. It was a
cave, and a stone lay upon it.
39Jesus said, Take ye away the stone.
Martha, the sister of him that was dead,
saith unto him, Lord, by this time he stinketh: for he hath been *dead* four days.
40Jesus saith unto her, Said I not unto
thee, that, if thou wouldest believe,
thou shouldest see the glory of God?
41Then they took away the stone
from the place where the dead was laid.
And Jesus lifted up *his* eyes, and said,
Father, I thank thee that thou hast
heard me.
42And I knew that thou hearest me
always: but because of the people which
stand by I said *it,* that they may believe
that thou hast sent me.
43And when he thus had spoken, he
cried with a loud voice, Lazarus, come
forth.
44And he that was dead came forth,
bound hand and foot with graveclothes:
and his face was bound about with a
napkin. Jesus saith unto them, Loose
him, and let him go.
45Then many of the Jews which came
to Mary, and had seen the things which
Jesus did, believed on him.
46But some of them went their ways
to the Pharisees, and told them what
things Jesus had done.

The Pharisees plan to kill the Lord

¶47Then gathered the chief priests
and the Pharisees a council, and said,
What do we? for this man doeth many
miracles.
48If we let him thus alone, all *men* will
believe on him: and the Romans shall
come and take away both our place and
nation.
49And one of them, *named* *Caiaphas,
being the high priest that same year,
said unto them, Ye know nothing at all,
50Nor consider that it is expedient
for us, that one man should die for the
people, and that the whole nation perish not.
51And this spake he not of himself:
but being high priest that year, he
prophesied that Jesus should die for
that nation;
52And not for that nation only, but that
also he should gather together in one
the children of God that were scattered
abroad.
53Then from that day forth they took
counsel together for to put him to
death.
54Jesus therefore walked no more
openly among the Jews; but went
thence unto a country near to the wilderness, into a city called *Ephraim,
and there continued with his disciples.
¶55And the Jews' passover was nigh
at hand: and many went out of the country up to Jerusalem before the passover,
to purify themselves.
56Then sought they for Jesus, and
spake among themselves, as they stood
in the temple, What think ye, that he
will not come to the feast?

11:38 groaning in himself. This could have been because of the unbelief of those who surrounded Him (vss. 37,39).

11:51 prophesied. This means that Caiaphas, the high priest, spoke God's message here. He probably did not realize the real meaning of his words, because he probably agreed with the others that Jesus must die so that He would not lead a rebellion, which might make the Romans take away the little freedom the Jewish people had left (vs. 48).

11:55 passover was nigh. This was the last *Passover of Jesus' life.

[57]Now both the chief priests and the Pharisees had given a commandment, that, if any man knew where he were, he should shew *it,* that they might take him.

The farewell supper at Bethany
(Matt. 26:6-13; Mark 14:3-9;
cf. Luke 7:37-38)

12 Then Jesus six days before the passover came to Bethany, where Lazarus was which had been dead, whom he raised from the dead.

[2]There they made him a supper; and Martha served: but Lazarus was one of them that sat at the table with him.

[3]Then took Mary a pound of ointment of *spikenard, very costly, and anointed the feet of Jesus, and wiped his feet with her hair: and the house was filled with the odour of the ointment.

[4]Then saith one of his disciples, *Judas Iscariot, Simon's *son,* which should betray him,

[5]Why was not this ointment sold for three hundred pence, and given to the poor?

[6]This he said, not that he cared for the poor; but because he was a thief, and had the *bag, and bare what was put therein.

[7]Then said Jesus, Let her alone: against the day of my burying hath she kept this.

[8]For the poor always ye have with you; but me ye have not always.

[9]Much people of the Jews therefore knew that he was there: and they came not for Jesus' sake only, but that they might see Lazarus also, whom he had raised from the dead.

¶[10]But the chief priests consulted that they might put Lazarus also to death;

[11]Because that by reason of him many of the Jews went away, and believed on Jesus.

Jesus enters Jerusalem
(Matt. 21:4-9; Mark 11:7-10;
Luke 19:35-38)

¶[12]On the next day much people that were come to the feast, when they heard that Jesus was coming to Jerusalem,

[13]Took branches of palm trees, and went forth to meet him, and cried, *Hosanna: Blessed *is* the King of *Israel that cometh in the name of the Lord.

[14]And Jesus, when he had found a young ass, sat thereon; as it is written,

[15]Fear not, daughter of *Sion: behold, thy King cometh, sitting on an ass's colt.

[16]These things understood not his disciples at the first: but when Jesus was glorified, then remembered they that these things were written of him, and *that* they had done these things unto him.

[17]The people therefore that was with him when he called Lazarus out of his grave, and raised him from the dead, bare record.

[18]For this cause the people also met him, for that they heard that he had done this miracle.

[19]The Pharisees therefore said among themselves, Perceive ye how ye prevail nothing? behold, the world is gone after him.

¶[20]And there were certain Greeks among them that came up to worship at the feast:

[21]The same came therefore to Philip,

12:6 the bag. Judas Iscariot was the treasurer and looked after the money of the Lord and the disciples. John also states that Judas was "a thief," so he took money from the funds for himself. Judas was extremely self-serving. We must examine ourselves to make sure that our motives are pure and we truly want God's will in our lives—not just what will make us feel good or will help us gain fame or fortune.

12:7 against the day of my burying. Mary realized that the Lord Jesus was going to die (see Matt. 26:6-13).

12:15 Fear not, daughter of Sion. Jesus was fulfilling Zechariah 9:9.

12:20 Greeks. See *Grecians.

which was of Bethsaida of Galilee, and
desired him, saying, Sir, we would see
Jesus.
22 Philip cometh and telleth Andrew:
and again Andrew and Philip tell Jesus.

Jesus foretells His death

¶23 And Jesus answered them, saying,
The hour is come, that the Son of man
should be glorified.
24 Verily, verily, I say unto you, Except
a corn of wheat fall into the ground and
die, it abideth alone: but if it die, it
bringeth forth much fruit.
25 He that loveth his life shall lose it;
and he that hateth his life in this world
shall keep it unto life eternal.
26 If any man serve me, let him follow
me; and where I am, there shall also
my servant be: if any man serve me,
him will *my* Father honour.
27 Now is my soul troubled; and what
shall I say? Father, save me from this
hour: but for this cause came I unto this
hour.
28 Father, glorify thy name. Then
came there a voice from *heaven, *saying,* I have both glorified *it,* and will glorify *it* again.
29 The people therefore, that stood by,
and heard *it,* said that it thundered: others said, An *angel spake to him.
30 Jesus answered and said, This voice
came not because of me, but for your
sakes.
31 Now is the *judgment of this world:
now shall the prince of this world be
cast out.
32 And I, if I be lifted up from the
earth, will draw all *men* unto me.
33 This he said, signifying what death
he should die.
34 The people answered him, We have
heard out of the law that Christ abideth
for ever: and how sayest thou, The Son
of man must be lifted up? who is this
Son of man?
35 Then Jesus said unto them, Yet a
little while is the light with you. Walk
while ye have the light, lest darkness
come upon you: for he that walketh in
darkness knoweth not whither he
goeth.
36 While ye have light, believe in the
light, that ye may be the children of
light. These things spake Jesus, and departed, and did hide himself from them.
¶37 But though he had done so many
*miracles before them, yet they be-
lieved not on him:
38 That the saying of Esaias the
prophet might be fulfilled, which he
spake, Lord, who hath believed our report? and to whom hath the arm of the
Lord been revealed?
39 Therefore they could not believe,
because that Esaias said again,
40 He hath blinded their eyes, and
hardened their heart; that they should
not see with *their* eyes, nor understand
with *their* heart, and be converted, and
I should heal them.
41 These things said Esaias, when he
saw his glory, and spake of him.
¶42 Nevertheless among the chief rulers also many believed on him; but because of the Pharisees they did not
*confess *him,* lest they should be put
out of the *synagogue:
43 For they loved the praise of men
more than the praise of God.
¶44 Jesus cried and said, He that
believeth on me, believeth not on me,
but on him that sent me.

12:31 Now is the judgment. "This world" means this world system, led at the time of the Lord by the Jews, as religious leaders, and the Romans, as political leaders. Both of these groups rejected and crucified the Lord Jesus Christ. Christ's death condemned or judged the world, because in putting Him to death, the leaders showed what they thought of the Son of God.

12:31 prince of this world. Satan, who is behind this whole wicked world system.

12:34 Christ abideth for ever. See Psalm 72:17.

12:35 light. The Lord Jesus Christ Himself (see John 1:9; see also John 8:12 note).

12:38 Esaias the prophet. Verses 38-41 are from Isaiah 53:1 and 6:10.

45And he that seeth me seeth him
that sent me.
46I am come a light into the world,
that whosoever believeth on me should
not abide in darkness.
47And if any man hear my words, and
believe not, I judge him not: for I came
not to judge the world, but to save the
world.
48He that rejecteth me, and receiveth
not my words, hath one that judgeth
him: the word that I have spoken, the
same shall judge him in the last day.
49For I have not spoken of myself; but
the Father which sent me, he gave me
a commandment, what I should say, and
what I should speak.
50And I know that his commandment
is life everlasting: whatsoever I speak
therefore, even as the Father said unto
me, so I speak.

IV. The Private Talks of Christ (13:1—17:26)

The last supper (Matt. 26:7-30; Mark 14:17-26; Luke 22:14-39)

13 Now before the feast of the
passover, when Jesus knew that
his hour was come that he should depart out of this *world unto the Father,
having loved his own which were in the
world, he loved them unto the end.

Jesus washes His disciples' feet

2And supper being ended, the *devil
having now put into the heart of Judas
Iscariot, Simon's *son,* to betray him;
3Jesus knowing that the Father had
given all things into his hands, and
that he was come from *God, and went
to God;
4He riseth from supper, and laid aside
his garments; and took a towel, and
girded himself.
5After that he poureth water into a
bason, and began to wash the disciples'
feet, and to wipe *them* with the towel
wherewith he was girded.
6Then cometh he to Simon *Peter:
and Peter saith unto him, Lord, dost
thou wash my feet?
7Jesus answered and said unto him,
What I do thou knowest not now; but
thou shalt know hereafter.
8Peter saith unto him, Thou shalt
never wash my feet. Jesus answered
him, If I wash thee not, thou hast no
part with me.
9Simon Peter saith unto him, Lord,
not my feet only, but also *my* hands and
my head.
10Jesus saith to him, He that is
washed needeth not save to wash *his*
feet, but is *clean every whit: and ye
are clean, but not all.

13:10 The Washing of Feet
The Lord Jesus Christ wanted to teach the disciples a very important truth, so He made use of an illustration that they would all understand, as He used parables. A man would go to the public baths and bathe, but as he came back to his house, his feet would become dusty again, and he would have to wash them just after he entered the house. Christians are cleansed from their sins by the blood of the Lord Jesus (1 John 1:7), but each day that they walk through this world they come in contact with evil, or they sin themselves, and need to be cleansed. This sin has to be confessed and forgiven (1 John 1:9), and this confession and forgiveness is the needed cleansing–the washing of the feet.

11For he knew who should betray
him; therefore said he, Ye are not all
clean.
12So after he had washed their feet,
and had taken his garments, and was set
down again, he said unto them, Know
ye what I have done to you?
13Ye call me Master and Lord: and ye
say well; for *so* I am.
14If I then, *your* Lord and Master,

12:45 seeth me. See John 1:18 note, "Seeing God."
12:47 I came not to judge the world. See John 9:39 first note.
12:50 life everlasting. See John 3:15-16 note, "Eternal Life."
13:1 unto the end. Unto the uttermost. He showed His love in every possible way.

have washed your feet; ye also ought to
wash one another's feet.
15 For I have given you an example,
that ye should do as I have done to you.
16 Verily, verily, I say unto you, The
servant is not greater than his lord;
neither he that is sent greater than he
that sent him.
17 If ye know these things, happy are
ye if ye do them.
¶18 I speak not of you all: I know
whom I have chosen: but that the scripture may be fulfilled, He that eateth
bread with me hath lifted up his heel
against me.
19 Now I tell you before it come, that,
when it is come to pass, ye may believe
that I am *he.*
20 Verily, verily, I say unto you, He
that receiveth whomsoever I send
receiveth me; and he that receiveth me
receiveth him that sent me.

Jesus foretells His betrayal
(Matt. 26:20-25; Mark 14:17-21;
Luke 22:21-22)

21 When Jesus had thus said, he was
troubled in spirit, and testified, and said,
Verily, verily, I say unto you, that one
of you shall betray me.
22 Then the disciples looked one on
another, doubting of whom he spake.
23 Now there was leaning on Jesus'
bosom one of his disciples, whom Jesus
loved.
24 Simon Peter therefore beckoned to
him, that he should ask who it should
be of whom he spake.
25 He then lying on Jesus' breast saith
unto him, Lord, who is it?
26 Jesus answered, He it is, to whom I
shall give a sop, when I have dipped *it.*
And when he had dipped the sop, he
gave *it* to Judas Iscariot, *the son* of
Simon.
27 And after the sop *Satan entered
into him. Then said Jesus unto him,
That thou doest, do quickly.
28 Now no man at the table knew for
what intent he spake this unto him.
29 For some *of them* thought, because Judas had the bag, that Jesus
had said unto him, Buy *those things*
that we have need of against the feast;
or, that he should give something to the
poor.
30 He then having received the sop
went immediately out: and it was night.
¶31 Therefore, when he was gone out,
Jesus said, Now is the Son of man glorified, and God is glorified in him.
32 If God be glorified in him, God shall
also glorify him in himself, and shall
*straightway glorify him.
33 Little children, yet a little while I
am with you. Ye shall seek me: and as I
said unto the Jews, Whither I go, ye
cannot come; so now I say to you.
34 A new commandment I give unto
you, That ye love one another; as I have
loved you, that ye also love one another.
35 By this shall all *men* know that ye
are my disciples, if ye have love one to
another.

Jesus foretells Peter's denial
(Matt. 26:33-35; Mark 14:29-31;
Luke 22:33-34)

¶36 Simon Peter said unto him, Lord,
whither goest thou? Jesus answered
him, Whither I go, thou canst not follow me now; but thou shalt follow me
afterwards.
37 Peter said unto him, Lord, why cannot I follow thee now? I will lay down
my life for thy sake.
38 Jesus answered him, Wilt thou lay
down thy life for my sake? Verily, verily, I say unto thee, The cock shall not
crow, till thou hast denied me thrice.

13:14 to wash one another's feet. We should be willing to do anything for the comfort and help of another Christian.
13:18 He that eateth bread. See Psalm 41:9.
13:23 one of his disciples. John, the writer of this Gospel, "whom Jesus loved." Jesus and John shared a special closeness.

The last talk: in the upper room

14 Let not your heart be troubled: ye believe in God, believe
also in me.

14:1 Jesus Comforts His Disciples
The Lord knew that He was about to die, but instead of asking for help and comfort, He spent these last hours in comforting His disciples. After He had talked with them (chaps. 14–16), He prayed for them (chap. 17), and then, after they had sung a hymn together, He went away separately in the Garden of Gethsemane (chap. 18) from which He was taken by the soldiers, and then He was crucified (chap. 19).

2 In my Father's house are many mansions: if *it were* not *so*, I would have told
you. I go to prepare a place for you.
3 And if I go and prepare a place for
you, I will come again, and receive you
unto myself; that where I am, *there* ye
may be also.
4 And whither I go ye know, and the
way ye know.
5 Thomas saith unto him, Lord, we
know not whither thou goest; and how
can we know the way?
6 Jesus saith unto him, I am the way,
the truth, and the life: no man cometh
unto the Father, but by me.
7 If ye had known me, ye should have
known my Father also: and from henceforth ye know him, and have seen him.
8 Philip saith unto him, Lord, shew us
the Father, and it sufficeth us.
9 Jesus saith unto him, Have I been so
long time with you, and yet hast thou
not known me, Philip? he that hath seen
me hath seen the Father; and how
sayest thou *then*, Shew us the Father?
10 Believest thou not that I am in the
Father, and the Father in me? the words
that I speak unto you I speak not of
myself: but the Father that dwelleth in
me, he doeth the works.
11 Believe me that I *am* in the Father,
and the Father in me: or else believe me
for the very works' sake.
12 Verily, verily, I say unto you, He
that believeth on me, the works that I
do shall he do also; and greater *works*
than these shall he do; because I go
unto my Father.
13 And whatsoever ye shall ask in my
name, that will I do, that the Father may
be glorified in the Son.
14 If ye shall ask any thing in my
name, I will do *it*.
¶ 15 If ye love me, keep my commandments.

The promise of the Holy Spirit

16 And I will pray the Father, and he
shall give you another Comforter, that
he may abide with you for ever;
17 *Even* the Spirit of truth; whom the
world cannot receive, because it seeth
him not, neither knoweth him: but ye
know him; for he dwelleth with you, and
shall be in you.
18 I will not leave you comfortless: I
will come to you.
19 Yet a little while, and the world

14:2 mansions. Rooms or abiding places.
14:3 I will come again. This was the first promise of Christ's return for His own (see 1 Thess. 4:14-17 and 4:13 note, "Hope for the Dead").
14:6 I am the way. Compare John 10:9.
14:9 he that hath seen me. See 1:18 note, "Seeing God."
14:12 greater works than these. Not greater miracles, but through Christ and the power of the Spirit, the ministry of His followers would have wider spiritual effects—reaching more people than Jesus' earthly ministry did.
14:13 in my name. See John 16:23 second note.
14:16 another Comforter. The word "comforter" means *one called alongside to help.* The Lord Jesus was promising to send the *Holy Spirit to "comfort" the disciples when He was gone. The Holy Spirit would dwell in believers and help them, just as the Lord had done when He was with them (see John 14:26; 15:26; 16:7-15).

seeth me no more; but ye see me: because I live, ye shall live also.
20At that day ye shall know that I *am*
in my Father, and ye in me, and I in you.
21He that hath my commandments,
and keepeth them, he it is that loveth
me: and he that loveth me shall be loved
of my Father, and I will love him, and
will manifest myself to him.
22Judas saith unto him, not Iscariot,
Lord, how is it that thou wilt manifest
thyself unto us, and not unto the world?
23Jesus answered and said unto him,
If a man love me, he will keep my
words: and my Father will love him, and
we will come unto him, and make our
abode with him.
24He that loveth me not keepeth not
my sayings: and the word which ye hear
is not mine, but the Father's which sent
me.
25These things have I spoken unto
you, being *yet* present with you.
26But the Comforter, *which is* the
Holy Ghost, whom the Father will send
in my name, he shall teach you all
things, and bring all things to your remembrance, whatsoever I have said
unto you.

The promise of peace

27Peace I leave with you, my peace I
give unto you: not as the world giveth,
give I unto you. Let not your heart be
troubled, neither let it be afraid.
28Ye have heard how I said unto you,
I go away, and come *again* unto you. If
ye loved me, ye would rejoice, because
I said, I go unto the Father: for my Father is greater than I.
29And now I have told you before it
come to pass, that, when it is come to
pass, ye might believe.
30Hereafter I will not talk much with
you: for the prince of this world cometh,
and hath nothing in me.
31But that the world may know that I
love the Father; and as the Father gave
me commandment, even so I do. Arise,
let us go hence.

On the way to the Garden of Gethsemane

15 I am the true vine, and my Father is the husbandman.
2Every branch in me that beareth not
fruit he taketh away: and every *branch*
that beareth fruit, he purgeth it, that it
may bring forth more fruit.
3Now ye are clean through the word
which I have spoken unto you.
4Abide in me, and I in you. As the
branch cannot bear fruit of itself, except
it abide in the vine; no more can ye,
except ye abide in me.
5I am the vine, ye *are* the branches:
He that abideth in me, and I in him, the
same bringeth forth much fruit: for
without me ye can do nothing.
6If a man abide not in me, he is cast
forth as a branch, and is withered; and
men gather them, and cast *them* into the
*fire, and they are burned.

14:19 because I live. See 14:6; 11:25-26.

14:22 Judas . . . not Iscariot. See Luke 6:16.

14:27 Peace I leave with you. This was a solemn farewell but one that promised peace and so was intended to comfort Christ's disciples.

14:28 my Father is greater than I. In their relationship as Father and Son, the Father was greater. Jesus obeyed His Father's will completely and subjected Himself to human limitations while He was on earth.

15:2 purgeth. A man who owns a vineyard, a husbandman, prunes his vines by cutting off much of the growth each year, because this causes the other branches to produce better grapes. God is our "husbandman"; He allows us to go through trouble and suffering if these things are needed in our lives to make us more fruitful for Him (see Heb. 12:5-12).

15:4 Abide in me. This means that the Christian must not allow anything in his or her life that would separate him or her from the Lord.

15:6 If a man abide not. The mark of the true believer is that he or she does abide in and stay close to the Lord (1 John 2:19).

7 If ye abide in me, and my words
abide in you, ye shall ask what ye will,
and it shall be done unto you.
8 Herein is my Father glorified, that
ye bear much fruit; so shall ye be my
disciples.
9 As the Father hath loved me, so have
I loved you: continue ye in my love.
10 If ye keep my commandments, ye
shall abide in my love; even as I have
kept my Father's commandments, and
abide in his love.
11 These things have I spoken unto
you, that my joy might remain in you,
and *that* your joy might be full.
12 This is my commandment, That ye
love one another, as I have loved you.
13 Greater love hath no man than this,
that a man lay down his life for his
friends.
14 Ye are my friends, if ye do whatsoever I command you.
15 Henceforth I call you not servants;
for the servant knoweth not what his
lord doeth: but I have called you friends;
for all things that I have heard of my
Father I have made known unto you.
16 Ye have not chosen me, but I have
chosen you, and ordained you, that ye
should go and bring forth fruit, and *that*
your fruit should remain: that whatsoever ye shall ask of the Father in my
name, he may give it you.
17 These things I command you, that
ye love one another.

The believer and the world

18 If the world hate you, ye know that
it hated me before *it hated* you.
19 If ye were of the world, the world
would love his own: but because ye are
not of the world, but I have chosen you
out of the world, therefore the world
hateth you.
20 Remember the word that I said
unto you, The servant is not greater
than his lord. If they have persecuted
me, they will also persecute you; if they
have kept my saying, they will keep
yours also.
21 But all these things will they do
unto you for my name's sake, because
they know not him that sent me.
22 If I had not come and spoken unto
them, they had not had *sin: but now
they have no cloke for their sin.
23 He that hateth me hateth my Father
also.
24 If I had not done among them the
works which none other man did, they
had not had sin: but now have they both
seen and hated both me and my Father.
25 But *this cometh to pass,* that the
word might be fulfilled that is written
in their *law, They hated me without a
cause.

The work of the Holy Spirit

26 But when the Comforter is come,
whom I will send unto you from the
Father, *even* the Spirit of truth, which
proceedeth from the Father, he shall
testify of me:
27 And ye also shall bear witness, because ye have been with me from the
beginning.

Warning of persecutions

16 These things have I spoken
unto you, that ye should not be
offended.
2 They shall put you out of the *synagogues: yea, the time cometh, that
whosoever killeth you will think that he
doeth God service.
3 And these things will they do unto
you, because they have not known the
Father, nor me.
4 But these things have I told you,
that when the time shall come, ye may

15:22 they had not had sin. If the Lord had not claimed to be the Messiah, the Jewish leaders, and others who rejected Christ, could have treated Him as a mere man; in that case, their rejection of Him would not have been a sin. His people had the opportunity to see Him as He really was; therefore, they were inexcusable.

15:25 hated me without a cause. A quotation from Psalm 35:19.

remember that I told you of them. And
these things I said not unto you at the
beginning, because I was with you.
5 But now I go my way to him that
sent me; and none of you asketh me,
Whither goest thou?
6 But because I have said these things
unto you, sorrow hath filled your heart.

The work of the Holy Spirit

7 Nevertheless I tell you the truth; It
is expedient for you that I go away: for
if I go not away, the Comforter will not
come unto you; but if I depart, I will
send him unto you.
8 And when he is come, he will reprove the world of sin, and of *righteousness, and of judgment:
9 Of sin, because they believe not on
me;
10 Of righteousness, because I go to
my Father, and ye see me no more;
11 Of judgment, because the prince of
this world is judged.
12 I have yet many things to say unto
you, but ye cannot bear them now.
13 Howbeit when he, the Spirit of
truth, is come, he will guide you into all
truth: for he shall not speak of himself;
but whatsoever he shall hear, *that* shall
he speak: and he will shew you things
to come.
14 He shall glorify me: for he shall
receive of mine, and shall shew *it* unto
you.
15 All things that the Father hath are
mine: therefore said I, that he shall take
of mine, and shall shew *it* unto you.

The return of the Lord Jesus

16 A little while, and ye shall not see
me: and again, a little while, and ye shall
see me, because I go to the Father.
17 Then said *some* of his disciples
among themselves, What is this that he
saith unto us, A little while, and ye shall
not see me: and again, a little while, and
ye shall see me: and, Because I go to
the Father?
18 They said therefore, What is this
that he saith, A little while? we cannot
tell what he saith.
19 Now Jesus knew that they were
desirous to ask him, and said unto them,
Do ye enquire among yourselves of
that I said, A little while, and ye shall
not see me: and again, a little while, and
ye shall see me?
20 Verily, verily, I say unto you, That
ye shall weep and lament, but the world
shall rejoice: and ye shall be sorrowful,
but your sorrow shall be turned into
joy.
21 A woman when she is in travail hath
sorrow, because her hour is come: but
as soon as she is delivered of the child,
she remembereth no more the anguish,
for joy that a man is born into the world.
22 And ye now therefore have sorrow:
but I will see you again, and your heart
shall rejoice, and your joy no man
taketh from you.
23 And in that day ye shall ask me
nothing. Verily, verily, I say unto you,
Whatsoever ye shall ask the Father in
my name, he will give *it* you.
24 Hitherto have ye asked nothing in
my name: ask, and ye shall receive, that
your joy may be full.
25 These things have I spoken unto
you in *proverbs: but the time cometh,
when I shall no more speak unto you in
proverbs, but I shall shew you plainly
of the Father.
26 At that day ye shall ask in my name:
and I say not unto you, that I will pray
the Father for you:
27 For the Father himself loveth you,

16:11 Of judgment. See John 12:31 first note.

16:23 ye shall ask me nothing. Jesus was saying, "You shall ask Me no questions." The Holy Spirit would guide Christ's followers and help them understand spiritual things.

16:23 in my name. A Christian prays in the name of the Lord Jesus. This is not as a fetish or charm, but because God loves the Lord so very much, He delights in answering prayers offered in His name, or "for Jesus' sake."

because ye have loved me, and have believed that I came out from God.

28 I came forth from the Father, and am come into the world: again, I leave the world, and go to the Father.

29 His disciples said unto him, Lo, now speakest thou plainly, and speakest no proverb.

30 Now are we sure that thou knowest all things, and needest not that any man should ask thee: by this we believe that thou camest forth from God.

31 Jesus answered them, Do ye now believe?

32 Behold, the hour cometh, yea, is now come, that ye shall be scattered, every man to his own, and shall leave me alone: and yet I am not alone, because the Father is with me.

33 These things I have spoken unto you, that in me ye might have peace. In the world ye shall have tribulation: but be of good cheer; I have overcome the world.

The prayer of the Lord Jesus

17 These words spake Jesus, and lifted up his eyes to heaven, and said, Father, the hour is come; glorify thy Son, that thy Son also may glorify thee:

2 As thou hast given him power over all *flesh, that he should give *eternal life to as many as thou hast given him.

3 And this is life eternal, that they might know thee the only true God, and Jesus *Christ, whom thou hast sent.

4 I have glorified thee on the earth: I have finished the work which thou gavest me to do.

5 And now, O Father, glorify thou me with thine own self with the glory which I had with thee before the world was.

6 I have manifested thy name unto the men which thou gavest me out of the world: thine they were, and thou gavest them me; and they have kept thy word.

7 Now they have known that all things whatsoever thou hast given me are of thee.

8 For I have given unto them the words which thou gavest me; and they have received *them,* and have known surely that I came out from thee, and they have believed that thou didst send me.

9 I pray for them: I pray not for the world, but for them which thou hast given me; for they are thine.

10 And all mine are thine, and thine are mine; and I am glorified in them.

11 And now I am no more in the world, but these are in the world, and I come to thee. Holy Father, keep through thine own name those whom thou hast given me, that they may be one, as we *are.*

12 While I was with them in the world, I kept them in thy name: those that thou gavest me I have kept, and none

---

17:1 GLORIFY

The Lord Jesus Christ asked six petitions:

1. that He might be glorified so He might glorify the Father (vs. 1);
2. that believers would be safe (vs. 11);
3. that believers would be sanctified (vs. 17);
4. that believers would be in unity with each other (vs. 21);
5. that future believers would also be safe, sanctified, and unified (vs. 20); and
6. that all believers would be with Christ throughout eternity so they could see and share His glory (vs. 24).

Christ asked God for all this on the basis of the Father's great love for the Son, which was "before the foundation of the world" (vs. 24).

16:32 ye . . . shall leave me alone. See Matthew 26:56.

17:4 I have finished the work. Jesus was looking to His death on the cross (see John 19:30).

of them is lost, but the son of perdition;
that the scripture might be fulfilled.
13 And now come I to thee; and these
things I speak in the world, that they
might have my joy fulfilled in themselves.
14 I have given them thy word; and the
world hath hated them, because they
are not of the world, even as I am not
of the world.
15 I pray not that thou shouldest take
them out of the world, but that thou
shouldest keep them from the evil.
16 They are not of the world, even as
I am not of the world.
17 Sanctify them through thy truth:
thy word is truth.
18 As thou hast sent me into the
world, even so have I also sent them
into the world.
19 And for their sakes I sanctify myself, that they also might be sanctified
through the truth.
20 Neither pray I for these alone, but
for them also which shall believe on me
through their word;
21 That they all may be one; as thou,
Father, *art* in me, and I in thee, that they
also may be one in us: that the world
may believe that thou hast sent me.
22 And the glory which thou gavest
me I have given them; that they may be
one, even as we are one:
23 I in them, and thou in me, that they
may be made perfect in one; and that
the world may know that thou hast sent
me, and hast loved them, as thou hast
loved me.
24 Father, I will that they also, whom
thou hast given me, be with me where I
am; that they may behold my glory, which
thou hast given me: for thou lovedst me
before the foundation of the world.
25 O righteous Father, the world hath
not known thee: but I have known thee,
and these have known that thou hast
sent me.
26 And I have declared unto them thy
name, and will declare *it:* that the love
wherewith thou hast loved me may be
in them, and I in them.

V. The Trial and Death of Christ (18:1—19:42)

In the garden (Matt. 26:36-46; Mark 14:32-42; Luke 22:39-46)

18 When Jesus had spoken these
words, he went forth with his
disciples over the brook Cedron, where
was a garden, into the which he entered, and his disciples.

The arrest of Jesus (Matt. 26:47-56; Mark 14:43-50; Luke 22:47-53)

2 And Judas also, which betrayed him,
knew the place: for Jesus ofttimes resorted thither with his disciples.
3 Judas then, having received a band
of men and officers from the chief
priests and *Pharisees, cometh thither
with lanterns and torches and weapons.
4 Jesus therefore, knowing all things
that should come upon him, went forth,
and said unto them, Whom seek ye?
5 They answered him, Jesus of Nazareth. Jesus saith unto them, I am *he.*
And Judas also, which betrayed him,
stood with them.
6 As soon then as he had said unto
them, I am *he,* they went backward, and
fell to the ground.
7 Then asked he them again, Whom
seek ye? And they said, Jesus of Nazareth.
8 Jesus answered, I have told you that
I am *he:* if therefore ye seek me, let
these go their way:
9 That the saying might be fulfilled,

17:12 son of perdition. Judas Iscariot.
17:12 that the scripture might be fulfilled. See Psalm 41:9 and John 13:18.
18:1 a garden. The Garden of Gethsemane (Matt. 26:36).
18:5 I am he. This refers back to the "I AM" of the Old Testament, for this was one of the *names of God.
18:9 the saying might be fulfilled, which he spake. In His prayer (John 17:12).

which he spake, Of them which thou gavest me have I lost none.
10Then Simon Peter having a sword drew it, and smote the high priest's servant, and cut off his right ear. The servant's name was Malchus.
11Then said Jesus unto Peter, Put up thy sword into the sheath: the cup which my Father hath given me, shall I not drink it?

The trial of Jesus: before Annas (Matt. 26:57-68; Mark 14:53-65; Luke 22:66-71)

12Then the band and the captain and officers of the Jews took Jesus, and bound him,
13And led him away to Annas first; for he was father in law to Caiaphas, which was the high priest that same year.
14Now Caiaphas was he, which gave counsel to the Jews, that it was expedient that one man should die for the people.

The failure of Peter (Matt. 26:69-75; Mark 14:66-72; Luke 22:54-62)

¶15And Simon Peter followed Jesus, and *so did* another disciple: that disciple was known unto the high priest, and went in with Jesus into the palace of the high priest.
16But Peter stood at the door without. Then went out that other disciple, which was known unto the high priest, and spake unto her that kept the door, and brought in Peter.
17Then saith the damsel that kept the door unto Peter, Art not thou also *one* of this man's disciples? He saith, I am not.
18And the servants and officers stood there, who had made a fire of coals; for it was cold: and they warmed themselves: and Peter stood with them, and warmed himself.

The trial of Jesus: before Caiaphas

¶19The high priest then asked Jesus of his disciples, and of his *doctrine.
20Jesus answered him, I spake openly to the world; I ever taught in the *synagogue, and in the temple, whither the Jews always resort; and in secret have I said nothing.
21Why askest thou me? ask them which heard me, what I have said unto them: behold, they know what I said.
22And when he had thus spoken, one of the officers which stood by struck Jesus with the palm of his hand, saying, Answerest thou the high priest so?
23Jesus answered him, If I have spoken evil, bear witness of the evil: but if well, why smitest thou me?
24Now Annas had sent him bound unto Caiaphas the high priest.
25And Simon Peter stood and warmed himself. They said therefore unto him, Art not thou also *one* of his disciples? He denied *it,* and said, I am not.
26One of the servants of the high priest, being *his* *kinsman whose ear Peter cut off, saith, Did not I see thee in the garden with him?
27Peter then denied again: and immediately the cock crew.

The trial of Jesus: before Pilate (Matt. 27:1-26; Mark 15:1-5; Luke 23:1-7, 13-25)

¶28Then led they Jesus from Caiaphas unto the hall of *judgment: and it

---

18:10 cut off his right ear. Luke tells us that the Lord healed the ear of Malchus (Luke 22:51).
18:14 Caiaphas. A *Sadducee, son-in-law of Annas (vs. 13), and a servant of Rome. Compare Luke 3:2.
18:15 another disciple. John, the writer of this Gospel.
18:27 the cock crew. The rooster crowed. See John 13:38.
18:28 hall of judgment. The palace or headquarters of the Roman government in Jerusalem. The Jews would not enter it because all the *leaven might not have been removed, and they might, therefore, be made *unclean for the *Passover.

was early; and they themselves went
not into the judgment hall, lest they
should be defiled; but that they might
eat the *passover.
29Pilate then went out unto them, and
said, What accusation bring ye against
this man?
30They answered and said unto him,
If he were not a malefactor, we would
not have delivered him up unto thee.
31Then said Pilate unto them, Take
ye him, and judge him according to your
law. The Jews therefore said unto him,
It is not lawful for us to put any man to
*death:
32That the saying of Jesus might be
fulfilled, which he spake, signifying
what death he should die.
33Then Pilate entered into the judgment hall again, and called Jesus, and
said unto him, Art thou the *King of the
Jews?
34Jesus answered him, Sayest thou
this thing of thyself, or did others tell
it thee of me?
35Pilate answered, Am I a Jew? Thine
own nation and the chief priests have
delivered thee unto me: what hast thou
done?
36Jesus answered, My *kingdom is
not of this world: if my kingdom were
of this world, then would my servants
fight, that I should not be delivered to
the Jews: but now is my kingdom not
from hence.
37Pilate therefore said unto him, Art
thou a king then? Jesus answered, Thou
sayest that I am a king. To this end was
I born, and for this cause came I into the
world, that I should bear witness unto
the truth. Every one that is of the truth
heareth my voice.
38Pilate saith unto him, What is
truth? And when he had said this, he
went out again unto the Jews, and saith
unto them, I find in him no fault *at all.*
39But ye have a custom, that I should
release unto you one at the passover:
will ye therefore that I release unto you
the King of the Jews?
40Then cried they all again, saying,
Not this man, but Barabbas. Now Barabbas was a robber.

The crown of thorns
(Matt. 27:27-30; Mark 15:16-20)

19 Then Pilate therefore took
Jesus, and scourged *him.*
2And the soldiers platted a crown of
thorns, and put *it* on his head, and they
put on him a purple robe,
3And said, Hail, King of the Jews! and
they smote him with their hands.
4Pilate therefore went forth again,
and saith unto them, Behold, I bring
him forth to you, that ye may know that
I find no fault in him.
5Then came Jesus forth, wearing the
crown of thorns, and the purple robe.
And *Pilate* saith unto them, Behold the
man!
6When the chief priests therefore and
officers saw him, they cried out, saying,
Crucify *him,* crucify *him.* Pilate saith
unto them, Take ye him, and crucify
him: for I find no fault in him.
7The Jews answered him, We have a
law, and by our law he ought to die,
because he made himself the Son of
*God.
¶8When Pilate therefore heard that
saying, he was the more afraid;
9And went again into the judgment
hall, and saith unto Jesus, Whence art
thou? But Jesus gave him no answer.
10Then saith Pilate unto him,
Speakest thou not unto me? knowest
thou not that I have power to crucify
thee, and have power to release thee?
11Jesus answered, Thou couldest

18:29 Pilate. The Roman governor.
18:31 It is not lawful. The Jews were under the authority of Rome. They did not have the right to condemn a person to death. This was their reason for bringing our Lord before Pilate—that Pilate might have Jesus put to death.
18:32 signifying what death. See John 12:32-33.
19:7 by our law. This was a reference to Leviticus 24:16.

have no power *at all* against me, except
it were given thee from above: therefore he that delivered me unto thee
hath the greater sin.
12And from thenceforth Pilate sought
to release him: but the Jews cried out,
saying, If thou let this man go, thou
art not Caesar's friend: whosoever
maketh himself a king speaketh against
Caesar.
¶13When Pilate therefore heard that
saying, he brought Jesus forth, and sat
down in the judgment seat in a place
that is called the Pavement, but in the
Hebrew, Gabbatha.
14And it was the preparation of the
passover, and about the sixth hour: and
he saith unto the Jews, Behold your
King!
15But they cried out, Away with *him,*
away with *him,* crucify him. Pilate saith
unto them, Shall I crucify your King?
The chief priests answered, We have no
king but Caesar.

The crucifixion (Matt. 27:33-54; Mark 15:22-39; Luke 23:33-47)

16Then delivered he him therefore
unto them to be crucified. And they
took Jesus, and led *him* away.
17And he bearing his cross went forth
into a place called *the place* of a
skull, which is called in the Hebrew
Golgotha:
18Where they crucified him, and two
others with him, on either side one, and
Jesus in the midst.
¶19And Pilate wrote a title, and put *it*
on the cross. And the writing was,
JESUS OF NAZARETH THE KING
OF THE JEWS.
20This title then read many of the
Jews: for the place where Jesus was
crucified was nigh to the city: and it was
written in Hebrew, *and* Greek, *and*
Latin.
21Then said the chief priests of the
Jews to Pilate, Write not, The King of
the Jews; but that he said, I am King of
the Jews.
22Pilate answered, What I have written I have written.
¶23Then the soldiers, when they had
crucified Jesus, took his garments, and
made four parts, to every soldier a part;
and also *his* coat: now the coat was
without seam, woven from the top
throughout.
24They said therefore among themselves, Let us not rend it, but cast lots
for it, whose it shall be: that the scripture might be fulfilled, which saith,
They parted my raiment among them,
and for my vesture they did cast lots.
These things therefore the soldiers
did.
¶25Now there stood by the cross of
Jesus his mother, and his mother's sister, Mary the *wife* of Cleophas, and
Mary Magdalene.
26When Jesus therefore saw his
mother, and the disciple standing by,
whom he loved, he saith unto his mother, Woman, behold thy son!
27Then saith he to the disciple, Behold thy mother! And from that hour
that disciple took her unto his own
home.
¶28After this, Jesus knowing that all
things were now accomplished, that the
scripture might be fulfilled, saith, I
thirst.
29Now there was set a vessel full of
vinegar: and they filled a spunge with

19:12 Caesar. Caesar, the Roman Emperor Tiberius.
19:13 the Pavement. An open court.
19:14 sixth hour. Six o'clock in the morning by Roman time.
19:17 bearing his cross. Bearing the cross for Himself; when He sank beneath the burden, He was given assistance (Matt. 27:32; Mark 15:21; Luke 23:26).
19:24 They parted my raiment. See Psalm 22:18.
19:26 disciple standing by, whom he loved. John the apostle, the writer of this book. Jesus gave His mother into John's care.
19:28 I thirst. See Psalm 69:21.

vinegar, and put *it* upon hyssop, and put
it to his mouth.

"It is finished"

30When Jesus therefore had received
the vinegar, he said, It is finished: and he
bowed his head, and gave up the ghost.
31The Jews therefore, because it was
the preparation, that the bodies should
not remain upon the cross on the *sabbath day, (for that sabbath day was an
high day,) besought Pilate that their
legs might be broken, and *that* they
might be taken away.
32Then came the soldiers, and brake
the legs of the first, and of the other
which was crucified with him.
33But when they came to Jesus, and
saw that he was dead already, they
brake not his legs:
34But one of the soldiers with a spear
pierced his side, and forthwith came
there out *blood and water.
35And he that saw *it* bare record, and
his record is true: and he knoweth that
he saith true, that ye might believe.
36For these things were done, that
the scripture should be fulfilled, A bone
of him shall not be broken.
37And again another scripture saith,
They shall look on him whom they
pierced.

The burial (Matt. 27:57-60; Mark 15:43-47; Luke 23:50-56)

¶38And after this *Joseph of Arimathaea, being a disciple of Jesus, but
secretly for fear of the Jews, besought
Pilate that he might take away the body
of Jesus: and Pilate gave *him* leave. He
came therefore, and took the body of
Jesus.
39And there came also Nicodemus,
which at the first came to Jesus by
night, and brought a mixture of myrrh
and aloes, about an hundred pound
weight.
40Then took they the body of Jesus,
and wound it in linen clothes with the
spices, as the manner of the Jews is to
bury.
41Now in the place where he was crucified there was a garden; and in the
garden a new sepulchre, wherein was
never man yet laid.
42There laid they Jesus therefore
because of the Jews' preparation *day;*
for the sepulchre was nigh at hand.

VI. The Resurrection of Christ (20:1-31) (Matt. 28:1-10; Mark 16:1-14; Luke 24:1-43)

20 The first *day* of the week
cometh Mary Magdalene early,
when it was yet dark, unto the sepulchre, and seeth the stone taken away
from the sepulchre.
2Then she runneth, and cometh to
Simon *Peter, and to the other disciple,
whom Jesus loved, and saith unto them,
They have taken away the Lord out of
the sepulchre, and we know not where
they have laid him.
3Peter therefore went forth, and that

19:29 spunge with vinegar, and put it upon hyssop. This was an act of compassion. The hyssop was probably the caper plant, which has stems that are three or four feet long.
19:30 It is finished. The work of atonement, of bearing the judgment of God against sin, was finished.
19:31 an high day. It was the first day of unleavened bread, a great festival (Exod. 12:16; Lev. 23:7).
19:31 legs might be broken. To hasten death so Jesus and the two thieves could be buried before the Sabbath began.
19:36 A bone of him shall not be broken. See Exodus 12:46; Numbers 9:12; Psalm 34:20 (see also Ps. 34:20 note, "No Broken Bones").
19:37 They shall look on him. See Zechariah 12:10 and its note, "Christ's Death."
20:1 first day of the week. The Jewish *Sabbath was the seventh day of the week, Saturday. Jesus Christ rose from the dead on the first day of the week, Sunday. We "keep" this day, therefore, in memory of Christ's resurrection (see 1 Cor. 16:2).
20:2 the other disciple. John.

other disciple, and came to the sepulchre.
4So they ran both together: and the
other disciple did outrun Peter, and
came first to the sepulchre.
5And he stooping down, *and looking
in,* saw the linen clothes lying; yet went
he not in.
6Then cometh Simon Peter following
him, and went into the sepulchre, and
seeth the linen clothes lie,
7And the napkin, that was about his
head, not lying with the linen clothes,
but wrapped together in a place by itself.
8Then went in also that other disciple, which came first to the sepulchre,
and he saw, and believed.
9For as yet they knew not the scripture, that he must rise again from the
dead.
10Then the disciples went away again
unto their own home.

Mary Magdalene, the first to see the risen Lord

¶11But Mary stood without at the
sepulchre weeping: and as she wept,
she stooped down, *and looked* into the
sepulchre,
12And seeth two *angels in white sitting, the one at the head, and the other
at the feet, where the body of Jesus had
lain.
13And they say unto her, Woman, why
weepest thou? She saith unto them,
Because they have taken away my
Lord, and I know not where they have
laid him.
14And when she had thus said, she
turned herself back, and saw Jesus
standing, and knew not that it was Jesus.
15Jesus saith unto her, Woman, why
weepest thou? whom seekest thou?
She, supposing him to be the gardener,
saith unto him, Sir, if thou have borne
him hence, tell me where thou hast laid
him, and I will take him away.
16Jesus saith unto her, Mary. She
turned herself, and saith unto him, Rab-
boni; which is to say, Master.
17Jesus saith unto her, Touch me not;
for I am not yet ascended to my Father:
but go to my brethren, and say unto
them, I ascend unto my Father, and your
Father; and *to* my God, and your God.
18Mary Magdalene came and told the
disciples that she had seen the Lord,
and *that* he had spoken these things
unto her.

Jesus appears to the disciples on the first Sunday evening (Luke 24:36-49)

¶19Then the same day at evening, being the first *day* of the week, when the
doors were shut where the disciples
were assembled for fear of the Jews,
came Jesus and stood in the midst, and
saith unto them, *Peace *be* unto you.
20And when he had so said, he
shewed unto them *his* hands and his
side. Then were the disciples glad,
when they saw the Lord.
21Then said Jesus to them again,
Peace *be* unto you: as *my* Father hath
sent me, even so send I you.
22And when he had said this, he
breathed on *them,* and saith unto them,
Receive ye the Holy Ghost:
23Whose soever sins ye remit, they
are remitted unto them; *and* whose
soever *sins* ye retain, they are retained.

20:9 knew not the scripture. This refers to Psalm 16:10.

20:17 Touch me not. The thought is, "Do not grasp or hold Me." There was to begin then, following Christ's resurrection, a new ministry when the risen and ascended Lord would act as our Advocate and Intercessor at the right hand of the Father.

20:22 breathed on them. Compare this with Genesis 2:7. Just as natural life was breathed into man by the Creator, so supernatural life, the new life, is given to all born-again believers through the Holy Spirit.

20:23 remitted . . . retained. Every *born-again person filled with the Holy Spirit has the privilege of presenting Christ to unbelievers. The message is that of Peter (Acts 2:38; 10:43 and its note), and of Paul (Acts 13:38).

Jesus appears again the next Sunday

¶[24]But Thomas, one of the twelve,
called Didymus, was not with them
when Jesus came.
[25]The other disciples therefore said
unto him, We have seen the Lord. But
he said unto them, Except I shall see in
his hands the print of the nails, and put
my finger into the print of the nails, and
thrust my hand into his side, I will not
believe.
¶[26]And after eight days again his disciples were within, and Thomas with
them: *then* came Jesus, the doors being
shut, and stood in the midst, and said,
Peace *be* unto you.
[27]Then saith he to Thomas, Reach
hither thy finger, and behold my hands;
and reach hither thy hand, and thrust *it*
into my side: and be not faithless, but
believing.

20:27 Christ's Body
Jesus had the same body after He had risen as He had before, but this risen body was triumphant over death and time and space. In His resurrection body our Lord could appear or disappear at will, and even enter a room where the doors and windows were shut (vs. 19). Our bodies will one day be just like His resurrection body (1 John 3:2).

[28]And Thomas answered and said
unto him, My Lord and my God.
[29]Jesus saith unto him, Thomas, because thou hast seen me, thou hast
believed: blessed *are* they that have not
seen, and *yet* have believed.

The reason for writing the Gospel

¶[30]And many other signs truly did
Jesus in the presence of his disciples,
which are not written in this book:
[31]But these are written, that ye might
believe that Jesus is the Christ, the Son
of God; and that believing ye might
have life through his name.

VII. The Days between the Resurrection and the Ascension (21:1-25)

21 After these things Jesus
shewed himself again to the disciples at the sea of Tiberias; and on this
wise shewed he *himself.*
[2]There were together Simon Peter,
and Thomas called Didymus, and Nathanael of Cana in Galilee, and the *sons*
of Zebedee, and two other of his disciples.

The disciples go fishing

[3]Simon Peter saith unto them, I go a
fishing. They say unto him, We also go
with thee. They went forth, and entered
into a ship immediately; and that night
they caught nothing.

The Lord appears to them

[4]But when the morning was now
come, Jesus stood on the shore: but the
disciples knew not that it was Jesus.
[5]Then Jesus saith unto them, Children, have ye any meat? They answered him, No.
[6]And he said unto them, Cast the net
on the right side of the ship, and ye shall
find. They cast therefore, and now they
were not able to draw it for the multitude of fishes.
[7]Therefore that disciple whom Jesus
loved saith unto Peter, It is the Lord.
Now when Simon Peter heard that it
was the Lord, he girt *his* fisher's coat
unto him, (for he was naked,) and did
cast himself into the sea.
[8]And the other disciples came in a
little ship; (for they were not far from
land, but as it were two hundred cubits,)
dragging the net with fishes.
[9]As soon then as they were come to
land, they saw a fire of coals there, and
fish laid thereon, and bread.
[10]Jesus saith unto them, Bring of the
fish which ye have now caught.
[11]Simon Peter went up, and drew the

21:1 sea of Tiberias. Sea of Galilee. See John 6:1.
21:2 Nathanael. See John 1:45-49 for his conversion.
21:5 have ye any meat? "Have you caught any fish to eat?"

net to land full of great fishes, an hundred and fifty and three: and for all there
were so many, yet was not the net broken.
12 Jesus saith unto them, Come *and*
dine. And none of the disciples durst
ask him, Who art thou? knowing that it
was the Lord.
13 Jesus then cometh, and taketh
bread, and giveth them, and fish likewise.
14 This is now the third time that
Jesus shewed himself to his disciples,
after that he was risen from the dead.

Jesus talks to Peter

¶ 15 So when they had dined, Jesus
saith to Simon Peter, Simon, *son* of
Jonas, lovest thou me more than these?
He saith unto him, Yea, Lord; thou
knowest that I love thee. He saith unto
him, Feed my lambs.

21:15 Jesus Questions Peter
Our Lord used a word indicating *to love deeply,* but Peter used one that meant *to be fond of.* It is as though Jesus said, "Do you really love Me, Peter–that is, very deeply?" And Peter, remembering His denial of the Lord on the night of His arrest, only dared to say, "Lord, You know that I am very fond of You." He was perhaps afraid to speak too strongly for fear that he might fail again, but Jesus showed how much He trusted him by telling him to care for the young Christians (the lambs) and the older ones (the sheep). The thrice-repeated question, "Lovest thou me?" suggests a tender allusion to the apostle's thrice-repeated denial.

16 He saith to him again the second
time, Simon, *son* of Jonas, lovest thou
me? He saith unto him, Yea, Lord; thou
knowest that I love thee. He saith unto
him, Feed my sheep.
17 He saith unto him the third time,
Simon, *son* of Jonas, lovest thou me?
Peter was grieved because he said unto
him the third time, Lovest thou me?
And he said unto him, Lord, thou
knowest all things; thou knowest that
I love thee. Jesus saith unto him, Feed
my sheep.
18 Verily, verily, I say unto thee, When
thou wast young, thou girdedst thyself,
and walkedst whither thou wouldest:
but when thou shalt be old, thou shalt
stretch forth thy hands, and another
shall gird thee, and carry *thee* whither
thou wouldest not.
19 This spake he, signifying by what
death he should glorify God. And when
he had spoken this, he saith unto him,
Follow me.
20 Then Peter, turning about, seeth
the disciple whom Jesus loved following; which also leaned on his breast at
supper, and said, Lord, which is he that
betrayeth thee?
21 Peter seeing him saith to Jesus,
Lord, and what *shall* this man *do?*
22 Jesus saith unto him, If I will that
he tarry till I come, what *is that* to thee?
follow thou me.
23 Then went this saying abroad
among the brethren, that that disciple
should not die: yet Jesus said not unto
him, He shall not die; but, If I will that
he tarry till I come, what *is that* to thee?

Conclusion

24 This is the disciple which testifieth
of these things, and wrote these things:
and we know that his testimony is
true.
25 And there are also many other
things which Jesus did, the which, if
they should be written every one, I
suppose that even the world itself could
not contain the books that should be
written. Amen.

21:12 Come and dine. Come and have breakfast, the first meal of the day.
21:14 third time. The first two times were John 20:19 and 20:26.
21:18 when thou shalt be old. It is believed that the apostle Peter, who was at least middle-aged at this time, was put to death about the year A.D. 67.
21:20 the disciple whom Jesus loved. The apostle John (see vs. 24).

The ACTS of the Apostles

BACKGROUND

This book, called The Acts of the Apostles, is a sequel to the Gospel of Luke. Its writer, Luke (see introduction to the Gospel according to Luke), continues in Acts the history of the work of the Lord Jesus Christ in the first century, but here the work is done by Him through the Holy Spirit, who came to dwell within believers on the Day of Pentecost, ten days after the ascension of our Lord.

THEME AND SUMMARY

The Acts of the Apostles is a book of beginnings. It tells of:

1. the Father's gift of the Spirit;
2. the establishment of the Church; and
3. the beginning of New Testament missionary work.

From chapter 1 to 9:43, Peter is the central personage of the book, Jerusalem is the center of the Church, and the ministry is confined almost entirely to Israel. From 10:1 to 28:31, Paul is the prominent figure, Antioch is the center of authority, and the ministry reaches out to the Gentiles. At 16:10 the narrative changes from "they" to "we" indicating that Luke began to accompany Paul at that point. The key verse of the book is found in 1:8.

God permitted persecution to scatter the early Christians from Jerusalem and the land of Palestine to the uttermost parts of the then known world. All of these early Christians seem to have been witnesses to Christ, and this is God's intent for all of us who are His.

THE TIME

The events in Acts cover a period of 34 years, from A.D. 30 to 63.

OUTLINE OF ACTS

I.	Introduction	Acts 1:1-26
II.	First Coming of the Holy Spirit on Believers through His Witnesses	Acts 2:1—11:18
III.	First Gentile Church	Acts 11:19-30
IV.	Parenthesis: Continued Persecution	Acts 12:1-25
V.	First Century Missions	Acts 13:1—28:31

I. Introduction (1:1-26)

1 The former treatise have I made, O Theophilus, of all that Jesus began both to do and teach,

2 Until the day in which he was taken up, after that he through the Holy Ghost had given commandments unto the *apostles whom he had chosen:

3 To whom also he shewed himself alive after his passion by many infallible proofs, being seen of them forty days, and speaking of the things pertaining to the *kingdom of God:

4 And, being assembled together with *them,* commanded them that they should not depart from *Jerusalem, but wait for the promise of the Father, which, *saith he,* ye have heard of me.

5 For John truly baptized with water; but ye shall be baptized with the Holy Ghost not many days hence.

6 When they therefore were come together, they asked of him, saying, Lord, wilt thou at this time restore again the kingdom to *Israel?

7 And he said unto them, It is not for you to know the times or the seasons, which the Father hath put in his own power.

8 But ye shall receive power, after that the Holy Ghost is come upon you: and ye shall be witnesses unto me both in Jerusalem, and in all Judaea, and in *Samaria, and unto the uttermost part of the earth.

9 And when he had spoken these things, while they beheld, he was taken up; and a cloud received him out of their sight.

10 And while they looked stedfastly toward *heaven as he went up, behold, two men stood by them in white apparel;

11 Which also said, Ye men of Galilee, why stand ye gazing up into heaven? this same Jesus, which is taken up from you into heaven, shall so come in like

1:5 The Spirit's Baptism

In Matthew 3:11, John the Baptist told of the future when Jesus would baptize "with the Holy Ghost, and with fire" (see Matt. 3:11 note, "Various Baptisms"). Some believe that this baptism of fire took place at the same time as the baptism of the Holy Spirit, that it was evidenced by the cloven tongues like fire (Acts 2:3). Some believe that the baptism of fire speaks of the burning zeal and power given to believers. In this verse (1:5) our Lord simply declared to His disciples that they would be baptized "with the Holy Ghost not many days hence."

1:1 former treatise. Treatise means *a letter* or *book of explanation*. The former treatise was the Gospel according to Saint Luke. See Luke 1:3 and its note, "Theophilus."

1:3 passion. The crucifixion and death of the Lord Jesus Christ.

1:3 kingdom of God. The rule of God in the hearts of people as well as over all of His created universe.

1:4 promise of the Father. The Holy Spirit is the "promise of the Father" that Christ said He would "pray the Father" to send to them when He went away. (See our Lord's words: Luke 24:49; John 14:16,26; 16:7,13.)

1:5 not many days hence. This was forty days after the Crucifixion and Resurrection. Other days were to pass (seven to ten), before the Day of *Pentecost would come.

1:7 not for you to know. No one but God the Father knows when He will restore Israel (Matt. 24:36,42).

1:8 witnesses. A witness is a person who saw something happen and therefore can truly say that it did happen. Jesus needed His early church members to spread the news of the gospel.

1:11 shall so come. The two angels told Christ's followers that this "same Jesus" shall come again in the same way that He went away. He went away in His glorified body. He will return with His glorified body. He went away as a person. He will return as a person. He was seen ascending. He will be seen descending. He was taken up in the cloud. He will return in the clouds. When He returns, angels and the believers of all ages will be with Him (Matt. 25:31; Jude 14; compare Deut. 33:2). The important thing is that Christians shall be witnessing and watching until He comes (1 Thess. 1:9-10).

manner as ye have seen him go into
heaven.
12 Then returned they unto Jerusalem
from the mount called Olivet, which
is from Jerusalem a *sabbath day's
journey.

1:12 Journey on the Sabbath
The rabbis allowed the Jewish people to go about two thousand cubits, or a little more than half a mile, on the Sabbath. In Joshua 3:4 they found their rule for this–two thousand cubits was the distance between the ark and the people on their march. The rabbis believed that this was the nearest distance between the tents of the people and the tabernacle, and that it was, therefore, all right to travel just that far.

13 And when they were come in, they
went up into an upper room, where
abode both *Peter, and James, and John,
and Andrew, Philip, and Thomas, Bartholomew, and Matthew, James *the son*
of Alphaeus, and Simon Zelotes, and
Judas *the brother* of James.
14 These all continued with one accord in *prayer and supplication, with
the women, and Mary the mother of
Jesus, and with his brethren.
¶ 15 And in those days Peter stood up
in the midst of the disciples, and said,
(the number of names together were
about an hundred and twenty,)
16 Men *and* brethren, this scripture
must needs have been fulfilled, which
the Holy Ghost by the mouth of *David spake before concerning Judas,
which was guide to them that took
Jesus.
17 For he was numbered with us, and
had obtained part of this ministry.
18 Now this man purchased a field
with the reward of iniquity; and falling
headlong, he burst asunder in the
midst, and all his bowels gushed out.
19 And it was known unto all the
dwellers at Jerusalem; insomuch as
that field is called in their proper
tongue, Aceldama, that is to say, The
field of blood.
20 For it is written in the book of
Psalms, Let his habitation be desolate,
and let no man dwell therein: and his
bishoprick let another take.
21 Wherefore of these men which
have companied with us all the time
that the Lord Jesus went in and out
among us,
22 Beginning from the *baptism of
John, unto that same day that he was
taken up from us, must one be ordained
to be a witness with us of his *resurrection.
23 And they appointed two, Joseph
called Barsabas, who was surnamed
Justus, and Matthias.
24 And they prayed, and said, Thou,
Lord, which knowest the hearts of all
men, shew whether of these two thou
hast chosen,
25 That he may take part of this ministry and apostleship, from which Judas
by transgression fell, that he might go
to his own place.
26 And they gave forth their lots; and
the lot fell upon Matthias; and he was
numbered with the eleven apostles.

II. First Coming of the Holy Spirit
(2:1—11:18)

*1) On Jewish *believers*

2 And when the day of Pentecost
was fully come, they were all with
one accord in one place.
2 And suddenly there came a sound
from heaven as of a rushing mighty

1:12 Olivet. The place from which Jesus ascended into heaven (see Zech. 14:4 note, "The Mount of Olives").
1:16 this scripture. Peter was referring to Psalm 41:9.
1:17 obtained. Shared in or received.
1:18 purchased a field. Read Zechariah 11:12 note, "A Picture of Christ's Coming."
1:20 it is written. Two psalms are referred to here—Psalms 69:25 and 109:8. Psalm 109:8 puts it simply: "Let another take his [Judas'] office."
1:26 the lot fell. The Jonah 1:7 note, "Casting Lots," will explain the word "lot."

2:1 The Sixth Dispensation: The Church Age

The church age is the period of time between the termination of Christ's earthly ministry and His return, during which God, who is no longer dealing with Israel nationally as He did in the Old Testament times, purposes to call out from among the nations a people for His name (Acts 15:14). This dispensation, which was initiated with the advent of the *Holy Spirit on the Day of *Pentecost, to dwell within the hearts of believers in Christ, will continue until the *church is taken from the earth at the *Rapture (1 Thess. 4:13-17; see also 4:13 note, "Hope for the Dead"). The church age is also known as the age of grace.

wind, and it filled all the house where
they were sitting.
3And there appeared unto them cloven tongues like as of fire, and it sat
upon each of them.
4And they were all filled with the
Holy Ghost, and began to speak with
other tongues, as the Spirit gave them
utterance.
5And there were dwelling at Jerusalem Jews, devout men, out of every
nation under heaven.
6Now when this was noised abroad,
the multitude came together, and were
confounded, because that every man
heard them speak in his own language.
7And they were all amazed and marvelled, saying one to another, Behold,
are not all these which speak Galilaeans?
8And how hear we every man in our
own tongue, wherein we were born?
9Parthians, and Medes, and Elamites,
and the dwellers in Mesopotamia, and
in Judaea, and Cappadocia, in Pontus,
and Asia,
10Phrygia, and Pamphylia, in *Egypt,
and in the parts of Libya about Cyrene,
and strangers of Rome, Jews and proselytes,
11Cretes and Arabians, we do hear
them speak in our tongues the wonderful works of God.
12And they were all amazed, and
were in doubt, saying one to another,
What meaneth this?
13Others mocking said, These men
are full of new *wine.
¶14But Peter, standing up with the
eleven, lifted up his voice, and said unto
them, Ye men of Judaea, and all *ye* that

2:1 PENTECOST

Pentecost was one of seven feast days of Israel. Each feast was a reminder to them of what the Lord had done for them or would do for them in the future. (Read Lev. 23:16 note, "The Feast of Pentecost.") Thus it happened that the disciples, who were devout Israelites, observed the Feast of Pentecost. God used this day to commission and empower the *church. Thus, He sent the Holy Spirit to baptize the disciples and to give them power to perform His work in the new way He had planned.

The children of Israel were familiar with certain signs as proofs that God gave them when He wanted to call their attention to the fact that He was speaking directly from heaven (Exod. 19:18; 1 Kings 19:11-12). On the Day of Pentecost the mighty rushing wind, the tongues like as of fire, and the voice of the Holy Spirit speaking through the disciples in other languages were all or signs that this was from God.

In the next few chapters of the Book of Acts, it is seen that the Holy Spirit was given to different groups under different conditions, but never twice in exactly the same way. The tongues like as of fire never appeared again. After the first century all of the signs ceased.

2:14 Peter. Simon Peter, who was once the disciple who denied Christ (John 18:15-27), now became a powerful preacher by the power of the Holy Spirit. From that time on he was a great, fearless witness and was faithful until his death. Tradition says that when he was put to death for his faith and preaching, he asked to be crucified head downward, because he did not feel worthy to die as the Lord had died.

dwell at Jerusalem, be this known unto
you, and hearken to my words:
15For these are not drunken, as ye
suppose, seeing it is *but* the third hour
of the day.
16But this is that which was spoken
by the *prophet Joel;
17And it shall come to pass in the last
days, saith God, I will pour out of my
Spirit upon all flesh: and your sons and
your daughters shall prophesy, and your
young men shall see visions, and your
old men shall dream dreams:
18And on my servants and on my
handmaidens I will pour out in those
days of my Spirit; and they shall prophesy:
19And I will shew wonders in heaven
above, and signs in the earth beneath;
blood, and fire, and vapour of smoke:
20The sun shall be turned into darkness, and the moon into blood, before
that great and notable day of the Lord
come:
21And it shall come to pass, *that*

2:20 The Day of the Lord
The Day of the Lord is sometimes called "that day" and "the great day." It is to begin when the Lord returns and is to end when the heavens and earth are purged by fire as the new heavens and new earth are prepared for eternal blessing (Isa. 65:17-19; 66:22; 2 Pet. 3:12-13; Rev. 21:1 and its note, "The New Earth"). During the Day of the Lord, there will take place the time of *Tribulation, the destruction of the *Beast and those who worship him, as well as the False Prophet (Rev. 19:20-21), the *judgment of the nations (Matt. 25:31-46), the *Millennium (Rev. 20:2-4), *Satan's revolt and final overthrow (Rev. 20:7-10), the second *resurrection and the final *judgment (Rev. 20:11-15).

COUNTRIES OF THE PEOPLE MENTIONED AT PENTECOST

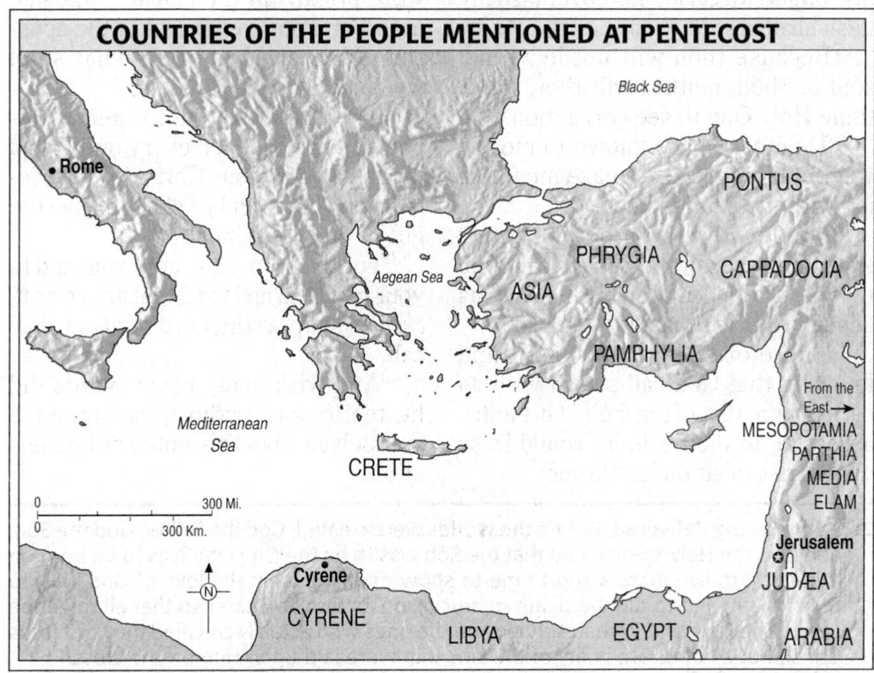

2:15 third hour. This was nine o'clock in the morning. Men did not become "drunk" in the morning.

2:16 Joel. The reference is to Joel 2:28-32 (see 2:28 note and 2:32 note, "A Remnant of Israel"). Peter reminded his hearers of this promise of the Spirit. The prophecy was only partly fulfilled at Pentecost. Before the Lord Jesus Christ returns in glory in the last days (vs. 17), it will all be fulfilled exactly as it was prophesied by the prophet Joel.

whosoever shall call on the name of the
Lord shall be saved.
22 Ye men of Israel, hear these words;
Jesus of Nazareth, a man approved of
God among you by *miracles and wonders and signs, which God did by him
in the midst of you, as ye yourselves
also know:
23 Him, being delivered by the determinate counsel and foreknowledge of
God, ye have taken, and by wicked
hands have crucified and slain:
24 Whom God hath raised up, having
loosed the pains of *death: because it
was not possible that he should be
holden of it.
25 For David speaketh concerning
him, I foresaw the Lord always before
my face, for he is on my right hand, that
I should not be moved:
26 Therefore did my heart rejoice, and
my tongue was glad; moreover also my
flesh shall rest in *hope:
27 Because thou wilt not leave my
soul in *hell, neither wilt thou suffer
thine Holy One to see corruption.
28 Thou hast made known to me the
ways of life; thou shalt make me full of
joy with thy countenance.
29 Men *and* brethren, let me freely
speak unto you of the patriarch David,
that he is both dead and buried, and his
sepulchre is with us unto this day.
30 Therefore being a prophet, and
knowing that God had sworn with an
oath to him, that of the fruit of his loins,
according to the flesh, he would raise
up *Christ to sit on his throne;
31 He seeing this before spake of the
resurrection of Christ, that his soul was
not left in hell, neither his flesh did see
corruption.
32 This Jesus hath God raised up,
whereof we all are witnesses.
33 Therefore being by the right hand
of God exalted, and having received of
the Father the promise of the Holy
Ghost, he hath shed forth this, which ye
now see and hear.
34 For David is not ascended into the
heavens: but he saith himself, The
LORD said unto my Lord, Sit thou on my
right hand,
35 Until I make thy foes thy footstool.
36 Therefore let all the house of Israel
know assuredly, that God hath made
that same Jesus, whom ye have crucified, both Lord and Christ.
¶37 Now when they heard *this*, they
were pricked in their heart, and said
unto Peter and to the rest of the apostles, Men *and* brethren, what shall
we do?
38 Then Peter said unto them, *Repent, and be baptized every one of you
in the name of Jesus Christ for the *remission of sins, and ye shall receive the
gift of the Holy Ghost.
39 For the promise is unto you, and to
your children, and to all that are afar off,
even as many as the Lord our God shall
call.
40 And with many other words did
he testify and *exhort, saying, Save
yourselves from this untoward generation.

2:23 Him, being delivered. Before the worlds were created, God the Father, God the Son, and God the Holy Spirit willed that the Son was to be the One who was to be born on the earth, to live there a short time to show mankind what the love of God was, to teach them, and to die the death of crucifixion as the Sin Bearer so that all might be saved. The Jews and Roman soldiers are the ones who actually crucified the Lord Jesus Christ, but all of us are guilty of the sins that were laid upon Him on the cross.

2:23 foreknowledge. See 1 Peter 1:2 first note and 1 Peter 1:20 first note.

2:25 For David speaketh. See Psalm 16:8-11.

2:27 hell. *Hades.

2:30 he would raise up Christ. Read 2 Samuel 7:1-17 to see God's promise (see also 2 Sam. 7:11 note, "The Davidic Covenant").

2:34 he saith himself. Read Psalm 110:1.

2:38 gift. The Holy Spirit was promised as a free gift to all those who repented and were baptized in the name of Christ for the remission of sins.

2) To three thousand believers

¶41Then they that gladly received his
word were baptized: and the same day
there were added *unto them* about three
thousand souls.
42And they continued stedfastly in
the apostles' *doctrine and fellowship,
and in breaking of bread, and in prayers.
43And fear came upon every soul: and
many wonders and signs were done by
the apostles.
44And all that believed were together,
and had all things common;
45And sold their possessions and
goods, and parted them to all *men,* as
every man had need.
46And they, continuing daily with one
accord in the temple, and breaking
bread from house to house, did eat their
meat with gladness and singleness of
heart,
47Praising God, and having favour
with all the people. And the Lord added
to the *church daily such as should
be saved.

3 Now Peter and John went up together
into the temple at the hour
of prayer, *being* the ninth *hour.*
2And a certain man lame from his
mother's womb was carried, whom
they laid daily at the gate of the temple
which is called Beautiful, to ask
alms of them that entered into the
temple;
3Who seeing Peter and John about to
go into the temple asked an alms.
4And Peter, fastening his eyes upon
him with John, said, Look on us.
5And he gave heed unto them, expecting
to receive something of them.
6Then Peter said, Silver and gold
have I none; but such as I have give I
thee: In the name of Jesus Christ of
Nazareth rise up and walk.
7And he took him by the right hand,
and lifted *him* up: and immediately his
feet and ankle bones received strength.
8And he leaping up stood, and
walked, and entered with them into the
temple, walking, and leaping, and praising
God.
9And all the people saw him walking
and praising God:
10And they knew that it was he which
sat for alms at the Beautiful gate of the
temple: and they were filled with wonder
and amazement at that which had
happened unto him.
11And as the lame man which was
healed held Peter and John, all the people
ran together unto them in the porch
that is called Solomon's, greatly wondering.
¶12And when Peter saw *it,* he answered
unto the people, Ye men of Israel,
why marvel ye at this? or why look
ye so earnestly on us, as though by our
own power or holiness we had made
this man to walk?
13The God of *Abraham, and of
*Isaac, and of *Jacob, the God of our
fathers, hath glorified his Son Jesus;

2:41 they. Those who believed were added to the church, not with any signs like those that came on the disciples earlier but simply by believing on Christ and being baptized. This is the second time that the Holy Spirit was given. See Acts 2:2-4; 8:17; 9:17 and its note, "The Gift of the Holy Spirit"; 10:44 and its note, "The Coming of the Holy Ghost"; 19:6.
2:42 doctrine. Teaching about spiritual thruths.
2:42 breaking of bread. This term has come to stand for the celebration of the Lord's Supper because of what the Lord Jesus Christ did and said on the night that He was betrayed (Luke 22:20; 1 Cor. 11:23-24 and 1 Cor. 11:24 note, "The Symbolic Body").
2:44 common. This is sometimes called "first-century communism." It is different from communism today. The early Christians were unselfish and reasoned "what is mine is yours." Today selfish communism claims "what is yours is mine."
2:47 church. This is the first mention of the New Testament *church in the Book of Acts.
3:1 the ninth hour. It was three o'clock.
3:11 the porch that is called Solomon's. This was a sort of hallway, open in front and on the sides. It was on the east side of the temple which Herod, not Solomon, had built.

whom ye delivered up, and denied him
in the presence of *Pilate, when he was
determined to let *him* go.
14But ye denied the Holy One and the
Just, and desired a murderer to be
granted unto you;
15And killed the Prince of life, whom
God hath raised from the dead; whereof
we are witnesses.
16And his name through *faith in his
name hath made this man strong, whom
ye see and know: yea, the faith which
is by him hath given him this perfect
soundness in the presence of you all.
17And now, brethren, I wot that
through ignorance ye did *it,* as *did* also
your rulers.
18But those things, which God before
had shewed by the mouth of all his
*prophets, that Christ should suffer, he
hath so fulfilled.
¶19Repent ye therefore, and be converted, that your sins may be blotted
out, when the times of refreshing shall
come from the presence of the Lord;
20And he shall send Jesus Christ,
which before was preached unto you:
21Whom the heaven must receive
until the times of restitution of all
things, which God hath spoken by the
mouth of all his holy prophets since the
*world began.
22For *Moses truly said unto the fathers, A prophet shall the Lord your
God raise up unto you of your brethren,
like unto me; him shall ye hear in all
things whatsoever he shall say unto
you.
23And it shall come to pass, *that* every
soul, which will not hear that prophet,
shall be destroyed from among the
people.
24Yea, and all the prophets from
*Samuel and those that follow after, as
many as have spoken, have likewise
foretold of these days.
25Ye are the children of the prophets,
and of the *covenant which God made
with our fathers, saying unto Abraham,
And in thy seed shall all the kindreds
of the earth be blessed.
26Unto you first God, having raised
up his Son Jesus, sent him to bless you,
in turning away every one of you from
his iniquities.

3:21 Promises Fulfilled
Jesus Christ will not return in glory until all the promises that the prophets have made by the command of God, about Israel being restored, have come to pass. They have said:
1. Israel will go back to the land of Palestine (Deut. 30:1-5); and
2. their country shall once more be a kingdom ruled by One who is descended from King David (2 Sam. 7:8-17). Read also the notes on the *covenant and the *kingdom.

4 And as they spake unto the people, the priests, and the captain of
the temple, and the *Sadducees, came
upon them,
2Being grieved that they taught the
people, and preached through Jesus the
resurrection from the dead.
3And they laid hands on them, and
put *them* in hold unto the next day: for
it was now eventide.
4Howbeit many of them which heard
the word believed; and the number of
the men was about five thousand.
¶5And it came to pass on the morrow,
that their rulers, and *elders, and
*scribes,
6And Annas the high priest, and *Ca-

3:14 Holy One and the Just. Peter was referring to the Saviour.
3:14 a murderer. Read about Barabbas in John 18:39-40. Barabbas was a murderer as well as a robber.
3:19 be converted. To turn around completely, away from sin.
3:19 times of refreshing. When Jesus Christ comes to reign (see *kingdom), there will be wonderful rest for His people.
3:20 And he shall send. A declaration as to Christ's coming to reign at the end of the *Tribulation. Peter's appeal here is to Israel the nation.
4:3 in hold. In prison.

iaphas, and John, and Alexander, and as
many as were of the kindred of the high
priest, were gathered together at Jerusalem.
7And when they had set them in the
midst, they asked, By what power, or by
what name, have ye done this?
8Then Peter, filled with the Holy
Ghost, said unto them, Ye rulers of the
people, and elders of Israel,
9If we this day be examined of the
good deed done to the impotent man,
by what means he is made whole;
10Be it known unto you all, and to all
the people of Israel, that by the name
of Jesus Christ of Nazareth, whom ye
crucified, whom God raised from the
dead, *even* by him doth this man stand
here before you whole.
11This is the stone which was set at
nought of you builders, which is become the head of the corner.
12Neither is there *salvation in any
other: for there is none other name
under heaven given among men,
whereby we must be saved.
¶13Now when they saw the boldness
of Peter and John, and perceived that
they were unlearned and ignorant men,
they marvelled; and they took knowledge of them, that they had been with
Jesus.
14And beholding the man which was
healed standing with them, they could
say nothing against it.
15But when they had commanded
them to go aside out of the council, they
conferred among themselves,
16Saying, What shall we do to these
men? for that indeed a notable *miracle hath been done by them *is* manifest
to all them that dwell in Jerusalem; and
we cannot deny *it*.
17But that it spread no further among
the people, let us straitly threaten
them, that they speak henceforth to no
man in this name.
18And they called them, and commanded them not to speak at all nor
teach in the name of Jesus.
19But Peter and John answered and
said unto them, Whether it be right in
the sight of God to hearken unto you
more than unto God, judge ye.
20For we cannot but speak the things
which we have seen and heard.
21So when they had further threatened them, they let them go, finding
nothing how they might punish them,
because of the people: for all *men* glorified God for that which was done.
22For the man was above forty years
old, on whom this miracle of healing
was shewed.
¶23And being let go, they went to
their own company, and reported all
that the chief priests and elders had said
unto them.
24And when they heard that, they lifted up their voice to God with one accord, and said, Lord, thou *art* God,
which hast made heaven, and earth, and
the sea, and all that in them is:
25Who by the mouth of thy servant
David hast said, Why did the heathen
rage, and the people imagine vain
things?
26The kings of the earth stood up,
and the rulers were gathered together against the Lord, and against his
Christ.
27For of a truth against thy holy child
Jesus, whom thou hast anointed, both
*Herod, and Pontius Pilate, with the
*Gentiles, and the people of Israel,
were gathered together,
28For to do whatsoever thy hand and
thy counsel determined before to be
done.
29And now, Lord, behold their

4:11 stone. The Lord Jesus Christ is the stone which the builders refused. See Psalm 118:22 and 1 Peter 2:4 first note.
4:25 by the mouth of thy servant David. Read all of Psalm 2.
4:25 heathen. Meaning the Gentile nations.
4:28 thy counsel determined before. See *predestination.

threatenings: and grant unto thy servants, that with all boldness they may
speak thy word,
30By stretching forth thine hand to
heal; and that signs and wonders may
be done by the name of thy holy child
Jesus.
¶31And when they had prayed, the
place was shaken where they were assembled together; and they were all
filled with the Holy Ghost, and they
spake the word of God with boldness.
¶32And the multitude of them that believed were of one heart and of one
soul: neither said any *of them* that ought
of the things which he possessed was
his own; but they had all things common.
33And with great power gave the
apostles witness of the resurrection of
the Lord Jesus: and great grace was
upon them all.
34Neither was there any among them
that lacked: for as many as were possessors of lands or houses sold them,
and brought the prices of the things that
were sold,
35And laid *them* down at the apostles'
feet: and distribution was made unto
every man according as he had need.
36And Joses, who by the apostles was
surnamed Barnabas, (which is, being
interpreted, The son of consolation,) a
Levite, *and* of the country of Cyprus,
37Having land, sold *it,* and brought
the money, and laid *it* at the apostles'
feet.

5 But a certain man named Ananias, with Sapphira his wife, sold a
possession,
2And kept back *part* of the price, his
wife also being privy *to it,* and brought
a certain part, and laid *it* at the apostles'
feet.
3But Peter said, Ananias, why hath
*Satan filled thine heart to lie to the
Holy Ghost, and to keep back *part* of the
price of the land?
4Whiles it remained, was it not thine
own? and after it was sold, was it not in
thine own power? why hast thou conceived this thing in thine heart? thou
hast not lied unto men, but unto God.
5And Ananias hearing these words
fell down, and gave up the ghost: and
great fear came on all them that heard
these things.
6And the young men arose, wound
him up, and carried *him* out, and buried *him.*
7And it was about the space of three
hours after, when his wife, not knowing
what was done, came in.
8And Peter answered unto her, Tell
me whether ye sold the land for so
much? And she said, Yea, for so much.
9Then Peter said unto her, How is it
that ye have agreed together to *tempt
the Spirit of the Lord? behold, the feet
of them which have buried thy husband
are at the door, and shall carry thee out.
10Then fell she down *straightway at
his feet, and yielded up the ghost: and
the young men came in, and found her
dead, and, carrying *her* forth, buried *her*
by her husband.
11And great fear came upon all the
church, and upon as many as heard
these things.
¶12And by the hands of the apostles

4:29 grant. Instead of praying that they would be protected from danger, the disciples prayed that they might be braver to speak the truth. God answered their prayer by giving them boldness and great power. He also empowered them with signs and wonders. Read about these in Acts 5:12-16.

4:33 grace. Compare this with Acts 6:8: "Full of faith and power." Joy and power follow the filling with the Holy Spirit (see vs. 31).

4:36 Barnabas. Later Barnabas accompanied Paul on his first missionary journey.

5:2 privy to. Aware of.

5:3 lie. Lying to the Holy Spirit is lying to God (see vs. 4). The punishment of Ananias and Sapphira was to be a lesson to the *church that God wanted only clean temples (see 1 Cor. 6:19) in which the Holy Spirit would live and work.

were many signs and wonders wrought
among the people; (and they were all
with one accord in Solomon's porch.
13 And of the rest durst no man join
himself to them: but the people magnified them.
14 And *believers were the more added to the Lord, multitudes both of men
and women.)
15 Insomuch that they brought forth
the sick into the streets, and laid *them*
on beds and couches, that at the least
the shadow of Peter passing by might
overshadow some of them.
16 There came also a multitude *out* of
the cities round about unto Jerusalem,
bringing sick folks, and them which
were vexed with *unclean spirits: and
they were healed every one.
¶ 17 Then the high priest rose up, and
all they that were with him, (which is
the sect of the Sadducees,) and were
filled with indignation,
18 And laid their hands on the apostles, and put them in the common
prison.
19 But the *angel of the Lord by night
opened the prison doors, and brought
them forth, and said,
20 Go, stand and speak in the temple
to the people all the words of this life.
21 And when they heard *that,* they
entered into the temple early in the
morning, and taught. But the high
priest came, and they that were with
him, and called the council together, and
all the senate of the children of Israel,
and sent to the prison to have them
brought.
22 But when the officers came, and
found them not in the prison, they returned, and told,
23 Saying, The prison truly found we
shut with all safety, and the keepers
standing without before the doors: but
when we had opened, we found no man
within.
24 Now when the high priest and the
captain of the temple and the chief
priests heard these things, they doubted of them whereunto this would grow.
25 Then came one and told them, saying, Behold, the men whom ye put in
prison are standing in the temple, and
teaching the people.
26 Then went the captain with the officers, and brought them without violence: for they feared the people, lest
they should have been stoned.
27 And when they had brought them,
they set *them* before the council: and
the high priest asked them,
28 Saying, Did not we straitly command you that ye should not teach in
this name? and, behold, ye have filled
Jerusalem with your doctrine, and intend to bring this man's blood upon us.
¶ 29 Then Peter and the *other* apostles
answered and said, We ought to obey
God rather than men.
30 The God of our fathers raised up
Jesus, whom ye slew and hanged on a
tree.
31 Him hath God exalted with his right
hand *to be* a Prince and a Saviour, for to
give *repentance to Israel, and forgiveness of sins.
32 And we are his witnesses of these
things; and *so is* also the Holy Ghost,
whom God hath given to them that obey
him.
¶ 33 When they heard *that,* they were
cut *to the heart,* and took counsel to slay
them.
34 Then stood there up one in the
council, a *Pharisee, named Gamaliel,
a doctor of the *law, had in reputation
among all the people, and commanded
to put the apostles forth a little space;
35 And said unto them, Ye men of Israel, take heed to yourselves what ye
intend to do as touching these men.
36 For before these days rose up Theu-
das, boasting himself to be somebody;

5:20 words of this life. That is, words bringing eternal life through Christ (John 3:16; see also John 3:15-16 note, "Eternal Life").

5:28 doctrine. Teaching about the Lord Jesus Christ.

to whom a number of men, about
four hundred, joined themselves: who
was slain; and all, as many as obeyed
him, were scattered, and brought to
nought.
37 After this man rose up Judas of
Galilee in the days of the taxing, and
drew away much people after him: he
also perished; and all, *even* as many as
obeyed him, were dispersed.
38 And now I say unto you, Refrain
from these men, and let them alone: for
if this counsel or this work be of men,
it will come to nought:
39 But if it be of God, ye cannot overthrow it; lest haply ye be found even to
fight against God.
40 And to him they agreed: and when
they had called the apostles, and beat-
en *them,* they commanded that they
should not speak in the name of Jesus,
and let them go.
¶ 41 And they departed from the presence of the council, rejoicing that they
were counted worthy to suffer shame
for his name.
42 And daily in the temple, and in
every house, they ceased not to teach
and preach Jesus Christ.

6 And in those days, when the number of the disciples was multiplied,
there arose a murmuring of the Grecians against the Hebrews, because
their widows were neglected in the
daily ministration.
2 Then the twelve called the multitude of the disciples *unto them,* and said,
It is not reason that we should leave the
word of God, and serve tables.
3 Wherefore, brethren, look ye out
among you seven men of honest report,
full of the Holy Ghost and wisdom,
whom we may appoint over this business.
4 But we will give ourselves continually to prayer, and to the ministry of the
word.
¶ 5 And the saying pleased the whole
multitude: and they chose Stephen, a
man full of faith and of the Holy Ghost,
and Philip, and Prochorus, and Nicanor,
and Timon, and Parmenas, and Nicolas
a proselyte of Antioch:

6:5 Stephen

The name means *crowned*. Stephen was the first Christian martyr. He and the six other Grecian Jews named here became the first deacons of the church. It was their duty to divide food and clothing among the poor and the widows.

6 Whom they set before the apostles:
and when they had prayed, they laid
their hands on them.
7 And the word of God increased; and
the number of the disciples multiplied
in Jerusalem greatly; and a great company of the priests were obedient to the
faith.
8 And Stephen, full of faith and power, did great wonders and *miracles
among the people.
¶ 9 Then there arose certain of the
*synagogue, which is called *the syna-
gogue* of the Libertines, and Cyrenians,
and Alexandrians, and of them of Cilicia and of Asia, disputing with Stephen.
10 And they were not able to resist the
wisdom and the spirit by which he
spake.
11 Then they suborned men, which

6:9 The Libertines

The Libertines were probably descendants of former prisoners of the Roman Consul Pompey, who were later freed, or set at liberty, under the next emperor, Tiberius. They worshipped in a synagogue of their own in Jerusalem.

5:37 in the days of the taxing. See Luke 2:1.

6:1 Grecians. Jews who spoke Greek, sometimes called "Hellenists."

6:5 proselyte. Nicolas was one of the many who, born as Gentiles, adopted the Jewish faith (see Acts 2:10).

6:6 laid their hands on them. The apostles set these men apart for service by prayer and laying hands on them, an ancient Jewish practice (Num. 27:23; Deut. 34:9).

said, We have heard him speak blasphemous words against Moses, and *against* God.

12 And they stirred up the people, and the elders, and the scribes, and came upon *him,* and caught him, and brought *him* to the council,

13 And set up false witnesses, which said, This man ceaseth not to speak blasphemous words against this holy place, and the law:

14 For we have heard him say, that this Jesus of Nazareth shall destroy this place, and shall change the customs which Moses delivered us.

15 And all that sat in the council, looking stedfastly on him, saw his face as it had been the face of an angel.

7 Then said the high priest, Are these things so?

2 And he said, Men, brethren, and fathers, hearken; The *God of glory appeared unto our father Abraham, when he was in Mesopotamia, before he dwelt in Charran,

3 And said unto him, Get thee out of thy country, and from thy kindred, and come into the land which I shall shew thee.

4 Then came he out of the land of the Chaldaeans, and dwelt in Charran: and from thence, when his father was dead, he removed him into this land, wherein ye now dwell.

5 And he gave him *none inheritance in it, no, not *so much as* to set his foot on: yet he promised that he would give it to him for a possession, and to his seed after him, when *as yet* he had no child.

6 And God spake on this wise, That his seed should sojourn in a strange land; and that they should bring them into bondage, and entreat *them* evil four hundred years.

7 And the nation to whom they shall be in bondage will I judge, said God: and after that shall they come forth, and serve me in this place.

8 And he gave him the covenant of *circumcision: and so *Abraham* begat Isaac, and circumcised him the eighth day; and Isaac *begat* Jacob; and Jacob *begat* the twelve patriarchs.

9 And the patriarchs, moved with envy, sold *Joseph into Egypt: but God was with him,

10 And delivered him out of all his afflictions, and gave him favour and wisdom in the sight of *Pharaoh king of Egypt; and he made him governor over Egypt and all his house.

11 Now there came a dearth over all the land of Egypt and Chanaan, and great affliction: and our fathers found no sustenance.

12 But when Jacob heard that there was corn in Egypt, he sent out our fathers first.

13 And at the second *time* Joseph was made known to his brethren; and Joseph's kindred was made known unto Pharaoh.

14 Then sent Joseph, and called his father Jacob to *him,* and all his kindred, threescore and fifteen souls.

15 So Jacob went down into Egypt, and died, he, and our fathers,

16 And were carried over into Sychem, and laid in the sepulchre that Abraham bought for a sum of money of the sons of Emmor *the father* of Sychem.

17 But when the time of the promise drew nigh, which God had sworn to Abraham, the people grew and multiplied in Egypt,

18 Till another king arose, which knew not Joseph.

19 The same dealt subtilly with our kindred, and evil entreated our fathers,

---

7:2 Charran. This is the Greek spelling of the word "Haran" when translated into English.
7:5 his seed. Abraham's descendants.
7:11 Chanaan. The Greek spelling of the word "Canaan."
7:14 all his kindred. Here Jacob's sons' wives are counted to make the number seventy-five. Read the Genesis 46:27 note.
7:17 the time of the promise. Read verses 6-7 for the promise.

so that they cast out their young children, to the end they might not live.
20 In which time Moses was born, and
was exceeding fair, and nourished up in
his father's house three months:
21 And when he was cast out,
Pharaoh's daughter took him up, and
nourished him for her own son.
22 And Moses was learned in all the
wisdom of the Egyptians, and was
mighty in words and in deeds.
23 And when he was full forty years
old, it came into his heart to visit his
brethren the children of *Israel.
24 And seeing one *of them* suffer
wrong, he defended *him,* and avenged
him that was oppressed, and smote the
Egyptian:
25 For he supposed his brethren would
have understood how that God by his
hand would deliver them: but they understood not.
26 And the next day he shewed himself unto them as they strove, and
would have set them at one again, saying, Sirs, ye are brethren; why do ye
wrong one to another?
27 But he that did his neighbour wrong
thrust him away, saying, Who made
thee a ruler and a judge over us?
28 Wilt thou kill me, as thou diddest
the Egyptian yesterday?
29 Then fled Moses at this saying, and
was a stranger in the land of Madian,
where he begat two sons.
30 And when forty years were expired, there appeared to him in the wilderness of mount Sina an angel of the
Lord in a flame of fire in a bush.
31 When Moses saw *it,* he wondered
at the sight: and as he drew near to
behold *it,* the voice of the Lord came
unto him,
32 *Saying,* I *am* the God of thy fathers,
the God of Abraham, and the God of
Isaac, and the God of Jacob. Then Moses trembled, and durst not behold.
33 Then said the Lord to him, Put off
thy shoes from thy feet: for the place
where thou standest is *holy ground.
34 I have seen, I have seen the affliction of my people which is in Egypt, and
I have heard their groaning, and am
come down to deliver them. And now
come, I will send thee into Egypt.
35 This Moses whom they refused,
saying, Who made thee a ruler and a
judge? the same did God send *to be* a
ruler and a deliverer by the hand of the
angel which appeared to him in the
bush.
36 He brought them out, after that he
had shewed wonders and signs in the
land of Egypt, and in the Red sea, and
in the wilderness forty years.
¶ 37 This is that Moses, which said
unto the children of Israel, A prophet
shall the Lord your God raise up unto
you of your brethren, like unto me; him
shall ye hear.
38 This is he, that was in the church
in the wilderness with the angel which
spake to him in the mount Sina, and
with our fathers: who received the
lively oracles to give unto us:
39 To whom our fathers would not obey,
but thrust *him* from them, and in their
hearts turned back again into Egypt,
40 Saying unto *Aaron, Make us gods
to go before us: for *as for* this Moses,
which brought us out of the land of
Egypt, we wot not what is become of
him.
41 And they made a calf in those days,
and offered *sacrifice unto the idol, and
rejoiced in the works of their own
hands.
42 Then God turned, and gave them
up to worship the host of *heaven; as
it is written in the book of the proph-

7:30 mount Sina. Mount Sinai.
7:38 church. The Greek word *ecclesia* means *called out.* As used here, this word means a group called out to worship God in the wilderness during the journey from Egypt to the Promised Land. It is not the New Testament *church.
7:38 lively oracles. The *living words,* the words of God (Rom. 3:1-3).

ets, O ye house of Israel, have ye offered to me slain beasts and sacrifices *by the space of* forty years in the wilderness?
[43]Yea, ye took up the *tabernacle of Moloch, and the star of your god Remphan, figures which ye made to worship them: and I will carry you away beyond *Babylon.
[44]Our fathers had the tabernacle of witness in the wilderness, as he had appointed, speaking unto Moses, that he should make it according to the fashion that he had seen.
[45]Which also our fathers that came after brought in with Jesus into the possession of the Gentiles, whom God drave out before the face of our fathers, unto the days of *David;
[46]Who found favour before God, and desired to find a tabernacle for the God of Jacob.
[47]But Solomon built him an house.
[48]Howbeit the most High dwelleth not in temples made with hands; as saith the prophet,
[49]Heaven *is* my throne, and earth *is* my footstool: what house will ye build me? saith the Lord: or what *is* the place of my rest?
[50]Hath not my hand made all these things?
¶[51]Ye stiffnecked and *uncircumcised in heart and ears, ye do always resist the Holy Ghost: as your fathers *did*, so *do* ye.
[52]Which of the prophets have not your fathers persecuted? and they have slain them which shewed before of the coming of the Just One; of whom ye have been now the betrayers and murderers:
[53]Who have received the law by the disposition of *angels, and have not kept *it*.
¶[54]When they heard these things, they were cut to the heart, and they gnashed on him with *their* teeth.
[55]But he, being full of the Holy Ghost, looked up stedfastly into heaven, and saw the glory of God, and Jesus standing on the right hand of God,
[56]And said, Behold, I see the heavens opened, and the Son of man standing on the right hand of God.
[57]Then they cried out with a loud voice, and stopped their ears, and ran upon him with one accord,
[58]And cast *him* out of the city, and stoned *him:* and the witnesses laid down their clothes at a young man's feet, whose name was Saul.
[59]And they stoned Stephen, calling upon *God*, and saying, Lord Jesus, receive my spirit.
[60]And he kneeled down, and cried

7:60 Falling Asleep
The expression "to fall asleep" was used to mean physical death. Jesus employed it about his friend Lazarus (John 11:11), whom He raised from the dead. Paul used it also when he wrote to the Thessalonian Christians (1 Thess. 4:13-18; see also 4:13 note, "Hope for the Dead") to comfort them about those who had died before the hoped-for coming of Christ.

7:42 the host of heaven. Not, of course, angels (Luke 2:13), but stars, planets, etc.
7:42 as it is written. See Amos 5:25-27.
7:43 Moloch . . . Remphan. Moloch was a fire god. Children were sacrificed by fire to Moloch. Remphan and Moloch were also worshipped along with the stars.
7:45 Jesus. Not out Lord, but Joshua, who succeeded Moses. Joshua is a shorter form of the Hebrew name Jehoshua. Jesus is the Greek name for Joshua, just as Henry is the English spelling of the German name Heinrich.
7:48 as saith the prophet. Read Isaiah 66:1-2.
7:58 Saul. The first mention of the man who would become the apostle to the Gentiles. Saul was his Hebrew name. Later he was called by the Roman or Gentile name of Paul, which means *little*.
7:59-60 receive my spirit . . . lay not this sin to their charge. The dying words of Stephen were much like those of the Lord Jesus Christ (Luke 23:34,46).

with a loud voice, Lord, lay not this *sin
to their charge. And when he had said
this, he fell asleep.

8 And Saul was consenting unto his
*death. And at that time there was
a great persecution against the *church
which was at *Jerusalem; and they
were all scattered abroad throughout
the regions of Judaea and *Samaria,
except the *apostles.

2 And devout men carried Stephen *to
his burial,* and made great lamentation
over him.

3 As for Saul, he made havock of the
church, entering into every house, and
haling men and women committed *them
to* prison.

4 Therefore they that were scattered
abroad went every where preaching the
word.

3) The Holy Spirit is given to the Samaritans

5 Then Philip went down to the city of
Samaria, and preached *Christ unto
them.

6 And the people with one accord gave
heed unto those things which Philip
spake, hearing and seeing the miracles
which he did.

7 For unclean spirits, crying with loud
voice, came out of many that were possessed *with them:* and many taken with
palsies, and that were lame, were
healed.

8 And there was great joy in that city.

9 But there was a certain man, called
Simon, which beforetime in the same
city used sorcery, and bewitched the
people of Samaria, giving out that himself was some great one:

10 To whom they all gave heed, from
the least to the greatest, saying, This
man is the great power of God.

11 And to him they had regard, because that of long time he had bewitched them with sorceries.

12 But when they believed Philip
preaching the things concerning the
*kingdom of God, and the name of Jesus
Christ, they were baptized, both men
and women.

13 Then Simon himself believed also:
and when he was baptized, he continued with Philip, and wondered, beholding the miracles and signs which were
done.

14 Now when the apostles which were
at Jerusalem heard that Samaria had
received the word of God, they sent
unto them *Peter and John:

15 Who, when they were come down,
prayed for them, that they might receive the Holy Ghost:

16 (For as yet he was fallen upon none
of them: only they were baptized in the
name of the Lord Jesus.)

17 Then laid they *their* hands on them,
and they received the Holy Ghost.

18 And when Simon saw that through
laying on of the apostles' hands the

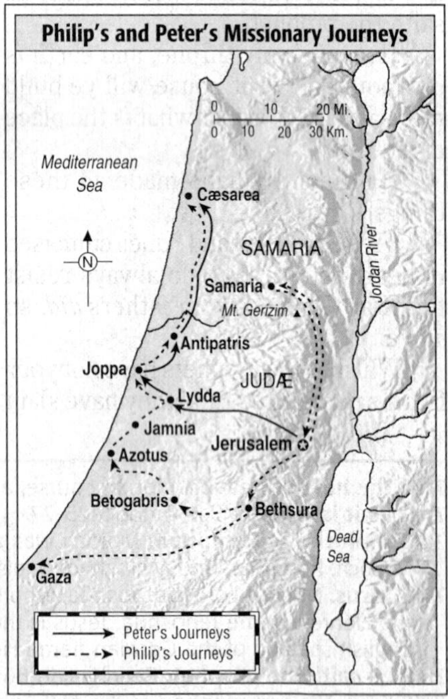

8:5 Philip. Philip was one of the first deacons, with Stephen (see Acts 6:5 and its note, "Stephen").

8:9 used sorcery. Simon was a magician who bewitched or amazed people.

Holy Ghost was given, he offered them
money,
[19]Saying, Give me also this power,
that on whomsoever I lay hands, he
may receive the Holy Ghost.
[20]But Peter said unto him, Thy money perish with thee, because thou hast
thought that the gift of God may be
purchased with money.
[21]Thou hast neither part nor lot in
this matter: for thy heart is not right in
the sight of God.
[22]*Repent therefore of this thy wickedness, and pray God, if perhaps the
thought of thine heart may be *forgiv-
en thee.
[23]For I perceive that thou art in the
gall of bitterness, and *in* the bond of iniquity.
[24]Then answered Simon, and said,
Pray ye to the Lord for me, that none
of these things which ye have spoken
come upon me.
[25]And they, when they had testified
and preached the word of the Lord, returned to Jerusalem, and preached the
*gospel in many villages of the *Samar-
itans.
[26]And the angel of the Lord spake
unto Philip, saying, Arise, and go toward the south unto the way that goeth
down from Jerusalem unto *Gaza,
which is desert.
[27]And he arose and went: and, behold, a man of Ethiopia, an eunuch of
great authority under Candace queen
of the Ethiopians, who had the charge
of all her treasure, and had come to Jerusalem for to worship,
[28]Was returning, and sitting in his
chariot read Esaias the *prophet.
[29]Then the Spirit said unto Philip,
Go near, and join thyself to this chariot.
[30]And Philip ran thither to *him,* and
heard him read the prophet Esaias, and
said, Understandest thou what thou
readest?
[31]And he said, How can I, except
some man should guide me? And he
desired Philip that he would come up
and sit with him.
[32]The place of the scripture which he
read was this, He was led as a sheep to
the slaughter; and like a lamb dumb
before his shearer, so opened he not his
mouth:
[33]In his humiliation his *judgment
was taken away: and who shall declare
his generation? for his life is taken from
the earth.
[34]And the eunuch answered Philip,
and said, I pray thee, of whom speaketh
the prophet this? of himself, or of some
other man?
[35]Then Philip opened his mouth, and
began at the same scripture, and
preached unto him Jesus.
[36]And as they went on *their* way, they
came unto a certain water: and the eunuch said, See, *here is* water; what doth
hinder me to be baptized?
[37]And Philip said, If thou believest
with all thine heart, thou mayest. And
he answered and said, I believe that
Jesus Christ is the Son of God.
[38]And he commanded the chariot to
stand still: and they went down both
into the water, both Philip and the eunuch; and he baptized him.
[39]And when they were come up out
of the water, the Spirit of the Lord
caught away Philip, that the eunuch saw
him no more: and he went on his way
rejoicing.
[40]But Philip was found at Azotus: and
passing through he preached in all the
cities, till he came to Caesarea.

4) The Holy Spirit given to Saul

9 And Saul, yet breathing out threatenings and slaughter against the

8:28 Esaias. The Greek form of the name Isaiah.

8:35 same scripture. The man was reading Isaiah 53, and Philip explained to him that the Lord Jesus Christ, who had died and risen again and ascended, was the Messiah of whom Isaiah had written centuries before.

disciples of the Lord, went unto the
high priest,
[2]And desired of him letters to *Damascus to the *synagogues, that if he
found any of this way, whether they
were men or women, he might bring
them bound unto Jerusalem.
[3]And as he journeyed, he came near
Damascus: and suddenly there shined
round about him a light from heaven:
[4]And he fell to the earth, and heard a
voice saying unto him, Saul, Saul, why
persecutest thou me?
[5]And he said, Who art thou, Lord?
And the Lord said, I am Jesus whom
thou persecutest: *it is* hard for thee to
kick against the pricks.
[6]And he trembling and astonished
said, Lord, what wilt thou have me to
do? And the Lord *said* unto him, Arise,
and go into the city, and it shall be told
thee what thou must do.
[7]And the men which journeyed with
him stood speechless, hearing a voice,
but seeing no man.
[8]And Saul arose from the earth; and
when his eyes were opened, he saw no
man: but they led him by the hand, and
brought *him* into Damascus.
[9]And he was three days without
sight, and neither did eat nor drink.
¶[10]And there was a certain disciple at
Damascus, named Ananias; and to him
said the Lord in a vision, Ananias. And
he said, Behold, I *am here,* Lord.
[11]And the Lord *said* unto him, Arise,
and go into the street which is called
Straight, and enquire in the house of
Judas for *one* called Saul, of Tarsus: for,
behold, he prayeth,
[12]And hath seen in a vision a man
named Ananias coming in, and putting
his hand on him, that he might receive
his sight.
[13]Then Ananias answered, Lord, I
have heard by many of this man, how
much evil he hath done to thy *saints
at Jerusalem:
[14]And here he hath authority from
the chief priests to bind all that call on
thy name.
[15]But the Lord said unto him, Go thy
way: for he is a chosen vessel unto me,
to bear my name before the Gentiles,
and kings, and the children of Israel:
[16]For I will shew him how great
things he must suffer for my name's
sake.
[17]And Ananias went his way, and entered into the house; and putting his
hands on him said, Brother Saul, the
Lord, *even* Jesus, that appeared unto
thee in the way as thou camest, hath
sent me, that thou mightest receive thy
sight, and be filled with the Holy Ghost.

9:17 The Gift of the Holy Spirit
This is the fourth time that the gift of the Holy Spirit was given under varying circumstances. Saul had believed on the Damascus Road when he heard the voice, but he did not receive the Holy Spirit until Ananias, a disciple, laid his hands on him. Then his sight was restored. He was then baptized and filled with the Holy Spirit. See Acts 10:44-48 (see 10:44 note, "The Coming of the Holy Ghost") for the next bestowing of the Holy Spirit on believers who were Gentiles.

[18]And immediately there fell from his
eyes as it had been scales: and he received sight forthwith, and arose, and
was baptized.
[19]And when he had received meat, he
was strengthened. Then was Saul certain days with the disciples which were
at Damascus.
[20]And straightway he preached
Christ in the synagogues, that he is the
Son of God.
[21]But all that heard *him* were amazed,
and said; Is not this he that destroyed
them which called on this name in Je-

9:2 of this way. The people who were "of this way" were the followers of the Lord Jesus Christ (see John 14:6).

9:5 to kick against the pricks. The word "pricks" means *goads,* which were sharp, pointed sticks used to make the oxen go forward. Kicking against them did no good; it merely injured the oxen.

rusalem, and came hither for that intent, that he might bring them bound
unto the chief priests?
22But Saul increased the more in
strength, and confounded the Jews
which dwelt at Damascus, proving that
this is very Christ.

9:22 Paul's Return to Damascus
In Paul's letter to the Galatian Christians (Gal. 1:17), he tells of having gone to Arabia immediately after his conversion, where he stayed for two years before returning to Damascus. It was there that God revealed to him the wonderful truths about the Scriptures, which he later preached and which are now written in his epistles.

¶23And after that many days were fulfilled, the Jews took counsel to kill him:
24But their laying await was known of
Saul. And they watched the gates day
and night to kill him.
25Then the disciples took him by
night, and let *him* down by the wall in a
basket.
26And when Saul was come to Jerusalem, he assayed to join himself to the
disciples: but they were all afraid of
him, and believed not that he was a disciple.
27But Barnabas took him, and
brought *him* to the apostles, and declared unto them how he had seen the
Lord in the way, and that he had spoken
to him, and how he had preached boldly at Damascus in the name of Jesus.
28And he was with them coming in
and going out at Jerusalem.
29And he spake boldly in the name of
the Lord Jesus, and disputed against the
*Grecians: but they went about to slay
him.
30*Which* when the brethren knew,
they brought him down to Caesarea,
and sent him forth to Tarsus.
31Then had the churches rest
throughout all Judaea and Galilee and
Samaria, and were edified; and walking
in the *fear of the Lord, and in the comfort of the Holy Ghost, were multiplied.
¶32And it came to pass, as Peter
passed throughout all *quarters,* he came
down also to the saints which dwelt at
Lydda.
33And there he found a certain man
named Æneas, which had kept his bed
eight years, and was sick of the palsy.
34And Peter said unto him, Æneas,
Jesus Christ maketh thee whole: arise,
and make thy bed. And he arose immediately.
35And all that dwelt at Lydda and
Saron saw him, and turned to the Lord.
¶36Now there was at Joppa a certain
disciple named Tabitha, which by interpretation is called Dorcas: this woman
was full of good works and almsdeeds
which she did.
37And it came to pass in those days,
that she was sick, and died: whom when
they had washed, they laid *her* in an
upper chamber.
38And forasmuch as Lydda was nigh
to Joppa, and the disciples had heard
that Peter was there, they sent unto
him two men, desiring *him* that he
would not delay to come to them.
39Then Peter arose and went with
them. When he was come, they brought
him into the upper chamber: and all the
widows stood by him weeping, and
shewing the coats and *garments which
Dorcas made, while she was with them.
40But Peter put them all forth, and
kneeled down, and prayed; and turning
him to the body said, Tabitha, arise. And
she opened her eyes: and when she saw
Peter, she sat up.
41And he gave her *his* hand, and lifted her up, and when he had called the

9:26 Jerusalem. This was the first of Paul's four visits to Jerusalem after his conversion. On this occasion he did not keep company with his former friends but hunted up the disciples to be with them. They did not trust Paul and were afraid that he was using some new scheme to continue his persecutions of Christians.

9:27 Barnabas. This is the Levite who, in Acts 4:36-37, sold all his land and gave the money to the disciples. He became a missionary to the Gentiles with Paul (13:2).

saints and widows, presented her alive.
42 And it was known throughout all
Joppa; and many believed in the Lord.
43 And it came to pass, that he tarried
many days in Joppa with one Simon a
tanner.

5) The Holy Spirit given to Gentiles

10 There was a certain man in
Caesarea called Cornelius, a
*centurion of the band called the Ital-
ian *band,*
2 A devout *man,* and one that feared
God with all his house, which gave
much alms to the people, and prayed to
God alway.
3 He saw in a vision evidently about
the ninth hour of the day an angel of
God coming in to him, and saying unto
him, *Cornelius.
4 And when he looked on him, he was
afraid, and said, What is it, Lord? And
he said unto him, Thy prayers and thine
alms are come up for a memorial before
God.
5 And now send men to Joppa, and call
for *one* Simon, whose surname is Peter:
6 He lodgeth with one Simon a tanner,
whose house is by the sea side: he shall
tell thee what thou oughtest to do.
7 And when the angel which spake
unto Cornelius was departed, he called
two of his household servants, and a
devout soldier of them that waited on
him continually;
8 And when he had declared all *these*
things unto them, he sent them to
Joppa.
¶9 On the morrow, as they went on
their journey, and drew nigh unto the
city, Peter went up upon the housetop
to pray about the sixth hour:
10 And he became very hungry, and
would have eaten: but while they made
ready, he fell into a trance,
11 And saw heaven opened, and a certain vessel descending unto him, as it
had been a great sheet knit at the four
corners, and let down to the earth:
12 Wherein were all manner of fourfooted beasts of the earth, and wild
beasts, and creeping things, and fowls
of the air.
13 And there came a voice to him,
Rise, Peter; kill, and eat.
14 But Peter said, Not so, Lord; for I
have never eaten any thing that is common or unclean.
15 And the voice *spake* unto him again
the second time, What God hath
cleansed, *that* call not thou common.
16 This was done thrice: and the vessel was received up again into heaven.
17 Now while Peter doubted in himself
what this vision which he had seen
should mean, behold, the men which
were sent from Cornelius had made
enquiry for Simon's house, and stood
before the gate,
18 And called, and asked whether Simon, which was surnamed Peter, were
lodged there.
¶19 While Peter thought on the vision,
the Spirit said unto him, Behold, three
men seek thee.
20 Arise therefore, and get thee down,
and go with them, doubting nothing: for
I have sent them.

10:1 Cornelius. Cornelius, a Roman centurion, was a Gentile. Gentiles were despised by Jews, who considered them as outcasts—away from God and not privileged to enjoy His blessings (Eph. 2:12).

10:3 ninth hour. This was three o'clock in the afternoon. It was a vision from God and not a dream at night.

10:6 lodgeth. In this verse, in verse 32, and in Acts 9:11, note again that God knows all about the details of our lives and actions.

10:9 sixth hour. Noon.

10:14 common. In the Law of Moses, the Israelites were commanded not to eat of certain unclean animals (Lev. 11). Peter had always obeyed this law, but God was teaching him a lesson (Acts 10:15), which Peter learned (vs. 28).

10:20 doubting nothing. When God asks His children to do His bidding, He goes ahead of them and prepares the way.

21 Then Peter went down to the men
which were sent unto him from Cornelius; and said, Behold, I am he whom ye
seek: what *is* the cause wherefore ye
are come?
22 And they said, Cornelius the centurion, a *just man, and one that
*feareth God, and of good report among
all the nation of the Jews, was warned
from God by an holy angel to send for
thee into his house, and to hear words
of thee.
23 Then called he them in, and lodged
them. And on the morrow Peter went
away with them, and certain brethren
from Joppa accompanied him.
24 And the morrow after they entered
into Caesarea. And Cornelius waited for
them, and had called together his kinsmen and near friends.
25 And as Peter was coming in, Cornelius met him, and fell down at his
feet, and worshipped *him.*
26 But Peter took him up, saying,
Stand up; I myself also am a man.
27 And as he talked with him, he went
in, and found many that were come together.
28 And he said unto them, Ye know
how that it is an unlawful thing for a
man that is a Jew to keep company, or
come unto one of another nation; but
God hath shewed me that I should not
call any man common or unclean.
29 Therefore came I *unto you* without
gainsaying, as soon as I was sent for: I
ask therefore for what intent ye have
sent for me?
30 And Cornelius said, Four days ago
I was fasting until this hour; and at the
ninth hour I prayed in my house, and,
behold, a man stood before me in bright
clothing,
31 And said, Cornelius, thy *prayer is
heard, and thine alms are had in remembrance in the sight of God.
32 Send therefore to Joppa, and call
hither Simon, whose surname is Peter;
he is lodged in the house of *one* Simon
a tanner by the sea side: who, when he
cometh, shall speak unto thee.
33 Immediately therefore I sent to
thee; and thou hast well done that thou
art come. Now therefore are we all here
present before God, to hear all things
that are commanded thee of God.
¶34 Then Peter opened *his* mouth, and
said, Of a truth I perceive that God is
no respecter of persons:
35 But in every nation he that feareth
him, and worketh *righteousness, is
accepted with him.
36 The word which *God* sent unto the
children of Israel, preaching *peace by
Jesus Christ: (he is Lord of all:)
37 That word, *I say,* ye know, which
was published throughout all Judaea,
and began from Galilee, after the *baptism which John preached;
38 How God anointed Jesus of Nazareth with the Holy Ghost and with power: who went about doing good, and
healing all that were oppressed of the
*devil; for God was with him.
39 And we are witnesses of all things
which he did both in the land of the
Jews, and in Jerusalem; whom they
slew and hanged on a tree:
40 Him God raised up the third day,
and shewed him openly;
41 Not to all the people, but unto witnesses chosen before of God, *even* to us,
who did eat and drink with him after he
rose from the dead.
42 And he commanded us to preach
unto the people, and to testify that it is
he which was ordained of God *to be* the
Judge of *quick and dead.

10:28 it is an unlawful thing. Read verses 1 and 14 notes.
10:34 God is no respecter of persons. Read Romans 3:29; 10:12-13.
10:38 How God anointed Jesus. Isaiah 61:1 (see 61:1 note, "The Advents of Christ") and John 1:32-34 tell more about the anointing of the Lord Jesus by the Holy Spirit.
10:39 witnesses. Notice that all of the disciples, and not only those who had seen the Lord Jesus in the body, were to be witnesses of the things mentioned in verses 39-43.
10:42 quick and dead. "Quick" refers to the *living,* thus the living and the dead.

[43]To him give all the *prophets witness, that through his name whosoever believeth in him shall receive remission of sins.

¶[44]While Peter yet spake these words, the Holy Ghost fell on all them which heard the word.

[45]And they of the circumcision which believed were astonished, as many as came with Peter, because that on the *Gentiles also was poured out the gift of the Holy Ghost.

[46]For they heard them speak with tongues, and magnify God. Then answered Peter,

[47]Can any man forbid water, that these should not be baptized, which have received the Holy Ghost as well as we?

[48]And he commanded them to be baptized in the name of the Lord. Then prayed they him to tarry certain days.

11 And the apostles and brethren that were in Judaea heard that the Gentiles had also received the word of God.

[2]And when Peter was come up to Jerusalem, they that were of the circumcision contended with him,

[3]Saying, Thou wentest in to men uncircumcised, and didst eat with them.

[4]But Peter rehearsed *the matter* from the beginning, and expounded *it* by order unto them, saying,

[5]I was in the city of Joppa praying: and in a trance I saw a vision, A certain vessel descend, as it had been a great sheet, let down from heaven by four corners; and it came even to me:

[6]Upon the which when I had fastened mine eyes, I considered, and saw fourfooted beasts of the earth, and wild beasts, and creeping things, and fowls of the air.

[7]And I heard a voice saying unto me, Arise, Peter; slay and eat.

[8]But I said, Not so, Lord: for nothing common or *unclean hath at any time entered into my mouth.

[9]But the voice answered me again from heaven, What God hath cleansed, *that* call not thou common.

[10]And this was done three times: and all were drawn up again into heaven.

[11]And, behold, immediately there were three men already come unto the house where I was, sent from Caesarea unto me.

[12]And the Spirit bade me go with them, nothing doubting. Moreover these six brethren accompanied me, and we entered into the man's house:

10:44 THE COMING OF THE HOLY GHOST

This is the fifth time the Holy Spirit was given, and the second time that signs accompanied it. Notice that it was different from the other times.

1. The Jews at Pentecost believed, received the Holy Spirit, and spoke with tongues (Acts 2:4).
2. The Samaritans believed and were baptized, but they did not receive the Holy Spirit until the hands of the apostles were laid on them (8:17), though they were already baptized (v. 8:12).
3. Saul believed and was baptized and was filled with the Holy Spirit when the hands of Ananias, God's chosen representative, were laid on him (9:17-18). Then he was baptized.
4. The Gentiles in the house of Cornelius received the Holy Spirit immediately when they believed and spoke with tongues (just as the Jews at Pentecost), before they were baptized with water.

At this fifth time, there was a special reason for giving Gentiles the sign of speaking in tongues as a proof that they had received the Holy Spirit. To receive the same sign which was first given to the Jews was a proof to the Jews that God had accepted the Gentiles just as He had accepted Jewish believers at *Pentecost. See Acts 19:6 for the next bestowing of the Holy Spirit in the early *church age. It was the last record in the Bible of the gift of tongues as a sign of the presence of the Holy Spirit.

10:43 remission. Remission means *pardon* or *forgiveness*. The only condition was to believe in Christ.

10:45 of the circumcision. Hebrew Christians are meant here (see also 11:2).

[13]And he shewed us how he had seen
an *angel in his house, which stood and
said unto him, Send men to Joppa, and
call for Simon, whose surname is Peter;
[14]Who shall tell thee words, whereby
thou and all thy house shall be saved.
[15]And as I began to speak, the Holy
Ghost fell on them, as on us at the beginning.
[16]Then remembered I the word of the
Lord, how that he said, John indeed
baptized with water; but ye shall be
baptized with the Holy Ghost.
[17]Forasmuch then as God gave them
the like gift as *he did* unto us, who believed on the Lord Jesus Christ; what
was I, that I could withstand God?
[18]When they heard these things, they
held their peace, and glorified God, saying, Then hath God also to the Gentiles
granted *repentance unto life.

III. First Gentile Church (11:19-30)

¶[19]Now they which were scattered
abroad upon the persecution that arose
about Stephen travelled as far as Phenice, and Cyprus, and Antioch, preaching the word to none but unto the Jews
only.
[20]And some of them were men of
Cyprus and Cyrene, which, when they
were come to Antioch, spake unto the
Grecians, preaching the Lord Jesus.
[21]And the hand of the Lord was with
them: and a great number believed, and
turned unto the Lord.
¶[22]Then tidings of these things came
unto the ears of the church which was
in Jerusalem: and they sent forth Barnabas, that he should go as far as Antioch.
[23]Who, when he came, and had seen
the *grace of God, was glad, and exhorted them all, that with purpose of heart
they would cleave unto the Lord.
[24]For he was a good man, and full of
the Holy Ghost and of *faith: and much
people was added unto the Lord.
[25]Then departed Barnabas to Tarsus,
for to seek Saul:
[26]And when he had found him, he
brought him unto Antioch. And it came
to pass, that a whole year they assembled themselves with the church, and
taught much people. And the disciples
were called Christians first in Antioch.

11:19-21 The Church Grows
In the very short period between the stoning of Stephen and this time during which the believers were scattered abroad, they became witnesses to the gospel wherever they went. Instead of only one church in Jerusalem, there were now churches in many cities and towns. The believers had traveled as far, for example, as Antioch, which is on the northeastern shore of the Mediterranean Sea. Barnabas became the first preacher of the church at Antioch. He brought Paul to Antioch to teach the people also. Antioch became the starting place for Paul's later missionary journeys.

11:26 The Name "Christian"
The name of Christian, *Christ's one,* was first given to the believers at Antioch. It was not conferred by our Lord but used by the world, which looks at external things only. Some people think today that all who live in a so-called Christian nation are Christians. The name should only be used of those who are believers in the Lord Jesus Christ as personal Saviour and live as true disciples.

¶[27]And in these days came prophets
from Jerusalem unto Antioch.
[28]And there stood up one of them
named Agabus, and signified by the
Spirit that there should be great dearth
throughout all the *world: which came
to pass in the days of Claudius *Caesar.
[29]Then the disciples, every man according to his ability, determined to

11:18 glorified God. The Jewish believers were now beginning to understand that God's plan for the church was that Gentiles as well as Jews were to receive the gospel and by the Holy Spirit were to become members with them of the *church.
11:28 great dearth. Famine.

send relief unto the brethren which
dwelt in Judaea:
30 Which also they did, and sent it to
the *elders by the hands of Barnabas
and Saul.

III. Continued Persecution (12:1-25)

12 Now about that time *Herod the
king stretched forth *his* hands
to vex certain of the church.
2 And he killed James the brother of
John with the sword.
3 And because he saw it pleased the
Jews, he proceeded further to take Peter also. (Then were the days of *unleavened bread.)
4 And when he had apprehended him,
he put *him* in prison, and delivered *him*
to four quaternions of soldiers to keep
him; intending after Easter to bring him
forth to the people.
5 Peter therefore was kept in prison:
but prayer was made without ceasing of
the church unto God for him.
6 And when Herod would have
brought him forth, the same night Peter was sleeping between two soldiers,
bound with two chains: and the keepers before the door kept the prison.
7 And, behold, the angel of the Lord
came upon *him,* and a light shined in the
prison: and he smote Peter on the side,
and raised him up, saying, Arise up
quickly. And his chains fell off from *his*
hands.
8 And the angel said unto him, Gird
thyself, and bind on thy sandals. And so
he did. And he saith unto him, Cast thy
garment about thee, and follow me.
9 And he went out, and followed him;
and *wist not that it was true which was
done by the angel; but thought he saw
a vision.
10 When they were past the first and
the second ward, they came unto the
iron gate that leadeth unto the city;
which opened to them of his own accord: and they went out, and passed on
through one street; and forthwith the
angel departed from him.
11 And when Peter was come to himself, he said, Now I know of a surety,
that the Lord hath sent his angel, and
hath delivered me out of the hand of
Herod, and *from* all the expectation of
the people of the Jews.
12 And when he had considered *the
thing,* he came to the house of Mary the
mother of John, whose surname was
Mark; where many were gathered together praying.
13 And as Peter knocked at the door
of the gate, a damsel came to hearken,
named Rhoda.
14 And when she knew Peter's voice,
she opened not the gate for gladness,
but ran in, and told how Peter stood
before the gate.
15 And they said unto her, Thou art mad.
But she constantly affirmed that it was
even so. Then said they, It is his angel.
16 But Peter continued knocking: and
when they had opened *the door,* and saw
him, they were astonished.

12:1 Herod. Herod Agrippa I, also called King Agrippa. He was the father of Herod Agrippa II, before whom Paul was taken.

12:4 quaternions. A quaternion was a Roman guard of four soldiers, detailed to act as sentries over a prisoner. In the strictest custody (as in the case of Peter), each hand of the prisoner was handcuffed to a separate soldier inside the cell, while the other two kept sentry outside the door. These four were relieved every three hours, day and night, so that there were four quaternions required for one day's service and four for the night watches.

12:4 Easter. This was the Passover time, when the Jewish people kept the feast in memory of the first Passover (see Exod. 12:3 note, "The Meaning of Passover"). They did not commemorate Easter as the Christian Jews did, and as we do, in memory of the resurrection of our Lord Jesus Christ.

12:10 the first and the second ward. "Ward" and "guard" are different spellings of the same word.

12:15 his angel. Read Matthew 18:10 and Hebrews 1:4 note, "Angels."

[17]But he, beckoning unto them with
the hand to hold their peace, declared
unto them how the Lord had brought
him out of the prison. And he said, Go
shew these things unto James, and to
the brethren. And he departed, and
went into another place.
[18]Now as soon as it was day, there
was no small stir among the soldiers,
what was become of Peter.
[19]And when Herod had sought for him,
and found him not, he examined the keepers, and commanded that *they* should be
put to death. And he went down from
Judaea to Caesarea, and *there* abode.
¶[20]And Herod was highly displeased
with them of *Tyre and Sidon: but they
came with one accord to him, and, having made Blastus the king's chamberlain their friend, desired peace; because
their country was nourished by the
king's *country.*
[21]And upon a set day Herod, arrayed
in royal apparel, sat upon his throne,
and made an oration unto them.
[22]And the people gave a shout, *saying, It is* the voice of a god, and not of a
man.
[23]And immediately the angel of the
Lord smote him, because he gave not
God the glory: and he was eaten of
worms, and gave up the ghost.
¶[24]But the word of God grew and
multiplied.
[25]And Barnabas and Saul returned
from Jerusalem, when they had fulfilled
their ministry, and took with them John,
whose surname was *Mark.

IV. First Century Missions (13:1—28:31)

13 Now there were in the church
that was at Antioch certain
prophets and teachers; as Barnabas,
and Simeon that was called Niger, and
Lucius of Cyrene, and Manaen, which
had been brought up with Herod the
*tetrarch, and Saul.
[2]As they ministered to the Lord, and
fasted, the Holy Ghost said, Separate

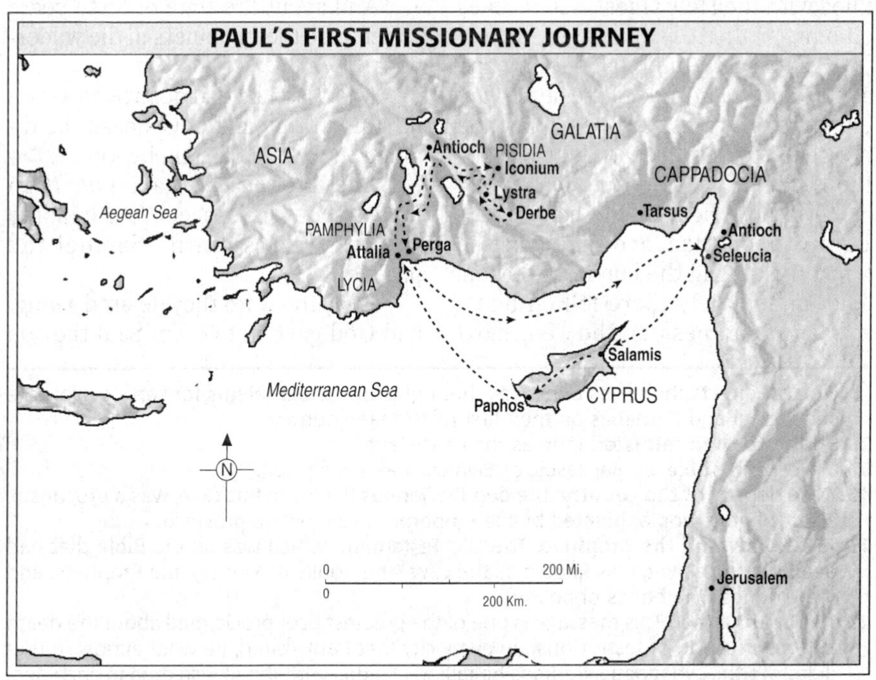

13:1 Manaen. Manaen, a Christian, was a foster brother of Herod Agrippa.
13:2 Holy Ghost. The Holy Spirit not only baptizes believers, lives in them, and fills them;

me Barnabas and Saul for the work
whereunto I have called them.
[3]And when they had fasted and
prayed, and laid *their* hands on them,
they sent *them* away.
¶[4]So they, being sent forth by the
Holy Ghost, departed unto Seleucia;
and from thence they sailed to Cyprus.
[5]And when they were at Salamis,
they preached the word of *God in the
*synagogues of the Jews: and they had
also John to *their* minister.
[6]And when they had gone through
the isle unto Paphos, they found a certain sorcerer, a false prophet, a Jew,
whose name *was* Bar-jesus:
[7]Which was with the deputy of the
country, Sergius Paulus, a prudent man;
who called for Barnabas and Saul, and
desired to hear the word of God.
[8]But Elymas the sorcerer (for so is
his name by interpretation) withstood
them, seeking to turn away the deputy
from the faith.
[9]Then Saul, (who also *is called* Paul,)
filled with the Holy Ghost, set his eyes
on him,
[10]And said, O full of all subtilty and
all mischief, *thou* child of the devil, *thou*
enemy of all righteousness, wilt thou
not cease to pervert the right ways of
the Lord?
[11]And now, behold, the hand of the
Lord *is* upon thee, and thou shalt be
blind, not seeing the sun for a season.
And immediately there fell on him a
mist and a darkness; and he went about
seeking some to lead him by the hand.
[12]Then the deputy, when he saw what
was done, believed, being astonished at
the *doctrine of the Lord.
[13]Now when Paul and his company
loosed from Paphos, they came to Perga in Pamphylia: and John departing
from them returned to Jerusalem.
¶[14]But when they departed from Perga, they came to Antioch in Pisidia, and
went into the *synagogue on the *sabbath day, and sat down.
[15]And after the reading of the *law
and the prophets the rulers of the synagogue sent unto them, saying, *Ye* men
and brethren, if ye have any word of
exhortation for the people, say on.
[16]Then Paul stood up, and beckoning
with *his* hand said, Men of *Israel, and
ye that fear God, give audience.
[17]The God of this people of Israel
chose our fathers, and exalted the people when they dwelt as strangers in the
land of *Egypt, and with an high arm
brought he them out of it.
[18]And about the time of forty years
suffered he their manners in the wilderness.
[19]And when he had destroyed seven
nations in the land of Chanaan, he divided their land to them by lot.
[20]And after that he gave *unto them*
judges about the space of four hundred
and fifty years, until *Samuel the
prophet.
[21]And afterward they desired a king:
and God gave unto them Saul the son

He also directs their lives and gives them gifts or certain talents for service. Here He sends Saul and Barnabas on their first missionary journey.

13:5 John to their minister. John as their assistant.

13:6 a certain sorcerer. Bar-Jesus, or Elymas, was a magician.

13:7 the deputy of the country. The deputy, Sergius Paulus in this case, was a proconsul, a sort of governor, appointed by the emperor to rule over a province.

13:15 the law and the prophets. The Old Testament, which was all the Bible that had been written as yet, was known as the Law (the books of Moses), the Prophets, and the Writings (the books of poetry).

13:16 Men of Israel. This message is one of the greatest ever proclaimed about the death and resurrection of Jesus Christ. In every city that Paul visited, he went almost immediately to the synagogue. Perhaps he talked like this with the Jewish men in each one. Because many would not believe, he went to the Gentiles, and thus Gentile churches were started in many places.

13:21 Cis. Kish, the father of Israel's first king, Saul.

of Cis, a man of the tribe of Benjamin,
by the space of forty years.
22And when he had removed him, he
raised up unto them *David to be their
king; to whom also he gave testimony,
and said, I have found David the *son* of
Jesse, a man after mine own heart,
which shall fulfil all my will.
23Of this man's seed hath God according to *his* promise raised unto Israel a Saviour, Jesus:
24When John had first preached before his coming the *baptism of repentance to all the people of Israel.
25And as John fulfilled his course, he
said, Whom think ye that I am? I am not
he. But, behold, there cometh one after
me, whose shoes of *his* feet I am not
worthy to loose.
26Men *and* brethren, children of the
stock of *Abraham, and whosoever
among you *feareth God, to you is the
word of this *salvation sent.
27For they that dwell at Jerusalem,
and their rulers, because they knew
him not, nor yet the voices of the prophets which are read every sabbath day,
they have fulfilled *them* in condemning
him.
28And though they found no cause of
death *in him,* yet desired they *Pilate
that he should be slain.
29And when they had fulfilled all that
was written of him, they took *him* down
from the tree, and laid *him* in a sepulchre.
30But God raised him from the dead:
31And he was seen many days of
them which came up with him from
Galilee to Jerusalem, who are his witnesses unto the people.
32And we declare unto you glad tidings, how that the promise which was
made unto the fathers,
33God hath fulfilled the same unto us
their children, in that he hath raised up
Jesus again; as it is also written in the
second psalm, Thou art my Son, this
day have I begotten thee.
34And as concerning that he raised
him up from the dead, *now* no more to
return to corruption, he said on this
wise, I will give you the sure mercies
of David.
35Wherefore he saith also in another
psalm, Thou shalt not suffer thine Holy
One to see corruption.
36For David, after he had served his
own generation by the will of God, fell
on sleep, and was laid unto his fathers,
and saw corruption:
37But he, whom God raised again,
saw no corruption.
¶38Be it known unto you therefore,
men *and* brethren, that through this
man is preached unto you the forgiveness of sins:
39And by him all that believe are justified from all things, from which ye
could not be justified by the law of
*Moses.
40Beware therefore, lest that come
upon you, which is spoken of in the
prophets;
41Behold, ye despisers, and wonder,
and perish: for I work a work in your days,
a work which ye shall in no wise believe,
though a man declare it unto you.

13:23 according to his promise. Read 2 Samuel 7:8-17 and 7:11 note, "The Davidic Covenant."
13:23 a Saviour. Read Romans 1:16 notes and 1:16-17 note, "Salvation by Faith."
13:24 John. John the Baptist (Matt. 3:1-2).
13:32 glad tidings. Read Luke 2:10-11.
13:33 in the second psalm. Read Psalm 2:7 and its note, "The First Begotten."
13:34 he said. Read Isaiah 55:3.
13:35 in another psalm. Psalm 16:10.
13:38 this man. The Lord Jesus Christ (Acts 13:23,33).
13:39 all that believe are justified. See *assurance.
13:39 ye could not be justified by. See *justification.
13:40 in the prophets. See Habakkuk 1:5 and its note, "Unbelievable Happenings."

42 And when the Jews were gone out of the synagogue, the Gentiles besought that these words might be preached to them the next sabbath.

43 Now when the congregation was broken up, many of the Jews and religious proselytes followed Paul and Barnabas: who, speaking to them, persuaded them to continue in the grace of God.

¶ 44 And the next sabbath day came almost the whole city together to hear the word of God.

45 But when the Jews saw the multitudes, they were filled with envy, and spake against those things which were spoken by Paul, contradicting and blaspheming.

46 Then Paul and Barnabas waxed bold, and said, It was necessary that the word of God should first have been spoken to you: but seeing ye put it from you, and judge yourselves unworthy of everlasting life, lo, we turn to the Gentiles.

47 For so hath the Lord commanded us, *saying,* I have set thee to be a light of the Gentiles, that thou shouldest be for salvation unto the ends of the earth.

48 And when the Gentiles heard this, they were glad, and glorified the word of the Lord: and as many as were ordained to *eternal life believed.

49 And the word of the Lord was published throughout all the region.

50 But the Jews stirred up the devout and honourable women, and the chief men of the city, and raised persecution against Paul and Barnabas, and expelled them out of their coasts.

51 But they shook off the dust of their feet against them, and came unto Iconium.

52 And the disciples were filled with joy, and with the Holy Ghost.

14 And it came to pass in Iconium, that they went both together into the synagogue of the Jews, and so spake, that a great multitude both of the Jews and also of the Greeks believed.

2 But the unbelieving Jews stirred up the Gentiles, and made their minds evil affected against the brethren.

3 Long time therefore abode they speaking boldly in the Lord, which gave testimony unto the word of his grace, and granted signs and wonders to be done by their hands.

4 But the multitude of the city was divided: and part held with the Jews, and part with the *apostles.

5 And when there was an assault made both of the Gentiles, and also of the Jews with their rulers, to use *them* despitefully, and to stone them,

6 They were ware of *it,* and fled unto Lystra and Derbe, cities of Lycaonia, and unto the region that lieth round about:

7 And there they preached the *gospel.

¶ 8 And there sat a certain man at Lystra, impotent in his feet, being a cripple from his mother's womb, who never had walked:

9 The same heard Paul speak: who stedfastly beholding him, and perceiving that he had faith to be healed,

10 Said with a loud voice, Stand upright on thy feet. And he leaped and walked.

11 And when the people saw what Paul had done, they lifted up their voices, saying in the speech of Lycaonia, The gods are come down to us in the likeness of men.

12 And they called Barnabas, Jupiter; and Paul, Mercurius, because he was the chief speaker.

13:47 the Lord commanded. Read Isaiah 42:6-7.
13:48 the Gentiles . . . believed. See *faith.
14:12 Jupiter . . . Mercurius. Two of the Roman gods, corresponding respectively to Zeus and Hermes, Greek gods. At first, the people of Lystra mistakenly thought Barnabas and Paul were these gods, but they set the people straight (vss. 14-17). Only days later, however, with some persuaded by Jews who wanted to discredit Paul, the people of Lystra turned on him, stoned him, and left him for dead (vs. 19; see its note).

[13]Then the priest of Jupiter, which
was before their city, brought oxen and
garlands unto the gates, and would have
done *sacrifice with the people.
[14]*Which* when the apostles, Barnabas
and Paul, heard *of,* they rent their
clothes, and ran in among the people,
crying out,
[15]And saying, Sirs, why do ye these
things? We also are men of like passions
with you, and preach unto you that ye
should turn from these vanities unto
the living God, which made *heaven,
and earth, and the sea, and all things
that are therein:
[16]Who in times past suffered all nations to walk in their own ways.
[17]Nevertheless he left not himself
without witness, in that he did good,
and gave us rain from heaven, and fruitful seasons, filling our hearts with food
and gladness.
[18]And with these sayings scarce restrained they the people, that they had
not done sacrifice unto them.
¶[19]And there came thither *certain*
Jews from Antioch and Iconium, who
persuaded the people, and, having
stoned Paul, drew *him* out of the city,
supposing he had been dead.
[20]Howbeit, as the disciples stood
round about him, he rose up, and came
into the city: and the next day he departed with Barnabas to Derbe.

14:19 Death by Stoning
Paul's suffering for Jesus Christ had begun. Death by stoning was very cruel and painful. The bones of the body were crushed with large boulders. After the stoning, the victim was dragged by the heels to the outskirts of the city and left for dogs and wild beasts to devour. To be left there outside the city as Paul must have been and then to rise up again and walk back was a miracle. Paul probably suffered much pain the rest of his life due to this incident. He refers to his physical suffering several times in his letters (see 2 Cor. 11:23-27 and 11:24 note, "A Severe Punishment"; 12:7-10 and 12:7-8 notes).

[21]And when they had preached the
gospel to that city, and had taught many,
they returned again to Lystra, and *to*
Iconium, and Antioch,
[22]Confirming the souls of the disciples, *and* exhorting them to continue in
the faith, and that we must through
much tribulation enter into the *kingdom of God.

14:22 Persecution of Jewish Believers
The Jewish believers who were suffering persecution could not understand it. In the past, obedience to God and the *Law of Moses was always rewarded by blessing and prosperity, not suffering. Paul tried to show them that the Lord was teaching them that belief in Him would cost them much. The Lord Jesus Himself had suffered much and had foretold that His disciples would suffer (John 15:18-25; 16:1-6,20-22). But He comforted His disciples with wonderful promises. Read John 16:33 and Matthew 28:20.

[23]And when they had ordained them
elders in every *church, and had prayed
with fasting, they commended them to
the Lord, on whom they believed.
[24]And after they had passed throughout Pisidia, they came to Pamphylia.
[25]And when they had preached the
word in Perga, they went down into
Attalia:
[26]And thence sailed to Antioch, from
whence they had been recommended to
the *grace of God for the work which
they fulfilled.
[27]And when they were come, and had
gathered the church together, they rehearsed all that God had done with
them, and how he had opened the door
of faith unto the Gentiles.
[28]And there they abode long time
with the disciples.

15 And certain men which came
down from Judaea taught the
brethren, *and said,* Except ye be circumcised after the manner of Moses,
ye cannot be saved.
[2]When therefore Paul and Barnabas
had no small dissension and disputation

15:1 The Issue of Circumcision
It was hard after centuries of obedience to the Law of Moses for Jewish Christians to believe that one could be saved and become a member of the church without observing certain ordinances of the Law. The Judaizers, as they were called, tried to make Gentiles keep Jewish customs, telling them, for example, that they could not be saved unless they were circumcised. The law of circumcision was given to Abraham (see Gen. 17:10 note, "Circumcision"), and repeated by Moses in Leviticus 12:3. Paul told these Jews that in the new age into which they were now entering, they were not under the *Law (Rom. 6:14).

with them, they determined that Paul
and Barnabas, and certain other of
them, should go up to *Jerusalem unto
the apostles and elders about this question.
3And being brought on their way by
the church, they passed through
Phenice and *Samaria, declaring the
conversion of the Gentiles: and they
caused great joy unto all the brethren.
4And when they were come to Jerusalem, they were received of the
church, and *of* the apostles and elders,
and they declared all things that God
had done with them.
5But there rose up certain of the sect
of the *Pharisees which believed, saying, That it was needful to circumcise
them, and to command *them* to keep the
law of Moses.
¶6And the apostles and elders came
together for to consider of this matter.
7And when there had been much disputing, *Peter rose up, and said unto
them, Men *and* brethren, ye know how
that a good while ago God made choice
among us, that the Gentiles by my
mouth should hear the word of the gospel, and believe.
8And God, which knoweth the hearts,
bare them witness, giving them the
Holy Ghost, even as *he did* unto us;
9And put no difference between us
and them, purifying their hearts by
faith.
10Now therefore why *tempt ye God,
to put a yoke upon the neck of the disciples, which neither our fathers nor we
were able to bear?
11But we believe that through the
grace of the Lord Jesus *Christ we shall
be saved, even as they.
¶12Then all the multitude kept silence, and gave audience to Barnabas
and Paul, declaring what *miracles and
wonders God had wrought among the
Gentiles by them.
¶13And after they had held their
peace, James answered, saying, Men
and brethren, hearken unto me:

15:13 James, the Brother of Jesus
James was the half brother of Jesus. James was the head of the church at Jerusalem. He spoke to the elders of the church with great wisdom. He seemed to understand the meaning of the *kingdom and the *church age. James explained that "at the first," or "for the first time" (vs. 14), God's purpose for this age was now told, for Peter (Simon) said that it is to take out of the Gentiles all over the world "a people for his name." After this age the Messiah will return and set up the kingdom on earth promised by the prophets, and then He will reign over the earth for a thousand years (Rev. 20:4).

14Simeon hath declared how God at
the first did visit the Gentiles, to take
out of them a people for his name.
15And to this agree the words of the
prophets; as it is written,
16After this I will return, and will build
again the *tabernacle of David, which is
fallen down; and I will build again the
ruins thereof, and I will set it up:
17That the residue of men might seek
after the Lord, and all the Gentiles,
upon whom my name is called, saith the
Lord, who doeth all these things.

15:15 the words of the prophets. See Amos 9:11-12 (see also 9:11 note, "An Everlasting Kingdom").

18Known unto God are all his works
from the beginning of the world.
19Wherefore my sentence is, that we
trouble not them, which from among
the Gentiles are turned to God:
20But that we write unto them, that
they abstain from pollutions of idols,
and *from* fornication, and *from* things
strangled, and *from* blood.
21For Moses of old time hath in every
city them that preach him, being read
in the synagogues every sabbath day.
22Then pleased it the apostles and
elders, with the whole church, to send
chosen men of their own company to
Antioch with Paul and Barnabas; *namely,* Judas surnamed Barsabas, and Silas,
chief men among the brethren:
23And they wrote *letters* by them after this manner; The apostles and elders and brethren *send* greeting unto
the brethren which are of the Gentiles
in Antioch and Syria and Cilicia:
24Forasmuch as we have heard, that
certain which went out from us have
troubled you with words, subverting
your souls, saying, *Ye must* be circumcised, and keep the law: to whom we
gave no *such* commandment:
25It seemed good unto us, being assembled with one accord, to send chosen men unto you with our beloved
Barnabas and Paul,
26Men that have hazarded their lives
for the name of our Lord Jesus Christ.
27We have sent therefore Judas and
Silas, who shall also tell *you* the same
things by mouth.
28For it seemed good to the Holy
Ghost, and to us, to lay upon you no greater burden than these necessary things;
29That ye abstain from meats offered
to idols, and from blood, and from things
strangled, and from fornication: from
which if ye keep yourselves, ye shall do
well. Fare ye well.
30So when they were dismissed, they
came to Antioch: and when they had
gathered the multitude together, they
delivered the epistle:
31*Which* when they had read, they
rejoiced for the consolation.
32And Judas and Silas, being prophets also themselves, exhorted the
brethren with many words, and confirmed *them.*
33And after they had tarried *there* a
space, they were let go in peace from
the brethren unto the apostles.
34Notwithstanding it pleased Silas to
abide there still.
35Paul also and Barnabas continued in
Antioch, teaching and preaching the
word of the Lord, with many others
also.
¶36And some days after Paul said
unto Barnabas, Let us go again and visit
our brethren in every city where we
have preached the word of the Lord,
and see how they do.
37And Barnabas determined to take
with them John, whose surname was
Mark.
38But Paul thought not good to take
him with them, who departed from
them from Pamphylia, and went not
with them to the work.
39And the contention was so sharp
between them, that they departed asunder one from the other: and so Barnabas took Mark, and sailed unto Cyprus;
40And Paul chose Silas, and departed,

15:24 subverting your souls. To subvert means *to turn upside down* or *to upset.* The Gentile Christians were becoming distressed in their souls because of the teachings of the Jewish Christians, who did not remember that they also had been saved by grace instead of the works of the Law. Since Ephesians 2:8-10 had not yet been written, Paul and Barnabas were sent to tell these Christians what the Holy Spirit had taught them.

15:26 hazarded their lives. Barnabas and Paul had risked their lives just a short time before this (Acts 13:50).

15:32 prophets. For a definition of a New Testament prophet, read 1 Corinthians 14:3.

15:40 Silas. Silas (or Silvanus) was a member of the church at Jerusalem. He was a faithful companion to Paul and is often mentioned in Paul's epistles.

15:37-38 Mark's Departure
Acts 12:25 gives the time of John Mark's joining with Barnabas and Paul in their ministry. For some unexplained reason, Mark left them at Pamphylia (Acts 13:13), and apparently Paul disapproved. We hear of Mark again, however, as having been with Peter in Babylon (1 Pet. 5:13) and still later visiting Paul in prison at Rome (Col. 4:10). Whatever the cause of Mark's earlier departure from Paul and Barnabas, apparently he returned and became a valuable helper to Paul in the closing days of his life (2 Tim. 4:11). He was also used by God to write the Gospel which bears his name.

being recommended by the brethren
unto the grace of God.
41 And he went through Syria and Cilicia, confirming the churches.

16 Then came he to Derbe and
Lystra: and, behold, a certain
disciple was there, named *Timotheus,
the son of a certain woman, which was
a Jewess, and believed; but his father
was a Greek:

16:1 Timothy
On this second journey, Paul met a young disciple named Timothy, whose mother and grandmother had been saved, probably on Paul's first visit to Lystra in Asia Minor. Timothy became one of Paul's dearest friends. Paul calls him his "son in the faith" (1 Tim. 1:2) and his "dearly beloved son" (2 Tim. 1:2). From Lystra Timothy traveled with Paul and Silas, and Paul soon trusted him with great responsibility. He became the leader of the church at Ephesus. It was to him that Paul wrote two epistles of the New Testament, 1 and 2 Timothy.

2 Which was well reported of by the
brethren that were at Lystra and Iconium.
3 Him would Paul have to go forth
with him; and took and circumcised him
because of the Jews which were in
those quarters: for they knew all that
his father was a Greek.
4 And as they went through the cities,
they delivered them the decrees for to
keep, that were ordained of the apostles
and elders which were at Jerusalem.
5 And so were the churches established in the faith, and increased in
number daily.
6 Now when they had gone throughout Phrygia and the region of Galatia,
and were forbidden of the Holy Ghost
to preach the word in Asia,
7 After they were come to Mysia, they
assayed to go into Bithynia: but the
Spirit suffered them not.

16:7 The Spirit's Guidance
The Holy Spirit was guiding His servants. He showed them where to go and also where not to go. They were forbidden to go to Asia by the Holy Ghost (vs. 6) because Paul had already reached the remnant there (13:44-46; Rom. 11:5) and the Holy Ghost led them elsewhere into uncharted territory (Rom. 15:20; 2 Cor. 10:16).

8 And they passing by Mysia came
down to Troas.
9 And a vision appeared to Paul in the
night; There stood a man of Macedonia,
and prayed him, saying, Come over into
Macedonia, and help us.
10 And after he had seen the vision,
immediately we endeavoured to go into
Macedonia, assuredly gathering that
the Lord had called us for to preach the
gospel unto them.
11 Therefore loosing from Troas, we
came with a straight course to
Samothracia, and the next *day* to Neapolis;
12 And from thence to Philippi, which
is the chief city of that part of Macedo-

16:10 we. This is the first mention of Luke, the writer of Acts. He joined Paul and his party here at Troas and traveled with them from that time almost constantly. Luke remained with Paul at the close of his life when Paul was a prisoner in Rome.

16:12 a colony. Philippi was under the rule of Rome. Philippi was a key city in the region of Macedonia.

16:12 Philippi
The first church of Europe was in the city of Philippi. The Christians at Philippi loved Paul and, although they were poor, they gave what they could to him. They also sent a gift of money with Paul to the Jerusalem church for their poor. In writing to the Corinthian church (2 Cor. 8:1-4), Paul tells why they were so very generous, and gives a fine rule for Christian giving: "They . . . first gave their own selves to the Lord" (2 Cor. 8:5).

nia, *and* a colony: and we were in that
city abiding certain days.
13And on the sabbath we went out of
the city by a river side, where *prayer
was wont to be made; and we sat down,
and spake unto the women which resorted *thither.*
¶14And a certain woman named Lyd-
ia, a seller of purple, of the city of Thyatira, which worshipped God, heard *us:*
whose heart the Lord opened, that she
attended unto the things which were
spoken of Paul.
15And when she was baptized, and
her household, she besought *us,* saying,
If ye have judged me to be faithful to the
Lord, come into my house, and abide
there. And she constrained us.
¶16And it came to pass, as we went
to prayer, a certain damsel possessed
with a spirit of divination met us, which
brought her masters much gain by
soothsaying:
17The same followed Paul and us, and
cried, saying, These men are the servants of the most high God, which shew
unto us the way of salvation.
18And this did she many days. But

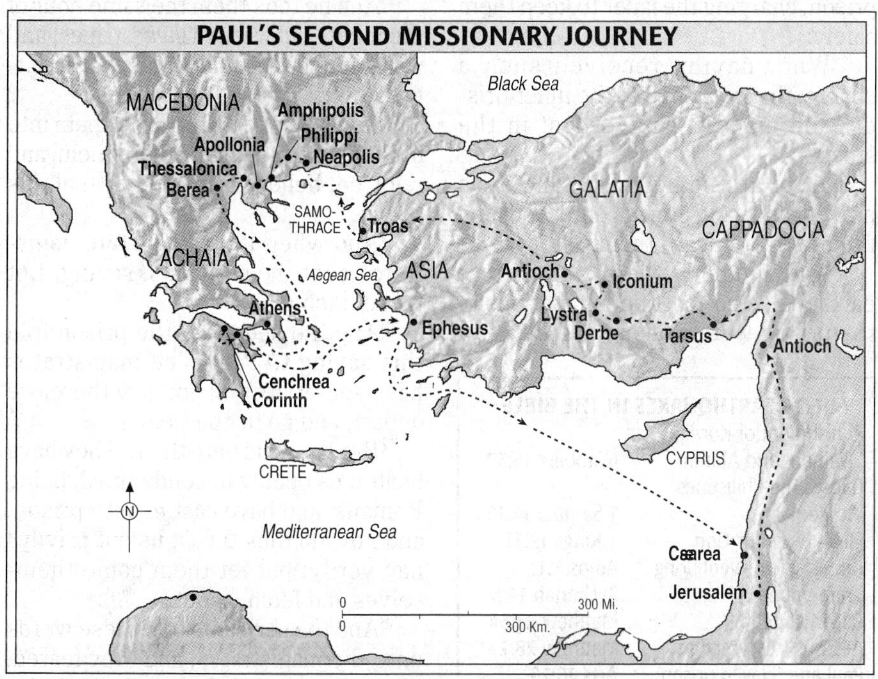

16:14 a seller of purple. Purple was an expensive dye made from certain shellfish. Lydia sold purple clothes that had been made and dyed in her native city, Thyatira, but she was converted to Christ in Philippi. She and her entire household were baptized (vs. 15).
16:14 of Paul. By Paul.
16:16 a spirit of divination . . . soothsaying. The girl was a fortune-teller. She had an evil spirit living in her (vs. 18). Some have thoughtlessly criticized Paul for old-fashioned views about womanhood. Note that here he defended a slave girl and was flogged within an inch of his life for her sake (vss. 22-23).

Paul, being grieved, turned and said to the spirit, I command thee in the name of Jesus Christ to come out of her. And he came out the same hour.

¶ 19 And when her masters saw that the *hope of their gains was gone, they caught Paul and Silas, and drew *them* into the marketplace unto the rulers,

20 And brought them to the magistrates, saying, These men, being Jews, do exceedingly trouble our city,

21 And teach customs, which are not lawful for us to receive, neither to observe, being Romans.

22 And the multitude rose up together against them: and the magistrates rent off their clothes, and commanded to beat *them.*

23 And when they had laid many *stripes upon them, they cast *them* into prison, charging the jailer to keep them safely:

24 Who, having received such a charge, thrust them into the inner prison, and made their feet fast in the stocks.

¶ 25 And at midnight Paul and Silas prayed, and sang praises unto God: and the prisoners heard them.

26 And suddenly there was a great earthquake, so that the foundations of the prison were shaken: and immediately all the doors were opened, and every one's bands were loosed.

27 And the keeper of the prison awaking out of his sleep, and seeing the prison doors open, he drew out his sword, and would have killed himself, supposing that the prisoners had been fled.

28 But Paul cried with a loud voice, saying, Do thyself no harm: for we are all here.

29 Then he called for a light, and sprang in, and came trembling, and fell down before Paul and Silas,

30 And brought them out, and said, Sirs, what must I do to be saved?

31 And they said, Believe on the Lord Jesus Christ, and thou shalt be saved, and thy house.

32 And they spake unto him the word of the Lord, and to all that were in his house.

33 And he took them the same hour of the night, and washed *their* stripes; and was baptized, he and all his, *straightway.

34 And when he had brought them into his house, he set meat before them, and rejoiced, believing in God with all his house.

35 And when it was day, the magistrates sent the serjeants, saying, Let those men go.

36 And the keeper of the prison told this saying to Paul, The magistrates have sent to let you go: now therefore depart, and go in *peace.

37 But Paul said unto them, They have beaten us openly uncondemned, being Romans, and have cast *us* into prison; and now do they thrust us out privily? nay verily; but let them come themselves and fetch us out.

38 And the serjeants told these words unto the magistrates: and they feared, when they heard that they were Romans.

16:26 EARTHQUAKES IN THE BIBLE

Punishment of Korah, Dathan and Abiram	Numbers 16:32
Causes the Philistines to flee	1 Samuel 14:15
Elijah waits for God	1 Kings 19:11
An historical event, long remembered	Amos 1:1; Zechariah 14:5
At Jesus' death	Matthew 27:54
At Jesus' resurrection	Matthew 28:2
Paul and Silas in prison	Acts 16:26
At the end times	Revelation 11:13

16:31 Believe. See *faith.

16:37 Romans. Paul was a Roman citizen; therefore, the many rights of a free Roman citizen belonged to him. The officials here in Philippi could have been punished severely if Paul had told those in power at Rome that he had been put into prison without even a trial and without any chance to speak for himself.

39 And they came and besought them,
and brought *them* out, and desired *them*
to depart out of the city.
40 And they went out of the prison,
and entered into *the house of* Lydia: and
when they had seen the brethren, they
comforted them, and departed.

17 Now when they had passed
through Amphipolis and Apollonia, they came to Thessalonica,
where was a synagogue of the Jews:
2 And Paul, as his manner was, went
in unto them, and three sabbath days
reasoned with them out of the scriptures,
3 Opening and alleging, that Christ
must needs have suffered, and risen again
from the dead; and that this Jesus, whom
I preach unto you, is Christ.
4 And some of them believed, and
consorted with Paul and Silas; and of
the devout Greeks a great multitude,
and of the chief women not a few.
¶ 5 But the Jews which believed not,
moved with envy, took unto them certain lewd fellows of the baser sort, and
gathered a company, and set all the city
on an uproar, and assaulted the house
of Jason, and sought to bring them out
to the people.
6 And when they found them not, they
drew Jason and certain brethren unto
the rulers of the city, crying, These that
have turned the *world upside down
are come hither also;
7 Whom Jason hath received: and
these all do contrary to the decrees of
*Caesar, saying that there is another
king, *one* Jesus.
8 And they troubled the people and
the rulers of the city, when they heard
these things.
9 And when they had taken security of
Jason, and of the other, they let them go.
¶ 10 And the brethren immediately
sent away Paul and Silas by night unto
Berea: who coming *thither* went into
the synagogue of the Jews.
11 These were more noble than those
in Thessalonica, in that they received
the word with all readiness of mind, and
searched the scriptures daily, whether
those things were so.
12 Therefore many of them believed;
also of honourable women which were
Greeks, and of men, not a few.
13 But when the Jews of Thessalonica had knowledge that the word of God
was preached of Paul at Berea, they
came thither also, and stirred up the
people.
14 And then immediately the brethren
sent away Paul to go as it were to the
sea: but Silas and Timotheus abode
there still.
15 And they that conducted Paul
brought him unto Athens: and receiving a commandment unto Silas and
Timotheus for to come to him with all
speed, they departed.
¶ 16 Now while Paul waited for them at
Athens, his spirit was stirred in him,
when he saw the city wholly given to
*idolatry.
17 Therefore disputed he in the synagogue with the Jews, and with the devout persons, and in the market daily
with them that met with him.
18 Then certain philosophers of the Epicureans, and of the Stoicks, encountered

---

17:1 Thessalonica. It is to the church at Thessalonica that Paul wrote his first letter, later in the journey, when he had reached Corinth.

17:1 synagogue. See Acts 9:20; 13:14.

17:3 must needs. The Lord Jesus Himself said that it was absolutely necessary that He die and rise from the dead if sinners were to be saved from their sins (read Luke 24:26,46; see also Rom. 1:16-17 note, "Salvation by Faith").

17:5 lewd. Vile.

17:18 Epicureans. Epicureans were philosophers (learned teachers), followers of Epicurus (341–270 B.C.). They believed that their own pleasure or happiness was the only thing worthwhile. Thus they were known for their self-indulgence.

17:18 Stoicks. The Stoicks (or Stoics) were a group of philosophers who repressed all

him. And some said, What will this babbler say? other some, He seemeth to be a setter forth of strange gods: because he preached unto them Jesus, and the *resurrection.

19 And they took him, and brought him unto Areopagus, saying, May we know what this new doctrine, whereof thou speakest, *is?*

20 For thou bringest certain strange things to our ears: we would know therefore what these things mean.

21 (For all the Athenians and strangers which were there spent their time in nothing else, but either to tell, or to hear some new thing.)

¶ 22 Then Paul stood in the midst of Mars' hill, and said, *Ye* men of Athens, I perceive that in all things ye are too superstitious.

23 For as I passed by, and beheld your devotions, I found an *altar with this inscription, TO THE UNKNOWN GOD. Whom therefore ye ignorantly worship, him declare I unto you.

24 God that made the world and all things therein, seeing that he is Lord of heaven and earth, dwelleth not in temples made with hands;

25 Neither is worshipped with men's hands, as though he needed any thing, seeing he giveth to all life, and breath, and all things;

26 And hath made of one blood all nations of men for to dwell on all the face of the earth, and hath determined the times before appointed, and the bounds of their habitation;

27 That they should seek the Lord, if haply they might feel after him, and find him, though he be not far from every one of us:

28 For in him we live, and move, and have our being; as certain also of your own poets have said, For we are also his offspring.

29 Forasmuch then as we are the offspring of God, we ought not to think that the Godhead is like unto gold, or silver, or stone, graven by art and man's device.

30 And the times of this ignorance God winked at; but now commandeth all men every where to repent:

31 Because he hath appointed a day, in the which he will judge the world in *righteousness by *that* man whom he

17:30 Repentance
Repentance in the New Testament means that a person has changed his mind. He no longer thinks about sin, God, or himself in the same way he did before. It is more than just being sorry that he has done wrong, although that often comes first. Sometimes a saved person has to repent; always an unsaved person has to repent and turn from sin before he can come to God in true believing faith.

---

feelings and condemned happiness of any sort as a weakness. They were indifferent to pleasure and to pain. The founder of this school of thought was a Greek, Zeno (335–263 B.C.). Their name, Stoics, came from the fact that they met often on the *Stoa Poikile* (the Painted Porch) at Athens.

17:19 Areopagus. Mars' Hill.

17:24 dwelleth not in temples made with hands. Years before, when Paul was not a Christian, he had heard Stephen speak just before he was stoned to death. Paul apparently never forgot the words that Stephen said, for he repeated some of them here (see Acts 7:48-50).

17:27 though he be not far. Read Psalm 139:7-10; Romans 10:8.

17:28 your own poets. Aratus and Cleanthes, two Greek poets, had said this. Paul made use of his unusually fine education in bearing testimony to the Lord Jesus Christ.

17:29 offspring of God. This speaks of the human race, created by God and descended from Adam. A god of gold or silver or stone could not make or create anything, and it would be foolish to worship such a god.

17:30 winked at. Overlooked.

17:31 a day . . . judge. See *Day of Judgment.

17:31 world. Inhabited earth.

hath ordained; *whereof* he hath given
*assurance unto all *men,* in that he hath
raised him from the dead.
¶ 32 And when they heard of the resurrection of the dead, some mocked:
and others said, We will hear thee again
of this *matter.*
33 So Paul departed from among them.
34 Howbeit certain men clave unto
him, and believed: among the which
was Dionysius the Areopagite, and a
woman named Damaris, and others
with them.

18 After these things Paul departed from Athens, and came to
Corinth;

18:1 The City of Corinth
Corinth was a city in Greece that was known for its sinful idolatry and evil living. In this city Paul wrote two epistles to the church at Thessalonica. After leaving Corinth, Paul sailed by way of Ephesus to Jerusalem, thus ending his second missionary journey. He had visited twenty cities and established many churches.

2 And found a certain Jew named Aquila, born in Pontus, lately come from
Italy, with his wife Priscilla; (because
that Claudius had commanded all Jews
to depart from Rome:) and came unto
them.
3 And because he was of the same
craft, he abode with them, and wrought:
for by their occupation they were
tentmakers.
4 And he reasoned in the synagogue
every sabbath, and persuaded the Jews
and the Greeks.
5 And when Silas and Timotheus were
come from Macedonia, Paul was
pressed in the spirit, and testified to the
Jews *that* Jesus *was* Christ.
6 And when they opposed themselves, and blasphemed, he shook *his*
raiment, and said unto them, Your blood
be upon your own heads; I *am* *clean:
from henceforth I will go unto the
*Gentiles.
¶ 7 And he departed thence, and entered into a certain *man's* house, named
Justus, *one* that worshipped God, whose
house joined hard to the synagogue.
8 And Crispus, the chief *ruler of the
synagogue, believed on the Lord with
all his house; and many of the Corinthians hearing believed, and were baptized.
9 Then spake the Lord to Paul in the
night by a vision, Be not *afraid, but
speak, and hold not thy peace:
10 For I am with thee, and no man
shall set on thee to hurt thee: for I have
much people in this city.
11 And he continued *there* a year and
six months, teaching the word of God
among them.
¶ 12 And when Gallio was the deputy
of Achaia, the Jews made insurrection
with one accord against Paul, and
brought him to the judgment seat,
13 Saying, This *fellow* persuadeth men
to worship God contrary to the law.
14 And when Paul was now about to
open *his* mouth, Gallio said unto the
Jews, If it were a matter of wrong or
wicked lewdness, O *ye* Jews, reason
would that I should bear with you:
15 But if it be a question of words and
names, and *of* your law, look ye *to it;* for
I will be no judge of such *matters.*
16 And he drave them from the judgment seat.
17 Then all the Greeks took Sosthenes, the chief ruler of the synagogue,
and beat *him* before the judgment seat.
And Gallio cared for none of those
things.
¶ 18 And Paul *after this* tarried *there* yet
a good while, and then took his leave of

18:5 pressed in the spirit. Paul was led by the Holy Spirit to bear testimony there.
18:8 believed, and were baptized. *Faith (belief in the Lord Jesus Christ) was all that was needed for salvation and membership in the true *church. Baptism is an act of obedience.
18:14 wicked lewdness. Villainy or crime.
18:17 Sosthenes. A believer (see 1 Cor. 1:1).

the brethren, and sailed thence into
Syria, and with him Priscilla and Aquila; having shorn *his* head in Cenchrea:
for he had a vow.
19 And he came to Ephesus, and left
them there: but he himself entered into
the synagogue, and reasoned with the
Jews.
20 When they desired *him* to tarry
longer time with them, he consented
not;
21 But bade them farewell, saying, I
must by all means keep this feast that
cometh in Jerusalem: but I will return
again unto you, if God will. And he
sailed from Ephesus.
22 And when he had landed at Caesarea, and gone up, and saluted the
church, he went down to Antioch.
¶23 And after he had spent some time
there, he departed, and went over *all* the
country of Galatia and Phrygia in order,
strengthening all the disciples.
24 And a certain Jew named *Apollos,
born at Alexandria, an eloquent man,
and mighty in the scriptures, came to
Ephesus.

18:24 Apollos
Apollos was a Jewish man who loved and worshipped God. He was born in Egypt. He preached the same message that John the Baptist had preached, "Repent ye: for the kingdom of heaven is at hand" (Matt. 3:2). He knew little about the Lord Jesus Christ and the gospel of grace. Aquila and Priscilla took Apollos in and taught him about Christ and "the way of God more perfectly" (vs. 26).

25 This man was instructed in the way
of the Lord; and being fervent in the
spirit, he spake and taught diligently
the things of the Lord, knowing only
the baptism of John.
26 And he began to speak boldly in the
synagogue: whom when *Aquila and
Priscilla had heard, they took him unto
them, and expounded unto him the way
of God more perfectly.
27 And when he was disposed to pass
into Achaia, the brethren wrote, exhorting the disciples to receive him: who,
when he was come, helped them much
which had believed through *grace:
28 For he mightily convinced the Jews,
and that publickly, shewing by the scriptures that Jesus was Christ.

6) Holy Spirit given at Ephesus

19 And it came to pass, that, while
Apollos was at Corinth, Paul
having passed through the upper coasts
came to Ephesus: and finding certain
disciples,

19:1 Disciples of Apollos
The phrase "certain disciples" refers to the disciples of Apollos, whom he had taught as much as he himself knew (see Acts 18:24-25). When Paul found these people, he taught them more fully, and when they had heard and believed, they were baptized in the name of the Lord Jesus. Notice that when Paul had laid hands on them they received the Holy Ghost. They then spoke with tongues and prophesied (Acts 19:6). This is the last time in the Book of Acts that the speaking with tongues occurred at the moment of belief as a sign of the presence of the Holy Spirit. Later on, in the early days of the church at Corinth, the "gift of tongues" was given to certain people in the church for the purpose of glorifying God, but not simply as a sign of the presence of the Holy Ghost.

2 He said unto them, Have ye received the Holy Ghost since ye believed? And they said unto him, We
have not so much as heard whether
there be any Holy Ghost.
3 And he said unto them, Unto what
then were ye baptized? And they said,
Unto John's baptism.
4 Then said Paul, John verily baptized

18:23 he departed. Paul began his third missionary journey by land.
18:25 the baptism of John. Acts 19:4 explains this.
19:2 since ye believed. Since the permanent indwelling of the Holy Ghost did not take place until after Pentecost, Paul asks these believers if they had received Him yet.

with the baptism of *repentance, saying unto the people, that they should believe on him which should come after him, that is, on Christ Jesus.
5When they heard *this,* they were baptized in the name of the Lord Jesus.
6And when Paul had laid *his* hands upon them, the Holy Ghost came on them; and they spake with tongues, and prophesied.
7And all the men were about twelve.
8And he went into the *synagogue, and spake boldly for the space of three months, disputing and persuading the things concerning the kingdom of *God.
9But when divers were hardened, and believed not, but spake evil of that way before the multitude, he departed from them, and separated the disciples, disputing daily in the school of one Tyrannus.
10And this continued by the space of two years; so that all they which dwelt in Asia heard the word of the Lord Jesus, both Jews and Greeks.
11And God wrought special *miracles by the hands of Paul:
12So that from his body were brought unto the sick handkerchiefs or aprons, and the diseases departed from them, and the evil spirits went out of them.
¶ 13Then certain of the vagabond Jews, exorcists, took upon them to call over them which had evil spirits the name of the Lord Jesus, saying, We adjure you by Jesus whom Paul preacheth.
14And there were seven sons of *one* Sceva, a Jew, *and* chief of the priests, which did so.
15And the evil spirit answered and said, Jesus I know, and Paul I know; but who are ye?
16And the man in whom the evil spirit was leaped on them, and overcame them, and prevailed against them, so that they fled out of that house naked and wounded.
17And this was known to all the Jews

PAUL'S THIRD MISSIONARY JOURNEY

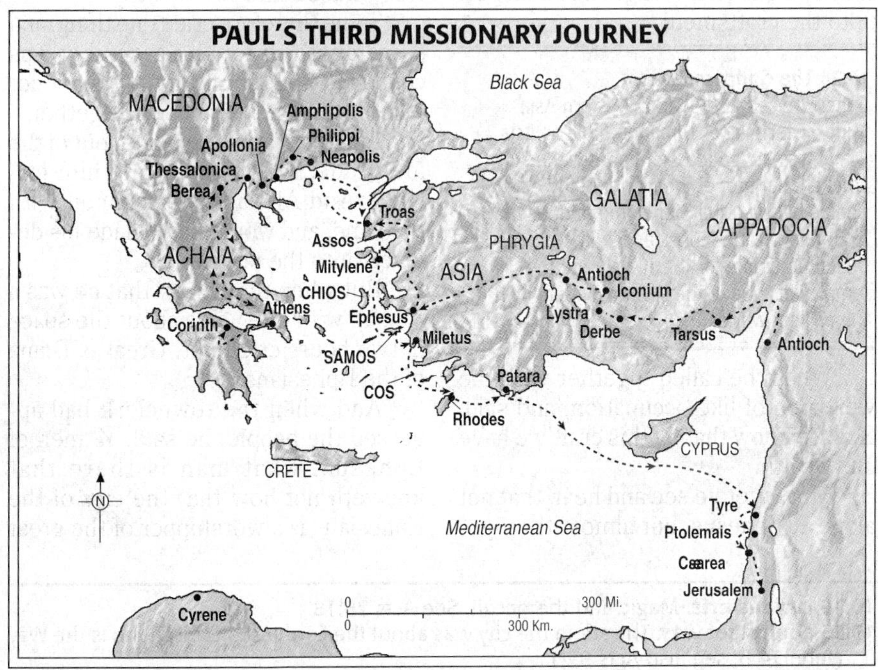

19:13 exorcists. Magicians, who by some satanic power, were able to cast out demons, as a sort of showmanship.

and Greeks also dwelling at Ephesus;
and *fear fell on them all, and the name
of the Lord Jesus was magnified.
18 And many that believed came, and
confessed, and shewed their deeds.
19 Many of them also which used curious arts brought their books together, and burned them before all *men:* and
they counted the price of them, and
found *it* fifty thousand *pieces* of silver.
20 So mightily grew the word of God
and prevailed.
¶21 After these things were ended,
Paul purposed in the spirit, when he had
passed through Macedonia and Achaia,
to go to Jerusalem, saying, After I have
been there, I must also see Rome.
22 So he sent into Macedonia two of
them that ministered unto him, *Timotheus and Erastus; but he himself
stayed in Asia for a season.
23 And the same time there arose no
small stir about that way.
24 For a certain *man* named Demetrius, a silversmith, which made silver
shrines for Diana, brought no small gain
unto the craftsmen;

19:24 The Goddess Diana
Ephesus was the capital of Western Asia Minor, which is known in the Bible as Asia. Diana was the goddess of Ephesus, and so of all that part of the world. Many people believed that her statue had fallen from heaven. The Ephesians built a beautiful temple for the statue, and the temple was one of the seven wonders of the ancient world.

25 Whom he called together with the
workmen of like occupation, and said,
Sirs, ye know that by this craft we have
our wealth.
26 Moreover ye see and hear, that not
alone at Ephesus, but almost throughout all Asia, this Paul hath persuaded
and turned away much people, saying
that they be no gods, which are made
with hands:
27 So that not only this our craft is in
danger to be set at nought; but also that
the temple of the great goddess Diana
should be despised, and her magnifi-
cence should be destroyed, whom all
Asia and the world worshippeth.
28 And when they heard *these sayings,*
they were full of wrath, and cried out,
saying, Great *is* Diana of the Ephesians.
29 And the whole city was filled with
confusion: and having caught Gaius and
*Aristarchus, men of Macedonia, Paul's
companions in travel, they rushed with
one accord into the theatre.
30 And when Paul would have entered
in unto the people, the disciples suffered him not.
31 And certain of the chief of Asia,
which were his friends, sent unto him,
desiring *him* that he would not adventure himself into the theatre.
32 Some therefore cried one thing, and
some another: for the assembly was
confused; and the more part knew not
wherefore they were come together.
33 And they drew Alexander out of the
multitude, the Jews putting him forward. And Alexander beckoned with
the hand, and would have made his defence unto the people.
34 But when they knew that he was a
Jew, all with one voice about the space
of two hours cried out, Great *is* Diana
of the Ephesians.
35 And when the townclerk had appeased the people, he said, *Ye* men of
Ephesus, what man is there that
knoweth not how that the city of the
Ephesians is a worshipper of the great

19:19 curious arts. Magic and the occult. See Acts 26:18.
19:23 about that way. The stir in the city was about the Lord Jesus Christ, who is the Way (John 14:6; see also Acts 9:2).
19:29 into the theatre. Public meetings were often held in the theaters or arenas, which were built in the open air without roofs. They were large enough to hold vast numbers of the people.

goddess Diana, and of the *image* which
fell down from Jupiter?
36Seeing then that these things cannot be spoken against, ye ought to be
quiet, and to do nothing rashly.
37For ye have brought hither these
men, which are neither robbers of
churches, nor yet blasphemers of your
goddess.
38Wherefore if Demetrius, and the
craftsmen which are with him, have a
matter against any man, the *law is
open, and there are deputies: let them
implead one another.
39But if ye enquire any thing concerning other matters, it shall be determined in a lawful assembly.
40For we are in danger to be called in
question for this day's uproar, there
being no cause whereby we may give
an account of this concourse.
41And when he had thus spoken, he
dismissed the assembly.

20 And after the uproar was
ceased, Paul called unto *him* the
disciples, and embraced *them,* and departed for to go into Macedonia.
2And when he had gone over those
parts, and had given them much exhortation, he came into Greece,
3And *there* abode three months. And
when the Jews laid wait for him, as he
was about to sail into Syria, he purposed
to return through Macedonia.
4And there accompanied him into
Asia Sopater of Berea; and of the Thessalonians, Aristarchus and Secundus;
and Gaius of Derbe, and Timotheus; and
of Asia, *Tychicus and Trophimus.
5These going before tarried for us at
Troas.
¶6And we sailed away from Philippi
after the days of *unleavened bread,
and came unto them to Troas in five
days; where we abode seven days.
7And upon the first *day* of the week,
when the disciples came together to
break bread, Paul preached unto them,
ready to depart on the morrow; and
continued his speech until midnight.
8And there were many lights in the
upper chamber, where they were gathered together.
9And there sat in a window a certain
young man named Eutychus, being fall-
en into a deep sleep: and as Paul was
long preaching, he sunk down with
sleep, and fell down from the third loft,
and was taken up dead.
10And Paul went down, and fell on
him, and embracing *him* said, Trouble
not yourselves; for his life is in him.
11When he therefore was come up
again, and had broken bread, and eaten,
and talked a long while, even till break
of day, so he departed.
12And they brought the young man
alive, and were not a little comforted.
¶13And we went before to ship, and
sailed unto Assos, there intending to
take in Paul: for so had he appointed,
minding himself to go afoot.
14And when he met with us at Assos,
we took him in, and came to Mitylene.
15And we sailed thence, and came the
next *day* over against Chios; and the
next *day* we arrived at Samos, and tarried at Trogyllium; and the next *day* we
came to Miletus.
16For Paul had determined to sail by
Ephesus, because he would not spend
the time in Asia: for he hasted, if it were
possible for him, to be at Jerusalem the
day of Pentecost.
¶17And from Miletus he sent to Ephesus, and called the *elders of the
*church.
18And when they were come to him,
he said unto them, Ye know, from the
first day that I came into Asia, after
what manner I have been with you at all
seasons,

20:6 the days of unleavened bread. This was the *Passover time.

20:7 upon the first day of the week. The Christians met together on the first day, Sunday, for their worship. On Saturday the Lord Jesus lay in the tomb; on Sunday He was raised.

19 Serving the Lord with all humility
of mind, and with many tears, and
*temptations, which befell me by the
lying in wait of the Jews:
20 *And* how I kept back nothing that
was profitable *unto you,* but have
shewed you, and have taught you
publickly, and from house to house,
21 Testifying both to the Jews, and
also to the Greeks, repentance toward
God, and *faith toward our Lord Jesus
Christ.
22 And now, behold, I go bound in the
spirit unto Jerusalem, not knowing the
things that shall befall me there:
23 Save that the Holy Ghost witnesseth in every city, saying that bonds and
afflictions abide me.
24 But none of these things move me,
neither count I my life dear unto myself, so that I might finish my course
with joy, and the ministry, which I have
received of the Lord Jesus, to testify
the *gospel of the *grace of God.
25 And now, behold, I know that ye all,
among whom I have gone preaching the
*kingdom of God, shall see my face no
more.
26 Wherefore I take you to record this
day, that I *am* pure from the blood of all
men.
27 For I have not shunned to declare
unto you all the counsel of God.
¶28 Take heed therefore unto yourselves, and to all the flock, over the
which the Holy Ghost hath made you
overseers, to feed the church of God,
which he hath purchased with his own
blood.
29 For I know this, that after my departing shall grievous wolves enter in
among you, not sparing the flock.
30 Also of your own selves shall men
arise, speaking perverse things, to
draw away disciples after them.
31 Therefore watch, and remember,
that by the space of three years I ceased
not to warn every one night and day
with tears.
32 And now, brethren, I commend you
to God, and to the word of his grace,
which is able to build you up, and to give
you an inheritance among all them
which are *sanctified.
33 I have coveted no man's silver, or
gold, or apparel.
34 Yea, ye yourselves know, that these
hands have ministered unto my necessities, and to them that were with me.
35 I have shewed you all things, how
that so labouring ye ought to support
the weak, and to remember the words
of the Lord Jesus, how he said, It is
more blessed to give than to receive.
¶36 And when he had thus spoken, he
kneeled down, and prayed with them
all.
37 And they all wept sore, and fell on
Paul's neck, and kissed him,
38 Sorrowing most of all for the words
which he spake, that they should see
his face no more. And they accompanied him unto the ship.

21 And it came to pass, that after
we were gotten from them, and
had launched, we came with a straight
course unto Coos, and the *day* following unto Rhodes, and from thence unto
Patara:
2 And finding a ship sailing over unto
Phenicia, we went aboard, and set forth.
3 Now when we had discovered Cyprus, we left it on the left hand, and
sailed into Syria, and landed at *Tyre:
for there the ship was to unlade her
*burden.
4 And finding disciples, we tarried
there seven days: who said to Paul
through the *Spirit, that he should not
go up to Jerusalem.

20:29 grievous wolves. Paul knew that false teachers would come to try to lead many of the flock away to destroy them. Sheep are not strong enough to fight against wolves. They must stay close to their Good Shepherd, who can always protect them from the wolves (see also 2 Cor. 11:13-15 and 11:14 note, "Satan's Disguise"; 2 Pet. 2:1-3; 3 John 3,10; Rev. 2:6,15).

21:3 discovered. This means that they *came in sight* of Cyprus.

[5]And when we had accomplished
those days, we departed and went our
way; and they all brought us on our way,
with wives and children, till *we were* out
of the city: and we kneeled down on the
shore, and prayed.
[6]And when we had taken our leave
one of another, we took ship; and they
returned home again.
[7]And when we had finished *our*
course from Tyre, we came to Ptolemais, and saluted the brethren, and abode
with them one day.
[8]And the next *day* we that were of
Paul's company departed, and came
unto Caesarea: and we entered into the
house of Philip the evangelist, which
was *one* of the seven; and abode with
him.
[9]And the same man had four daughters, virgins, which did prophesy.
[10]And as we tarried *there* many days,
there came down from Judaea a certain
*prophet, named Agabus.
[11]And when he was come unto us, he
took Paul's girdle, and bound his own
hands and feet, and said, Thus saith the
Holy Ghost, So shall the Jews at *Jerusalem bind the man that owneth this
girdle, and shall deliver *him* into the
hands of the Gentiles.
[12]And when we heard these things,
both we, and they of that place, besought him not to go up to Jerusalem.
[13]Then Paul answered, What mean ye
to weep and to break mine heart? for I
am ready not to be bound only, but also
to die at Jerusalem for the name of the
Lord Jesus.
[14]And when he would not be persuaded, we ceased, saying, The will of the
Lord be done.
¶[15]And after those days we took up
our carriages, and went up to Jerusalem.
[16]There went with us also *certain* of
the disciples of Caesarea, and brought
with them one Mnason of Cyprus, an
old disciple, with whom we should
lodge.
[17]And when we were come to Jerusalem, the brethren received us gladly.

21:17 The Brethren
The brethren were the believers of the Jerusalem church of which James, the half brother of the Lord, was leader. The spread of Christianity over the Roman Empire was progressing so rapidly that it threatened to wipe out Judaism. The Jewish leaders realized that the people were turning away from them. They did not know that in fighting Christianity they were fighting God, for God had ordained that Judaism should cease and that the church age (see *dispensation) should begin. (See the speech of James in Acts 15:13-18.)

[18]And the *day* following Paul went in
with us unto James; and all the elders
were present.
[19]And when he had saluted them, he
declared particularly what things God
had wrought among the Gentiles by his
ministry.
[20]And when they heard *it,* they glorified the Lord, and said unto him, Thou
seest, brother, how many thousands of
Jews there are which believe; and they
are all zealous of the law:
[21]And they are informed of thee, that
thou teachest all the Jews which are
among the Gentiles to forsake *Moses,
saying that they ought not to circumcise *their* children, neither to walk after the customs.
[22]What is it therefore? the multitude
must needs come together: for they will
hear that thou art come.
[23]Do therefore this that we say to
thee: We have four men which have a
vow on them;

21:8 one of the seven. Acts 6:3,5 tells us who all of the seven were and something of what they did.
21:15 took up our carriages. Packed our baggage.
21:16 an old disciple. An *early* disciple.
21:23 a vow. Read Numbers 6:1-7 (see also 6:2 note, "A Nazarite"), which tells of the

24 Them take, and purify thyself with them, and be at charges with them, that they may shave *their* heads: and all may know that those things, whereof they were informed concerning thee, are nothing; but *that* thou thyself also walkest orderly, and keepest the law.

25 As touching the Gentiles which believe, we have written *and* concluded that they observe no such thing, save only that they keep themselves from *things* offered to idols, and from blood, and from strangled, and from fornication.

26 Then Paul took the men, and the next day purifying himself with them entered into the temple, to signify the accomplishment of the days of purification, until that an *offering should be offered for every one of them.

¶27 And when the seven days were almost ended, the Jews which were of Asia, when they saw him in the temple, stirred up all the people, and laid hands on him,

28 Crying out, Men of *Israel, help: This is the man, that teacheth all *men* every where against the people, and the law, and this place: and further brought Greeks also into the temple, and hath polluted this holy place.

29 (For they had seen before with him in the city Trophimus an Ephesian, whom they supposed that Paul had brought into the temple.)

30 And all the city was moved, and the people ran together: and they took Paul, and drew him out of the temple: and forthwith the doors were shut.

31 And as they went about to kill him, tidings came unto the chief captain of the band, that all Jerusalem was in an uproar.

32 Who immediately took soldiers and *centurions, and ran down unto them: and when they saw the chief captain and the soldiers, they left beating of Paul.

33 Then the chief captain came near, and took him, and commanded *him* to be bound with two chains; and demanded who he was, and what he had done.

34 And some cried one thing, some another, among the multitude: and when he could not know the certainty for the tumult, he commanded him to be carried into the castle.

35 And when he came upon the stairs, so it was, that he was borne of the soldiers for the violence of the people.

36 For the multitude of the people followed after, crying, Away with him.

37 And as Paul was to be led into the castle, he said unto the chief captain, May I speak unto thee? Who said, Canst thou speak Greek?

38 Art not thou that Egyptian, which before these days madest an uproar, and leddest out into the wilderness four thousand men that were murderers?

39 But Paul said, I am a man *which am* a Jew of Tarsus, *a city* in Cilicia, a citizen of no mean city: and, I beseech thee, suffer me to speak unto the people.

40 And when he had given him licence, Paul stood on the stairs, and beckoned with the hand unto the people. And when there was made a great silence, he spake unto *them* in the Hebrew tongue, saying,

22 Men, brethren, and fathers, hear ye my defence *which I make* now unto you.

2 (And when they heard that he spake in the Hebrew tongue to them, they kept the more silence: and he saith,)

3 I am verily a man *which am* a Jew, born in Tarsus, *a city* in Cilicia, yet brought up in this city at the feet of Gamaliel, *and* taught according to the perfect manner of the law of the fathers, and was zealous toward God, as ye all are this day.

4 And I persecuted this way unto the

Nazarite vow or promise that the Jewish men observed in the past in order to show in this way that they belonged to God and wished to serve Him.

21:24 be at charges with them. Paul was told to pay the expenses of the four men.

death, binding and delivering into prisons both men and women.
5 As also the high priest doth bear me
witness, and all the estate of the elders:
from whom also I received letters unto
the brethren, and went to *Damascus,
to bring them which were there bound
unto Jerusalem, for to be punished.
6 And it came to pass, that, as I made
my journey, and was come nigh unto
Damascus about noon, suddenly there
shone from *heaven a great light round
about me.
7 And I fell unto the ground, and heard
a voice saying unto me, Saul, Saul, why
persecutest thou me?
8 And I answered, Who art thou,
Lord? And he said unto me, I am Jesus
of Nazareth, whom thou persecutest.
9 And they that were with me saw indeed the light, and were afraid; but they
heard not the voice of him that spake
to me.
10 And I said, What shall I do, Lord?
And the Lord said unto me, Arise, and
go into Damascus; and there it shall be
told thee of all things which are appointed for thee to do.
11 And when I could not see for the
glory of that light, being led by the hand
of them that were with me, I came into
Damascus.
12 And one Ananias, a devout man
according to the law, having a good report of all the Jews which dwelt *there,*
13 Came unto me, and stood, and said
unto me, Brother Saul, receive thy
sight. And the same hour I looked up
upon him.
14 And he said, The God of our fathers
hath chosen thee, that thou shouldest
know his will, and see that Just One, and
shouldest hear the voice of his mouth.
15 For thou shalt be his witness unto
all men of what thou hast seen and
heard.
16 And now why tarriest thou? arise,
and be baptized, and wash away thy
sins, calling on the name of the Lord.
17 And it came to pass, that, when I
was come again to Jerusalem, even
while I prayed in the temple, I was in a
trance;
18 And saw him saying unto me, Make
haste, and get thee quickly out of Jerusalem: for they will not receive thy testimony concerning me.
19 And I said, Lord, they know that I
imprisoned and beat in every synagogue them that believed on thee:
20 And when the blood of thy martyr
Stephen was shed, I also was standing
by, and consenting unto his death, and
kept the raiment of them that slew him.
21 And he said unto me, Depart: for I
will send thee far hence unto the Gentiles.
22 And they gave him audience unto
this word, and *then* lifted up their
voices, and said, Away with such a *fel-*
low from the earth: for it is not fit that
he should live.
23 And as they cried out, and cast off
their clothes, and threw dust into the air,
24 The chief captain commanded him
to be brought into the castle, and bade
that he should be examined by scourging; that he might know wherefore they
cried so against him.
25 And as they bound him with thongs,
Paul said unto the *centurion that
stood by, Is it lawful for you to scourge
a man that is a Roman, and uncondemned?
26 When the centurion heard *that,* he
went and told the chief captain, saying,

22:9 heard not the voice. The men with Paul did not hear with the understanding—it was a sound to them, not words (see Acts 9:7).

22:16 wash away thy sins. It was not the baptizing that washed away the sins. Paul called upon the name of the Lord, whose blood washed away his sins. The baptism, a symbol, witnessed that Paul's sins had been taken by the Lord Jesus.

22:21 Gentiles. Here was the supreme issue. Christ for the Jews?—yes! But Christ for the world, for the Gentiles?—the Jews were aghast. They could not believe that the God of Israel would reach out to Gentile "dogs" with the message of redemption.

Take heed what thou doest: for this man
is a Roman.
[27]Then the chief captain came, and
said unto him, Tell me, art thou a Roman? He said, Yea.
[28]And the chief captain answered,
With a great sum obtained I this freedom. And Paul said, But I was *free* born.
[29]Then *straightway they departed
from him which should have examined him: and the chief captain also was afraid, after he knew that he was a Roman, and because he had bound him.
[30]On the morrow, because he would
have known the certainty wherefore he was accused of the Jews, he loosed him from *his* bands, and commanded the chief priests and all their council to appear, and brought Paul down, and set him before them.

23
And Paul, earnestly beholding the council, said, Men *and* brethren, I have lived in all good conscience before God until this day.
[2]And the high priest Ananias com-
manded them that stood by him to smite him on the mouth.
[3]Then said Paul unto him, God shall
smite thee, *thou* whited wall: for sittest thou to judge me after the law, and commandest me to be smitten contrary to the law?
[4]And they that stood by said, Revilest
thou God's high priest?
[5]Then said Paul, I *wist not, breth-
ren, that he was the high priest: for it is written, Thou shalt not speak evil of the ruler of thy people.
[6]But when Paul perceived that the
one part were *Sadducees, and the other Pharisees, he cried out in the council, Men *and* brethren, I am a *Pharisee, the son of a Pharisee: of the *hope and *resurrection of the dead I am called in question.
[7]And when he had so said, there
arose a dissension between the Pharisees and the Sadducees: and the multitude was divided.
[8]For the Sadducees say that there is
no resurrection, neither *angel, nor spirit: but the Pharisees *confess both.
[9]And there arose a great cry: and the
*scribes *that were* of the Pharisees' part arose, and strove, saying, We find no evil in this man: but if a spirit or an angel hath spoken to him, let us not fight against God.
[10]And when there arose a great dis-
sension, the chief captain, fearing lest Paul should have been pulled in pieces of them, commanded the soldiers to go down, and to take him by force from among them, and to bring *him* into the castle.
[11]And the night following the Lord
stood by him, and said, Be of good cheer, Paul: for as thou hast testified of me in Jerusalem, so must thou bear witness also at Rome.
[12]And when it was day, certain of the
Jews banded together, and bound themselves under a curse, saying that they would neither eat nor drink till they had killed Paul.
[13]And they were more than forty
which had made this conspiracy.
[14]And they came to the chief priests
and elders, and said, We have bound ourselves under a great curse, that we will eat nothing until we have slain Paul.
[15]Now therefore ye with the council
signify to the chief captain that he bring him down unto you to morrow, as though ye would enquire something more perfectly concerning him: and we, or ever he come near, are ready to kill him.
[16]And when Paul's sister's son heard
of their lying in wait, he went and entered into the castle, and told Paul.
[17]Then Paul called one of the centu-
rions unto *him,* and said, Bring this young man unto the chief captain: for he hath a certain thing to tell him.
[18]So he took him, and brought *him* to
the chief captain, and said, Paul the prisoner called me unto *him,* and prayed me

---

23:5 it is written. We find this in Exodus 22:28.

to bring this young man unto thee, who hath something to say unto thee.

19 Then the chief captain took him by the hand, and went *with him* aside privately, and asked *him,* What is that thou hast to tell me?

20 And he said, The Jews have agreed to desire thee that thou wouldest bring down Paul to morrow into the council, as though they would enquire somewhat of him more perfectly.

21 But do not thou yield unto them: for there lie in wait for him of them more than forty men, which have bound themselves with an oath, that they will neither eat nor drink till they have killed him: and now are they ready, looking for a promise from thee.

22 So the chief captain *then* let the young man depart, and charged *him, See thou* tell no man that thou hast shewed these things to me.

23 And he called unto *him* two centurions, saying, Make ready two hundred soldiers to go to Caesarea, and horsemen threescore and ten, and spearmen two hundred, at the third hour of the night;

24 And provide *them* beasts, that they may set Paul on, and bring *him* safe unto Felix the governor.

25 And he wrote a letter after this manner:

26 Claudius Lysias unto the most excellent governor Felix *sendeth* greeting.

27 This man was taken of the Jews, and should have been killed of them: then came I with an army, and rescued him, having understood that he was a Roman.

28 And when I would have known the cause wherefore they accused him, I brought him forth into their council:

29 Whom I perceived to be accused of questions of their law, but to have nothing laid to his charge worthy of death or of bonds.

30 And when it was told me how that the Jews laid wait for the man, I sent straightway to thee, and gave commandment to his accusers also to say before thee what *they had* against him. Farewell.

31 Then the soldiers, as it was commanded them, took Paul, and brought *him* by night to Antipatris.

32 On the morrow they left the horsemen to go with him, and returned to the castle:

33 Who, when they came to Caesarea, and delivered the epistle to the governor, presented Paul also before him.

34 And when the governor had read *the letter,* he asked of what province he was. And when he understood that *he was* of Cilicia;

35 I will hear thee, said he, when thine accusers are also come. And he commanded him to be kept in *Herod's judgment hall.

24

And after five days Ananias the high priest descended with the elders, and *with* a certain orator *named* Tertullus, who informed the governor against Paul.

2 And when he was called forth, Tertullus began to accuse *him,* saying, Seeing that by thee we enjoy great quietness, and that very worthy deeds are done unto this nation by thy providence,

3 We accept *it* always, and in all places, most noble Felix, with all thankfulness.

4 Notwithstanding, that I be not further tedious unto thee, I pray thee that thou wouldest hear us of thy clemency a few words.

5 For we have found this man *a* pestilent *fellow,* and a mover of sedition among all the Jews throughout the *world, and a ringleader of the sect of the Nazarenes:

6 Who also hath gone about to profane the temple: whom we took, and would have judged according to our law.

7 But the chief captain Lysias came *upon us,* and with great violence took *him* away out of our hands,

---

23:35 Herod's judgment hall. This was part of Herod's beautiful palace.

8Commanding his accusers to come
unto thee: by examining of whom thyself mayest take knowledge of all these
things, whereof we accuse him.
9And the Jews also assented, saying
that these things were so.
10Then Paul, after that the governor
had beckoned unto him to speak, answered, Forasmuch as I know that thou
hast been of many years a judge unto
this nation, I do the more cheerfully
answer for myself:
11Because that thou mayest understand, that there are yet but twelve
days since I went up to Jerusalem for
to worship.
12And they neither found me in the
temple disputing with any man, neither
raising up the people, neither in the
synagogues, nor in the city:
13Neither can they *prove the things
whereof they now accuse me.
14But this I confess unto thee, that
after the way which they call heresy, so
worship I the God of my fathers, believing all things which are written in the
law and in the *prophets:
15And have hope toward God, which
they themselves also allow, that there
shall be a resurrection of the dead, both
of the just and unjust.
16And herein do I exercise myself, to
have always a conscience void of offence toward God, and *toward* men.
17Now after many years I came to
bring alms to my nation, and *offerings.
18Whereupon certain Jews from Asia
found me purified in the temple, neither
with multitude, nor with tumult.
19Who ought to have been here before thee, and object, if they had ought
against me.
20Or else let these same *here* say, if
they have found any evil doing in me,
while I stood before the council,
21Except it be for this one voice, that
I cried standing among them, Touching
the resurrection of the dead I am called
in question by you this day.
¶22And when Felix heard these
things, having more perfect knowledge
of *that* way, he deferred them, and said,
When Lysias the chief captain shall
come down, I will know the uttermost
of your matter.
23And he commanded a centurion to
keep Paul, and to let *him* have liberty,
and that he should forbid none of his
acquaintance to minister or come unto
him.
¶24And after certain days, when Felix
came with his wife Drusilla, which was
a Jewess, he sent for Paul, and heard
him concerning the faith in *Christ.
25And as he reasoned of *righteousness, temperance, and *judgment to
come, Felix trembled, and answered,
Go thy way for this time; when I have a
convenient season, I will call for thee.
26He hoped also that money should
have been given him of Paul, that he
might loose him: wherefore he sent for
him the oftener, and communed with
him.
27But after two years Porcius Festus
came into Felix' room: and Felix, willing to shew the Jews a pleasure, left
Paul bound.

25

Now when Festus was come into the province, after three
days he ascended from Caesarea to Jerusalem.
2Then the high priest and the chief of
the Jews informed him against Paul, and
besought him,
3And desired favour against him, that
he would send for him to Jerusalem,
laying wait in the way to kill him.
4But Festus answered, that Paul
should be kept at Caesarea, and that

24:22 of that way. Felix knew much about the Lord Jesus and His teachings and that He was the Way (John 14:6), but he was a coward, afraid of the Jewish people, and turned away the greatest thing that could have come into his life (vss. 25-27). See also Acts 9:2 and 19:23 notes.

24:27 Felix' room. Porcius Festus became the governor in place of Felix, who, to please the Jews, left Paul there in prison.

he himself would depart shortly *thither.*
[5]Let them therefore, said he, which
among you are able, go down with *me,*
and accuse this man, if there be any
wickedness in him.
[6]And when he had tarried among
them more than ten days, he went down
unto Caesarea; and the next day sitting
on the judgment seat commanded Paul
to be brought.
[7]And when he was come, the Jews
which came down from Jerusalem stood
round about, and laid many and grievous complaints against Paul, which they
could not prove.
[8]While he answered for himself, Neither against the *law of the Jews, neither against the temple, nor yet against
Caesar, have I offended any thing at all.
[9]But Festus, willing to do the Jews a
pleasure, answered Paul, and said, Wilt
thou go up to Jerusalem, and there be
judged of these things before me?
[10]Then said Paul, I stand at Caesar's
judgment seat, where I ought to be
judged: to the Jews have I done no
wrong, as thou very well knowest.
[11]For if I be an offender, or have committed any thing worthy of death, I refuse not to die: but if there be none of
these things whereof these accuse me,
no man may deliver me unto them. I
appeal unto Caesar.
[12]Then Festus, when he had conferred with the council, answered, Hast
thou appealed unto Caesar? unto Caesar shalt thou go.
¶[13]And after certain days king Agrippa and Bernice came unto Caesarea to
salute Festus.
[14]And when they had been there
many days, Festus declared Paul's
cause unto the king, saying, There is a
certain man left in bonds by Felix:
[15]About whom, when I was at Jerusalem, the chief priests and the elders
of the Jews informed *me,* desiring *to*
have judgment against him.
[16]To whom I answered, It is not the
manner of the Romans to deliver any
man to die, before that he which is accused have the accusers face to face,
and have licence to answer for himself
concerning the crime laid against him.
[17]Therefore, when they were come
hither, without any delay on the morrow I sat on the judgment seat, and
commanded the man to be brought
forth.
[18]Against whom when the accusers
stood up, they brought none accusation
of such things as I supposed:
[19]But had certain questions against
him of their own superstition, and of
one Jesus, which was dead, whom Paul
affirmed to be alive.
[20]And because I doubted of such
manner of questions, I asked *him*
whether he would go to Jerusalem, and
there be judged of these matters.
[21]But when Paul had appealed to be
reserved unto the hearing of Augustus,
I commanded him to be kept till I might
send him to Caesar.

25:21 Caesar Augustus
This Augustus was Caesar Augustus, not the Augustus of Luke 2:1 who had been long dead. The Greek name Augustus, meaning *venerable,* was used as a title by several emperors.

[22]Then Agrippa said unto Festus, I
would also hear the man myself. To
morrow, said he, thou shalt hear him.
¶[23]And on the morrow, when Agrippa was come, and Bernice, with great
pomp, and was entered into the place
of hearing, with the chief captains, and
principal men of the city, at Festus'
commandment Paul was brought forth.
[24]And Festus said, King Agrippa, and

25:8 Caesar. Caesar was the title of the Emperor Augustus. He was the chief ruler of the world at that time. Festus and Agrippa (vs. 13) were both under Caesar's rule.
25:13 Agrippa. Herod Agrippa II, son of Herod Agrippa I (Acts 12:1) and great-grandson of Herod the Great (Matt. 2:1).

all men which are here present with us,
ye see this man, about whom all the
multitude of the Jews have dealt with
me, both at Jerusalem, and *also* here,
crying that he ought not to live any
longer.
25But when I found that he had committed nothing worthy of death, and
that he himself hath appealed to Augustus, I have determined to send him.
26Of whom I have no certain thing to
write unto my lord. Wherefore I have
brought him forth before you, and specially before thee, O king Agrippa, that,
after examination had, I might have
somewhat to write.
27For it seemeth to me unreasonable
to send a prisoner, and not withal to signify the crimes *laid* against him.

26 Then Agrippa said unto Paul,
Thou art permitted to speak for
thyself. Then Paul stretched forth the
hand, and answered for himself:
2I think myself happy, king Agrippa,
because I shall answer for myself this
day before thee touching all the things
whereof I am accused of the Jews:
3Especially *because I know* thee to be
expert in all customs and questions
which are among the Jews: wherefore
I beseech thee to hear me patiently.
4My manner of life from my youth,
which was at the first among mine
own nation at Jerusalem, know all the
Jews;
5Which knew me from the beginning,
if they would testify, that after the most
straitest sect of our *religion I lived a
*Pharisee.
6And now I stand and am judged for
the hope of the promise made of *God
unto our fathers:
7Unto which *promise* our twelve
tribes, instantly serving *God* day and
night, hope to come. For which hope's
sake, king Agrippa, I am accused of the
Jews.
8Why should it be thought a thing
incredible with you, that God should
raise the dead?
9I verily thought with myself, that I
ought to do many things contrary to the
name of Jesus of Nazareth.
10Which thing I also did in Jerusalem:
and many of the *saints did I shut up in
prison, having received authority from
the chief priests; and when they were
put to death, I gave my voice against
them.
11And I punished them oft in every
*synagogue, and compelled *them* to
blaspheme; and being exceedingly mad
against them, I persecuted *them* even
unto strange cities.
12Whereupon as I went to Damascus
with authority and commission from
the chief priests,
13At midday, O king, I saw in the way
a light from heaven, above the brightness of the sun, shining round about me
and them which journeyed with me.
14And when we were all fallen to the
earth, I heard a voice speaking unto me,
and saying in the Hebrew tongue, Saul,
Saul, why persecutest thou me? *it is*
hard for thee to kick against the pricks.
15And I said, Who art thou, Lord? And
he said, I am Jesus whom thou persecutest.
16But rise, and stand upon thy feet:
for I have appeared unto thee for this
purpose, to make thee a minister and a
witness both of these things which thou
hast seen, and of those things in the
which I will appear unto thee;
17Delivering thee from the people,
and *from* the *Gentiles, unto whom now
I send thee,
18To open their eyes, *and* to turn
them from darkness to light, and *from*

26:3 I know thee to be expert. Herod Agrippa II, who was nominally Jewish, as were actually all of the Herods, would know the customs and the laws of the Jews.

26:6 the promise made of God. The promise of the Messiah had been given to the "fathers," Abraham (Gen. 22:18), Isaac, and Jacob (Gen. 49:10; see also its note, "The Promise of Christ"). Paul declared that Jesus was the Messiah thus promised.

the power of *Satan unto God, that they
may receive forgiveness of sins, and
inheritance among them which are
sanctified by *faith that is in me.
19 Whereupon, O king Agrippa, I was
not disobedient unto the heavenly vision:
20 But shewed first unto them of Damascus, and at Jerusalem, and throughout all the coasts of Judaea, and *then* to
the Gentiles, that they should *repent
and turn to God, and do works meet for
*repentance.
21 For these causes the Jews caught
me in the temple, and went about to
kill *me.*
22 Having therefore obtained help of
God, I continue unto this day, witnessing both to small and great, saying none
other things than those which the
prophets and Moses did say should
come:
23 That Christ should suffer, *and* that
he should be the first that should rise
from the dead, and should shew light
unto the people, and to the Gentiles.
¶ 24 And as he thus spake for himself,
Festus said with a loud voice, Paul, thou
art beside thyself; much learning doth
make thee mad.
25 But he said, I am not mad, most
noble Festus; but speak forth the words
of truth and soberness.
26 For the king knoweth of these
things, before whom also I speak freely: for I am persuaded that none of these
things are hidden from him; for this
thing was not done in a corner.
27 King Agrippa, believest thou the
prophets? I know that thou believest.
28 Then Agrippa said unto Paul, Almost thou persuadest me to be a Christian.
29 And Paul said, I would to God, that
not only thou, but also all that hear me
this day, were both almost, and altogether such as I am, except these
bonds.
30 And when he had thus spoken, the
king rose up, and the governor, and
Bernice, and they that sat with them:
31 And when they were gone aside,
they talked between themselves, saying, This man doeth nothing worthy of
death or of bonds.
32 Then said Agrippa unto Festus,
This man might have been set at liberty, if he had not appealed unto Caesar.

27 And when it was determined
that we should sail into Italy,
they delivered Paul and certain other
prisoners unto *one* named Julius, a
*centurion of Augustus' band.
2 And entering into a ship of Adramyttium, we launched, meaning to sail by
the coasts of Asia; *one* *Aristarchus, a
Macedonian of Thessalonica, being
with us.
3 And the next *day* we touched at Sidon. And Julius courteously entreated
Paul, and gave *him* liberty to go unto his
friends to refresh himself.
4 And when we had launched from
thence, we sailed under Cyprus, because the winds were contrary.
5 And when we had sailed over the sea
of Cilicia and Pamphylia, we came to
Myra, *a city* of Lycia.
6 And there the centurion found a ship
of Alexandria sailing into Italy; and he
put us therein.
7 And when we had sailed slowly
many days, and scarce were come over
against Cnidus, the wind not suffering
us, we sailed under Crete, over against
Salmone;
8 And, hardly passing it, came unto a
place which is called The fair havens;
nigh whereunto was the city *of* Lasea.
¶ 9 Now when much time was spent,

26:24 beside thyself. Out of your mind.

26:28 Almost thou persuadest. Paul was extremely persuasive. So much so that King Agrippa was moved by his scriptural arguments concerning Christ. However, this verse conveys a very sad truth—someone that is *almost* convinced is still *completely* lost. The king would have released him had he not appealed to Caesar.

and when sailing was now dangerous,
because the fast was now already past,
Paul admonished *them,*
10And said unto them, Sirs, I perceive
that this voyage will be with hurt and
much damage, not only of the lading and
ship, but also of our lives.
11Nevertheless the centurion believed the master and the owner of the
ship, more than those things which
were spoken by Paul.
12And because the haven was not
commodious to winter in, the more part
advised to depart thence also, if by any
means they might attain to Phenice,
and there to winter; *which is* an haven
of Crete, and lieth toward the south
west and north west.
13And when the south wind blew
softly, supposing that they had obtained
their purpose, loosing *thence,* they
sailed close by Crete.
14But not long after there arose
against it a tempestuous wind, called
Euroclydon.
15And when the ship was caught, and
could not bear up into the wind, we let
her drive.
16And running under a certain island
which is called Clauda, we had much
work to come by the boat:
17Which when they had taken up,
they used helps, undergirding the ship;
and, fearing lest they should fall into the
quicksands, strake sail, and so were
driven.
18And we being exceedingly tossed
with a tempest, the next *day* they lightened the ship;
19And the third *day* we cast out with
our own hands the tackling of the ship.
20And when neither sun nor stars in
many days appeared, and no small tempest lay on *us,* all hope that we should
be saved was then taken away.
21But after long abstinence Paul stood

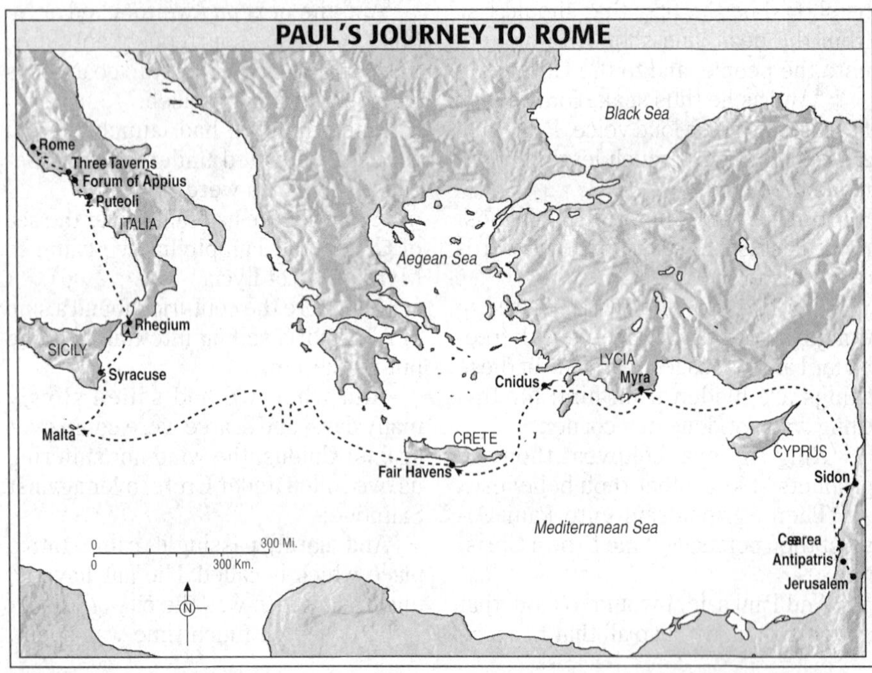

27:9 the fast. The fast was on the tenth day of the seventh *month, October (Lev. 23:27-29).

27:14 Euroclydon. This was an ENE (east northeast) wind. In that time of year, on the Mediterranean Sea, a south wind (vs. 13) often switches around suddenly to become a violent north wind.

forth in the midst of them, and said, Sirs,
ye should have hearkened unto me, and
not have loosed from Crete, and to have
gained this harm and loss.
22 And now I *exhort you to be of good
cheer: for there shall be no loss of *any*
man's life among you, but of the ship.
23 For there stood by me this night the
angel of God, whose I am, and whom I
serve,
24 Saying, Fear not, Paul; thou must
be brought before Caesar: and, lo, God
hath given thee all them that sail with
thee.
25 Wherefore, sirs, be of good cheer:
for I believe God, that it shall be even
as it was told me.
26 Howbeit we must be cast upon a
certain island.
27 But when the fourteenth night was
come, as we were driven up and down
in Adria, about midnight the shipmen
deemed that they drew near to some
country;
28 And sounded, and found *it* twenty
fathoms: and when they had gone a little further, they sounded again, and
found *it* fifteen fathoms.
29 Then fearing lest we should have
fallen upon rocks, they cast four anchors
out of the stern, and wished for the day.
30 And as the shipmen were about to
flee out of the ship, when they had let
down the boat into the sea, under
colour as though they would have cast
anchors out of the foreship,
31 Paul said to the centurion and to the
soldiers, Except these abide in the ship,
ye cannot be saved.
32 Then the soldiers cut off the ropes
of the boat, and let her fall off.
33 And while the day was coming on,
Paul besought *them* all to take meat,
saying, This day is the fourteenth day
that ye have tarried and continued fasting, having taken nothing.
34 Wherefore I pray you to take *some*
meat: for this is for your health: for
there shall not an hair fall from the head
of any of you.
35 And when he had thus spoken, he
took bread, and gave thanks to God in
presence of them all: and when he had
broken *it,* he began to eat.
36 Then were they all of good cheer,
and they also took *some* meat.
37 And we were in all in the ship two
hundred threescore and sixteen souls.
38 And when they had eaten enough,
they lightened the ship, and cast out the
wheat into the sea.
39 And when it was day, they knew not
the land: but they discovered a certain
creek with a shore, into the which they
were minded, if it were possible, to
thrust in the ship.
40 And when they had taken up the
anchors, they committed *themselves*
unto the sea, and loosed the rudder
bands, and hoised up the mainsail to the
wind, and made toward shore.
41 And falling into a place where two
seas met, they ran the ship aground;
and the forepart stuck fast, and remained unmoveable, but the hinder
part was broken with the violence of the
waves.
42 And the soldiers' counsel was to kill
the prisoners, lest any of them should
swim out, and escape.
43 But the centurion, willing to save
Paul, kept them from *their* purpose; and
commanded that they which could
swim should cast *themselves* first *into*
the sea, and get to land:
44 And the rest, some on boards, and
some on *broken pieces* of the ship. And
so it came to pass, that they escaped all
safe to land.

28 And when they were escaped,
then they knew that the island
was called Melita.

27:24 Fear not. God reveals to His own children plans and guidance that they could not know otherwise and which even others who have been trained cannot know.
27:28 fathoms. One fathom is six feet.
27:30 shipmen. Sailors.

2 And the barbarous people shewed us no little kindness: for they kindled a fire, and received us every one, because of the present rain, and because of the cold.

3 And when Paul had gathered a bundle of sticks, and laid *them* on the fire, there came a viper out of the heat, and fastened on his hand.

4 And when the barbarians saw the *venomous* beast hang on his hand, they said among themselves, No doubt this man is a murderer, whom, though he hath escaped the sea, yet vengeance suffereth not to live.

5 And he shook off the beast into the fire, and felt no harm.

6 Howbeit they looked when he should have swollen, or fallen down dead suddenly: but after they had looked a great while, and saw no harm come to him, they changed their minds, and said that he was a god.

¶ 7 In the same quarters were possessions of the chief man of the island, whose name was Publius; who received us, and lodged us three days courteously.

8 And it came to pass, that the father of Publius lay sick of a fever and of a bloody flux: to whom Paul entered in, and prayed, and laid his hands on him, and healed him.

9 So when this was done, others also, which had diseases in the island, came, and were healed:

10 Who also honoured us with many honours; and when we departed, they laded *us* with such things as were necessary.

¶ 11 And after three months we departed in a ship of Alexandria, which had wintered in the isle, whose sign was Castor and Pollux.

12 And landing at Syracuse, we tarried *there* three days.

13 And from thence we fetched a compass, and came to Rhegium: and after one day the south wind blew, and we came the next day to Puteoli:

14 Where we found brethren, and were desired to tarry with them seven days: and so we went toward Rome.

15 And from thence, when the brethren heard of us, they came to meet us as far as Appii forum, and The three taverns: whom when Paul saw, he thanked God, and took courage.

16 And when we came to Rome, the centurion delivered the prisoners to the captain of the guard: but Paul was suf-

28:16 PAUL IN ROME

It was in the spring of A.D. 61 that Paul, with Luke, arrived in Rome. He was well treated by the authorities. Luke tells of Paul's living "in his own hired house" (vs. 30), where he was visited by the Christians. It was probably from Rome that Paul wrote letters to the churches (Colossians, Ephesians, Philippians), and a personal letter to his friend, Philemon, who lived in Colosse.

It is possible that he was released for a year when he again visited Macedonia (Phil. 2:24), Asia Minor (Philem. 22), and perhaps Spain (Rom. 15:24). His first epistle to Timothy and his letter to Titus were probably written from Macedonia and Ephesus during his freedom (Titus 3:12). After a year he was again put in prison in Rome, and it is believed that this time he was cast into a dungeon. During this last imprisonment, he wrote his last letter, which was to Timothy. There is a note of sadness in it, for many of the disciples who had visited him during his first Roman imprisonment failed to come to him on this occasion. Luke alone remained with Paul.

Historians date Paul's death in the summer of A.D. 68, seven years after he first went to Rome. Tradition tells us that it was during the great and terrible Roman persecution of the Christians by the Emperor Nero that Paul's head was cut off, somewhere on the Ostian Road outside of Rome. His "crowns for service," of which he wrote to the churches, are laid up in heaven until the judgment seat of Christ.

28:4 vengeance. Justice.
28:15 Appii forum. The marketplace of Appii.
28:16 kept. Guarded.

fered to dwell by himself with a soldier
that kept him.
¶[17]And it came to pass, that after
three days Paul called the chief of the
Jews together: and when they were
come together, he said unto them, Men
and brethren, though I have committed
nothing against the people, or customs
of our fathers, yet was I delivered prisoner from Jerusalem into the hands of
the Romans.
[18]Who, when they had examined me,
would have let *me* go, because there
was no cause of death in me.
[19]But when the Jews spake against *it,*
I was constrained to appeal unto Caesar; not that I had ought to accuse my
nation of.
[20]For this cause therefore have I
called for you, to see *you,* and to speak
with *you:* because that for the hope of
Israel I am bound with this chain.
[21]And they said unto him, We neither
received letters out of Judaea concerning thee, neither any of the brethren
that came shewed or spake any harm of
thee.
[22]But we desire to hear of thee what
thou thinkest: for as concerning this
sect, we know that every where it is
spoken against.
[23]And when they had appointed him
a day, there came many to him into *his*
lodging; to whom he expounded and
testified the kingdom of God, persuading them concerning Jesus, both out of
the law of Moses, and *out of* the prophets, from morning till evening.
[24]And some believed the things
which were spoken, and some believed
not.
[25]And when they agreed not among
themselves, they departed, after that
Paul had spoken one word, Well spake
the Holy Ghost by Esaias the prophet
unto our fathers,
[26]Saying, Go unto this people, and
say, Hearing ye shall hear, and shall not
understand; and seeing ye shall see,
and not perceive:
[27]For the heart of this people is
waxed gross, and their ears are dull of
hearing, and their eyes have they
closed; lest they should see with *their*
eyes, and hear with *their* ears, and understand with *their* heart, and should be
converted, and I should heal them.
[28]Be it known therefore unto you,
that the salvation of God is sent unto
the Gentiles, and *that* they will hear it.
[29]And when he had said these words,
the Jews departed, and had great reasoning among themselves.
¶[30]And Paul dwelt two whole years
in his own hired house, and received all
that came in unto him,
[31]Preaching the kingdom of God, and
teaching those things which concern
the Lord Jesus Christ, with all confidence, no man forbidding him.

28:20 the hope of Israel. Read the Acts 26:6 note.
28:25 by Esaias the prophet. Read Isaiah 6:9-10.

The Epistle of Paul the Apostle to the

ROMANS

BACKGROUND AND SUMMARY

Suppose that a judge entrusted by society with guardianship of the law should say to a convicted criminal: "I have nothing against you. You are as free as if you had never committed a crime. You may go." What an outrage against justice that would be! The judge, who above all people should uphold the law, would be breaking the law. The public would be endangered, for the criminal would go free only to commit more crimes.

Every man is a sinner in God's sight, under sentence of death, eternal death. Yet God, the only really righteous Judge, can set free any sinner without breaking His holy Law or endangering others. The book of Romans tells how He can do it, and still be righteous: He took His own Son, the Lord Jesus Christ, and caused Him to suffer the full death penalty for all the sin of all the world; that satisfied His Law's demands. Then He raised up His Son from the dead to His own throne and now offers the very life of His Son, His own righteous nature, as a gift to any who will receive Him. This gives the former sinner not only the *desire,* but the *power* to live righteously forever after.

THE WRITER AND TIME

Romans is an epistle that Paul the apostle wrote about A.D. 57–58 to Christians in Rome.

STRUCTURE

The book of Romans is divided in seven sections (see outline). Sections I and VII are greetings. Section II explains what sinners we are by nature, and Section III explains how to become a Christian. Section IV tells how to live the Christian life, that is, how to get victory over sin. In Section V Paul explains why God's own nation Israel has not attained righteousness. Section VI describes how to serve God in practical ways.

OUTLINE OF ROMANS

I.	Greetings	Romans 1:1-16
II.	No Righteousness *in* Us	Romans 1:17—3:20
III.	God's Righteousness *on* Us	Romans 3:21—5:11
IV.	God's Righteousness *in* Us	Romans 5:12—8:39

V.	God's Righteousness versus Man's Righteousness	Romans 9:1—11:36
VI.	God's Righteousness *through* Us	Romans 12:1—15:33
VII.	Greetings	Romans 16:1-27

I. Greetings (1:1-16)

1 Paul, a servant of Jesus *Christ,
called *to be* an *apostle, separated
unto the *gospel of *God,
2(Which he had promised afore by his
*prophets in the holy scriptures,)
3Concerning his Son Jesus Christ our
Lord, which was made of the seed of
*David according to the flesh;
4And declared *to be* the Son of God
with power, according to the spirit of
holiness, by the *resurrection from the
dead:
5By whom we have received *grace
and apostleship, for obedience to the
*faith among all nations, for his
name:
6Among whom are ye also the called
of Jesus Christ:
7To all that be in Rome, beloved of
God, called *to be* *saints: Grace to you
and *peace from God our Father, and
the Lord Jesus Christ.
¶8First, I thank my God through Jesus
Christ for you all, that your faith is spoken of throughout the whole *world.
9For God is my witness, whom I
serve with my spirit in the gospel of his
Son, that without ceasing I make mention of you always in my prayers;
10Making request, if by any means
now at length I might have a prosperous journey by the will of God to come
unto you.
11For I long to see you, that I may
impart unto you some spiritual gift, to
the end ye may be established;
12That is, that I may be comforted
together with you by the mutual faith
both of you and me.
13Now I would not have you ignorant,
brethren, that oftentimes I purposed to
come unto you, (but was let hitherto,)
that I might have some fruit among you
also, even as among other *Gentiles.
14I am debtor both to the Greeks, and
to the Barbarians; both to the wise, and
to the unwise.
15So, as much as in me is, I am ready
to preach the gospel to you that are at
Rome also.

1:7 The Saints of God

"Saints" is the word that God uses for those who have taken Jesus Christ as their Saviour. It means *set-apart ones* (Num. 6:2). In Greek it is the same word as "holy," "consecrated," or "sanctified." It has nothing to do with a person's own efforts at godliness. Saints are not special Christians addressed as "Saint" who are adored and appear in pictures, stained-glass windows, and altars. Rather, for His own purpose, God has set apart for Himself (Rom. 8:29 and its note, "Predestination") all who have believed in Jesus Christ as their Saviour. He calls them saints, though they are in themselves no better than other people. Other names for saints are Christians, children of God, sons of God, the church of God, the church of Christ, born-again believers.

1:3 Concerning his Son. God made many promises (vs. 2) about the Saviour who would come; for instance, He spoke through Moses (Deut. 18:18) and Isaiah (Isa. 53:6).

1:3 which was made of the seed of David. The Lord Jesus Christ descended from King David through His mother (Luke 3:23).

1:14 debtor. Paul was a debtor because he had something—the gospel—that God gave him to give to everyone with whom Paul came in contact. Everybody who knows the gospel is a debtor in this sense (Eph. 3:1-3).

1:14 Greeks, and to the Barbarians. In Paul's days, the Greeks were the cultured, educated people; the Barbarians were all who were not Greeks.

[16]For I am not ashamed of the gospel of Christ: for it is the power of God unto *salvation to every one that believeth; to the Jew first, and also to the Greek.

II. No Righteousness in Us (1:17—3:20)

[17]For therein is the *righteousness of God revealed from faith to faith: as it is written, The *just shall live by faith.

¶[18]For the wrath of God is revealed from *heaven against all ungodliness and unrighteousness of men, who hold the truth in unrighteousness;

[19]Because that which may be known of God is manifest in them; for God hath shewed *it* unto them.

[20]For the invisible things of him from the creation of the world are clearly seen, being understood by the things that are made, *even* his eternal power and Godhead; so that they are without excuse:

[21]Because that, when they knew God, they glorified *him* not as God, neither were thankful; but became vain in their imaginations, and their foolish heart was darkened.

[22]Professing themselves to be wise, they became *fools,

[23]And changed the glory of the uncorruptible God into an image made like to corruptible man, and to *birds, and fourfooted beasts, and creeping things.

¶[24]Wherefore God also gave them up to uncleanness through the *lusts of

1:16-17 Salvation by Faith

Salvation is in three tenses: past–every believer has been saved from the guilt and penalty of sin (Rom. 3:19); present–every believer is being saved daily from the power of sin in his life (Rom. 6:14); future–every believer will be saved from even the presence of sin in his nature, so that in heaven he will be without sin and become more like the Lord Jesus Christ (Rom. 13:11).

In bestowing salvation on us, God uses the way of faith instead of the way of works. He offers His righteousness only to those who believe (Rom. 3:22). Faith, in the cases of salvation and righteousness, is distrusting self and trusting another–in this case, God. It is believing that what He says is true before we see that it is.

1:16 gospel. The gospel is God's good news to sinners that His Son Jesus Christ has taken their sins on Himself and satisfied God's justice by bearing the full death penalty for them; and not only that, but He rose from the dead to give them eternal life.

1:16 to the Jew first. The gospel was offered first to the Jews until they rejected it and God turned to the Gentiles. See Acts 13:46; 18:5-6; 28:28.

1:16 Greek. Used in the singular this word means *Gentile,* any Gentile.

1:17 therein. In the gospel. God could have shown His righteousness in a way that would not have been good news. He could have destroyed the whole human race, for all were sinners, but He chose to show it in a way that revealed His love.

1:17 as it is written. Read Habakkuk 2:4 and its note, "God's Grace."

1:18 hold the truth in unrighteousness. This refers to people who know the truth but will not believe it themselves or teach it to others.

1:20 without excuse. No one can excuse his unbelief by saying that he did not know. God shows something of the truth about Himself to every person. Everyone really knows that there must be a God, the eternal Creator, to whom they are responsible. Even atheists call upon God, or curse Him, in times of trouble.

1:23 image. This refers to the beginning of idol worship. Heathen, barbarous nations became so by turning against God. Primitive nations were not barbarous, for the worship of God began with the first man, Adam.

1:24 gave them up. Read in Genesis 11 how the nations rebelled against God and built a temple to the things He had created instead of to Him. God "gave them up," but at the same time He chose Abram, through whose seed all nations would be blessed (Gen. 12:1-3; see also Gen. 12:1 note, "The Abrahamic Covenant" and Gen. 12:3 note).

1:24 to uncleanness. People sink lower and lower into sin when they go their own way,

their own hearts, to dishonour their
own bodies between themselves:
[25]Who changed the truth of God into
a lie, and worshipped and served the
creature more than the Creator, who is
blessed for ever. *Amen.
[26]For this cause God gave them up
unto vile affections: for even their
women did change the natural use into
that which is against nature:
[27]And likewise also the men, leaving
the natural use of the woman, burned
in their *lust one toward another; men
with men working that which is unseemly,
and receiving in themselves
that recompence of their error which
was meet.
[28]And even as they did not like to retain
God in *their* knowledge, God gave
them over to a reprobate mind, to do
those things which are not convenient;
[29]Being filled with all unrighteousness,
fornication, wickedness, covetousness,
maliciousness; full of envy,
murder, debate, deceit, malignity;
whisperers,
[30]Backbiters, haters of God, despiteful,
proud, boasters, inventors of evil
things, disobedient to parents,
[31]Without understanding, covenantbreakers,
without natural affection,
implacable, unmerciful:
[32]Who knowing the *judgment of
God, that they which commit such
things are worthy of *death, not only do
the same, but have pleasure in them
that do them.

2 Therefore thou art inexcusable,
O man, whosoever thou art that
judgest: for wherein thou judgest another,
thou condemnest thyself; for
thou that judgest doest the same things.
[2]But we are sure that the judgment
of God is according to truth against
them which commit such things.
[3]And thinkest thou this, O man, that
judgest them which do such things, and
doest the same, that thou shalt escape
the judgment of God?
[4]Or despisest thou the riches of his
goodness and forbearance and longsuffering;
not knowing that the goodness
of God leadeth thee to *repentance?
[5]But after thy hardness and impenitent
heart treasurest up unto thyself
wrath against the day of wrath and *revelation
of the righteous judgment of
God;
[6]Who will *render to every man according
to his deeds:
[7]To them who by patient continuance
in well doing seek for glory and honour
and immortality, *eternal life:
[8]But unto them that are contentious,
and do not obey the truth, but obey unrighteousness,
indignation and wrath,
[9]Tribulation and anguish, upon every
soul of man that doeth evil, of the Jew
first, and also of the Gentile;
[10]But glory, honour, and peace, to
every man that worketh good, to the
Jew first, and also to the Gentile:
[11]For there is no respect of persons
with God.

---

apart from God. But God never ceases to plead with a soul until that one has either believed in Him or definitely and finally turned away from Him.

2:1 thou art that judgest. Many so-called "good" people will say, "Of course, those are terrible sins, but I don't do those things." Yet the poison of sin is in every person, although it may show itself in different forms in different people.

2:5 against the day of wrath. In the *Day of the Lord.

2:6 according to his deeds. Those who have let the Lord Jesus Christ take away their sins are given God's righteousness and are judged for Christ's deeds, not their own (2 Cor. 5:21). But let us also remember that since we are robed in God's righteousness in Christ, we have a responsibility, since we are "created in Christ Jesus unto good works" (Eph. 2.10).

2:7 well doing. See in John 6:28-29 what our Lord calls "well doing."

2:9 of the Jew first. They had the greatest privileges, in first knowing God's will.

2:10 worketh good. No one of himself can do good works, that is, good enough in God's sight to merit salvation (compare Rom. 8:8).

12 For as many as have sinned without *law shall also perish without law: and as many as have sinned in the law shall be judged by the law;

13 (For not the hearers of the law *are* just before God, but the doers of the law shall be justified.

14 For when the Gentiles, which have not the law, do by nature the things contained in the law, these, having not the law, are a law unto themselves:

> **2:14-15 Man's Conscience**
> Every person, however ignorant, has a standard of right and wrong. He has a conscience, though it may be defective. A cannibal who has never heard of the Ten Commandments may have a strict code, let us say, in respect to fidelity to his wife. God will judge such a person on the basis of what he knows—but he will not be saved on that basis, for no one can completely fulfill the law's righteousness (James 2:10).

15 Which shew the work of the law written in their hearts, their conscience also bearing witness, and *their* thoughts the mean while accusing or else excusing one another;)

16 In the day when God shall judge the secrets of men by Jesus Christ according to my gospel.

¶ 17 Behold, thou art called a Jew, and restest in the law, and makest thy boast of God,

18 And knowest *his* will, and approvest the things that are more excellent, being instructed out of the law;

19 And art confident that thou thyself art a guide of the blind, a light of them which are in darkness,

20 An instructor of the foolish, a teacher of babes, which hast the form of knowledge and of the truth in the law.

21 Thou therefore which teachest another, teachest thou not thyself? thou that preachest a man should not steal, dost thou steal?

22 Thou that sayest a man should not commit adultery, dost thou commit adultery? thou that abhorrest idols, dost thou commit sacrilege?

23 Thou that makest thy boast of the law, through breaking the law dishonourest thou God?

24 For the name of God is blasphemed among the Gentiles through you, as it is written.

25 For *circumcision verily profiteth, if thou keep the law: but if thou be a breaker of the law, thy circumcision is made uncircumcision.

26 Therefore if the uncircumcision keep the righteousness of the law, shall not his uncircumcision be counted for circumcision?

27 And shall not uncircumcision which is by nature, if it fulfil the law, judge thee, who by the letter and circumcision dost transgress the law?

28 For he is not a Jew, which is one outwardly; neither *is that* circumcision, which is outward in the flesh:

29 But he *is* a Jew, which is one inwardly; and circumcision *is that* of the heart, in the spirit, *and* not in the letter; whose praise *is* not of men, but of God.

3 What advantage then hath the Jew? or what profit *is there* of circumcision?

2 Much every way: chiefly, because that unto them were committed the oracles of God.

2:12 without law. The Gentiles did not know God's law as the Jews knew it through Moses.
2:15 work of the law . . . their conscience also bearing witness. They are convicted of sin.
2:16 judge the secrets. See Romans 2:6 note; see also John 5:24.
2:17 thou . . . makest thy boast of God. God is speaking here to Jews who, like the "good" Gentiles, think, "We are better than they."
2:24 as it is written. See Isaiah 52:5.
2:27 if it fulfil. No Gentile (or Jew either) was ever able to keep the Law perfectly. See Romans 2:14-15 note, "Man's Conscience."
2:29 circumcision is that of the heart. See Deuteronomy 10:16 note.
3:2 oracles. The will of God, His very words, given through Moses and all the prophets.

3 For what if some did not believe?
shall their unbelief make the faith of
God without effect?
4 God forbid: yea, let God be true, but
every man a liar; as it is written, That
thou mightest be justified in thy sayings, and mightest overcome when
thou art judged.
5 But if our unrighteousness commend the righteousness of God, what
shall we say? *Is* God unrighteous who
taketh vengeance? (I speak as a man)
6 God forbid: for then how shall God
judge the world?
7 For if the truth of God hath more
abounded through my lie unto his
glory; why yet am I also judged as a
sinner?
8 And not *rather,* (as we be slanderously reported, and as some affirm that we
say,) Let us do evil, that good may
come? whose damnation is just.
¶ 9 What then? are we better *than
they?* No, in no wise: for we have before
proved both Jews and Gentiles, that
they are all under *sin;
10 As it is written, There is none
righteous, no, not one:
11 There is none that understandeth,
there is none that seeketh after God.
12 They are all gone out of the way,
they are together become unprofitable; there is none that doeth good,
no, not one.
13 Their throat *is* an open sepulchre;
with their tongues they have used deceit; the poison of asps *is* under their
lips:
14 Whose mouth *is* full of cursing and
bitterness:
15 Their feet *are* swift to shed blood:
16 Destruction and misery *are* in their
ways:
17 And the way of peace have they not
known:
18 There is no *fear of God before
their eyes.
¶ 19 Now we know that what things
soever the law saith, it saith to them
who are under the law: that every
mouth may be stopped, and all the
world may become guilty before God.
20 Therefore by the deeds of the law
there shall no flesh be justified in his
sight: for by the law *is* the knowledge
of sin.

III. God's Righteousness on Us (3:21—5:11)

¶ 21 But now the righteousness of God
without the law is manifested, being
witnessed by the law and the prophets;
22 Even the righteousness of God
which is by faith of Jesus Christ unto all
and upon all them that believe: for there
is no difference:
23 For all have sinned, and come short
of the glory of God;

3:22 God's Righteousness
God's righteousness, which He offers as a free gift to any sinner who will receive it, is very different from the righteousness that man would have if he could keep the Law perfectly; because God never had to earn His righteousness, and He can never lose it. Righteousness is His very nature. It is His own righteousness, His own nature—which is Christ Himself—that He gives to believing sinners.

3:3 faith. Faithfulness.
3:4 man a liar. Let us believe all men on earth to have broken their word, rather than believe God has broken His.
3:4 as it is written. See Psalm 51:4.
3:5 commend. Paul is using the crooked reasoning of Jewish minds. "If our sinfulness," they say, "shows how wonderful God's righteousness is, why does God punish us for sinning?"
3:19 become guilty. Or "having been proved guilty," may await sentence.
3:20 by the deeds of the law. The Law makes sin show up, as a mirror shows a person if his face is dirty. The mirror cannot make the face clean; the Law cannot take the sins away.

3:25 Propitiation
The word "propitiation" is translated "mercy seat" in Hebrews 9:5. To understand this, we must go back to Leviticus 16. The entrance of the high priest into the presence of God once a year was made possible by the blood of the sacrifice which he brought. He sprinkled the blood on the *ark of the covenant, which symbolized the throne of God. That throne would have been a throne of judgment, but the blood showed that someone had already been judged; thus, the throne became a throne of mercy. The Lord Jesus Christ Himself is said to be the place where the believing sinner may meet God.

24Being justified freely by his grace
through the *redemption that is in
Christ Jesus:
25Whom God hath set forth *to be* a
propitiation through faith in his blood,
to declare his righteousness for the
*remission of sins that are past,
through the forbearance of God;
26To declare, *I say,* at this time his
righteousness: that he might be just,
and the justifier of him which believeth
in Jesus.
27Where *is* boasting then? It is excluded. By what law? of works? Nay:
but by the law of faith.
28Therefore we conclude that a man
is justified by faith without the deeds of
the law.
29*Is he* the God of the Jews only? *is
he* not also of the Gentiles? Yes, of the
Gentiles also:
30Seeing *it is* one God, which shall
justify the circumcision by faith, and
uncircumcision through faith.
31Do we then make void the law
through faith? God forbid: yea, we establish the law.

4 What shall we say then that Abraham our father, as pertaining to the
flesh, hath found?
2For if *Abraham were justified by
works, he hath *whereof* to glory; but not
before God.
3For what saith the scripture? Abraham believed God, and it was counted
unto him for righteousness.
4Now to him that worketh is the *reward not reckoned of grace, but of debt.
5But to him that worketh not, but
believeth on him that justifieth the ungodly, his faith is counted for righteousness.
6Even as David also describeth the
blessedness of the man, unto whom
God imputeth righteousness without
works,
7*Saying,* Blessed *are* they whose iniquities are *forgiven, and whose sins
are covered.
8Blessed *is* the man to whom the
Lord will not impute sin.
9*Cometh* this blessedness then upon
the circumcision *only,* or upon the uncircumcision also? for we say that faith
was reckoned to Abraham for righteousness.
10How was it then reckoned? when

3:24 justified. There is no English verb that means "to righteous" a person; we use the word "justify." It means to *account* or *consider righteous* a person who is not righteous.

3:24 redemption. To redeem means *to buy back* what was once yours. See Exodus 6:6 note, "God's Promise to Redeem."

3:26 just, and the justifier. God's gift of righteousness allows Him to be just.

3:31 establish. That is, in the Law's correct use, according to 1 Timothy 1:8-10. See Romans 3:20 note.

4:1 Abraham. The Jews believed that if anyone were righteous, it was Abraham. The question is, On what grounds did God count him righteous—his works or his faith?

4:3 For what saith the scripture? See Genesis 15:6 and its note, "Abraham's Faith."

4:5 justifieth the ungodly. God counts a sinner as righteous, when He gives him His own righteousness, Christ Himself. The sinner's faith is "counted for righteousness," just as Abraham's was.

4:6 imputeth. Credited to.

4:7 Blessed are they. See Psalm 32:2.

4:11 Outward Signs
The sign of circumcision was given to Abraham when he was ninety-nine years old (see Gen. 17:10 and its note, "Circumcision"). He was counted righteous by God about fifteen years before that (see Gen. 15:6 and its note, "Abraham's Faith"). Therefore, Paul proves that an outward sign or ceremony has nothing whatever to do with whether God counts a person righteous. He counts righteous the ungodly who put their trust in the Lord Jesus Christ. It is in Christ that outward signs, such as baptism, taking Communion, and joining the church become significant.

he was in circumcision, or in uncircumcision? Not in circumcision, but in
uncircumcision.
11 And he received the sign of circumcision, a seal of the righteousness of the
faith which *he had yet* being *uncircumcised: that he might be the father of all
them that believe, though they be not
circumcised; that righteousness might
be imputed unto them also:
12 And the father of circumcision to
them who are not of the circumcision
only, but who also walk in the steps of
that faith of our father Abraham, which
he had being *yet* uncircumcised.
13 For the promise, that he should be
the heir of the world, *was* not to Abraham, or to his seed, through the law, but
through the righteousness of faith.
14 For if they which are of the law *be*
heirs, faith is made void, and the promise made of none effect:
15 Because the law worketh wrath: for
where no law is, *there is* no transgression.
16 Therefore *it is* of faith, that *it might
be* by grace; to the end the promise
might be sure to all the seed; not to that
only which is of the law, but to that also
which is of the faith of Abraham; who
is the father of us all,
17 (As it is written, I have made thee
a father of many nations,) before him
whom he believed, *even* God, who
*quickeneth the dead, and calleth those
things which be not as though they
were.
18 Who against *hope believed in
hope, that he might become the father
of many nations; according to that
which was spoken, So shall thy seed be.
19 And being not weak in faith, he considered not his own body now dead,
when he was about an hundred years
old, neither yet the deadness of Sarah's
womb:
20 He staggered not at the promise of
God through unbelief; but was strong in
faith, giving glory to God;
21 And being fully persuaded that,
what he had promised, he was able also
to perform.
22 And therefore it was imputed to
him for righteousness.
23 Now it was not written for his sake
alone, that it was imputed to him;
24 But for us also, to whom it shall be
imputed, if we believe on him that
raised up Jesus our Lord from the dead;
25 Who was delivered for our offences,
and was raised again for our justification.

4:15 no transgression. If the owner of a great estate does not put up a sign, "No Trespassing," and there is not even a fence around his grounds, a man cannot justly be arrested for trespassing if he walks through the estate.

4:17 (As it is written . . . . Wherever there are parentheses, always read the text through once, skipping the words between parentheses, to get the sense. This verse is found in Genesis 17:5.

4:18 Who. Abraham.

4:18 according to that which was spoken. Abraham believed God's promise in Genesis 15:5.

4:25 raised again for our justification. The Lord Jesus Christ was raised from the dead after He had been crucified for our sins, thus proving that God accepted His death as the payment of our penalty.

The seven results of justification

5 Therefore being justified by faith,
we have peace with God through
our Lord Jesus Christ:
2By whom also we have access by
faith into this grace wherein we stand,
and rejoice in hope of the glory of God.
3And not only *so,* but we glory in
tribulations also: knowing that tribulation worketh patience;
4And patience, experience; and experience, hope:
5And hope maketh not ashamed; because the love of God is shed abroad in
our hearts by the Holy Ghost which is
given unto us.
6For when we were yet without
strength, in due time Christ died for the
ungodly.
7For scarcely for a righteous man will
one die: yet peradventure for a good
man some would even dare to die.
8But God commendeth his love toward us, in that, while we were yet sinners, Christ died for us.
9Much more then, being now justified
by his blood, we shall be saved from
wrath through him.
10For if, when we were enemies, we
were *reconciled to God by the death
of his Son, much more, being reconciled, we shall be saved by his life.
11And not only *so,* but we also joy in
God through our Lord Jesus Christ, by
whom we have now received the
*atonement.

IV. God's Righteousness in Us (5:12—8:39)

¶12Wherefore, as by one man sin entered into the world, and death by sin;
and so death passed upon all men, for
that all have sinned:

5:12 By One Man
It was one man's–Adam's–sin that brought a death sentence upon all of his descendants. It was the one Man, Christ, who brought life to all of His descendants, that is, to everyone who believes God's Word and is born of God. Notice through this section how many times Adam and Christ are contrasted by use of the words "by one man." Christ is called the "last Adam" in 1 Corinthians 15:45-47, because in rising from the dead He became the head of a new race of people, those born twice, born from above by believing in Him.

13(For until the law sin was in the
world: but sin is not imputed when
there is no law.
14Nevertheless death reigned from
*Adam to *Moses, even over them that
had not sinned after the similitude of
Adam's transgression, who is the figure
of him that was to come.
15But not as the offence, so also *is* the
free gift. For if through the offence of
one many be dead, much more the
*grace of God, and the gift by grace,
which is by one man, Jesus Christ, hath
abounded unto many.
16And not as *it was* by one that
sinned, *so is* the gift: for the judgment

5:1 peace with God. This is not peace of mind, but peace between God and man. Christ put away our sin, thus making peace possible.

5:9 shall be saved. This is the future tense of salvation (see Rom. 1:16-17 note, "Salvation by Faith").

5:10 shall be saved. This is the present tense of salvation, meaning we are saved daily from the power of sin, by the Holy Spirit giving us His power and strength to overcome sin (see Romans 1:16-17 note, "Salvation by Faith").

5:13 until. God's Law was not given through Moses until hundreds of years after Adam.

5:14 death reigned. The fact that everyone died, even before the Law was given at Mount Sinai, is proof that, Law or no Law, everyone is a sinner by nature. Even babies, who never heard of the Law and know nothing of right or wrong, never need to be taught to do wrong. They come by it naturally. Since the Fall, we are all born with a sinful nature.

5:15 But not as. The meaning is simpler than the sentence sounds. Count how many times Paul uses the words "much more" in this chapter. Whatever was death to the First Adam, much more is life to the Second Adam, that is, Christ.

was by one to *condemnation, but the
free gift *is* of many offences unto justification.
17For if by one man's offence death
reigned by one; much more they which
receive abundance of grace and of the
gift of righteousness shall reign in life
by one, Jesus Christ.)
18Therefore as by the offence of one
judgment came upon all men to condemnation; even so by the righteousness of
one *the free gift came* upon all men unto
justification of life.
19For as by one man's disobedience
many were made sinners, so by the obedience of one shall many be made righteous.
20Moreover the law entered, that the
offence might abound. But where sin
abounded, grace did much more abound:
21That as sin hath reigned unto death,
even so might grace reign through righteousness unto *eternal life by Jesus
Christ our Lord.

6 What shall we say then? Shall we
continue in sin, that grace may
abound?
2God forbid. How shall we, that are
dead to sin, live any longer therein?
3Know ye not, that so many of us as
were baptized into Jesus Christ were
baptized into his death?
4Therefore we are buried with him by
*baptism into death: that like as Christ
was raised up from the dead by the
glory of the Father, even so we also
should walk in newness of life.
5For if we have been planted together in the likeness of his death, we
shall be also *in the likeness* of *his* resurrection:

6:3 The Word "Baptized"
Since there is no English word for the Greek *baptizo,* the translators brought it into English. A good illustration of what it means is in 1 Corinthians 10:1-2. (The full story is in Exodus 14.) Because the Israelites shared with Moses the experience of trusting through terror, it is said that they were "baptized unto Moses." They were drawn into oneness with him that night as they never would have been had they not gone through the same experience together. Since God reckons that every Christian has died with Christ on the cross, He says that every Christian has been "baptized into Jesus Christ." We are so one with Him, having received His very life, that God says that we are members of His body (1 Cor. 12:12-13). The Christian ceremony of baptism is an outward sign that a Christian believes this in his heart.

6Knowing this, that our old man is
crucified with *him,* that the body of sin
might be destroyed, that henceforth we
should not serve sin.
7For he that is dead is freed from sin.
8Now if we be dead with Christ, we
believe that we shall also live with him:
9Knowing that Christ being raised
from the dead dieth no more; death hath
no more dominion over him.
10For in that he died, he died unto sin
once: but in that he liveth, he liveth
unto God.
11Likewise reckon ye also yourselves
to be dead indeed unto sin, but alive
unto God through Jesus Christ our
Lord.
12Let not sin therefore reign in your
mortal body, that ye should obey it in
the *lusts thereof.
13Neither yield ye your members *as*

5:20 the law entered. It came to show mankind their sin.
6:2 dead to sin. Remember that death does not mean that the dead thing does not exist anymore; it is simply in a different realm. A Christian has died to the realm where sin reigns; he has been born from above into a realm where there is no sin. The old sinful nature is still in him, but he has also a new nature, distinct from the old. The two have nothing in common.
6:6 old man. The old, corrupt, sinful nature.
6:11 reckon. Reckon does not mean *realize* or *feel.* It means *count* and is a word that has to do with bookkeeping. You may not "realize" or "feel" that you have a million dollars, but if the bankbook tells you so, you count ("reckon") on it and use it.

instruments of unrighteousness unto
sin: but yield yourselves unto God, as
those that are alive from the dead, and
your members *as* instruments of righteousness unto God.
14 For sin shall not have dominion
over you: for ye are not under the law,
but under grace.
15 What then? shall we sin, because
we are not under the law, but under
grace? God forbid.
16 Know ye not, that to whom ye yield
yourselves servants to obey, his servants ye are to whom ye obey; whether
of sin unto death, or of obedience unto
righteousness?
17 But God be thanked, that ye were
the servants of sin, but ye have obeyed
from the heart that form of *doctrine
which was delivered you.
18 Being then made free from sin, ye
became the servants of righteousness.
19 I speak after the manner of men
because of the infirmity of your flesh:
for as ye have yielded your members
servants to uncleanness and to iniquity unto iniquity; even so now yield your
members servants to righteousness
unto holiness.
20 For when ye were the servants of
sin, ye were free from righteousness.
21 What fruit had ye then in those
things whereof ye are now ashamed?
for the end of those things *is* death.
22 But now being made free from sin,
and become servants to God, ye have
your fruit unto holiness, and the end
everlasting life.
23 For the wages of sin *is* death; but
the gift of God *is* eternal life through
Jesus Christ our Lord.

7 Know ye not, brethren, (for I speak
to them that know the law,) how
that the law hath dominion over a man
as long as he liveth?
2 For the woman which hath an husband is bound by the law to *her* husband
so long as he liveth; but if the husband
be dead, she is loosed from the law of
her husband.
3 So then if, while *her* husband liveth,
she be married to another man, she

6:18 Free from Sin

The Christian is not free from the *presence* of sin, for as long as we live on earth the old sinful nature is still within each of us, showing itself whenever the believer ceases for one moment to yield his will to Christ. The believer is free, however, from the *bondage* to sin, free to do God's will.

The Christian can know what it is to walk in habitual victory over sin by:

1. realizing and counting on the fact that what God says is true (vs. 11); and
2. yielding to Him constantly by giving his or her hands, feet, eyes, ears, mind, voice, and everything else as tools for His use.

6:14 law. God's Law demanded a holy life. God's grace demands it also, for God will not lower His standards. But grace makes a holy life possible, as the Law could not (see Rom. 3:20,31; 5:20 notes), by freely giving Christ's own life to believers.

6:16 Know ye not . . . ? See Romans 6:3 (and its note, "The Word 'Baptized'") and 7:1 (and its note). These words divide the sixth and seventh chapters into three parts. The first part tells God's plan for the believer's victory over sin. The second gives a servant-and-master illustration of it. The third gives a wife-and-husband illustration of it.

6:18 became. Suppose you have been working for a difficult employer and suddenly the company changes hands. You then become the employee of the new owner. Even though you see the old owner often, you no longer need to obey him. You have died to him as your master. Sin was the master of every person, and the Law was sin's foreman, or taskmaster. But Christ has redeemed us from the "curse of the law" (Gal. 3:13).

6:19 servants to righteousness. This is our service of love out of devotion to a loving, living Christ within our hearts.

6:22 free from sin. See Romans 6:18 note, "Free from Sin."

7:1 Know ye not . . . ? See 6:16 note. Here is Paul's second illustration of how God makes Christians free from the power of sin by counting them dead with Christ. Believers share the life of the risen Christ and are free to serve Him out of sheer love.

shall be called an adulteress: but if her husband be dead, she is free from that law; so that she is no adulteress, though she be married to another man.

4 Wherefore, my brethren, ye also are become dead to the law by the *body of *Christ; that ye should be married to another, *even* to him who is raised from the dead, that we should bring forth fruit unto *God.

5 For when we were in the flesh, the motions of sins, which were by the law, did work in our members to bring forth fruit unto *death.

6 But now we are delivered from the law, that being dead wherein we were held; that we should serve in newness of spirit, and not *in* the oldness of the letter.

¶7 What shall we say then? *Is* the law sin? God forbid. Nay, I had not known sin, but by the law: for I had not known *lust, except the law had said, Thou shalt not covet.

8 But sin, taking occasion by the commandment, wrought in me all manner of concupiscence. For without the law sin *was* dead.

9 For I was alive without the law once: but when the commandment came, sin revived, and I died.

10 And the commandment, which *was ordained* to life, I found *to be* unto death.

11 For sin, taking occasion by the commandment, deceived me, and by it slew *me*.

12 Wherefore the law *is* *holy, and the commandment holy, and *just, and good.

13 Was then that which is good made death unto me? God forbid. But sin, that it might appear sin, working death in me by that which is good; that sin by the commandment might become exceeding sinful.

7:14 Carnal

"Carnal" and "fleshly" are words that Paul used for the old sinful nature that is in every person. Romans 8:7 shows that it is incurable; it will never change. Our only hope is the new nature, Christ's own nature, which is given to every believer in Him.

14 For we know that the law is spiritual: but I am carnal, sold under sin.

15 For that which I do I allow not: for what I would, that do I not; but what I hate, that do I.

16 If then I do that which I would not, I consent unto the law that *it is* good.

17 Now then it is no more I that do it, but sin that dwelleth in me.

18 For I know that in me (that is, in my flesh,) dwelleth no good thing: for to will is present with me; but *how* to perform that which is good I find not.

19 For the good that I would I do not: but the evil which I would not, that I do.

20 Now if I do that I would not, it is no more I that do it, but sin that dwelleth in me.

21 I find then a law, that, when I would do good, evil is present with me.

7:5 when we were in the flesh. When we were still in sin, before we were born from above.

7:6 being dead wherein we were held. That is, dead to the Law. The Law did not die—we as Christians died and are alive again, to serve God by our new lives.

7:7 Thou shalt not covet. See Exodus 20:17.

7:8 concupiscence. Covetous desire.

7:9 without the law. Before Paul understood the real spiritual meaning of the Law.

7:9 I died. Paul found that the Law put him under the sentence of eternal spiritual death.

7:11 slew me. The Law killed all hope of Paul making himself good by his own efforts.

7:13 might become. Might be seen to be.

7:14 law is spiritual. Though Israel was directed to obey the Law by outward forms, when Jesus Christ came, He always made it plain that God meant for obedience to spring from within our hearts—not just to be a sense of duty.

7:16 consent unto. Admit that.

7:20 no more I. This is not an excuse for sinning. It is just an explanation of the fact that

7:21 Law
The word law is used in two senses in this section. It is not difficult to tell from the context which is meant.
1. Law meaning commandments, as Law of God, Law of Moses (sometimes simply Law).
2. Law as a principle, as the law of sin and death, the law of the Spirit. The word "law" is often used outside of the Bible in this latter sense, as for instance, the law of gravity.

22 For I delight in the law of God after
the inward man:
23 But I see another law in my members, warring against the law of my
mind, and bringing me into captivity to
the law of sin which is in my members.
24 O wretched man that I am! who
shall deliver me from the body of this
death?
25 I thank God through Jesus Christ
our Lord. So then with the mind I myself serve the law of God; but with the
flesh the law of sin.
8 *There is* therefore now no condemnation to them which are in
Christ Jesus, who walk not after the
flesh, but after the Spirit.
2 For the *law of the Spirit of life in
Christ Jesus hath made me free from
the law of sin and death.
3 For what the law could not do, in that
it was weak through the flesh, God
sending his own Son in the likeness of
sinful flesh, and for sin, condemned sin
in the flesh:
4 That the *righteousness of the law
might be fulfilled in us, who walk not
after the flesh, but after the Spirit.
5 For they that are after the flesh do
mind the things of the flesh; but they
that are after the Spirit the things of the
Spirit.
6 For to be carnally minded *is* death;
but to be spiritually minded *is* life and
*peace.
7 Because the carnal mind *is* enmity
against God: for it is not subject to the
law of God, neither indeed can be.
8 So then they that are in the flesh
cannot please God.
9 But ye are not in the flesh, but in the
Spirit, if so be that the Spirit of God
dwell in you. Now if any man have not
the Spirit of Christ, he is none of his.
10 And if Christ *be* in you, the body *is*
dead because of sin; but the Spirit *is* life
because of righteousness.
11 But if the Spirit of him that raised
up Jesus from the dead dwell in you, he
that raised up Christ from the dead shall
also quicken your mortal bodies by his
Spirit that dwelleth in you.
¶ 12 Therefore, brethren, we are debtors, not to the flesh, to live after the
flesh.
13 For if ye live after the flesh, ye
shall die: but if ye through the Spirit do
mortify the deeds of the body, ye shall
live.
14 For as many as are led by the Spirit
of God, they are the sons of God.
15 For ye have not received the spirit
of bondage again to fear; but ye have

now Paul had a new nature in which the new "I" lived. Sin still lived in the old nature, as it does in every Christian. It is the continuous fight between the old "I" and the new "I" that brings about the inward struggle.

7:25 So then. This sentence is not an answer; it is a summing up of the situation.

8:2 Spirit. "I," "me," or "my" appear nearly fifty times in the chapter 7 struggle (vss. 7-25), and the Holy Spirit is not mentioned once; in chapter 8 the "I" is practically out of sight, and the Holy Spirit is spoken of nearly twenty times.

8:7 law of God. See Romans 7:21 note.

8:11 quicken. Make alive, give life to. This quickening of our bodies will be at His coming (1 Thess. 4:13-18 and see 1 Thess. 4:13 note, "Hope for the Dead"; 1 Cor. 15:51-57 and see 1 Cor. 15:52 note, "A Final Resurrection").

8:13 ye shall die. If a Christian persists in disobeying God, he may be called "home," like a naughty child who is disgracing his father. We are continually warned concerning the consequences of defiling the temple of God (1 Cor. 3:17).

received the Spirit of *adoption, whereby we cry, Abba, Father.
16 The Spirit itself beareth witness
with our spirit, that we are the children
of God:
17 And if children, then heirs; heirs of
God, and joint-heirs with Christ; if so
be that we suffer with *him,* that we may
be also glorified together.
¶ 18 For I reckon that the sufferings of
this present time *are* not worthy *to
be compared* with the glory which shall
be revealed in us.
19 For the earnest expectation of the
creature waiteth for the manifestation
of the sons of God.
20 For the creature was made subject
to *vanity, not willingly, but by reason of
him who hath subjected *the same* in hope,

8:20 A Mystery
God made the creation subject to death, after man sinned, in the hope of glory. He does not plan evil or suffering, but He allows it in order to bring glory out of it. This is a mystery that not even Christians can understand, but it is plainly taught in the Bible and in all human experience. See John 12:28-29. The glory, the gain, will come when Man–the Man Christ Jesus–rules the earth.

21 Because the creature itself also
shall be delivered from the bondage of
corruption into the glorious liberty of
the children of God.
22 For we know that the whole creation groaneth and travaileth in pain
together until now.
23 And not only *they,* but ourselves
also, which have the firstfruits of the
Spirit, even we ourselves groan within
ourselves, waiting for the adoption, *to
wit,* the *redemption of our body.
24 For we are saved by hope: but hope
that is seen is not hope: for what a man
seeth, why doth he yet hope for?
25 But if we hope for that we see not,
then do we with patience wait for *it.*
26 Likewise the Spirit also helpeth our
infirmities: for we know not what we
should pray for as we ought: but the
Spirit itself maketh intercession for us
with groanings which cannot be uttered.
27 And he that searcheth the hearts
knoweth what *is* the mind of the Spirit,
because he maketh intercession for the
*saints according to *the will of* God.
28 And we know that all things work
together for good to them that love
God, to them who are the called according to *his* purpose.
29 For whom he did foreknow, he also
did *predestinate *to be* conformed to the
image of his Son, that he might be the
firstborn among many brethren.
30 Moreover whom he did predestinate, them he also called: and whom he
called, them he also justified: and whom
he justified, them he also glorified.
31 What shall we then say to these
things? If God *be* for us, who *can be*
against us?
32 He that spared not his own Son, but
delivered him up for us all, how shall he
not with him also freely give us all
things?

8:15 Abba. The Aramaic word for "Father" or even "Daddy," an even more intimate term for our loving Father God. See Galatians 4:6 and its note, "Abba."

8:16 The Spirit itself. The Holy Spirit is one of the three persons of the Godhead. See John 15:26 for the reason "itself" is used here. The "Comforter" was going to elevate Christ, not Himself.

8:19 creature. The whole creation: birds, trees, beasts, rivers, mountains, etc.

8:19 the manifestation of. The revealing of. Read Romans 8:23 note about the celebration that will take place in heaven someday for the whole universe to see.

8:23 adoption. There is a sense in which those who have been born again are sons, or children, of God. That is our position as believers. But the manifestation of our acceptance as full-grown sons, daughters, and heirs awaits the day when we shall be caught up to be with Christ, when our bodies will be redeemed and fashioned like His glorious body. See Galatians 4:5; Ephesians 1:5; and 1 John 3:2.

8:24 by hope. In that hope, the hope of our redemption–on this earth and in eternity.

8:29 Predestination
The word "predestinate" is used only here and in Ephesians 1:5,11, where the meaning is the same as here (see Eph. 1:5 note, "Adoption" and Eph. 1:11 note, "Predestination"). It means *to plan beforehand.* Just as earthly parents make delightful plans for the future of their children, so God does for His children. The verse does not say that He planned that certain people would become His children. It says that He planned that all His children would be like His beloved Son, Jesus Christ. He made plans for "whom he did foreknow." He looked ahead from the beginning of time to the end of time and saw His Son, and in Him all believers. This does not in any sense whatsoever take away from the fact that each person who is born into the world has a free will to receive or reject Jesus Christ as Saviour.

33Who shall lay any thing to the
charge of God's *elect? *It is* God that
justifieth.
34Who *is* he that condemneth? *It is*
Christ that died, yea rather, that is risen again, who is even at the right hand
of God, who also maketh intercession
for us.
35Who shall separate us from the love
of Christ? *shall* tribulation, or distress,
or persecution, or famine, or nakedness, or peril, or sword?
36As it is written, For thy sake we are
killed all the day long; we are accounted as sheep for the slaughter.
37Nay, in all these things we are
more than conquerors through him that
loved us.
38For I am persuaded, that neither
death, nor life, nor *angels, nor principalities, nor powers, nor things present,
nor things to come,
39Nor height, nor depth, nor any
other creature, shall be able to separate
us from the love of God, which is in
Christ Jesus our Lord.

V. God's Righteousness versus Man's Righteousness (9:1—11:36)

*God's past dealings with *Israel*

9 I say the truth in Christ, I lie not,
my conscience also bearing me
witness in the Holy Ghost,
2That I have great heaviness and continual sorrow in my heart.
3For I could wish that myself were
accursed from Christ for my brethren,
my kinsmen according to the flesh:
4Who are Israelites; to whom *pertaineth* the adoption, and the glory, and
the covenants, and the giving of the law,
and the service *of God,* and the promises;
5Whose *are* the fathers, and of whom
as concerning the flesh Christ *came,*
who is over all, God blessed for ever.
*Amen.

8:33 It is God that justifieth. Or, "God will not [lay anything to our charge], for He is the One who first counted us righteous."
8:34 It is Christ that died. Or, "Christ will not [condemn us], for He is the One who died to save us."
9:4 adoption. This is a national adoption, not an individual one. Whenever God speaks of it, He refers to the nation Israel, as in Exodus 4:22. Contrast with this the personal adoption described in the Romans 8:23 note.
9:4 glory. The glory of the LORD was present with them in the Shekinah cloud (Exod. 40:34-38).
9:4 covenants. There is no record that God ever made a covenant with a single Gentile nation.
9:4 giving of the law. This was never given to Gentiles.
9:4 service of God. This refers to the directions for the priesthood in Leviticus, never given to Gentiles.
9:4 promises. Thousands of promises were given to Israel as a nation; none have ever been given to a single Gentile nation. The gospel, now offered to individuals, Jew or Gentile, is not a promise but a fact to be believed. All "spiritual blessings" (including promises) belong to believers (Eph. 1:3; see also its note, "Heavenly Places").
9:5 fathers. Abraham, Isaac, Jacob, etc.

9:4 God's Promise to the Israelites
Paul's love for the Jews shows Christ's own feeling toward His chosen people. Although they have refused His grace, He still loves them and will bring them as a nation to see their sin and to hate it. There was a time when Gentiles, too, turned their backs on God, yet He still loves them and is offering them salvation. Individual salvation is offered to the Jew on the same basis. There is no place in the heart of any Christian for anti-Semitism (hatred toward Jews). The fact that God offers salvation to the Gentiles and gives them promises of heavenly glory does not mean that He has forgotten or broken His promises for earthly blessing to His earthly people Israel, but they tried to gain His favor in the wrong way (Rom. 9:31-32).

¶6Not as though the word of God hath
taken none effect. For they *are* not all
Israel, which are of Israel:
7Neither, because they are the seed
of Abraham, *are they* all children: but, In
*Isaac shall thy seed be called.
8That is, They which are the children
of the flesh, these *are* not the children
of God: but the children of the promise
are counted for the seed.
9For this *is* the word of promise, At
this time will I come, and Sarah shall
have a son.
10And not only *this;* but when Re-
becca also had conceived by one, *even*
by our father Isaac;
11(For *the children* being not yet born,
neither having done any good or evil,
that the purpose of God according to
*election might stand, not of works, but
of him that calleth;)
12It was said unto her, The elder shall
serve the younger.
13As it is written, *Jacob have I loved,
but *Esau have I hated.
¶14What shall we say then? *Is there*
unrighteousness with God? God forbid.
15For he saith to Moses, I will have
*mercy on whom I will have mercy, and
I will have compassion on whom I will
have compassion.
16So then *it is* not of him that willeth,
nor of him that runneth, but of God that
sheweth mercy.
17For the scripture saith unto *Pharaoh, Even for this same purpose have
I raised thee up, that I might shew my

9:11 Election: God's Choosing
Election means *choosing, appointing*. God's choosing is always based on His foreknowledge (1 Pet. 1:2). Nowhere does the Bible say that God chooses to save some and to damn others. Here it does say that God chose Isaac to be one of His nation and not Ishmael, Jacob and not Esau, and that His choosing had nothing whatever to do with their own goodness. As a matter of fact, Jacob's life does not show any more good works—in man's sight, at least—than Esau's. God's choice of Jacob to be one of His nation does not mean that Esau could not have been saved, if he had cared to be. God saves individual Gentiles at any time if they will come to Him in the way that He directs. For instance, Ruth, a Gentile, was saved by accepting the God of Israel as her own (Ruth 1:16).

9:5 Christ. The One who is the eternal God who came to earth in a body of Jewish flesh.
9:6 not all Israel. Not every descendant of Abraham belongs to God's people, the Lord says through Paul. Only those who believe are counted so, as Abraham was. For instance, Ishmael was not counted as one of God's nation, or, later, Esau (see also John 8:37-44).
9:7 In Isaac shall. See Genesis 21:12.
9:9 the word of promise. See Genesis 18:10.
9:12 The elder shall serve. See Genesis 25:23 (see also Gen. 25:25-26 note, "Jacob and Esau").
9:13 Jacob have I loved. See Malachi 1:2 last note and 1:3 note.
9:17 Even for this same purpose. See Exodus 9:16.
9:17 raised thee up. Not brought Pharaoh into being but, knowing his heart, raised him up to a position of prominence so that all men might see how God deals with rebels against His will.

power in thee, and that my name might
be declared throughout all the earth.
18Therefore hath he mercy on whom
he will *have mercy,* and whom he will he
hardeneth.
19Thou wilt say then unto me, Why
doth he yet find fault? For who hath
resisted his will?
20Nay but, O man, who art thou that
repliest against God? Shall the thing
formed say to him that formed *it,* Why
hast thou made me thus?
21Hath not the potter power over the
clay, of the same lump to make one vessel unto honour, and another unto dishonour?
22*What* if God, willing to shew *his*
wrath, and to make his power known,
endured with much longsuffering the
vessels of wrath fitted to destruction:
23And that he might make known the
riches of his glory on the vessels of
mercy, which he had afore prepared
unto glory,
24Even us, whom he hath called, not
of the Jews only, but also of the *Gentiles?
25As he saith also in Osee, I will call
them my people, which were not my
people; and her beloved, which was not
beloved.
26And it shall come to pass, *that* in the
place where it was said unto them, Ye
are not my people; there shall they be
called the children of the living God.
27Esaias also crieth concerning Israel, Though the number of the children of Israel be as the sand of the sea,
a *remnant shall be saved:
28For he will finish the work, and cut
it short in righteousness: because a
short work will the Lord make upon the
earth.
29And as Esaias said before, Except
the Lord of Sabaoth had left us a seed,
we had been as Sodoma, and been made
like unto Gomorrha.
30What shall we say then? That the
Gentiles, which followed not after righteousness, have attained to righteousness, even the righteousness which is
of *faith.
31But Israel, which followed after the
law of righteousness, hath not attained
to the law of righteousness.
32Wherefore? Because *they sought it*
not by faith, but as it were by the works
of the law. For they stumbled at that
stumblingstone;
33As it is written, Behold, I lay in
*Sion a stumblingstone and rock of of-
fence: and whosoever believeth on him
shall not be ashamed.

God's present dealings with Israel

10 Brethren, my heart's desire and
*prayer to God for Israel is, that
they might be saved.
2For I bear them record that they
have a zeal of God, but not according to
knowledge.
3For they being ignorant of God's
righteousness, and going about to establish their own righteousness, have

---

9:18 he hardeneth. Compare Exodus 4:21 (see also its note, "Pharaoh's Hardened Heart") with Exodus 8:15,19,32. Notice that it was not God's judgment but His mercy that hardened Pharaoh's heart each time.

9:23 vessels of mercy. Not because the people deserved glory but to show forth God's grace. All have sinned; all need mercy; God offers it to all, but some refuse it, and thus become fit only for God's wrath.

9:25 Osee. Greek for Hosea (Hos. 1:9-10).

9:26 not my people. Gentiles.

9:27 Esaias. Greek for Isaiah. The verse refers to Isaiah 10:22-23.

9:28 work . . . a short work. The work of judging both Jews and Gentiles who rebel against God.

9:29 Except the Lord of Sabaoth. See Isaiah 1:9.

9:32 stumblingstone. As in 1 Peter 2:8. The stone is Christ, come down so low that the Jews did not see Him as their Messiah. They were looking only for a king.

not submitted themselves unto the
righteousness of God.
4For Christ *is* the end of the law for
righteousness to every one that believeth.
5For Moses describeth the righteousness which is of the law, That the man
which doeth those things shall live by
them.
6But the righteousness which is of faith
speaketh on this wise, Say not in thine
heart, Who shall ascend into *heaven?
(that is, to bring Christ down *from above:*)
7Or, Who shall descend into the
deep? (that is, to bring up Christ again
from the dead.)
8But what saith it? The word is nigh
thee, *even* in thy mouth, and in thy
heart: that is, the word of faith, which
we preach;
9That if thou shalt *confess with thy
mouth the Lord Jesus, and shalt believe
in thine heart that God hath raised him
from the dead, thou shalt be saved.
10For with the heart man believeth
unto righteousness; and with the mouth
confession is made unto *salvation.
11For the scripture saith, Whosoever
believeth on him shall not be ashamed.
12For there is no difference between
the Jew and the Greek: for the same
Lord over all is rich unto all that call
upon him.
13For whosoever shall call upon the
name of the Lord shall be saved.
14How then shall they call on him in
whom they have not believed? and how
shall they believe in him of whom they
have not heard? and how shall they hear
without a preacher?
15And how shall they preach, except
they be sent? as it is written, How
beautiful are the feet of them that
preach the *gospel of peace, and bring
glad tidings of good things!
16But they have not all obeyed the
gospel. For Esaias saith, Lord, who hath
believed our report?
17So then faith *cometh* by hearing, and
hearing by the word of God.
18But I say, Have they not heard? Yes
verily, their sound went into all the

10:6 A CONVERSATION

Verses 6-21 give an imaginary conversation between a Jew who says that he wants to be saved and a Christian Jew who is already saved.
Jew: "Who will go up to heaven and bring down our Messiah?"
Christian: "He has come. He is Jesus."
Jew: "But He died. Who will bring Him up from the dead?"
Christian: "He has risen. If you will tell God that you believe sincerely from your heart that Jesus has risen, you will be saved. God will save anybody who asks Him. You say that some cannot ask because they have never heard of Him. It is not that they have not heard; everyone has heard of God (Rom. 1:19-20), but they will not believe. And Israel has certainly heard of her Messiah but has refused Him, and God is saving Gentiles."

10:4 end of the law. Christ fulfilled all the Law perfectly and completely, and then put it away as, for example, an artist finishes a picture and puts it aside, since there is nothing more to be done to it. If anyone tries to add to the Law or the Word of God, it is wrong and an insult.
10:5 That the man. See Leviticus 18:5.
10:6 Who shall ascend . . . ? See Deuteronomy 30:12-13.
10:8 The word is nigh thee. See Deuteronomy 30:14.
10:11 the scripture saith. See Isaiah 28:16 (see also its note, "A Sure Foundation"); 49:23.
10:13 whosoever shall call. See Joel 2:32 and its note, "A Remnant of Israel."
10:15 as it is written. See Isaiah 52:7; Nahum 1:15 (see also its note, "A Future Peace").
10:16 Esaias saith. See Isaiah 53:1.
10:18 their sound went. See Psalm 19:4.

earth, and their words unto the ends of
the *world.
[19]But I say, Did not Israel know? First
Moses saith, I will provoke you to jealousy by *them that are* no people, *and* by
a foolish nation I will anger you.
[20]But Esaias is very bold, and saith,
I was found of them that sought me not;
I was made manifest unto them that
asked not after me.
[21]But to Israel he saith, All day long
I have stretched forth my hands unto a
disobedient and gainsaying people.

God's future dealings with Israel

11 I say then, Hath God cast away
his people? God forbid. For I
also am an Israelite, of the seed of
*Abraham, *of* the tribe of Benjamin.
[2]God hath not cast away his people
which he foreknew. Wot ye not what the
scripture saith of *Elias? how he
maketh intercession to God against Israel, saying,
[3]Lord, they have killed thy *prophets, and digged down thine altars; and I
am left alone, and they seek my life.
[4]But what saith the answer of God
unto him? I have reserved to myself
seven thousand men, who have not
bowed the knee to *the image of* *Baal.
[5]Even so then at this present time
also there is a remnant according to the
election of *grace.
[6]And if by grace, then *is it* no more
of works: otherwise grace is no more
grace. But if *it be* of works, then is it no
more grace: otherwise work is no more
work.
¶[7]What then? Israel hath not obtained that which he seeketh for; but
the election hath obtained it, and the
rest were blinded
[8](According as it is written, God
hath given them the spirit of slumber,
eyes that they should not see, and ears
that they should not hear;) unto this
day.
[9]And *David saith, Let their table be
made a snare, and a trap, and a stumblingblock, and a recompence unto
them:
[10]Let their eyes be darkened, that
they may not see, and bow down their
back alway.
[11]I say then, Have they stumbled that
they should fall? God forbid: but *rather*
through their fall salvation *is come* unto
the Gentiles, for to provoke them to
jealousy.
[12]Now if the fall of them *be* the riches
of the world, and the diminishing of
them the riches of the Gentiles; how
much more their fulness?
¶[13]For I speak to you Gentiles, inasmuch as I am the *apostle of the Gentiles, I magnify mine office:
[14]If by any means I may provoke to
emulation *them which are* my flesh, and
might save some of them.
[15]For if the casting away of them *be*
the reconciling of the world, what *shall*

10:19 Moses saith. See Deuteronomy 32:21.
10:20 Esaias is very bold. See Isaiah 65:1; 42:6-7; 65:2.
11:1 Hath God cast away his people? See Psalm 94:14.
11:2 foreknew. See Romans 9:11 note, "Election: God's Choosing."
11:3 Lord, they have killed. See 1 Kings 19:10,14.
11:4 I have reserved to myself. See 1 Kings 19:18.
11:6 if by grace. This verse is like saying, "If a thing is black, it cannot be white; if it is white, it cannot be black." Salvation cannot be a free gift from God and at the same time be something that can be earned.
11:7 Israel. The whole nation.
11:7 blinded. Many who long for their Messiah cannot see that Jesus Christ is He.
11:8 According as it is written. See Isaiah 29:10.
11:9 David saith. See Psalm 69:22.
11:12 the fall of them. The punishment is not forever, and what a blessing when Israel repents! With the Jews rejecting Christ, the Gentiles will receive His riches. How much more when Israel receives Him will they also receive His blessings and riches!

the receiving *of them be,* but life from
the dead?
16For if the firstfruit *be* holy, the lump
is also *holy:* and if the root *be* holy, so *are*
the branches.
17And if some of the branches be broken off, and thou, being a wild olive
tree, wert graffed in among them, and
with them partakest of the root and fatness of the olive tree;
18Boast not against the branches. But
if thou boast, thou bearest not the root,
but the root thee.
19Thou wilt say then, The branches
were broken off, that I might be graffed
in.
20Well; because of unbelief they were
broken off, and thou standest by faith.
Be not highminded, but *fear:
21For if God spared not the natural
branches, *take heed* lest he also spare
not thee.
22Behold therefore the goodness and
severity of God: on them which fell,
severity; but toward thee, goodness, if
thou continue in *his* goodness: otherwise thou also shalt be cut off.
23And they also, if they abide not still
in unbelief, shall be graffed in: for God
is able to graff them in again.
24For if thou wert cut out of the olive
tree which is wild by nature, and wert
graffed contrary to nature into a good
olive tree: how much more shall these,
which be the natural *branches,* be
graffed into their own olive tree?
¶25For I would not, brethren, that ye
should be ignorant of this *mystery,
lest ye should be wise in your own conceits; that blindness in part is happened
to Israel, until the fulness of the Gentiles be come in.
26And so all Israel shall be saved: as
it is written, There shall come out of
Sion the Deliverer, and shall turn away
ungodliness from Jacob:
27For this *is* my *covenant unto
them, when I shall take away their sins.
28As concerning the gospel, *they are*
enemies for your sakes: but as touching the election, *they are* beloved for the
fathers' sakes.
29For the gifts and calling of God *are*
without *repentance.
30For as ye in times past have not
believed God, yet have now obtained
mercy through their unbelief:
31Even so have these also now not
believed, that through your mercy they
also may obtain mercy.
32For God hath concluded them all in
unbelief, that he might have mercy
upon all.
¶33O the depth of the riches both of
the wisdom and knowledge of God! how
unsearchable *are* his judgments, and his
ways past finding out!
34For who hath known the mind of

11:15 life from the dead. See Isaiah 26:16-19; Ezekiel 37:1-14; Hosea 6:1-3.
11:16 firstfruit. The Jews who were saved during the lifetime of Jesus Christ on this earth are a proof that God has not given up on the nation altogether (Isa. 54:7-8).
11:17 some of the branches. Some Israelites.
11:17 thou, being a wild olive tree. Gentile Christians.
11:17 partakest of the root. The Lord Jesus Christ.
11:21 spare not thee. No true believer will ever be cut off from Christ (Rom. 8:39; 1 Cor. 12:27), but the Gentiles (vs. 13) as a group will be cut off when the nation of Israel is graffed back in (vs. 23) after the rapture of the church.
11:23 if they abide not still in unbelief. See Jeremiah 3:21-25; 50:1-5.
11:25 fulness of the Gentiles. When God's purposed number of Gentiles are saved, they and Christian Jews will be taken out of the world in the *Rapture (1 Thess. 4:13-18). In that day, the blindness will be removed from Israel as a nation, and they will be His witnesses.
11:26 as it is written. The real Israel will be saved in the way that it was prophesied that they would be, that is, by the coming out of Zion—not out of Bethlehem this time—of the Lord Jesus Christ (see Isa. 59:20-21).
11:29 without repentance. God never changes His mind when He makes a promise.

the Lord? or who hath been his counsellor?
35Or who hath first given to him, and
it shall be recompensed unto him again?
36For of him, and through him, and to
him, *are* all things: to whom *be* glory for
ever. Amen.

VI. God's Righteousness through Us (12:1—15:33)

12 I beseech you therefore, brethren, by the mercies of God, that
ye present your bodies a living *sacrifice, holy, acceptable unto God, *which is*
your reasonable service.
2And be not conformed to this world:
but be ye transformed by the renewing
of your mind, that ye may *prove what
is that good, and acceptable, and *perfect, will of God.

Service toward other Christians

¶3For I say, through the grace given
unto me, to every man that is among
you, not to think *of himself* more highly
than he ought to think; but to think soberly, according as God hath dealt to
every man the measure of faith.
4For as we have many members in
one body, and all members have not the
same office:
5So we, *being* many, are one body in
Christ, and every one members one of
another.
6Having then gifts differing according
to the grace that is given to us, whether
*prophecy, *let us prophesy* according to
the proportion of faith;
7Or ministry, *let us wait* on *our* ministering: or he that teacheth, on teaching;
8Or he that exhorteth, on exhortation: he that giveth, *let him do it* with
simplicity; he that ruleth, with diligence; he that sheweth mercy, with
cheerfulness.
¶9*Let* love be without dissimulation.
Abhor that which is evil; cleave to that
which is good.
10*Be* kindly affectioned one to another with brotherly love; in honour
preferring one another;
11Not slothful in business; fervent in
spirit; serving the Lord;
12Rejoicing in *hope; patient in tribulation; continuing instant in prayer;
13Distributing to the necessity of
saints; given to hospitality.
14Bless them which persecute you:
bless, and curse not.
15Rejoice with them that do rejoice,
and weep with them that weep.
16*Be* of the same mind one toward
another. Mind not high things, but condescend to men of low estate. Be not
wise in your own conceits.

Service toward the rest of the world

17Recompense to no man evil for evil.
Provide things honest in the sight of all
men.
18If it be possible, as much as lieth in
you, live peaceably with all men.
19Dearly beloved, avenge not yourselves, but *rather* give place unto wrath:
for it is written, Vengeance *is* mine; I
will repay, saith the Lord.
20Therefore if thine enemy hunger,
feed him; if he thirst, give him drink: for
in so doing thou shalt heap coals of fire
on his head.
21Be not overcome of evil, but overcome evil with good.

13 Let every soul be subject unto
the higher powers. For there is
no power but of *God: the powers that
be are ordained of God.

12:5 one body in Christ. See 1 Corinthians 12:12-31.
12:6 gifts. Gifts for service to God and others. See 1 Corinthians 12:1-11,28-31.
12:9 dissimulation. Hypocrisy—a show of love where there is none
12:19 Vengeance is mine. See Deuteronomy 32:35.
13:1 be subject. This is possible for a Christian even though the higher powers may require something his Christian conscience cannot approve, for he can take the alternative punishment without complaint.
13:1 ordained of God. This does not mean that He approves everything that the higher

2 Whosoever therefore resisteth the power, resisteth the ordinance of God: and they that resist shall receive to themselves damnation.

3 For rulers are not a terror to good works, but to the evil. Wilt thou then not be afraid of the power? do that which is good, and thou shalt have praise of the same:

4 For he is the minister of God to thee for good. But if thou do that which is evil, be afraid; for he beareth not the sword in vain: for he is the minister of God, a revenger to *execute* wrath upon him that doeth evil.

5 Wherefore *ye* must needs be subject, not only for wrath, but also for conscience sake.

6 For for this cause pay ye tribute also: for they are God's ministers, attending continually upon this very thing.

7 *Render therefore to all their dues: tribute to whom tribute *is due;* custom to whom custom; fear to whom fear; honour to whom honour.

8 Owe no man any thing, but to love one another: for he that loveth another hath fulfilled the law.

9 For this, Thou shalt not commit adultery, Thou shalt not kill, Thou shalt not steal, Thou shalt not bear false witness, Thou shalt not covet; and if *there be* any other commandment, it is briefly comprehended in this saying, namely, Thou shalt love thy neighbour as thyself.

10 Love worketh no ill to his neighbour: therefore love *is* the fulfilling of the law.

11 And that, knowing the time, that now *it is* high time to awake out of sleep: for now *is* our salvation nearer than when we believed.

12 The night is far spent, the day is at hand: let us therefore cast off the works of darkness, and let us put on the armour of light.

13 Let us walk honestly, as in the day; not in rioting and drunkenness, not in chambering and wantonness, not in strife and envying.

14 But put ye on the Lord Jesus *Christ, and make not provision for the *flesh, to *fulfil* the *lusts *thereof.*

14 Him that is weak in the faith receive ye, *but* not to doubtful disputations.

2 For one believeth that he may eat all things: another, who is weak, eateth herbs.

3 Let not him that eateth despise him that eateth not; and let not him which eateth not judge him that eateth: for God hath received him.

4 Who art thou that judgest another man's servant? to his own master he standeth or falleth. Yea, he shall be holden up: for God is able to make him stand.

5 One man esteemeth one day above another: another esteemeth every day *alike.* Let every man be fully persuaded in his own mind.

---

powers do. Sometimes God's attitude toward them is like that which he had toward Pharaoh (see Rom. 9:17 and its note).

13:2 damnation. Condemnation or judgment of the law of the land.

13:9 For this. See Exodus 20:13-17; Leviticus 19:18.

13:10 love is the fulfilling of the law. Or, the "fullness of the law," like the righteous essence of the Law (Rom. 8:4). No Christian is under the Law, but a Christian who lets the love of God flow through him demonstrates this love by keeping his testimony pure by abiding by the "thou shalt not's" listed here.

13:11 salvation nearer. See Romans 1:16-17 note, "Salvation by Faith," for the future aspect of salvation.

14:1 not to doubtful disputations. Do not discuss questions that are not taught in the Bible and about which even sincere and mature Christians disagree. Don't pass judgment on matters that are of opinion only. It's a waste of time and energy—Christians should be "redeeming the time" (Eph. 5:16; Col. 4:5) and encouraging one another.

14:2 eateth herbs. Vegetables. See Romans 14:20 note, "Eating Meat."

14:5 alike. Many questions still remain unresolved concerning how to apply Sabbath

6He that regardeth the day, regardeth
it unto the Lord; and he that regardeth
not the day, to the Lord he doth not regard *it*. He that eateth, eateth to the
Lord, for he giveth God thanks; and he
that eateth not, to the Lord he eateth
not, and giveth God thanks.
7For none of us liveth to himself, and
no man dieth to himself.
8For whether we live, we live unto
the Lord; and whether we die, we die
unto the Lord: whether we live therefore, or die, we are the Lord's.
9For to this end Christ both died, and
rose, and revived, that he might be Lord
both of the dead and living.
10But why dost thou judge thy
brother? or why dost thou set at nought
thy brother? for we shall all stand before the judgment seat of Christ.

14:10 The Judgment Seat
In Greek this is the word for the judges' stand at the Olympic races. Just as the Olympic contestants stood before the judges' stand to receive their laurels, so every Christian shall stand before Christ to receive any *rewards he may have earned. Contestants (Christians) should certainly not try to judge each other (Matt. 7:1-5).

11For it is written, *As* I live, saith the
Lord, every knee shall bow to me, and
every tongue shall *confess to God.
12So then every one of us shall give
account of himself to God.
13Let us not therefore judge one
another any more: but judge this
rather, that no man put a stumblingblock or an occasion to fall in *his*
brother's way.
14I know, and am persuaded by the
Lord Jesus, that *there is* nothing *unclean of itself: but to him that esteemeth any thing to be unclean, to him
it is unclean.
15But if thy brother be grieved with
thy meat, now walkest thou not chari-
tably. Destroy not him with thy meat,
for whom Christ died.
16Let not then your good be evil spoken of:
17For the *kingdom of God is not
meat and drink; but *righteousness,
and *peace, and joy in the Holy Ghost.
18For he that in these things serveth
Christ *is* acceptable to God, and approved of men.
19Let us therefore follow after the
things which make for peace, and things
wherewith one may edify another.
20For meat destroy not the work of
God. All things indeed *are* pure; but *it
is* evil for that man who eateth with offence.
21*It is* good neither to eat flesh, nor
to drink *wine, nor *any thing* whereby
thy brother stumbleth, or is offended,
or is made weak.
22Hast thou faith? have *it* to thyself
before God. Happy *is* he that condemneth not himself in that thing which
he alloweth.
23And he that doubteth is damned if
he eat, because *he eateth* not of faith: for
whatsoever *is* not of faith is *sin.

15 We then that are strong ought to
bear the infirmities of the weak,
and not to please ourselves.
2Let every one of us please *his* neighbour for *his* good to edification.
3For even Christ pleased not himself;

---

principles. Where one person considers one day of the week specifically the Lord's, another considers that every day belongs to God on the basis of Romans 12:1 and Colossians 3:23. God receives the service and devotion of each person according to the way each one sees the question.

14:11 every knee shall bow. See Isaiah 45:23 and its note, "Universal Recognition of Christ."

14:14 unclean. The Jews used the word "unclean" to refer especially to meats not allowed by the Law (see Lev. 11 and Acts 10). God, who gave the laws about food in Leviticus, had taken Peter out from under those laws in Acts.

14:23 not of faith. Faith begins when one despairs of self. Any act, then, which comes from confidence in self instead of trusting in God is sin.

but, as it is written, The reproaches of
them that reproached thee fell on me.
4For whatsoever things were written
aforetime were written for our learning,
that we through patience and comfort
of the scriptures might have hope.
5Now the God of patience and consolation grant you to be likeminded one
toward another according to Christ
Jesus:
6That ye may with one mind *and* one
mouth glorify God, even the Father of
our Lord Jesus Christ.
¶7Wherefore receive ye one another,
as Christ also received us to the glory
of God.
8Now I say that Jesus Christ was a
minister of the *circumcision for the
truth of God, to confirm the promises
made unto the fathers:
9And that the *Gentiles might glorify God for *his* *mercy; as it is written,
For this cause I will confess to thee
among the Gentiles, and sing unto thy
name.
10And again he saith, Rejoice, ye
Gentiles, with his people.
11And again, Praise the Lord, all ye
Gentiles; and laud him, all ye people.
12And again, Esaias saith, There shall
be a root of Jesse, and he that shall rise
to reign over the Gentiles; in him shall
the Gentiles *trust.
13Now the God of hope fill you with
all joy and peace in believing, that ye
may abound in hope, through the power
of the Holy Ghost.
14And I myself also am persuaded of
you, my brethren, that ye also are full
of goodness, filled with all knowledge,
able also to admonish one another.
15Nevertheless, brethren, I have
written the more boldly unto you in
some sort, as putting you in mind, because of the grace that is given to me
of God,
16That I should be the minister of
Jesus Christ to the Gentiles, ministering the gospel of God, that the *offering up of the Gentiles might be
acceptable, being sanctified by the Holy
Ghost.
17I have therefore whereof I may
glory through Jesus Christ in those
things which pertain to God.
18For I will not dare to speak of any

14:20 EATING MEAT

God is now teaching the good news that man has favor with Him through Christ's precious blood alone; therefore, one must not dim the glory of Christ by making a man think that he can gain or lose that favor by such an outward triviality as eating or not eating meat.

A subject that caused heated argument in the early church was whether it was right or wrong to eat meat that had been offered in an idol's temple. Such meat was sold at lower prices in the markets afterward, and many took advantage of that, saying that there was no such person as an idol, so it made no difference. Others contended that one who ate such meat was sharing in the idol worship, so they made it a rule never to eat meat at all, worrying that sometime when they were out to dinner, they would eat it without knowing that it had been offered to an idol, and thus they would dishonor God. The Spirit of God says that, as in verses 2-6, such questions must be settled individually, between God and man.

15:3 The reproaches of them. See Psalm 69:9.

15:8 minister of the circumcision. God had promised a Messiah to Israel. Therefore, He sent Jesus Christ, whose earthly ministry began with the people of the circumcision (Jews). It was not until the Jews rejected Him as their Messiah that God turned to the Gentiles and offered them Christ, whom most Jews refused.

15:9 For this cause. See Psalm 18:49; Isaiah 42:6-7.

15:10 Rejoice, ye Gentiles. See Deuteronomy 32:43.

15:11 Praise the Lord. See Psalm 117:1.

15:12 There shall be a root. See Isaiah 11:1,10 (see also Isa. 11:1 note, "The Branch of Jesse").

of those things which Christ hath not
wrought by me, to make the Gentiles
obedient, by word and deed,
[19]Through mighty signs and wonders, by the power of the Spirit of God;
so that from *Jerusalem, and round
about unto Illyricum, I have fully
preached the gospel of Christ.
[20]Yea, so have I strived to preach the
gospel, not where Christ was named,
lest I should build upon another man's
foundation:
[21]But as it is written, To whom he
was not spoken of, they shall see: and
they that have not heard shall understand.
[22]For which cause also I have been
much hindered from coming to you.
[23]But now having no more place in
these parts, and having a great desire
these many years to come unto you;
[24]Whensoever I take my journey into
Spain, I will come to you: for I trust to
see you in my journey, and to be
brought on my way thitherward by you,
if first I be somewhat filled with your
company.
[25]But now I go unto Jerusalem to
minister unto the *saints.
[26]For it hath pleased them of Macedonia and Achaia to make a certain contribution for the poor saints which are
at Jerusalem.
[27]It hath pleased them verily; and
their debtors they are. For if the Gentiles have been made *partakers of
their spiritual things, their duty is also
to minister unto them in *carnal things.
[28]When therefore I have performed
this, and have sealed to them this fruit,
I will come by you into Spain.
[29]And I am sure that, when I come
unto you, I shall come in the *fulness
of the blessing of the gospel of Christ.
¶[30]Now I beseech you, brethren, for
the Lord Jesus Christ's sake, and for
the love of the Spirit, that ye strive together with me in *your* prayers to God
for me;
[31]That I may be delivered from them
that do not believe in Judaea; and that
my service which *I have* for Jerusalem
may be accepted of the saints;
[32]That I may come unto you with joy
by the will of God, and may with you be
refreshed.
[33]Now the God of peace *be* with you
all. *Amen.

VII. Greetings (16:1-27)

16 I commend unto you Phebe our
sister, which is a servant of the
church which is at Cenchrea:
[2]That ye receive her in the Lord, as
becometh saints, and that ye assist her
in whatsoever business she hath need
of you: for she hath been a succourer of
many, and of myself also.
[3]Greet Priscilla and Aquila my helpers in Christ Jesus:
[4]Who have for my life laid down their
own necks: unto whom not only I give
thanks, but also all the churches of the
Gentiles.
[5]Likewise *greet* the church that is in
their house. Salute my wellbeloved
Epaenetus, who is the firstfruits of
Achaia unto Christ.

16:5 The Home Church
Groups of believers met in ordinary private home in those days, partly because of poverty, partly for fear of those who hated them. It is possible that the *church age will end as it began, but where two or three are gathered together in Christ's name, He is in the midst (Matt. 18:20).

[6]Greet Mary, who bestowed much
labour on us.
[7]Salute Andronicus and Junia, my
kinsmen, and my fellowprisoners, who
are of note among the apostles, who
also were in Christ before me.

15:21 To whom he was not spoken of. See Isaiah 52:15.
15:27 carnal things. Things for the body, as food, clothing, and shelter, etc.
16:1 servant. Sometimes rendered "deaconess."

[8]Greet Amplias my beloved in the
Lord.
[9]Salute Urbane, our helper in Christ,
and Stachys my beloved.
[10]Salute Apelles approved in Christ.
Salute them which are of Aristobulus'
household.
[11]Salute Herodion my kinsman.
Greet them that be of the *household* of
Narcissus, which are in the Lord.
[12]Salute Tryphena and Tryphosa,
who labour in the Lord. Salute the beloved Persis, which laboured much in
the Lord.
[13]Salute Rufus chosen in the Lord,
and his mother and mine.
[14]Salute Asyncritus, Phlegon, Her-
mas, Patrobas, Hermes, and the brethren which are with them.
[15]Salute Philologus, and Julia, Ne-
reus, and his sister, and Olympas, and
all the saints which are with them.
[16]Salute one another with an holy
kiss. The churches of Christ salute
you.
¶[17]Now I beseech you, brethren,
mark them which cause divisions and
offences contrary to the doctrine which
ye have learned; and avoid them.
[18]For they that are such serve not our
Lord Jesus Christ, but their own belly;
and by good words and fair speeches
deceive the hearts of the simple.
[19]For your obedience is come abroad
unto all *men.* I am glad therefore on
your behalf: but yet I would have you
wise unto that which is good, and simple concerning evil.
[20]And the God of peace shall bruise
Satan under your feet shortly. The
grace of our Lord Jesus Christ *be* with
you. Amen.
¶[21]Timotheus my workfellow, and
Lucius, and Jason, and Sosipater, my
kinsmen, salute you.
[22]I Tertius, who wrote *this* epistle,
salute you in the Lord.
[23]Gaius mine host, and of the whole
church, saluteth you. Erastus the chamberlain of the city saluteth you, and
Quartus a brother.
[24]The grace of our Lord Jesus Christ
be with you all. Amen.
¶[25]Now to him that is of power to
stablish you according to my gospel,
and the preaching of Jesus Christ, according to the revelation of the mystery,
which was kept secret since the world
began,
[26]But now is made manifest, and by
the scriptures of the prophets, according to the commandment of the everlasting God, made known to all nations
for the obedience of faith:
[27]To God only wise, *be* glory through
Jesus Christ for ever. Amen.

16:21 Timotheus. *Timothy.
16:22 Tertius, who wrote this epistle. Paul dictated the letter to Tertius.

The First Epistle of Paul the Apostle to the

CORINTHIANS

BACKGROUND

Corinth was a large, wealthy, business city, famous for its learning. It was also a very wicked city, a seaport situated in Greece in the Isthmus of Corinth. It had a mixed population which included Romans, Jews, and Greeks.

The story of Paul's first visit to the city is told in Acts 18. He lived there for about eighteen months, working as a tentmaker, and giving his other time to preaching the Word of God. Many people were saved, a church was formed, and this epistle is one of the letters which Paul wrote to the Christians there.

Wherever the Holy Spirit is at work, it is certain that the devil is also busy. In Corinth the converts began to quarrel among themselves. This led to "divisions," and the separating of themselves into unfriendly parties around different leaders. Apollos, for example, had a following among those who liked his clever speaking. Foolishly they thought that Paul was by no means so attractive (see 2 Corinthians 10:10). Again, some favored Paul, and yet others formed themselves into a "Peter party." Such a state of affairs meant a very low level of spiritual life, and it's not surprising that some believers were overcome by sin. After a time, they wrote to Paul about many of these difficulties, and this letter was his reply. In it he answered many questions, and with loving faithfulness pointed out things that were wrong.

THEMES

The Greeks were proud of their learning. Paul began his letter by showing the difference between earthly wisdom and heavenly wisdom. A clever man may be foolish in the eyes of God. One short verse gives the central thought of the epistle (1 Corinthians 6:17): The Christian is in vital union with Christ. Evil can be overcome and God's will be done *only* as that glorious truth is believed and lived out.

THE TIME

Paul wrote 1 Corinthians in A.D. 57 at the end of his three years of ministry in Ephesus (Acts 20:31; 1 Corinthians 16:5-8).

STRUCTURE

In 2 Timothy 3:16 we read that the Word of God reproves, corrects, and instructs. This letter divides itself into those three sections.

OUTLINE

I.	Reproof	1 Corinthians 1:1—6:20
II.	Correction	1 Corinthians 7:1—11:34
III.	Instruction	1 Corinthians 12:1—16:24

I. Reproof (1:1—6:20)
*Paul greets the *saints*

1 Paul, called *to be* an *apostle of
Jesus *Christ through the will of
God, and Sosthenes *our* brother,
2Unto the *church of God which is at
Corinth, to them that are sanctified in
Christ Jesus, called *to be* *saints, with
all that in every place call upon the
name of Jesus Christ our Lord, both
theirs and ours:
3Grace *be* unto you, and *peace, from
God our Father, and *from* the Lord Jesus
Christ.
¶4I thank my God always on your behalf, for the *grace of God which is
given you by Jesus Christ;
5That in every thing ye are enriched
by him, in all utterance, and *in* all knowledge;
6Even as the testimony of Christ was
confirmed in you:
7So that ye come behind in no gift;
waiting for the coming of our Lord Jesus
Christ:
8Who shall also confirm you unto the
end, *that ye may be* *blameless in the
day of our Lord Jesus Christ.
9God *is* faithful, by whom ye were
called unto the fellowship of his Son
Jesus Christ our Lord.

Divisions among the saints

¶10Now I beseech you, brethren, by
the name of our Lord Jesus Christ, that
ye all speak the same thing, and *that*
there be no divisions among you; but
that ye be perfectly joined together in
the same mind and in the same *judgment.
11For it hath been declared unto me
of you, my brethren, by them *which are
of the house* of Chloe, that there are contentions among you.
12Now this I say, that every one of
you saith, I am of Paul; and I of *Apollos; and I of Cephas; and I of Christ.

1:7-8 Christ's Coming
The phrases, "the coming of our Lord Jesus Christ," and "the day of our Lord Jesus Christ," refer to the time when Christ will appear a second time. He promised to come again (John 14:3). The day of our Lord Jesus Christ or Day of Christ (1 Cor. 1:8; 5:5; 2 Cor. 1:14; Phil. 1:6,10; 2:16) will be a time of blessing and reward for believers, just as the *Day of the Lord will be a time of judgment for unbelievers.

1:12 Separate Parties
The phrases "I am of Paul," "I of Apollos," and "I of Cephas" were the divisions (or parties) referred to in verse 10. Notice that even those who boasted that they were of Christ were as guilty of the "party spirit" as the others. Differences of opinion within the church should not be allowed to become personal differences. All believers should be "perfectly joined together" (vs. 10). Beware of anything unscriptural that separates Christians from each other.

1:1 Paul . . . apostle of Jesus Christ through the will of God. Some questioned Paul's right to be called an apostle, for he was not one of the original Twelve. See 1 Corinthians 9:1-6 (see also 1 Cor. 9:1-2 note, "Apostles"); 2 Corinthians 1:1.
1:1 Sosthenes our brother. The chief ruler of the synagogue (Acts 18:17) and a Christian brother, as Paul refers to him in this verse.
1:12 Apollos. See Acts 18:24-28 (see also Acts 18:24 note, "Apollos"); 19:1.
1:12 Cephas. This was another name for Simon Peter, given him by Jesus (John 1:42).

13 Is Christ divided? was Paul crucified for you? or were ye baptized in the name of Paul?

14 I thank God that I baptized none of you, but Crispus and Gaius;

15 Lest any should say that I had baptized in mine own name.

16 And I baptized also the household of Stephanas: besides, I know not whether I baptized any other.

17 For Christ sent me not to baptize, but to preach the *gospel: not with wisdom of words, lest the cross of Christ should be made of none effect.

The world's wise are foolish

¶ 18 For the preaching of the cross is to them that perish foolishness; but unto us which are saved it is the power of God.

19 For it is written, I will destroy the wisdom of the wise, and will bring to nothing the understanding of the prudent.

20 Where *is* the wise? where *is* the *scribe? where *is* the disputer of this world? hath not God made foolish the wisdom of this world?

God's foolish are wise

21 For after that in the wisdom of God the world by wisdom knew not God, it pleased God by the foolishness of preaching to save them that believe.

22 For the Jews require a sign, and the Greeks seek after wisdom:

23 But we preach Christ crucified, unto the Jews a stumblingblock, and unto the Greeks foolishness;

24 But unto them which are called, both Jews and Greeks, Christ the power of God, and the wisdom of God.

25 Because the foolishness of God is wiser than men; and the weakness of God is stronger than men.

26 For ye see your calling, brethren, how that not many wise men after the *flesh, not many mighty, not many noble, *are called:*

27 But God hath chosen the foolish things of the world to confound the wise; and God hath chosen the weak things of the world to confound the things which are mighty;

28 And base things of the world, and things which are despised, hath God chosen, *yea,* and things which are not, to bring to nought things that are:

29 That no flesh should glory in his presence.

30 But of him are ye in Christ Jesus, who of God is made unto us wisdom, and *righteousness, and sanctification, and *redemption:

31 That, according as it is written, He that glorieth, let him glory in the Lord.

Paul's wisdom from God

2 And I, brethren, when I came to you, came not with excellency of speech or of wisdom, declaring unto you the testimony of God.

2 For I determined not to know any thing among you, save Jesus Christ, and him crucified.

3 And I was with you in weakness,

1:13 Is Christ divided? No! He is the one head of the one body, composed of all truly born-again people.

1:19 it is written. See Isaiah 29:14.

1:20 wise. Probably the Greek philosophers and teachers.

1:20 scribe. The scribes were Hebrew lawyers and learned men.

1:21 the foolishness of preaching. The preaching of the gospel, although thought to be foolish by many, carries the great message by which those who believe are saved.

1:26 not many wise. Note that Paul does not say, "Not any." Great learning can be used for God, but it is not necessary in order to understand God's truth (1 Cor. 2:14).

1:27 God hath chosen the weak things. Not because there is virtue in being weak, but human weakness magnifies His strength.

2:2 Jesus Christ, and him crucified. The death of the cross (Phil. 2:8) is central to the gospel. Only by *atonement for sin will a holy God save guilty sinners.

2:3 I was with you in weakness. No doubt the apostle is referring to his fragile body. See 2 Corinthians 12:7 and Galatians 4:13.

and in fear, and in much trembling.
4And my speech and my preaching
was not with enticing words of man's
wisdom, but in demonstration of the
Spirit and of power:
5That your *faith should not stand
in the wisdom of men, but in the power
of God.
6Howbeit we speak wisdom among
them that are *perfect: yet not the wisdom of this world, nor of the princes of
this world, that come to nought:
7But we speak the wisdom of God in
a *mystery, *even* the hidden *wisdom,*
which God ordained before the world
unto our glory:
8Which none of the princes of this
world knew: for had they known *it,* they
would not have crucified the Lord of
glory.

All true wisdom is from God

9But as it is written, Eye hath not
seen, nor ear heard, neither have entered into the heart of man, the things
which God hath prepared for them that
love him.
10But God hath revealed *them* unto us
by his Spirit: for the Spirit searcheth all
things, yea, the deep things of God.
11For what man knoweth the things
of a man, save the spirit of man which
is in him? even so the things of God
knoweth no man, but the Spirit of God.
12Now we have received, not the
spirit of the world, but the spirit which
is of God; that we might know the
things that are freely given to us of
God.
13Which things also we speak, not
in the words which man's wisdom
teacheth, but which the Holy Ghost
teacheth; comparing spiritual things
with spiritual.
14But the natural man receiveth not
the things of the Spirit of God: for they
are foolishness unto him: neither can he
know *them,* because they are spiritually
discerned.
15But he that is spiritual judgeth all
things, yet he himself is judged of no
man.
16For who hath known the mind of
the Lord, that he may instruct him? But
we have the mind of Christ.

Babes in Christ

3 And I, brethren, could not speak
unto you as unto spiritual, but as
unto carnal, *even* as unto babes in
Christ.
2I have fed you with milk, and not

2:4 not with enticing words. Not "flowery" or persuasive language but the "demonstration of the Spirit" is necessary for truly spiritual preaching (see vs. 5).
2:6 princes of this world. Rulers of this age.
2:7 ordained. Predestinated. God Himself planned the way of salvation for us before the ages began. Then when the "fulness of the time was come" (Gal. 4:4), He carried out His plan through our Lord Jesus Christ. See also Romans 8:29 note, "Predestination."
2:9 the things which God hath prepared. This does not only speak of the future glories of heaven but also the present blessings of salvation. These are known and enjoyed through the Holy Spirit (vss. 10-12), who alone can reveal and teach divine truth.
2:13 comparing spiritual things with spiritual. The great doctrines of the faith should be studied by comparing one part of Scripture with another. They never contradict each other but lead the student into full understanding. See *inspiration.
2:14 the natural man. Man, just as he is by birth, before he is born again.
2:16 we have the mind of Christ. As Christ dwells and fills the believer, so the mind is renewed and becomes the channel for His thoughts.
3:1 not . . . spiritual, but as unto carnal. Believers are divided by Paul into two classes: carnal and spiritual. The carnal Christian possesses the Holy Spirit but is unconsecrated. He lives just like the people of the world, as if he were not born again. The spiritual man is filled with the Spirit and can feed on the "deep things of God" (1 Cor. 2:10).
3:1 as unto babes in Christ. A carnal Christian is not necessarily disobedient or sinful, although "carnal" could mean that as well. "Carnality" may mean *lack of growth.* Spiritual babies should develop into spiritual men and women. Just as babies need food if

with meat: for hitherto ye were not able
to bear it, neither yet now are ye able.
¶3For ye are yet carnal: for whereas
there is among you envying, and strife,
and divisions, are ye not carnal, and
walk as men?
4For while one saith, I am of Paul;
and another, I *am* of Apollos; are ye not
carnal?
5Who then is Paul, and who *is* Apollos, but ministers by whom ye believed,
even as the Lord gave to every man?

Christian growth

6I have planted, Apollos watered; but
God gave the increase.
7So then neither is he that planteth
any thing, neither he that watereth; but
God that giveth the increase.
8Now he that planteth and he that
watereth are one: and every man shall
receive his own reward according to his
own labour.

3:8 Rewards for Service
Salvation is not a reward—Christians can do nothing to deserve salvation; it is the gift of God (Eph. 2:8-9). After a Christian is saved, however, by accepting God's free gift, his heavenly Father longs to bestow further blessings upon him and promise him certain rewards for faithful service. See Daniel 12:3; Matthew 5:11-12; 6:1-6; 10:41-42; 16:27; Luke 6:35; 1 Corinthians 3:8,14; 9:17-18; Philippians 4:1; Colossians 3:24; 1 Thessalonians 2:19; 2 Timothy 4:8; Hebrews 11:6; James 1:12; 1 Peter 5:4; 2 John 8; Revelation 2:10; 3:11,21; 11:18; 22:12. Notice how many times the rewards are called "crowns."

3:12 Building Materials
Gold, silver, precious stones, wood, hay, and stubble are the materials with which Christians build. The first three are good because they stand the test of the fire. Such service will endure through all eternity. The latter three are bad because the fire will destroy them. These refer to unworthy service, performed perhaps with a selfish or improper motive or grudgingly. Thus a Christian may suffer loss (vs. 15) instead of receiving a reward (vs. 14). His salvation, of course, is not affected, for that rests upon the finished work of Christ. Some, however, will be saved "so as by fire" (vs. 15). In this building it is not the size of the work that matters but the sort of work one has done.

Christian service

9For we are labourers together with
God: ye are God's husbandry, *ye are*
God's building.

The Gospel foundation

10According to the grace of God
which is given unto me, as a wise mas-
terbuilder, I have laid the foundation,
and another buildeth thereon. But let
every man take heed how he buildeth
thereupon.
11For other foundation can no man lay
than that is laid, which is Jesus Christ.

The testing of service

12Now if any man build upon this
foundation gold, silver, precious stones,
wood, hay, stubble;
13Every man's work shall be made

---

they are to grow, so newborn Christians need food—the Word of God. See previous note.

3:3 ye are yet carnal. Carnality often leads to strife and divisions. The Holy Spirit never unnecessarily divides Christians but unites them into oneness of life and purpose.

3:6-7 I have planted . . . he that planteth . . . God that giveth the increase. The gardener plants the seed and waters it, but God alone can quicken it into life. The Christian teacher and worker must do their parts, but it is God's part to give eternal life.

3:12 if any man build. Though saved by grace (Eph. 2:8), every Christian is also saved "unto good works" (Eph. 2:10). This is the building. Jesus Christ is the one true "foundation" (1 Cor. 3:11). "How he buildeth thereupon" is what matters for the Christian (vs. 10). He will be judged (not for his sins, for these have already been judged at Calvary) for his work and service. See 2 Corinthians 5:10; see also Romans 14:10 and its note, "The Judgment Seat."

manifest: for the day shall declare it,
because it shall be revealed by *fire;
and the fire shall try every man's work
of what sort it is.
14If any man's work abide which he
hath built thereupon, he shall receive a
reward.
15If any man's work shall be burned,
he shall suffer loss: but he himself shall
be saved; yet so as by fire.

God's temple of living stones

16Know ye not that ye are the temple of God, and *that* the Spirit of God
dwelleth in you?
17If any man defile the temple of God,
him shall God destroy; for the temple
of God is holy, which *temple* ye are.
¶18Let no man deceive himself. If any
man among you seemeth to be wise in
this world, let him become a fool, that
he may be wise.
19For the wisdom of this world is foolishness with God. For it is written, He
taketh the wise in their own craftiness.
20And again, The Lord knoweth the
thoughts of the wise, that they are vain.
21Therefore let no man glory in men.
For all things are yours;
22Whether Paul, or Apollos, or Cephas,
or the world, or life, or *death, or things
present, or things to come; all are yours;
23And ye are Christ's; and Christ *is*
God's.

Faithfulness in service

4 Let a man so account of us, as of
the ministers of Christ, and stewards of the *mysteries of God.
2Moreover it is required in stewards,
that a man be found faithful.
3But with me it is a very small thing
that I should be judged of you, or of
man's judgment: yea, I judge not mine
own self.
4For I know nothing by myself; yet
am I not hereby justified: but he that
judgeth me is the Lord.
5Therefore judge nothing before the
time, until the Lord come, who both will
bring to light the hidden things of darkness, and will make manifest the counsels of the hearts: and then shall every
man have praise of God.

The example of Paul and Apollos

6And these things, brethren, I have in
a figure transferred to myself and *to*
*Apollos for your sakes; that ye might
learn in us not to think *of men* above
that which is written, that no one of you
be puffed up for one against another.
7For who maketh thee to differ *from*
another? and what hast thou that thou
didst not receive? now if thou didst receive *it,* why dost thou glory, as if thou
hadst not received *it?*
8Now ye are full, now ye are rich, ye
have reigned as kings without us: and I
would to God ye did reign, that we also
might reign with you.
9For I think that God hath set forth
us the *apostles last, as it were appointed to death: for we are made a spectacle unto the world, and to *angels, and
to men.
10We *are* fools for Christ's sake, but
ye *are* wise in Christ; we *are* weak, but

3:16 the Spirit of God dwelleth in you. Since every Christian possesses the Holy Spirit (see Rom. 8:9), his body is the temple of God.

3:17 him shall God destroy. To misuse or neglect the body is a sin against God, and it will destroy or degrade it for usefulness in God's service.

3:19 it is written. See Job 5:13; Psalm 94:11.

4:1 stewards of the mysteries of God. A mystery in the New Testament is not something mysterious, but a secret of divine truth that the Holy Spirit reveals to His stewards (believing servants) and enables them to pass on to others (compare Matt. 13:11 and its note, "Mysteries of the Kingdom"; 1 Cor. 15:51).

4:7 what hast thou that thou didst not receive? Special gifts and talents (or other blessings) that a Christian may possess have all been given to him by God and give him no reason for being "puffed up" (vs. 6).

ye *are* strong; ye *are* honourable, but we
are despised.
11Even unto this present hour we
both hunger, and thirst, and are naked,
and are buffeted, and have no certain
dwellingplace;
12And labour, working with our own
hands: being reviled, we bless; being
persecuted, we suffer it:
13Being defamed, we intreat: we are
made as the filth of the world, *and*
are the offscouring of all things unto this
day.
14I write not these things to shame
you, but as my beloved sons I warn *you*.
15For though ye have ten thousand
instructers in Christ, yet *have ye* not
many fathers: for in Christ Jesus I have
begotten you through the gospel.
16Wherefore I beseech you, be ye followers of me.
17For this cause have I sent unto you
*Timotheus, who is my beloved son,
and faithful in the Lord, who shall bring
you into remembrance of my ways
which be in Christ, as I teach every
where in every church.
18Now some are puffed up, as though
I would not come to you.
19But I will come to you shortly, if the
Lord will, and will know, not the speech
of them which are puffed up, but the
power.
20For the *kingdom of God *is* not in
word, but in power.
21What will ye? shall I come unto you
with a rod, or in love, and *in* the spirit
of meekness?

The uncovering of immorality

5 It is reported commonly *that there*
is fornication among you, and such
fornication as is not so much as named
among the *Gentiles, that one should
have his father's wife.
2And ye are puffed up, and have not
rather mourned, that he that hath done
this deed might be taken away from
among you.
3For I verily, as absent in body, but
present in spirit, have judged already, as
though I were present, *concerning* him
that hath so done this deed,
4In the name of our Lord Jesus
Christ, when ye are gathered together,
and my spirit, with the power of our
Lord Jesus Christ,
5To deliver such an one unto Satan for
the destruction of the flesh, that the
spirit may be saved in the day of the
Lord Jesus.

5:5 God Uses Satan
When a Christian has sinned, God uses Satan to punish him. The "flesh" does not refer to the body, but to the self-nature which must be destroyed, that is, put behind the believer. This may be done by the believer allowing the Holy Spirit to control him, but if that is refused, God may allow Satan to have his way with a Christian until the self-life is dealt with (see Ps. 109:6). He does not become Satan's final property, however.

6Your glorying *is* not good. Know ye
not that a little leaven leaveneth the
whole lump?
7Purge out therefore the old leaven,
that ye may be a new lump, as ye are
unleavened. For even Christ our *passover is sacrificed for us:
8Therefore let us keep the feast, not
with old leaven, neither with the leaven
of malice and wickedness; but with the
unleavened *bread* of sincerity and truth.
9I wrote unto you in an epistle not to
company with fornicators:
10Yet not altogether with the fornicators of this world, or with the covetous,
or extortioners, or with idolaters; for
then must ye needs go out of the world.

4:19 if the Lord will. Plans for the future should always be subject to the will of God (see James 4:15).
4:21 with a rod. As a father prepared to punish a child for disobedience.
5:6 a little leaven leaveneth the whole lump. Leaven in Scripture refers to evil. If allowed to remain, it will spread its defilement. Sin must be purged out of the believer at once.

[11]But now I have written unto you
not to keep company, if any man that
is called a brother be a fornicator, or
covetous, or an idolater, or a railer, or a
drunkard, or an extortioner; with such
an one no not to eat.
[12]For what have I to do to judge them
also that are without? do not ye judge
them that are within?
[13]But them that are without God
judgeth. Therefore put away from
among yourselves that wicked person.

Saints forbidden to go to law against other saints

6 Dare any of you, having a matter
against another, go to law before
the unjust, and not before the saints?
[2]Do ye not know that the saints shall
judge the world? and if the world shall
be judged by you, are ye unworthy to
judge the smallest matters?
[3]Know ye not that we shall judge
angels? how much more things that
pertain to this life?
[4]If then ye have judgments of things
pertaining to this life, set them to judge
who are least esteemed in the church.
[5]I speak to your shame. Is it so, that
there is not a wise man among you? no,
not one that shall be able to judge between his brethren?
[6]But brother goeth to law with
brother, and that before the *unbelievers.
[7]Now therefore there is utterly a fault
among you, because ye go to law one
with another. Why do ye not rather take
wrong? why do ye not rather *suffer
yourselves to* be defrauded?
[8]Nay, ye do wrong, and defraud, and
that *your* brethren.

The temple of the Lord to be used for Him

[9]Know ye not that the unrighteous
shall not inherit the kingdom of God?
Be not deceived: neither fornicators,
nor idolaters, nor adulterers, nor effeminate, nor abusers of themselves
with mankind,
[10]Nor thieves, nor covetous, nor
drunkards, nor revilers, nor extortioners, shall inherit the kingdom of God.
[11]And such were some of you: but ye
are washed, but ye are sanctified, but ye
are justified in the name of the Lord
Jesus, and by the Spirit of our God.
¶[12]All things are lawful unto me, but
all things are not expedient: all things
are lawful for me, but I will not be
brought under the power of any.
[13]Meats for the belly, and the belly for
meats: but God shall destroy both it and
them. Now the body *is* not for fornication, but for the Lord; and the Lord for
the body.
[14]And God hath both raised up the
Lord, and will also raise up us by his
own power.
[15]Know ye not that your bodies are
the members of Christ? shall I then
take the members of Christ, and make
them the members of an harlot? God
forbid.
[16]What? know ye not that he which
is joined to an harlot is one body? for
two, saith he, shall be one flesh.
[17]But he that is joined unto the Lord
is one spirit.

5:13 put away from among yourselves. This speaks of the necessity for *separation by Christians from worldly, sinful people, as well as from the things of the world.

6:11 but ye are washed. In verses 9-10 sin is rebuked as belonging to the kingdom of Satan. But the Christian, who has been cleansed by the blood, is both sanctified and justified. He is set apart for God and must live righteously before an unholy world, as one who has been made righteous before a holy God.

6:13 the body is . . . for the Lord. Two great sins are here mentioned—gluttony and impurity. These are sins against the body, which ought to be kept holy because it belongs to the Lord and is the "temple of the Holy Ghost" (vs. 19). It has been redeemed at a great price (vs. 20) and must therefore glorify God.

6:16 two, saith he, shall be one flesh. See Genesis 2:24.

[18]Flee fornication. Every *sin that a
man doeth is without the body; but he
that committeth fornication sinneth
against his own body.
[19]What? know ye not that your body
is the temple of the Holy Ghost *which*
is in you, which ye have of God, and ye
are not your own?
[20]For ye are bought with a price:
therefore glorify God in your body, and
in your spirit, which are God's.

II. Correction (7:1—11:34)
Paul answers questions asked of him

7 Now concerning the things where
of ye wrote unto me: *It is* good for
a man not to touch a woman.
[2]Nevertheless, *to avoid* fornication,
let every man have his own wife, and let
every woman have her own husband.
[3]Let the husband *render unto the
wife due benevolence: and likewise also
the wife unto the husband.
[4]The wife hath not power of her own
body, but the husband: and likewise also
the husband hath not power of his own
body, but the wife.
[5]Defraud ye not one the other, except
it be with consent for a time, that ye
may give yourselves to fasting and
*prayer; and come together again, that
Satan *tempt you not for your inconti-
nency.
[6]But I speak this by permission, *and*
not of commandment.
[7]For I would that all men were even
as I myself. But every man hath his
proper gift of *God, one after this manner, and another after that.
¶[8]I say therefore to the unmarried
and widows, It is good for them if they
abide even as I.
[9]But if they cannot contain, let them
marry: for it is better to marry than to
burn.
[10]And unto the married I command,
yet not I, but the Lord, Let not the wife
depart from *her* husband:
[11]But and if she depart, let her remain
unmarried, or be *reconciled to *her*
husband: and let not the husband put
away *his* wife.
[12]But to the rest speak I, not the Lord:
If any brother hath a wife that believeth
not, and she be pleased to dwell with
him, let him not put her away.
[13]And the woman which hath an husband that believeth not, and if he be
pleased to dwell with her, let her not
leave him.
[14]For the unbelieving husband is
sanctified by the wife, and the unbelieving wife is sanctified by the husband:
else were your children *unclean; but
now are they holy.
[15]But if the unbelieving depart, let
him depart. A brother or a sister is not
under bondage in such *cases:* but God
hath called us to peace.
[16]For what knowest thou, O wife,
whether thou shalt save *thy* husband?
or how knowest thou, O man, whether
thou shalt save *thy* wife?
[17]But as God hath distributed to
every man, as the Lord hath called
every one, so let him walk. And so ordain I in all churches.
[18]Is any man called being circum-

6:20 bought with a price. The price is the precious blood of the Lord Jesus Christ (1 Pet. 1:18-19).

7:1 concerning the things. In this chapter and the following ones, Paul deals with certain matters about which the Corinthian Christians had written him.

7:10,12 not I, but the Lord . . . speak I, not the Lord. In the first matter, the Saviour Himself had directly spoken (Mark 10:12). In the second, Paul makes a practical application of the Lord's teaching. A deeply spiritual man, Paul thus dedicates spiritual common sense to the problem at hand.

7:14 the unbelieving husband is sanctified. The word "sanctified" is not used here in the sense of being saved. The teaching is that if either husband or wife is converted after marriage, the way is prepared for the conversion of the other also by such a one being brought into a place of special privilege.

cised? let him not become uncircumcised. Is any called in uncircumcision?
let him not be circumcised.
19 *Circumcision is nothing, and uncircumcision is nothing, but the keeping of the commandments of God.
20 Let every man abide in the same
calling wherein he was called.
21 Art thou called *being* a servant?
care not for it: but if thou mayest be
made free, use *it* rather.
22 For he that is called in the Lord,
being a servant, is the Lord's freeman:
likewise also he that is called, *being*
free, is *Christ's servant.
23 Ye are bought with a price; be not
ye the servants of men.
24 Brethren, let every man, wherein
he is called, therein abide with God.
¶25 Now concerning virgins I have no
commandment of the Lord: yet I give my
judgment, as one that hath obtained
*mercy of the Lord to be faithful.
26 I suppose therefore that this is good
for the present distress, *I say,* that *it is*
good for a man so to be.
27 Art thou bound unto a wife? seek
not to be loosed. Art thou loosed from
a wife? seek not a wife.
28 But and if thou marry, thou hast not
sinned; and if a virgin marry, she hath
not sinned. Nevertheless such shall
have trouble in the *flesh: but I spare
you.
29 But this I say, brethren, the time *is*
short: it remaineth, that both they that
have wives be as though they had none;
30 And they that weep, as though they
wept not; and they that rejoice, as
though they rejoiced not; and they that
buy, as though they possessed not;
31 And they that use this *world, as
not abusing *it:* for the fashion of this
world passeth away.
32 But I would have you without carefulness. He that is unmarried careth for
the things that belong to the Lord, how
he may please the Lord:
33 But he that is married careth for the
things that are of the world, how he may
please *his* wife.
34 There is difference *also* between a
wife and a virgin. The unmarried woman careth for the things of the Lord, that
she may be holy both in body and in
spirit: but she that is married careth for
the things of the world, how she may
please *her* husband.
35 And this I speak for your own profit; not that I may cast a snare upon you,
but for that which is comely, and that ye
may attend upon the Lord without dis-
traction.
36 But if any man think that he
behaveth himself uncomely toward
his virgin, if she pass the flower of *her*
age, and need so require, let him do
what he will, he sinneth not: let them
marry.
37 Nevertheless he that standeth stedfast in his heart, having no necessity, but
hath power over his own will, and hath
so decreed in his heart that he will keep
his virgin, doeth well.
38 So then he that giveth *her* in marriage doeth well; but he that giveth *her*
not in marriage doeth better.
39 The wife is bound by the law as long
as her husband liveth; but if her husband
be dead, she is at liberty to be married
to whom she will; only in the Lord.
40 But she is happier if she so abide,
after my judgment: and I think also that
I have the Spirit of God.

Paul answers another question

8 Now as touching things offered
unto idols, we know that we all have

7:23 be not ye the servants of men. Christians, having been purchased by the blood of Christ, are His servants first of all and should try to please Him rather than men.
7:25 virgins. Unmarried people who are still chaste.
7:39 only in the Lord. A believer must not marry an unsaved person (2 Cor. 6:14; see also its note and 2 Cor. 6:17 note, "Separation").
8:1 as touching things offered. In chapters 8–10 Paul answers another question that he

knowledge. Knowledge puffeth up, but
charity edifieth.
2And if any man think that he
knoweth any thing, he knoweth nothing yet as he ought to know.
3But if any man love God, the same
is known of him.
4As concerning therefore the eating
of those things that are offered in *sacrifice unto idols, we know that an idol
is nothing in the world, and that *there*
is none other God but one.
5For though there be that are called
gods, whether in *heaven or in earth,
(as there be gods many, and lords many,)

8:5 False Gods in New Testament Times

Name	Worshipped by	Reference
Castor, Pollux	the Greeks	Acts 28:11
Diana (Artemis)	all of Asia	Acts 19:28
Jupiter	the Greeks	Acts 14:12
Mercurius	the Greeks	Acts 14:12

6But to us *there is but* one God, the
Father, of whom *are* all things, and we
in him; and one Lord Jesus Christ, by
whom *are* all things, and we by him.
7Howbeit *there is* not in every man
that knowledge: for some with conscience of the idol unto this hour eat *it*
as a thing offered unto an idol; and their
conscience being weak is defiled.
8But meat commendeth us not to
God: for neither, if we eat, are we the
better; neither, if we eat not, are we the
worse.
9But take heed lest by any means this
liberty of yours become a stumblingblock to them that are weak.
10For if any man see thee which hast
knowledge sit at meat in the idol's
temple, shall not the conscience of
him which is weak be emboldened to eat
those things which are offered to idols;
11And through thy knowledge shall
the weak brother perish, for whom
Christ died?
12But when ye sin so against the
brethren, and wound their weak conscience, ye sin against Christ.
13Wherefore, if meat make my
brother to *offend, I will eat no flesh
while the world standeth, lest I make
my brother to offend.

Paul speaks of his Apostleship

9 Am I not an *apostle? am I not free?
have I not seen Jesus Christ our
Lord? are not ye my work in the Lord?
2If I be not an apostle unto others, yet
doubtless I am to you: for the seal of
mine apostleship are ye in the Lord.

9:1-2 Apostles

The word "apostle" is from the Greek, meaning *one who is sent forth, a delegate*. The word is used especially of the Twelve, but also of Paul. All the apostles had seen the Lord, and this was an essential qualification of apostleship in a strict technical sense (Acts 1:21-26; 1 Cor. 9:1-2). Under this limitation, the term was freely applied to prominent teachers in the early Christian church, notably to Barnabas. In two passages Paul places apostles first among the various orders of the church's ministry (1 Cor. 12:28; Eph. 4:11). The word is once applied to Christ Himself (Heb. 3:1).

was asked. Was it right for a Christian to eat the flesh of animals that had been used as a sacrifice to idols?

8:1 charity edifieth. Love builds up.

8:9 take heed. There are some things which, although not perhaps sinful in themselves, should be shunned because the weaker Christian might be made to stumble by them (vs. 13).

8:13 offend. Stumble or fall into sin.

9:1 have I not seen Jesus Christ . . . ? Paul saw the Saviour at his conversion on the Damascus Road (Acts 9:17; 26:16; 1 Cor. 15:8).

9:6 have not we power to forbear working? Paul earned his own living by working with his hands. Yet he had a perfect right to expect to "forbear working" and be supported by those to whom he ministered (see Matt. 10:10). Putting into practice his own teaching, Paul did not always claim his rights (1 Cor 9:15).

3 Mine answer to them that do examine me is this,
4 Have we not power to eat and to
drink?

Paul's right to marry

5 Have we not power to lead about a
sister, a wife, as well as other apostles,
and *as* the brethren of the Lord, and
*Cephas?

Paul's right to receive a salary for his ministry

6 Or I only and Barnabas, have not we
power to forbear working?
7 Who goeth a warfare any time at his
own charges? who planteth a vineyard,
and eateth not of the fruit thereof? or
who feedeth a flock, and eateth not of
the milk of the flock?
8 Say I these things as a man? or saith
not the law the same also?
9 For it is written in the law of *Moses, Thou shalt not muzzle the mouth
of the ox that treadeth out the corn.
Doth God take care for oxen?
10 Or saith he *it* altogether for our
sakes? For our sakes, no doubt, *this* is
written: that he that ploweth should
plow in *hope; and that he that
thresheth in hope should be partaker of
his hope.
11 If we have sown unto you spiritual
things, *is it* a great thing if we shall reap
your carnal things?
12 If others be *partakers of *this*
power over you, *are* not we rather?
Nevertheless we have not used this
power; but suffer all things, lest we
should hinder the *gospel of Christ.
13 Do ye not know that they which
minister about *holy things live *of the
things* of the temple? and they which
wait at the *altar are partakers with the
altar?
14 Even so hath the Lord ordained that
they which preach the gospel should
live of the gospel.
15 But I have used none of these
things: neither have I written these
things, that it should be so done unto
me: for *it were* better for me to die, than
that any man should make my glorying
void.
16 For though I preach the gospel, I
have nothing to glory of: for necessity
is laid upon me; yea, woe is unto me, if
I preach not the gospel!
17 For if I do this thing willingly, I have
a *reward: but if against my will, a dispensation *of the gospel* is committed
unto me.
18 What is my reward then? *Verily*
that, when I preach the gospel, I may
make the gospel of Christ without
charge, that I abuse not my power in the
gospel.

Paul refuses his privileges in order that some may be saved

19 For though I be free from all *men,*
yet have I made myself servant unto all,
that I might gain the more.
20 And unto the Jews I became as a
Jew, that I might gain the Jews; to them
that are under the law, as under the law,
that I might gain them that are under
the law;
21 To them that are without law, as
without law, (being not without law to
God, but under the law to Christ,) that
I might gain them that are without
law.
22 To the weak became I as weak, that
I might gain the weak: I am made all
things to all *men,* that I might by all
means save some.
23 And this I do for the gospel's sake,
that I might be partaker thereof with
you.

9:9 it is written. See Deuteronomy 25:4.
9:11 carnal. Fleshly, of the world (see 1 Cor. 3:1 notes).
9:13 live. Eat (see Lev. 10:12-15).
9:20 unto the Jews I became as a Jew. While Paul was ever faithful to God in his message (being "under law to Christ," vs. 21), yet he adapted himself to different conditions and people, becoming "all things to all men" (vs. 22).

The Christian race

24 Know ye not that they which run in
a race run all, but one receiveth the
prize? So run, that ye may obtain.
25 And every man that striveth for the
mastery is temperate in all things. Now
they *do it* to obtain a corruptible crown;
but we an incorruptible.
26 I therefore so run, not as uncer-
tainly; so fight I, not as one that beateth
the air:
27 But I keep under my body, and
bring *it* into subjection: lest that by any
means, when I have preached to others,
I myself should be a castaway.

Examples for the believer

10 Moreover, brethren, I would not
that ye should be ignorant, how
that all our fathers were under the cloud,
and all passed through the sea;
2 And were all baptized unto Moses in
the cloud and in the sea;
3 And did all eat the same spiritual
meat;
4 And did all drink the same spiritual
drink: for they drank of that spiritual Rock that followed them: and that
Rock was Christ.
5 But with many of them God was not
well pleased: for they were overthrown
in the wilderness.

Steps in backsliding
1) Desire for evil things

6 Now these things were our examples, to the intent we should not *lust
after evil things, as they also lusted.

2) The setting up of that desire as an idol

7 Neither be ye idolaters, as *were*
some of them; as it is written, The people sat down to eat and drink, and rose
up to play.

3) Fellowship with the world

8 Neither let us commit fornication, as
some of them committed, and fell in one
day three and twenty thousand.

4) Unfaithfulness to Christ

9 Neither let us *tempt Christ, as
some of them also tempted, and were
destroyed of serpents.

5) Turning completely to the world

10 Neither murmur ye, as some of
them also murmured, and were destroyed of the destroyer.
11 Now all these things happened unto

9:25 temperate in all things. The Christian life is like running in a race (vs. 24). The good athlete refuses anything that would hinder his pace or endurance. So Christians, whose prize is an eternal one, should say no to all appetites that are harmful.

9:25 crown. Paul desired the incorruptible crown, obtained as a reward for winning men to Christ (1 Thess. 2:19).

9:27 I myself should be a castaway. Just as a tool which is defective would be left off to one side, so it is possible to become a castaway or rejected in God's service. No question of loss of salvation is involved here.

10:1 were under the cloud, and all passed through the sea. That is, the pillar of cloud that guided the Israelites, and the Red Sea through which they passed. Being "baptized unto Moses" (vs. 2) means that they promised to obey and follow him as God's leader for them. See Exodus 14.

10:4 that spiritual Rock that followed them. It is not that the rock or its stream followed them literally. "That Rock was Christ," and He was always with His people in their journeyings.

10:6 our examples. The history of God's ancient people is meant to illustrate spiritual truth for Christians today. They are *types (see also vs. 11).

10:7 as it is written. See Exodus 32:6.

10:8 fell in one day. In Numbers 25:9 the number of deaths given is 24,000, which reflects the total number of deaths "in the plague"; whereas, here is the total number of deaths "in one day"—23,000. This is one of the Bible passages that some believe contains a contradiction between the Old and New Testaments.

10:9 destroyed of serpents. See Numbers 21:6.

them for ensamples: and they are written for our admonition, upon whom the ends of the world are come.

The believer's responsibility

12Wherefore let him that thinketh he standeth take heed lest he fall.
13There hath no temptation taken you but such as is common to man: but God *is* faithful, who will not suffer you to be tempted above that ye are able; but will with the temptation also make a way to escape, that ye may be able to bear *it.*
¶14Wherefore, my dearly beloved, flee from *idolatry.
15I speak as to wise men; judge ye what I say.
16The cup of blessing which we bless, is it not the communion of the *blood of Christ? The bread which we break, is it not the communion of the *body of Christ?
17For we *being* many are one bread, *and* one body: for we are all partakers of that one bread.
18Behold *Israel after the flesh: are not they which eat of the sacrifices partakers of the altar?
19What say I then? that the idol is any thing, or that which is offered in sacrifice to idols is any thing?
20But *I say,* that the things which the Gentiles sacrifice, they sacrifice to devils, and not to God: and I would not that ye should have fellowship with devils.
21Ye cannot drink the cup of the Lord, and the cup of devils: ye cannot be partakers of the Lord's table, and of the table of devils.
22Do we provoke the Lord to jealousy? are we stronger than he?

The law of love

23All things are lawful for me, but all things are not expedient: all things are lawful for me, but all things edify not.
24Let no man seek his own, but every man another's *wealth.*
25Whatsoever is sold in the shambles, *that* eat, asking no question for conscience sake:
26For the earth *is* the Lord's, and the fulness thereof.
27If any of them that believe not bid you *to a feast,* and ye be disposed to go; whatsoever is set before you, eat, asking no question for conscience sake.
28But if any man say unto you, This is offered in sacrifice unto idols, eat not for his sake that shewed it, and for conscience sake: for the earth *is* the Lord's, and the fulness thereof:
29Conscience, I say, not thine own, but of the other: for why is my liberty judged of another *man's* conscience?
30For if I by *grace be a partaker, why am I evil spoken of for that which I give thanks?
31Whether therefore ye eat, or drink, or whatsoever ye do, do all to the glory of God.
32Give none offence, neither to the Jews, nor to the Gentiles, nor to the *church of God:

10:11 world. Age.
10:13 God is faithful. God allows every temptation and gives strength "that ye may be able to bear it." Therefore no Christian ever needs to be defeated.
10:13 will not suffer you. Will not let or allow you.
10:16 The cup of blessing which we bless. This refers to the commemoration of the Lord's Supper, in which "the cup" and the "bread which we break" express the true union of all believers and speak of the Saviour's blood shed and His body given for us all.
10:20 Gentiles. In this verse, the unbelievers.
10:20 fellowship. Communion, as in verse 16.
10:21 Ye cannot. This verse with verse 20 speaks again of the necessity for Christian *separation (see 2 Cor. 6:17 note, "Separation").
10:26 the earth is the Lord's. See Psalm 24:1.
10:31 do all to the glory of God. All questionable things can be decided by the test of whether something will glorify God.

33Even as I please all *men* in all
things, not seeking mine own profit, but
the *profit* of many, that they may be
saved.

The dress of Christians as they meet for worship

11 Be ye followers of me, even as
I also *am* of Christ.
¶2Now I praise you, brethren, that ye
remember me in all things, and keep
the ordinances, as I delivered *them*
to you.
3But I would have you know, that
the head of every man is Christ; and the
head of the woman *is* the man; and the
head of Christ *is* God.
4Every man praying or prophesying,
having *his* head covered, dishonoureth
his head.
5But every woman that prayeth or
prophesieth with *her* head uncovered
dishonoureth her head: for that is even
all one as if she were shaven.
6For if the woman be not covered, let
her also be shorn: but if it be a shame
for a woman to be shorn or shaven, let
her be covered.
7For a man indeed ought not to cover *his* head, forasmuch as he is the image and glory of God: but the woman is
the glory of the man.
8For the man is not of the woman; but
the woman of the man.
9Neither was the man *created for
the woman; but the woman for the
man.
10For this cause ought the woman to
have power on *her* head because of the
*angels.
11Nevertheless neither is the man
without the woman, neither the woman without the man, in the Lord.
12For as the woman *is* of the man,
even so *is* the man also by the woman;
but all things of God.
13Judge in yourselves: is it comely
that a woman pray unto God uncovered?
14Doth not even nature itself teach
you, that, if a man have long hair, it is a
shame unto him?
15But if a woman have long hair, it is
a glory to her: for *her* hair is given her
for a covering.
16But if any man seem to be contentious, we have no such custom, neither
the churches of God.
¶17Now in this that I declare *unto you*
I praise *you* not, that ye come together
not for the better, but for the worse.
18For first of all, when ye come together in the church, I hear that there
be divisions among you; and I partly
believe it.
19For there must be also heresies
among you, that they which are approved may be made manifest among
you.

The order to be followed in celebrating the Lord's Supper

20When ye come together therefore
into one place, *this* is not to eat the
Lord's supper.
21For in eating every one taketh before *other* his own supper: and one is
hungry, and another is drunken.
22What? have ye not houses to eat
and to drink in? or despise ye the
church of God, and shame them that
have not? What shall I say to you?

11:10 power on her head. The woman ought to be under authority, and the head covering, in Corinth, was a sign of her submission to the authority of her husband (Eph. 5:21-24).
11:10 because of the angels. Because of the presence of the angels.
11:13 comely. Suitable or proper.
11:19 heresies. Factions and sects.
11:20 this is not to eat the Lord's supper. The early Christians held a love feast before the Lord's Supper, and the food they each brought was shared by all. Some were greedy and selfish, however, and this caused a bad spirit for the remembrance feast (Communion) that followed.

shall I praise you in this? I praise
you not.
[23]For I have received of the Lord that
which also I delivered unto you, That
the Lord Jesus the *same* night in which
he was betrayed took bread:
[24]And when he had given thanks, he
brake *it,* and said, Take, eat: this is my
body, which is broken for you: this do
in remembrance of me.

11:24 The Symbolic Body
The Saviour Himself is at God's right hand in His glorified body, but the broken bread is a symbol to remind Christians of His body, which was given for them. The drinking of the cup (vs. 25) is in remembrance of His precious blood shed for the remission of sins. This feast should be partaken of only by those whose faith is in Christ, and it is to continue until He comes (vs. 26).

[25]After the same manner also *he took*
the cup, when he had supped, saying,
This *cup is the new *testament in my
blood: this do ye, as oft as ye drink *it,*
in remembrance of me.
[26]For as often as ye eat this bread,
and drink this cup, ye do shew the
Lord's *death till he come.
[27]Wherefore whosoever shall eat this
bread, and drink *this* cup of the Lord,
unworthily, shall be guilty of the body
and blood of the Lord.
[28]But let a man examine himself, and
so let him eat of *that* bread, and drink
of *that* cup.
[29]For he that eateth and drinketh
unworthily, eateth and drinketh *damnation to himself, not discerning the
Lord's body.
[30]For this cause many *are* weak and
sickly among you, and many sleep.
[31]For if we would judge ourselves, we
should not be judged.
[32]But when we are judged, we are
*chastened of the Lord, that we should
not be condemned with the world.
[33]Wherefore, my brethren, when ye
come together to eat, tarry one for another.
[34]And if any man hunger, let him eat
at home; that ye come not together
unto *condemnation. And the rest will
I set in order when I come.

III. Instruction (12:1—16:24)
Concerning spiritual gifts

12 Now concerning spiritual *gifts,*
brethren, I would not have you
ignorant.
[2]Ye know that ye were *Gentiles,
carried away unto these dumb idols,
even as ye were led.
[3]Wherefore I give you to understand,
that no man speaking by the Spirit of
God calleth Jesus accursed: and *that* no
man can say that Jesus is the Lord, but
by the Holy Ghost.
[4]Now there are diversities of gifts,
but the same Spirit.

12:4 Various Gifts
Many people profess to have gifts (special powers) to work miracles, etc., but they may not come from God. If the gifts are truly given by the Spirit (see vss. 8-10), they will exalt Jesus as Lord (vs. 3) and not merely create excitement or sensation and heightened emotions.

11:23 I have received of the Lord. This precious message from the Lord was especially given to the apostle to be passed on to the church.
11:29 eateth and drinketh damnation. The word "damnation" means *judgment.* It does not refer to the eternal condemnation of unbelievers. Partaking unworthily of the Lord's Table may bring some sort of chastisement upon the Christian. This is referred to in verse 30.
11:31 if we would judge ourselves. This means that if Christians would examine themselves and confess their sins before God, the sins would be forgiven and forgotten, and the sinner would escape the judgments of verse 30.
12:1 spiritual gifts. Gifts given by and through the power of the Holy Spirit to strengthen and build up the church and its members.

5 And there are differences of administrations, but the same Lord.

6 And there are diversities of operations, but it is the same God which worketh all in all.

7 But the manifestation of the Spirit is given to every man to profit withal.

8 For to one is given by the Spirit the word of wisdom; to another the word of knowledge by the same Spirit;

9 To another *faith by the same Spirit; to another the gifts of healing by the same Spirit;

10 To another the working of *miracles; to another *prophecy; to another discerning of spirits; to another *divers* kinds of tongues; to another the interpretation of tongues:

11 But all these worketh that one and the selfsame Spirit, dividing to every man severally as he will.

The spiritual Church is one

12 For as the body is one, and hath many members, and all the members of that one body, being many, are one body: so also *is* Christ.

13 For by one Spirit are we all baptized into one body, whether *we be* Jews or Gentiles, whether *we be* bond or free; and have been all made to drink into one Spirit.

14 For the body is not one member, but many.

15 If the foot shall say, Because I am not the hand, I am not of the body; is it therefore not of the body?

16 And if the ear shall say, Because I am not the eye, I am not of the body; is it therefore not of the body?

17 If the whole body *were* an eye, where *were* the hearing? If the whole *were* hearing, where *were* the smelling?

18 But now hath God set the members every one of them in the body, as it hath pleased him.

19 And if they were all one member, where *were* the body?

20 But now *are they* many members, yet but one body.

21 And the eye cannot say unto the hand, I have no need of thee: nor again the head to the feet, I have no need of you.

22 Nay, much more those members of the body, which seem to be more feeble, are necessary:

23 And those *members* of the body, which we think to be less honourable, upon these we bestow more abundant honour; and our uncomely *parts* have more abundant comeliness.

24 For our comely *parts* have no need: but God hath tempered the body together, having given more abundant honour to that *part* which lacked:

25 That there should be no schism in the body; but *that* the members should have the same care one for another.

26 And whether one member suffer, all the members suffer with it; or one member be honoured, all the members rejoice with it.

27 Now ye are the body of Christ, and members in particular.

28 And God hath set some in the church, first *apostles, secondarily *prophets, thirdly teachers, after that miracles, then gifts of healings, helps, governments, diversities of tongues.

29 *Are* all apostles? *are* all prophets? *are* all teachers? *are* all workers of miracles?

30 Have all the gifts of healing? do all speak with tongues? do all interpret?

31 But covet earnestly the best gifts: and yet shew I unto you a more excellent way.

A love-song of victory

13 Though I speak with the tongues of men and of angels,

12:10 prophecy. See 1 Corinthians 14:1 note.
12:25 schism. Division.
12:31 a more excellent way. Love. See chapter 13.
13:1 charity. Love. Without love in the heart, the exercise of gifts or ability is only useless noise.

and have not charity, I am become *as*
sounding brass, or a tinkling cymbal.
2 And though I have *the gift of* prophecy, and understand all *mysteries,
and all knowledge; and though I have
all faith, so that I could remove mountains, and have not charity, I am nothing.
3 And though I bestow all my goods to
feed *the poor,* and though I give my body
to be burned, and have not charity, it
profiteth me nothing.
4 Charity suffereth long, *and* is kind;
charity envieth not; charity vaunteth
not itself, is not puffed up,
5 Doth not behave itself unseemly,
seeketh not her own, is not easily provoked, thinketh no evil;
6 Rejoiceth not in iniquity, but rejoiceth in the truth;
7 Beareth all things, believeth all
things, hopeth all things, endureth all
things.
8 Charity never faileth: but whether
there be prophecies, they shall fail;
whether *there be* tongues, they shall
cease; whether *there be* knowledge, it
shall vanish away.
9 For we know in part, and we prophesy in part.
10 But when that which is perfect is
come, then that which is in part shall be
done away.
11 When I was a child, I spake as a
child, I understood as a child, I thought
as a child: but when I became a man, I
put away childish things.
12 For now we see through a glass,
darkly; but then face to face: now I
know in part; but then shall I know even
as also I am known.
13 And now abideth faith, hope, charity, these three; but the greatest of
these *is* charity.

Prophecy, the greatest gift

14 Follow after charity, and desire
spiritual *gifts,* but rather that ye
may prophesy.
2 For he that speaketh in an *unknown*
tongue speaketh not unto men, but unto
*God: for no man understandeth *him;*
howbeit in the spirit he speaketh mysteries.
3 But he that prophesieth speaketh
unto men *to* edification, and exhortation, and comfort.
4 He that speaketh in an *unknown*
tongue edifieth himself; but he that
prophesieth edifieth the church.
5 I would that ye all spake with
tongues, but rather that ye prophesied:
for greater *is* he that prophesieth than
he that speaketh with tongues, except
he interpret, that the church may receive edifying.
6 Now, brethren, if I come unto you
speaking with tongues, what shall I
profit you, except I shall speak to you
either by *revelation, or by knowledge,
or by prophesying, or by *doctrine?
7 And even things without life giving
sound, whether pipe or harp, except
they give a distinction in the sounds,
how shall it be known what is piped or
harped?
8 For if the trumpet give an uncertain
sound, who shall prepare himself to the
battle?
9 So likewise ye, except ye utter by
the tongue words easy to be understood, how shall it be known what is
spoken? for ye shall speak into the air.

13:4 Charity suffereth long. Notice eight things (vss. 4-6) which love is not: jealous, headstrong, proud, unseemly or inappropriate acting, selfish, irritable, spiteful, or mischievous. It is kind, patient, appreciative, optimistic, and gracious.

13:13 And now abideth. Special gifts may disappear, but these three graces—faith, hope, and love—are given to all believers at all times. Love is the greatest because it will live on into eternity, while faith and hope only endure for the time we're on earth.

14:1 that ye may prophesy. The word "prophesy" here does not mean foretelling the future. Rather, it is the power to understand and to give forth God's truth (1 Thess. 5:20), for edification, exhortation, and comfort (vs. 3).

14:2 unknown tongue. See Acts 2 notes.

[10]There are, it may be, so many kinds
of voices in the *world, and none of
them *is* without signification.
[11]Therefore if I know not the meaning of the voice, I shall be unto him that
speaketh a barbarian, and he that
speaketh *shall be* a barbarian unto me.
[12]Even so ye, forasmuch as ye are
zealous of spiritual *gifts,* seek that ye
may excel to the edifying of the church.
[13]Wherefore let him that speaketh in
an *unknown* tongue pray that he may
interpret.
[14]For if I pray in an *unknown* tongue,
my spirit prayeth, but my understanding is unfruitful.
[15]What is it then? I will pray with the
spirit, and I will pray with the understanding also: I will sing with the spirit,
and I will sing with the understanding
also.
[16]Else when thou shalt bless with
the spirit, how shall he that occupieth
the room of the unlearned say *Amen
at thy giving of thanks, seeing he understandeth not what thou sayest?
[17]For thou verily givest thanks well,
but the other is not edified.
[18]I thank my God, I speak with
tongues more than ye all:
[19]Yet in the church I had rather speak
five words with my understanding, that
by my voice I might teach others also,
than ten thousand words in an *unknown*
tongue.
[20]Brethren, be not children in understanding: howbeit in malice be ye children, but in understanding be men.
[21]In the *law it is written, With *men
of* other tongues and other lips will I
speak unto this people; and yet for all
that will they not hear me, saith the
Lord.

The sign of tongues

[22]Wherefore tongues are for a sign,
not to them that believe, but to them
that believe not: but prophesying *serveth*
not for them that believe not, but for
them which believe.
[23]If therefore the whole church be
come together into one place, and all
speak with tongues, and there come in
those that are unlearned, or *unbelievers, will they not say that ye are mad?
[24]But if all prophesy, and there come
in one that believeth not, or *one* unlearned, he is convinced of all, he is
judged of all:
[25]And thus are the secrets of his
heart made manifest; and so falling
down on *his* face he will worship God,
and report that God is in you of a truth.
[26]How is it then, brethren? when ye
come together, every one of you hath a
psalm, hath a doctrine, hath a tongue,
hath a revelation, hath an interpretation. Let all things be done unto edifying.
[27]If any man speak in an *unknown*
tongue, *let it be* by two, or at the most
by three, and *that* by course; and let one
interpret.
[28]But if there be no interpreter, let
him keep silence in the church; and let
him speak to himself, and to God.
[29]Let the prophets speak two or
three, and let the other judge.
[30]If *any thing* be revealed to another
that sitteth by, let the first hold his
peace.
[31]For ye may all prophesy one by one,
that all may learn, and all may be comforted.
[32]And the spirits of the prophets are
subject to the prophets.
[33]For God is not *the author* of confusion, but of peace, as in all churches of
the *saints.
[34]Let your women keep silence in the
churches: for it is not permitted unto
them to speak; but *they are commanded* to be under obedience, as also saith
the law.
[35]And if they will learn any thing, let
them ask their husbands at home: for

14:21 it is written. See Isaiah 28:11.
14:27 by course. In order, each in turn.

it is a shame for women to speak in the
church.
36 What? came the word of God out
from you? or came it unto you only?
37 If any man think himself to be a
*prophet, or spiritual, let him acknowl-
edge that the things that I write unto you
are the commandments of the Lord.
38 But if any man be ignorant, let him
be ignorant.
39 Wherefore, brethren, covet to
prophesy, and forbid not to speak with
tongues.
40 Let all things be done decently and
in order.

The Gospel of the Resurrection

15 Moreover, brethren, I declare
unto you the *gospel which I
preached unto you, which also ye have
received, and wherein ye stand;
2 By which also ye are saved, if ye
keep in memory what I preached unto
you, unless ye have believed in vain.
3 For I delivered unto you first of all
that which I also received, how that
*Christ died for our sins according to
the scriptures;
4 And that he was buried, and that he
rose again the third day according to the
scriptures:
5 And that he was seen of *Cephas,
then of the twelve:
6 After that, he was seen of above five
hundred brethren at once; of whom the
greater part remain unto this present,
but some are fallen asleep.
7 After that, he was seen of James;
then of all the apostles.
8 And last of all he was seen of me
also, as of one born out of due time.
9 For I am the least of the apostles, that
am not meet to be called an *apostle,
because I persecuted the church of God.
10 But by the *grace of God I am what
I am: and his grace which *was bestowed*
upon me was not in vain; but I laboured
more abundantly than they all: yet not I,
but the grace of God which was with me.
11 Therefore whether *it were* I or they,
so we preach, and so ye believed.
12 Now if Christ be preached that he
rose from the dead, how say some
among you that there is no *resurrection of the dead?
13 But if there be no resurrection of
the dead, then is Christ not risen:
14 And if Christ be not risen, then *is*
our preaching vain, and your faith *is* also
vain.
15 Yea, and we are found false witnesses of God; because we have testified of God that he raised up Christ:
whom he raised not up, if so be that the
dead rise not.
16 For if the dead rise not, then is not
Christ raised:
17 And if Christ be not raised, your
faith *is* vain; ye are yet in your sins.
18 Then they also which are fallen
asleep in Christ are perished.
19 If in this life only we have *hope
in Christ, we are of all men most miserable.

14:37 the commandments of the Lord. Paul had written this letter to the Corinthians by *inspiration.

15:4 he rose again. By the death of Christ on the cross, God's righteous demands are fully satisfied. Because of His resurrection, guilty sinners may receive the salvation that He purchased (see Rom. 4:25).

15:8 he was seen of me also. See 1 Corinthians 9:1 note and 1 Corinthians 9:1-2 note, "Apostles."

15:8 born out of due time. Paul knew that Israel as a nation was to be born again through their belief in Jesus Christ at some future time (see Matt. 23:39). Paul was born again before that time of national belief.

15:14 if Christ be not risen. Obviously, a dead Christ is powerless to save sinners. In raising Him from the dead, God showed His satisfaction with the Saviour's finished work on the cross.

15:18 they also which are fallen asleep. If Christ had not risen from the dead, then nobody else could be raised.

The order of resurrections

[20]But now is Christ risen from the
dead, *and* become the firstfruits of
them that slept.
[21]For since by man *came* death, by
man *came* also the resurrection of the
dead.
[22]For as in *Adam all die, even so in
Christ shall all be made alive.
[23]But every man in his own order:
Christ the firstfruits; afterward they
that are Christ's at his coming.
[24]Then *cometh* the end, when he shall
have delivered up the *kingdom to God,
even the Father; when he shall have put
down all rule and all authority and
power.
[25]For he must reign, till he hath put
all enemies under his feet.
[26]The last enemy *that* shall be destroyed *is* death.
[27]For he hath put all things under his
feet. But when he saith, all things are
put under *him, it is* manifest that he is
excepted, which did put all things under him.
[28]And when all things shall be subdued unto him, then shall the Son also
himself be subject unto him that put all
things under him, that God may be all
in all.
[29]Else what shall they do which are
baptized for the dead, if the dead rise
not at all? why are they then baptized
for the dead?

15:24 The Kingdom
Christ is now seated at the right hand of God, but after He comes for His own (1 Thess. 4:17), He will return in power with them to set up His kingdom on earth. See *Rapture and *Second Coming. The promise given to David (2 Sam. 7:1-17; see also 2 Sam. 7:11 note, "The Davidic Covenant") will be fulfilled, for Christ, in His humanity through His mother Mary, is descended from David. Israel will be gathered once again as a nation, and Jesus Christ will reign as King for one thousand years, the *Millennium (Matt. 24:27-30; Luke 1:31-33; Acts 15:14-17; Rev. 20:1-10). At the end of this time, the Son will turn the kingdom over to the Father, that God may be "all in all" (vs. 28). The throne will then be that of "God and of the Lamb" (Rev. 22:1). See further notes on *kingdom.

[30]And why stand we in jeopardy
every hour?
[31]I protest by your rejoicing which I
have in Christ Jesus our Lord, I die
daily.
[32]If after the manner of men I have
fought with beasts at Ephesus, what
advantageth it me, if the dead rise not?
let us eat and drink; for to morrow we
die.
[33]Be not deceived: evil communications corrupt good manners.
[34]Awake to *righteousness, and *sin
not; for some have not the knowledge
of God: I speak *this* to your shame.

15:20 the firstfruits of them that slept. Christ was the first to be raised into an endless life over which death could have no power. Some had been raised from the dead previously, but they tasted death again. (Death had no dominion over Christ because He was sinless.) He is the resurrection *firstfruits, and the raising of believers will be the resurrection harvest.

15:22 as in Adam all die. By natural birth all are in Adam and are therefore dead in sins (Eph. 2:1). By being born again we are made alive in Christ. The unsaved person is still in Adam and dead in his sins. The saved person is in Christ.

15:25 he must reign. The great purpose of redemption is not only that we might be saved, but that Christ may reign supreme. He is the mighty conqueror of every enemy, even death itself (vs. 26). His full victory will be known in the world at the end of time and the beginning of eternity.

15:31 I die daily. Paul means that he was constantly exposed to death for Christ's sake. Remember also that "self" must also "die daily," even moment by moment, if Christ is to fill the throne of the heart. See also Galatians 2:20. "Crucifixion" means *death*.

15:32 let us eat and drink. Paul is quoting Isaiah 22:13.

How the dead are raised

¶35But some *man* will say, How are
the dead raised up? and with what body
do they come?
36*Thou* fool, that which thou sowest
is not quickened, except it die:
37And that which thou sowest, thou
sowest not that body that shall be, but
bare grain, it may chance of wheat, or
of some other *grain:*
38But God giveth it a body as it hath
pleased him, and to every seed his own
body.
39All flesh *is* not the same flesh: but
there is one *kind of* flesh of men, another
flesh of beasts, another of fishes, *and*
another of *birds.
40*There are* also celestial bodies, and
bodies terrestrial: but the glory of the
celestial *is* one, and the *glory* of the terrestrial *is* another.
41*There is* one glory of the sun, and
another glory of the moon, and another
glory of the stars: for *one* star differeth
from *another* star in glory.
42So also *is* the resurrection of the
dead. It is sown in corruption; it is
raised in incorruption:
43It is sown in dishonour; it is raised
in glory: it is sown in weakness; it is
raised in power:
44It is sown a natural body; it is raised
a spiritual body. There is a natural body,
and there is a spiritual body.
45And so it is written, The first man
Adam was made a living soul; the *last
Adam *was made* a quickening spirit.
46Howbeit that *was* not first which is
spiritual, but that which is natural; and
afterward that which is spiritual.
47The first man *is* of the earth,
earthy: the second man *is* the Lord from
*heaven.
48As *is* the earthy, such *are* they also
that are earthy: and as *is* the heavenly,
such *are* they also that are heavenly.
49And as we have borne the image of
the earthy, we shall also bear the *image of the heavenly.
50Now this I say, brethren, that flesh

15:29 A CLARIFICATION

Verses 20-28 are parenthetical; verse 29 follows verse 19 in thought: "If in this life only we have hope in Christ, we are of all men most miserable. . . . Else what shall they do which are baptized for the dead, if the dead rise not at all? why are they then baptized for the dead?" Many had died for Christ's sake under persecution; other believers had gone to their graves in a normal way; but all of these had their hope fixed in the Lord, faithfully believing that by His resurrection, their resurrection–the resurrection of the dead in Christ–was assured.

As one by one Christians died or were slain, others came along in place of the dead to make up the living organism on earth, the remnant on earth, the *church, who would bear testimony to Jesus' name. If in this life only there was hope in Christ (vs. 19), why would generation after generation be baptized in the place of the dead? If in this life only there is hope, why identify oneself with Christ by baptism, and in this way invite persecution? The next verse goes on with this thought: "And why stand we in jeopardy every hour?" (vs. 30).

15:35 with what body do they come? This verse proves the actual resurrection of the body. But here is a mystery: While the same body is raised, yet it is transformed from a natural body into a spiritual body (vs. 44).
15:36 quickened. Made alive.
15:42 So also is the resurrection. While all Christians possess resurrection life and will therefore possess spiritual bodies (Phil. 3:21), not all will enjoy an equal measure of eternal glory (1 Cor. 15:41). Glory there depends upon grace here.
15:45 And so it is written. See Genesis 2:7.
15:45 was made. Adam became.
15:45 a quickening spirit. We also have been quickened because of Christ's work (Eph. 2:1). The Last Adam, Jesus Christ, is a life-giving Spirit.

and blood cannot inherit the *kingdom
of God; neither doth corruption inherit
incorruption.

Victory over death

[51]Behold, I shew you a *mystery; We
shall not all sleep, but we shall all be
changed,
[52]In a moment, in the twinkling of an
eye, at the last trump: for the trumpet
shall sound, and the dead shall be raised
incorruptible, and we shall be changed.
[53]For this corruptible must put on
incorruption, and this mortal *must* put
on immortality.
[54]So when this corruptible shall have
put on incorruption, and this mortal
shall have put on immortality, then shall
be brought to pass the saying that is
written, Death is swallowed up in victory.
[55]O death, where *is* thy sting? O grave,
where *is* thy victory?
[56]The sting of death *is* sin; and the
strength of sin *is* the law.
[57]But thanks *be* to God, which giveth
us the victory through our Lord Jesus
Christ.
[58]Therefore, my beloved brethren, be
ye stedfast, unmovable, always abounding in the work of the Lord, forasmuch
as ye know that your labour is not in
vain in the Lord.

The offering for the saints

16 Now concerning the collection
for the saints, as I have given
order to the churches of Galatia, even
so do ye.
[2]Upon the first *day* of the week let
every one of you lay by him in store, as
God hath prospered him, that there be
no gatherings when I come.
[3]And when I come, whomsoever ye
shall approve by *your* letters, them will
I send to bring your liberality unto Jerusalem.
[4]And if it be meet that I go also, they
shall go with me.
[5]Now I will come unto you, when I

15:52 A FINAL RESURRECTION

God revealed to Moses, to Job, to David, to Isaiah, and to Daniel the fact that there would be a resurrection (see Gen. 22:5 with Heb. 11:19; Job 19:25-27; Pss. 16:9-11; 17:14-15; Isa. 26:19; Dan. 12:2). There were dead who were raised by miracles in Old Testament times as well as in New Testament times (2 Kings 4:32-35; 13:21; Matt. 9:25; Luke 7:12-15; John 11:43-44). Jesus Christ said that He would arise from the dead (John 10:18; Luke 24:1-8), and He gave His apostles power to raise the dead (Matt. 10:8), which they did do (Acts 9:36-41; 20:9-10).

At the time that the Lord Himself was raised, there was a resurrection of bodies of others who had died (Matt. 27:52-53). When Christ comes for His own (1 Cor. 15:23), there will be a resurrection "of life" of all those who have died in Christ (1 Thess. 4:16). One thousand years later there will be a resurrection "of judgment" (Rev. 20:5,11-13) of unbelievers. However, some who are alive on the earth at the time of 1 Corinthians 15:23 and who are not believers will be saved during the coming *Tribulation and will die as martyrs during that awful time. These will be raised at the end of that period and will be counted as having a part in the first resurrection (Rev. 20:4).

Sickness and death will have no power over the glorious resurrection bodies of believers, for they will be as our Lord is (1 John 3:2). No one knows what the raised bodies of believers will be like, except that they will be like the Lord's resurrection body.

15:50 flesh and blood cannot inherit. Human flesh and blood are defiled by sin. One must have a sinless body in order to live in a sinless heaven.

15:51 We shall not all sleep. This refers to the *Rapture, the catching away of believers at His coming (1 Thess. 4:15-17). One generation of believers, alive on the earth at the time, escape death. Whether they sleep or not, however, all will be changed. The word "mortal" refers to those who are alive, "corruptible" to those who sleep.

16:2 Upon the first day of the week. Giving money to God's work should be done with method, not carelessly as to time or amount.

16:2 gatherings. Collections of money for offerings.

shall pass through Macedonia: for I do
pass through Macedonia.
6And it may be that I will abide, yea,
and winter with you, that ye may bring
me on my journey whithersoever I go.
7For I will not see you now by the
way; but I trust to tarry a while with
you, if the Lord permit.
8But I will tarry at Ephesus until Pentecost.
9For a great door and effectual is
opened unto me, and *there are* many
adversaries.

Final instructions

10Now if Timotheus come, see that
he may be with you without fear: for
he worketh the work of the Lord, as I
also *do.*
11Let no man therefore despise him:
but conduct him forth in peace, that he
may come unto me: for I look for him
with the brethren.
12As touching *our* brother Apollos, I
greatly desired him to come unto you
with the brethren: but his will was not
at all to come at this time; but he will
come when he shall have convenient
time.
13Watch ye, stand fast in the faith,
quit you like men, be strong.
14Let all your things be done with
charity.
15I beseech you, brethren, (ye know
the house of Stephanas, that it is the
firstfruits of Achaia, and *that* they have
addicted themselves to the ministry of
the saints,)
16That ye submit yourselves unto
such, and to every one that helpeth with
us, and laboureth.
17I am glad of the coming of Stephanas and Fortunatus and Achaicus: for
that which was lacking on your part
they have supplied.
18For they have refreshed my spirit
and yours: therefore acknowledge ye
them that are such.

Closing greetings

¶19The churches of Asia salute you.
Aquila and Priscilla salute you much in
the Lord, with the church that is in their
house.
20All the brethren greet you. Greet
ye one another with an holy kiss.

A postscript written by Paul's own hand

21The salutation of *me* Paul with mine
own hand.
22If any man love not the Lord Jesus
Christ, let him be Anathema Maranatha.

16:22 A Postscript
This little postscript to a dictated letter, added in Paul's own handwriting, refers to the terrible danger of not loving Christ. "Anathema" means *cast away;* "Maranatha" means *the Lord cometh.* The two words joined would suggest the judgment of unbelievers at the coming of the Lord. His coming will mean either salvation or judgment, depending on the state of each person's heart.

23The grace of our Lord Jesus Christ
be with you.
24My love *be* with you all in Christ
Jesus. Amen.

16:15 Stephanas. A Christian at Corinth, whose family Paul baptized (1 Cor. 1:16). Fortunatus and Achaicus (vs. 17) probably belonged to this family.

The Second Epistle of Paul the Apostle to the

CORINTHIANS

BACKGROUND

It is agreed that Paul wrote this second letter, probably at Philippi, to the Corinthians as an *apologist.* This does not mean that he had something for which to apologize! Certain charges had been brought against him, and he defended himself in these answers. His *apology,* in this sense, was a defense of his ministry and of himself as a servant of the Lord. The epistle shows that God was his Defense and Comforter amid all the unkind attacks that were made upon his character and conduct. See 2 Corinthians 1:12-24; 2:17; 3:1-6; 4:1-5; 6:3-10; 7:2; 10:1—12:13.

THE TIME

This book was written in A.D. 58.

OUTLINE OF 2 CORINTHIANS

The letter does not divide easily into sections, but it may be roughly outlined as follows:

I.	Explanation	2 Corinthians 1:1—7:16
II.	Exhortation	2 Corinthians 8:1—9:15
III.	Vindication	2 Corinthians 10:1—13:14

I. Explanation (1:1—7:16)

*Joy in *Christ even in tribulation*

1 Paul, an *apostle of Jesus Christ
by the will of God, and *Timothy
our brother, unto the church of God
which is at Corinth, with all the *saints
which are in all Achaia:
2*Grace *be* to you and *peace from
God our Father, and *from* the Lord Jesus
Christ.
¶3Blessed *be* God, even the Father of
our Lord Jesus Christ, the Father of
mercies, and the God of all comfort;
4Who comforteth us in all our tribulation, that we may be able to comfort
them which are in any trouble, by the
comfort wherewith we ourselves are
comforted of God.
5For as the sufferings of Christ
abound in us, so our consolation also
aboundeth by Christ.
6And whether we be afflicted, *it is* for
your consolation and *salvation, which
is effectual in the enduring of the same
sufferings which we also suffer: or
whether we be comforted, *it is* for your
consolation and salvation.
7And our *hope of you *is* stedfast,
knowing, that as ye are *partakers of
the sufferings, so *shall ye be* also of the
consolation.
8For we would not, brethren, have

1:1 unto the church . . . at Corinth. See the introduction to 1 Corinthians.

1:5 the sufferings of Christ. Persecutions because of faithfulness to the Lord Jesus Christ.

1:6-8 Suffering for Christ
What Paul himself suffered for the sake of the Lord Jesus Christ and His people, and the comfort he received, were intended to encourage others to also suffer for Christ's sake. Throughout this letter "comfort" means *encouragement*.

The great trouble mentioned in verse 8 occurred while Paul was in Asia. It probably resulted in great physical strain and severe illness for the apostle.

you ignorant of our trouble which came
to us in Asia, that we were pressed out
of measure, above strength, insomuch
that we despaired even of life:
9 But we had the sentence of *death
in ourselves, that we should not *trust
in ourselves, but in God which raiseth
the dead:
10 Who delivered us from so great a
death, and doth deliver: in whom we
trust that he will yet deliver *us;*
11 Ye also helping together by *prayer
for us, that for the gift *bestowed* upon us
by the means of many persons thanks
may be given by many on our behalf.

Paul explains his failure to visit the Corinthians

¶ 12 For our rejoicing is this, the testimony of our conscience, that in simplicity and godly sincerity, not with fleshly
wisdom, but by the *grace of God, we
have had our *conversation in the
*world, and more abundantly to you-
ward.
13 For we write none other things
unto you, than what ye read or acknowledge; and I trust ye shall acknowledge
even to the end;
14 As also ye have acknowledged us in
part, that we are your rejoicing, even as
ye also *are* ours in the day of the Lord
Jesus.
¶ 15 And in this confidence I was
minded to come unto you before, that ye
might have a second benefit;
16 And to pass by you into Macedonia,
and to come again out of Macedonia
unto you, and of you to be brought on
my way toward Judaea.
17 When I therefore was thus minded,
did I use lightness? or the things that I
purpose, do I purpose according to the
flesh, that with me there should be yea
yea, and nay nay?
18 But *as* God *is* true, our word toward
you was not yea and nay.
19 For the Son of God, Jesus Christ,
who was preached among you by us,
even by me and *Silvanus and *Timotheus, was not yea and nay, but in him
was yea.
20 For all the promises of God in him
are yea, and in him *Amen, unto the
glory of God by us.
21 Now he which stablisheth us with
you in Christ, and hath anointed us,
is God;
22 Who hath also sealed us, and given
the earnest of the Spirit in our hearts.
23 Moreover I call God for a record
upon my soul, that to spare you I came
not as yet unto Corinth.
24 Not for that we have dominion over
your *faith, but are helpers of your joy:
for by faith ye stand.

1:10 Who delivered us from so great a death. Paul evidently thought that the end of his time upon earth had come, but God had further work for Paul to do.
1:12 in the world. Among mankind.
1:15 I was minded to come unto you before. See 1 Corinthians 16:5.
1:17 do I purpose according to the flesh . . . ? The will of God, not his own personal pleasure or convenience, was the one thing that mattered to the apostle Paul.
1:20 the promises of God in him are yea, and in him Amen. "Yea" refers to the definite promise, and "Amen" (which means *so be it*) is the fulfillment of the promise. Both are sure in Him.
1:22 the earnest of the Spirit. The promise or pledge of the Spirit.
1:24 Not for that we have dominion. The Corinthians were responsible to God, not to Paul, just as any Christian is only responsible to God in matters of faith.

The moral condition of
the Corinthians

2 But I determined this with myself,
that I would not come again to you
in heaviness.
2 For if I make you sorry, who is he
then that maketh me glad, but the same
which is made sorry by me?
3 And I wrote this same unto you, lest,
when I came, I should have sorrow from
them of whom I ought to rejoice; having confidence in you all, that my joy is
the joy of you all.
4 For out of much affliction and anguish of heart I wrote unto you with
many tears; not that ye should be
grieved, but that ye might know the
love which I have more abundantly unto
you.

Forgiveness follows true repentance

5 But if any have caused grief, he hath
not grieved me, but in part: that I may
not overcharge you all.
6 Sufficient to such a man *is* this
punishment, which *was inflicted* of
many.
7 So that contrariwise ye *ought* rather to forgive *him,* and comfort *him,* lest
perhaps such a one should be swallowed up with overmuch sorrow.
8 Wherefore I beseech you that ye
would confirm *your* love toward him.
9 For to this end also did I write, that
I might know the proof of you, whether ye be obedient in all things.
10 To whom ye forgive any thing, I *forgive* also: for if I forgave any thing, to
whom I forgave *it,* for your sakes *forgave I it* in the person of Christ;
11 Lest *Satan should get an advantage of us: for we are not ignorant of his
devices.

Paul ministers the Word as led
by the Spirit

12 Furthermore, when I came to Troas to *preach* Christ's *gospel, and a door
was opened unto me of the Lord,
13 I had no rest in my spirit, because I
found not *Titus my brother: but taking my leave of them, I went from
thence into Macedonia.

Minister in triumph

14 Now thanks *be* unto God, which always causeth us to triumph in Christ,
and maketh manifest the savour of his
knowledge by us in every place.

2:14 The Triumph
Verse 14 is a verse with a vision. The writer sees in his mind's eye a Roman conqueror leading a homeward march of triumph after the battle. Paul declares himself to be one of Christ's captives, and following his great Captain, is led on from place to place in the triumphant march. The victory was being celebrated in different places. So the Christian enjoys a victory already won by the Saviour.

15 For we are unto God a sweet savour
of Christ, in them that are saved, and in
them that perish:
16 To the one *we are* the savour of
death unto death; and to the other the
savour of life unto life. And who *is* sufficient for these things?
17 For we are not as many, which corrupt the word of God: but as of sincerity, but as of God, in the sight of God
speak we in Christ.

The Corinthians are Paul's letters
of recommendation

3 Do we begin again to commend
ourselves? or need we, as some
others, epistles of commendation to you,

2:1 in heaviness. To reproach you.
2:4 I wrote. Paul is speaking of his first epistle to the Corinthians.
2:6 punishment. This means *censure* or *blame.*
2:11 we are not ignorant of his devices. Christians must always remember that Satan is a very wily enemy, and we should see to it that he does not "get an advantage" (compare 1 Cor. 5:5; see also its note, "God Uses Satan").
2:16 To the one we are the savour of death. The same glorious gospel that proclaims life to the believer is also a message of judgment and death to the unbeliever.

or *letters* of commendation from you?

2 Ye are our epistle written in our hearts, known and read of all men:

3 *Forasmuch as ye are* manifestly declared to be the epistle of Christ ministered by us, written not with ink, but with the Spirit of the living God; not in tables of stone, but in fleshy tables of the heart.

¶4 And such trust have we through Christ to God-ward:

5 Not that we are sufficient of ourselves to think any thing as of ourselves; but our sufficiency *is* of God;

Minister in boldness

6 Who also hath made us able ministers of the new *testament; not of the letter, but of the spirit: for the letter killeth, but the spirit giveth life.

7 But if the ministration of death, written *and* engraven in stones, was glorious, so that the children of *Israel could not stedfastly behold the face of *Moses for the glory of his countenance; which *glory* was to be done away:

8 How shall not the ministration of the spirit be rather glorious?

9 For if the ministration of *condemnation *be* glory, much more doth the ministration of *righteousness exceed in glory.

10 For even that which was made glorious had no glory in this respect, by reason of the glory that excelleth.

11 For if that which is done away *was* glorious, much more that which remaineth *is* glorious.

12 Seeing then that we have such hope, we use great plainness of speech:

13 And not as Moses, *which* put a vail over his face, that the children of Israel could not stedfastly look to the end of that which is abolished:

14 But their minds were blinded: for until this day remaineth the same vail untaken away in the reading of the old testament; which *vail* is done away in Christ.

15 But even unto this day, when Moses is read, the vail is upon their heart.

16 Nevertheless when it shall turn to the Lord, the vail shall be taken away.

17 Now the Lord is that Spirit: and where the Spirit of the Lord *is,* there *is* liberty.

18 But we all, with open face beholding as in a glass the *glory of the Lord, are changed into the same image from glory to glory, *even* as by the Spirit of the Lord.

Minister in honesty

4 Therefore seeing we have this ministry, as we have received *mercy, we faint not;

2 But have renounced the hidden things of dishonesty, not walking in craftiness, nor handling the word of

---

3:2 Ye are our epistle. The day-by-day life of every Christian is an epistle (or letter) that other people read.

3:6 the letter killeth, but the spirit giveth life. The *Law shows the sinfulness of the sinner and therefore condemns him; but grace brings life and salvation.

3:7 the ministration of death. The *Law; see verse 6 note. See also Exodus 34:29-35.

3:7 was glorious. Began with glory.

3:14 until this day remaineth the same vail. The unbelieving Jews are still blinded to the glory of the gospel because they do not accept the New Testament as the fulfillment and explanation of the Old. The veil is removed when the Lord is personally received (vs. 16).

3:16 it. The heart.

3:17 the Lord is that Spirit. The Spirit of verse 6, who giveth life.

3:18 changed into the same image. As a believer keeps his eye on the Saviour, so he becomes more holy and Christlike. He reflects the divine glory as a mirror reflects the sunshine.

4:1 as we have received mercy, we faint not. Those who have received Christ can be victorious over all fears as they proclaim the gospel, but they cannot give it out to others until they have themselves received it.

God deceitfully; but by manifestation of
the truth commending ourselves to
every man's conscience in the sight
of God.
3But if our gospel be hid, it is hid to
them that are lost:
4In whom the god of this world hath
blinded the minds of them which believe not, lest the light of the glorious
gospel of Christ, who is the image of
God, should shine unto them.
5For we preach not ourselves, but
Christ Jesus the Lord; and ourselves
your servants for Jesus' sake.
6For God, who commanded the light
to shine out of darkness, hath shined
in our hearts, to *give* the light of the
knowledge of the glory of God in the
face of Jesus Christ.
¶7But we have this treasure in earth-
en vessels, that the excellency of the
power may be of God, and not of us.

Afflictions light for Christ (Rom. 8:18)

8*We are* troubled on every side, yet
not distressed; *we are* perplexed, but
not in despair;
9Persecuted, but not forsaken; cast
down, but not destroyed;
10Always bearing about in the body
the dying of the Lord Jesus, that the life
also of Jesus might be made manifest in
our body.
11For we which live are alway delivered unto death for Jesus' sake, that the
life also of Jesus might be made manifest in our mortal flesh.
12So then death worketh in us, but life
in you.
13We having the same spirit of faith,
according as it is written, I believed, and
therefore have I spoken; we also believe, and therefore speak;
14Knowing that he which raised up
the Lord Jesus shall raise up us also by
Jesus, and shall present *us* with you.
15For all things *are* for your sakes,
that the abundant grace might through
the thanksgiving of many redound to
the glory of God.
16For which cause we faint not; but
though our outward man perish, yet the
inward *man* is renewed day by day.
17For our light affliction, which is
but for a moment, worketh for us a far
more exceeding *and* eternal weight of
glory;
18While we look not at the things
which are seen, but at the things which
are not seen: for the things which are
seen *are* temporal; but the things which
are not seen *are* eternal.

Christians need not fear death

5 For we know that if our earthly
house of *this* *tabernacle were dissolved, we have a building of God, an
house not made with hands, eternal in
the heavens.
2For in this we groan, earnestly de-

4:2 manifestation. A clear, true statement of the gospel.
4:3 if our gospel be hid. The unsaved are blinded by Satan; therefore, they cannot see the glory of the gospel (vs. 4).
4:4 the god of this world. This refers to Satan. Compare the Lord's own words in John 12:31; 14:30; 16:11. See also Ephesians 2:2.
4:5 we preach not ourselves, but Christ Jesus the Lord. The lordship of Christ, as well as His power to save from sin, should be the theme of every true minister.
4:6 God, who commanded the light. See John 1:5,9.
4:7 earthen vessels. Our human bodies.
4:10 bearing about in the body the dying of the Lord Jesus. First of all, this refers to the apostle's physical sufferings for Christ's sake, but it also suggests that the self-life must be mortified and put to death daily so that the mortal body may show forth the life of Jesus also (vs. 11). See 2 Corinthians 5:14 note; see also 1 Corinthians 15:31 note.
4:13 according as it is written. See Psalm 116:10.
5:1 an house not made with hands. This is the spiritual body that believers receive at the resurrection, in contrast to the earthly house (the natural body), which is like a tent in the sense that it is just a temporary abiding place (see 1 Cor. 15:40,42-44).

siring to be clothed upon with our
house which is from *heaven:
[3]If so be that being clothed we shall
not be found naked.
[4]For we that are in *this* tabernacle do
groan, being burdened: not for that we
would be unclothed, but clothed upon,
that mortality might be swallowed up
of life.
[5]Now he that hath wrought us for
the selfsame thing *is* God, who also
hath given unto us the *earnest of the
Spirit.
[6]Therefore *we are* always confident,
knowing that, whilst we are at home in
the body, we are absent from the Lord:
[7](For we walk by faith, not by sight:)
[8]We are confident, *I say,* and willing
rather to be absent from the body, and
to be present with the Lord.
[9]Wherefore we labour, that, whether
present or absent, we may be accepted
of him.
[10]For we must all appear before the
*judgment seat of Christ; that every
one may receive the things *done* in *his*
body, according to that he hath done,
whether *it be* good or bad.
¶[11]Knowing therefore the terror of
the Lord, we persuade men; but we are
made manifest unto God; and I trust
also are made manifest in your consciences.
[12]For we commend not ourselves
again unto you, but give you occasion
to glory on our behalf, that ye may have
somewhat to *answer* them which glory
in appearance, and not in heart.
[13]For whether we be beside ourselves, *it is* to God: or whether we be
sober, *it is* for your cause.

Minister in love

[14]For the love of Christ constraineth
us; because we thus judge, that if one
died for all, then were all dead:
[15]And *that* he died for all, that they
which live should not henceforth live
unto themselves, but unto him which
died for them, and rose again.
[16]Wherefore henceforth know we no
man after the flesh: yea, though we
have known Christ after the flesh, yet
now henceforth know we *him* no more.
[17]Therefore if any man *be* in Christ,
he is a new creature: old things are
passed away; behold, all things are become new.
[18]And all things *are* of God, who hath
reconciled us to himself by Jesus
Christ, and hath given to us the ministry of reconciliation;
[19]To wit, that God was in Christ, reconciling the world unto himself, not
imputing their trespasses unto them;
and hath committed unto us the word
of reconciliation.
[20]Now then we are ambassadors for

5:3 we shall not be found naked. Nakedness is the result of sin. Unbelievers are spiritually naked and can never be clothed with the glorified body that Christians will enjoy.
5:9 labour. Are ambitious—make it a point of honor.
5:9 accepted of him. Well pleasing to God.
5:10 we must all appear before the judgment seat. This must not be confused with the Great White Throne Judgment before which unbelievers will appear. All Christians will appear before the judgment seat of Christ (see 1 Cor. 3:12 notes, especially "Building Materials").
5:14 if one died for all, then were all dead. All believers are regarded by God as having died with Christ upon the cross (Rom. 6:6). The old self-life must therefore be considered dead by faith (Rom. 6:11).
5:16 know we him no more. We have entered a new relationship with Christ through the Spirit, so the old fleshly relationship (or lack of relationship) is over.
5:17 creature. Creation.
5:18 the ministry of reconciliation. All Christians should share this ministry, that is, the privilege of telling sinners that they may be "reconciled to God" (vs. 20).
5:19 the world. Mankind.
5:20 ambassadors. Speaking the Word of and working as led by Christ our King.

Christ, as though God did beseech *you*
by us: we pray *you* in Christ's stead, be
ye reconciled to God.
21For he hath made him *to be* *sin for
us, who knew no sin; that we might be
made the righteousness of God in him.

A true minister of the gospel

6 We then, *as* workers together *with
him,* beseech *you* also that ye receive not the *grace of God in vain.
2(For he saith, I have heard thee in a
time accepted, and in the day of salvation have I succoured thee: behold, now
is the accepted time; behold, now *is* the
day of salvation.)
3Giving no offence in any thing, that
the ministry be not blamed:
4But in all *things* approving ourselves
as the ministers of God, in much patience, in afflictions, in necessities, in
distresses,
5In *stripes, in imprisonments, in
tumults, in labours, in watchings, in
fastings;
6By pureness, by knowledge, by
longsuffering, by kindness, by the Holy
Ghost, by love unfeigned,
7By the word of truth, by the power
of God, by the armour of righteousness
on the right hand and on the left,
8By honour and dishonour, by evil
report and good report: as deceivers,
and *yet* true;
9As unknown, and *yet* well known; as
dying, and, behold, we live; as *chastened, and not killed;
10As sorrowful, yet alway rejoicing;
as poor, yet making many rich; as having nothing, and *yet* possessing all
things.

Christian separation

¶11O *ye* Corinthians, our mouth is
open unto you, our heart is enlarged.
12Ye are not straitened in us, but ye
are straitened in your own bowels.
13Now for a recompence in the same,
(I speak as unto *my* children,) be ye also
enlarged.
14Be ye not unequally yoked together
with *unbelievers: for what fellowship
hath righteousness with unrighteousness? and what communion hath light
with darkness?
15And what concord hath Christ with
Belial? or what part hath he that believeth with an infidel?
16And what agreement hath the temple of God with idols? for ye are the
temple of the living God; as God hath
said, I will dwell in them, and walk in
them; and I will be their God, and they
shall be my people.

5:20 reconciled. This means *to be thoroughly changed.* It speaks of the sinner becoming a new creature through Christ before he can meet with God.
6:1 receive not the grace of God in vain. Grace provides salvation for all, but for those who refuse the gift, it is in "vain."
6:2 he saith. See Isaiah 49:8.
6:4 approving ourselves as the ministers. Showing ourselves as the servants.
6:7 by the armour of righteousness. See *garments.
6:8 By honour and dishonour. Compare 2 Corinthians 11:24-30.
6:8 as deceivers, and yet true. See John 7:12 where our Lord was called a deceiver.
6:10 possessing all things. "No good thing will he withhold from them that walk uprightly" (Ps. 84:11).
6:12 Ye are not straitened in us. The Apostle Paul was telling them: "We are not withholding [restricting] our affection from you, but you are withholding yours from us." Paul's heart was large enough to love and hold all the Corinthians. He asked them to make room in their hearts for him (vs. 13; 7:12).
6:14 Be ye not unequally yoked together. This applies to all relationships of life, including intimate friendships, marriage, business, and ecclesiastical affiliations.
6:15 Belial. *Belial, in opposition to Christ, stands for all that is against Him. The word means *worthlessness*.
6:15 infidel. Unbeliever.
6:16 as God hath said. See Leviticus 26:12; Isaiah 52:11; Jeremiah 31:33.

[17]Wherefore come out from among
them, and be ye separate, saith the
Lord, and touch not the *unclean *thing;*
and I will receive you,

6:17 Separation
The context of this verse proves that this refers to separation from all that is unclean, that is, unholy things and evil people. That is one side of separation, but the Christian is also to be separated *to* God. A person living in the world cannot live entirely apart from the evil in the world, but he can refuse to have any part in that evil. It was the world that crucified the Christian's Saviour. Not until the Christian lives the truly separated life can he have full fellowship with God, his heavenly Father, and not until then will his service bear fruit for the Lord (2 Tim. 2:21; Heb. 13:13-15).

[18]And will be a Father unto you, and
ye shall be my sons and daughters, saith
the Lord Almighty.

Christian cleansing

7 Having therefore these promises,
dearly beloved, let us cleanse ourselves from all filthiness of the *flesh
and spirit, perfecting holiness in the
*fear of God.

Human interests and affections in the Lord

¶[2]Receive us; we have wronged no
man, we have corrupted no man, we
have defrauded no man.
[3]I speak not *this* to condemn *you:* for
I have said before, that ye are in our
hearts to die and live with *you.*
[4]Great *is* my boldness of speech toward you, great *is* my glorying of you: I
am filled with comfort, I am exceeding
joyful in all our tribulation.
[5]For, when we were come into Macedonia, our flesh had no rest, but we
were troubled on every side; without
were fightings, within *were* fears.
[6]Nevertheless God, that comforteth
those that are cast down, comforted us
by the coming of *Titus;
[7]And not by his coming only, but by
the consolation wherewith he was comforted in you, when he told us your earnest desire, your *mourning, your
fervent mind toward me; so that I rejoiced the more.
[8]For though I made you sorry with a
letter, I do not repent, though I did repent: for I perceive that the same
epistle hath made you sorry, though *it
were* but for a season.
[9]Now I rejoice, not that ye were made
sorry, but that ye sorrowed to *repentance: for ye were made sorry after a
godly manner, that ye might receive
damage by us in nothing.
[10]For godly sorrow worketh repentance to *salvation not to be repented
of: but the sorrow of the world worketh
*death.
[11]For behold this selfsame thing, that
ye sorrowed after a godly sort, what
carefulness it wrought in you, yea, *what*
clearing of yourselves, yea, *what* indignation, yea, *what* fear, yea, *what* vehement desire, yea, *what* zeal, yea, *what*
revenge! In all *things* ye have approved
yourselves to be clear in this matter.
[12]Wherefore, though I wrote unto
you, *I did it* not for his cause that had
done the wrong, nor for his cause that
suffered wrong, but that our care for
you in the sight of God might appear
unto you.
[13]Therefore we were comforted in
your comfort: yea, and exceedingly
the more joyed we for the joy of Titus, because his spirit was refreshed
by you all.
[14]For if I have boasted any thing to
him of you, I am not ashamed; but as we
spake all things to you in truth, even so

7:1 let us cleanse ourselves. While God alone can cleanse from sin, we must be willing to receive the cleansing and to walk in the light day by day.
7:8 repent. Regret.
7:9 sorry after a godly manner. Godly sorrow does not rob a Christian of his joy in the Lord; it prompts him to repent, turn from the sinful behavior, and be even more fruitful for the Lord. It also restores communion with the Lord.

our boasting, which *I made* before
Titus, is found a truth.
15And his inward affection is more
abundant toward you, whilst he remembereth the obedience of you all, how
with fear and trembling ye received
him.
16I rejoice therefore that I have confidence in you in all *things*.

II. Exhortation (8:1—9:15)

*Giving *money for the work of the Lord*

8 Moreover, brethren, we do you to
wit of the *grace of God bestowed
on the churches of Macedonia;

8:1 God's Grace
The grace of God here refers to a gift of money, and was, therefore, a token of spiritual grace (2 Cor. 6:1). Agabus had predicted a famine (Acts 11:28), which had come and caused suffering among believers in Judaea. When Paul was in Jerusalem, he promised that he would try to get help for the church's poor in Jerusalem (Gal. 2:10).

2How that in a great trial of affliction
the abundance of their joy and their
deep poverty abounded unto the riches
of their liberality.
3For to *their* power, I bear record, yea,
and beyond *their* power *they were* willing of themselves;
4Praying us with much intreaty that
we would receive the gift, and *take upon
us* the fellowship of the ministering to
the *saints.
5And *this they did,* not as we hoped,
but first gave their own selves to the
Lord, and unto us by the will of God.
6Insomuch that we desired Titus,
that as he had begun, so he would also
finish in you the same grace also.
7Therefore, as ye abound in every
thing, in *faith, and utterance, and
knowledge, and *in* all diligence, and *in*
your love to us, *see* that ye abound in
this grace also.
8I speak not by commandment, but by
occasion of the forwardness of others,
and to prove the sincerity of your love.
9For ye know the grace of our Lord
Jesus *Christ, that, though he was rich,
yet for your sakes he became poor, that
ye through his poverty might be rich.
10And herein I give *my* advice: for this
is expedient for you, who have begun
before, not only to do, but also to be
forward a year ago.
11Now therefore perform the doing *of
it;* that as *there was* a readiness to will,
so *there may be* a performance also out
of that which ye have.
12For if there be first a willing mind, *it
is* accepted according to that a man hath,
and not according to that he hath not.
13For *I mean* not that other men be
eased, and ye burdened:
14But by an equality, *that* now at this
time your abundance *may be a supply* for
their want, that their abundance also
may be *a supply* for your want: that
there may be equality:
15As it is written, He that *had gathered* much had nothing over; and he that
had gathered little had no lack.
16But thanks *be* to God, which put the
same earnest care into the heart of Titus for you.
17For indeed he accepted the exhortation; but being more forward, of his
own accord he went unto you.
18And we have sent with him the
brother, whose praise *is* in the *gospel
throughout all the churches;

8:5 not as we hoped. The Macedonians gave above and beyond Paul's hopes. God loves a cheerful giver (2 Cor. 9:7).
8:5 first gave their own selves to the Lord. God wants our hearts before our gifts (see also vs. 12). It is the quality of the gift that matters more than the quantity.
8:15 As it is written. See Exodus 16:18.
8:17 being more forward. Anxious to come to your assistance.
8:18 we have sent with him. It is thought that Luke and Trophimus were those who went with Titus (see also vs. 22), not because he could not be trusted, but in order that verses 20-21 might be fulfilled.

[19]And not *that* only, but who was also
chosen of the churches to travel with us
with this grace, which is administered
by us to the glory of the same Lord, and
declaration of your ready mind:
[20]Avoiding this, that no man should
blame us in this abundance which is
administered by us:
[21]Providing for honest things, not
only in the sight of the Lord, but also
in the sight of men.
[22]And we have sent with them our
brother, whom we have oftentimes
proved diligent in many things, but now
much more diligent, upon the great
confidence which *I have* in you.
[23]Whether *any do enquire* of Titus, *he*
is my partner and fellowhelper concerning you: or our brethren *be en-*
quired of, they are the messengers of the
churches, *and* the glory of Christ.
[24]Wherefore shew ye to them, and
before the churches, the proof of your
love, and of our boasting on your behalf.

Giving money (continued)

9 For as touching the ministering to
the saints, it is superfluous for me
to write to you:
[2]For I know the forwardness of your
mind, for which I boast of you to them
of Macedonia, that Achaia was ready a
year ago; and your zeal hath provoked
very many.
[3]Yet have I sent the brethren, lest our
boasting of you should be in vain in this
behalf; that, as I said, ye may be ready:
[4]Lest haply if they of Macedonia
come with me, and find you unprepared, we (that we say not, ye) should
be ashamed in this same confident
boasting.
[5]Therefore I thought it necessary to
*exhort the brethren, that they would
go before unto you, and make up beforehand your bounty, whereof ye had notice before, that the same might be
ready, as *a matter of* bounty, and not as
of covetousness.
[6]But this *I say,* He which soweth
sparingly shall reap also sparingly; and
he which soweth bountifully shall reap
also bountifully.
[7]Every man according as he pur-
poseth in his heart, *so let him give;* not
grudgingly, or of necessity: for God
loveth a cheerful giver.
[8]And God *is* able to make all grace
abound toward you; that ye, always having all sufficiency in all *things,* may
abound to every good work:
[9](As it is written, He hath dispersed
abroad; he hath given to the poor: his
*righteousness remaineth for ever.
[10]Now he that ministereth seed to the
sower both minister bread for *your* food,
and multiply your seed sown, and increase the fruits of your righteousness;)
[11]Being enriched in every thing to all
bountifulness, which causeth through
us thanksgiving to God.
[12]For the administration of this service not only supplieth the want of the
saints, but is abundant also by many
thanksgivings unto God;
[13]Whiles by the experiment of this
ministration they glorify God for your
professed subjection unto the gospel of
Christ, and for *your* liberal distribution
unto them, and unto all *men;*
[14]And by their *prayer for you, which
long after you for the exceeding *grace
of God in you.
[15]Thanks *be* unto God for his unspeakable gift.

III. Vindication (10:1—13:14)
Paul's Apostleship from God

10 Now I Paul myself beseech you
by the meekness and gentleness

9:6 bountifully. With blessings.
9:9 As it is written. See Psalm 112:9.
9:9 his righteousness. His liberality and generosity.
9:10 he that ministereth seed to the sower. God promises a special blessing to the generous giver. He will be enriched in everything (vs. 11).

of Christ, who in presence *am* base
among you, but being absent am bold
toward you:
2But I beseech *you,* that I may not be
bold when I am present with that confidence, wherewith I think to be bold
against some, which think of us as if we
walked according to the flesh.
3For though we walk in the flesh, we
do not war after the flesh:
4(For the weapons of our warfare *are*
not *carnal, but mighty through God to
the pulling down of strong holds;)
5Casting down imaginations, and
every high thing that exalteth itself
against the knowledge of God, and
bringing into captivity every thought to
the obedience of Christ;
6And having in a readiness to revenge
all disobedience, when your obedience
is fulfilled.
7Do ye look on things after the outward appearance? If any man trust to
himself that he is Christ's, let him of
himself think this again, that, as he *is*
Christ's, even so *are* we Christ's.
8For though I should boast somewhat
more of our authority, which the Lord
hath given us for edification, and not for
your destruction, I should not be
ashamed:
9That I may not seem as if I would
terrify you by letters.
10For *his* letters, say they, *are*
weighty and powerful; but *his* bodily
presence *is* weak, and *his* speech contemptible.
11Let such an one think this, that,
such as we are in word by letters when
we are absent, such *will we be* also in
deed when we are present.
12For we dare not make ourselves of
the number, or compare ourselves with
some that commend themselves: but
they measuring themselves by themselves, and comparing themselves
among themselves, are not wise.
13But we will not boast of things
without *our* measure, but according to
the measure of the rule which God hath
distributed to us, a measure to reach
even unto you.
14For we stretch not ourselves beyond *our measure,* as though we
reached not unto you: for we are come
as far as to you also in *preaching* the
gospel of Christ:
15Not boasting of things without *our*
measure, *that is,* of other men's
labours; but having *hope, when your
faith is increased, that we shall be enlarged by you according to our rule
abundantly,
16To preach the gospel in the *regions*
beyond you, *and* not to boast in another
man's line of things made ready to our
hand.
17But he that glorieth, let him glory
in the Lord.
18For not he that commendeth himself is approved, but whom the Lord
commendeth.

Paul's faithful witness

11 Would to God ye could bear
with me a little in *my* folly: and
indeed bear with me.
2For I am jealous over you with

10:1 who in presence am base among you. Paul refers here to his personal appearance, which was possibly unimpressive (2 Cor. 10:10).
10:3 walk in the flesh. Are men.
10:4 the weapons of our warfare are not carnal. Spiritual warfare can only be fought with spiritual weapons, such as God's Word and prayer (see Eph. 6:10-18).
10:7 things after the outward appearance. Judging others by appearances is neither kind nor safe.
10:8 edification. Building up.
10:8 destruction. Overthrowing.
10:13 without our measure. Beyond our limit. Corinth was part of the "district" that had been given to Paul for his ministry. Other men (vs. 15) were given other districts. Paul claimed no credit for the work being done beyond the field of his missionary tours.

godly jealousy: for I have espoused you
to one husband, that I may present *you*
as a chaste virgin to Christ.
3 But I fear, lest by any means, as the
serpent beguiled Eve through his subtilty, so your minds should be corrupted from the simplicity that is in Christ.
4 For if he that cometh preacheth another Jesus, whom we have not preached,
or *if* ye receive another spirit, which ye
have not received, or another gospel,
which ye have not accepted, ye might
well bear with *him*.
5 For I suppose I was not a whit behind the very chiefest *apostles.
6 But though *I be* rude in speech, yet
not in knowledge; but we have been
throughly made manifest among you in
all things.
7 Have I committed an offence in
abasing myself that ye might be exalted, because I have preached to you the
gospel of God freely?
8 I robbed other churches, taking
wages *of them,* to do you service.
9 And when I was present with you,
and wanted, I was chargeable to no
man: for that which was lacking to me
the brethren which came from Macedonia supplied: and in all *things* I have kept
myself from being burdensome unto
you, and *so* will I keep *myself.*
10 As the truth of Christ is in me, no
man shall stop me of this boasting in the
regions of Achaia.
11 Wherefore? because I love you not?
God knoweth.
12 But what I do, that I will do, that I
may cut off occasion from them which
desire occasion; that wherein they glory, they may be found even as we.

False teachers

13 For such *are* false apostles, deceitful workers, transforming themselves
into the apostles of Christ.
14 And no marvel; for *Satan himself
is transformed into an *angel of light.

11:14 Satan's Disguise
Satan can, and often does, disguise himself as an angel of light. He is a deceiver. Notice that the Devil is a real person, not just an evil power.

15 Therefore *it is* no great thing if his
ministers also be transformed as the
ministers of righteousness; whose end
shall be according to their works.

Paul's painful duty to speak of himself

¶ 16 I say again, Let no man think me a
fool; if otherwise, yet as a fool receive
me, that I may boast myself a little.
17 That which I speak, I speak *it* not
after the Lord, but as it were foolishly,
in this confidence of boasting.
18 Seeing that many glory after the
flesh, I will glory also.
19 For ye suffer fools gladly, seeing ye
yourselves are wise.
20 For ye suffer, if a man bring you into
bondage, if a man devour *you,* if a man

11:2 godly jealousy. Jealousy is usually sinful because it is selfish. There is a godly jealousy, which is concerned about the interests of the Saviour and the kingdom of God.
11:2 espoused you to one husband. The believer's union with Christ is likened to the union of marriage (see Eph. 5:25-33).
11:3 as the serpent beguiled Eve. See Genesis 3:1-5 (see Gen. 3:1 note, "The Role of the Serpent").
11:4 preacheth another Jesus. This refers to false teachers who misrepresent the Lord Jesus Christ and who do not preach the true Saviour of the Bible.
11:6 rude in speech. Not eloquent–simple and plain, unskilled in speaking.
11:8 I robbed other churches. Paul did not mean that he stole money but that he accepted these gifts in order to be able to do service for the Corinthians.
11:11 God knoweth. He knew that Paul loved the Corinthians very much.
11:16 I say again. Paul returns to the thought of verse 1.
11:17 not after the Lord. Not commanded of Him, but permitted by Him.
11:20 suffer. Accept or put up with.

take *of you,* if a man exalt himself, if a
man smite you on the face.
21 I speak as concerning reproach, as
though we had been weak. Howbeit
whereinsoever any is bold, (I speak
foolishly,) I am bold also.
22 Are they Hebrews? so *am* I. Are
they Israelites? so *am* I. Are they the
seed of *Abraham? so *am* I.
23 Are they ministers of Christ? (I
speak as a fool) I *am* more; in labours
more abundant, in *stripes above measure, in prisons more frequent, in
deaths oft.
24 Of the Jews five times received I
forty *stripes* save one.

11:24 A Severe Punishment
The law for certain offences was forty stripes, but there was a severe penalty attached if even one more than forty were given. To be sure that there was no mistake made in counting, offenders were given one less than forty.

25 Thrice was I beaten with rods, once
was I stoned, thrice I suffered shipwreck, a night and a day I have been in
the deep;
26 *In* journeyings often, *in* perils of
waters, *in* perils of robbers, *in* perils
by *mine own* countrymen, *in* perils by
the heathen, *in* perils in the city, *in*
perils in the wilderness, *in* perils in
the sea, *in* perils among false brethren;
27 In weariness and painfulness, in
watchings often, in hunger and thirst,
in fastings often, in cold and nakedness.
28 Beside those things that are without, that which cometh upon me daily,
the care of all the churches.
29 Who is weak, and I am not weak?
who is offended, and I burn not?
30 If I must needs glory, I will glory of
the things which concern mine infirmities.
31 The God and Father of our Lord
Jesus Christ, which is blessed for evermore, knoweth that I lie not.
32 In *Damascus the governor under
Aretas the king kept the city of the
Damascenes with a garrison, desirous
to apprehend me:
33 And through a window in a basket
was I let down by the wall, and escaped
his hands.

Paul speaks of himself (continued)

12 It is not expedient for me
doubtless to glory. I will come
to visions and revelations of the Lord.
2 I knew a man in Christ above fourteen years ago, (whether in the body, I
cannot tell; or whether out of the body,
I cannot tell: God knoweth;) such an
one caught up to the third *heaven.
3 And I knew such a man, (whether in
the body, or out of the body, I cannot
tell: God knoweth;)
4 How that he was caught up into
paradise, and heard unspeakable words,
which it is not lawful for a man to
utter.

12:3-4 Paradise
The word "paradise" is probably from a Persian word signifying a park and used as a translation of the Hebrew word for "Eden." The word occurs three times in the New Testament. The later Jewish scholars recognized two distinct regions in hades (the common abode of the dead): paradise and gehenna. It is probably in reference to this belief that our Lord uses the word "paradise" in His assurance to the dying robber (Luke 23:43; compare 16:23 and its note, "A Place Called Hell"). In the other two passages, both of which are highly symbolic, the word points to some region of heavenly blessedness (2 Cor. 12:3-4; Rev. 2:7).

12:2 I knew a man. Here Paul speaks of himself (vs. 7).
12:2 third heaven. God's abiding place.
12:4 paradise. Into the presence of God (compare vs. 2; Luke 23:43).
12:4 lawful. Permitted.

5 Of such an one will I glory: yet of myself I will not glory, but in mine infirmities.

6 For though I would desire to glory, I shall not be a fool; for I will say the truth: but *now* I forbear, lest any man should think of me above that which he seeth me *to be,* or *that* he heareth of me.

7 And lest I should be exalted above measure through the abundance of the revelations, there was given to me a thorn in the flesh, the messenger of Satan to buffet me, lest I should be exalted above measure.

8 For this thing I besought the Lord thrice, that it might depart from me.

9 And he said unto me, My grace is sufficient for thee: for my strength is made perfect in weakness. Most gladly therefore will I rather glory in my infirmities, that the power of Christ may rest upon me.

10 Therefore I take pleasure in infirmities, in reproaches, in necessities, in persecutions, in distresses for Christ's sake: for when I am weak, then am I strong.

¶ 11 I am become a fool in glorying; ye have compelled me: for I ought to have been commended of you: for in nothing am I behind the very chiefest apostles, though I be nothing.

12 Truly the signs of an *apostle were wrought among you in all patience, in signs, and wonders, and mighty deeds.

13 For what is it wherein ye were inferior to other churches, except *it be* that I myself was not burdensome to you? forgive me this wrong.

14 Behold, the third time I am ready to come to you; and I will not be burdensome to you: for I seek not yours, but you: for the children ought not to lay up for the parents, but the parents for the children.

15 And I will very gladly spend and be spent for you; though the more abundantly I love you, the less I be loved.

16 But be it so, I did not burden you: nevertheless, being crafty, I caught you with guile.

17 Did I make a gain of you by any of them whom I sent unto you?

18 I desired *Titus, and with *him* I sent a brother. Did Titus make a gain of you? walked we not in the same spirit? *walked we* not in the same steps?

Final warnings

19 Again, think ye that we excuse ourselves unto you? we speak before God in Christ: but *we do* all things, dearly beloved, for your edifying.

20 For I fear, lest, when I come, I shall not find you such as I would, and *that* I shall be found unto you such as ye would not: lest *there be* debates, envyings, wraths, strifes, backbitings, whisperings, swellings, tumults:

21 *And* lest, when I come again, my God will humble me among you, and *that* I shall bewail many which have sinned already, and have not repented of the uncleanness and fornication and lasciviousness which they have committed.

13 This *is* the third *time* I am coming to you. In the mouth of

---

12:7 a thorn in the flesh. Probably some kind of bodily affliction. A thorn suggests that it was painful. The very fact that it is not described is a message to comfort those who must bear any affliction whatsoever.

12:7 the messenger of Satan. Caused by Satan but allowed by God for Paul's spiritual good.

12:8 I besought the Lord thrice. Paul literally pleaded with the Lord three times to remove the affliction. His prayer was answered, not by the removal of the thorn, but by the gift of necessary grace to bear it (vs. 9).

12:9 rest upon me. Envelop me.

12:15 for you. For your souls.

12:18 spirit . . . steps. This speaks of the inward leading of the Spirit and the outward evidences of that leading.

two or three witnesses shall every
word be established.
[2]I told you before, and foretell you, as
if I were present, the second time; and
being absent now I write to them which
heretofore have sinned, and to all other,
that, if I come again, I will not spare:
[3]Since ye seek a proof of Christ
speaking in me, which to you-ward is
not weak, but is mighty in you.
[4]For though he was crucified through
weakness, yet he liveth by the power
of God. For we also are weak in him, but
we shall live with him by the power of
God toward you.
[5]Examine yourselves, whether ye be
in the faith; prove your own selves.
Know ye not your own selves, how that
Jesus Christ is in you, except ye be reprobates?
[6]But I trust that ye shall know that
we are not reprobates.
[7]Now I pray to God that ye do no evil;
not that we should appear approved, but
that ye should do that which is honest,
though we be as reprobates.
[8]For we can do nothing against the
truth, but for the truth.
[9]For we are glad, when we are weak,
and ye are strong: and this also we wish,
even your perfection.
[10]Therefore I write these things being absent, lest being present I should
use sharpness, according to the power
which the Lord hath given me to edification, and not to destruction.

Conclusion

¶[11]Finally, brethren, farewell. Be perfect, be of good comfort, be of one mind,
live in peace; and the God of love and
peace shall be with you.
[12]Greet one another with an holy
kiss.
¶[13]All the saints salute you.
[14]The grace of the Lord Jesus Christ,
and the love of God, and the communion
of the Holy Ghost, *be* with you all. Amen.

13:1 two or three witnesses. It was Jewish Law that any case had to be established by more than one witness (compare Deut. 19:15).

13:2 heretofore have sinned. Some of the Corinthians continued in their old sins on a habitual basis.

The Epistle of Paul the Apostle to the

GALATIANS

THE WRITER AND TIME

Paul, the apostle to the Gentiles, wrote this letter to the Christians in Galatia about A.D. 58.

BACKGROUND

Paul had preached to the Galatians on his first and second journeys (Acts 13:14—14:28; 16:1-6). After he had left, other preachers came down from Jerusalem and taught many false ideas which some of the Galatians accepted. The false teaching mixed Jewish religion with the Christian gospel by saying that:

1. Salvation depended not only on belief in the Lord Jesus Christ, but also on abiding by Jewish Law
2. Sanctification, or leading a separate Christian life, required the keeping of the Law, as well as Jewish ritual and the help of the Holy Spirit.

THEME

Paul wrote this letter to expose the errors, and to defend the pure gospel that he had taught the Galatians. He insisted, first, that he was a true apostle whose message came from God, and second, that the gospel was a revelation from God and that it rests upon a promise made to Abraham hundreds of years before the Law was given. The lesson is needed today. People still need to be taught that being saved or born again is *by belief* on the Lord Jesus Christ and *not* by "doing one's best," and that the Christian life depends not on trying to be good, but by trusting in the inner working of the Holy Spirit.

OUTLINE OF GALATIANS

I.	Greetings	Galatians 1:1-5
II.	The Reason for the Letter	Galatians 1:6-9
III.	Paul's Defense of Himself	Galatians 1:10—2:21
IV.	Paul's Defense of the Gospel	Galatians 3:1—5:15
V.	The True Way of Holiness	Galatians 5:16—6:14
VI.	Closing Greetings	Galatians 6:15-18

I. Greetings (1:1-5)

1 Paul, an apostle, (not of men, neither by man, but by Jesus *Christ,
and *God the Father, who raised him
from the dead;)
2 And all the brethren which are with
me, unto the churches of Galatia:
3 *Grace *be* to you and *peace from
God the Father, and *from* our Lord Jesus
Christ,
4 Who gave himself for our sins, that
he might deliver us from this present
evil *world, according to the will of God
and our Father:
5 To whom *be* glory for ever and ever.
*Amen.

II. The Reason for the Letter (1:6-9)

¶6 I marvel that ye are so soon removed from him that called you into the
grace of Christ unto another *gospel:
7 Which is not another; but there be
some that trouble you, and would pervert the gospel of Christ.
8 But though we, or an *angel from
*heaven, preach any other gospel unto
you than that which we have preached
unto you, let him be accursed.
9 As we said before, so say I now
again, If any *man* preach any other gospel unto you than that ye have received,
let him be accursed.

III. Paul's Self-Defense (1:10—2:21)

¶10 For do I now persuade men, or
God? or do I seek to please men? for if
I yet pleased men, I should not be the
servant of Christ.
11 But I certify you, brethren, that the
gospel which was preached of me is not
after man.
12 For I neither received it of man,
neither was I taught *it,* but by the revelation of Jesus Christ.
13 For ye have heard of my conversation in time past in the Jews' religion, how that beyond measure I
persecuted the *church of God, and
wasted it:
14 And profited in the Jews' religion
above many my equals in mine own
nation, being more exceedingly zealous
of the *traditions of my fathers.

1:14 Traditions

Traditions are practices of long standing invented by men, some of which were religious. Traditions were usually carried on from one generation to the next (not always with good reason). The Bible is not a tradition; it's a revelation from God. See Matthew 15:1-9 for some of the Jewish traditions that the Lord condemned (see also Matt. 15:2 note, "The Tradition of the Elders").

15 But when it pleased God, who separated me from my mother's womb, and
called *me* by his grace,
16 To reveal his Son in me, that I might
preach him among the heathen; immediately I conferred not with flesh and
blood:
17 Neither went I up to *Jerusalem to
them which were *apostles before me;
but I went into Arabia, and returned
again unto *Damascus.
18 Then after three years I went up to

1:1 not of men. Paul emphasized this fact because the false teachers had tried to discredit him, saying that he was not a proper apostle, since he had not become one until long after our Lord's ascension.

1:1 raised him from the dead. See 1 Corinthians 15 notes, including verse 52 note, "A Final Resurrection."

1:12 revelation. "Revelation" means *something uncovered.* The Lord Jesus Christ revealed or showed Himself to Paul at his conversion on the road to Damascus (Acts 9:3-20).

1:13 conversation. Attitude or way of life.

1:13 religion. "Religion" is a comprehensive word for forms of worship, ceremonies, and outward conduct (James 1:26-27). People may be very religious without knowing Christ as their Saviour.

1:17 Arabia. This period of Paul's life is not mentioned in Acts. It must have come between that which is recorded in Acts 9:21 and 9:22 (see also Acts 9:22 note, "Return to Damascus").

Jerusalem to see *Peter, and abode with
him fifteen days.
19But other of the apostles saw I
none, save James the Lord's brother.
20Now the things which I write unto
you, behold, before God, I lie not.
21Afterwards I came into the regions
of Syria and Cilicia;
22And was unknown by face unto the
churches of Judaea which were in
Christ:
23But they had heard only, That he
which persecuted us in times past now
preacheth the *faith which once he destroyed.
24And they glorified God in me.
2 Then fourteen years after I went
up again to Jerusalem with Barnabas, and took *Titus with *me* also.
2And I went up by revelation, and
communicated unto them that gospel
which I preach among the *Gentiles,
but privately to them which were of
reputation, lest by any means I should
run, or had run, in vain.
3But neither Titus, who was with me,
being a Greek, was compelled to be circumcised:
4And that because of false brethren
unawares brought in, who came in privily to spy out our liberty which we have
in Christ Jesus, that they might bring
us into bondage:
5To whom we gave place by subjection, no, not for an hour; that the truth
of the gospel might continue with you.
6But of these who seemed to be
somewhat, (whatsoever they were, it
maketh no matter to me: God accepteth
no man's person:) for they who seemed
to be somewhat in conference added
nothing to me:
7But contrariwise, when they saw
that the gospel of the uncircumcision
was committed unto me, as *the gospel* of
the *circumcision *was* unto Peter;
8(For he that wrought effectually in
Peter to the apostleship of the circumcision, the same was mighty in me toward the Gentiles:)
9And when James, *Cephas, and
John, who seemed to be pillars, perceived the grace that was given unto
me, they gave to me and Barnabas the
right hands of fellowship; that we
should go unto the heathen, and they
unto the circumcision.
10Only *they would* that we should remember the poor; the same which I
also was forward to do.
11But when Peter was come to Antioch, I withstood him to the face, because he was to be blamed.
12For before that certain came from
James, he did eat with the Gentiles: but
when they were come, he withdrew and
separated himself, fearing them which
were of the circumcision.
13And the other Jews dissembled
likewise with him; insomuch that Barnabas also was carried away with their
dissimulation.
14But when I saw that they walked
not uprightly according to the truth of
the gospel, I said unto Peter before
them all, If thou, being a Jew, livest after the manner of Gentiles, and not as
do the Jews, why compellest thou the
Gentiles to live as do the Jews?
15We *who are* Jews by nature, and not
sinners of the Gentiles,
16Knowing that a man is not justified
by the works of the *law, but by the faith
of Jesus Christ, even we have believed
in Jesus Christ, that we might be justified by the faith of Christ, and not by the

---

2:1 fourteen years after. Verses 1-10 describe Paul's view of the events of Acts 15.

2:7 the gospel of the uncircumcision. As a general term, "circumcision" means the Jews, and "uncircumcision" the Gentiles.

2:11 I withstood him. This incident must have occurred after the council of Jerusalem of Acts 15; see Acts 10:28; 11:2-3. Paul and Peter differed here in policy: They were still brethren beloved in the Lord; see 2 Peter 3:15. Notice in Galatians 2:15-21 that Paul acknowledged that he and Peter were in accord as to the doctrine of salvation and justification by faith.

works of the law: for by the works of the
law shall no flesh be justified.
17But if, while we seek to be justified
by Christ, we ourselves also are found
sinners, *is* therefore Christ the minister of *sin? God forbid.
18For if I build again the things which
I destroyed, I make myself a transgressor.
19For I through the law am dead to
the law, that I might live unto God.

2:19 Dead to the Law
Paul, under the Law, would have had to die for his sins, but Christ had died to pay his penalty, and Paul was dead to the Law. When Christ died upon the cross, it was as if all the sins, all the evil, all the unbelief for which any believer in the Lord Jesus Christ could have been held responsible were nailed with Him there (Col. 2:14; see also its note, "A Cancelled Bond"). This is why we are no longer "under the law" (Rom. 6:14).

20I am crucified with Christ: nevertheless I live; yet not I, but Christ liveth
in me: and the life which I now live in
the flesh I live by the faith of the Son of
God, who loved me, and gave himself
for me.
21I do not frustrate the *grace of God:
for if *righteousness *come* by the law,
then Christ is dead in vain.

IV. Paul's Defense of the Gospel (3:1—5:15)

3 O foolish Galatians, who hath bewitched you, that ye should not
obey the truth, before whose eyes
Jesus Christ hath been evidently set
forth, crucified among you?
2This only would I learn of you, Received ye the Spirit by the works of the
law, or by the hearing of faith?
3Are ye so foolish? having begun in
the Spirit, are ye now made perfect by
the flesh?

3:3 Being Perfected
We are made righteous "in Christ" in a moment of time. This is done while we are still sinful; then the Holy Spirit begins to "perfect" us. Since to be perfect means to be mature or full-grown (Phil. 3:12, 15), this comes about by a gradual growth that we can help or hinder. If we do not study the Word and yield to the Holy Spirit, our growth will be slight, if we grow at all.

4Have ye suffered so many things in
vain? if *it be* yet in vain.
5He therefore that ministereth to
you the Spirit, and worketh *miracles among you, *doeth he it* by the
works of the law, or by the hearing of
faith?
6Even as *Abraham believed God,
and it was accounted to him for righteousness.
¶7Know ye therefore that they which
are of faith, the same are the children
of Abraham.
8And the scripture, foreseeing that
God would justify the heathen through
faith, preached before the gospel unto

2:17 if . . . we ourselves also are found sinners. Paul is saying here, "If we who are Jews receive Christ's salvation and acknowledge that He paid our debt of sin, and then act as if we are still sinners bound by the Law, as are those who have not believed, we do it apart from Christ." The Law is perfect, but man is powerless to keep it perfectly. Christ came to fulfill the Law perfectly. If the Law is picked up again, we bind ourselves to the old Law and the old traditions.

2:20 Christ liveth in me. One of the *mysteries, or reveled secrets, of the gospel is that Christ dwells in each believer (Col. 1:27 and its note, "Christ Lives in Us").

2:21 if righteousness come by the law. If people could have been saved by doing good works, then Christ's death would not have been necessary.

3:1 evidently set forth. Jesus Christ was clearly and openly set forth as the Truth—by the Word, by God Himself, by the Holy Spirit, by His own life and testimony, and by His crucifixion, resurrection, and ascension.

3:7 children of Abraham. Because of the fulfilled promise of Genesis 12:3, repeated here in verse 8, Christians are the spiritual seed or descendants of Abraham (see vs. 29). They are children by faith.

Abraham, *saying,* In thee shall all nations be blessed.
9So then they which be of faith are
blessed with faithful Abraham.
10For as many as are of the works of
the law are under the curse: for it is
written, Cursed *is* every one that continueth not in all things which are written in the book of the law to do them.

3:10 Curse or Blessing
To be "under the curse" is simply to fall under God's judgment instead of having His blessing. The quotation comes from Deuteronomy 27:26. The Law promised righteousness to all those who kept it perfectly. Those who did not keep it were condemned to death. Man could not keep it perfectly, because he was imperfect, but Christ took the condemnation and redeemed the believer. That did not mean that the Law was not good. It meant that it was perfectly just and perfectly good. Our Lord proved that by fulfilling it.

11But that no man is justified by the
law in the sight of God, *it is* evident: for,
The *just shall live by faith.
12And the law is not of faith: but, The
man that doeth them shall live in them.
13Christ hath *redeemed us from the
curse of the law, being made a curse for
us: for it is written, Cursed *is* every one
that hangeth on a tree:
14That the blessing of Abraham
might come on the Gentiles through
Jesus Christ; that we might receive the
promise of the Spirit through faith.
15Brethren, I speak after the manner
of men; Though *it be* but a man's *covenant, yet *if it be* confirmed, no man
disannulleth, or addeth thereto.
16Now to Abraham and his seed were
the promises made. He saith not, And
to seeds, as of many; but as of one, And
to thy seed, which is Christ.
17And this I say, *that* the covenant,
that was confirmed before of God in
Christ, the law, which was four hundred
and thirty years after, cannot disannul,
that it should make the promise of none
effect.
18For if the inheritance *be* of the law,
it is no more of promise: but God gave
it to Abraham by promise.
19Wherefore then *serveth* the law? It
was added because of transgressions,
till the seed should come to whom the
promise was made; *and it was* ordained
by *angels in the hand of a *mediator.
20Now a mediator is not *a mediator* of
one, but God is one.
21*Is* the law then against the promises
of God? God forbid: for if there had been
a law given which could have given life,
verily righteousness should have been
by the law.
22But the scripture hath concluded all
under sin, that the promise by faith of

3:11 The just shall live by faith. Read Habakkuk 2:4 (see also its note, "God's Grace").
3:13 it is written. See Deuteronomy 21:23.
3:13 Cursed is every one that hangeth on a tree. When the Lord Jesus was crucified, He hung upon a tree and was made a curse for us. See verse 10 note, "Curse or Blessing."
3:15 after the manner of men. To use a human illustration.
3:15 covenant. Paul is referring to the *covenant made between God and Abraham.
3:16 to Abraham and his seed. The promise to Abraham is found in Genesis 12; the promise to his seed (Christ) is found in Genesis 22. Paul's whole argument is based on the difference between a singular and a plural noun. Here is a great illustration of the verbal *inspiration of Scripture.
3:19 Wherefore then serveth the law? The Law was perfect and, by observing its perfection, man could see that he himself was imperfect and thus a sinner short of the glory and perfection of God. Thus the Law in its perfection should bring man to see his need of a Saviour, who is Christ.
3:19 seed. See verse 16 note.
3:19 mediator. A mediator is a person who acts for two people in a dispute. Moses was the mediator between God and the Israelites. Christ is the Mediator between God and men. See 1 Timothy 2:5.

Jesus Christ might be given to them
that believe.
¶23But before faith came, we were
kept under the law, shut up unto the
faith which should afterwards be revealed.
24Wherefore the law was our schoolmaster *to bring us* unto Christ, that we
might be justified by faith.

3:24 Slaves as "Schoolmasters"
In the time of Paul, educated slaves used to look after young children, especially when going through the streets to and from school. It was the duty of these "schoolmasters" (as they were called), to teach the children what was right and wrong for them to do and to keep them in the right paths. When the children were grown, they no longer had the schoolmasters to obey, but they answered to their fathers. So the Christian is not under schoolmaster Law, but under the Father God.

25But after that faith is come, we are
no longer under a schoolmaster.
26For ye are all the children of God by
faith in Christ Jesus.
27For as many of you as have been
baptized into Christ have put on Christ.
28There is neither Jew nor Greek,
there is neither bond nor free, there is
neither male nor female: for ye are all
one in Christ Jesus.
29And if ye *be* Christ's, then are ye
Abraham's seed, and heirs according to
the promise.

4 Now I say, *That* the heir, as long
as he is a child, differeth nothing
from a servant, though he be lord of all;
2But is under tutors and governors
until the time appointed of the father.
3Even so we, when we were children,
were in bondage under the elements of
the world:
4But when the fulness of the time
was come, God sent forth his Son, made
of a woman, made under the law,
5To *redeem them that were under
the law, that we might receive the
*adoption of sons.

4:6 Abba
Abba is the Aramaic word for "Father" (compare Bar-Abbas, son of the father). Aramaic was the familiar language of the people and was spoken by Christ (see Mark 14:36). One who has been born again can come to his heavenly Father as freely and familiarly as a little child who runs to his daddy. God is our heavenly Father–our perfect, loving Daddy.

6And because ye are sons, God hath
sent forth the Spirit of his Son into your
hearts, crying, Abba, Father.
7Wherefore thou art no more a servant, but a son; and if a son, then an heir
of God through Christ.
¶8Howbeit then, when ye knew not
God, ye did service unto them which by
nature are no gods.
9But now, after that ye have known
God, or rather are known of God, how
turn ye again to the weak and beggarly
elements, whereunto ye desire again to
be in bondage?
10Ye observe days, and months, and
times, and years.

3:27 baptized. Baptism of the Holy Spirit by which Christians are made a part of the body of Christ. See 1 Corinthians 12:13.

3:28 ye are all one. In Christ, all have the same privileges and responsibilities, for in Him all are children of God (vs. 26; John 1:12) and heirs with Christ (vs. 29; James 2:5).

4:4 the fulness of the time. This was prophesied in Daniel 9:25. It was because Anna and Simeon knew that the time had come that they were awaiting the Messiah in the temple (Luke 2:25-38).

4:4 made of a woman. See Genesis 3:15 note, "The Promise of a Saviour," for the first promise about the Saviour and His birth.

4:9 beggarly elements. This means *miserable principles or ideas.* When Jewish believers accepted the wrong ideas of the false preachers (see the introduction to this book), they went back to the Jewish Law, believing that they must work on their own righteousness instead of accepting the righteousness of Christ.

4:10 Ye observe days. The Galatians were going back to old feasts and holidays that were

11 I am afraid of you, lest I have bestowed upon you labour in vain.

¶ 12 Brethren, I beseech you, be as I
am; for I *am* as ye *are:* ye have not injured me at all.

4:12 God's Acceptance
Paul here asked the foolish Galatians to take the position which he held, that he was a sinner justified by faith in Jesus Christ and free from the bondage of trying to be saved by works and ceremonies. He added, however, "I am as ye are," for since the Galatians had really been justified by faith, God had accepted them. Even those who are unsure of their salvation after they are born again are nevertheless saved in the sight of God.

13 Ye know how through infirmity of
the flesh I preached the gospel unto you
at the first.

14 And my *temptation which was in
my flesh ye despised not, nor rejected;
but received me as an angel of God, *even*
as Christ Jesus.

15 Where is then the blessedness ye
spake of? for I bear you record, that, if
it had been possible, ye would have
plucked out your own eyes, and have
given them to me.

16 Am I therefore become your enemy, because I tell you the truth?

17 They zealously affect you, *but* not
well; yea, they would exclude you, that
ye might affect them.

18 But *it is* good to be zealously affected always in *a* good *thing,* and not only
when I am present with you.

19 My little children, of whom I travail
in birth again until Christ be formed
in you,

20 I desire to be present with you now,
and to change my voice; for I stand in
doubt of you.

¶ 21 Tell me, ye that desire to be under the law, do ye not hear the law?

22 For it is written, that Abraham had
two sons, the one by a bondmaid, the
other by a freewoman.

23 But he *who was* of the bondwoman
was born after the flesh; but he of the
freewoman *was* by promise.

24 Which things are an allegory: for
these are the two covenants; the one
from the mount *Sinai, which gendereth to bondage, which is Agar.

25 For this Agar is mount Sinai in Arabia, and answereth to Jerusalem which
now is, and is in bondage with her children.

26 But Jerusalem which is above is
free, which is the mother of us all.

27 For it is written, Rejoice, *thou* barren that bearest not; break forth and
cry, thou that travailest not: for the desolate hath many more children than she
which hath an husband.

28 Now we, brethren, as *Isaac was,
are the children of promise.

29 But as then he that was born after

---

given by God as *types of Christ, before He came. In Him the types were fulfilled.

4:14 temptation. Paul referred to the illness from which he suffered all of the time (2 Cor. 12:7). It probably was a test of faith, or "temptation," to the Galatians, for he had healed others but could not heal himself.

4:15 blessedness. The Holy Spirit witnessing in their hearts (Rom. 8:16).

4:15 plucked out your own eyes. In love for Paul they would have given up their dearest possession if it would have been of help to him.

4:17 They zealously affect you. The false teachers are spoken of here.

4:21 hear the law. Listen to it and learn from it, for it points to the Lord Jesus.

4:22 two sons. Ishmael and Isaac (Gen. 16:15; 21:3; see also Gen. 21:3 note, "Isaac: A Type of Christ"). Hagar, the slave mother, and Sarah, the free mother, stood for two covenants—work and grace, or the Law given at Mount Sinai and the grace of the new Jerusalem (Rev. 21:1-2; see also Rev. 21:1 note, "The New Earth").

4:24 an allegory. This is a description of one thing by using an image of another; for instance, instead of calling a man brave, one might tell a story in which the man appears as a lion.

4:24 Agar. Hagar. The Arabic name for Mount Sinai is Hagar, meaning *a stone.*

the flesh persecuted him *that was born*
after the Spirit, even so *it is* now.
30 Nevertheless what saith the scripture? Cast out the bondwoman and her
son: for the son of the bondwoman shall
not be heir with the son of the freewoman.
31 So then, brethren, we are not children of the bondwoman, but of the free.
5 Stand fast therefore in the liberty
wherewith Christ hath made us
free, and be not entangled again with
the yoke of bondage.
¶ 2 Behold, I Paul say unto you, that if
ye be circumcised, Christ shall profit
you nothing.
3 For I testify again to every man that
is circumcised, that he is a debtor to do
the whole law.
4 Christ is become of no effect unto
you, whosoever of you are justified by
the law; ye are fallen from grace.
5 For we through the Spirit wait for
the *hope of righteousness by faith.
6 For in Jesus Christ neither circumcision availeth any thing, nor uncircumcision; but faith which worketh by
love.
7 Ye did run well; who did hinder you
that ye should not obey the truth?
8 This persuasion *cometh* not of him
that calleth you.
9 A little *leaven leaveneth the whole
lump.
10 I have confidence in you through
the Lord, that ye will be none otherwise minded: but he that troubleth you
shall bear his *judgment, whosoever
he be.
11 And I, brethren, if I yet preach circumcision, why do I yet suffer persecution? then is the offence of the cross
ceased.
12 I would they were even cut off
which trouble you.
¶ 13 For, brethren, ye have been called
unto liberty; only *use* not liberty for an
occasion to the flesh, but by love serve
one another.
14 For all the law is fulfilled in one
word, *even* in this; Thou shalt love thy
neighbour as thyself.
15 But if ye bite and devour one another, take heed that ye be not consumed one of another.

V. The Way of Holiness (5:16—6:14)

16 *This* I say then, Walk in the Spirit,
and ye shall not fulfil the lust of the
flesh.
17 For the flesh lusteth against the
Spirit, and the Spirit against the flesh:
and these are contrary the one to the
other: so that ye cannot do the things
that ye would.
18 But if ye be led of the Spirit, ye are
not under the law.
19 Now the works of the flesh are
manifest, which are *these;* Adultery, for-

4:29 persecuted him. Read Genesis 21:9.

5:3 debtor to do the whole law. If a man tried to keep one point of the Law in order to be saved, that one thing would make it necessary for him to keep the whole Law, if that were the basis of his salvation.

5:4 ye are fallen from grace. See Romans 5:2: "grace wherein we stand."

5:6 worketh by love. We are saved by faith, not by works. If we truly believe and have been born again, we shall love God and make an effort to do the works that will please Him (Rom. 5:5; Eph. 1:15; James 2:17). See also Ephesians 2:8-10.

5:11 the offence of the cross. The cross is always offensive and hateful to those who are not willing to accept God's provision for them (1 Cor. 1:23).

5:13 an occasion to the flesh. Do not use your liberty in Christ to be lazy, selfish Christians.

5:13 flesh. Human nature apart from God.

5:16 Walk in the Spirit, and ye shall not fulfil. The old nature is still in the believer, but by the power of the Holy Spirit, he can overcome the old, bad desires. "Walk" refers to attitude of life as does "conversation" in Galatians 1:13.

5:16 lust. Desire; lust usually refers to evil desire.

nication, uncleanness, lasciviousness,
[20]*Idolatry, witchcraft, hatred, variance, emulations, wrath, strife, seditions, heresies,
[21]Envyings, murders, drunkenness, revellings, and such like: of the which I tell you before, as I have also told *you* in time past, that they which do such things shall not inherit the *kingdom of God.
[22]But the fruit of the Spirit is love, joy, peace, longsuffering, gentleness, goodness, faith,
[23]Meekness, temperance: against such there is no law.

5:22-23 The Fruit of the Spirit
When the Spirit controls a life, He causes the graces named here to grow in that life. Growth is gradual, and more growth will appear in some believers than in others. This is the abiding, joyful life of John 15:1-11. For true growth, we must abide; that is, keep fully yielded to the Spirit all of the time. If we sin, we can have forgiveness at once (1 John 1:9), but such failures keep us from growing.

[24]And they that are Christ's have crucified the flesh with the affections and *lusts.
[25]If we live in the Spirit, let us also walk in the Spirit.
[26]Let us not be desirous of vain glory, provoking one another, envying one another.

6 Brethren, if a man be overtaken in a fault, ye which are spiritual, restore such an one in the spirit of meekness; considering thyself, lest thou also be tempted.
[2]Bear ye one another's burdens, and so fulfil the law of Christ.
[3]For if a man think himself to be something, when he is nothing, he deceiveth himself.
[4]But let every man prove his own work, and then shall he have rejoicing in himself alone, and not in another.
[5]For every man shall bear his own burden.
[6]Let him that is taught in the word communicate unto him that teacheth in all good things.
[7]Be not deceived; God is not mocked: for whatsoever a man soweth, that shall he also reap.
[8]For he that soweth to his flesh shall of the flesh reap corruption; but he that soweth to the Spirit shall of the Spirit reap life everlasting.
[9]And let us not be weary in well doing: for in due season we shall reap, if we faint not.
[10]As we have therefore opportunity, let us do good unto all *men*, especially unto them who are of the household of faith.
¶[11]Ye see how large a letter I have written unto you with mine own hand.

6:11 Letter Writing
Paul's infirmity of the eyes made it very difficult for him to write long letters; however, he wrote this letter himself. It is believed that Paul had a severe eye disease and that he was nearly blind. Usually he dictated his letters and just signed them himself (Col. 4:18; 2 Thess. 3:17), but in this letter of warning he wanted to show his special love for the Galatians.

5:21 shall not inherit. Read Revelation 21:8.
5:24 crucified. Crucifixion is a slow death. The sinful desires do not die easily. The Holy Spirit will not give us victory over them until we decide that they are wrong and that they must die.
5:25 walk. See 5:16 first note.
6:2 Bear ye one another's burdens. Compare this with verse 5. Verse 2 speaks of the burdens which can be shared: sorrow, misfortune, etc.; verse 5 speaks of those that cannot be taken by anyone else: physical illness, a painful duty, etc.
6:4 prove. Test.
6:6 communicate. In this verse, "communicate" means *to share*.

[12]As many as desire to make a fair
shew in the flesh, they constrain you to
be circumcised; only lest they should
suffer persecution for the cross of
Christ.
[13]For neither they themselves who
are circumcised keep the law; but desire to have you circumcised, that they
may glory in your flesh.
[14]But God forbid that I should glory,
save in the cross of our Lord Jesus
Christ, by whom the world is crucified
unto me, and I unto the world.

6:15 New Creatures in Christ
The new birth is an act of creation, and only God can create; it is a work of God (John 1:12), brought about by the Word—the seed of the new birth (1 Pet. 1:23), by the Holy Spirit (John 3:5). Those who are born again are given new life—eternal life (John 10:28), and become new creatures (2 Cor. 5:17). Christ did not die to promote a ceremony but to make us new men and women.

VI. Closing Greetings (6:15-18)

[15]For in Christ Jesus neither circumcision availeth any thing, nor uncircumcision, but a new creature.
[16]And as many as walk according to
this rule, peace *be* on them, and mercy,
and upon the Israel of God.

6:16 The Israel of God
Not all of the children of Abraham became Israelites. This term was first applied to Jacob (Gen. 32:28). Esau was a grandson of Abraham, as was Jacob, but Esau never became an Israelite because he rejected God's plan for him. The true "Israel of God" is made up of all true believers, Jews and Gentiles alike (Rom. 9:6-16). All of the promises that God made to Abraham, or to Israel, will be fulfilled.

¶[17]From henceforth let no man trouble me: for I bear in my body the marks
of the Lord Jesus.
¶[18]Brethren, the grace of our Lord
Jesus Christ *be* with your spirit. Amen.

6:14 world is crucified. The world was dead to Paul.

6:17 the marks of the Lord Jesus. Slaves' bodies were branded to show to whom they belonged. Paul, the slave of the Lord Jesus Christ (Rom. 1:1), bore His marks (see 2 Cor. 11:23-27).

6:18 Brethren. Believers all become part of the family of God the moment they accept Christ. They become the born sons and daughters of God and brothers and sisters of the Lord Jesus Christ, for He is called the "firstborn among many brethren" (Rom. 8:29; see also its note, "Predestination").

The Epistle of Paul the Apostle to the

EPHESIANS

THE WRITER AND TIME

Ephesians was a letter written in about A.D. 62, by the Apostle Paul to the church at Ephesus, the Greek city where the great temple of Diana was (Acts 19:24).

BACKGROUND

Paul had preached the gospel in Ephesus ten years before, and had built up a large and flourishing church there (see Acts 19; 20:17-38). This letter may be the one that is mentioned in Colossians 4:16 as a letter to be read to the Laodiceans. It is probably true that it was a sort of circular letter intended for the true *church, not only at Ephesus, but at Laodicea, too. Since these believers had been taught by Paul for about three years, they were well able to understand the deepest truths of Christianity.

THINGS TO NOTE

There is a close relationship between the message of the book of Joshua in respect to the children of Israel, and the message of the book of Ephesians in respect to the church. The *heavenly places of the Christian were pictured to the Israelites in their promised land of Canaan. In both cases we see conflict and even failure, but we can also see the joys of true victory and true possession of the promised blessings of the Lord.

THEME

The theme of this epistle is salvation by grace and the unity in Christ of both Jews and Gentiles.

OUTLINE OF EPHESIANS

I.	God's Plan for Salvation	Ephesians 1:1-23
II.	God's Way of Salvation	Ephesians 2:1-22
III.	Paul's Revelation of God's Plan	Ephesians 3:1-21
IV.	The High Calling of Believers	Ephesians 4:1-16
V.	The Suitable Behavior of Believers	Ephesians 4:17—6:9
VI.	The Warfare of Believers	Ephesians 6:10-24

I. God's Plan for Salvation (1:1-23)
The greeting

1 Paul, an *apostle of Jesus *Christ
by the will of *God, to the saints
which are at Ephesus, and to the faithful in Christ Jesus:
2*Grace *be* to you, and *peace, from
God our Father, and *from* the Lord Jesus
Christ.
¶3Blessed *be* the God and Father of
our Lord Jesus Christ, who hath
blessed us with all spiritual blessings in
heavenly *places* in Christ:

1:3 Heavenly Things
"Heavenly places" means *the heavenlies* or the realm of heavenly things as contrasted with earthly things. God blessed the Jews, His earthly people, with earthly blessings such as long life, wealth, and prosperity; and they were to be enjoyed here on the earth. But now, since Jesus Christ came, God has blessed His people, the Christians, with spiritual blessings, such as forgiveness of sins, peace with God, and true happiness, all of which can be enjoyed whether earthly blessings are included or not. What really counts for the Christian are the heavenly things.

4According as he hath chosen us in
him before the foundation of the
*world, that we should be *holy and
without blame before him in love:
5Having predestinated us unto the
adoption of children by Jesus Christ to
himself, according to the good pleasure
of his will,
6To the praise of the glory of his
grace, wherein he hath made us accepted in the beloved.

1:5 Adoption
When a child is born, he is counted as a child of his parents right away, but there are certain things he is not allowed to do until he is grown. Just as soon as a person believes in Christ as His Saviour from the guilt and punishment of sin, he is born again and becomes a child of God (John 1:12), but he does not have to wait many years for his rights and privileges, for he is adopted at once into these blessings. It is as if God were pointing out that the one who believes is as much His child as is our Lord, our Father's only begotten Son.

7In whom we have *redemption
through his *blood, the forgiveness of
sins, according to the riches of his
grace;
8Wherein he hath abounded toward
us in all wisdom and prudence;
9Having made known unto us the
*mystery of his will, according to his
good pleasure which he hath purposed
in himself:
10That in the dispensation of the
fulness of times he might gather together in one all things in Christ, both
which are in *heaven, and which are on
earth; *even* in him:

1:10 The Seventh Dispensation
The "dispensation of the fulness of times" is the last of the *dispensations or periods of God's dealings with men. It will be a time of blessing, the *Millennium, when heaven and earth will unite under the kingship of the Lord Jesus Christ. It is the time of Colossians 1:20 (see also its note, "Reconciliation").

1:1 saints . . . and to the faithful. A saint is not a sinless person but a saved sinner. A sinner becomes a saint when he believes on the Lord Jesus Christ as his Saviour. "Faithful in Christ Jesus" is another way of describing the Christians, for they were people who had trusted or had faith in the Lord.

1:5 predestinated. This word means that God determined beforehand that everyone who believed on Jesus Christ as Saviour would become His son or daughter and a member of His family and would have certain blessings. Here it is the blessing of adoption in Christ that is promised (see John 1:12; Rom. 8:15; Gal. 4:5). See verse 11 note, "Predestination."

1:6 the beloved. This is the Lord Jesus Christ. God accepts us, not because of anything that we have done but because of the love that He has for Jesus Christ, our Saviour, and through Him, for us.

11 In whom also we have obtained an
inheritance, being predestinated according to the purpose of him who
worketh all things after the counsel of
his own will:
12 That we should be to the praise of
his glory, who first trusted in Christ.
13 In whom ye also *trusted,* after that
ye heard the word of truth, the *gospel
of your *salvation: in whom also after
that ye believed, ye were sealed with
that *holy Spirit of promise,
14 Which is the earnest of our inheritance until the redemption of the purchased possession, unto the praise of
his glory.

Paul's prayer for the Christians

¶ 15 Wherefore I also, after I heard of
your *faith in the Lord Jesus, and love
unto all the saints,
16 Cease not to give thanks for you,
making mention of you in my prayers;
17 That the God of our Lord Jesus
Christ, the Father of glory, may give
unto you the spirit of wisdom and *revelation in the knowledge of him:
18 The eyes of your understanding
being enlightened; that ye may know
what is the *hope of his calling, and
what the riches of the glory of his inheritance in the saints,
19 And what *is* the exceeding greatness of his power to us-ward who believe, according to the working of his
mighty power,
20 Which he wrought in Christ, when
he raised him from the dead, and set
him at his own right hand in the heavenly *places,*
21 Far above all principality, and power, and might, and dominion, and every
name that is named, not only in this
world, but also in that which is to come:
22 And hath put all *things* under his
feet, and gave him *to be* the head over
all *things* to the *church,
23 Which is his body, the fulness of
him that filleth all in all.

II. God's Way of Salvation (2:1-22)

2 And you *hath he quickened,* who
were dead in trespasses and sins;
2 Wherein in time past ye walked according to the course of this world, according to the prince of the power of the

1:11 PREDESTINATION

Predestination speaks of *being marked out*. The word, in its different forms, appears in only three passages in the Bible, and never does it suggest that a person is predestined or marked out to be lost or to be saved. It always speaks about those who are saved.

In Romans 8:29-30 (and Rom. 8:29 note, "Predestination"), we find that those predestined are those who are marked out to be conformed to the image of the Son of God. In Ephesians 1:5, it is written that those who have been chosen in Christ have been marked out for the place of children; and in Ephesians 1:11-12, we learn that Christ's own have been marked out to praise His glory.

Someone has said that "election" has to do with what the Christian has been chosen *from,* while "predestination" has to do with what the Christian has been marked out *to*. The former speaks of what we came from; the latter has to do with what we are and where we are going to be.

1:13 sealed. Sealing in the Bible suggests: 1) Ownership. We are owned by God when we trust Jesus Christ; and the Holy Spirit dwelling in us is the seal that shows this. 2) Security. When an agreement is made, the document is sealed with a special seal. The Holy Spirit in us is the seal that our salvation is a completed agreement (see 4:30; 2 Tim. 2:19).

1:14 earnest. This was the first payment made on a purchase by the buyer, as on a house. It was a promise that the rest of the payment would be made. The Holy Spirit is the earnest given to us by God to promise us that He will one day complete our redemption from this world of sin and suffering and take us to be with Him in heaven.

1:23 his body. See *church.

2:2 prince of the power of the air. *Satan. "Power of the air" speaks of the region of evil spirits over which Satan rules.

air, the spirit that now worketh in the
children of disobedience:
3Among whom also we all had our conversation in times past in the *lusts of our
*flesh, fulfilling the desires of the flesh
and of the mind; and were by nature the
children of wrath, even as others.
4But God, who is rich in *mercy, for
his great love wherewith he loved us,
5Even when we were dead in sins,
hath quickened us together with Christ,
(by grace ye are saved;)
6And hath raised *us* up together, and
made *us* sit together in heavenly *places*
in Christ Jesus:
7That in the ages to come he might
shew the exceeding riches of his grace
in *his* kindness toward us through
Christ Jesus.
8For by grace are ye saved through
faith; and that not of yourselves: *it is* the
gift of God:
9Not of works, lest any man should
boast.
10For we are his workmanship, *created in Christ Jesus unto good works,
which God hath before ordained that we
should walk in them.

The position of Gentiles before conversion

¶11Wherefore remember, that ye *being* in time past Gentiles in the flesh,
who are called Uncircumcision by that
which is called the *Circumcision in the
flesh made by hands;
12That at that time ye were without
Christ, being aliens from the commonwealth of *Israel, and strangers from
the covenants of promise, having no
hope, and without God in the world:

The position of Gentiles after conversion

13But now in Christ Jesus ye who
sometimes were far off are made nigh
by the blood of Christ.
14For he is our peace, who hath made
both one, and hath broken down the
middle wall of partition *between us;*
15Having abolished in his flesh the
enmity, *even* the *law of commandments *contained* in ordinances; for to
make in himself of twain one new man,
so making peace;
16And that he might *reconcile both
unto God in one body by the cross, having slain the enmity thereby:
17And came and preached peace to
you which were afar off, and to them
that were nigh.
18For through him we both have access by one Spirit unto the Father.

The Church a temple for God

19Now therefore ye are no more
strangers and foreigners, but fellowcitizens with the saints, and of the
household of God;
20And are built upon the foundation
of the *apostles and *prophets, Jesus
Christ himself being the chief corner
stone;
21In whom all the building fitly
framed together groweth unto an holy
temple in the Lord:
22In whom ye also are builded togeth-

2:11 The Gentiles
Gentiles is a general term for all people who were not born Jews. The Jews looked down on Gentiles and never had anything to do with them. Paul goes on to explain that the gospel united both peoples to one new group, the *church. He compares it to the great temple at Jerusalem—each Christian being like a stone, fitting the one into the other, with the Lord Jesus as the chief cornerstone (see 1 Pet. 2:4-6).

2:5 dead. People who are not Christians are looked upon as spiritually dead. They need the new birth to bring them to life toward God (see John 3:3 note, "Born Again"). If they are never born again, they go on being dead toward God and are eternally separated from Him. This separation is called "the second death" (Rev. 20:6,14; see also 20:12 note, "The Dead," and Rev. 20:14 note).
2:13 sometimes. Once.
2:15 one new man. The church (see vs. 11 note, "The Gentiles").

er for an habitation of God through the
Spirit.

III. Revelation of God's Plan (3:1-21)

3 For this cause I Paul, the prisoner
of Jesus Christ for you Gentiles,
2 If ye have heard of the dispensation
of the *grace of God which is given me
to you-ward:
3 How that by revelation he made
known unto me the *mystery; (as I
wrote afore in few words,
4 Whereby, when ye read, ye may understand my knowledge in the mystery
of Christ)
5 Which in other ages was not made
known unto the sons of men, as it is
now revealed unto his holy apostles and
prophets by the Spirit;
6 That the Gentiles should be fellow-
heirs, and of the same body, and *partakers of his promise in Christ by the
gospel:
7 Whereof I was made a minister, according to the gift of the grace of God
given unto me by the effectual working
of his power.
8 Unto me, who am less than the least
of all saints, is this grace given, that I
should preach among the Gentiles the
unsearchable riches of Christ;
9 And to make all *men* see what *is* the
fellowship of the mystery, which from
the beginning of the world hath been
hid in God, who created all things by
Jesus Christ:
10 To the intent that now unto the
principalities and powers in heavenly
places might be known by the church
the manifold wisdom of God,
11 According to the eternal purpose
which he purposed in Christ Jesus our
Lord:
12 In whom we have boldness and access with confidence by the faith of him.

Paul's second prayer for the Christians

13 Wherefore I desire that ye faint not
at my tribulations for you, which is your
glory.
14 For this cause I bow my knees unto
the Father of our Lord Jesus Christ,
15 Of whom the whole family in heav-
en and earth is named,
16 That he would grant you, according
to the riches of his glory, to be strengthened with might by his Spirit in the inner man;
17 That Christ may dwell in your
hearts by faith; that ye, being rooted
and grounded in love,
18 May be able to comprehend with all

3:3 MYSTERIES OF THE BIBLE

1. The mystery of the kingdom of heaven (Matt. 13:11; see also its note, "The Mysteries of the Kingdom")
2. The mystery of the Jewish "blindness" (Rom. 11:25)
3. The mystery of the raising of believers—the *Rapture (1 Cor. 15:51-52; see also 1 Cor. 15:52 note, "A Final Resurrection")
4. The mystery of the church, as revealed in this passage (Eph. 3:1-11)
5. The mystery of the church, the bride of Christ (Eph. 5:25,32; see also Eph. 5:32 note, "The Church")
6. The mystery of the gospel (Eph. 6:19)
7. The mystery of Christ in the believer (Col. 1:27 and its note, "Christ Lives in Us")
8. The mystery of God—Christ (Col. 2:2, 9)
9. The mystery of godliness (1 Tim. 3:16)
10. The mystery of iniquity (2 Thess. 2:7)
11. The mystery of the seven stars (Rev. 1:20 and its note, "Angels")
12. The mystery of Babylon (Rev. 17:5,7)

3:2 dispensation . . . which is given me. In this verse "dispensation" means *a special privilege*.
3:9 created all things by Jesus Christ. See John 1:3.

saints what *is* the breadth, and length, and depth, and height;

19 And to know the love of Christ, which passeth knowledge, that ye might be filled with all the fulness of God.

¶ 20 Now unto him that is able to do exceeding abundantly above all that we ask or think, according to the power that worketh in us,

21 Unto him *be* glory in the church by Christ Jesus throughout all ages, world without end. *Amen.

IV. The High Calling of Believers (4:1-16)

4 I therefore, the prisoner of the Lord, beseech you that ye walk worthy of the vocation wherewith ye are called,

2 With all lowliness and meekness, with longsuffering, forbearing one another in love;

3 Endeavouring to keep the unity of the Spirit in the bond of peace.

The seven "ones"

4 *There is* one body, and one Spirit, even as ye are called in one hope of your calling;

5 One Lord, one faith, one *baptism,

6 One God and Father of all, who *is* above all, and through all, and in you all.

The gifts of Christ to the Christians

7 But unto every one of us is given grace according to the measure of the gift of Christ.

8 Wherefore he saith, When he ascended up on high, he led captivity captive, and gave gifts unto men.

9 (Now that he ascended, what is it but that he also descended first into the lower parts of the earth?

10 He that descended is the same also that ascended up far above all heavens, that he might fill all things.)

11 And he gave some, apostles; and some, prophets; and some, evangelists; and some, pastors and teachers;

12 For the perfecting of the saints, for the work of the ministry, for the edifying of the *body of Christ:

13 Till we all come in the unity of the faith, and of the knowledge of the Son of God, unto a perfect man, unto the measure of the stature of the *fulness of Christ:

14 That we *henceforth* be no more children, tossed to and fro, and carried about with every wind of *doctrine, by the sleight of men, *and* cunning craftiness, whereby they lie in wait to deceive;

15 But speaking the truth in love, may grow up into him in all things, which is the head, *even* Christ:

16 From whom the whole body fitly joined together and compacted by that which every joint supplieth, according to the effectual working in the measure of every part, maketh increase of the body unto the edifying of itself in love.

V. Behavior of Believers (4:17—6:9)

¶ 17 This I say therefore, and testify in the Lord, that ye henceforth walk not

---

4:1 vocation. A vocation is a *calling* or a *life work*. To live for Christ is the chief "business" of the Christian.

4:2 forbearing one another. Accepting and loving each other in Christ.

4:4 one body. The body of Christ (compare 1 Cor. 12:13).

4:5 one faith. This is *the* faith, faith in Christ—the one great standard of truth, or Christian teaching, which God has given to the world.

4:5 one baptism. By the use of water.

4:6 Father of all. This speaks of God, the Creator of all men.

4:8 When he ascended. A quotation from Psalm 68:18, which refers to the Lord Jesus Christ and tells of His coming down to earth, His death ("descended first into the lower parts of the earth"), and His ascension to be with God.

4:8 led captivity captive. He conquered the very power, Satan, that had for so long held men in bondage (compare Heb. 2:15).

4:8 gave gifts unto men. This refers to the gifts of teaching, prophesying, etc., that He gave to the apostles and early Christians, and that He gives to Christians today.

as other Gentiles walk, in the *vanity
of their mind,
18Having the understanding darkened, being alienated from the life of
God through the ignorance that is in
them, because of the blindness of their
heart:
19Who being past feeling have given
themselves over unto lasciviousness, to
work all uncleanness with greediness.
20But ye have not so learned Christ;
21If so be that ye have heard him, and
have been taught by him, as the truth
is in Jesus:
22That ye put off concerning the former conversation the old man, which is
corrupt according to the deceitful lusts;
23And be renewed in the spirit of your
mind;
24And that ye put on the new man,
which after God is created in *righteousness and true holiness.
¶25Wherefore putting away lying,
speak every man truth with his neighbour: for we are members one of another.
26Be ye angry, and *sin not: let not
the sun go down upon your wrath:
27Neither give place to the *devil.
28Let him that stole steal no more:
but rather let him labour, working with
his hands the thing which is good,
that he may have to give to him that
needeth.
29Let no corrupt communication proceed out of your mouth, but that which
is good to the use of edifying, that it
may minister grace unto the hearers.
30And grieve not the *holy Spirit of
God, whereby ye are sealed unto the
day of *redemption.
31Let all bitterness, and wrath, and
anger, and clamour, and evil speaking,
be put away from you, with all malice:
32And be ye kind one to another, ten-
derhearted, forgiving one another, even
as God for Christ's sake hath *forgiven
you.

5 Be ye therefore followers of God,
as dear children;
2And walk in love, as Christ also hath
loved us, and hath given himself for us
an *offering and a *sacrifice to God for
a sweetsmelling savour.
3But fornication, and all uncleanness, or covetousness, let it not be
once named among you, as becometh
saints;
4Neither filthiness, nor foolish talking, nor jesting, which are not convenient: but rather giving of thanks.
5For this ye know, that no whore-
monger, nor *unclean person, nor covetous man, who is an idolater, hath any
inheritance in the *kingdom of Christ
and of God.
6Let no man deceive you with vain
words: for because of these things
cometh the wrath of God upon the children of disobedience.
7Be not ye therefore partakers with
them.
8For ye were sometimes darkness,
but now *are ye* light in the Lord: walk
as children of light:
9(For the fruit of the Spirit *is* in all
goodness and righteousness and truth;)
10Proving what is acceptable unto the
Lord.
11And have no fellowship with the
unfruitful works of darkness, but rather reprove *them.*

4:18 blindness. Hardness; numbness.

4:20 not so learned Christ. Here Paul was speaking of our Lord as the Risen One who is sitting at the right hand of God.

4:21 the truth . . . in Jesus. See John 14:6.

4:22 the old man. What we were before we were saved. As Christians we must have nothing more to do with that old self. It is the old "I" which has been crucified with Christ (Gal. 2:20), and must be so counted (Col. 3:8-14); old things must be "put away" (vss. 25-31).

4:23 be renewed. Being renewed. The mind, like the body, is renewed by feeding. The Christian's food for his mind is the Word of God, the Bible, and also fellowship and communion with the Lord and with other Christians.

12 For it is a shame even to speak of
those things which are done of them in
secret.
13 But all things that are reproved are
made manifest by the light: for whatsoever doth make manifest is light.
14 Wherefore he saith, Awake thou
that sleepest, and arise from the dead,
and Christ shall give thee light.
15 See then that ye walk circumspectly, not as *fools, but as wise,
16 Redeeming the time, because the
days are evil.
17 Wherefore be ye not unwise, but
understanding what the will of the
Lord *is*.
18 And be not drunk with *wine,
wherein is excess; but be filled with the
Spirit;
19 Speaking to yourselves in psalms
and hymns and spiritual songs, singing
and making melody in your heart to the
Lord;
20 Giving thanks always for all things
unto God and the Father in the name of
our Lord Jesus Christ;

Husbands and wives

21 Submitting yourselves one to another in the *fear of God.
22 Wives, submit yourselves unto
your own husbands, as unto the Lord.
23 For the husband is the head of the
wife, even as Christ is the head of the
church: and he is the saviour of the
body.
24 Therefore as the church is subject
unto Christ, so *let* the wives *be* to their
own husbands in every thing.
25 Husbands, love your wives, even as
Christ also loved the church, and gave
himself for it;
26 That he might sanctify and cleanse
it with the washing of water by the
word,
27 That he might present it to himself a glorious church, not having spot,
or wrinkle, or any such thing; but that
it should be holy and without blemish.
28 So ought men to love their wives as
their own bodies. He that loveth his
wife loveth himself.
29 For no man ever yet hated his own
flesh; but nourisheth and cherisheth it,
even as the Lord the church:
30 For we are members of his body, of
his flesh, and of his bones.
31 For this cause shall a man leave his
father and mother, and shall be joined
unto his wife, and they two shall be one
flesh.
32 This is a great *mystery: but I
speak concerning Christ and the
church.
33 Nevertheless let every one of you
in particular so love his wife even as
himself; and the wife *see* that she reverence *her* husband.

Children and servants

6 Children, obey your parents in the
Lord: for this is right.
2 Honour thy father and mother;

5:32 THE CHURCH

1. The church is not a building or group; it is composed of every believer of Jesus Christ from Pentecost to the first resurrection. It is called the body of Christ (Eph. 1:22-23), to show how close the members are to each other and to Christ; the Temple of God (Eph. 2:21-22), to show its purpose to worship God; and the bride of Christ (Eph. 5:25-32; compare Rev. 21:2,9), to show His great love for it.
2. The visible church is that organization that can be seen, and it consists of everyone who professes to be a Christian. Many in this church have not been born again. It is the history of this outward church that Revelation 2 and 3 present. It is divided into different groups, forms of government, and sets of doctrine.
3. The local church is the visible church in its local groups. In Paul's time it was all the believers in one place who gathered for breaking of bread, worship, preaching, prayer, and testimony. They could claim the promise of Matthew 18:20.

(which is the first commandment with
promise;)
3 That it may be well with thee, and
thou mayest live long on the earth.
4 And, ye fathers, provoke not your
children to wrath: but bring them up in
the nurture and admonition of the Lord.
5 Servants, be obedient to them that
are *your* masters according to the flesh,
with fear and trembling, in singleness
of your heart, as unto Christ;
6 Not with eyeservice, as menpleasers; but as the servants of Christ,
doing the will of God from the heart;
7 With good will doing service, as to
the Lord, and not to men:
8 Knowing that whatsoever good thing
any man doeth, the same shall he receive
of the Lord, whether *he be* bond or free.
9 And, ye masters, do the same things
unto them, forbearing threatening:
knowing that your Master also is in
heaven; neither is there respect of persons with him.

VI. The Warfare of Believers (6:10-24)

¶10 Finally, my brethren, be strong in
the Lord, and in the power of his might.
11 Put on the whole armour of God,
that ye may be able to stand against the
wiles of the devil.
12 For we wrestle not against flesh
and blood, but against principalities,
against powers, against the rulers of the
darkness of this world, against spiritual wickedness in high *places*.
13 Wherefore take unto you the whole
armour of God, that ye may be able to
withstand in the evil day, and having
done all, to stand.
14 Stand therefore, having your loins
girt about with truth, and having on the
breastplate of righteousness;
15 And your feet shod with the preparation of the gospel of peace;
16 Above all, taking the shield of faith,
wherewith ye shall be able to quench all
the fiery darts of the wicked.
17 And take the helmet of salvation,
and the sword of the Spirit, which is the
word of God:
18 Praying always with all prayer and
supplication in the Spirit, and watching
thereunto with all perseverance and
supplication for all saints;
19 And for me, that utterance may be
given unto me, that I may open my
mouth boldly, to make known the mystery of the gospel,
20 For which I am an ambassador in
bonds: that therein I may speak boldly,
as I ought to speak.
¶21 But that ye also may know my affairs, *and* how I do, Tychicus, a beloved
brother and faithful minister in the
Lord, shall make known to you all
things:
22 Whom I have sent unto you for the
same purpose, that ye might know our
affairs, and *that* he might comfort your
hearts.
¶23 Peace *be* to the brethren, and love
with faith, from God the Father and the
Lord Jesus Christ.
24 Grace *be* with all them that love our
Lord Jesus Christ in sincerity. Amen.

6:2 first commandment with promise. See Exodus 20:12.
6:5 Servants. This was not just addressed to slaves but to anyone who has one in authority over him—such as any employees (see vs. 8).
6:6 eyeservice. Working only when one is being watched.
6:10 be strong in the Lord. Be strengthened daily in the Lord's strength.
6:11 wiles of the devil. The crafty methods and schemes by which the Devil tries to deceive even Christians into thinking that he and his plans are all right.
6:12 spiritual wickedness. A fact that is still true today and that we must face.
6:13 to stand. To stand firmly because of Christ's finished work.
6:16 the wicked. The Wicked One, Satan.
6:17 word of God. The Bible, when it is used under the guidance of the Holy Spirit, is the sword of the Spirit. We must use all the spiritual armor with which the Lord has supplied us to live in victory, by being totally dependent on our Lord and His Word.

The Epistle of Paul the Apostle to the

PHILIPPIANS

THE WRITER AND TIME

This letter was written by the Apostle Paul to the Christians at Philippi while he was in prison in Rome. The date of writing is, presumably, A.D. 63.

BACKGROUND

Philippi was a city of Macedonia at the northern end of the Aegean Sea, which lies on the east of Greece. Paul visited Philippi three times (Acts 16:12-40; 20:5,6; 2 Corinthians 13:1). On his first visit there he was imprisoned because he was used of the Lord to cast out a demon from a slave-girl. But through that imprisonment the Philippian jailor and his family were saved, and a church grew up in that city.

THINGS TO NOTE

This letter acknowledges a gift of money which the Philippian Christians sent to Paul by Epaphroditus (Philippians 2:25). The words "you," "your," "ye," occur seventy-six times, showing that this is a personal letter. Though imprisoned, Paul was full of joy, for the words "joy" and "rejoice," or some other forms of these words, are found eighteen times.

OUTLINE OF PHILIPPIANS

Keeping the four chapters as the main parts, the book may be outlined in this way:

I.	Christian Friendship	Philippians 1:1-30
II.	Christian Living	Philippians 2:1-30
III.	Christian Righteousness	Philippians 3:1-21
IV.	Christian Peace	Philippians 4:1-23

I. Christian Friendship (1:1-30)

1 Paul and Timotheus, the servants
of Jesus *Christ, to all the *saints
in Christ Jesus which are at Philippi,
with the bishops and deacons:
2 *Grace *be* unto you, and peace, from
*God our Father, and *from* the Lord
Jesus Christ.

Paul's love for the Philippians

¶3 I thank my God upon every remembrance of you,

1:1 Timotheus. This is the Greek form of the name Timothy, to whom Paul wrote two letters, 1 and 2 Timothy.

1:2 peace. Romans 5:1 tells the one method by which we may gain real peace.

1:1 Bishops and Deacons
Bishops were overseers (as were elders) and were the spiritual leaders of the church. The deacons were usually younger men and looked after the ordinary, practical business connected with the church.

4 Always in every *prayer of mine for
you all making request with joy,
5 For your fellowship in the *gospel
from the first day until now;
6 Being confident of this very thing,
that he which hath begun a good work
in you will perform *it* until the day of
Jesus Christ:
7 Even as it is meet for me to think
this of you all, because I have you in my
heart; inasmuch as both in my bonds,
and in the defence and confirmation of
the gospel, ye all are *partakers of my
grace.
8 For God is my record, how greatly
I long after you all in the bowels of Jesus
Christ.
9 And this I pray, that your love may
abound yet more and more in knowledge and *in* all judgment;
10 That ye may approve things that
are excellent; that ye may be sincere
and without offence till the day of
Christ;
11 Being filled with the fruits of *righteousness, which are by Jesus Christ,
unto the glory and praise of God.

Paul's joy in prison

¶12 But I would ye should understand,
brethren, that the things *which happened* unto me have fallen out rather
unto the furtherance of the gospel;
13 So that my bonds in Christ are
manifest in all the palace, and in all
other *places;*
14 And many of the brethren in the
Lord, waxing confident by my bonds,
are much more bold to speak the word
without fear.
15 Some indeed preach Christ even
of envy and strife; and some also of
good will:
16 The one preach Christ of contention, not sincerely, supposing to add affliction to my bonds:
17 But the other of love, knowing
that I am set for the defence of the
gospel.
18 What then? notwithstanding, every
way, whether in pretence, or in truth,
Christ is preached; and I therein do rejoice, yea, and will rejoice.

Paul's trust in Christ

19 For I know that this shall turn to my
salvation through your prayer, and the
supply of the Spirit of Jesus Christ,
20 According to my earnest expectation and *my* *hope, that in nothing I
shall be ashamed, but *that* with all boldness, as always, *so* now also Christ shall

---

1:6 he . . . will perform it. God will keep His people (1 Cor. 10:13; 2 Thess. 3:3; 1 Pet. 1:5; Jude 24; see also Jude 24 note, "Being Faultless"). See *assurance.
1:6 day of Jesus Christ. The time when Jesus will return to reward His people. See Revelation 22:12.
1:8 bowels. Love and tenderness.
1:10 day of Christ. See verse 6 second note.
1:11 the fruits of righteousness, which are by Jesus Christ. See Galatians 5:22-23 and its note, "The Fruit of the Spirit."
1:12 fallen out rather unto the furtherance. The things that had happened to Paul caused the gospel to be advanced and spread farther (Rom. 8:28).
1:13 the palace. Caesar's court.
1:14 waxing confident by my bonds. The glory of Paul's courage in Christ filled the other Christian brethren with the same courage. When his voice was silenced, other witnesses became braver.
1:15 envy and strife. Some preached the gospel in order to have the honor that Paul deservedly had.
1:19 my salvation. Paul spoke of his present victory in the midst of trial (and blessing for him, in spite of the trial) since he had no doubt of his eternal salvation.

be magnified in my body, whether *it be*
by life, or by *death.
[21]For to me to live *is* Christ, and to
die *is* gain.
[22]But if I live in the *flesh, this *is* the
fruit of my labour: yet what I shall
choose I wot not.
[23]For I am in a strait betwixt two,
having a desire to depart, and to be with
Christ; which is far better:
[24]Nevertheless to abide in the flesh
is more needful for you.
[25]And having this confidence, I know
that I shall abide and continue with
you all for your furtherance and joy of
*faith;
[26]That your rejoicing may be more
abundant in Jesus Christ for me by my
coming to you again.

Paul's example to the Philippians

[27]Only let your *conversation be as
it becometh the gospel of Christ: that
whether I come and see you, or else be
absent, I may hear of your affairs, that
ye stand fast in one spirit, with one
mind striving together for the faith of
the gospel;
[28]And in nothing terrified by your
adversaries: which is to them an evident token of perdition, but to you of
salvation, and that of God.
[29]For unto you it is given in the behalf of Christ, not only to believe on
him, but also to suffer for his sake;
[30]Having the same conflict which ye
saw in me, and now hear *to be* in me.

II. Christian Living (2:1-30)

2 If *there be* therefore any consolation in Christ, if any comfort of
love, if any fellowship of the Spirit, if
any bowels and mercies,
[2]Fulfil ye my joy, that ye be likeminded, having the same love, *being* of
one accord, of one mind.
[3]*Let* nothing *be done* through strife or
vainglory; but in lowliness of mind let
each esteem other better than themselves.
[4]Look not every man on his own
things, but every man also on the things
of others.

Being humble like Christ Jesus

[5]Let this mind be in you, which was
also in Christ Jesus:
[6]Who, being in the form of God,
thought it not robbery to be equal with
God:

2:6 The Form of God
The "form of God" speaks of the glorious appearance that the Lord Jesus Christ had: "the glory which I had with thee" (John 17:5). When He came to the earth to live, He did not empty Himself of any part of His divine nature, although He was made in the likeness of men (vs. 7). That means only that He emptied Himself of the outward glory that was a mark of His godhead and majesty. The eyes of men could not have looked upon His glory.

[7]But made himself of no reputation,
and took upon him the form of a servant,

1:21 to live is Christ and to die is gain. On this earth Christ was everything to Paul (vss. 7-8), but in heaven the actual presence of the Lord Jesus Christ will be far better (vs. 23; John 14:1-3; Rev. 21:4; 22:3-5).

2:1 If there be therefore any consolation. This does not mean that the Philippians did not have these qualities, but since they had these qualities through Christ, they should encourage each other and become more unified and be "of one mind" (vs. 2). Note the four blessings God had given them: consolation (encouragement), comfort, communion, compassion (love). The Philippian church seemed to be a very loving, giving group of believers. Paul also had great love for them.

2:3 vainglory. Pride or conceit.

2:6 thought it not robbery. Our Lord was not grasping at something that was not His by divine right; it was rightfully His, for He is God.

2:7 made himself of no reputation. Emptied Himself.

and was made in the likeness of men:
[8]And being found in fashion as a man,
he humbled himself, and became obedient unto death, even the death of the
cross.
[9]Wherefore God also hath highly exalted him, and given him a name which
is above every name:
[10]That at the name of Jesus every
knee should bow, of *things* in *heaven,
and *things* in earth, and *things* under the
earth;
[11]And *that* every tongue should confess that Jesus Christ *is* Lord, to the
glory of God the Father.

Letting others see the new life

¶[12]Wherefore, my beloved, as ye
have always obeyed, not as in my presence only, but now much more in my
absence, work out your own salvation
with fear and trembling.
[13]For it is God which worketh in you
both to will and to do of *his* good pleasure.
[14]Do all things without murmurings
and disputings:
[15]That ye may be *blameless and
harmless, the sons of God, without rebuke, in the midst of a crooked and perverse nation, among whom ye shine as
lights in the *world;
[16]Holding forth the word of life; that
I may rejoice in the day of Christ, that I
have not run in vain, neither laboured
in vain.
[17]Yea, and if I be offered upon the
*sacrifice and service of your faith, I joy,
and rejoice with you all.
[18]For the same cause also do ye joy,
and rejoice with me.

The example of Timothy

¶[19]But I *trust in the Lord Jesus to
send *Timotheus shortly unto you, that
I also may be of good comfort, when I
know your state.
[20]For I have no man likeminded, who
will naturally care for your state.
[21]For all seek their own, not the
things which are Jesus Christ's.
[22]But ye know the proof of him, that,
as a son with the father, he hath served
with me in the gospel.
[23]Him therefore I hope to send presently, so soon as I shall see how it will
go with me.
[24]But I trust in the Lord that I also
myself shall come shortly.

The example of Epaphroditus

[25]Yet I supposed it necessary to send
to you Epaphroditus, my brother, and
companion in labour, and fellowsoldier,

2:8 found in fashion. Living in human form as a Man on earth (Matt. 8:20 and its note, "The Son of Man"; John 7:46).

2:10 every knee should bow. This has not yet come to pass, but it will definitely happen when Christ comes again to reign (Rev. 5:13).

2:12 work out. This does not mean working to earn our salvation, which is "not of works" (Eph. 2:8-9). Verse 12 shows that it is God working "in" us "to will and to do his good pleasure." We are to work "out" what God has worked "in" us. Notice the verse does not say or imply that we are to work "for" our salvation.

2:15 without rebuke. We should not give others an opportunity or cause to say anything against us as Christians; we are to live pure and "blameless" lives by the Spirit's power in us.

2:15 perverse nation. All people opposed to God are perverse, serving Satan, whether they realize it or not.

2:15 lights. Christ is *the* Light of the World (John 8:12), but He also calls His people the light of the world (Matt. 5:14-16).

2:15 world. Mankind.

2:17 if I be offered. It was the custom to pour wine on burnt sacrifices as an additional offering. The Philippians gave faith and service to God as their offering. Paul was willing to pour out his life as an additional offering. See John 15:13.

2:25 fellowsoldier. Not in the Roman army but a soldier of the Lord. Epaphroditus was serving with Paul in Christ's army. See Paul's advice to Timothy (2 Tim. 2:3-4).

but your messenger, and he that ministered to my wants.
26 For he longed after you all, and was
full of heaviness, because that ye had
heard that he had been sick.
27 For indeed he was sick nigh unto
death: but God had *mercy on him;
and not on him only, but on me also,
lest I should have sorrow upon sorrow.
28 I sent him therefore the more carefully, that, when ye see him again, ye
may rejoice, and that I may be the less
sorrowful.
29 Receive him therefore in the Lord
with all gladness; and hold such in reputation:
30 Because for the work of Christ he
was nigh unto death, not regarding his
life, to supply your lack of service toward me.

III. Christian Righteousness (3:1-21)

3 Finally, my brethren, rejoice in the
Lord. To write the same things to
you, to me indeed *is* not grievous, but
for you *it is* safe.
¶2 Beware of dogs, beware of evil
workers, beware of the concision.
3 For we are the circumcision, which
worship God in the spirit, and rejoice in
Christ Jesus, and have no confidence in
the flesh.

Paul trusts only in Christ

4 Though I might also have confidence in the flesh. If any other man
thinketh that he hath whereof he might
trust in the flesh, I more:
5 Circumcised the eighth day, of the
stock of *Israel, *of* the tribe of Benjamin, an Hebrew of the Hebrews; as
touching the *law, a *Pharisee;
6 Concerning zeal, persecuting the
*church; touching the righteousness
which is in the law, blameless.
7 But what things were gain to me,
those I counted loss for Christ.
8 Yea doubtless, and I count all things
but loss for the excellency of the knowledge of Christ Jesus my Lord: for whom
I have suffered the loss of all things, and
do count them *but* dung, that I may win
Christ,
9 And be found in him, not having
mine own righteousness, which is of
the law, but that which is through the
faith of Christ, the righteousness which
is of God by faith:
10 That I may know him, and the
power of his *resurrection, and the fel-

2:30 supply your lack of service. Epaphroditus risked his life to help Paul and to do what he could for him, since the Philippians were not there.

3:2 dogs. Evil men. See also Psalm 22:16; Isaiah 56:10-11; 2 Peter 2:22.

3:2 concision. These were people who mutilated their own flesh, as the heathen did, trying to earn favor with God in a way He had already soundly condemned (Lev. 21:5; Deut. 14:1). They followed Mosaic practices too but had no heart for God.

3:3 we are the circumcision. Paul is here speaking not of the Jews in Old Testament times; he was talking about true Christians, who worship God sincerely (John 4:24), who trust only in Christ, knowing there is nothing good in themselves (Rom. 7:18-19).

3:6 persecuting the church. Acts 9:1; 22:4-5; 26:9-11 give instances of Paul's former persecution of Christians.

3:6 blameless. Paul had kept the Old Testament laws as his Jewish teachers had explained them and as he understood them.

3:7 gain . . . loss. Since he now knew that all his education, his family, and his own goodness could not save him, he no longer trusted these things; he only trusted the Lord Jesus Christ and was willing to give them all up for His sake.

3:8 dung. Refuse or rubbish, absolutely worthless.

3:10 power of his resurrection. Because of the resurrection of Christ, believers are sure of forgiveness (Rom. 4:25), of power in this life (Rom. 6:4), and of being raised from the dead (Rom. 8:11).

lowship of his sufferings, being made
conformable unto his death;
[11]If by any means I might attain unto
the resurrection of the dead.
[12]Not as though I had already attained, either were already perfect: but
I follow after, if that I may apprehend
that for which also I am apprehended of
Christ Jesus.
[13]Brethren, I count not myself to
have apprehended: but *this* one thing *I*
do, forgetting those things which are
behind, and reaching forth unto those
things which are before,
[14]I press toward the mark for the
prize of the high calling of God in Christ
Jesus.

Looking for the Lord Jesus Christ

[15]Let us therefore, as many as be
perfect, be thus minded: and if in any
thing ye be otherwise minded, God
shall reveal even this unto you.
[16]Nevertheless, whereto we have already attained, let us walk by the same
rule, let us mind the same thing.
[17]Brethren, be followers together of
me, and mark them which walk so as ye
have us for an ensample.
[18](For many walk, of whom I have
told you often, and now tell you even
weeping, *that they are* the enemies of
the cross of Christ:
[19]Whose end *is* destruction, whose
God *is their* belly, and *whose* glory *is*
in their shame, who mind earthly
things.)
[20]For our conversation is in heaven;
from whence also we look for the Saviour, the Lord Jesus Christ:
[21]Who shall change our vile body, that
it may be fashioned like unto his glorious body, according to the working
whereby he is able even to subdue all
things unto himself.

IV. Christian Peace
(4:1-23)

4 Therefore, my brethren dearly beloved and longed for, my joy and
crown, so stand fast in the Lord, *my*
dearly beloved.
[2]I beseech Euodias, and beseech
Syntyche, that they be of the same mind
in the Lord.
[3]And I intreat thee also, true yokefellow, help those women which laboured
with me in the gospel, with Clement

3:10 conformable. Christians are to live as those who have died with Christ (Rom. 6:6,8) and have a new life in Him.

3:11 attain. Paul was speaking of "resurrection perfection," that perfection which will be the condition of every Christian when he sees Jesus Christ at the *Rapture (see 1 John 3:2-3). Paul sought every day to live in such a way as to attain that perfection.

3:12 apprehend. Seize or lay hold of (compare Eph. 3:18).

3:14 press toward the mark. Like a runner in a race. This was an illustration often used by Paul (1 Cor. 9:24; Gal. 5:7; 2 Tim. 4:7).

3:14 high calling. The complete and perfect Christian life, which we begin to live here through the power of Christ and which we shall know fully in heaven (Col. 3:1-3; 2 Tim. 1:9-10; Heb. 3:1).

3:15 perfect. This was as though Paul were saying, "Let us who are full-grown Christians keep these things in mind."

3:17 ensample. Example.

3:21 change our vile body. Christ will change our worthless human bodies so that they will be perfect and live forever (1 Cor. 15:42-44, 49-54; see also 1 Cor. 15:52 note, "A Final Resurrection"; 1 John 3:2).

4:1 my joy and crown. The Philippians whom Paul had won to Christ were not only a great joy to him but would be a reward for him, like a crown, at the second coming of the Lord (1 Thess. 2:19).

4:2 Euodias, and beseech Syntyche. Paul was asking two women who had disagreed to come to an agreement as Christians. Women were the first converts of Philippi (Acts 16:13-14).

4:3 true yokefellow. One of Paul's helpers, of whose name we are not certain.

also, and *with* other my fellowlabourers,
whose names *are* in the book of life.

Peace through prayer

4Rejoice in the Lord alway: *and* again
I say, Rejoice.
5Let your moderation be known unto
all men. The Lord *is* at hand.
6Be careful for nothing; but in every
thing by prayer and supplication with
thanksgiving let your requests be made
known unto God.
7And the peace of God, which passeth
all understanding, shall keep your
hearts and minds through Christ Jesus.

Peace through pure thoughts

8Finally, brethren, whatsoever things
are true, whatsoever things *are* honest,
whatsoever things *are* just, whatsoever
things *are* pure, whatsoever things *are*
lovely, whatsoever things *are* of good
report; if *there be* any virtue, and if *there
be* any praise, think on these things.
9Those things, which ye have both
learned, and received, and heard, and
seen in me, do: and the God of peace
shall be with you.

Peace through trust in God

¶ 10But I rejoiced in the Lord greatly,
that now at the last your care of me hath
flourished again; wherein ye were also
careful, but ye lacked opportunity.
11Not that I speak in respect of want:
for I have learned, in whatsoever state
I am, *therewith* to be content.
12I know both how to be abased, and
I know how to abound: every where and
in all things I am instructed both to be
full and to be hungry, both to abound and
to suffer need.
13I can do all things through Christ
which strengtheneth me.
14Notwithstanding ye have well
done, that ye did communicate with my
affliction.
15Now ye Philippians know also, that
in the beginning of the gospel, when I
departed from Macedonia, no church
communicated with me as concerning
giving and receiving, but ye only.
16For even in Thessalonica ye sent
once and again unto my necessity.
17Not because I desire a gift: but I
desire fruit that may abound to your
account.
18But I have all, and abound: I am full,
having received of Epaphroditus the
things *which were sent* from you, an
odour of a sweet smell, a sacrifice acceptable, wellpleasing to God.
19But my God shall supply all your
need according to his riches in glory by
Christ Jesus.

Peace through the grace of Christ

20Now unto God and our Father *be*
glory for ever and ever. Amen.
¶21Salute every saint in Christ Jesus.
The brethren which are with me greet
you.
22All the saints salute you, chiefly
they that are of Caesar's household.
¶23The grace of our Lord Jesus
Christ *be* with you all. Amen.

4:3 book of life. See Revelation 3:5; 13:8; 20:15; 21:27; 22:19.

4:5 at hand. Near. The Lord Jesus Christ could come at any moment (James 5:7-9).

4:6 Be careful for nothing. Don't be anxious or worried about anything.

4:6 supplication. Especially earnest prayer and petition (Ps. 142:1-2; Hos. 12:4; Heb. 5:7-8).

4:14 communicate. The Philippians had shared with and helped Paul in his trouble (see vs. 10) by their gifts.

4:17 I desire fruit. Paul wanted them to learn the blessing that comes from giving (Acts 20:35).

4:18 odour of a sweet smell. This illustration comes from the Old Testament sacrifices (Gen. 8:20-21; Exod. 29:18). See also Romans 12:1; 2 Corinthians 2:14-15.

4:22 Caesar's household. Paul was referring to some of the servants and perhaps some of the men and women who had higher positions in the Roman emperor's palace. These people had believed the gospel.

The Epistle of Paul the Apostle to the

COLOSSIANS

THE WRITER AND TIME

This letter by the Apostle Paul was written in A.D. 62 to believers in Colosse, a city of Asia Minor in a region known as Phrygia.

BACKGROUND

Paul traveled through Phrygia (Acts 16:6; 18:23), but we do not read of his visiting Colosse. Another missionary, Epaphras (1:7; 4:12), appears to have been the one who first brought the gospel to the Colossians, who also took the letter to Philemon (Philemon 23).

The Colossians were for the most part Gentiles, but, like their Galatian neighbors, were troubled over the question as to whether they should worship angels and follow old Jewish customs. Paul wrote this epistle to make it very clear that the Lord Jesus Christ is above all, and that Christians may come to God freely through faith in Him alone.

THINGS TO NOTE

The writer mentions many things God has done for believers in Christ:

1. He has made us partakers of the inheritance of the saints; Colossians 1:12
2. He has delivered us from the power of darkness; Colossians 1:13
3. He has redeemed us and forgives our sins; Colossians 1:14
4. He gives us peace and reconciles all things; Colossians 1:20
5. He reconciles us to ourselves; Colossians 1:21
6. He makes us holy, unblameable, and unreproveable; Colossians 1:22
7. He gives us the riches and hope of glory; Colossians 1:27
8. He roots us, builds us up, and establishes our faith; Colossians 2:7
9. He makes us complete in him; Colossians 2:10
10. He has raised us with him; Colossians 2:12
11. He has let us put on the new man, renewed in knowledge, created in his image; Colossians 3:10
12. He has forgiven us. Colossians 3:13

OUTLINE OF COLOSSIANS

I.	Christ above All	Colossians 1:1-29
II.	The Good News of Life in Christ	Colossians 2:1-23
III.	How to Live the Christian Life	Colossians 3:1-25
IV.	Christian Fellowship	Colossians 4:1-18

I. Christ above All
(1:1-29)

1 Paul, an *apostle of Jesus *Christ
by the will of *God, and *Timotheus *our* brother,
2 To the *saints and faithful brethren
in Christ which are at Colosse: Grace
be unto you, and *peace, from God our
Father and the Lord Jesus Christ.

Paul's prayer for the Colossians

¶3 We give thanks to God and the Father of our Lord Jesus Christ, praying
always for you,
4 Since we heard of your *faith in
Christ Jesus, and of the love *which ye
have* to all the saints,
5 For the *hope which is laid up for
you in *heaven, whereof ye heard before in the word of the truth of the *gospel;
6 Which is come unto you, as *it is* in
all the *world; and bringeth forth fruit,
as *it doth* also in you, since the day ye
heard *of it,* and knew the grace of God
in truth:
7 As ye also learned of *Epaphras our
dear fellowservant, who is for you a
faithful minister of Christ;
8 Who also declared unto us your love
in the Spirit.
9 For this cause we also, since the day
we heard *it,* do not cease to pray for
you, and to desire that ye might be filled
with the knowledge of his will in all
wisdom and spiritual understanding;
10 That ye might walk worthy of the
Lord unto all pleasing, being fruitful in
every good work, and increasing in the
knowledge of God;
11 Strengthened with all might, according to his glorious power, unto all
patience and longsuffering with joyfulness;

Paul's praise of the Lord Jesus Christ

12 Giving thanks unto the Father,
which hath made us meet to be *partakers of the inheritance of the saints in
light:
13 Who hath delivered us from the
power of darkness, and hath translated
us into the *kingdom of his dear Son:
14 In whom we have *redemption
through his *blood, *even* the forgiveness of sins:
15 Who is the image of the invisible
God, the firstborn of every creature:
16 For by him were all things *created, that are in heaven, and that are in
earth, visible and invisible, whether
they be thrones, or dominions, or principalities, or powers: all things were
created by him, and for him:

1:6 The Grace of God
Nobody—man, woman, or child—deserves to have the love of God; nevertheless, God loves even the sinner and has provided the way of salvation for him (Rom. 5:8). This love of God, bestowed upon those who do not deserve it, is the manifestation of God's grace. It is His free gift (Eph. 2:8).

1:9 spiritual understanding. The mind of a "born again" person, who is helped by the Spirit of God. It is different from the mind of the unsaved person, from the natural mind (1 Cor. 2:14) which cannot understand spiritual things.
1:10 walk. Live.
1:12 made us meet. Qualified us.
1:13 power of darkness. The power of Satan and all that is evil in this world (Luke 22:53; Eph. 6:12).
1:13 his dear Son. The Son of the Father's love.
1:15 image. It is only in the Lord Jesus Christ, the Man who lived on earth and who is now living in heaven, that we see God (John 1:18 and its note, "Seeing God"; John 14:9; 1 Tim. 3:16). The *theophanies of God in the Old Testament were appearances of the Son in physical form.
1:15 firstborn. The next two verses and other passages (see Rev. 3:14) help to explain this great mystery. The Lord Jesus Christ was with God the Father before anything or anyone was created (John 17:5; Heb.1:6; see also *God—the Trinity).

17And he is before all things, and by
him all things consist.
18And he is the head of the body, the
*church: who is the beginning, the first-
born from the dead; that in all *things* he
might have the preeminence.
19For it pleased *the Father* that in him
should all fulness dwell;
20And, having made peace through
the blood of his cross, by him to reconcile all things unto himself; by him, *I
say,* whether *they be* things in earth, or
things in heaven.

1:20 Reconciliation
To reconcile means that Christ will bring back to Himself the earth, which has been damaged by sin (Gen. 3:17-18; Isa. 55:8-13; Rom. 8:22-23); and He will bring to Himself all sinners who believe on Him as Saviour (2 Cor. 5:18-20; 1 Pet. 3:18). "Reconciliation" means *to change thoroughly from*. It is found in Romans 5:10; 11:15; 1 Corinthians 7:11; 2 Corinthians 5:18-20. *God* is not reconciled—the debt of man's sin was paid to Him by the Lord Jesus Christ so that *mankind*—sinners—might be reconciled, or thoroughly changed, in God's sight.

21And you, that were sometime alienated and enemies in *your* mind by wicked works, yet now hath he reconciled
22In the body of his *flesh through
*death, to present you *holy and unblame-
able and unreproveable in his sight:

Paul's preaching

23If ye continue in the faith grounded
and settled, and *be* not moved away
from the hope of the gospel, which ye
have heard, *and* which was preached to
every creature which is under heaven;
whereof I Paul am made a minister;
24Who now rejoice in my sufferings
for you, and fill up that which is behind
of the afflictions of Christ in my flesh
for his body's sake, which is the church:
25Whereof I am made a minister, according to the dispensation of God
which is given to me for you, to fulfil the
word of God;
26*Even* the *mystery which hath been
hid from ages and from generations, but
now is made manifest to his saints:
27To whom God would make known
what *is* the riches of the glory of this
mystery among the *Gentiles; which is
Christ in you, the hope of glory:
28Whom we preach, warning every
man, and teaching every man in all

1:24 The Afflictions of Christ
Paul is here speaking of the *church, the body, of which Christ is the Head. The Lord suffered for sin on the cross, and the church cannot take part in this suffering. But the church must bear a certain amount of suffering (Isa. 63:9; Acts 9:4; Rom. 8:17; 2 Cor. 1:5; 2 Tim. 2:12; 3:12; 1 Pet. 3:18).

1:27 Christ Lives in Us
Christ living in us is the great and glorious truth of the gospel, not known and not even possible until Jesus Christ died and rose again. Because He is within the one who has been born again, that one has eternal life, can overcome temptation in this life, and looks forward to eternity in heaven (John 17:22-23; Col. 3:4).

1:17 before. Compare this with the wonderful words of our Lord to the Jews (John 8:58).
1:17 by him. Not only did Christ create all things, but all things are kept, or consist as they are, by Him.
1:19 fulness. This refers to the fullness of the Godhead, which is God, the Father; God, the Son; and God, the Holy Spirit (Col. 2:9). Jesus Christ was filled with God the Holy Spirit (Isa. 42:1—a prophecy about Christ; see also Isa. 42:1 note, "Christ as Servant"; John 3:34), and God the Father dwelled within Him (John 17:21-23).
1:21 sometime. In the past.
1:22 body of his flesh. The human body of our Lord.
1:25 dispensation. The particular task or responsibility of the stewardship of the gospel given to him by God.
1:25 fulfil. Make fully known.

wisdom; that we may present every
man *perfect in Christ Jesus:
29 Whereunto I also labour, striving according to his working, which worketh
in me mightily.

II. The Good News of Life in Christ (2:1-23)

2 For I would that ye knew what
great conflict I have for you, and *for*
them at Laodicea, and *for* as many as
have not seen my face in the flesh;
2 That their hearts might be comforted, being knit together in love, and unto
all riches of the full *assurance of understanding, to the acknowledgement
of the mystery of God, and of the Father,
and of Christ;
3 In whom are hid all the treasures of
wisdom and knowledge.
4 And this I say, lest any man should
beguile you with enticing words.
5 For though I be absent in the flesh,
yet am I with you in the spirit, joying
and beholding your order, and the
stedfastness of your faith in Christ.

The wonderful salvation in Christ

¶6 As ye have therefore received
Christ Jesus the Lord, *so* walk ye in him:
7 Rooted and built up in him, and
stablished in the faith, as ye have been
taught, abounding therein with thanksgiving.
8 Beware lest any man spoil you
through philosophy and vain deceit, after the *tradition of men, after the rudiments of the world, and not after
Christ.
9 For in him dwelleth all the fulness
of the Godhead bodily.
10 And ye are complete in him, which is
the head of all principality and power:
11 In whom also ye are circumcised
with the *circumcision made without
hands, in putting off the body of the
sins of the flesh by the circumcision of
Christ:
12 Buried with him in *baptism, wherein also ye are risen with *him* through
the faith of the operation of God, who
hath raised him from the dead.
13 And you, being dead in your sins
and the uncircumcision of your flesh,
hath he quickened together with him,
having *forgiven you all trespasses;
14 Blotting out the handwriting of ordinances that was against us, which was
contrary to us, and took it out of the
way, nailing it to his cross;

2:14 A Cancelled Bond
In the East, a bond is cancelled by being nailed to a post. So the bond of guilt against the sinner was nailed to the cross of Christ. The guilt of those sins is blotted out just as if they had never been committed.

1:29 his working. See Zechariah 4:6; Philippians 1:6; 4:13.
2:1 great conflict. Paul spoke here of his continual, earnest prayer for the Colossians and the church at Laodicea.
2:2 mystery of God. The Lord Jesus is meant here.
2:6 As . . . so. As Christ is received by faith, so Christians are to walk, or to live, by faith (John 1:12; 2 Cor. 5:7; Eph. 2:8; Gal. 2:20; 5:16).
2:7 Rooted and built up in him. See John 15:5; Ephesians 2:19-22; 1 Peter 2:5.
2:8 philosophy and vain deceit. Mere human teaching, not in agreement with the Scriptures.
2:8 rudiments. Religious rituals and principles not in accord with the Word of God.
2:10 complete in him. Made what they ought to be and filled with all the necessary power by Christ.
2:11 In whom also. Verses 11-15 describe the change that takes place when the sinner is *born again: first, the forgiveness and turning away from sin; then, the coming in of the new life, which is everlasting, and which God can now give to those who believe, because Christ rose from the dead. See Ephesians 2:1, 5-6; 1 Peter 2:24.
2:13 dead in your sins. Spiritual *death.
2:13 quickened. Made alive.

15*And* having spoiled principalities
and powers, he made a shew of them
openly, triumphing over them in it.

The freedom of life in Christ

16Let no man therefore judge you in
meat, or in drink, or in respect of an
holyday, or of the *new moon, or of the
*sabbath *days:*
17Which are a shadow of things to
come; but the body *is* of Christ.
18Let no man beguile you of your reward in a voluntary humility and worshipping of *angels, intruding into
those things which he hath not seen,
vainly puffed up by his fleshly mind,
19And not holding the Head, from
which all the body by joints and bands
having nourishment ministered, and
knit together, increaseth with the increase of God.
¶20Wherefore if ye be dead with
Christ from the rudiments of the world,
why, as though living in the world, are
ye subject to ordinances,
21(Touch not; taste not; handle not;
22Which all are to perish with the
using;) after the commandments and
doctrines of men?
23Which things have indeed a shew
of wisdom in will worship, and humility, and neglecting of the body; not in
any honour to the satisfying of the
flesh.

III. How to Live the Christian Life (3:1-25)

3 If ye then be risen with Christ,
seek those things which are above,
where Christ sitteth on the right hand
of God.
2Set your affection on things above,
not on things on the earth.
3For ye are dead, and your life is hid
with Christ in God.
4When Christ, *who is* our life, shall
appear, then shall ye also appear with
him in glory.

The Christian character

¶5Mortify therefore your members
which are upon the earth; fornication,

2:15 spoiled. Disarmed.

2:15 principalities and powers. See Col. 1:13 first note; see also Ephesians 6:12.

2:16 judge. Criticize or condemn. Paul told the Colossian Christians that they did not need to be troubled by those who criticized them because of what they ate or drank or because they no longer kept the Jewish Sabbath—the seventh day—and other Jewish holidays. The three kinds of days are mentioned in 1 Chronicles 23:31.

2:17 a shadow of things to come. Much of the Old Testament laws and rituals were examples or illustrations of what Christ would be or do for the sinner. Since He has come, the symbols are no longer needed (Heb. 8:5; 10:1).

2:18 Let no man beguile you. Paul warns against false teachers who taught that our Lord was only the highest One among the angels and that the angels were to be worshipped.

2:19 not holding. Not believing that the Lord Jesus Christ is above all others.

2:19 joints and bands. Joints and ligaments. Each part of the true *church is joined to every other part, as are the various parts of the human body.

2:19 increase of God. The growth and blessing that God gives.

2:21 Touch not. Three kinds of man-made ordinances from which the Christian is liberated. Rules about not touching, tasting, and handling are still tests of holiness in certain Oriental religions, such as Hinduism and Islam.

2:23 not in any honour. A paraphrase: "Which do not really honour God, but only satisfy the flesh"; because keeping these ordinances gives men a reputation for holiness.

3:1 risen with Christ. See Romans 6:4-5; Ephesians 2:6; Colossians 2:12.

3:1 seek. Have your heart set on heavenly things. The Lord Jesus used the same word (Matt. 6:33).

3:3 dead. Not dead physically, but dead to sin. Read Romans 6:2.

3:4 our life. See John 1:4; 14:6.

3:4 appear. See John 14:3; Acts 1:11; 1 Thessalonians 4:14-17.

3:5 Mortify. Put to death—in this case, evil desires (Rom. 8:13; Gal. 5:24).

uncleanness, inordinate affection, evil
concupiscence, and covetousness,
which is *idolatry:
6For which things' sake the wrath of
God cometh on the children of disobedience:
7In the which ye also walked some
time, when ye lived in them.
8But now ye also put off all these;
anger, wrath, malice, blasphemy, filthy
communication out of your mouth.
9Lie not one to another, seeing that
ye have put off the old man with his
deeds;
10And have put on the *new *man,*
which is renewed in knowledge after
the *image of him that created him:
11Where there is neither Greek nor
Jew, circumcision nor uncircumcision,
Barbarian, Scythian, bond *nor* free: but
Christ *is* all, and in all.
12Put on therefore, as the *elect of
God, holy and beloved, bowels of mercies, kindness, humbleness of mind,
meekness, longsuffering;
13Forbearing one another, and forgiving one another, if any man have a quarrel against any: even as Christ forgave
you, so also *do* ye.
14And above all these things *put on*
*charity, which is the bond of perfect-
ness.
15And let the peace of God rule in
your hearts, to the which also ye are
called in one body; and be ye thankful.
16Let the word of Christ dwell in
you richly in all wisdom; teaching and
admonishing one another in psalms
and hymns and spiritual songs, singing with grace in your hearts to the
Lord.
17And whatsoever ye do in word or
deed, *do* all in the name of the Lord
Jesus, giving thanks to God and the
Father by him.

The Christian family

¶18Wives, submit yourselves unto
your own husbands, as it is fit in the
Lord.
19Husbands, love *your* wives, and be
not bitter against them.
20Children, obey *your* parents in all
things: for this is well pleasing unto the
Lord.
21Fathers, provoke not your children
to anger, lest they be discouraged.
22Servants, obey in all things *your*
masters according to the flesh; not with
eyeservice, as menpleasers; but in singleness of heart, *fearing God:

The Christian rule of life

23And whatsoever ye do, do *it* heartily, as to the Lord, and not unto men;
24Knowing that of the Lord ye shall
receive the reward of the inheritance:
for ye serve the Lord Christ.
25But he that doeth wrong shall
receive for the wrong which he hath
done: and there is no respect of persons.

IV. Christian Fellowship (4:1-18)

4 Masters, give unto *your* servants
that which is just and equal;
knowing that ye also have a Master in
heaven.

3:10 the new man. This is who we have become because of the new nature, received at the new birth (2 Cor. 5:17), in contrast to the old man (vs. 9). See also the *old nature.

3:10 him that created. The Lord Jesus Christ.

3:11 Barbarian. The Greeks called all people Barbarians who did not speak Greek.

3:11 Scythian. Uncivilized people who lived in Scythia, north of the Black Sea.

3:14 bond of perfectness. Love binds together all the good things just mentioned in verses 12-13 (see also 1 Cor. 13:13).

3:22 to the flesh. This word used with "masters" refers to earthly "masters" (or employers).

3:22 eyeservice. Christian servants and employees should work hard and faithfully, not just because it looks good, and in order to please men, but because they belong to God and are to please Him first (Matt. 6:24; Gal. 1:10).

The Christian's fellowship in prayer

¶ 2 Continue in prayer, and watch in
the same with thanksgiving;
3 Withal praying also for us, that God
would open unto us a door of utterance,
to speak the mystery of Christ, for
which I am also in bonds:
4 That I may make it manifest, as I
ought to speak.

The Christian's testimony

5 Walk in wisdom toward them that
are without, redeeming the time.
6 Let your speech *be* alway with grace,
seasoned with salt, that ye may know
how ye ought to answer every man.

The Christian's fellowship on earth

¶ 7 All my state shall Tychicus declare
unto you, *who is* a beloved brother, and
a faithful minister and fellowservant in
the Lord:
8 Whom I have sent unto you for the
same purpose, that he might know your
estate, and comfort your hearts;
9 With Onesimus, a faithful and beloved brother, who is *one* of you. They
shall make known unto you all things
which *are done* here.
¶ 10 Aristarchus my fellowprisoner
saluteth you, and Marcus, sister's son
to Barnabas, (touching whom ye received commandments: if he come unto
you, receive him;)
11 And Jesus, which is called Justus,
who are of the circumcision. These
only *are my* fellowworkers unto the
kingdom of God, which have been a
comfort unto me.
12 Epaphras, who is *one* of you, a servant of Christ, saluteth you, always
labouring fervently for you in prayers,
that ye may stand perfect and complete
in all the will of God.
13 For I bear him record, that he hath
a great zeal for you, and them *that are*
in Laodicea, and them in Hierapolis.
14 Luke, the beloved physician, and
Demas, greet you.
15 Salute the brethren which are in
Laodicea, and Nymphas, and the church
which is in his house.
16 And when this epistle is read among
you, cause that it be read also in the
church of the Laodiceans; and that ye
likewise read the *epistle* from Laodicea.
17 And say to Archippus, Take heed to
the ministry which thou hast received
in the Lord, that thou fulfil it.
¶ 18 The salutation by the hand of me
Paul. Remember my bonds. Grace *be*
with you. Amen.

4:2 watch. Be alert or wide awake; pay attention to what you are saying in prayer, and be persistent in praying (Matt. 26:41; 1 Cor. 16:13; 1 Pet. 4:7).

4:3 door of utterance. Paul was asking the Colossians to pray that God would make it possible for him to preach the gospel. Paul's greatest desire was to see people saved. His appeal anticipates our own, especially where countries are closed to the gospel.

4:3 in bonds. In prison. (See the introduction to Philippians.)

4:5 them that are without. All those who are not Christians.

4:5 redeeming the time. The word means buying back. We are to make good use of our time—not wasting it (Eph. 5:15-16).

4:6 seasoned with salt. Doing good to those who hear (Matt. 5:13; Mark 9:50; Eph. 4:29).

4:6 answer. Not only to know how to answer questions, but to know what to say under various and different circumstances. Answer is sometimes used in Scripture where no question is asked (Luke 8:50; 14:3,5; John 16:29-31; 1 Pet. 3:15).

4:7 Tychicus. One of the eight men, mentioned in the last twelve verses of this letter, who was with Paul in Rome. Tychicus was from a province of Asia (in Asia Minor), Acts 20:4, and was one of the bearers of this letter to the Colossians.

4:9 Onesimus. See vs. 7 note. A runaway slave of Philemon's, whom Paul had brought to the Lord Jesus Christ, and whose story is told in the book of Philemon.

4:10 Aristarchus. A Thessalonian Greek, who was in prison with Paul. See Acts 19:29; 20:4; 27:2; Philemon 24.

The First Epistle of Paul the Apostle to the

THESSALONIANS

BACKGROUND

In Macedonia there is a city named Salonica. In Paul's day it was called Thessalonica. On his second missionary journey Paul visited this city and founded a church, but was driven out by unbelieving Jews. Being unable to return to Thessalonica, he sent Timothy to visit the church. He brought back an excellent report, which warmed the apostle's heart, and moved him to write them this letter.

THINGS TO NOTE

First Thessalonians is the first of the letters written by apostles to the churches. It is one of the earliest documents of the New Testament, having been committed to paper before the four Gospels themselves. The date, A.D. 54, of the epistle is important because its first verse, actually the first written words of the Apostle Paul, contain the words "Lord Jesus Christ." It follows that the Deity of Jesus was not a later development of faith among the early Christians, who from the very beginning had never thought of Him as other than God the Son.

THEMES

The epistle shows the rapid progress and flourishing condition of an early church. Paul had much to praise and nothing to blame.

First, he reviewed with the new believers the great doctrines he had taught them (1 Thessalonians 1; 2).

Second, he encouraged them to stand fast in spite of persecution and to go on to holier living (1 Thessalonians 3:1—4:12).

Third, he comforted them about the Christians who had died and reminded them of the hope of the Lord's coming (1 Thessalonians 4:13).

OUTLINE OF 1 THESSALONIANS

I.	The Obedient Church Praised for Faith, Love, and Hope	1 Thessalonians 1:1-10
II.	The Thankful Servant and His Reward	1 Thessalonians 2:1-20
III.	The Obedient Servant, His Joy and Comfort in the Holy Living of Believers	1 Thessalonians 3:1-13
IV.	The Believer's Life	1 Thessalonians 4:1-12
V.	The Believer's Hope	1 Thessalonians 4:13-18
VI.	The Day of the Lord and Its Practical Effect on Believers	1 Thessalonians 5:1-28

I. The Obedient Church Praised for Faith, Love, and Hope (1:1-10)

1 Paul, and Silvanus, and *Timotheus, unto the *church of the
Thessalonians *which is* in *God the
Father and *in* the Lord Jesus *Christ:
*Grace *be* unto you, and *peace, from
God our Father, and the Lord Jesus
Christ.
¶2We give thanks to God always for
you all, making mention of you in our
prayers;
3Remembering without ceasing your
work of *faith, and labour of love, and
patience of *hope in our Lord Jesus
Christ, in the sight of God and our Father;

1:3 Three Principles to Live By
There are three wonderfully interesting verses in this first chapter, which give the three ruling principles of the Christian life. We find the principles announced in verse 3, and the ways to carry out the principles in verses 9-10:

1. The "work of faith" is to turn "to God from idols" (vs. 9);
2. The "labour of love" is "to serve the living and true God" (vs. 9); and
3. The "patience of hope" is "to wait for his Son from heaven" (vs. 10).

4Knowing, brethren beloved, your
*election of God.
5For our *gospel came not unto you
in word only, but also in power, and in
the Holy Ghost, and in much *assurance; as ye know what manner of men
we were among you for your sake.
6And ye became followers of us, and
of the Lord, having received the word
in much affliction, with joy of the Holy
Ghost:
7So that ye were ensamples to all that
believe in Macedonia and Achaia.
8For from you sounded out the word
of the Lord not only in Macedonia and
Achaia, but also in every place your
faith to God-ward is spread abroad; so
that we need not to speak any thing.
9For they themselves shew of us
what manner of entering in we had unto
you, and how ye turned to God from
idols to serve the living and true God;
10And to wait for his Son from *heav-
en, whom he raised from the dead, *even*
Jesus, which delivered us from the
wrath to come.

II. The Thankful Servant and His Reward (2:1-20)

2 For yourselves, brethren, know
our entrance in unto you, that it
was not in vain:
2But even after that we had suffered
before, and were shamefully entreated,
as ye know, at Philippi, we were bold in
our God to speak unto you the gospel
of God with much contention.
3For our exhortation *was* not of deceit, nor of uncleanness, nor in guile:
4But as we were allowed of God to be
put in trust with the gospel, even so we
speak; not as pleasing men, but God,
which trieth our hearts.
5For neither at any time used we flattering words, as ye know, nor a cloke of
covetousness; God *is* witness:
6Nor of men sought we glory, neither
of you, nor *yet* of others, when we might
have been burdensome, as the *apostles of Christ.
7But we were gentle among you,
even as a nurse cherisheth her children:
8So being affectionately desirous of
you, we were willing to have imparted
unto you, not the gospel of God only, but
also our own souls, because ye were
dear unto us.
9For ye remember, brethren, our
labour and travail: for labouring night
and day, because we would not be

1:1 Silvanus. This was Silas (see Acts 15:22-40; 16:25; 17:10; 2 Cor. 1:19; 2 Thess. 1:1).
1:7 ensamples. Examples.
2:2 Philippi. Look up the account in Acts 16:12-40 (see also Acts 16:12 note, "Philippi").
2:7 cherisheth her children. Takes loving care of her own children.

chargeable unto any of you, we preached
unto you the gospel of God.
10 Ye *are* witnesses, and God *also,* how
holily and justly and unblameably we
behaved ourselves among you that believe:
11 As ye know how we exhorted and
comforted and charged every one of
you, as a father *doth* his children,
12 That ye would walk worthy of God,
who hath called you unto his *kingdom
and glory.
¶ 13 For this cause also thank we God
without ceasing, because, when ye received the word of God which ye heard
of us, ye received *it* not *as* the word of
men, but as it is in truth, the word of
God, which effectually worketh also in
you that believe.
14 For ye, brethren, became followers
of the churches of God which in Judaea
are in Christ Jesus: for ye also have
suffered like things of your own countrymen, even as they *have* of the Jews:
15 Who both killed the Lord Jesus, and
their own *prophets, and have persecuted us; and they please not God, and
are contrary to all men:
16 Forbidding us to speak to the *Gentiles that they might be saved, to fill up
their sins alway: for the wrath is come
upon them to the uttermost.
¶ 17 But we, brethren, being taken from
you for a short time in presence, not in
heart, endeavoured the more abundantly to see your face with great desire.
18 Wherefore we would have come
unto you, even I Paul, once and again;
but Satan hindered us.
19 For what *is* our hope, or joy, or
crown of rejoicing? *Are* not even ye in
the presence of our Lord Jesus Christ
at his coming?
20 For ye are our glory and joy.

III. The Obedient Servant: His Joy and Comfort in the Holy Living of Believers (3:1-13)

3 Wherefore when we could no longer forbear, we thought it good to
be left at Athens alone;
2 And sent Timotheus, our brother,
and minister of God, and our fellowlabourer in the gospel of Christ, to
establish you, and to comfort you concerning your faith:
3 That no man should be moved by
these afflictions: for yourselves know
that we are appointed thereunto.
4 For verily, when we were with you,
we told you before that we should suffer tribulation; even as it came to pass,
and ye know.
5 For this cause, when I could no longer forbear, I sent to know your faith,
lest by some means the tempter have
tempted you, and our labour be in vain.
6 But now when Timotheus came
from you unto us, and brought us good
tidings of your faith and *charity, and
that ye have good remembrance of us
always, desiring greatly to see us, as we
also *to see* you:
7 Therefore, brethren, we were comforted over you in all our affliction and
distress by your faith:
8 For now we live, if ye stand fast in
the Lord.
9 For what thanks can we *render to
God again for you, for all the joy wherewith we joy for your sakes before our
God;

2:18 Satan. See the account of the fall of Lucifer in Isaiah 14:12-14 (see also 14:12 note, "Lucifer").

2:19 crown of rejoicing. See *reward.

2:19 at his coming. Paul alludes to Christ's *second coming five times in this book: 1:10; 2:19; 3:13; 4:15-16; and, by implication, 5:2-3. The reader must determine whether the references are to His coming for His *church or to set up His *kingdom.

3:1 Athens. Look up Acts 17:15.

3:4 tribulation. This means *persecution and suffering.* Paul was afraid that the persecution might have caused some of the Christians to depart from the faith (vs. 5).

3:5 tempter. Satan.

10 Night and day praying exceedingly
that we might see your face, and might
*perfect that which is lacking in your
faith?
11 Now God himself and our Father,
and our Lord Jesus Christ, direct our
way unto you.
12 And the Lord make you to increase
and abound in love one toward another,
and toward all *men,* even as we *do* toward you:
13 To the end he may stablish your
hearts unblameable in holiness before
God, even our Father, at the coming of
our Lord Jesus Christ with all his
*saints.

IV. The Believer's Life (4:1-12)

4 Furthermore then we beseech
you, brethren, and *exhort *you* by
the Lord Jesus, that as ye have received
of us how ye ought to walk and to please
God, *so* ye would abound more and
more.
2 For ye know what commandments
we gave you by the Lord Jesus.
3 For this is the will of God, *even* your
sanctification, that ye should abstain
from fornication:
4 That every one of you should know
how to possess his vessel in sanctification and honour;
5 Not in the lust of concupiscence,
even as the Gentiles which know not
God:
6 That no *man* go beyond and defraud
his brother in *any* matter: because that
the Lord *is* the avenger of all such, as
we also have forewarned you and testified.
7 For God hath not called us unto uncleanness, but unto holiness.
8 He therefore that despiseth,
despiseth not man, but God, who hath
also given unto us his *holy Spirit.
9 But as touching brotherly love ye
need not that I write unto you: for ye
yourselves are taught of God to love
one another.
10 And indeed ye do it toward all the
brethren which are in all Macedonia:
but we beseech you, brethren, that ye
increase more and more;
11 And that ye study to be quiet, and
to do your own business, and to work
with your own hands, as we commanded you;
12 That ye may walk honestly toward
them that are without, and *that* ye may
have lack of nothing.

V. The Believer's Hope (4:13-18)

¶13 But I would not have you to be ignorant, brethren, concerning them
which are asleep, that ye sorrow not,
even as others which have no hope.

4:13 Hope for the Dead
Some of the Christians had died, and their friends feared that they would lose out at the return of the Lord Jesus Christ, missing His rewards. Paul therefore explained that:
1. All dead saints will rise first (vs. 16); and
2. All living saints will be caught up with them to meet the Lord in the air when the *Rapture takes place.

It will be the first resurrection. See also 1 Corinthians 15:51-52 notes, including verse 52 note, "A Final Resurrection."

14 For if we believe that Jesus died
and rose again, even so them also which
sleep in Jesus will God bring with
him.
15 For this we say unto you by the
word of the Lord, that we which are
alive *and* remain unto the coming of the
Lord shall not prevent them which are
asleep.
16 For the Lord himself shall descend
from heaven with a shout, with the
voice of the archangel, and with the

4:8 despiseth. Rejects.
4:11 study to be quiet. Make it the ambition of life to apply oneself to lead a quiet, godly life.
4:15 prevent. Go before. "Prevent" is an old word meaning *precede*.

trump of God: and the dead in Christ shall rise first:

17 Then we which are alive *and* remain shall be caught up together with them in the clouds, to meet the Lord in the air: and so shall we ever be with the Lord.

18 Wherefore comfort one another with these words.

VI. The Day of the Lord and Its Practical Effect on Believers (5:1-28)

5 But of the times and the seasons, brethren, ye have no need that I write unto you.

2 For yourselves know perfectly that the day of the Lord so cometh as a thief in the night.

3 For when they shall say, Peace and safety; then sudden destruction cometh upon them, as travail upon a woman with child; and they shall not escape.

4 But ye, brethren, are not in darkness, that that day should overtake you as a thief.

5 Ye are all the children of light, and the children of the day: we are not of the night, nor of darkness.

6 Therefore let us not sleep, as *do* others; but let us watch and be sober.

7 For they that sleep sleep in the night; and they that be drunken are drunken in the night.

8 But let us, who are of the day, be sober, putting on the breastplate of faith and love; and for an helmet, the hope of salvation.

9 For God hath not appointed us to wrath, but to obtain salvation by our Lord Jesus Christ,

10 Who died for us, that, whether we wake or sleep, we should live together with him.

11 Wherefore comfort yourselves together, and edify one another, even as also ye do.

¶ 12 And we beseech you, brethren, to know them which labour among you, and are over you in the Lord, and admonish you;

13 And to esteem them very highly in love for their work's sake. *And* be at peace among yourselves.

14 Now we exhort you, brethren, warn them that are unruly, comfort the feebleminded, support the weak, be patient toward all *men.*

15 See that none render evil for evil unto any *man;* but ever follow that which is good, both among yourselves, and to all *men.*

16 Rejoice evermore.

17 Pray without ceasing.

18 In every thing give thanks: for this is the will of God in Christ Jesus concerning you.

19 Quench not the Spirit.

20 Despise not prophesyings.

21 Prove all things; hold fast that which is good.

22 Abstain from all appearance of evil.

23 And the very God of peace sanctify

5:23 The Three Parts of Man
Man was made in the image of God. Man, like God, is thus a trinity, that is, three in one. He is body, soul, and spirit. His body is the house in which he lives and through which he can be seen and known. Through his soul he has memory, affection, ambition, will, love, hate, etc. But most important of all is a man's spirit through which he can know and worship God. Sin can defile the body and spirit; therefore, Paul prayed (vs. 23) that the God of peace would sanctify the people wholly. See also Genesis 1:26 note and Genesis 1:27 note, "In God's Image."

5:1 times and the seasons. Paul is saying that no one knows just when the Lord will come.
5:8 the breastplate of faith and love. See *garments and Ephesians 6:11-18.
5:20 prophesyings. This does not necessarily mean foretelling the future. A prophecy is really a message from God and may be about the past, present, or future. The believers were to listen respectfully to those who gave them God's messages.
5:21 Prove all things. Test everything by the Word of God.

you wholly; and *I pray God* your whole
spirit and soul and body be preserved
blameless unto the coming of our Lord
Jesus Christ.
24 Faithful *is* he that calleth you, who
also will do *it*.
¶25 Brethren, pray for us.
¶26 Greet all the brethren with an holy
kiss.
27 I charge you by the Lord that this
epistle be read unto all the holy brethren.
¶28 The grace of our Lord Jesus
Christ *be* with you. Amen.

The Second Epistle of Paul the Apostle to the

THESSALONIANS

BACKGROUND

The Second Epistle to the Thessalonians seems to have been written soon after the first epistle, for we recognize in 2 Thessalonians 1:4,5 the same persecution and affliction existing as that endured and spoken of by Paul in his first letter. No doubt these very trials were the occasion for his first message and now became the reason for this call to courage to "be not soon shaken in mind or be troubled" (2 Thessalonians 2:2).

THE WRITER AND TIME

The epistle was written during Paul's stay at Corinth, when he was there for a year and a half (Acts 18:11); Timothy and Silas (2 Thessalonians 1:1) were with him during that stay and were not with him again for a long time. The date of writing is A.D. 54.

SUMMARY

There is a two-fold purpose in this second letter to the church in Thessalonica:

1. to correct the confusion in the minds of these patiently suffering Christians about the coming of the Lord Jesus Christ; and

2. to give them further teachings about the *Day of the Lord, showing that before the Second Coming there will be a terrible falling away as the events of 2:3 (see its note) take place. Believers were to follow his example of serving as they waited (1 Thessalonians 1:9,10; 2 Thessalonians 3:7-10).

OUTLINE OF 2 THESSALONIANS

I.	Thanksgiving for a Growing Faith in the Midst of Persecution	2 Thessalonians 1:1-12
II.	The Man of Sin Revealed	2 Thessalonians 2:1-17
III.	Exhortation to Orderly Conduct	2 Thessalonians 3:1-15
IV.	Prayer, Salutation, Blessing	2 Thessalonians 3:16-18

I. Thanksgiving for a Growing Faith in the Midst of Persecution (1:1-12)

1 Paul, and *Silvanus, and *Timotheus, unto the *church of the
Thessalonians in God our Father and
the Lord Jesus *Christ:

2 *Grace unto you, and *peace, from
God our Father and the Lord Jesus
Christ.

¶3 We are bound to thank God always
for you, brethren, as it is meet, because
that your *faith groweth exceedingly,

and the *charity of every one of you all
toward each other aboundeth;
4 So that we ourselves glory in you in
the churches of God for your patience
and faith in all your persecutions and
tribulations that ye endure:
5 *Which is* a manifest token of the
righteous *judgment of God, that ye
may be counted worthy of the *kingdom of God, for which ye also suffer:
6 Seeing *it is* a righteous thing with
God to recompense tribulation to them
that trouble you;
7 And to you who are troubled rest
with us, when the Lord Jesus shall be
revealed from *heaven with his mighty
*angels,
8 In flaming *fire taking vengeance on
them that know not God, and that obey
not the *gospel of our Lord Jesus
Christ:
9 Who shall be punished with everlasting destruction from the presence
of the Lord, and from the glory of his
power;
10 When he shall come to be glorified
in his *saints, and to be admired in all
them that believe (because our testimony among you was believed) in that
day.
11 Wherefore also we pray always for
you, that our God would count you worthy of *this* calling, and fulfil all the good
pleasure of *his* goodness, and the work
of faith with power:
12 That the name of our Lord Jesus
Christ may be glorified in you, and ye
in him, according to the grace of our
God and the Lord Jesus Christ.

II. The Man of Sin Revealed (2:1-17)

2 Now we beseech you, brethren, by
the coming of our Lord Jesus
Christ, and *by* our gathering together
unto him,
2 That ye be not soon shaken in mind,
or be troubled, neither by spirit, nor by
word, nor by letter as from us, as that
the day of Christ is at hand.
3 Let no man deceive you by any
means: for *that day shall not come,* except there come a falling away first, and
that man of *sin be revealed, the son of
perdition;
4 Who opposeth and exalteth himself
above all that is called God, or that is

2:3 BEFORE THE LORD COMES

Before the Lord comes to set up His *kingdom there will be:

1. lawlessness working all over the earth (vs. 7); which leads to
2. a time of great sin—the apostasy or falling-away time, when even professing Christians will forsake the Lord and His teachings (vs. 3);
3. the Holy Spirit, who has been a restraining influence sent by God to turn men's hearts to Him and to keep Satan from doing just as he pleased upon the earth, will be removed as a restrainer (vs. 7), because the Holy Spirit's temples, the believers (1 Cor. 6:19), will have gone to be with the Lord in the *Rapture (1 Thess. 4:14-17);
4. the *Antichrist will reveal himself and will be worshipped (vss. 3, 8-10; Rev. 13);
5. the destruction of this wicked one by the Lord (vs. 8; Rev. 19:19-20; see also Rev. 19:19 note, "Armageddon"); and
6. the *Day of the Lord.

1:7 when the Lord Jesus shall be revealed. This speaks of the coming of the Lord in judgment (see vs. 8 and Rev. 19:11-16).

2:2 by spirit, nor by word, nor by letter. Some of those who were teaching that the Lord would come at any minute and that Christians must, therefore, cease from work to watch for Him, said that the Holy Spirit had told them; others said that Paul had said this when he was with them; and still others said that Paul had written a letter teaching this. Such a letter, said to be from Paul, was passed around among the believers. That is why Paul guaranteed his letters with his own signature (see 2 Thess. 3:17 and its note).

worshipped; so that he as God sitteth
in the temple of God, shewing himself
that he is God.
5Remember ye not, that, when I was
yet with you, I told you these things?
6And now ye know what withholdeth
that he might be revealed in his time.
7For the *mystery of iniquity doth
already work: only he who now letteth
will let, until he be taken out of the way.
8And then shall that Wicked be revealed, whom the Lord shall consume
with the spirit of his mouth, and shall
destroy with the brightness of his
coming:
9*Even him,* whose coming is after the
working of *Satan with all power and
signs and lying wonders,
10And with all deceivableness of unrighteousness in them that perish;
because they received not the love of
the truth, that they might be saved.
11And for this cause God shall send
them strong delusion, that they should
believe a lie:
12That they all might be damned who
believed not the truth, but had pleasure
in unrighteousness.
¶13But we are bound to give thanks
alway to God for you, brethren beloved
of the Lord, because God hath from the
beginning chosen you to *salvation
through sanctification of the Spirit and
belief of the truth:
14Whereunto he called you by our
gospel, to the obtaining of the glory of
our Lord Jesus Christ.
15Therefore, brethren, stand fast,
and hold the *traditions which ye have
been taught, whether by word, or our
epistle.
16Now our Lord Jesus Christ himself,
and God, even our Father, which hath
loved us, and hath given *us* everlasting
consolation and good *hope through
grace,
17Comfort your hearts, and stablish
you in every good word and work.

2:11 A Strong Delusion
Those who are then living who have willfully rejected Christ up to the time of the *Rapture will not turn to the Lord during the period of the coming *Tribulation before the Lord Jesus comes in power, but God will send them a strong delusion, so that they will believe a lie instead of the truth. They *would* not receive when they *could* have (vs. 10).

2:15 THE DOCTRINES OF THE FAITH

The Thessalonian Christians had been taught all of the great doctrine or truths of their faith. They had learned about:

1. the Lord's choosing, or *election (1 Thess. 1:4);
2. the Holy Spirit and His work (1 Thess. 1:5-6; 4:8; 5:19);
3. their safety as believers, or *assurance (1 Thess. 1:5);
4. the *Trinity (1 Thess. 1:1,5-6);
5. the Christian's manner of living (1 Thess. 1:9; 2:12; 4:1);
6. the *Second Coming (1 Thess. 1:10; 2:19; 3:13; 4:14-17; 5:23);
7. holy, separated living, or sanctification (1 Thess. 4:3; 5:23);
8. the *Day of the Lord (1 Thess. 5:1-3);
9. the *Resurrection (1 Thess. 4:14-18); and
10. the created-in-the image-of-God nature of man (1 Thess. 5:23; see also its note, "The Three Parts of Man").

2:6 what withholdeth. That which holds back. The Man of Sin (vs. 3) is restrained until the time comes for him to be revealed (vs. 8).
2:7 he who now letteth. The Holy Spirit is the One restraining the Man of Sin. See verse 3 note, "Before the Lord Comes."
2:7 he who now letteth will let. He who restrains will continue to do so.
2:8 Wicked. Wicked one—he is called the *Beast in Revelation 13:11.
2:12 damned. Judged and condemned.

III. Exhortation to Orderly Conduct
(3:1-15)

3 Finally, brethren, pray for us, that
the word of the Lord may have *free*
course, and be glorified, even as *it is*
with you:
2 And that we may be delivered from
unreasonable and wicked men: for all
men have not faith.
3 But the Lord is faithful, who shall
stablish you, and keep *you* from evil.
4 And we have confidence in the
Lord touching you, that ye both do and
will do the things which we command
you.
5 And the Lord direct your hearts into
the love of God, and into the patient
waiting for Christ.
¶ 6 Now we command you, brethren,
in the name of our Lord Jesus Christ,
that ye withdraw yourselves from
every brother that walketh disorderly,
and not after the tradition which he received of us.
7 For yourselves know how ye ought
to follow us: for we behaved not ourselves disorderly among you;
8 Neither did we eat any man's bread
for nought; but wrought with labour and
travail night and day, that we might not
be chargeable to any of you:
9 Not because we have not power, but
to make ourselves an ensample unto
you to follow us.
10 For even when we were with you,
this we commanded you, that if any
would not work, neither should he eat.
11 For we hear that there are some
which walk among you disorderly,
working not at all, but are busybodies.
12 Now them that are such we command and exhort by our Lord Jesus
Christ, that with quietness they work,
and eat their own bread.
13 But ye, brethren, be not weary in
well doing.
14 And if any man obey not our word
by this epistle, note that man, and have
no company with him, that he may be
ashamed.
15 Yet count *him* not as an enemy, but
admonish *him* as a brother.

IV. Salutation (3:16-18)

16 Now the Lord of peace himself give
you peace always by all means. The
Lord *be* with you all.
¶ 17 The salutation of Paul with mine
own hand, which is the token in every
epistle: so I write.
18 The grace of our Lord Jesus Christ
be with you all. Amen.

3:12 work, and eat their own bread. Some Christians at Thessalonica had ceased working as they waited for the Lord to come.

3:17 salutation of Paul with mine own hand. See 2 Thessalonians 2:2 first note.

The First Epistle of Paul the Apostle to

TIMOTHY

THE WRITER AND TIME

This epistle, and the one which follows, were written by Paul to his friend, Timothy, in A.D. 64 and 67 respectively. The first letter to Timothy was written from Laodicea, which is the chief city of Phrygia, Pacatiana.

BACKGROUND

The name Timothy (or Timotheus) means *honoring God.* Timothy was named in Greek, because of his father, but his mother, Eunice, and his grandmother, Lois (2 Timothy 1:5), were of the Jewish faith (Acts 16:1-3).

The story of how the young man, Timothy, was saved can easily be pieced together from Acts 14:6-23; 16:1; 2 Timothy 1:5. Paul loved Timothy like his own son, and Timothy was devoted to Paul. It was, therefore, arranged that Timothy should travel with Paul on his preaching tours. Later when Paul had to go to Macedonia (1 Timothy 1:3), he left Timothy in charge of the churches in Asia Minor.

THEME

Paul wrote often to the young man, Timothy, both to encourage him, and to tell him how to direct the affairs of the churches; this is God's direction for the churches today, as well. This letter, summed up, says that the main duty of an overseer of a church is to guard the truth.

OUTLINE OF 1 TIMOTHY

I.	Opening Greeting	1 Timothy 1:1-2
II.	Timothy to Silence False Teachers	1 Timothy 1:3—6:20

- A. By Refusing Any Other Teaching as Gospel Truth, Especially "Saved by Good Works"
- B. By Keeping an Atmosphere of Quiet Order in Church Gatherings
- C. By Refusing New Teachings that Women Sometimes Claim to Have Received from God
- D. By Keeping to the Highest Standards for Those Who Direct Church Affairs
- E. By Remembering the Danger of False Teachers
- F. By Keeping the Personal Life Right before God
- G. By Loving Attitudes toward the Weak
- H. By Rewarding Faithful Teachers, without Favoritism

I. By Caution in Appointing Overseers
J. By Teaching Christians to Be Content in Even the Lowest Places in Life
K. By a True Sense of the Small Value of Riches in Comparison to Eternal Things
L. By Not Believing Teaching Which Disagrees with God's Word

III. Final Blessings 1 Timothy 6:21

I. Opening Greeting (1:1-2)

1 Paul, an *apostle of Jesus *Christ
by the commandment of *God our
Saviour, and Lord Jesus Christ, *which is*
our *hope;
2Unto Timothy, *my* own son in the
faith: *Grace, *mercy, *and* *peace, from
God our Father and Jesus Christ our
Lord.

II. Silence False Teachers (1:3—6:20)

*A. By Refusing Any Other Teaching as *Gospel Truth, Especially "Saved by Good Works"*

¶3As I besought thee to abide still at
Ephesus, when I went into Macedonia,
that thou mightest charge some that
they teach no other *doctrine,
4Neither give heed to fables and endless *genealogies, which minister
questions, rather than godly edifying
which is in faith: *so do.*
5Now the end of the commandment
is *charity out of a pure heart, and *of* a
good conscience, and *of* faith unfeigned:
6From which some having swerved
have turned aside unto vain jangling;
7Desiring to be teachers of the *law;
understanding neither what they say,
nor whereof they affirm.
8But we know that the law *is* good, if
a man use it lawfully;
9Knowing this, that the law is not
made for a righteous man, but for the
lawless and disobedient, for the ungodly and for sinners, for unholy and profane, for murderers of fathers and
murderers of mothers, for manslayers,
10For whoremongers, for them that
defile themselves with mankind, for
menstealers, for liars, for perjured persons, and if there be any other thing
that is contrary to sound doctrine;
11According to the glorious gospel of
the blessed God, which was committed
to my trust.
12And I thank Christ Jesus our Lord,
who hath enabled me, for that he counted me faithful, putting me into the ministry;
13Who was before a blasphemer, and
a persecutor, and injurious: but I obtained mercy, because I did *it* ignorantly
in unbelief.
14And the grace of our Lord was exceeding abundant with faith and love
which is in Christ Jesus.
15This *is* a faithful saying, and worthy
of all acceptation, that Christ Jesus
came into the *world to save sinners;
of whom I am chief.
16Howbeit for this cause I obtained
mercy, that in me first Jesus Christ
might shew forth all longsuffering,
for a pattern to them which should

1:2 Unto Timothy. Note that Timothy is often given the Greek form of his name, Timotheus, in Paul's other epistles (see Col. 1:1).
1:2 own son. He was born again through Paul's ministry, so he was Paul's spiritual son.
1:6 vain jangling. Foolish discussions and empty babblings, like the drivel of idiots.
1:9 the law. Law here means any law–God's law or the law of a country.
1:16 for a pattern. Paul was a wonderful example of God's grace and mercy. Anyone who

hereafter believe on him to life everlasting.
17 Now unto the King eternal, immor-
tal, invisible, the only wise God, *be*
honour and glory for ever and ever.
*Amen.
18 This charge I commit unto thee, son
Timothy, according to the prophecies
which went before on thee, that thou
by them mightest war a good warfare;
19 Holding faith, and a good conscience; which some having put away
concerning faith have made shipwreck:
20 Of whom is Hymenaeus and Alexander; whom I have delivered unto
*Satan, that they may learn not to blas-
pheme.

B. By Keeping an Atmosphere of Quiet Order in Church Gatherings

2 I *exhort therefore, that, first of all,
supplications, prayers, interces-
sions, *and* giving of thanks, be made for
all men;
2 For kings, and *for* all that are in
authority; that we may lead a quiet
and peaceable life in all godliness and
honesty.
3 For this *is* good and acceptable in the
sight of God our Saviour;
4 Who will have all men to be saved,
and to come unto the knowledge of the
truth.
5 For *there is* one God, and one mediator between God and men, the man
Christ Jesus;
6 Who gave himself a ransom for all,
to be testified in due time.
7 Whereunto I am ordained a preacher, and an apostle, (I speak the truth in
Christ, *and* lie not;) a teacher of the
*Gentiles in faith and verity.
8 I will therefore that men pray every
where, lifting up holy hands, without
wrath and doubting.
9 In like manner also, that women
adorn themselves in modest apparel,
with shamefacedness and sobriety; not
with broided hair, or gold, or pearls, or
costly array;
10 But (which becometh women professing godliness) with good works.
11 Let the woman learn in silence with
all subjection.

C. By Refusing New Teachings that Women Sometimes Claim to Have Received from God

12 But I suffer not a woman to teach,
nor to usurp authority over the man,
but to be in silence.

---

thinks he has sinned so much that God cannot forgive him needs to remember how He showed mercy to Paul even after the terrible way that he tormented Christians (see Acts 8:3).

1:18 war. The war is to be against the Christian's three enemies: the world, the flesh, (the old sinful nature), and the Devil (see Eph. 6:12; Jude 3).

1:19 a good conscience. Sin in the life does not seem to be the question here; the conscience is to be kept clear concerning what the Christian believes, as well as in the matter of conduct.

1:19 shipwreck. Fallen into spiritual disaster, having wrecked their faith.

1:20 Hymenaeus. Read more about him and what he taught in 2 Timothy 2:17-18.

1:20 delivered unto Satan. See 1 Corinthians 5:5 note, "God Uses Satan."

2:4 Who will have. It is God's desire that all should be saved (2 Pet. 3:9).

2:5 mediator. See Job 9:33 note.

2:6 ransom. See Exodus 6:6 note, "God's Promise to Redeem."

2:8 lifting up holy hands. The Jewish attitude of prayer.

2:8 holy hands. Prayer will not be answered if an unholy life is allowed (Isa. 59:1-2; James 4:3-4).

2:11 silence. Quietness (also in vs. 12).

2:11 subjection. Submission and true yielding to the truth.

2:12 usurp authority. God has given a perfect illustration of the right relationship of man and wife in His picture of Christ and His bride, the *church. See Ephesians 5:21-33; Revelation 19:7-8. Although the woman is just as near and dear to God, and has just

[13]For *Adam was first formed, then
Eve.
[14]And Adam was not deceived, but
the woman being deceived was in the
transgression.
[15]Notwithstanding she shall be saved
in childbearing, if they continue in
faith and charity and holiness with sobriety.

D. By Keeping to the Highest Standards for Those Who Direct Church Affairs

3 This *is* a true saying, If a man desire the office of a bishop, he
desireth a good work.
[2]A bishop then must be blameless,
the husband of one wife, vigilant, sober,
of good behaviour, given to hospitality,
apt to teach;
[3]Not given to *wine, no striker, not
greedy of filthy lucre; but patient, not a
brawler, not covetous;
[4]One that ruleth well his own house,
having his children in subjection with
all gravity;
[5](For if a man know not how to rule
his own house, how shall he take care
of the *church of God?)
[6]Not a novice, lest being lifted up
with pride he fall into the *condemnation of the *devil.
[7]Moreover he must have a good report of them which are without; lest he
fall into reproach and the snare of the
devil.
[8]Likewise *must* the deacons *be* grave,
not doubletongued, not given to much
wine, not greedy of filthy lucre;

2:12 WOMEN AND TEACHING

This verse seems puzzling at first when we remember how greatly God has blessed women Bible teachers. Acts 18:26 shows that Paul cannot mean that women are not to teach the truth that has been revealed. He means that it is not given to women, especially the Ephesian women, to receive and give out new truth such as Paul and the other disciples were doing. (Even men may not do it now, since the Bible's revelation of truth is complete.) From the following verses, we see that women are more easily deceived than men and are therefore not chosen for this service.

This Scripture was especially directed toward the women in Ephesus who were new believers. The Ephesian church had a problem with false teachers, and the women had been more susceptible to being deceived than the men. The women were also flaunting their newfound freedom in the Lord by wearing inappropriate clothing (see vs. 9). The Ephesian women simply did not have the Christian maturity or knowledge to be in positions of teaching others. There were, however, many great women workers in the first-century church, including Priscilla (Acts 18:26), Phebe and Mary, Tryphena, and Tryphosa (Rom. 16:6,12).

as exalted a position in God's family as any man (Gal. 3:28), the Ephesian women were not to speak with authority in church worship and government. Paul himself acknowledged that women publicly prayed and prophesied (1 Cor. 11:5). He obviously approved of that, or he would have instructed the Corinthian church to keep the women from publicly speaking out for God in these ways.

3:1 desire. Because he longs to serve the Lord.
3:1 bishop. Overseer. One who takes the responsibility of directing and teaching in the local church. See Acts 20:28.
3:2 blameless. Without sins that he knows and allows in his life.
3:2 one wife. Only one wife.
3:3 no striker. Not violent or easily provoked to anger or a physical fight.
3:3 greedy of filthy lucre. A lover of money, grasping for riches (see also vs. 8).
3:3 not covetous. In God's sight, a man who desired the office for his own glory or his own interests would not be eligible at all.
3:4 gravity. Not trivial or flippant—a man who is easy to respect.
3:6 Not a novice. Not inexperienced or a recent convert.
3:6 condemnation of the devil. Satan was condemned for his pride (Ezek. 28:17).
3:6 devil. See *Satan. (See also Isa. 14:12-15 and Isa. 14:12 note, "Lucifer.")
3:8 deacons. The word "deacon" means *servant* or *minister* and may apply to any form

9Holding the *mystery of the faith in
a pure conscience.
10And let these also first be proved;
then let them use the office of a deacon,
being *found* blameless.
11Even so *must their* wives *be* grave,
not slanderers, sober, faithful in all
things.
12Let the deacons be the husbands of
one wife, ruling their children and their
own houses well.
13For they that have used the office
of a deacon well purchase to themselves a good degree, and great boldness in the faith which is in Christ
Jesus.
14These things write I unto thee,
hoping to come unto thee shortly:
15But if I tarry long, that thou mayest
know how thou oughtest to behave thyself in the house of God, which is the
church of the living God, the pillar and
ground of the truth.
16And without controversy great is
the mystery of godliness: God was
manifest in the flesh, justified in the
Spirit, seen of *angels, preached unto
the Gentiles, believed on in the world,
received up into glory.

E. By Remembering the Danger of False Teachers

4 Now the Spirit speaketh expressly, that in the latter times
some shall depart from the faith, giving
heed to seducing spirits, and doctrines
of devils;
2Speaking lies in hypocrisy; having
their conscience seared with a hot
iron;
3Forbidding to marry, *and commanding* to abstain from meats, which God

3:8 TEACHINGS ABOUT DRINKING

1. Wine is a symbol of the lifeblood of Jesus Christ (Matt. 26:27-28; John 15:1; 1 Cor. 11:25).
2. Wine is further used as a symbol of the joy of living (Ps. 104:15). But the joy it gives may be deceitful (Prov. 20:1); it does not last (Prov. 23:29-32); it makes a person lose control of himself (Prov. 23:33-35; Gen. 9:21; 19:32-35).
3. Wine was originally given to man to be used (Ps. 104:14-15):
   (a) In celebration (Gen. 14:18; John 2:8-9; Deut. 14:22-26). *Fermented* wine will not be used in this way during the *Millennium (Joel 3:18; Amos 9:13).
   (b) As medicine (Luke 10:34; 1 Tim. 5:23; Prov. 31:6).
   (c) As an offering to God—always poured out, never drunk (Num. 28:7).
4. It is not wise for persons in any position of responsibility to drink it (Prov. 31:4-5).
5. Those who want to be alert to know and do God's will are forbidden to drink it (Luke 1:15; Lev. 10:9-11; Num. 6:3).
6. Those who are careful not to lead others astray will not drink it (Rom. 14:21), because while God evidently meant it to be used in the three ways given above, man has abused this privilege.
7. Jesus Christ said that He will not drink it until He can share His joy with His bride (Matt. 26:29), because it is a symbol of joy.

of ministry for the Lord. All who are engaged in service for the Lord should live in a way that is as godly and holy as bishops or pastors. The deacons should also live up to the requirements given in verses 1-7.

3:13 purchase to themselves. They do not obtain salvation, which is a free gift; they obtain *rewards for service, as well as good standing and respect in the church, all of which must be earned.

4:1 latter times. The latter days, or latter times, began with Christ's resurrection and will continue until His return, when He will set up His kingdom.

4:1 devils. The Greek word used here means *demons* or *evil spirits*. We know only one as the Devil, Satan, the enemy of God. The demons are angels who sinned with Satan.

4:2 seared. As the scar of a burn has little or no sensation in it, so are the consciences of those who have burned them by lying, that is, by teaching false doctrines.

4:3 About Celibacy
False teachers were advocating celibacy, forbidding marriage. It is true that if a Christian wants to belong so entirely to the Lord that he does not choose to share devotion to Him even with a mate, God accepts that as a kind of "whole burnt offering." There is no rule in Scripture against marriage in the church, whether clergy or laity. God never requires celibacy (Lev. 21:7; Deut. 24:5), nor does He desire that all should practice it (compare 1 Cor. 7:25-40).

hath created to be received with
thanksgiving of them which believe and
know the truth.
4 For every creature of God *is* good,
and nothing to be refused, if it be received with thanksgiving:
5 For it is sanctified by the word of
God and *prayer.
6 If thou put the brethren in remembrance of these things, thou shalt be a
good minister of Jesus Christ, nourished up in the words of faith and of
good doctrine, whereunto thou hast attained.
7 But refuse profane and old wives'
fables, and exercise thyself *rather* unto
godliness.
8 For bodily exercise profiteth little:
but godliness is profitable unto all
things, having promise of the life that
now is, and of that which is to come.
9 This *is* a faithful saying and worthy
of all acceptation.
10 For therefore we both labour and
suffer reproach, because we trust in
the living God, who is the Saviour of
all men, specially of those that believe.

F. By Keeping the Personal Life Right before God

¶ 11 These things command and teach.
12 Let no man despise thy youth; but
be thou an example of the *believers,
in word, in *conversation, in *charity,
in spirit, in faith, in purity.
13 Till I come, give attendance to reading, to exhortation, to doctrine.
14 Neglect not the gift that is in thee,
which was given thee by *prophecy,
with the laying on of the hands of the
presbytery.
15 Meditate upon these things; give
thyself wholly to them; that thy profiting may appear to all.
16 Take heed unto thyself, and unto
the doctrine; continue in them: for in
doing this thou shalt both save thyself,
and them that hear thee.

5 Rebuke not an elder, but intreat
him as a father; *and* the younger
men as brethren;
2 The elder women as mothers; the
younger as sisters, with all purity.
3 Honour widows that are widows indeed.
4 But if any widow have children or
nephews, let them learn first to shew
piety at home, and to requite their parents: for that is good and acceptable
before God.
5 Now she that is a widow indeed, and
desolate, trusteth in God, and continueth in supplications and prayers night
and day.
6 But she that liveth in pleasure is
dead while she liveth.

4:8 profiteth little. This means *is of some value,* but spiritual "fitness" is more important than physical fitness.
4:10 Saviour of all men. This does not mean that all men are saved (see Matt. 7:13; 25:41). It means that in Christ salvation for all has been provided and is available.
4:16 save thyself. Salvation is in three tenses. See Romans 1:16-17 note, "Salvation by Faith." In this verse the present tense is meant: You do save yourself and others from wrong beliefs and therefore from wrong ways by this continual reminder.
5:3 widows indeed. Those who are very poor and without support from relatives (see also vss. 5 and 16) had to be supported by the church.
5:4 nephews. Any descendants, children, nephews, or grandchildren.
5:4 let them. Let the children or descendants take care of their widows.

G. By Loving Attitudes toward the Weak

[7]And these things give in charge, that
they may be blameless.
[8]But if any provide not for his own,
and specially for those of his own
house, he hath denied the faith, and is
worse than an *infidel.
[9]Let not a widow be taken into the
number under threescore years old,
having been the wife of one man,

5:9 The List of Widows
The "number" was a certain list of widows who were dependent on the church for support and who had promised to give the rest of their lives to working for the church in exchange for that support. The work, which consisted of bringing up orphans, taking care of the sick, etc. (vs. 10), required trained workers. If a young widow was taken and trained, she might soon change her mind and marry again, so the widows had to be at least sixty years old to be qualified for the "number." In the case of the young widows, it would not be fair to give her the support that the really needy required.

[10]Well reported of for good works; if
she have brought up children, if she
have lodged strangers, if she have
washed the *saints' feet, if she have
relieved the afflicted, if she have diligently followed every good work.
[11]But the younger widows refuse: for
when they have begun to wax wanton
against Christ, they will marry;
[12]Having damnation, because they
have cast off their first faith.
[13]And withal they learn *to be* idle,
wandering about from house to house;
and not only idle, but tattlers also and
busybodies, speaking things which they
ought not.
[14]I will therefore that the younger
women marry, bear children, guide the
house, give none occasion to the adversary to speak reproachfully.
[15]For some are already turned aside
after Satan.

H. By Rewarding Faithful Teachers, without Favoritism

[16]If any man or woman that believeth
have widows, let them relieve them,
and let not the church be charged; that
it may relieve them that are widows
indeed.
[17]Let the *elders that rule well be
counted worthy of double honour, especially they who labour in the word and
doctrine.
[18]For the scripture saith, Thou shalt
not muzzle the ox that treadeth out the
corn. And, The labourer *is* worthy of his
reward.
[19]Against an elder receive not an accusation, but before two or three witnesses.
[20]Them that *sin rebuke before all,
that others also may *fear.

I. By Caution in Appointing Overseers

[21]I charge *thee* before God, and the
Lord Jesus Christ, and the *elect angels, that thou observe these things
without preferring one before another,
doing nothing by partiality.
[22]Lay hands suddenly on no man,

5:9 one man. That is, not having had more than one husband.

5:11 they will marry. Remarriage was not wrong (vs. 14), but the work entrusted to this list of women (see vs. 9 note, "The List of Widows") required experience and character. Unless a widow really accepted the call to self-denial, she might be led to be "wanton" and follow her natural impulses, giving more attention to her own desires than Christ's will for her life.

5:12 Having damnation. Condemnation—being guilty of breaking their promise to give their whole lives to the work of the Lord (see vs. 9 note, "The List of Widows").

5:18 the scripture saith. See Deuteronomy 25:4; 1 Corinthians 9:7-11; Luke 10:7. The preachers and teachers of the Word were to receive honor and be taken care of financially by the church for which they worked so diligently.

5:22 Lay hands suddenly. Do not be hasty in ordaining men to office in the church. The

neither be partaker of other men's sins:
keep thyself pure.
23Drink no longer water, but use a little wine for thy stomach's sake and
thine often infirmities.
24Some men's sins are open beforehand, going before to judgment; and
some *men* they follow after.
25Likewise also the good works *of*
some are manifest beforehand; and they
that are otherwise cannot be hid.

J. By Teaching Christians to Be Content in Even the Lowest Places in Life

6 Let as many servants as are under
the yoke count their own masters
worthy of all honour, that the name of
God and *his* doctrine be not blasphemed.
2And they that have believing masters, let them not despise *them,* because they are brethren; but rather do
them service, because they are faithful
and beloved, partakers of the benefit.
These things teach and exhort.
¶3If any man teach otherwise, and
consent not to wholesome words, *even*
the words of our Lord Jesus Christ, and
to the doctrine which is according to
godliness;
4He is proud, knowing nothing, but
doting about questions and strifes of
words, whereof cometh envy, strife,
railings, evil surmisings,

K. By a True Sense of the Small Value of Riches in Comparison to Eternal Things

5Perverse disputings of men of corrupt minds, and destitute of the truth,
supposing that gain is godliness: from
such withdraw thyself.
6But godliness with contentment is
great gain.
7For we brought nothing into *this*
world, *and it is* certain we can carry
nothing out.
8And having food and raiment let us
be therewith content.
9But they that will be rich fall into
temptation and a snare, and *into* many
foolish and hurtful lusts, which drown
men in destruction and perdition.
10For the love of money is the root of
all evil: which while some coveted after, they have erred from the faith, and
pierced themselves through with many
sorrows.
11But thou, O man of God, flee these
things; and follow after righteousness,
godliness, faith, love, patience, meekness.
12Fight the good fight of faith, lay hold
on eternal life, whereunto thou art also
called, and hast professed a good profession before many witnesses.
13I give thee charge in the sight of
God, who quickeneth all things, and
before Christ Jesus, who before Pontius Pilate witnessed a good confession;
14That thou keep *this* commandment
without spot, unrebukeable, until the
appearing of our Lord Jesus Christ:
15Which in his times he shall shew,
who is the blessed and only Potentate,
the King of kings, and Lord of lords;
16Who only hath immortality, dwelling

---

custom was for the men already in office to lay their hands on the new officers' heads, in a solemn ceremony as a sign that the new officers now shared in the responsibilities.

5:23 Drink no longer water. Do not drink only water.

5:23 wine. See 1 Timothy 3:8 note, "Teachings about Drinking."

6:2 despise. Disregard.

6:9 will be rich. Desire to be rich.

6:10 the root of all evil. The love of money is the most destructive force in society.

6:10 erred from the faith. Not lost their faith but taken the wrong path for a time. God has to send sorrows to draw them back.

6:12 lay hold on. Paul is urging Timothy to possess eternal life more practically, more fully, and more confidently.

6:13 before Pontius Pilate. See John 18:36-37.

in the light which no man can approach
unto; whom no man hath seen, nor can
see: to whom *be* honour and power
everlasting. Amen.
[17]Charge them that are rich in this
world, that they be not highminded, nor
trust in uncertain riches, but in the living God, who giveth us richly all things
to enjoy;
[18]That they do good, that they be rich
in good works, ready to distribute, willing to communicate;
[19]Laying up in store for themselves
a good foundation against the time to
come, that they may lay hold on eternal life.

L. By not Believing Teaching which Disagrees with God's Word

[20]O Timothy, keep that which is committed to thy trust, avoiding profane
and vain babblings, and oppositions of
science falsely so called:

III. Final Blessing (6:21)

[21]Which some professing have erred
concerning the faith. Grace *be* with
thee. Amen.

6:19 they may lay hold on eternal life. All Christians possess eternal life, but not all Christians lay hold on its blessings.

6:21 some professing have erred. Some foolish people listen to unproved theories and believe them instead of God's Word. A good passage in the Bible for them to read is 1 Corinthians 1:19-31.

The Second Epistle of Paul the Apostle to

TIMOTHY

THE WRITER AND TIME

For an account of Timothy see the introduction to 1 Timothy. Timothy was ordained the first bishop of the church at Ephesus.

The Second Epistle to Timothy was written from Rome, when Paul was brought before Nero the second time. It was written towards the end of the Emperor Nero's reign, about A.D. 67.

MESSAGE

There is much sentiment attached to the last message of a friend, and this second letter of Paul to his "son in the faith" is especially sacred, since it is believed to be the last to leave Paul's mighty pen. The object of Paul's "last will and testament" was to inform young Timothy of the dangers threatening the apostle, and to fortify his courage, asking him to hurry to his aged friend, bringing Mark with him. Because it belongs to his old age, this epistle bears Paul's mature thought.

Second Timothy is loaded with advice regarding all necessary equipment for Christian service. Paul's counsel came from a very tender heart, for he was writing to his son in the faith.

OUTLINE OF 2 TIMOTHY

I.	Christians and Their Mission	2 Timothy 1:1-18
II.	Christians and Their Master	2 Timothy 2:1-26
III.	Christians and Their Message	2 Timothy 3:1-17
IV.	Christians and Their Motive	2 Timothy 4:1-22

I. Christians and Their Mission (1:1-18)

Value of a Godly heritage

1 Paul, an *apostle of Jesus *Christ
by the will of *God, according to
the promise of life which is in Christ
Jesus,
2To *Timothy, *my* dearly beloved son:
*Grace, *mercy, *and* *peace, from
God the Father and Christ Jesus our
Lord.
¶3I thank God, whom I serve from *my*
forefathers with pure conscience, that
without ceasing I have remembrance of
thee in my prayers night and day;

1:2 my dearly beloved son. See 1 Timothy 1:2 second note. Probably Timothy was converted during Paul's first visit to Timothy's hometown of Lystra.

[4]Greatly desiring to see thee, being
mindful of thy tears, that I may be filled
with joy;
[5]When I call to remembrance the
unfeigned *faith that is in thee, which
dwelt first in thy grandmother Lois, and
thy mother Eunice; and I am persuaded that in thee also.

Maintaining the flame of power

[6]Wherefore I put thee in remembrance that thou stir up the gift of God,
which is in thee by the putting on of my
hands.
[7]For God hath not given us the spirit
of fear; but of power, and of love, and of
a sound mind.
[8]Be not thou therefore ashamed of
the testimony of our Lord, nor of me his
prisoner: but be thou partaker of the
afflictions of the *gospel according to
the power of God;

Calling, committings, and keepings

[9]Who hath saved us, and called *us*
with an *holy calling, not according to
our works, but according to his own
purpose and grace, which was given
us in Christ Jesus before the world
began,
[10]But is now made manifest by the
appearing of our Saviour Jesus Christ,
who hath abolished *death, and hath
brought life and immortality to light
through the gospel:
[11]Whereunto I am appointed a
preacher, and an apostle, and a teacher
of the *Gentiles.
[12]For the which cause I also suffer
these things: nevertheless I am not
ashamed: for I know whom I have believed, and am persuaded that he is able
to keep that which I have committed
unto him against that day.
[13]Hold fast the form of sound words,
which thou hast heard of me, in faith
and love which is in Christ Jesus.
[14]That good thing which was committed unto thee keep by the Holy Ghost
which dwelleth in us.

Unworthy and worthy friends

[15]This thou knowest, that all they
which are in Asia be turned away from
me; of whom are Phygellus and Hermogenes.
[16]The Lord give mercy unto the
house of Onesiphorus; for he oft refreshed me, and was not ashamed of my
chain:
[17]But, when he was in Rome, he
sought me out very diligently, and
found *me*.
[18]The Lord grant unto him that he
may find mercy of the Lord in that day:
and in how many things he ministered
unto me at Ephesus, thou knowest very
well.

II. Christians and Their Master (2:1-26)

Sons must be soldiers

2 Thou therefore, my son, be strong
in the grace that is in Christ Jesus.
[2]And the things that thou hast heard
of me among many witnesses, the same
commit thou to faithful men, who shall
be able to teach others also.
[3]Thou therefore endure hardness, as
a good soldier of Jesus Christ.
[4]No man that warreth entangleth
himself with the affairs of *this* life; that
he may please him who hath chosen
him to be a soldier.

1:5 Eunice. See the introduction to 1 Timothy.
1:6 putting on of my hands. See 1 Timothy 5:22 and its note.
1:9 world. Ages.
1:13 form of sound words. Pattern of sound teaching and doctrine.
1:15 Phygellus and Hermogenes. These two, along with some others, left Paul while he was in prison because they were ashamed of his being there (vs.16). They seem to have caused Paul a great degree of grief and surprise. See also 4:16.
1:16 Onesiphorus. Onesiphorus means *bringing advantage*. This friend lived his name.
1:16 chain. Chain is another way of saying that Paul was a prisoner.

Believers must be sufferers and laborers

[5]And if a man also strive for mas-
teries, *yet* is he not crowned, except he
strive lawfully.
[6]The husbandman that laboureth
must be first partaker of the fruits.
[7]Consider what I say; and the Lord
give thee understanding in all things.
[8]Remember that Jesus Christ of the
seed of *David was raised from the dead
according to my gospel:
[9]Wherein I suffer trouble, as an evil
doer, *even* unto bonds; but the word of
God is not bound.
[10]Therefore I endure all things for the
*elect's sakes, that they may also ob-
tain the *salvation which is in Christ
Jesus with eternal glory.
[11]*It is* a faithful saying: For if we be dead
with *him,* we shall also live with *him:*
[12]If we suffer, we shall also reign
with *him:* if we deny *him,* he also will
deny us:
[13]If we believe not, *yet* he abideth
faithful: he cannot deny himself.
[14]Of these things put *them* in remembrance, charging *them* before the Lord
that they strive not about words to
no profit, *but* to the subverting of the
hearers.
[15]Study to shew thyself approved
unto God, a workman that needeth not
to be ashamed, rightly dividing the
word of truth.

Vassals must be vessels

[16]But shun profane *and* vain babblings: for they will increase unto more
ungodliness.
[17]And their word will eat as doth a
canker: of whom is Hymenaeus and
Philetus;
[18]Who concerning the truth have
erred, saying that the *resurrection is
past already; and overthrow the faith of
some.
[19]Nevertheless the foundation of God
standeth sure, having this seal, The
Lord knoweth them that are his. And,
Let every one that nameth the name of
Christ depart from iniquity.
[20]But in a great house there are not
only vessels of gold and of silver, but
also of wood and of earth; and some to
honour, and some to dishonour.
[21]If a man therefore purge himself
from these, he shall be a vessel unto
honour, sanctified, and meet for the
master's use, *and* prepared unto every
good work.
[22]Flee also youthful *lusts: but follow
*righteousness, faith, *charity, peace,
with them that call on the Lord out of a
pure heart.
[23]But foolish and unlearned questions avoid, knowing that they do gender strifes.
[24]And the servant of the Lord must
not strive; but be gentle unto all *men,*
apt to teach, patient,
[25]In meekness instructing those
that oppose themselves; if God
peradventure will give them *repentance to the acknowledging of the
truth;
[26]And *that* they may recover themselves out of the snare of the *devil,
who are taken captive by him at his
will.

2:6 husbandman. The farmer must work before partaking of the fruits.

2:8 my gospel. This is equivalent to Paul's emphasis upon the death and resurrection of the Lord Jesus Christ.

2:9 suffer . . . even unto bonds. Paul was in prison because he preached Christ.

2:11 be dead with him. Have died with Christ (see Gal. 2:20).

2:13 believe not. Are unfaithful.

2:15 Study. Do your best and exercise yourself in the Word; make it your ambition to know the truth of the Scriptures.

2:19 the foundation of God. Those who are righteous in God's sight because they have accepted Jesus Christ as Saviour are an "everlasting foundation" (see Prov. 10:25).

III. The Christians' Message (3:1-17)

Signs of the times

3 This know also, that in the last
days perilous times shall come.
2For men shall be lovers of their own
selves, covetous, boasters, proud, blasphemers, disobedient to parents,
unthankful, unholy,
3Without natural affection, truce-
breakers, false accusers, incontinent,
fierce, despisers of those that are good,
4Traitors, heady, highminded, lovers
of pleasures more than lovers of God;
5Having a form of godliness, but denying the power thereof: from such
turn away.
6For of this sort are they which creep
into houses, and lead captive silly
women laden with sins, led away with
divers lusts,
7Ever learning, and never able to
come to the knowledge of the truth.
8Now as Jannes and Jambres withstood *Moses, so do these also resist
the truth: men of corrupt minds, reprobate concerning the faith.
9But they shall proceed no further:
for their folly shall be manifest unto all
men, as theirs also was.

Follow the faithful

10But thou hast fully known my *doctrine, manner of life, purpose, faith,
longsuffering, charity, patience,
11Persecutions, afflictions, which
came unto me at Antioch, at Iconium, at
Lystra; what persecutions I endured: but
out of *them* all the Lord delivered me.
12Yea, and all that will live godly in
Christ Jesus shall suffer persecution.

3:16 INSPIRATION OF THE SCRIPTURES

The Scriptures are the result of the Holy Spirit acting on the minds of certain chosen men so that what they wrote was the Word of God. Just as Jesus Christ is wholly God and wholly Man, the Living Word (John 1:1-14; see also John 1:1 note, "The Word"), so the written Word is perfectly divine and perfectly human. It is divine so that it may be our faultless guide; it is human so that we may understand it.

Although the Holy Spirit was the inspiration, He allowed the writers to use their various styles: What Isaiah wrote does not sound like Matthew's writing; what Moses wrote does not sound like Paul (see 1 Cor. 14:32; 2 Cor. 13:10). There is divine unity, however, which is one proof of its divine inspiration. The writers themselves knew that they were being used of God (see 1 Cor. 14:37; 2:13; Zech. 9:1; Mal. 1:1).

Jesus Christ prepared the way for the writing of the New Testament when He promised His disciples that the Holy Spirit would be their memory (John 14:26; 15:26; 16:13-14). Not just a part of the Scriptures is inspired, as we know from this verse in 2 Timothy (3:16). "All" literally means *every* Scripture, or *every* portion. The inspired writers did not always understand everything they were recording (1 Pet. 1:11 and its note, "Christ's Suffering and Glory"), but they still wrote. Just because the writers recorded wicked men's deeds or words does not mean that God approved of those actions; rather, it is proof of His truth and of the Bible being a truthful record. The Lord Jesus Christ testified that the Old Testament is the Word of God (Luke 4:1-12,21; 24:25-27; John 5:39). Note also that the prophecies which have been fulfilled in detail are wonderful proof of the inspiration of our Holy Bible. And while there are prophecies still to be fulfilled, nothing more will be added to the Scriptures (see Rev. 22:18-19). See also *How We Got Our English Bible*, p. xxiii.

3:1 last days. The last days are the period from Paul's day right on until the immediate days before Jesus Christ returns in the air for those who are His own, and to the earth in power and great glory (see 1 Thess. 4:13-18 and 1 Thess. 4:13 note, "Hope for the Dead"; Rev. 19:11-16).

3:8 Jannes and Jambres. These men, probably brothers, were Egyptian magicians with whom Moses had contact in Pharaoh's palace (Exod. 7:11-12,22; 8:7; 9:11).

3:11 Persecutions. Read about some of these in Acts 13 and 14 (see also Acts 14:19 note, "Death by Stoning," and Acts 14:22 note, "Persecution of Jewish Believers").

[13]But evil men and seducers shall
wax worse and worse, deceiving, and
being deceived.

Abide in the truth

[14]But continue thou in the things
which thou hast learned and hast been
assured of, knowing of whom thou hast
learned *them;*
[15]And that from a child thou hast
known the holy scriptures, which are
able to make thee wise unto salvation
through faith which is in Christ Jesus.
[16]All scripture *is* given by *inspiration of God, and *is* profitable for doctrine, for reproof, for correction, for
instruction in righteousness:
[17]That the man of God may be *perfect, throughly furnished unto all good
works.

IV. Christians and Their Motive (4:1-22)

Christ's return, and faithfulness

4 I charge *thee* therefore before God,
and the Lord Jesus Christ, who
shall judge the quick and the dead at his
appearing and his kingdom;
[2]Preach the word; be instant in season, out of season; reprove, rebuke,
exhort with all longsuffering and doctrine.
[3]For the time will come when they
will not endure sound doctrine; but after their own lusts shall they heap to
themselves teachers, having itching
ears;
[4]And they shall turn away *their* ears
from the truth, and shall be turned unto
fables.

The evangelist and his rewards

[5]But watch thou in all things, endure
afflictions, do the work of an evangelist,
make full proof of thy ministry.
[6]For I am now ready to be offered,
and the time of my departure is at hand.
[7]I have fought a good fight, I have
finished *my* course, I have kept the
faith:
[8]Henceforth there is laid up for me a
crown of righteousness, which the
Lord, the righteous judge, shall give me
at that day: and not to me only, but unto
all them also that love his appearing.
¶[9]Do thy diligence to come shortly
unto me:
[10]For Demas hath forsaken me, having loved this present world, and is departed unto Thessalonica; Crescens to
Galatia, Titus unto Dalmatia.
[11]Only Luke is with me. Take *Mark,
and bring him with thee: for he is profitable to me for the ministry.
[12]And Tychicus have I sent to
Ephesus.

A cure for discontent

[13]The cloke that I left at Troas with
Carpus, when thou comest, bring *with*

3:14 continue thou. Paul was encouraging Timothy to hold tightly to his faith in Christ and the spiritual truths he'd been taught, despite any opposition.
4:1 quick. Living, Hebrews 4:12.
4:2 reprove. Correct or convict.
4:3 itching ears. Ears that are tired of hearing the truth—their owners long for new teachings, even if they are false, that will make these people feel good about themselves. They don't want to hear things that convict or reprove them.
4:7 a good fight. *The* good fight—the only one that matters—living wholeheartedly for Christ, no matter what.
4:8 crown of righteousness. See *reward.
4:10 Crescens. One of Paul's helpers.
4:10 Titus. One whom Paul led to the Lord and to whom he wrote a letter (see Titus 1:4).
4:11 Luke . . . Mark. Writers of the two Gospels called by their names. Note the change in young Mark, so that he could be used in the Lord's service (compare Acts 15:37-41).
4:12 Tychicus. One of Paul's companions (Acts 20:4).
4:13 Carpus. A trusted Christian friend at Troas. It is said that he later became bishop of Berytus in Thrace.

thee, and the books, *but* especially the
parchments.
14 Alexander the coppersmith did me
much evil: the Lord reward him according to his works:
15 Of whom be thou ware also; for
he hath greatly withstood our
words.
16 At my first answer no man stood
with me, but all *men* forsook me: *I
pray God* that it may not be laid to
their charge.
17 Notwithstanding the Lord stood
with me, and strengthened me; that
by me the preaching might be fully
known, and *that* all the Gentiles might
hear: and I was delivered out of the
mouth of the lion.
18 And the Lord shall deliver me from
every evil work, and will preserve *me*
unto his heavenly kingdom: to whom *be*
glory for ever and ever. Amen.
¶ 19 Salute Prisca and Aquila, and the
household of Onesiphorus.
20 Erastus abode at Corinth: but
Trophimus have I left at Miletum sick.
21 Do thy diligence to come before
winter. Eubulus greeteth thee, and Pudens, and Linus, and Claudia, and all the
brethren.
¶ 22 The Lord Jesus Christ *be* with thy
spirit. Grace *be* with you. Amen.

4:13 books . . . parchments. The books were papyrus rolls, but the parchments may have been some of his inspired epistles, as well as the Old Testament Scriptures, which Paul loved to read in prison and out of prison.

4:14 Alexander. The coppersmith at Ephesus. See 1 Timothy 1:20; Acts 19:33-34.

4:17 strengthened. The expression means literally *infused power into me.*

4:17 delivered out of the mouth of the lion. This was another way of saying that Paul had been delivered from a terrible danger. He may have been speaking of his deliverance from the Emperor Nero.

4:19 Prisca and Aquila. Prisca was a name for Priscilla. See also Romans 16:3; 1 Corinthians 16:19; Acts 18:2,26 for what this husband-and-wife team did for the Lord.

4:20 Erastus. He was chamberlain, or city steward, and treasurer of Corinth (Rom. 16:23).

4:20 Trophimus. He was a Gentile of Ephesus (Acts 21:29), who went with Paul on his third missionary journey. He probably accompanied Titus and Luke in carrying Paul's second letter to the Corinthians (see 2 Cor. 8:18 note). It is said that he was beheaded by Nero.

4:21 Eubulus. A Christian at Rome. Some think that he was Aristobulus, said to be the first evangelist of Britain.

4:21 Pudens. A loyal Roman Christian. An interesting tradition says that King Cogidnubus of Britain had a daughter, named Claudia after the Emperor Tiberias Claudius, and that this princess was married to Pudens. Their son is said to have been Linus, here mentioned, who later became bishop of Rome.

The Epistle of Paul the Apostle to

TITUS

THE WRITER

Titus was written by Paul the apostle (Titus 1:1). It was written to Titus, ordained the first bishop of the church of the Cretians, from the city of Nicopolis in Macedonia.

BACKGROUND

Titus, to whom this letter was addressed, was one of Paul's converts (Titus 1:4). He was a companion of Paul and Barnabas when they went to Jerusalem at the end of the first missionary journey (Galatians 2:1). He was a Gentile by birth (Galatians 2:3). He often served Paul, both as a traveling companion on his missionary journeys, and as his messenger (2 Corinthians 8:23; 12:18).

According to this letter, he was put in charge of the church on the island of Crete (Titus 1:5). Paul gave the Cretans a very bad character (Titus 1:10-16). They were difficult people for the Romans to subdue and colonize, partly because they were a mixture of races. Paul urged Titus to get them to "obey magistrates" (Titus 3:1). The very difficulty of the task gives us some idea of Paul's high estimate of the character and qualities of Titus.

The circumstances under which this letter was written were probably as follows:

1. Paul was released from his first imprisonment, A.D. 63.
2. He visited Ephesus. There he left Timothy to supervise the church, while he went on to Corinth.
3. From Corinth he wrote 1 Timothy to encourage and instruct Timothy.
4. He visited Crete with Titus and left Titus there to supervise the church, while he went on to Nicopolis (in Macedonia).
5. From Nicopolis, probably A.D. 64, he wrote this letter to encourage and instruct Titus. Shortly after this he paid a short visit to Troas where he was suddenly arrested and taken to Rome. From Rome he wrote his last letter—2 Timothy—just before his death, probably by beheading.

This letter and the one written by James should be read with Romans and Galatians. Titus and James deal especially with the place of works in the plan of salvation, while Romans and Galatians deal with that of faith.

OUTLINE OF TITUS

I. How a Church Should Be Organized — Titus 1:1-16
- A. Whom to Ordain
  - 1. The Elder in his home

2. The Elder in himself
3. The Elder in the church

B. Whom to Rebuke
1. Bad teachers
2. Bad followers of the bad teachers

II. What and How the Church Should Teach — Titus 2:1-15
III. How the Members Should Behave — Titus 3:1-15

A. The Two-fold Duty of Christians
1. Conduct as citizens
2. Character as Christians

B. God's Help
C. Satan's Hindrances

I. How a Church Should Be Organized (1:1-16)

1 Paul, a servant of God, and an
*apostle of Jesus *Christ, accord-
ing to the *faith of God's *elect, and the
acknowledging of the truth which is
after godliness;
2In hope of eternal life, which God,
that cannot lie, promised before the
world began;
3But hath in due times manifested his
word through preaching, which is committed unto me according to the commandment of God our Saviour;
4To *Titus, *mine* own son after the
common faith: Grace, mercy, *and* peace,
from God the Father and the Lord Jesus
Christ our Saviour.

Why Titus was left in Crete

¶5For this cause left I thee in Crete,
that thou shouldest set in order the
things that are wanting, and ordain *elders in every city, as I had appointed
thee:

A. Whom to Ordain

1. The Elder in his home

6If any be *blameless, the husband of
one wife, having faithful children not
accused of riot or unruly.

2. The Elder in himself

7For a bishop must be blameless, as
the steward of God; not selfwilled, not
soon angry, not given to *wine, no
striker, not given to filthy lucre;

1:1 servant of God. This is the only time that Paul applies this title to himself. Elsewhere he describes himself as a "servant of Jesus Christ."

1:1 according to the faith of God's elect. Paul occupied the office of an apostle, or messenger, of the Lord Jesus Christ to increase the faith of God's elect, or chosen, people.

1:2 In hope of eternal life. The work of God by His Holy Spirit has in it always an eternal purpose, "promised before the world began" and manifested "in due [appointed] times" (vs. 3).

1:2 world. Ages.

1:3 committed unto me. Preaching is a work appointed by God.

1:4 Titus, mine own son. The expression means that Titus, like Timothy (1 Tim. 1:2), had been brought to Christ by Paul. Later Paul calls Titus "brother" (2 Cor. 2:13), and "partner and fellowhelper" (2 Cor. 8:23).

1:4 Grace, mercy, and peace. Grace is the favor of God. Mercy is the fruit of that favor. Peace is the fruit of mercy.

1:5 things that are wanting. Titus was to complete what Paul had left unfinished because of the shortness of his stay.

1:7 For a bishop. From verse 7, we can see that Paul is speaking of the bishop and the

1:5 Ordained Elders
Overseers from among the older and more experienced Christians. There were such people in the churches, but they had not been ordained, or set apart, by authority. Titus was to do this. They were appointed to be the ruling body in the local churches (1 Tim. 3:5; 5:17), to keep the Word of God free from wrong interpretations, to preach only the truth (Titus 1:9), to watch over the congregations just as a shepherd guards his sheep (Acts 20:28; 1 Pet. 5:2).

8But a lover of hospitality, a lover of
good men, sober, *just, *holy, temperate;

3. The Elder in the church

9Holding fast the faithful word as he
hath been taught, that he may be able
by sound *doctrine both to *exhort and
to convince the gainsayers.

B. Whom to Rebuke
1. Bad teachers

10For there are many unruly and vain
talkers and deceivers, specially they of
the *circumcision:
11Whose mouths must be stopped,
who subvert whole houses, teaching
things which they ought not, for filthy
lucre's sake.

2. Bad followers of the bad teachers

12One of themselves, *even* a *prophet of their own, said, The Cretians *are*
alway liars, evil beasts, slow bellies.
13This witness is true. Wherefore
rebuke them sharply, that they may be
sound in the faith;
14Not giving heed to Jewish fables,
and commandments of men, that turn
from the truth.
15Unto the pure all things *are* pure:
but unto them that are defiled and unbelieving *is* nothing pure; but even their
mind and conscience is defiled.
16They profess that they know God;
but in works they deny *him,* being
abominable, and disobedient, and unto
every good work reprobate.

II. What and How the Church Should Teach (2:1-15)

2 But speak thou the things which
become sound doctrine:
2That the aged men be sober, grave,
temperate, sound in faith, in *charity, in
patience.
3The aged women likewise, that *they*
be in behaviour as becometh holiness,
not false accusers, not given to much
wine, teachers of good things;
4That they may teach the young
women to be sober, to love their husbands, to love their children,
5*To be* discreet, chaste, keepers at
home, good, obedient to their own husbands, that the word of God be not blasphemed.
6Young men likewise exhort to be
sober minded.

---

elder (vs. 5) as having the same office. The word "bishop" comes from the Greek *episcopus,* meaning *overseer.*

1:7 blameless, as the steward of God. Of irreproachable character as God's ambassador.

1:10 specially they of the circumcision. The most dangerous teachers were the Jews who mixed Jewish laws with Christian liberty.

1:11 for filthy lucre's sake. Their object was to make money for themselves.

1:12 One of themselves. Paul was quoting a Cretan poet named Epimenides.

1:12 liars. A common phrase was "to play the Cretan," which meant to be a liar.

1:12 slow bellies. Lazy gluttons.

1:15 Unto the pure all things are pure. Even meats marked as *unclean in Jewish Law, and therefore forbidden, were now pure, that is, lawful to be used.

1:16 abominable, and disobedient . . . reprobate. "Abominable" means *offensive.* "Unto every good work reprobate" means incapable of forming true judgments concerning what was right and wrong.

2:3 not false accusers. Avoiding gossip or scandal.

2:5 blasphemed. Spoken evil of.

[7]In all things shewing thyself a pattern of good works: in doctrine *shewing*
uncorruptness, gravity, sincerity,
[8]Sound speech, that cannot be condemned; that he that is of the contrary
part may be ashamed, having no evil
thing to say of you.
[9]*Exhort* servants to be obedient unto
their own masters, *and* to please *them*
well in all *things;* not answering again;
[10]Not purloining, but shewing all
good fidelity; that they may adorn the
doctrine of God our Saviour in all
things.
[11]For the *grace of God that bringeth
*salvation hath appeared to all men,
[12]Teaching us that, denying ungodliness and worldly *lusts, we should live
soberly, righteously, and godly, in this
present world;
[13]Looking for that blessed hope, and
the glorious appearing of the great God
and our Saviour Jesus Christ;
[14]Who gave himself for us, that he
might *redeem us from all iniquity, and
purify unto himself a peculiar people,
zealous of good works.
[15]These things speak, and exhort,
and rebuke with all authority. Let no
man despise thee.

III. How the Members of the Church Should Behave (3:1-15)

A. The Two-fold Duty of Christians

1. Conduct as citizens

3 Put them in mind to be subject to
principalities and powers, to obey
magistrates, to be ready to every good
work,

2. Character as Christians

[2]To speak evil of no man, to be no
brawlers, *but* gentle, shewing all meekness unto all men.
[3]For we ourselves also were some-

2:1 TITUS' TEACHING

Titus was to deliver the message of God to five special sets of people: "aged men" (vs. 2); "aged women" (vs. 3); "young women" (vs. 4); "young men" (vs. 6); and "servants" (vs. 9).

Titus' teaching was to be marked by five characteristics: It was to be true, serious, sincere (vs. 7), convincing, and unquestionable (vs. 8).

Titus himself was to be an example to his listeners and learners (vs. 7).

The content of his teaching was to be threefold: what we must leave (vs. 12), how we should live (vs. 12), and what we should look for (vs. 13). His teaching had to be based upon the threefold work of Christ for His people as a result of His death upon the cross: He set us free–redeemed "us from all iniquity" (vs. 14); He set us apart–purified "unto himself a peculiar people" (vs. 14); He set us on fire–made us "zealous of good works" (vs. 14).

2:7 In all things. Above everything else.
2:9 servants. Slaves.
2:10 purloining. Pilfering, stealing.
2:10 adorn the doctrine. Recommend the teaching and make it attractive; live so that there may be an outward manifestation of the faith believed in.
2:12 denying ungodliness and worldly lusts. Refusing to follow everything unworthy of God, as well as all worldly ambitions.
2:13 Looking for. Looking out for, living in expectation of.
2:14 a peculiar people. Christ's own special people.
2:15 exhort. Encourage.
2:15 despise. Condescend to or speak badly of.
3:1 to be subject to principalities and powers, to obey magistrates. Rome conquered Crete in 67 B.C., and thus had been ruling there for 125 years. The Cretans had often been unruly, and they were told to substitute "every good work" for useless revolt.
3:1 ready to every good work. Notice that three times in this final chapter Paul referred to good works–here and in verses 8 and 14.
3:3 sometimes. Once, used to be.

times foolish, disobedient, deceived,
serving divers lusts and pleasures, living in malice and envy, hateful, *and* hating one another.

B. God's Help

4But after that the kindness and love
of God our Saviour toward man appeared,
5Not by works of righteousness
which we have done, but according to
his mercy he saved us, by the washing
of regeneration, and renewing of the
Holy Ghost;
6Which he shed on us abundantly
through Jesus Christ our Saviour;
7That being justified by his grace, we
should be made heirs according to the
hope of eternal life.
8*This is* a faithful saying, and these
things I will that thou affirm constantly, that they which have believed in God
might be careful to maintain good
works. These things are good and profitable unto men.

C. Satan's Hindrances

9But avoid foolish questions, and
genealogies, and contentions, and strivings about the law; for they are unprofitable and vain.
10A man that is an heretick after the
first and second admonition reject;
11Knowing that he that is such is subverted, and sinneth, being condemned
of himself.

Conclusion

¶12When I shall send Artemas unto
thee, or Tychicus, be diligent to come
unto me to Nicopolis: for I have determined there to winter.
13Bring Zenas the lawyer and Apollos on their journey diligently, that
nothing be wanting unto them.
14And let ours also learn to maintain
good works for necessary uses, that
they be not unfruitful.
¶15All that are with me salute thee.
Greet them that love us in the faith.
Grace *be* with you all. Amen.

3:4 after that. When.
3:4 appeared. Came to light; were made manifest.
3:5 the washing of regeneration. That cleansing which was a new birth. See John 1:13, 1 Corinthians 6:11 note.
3:5 renewing of the Holy Ghost. The restoring power of the Holy Spirit.
3:7 justified by his grace. Made right with God through His loving-kindness.
3:7 we should be made heirs according to the hope of eternal life. We will come into our inheritance of eternal life in accordance with our expectation and God's promise in Christ.
3:9 avoid. Titus was to avoid useless discussions, controversies, human additions to, explanations of, and arguments about the Law.
3:10 an heretick. One who caused divisions and who had been warned was to be rejected, that is, not to be argued with further.
3:11 subverted. Warped in his thinking and become a backslider. He lived in sin, despite his own conscience telling him it was sin.
3:12 When I shall send. Whenever I am able to send.
3:12 Artemas. In tradition, he was the bishop of Lystra.
3:13 Zenas the lawyer. The teacher of the Law. The name is a contraction of Zenodorus, a Jewish *scribe, who kept his title even after he was converted.
3:14 let ours also learn to maintain good works for necessary uses. Encourage all our people to practice giving generously to whatever necessities may arise.
3:15 salute thee. Send greetings.
3:15 Greet them that love us in the faith. This closing salutation is different from any other in Paul's epistles. It does not disprove the genuineness of his authorship, however. On the contrary, a writer trying to sound like Paul would certainly have copied from the other epistles of Paul.

The Epistle of Paul the Apostle to

PHILEMON

BACKGROUND

To understand this wonderful little letter something should be known of the circumstances which led to its writing. In his later years the Apostle Paul, probably while a prisoner at Rome, had met a runaway slave named Onesimus. Slavery was one of the curses of the Roman Empire, and, because of the abuses which resulted from it, one of the causes for the Empire's downfall. According to Gibbon, one-half the population in the Empire were slaves, and later estimates run to three-fourths. Roman law, declaring the slave to have no rights, put him in the place of a mere possession of his master. Thus for a slave to run away or steal was a crime punishable even by death. For such a transgressor the law held but one hope—for him to find someone to intercede for his reinstatement. A letter of such intercession is the epistle to Philemon.

As we read between the lines we see that Onesimus was a fugitive from justice, having stolen from his master, Philemon. We see also that Paul had led Onesimus to Christ. In fact the whole chain of circumstances behind this epistle is a marvelous illustration of God's gracious providence. It was not by chance that Onesimus met Paul; nor was it by chance that Paul was acquainted with Philemon, a Christian and a member of the church at Colosse.

STRUCTURE

In reading and studying this personal letter, it should be remembered that literary critics consider it one of the supreme masterpieces of letter writing. No one has ever surpassed the exquisite tact and courtesy of Paul, the Christian gentleman, as he writes in behalf of Onesimus. But the epistle is more than a literary masterpiece, for spiritual-minded Bible scholars see in it a touching parable of redemption through the Lord Jesus Christ.

THE TIME

The date of writing is about A.D. 62.

OUTLINE

To outline such a compactly living piece of literature is unnecessary; it is so short as to demand reading as a unit.

1 Paul, a prisoner of Jesus Christ, and
Timothy *our* brother, unto Philemon
our dearly beloved, and fellowlabourer,
2 And to *our* beloved Apphia, and Archippus our fellowsoldier, and to the
church in thy house:
3 Grace to you, and peace, from God
our Father and the Lord Jesus Christ.
¶ 4 I thank my God, making mention
of thee always in my prayers,
5 Hearing of thy love and faith, which
thou hast toward the Lord Jesus, and toward all *saints;
6 That the communication of thy faith
may become effectual by the acknowledging of every good thing which is in
you in Christ Jesus.
7 For we have great joy and consolation in thy love, because the bowels
of the saints are refreshed by thee,
brother.
8 Wherefore, though I might be much
bold in Christ to enjoin thee that which
is convenient,
9 Yet for love's sake I rather beseech
thee, being such an one as Paul the
aged, and now also a prisoner of Jesus
Christ.
10 I beseech thee for my son Onesimus, whom I have begotten in my
bonds:
11 Which in time past was to thee unprofitable, but now profitable to thee
and to me:
12 Whom I have sent again: thou
therefore receive him, that is, mine own
bowels:
13 Whom I would have retained with
me, that in thy stead he might have
ministered unto me in the bonds of the
gospel:
14 But without thy mind would I do
nothing; that thy benefit should not
be as it were of necessity, but willingly.
15 For perhaps he therefore departed
for a season, that thou shouldest receive him for ever;

---

1 prisoner of Jesus Christ. Paul does not, as in most of his epistles, begin by referring to himself as an apostle. This is a personal letter, and so he identifies himself simply as a prisoner of Jesus Christ.

1 Philemon. Names of Bible characters sometimes, but not always, have significant meanings. Philemon means *friendly*.

2 Apphia. A woman's name; it probably referred to Philemon's wife.

2 Archippus. Supposed to have been Philemon's son.

2 the church in thy house. The Christian church began in private homes. Separate buildings for worship were not erected for several hundred years.

6 That the communication of thy faith. The meaning of the clauses of this verse, is this: Paul is praying that those helped by Philemon might acknowledge Philemon's good deeds as done from Christ Jesus.

8-9 much bold in Christ to enjoin thee . . . Yet for love's sake I rather beseech thee. As the God-appointed apostle to the Gentiles, Paul might have commanded Philemon to do his bidding. It is a strong man who is big enough to lay aside his authority and rely only upon the persuasive power of love.

10 my son Onesimus. This story is a beautiful example of justification by faith. Paul acts as a human mediator between the one wronged and the sinner, just as Christ is our mediator with the Father (1 Tim. 2:5).

11 unprofitable, but now profitable. "Onesimus" means *profitable*. Paul indulged in a bit of humor as he played on the meaning of Onesimus' name and gently covered up the fugitive's sin with a pun.

13 Whom I would have retained with me. With almost every sentence in this masterful little letter, Paul was entwining himself and Onesimus around the heart of Philemon.

15 departed for a season. This is the most delicate description of a runaway thief in all the literature of the world. It is as if Paul had said, "Perhaps he took a brief vacation so that you might take him back for good."

16 Not now as a servant, but above
a servant, a brother beloved, specially to me, but how much more unto
thee, both in the flesh, and in the
Lord?
17 If thou count me therefore a partner, receive him as myself.
18 If he hath wronged thee, or oweth
thee ought, put that on mine account;
19 I Paul have written *it* with mine
own hand, I will repay *it:* albeit I do not
say to thee how thou owest unto me
even thine own self besides.
20 Yea, brother, let me have joy of thee
in the Lord: refresh my bowels in the
Lord.
¶ 21 Having confidence in thy obedience I wrote unto thee, knowing that
thou wilt also do more than I say.
22 But withal prepare me also a lodging: for I trust that through your prayers
I shall be given unto you.
¶ 23 There salute thee *Epaphras, my
fellowprisoner in Christ Jesus;
24 *Marcus, *Aristarchus, *Demas,
Lucas, my fellowlabourers.
¶ 25 The grace of our Lord Jesus
Christ *be* with your spirit. Amen.

19 PAUL'S PROMISSORY NOTE

The aged apostle, possibly half blind, seldom wrote with his own hand. Sometimes he managed to do this by using very large letters of the alphabet (Gal. 6:11). His reason for a handwritten letter to Philemon was that here was his promissory note. According to Roman law, the debt of another could be assumed only by written contract. In this way, Paul, prisoner though he was, legally took upon himself the debt of Onesimus.

So the Lord Jesus Christ has taken upon Himself the debt of our sin. The book of Philemon is above all else a striking parable of redemption. The wronged master, Philemon, stands for God, against whom every one of us has sinned. Onesimus, the fugitive slave, stands for us as sinners, bound to our sin with chains no human power can ever break. Paul, the interceding friend, stands for the Lord Jesus Christ, who says of every sinner's guilt, "I Christ have written it (the payment of the debt of sin) with My own blood. I have repaid it."

16 above a servant. This epistle has been appropriately called "the first emancipation proclamation." Although it does not contain a word against slavery, the spirit that breathes through it is opposed to slavery. Philemon and Onesimus, though master and slave, were now brothers in the Lord. Spiritual relationships transcend human relationships—all people are equal in God's eyes and in Christ.

18 put that on mine account. In this place Paul makes use of a Greek verb which appears only one other time in the New Testament (Rom. 5:13), where it is rendered "imputed." Imputation is another way of expressing the idea of crediting something or charging it. When God saves a sinner, He charges to the sinner's credit Christ's perfect righteousness.

19 thou owest. Philemon owed his conversion to Paul's ministry. Paul had led Philemon to Christ.

24 Lucas. Luke, the beloved physician and loyal companion of Paul, author of the third Gospel and Acts (Col. 4:14; 2 Tim. 4:11).

The Epistle of Paul the Apostle to the

HEBREWS

THE WRITER AND TIME

Hebrews appears to have been written in Italy (Hebrews 13:24) about A.D. 62 to 64. No one knows positively who wrote the epistle. The author is not mentioned, as in Romans 1:1; 1 Peter 1:1; and James 1:1. But many believe that it is by Paul, not only because it seems like Paul's writing, but because of the reference in 2 Peter 3:15, and because it ends with the special "token" with which, as he declared in 2 Thessalonians 3:17-18, Paul closed his various letters.

Compare Hebrews 13:25 with:

Romans 16:24	1 Thessalonians 5:28
1 Corinthians 16:23-24	2 Thessalonians 3:18
2 Corinthians 13:14	1 Timothy 6:21
Galatians 6:18	2 Timothy 4:22
Ephesians 6:24	Titus 3:15
Philippians 4:23	Philemon 25
Colossians 4:18	

BACKGROUND

The epistle was addressed, in the first place, to Hebrew Christians of Palestine and the East, to guard them against unbelief and to strengthen their faith in the Lord Jesus Christ. It contains a "word of exhortation" (Hebrews 13:22), or warning.

These Jewish Christians had been brought up in Judaism, with its system of sacrifices, under the old *covenant with Moses. This covenant was the promise of God made to the children of Israel through Moses. The old covenant required regular sacrifices for sins, and a high priest to present the blood of the slain animals as sacrifices to God on behalf of the sinners. Because these sacrifices could not take away sin, but were only reminders of the need for taking away sin, they were repeated every year as *types of God's way of salvation.

The old covenant was, in every way, a picture of the new covenant, in which God's promise is given to His people through the Lord Jesus Christ. These Old Testament pictures are just shadows, or outlines, which are filled in and made complete in the new covenant. Because the blood of lambs and of goats could never take away sin, God sent His only Son—a "Lamb" without sin—to bear the sin of the world; not yearly, as in the old covenant, but, because the Lord Jesus was perfect, His death on the cross was the one perfect sacrifice for sin.

THINGS TO NOTE

Apart from the epistle to the Hebrews, the Word of God tells very little, indeed, of the present ministry of the Son of God in the presence of God, or of His constant office as High Priest. The key word is "better." The promises of God in Christ are "better" than His promises to His people through Moses.

OUTLINE OF HEBREWS

I.	The Lord Jesus Christ Superior to Angels	Hebrews 1:1—2:18
II.	The Lord Jesus Christ Superior to Moses	Hebrews 3:1—4:13
III.	The Lord Jesus Christ Superior to the High Priests	Hebrews 4:14—10:39
IV.	Heroes of Faith	Hebrews 11:1-40
V.	Life of Believers under the New Covenant	Hebrews 12:1—13:25

I. The Lord Jesus Christ Superior to Angels (1:1-2:18)

1 *God, who at sundry times and in
divers manners spake in time past
unto the fathers by the *prophets,
2 Hath in these last days spoken unto
us by *his* Son, whom he hath appointed
heir of all things, by whom also he made
the worlds;
3 Who being the brightness of *his* glory, and the express *image of his person, and upholding all things by the
word of his power, when he had by himself purged our sins, sat down on the
right hand of the Majesty on high;
4 Being made so much better than the
*angels, as he hath by inheritance ob-
tained a more excellent name than they.

1:2 God's Son
God the Father allowed His Son to speak everything into existence (Gen. 1:3), using Him to even create all things (Col. 1:16). All things were created by Him for Him. The name by which the Saviour is most frequently called in this epistle is the historical name, Jesus. The Son is spoken of as existing in three estates: His present condition of honor and glory; His earthly life, or the days of His flesh; and His state of preexistence before coming into the world.

5 For unto which of the angels said he
at any time, Thou art my Son, this day
have I begotten thee? And again, I will
be to him a Father, and he shall be to me
a Son?

1:1 at sundry times and in divers manners. An many times and in various ways.
1:2 these last days. Since the coming of Christ, even up to today.
1:2 worlds. Universe.
1:3 brightness. Radiance.
1:3 express image of his person. The term "express image" means the *exact representation* of God. It refers to what is engraved on any object, as a seal; it speaks therefore, of distinct, sharply defined features of mind or body by which any thing or any person may be distinguished, in this case, God represented by Christ.
1:3 purged our sins. Believers are washed from their sins in Christ's own blood (1 Cor. 6:11; Rev. 1:5).
1:3 on the right hand of the Majesty on high. This phrase taken from Psalm 110:1 is used to describe the present dignity of the Son (see also Eph. 1:20-21). He occupies the place of honor (1 Kings 2:19; Ps. 45:9) in the universe, a place of influence and rule (Heb. 1:4; 2:9).
1:5 Thou art my Son. See Psalm 2:7 and its note, "The First Begotten."
1:5 I will be to him a Father. See 2 Samuel 7:14.

[6]And again, when he bringeth in the
firstbegotten into the world, he saith,
And let all the angels of God worship
him.
[7]And of the angels he saith, Who
maketh his angels spirits, and his ministers a flame of *fire.
[8]But unto the Son *he saith,* Thy
throne, O God, *is* for ever and ever: a
sceptre of righteousness *is* the sceptre
of thy *kingdom.
[9]Thou hast loved righteousness, and
hated iniquity; therefore God, *even* thy
God, hath anointed thee with the oil of
gladness above thy fellows.
[10]And, Thou, Lord, in the beginning
hast laid the foundation of the earth; and
the heavens are the works of thine
hands:
[11]They shall perish; but thou remainest; and they all shall wax old as
doth a garment;
[12]And as a vesture shalt thou fold
them up, and they shall be changed: but
thou art the same, and thy years shall
not fail.
[13]But to which of the angels said he
at any time, Sit on my right hand, until
I make thine enemies thy footstool?
[14]Are they not all ministering spirits,
sent forth to minister for them who
shall be heirs of *salvation?

2 Therefore we ought to give the
more earnest heed to the things
which we have heard, lest at any time
we should let *them* slip.
[2]For if the word spoken by angels was
stedfast, and every transgression and

1:4 ANGELS

"Angels" means *messengers*. The Word of God very plainly teaches that God created angels, who are spiritual beings who do the service of God (vs. 14). They carried God's messages to men and still carry out His will in various ways. Some of the angels fell into sin with Satan, who was also an angel (Jude 6).

The Scriptures reveal some angels by name: Michael (Dan. 12:1), the archangel or chief angel (Jude 9); and Gabriel (Luke 1:26). Other angels are revealed by titles that indicate their type of service: *seraphims and *cherubims. Sometimes the word "angel" refers to human messengers (1 Kings 19:2; Luke 7:24), and some of the prophets were spoken of as God's angels or messengers (see Hag. 1:13). Sometimes the heavenly angels are called "holy ones" or "watchers." They meet in council with God and make up His hosts.

Occasionally angels have taken human form and been mistaken for men (Gen. 18:2,16), and some of these appearances were really *theophanies. We never read of their looking like women or of their having wings, except for the orders of cherubims and seraphims, however, who are winged beings (see Exod. 25:20; Isa. 6:2 and its note, "Seraphims").

No one becomes an angel when he or she dies. Angels were created by God to be angels forever.

1:6 world. The inhabited earth.
1:6 And let all. The angelic beings were created for the specific purpose of worshipping God.
1:7 Who maketh his angels spirits. See Psalm 104:4.
1:8 Thy throne, O God. Compare this verse and the next with Psalm 45:6-7.
1:8 righteousness. Godly living and uprightness.
1:10 Thou, Lord. Compare verses 10-12 with Psalm 102:25-27.
1:12 vesture. Robe.
1:13 But to which. Verses 13-14 mark the final contrast between the place of the Son and that of the angels in the saving work of the Lord Jesus Christ.
1:13 Sit on my right hand. Compare with Psalm 110:1; see also Hebrews 1:3 and its note.
2:1 Therefore. That is, because of what has just been said concerning the Son.
2:1 let them slip. Drift away. We should not worry that the words will slip away from us, but that we might fail to heed God's Word and we would slip or drift away from God, especially into false teaching.

disobedience received a *just recompence of *reward;
3How shall we escape, if we neglect
so great salvation; which at the first
began to be spoken by the Lord, and
was confirmed unto us by them that
heard *him;*
4God also bearing *them* witness, both
with signs and wonders, and with divers
*miracles, and gifts of the Holy Ghost,
according to his own will?

The Lord Jesus Christ to be over the earth

¶5For unto the angels hath he not put
in subjection the world to come, whereof we speak.
6But one in a certain place testified,
saying, What is man, that thou art mindful of him? or the son of man, that thou
visitest him?
7Thou madest him a little lower than
the angels; thou crownedst him with
glory and honour, and didst set him over
the works of thy hands:
8Thou hast put all things in subjection
under his feet. For in that he put all in
subjection under him, he left nothing
that is not put under him. But now we
see not yet all things put under him.

The Lord Jesus Christ was made, for a season, lower than the angels

9But we see Jesus, who was made a
little lower than the angels for the suffering of *death, crowned with glory and
honour; that he by the *grace of God
should taste death for every man.
10For it became him, for whom *are* all
things, and by whom *are* all things, in
bringing many sons unto glory, to make
the captain of their salvation perfect
through sufferings.
11For both he that sanctifieth and
they who are sanctified *are* all of one:
for which cause he is not ashamed to
call them brethren,
12Saying, I will declare thy name unto
my brethren, in the midst of the
*church will I sing praise unto thee.
13And again, I will put my *trust in
him. And again, Behold I and the children which God hath given me.
14Forasmuch then as the children are
*partakers of flesh and blood, he also
himself likewise took part of the same;
that through death he might destroy
him that had the power of death, that is,
the *devil;
15And deliver them who through
*fear of death were all their lifetime
subject to bondage.
16For verily he took not on *him the
nature of* angels; but he took on *him* the
seed of *Abraham.
17Wherefore in all things it behoved
him to be made like unto *his* brethren,
that he might be a merciful and faithful
high priest in things *pertaining* to God,
to make *reconciliation for the sins of
the people.

2:17 The Faithful High Priest
The people of God, though redeemed, pardoned, reconciled, and forever freed from the condemnation of sin, are still exposed to temptation and are likely to sin. To meet this need, God has provided for His people "a merciful and faithful high priest," who makes reconciliation, or propitiation, for their sins. Except for this, the people of God could not come into His presence for worship.

2:6 What is man . . . ? See Psalm 8:4-6.
2:9 a little. In becoming human, Christ was made lower than the angels, but it was only for a short time.
2:10 captain. The Lord Jesus Christ, the Pioneer and Leader of our salvation.
2:12 I will declare. Compare this verse with Psalm 22:22.
2:13 I will put my trust. This is taken from the Septuagint (see *How We Got Our English Bible*, p. xxiii) translation of Isaiah 8:17.
2:13 Behold I and the children. Spoken by Isaiah in 8:18.
2:16 he took not on him. Christ did not come to be the Saviour of fallen angels; He came to be the Saviour of fallen mankind.

18 For in that he himself hath suffered
being *tempted, he is able to succour
them that are tempted.

II. The Lord Jesus Christ Superior
to Moses (3:1—4:13)

3 Wherefore, holy brethren, partakers of the heavenly calling, consider the *Apostle and High Priest of
our profession, *Christ Jesus;
2 Who was faithful to him that appointed him, as also *Moses *was faithful* in
all his house.
3 For this *man* was counted worthy of
more glory than Moses, inasmuch as he
who hath builded the house hath more
honour than the house.
4 For every house is builded by some
man; but he that built all things *is* God.
5 And Moses verily *was* faithful in all
his house, as a servant, for a *testimony
of those things which were to be spoken after;
6 But Christ as a son over his own
house; whose house are we, if we hold
fast the confidence and the rejoicing of
the *hope firm unto the end.
7 Wherefore (as the Holy Ghost saith,
To day if ye will hear his voice,
8 *Harden not your hearts, as in the
provocation, in the day of *temptation
in the wilderness:
9 When your fathers tempted me,
proved me, and saw my works forty
years.
10 Wherefore I was grieved with that
generation, and said, They do alway
*err in *their* heart; and they have not
known my ways.
11 So I sware in my wrath, They shall
not enter into my rest.)
12 Take heed, brethren, lest there be
in any of you an evil heart of unbelief,
in departing from the living God.
13 But *exhort one another daily,
while it is called To day; lest any of you
be hardened through the deceitfulness
of *sin.
14 For we are made partakers of
Christ, if we hold the beginning of our
confidence stedfast unto the end;
15 While it is said, To day if ye will
hear his voice, harden not your hearts,
as in the provocation.
16 For some, when they had heard, did
provoke: howbeit not all that came out
of *Egypt by Moses.
17 But with whom was he grieved forty years? *was it* not with them that had
sinned, whose carcases fell in the wilderness?
18 And to whom sware he that they
should not enter into his rest, but to
them that believed not?
19 So we see that they could not enter in because of unbelief.

Rest for the believer

4 Let us therefore fear, lest, a promise being left *us* of entering into his
rest, any of you should seem to come
short of it.
2 For unto us was the *gospel preached,
as well as unto them: but the word
preached did not profit them, not being
mixed with *faith in them that heard *it.*
3 For we which have believed do enter into rest, as he said, As I have sworn

---

3:1 partakers. Companions; to take part.
3:1 profession. Confession.
3:2 Moses was faithful. See Numbers 12:7.
3:7 To day if ye will. Verses 7-11 and also verse 15 are taken from Psalm 95:7-11.
3:13 while it is called To day. This is the period during which we "hear"; the period fixed by God for entering into His rest (as in Heb. 4:7)—the period until Christ will come again.
3:14 of Christ. See Ephesians 3:6.
3:16 For some, when they had heard, did provoke: howbeit not all. Both the Hebrews, to whom the apostle was writing here, and Israel, heard the Lord's voice (3:7; 4:2); when Israel heard, they were provoked; and the danger of these Hebrews falling into the same example (4:11) is seen from the fact that Israel's defection was universal and that it happened when the memory of their deliverance from Egypt was still fresh.
4:3 As I have sworn. Compare with Psalm 95:11.

in my wrath, if they shall enter into my
rest: although the works were finished
from the foundation of the world.
4For he spake in a certain place of the
seventh *day* on this wise, And God did
rest the seventh day from all his works.
5And in this *place* again, If they shall
enter into my rest.
6Seeing therefore it remaineth that
some must enter therein, and they to
whom it was first preached entered not
in because of unbelief:
7Again, he limiteth a certain day, saying in *David, To day, after so long a
time; as it is said, To day if ye will hear
his voice, harden not your hearts.
8For if Jesus had given them rest,
then would he not afterward have spoken of another day.

Redemption-rest

9There remaineth therefore a rest to
the people of God.
10For he that is entered into his rest,
he also hath ceased from his own
works, as God *did* from his.
11Let us labour therefore to enter
into that rest, lest any man fall after the
same example of unbelief.
12For the word of God *is* *quick, and
powerful, and sharper than any twoedged sword, piercing even to the dividing asunder of soul and spirit, and
of the joints and marrow, and *is* a dis-

4:3 ENTERING GOD'S REST

The reasoning of the writer of the epistle to the Hebrews about the rest of God is based on two passages which he combines: "And [God] rested" (Gen. 2:2) and "they [shall] not enter into my rest" (Ps. 95:11). The writer implies that there is a "rest of God," which He Himself enjoys and that He entered into it when the work of creation was finished (Heb. 4:3,10). It is clear that this rest of God has not yet come for Christians, but God has entered into Himself.

The term "rest" does not mean that God was tired from His work of creation, merely that He ceased from it; nor does it mean that since then He has been doing nothing. It means that after His work of creation was finished, He enjoyed satisfaction in His completed work, as well as the sense of rest.

From the other passage, "They [shall] not enter into my rest," the writer implies that it was God's wish that man should enter into His rest and share it with Him. God desired to see fulfilled in Israel His purpose that man should enter with Him into His rest. Though Israel came short through disobedience, their unbelief could not make the faithfulness of God without effect (Rom. 3:3). His gracious design that "some must enter therein" (Heb. 4:6) still remained, and a long time afterward He gave the promise again, even setting a time for the entering into the rest when He said, "To day if ye will hear [My] voice, harden not your hearts" (compare Ps. 95:7; Heb. 4:7).

4:3 world. Earth.
4:4 God did rest the seventh day. See Genesis 2:2.
4:6 it was first preached. It (the gospel) after the Exodus, was simply trusting God's promises to the Israelites. The gospel of Christ had not come yet, therefore the *content of their faith* differed from ours.
4:7 limiteth. Fixed or set.
4:7 To day if ye will hear. See Psalm 95:7-8.
4:8 Jesus. Not the Lord Jesus Christ. Here we have the Greek form for Joshua. Joshua could not lead all of the children of Israel into their rest in Canaan, for God had ruled that many of them, because of their unbelief, could not enter there; but this looks ahead to the eternal rest in Christ, and all—Jews and Gentiles—are invited to enter there.
4:11 Let us labour. Read what this labor consists of in 2 Peter 1:10.
4:11 unbelief. Disobedience.
4:12 For the word of God. Compare this verse with Isaiah 49:2.
4:12 quick, and powerful. God's Word is living ("quick") and life-changing, because it is a spoken and heard Word; it is active and it works in us if we allow it to—it can help shape our lives into godly lives.

cerner of the thoughts and intents of the heart.
[13]Neither is there any creature that is not manifest in his sight: but all things *are* naked and opened unto the eyes of him with whom we have to do.

III. The Lord Jesus Christ Superior to the High Priest (4:14—10:39)

[14]Seeing then that we have a great high priest, that is passed into the heavens, Jesus the Son of God, let us hold fast *our* profession.
[15]For we have not an high priest which cannot be touched with the feeling of our infirmities; but was in all points tempted like as *we are, yet* without sin.
[16]Let us therefore come boldly unto the throne of grace, that we may obtain *mercy, and find grace to help in time of need.

The Lord Jesus Christ, a High Priest

5 For every high priest taken from among men is ordained for men in things *pertaining* to God, that he may offer both gifts and sacrifices for sins:
[2]Who can have compassion on the ignorant, and on them that are out of the way; for that he himself also is compassed with infirmity.
[3]And by reason hereof he ought, as for the people, so also for himself, to offer for sins.
[4]And no man taketh this honour unto himself, but he that is called of God, as *was* *Aaron.
[5]So also Christ glorified not himself to be made an high priest; but he that said unto him, Thou art my Son, to day have I begotten thee.
[6]As he saith also in another *place,* Thou *art* a priest for ever after the order of *Melchisedec.
[7]Who in the days of his flesh, when he had offered up prayers and supplications with strong crying and tears unto him that was able to save him from death, and was heard in that he feared;
[8]Though he were a Son, yet learned he obedience by the things which he suffered;

4:13 him with whom we have to do. With whom (God) we must give account of ourselves.
4:14 passed into the heavens. Compare with Hebrews 9:12,24.
4:15 be touched with the feeling of our infirmities. Sympathize with our weaknesses, since He became human and lived through the full range of human emotions, but without sin.
4:15 like as we are. Tempted in the same way we are.
4:15 yet without sin. Apart from sin. The Lord Jesus Christ could not sin, but He was tempted, or tested, in other ways, such as by loneliness, by being misunderstood, by having no place to lay His head, etc. He was fully human; He felt pain (especially on the cross but emotional pain as well); He got tired, hungry, thirsty. He became one of us so He could "walk in our shoes," so to speak, the difference being that though Christ could be tempted, He could not sin. Only the Sinless One could be qualified to pay for our sins.
4:16 Let us therefore come boldly. Draw near with glad confidence since Christ is our High Priest and Friend and God loves us—so much that He sacrificed His Son.
5:2 compassed with infirmity. Subject to weakness.
5:4 called of God, as was Aaron. First told in Exodus 28:1; Numbers 16:40.
5:5 but he that said. This means that Christ did not glorify Himself; God, who said the next words, was the One who did the glorifying.
5:5 Thou art my Son. See Psalm 2:7 and its note, "The First Begotten."
5:6 Thou art a priest. Compare verses 5-6 with Psalm 110:4.
5:6 Melchisedec. See *Melchizedek.
5:7 prayers. See Matthew 26:39,41.
5:7 in that he feared. Because of Christ's piety or godly fear.
5:8 obedience. Described in Philippians 2:8.

9 And being made perfect, he became
the author of eternal salvation unto all
them that obey him;
10 Called of God an high priest after
the order of Melchisedec.
¶ 11 Of whom we have many things to
say, and hard to be uttered, seeing ye
are dull of hearing.
12 For when for the time ye ought to
be teachers, ye have need that one
teach you again which *be* the first principles of the oracles of God; and are
become such as have need of milk, and
not of strong meat.
13 For every one that useth milk *is*
unskilful in the word of righteousness:
for he is a babe.
14 But strong meat belongeth to them
that are of full age, *even* those who by
reason of use have their senses exercised to discern both good and evil.

6 Therefore leaving the principles
of the *doctrine of Christ, let us go
on unto perfection; not laying again the
foundation of *repentance from dead
works, and of faith toward God,
2 Of the doctrine of baptisms, and of
laying on of hands, and of *resurrection
of the dead, and of eternal *judgment.
3 And this will we do, if God permit.
4 For *it is* impossible for those who
were once enlightened, and have tasted of the heavenly gift, and were made
partakers of the Holy Ghost,
5 And have tasted the good word of
God, and the powers of the world to
come,
6 If they shall fall away, to renew them
again unto repentance; seeing they
crucify to themselves the Son of God
afresh, and put *him* to an open shame.
7 For the earth which drinketh in the
rain that cometh oft upon it, and

6:7 A Parable of the Ground
Verses 7-8 give a *parable of two pieces of ground: Both have been cultivated in the same way, sharing the same sun and rain; but one produces useful herbs for those who till it, thus partaking of blessing from God, as described in Psalm 65:10. The other produces only the fruit of the Curse–thorns and briers; it is worthless and in danger of being completely given up when its good-for-nothing fruit is burned. In one case, we see the good soil into which good seed has fallen; in the other, barren soil in which the good seed could not bear fruit.

5:9 being made perfect. Christ was always perfect, but He proved it to us through His obedience, even though it included terrible suffering. See Hebrews 2:10.
5:10 Called of God an high priest. Not called *to be* a High Priest, but *addressed* as a High Priest. As our High Priest, Jesus Christ is our Intercessor to God.
5:11 Of whom. That is, of Christ, not of Melchizedek.
5:11 hard to be uttered. Hard to explain.
5:12 for the time. That is, in consideration of the length of time since they had received the truth; the ones who received this epistle should've already been more spiritually mature.
5:12 milk. As for spiritual babies. See 1 Corinthians 3:1-3.
5:12 not of strong meat. They were unable to receive the solid food of the Word.
5:13 that useth milk. That is, one who habitually feeds or lives on milk only.
5:13 unskilful in. Without experience of, unable to understand.
6:1 principles of the doctrine of Christ. Elementary teachings about Christ.
6:1 let us go on. Compare this and the following verse with the principles brought together in Acts 2:38; 3:19-21; and 26:20. Notice also the principles by which the godly Jews were guided, contrasted with the truths of Christianity.
6:4 For it is impossible. Verses 4-8 speak of professed believers who almost come to the place of faith in Christ, and who even recognize the work of the Holy Spirit, but they do not have faith. Like the spies at Kadesh-barnea (Deut. 1:19-26), though they saw the Promised Land and partook of its fruit, they turned back in unbelief.
6:4 once enlightened. The general effect of Christian truth upon the mind. "Once" implies a distinct historical fact.
6:4 were made partakers of. Shared in.

bringeth forth herbs meet for them by
whom it is dressed, receiveth blessing
from God:
8 But that which beareth thorns and
briers *is* rejected, and *is* nigh unto cursing; whose end *is* to be burned.
9 But, beloved, we are persuaded
better things of you, and things that
accompany salvation, though we thus
speak.
10 For God *is* not unrighteous to forget your work and labour of love, which
ye have shewed toward his name, in that
ye have ministered to the *saints, and
do minister.
11 And we desire that every one of
you do shew the same diligence to the
full *assurance of hope unto the end:
12 That ye be not slothful, but followers of them who through faith and patience inherit the promises.
13 For when God made promise to
Abraham, because he could swear by no
greater, he sware by himself,
14 Saying, Surely blessing I will bless
thee, and multiplying I will multiply
thee.
15 And so, after he had patiently endured, he obtained the promise.
16 For men verily swear by the greater: and an oath for confirmation *is* to
them an end of all strife.
17 Wherein God, willing more abundantly to shew unto the heirs of promise the immutability of his counsel,
confirmed *it* by an oath:
18 That by two immutable things, in
which *it was* impossible for God to lie,
we might have a strong consolation,
who have fled for refuge to lay hold
upon the hope set before us:
19 Which *hope* we have as an anchor of
the soul, both sure and stedfast, and
which entereth into that within the
veil;
20 Whither the forerunner is for us
entered, *even* Jesus, made an high priest
for ever after the order of Melchisedec.

6:17 God's Oath

"Confirmed" here means *intervened* or *interposed* Himself. When men appeal to God, the greater One, they bring Him in as surety or promise between themselves and those to whom they make a promise or affirmation. Since, however, God was unable to appeal to anyone greater than Himself, God brought in Himself as surety. He mediated or came in between men and Himself, through the oath by Himself.

Melchisedec, a type of Christ

7 For this Melchisedec, king of Salem, priest of the most high *God,
who met Abraham returning from the
slaughter of the kings, and blessed him;
2 To whom also Abraham gave a tenth
part of all; first being by interpretation
King of *righteousness, and after that
also King of Salem, which is, King of
*peace;
3 Without father, without mother,
without descent, having neither beginning of days, nor end of life; but

6:9 better things of you, and things that accompany salvation. Those to whom this epistle is written are considered true believers in Christ.
6:10 your work and labour of love. Compare this with Matthew 25:40.
6:13 For when God made promise . . . he sware. The promise and the oath were given at the same time: God, when He promised . . . sware (see Gen. 22:16).
6:14 blessing. The patriarchal form of blessing, as in Genesis 22:16-17.
6:17 heirs of promise. As told in Hebrews 11:9 and Romans 8:17.
6:18 two immutable things. The two unchangeable things are God's nature and God's oath. Since God is Truth, He cannot lie.
6:18 consolation. Encouragement.
6:19 within the veil. Compare with Leviticus 16:15.
6:20 Whither. Where, which is within the veil, as in Hebrews 4:14.
7:3 Without. That is, without record of.
7:3 descent. Genealogy or register of descent.

made like unto the Son of God; abideth
a priest continually.

Melchisedec's priesthood greater than Aaron's

4 Now consider how great this man
was, unto whom even the patriarch
Abraham gave the tenth of the spoils.
5 And verily they that are of the sons
of Levi, who receive the office of the
priesthood, have a commandment to
take *tithes of the people according to
the *law, that is, of their brethren,
though they come out of the loins of
Abraham:
6 But he whose descent is not counted from them received tithes of Abraham, and blessed him that had the
promises.
7 And without all contradiction the
less is blessed of the better.
8 And here men that die receive
tithes; but there he *receiveth them,* of
whom it is witnessed that he liveth.
9 And as I may so say, Levi also,
who receiveth tithes, payed tithes in
Abraham.
10 For he was yet in the loins of his
father, when Melchisedec met him.
11 If therefore perfection were by the
Levitical priesthood, (for under it the
people received the law,) what further
need *was there* that another priest
should rise after the order of Melchisedec, and not be called after the
order of Aaron?
12 For the priesthood being changed,
there is made of necessity a change also
of the law.
13 For he of whom these things are
spoken pertaineth to another tribe, of
which no man gave attendance at the
*altar.
14 For *it is* evident that our Lord
sprang out of Juda; of which tribe Moses spake nothing concerning priesthood.
15 And it is yet far more evident: for
that after the similitude of Melchisedec
there ariseth another priest,
16 Who is made, not after the law of a
*carnal commandment, but after the
power of an endless life.
17 For he testifieth, Thou *art* a priest
for ever after the order of Melchisedec.
18 For there is verily a disannulling of
the commandment going before for the
weakness and unprofitableness thereof.
19 For the law made nothing perfect,
but the bringing in of a better hope *did;*
by the which we draw nigh unto God.
20 And inasmuch as not without an
oath *he was made priest:*
21 (For those priests were made without an oath; but this with an oath by him
that said unto him, The Lord sware and
will not *repent, Thou *art* a priest for
ever after the order of Melchisedec:)

7:3 made like unto the Son of God. In this particular, that Melchizedek and Christ had neither beginning of days nor end of life.
7:3 abideth a priest continually. The priesthood was continuous because the priest was one who had neither beginning of days nor end of life.
7:5 sons of Levi. See Numbers 18:21,26.
7:6 received tithes. Told in Genesis 14:20.
7:8 here. Of the Aaronic priesthood.
7:8 there. Of the Melchizedek priesthood.
7:8 of whom. See Hebrews 5:6; Revelation 1:18.
7:13 pertaineth to another tribe. Christ was of the tribe of Judah (see vs. 14), not the tribe of Levi, from which the earthly priests came.
7:13 gave attendance. Had been attached to the service of.
7:14 evident. As set forth in Genesis 49:8,10.
7:16 Who is made. Who has become priest.
7:18 disannulling. Annulling or setting aside.
7:19 For the law. Literally, "For the law perfected nothing, but it was the bringer in of a better hope."
7:21 The Lord sware. See Psalm 110:4.

22 By so much was Jesus made a surety of a better *testament.

23 And they truly were many priests, because they were not suffered to continue by reason of death:

24 But this *man,* because he continueth ever, hath an unchangeable priesthood.

25 Wherefore he is able also to save them to the uttermost that come unto God by him, seeing he ever liveth to make intercession for them.

26 For such an high priest became us, *who is* holy, harmless, undefiled, separate from sinners, and made higher than the heavens;

27 Who needeth not daily, as those high priests, to offer up *sacrifice, first for his own sins, and then for the people's: for this he did once, when he offered up himself.

28 For the law maketh men high priests which have infirmity; but the word of the oath, which was since the law, *maketh* the Son, who is consecrated for evermore.

8 Now of the things which we have spoken *this is* the sum: We have such an high priest, who is set on the right hand of the throne of the Majesty in the heavens;

2 A minister of the sanctuary, and of the true tabernacle, which the Lord pitched, and not man.

3 For every high priest is ordained to offer gifts and sacrifices: wherefore *it is* of necessity that this man have somewhat also to offer.

4 For if he were on earth, he should not be a priest, seeing that there are priests that offer gifts according to the law:

5 Who serve unto the example and shadow of heavenly things, as Moses was admonished of God when he was about to make the tabernacle: for, See, saith he, *that* thou make all things according to the pattern shewed to thee in the mount.

Christ negotiates a better covenant

6 But now hath he obtained a more excellent ministry, by how much also he is the *mediator of a better *covenant, which was established upon better promises.

The new covenant better than the old

7 For if that first *covenant* had been faultless, then should no place have been sought for the second.

8 For finding fault with them, he saith, Behold, the days come, saith the Lord, when I will make a new covenant with the house of *Israel and with the house of *Judah:

9 Not according to the covenant that I made with their fathers in the day when I took them by the hand to lead them out of the land of Egypt; because they continued not in my covenant, and I regarded them not, saith the Lord.

10 For this *is* the covenant that I will make with the house of Israel after those days, saith the Lord; I will put my *laws into their mind, and write them in their hearts: and I will be to them a God, and they shall be to me a people:

11 And they shall not teach every man his neighbour, and every man his

---

7:22 surety of a better testament. Guarantee of a better covenant.
7:25 to the uttermost. Completely. Not simply salvation from every kind of sin, but even greater than that—salvation forevermore, throughout eternity.
7:28 consecrated. Perfected.
8:1 the sum. The main point.
8:2 sanctuary. Holy things.
8:2 true tabernacle. The body of Christ. See Hebrews 10:21; 1 Timothy 3:15.
8:5 example. Representation or pattern.
8:5 See, saith he. God said to Moses. Read Exodus 25:40.
8:7 that first covenant. Described in Exodus 3:8; 19:5.
8:10 I will be to them a God. As promised in Jeremiah 31:33-34.

brother, saying, Know the Lord: for all
shall know me, from the least to the
greatest.
12 For I will be merciful to their unrighteousness, and their sins and their
iniquities will I remember no more.
13 In that he saith, A new *covenant,* he
hath made the first old. Now that which
decayeth and waxeth old *is* ready to
vanish away.

9 Then verily the first *covenant* had
also ordinances of divine service,
and a worldly sanctuary.
2 For there was a tabernacle made;
the first, wherein *was* the *candlestick,
and the table, and the *shewbread;
which is called the sanctuary.
3 And after the second veil, the tabernacle which is called the Holiest of all;
4 Which had the golden *censer, and
the *ark of the covenant overlaid round
about with gold, wherein *was* the golden
pot that had *manna, and Aaron's rod
that budded, and the tables of the covenant;
5 And over it the cherubims of glory
shadowing the mercyseat; of which we
cannot now speak particularly.
6 Now when these things were thus
ordained, the priests went always into
the first tabernacle, accomplishing the
service *of God.*
7 But into the second *went* the high
priest alone once every year, not without *blood, which he offered for himself, and *for* the errors of the people:
8 The Holy Ghost this signifying, that
the way into the holiest of all was not
yet made manifest, while as the first
tabernacle was yet standing:

8:8 THE NEW COVENANT

A new covenant was promised in Jeremiah 31:31-34; Isaiah 61:8. The old covenant was a shadow (Heb. 8:5) of the new covenant–that is, it was a shadow, just as a photograph of a house only shows what the house is like. The new covenant is like taking possession of the house with all the joy of the home. The Hebrew believers had been satisfied with the Law, which was just the shadow of heavenly things. The new or "better" covenant (vs. 6) is found in verse 10, and the new and better promises are found in verses 10-12.

The new covenant is better than the *covenant with Moses in its effective power (Heb. 7:19 and its note; Rom. 8:3-4). It was established on unconditional promises (compare Exod. 19:5 with Heb. 8:10,12). Under the new covenant, obedience was not through fear but because of a willing heart and mind (compare Heb. 2:2; 12:25-27 with 8:10). Every believer may know the Lord personally, for His Law is written on the heart of the Christian (8:11). The believer's sins are forgotten forever by the Lord (compare 10:3 with 8:12; 10:17). The new covenant rests upon the finished work of the Lord Jesus Christ (Matt. 26:27-28; 1 Cor. 11:25; Heb. 9:11-12,18-23; see also Heb. 9:11 note, "Christ as High Priest."). Under the new covenant, Israel is established forever, and their future conversion and blessings are promised (Jer. 31:31-40; 2 Sam. 7:8-17; see also 2 Sam. 7:11 note, "The Davidic Covenant").

8:13 decayeth and waxeth old is ready to vanish away. Obsolete and growing old. As far back as the days of Jeremiah, the first covenant was made old by the mention of a new one; that which is old is ready to vanish away. The writer does not say here that the Law is annulled or to be put aside; he says that it is expiring of old age.

9:1 worldly sanctuary. Belonging to this world, earthly.

9:3 after. Behind.

9:3 Holiest of all. *Holy of Holies.

9:4 golden pot. Its use is explained in Exodus 16:33.

9:4 Aaron's rod. See Numbers 17:10.

9:4 tables of the covenant. Stone tablets with the Ten Commandments on them (Exod. 34:29; Deut.10:2,5).

9:5 cherubims of glory. The glory is that of God, who dwelled and appeared on the *cherubims, which are representations of cherubs around the *mercy seat.

9:5 particularly. In detail.

9:7 errors. Sins of ignorance.

9Which *was* a figure for the time then
present, in which were offered both
gifts and sacrifices, that could not make
him that did the service perfect, as pertaining to the conscience;
10*Which stood* only in meats and
drinks, and divers washings, and carnal
ordinances, imposed *on them* until the
time of reformation.

The sanctuary and sacrifice of the New Covenant are realities

11But *Christ being come an high
priest of good things to come, by a
greater and more perfect tabernacle,
not made with hands, that is to say, not
of this building;
12Neither by the blood of goats and
calves, but by his own blood he entered
in once into the holy place, having obtained eternal *redemption *for us.*
13For if the blood of bulls and of goats,
and the ashes of an heifer sprinkling the
*unclean, sanctifieth to the purifying of
the flesh:
14How much more shall the blood of
Christ, who through the eternal Spirit
offered himself without spot to God,
purge your conscience from dead works
to serve the living God?
15And for this cause he is the mediator of the new testament, that by means
of *death, for the redemption of the
transgressions *that were* under the first
testament, they which are called might
receive the promise of eternal inheritance.

9:11 CHRIST AS HIGH PRIEST

According to Old Testament ideas, which the epistle follows, the slaying of the victim and the entering of the high priest into the Holy of Holies with the blood constituted one act of sacrifice. The sacrifice was not just an offering–it was the realization, through the offering, of the continued covenant relationship of the Lord and His people. This was shown in the entering of the high priest, the representative of the people, with blood into the Holy of Holies, the very presence of God. Yet the priest did not enter because of an offering already made, as if the mere slaying of the victim were the offering. It was the blood that atoned. The sacrifice was not yet made until the life, the blood, was *offered* (Heb. 9:7) before the Lord and received by Him. The high priest and the blood went in together. This was a double act, or two acts in one. Carrying in the blood, he made atonement; and he could go in because of the atonement that he made, for he was the representative of the people before the Lord.

The book of Hebrews transfers all this to the ministry of the Son. He entered through His blood into the true Holy of Holies, God's dwelling place, and obtained "eternal redemption" (9:12), and in virtue of the redemption obtained, He appeared before the face and in the presence of God for us (9:24). As He sat down at the right hand of God and came no more out from His presence, He realized in Himself, as the representative of the people, an eternal fellowship of service on the one hand (9:14) and help on the other (4:16; 13:21) between the people and God.

9:9 in which. In the Holy Place.
9:10 reformation. The new order brought by Christ.
9:11 building. Creation, that is, the true tabernacle is created by God.
9:12 Neither by the blood. The high priest entered through the blood of goats and calves—Christ through His own blood (1 Pet. 1:18-19). The high priest went in once a year—Christ did it once for all time.
9:14 How much more . . . ? The crux of the argument. Christ, as High Priest, is Himself the offering, dealing adequately with sin by actually bringing man into redeemed and life-giving relationship with our loving Father.
9:14 serve. Worship.
9:15 And for this cause. The Son, because His blood purifies the conscience, is the *Mediator of a new covenant.

The New Covenant is sealed by Christ's Blood

16For where a testament *is,* there
must also of necessity be the death of
the testator.
17For a testament *is* of force after
men are dead: otherwise it is of no
strength at all while the testator liveth.
18Whereupon neither the first *testament* was dedicated without blood.
19For when *Moses had spoken
every precept to all the people according to the law, he took the blood of
calves and of goats, with water, and
scarlet wool, and *hyssop, and sprinkled both the book, and all the people,
20Saying, This *is* the blood of the testament which God hath enjoined unto
you.
21Moreover he sprinkled with blood
both the tabernacle, and all the vessels
of the ministry.
22And almost all things are by the law
purged with blood; and without shedding of blood is no *remission.
23*It was* therefore necessary that the
patterns of things in the heavens should
be purified with these; but the heavenly things themselves with better sacrifices than these.
24For Christ is not entered into the
holy places made with hands, *which are*
the figures of the true; but into *heav-
en itself, now to appear in the presence
of God for us:

The one sacrifice of the New Covenant is better than the many of the Old

25Nor yet that he should offer himself
often, as the high priest entereth into
the holy place every year with blood of
others;
26For then must he often have suffered since the foundation of the *world:
but now once in the end of the world

9:27 PHYSICAL AND SPIRITUAL DEATH

Death was foretold as a consequence of sin in Genesis 3:19, and the theme runs throughout the Bible. In this verse, "to die" refers to physical death.

The word is used in several senses in the Bible:

1. It speaks of the actual physical act of dying (Gen. 5:5 and its note, "Death Comes to All Men");
2. It speaks of the period after one has died (Gen. 27:7);
3. It speaks of poison or that which could cause one to die (2 Kings 4:40);
4. It speaks of those who are in danger of dying (Judg. 15:18; 2 Cor. 11:23); and
5. It is addressed as if it were a person (1 Cor. 15:55).

Spiritual death is the loss of spiritual life (Rom. 8:6). The final state of those who are not born again is called the "second death" (Rev. 20:14).

Physical death that is the result of sin does not affect only the body, because a person who has died is still conscious, whether he is in hell or in heaven (Luke 16:19-31). All physical death will end in the resurrection of the body (1 Cor. 15:52; see also its note, "A Final Resurrection"), but not all bodies will die or have died (Gen. 5:24; 1 Cor. 1:51-52; 1 Thess. 4:15-17). Death for the believer is called "sleep," because his body may be awakened at any minute when Jesus Christ comes for His own (1 Thess. 4:15-18), and until that time the believer's spirit is with the Lord (Luke 23:43; Phil. 1:21,23).

9:16 testator. He who made the will or testament.
9:18 dedicated. Inaugurated.
9:20 This is the blood. Compare this verse with Matthew 26:28.
9:21 he sprinkled. See Exodus 29:12,36.
9:22 remission. Forgiveness.
9:23 patterns. Symbols.
9:24 the figures. Copies.
9:25 of others. Not his own.
9:26 end of the world. Completion of the ages at Christ's return.

hath he appeared to put away *sin by the
sacrifice of himself.
27And as it is appointed unto men
once to die, but after this the judgment:
28So Christ was once offered to bear
the sins of many; and unto them that
look for him shall he appear the second
time without sin unto *salvation.
10 For the law having a shadow of
good things to come, *and* not
the very image of the things, can never
with those sacrifices which they offered
year by year continually make the comers thereunto perfect.
2For then would they not have ceased
to be offered? because that the worshippers once purged should have had no
more conscience of sins.
3But in those *sacrifices there is* a remembrance again *made* of sins every
year.
4For *it is* not possible that the blood
of bulls and of goats should take away
sins.
5Wherefore when he cometh into the
world, he saith, Sacrifice and *offering
thou wouldest not, but a body hast thou
prepared me:
6In burnt-offerings and *sacrifices* for
sin thou hast had no pleasure.
7Then said I, Lo, I come (in the volume of the book it is written of me,) to
do thy will, O God.
8Above when he said, Sacrifice and
offering and burnt-offerings and *offering*
for sin thou wouldest not, neither hadst
pleasure *therein;* which are offered by
the law;
9Then said he, Lo, I come to do thy
will, O God. He taketh away the first,
that he may establish the second.
10By the which will we are sanctified
through the offering of the body of Jesus
Christ once *for all.*
11And every priest standeth daily
ministering and offering oftentimes the
same sacrifices, which can never take
away sins:
12But this man, after he had offered
one sacrifice for sins for ever, sat down
on the right hand of God;
13From henceforth expecting till his
enemies be made his footstool.
14For by one offering he hath perfected for ever them that are sanctified.
15*Whereof* the Holy Ghost also is a

10:3 THE NEED TO REMEMBER

"Remembrance" means *recognition, calling to mind, acknowledgment.* Each of the yearly sacrifices under the Law was like a promissory note that is renewed every year when the person in debt is unable to pay. The note has no real value in itself; nor did the sacrifice have any moral value in the sight of God. But in that note there is an acknowledgment of the debt from year to year. If someone who is able to pay should endorse the note, then when it was due to be paid it would be referred to the one who endorsed it for settlement, and he would pay the money. The application is clear. It was not possible that the blood of bulls and goats should take away sins, but each time a believing Israelite brought his sacrifice to the altar, he was "giving his note" to God. He acknowledged his responsibility for the same. This was all he could do; he could not pay. But the preincarnate Christ endorsed every one of the notes and in the fullness of time came prepared to settle in full for all.

9:27 judgment. The *Day of Judgment.
9:28 without sin. Apart from sin.
10:1 comers. Those who draw near, that is, worshippers of God.
10:5 world. To mankind.
10:5 Sacrifice and offering. Compare verses 5-7 with Psalm 40:6-8.
10:9 the first . . . the second. The Law and God's will, the new covenant under Christ's blood, so that the blood of animals did not need to be sacrificed anymore.
10:10 we. Those mentioned in verse 14, "them that are sanctified."
10:12 on the right hand of God. See Psalm 110:1.
10:14 them that are sanctified. The "we" of verse 10.

witness to us: for after that he had said
before,
[16]This *is* the covenant that I will
make with them after those days, saith
the Lord, I will put my laws into their
hearts, and in their minds will I write
them;
[17]And their sins and iniquities will I
remember no more.
[18]Now where remission of these *is,*
there is no more offering for sin.

The believer worships in the holiest

¶[19]Having therefore, brethren, boldness to enter into the holiest by the
blood of Jesus,
[20]By a new and living way, which he
hath consecrated for us, through the
veil, that is to say, his flesh;
[21]And *having* an high priest over the
house of God;
[22]Let us draw near with a true heart
in full *assurance of *faith, having our
hearts sprinkled from an evil conscience, and our bodies washed with
pure water.
[23]Let us hold fast the *profession of
our faith without wavering; (for he *is*
faithful that promised;)
[24]And let us consider one another to
provoke unto love and to good works:
[25]Not forsaking the assembling of
ourselves together, as the manner of
some *is;* but exhorting *one another:* and
so much the more, as ye see the day
approaching.
[26]For if we sin wilfully after that we
have received the knowledge of the
truth, there remaineth no more sacrifice for sins,
[27]But a certain fearful looking for of
judgment and fiery indignation, which
shall devour the adversaries.
[28]He that despised Moses' law died
without *mercy under two or three
witnesses:
[29]Of how much sorer punishment,
suppose ye, shall he be thought worthy,
who hath trodden under foot the Son of
God, and hath counted the blood of the
covenant, wherewith he was sanctified,

10:22 Assurance of Faith
Assurance speaks of the Christians' joyous faith because of our fearless trust in God and His sure Word. Jesus Christ used the word "amen" or "verily" to express the certainty of His words and their trustworthiness. Our confidence is not based on "works of righteousness which we have done" (Titus 3:4-5), but on Christ's sacrifice and High Priesthood (Heb. 10:21-22). Assurance is our understanding that our souls are freed through Christ's finished work–freed from the power of evil and from the judgment upon evil. It is not self-confidence; it is confidence in Christ. See Colossians 2:1-10.

10:16 This is the covenant. Compare verses 16-17 with Jeremiah 31:33-34.
10:19 boldness. This word means *all speech,* that is, freedom of speech, speaking everything with no concealment and in perfect liberty. But the confession is twofold: owning our sins and also confessing Christ's glories.
10:20 living way. Told in John 14:6; Hebrews 7:24.
10:20 consecrated. In this verse, "consecrated" means *opened.* Christ opened the way for us to come "through the veil" of "his flesh"–His blood– into the presence of God our Father.
10:25 the assembling of ourselves together. The meeting of Christians with one another for worship, preaching, study of the Word, and mutual encouragement and edification.
10:25 as the manner of some is. Some believers neglected to assemble for fear of persecution, but see Matthew 10:32.
10:25 exhorting. Encouraging.
10:25 as ye see the day approaching. The *Day of the Lord. See Matthew 24.
10:26 wilfully. See the result of this in 2 Peter 2:20-21 (see also 2 Pet. 2:20 note, "Of Wicked Men").
10:29 an unholy thing. A common or unclean thing.

an unholy thing, and hath done despite
unto the Spirit of *grace?
30For we know him that hath said,
Vengeance *belongeth* unto me, I will recompense, saith the Lord. And again,
The Lord shall judge his people.
31*It is* a fearful thing to fall into the
hands of the living God.
32But call to remembrance the former days, in which, after ye were illuminated, ye endured a great fight of
afflictions;
33Partly, whilst ye were made a
gazingstock both by reproaches and afflictions; and partly, whilst ye became
companions of them that were so used.
34For ye had compassion of me in my
bonds, and took joyfully the spoiling of
your goods, knowing in yourselves that
ye have in heaven a better and an enduring substance.
35Cast not away therefore your confidence, which hath great recompence
of reward.
36For ye have need of patience, that,
after ye have done the will of God, ye
might receive the promise.
37For yet a little while, and he that
shall come will come, and will not tarry.
38Now the *just shall live by faith: but
if *any man* draw back, my soul shall
have no pleasure in him.
39But we are not of them who draw
back unto perdition; but of them that
believe to the saving of the soul.

IV. Heroes of Faith (11:1-40)

The sphere of faith

11 Now faith is the substance of
things hoped for, the evidence
of things not seen.

11:1 Faith
Faith is simply taking God at His word. This description of faith leads the writer of the epistle to unfold the long and famous "honor roll" of Old Testament persons who lived, endured, and died in faith, and had from God the testimony that they were pleasing to Him. It is important to remember that God has never had two ways of saving men. Faith has always been the way to salvation–faith in God in the Old Testament (old covenant) and faith in the blood of Christ in the New Testament (new covenant).

2For by it the *elders obtained a good
report.
3Through faith we understand that
the worlds were framed by the word of
God, so that things which are seen were
not made of things which do appear.

11:3 Faith Brings Understanding
Scholars and scientists throughout the centuries have theorized and speculated as to the origin of the universe–how did it come into being in the first place? To those who have faith in God, there is no mystery. They believe the Word of God and that He created all things. The most uneducated Christian is troubled less about the mysteries of life and matter than the greatest non-Christian scientist, for the Christian knows by faith that God's Word is true, and that is enough for him.

Abel

4By faith *Abel offered unto God a
more excellent sacrifice than Cain, by
which he obtained witness that he was
righteous, God testifying of his gifts:
and by it he being dead yet speaketh.

10:29 the Spirit of grace. That is, in salvation.
10:30 Vengeance belongeth unto me. See Deuteronomy 32:35-36.
10:32 fight of afflictions. A struggle of sufferings.
10:34 knowing in yourselves. Knowing that you have for yourselves.
10:38 the just shall live by faith. It is interesting to read this verse with Habakkuk 2:3-4 (see also a Hab. 2:4 note, "God's Grace").
11:1 substance. Assurance.
11:1 evidence. Conviction of the heart.
11:3 worlds were framed. Universe was created.
11:4 by which. Through Abel's faith.

Enoch

[5]By faith Enoch was translated that
he should not see death; and was not
found, because God had translated him:
for before his translation he had this
testimony, that he pleased God.
[6]But without faith *it is* impossible to
please *him:* for he that cometh to God
must believe that he is, and *that* he is a
rewarder of them that diligently seek
him.

Noah

[7]By faith Noah, being warned of God
of things not seen as yet, moved with
fear, prepared an ark to the saving of his
house; by the which he condemned the
world, and became heir of the righteousness which is by faith.

Abraham

[8]By faith *Abraham, when he was
called to go out into a place which he
should after receive for an inheritance,
obeyed; and he went out, not knowing
whither he went.
[9]By faith he sojourned in the land of
promise, as *in* a strange country, dwelling in tabernacles with *Isaac and *Jacob, the heirs with him of the same
promise:
[10]For he looked for a city which hath
foundations, whose builder and maker
is God.

Sara

[11]Through faith also Sara herself received strength to conceive seed, and
was delivered of a child when she was
past age, because she judged him faithful who had promised.
[12]Therefore sprang there even of
one, and him as good as dead, *so many*
as the stars of the sky in multitude, and
as the sand which is by the sea shore
innumerable.
[13]These all died in faith, not having
received the promises, but having seen
them afar off, and were persuaded of
them, and embraced *them,* and confessed that they were strangers and
pilgrims on the earth.
[14]For they that say such things declare plainly that they seek a country.
[15]And truly, if they had been mindful

11:5 By faith Enoch was translated. Read Genesis 5:22,24. Enoch's faith and his translation were associated in this way: His victory over death was not a consequence of his faith but God's witness to Enoch's faith.
11:5 translated. Taken up to heaven without death. The only other person in the Old Testament taken by God without dying was Elijah (2 Kings 2:11; see also its note, "A Preview of the Rapture").
11:7 Noah. Read Genesis 6:14,22.
11:7 things not seen as yet. See Genesis 2:6, 7:4. In the account of Noah rain is mentioned for the first time.
11:7 saving. Salvation.
11:7 condemned the world. Every tap of Noah's hammer declared him to be a man of faith, and further, it condemned that generation who did not believe God and whose wickedness brought the judgment of the Flood.
11:7 world. Mankind.
11:9 strange country. A land not his own.
11:9 dwelling in tabernacles. Living in tents. See Genesis 13:3,18.
11:10 looked for. Waited for and looked forward to.
11:10 builder. God is the architect and builder.
11:11 Sara. Read Genesis 21:1-2.
11:12 stars of the sky. Genesis 22:17 gives the promise.
11:13 the promises. Recorded in Genesis 3:15 (see also its note, "The Promise of a Saviour"); 12:7.
11:13 persuaded of them, and embraced them. Acted upon the promises.
11:14 a country. A country of their own, a homeland.

of that *country* from whence they came
out, they might have had opportunity to
have returned.
[16]But now they desire a better *country,* that is, an heavenly: wherefore God
is not ashamed to be called their God:
for he hath prepared for them a city.
[17]By faith Abraham, when he was
tried, offered up Isaac: and he that had
received the promises offered up his
only begotten *son,*
[18]Of whom it was said, That in Isaac
shall thy seed be called:
[19]Accounting that God *was* able to
raise *him* up, even from the dead; from
whence also he received him in a figure.

Isaac

[20]By faith Isaac blessed Jacob and
*Esau concerning things to come.

Jacob

[21]By faith Jacob, when he was a dying, blessed both the sons of *Joseph;
and worshipped, *leaning* upon the top
of his staff.

Joseph

[22]By faith Joseph, when he died,
made mention of the departing of the
children of Israel; and gave commandment concerning his bones.

The parents of Moses

[23]By faith Moses, when he was born,
was hid three months of his parents,
because they saw *he was* a proper child;
and they were not afraid of the king's
commandment.

Moses

[24]By faith Moses, when he was come
to years, refused to be called the son of
*Pharaoh's daughter;
[25]Choosing rather to suffer affliction
with the people of God, than to enjoy
the pleasures of sin for a season;
[26]Esteeming the reproach of Christ
greater riches than the treasures in
*Egypt: for he had respect unto the
recompence of the reward.
[27]By faith he forsook Egypt, not fearing the wrath of the king: for he endured, as seeing him who is invisible.
[28]Through faith he kept the *passover, and the sprinkling of blood, lest he
that destroyed the firstborn should
touch them.
[29]By faith they passed through the
Red sea as by dry *land:* which the Egyptians assaying to do were drowned.

Joshua

[30]By faith the walls of Jericho fell
down, after they were compassed about
seven days.

11:15 that country. See Genesis 11:31.
11:17 tried. Tested. See Genesis 22:1 (see also its note, "Testing Versus Tempting"); James 2:21 (see also James 2:21-25 note, "Demonstrations of Faith").
11:18 Of whom. To whom, that is, this was said to Abraham in Genesis 21:12.
11:19 even from the dead. A picture of resurrection. See Genesis 22 and Matthew 20:19.
11:19 in a figure. Figuratively speaking, a *parable.
11:20 Isaac. See Genesis 27:27.
11:21 leaning upon the top of his staff. Here is a little more of the story than was told in Genesis 47:31.
11:23 hid three months of his parents. Compare Exodus 2:2, where the mother is spoken of as hiding the child; here both his parents are mentioned. The hiding of the child was an act of faith.
11:23 proper. Beautiful.
11:26 the reproach of Christ. The same reproach as Christ bore: the hatred and persecution of the world. Moses, once a prince of Egypt, gladly endured worldly disgrace for his faith in God.
11:29 through the Red sea. See Exodus 14:22; Jude 5.
11:30 the walls of Jericho. Here the faith of the whole people is again shown. See Joshua 6:12,20.

11:1 GREAT HEROES OF THE FAITH

Name	Description	Act of Faith	Reference
Abel	The second son of Adam and Eve. He was murdered by his brother, Cain.	Offered the best lamb as a sacrifice to God.	Genesis 4:1-16
Enoch	A God-fearing man who did not die but was taken to heaven.	He walked with God.	Genesis 5:21-26
Noah	A righteous, God-fearing man who obeyed God's order to build an ark thus saving himself, his family and the living creatures on earth from a devastating flood.	He believed God and obeyed Him without questioning.	Genesis 6:1–9:17
Abraham	A man chosen by God to become the father of the great nation Israel. God promised Abraham that he would have descendants as numerous as the stars in the heavens.	Abraham trusted God, leaving the security of homeland to follow God's command.	Genesis 12:1-9; 17:1-8.
Sara	The wife of Abraham who conceived and gave birth to Isaac in her old age.	Sara believed God would be faithful to His promise to make Abraham into a great nation.	Genesis 18:1-15; 21:1-8
Isaac	The son of Abraham and Sara, born when they were both very old. His birth was foretold by an angel of the Lord and fulfilled the promise God had made to his father. He married Rebekah, was the father of Jacob and Esau, and inherited the covenant promise.	He blessed his sons.	Genesis 27:1-40
Jacob	The younger son of Isaac and Rebekah and twin brother of Esau. His name was later changed to Israel. God's covenant was repeated to him. The twelve tribes of Israel were named after his sons.	Blessed his sons and Ephraim and Manasseh, his grandsons.	Genesis 48:1-22
Joseph	Favorite son of Jacob who was hated by his brothers and sold into slavery in Egypt. God rewarded Joseph for his obedience by making him a great ruler in Egypt, thus enabling him to save his family from starvation during a great famine.	Believed that God would someday deliver His people from Egypt and return them to their land.	Genesis 37–50
Jochebed and her husband	The parents of Moses.	They hid their son to save him from being killed.	Exodus 2:1-3
Moses	The great leader of the Israelites who led them out of slavery in Egypt to the Promised Land.	He refused to be identified with the royalty of Egypt. Left the comforts of Egypt to lead God's people. Observed the Passover and led the people through the Red sea.	Exodus 1–15; 19–34
Rahab	A prostitute from Jericho who helped the Israelite spies. She and her family were spared when Jericho was destroyed.	She helped the spies of Israel.	Joshua 2:1,3; 6:21-25
Gedeon, Barak, Samson, Jephthae	Judges of the Israelites who delivered the people from the oppression of their enemies.	They performed heroic tasks and found their strength came from God.	Judges 4–16
David	The youngest son of Jesse. He was a man after God's own heart who was a brave warrior and the greatest king of Israel.	He killed the giant Goliath and followed the Lord.	1 Samuel 16:1; 17; 1 Kings 2:11
Samuel	Son of Elkanah and Hannah who grew up in the service of the Lord at Shiloh. As a great leader and judge of Israel he anointed Saul as the first king of Israel.	He led the people of Israel in the ways of the Lord.	1 Samuel 1:1–25:1

Rahab

[31]By faith the harlot *Rahab perished
not with them that believed not, when
she had received the spies with peace.

Others

[32]And what shall I more say? for the
time would fail me to tell of Gedeon,
and *of* Barak, and *of* Samson, and *of*
Jephthae; *of* *David also, and *Samuel,
and *of* the *prophets:
[33]Who through faith subdued kingdoms, wrought righteousness, obtained
promises, stopped the mouths of lions,
[34]Quenched the violence of fire, escaped the edge of the sword, out of
weakness were made strong, waxed
valiant in fight, turned to flight the armies of the aliens.
[35]Women received their dead raised
to life again: and others were tortured,
not accepting deliverance; that they
might obtain a better resurrection:
[36]And others had trial of *cruel* mockings and scourgings, yea, moreover of
bonds and imprisonment:
[37]They were stoned, they were sawn
asunder, were tempted, were slain with
the sword: they wandered about in
sheepskins and goatskins; being destitute, afflicted, tormented;
[38](Of whom the world was not worthy:) they wandered in deserts, and *in*
mountains, and *in* dens and caves of the
earth.
[39]And these all, having obtained a
good report through faith, received not
the promise:
[40]God having provided some better
thing for us, that they without us should
not be made perfect.

V. Life of Believers under the New Covenant (12:1—13:25)

12 Wherefore seeing we also are
compassed about with so great
a cloud of witnesses, let us lay aside
every weight, and the sin which doth so

11:31 Rahab. See Joshua 6:23; James 2:25 (see also James 2:21-25 note, "Demonstrations of Faith").
11:32 Gedeon. Gideon. See Judges 6:11.
11:32 Barak. See Judges 4:6.
11:32 Samson. See Judges 15:16.
11:32 Jephthae. Jephthah. See Judges 11:32.
11:32 Samuel. See 1 Samuel 7:9.
11:35 raised to life again. See 1 Kings 17:22; 2 Kings 4:35.
11:35 not accepting deliverance. This is explained in verses 24-25.
11:37 stoned. This is true of Zechariah (2 Chron. 24:20-22; Matt. 23:35). Stoning was a common mode of capital punishment among the Jews (see Deut. 13:10; Josh. 7:25, see also its note, "A Form of Punishment"; Matt. 21:35; Acts 7, especially vss. 54-60).
11:37 were sawn asunder. Sawed in two. Both Jewish and Christian tradition says that Isaiah was martyred in this way. See 2 Samuel 12:31; 1 Chronicles 20:1-3.
11:37 tempted. Tested under trial, perhaps tortured.
11:37 slain with the sword. Read about Urijah the prophet (Jer. 26:23).
11:38 caves. The land of Palestine, from its limestone formation, was full of caves (1 Kings 18:4,13; 19:9).
12:1 Wherefore. This word connects what is to come with the previous chapter, especially with its closing words.
12:1 compassed about. Surrounded.
12:1 cloud of witnesses. The heroes of the faith enumerated in chapter 11 and all those who have gone on before whose faith was in God's Word.
12:1 lay aside every weight. First Peter 5:7 tells us how to do this. Weight is not always sin in itself. It is whatever adds to the difficulty of our spiritual progress. The weights are not necessarily external; they are, first of all, in the heart. The moment a thing that is not in God's purpose for a Christian finds a place in the heart and mind, it becomes a weight, no matter what it is. And the result—lack of spiritual growth and peace with God—is soon obvious.

easily beset *us,* and let us run with patience the race that is set before us,
2 Looking unto Jesus the author and
finisher of *our* faith; who for the joy that
was set before him endured the cross,
despising the shame, and is set down at
the right hand of the throne of God.
3 For consider him that endured such
contradiction of sinners against himself,
lest ye be wearied and faint in your
minds.
4 Ye have not yet resisted unto blood,
striving against sin.
5 And ye have forgotten the exhortation which speaketh unto you as unto
children, My son, despise not thou the
chastening of the Lord, nor faint when
thou art rebuked of him:
6 For whom the Lord loveth he chasteneth, and scourgeth every son whom
he receiveth.
7 If ye endure chastening, God dealeth
with you as with sons; for what son is
he whom the father *chasteneth not?
8 But if ye be without chastisement,
whereof all are *partakers, then are ye
bastards, and not sons.
9 Furthermore we have had fathers of
our flesh which corrected *us,* and we
gave *them* reverence: shall we not much
rather be in subjection unto the Father
of spirits, and live?
10 For they verily for a few days
*chastened *us* after their own pleasure;
but he for *our* profit, that *we* might be
partakers of his holiness.
11 Now no chastening for the present
seemeth to be joyous, but grievous:
nevertheless afterward it yieldeth the
peaceable fruit of righteousness unto
them which are exercised thereby.
12 Wherefore lift up the hands which
hang down, and the feeble knees;
13 And make straight paths for your
feet, lest that which is lame be turned
out of the way; but let it rather be
healed.
14 Follow peace with all *men,* and holiness, without which no man shall see
the Lord:
15 Looking diligently lest any man fail
of the *grace of God; lest any root of
bitterness springing up trouble *you,* and
thereby many be defiled;
16 Lest there *be* any fornicator, or profane person, as Esau, who for one morsel of meat sold his *birthright.
17 For ye know how that afterward,
when he would have inherited the
blessing, he was rejected: for he found
no place of *repentance, though he
sought it carefully with tears.

Final contrast of the two covenants

18 For ye are not come unto the mount
that might be touched, and that burned
with fire, nor unto blackness, and darkness, and tempest,

12:1 easily beset us. Ensnares or traps us, like a close-fitting cloak or garment that clings to the one who wears it and impedes progress and freedom of motion.
12:1 set before us. It is an appointed race. Each step of the course has been marked for us.
12:2 author and finisher. Pioneer and Perfecter.
12:3 consider. Think about the great thing the Lord Jesus Christ has done for us, and the things with which He had to struggle by becoming human—He endured horrific pain on the cross and death to bring us into the kingdom of God.
12:5 children. Sons. Compare this verse and verse 6 with Proverbs 3:11-12 (see also Prov. 3:11-12 note, "The Chastening of the LORD").
12:7 what son is he . . . ? See Proverbs 13:24.
12:10 after their own pleasure. What they thought was best.
12:12 lift up the hands. See Isaiah 35:3. "Feeble" means *failing* or *weak* knees.
12:13 straight. Even.
12:15 fail. Fall short.
12:17 it. The blessing.
12:18 the mount. Mount Sinai could be touched except when it became the place where God met Moses (see Exod. 19, especially vs. 12).

19 And the sound of a trumpet, and the
voice of words; which *voice* they that
heard intreated that the word should
not be spoken to them any more:
20 (For they could not endure that
which was commanded, And if so much
as a beast touch the mountain, it shall
be stoned, or thrust through with a dart:
21 And so terrible was the sight, *that*
Moses said, I exceedingly fear and
quake:)
22 But ye are come unto mount *Sion,
and unto the city of the living God, the
heavenly *Jerusalem, and to an innumerable company of *angels,
23 To the general assembly and
*church of the firstborn, which are writ-
ten in heaven, and to God the Judge of
all, and to the spirits of just men made
*perfect,
24 And to Jesus the *mediator of the
new covenant, and to the blood of sprinkling, that speaketh better things than
that of Abel.
25 See that ye refuse not him that
speaketh. For if they escaped not who
refused him that spake on earth,
much more *shall not* we *escape,* if we
turn away from him that *speaketh* from
heaven:
26 Whose voice then shook the earth:
but now he hath promised, saying, Yet
once more I shake not the earth only,
but also heaven.
27 And this *word,* Yet once more, sig-
nifieth the removing of those things
that are shaken, as of things that are
made, that those things which cannot
be shaken may remain.
28 Wherefore we receiving a *kingdom
which cannot be moved, let us have
grace, whereby we may serve God acceptably with reverence and godly fear:
29 For our God *is* a consuming fire.

13 Let brotherly love continue.
2 Be not forgetful to entertain
strangers: for thereby some have entertained angels unawares.
3 Remember them that are in bonds,
as bound with them; *and* them which
suffer adversity, as being yourselves
also in the body.
4 Marriage *is* honourable in all, and
the bed undefiled: but whoremongers
and adulterers God will judge.
5 *Let your* conversation *be* without
covetousness; *and be* content with such
things as ye have: for he hath said, I will
never leave thee, nor forsake thee.
6 So that we may boldly say, The Lord
is my helper, and I will not fear what
man shall do unto me.
¶7 Remember them which have the
rule over you, who have spoken unto
you the word of God: whose faith follow,
considering the end of *their* conversation.
8 Jesus Christ the same yesterday,
and to day, and for ever.
9 Be not carried about with divers and
strange doctrines. For *it is* a good thing
that the heart be established with
grace; not with meats, which have not
profited them that have been occupied
therein.

Christian separation and worship

10 We have an altar, whereof they have
no right to eat which serve the tabernacle.

12:19 voice. God's voice (Exod. 19:18-19).
12:23 spirits of just men. The Old Testament saints, now already in heaven and made perfect through the offering of the Son.
12:24 the blood of sprinkling. See Exodus 24:8.
12:26 Yet once more. See Haggai 2:6 (see also its note, "The Final Shaking").
12:28 moved. Shaken. Therefore, "have" or "hold fast" grace.
13:3 bonds. In prison. See our Lord's word about this in Matthew 25:36,39-40.
13:5 he. God spoke these words through Moses. See Deuteronomy 31:6.
13:6 The Lord is my helper. Compare with Psalms 56:11; 118:6.
13:8 for ever. To the ages to come, throughout eternity.
13:9 carried about. Do not be carried "away."

11 For the bodies of those beasts,
whose blood is brought into the sanctuary by the high priest for sin, are
burned without the camp.
12 Wherefore Jesus also, that he might
sanctify the people with his own blood,
suffered without the gate.
13 Let us go forth therefore unto him
without the camp, bearing his reproach.
14 For here have we no continuing
city, but we seek one to come.

The Christian's sacrifice and obedience

15 By him therefore let us offer the
sacrifice of praise to God continually,
that is, the fruit of *our* lips giving thanks
to his name.
16 But to do good and to communicate
forget not: for with such sacrifices God
is well pleased.
17 Obey them that have the rule over
you, and submit yourselves: for they
watch for your souls, as they that must
give account, that they may do it with
joy, and not with grief: for that *is* unprofitable for you.

Benediction

¶ 18 Pray for us: for we trust we have
a good conscience, in all things willing
to live honestly.
19 But I beseech *you* the rather to do
this, that I may be restored to you the
sooner.
20 Now the God of peace, that brought
again from the dead our Lord Jesus, that
great shepherd of the sheep, through
the blood of the everlasting covenant,
21 Make you perfect in every good
work to do his will, working in you that
which is wellpleasing in his sight,
through Jesus Christ; to whom *be* glory
for ever and ever. Amen.
22 And I beseech you, brethren, suffer
the word of exhortation: for I have written a letter unto you in few words.
23 Know ye that *our* brother Timothy
is set at liberty; with whom, if he come
shortly, I will see you.
¶ 24 Salute all them that have the rule
over you, and all the saints. They of
Italy salute you.
¶ 25 Grace *be* with you all. Amen.

13:11 without the camp. According to the Law of the offering of the *Day of Atonement, and those offerings whose blood was brought by the high priest into the Holy of Holies, the flesh of such offerings was not partaken of by the priests; it was removed outside the camp and consumed by fire. So the Lord Jesus, the Lamb of God, was sacrificed outside the city.

13:12 with his own blood. By the sacrifice of Himself.

13:13 Let us go forth. To partake in and share the benefits of the true *sin offering, we must abandon the "camp," the abode of unbelieving Israel, where its religious life and ordinances rule; we must go forth to Christ, sharing His reproach and rejection (Acts 5:41).

13:14 continuing. Lasting.

13:16 communicate. Share what you have with others. Compare Romans 12:13; Galatians 6:6.

13:16 sacrifices. See Philippians 4:18.

13:17 have the rule over you. Lead and guide you, spiritual leaders, as pastors.

13:19 the rather. Urge you earnestly.

13:20 God of peace. See Romans 15:33; 16:20.

13:20 through. In the power of or in virtue of.

13:21 Make you perfect. Equip you.

13:21 work. Thing.

13:22 word of exhortation. This letter or epistle.

13:25 Grace be with you all. Amen. The closing benediction found in all of Paul's letters. (See "The Writer and Time" in the introduction to Hebrews.)

The General Epistle of

JAMES

THE WRITER AND TIME

This letter was written by the man named James who was called "James the Just," one of the brothers of our Lord. He presided over the church at Jerusalem (Acts 12:17; 15:13). The letter is believed to be the earliest of all the writings of the New Testament, its date being about A.D. 45. The writer, who was not the Apostle James, was himself martyred in A.D. 63.

THEME

The letter is written particularly to Jewish Christians (James 1:1) to warn them against certain faults which they showed, and to instruct them as to how to grow in the Christian faith so that their Christianity would be matured and, therefore, an honor to Him whom they professed to follow. The faults referred to were those which might be expected in Christians who had been Jews and who were now suffering persecution for their faith. The persecution referred to was probably that under Herod Agrippa I in which the Apostle James was martyred (Acts 12:1-2).

OUTLINE OF JAMES

I.	Trials and Temptations	James 1:1-27
II.	Faults and Failings	James 2:1—5:6
III.	Commands and Prohibitions	James 5:7-18
IV.	Postscript	James 5:19-20

I. Trials and Temptations
(1:1-27)

1. A test of character

1 James, a servant of *God and of
the Lord Jesus *Christ, to the
twelve tribes which are scattered
abroad, greeting.

¶2My brethren, count it all joy when
ye fall into divers temptations;
3Knowing *this,* that the trying of your
*faith worketh patience.
4But let patience have *her* perfect
work, that ye may be perfect and entire,
wanting nothing.

1:1 servant of God and of the Lord Jesus Christ. "Servant" conveys the meaning of *slave* or *bondslave*. Note that the same word is used to denote James' attitude to Jesus as to God, showing his belief in the deity of the Lord Jesus. Notice especially that James, the Lord's half brother of the flesh, is not ashamed to speak thus of the Lord Jesus.

1:1 to the twelve tribes which are scattered abroad. The head of the mother church in Jerusalem is writing to his Jewish fellow believers living among the tribes of Israel scattered throughout the world.

1:2 fall into divers temptations. Be surrounded by various trials. The temptations are not allurements to sin but tests of character. (Some to whom James writes were afflicted and sick; see 5:13-15; see also 5:15 notes, especially "Prayer for the Sick.")

1:3 patience. Not waiting for something to happen but enduring, with the grace of God, what is happening.

1:4 perfect work. Full effect, enduring to the end (Matt. 10:22).

1:4 perfect and entire. Mature and complete with nothing essential lacking.

5 If any of you lack wisdom, let him
ask of God, that giveth to all *men* liberally, and upbraideth not; and it shall be
given him.
6 But let him ask in faith, nothing
wavering. For he that wavereth is like
a wave of the sea driven with the wind
and tossed.
7 For let not that man think that he
shall receive any thing of the Lord.
8 A double minded man *is* unstable in
all his ways.
9 Let the brother of low degree rejoice
in that he is exalted:
10 But the rich, in that he is made low:
because as the flower of the grass he
shall pass away.
11 For the sun is no sooner risen with
a burning heat, but it withereth the
grass, and the flower thereof falleth,
and the grace of the fashion of it
perisheth: so also shall the rich man
fade away in his ways.
12 Blessed *is* the man that endureth
*temptation: for when he is tried, he
shall receive the crown of life, which
the Lord hath promised to them that
love him.

2. Temptations to sin

13 Let no man say when he is tempted, I am tempted of God: for God cannot
be tempted with evil, neither tempteth
he any man:
14 But every man is tempted, when he
is drawn away of his own *lust, and enticed.
15 Then when lust hath conceived, it
bringeth forth *sin: and sin, when it is
finished, bringeth forth *death.
16 Do not *err, my beloved brethren.
17 Every good gift and every perfect
gift is from above, and cometh down
from the Father of lights, with whom is
no variableness, neither shadow of
turning.
18 Of his own will begat he us with the
word of truth, that we should be a kind
of firstfruits of his creatures.

3. The inference from all this

¶19 Wherefore, my beloved brethren,

1:5 lack. God desires to give wisdom to every child of God. This verse conveys the thought: "If any of you want wisdom." Read about Solomon's desire for wisdom in 1 Kings 3:5-12.

1:5 liberally, and upbraideth not. Generously and without reproach. God is pleased when we ask Him for wisdom, and this verse affirms that He will give it to us if we only ask Him—a wonderful promise!

1:6 wavering. Doubting. It speaks of going back and forth, seemingly, between faith and unbelief—being spiritually wishy-washy.

1:7 that man. The one who wavers or doubts.

1:9 exalted. By being an heir of God.

1:10 made low. Robbed of his goods for Christ's sake, or reduced in circumstances as a test of character.

1:11 burning heat. Hot wind from the south. Scorching wind often comes at sunrise (Jon. 4:8).

1:11 the grace of the fashion. The outward appearance of beauty.

1:12 when he is tried. When he has proved himself, having passed through the testing.

1:12 the crown of life. The crown of life, the garland of the victor, unfading in contrast to "the flower of the grass" (vs. 10). This refers to eternal life but also to temptation. See *reward.

1:13 when he is tempted. The writer passes now from testing by affliction to temptation to sin. God sends trials only to make us stronger. Our own selfish desires are the source of evil. We are drawn away by them. The cause of sin is in us. "Enticed" (vs. 14) means taken with bait, like fish.

1:15 death. Spiritual death, separation from God (Gen. 2:17). Death stands in striking contrast to the "crown of life" (vs. 12).

1:16 Do not err. Do not be deceived.

1:19 Wherefore . . . swift to hear, slow to speak, slow to wrath. Therefore, as all evil comes from ourselves and all good comes from God, Christians should rely on the

1:18 New Birth
Our *new birth is the highest example of the good gifts that come from God. The Word of Truth, the message based upon God's faithfulness, the gospel, is the means of our new birth. Faith takes what the gospel brings. Because of the Resurrection, Christ is the *firstfruits (1 Cor. 15:20,23). We by our new birth are a kind of firstfruits, a pledge that one day all creation will be made new (Rom. 8:19,23).

let every man be swift to hear, slow to
speak, slow to wrath:
20For the wrath of man worketh not
the *righteousness of God.
21Wherefore lay apart all filthiness
and superfluity of naughtiness, and
receive with meekness the engrafted
word, which is able to save your
souls.
22But be ye doers of the word, and not
hearers only, deceiving your own
selves.
23For if any be a hearer of the word,
and not a doer, he is like unto a man beholding his natural face in a glass:
24For he beholdeth himself, and
goeth his way, and *straightway forgetteth what manner of man he was.
25But whoso looketh into the perfect
law of liberty, and continueth *therein,* he
being not a forgetful hearer, but a doer
of the work, this man shall be blessed
in his deed.
26If any man among you seem to be
religious, and bridleth not his tongue,
but deceiveth his own heart, this man's
*religion *is* vain.
27Pure religion and undefiled before
God and the Father is this, To visit the
fatherless and widows in their affliction,
and to keep himself unspotted from the
*world.

II. Faults and Failings (2:1—5:6)
*1. Social distinctions in the *church*

2 My brethren, have not the faith of
our Lord Jesus Christ, *the Lord* of
glory, with respect of persons.
2For if there come unto your assembly a man with a gold ring, in goodly
apparel, and there come in also a poor
man in vile raiment;
3And ye have respect to him that
weareth the gay clothing, and say unto
him, Sit thou here in a good place; and
say to the poor, Stand thou there, or sit
here under my footstool:
4Are ye not then partial in yourselves, and are become judges of evil
thoughts?

Holy Spirit to help us be balanced. We should listen more than we talk, caring more for our effect upon others. We should not be quick to become angry or enraged when we don't get our own selfish desires.

1:20 worketh not. Does not produce.

1:21 lay apart. Put off and put away, once and for all, as a filthy garment. The "superfluity of naughtiness" is the failure to check evil, and then wickedness can overflow in our lives. This can only be checked by humbly welcoming the gospel: "the expulsive power of a new affection."

1:21 engrafted word. The Law admonished man only from without. The gospel is an inward, implanted power, like a fruitful shoot grafted upon a wild stock.

1:22 be ye doers of the word. Make a habit of obeying the Word, not just hearing it.

1:23 beholding his natural face in a glass. Observing in a mirror. In the same way, the hearer sees his moral condition in the Word of God.

1:25 looketh into. Gazes. A glance leads to forgetting; a gaze leads to doing.

1:25 the perfect law of liberty. The standard set by the gospel in Christ.

1:25 doer of the work. Doer of work; one who translates what he believes into actions.

2:1 have not the faith . . . with respect of persons. The meaning is: "Do you, who believe in the Lord Jesus Christ, treat some people with more respect and partiality than others just because they are rich or have high worldly positions?"

2:3 under my footstool. Down by my footstool; that would be the lowest place.

2:4 judges of evil thoughts. Judges with evil thoughts, possessed of low standards according to their human judgment.

2:2 An Assembly of Believers
An assembly was the synagogue; the Christian place of worship was still called by the Jewish word; it later was discarded in favor of the word "church." In the Jewish synagogue people often sat according to rank. Christian churches originally took their shape from the Jewish synagogue, the communion table taking the place of the ark at the east end. Any place where two or more gather for worship might be termed an "assembly."

5Hearken, my beloved brethren,
Hath not God chosen the poor of this
world rich in faith, and heirs of the
*kingdom which he hath promised to
them that love him?
6But ye have despised the poor. Do
not rich men oppress you, and draw you
before the judgment seats?
7Do not they blaspheme that worthy
name by the which ye are called?
8If ye fulfil the royal law according to
the scripture, Thou shalt love thy
neighbour as thyself, ye do well:
9But if ye have respect to persons, ye
commit sin, and are convinced of the
law as transgressors.
10For whosoever shall keep the
whole law, and yet offend in one *point,*
he is guilty of all.
11For he that said, Do not commit
adultery, said also, Do not kill. Now
if thou commit no adultery, yet if thou
kill, thou art become a transgressor of
the law.
12So speak ye, and so do, as they that
shall be judged by the law of liberty.
13For he shall have judgment without
*mercy, that hath shewed no mercy;
and mercy rejoiceth against judgment.

2. Faith not followed by fruits

14What *doth it* profit, my brethren,
though a man say he hath faith, and
have not works? can faith save him?
15If a brother or sister be naked, and
destitute of daily food,
16And one of you say unto them, Depart in peace, be *ye* warmed and filled;
notwithstanding ye give them not those
things which are needful to the body;
what *doth it* profit?
17Even so faith, if it hath not works,
is dead, being alone.
18Yea, a man may say, Thou hast faith,
and I have works: shew me thy faith
without thy works, and I will shew thee
my faith by my works.

2:6 before the judgment seats. They were dragged there violently and persecuted for their faith in Christ.
2:7 Do not they blaspheme . . . ? Isn't it the rich people who blaspheme?
2:8 royal law. The Law that is king of all the Laws, found in Leviticus 19:18 (compare Matt. 22:35-40).
2:9 convinced of the law. Convicted by the Law.
2:10 offend. Conveys the thought of stumbling, but not falling.
2:10 guilty of all. A garment torn in one part is a torn garment; a harmony with one discordant note is a ruined harmony; a chain with one broken link is a broken chain.
2:11 Do not commit adultery . . . Do not kill. See Exodus 20:13-14.
2:12 So speak ye, and so do . . . by the law of liberty. This refers to James 1:19-26.
2:13 mercy rejoiceth against judgment. Those who practice mercy ("love," as in vs. 8) do not fear judgment; it cannot condemn them.
2:14 though a man say he hath faith. Though a man should make a profession of having faith. Such was Simon the sorcerer (Acts 8:12,20).
2:14 can faith save him? Can that kind of faith—intellectual belief without a change of heart and life—save him?
2:15 a brother or sister. A fellow Christian—one whom we especially ought to help.
2:17 faith . . . is dead, being alone. Faith merely professed is a dead thing, as a body would be dead if separated from the spirit (vs. 26).
2:18 shew me thy faith without thy works. *Exhibit* or *let me see,* not *prove to me*. To show faith to man, works of some kind are necessary. We are justified in the sight of

[19]Thou believest that there is one
God; thou doest well: the devils also
believe, and tremble.
[20]But wilt thou know, O vain man,
that faith without works is dead?
[21]Was not *Abraham our father justified by works, when he had offered
*Isaac his son upon the *altar?
[22]Seest thou how faith wrought with
his works, and by works was faith made
perfect?
[23]And the scripture was fulfilled
which saith, Abraham believed God,
and it was imputed unto him for righteousness: and he was called the Friend
of God.
[24]Ye see then how that by works a
man is justified, and not by faith only.
[25]Likewise also was not *Rahab the
harlot justified by works, when she had
received the messengers, and had sent
them out another way?
[26]For as the body without the spirit
is dead, so faith without works is dead
also.

3. Failure to control tongue and temper

3 My brethren, be not many masters, knowing that we shall receive
the greater *condemnation.
[2]For in many things we offend all. If
any man offend not in word, the same
is a perfect man, *and* able also to bridle
the whole body.
[3]Behold, we put bits in the horses'
mouths, that they may obey us; and we
turn about their whole body.
[4]Behold also the ships, which though
they be so great, and *are* driven of fierce
winds, yet are they turned about with
a very small helm, whithersoever the
governor listeth.
[5]Even so the tongue is a little member, and boasteth great things. Behold, how great a matter a little fire
kindleth!
[6]And the tongue *is* a fire, a world of
iniquity: so is the tongue among our
members, that it defileth the whole
body, and setteth on fire the course of
nature; and it is set on fire of *hell.

2:21,25 DEMONSTRATIONS OF FAITH

The question in verse 21 is not as to the ground upon which Abraham was justified or declared righteous by God, but as to the outward demonstration of his faith. God put Abraham's faith to the test of demonstration (Gen. 22:1; see also its note, "Testing Versus Tempting"). Abraham was justified in his trusting God's promise of an heir. That justification was demonstrated to men by his offering Isaac forty years later. A tree shows by its fruits that it is alive.

Rahab (vs. 25) believed what logically was most improbable: that a few people untrained in war would conquer a well-armed military. Because of that belief she hid the spies at the risk of her life (see Josh. 2:1; see also its note, "Rahab"). Abraham was an illustrious Jew; Rahab an inconspicuous Gentile. In both cases, deeds exhibited the reality of faith.

God when He sees our faith (which He alone can see). We are justified in the sight of men when they see our good works—fruits of faith.

2:20 vain man. Foolish man.

2:22 faith wrought with his works. Faith worked side by side with Abraham's action (in offering Isaac) and was made perfect, or received its realization, through Abraham's willingness to offer his promised son; it was more than mere obedience; it was faith.

2:23 Abraham believed God. See Genesis 15:6 and its note, "Abraham's Faith."

2:24 not by faith only. That is, not by faith cut off from obedience, its fruit.

3:1 be not many masters. Not many of you should become teachers, for we who teach will be judged more strictly.

3:2 we offend all. We all make mistakes, every one of us.

3:2 If any man offend not in word. If any man never makes a slip with his tongue.

3:4 the governor. The pilot, the man at the helm.

3:6 a fire. Like a spark the tongue can cause great sin, mischief, or damage.

3:6 it defileth the whole body. It stains our whole being. The "course of nature" is every influence or part of our lives.

7 For every kind of beasts, and of
birds, and of serpents, and of things in
the sea, is tamed, and hath been tamed
of mankind:
8 But the tongue can no man tame;
it is an unruly evil, full of deadly poison.
9 Therewith bless we God, even the
Father; and therewith curse we men,
which are made after the similitude
of God.
10 Out of the same mouth proceedeth
blessing and cursing. My brethren,
these things ought not so to be.
11 Doth a fountain send forth at the
same place sweet *water* and bitter?
12 Can the *fig tree, my brethren, bear
olive berries? either a vine, figs? so *can*
no fountain both yield salt water and
fresh.
13 Who *is* a wise man and endued with
knowledge among you? let him shew
out of a good *conversation his works
with meekness of wisdom.
14 But if ye have bitter envying and
strife in your hearts, glory not, and lie
not against the truth.
15 This wisdom descendeth not from
above, but *is* earthly, sensual, devilish.
16 For where envying and strife *is,*
there *is* confusion and every evil
work.
17 But the wisdom that is from above
is first pure, then peaceable, gentle, *and*
easy to be intreated, full of mercy and
good fruits, without partiality, and without hypocrisy.
18 And the fruit of righteousness is
sown in peace of them that make peace.

4. Contention and strife

4 From whence *come* wars and
fightings among you? *come they* not
hence, *even* of your *lusts that war in
your members?
2 Ye *lust, and have not: ye kill, and
desire to have, and cannot obtain: ye
fight and war, yet ye have not, because
ye ask not.
3 Ye ask, and receive not, because ye
ask amiss, that ye may consume *it* upon
your lusts.
4 Ye adulterers and adulteresses,
know ye not that the friendship of the
world is enmity with God? whosoever
therefore will be a friend of the world
is the enemy of God.
5 Do ye think that the scripture saith

3:9 made after the similitude of God. Made in God's likeness (see Gen. 1:26-27; see also Gen. 1:27 note, "In God's Image").

3:13 with meekness of wisdom. With the humility that always goes with true wisdom.

3:14 glory not, and lie not against the truth. Do not boast. To boast about yourselves while you have such things in your hearts is to lie.

3:15 earthly, sensual, devilish. Belongs to this world; agrees with the physical senses; comes from below. (Here are man's three enemies: the world, the flesh, and the Devil.)

3:16 confusion. Disorder.

3:17 pure . . . easy to be intreated . . . without hypocrisy. Free from all that is earthly, sensual, and devilish; open to reason and kind in its treatment of a neighbor's faults; without pretence, real.

3:18 is sown in peace of them that make peace. This fruit is peace; the peacemakers who sow peace will reap, of course, peace.

4:1 come they not hence, even of your lusts . . . ? Do they not come from wanting to please yourself—from being selfish?

4:2 Ye lust, and have not. You set your heart upon certain pleasures, but you are not enriched by them. You are so self-centered that you try to push others out of your way so that you can please only yourself and are thus, in God's sight, murderers.

4:2 ye have not, because ye ask not. If you prayed correctly, there would be no conflict of desires.

4:3 Ye ask, and receive not, because ye ask amiss. When you do pray, you get nothing because you pray with the wrong motive, namely, to add to your own pleasures.

4:4 Ye adulterers and adulteresses. You faithless people.

4:4 whosoever therefore will be. Whoever is determined to be.

in vain, The spirit that dwelleth in us
lusteth to envy?
6But he giveth more grace. Wherefore he saith, God resisteth the proud,
but giveth grace unto the humble.
7Submit yourselves therefore to
God. Resist the *devil, and he will flee
from you.
8Draw nigh to God, and he will draw
nigh to you. Cleanse *your* hands, *ye* sinners; and purify *your* hearts, *ye* double
minded.
9Be afflicted, and mourn, and weep:
let your laughter be turned to *mourning, and *your* joy to heaviness.
10Humble yourselves in the sight of
the Lord, and he shall lift you up.
11Speak not evil one of another,
brethren. He that speaketh evil of *his*
brother, and judgeth his brother,
speaketh evil of the law, and judgeth the
law: but if thou judge the law, thou art
not a doer of the law, but a judge.
12There is one lawgiver, who is able
to save and to destroy: who art thou
that judgest another?

5. Independence of God

¶13Go to now, ye that say, To day or
to morrow we will go into such a city,
and continue there a year, and buy and
sell, and get gain:
14Whereas ye know not what *shall
be* on the morrow. For what *is* your
life? It is even a vapour, that appeareth
for a little time, and then vanisheth
away.
15For that ye *ought* to say, If the Lord
will, we shall live, and do this, or that.
16But now ye rejoice in your boast-
ings: all such rejoicing is evil.
17Therefore to him that knoweth to
do good, and doeth *it* not, to him it is sin.

6. Oppression of the poor by the rich

5 Go to now, *ye* rich men, weep and
howl for your miseries that shall
come upon *you*.
2Your riches are corrupted, and your
garments are motheaten.
3Your gold and silver is cankered; and
the rust of them shall be a witness
against you, and shall eat your flesh as

4:5 in vain . . . ? Do you imagine that there is no meaning in or reason for the Scripture when it says these things? The latter portion of this verse conveys this thought: "The spirit [that is, the Holy Spirit] that dwelleth in us yearns jealously over us." The indwelling Spirit would guard Christians from committing sin. (See 1 Cor. 6:15,19-20; 2 Cor. 6:16-17; see also 2 Cor. 6:17 note, "Separation.")
4:6 But he giveth more grace. God continually grants more and more grace as we resist the spirit to envy, to lust, and to sin.
4:8 Draw nigh. Come close or near.
4:8 double minded. Wavering between God and the world. A Christian trying to do this will live in constant defeat and will lack communion and peace with God—in short, that person will be miserable until he makes up his mind to follow God with a whole heart.
4:9 Be afflicted, and mourn, and weep. Be miserable, grieve and mourn and lament over sin.
4:11 speaketh evil of the law. The Law says, "Love thy neighbor as thyself" (Lev. 19:18).
4:12 There is one lawgiver. There is only One who is Lawgiver, Judge, and King (Isa. 33:22): God Himself who is able both to save and to destroy.
4:12 who art thou that judgest another? The order of the words in the original Greek is emphatic. "Thou, who art thou that . . . ?" Judgment belongs to God; leave it to Him.
4:13 Go to now. An expression to arrest attention: "Come now!" or "See here!"
4:15 For that ye ought to say. Instead you should say.
5:1 ye rich men. The words, though always true, were addressed specifically to rich, unbelieving Jews. But they will be read by poor believers and are meant to carry encouragement to them. The miseries were to come at the destruction of Jerusalem (A.D. 70).
5:2 Your riches are corrupted. The riches you have accumulated by your oppression of the poor are rotten and about to disappear. Moth-eaten garments are an example of disappearing property, as is the rusted "gold and silver" of verse 3.

it were fire. Ye have heaped treasure
together for the last days.
[4]Behold, the hire of the labourers
who have reaped down your fields,
which is of you kept back by fraud,
crieth: and the cries of them which have
reaped are entered into the ears of the
Lord of sabaoth.
[5]Ye have lived in pleasure on the
earth, and been wanton; ye have
nourished your hearts, as in a day of
slaughter.
[6]Ye have condemned *and* killed the
just; *and* he doth not resist you.

III. Commands and Prohibitions (5:7-18)

1. A command to be patient

¶[7]Be patient therefore, brethren,
unto the coming of the Lord. Behold,
the husbandman waiteth for the precious fruit of the earth, and hath long
patience for it, until he receive the early
and latter rain.
[8]Be ye also patient; stablish your
hearts: for the coming of the Lord
draweth nigh.

2. A prohibition against judging others

[9]Grudge not one against another,
brethren, lest ye be condemned: behold, the judge standeth before the
door.
[10]Take, my brethren, the prophets,
who have spoken in the name of the
Lord, for an example of suffering affliction, and of patience.
[11]Behold, we count them happy
which endure. Ye have heard of the patience of Job, and have seen the end of
the Lord; that the Lord is very pitiful,
and of tender mercy.

3. A prohibition against taking oaths

[12]But above all things, my brethren,
swear not, neither by heaven, neither
by the earth, neither by any other oath:
but let your yea be yea; and *your* nay,
nay; lest ye fall into condemnation.

5:3 for the last days. *In* the last days, that is, in these days immediately preceding the catastrophe of A.D. 70. This could certainly also apply to people today who have gotten rich by taking advantage of the poor.

5:4 the Lord of sabaoth. This title for God is used only here and in Romans 9:29. It is used many times in its Hebrew form in the Old Testament, for it means the *Lord of Hosts*. See *names of God.

5:5 as in a day of slaughter. As animals enjoy feeding on the very day on which they are to be killed, unconscious of what is coming, so were these people concerned and consumed only with their own pleasures.

5:6 Ye have condemned and killed the just. This was true in the death of Christ (see Acts 3:14), and it was later true of His followers made "just" and righteous in Him.

5:7 unto the coming of the Lord. Until Christ's personal return at the end of the age, when the need for patient waiting will end.

5:7 Behold, the husbandman waiteth. James used a *parable, this one about a farmer, as an illustration, as our Lord so often did.

5:7 the early and latter rain. The early rain fell at sowing time, about November; the latter rain fell about March, in time to swell the grain.

5:8 stablish your hearts. Establish and keep your hearts steady, patiently waiting for and trusting in God.

5:9 Grudge not one against another, brethren. Do not keep on grumbling impatiently. First, James encouraged them to bear the persecution of unbelievers; here, he encouraged them to bear patiently the irritations from their brethren and fellow believers, which are sometimes less easy to bear.

5:9 the judge standeth before the door. The Judge, the Lord Jesus Christ, is about to come through the "everlasting doors" (Ps. 24:7).

5:11 the end of the Lord. The happy end God gave Job after his long endurance (Job 42:10,12-17).

5:11 very pitiful. Full of pity.

5:12 swear not. Swearing is alien to the Christian. A Christian should not lie, exaggerate,

4. A command to pray

13Is any among you afflicted? let him
pray. Is any merry? let him sing psalms.
14Is any sick among you? let him call
for the elders of the church; and let
them pray over him, anointing him with
oil in the name of the Lord:
15And the prayer of faith shall save
the sick, and the Lord shall raise him
up; and if he have committed sins, they
shall be forgiven him.
16Confess *your* faults one to another, and pray one for another, that
ye may be healed. The effectual fervent
prayer of a righteous man availeth
much.
17Elias was a man subject to like passions as we are, and he prayed earnestly that it might not rain: and it rained
not on the earth by the space of three
years and six months.
18And he prayed again, and the heav-
en gave rain, and the earth brought
forth her fruit.

IV. Postscript (5:19-20)

19Brethren, if any of you do err from
the truth, and one convert him;
20Let him know, that he which converteth the sinner from the error of his
way shall save a soul from death, and
shall hide a multitude of sins.

5:15 Prayer for the Sick

Sickness is not necessarily a punishment for, or the result of, specific sins, though it may be. In such a case, if the sickness is the result of sin, the prayer answered for healing will also be answered for the forgiveness of sin or sins committed. The forgiveness is, of course, through the blood of Jesus Christ (Heb. 9:14-22).

Much illness, of course, is simply the result of living in a fallen world. Jesus cares about our bodies just as He does our spirits. The members of a church should always be ready and willing to give encouragement, support (of whatever kind is needed), love, and prayer to those who are ill. God will heal the ill person if it's in His sovereign will. All prayers are subject to God's will.

---

or use profane language (see 1 Tim. 4:7; 2 Tim. 2:16). See our Lord's command in Matthew 5:34-37. The right use of the tongue follows in verse 13: "pray."

5:12 let your yea be yea. A Christian's word should be an unbreakable bond.

5:14 call for the elders. Such definitely appointed church officers already existed. They would represent the whole church in this ministry.

5:14 anointing him with oil. This appears to be associated with the period of miracle-working in the early church. Among the Jews, oil was used as a medicine (see Mark 6:13); so it is appropriate here. It is also a *type of the *Holy Spirit, through whom all our prayers are answered.

5:15 the prayer of faith shall save. The oil was only the symbol. The prayer did not save his soul from sin but his body from sickness. This sickness may have been the result of chastening, but that is certainly not always the case. See note above, "Prayer for the Sick."

5:16 Confess your faults one to another. The guilty one should own up to the one he has wronged. Christians can also gain strength by sharing their struggles with sin with mature Christians they can trust, who will pray for them and encourage them, assuring them of God's forgiveness if the one who sinned has asked His forgiveness but still feels guilty. This is one of Satan's tools to keep believers discouraged and from living victorious lives.

5:16 The effectual fervent prayer. An effective prayer energized by the Holy Spirit will accomplish a great deal.

5:17 he prayed earnestly. "He prayed with prayer," a Hebrew expression for intense prayer. (For an illustration, see 1 Kings 17–18; see also 1 Kings 17:17 note, "Elijah's Power.")

5:18 her fruit. It had been withheld because of sin.

5:19 the truth. The message of the gospel.

5:20 death. Separation from God, spiritual death.

5:20 shall hide a multitude of sins. The one who deals with the sinner does not hide his own sins but the sins of the one converted. Here is an inspired encouragement to the soul-winner.

The First Epistle General of

PETER

THE WRITER AND TIME

The Apostle Peter wrote this epistle especially to Christian Jews who were in five provinces of Asia Minor, north of Palestine (1 Peter 1:1). But he also wrote to Gentile Christians (1 Peter 2:10). This is the same Peter who was a disciple of the Lord Jesus Christ during His life on earth. John tells how he became a disciple (John 1:40-42). Peter was with our Lord when some very important things happened (Matthew 16:16-18; 17:1-2; 26:36-37; John 21:15), and he became a leader among the disciples (Acts 1:15; 2:14; 4:8-12; 15:7). The date of writing is thought to be A.D. 63.

THEME

The letter tells of the wonderful salvation in Christ and teaches Christians that they must live holy lives; that they will suffer because they are Christians, but that there is great comfort in their Lord; that they should be kind to one another, preach and teach gladly, and be humble before God, casting their care upon Him.

OUTLINE OF 1 PETER

I.	The New Birth	1 Peter 1:1-25
II.	The New People	1 Peter 2:1-25
III.	The New Way to Live	1 Peter 3:1-22
IV.	The New Way to Suffer	1 Peter 4:1-19
V.	The New Way to Serve	1 Peter 5:1-14

I. The New Birth (1:1-25)

Greetings

1 *Peter, an *apostle of Jesus
*Christ, to the strangers scattered
throughout Pontus, Galatia, Cappadocia, Asia, and Bithynia,
2*Elect according to the foreknowledge of *God the Father, through sanctification of the Spirit, unto obedience
and sprinkling of the *blood of Jesus
Christ: *Grace unto you, and *peace, be
multiplied.

The great salvation

¶3Blessed *be* the God and Father of
our Lord Jesus Christ, which according

1:1 strangers. Jewish Christians scattered among the Gentiles (John 7:35; James 1:1).

1:1 Asia. A province in Asia Minor bordering on the Aegean Sea. In it were Mysia, Phrygia, and other districts mentioned in the New Testament (Acts 2:9; Rev. 1:11).

1:2 foreknowledge. What God knows beforehand.

1:2 sprinkling. The word "sprinkle" is used many times in the Old Testament in connection with the blood of the animal sacrifices. As these sacrifices were illustrations of the sacrifice of the Lord Jesus Christ on the cross, this same word is used in connection with His blood (Lev. 16:14; Heb. 9:13-14,19-21; 10:22 and its note, "Assurance of Faith"; 12:24).

to his abundant *mercy hath begotten
us again unto a lively *hope by the *resurrection of Jesus Christ from the dead,
4To an inheritance incorruptible, and
undefiled, and that fadeth not away, reserved in *heaven for you,
5Who are kept by the power of God
through *faith unto *salvation ready to
be revealed in the last time.
6Wherein ye greatly rejoice, though
now for a season, if need be, ye are in
heaviness through manifold *temptations:
7That the trial of your faith, being
much more precious than of gold that
perisheth, though it be tried with fire,
might be found unto praise and honour
and glory at the appearing of Jesus
Christ:
8Whom having not seen, ye love; in
whom, though now ye see *him* not, yet
believing, ye rejoice with joy unspeakable and full of glory:
9Receiving the end of your faith, *even*
the salvation of *your* souls.
10Of which salvation the *prophets
have inquired and searched diligently,
who prophesied of the grace *that should
come* unto you:
11Searching what, or what manner of
time the Spirit of Christ which was in
them did signify, when it testified beforehand the sufferings of Christ, and
the glory that should follow.

1:11 Christ's Sufferings and Glory
The Old Testament prophets, writing several hundred years before the Lord Jesus Christ came to earth, could not see clearly all that their own prophecies meant. They wrote of His crucifixion, for example (Isa. 53), but did not fully understand His resurrection, His return to heaven, and that His reign in power would be, not at His first coming to earth, but at His second coming.

12Unto whom it was revealed, that
not unto themselves, but unto us they
did minister the things, which are now
reported unto you by them that have
preached the *gospel unto you with the
Holy Ghost sent down from heaven;
which things the *angels desire to look
into.

1:3 begotten. Given us new life; caused us to be born again.
1:3 lively. Living, real.
1:3 resurrection. Our Saviour rose from the tomb, overcoming death—and all who believe in Him will be raised from the dead (John 11:25; Rom. 6:8-9; 1 Cor. 15).
1:4 inheritance. Eternal life through faith in Christ as our Saviour.
1:4 incorruptible. Imperishable, that which will never die.
1:5 kept. Guarded.
1:5 revealed. Salvation will be complete when Jesus Christ comes again in the "last time," for then all who believed in Him will be raised, and those who are still alive will be caught up to be with Him (1 Cor. 15:22-23,51-53 and see 1 Cor. 15:52 note, "A Final Resurrection"; 1 Thess. 4:16-17).
1:6 manifold temptations. Various trials and troubles that test faith and show whether it is really trust in God.
1:7 gold. When gold is put into the fire, the fire separates it from all the other things that are found with it in the earth. Tried in the fire, gold is purified, but faith in God is more precious than gold, and it, too, is tested by trials which seem like fire, that it may be made more pure.
1:7 found unto praise. When Jesus Christ comes again, all who are redeemed will praise and honor and give glory to Him for His power in saving sinners (Eph. 2.6-7; Phil. 2:10-11; Rev. 4:11; 5:11-13).
1:9 end. The goal—the "salvation of [our] souls," as explained in the last part of the verse.
1:10 inquired and searched. Though the writers of the books of prophecy in the Old Testament wrote concerning the Lord Jesus, as God told them to do, they did not fully understand all that these prophecies meant; so they were eager to learn more about the meaning of the words they had written.
1:12 minister. Serve. The prophets were not serving the people of their own time, or themselves, as much as they were serving us.

Why Christians should be holy

¶ 13Wherefore gird up the loins of your
mind, be sober, and hope to the end for
the grace that is to be brought unto you
at the *revelation of Jesus Christ;

1:13 A Custom Explained
The people of that day wore loose robes held in place by girdles or belts. When they had hard work to do, they would fasten the belts more tightly to keep the robes from getting in their way. This expression, "gird up the loins of your mind," comes from that custom, and it means to be serious and thoughtful, remembering that the Lord Jesus Christ is coming again (Luke 12:35-36; 17:8; Acts 12:8).

14As obedient children, not fashioning yourselves according to the former
*lusts in your ignorance:
15But as he which hath called you is
holy, so be ye holy in all manner of *conversation;
16Because it is written, Be ye holy;
for I am holy.
17And if ye call on the Father, who
without respect of persons judgeth according to every man's work, pass the
time of your sojourning *here* in fear:
18Forasmuch as ye know that ye were
not *redeemed with corruptible things,
as silver and gold, from your vain conversation *received* by *tradition from
your fathers;
19But with the precious blood of
Christ, as of a lamb without blemish and
without spot:
20Who verily was foreordained before
the foundation of the *world, but was
manifest in these last times for you,
21Who by him do believe in God, that
raised him up from the dead, and gave
him glory; that your faith and hope
might be in God.

The power of God's word

22Seeing ye have purified your souls
in obeying the truth through the Spirit
unto unfeigned love of the brethren, *see
that ye* love one another with a pure
heart fervently:
23Being *born again, not of corruptible seed, but of incorruptible, by the
word of God, which liveth and abideth
for ever.
24For all *flesh *is* as grass, and all the
glory of man as the flower of grass. The
grass withereth, and the flower thereof
falleth away:
25But the word of the Lord endureth
for ever. And this is the word which by
the gospel is preached unto you.

1:13 the revelation. The coming of our Lord.
1:14 fashioning. Not taking as a pattern or model for your lives the things you once did (Rom. 12:1-2; Col. 3:1-3).
1:15 be ye holy in all manner of conversation. Be holy and Christlike in all that you do—all your behavior and conduct.
1:16 Be ye holy. See Leviticus 11:44; 2 Corinthians 6:17-18 (see also 2 Cor. 6:17 note, "Separation").
1:17 without respect of persons. God judges all men as they really are, not according to what men think of them (1 Sam. 16:7; Acts 10:34-35).
1:17 fear. The fear of God, reverence for God (Ps. 111:10).
1:18 vain conversation. An empty life without aim or purpose.
1:19 as of a lamb. Read Exodus 12:5; Leviticus 9:3; Numbers 28:3.
1:20 foreordained. Before the world was created, God, foreseeing sin, planned that Christ should die for sinners (John 17:24; Eph.1:4; Rev. 13:8).
1:20 manifest. Made known, revealed.
1:23 born again. See John 3:3-7 and John 3:3 note, "Born Again."
1:23 corruptible seed. Seed that may be destroyed. It is through faith in God's Word concerning His Son Jesus Christ that people are born again (John 5:24; Rom. 1:1,3,16 and see Rom. 1:16-17 note, "Salvation by Faith"; 10:17). His Word is "incorruptible seed," that is, seed that will not die (Luke 8:11).
1:24 all flesh is as grass. Quoted from Isaiah 40:6-8.

II. The New People (2:1-25)

2 Wherefore laying aside all malice,
and all guile, and hypocrisies, and
envies, and all evil speakings,
2As newborn babes, desire the sincere milk of the word, that ye may grow
thereby:
3If so be ye have tasted that the Lord
is gracious.
4To whom coming, *as unto* a living
stone, disallowed indeed of men, but
chosen of God, *and* precious,
5Ye also, as lively stones, are built up
a spiritual house, an holy priesthood, to
offer up spiritual sacrifices, acceptable
to God by Jesus Christ.
6Wherefore also it is contained in the
scripture, Behold, I lay in *Sion a chief
corner stone, elect, precious: and he
that believeth on him shall not be confounded.
7Unto you therefore which believe *he*
is precious: but unto them which be
disobedient, the stone which the builders disallowed, the same is made the
head of the corner,
8And a stone of stumbling, and a rock
of offence, *even to them* which stumble
at the word, being disobedient: whereunto also they were appointed.

God's own people

9But ye *are* a chosen generation, a
royal priesthood, an holy nation, a peculiar people; that ye should shew forth
the praises of him who hath called you
out of darkness into his marvellous
light:
10Which in time past *were* not a people, but *are* now the people of God:
which had not obtained mercy, but now
have obtained mercy.

Strangers and pilgrims

¶11Dearly beloved, I beseech *you* as
strangers and pilgrims, abstain from
fleshly lusts, which war against the
soul;
12Having your conversation honest
among the *Gentiles: that, whereas
they speak against you as evildoers, they
may by *your* good works, which they
shall behold, glorify God in the day of
visitation.

2:1 Wherefore. This word refers to chapter 1; that is, *because* you have been born again (1:22-23), lay aside all malice, etc.

2:2 sincere milk of the word. The plain, pure, and simple truths of the Bible.

2:3 tasted. Learned by experience.

2:4 living stone. In verses 4-8 stones are spoken of as illustrations of Christ and His people. He is the living stone, the foundation and cornerstone (vs. 6; 1 Cor. 3:11), not of a visible edifice or organization, but of a "spiritual house," His church (vs. 5).

2:4 disallowed. Rejected or refused by men (Ps. 118:22; John 1:11).

2:5 spiritual house. The church of God, of which every believer in Christ is a member (Acts 20:28; 2 Cor. 6:16; Eph. 2:19-22; Col. 1:18,24).

2:5 priesthood. In Christ we are as priests because we have direct access to God (Rev. 1:6; 20:6). See also Hebrews 9:7.

2:5 spiritual sacrifices. Not burnt offerings as in Mosaic times but the yielding of ourselves to God for His service (Ps. 51:17; Rom. 12:1-2).

2:6 it is contained in the scripture. See Isaiah 28:16 (see also its note, "A Sure Foundation").

2:6 confounded. Put to shame.

2:9 a peculiar people. Not peculiar in the usual sense of the word, but a people set apart for God who belong to Him (2 Cor. 6:17-18; see also 2 Cor. 6:17 note, "Separation"), just as those in the military are set apart for special service.

2:11 as strangers and pilgrims. As *aliens* and *exiles* who do not belong primarily to this earth but who are just passing through it to the home in heaven (John 14:1-3; Phil. 3:20).

2:11 war against the soul. Draw the soul away from fellowship with God, weakening our spiritual life.

2:12 day of visitation. The day when God's judgment will fall upon those who do not

¶[13]Submit yourselves to every ordinance of man for the Lord's sake: whether it be to the king, as supreme;
[14]Or unto governors, as unto them that are sent by him for the punishment of evildoers, and for the praise of them that do well.
[15]For so is the will of God, that with well doing ye may put to silence the ignorance of foolish men:
[16]As free, and not using *your* liberty for a cloke of maliciousness, but as the servants of God.
[17]Honour all *men.* Love the brotherhood. Fear God. Honour the king.

Followers of the Lord Jesus Christ

[18]Servants, *be* subject to *your* masters with all fear; not only to the good and gentle, but also to the froward.
[19]For this *is* thankworthy, if a man for conscience toward God endure grief, suffering wrongfully.
[20]For what glory *is it,* if, when ye be buffeted for your faults, ye shall take it patiently? but if, when ye do well, and suffer *for it,* ye take it patiently, this *is* acceptable with God.
[21]For even hereunto were ye called: because Christ also suffered for us, leaving us an example, that ye should follow his steps:
[22]Who did no *sin, neither was guile found in his mouth:
[23]Who, when he was reviled, reviled not again; when he suffered, he threatened not; but committed *himself* to him that judgeth righteously:
[24]Who his own self bare our sins in his own body on the tree, that we, being dead to sins, should live unto *righteousness: by whose *stripes ye were healed.
[25]For ye were as sheep going astray; but are now returned unto the Shepherd and Bishop of your souls.

III. The New Way to Live (3:1-22)

3 Likewise, ye wives, *be* in subjection to your own husbands; that, if any obey not the word, they also may without the word be won by the conversation of the wives;
[2]While they behold your chaste conversation *coupled* with fear.
[3]Whose adorning let it not be that

---

believe, here referred to as "Gentiles," and they will realize that the Christians whom they criticized and persecuted were right.

2:13 every ordinance of man. Earthly rulers and those in authority and the laws they make (Matt. 22:21; Rom. 13:1,7).

2:15 put to silence. When Christians obey the laws of the countries in which they live, others find very little for which to criticize them (see vs. 12; see also the example of the Lord Jesus Christ, vss. 21-22, and Luke 23:4,14).

2:16 free. Set free from the power of Satan and old evil habits by the power of the Lord Jesus Christ (Gal. 5:1).

2:16 cloke of maliciousness. Covering for evil. Peter is saying to the Christians to whom he is writing that they must not think they can break men's laws just because the Lord has set them free. They were not to talk and act as though they were holy and then do wrong.

2:17 brotherhood. All Christians.

2:18 with all fear. With respect and a real desire to please them.

2:18 froward. Those who may be harsh, unkind, and expect too much.

2:23 when he was reviled. See Matthew 27:29-31,40-44.

2:23 committed himself to him that judgeth righteously. Jesus Christ submitted Himself entirely to the Father's will, even under the agony of the cross (Mark 14:36; Luke 23:46).

2:24 the tree. The cross upon which our Lord died in our place.

2:24 stripes. The wounds of the Saviour (the same Greek word as used in Isa. 53:5 in Septuagint). See Acts 16:23; 2 Corinthians 11:23 for a similar thought.

2:25 the Shepherd and Bishop. The Lord Jesus Christ.

3:2 fear. Reverence for their husbands (Eph. 5:33).

outward *adorning* of plaiting the hair,
and of wearing of gold, or of putting on
of apparel;
4But *let it be* the hidden man of the
heart, in that which is not corruptible,
even the ornament of a meek and quiet
spirit, which is in the sight of God of
great price.

3:4 The Inner Person
The "hidden man of the heart" is the real person inside the body (whether man or woman) who has been born again through faith in Jesus Christ (2 Cor. 5:17). The change that God works in the heart does more to make a person attractive than fine clothing can ever do (Rom. 12:2).

5For after this manner in the old time
the holy women also, who trusted in
God, adorned themselves, being in subjection unto their own husbands:
6Even as Sarah obeyed *Abraham,
calling him lord: whose daughters ye
are, as long as ye do well, and are not
afraid with any amazement.
7Likewise, ye husbands, dwell with
them according to knowledge, giving
honour unto the wife, as unto the weaker vessel, and as being heirs together
of the grace of life; that your prayers be
not hindered.

The love and patience of brethren

8Finally, *be ye* all of one mind, having
compassion one of another, love as
brethren, *be* pitiful, *be* courteous:
9Not rendering evil for evil, or railing for railing: but contrariwise blessing; knowing that ye are thereunto
called, that ye should inherit a blessing.
10For he that will love life, and see
good days, let him refrain his tongue
from evil, and his lips that they speak
no guile:
11Let him eschew evil, and do good;
let him seek peace, and ensue it.
12For the eyes of the Lord *are* over
the righteous, and his ears *are open*
unto their prayers: but the face of the
Lord *is* against them that do evil.
¶13And who *is* he that will harm you,
if ye be followers of that which is good?

Suffering for righteousness' sake

14But and if ye suffer for righteousness' sake, happy *are ye:* and be not
*afraid of their terror, neither be trou-
bled;
15But sanctify the Lord God in your
hearts: and *be* ready always to *give* an
answer to every man that asketh you a
reason of the hope that is in you with
meekness and fear:

3:3 adorning. This word, used twice in this verse, is explained by the verse itself and by verse 4.
3:6 whose daughters ye are. In Galatians 3:7 those who believe in God are called "children of Abraham," even though they are not Jews; so here, those women who imitate Sara (Gen. 18) by obeying their husbands are called her daughters.
3:7 heirs together. When both husband and wife are Christians, they are "heirs of God, and joint-heirs with Christ" (Rom. 8:17), and together they inherit eternal life (Heb. 1:14, James 2:5; 1 Pet. 1:4,13).
3:8 pitiful. Kindhearted.
3:9 but contrariwise blessing. Instead of "railing" (being insulting) or trying to "get even," be kind to those who speak or act evilly toward you (Matt. 5:44-45).
3:11 eschew evil. Turn away from evil.
3:11 ensue it. Pursue, follow after, peace.
3:12 the eyes of the Lord. The words of verses 10-12 recall Psalm 34:12-16.
3:14 happy are ye. The same Greek word that means *blessed*.
3:14 be not afraid. Do not let the enemies of the gospel make you afraid (Ps. 27:1; Heb. 13:6). Peter had denied our Lord three times (Matt. 26:69-75), but in Christ he had become bold (Acts 4:13).
3:15 the hope. The hope of eternal life that the gospel brings us (Rom. 8:24; Titus 3:7).
3:15 with meekness and fear. Gentleness and respect. Don't give your answer proudly but humbly and with reverent fear of God—but not with fear of men.

[16]Having a good conscience; that, whereas they speak evil of you, as of evildoers, they may be ashamed that falsely accuse your good conversation in Christ.
[17]For *it is* better, if the will of God be so, that ye suffer for well doing, than for evil doing.

The example of the Lord Jesus Christ

[18]For Christ also hath once suffered for sins, the *just for the unjust, that he might bring us to God, being put to *death in the flesh, but quickened by the Spirit:
[19]By which also he went and preached unto the spirits in prison;
[20]Which sometime were disobedient, when once the longsuffering of God waited in the days of Noah, while the *ark was a preparing, wherein few, that is, eight souls were saved by water.
[21]The like figure whereunto *even* *baptism doth also now save us (not the putting away of the filth of the flesh, but the answer of a good conscience toward God,) by the resurrection of Jesus Christ:
[22]Who is gone into heaven, and is on the right hand of God; angels and authorities and powers being made subject unto him.

3:21 Baptism
Verse 21 makes it clear that it is not baptism by water that saves anyone. Salvation comes only through faith in Christ. Only this faith in Him can give "a good conscience" or a conscience at peace with God (Rom. 5:1). Baptism is a symbol of judgment–death–and that is what the Flood was.

IV. The New Way to Suffer (4:1-19)

4 Forasmuch then as Christ hath suffered for us in the flesh, arm yourselves likewise with the same mind: for he that hath suffered in the flesh hath ceased from sin;
[2]That he no longer should live the rest of *his* time in the flesh to the *lusts of men, but to the will of God.
[3]For the time past of *our* life may suffice us to have wrought the will of the Gentiles, when we walked in lasciviousness, lusts, excess of *wine, revellings, banquetings, and abominable idolatries:
[4]Wherein they think it strange that ye run not with *them* to the same excess of riot, speaking evil of *you:*

3:18 once suffered. Christ suffered for sins but not for His own, for He is God, and He did not sin (see 1 Pet. 2:22). That is why it says "the just for the unjust"; the Lord Jesus Christ–who is holy and righteous and just–suffered on the cross for us who are unjust, that He, through taking our place as sinners, might give us His place as righteous.
3:18 quickened. Made alive again (Rom. 6:4; 8:11).
3:19 By which also he went and preached . . . in prison. The traditional interpretation of this verse is that, between His death and resurrection, Christ went to proclaim salvation to God's followers from the Old Testament era (and any who believed in God and died before the Cross). See Matthew 27:52-53. Others think that Jesus Christ, by the Holy Spirit, preached through Noah to the sinful people of his time, as He preached also through the prophets (1 Pet. 1:10-11; see also 1 Pet. 1:11 note, "Christ's Sufferings and Glory").
3:20 the longsuffering of God waited. It was 120 years from the time God said that He would destroy man until the Flood came (Gen. 6:3), and during that time men had a chance to repent of their sins and turn to God.
3:20 eight souls. For the people who went into the ark, see Genesis 6:10; 7:7.
3:21 The like figure. The saving of Noah and his family in the ark is an illustration of salvation today through faith in Jesus Christ.
4:1 arm yourselves likewise with the same mind. Strengthen yourselves with the same willingness to do God's will and the same trust in God that Christ had (Phil. 2:5).
4:3 may suffice us. We have wasted enough time in worldliness.
4:3 lasciviousness, lusts. The verse describes the degradation of paganism and applies to paganism in every era.

[5]Who shall give account to him that is
ready to judge the *quick and the dead.
[6]For for this cause was the gospel
preached also to them that are dead,
that they might be judged according to
men in the flesh, but live according to
God in the spirit.

Living for others

¶[7]But the end of all things is at hand:
be ye therefore sober, and watch unto
*prayer.
[8]And above all things have fervent
charity among yourselves: for charity
shall cover the multitude of sins.
[9]Use hospitality one to another without grudging.
[10]As every man hath received the
gift, *even so* minister the same one to
another, as good stewards of the manifold *grace of God.
[11]If any man speak, *let him speak* as
the oracles of God; if any man minister,
let him do it as of the ability which God
giveth: that God in all things may be
glorified through Jesus Christ, to whom
be praise and dominion for ever and
ever. *Amen.

Rejoicing in suffering

¶[12]Beloved, think it not strange concerning the fiery trial which is to try
you, as though some strange thing happened unto you:
[13]But rejoice, inasmuch as ye are
partakers of Christ's sufferings; that,
when his glory shall be revealed, ye
may be glad also with exceeding joy.
[14]If ye be reproached for the name
of Christ, happy *are ye;* for the spirit of
glory and of God resteth upon you: on
their part he is evil spoken of, but on
your part he is glorified.
[15]But let none of you suffer as a murderer, or *as* a thief, or *as* an evildoer,
or as a busybody in other men's matters.
[16]Yet if *any man suffer* as a Christian,
let him not be ashamed; but let him glorify God on this behalf.
[17]For the time *is come* that judgment
must begin at the house of God: and if
it first *begin* at us, what shall the end
be of them that obey not the gospel of
God?
[18]And if the righteous scarcely be

4:5 give account. They will have to appear before God to be judged for their wickedness (Luke 10:14; Rom. 2:5-6; 2 Tim. 4:1; Rev. 20:11-12).
4:7 the end of all things. The second coming of Jesus Christ, which will end this present age or *dispensation (Matt. 24:42; Phil. 4:5; James 5:7-9).
4:7 watch unto prayer. Take time to pray, and pray earnestly (Matt. 26:41; Col. 4:2).
4:8 charity shall cover. Charity is a type of love, and true love for others overlooks many weaknesses (1 Cor. 13:4,5,13).
4:10 the gift. One must minister (use) for the good of others whatever special talent or skill God has given to him (Rom. 12:6-8).
4:10 as good stewards. In Christ we do not own life and property—they are trusts, and we are to manage them well (1 Cor. 4:1-2; 1 Tim. 6:17-18; compare Matt. 25:14-30).
4:11 as the oracles of God. As speaking God's very words as given to us by Him, so that speaking for Christ is not expressing a personal opinion. It is delivering God's message.
4:11 dominion. Power over all.
4:12 to try you. To test and prove you.
4:13 partakers of. Have a part or share in.
4:13 when his glory shall be revealed. When He comes again in glory (2 Tim. 2:12).
4:16 on this behalf. Because he does suffer as a Christian.
4:17 judgment must begin at the house of God. The house of God means the *church, made up of all Christian people. They should be the first to confess their sins to God, repent, and turn away from sin (2 Cor. 6:17-18 and see also 2 Cor. 6:17 note, "Separation"; 7:1).
4:18 scarcely. With difficulty. It cost God the life of His Son that we might be made righteous; surely then, those who are unrighteous, ungodly sinners who have rejected Christ cannot be saved.

saved, where shall the ungodly and the
sinner appear?
19Wherefore let them that suffer according to the will of God commit the
keeping of their souls *to him* in well
doing, as unto a faithful Creator.

V. The New Way to Serve (5:1-14)

5 The elders which are among you
I exhort, who am also an elder, and
a witness of the sufferings of Christ,
and also a partaker of the glory that
shall be revealed:
2Feed the flock of God which is
among you, taking the oversight *thereof,*
not by constraint, but willingly; not for
filthy lucre, but of a ready mind;
3Neither as being lords over *God's*
heritage, but being ensamples to the
flock.
4And when the chief Shepherd shall
appear, ye shall receive a crown of glory
that fadeth not away.

Being humble and trusting God

5Likewise, ye younger, submit yourselves unto the elder. Yea, all *of you* be
subject one to another, and be clothed
with humility: for God resisteth the
proud, and giveth grace to the humble.
¶6Humble yourselves therefore under the mighty hand of God, that he may
exalt you in due time:

5:5 Clothed in Humility

The expression used here means *to put on humility* as a girdle, or a slave's work apron, as Jesus Christ wrapped Himself with a towel when He washed the disciples' feet (John 13:4-5). Clothing very often symbolizes, or pictures, character in the Bible. For example, in the Garden of Eden, Adam and Eve's attempt to clothe themselves with fig leaves stands for their self-righteousness (Gen. 3:7); see also Isaiah 64:6. When God made *coats of skins for Adam and Eve (Gen. 3:21), it was a picture of the death and shed blood of the Lord Jesus Christ, the Lamb of God, and of their being dressed in God's righteousness as the Christian must be (Job 29:14; Ps. 132:9; Isa. 11:5; 59:17; 61:10; Rom. 3:22–"righteousness . . . upon all that believe"; see also Rom. 3:22 note, "God's Righteousness"; Rev. 19:8). See more about the "garments" of a believer in Ephesians 6:11-17.

7Casting all your care upon him; for
he careth for you.
8Be sober, be vigilant; because your
adversary the devil, as a roaring lion,
walketh about, seeking whom he may
devour:
9Whom resist stedfast in the faith,
knowing that the same afflictions are
accomplished in your brethren that are
in the world.
10But the God of all grace, who hath
called us unto his eternal glory by

5:1 partaker of the glory. Peter, with other believers who have died, will be with the Lord when He comes again in glory (Rom. 8:17-18; 1 Thess. 4:14-16; Jude 14).

5:2 Feed the flock of God. Preach, not only from the pulpit, but in personal contacts and by our lives, the truths of God's Word to Christians (John 21:15-17; see also John 21:15 note, "Jesus Questions Peter").

5:2 filthy lucre. An earthly reward, such as money, especially dishonest gain.

5:3 Neither as being lords. Not acting like proud masters or condescending to Christ's church.

5:3 God's heritage. God's people entrusted to earthly shepherds or leaders (Deut. 32:9).

5:3 ensamples. Examples.

5:4 the chief Shepherd. The Lord Jesus Christ (John 10:11, 14; Heb. 13:20), the only Head of the church.

5:4 crown of glory. Other crowns are spoken of as rewards in Scripture (1 Thess. 2:19; 2 Tim. 4:8; James 1:12; Rev. 2:10).

5:9 Whom resist stedfast in the faith. Only by the power of the Spirit of God and His Word can we overcome Satan and stand firm against him. See how the Lord Jesus used God's Word against Satan (Matt. 4:4,7,10; note also Eph. 6:10-18).

5:9 accomplished. Other Christians are facing the same temptations and trials (1 Cor. 10:13) that the world of unbelievers faces.

Christ Jesus, after that ye have suffered
a while, make you perfect, stablish,
strengthen, settle *you*.
11 To him *be* glory and dominion for
ever and ever. Amen.

Personal messages

¶ 12 By Silvanus, a faithful brother
unto you, as I suppose, I have written
briefly, exhorting, and testifying that
this is the true grace of God wherein
ye stand.
13 The *church that is* at Babylon, elect-
ed together with *you*, saluteth you; and
so doth Marcus my son.
14 Greet ye one another with a kiss of
charity. Peace *be* with you all that are in
Christ Jesus. Amen.

5:10 make you perfect. God will complete the work that He has begun in the Christian (Phil. 1:6).

5:12 Silvanus. The man by whom Peter sent this first letter. He is thought to be the same as Silas (Acts 16:19,23,25; 18:5; 2 Cor. 1:19).

5:13 Marcus my son. John Mark, the writer of the Gospel that bears his name, was not Peter's natural son (that is, Peter was not his father), but he had come to know the Lord Jesus as Saviour through Peter; so he was called his "son in the faith."

5:14 kiss of charity. This was a custom more common among the people of Palestine in the time of the apostles than it is among us. Christians followed this custom in purity and holiness and with respect for one another (Acts 20:37; Rom. 16:16).

The Second Epistle General of

PETER

THE WRITER AND TIME

The Apostle Peter wrote this second letter three years after the first, that is, A.D. 66. A few of the main facts of Peter's life, with references, may be found in the introduction to First Peter.

THEMES

The First Epistle was written especially to Christian *Jews*; the Second is addressed to *all* Christians: "them that have obtained like precious faith" (vs. 1). In his Second Epistle, Peter writes of the virtues, or good qualities, that every Christian should have; of his approaching death; of the transfiguration of the Lord Jesus Christ, which he had seen; and of the Scriptures, written by men inspired of God. He warns Christians against false teachers, who will appear in the last days of this age. He urges believers not to make the mistake of unbelievers, who think that the Lord Jesus Christ is not coming back again, but encourages them, rather, to live holy lives and to look forward to the return of the Lord to the earth.

OUTLINE OF 2 PETER

I.	The Blessings God Has Given Us	2 Peter 1:1-21
II.	Warnings Concerning False Teachers	2 Peter 2:1-22
III.	The Return of the Lord Jesus Christ	2 Peter 3:1-18

I. God's Blessings to Us (1:1-21)

Greeting

1 Simon *Peter, a servant and an
*apostle of Jesus *Christ, to them
that have obtained like precious *faith
with us through the *righteousness of
God and our Saviour Jesus Christ:
2 Grace and peace be multiplied unto
you through the knowledge of God, and
of Jesus our Lord,

Partakers of the divine nature

3 According as his divine power hath
given unto us all things that *pertain* unto
life and godliness, through the knowledge of him that hath called us to glory
and virtue:
4 Whereby are given unto us exceeding great and precious promises: that by
these ye might be *partakers of the
divine nature, having escaped the cor-

1:2 be multiplied. The better we know God and the Lord Jesus Christ, the more our hearts will be filled with His grace and peace (see John 1:17 and its notes, including "The Law"; Rom. 5:1; Titus 3:4-7).

1:3 all things that pertain unto life and godliness. All that anyone needs to live the Christian life: first the life itself through the new birth; then the power to live that life through the Holy Spirit (Rom. 8:1-4; Eph. 1:3 and its note, "Heavenly Places"; 1 John 5:11-12).

1:3 to glory and virtue. Or "by His own glory and virtue." Thus sinners are drawn to God (Ps. 63:1-2; Rom. 2:4; Eph. 1:17-19).

1:4 The Divine Nature
It is by believing and receiving for ourselves the promises of God that Christians receive more and more of the holiness of God. The moment we are *born again we receive a new life, the life of Christ Himself. Thus we are made partakers of the divine nature. As we appropriate and use this great gift by yielding to the indwelling Spirit, we become more and more conformed to the divine image of Christ—more like Jesus.

ruption that is in the *world through
*lust.
5And beside this, giving all diligence,
add to your faith virtue; and to virtue
knowledge;
6And to knowledge temperance; and
to temperance patience; and to patience
godliness;
7And to godliness brotherly kindness; and to brotherly kindness *charity.
8For if these things be in you, and
abound, they make *you that ye shall* neither *be* barren nor unfruitful in the
knowledge of our Lord Jesus Christ.
9But he that lacketh these things is
blind, and cannot see afar off, and hath
forgotten that he was purged from his
old sins.
10Wherefore the rather, brethren,
give diligence to make your calling and
*election sure: for if ye do these things,
ye shall never fall:
11For so an entrance shall be ministered unto you abundantly into the
everlasting *kingdom of our Lord and
Saviour Jesus Christ.

Peter's approaching death

¶12Wherefore I will not be negligent
to put you always in remembrance of
these things, though ye know *them*, and
be established in the present truth.
13Yea, I think it meet, as long as I am
in this tabernacle, to stir you up by putting *you* in remembrance;
14Knowing that shortly I must put off
this my tabernacle, even as our Lord
Jesus Christ hath shewed me.
15Moreover I will endeavour that ye
may be able after my decease to have
these things always in remembrance.

The transfiguration

16For we have not followed cunningly
devised fables, when we made known
unto you the power and coming of our
Lord Jesus Christ, but were eyewit-
nesses of his majesty.
17For he received from God the Father honour and glory, when there came
such a voice to him from the excellent
glory, This is my beloved Son, in whom
I am well pleased.
18And this voice which came from
*heaven we heard, when we were with
him in the *holy mount.

The light in a dark place

19We have also a more sure word of
*prophecy; whereunto ye do well that
ye take heed, as unto a light that

1:5 giving all diligence. Note that in verses 5-7 eight qualities (besides diligence) are named, which recall the fruit of the Spirit in Galatians 5:22-23 (see also its note, "The Fruit of the Spirit"). See also 2 Peter 1:10 and its note.
1:6 temperance. The word means *self-control* (1 Cor. 9:25).
1:8 barren. Useless, like a fruit tree that bears no fruit.
1:9 purged from his old sins. Cleansed by our Lord's most precious blood (see 1 Cor. 6:11; Heb. 9:14; 10:22 and its note, "Assurance of Faith"; Rev. 1:5).
1:10 give diligence. They believed in Christ as Saviour; now they were to show that belief by their conduct.
1:13 this tabernacle. This body.
1:16 the power and coming of our Lord Jesus Christ. From this point on through verse 18 Peter is recalling the Transfiguration of Jesus Christ on the mountain. See Matthew 17:1-8 (see also Matt. 17:2 note, "The Transfiguration").
1:19 a more sure word of prophecy. The disciples had known many things concerning Jesus by faith in the Old Testament prophecies. At the Transfiguration, and during the

shineth in a dark place, until the day
dawn, and the day star arise in your
hearts:
[20]Knowing this first, that no prophecy of the scripture is of any private interpretation.
[21]For the prophecy came not in old
time by the will of man: but holy men
of God spake *as they were* moved by the
Holy Ghost.

II. Concerning False Teachers (2:1-22)

2 But there were false *prophets also
among the people, even as there
shall be false teachers among you, who
privily shall bring in damnable heresies,
even denying the Lord that bought
them, and bring upon themselves swift
destruction.
[2]And many shall follow their pernicious ways; by reason of whom the way
of truth shall be evil spoken of.
[3]And through covetousness shall
they with feigned words make merchandise of you: whose judgment now
of a long time lingereth not, and their
damnation slumbereth not.

Punishment and deliverance

[4]For if God spared not the *angels
that sinned, but cast *them* down to *hell,
and delivered *them* into chains of darkness, to be reserved unto judgment;
[5]And spared not the old world, but
saved Noah the eighth *person,* a
preacher of righteousness, bringing
in the flood upon the world of the ungodly;
[6]And turning the cities of Sodom and
Gomorrah into ashes condemned *them*
with an overthrow, making *them* an
*ensample unto those that after should
live ungodly;
[7]And delivered just Lot, vexed with
the filthy *conversation of the wicked:
[8](For that righteous man dwelling

---

life of our Lord on earth, they saw and heard things that confirmed the prophecies, or made those prophecies more certain.

1:19 until the day dawn, and the day star arise. Until that glorious day when the Lord Jesus Christ shall come back again. He is called the "morning star" in Revelation 22:16 (see also its note, "The Bright Morning Star") and the "Sun of righteousness" in Malachi 4:2.

1:20 any private interpretation. No prophecy should be taken by itself but should be compared with other parts of Scripture in order to learn its full meaning. Christians should also not impose what they want Scripture to mean for their own interests or desires. They should study the whole Word of God, asking the Holy Spirit to give them understanding.

1:21 moved by the Holy Ghost. This is one of the important passages of Scripture, showing that the Bible is not a man-inspired book. Every word of it came from God through men who were guided and kept from error in their writing by the Holy Spirit (Exod. 4:15; 19:6; 20:1 and its note, "The Mosaic Covenant"; Isa.1:2 and its note, "Isaiah's Call to Repent"; Jer. 1:2; 2 Tim. 3:16 and its note, "Inspiration of the Scriptures"). See *inspiration.

2:1 false prophets. See Jeremiah 5:31.

2:1 false teachers. In the last days of this present age, before the return of the Lord, there will be teachers—even now there are many of them—who teach what is not true (Matt. 24:5, 24; Acts 20:29-30; 1 Tim. 4:1).

2:1 damnable heresies. Destructive teachings that are contrary to the Word of God.

2:3 make merchandise of you. They will exploit you and lead you astray in order to gain wealth or high positions for themselves.

2:3 whose judgment . . . and their damnation. God will punish them at the right time (2 Thess. 1:7-9).

2:4 For if God spared not the angels. The end of this long sentence beginning "For if" is found in verses 9-10; verse 9 helps to explain the "if." Since God has punished wicked men and angels and saved His own people in the past, He will surely do so again. Compare Jude 6,14-15.

2:4 to be reserved unto judgment. To be kept until the final judgment (Rev. 20:10-15).

among them, in seeing and hearing,
vexed *his* righteous soul from day to
day with *their* unlawful deeds;)
9The Lord knoweth how to deliver
the godly out of *temptations, and to
reserve the unjust unto the day of judgment to be punished:

Those who walk after the flesh

10But chiefly them that walk after the
*flesh in the lust of uncleanness, and
despise government. Presumptuous
are they, selfwilled, they are not afraid
to *speak evil of dignities.
11Whereas angels, which are greater
in power and might, bring not railing
accusation against them before the
Lord.
12But these, as natural brute beasts,
made to be taken and destroyed, speak
evil of the things that they understand
not; and shall utterly perish in their own
corruption;
13And shall receive the reward of
unrighteousness, *as* they that count it
pleasure to riot in the day time. Spots
they are and blemishes, sporting themselves with their own deceivings while
they feast with you;
14Having eyes full of adultery, and
that cannot cease from *sin; beguiling
unstable souls: an heart they have exercised with covetous practices; cursed
children:
15Which have forsaken the right way,
and are gone astray, following the way
of *Balaam *the son* of Bosor, who loved
the wages of unrighteousness;
16But was rebuked for his iniquity:
the dumb ass speaking with man's voice
forbad the madness of the *prophet.
17These are wells without water,
clouds that are carried with a tempest;
to whom the mist of darkness is reserved for ever.
18For when they speak great swelling
words of *vanity, they allure through the
*lusts of the flesh, *through much* wantonness, those that were *clean escaped from them who live in error.
19While they promise them liberty,
they themselves are the servants of
corruption: for of whom a man is overcome, of the same is he brought in
bondage.
20For if after they have escaped the
pollutions of the world through the
knowledge of the Lord and Saviour
Jesus Christ, they are again entangled
therein, and overcome, the latter end is
worse with them than the beginning.
21For it had been better for them not
to have known the way of righteousness, than, after they have known *it,* to
turn from the holy commandment delivered unto them.
22But it is happened unto them according to the true proverb, The dog *is*

2:9 deliver the godly. Compare these words of Peter with Paul's words in 1 Corinthians 10:13; 2 Timothy 4:17-18.
2:10 despise government. Having no respect for those in authority, whether they are kings, presidents, governors, teachers, or parents (2 Tim. 3:1-2).
2:11 railing accusation. Accusing them with insults and rude language (Num. 12:1,8; Jude 9).
2:13 Spots they are and blemishes. The false teachers bring disgrace to the cause that they are supposed to represent.
2:13 their own deceivings. Enjoying so-called pleasures, which last only a short time, and which deceive not only others but themselves also (Matt. 13:22; Eph. 4:22).
2:14 eyes full of adultery. Eyes and hearts full of evil desires.
2:14 cursed children. Not little children, of course, but men who curse others and who are cursed themselves, because they have not believed the gospel (Gal. 3:10; see also its note, "Curse or Blessing").
2:15 the way of Balaam. See Jude 11 note about the "error of Balaam."
2:16 the dumb ass speaking. See Numbers 22:28-30.
2:17 darkness is reserved. Darkness is often used to describe the condition of sinners, both in this life and after death (Matt. 8:12; Eph. 5:8,11; Col. 1:13).
2:22 the true proverb. Part of this proverb comes from Proverbs 26:11.

2:20 Of Wicked Men
In the greater part of this chapter, Peter has been speaking of wicked men, who sin continually, and of those whom they lead astray. Some may have escaped from the evil of the world for a time, through hearing of Christ and knowing something about Him. But Peter is not speaking here of those who were truly saved, for Jesus Christ said that those who are His sheep (through the new birth) shall never perish (John 5:24; 10:28-29). See *assurance.

turned to his own vomit again; and the
sow that was washed to her wallowing
in the mire.

III. Christ's Return (3:1-18)
"Be mindful"

3 This second epistle, beloved, I
now write unto you; in *both* which
I stir up your pure minds by way of remembrance:
[2]That ye may be mindful of the words
which were spoken before by the holy
prophets, and of the commandment of
us the apostles of the Lord and Saviour:
[3]Knowing this first, that there shall
come in the last days scoffers, walking
after their own lusts,
[4]And saying, Where is the promise of
his coming? for since the fathers fell
asleep, all things continue as *they were*
from the beginning of the creation.
[5]For this they willingly are ignorant
of, that by the word of God the heavens
were of old, and the earth standing out
of the water and in the water:
[6]Whereby the world that then was,
being overflowed with water, perished:
[7]But the heavens and the earth,
which are now, by the same word are
kept in store, reserved unto fire against
the day of judgment and perdition of
ungodly men.

"Beloved . . . be not ignorant"

[8]But, beloved, be not ignorant of this
one thing, that one day *is* with the Lord
as a thousand years, and a thousand
years as one day.
[9]The Lord is not slack concerning his
promise, as some men count slackness;
but is longsuffering to us-ward, not will-

3:2 words which were spoken before by the holy prophets. Here Peter refers to the Old Testament. The balance of the verse, however, speaks of the commands of the apostles. Since Peter's time these words are written in the New Testament. Thus the whole Bible is meant here. We should remember to read, study, and think about the truths of the Bible.
3:3 scoffers. Those who laugh at the truths of God's Word and the love of Christ. They will laugh at Christians as well.
3:4 Where is the promise of his coming? The thought of these scoffers (vs. 3) is this: "Since He has not yet come back to this earth, we do not believe He is coming at all." But God's Word is still true, and there are many promises in the Word concerning the second coming of Christ (Matt. 5:18; Acts 1:11).
3:4 since the fathers fell asleep. Since the first men on this earth died.
3:5 they willingly are ignorant of. These scoffers are like this because they do not want to know the truth (Eph. 4:18).
3:5 by the word of God. Peter is here speaking of the creation of the world. Every part of the creation came into being because "God said" (Gen. 1:6,9).
3:6 overflowed with water. It was by the same almighty word of God that the Flood came upon the earth and drowned all men except Noah and his seven family members in the ark (Gen. 6:13; 7:7,10,21,23).
3:7 kept in store, reserved unto fire. See 2 Peter 3:12; 2 Thessalonians 1:7-9.
3:7 perdition. Destruction.
3:8 one day . . . as a thousand years. Our years are but instants in the flow of time in the universe. God is eternal, and a thousand years are short in His sight (Pss. 90:2,4; 93:2; 103:15-16).
3:9 longsuffering to us-ward. Patient toward all of us. God is still giving men the chance to receive Jesus Christ as their Saviour, before He returns as the Judge of this earth. John 3:16 is a good verse to compare with this one. See also 2 Peter 3:15.

ing that any should perish, but that all
should come to repentance.
[10]But the day of the Lord will come as
a thief in the night; in the which the
heavens shall pass away with a great
noise, and the elements shall melt with
fervent heat, the earth also and the works
that are therein shall be burned up.
[11]*Seeing* then *that* all these things
shall be dissolved, what manner *of persons*
ought ye to be in *all* holy conversation
and godliness,
[12]Looking for and hasting unto the
coming of the day of God, wherein the
heavens being on fire shall be dissolved,
and the elements shall melt with fervent
heat?
[13]Nevertheless we, according to his
promise, look for new heavens and a
new earth, wherein dwelleth righteousness.

"Beloved . . . be diligent"

[14]Wherefore, beloved, seeing that ye
look for such things, be diligent that ye
may be found of him in peace, without
spot, and blameless.
[15]And account *that* the longsuffering
of our Lord *is* salvation; even as our
beloved brother Paul also according to
the wisdom given unto him hath written
unto you;
[16]As also in all *his* epistles, speaking
in them of these things; in which
are some things hard to be understood,
which they that are unlearned and
unstable wrest, as *they do* also the
other scriptures, unto their own destruction.

"Beloved . . . beware"

[17]Ye therefore, beloved, seeing ye
know *these things* before, beware lest ye
also, being led away with the error of
the wicked, fall from your own stedfastness.
[18]But grow in grace, and *in* the
knowledge of our Lord and Saviour
Jesus Christ. To him *be* glory both now
and for ever. Amen.

3:10 day of the Lord. Not twenty-four hours, but a period of time beginning when Jesus Christ returns to establish His righteous kingdom and ends with the cleansing of the heavens and the earth by fire (Matt. 24:29-30; 25:31-32; Rev. 20:4-6). It is after the coming of the Lord Jesus Christ for His *church in the *Rapture (1 Thess. 4:15-17; Titus 2:13).

3:10 as a thief in the night. The people of the world will not expect Him and will be taken by surprise.

3:12 hasting unto the coming. Awaiting eagerly, wanting to hasten the coming of the Lord.

3:13 new heavens and a new earth. See Revelation 21:1 (see also its note, "The New Earth"), 27; 22:3-5.

3:16 unlearned and unstable. Those who are not taught in and are ignorant of the Word of God and who do not have a firm faith in it.

3:16 wrest. Twist, giving the Scriptures the wrong meaning.

3:17 the error of the wicked. The error of denying the return of the Lord Jesus Christ, since He has not yet come (vss. 3-4).

The First Epistle General of

JOHN

THE WRITER AND TIME

The Apostle John, who also wrote the Gospel According to Saint John, wrote this epistle, as the contents of the two books clearly show.

Compare: John 1:1 with 1 John 1:1
John 16:24 with 1 John 1:4
John 14:15 with 1 John 2:3
John 17:2 with 1 John 2:25

The date of writing was after A.D. 90.

SUMMARY AND THEME

The First Epistle of John is a letter containing a heart-to-heart message such as a father might write to his children. It is filled with expressions of love, with advice, and with warnings. The persons to whom God is directly speaking through the apostle are those who have received the Lord Jesus Christ as Saviour, those who are called "sons" in John 1:12.

THINGS TO NOTE

John's Gospel tells how one may become a child of God; John's First Epistle tells how the born-again one, the child of God, should conduct himself in relation to the Father and to others of the children. Fathers are accustomed to speak with authority, and in this family letter, one forceful word is repeated many times. The word is "know." First John 2:3 is one of the many verses in which it is found.

The key verse of the epistle is 1 John 5:13.

OUTLINE OF 1 JOHN

I. The Family Enjoying Fellowship with the Father — 1 John 1:1—3:24
   A. Through the Lord Jesus Christ, the Saviour
   B. By Walking (or Living) in the Light
   C. By Having the Right Attitude about Sin
   D. By Depending upon the Lord Jesus Christ
   E. By Meeting the Tests of Fellowship Obedience and Love

II. The Family Warned of Dangers in the World — 1 John 4:1—5:21

I. Fellowship (1:1—3:24)

1 That which was from the beginning, which we have heard, which
we have seen with our eyes, which we
have looked upon, and our hands have
handled, of the Word of life;

1:1 The Word of Life
Words are used by human beings to express thoughts. The Lord Jesus Christ is called "the Word" several times in the New Testament (John 1:1 and its note, "The Word," 14; Rev. 19:13); that is, He Himself, being God (John 1:1), has become, for men, the means of their understanding the nature and purpose of God the Father, God the Son, and God the Holy Spirit. The Bible is the *written* Word of God; Jesus Christ is the *living* Word of God. Coming to earth to be the Saviour of sinners, the Lord Jesus Christ, in a special way, became the expression of God's attitude toward sin and redemption: God hates sin, but He loves the sinner (Rom. 5:8; John 3:16; see also John 3:15-16 note, "Eternal Life"); it is through Christ and His redemptive work alone that the sinner can be forgiven.

2 (For the life was manifested, and we
have seen *it*, and bear witness, and
shew unto you that *eternal life, which
was with the Father, and was manifested unto us;)
3 That which we have seen and heard
declare we unto you, that ye also may
have fellowship with us: and truly our
fellowship *is* with the Father, and with
his Son Jesus *Christ.
4 And these things write we unto you,
that your joy may be full.

Fellowship by walking or living in the light

¶5 This then is the message which we
have heard of him, and declare unto
you, that *God is light, and in him is no
darkness at all.
6 If we say that we have fellowship
with him, and walk in darkness, we lie,
and do not the truth:
7 But if we walk in the light, as he is
in the light, we have fellowship one with
another, and the *blood of Jesus Christ
his Son cleanseth us from all *sin.

Fellowship by having the right attitude about sin

8 If we say that we have no sin, we
deceive ourselves, and the truth is not
in us.
9 If we *confess our sins, he is faithful and *just to forgive us *our* sins, and
to cleanse us from all unrighteousness.
10 If we say that we have not sinned,
we make him a liar, and his word is not
in us.

1:1 from the beginning. The Lord Jesus Christ lived eternally—before He came to earth as the God-man, even before the creation of the universe. Read John 1:1,2,14 with the notes on these verses (which includes John 1:1 note, "The Word"), and also the note on Genesis 1:26 (see also Gen. 11:7 note, "The Trinity"). The existence of God cannot be measured in years; it is continual, without beginning and without end.
1:2 with the Father. See John 1:1,18 (see also John 1:18 note, "Seeing God"); 16:28.
1:3 fellowship with us. Fellowship means *having in common*—it is more than friendship; it is communion, a very close understanding. David and Jonathan had fellowship (1 Sam. 18:1).
1:6 do not. Practice not; that is, we do not make it a habit to practice the truth.
1:7 walk in the light. Here we are told both where to walk and how to walk—"in the light, as he is in the light."
1:7 blood. See *sacrifice.
1:8 If we say that we have no sin. Christ alone could truthfully say that (John 8:29,46; 14:30). The more that men understand the fact that God is light (1 John 1:5), the more they are aware of their own impurity and sinfulness.
1:8 we deceive ourselves. Not merely meaning *we are mistaken,* but *we lead ourselves astray.*
1:9 faithful and just. God is faithful (entirely true) to His promises and to His people, and at the same time He is just (righteous) in forgiving sin, because the penalty was met at Calvary.
1:10 we make him a liar. See 1 John 5:10.

Fellowship by dependence upon the Saviour

2 My little children, these things
write I unto you, that ye sin not.
And if any man sin, we have an advocate with the Father, Jesus Christ the
righteous:

> **2:1 Our Advocate**
> An advocate is one who is called to help another; one who pleads the cause of another, as a lawyer may do in court. Because Jesus Christ made atonement (see Exod. 29:33 note, "Atonement") for all sin on the cross of Calvary, He has the right to act as Advocate in the presence of God for any person who commits sin after he has received the Lord as Saviour. The same word which is translated "advocate" in this passage is used in John 14:16-17,26; 15:26; 16:7, and is there translated "Comforter." The Holy Spirit is our Helper on earth, while Jesus is our Helper in heaven.

2 And he is the propitiation for our
sins: and not for ours only, but also for
the sins of the whole world.

The tests of fellowship: obedience and love

3 And hereby we do know that we
know him, if we keep his commandments.
4 He that saith, I know him, and keepeth not his commandments, is a liar, and
the truth is not in him.
5 But whoso keepeth his word, in him
verily is the love of God perfected:
hereby know we that we are in him.
6 He that saith he abideth in him
ought himself also so to walk, even as
he walked.
¶ 7 Brethren, I write no new commandment unto you, but an old commandment which ye had from the
beginning. The old commandment is
the word which ye have heard from the
beginning.
8 Again, a new commandment I write
unto you, which thing is true in him and
in you: because the darkness is past,
and the true light now shineth.
9 He that saith he is in the light, and
hateth his brother, is in darkness even
until now.

2:1 And if any man sin. Sin in the life of anyone who is a believer in Jesus Christ does not change his *relationship* to God, for he is still a child of God; but it does break his *fellowship* with God. If any earthly child disobeys his father or mother, he is still the son of his parents, but his communion with them is broken until the disobedience is made right, through confession on his part and forgiveness on the part of the parents.

2:2 propitiation. Jesus Christ is the One and only One through whom the righteous God can show mercy to sinners. This verse reveals Christ as "the atoning sacrifice." The work of *atonement has already been accomplished.

2:2 of the whole world. The blood that Christ shed on Calvary was sufficient to have covered the sins of everybody who has ever lived or will ever live, but it is possible for people to reject Him and His salvation. Those who act that way cannot be saved (John 3:18; 12:48).

2:3 commandments. This does not mean the Ten Commandments. In this epistle, John uses a word which means *the will* or *the commands* of God as revealed in the Bible. A Christian is supposed to keep the "law of Christ" (see John 15:10-12; Gal. 6:2); this proves that he knows Jesus Christ as Saviour.

2:5 perfected. Fully developed. Christians will not be perfect, that is, sinless, until they are in heaven, but they can be perfect in the sense of being fully developed. Fruit that is not yet ripe, for example, is not perfect from the viewpoint of the one who wishes to eat it, but it may be perfect at its stage of growth and will develop into perfection (see Matt. 5:48; Eph. 4:12-13).

2:6 to walk. To live.

2:7 which ye had from the beginning. First John 3:11 tells what this commandment is.

2:8 a new commandment. John remembered the words of Jesus, which can be found in John 15:12. It was an old command (1 John 3:11); but it is new, because when a person becomes a Christian there is a new love in his or her heart.

2:8 the true light. John 8:12 tells who this is.

[10]He that loveth his brother abideth
in the light, and there is none occasion
of stumbling in him.
[11]But he that hateth his brother is in
darkness, and walketh in darkness, and
knoweth not whither he goeth, because
that darkness hath blinded his eyes.
[12]I write unto you, little children,
because your sins are *forgiven you for
his name's sake.
[13]I write unto you, fathers, because
ye have known him *that is* from the
beginning. I write unto you, young men,
because ye have overcome the wicked
one. I write unto you, little children,
because ye have known the Father.
[14]I have written unto you, fathers,
because ye have known him *that is* from
the beginning. I have written unto you,
young men, because ye are strong, and
the word of God abideth in you, and ye
have overcome the wicked one.
[15]Love not the world, neither the
things *that are* in the world. If any man
love the world, the love of the Father
is not in him.
[16]For all that *is* in the world, the lust
of the flesh, and the lust of the eyes, and
the pride of life, is not of the Father, but
is of the world.
[17]And the world passeth away, and
the lust thereof: but he that doeth the
will of God abideth for ever.
¶[18]Little children, it is the last time:
and as ye have heard that antichrist
shall come, even now are there many
antichrists; whereby we know that it is
the last time.

2:15 Don't Love the World
Do not give first place in your affections and interests to anything that belongs only to the world system that we can see or to the age in which we live–to worldly amusements and habits that do not glorify God. Choose, rather, that which will abide forever (vs. 17). God loved the world, mankind, and gave His Son for it (John 3:16; see also John 3:15-16 note, "Eternal Life"). We may love the world in that way, being willing to give even our lives, if need be, in order that we might lead others to the Lord. See *world and *separation.

2:18 The Antichrist
The word "antichrist" means *an opponent* or *enemy of Messiah,* one who is against Christ, and it refers here to any person who sets himself against the Lord Jesus Christ, the Saviour. The many antichrists mentioned in this verse and the spirit of antichrist (1 John 4:3) prepare the way for *the* Antichrist, an individual who will speak and act in more terrible rebellion against God than any other man. This Wicked One is described by other names (see 2 Thess. 2:3-4; Rev. 13:1-8; 16:13 and its note, "The Satanic Trinity"; 19:20; 20:10). See *Antichrist.

[19]They went out from us, but they
were not of us; for if they had been of
us, they would *no doubt* have continued
with us: but *they went out,* that they
might be made manifest that they were
not all of us.
[20]But ye have an unction from the
Holy One, and ye know all things.
[21]I have not written unto you because

2:10 occasion of stumbling. Stumbling block. There should be nothing in the one who walks in the light that will cause his brother or sister to stumble or fall into sin.
2:11 darkness. A symbol of sin.
2:13 because ye have overcome the wicked one. This is only possible because Christ has overcome Satan (though this is not yet fully apparent in the world). We are shielded against Satan with the armor of God (see Heb. 2:14; Eph. 6:11; 1 John 4:4).
2:16 lust of the flesh. The desires of the sinful human nature. The notes on Romans 7:14 and Romans 7:17, "The Two Natures," will explain more about this. See *flesh.
2:19 They went out from us. Those who are against Christ in their hearts are really separated from true believers, though they may still be listed as church members.
2:20 the Holy One. The Holy Spirit has come upon you.
2:20 ye know all things. All things believers need to live and behave in a righteous way that honors God are provided by the Holy Spirit who dwells in Christians. It is through the Comforter and Helper that we have the power to overcome sin.

2:20 A Holy Unction
A special, spiritual appointment or anointing. In Old Testament times, certain objects and individuals were appointed or set apart for holy service and were anointed with oil as an indication of this fact. We know what the holy anointing oil was composed of (Exod. 30:23-35) and its special purpose (Exod. 30:26-30). Kings, priests, and prophets were anointed with oil (Exod. 30:30; 1 Sam. 10:1, 24; 16:1, 13; 1 Kings 19:16). For the believer in the Lord Jesus Christ, the *Holy Spirit Himself is the anointing by which the born-again one is set apart for service to the Lord (Acts 1:8).

ye know not the truth, but because ye
know it, and that no lie is of the truth.
22Who is a liar but he that denieth
that Jesus is the Christ? He is antichrist, that denieth the Father and the
Son.
23Whosoever denieth the Son, the
same hath not the Father: *[but] he that
acknowledgeth the Son hath the Father
also.*
24Let that therefore abide in you,
which ye have heard from the beginning. If that which ye have heard from
the beginning shall remain in you, ye
also shall continue in the Son, and in the
Father.
25And this is the promise that he hath
promised us, *even* eternal life.
26These *things* have I written unto
you concerning them that seduce you.
27But the anointing which ye have
received of him abideth in you, and ye
need not that any man teach you: but as
the same anointing teacheth you of all
things, and is truth, and is no lie, and
even as it hath taught you, ye shall
abide in him.
28And now, little children, abide in
him; that, when he shall appear, we may
have confidence, and not be ashamed
before him at his coming.
29If ye know that he is righteous, ye
know that every one that doeth *righteousness is born of him.

3 Behold, what manner of love the
Father hath bestowed upon us, that
we should be called the sons of God:
therefore the world knoweth us not,
because it knew him not.
2Beloved, now are we the sons of
God, and it doth not yet appear what
we shall be: but we know that, when he
shall appear, we shall be like him; for we
shall see him as he is.
3And every man that hath this *hope
in him purifieth himself, even as he is
pure.
4Whosoever committeth sin transgresseth also the *law: for sin is the
transgression of the law.
5And ye know that he was manifested
to take away our sins; and in him is
no sin.

2:22 denieth that Jesus is the Christ. Compare 1 John 4:3.
2:22 denieth the Father and the Son. Compare John 14:9-11.
2:25 promise . . . eternal life. For this wonderful promise see John 3:16 (see also John 3:15-16 note, "Eternal Life"); 17:2-3.
2:26 them that seduce you. This phrase means *deceive you* or *lead you astray*.
2:27 anointing. See verse 20 note above, "A Holy Unction."
2:28 when he shall appear. We do not know when this will be, but we know that it *will* be—it will definitely happen. The Christian must be serving God while he is waiting for Jesus Christ if he is not to be ashamed at the Lord's coming (1 Thess. 1:9-10; 2:12; 4:16-18). See *Christ—Second Coming and *reward.
2:29 doeth righteousness. Practices right living, acts righteously.
3:1 sons. Children (as in Matt. 5:45; John 1:12; 1 John 3:10; 5:2).
3:2 when he shall appear. Jesus Christ is coming for His own (1 Thess. 4:16-18) and, later, He is coming *with* them (Jude 14-15).
3:3 in him. In Christ.
3:3 as he is pure. There is no uncleanness of any kind in Jesus Christ. The Christian's real home is not this earth (Eph. 2:5-6). He should live, therefore, as a citizen of heaven.
3:5 take away our sins. As the Lamb of God (John 1:29; Heb. 9:26).

6 Whosoever abideth in him sinneth
not: whosoever sinneth hath not seen
him, neither known him.
7 Little children, let no man deceive
you: he that doeth righteousness is
righteous, even as he is righteous.
8 He that committeth sin is of the
*devil; for the devil sinneth from the
beginning. For this purpose the Son of
God was manifested, that he might destroy the works of the devil.
9 Whosoever is born of God doth not
commit sin; for his seed remaineth in
him: and he cannot sin, because he is
born of God.

3:9 Avoiding Sin
The phrase "commit sin" in this verse means *to practice sin* or *to go on sinning.* See verses 4, 6, and 8. Christians may fall into sin because of our old sinful nature, but we do not practice it or continue in it willfully. We have a new nature because we are born of God and that new nature does not lead us to sin. "Cannot sin" means that if we are born again, it is not possible to go on sinning willfully, because the Holy Spirit will convict us of sin, and we will want to turn away from it to stay close to God. If we do continue to sin, we should search our hearts to be sure that we are Christians.

10 In this the children of God are manifest, and the children of the devil: whosoever doeth not righteousness is not
of God, neither he that loveth not his
brother.
11 For this is the message that ye
heard from the beginning, that we
should love one another.
12 Not as Cain, *who* was of that wicked one, and slew his brother. And
wherefore slew he him? Because his
own works were evil, and his brother's
righteous.
¶13 Marvel not, my brethren, if the
world hate you.
14 We know that we have passed from
*death unto life, because we love the
brethren. He that loveth not *his* brother
abideth in death.
15 Whosoever hateth his brother is a
murderer: and ye know that no murderer hath eternal life *abiding in him.
16 Hereby perceive we the love *of
God,* because he laid down his life for
us: and we ought to lay down *our* lives
for the brethren.
17 But whoso hath this world's good,
and seeth his brother have need, and
shutteth up his *bowels *of compassion*
from him, how dwelleth the love of God
in him?
18 My little children, let us not love in
word, neither in tongue; but in deed and
in truth.
19 And hereby we know that we are of
the truth, and shall assure our hearts
before him.
20 For if our heart condemn us, God is
greater than our heart, and knoweth all
things.
21 Beloved, if our heart condemn us

3:6 abideth in him. See verse 24 for a test as to whether or not you are abiding in Him.

3:7 he that doeth righteousness. In the passages where righteousness is mentioned in this epistle, the word means the righteous life that is given to a person when he believes in Christ and is thus born again and then has the Holy Spirit living in him (Rom. 3:22; 10:10).

3:12 Not as Cain. See Genesis 4:8; Hebrews 11:4.

3:16 perceive we the love of God. We do know and realize the love of God for us.

3:16 to lay down our lives. There have been many people who were willing to lay down their lives for Christ's sake. See Acts 7:59-60; Romans 16:3-4. Read also Hebrews 11:32-38. Compare Matthew 25:31-40.

3:17 this world's good. This means *the world's goods* or *material things* that are bought and sold.

3:18 let us not love in word. Compare James 2:15-16.

3:20 For if our heart condemn us. When the believer's conscience tells him that he has done wrong, he may turn at once as the "child" or "son" (John 1:12) he is of the One who "knoweth all things" and receive help and comfort and forgiveness, if need be.

not, *then* have we confidence toward
God.
22 And whatsoever we ask, we receive
of him, because we keep his commandments, and do those things that are
pleasing in his sight.
23 And this is his commandment, That
we should believe on the name of his
Son Jesus Christ, and love one another,
as he gave us commandment.
24 And he that keepeth his commandments dwelleth in him, and he in him.
And hereby we know that he abideth in
us, by the Spirit which he hath given us.

II. Dangers in the World (4:1—5:21)

4 Beloved, believe not every spirit,
but try the spirits whether they are
of God: because many false *prophets
are gone out into the world.
2 Hereby know ye the Spirit of God:
Every spirit that confesseth that Jesus
Christ is come in the flesh is of God:
3 And every spirit that confesseth not
that Jesus Christ is come in the flesh is
not of God: and this is that *spirit* of antichrist, whereof ye have heard that it
should come; and even now already is
it in the world.
4 Ye are of God, little children, and
have overcome them: because greater
is he that is in you, than he that is in the
world.
5 They are of the world: therefore
speak they of the world, and the world
heareth them.
6 We are of God: he that knoweth God
heareth us; he that is not of God heareth
not us. Hereby know we the spirit of
truth, and the spirit of error.
¶7 Beloved, let us love one another:
for love is of God; and every one that
loveth is born of God, and knoweth God.
8 He that loveth not knoweth not God;
for God is love.
9 In this was manifested the love of
God toward us, because that God sent
his only begotten Son into the world,
that we might live through him.
10 Herein is love, not that we loved
God, but that he loved us, and sent his
Son *to be* the propitiation for our sins.
11 Beloved, if God so loved us, we
ought also to love one another.

3:21 then have we confidence. Confidence here means *boldness*—that is, freedom to approach God the Father fearlessly because of a right relationship with Him through Jesus.

3:22 whatsoever we ask. Believers may ask and receive when certain conditions are met. One condition, keeping His commandments, is given here. Read also John 14:13—ask in the name of the Lord Jesus, and 15:7; 16:23; Hebrews 11:6; Mark 11:23; Psalm 66:18; 1 John 5:14-15; Philippians 4:6; Ephesians 6:18.

3:23 his commandment. The verse shows that this commandment has two parts: faith and love. We cannot truly love believers unless we, too, have faith in Jesus, nor can we truly believe in Him without love.

3:24 dwelleth in him, and he in him. Christ is in the believer, and the believer is in Christ (John 17:21-23; Gal. 2:20; Col. 1:27 and its note, "Christ Lives in Us"; Rev. 3:20).

4:1 try the spirits. *Prove* or *test* the spirits. The tests that are to be applied are found in verses 2-3. No matter how holy men's teachings may appear to be, they must be tested by the Word of God.

4:1 false prophets. False teachers.

4:3 antichrist. See 1 John 2:18 note, "The Antichrist."

4:4 he that is in the world. Satan, "the prince of this world" (John 14:30; 16:11). See *Devil.

4:6 he that knoweth God heareth us. He who knows God as his Father, because that one is a child of God through faith in Jesus Christ (John 1:12), will listen to the teachers who speak God's truth.

4:10 not that we loved God. The love was all on God's part, not on ours. The verse conveys this meaning: "Not that we did any act of love at any time to God, but that He did the act of love to us in sending Christ."

4:11 if. The word "if" used in this way means *because* or *since*.

[12]No man hath seen God at any time.
If we love one another, God dwelleth in
us, and his love is perfected in us.

4:12 Seeing God
No man has seen the triune God–Father, Son, and Holy Spirit. See *God–the Trinity. In Jesus Christ dwells "the fulness of the Godhead" (Col. 2:9), however, and men have seen Him. Now, absent from earth, He is the One whom "having not seen, ye love" (1 Pet. 1:8). Christ gave a surprising answer to a disciple's question concerning this matter (see John 14:9).

[13]Hereby know we that we dwell in
him, and he in us, because he hath given
us of his Spirit.
[14]And we have seen and do testify
that the Father sent the Son *to be* the
Saviour of the world.
[15]Whosoever shall *confess that
Jesus is the Son of God, God dwelleth
in him, and he in God.
[16]And we have known and believed
the love that God hath to us. God is
love; and he that dwelleth in love
dwelleth in God, and God in him.
[17]Herein is our love made *perfect,
that we may have boldness in the day
of *judgment: because as he is, so are
we in this world.
[18]There is no fear in love; but perfect
love casteth out fear: because fear hath
torment. He that feareth is not made
perfect in love.
[19]We love him, because he first
loved us.
[20]If a man say, I love God, and hateth
his brother, he is a liar: for he that
loveth not his brother whom he hath
seen, how can he love God whom he
hath not seen?
[21]And this commandment have we
from him, That he who loveth God love
his brother also.

5 Whosoever believeth that Jesus
is the Christ is born of God: and
every one that loveth him that begat
loveth him also that is begotten of him.
[2]By this we know that we love the
children of God, when we love God, and
keep his commandments.
[3]For this is the love of God, that we
keep his commandments: and his commandments are not grievous.
[4]For whatsoever is born of God overcometh the world: and this is the victory that overcometh the world, *even*
our faith.
[5]Who is he that overcometh the
world, but he that believeth that Jesus
is the Son of God?
[6]This is he that came by water and
blood, *even* Jesus Christ; not by water
only, but by water and blood. And it is
the Spirit that beareth witness, because
the Spirit is truth.

5:6 Water and Blood
These words present two pictures. First, we see the Lord Jesus Christ, the Sinless One, being baptized of John the Baptist in the Jordan River (Matt. 3:13-17; Mark 1:9-11 and Mark 1:9 note, "The Baptism of Jesus"; Luke 3:21-22). The word "water" brings to mind that wonderful scene, and especially the message from heaven that was heard that day. The second picture is at Calvary, where Christ shed His blood to make atonement for our sins.

[7]For there are three that bear record
in heaven, the Father, the Word, and the
Holy Ghost: and these three are one.
[8]And there are three that bear witness in earth, the Spirit, and the water,

---

4:18 made perfect in love. See 1 John 2:5 note.
5:2 By this. Our love for fellow believers in Christ is the outward sign of our inner love to God.
5:3 For this is the love of God. Real love for God in our hearts will cause us to keep His commandments. "Of" in this context means *for* or *toward*.
5:3 commandments are not grievous. That is, they are not difficult to follow. The reason is given in Philippians 4:13 and Matthew 11:30. It is the way of the transgressor, or evildoer, who insists on going his own way, that is hard (Prov. 13:15).

and the blood: and these three agree
in one.
9 If we receive the witness of men, the
witness of God is greater: for this is the
witness of God which he hath testified
of his Son.
10 He that believeth on the Son of God
hath the witness in himself: he that
believeth not God hath made him a liar;
because he believeth not the record
that God gave of his Son.
11 And this is the record, that God
hath given to us eternal life, and this life
is in his Son.
12 He that hath the Son hath life; *and*
he that hath not the Son of God hath
not life.
13 These things have I written unto
you that believe on the name of the Son
of God; that ye may know that ye have
eternal life, and that ye may believe on
the name of the Son of God.
14 And this is the confidence that we
have in him, that, if we ask any thing
according to his will, he heareth us:
15 And if we know that he hear us,
whatsoever we ask, we know that we
have the petitions that we desired of
him.
16 If any man see his brother sin a sin
which is not unto death, he shall ask,
and he shall give him life for them that
sin not unto death. There is a sin unto
death: I do not say that he shall pray
for it.
17 All unrighteousness is sin: and
there is a sin not unto death.
18 We know that whosoever is born of
God sinneth not; but he that is begotten of God keepeth himself, and that
wicked one toucheth him not.
19 *And* we know that we are of God,
and the whole world lieth in wickedness.
20 And we know that the Son of God
is come, and hath given us an understanding, that we may know him that is
true, and we are in him that is true, *even*
in his Son Jesus Christ. This is the true
God, and eternal life.
21 Little children, keep yourselves
from idols. Amen.

5:10 hath the witness in himself. The Christian has the Spirit of God dwelling in him. See 1 John 3:24 note and John 14:16 note.

5:16 his brother. When the Christian receives Jesus Christ as his Saviour, he becomes a child of God (John 1:12). This, of course, means that God is his Father, and that all other fellow believers in Christ are his brothers (and sisters).

5:16 There is a sin unto death. This speaks of believers—not of spiritual *death, but of physical death, as chastisement for some sin that remains persistent. Read about Ananias and Sapphira (Acts 5:1-11), and see also James 5:15 and its note, "Prayer for the Sick."

5:18 whosoever is born of God sinneth not. See 1 John 3:9 note, "Avoiding Sin."

5:18 keepeth himself. The believer's part in the keeping is to yield to the *Holy Spirit who dwells in him. His old nature, called the "natural man" (1 Cor. 2:14), is still present, still able to sin, but the believer can have the victory over "that wicked one," Satan, and his old nature through Christ (Rom. 7:24-25).

5:21 keep yourselves from idols. Guard yourselves; be on the watch against any object of worship other than the Lord.

The Second Epistle of

JOHN

THE WRITER AND TIME

This epistle was written by the Apostle John after A.D. 90.

THEME

John's Second Epistle was written to emphasize the importance of the "truth," to help the believers to walk or live correctly in times of evil teaching or doctrine. Read the introduction to 1 John.

OUTLINE OF 2 JOHN

I.	Truth and Love in the Christian Walk	2 John 1-6
II.	The Danger of Unscriptural Ways	2 John 7-11
III.	Greetings	2 John 12-13

I. Truth and Love (1-6)

1The *elder unto the *elect lady and
her children, whom I love in the truth;
and not I only, but also all they that have
known the truth;
2For the truth's sake, which dwelleth
in us, and shall be with us for ever.
3Grace be with you, mercy, *and*
peace, from God the Father, and from
the Lord Jesus Christ, the Son of the
Father, in truth and love.
¶4I rejoiced greatly that I found of thy
children walking in truth, as we have
received a commandment from the Father.
5And now I beseech thee, lady, not as
though I wrote a new commandment
unto thee, but that which we had from
the beginning, that we love one another.
6And this is love, that we walk after
his commandments. This is the commandment, That, as ye have heard from
the beginning, ye should walk in it.

II. Danger of Unscriptural Ways (7-11)

7For many deceivers are entered into
the world, who confess not that Jesus
Christ is come in the flesh. This is a
deceiver and an antichrist.
8Look to yourselves, that we lose not
those things which we have wrought,
but that we receive a full reward.
9Whosoever transgresseth, and
abideth not in the doctrine of Christ,
hath not God. He that abideth in the

---

1 The elder. John spoke here of himself.
1 the elect lady. Some scholars believe that John wrote this epistle to the *church, the "elect lady," but many others believe that it was addressed to a real Christian woman and her children.
2 which dwelleth in us. The Word of God (see Col. 3:16; 1 Pet. 1:23).
4 walking in truth. Living according to God's Word and yielding to the Holy Spirit.
5 love one another. This is the keynote of John's teaching. See 1 John 4:11,16; 2 John 6.
7 an antichrist. As used here, the name means someone who is an enemy of and purposely opposes the Lord Jesus Christ. See 1 John 2:18. Do not confuse this with the *Antichrist of Revelation 13:1-8.

doctrine of Christ, he hath both the Father and the Son.

10 If there come any unto you, and bring not this doctrine, receive him not into *your* house, neither bid him God speed:

11 For he that biddeth him God speed is partaker of his evil deeds.

III. Greetings (12-13)

¶ 12 Having many things to write unto you, I would not *write* with paper and ink: but I trust to come unto you, and speak face to face, that our joy may be full.

13 The children of thy elect sister greet thee. Amen.

The Third Epistle of

JOHN

THE WRITER AND TIME

This third epistle was written by the Apostle John after A.D. 90.

THEME

The Third Epistle of John, addressed to Gaius, a Christian, emphasized the importance of the "truth," or the Scriptures, in days of difficulty within the church. John had evidently written an earlier letter (3 John 9) to this church, but a domineering brother named Diotrephes had refused to receive it and had also refused to receive other brethren. This shows the beginning, even before the end of the first century, of attempts to spoil the simple order of the early church by ambitious men who tried to get too much authority. See the introduction to 1 John.

OUTLINE OF 3 JOHN

I.	Greetings	3 John 1-4
II.	Advice	3 John 5-8
III.	The Domineering Diotrephes	3 John 9-11
IV.	The Good Demetrius	3 John 12-14

I. Greetings (1-4)

1The *elder unto the wellbeloved
Gaius, whom I love in the truth.

¶2Beloved, I wish above all things
that thou mayest prosper and be in
health, even as thy soul prospereth.

3For I rejoiced greatly, when the
brethren came and testified of the truth
that is in thee, even as thou walkest in
the truth.

4I have no greater joy than to hear
that my children walk in truth.

II. Advice (5-8)

5Beloved, thou doest faithfully whatsoever thou doest to the brethren, and
to strangers;

6Which have borne witness of thy
charity before the *church: whom if
thou bring forward on their journey after a godly sort, thou shalt do
well:

7Because that for his name's sake
they went forth, taking nothing of the
Gentiles.

8We therefore ought to receive such,
that we might be fellowhelpers to the
truth.

III. The Domineering Diotrephes (9-11)

¶9I wrote unto the church: but Diotrephes, who loveth to have the preeminence among them, receiveth us
not.

---

2 above all things. The writer's greatest desire is for the reader to prosper.

4 my children. Christians who had been converted through the apostle or who had been greatly helped by him. Compare 1 Corinthians 4:15.

4 walk in truth. Live according to the will of God.

6 charity. A type of love. See 1 Corinthians 13; see also *charity.

[10]Wherefore, if I come, I will remember his deeds which he doeth,
prating against us with malicious
words: and not content therewith,
neither doth he himself receive the
brethren, and forbiddeth them that
would, and casteth *them* out of the
church.

¶[11]Beloved, follow not that which is
evil, but that which is good. He that
doeth good is of God: but he that doeth
evil hath not seen God.

IV. The Good Demetrius (12-14)

[12]Demetrius hath good report of all
men, and of the truth itself: yea, and we
also bear record; and ye know that our
record is true.

¶[13]I had many things to write, but I
will not with ink and pen write unto
thee:

[14]But I trust I shall shortly see thee,
and we shall speak face to face. Peace
be to thee. *Our* friends salute thee.
Greet the friends by name.

The General Epistle of

JUDE

THE WRITER AND TIME

Jude, formerly called Judas, must not be confused with Judas Iscariot. One rarely, if ever, hears of a person today named Judas, because of the stigma attached to the name on account of Judas Iscariot's sin. Jude was probably the half brother of Jesus. The date of the epistle is A.D. 66.

THEME

As Jude was planning to write an epistle to explain the way of salvation, he heard that false teachers had slyly crept in among the believers. He changed his original plan and wrote this letter which bears his name (vss. 3-4). In the last days of this age (see *dispensations), before the Lord Jesus Christ comes back to judge and rule the earth, there will be a great outbreak of false teachers right within the churches. The placement of Jude near the end of the Bible suggests that it was written especially for those people who live in the last days. Many false teachers are now in the churches! The letter describes the false teachers, foretells their sure destruction, and tells believers that they must "earnestly contend for the faith" (vs. 3).

OUTLINE OF JUDE

I.	Danger of False Teachers	Jude 1-16
II.	Duty to Fight for God's Truth	Jude 17-25

I. Danger of False Teachers (1-16)

[1]Jude, the servant of Jesus Christ,
and brother of James, to them that are
sanctified by God the Father, and preserved in Jesus Christ, *and* called:
[2]Mercy unto you, and peace, and
love, be multiplied.
¶[3]Beloved, when I gave all diligence
to write unto you of the common *salvation, it was needful for me to write
unto you, and exhort *you* that ye should
earnestly contend for the faith which
was once delivered unto the saints.
[4]For there are certain men crept in
unawares, who were before of old ordained to this condemnation, ungodly men, turning the grace of our God
into lasciviousness, and denying the

---

1 preserved. Kept by God. God uses this word to describe the believer's *assurance in Christ.

3 common salvation. Common to, or shared by, every believer.

3 contend. To contend does not mean to be contentious, or to argue; it does mean to *stand for the faith at all costs*.

3 once. Once for all; that is, never to be changed or added to.

4 ordained to this condemnation. The prophets predicted the condemnation of these men; see verses 14-15.

4 lasciviousness. Unclean greediness. They say, "If we are saved by grace, and not by works, then we can sin as much as we please!" Those who say such a thing are not saved, for true believers are not "pleased" to sin.

only Lord God, and our Lord Jesus
Christ.

False teachers shall be destroyed:
1. As were the unbelieving Israelites

5 I will therefore put you in remembrance, though ye once knew this, how that the Lord, having saved the people out of the land of Egypt, afterward destroyed them that believed not.

2. As will be the fallen angels

6 And the *angels which kept not their first estate, but left their own habitation, he hath reserved in everlasting chains under darkness unto the judgment of the great day.

3. As were the sinners of Sodom and Gomorrha

7 Even as Sodom and Gomorrha, and the cities about them in like manner, giving themselves over to fornication, and going after strange flesh, are set forth for an example, suffering the vengeance of eternal fire.
8 Likewise also these *filthy* dreamers defile the flesh, despise dominion, and speak evil of dignities.
9 Yet Michael the archangel, when contending with the devil he disputed about the body of Moses, durst not bring against him a railing accusation, but said, The Lord rebuke thee.
10 But these speak evil of those things which they know not: but what they know naturally, as brute beasts, in those things they corrupt themselves.

4. As were Cain and Balaam and Core

11 Woe unto them! for they have gone in the way of Cain, and ran greedily after the error of Balaam for reward, and perished in the gainsaying of Core.
12 These are spots in your feasts of charity, when they feast with you, feeding themselves without fear: clouds *they are* without water, carried about of winds; trees whose fruit withereth, without fruit, twice dead, plucked up by the roots;
13 Raging waves of the sea, foaming out their own shame; wandering stars, to whom is reserved the blackness of darkness for ever.

---

6 first estate. The word "estate" here means the conditions under which the angels were created and their original position in heaven.
6 left their own habitation. They left their home, in this case, heaven.
6 the judgment of the great day. This speaks of the *Day of the Lord when Satan and the fallen angels will be judged, just before the final judgment. See *judgment.
8 speak evil of dignities. One way people do this is by making fun of the idea that there is a person called Satan. Though he is so wicked, he is of high angelic rank. See also 2 Peter 2:10.
9 Yet Michael. See 2 Peter 2:11. The great archangel Michael refused to take authority that was not his.
9 body of Moses. There is no record of this dispute. It probably took place at the time of Moses' secret burial (Deut. 34:5-6).
11 way of Cain. See Genesis 4:1-12. Cain wanted to worship God in his own way—not in God's way. He rejected the truth of pardon by an atoning sacrifice. Some who despise the Lamb of God, in this day, fall into the same sin.
11 error of Balaam. Balaam *hired himself out* as a prophet! See Numbers 22–24; 31:16.
11 gainsaying of Core. Gainsaying means *against the Word.* Core (Hebrew *Korah*) rebelled against Aaron, God's appointed high priest. See Numbers 16.
12 spots. False teachers.
12 feasts of charity. Love feasts prior to the Lord's Supper (Communion), or special gatherings of Christians in loving fellowship.
12 feeding themselves. The context shows that they are: "Shepherds that without fear feed themselves," instead of the sheep. A "teacher" (these were false teachers) who denies or withholds from his people our Lord Jesus Christ as the Son of God and the Bread of Life falls under this solemn condemnation.

5. As Enoch prophesied

14And Enoch also, the seventh from
Adam, prophesied of these, saying, Behold, the Lord cometh with ten thousands of his saints,
15To execute *judgment upon all, and
to convince all that are ungodly among
them of all their ungodly deeds which
they have ungodly committed, and of all
their hard *speeches* which ungodly sinners have spoken against him.
16These are murmurers, complain-
ers, walking after their own *lusts; and
their mouth speaketh great swelling
words, having men's persons in admiration because of advantage.

II. Duty to Fight for God's Truth (17-25)

¶17But, beloved, remember ye the
words which were spoken before of the
*apostles of our Lord Jesus Christ;
18How that they told you there should
be mockers in the last time, who should
walk after their own ungodly lusts.
19These be they who separate themselves, sensual, having not the Spirit.
20But ye, beloved, building up yourselves on your most holy faith, praying
in the Holy Ghost,
21Keep yourselves in the love of God,
looking for the mercy of our Lord Jesus
Christ unto eternal life.
22And of some have compassion,
making a difference:

23 Spotted by the Flesh
A garment is that which covers, like clothing. A friendly manner may cover a heart not right with God. If things that are quite all right in themselves have been spotted by the world, the Christian must have nothing to do with them. Brass is a good metal; God commanded that the brazen serpent be made (Num. 21:8-9; see Num. 21:8 note, "The Fiery Serpent"); but when the Israelites worshipped the serpent it was "spotted by the flesh," and Hezekiah destroyed it (2 Kings 18:4). See *flesh.

23And others save with fear, pulling
them out of the fire; hating even the
garment spotted by the *flesh.
¶24Now unto him that is able to keep
you from falling, and to present *you*
faultless before the presence of his
glory with exceeding joy,
25To the only wise God our Saviour,
be glory and majesty, dominion and
power, both now and ever. Amen.

24 Being Faultless
To be faultless is better than to be merely blameless. As long as Christians are on earth with our old sinful natures, we shall have faults, but God will not blame us for them since He has already laid the blame on Christ. One day, however, when we are glorified, these sinful natures will be gone forever; then we shall not only be blameless but without fault. Then we shall be perfectly conformed to the image of the Lord Jesus Christ.

---

17 remember ye the words. Jude does not seem to have been an apostle. See Acts 20:29; 1 Timothy 4:1-2; 2 Timothy 3:1; 2 Peter 3:2.
18 they told you. Peter, among others, had made it very plain (2 Pet. 3:1-4).
19 separate themselves. Not from the world or from unbelief, as Christians should do, but instead they separate themselves from true, earnest Christians.
19 sensual. Worldly minded.
20 praying in the Holy Ghost. One who is willing that God should have His way at all costs can be fully controlled by the Holy Spirit so that he really desires and prays for what is in the will of God. Such prayer is always answered.
21 Keep yourselves in the love of God. It is not that we must keep God loving us! We are to keep our footsteps in the way that His love directs. We are also to stay away from and not listen to false teaching.
22 of some. We must be careful to distinguish between those who have only been deceived for a time with false doctrine and those who are willfully rebellious against God's truth. Second John 10 tells how to treat the latter.
23 with fear. Contact with false teaching is dangerous for the Christian.
24 falling. Stumbling. The Lord not only keeps us from falling in our Christian walk, He keeps us even from stumbling.

The REVELATION *of Saint John*

THE WRITER AND TIME

The Apostle John, the last surviving apostle, wrote the last Gospel, the last epistle, and the last book in the New Testament. He was exiled to Patmos, a rocky island in the Mediterranean, during a time of persecution, and there he saw this vision. The date of writing was about A.D. 96.

BACKGROUND

Some people think that this is a book that cannot be understood, but the Spirit of God in verse 1 calls it a "revelation." A revelation is something that uncovers, or reveals. This book, then, tells something God wants us to know. He promises in Revelation 1:3 a special blessing for reading this book. Much of it is written in sign language because we on earth know very little of the language of heaven and the unseen world. Therefore, when God wants to tell of things in heaven, He uses signs or symbols; every one of them is used and explained somewhere else in the Bible, so that we shall be sure not to misunderstand Him.

THINGS TO NOTE

There are four things to notice and remember as we read the Revelation:

1. Its True Name. It is not *Revelations*, as it is so often called, but *Revelation,* one great unveiling. The Gospels showed the Lord Jesus as He was on earth, a Saviour, dying for sinners. The Revelation shows Him as He is now and will be, a Priest-King, judging sin. Because this book is the Revelation of Jesus Christ, everything in it centers around Him.

2. Its Subject: Judgment, in the sense of setting things right. Sin must be judged before righteousness and peace can come into the world to stay. This book shows the Lord Jesus Christ judging first the church's witness in this world, then the sin of the world, then Satan. Judgment prepares the way for His everlasting kingdom.

3. Its Order. From chapter 4 on, the events move along very much as they do in a novel; that is, the story goes to a certain point, then takes us to another scene to pick up on other characters and tell what was happening in the meantime to them. The scene shifts often from heaven to earth and back again. Now and then a hint is given of something that is to happen much later in the story.

4. Its Outline: Given by the Lord Jesus Christ Himself in His command to the Apostle John, in Revelation 1:19.

OUTLINE OF REVELATION

I.	The Vision that John had just seen of Christ ("The Things Which Thou Hast Seen")	Revelation 1:1-20
II.	The Spiritual Condition of the Church during the Whole Church Age, from the descent of the Holy Spirit (Acts 2) to the taking up of the Church (1 Thessalonians 4) ("The Things Which Are")	Revelation 2:1—3:22
III.	The Things that Will Happen after the Church is Taken up out of the World. ("The Things Which Shall Be Hereafter ")	Revelation 4:1—22:21

I. "The Things Which Thou Hast Seen" (1:1-20)

Introduction

1 The *Revelation of Jesus *Christ,
which *God gave unto him, to
shew unto his servants things which
must shortly come to pass; and he sent
and signified *it* by his *angel unto his
servant John:
2Who bare record of the word of God,
and of the testimony of Jesus Christ,
and of all things that he saw.
3Blessed *is* he that readeth, and
they that hear the words of this *prophecy, and keep those things which are
written therein: for the time *is* at
hand.
4John to the seven churches which
are in Asia: *Grace *be* unto you, and
*peace, from him which is, and which
was, and which is to come; and from the
seven Spirits which are before his
throne;
5And from Jesus Christ, *who is* the
faithful witness, *and* the first begotten
of the dead, and the prince of the kings
of the earth. Unto him that loved us, and
washed us from our sins in his own
*blood,
6And hath made us kings and priests
unto God and his Father; to him *be* glory and dominion for ever and ever.
*Amen.
7Behold, he cometh with clouds; and
every eye shall see him, and they *also*
which pierced him: and all kindreds of
the earth shall wail because of him.
Even so, Amen.
8I am Alpha and Omega, the beginning and the ending, saith the Lord,

1:1 shortly come to pass. When the events begin to occur, they will occur rapidly. "Shortly" is translated from the Greek word from which we get our English word "tachometer," which measures speed. "Shortly" is to be interpreted by eternal standards (see Ps. 90:4).

1:3 the time is at hand. We live in the same *dispensation in which John was living when he wrote. When the dispensation ends, "the things which shall be" (Rev. 1:19) will begin to happen.

1:4 seven Spirits. There are not seven Holy Spirits. John was speaking of one Spirit in His perfect fullness, because seven is the number of perfection—compare 1 Corinthians 12:4,13; Isaiah 11:2.

1:7 every eye. When the Lord Jesus Christ returns publicly to set up His *kingdom.

1:8 Alpha and Omega. The first and last letters of the Greek alphabet. In English this

which is, and which was, and which is
to come, the Almighty.

The vision

¶ 9 I John, who also am your brother,
and companion in tribulation, and in the
*kingdom and patience of Jesus Christ,
was in the isle that is called Patmos, for
the word of God, and for the testimony
of Jesus Christ.
10 I was in the Spirit on the Lord's day,
and heard behind me a great voice, as
of a trumpet,
11 Saying, I am Alpha and Omega, the
first and the last: and, What thou seest,
write in a book, and send *it* unto the seven
churches which are in Asia; unto Ephesus, and unto Smyrna, and unto Pergamos, and unto Thyatira, and unto Sardis,
and unto Philadelphia, and unto Laodicea.
12 And I turned to see the voice that
spake with me. And being turned, I saw
seven golden candlesticks;
13 And in the midst of the seven
candlesticks *one* like unto the Son of
man, clothed with a garment down to
the foot, and girt about the paps with a
golden girdle.
14 His head and *his* hairs *were* white
like wool, as white as snow; and his
eyes *were* as a flame of fire;
15 And his feet like unto fine brass, as
if they burned in a furnace; and his
voice as the sound of many waters.
16 And he had in his right hand seven
stars: and out of his mouth went a
sharp twoedged sword: and his countenance *was* as the sun shineth in his
strength.
17 And when I saw him, I fell at his
feet as dead. And he laid his right hand
upon me, saying unto me, Fear not; I am
the first and the last:
18 *I am* he that liveth, and was dead;
and, behold, I am alive for evermore,
Amen; and have the keys of hell and of
*death.
¶ 19 Write the things which thou hast
seen, and the things which are, and the
things which shall be hereafter;
20 The *mystery of the seven stars
which thou sawest in my right hand,
and the seven golden candlesticks. The
seven stars are the angels of the seven
churches: and the seven candlesticks
which thou sawest are the seven
churches.

II. "The Things Which Are" (2:1—3:21)

*1. The Message to Ephesus: the early years of the *Church*

2 Unto the angel of the church of
Ephesus write; These things saith
he that holdeth the seven stars in his

---

would read "I am A to Z," that is, the whole alphabet—or the beginning and end of all things. Christ is everything.

1:13 like unto the Son of man. This is not a picture of what the Lord Jesus Christ actually looked like. Every detail of John's vision is a symbol of some quality which struck John particularly as he looked. For instance, "His head . . . white as snow" speaks of purity and age—the fact that He is eternal; and "his eyes were as a flame of fire" (vs. 14), showing the searching intensity of His judgment.

1:13 girt about the paps. Band around the chest. A girdle was worn in this way in Eastern countries by either a king or a priest. The Lord Jesus Christ is both. As a Priest, He must judge the sins of His people; as King, He must judge rebels and set up His *kingdom. In the Revelation He is seen doing both.

1:16 seven stars. Verse 20 explains what these are. His right hand is a place of safety.

1:16 sword. The sword in Christ's mouth shows the power of the message and that His words of judgment are sharp as swords (Isa. 49:2; Eph. 6:17; Heb. 4:12).

1:18 have the keys of hell. Hell here is *Hades.

1:20 candlesticks. Or *lampstands*. In those times, people used oil lamps to light their homes. The lamps could be carried or set down. The lampstand was a pedestal about the height of a floor lamp, on which the lamp was placed to throw light over the whole room.

2:1 Ephesus. See Revelation 3:6 note, "The Seven Churches."

1:20 Angels
These are *literally* angels, just as in John's other seventy references to angels in this book. Much like the angel used to give the revelation to John (see Rev. 1:1), these angels communicate the message of God to these literal churches of the future. In the future, God is going to frequently use angels in a more visibly supernatural way. For example, Rev. 14:6 refers to an angel that will have the everlasting gospel. Children have angels (Matt. 18:10), God sent His angel to Peter (Acts 12:11)—why not to the churches?

right hand, who walketh in the midst of
the seven golden candlesticks;
2 I know thy works, and thy labour,
and thy patience, and how thou canst
not bear them which are evil: and thou
hast tried them which say they are
*apostles, and are not, and hast found
them liars:
3 And hast borne, and hast patience,
and for my name's sake hast laboured,
and hast not fainted.
4 Nevertheless I have *somewhat*
against thee, because thou hast left thy
first love.
5 Remember therefore from whence
thou art fallen, and *repent, and do the
first works; or else I will come unto
thee quickly, and will remove thy
candlestick out of his place, except thou
repent.
6 But this thou hast, that thou hatest
the deeds of the Nicolaitans, which I
also hate.
7 He that hath an ear, let him hear
what the Spirit saith unto the churches;
To him that overcometh will I give to
eat of the *tree of life, which is in the
midst of the *paradise of God.

2. The message to Smyrna: the period of great persecutions (A.D. 100-300)

¶8 And unto the angel of the church in
Smyrna write; These things saith the
first and the last, which was dead, and
is alive;
9 I know thy works, and tribulation,
and poverty, (but thou art rich) and *I
know* the blasphemy of them which say
they are Jews, and are not, but *are* the
*synagogue of *Satan.
10 Fear none of those things which
thou shalt suffer: behold, the *devil shall
cast *some* of you into prison, that ye may
be tried; and ye shall have tribulation
ten days: be thou faithful unto death,
and I will give thee a crown of life.
11 He that hath an ear, let him hear
what the Spirit saith unto the churches;

2:1 THE MESSAGES TO THE CHURCHES

These messages to the churches should be read in four ways:

1. as messages to seven particular churches at the time when John wrote;
2. as a history of the whole church from the beginning to the end of its stay on the earth;
3. as messages to the whole church during the whole church age, for the same kinds of temptations and failures and victories can always be found in various sections of the whole church as long as it is on earth; and
4. as personal messages to each believer. It is important to remember the distinction between "the church"—all the people who say they are Christians, and the "true *church"—those who are really born again. A "local church" means a group of both true and professing Christians who "belong" to a certain church in a certain town.

2:5 remove. This does not mean that any persons who are born of God can ever be lost; that would contradict other parts of the Bible. The Lord Jesus means that He will not use that church anymore as a lamp to shine for Him.

2:6 Nicolaitans. We have no certain information about these people. The word "nicolaitans" comes from two Greek words, meaning *to conquer* and *the people.* It seems to indicate that there were some church leaders even in these early days who wanted to hold office and get power over the people. They distinguished between themselves and the people as "the clergy" and "the laity."

2:8 Smyrna. See Revelation 3:6 note, "The Seven Churches."

He that overcometh shall not be hurt of
the *second death.

3. The message to Pergamos: the period when the Church joined the world (about A.D. 300-500)

¶12And to the angel of the church in
Pergamos write; These things saith he
which hath the sharp sword with two
edges;
13I know thy works, and where thou
dwellest, *even* where Satan's seat *is:*
and thou holdest fast my name, and hast
not denied my faith, even in those days
wherein Antipas *was* my faithful martyr, who was slain among you, where
Satan dwelleth.
14But I have a few things against
thee, because thou hast there them that
hold the *doctrine of *Balaam, who
taught Balac to cast a stumblingblock
before the children of *Israel, to eat
things sacrificed unto idols, and to commit fornication.
15So hast thou also them that hold the
doctrine of the Nicolaitans, which thing
I hate.
16Repent; or else I will come unto
thee quickly, and will fight against them
with the sword of my mouth.
17He that hath an ear, let him hear
what the Spirit saith unto the churches;
To him that overcometh will I give to
eat of the hidden *manna, and will give

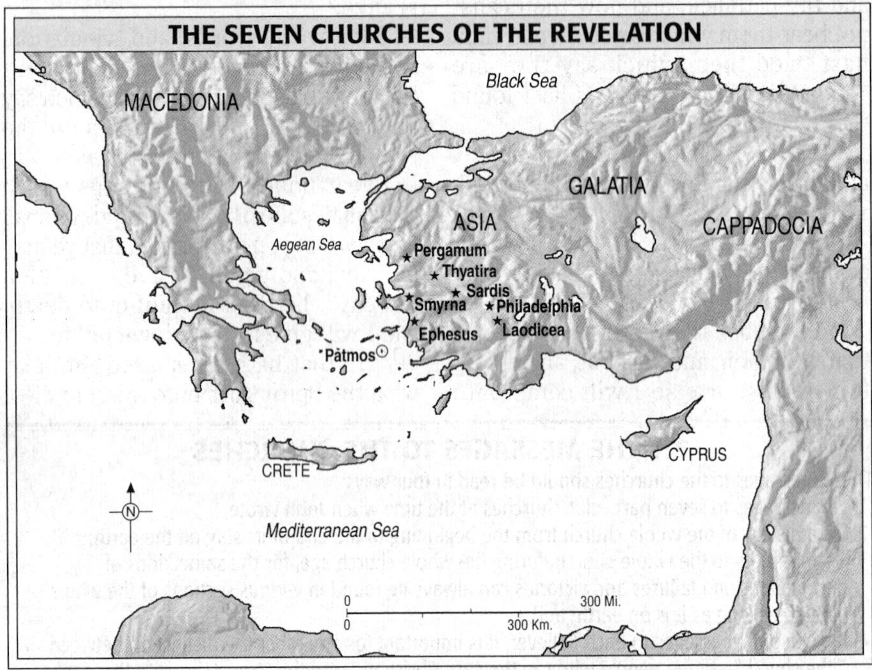

2:12 Pergamos. See Revelation 3:6 note, "The Seven Churches."
2:13 Satan's seat. This means the center of heathen religion with which the church was now in close contact since the recognition by Constantine.
2:13 martyr. A martyr is one who is slain for his faith in a cause. The word for "witness" in the Greek is *martys*—it is the root from which we get our word "martyr." So many believers, witnesses for Christ, were slain in these days that the words "martyr" and "witness" became somewhat synonymous.
2:14 doctrine of Balaam. Balaam was a man who pretended to follow God's commands, but he taught the children of Israel to try to get around them and thus have their own way. See Numbers 22–24; 31:15-17.
2:15 doctrine of the Nicolaitans. See 2:6 note. What formerly were deeds or acts had become a doctrine, a teaching of the church.

him a white stone, and in the stone a
new name written, which no man
knoweth saving he that receiveth *it.*

4. The message to Thyatira: the period of Roman power over the Church (about A.D. 500-1500)

¶18 And unto the angel of the church
in Thyatira write; These things saith
the Son of God, who hath his eyes like
unto a flame of fire, and his feet *are* like
fine brass;
19 I know thy works, and *charity, and
service, and faith, and thy patience, and
thy works; and the last *to be* more than
the first.
20 Notwithstanding I have a few things
against thee, because thou sufferest that
woman Jezebel, which calleth herself a
prophetess, to teach and to seduce my
servants to commit fornication, and to
eat things sacrificed unto idols.
21 And I gave her space to repent of
her fornication; and she *repented not.
22 Behold, I will cast her into a bed,
and them that commit adultery with her
into *great tribulation, except they repent of their deeds.
23 And I will kill her children with
death; and all the churches shall know
that I am he which searcheth the reins
and hearts: and I will give unto every
one of you according to your works.
24 But unto you I say, and unto the rest
in Thyatira, as many as have not this
doctrine, and which have not known the
depths of Satan, as they speak; I will put
upon you none other burden.
25 But that which ye have *already* hold
fast till I come.
26 And he that overcometh, and
keepeth my works unto the end, to him
will I give power over the nations:
27 And he shall rule them with a rod
of iron; as the vessels of a potter shall
they be broken to shivers: even as I
received of my Father.
28 And I will give him the morning star.
29 He that hath an ear, let him hear
what the Spirit saith unto the churches.

5. The message to Sardis: the period of the Reformations (from about A.D. 1500 on)

3 And unto the angel of the church
in Sardis write; These things saith
he that hath the seven Spirits of God,
and the seven stars; I know thy works,
that thou hast a name that thou livest,
and art dead.
2 Be watchful, and strengthen the
things which remain, that are ready to
die: for I have not found thy works *perfect before God.
3 Remember therefore how thou hast
received and heard, and hold fast, and
repent. If therefore thou shalt not
watch, I will come on thee as a thief,
and thou shalt not know what hour I will
come upon thee.

2:17 hidden manna. Jesus Christ is the Bread that came down from heaven, the antitype of the manna of the wilderness. "Hidden" may refer to the fact that those who do not know Him cannot understand the joy that the believer has in Him.
2:17 white stone. The custom of voting affirmatively with small white stones, and negatively with black stones, dates back to the ceremonial court held in Athens at the Areopagus. A judge voting for acquittal put in the white stone; for guilt, the black stone. This fashion has carried down through the centuries and is used today in many fraternal organizations, and the like, for elections. The "white stone" speaks of our acquittal in the matter of our sins, which were placed upon Jesus Christ on the cross.
2:18 Thyatira. See Revelation 3:6 note, "The Seven Churches."
2:25 till I come. This is the first promise in these messages of His coming. It is given to faithful believers who love the Lord and hate evil.
2:27 rule. In the *kingdom of the Lord on earth, sin will be judged instantly and righteously.
3:1 Sardis. See verse 6 note, "The Seven Churches."
3:3 as a thief. These are not the words of the heavenly bridegroom to the true church, His bride, but the warning of the Lord to those who say that they are Christians but are unfaithful to Him.

[4]Thou hast a few names even in Sardis which have not defiled their garments; and they shall walk with me in white: for they are worthy.
[5]He that overcometh, the same shall be clothed in white raiment; and I will not blot out his name out of the book of life, but I will *confess his name before my Father, and before his angels.
[6]He that hath an ear, let him hear what the Spirit saith unto the churches.

3:6 THE SEVEN CHURCHES

1. Ephesus (2:1): Ephesus means *full-purposed* or *desirable*. God had a purpose in forming the true church, and, though the local church may fail, He will surely complete His purpose. The local church at Ephesus failed because they ceased to love Jesus Christ more than anything else. Ephesus pictures the first few years of church history before the persecutions began to be severe.
2. Smyrna (2:8): Smyrna speaks of *bitterness* or *suffering*. This church pictures the time when the Roman emperors persecuted the true church. Many Christians were thrown to the lions and many were burned at the stake. But the more they suffered for Christ, the more joyous they were in their fellowship with Him and their witness for Him.
3. Pergamos (2:12): Pergamos means *mixed marriage*. God intends that the church shall be the bride of Christ (see 2 Cor. 11:2-3), but about A.D. 300 the Roman Emperor Constantine said that he was going to be a Christian, so he stopped the persecutions and commanded everyone in his empire to accept Christianity. He offered to build beautiful churches and to give a great deal of money to them. The church leaders accepted his offer, for it sounded very fine. Thousands of heathen priests who would have been out of office pretended to obey the command. Without any real repentance from sin or belief in Jesus Christ as Saviour, millions of heathen began to call themselves Christians. The church thought how wonderful it was that all these people were becoming Christians. They gave up looking for the early return of Jesus and settled down to enjoy heathen pleasures and power in this world. It was as if the church became "married" to the *world. Many heathen customs and ceremonies soon became a part of church services almost without the true Christians realizing it. The real truth of the gospel was almost hidden under a mass of ceremony, untruth, and traditions of men.
4. Thyatira (2:18): The name means *continual sacrifice* and indicates the error into which the church fell in this period, in ignoring the fact that the one sacrifice of Christ on the cross was sufficient to forgive all sin (Heb. 10:12). In prophetic-historic meaning, Thyatira speaks of the period in which the rule over the church was given to one man as its head around A.D. 500. Christ is the Head of the church, and no man has a right to usurp His authority (see 1 Tim. 2:5).
5. Sardis (3:1): Sardis means *those escaped*. The message describes those in the whole *church who protested against erroneous teaching begun in Pergamos and carried on in Thyatira, and these protesters tried to reform the church. The protest started about A.D. 1500 when the Spirit of God began to raise up, from time to time, servants of His to bring to light many truths of the Bible, which had been lost to the church as a whole by being buried under untruths. The danger into which the Protestant churches fell was of professing to believe all the doctrines of the Bible but of failing to carry them out in their own lives. This is why the Lord said to them: "Thou hast a name that thou livest, and art dead" (Rev. 3:1).
6. Philadelphia (3:7): Philadelphia means *brotherly love*. During this period, following the Reformation (Sardis), the Holy Spirit began to revive many believers and to draw them closer together in brotherly love, even though Europe as a whole was being torn apart by fearful religious wars. The Holy Spirit could do this because the people truly loved the Lord Jesus Christ and His Word. The test is "Thou . . . hast kept my word, and hast not denied my name" (Rev. 3:8).
7. Laodicea (3:14): Laodicea means *the people speak*. This message is for the *church at a time when they cared more for the words of man than for the Word of God. The city of Laodicea was noted for its warm springs, pleasant for bathing but sickening to drink, and it is a picture of the church just before her Lord returns. Though some were warmly devoted and some utterly cold, most were the mixture of lukewarmness that is disgusting to the Lord.

6. The message to Philadelphia: the period when true believers stand out against unbelief in the Church (about A.D. 1800 onwards)

¶7 And to the angel of the church in Philadelphia write; These things saith he that is *holy, he that is true, he that hath the key of *David, he that openeth, and no man shutteth; and shutteth, and no man openeth;

8 I know thy works: behold, I have set before thee an open door, and no man can shut it: for thou hast a little strength, and hast kept my word, and hast not denied my name.

9 Behold, I will make them of the synagogue of Satan, which say they are Jews, and are not, but do lie; behold, I will make them to come and worship before thy feet, and to know that I have loved thee.

10 Because thou hast kept the word of my patience, I also will keep thee from the hour of *temptation, which shall come upon all the *world, to try them that dwell upon the earth.

11 Behold, I come quickly: hold that fast which thou hast, that no man take thy crown.

3:10 The Hour of Temptation
The hour of temptation is the *Tribulation that is described in Revelation 6–19. This verse seems to promise that the "true church" will be taken out of the world before that time–to be with the Lord. Of course, most of the true church would not go through it, for they have already finished their earthly lives. This promise is to believers who are on the earth at the end of the *church age (see 1 Thess. 5:5-9).

12 Him that overcometh will I make a pillar in the temple of my God, and he shall go no more out: and I will write upon him the name of my God, and the name of the city of my God, *which is* new *Jerusalem, which cometh down out of *heaven from my God: and *I will write upon him* my new name.

13 He that hath an ear, let him hear what the Spirit saith unto the churches.

7. The message to Laodicea: the period at the very end of the Church Age

¶14 And unto the angel of the church of the Laodiceans write; These things saith the Amen, the faithful and true witness, the beginning of the creation of God;

15 I know thy works, that thou art neither cold nor hot: I would thou wert cold or hot.

16 So then because thou art lukewarm, and neither cold nor hot, I will spue thee out of my mouth.

17 Because thou sayest, I am rich, and increased with goods, and have need of nothing; and knowest not that thou art wretched, and miserable, and poor, and blind, and naked:

18 I counsel thee to buy of me gold tried in the fire, that thou mayest be rich; and white raiment, that thou mayest be clothed, and *that* the shame of thy nakedness do not appear; and anoint thine eyes with eyesalve, that thou mayest see.

19 As many as I love, I rebuke and *chasten: be zealous therefore, and repent.

20 Behold, I stand at the door, and knock: if any man hear my voice, and

3:7 Philadelphia. See verse 6 note, "The Seven Churches."
3:7 the key of David. See Isaiah 22:22.
3:14 Laodiceans. See verse 6 note, "The Seven Churches."
3:18 buy. This does not mean that salvation can be bought. The Lord Jesus Christ is urging them to exchange worldly wealth for heavenly glory.
3:18 eyesalve. The city of Laodicea was famous for its school of medicine, where eye doctors had discovered a wonderful salve that cured some kinds of blindness. The Lord spoke to those people in a way that they could understand if they chose to.
3:20 at the door. Our Lord pictures Himself at the end of the church age as outside the church (though not outside the true church, of course). Even so, He is still willing to be gracious to anyone who will let Him into his or her heart. This gracious invitation is

open the door, I will come in to him, and
will sup with him, and he with me.
21 To him that overcometh will I grant
to sit with me in my throne, even as I
also overcame, and am set down with
my Father in his throne.
22 He that hath an ear, let him hear
what the Spirit saith unto the churches.

III. "The Things Which Shall Be Hereafter" (4:1—22:21)

The first supernatural warning (see outline, 6:1)

4 After this I looked, and, behold, a
door *was* opened in heaven: and the
first voice which I heard *was* as it were
of a trumpet talking with me; which
said, Come up hither, and I will shew
thee things which must be hereafter.
2 And immediately I was in the spirit:
and, behold, a throne was set in heaven,
and *one* sat on the throne.
3 And he that sat was to look upon like
a jasper and a sardine stone: and *there*
was a rainbow round about the throne,
in sight like unto an emerald.
4 And round about the throne *were*
four and twenty seats: and upon the
seats I saw four and twenty *elders sitting,
clothed in white raiment; and they
had on their heads crowns of gold.
5 And out of the throne proceeded
lightnings and thunderings and voices:
and *there were* seven lamps of fire burning
before the throne, which are the
seven Spirits of God.
6 And before the throne *there was* a
sea of glass like unto crystal: and in the
midst of the throne, and round about the
throne, *were* four *beasts full of eyes
before and behind.
7 And the first beast *was* like a lion,
and the second beast like a calf, and the
third beast had a face as a man, and the
fourth beast *was* like a flying eagle.

Worship because of creation

8 And the four beasts had each of
them six wings about *him;* and *they were*
full of eyes within: and they rest not day
and night, saying, Holy, holy, holy, Lord
God Almighty, which was, and is, and is
to come.
9 And when those beasts give glory
and honour and thanks to him that sat on
the throne, who liveth for ever and ever,
10 The four and twenty elders fall
down before him that sat on the throne,
and worship him that liveth for ever and

4:1 The Trumpet Call
This call seems to indicate the fulfillment of the *Rapture (1 Thess. 4:13-17; see also vs. 13 note, "Hope for the Dead"). John, to whom the call came, represents believers who will be on earth when the Lord Jesus returns for His church, which is not seen again as taking part in the events following the trumpet call until chapter 19, when the *Great Tribulation is all over. The removal of the church is the first of four supernatural warnings by which God will indicate that judgment is about to fall. The warnings will be given in the four corners of the earth so that everyone will have an adequate chance to repent of his sin and be saved. The time between the first supernatural warning and the second is three-and-one-half years. The time between the second and third is again three-and-one-half years. The fourth warning is probably a few weeks after the third, and the return of the Lord Jesus Christ is shortly after the fourth (see 6:1 note, "The Outline for Revelation 6–20.")

---

for everyone who will hear His voice. Here, as He gives this last invitation, the time He calls "today" (Heb. 3:13) is just about over!

4:4 elders. Elders in the Bible are the representatives of the people. These represent God's saved ones who will be priests and kings like their Lord. The twenty-four may well represent both Old Testament and New Testament believers: the twelve tribes of Israel and the twelve apostles.

4:5 seven. See Revelation 1:4 and its note.

4:6 beasts. This word can read "living ones"; it is best to read it that way all through the Revelation. These living ones are the *cherubim.

4:8 rest not. They never tire of praising Him.

ever, and cast their crowns before the
throne, saying,
11Thou art worthy, O Lord, to receive
glory and honour and power: for thou
hast *created all things, and for thy
pleasure they are and were created.

The seven-sealed book

5 And I saw in the right hand of him
that sat on the throne a book written within and on the backside, sealed
with seven seals.

5:1 The Sealed Book
This book, or literally, a *scroll* (they did not have books like ours in those days), so thoroughly sealed, like a legal paper, is the title deed to this earth. Go back to Genesis 1 and 3, and to the references mentioned in the notes there, and read how the right to rule the earth was given by God to man (Adam), who forfeited it to Satan. At the cross Jesus Christ, as the Son of Man, conquered Satan to get it back for man, but He has never actually taken "the deed" and will not until this time comes. Until then, Satan is the "prince of this world" (John 14:30).

2And I saw a strong angel proclaiming with a loud voice, Who is worthy to
open the book, and to loose the seals
thereof?
3And no man in heaven, nor in
earth, neither under the earth, was
able to open the book, neither to look
thereon.
4And I wept much, because no man
was found worthy to open and to read
the book, neither to look thereon.

Christ in His Kingly character

5And one of the elders saith unto me,
Weep not: behold, the Lion of the tribe
of Juda, the Root of David, hath prevailed to open the book, and to loose the
seven seals thereof.
6And I beheld, and, lo, in the midst of
the throne and of the four beasts, and
in the midst of the elders, stood a Lamb
as it had been slain, having seven horns
and seven eyes, which are the seven
Spirits of God sent forth into all the
earth.

Worship because of redemption

7And he came and took the book out
of the right hand of him that sat upon
the throne.
8And when he had taken the book,
the four beasts and four *and* twenty elders fell down before the Lamb, having
every one of them harps, and golden
*vials full of odours, which are the
prayers of *saints.
9And they sung a new song, saying,
Thou art worthy to take the book, and
to open the seals thereof: for thou wast

5:4 wept. John wept because he had a sudden vision of what it would mean if Satan had the right to rule this world forever.

5:5 Lion of the tribe of Juda. The lion is the king of beasts. In Genesis 49:10 (see its note, "The Promise of Christ"), Jacob prophesied that the King of Israel and of the world should be born of the tribe of Judah. The prophecy was fulfilled, for Mary, the mother of the Lord Jesus Christ, was of the tribe of Judah.

5:5 Root of David. Jesus Christ was of the house of David.

5:6 Lamb. See Genesis 3:21 and John 1:29. The Lord Jesus Christ is the Lion, the King of Kings, only because He was first willing to be the Lamb slain for sinners.

5:6 seven horns. Horns always symbolize the power to rule.

5:6 seven eyes. The "seven eyes, which are the seven Spirits of God" mean that the Lord Jesus sees all things and is able by His Spirit to look even into hearts (see Zech. 3:8-9; 4:10; see its note, "An Alternate Reading").

5:7 he came. Daniel saw a little part of this same vision (Dan. 7:13).

5:9 a new song. This song is another scriptural reason that we have for believing that the "four and twenty elders" (see Rev. 4:4 note) refers to the whole body of Old Testament and New Testament believers, for no one but those who have been saved by faith in the Lamb of God can sing this song.

slain, and hast *redeemed us to God by
thy blood out of every kindred, and
tongue, and people, and nation;
10 And hast made us unto our God
kings and priests: and we shall reign on
the earth.
11 And I beheld, and I heard the voice
of many angels round about the throne
and the beasts and the elders: and the
number of them was ten thousand
times ten thousand, and thousands of
thousands;
12 Saying with a loud voice, Worthy is
the Lamb that was slain to receive
power, and riches, and wisdom, and
strength, and honour, and glory, and
blessing.
13 And every creature which is in
heaven, and on the earth, and under the
earth, and such as are in the sea, and all
that are in them, heard I saying, Blessing, and honour, and glory, and power,
be unto him that sitteth upon the
throne, and unto the Lamb for ever and
ever.
14 And the four beasts said, Amen.
And the four *and* twenty elders fell
down and worshipped him that liveth
for ever and ever.

The Seven Seals

1. The spirit of conquest

6 And I saw when the Lamb opened
one of the seals, and I heard, as it
were the noise of thunder, one of the
four beasts saying, Come and see.
2 And I saw, and behold a white horse:
and he that sat on him had a bow; and a
crown was given unto him: and he went
forth conquering, and to conquer.

2. No peace left on earth

3 And when he had opened the second
seal, I heard the second beast say, Come
and see.
4 And there went out another horse
that was red: and *power* was given to
him that sat thereon to take peace from
the earth, and that they should kill one
another: and there was given unto him
a great sword.

3. Famine

5 And when he had opened the third
seal, I heard the third beast say, Come
and see. And I beheld, and lo a black
horse; and he that sat on him had a pair
of balances in his hand.
6 And I heard a voice in the midst of
the four beasts say, A measure of wheat
for a penny, and three measures of barley for a penny; and *see* thou hurt not
the oil and the wine.

4. Death

7 And when he had opened the fourth
seal, I heard the voice of the fourth
beast say, Come and see.
8 And I looked, and behold a pale
horse: and his name that sat on him
was Death, and Hell followed with
him. And power was given unto them
over the fourth part of the earth, to
kill with sword, and with hunger, and

5:13 every creature. Here is one of the hints that John gives of what will happen much later. It shows the fulfillment of Philippians 2:10-11.

6:1 I saw. Because John was in heaven, in the spirit, he could see things that people on earth call invisible. He tells some things that will not be seen by those on earth when they happen. If you want to know how it will be for those who live on earth during the *Tribulation, read chapters 6–19, and keep turning back to the outline on the next page. Some of the events in the outline are scarcely mentioned in the Revelation, but see the references for more about them.

6:1 Come. The living one is not speaking to John, but to the rider on the horse, as if to say, "Come; it is time to do what you are about to do!" See also verses 3, 5, and 7.

6:6 penny. The word that is translated "penny" is the denarius, which was equal to a full day's wage.

6:8 Hell. Hades. See Luke 16:23 note, "The Place Called Hell." The place of the dead is pictured here as a terrible monster about to seize people.

6:1 THE OUTLINE FOR REVELATION 6 TO 20

Note: Do not try to read "across," that is, to find in every case a certain event on earth corresponding to a certain event in heaven. Events are placed in order, but many happen together, or go on for a long period, for example, the rise of the Roman Empire.

What Those on Earth Do Not See

The true church caught up (1 Thess. 4:13-17; 1 Cor. 15:51-54)

Seal five opened: martyrs calling for judgment (Rev. 6:9-11)

Seal six opened: warning of judgment (Rev. 6:12-17)

Satan cast out of first heaven (Rev. 12:9)

Believing Jews "sealed" (Rev. 7:2-8)

Seal seven opened: silence to hear prayers and answer (Rev. 8:1)

Prayer of saints for judgment (Rev. 8:4)

Seven trumpets announce judgment (Rev. 8:6–11:18)

Seven thunders (Rev. 10:4)

Seventh trumpet announces coronation in heaven of the Lord Jesus Christ (Rev. 11:15)

Son of Man reaps the earth (Rev. 14:14-16)

Angel gathers "vine of the earth" for judgment (Rev. 14:19; 16:16)

Seven bowls of wrath poured out (Rev. 16:1-21)

Heaven rejoices over fall of "Babylon" (Rev. 19:1-3)

Marriage supper of Lamb (Rev. 19:7-9)

King of Kings leaves heaven with His followers (Rev. 19:11-16)

Beast and False Prophet destroyed (Rev. 19:20)

Binding of Satan (Rev. 20:1-3)

Messiah's throne set up (Rev. 20:4)

Resurrection and rewarding of Tribulation martyrs (Rev. 20:4-6)

Beginning of Sorrows (Matt. 24:8)

Jacob's Trouble (Jer. 30:7)

What Those on Earth Do See

First Supernatural Warning:

Disappearance of Christians (1 Thess. 4:14-17)

Man of Sin (Antichrist) revealed (2 Thess. 2:3,8)

Rise of Roman Empire (Rev. 13:1)

Rise of Israel (Isa. 11:11)

Antichrist's covenant with Israel (Dan. 9:27)

Rise of "Babylon" (Rev. 17:1-7)

War, famines, plagues, etc. (Matt. 24:6-7)

Second Supernatural Warning:

Heaven opened; signs in sun, moon, etc. (Rev. 6:12-17)

Covenant with Israel broken (Dan. 9:27)

"Abomination" set up (Matt. 24:15)

Jews flee (Matt. 24:16; Rev. 12:6)

Two witnesses preach forty-two months and are slain (Rev. 11:3)

Limited judgments on trees (Rev. 8:7, a picture of man rising up in pride; Nebuchadnezzar compared to a great tree, Dan. 4:10-28)

Third Supernatural Warning

Two witnesses rise and are caught up to heaven (Rev. 11:11-12)

Fourth Supernatural Warning:

Three angels preach from the sky (Rev. 14:6-11)

Gathering to Armageddon (Rev. 16:16; 14:19-20; 19:19)

Seven plagues in quick succession (Rev. 16:1-21)

Fall of "Babylon" (Rev. 18:9-19)

Siege of Jerusalem (Isa. 10:28)

United rebellion against God and Christ (Ps. 2:2; Rev. 19:19)

Personal appearance of the King of Kings

(Rev. 19:11-16; Matt. 24:30; Zech. 14:3-5)

with death, and with the beasts of the earth.

5. Martyrs pray in heaven

9 And when he had opened the fifth seal, I saw under the *altar the souls of them that were slain for the word of God, and for the testimony which they held:

10 And they cried with a loud voice, saying, How long, O Lord, holy and true, dost thou not judge and avenge our blood on them that dwell on the earth?

11 And white robes were given unto every one of them; and it was said unto them, that they should rest yet for a little season, until their fellowservants also and their brethren, that should be killed as they *were,* should be fulfilled.

6. The second supernatural warning (see 4:1, note; 6:1, outline)

12 And I beheld when he had opened the sixth seal, and, lo, there was a great earthquake; and the sun became black as sackcloth of hair, and the moon became as blood;

13 And the stars of heaven fell unto the earth, even as a *fig tree casteth her untimely figs, when she is shaken of a mighty wind.

14 And the heaven departed as a scroll when it is rolled together; and every mountain and island were moved out of their places.

15 And the kings of the earth, and the great men, and the rich men, and the chief captains, and the mighty men, and every bondman, and every free man, hid themselves in the dens and in the rocks of the mountains;

16 And said to the mountains and rocks, Fall on us, and hide us from the face of him that sitteth on the throne, and from the wrath of the Lamb:

17 For the great day of his wrath is come; and who shall be able to stand?

The saved of the Tribulation period

7 And after these things I saw four *angels standing on the four corners of the earth, holding the four winds of the earth, that the wind should not blow on the earth, nor on the sea, nor on any tree.

> **7:1 A Special Group Saved**
> After the warnings and testings of the first three-and-one-half years, John is looking ahead here and gives a picture of the great company of Jews and Gentiles who are to be saved during the *Great Tribulation. These people are not members of the *church, nor are they people who have a second chance to be saved. They are the people who will turn to God during the next age and have a special work to do in that age.

2 And I saw another angel ascending from the east, having the seal of the living *God: and he cried with a loud voice to the four angels, to whom it was given to hurt the earth and the sea,

3 Saying, Hurt not the earth, neither the sea, nor the trees, till we have sealed the servants of our God in their foreheads.

4 And I heard the number of them which were sealed: *and there were* sealed an hundred *and* forty *and* four thousand of all the tribes of the children of Israel.

5 Of the tribe of Juda *were* sealed twelve thousand. Of the tribe of Reuben *were* sealed twelve thousand. Of the

---

6:9 altar. This sign is explained in Leviticus 4:25. John means that because of the way in which they died, the Christian martyrs are like the Old Testament sacrifices whose blood was poured out at the bottom of the altar.

6:14 heaven. Probably a tremendous supernatural change in the sky will startle the people on earth into realizing that God is on His throne watching them, and that Jesus Christ, God's Lamb, is there too.

6:15 hid. See Isaiah's prophecy (Isa. 2:19,21; see also Isa. 2:12 note, "The Day of the LORD").

tribe of Gad *were* sealed twelve thousand.
[6]Of the tribe of Aser *were* sealed
twelve thousand. Of the tribe of Nepthalim *were* sealed twelve thousand. Of the tribe of Manasses *were* sealed twelve thousand.
[7]Of the tribe of Simeon *were* sealed
twelve thousand. Of the tribe of Levi *were* sealed twelve thousand. Of the tribe of Issachar *were* sealed twelve thousand.
[8]Of the tribe of Zabulon *were* sealed
twelve thousand. Of the tribe of *Joseph *were* sealed twelve thousand. Of the tribe of Benjamin *were* sealed twelve thousand.
[9]After this I beheld, and, lo, a great
multitude, which no man could number, of all nations, and kindreds, and people, and tongues, stood before the throne, and before the Lamb, clothed with white robes, and palms in their hands;
[10]And cried with a loud voice, saying,
*Salvation to our God which sitteth upon the throne, and unto the Lamb.
[11]And all the angels stood round
about the throne, and *about* the elders and the four beasts, and fell before the throne on their faces, and worshipped God,
[12]Saying, *Amen: Blessing, and glo-
ry, and wisdom, and thanksgiving, and honour, and power, and might, *be* unto our God for ever and ever. Amen.
[13]And one of the elders answered,
saying unto me, What are these which are arrayed in white robes? and whence came they?
[14]And I said unto him, Sir, thou know-
est. And he said to me, These are they which came out of *great tribulation, and have washed their robes, and made them white in the *blood of the Lamb.
[15]Therefore are they before the
throne of God, and serve him day and night in his temple: and he that sitteth on the throne shall dwell among them.
[16]They shall hunger no more, neither
thirst any more; neither shall the sun light on them, nor any heat.
[17]For the Lamb which is in the midst
of the throne shall feed them, and shall lead them unto living fountains of waters: and God shall wipe away all tears from their eyes.

7. The seven trumpets come out of the seventh seal

8 And when he had opened the sev-
enth seal, there was silence in heaven about the space of half an hour.
[2]And I saw the seven angels which
stood before God; and to them were given seven trumpets.
[3]And another angel came and stood
at the altar, having a golden *censer; and there was given unto him much *incense, that he should offer *it* with the prayers of all saints upon the golden altar which was before the throne.
[4]And the smoke of the incense, *which*
came with the prayers of the saints, ascended up before God out of the angel's hand.
[5]And the angel took the censer, and
filled it with *fire of the altar, and cast *it* into the earth: and there were voices, and thunderings, and lightnings, and an earthquake.
[6]And the seven angels which had the
seven trumpets prepared themselves to sound.

The first trumpet

¶[7]The first angel sounded, and there
followed hail and fire mingled with blood, and they were cast upon the earth: and the third part of trees was burnt up, and all green grass was burnt up.

The second trumpet

[8]And the second angel sounded, and
as it were a great mountain burning

8:2 trumpets. Note that there are seven seals, seven trumpets, and seven vials of wrath. The opening of the seals seems to *prepare* for final judgment; the blowing of the trumpets seems to *announce* final judgment; the pouring of the vials *is* final judgment.

with fire was cast into the sea: and the
third part of the sea became blood;
9And the third part of the creatures
which were in the sea, and had life,
died; and the third part of the ships
were destroyed.

The third trumpet

10And the third angel sounded, and
there fell a great star from heaven,
burning as it were a lamp, and it fell
upon the third part of the rivers, and
upon the fountains of waters;
11And the name of the star is called
*Wormwood: and the third part of the
waters became wormwood; and many
men died of the waters, because they
were made bitter.

The fourth trumpet

12And the fourth angel sounded, and
the third part of the sun was smitten,
and the third part of the moon, and the
third part of the stars; so as the third
part of them was darkened, and the day
shone not for a third part of it, and the
night likewise.
¶13And I beheld, and heard an angel
flying through the midst of heaven, saying with a loud voice, Woe, woe, woe,
to the inhabiters of the earth by reason
of the other voices of the trumpet of the
three angels, which are yet to sound!

The fifth trumpet: the first woe

9 And the fifth angel sounded, and I
saw a star fall from *heaven unto
the earth: and to him was given the key
of the bottomless pit.
2And he opened the bottomless pit;
and there arose a smoke out of the *pit,
as the smoke of a great furnace; and the
sun and the air were darkened by reason of the smoke of the pit.
3And there came out of the smoke
locusts upon the earth: and unto them
was given power, as the *scorpions of
the earth have power.
4And it was commanded them that
they should not hurt the grass of the
earth, neither any green thing, neither
any tree; but only those men which have
not the seal of God in their foreheads.
5And to them it was given that they
should not kill them, but that they
should be tormented five months: and
their torment *was* as the torment of a
scorpion, when he striketh a man.
6And in those days shall men seek
*death, and shall not find it; and shall
desire to die, and death shall flee from
them.
7And the shapes of the locusts *were*
like unto horses prepared unto battle;
and on their heads *were* as it were
crowns like gold, and their faces *were* as
the faces of men.
8And they had hair as the hair of
women, and their teeth were as *the teeth*
of lions.
9And they had breastplates, as it were
breastplates of iron; and the sound of
their wings *was* as the sound of chariots of many horses running to battle.
10And they had tails like unto scorpions, and there were stings in their tails:
and their power *was* to hurt men five
months.
11And they had a king over them,
which is the angel of the bottomless pit,
whose name in the Hebrew tongue *is*
Abaddon, but in the Greek tongue hath
his name Apollyon.
12One woe is past; *and,* behold, there
come two woes more hereafter.

The sixth trumpet

¶13And the sixth angel sounded, and
I heard a voice from the four horns of
the golden altar which is before God,

9:1 star. Angels, good or bad, are sometimes referred to as stars (see Isa. 14:12 and its note, "Lucifer").

9:1 bottomless pit. The Abyss.

9:3 locusts. Symbolic, probably, of demons, because they come from the bottomless pit, which means the domain of Satan, and their "king over them" (vs. 11) is called "Apollyon," which is another name for Satan.

14 Saying to the sixth angel which had the trumpet, Loose the four angels which are bound in the great river Euphrates.

15 And the four angels were loosed, which were prepared for an hour, and a day, and a month, and a year, for to slay the third part of men.

16 And the number of the army of the horsemen *were* two hundred thousand thousand: and I heard the number of them.

17 And thus I saw the horses in the vision, and them that sat on them, having breastplates of fire, and of jacinth, and brimstone: and the heads of the horses *were* as the heads of lions; and out of their mouths issued fire and smoke and brimstone.

18 By these three was the third part of men killed, by the fire, and by the smoke, and by the brimstone, which issued out of their mouths.

19 For their power is in their mouth, and in their tails: for their tails *were* like unto serpents, and had heads, and with them they do hurt.

20 And the rest of the men which were not killed by these plagues yet *repented not of the works of their hands, that they should not worship devils, and idols of gold, and silver, and brass, and stone, and of wood: which neither can see, nor hear, nor walk:

21 Neither repented they of their murders, nor of their sorceries, nor of their fornication, nor of their thefts.

Events in heaven
The little book

10 And I saw another mighty angel come down from heaven, clothed with a cloud: and a rainbow *was* upon his head, and his face *was* as it were the sun, and his feet as pillars of fire:

2 And he had in his hand a little book open: and he set his right foot upon the sea, and *his* left *foot* on the earth,

3 And cried with a loud voice, as *when* a lion roareth: and when he had cried, seven thunders uttered their voices.

4 And when the seven thunders had uttered their voices, I was about to write: and I heard a voice from heaven saying unto me, Seal up those things which the seven thunders uttered, and write them not.

5 And the angel which I saw stand upon the sea and upon the earth lifted up his hand to heaven,

6 And sware by him that liveth for ever and ever, who *created heaven, and the things that therein are, and the earth, and the things that therein are, and the sea, and the things which are therein, that there should be time no longer:

7 But in the days of the voice of the seventh angel, when he shall begin to sound, the *mystery of God should be finished, as he hath declared to his servants the *prophets.

8 And the voice which I heard from heaven spake unto me again, and said, Go *and* take the little book which is open in the hand of the angel which standeth upon the sea and upon the earth.

9 And I went unto the angel, and said unto him, Give me the little book. And he said unto me, Take *it,* and eat it up; and it shall make thy belly bitter, but it shall be in thy mouth sweet as honey.

10 And I took the little book out of the angel's hand, and ate it up; and it was in my mouth sweet as honey: and as soon as I had eaten it, my belly was bitter.

11 And he said unto me, Thou must prophesy again before many peoples, and nations, and tongues, and kings.

Events of the forty-two months
(see 6:1, outline)

11 And there was given me a reed like unto a rod: and the angel

---

9:15 an hour. A certain hour, which God had appointed long before it happened.
10:6 time. Delay.

stood, saying, Rise, and measure the
temple of God, and the altar, and them
that worship therein.
2 But the court which is without the
temple leave out, and measure it not;
for it is given unto the *Gentiles: and
the *holy city shall they tread under
foot forty *and* two months.
3 And I will give *power* unto my two
witnesses, and they shall prophesy a
thousand two hundred *and* threescore
days, clothed in sackcloth.
4 These are the two olive trees, and
the two candlesticks standing before
the God of the earth.
5 And if any man will hurt them, fire
proceedeth out of their mouth, and
devoureth their enemies: and if any
man will hurt them, he must in this
manner be killed.
6 These have power to shut heaven,
that it rain not in the days of their
*prophecy: and have power over waters
to turn them to blood, and to smite the
earth with all plagues, as often as they
will.
7 And when they shall have finished
their testimony, the beast that
ascendeth out of the bottomless pit
shall make war against them, and shall
overcome them, and kill them.
8 And their dead bodies *shall lie* in the
street of the great city, which spiritually is called Sodom and *Egypt, where
also our Lord was crucified.
9 And they of the people and kindreds
and tongues and nations shall see their
dead bodies three days and an half, and
shall not suffer their dead bodies to be
put in graves.
10 And they that dwell upon the earth
shall rejoice over them, and make merry, and shall send gifts one to another;
because these two prophets tormented
them that dwelt on the earth.

Third supernatural warning

11 And after three days and an half the
Spirit of life from God entered into
them, and they stood upon their feet;
and great *fear fell upon them which
saw them.
12 And they heard a great voice from
heaven saying unto them, Come up hither. And they ascended up to heaven in a
cloud; and their enemies beheld them.

The second woe

13 And the same hour was there a
great earthquake, and the tenth part of
the city fell, and in the earthquake were
slain of men seven thousand: and the
*remnant were affrighted, and gave glo-
ry to the God of heaven.
14 The second woe is past; *and,* behold, the third woe cometh quickly.

The seventh trumpet

15 And the seventh angel sounded;
and there were great voices in heaven,

11:2 temple. As soon as the "beast" (see Rev. 13:1) makes the covenant with the nation of Israel, agreeing to let them hold their temple worship again (see Dan. 9:27; see Dan. 9:24-27 note, "A Central Prophecy"), they will rebuild their temple on Mount Zion. John is told to measure it, because taking the measure of a thing means calculating its value, or weighing its worth, to see if it comes up to God's standard.

11:2 measure it not. During Herod's time, for the first time in history, Gentiles were allowed to come into an outer court of the temple he built, but they were not expected to take part in the Mosaic services. This was never expected of them; therefore, God does not judge or measure them according to the Mosaic standard here. (See Rom. 2:12-14.)

11:4 candlesticks. Lampstands. This means that these men (perhaps more than two, the number being the number of testimony, Deut. 19:15) shall give out God's truth with power because they receive the power directly from God who dwells in men, as if an olive tree were lit and burning the olive oil that is in it.

11:7 beast. See Revelation 13:1-8.

11:8 the great city. Jerusalem.

11:13 the city. Jerusalem.

saying, The kingdoms of this *world are
become *the kingdoms* of our Lord, and
of his *Christ; and he shall reign for
ever and ever.
16And the four and twenty *elders,
which sat before God on their seats, fell
upon their faces, and worshipped God,
17Saying, We give thee thanks,
O Lord God Almighty, which art, and
wast, and art to come; because thou
hast taken to thee thy great power, and
hast reigned.
18And the nations were angry, and thy
wrath is come, and the time of the dead,
that they should be judged, and that
thou shouldest give reward unto thy
servants the prophets, and to the
*saints, and them that fear thy name,
small and great; and shouldest destroy
them which destroy the earth.
19And the temple of God was
opened in heaven, and there was seen
in his temple the *ark of his *testament:
and there were lightnings, and
voices, and thunderings, and an earthquake,
and great hail.

The history of the Jews

12 And there appeared a great
wonder in heaven; a woman
clothed with the sun, and the moon
under her feet, and upon her head a
crown of twelve stars:

The woman: Israel

2And she being with child cried, travailing
in birth, and pained to be delivered.

The dragon: Satan

3And there appeared another wonder
in heaven; and behold a great red dragon,
having seven heads and ten horns,
and seven crowns upon his heads.
4And his tail drew the third part of
the stars of heaven, and did cast them
to the earth: and the dragon stood before
the woman which was ready to be
delivered, for to devour her child as
soon as it was born.

The man-child: Christ

5And she brought forth a man child,
who was to rule all nations with a rod
of iron: and her child was caught up
unto God, and *to* his throne.
6And the woman fled into the wilderness,
where she hath a place prepared
of God, that they should feed her there
a thousand two hundred *and* threescore
days.

The archangel: Michael

7And there was war in heaven: Michael
and his angels fought against the
dragon; and the dragon fought and his
angels,

11:16 seats. Thrones.
11:19 ark. See *ark of the covenant.
12:1 And. John stops telling the order of events during the time of *Tribulation in order to give a survey of the whole history of Satan's fight against the Jews, God's earthly people.
12:2 cried. This probably refers to the suffering of Israel ever since they have been a nation, in Egypt, and in the Captivity, and until the Messiah was born.
12:3 seven. Notice that Satan is here described in the same fashion as his man, the Beast, in Revelation 13:1 and 17:3.
12:4 stars. These are the *angels who followed Satan in his rebellion against God. See Revelation 9:1 and its note; see also Genesis 6:2 note, "The Sons of God."
12:4 to devour. See Matthew 2:16.
12:5 caught up unto God. This looks back to the ascension of Christ after His death and resurrection. It may also allude to the *Rapture of the *church (the body of Christ).
12:6 fled. Between verses 5-6 occurs the church period in which the Jews, as such, do not figure. Verse 6 starts with their history after the church has gone to heaven. They will have three-and-one-half years of peace when the *Beast will make a covenant with them allowing them to set up their temple worship again. Then three-and-one-half years of terrible persecution will break out as described in verse 13.
12:7 Michael. The great angel whose special rule is the Jewish nation. See *angels.

8And prevailed not; neither was their
place found any more in heaven.
9And the great dragon was cast out,
that old serpent, called the *Devil, and
*Satan, which deceiveth the whole
world: he was cast out into the earth,
and his angels were cast out with him.
10And I heard a loud voice saying in
heaven, Now is come salvation, and
strength, and the *kingdom of our God,
and the power of his Christ: for the accuser of our brethren is cast down,
which accused them before our God day
and night.
11And they overcame him by the
blood of the Lamb, and by the word of
their testimony; and they loved not
their lives unto the death.
12Therefore rejoice, *ye* heavens, and
ye that dwell in them. Woe to the inhabiters of the earth and of the sea! for the
devil is come down unto you, having
great wrath, because he knoweth that
he hath but a short time.
13And when the dragon saw that he
was cast unto the earth, he persecuted
the woman which brought forth the
man *child*.
14And to the woman were given two
wings of a great eagle, that she might
fly into the wilderness, into her place,
where she is nourished for a time, and
times, and half a time, from the face of
the serpent.
15And the serpent cast out of his
mouth water as a flood after the woman, that he might cause her to be carried away of the flood.
16And the earth helped the woman,
and the earth opened her mouth, and
swallowed up the flood which the dragon cast out of his mouth.

The believing Jews

17And the dragon was wroth with the
woman, and went to make war with the
remnant of her seed, which keep the
commandments of God, and have the
testimony of Jesus Christ.

The Beast out of the sea

13 And I stood upon the sand of
the sea, and saw a beast rise up
out of the sea, having seven heads and
ten horns, and upon his horns ten
crowns, and upon his heads the name
of blasphemy.

13:1 A Beast from the Sea
Both the Old and New Testaments tell of a great superman who will one day gain control of the reformed Roman Empire of ten nations, and, showing his great power, demand actual worship as if he were God. This will be the Antichrist (1 John 2:18 and its note, "The Antichrist), also called "that man of sin" (2 Thess. 2:3,10; see also 2 Thess. 2:3 note, "Before the Lord Comes"). Read about him in Daniel 7:7-8 (and Dan. 7:8 note, "The Meaning of a Little Horn"). Sometimes "the Beast" (the *Antichrist) refers to the man, sometimes his empire; he will so thoroughly control his empire that either will be true. He will have the support of the second "beast" that will come out of the earth (Rev. 13:11; see Rev. 13:14 note, "The Beast from the Earth"), who will be the False Prophet. See Revelation 16:13 and note, "The Satanic Trinity."

2And the beast which I saw was like
unto a leopard, and his feet were as *the*
feet of a bear, and his mouth as the
mouth of a lion: and the dragon gave
him his power, and his seat, and great
authority.
3And I saw one of his heads as it were
wounded to death; and his deadly
wound was healed: and all the world
wondered after the beast.
4And they worshipped the dragon
which gave power unto the beast: and
they worshipped the beast, saying, Who
is like unto the beast? who is able to
make war with him?
5And there was given unto him a
mouth speaking great things and blas-

13:3 wounded to death. A suggestion that the Roman Empire came to an end and its parts became separate kingdoms. These will be united again and there will be an emperor again over them—the Beast or Antichrist, inspired by Satan.

phemies; and power was given unto
him to continue forty *and* two months.
[6]And he opened his mouth in blasphemy against *God, to blaspheme his
name, and his *tabernacle, and them
that dwell in heaven.
[7]And it was given unto him to make
war with the saints, and to overcome
them: and power was given him over all
kindreds, and tongues, and nations.
[8]And all that dwell upon the earth
shall worship him, whose names are not
written in the book of life of the Lamb
slain from the foundation of the world.
[9]If any man have an ear, let him hear.
[10]He that leadeth into captivity shall
go into captivity: he that killeth with the
sword must be killed with the sword.
Here is the patience and the *faith of
the saints.

The Beast out of the earth

[11]And I beheld another beast coming
up out of the earth; and he had two horns
like a lamb, and he spake as a dragon.
[12]And he exerciseth all the power of
the first beast before him, and causeth
the earth and them which dwell therein
to worship the first beast, whose deadly wound was healed.
[13]And he doeth great wonders, so
that he maketh fire come down from
heaven on the earth in the sight of men,
[14]And deceiveth them that dwell on
the earth by *the means of* those *miracles which he had power to do in the
sight of the beast; saying to them that
dwell on the earth, that they should
make an image to the beast, which

13:14 The Beast from the Earth
As the first Beast (vs. 1); came out of "the sea," which stands for the nations of the world, this Beast comes out of "the earth," a symbol of Palestine. He will be a Jew and will plot evil with the other Beast, the Roman emperor who will be the Antichrist (see Rev. 13:13 and Rev. 13:1 note, "The Beast from the Sea"). This will be "the false prophet" (Rev. 16:13; 19:20; 20:10), and the False Prophet will work signs and wonders and will serve the Antichrist and cause people to worship the Antichrist. See Revelation 16:13 and its note, "The Satanic Trinity."

had the wound by a sword, and did live.
[15]And he had power to give life unto
the image of the beast, that the image
of the beast should both speak, and
cause that as many as would not worship the image of the beast should be
killed.
[16]And he causeth all, both small and
great, rich and poor, free and bond, to
receive a mark in their right hand, or in
their foreheads:
[17]And that no man might buy or sell,
save he that had the mark, or the name
of the beast, or the number of his name.
[18]Here is wisdom. Let him that hath
understanding count the number of the
beast: for it is the number of a man; and
his number *is* Six hundred threescore
and six.

The Lamb victorious with His faithful Jewish remnant

14 And I looked, and, lo, a Lamb
stood on the mount *Sion, and

13:5 forty and two months. Three-and-one-half years, the second half of the coming *Tribulation. The Antichrist rose to power during the first half. He continues during the second half.

13:14 image. This will probably be set up at Jerusalem. At the beginning of the coming *Tribulation, the Beast, the Antichrist, will sign a treaty with the Jews, allowing them to worship once more in their temple undisturbed. At the end of three-and-one-half years, the Beast will break the treaty and will cause his own image to be set up to be worshipped. That is the sign for Jews to flee from the city (see Dan. 9:27 and 9:24-27 note, "A Central Prophecy"; Matt. 24:15).

14:1 lo. John says, "Look!" because this scene is the close of the great centuries-old struggle between Satan and God's people, Israel. The Lord Jesus Christ, Israel's Messiah, is seen here gloriously triumphant over Satan.

13:18 The Number of the Beast
No doubt believers living at the time when the Beast rules will understand what "the number of the beast" is; but it is not necessary to know it ahead of time. It has been suggested, however, that because some languages use alphabet letters for figures, and so every word is a sum in arithmetic, that the name of the Beast will be such a sum, adding up to 666.

Seven is God's number, that of perfection; six is the number of man, less than perfect, Here is suggested the trinity of evil through man under Satan.

with him an hundred forty *and* four
thousand, having his Father's name
written in their foreheads.
2 And I heard a voice from heaven, as
the voice of many waters, and as the
voice of a great thunder: and I heard the
voice of harpers harping with their
harps:
3 And they sung as it were a new song
before the throne, and before the four
beasts, and the elders: and no man
could learn that song but the hundred
and forty *and* four thousand, which
were *redeemed from the earth.
4 These are they which were not defiled with women; for they are virgins.
These are they which follow the Lamb
whithersoever he goeth. These were
redeemed from among men, *being* the
firstfruits unto God and to the Lamb.
5 And in their mouth was found no
guile: for they are without fault before
the throne of God.

Fourth supernatural warning

¶6 And I saw another *angel fly in
the midst of heaven, having the everlasting *gospel to preach unto them
that dwell on the earth, and to every
nation, and kindred, and tongue, and
people,
7 Saying with a loud voice, Fear God,
and give glory to him; for the hour of
his *judgment is come: and worship
him that made heaven, and earth, and
the sea, and the fountains of waters.

Fall of Babylon and doom of Beast-worshippers announced

8 And there followed another angel,
saying, *Babylon is fallen, is fallen, that
great city, because she made all nations
drink of the wine of the wrath of her
fornication.
9 And the third angel followed them,
saying with a loud voice, If any man
worship the beast and his image, and
receive *his* mark in his forehead, or in
his hand,
10 The same shall drink of the wine of
the wrath of God, which is poured out
without mixture into the cup of his indignation; and he shall be tormented
with *fire and brimstone in the presence of the holy *angels, and in the
presence of the Lamb:
11 And the smoke of their torment
ascendeth up for ever and ever: and
they have no rest day nor night, who
worship the beast and his image, and
whosoever receiveth the mark of his
name.
12 Here is the patience of the saints:
here *are* they that keep the commandments of God, and the faith of Jesus.

The blessedness of the martyrs

13 And I heard a voice from heaven
saying unto me, Write, Blessed *are* the

14:6 another angel. The last angel of whom John spoke was the seventh trumpeter (11:15). Then John left the story to give the history of Satan's fight against Israel. Now John goes on with the next events.
14:6 midst. In mid-heaven. This will be God's fourth and last startling, supernatural warning.
14:6 gospel. The everlasting gospel, from what the angel says, is the good news that God, the Creator, is about to set things right in His creation. There is only a moment left to turn from sin and worship Him (vs. 7).
14:8 Babylon. See 17:1 note.

dead which die in the Lord from henceforth: Yea, saith the Spirit, that they may rest from their labours; and their works do follow them.

Vision of Armageddon

¶[14]And I looked, and behold a white
cloud, and upon the cloud *one* sat like
unto the Son of man, having on his head
a golden crown, and in his hand a sharp
sickle.
[15]And another angel came out of the
temple, crying with a loud voice to him
that sat on the cloud, Thrust in thy sickle, and reap: for the time is come for
thee to reap; for the harvest of the earth
is ripe.
[16]And he that sat on the cloud thrust
in his sickle on the earth; and the earth
was reaped.
[17]And another angel came out of the
temple which is in heaven, he also having a sharp sickle.
[18]And another angel came out from
the *altar, which had power over fire;
and cried with a loud cry to him that had
the sharp sickle, saying, Thrust in thy
sharp sickle, and gather the clusters of
the vine of the earth; for her grapes are
fully ripe.
[19]And the angel thrust in his sickle
into the earth, and gathered the vine of
the earth, and cast *it* into the great
winepress of the wrath of God.
[20]And the winepress was trodden
without the city, and blood came out of
the winepress, even unto the horse
bridles, by the space of a thousand *and*
six hundred furlongs.

The seven vials

15 And I saw another sign in heaven, great and marvellous, seven
angels having the seven last plagues;
for in them is filled up the wrath of
God.
[2]And I saw as it were a sea of glass
mingled with fire: and them that had
gotten the victory over the beast, and
over his image, and over his mark, *and*
over the number of his name, stand
on the sea of glass, having the harps
of God.
[3]And they sing the song of *Moses
the servant of God, and the song of the
Lamb, saying, Great and marvellous *are*
thy works, Lord God Almighty; *just
and true *are* thy ways, thou King of
saints.
[4]Who shall not fear thee, O Lord, and
glorify thy name? for *thou* only *art* holy:
for all nations shall come and worship
before thee; for thy judgments are
made manifest.
[5]And after that I looked, and, behold,
the temple of the tabernacle of the testimony in *heaven was opened:
[6]And the seven angels came out of
the temple, having the seven plagues,
clothed in pure and white linen, and
having their breasts girded with golden
girdles.
[7]And one of the four beasts gave unto
the seven angels seven golden vials full
of the wrath of God, who liveth for ever
and ever.
[8]And the temple was filled with
smoke from the glory of God, and from
his power; and no man was able to enter
into the temple, till the seven plagues
of the seven angels were fulfilled.

The first vial

16 And I heard a great voice out of the temple saying to the
seven angels, Go your ways, and pour

14:13 dead. John is talking about those who die as martyrs during the *Great Tribulation. Of course it is true that all who die in the Lord are happy, yet these are to have special blessing because it will be harder during their lifetime to stand for the truth of God's Word than at any time in history.
14:20 furlongs. One furlong is 606 feet.
15:6 white. White stands for righteousness.
15:7 vials. Bowls. God's wrath is pictured here as if it were liquid fire that could be poured out of a bowl.

out the vials of the wrath of God upon
the earth.
2And the first went, and poured out
his vial upon the earth; and there fell a
noisome and grievous sore upon the
men which had the mark of the beast,
and *upon* them which worshipped his
image.

The second vial

3And the second angel poured out his
vial upon the sea; and it became as the
blood of a dead *man:* and every living
soul died in the sea.

The third vial

4And the third angel poured out his
vial upon the rivers and fountains of
waters; and they became blood.
5And I heard the angel of the waters
say, Thou art righteous, O Lord, which
art, and wast, and shalt be, because thou
hast judged thus.
6For they have shed the blood of
saints and prophets, and thou hast given
them blood to drink; for they are worthy.
7And I heard another out of the altar
say, Even so, Lord God Almighty, true
and righteous *are* thy judgments.

The fourth vial

8And the fourth angel poured out his
vial upon the sun; and power was given
unto him to scorch men with fire.
9And men were scorched with great
heat, and blasphemed the name of God,
which hath power over these plagues:
and they repented not to give him
glory.

The fifth vial

10And the fifth angel poured out his
vial upon the seat of the beast; and his
kingdom was full of darkness; and they
gnawed their tongues for pain,
11And blasphemed the God of heaven
because of their pains and their
sores, and repented not of their deeds.

The sixth vial

12And the sixth angel poured out his
vial upon the great river Euphrates; and
the water thereof was dried up, that the
way of the kings of the east might be
prepared.
13And I saw three *unclean spirits
like frogs *come* out of the mouth of the
dragon, and out of the mouth of the
beast, and out of the mouth of the false
*prophet.

16:13 The Satanic Trinity
Here the satanic trinity unite their power against God. Remember that Satan has always tried to imitate what God is and does, but his imitations are poor substitutes. Satan's "trinity" is composed of the dragon, Satan himself; the Beast, who is the Antichrist and the head of the revived Roman Empire; and the False Prophet, who causes all to worship the Antichrist.

14For they are the spirits of devils,
working *miracles, *which* go forth unto
the kings of the earth and of the whole
world, to gather them to the battle of
that great day of God Almighty.
15Behold, I come as a thief. Blessed
is he that watcheth, and keepeth his
*garments, lest he walk naked, and
they see his shame.

16:3 every. Compare this with what happened in Revelation 8:8-9. There the judgment was a warning, for it was limited to one-third. These bowl judgments are final and unlimited.

16:8 scorch. Those in the Tribulation will have such hardened hearts that they will not turn to the Lord no matter the judgment He brings. The next verse says that they will blaspheme the name of God after He scorches them.

16:9 repented not. Compare with 9:21.

16:12 way of the kings. In order that the Eastern kings may easily transport their troops to *Armageddon.

16:15 Behold. This verse is like the voice of Jesus Christ breaking through the horror for an instant, calling warning to rebels and encouragement to those who trust Him.

[16]And he gathered them together
into a place called in the Hebrew tongue
Armageddon.

The seventh vial

[17]And the seventh angel poured out
his vial into the air; and there came a
great voice out of the temple of heav-
en, from the throne, saying, It is done.
[18]And there were voices, and thunders, and lightnings; and there was a
great earthquake, such as was not since
men were upon the earth, so mighty an
earthquake, *and* so great.
[19]And the great city was divided into
three parts, and the cities of the nations
fell: and great Babylon came in remembrance before God, to give unto her the
cup of the wine of the fierceness of his
wrath.
[20]And every island fled away, and the
mountains were not found.
[21]And there fell upon men a great hail
out of heaven, *every stone* about the
weight of a talent: and men blasphemed
God because of the plague of the hail; for
the plague thereof was exceeding great.

The seven dooms:
1. Doom of Babylon

17 And there came one of the
seven angels which had the
seven vials, and talked with me, saying
unto me, Come hither; I will shew unto
thee the judgment of the great *whore
that sitteth upon many waters:
[2]With whom the kings of the earth
have committed fornication, and the
inhabitants of the earth have been made
drunk with the wine of her fornication.
[3]So he carried me away in the spirit
into the wilderness: and I saw a woman sit upon a scarlet coloured beast, full
of names of blasphemy, having seven
heads and ten horns.

17:3 A Scarlet-Colored Beast
The false church, the religious power, is pictured here as seated upon the Beast, the political power. That means that the false religious power shall control the secular or political power for awhile. Verse 16 tells how the whole Roman Empire will finally throw off even the pretense at religion and adopt the worship of the Beast, the Antichrist. It is to be observed that the Beast and the woman go together. Since the union is the apostate ecclesiastical system that reaches into all Christendom, it is quite evident that the revived Roman Empire will include all Christendom, including North and South America.

[4]And the woman was arrayed in purple and scarlet colour, and decked with
gold and precious stones and pearls,
having a golden cup in her hand full of
abominations and filthiness of her fornication:
[5]And upon her forehead *was* a name
written, MYSTERY, BABYLON THE
GREAT, THE MOTHER OF HAR-
LOTS AND ABOMINATIONS OF
THE EARTH.
[6]And I saw the woman drunken with
the blood of the *saints, and with the
blood of the martyrs of Jesus: and when
I saw her, I wondered with great admiration.

16:16 Armageddon. This word means the *Mount of Slaughter*. Many great battles of the world have been fought there. See Revelation 19:19 note, "The Battle of Armageddon."
16:17 done. The next three chanters do not tell *more* events that must happen before the actual setting up of the *kingdom; they only describe fully what happened after the pouring out of the seventh vial.
16:19 Babylon. This is the name God uses for Satan's great earthly system of government and religion.
16:21 talent. A talent was a weight equal to seventy-five pounds.
17:1 Come hither. John stops the story again here to show what the false church has been doing since the true *church was taken out of the world. This false church, Babylon, pretends to be Christ's but is in reality like an extremely sinful woman.
17:6 admiration. John looked at her with *wonder* and *astonishment*.

[7]And the angel said unto me, Wherefore didst thou marvel? I will tell thee
the mystery of the woman, and of the
beast that carrieth her, which hath the
seven heads and ten horns.

The Roman Empire Revived

[8]The beast that thou sawest was, and
is not; and shall ascend out of the bottomless pit, and go into perdition: and
they that dwell on the earth shall wonder, whose names were not written in
the book of life from the foundation of
the *world, when they behold the beast
that was, and is not, and yet is.
[9]And here *is* the mind which hath
wisdom. The seven heads are seven
mountains, on which the woman
sitteth.
[10]And there are seven kings: five are
fallen, and one is, *and* the other is not
yet come; and when he cometh, he
must continue a short space.
[11]And the beast that was, and is not,
even he is the eighth, and is of the
seven, and goeth into perdition.
[12]And the ten horns which thou
sawest are ten kings, which have received no kingdom as yet; but receive
power as kings one hour with the beast.
[13]These have one mind, and shall
give their power and strength unto the
beast.
[14]These shall make war with the
Lamb, and the Lamb shall overcome
them: for he is Lord of lords, and King
of kings: and they that are with him *are*
called, and chosen, and faithful.
[15]And he saith unto me, The waters
which thou sawest, where the whore
sitteth, are peoples, and multitudes,
and nations, and tongues.
[16]And the ten horns which thou
sawest upon the beast, these shall hate
the whore, and shall make her desolate
and naked, and shall eat her flesh, and
burn her with fire.
[17]For God hath put in their hearts to
fulfil his will, and to agree, and give
their kingdom unto the beast, until the
words of God shall be fulfilled.
[18]And the woman which thou sawest
is that great city, which reigneth over
the kings of the earth.

God views Babylon

18 And after these things I saw
another angel come down from
heaven, having great power; and the
earth was lightened with his glory.
[2]And he cried mightily with a strong
voice, saying, Babylon the great is fall-
en, is fallen, and is become the habitation of devils, and the hold of every foul
spirit, and a cage of every unclean and
hateful bird.
[3]For all nations have drunk of the
wine of the wrath of her fornication, and
the kings of the earth have committed
fornication with her, and the merchants
of the earth are waxed rich through the
abundance of her delicacies.
[4]And I heard another voice from
heaven, saying, Come out of her, my
people, that ye be not *partakers of her
sins, and that ye receive not of her
plagues.
[5]For her sins have reached unto

17:8 beast. Here is another (see Rev. 13:3) description of the way in which the Roman Empire flourished, disappeared, and will be revived again by satanic power.

17:9 seven mountains. Rome, the capital of the Beast's empire, is built on seven mountains. The city, the religious power, and the political power are all called Babylon, meaning *confusion* (see verse 1 note).

17:10 seven kings. The seven heads of the Beast also represent seven kings, or seven forms of government in the Roman Empire. At the time John was writing, five of these had already come and gone, one was ruling, and the last had not come yet. Compare with Revelation 13:3.

17:12 ten kings. Ten nations will form the future Roman Empire ruled by the Antichrist. (See Rev. 13:1 note, "A Beast from the Sea," and Dan. 2 and 7.)

17:16 hate. The political power will finally throw off the pretense of religion and substitute the worship of the Beast.

heaven, and God hath remembered her
iniquities.
6 Reward her even as she rewarded
you, and double unto her double according to her works: in the cup which she
hath filled fill to her double.
7 How much she hath glorified herself, and lived deliciously, so much torment and sorrow give her: for she saith
in her heart, I sit a queen, and am no
widow, and shall see no sorrow.
8 Therefore shall her plagues come in
one day, *death, and *mourning, and
famine; and she shall be utterly burned
with fire: for strong *is* the Lord God who
judgeth her.

The human view of Babylon

9 And the kings of the earth, who have
committed fornication and lived deliciously with her, shall bewail her, and
lament for her, when they shall see the
smoke of her burning,
10 Standing afar off for the *fear of her
torment, saying, Alas, alas, that great
city Babylon, that mighty city! for in
one hour is thy judgment come.
11 And the merchants of the earth shall
weep and mourn over her; for no man
buyeth their merchandise any more:
12 The merchandise of gold, and silver, and precious stones, and of pearls,
and fine linen, and purple, and silk, and
scarlet, and all thyine wood, and all
manner vessels of ivory, and all manner
vessels of most precious wood, and of
brass, and iron, and marble,
13 And cinnamon, and odours, and
ointments, and frankincense, and wine,
and oil, and fine flour, and wheat, and
beasts, and sheep, and horses, and chariots, and slaves, and souls of men.
14 And the fruits that thy soul lusted
after are departed from thee, and all
things which were dainty and goodly
are departed from thee, and thou shalt
find them no more at all.
15 The merchants of these things,
which were made rich by her, shall
stand afar off for the fear of her torment,
weeping and wailing,
16 And saying, Alas, alas, that great
city, that was clothed in fine linen, and
purple, and scarlet, and decked with
gold, and precious stones, and pearls!
17 For in one hour so great riches is
come to nought. And every shipmaster,
and all the company in ships, and sailors, and as many as trade by sea, stood
afar off,
18 And cried when they saw the
smoke of her burning, saying, What *city*
is like unto this great city!
19 And they cast dust on their heads,
and cried, weeping and wailing, saying,
Alas, alas, that great city, wherein were
made rich all that had ships in the sea
by reason of her costliness! for in one
hour is she made desolate.

The heavenly view of Babylon

20 Rejoice over her, *thou* heaven, and
ye holy *apostles and prophets; for God
hath avenged you on her.
21 And a mighty angel took up a stone
like a great millstone, and cast *it* into
the sea, saying, Thus with violence
shall that great city Babylon be thrown
down, and shall be found no more
at all.
22 And the voice of harpers, and musicians, and of pipers, and trumpeters,
shall be heard no more at all in thee; and
no craftsman, of whatsoever craft *he be,*
shall be found any more in thee; and the
sound of a millstone shall be heard no
more at all in thee;
23 And the light of a candle shall shine
no more at all in thee; and the voice of
the *bridegroom and of the bride shall
be heard no more at all in thee: for thy
merchants were the great men of the
earth; for by thy sorceries were all nations deceived.
24 And in her was found the blood of
prophets, and of saints, and of all that
were slain upon the earth.

The alleluias of the saints

19 And after these things I heard
a great voice of much people in
heaven, saying, Alleluia; *Salvation,

and glory, and honour, and power, unto
the Lord our *God:
[2]For true and righteous *are* his judgments: for he hath judged the great
whore, which did corrupt the earth with
her fornication, and hath avenged the
blood of his servants at her hand.
[3]And again they said, Alleluia. And
her smoke rose up for ever and ever.
[4]And the four and twenty *elders and
the four beasts fell down and worshipped God that sat on the throne, saying, *Amen; Alleluia.
[5]And a voice came out of the throne,
saying, Praise our God, all ye his servants, and ye that fear him, both small
and great.
[6]And I heard as it were the voice of a
great multitude, and as the voice of
many waters, and as the voice of mighty
thunderings, saying, Alleluia: for the
Lord God omnipotent reigneth.

The marriage of the Lamb

[7]Let us be glad and rejoice, and give
honour to him: for the marriage of the
Lamb is come, and his wife hath made
herself ready.
[8]And to her was granted that she
should be arrayed in fine linen, clean
and white: for the fine linen is the *righteousness of saints.
[9]And he saith unto me, Write,
Blessed *are* they which are called unto
the marriage supper of the Lamb. And
he saith unto me, These are the true
sayings of God.
[10]And I fell at his feet to worship
him. And he said unto me, See *thou
do it* not: I am thy fellowservant, and
of thy brethren that have the testimony of Jesus: worship God: for the testimony of Jesus is the spirit of *prophecy.

19:11 The Tribulation

The Tribulation is a period of approximately seven years, equivalent to Daniel's Seventieth Week (Dan. 9), the time just before the return of the Lord Jesus in glory and power to reign over the earth (Rev. 19:11-16). During the first half of the Tribulation, the Antichrist will be revealed (Dan. 9:26-27) and he will make a covenant with Israel.

The *Great* Tribulation is the last half of Daniel's Seventieth Week, three-and-a-half years long, specifically called the Time of *Jacob's Trouble (Jer. 30:7 and its note, "Future Trouble"), though it will involve the whole world (Rev. 3:10; see its note, "The Hour of Temptation"). The Tribulation is fully described in Revelation 6–19; see also Matthew 24–25.

*The Second Coming of the Lord
Jesus Christ in glory*

[11]And I saw heaven opened, and behold a white horse; and he that sat upon
him *was* called Faithful and True, and
in righteousness he doth judge and
make war.
[12]His eyes *were* as a flame of fire, and
on his head *were* many crowns; and he
had a name written, that no man knew,
but he himself.
[13]And he *was* clothed with a vesture
dipped in blood: and his name is called
The Word of God.
[14]And the armies *which were* in heaven followed him upon white horses,
clothed in fine linen, white and clean.
[15]And out of his mouth goeth a sharp
sword, that with it he should smite the
nations: and he shall rule them with a
rod of iron: and he treadeth the wine-

19:7 his wife. This is a picture of the true *church in heaven and of her happiness and triumph with the Lamb—the Lord Jesus Christ.

19:11 saw. Be sure to keep in mind the difference between the return of the Lord to take the *church to heaven, the *Rapture described in 1 Thessalonians 4:16, and His visible return to set up His *kingdom, the Second Coming.

19:15 winepress. In the East the grapes are placed in a great box or vat where the workmen tread them with their bare feet to press out the grape juice. This is often used in the Bible as a picture of judgment. See Revelation 14:20 and Isaiah 63:1-6 (see also Isa. 63:1 note, "Christ's Coming").

press of the fierceness and wrath of
Almighty God.
16And he hath on *his* vesture and on
his thigh a name written, KING OF
KINGS, AND LORD OF LORDS.
¶17And I saw an angel standing in the
sun; and he cried with a loud voice, saying to all the fowls that fly in the midst
of heaven, Come and gather yourselves
together unto the supper of the great
God;
18That ye may eat the flesh of kings,
and the flesh of captains, and the flesh
of mighty men, and the flesh of horses,
and of them that sit on them, and the
flesh of all *men, both* free and bond, both
small and great.
19And I saw the beast, and the kings
of the earth, and their armies, gathered
together to make war against him that
sat on the horse, and against his army.

> **19:19 The Battle of Armageddon**
> This great battle of Armageddon is not just another battle between the nations of the earth. It is a united attack by nations of the earth against God and the Lord Jesus Christ, who at this time will be represented by the believing Jews. The attitude of the nations is described in Psalm 2. The battle is scarcely described at all here in Revelation, for the important thing is not the battle, but the triumph of Christ. The Old Testament prophets tell many details about the battle. Read Zechariah 14:1-5 and Joel 2:1-21.

2. Doom of the beast
3. Doom of the False Prophet

20And the beast was taken, and with
him the false prophet that wrought
*miracles before him, with which he
deceived them that had received the
mark of the *beast, and them that worshipped his image. These both were
cast alive into a lake of fire burning with
brimstone.

4. Doom of the kings

21And the *remnant were slain with
the sword of him that sat upon the
horse, which *sword* proceeded out of his
mouth: and all the fowls were filled with
their flesh.

The Millennium

20 And I saw an *angel come down
from heaven, having the key of
the bottomless pit and a great chain in
his hand.
2And he laid hold on the dragon, that
old serpent, which is the *Devil, and
*Satan, and bound him a *thousand
years,
3And cast him into the bottomless pit,
and shut him up, and set a seal upon
him, that he should deceive the nations
no more, till the thousand years should
be fulfilled: and after that he must be
loosed a little season.

The first resurrection

4And I saw thrones, and they sat upon
them, and *judgment was given unto
them: and *I saw* the souls of them that
were beheaded for the witness of Jesus,
and for the word of God, and which had
not worshipped the beast, neither his
image, neither had received *his* mark
upon their foreheads, or in their hands;

19:20 lake of fire. See Revelation 20:14 note. The Beast and the False Prophet are the first persons ever to be put into the lake of fire.
19:21 sword. See Revelation 1:16 second note.
20:2 thousand years. Satan will be bound and harmless during the whole reign of Jesus Christ on this earth, known as the *Millennium, because of its duration of one thousand years.
20:3 loosed. See 20:7.
20:4 thrones. Here is the actual beginning of the *kingdom *dispensation. Jeremiah 31:31 tells of the covenant that God made with His people Israel at that time. The "Sermon on the Mount" (Matt. 5–7) gives the principles on which the Lord Jesus Christ will set up His kingdom. Isaiah 11–12 describe life as it will be in the kingdom.
20:4 beheaded. This verse shows how the martyrs of the *Great Tribulation (Rev. 14:13 and its note) are to be rewarded.

and they lived and reigned with *Christ
a thousand years.
5But the rest of the dead lived not
again until the thousand years were finished. This *is* the first *resurrection.

20:5-6 The First Resurrection
The phrase "the first resurrection" does not mean that this will be the first time anyone was ever raised from the dead! It means that this completes the "first resurrection." The first resurrection includes all who rise from the dead before the *Millennium. The first to rise was Christ Himself, called the "firstfruits" (1 Cor. 15:20). (Lazarus, Jarius' daughter, the son of the widow of Nain, Dorcas in Acts 9:39-41, and the one or two raised in Old Testament times were raised from the dead, but not in the same sense, for they died again.) The next to rise will be the dead in Christ at the *Rapture of the *church. The last to rise in the first resurrection will be those who have been saved during the Tribulation. Notice that no unbelievers are in any of these groups. Unbelievers are "the rest of the dead" in verse 5.

6Blessed and holy *is* he that hath part
in the first resurrection: on such the
*second death hath no power, but they
shall be priests of God and of Christ,
and shall reign with him a thousand
years.

5. Doom of Gog and Magog

7And when the thousand years are
expired, Satan shall be loosed out of his
prison,
8And shall go out to deceive the nations which are in the four quarters of
the earth, Gog and Magog, to gather
them together to battle: the number of
whom *is* as the sand of the sea.
9And they went up on the breadth of
the earth, and compassed the camp of
the saints about, and the beloved city:
and *fire came down from God out of
heaven, and devoured them.

6. Doom of Satan

10And the devil that deceived them
was cast into the lake of fire and brimstone, where the beast and the false
prophet *are*, and shall be tormented day
and night for ever and ever.

The last judgment
7. Doom of unbelievers

¶11And I saw a great white throne,
and him that sat on it, from whose face
the earth and the heaven fled away; and
there was found no place for them.
12And I saw the dead, small and great,
stand before God; and the books were
opened: and another book was opened,
which is *the book* of life: and the dead
were judged out of those things which
were written in the books, according to
their works.

20:12 The Dead
The dead are those who were not raised at the first resurrection (see vss. 5-6 note), as well as those who have rebelled against Christ during the *Millennium and have therefore been punished by death. No saved ones of any age will be judged at the Great White Throne, because those who believe "shall not come into condemnation [judgment]" (John 5:24). The Lord Jesus Christ has taken their judgment on the cross. This judgment has to do only with those who refused Him as their Saviour.

They will be judged "according to their works," and will be condemned because their names are not written in the Book of Life.

13And the sea gave up the dead which
were in it; and death and *hell delivered
up the dead which were in them: and
they were judged every man according
to their works.

20:6 second death. See verse 14 note.
20:8 Gog and Magog. These names were given in Ezekiel 38:2 (see its note, "Gog and Magog"). A similar power will lead, under Satan, the last rebellion against the Lord Jesus Christ at some future day.
20:10 devil. Satan is first seen in Genesis 3. His evil trail can be followed straight through the Bible, but here it ends forever.
20:11 great white throne. This throne is set up for the final judgment of men and angels.

14And death and hell were cast into
the lake of fire. This is the second
death.
15And whosoever was not found written in the book of life was cast into the
lake of fire.

The new Heaven and new earth

21 And I saw a new *heaven and a
new earth: for the first heaven
and the first earth were passed away;
and there was no more sea.

21:1 The New Earth
Peter tells us (2 Pet. 3:4-13) that while God once cleansed the former earth by water (see Gen. 1:2), He will cleanse it once more, by fire. As there are some disease germs that cannot be killed except by fire, so it is with sin. But as the earth of Genesis 1:1 did not cease to exist when it was destroyed, so it appears that it will not cease to exist in the future destruction by fire, but will simply be melted and remade, a new earth, where sin will never enter (Ps. 119:90; Eccles. 1:4 and its note, "The Earth Endures").

The new city, Jerusalem

2And I John saw the *holy city, new
*Jerusalem, coming down from God out
of heaven, prepared as a bride adorned
for her husband.
3And I heard a great voice out of
heaven saying, Behold, the *tabernacle
of God *is* with men, and he will dwell
with them, and they shall be his people,
and God himself shall be with them, *and
be* their God.
4And God shall wipe away all tears
from their eyes; and there shall be no
more death, neither sorrow, nor crying,
neither shall there be any more pain: for
the former things are passed away.
5And he that sat upon the throne said,
Behold, I make all things new. And he
said unto me, Write: for these words are
true and faithful.
6And he said unto me, It is done. I am
*Alpha and Omega, the beginning and
the end. I will give unto him that is
athirst of the fountain of the water of life
freely.
7He that overcometh shall inherit all
things; and I will be his God, and he
shall be my son.
8But the fearful, and unbelieving,
and the abominable, and murderers, and
whoremongers, and sorcerers, and
idolaters, and all liars, shall have their
part in the lake which burneth with fire
and brimstone: which is the second
death.
¶9And there came unto me one of the
seven *angels which had the seven *vials full of the seven last plagues, and
talked with me, saying, Come hither, I will
shew thee the bride, the Lamb's wife.
10And he carried me away in the spirit to a great and high mountain, and
shewed me that great city, the holy Jerusalem, descending out of heaven
from God,
11Having the glory of God: and her
light *was* like unto a stone most precious, even like a jasper stone, clear as
crystal;
12And had a wall great and high, *and*
had twelve gates, and at the gates
twelve angels, and names written thereon, which are *the names* of the twelve
tribes of the children of *Israel:
13On the east three gates; on the
north three gates; on the south three
gates; and on the west three gates.
14And the wall of the city had twelve

20:14 second death. The second death and the lake of fire mean the same thing—everlasting separation from God in torment, which is the punishment of all who have already died physically in unbelief and rebellion against God. Jesus Christ Himself speaks of this second death (Matt. 25:41) very solemnly and sadly, we may be sure, for He does not desire that any should be lost (2 Pet. 3:9).
21:2 new Jerusalem. This city is not the new earth; it is a heavenly city.
21:9 shew thee. Beginning here in verse 9, it appears that we are taken back to the *Millennium to see the millennial city. As Babylon was both a city and a woman (Rev. 17:1-18), so the new Jerusalem is both the city and the home of the bride of Christ.

foundations, and in them the names of
the twelve apostles of the Lamb.
15 And he that talked with me had a
golden reed to measure the city, and the
gates thereof, and the wall thereof.
16 And the city lieth foursquare, and
the length is as large as the breadth: and
he measured the city with the reed,
twelve thousand *furlongs. The length
and the breadth and the height of it are
equal.
17 And he measured the wall thereof,
an hundred *and* forty *and* four *cubits,
according to the measure of a man, that
is, of the angel.
18 And the building of the wall of it
was *of* jasper: and the city *was* pure
gold, like unto clear glass.
19 And the foundations of the wall of
the city *were* garnished with all manner
of precious stones. The first foundation
was jasper; the second, sapphire; the
third, a chalcedony; the fourth, an emerald;
20 The fifth, sardonyx; the sixth,
sardius; the seventh, chrysolite; the
eighth, beryl; the ninth, a topaz; the
tenth, a chrysoprasus; the eleventh, a
jacinth; the twelfth, an amethyst.
21 And the twelve gates *were* twelve
pearls; every several gate was of one
pearl: and the street of the city *was* pure
gold, as it were transparent glass.
22 And I saw no temple therein: for
the Lord God Almighty and the Lamb
are the temple of it.
23 And the city had no need of the sun,
neither of the moon, to shine in it: for
the glory of God did lighten it, and the
Lamb *is* the light thereof.
24 And the nations of them which are
saved shall walk in the light of it: and
the kings of the earth do bring their
glory and honour into it.
25 And the gates of it shall not be shut
at all by day: for there shall be no night
there.
26 And they shall bring the glory and
honour of the nations into it.
27 And there shall in no wise enter
into it any thing that defileth, neither
whatsoever worketh *abomination, or
maketh a lie: but they which are written in the Lamb's book of life.

The new Paradise

22 And he shewed me a pure river
of water of life, clear as crystal,
proceeding out of the throne of God and
of the Lamb.
2 In the midst of the street of it, and
on either side of the river, *was there* the
tree of life, which bare twelve *manner
of* fruits, *and* yielded her fruit every
month: and the leaves of the tree *were*
for the healing of the nations.
3 And there shall be no more curse:
but the throne of God and of the Lamb
shall be in it; and his servants shall
serve him:
4 And they shall see his face; and his
name *shall be* in their foreheads.
5 And there shall be no night there;
and they need no candle, neither light
of the sun; for the Lord God giveth them
light: and they shall reign for ever and
ever.
¶ 6 And he said unto me, These sayings *are* faithful and true: and the Lord
God of the holy prophets sent his angel
to shew unto his servants the things
which must shortly be done.
7 Behold, I come quickly: blessed *is*
he that keepeth the sayings of the
prophecy of this book.
8 And I John saw these things, and
heard *them*. And when I had heard and
seen, I fell down to worship before the
feet of the angel which shewed me
these things.

21:24 nations. There will be kings on earth at that time, ruling under God in righteousness and peace.

22:2 tree of life. This tree was kept from man after he sinned (Gen. 3:22-24), but now it is given back to the redeemed. It is an interesting study to compare the books of Genesis and the Revelation to see how many things and persons have their beginning in Genesis and their end or fulfillment in Revelation.

[9]Then saith he unto me, See *thou do*
it not: for I am thy fellowservant, and
of thy brethren the prophets, and of
them which keep the sayings of this
book: worship God.
[10]And he saith unto me, Seal not the
sayings of the prophecy of this book: for
the time is at hand.
[11]He that is unjust, let him be unjust
still: and he which is filthy, let him be
filthy still: and he that is righteous, let
him be righteous still: and he that is
holy, let him be holy still.
[12]And, behold, I come quickly; and
my reward *is* with me, to give every
man according as his work shall be.
[13]I am Alpha and Omega, the beginning and the end, the first and the last.
[14]Blessed *are* they that do his commandments, that they may have right
to the tree of life, and may enter in
through the gates into the city.
[15]For without *are* dogs, and sorcerers, and whoremongers, and murderers, and idolaters, and whosoever
loveth and maketh a lie.
¶[16]I Jesus have sent mine angel to
testify unto you these things in the
churches. I am the root and the offspring of David, *and* the bright and
morning star.
¶[17]And the Spirit and the bride say,
Come. And let him that heareth say,
Come. And let him that is athirst come.
And whosoever will, let him take the
water of life freely.
¶[18]For I testify unto every man that
heareth the words of the prophecy of
this book, If any man shall add unto
these things, God shall add unto him
the plagues that are written in this
book:
[19]And if any man shall take away from
the words of the book of this prophecy,
God shall take away his part out of the
book of life, and out of the holy city, and
from the things which are written in this
book.
¶[20]He which testifieth these things
saith, Surely I come quickly. Amen.
Even so, come, Lord Jesus.
¶[21]The grace of our Lord Jesus
Christ *be* with you all. Amen.

22:16 The Bright Morning Star
The last word of God to Israel in the Old Testament was that the Lord would come to them one day as the "Sun of righteousness" (Mal. 4:2). His last word here is that He will soon come as the "bright and morning star." The morning star rises just before the sun rises. We may look for Him to call His *church to Himself at any time, certainly before He comes to rule as the Son of David, Israel's Messiah.

22:10 at hand. See Revelation 1:3.

22:11 let. This means that when the things written in this book have taken place, there will be no more opportunity for men to be saved and changed into the likeness of the Lord Jesus Christ. Whatever they are at the end of this time, they will be for all eternity.

22:17 Come. This is the invitation the Holy Spirit is giving to everyone, through the *church and through the Bible.

22:18 add. This most solemn warning, while applying specifically to "the prophecy of this book," the Revelation, reaches beyond to the whole Bible, for the Revelation and the rest of the Bible are so bound together that they cannot be thought of separately. See *inspiration.

22:19 book of life. There is surely room in the Book of Life for every soul ever born, but those who refuse to take the eternal life that God offers in His Son, our Lord Jesus Christ, will not find their names written there.

INDEXES AND MAPS

SUBJECT INDEX
to the New Pilgrim Bible *1807*

The New Oxford Bible
CONCORDANCE
The King James Bible *1843*

THE NEW OXFORD BIBLE MAPS
Index to Maps *2049*
Maps

SUBJECT INDEX
TO THE NEW PILGRIM BIBLE

Aaron
Lev. 8:2
Num. 12:1
Num. 17:2

Aaron's rod
Num. 17:2,8

Abba
Gal. 4:4

Abel
Gen. 4:4

Abiding
John 15:4
John 15:6
1 John 3:6

Abijam
1 Kings 15:1-4

Abimelech
Ps. 24

Abomination
Exod. 8:26
Lev. 7:18
Isa. 44:19
Dan. 9:27

Abraham
Gen. 17:5
Gen. 18 (map)
Gen. 13:1
Gen. 22:17 (chart)
1 Chron. 1:27
John 8:33
Rom. 4:1
Gal. 3:7
James 2:21

Acrostic
Ps. 25
Ps. 145:1

Achish, the king of Gath
1 Sam. 21:10

Adam
Rom. 5:12
1 Cor. 15:22

Adamant stone
Zech. 7:12

Adonijah
1 Kings 1:5

Adoni-Bezek
Judg. 1:5

Adoption
Rom. 8:23
Rom. 9:4
Eph. 1:5

Advent
Isa. 61:1

Advocate
1 John 2:1

Affliction
Job 32:1,2
Job 42:6
Prov. 3:11-12
Col. 1:24

Affliction and iron
Ps. 107:10

Afraid, be not
1 Pet. 3:14

Ahab
1 Kings 16:29

Ahasuerus
Ezra 1:1
Esther 1:1

Alabaster box
Mark 14:3

Alamoth
1 Chron. 15:20
Ps. 6 (table)

Alpha and Omega
Rev. 1:8

Altar
2 Chron. 6:12
Gen. 8:20
Exod. 24:4
Exod. 27:1
Josh. 8:31
Josh. 22:10
Josh. 22:19
2 Kings 16:10

Al-taschith
Ps. 57

Amalek
Exod. 17:8
Gen. 36:1
1 Chron. 4:43
Esther 3:1

Amen
Deut. 27:15
Jer. 11:5

Ammon
Judg. 10:7
Amos 1:13

Amorite
Amos 2:9

Anakims, The
Josh. 11:21

Angel
Heb. 1:4
Exod. 14:19
1 Kings 13:18
Ps. 91:11
Isa. 6:2

Dan. 4:13
Dan. 10:21
Mark 12:25
Mark 16:5
Luke 24:4
Rev. 1:20
Rev. 14:6

of the Lord
Exod. 3:2
Exod. 23:5
2 Kings 4:16

Anger of the LORD
1 Kings 11:9
2 Kings 13:3

Animals
Lev. 11:47 (chart)
Gen. 7:2 (clean beasts)
Lev. 11:2 (beasts)
Lev. 11:5 (coney/rabbit)
Lev. 11:6 (hare)
Num. 23:22 (unicorn)
Deut. 14:5 (pygarg)
Deut. 14:7 (coney/rabbit)
Judg. 15:4 (foxes)
1 Sam. 6:4 (mice)
Job 39:10 (unicorn)
Job 40:15 (behemoth)
Job 41:1 (leviathan)
Ps. 42:1 (hart)
Isa. 35:7 (dragon)
Jer. 17:3 (eagle)
Jer. 19:2 (lion)
Zech. 1:8 (horse)

Anna
Luke 2:36

Anoint
James 5:14
1 Sam. 9:16
1 Sam. 24:6
Ps. 2:2
Ps. 20:6
Ps. 23:5
Ps. 84:9
1 John 2:20

Anointed One
1 Sam. 2:10

Antichrist
1 John 2:18
Ps. 55:9
Jer. 30:8
Dan. 11:36
2 John 7

Apollos
Acts 18:24
Acts 19:1

Apology (apologetics)
Introduction to 2 Corinthians

Apostle
Luke 6:13
1 Cor. 9:1-2

Apple of His eye
Zech. 2:8

Aquila and Priscilla
2 Tim. 4:19

Aristarchus
Col. 4:10

Ark (of the Covenant)
1 Chron. 15:28
Exod. 25:10
1 Sam. 4:3
1 Sam. 6:19
1 Sam. 14:18
2 Sam. 6:2
2 Sam. 6:3-7
2 Sam. 6:13
2 Sam. 6:19
2 Sam. 7:1
1 Kings 8:9
1 Chron. 13:7
1 Chron. 16:37

Ark (Noah's)
Gen. 6:14

Armageddon
Rev. 16:16
2 Kings 23:29
Isa. 15:1
Isa. 26:21
Joel 3:2
Joel 3:9
Zech. 10:3
Rev. 16:12
Rev. 19:19

Armor
Exod. 39:23
1 Sam. 17:6
1 Kings 20:11
2 Cor. 10:4

Artaxerxes
Neh. 2:1
Ezra 1:1

Asa
1 Kings 15:9

Asaph
1 Chron. 6:39

Ashkelon
1 Sam. 5:1
Zech. 9:5

Ashtaroth
Deut. 12:3
Josh. 10:13
Judg. 2:13
1 Sam. 31:10
Jer. 7:18

Ass colts, Rode on
Judg. 10:4

Asshur
Hos. 14:3

Assurance
Heb. 10:22
Ps. 94:14
Isa. 45:17
John 6:37
1 Cor. 9:27
Phil. 1:6
2 Pet. 2:20

Assyria
Isa. 36 (map)

Atonement
Exod. 29:33
Lev. 6:30
Lev. 16:30

Lev. 17:11
Job 33:24
Prov. 16:6
1 Cor. 2:2
Col. 1:20
Heb. 1:3

Avenger of blood
Josh. 20:3
Num. 35:6
2 Sam. 14:11

Baal
1 Kings 18:26
Num. 25:3
Judg. 2:11
Judg. 8:33
1 Kings 18:22
Isa. 46:1
Jer. 50:2
Zeph. 1:4
Matt. 10:25
Mark 3:22
Luke 11:15

Babylon
Dan. 1 (map)
Exile to
Ps. 137:1
Isa. 39:6
Prophecy about
Isa. 13:1
Isa. 13:17
Isa. 21:9
Isa. 39:6
Jer. 39:7
Jer. 50:2
Jer. 51:64
Zech. 2:6
Rev. 16:19

Backsliding
Jer. 3:14

Balaam
Num. 22:5
Jude 11
Rev. 2:14

Balm of Gilead
Jer. 8:22

Baptism
Rom. 6:3
Matt. 3:11
Mark 1:9
John 1:5
Acts 18:8
1 Cor. 15:29
1 Pet. 3:21

Baruch
Jer. 45:1

Bashan
Amos 4:1
Ps. 22:12
Isa. 33:9
Nah. 1:4

Bath
Isa. 5:10

Bear the iniquity
Exod. 28:38

Beasts, These are the
Lev. 11:2

Beast
Rev. 13:1
Ps. 55:20
Dan. 7:8
Dan. 7:11
Dan. 9:24
Ezek. 28:2
Hab. 2:19
Zech. 11:16,17
2 Thess. 2:8
Rev. 13:14
Rev. 13:18
Rev. 17:3
Rev. 17:8
Rev. 17:10

Bedchamber
2 Kings 11:2

Beelzebub
Matt. 10:25
Mark 3:22

Beer-sheba
Gen. 21:31

Bel
Isa. 46:1

Belial, Children of
Deut. 13:13
2 Cor. 6:15

Believers
in the Body
Gal. 6:18
Mal. 3:16
Luke 20:35
Acts 21:17
Eph. 5:32
Heb. 10:25
James 2:2
Character of
Ps. 24:4
Acts 14:22
1 Cor. 1:12
Introduction to James
Introduction to 2 Peter
Chosen
Ps. 33:12
Ps. 139:16
Rev. 22:19
Christ in the
Gal. 2:20
1 John 3:24
Death of
1 Cor. 15:29
Devoted
Luke 8:21
John 15:4
Rom. 7:17
1 John 5:18
Disciplined
Prov. 16:3
Jer. 3:14
Rom. 13:1
Guided
Prov. 3:5-6
Col. 1:9
Identity of
Gal. 6:15
Gal. 3:7
Gal. 3:28
Gal. 6:18
Titus 3:7

1 Pet. 2:9
1 Pet. 2:11
Life of
2 Cor. 3:2
1 Cor. 9:25
1 Thess. 1:3
Loved
Num. 23:21
Ps. 34:9
Ps. 139:10
1 Cor. 13:13
Rewarded
1 Cor. 3:8
Righteoussness of
1 John 2:20
Rom. 6:18
Rom. 6:19
1 Cor. 6:11
2 Cor. 6:10
2 Cor. 6:14
Heb. 12:1
James 5:12
Jude 24
1 John 3:9
Sanctified
1 Cor. 2:16
Lev. 8:4
John 13:10
Rom. 2:6
1 Cor. 15:31
2 Cor. 3:18
1 Pet. 3:4
2 Pet. 1:4
Saved
Rom. 6:2
Exod. 19:6
1 Sam. 25:29
Mark 3:35
Mark 4:26
John 6:37
Rom. 7:6
Gal. 2:19
1 John 2:1
As a Witness
Acts 11:26
John 20:23
Phil. 2:15
Works of
1 Cor. 3:12

Bel . . . Merodach
Jer. 50:2

Beloved
Song 1:9
Isa. 5:1

Belshazzar
Dan. 5:1

Ben-hadad
1 Kings 15:18
1 Kings 20:1

Benjamin, tribe of
Judg. 21:2-3
1 Chron. 7:6

Beth-aven
Hos. 4:15

Beth-el
Gen. 12:8
Gen. 35:1
2 Kings 23:4
2 Kings 23:15

Bethphage
Mark 11:1

Beth-shemesh
Jer. 43:13

Bible
Introduction to 1 Chronicles
Introduction to Job
2 Tim. 4:13
Heb. 5:12
Luke 24:27
Inspiration of the
2 Tim. 3:16
Gen. 20:1
Josh. 24:27
Isa. 21:9
Isa. 40:22
Isa. 44:28
Jer. 1:5
Jer. 30:2
Matt. 5:1
1 Cor. 2:13
1 Cor. 14:37
Gal. 3:16
2 Pet. 1:21
Rev. 22:18
the Law
Exod. 19:25
2 Kings 11:12
2 Chron. 34:15
Ezra 6:18
Ps. 119:1
Jer. 15:16
James 1:21
2 Pet. 3:2
Prophecy
Isa. 34:16
Jer. 51:64
Dan. 9:2
Rev. 22:18
Word of God
2 Tim. 3:16
Jer. 23:29
Zech. 5:1
Eph. 6:17
Heb. 4:12

Birds
Num. 11:31
Deut. 14:12,13
Deut. 14:18
Zech. 5:9

Birth
2 Kings 4:16 (chart)

Birthright
Gen. 25:31

Bishop
Phil. 1:1
1 Tim. 3:1
Titus 1:7

Bitter
2 Sam. 6:21

Blameless
Phil. 3:6
1 Tim. 3:2
Jude 24

Blessing
2 Chron. 7:14
Deut. 33:1

Josh. 23:15
Ps. 1:1
Ezek. 47:1-3

Blood
Lev. 1:5
Lev. 8:23
Lev. 17:10,11
Job 16:18
Zech. 9:7
Mark 14:24
Heb. 9:12
Heb. 13:12
1 Pet. 1:2
1 John 5:6

Blue
Exod. 26:1
Num. 15:38

Boaz
1 Kings 7:21

Body of Christ
Eph. 5:32

Body, this is My
Mark 14:22
1 Cor. 11:24

Book of life
Ps. 139:16
Mal. 3:16

Book of (the law of) Moses
Ezra 6:18
Neh. 8:1 (chart)
Jer. 15:16

Book of Nathan
1 Chron. 29:29

Born again
John 3:3
John 5:21
John 10:10
Col. 2:11
2 Pet. 1:4

Borrow
Exod. 3:22

Bottles
Mark 2:22
Josh. 9:4
2 Sam. 16:1
Ps. 119:83

Bowels
Gen. 43:30
Song 5:4
Phil. 1:8

Branch, a
Isa. 11:1
Zech. 3:8
Zech. 6:12

Branch of Jesse
Isa. 11:1

Bread
Eccles. 11:1

Breaking of bread
Acts 2:42

Bride of Christ
Eph. 5:32

Bridegroom, The
Mark 2:19

Broken bones
Ps. 34:20

Brutish man
Ps. 92:6

Buckler
Ps. 18:2

Burden
2 Kings 9:25
Isa. 13:1
Jer. 23:33

Burnt-offering
Lev. 1:4

Butter
Judg. 5:25

Cab
2 Kings 6:25

Cabul
1 Kings 9:13

Caesar
Luke 2:1
Matt. 22:17
Mark 12:17
John 19:12
Acts 25:21
Acts 25:8
Phil. 4:22

Caiaphas
John 18:14

Caleb
Num. 14:24
Num. 14:30
Josh. 14:6
Judg. 1:12

Calendar
Gen. 7:11

Calling (God's)
Judg. 6:15

Canaan
Gen. 9:25
Deut. 11:10
Josh. 8 (map)
Josh. 12 (map)
Josh. 9:1
Mark 7:5-30

Candlestick(s)
Zeph. 1:12
Rev. 1:20

Canticle
Song (all chpts.)

Captivity
Jer. 25:11
Deut. 28:36
Introduction to 1 Kings
1 Chron. 9:1
Introduction to Ezra
Ezra 8:32
Isa. 44:28
Ps. 137:1
Introduction to Ezekiel

Carmel
1 Sam. 25:2
Isa. 33:9
Amos 1:2

Carnal
Rom. 7:14

Rom. 8:6
Rom. 15:27
1 Cor. 3:1
1 Cor. 9:11

Celibacy
1 Tim. 4:3

Censer
Num. 16:6

Centurion
Matt. 8:5

Cephas
1 Cor. 1:12

Chapiter
Exod. 36:38
1 Kings 7:16

Charity
1 Cor. 8:1
1 Cor. 13:1,4
1 Pet. 4:8

Chasten
Prov. 3:11
Deut. 8:5
2 Kings 6:33
Introduction to Ruth
Job 5:18
Job 23:10
Job 42:6
Amos 4:6
1 John 5:16

Chemosh
Judg. 11:24

Cherethites and the Pelethites
2 Sam. 8:18

Cherubims
Gen. 3:24
Exod. 25:18
Ps. 99:1
Ezek. 1:1
Ezek. 10:8
Heb. 9:5

Child
Mark 9:36
Mark 10:14

Chimham
Jer. 41:17

Chinnereth (Chinneroth)
Josh. 12:3

Chittim
Num. 24:24

Choler
Dan. 8:7

Christ
John 5:18
Ps. 1:1
Ps. 2:7
Prov. 7:19
Isa. 42:1
Isa. 44:6
Dan. 7:9
Matt. 2 (map)
Matt. 3 (map)
Matt. 17:2
Mark 5 (map)
John 1:1
John 5:19
John 6 (map)
John 6:32
Rom. 9:5
1 Cor. 1:13
Heb. 1:3
Heb. 5:9
1 John 3:3
Rev. 2:17
Rev. 5:5

Authority of
Mark 1:22
Mark 6:48

in David's Line
1 Chron. 3:5
Isa. 22:22
Luke 3:23

Death and suffering of
Isa. 53:1
Ps. 22
Ps. 22:1
Ps. 40:12
Ps. 102:23
Isa. 50:6
Isa. 52:13
Zech. 12:10
Mark 15:17
Mark 15:34 (chart)
Luke 12:50
1 Pet. 2:23
1 Pet. 3:18

Deity
John 10:30
Isa. 43:15
Ezek. 43:2
Matt. 2:11
Mark 10:18
Luke 2:49
1 John 1:1

Emmanuel
Matt. 1:23

First Coming
Isa. 61:1
Isa. 49:5
Isa. 63:1
Zech. 11:12
Mal. 3:1
Matt. 5:17
Luke 1:35
Luke 2:28

Humanity of
Matt. 1:1
Mark 1:13
Mark 6:3
Luke 9:58
Phil. 2:6

King
Isa. 32:1
Ps. 20:9
Ps. 110:1
Isa. 10:26
Isa. 33:22
Jer. 3:17
Jer. 30:9
Ezek. 21:27
Ezek. 37:16
Ezek. 43:2
Dan. 2:45
Zech. 6:11
Zech. 14:16

Acts 3:20
Love of
Luke 13:24
John 17:1
Eph. 1:6
Messiah
John 4:25
1 Sam. 2:10
Ps. 20:6
Mark 8:29
Luke 2:32
Acts 26:6
Rom. 15:8
Rev. 22:16
Priest
Heb. 9:11
Deut. 14:1
1 Sam. 2:35
Jer. 30:21
Matt. 3:15
Mark 16:19
Heb. 2:17
Heb. 5:10
Prophet
Deut. 18:15
Prophecy
Mic. 5:2
Num. 9:12
Ps. 2:6
Ps. 22:14
Ps. 34:20
Isa. 7:14
Isa. 9:2
Isa. 11:1
Isa. 40:1
Isa. 49:5
Isa. 53:7
Isa. 60:19
Lam. 3:30
Hos. 11:1
Nah. 1:5
Zech. 1:8
Zech. 3.8
Zech. 6:12
Zech. 9:9
Introduction to Malachi
John 5:46
Acts 26:6
Resurrection
John 20:27
Ps. 16:10
Luke 24:3
1 Cor. 15:20
Reign of
Jer. 30:9
Saviour
John 4:42
1 Sam. 25:29
Jer. 10:23
Mic. 5:5
Mark 1:1
Mark 14:22
Luke 2:11
John 1:29
John 6:51
Rom. 5:12
Rom. 10:6
1 Cor. 11:24
1 Tim. 4:10
Heb. 10:20
1 John 2:1
Rev. 5:6
Second Coming
Matt. 24:3
Gen. 49:10
Ps. 45:5
Isa. 60:13
Isa. 61:1
Isa. 63:1
Jer. 25:30
Ezek. 8:4
Hos. 6:3
Zeph. 3:15
Hag. 2:7
Zech. 12:10
Zech. 14:4
Matt. 3:12
Mark 9:2
Mark 14:62
Luke 9:29
Luke 18:8
Acts 1:11
1 Cor. 1:7-8
1 Cor.15:24
2 Thess. 2:3
1 Pet. 1:13
1 Pet. 4:7
2 Pet. 3:10
1 John 2:28
1 John 3:2
Rev. 2:25
Rev. 19:11
Son of God
Isa. 9:6
Prov. 30:4
Isa. 6:1
Luke 2:49
Luke 3:22
John 1:3
Acts 2:23
Heb. 1:2
Son of man
Matt. 8:20
Mark 13:26
Rev. 1:13
Stone
Isa. 28:16
Ps. 118:22
Dan. 2:34,35
Dan. 2:45
Zech. 3:9
Zech. 10:4
Zech. 4:7
Matt. 21:42
Luke 20:17
Acts 4:11
Rom. 9:32
1 Pet. 2:4,7,8
1 Pet. 2:7
1 Pet. 2:7
1 Pet. 2:7,8
Victory in
2 Cor. 2:14
Word
John 1:1

Church

Acts 7:38
Acts 2:47
Acts 18:8
Introduction to Ephesians
Eph. 3:3

Eph. 5:32
Col. 2:19
Christ and the
John 10:16
Rev. 19:7
Dispensational
Dan. 9:24
Acts 15:13
in the New Testament
Eph. 5:32
Acts 11:19-21
Rom. 16:5
1 Cor. 1:12
1 Tim. 5:9
Philem. 2
Rev. 2:1—3:22 (map)
Purposes for
Acts 11:18
Isa. 59:20
Acts 15:13
1 Pet. 4:17
Types of
Eph. 2:11
Gen. 24:4 (wife)
Ps. 45:title (bride)
Ps. 45:9 (queen)
Ps. 45:12 (temple)
Ps. 50:5 (Israel)
Rev. 2:1
Rev. 2:1—3:22

Church Age
Gen. 1:28
Acts 2:1

Cieled
Ezek. 41:16

Circumcision
Gen. 17:10
Deut. 10:16
Josh. 5:2
Jer. 6:10
Acts 15:1
Rom. 4:10
Rom. 2:29
Titus 1:10

Cities of refuge
Num. 35:6
Deut. 4:42
Josh. 20:2

City of palm trees
Judg. 1:16

Clean
Gen. 7:2
Lev. 14:2
Lev. 11:47
Num. 19:9
Luke 5:14

Cleansing
Lev. 14:2

Clothed with humility
1 Pet. 5:5

Cloudy pillar
Exod. 13:21

Coats of skins
Gen. 3:21

Common
Acts 2:44
Acts 10:14

Complaint
Num. 11:4 (chart)

Company of prophets
1 Sam. 10:5

Concubine
Judg. 8:31

Condemnation
Ps. 10:13
Ps. 15:4

Confess
Gen. 3:11
Neh. 9:3
James 5:16

Conscience
Rom. 2:14-15

Consecrate
Exod. 28:3
1 Chron. 29:5

Constellations
Job 38:31-32

Conversation
Gal. 1:13
1 Pet. 1:15

Convocation
Exod. 12:16
Num. 28:18

Cor
Ezek. 45:14

Corban
Mark 7:11

Corinth
Acts 18:1
Introduction to 1 Corinthians

Corruptible seed
1 Pet. 1:23

Covenant
Gen. 1:28
Introduction to Hebrews
Abrahamic
Deut. 29:1
Gen. 12:1
Gen. 13:1
Gen. 28:14
Josh. 21:45
Isa. 14:1
with the Beast
Ps. 55:20
of Christ
Gen. 17:19
Heb. 8:8
Davidic
2 Sam. 7:11
1 Chron. 17:7
1 Chron. 17:14
2 Chron. 22:10
Ps. 89:19
Amos 9:11
Luke 1:33
with God
Heb. 8:8
Deut. 29:1
Ps. 25:10
Jer. 31:1
Jer. 34:18
Ezek. 16:60

Ezek. 36:24
Zech. 9:11
Mal. 2:5
Acts 3:21
Rom. 9:4
Noahic
Gen. 9:1
between Men
1 Sam. 11:1
Mosaic
Exod. 20:1
2 Chron. 13:5
Jer. 11:2
of Salt
2 Chron. 13:5

Created
Gen. 1:19 (Chart)
Gen. 1:27

Crossing the Jordan
Josh. 3:17

Crown of thorns
Mark 15:17

Cubits
Gen. 7:20

Cunning work
Exod. 28:15

Cup is the New Testament
1 Cor. 10:16
Mark 14:22-24

Cup, this
Mark 14:36

Curious
Exod. 28:8

Curse
Josh. 23:15
Gal. 3:10

Cyrus
Ezra 1:1
Introduction to Nehemiah
Isa. 44:28

Damascus
Isa. 17:1
Jer. 49:23

Damnation
1 Cor. 11:29
Rom. 3:8
Rom. 13:2
1 Tim. 5:12

Dan, tribe of
Judg. 18:1

Dan . . . to Beersheba
Judg. 20:1

Daniel
Ezek. 14:14
Introduction to Daniel
Dan. 1:7

Darius
Ezra 1:1
Dan. 5:31
Zech. 1:1

David
1 Chron. 14:10
1 Sam. 17:5
1 Sam. 22 (map)
Introduction to 2 Samuel
2 Sam. 3 (chart)
2 Sam. 3:2
2 Sam. 7:13
2 Sam. 10:2 (map)
2 Sam. 23:1
1 Kings 2:11 (chart)
1 Kings 8:20
2 Kings 14:3
1 Chron. 14:17
1 Chron. 17:16
1 Chron. 20:1
1 Chron. 21:13-14
2 Chron. 33:7
Matt. 12:3

Day of Atonement
Num. 29:7-11
Lev. 16:30

Day of Christ
Isa. 28:5

Day of His wrath
Ps. 110:5

Day of judgment
Matt. 12:36
Job 21:30
Prov. 16:4
Obad. 1:15
Luke 16:23

Day of Christ, the
1 Cor. 1:78

Day of Pentecost
Acts 2:1

Day of redemption
Eph. 4:30

Day of slaughter
James 5:5

Day of the LORD
Isa. 2:12
Ps. 110:5
Isa. 10:20
Isa. 13:9
Introduction to Joel
Joel 1:15
Joel 2:1
Joel 3:14
Obad. 15
Zech. 6:1
Zech. 12:8
Zech. 14:6
Luke 17:31
Acts 2:20
2 Pet. 3:10
Jude 6

Day of wrath
Ps. 110:5
Zeph. 3:8

Day shall not come, that
2 Thess. 2:3

Day's journey
Num. 11:31

Daysman
Job 9:33
Job 16:21

Deacons
Phil. 1:1
1 Tim. 3:8

Death
John 8:51
Figurative
1 Cor. 15:31
Phil. 3:10
Physical
Heb. 9:27
Gen. 3:4
Gen. 23:1-19
Num. 27:13
Job 7:21
Mark 5:39
Acts 7:60
Rom. 7:24
1 Cor. 15:18
1 Thess. 4:13
1 John 5:16
and Sin
Gen. 5:5
Ps. 90:7
Rom. 5:14
Rom. 8:13
James 5:20
Spiritual
Heb. 9:27
Ps. 30:3
Luke 9:60
John 5:25
Rom. 7:9
Col. 2:13
James 1:15
Victory over
Isa. 25:8

Deism
Eccles. 3:16
Eccles. 4:1

Delusion, strong
2 Thess. 2:11

Demas
Col. 4:14

Demon
1 Tim. 4:1
Mark 5:2
Luke 11:14
Rev. 9:3

Den of thieves
Mark 11:17

Deny himself
Mark 8:34

Devil
Isa. 14:12
Job 1:14
Job 2:2
Isa. 27:1
Ezek. 28:2
Ezek. 28:12
Hos. 4:19
Zech. 3:1
John 12:31
2 Cor. 11:14
Eph. 6:11
1 Pet. 5:9
Mark 3:27
Luke 11:21
Rev. 16:13
Rev. 20:10

Devotion
Num. 14:12

Diana
Acts 19:24

Disciple
Luke 10:1
John 14:1
Acts 19:1

Dispensations
Gen. 1:28 (First)
Gen. 3:23 (Second)
Gen. 10:8 (Third)
Gen. 12:1 (Fourth)
Exod. 19:3-5 (Fifth)
Dan. 9:24-27
Acts 2:1 (Sixth)
Eph. 1:10 (Fullness of Times)
Rev. 1:3
Rev. 20:4 (Seventh)

Divided Kingdom
1 Kings 11 (map)
Introduction to 2 Kings
Hos. 1:1

Divination, Magic, and Witchcraft
1 Sam. 6:2

Doctrine
Acts 2:42
Acts 5:28
2 Thess. 2:15

Drams
Ezra 2:69

Drink-offering
Gen. 35:14
1 Sam. 7:6

Dung
Jer. 8:2
Phil. 3:8

Dung port
Neh. 2:13

Earing time, in
Exod. 34:21

Earnest of the spirit
2 Cor. 1:22
Eph. 1:14

Eat upon the mountains
Ezek. 18:6

Eden
Gen. 2:8-15
Gen. 3:17

Edom
Gen. 25:30
Deut. 23:7
Josh. 12:7
2 Kings 8:22
Ezek. 25:12
Ps. 60:8
Ps. 83:6
Jer. 49:10
Introduction to Obadiah

Egypt
Exod. 1:8

Exod. 12:12 (chart)
Exod. 15 (map)
2 Kings 25:26
Ezek. 29:2

Elders
Titus 1:5
Ruth 4:2
Job 12:20
Ps. 69:12
Matt. 15:2
Mark 7:3
James 5:14
Rev. 4:4

Elect, the
Mark 13:20
Titus 1:1

Election
Isa. 65:9
Rom. 9:11
Titus 1:1

El-Elohe-Israel
Gen. 33:20

Elias
Mark 6:15
Matt. 11:14
Mark 9:4
Luke 1:17

Elijah, the Tishbite
1 Kings 17:1
1 Kings 17:7
1 Kings 18 (map)
1 Kings 19:5
2 Kings 1:3

Elisha
1 Kings 19:19
2 Kings 2:24

Emerods
1 Sam. 5:6

Ensample
Phil. 3:17
1 Thess. 1:7

Ephah
Exod. 16:36
Amos 8:5

Ephod
Exod. 25:7
1 Sam. 21:9
1 Sam. 23:9

Ephraim
Hos. 7:8
Judg. 8:1
Josh. 17:14
2 Chron. 25:7
2 Chron. 30:1
Ps. 78:9
Ps. 78:67
Ps. 80:2
Isa. 7:2
Zech. 10:7

Err
Mark 12:24
1 Tim. 6:21

Esau
Obad. 6
Jer. 49:10
Gal. 6:16

Eternal life
John 3:15-16
Acts 5:20
1 Tim. 6:19
1 Pet. 3:15

Evil continually, only
Gen. 6:5

Exhort
Titus 2:15

Exile
2 Chron. 32 (map)
2 Chron. 36 (map)
Ezra 2 (map)
Introduction to Esther
Ps. 137:1
Isa. 39:6

Ezekiel
Ezek. 2:1
Ezek. 1:3
Ezek. 24:18

Ezra
Introduction to 1 Chronicles
Introduction to Nehemiah

Faith
Heb. 11:1 (chart)
Rom. 1:16-17
Heb. 10:22
Heb. 11:3
James 2:17
Examples of
Gen. 3:20
Gen. 22:5
Ezra 8:32
Luke 1:68
Luke 7:50
Heb. 11:5
James 2:21-25
Rewarded
Gen. 15:6
Josh. 1:11
Mark 10:52
Luke 17:14
in God
Deut. 11:2
Mark 11:22
1 Pet. 1:7
of a Believer
Eph. 4:5
Col. 2:6
James 2:18
Salvation by
Rom. 1:16-17
Josh. 2:18
Ps. 130:1
Hab. 2:4
Luke 13:26-27
Acts 18:8

Fall of man
Gen. 3:6
Gen. 3:1

Falsehood
1 Sam. 20:6
1 Sam. 22:22

False Prophet
Dan. 11:36

False teachers
2 Pet. 2:6

Introduction to Jude

Familiar spirits
1 Sam. 28:3
2 Kings 21:6

Famine
Jer. 14:16 (chart)

Farthing
Matt. 10:29

Fatalism
Eccles. 3:1

Fatherhood of God
Isa. 63:16

Fathoms
Acts 27:28

Fear
Prov. 1:7
Ps. 19:9
Jon. 1:9
Luke 12:5
2 Kings 17:33

Feasts
Num. 10:10
Num. 29:39
Exod. 23:16 (of Weeks)
Lev. 23:4 (of Tabernacles)
Lev. 16:30 (of the Day of Atonement)
Lev. 23:5 (of the Passover)
Lev. 23:7 (of the Day of Atonement)
Lev. 23:10 (of Firstfruits)
Lev. 23:16 (of Pentecost)
Lev. 23:16 (of the Wave Loaves)
Lev. 23:34 (of the Trumpets)
1 Kings 9:25
Ezra 3:4
Neh. 8:14 (of Tabernacles)
Esther 9:24 (of Purim)
Zech. 14:16 (of Tabernacles)
Luke 22:1 (of the Unleavened Bread)
John 7:37 (Great Day of the)
John 10:22 (of dedication)
Jude 12 (of Charity)

Festival
Num. 10:10

Fiery Serpent
Num. 21:8

Fig tree
Jer. 8:13

Fillets
Exod. 27:10

Fining pot
Prov. 17:3
1 Pet. 1:7

Fire
Lev. 1:8
2 Chron. 7:1
Jer. 23:29
Luke 12:49

Firstborn
Num. 3:40
Ruth 4:5
Ps. 89:19

Firkins
John 2:6

First day of the week
Matt. 12:2
Mark 16:2
John 20:1
Acts 20:7

Firstfruits of your harvest
Lev. 23:10
2 Kings 4:42
1 Cor. 15:20

Flesh
Rom. 7:14
Josh. 17:12
Judg. 3:12
Rom. 7:5
Gal. 5:13
1 John 2:16
Jude 23

Flowing with milk and honey
Exod. 3:8

Floods lift up their waves
Ps. 93:3

Food
Lev. 11:2
Rom. 14:20

Foolishness
Prov. 1:22
Eccles. 2:1

Forbid then not
Mark 10:14

Forgiveness
Matt. 12:31
Mark 2:7
Acts 10:43

Rain
Joel 2:23

Free-will offering
Lev. 1:3

Friendship
Num. 33:55
Job 2:11-13
Job 6:15

From the tower . . . to the fenced city
2 Kings 17:9

Frontlets
Matt. 23:5
Deut. 6:8

Froward
Prov. 2:12
Prov. 21:8
1 Pet. 2:18

Fruit
Ps. 1:3
Phil. 1:11

Fruit of the Spirit
Gal. 5:22-23

Fulness
Col. 1:19

Furlongs
Rev. 14:20

Gaal
Judg. 9:26

Gabriel
Dan. 8:16

Galilee
John 6 (map)

Gall and wormwood
Deut. 29:18

Garments
1 Pet. 5:5
Gen. 3:7
Gen. 3:21
Exod. 28:2
2 Kings 2:8
2 Kings 10:22
Isa. 59:6
Zech. 3:3
Zech. 3:5
Luke 23:11
1 Pet. 1:13
1 Pet. 2:16
Jude 23

Gate
Job 29:7
Ps. 9:14

Gath
2 Kings 12:17

Gaza
Zeph. 2:4

Genealogies
1 Chron. 1:1
1 Chron. 3:5
1 Chron. 7:6
1 Chron. 9:35

Genealogy of Christ
Matt. 1:1
Luke 3:23

Generation, this
Matt. 24:34
Mark 13:30

Gentiles
1 Sam. 14:6
John 10:16
Eph. 2:11

Gerah
Exod. 30:13

Gethsemane
Mark 14:32
Luke 22:39

Giants
Num. 13:22
Deut. 3:11
Josh. 11:21

Gideon
Judg. 7 (map)

Gifts
Acts 2:38
1 Cor. 12:4
Eph. 4:8

Gift, a
Mark 7:11

Gilead
Jer. 22:6

Gilgal
1 Sam. 11:15

Gins
Ps. 140:5

Gird up now thy loins
Job 38:3

Gittith
Ps. 8:title

Give ye them to eat
Mark 6:37

Glory of God
Ezek. 1:1
Ps. 29:1
Ezek. 8:4
Ezek. 43:2
Zech. 2:8

Goats' hair
Exod. 26:7

God
Gen. 1:1
Isa. 63:16
Ps. 18:25
Isa. 64:8
Jer. 10:16
John 14:28
Eph. 4:6
2 Pet. 3:5

Anger of
2 Kings 13:3

Grace of
Eccles. 2:26
Ezek. 36:21
Heb. 4:3

Holiness of
Lev. 19:2
Num. 4:15
1 Kings 11:9

Justice of
1 Kings 11:9
2 Kings 6:33
Ps. 50:1
Isa. 13:9
James 4:12
1 John 1:9

Love of
Num. 23:21
Ps. 24:6
Introduction to Hosea

Manifestation of
John 1:18
Exod. 24:10
Phil. 2:6
1 John 4:12

Mercy
2 Sam. 9:3
Ps. 136:1
2 Pet. 3:9

Omnipotence of
1 Sam. 2:2
1 Kings 20:23
Job 26:14
Amos 9:5

Luke 12:5
Omnipresence of
Gen. 3:8
Ps. 139:7
Jon. 1:3
Omniscience of
Ps. 139:1
Prov. 2:5
Prov. 15:11
Presence
Ezek. 48:35
Hab. 2:20
Sovereignty
Num. 3:41
Job 1:8
Ezek. 6:7
Zeph. 3:8
Trinity
Gen. 11:7
Gen. 1:2
Gen. 1:26
Prov. 6:22
Isa. 42:1
Jer. 50:20
Matt. 3:16
Luke 3:22
John 1:3
John 1:18
1 John 4:12
Vengence of
Ps. 94:1
Isa. 10:13
Heb. 10:30
Work of
Prov. 6:22

Gog, the land of Magog
Ezek. 38:2
Rev. 20:8

Goliath
1 Sam. 17:1

Gold
2 Chron. 8:18
Dan. 3:1

Golden Rule
Prov. 24:29

Gomer
Ezek. 38:6

Good Master
Mark 10:17

Gospel
Introduction to Matthew
Mark 1:1
Rom. 1:16
Introduction to Galatians
Rev. 14:6

Go to now
James 4:13

Grace of God
Col. 1:6
Hab. 2:4
John 1:17
Acts 4:33
Rom. 9:23
Rom. 11:6
2 Cor. 6:1
2 Cor. 8:1
Titus 1:4
James 4:6

Grave
Eccles. 9:10

Graven Image
Judg. 17:3
Dan. 2:31
Dan. 3:1

Great cry
Exod. 11:6

Great Tribulation
Deut. 4:30
Isa. 3:1
Zech. 6:5
Mark 13:13
Mark 13:19,20
Rev. 7:1
Rev. 13:5

Grecians
Acts 6:1

Grove
Deut. 12:3

Habergeon
Exod. 39:23

Hades
Luke 16:23
Rev. 6:8

Hallel
Ps. 113:title

Haman
Esther 3:1

Harden Heart
Exod. 4:21

Hardened their necks
2 Kings 17:14
Jer. 7:26

Hare
Lev. 11:6

Hazael
1 Kings 19:15
2 Kings 8:11,15

Heart
Prov. 4:23
Prov. 22:11
1 Pet. 3:4

Heath
Jer. 17:6

Heaven
Gen. 1:6
Isa. 65:17
2 Cor. 12:2
Eph. 1:3

Heavenly places
Eph. 1:3

Heave-offering
Exod. 29:27

Heifer, red
Num. 19:2

Hell
Luke 16:23
2 Sam. 22:6
Job 7:9
Job 17:16
Isa. 5:14

Hab. 2:5
Matt. 5:22
Mark 9:44
Rev. 6:8
Rev. 20:14

Heman
1 Chron. 6:33

Herod
Matt. 2:1
Matt. 22:16
Mark 6:14
Luke 3:1
Acts 12:1

Herodians
Matt. 22:16
Mark 3:6

Hezekiah
2 Kings 16:20

High places
Lev. 26:30
1 Kings 3:4
2 Chron. 6:12
Heb. 2:17

Hin
Exod. 29:40

Hind's feet
Hab. 3:19

Hinnom, Valley of the Son of
Jer. 19:2

Hiram, King of Tyre
1 Kings 5:1
2 Chron. 2:3

Hiram out of Tyre
1 Kings 7:13
2 Chron. 4:11

His own voluntary will
Lev. 1:3

Hittites
Judg. 1:26

Hobab
Num. 10:29

Holy
1 Sam. 2:2
1 Sam. 2:10
2 Sam. 6:3-7
Zech. 8:3

Holy city
Neh. 11:1

Holy Garments
Exod. 28:2

Holy of holies
Exod. 26:34
Heb. 9:3
2 Chron. 4:20

Holy Spirit
Mal. 2:15
Luke 11:13
John 3:8
Rev. 1:4
in the Believer
Acts 13:2
1 Cor. 3:16
Acts 1:5
Acts 16:7
Gal. 5:22-23
1 John 2:20
1 John 5:18
Holy Ghost
Acts 10:44
Luke 2:25
Acts 1:5
Acts 13:2
Gift of the
Acts 2:38
John 20:22
Acts 1:4
Acts 2:41
Acts 9:17
Acts 19:1
1 Cor. 12:4
Power of
Num. 11:25
Speaking through man
1 Sam. 10:10
2 Pet. 1:21
Speaking to man
1 Chron. 28:12
in the Trinity
Gen. 1:2
Type of
Deut. 32:11

Homer
Lev. 27:16

Hope
Job 14:10

Horeb
Deut. 4:10

Horn
1 Kings 1:50
Job 16:15
1 Sam. 2:1
Dan. 7:7
Zech. 1:18
Zech. 1:19
Luke 1:69

Hosanna
Mark 11:9
Ps. 118:25
Matt. 21:9

Hough
Josh. 11:6

House of the forest of Lebanon
1 Kings 7:2

House of the LORD
1 Kings 6:1
Hos. 8:1

Huldah
2 Kings 22:14

Hur
Exod. 17:10

Husbandmen
Mark 12:1

Hymenaeus
1 Tim. 1:20

Hyssop
Exod. 12:22

Idol Groves
Deut. 12:3

Idolatry
Num. 25:2

Judg. 17:3
Jer. 10:8
Amos 4:4
2 Chron. 25:1 (chart)
Rom. 1:23
Dangers of
Ps. 135:15
Examples of
Exod. 12:12 (chart)
Exod. 32:4
Lev. 26:30
Deut. 12:3
Deut. 18:10
1 Sam. 5:2
2 Kings 17:16
2 Chron. 11:15
Ps. 16:4
Isa. 1:29
Isa. 34:14
Isa. 41:7
Isa. 57:8
Jer. 2:27
Jer. 3:2
Jer. 23:10
Jer. 43:13
Jer. 48:13
Ezek. 6:9
Ezek. 8:14
Hos. 4:13
Hos. 4:19
Hos. 10:1
Hos. 10:5
Amos 5:26
Mic. 1:5
Acts 19:24
1 Cor. 8:5 (chart)
God's punishment for
Lev. 26:1
Deut. 2:34
2 Kings 17:18
Amos 3:14

Image of God
Gen. 1:27
Prov. 20:27
1 Thess. 5:23

Image and superscription
Mark 12:16

Immanuel
Isa. 7:14

Imputeth
Rom. 4:6
Philem. 18

Incense
Exod. 30:1

Infidel
2 Cor. 6:15

Inn, the
Gen. 43:21

Inspiration
2 Tim. 3:16
Gen. 20:1
Josh. 24:27
Isa. 21:9
Isa. 40:22
Isa. 44:28
Jer. 1:5
Jer. 30:2
Matt. 5:1
1 Cor. 2:13
1 Cor. 14:37
Gal. 3:16
2 Pet. 1:21
Rev. 22:18

Intermarriage
Deut. 2:34
Ezra 10:3

Isaac
Gen 21:3

Isaiah
Introduction to Isaiah
Isa. 56 (chart)

Isles
Gen. 10:5

Israel
Disobedience of
Ezek. 22:2
Gen. 46:3
Num. 11:4
Introduction to Judges
Ezek. 15:2
Ezek. 33:31
Ezek. 36:20
Introduction to Amos
Amos 9:8
Mark 11:13
Divided
1 Kings 11:20
2 Chron. 10:16
God's chosen
Amos 3:2
Ps. 33:12
Mic. 5:7
Mark 12:1
Rom. 1:16
God's Promises to
Rom. 9:4
Gen. 12:1
Gen. 15:18
Exod. 1:7
Josh. 1:6
Josh. 1:11
Jer. 16:15
Jer. 24:10
Jer. 31:1
Ezek. 33:31
Amos 9:7
Mark 13:30
Jacob, renamed
Gen. 28:10
Messiah from
Isa. 43:21
Isa. 44:1
Isa. 49:5
Names of
Isa. 54:5
Ezek. 23:4
Hos. 11:1
Amos 5:15
Origins of
Gen. 11:10
Gal. 6:16
Punishment of
Jer. 49:12

2 Kings 17:18
Jer. 3:6
Jer. 13:12
Jer. 18:3
Hos. 2:22
Amos 3:12
Regathering and Restoration of
Amos 9:13
Deut. 30:1-10
Ps. 107:4
Isa. 18:7
Isa. 27:12
Isa. 41:8
Jer. 3:18
Ezek. 37:1
Zeph. 3:20
Isa. 62:3
Isa. 65:9
Jer. 3:18
Ezek. 28:25
Ezek. 37:1
Introduction to Haggai
Zech. 10:10
Mark 13:27
Refusal of Christ
John 1:11
2 Cor. 3:14
Tribes of
Gen. 29:32
Gen. 49:1
Num. 32:1-5
Josh. 16 (map)
Ps. 68:27
Hos. 1:1
Unfaithfulness
Isa. 54:5
Ezek. 23:4
Hos. 2:2
ssue of blood, an
Mark 5:25
achin
1 Kings 7:21
acob
Gen. 28:10
Gen. 27:36
Gen. 30 (map)
Gen. 32:25
Mal. 1:2
Jacob and Esau
Gen. 25:25-26
Jacob's trouble, the time of
Jer. 30:7
James
Acts 15:13
Jasher, the book of
Josh. 10:13
Jealous God
Exod. 20:5
Zeph. 1:18
Zeph. 3:8
Jebusites
2 Sam. 5:6
Jechonias
Matt. 1:11
Jeduthun
Ps. 39:title
Jehoiada
2 Kings 11:4
Jehoshua
Num. 13:16
Jehu
2 Kings 9:2
Jeremiah, the prophet
Introduction to Jeremiah
Introduction to Lamentations
Jer. 26:20
Jer. 37:12
Jer. 43:6
Jerubbaal
Judg. 6:32
Jerusalem
Josh. 10:1
1 Chron. 11:5
Neh. 11:1
Jer. 22:23
Hos. 13 (map)
Zech. 1:17
Luke 20 (map)
Capital
Isa. 2:3
Jer. 3:17
Zech. 9:8
Destruction of
Amos 2:5
Mic. 3:12
Matt. 24:2
Luke 21:20
Prophecy about
Isa. 29:1
Jer. 5:1
Mic. 3:12
Matt. 24:2
Luke 21:20
Sin of
Isa. 4:4
Jer. 9:2
Jewels
Gen. 24:22
Exod. 35:22
Jeshurun
Deut. 32:15
Joab
2 Sam. 20:10
Job
Job 42:10 (chart)
Joash
2 Kings 11:2
John (the apostle)
Introduction to John
Introduction to 1 John
Introduction to Revelation
John the Baptist
Isa. 40:3
Mal. 3:1
Jonah
Jon. 2 (map)
Jon. 4:1

Joseph
Gen. 37:2
Gen. 39 (map)

Joseph of Arimathaea
Mark 15:43

Joshua
Introduction to Joshua
Josh. 1:1
Exod. 17:9
Num. 13:16
Josh. 11:18
Josh. 19:49

Josiah
2 Kings 21:24
2 Chron. 22:10

Jot
Matt. 5:18

Joy
Hab. 3:17

Jubile(e)
Lev. 25:4-5
Josh. 6:4
Jer. 34:16
Ezek. 7:13

Judah
Judg. 1:2
2 Chron. 2:3
2 Kings 25:21
2 Chron. 36:20
Neh. 4:10

Judas Iscariot
Ps. 55:13
Ps. 109:8
Luke 22:3
John 17:12

Judges
Judg. 2:18

Judgment
Matt. 12:36
John 9:39
Christ's
Jer. 25:30
Ezek. 20:35
Luke 17:31
Example of
Num. 16:31-35
2 Sam. 6:3-7
Final
Ezek. 20:35
John 5:22
2 Cor. 5:10
Rev. 8:2
Rev. 16:3
Rev. 20:11
Rev. 20:12
of the Innocent
Ps. 7:11
James 2:13
Israel a tool of God's
Ps. 149:7
Mic. 5:7
as Justice
Ps. 7:6
of the Nations
Ezek. 25:2
Isa. 23:15
Isa. 34:2
Isa. 66:24
Introduction to Nahum
Zeph. 3:9
Zech. 5:7
Mal. 3:18
Matt. 25:32
of his People
Ps. 50:1
Lam. 4:6
Ezek. 34:17
Amos 9:7
Mic. 1:2
Introduction to Zephaniah
1 Cor. 16:22
Seven Great
Matt. 12:36
Symbols of
Lev. 1:8
2 Kings 1:10
2 Chron. 7:1
Ps. 21:12
Isa. 6:6
Jer. 13:1
Jer. 14:1-4
Ezek. 10:2
Nature of God's
Lam. 2:2
Ps. 58:9
John 19:30
1 Sam. 2:10

Judgment Seat of Christ
Rom. 14:10
2 Cor. 5:10

Jupiter . . . Mercurius
Acts 14:12

Just
Job 9:2
Rom. 3:24
Rom. 4:5
Titus 3:7

Kedar
Isa. 42:11
Jer. 49:28

Kenite
Num. 24:21

Kin
Ruth 1:11

King of Persia
Ezra 1:1
Ezra 4:5-7
Neh. 2:1
Esther 1:1

Kingdom
Rev. 20:4
Millennial
1 Cor. 15:24
2 Chron. 9:22
Isa. 28:5
Ezek. 43:19
Mysteries of the
Matt. 13:11
Nature of
Amos 9:13
Isa. 4:5
Ezek. 34:11

Joel 3:10
Zech. 3:10
Acts 3:19
Foretold
Acts 3:21
2 Sam. 7:11
Ps. 72:1
Ps. 138:4
Zech. 9:8
Amos 9:11
Government
Isa. 33:22
Isa. 1:26
Isa. 2:3

Kingdom of God
Matt. 6:33
Acts 1:3

Kingdom of Heaven
Matt. 11:11
Matt. 3:2
Mark 4:30
Matt. 16:19

King of the Jews, the
Mark 15:2
Mark 15:26

Kinsman
Ruth 1:11
Ruth 2:20

Knops
Exod. 25:31

Korah
Num. 16:1-3
Num. 26:11

Lachish
2 Kings 14:19

Laid their hands on them
Acts 6:6

Land
Josh. 16 (map)
Josh. 21:54

Landmark
Deut. 19:14
Prov. 22:28

Last Adam
Rom. 5:12

Last days, but in the
Mic. 4:1
Joel 2:28
2 Tim. 3:1

Latter day, at the
Job 19:25
Jer. 30:24
1 Tim. 4:1

Laver
Exod. 30:18

Law
John 1:17
Ps. 119
Luke 10:27
Rom. 7:21
Gal. 3:19
Human
Gen. 14:1
Luke 11:52
Age of
Exod. 19:3-5
Fulfilled
Rom. 10:4
Gal. 3:10
Heb. 6:17
Perfection demanded by the
Exod. 19:8
Matt. 19:17
Rom. 3:20
Rom. 6:14
2 Cor. 3:6
Gal. 2:19
of Moses
Exod. 19:25
Exod. 20:1
Exod. 20:2
Introduction to Deuteronomy
Acts 13:15
Legalism and the
Matt. 15:2
Mark 7:3
Mark 12:28
Acts 1:12
Neglect of the
2 Chron. 12:1
Natural
Job 26:10
Obedience to the
Josh. 1:2
2 Chron. 12:1
2 Chron. 34:15
Jer. 15:16
Rom. 7:14
Gal. 5:3

Leaven
1 Cor. 5:6
Lev. 7:13
Mark 8:15

Lebanon
Hab. 2:17
Zech. 11:1

Lees, settled on his
Jer. 48:11

Legion
Mark 5:9

Leper/Leprosy
Lev. 13:2
2 Kings 7:3
Mark 2:40

Leviathan
Job 41:1

Levites
Josh. 21:3
1 Chron. 23:3,28

Libertines
Acts 6:9

Light
Gen. 1:3
Gen. 1:14
Isa. 60:19
Zech. 14:6

Linen
Exod. 26:1

Log
Lev. 14:10

LORD appeared
Gen. 12:7

LORD of hosts
1 Sam. 1:3

Lost years
Num. 20:1

Lot
Gen. 13:10

Lots, casting
Jon. 1:7
1 Sam. 14:41-42

Love
Num. 23:21
Song 1:9

Lubims
2 Chron. 12:3

Lucifer
Introduction to Genesis
Isa. 14:12
(See also Satan)

Luke
Introduction to Luke
Introduction to Acts

Lust
Gal. 5:16
1 John 2:16

Magic
(See witch)

Mahanaim
2 Sam. 2:8

Manasseh
Gen. 41:51
2 Kings 10:33
Josh. 17:14

Manna
Exod. 16:15

Mark (Marcus)
Introduction to Mark
Acts 15:37-38
Col. 4:10

Marriage
Matt. 25:1-3
1 Tim. 4:3

Mary
Luke 1:47

Maschil
Ps. 32:title

Materialism
Eccles. 2:12

Measure
Gen. 7:20 (Cubit)
Exod. 16:16 (Omer)
Exod. 16:36 (Ephah)
Exod. 28:16 (Span)
Exod. 29:40 (Deal)
Lev. 14:10 (Log)
Lev. 27:16 (Homer)
1 Sam. 17:7 (Shekel)
1 Sam. 25:8 (Measure)
2 Sam. 6:13 (Paces)
1 Kings 5:11 (Measure)
2 Kings 6:25 (Cab)
Ezra 2:69 (Dram)
Isa. 5:10 (Bath)
Ezek. 40:3 (Reed)
Ezek. 45:14 (Cor)
Amos 7:7 (Plumbline)
Zech. 5:7 (Talent)
John 2:6 (Firkin)
Acts 27:28 (Fathoms)
Rev. 14:20 (Furlongs)

Meat-offering
Lev. 2:1

Medes and Persians
Esther 2 (map)
Dan. 5:28

Mediator
Job 9:33
Gal. 3:19

Megiddo
2 Kings 23:29

Melchizedek (Melchisedec)
Gen. 14:18
Heb. 7:3

Mephibosheth
2 Sam. 9:3

Mercy
Ps. 5:7
Ps. 71:15
Rom. 3:25

Mercy seat
Exod. 25:17

Meshech and Tubal
Ezek. 27:13

Mesopotamia
Judg. 3:8

Messiah
1 Sam. 2:10
Isa. 40:1
Isa. 49:1
Ezek. 17:22
Ezek. 34:23
Zech. 3:8
Zech. 6:12
John 4:25

Michtam
Ps. 16:title

Midian
Exod. 2:15
Num. 22:3
Judg. 6:1

Mill
Exod. 11:5
Deut. 24:6

Millennium
1 Cor. 15:24
Isa. 35:1
Isa. 45:17
Isa. 56:7
Jer. 30:9
Ezek. 34:17
Ezek. 48:1
Ezek. 48:35
Zeph. 3:13
Rev. 21:9

Millo
2 Sam. 5:9

Miracle
Mark 8:22-26
Josh. 3:17 (chart)
Josh. 10:13
1 Sam. 6:12
1 Kings 17:17
2 Kings 1:10

2 Kings 4:44
Ps. 78:12
Isa. 38:8
Jon. 1:17
Mark 5:31
Mark 8:4
Mark 8:11
Mark 15:38

Miriam
Exod. 15:20
Num. 12:1

Mites, which make a Farthing, Two
Mark 12:42

Moab
Ruth 1:1
Gen. 19:37
Num. 22:3
2 Kings 1:1
Ezek. 25:8
Amos 1:13

Molech (Moloch)
Lev. 20:2
2 Kings 16:3
2 Kings 23:10
Jer. 49:1
Acts 7:43

Money
Exod. 25:34 (Talent)
Exod. 30:13 (Shekel of Silver)
Exod. 38:26 (Bekah)
Ezra 2:69 (Dram)
Ezek. 45:12 (Maneh)
Matt. 10:29 (Farthing)
Matt. 18:28 (Pence)
Mark 6:37 (Pennyworth)
Mark 12:15 (Penny)
Mark 12:42 (Mite)
Luke 12:6 (Farthing)
Luke 19:13 (Pound)

Month
Gen. 7:11

Moses
Exod. 2:10
Num. 12:7
Num. 14:12
Num. 20:12
Introduction to Deuteronomy
Ezra 6:18

Mount Sinai
(See Sinai)

Mountain
Ps. 72:3
Jer. 51:25
Mic. 4:1,2

Mount of Olives
1 Kings 11:7
Zech. 14:4
Luke 22:39

Mount Zion
Ps. 48:2

Mourning
Jer. 6:26
Deut. 14:1
1 Sam. 4:12
2 Sam. 1:2
2 Sam. 13:19
Job 1:20
Job 16:15
Ps. 56:8
Jer. 41:5
Amos 5:16
Jon. 3:6
Mic.1:16
Matt. 9:23
Mark 5:38

Music
1 Chron. 25:1
Exod. 15:20
Deut. 32:1 (chart)
1 Sam. 10:5
2 Kings 3:15
1 Chron. 15:20
2 Chron. 5:12
Job 30:31
Ps. 4:title
Ps. 6:10
Hab. 3:1
Hab. 3:3

Muthlabben
Ps. 9:title

Mystery
Matt. 13:11
Rom. 8:20
1 Cor. 4:1
Eph. 3:3

Naboth
1 Kings 21:3

Nadab and Abihu
Lev. 10:1

Nahash the Ammonite
1 Sam. 11:1

Nail
Zech. 10:4

Name of the Lord, in the
1 Sam. 17:45

Names of God
Gen. 1:1 (God—Elohim)
Gen. 2:4 (Chart)
Gen. 3:5 (Gods)
Gen. 14:18 (Most High God—El Elyon)
Gen. 15:2 (Lord God—Adonai Jehovah)
Gen. 17:1 (Almighty God—El Shadai)
Gen. 21:33 (Everlasting God—El Olam)
Gen. 22:14 (Jehovah-jireh)
Gen. 35:11 (God Almighty)
Exod. 3:14 (I AM)
Exod. 6:3 (Jehovah)
Exod. 15:26 (LORD that healeth thee)
Exod. 17:15 (Jehovah-nissi)
Judg. 6:24 (Jehovah-Shalom)

1 Sam. 1:3 (LORD of Hosts—Jehovah—Sabaoth)
Ps. 68:4 (Jah)
Isa. 7:14 (Immanuel)
Isa. 9:6 (Son)
Isa. 10:17 (Light of Israel)
Isa. 45:23 (Lord)
Isa. 63:16 (Father)
Ezek. 20:12 (LORD that sanctify them)
Dan. 7:9 (Ancient of Days)
Hos. 2:16 (Ishi)
Zech. 1:1 (LORD)
Matt. 1:23 (Emmanuel)
Matt. 5:33 (LORD)
Luke 2:21 (Jesus)
Luke 2:25 (Consolation of Israel)
John 1:1 (Word)
John 8:58 (I AM)
John 18:5 (I am He)
Rom. 8:15 (Abba)
Gal. 4:6 (Abba)
James 5:4 (LORD of Sabaoth)
1 John 2:1 (Advocate)
Rev. 1:8 (Alpha and Omega)

Naomi
(Introduction to Ruth)

Natural man
1 Cor. 2:14

Nature
Ps. 138:2

Nazarite
Num. 6:2
Judg. 16:7
1 Sam. 1:11

Nebuchadnezzar . . .
My servant
2 Kings 25 (map)
Jer. 27:6

Nehemiah
Introduction to Nehemiah
Neh. 13:7

Neginoth
Ps. 4:title

Nethinims
Ezra 2:43

New Birth
Ezek. 18:31
James 1:18

New Creature (Creation)
Gal. 6:15
1 John 3:9

New man
Ps. 8:2
Eph. 4:24
Col. 3:10

New moon
1 Sam. 20:5
Amos 8:5

Nineveh
Jon. 4:11
Nah. 2:4

Noash
2 Kings 13:9

None inheritance
Josh. 13:14

Noph
Jer. 2:16

Numbering
2 Sam. 24:2
Introduction to Numbers
Num. 1:2
Num. 1:18
Num. 3:40
Num. 26:51
Josh. 8:10
1 Chron. 21:1
Luke 2:1

Numbers in the Bible
1 Kings 8:31
Josh. 6:4
Ps. 119:164
Rev. 1:4

Obadiah
1 Kings 18:3

Obed
Ruth 4:17

Obedience
1 Chron. 13:7
Gen. 46:3
1 Kings 13:18

Oblation
Lev. 2:4

Observed times
2 Kings 21:6

Offend
James 2:10
Matt. 5:29
1 Cor. 8:13

Offering(s)
Num. 15:9
Gen. 35:14 (Drink)
Lev. 1:2
Lev. 1:3
Lev. 1:4 (Burnt)
Lev. 2:1 (Meat or Meal)
Lev. 3:1 (Peace)
Lev. 4:3 (Sin)
Lev. 5:6
Lev. 27:2
2 Sam. 24:24
1 Chron. 29:5
Matt. 6:1
Mark 12:43
Luke 11:41
2 Cor. 8:5
2 Cor. 9:10
Titus 3:14

Oil
1 Kings 1:39
2 Kings 4:2

Old man, The
Eph. 4:22
Josh. 3:1
Josh. 23:13

Rom. 6:6

)ld nature, the
1 John 5:18
Rom. 7:24

)mer
Exod. 16:16

)mri
1 Kings 16:23

)nesiphorus
2 Tim. 1:16

)phir
Job 22:24

)racle
2 Chron. 4:20

)uches
Exod. 28:11

)ur Father Which Art n Heaven
Matt. 6:9

'alace—Solomon's
1 Kings 7:1

'arable
Mark 4:2
Judg. 9:8
2 Sam. 14:5
2 Kings 14:9
Prov. 26:9
Eccles. 9:15
Isa. 5:1
Ezek. 17:2
Ezek. 19:1,2
Ezek. 24:3
Mark 4:30
Luke 19:12
Heb. 6:7
James 5:7

'aradise
2 Cor. 12:3-4
Luke 23:43

'artakers
Heb. 3:1
Heb. 6:4

'assover
Exod. 12:3
Lev. 23:5
2 Kings 23:22 (chart)
2 Chron. 30:1-20
2 Chron. 35:18
Luke 22:7
Luke 22:15
John 1:29
Acts 12:4

Paul
Acts 9:22
Acts 13 (map)
Acts 16 (map)
Acts 19 (map)
Acts 27 (map)
Acts 28:16
Gal. 6:11
Introduction to 2 Timothy
Philem. 19

Peace
Matt. 10:34
Joel 3:10
Nah. 1:15
Luke 24:36
Rom. 5:1
Phil. 1:2

Peace-offering
Lev. 3:1
1 Kings 8:63

Peculiar
Deut. 14:2
1 Pet. 2:9

Penny (Pence)
Mark 12:15

Pentecost, Day of
Acts 2 (map)
Acts 2:1
Luke 11:13
Luke 12:49
Acts 2:1

Perfection
1 John 2:5
Gen. 17:1
2 Kings 20:3
Job 1:1
Gal. 3:3
Phil. 3:11
Phil. 3:15
Jude 24

Persecution
Introduction to 2 Thessalonians

Persians, Medes and
Esther 2 (map)
Dan. 5:28

Peter
Matt. 16:18
John 21:15
John 21:1
Acts 2:14
Acts 8 (map)

Pharaoh
Gen. 12:15
Exod. 4:21
Exod. 8:25
Isa. 52:4

Pharisee
Matt. 3:7
Mark 8:15

Philip
Acts 8 (map)

Philippi
Acts 16:12
Introduction to Philippians

Philistines
Judg. 13:1
Ezek. 25:15
Amos 1:8
Mic. 1:10

Phinehas
Josh. 22:13
Judg. 20:28

Piercing
Deut. 15:17

Pilate
John 18:29

Pillar
2 Kings 11:14

Pit, the
Job 17:16

Plagues
Exod. 9:27 (chart)
2 Sam. 24:15 (chart)

Plants
Exod. 12:22 (Hyssop)
Exod. 25:5 (Shittim Wood)
Num. 24:6 (Lign Aloe)
Ruth 2:2 (Corn)
1 Kings 10:11 (Almug Trees)
2 Chron. 2:8 (Almug Trees)
Ps. 37:35 (Green Bay Tree)
Isa. 6:13 (Teil Tree)
Isa. 28:25 (Black Poppy)
Isa. 41:19 (Shittah Tree)
Isa. 41:19 (Oil Tree)
Isa. 43:24 (Sweet Cane)
Jer. 17:6 (Tamarisk)
Amos 7:14 (Sycamore)
Nah. 2:3 (Fir Tree)
Matt. 23:23 (Cummin)

Plumbline
Amos 7:7

Plummet
Zech. 4:10

Poor
Eccles. 4:1

Porters
1 Chron. 26:1
2 Chron. 31:14

Portion have we in David?, what
1 Kings 12:16

Potsherd
Job 2:8

Potter and the Clay
Jer. 18:3

Power and glory, great
Mark 13:26

Praise ye the LORD
Ps. 106:1
Ps. 146:1
Ps. 150:1

Prayer
Answered
Jude 20
Ps. 72:20
Acts 4:29
Examples of
Matt. 6:9
1 Chron. 4:9
Eccles. 5:2
Lam. 5:1
Mic. 7:7
Col. 2:1
God's response to
Jer. 7:16
Ezek. 22:30
1 Tim. 2:8
Importance of
1 Kings 8:22
James 5:16
Imprecatory
Ps. 5:10
Ps. 109:1
Ps. 137:9
the Lord's
Matt. 6:9
Should be
John 16:23
Mark 9:29
Luke 11:8
Luke 18:1
Col. 4:2
James 4:3
James 5:15
1 Pet. 4:7
1 John 3:21
1 John 3:22
Transformation by
Jon. 2:7
Types of
Mic. 7:7
Phil. 4:6
Heb. 10:19

Predestination
Eph. 1:11
Rom. 8:29
Rom. 9:11
1 Cor. 2:7
Eph. 1:5

Presumptuously, the soul that doeth ought
Num. 15:30
Deut. 1:45

Prevent(ed)
1 Thess. 4:15
Matt. 17:25

Priest
Exod. 28:2
1 Chron. 24:10
Heb. 9:11

Priesthood
Lev. 8:24

Profession
Heb. 3:1

Promise
Rom. 9:4
Gen. 3:15
Gen. 12:1
Gen. 15:18
Gen. 49:10
Exod. 1:7
Deut. 4:31
Deut. 28:36
Josh. 1:6
Judg. 21:45
1 Kings 3:14
1 Kings 11:36
1 Kings 13:2
Ps. 103:3
Jer. 16:15
Ezek. 33:31
Mark 13:30

Prophecy
Isa. 46:10
1 Sam. 10:10
1 Chron. 25:1
Jer. 46:26
Ezek. 25:2

Dan. 7:8
Dan. 8:1
Dan. 8:9
Dan. 9:24-27
Acts 2:16
1 Cor. 14:1
1 Thess. 5:20
2 Thess. 2:11
1 Pet. 1:11

Fulfilled—Christ
Mic. 5:2
Matt. 2:33
Mark 12:10
Mark 14:49
Mark 15:27
Mark 15:36
Mark 15:46
Luke 2:4
Luke 23:32
Luke 23:53
Luke 24:26
Luke 4:18
Acts 3:21
John 7:42
John 17:12
John 19:36
Rom. 1:3
Gal. 4:4

Fulfilled—Individuals
1 Kings 21:19
2 Kings 9:10
2 Kings 10:7
2 Kings 15:10
Jer. 39:7

Fulfilled—Israel
Zech. 6:15
Deut. 4:27
Deut. 28:36
Deut. 28:49
Deut. 28:64
Isa. 39:6
Jer. 1:13
Jer. 11:2
Jer. 25:11
Ezek. 15:6

Fulfilled—Nations
Isa. 21:9
1 Kings 16:34
2 Kings 8:22
2 Kings 19:25
1 Chron. 1:31
Isa. 13:17
Isa. 16:14
Isa. 23:1
Isa. 45:4
Ezek. 26:2
Dan. 2:31

Prophet
1 Sam. 19:24
1 Kings 19:19
Isa. 22:1 (chart)
Ezek. 12:3
Amos 3:7
Mic. 7:7
Zech. 1:4

Propitiation
Rom. 3:25
Luke 18:13
1 John 2:2

Proselyte
Acts 6:5

Prove(th)
Deut. 8:2
Gal. 6:4
1 Thess. 5:21

Proverbs
Introduction to Proverbs
Prov. 1:1
Eccles. 12:9

Psalms
Introduction to Psalms
Ps. 63:1 (chart)

Psaltery
1 Sam. 10:5
2 Chron. 5:12

Publican
Matt. 9:10

Queen of Heaven
Jer. 7:18

Queen of Sheba
1 Kings 10:1

Queen of the South
Matt. 12:42

Quick
2 Tim. 4:1
Acts 10:42

Quicken
1 Pet. 3:18
Col. 2:13

Quickeneth
John 5:21

Rahab
Josh. 2:1

Rain
Deut. 11:14
Joel 2:23
Zech. 10:1
James 5:7

Ransom
Job 33:24

Ransomed
Job 33:24

Rapture
1 Thess. 4:13
2 Kings 2:11
1 Cor. 15:51
Rev. 4:1

Reassurance
Num. 18:1

Receipt of custom
Matt. 9:9
Mark 2:14

Reconciliation
Col. 1:20
Lev. 6:30
2 Cor. 5:20

Redeemer
Isa. 47:4
Job 19:25
Isa. 59:20

Redemption
Exod. 6:6
Exod. 30:13
Ruth 1:11
Neh. 1:10
Job 19:25
Hos. 3:2
Rom. 3:24

Reed
Ezek. 40:3

Rehoboam
1 Kings 12:1

Reins, my
Ps. 7:9

Rejected
Mark 12:10

Religion
Eccles. 5:1
Gal. 1:13

Remission
Acts 10:43
Heb. 9:22

Remnant
Amos 9:8
Ezra 1:3
Ps. 89:36-51
Isa. 6:13
Isa. 7:3
Isa. 26:2
Jer. 14:1
Ezek. 34:11
Joel 2:32
Mic. 5:7
Zech. 9:7
Zech. 13:9
Mark 13:20

Render
Mark 12:17

Rent his mantle
Job 1:20

Repentance
Acts 17:30
Isa. 1:2
Jer. 2:2
Jer. 3:6
Jer. 7:2
Hos. 6:2
Zech. 8:14
Mark 1:4
John 5:14

Rereward
Isa. 52:12

Rest
Heb. 4:3

Resurrection
1 Cor. 15:52
Col. 1:27
Rev. 20:5
Types of
Josh. 4:2
Ps. 16:10
Jer. 1:11
Mark 16:2
Christ and
1 Cor. 15:4
Job 14:10
Isa. 25:8
Matt. 22:30
John 20:27
1 Cor. 15:14
1 Cor. 15:18
1 Pet. 1:3
of Believers
1 Thess. 4:13
Isa. 26:14
Isa. 26:19
Luke 14:14
John 6:40
1 Cor. 15:35
1 Cor. 15:42
1 Cor. 15:52
2 Cor. 5:1
Phil. 3:10
Rev. 20:5-6
Rev. 20:12

Revelation
Gal. 1:12
Introduction to Revelation
Rev. 2 (map)
Rev. 6 (outline)

Revenge
2 Sam. 14:11

Reverence
Num. 4:15

Reward
1 Cor. 3:8
Rom. 14:10
1 Cor. 9:25
2 Cor. 5:10
Phil. 4:1
1 Tim. 3:13
James 1:12
1 Pet. 5:4

Rezin
Isa. 8:6

Riches enter, how hardly shall they that have
Mark 10:23

Riding on a colt
Judg. 10:4

Righteousness
Rom. 3:22
Gen. 7:1
Gen. 24:65
Deut. 6:25
Ps. 7:8
Ezek. 18:22
Gal. 3:24
1 John 3:7
Rev. 15:6

Rock
Job 18:4
1 Sam. 2:2
Ps. 61:2
1 Cor. 10:4

Roman Empire
Dan. 2:31
Deut. 28:49
Dan. 11:35
Rev. 17:12

Rudiments
Col. 2:8

Rulers
Hab. 1:11

Mark 12:14
Ruth
Ruth 2 (map)
Rush, Branch and
Isa. 9:14
Sabbath
Matt. 12:2
Lev. 25:4
Deut. 5:12
John 20:1
Sabbath Day's journey
Acts 1:12
Sackcloth . . . ashes
Jer. 6:26
Sacrifice
Lev. 1:3-5
Heb. 10:3
1 Pet. 1:2
Sadducee
Matt. 3:7
Mark 8:15
Saints
Rom. 1:7
Deut. 33:2
Ps. 45:7
Dan. 7:18
Eph. 1:1
Heb. 12:23
Salt
Matt. 5:13
Lev. 2:1
2 Kings 2:21
Salvation
1 Cor. 1:21
Heb. 7:25
Jude 3
Rev. 3:20
through Christ
1 John 2:2
John 1:5
John 3:33
John 11:25
Acts 17:3
Acts 22:16
Rom. 5:12
1 Pet. 1:5
by Faith
Rom. 1:16-17
Acts 18:8
Rom. 5:9-10
from God
John 3:3
Jer. 3:6
Luke 13:23
John 3:33
Jews and
Luke 2:32
John 4:22
Types of
Josh. 3:17
Samaria
2 Kings 13:6
Ezra 4:1
Samaritan
Isa. 7:2
Neh. 6:1
Samuel
Introduction to 1 Samuel
1 Sam. 1:20
Samson
Judg. 16:17
Judg. 16:31
Sanballat . . . Tobiah
Neh. 2:10
Neh. 6:1
Sanctification
Exod. 13:2
Gen. 2:3
Sanctuary
Ps. 8:14
Isa. 8:14
Heb. 8:2
Sanhedrin
Matt. 26:59
Satan
Gen. 3:1
Isa. 14:12
Ezek. 28:12
1 Cor. 5:5
2 Cor. 11:14
Rev. 16:13
Saul
1 Sam. 15:14
2 Sam. 1:10
1 Chron. 10:13
Saul and David
1 Sam. 22:9 (map)
1 Sam. 26:25
1 Sam. 26 (chart)
Saviour
John 4:42
1 Sam. 25:29
Jer. 10:23
Mic. 5:5
Mark 1:1
Mark 14:22
Luke 2:11
John 1:29
John 6:51
Rom. 5:12
Rom. 10:6
1 Cor. 11:24
1 Tim. 4:10
Heb. 10:20
1 John 2:1
Rev. 5:6
Scarlet thread
Josh. 2:18
Scatter(ed) them
Zech. 7:14
Scorpion
1 Kings 12:11
Scribe
Matt. 2:4
Scrip
Mark 6:8
Sea of the Plain
Deut. 4:49
Josh 12:3
Sealed
Eph. 1:13
Rev. 5:1

Second Coming, see Christ, Second Coming

Second Death
Rev. 20:14

Seed
Gen. 4:25

Seir
Josh. 12:7

Selah
Hab. 3:3 or Ps. 6:10

Separate
2 Cor. 6:17
Exod. 8:25
Exod. 10:24
Deut. 22:9-11
Josh. 23:7
1 Sam. 8:20
Prov. 25:26
Ezra 9:1
Neh. 9:2
Mal. 2:11
Rom. 14:20
1 Cor. 5:13
1 John 2:15

Seraphim
Isa. 6:2

Sermon on the Mount
Matt. 5:1
Matt. 5:3-16

Servant
Deut. 15:17

Servant, my
Isa. 42:1
Isa. 52:13
Jer. 27:6

Set feasts
Num. 29:39

Seventy weeks
Dan. 9:24

Sharon
Isa. 33:9

Sheba
1 Kings 10:1

Shechem
Judg. 9:1
1 Kings 12:1

Sheep gate
Neh. 3:1

Shekel . . . silver
Exod. 30:13

Shekels of brass
2 Sam. 21:16

Shekinah
Ezek. 8:4
Gen. 15:17
Isa. 4:5
Zech. 2:8

Sheminith
Ps. 6

Shepherd
Ps. 80:1 (chart)
Mic. 2:12

Sherd
Isa. 30:14

Shewbread
Exod. 25:30
1 Sam. 21:5-6
Mal. 1:7

Shiloh
Josh. 18:1
1 Sam. 1:3

Shittim wood
Exod. 25:5

Shoes
Ps. 60:8

Shoshannim
Ps. 45:0

Shushan
Esther 1:2

Sick of love
Song 2:5

Sihor
Isa. 23:3

Silvanus
1 Thess. 1:1
1 Pet. 5:12

Silver
Exod. 30:13

Sin
Introduction to Genesis
Ps. 51:3
Ps. 103:3
Isa. 59:6
Jer. 18:4
Eph. 4:26
1 John 1:8
1 John 3:9

Consequences of
Exod. 20:5
Num. 11:34
Num. 15:30
Deut. 1:45
2 Sam. 12:10
1 Chron. 10:13
Isa. 59:2
Jer. 16:2
Lam. 1:5
Lam. 2:2
Ezek. 4:1
Ezek. 5:1
Hos. 13:16
Amos 3:3

Examples of
Gen. 11:4
Num. 7:1
Rom. 14:23

Forgiveness of
Jer. 30:12
Col. 2:14

Judgment of
Ps. 22:2
Num. 32:23
Isa. 5:8

Types of
Song 2:15
Jer. 13:1
Zech. 5:4

Unpardonable
Matt. 12:31

Victory over
Rom. 6:18

Sin-offering
Lev. 4:1
Gen. 4:3
Gen. 8:21
Lev. 1:9
Lev. 4:12
Heb. 13:13

Sin, unpardonable
Matt. 12:31

Sinai
Ps. 81:7
Exod. 3:1
Exod. 18:5
Ps. 68:8
Acts 7:30
Heb. 12:8

Sion (Zion)
1 Chron. 11:5
Zech. 1:17

Sisera
Judg. 4:2

Slavery
Exod. 1:13
Gal. 3:24
Introduction to Phile-mon

Snare
Deut. 7:16

Snuffers
2 Kings 12:13

Sodom and Gomorrah
Gen. 19:24

Solomon
1 Kings 3:7
1 Kings 4:26
1 Kings 11:42
2 Chron. 9:22
Introduction to Ecclesiastes
Introduction to Song of Solomon

Songs
Deut. 32:1 (chart)

Song of degrees
Ps. 120

Son of David
Matt. 1:1

Son of God
Isa. 9:6-7
Heb. 1:2

Son of Man
Matt. 8:20

Sons of Korah
Ps. 42 title

Sons of Zadok
Ezek. 44:15

Span
Exod. 28:16

Speak evil of dignities
Jude 8

Spikenard
Mark 14:3

Spirit (of God)
See Holy Spirit

Spirit (of man)
Prov. 20:27
Eccles. 1:14
1 Thess. 5:23

Spirit (spirit)
1 Sam. 28:3

Stephen
Acts 6:5

Stock. . .stone
Jer. 2:27

Stone (rejected)
Isa. 28:16

Stoning
Josh. 7:25

Straightway
Prov. 7:22
Mark 1:10

Stripes
Prov. 17:10

Stumblingstone
Rom. 9:32

Syria
1 Kings 20:23

Succoth
Judg. 8:5

Suffering
Job 42:6
Isa. 50:6
Hos. 3:1
John 11:35
Acts 14:19
Acts 14:22
1 Cor. 1:6-8
2 Cor. 11:24
1 Pet. 1:11

Sum, take ye the
Num. 1:2

Superscription
Mark 15:26

Sweet savour
Gen. 8:21
Lev. 1:9

Synagogue
Ps. 74:8
John 9:22

Tabernacle
Exod. 25:9
Exod. 26:1
Exod. 27:14 (chart)
Lev. 1:1
1 Sam. 1:9
1 Sam. 3:3
1 Chron. 23:28
2 Chron. 1:3

Tabret
1 Sam. 10:5

Taches
Exod. 26:6

Tadmor
1 Kings 9:18

Tarshish
Jon. 1:3

Tax Money
Judg. 1:28
Mark 12:14

Temple of the Lord
2 Chron. 31:10

1 Sam. 1:9
Ps. 30
Ps. 74:3
Jer. 52:17 (chart)
Mark 11:17
John 2:17

Temple—Millennial
Ezek. 40:5
Jer. 30:18
Ezek. 43:19
Hab. 2:20
Hag. 2:9

Temple—Solomon's
1 Kings 6:1
1 Kings 6:12

Temptation
Gen. 22:1
Mark 1:13
Luke 4:10
Heb. 11:37
1 Pet. 1:6
Rev. 3:10

Ten Commandments
Exod. 20:2
Deut. 5:6

Tenons
Exod. 26:17

Tenth deal
Exod. 29:40

Teraphim
Judg. 17:3

Testament
Mark 14:24

Tetrarch
Luke 3:1

Theophany
Gen. 35:9
Gen. 12:7
Gen. 32:20
Exod. 3:2
Josh. 5:13-15
Dan. 3:25
Zech. 1:8
Zech. 3:1
Col. 1:15

Theophilus
Luke 1:3

Thousand years
Rev. 20:2

Three tabernacles
Mark 9:5

Throne, Great White
Rev. 20:11

Timbrels
Exod. 15:20

Times of the Gentiles
Luke 21:24
Isa. 29:1
Jer. 27:6
Jer. 39:5
Jer. 50:2
Dan. 2:31
Luke 21:20

Timotheus (Timothy)
Acts 16:1
Phil. 1:1
Introduction to
1 Timothy

Tirshatha
Ezra 2:63

Tithes
Gen. 14:20
Lev. 27:30
Num. 18:24

Titus
2 Tim. 4:10
Introduction to Titus
Titus 1:4
Titus 2:1

Tobiah, Sanballat and
Neh. 2:10

Togarmah
Ezek. 27:14

Tools
Deut. 15:17
1 Sam. 13:20
1 Sam. 13:21

Tophet
Jer. 19:6
2 Kings 23:10
Jer. 7:31

Touched Me, who
Mark 5:31

Tower of Meah . . . Hananeel
Neh. 3:1

Tower of the furnaces
Neh. 3:11

Tradition
Gal. 1:14
2 Thess. 2:15

Transfigured
Matt. 17:2
Mark 9:2

Treasury, the
Mark 12:41

Tree
Gen. 2:9 (of life/tree of knowledge)
1 Kings 10:11 (almug)
Isa. 6:13 (teil)
Jer. 1:11 (almond)
Jer. 8:13 (fig)
Matt. 21:19 (fig)
Mark 11:13(fig)
Rev. 22:2 (of life)

Trespass
Lev. 6:5
Luke 17:3

Trespass-offering
Lev. 5:6

Tribe
Gen. 29:32
Gen. 49:1
Num. 2:2
Num. 32:1-5
Ps. 68:27
Hos. 1:1

Tribulation, the
Rev. 19:11-16

Isa. 29:1
Dan. 9:24
Mark 13:7
Mark 13:19-20
Rev. 6:11

Beast and the
Rev. 13:14
Ps. 55:20
Dan. 3:1

Believers and the
Rev. 3:10
Gen. 5:5
Mark 13:13-14
Mark 13:24
Rev. 13:5
Rev. 14:13

Earth and the
Isa. 24:1
Jer. 4:23

Israel and the
Jer. 30:7
Deut. 4:30
Ps. 44:4
Isa. 3:1
Hos. 6:11
Mic. 5:3
Matt. 24:3

Nations and the
Isa. 34:2

Unbelievers and the
2 Thess. 2:11
Rev. 7:1

Tribute
Matt. 17:24

Trinity
Gen. 11:7
Gen. 1:2
Gen. 1:26
Prov. 6:22
Isa. 42:1
Jer. 50:20
Matt. 3:16
Luke 3:22
John 1:3
John 1:18
1 John 4:12

Trust
2 Kings 18:5
Ruth 2:12
Prov. 18:10
Nah. 1:7

Tubal, Meshech and
Ezek. 27:13
Ezek. 38:2

Two wives
1 Sam. 1:2

Tychicus
Col. 4:7
2 Tim. 4:12

Type
Gen. 2:9
Gen. 4:25 (sons of Adam)
Gen. 6:14 (ark/Jesus Christ)
Gen. 7:16 (door of ark/safety in Christ)
Gen. 8:21 (meat-offering/Christ)
Gen. 14:18 (Melchizedek/Christ)
Gen. 21:3 (Isaac/Christ)
Gen. 22:13 (ram/Christ)
Gen. 28:10 (Jacob/nation of Israel)
Gen. 35:14 (drink-offering/Christ)
Gen. 35:18 (Ben-oni/Christ)
Gen. 37:2 (Joseph/Christ)
Exod. 12:3 (Passover)
Exod. 15:22 (40 years in wilderness/life)
Exod. 16:15 (manna)
Exod. 25:9 (tabernacle/Christ)
Exod. 26:1 (tabernacle)
Exod. 27:16 (gate/Christ)
Exod. 27:20 (oil/Holy Spirit)
Exod. 30:1 (incense/prayer)
Lev. 2:1 (meal-offering/Christ)
Lev. 2:11 (honey/Christ)
Lev. 3:1 (peace-offering/Christ's death)
Lev. 5:6 (trespass-offering/Christ)
Lev. 13:2 (leprosy/sin)
Lev. 14:2 (law/cleansing)
Lev. 21:17 (priests/Christ)
Lev. 23:17 (wave loaves/Christ)
Num. 13:16 (Joshua/Christ)
Num. 19:2 (sacrifices/death of Christ)
Num. 21:8 (fiery serpent/sin)
Josh. 1:1 (Joshua/Christ)
Josh. 1:2 (Moses/Law and Joshua/Saviour)
Josh. 2:18 (scarlet thread/gospel)
Josh. 3:1 (Jordan River/death of believer)
Josh. 3:17 (Jordan River/death of Christ)
Josh. 17:12 (Canaanites/flesh)
Josh. 22:19 (altar/cross)
Judg. 3:12 (Moabites/flesh)
Judg. 4:2 (Sisera's death/defeat of devil)
Judg. 10:7 (Ammon/rejection of Christ)
Ruth 2:20 (Boaz/Christ)
1 Sam. 21:5-6 (shewbread/God)
1 Kings 1:39 (oil/Holy Spirit)
2 Kings 2:11 (Elijah and Enoch/Rapture)

2 Kings 25:13 (vessels/ glory of Christ)
1 Chron. 12:22 (David/ Christ)
2 Chron. 9:22 (Solomon/ Christ)
Ps. 135:14 (Deliverance)
Isa. 45:1 (Cyrus/Christ)
Jer. 11:21 (Jeremiah/ Christ)
Ezek. 28:12 (Ethbaal II/ Beast)
Dan. 8:9 (Antiochus Epiphanes/little horn)
Hos. 12:10
Hag. 2:23 (Zerubbabel/ Christ)
Zech. 4:3 (olive trees/ Zerubbabel and Joshua)
Matt. 5:17 (Christ/ antitype of Law)
Mark 1:40 (leper/sinner)
1 Cor. 10:6 (Israelites/ Christians)

Tyre
Josh. 11:8
Ps. 45:12
Isa. 23:1
Isa. 23:15
Ezek. 26:2
Ezek. 28:21

Unbelievers
Rom. 1:20
Ps. 5:5
Ps. 28:3
Ps. 55:15
Prov. 1:22
Prov. 14:10
Isa. 66:24
Gal. 3:10
2 Pet. 2:20

Uncircumcised
1 Sam. 14:6

Unclean and the clean
Rom. 14:14
Lev. 11:2
Lev. 11:47 (chart)
Num. 9:6
Deut. 12:15
Deut. 14:3
Ezek. 4:15
Titus 1:15

Under every green tree
2 Kings 16:4

Unicorn
Job 39:10

Unity
Introduction to 1 Corinthians
1 Cor. 1:12

Unleavened bread
Gen. 19:3

"Unpardonable" sin
Matt. 12:31

Urim and Thummim
Deut. 33:8
1 Sam. 14:18
1 Sam. 23:9

Usurer
Exod. 22:25

Usury
Ps. 15:5

Vail (Veil)
Exod. 26:31

Valley of salt
1 Chron. 18:12

Vanity
Eccles. 1:2

Veil of the Temple
Mark 15:38

Vexation of spirit
Eccles. 1:14

Vials
Rev. 15:7

Vinegar
Ruth 2:14
Matt. 27:34

Vineyard
Mark 12:1
Isa. 5:1

Virtuous Woman
Prov. 31:10

Voluntary will, His own
Lev. 1:3

Vow
Lev. 27:2
Judg. 11:30

Wandering, Years of
Num. 15:2

Wash . . . feet
Gen. 18:4
John 13:10

Water
Isa. 36:2
1 John 5:6

Water of gall
Jer. 8:14

Wave-offering
Exod. 29:27

Weights
Exod. 30:13 (Shekel)
2 Kings 8:9 (Camel's Burden)
Rev. 16:21 (Talent)

Whirlwind, out of the
Job 38:1

Whole, they that are
Mark 2:17

Whore
Prov. 23:27
Judg. 8:27
Ezek. 6:9
Hos. 1:2

Wicked Men
2 Pet. 2:20

Wilderness
Exod. 15:22
Num. 33:13
Deut. 1:2

Window
Judg. 5:28

Wine
1 Tim. 3:8
1 Tim. 5:23

Winketh with his eyes
Prov. 6:13

Wisdom
Prov. 8:22
2 Chron. 1:10
Prov. 2:5
Prov. 4:7
Prov. 8:1 (chart)
Luke 7:35

Wist not
Exod. 34:29

Witch
Exod. 22:18
1 Sam. 6:2
Acts 16:16

Witness
John 5:31-33, 36-39

Women
1 Tim. 2:12

Word of God
Eccles. 12:13
Jer. 30:2
Jer. 36:2

Word of Life
1 John 1:1

Words, these are the
Exod. 19:6

World
John 12:31
1 John 2:15
Ages
Matt. 28:20
Mark 10:30
1 Cor. 10:11
2 Cor. 4:4
2 Tim. 1:9
Titus 1:2
Titus 2:12
Earth
Eccles. 1:4
Isa. 24:1-3
Jer. 4:23
Acts 17:31
Heb. 1:6
Heb. 4:3
Rev. 21:1
Love for the
1 John 2:15
Mankind
Isa. 13:11
Matt. 13:35
John 3:16
2 Cor. 1:12
Phil. 2:15
Heb. 10:5

Wormwood
Deut. 29:18

Worship
Introduction to Leviticus
Ps. 16:4
Ps. 105:1
Ps. 106:1
Ps. 120
Amos 8:5

Worshipped . . . the host of heaven
2 Kings 17:16

Ye shall know that I am the LORD
Ezek. 6:7

Year of Jubilee
Lev. 25:4-5

Zadok
1 Sam. 2:35

Zechariah
Zech. 1:1

Zedekiah
Jer. 21:1
Jer. 39:7

Zerubbabel
Zech. 4:6
Ezra 1:8
Hag. 2:23

Zion (Sion)
1 Chron. 11:5
Zech. 1:17

Zoan
Isa. 19:11

THE NEW OXFORD BIBLE

CONCORDANCE

THE KING JAMES BIBLE

BASE. Ezek. 21:26, and *a.* him that is high.
Dan. 4:37, walk in pride, he is able to *a.*
Mt. 23:12; Lk. 14:11; 18:14, whosoever exalteth himself shall be *a.*
Phil. 4:12, I know how to be *a.*
See Job 40:11; Isa. 31:4; 2Cor. 11:7.
BATED. Gen. 8:3; Lev. 27:18; Dt. 34:7; Jud. 8:3.
BHOR. Ex. 5:21, made our savour to be *a.*
Job 19:19, my inward friends *a.*
Ps. 78:59, Lord wroth, and *a.* Israel.
89:38, thou hast cast off and *a.*
107:18, soul *a.* all manner of meat.
119:163, I hate and *a.* lying.
Prov. 22:14, *a.* of the Lord shall fall there.
Isa. 7:16, land thou *a.* shall be forsaken.
66:24, they shall be an *a.* unto all flesh.
Ezek. 16:25, made thy beauty to be *a.*
Amos 6:8, I *a.* the excellency of Jacob.
See Lev. 26:11; Job 42:6; Rom. 12:9.
BIDE. Gen. 44:33, let servant *a.* instead of lad.
Ex. 16:29, *a.* every man in his place.
Num. 24:2, he saw Israel *a.* in tents.
31:19, *a.* without camp seven days.
1Sam. 5:7, ark of God not *a.* with us.
Job 24:13, nor *a.* in the paths thereof.
Ps. 15:1, Lord, who shall *a.* in thy tabernacle.
91:1, shall *a.* under the shadow.
Prov. 15:31, reproof *a.* among wise.
Eccl. 1:4, the earth *a.* for ever.
Jer. 42:10, if ye will still *a.* in this land.
49:18, 33; 50:40, there shall no man *a.*
Hos. 3:3, thou shalt *a.* many days.
Joel 2:11, day very terrible, who can *a.* it.
Mt. 10:11; Mk. 6:10; Lk. 9:4, there *a.* till ye go.
Lk. 2:8, shepherds *a.* in field.
19:5, to day I must *a.* at thy house.
24:29, *a.* with us, it is toward evening.
Jn. 3:36, wrath of God *a.* on him.
5:38, not his word *a.* in you.
14:16, another Comforter that he may *a.*
15:4, *a.* in me.
5, he that *a.* in me bringeth.
10, *a.* in my love.
Acts 16:15, come to my house and *a.*
1Cor. 3:14, if any man's work *a.*
13:13, now *a.* faith, hope, charity.
2Tim. 2:13, if we believe not he *a.*
See Gen. 29:19; Num. 35:25; Eccl. 8:15.
BILITY. Ezra 2:69, they gave after their *a.*
Dan. 1:4, had *a.* to stand in the palace.
Mt. 25:15, to teach according to *a.*
1Pet. 4:11, as of the *a.* God giveth.
See Lev. 27:8; Neh. 5:8; Acts 11:29.
BJECTS. Ps. 35:15, the *a.* gathered themselves together.

ABLE. Dt. 16:17, every man give as he is *a.*
Josh. 23:9, no man *a.* to stand before you.
1Sam. 6:20, who is *a.* to stand before God.
1Ki. 3:9, who is *a.* to judge.
2Chr. 2:6, who is *a.* to build.
Prov. 27:4, who is *a.* to stand before envy.
Amos 7:10, land not *a.* to bear his words.
Mt. 3:9, God is *a.* of these stones.
9:28, believe ye that I am *a.*
20:22, are ye *a.* to drink of cup.
Lk. 12:26, not *a.* to do least.
Acts 6:10, not *a.* to resist wisdom.
Rom. 4:21, what he had promised he was *a.*
8:39, *a.* to separate us from love of God.
1Cor. 10:13, tempted above that ye are *a.*
2Cor. 3:6, *a.* ministers of new testament.
Eph. 3:18, *a.* to comprehend with all saints.
Phil. 3:21, *a.* to subdue all things.
Heb. 2:18, *a.* to succour tempted.
Jas. 4:12, *a.* to save and destroy.
Jude 24, *a.* to keep you from falling.
Rev. 5:3, no man *a.* to open book.
6:17, who shall be *a.* to stand.
See Ex. 18:21.
ABOARD. Acts 21:2.
ABODE (*n.*). Jn. 14:23, we will come and make our *a.*
See 2Ki. 19:27; Isa. 37:28.
ABODE (*v.*). Gen. 49:24, his bow *a.* in strength.
Ex. 24:16, glory of the Lord *a.* on Sinai.
Jud. 21:2, the people *a.* there before God.
Lk. 1:56, Mary *a.* with her three months.
Jn. 1:32, the Spirit, and it *a.* on him.
39, they came and *a.* with him.
8:44, a murderer, and *a.* not in truth.
Acts 14:3, long time *a.*, speaking boldly.
18:3, Paul *a.* with them and wrought.
See 1Sam. 7:2; Ezra 8:15.
ABOLISH. 2Cor. 3:13, the end of that which is *a.*
Eph. 2:15, *a.* in his flesh the enmity.
2Tim. 1:10, Christ, who hath *a.* death.
See Isa. 2:18; 51:6; Ezek. 6:6.
ABOMINABLE. 1Ki. 21:26, Ahab *a.* in following idols.
Job 15:16, how much more *a.* is man.
Ps. 14:1; 53:1, they have done *a.* works.
Isa. 14:19, cast out like *a.* branch.
65:4; Jer. 16:18, broth of *a.* things.
Jer. 44:4, this *a.* thing that I hate.
Ti. 1:16, in works they deny him, being *a.*
1Pet. 4:3, walked in *a.* idolatries.
See Lev. 11:43; Dt. 14:3; Rev. 21:8.
ABOMINATION. Gen. 43:32; 46:34, *a.* to Egyptians.
Lev. 18:26, shall not commit any *a.*
Dt. 7:26, nor bring *a.* into house.

18:9, after the *a.* of nations.
12, because of *a.* the Lord doth drive.
25:16, do unrighteously are *a.* to God.
1Sam. 13:4, Israel had in *a.* with Philistines.
Prov. 3:32; 11:20, froward *a.* to the Lord.
8:7, wickedness an *a.* to my lips.
15, 8, 9, 26; 21:27, sacrifice, etc. of wicked are *a.*
28:9, even his prayer shall be *a.*
Isa. 44:19, residue thereof an *a.*
Jer. 4:1, put away thine *a.* out of sight.
6:15; 8:12, ashamed when committed *a.*
Ezek. 5:9, the like, because of all thine *a.*
33:29, land desolate because of *a.*
Dan. 11:31; Mt. 24:15; Mk. 13:14, *a.* of desolation.
Lk. 16:15, esteemed among men *a.* with God.
Rev. 21:27, in no wise enter that worketh *a.*
See Lev. 7:18; 11:41; Mal. 2:11; Rev. 17:4.
ABOUND. Prov. 28:20, faithful shall *a.* with blessings.
Rom. 15:13, that ye may *a.* in hope.
1Cor. 15:58, always *a.* in work.
2Cor. 1:5, as sufferings *a.* so consolation *a.*
See Rom. 3:7; 5:15; Phil. 4:12.
ABOVE. Dt. 28:13, *a.* only and not beneath.
Job 31:2, portion of God from *a.*
Prov. 15:24, way of life *a.* to wise.
Mt. 10:24; Lk. 6:40, disciple not *a.* master.
Jn. 3:31, cometh from *a.* is *a.* all.
8:23, I am from *a.*
Rom. 14:5, one day *a.* another.
1Cor. 4:6, *a.* that which is written.
Gal. 4:26, Jerusalem *a.* is free.
See Gen. 48:22; Ps. 138:2; Jas. 1:17.
ABSENT. 1Cor. 5:3; Col. 2:5, *a.* in body.
2Cor. 5:6, *a.* from Lord.
See Gen. 31:49; 2Cor. 10:1.
ABSTAIN. Acts 15:20, 29, *a.* from pollutions of idols.
1Th. 5:22, *a.* from all appearance of evil.
1Pet. 2:11, *a.* from fleshly lusts.
See 1Th. 4:3; 1Tim. 4:3.
ABSTINENCE. Acts 27:21, after long *a.* Paul stood forth.
ABUNDANCE. 1Sam. 1:16, out of *a.* of my complaint.
1Ki. 18:41, sound of *a.* of rain.
1Chr. 29:21, offered sacrifices in *a.*
Ps. 52:7, trusted in *a.* of riches.
72:7; Jer. 33:6, *a.* of peace.
Eccl. 5:10, loveth *a.* with increase.
12, *a.* of rich not suffer to sleep.
Mt. 12:34; Lk. 6:45, out of *a.* of heart.
13:12; 25:29, he shall have more *a.*
Lk. 12:15, life consisteth not in *a.*
2Cor. 8:2, of affliction the *a.* of their joy.
12:7, through *a.* of revelations.
See Job 36:31; Rom. 5:17; Rev. 18:3.
ABUNDANT. Job 36:28, clouds drop and distil *a.*
Ps. 145:7, *a.* utter the memory.
Isa. 56:12, as this day and more *a.*
1Cor. 15:10; 2Cor. 11:23, laboured more *a.* than all.
1Tim. 1:14, grace was exceeding *a.*
Ti. 3:6, shed *a.* through Jesus Christ.
2Pet. 1:11, entrance administered *a.*
See Ex. 31:6; Isa. 55:7; 1Pet. 1:3.
ABUSE. 1Cor. 7:31, use world as not *a.*
9:18, that I *a.* not my power.
See 1Sam. 31:4; 1Chr. 10:4.
ACCEPT. Gen. 4:7, shalt thou not be *a.*
Ex. 28:38; Lev. 10:19, *a.* before the Lord.
Dt. 33:11, *a.* the work of his hands.
1Sam. 18:5, *a.* in sight of all people.
2Sam. 24:23, the Lord thy God *a.* thee.
Est. 10:3, *a.* of his brethren.
Job 13:8; 32:21, will ye *a.* his person.
42:8, 9, him will I *a.*
Prov. 18:5, not good to *a.* wicked.
Jer. 14:12; Amos 5:22, I will not *a.* them.
37:20; 42:2, supplication be *a.*
Ezek. 20:40; 43:27, I will *a.*
Mal. 1:13, should I *a.* this.
Lk. 4:24, no prophet is *a.*
Acts 10:35, he that worketh righteousness is *a.*
Rom. 15:31, service *a.* of saints.
2Cor. 5:9, present or absent we may be *a.*
See Ps. 119:108; Eccl. 12:10; Mal. 1:8.
ACCESS. Rom. 5:2; Eph. 2:18; 3:12.
ACCOMPLISH. Job 14:6, *a.* as an hireling.
Ps. 64:6, they *a.* diligent search.
Prov. 13:19, desire *a.* is sweet.
Isa. 40:2, her warfare is *a.*
Lk. 12:50, straitened till it be *a.*
1Pet. 5:9, afflictions are *a.* in brethren.
See Isa. 55:11; Lk. 18:31; 22:37.
ACCORD. Acts 1:14; 4:24; 8:6; Phil. 2:2.
ACCORDING. Ex. 12:25, *a.* as he hath promised.
Dt. 16:10, *a.* as God hath blessed thee.
Job 34:11; Jer. 17:10; 25:14; 32:19, *a.* to ways.
Mt. 16:27; Rom. 2:6; 2Tim. 4:14, *a.* to works.
Jn. 7:24, *a.* to the appearance.
Rom. 8:28, called *a.* to his purpose.
12:6, gifts differing *a.* to grace.
2Cor. 8:12, *a.* to that a man hath.
See Mt. 9:29; Ti. 3:5.
ACCOUNT. Mt. 12:36, give *a.* in day of judgment.
Lk. 16:2, give *a.* of stewardship.
Lk. 20:35, *a.* worthy to obtain.
Rom. 14:12, every one give *a.* to God.
Gal. 3:6, *a.* to him for righteousness.
Heb. 13:17, watch as they that give *a.*
See Job 33:13; Ps. 144:3; 1Pet. 4:5.
ACCURSED. Josh. 6:18; 7:1; 22:20; 1Chr. 2:7, *a.* thing.
Rom. 9:3, wish myself *a.* from Christ.
1Cor. 12:3, no man calleth Jesus *a.*
Gal. 1:8, 9, preach other gospel, let him be *a.*
See Dt. 21:23; Josh. 6:17; Isa. 65:20.
ACCUSATION. Lk. 19:8, anything by false *a.*
1Tim. 5:19, against elder receive not *a.*
2Pet. 2:11; Jude 9, railing *a.*
See Mt. 27:37; Mk. 15:26; Lk. 6:7.
ACCUSE. Prov. 30:10, *a.* not servant to his master.
Mt. 27:12, when *a.* he answered nothing.
Lk. 16:1, was *a.* that he had wasted.

Jn. 5:45, I will *a.* you to the Father.
Ti. 1:6, not *a.* of riot or unruly.
See Mt. 12:10; Mk. 3:2; Lk. 11:54; Rev. 12:10.
CKNOWLEDGE. Ps. 32:5; 51:3, I *a.* my sin.
Prov. 3:6, in all thy ways *a.* him.
Isa. 63:16, though Israel *a.* us not.
1Jn. 2:23, he that *a.* the Son.
See Dan. 11:39; Hos. 5:15.
CQUAINT. Job 22:21; Ps. 139:3; Eccl. 2:3; Isa. 53:3.
CQUAINTANCE. Job. 19:13; Ps. 31:11; 55:13.
CQUIT. Job 10:14; Nah. 1:3.
CTIONS. 1Sam. 2:3.
CTIVITY. Gen. 47:6.
DDER. Gen. 49:17; Ps. 58:4; 91:13; 140:3; Prov. 23:32.
DDICTED. 1Cor. 16:15.
DDITION. 1Ki. 7:29, 30, 36.
DJURE. Josh. 6:26; 1Sam. 14:24; 1Ki. 22:16; 2Chr. 18:15; Mt. 26:63; Mk. 5:7; Acts 19:13.
DMINISTER. 1Cor. 12:5; 2Cor. 8:19, 20; 9:12.
DMIRE. 2Th. 1:10; Jude 16; Rev. 17:6.
DMONISH. Acts 27:9, Paul *a.* them.
Rom. 15:14; Col. 3:16, *a.* one another.
1Th. 5:12, over you in Lord, and *a.* you.
2Th. 3:15, *a.* him as a brother.
Heb. 8:5, Moses was *a.* of God.
See Eccl. 4:13; 12:12; Jer. 42:19.
DMONITION. 1Cor. 10:11; Eph. 6:4; Ti. 3:10.
DO. Mk. 5:39.
DOPTION. Rom. 8:15, 23; 9:4; Gal. 4:5; Eph. 1:5.
DORN. Isa. 61:10; Rev. 21:2, bride *a.* herself.
1Tim. 2:9; 1Pet. 3:3, 5, women *a.*
Ti. 2:10. *a.* doctrine of God.
See Jer. 31:4; Lk. 21:5.
DVANCED. 1Sam. 12:6; Est. 3:1; 5:11; 10:2.
DVANTAGE. Lk. 9:25, what is a man *a.*
Rom. 3:1; 1Cor. 15:32, what *a.*?
2Cor. 2:11, lest Satan get *a.*
See Job 35:3; Jude 16.
DVENTURE. Dt. 28:56; Jud. 9:17; Acts 19:31.
DVERSARY. Dt. 32:43; Ps. 89:42; Isa. 59:18; Jer. 46:10; Nah. 1:2; Lk. 13:17, his *a.*
Ex. 23:22, I will be *a.* to thy *a.*
Num. 22:22, angel stood for *a.*
1Ki. 5:4, neither *a.* nor evil.
11:14, 23, Lord stirred up *a.*
Job 31:35, that mine *a.* had written.
Ps. 38:20; 69:19; 109:4, 20, 29; Isa. 1:24, my *a.*
74:10, how long shall *a.* reproach.
Isa. 50:8, who is mine *a.*
64:2; Jer. 30:16; Mic. 5:9, thy *a.*
Amos 3:11, *a.* shall be round the land.
Mt. 5:25, agree with thine *a.*
Lk. 12:58, when thou goest with thine *a.*
1Cor. 16:9, there are many *a.*
Phil. 1:28, terrified by your *a.*
1Tim. 5:14, give no occasion to *a.*
Heb. 10:27, indignation shall devour *a.*
1Pet. 5:8, 9, because your *a.* the devil.
See 1Sam. 2:10; Isa. 9:11; 11:13.
DVERSITY. 1Sam. 10:19; 2Sam. 4:9; 2Chr. 15:6, all *a.*
Ps. 10:6, I shall never be in *a.*
94:13; Prov. 24:10; Eccl. 7:14, day of *a.*
Prov. 17:17, brother is born for *a.*
Isa. 30:20, bread of *a.*
Heb. 13:3, remember them which suffer *a.*
See Ps. 31:7; 35:15.
ADVERTISE. Num. 24:14; Ruth 4:4.
ADVICE. 1Sam. 25:33, blessed be thy *a.*
2Sam. 19:43, that our *a.* should not be first.
2Chr. 10:9, 14, what *a.* give ye.
Prov. 20:18, with good *a.* make war.
2Cor. 8:10, herein I give my *a.*
See Jud. 19:30; 20:7; 2Chr. 25:17.
ADVISE. Prov. 13:10, with the well *a.* is wisdom.
Acts 27:12, the more part *a.* to depart.
See 2Sam. 24:13; 1Ki. 12:6; 1Chr. 21:12.
ADVISEMENT. 1Chr. 12:19.
ADVOCATE. 1Jn. 2:1, an *a.* with the Father.
AFAR-OFF. Jer. 23:23, a God *a.*
30:10; 46:27, I will save them from *a.*
Mt. 26:58; Mk. 14:54; Lk. 22:54, followed *a.*
Acts 2:39, promise to all *a.*
Eph. 2:17, preached to you *a.*
Heb. 11:13, seen the promises *a.*
See Gen. 22:4; Ezra 3:13.
AFFAIRS. 1Chr. 26:32, pertaining to God and *a.* of king.
2Tim. 2:4, entangleth himself with *a.*
See Dan. 2:49; 3:12; Eph. 6:21, 22.
AFFECTED. Acts 14:2, minds evil *a.* against brethren.
Gal. 4:17, 18 zealously *a.*
See Lam. 3:51.
AFFECTION. 1Chr. 29:3, have set *a.* to house of God.
Rom. 1:26, vile *a.*
31; 2Tim. 3:3, without natural *a.*
12:10, be kindly *a.* one to another.
Gal. 5:24, crucified with *a.*
Col. 3:2, set your *a.* on things above.
5, inordinate *a.*
See 2Cor. 7:15.
AFFINITY. 1Ki. 3:1; 2Chr. 18:1; Ezra 9:14.
AFFIRM. Acts 25:19, Jesus, whom Paul *a.* to be alive.
See Rom. 3:8; 1Tim. 1:7; Ti. 3:8.
AFFLICT. Lev. 16:29, 31; Num. 29:7; Isa. 58:3, 5, *a.* your souls.
Num. 11:11, wherefore hast thou *a.*
Ruth 1:21, Almighty hath *a.* me.
1Ki. 11:39, I will *a.* seed of David.
2Chr. 6:26; 1Ki. 8:35, turn when thou dost *a.*
Job 6:14, to *a.* pity should be showed.
Ps. 44:2, how thou didst *a.* people.
55:19, God shall hear and *a.*
82:3, do justice to the *a.*
90:15, the days wherein thou hast *a.*
119:67, before I was *a.*
140:12, maintain cause of *a.*
Prov. 15:15, days of the *a.* evil.
22:22, neither oppress the *a.*
31:5, pervert judgment of *a.*
Isa. 51:21, hear thou *a.* and drunken.

53:4, 7, smitten of God and *a.*
54:11, thou *a.* tossed with tempest.
63:9, in all their *a.* he was *a.*
Lam. 1:5, 12, the Lord hath *a.*
Nah. 1:12, I will *a.* no more.
Zeph. 3:12, I will leave an *a.* people.
2Cor. 1:6, *a.* it is for consolation.
1Tim. 5:10, if she have relieved the *a.*
Heb. 11:37, destitute, *a.*, tormented.
Jas. 4:9, be *a.* and mourn and weep.
5:13, is any *a.*, let him pray.
See Ex. 1:11, 12; 22:22, 23.
AFFLICTION. Gen. 29:32; Dt. 26:7; Ps. 25:18, looked on *a.*
Ex. 3:7; Acts 7:10, 11, 34, have seen *a.* of people.
Dt. 16:3; 1Ki. 22:27; 2Chr. 18:26, bread of *a.*
2Chr. 20:9, cry to thee in *a.*
33:12, in *a.* besought the Lord.
Job 5:6, *a.* cometh not forth of the dust.
30:16, 27, days of *a.*
Job 36:8, cords of *a.*
Ps. 34:19, many are *a.* of righteous.
119:50, this my comfort in *a.*
132:1 remember David and all his *a.*
Isa. 30:20, water of *a.*
48:10, furnace of *a.*
Jer. 16:19, refuge in day of *a.*
Lam. 3:1 man that hath seen *a.*
Hos. 5:15, in their *a.* they will seek.
Mk. 4:17, *a.* ariseth for the word's sake.
Acts 20:23, bonds and a abide me.
2Cor. 2:4, out of much *a.* I wrote.
4:17, light *a.* for moment.
8:2, great trial of *a.*
Phil. 1:16, add *a.* to bonds.
Heb. 10:32, great fight of *a.*
11:25, suffer *a.* with people.
Jas. 1:27, visit fatherless in *a.*
See 2Ki. 14:26; Col. 1:24.
AFFRIGHT. Isa. 21:4, fearfulness *a.* me.
Mk. 16:5; Lk. 24:37, they were *a.*
Mk. 16:6, be not *a.* ye seek Jesus.
See Dt. 7:21; 2Chr. 32:18; Jer. 51:32.
AFOOT. Mk. 6:33; Acts 20:13.
AFORETIME. Dan. 6:10, prayed as *a.*
Rom. 15:4, things were written *a.*
See Isa. 52:4; Jer. 30:20.
AFRAID. Mt. 14:27; Mk. 5:36; 6:50; Jn. 6:20, be not *a.*
Gen. 20:8; Ex. 14:10; Mk. 9:6; Lk. 2:9, sore *a.*
Lev. 26:6; Job 11:19; Isa. 17:2; Ezek. 34:28; Mic. 4:4; Zeph. 3:13, none make *a.*
Jud. 7:3, whosoever is fearful and *a.*
1Sam. 18:29, Saul yet the more *a.*
Neh. 6:9, they all made us *a.*
Job 3:25, that I was *a.* of is come.
9:28, I am *a.* of sorrows.
Ps. 27:1, of whom shah I be *a.*
56:3, 11, what time I am *a.*
65:8, *a.* at thy tokens.
91:5, *a.* for terror by night.
112:7, *a.* of evil tidings.
Isa. 51:12, be *a.* of a man that shall die.
Mk. 9:32; 10:32, *a.* to ask him.
Jn. 19:8, Pilate was more *a.*
Gal. 4:11, I am *a.* of you.
Heb. 11:23, not *a.* of commandment.
See Dt. 1:17; Ps. 3:6.
AFRESH. Heb. 6:6.
AFTERNOON. Jud. 19:8.
AFTERWARDS. 1Sam 24:5, *a.* David's heart smote him.
Ps. 73:24, *a.* receive me to glory.
Prov. 20:17, deceit sweet, but *a.*
24:27, prepare work and *a.* build.
29:11, wise man keepeth till *a.*
Jn. 13:36, thou shalt follow me *a.*
1Cor. 15:23, *a.* they that are Christ's.
See Ex. 11:1; Mt. 21:32; Gal. 3:23.
AGAINST. Lk. 2:34; Acts 19:36; 28:22, spoken *a.*
See Gen. 16:12; Mt. 12:30; Lk. 11:23.
AGATE. Ex. 28:19; 39:12, an *a.*
Isa. 54:12, make thy windows of *a.*
Ezek. 27:16, and *a.*
AGED. 2Sam. 19:32; Job 15:10; Ti. 2:2, *a.* men.
Phile. 9, Paul the *a.*
See Job 12:20; 29:8; 32:9.
AGES. Eph. 2:7; 3:5, 21; Col. 1:26.
AGONE. 1Sam. 30:13.
AGONY. Lk. 22:44.
AGREE. Amos 3:3, except they be *a.*
Mt. 5:25, *a.* with adversary.
18:19, two of you shall *a.*
Mk. 14:56, 59, witness *a.* not.
Acts 15:15, to this *a.* words of the prophets.
1Jn. 5:8, these three *a.* in one.
See Mt. 20:2; Lk. 5:36; Acts 5:9; Rev. 17:17.
AGREEMENT. Isa. 28:15; 2Cor. 6:16.
AGROUND. Acts 27:41.
AHA. Ps. 35:21; 40:15; 70:3; Isa. 44:16; Ezek. 25:3; 26:2; 36:2.
AILETH. Gen. 21:17; Jud. 18:23; 1Sam. 11:5; 2Sam 14:5; Ps. 114:5; Isa. 22:1.
AIR. Job 41:16, no *a.* can come between.
1Cor. 9:26, as one that beateth the *a.*
14:9, ye shall speak into *a.*
1Th. 4:17, meet Lord in *a.*
See 2Sam. 21:10; Eccl. 10:20; Acts 22:23; Rev. 9:2.
ALARM (how sounded). Num. 10:5, when ye blow an *a.*
Jer. 4:19; 49:2, *a.* of war.
Joel 2:1, sound *a.* in holy mountain.
See 2Chr. 13:12; Zeph. 1:16.
ALAS. 2Ki. 6:5, 15, *a.* my master.
Ezek. 6:11, stamp and say *a.*
See Num. 24:23; Jer. 30:7; Rev. 18:10.
ALBEIT. Ezek. 13:7; Phile. 19.
ALIEN. Dt. 14:21, sell it to an *a.*
Ps. 69:8, an *a.* unto my mother's children.
Eph. 2:12, *a.* from commonwealth.
Heb. 11:34, armies of the *a.*
See Ex. 18:3; Job 19:15; Isa. 61:5; Lam. 5:2.
ALIENATED. Ezek. 23:17; Eph. 4:18; Col. 1:21.
ALIKE. Job 21:26, lie down *a.* in dust.
Ps. 33:15, fashioneth hearts *a.*

Eccl. 9:2, things cometh *a.* to all.
See Ps. 139:12; Eccl. 11:6; Rom. 14:5.
LIVE. Lev. 16:10, scapegoat presented *a.*
Num. 16:33, went down *a.* into pit.
Dt. 4:4, are *a.* every one of you.
32:39; 1Sam. 2:6, I kill and I make *a.*
Ezek. 13:18; 18:27, save soul *a.*
Mk. 16:11, heard that he was *a.*
Lk. 15:24, 32, son was dead and is *a.*
24:23, angels who. said he was *a.*
Acts 1:3, showed himself *a.*
Rom. 6:11, 13 *a.* to God.
1Cor. 15:22, all be made *a.*
1Th. 4:15, we who are *a.* and remain.
Rev. 1:18, I am *a.* for evermore.
See 2Ki. 5:7; Dan. 5:19; Rev. 2:8; 19:20.
LLEGING. Acts 17:3.
LLEGORY. Gal. 4:24, which things are an *a.*
LLOW. Lk. 11:48; Acts 24:25; Rom. 7:15; 14:22.
LLOWANCE. 2Ki. 25:30.
LL THINGS. 1Cor. 6:12, *a.* are lawful, but not expedient.
LLURE. Hos. 2:14; 2Pet. 2:18.
LMIGHTY. Ex. 6:3, by the name of God *A.*
Job 11:7, canst thou find out the *A.*
29:5, when *A.*was yet with me.
Ezek. 1:24; 10:5, I heard as voice of *A.*
Rev. 1:8; 4:8; 11:17, *A.* who was, and is.
See Gen. 17:1; Job 21:15; Ps. 91:1.
LMS. Mt. 6:1; Lk. 11:41; 12:33; Acts 10:2.
LMOND. Num. 17:8, and yielded *a.*
Jer. 1:11, a rod of an *a.* tree.
Eccl. 12:5, *a.* tree shall flower.
LOES. Ps. 45:8, smell of .... and *a.*
Song 4:14, *a.*, with all the chief spices.
Jn. 19:39, a mixture of myrrh and *a.*
LONE. Num. 11:14; Dt. 1:9, bear all these people *a.*
1Ki. 11:29, they two *a.* in field.
Job 1:15, escaped *a.* to tell.
Ps. 136:4, *a.* doeth great wonders.
Mt. 4:4; Lk. 4:4, not live by bread *a.*
Lk. 9:18, 36; Jn. 6:15, Jesus was *a.*
13:8, let *a.* this year also.
See Gen. 2:18; Mt. 18:15; Jas. 2:17.
LREADY. Eccl. 1:10; Mal. 2:2; Jn. 3:18; Phil. 3:16.
LTAR. Mt. 5:23, bring gift to *a.*
23:18, swear by *a.*
1Cor. 9:13; 10:18, wait at *a.*
Heb. 13:10, we have an *a.*
See 1Ki. 13:2; Isa. 19:19; Acts 17:23.
LTER. Ps. 89:34, nor *a.* thing gone out of my lips.
Lk. 9:29, fashion of countenance *a.*
See Lev. 27:10; Dan. 6:8.
LTOGETHER. Ps. 14:3; 53:3, *a.* become filthy.
Ps. 50:21, *a.* such an one as thyself.
Song 5:16, he is *a.* lovely.
See Ps. 19:9; 39:5; 139:4.
LWAYS. Job 7:16, I would not live *a.*
Ps. 103:9, not *a.* chide.
Mt. 28:20, I am with you *a.*
Mk. 14:7; Jn. 12:8, me ye have not *a.*
Phil. 4:4, rejoice in Lord *a.*
See Ps. 16:8; Isa. 57:16; Jn. 11:42.
AMAZED. Mt. 19:25, disciples exceedingly *a.*
Mk. 2:12; Lk. 5:26, *a.*, and glorified God.
14:33, he began to be sore *a.*
Lk. 9:43, *a.* at mighty power of God.
See Ezek. 32:10; Acts 3:10; 1Pet. 3:6.
AMBASSADORS. 2Chr. 32:31, the business of the *a.*
2Cor. 5:20, we are *a.* for Christ.
See Prov. 13:17; Isa. 18:2; 33:7; Jer. 49:14; Obad. 1; Eph. 6:20.
AMBER. Ezek. 1:4, 27; 8:2, as the colour of *a.*
AMEN (tantamount to an oath). Num. 5:22, the woman shall say, *A.*
Dt. 27:15-26, the people shall say, *A.*
Ps. 41:13; 72:19; 89:52, *A.* and *A.*
106:48, let all the people say, *A.*
Mt. 6:13, and the glory for ever, *A.*
1Cor. 14:16, of the unlearned say, *A.*
2Cor. 1:20, and in him, *A.*
Rev. 3:14, These things saith the *A.*
See Rev. 22:20.
AMEND. Jer. 7:3; 26:13; 35:15; Jn. 4:52.
AMIABLE. Ps. 84:1.
AMISS. 2Chr. 6:37; Dan. 3:29; Lk. 23:41; Jas. 4:3.
ANCHOR. Heb. 6:19, have as an *a.* of the soul.
ANCIENT OF DAYS. Dan. 7:22, until the *a.* came.
ANGEL. Gen. 48:16, the *A.* who redeemed me.
Ps. 34:7, *a.* of Lord encampeth.
78:25, man did eat *a.* food.
Eccl. 5:6, nor say before *a.* it was error.
Isa. 63:9, *a.* of his presence saved them.
Hos. 12:4, he had power over *a.*
Mt. 13:39, reapers are the *a.*
Mk. 12:25; Lk. 20:36, are as *a.* in heaven.
Lk. 22:43, an *a.* strengthening him.
Jn. 5:4, *a.* went down at a certain season.
Acts 12:15, it is his *a.*
1Cor. 6:3, we shall judge *a.*
2Cor. 11:14, transformed into *a.* of light.
Heb. 2:2, word spoken by *a.*
16, not nature of *a.*
13:2, entertained *a.* unawares.
1Pet. 1:12, *a.* desire to look into.
See Gen. 19:1; Ps. 8:5; Mt. 25:41; Heb. 2:7.
ANGER. Gen. 49:7, cursed be their *a.*
Neh. 9:17, slow to *a.*
Ps. 6:1; Jer. 10:24, rebuke me not in *a.*
30:5, *a.* endureth but a moment.
Prov. 15:1, grievous words stir up *a.*
19:11, discretion deferreth *a.*
Eccl. 7:9, *a.* resteth in bosom of fools.
Mk. 3:5, he looked on them with *a.*
Col. 3:8, put off *a.*, wrath, malice.
See Ps. 37:8; 85:3; 90:7; Prov. 16:32.
ANGRY. Ps. 7:11, God is *a.* with the wicked.
Prov. 14:17, he that is soon *a.*
22:24, make no friendship with *a.* man.
25:23, so doth an *a.* countenance.
Jon. 4:4, doest thou well to be *a.*
Mat 5:22, whosoever is *a.* with brother.
Jn. 7:23, are ye *a.* at me.
Eph. 4:26, be *a.* and sin not.
Ti. 1:7, bishop not soon *a.*

See Gen. 18:30; Prov. 21:19; Eccl. 5:6; 7:9.
ANGUISH. Ex. 6:9, hearkened not for *a.*
Job 7:11, I will speak in *a.* of spirit.
Rom. 2:9, tribulation and *a.* on every soul.
2Cor. 2:4, out of much *a.* of heart.
See Gen. 42:21; Isa. 8:22; Jn. 16:21.
ANOINT. Dt. 28:40; 2Sam. 14:2, *a.* not thyself.
Isa. 21:5, arise and *a.* shield.
61:1; Lk. 4:18, *a.* to preach.
Mk. 14:8, *a.* my body to burying.
Lk. 7:46, my head thou didst not *a.*
Jn. 9:6, *a.* eyes of blind man.
12:3, Mary *a.* feet of Jesus.
2Cor. 1:21, he which *a.* us is God.
1Jn. 2:27, the same *a.* teacheth.
Rev. 3:18, *a.* thine eyes with eyesalve.
See Jud. 9:8; Ps. 2:2; 84:9; Jas. 5:14.
ANOINTED. 1Sam. 26:9.
ANOINTING OIL. Ex. 30:25, it shall be an holy *a.*
37:29, he made the holy *a.*
ANON. Mt. 13:20; Mk. 1:30.
ANOTHER. Prov. 27:2, let *a.* praise thee.
2Cor. 11:4; Gal. 1:6, 7, *a.* gospel.
Jas. 5:16, pray one for *a.*
See 1Sam. 10:6; Job 19:27; Isa. 42:8; 48:11.
ANSWER (*n.*). Job 19:16; 32:3; Song 5:6; Mic. 3:7; Jn. 19:9, no *a.*
Prov. 15:1, a soft *a.* turneth.
16:1 *a.* of tongue from the Lord.
1Pet. 3:15, be ready to give *a.*
21, *a.* of good conscience.
See Job 35:12; Lk. 2:47; 2Tim. 4:16.
ANSWER (*v.*). Job 11:2, multitude of words be *a.*
Ps. 65:5, by terrible things wilt thou *a.*
Prov. 1:28, I will not *a.*
18:13, *a.* a matter before he heareth.
26:4, 5, *a.* not a fool.
Eccl. 10:19, money *a.* all things.
Lk. 21:14, meditate not what to *a.*
2Cor. 5:12, somewhat to *a.*
Col. 4:6, how ye ought to *a.*
Ti. 2:9, not *a.* again.
See 1Ki. 18:29; Ps. 138:3; Isa. 65:12, 24.
ANTIQUITY. Isa. 23:7.
APART. Mt. 14:13, desert place *a.*
23; 17:1; Lk. 9:28, mountain *a.*
Mk. 6:31, come ye yourselves *a.*
See Ps. 4:3; Zech. 12:12; Jas. 1:21.
APPARENTLY. Num. 12:8.
APPEAR. Col. 3:4; 1Tim. 6:14; 2Tim. 1:10; 4:8; Ti. 2:13; Heb. 9:28; 1Pet. 1:7, *a.* of Christ.
1Sam. 16:7, man looketh on the outward *a.*
Ps. 42:2, when shall I *a.* before God.
90:16, let thy work *a.*
Song 2:12, flowers *a.* on earth.
Mt. 6:16, *a.* to men to fast.
23:28, outwardly *a.* righteous.
Rom. 7:13, that it might *a.* sin.
2Cor. 5:10, we must all *a.*
12, glory in *a.*
1Th. 5:22, *a.* of evil.
1Tim. 4:15, profiting may *a.*
See Ex. 23:15; Mt. 24:30; Lk. 19:11.
APPEASE. Gen. 32:20; Prov. 15:18; Acts 19:35.
APPERTAIN. Num. 16:30; Jer. 10:7; Rom. 4:1.
APPETITE. Job 38:39; Prov. 23:2; Eccl. 6:7; Isa. 29:8.
APPLY. Ps. 90:12; Prov. 2:2; 22:17; 23:12; Eccl. 7:25
APPOINT. Job 7:3, wearisome nights are *a.*
14:5, thou hast *a.* bounds.
30:23, house *a.* for all living.
Ps. 79:11; 102:20, preserve those *a.* to die.
Mt. 24:51; Lk. 12:46, *a.* him his portion.
Acts 6:3, seven men whom we may *a.*
1Th. 5:9, not *a.* to wrath.
See Job 14:13; Ps. 104:19; Acts 17:31.
APPREHEND. Acts 12:4; 2Cor. 11:32; Phil. 3:12.
APPROACH. Isa. 58:2, take delight in *a.* God.
Lk. 12:33, where no thief *a.*
1Tim. 6:16, light no man can *a.*
Heb. 10:25, as ye see the day *a.*
See Dt. 31:14; Job. 40:19; Ps. 65:4.
APPROVE. Acts 2:22, a man *a.* of God.
Rom. 16:10, *a.* in Christ.
Phil. 1:10, *a.* things that are excellent.
2Tim. 2:15, show thyself *a.*
See Ps. 49:13; 1Cor. 11:19; Phil. 1:10.
APT. 2Ki. 24:16; 1Tim. 3:2; 2Tim. 2:24.
ARCHANGEL. 1Th. 4:16, voice of *a.*
Jude 9, Michael the *a.* contending.
ARCHERS. Gen. 21:20, and became an *a.*
49:23, the *a.* have sorely grieved him.
1Sam. 31:3, and the *a.* hit him.
2Chr. 35:23, and the *a.* shot at king Josiah.
Job 16:13, his *a.* compass me.
See 1Ki. 22:34.
ARGUING. Job 6:25.
ARGUMENTS. Job 23:4.
ARIGHT. Ps. 50:23; 78:8; Prov. 15:2; 23:31.
ARISE. 1Ki. 18:44, there *a.* a little cloud.
Neh. 2:20, *a.* and build.
Ps. 68:1, let God *a.*
88:10, dead *a.* and praise thee.
112:4, to upright *a.* light.
Mal. 4:2, Sun of righteousness *a.*
Mk. 2:11; Lk. 7:14; 8:54; Acts 9:40, I say *a.*
Lk. 15:18, I will *a.* and go.
Eph. 5:14, *a.* from the dead.
2Pet. 1:19, till daystar *a.*
See Isa. 26:19; Jer. 2:27.
ARMOUR (Goliath's). 1Sam. 17:54, but he put his *a.* in his tent.
1Ki. 22:38, and their washed his *a.*
Isa. 22:8, didst look in that day to *a.*
Lk. 11:22, his *a.* wherein he trusted.
Rom. 13:12, let us put on *a.* of light.
2Cor. 6:7, approving by *a.* of righteousness.
Eph. 6:11, 13, put on the *a.* of God.
See 2Cor. 10:3; 1Th. 5:8.
ARMS. Dt. 33:27, underneath are the everlasting *a.*
See Gen. 49:24; Job 22:9; Ps. 37:17; Mk. 10:16.
ARMY. 1Sam. 17:10, I defy the *a.* of Israel.
Job 25:3, is there any number of his *a.*
Lk. 21:20, Jerusalem compassed with *a.*
Acts 23:27, then came I with an *a.*

Heb. 11:34, *a.* of the aliens.
See Song 6:4; Ezek. 37:10.
RRAY. Jer. 43:12, shall *a.* himself with land.
Mt. 6:29; Lk. 12:27, *a.* like one of these.
1Tim. 2:9, not with costly *a.*
Rev. 7:13, *a.* in white robes.
See Job 40:10; Rev. 17:4; 19:8.
RRIVED. Lk. 8:26; Acts 20:15.
RROGANCY. 1Sam. 2:3; Prov. 8:13; Isa. 13:11; Jer. 48:29.
RROW. Num. 24:8, pierce through with *a.*
Ps. 38:2, thine *a.* stick fast.
76:3, brake the *a.* of the bow.
91:5, *a.* that flieth by day.
Prov. 25:18, false witness sharp *a.*
26:18, casteth *a.* and death.
Ezek. 5:16, evil *a.* of famine.
See Dt. 32:23; 2Sam. 22:15; Job 6:4; 41:28.
RTIFICER. Gen. 4:22; 1Chr. 29:5; 2Chr. 34:11; Isa. 3:3.
RTILLERY. 1Sam. 20:40.
SCEND. Ps. 68:18; Rom. 10:6; Eph. 4:8, *a.* on high.
Jn. 1:51, angels of God *a.*
3:13, no man hath *a.* to heaven.
20:17, I am not yet *a.*
Rev. 8:4, smoke of incense *a.*
11:12, they *a.* up to heaven.
See Ps. 24:3; 139:8.
SCRIBE. Dt. 32:3; Job 36:3; Ps. 68:34.
SHAMED. Job 11:3, shall no man make *a.*
Ps. 25:3, let none that wait be *a.*
31:1, let me never be *a.*
34:5, their faces were not *a.*
Isa. 45:17, not *a.* world without end.
65:13, ye shall be *a.*
Jer. 2:26, as a thief is *a.*
6:15; 8:12, were their *a.*
12:13, *a.* of your revenues.
14:4, plowmen were *a.*
Lk. 16:3, to beg. I am *a.*
Rom. 1:16, not *a.* of Gospel.
5:5, hope maketh not *a.*
9:33; 10:11, believeth shall not be *a.*
2Tim. 1:8, not *a.* of testimony.
2:15, workman that needeth not to be *a.*
Heb. 2:11, not *a.* to call them brethren.
11:16, not *a.* to be called their God.
1Pet. 4:16, suffer as Christian, not be *a.*
See Gen. 2:25; 2Tim. 1:12.
SHES. Gen. 18:27, which am but dust and *a.*
Job 2:8, and he sat down among the *a.*
13:12, remembrances are like unto *a.*
30:19, and become like dust and *a.*
42:6, and repent in dust and *a.*
Ps. 102:9, I have eaten *a.* like bread.
Isa. 44:20, he feedeth on *a.*
Jon. 3:6, king sat in *a.*
Heb. 9:13, if the *a.* of an heifer.
See 2Sam. 13:19; Est. 4:1; Isa. 58:5; Mt. 11:21.
SIDE. 2Ki. 4:4; Mk. 7:33; Heb. 12:1.
SK. Ps. 2:8; Isa. 45:11, *a.* of me.
Isa. 65:1, sought of them that *a.* not.
Mt. 7:7; Lk. 11:9, *a.* and it shall be given.
21:22, whatsoever ye *a.*
Mk. 6:22, *a.* what thou wilt.
Jn. 14:13; 15:16, *a.* in my name.
Jas. 1:5, let him *a.* of God.
1Pet. 3:15, *a.* reason of hope.
1Jn. 3:22; 5:14, whatsoever we *a.*
See Dt. 32:7; Jn. 4:9, 10; 1Cor. 14:35.
ASLEEP. Mt. 8:24; Mk. 4:38, but he was *a.*
26:40; Mk. 14:40, disciples *a.*
1Cor. 15:6, some are fallen *a.*
1Th. 4:13, 15, them that are *a.*
2Pet. 3:4, since fathers fell *a.*
See Song 7:9.
ASP. Dt. 32:33, the cruel venom of *a.*
Job 20:14, 16, it is the gall of *a.*
Isa. 11:8, play on the hole of the *a.*
Rom. 3:13, the poison of *a.*
ASS. Num. 22:30, am not I thine *a.*
Prov. 26:3, bridle for *a.*
Isa. 1:3, *a.* his master's crib.
Jer. 22:19, burial of an *a.*
Zech. 9:9; Mt. 21:5, riding on *a.*
Lk. 14:5, *a.* fallen into pit.
2Pet. 2:16, dumb *a.* speaking.
See Gen. 49:14; Ex. 23:4; Dt. 22:10.
ASSAULT. Est. 8:11; Acts 14:5; 17:5.
ASSAY. Acts 9:26, Saul *a.* to join disciples.
16:7, their *a.* to go to Bithynia.
Heb. 11:29, Egyptians *a.* to do.
See Dt. 4:34; 1Sam. 17:39; Job 4:2.
ASSENT. 2Chr. 18:12; Acts 24:9.
ASSIGNED. Gen. 47:22; Josh. 20:8; 2Sam. 11:16.
ASSIST. Rom. 16:2.
ASSOCIATE. Isa. 8:9.
ASSURANCE. Isa. 32:17, effect of righteousness *a.*
Col. 2:2, full *a.* of understanding.
1Th. 1:5, gospel came in much *a.*
Heb. 6:11; 10:22, full *a.* of hope.
See Dt. 28:66; Acts 17:31.
ASSURE. 2Tim. 3:14; 1Jn. 3:19.
ASSWAGE. Gen. 8:1; Job 16:5.
ASTONIED. Ezra 9:3; Job 17:8; Dan. 3:24; 4:19.
ASTONISHED. Mt. 7:28; 22:33; Mk. 1:22; 6:2; 11:18; Lk. 4:32, *a.* at his doctrine.
Lk. 2:47, *a.* at his understanding.
5:9, *a.* at draught of fishes.
24:22, women made us *a.*
Acts 9:6, Saul trembling and *a.*
12:16, saw Peter, they were *a.*
13:12, deputy believed, being *a.*
See Job 26:11; Jer. 2:12.
ASTONISHMENT. 2Chr. 29:8; Jer. 25:9, *a.* and hissing.
Ps. 60:3, made us drink wine of *a.*
Jer. 8:21, *a.* hath taken hold.
See Dt. 28:28, 37; Ezek. 5:15.
ASTROLOGERS. Isa. 47:13, let now the *a.*
Dan. 2:2; 4:7; 5:7, the *a.*
ATHIRST. Mt. 25:44; Rev. 21:6; 22:17.
ATONEMENT. Lev. 23:28; 25:9, a day of *a.*
2Sam. 21:3, wherewith shall I make *a.*
Rom. 5:11, by whom we received *a.*
See Lev. 4:20; 16:17; Num. 8:21.

ATTAIN. Ps. 139:6, I cannot *a.* to it.
2Sam. 23:19; 1Chr. 11:26, he *a.* not to first three.
Rom. 9:30, Gentiles *a.* to righteousness.
Phil. 3:11, 12, 16, that I might *a.*
See Gen. 47:9; Prov. 1:5; Ezek. 46:7; 1Tim. 4:6.
ATTEND. Ps. 17:1; 61:1; 142:6, *a.* to my cry.
Prov. 4:20, my son *a.* to my words.
See Ps. 55:2; 86:6.
ATTENDANCE. 1Tim. 4:13; Heb. 7:13.
ATTENT. 2Chr. 6:40; 7:15.
ATTENTIVE. Neh. 1:6; Job 37:2; Ps. 130:2; Lk. 19:48.
ATTIRE. Jer. 2:32; Ezek. 23:15.
AUDIENCE. 1Chr. 28:8, in *a.* of our God.
Lk. 7:1; 20:45, in *a.* of people.
Acts 13:16, ye that fear God give *a.*
See Ex. 24:7; Acts 15:12.
AUGMENT. Num. 32:14.
AUSTERE. Lk. 19:21.
AUTHOR. 1Cor. 14:33; Heb. 5:9; 12:2.
AUTHORITY. Mt. 7:29; Mk. 1:22, as one having *a.*
8:9; Lk. 7:8, I am a man under *a.*
21:23; Lk. 4:36, by what *a.*
Lk. 9:1, power and *a.* over devils.
19:17, have *a.* over ten cities.
Jn. 5:27, *a.* to execute judgment.
1Cor. 15:24, put down all *a.*
1Tim. 2:2, kings and all in *a.*
12, suffer not a woman to usurp *a.*
Ti. 2:15, rebuke with all *a.*
1Pet. 3:22, angels and *a.* subject.
See Prov. 29:2; 2Cor. 10:8; Rev. 13:2.
AVAILETH. Est. 5:13; Gal. 5:6; Jas. 5:16.
AVENGE. Dt. 32:43, he will *a.* blood.
Josh. 10:13, sun stayed till people *a.*
1Sam. 24:12, the Lord judge and *a.*
2Sam. 22:48; Ps. 18:47, it is God that *a.* me.
Est. 8:13, Jews *a.* themselves.
Isa. 1:24, I will *a.* me of mine enemies.
Lk. 18:3, *a.* me of my adversary.
See Gen. 4:24; Lev. 19:18; Jer. 5:9; 9:9.
AVENGER. Ps. 8:2; 44:16, enemy and *a.*
1Th. 4:6, the Lord is. the *a.*
See Num. 35:12; Dt. 19:6; Josh. 20:5.
AVERSE. Mic. 2:8.
AVOID. Prov. 4:15, *a.* it, pass not by it.
1Tim. 6:20; 2Tim. 2:23; Ti. 3:9, *a.* babblings.
See Rom. 16:17; 2Cor. 8:20.
AVOUCHED. Dt. 26:17, 18.
AWAKE. Ps. 17:15, when I *a.*, with thy likeness.
73:20, as a dream when one *a.*
Prov. 23:35, *a.* I will seek it again.
Isa. 51:9, *a.*, *a.*, put on strength.
Joel 1:5, *a.* ye drunkards.
Zech. 13:7, *a.* O sword.
Lk. 9:32, when *a.* they saw his glory.
Rom. 13:11, high time to *a.*
1Cor. 15:34, *a.* to righteousness.
Eph. 5:14, *a.* thou that sleepest.
See Jer. 51:57; Jn. 11:11.
AWARE. Song 6:12; Jer. 50:24; Lk. 11:44.
AWE. Ps. 4:4; 33:8; 119:161.
AWL. Ex. 21:6; Dt. 15:17.
AXE. Ps. 74:5, famous as he had lifted up *a.*
Isa. 10:15, shall the *a.* boast.
Mt. 3:10; Lk. 3:9, the *a.* is laid to root.
See 1Sam. 13:20; 1Ki. 6:7; 2Ki. 6:5.
BABBLER. Eccl. 10:11; Acts 17:18.
BABBLING. Prov. 23:29; 1Tim. 6:20; 2Tim. 2:16.
BABE. Ps. 8:2; Mt. 21:16, out of mouth of *b.*
17:14, leave their substance to *b.*
Isa. 3:4, *b.* shall rule over them.
Mt. 11:25; Lk. 10:21, revealed to *b.*
Rom. 2:20, teacher of *b.*
1Cor. 3:1, *b.* in Christ.
1Pet. 2:2, newborn *b.*
See Ex. 2:6; Lk. 2:12, 16; Heb. 5:13.
BACK. Josh. 8:26, drew not his hand *b.*
1Sam. 10:9, he turned his *b.*
Neh. 9:26, cast law behind *b.*
Ps. 129:3, plowers plowed upon my *b.*
Prov. 10:13; 19:29; 26:3, rod for *b.*
Isa. 38:17, cast sins behind *b.*
50:6, gave *b.* to smiters.
See Num. 24:11; 2Sam. 19:10; Job 26:9.
BACKBITERS. Rom. 1:30.
BACKBITING. Ps. 15:3; Prov. 25:23; 2Cor. 12:20.
BACKSLIDER. Prov. 14:14, *b.* in heart filled with his own ways.
Jer. 3:6, 8, 11, 12, *b.* Israel.
8:5, perpetual *b.*
14:7, our *b.* are many.
Hos. 4:16, as a *b.* heifer.
11:7, bent to *b.* from me.
14:4, will heal their *b.*
See Jer. 2:19; 5:6; 31:22; 49:4.
BACKWARD. 2Ki. 20:10; Isa. 38:8, let shadow return *b.*
Job 23:8, *b.*, but I cannot perceive.
Ps. 40:14; 70:2, driven *b.*
Isa. 59:14, judgment is turned *b.*
Jer. 7:24, they went *b.* and not forward.
See Gen. 9:23; 49:17; Jn. 18:6.
BAD. Gen. 24:50; 31:24, 29; Lev. 27:12, 14, 33; Num. 13:19; 24:13; 2Sam. 13:22; 14:17; 1Ki. 3:9; Mt. 22:10; 2Cor. 5:10, good or *b.*
See Lev. 27:10; Ezra 4:12; Jer. 24:2; Mt. 31:48.
BADGERS' SKINS. Ex. 25:5, and *b.*
26:14, a covering above of *b.*
BADNESS. Gen. 41:19.
BAG. Dt. 25:13; Prov. 16:11; Mic. 6:11, *b.* of weights.
Job 14:17, transgression sealed in *b.*
Isa. 46:6, lavish gold out of *b.*
Hag. 1:6, *b.* with holes.
Lk. 12:33, *b.* that wax not old.
Jn. 12:6; 13:29, a thief, and had the *b.*
See 1Sam. 17:40; 2Ki. 5:23; Prov. 7:20.
BAKE. Gen. 19:3; Lev. 26:26; 1Sam. 28:24; Isa. 44:15, *b.* bread.
Ex. 12:39; Lev. 24:5, *b.* cakes.
See Gen. 40:17; Ex. 16:23; Lev. 2:4; Num. 11:8.
BAKER. Gen. 40:1; 41:10; 1Sam. 8:13; Jer. 37:21; Hos. 7:4.
BALANCE. Lev. 19:36; Prov. 16:11; Ezek. 45:10, just *b.*

Job 37:16, the *b.* of clouds.
Ps. 62:9, laid in *b.*, lighter than vanity.
Prov. 11:1; 20:23; Hos. 12:7; Amos 8:5; Mic. 6:11, false *b.*
Isa. 40:12, 15, weighed hills in *b.*
46:6, weigh silver in the *b.*
Rev. 6:5, a pair of *b.*
See Job 6:2; 31:6; Jer. 32:10.
ALD. 2Ki. 2:23, go up, thou *b.* head.
Jer. 48:37; Ezek. 29:18, every head *b.*
See Lev. 13:40; Jer. 16:6; Ezek. 27:31.
ALDNESS. Isa. 3:24, instead of well set hair *b.*
22:12, call to weeping and *b.*
Mic. 1:16, enlarge thy *b.* as eagle.
See Lev. 21:5; Dt. 14:1; Ezek. 7:18; Amos 8:10.
ALL. Isa. 22:18.
ALM. Jer. 8:22; 46:11, *b.* in Gilead.
See Gen. 37:25; 43:11; Jer. 51:8; Ezek. 27:17.
ANDS. Ps. 2:3; 107:14, break their *b.* asunder.
73:4, there are no *b.* in their death.
Hos. 11:4, drew them with *b.* of love.
Zech. 11:7, two staves, Beauty and *B.*
Mt. 27:27; Mk. 15:16, gathered to him whole *b.*
See Job 38:31; Eccl. 7:26; Lk. 8:29; Col. 2:19.
ANISHED. 2Sam. 14:13; Ezra 7:26; Lam. 2:14.
ANK. Lk. 19:23, gavest not money into *b.*
See Gen. 41:17; 2Sam. 20:15; Ezek. 47:7.
ANNER. Ps. 20:5, in name of God set up *b.*
See Ps. 60:4; Song 2:4; 6:4; Isa. 13:2.
ANQUET. Est. 5:4; Job 41:6; Song 2:4; Dan. 5; Amos 6:7.
APTISM. Mt. 20:22; Mk. 10:38; Lk. 12:50, to be baptized with *b.*
21:25; Mk. 11:30; Lk. 7:29; 20:4; Acts 1:22; 18:25; 19:3, *b.* of John.
Mk. 1:4; Lk. 3:3; Acts 13:24; 19:4, *b.* of repentance.
Rom. 6:4; Col. 2:12, buried with him by *b.*
Eph. 4:5, one Lord, one faith, one *b.*
Heb. 6:2, doctrine of *b.*
See Mt. 3:7; 1Pet. 3:21.
APTIZE. Mt. 3:11; Mk. 1:8; Lk. 3:16; Jn. 1:26, *b.* with Holy Ghost.
14, I have need to be *b.*
16, Jesus when *b.* went up.
Mk. 16:16, he that believeth and is *b.*
Lk. 3:7, multitude came to be *b.*
12; 7:29, publicans to be *b.*
21, Jesus being *b.*, and praying.
7:30, Pharisees and lawyers being not *b.*
Jn. 1:33, he that sent me to *b.*
3:22, 23, tarried with them and *b.*
4:1, 2, Jesus made and *b.* more.
Acts 2:38, repent and be *b.*
41, gladly received word were *b.*
8:12, *b.* both men and women.
16, *b.* in name of Jesus.
36, what doth hinder to be *b.*
9:18, Saul arose and was *b.*
10:47, can any forbid *b.*
16:15, 33, *b.* and household.
18:8, many believed and were *b.*
22:16, be *b.* and wash away thy sins.
Rom. 6:3; Gal. 3:27, were *b.* into Jesus.
1Cor. 1:13, were ye *b.* in name of Paul.
10:2, were all *b.* in cloud.
12:13, all *b.* into one body.
15:29, *b.* for the dead.
See Mt. 28:19; Jn. 1:25, 28, 31.
BARBARIANS. Acts 28:4; Rom. 1:14; 1Cor. 14:11.
BARBAROUS. Acts 28:2.
BARBED. Job 41:7.
BARBER. Ezek. 5:1.
BARE (*v.*). Ex. 19:4; Dt. 1:31; Isa. 53:12; 63:9; Mt. 8:17; 1Pet. 2:24.
BARE (*ad.*). Isa. 52:10; 1Cor. 15:37.
BARLEY. Ex. 9:31, *b.* was in the ear.
Dt. 8:8, a land of wheat and *b.*
Ruth 1:22, beginning of *b.* harvest.
Jn. 6:9, five *b.* loaves.
Rev. 6:6, three measures of *b.*
BARKED. Joel 1:7.
BARN. Job 39:12, gather thy seed into *b.*
Mt. 6:26; Lk. 12:24, nor gather into *b.*
13:30, gather wheat into *b.*
Lk. 12:18, pull down my *b.*
See 2Ki. 6:27; Joel 1:17; Hag. 2:19.
BARREL. 1Ki. 17:12, 14; 18:33.
BARREN. 2Ki. 2:19, water naught and ground *b.*
Ps. 107:34, turneth fruitful land into *b.*
Isa. 54:1, sing, O *b.*, thou that didst not bear.
2Pet. 1:8, neither *b.* nor unfruitful.
See Ex. 23:26; Job 24:21; Lk. 23:29.
BARS. Job 17:16, down to the *b.* of the pit.
Ezek. 38:11, having neither *b.* nor gates.
See 1Sam. 23:7; Job 38:10; Ps. 107:16; Isa. 45:2.
BASE. Job 30:8, children of *b.* men.
Mal. 2:9, I have made you *b.*
Acts 17:5, fellows of *b.* sort.
1Cor. 1:28, *b.* things of the world.
2Cor. 10:1, in presence am *b.*
See 2Sam. 6:22; Isa. 3:5; Ezek. 17:14; Dan. 4:17.
BASKET. Dt. 28:5, 17, blessed be thy *b.*
Amos 8:1, *b.* of summer fruit.
Mt. 14:20; Mk. 6:43; Lk. 9:17; Jn. 6:13, twelve *b.*
15:37; Mk. 8:8, seven *b.*
16:9; Mk. 8:19, how many *b.*
See Gen. 40:16; Ex. 29:23; Jud. 6:19; Jer. 24:2.
BASON. Jn. 13:5, poureth water into a *b.*
See Ex. 12:22; 24:6; 1Chr. 28:17; Jer. 52:19.
BASTARD. Dt. 23:2, a *b.* shall not enter.
Zech. 9:6, *b.* shall dwell in Ashdod.
Heb. 12:8, *b.* and not sons.
BATH (a measure). 1Ki. 7:26, it contained two thousand *b.*
2Chr. 2:10, twenty thousand *b.* of. wine.
Ezra 7:22, an hundred *b.* of wine.
Isa. 5:10, shall yield one *b.*
BATHE. Lev. 15:5; 17:16; Num. 19:7; Isa. 34:5.
BATS. Lev. 11:19; Dt. 14:18; Isa. 2:20.
BATTLE, 1Sam. 17:20, host shouted for *b.*
47; 2Chr. 20:15, the *b.* is the Lord's.
1Chr. 5:20, they cried to God in *b.*
Ps. 18:39, strength to *b.*
55:18, delivered my soul from *b.*
Eccl. 9:11, nor *b.* to strong.

Jer. 50:22, sound of *b.* in land.
See Job 39:25; 41:8; Ps. 76:3; 140:7.
BATTLEMENTS. Dt. 22:8; Jer. 5:10.
BAY TREE. Ps. 37:35.
BEACON. Isa. 30:17.
BEAM. Ps. 104:3, who layeth *b.* in waters.
Mt. 7:5; Lk. 6:42, cast out *b.*
See Jud. 16:14; 2Ki. 6:2; Hab. 2:11.
BEAR (*v.*). Gen. 4:13, greater than I can *b.*
13:6; 36:7, land not able to *b.*
43:9; 44:32, let me b blame.
Ex. 20:16; 1Ki. 21:10; Lk. 11:48; Jn. 1:7; 5:31; 8:19; 15:27; Acts 23:11; Rom. 8:16; 1Jn. 1:2; 5:8, *b.* witness.
28:12, Aaron *b.* names before Lord.
Lev. 24:15; Ezek. 23:49; Heb. 9:28, *b.* sin.
Num. 11:14; Dt. 1:9, not able to *b.* people.
Est. 1:22; Jer. 5:31; Dan. 2:39, *b.* rule.
Ps. 91:12; Mt. 4:6; Lk. 4:11, they shall *b.* thee up.
Prov. 18:14, wounded spirit who can *b.*
Isa. 52:11, clean that *b.* vessels.
Jer. 31:19, *b.* reproach of youth.
Lam. 3:27, good to *b.* yoke in youth.
Mt. 3:11, not worthy to *b.*
27:32; Mk. 15:21; Lk. 23:26, *b.* cross.
Jn. 16:12, cannot *b.* them now.
Rom. 13:4, *b.* not sword in vain.
15:1, *b.* infirmities of the weak.
1Cor. 13:7, charity *b.* all things.
15:49, *b.* image of the heavenly.
Gal. 6:2, 5, *b.* burdens.
17, *b.* in my body.
See Ex. 28:38; Dt. 1:31; Prov. 12:24.
BEAR (*n.*). Isa. 11:7, cow and *b.* shall feed.
59:11, roar like *b.*
Hos. 13:8, as a *b.* bereaved.
Amos 5:19, as if a man did flee from *b.*
See 1Sam. 17:34; 2Sam. 17:8; Prov. 17:12.
BEARD. 2Sam. 10:5; 1Chr. 19:5, till *b.* be grown.
Ps. 133:2, even Aaron's *b.*
Ezek. 5:1, cause razor to pass on *b.*
See Lev. 13:29; 1Sam. 21:13; 2Sam. 20:9.
BEARING. Ps. 126:6, *b.* precious seed.
Jn. 19:17, *b.* cross.
Rom. 2:15; 9:1, conscience *b.* witness.
2Cor. 4:10, *b.* about in body dying of Jesus.
Heb. 13:13, *b.* his reproach.
See Gen. 1:29; Num. 10:17; Mk. 14:13.
BEAST. Job 12:7, ask *b.*, they shall teach.
Job 18:3, counted as *b.*
Ps. 49:12, like *b.* that perish.
73:22, as *b.* before thee.
Prov. 12:10, regardeth life of *b.*
Eccl. 3:19, no pre-eminence above *b.*
1Cor. 15:32, fought with *b.*
Jas. 3:7, every kind of *b.* is tamed.
2Pet. 2:12, as natural brute *b.*
See Lev. 11:47; Ps. 50:10; 147:9; Rom. 1:23.
BEAT. Isa. 2:4; Joel 3:10; Mic. 4:3, *b.* swords.
Lk. 12:47, *b.* with many stripes.
1Cor. 9:26, as one that *b.* the air.
See Prov. 23:14; Mic. 4:13; Mk. 12:5; 13:9.
BEAUTIFUL. Ps. 48:2, *b.* for situation is Zion.
Eccl. 3:11, everything *b.* in his time.
Song 6:4, thou art *b.*, O my love.
Isa. 4:2, the branch of the Lord be *b.*
52:1, O Zion, put on thy *b.* garments.
7; Rom. 10:15, how *b.* are the feet.
64:11, *b.* house is burnt up.
Jer. 13:20, where is thy *b.* flock?
Mt. 23:27, sepulchres which appear *b.*
Acts 3:2, 10, at the gate called *B.*
BEAUTY. 1Chr. 16:29; 2Chr. 20:21; Ps. 29:2; 96:9; 110:3, *b.* of holiness.
Ezra 7:27, to *b.* the Lord's house.
Ps. 27:4, behold *b.* of the Lord.
39:11, *b.* to consume away.
50:2, perfection of *b.*
Prov. 31:30, *b.* is vain.
See 2Sam. 1:19; Ps. 90:17; Zech. 9:17.
BEAUTY AND BANDS. Zech. 11:7, two staves, *B.*
BECKON. Lk. 1:22; Jn. 13:24; Acts 12:17; 21:40.
BECOMETH. Ps. 93:5, holiness *b.* thy house.
Rom. 16:2; Eph. 5:3, as *b.* saints.
Phil. 1:27; 1Tim. 2:10; Ti. 2:3, as *b.* gospel.
See Prov. 17:7; Mt. 3:15.
BED. Job 7:13, when I say my *b.* shall comfort.
33:15, in slumberings upon *b.*
Ps. 63:6, when I remember thee upon my *b.*
Mt. 9:6; Mk. 2:9; Jn. 5:11, take up *b.*
See 2Ki. 4:10; Isa. 28:20; Mk. 4:21; Lk. 8:16.
BEDSTEAD. Dt. 3:11, was a *b.* of iron.
BEES. Dt. 1:44; Jud. 14:8; Ps. 118:12; Isa. 7:18.
BEEVES. Lev. 22:19; Num. 31:28, 38.
BEFALL. Gen. 42:4; 44:29, mischief *b.* him.
49:1; Dt. 31:29; Dan. 10:14, *b.* in last days.
Jud. 6:13, why is all this *b.* us?
Ps. 91:10, no evil *b.* thee.
Eccl. 3:19, *b.* men, *b.* beasts, one thing *b.*
See Lev. 10:19; Dt. 31:17; Acts 20:19.
BEG. Ps. 37:25; 109:10; Prov. 20:4; Lk. 16:3.
BEGGARLY. Gal. 4:9.
BEGIN. Ezek. 9:6, *b.* at my sanctuary.
1Pet. 4:17, judgment *b.* at house of God.
See 1Sam. 3:12; 2Cor. 3:1.
BEGINNING. Gen. 1:1, in the *b.* God created heaven.
Job 8:7, though thy *b.* was small.
Ps. 111:10; Prov. 1:7; 9:10, *b.* of wisdom.
119:160, word true from *b.*
Eccl. 7:8, better end than *b.*
Mt. 19:8, from *b.* not so.
Lk. 24:47, *b.* at Jerusalem.
Jn. 1:1, in the *b.* was the Word.
2:11, this *b.* of miracles.
Heb. 3:14, hold *b.* of confidence.
Rev. 1:8; 21:6; 22:13, I am the *b.*
See 1Chr. 17:9; Prov. 8:22, 23; Col. 1:18.
BEGOTTEN. Ps. 2:7; Acts 13:33; Heb. 1:5; 5:5, thi day have I *b.* thee.
1Pet. 1:3, *b.* to a lively hope.
See Job 38:28; 1Cor. 4:15; Phile. 10.
BEGUILE. Gen. 29:25; Josh. 9:22, wherefore hast thou *b.* me.
2Pet. 2:14, *b.* unstable souls.
See Num. 25:18; 2Cor. 11:3.

EGUN. Gal. 3:3, having *b.* in Spirit.
Phil. 1:6, hath *b.* good work.
See Dt. 3:24; 2Cor. 8:16; 1Tim. 5:11.
EHALF. Job 36:2, speak on God's *b.*
Phil. 1:29, in *b.* of Christ.
See 2Chr. 16:9; 2Cor. 1:11; 5:12.
EHAVE. 1Sam. 18:5, 14, 15, 30, David *b.* wisely.
1Chr. 19:13, *b.* ourselves valiantly.
Ps. 101:2, I will *b.* wisely.
Isa. 3:5, child shall *b.* proudly.
1Th. 2:10, how unblameably we *b.*
1Tim. 3:2, bishop of good *b.*
See Ps. 131:2; 1Cor. 13:5; Ti. 2:3.
EHEADED. Mt. 14:10; Mk. 6:16; Lk. 9:9; Rev. 20:4.
EHIND. Ex. 10:26, not hoof be left *b.*
Phil. 3:13, things which are *b.*
Col. 1:24, fill up what is *b.*
See 1Ki. 14:9; Neh. 9:26; 2Cor. 11:5.
EHOLD. Ps. 37:37, *b.* the upright.
Mt. 18:10, their angels always *b.*
Jn. 17:24, that they may *b.* glory.
2Cor. 3:18, *b.* as in a glass.
See Num. 24:17; Ps. 91:8; 119:37.
EHOVED. Lk. 24:46; Heb. 2:17.
ELIEF. 2Th. 2:13.
ELIEVE. Num. 14:11, how long ere they *b.* me.
2Chr. 20:20, *b.* Lord, *b.* prophets.
Ps. 78:22, they *b.* not in God.
Prov. 14:15, simple *b.* every word.
Mt. 8:13, as thou hast *b.* so be it.
9:28, *b.* ye that I am able.
21:25; Mk. 11:31, why then did ye not *b.*
27:42, come down and we will *b.*
Mk. 5:36; Lk. 8:50, only *b.*
9:23, canst *b.* all things possible.
11:24, *b.* that ye receive.
16:13, neither *b.* they them.
Lk. 1:1, things most surely *b.*
8:13, which for a while *b.*
24:25, slow of heart to *b.*
41, *b.* not for joy.
Jn. 1:7, all through him might *b.*
2:22, they *b.* the scripture.
3:12 *b.* heavenly things.
5:44, how can ye *b.* which receive honour.
47, how shall ye *b.* my words.
6:36, seen me and *b.* not.
7:5, neither did his brethren *b.*
48, have any of the rulers *b.*?
10:38, *b.* the works.
11:15, to intent ye may *b.*
26, never die, *b.* thou this?
48, all men will. *b.*
12:36, *b.* in the light.
17:21, the world may *b.*
20:25, I will not *b.*
29, have not seen yet have *b.*
Acts 4:32, multitude of them that *b.*
13:39, all that *b.* are justified.
48, ordained to eternal life *b.*
16:34, *b.* with all his house.
Rom. 4:11, father of all that *b.*
18, against hope *b.* in hope.
9:33, *b.* not ashamed.
10:14, how shall they *b.*
1Cor. 7:12, wife that. *b.* not.
2Cor. 4:13, we *b.* and therefore speak.
Gal. 3:22, promise to them that *b.*
2Th. 1:10, admired in all that *b.*
Heb. 10:39, b, to saving of soul.
11:6, must *b.* that he is.
Jas. 2:19, devils *b.* and tremble.
1Pet. 2:6, he that *b.* shall not be confounded.
See Ex. 4:5; 19:9; Isa. 43:10; Mt. 21:22; Jn. 8:24; 10:37; Acts 9:26.
BELLY. Gen. 3:14; Job 15:2; Mt. 15:17; Mk. 7:19; Jn. 7:38; Rom. 16:18; Phil. 3:19; Ti. 1:12.
BELONGETH. Dt. 32:35; Ps. 94:1; Heb. 10:30.
BELOVED. Dt. 33:12, *b.* dwell in safety.
Ps. 127:2, giveth his *b.* sleep.
Dan. 9:23; 10:11, 19, greatly *b.*
Mt. 3:17; 17:5; Mk. 1:11; 9:7; Lk. 3:22; 9:35; 2Pet. 1:17, *b.* son.
Rom. 11:28, *b.* for fathers' sakes.
Eph. 1:6, accepted in the *b.*
Col. 4:9; Phile. 16, *b.* brother.
See Neh. 13:26; Song 2:16; Rom. 16:9.
BEMOAN. Job 42:11; Jer. 15:5; Nah. 3:7.
BEND. Ps. 11:2; Isa. 60:14; Ezek. 17:7.
BENEATH. Prov. 15:24, depart from hell *b.*
Isa. 14:9, hell from *b.* is moved.
Jn. 8:23, ye are from *b.*
See Dt. 4:39; Jer. 31:37.
BENEFACTORS. Lk. 22:25.
BENEFIT. Ps. 68:19, loadeth us with *b.*
1Tim. 6:2, partakers of the *b.*
See 2Chr. 32:25; Ps. 103:2; 2Cor. 1:15; Phile. 14.
BENEVOLENCE. 1Cor. 7:3.
BEREAVE. Gen. 42:36; 43:14, *b.* of children.
Eccl. 4:8, *b.* my soul of God.
Jer. 15:7; 18:21, I will *b.* thee.
See Ezek. 5:17; 36:12; Hos. 13:8.
BESEECH. Job 42:4, hear I *b.* thee.
Mt. 8:5; Lk. 7:3, centurion *b.* him.
Lk. 9:38, I *b.* thee, look on my son.
2Cor. 5:20, as though God did *b.* you.
Eph. 4:1, *b.* you to walk.
Phile. 9, for love's sake *b.* thee.
See Ex. 33:18; Jon. 1:14; Rom. 12:1.
BESET. Ps. 22:12; 139:5; Hos. 7:2; Heb. 12:1.
BESIDE. Mk. 3:21; Acts 26:24; 2Cor. 5:13.
BESIEGE. Dt. 28:52; Eccl. 9:14; Isa. 1:8.
BESOUGHT. Ex. 32:11; Dt. 3:23; 1Ki. 13:6; 2Chr. 33:12; Jer. 26:19, *b.* the Lord.
Mt. 8:31; Mk. 5:10; Lk. 8:31, devils *b.* him.
34; Lk. 8:37, *b.* him to depart.
Jn. 4:40, *b.* that he would tarry.
2Cor. 12:8, I *b.* the Lord thrice.
See Gen. 42:21; Est. 8:3.
BEST. 1Sam. 15:9, 15, spared *b.* of sheep.
Ps. 39:5, at *b.* state vanity.
Lk. 15:22, *b.* robe.
1Cor. 12:31, *b.* gifts.
See Gen. 43:11; Dt. 23:16; 2Sam. 18:4.

BESTEAD. Isa. 8:21.
BESTIR. 2Sam. 5:24.
BESTOW. Lk. 12:17, no room to *b.* my fruits.
1Cor. 15:10, grace *b.* on us not in vain.
Gal. 4:11, lest I have *b.* labour in vain.
1Jn. 3:1, manner of love Father *b.*
See 1Chr. 29:25; Isa. 63:7; Jn. 4:38.
BETHINK. 1Ki. 8:47; 2Chr. 6:37.
BETIMES. Gen. 26:31; 2Chr. 36:15; Job 8:5; Prov. 13:24.
BETRAY. Mt. 26:16; Mk. 14:11; Lk. 22:21, 22, opportunity to *b.*
27:4, I *b.* innocent blood.
1Cor. 11:23, same night he was *b.*
See Mt. 24:10; Mk. 14:18; Jn. 6:64; 21:20.
BETROTH. Hos. 2:19, 20.
BETTER. 1Sam. 15:22, to obey *b.* than sacrifice.
1Ki. 19:4, I am not *b.* than my fathers.
Ps. 63:3, lovingkindness *b.* than life.
Eccl. 4:9, two are *b.* than one.
7:10, former days *b.* than these.
Mt. 12:12, man b, than a sheep.
Lk. 5:39, he saith, the old is *b.*
Phil. 2:3, each esteem other *b.* than himself.
Heb. 1:4, much *b.* than angels.
11:16, a *b.* country.
2Pet. 2:21, *b.* not have known the way.
See Eccl. 2:24; Song 1:2; Jon. 4:3.
BEWAIL. Lk. 8:52, all wept and *b.* her.
Lk. 23:27, of women which also *b.*
2Cor. 12:21, *b.* many who have sinned.
See Dt. 21:13; Jud. 11:37; Rev. 18:9.
BEWARE. Jud. 13:4, *b.* and drink not wine.
Job 36:18, *b.* lest he take thee away.
Mt. 16:6; Mk. 8:15; Lk. 12:1, *b.* of leaven.
Mk. 12:38; Lk. 20:46, *b.* of scribes.
Lk. 12:15, *b.* of covetousness.
Phil. 3:2, *b.* of dogs, *b.* of evil workers.
See Dt. 6:12; 8:11; 15:9.
BEWITCHED. Acts 8:9; Gal. 3:1.
BEWRAY. Isa. 16:3; Prov. 27:16; 29:24; Mt. 26:73.
BEYOND. Num. 22:18; 2Cor. 8:3; Gal. 1:13; 1Th. 4:6.
BIER, 2Sam. 3:31; Lk. 7:14.
BILLOWS. Ps. 42:7; Jon. 2:3.
BIND. Prov. 6:21, *b.* them continually upon heart.
Isa. 61:1, *b.* up brokenhearted.
Mt. 12:29; Mk. 3:27, *b.* strong man.
16:19; 18:18, *b.* on earth.
See Num. 30:2; Job 26:8; 38:31.
BIRD. 2Sam. 21:10, suffered not *b.* to rest.
Song 2:12, time of the singing of *b.*
Jer. 12:9, heritage like a speckled *b.*
Mt. 8:20; Lk. 9:58, *b.* of the air have nests.
See Ps. 11:1; 124:7; Prov. 1:17; Eccl. 10:20.
BIRTH. Jn. 9:1, blind from *b.*
Gal. 4:19, of whom I travail in *b.*
See Eccl. 7:1; Isa. 66:9; Lk. 1:14.
BIRTHDAY. Gen. 40:20, which was Pharaoh's *b.*
Mt. 14:6; Mk. 6:21, when Herod's *b.* was kept.
BIRTHRIGHT. Gen. 25:31; 27:36; Heb. 12:16.
BISHOP (qualifications of). 1Tim. 3:1, if a man desire office of *b.*
Ti. 1:7, *b.* must be blameless.
1Pet. 2:25, Shepherd and *B.* of your souls.
See Acts 1:20; Phil. 1:1.
BIT. Ps. 32:9; Jas. 3:3.
BITE, Prov. 23:32, at last it *b.* like serpent.
Mic. 3:5, prophets that *b.* with teeth.
Gal. 5:15, if ye *b.* and devour one another.
See Eccl. 10:8; Amos 5:19; 9:3.
BITTER. Ex. 12:8; Num. 9:11, with *b.* herbs.
Dt. 32:24, devoured with *b.* destruction.
Job. 13:26, writest *b.* things.
Isa. 5:20, that put *b.* for sweet.
24:9, drink *b.* to them that drink it.
Jer. 2:19, an evil thing and *b.*
Mt. 26:75; Lk. 22:62, Peter wept *b.*
Col. 3:19, be not *b.* against them.
See Ex. 1:14; 15:23, 2Ki. 14:26.
BITTERNESS. Job 10:1; 21:25; Isa. 38:15, in *b.* of soul.
Prov. 14:10, heart knoweth own *b.*
Acts 8:23, in the gall. of *b.*
Eph. 4:31, let all *b.* be put away.
Heb. 12:15, lest any root of *b.*
See 1Sam. 15:32; Prov. 17:25; Rom. 3:14.
BLACK. Mt. 5:36; Jude 13; Rev. 6:5.
BLADE. Jud. 3:22; Mt. 13:26; Mk. 4:28.
BLAME. 2Cor. 6:3; 8:20; Gal. 2:11; Eph. 1:4.
BLAMELESS. 1Cor. 1:8, be *b.* in day of the Lord.
Phil. 2:15, that ye may be *b.*
See Mt. 12:5; Phil. 3:6; Ti. 1:6, 7.
BLASPHEME. 2Sam. 12:14, occasion to enemies to *b.*
Isa. 52:5, my name continually is *b.*
Mt. 9:3, scribes said, this man *b.*
Mk. 3:29, *b.* against Holy Ghost.
Acts 26:11, I compelled them to *b.*
Rom. 2:24, name of God is *b.* through you.
Jas. 2:7, *b.* that worthy name.
See 1Ki. 21:10; Ps. 74:10, 18; 1Tim. 1:20.
BLASPHEMY. Mt. 12:31, all manner of *b.*
26:65; Mk. 14:64, he hath spoken *b.*
Lk. 5:21, who is this which speaketh. *b.*?
See 2Ki. 19:3; Ezek. 35:12; Mt. 15:19.
BLAST. Gen. 41:6; Dt. 28:22; 1Ki. 8:37.
BLAZE. Mk. 1:45.
BLEATING. Jud. 5:16; 1Sam. 15:14.
BLEMISH. Dan. 1:4, children in whom was no *b.*
Eph. 5:27, holy and without *b.*
1Pet. 1:19, a lamb without *b.* and spot.
See Lev. 21:17; Dt. 15:21; 2Sam. 14:25.
BLESS. Dt. 28:3, *b.* in city, *b.* in field.
1Chr. 4:10, Oh that thou wouldest *b.* me.
Prov. 10:7, memory of just is *b.*
Isa. 32:20, *b.* are ye that sow.
65:16, *b.* himself in God of truth.
Mt. 5:44; Lk. 6:28; Rom. 12:14, *b.* them that curse.
Acts 20:35, more *b.* to give than receive.
2Cor. 11:32, *b.* for evermore.
Ti. 2:13, looking for that *b.* hope.
Rev. 14:12, *b.* are dead that die in Lord.
See Gen. 22:17; Hag. 2:19; Jas. 3:9, 10.
BLESSING. Dt. 23:5; Neh. 13:2, turned curse into *b.*

Job 19:13, *b.* of him that was ready to perish.
Prov. 10:22, *b.* of Lord maketh rich.
28:20, faithful man shall abound with *b.*
Isa. 65:8, destroy it not, a *b.* is in it.
Mal. 2:2, I will curse your *b.*
3:10, pour you out a *b.*
Rom. 15:29, fulness of *b.* of Gospel.
1Cor. 10:16, cup of *b.* which we bless.
Jas. 3:10, proceed *b.* and cursing.
Rev. 5:12, worthy to receive honour and *b.*
See Gen. 27:35; 39:5; Dt. 11:26, 29.
BLIND (*v.*). Ex. 23:8, the gift *b.* the wise.
2Cor. 3:14; 4:4, their minds were *b.*
1Jn. 2:11, darkness hath *b.*
See Dt. 16:19; 1Sam. 12:3.
BLINDNESS. Eph. 4:18, because of *b.* of their heart.
See Dt. 28:28; 2Ki. 6:18; Zech. 12:4.
BLOOD. Gen. 9:6, whoso sheddeth man's *b.*
Josh. 2:19; 1Ki. 2:32, *b.* on head.
Ps. 51:14, deliver me from *b.* guiltiness.
72:14, precious shall *b.* be in his sight.
Prov. 29:10, the *b.* thirsty hate upright.
Isa. 9:5, garments rolled in *b.*
Jer. 2:34, the *b.* of poor innocents.
Ezek. 9:9, land is full of *b.*
18:13; 33:5, his *b.* be upon him.
Hab. 2:12, buildeth a town with *b.*
Mt. 9:20; Mk. 5:25; Lk. 8:43, issue of *b.*
16:17, flesh and *b.* hath not revealed.
27:4, I have betrayed innocent *b.*
25, his *b.* be on us and our children.
Mk. 14:24; Lk. 22:20, my *b.* shed.
Lk. 22:20; 1Cor. 11:25, new testament in my *b.*
44, sweat as drops of *b.* falling.
Jn. 1:13, born not of *b.*
6:54, 55, 56, drinketh my *b.*
Acts 15:20; 21:25, abstain from *b.*
17:26, made of one *b.*
20:28, church purchased with his *b.*
Rom. 3:25, through faith in his *b.*
5:9, justified by his *b.*
1Cor. 10:16, communion of *b.* of Christ.
11:27, guilty of body and *b.* of the Lord.
15:50, flesh and *b.* cannot inherit.
Eph. 1:7; Col. 1:14, redemption through his *b.*
Heb. 9:22, without shedding of *b.*
10:29; 13:20, *b.* of the covenant.
1Pet. 1:19, with precious *b.* of Christ.
Rev. 7:14; 12:11, in the *b.* of the Lamb.
See Gen. 9:4; Ex. 4:9; 12:13; Lev. 3:17; Ps. 55:23; Rev. 16:6; 17:6.
BLOSSOM. Isa. 35:1, desert shall *b.* as the rose.
Hab. 3:17, fig tree shall not *b.*
See Gen. 40:10; Num. 17:5; Isa. 27:6.
BLOT. Ex. 32:32; Ps. 69:28; Rev. 3:5, *b.* out of book.
Isa. 44:22, *b.* out as thick cloud.
Acts 3:19, repent that sins may be *b.* out.
Col. 2:14, *b.* out handwriting.
See Dt. 9:14; 2Ki. 14:27; Jer. 18:23.
BLUSH. Ezra 9:6; Jer. 6:15; 8:12.
BOAST (*n.*). Ps. 34:2; Rom. 2:17, 23; 3:27.
BOAST (*v.*). 1Ki. 20:11, not *b.* as he that putteth it off.
Ps. 49:6; 94:4, *b.* themselves.
Prov. 27:1, *b.* not of to-morrow.
2Cor. 11:16, that I may *b.* myself a little.
Eph. 2:9, lest any man should *b.*
Jas. 3:5, tongue *b.* great things.
See 2Chr. 25:19; Prov. 20:14; Jas. 4:16.
BOATS. Jn. 6:22; Acts 27:16, 30.
BODY. Job 19:26, worms destroy this *b.*
Prov. 5:11, when thy flesh and *b.* are consumed.
Mt. 5:29, *b.* cast into hell.
Mt. 6:22; Lk. 11:34, *b.* full of light.
25; Lk. 12:22, take no thought for *b.*
Mk. 5:29, felt in *b.* that she was healed.
Lk. 17:37, wheresoever the *b.* is.
Jn. 2:21, the temple. of his *b.*
Acts 19:12, from his *b.* were brought.
Rom. 6:6, *b.* of sin destroyed.
7:24, *b.* of this death.
12:1, present your *b.* a living sacrifice.
4; 1Cor. 12:14, many members, one *b.*
1Cor. 9:27, I keep under my *b.*
13:3, though I give my *b.* to. be burned.
2Cor. 5:8, absent from the *b.*
12:2, whether in *b.* or out of the *b.*
Gal. 6:17, I bear in *b.* marks.
Phil. 3:21, like to his glorious *b.*
1Pet. 2:24, in his own *b.* on tree.
See Gen. 47:18; Dt. 28:4; Rom. 12:5.
BODILY. Lk. 3:22; 2Cor. 10:10; Col. 2:9; 1Tim. 4:8.
BOLD. Eccl. 8:1, the *b.* of face changed.
Jn. 7:26, he speaketh *b.*
2Cor. 10:2, I may not be *b.*
Eph. 3:12, we have *b.* and access.
Heb. 4:16, let us come *b.* to throne.
1Jn. 4:17, have *b.* in day of judgment.
See Prov. 28:1; Acts 13:46; Rom. 10:20.
BOND. Acts 8:23, in *b.* of iniquity.
Eph. 4:3, *b.* of peace.
Col. 3:14, *b.* of perfectness.
See Num. 30:2; Ezek. 20:37; Lk. 13:16.
BONDAGE. Jn. 8:33, never in *b.* to any man.
See Rom. 8:15; Gal. 5:1; Heb. 2:15.
BONDMAID. Lev. 19:20, a woman that is a *b.*
25:44, and thy *b.*
BONDMAN. Dt. 15:15; 16:12; 24:18.
BONDMEN. Lev. 25:39, both thy *b.*
BONDWOMAN. Gen. 21:10; Gal. 4:30.
BONE. Ex. 12:46; Num. 9:12, neither shall ye break a *b.* thereof.
Job 20:11, *b.* full of sin.
40:18, *b.* as pieces of brass.
Ps. 51:8, the *b.* broken may rejoice.
Prov. 12:4, as rottenness in his *b.*
Mt. 23:27, full of dead men's *b.*
Lk. 24:39, spirit hath not flesh and *b.*
See Gen. 2:23; Ezek. 37:7; Jn. 19:36.
BOOK. Job 19:23, printed in a *b.*
31:35, adversary had written a *b.*
Isa. 34:16, seek out of the *b.* of the Lord.
Mal. 3:16, *b.* of remembrance.
Lk. 4:17, when he had opened *b.*
Jn. 21:25, world could not contain *b.*
Phil. 4:3; Rev. 3:5; 13:8; 17:8; 20:12; 21:27;

22:19, *b.* of life.
Rev. 22:19, take away from words of *b.*
See Ex. 17:14; Ezra 4:15; Acts 19:19; 2Tim. 4:13.
BOOTH. Job 27:18; Jon. 4:5.
BOOTHS. Lev. 23:42, ye shall dwell in *b.*
Neh. 8:14, Israel shall dwell in *b.*
BOOTY. Num. 31:32; Jer. 49:32; Hab. 2:7; Zeph. 1:13.
BORN. Job 5:7, man *b.* to trouble.
14:1; 15:14; 25:4; Mt. 11:11, *b.* of a woman.
Ps. 87:4, this man was *b.* there.
Isa. 9:6, unto us a child is *b.*
66:8, shall a nation be *b.* at once.
Jn. 1:13; 1Jn. 4:7; 5:1, 4, 18, *b.* of God.
3:3; 1Pet. 1:23, *b.* again.
6:8, *b.* of Spirit.
1Cor. 15:8, as one *b.* out of due time.
1Pet. 2:2, as new-*b.* babes.
See Job 3:3; Prov. 17:17; Eccl. 3:2.
BORNE. Ps. 55:12, an enemy, then I could have *b.* it.
Isa. 53:4, *b.* our griefs, carried our sorrows.
Mt. 23:4; Lk. 11:46, grievous to be *b.*
See Job 34:31; Lam. 5:7; Mt. 20:12.
BORROW. Dt. 15:6; 28:12, lend but not *b.*
Ps. 37:21, wicked *b.* and payeth not.
Prov. 22:7, the *b.* is servant.
Mt. 5:42, him that would *b.* of thee.
See Ex. 3:22; 11:2; 22:14; 2Ki. 4:3.
BOSOM. Ps. 35:13, prayer returned into own *b.*
Prov. 6:27, take fire in his *b.*
Isa. 40:11, carry lambs in *b.*
Lk. 16:22, carried into Abraham's *b.*
Jn. 1:18, in the *b.* of the Father.
13:23, leaning on Jesus' *b.*
See Ex. 4:6; Dt. 13:6; Job 31:33.
BOSSES. Job 15:26.
BOTCH. Dt. 28:27, 35.
BOTTLE. Jud. 4:19, a *b.* of milk.
1Sam. 1:24; 10:3; 16:20; 2Sam. 16:1, a *b.* of wine.
Ps. 56:8, put thou my tears into thy *b.*
119:83, like a *b.* in the smoke.
See Gen. 21:14, 15; Hab. 2:15.
BOTTLES. Josh. 9:13, these *b.* of wine.
1Sam. 25:18, and two *b.* of wine.
Job 32:19, ready to burst like new *b.*
Hos. 7:5, sick with *b.* of wine.
Mt. 9:17; Mk. 2:22; Lk. 5:37, new wine in old *b.*
BOTTOMLESS. Rev. 9:1; 11:7; 17:8; 20:1, 2, the *b.* pit.
BOUGH. Gen. 49:22; Jud. 9:48; Dt. 24:20; Job 14:9; Ps. 80:10; Ezek. 31:30.
BOUGHT. Lk. 14:18; 1Cor. 6:20; 7:23; 2Pet. 2:1.
BOUND. Ps. 107:10, being *b.* in affliction.
Prov. 22:15, foolishness *b.* in heart of child.
Acts 20:22, *b.* in spirit to Jerusalem.
1Cor. 7:27, art thou *b.* to a wife.
2Tim. 2:9, word of God is not *b.*
Heb. 13:3, in bonds as *b.* with them.
See Gen. 44:30; Mt. 16:19; Mk. 5:4.
BOUNTY. 1Ki. 10:13; 2Cor. 9:5.
BOUNTIFUL. Prov. 22:9, a *b.* eye shall be blessed.
Isa. 32:5, nor churl said to be *b.*
See Ps. 13:6; 116:7; 119:17; 2Cor. 9:6.
BOWELS. Gen. 43:30, his *b.* did yearn.
Isa. 63:15, where is sounding of thy *b.*
2Cor. 6:12, straitened in *b.*
Col. 3:12, *b.* of mercies.
Phil. 1:8, after you in *b.* of Christ.
2:1, if there be any *b.*
1Jn. 3:17, *b.* of compassion.
See Acts 1:18; Phile. 12.
BOWLS. Num. 7:25, one silver *b.*
Eccl. 12:6, golden *b.* be broken.
Amos 6:6, that drink wine in *b.*
Zech. 4:2, with a *b.* upon the top of it.
BRACELET. Gen. 24:30; Ex. 35:22; Isa. 3:19.
BRAKE. 2Ki. 23:14; 2Chr. 34:4, Josiah *b.* images.
Mt. 14:19; 15:36; 26:26; Mk. 6:41; 8:6; 14:22; Lk. 9:16; 22:19; 24:30; 1Cor. 11:24, blessed and *b.*
See Ex. 32:19; 1Sam. 4:18; Lk. 5:6; Jn. 19:32.
BRAMBLE. Jud. 9:14; Isa. 34:13; Lk. 6:44.
BRANCH. Job 14:7, tender *b.* not cease.
Prov. 11:28, righteous flourish as *b.*
Jer. 23:5, will raise a righteous *b.*
Mt. 13:32; Lk. 13:19, birds lodge in *b.*
21:8; Mk. 11:8; Jn. 12:13, cut down *b.*
See Zech. 3:8; 6:12; Jn. 15:2, 4, 5, 6; Rom. 11:16.
BRAND. Jud. 15:5, set the *b.* on fire.
Zech. 3:2, as a fire *b.* plucked out.
BRASS. Dt. 8:9; 28:23; 1Cor. 13:1.
BRAVERY. Isa. 3:18.
BRAWLER. Prov. 25:24; 1Tim. 3:3; Ti. 3:2.
BRAY. Job 6:5; 30:7; Prov. 27:22.
BREACH. Isa. 58:12, the repairer of the *b.*
Lam. 2:13, thy *b.* is great like the sea.
See Lev. 24:20; Ps. 106:23; Amos 4:3; 6:11.
BREAD. Dt. 8:3; Mt. 4:4; Lk. 4:4, not live by *b.* alone.
Ruth 1:6, visited people in giving them *b.*
1Ki. 17:6, ravens brought *b.* and flesh.
Job 22:7, withholden *b.* from hungry.
33:20, soul abhorreth *b.*
Ps. 132:15, satisfy poor with *b.*
Prov. 9:17, *b.* eaten in secret.
12:11; 20:13; 28:19, satisfied with *b.*
Prov. 31:27, eateth not *b.* of idleness.
Eccl. 11:1, cast *b.* on waters.
Isa. 33:16, *b.* given and waters sure.
55:2, money for that which is not *b.*
10, seed to sower, *b.* to eater.
Mt. 4:3; Lk. 4:3, stones made *b.*
6:11; Lk. 11:11, give us daily *b.*
15:26; Mk. 7:27, take children's *b.*
Lk. 24:35, known in breaking *b.*
Acts 2:42; 20:7; 27:35, breaking *b.*
2Th. 3:8, eat any man's *b.* for nought.
See Ex. 16:4; 23:25; Josh. 9:5; Jud. 7:13.
BREAK. Song 2:17; 4:6, day *b.* and shadows flee.
Isa. 42:3; Mt. 12:20, bruised reed shall he not *b.*
Jer. 4:3; Hos. 10:12, *b.* up fallow ground.
Acts 21:13, to weep and *b.* my heart.
See Ps. 2:3; Mt. 5:19; 9:17; 1Cor. 10:16.
BREATH. Gen. 2:7; 6:17; 7:15, *b.* of life.
Isa. 2:22, cease from man whose *b.*
Ezek. 37:5, 10, I will cause *b.* to enter.

Acts 17:25, he giveth to all life and *b.*
See Job 12:10; 33:4; Ps. 146:4; 150:6.
BREATHE. Ps. 27:12; Ezek. 37:9; Jn. 20:22.
BREECHES. Ex. 28:42; Lev. 6:10; 16:4; Ezek. 44:18.
BRETHREN. Mt. 23:8, all ye are *b.*
Mk. 10:29; Lk. 18:29, no man left house or *b.*
Col. 1:2, faithful *b.* in Christ.
1Jn. 3:14, because we love the *b.*
See Gen. 42:8; Prov. 19:7; Jn. 7:5.
BRIBE. 1Sam. 12:3, have I received any *b.*
Ps. 26:10, right hand is full of *b.*
See 1Sam. 8:3; Isa. 33:15; Job 15:34.
BRICK. Gen. 11:3; Ex. 1:14; 5:7; Isa. 9:10; 65:3.
BRIDE. Isa. 61:10; Jer. 2:32; Rev. 21:2; 22:17.
BRIDEGROOM. Mt. 25:1, to meet the *b.*
Jn. 3:29, because of *b.* voice.
See Ps. 19:5; Isa. 62:5; Mt. 9:15.
BRIDLE. Prov. 26:3, a *b.* for the ass.
Jas. 1:26, *b.* not his tongue.
3:2, able to *b.* whole body.
See 2Ki. 19:28; Ps. 39:1; Isa. 37:29.
BRIGANDINE. Jer. 46:4; 51:3.
BRIGHT. Job 37:21, *b.* light in the clouds.
Isa. 60:3, to *b.* of thy rising.
62:1, righteousness go forth as *b.*
Mt. 17:5, *b.* cloud overshadowed.
2Th. 2:8, *b.* of his coming.
Heb. 1:3, the *b.* of his glory.
Rev. 22:16, the *b.* and morning star.
See Lev. 13:2; Jer. 51:11; Zech. 10:1.
BRIMSTONE. Gen. 19:24, rained upon Sodom and Gomorrah *b.*
Isa. 30:33, like a stream of *b.*
Rev. 9:17, issued fire and *b.*
14:10, tormented with fire and *b.*
19:20, a lake of fire and *b.*
BRINK. Gen. 41:3; Ex. 2:3; 7:15; Josh. 3:8.
BROAD. Ps. 119:96; Mt. 7:13; 23:5.
BROIDERED. Ezek. 16:10, 13; 27:7, 16, 24, *b.* work.
See Ex. 28:4; 1Tim. 2:9.
BROILED. Lk. 24:42.
BROKEN. Ps. 34:18; 51:17; 69:20, *b.* heart.
Jn. 10:35, scripture cannot be *b.*
19:36, bone shall not be *b.*
Eph. 2:14, *b.* down middle wall.
See Job 17:11; Prov. 25:19; Jer. 2:13.
BROOD. Lk. 13:34.
BROOK. 1Sam. 17:40; Ps. 42:1; 110:7.
BROTH. Jud. 6:19; Isa. 65:4.
BROTHER. Prov. 17:17, *b.* born for adversity.
18:9, slothful *b.* to waster.
19, *b.* offended harder to be won.
24. friend closer than *b.*
Eccl. 4:8, neither child nor *b.*
Mt. 10:21, *b.* shall deliver up *b.*
1Cor. 6:6, *b.* goeth to law with *b.*
2Th. 3:15, admonish as *b.*
See Gen. 4:9; Mt. 5:23; 12:50; Mk. 3:35.
BROTHERLY. Rom. 12:10; 1Th. 4:9; Heb. 13:1, *b.* love.
See Amos 1:9; 2Pet. 1:7.

BROW. Isa. 48:4; Lk. 4:29.
BRUISE (*n.*). Isa. 1:6; Jer. 30:12; Nah. 3:19.
BRUISE (*v.*). 2Ki. 18:21, staff of this *b.* reed.
Isa. 42:3; Mt. 12:20, *b.* reed shall he not break.
53:5, *b.* for our iniquities.
See Gen. 3:15; Isa. 53:10; Rom. 16:20.
BRUIT. Jer. 10:22; Nah. 3:19.
BRUTISH. Ps. 92:6, a *b.* man knoweth not.
Prov. 30:2, I am more *b.* than any.
Jer. 10:21, pastors are become *b.*
See Ps. 49:10; Jer. 10:8; Ezek. 21:31.
BUCKET. Num. 24:7; Isa. 40:15.
BUCKLER. 2Sam. 22:31; Ps. 18:2; 91:4; Prov. 2:7.
BUD. Num. 17:8. Isa. 18:5; 61:11; Hos. 8:7.
BUFFET. Mt. 26:67; 1Cor. 4:11; 2Cor. 12:7; 1Pet. 2:20.
BUILD. Ps. 127:1, labour in vain that *b.*
Eccl. 3:3, a time to *b.* up.
Isa. 58:12, *b.* old waste places.
Mt. 7:24; Lk. 6:48, wise man *b.* on rock.
Lk. 14:30, began to *b.*, not able to finish.
Acts 20:32, able to *b.* you up.
Rom. 15:20, lest I *b.* on another.
1Cor. 3:12, if any *b.* on this foundation.
Eph. 2:22, in whom ye are *b.* together.
See 1Chr. 17:12; 2Chr. 6:9; Eccl. 2:4.
BUILDER. Ps. 118:22; Mt. 21:42; Mk. 12:10; Lk. 20:17; Acts 4:11; 1Pet. 2:7, *b.* refused.
1Cor. 3:10, as a wise master-*b.*
Heb. 11:10, whose *b.* and maker is God.
See 1Ki. 5:18; Ezra 3:10.
BUILDING. 1Cor. 3:9; 2Cor. 5:1; Eph. 2:21; Col. 2:7.
BULRUSH. Ex. 2:3; Isa. 18:2; 58:5.
BULWARK, Isa. 26:1, salvation for walls and *b.*
See Dt. 20:20; Ps. 48:13; Eccl. 9:14.
BUNDLE. Gen. 42:35; 1Sam. 25:29; Mt. 13:30; Acts 28:3.
BURDEN. Ps. 55:22, cast thy *b.* on the Lord.
Eccl. 12:5, grasshopper shall be a *b.*
Mt. 11:30, my *b.* is light.
20:12, borne *b.* and heat of day.
23:4; Lk. 11:46, bind heavy *b.*
Gal. 6:2, 5, bear his own *b.*
See Num. 11:11; Acts 15:28; 2Cor. 12:16.
BURDENSOME. Zech. 12:3; 2Cor. 11:9; 1Th. 2:6.
BURIAL. Eccl. 6:3; Jer. 22:19; Mt. 26:12; Acts 8:2.
BURN. Ps. 39:3, musing the fire *b.*
Prov. 26:23, *b.* lips and wicked heart.
Isa. 9:18, wickedness *b.* as fire.
33:14, dwell with everlasting *b.*
Mal. 4:1, day that shall *b.* as oven.
Mt. 13:30, bind tares to *b.* them.
Lk. 3:17, chaff *b.* with fire unquenchable.
12:35, loins girded and lights *b.*
24:32, did not our heart *b.*
Jn. 5:35, he was a *b.* and shining light.
1Cor. 13:3, give my body to be *b.*
Heb. 6:8, whose end is to be *b.*
Rev. 4:5, lamps b, before throne.
19:20, into a lake *b.*
See Gen. 44:18; Ex. 3:2; 21:25.
BURNT-OFFERING. Ps. 40:6, *b.* thou hast not required.

Isa. 61:8, I hate robbery for *b.*
Jer. 6:20, your *b.* not acceptable.
Hos. 6:6, knowledge more than *b.*
Mk. 12:33, love neighbour more than *b.*
See Gen. 22:7; Lev. 1:4; 6:9.
BURST. Job 32:19; Prov. 3:10; Mk. 2:22; Lk. 5:37.
BURY. Mt. 8:21; Lk. 9:59, suffer me to *b.* my father.
22; Lk. 9:60, let dead *b.* dead.
Jn. 19:40, manner of the Jews is to *b.*
Rom. 6:4; Col. 2:12, *b.* with him by baptism.
1Cor. 15:4, he was *b.* and rose again.
See Gen. 23:4; 47:29; Mt. 14:12.
BUSHEL. Mt. 5:15; Mk. 4:21; Lk. 11:38.
BUSINESS. 1Sam. 21:8, king's *b.* requireth haste.
Ps. 107:23, do *b.* in great waters.
Prov. 22:29, diligent in *b.*
Lk. 2:49, about my Father's *b.*
Rom. 12:11, not slothful in *b.*
1Th. 4:11, study to do your own *b.*
See Josh. 2:14; Jud. 18:7; Neh. 13:30.
BUSYBODIES. 2Th. 3:11, but. are *b.*
1Tim. 5:13, tattlers also and *b.*
1Pet. 4:15, *b.* in other men's matters.
See Prov. 20:3; 26:17; 1Th. 4:11.
BUTLER. Gen. 40:1; 41:9.
BUTTER. Isa. 7:15, 22, *b.* and honey shall he eat.
See Jud. 5:25; Job 29:6; Ps. 55:21; Prov. 30:33.
BUY. Lev. 22:11, *b.* any soul with money.
Prov. 23:23, *b.* the truth.
Isa. 55:1, *b.* and eat, *b.* wine and milk.
Mt. 25:9, go to them that sell and *b.*
Jn. 4:8, disciples were gone to *b.* meat.
Jas. 4:13, we will *b.* and sell and get gain.
Rev. 3:18, *b.* of me gold tried.
13:17, no man b, save he that had mark.
18:11, no man *b.* her merchandise.
See Gen. 42:2; 47:19; Ruth 4:4; Mt. 13:44.
BUYER. Prov. 20:14; Isa. 24:2; Ezek. 7:12.
BY-AND-BY. Mt. 13:21; Mk. 6:25; Lk. 17:7; 21:9.
BYWAYS. Jud. 5:6.
BYWORD. Job 17:6; 30:9, a *b.* of the people.
Ps. 44:14, a *b.* among the heathen.
See Dt. 28:37; 1Ki. 9:7; 2Chr. 7:20.
CABINS. Jer. 37:16.
CAGE. Jer. 5:27; Rev. 18:2.
CAKE. 2Sam. 6:19, to every man a *c.* of bread.
1Ki. 17:13, to make me a little *c.* first.
See Jud. 7:13; Jer. 7:18; 44:19; Hos. 7:8.
CALAMITY. Dt. 32:35; 2Sam. 22:19; Ps. 18:18, day of *c.*
Ps. 57:1, until *c.* be overpast.
Prov. 1:26, I will laugh at your *c.*
17:5, he that is glad at *c.*
19:13, foolish son *c.* of father.
27:10, brother's house in day of *c.*
See Job 6:2; Prov. 24:22.
CALF. Ex. 32:4; Isa. 11:6; Lk. 15:23.
CALKERS. Ezek. 27:9, 27.
CALLING. Rom. 11:29, *c.* of God without repentance.
1Cor. 7:20, abide in same. *c.*
Eph. 1:18, the hope of his *c.*
Phil. 3:14, prize of high *c.*
2Th. 1:11, worthy of this *c.*
2Tim. 1:9, called us with holy *c.*
Heb. 3:1, partakers of heavenly *c.*
2Pet. 1:10, make *c.* and election sure.
See Acts 7:59; 22:16; 1Cor. 1:26.
CALM. Ps. 107:29; Jon. 1:11; Mt. 8:26; Mk. 4:39; Lk. 8:24.
CALVES. 1Ki. 12:28, made two *c.* of gold.
See Hos. 14:2; Mal. 4:2.
CAMEL'S HAIR. Mt. 3:4, raiment of *c.*
CAMELS. Isa. 60:6, the multitude of *c.* shall cover thee.
Mt. 19:24, it is easier for a *c.*
23:24, strain at a gnat, swallow a *c.*
See Gen. 24:64; Ex. 9:3; Lev. 11:4; Dt. 14:7; 1Chr. 5:21; Job 1:3.
CAMP (*n.*). Ex. 14:19, angel went before *c.*
16:13, quails covered the *c.*
Num. 1:52, every man by his own *c.*
Dt. 23:14, Lord walketh in midst of *c.*
See 1Sam. 4:6, 7; Heb. 13:13.
CAMP (*v.*). Isa. 29:3; Jer. 50:29; Nah. 3:17.
CANDLE. Job 29:3, when his *c.* shined upon my head.
Ps. 18:28, thou wilt light my *c.*
Prov. 20:27, spirit of man, *c.* of the Lord.
Zeph. 1:12, search Jerusalem with *c.*
Mt. 5:15; Mk. 4:21; Lk. 8:16; 11:33, lighted a *c.*
Rev. 18:23, *c.* shine no more in thee.
22:5, need no *c.* nor light.
See Job 18:6; 21:17; Prov. 24:20.
CANDLESTICK. 2Ki. 4:10, let us set for him a *c.*
See Mk. 4:21; Heb. 9:2; Rev. 2:5.
CANKERED. 2Tim. 2:17; Jas. 5:3.
CAPTIVE. Ex. 12:29, firstborn of *c.* in dungeon.
Isa. 51:14, *c.* exile hasteneth.
52:2, O *c.* daughter of Zion.
2Tim. 2:26, taken *c.* at his will.
3:6, lead *c.* silly women.
See 2Ki. 5:2; Isa. 14:2; 61:1; Lk. 4:18.
CAPTIVITY. Rom. 7:23, into *c.* to law of sin.
2Cor. 10:5, bringing into *c.* every thought.
See Job 42:10; Ps. 14:7; 85:1; 126:1.
CARCASE. Isa. 66:24; Mt. 24:28; Heb. 3:17.
CARE (*n.*). Jer. 49:31, nation that dwelleth without
Mt. 13:22; Mk. 4:19, *c.* of this world.
Lk. 8:14; 21:34, choked with *c.*
1Cor. 9:9, doth God take *c.* for oxen.
12:25, have same *c.* one for another.
2Cor. 11:28, the *c.* of all the churches.
1Pet. 5:7. casting all your *c.* on him.
See 1Sam. 10:2; 2Ki. 4:13; 2Cor. 7:12.
CARE (*v.*). Ps. 142:4, no man *c.* for my soul.
Jn. 12:6, not that he *c.* for poor.
Acts 18:17, Gallio *c.* for none of those things.
Phil. 2:20, naturally *c.* for your state.
See 2Sam. 18:3; Lk. 10:40.
CAREFUL. Jer. 17:8, not be *c.* in year of drought.
Dan. 3:16, we are not *c.* to answer.
Lk. 10:41, thou art *c.* about many things.
Phil. 4:6, be *c.* for nothing.
Heb. 12:17, he sought it *c.* with tears.
See 2Ki. 4:13; Phil. 4:10; Ti. 3:8.

AREFULNESS. Ezek. 12:18; 1Cor. 7:32; 2Cor. 7:11.
ARELESS. Jud. 18:7; Isa. 32:9; 47:8; Ezek. 39:6.
ARNAL. Rom. 7:14, *c.*, sold under sin.
8:7, *c.* mind is enmity.
1Cor. 3:1, not speak but as to *c.*
2Cor. 10:4, weapons of our warfare not *c.*
See 1Cor. 9:11; Col. 2:18; Heb. 7:16; 9:10.
ARPENTER'S SON. Mt. 13:55; Mk. 6:3, is not this the *c.*?
ARPENTERS. 2Sam. 5:11, and cedar trees and *c.*
Zech. 1:20, and the Lord shewed me four *c.*
ARRIAGE. Jud. 18:21; Isa. 10:28; 46:1; Acts 21:15.
ARRY. 1Ki. 18:12, Spirit of the Lord shall *c.* thee.
Isa. 40:11, *c.* lambs in his bosom.
53:4, *c.* our sorrows.
63:9, *c.* them all days of old.
Ezek. 22:9, men *c.* tales to shed blood.
Mk. 6:55, began to *c.* about in beds.
Jn. 5:10, not lawful to *c.* thy bed.
21:18, and *c.* thee whither thou wouldest not.
Eph. 4:14, *c.* about with every wind.
1Tim. 6:7, we can *c.* nothing out.
Heb. 13:9, not *c.* about with divers.
2Pet. 2:17, clouds *c.* with a tempest.
Jude 12, clouds *c.* about of winds.
See Ex. 33:15; Num. 11:12; Dt. 14:24.
ART. Isa. 5:18, draw sin as with a *c.* rope.
Amos 2:13, *c.* full of sheaves.
See 1Sam. 6:7; 2Sam. 6:3; 1Chr. 13:7; Isa. 28:28.
ASE. Ps. 144:15, happy people in such a *c.*
Mt. 5:20, in no *c.* enter heaven.
Jn. 5:6, long time in that *c.*
See Ex. 5:19; Dt. 19:4; 24:13.
ASSIA. Ex. 30:24, of *c.* five hundred shekels.
Ps. 45:8, thy garments smell of *c.*
AST. Prov. 16:33, lot is *c.* into lap.
Mt. 5:29; Mk. 9:45, whole body *c.* into hell.
Mk. 9:38; Lk. 9:49, one *c.* out devils.
Lk. 21:1, *c.* gifts into treasury.
Jn. 8:7, first *c.* stone at her.
2Cor. 10:5, *c.* down imaginations.
1Pet. 5:7, c, all care upon him.
1Jn. 4:18, love *c.* out fear.
See Ps. 76:6; Prov. 26:18; 3Jn. 10.
ASTAWAY. 1Cor. 9:27, lest I be a *c.*
ASTLE. Num. 31:10; Prov. 18:19; Acts 21:34.
ATCH. Ps. 10:9, to *c.* the poor.
Mt. 13:19, devil *c.* away what was sown.
Lk. 5:10, from henceforth thou shalt *c.* men.
Jn. 10:12, wolf *c.* and scattereth sheep.
See 2 Ki. 7:12; Ezek. 19:3; Mk. 12:13.
ATTLE. Gen. 46:32, their trade to feed *c.*
Ex. 10:26, our *c.* shall go with us.
Dt. 2:35; 3:7; Josh. 8:2, the *c.* ye shall take for prey.
Ps. 50:10, *c.* upon a thousand hills.
See Gen. 1:25; 30:43; Jon. 4:11.
AUGHT. Gen. 22:13, ram *c.* by horns.
Jn. 21:3, that night they *c.* nothing.
2Cor. 12:2, *c.* up to third heaven.
16, I *c.* you with guile.
1Th. 4:17, be *c.* up together with them.
See 2Sam. 18:9; Prov. 7:13; Rev. 12:5.
CAUSE (*n.*). Mt. 19:5; Mk. 10:7; Eph. 5:31, for this *c.* shall a man leave.
1Cor. 11:30, for this *c.* many are sickly.
1Tim. 1:16, for this *c.* I obtained mercy.
See Prov. 18:17; 2Cor. 4:16; 5:13.
CAUSE (*v.*). Ezra 6:12, God *c.* his name to dwell.
Ps. 67:1; 80:3, *c.* his face to shine.
Rom. 16:17, them. who *c.* divisions.
See Dt. 1:38; 12:11; Job 6:24.
CAUSELESS. 1Sam. 25:31; Prov. 26:2.
CAVES. 1Ki. 18:4, Obadiah hid them by fifty in *c.*
19:9, and he came thither into a *c.*
Isa. 2:19, go into a *c.* for fear of the Lord.
See Gen. 19:30; 23:19; 49:29; Josh. 10:16; 1Sam. 13:6; 22:1; 24:10.
CEASE. Dt. 15:11, poor never *c.* out of land.
Job 3:17, the wicked *c.* from troubling.
Ps. 46:9, he maketh wars to *c.*
Prov. 26:20, strife *c.*
Eccl. 12:3, grinders *c.* because few.
Acts 20:31, I *c.* not to warn.
1Cor. 13:8, tongues they shall. *c.*
1Th. 5:17, pray without *c.*
1Pet. 4:1, hath *c.* from sin.
See Gen. 8:22; Isa. 1:16; 2:22.
CEDAR. 1Ki. 5:6, they hew me *c.* trees out of Lebanon.
6:15, with boards of *c.*
Job 40:17, he moveth his tail like a *c.*
Ps. 92:12, grow like a *c.* in Lebanon.
CEDARS (of Lebanon). Jud. 9:15, devour the *c.* of Lebanon.
Isa. 2:13, upon all the *c.* of Lebanon.
See Ps. 104:16; 148:9; Song 5:15; Ezek. 17:3.
CELEBRATE. Lev. 23:32; Isa. 38:18.
CELESTIAL. 1Cor. 15:40.
CENSER. Ezek. 8:11, every man his *c.*
Heb. 9:4, holiest had the golden *c.*
Rev. 8:3, angel having a golden *c.*
5, angel took the *c.* and filled.
See Lev. 10:1; 16:12; Num. 16:36; 1Ki. 7:30.
CEREMONIES. Num. 9:3.
CERTAIN. Ex. 3:12, *c.* I will be with thee.
1Cor. 4:11, no *c.* dwelling-place.
Heb. 10:27, a *c.* looking for of judgment.
See Dt. 13:14; 1Ki. 2:37; Dan. 2:45.
CERTIFY. 2Sam. 15:28; Gal. 1:11.
CHAFF. Mt. 3:12; Lk. 3:17, burn up *c.* with fire.
See Jer. 23:28; Hos. 13:3; Zeph. 2:2.
CHAIN. Mk. 5:3, no, not with *c.*
Acts 12:7, Peter's *c.* fell off.
2Tim. 1:16, not ashamed of my *c.*
2Pet. 2:4, into *c.* of darkness.
Jude 6, everlasting *c.* under darkness.
See Ps. 73:6; Lam. 3:7; Isa. 40:19.
CHALCEDONY. Rev. 21:19, the third, a *c.*
CHALLENGETH. Ex. 22:9.
CHAMBER. 2Ki. 4:10, little *c.* on wall.
Ps. 19:5, as bridegroom coming out of *c.*
Isa. 26:20, enter into thy *c.*
Ezek. 8:12, *c.* of imagery.
Mt. 24:26, in secret *c.*

Acts 9:37; 20:8 in upper *c.*
See Dan. 6:10; Joel 2:16; Prov. 7:27.
CHAMPION. 1Sam. 17:4, 51.
CHANCE. 1Sam. 6:9; 2Sam. 1:6; Eccl. 9:11; Lk. 10:31.
CHANGE (*n.*). Job 14:14, till my *c.* come.
Prov. 24:21, meddle not with them given to *c.*
See Jud. 14:12; Zech. 3:4; Heb. 7:12.
CHANGE (*v.*). Ps. 15:4, sweareth and *c.* not.
102:26, as vesture shalt thou *c.* them.
Lam. 4:1, fine gold. *c.*
Mal. 3:6, I the Lord *c.* not.
Rom. 1:23, *c.* glory of uncorruptible God.
1Cor. 15:51, we shall all be *c.*
2Cor. 3:18, *c.* from glory to glory.
See Job 17:12; Jer. 2:36; 13:23.
CHANT. Amos 6:5.
CHAPEL. Amos 7:13, for it is the king's *c.*
CHAPMEN. 2Chr. 9:14.
CHAPT. Jer. 14:4.
CHARGE. Job 1:22, nor *c.* God foolishly.
4:18, angels he *c.* with folly.
Mt. 9:30; Mk. 5:43; Lk. 9:21, Jesus *c.* them.
Acts 7:60; 2Tim. 4:16, lay not sin to their *c.*
Rom. 8:33, who shall lay any thing to *c.*
1Cor. 9:18, gospel without *c.*
1Tim. 1:3, *c.* that they teach no other.
5:21; 2Tim. 4:1, I *c.* thee before God.
6:17, *c.* them that are rich.
See Ex. 6:13; Ps. 35:11; 91:11; Mk. 9:25.
CHARGEABLE. 2Sam. 13:25; 2Cor. 11:9; 1Th. 2:9.
CHARIOT. 2Ki. 2:11, there appeared a *c.* of fire.
CHARIOTS. Ex. 14:6, he made ready his *c.*
1Sam. 13:5, Philistines gathered thirty thousand *c.*
2Sam. 10:18, David slew the men of seven hundred *c.*
Ps. 20:7, some trust in *c.*
Nah. 3:2, and of the jumping *c.*
See 2Ki. 6:14, 17; Ps. 68:17.
CHARITY. Rom. 14:15, now walkest not *c.*
Col. 3:14, put on *c.*
2Th. 1:3, *c.* aboundeth.
1Tim. 1:5, end of commandment is *c.*
2Tim. 2:22, follow faith, *c.*, peace.
Ti. 2:2, sound in faith, in *c.*
1Pet. 4:8, *c.* cover sins.
2Pet. 1:7, to brotherly kindness *c.*
Jude 12, spots in feasts of *c.*
See 1Cor. 8:1; 13:1; 14:1; 16:14; Rev. 2:19.
CHARMER. Dt. 18:11; Ps. 58:5; Jer. 8:17.
CHASE. Lev. 26:8, five *c.* hundred.
Dt. 32:30; Josh. 23:10, one *c.* thousand.
See Job 18:18; Ps. 35:5; Lam. 3:52.
CHASTE. 2Cor. 11:2; Ti. 2:5; 1Pet. 3:2.
CHASTEN. Dt. 8:5, as a man *c.* son.
Ps. 6:1; 38:1, nor *c.* me in displeasure.
94:12, blessed is the man whom thou *c.*
Prov. 19:18, *c.* thy son while there is hope.
2Cor. 6:9, as *c.* and not killed.
Heb. 12:6; Rev. 3:19, whom the Lord loveth he *c.*
11, no *c.* seemeth to be joyous.
See Ps. 69:10; 73:14; 118:18.
CHASTISEMENT. Dt. 11:2; Job 34:31; Isa. 53:5.
CHATTER. Isa. 38:14.
CHEEK. Mt. 5:39; Lk. 6:29, smiteth on right *c.*
See Job 16:10; Isa. 50:6; Lam. 3:30.
CHEER. Prov. 15:13, maketh a *c.* countenance.
Zech. 9:17, corn make young men *c.*
Jn. 16:33, be of good *c.*, I have overcome.
Acts 23:11; 27:22, 25, be of good *c.*
Rom. 12:8, he that showeth mercy with *c.*
2Cor. 9:7, God loveth a *c.* giver.
See Jud. 9:13; Mt. 9:2; 14:27; Mk. 6:50.
CHERISHETH. Eph. 5:29; 1Th. 2:7.
CHICKENS. Mt. 23:37.
CHIDE. Ex. 17:2; Jud. 8:1; Ps. 103:9.
CHIEFEST. Song 5:10; Mk. 10:44; 2Cor. 11:5.
CHILD. Gen. 42:22, do not sin against the *c.*
Ps. 131:2, quieted myself as a weaned *c.*
Prov. 20:11, a *c.* is known by his doings.
Prov. 22:6, train up a *c.* in way.
15, foolishness in heart of *c.*
Isa. 9:6, to us a *c.* is born.
65:20, *c.* shall die an hundred years old.
Lk. 1:66, what manner of *c.*
Jn. 4:49, come ere my *c.* die.
1Cor. 13:11, when I was a *c.*
2Tim. 3:15, from a *c.* hast known.
See Ex. 2:2; Eccl. 4:13; 10:16; Heb. 11:23.
CHILDREN. 1Sam. 16:11, are here all thy *c.*
Ps. 34:11, come ye *c.* hearken to me.
45:16, instead of fathers shall be *c.*
128:3, thy *c.* like olive plants.
Isa. 8:18; Heb. 2:13, I and *c.* given me.
30:9, lying *c.*, *c.* that will not hear.
63:8, *c.* that will not lie.
Jer. 31:15; Mt. 2:18, Rachel weeping for her *c.*
Ezek. 18:2, *c.* teeth on edge.
Mt. 15:26; Mk. 7:27; not take *c.* bread.
17:26, then are the *c.* free.
19:14; Mk. 10:14; Lk. 18:16, suffer little *c.*
Lk. 16:8, *c.* of this world wiser than *c.* of light.
20:36, *c.* of God and the resurrection.
Jn. 12:36; Eph. 5:8; 1Th. 5:5, *c.* of light.
Rom. 8:16; Gal. 3:26; 1Jn. 3:10, witness that we are the *c.* of God.
Eph. 4:14, be henceforth no more *c.*
5:6; Col. 3:6, *c.* of disobedience.
6:1; Col. 3:20, *c.* obey your parents.
1Tim. 3:4, having his *c.* in subjection.
See Num. 16:27; Est. 3:13; Mt. 14:21.
CHODE. Gen. 31:36; Num. 20:3.
CHOICE. 1Sam. 9:2, Saul a *c.* young man.
Acts 15:7, God made *c.* among us.
See Gen. 23:6; 2Sam. 10:9; Prov. 8:10.
CHOKE. Mt. 13:22; Mk. 4:19; Lk. 8:14.
CHOLER. Dan. 8:7; 11:11.
CHOSE. Ps. 33:12, people *c.* for his inheritance.
89:19, exalted one *c.* out of people.
Prov. 16:16; 22:1, rather to be *c.*
Jer. 8:3, death *c.* rather than life.
Mt. 20:16; 22:14, many called, few *c.*
Lk. 10:42, hath *c.* that good part.
14:7, they *c.* the chief rooms.
Jn. 15:16, ye have not *c.* me.

Acts 9:15, he is a *c.* vessel.
Rom. 16:13, *c.* in the Lord.
1Cor. 1:27, 28, God hath *c.* foolish things.
Eph. 1:4, according as he hath *c.* us.
1Pet. 2:4, *c.* of God and precious.
9, a *c.* generation.
See Ex. 18:25; 2Sam. 6:21; 1Chr. 16:13.
CHRIST. Mt. 16:16, thou art the *C.*
24:5, many shall come, saying, I am *C.*
Jn. 4:25, the Messias which is called *C.*
29, is not this the *C.*?
6:69, we are sure that thou art that *C.*
Phil. 1:15, 16, some preach *C.* of contention.
1Pet. 1:11, the Spirit of *C.* did signify.
1Jn. 2:22, denieth that Jesus is the *C.*?
5:1, whoso believeth Jesus is the *C.*
Rev. 20:4, they reigned with *C.* a thousand years.
6, priests of God and *C.*
See Mt. 1:16; 2:4; Lk. 2:26.
CHRISTIAN. Acts 11:26; 26:28; 1Pet. 4:16.
CHRYSOLITE. Rev. 21:20, the seventh *c.*
CHRYSOPRASUS. Rev. 21:20, the tenth, a *c.*
CHURCH. Mt. 18:17, tell it to the *c.*
Acts 2:47, added to *c.* daily.
7:38, the *c.* in the wilderness.
19:37, neither robbers of *c.*
20:28, feed the *c.* of God.
Rom. 16:5; 1Cor. 16:19; Phile. 2, *c.* in house.
1Cor. 14:28, 34, keep silence in the *c.*
Eph. 5:24, the *c.* is subject to Christ.
25, as Christ loved the *c.*
Col. 1:18, 24, head of the body the *c.*
Heb. 12:23, the *c.* of the firstborn.
See Mt. 16:18; Rev. 1:4; 2:1; 22:16.
CHURLISH. 1Sam. 25:3, but the man was *c.*
CIELED. 2Chr. 3:5; Jer. 22:14; Hag. 1:4.
CIRCLE. Isa. 40:22.
CIRCUIT. 1Sam. 7:16; Job 22:14; Ps. 19:6; Eccl. 1:6.
CIRCUMCISE. Rom. 4:11, though not *c.*
Gal. 5:2, if ye be *c.* Christ shall profit nothing.
Phil. 3:5, *c.* the eighth day.
See Dt. 30:6; Jn. 7:22; Acts 15:1.
CIRCUMCISION. Rom. 3:1, what profit is there of *c.*
15:8, Jesus Christ minister of *c.*
Gal. 5:6; 6:15, in Christ neither *c.* availeth.
Phil. 3:3, the *c.* which worship God.
Col. 2:11, *c.* without hands.
3:11, neither *c.* nor uncircumcision.
See Ex. 4:26; Jn. 7:22; Acts 7:8.
CIRCUMSPECT. Ex. 23:13; Eph. 5:15.
CISTERN. Eccl. 12:6, the wheel broken at the *c.*
Jer. 2:13, hewed out *c.*, broken *c.*
See 2Ki. 18:31; Prov. 5:15; Isa. 36:16.
CITIZEN. Lk. 15:15; 19:14; Acts 21:39; Eph. 2:19.
CITY. Num. 35:6; Josh. 15:59, *c.* of refuge.
2Sam. 19:37, I may die in mine own *c.*
Ps. 46:4, make glad the *c.* of God.
107:4, found no *c.* to dwell in.
127:1, except Lord build *c.*
Prov. 8:3, wisdom crieth in *c.*
16:32, than he that taketh a *c.*
Eccl. 9:14, a little *c.* and few men.
Isa. 33:20, *c.* of solemnities.
Zech. 8:3, a *c.* of truth.
Mt. 5:14, *c.* set on a hill.
21:10, all the *c.* was moved.
Lk. 24:49, tarry in the *c.*
Acts 8:8, great joy in that *c.*
Heb. 11:10, a *c.* that hath foundations.
12:22, the *c.* of living God.
13:14, no continuing *c.*
Rev. 16:19, the *c.* of the nations fell.
20:9, compassed the beloved *c.*
See Gen. 4:17; 11:4; Jon. 1:2; Rev. 14:8; 21:10.
CLAD. 1Ki. 11:29; Isa 59:17.
CLAMOUR. Prov. 9:13; Eph. 4:31.
CLAP. Ps. 47:1, *c.* your hands all ye people.
98:8, let the floods *c.* their hands.
Isa. 55:12, the trees shall *c.* their hands.
Lam. 2:15, all that pass by *c.* their hands.
See 2Ki. 11:12; Job 27:23; 34:37.
CLAVE. Ruth 1:14, Ruth *c.* to her mother-in-law.
2Sam. 23:10, his hand *c.* to the sword.
Neh. 10:29, they *c.* to their brethren.
Acts 17:34, certain men *c.* to Paul.
See Gen. 22:3; Num. 16:31; 1Sam. 6:14.
CLAWS. Dt. 14:6; Dan. 4:33; Zech. 11:16.
CLAY. Job 10:9, thou hast made me as *c.*
13:12, bodies like to bodies of *c.*
33:6, I also am formed out of *c.*
Ps. 40:2, out of the miry *c.*
Dan. 2:33, part of iron, part of *c.*
Jn. 9:6, made *c.* and anointed.
Rom. 9:21, power over the *c.*
See Isa. 29:16; 41:25; 45:9; 64:8; Jer. 18:4.
CLEAN. 2Ki. 5:12, may I not wash and be *c.*
Job 14:4, who can bring *c.* out of unclean.
15:15, heavens not *c.* in his sight.
Ps. 24:4, he that hath *c.* hands.
51:10, create in me a *c.* heart.
77:8, is his mercy *c.* gone for ever?
Prov. 16:2, *c.* in his own eyes.
Isa. 1:16, wash you, make you *c.*
52:11, be *c.* that bear vessels of the Lord.
Ezek. 36:25, then will I sprinkle *c.* water.
Mt. 8:2; Mk. 1:40; Lk. 5:12, thou canst make me *c.*
23:25; Lk. 11:39, make *c.* the outside.
Lk. 11:41, all things *c.* unto you.
Jn. 13:11, ye are not all *c.*
Jn. 15:3, *c.* through word I have spoken.
Acts 18:6, I am *c.*
Rev. 19:8, arrayed in fine linen *c.* and white.
See Lev. 23:22; Josh. 3:17; Prov. 14:4.
CLEANNESS. 2Sam. 22:21; Ps. 18:20; Amos 4:6.
CLEANSE. Ps. 19:12, *c.* me from secret faults.
73:13, I have *c.* my heart in vain.
Prov. 20:30, blueness of wound *c.* evil.
Mt. 8:3, immediately his leprosy was *c.*
10:8; 11:5; Lk. 7:22, *c.* lepers.
23:26, *c.* first that which is within.
Lk. 4:27, none was *c.* saving Naaman.
17:17, were not ten *c.*
Acts 10:15; 11:9, what God hath *c.*
2Cor. 7:1, let us *c.* ourselves.
Jas. 4:8, *c.* your hands, ye sinners.

1Jn. 1:7, 9, *c.* us from all sin.
See Ezek. 36:25; Mk. 1:44.
CLEAR. Gen. 44:16, how shall we *c.* ourselves?
Ex. 34:7, by no means *c.* the guilty.
2Sam. 23:4, *c.* shining after rain.
Job 11:17, age shall be *c.* than noonday.
Ps. 51:4, be *c.* when thou judgest.
Mt. 7:5; Lk. 6:42, see *c.* to pull out mote.
Mk. 8:25, saw every man *c.*
Rom. 1:20, things from creation *c.* seen.
Rev. 21:11; 22:1, light *c.* as crystal.
See Gen. 24:8; Song 6:10; Zech. 14:6.
CLEAVE. Josh. 23:8, *c.* to the Lord your God.
2Ki. 5:27, leprosy shall *c.* to thee.
Job 29:10; Ps. 137:6; Ezek. 3:26, *c.* to roof of mouth.
Ps. 119:25, my soul *c.* to dust.
Eccl. 10:9, he that *c.* wood shall be endangered.
Acts 11:23, with purpose of heart *c.*
Rom. 12:9, *c.* to that which is good.
See Gen. 2:24; Mt. 19:5; Mk. 10:7.
CLEFTS. Song 2:14; Isa. 2:21; Jer. 49:16; Amos 6:11; Obad. 3.
CLEMENCY. Acts 24:4.
CLERK. Acts 19:35.
CLIMB. Jn. 10:1, but *c.* up some other way.
See 1Sam. 14:13; Amos 9:2; Lk. 19:4.
CLODS. Job 21:33, the *c.* of the valley shall be sweet.
See Job 7:5; Isa. 28:24; Hos. 10:11; Joel 1:17.
CLOKE. Mt. 5:40; Lk. 6:29, let him have thy *c.* also.
1Th. 2:5, a *c.* of covetousness.
1Pet. 2:16, a *c.* of maliciousness.
CLOSE (*v.*). Gen. 2:21; Isa. 29:10; Mt. 13:15.
CLOSE. Prov. 18:24, sticketh *c.* than a brother.
Lk. 9:36, they kept it *c.*
See Num. 5:13; 1Chr. 12:1; Job 28:21.
CLOSET. Mt. 6:6; Lk. 12:3.
CLOTH. 1Sam. 19:13; 21:9; Mt. 9:16; Mk. 2:21.
CLOTHE. Ps. 65:13, pastures *c.* with flocks.
109:18, *c.* himself with cursing.
132:9, *c.* with righteousness.
16, *c.* with salvation.
Prov. 23:21, drowsiness shall *c.* a man.
31:21, household *c.* with scarlet.
Isa. 50:3, *c.* heavens with blackness.
61:10, *c.* with garments of salvation.
Mt. 6:30; Lk. 12:28, *c.* grass of field.
31, wherewithal shall we be *c.*
11:8; Lk. 7:25, man *c.* in soft raiment.
25:36, 43, naked and ye *c.* me.
Mk. 1:6, *c.* with camel's hair.
5:15; Lk. 8:35, *c.* and in right mind.
15:17, *c.* Jesus with purple.
Lk. 16:19, *c.* in purple and fine linen.
2Cor. 5:2, desiring to be *c.* upon.
1Pet. 5:5, be *c.* with humility.
Rev. 3:18, that thou mayest be *c.*
12:1, woman *c.* with the sun.
19:13, *c.* with a vesture dipped in blood.
See Gen. 3:21; Ex. 40:14; Est. 4:4.
CLOTHES. Dt. 29:5; Neh. 9:21, *c.* not waxen old.
Mk. 5:28, if I touch but his *c.*
Lk. 2:7, in swaddling *c.*
Lk. 8:27, a man that ware no *c.*
19:36, spread *c.* in the way.
24:12; Jn. 20:5, linen *c.* laid.
Jn. 11:44, bound with grave-*c.*
Acts 7:58, laid down *c.* at Saul's feet.
22:23, cried out and cast off *c.*
See Gen. 49:11; 1Sam. 19:24; Neh. 4:23.
CLOTHING. Ps. 45:13, her *c.* of wrought gold.
Prov. 27:26, lambs are for thy *c.*
31:22, her *c.* is silk and purple.
25, strength and honour are her *c.*
Isa. 3:7, in my house is neither bread nor *c.*
23:18, merchandise for durable *c.*
59:17, garments of vengeance for *c.*
Mt. 7:15, in sheep's *c.*
Mk. 12:38, love to go in long *c.*
Acts 10:30, a man in bright *c.*
Jas. 2:3, to him that weareth gay *c.*
See Job 22:6; 24:7; 31:19; Ps. 35:13.
CLOUD. Ex. 13:21; 14:24; Neh. 9:19, a pillar of *c.*
1Ki. 18:44, 45, a little *c.*
Ps. 36:5, faithfulness reacheth to *c.*
97:2, *c.* and darkness round about him.
99:7, spake in *c.* pillar.
Prov. 3:20, *c.* dropped down dew.
Eccl. 11:4, regardeth the *c.* not reap.
12:2, nor *c.* return after rain.
Isa. 5:6, command *c.* rain not.
44:22, blotted out as thick *c.*
60:8, fly as a *c.*
Dan. 7:13; Lk. 21:27, Son of man with *c.*
Hos. 6:4; 13:3, goodness as morning *c.*
Mt. 17:5; Mk. 9:7; Lk. 9:34, *c.* overshadowed.
24:30; 26:64; Mk. 13:26; 14:62, in *c.* with power.
1Cor. 10:1, fathers under *c.*
1Th. 4:17, caught up in *c.*
2Pet. 2:17, *c.* carried with tempest.
Jude 12, *c.* without water.
Rev. 1:7, he cometh with *c.*
14:14-16, white *c.*
See Gen. 9:13; Ex. 24:15; 40:34.
CLOUT. Josh. 9:5; Jer. 38:11.
CLOVEN. Lev. 11:3; Dt. 14:7; Acts 2:3.
CLUSTER. Isa. 65:8, new wine in *c.*
See Num. 13:23; Song 1:14; Rev. 14:18.
COAL. Prov. 6:28, hot *c.* and not be burned.
25:22; Rom. 12:20, heap *c.* of fire.
Jn. 18:18; 21:9, fire of *c.*
See Job 41:21; Ps. 18:8; Isa. 6:6.
COAST. 1Chr. 4:10; Mt. 8:34; Mk. 5:17.
COAT. Mt. 5:40, take away thy *c.*
10:10; Mk. 6:9, neither provide two *c.*
Lk. 6:29, thy *c.* also.
Jn. 19:23, *c.* without seam.
21:7, fisher's *c.*
Acts 9:39, the *c.* which Dorcas made.
See Gen. 3:21; 37:3; 1Sam. 2:19.
COCK. Mt. 26:34; Mk. 13:35; 14:30; Lk. 22:34.
COCKATRICE. Isa. 11:8; 14:29; 59:5.
COCKLE. Job 31:40.
COFFER. 1Sam. 6:8, 11, 15.

OFFIN. Gen. 50:26.
OGITATIONS. Dan. 7:28.
OLD. Prov. 20:4, by reason of *c.*
25:13, *c.* of snow in harvest.
20, garment in *c.* weather.
25, *c.* waters to thirsty soul.
Mt. 10:42, cup of *c.* water.
24:12, love of many wax *c.*
2Cor. 11:27, in *c.* and nakedness.
Rev. 3:15, neither *c.* nor hot.
See Gen. 8:22; Job 24:7; 37:9; Ps. 147:17.
OLLECTION. 2Chr. 24:6; Acts 11:29; Rom. 15:26; 1Cor. 16:1.
OLLEGE. 2Ki. 22:14; 2Chr. 34:22.
OLOUR. Prov. 23:31, *c.* in the cup.
Acts 27:30, under *c.* as though.
See Gen. 37:3; Ezek. 1:4; Dan. 10:6.
OMELY. Ps. 33:1, praise is *c.*
1Cor. 11:13, is it *c.* that a woman.
See 1Sam. 16:18; Prov. 30:29; Isa. 53:2.
OMFORT (*n.*). Mt. 9:22; Mk. 10:49; Lk. 8:48.
2Cor. 13:11, be of good *c.*
Acts 9:31, *c.* of Holy Ghost.
Rom. 15:4, patience and *c.* of scriptures.
2Cor. 1:3, God of all *c.*
7:13, were comforted in your *c.*
Phil. 2:1, if any *c.* of love.
See Job 10:20; Ps. 94:19; 119:50; Isa. 57:6.
OMFORT (*v.*). Gen. 37:35; Ps. 77:2; Jer. 31:15, refused to be *c.*
Ps. 23:4, rod and staff *c.*
Isa. 40:1, *c.* ye, *c.* ye my people.
49:13; 52:9, God hath *c.* his people.
61:2, *c.* all that mourn.
66:13, as one whom his mother *c.*
Mt. 5:4, they shall be *c.*
Lk. 16:25, he is *c.*, and thou art tormented.
Jn. 11:19, to *c.* concerning their brother.
2Cor. 1:4, able to *c.* them.
1Th. 4:18, *c.* one another with these words.
5:11, wherefore *c.* yourselves together.
14, *c.* the feeble-minded.
See Gen. 5:29; 18:5; 37:35.
OMFORTABLE. Isa. 40:2; Hos. 2:14; Zech. 1:13.
OMFORTER. Job 16:2, miserable *c.* are ye all.
Ps. 69:20, looked for *c.* but I found none.
Jn. 14:16, give you another *C.*
15:26, when the *C.* is come.
16:7, *C.* will not come.
See 2Sam. 10:3; 1Chr. 19:3.
OMFORTLESS. Jn. 14:18.
OMMAND. Ps. 33:9, he *c.* and it stood fast.
Lk. 8:25, he *c.* even the winds.
9:54, *c.* fire from heaven.
Jn. 15:14, if ye do what I *c.* you.
Acts 17:30, *c.* all men everywhere.
See Gen. 18:19; Dt. 28:8.
OMMANDER. Isa. 55:4.
OMMANDMENT. Ps. 119:86, *c.* are faithful.
96, *c.* exceeding broad.
127, I love thy *c.*
143, thy *c.* are my delight.
Mt. 15:9; Mk. 7:7; Col. 2:22, the *c.* of men.
Lk. 23:56, rested according to *c.*
Jn. 13:34; 1Jn. 2:7; 2Jn. 5, a new *c.*
Rom. 7:12, *c.* is holy, just, and good.
1Cor. 7:6; 2Cor. 8:8, by permission, not by *c.*
Eph. 6:2, first *c.* with promise.
1Tim. 1:5, end of the *c.* is charity.
See Est. 3:3.
COMMEND. Lk. 16:8, *c.* unjust steward.
23:46, into thy hands I *c.*
Rom. 3:5, unrighteousness *c.* righteousness of God.
5:8, God *c.* his love toward us.
1Cor. 8:8, meat *c.* us not.
2Cor. 3:1; 5:12, *c.* ourselves.
4:2, *c.* to every man's conscience.
10:18, not he that *c.* himself is approved.
See Prov. 12:8; Eccl. 8:15; Acts 20:32.
COMMISSION. Ezra 8:36; Acts 26:12.
COMMIT. Ps. 37:5, *c.* thy way to the Lord.
Jer. 2:13, have *c.* two evils.
Jn. 2:24, Jesus did not *c.* himself to them.
5:22, hath *c.* judgment to Son.
Rom. 3:2, were *c.* oracles of God.
2Cor. 5:19, had *c.* to us word of reconciliation.
1Tim. 6:20, keep what is *c.* to thee.
2Tim. 2:2, *c.* thou to faithful men.
1Pet. 2:23, *c.* himself to him that judgeth.
See Job 5:8; Ps. 31:5; 1Cor. 9:17.
COMMODIOUS. Acts 27:12.
COMMON. Eccl. 6:1, evil, and it is *c.* among men.
Mk. 12:37, the *c.* people heard him gladly.
Acts 2:44; 4:32, all things *c.*
10:14; 11:8, never eaten any thing *c.*
15; 11:9, call not thou *c.*
1Cor. 10:13, temptation *c.* to men.
Eph. 2:12, aliens from *c.*-wealth.
See Lev. 4:27; Num. 16:29; 1Sam. 21:4.
COMMOTION. Jer. 10:22; Lk. 21:9.
COMMUNE. Job 4:2, if we *c.* with thee.
Ps. 4:4; 77:6; Eccl. 1:16, *c.* with own heart.
Zech. 1:14, angel that *c.* with me.
See Ex. 25:22; 1Sam. 19:3; Lk. 22:4.
COMMUNICATE. Gal. 6:6, let him that is taught *c.*
1Tim. 6:18, be willing to *c.*
Heb. 13:16, do good and *c.*
See Gal. 2:2; Phil. 4:14, 15.
COMMUNICATION. Mt. 5:37, let your *c.* be yea.
Lk. 24:17, what manner of *c.*
1Cor. 15:33, evil *c.* corrupt good manners.
Eph. 4:29, let no corrupt *c.* proceed.
See 2Ki. 9:11; Phile. 6.
COMMUNION. 1Cor. 10:16; 2Cor. 6:14; 13:14.
COMPACT. Ps. 122:3; Eph. 4:16.
COMPANY. 1Sam. 10:5; 19:20, a *c.* of prophets.
Ps. 55:14, walked to house of God in *c.*
68:11, great was the *c.* of those.
Mk. 6:39; Lk. 9:14, sit down by *c.*
2Th. 3:14, have no *c.* with him.
Heb. 12:22, innumerable *c.* of angels.
See Num. 16:6; Jud. 9:37; 18:23.
COMPANION. Job 30:29, a *c.* to owls.
Ps. 119:63, a *c.* to them that fear thee.
Prov. 13:20, *c.* of fools shall be destroyed.

28:7, *c.* of riotous men.
24, the *c.* of a destroyer.
Acts 19:29, Paul's *c.* in travel.
Phil. 2:25; Rev. 1:9, brother and *c.* in labour.
See Ex. 32:27; Jud. 11:38; 14:20.
COMPARE. Prov. 3:15; 8:11, not to be *c.* to wisdom.
Isa. 40:18, what likeness will ye *c.* to him?
46:5, to whom will ye *c.* me.
Lam. 4:2, *c.* to fine gold.
Rom. 8:18, not worthy to be *c.* with glory.
1Cor. 2:13, *c.* spiritual things with spiritual.
See Ps. 89:6; 2Cor. 10:12.
COMPARISON. Jud. 8:2; Hag. 2:3; Mk. 4:30.
COMPASS (*n.*). 2Sam. 5:23; 2Ki. 3:9; Isa. 44:13; Acts 28:13.
COMPASS (*v.*). 2Sam. 22:5; Ps. 18:4; 116:3, waves of death *c.* me.
6; Ps. 18:5, sorrows of hell *c.* me.
Ps. 5:12, with favour *c.* as with a shield.
32:7, *c.* with songs of deliverance.
10, mercy shall *c.* him about.
Isa. 50:11, *c.* yourselves with sparks.
Mt. 23:15, *c.* sea and land.
Lk. 21:20, Jerusalem *c.* with armies.
Heb. 5:2, he also is *c.* with infirmity.
12:1, *c.* about with cloud of witnesses.
See Josh. 6:3; Job 16:13; Jer. 31:22.
COMPASSION. Isa. 49:15, that she should not have *c.*
Lam. 3:22, his *c.* fail not.
32; Mic. 7:19, yet will he have *c.*
Mt. 9:36; 14:14; Mk. 1:41; 6:34, Jesus moved with *c.*
18:33, *c.* on thy fellowservant.
20:34, had *c.* on them and touched.
Mk. 5:19, the Lord hath had *c.*
9:22, have *c.*, and help us.
Lk. 10:33, the Samaritan had *c.*
15:20, father had *c.*, and ran.
Rom. 9:15, I will have *c.* on whom I will.
Heb. 5:2, have *c.* on ignorant.
1Pet. 3:8, of one mind, having *c.*
1Jn. 3:17, shutteth up bowels of *c.*
Jude 22, of some have *c.*, making a difference.
See Ps. 78:38; 86:15; 111:4; 112:4.
COMPEL. Mt. 5:41, *c.* thee to go a mile.
27:32; Mk. 15:21, *c.* to bear cross.
Lk. 14:23, *c.* to come in.
Acts 26:11, I *c.* them to blaspheme.
See Lev. 25:39; 2Cor. 12:11; Gal. 2:3.
COMPLAIN. Ps. 144:14, no *c.* in our streets.
Lam. 3:39, wherefore doth a living man *c.*
Jude 16, these murmurers, *c.*
See Num. 11:1; Jud. 21:22; Job 7:11.
COMPLAINT. Job 23:2, to-day is my *c.* bitter.
Ps. 142:2, I poured out my *c.* before him.
See 1Sam. 1:16; Job 7:13; 9:27; 10:1.
COMPLETE. Lev. 23:15; Col. 2:10; 4:12.
COMPREHEND. Job 37:5; Isa. 40:12; Jn. 1:5; Eph. 3:18.
CONCEAL. Prov. 12:23, prudent man *c.* knowledge.
25:2, glory of God to *c.* a thing.
Jer. 50:2, publish and *c.* not.
See Gen. 37:26; Dt. 13:8.
CONCEIT. Rom. 11:25; 12:16, wise in your own *c.*
CONCEIT (reproved). Prov. 3:7; 12:15; 18:11; 20:5; 28:11;
Isa. 5:21.
CONCEIVE. Ps. 7:14, *c.* mischief, brought forth falsehood.
Ps. 51:5, in sin did my mother *c.* me.
Acts 5:4, why hast thou *c.* this thing.
Jas. 1:15, when lust *c.* it bringeth forth.
See Job 15:35; Isa. 7:14; 59:4.
CONCERN. Lk. 24:27, things *c.* himself.
Rom. 9:5, as *c.* the flesh Christ came.
16:19, simple *c.* evil.
Phil. 4:15, *c.* giving and receiving.
1Tim. 6:21, have erred *c.* the faith.
1Pet. 4:12, *c.* fiery trial.
See Lev. 6:3; Num. 10:29; Ps. 90:13; 135:14.
CONCISION. Phil. 3:2.
CONCLUDE. Rom. 3:28; 11:32; Gal. 3:22.
CONCLUSION. Eccl. 12:13.
CONCORD. 2Cor. 6:15.
CONCUPISCENCE. Col. 3:5; 1Th. 4:5, mortify evil *c.*
CONDEMN. Job 10:2, I will say to God, do not *c.* me.
Amos 2:8, drink wine of the *c.*
Mt. 12:7, ye would not have *c.* the guiltless.
37, by thy words shalt be *c.*
42; Lk. 11:31, rise in judgment and *c.*
20:18, shall *c.* him to death.
27:3, Judas when he saw he was *c.*
Mk. 14:64, all *c.* him to be guilty.
Lk. 6:37, *c.* not and ye shall not be *c.*
Jn. 3:17, God sent not his Son to *c.*
18, believe not is *c.*
8:10, hath no man *c.* thee?
11, neither do I *c.* thee.
Rom. 2:1, thou *c.* thyself.
8:3, *c.* sin in the flesh.
34, who is he that *c.*?
14:22, that *c.* not himself.
Ti. 2:8, sound speech that cannot be *c.*
Jas. 5:6, ye *c.* and killed the just.
9, grudge not lest ye be *c.*
1Jn. 3:21, if our heart *c.* us not.
See Job 9:20; 15:6; Mt. 12:41.
CONDEMNATION. Jn. 3:19, this is the *c.*, that light
2Cor. 3:9, the ministration of *c.*
1Tim. 3:6, the *c.* of the devil.
Jas. 5:12, lest ye fall into *c.*
Jude 4, of old ordained to this *c.*
See Lk. 23:40; Rom. 5:16; 8:1.
CONDESCEND. Rom. 12:16.
CONDITION. 1Sam. 11:2; Lk. 14:32.
CONDUIT. 2Ki. 18:17; 20:20; Isa. 7:3; 36:2.
CONEY. Lev. 11:5; Ps. 104:18; Prov. 30:26.
CONFECTION. Ex. 30:35; 1Sam. 8:13.
CONFEDERATE. Gen. 14:13; Isa. 7:2; 8:12; Obad. 7.
CONFERENCE. Gal. 2:6.
CONFERRED. Gal. 1:16.
CONFESS. Prov. 28:13, whoso *c.* and forsaketh.

Mt. 10:32; Lk. 12:8, *c.* me before men.
Jn. 9:22, if any man did *c.*
12:42, rulers did not *c.* him.
Acts 23:8, Pharisees *c.* both.
Rom. 10:9, shall *c.* with thy mouth.
14:11; Phil. 2:11, every tongue *c.*
Heb. 11:13, *c.* they were strangers.
Jas. 5:16, *c.* your faults one to another.
1Jn. 1:9, if we *c.* our sins.
4:2, every spirit that *c.* Christ.
15, whoso shall *c.* that Jesus is the Christ.
Rev. 3:5, I will *c.* his name before my Father.
See Lev. 16:21; 1Ki. 8:33; 2Chr. 6:24.
CONFESSION. Rom. 10:10; 1Tim. 6:13.
CONFIDENCE. Ps. 65:5, the *c.* of all the ends of the earth.
118:8, 9, than to put *c.* in man.
Prov. 3:26, the Lord shall be thy *c.*
14:26, in fear of the Lord is strong *c.*
Isa. 30:15, in *c.* shall be your strength.
Jer. 2:37, hath rejected thy *c.*
Eph. 3:12, access with *c.* by the faith of him.
Phil. 3:3, 4, no *c.* in flesh.
Heb. 3:6, 14, hold fast *c.*
10:35, cast not away *c.*
1Jn. 2:28, we may have *c.*
3:21, we have *c.* toward God.
5:14, this is the *c.* we have in him.
See Job 4:6; 18:14; 31:24; Prov. 25:19.
CONFIDENT. Ps. 27:3; Prov. 14:16; 2Cor. 5:6; Phil. 1:6.
CONFIRM. Isa. 35:3, *c.* the feeble knees.
Mk. 16:20, *c.* the word with signs.
Acts 14:22, *c.* the souls of the disciples.
15:32, 41, exhorted brethren, and *c.* them.
Rom. 15:8, *c.* the promises made to fathers.
See 2Ki. 15:19.
CONFIRMATION. Phil. 1:7; Heb. 6:16.
CONFISCATION. Ezra 7:26.
CONFLICT. Phil. 1:30; Col. 2:1.
CONFORM. Rom. 8:29; 12:2; Phil. 3:10.
CONFOUND. Ps. 22:5, fathers trusted and were not *c.*
40:14; 70:2, ashamed and *c.*
Acts 2:6, multitude were *c.*
9:22, Saul *c.* the Jews.
See Gen. 11:7; Ps. 71:13; 129:5.
CONFUSED. Isa. 9:5; Acts 19:32.
CONFUSION. Dan. 9:7, to us belongeth *c.* of faces.
Acts 19:29, city was filled with *c.*
1Cor. 14:33, God not author of *c.*
See Ps. 70:2; 71:1; 109:29; Isa. 24:10.
CONGEALED. Ex. 15:8.
CONGRATULATE. 1Chr. 18:10.
CONGREGATION. Num. 14:10, all the *c.* bade stone them.
Neh. 5:13, all the *c.* said Amen.
Ps. 1:5, nor sinners in the *c.* of the righteous.
26:12, in the *c.* will I bless the Lord.
Prov. 21:16, in the *c.* of the dead.
Joel 2:16, sanctify the *c.*
Acts 13:43, when the *c.* was broken up.
See Ex. 12:6; 16:2; 39:32; Lev. 4:13.
CONIES. Ps. 104:18, the rocks for the *c.*
Prov. 30:26, the *c.* are but a feeble folk.
See Lev. 11:5; Dt. 14:7.
CONQUERORS. Rom. 8:37; Rev. 6:2.
CONSCIENCE. Acts 24:16, *c.* void of offence.
Rom. 2:15; 9:1; 2Cor. 1:12, *c.* bearing witness.
13:5; 1Cor. 10:25, 27, 28, for *c.* sake.
1Cor. 8:10, 12, weak *c.*
1Tim. 1:5, 19; Heb. 13:18; 1Pet. 3:16, a good *c.*
3:9, mystery of faith in pure *c.*
4:2, *c.* seared with hot iron.
Heb. 9:14, purge *c.* from dead works.
10:22, hearts sprinkled from evil *c.*
See Jn. 8:9; Acts 23:1; 2Cor. 4:2.
CONSECRATE. 1Chr. 29:5, to *c.* his service to the Lord.
Mic. 4:13, I will *c.*
Heb. 7:28, who is *c.* for evermore.
10:20, living way which he hath *c.*
See Ex. 28:3; 29:35; 32:29; Lev. 7:37.
CONSENT. Ps. 50:18, a thief thou *c.* with him.
Prov. 1:10, if sinners entice thee *c.* not.
Zeph. 3:9, to serve with one *c.*
Lk. 14:18, with one *c.* began to make excuse.
See Dt. 13:8; Acts 8:1; Rom. 7:16.
CONSIDER. Ps. 8:3, when I *c.* the heavens.
41:1, blessed is he that *c.* the poor.
48:13, *c.* her palaces.
50:22, *c.* this, ye that forget God.
Prov. 6:6, *c.* her ways and be wise.
23:1, *c.* diligently what is before thee.
24:12, doth not he *c.* it.?
28:22, and *c.* not that poverty.
Eccl. 5:1, they *c.* not that they do evil.
7:14, in day of adversity *c.*
Isa. 1:3, my people doth not *c.*
Jer. 23:20; 30:24, in latter days ye shall *c.*
Ezek. 12:3, it may be they will *c.*
Hag. 1:5, 7, *c.* your ways.
Mt. 6:28; Lk. 12:27, *c.* lilies of the field.
7:3, *c.* not the beam.
Lk. 12:24, *c.* the ravens.
Gal. 6:1, *c.* thyself lest thou also be tempted.
Heb. 3:1, *c.* the Apostle and High Priest.
7:4, now *c.* how great this man was.
10:21, *c.* one another to provoke.
12:3, *c.* him that endured.
13:7, *c.* the end of their conversation.
See Dt. 32:29; Jud. 18:14; 1Sam. 12:24.
CONSIST. Lk. 12:15; Col. 1:17.
CONSOLATION. Job 15:11, are the *c.* of God small.
Lk. 6:24, ye have received your *c.*
Rom. 15:5, the God of *c.*
Phil. 2:1, if there be any *c.* in Christ.
2Th. 2:16, everlasting *c.*
Heb. 6:18, strong *c.*
See Jer. 16:7; Lk. 2:25; Acts 4:36.
CONSPIRACY. 2Sam. 15:2; Jer. 11:9; Acts 23:13.
CONSTANTLY. 1Chr. 28:7; Prov. 21:28; Ti. 3:8.
CONSTRAIN. Job 32:18; Lk. 24:29; 2Cor. 5:14; 1Pet. 5:2.
CONSULT. Ps. 83:3; Mk. 15:1; Lk. 14:31; Jn. 12:10.
CONSUME. Ex. 3:2, bush was not *c.*

Dt. 4:24; 9:3; Heb. 12:29, a *c.* fire.
1Ki. 18:38; 2Chr. 7:1, fire fell and *c.* the sacrifice.
Job 20:26, fire not blown shall *c.* him.
Ps. 39:11, *c.* away like a moth.
Mal. 3:6, therefore ye are not *c.*
Lk. 9:54, *c.* them as Elias did.
Gal. 5:15, take heed ye be not *c.*
Jas. 4:3, that ye may *c.* it on your lusts.
See Ex. 32:10; 33:3; Dt. 5:25; Josh. 24:20.
CONSUMMATION. Dan. 9:27.
CONSUMPTION. Lev. 26:16; Dt. 28:22; Isa. 10:22.
CONTAIN. 1Ki. 8:27; 2Chr. 2:6; 6:18; 1Cor. 7:9.
CONTEMN. Ps. 10:13; 15:4; 107:11; Ezek. 21:10.
CONTEMPT. Prov. 18:3, wicked cometh, then cometh *c.*
Dan. 12:2, awake to everlasting *c.*
See Est. 1:18; Job 31:34; Ps. 119:22.
CONTEMPTIBLE. Mal. 1:7, 12; 2:9; 2Cor. 10:10.
CONTEND. Isa. 49:25, I will *c.* with him that *c.*
50:8, who will *c.* with me.
Jer. 12:5, how canst thou *c.* with horses.
See Job 10:2; 13:8; Eccl. 6:10; Jude 3, 9.
CONTENT. Mk. 15:15, willing to *c.* the people.
Lk. 3:14, be *c.* with your wages.
Phil. 4:11, I have learned to be *c.*
1Tim. 6:6, godliness with *c.* is great gain.
8, having food let us be *c.*
Heb. 13:5, be *c.* with such things as ye have.
See Gen. 37:27; Josh. 7:7; Job 6:28; Prov. 6:35.
CONTENTION. Prov. 18:18, the lot causeth *c.* to cease.
19:13; 27:15, *c.* of a wife.
23:29, who hath *c.*
Acts 15:39, the *c.* was sharp.
1Cor. 1:11, there are *c.* among you.
Phil. 1:16, preach Christ of *c.*
1Th. 2:2, to speak with much *c.*
Ti. 3:9, avoid *c.* and strivings.
See Prov. 13:10; 17:14; 18:6; 22:10.
CONTENTIOUS. Prov. 21:19; 26:21; 27:15; Rom. 2:8; 1Cor. 11:16.
CONTINUAL. Ps. 34:1; 71:6, praise *c.* in my mouth.
40:11, let thy truth *c.* preserve me.
73:23, I am *c.* with thee.
Prov. 6:21, bind them *c.* on thine heart.
15:15, merry heart hath a *c.* feast.
Isa. 14:6, smote with a *c.* stroke.
52:5, my name is *c.* blasphemed.
Lk. 18:5, lest by her *c.* coming.
24:53, were *c.* in the temple.
Acts 6:4, give ourselves *c.* to prayer.
Rom. 9:2, I have *c.* sorrow in my heart.
Heb. 7:3, abideth a priest *c.*
See Ex. 29:42; Num. 4:7; Job 1:5.
CONTINUANCE. Dt. 28:59; Ps. 139:16; Isa. 64:5; Rom. 2:7.
CONTINUE. Job 14:2, as a shadow and *c.* not.
Ps. 72:17, name shall *c.* as long as the sun.
Isa. 5:11, *c.* till wine inflame them.
Jer. 32:14, evidences may *c.* many days.
Lk. 6:12, he *c.* all night in prayer.
22:28, that *c.* with me in my temptation.
Jn. 8:31, if ye *c.* in my word.
15:9, *c.* ye in my love.
Acts 1:14; 2:46, *c.* with one accord.
12:16, Peter *c.* knocking.
13:43, to *c.* in grace of God.
14:22, exhorting them to *c.* in faith.
26:22, I *c.* unto this day.
Rom. 6:1, shall we *c.* in sin?
12:12; Col. 4:2, *c.* in prayer.
Gal. 3:10, that *c.* not in all things.
Col. 1:23; 1Tim. 2:15, if ye *c.* in the faith.
1Tim. 4:16; 2Tim. 3:14, *c.* in them.
Heb. 7:23, not suffered to *c.* by reason.
24, this man *c.* ever.
13:1, let brotherly love *c.*
14, here have we no *c.* city.
Jas. 4:13, and *c.* there a year.
2Pet. 3:4, all things *c.* as they were.
1Jn. 2:19, no doubt have *c.* with us.
See 1Sam. 12:14; 13:14; 2Sam. 7:29.
CONTRADICTION. Heb. 7:7; 12:3.
CONTRARIWISE. 2Cor. 2:7; Gal. 2:7; 1Pet. 3:9.
CONTRARY. Acts 18:13, *c.* to the law.
26:9, many things *c.* to name of Jesus.
Gal. 5:17, *c.* the one to the other.
1Th. 2:15, *c.* to all men.
1Tim. 1:10, *c.* to sound doctrine.
Ti. 2:8, he of the *c.* part may be ashamed.
See Lev. 26:21; Est. 9:1; Mt. 14:24; Acts 17:7.
CONTRIBUTION. Rom. 15:26.
CONTRITE. Ps. 34:18; 51:17; Isa. 57:15; 66:2.
CONTROVERSY. Jer. 25:31, a *c.* with the nations.
Mic. 6:2, hath a *c.* with his people.
1Tim. 3:16, without *c.* great is the mystery.
See Dt. 17:8; 19:17; 21:5; 25:1.
CONVENIENT. Prov. 30:8, feed me with food *c.*
Acts 24:25, when I have a *c.* season.
Rom. 1:28, things which are not *c.*
Eph. 5:4, talking, jesting, are not *c.*
See Jer. 40:4; Mk. 6:21; 1Cor. 16:12.
CONVERSANT. Josh. 8:35; 1Sam. 25:15.
CONVERSATION. Ps. 37:14, such as be of upright *c.*
50:23, that ordereth his *c.* aright.
Phil. 1:27, *c.* as becometh the gospel.
3:20, our *c.* is in heaven.
1Tim. 4:12, an example in *c.*
Heb. 13:5, *c.* without covetousness.
7, considering end of their *c.*
1Pet. 1:15; 2Pet. 3:11, holy *c.*
18, redeemed from vain *c.*
2:12, your *c.* honest among Gentiles.
3:1, won by *c.* of wives.
2Pet. 2:7, vexed with filthy *c.*
See Gal. 1:13; Eph. 2:3; 4:22; Jas. 3:13.
CONVERSION. Acts 15:3.
CONVERT. Ps. 19:7, perfect, *c.* the soul.
Isa. 6:10; Mt. 13:15; Mk. 4:12; Jn. 12:40; Acts 28:27,
lest they *c.*
Mt. 18:3, except ye be *c.*
Lk. 22:32, when *c.* strengthen thy brethren.
Acts 3:19, repent and be *c.*
Jas. 5:19, 20, and one *c.* him.

See Ps. 51:13; Isa. 1:27; 60:5.
CONVICTED. Jn. 8:9.
CONVINCE. Jn. 8:46, which of you *c.* me of sin.
Ti. 1:9, able to *c.* gainsayers.
See Job 32:12; Acts 18:28; 1Cor. 14:24.
CONVOCATION. Ex. 12:16; Lev. 23:2; Num. 28:26.
COOK. 1Sam. 8:13; 9:23, 24.
COOL. Gen. 3:8; Lk. 16:24.
COPPER. Ezra 8:27; 2Tim. 4:14.
COPY. Dt. 17:18; Josh. 8:32; Prov. 25:1.
CORBAN. Mk. 7:11, it is *c.*
CORD. Prov. 5:22, holden with the *c.* of sins.
Eccl. 4:12, a threefold *c.*
12:6, silver *c.* loosed.
Isa. 5:18, draw iniquity with *c.*
54:2, lengthen *c.*
Hos. 11:4, the *c.* of a man.
Jn. 2:15, scourge of small *c.*
See Jud. 15:13; Ps. 2:3; 118:27; Jer. 38:6.
CORN. Gen. 42:2; Acts 7:12, *c.* in Egypt.
Dt. 25:4; 1Cor. 9:9; 1Tim. 5:18, ox treadeth *c.*
Jud. 15:5, foxes into standing *c.*
Job 5:26, like as a shock of *c.*
Ps. 4:9, in time their *c.* increased.
65:7, prepared them *c.*
13, valleys covered over with *c.*
72:16, handful of *c.* in the earth.
Prov. 11:26, he that withholdeth *c.*
Zech. 9:17, *c.* shall make men cheerful.
Mt. 12:1; Mk. 2:23; Lk. 6:1, pluck *c.*
Mk. 4:28, full *c.* in the ear.
Jn. 12:24, a *c.* of wheat fall into ground.
See Gen. 27:28; 41:57; Dt. 33:28; Isa. 36:17.
CORNER. Ps. 118:22; Eph. 2:20, head stone of *c.*
144:12, daughters as *c.* stones.
Isa. 28:16; 1Pet. 2:6, a precious *c.* stone.
Mt. 6:5, pray in *c.* of the streets.
Rev. 7:1, on four *c.* of the earth.
See Job 1:19; Prov. 7:8; 21:9.
CORNET. 2Sam. 6:5; 1Chr. 15:28; Dan. 3:5.
CORPSE. 2Ki. 19:35; Isa. 37:36; Nah. 3:3; Mk. 6:29.
CORRECT. Prov. 3:12, whom the Lord loveth he *c.*
29:17, *c.* thy son.
19, servant will not be *c.* by words.
Jer. 10:24, *c.* me, but with judgment.
30:11; 46:28, I will *c.* thee in measure.
Heb. 12:9, we have had fathers which *c.* us.
See Job 5:17; Ps. 39:11; 94:10.
CORRECTION. Prov. 22:15, rod of *c.* shall drive it.
Jer. 2:30; 5:3; 7:28; Zeph. 3:2, receive *c.*
2Tim. 3:16, scripture profitable for *c.*
See Job 37:13; Prov. 3:11; 7:22; 15:10.
CORRUPT. Dt. 4:16, take heed lest ye *c.*
31:29, after my death ye will *c.*
Mt. 6:19; Lk. 12:33, moth *c.*
7:17; 12:33; Lk. 6:43, a *c.* tree.
1Cor. 15:33, evil communications *c.*
2Cor. 2:17, not as many, which *c.* the word.
7:2, we have *c.* no man.
11:2, lest your minds be *c.*
Eph. 4:22, put off old man which is *c.*
29, let no *c.* communication.
1Tim. 6:5; 2Tim. 3:8, men of *c.* minds.
Jas. 5:1, your riches are *c.*
See Gen. 6:11; Job 17:1; Prov. 25:26.
CORRUPTERS. Isa. 1:4; Jer. 6:28.
CORRUPTIBLE. Rom. 1:23; 1Cor. 9:25; 15:53; 1Pet. 1:18; 3:4.
CORRUPTION. Ps. 16:10; 49:9; Acts 2:27; 13:35, not see *c.*
Jon. 2:6, brought up life from *c.*
Rom. 8:21, from bondage of *c.*
1Cor. 15:42, 50, sown in *c.*
Gal. 6:8, of flesh reap *c.*
2Pet. 1:4, the *c.* that is in world.
2:12, perish in their own *c.*
See Lev. 22:25; Job 17:14; Isa. 38:17.
CORRUPTLY. 2Chr. 27:2; Neh. 1:7.
COST. 2Sam. 24:24; 1Chr. 21:24, offer of that which *c.* nothing.
Lk. 14:28, sitteth down and counteth *c.*
See 2Sam. 19:42; 1Ki. 5:17; Jn. 12:3; 1Tim. 2:9.
COTTAGE. Isa. 1:8; 24:20; Zeph. 2:6.
COUCH. Lk. 5:19, let him down with *c.*
24, take up thy *c.*
Acts 5:15, laid sick on *c.*
See Gen. 49:11; Job 7:13; 38:40; Ps. 6:6; Amos 6:4.
COULD. Isa. 5:4; Mk. 6:19; 9:18; 14:8.
COULTER. 1Sam. 13:20, 21.
COUNCIL. Mt. 5:22; 10:17; Acts 5:27; 6:12.
COUNSEL. Neh. 4:15, brought their *c.* to nought.
Job 38:2; 42:3, darkeneth *c.* by words.
Ps. 1:1, *c.* of the ungodly.
33:11; Prov. 19:21, *c.* of Lord standeth.
55:14, took sweet *c.* together.
73:24, guide me with thy *c.*
Prov. 1:25, 30, set at nought all my *c.*
11:14, where no *c.* is, people fall.
15:22, without *c.* purposes are disappointed.
21:30, there is no *c.* against the Lord.
Eccl. 8:2, I *c.* thee keep king's commandment.
Isa. 28:29, wonderful in *c.*
30:1, that take *c.*, but not of me.
40:14, with whom took he *c.*
46:10, my *c.* shall stand.
Jer. 32:19 great in *c.*, mighty in working.
Hos. 10:6, ashamed of his own *c.*
Mk. 3:6; Jn. 11:53, took *c.* against Jesus.
Acts 2:23, determinate *c.* of God.
4:28, what thy *c.* determined before.
5:38, if this *c.* be of men.
20:27, declare all *c.* of God.
1Cor. 4:5, make manifest *c.* of the heart.
Eph. 1:11, after the *c.* of his own will.
Heb. 6:17, the immutability of his *c.*
Rev. 3:18, I *c.* thee to buy gold tried in fire.
See Ex. 18:19; Josh. 9:14; 2Sam. 15:31.
COUNSELLOR. Prov. 11:14; 15:22; 24:6, in multitude of *c.*
12:20, to *c.* of peace is joy.
Mic. 4:9, is thy *c.* perished?
Mk. 15:43; Lk. 23:50, an honourable *c.*
Rom. 11:34, who hath been his *c.*
See 2Chr. 22:3; Job 3:14; 12:17.
COUNT. Gen. 15:6; Ps. 106:31; Rom. 4:3; Gal. 3:6, *c.*

for righteousness.
Ps. 44:22, *c.* as sheep for the slaughter.
Prov. 17:28, even a fool is *c.* wise.
Isa. 32:15, field be *c.* for a forest.
Mt. 14:5; Mk. 11:32, they *c.* him as a prophet.
Lk. 21:36; Acts 5:41; 2Th. 1:5, 11; 1Tim. 5:17, *c.* worthy.
Acts 20:24, neither *c.* I my life dear.
Phil. 3:7, 8, I *c.* loss for Christ.
13, I *c.* not myself to have apprehended.
Heb. 10:29, *c.* blood an unholy thing.
Jas. 1:2, *c.* it all joy.
2Pet. 3:9, as some men *c.* slackness.
See Num. 23:10; Job 31:4; Ps. 139:18, 22.
COUNTENANCE. 1Sam. 16:7, look not on his *c.* or stature.
12; 17:42, David of beautiful *c.*
Neh. 2:2, why is thy *c.* sad?
Job 14:20, thou changest his *c.*
Ps. 4:6; 44:3; 89:15; 90:8, light of thy *c.*
Prov. 15:13, merry heart maketh cheerful *c.*
27:17, sharpeneth *c.* of his friend.
Eccl. 7:3, by sadness of *c.* heart made better.
Isa. 3:9, their *c.* doth witness against them.
Mt. 6:16, hypocrites of a sad *c.*
28:3; Lk. 9:29, *c.* like lightning.
Rev. 1:16, his *c.* as the sun shineth.
See Gen. 4:5; Num. 6:26; Jud. 13:6.
COUNTRY. Prov. 25:25, good news from a far *c.*
Mt. 13:57; Mk. 6:4; Lk. 4:24; Jn. 4:44, in his own *c.*
21:33; 25:14; Mk. 12:1, went to far *c.*
Lk. 4:23, do also here in thy *c.*
Acts 12:20, their *c.* nourished by king's *c.*
Heb. 11:9, sojourned as in strange *c.*
16, desire a better *c.*
See Gen. 12:1; 24:4; Josh. 9:6; Lk. 15:13.
COUNTRYMEN. 2Cor. 11:26; 1Th. 2:14.
COUPLED. 1Pet. 3:2.
COURAGE. Dt. 31:6; 7:23; Josh. 10:25; Ps. 27:14; Acts 28:15, thanked God and took *c.*
See Num. 13:20; Josh. 1:7; 2:11; 2Sam. 13:28.
COURSE. Acts 20:24; 2Tim. 4:7, finished my *c.*
2Th. 3:1, may have free *c.*
Jas. 3:6, setteth on fire the *c.* of nature.
See Jud. 5:20; Ps. 82:5; Acts 13:25.
COURT. Ex. 27:9, thou shalt make the *c.* of the tabernacle.
38:9, and he made the *c.*
Ps. 65:4, that he may dwell in thy *c.*
84:2, fainteth for the *c.* of the Lord.
92:13, flourish in the *c.* of our God.
100:4, enter into his *c.* with praise.
Isa. 1:12, who required this to tread my *c.*?
Lk. 7:25, live delicately are in kings' *c.*
See Isa. 34:13; Jer. 19:14; Ezek. 9:7.
COURTEOUS. Acts 27:3; 28:7; 1Pet. 3:8.
COUSIN. Lk. 1:36, 58.
COVENANT. Num. 18:19; 2Chr. 13:5, *c.* of salt.
25:12, my *c.* of peace.
Ps. 105:8; 106:45, he remembereth his *c.* for ever.
111:5, ever mindful of his *c.*
Isa. 28:18, your *c.* with death disannulled.
Mt. 26:15; Lk. 22:5, they *c.* with him.
Acts 3:25, children of the *c.*
Rom. 9:4, to whom pertaineth the *c.*
Eph. 2:12, strangers from *c.* of promise.
Heb. 8:6, mediator of a better *c.*
12:24, mediator of the new *c.*
13:20, blood of the everlasting *c.*
See Gen. 9:15; Ex. 34:28; Job 31:1; Jer. 50:5.
COVER. Ex. 15:5, depths *c.* them, sank as stone.
33:32, I will *c.* them.
1Sam. 28:14, an old man *c.* with a mantle.
Est. 7:8, they *c.* Haman's face.
Ps. 32:1; Rom. 4:7, blessed whose sin is *c.*
73:6, violence *c.* them as a garment.
91:4, he shall *c.* thee with his feathers.
Ps. 104:6, thou *c.* it with the deep.
Prov. 10:6, 11, violence *c.* mouth of the wicked.
12, love *c.* all sins.
12:16, a prudent man *c.* shame.
17:9, he that *c.* transgression seeketh love.
28:13, he that *c.* sins shall not prosper.
Isa. 26:21, earth no more *c.* her slain.
Mt. 8:24, ship *c.* with waves.
10:26; Lk. 12:2, there is nothing *c.*
1Cor. 11:4, having his head *c.*
6, if women be not *c.*
7, a man ought not to *c.* his head.
1Pet. 4:8, charity shall *c.* multitude of sins.
See Gen. 7:19; Ex. 8:6; 21:33; Lev. 16:13.
COVERING. Job 22:14, thick clouds are a *c.* to him.
24:7, naked have no *c.* in the cold.
26:6, destruction hath no *c.*
31:19, if I have seen any poor without *c.*
Isa. 28:20, *c.* narrower than he can wrap.
See Gen. 8:13; Lev. 13:45; 2Sam. 17:19.
COVERT. Ps. 61:4; Isa. 4:6; 16:4; 32:2.
COVET. Prov. 21:26, he *c.* greedily all the day.
Hab. 2:9, *c.* an evil covetousness.
Acts 20:33, I have *c.* no man's silver.
1Cor. 12:31, *c.* earnestly the best gifts.
1Tim. 6:10, while some *c.* after, they erred.
See Ex. 20:17; Dt. 5:21; Rom. 7:7; 13:9.
COVETOUS. Prov. 28:16, he that hateth *c.* shall prolong.
Ezek. 33:31, their heart goeth after *c.*
Mk. 7:22, out of heart proceedeth *c.*
Rom. 1:29, filled with all *c.*
1Cor. 6:10; Eph. 5:5, nor *c.* inherit kingdom.
Eph. 5:3, but *c.*, let it not be named.
2Tim. 3:2, men shall be *c.*
Heb. 13:5, conversation without *c.*
2Pet. 2:3, through *c.* make merchandise.
14, exercised with *c.* practices.
See Ps. 10:3; 119:36; 1Cor. 5:10.
COW. Lev. 22:28; Job 21:10; Isa. 11:7.
CRACKLING. Eccl. 7:6.
CRAFT. Job 5:13; 1Cor. 3:19, taketh wise in their *c.*
Lk. 20:23, he perceived their *c.*
Acts 19:25, by this *c.* we have our wealth.
27, our *c.* is in danger.
2Cor. 4:2, not walking in *c.*
12:16, being *c.* I caught you.

Eph. 4:14, carried away with cunning *c.*
See Dan. 8:25; Acts 18:3; Rev. 18:22.
RAG. Job 39:28.
RANE. Isa. 38:14; Jer. 8:7.
RASHING. Zeph. 1:10.
RAVE. Prov. 16:26; Mk. 15:43.
REATE. Isa. 40:26, who hath *c.* these things?
43:7, *c.* him for my glory.
65:17, I *c.* new heavens and new earth.
Jer. 31:22, the Lord hath *c.* a new thing.
Amos 4:13, he that *c.* wind.
Mal. 2:10, hath not one God *c.* us?
1Cor. 11:9, neither was man *c.* for woman.
Eph. 2:10, *c.* in Christ Jesus.
4:24, after God is *c.* in righteousness.
Col. 1:16, by him were all things *c.*
1Tim. 4:3, which God *c.* to be received.
See Gen. 1:1; 6:7; Dt. 4:32; Ps. 51:10.
REATION. Mk. 10:6; 13:19; Rom. 1:20; 8:22; 2Pet. 3:4.
REATOR. Eccl. 12:1; Isa. 40:28; Rom. 1:25; 1Pet. 4:19.
REATURE. Mk. 16:15; Col. 1:23, preach to every *c.*
Rom. 8:19, expectation of the *c.*
2Cor. 5:17; Gal. 6:15, new *c.*
Col. 1:15, firstborn of every *c.*
1Tim. 4:4, every *c.* of God is good.
See Gen. 1:20; 2:19; Isa. 13:21; Ezek. 1:20; Eph. 2:10; 4:24.
REATURES. Ezek. 1:5, came the likeness of four living *c.*
REDITOR. Dt. 15:2; 2Ki. 4:1; Isa. 50:1; Mt. 18:23; Lk. 7:41.
REEK. Acts 27:39.
REEP. Ps. 104:20, beasts of the forest *c.* forth.
25, in sea are *c.* things.
Ezek. 8:10, form of *c.* things portrayed.
Acts 10:12; 11:6, Peter saw *c.* things.
2Tim. 3:6, they *c.* into houses.
Jude 4, certain men *c.* in unawares.
See Gen. 1:25; 7:8; Lev. 11:41; Dt. 4:18.
REW. Mt. 26:74; Mk. 14:68; Lk. 22:60.
RIB. Job 39:9; Prov. 14:4; Isa. 1:3.
RIMSON. 2Chr. 2:7; Isa. 1:18; Jer. 4:30.
RIPPLE. Acts 14:8.
ROOKED. Eccl. 1:15; 7:13, *c.* cannot be made straight.
Isa. 40:4; 42:16; Lk. 3:5, *c.* shall be made straight.
45:2, make the *c.* places straight.
59:8; Lam. 3:9, *c.* paths.
Phil. 2:15, in midst of a *c.* nation.
See Lev. 21:20; Dt. 32:5; Job 26:13.
ROPS. Lev. 1:16; Ezek. 17:22.
ROSS. Mt. 16:24; Mk. 8:34; 10:21; Lk. 9:23, take up *c.*
27:32; Mk. 15:21; Lk. 23:26, compelled to bear *c.*
40; Mk. 15:30, come down from *c.*
Jn. 19:25, there stood by *c.*
1Cor. 1:17; Gal. 6:12; Phil. 3:18, *c.* of Christ.
18, preaching of the *c.*
Gal. 5:11, offence of the *c.*
6:14, glory save in the *c.*
Eph. 2:16, reconcile both by the *c.*
Phil. 2:8, the death of the *c.*
Col. 1:20, peace through blood of the *c.*
Col. 2:14, nailing it to his *c.*
Heb. 12:2, for joy endured the *c.*
See Obad. 14; Mt. 10:38; Jn. 19:17, 19.
CROUCH. 1Sam. 2:36; Ps. 10:10.
CROWN. Job 19:9, taken the *c.* from my head.
Ps. 8:5; Heb. 2:7, 9, *c.* with glory and honour.
65:11, thou *c.* the year.
103:4, *c.* thee with lovingkindness.
Prov. 4:9, a *c.* of glory shall she deliver.
12:4, virtuous woman is a *c.*
14:18, prudent *c.* with knowledge.
16:31, hoary head a *c.* of glory.
17:6, children's children are the *c.* of old men.
Isa. 28:1, woe to the *c.* of pride.
Mt. 27:29; Mk. 15:17; Jn. 19:2, a *c.* of thorns.
1Cor. 9:25, to obtain a corruptible *c.*
Phil. 4:1, my joy and *c.*
1Th. 2:19, a *c.* of rejoicing.
2Tim. 2:5, not *c.* except he strive.
4:8, a *c.* of righteousness.
Jas. 1:12; Rev. 2:10, *c.* of life.
1Pet. 5:4, a *c.* of glory.
Rev. 3:11, hold fast, that no man take try *c.*
4:10, cast *c.* before throne.
19:12, on head were many *c.*
See Ex. 25:25; 29:6; Job 31:36.
CRUCIFY. Mt. 27:22, all said, let him be *c.*
Mk. 15:13; Lk. 23:21; Jn. 19:6, 15, *c.* him.
Acts 2:23, by wicked hands ye have *c.*
Rom. 6:6, old man is *c.* with him.
1Cor. 1:13, was Paul *c.* for you.
23, we preach Christ *c.*
2:2, save Jesus Christ and him *c.*
2Cor. 13:4, though he was *c.* through weakness.
Gal. 2:20, I am *c.* with Christ.
3:1, Christ set forth *c.*
5:24, have *c.* the flesh.
6:14, the world is *c.* unto me.
Heb. 6:6, *c.* to themselves afresh.
See Mt. 20:19; 23:34; 27:31; Mk. 15:20.
CRUEL. Ps. 25:19, with *c.* hatred.
27:12, breathe out *c.*
74:20, full of the habitations of *c.*
Prov. 5:9, give thy years to the *c.*
11:17, *c.* troubleth his own flesh.
12:10, tender mercies of the wicked are *c.*
27:4, wrath is *c.*
Song 8:6, jealousy is *c.*
Heb. 11:36, trials of *c.* mockings.
See Gen. 49:7; Ex. 6:9; Dt. 32:33.
CRUMBS. Mt. 15:27; Mk. 7:28; Lk. 16:21.
CRUSE. 1Sam. 26:11; 1Ki. 14:3; 17:12; 19:6.
CRUSH. Job 5:4, children are *c.* in the gate.
39:15, forgetteth that the foot may *c.* them.
See Lev. 22:24; Num. 22:25; Dt. 28:33.
CRY (*n.*). 1Sam. 5:12, *c.* of the city went up to heaven.
Job 34:28, he heareth the *c.* of the afflicted.

Ps. 9:12, forgetteth not *c.* of the humble.
34:15, ears are open to their *c.*
Prov. 21:13, stoppeth his ears at the *c.* of the poor.
Mt. 25:6, at midnight there was a *c.* made.
See Gen. 18:20; Ex. 2:23; Num. 16:34.
CRY (*v.*). Ex. 14:15, wherefore *c.* thou unto me?
Lev. 13:45, cover his lip, and *c.* unclean.
Job 29:12, I delivered poor that *c.*
Ps. 147:9, food to young ravens which *c.*
Prov. 8:1, doth not wisdom *c.*
Isa. 58:1, *c.* aloud, spare not.
Mt. 12:19, he shall not strive nor *c.*
20:31; Mk. 10:48; Lk. 18:39, they *c.* the more.
Lk. 18:7, elect who *c.* day and night.
Jn. 7:37, Jesus *c.*, if any man thirst.
Acts 19:32; 21:34, some *c.* one thing and some another.
See Ex. 5:8; 32:18; 2Ki. 8:3.
CRYING. Prov. 19:18; Isa. 65:19; Heb. 5:7; Rev. 21:4.
CRYSTAL. Job 28:17; Ezek. 1:22; Rev. 4:6; 21:11; 22:1.
CUBIT. Mt. 6:27; Lk. 12:25.
CUCUMBERS. Num. 11:5; Isa. 1:8.
CUMBER. Dt. 1:12; Lk. 10:40; 13:7.
CUNNING. Ps. 137:5, let my hand forget her *c.*
Jer. 9:17, send for *c.* women.
Eph. 4:14, carried about by *c.* craftiness.
2Pet. 1:16, not follow *c.* devised fables.
See Gen. 25:27; Ex. 38:23; 1Sam. 16:16; Dan. 1:4.
CUP. Ps. 116:13, take *c.* of salvation.
Mt. 10:42; Mk. 9:41, *c.* of cold water.
20:22; Mk. 10:39, drink of my *c.*
23:25, make clean outside of *c.*
26:27; Mk. 14:23; Lk. 22:17; 1Cor 11:25, took *c.*
39; Mk. 14:36; Lk. 22:42, let this *c.* pass.
Luke 22:20; 1Cor. 11:25 this *c.* is new testament.
Jn. 18:11, *c.* which my father hath given.
1Cor. 10:16, *c.* of blessing we bless.
11:26, as often as ye drink this *c.*
27, drink this *c.* unworthily.
See Gen. 40:11; 44:2; Prov. 23:31.
CURDLED. Job 10:10.
CURE. Lk. 7:21, in that hour he *c.* many.
9:1, power to *c.* diseases.
13:32, I do *c.* to-day.
See Jer. 33:6; 46:11; Hos. 5:13; Mt. 17:16.
CURIOUS. Ex. 28:8; Ps. 139:15; Acts 19:19.
CURRENT. Gen. 23:16.
CURSE (*n.*). Dt. 11:26, I set before you blessing and *c.*
23:5, turned *c.* into blessing.
Mal. 3:9, ye are cursed with a *c.*
Gal. 3:10, are under the *c.*
Rev. 22:3, no more *c.*
See Gen. 27:12; Num. 5:18.
CURSE (*v.*). Lev. 19:14, not *c.* the deaf.
Num. 23:8, how shall I *c.* whom God hath not.
Jud. 5:23, *c.* ye Meroz, *c.* ye bitterly.
Job 2:9, *c.* God, and die.
Ps. 62:4, they bless, but *c.* inwardly.
Mal. 2:2, I will *c.* your blessing.
Mt. 5:44; Lk. 6:28; Rom. 12:14, bless them that *c.* you.
26:74; Mk. 14:71, he began to *c.*
Mk. 11:21, fig tree thou *c.*
Jn. 7:49, knoweth not the law are *c.*
Gal. 3:10, *c.* is every one that continueth not.
Jas. 3:9, therewith *c.* we men.
See Gen. 8:21; 12:3; Num. 22:6.
CURTAIN. Ex. 26:36, the length of one *c.*
CUSTOM. Mt. 9:9; Mk. 2:14; Lk. 5:27, receipt of *c.*
Mt. 17:25, of whom do kings take *c.*
Lk. 4:16, as his *c.* was, went into synagogue.
Jn. 18:39, ye have a *c.*
Acts 16:21, teach *c.* which are not lawful.
Rom 13:7, *c.* to whom *c.*
1Cor. 11:16, we have no such *c.*
See Gen. 31:35; Jud. 11:39; Jer. 10:3.
CUTTING. Ex. 31:5; 35:33; Isa. 38:10; Mk. 5:5.
CYMBAL. 1Cor 13:1.
CYMBALS. 2Sam 6:5, on cornets and on *c.*
1Chr. 15:16, harps and *c.*
16:5, Asaph made a noise with *c.*
Ps. 150:5, praise him upon the loud *c.*
DAGGER. Jud. 3:16, 21:22.
DAILY. Ps. 13:2, sorrow in my heart *d.*
68:19, *d.* loadeth us.
Prov. 8:30, I was *d.* his delight.
Dan. 8:11; 11:31; 12:11, *d.* sacrifice taken away.
Mt. 6:11; Lk. 11:3, our *d.* bread.
Lk. 9:23, take up cross *d.*
Acts 2:47, added to church *d.*
6:1, the *d.* ministration.
16:5, churches increased *d.*
17:11, searched the scriptures *d.*
1Cor. 15:31, I die *d.*
Jas. 2:15, destitute of *d.* food.
See Num. 4:16; 28:24; Neh. 5:18; Dan. 1:5.
DAINTY. Ps. 141:4, let me not eat of their *d.*
Prov. 23:3, be not desirous of his *d.*
See Gen. 49:20; Job 33:20; Rev. 18:14.
DALE. Gen. 14:17; 2Sam. 18:18.
DAM. Ex. 22:30; Lev. 22:27; Dt. 22:6.
DAMAGE. Prov. 26:6, drinketh *d.*
Acts 27:10, voyage will be with much *d.*
2Cor. 7:9, receive *d.* by us in nothing.
See Ezra 4:22; Est. 7:4; Dan. 6:2.
DAMNABLE. 2 Pet. 2:1.
DAMNATION. Mt. 23:33, can ye escape the *d.* of hell.
Mk. 3:29, in danger of eternal *d.*
Jn. 5:29, the resurrection of *d.*
Rom. 13:2, receive to themselves *d.*
1Cor. 11:29, eateth and drinketh *d.*
2Pet. 2:3, their *d.* slumbereth not.
See Mt. 23:14; Mk. 12:40; Lk. 20:47; Rom. 3:8.
DAMNED. Mk. 16:16; Rom 14:23; 2Th. 2:12.
DAMSEL. Ps. 68:25, among them were the *d.* playing.
Mt. 14:11, Mk. 6:28, given to the *d.*
26:69; Jn. 18:17, *d.* came to Peter.
Mk. 5:39, the *d.* is not dead.

Acts 12:13, a *d.* came to hearken.
16:16, *d.* possessed with a spirit.
See Gen. 24:55; 34:3; Jud. 5:30; Ruth 2:5.
ANCE. Ex. 32:19, he saw the calf and *d.*
1Sam. 18:6, came out singing and *d.*
2Sam. 6:14, David *d.* before the Lord.
Job 21:11, their children *d.*
Ps. 30:11, turned my mourning into *d.*
149:3; 150:4, praise him in the *d.*
Eccl. 3:4, a time to *d.*
Mt. 11:17; Lk. 7:32, piped, and ye have not *d.*
14:6; Mk. 6:22, daughter of Herodias *d.*
See Jud. 21:23; Jer. 31:13; Lam 5:15.
ANDLED. Isa. 66:12.
ANGER. Mt. 3:21; Mk. 5:29; Acts 19:27; 27:9.
ARE. Rom 5:7, some would even *d.* to die.
See Job 41:10; Rom. 15:18; 1Cor. 6:1; 2Cor. 10:12.
ARK. Job 12:25, they grope in the *d.*
22:13, can he judge through *d.* cloud?
24:16, in the *d.* they dig.
38:2, that *d.* counsel by words.
Ps. 49:4; Prov. 1:6, *d.* sayings.
69:23; Rom. 11:10, let their eyes be *d.*
88:12, wonders be know in the *d.*
Eccl. 12:2, stars be not *d.*
3, look out of windows be *d.*
Zech. 14:6, shall not be clear nor *d.*
Mt. 24:29; Mk. 13:24, sun be *d.*
Lk. 23:45, sun *d.* and vail rent.
Jn. 20:1, early, when it was yet *d.*
Rom. 1:21, foolish heart was *d.*
Eph. 4:18, understanding *d.*
See Gen. 15:17; Ex. 10:15; Num. 12:8; Joel 2:10.
ARKNESS. Dt. 5:22, spake out of thick *d.*
28:29, grope as the blind in *d.*
1Sam. 2:9, wicked shall be silent in *d.*
2Sam. 22:10; Ps. 18:9, *d.* under his feet.
29; Ps. 18:28, Lord will enlighten my *d.*
1Ki. 8:12; 2Chr. 6:1, dwell in thick *d.*
Job 3:5; Ps. 10:10, *d.* and shadow of death.
10:22, land where the light is as *d.*
30:26, waited for light there came *d.*
Ps. 91:6, pestilence that walketh in *d.*
97:2, clouds and *d.* are round about him.
112:4, to upright ariseth light in *d.*
139:12, *d.* and light alike to thee.
Prov. 20:20, lamp be put out in *d.*
Eccl. 2:13, as far as light excelleth *d.*
14, fool walketh in *d.*
Isa. 58:10, thy *d.* as noon day.
60:2, *d.* cover the earth, gross *d.*
Joel 2:2, day of clouds and thick *d.*
Mt. 6:23; Lk. 11:34, body full of *d.*
8:12; 22:13; 25:30, outer *d.*
10:27; Lk. 12:3, what I tell in *d.* speak.
Lk. 1:79; Rom. 2:19, light to them that sit in *d.*
Lk. 22:53; Col. 1:13, the power of *d.*
23:44, *d.* over all the earth.
Jn. 1:5, *d.* comprehended it not.
3:19, loved *d.* rather than light.
12:35, walk while ye have light, lest *d.*
Acts 26:18, turn from *d.* to light.
Rom. 13:12; Eph. 5:11, works of *d.*
1Cor. 4:5, hidden things of *d.*
2Cor. 4:6, light to shine out of *d.*
6:14, what communion hath light with *d.*
Eph. 6:12, rulers of the *d.* of this world.
1Th. 5:5, not of the night nor of *d.*
Heb. 12:18, to blackness and *d.*
1Pet. 2:9, out of *d.* into marvellous light.
2Pet. 2:4, into chains of *d.*
1Jn. 1:5, in him is no *d.* at all.
6, and walk in *d.* we lie.
2:8, the *d.* is past.
9, hateth his brother, is in *d.*
11, *d.* hath blinded his eyes.
Rev. 16:10, kingdom full of *d.*
See Gen. 1:2; 15:12; Ex. 10:21; 20:21.
DARLING. Ps. 22:20; 35:17.
DART. Job 41:26; Prov. 7:23; Eph. 6:16.
DASH. Ps. 2:9; Isa. 13:16; Hos. 13:16, *d.* in pieces.
91:12; Mt. 4:6; Lk. 4:11, *d.* thy foot.
137:9, that *d.* thy little ones.
See Ex. 15:6; 2Ki. 8:12; Jer. 13:14.
DAUB. Ex. 2:3; Ezek. 13:10; 22:28.
DAUGHTER. Gen. 24:23, 47; Jud. 11:34, whose *d.* art thou?
27:46, weary of life because of *d.* of Heth.
Dt. 28:53, eat flesh of sons and *d.*
2Sam. 1:20, lest *d.* of Philistines rejoice.
12:3, lamb was unto him as a *d.*
Ps. 45:9, kings' *d.* among honourable women.
144:12, our *d.* as corner-stones.
Prov. 30:15, horseleech hath two *d.*
31:29, many *d.* have done virtuously.
Eccl. 12:4, the *d.* of music.
Isa. 22:4; Jer. 9:1, Lam. 2:11; 3:48, spoiling of the *d.*
Jer. 6:14, healed hurt of *d.* of my people.
8:21, for hurt of *d.* am I hurt
9:1, weep for slain of *d.* of my people.
Mic. 7:6; Mt. 10:35; Lk. 12:53, *d.* riseth against mother.
Mt. 15:28, her *d.* was made whole.
Lk. 8:42, one only *d.* about twelve years of age.
13:16, this woman *d.* of Abraham.
Heb. 11:24, refused to be son of Pharaoh's *d.*
See Gen. 6:1; Ex. 1:16; 21:7; Num. 27:8.
DAWN. Ps. 119:147, I prevented the *d.* of the morning.
2Pet. 1:19, till the day *d.*
See Josh. 6:15; Jud. 19:26; Job 3:9; 7:4.
DAY. Gen. 41:9, I do remember my faults this *d.*
Dt. 4:32, ask of the *d.* that are past.
1Sam. 25:8, come in a good *d.*
2Ki. 7:9, this *d.* is a *d.* of good tidings.
1Chr. 23:1, 28; 2Chr. 24:15, full of *d.*
29:15; Job 8:9, our *d.* as a shadow.
Neh. 4:2, will they make an end in a *d.*
Job 7:1, *d.* like the *d.* of an hireling.
14:6, till he accomplish his *d.*
19:25, stand at latter *d.* upon the earth.
21:30, reserved to *d.* of destruction.
32:7, I said *d.* should speak.
Ps. 2:7; Acts 13:33; Heb 1:5, this *d.* have I

begotten thee.
19:2, *d.* unto *d.* uttereth speech.
84:10, a *d.* in thy courts.
Prov. 3:2, 16, length of *d.*
4:18, more and more to perfect *d.*
27:1, what a *d.* may bring forth.
Eccl. 7:1, *d.* of death better than *d.* of birth.
12:1, while the evil *d.* come not.
Isa. 2:12; 13:6, 9; Joel 1:15; 2:1; Zeph. 1:7; Zech. 14:1, *d.* of the Lord.
10:3, in the *d.* of visitation.
27:3, the Lord will keep it night and *d.*
58:5, acceptable *d.* to the Lord.
Isa. 65:20, an infant of *d.*
Joel 2:11, 31; Zeph. 1:14; Mal. 4:5; Acts 2:20, great *d.* of the Lord.
Zech. 4:10, despised *d.* of small things.
Mal. 3:2, who may abide *d.* of his coming.
Mt. 7:22, many will say in that *d.*
24:36; Mk. 13:32, that *d.* knoweth no man.
50; Lk. 12:46, in a *d.* looked not for.
25:13, ye know not the *d.* nor the hour.
Lk. 21:34, that *d.* come unawares.
23:43, to-*d.* shalt thou be with me.
Jn. 6:39, raise it again at last *d.*
8:56, Abraham rejoiced to see my *d.*
9:4, I must work while it is *d.*
Acts 17:31, he hath appointed a *d.*
Rom. 2:5, wrath against *d.* of wrath.
14:5, esteemeth every *d.* alike.
2Cor. 6:2, the *d.* of salvation.
Phil. 1:6, perform it until *d.* of Christ.
1Th. 5:2; 2Pet. 3:10, *d.* cometh as a thief.
5, children of the *d.*
Heb. 13:8, Jesus Christ same to-*d.* and for ever.
2Pet. 3:8, one *d.* as a thousand years.
See Gen. 1:5, 27:2; Job 1:4; Ps. 77:5; 118:24; Jn. 11:24; 12:48; 1Cor. 3:13; Rev. 6:17; 16:14; 20:10.

DAYS (last). Isa. 2:2, it shall come to pass in the last *d.*
See Mic. 4:1; Acts 2:17; 2Tim. 3:1; Heb. 1:2; Jas. 5:3; 2Pet. 3:3.

DAYSMAN. Job 9:33.

DAYSPRING. Job 38:12, *d.* to know his place.
Lk. 1:78, *d.* from on high hath visited us.

DAYSTAR. 2Peter 1:19, *d.* arise in your hearts.

DEAD. Lev. 19:28, cuttings for the *d.*
Ruth 1:8, as ye have dealt with *d.*
1Sam. 24:14; 2Sam 9:8; 16:9, *d.* dog.
Ps. 31:12, forgotten as a *d.* man.
115:17, *d.* praise not the Lord.
Prov. 9:18, knoweth not that the *d.* are there.
Eccl. 4:2, the *d.* which are already *d.*
9:4, living dog better than *d.* lion.
5, *d.* know not any thing.
10:1, *d.* flies cause ointment.
Isa. 26:19, thy *d.* men shall live.
Jer. 22:10, weep not for the *d.*
Mt. 8:22, let the *d.* bury their *d.*
9:24, Mk. 5:39; Lk. 8:52, not *d.* but sleepeth.
11:5; Lk. 7:22, deaf hear *d.* raised.
22:32, not God of the *d.*
23:27, full of *d.* men's bones.
Mk. 9:10, rising from *d.* should mean.
Lk. 15:24, 32; Rev. 1:18, *d.* and is alive again.
16:31, though one rose from the *d.*
Jn. 5:25, *d.* shall hear.
6:49, did eat manna, and are *d.*
11:25, though *d.* yet shall he live.
44, he that was *d.* came forth.
Acts 10:42; 2Tim. 4:1, judge of quick and *d.*
26:23, first that should rise from *d.*
Rom. 6:2, 11; 1Pet. 2:24, *d.* to sin.
7:4; Gal. 2:19, *d.* to the law.
14:9, Lord both of *d.* and living.
1Cor. 15:15, if the *d.* rise not.
35, how are the *d.* raised.
2Cor. 1:9, trust in God who raiseth *d.*
5:14, then were all *d.*
Eph. 2:1; Col. 2:13, *d.* in trespasses and sins.
5:14, arise from the *d.*
Col. 1:18, firstborn from the *d.*
2:20; 2Tim. 2:11, *d.* with Christ.
1Th. 4:16, *d.* in Christ shall rise first.
1Tim. 5:6, *d.* while she liveth.
Heb. 6:1; 9:14, from *d.* works.
11:4, being *d.*, yet speaketh.
13:20, brought again from the *d.*
Jas. 2:17, 20, 26, faith *d.*
1Pet. 4:6, preached to them that are *d.*
Jude 12, twice *d.*
Rev. 1:5, first-begotten of the *d.*
Rev. 3:1, a name that thou livest, and art *d.*
14:13, blessed are the *d.*
20:5, rest of *d.* lived not again.
12, the *d.* small and great.
13, sea gave up *d.*
See Gen. 23:3; Ex. 12:30; Mk. 9:26; Rev 1:18.

DEADLY. Mk. 16:18, drink any *d.* thing.
Jas. 3:8, tongue full of *d.* poison.
See 1Sam. 5:11; Ps. 17:9 Ezek. 30:24.

DEAF. Ps. 58:4, like *d.* adder that stoppeth.
Isa. 29:18, shall the *d.* hear the words.
Mt. 11:5; Lk. 7:22, the *d.* hear.
Mk. 7:37, he maketh the *d.* to hear.
9:25, thou *d.* spirit, come out.
See Ex. 4:11; Lev. 19:14; Isa. 42:18; 43:8.

DEAL (a measure). Ex. 29:40, with the one lamb, a tenth *d.* of flour.
Lev. 14:10, three tenth *d.* of fine flour for a meat offering.

DEAL. Lev. 19:11, nor *d.* falsely.
Job 42:8, *d.* with you after folly.
Ps. 75:4, *d.* not foolishly.
Prov. 12:22, they that *d.* truly his delight.
Isa. 21:2; 24:16, treacherous dealer *d.* treacherously.
26:10, in land of uprightness *d.* unjustly.
Jer. 6:13; 8:10, every one *d.* falsely.
Hos. 5:7, have *d.* treacherously against the Lord
Zech. 1:6, as Lord thought, so hath he *d.*
Mk. 7:36; 10:48, the more a great *d.*
Lk. 2:48, why hast thou thus *d.* with us?
Rom. 12:3, according as God hath *d.*
See Gen. 32:9; Ex. 1:10; Dt. 7:5; 2Chr. 2:3.

EALING. 1Sam. 2:23; Ps. 7:16; Jn. 4:9.
EAR. Jer. 31:20, is Ephraim my *d.* son.
Acts 20:24, neither count I my life *d.*
Rom. 12:19; 1Cor 10:14; 2Cor. 7:1; 12:19; Phil. 4:1; 2Tim. 1:2; 1Pet. 2:11, *d.* beloved.
Eph. 5:1, followers of God as *d.* children.
Col. 1:13, into kingdom of his *d.* Son.
1Th. 2:8, because ye were *d.* unto us.
See Jer. 12:7; Lk. 7:2; Phile. 1.
EARTH. 2Chr. 6:28, if there be a *d.* in the land.
Neh. 5:3, buy corn because of *d.*
Acts 11:28, Agabus signified a great *d.*
See Gen. 41:54; 2Ki. 4:38; Jer. 14:1; Acts 7:11.
EATH. Num. 16:29, if these men die common *d.*
23:10, let me die *d.* of righteous.
Jud. 5:18, jeoparded lives to the *d.*
16:16, soul was vexed to *d.*
30, which he slew at his *d.* were more.
Ruth 1:17, if ought but *d.* part thee and me.
1Sam. 15:32, the bitterness of *d.* past.
20:3, but a step between me and *d.*
2Sam. 1:23, in *d.* not divided.
22:5; Ps. 18:4; 116:8, waves of *d.* compassed.
Job 3:21, long for *d.* but it cometh not.
7:15, my soul chooseth *d.*
30:23, thou wilt bring me to *d.*
Ps. 6:5, in *d.* no remembrance.
13:3, lest I sleep the sleep of *d.*
23:4, valley of shadow of *d.*
48:14, our guide even unto *d.*
68:20, the issues from *d.*
89:48, what man shall not see *d.*
102:20, loose those appointed to *d.*
107:10, in darkness and shadow of *d.*
116:15, precious is *d.* of his saints.
Prov. 7:27, to chambers of *d.*
8:36, that hate me love *d.*
14:32, righteous hath hope in his *d.*
24:11, deliver them drawn to *d.*
Song 8:6, love is strong as *d.*
Isa. 9:2; Jer. 2:6, land of the shadow of *d.*
25:8; 1Cor. 15:56, swallow up *d.* in victory.
38:18, for *d.* cannot celebrate thee.
Jer. 8:3, *d.* chosen rather than life.
9:21, *d.* come up to our windows.
Ezek. 18:32; 33:11, no pleasure in *d.*
Hos. 13:14, O *d.* I will be thy plagues.
Mt. 15:4; Mk. 7:10, let him die the *d.*
16:28; Mk. 9:1; Lk. 9:27, not taste of *d.*
26:38; Mk. 14:34, my soul is sorrowful to *d.*
Mk. 5:23; Jn. 4:47, lieth at point of *d.*
Lk. 2:26, should not see *d.* before.
22:33, will go to prison and *d.*
Jn. 5:24; 1 Jn. 3:14, passed from *d.* to life.
8:51, 52, keep my saying, shall never see *d.*
11:4, sickness not unto *d.*
12:33; 18:32; 21:19, signifying what *d.*
Acts 2:24, having loosed pains of *d.*
Rom. 1:32, such things are worthy of *d.*
5:10; Col. 1:22, reconciled by the *d.*
12, *d.* by sin and so *d.* passed on all.
14:17, *d.* reigned from Adam to Moses.
6:5, planted in likeness of his *d.*
21, end of those things is *d.*
23, wages of sin is *d.*
8:2, law of sin and *d.*
1Cor. 3:22, life or *d.* all are yours.
11:26, show the Lord's *d.* till he come.
15:21, by man came *d.*
55:56, O *d.* where is thy sting?
2Cor. 1:9, sentence of *d.* in ourselves.
2:16, savour of *d.* unto *d.*
4:12, *d.* worketh in us.
11:23, in *d.* oft.
Phil. 2:8, *d.*, even *d.* of the cross.
Heb. 2:9, taste *d.* for every man.
15, through fear of *d.* were.
Jas. 1:15, sin bringeth forth *d.*
1Jn. 5:16, a sin unto *d.*
Rev. 1:18, keys of hell and of *d.*
2:10, be faithful unto *d.*
11; 6:14, second *d.*
6:8, his name that sat on him was *d.*
9:6, seek *d.* and *d.* shall flee.
20:16, *d.* and hell delivered up.
21:4, no more *d.*
See Prov. 14:12; 16:25; Jn. 18:31; Jas. 5:20.
DEBASE. Isa. 57:9.
DEBATE. Prov. 25:9; Isa. 58:4; Rom. 1:29; 2Cor. 12:20.
DEBT. 2Ki. 4:7, go, pay thy *d.* and live.
Neh. 10:31, leave the exaction of every *d.*
Prov. 22:26, be not sureties for *d.*
Mt. 18:27, forgave him the *d.*
See 1Sam 22:2; Mt. 6:12; Rom. 4:4.
DEBTOR. Mt. 6:12, as we forgive our *d.*
Lk. 7:41, creditor which had two *d.*
Rom. 1:14, I am *d.* to the Greeks.
8:12, we are *d.*, not to the flesh.
15:27, their *d.* they are.
Gal. 5:3, *d.* to do the whole law.
See Ezek. 18:7; Mt. 18:21; 23:16; Lk. 16:5.
DECAY. Lev. 25:35; Neh. 4:10; Heb. 8:13.
DECEASE. Isa. 26:14; Mt. 22:25; Lk. 9:31; 2Pet. 1:15
DECEIT. Ps. 10:7, mouth full of *d.* and fraud.
36:3, words are iniquity and *d.*
55:23, *d.* men shall not live half their days.
Prov. 12:5, counsels of wicked are *d.*
20:17, bread of *d.* is sweet.
27:6, kisses of an enemy are *d.*
31:30, favour is *d.* and beauty vain.
Jer. 14:14; 23:26, prophesy the *d.* of their heart.
17:9, heart is *d.* above all things.
48:10, that doeth work of the Lord *d.*
Hos. 11:12, compasseth me with *d.*
Amos. 8:5, falsifying balances by *d.*
Zeph. 1:9, fill their masters' houses with *d.*
Mt. 13:22; Mk. 4:19, the *d.* of riches.
Mk. 7:22, out of heart proceed *d.*
Rom. 3:13, they have used *d.*
2Cor. 4:2, handling word of God *d.*
11:13, false apostles, *d.* workers.
Eph. 4:22, according to *d.* lusts.
Col. 2:8, vain *d.*, after tradition.
See Ps. 50:19; Prov. 12:20; Jer. 5:27; Mic. 6:11.

DECEIVE. Dt. 11:16, take heed that your heart be not *d.*
2Ki. 19:10; Isa. 37:10, let not thy God *d.* thee.
Job 12:16, the *d.* and the *d.* are his.
Jer. 20:7, thou hast *d.* me and I was *d.*
37:9, *d.* not yourselves.
Obad. 3, pride of heart hath *d.* thee.
Mt. 24:24, if possible *d.* the very elect.
27:63, remember that that *d.* said.
Jn. 7:12, nay, but he *d.* the people.
47, are ye also *d.*?
1Cor. 6:9; 15:33; Gal. 6:7, be not *d.*
2Cor. 6:8, as *d.*, and yet true.
Eph. 4:14, whereby they lie in wait to *d.*
5:6, 2Th. 2:3; 1Jn. 3:7, let no man *d.* you.
1Tim. 2:14, Adam was not *d.*
2Tim. 3:13, worse and worse, *d.* and being *d.*
1Jn. 1:8, no sin, we *d.* ourselves.
2Jn. 7, many *d.* entered into world.
See Gen. 31:7; Isa. 44:20; Ezek. 14:9; Rev. 12:9; 19:20.
DECENTLY. 1Cor. 14:40.
DECISION. Joel 3:14.
DECK. Job 40:10, *d.* thyself with majesty.
Isa. 61:10, as a bridegroom *d.* himself.
Jer. 4:30, though thou *d.* thee with ornaments.
10:4, they *d.* it with silver.
See Prov. 7:16; Ezek. 16:11; Rev. 17:4; 18:16.
DECLARATION. Est. 10:2; Job 13:17; Lk. 1:1; 2Cor. 8:19.
DECLARE. 1Chr. 16:24; Ps. 96:3, *d.* glory among heathen.
Job 21:31, who shall *d.* his way to his face.
31:37, I would *d.* number of my steps.
Ps. 2:7, I will *d.* decree.
9:11, *d.* among the people his doings.
19:1, heavens *d.* glory of God.
30:9, shall dust *d.* thy truth.
40:10, I have *d.* what he hath done.
66:16, I will *d.* for ever.
75:9, I will *d.* for ever.
118:17, live and *d.* the works of the Lord.
145:4, one generation shall *d.* thy mighty acts.
Isa. 3:9, they *d.* their sin as Sodom.
41:26; 45:21, who hath *d.* from beginning.
45:19, I *d.* things that are right.
46:10, *d.* end from the beginning.
53:8; Acts 8:33, who shall *d.* his generation.
66:19, *d.* my glory among Gentiles.
Jn. 17:26 have *d.* thy name and will *d.* it.
Acts 13:32, we *d.* to you glad tidings.
17:23, him *d.* I unto you.
20:27, *d.* the counsel of God.
Rom. 1:4, *d.* to be Son of God with power.
1Cor. 3:13, day shall *d.* it.
See Josh. 20:4; Jn. 1:18; Heb. 11:14; 1Jn. 1:3.
DECLINE. Dt. 17:11, thou shalt not *d.* from sentence.
2Chr. 34:2, *d.* neither to right nor left.
Ps. 102:11; 109:23, days like a shadow that *d.*
119:51, 157, not *d.* from thy law.
See Ex. 23:2; Job 23:11; Prov. 4:5; 7:25.
DECREASE. Gen. 8:5, Ps. 107:38; Jn. 3:30.
DECREE. Job 22:28, thou shalt *d.* a thing and it shall be.
28:26, made a *d.* for the rain.
Ps. 148:6, a *d.* which shall not pass.
Prov. 8:15, by me princes *d.* justice.
29, he gave to the sea his *d.*
Isa. 10:1, that *d.* unrighteous *d.*
Acts 16:4, delivered the *d.* to keep.
See Dan. 2:9; 6:8; Acts 17:7; 1Cor 7:37.
DEDICATE. Dt. 20:5, lest he die and another *d.* it.
Jud. 17:3, wholly *d.* silver to the Lord.
1Chr. 26:27, of spoil they did *d.*
Ezek. 44:29, every *d.* thing shall be theirs.
See 1Ki. 7:51, 8:63; 15:15; 1Chr. 18:11; Heb 9:18
DEED. Ex. 9:16; 1Sam 25:34; 26:4, in very *d.*
2Sam 12:14, by this *d.* hast given occasion.
Ezra 9:13, come upon us for our evil *d.*
Neh. 13:14, wipe not out my good *d.*
Ps. 28:4; Isa. 59:18; Jer. 25:14; Rom. 2:6, according to their *d.*
Lk. 11:48, ye allow the *d.* of your fathers.
23:41, due reward of our *d.*
24:19, a prophet might in *d.*
Jn. 3:19, because their *d.* were evil.
8:41, ye do the *d.* of your father.
Acts 7:22, Moses, mighty in word and *d.*
Rom. 3:20, by *d.* of law, no flesh justified.
28, justified without *d.* of the law.
Col. 3:9, put off old man with his *d.*
17, whatsoever ye do in word or *d.*
Jas. 1:25, shall be blessed in his *d.*
1Jn. 3:18, not love in word, but in *d.*
See Gen. 44:15; Lk. 23:51; Acts 19:18.
DEEMED. Acts 27:27.
DEEP. Gen. 7:11; 8:2, fountains of *d.*
Dt. 33:13, the *d.* that coucheth beneath.
Job 38:30, face of *d.* is frozen.
41:31, maketh the *d.* boil like a pot.
Ps. 36:6, thy judgments are a great *d.*
42:7, *d.* calleth to *d.*
Ps. 95:4, in his hand are the *d.* places.
107:24, see his wonders in the *d.*
Prov. 22:14; 23:27, strange women *d.* pit.
Isa. 63:13, led them through *d.*
Mt. 13:5, no *d.* of earth.
Lk. 5:4, launch into *d.*
6:48, digged *d.* and laid foundations.
8:31, command to go into the *d.*
Jn. 4:11, the well is *d.*
1Cor. 2:10, searcheth *d.* things of God.
See Job 4:13; 33:15; Prov. 19:15; Rom. 10:7.
DEER. Dt. 14:5; 1Ki. 4:23.
DEFAME. Jer. 20:10; 1Cor. 4:13.
DEFEAT. 2Sam. 15:34; 17:14.
DEFENCE. Job 22:25, the Almighty shall be thy *d.*
Ps. 7:10, my *d.* is of God
59:9, 17; 62:2, for God is my *d.*
89:18; 94:22, Lord is *d.*
Eccl. 7:12, wisdom a *d.* money a *d.*
Isa. 33:16, place of *d.* munitions of rocks.
Phil. 1:7, 17, in *d.* of the Gospel.
See Num. 14:9; Acts 19:33; 22:1.

EFEND. Ps. 5:11, shout for joy, because thou *d.* them.
82:3, *d.* the poor and fatherless.
Zech. 9:15, Lord of hosts shall *d.* them.
Acts 7:24, *d.* him and avenged the oppressed.
See Ps. 20:1; 59:1; Is. 31:5.
EFILE. Ex. 31:14, that *d.* sabbath be put to death.
Num. 35:33, blood *d.* the land.
2Ki. 23:13, high places did king *d.*
Neh. 13:29, they have *d.* the priesthood.
Ps. 74:7; 79:1, *d.* dwelling-place of thy name.
106:39, *d.* with their won works.
Isa. 59:3, your hands are *d.* with blood.
Jer. 2:7; 16:18, ye *d.* my land.
Ezek. 4:13, eat their *d.* bread.
23:38, they have *d.* my sanctuary.
36:17, they *d.* it by their own ways.
Dan. 1:8, would not *d.* himself with meat.
Mt. 15:11, 18:20; Mk. 7:15, 20, 23, *d.* a man.
Jn. 18:28, lest they should be *d.*
1Cor. 3:17, if any man *d.* temple of God.
8:7, conscience being weak is *d.*
1Tim. 1:10, law for them that *d.* themselves.
Ti. 1:15, to *d.* nothing pure, even conscience *d.*
Heb. 12:15, thereby many be *d.*
Jude 8, filthy dreamers *d.* flesh.
Rev. 3:4, few not *d.* their garments.
See Ex. 31:41; Lev. 21:4; Jas. 3:6; Rev. 21:27.
EFRAUD. 1Sam. 12:3,4, whom have I *d.*?
Mk. 10:19; 1Cor. 7:5, *d.* not.
1Cor. 6:7, rather suffer to be *d.*
8, do wrong and *d.* your brethren.
2Cor. 7:2, we have *d.* no man.
See Lev. 19:13; 1Th. 4:6.
EGENERATE. Jer. 2:21.
EGREE. Ps. 62:9, men of low *d.*, high *d.*
1Tim. 3:13, purchase to themselves good *d.*
Jas. 1:9, brother of low *d.* rejoice.
See 2Ki. 20:9; 1Chr. 17:17; Isa. 38:8; Lk. 1:52.
ELAY. Mt. 24:48; Lk. 12:45, my lord *d.* his coming.
Acts 9:38, that he would not *d.* to come.
See Ex. 22:29; 32:1; Acts 25:17.
ELECTABLE. Isa. 44:9.
ELICACY. Rev. 18:3.
ELICATE. 1Sam 15:32, Agag came to him *d.*
Prov. 29:21, he that *d.* bringeth up servant.
Isa. 47:1, no more called tender and *d.*
Lam. 4:5, that did feed *d.* are desolate.
Lk. 7:25, that live *d.* are kings' courts.
See Dt. 28:54, 56; Jer. 6:2; Mic. 1:16.
ELICIOUSLY. Rev. 18:7.
ELIGHT (*n.*). Dt. 10:15, Lord had a *d.* in thy fathers.
1Sam. 15:22, hath Lord as great *d.* in offerings.
2Sam 15:26, I have no *d.* in thee.
Job 22:26, shalt thou have *d.* in the Almighty.
Ps. 1:2, his *d.* is in law of Lord.
16:3, to excellent in whom is my *d.*
119:24, testimonies my *d.* and counsel.
77, 92, 174, thy law is my *d.*
143, thy commandments are my *d.*
Prov. 8:30, I was daily his *d.*
31, my *d.* were with sons of men.
Prov. 18:2, fool hath no *d.* in understanding.
19:10, *d.* not seemly for a fool.
Song 2:3, under his shadow with great *d.*
Isa. 58:13, call sabbath a *d.*
See Prov. 11:1; 12:22; 15:8; 16:13.
DELIGHT (*v.*). Job 27:10, will he *d.* himself in the Almighty?
Ps. 37:4, *d.* also in the Lord.
11, meek shall *d.* in abundance of peace.
51:16, thou *d.* not in burnt offering.
94:19, thy comforts *d.* my soul.
Isa. 42:1, elect in whom my soul *d.*
55:2, soul *d.* itself in fatness.
62:4, the Lord *d.* in thee.
Mic. 7:18, he *d.* in mercy.
Rom. 7:22, I *d.* after the inward man.
See Num. 14:8; Prov. 1:22; 2:14; Mal. 3:1
DELIGHTSOME. Mal. 3:12.
DELIVER. Ex. 3:8; Acts 7:34, I am come down to *d.* them.
Num. 35:25, congregation shall *d.* slayer.
Dt. 32:39; Isa. 43:13, any *d.* out of my hand.
2Chr. 32:13, were gods able to *d.* their lands.
Job 5:19, shall *d.* thee in six troubles.
36:18, great ransom cannot *d.*
Ps. 33:17, nor *d.* any by great strength.
56:13, *d.* my feet from falling.
144:10, *d.* David from hurtful sword.
Prov. 24:11, forbear to *d.* them.
Eccl. 9:15, by wisdom *d.* city.
Isa. 50:2, have I no power to *d.*?
Jer. 1:8, I am with thee to *d.* thee.
39:17, I will *d.* in that day.
Dan. 3:17, for God is able to *d.* and will *d.*
6:14, king set heart on Daniel to *d.*
Amos. 2:14, neither shall mighty *d.*
9:1, he that escapeth shall not be *d.*
Mal. 3:15, they that tempt God are *d.*
Mt. 6:13; Lk. 11:4, *d.* us from evil.
11:27; Lk. 10:22, all things *d.* to me of my Father.
26:15, I will *d.* him to you.
Acts 2:23, being *d.* by the counsel of God.
Rom. 4:25, was *d.* for our offences.
7:6, we are *d.* from the law.
8:21, creature shall be *d.*
2Cor. 4:11, *d.* to death for Jesus' sake.
2Tim. 4:18, *d.* me from every evil work.
Jude 3, faith once *d.* to saints.
See Rom. 8:32; 2Cor. 1:10; Gal. 1:4; 2Pet. 2:7.
DELIVERANCE. 2Ki. 5:1, by him had given *d.* to Syria.
1Chr. 11:14, saved by great *d.*
Ps. 32:7, compass me with songs of *d.*
Lk. 4:18, preach *d.* to the captives.
Heb. 11:35, not accepting *d.*
See Gen. 45:7; Joel 2:32; Obad. 17.
DELUSION. Isa. 66:4; 2Th. 2:11.
DEMAND. Dan. 4:17; Mt. 2:4; Lk. 3:14.
DEMONSTRATION. 1Cor. 2:4.
DEN. Job 37:8, then the beasts go into *d.*
Isa. 11:8, put hand on cocatrice *d.*
Jer. 7:11, is this house a *d.* of robbers.

Mt. 21:13; Mk. 11:17, a *d.* of thieves.
Heb. 11:38, in deserts and in *d.*
See Jud. 6:2; Dan. 6:7; Amos 3:4.
DENOUNCE. Dt. 30:18.
DENY. Josh. 24:27, lest ye *d.* your God.
Prov. 30:9, lest I be full and *d.* thee.
Lk. 20:27, which *d.* resurrection.
2Tim 2:13, he cannot *d.* himself.
Ti. 1:16, in works they *d.* him.
See 1Tim 5:8; 2Tim. 3:5; Ti. 2:12.
DEPART. Gen. 49:10, sceptre shall not *d.* from Judah.
2Sam 22:22; Ps. 18:21, have not *d.* from my God.
Job 21:14; 22:17, they say to God, *d.*
28:28, to *d.* from evil is understanding.
Ps. 6:8; Mt. 7:23; Lk. 13:27, *d.* ye workers of iniquity.
34:14; 37:27, *d.* from evil, and do good.
105:38, Egypt was glad when they *d.*
Prov. 15:24, he may *d.* from hell beneath.
22:6, when old he will not *d.* from it.
27:22, yet will not foolishness *d.*
Mt. 14:16, they need not *d.*
25:41, *d.* from me, ye cursed.
Lk. 2:29, lettest thou thy servant *d.* in peace.
Lk. 4:13, devil *d.* for a season.
21:21, let them in midst *d.*
Jn. 13:1, when Jesus knew he should *d.*
2Cor. 12:8, besought that it might *d.* from me.
Phil. 1:23, desire to *d.*
1Tim. 4:1, some shall *d.* from the faith.
2Tim. 2:19, nameth Christ *d.* from iniquity.
See Isa. 54:10; Mic. 2:10; 2Tim. 4:6; Heb. 3:12.
DEPOSED. Dan. 5:20.
DEPRIVED. Gen. 27:45; Job 39:17; Isa. 38:10.
DEPTH. Job 28:14, *d.* saith, it is not in me.
Ps. 33:7, he layeth up *d.* in storehouses.
77:16, waters afraid *d.* troubled.
106:9, led through *d.* as through wilderness.
107:26, they go down again to *d.*
Prov. 8:24, when no *d.* I was brought forth.
25:3, heaven for height, earth for *d.*
Mt. 18:6, better drowned in *d.* of sea.
Mk. 4:5, no *d.* of earth.
Rom. 11:33, the *d.* of the riches.
See Isa. 7:11; Mic. 7:19; Rom. 8:39.
DEPUTED. 2Sam. 15:3.
DEPUTY. 1Ki. 22:47; Acts 13:7; 18:12; 19:38.
DERIDE. Hab. 1:10; Lk. 16:14; 23:35.
DERISION. Job 30:1, younger than I have me in *d.*
Ps. 2:4, the Lord shall have them in *d.*
44:13; 79:4, a *d.* to them round us.
Jer. 20:7, 8, in *d.* daily.
Lam. 3:14, I was a *d.* to my people.
See Ps. 119:51; Ezek. 23:32; 36:4; Hos. 7:16.
DESCEND. Ezek. 26:20; 31:16, with them that *d.* into pit.
Mt. 7:25, 27, rain *d.* and floods came.
Mk. 1:10; Jn. 1:32, 33, Spirit *d.*
15:32, let Christ now *d.* from cross.
Rom. 10:7, who shall *d.* into the deep?
Eph. 4:10, he that *d.* is same that ascended.
Jas. 3:15, this wisdom *d.* not.
Rev. 21:10, great city *d.* out of heaven.
See Gen. 28:12; Ps. 49:17; 133:3; Prov. 30:4.
DESCENT. Lk. 19:37; Heb. 7:3, 6.
DESCRIBE. Josh. 18:4; Jud. 8:14; Rom. 4:6; 10:5.
DESCRY. Jud. 1:23.
DESERT. Ps. 78:40, oft did they grieve him in *d.*
102:6, like an owl of the *d.*
Isa. 35:1, the *d.* shall rejoice.
6; 43:19, streams in the *d.*
Isa. 40:3, in *d.* a highway for our God.
Jer. 2:6, led us through land of *d.*
17:6, like the heath in the *d.*
25:24, people that dwell in *d.* shall drink.
Mt. 24:26, say, behold, he is in the *d.*
Lk. 1:80, John in *d.* till his showing.
9:10, aside privately into *d.* place.
Jn. 6:31, did eat manna in *d.*
See Ex. 5:3; 19:2; Isa. 51:3; Mk. 6:31.
DESERTS. Ps. 28:4; Ezek. 7:27.
DESERVE. Jud. 9:16; Ezra 9:13; Job 11:6.
DESIRABLE. Ezek. 23:6, 12, 23.
DESIRE (*n.*). 2Chr. 15:15, sought him with their whole *d.*
Job 34:36, my *d.* is that Job may be tried.
Ps. 10:3; 21:2; Rom. 10:1, heart's *d.*
37:4, he shall give thee the *d.* of thine heart.
54:7; 59:10; 92:11; 112:8, *d.* on enemies.
92:11; 112:10; 140:8, *d.* of the wicked.
145:16, the *d.* of every living things.
Prov. 10:24; 11:23, the *d.* of righteous.
13:12, when *d.* cometh, it is a tree of life.
19:22, the *d.* of a man is his kindness.
21:25, the *d.* of slothful killeth him.
Eccl. 12:5, *d.* shall fail.
Ezek. 24:16, 21, 25, the *d.* of thine eyes.
Mic. 7:3, great man uttereth mischievous *d.*
Hab. 2:5, enlargeth *d.* as hell.
Hag. 2:7, the *d.* of all nations.
Lk. 22:15, with *d.* I have *d.* to eat.
Eph. 2:3, fulfilling *d.* of flesh and mind.
Phil. 1:23, having a *d.* to depart.
See Gen. 3:16; Job 14:15; 31:16.
DESIRE (*v.*). Dt. 14:26, bestow for whatsoever thy soul *d.*
1Sam. 2:16, take as much as thy soul *d.*
12:13, behold the king whom ye *d.*
Neh. 1:11, servants who *d.* to fear thy name.
Job 13:3, I *d.* to reason with God.
Ps. 19:10, more to be *d.* than gold.
27:4, one thing I *d.* of the Lord.
34:12, that *d.* life and loveth many days.
40:6, sacrifice and offering thou didst not *d.*
45:11, king greatly *d.* thy beauty.
73:25, none on earth I *d.* beside thee.
107:30, to their *d.* haven.
Prov. 3:15, 8:11, all thou canst *d.* not to be compared.
13:4, soul of sluggard *d.*, and hath not.
Eccl. 2:10, what my eyes *d.* I kept not.
Isa. 53:2, no beauty that we should *d.*
Hos. 6:6, I *d.* mercy and not sacrifice.
Mic. 7:1, soul *d.* first-ripe fruit.
Zeph. 2:1, gather together, O nation not *d.*

Mt. 12:46; Lk. 8:20, his brethren *d.*
13:17, have *d.* to see those things.
20:20, *d.* a certain thing of him.
Mk. 9:35, if any *d.* to be first.
10:35, do for us whatsoever we *d.*
11:24, what things ye *d.* when ye pray.
15:6; Lk. 23:25, prisoner whom they *d.*
Lk. 9:9, who is this, and he *d.* to see him.
10:24, kings have *d.* to see.
16:21, *d.* to be fed with crumbs.
20:46, scribes *d.* to walk in long robes.
22:15, have *d.* to eat this passover.
31, Satan hath *d.* to have you.
Acts 3:14, *d.* a murderer to be granted.
1Cor. 14:1, and *d.* spiritual gifts.
2Cor. 5:2, *d.* to be clothed upon.
Gal. 4:9, ye *d.* again to be in bondage.
21, ye that *d.* to be under the law.
6:12, many *d.* to make show in the flesh.
Eph. 3:13, I *d.* that ye faint not.
Phil. 4:17, not because I *d.* a gift; I *d.* fruit.
1Tim. 3:1, he *d.* a good work.
Heb. 11:16, they *d.* a better country.
Jas. 4:2, ye *d.* to have, and cannot obtain.
1Pet. 1:12, the angels *d.* to look into.
2:2, as babes *d.* sincere milk of word.
1Jn. 5:15, we have petitions we *d.*
See Gen. 3:6; Job 7:2; Ps. 51:6; Lk. 5:39.
ESIROUS. Prov. 23:3; Lk. 23:8; Jn. 16:19; Gal. 5:26.
ESOLATE. Ps. 25:16, have mercy, for I am *d.*
40:15, let them be *d.* for reward.
143:4, my heart within me is *d.*
Isa. 54:1; Gal. 4:27, more are children of *d.*
62:4, nor shall thy land any more be termed *d.*
Jer. 2:12, be ye very *d.*, saith the Lord.
32:43; 33:12, *d.* without man or beast.
Ezek. 6:6, your altars may be made *d.*
Dan. 11:31; 12:11, abomination that maketh *d.*
Mal. 1:4, return and build the *d.* places.
Mt. 23:38; Lk. 13:35, house left to you *d.*
Acts 1:20, let his habitation be *d.*
1Tim. 5:5, widow indeed, and *d.*
Rev. 18:19, in one hour is she made *d.*
See Ps. 34:22; Jer. 12:10; Joel 2:3; Zech. 7:14.
ESOLATION. 2Ki. 22:19, they should become a *d.* and a curse.
Ps. 46:8, what *d.* he hath made in the earth.
74:3; Jer. 25:9; Ezek. 35:9, perpetual *d.*
Prov. 1:27, when your fear cometh as *d.*
3:25, the *d.* of the wicked.
Isa. 61:4, raise up former *d.*, the *d.* of many generations.
Dan. 9:26, to end of war *d.* are determined.
Zeph 1:15, a day of wrath, wasting, and *d.*
Mt. 12:25; Lk. 11:17, house divided brought to *d.*
Lk. 21:20, then know *d.* is nigh.
See Lev. 26:31; Josh. 8:28; Job 30:14.
ESPAIR. 1Sam. 27:1; Eccl. 2:20; 2Cor. 4:8.
ESPERATE. Job 6:26; Isa. 17:11; Jer. 17:9.
ESPISE. Num. 11:20, ye have *d.* the Lord.
15:31; Prov. 13:13; Isa. 5:24; 30:12, *d.* the word.
1Sam. 2:30, that *d.* me shall be lightly esteemed.
Neh. 4:4, hear, O God, for we are *d.*
Est. 1:17, so that they *d.* their husbands.
Job 5:17; Prov. 3:11; Heb. 12:5, *d.* not chastening.
19:18, young children *d.* me.
36:5, God is mighty and *d.* not any.
Ps. 51:17, contrite heart thou wilt not *d.*
53:5, put to shame, because God *d.* them.
73:20, thou shalt *d.* their image.
102:17, he will not *d.* their prayer.
Prov. 1:7, fools *d.* wisdom.
30:5, 12, *d.* reproof.
6:30, men do not *d.* a thief.
15:5, fool *d.* father's instruction.
20, foolish man *d.* his mother.
32, refuseth instruction *d.* own soul.
19:16, he that *d.* his ways shall die.
30:17, *d.* to obey his mother, ravens shall.
Eccl. 9:16, poor man's wisdom is *d.*
Isa. 33:15, he that *d.* gain of oppressions.
49:7, saith Lord to him whom man *d.*
Jer. 49:15, I will make thee small and *d.*
Ezek. 20:13, 16, they *d.* my judgments.
22:8, thou hast *d.* holy things.
Amos 2:4, they *d.* they law of the Lord.
Zech. 4:10, who hath *d.* day of small things.
Mal. 1:6, wherein have we *d.* thy name?
Mt. 6:24, Lk. 16:13, hold to one, *d.* the other.
18:10, *d.* not one of these little ones.
Lk. 10:16, *d.* you, *d.* me; *d.* him that sent me.
18:9, righteous, and *d.* others.
Rom. 2:4, *d.* thou the riches of his goodness.
1Cor. 1:28, things *d.* God hath chosen.
4:10, ye are honourable, but we are *d.*
11:22, *d.* ye the church of God.
16:11, let no man therefore *d.* him.
1Th. 4:8, *d.* not man, but God.
5:20, *d.* not prophesyings.
1Tim. 4:12, let no man *d.* thy youth.
6:2, not *d.* because brethren.
Ti. 2:15, let no man *d.* thee.
Heb. 12:2, endured cross, *d.* the shame.
Jas. 2:6, ye have *d.* the poor.
See Gen. 16:4; 25:34; 2Sam. 6:16; Rom. 14:3.
DESPISERS. Acts 13:41; 2Tim. 3:3.
DESPITE. Ezek. 25:6, 15; 36:5; Rom. 1:30; Heb. 10:29.
DESPITEFULLY. Mt. 5:44; Lk. 6:28; Acts 14:5.
DESTITUTE. Ps. 102:17, will regard prayer of *d.*
Prov. 15:21, folly is joy to him that is *d.* of wisdom.
1Tim. 6:5, *d.* of the truth.
Heb. 11:37, being *d.*, afflicted, tormented.
See Gen. 24:27; Ezek. 32:15; Jas. 2:15.
DESTROY. Gen. 18:23, *d.* righteous with the wicked.
Ex. 22:20, he shall be utterly *d.*
Dt. 9:14, let me alone that I may *d.* them.
1Sam. 15:6, depart, lest I *d.* you with them.
2Sam. 1:14, *d.* Lord's anointed.
Job 2:3, movedst me to *d.* without cause.
10:8, made me, yet thou dost *d.* me.

19:10, he hath *d.* me on every side.
26, though worms *d.* his body.
Ps. 40:14; 63:9, seek my soul to *d.* it.
145:20, all the wicked will be *d.*
Prov. 1:32, prosperity of fools shall *d.* them.
13:23, is *d.* for want of judgment.
31:3, that which *d.* kings.
Eccl. 9:18, one sinner *d.* much good.
Isa. 10:7, it is in his heart to *d.*
11:9; 65:25, *d.* in holy mountain.
19:3, I will *d.* the counsel thereof.
28:2, as a *d.* storm.
Jer. 13:14, I will not spare but *d.* them.
17:18, *d.* them with double destruction.
23:1, woe to pastors that *d.* the sheep.
Ezek. 9:1, with *d.* weapon in his hand.
22:27, *d.* souls to get dishonest gain.
Dan. 8:24, he shall *d.* wonderfully.
Hos. 13:9, thou hast *d.* thyself.
Mt. 5:17, not to *d.* but to fulfil.
10:28, fear him that is able to *d.*
12:14; Mk. 3:6; 11:18, they might *d.* him.
21:41, he will miserably *d.* those.
22:7, and *d.* those murderers.
27:20, ask Barabbas and *d.* Jesus.
Mk. 1:24; Lk. 4:34, art thou come to *d.*
12:9, Lk. 20:16, *d.* the husbandmen.
14:58, say, I will *d.* this temple.
15:29, thou that *d.* the temple.
Lk. 6:9, is it lawful to save life or *d.*
9:56, is not come to *d.* men's lives.
17:27, flood came and *d.* them all.
Jn. 2:19, Jesus said, *d.* this temple.
Rom. 14:15, *d.* not him with thy meat.
1Cor. 6:13, God shall *d.* both it and them.
Gal. 1:23, preacheth the faith he once *d.*
2:18, if I build the things which I *d.*
2Th. 2:8, *d.* with brightness of his coming.
Heb. 2:14, *d.* him that had the power.
Jas. 4:12, able to save and to *d.*
1pJn. 3:8, *d.* the works of the devil.
See Gen. 6:17; Isa. 65:8; Rom. 6:6; 2Pet. 2:12; Jude 5.
DESTROYER. Ex. 12:23, not suffer *d.* to some.
Jud. 16:24, delivered the *d.* of our country.
Job 15:21, in prosperity the *d.* shall come.
Ps. 17:4, kept from paths of the *d.*
Prov. 28:24, the companion of a *d.*
See Job 33:22; Isa. 49:17; Jer. 22:7; 50:11.
DESTRUCTION. 2Chr. 22:4, his counsellors to his *d.*
26:16, heart lifted up to *d.*
Est. 8:6, endure to see *d.* of my kindred.
Job 5:21, neither be afraid of *d.*
21:17, how oft cometh *d.*
26:6, *d.* hath no covering.
31:3, is not *d.* to the wicked.
Ps. 9:6, *d.* are come to a perpetual end.
35:8, into that very *d.* let him fall.
73:18, thou castedst them down to *d.*
90:3, turnest man to *d.*
91:6, the *d.* that wasteth at noon day.
103:4, redeemeth thy life from *d.*
Prov. 1:27, your *d.* cometh as a whirlwind.
10:14, mouth of foolish near *d.*
15, *d.* of poor is their poverty.
14:28, want of people *d.* of the prince.
16:18, pride goeth before *d.*
17:19, exalteth gate seeketh *d.*
18:7, fool's mouth is his *d.*
27:20, hell and *d.* never full.
31:8, such as are appointed to *d.*
Isa. 14:23, the besom of *d.*
19:18, the city of *d.*
59:7, wasting and *d.* in their paths.
60:18, *d.* be no more heard.
Jer. 17:18, destroy with double *d.*
46:20, *d.* cometh out of north.
50:22, sound of great *d.* in the land.
Lam. 2:11; 3:48; 4:10, *d.* of the daughter of my people.
Hos. 13:14, O grave, I will be thy *d.*
Mt. 7:13, broad way leadeth to *d.*
Rom. 3:16, *d.* and misery in their ways.
9:22, vessels fitted to *d.*
Phil. 3:18, 19, many walk whose end is *d.*
1Th. 5:3, then sudden *d.* cometh.
2Th. 1:9, punished with everlasting *d.*
1Tim. 6:9, lusts drown men in *d.*
2Pet. 2:1, bring on themselves swift *d.*
3:16, wrest to their own *d.*
See Job 21:20; 31:23; Prov. 10:29; 21:15.
DETAIN. Jud. 13:15, 16; 1Sam 21:7.
DETERMINATE. Acts. 2:23.
DETERMINATION. Zeph. 3:8.
DETERMINE. Ex. 21:22, pay as the judges *d.*
1Sam. 20:7, be sure evil is *d.* by him.
Job 14:5, seeing his days are *d.*
Dan. 11:36, that that is *d.* shall be done.
Lk. 22:22, Son of man goeth as it was *d.*
Acts 3:13, Pilate was *d.* to let him go.
17:26, hath *d.* the times appointed.
1Cor. 2:2, I *d.* not to know anything.
See 2Chr. 2:1; 25:16; Isa. 19:17; Dan. 9:24.
DETEST. Dt. 7:26.
DETESTABLE. Jer. 16:18; Ezek. 5:11; 7:20; 11:18; 37:23.
DEVICE. Est. 9:25, *d.* return on his own head.
Ps. 10:2, let them be taken in the *d.*
33:10, maketh *d.* of the people of none effect
37:7, bringeth wicked *d.* to pass.
Prov. 1:31, be filled with their own *d.*
12:2, man of wicked *d.* will he condemn.
19:21, many *d.* in a man's heart.
Eccl. 9:10, no work nor *d.* in grave.
Jer. 18:12, will walk after our own *d.*
Dan. 11:24, 25, he shall forecast *d.*
Acts 17:29, like stone graven by man's *d.*
2Cor. 2:11, not ignorant of his *d.*
See 2Chr. 2:14; Est. 8:3; Job 5:12.
DEVILISH. Jas. 3:15.
DEVILS (Sacrifices offered to). Lev. 17:7, offer thei[r] sacrifices unto *d.*
See Dt. 32:17; 2Chr. 11:15; Ps. 106:37; 1Cor. 10:20; Rev. 9:20.
DEVILS (confess Jesus to be Christ). Mt. 8:29; Mk

1:24; 3:11; 5:7; Lk. 4:34, 41; Acts 19:15.
Jas. 2:19, the *d.* also believe and tremble.
EVISE. Ex. 31:4; 35:32, 35, *d.* works in gold.
Ps. 35:4, to confusion that *d.* my hurt.
36:4, he *d.* mischief on his bed.
41:7, against me do they *d.* my hurt.
Prov. 3:29, *d.* not evil against thy neighbour.
6:14, he *d.* mischief continually.
18, a heart that *d.* wicked imaginations.
14:22, err that *d.* evil, *d.* good.
16:9, man's heart *d.* his way.
Isa. 32:7, *d.* wicked devices to destroy poor.
8, the liberal *d.* liberal things.
2Pet. 1:16, cunningly *d.* fables.
See 2Sam. 14:14; Jer. 51:12; Lam. 2:17; Mic. 2:1.
EVOTE. Lev. 27:21, 28; Num. 18:14; Ps. 119:38.
EVOTIONS. Acts 17:23.
EVOUR. Gen. 37:20, some evil beast hath *d.* him.
41:7, 24, seven thin *d.* the seven rank.
Ex. 24:17; Isa. 29:6; 30:27, 30; 33:14, *d.* fire.
Lev. 10:2, fire from Lord *d.* them.
Dt. 32:24, *d.* with burning heat.
2Sam. 11:25, sword *d.* one as well as another.
18:8, wood *d.* more than sword *d.*
22:9; Ps. 18:8, fire out of his mouth *d.*
Job 18:13, death shall *d.* his strength.
Ps. 80:13, beasts of field *d.* it.
Prov. 20:25, man who *d.* that which is holy.
30:14, jaw teeth as knives to *d.*
Isa. 1:7, strangers *d.* it in your presence.
20, if ye rebel, be *d.* with sword.
Jer. 2:30, your sword hath *d.* prophets.
3:24, shame *d.* labour of our fathers.
30:16, that *d.* thee shall be *d.*
Ezek. 15:7, fire shall *d.* them.
23:37, pass through fire to *d.* them.
Hos. 8:14; Amos 1:14; 2:2, it shall *d.* palaces.
Joel 2:3, a fire *d.* before them.
Amos 4:9, fig trees, palmer-worm *d.* them.
Hab. 1:13, wicked *d.* man that is more righteous.
Zeph. 1:18; 3:8, *d.* by fire of jealousy.
Mal. 3:11, will rebuke the *d.* for your sakes.
Mt. 13:4; Mk. 4:4; Lk. 8:5, fowls *d.* them.
23:14; Mk. 12:40; Lk. 20:47, *d.* widows' houses.
Lk. 15:30, thy son hath *d.* thy living.
2Cor. 11:20, if a man *d.* you.
Gal. 5:15, ye bite and *d.* one another.
Heb. 10:27, which shall *d.* adversaries.
1Pet. 5:8, seeking whom he may *d.*
See Gen. 31:15; 2Sam 2:26; Ps. 50:3; 52:4.
EVOUT. Lk. 2:25, Simeon was just and *d.*
Acts 2:5; 8:2, *d.* men.
See Acts 10:2; 13:50; 17:4, 17; 22:12.
EW. Gen. 27:28, God give thee the *d.* of heaven.
Dt. 32:2, my speech shall distil as the *d.*
33:13, for the *d.*, and for the deep.
Jud. 6:37, if the *d.* be on the fleece only.
2Sam. 1:21, let there be no *d.*
17:12, we will light on him as *d.* falleth.
1Ki. 17:1, there shall not be *d.* nor rain.
Job 38:28, who hath begotten drops of *d.*
Prov. 3:20, clouds drop down *d.*
Isa. 18:4, like *d.* in heat of harvest.
Dan. 4:15, 23, 25, 33, wet with *d.* of heaven.
Hos. 6:4; 13:3, goodness as early *d.*
Hag. 1:10, heaven is stayed from *d.*
See Ex. 16:13; Num. 11:9; Job 29:19; Ps. 110:3; 133:3; Prov. 19:12; Isa. 26:19; Hos. 14:5.
DIADEM. Job 29:14; Isa. 28:5; 62:3; Ezek. 21:26.
DIAL. 2Ki. 20:11, it had gone down in the *d.* of Ahaz.
Isa. 38:8, gone down in the sun *d.* of Ahaz.
DIAMOND (in high priest's breastplate). Ex. 28:18; 39:11.
See Jer. 17:1; Ezek. 28:13.
DID. Mt. 13:58, he *d.* not many mighty works.
Jn. 4:29, all things that ever I *d.*
9:26, what *d.* he to thee?
15:24, works which none other man *d.*
See Gen. 6:22; 1Sam. 1:7; Job 1:5; 1Pet. 2:22.
DIE. Gen. 2:17; 20:7; 1Sam. 14:44; 22:16; 1Ki. 2:37, 42; Jer. 26:8; Ezek. 3:18; 33:8, 14, surely *d.*
3:3; Lev. 10:6; Num. 18:32, lest ye *d.*
27:4; 45:28; Prov. 30:7, before I *d.*
Ex. 21:12, smiteth a man that he *d.*
Lev. 7:24; 22:8; Dt. 14:21; Ezek. 4:14, that *d.* of itself.
Num. 16:29, if these *d.* common death.
23:10, let me *d.* death of righteous.
Dt. 31:14, days approach that thou must *d.*
Ruth 1:17, where thou *d.* will I *d.*
2Sam. 3:33, *d.* Abner as a fool *d.*?
2Ki. 20:1; Isa. 38:1, shalt *d.* and not live.
2Chr. 25:4; Jer. 31:30, every man *d.* for own sin.
Job 2:9, his wife said, curse God and *d.*
3:11, why *d.* I not from the womb.
Job 12:2, wisdom shall *d.* with you.
14:4, if a man *d.*, shall he live again?
21:23, one *d.* in full strength.
25, another *d.* in bitterness of soul.
29:18, I shall *d.* in my nest.
Ps. 41:5, when shall he *d.* and name perish?
49:10, wise men *d.*, likewise the fool.
17, when he *d.* carry nothing away.
Prov. 5:23, he shall *d.* without instruction.
10:21, fools *d.* for want of wisdom.
11:7, *d.* his expectation perish.
Eccl. 2:16, how *d.* the wise man
7:17, why shouldest thou *d.* before thy time?
9:5, living know they shall *d.*
Isa. 66:24; Mk. 9:44, worm shall not *d.*
Jer. 27:13; Ezek. 18:31; 33:11, why will ye *d.*
28:16, this year thou shalt *d.*
34:5, thou shalt *d.* in peace.
Ezek. 18:4, 20, soul that sinneth shall *d.*
32, no pleasure in death of him that *d.*
33:8, wicked man shall *d.* in iniquity.
Amos. 6:9, if ten men in house they shall *d.*
9:10, sinners of my people shall *d.*
Jon. 4:3, 8, it is better to *d.* than live.
Mt. 15:4; Mk. 7:10, let him *d.* the death.
22:27; Mk. 12:22; Lk. 20:32, woman *d.* also.
26:35; Mk. 14:31, though I *d.* with thee.
Lk. 7:2, servant was ready to *d.*
16:22, beggar *d.*, rich man also *d.*
20:36, nor can they *d.* any more.

Jn. 4:49, come down ere my child *d.*
11:21, 32, my brother had not *d.*
37, that even this man should not have *d.*
50; 18:4, that one man *d.* for people.
51, that Jesus should *d.* for nation.
12:24, except a corn of wheat *d.*
19:7, by our law he ought to *d.*
Acts 9:37, Dorcas was sick and *d.*
21:13, ready also to *d.* at Jerusalem.
25:11, I refuse not to *d.*
Rom. 5:7, for righteous man will one *d.*
7:9, sin revived and I *d.*
8:34, it is Christ that *d.*
14:7, no man *d.* to himself.
9, Christ both *d.,* rose, and revived.
15; 1Cor. 8:11, for whom Christ *d.*
1Cor. 15:3, Christ *d.* for our sins.
22, as in Adam all *d.*
31, I *d.* daily.
36, not quickened except it *d.*
2Cor. 5:14, if one *d.* for all.
Phil. 1:21, to *d.* is gain.
1Th. 4:14, we believe that Jesus *d.*
5:10, who *d.* for us that we should live.
Heb. 7:8, here men that *d.* receive tithes.
9:27, appointed unto men once to *d.*
11:13, these all *d.* in faith.
Rev. 3:2, things that are ready to *d.*
9:6, men shall desire to *d.*
14:13, the dead that *d.* in the Lord.
See Job 14:10; Ps. 118:7; Rom. 5:6; 6:10.
DIET. Jer. 52:34.
DIFFER. Rom. 12:6; 1Cor. 4:7; 15:41; Gal. 4:1.
DIFFERENCE. Lev. 10:10; Ezek. 44:23, a *d.* between holy and unholy.
11:47; 20:25, *d.* between clean and unclean.
Ezek. 22:26, they have put no *d.* between.
Acts 15:9, put no *d.* between us.
Rom. 3:22; 10:12, for there is no *d.*
See Ex. 11:7; 1Cor. 12:5; Jude 22.
DIG. Ex. 21:33, *d.* a pit and not cover it.
Dt. 6:11; Neh. 9:25, wells *d.* which thou *d.* not.
8:9, out of hills mayest *d.* brass.
Job 6:27, ye *d.* a pit for your friend.
24:16, in the dark they *d.*
Ps. 7:15; 57:6, *d.* a pit and is fallen.
Isa. 51:1, hole of pit whence ye are *d.*
Mt. 21:33, and *d.* a winepress.
25:18, *d.* in the earth and hid.
Lk. 13:8, till I *d.* about it.
16:3, I cannot *d.*, to beg I am ashamed.
See Job 3:21; Ezek. 8:8; 12:5; Lk. 6:48.
DIGNITY. Eccl. 10:6, folly set in great *d.*
2Pet. 2:10; Jude 8, speak evil of *d.*
See Gen. 49:3; Est. 6:3; Hab. 1:7.
DILIGENCE. Prov. 4:23; 2Tim. 4:9; Jude 3.
DILIGENT. Josh. 22:5, take *d.* heed to commandment.
Ps. 64:6, accomplish a *d.* search.
Lk. 15:8, seek *d.* till she find it.
Acts 18:25, taught *d.* the things of the Lord.
2Tim. 1:17, in Rome sought me *d.*
Heb. 12:15, looking *d.* lest any man fail.
See Dt. 19:18; Prov. 11:27; 23:1; Mt. 2:7.
DIM. Dt. 34:7, eye not *d.* nor force abated.
Job 17:7, eye also *d.* by reason of sorrow.
Lam. 4:1, gold become *d.*
See Gen. 27:1; 48:10; 1Sam. 3:2; Isa. 8:22.
DIMINISH. Dt. 4:2; 12:32, nor *d.* ought from it.
Prov. 13:11, gotten by vanity shall be *d.*
Rom. 11:12, *d.* of them be riches of Gentiles.
See Ex. 5:8; Lev. 25:16; Jer. 26:2; Ezek. 16:27.
DINE. Gen. 43:16; Lk. 11:37; Jn. 21:12, 15.
DINNER. Prov. 15:17; Mt. 22:4; Lk. 11:38; 14:12.
DIP. Lev. 4:6; 9:9; 17:14, priest shall *d.* his finger.
Ruth 2:14, *d.* morsel in vinegar.
1Sam. 14:27, *d.* rod in honeycomb.
2Ki. 5:14, Naaman *d.* in Jordan.
Mt. 26:23; Mk. 14:20, *d.* hand in dish.
Jn. 13:26, when he had *d.* the sop.
Rev. 19:13, a vesture *d.* in blood.
See Gen. 37:31; Josh. 3:15; Lk. 16:24.
DIRECT. Job 32:14, he hath not *d.* his words.
37:3, he *d.* it under the whole heaven.
Ps. 5:3, in morning will I *d.* my prayer.
119:5, O that my ways were *d.* to keep.
Prov. 3:6, he shall *d.* thy paths.
11:5, righteousness shall *d.* his way.
16:9, the Lord *d.* his steps.
21:29, as for upright he *d.* his way.
Eccl. 10:10, wisdom profitable to *d.*
Isa. 40:13, who hath *d.* Spirit of the Lord.
Jer. 10:23, not in man to *d.* his steps.
2Th. 3:5, *d.* your hearts into love of God.
See Gen. 46:28; Isa. 45:13; 61:8; 1Th. 3:11.
DIRECTION. Num. 21:18
DIRECTLY. Num. 19:4; Ezek. 42:12.
DIRT. Jud. 3:22; Ps. 18:42; Isa. 57:20.
DISALLOWED. Num. 30:5, 8, 11; 1Pet. 2:4, 7.
DISANNUL. Isa. 14:27, Lord purposed, who shall *d.* it?
28:18, your covenant with death shall be *d.*
Gal. 3:15, 17, covenant no man *d.*
See Job 40:8; Heb. 7:18.
DISAPPOINT. Job 5:12; Ps. 17:13; Prov. 15:22
DISCERN. 2Sam. 19:35, can I *d.* between good and evil?
1Ki. 3:9, that I may *d.* between good and bad.
3:11, understanding to *d.* judgment.
Ezra 3:13, could not *d.* noise of joy.
Job 4:16, could not *d.* form thereof.
6:30, cannot my taste *d.* perverse things?
Prov. 7:7, I *d.* among the youths.
Eccl. 8:5, wise man's heart *d.* time.
Jon. 4:11, cannot *d.* between right and left.
Mal. 3:18, *d.* between righteous and wicked.
Mt. 16:3; Lk. 12:56, *d.* face of sky.
1Cor. 2:14, they are spiritually *d.*
11:29, not *d.* the Lord's body.
12:10, to another is given *d.* of spirits.
Heb. 4:12, the word is a *d.* of the thoughts.
5:14, exercised to *d.* good and evil.
See Gen. 27:23; 31:32; 38:25; 2Sam. 14:17
DISCHARGE. 1Ki. 5:9; Eccl. 8:8.
DISCIPLE. Isa. 8:16, seal law among my *d.*
Mt. 10:1; Lk. 6:13, called his twelve *d.*

24; Lk. 6:40, *d.* not above his master.
Mt. 10:42, give cup of water in the name of a *d.*
12:2, thy *d.* do that which is not lawful.
15:2, why do *d.* transgress tradition.
17:16, brought to thy *d.*, and they could not cure.
19:13; Mk. 10:13, the *d.* rebuked them.
20:17, Jesus took *d.* apart.
22:16, Pharisees sent their *d.*
26:18; Mk. 14:14; Lk. 22:11, keep passover with *d.*
35, likewise also said the *d.*
56, all the *d.* forsook him and fled.
28:7, tell his *d.* he is risen.
13, say ye, his *d.* came by night.
Mk. 2:18; Lk. 5:33, why do *d.* of John fast?
4:34, he expounded all things to *d.*
7:2, *d.* eat with unwashen hands.
5, why walk not *d.* according to tradition?
Lk. 5:30, Pharisees murmured against *d.*
6:20, lifted up eyes on *d.*
11:1, as John taught his *d.*
14:26, 27, 33, cannot be my *d.*
19:37, *d.* began to rejoice and praise God.
39, Master, rebuke thy *d.*
Jn. 2:11, his *d.* believed on him.
4:2, Jesus baptized not, but his *d.*
6:22, his *d.* were gone away alone.
66, many of his *d.* went back.
7:3, that thy *d.* may see works.
8:31; 13:35, then are ye my *d.* indeed.
9:27, will ye also be his *d.*?
28, thou art his *d.*, we are Moses' *d.*
13:5, began to wash *d.* feet.
15:8, so shall ye be my *d.*
18:15, 16, that *d.* was known.
17, 25, art not thou one of his *d.*?
19:26; 20:2; 21:7, 20, *d.* whom Jesus loved.
38, a *d.* of Jesus, but secretly for fear.
20:18, told *d.* she had seen the Lord.
21:23, that that *d.* should not die.
24, this is the *d.* which testifieth.
Acts 9:1, slaughter against *d.*
26, essayed to join himself to *d.*
11:26, *d.* called Christians first.
20:7, *d.* came together to break bread.
30, to draw away *d.* after them.
21:16, an old *d.* with whom we should lodge.
See Mt. 11:1; Jn. 3:25; 18:1, 2; 20:26.
ISCIPLINE. Job 36:10.
ISCLOSE. Isa. 26:21.
ISCOMFITED. Jud. 4:15, Lord *d.* Sisera.
8:12, Gideon *d.* all the host.
2Sam. 22:15; Ps. 18:14, lightnings, and *d.* them.
Isa. 31:8, his young men shall be *d.*
See Ex. 17:13; Num. 14:45; Josh. 10:10
ISCOMFITURE. 1Sam. 14:20.
ISCONTENTED. 1Sam. 22:2.
ISCONTINUE. Jer. 17:4.
ISCORD. Prov. 6:14, 19.
ISCOURAGE. Num. 32:7, wherefore *d.* the heart of the children of Israel.
Dt. 1:21, fear not, nor be *d.*
28, our brethren have *d.* our heart.
Col. 3:21, your children, lest they be *d.*
See Num. 21:4; 32:9; Isa. 42:4.
DISCOVER. 1Sam. 14:8, 11, we will *d.* ourselves to them.
2Sam. 22:16; Ps. 18:15, foundations of the world *d.*
Job 12:22, he *d.* deep things.
41:13, who can *d.* face of his garment?
Prov. 25:9, *d.* not a secret to another.
Ezek. 21:24, your transgressions are *d.*
See Ps. 29:9; Hos. 7:1; Hab. 3:13; Acts 21:3.
DISCREET. Gen. 41:33, 39; Mk. 12:34; Ti. 2:5.
DISCRETION. Ps. 112:5; Prov. 11:22; Isa. 28:26; Jer. 10:12.
DISDAINED. 1Sam. 17:42; Job 30:1.
DISEASE. Ex. 15:26; Dt. 7:15, none of these *d.* on you.
Dt. 28:60, bring on thee all *d.* of Egypt.
2Ki. 1:2; 8:8, 9, recover of *d.*
2Chr. 16:12, in *d.* sought not the Lord.
Job 30:18, by force of my *d.*
Ps. 103:3, who healeth all thy *d.*
Eccl. 6:2, vanity, and it is an evil *d.*
Ezek. 34:4, *d.* have ye not strengthened.
21, have pushed *d.* with your horns.
See Mt. 4:23; 14:35; Lk. 9:1; Acts 28:9.
DISFIGURE. Mt. 6:16.
DISGRACE. Jer. 14:21.
DISGUISE. 1Sam. 28:8; 1Ki. 14:2; 20:38; 22:30; 2Chr. 18:29; 35:22; Job 24:15.
DISH. Jud. 5:25; 2Ki. 21:13; Mt. 26:23; Mk. 14:20.
DISHONESTY. 2Cor. 4:2.
DISHONOUR. Ps. 35:26; 71:13, clothed with shame and *d.*
Prov. 6:33, a wound and *d.* shall he get.
Mic. 7:6, son *d.* father.
Jn. 8:49, I honour my father, ye *d.* me.
Rom. 9:21, one vessel to honour, another to *d.*
1Cor. 15:43, sown in *d.*
2Cor. 6:8, by honour and *d.*
2Tim. 2:20, some to honour, some to *d.*
See Ezra 4:14; Rom. 1:24; 2:23; 1Cor. 11:4, 5.
DISINHERIT. Num. 14:12.
DISMAYED. Dt. 31:8; Josh. 1:9; 8:1; 10:25; 1Chr. 22:13; 28:20; 2Chr. 20:15, 17; 32:7; Isa. 41:10; Jer. 1:17; 10:2; 23:4; 30:10; 46:27; Ezek. 2:6; 3:9, fear not nor be *d.*
Jer. 17:18, let them be *d.*, let not me be *d.*
See 1Sam. 17:11; Jer. 8:9; 46:5; Obad. 9.
DISMISSED. 2Chr. 23:8; Acts 15:30; 19:41.
DISOBEDIENCE. Rom. 5:19; Eph. 2:2; 5:6; Heb. 2:2.
DISOBEDIENT. Lk. 1:17, turn *d.* to wisdom of just.
Acts 26:19, not *d.* to heavenly vision.
Rom. 1:30; 2Tim. 3:2, *d.* to parents.
1Tim. 1:9, law for lawless and *d.*
Ti. 3:3, we ourselves were sometimes *d.*
1Pet. 2:7, to them which be *d.*
3:20, spirits, which sometime were *d.*
See 1Ki. 13:26; Neh. 9:26; Rom. 10:21.
DISORDERLY. 1Th. 5:14; 2Th. 3:6, 7, 11.
DISPENSATION. 1Cor. 9:17, a *d.* of the gospel is

committed me.
Eph. 1:10, in the *d.* of the fulness of times.
3:2, the *d.* of the grace of God.
Col. 1:25, according to the *d.* of God.
DISPERSE. Prov. 15:7, lips of wise *d.* knowledge.
See Ps. 112:9; Jer. 25:34; Ezek. 12:15; 20:23.
DISPERSED. Est. 3:8, and *d.* among the people.
Isa. 11:12, the *d.* of Judah.
Jn. 7:35, go unto the *d.* among the Gentiles.
DISPERSED (prophecies concerning). Jer. 25:24; Ezek. 36:19; Zeph. 3:10.
DISPLAYED. Ps. 60:4.
DISPLEASE. Num. 11:1, it *d.* the Lord.
22:34, if it *d.* thee, I will get me back.
2Sam. 11:27, thing David had done *d.* the Lord.
1Ki. 1:6, father had not *d.* him at any time.
Ps. 60:1, thou hast been *d.*
Prov. 24:18, lest the Lord see it, and it *d.* him.
Isa. 59:15, it *d.* him there was no judgment.
Jon. 4:1, it *d.* Jonah exceedingly.
Mt. 21:15, scribes saw it, they were *d.*
Mk. 10:14, Jesus was much *d.*
41, much *d.* with James and John.
See Gen. 48:17; 1Sam. 8:6; 18:8; Zech. 1:2.
DISPLEASURE. Dt. 9:19; Jud. 15:3; Ps. 2:5; 6:1; 38:1.
DISPOSE. Job 34:13; 37:15; Prov. 16:33; 1Cor. 10:27.
DISPOSITION. Acts 7:53.
DISPOSSESS. Num. 33:53; Dt. 7:17; Jud. 11:23.
DISPUTATION. Acts 15:2; Rom. 14:1
DISPUTE. Job 23:7, the righteous might *d.* with him.
Mk. 9:33, what was it ye *d.* of by the way?
1Cor. 1:20, where is the *d.* of this world?
Phil. 2:14, do all things without *d.*
1Tim. 6:5, perverse *d.*
See Acts 9:29; 15:7; 17:17; Jude 9.
DISQUIET. 1Sam. 28:15, why *d.* to bring me up?
Ps. 42:5, 11; 43:5, why art thou *d.* within me?
See Ps. 38:8; 39:6; Jer. 50:34.
DISSEMBLE. Josh. 7:11; Ps. 26:4; Prov. 26:24; Jer. 42:20; Gal. 2:13.
DISSENSION. Acts 15:2; 23:7, 10.
DISSIMULATION. Rom. 12:9; Gal. 2:13.
DISSOLVE. Isa. 34:4, host of heaven shall be *d.*
Dan. 5:16, thou canst *d.* doubts.
2Cor. 5:1, house of tabernacle *d.*
2Pet. 3:11, all these things shall be *d.*
12, heavens being on fire shall be *d.*
See Job 30:22; Ps. 75:3; Isa. 14:31; 24:19; Dan. 5:12; Nah. 2:6.
DISTAFF. Prov. 31:19.
DISTIL. Dt. 32:2; Job 36:28.
DISTINCTION. 1Cor. 14:7.
DISTINCTLY. Neh. 8:8.
DISTRACT. Ps. 88:15; 1Cor. 7:35.
DISTRESS. Gen. 42:21, therefore is this *d.* come upon us.
Jud. 11:7, why are ye come when ye are in *d.*?
1Sam. 22:2, every one in *d.* came to David.
2Sam. 22:7; Ps. 18:6; 118:5; 120:1, in *d.* I called.
1Ki. 1:29, redeemed my soul out of all *d.*
2Chr. 28:22, in *d.* Ahaz trespassed more.
Neh. 2:17, ye see the *d.* we are in.
Ps. 25:17; 107:6, 13, 19, 28, out of *d.*
Prov. 1:27, mock when *d.* cometh.
Isa. 25:4, a strength to needy in *d.*
Obad. 12:14; Zeph. 1:15, day of *d.*
Lk. 21:23, shall be great *d.* in the land.
25, on earth *d.* of nations.
Rom. 8:35, shall *d.* separate us?
1Cor. 7:26, good for present *d.*
2Cor. 6:4, approving ourselves in *d.*
12:10, take pleasure in *d.*
See Gen. 35:3; Neh. 9:37; 2Cor. 4:8; 1Th. 3:7.
DISTRIBUTE. Neh. 13:13, office was to *d.* to brethren.
Job. 21:17, God *d.* sorrows in his anger.
Lk. 18:22, sell and *d.* to poor.
Jn. 6:11, given thanks, he *d.*
Rom. 12:13, *d.* to necessity of saints.
1Cor. 7:17, as God hath *d.* to every man.
2Cor. 9:13, your liberal *d.*
See Josh. 13:32; Acts 4:35; 2Cor. 10:13; 1Tim. 6:18.
DITCH. Ps. 7:15, fallen into *d.* he made.
Mt. 15:14; Lk. 6:39, both fall into *d.*
See 2Ki. 3:16; Job 9:31; Prov. 23:27; Isa. 22:11.
DIVERS. Dt. 22:9, sow vineyard with *d.* kinds.
11, garment of *d.* sorts.
25:13, not have in bag *d.* weights.
14, *d.* measures, great and small.
Prov. 20:10, 23, *d.* weights and measures abomination.
Mt. 4:24; Mk. 1:34; Lk. 4:40, *d.* diseases.
24:7; Mk. 13:8; Lk. 21:11, in *d.* places.
Mk. 8:3, for *d.* of them came from far.
1Cor. 12:10, to another *d.* kinds of tongues.
2Tim. 3:6; Ti. 3:3, led away with *d.* lusts.
Jas. 1:2, joy in *d.* temptations.
See Eccl. 5:7; Heb. 1:1; 2:4; 9:10; 13:9.
DIVERSE. Est. 3:8, laws *d.* from all people.
1Cor. 12:6, *d.* of operations, but same God.
See Est. 1:7; 1Cor. 12:4, 28.
DIVIDE. Lev. 11:4, 5, 6, 7, 26; Dt. 14:7, not eat these of them that *d.* the hoof.
Josh. 19:49, and end of *d.* the land.
1Ki. 3:25, *d.* living child in two.
Job 27:17, innocent shall *d.* silver.
Ps. 68:12; Prov. 16:19; Isa. 9:3; 53:12, *d.* spoil.
Amos 7:17, thy land shall be *d.* by line.
Mt. 12:25; Mk. 3:24; Lk. 11:17, kingdom or house *d.*
26; Mk. 3:26; Lk. 11:18, *d.* against himself.
Lk. 12:13, that he *d.* inheritance with me.
14, who made me a *d.*?
52, five in one house *d.*
53, father *d.* against son.
15:12, he *d.* unto them his living.
Acts 14:4; 23:7, multitude *d.*
1Cor. 1:13, is Christ *d.*?
12:11, *d.* to every man severally as he will.
2Tim. 2:15, rightly *d.* word of truth.
Heb. 4:12, piercing to *d.* asunder.
See Dan. 7:25; Hos. 10:2; Mt. 25:32; Lk. 22:17.

•IVINATION. Num. 23:23, neither is any *d.* against Israel.
Acts. 16:16, damsel with a spirit of *d.*
See Dt. 18:10; 2Ki. 17:17; Ezek. 13:23.
•IVINE (*v.*). Gen. 44:15, wot ye not that I can *d.*?
1Sam. 28:8, *d.* unto me by the familiar spirit.
Ezek. 13:9, prophets that *d.* lies.
21:29, they *d.* lies unto thee.
Mic. 3:11, prophets *d.* for money.
See Gen. 44:5; Ezek. 22:28; Mic. 3;6.
•IVINE (*ad.*). Prov. 16:10; Heb. 9:1; 2Pet. 1:3, 4.
•IVINER. 1Sam. 6:2; Isa. 44:25; Jer. 27:9; 29:8.
•IVISION. Ex. 8:23, will put a *d.* between my people.
Jud. 5:15, for *d.* of Reuben great thoughts of heart.
Lk. 12:51, I tell you nay, but rather *d.*
Jn. 7:43; 9:16; 10:19, *d.* because of him.
Rom. 16:17, mark them which cause *d.*
See 1Cor. 1:10; 3:3; 11:18.
•O. Ruth 3:5, all thou sayest I will *d.*
Eccl. 3:12, for a man to *d.* good.
Isa. 46:11, I will also *d.* it.
Hos. 6:4, what shall I *d.* unto thee?
Mt. 7:12, men should *d.* to you, *d.* ye even so.
23:3, they say, and *d.* not.
Lk. 10:28, this *d.* and thou shalt live.
22:19; 1Cor. 11:24, this *d.* in remembrance.
Jn. 15:5, without me ye can *d.* nothing.
Rom. 7:15, what I would, that *d.* I not.
2Cor. 11:12, what I *d.* that I will *d.*
Gal. 5:17, ye cannot *d.* the things ye would.
Phil. 4:13, I can *d.* all things through Christ.
Heb. 4:13, with whom we have to *d.*
Jas. 1:23, a hearer, not a *d.* of the word.
See Jn. 6:38; 10:37; Rev. 19:10; 22:9.
•OCTOR. Acts 5:34, Gamaliel, a *d.* of the law.
Lk. 2:46, sitting in the midst of the *d.*
5:17, *d.* of the law sitting by.
•OCTRINE. Prov. 4:2, I give you good *d.*
Isa. 28:9, made to understand *d.*
Jer. 10:8, the stock is a *d.* of vanities.
Mt. 15:9; Mk. 7:7, teaching for *d.* commandments of men.
16:12, the *d.* of the Pharisees.
Mk. 1:27; Acts 17:19, what new *d.* is this?
Jn. 7:17, do his will shall know of the *d.*
Acts 2:42, continued in apostles' *d.*
5:28, filled Jerusalem with your *d.*
Rom. 6:17, obeyed that form of *d.*
16:17, contrary to the *d.*
1Cor. 14:26, every one hath a *d.*
Eph. 4:14, every wind of *d.*
1Tim. 1:10, contrary to sound *d.*
4:6, nourished in words of good *d.*
13, give attendance to *d.*
16, take heed to thyself and *d.*
2Tim. 3:10, hast fully known my *d.*
16, scripture profitable for *d.*
4:2, exhort with all longsuffering and *d.*
Ti. 1:9, by sound *d.* to exhort and convince.
2:1, things which become sound *d.*
7, in *d.* showing uncorruptness.
10, adorn the *d.* of God our Saviour.
Heb. 6:1, principles of the *d.*
2, the *d.* of baptisms.
13:9, not carried about with strange *d.*
2Jn. 9, abideth in *d.* of Christ.
See Dt. 32:2; Job 11:4; Jn. 7:16; 1Tim. 5:17.
DOG. Ex. 11:7, against Israel not a *d.* move.
Dt. 23:18, not bring price of *d.* into house.
Jud. 7:5, that lappeth as *d.* lappeth.
1Sam. 17:43; 24:14; 2Sam. 3:8, am I a *d.*?
2Sam. 9:8, upon such a dead *d.* as I am.
2Ki. 8:13, what, is thy servant a *d.*?
Job 30:1, disdained to set with *d.*
Ps. 22:20, darling from power of the *d.*
59:6, they make noise like a *d.*
Prov. 26:11; 2Pet. 2:22, as a *d.* returneth.
Prov. 26:17, like one that taketh a *d.* by ears.
Eccl. 9:4, living *d.* better than dead lion.
Isa. 56:10, they are all dumb *d.*
66:3, as if he cut off a *d.* neck.
Mt. 7:6, give not that which is holy to *d.*
15:27; Mk. 7:28, the *d.* eat of crumbs.
Phil. 3:2, beware of *d.*
Rev. 22:15, without are *d.*
See Ex. 22:31; 1Ki. 14:11; 21:23; 22:28.
DOING. Ex. 15:11, fearful in praises, *d.* wonders.
Jud. 2:19, ceased not from their own *d.*
1Sam. 25:3, churlish and evil in his *d.*
1Chr. 22:16, arise, and be *d.*
Neh. 6:3, I am *d.* a great work.
Ps. 9:11; Isa. 12:4, declare his *d.*
66:5, terrible in *d.* toward children of men.
77:12, I will talk of thy *d.*
118:23; Mt. 21:42; Mk. 12:11, the Lord's *d.*
Mic. 2:7, are these his *d.*?
Mt. 24:46; Lk. 12:43, shall find so *d.*
Acts 10:38, went about *d.* good.
Rom. 2:7, patient continuance in well *d.*
2Cor. 8:11, perform the *d.* of it.
Gal. 6:9; 2Th. 3:13, weary in well *d.*
Eph. 6:6, *d.* will of God from heart.
1Pet. 2:15, with well *d.* put to silence.
3:17, suffer for well *d.*
4:19, commit souls in well *d.*
See Lev. 18:3; Prov. 20:11; Isa. 1:16; Jer. 4:4.
DOLEFUL. Isa. 13:21; Mic. 2:4.
DOMINION. Gen. 27:40, when thou shalt have *d.*
37:8, shalt thou have *d.* over us?
Num. 24:19, come he that shall have *d.*
Job. 25:2, *d.* and fear are with him.
38:33, canst thou set the *d.* thereof?
Ps. 8:6, *d.* over works of thy hands.
19:13; 119:133, let them not have *d.* over me.
72:8; Zech. 9:10, *d.* from sea to sea.
Isa. 26:13, other lords have had *d.* over us.
Dan. 4:34; 7:14, *d.* is an everlasting *d.*
Mt. 20:25, princes of Gentiles exercise *d.*
Rom 6:9, death hath no more *d.*
14, sin shall not have *d.*
7:1, law hath *d.* over a man.
2Cor. 1:24, not *d.* over your faith.
Eph. 1:21, above all *d.*
Col. 1:16, whether they be thrones or *d.*

See Dan. 6:26; 1Pet. 4:11; Jude 25; Rev. 1:6.
DOOR. Gen. 4:7, sin lieth at the *d.*
Ex. 12:7, strike blood on *d.* posts.
33:8; Num. 11:10, every man at tent *d.*
Jud. 16:3, Samson took *d.* of the gate.
Job 31:9, laid wait at neighbour's *d.*
32, I opened my *d.* to the travellers.
38:17, the *d.* of the shadow of death.
41:14, who can open *d.* of his face?
Ps. 24:7, ye everlasting *d.*
78:23, opened the *d.* of heaven.
84:10, rather be *d.*-keeper.
141:3, keep the *d.* of my lips.
Prov. 5:8, come not nigh *d.* of her house.
8:3, wisdom crieth at *d.*
26:14, as *d.* turneth on hinges.
Eccl. 12:4, *d.* shall be shut in the streets.
Isa. 6:4, posts of the *d.* moved.
26:20, enter, and shut thy *d.* about thee.
Hos. 2:15, for a *d.* of hope.
Mal. 1:10, who would shut the *d.* for nought?
Mt. 6:6, when thou hast shut thy *d.*
24:33; Mk. 13:29, near, even at the *d.*
25:10, and the *d.* was shut.
27:60; 28:2; Mk. 15:46, *d.* of sepulchre.
Mk. 1:33, city gathered at the *d.*
2:2, not so much as about the *d.*
Lk. 13:25, master hath shut to the *d.*
Jn. 10:1, 2, entereth not by *d.*
7:9, I am the *d.*
Jn. 18:16, Peter stood at the *d.* without.
17, damsel that kept the *d.*
20:19, 26, when *d.* were shut, Jesus came.
Acts 5:9, feet at the *d.* to carry thee out.
14:27, opened the *d.* of faith.
1Cor. 16:9, great *d.* and effectual.
2Cor. 2:12, *d.* opened to me of the Lord.
Col. 4:3, open a *d.* of utterance.
Jas. 5:9, judge standeth before the *d.*
Rev. 3:8, set before thee an open *d.*
20, I stand at *d.* and knock.
4:1, behold a *d.* opened in heaven.
See Ex. 21:6; Dt. 11:20; Isa. 57:8; Acts 5:19; 16:26.
DOTE. Jer. 50:36; Ezek. 23:5; 1Tim. 6:4.
DOUBLE. Gen. 43:12, 15, take *d.* money in hand.
Ex. 22:4, 7, 9, he shall restore *d.*
Dt. 15:18, worth a *d.* hired servant.
2Ki. 2:9, a *d.* portion of thy spirit.
1Chr. 12:33; Ps. 12:2, a *d.* heart.
Isa. 40:2, received *d.* for all her sins.
Jer. 16:18, recompense their sin *d.*
1Tim. 3:8, deacons not *d.* tongued.
5:17, worthy of *d.* honour.
Jas. 1:8, a *d.* minded man unstable.
4:8, purify your hearts, ye *d.* minded.
See Gen. 41:32; Isa. 61:7; Ezek. 21:14; Rev. 18:6.
DOUBT. Dt. 28:66, thy life shall hang in *d.*
Job. 12:2, no *d.* ye are the people.
Ps. 126:6, shall *d.* come again, rejoicing.
Dan. 5:12, 16, dissolving of *d.*
Mt. 14:31, wherefore didst thou *d.*?
21:21, if ye have faith, and *d.* not.
Mk. 11:23, shall not *d.* in his heart.
Lk. 11:20, no *d.* kingdom of God is come.
Jn. 10:24, how long dost thou make us to *d.*?
Acts 5:24, they *d.* whereunto this would grow.
28:4, no *d.* this man is a murderer.
Rom. 14:23, he that *d.* is damned if he eat.
Gal. 4:20, I stand in *d.* of you.
1Tim. 2:8, pray without wrath and *d.*
1Jn. 2:19, would no *d.* have continued.
See Lk. 12:29; Acts 2:12; Phil. 3:8.
DOUGH. Num. 15:20, a cake of the first of your *d.*
Neh. 10:37, the firstfruits of our *d.*
Ezek. 44:30, give unto the priest the first of your *d.*
DOVE. Ps. 55:6, that I had wings like a *d.*
Isa. 59:11, mourn sore like *d.*
60:8, flee as *d.* to their windows.
Mt. 10:16, be harmless as *d.*
21:12; Mk. 11:15; Jn. 2:14, them that sold *d.*
See Jer. 48:28; Hos. 7:11; Mt. 3:16; Mk. 1:10.
DOWN. 2Sam. 3:35, if I taste ought till sun be *d.*
2Ki. 19:30; Isa. 37:31, again take root *d.*
Ps. 59:15, let them wander up and *d.*
109:23, I am tossed up and *d.*
Eccl. 3:21, spirit of the beast that goeth *d.*
Zech. 10:12, walk up and *d.* in his name.
See Josh. 8:29; Ps. 139:2; Ezek. 38:14.
DOWRY. Gen. 30:20; 34:12; Ex. 22:17; 1Sam. 18:25
DRAG. Hab. 1:15, 16; Jn. 21:8.
DRAGON. Dt. 32:33, their wine is the poison of *d.*
Neh. 2:13, before the *d.* well.
Job 30:29, I am a brother to *d.*
Ps. 91:13, the *d.* shalt thou trample.
148:7, praise the Lord, ye *d.*
Isa. 43:20, the *d.* and owls shall honour me.
Jer. 9:11, will make Jerusalem a den of *d.*
Rev. 20:2, the *d.*, that old serpent.
See Rev. 12:3; 13:2, 11; 16:13.
DRANK. 1Sam. 30:12, nor *d.* water three days and nights.
2Sam. 12:3, and *d.* of his own cup.
1Ki. 17:6, and he *d.* of the brook.
Dan. 1:5, appointed of the wine he *d.*
5:4, they *d.* wine, and praised the gods.
Mk. 14:23, and they all *d.* of it.
Lk. 17:27, 28, they *d.*, they married.
Jn. 4:12, than our father, who *d.* thereof.
1Cor. 10:4, for they *d.* of that spiritual Rock.
See Gen. 9:21; 24:46; 27:25; Num. 20:11.
DRAUGHT. Mt. 15:17; Mk. 7:19; Lk. 5:4, 9; 21:6, 11
DRAVE. Ex. 14:25; Josh. 24:12; Jud. 6:9.
DRAW. Job 40:23, trusteth he can *d.* up Jordan.
41:1, canst thou *d.* out leviathan?
Ps. 28:3, *d.* me not away with wicked.
37:14, wicked have *d.* out sword.
55:21, yet were they *d.* swords.
88:3, my life *d.* nigh unto the grave.
Eccl. 12:1, nor years *d.* nigh.
Song 1:4, *d.* me. will run after thee.
Isa. 5:18, *d.* iniquity with cords.
12:3, *d.* water from wells of salvation.
Jer. 31:3, with lovingkindness have I *d.* thee.
Mt. 15:8, people *d.* nigh me with their mouth.

Lk. 21:8, the time *d.* near.
28, your redemption *d.* nigh.
Jn. 4:11, thou hast nothing to *d.* with.
15, thirst not, neither come hither to *d.*
Jn. 6:44, except the Father *d.* him.
12:32, if lifted up, will *d.* all men.
Heb. 10:22, *d.* near with true heart.
38, 39, if any *d.* back.
Jas. 4:8, *d.* nigh to God, he will *d.*
See Acts 11:10; 20:30; Heb 7:19; Jas. 2:6.
RAWER. Dt. 29:11; Josh 9:21
READ. Gen. 28:17, how *d.* is this place!
Dt. 2:25; 11:25, begin to put *d.* of thee.
Isa. 8:13, let him be your *d.*
Mal. 4:5, the great and *d.* day.
See Gen. 9:2; Ex. 15:16, Dan. 9:4.
REAM. Job 20:8, shall fly away as a *d.*
33:15, 16, in a *d.* he openeth the ears.
Ps. 73:20, as a *d.* when one awaketh.
126:1, we were like them that *d.*
Eccl. 5:3, a *d.* cometh through much business.
Jer. 23:28, prophet that hath a *d.*
Joel 2:28; Acts 2:17, old men *d.* *d.*
Jude 8, filthy *d.* defile the flesh.
See Job 7:14; Isa. 29:8; Jer. 27:9.
REGS. Ps. 75:8; Isa. 51:17.
RESS. Gen. 2:15, put man in garden to *d.* it.
Dt. 28:39, plant vineyards and *d.* them.
2Sam. 12:4, poor man's lamb and *d.* it.
See Ex. 30:7; Lk. 13:7; Heb. 6:7.
REW. Gen. 47:29, time *d.* nigh that Israel must die.
Ex. 2:10, because I *d.* him out of the water.
Josh. 8:26, Joshua *d.* not his hand back.
1Ki. 22:34; 2Chr. 18:33, man *d.* a bow.
2Ki. 9:24, Jehu *d.* bow with full strength.
Hos. 11:4, *d.* them with cords of a man.
Zeph. 3:2, she *d.* not near to her God.
Mt. 21:34, when time of fruit *d.* near.
Lk. 24:15, Jesus himself *d.* near.
Acts 5:37, and *d.* away much people.
See Est. 5:2; Lam. 3:57; Acts 7:17.
RINK (*n.*). Lev. 10:9, do not drink strong *d.* when ye go.
Num. 6:3, separate himself from strong *d.*
Dt. 14:26, bestow money for strong *d.*
29:6, strong *d.* these forty years.
Prov. 20:1, strong *d.* is raging.
31:4, not for princes to drink strong *d.*
6, give strong *d.* to him that is ready to perish.
Isa. 24:9, strong *d.* shall be bitter.
28:7, erred through strong *d.*
Mic. 2:11, prophesy of wine and strong *d.*
Hab. 2:15, that giveth his neighbour *d.*
Hag. 1:6, ye are not filled with *d.*
Mt. 25:35, 37, 42, thirsty, and ye gave me *d.*
Jn. 4:9, a Jew, askest *d.* of me.
6:55, my blood is *d.* indeed.
Rom 12:20, if thine enemy thirst, give him *d.*
14:17, the kingdom of god is not meat and *d.*
1Cor. 10:4, same spiritual *d.*
Col. 2:16, judge you in meat or in *d.*
See Gen. 21:19; Isa. 5:11, 22; 32:6; 43:20. Lk. 1:15; 1Tim. 5:23.
DRINK (*v.*). Ex. 15:24, what shall we *d.*?
17:1, no water for people to *d.*
2Sam. 23:16; 1Chr. 11:18; David would not *d.*
Ps. 36:8, *d.* of the river of thy pleasures.
60:3, *d.* the wine of astonishment.
80:5, gavest them tears to *d.*
110:7, he shall *d.* of the brook in the way.
Prov. 5:15, *d.* waters of thine own cistern.
31:5, lest they *d.* and forget the law.
7, let him *d.*, and forget his poverty.
Eccl. 9:7, *d.* wine with merry heart.
Song 5:1, *d.*, yea, *d.* abundantly.
Isa. 5:22, mighty to *d.* wine.
65:13, my servants shall *d.*, but ye.
Jer. 35:2, give Rechabites wine to *d.*
6, we will *d.* no wine.
14, to this day they *d.* none.
Ezek. 4:11, thou shalt *d.* water by measure.
Amos. 2:8, *d.* the wine of the condemned.
Zech. 9:15, they shall *d.*, and make a noise
Mt. 10:42, whoso shall give to *d.*
20:22; Mk. 10:38, are ye able to *d.*?
26:27, saying, *d.* ye all of it.
29; Mk. 14:25; Lk. 22:18, when I *d.* it new.
42, may not pass except I *d.*
Mk. 9:41, shall give you cup of water to *d.*
16:18, if they *d.* any deadly thing.
Jn. 4:10, give me to *d.*
7:37, let him come to me, and *d.*
18:11, cup given me, shall I not *d.* it?
Rom 14:21, not good to *d.* wine.
1Cor. 10:4, did all *d.* same spiritual drink.
11:25, as oft as ye *d.* it.
12:13, made to *d.* into one Spirit.
See Mk. 2:16; Lk. 7:33; 10:7.
DRIVE. Gen. 4:14, thou hast *d.* me out.
Ex. 23:28, hornets shall *d.* out Hivite.
Dt. 4:19, lest thou be *d.* to worship them.
Job 24:3, they *d.* away ass of the fatherless.
30:5, they were *d.* forth from among men.
Prov. 14:32, wicked *d.* away in his wickedness.
22:15, rod shall *d.* it away.
25:23, north wind *d.* away rain.
Jer. 46:15, stood not, because Lord did *d.* them.
Dan. 4:25; 5:21, they shall *d.* thee from men.
Hos. 13:3, as chaff *d.* with whirlwind.
Lk. 8:29, he was *d.* of the devil.
Jas. 1:6, wave *d.* with the wind.
See 2Ki. 9:20; Jer. 8:3; Ezek. 31:11.
DROMEDARIES. 1Ki. 4:28, straw for the horses and *d.*
Est. 8:10, and young *d.*
Isa. 60:6, the *d.* of Midian and Ephah.
Jer. 2:23, thou art a swift *d.* traversing her ways.
DROP (*n.*). Job 36:27, maketh small the *d.* of water.
Isa. 40:15, as the *d.* of a bucket.
See Job 38:28; Song 5:2; Lk. 22:44.
DROP (*v.*). Dt. 32:2, doctrine shall *d.* as the rain.
Job 29:22, my speech *d.* upon them.
Ps. 65:11, paths *d.* fatness.
68:8 heavens *d.* at presence of God.
Eccl. 10:18, through idleness house *d.* through.

Isa. 45:8, *d.* down, ye heavens.
Ezek. 20:46, *d.* thy word toward the south.
See 2Sam. 21:10; Joel 3:18; Amos 9:13.
DROPSY. Lk. 14:2, a man which had the *d.*
DROSS. Ps. 119:119; Prov. 25:4; 26:23; Isa. 1:22, 25; Ezek. 22:18.
DROUGHT. Dt. 28:24; 1Ki. 17; Isa. 58:11; Jer. 17:8; Hos. 13:5; Hag. 1:11.
DROVE. Gen. 3:24; 15:11; 32:16; 33:8; Jn. 2:15.
DROWN. Song 8:7, neither can floods *d.* it.
1Tim 6:9, that *d.* men in perdition.
See Ex. 15:4; Mt. 18:6; Heb. 11:29.
DROWSINESS. Prov. 23:21.
DRUNK. 2Sam. 11:13, David made Uriah *d.*
1Ki. 20:16, was drinking himself *d.*
Job 12:25; Ps. 107:27, stagger like a *d.* man.
Jer. 23:9, I am like a *d.* man.
Lam. 5:4, we have *d.* water for money.
Hab. 2:15, makest him *d.* also.
Mt. 24:49; Lk. 12:45, drink with the *d.*
Acts 2:15, these are not *d.*
1Cor. 11:21, one is hungry, and another *d.*
1Th. 5:7, they that be *d.* are *d.* in the night.
See Lk. 5:39; Jn. 2:10; Eph. 5:18; Rev. 17:6
DRUNKARD. Dt. 21:20, our son is a glutton and a *d.*
Prov. 23:21, *d.* and glutton come to poverty.
26:9, as a thorn goeth into hand of *d.*
1Cor. 6:10, nor *d.* shall inherit.
See Ps. 69:12; Isa. 24:20; Joel 1:5; Nah. 1:10.
DRUNKENNESS. Dt. 29:19, to add *d.* to thirst.
Eccl. 10:17, eat for strength, not for *d.*
Ezek. 23:33, shalt be filled with *d.*
See Lk. 21:34; Rom. 13:13; Ga. 5:21.
DRY. Prov. 17:22, a broken spirit *d.* the bones.
Isa. 44:3, pour floods on *d.* ground.
Mt. 12:43; Lk. 11:24, through *d.* places.
Mk. 5:29, fountain of blood *d.* up.
See Ps. 107:33, 35; Isa. 53:2; Mk. 11:20.
DUE. Lev. 10:13, 14, it is thy *d.*, and thy sons' *d.*
26:4; Dt. 11:14, rain in *d.* season.
Ps. 104:27; 145:15; Mt. 24:45; Lk. 14:42, meat in *d.* season.
Prov. 15:23, word spoken in *d.* season.
Mt. 18:34, pay all that was *d.*
Lk. 23:41, the *d.* reward of our deeds.
Rom. 5:6, in *d.* time Christ died.
Gal. 6:9, in *d.* season we shall reap.
See Prov. 3:27; 1Cor. 15:8; Ti. 1:3; 1Pet. 5:6.
DULL. Mt. 13:15; Acts 28:27; Heb. 5:11.
DUMB. Ex. 4:11, who maketh the *d.*?
Prov. 31:8, open thy mouth for the *d.*
Isa. 35:6, the tongue of the *d.* shall sing.
53:7; Acts 8:32, as sheep before shearers is *d.*
56:10, they are all *d.* dogs.
Ezek. 3:26, be *d.*, and shalt not be a reprover.
Hab. 2:19, woe to him that saith to *d.* stone.
Mt. 9:32; 12:22; 15:30; Mk. 7:37; 9:17; *d.* man.
See Ps. 39:2; Dan. 10:15; Lk. 1:20; 11:14; 2Pet. 2:16.
DUNG. 1Sam 2:8; Ps. 113:7, lifteth beggar from *d.*-hill.
Lk. 13:8, till I dig about it, and *d.* it.
14:35, neither fit for land nor *d.*-hill.
Phil. 3:8, count all things but *d.*
See Neh. 2:13; Lam. 4:5; Mal. 2:3.
DUNGEON. Gen. 40:15; 41:14; Ex. 12:29; Jer. 38:6 Lam. 3:53.
DURABLE. Prov. 8:18; Isa. 23:18.
DURETH. Mt. 13:21.
DURST. Mt. 22:46; Mk. 12:34; Lk. 20:40, nor *d.* ask questions.
Jn. 21:12, none of disciples *d.* ask.
See Est. 7:5; Job 32:6; Acts 5:13; Jude 9.
DUST. Gen. 2:7, Lord God formed man of *d.*
3:14, *d.* shalt thou eat.
19, *d.* thou art.
18:27, who am but *d.* and ashes.
Job 10:9, wilt thou bring me into *d.* again?
22:24; 27:16, lay up gold as *d.*
34:15, man shall turn again to *d.*
42:6, I repent in *d.* and ashes.
Ps. 30:9, shall the *d.* praise thee?
102:14, servants favour *d.* thereof.
103:14, remembereth that we are *d.*
104:29, they die and return to their *d.*
Eccl. 3:20, all are of the *d.* and turn to *d.* again.
12:7, then shall the *d.* return to the earth.
Isa. 40:12, comprehended *d.* of the earth.
65:25, *d.* shall be serpent's meat.
Lam. 3:29, he putteth his mouth in the *d.*
Dan. 12:2, many that sleep in *d.* shall awake.
Mic. 7:17, lick the *d.* like a serpent.
Mt. 10:14; Mk. 6:11; Lk. 9:5, shake off *d.* from feet.
Lk. 10:11, even *d.* of your city.
Acts 22:23, as they threw *d.* into the air.
See Ex. 8:16; Num. 23:10; Dt. 9:21; Josh. 7:6; Jo 2:12; 39:14; Lam. 2:10.
DUTY. Eccl. 12:13, the whole *d.* of man.
Lk. 17:10, that which was our *d.* to do.
Rom. 15:27, their *d.* is to minister.
See Ex. 21:10; Dt. 25:5; 2Chr. 8:14; Ezra 3:4.
DWELL. Dt. 12:11, cause his name to *d.* there.
1Sam. 4:4; 2Sam. 6:2; 1Chr. 13:6, *d.* between th cherubims.
1Ki. 8:30; 2Chr. 6:21, heaven thy *d.* place
Ps. 23:6, will *d.* in house of the Lord.
37:3, so shalt thou *d.* in the land.
84:10, than to *d.* in tents of wickedness.
132:14, here will I *d.*
133:1, good for brethren to *d.* together.
Isa. 33:14, who shall *d.* with devouring fire?
16, he shall *d.* on high.
57:15, I *d.* in the high and holy place.
Jn. 6:56, *d.* in me, and I in him.
14:10, the Father that *d.* in me.
17, for he *d.* with you, and shall be in you.
Rom. 7:17, sin that *d.* in me.
Col. 2:9, in him *d.* fulness of Godhead.
3:16, word of Christ *d.* in you richly.
1Tim. 6:16, *d.* in the light.
2Pet. 3:13, wherein *d.* righteousness.
1Jn. 3:17, how *d.* the love of God in him?
4:12, God *d.* in us.
See Rom. 8:9; 2Cor. 6:16; Jas. 4:5

'ED. Ex. 25:5; Isa. 63:1; Ezek. 23:15
'ING. 2Cor. 4:10, the *d.* of Lord Jesus.
2Cor. 6:9, as *d.* and behold we live.
See Num. 17:13; Lk. 8:42; Heb. 11:21.
ACH. Isa. 57:2, *e.* one walking in his uprightness.
Ezek. 4:6, *e.* day for a year.
Acts 2:3, cloven tongues sat on *e.*
Phil. 2:3, let *e.* esteem other.
See Ex. 18:7; Ps. 85:10; 2Th. 1:3
AGLE. Ex. 19:4, how I bare you on *e.* wings.
2Sam. 1:23, were swifter than *e.*
Job 9:26, *e.* that hasteth to prey.
39:27, doth the *e.* mount up?
Ps. 103:5, youth renewed like *e.*
Isa. 40:31, mount up with wings as *e.*
Ezek. 1:10, they four also had the face of an *e.*
17:3, a great *e.* with great wings.
Obad. 4, thou shalt exalt thyself as the *e.*
Mt. 24:28; Lk. 17:37, *e.* be gathered.
Rev. 4:7, the fourth beast was like a flying *e.*
See Dan. 4:33; Rev. 12:14.
AR (*n.*). Neh. 1:6, let thine *e.* be attentive.
Job 12:11; 34:3, doth not *e.* try words?
29:11, when the *e.* heard me, it blessed me.
42:5, heard of thee by the hearing of the *e.*
Ps. 45:10, and incline thine *e.*
58:4, like the deaf adder that stoppeth her *e.*
78:1, give *e.*, O my people.
94:9, he that planted the *e.*, shall he not hear?
Prov. 15:31, the *e.* that heareth the reproof.
17:4, liar giveth *e.* to naughty tongue.
18:15, *e.* of wise seeketh knowledge.
20:12, hearing *e.* seeing eye, Lord made.
20:17, bow down thine *e.*
25:12, wise reprover on obedient *e.*
Eccl. 1:8, nor the *e.* filled with hearing.
Isa. 48:8, from that time thine *e.* not opened.
50:4, he wakeneth my *e.* to hear.
55:3, incline your *e.* and come unto me.
59:1, nor his *e.* heavy, that it cannot.
Jer. 9:20, let your *e.* receive word of the Lord.
Amos 3:12, out of mouth of lion piece of an *e.*
1Cor. 2:9, nor *e.* heard.
12:16, if *e.* say, because I am not the eye.
See Rev. 2:7.
AR (*v.*). Ex. 34:21; Dt. 21:4; 1Sam 8:12.
ARLY. Ps. 46:5, and that right *e.*
63:1, *e.* will I seek thee.
90:14, satisfy us *e.* with thy mercy.
Prov. 1:28; 8:17, seek me *e.* shall find me.
Song 7:12, get up *e.* to vineyards.
Hos. 6:4; 13:3, as *e.* dew.
Jas. 5:7, the *e.* and latter rain.
See Jud. 7:3; Lk. 24:22; Jn. 20:1.
ARNEST. Job 7:2, as servant *e.* desireth shadow.
Jer. 31:20, I do *e.* remember him still.
Mic. 7:3, do evil with both hands *e.*
Lk. 22:44, in agony he prayed more *e.*
Rom. 8:19, the *e.* expectation of the creature.
1Cor. 12:31, covet *e.* best gifts.
2Cor. 1:22; 5:5, the *e.* of the Spirit.
5:2, *e.* desiring to be clothed.
Eph. 1:14, the *e.* of our inheritance.
Phil. 1:20, to my *e.* expectation and hope.
Jude 3, *e.* contend for the faith.
See Acts 3:12; Heb. 2:1; Jas. 5:17.
EARNETH. Hag. 1:6.
EARS. Ex. 10:2, tell it in *e.* of thy son.
1Sam. 3:11; 2Ki. 21:12; Jer. 19:3, at which *e.* shall tingle.
2Sam. 7:22, we have heard with our *e.*
Job 15:21, dreadful sound is in his *e.*
28:22, heard fame with our *e.*
Ps. 18:6, my cry came even into his *e.*
34:15, his *e.* are open unto their cry.
115:6; 135:17, they have *e.*, but hear not.
Prov. 21:13, stoppeth *e.* at cry of the poor.
23:9, speak not in *e.* of a fool.
26:17, one that taketh dog by the *e.*
Isa. 6:10; Mt. 13:15; Acts 28:27, make *e.* heavy.
Mt. 10:27, what ye hear in *e.*, preach.
13:16, blessed are your *e.*
26:51; Mk. 14:47, smote off *e.*
Mk. 7:33, put his fingers into *e.*
8:18, having *e.*, hear ye not?
Acts 7:51, uncircumcised in heart and *e.*
17:20, strange things to our *e.*
2Tim. 4:3, having itching *e.*
Jas. 5:4, entered into *e.* of the Lord.
1Pet. 3:12, his *e.* are open to prayer.
See Mt. 11:15; Mk. 4:9.
EARS (*of corn*). Dt. 23:25; Mt. 12:1.
EARTH. Gen. 8:22, while *e.* remaineth.
10:25, in his days was *e.* divided.
18:25, shall not Judge of all the *e.* do right?
Num. 14:21, all *e.* filled with glory.
16:30, if the *e.* open her mouth.
Dt. 32:1, O *e.* hear the words of my mouth.
Josh. 3:11; Zech. 6:5, Lord of all the *e.*
23:14, going way of all the *e.*
1Ki. 8:27; 2Chr. 6:18, will God dwell on the *e.*?
2Ki. 5:17, two mules' burden of *d.*
Job 7:1, appointed time to man upon *e.*
9:24, *e.* given into hand of wicked.
19:25, stand at latter day upon *e.*
26:7, hangeth *e.* upon nothing.
38:4, when I laid foundations of the *e.*
41:33, on *e.* there is not his like.
Ps. 2:8, uttermost parts of *e.*
8:1, excellent is thy name in *e.*
16:3, to saints that are in the *e.*
25:13, his seed shall inherit the *e.*
33:5, the *e.* is full of the goodness.
34:16, cut off remembrance from the *e.*
37:9, 11, 22, wait on Lord shall inherit *e.*
41:2, shall be blessed upon the *e.*
46:2, not fear, though *e.* be removed.
6, uttered voice, the *e.* melted.
8, desolations made in the *e.*
10, will be exalted in the *e.*
47:9, shields of the *e.* belong to God.
48:2, joy of the whole *e.*
50:4, call to *e.*, that he may judge.
57:5; 108:5, glory above all the *e.*
Ps. 58:11, a God that judgeth in the *e.*
60:2, made the *e.* to tremble.

63:9, lower parts of the *e.*
65:8, dwell in uttermost parts of *e.*
9, visitest *e.*, and waterest it.
67:6; Ezek. 34:27, *e.* yield increase.
68:8, *e.* shook, heavens dropped.
71:20, bring me up from depths of the *e.*
72:6, showers that water the *e.*
16, handful of corn in the *e.*
73:9, tongue walketh through *e.*
25, none on *e.* I desire beside thee.
75:3; Isa. 24:19, *e.* dissolved.
83:18; 97:9, most high over all *e.*
90:2, or ever thou hadst formed the *e.*
97:1, Lord reigneth, let *e.* rejoice.
99:1, Lord reigneth, let *e.* be moved.
102:25; 104:5; Prov. 8:29; Isa. 48:13, laid foundation of *e.*
104:13, the *e.* is satisfied.
24, the *e.* is full of thy riches.
112:2, seed mighty upon *e.*
115:16, *e.* given to children of men.
119:19, stranger in the *e.*
64, the *e.* full of thy mercy.
90, established the *e.*, it abideth.
146:4, he returneth to the *e.*
147:8, prepareth rain for the *e.*
148:13, glory above *e.* and heaven.
Prov. 3:19; Isa. 24:1, Lord founded the *e.*
8:23, set up from everlasting, or ever *e.* was.
26, he had not yet made *e.*, nor fields.
11:31, righteous recompensed in *e.*
25:3, the *e.* for depth.
30:14, teeth as knives to devour poor from *e.*
16, the *e.* not filled with water.
21, for three things *e.* is disquieted.
24, four things little upon *e.*
Eccl. 1:4, the *e.* abideth for ever.
3:21, spirit of beast goeth to *e.*
5:9, profit of the *e.* for all.
12:7, dust return to *e.*
Isa. 4:2, fruit of *e.* excellent.
11:9, *e.* full of knowledge of the Lord.
13:13, *e.* shall remove out of her place.
14:16, is this the man that made *e.* tremble?
26:9, when thy judgments are in the *e.*
21, *e.* shall disclose her blood.
34:1, let the *e.* hear.
40:22, sitteth on circle of the *e.*
28, Creator of ends of *e.* fainteth not.
44:24, spreadeth abroad *e.* by myself.
45:22, be saved, all ends of the *e.*
49:13, be joyful, O *e.*
51:6, the *e.* shall wax old.
66:1, the *e.* is my footstool.
8, shall *e.* bring forth in one day?
Jer. 15:10, man of contention to whole *e.*
22:29, O *e.*, *e.*, *e.*, hear word of Lord.
31:22, hath created new thing in *e.*
51:15, made the *e.* by his power.
Ezek. 9:9, the Lord hath forsaken the *e.*
43:2, the *e.* shined with his glory.
Hos. 2:22, the *e.* shall hear the corn.
Amos 3:5, bird fall in snare on *e.*
8:9, darken *e.* in the clear day.
9:9, least grain fall upon the *e.*
Jon. 2:6, *e.* with bars about me.
Mic. 6:2, ye strong foundations of the *e.*
7:2, good man perished out of the *e.*
17, move like worms of the *e.*
Nah. 1:5, *e.* burnt up at his presence
Hab. 2:14, *e.* filled with knowledge.
3:3, the *e.* full of his praise.
Hag. 1:10, *e.* stayed from her fruit.
Zech. 4:10, eyes of Lord run through *e.*
Mal. 4:6, lest I smite *e.* with a curse.
Mt. 5:5, meek shall inherit *e.*
Mt. 5:35, swear not by the *e.*
6:19, treasures upon *e.*
9:6; Mk. 2:10; Lk. 5:24, power on *e.* to forgive.
10:34, to send peace on *e.*
13:5, Mk. 4:5, not much *e.*
16:19, 18:18, shalt bind on *e.*
18:19, shall agree on *e.*
23:9, call no man father on *e.*
25:18, 25, digged in the *e.*
Mk. 4:28, *e.* bringeth forth fruit of herself.
31, less than all seeds in the *e.*
9:3, no fuller on *e.* can white them.
Lk. 2:14, on *e.* peace.
23:44, darkness over all *e.*
Jn. 3:12, I have told you *e.* things.
31, of *e.* is *e.*, and speaketh of the *e.*
12:32, lifted up from the *e.*
17:4, I have glorified thee on the *e.*
Acts 8:33, life taken from the *e.*
9:4, 8; 26:14, Saul fell to the *e.*
22:22, away with such a fellow from *e.*
Rom. 10:18, sound went into all *e.*
1Cor. 15:47, first man is of the *e.*, *e.*
48, as is the *e.*, such are they that are *e.*
49, the image of the *e.*
2Cor. 4:7, treasure in *e.* vessels.
Col. 3:2, affection not on things on *e.*
Phil. 3:19, who mind *e.* things.
Heb. 6:7, *e.* drinketh in the rain.
8:4, if he were on *e.*
11:13, strangers on the *e.*
12:25, refused him that spake on *e.*
26, voice then shook the *e.*
Jas. 3:15, this wisdom is *e.*
5:5, lives in pleasure on *e.*
7, the precious fruit of the *e.*
18, and the *e.* brought forth her fruit.
2Pet. 3:10, the *e.* shall be burnt up.
Rev. 5:10, we shall reign on the *e.*
7:3, hurt not the *e.*
18:1, *e.* lightened with his glory.
20:11, from whose face the *e.* fled.
21:1, a new *e.*
See Gen. 1:1, 11; 3:17; 7:10; Ex. 9:29; Job 12:8; Ps. 24:1;
Isa. 65:16; Mic. 1:4; Zeph. 3:8; 2Pet. 3:7, 13; Rev. 20:9.

EARTHQUAKE. 1Ki. 19:11; Isa. 29:6; Amos 1:1; Zech. 14:5; Mt. 24:7; 27:54; Acts 16:26; Rev

6:12; 8:5; 11:13; 16:18.
ASE. Ex. 18:22, so shall it be *e.* for thyself.
Dt. 28:65, among nations find no *e.*
Job 12:5, thought of him that is at *e.*
16:6, though I forbear, what am I *e.*?
21:23, dieth, being wholly at *e.*
Ps. 25:13, his soul shall dwell at *e.*
Isa. 32:9, 11, women that are at *e.*
Amos. 6:1, woe to them that are at *e.*
Mt. 9:5; Mk. 2:9; Lk. 5:23, is *e.* to say.
19:24; Mk. 10:25; Lk. 18:25, *e.* for camel.
1Cor. 13:5, not *e.* provoked.
Heb. 12:1, sin which doth so *e.* beset.
See Jer. 46:27; Zech. 1:15; Lk. 12:19.
AST. Gen. 41:6; 23:27, blasted with *e.* wind.
Ex. 10:13, Lord brought an *e.* wind.
Job 1:3, greatest of all men of the *e.*
15:2, fill his belly with *e.* wind.
27:21, *e.* wind carrieth him away.
38:24, scattereth *e.* wind on the earth.
Ps. 48:7, breakest ships with *e.* wind.
75:6, promotion cometh not from *e.*
103:12, as far as *e.* from west.
Isa. 27:8, stayeth rough wind in day of *e.* wind.
Ezek. 19:12, the *e.* wind drieth up her fruit.
43:2, glory of God of Israel came from way of *e.*
47:1, house stood toward the *e.*
Hos. 12:1, Ephraim followeth *e.* wind.
13:15, though fruitful, an *e.* wind shall come.
See Jon. 4:5, 8; Mt. 2:1; 8:11; 24:27.
ASTER. Acts 12:4, intending after *E.* to bring him forth.
ASY. Prov. 14:6; Mt. 11:30; 1Cor. 14:9; Jas. 3:17.
AT. Gen. 2:17, in day thou *e.* thou shalt die.
9:4; Lev. 19:26; Dt. 12:16, blood not *e.*
24:33, not *e.* till I have told.
43:32, Egyptians might not *e.* with Hebrews.
Ex. 12:16, no work, save that which man must *e.*
23:11, that the poor may *e.*
29:34, shall not be *e.*, because holy.
Lev. 25:20, what shall we *e.* seventh year?
Num. 13:32, a land that *e.* up inhabitants.
Josh. 5:11, 12, *e.* of old corn of the land.
1Sam. 14:30, if haply people had *e.* freely.
28:20, had *e.* no bread all day.
22, *e.*, that thou mayest have strength.
2Sam. 19:42, have we *e.* at all of the king's cost?
1Ki. 19:5; Acts 10:13; 11:7, angel said, Arise and *e.*
2Ki. 4:43, 44, they shall *e.*, and leave thereof.
6:28, give thy son, that we may *e.* him.
Neh. 5:2, corn, that we may *e.*, and live.
Job 3:24, my sighing cometh before I *e.*
5:5, whose harvest the hungry *e.* up.
6:6, *e.* without salt.
21:25, another never *e.* with pleasure.
31:17, have *e.* my morsel alone.
Ps. 22:26, meek shall *e.* and be satisfied.
69:9; Jn. 2:17, zeal hath *e.* me up.
102:9, have *e.* ashes like bread.
Prov. 1:31; Isa. 3:10, *e.* fruit of their own way.
13:25, *e.* to satisfying of soul.
18:21, they that love it shall *e.* the fruit.
23:1, sittest to *e.* with ruler.
24:13, *e.* honey, because it is good.
25:27, not good to *e.* much honey.
Eccl. 2:25, who can *e.* more than I?
4:5, fool *e.* his own flesh.
5:11, goods increase, they increased that *e.*
12, sleep be sweet, whether he *e.* little or much
17, all his days also he *e.* in darkness.
19; 6:2, not power to *e.* thereof.
10:16, thy princes *e.* in the morning.
17, blessed when princes *e.* in due season.
Isa. 4:1, we will *e.* our own bread.
7:15, 22, butter and honey shall he *e.*
11:7; 65:25, lion *e.* straw like ox.
29:8, he *e.*, awaketh, and is hungry.
51:8, worm shall *e.* them like wool.
55:1, come ye, buy and *e.*
2, *e.* ye that which is good.
10, give bread to the *e.*
65:13, my servants shall *e.*, but ye shall be.
Jer. 5:17, they shall *e.* up thine harvest.
15:16, words were found, and I did *e.* them.
24:2; 29:17, figs could not be *e.*
31:29; Ezek. 18:2, the fathers have *e.* sour grapes.
Ezek. 3:1, 2, 3, *e.* this roll.
4:10, *e.* by weight.
Dan. 4:33, *e.* grass as oxen.
Hos. 4:10; Mic. 6:14; Hag. 1:6, *e.*, and not have enough.
10:13, have *e.* the fruit of lies.
Mic. 7:1, there is not cluster to *e.*
Mt. 6:25; Lk. 12:22, what ye shall *e.*
9:11; Mk. 2:16; Lk. 15:2, why *e.* with publicans?
12:1, ears of corn, and *e.*
4, *e.* shewbread, which was not lawful to *e.*
14:16; Mk. 6:37; Lk. 9:13, give ye them to *e.*
15:20, to *e.* with unwashen hands
15:27; Mk. 7:28, dogs *e.* of crumbs.
32; Mk. 8:1, multitude have nothing to *e.*
24:49, to *e.* and drink with the drunken.
Mk. 2:16, when they saw him *e.* with.
6:31, no leisure so much as to *e.*
11:14, no man *e.* fruit of thee.
Lk. 5:33, but thy disciples *e.* and drink.
10:8, *e.* such things as are set before you.
12:19, take thine ease, *e.*, drink.
13:26, we have *e.* and drunk in thy presence.
Lk. 15:23, let us *e.* and be merry.
22:30, that ye may *e.* at my table.
24:43, he took it, and did *e.* before them.
Jn. 4:31, Master, *e.*
32, meat to *e.* ye know not of.
6:26, because ye did *e.* of loaves.
52, can this man give us his flesh to *e.*?
53, except ye *e.* the flesh.
Acts 2:46, did *e.* their meat with gladness.
9:9, Saul did neither *e.* nor drink.
11:3, thou didst *e.* with them.
23:14, will *e.* nothing until we have slain Paul.

Rom. 14:2, one believeth he may *e.* all things; weak *e.* herbs.
6, *e.* to the Lord.
20, who *e.* with offence.
21, neither to *e.* flesh nor drink wine.
1Cor. 5:11, with such an one no not to *e.*
8:7, *e.* it as a thing offered to idol.
8, neither if we *e.* are we better.
13, I will *e.* no flesh while world.
9:4, have we not power to *e.*?
10:3, all *e.* same spiritual meat.
27, *e.*, asking no question.
31, whether ye *e.* or drink.
11:29, he that *e.* unworthily.
2Th. 3:10, work not, neither should he *e.*
Heb. 13:10, whereof they have no right to *e.*
Rev. 2:7, *e.* of the tree of life.
17, will give to *e.* of hidden manna.
19:18, *e.* flesh of kings.
See Jud. 14:14; Prov. 31:27; Isa. 1:19; 65:4.
EDGE. Prov. 5:4; Heb. 4:12; Eccl. 10:10.
EDIFY. Rom. 14:19, wherewith one may *e.*
15:2, please his neighbour to *e.*
1Cor. 8:1, charity *e.*
14:3, he that prophesieth speaketh to *e.*
4, *e.* himself, *e.* the church.
10:23, all things lawful, but *e.* not.
Eph. 4:12, for *e.* of the body of Christ.
See 2Cor. 10:8; 13:10; 1Tim. 1:4.
EFFECT. Num. 30:8, make vow of none *e.*
2Chr. 7:11, Solomon prosperously *e.* all.
Ps. 33:10, devices of the people of none *e.*
Isa. 32:17, the *e.* of righteousness quietness.
Mt. 15:6; Mk. 7:13, commandment of God of none *e.*
1Cor. 1:17, lest cross be of none *e.*
Gal. 5:4, Christ is become of none *e.*
See Rom. 3:3; 4:14; 9:6; Gal. 3:17.
EFFECTUAL. 1Cor. 16:9, a great door and *e.* is opened.
Eph. 3:7; 4:16, the *e.* working.
Jas. 5:16, *e.* prayer of righteous man.
See 2Cor. 1:6; Gal. 2:8; 1Th. 2:13.
EFFEMINATE. 1Cor. 6:9.
EGG. Job 6:6, taste in the white of an *e.*
39:14, ostrich leaveth *e.* in earth.
Lk. 11:12, if he ask an *e.*
See Dt. 22:6; Isa. 10:14; 59:5; Jer. 17:11.
EITHER. Gen. 31:24, speak not *e.* good or bad.
Eccl. 11:6, prosper, *e.* this or that.
Mt. 6:24; Lk. 16:13, *e.* hate the one.
Jn. 19:18, on *e.* side one.
Rev. 22:2, on *e.* side the river.
See Dt. 17:3; 28:51; Isa. 7:11; Mt. 12:33.
ELDER. 1Sam. 15:30, honour me before *e.* of people.
Job 15:10, aged men, much *e.* than thy father.
32:4, waited, because they were *e.* than he.
Prov. 31:23, husband known among *e.*
Mt. 15:2; Mk. 7:3, tradition of the *e.*
1Tim. 5:17, let *e.* that rule be worthy.
Ti. 1:5, ordain *e.* in every city.
Heb. 11:2, the *e.* obtained good report.
Jas. 5:14, call for *e.* of the church.
1Pet. 5:1, the *e.* I exhort, who am an *e.*
5, younger submit to the *e.*
See Jn. 8:9 1Tim. 5:2; 2Jn. 1; 3Jn. 1.
ELECT. Isa. 42:1, mine *e.*, in whom my soul delighteth.
Isa. 45:4, mine *e.* I have called by name.
65:9, 22, mine *e.* shall inherit.
Mt. 24:22; Mk. 13:20, for *e.* sake days shortened
24; Mk. 13:22, deceive very *e.*
31; Mk. 13:27, gather together his *e.*
Lk. 18:7, avenge his own *e.*
Rom. 8:33, to charge of God's *e.*
Col. 3:12, put on as the *e.* of God.
1Tim. 5:21, charge thee before *e.* angels.
1Pet. 1:2, *e.* according to foreknowledge.
2:6, corner stone, *e.*, precious.
See 2Tim. 2:10; Ti. 1:1; 1Pet. 5:13; 2Jn. 1:13.
ELECTION. Rom. 9:11; 11:5; 1Th. 1:4; 2Pet. 1:10.
ELEMENTS. Gal. 4:3, 9; 2Pet. 3:10.
ELEVEN. Gen. 32:22, Jacob took his *e.* sons.
37:9, and *e.* stars made obeisance.
Acts 1:26, he was numbered with the *e.*
See Mt. 28:16; Mk. 16:14; Lk. 24:9.
ELOQUENT. Ex. 4:10; Isa. 3:3; Acts 18:24.
EMBALMED. Gen. 50:2, the days of those which are *e.*
26, and they *e.* him.
See Jn. 19:39.
EMBOLDEN. Job 16:3; 1Cor. 8:10.
EMBRACE. Job 24:8, *e.* rock for want of shelter.
Eccl. 3:5, a time to *e.*
Heb. 11:13, seen and *e.* promises.
See Prov. 4:8; 5:20; Lam. 4:5; Acts 20:1.
EMBROIDER. Ex. 28:39; 35:35; 38:23.
EMERALDS. Ex. 28:18; 39:11; Rev. 4:3; 21:19.
EMERODS. Dt. 28:27, and with *e.*
1Sam. 5:6, and smote them with *e.*
EMINENT. Ezek. 16:24, 31, 39; 17:22.
EMPIRE. Est. 1:20.
EMPLOY. Dt. 20:19; 1Chr. 9:3; Ezra. 10:15; Ezek. 39:14.
EMPTY. Gen. 31:42; Mk. 12:3; Lk. 1:53; 20:10, sen *e.* away.
Ex. 3:21, ye shall not go *e.*
23:15; 34:20; Dt. 16:16, appear before me *e.*
Dt. 15:13, not let him go away *e.*
Job 22:9, thou hast sent widows away *e.*
Eccl. 11:3, clouds *e.* themselves on the earth.
Isa. 29:8, awaketh, and his soul is *e.*
Jer. 48:11, Moab *e.* from vessel to vessel.
Nah. 2:2, the emptiers have *e.* them out.
Mt. 12:44, come, he findeth it *e.*
See 2Sam. 1:22; 2Ki. 4:3; Hos. 10:1.
EMULATION. Rom. 11:14; Gal. 5:20.
ENABLED. 1Tim. 1:12.
ENCAMP. Ps. 27:3, though host *e.* against me.
34:7, angel of Lord *e.* round.
See Num. 10:31; Job 19:12; Ps. 53:5.
ENCOUNTERED. Acts 17:18.
ENCOURAGE. Dt. 1:38; 3:28; 2Sam. 11:25, *e.* him.
Ps. 64:5, they *e.* themselves in an evil matter.
See 1Sam. 30:6; 2Chr. 31:4; 35:2; Isa. 41:7

ND. Gen. 6:13, the *e.* of all flesh before me.
Ex. 23:16; Dt. 11:12, in the *e.* of the year.
Num. 23:10, let my last *e.* be like his.
Dt. 8:16, do thee good at thy latter *e.*
32:29, consider their latter *e.*
Job 6:11, what is mine *e.*, that I should prolong?
8:7; 42:12, thy latter *e.* shall increase.
16:3, shall vain words have an *e.*?
26:10, till day and night come to an *e.*
Ps. 7:9, wickedness of wicked come to an *e.*
9:6, destructions come to perpetual *e.*
37:37, the *e.* of that man is peace.
39:4, make me to know my *e.*
73:17, then understood I their *e.*
102:27, the same, thy years have no *e.*
107:27, are at their wit's *e.*
119:96, an *e.* on all perfection.
Prov. 14:12, the *e.* thereof are ways of death.
17:24, eyes of fool in *e.* of earth.
19:20, be wise in thy latter *e.*
25:8, lest thou know not what to do in *e.*
Eccl. 3:11, find out from beginning to the *e.*
4:8, no *e.* of all his labour.
Eccl. 4:16, no *e.* of all the people.
7:2, that is the *e.* of all men.
8, better the *e.* of a thing.
10:13, the *e.* of his talk is madness.
12:12, of making books there is no *e.*
Isa. 9:7, of his government shall be no *e.*
46:10, declaring *e.* from beginning.
Jer. 5:31, what will ye do in *e.* thereof?
8:20, harvest past, summer *e.*
17:11, at his *e.* shall be a fool.
29:11, to give you an expected *e.*
31:17, there is hope in thine *e.*
Lam. 1:9, remembereth not her last *e.*
4:18; Ezek. 7:2, our *e.* is near, *e.* is come.
Ezek. 21:25; 35:5, iniquity shall have an *e.*
Dan. 8:17, 19; 11:27, at the time of *e.*
11:45, he shall come to his *e.*, and none shall help him.
12:8, what shall be the *e.*?
13, go thy way till the *e.* be.
Hab. 2:3, at the *e.* it shall speak.
Mt. 10:22; 24:13; Mk. 13:13, endureth to *e.*
13:39, harvest is *e.* of the world.
24:3, what sign of the *e.* of the world?
6; Mk. 13:7; Lk. 21:9, the *e.* is not yet.
14, then shall the *e.* come.
31, gather from one *e.* of heaven.
26:58, Peter sat to see the *e.*
28:20, I am with you, even unto the *e.*
Mk. 3:26, cannot stand, but hath an *e.*
Lk. 1:33, of his kingdom there shall be no *e.*
22:37, things concerning me have an *e.*
Jn. 13:1, he loved them unto the *e.*
18:37, to this *e.* was I born.
Rom. 6:21, the *e.* of those things is death.
22, the *e.* everlasting life.
10:4, the *e.* of the law for righteousness.
1Cor. 10:11, on whom *e.* of world are come.
Phil. 3:19, whose *e.* is destruction.
1Tim. 1:5, the *e.* of the commandment.
Heb. 6:8, whose *e.* is to be burned.
16, an oath an *e.* of strife.
7:3, neither beginning nor *e.* of life.
9:26, once in the *e.* hath he appeared.
13:7, considering *e.* of their conversation.
Jas. 5:11, ye have seen *e.* of the Lord.
1Pet. 1:9, receiving the *e.* of your faith.
13, be sober, and hope to the *e.*
4:7, the *e.* of all things is at hand.
17, what shall the *e.* be of them that obey not?
Rev. 2:26, keepeth my works unto *e.*
21:6; 22:13, the beginning and the *e.*
See Ps. 19:6; 65:5; Isa. 45:22; 52:10; Jer. 4:27
ENDAMAGE. Ezra. 4:13.
ENDANGER. Eccl. 10:9; Dan 1:10.
ENDEAVOUR. Ps. 28:4; Eph. 4:3; 2Pet. 1:15.
ENDLESS. 1Tim. 1:4; Heb. 7:16.
ENDUE. Gen. 30:20; 2Chr. 2:12; Lk. 24:49; Jas. 3:13.
ENDURE. Gen. 33:14, as the children be able to *e.*
Est. 8:6, how can I *e.* to see evil?
Job 8:15, hold it fast, but it shall not *e.*
31:23, I could not *e.*
Ps. 9:7; 102:12; 104:31, Lord shall *e.* for ever.
30:5, anger *e.* a moment, weeping *e.* for a night.
52:1, goodness of God *e.* continually.
72:5, as long as sun and moon *e.*
17, his name shall *e.* for ever.
100:5, his truth *e.* to all generations.
106:1; 107:1; 118:1; 136:1; 138:8; Jer. 33:11, his mercy *e.* for ever.
111:3; 112:3, 9, his righteousness *e.* for ever.
119:160, every one of thy judgments *e.*
135:13, thy name, O Lord, *e.* for ever.
145:13, thy dominion *e.*
Prov. 27:24, doth *e.* to every generation.
Ezek. 22:14, can thy heart *e.*?
Mt. 10:22; 24:13; Mk. 13:13, *e.* to the end.
Mk. 4:17, so *e.* but for a time.
Jn. 6:27, meat that *e.* unto life.
Rom. 9:22, God *e.* with much longsuffering.
1Cor. 13:7, charity *e.* all things.
2Tim. 2:3, *e.* hardness as good soldier.
4:3, they will not *e.* sound doctrine.
5, watch, *e.* afflictions.
Heb. 10:34, in heaven a better and *e.* substance.
12:7, if ye *e.* chastening.
Jas. 1:12, blessed is man that *e.* temptation.
5:11, we count them happy which *e.*
1Pet. 1:25, the word of the Lord *e.* for ever.
2:19, if a man for conscience *e.* grief.
See Heb. 10:32; 11:27; 12:2, 3.
ENEMY. Ex. 23:22, I will be *e.* to thine *e.*
Dt. 32:31, our *e.* themselves being judges.
Josh. 7:12, Israel turned backs before *e.*
Jud. 5:31, so let all thy *e.* perish.
1Sam. 24:19, if man find *e.*, will he let him go?
1Ki. 21:20, hast thou found me, O mine *e.*?
Job 13:24, wherefore holdest thou me for *e.*?
Ps. 8:2, still the *e.* and avenger.
23:5, in presence of mine *e.*

38:19, mine *e.* are lively.
61:3, a strong tower from the *e.*
72:9, his *e.* shall lick the dust.
119:98, wise than mine *e.*
127:5, speak with *e.* in the gate.
139:22, I count them mine *e.*
Prov. 16:7, maketh his *e.* at peace.
24:17, rejoice not when *e.* falleth.
25:21; Rom. 12:20, if *e.* hunger, give bread.
27:6, kisses of *e.* deceitful.
Isa. 9:11, Lord shall join *e.* together.
59:19, when *e.* shall come in like a flood.
63:10, he was turned to be their *e.*
Jer. 15:11, will cause *e.* to entreat thee well.
30:14, wounded thee with wound of *e.*
Mic. 7:6, man's *e.* men of his own house.
Mt. 5:43, said, thou shalt hate thine *e.*
44; Lk. 6:27, 35, I say, love your *e.*
13:25, 28, 39, his *e.* sowed tares.
Lk. 19:43, thine *e.* shall cast a trench.
Acts 13:10, thou *e.* of all righteousness.
Rom. 5:10, if when *e.* we were reconciled.
11:28, concerning the gospel they are *e.*
Gal. 4:16, am I become your *e.*?
Phil. 3:18, the *e.* of the cross.
Col. 1:21, were *e.* in your mind.
2Th. 3:15, count him not as an *e.*
Jas. 4:4, friend of the world is the *e.* of God.
See Ps. 110:1; Isa. 62:8; Jer. 15:14; Heb. 10:13.
ENGAGED. Jer. 30:21.
ENGINES. 2Chr. 26:15, and he made in Jerusalem *e.*
Ezek. 26:9, and he shall set *e.* of war.
ENGRAFTED. Jas. 1:21.
ENGRAVE. Ex. 28:11; 35:35; 38:23; Zech. 3:9; 2Cor. 3:7.
ENJOIN. Job 36:23; Phile. 8; Heb. 9:20.
ENJOY. Lev. 26:34; 2Chr. 36:21, land shall *e.* her sabbaths.
Eccl. 2:1, *e.* pleasure, this also is vanity.
24; 3:13; 5:18, soul *e.* good.
1Tim. 6:17, giveth us all things to *e.*
See Num. 36:8; Isa. 65:22; Heb. 11:25.
ENLARGE. Dt. 12:20, when the Lord shall *e.* thy border.
Ps. 4:1, thou hast *e.* me in distress.
25:17, troubles of heart *e.*
119:32, when thou shalt *e.* my heart.
Isa. 5:14, hell hath *e.* herself.
2Cor. 6:11, 13; 10:15, our heart is *e.*
See Isa. 54:2; Hab. 2:5; Mt. 23:5.
ENLIGHTEN. Ps. 19:8; Eph. 1:18; Heb. 6:4.
ENMITY. Rom. 8:7, carnal mind is *e.*
Eph. 2:15, 16, having abolished the *e.*
Jas. 4:4, friendship of world *e.* with God.
See Gen. 3:15; Num. 35:21; Lk. 23:12.
ENOUGH. Gen. 33:9, 11, I have *e.*, my brother.
45:28, it is *e.*, Joseph is alive.
Ex. 36:5, people bring more than *e.*
2Sam. 24:16; 1Ki. 19:4; 1Chr. 21:15; Mk. 14:41; Lk. 22:38, it is *e.*, stay thine hand.
Prov. 28:19, shall have poverty *e.*
30:15, four things say not, it is *e.*
16, fire saith not, it is *e.*
Isa. 56:11, dogs which can never have *e.*
Jer. 49:9, will destroy till they have *e.*
Hos. 4:10, eat, and not have *e.*
Obad. 5, stolen till they had *e.*
Mal. 3:10, room *e.* to receive it.
Mt. 10:25, *e.* for disciple.
25:9, lest there be not *e.*
See Dt. 1:6; 2Chr. 31:10; Hag. 1:6; Lk. 15:17.
ENQUIRE. Ex. 18:15, people come to me to *e.* of God.
2Sam. 16:23, as if a man had *e.* of oracle.
2Ki. 3:11, is there not a prophet to *e.*?
Ps. 78:34, returned and *e.* early after God.
Ezek. 14:3, should I be *e.* of at all by them?
20:3, 31, I will not be *e.*
36:37, I will yet for this be *e.* of.
Zeph. 1:6, those that have not *e.* for.
Mt. 10:11, *e.* who in it is worthy.
1Pet. 1:10, of which salvation the prophets *e.*
See Dt. 12:30; Isa. 21:12; Jn. 4:52.
ENRICH. 1Sam. 17:25; Ps. 65:9; Ezek. 27:33; 1Cor. 1:5; 2Cor. 9:11.
ENSAMPLE. 1Cor. 10:11, happened to them for *e.*
Phil. 3:17, as ye have us for an *e.*
2Th. 3:9, to make ourselves an *e.*
See 1Th. 1:7; 1Pet. 5:3; 2Pet. 2:6.
ENSIGN. Ps. 74:4; Isa. 5:26; 11:10; 18:3; 30:17.
ENSNARED. Job 34:30.
ENSUE. 1Pet. 3:11
ENTANGLE. Ex. 14:3; Mt. 22:15; Ga. 5:1
ENTER. Ps. 100:4, *e.* his gates with thanksgiving.
119:130, the *e.* of thy word giveth light.
Isa. 26:2, righteous nation may *e.* in.
20, *e.* thou into thy chambers.
Ezek. 44:5, mark well *e.* in of the house.
Mt. 6:6, prayest, *e.* into thy closet.
7:13; Lk. 13:24, *e.* in at strait gate.
10:11; Lk. 10:8, 10, what city ye *e.*
18:8; Mk. 9:43, better to *e.* into life.
19:17, if thou wilt *e.* into life, keep.
25:21, well done, *e.* into joy.
Mk. 5:12; Lk. 8:32, we may *e.* into swine.
14:38; Lk. 22:46, lest ye *e.* into temptation.
Lk. 9:34, feared as they *e.* cloud.
13:24, many will seek to *e.*
Jn. 3:4, can he *e.*?
4:38, ye are *e.* into their labours.
10:1, 2, *e.* not by the door.
Rom. 5:12, sin *e.* into world.
1Cor. 2:9, neither have *e.* into heart of man.
Heb. 3:11, 18, shall not *e.* into rest.
4:10, he that is *e.* into rest.
6:20, forerunner is for us *e.*
2Pet. 1:11, so an *e.* shall be ministered.
See Ps. 143:2; Prov. 17:10; Mt. 15:17.
ENTICE. Jud. 14:15; 16:5, *e.* husband that he may declare.
2Chr. 18:19, Lord said, who shall *e.* Ahab?
Prov. 1:10, if sinners *e.* thee.
1Cor. 2:4; Col. 2:4, with *e.* words.
See Job 31:27; Prov. 16:29; Jas. 1:14.
ENTIRE. Jas. 1:4.
ENTREAT. Mt. 22:6; Lk. 18:32, *e.* them spitefully.

ᴎTRY. 1Chr. 9:19; Prov. 8:3; Ezek. 8:5; 40:38.
ᴎVIRON. Josh. 7:9.
ᴎVY. Job 5:2, *e.* slayeth the silly one.
Ps. 73:3, I was *e.* at the foolish.
Prov. 3:31, *e.* not the oppressor.
14:30, *e.* is rottenness of the bones.
23:17, let not heart *e.* sinners.
24:1, 19, be not *e.* against evil men.
27:4, who is able to stand before *e.*?
Eccl. 4:4, for this a man is *e.*
9:6, their love, hatred, and *e.* is perished.
Mt. 27:18; Mk. 15:10, for *e.* they delivered.
Acts 7:9, patriarchs moved with *e.*
13:45; 17:5, Jews filled with *e.*
Rom. 1:29, full of *e.*, murder.
13:13, walk honestly, not in *e.*
1Cor. 3:3, among you *e.* and strife.
13:4, charity *e.* not.
2Cor. 12:20, I fear lest there be *e.*
Gal. 5:21, works of flesh are *e.*, murders.
26, *e.* one another.
Phil. 1:15, preach Christ even of *e.*
1Tim. 6:4, whereof cometh *e.*
Ti. 3:3, living in malice and *e.*
Jas. 4:5, spirit in us lusteth to *e.*
See Gen. 37:11; Ps. 106:16; Ezek. 31:9; 35:11.
ᴘHAH. Ex. 16:36, now an omer is the tenth part of an *e.*
Lev. 19:36, a just *e.* shall ye have.
Ezek. 45:10, ye shall have just balances, and a just *e.*
Zech. 5:6, this is an *e.* that goeth forth.
ᴘHOD. Ex. 28:6, they shall make the *e.* of gold.
Ex. 39:2, and he made the *e.* of gold.
Jud. 8:27, and Gideon made an *e.* thereof.
17:5, and made an *e.*
ᴘISTLE. 2Cor. 3:1, nor need *e.* of commendation.
2, ye are our *e.*
3, to be the *e.* of Christ.
2Th. 2:15; 3:14, by word or *e.*
2Pet. 3:16, as also in all his *e.*
See Acts 15:30; 23:33; 2Cor. 7:8; 2Th. 3:17.
QUAL. Ps. 17:2, eyes behold things that are *e.*
55:13, a man mine *e.*, my guide.
Prov. 26:7, legs of lame not *e.*
Isa. 40:25; 46:5, to whom shall I be *e.*?
Ezek. 18:25, 29; 33:17, 20, is not my way *e.*?
Mt. 20:12, hast made him *e.* to us.
Lk. 20:36, are *e.* to angels.
Jn. 5:18; Phil. 2:6, *e.* with God.
Col. 4:1, give servants what is *e.*
See Ex. 36:22; 2Cor. 8:14; Gal. 1:14.
QUITY. Ps. 98:9, judge the people with *e.*
Prov. 1:3, receive instruction of *e.*
2:9, understand judgment and *e.*
17:26, not good to strike princes for *e.*
Eccl. 2:21, a man whose labour is in *e.*
See Isa. 11:4; 59:14; Mic. 3:9; Mal. 2:6.
RECTED. Gen. 33:20.
RR. Ps. 95:10, people that do *e.* in their heart.
119:21, do *e.* from thy commandments.
Isa. 3:12; 9:16, lead the cause to *e.*
28:7, they *e.* in vision.
35:8, wayfaring men shall not *e.*
Mt. 22:29; Mk. 12:24, *e.*, not knowing scriptures.
1Tim. 6:10, have *e.* from the faith.
21, have *e.* concerning the faith.
Jas. 1:16, do not *e.* beloved brethren.
5:19, if any do *e.* from truth.
See Isa. 28:7; 29:24; Ezek. 45:20.
ERRAND. Gen. 24:33; Jud. 3:19; 2Ki. 9:5.
ERROR. Ps. 19:12, who can understand his *e.*?
Eccl. 5:6, neither say thou, it was an *e.*
10:5, evil which I have seen as an *e.*
Mt. 27:64, last *e.* worse than first.
Jas. 5:20, converteth sinner from *e.*
2Pet. 3:17, led away with *e.* of wicked.
1Jn. 4:6, the spirit of *e.*
See Job 19:4; Rom. 1:27; Heb. 9:7; Jude 11.
ESCAPE. Gen. 19:17, *e.* for thy life, *e.* to mountain.
1Ki. 18:40; 2Ki. 9:15, let none of them. *e.*
Est. 4:13, think not thou shalt *e.* in king's house.
Job 11:20, wicked shall not *e.*
19:20, *e.* with skin of my teeth.
Ps. 55:8, I would hasten my *e.*
Prov. 19:5, speaketh lies shall not *e.*
Eccl. 7:26, whoso pleaseth God shall *e.*
Isa. 20:6; Heb. 2:3, how shall we *e.*?
Ezek. 33:21, one that had *e.* came to me.
Amos. 9:1, he that *e.* shall not be delivered.
Mt. 23:33, how can ye *e.* damnation?
Lk. 21:36, worthy to *e.*
Jn. 10:39, he *e.* out of their hands.
Acts 27:44, they *e.* all safe to land.
28:4, he *e.* sea, yet vengeance.
Heb. 11:34, through faith *e.* edge of sword.
12:25, if they *e.* not who refused.
2Pet. 1:4, *e.* corruption in the world.
20, after they *e.* pollutions.
See Dt. 23:15; Ps. 124:7; 1Cor. 10:13.
ESCHEW. Job 1:1; 2:3; 1Pet. 3:11.
ESPECIALLY. Gal. 6:10; 1Tim. 4:10; 5:8; Phile. 16.
ESPOUSE. Song 3:11; Jer. 2:2; 2Cor. 11:2.
ESPY. Gen. 42:27; Josh. 14:7; Jer. 48:19; Ezek. 20:6.
ESTABLISH. Ps. 40:2, and *e.* my goings.
90:17, *e.* work of our hands.
Prov. 4:26, let thy ways be *e.*
12:19, lip of truth *e.* for ever.
16:12, throne *e.* by righteousness.
20:18, every purpose *e.* by counsel.
24:3, by understanding is house *e.*
29:4, king by judgment *e.* the land.
Isa. 7:9, if ye will not believe, ye shall not be *e.*
16:5, in mercy shall the throne be *e.*
Jer. 10:12; 51:15, he *e.* world by wisdom.
Mt. 18:16, two witnesses every word *e.*
Rom. 3:31, yea, we *e.* the law.
10:3, to *e.* their own righteousness.
Heb. 13:9, the heart be *e.* with grace.
2Pet. 1:12, be *e.* in the present truth.
See Amos 5:15; Hab. 2:12; Acts 16:5.
ESTATE. Ps. 136:23, remembered us in low *e.*
Eccl. 1:16, lo, I am come to great *e.*
Mk. 6:21, Herod made supper to chief *e.*
Rom. 12:16, condescend to me of low *e.*
Jude 6, angels kept not first *e.*

See Ezek. 36:11; Dan. 11:7; Lk. 1:48.
ESTEEM. Dt. 32:15, lightly *e.* rock of salvation.
1Sam. 2:30, despise me shall be lightly *e.*
18:23, I am a poor man, and lightly *e.*
Job 23:12, I have *e.* the words of his mouth.
36:19, will he *e.* thy riches?
41:27, he *e.* iron as straw.
Ps. 119:128, I *e.* all thy precepts.
Isa. 53:4, did *e.* him smitten.
Lam. 4:2, *e.* as earthen pitchers.
Lk. 16:15, highly *e.* among men.
Rom. 14:5, one man *e.* one day above another.
14, that *e.* any thing unclean.
Phil. 2:3, let each *e.* other better.
1Th. 5:13, *e.* highly for work's sake.
Heb. 11:26, *e.* reproach greater riches.
See Prov. 17:28; Isa. 29:17; 1Cor. 6:4.
ESTIMATION. Lev. 27:2-8, 13; Num. 18:16.
ESTRANGED. Job 19:13; Ps. 78:30; Jer. 19:4; Ezek. 14:5.
ETERNAL. Dt. 33:27, the *e.* God is thy refuge.
Isa. 60:15, will make thee an *e.* excellency.
Mt. 19:16; Mk. 10:17; Lk. 10:25; 18:18, what shall I do that I may have *e.* life?
25:46, righteous into life *e.*
Mk. 3:29, is in danger of *e.* damnation.
10:30, receive in world to come *e.* life.
Jn. 3:15, believeth in him have *e.* life.
4:36, gathereth fruit unto life *e.*
5:39, scriptures, in them *e.* life.
6:54, drinketh my blood hath *e.* life.
68, thou hast words of *e.* life.
10:28, give sheep *e.* life.
12:25, hateth life, shall keep it to life *e.*
17:2, give *e.* life to as many.
3, this is life *e.*, that they might know thee.
Acts 13:48, many as were ordained to *e.* life.
Rom. 2:7, who seek for glory, *e.* life.
5:21, grace reign to *e.* life.
6:23, gift of God is *e.* life.
2Cor. 4:17, an *e.* weight of glory.
2 Cor. 4:18, things not seen are *e.*
5:1, house *e.* in the heavens.
Eph. 3:11, according to *e.* purpose.
1Tim. 6:12, 19, lay hold on *e.* life.
Ti. 1:2; 3:7, in hope of *e.* life.
Heb. 5:9, author of *e.* salvation.
6:2, doctrine of *e.* judgment.
9:15, promise of *e.* inheritance.
1Pet. 5:10, called to *e.* glory by Christ.
1Jn. 1:2, *e.* life, which was with the Father.
2:25, this is the promise, even *e.* life.
3:15, no murderer hath *e.* life.
5:11, record, that God hath given to us *e.* life.
13, know that ye have *e.* life.
20, this is true God, and *e.* life.
Jude 7, vengeance of *e.* fire.
See Rom. 1:20; 1Tim. 1:17; 2Tim. 2:10; Jude 21.
ETERNITY. Isa. 57:15.
EUNUCHS. Isa. 56:4, for thus saith the Lord to the *e.*
Mt. 19:12, for there are some *e.*
Acts 8:27, an *e.* of great authority.
See Isa. 56:3.
EVANGELIST. Acts 21:8; Eph. 4:11; 2Tim. 4:5.
EVENING. 1Sam. 14:24, cursed that eateth till *e.*
1Ki. 17:6, brought bread morning and *e.*
Ps. 90:6, in *e.* cut down and withereth.
104:23, goeth to his labour until the *e.*
141:2, prayer as the *e.* sacrifice.
Eccl. 11:6, in *e.* withhold not thine hand.
Jer. 6:4, shadows of *e.* stretched out.
Hab. 1:8; Zeph. 3:3, *e.* wolves.
Zech. 14:7, at *e.* time shall be light.
Mt. 14:23, when *e.* was come, he was there alone.
Lk. 24:29, abide, for it is toward *e.*
See Gen. 30:16; Ps. 65:8; Mt. 16:2; Mk. 14:17.
EVENT. Eccl. 2:14; 9:2, 3.
EVER. Gen. 3:22, lest he eat, and live for *e.*
43:9; 44:32, let me bear blame for *e.*
Ex. 14:13, ye shall see them no more for *e.*
Lev. 6:13, fire *e.* burning on altar.
Dt. 5:29; 12:28, be well with them for *e.*
13:16, a heap for *e.*
32:40, lift up hand and say, I live for *e.*
Job 4:7, who *e.* perished?
Ps. 9:7, Lord shall endure for *e.*
12:7, thou wilt preserve them for *e.*
22:26, your heart shall live for *e.*
23:6, dwell in house of the Lord for *e.*
29:10, Lord sitteth king for *e.*
33:11, counsel of Lord standeth for *e.*
37:26, he is *e.* merciful, and lendeth.
48:14, our God for *e.* and *e.*
49:9, that he should still live for *e.*
51:3, my sin is *e.* before me.
52:8, trust in mercy of God for *e.* and *e.*
61:4, will abide in tabernacle for *e.*
73:26, my strength and portion for *e.*
74:19, forget not congregation of poor for *e.*
81:15, their time should have endured for *e.*
92:7, they shall be destroyed for *e.*
93:5, holiness becometh thine house for *e.*
102:12, thou shalt endure for *e.*
103:9, not keep his anger for *e.*
105:8, remember his covenant for *e.*
119:89, for *e.* thy word is settled.
132:14, this is my rest for *e.*
146:6, Lord keepeth truth for *e.*
10, Lord shall reign for *e.*
Prov. 27:24, riches not for *e.*
Eccl. 3:14, whatsoever God doeth shall be for *e.*
Isa. 26:4, trust in Lord for *e.*
32:17, assurance for *e.*
34:10; Rev. 14:11; 19:3, smoke shall go up fo
e.
40:8, word of God shall stand for *e.*
57:16, will not contend for *e.*
Lam. 3:31, Lord will not cast off for *e.*
Mt. 6:13, thine is the glory for *e.*
Mt. 21:19; Mk. 11:14, no fruit grow on thee for
Jn. 8:35, servant abideth not for *e.*
12:34, heard that Christ abideth for *e.*
14:16, Comforter abide for *e.*
Rom. 9:5, God blessed for *e.*

1Th. 4:17, so shall we *e.* be with the Lord.
5:15, *e.* follow good.
2Tim. 3:7, *e.* learning.
Heb. 7:25, he *e.* liveth to make.
13:8, same yesterday, to day, and for *e.*
See Mt. 24:21; Lk. 15:31; Jn. 10:8.
EVERLASTING. Ex. 40:15; Num. 25:13, an *e.* priesthood.
Ps. 90:2, from *e.* to *e.* thou art God.
139:24, lead me in way *e.*
Prov. 8:23, I was set up from *e.*
10:25, righteous in an *e.* foundation.
Isa. 9:6, called the *e.* Father.
26:4, in the Lord is *e.* strength.
33:14, with *e.* burnings.
35:10; 51:11; 61:7, *e.* joy.
45:17, with *e.* salvation.
54:8, with *e.* kindness.
55:13, for an *e.* sign.
56:5; 63:12, an *e.* name.
60:19, 20, an *e.* light.
Jer. 31:3, with an *e.* love.
Hab. 3:6, the *e.* mountains.
Mt. 18:8; 25:41, into *e.* fire.
19:29, inherit *e.* life.
25:46, into *e.* punishment.
Lk. 16:9, into *e.* habitations.
18:30, in world to come *e.* life.
Jn. 3:16, 36, believeth shall have *e.* life.
4:14, water springing up into *e.* life.
5:24, heareth my word hath *e.* life.
6:27, meat which endureth to *e.* life.
40, seeth Son may have *e.* life.
12:50, his commandment is life *e.*
Acts 13:46, unworthy of *e.* life.
Rom. 6:22, free from sin, the end *e.* life.
Gal. 6:8, of Spirit reap life *e.*
2Th. 1:9, punished with *e.* destruction.
2:16, given us *e.* consolation.
Jude 6, reserved in *e.* chains.
Rev. 14:6, having the *e.* gospel.
See Dan. 4:3; 7:27; 2Pet. 1:11.
EVERMORE. Ps. 16:11, pleasures for *e.*
37:27, do good and dwell for *e.*
121:8, preserve thy going out for *e.*
133:3, the blessing, life for *e.*
Jn. 6:34, *e.* give us this bread.
1Th. 5:16, rejoice *e.*
Heb. 7:28, consecrated for *e.*
Rev. 1:18, I am alive for *e.*
See 2Ki. 17:37; Ps. 77:8; 106:31.
EVERY. Gen. 4:14, *e.* one that findeth me shall slay me.
6:5, *e.* imagination of heart evil.
Lev. 19:10, neither shalt gather *e.* grape.
Dt. 4:4, alive *e.* one of you this day.
2Ki. 18:31, eat *e.* one of his fig tree.
2Chr. 30:18, pardon *e.* one.
Ps. 29:9, *e.* one doth speak of glory.
32:6, for this shall *e.* one that is godly.
68:30, till *e.* one submit himself.
119:101, refrained from *e.* evil way.
Prov. 2:9, *e.* good path.
7:12, in *e.* corner.
14:15, simple believeth *e.* word.
20:3, *e.* fool will be meddling.
30:5, *e.* word of God is pure.
Eccl. 10:3, saith to *e.* one he is a fool.
Jer. 51:29, *e.* purpose of the Lord.
Mt. 4:4, by *e.* word that proceedeth.
7:8; Lk. 11:10, *e.* one that asketh.
Mk. 1:45, came from *e.* quarter.
Lk. 19:26, to *e.* one which hath shall be given.
Rom. 14:11, *e.* knee bow, *e.* tongue confess.
2Cor. 10:5, *e.* thought.
Eph. 1:21; Phil. 2:9, far above *e.* name.
1Tim. 4:4, *e.* creature of God.
2Tim. 2:19, *e.* one that nameth.
21, *e.* good work.
Heb. 12:1, *e.* weight.
Jas. 1:17, *e.* good and perfect gift.
1Pet. 2:13, *e.* ordinance of man.
1Jn. 4:1, believe not *e.* spirit.
7, *e.* one that loveth.
Rev. 6:11, robes given to *e.* one.
See Gen. 27:29; Acts 2:38; 17:27; 20:31.
EVIDENCE. Jer. 32:10; Heb. 11:1.
EVIDENT. Gal. 3:1, Christ hath been *e.* set forth.
11, that no man is justified is *e.*
Phil. 1:28, an *e.* token of perdition.
See Job 6:28; Heb. 7:14, 15.
EVIL. Gen. 6:5; 8:21, thoughts of heart only *e.*
47:9, few and *e.* have the days.
Ex. 32:14; 2Sam. 24:16; 1Chr. 21:15, repented of the *e.*
Dt. 28:54, eye *e.* towards his brother.
56, her eye *e.* towards husband.
Job 2:10, receive good, and not *e.*
30:26, looked for good, then *e.* came.
Ps. 34:14; 37:27; Prov. 3:7, depart from *e.*
35:12; 109:5, they rewarded me *e.*
40:12, innumerable *e.* have compassed.
Prov. 14:19, *e.* bow before the good.
15:3, beholding the *e.* and good.
17:13, whoso rewardeth *e.* for good.
Isa. 1:4, a seed of *e.*-doers.
5:20, that call *e.* good, and good *e.*
7:15, 16, refuse the *e.* and choose the good.
Jer. 2:13, have committed two *e.*
19, know it is an *e.* thing and bitter.
24:3; 29:17, *e.* figs, very *e.*
42:6, whether good or *e.*, we will obey.
Mt. 5:45, rise on *e.* and good.
6:34, sufficient unto the day is the *e.* thereof.
7:11; Lk. 11:13, if ye, being *e.*
18, good tree cannot bring forth *e.*
9:4, wherefore think *e.* in your hearts?
Mk. 9:39, lightly speak *e.* of me.
Lk. 6:22, cast out your name as *e.*
35, he is kind to the *e.*
Lk. 6:45, *e.* man bringeth forth *e.*
Jn. 3:20, doeth *e.* hateth light.
18:23, if I have spoken *e.*
Acts 23:5, not speak *e.* of ruler.
Rom. 7:19, the *e.* I would not.
12:9, abhor that which is *e.*

17, recompense to no man *e.* for *e.*
21, overcome *e.* with good.
1Th. 5:22, appearance of *e.*
1Tim. 6:10, the root of all *e.*
2Tim. 4:18; Jas. 3:16, every *e.* work.
Ti. 3:2, speak *e.* of no man.
Jas. 3:8, tongue an unruly *e.*
1Pet. 3:9, not rendering *e.* for *e.*
See Prov. 13:21; Isa. 45:7; Eccl. 12:1; Eph 5:16; 6:13.
EXACT. Dt. 15:2, shall not *e.* it of neighbour.
Neh. 5:7, 10, 11, you *e.* usury.
10:31, leave the *e.* of every debt.
Job 11:6, God *e.* of thee less.
Lk. 3:13, *e.* not more than what is.
See Ps. 89:22; Isa. 58:3; 60:17.
EXALT. 1Chr. 29:11, *e.* as head above all.
Ps. 12:8, when vilest men are *e.*
34:3, let us *e.* his name together.
92:10, my horn shalt thou *e.*
97:9, *e.* far above all gods.
Prov. 4:8, *e.* her, and she shall promote thee.
11:11, by blessing of upright the city is *e.*
14:29, he that is hasty of spirit *e.* folly.
34, righteousness *e.* a nation.
17:19, he that *e.* his gate.
Isa. 2:2; Mic. 4:1, mountain of Lord's house *e.*
Isa. 40:4, every valley shall be *e.*
Ezek. 21:26, *e.* him that is low.
Mt. 11:23; Lk. 10:15, *e.* to heaven.
23:12; Lk. 14:11; 18:14, *e.* himself shall be abased.
2Cor. 11:20, if a man *e.* himself.
12:7, *e.* above measure.
Phil. 2:9, God hath highly *e.* him.
2Th. 2:4, *e.* himself above all that is called.
1Pet. 5:6, he may *e.* in due time.
See Ex. 15:2; Job 24:24; Lk. 1:52; Jas. 1:9.
EXAMINE. Ps. 26:2, *e.* me, O Lord.
Acts 4:9, if we this day be *e.*
22:24, 29, *e.* by scourging.
1Cor. 11:28, let a man *e.* himself.
2Cor. 13:5, *e.* yourselves.
See Ezra 10:16; Acts 24:8; 25:26; 1Cor. 9:3.
EXAMPLE. Jn. 13:15, I have given you an *e.*
1Tim. 4:12, be thou an *e.* of believers.
1Pet. 2:21, Christ suffered, leaving an *e.*
Jude 7, an *e.*, suffering vengeance.
See Mt. 1:19; 1Cor. 10:6; Heb. 4:11; 8:5.
EXCEED. Mt. 5:20, except righteousness *e.*
2Cor. 3:9, ministration doth *e.* in glory.
See 1Sam. 20:41; 2Chr. 9:6; Job 36:9.
EXCEEDING. Gen. 15:1, thy *e.* great reward.
27:34, an *e.* bitter cry.
Num. 14:7, land is *e.* good.
1Sam. 2:3, so *e.* proud.
Ps. 21:6, *e.* glad with thy countenance.
43:4, God my *e.* joy.
119:96, commandment *e.* broad.
Prov. 30:24, four things *e.* wise.
Jon. 1:16, men feared the Lord *e.*
4:6, *e.* glad of the gourd.
Mt. 2:10, with *e.* great joy.
4:8, an *e.* high mountain.
5:12, rejoice and be *e.* glad.
8:28, possessed with devils, *e.* fierce.
17:23; 26:22, they were *e.* sorry.
19:25, they were *e.* amazed.
26:38; Mk. 14:34, my soul is *e.* sorrowful.
Mk. 6:26, king *e.* sorry.
9:3, raiment *e.* white.
Lk. 23:8, Herod was *e.* glad.
Acts 7:20, Moses was *e.* fair.
26:11, being *e.* mad against them.
Rom. 7:13, sin might become *e.* sinful.
2Cor. 4:17, *e.* weight of glory.
7:4, *e.* joyful in our tribulation.
Gal. 1:14, *e.* zealous of traditions.
Eph. 1:19, the *e.* greatness of his power.
2:7, the *e.* riches of his grace.
3:20, able to do *e.* abundantly.
2Th. 1:3, your faith groweth *e.*
2Pet. 1:4, *e.* great and precious promises.
Jude 24, present you faultless with *e.* joy.
See 1Sam. 26:21; Jonah 3:3; Heb. 12:21.
EXCEL. Gen. 49:4, thou shalt not *e.*
Prov. 31:29, thou *e.* them all.
Eccl. 2:13, wisdom *e.* folly.
2Cor. 3:10, the glory that *e.*
See Ps. 103:20; 1Cor. 14:12.
EXCELLENCY. Ex. 15:7, the greatness of thine *e.*
Job 4:21, doth not their *e.* go away?
13:11, shall not his *e.* make you afraid?
Isa. 60:15, will make thee an eternal *e.*
1Cor. 2:1, not with *e.* of speech.
2Cor. 4:7, that the *e.* of the power.
Phil. 3:8, loss for the *e.* of Christ.
See Gen. 49:3; Ex. 15:7; Eccl. 7:12; Ezek. 24:21
EXCELLENT. Job 37:23, *e.* in power.
Ps. 8:1, 9, how *e.* is thy name!
16:3, to the *e.*, in whom is my delight.
36:7, how *e.* thy lovingkindness!
Prov. 8:6; 22:20, I will speak of *e.* things.
12:26, righteous more *e.* than neighbour.
17:7, *e.* speech becometh not a fool.
Prov. 17:27, of an *e.* spirit.
Isa. 12:5, he hath done *e.* things.
28:29, is *e.* in working.
Dan. 5:12; 6:3, *e.* spirit found in Daniel.
Rom. 2:18; Phil. 1:10, things more *e.*
1Cor. 12:31, a more *e.* way.
2Pet. 1:17, voice from the *e.* glory.
See Song 5:15; Lk. 1:3; Heb. 1:4; 8:6; 11:4.
EXCEPT. Gen. 32:26, *e.* thou bless me.
Dt. 32:30, *e.* their Rock had sold them.
Ps. 127:1, *e.* Lord build house.
Amos 3:3, *e.* they be agreed.
Mt. 5:20, *e.* your righteousness exceed.
18:3, *e.* ye be converted.
24:22; Mk. 13:20, *e.* days be shortened.
Mk. 7:3, Pharisees *e.* they wash oft.
Lk. 13:3; Rev. 2:5, 22, *e.* ye repent.
Jn. 3:2, *e.* God be with him.
5, *e.* man be born again.
4:48, *e.* ye see signs and wonders.
20:25, *e.* I see print of nails.

Acts 26:29, *e.* these bonds.
Rom. 10:15, how preach, *e.* they be sent?
1Cor. 15:36, *e.* it die.
2Tim. 2:5, *e.* he strive lawfully.
See Rom. 7:7; 1Cor. 14:5; 15:27; 2Th. 2:3.
XCESS. Mt. 23:25; Eph. 5:18; 1Pet. 4:3,4.
XCHANGE. Mt. 16:26; Mk. 8:37, in *e.* for his soul.
25:27, put money to *e.*
See Gen. 47:17; Lev. 27:10; Ezek. 48:14.
XCLUDE. Rom. 3:27; Gal. 4:17.
XCUSE. Lk. 14:18; Rom. 1:20; 2:15; 2Cor. 12:19.
XECRATION. Jer. 42:18; 44:12.
XECUTE. Dt. 33:21, he *e.* the justice of the Lord.
1Chr. 6:10; 24:2; Lk. 1:8, *e.* priest's office.
Ps. 9:16, Lord known by the judgment he *e.*
103:6, Lord *e.* righteousness and judgment.
Jer. 5:1, if any *e.* judgment, I will pardon.
Jn. 5:27, authority to *e.* judgment.
Rom. 13:4, minister of God to *e.* wrath.
See Hos. 11:9; Mic. 5:15; Joel 2:11.
XERCISE. Ps. 131:1, *e.* myself in things too high.
Jer. 9:24, *e.* lovingkindness.
Mt. 20:25; Mk. 10:42; Lk. 22:25, *e.* dominion.
Acts 24:16, I *e.* myself to have a conscience.
1Tim. 4:7, *e.* thyself unto godliness.
Heb. 5:14, *e.* to discern good and evil.
12:11, to them which are *e.* thereby.
2Pet. 2:14, heart *e.* with covetous practices.
See Eccl. 1:13; 3:10; Ezek. 22:29; Rev. 13:12.
XHORT. Lk. 3:18, many things in his *e.*
Acts 13:15, any words of *e.*
Rom 12:8, he that *e.*, on *e.*
1Tim. 6:2, these things *e.* and teach.
Ti. 1:9, may be able to *e.*
2:15, *e.* and rebuke with authority.
Heb. 3:13; 10:25, *e.* one another daily.
13:22, suffer word of *e.*
See Acts 11:23; 2Cor. 9:5; Ti. 2:6, 9.
XILE. 2Sam. 15:19; Isa. 51:14.
XPECTATION. Ps. 9:18, the *e.* of the poor.
62:5, my *e.* is from him.
Prov. 10:28; 11:7, 23, *e.* of the wicked.
Isa. 20:5, ashamed of their *e.*
6, such is our *e.*
Rom. 8:19, the *e.* of the creature.
Phil. 1:20, my earnest *e.* and hope.
See Jer. 29:11; Acts 3:5; Heb. 10:13.
XPEL. Josh. 23:5; Jud. 11:7; 2Sam. 14:14.
XPENSES. Ezra 6:4, 8.
XPERIENCE. Gen. 30:27; Eccl. 1:16; Rom. 5:4.
XPLOITS. Dan. 11:28, 32.
XPOUND. Jud. 14:14, 19, could not *e.* riddle.
Mk. 4:34, when they were alone, he *e.* all things
Lk. 24:27, *e.* the scriptures.
See Acts 11:4; 18:26; 28:23.
XPRESS. Heb. 1:3.
XPRESSLY. 1Sam. 20:21; Ezek. 1:3; 1Tim. 4:1.
XTEND. Ps. 16:2; 109:12; Isa. 66:12.
XTINCT. Job 17:1; Isa. 43:17.
XTOL. Ps. 30:1; 145:1, I will *e.* thee
68:4, *e.* him that rideth.
See Ps. 66:17; Isa. 52:13; Dan. 4:37.
XTORTION. Ezek. 22:12; Mt. 23:25.
EXTORTIONER. Ps. 109:11, let *e.* catch all he hath.
Isa. 16:4, the *e.* is at an end.
1Cor. 5:11, if any man be an *e.*
See Lk. 18:11; 1Cor. 5:10; 6:10.
EXTREME. Dt. 28:22; Job 35:15.
EYE. Gen. 3:6, pleasant to the *e.*
7, *e.* of both were opened.
27:1, his *e.* were dim.
49:12, his *e.* shall be red with wine.
Num. 10:31, be to us instead of *e.*
16:14, wilt thou put out *e.*?
24:3, 15, man whose *e.* are open said.
Dt. 3:27, lift up *e.*, behold with thine *e.*
12:8; Jud. 17:6; 21:25, right in own *e.*
16:19, gift blind *e.* of wise.
28:32, *e.* look, and fail with longing.
32:10, kept him as apple of *e.*
34:7, his *e.* was not dim.
1Ki. 1:20, *e.* of all Israel upon thee.
8:29, 52; 2Chr. 6:20, 40, *e.* open towards this house.
20:6, whatsoever is pleasant in thine *e.*
2Ki. 6:17, Lord opened *e.* of young man.
20, open the *e.* of these men.
2Chr. 16:9; Zech. 4:10, *e.* of Lord run to and fro.
34:28, nor thine *e.* see all the evil.
Job 7:8; 20:9, *e.* that hath seen me.
11:20, the *e.* of wicked shall fail.
15:12, what do thine *e.* wink at?
19:27, mine *e.* shall behold, and not another.
28:7, path vulture's *e.* hath not seen.
10, his *e.* seeth every precious thing.
29:11, when the *e.* saw me.
15, I was *e.* to the blind.
31:16, caused *e.* of widow to fail.
Ps. 11:4, his *e.* try children of men.
15:4, in whose *e.* a vile person.
19:8, enlightening the *e.*
33:18, *e.* of Lord on them that fear him.
34:15; 1Pet. 3:12, *e.* of Lord on the righteous.
36:1, no fear of God before his *e.*
69:3; 119:82, 123; Lam. 2:11, mine *e.* fail.
77:4, holdest mine *e.* waking.
116:8, delivered mine *e.* from tears.
119:18, open mine *e.*
132:4, not give sleep to mine *e.*
Prov. 10:26, as smoke to the *e.*
20:12, the seeing *e.*
22:9, a bountiful *e.*
23:29, redness of *e.*
27:20, the *e.* of man never satisfied.
30:17, the *e.* that mocketh.
Eccl. 1:8, *e.* is not satisfied with seeing.
2:14, wise man's *e.* are in his head.
6:9, better sight of *e.* than wandering of desire.
11:7, for the *e.* to behold the sun.
Isa. 1:16, I will hide mine *e.* from you.
29:10, the Lord hat closed *e.*
33:17, thine *e.* shall see the king in his beauty.
40:26; Jer. 13:20, lift up your *e.* on high.
Jer. 5:21; Ezek. 12:2, have *e.* and see not.

9:1, mine *e.* a fountain of tears.
13:17, mine *e.* shall weep sore.
14:17, let mine *e.* run down with tears.
24:6, set mine *e.* upon them for good.
Lam. 2:18, let not apple of *e.* cease.
Ezek. 24:16, 25, the desire of thine *e.*
Hab. 1:13, of purer *e.* than to behold evil.
Mt. 5:29, if right *e.* offend thee.
13:16, blessed are your *e.*
18:9; Mk. 9:47, to enter with one *e.*
Mk. 8:18, having *e.*, see ye not?
Lk. 1:2, from beginning were *e.*-witnesses.
24:16, their *e.* were holden.
Jn. 11:37, could not this man, which opened *e.*
Gal. 4:15, have plucked out your *e.*
Eph. 1:18, the *e.* of your understanding.
2Pet. 2:14, having *e.* full of adultery.
1Jn. 2:16, the lust of the *e.*
See Dt. 11:12; Ezra 5:5; Ps. 32:8; Prov. 3:7; 12:15; 15:3; 16:2; 21:2; Mt. 20:33; Jn. 10:21; 1Pet. 3:12.
EYESERVICE. Eph. 6:6; Col. 3:22, not with *e.* as menpleasers.
FABLES. 1Tim. 1:4; 4:7; 2Tim. 4:4; Ti. 1:14; 2Pet. 1:16.
FACE. Gen. 4:14, from thy *f.* shall I be hid.
32:30, I have seen God *f.* to *f.*
Ex. 33:11, Lord spake to Moses *f.* to *f.*
34:29, skin of *f.* shone.
33; 2Cor. 3:13, put vail on *f.*
Lev. 19:32, shall honour the *f.* of the old man.
Dt. 25:9, spit in *f.*, saying.
1Sam. 5:3, Dagon was fallen on his *f.*
2Ki. 4:29, 31, lay staff on *f.* of child.
14:8, let us look one another in *f.*
Ezra 9:7; Dan. 9:7, confusion of *f.*
Neh. 8:6, worshipped with *f.* to ground.
Job 1:11; 2:5, curse thee to thy *f.*
4:15, spirit passed before my *f.*
13:24; Ps. 44:24; 88:14, wherefore hidest thou thy *f.*?
Ps. 13:1, how long wilt thou hide thy *f.*?
27:9; 69:17; 102:2; 143:7, hide not thy *f.*
34:5, *f.* not ashamed.
59:2, sins have hid his *f.* from you.
84:9, look upon *f.* of anointed.
Prov. 27:19, in water *f.* answereth to *f.*
Eccl. 8:1, wisdom maketh *f.* to shine.
Isa. 3:15, ye grind *f.* of the poor.
25:8, wipe tears from off all *f.*
50:7, set my *f.* like flint.
Jer. 2:27, turned their back, and not *f.*
5:3, their *f.* harder than a rock.
30:6, all *f.* turned into paleness.
Dan. 10:6, *f.* as appearance of lightning.
Hos. 5:5, testifieth to his *f.*
Mt. 6:17, wash thy *f.*
11:10; Mk. 1:2; Lk. 7:27, messenger before *f.*
16:3; Lk. 12:56, discern *f.* of sky.
17:2, his *f.* did shine as sun.
18:10, angels behold *f.* of my father.
Lk. 2:31, before *f.* of all people.
9:51, 53, set his *f.* to Jerusalem.
22:64, struck him on *f.*
1Cor. 13:12, then *f.* to *f.*
2Cor. 3:18, all, with open *f.*
Gal. 1:22, I was unknown by *f.*
2:11, withstood him to the *f.*
Jas. 1:23, beholding *f.* in glass.
Rev. 20:11, from whose *f.* earth fled away.
See 1Ki. 19:13; Dan. 1:10; Acts 6:15; 20:25.
FADE. Isa. 1:30, whose leaf *f.*
24:4, earth mourneth and *f.*, the world *f.*
40:7, the flower *f.*
64:6, all *f.* as a leaf.
Jer. 8:13, and the leaf shall *f.*
Ezek. 47:12, whose leaf shall not *f.*
1Pet. 1:4; 5:4, inheritance that *f.* not away.
Jas. 1:11, rich man shall *f.* away.
See 2Sam. 22:46; Ps. 18:45; Isa. 28:1.
FAIL. Gen. 47:16, if money *f.*
Dt. 28:32, thine eyes shall *f.* with longing.
Josh. 21:45; 23:14; 1Ki. 8:56, there *f.* not any good thing.
1Sam. 17:32, let no man's heart *f.* him.
1Ki. 2:4; 8:25, shall not *f.* a man on throne.
17:14, neither shall cruse of oil *f.*
Ezra 4:22, take heed that ye *f.* not.
Job. 14:11, as waters *f.* from sea.
19:14, my kinsfolk have *f.*
Ps. 12:1, the faithful *f.* among men.
31:10; 38:10, my strength *f.* me.
77:8, doth his promise *f.*
89:33, nor suffer my faithfulness to *f.*
142:4, refuge *f.* me.
Eccl. 10:3, his wisdom *f.* him.
12:5, desire shall *f.*
Isa. 15:6, the grass *f.*
19:5, waters shall *f.*
31:3, they shall all *f.* together.
32:6, cause drink of thirsty to *f.*
10, the vintage shall *f.*
34:16, no one of these shall *f.*
38:14, eyes *f.* with looking upward.
41:17, tongue *f.* for thirst.
59:15, truth *f.*
Jer. 14:6, their eyes did *f.*
15:18, as waters that *f.*
48:33, I caused wine to *f.*
Lam. 3:22, his compassions *f.* not.
4:17, our eyes as yet *f.*
Ezek. 12:22, every vision *f.*
Amos 8:4, make poor of land to *f.*
Hab. 3:17, labour of olive shall *f.*
Lk. 12:33, treasure that *f.* not.
16:9, when ye *f.* they may receive you.
17, one tittle of law *f.*
21:26, hearts *f.* them for fear.
22:32, that thy faith *f.* not.
1Cor. 13:8, charity never *f.*
Heb. 1:12, thy years shall not *f.*
11:32, time would *f.* me to tell.
12:15, lest any man *f.* of grace of God.
See Dt. 31:6; Ps. 40:12; 143:7; Isa. 44:12.
FAIN. Job 27:22; Lk. 15:16.
FAINT. Gen. 25:29, 30, came from field, and he

was *f.*
45:26, Jacob's heart *f.*
Jud. 8:4, *f.* yet pursuing.
Job 4:5, now it is come, and thou *f.*
Ps. 27:13, I had *f.* unless I had believed.
107:5, their soul *f.* in them.
Prov. 24:10, if thou *f.* in day of adversity.
Isa. 1:5, whole heart *f.*
10:18, as when a standardbearer *f.*
40:28, Creator of earth *f.* not.
29, giveth power to the *f.*
30; Amos 8:13, even youths shall *f.*
31, walk, and not *f.*
44:12, he drinketh no water, and is *f.*
Jer. 8:18; Lam. 1:22; 5:17, my heart is *f.*
Mt. 15:32; Mk. 8:3, lest they *f.* by the way.
Lk. 18:1, pray, and not to *f.*
2Cor. 4:1, 16, as we have received mercy, we *f.* not.
Gal. 6:9, reap, if we *f.* not.
Heb. 12:3, wearied and *f.* in your minds.
5, nor *f.* when thou art rebuked.
See Dt. 20:8; Ps. 84:2; 119:81; Mt. 9:36.
AIR. Job 37:22, *f.* weather out of the north.
Ps. 45:2, *f.* than children of men.
Prov. 11:22, a *f.* woman without discretion.
26:25, when he speaketh *f.*, believe not.
Song 1:8; 5:9; 6:1, thou *f.* among women
6:10, *f.* as the moon.
Isa. 5:9, houses great and *f.*
Jer. 4:30, in vain shalt thou make thyself *f.*
12:6, though they speak *f.* words.
Dan. 1:15, their countenances appeared *f.*
Mt. 16:2, it will be *f.* weather.
Acts 7:20, Moses was exceeding *f.*
Rom. 16:18, by *f.* speeches deceive.
See Gen. 6:2; Isa. 54:11; Ezek. 27:12.
AITH. Dt. 32:20, children in whom is no *f.*
Mt. 6:30; 8:26; 14:31; 16:8; Lk. 12:28, ye of little *f.*
8:10; Lk. 7:9, so great *f.*
9:2; Mk. 2:5; Lk. 5:20, seeing their *f.*
22; Mk. 5:34; 10:52; Lk. 8:48; 17:19, thy *f.* hath made thee whole.
Mt. 9:29, according to your *f.*
15:28, great is thy *f.*
17:20, *f.* as a grain of mustard seed.
21:21, if ye have *f.*, ye shall not only do this.
23:23, omitted judgment, mercy, and *f.*
Mk. 4:40, how is it ye have no *f.*?
11:22, have *f.* in God.
Lk. 7:50, thy *f.* hath saved thee.
8:25, where is your *f.*?
17:5, increase our *f.*
18:8, shall he find *f.* on the earth?
22:32, that thy *f.* fail not.
Acts 3:16, the *f.* which is by him.
6:5; 11:24, a man full of *f.*
14:9, perceiving he had *f.* to be healed.
27, opened the door of *f.*
15:9, purifying their hearts by *f.*
16:5, established in the *f.*
26:18, sanctified by *f.*
Rom. 1:5, grace for obedience to *f.*
17, revealed from *f.* to *f.*
3:27, boasting excluded by *f.*
28; 5:1; Gal. 2:16; 3:24, justified by *f.*
4:5, *f.* counted for righteousness.
16, it is of *f.*, which is of the *f.* of Abraham.
19, 20, being not weak in *f.*
5:2, we have access by *f.*
10:8, the word of *f.*, which we preach.
17, *f.* cometh by hearing.
12:3, the measure of *f.*
6, prophesy according to proportion of *f.*
14:1, weak in *f.* receive ye.
22, hast thou *f.*?
23, what is not of *f.* is sin.
1Cor. 2:5, your *f.* should not stand is wisdom.
13:2, though I have all *f.*
13, now abideth *f.*
15:14, and your *f.* is also vain.
16:13, stand fast in the *f.*
2Cor. 1:24, not have dominion over *f.*
4:13, same spirit of *f.*
5:7, we walk by *f.*
13:5, examine whether ye be in the *f.*
Gal. 2:20, I live by the *f.* of Son of God.
3:2, by the hearing of *f.*
12, law is not of *f.*
23, before *f.* came.
5:6, *f.* which worketh by love.
6:10, the household of *f.*
Eph. 3:12, access by *f.* of him.
17, dwell in your hearts by *f.*
4:5, one Lord, one *f.*
13, in the unity of the *f.*
6:16, the shield of *f.*
Phil. 1:27, striving together for the *f.* of the gospel.
Col. 1:23, if ye continue in the *f.*
2:5, the stedfastness of your *f.*
1Th. 1:3; 2Th. 1:11, your work of *f.*
5:8, the breastplate of *f.*
2Th. 3:2, all men have not *f.*
1Tim. 1:2; Ti. 1:4, my own son in the *f.*
5; 2Tim. 1:5, *f.* unfeigned.
2:15, if they continue in *f.*
3:13, great boldness in the *f.*
4:1, shall depart from the *f.*
5:8, he hath denied the *f.*
6:10, 21, erred from the *f.*
12, fight the good fight of *f.*
2Tim. 3:8, reprobate concerning the *f.*
4:7, I have kept the *f.*
Ti. 1:1, the *f.* of God's elect.
Heb. 4:2, not being mixed with *f.*
6:1, not laying again the foundation of *f.*
12, through *f.* inherit the promises.
10:22, in full assurance of *f.*
11:1, *f.* is substance of things hoped for.
4, 5, 7, 8, 9, etc., by *f.* Abel, etc.
Heb. 11:6, without *f.* it is impossible.
13, these all died in *f.*
33, through *f.* subdued kingdoms.
39, a good report through *f.*

12:2, author and finisher of our *f.*
13:7, whose *f.* follow.
Jas. 1:3; 1Pet. 1:7, the trying of your *f.*
6, let them ask in *f.*
2:1, I have not *f.* with respect of persons.
5, rich in *f.*
14, man say he hath *f.*, can *f.* save him?
17, *f.* without works is dead.
18, thou hast *f.*, and I have works.
22, *f.* wrought with his works.
5:15, the prayer of *f.* shall save.
1Pet. 1:9, the end of your *f.*
5:9, resist stedfast in the *f.*
2Pet. 1:1, like precious *f.*
5, add to your *f.* virtue.
1Jn. 5:4, overcometh the world, even our *f.*
Jude 3, earnestly contend for the *f.*
20, your most holy *f.*
Rev. 2:13, hast not denied my *f.*
19, I know thy works and *f.*
13:10, patience and *f.* of the saints.
14:12, they that keep the *f.* of Jesus.
See Hab. 2:4; Rom. 1:12; 1Tim. 4:6.
FAITHFUL. 2Sam. 20:19, one of them that are *f.* in Israel.
Neh. 7:2, a *f.* man, and feared God.
9:8, his heart *f.* before thee.
13:13, counted *f.* to distribute.
Ps. 12:1, the *f.* fail among men.
89:37, a *f.* witness in heaven.
101:6, the *f.* of the land.
119:86, commandments *f.*
138, testimonies *f.*
Prov. 11:13, *f.* spirit concealeth.
13:17, *f.* ambassador is health.
14:5; Isa. 8:2; Jer. 42:5, a *f.* witness.
20:6, a *f.* man who can find?
25:13, as snow in harvest, so is a *f.* messenger.
27:6, *f.* are wounds of a friend.
28:20, *f.* man shall abound.
Isa. 1:21, 26, *f.* city.
Mt. 24:45; Lk. 12:42, who is a *f.* and wise servant?
25:21, good and *f.* servant.
23; Lk. 19:17, *f.* in a few things.
Lk. 16:10, *f.* in least *f.* in much.
Acts 16:15, if ye have judged me *f.*
1Cor. 4:2, required in stewards that a man be *f.*
17, Timothy *f.* in the Lord.
Gal. 3:9, blessed with *f.* Abraham.
Eph. 6:21; Col. 1:7; 4:7, a *f.* minister.
1Th. 5:24, *f.* is he that calleth you.
2Th. 3:3, Lord is *f.*, who shall stablish you.
1Tim. 1:15; 4:9; 2Tim. 2:11; tit. 3:8, a *f.* saying.
3:11, wives *f.* in all things.
2Tim. 2:2, commit to *f.* men.
13, yet he abideth *f.*
Heb. 2:17, a *f.* high priest.
3:2, *f.* to him that appointed him.
10:23; 11:11, he is *f.* that promised.
1Pet. 4:19, as unto a *f.* Creator.
1Jn. 1:9, he is *f.* and just to forgive.
Rev. 2:10, be thou *f.* unto death.
13, my *f.* martyr.
17:14, called and chosen, and *f.*
21:5; 22:6, these words are true and *f.*
See Dt. 7:9; Dan. 6:4; Rev. 1:5; 3:14; 19:11.
FAITHFULLY. 2Chr. 19:9; 34:12; Jer. 23:28; 3Jn. 5.
FAITHFULNESS. Ps. 5:9, no *f.* in their mouths.
36:5, thy *f.* reacheth unto the clouds
40:10; 88:11, declared thy *f.*
89:33, nor suffer my *f.* to fail.
92:2, show forth thy *f.* every night.
Isa. 11:5, *f.* the girdle of his reins.
Lam. 3:23, great is thy *f.*
See 1Sam. 26:23; Ps. 119:75; 143:1.
FAITHLESS. Mt. 17:17; Mk. 9:19; Lk. 9:41; Jn. 20:27.
FALL (*n.*). Prov. 16:18, haughty spirit before a *f.*
Mt. 7:27, great was the *f.* of it.
Lk. 2:34, set for the rise and *f.* of many.
Rom. 11:12, if the *f.* of them be the riches.
See Jer. 49:21; Ezek. 26:15; 31:16; 32:10.
FALL (*v.*). Gen. 45:24, see ye *f.* not out by the way.
Lev. 25:35, thy brother be *f.* in decay.
1Sam. 3:19, let none of his words *f.*
2Sam. 1:19, 25, 27, how are the mighty *f.*!
3:38, great man *f.* this day.
24:14; 1Chr. 21:13, *f.* into hands of God.
2Ki. 14:10, why meddle that thou shouldest *f.*?
Job 4:13; 33:15, deep sleep *f.* on men.
Ps. 5:10, let them *f.* by their own counsels.
7:15, is *f.* into ditch.
16:6, lines *f.* in pleasant places.
37:24, though he *f.*, not utterly cast down.
56:13; 116:8, deliver my feet from *f.*
72:11, kings shall *f.* down before him.
91:7, a thousand shall *f.* at thy side.
Prov. 10:8, 10, a prating fool shall *f.*
11:14, where no counsel is, the people *f.*
28, he that trusteth in riches shall *f.*
13:17; 17:20; 24:16, *f.* into mischief.
24:16, just man *f.* seven times.
17, rejoice not when thine enemy *f.*
26:27; Eccl. 10:8, diggeth a pit shall *f.* therei
Eccl. 4:10, woe to him that is alone when he *f.*
11:3, where the tree *f.*, there it shall be.
Isa. 14:12, how art thou *f.*!
34:4, as the leaf *f.* from the vine.
40:30, the young men shall utterly *f.*
Jer. 49:26; 50:30, young men *f.* in her streets.
Ezek. 24:6, let no lot *f.* on it.
Dan. 3:5; 11:26; Mt. 4:9, *f.* down and worship.
Hos. 10:8; Lk. 23:30; Rev. 6:16, say to hills, *f.* on us.
Mic. 7:8, when I *f.*
Zech. 11:2, the cedar is *f.*
Mt. 10:29, sparrow *f.* on ground.
12:11, *f.* into pit on sabbath day.
15:14; Lk. 6:39, both *f.* into the ditch.
21:44; Lk. 20:18, *f.* on this stone.
24:29; Mk. 13:25, stars *f.* from heaven.
Lk. 8:13, in time of temptation *f.* away.
10:18, Satan as lightning, *f.* from heaven.
Rom. 14:4, to his master he standeth or *f.*

13, occasion to *f.*
1Cor. 10:12, take heed lest he *f.*
15:6, 18, some are *f.* asleep.
Gal. 5:4, ye are *f.* from grace.
1Tim. 3:6, *f.* into the condemnation.
7, lest he *f.* into reproach.
6:9, rich *f.* into temptation.
Heb. 4:11, lest any *f.* after same example.
6:6, if they *f.* away.
10:31, to *f.* into hands of living God.
Jas. 1:2, joy when ye *f.* into temptation.
11; 1Pet. 1:24, flower thereof *f.*
5:12, lest ye *f.* into condemnation.
2Pet. 1:10, ye shall never *f.*
3:17, lest ye *f.* from stedfastness.
See Isa. 21:9; Lam 5:16; Rev. 14:8; 18:2.
ALLING. Job 4:4; 2Th. 2:3; Jude 24.
ALLOW. Jer. 4:3; Hos. 10:12.
ALSE. Ex. 20:16; Dt. 5:20; Mt. 19:18, shalt not bear *f.* witness.
23:1, shalt not raise a *f.* report.
2Ki. 9:12, it is *f.*, tell us now.
Ps. 119:104, 128, I hate every *f.* way.
120:3, thou *f.* tongue.
Prov. 6:19; 12:17; 14:5; 19:5; 21:28; 25:18, a *f.* witness.
11:1; 20:23, a *f.* balance.
Mt. 15:19, out of heart proceed *f.* witness.
24:24; Mk. 13:22, *f.* Christs and *f.* prophets.
26:59, 60; Mk. 14:56, 57, *f.* witness against Christ.
Mk. 13:22, *f.* prophets shall rise.
Lk. 19:8, any thing by *f.* accusation.
1Cor. 15:15, found *f.* witnesses of God.
2Cor. 11:13, such are *f.* apostles.
11:26, perils among *f.* brethren.
2Tim. 3:3; Ti. 2:3, *f.* accusers.
See Gal. 2:4; 2Pet. 2:1; 1Jn. 4:1.
ALSEHOOD. Job 21:34, in answers remaineth *f.*
Ps. 7:14, hath brought forth *f.*
144:8, 11, right hand of *f.*
Isa. 28:15, under *f.* have we hid ourselves.
57:4, a seed of *f.*
59:13, words of *f.*
Mic. 2:11, walking in the spirit and *f.*
See 2Sam. 18:13; Jer. 13:25; Hos. 7:1.
ALSELY. Lev. 6:3, 5; 19:12; Jer. 5:2; 7:9; Zech. 5:4, swear *f.*
Jer. 5:31; 29:9, prophets prophesy *f.*
Mt. 5:11, evil *f.*, for my sake.
1Tim. 6:20, science *f.* so called.
See Jer. 43:2; Lk. 3:14; 1Pet. 3:16.
AME. Josh. 9:9, we heard the *f.* of God.
1Ki. 10:1; 2Chr. 9:1, *f.* of Solomon.
Zeph. 3:19, get them *f.* in every land.
Mt. 4:24; Mk. 1:28; Lk. 4:14, 37; 5:15, *f.* of Jesus.
9:31, spread abroad his *f.*
14:1, Herod heard of the *f.*
See Gen. 45:16; Num. 14:15; Job 28:22; Isa. 66:19.
AMILIAR. Job 19:14; Ps. 41:9; Jer. 20:10.
AMILY. Gen. 12:3; 28:14, in thee all *f.* be blessed.
25:10, return every man to his *f.*
Dt. 29:18, lest a *f.* turn away from God.
1Sam. 9:21, my *f.* the least.
18:18, what is my father's *f.*?
1Chr. 4:38, princes in their *f.*
Ps. 68:6, setteth the solitary in *f.*
Jer. 3:14, one of a city, and two of a *f.*
10:25, on *f.* that call not.
31:1, God of all the *f.* of Israel.
Zech. 12:12, every *f.* apart.
Eph. 3:15, whole *f.* in heaven and earth.
See Num. 27:4; Jud. 1:25; Amos 3:2.
FAMINE. 2Sam. 21:1, a *f.* in days of David.
1Ki. 8:37; 2Chr. 20:9, if there be *f.*
18:2; 2Ki. 6:25, sore *f.* in Samaria.
2Ki. 8:1, the Lord hath called for a *f.*
Job 5:20, in *f.* he shall redeem thee.
22, at *f.* thou shalt laugh.
Ps. 33:19, to keep them alive in *f.*
37:19, in the days of *f.* shall be satisfied.
Jer. 24:10; 29:17, will send *f.* among them.
42:16, *f.* shall follow close.
Lam. 5:10, black because of *f.*
Ezek. 5:16, evil arrows of *f.*
36:29, I will lay no *f.* upon you.
Amos 8:11, a *f.*, not of bread.
Mt. 24:7; Mk. 13:8; Lk. 21:11, *f.* in divers places.
See Gen. 12:10; 41:27; 47:13; Lk. 15:14; Rom. 8:35.
FAMISH. Gen. 41:55; Prov. 10:3; Isa. 5:13; Zeph. 2:11.
FAMOUS. Ruth 4:11, 14; 1Chr. 5:24; Ps. 74:5; Ezek. 23:10.
FAN. Isa. 30:24; Jer. 15:7; 51:2; Mt. 3:12.
FAR. Gen. 18:25; 1Sam. 20:9, that be *f.* from thee.
Dt. 12:21; 14:24, if place too *f.* from thee.
Jud. 19:11; Mk. 6:35; Lk. 24:29, day *f.* spent.
1Sam. 2:30; 22:15; 2Sam. 20:20; 23:17, be it *f.* from me.
Job 5:4, children *f.* from safety.
11:14; 22:23, put iniquity *f.* away.
19:13, put my brethren *f.* from me.
34:10, *f.* be it from God to do wickedness.
Ps. 10:5, thy judgments are *f.* out of sight.
22:11; 35:22; 38:21; 71:12, be not *f.* from me.
97:9, *f.* above all gods.
103:12, *f.* as east from west.
Prov. 31:10, *f.* above rubies.
Isa. 43:6; 60:4, 9, sons from *f.*
46:12, *f.* from righteousness.
57:19, peace to him that is *f.* off.
Amos 6:3, put *f.* away evil day.
Mt. 16:22, be it *f.* from thee, Lord.
Mk. 12:34, not *f.* from the kingdom.
13:34, as a man taking a *f.* journey.
Jn. 21:8, they were not *f.* from land.
Acts 17:27, not *f.* from every one of us.
Rom. 13:12, the night is *f.* spent.
2Cor. 4:17, a *f.* more exceeding.
Eph. 1:21, *f.* above all principality.
2:13, *f.* off made nigh.
4:10, *f.* above all heavens.
Phil. 1:23, which is *f.* better.
Heb. 7:15, it is yet *f.* more evident.

See Isa. 33:17; Mt. 15:8; Mk. 8:3.
FARE. 1Sam. 17:18; Jon. 1:3; Lk. 16:19.
FAREWELL. Lk. 9:61; Acts 18:21; 2Cor. 13:11.
FARM. Mt. 22:5.
FARTHING. Mt. 5:26; 10:29; Mk. 12:42; Lk. 12:6.
FASHION. Job 10:8; Ps. 119:73, thine hands have *f.* me.
31:15, did not one *f.* us?
Ps. 33:15, he *f.* hearts alike.
139:16, in continuance were *f.*
Isa. 45:9, say to him that *f.* it.
Mk. 2:12, never saw it on this *f.*
Lk. 9:29, the *f.* of his countenance.
1Cor. 7:31, the *f.* of this world passeth.
Phil. 2:8, found in *f.* as a man.
See Gen. 6:15; Ex. 32:4; Ezek. 42:11; Jas. 1:11.
FAST. 2Sam. 12:23, he is dead, wherefore should I *f.*?
Ps. 33:9, he commanded, and it stood *f.*
65:6, setteth *f.* the mountains.
Isa. 58:3, why have we *f.*, and thou seest not?
4, ye *f.* for strife.
5, wilt thou call this a *f.*?
6, is not this the *f.* that I have chosen?
Joel 1:14, sanctify a *f.*?
Zech. 7:5, did ye at all *f.* unto me?
Mt. 6:16, when ye *f.*, be not.
18, appear not to *f.*
Mk. 2:19, can children of bridechamber *f.*
Lk. 18:12, I *f.* twice in the week.
See Jer. 14:12; Mt. 4:2; Acts 13:2.
FASTEN. Eccl. 12:11, as nails *f.* by the masters.
Isa. 22:23, 25, I will *f.* him as a nail.
Lk. 4:20, eyes of all were *f.* on him.
Acts 11:6, when I had *f.* mine eyes.
See 1Sam. 31:10; Job 38:6; Acts 3:4; 28:3.
FASTING. Ps. 35:13, I humbled myself with *f.*
109:24, knees weak through *f.*
Jer. 36:6, upon the *f.* day.
Mk. 8:3, send them away *f.*
1Cor. 7:5, give yourselves to *f.* and prayer.
2Cor. 6:5, in stripes, in *f.*
11:27, in *f.* oft.
See Dan. 6:18; 9:3; Mt. 17:21; Mk. 9:29.
FAT. Gen. 45:18, shall eat the *f.* of the land.
49:20, his bread shall be *f.*
Dt. 32:15, Jeshurun waxed *f.*, and kicked.
Neh. 8:10, eat the *f.*, and drink the sweet.
9:25, 35, took a *f.* land, and became *f.*
Ps. 17:10, inclosed in their own *f.*
92:14, shall be *f.* and flourishing.
119:70, heart *f.* as grease.
Prov. 11:25, liberal soul made *f.*
13:4, soul of diligent made *f.*
15:30, good report maketh the bones *f.*
Isa. 10:16, among his *f.* ones leanness.
25:6, feast of *f.* things.
Hab. 1:16, by them their portion if *f.*
See Gen. 41:2; Ex. 29:13; Lev. 3:3, 17; 7:22; Num. 13:20;
Jud. 3:17.
FATHER. Gen. 15:15, go to thy *f.* in peace.
17:4; Rom. 4:17, a *f.* of nations.
Ex. 15:2, he is my *f.* God, I will exalt him.
20:5; Num. 14:18, iniquity of *f.* upon children
21:15, he that smiteth his *f.*
17; Lev. 20:9, he that curseth his *f.*
Jud. 17:10; 18:19, be to me a *f.* and a priest.
1Sam. 10:12, who is their *f.*?
2Sam. 10:2; 1Chr. 19:2, as his *f.* showed kindness.
1Ki. 19:4, no better than my *f.*
2Ki. 2:12; 13:14, Elisha cried, my *f.*, my *f.*
6:21, my *f.*, shall I smite them?
1Chr. 28:9, know thou the God of thy *f.*
2Chr. 32:13, what I and my *f.* have done.
Ezra 7:27, blessed be the Lord God of our *f.*
Job 29:16, I was a *f.* to the poor.
31:18, brought up with me as with a *f.*
38:28, hath the rain a *f.*?
Ps. 27:10, when my *f.* and mother forsake me.
39:12, as all my *f.* were.
68:5, *f.* of fatherless.
95:9; Heb. 3:9, your *f.* tempted me.
103:13, as a *f.* pitieth his children.
Prov. 4:1, the instruction of a *f.*
3, I was my *f.* son.
10:1; 15:20, wise son maketh a glad *f.*
17:21, the *f.* of a fool hath no joy.
25; 19:13, foolish son grief to his *f.*
Isa. 9:6, the everlasting *F.*
49:23, kings shall be thy nursing *f.*
63:16; 64:8, doubtless thou art our *f.*
Jer. 3:4, wilt thou not cry, my *f.*?
31:9, I am a *f.* to Israel.
29; Ezek. 18:2, *f.* have eaten sour grapes.
Ezek. 18:4, as the soul of the *f.*
22:7, set light by *f.* and mother.
Mal. 1:6, if I be a *f.*, where is mine honour?
2:10, have we not all one *f.*?
Mt. 5:16, 45, 48, your *F.* in heaven.
6:8, 32; Lk. 12:30, your *F.* knoweth.
9; Lk. 11:2, our *F.* which art in heaven.
7:21; 12:50, the will of my *F.*
8:21; Lk. 9:59, to go and bury my *f.*
10:21, *f.* deliver up the child.
37, he that loveth *f.* or mother.
18:10, behold the face of my *F.*
14, not the will of your *F.*
23:9, call no man *f.* on earth.
25:34, ye blessed of my *F.*
Mk. 14:36; Rom. 8:15; Gal. 4:6, Abba, *F.*
Lk. 2:49, about my *F.* business.
6:36, as your *F.* is merciful.
11:11, of any that is a *f.*
12:32, it is your *F.* good pleasure.
15:21, *f.*, I have sinned.
16:27, send him to my *f.* house.
22:42, *F.* if thou be willing.
23:34, *F.*, forgive them.
46, *F.*, into thy hand.
Jn. 1:14, as of the only begotten of the *F.*
5:21, as the *F.* raiseth up the dead.
22, the *F.* judgeth no man.
23, even as they honour the *F.*
37:8, 16; 12:49; 14:24, the *F.* which hath

sent me.
6:37, all the *F.* giveth me.
46; 14:8, 9, hath seen the *F.*
8:41, we have one *F.*, even God.
44, devil is a liar, and the *f.* of it.
49, I honour my *F.*
10:15, as the *F.* knoweth me.
29, my *F.* is greater than all.
12:27, *F.* save me from this hour.
28, *F.*, glorify thy name.
13:1, should depart unto the *F.*
14:6, no man cometh to the *F.*, but by me.
16; 16:26, I will pray the *F.*
28, I am come from the *F.*
15:1, my *F.* is the husbandman.
16, whatsoever ye ask of the *F.*
16:16, because I go to the *F.*
32, the *F.* is with me.
17:1, *F.*, the hour is come.
20:17, I ascend to my *F.* and your *F.*
Acts 24:14, so worship I the God of my *f.*
Rom. 4:11, the *f.* of all that believe.
1Cor. 4:15, yet have we not many *f.*
2Cor. 1:3, *F.* of mercies, God of all comfort.
Gal. 1:14, zealous of the traditions of my *f.*
4:2, the time appointed of the *f.*
Eph. 4:6, one God and *F.* of all.
6:4, *f.*, provoke not your children.
Phil. 2:11, to the glory of the *F.*
22, as a son with the *f.*
Col. 1:19, it pleased the *F.* that in him.
1Tim. 5:1, entreat him as a *f.*
Heb. 1:5, I will be to him a *F.*
7:3, without *f.*, without mother.
12:9, the *F.* of spirits.
Jas. 1:17, the *F.* of lights.
2Pet. 3:4, since the *f.* fell asleep.
1Jn. 1:3, fellowship with the *F.*
2:1, an advocate with the *F.*
13, I write unto you, *f.*
15, the love of the *F.* is not in him.
23, hath not the *F.*
3:1, what manner of love the *F.* hath.
5:7, the *F.*, the Word, and Holy Ghost.
See 1Chr. 29:10; Lk. 11:2; Jn. 5:26; 20:7; Acts 1:4; 15:10; Rom. 4:16.

ATHERLESS. Ps. 10:14, the helper of the *f.*
Prov. 23:10, the fields of the *f.*
Isa. 1:23, they judge not the *f.*
10:2, that they may rob the *f.*
Jer. 49:11, leave thy *f.* children.
Hos. 14:3, in thee the *f.* findeth mercy.
Mal. 3:5, against those that oppress *f.*
Jas. 1:27, to visit the *f.* and widows.
See Ex. 22:22; Dt. 10:18; 14:29; 24:17; Job 31:17.

ATNESS. Ps. 36:8, the *f.* of thine house.
63:5, as with marrow and *f.*
65:11, thy paths drop *f.*
73:7, eyes stand out with *f.*
Isa. 55:2, soul delight itself in *f.*
See Gen. 27:28; Jud. 9:9; Rom. 11:17.

AULT. Gen. 41:9, I remember my *f.* this day.
Ps. 19:12, cleanse me from secret *f.*
Dan. 6:4, find none occasion nor *f.* in him.
Mt. 18:15, tell him his *f.*
Lk. 23:4; Jn. 18:38; 19:4, 6, I find no *f.*
Rom. 9:19, why doth he yet find *f.*?
Gal. 6:1, overtaken in a *f.*
Jas. 5:16, confess your *f.*
Rev. 14:5, are without *f.* before throne.
See Dt. 25:2; 1Sam. 29:3; 2Sam. 3:8.

FAULTLESS. Heb. 8:7; Jude 24.

FAULTY. 2Sam. 14:13; Hos. 10:2.

FAVOUR. Gen. 39:21, *f.* in the sight of the keeper.
Ex. 3:21; 11:3; 12:36, *f.* in sight of Egyptians.
Dt. 33:23, satisfied with *f.*
Ps. 5:12, with *f.* wilt thou compass him.
30:5, his *f.* is life.
102:13, the set time to *f.* her.
14, *f.* the dust thereof.
112:5, a good man showeth *f.*
Prov. 13:15, good understanding giveth *f.*
14:35; 19:12, the king's *f.*
18:22, obtaineth *f.* of the Lord.
31:30 *f.* is deceitful.
Lk. 2:52, increased in *f.* with God and man.
Acts 2:47, having *f.* with all people.
See Prov. 8:35; 12:2; Eccl. 9:11; Dan. 1:9.

FAVOURABLE. Jud. 21:22; Job 33:26; Ps. 77:7; 85:1.

FEAR (*n.*). Gen. 9:2, the *f.* of you on every beast.
20:11, *f.* of God not in this place.
Dt. 2:25; 11:25; 1Chr. 14:17, *f.* of thee on nations.
Job 4:6, is not this thy *f.*?
15:4, thou castest off *f.*
39:22, he mocketh at *f.*
Ps. 5:7, in thy *f.* will I worship.
14:5, there were they in great *f.*
19:9, *f.* of the Lord is clean.
Ps. 34:11, I will teach you the *f.* of the Lord.
36:1; Rom. 3:18, no *f.* of God before his eyes.
53:5, in *f.*, where no *f.* was.
111:10; Prov. 1:7; 9:10, *f.* beginning of wisdom.
Prov. 1:26, 27, mock when your *f.* cometh.
3:25, not afraid of sudden *f.*
10:21, *f.* of Lord prolongeth days.
14:26, in *f.* of Lord is strong confidence.
27, *f.* of Lord a fountain of life.
15:16, better little with *f.* of Lord.
19:23, *f.* of Lord tendeth to life.
29:25, *f.* of man bringeth a snare.
Eccl. 12:5, when *f.* shall be in the way.
Isa. 8:12, neither fear ye their *f.*
14:3, Lord give thee rest from *f.*
29:13, *f.* toward me taught by men.
Jer. 30:5, a voice of *f.*, not of peace.
32:40, I will put my *f.* in their hearts.
Mal. 1:6, where is my *f.*?
Mt. 14:26, disciples cried for *f.*
Lk. 21:26, hearts failing them for *f.*
Jn. 7:13; 19:38; 20:19, for *f.* of the Jews.
1Cor. 2:3, with you in weakness and *f.*
2Cor. 7:11, what *f.*, what desire.
Eph. 6:5; Phil. 2:12, with *f.* and trembling.
Heb. 2:15, *f.* of death.
11:7, Noah moved with *f.*

12:28, with reverence and godly *f.*
Jude 12, feeding themselves without *f.*
23, others save with *f.*
See Ps. 2:11; 2Cor. 7:5, 15; 1Pet. 2:18; 3:2.
FEAR (*v.*). Gen. 22:12, I know that thou *f.* God.
42:18, this do, and live, for I *f.* God.
Ex. 1:21, because they *f.* God.
14:13, *f.* not, stand still, and see.
18:21, able men, such as *f.* God.
20:20, *f.* God is come to prove.
Dt. 4:10, that they may learn to *f.*
5:29, O that they would *f.* me.
28:58, *f.* this glorious name.
66, thou shalt *f.* day and night.
1Chr. 16:30; Ps. 96:9, *f.* before him all earth.
Neh. 7:2, he *f.* God above many.
Job 1:9, doth Job *f.* God for nought?
11:15, put iniquity away, thou shalt not *f.*
Ps. 27:1, whom shall I *f.*?
3, my heart shall not *f.*
31:19, laid up for them that *f.* thee.
34:9, *f.* the Lord, ye his saints.
56:4; 118:6, will not *f.* what flesh can do.
66:16, come all ye that *f.* God.
76:7, thou art to be *f.*
86:11, unite my heart to *f.* thy name.
115:11, ye that *f.* the Lord, trust.
119:74, they that *f.* thee will be glad.
Prov. 3:7; 24:21, *f.* the Lord, and depart.
28:14, happy is the man that *f.* always.
31:30, woman that *f.* the Lord.
Eccl. 3:14, that men should *f.* before him.
5:7, but *f.* thou God.
9:2, as he that *f.* an oath.
12:13, *f.* God, and keep his commandments.
Isa. 8:12, neither *f.* ye their fear.
35:4, to them of fearful heart *f.* not.
41:10; 43:5, *f.* thou not, I am with thee.
14, *f.* not, thou worm Jacob.
Jer. 5:24, neither say they, let us *f.* the Lord.
10:7, who would not *f.* thee, King of nations?
33:9, they shall *f.* and tremble.
Dan. 6:26, that men *f.* before the God of Daniel.
Zeph. 3:7, I said, surely thou wilt *f.* me.
Mal. 3:16, they that *f.* the Lord spake.
4:2, to you that *f.* my name.
Mt. 1:20, *f.* not to take to thee.
10:28; Lk. 12:5, *f.* him who is able.
14:5; 21:46, Herod *f.* the multitude.
21:26; Mk. 11:32; Lk. 20:19, we *f.* the people.
Mk. 4:41, they *f.* exceedingly.
5:33, woman *f.* and trembling came.
11:18, scribes *f.* Jesus.
Lk. 9:31, *f.* as they entered cloud.
12:32, *f.* not, little flock.
18:2, judge which *f.* not God.
19:21, I *f.* thee, because thou art.
23:40, dost not thou *f.* God?
Jn. 9:22, because they *f.* the Jews.
Acts 10:22, just, and one that *f.* God.
35, he that *f.* is accepted.
13:26, whosoever among you *f.* God.
Rom. 8:15, bondage again to *f.*
11:20, not highminded, but *f.*
2Cor. 11:3; 12:20, I *f.* lest.
1Tim. 5:20, rebuke, that others may *f.*
Heb. 5:7, heard in that he *f.*
13:6, I will not *f.* what man.
1Jn. 4:18, that *f.* not perfect in love.
See 1Ki. 18:12; Col. 3:22; Heb. 4:1.
FEARFUL. Ex. 15:11, *f.* in praises.
Ps. 139:14, *f.* and wonderfully made.
Isa. 35:4, to them of a *f.* heart.
Mt. 8:26; Mk. 4:40, why are ye *f.*?
Heb. 10:27, *f.* looking for of judgment.
31, *f.* thing to fall into the hands.
See Dt. 20:8; Jud. 7:3; Lk. 21:11; Rev. 21:8.
FEARFULNESS. Ps. 55:5; Isa. 21:4; 33:14.
FEAST. Job 1:4, his sons went and *f.* in their house
Ps. 35:16, hypocritical mockers in *f.*
Prov. 15:15, merry heart continual *f.*
Eccl. 7:2; Jer. 16:8, the house of *f.*
10:19, *f.* is made for laughter.
Isa. 1:14, you appointed *f.* my soul hateth.
Amos 5:21, I despise your *f.* days.
8:10, turn your *f.* into mourning.
Mt. 23:6; Mk. 12:39; Lk. 20:46, uppermost rooms at *f.*
26:5; Mk. 14:2, not on the *f.* day.
Lk. 2:42, after the custom of the *f.*
14:13, when thou makest a *f.*
Jn. 7:8, go ye up to this *f.*
14, about the midst of the *f.*
37, that great day of the *f.*
13:29, buy what we need against the *f.*
Acts 18:21, I must by all means keep this *f.*
1Cor. 5:8, let us keep the *f.*
10:27, if any bid you to a *f.*
See Jud. 14:10; Est. 9:17; Mal. 2:3; Jude 12.
FEATHERS. Job 39:13; Ps. 91:4; Dan. 4:33.
FED. Gen. 48:15, who *f.* me all my life long.
Ps. 37:3, verily thou shalt be *f.*
Ezek. 34:8, shepherds *f.* themselves, not flock.
Mt. 25:37, hungred, and *f.* thee.
1Cor. 3:2, I have *f.* you with milk.
See Dt. 8:3; Ps. 78:72; 81:16; Lk. 16:21.
FEEBLE. Neh. 4:2, what do these *f.* Jews?
Job 4:4; Isa. 35:3; Heb. 12:12, strengthened the knees.
Ps. 105:37, not one *f.* person.
Prov. 30:26, comes a *f.* folk.
Ezek. 7:17; 21:7, all hands shall be *f.*
1Th. 5:14, comfort the *f.* minded.
See Gen. 30:42; Jer. 47:3; 1Cor. 12:22.
FEED. Gen. 46:32, trade hath been to *f.* cattle.
1Ki. 17:4, commanded ravens to *f.* thee.
22:27, *f.* him with bread of affliction.
Ps. 28:9, *f.* them, and lift them up for ever.
Prov. 15:14, mouth *f.* on foolishness.
30:8, *f.* me with food convenient.
Isa. 5:17, lambs shall *f.* after their manner.
11:7; 27:10, cow and bear shall *f.*
44:20, he *f.* on ashes.
61:5, strangers shall *f.* your flocks.
65:25, the wolf and lamb shall *f.*
Jer. 3:15, pastors *f.* you with knowledge.

6:3, *f.* every one in his place.
Hos. 12:1, Ephraim *f.* on wind.
Zech. 11:4, *f.* the flock of the slaughter.
Mt. 6:26, your heavenly Father *f.* them.
Lk. 12:24, sow not, yet God *f.* them.
Jn. 21:15, 16, 17, *f.* my lambs.
Rom. 12:20, if enemy hunger, *f.* him.
1Pet. 5:2, *f.* the flock of God.
See Song 1:7; Acts 20:28; Rev. 7:17.
FEEL. Gen. 27:12, 21, my father will *f.* me.
Acts 17:27, if haply they might *f.* after.
See Jud. 16:26; Job 20:20; Eccl. 8:5.
FEELING. Eph. 4:19, being past *f.*
Heb. 4:15, touched with *f.* of infirmities.
FEET. Gen. 49:10, lawgiver from between his *f.*
Dt. 2:28, I will pass through on my *f.*
Josh. 3:15, *f.* of priests dipped in Jordan.
14:9, land whereon *f.* have trodden.
Ruth 3:14, she lay at his *f.*
1Sam. 2:9, keep *f.* of his saints.
2Sam. 22:37; Ps. 18:36, my *f.* did not slip.
2Ki. 6:32, sound of his master's *f.*
13:21, dead man stood on his *f.*
Neh. 9:21, their *f.* swelled not.
Job 29:15, *f.* was I to the lame.
Ps. 8:6; 1Cor. 15:27; Eph. 1:22, all things under his *f.*
22:16, pierced my hands and my *f.*
31:8, set my *f.* in a large room.
40:2, my *f.* on a rock.
56:13; 116:8, deliver my *f.* from falling.
66:9, suffered not our *f.* to be moved.
73:2, my *f.* were almost gone.
115:7, *f.* have they, but walk not.
119:105, a lamp to my *f.*
122:2, our *f.* shall stand within thy gates.
Prov. 1:16; 6:18; Isa. 59:7, *f.* run to evil.
4:26, ponder path of thy *f.*
5:5, her *f.* go down to death.
6:13, speaketh with his *f.*
28, and his *f.* not be burnt.
7:11, her *f.* abide not in house.
19:2, he that hasteth with his *f.*
Song 5:3, washed my *f.*, how shall I defile?
7:1; Isa. 52:7, how beautiful are *f.*
Isa. 3:16, tinkling with *f.*
6:2, with twain he covered is *f.*
23:7, her own *f.* shall carry her.
26:6, the *f.* of the poor.
49:23; Mt. 10:14; Mk. 6:11; Lk. 9:5; Acts 13:51, dust of *f.*
52:7; Nah. 1:15, the *f.* of him that bringeth.
60:13, place of my *f.* glorious.
Lam. 3:34, crush under *f.* prisoners.
Ezek. 2:1, 2; 3:24, stand upon thy *f.*
24:17, 23, shoes upon thy *f.*
25:6, stamped with thy *f.*
32:2, troublest waters with thy *f.*
34:18, 19, foul residue with *f.*
Dan. 2:33, 42, *f.* part iron and part clay.
Dan. 10:6; Rev. 1:15; 2:18, *f.* like polished brass.
Nah. 1:3, clouds are the dust of his *f.*
Zech. 14:4, *f.* shall stand on Zion.
Mt. 7:6, trample them under *f.*
18:8, rather than having two *f.*
28:9, they held him by the *f.*
Lk. 1:79, guide our *f.* into way of peace.
7:38, she kissed his *f.*, and anointed them.
8:35, sitting at the *f.* of Jesus.
10:39, Mary sat at Jesus' *f.*
24:39, 40, behold my hands and my *f.*
Jn. 11:2; 12:3, wiped *f.* with her hair.
12:3, anointed the *f.* of Jesus.
13:5, began to wash disciples' *f.*
6, dost thou wash my *f.*?
8, thou shalt never wash my *f.*
10, needeth not save to wash his *f.*
20:12, one angel at head, other at *f.*
Acts 3:7, his *f.* received strength.
4:35, 37; 5:2, laid at apostles' *f.*
5:9, *f.* of them that buried thy husband.
Acts 14:8, a man impotent in his *f.*
21:11, Agabus bound his own hands and *f.*
222:3, at *f.* of Gamaliel.
Rom. 3:15, *f.* swift to shed blood.
10:15, the *f.* of them that preach.
16:20, bruise Satan under your *f.*
1Cor. 12:21, nor head to the *f.*, I have no need.
Eph. 6:15, your *f.* shod with preparation.
Rev. 1:17, I fell at his *f.* as dead.
13:2, *f.* as *f.* of a bear.
19:10; 22:8, at his *f.* to worship.
See 2Sam. 4:4; 2Ki. 9:35; 1Tim. 5:10.
FEIGN. 1Sam. 21:13, David *f.* himself mad.
Ps. 17:1, prayer not out of *f.* lips.
Jer. 3:10, turned to me *f.*
Lk. 20:20, *f.* themselves just men.
See 2Sam. 14:2; 1Ki. 14:5, 6; Neh. 6:8.
FELL. Gen. 4:5, his countenance *f.*
Josh. 6:20, the wall *f.* flat.
1Ki. 18:38, fire of Lord *f.*, and consumed.
2Ki. 6:5, as one was *f.* a beam.
Dan. 4:31, then *f.* a voice from heaven.
Jon. 1:7, lot on Jonah.
Mt. 7:25; Lk. 6:49, house *f.* not.
Lk. 8:23, Jesus *f.* asleep.
10:30, 36, *f.* among thieves.
13:4, upon whom tower *f.*
Acts 1:25, from which Judas *f.*
26, lot *f.* on Matthias.
13:36, *f.* on sleep.
2Pet. 3:4, since fathers *f.* asleep.
Rev. 16:19, cities of the nations *f.*
See Mt. 13:4; Acts 10:44; 19:35; 20:9.
FELLOW. Ex 2:13, wherefore smitest thou thy *f.*?
1Sam. 21:15, this *f.* to play the madman.
2Sam. 6:20, as one of the vain *f.*
2Ki. 9:11, wherefore came this mad *f.*?
Ps. 45:7; Heb. 1:9, oil of gladness above thy *f.*
Eccl. 4:10, one shall lift up his *f.*
Zech. 13:7, the man that is my *f.*
Mt. 11:16, like children calling to their *f.*
24:49, begin to smite his *f.*-servants.
26:61, this *f.* said, I am able to destroy.
71; Lk. 22:59, this *f.* was also with Jesus.
Lk. 23:2, found this *f.* perverting.

Jn. 9:29, as for this *f.*
Acts 17:5, lewd *f.* of the baser sort.
22:22, away with such a *f.*
24:5, this man a pestilent *f.*
Eph. 2:19, *f.*-citizens with the saints.
3:6, Gentiles *f.*-heirs.
Phil. 4:3; 1Th. 3:2; Philem 24, *f.*-labourers.
3Jn. 8, *f.*-helpers to the truth.
See Col. 4:11; Phile. 2; Rev. 19:10; 22:9.
FELLOWSHIP. Acts 2:42, in doctrine and *f.*
1Cor. 1:9, called to the *f.* of his Son.
10:20, not have *f.* with devils.
2Cor. 6:14, what *f.* hath righteousness?
Eph. 3:9, the *f.* of mystery.
5:11, have no *f.* with.
Phil. 1:5, your *f.* in the gospel.
2:1, if any *f.* of the Spirit.
3:10, the *f.* of his sufferings.
1Jn. 1:3, our *f.* is with the Father.
7, we have *f.* one with another.
See Lev. 6:2; Ps. 94:20; 2Cor. 8:4, 13, 14; Gal. 2:9.
FELT. Ex. 10:21; Prov. 23:35; Mk. 5:29; Acts 28:5.
FEMALE. Mt. 19:4; Mk. 10:6, made them male and *f.*
Gal. 3:28, in Christ neither male nor *f.*
See Gen. 7:16; Lev. 3:1; 27:4; Dt. 4:16.
FENCE. Job 10:11; 19:8; Ps. 62:3; Isa. 5:2.
FERVENT. Acts 18:25; Rom. 12:11, *f.* in spirit.
Jas. 5:16, *f.* prayer availeth much.
1Pet. 1:22, with a pure heart *f.*
2Pet. 3, 10, 12, melt with *f.* heat.
See 2Cor. 7:7; Col. 4:12; 1Pet. 4:8.
FETCH. Num. 20:10, must we *f.* water?
Job 36:3, I will *f.* my knowledge from afar.
Isa. 56:12, I will *f.* wine.
Acts 16:37, come themselves and *f.* us out.
See Dt. 19:5; 2Sam. 14:3; Acts 28:13.
FETTERS. Jud. 16:21; Ps. 105:18; 149:8; Mk. 5:4; Lk. 8:29.
FEVER. Dt. 28:22, the Lord shall smite thee with a *f.*
Mt. 8:14; Mk. 1:30, Simon's wife's mother lay sick of a *f.*
Jn. 4:52, at the seventh hour the *f.* left him.
FEW. Gen. 29:20, they seemed but a *f.* days.
47:9, *f.* and evil have the days of my life.
1Sam. 14:6, to save by many or *f.*
17:28, with whom left those *f.* sheep?
2Ki. 4:3, borrow not a *f.*
Neh. 7:4, city large, people *f.*
Job 14:1, man is of *f.* days.
16:22, when a *f.* years are come.
Eccl. 5:2, let thy words be *f.*
Mt. 7:14, *f.* there be that find it.
9:37; Lk. 10:2, the labourers are *f.*
15:34; Mk. 8:7, a *f.* little fishes.
20:16; 22:14, many called, *f.* chosen.
25:21, faithful in a *f.* things.
Mk. 6:5, laid hands on a *f.* sick folk.
Lk. 12:48, beaten with *f.* stripes.
13:23, are there *f.* that be saved?
Rev. 3:4, a *f.* names even in Sardis.
See Dt. 7:7; Ps. 109:8; Heb. 12:10.
FIDELITY. Ti. 2:10, showing good *f.*
FIELD. Dt. 21:1, if one be found slain in *f.*
1Sam. 22:7, will he give every one of you *f.*?
Prov. 24:30, the *f.* of the slothful.
Isa. 5:8, that lay *f.* to *f.*
Mt. 13:38, the *f.* is the world.
44, treasure hid in a *f.*
Jn. 4:35, look on the *f.*
Jas. 5:4, labourers which reaped your *f.*
See Mt. 6:28; 27:7; Acts 1:19.
FIERCE. Gen. 49:7, anger, for it was *f.*
Dt. 28:50, a nation of a *f.* countenance.
Mt. 8:28, exceeding *f.*
Lk. 23:5, and they were more *f.*
2Tim. 3:3, men shall be incontinent, *f.*
Jas. 3:4, driven of *f.* winds.
See 2Sam. 19:43; Isa. 33:19; Dan. 8:23.
FIERY. Dt. 33:2, a *f.* law for them.
Dan. 3:6, a *f.* furnace.
Eph. 6:16, the *f.* darts of the wicked.
Heb. 10:27, judgment and *f.* indignation.
1Pet. 4:12, concerning the *f.* trial.
See Num. 21:6; Dt. 8:15; Isa. 14:29.
FIG. 1Ki. 4:25; Mic. 4:4, dwelt under his *f.* tree.
2Ki. 18:31; Isa. 36:16, eat every one of his *f.* tre
20:7, Isaiah said, Take a lump of *f.*
Isa. 38:21, let them take a lump of *f.*
Jer. 24:1, two baskets of *f.* were set before the temple.
Hab. 3:17, although *f.* tree shall not blossom.
Mt. 7:16; Lk. 6:44, do men gather *f.* of thistles?
Lk. 21:29, behold the *f.* tree.
Jas. 3:12, can the *f.* tree bear olive berries?
Rev. 6:13, casteth untimely *f.*
See Jud. 9:10; Jer. 8:13; Lk. 13:6; Jn. 1:48.
FIGHT. Ex. 14:14; Dt. 1:30; 3:22; 20:4, Lord *f.* for you.
Josh. 23:10, he it is that *f.* for you.
1Sam. 25:28, *f.* the battles of the Lord.
2Ki. 10:3, *f.* for your master's house.
Neh. 4:14, *f.* for your brethren, sons, and wives.
Ps. 144:1, teacheth my fingers to *f.*
Jn. 18:36, then would my servants *f.*
Acts 5:39; 23:9, *f.* against God.
1Cor. 9:26, so *f.* I.
2Cor. 7:5, without were *f.*
1Tim. 6:12; 2Tim. 4:7, the good *f.*
Heb. 10:32, great *f.* of afflictions.
11:34, valiant in *f.*
Jas. 4:1, wars and *f.* among you.
2, ye *f.* and war.
See Zech. 10:5; 14:14; Rev. 2:16.
FIG-TREE. Mt. 21:19, presently the *f.* withered away.
Mk. 11:13, seeing a *f.* afar off.
FIG-TREE (parable of). Mt. 24:32; Lk. 21:29.
FIGURE. Dt. 4:16; Rom. 5:14; 1Cor. 4:6; Heb. 9:9; 1Pet. 3:21.
FILL. Num. 14:21; Ps. 72:19; Hab. 2:14, earth *f.* wi glory.
Job 23:4, *f.* my mouth with arguments.
Ps. 81:10, open mouth, I will *f.* it.

104:28, they are *f.* with good.
Prov. 3:10, barns *f.* with plenty.
14:14, *f.* with his own ways.
30:22, a fool when *f.* with meat.
Isa. 65:20, who hath not *f.* his days.
Mt. 5:6; Lk. 6:21, they shall be *f.*
Mk. 7:27, let the children first be *f.*
Lk. 1:15; Acts 4:8; 9:17; 13:9, *f.* with Holy Ghost.
14:23, that my house may be *f.*
Jn. 16:6, sorrow hath *f.* your heart.
Acts 5:28, ye have *f.* Jerusalem with your doctrine.
14:17, *f.* our hearts with food and gladness.
Rom. 1:29, *f.* with all unrighteousness.
15:14, *f.* with all knowledge.
Eph. 1:23, him that *f.* all in all.
3:19, *f.* with fulness of God.
5:18, be *f.* with the Spirit.
Phil. 1:11, *f.* with fruits of righteousness.
Col. 1:24, *f.* up what is behind.
Jas. 2:16, be ye warned and *f.*
Rev. 15:1, in them is *f.* up wrath of God.
See Dan 2:35; Lk. 2:40; 15:16; Jn. 2:7.
LTH. Isa. 4:4, washed away the *f.* of Zion.
1Cor. 4:13, as the *f.* of the world.
LTHINESS. 2Cor. 7:1, cleanse from all *f.* of flesh.
Eph. 5:4, nor let *f.* be named.
Jas. 1:21, lay apart all *f.*
See Ezek. 33:15; 36:25.
LTHY. Job 15:16, how much more *f.* is man?
Ps. 14:3; 53:3, altogether become *f.*
Isa. 64:6, as *f.* rags.
Zech. 3:3, clothed with *f.* garments.
Col. 3:8, put off *f.* communication.
1Tim. 3:3; Ti. 1:7; 1Pet. 5:2, *f.* lucre.
2Pet. 2:7, vexed with *f.* conversation.
Jude 8, *f.* dreamers.
Rev. 22:11, he that is *f.*, let him be *f.*
NALLY. 2Cor. 13:11; Eph. 6:10; Phil. 3:1;4:8; 2Th. 3:1; 1Pet. 3:8.
ND. Num. 32:23, be sure your sin will *f.* you out.
Job 9:10; Rom. 11:33, things past *f.* out.
23:3, where I might *f.* him.
Prov. 4:22, life to those that *f.* them.
8:17; Jer. 29:13, seek me early shall *f.* me.
35, whoso *f.* me, *f.* life.
18:22, *f.* a wife, *f.* a good thing.
Eccl. 9:10, thy hand *f.* to do, do it.
11:1, *f.* it after many days.
Isa. 58:13, *f.* thine own pleasure.
Jer. 6:16; Mt. 11:20, *f.* rest to your souls.
Mt. 7:7; Lk. 11:9, seek, and ye shall *f.*
7:14, few there be that *f.* it.
10:39, loseth his life shall *f.* it.
22:9, as many as ye shall *f.*
Mk. 11:13, he might *f.* any thing thereon.
13:36, he *f.* you sleeping.
Lk. 15:4, 8, till he *f.* it.
18:8, shall he *f.* faith on earth?
Jn. 1:41, first *f.* his brother.
Rom. 7:21, I *f.* a law that when I would.
Heb. 4:16, *f.* grace to help.
See Jn. 7:34; 2Tim. 1:18; Rev. 9:6.

FINE. Ps. 19:10, more to be desire than *f.* gold.
81:16; 147:14, the *f.* of the wheat.
Prov. 25:12, as an ornament of *f.* gold.
Lam. 4:1, how is the *f.* gold changed!
Mk. 15:46, Joseph brought *f.* linen.
See Job 28:1, 17; Lk. 16:19; Rev. 18:12; 19:8
FINGER. Ex. 8:19, this is the *f.* of God.
Ex. 31:18; Dt. 9:10, written with the *f.* of God.
1Ki. 12:10; 2Chr. 10:10, little *f.* thicker.
Prov. 7:3, bind them on thy *f.*
Isa. 58:9, the putting forth of the *f.*
Dan. 5:5, the *f.* of a man's hand.
Mt. 23:4; Lk. 11:46, not move with *f.*
Lk. 16:24, the tip of his *f.*
Jn. 8:6, with his *f.* wrote on ground.
20:25, put my *f.* into print of nails.
27, reach hither thy *f.*
See Ps. 8:3; Prov. 6:13; Isa. 2:8; 59:3; Lk. 11:20.
FINISH. 1Chr. 28:20, till thou hast *f.*
Neh. 6:15, so the wall was *f.*
Lk. 14:28, 29, 30, whether sufficient to *f.*
Jn. 4:34, to do his will, and *f.* his work.
5:36, which the Father hath given me to *f.*
17:4, have *f.* the work.
19:30, it is *f.*
Acts 20:24; 2Tim. 4:7, that I might *f.* my course.
2Cor. 8:6, *f.* in you the same grace.
Heb. 12:2, Jesus, author and *f.* of our faith.
Jas. 1:15, sin, when it is *f.*
See Dan. 9:24; Rev. 19:7; 11:7; 20:5.
FIRE. Gen. 22:7, behold the *f.* and the wood.
Ex. 3:2, bush burned with *f.*
22:6, he that kindled *f.* shall make restitution.
Lev. 10:2, *f.* from the Lord.
18:21; Dt. 19:10; 2Ki. 17:17; 23:10, pass through *f.*
Jud. 15:5, brands on *f.*, and burnt corn.
1Ki. 18:24, that answereth by *f.*
19:12, the Lord was not in the *f.*
1Chr. 21:26, Lord answered him by *f.*
Ps. 39:3, musing, the *f.* burned.
74:7, they have cast *f.* into thy sanctuary.
Prov. 6:27, can a man take *f.*?
26:18, mad man who casteth *f.*-brands.
20, no wood, the *f.* goeth out.
21, as wood is to *f.*, so is a contentious man.
Isa. 9:19, as the fuel of the *f.*
24:15, glorify the Lord in the *f.*
43:2, walkest through *f.* not be burned.
44:16, I have seen the *f.*
64:2, the melting *f.* burneth.
66:15, the Lord will come with *f.*
16, by *f.* will the Lord plead.
24; Mk. 9:44, neither their *f.* quenched.
Jer. 20:9, word as a *f.* in my bones.
Ezek. 36:5, in the *f.* of my jealousy.
Dan. 3:27, the *f.* had no power.
Amos 4:11, as a *f.*-brand plucked out.
Nah. 1:6, fury poured out like *f.*
Zech. 2:5, a wall of *f.* round about.
3:2, a brand plucked out of the *f.*
Mal. 3:2, like a refiner's *f.*
Mt. 3:10; 7:19; Lk. 3:9; Jn. 15:6, tree cast into *f.*

11; Lk. 3:16, baptize with *f.*
13:42, cast them into furnace of *f.*
18:8; 25:41; Mk. 9:43, 46, everlasting *f.*
Lk. 9:54, wilt thou that we command *f.*?
12:49, come to send *f.* on earth.
17:29, same day it rained *f.* and brimstone.
Acts 2:3, cloven tongues like as of *f.*
1Cor. 3:13, revealed by *f.* and the *f.* shall try.
15, saved, yet so as by *f.*
2Th. 1:8, in flaming *f.* taking vengeance.
Heb. 1:7, his ministers a flame of *f.*
11:34, quenched violence of *f.*
Jas. 3:5, a little *f.* kindleth.
6, the tongue is a *f.*
1Pet. 1:7, gold tried with *f.*
2Pet. 3:7, reserved unto *f.*
12, heavens being on *f.*
Jude 7, vengeance of eternal *f.*
23, pulling them out of the *f.*
Rev. 3:18, buy gold tried in the *f.*
20:9, *f.* came down from God.
10, devil cast into lake of *f.*
Rev. 20:14, death and hell cast into *f.*
21:8, the lake that burneth with *f.*
See Isa. 33:14; Jer. 23:29; Heb. 12:29.
FIRM. Josh. 3:17; Job 41:24; Ps. 73:4; Heb. 3:6.
FIRMAMENT. Gen. 1:6, let there be a *f.*
Ps. 19:1, the *f.* sheweth his handywork.
Ezek. 1:22, the likeness of the *f.*
Dan. 12:3, shine as the brightness of the *f.*
FIRST. 1 Ki. 17:13, make a little cake *f.*
Ezra 3:12; Hag. 2:3, the glory of the *f.* house.
Job 15:7, art thou the *f.* man born?
Prov. 3:9, honour the Lord with *f.*-fruits.
18:17, *f.* in his own cause.
Isa. 43:27, try *f.* father hath sinned.
Mt. 5:24, *f.* be reconciled.
6:33, seek ye *f.* the kingdom.
7:5, *f.* cast out the beam.
12:29; Mk. 3:27, except he *f.* bind strong man.
45, last state of that man worse than *f.*
17:10, 11; Mk. 9:12, Elias must *f.* come.
20:10, when the *f.* came, they supposed.
22:38; Mk. 12:28, 29, 30, the *f.* commandment.
Mk. 4:28, *f.* the blade.
9:35, if any desire to be *f.*, same shall be last.
13:10, gospel must *f.* be published.
Lk. 14:28, sitteth not down *f.*
17:25, but *f.* must he suffer many things.
Jn. 1:41, *f.* findeth his brother Simon.
5:4, whosoever *f.* stepped in.
8:7, let him *f.* cast a stone.
Acts 11:26, called Christians *f.* at Antioch.
Rom. 2:9, 10, of the Jew *f.*
8:23, the *f.*-fruits of the Spirit.
29, *f.*-born among many brethren.
11:16, if the *f.*-fruit be holy.
1 Cor. 12:28, *f.* apostles, secondarily prophets.
14:30, let the *f.* hold peace.
15:20, 23, Christ the *f.*-fruits,
45, the *f.* man was made a living soul.
46, not *f.* which is spiritual.
47, *f.* man is of the earth.
2 Cor. 8:5, *f.* gave their own selves.
12, if there be *f.* a willing mind.
Eph. 6:2, the *f.* commandment with promise.
Col. 1:15, 18, the *f.*-born of every creature.
1 Th. 4:16, dead in Christ shall rise *f.*
2 Th. 2:3, a falling away *f.*
1 Tim. 1:16, that in me *f.*
2:13, Adam was *f.* formed.
3:10, let these *f.* be proved.
5:4, learn *f.* to show piety at home.
12, cast off their *f.* faith.
2 Tim. 4:16, at my *f.* answer no man.
Ti. 3:10, after *f.* and second admonition.
Heb. 5:12, which be the *f.* principles.
7:27, *f.* for his own sins.
10:9, taketh away the *f.*
Jas. 3:17, *f.* pure, then peaceable.
1 Pet. 4:17, if judgment *f.* begin at us.
1 Jn. 4:19, because he *f.* loved us.
Jude 6, kept not their *f.* estate.
Rev. 2:4, left thy *f.* love.
5, do thy *f.* works.
20:5, this is the *f.* resurrection.
21:1, *f.* heaven and *f.* earth passed away.
See Ex. 4:8; Num. 18:13; Jn. 12:16.
FIR TREE. Isa. 41:19, I will set in the desert the *f.*
55:13, instead of the thorn shall come up the *f.*
60:13, the *f.*
Hos. 14:8, I am like a green *f.*
FISH. Eccl. 9:12, *f.* taken in an evil net.
Hab. 1:14, men as the *f.* of the sea.
Mt. 7:10, if he ask a *f.*
14:17; Mk. 6:38; Lk. 9:13, five loaves and two *f.*
Jn. 21:3, Peter saith, I go a *f.*
1 Cor. 15:39, one flesh of beasts, another of *f.*
See Jer. 16:16; Mt. 4:19; Mk. 1:17; Lk. 24:42.
FISHERS. Mt. 4:18; Mk. 1:16, for they were *f.*
Jn. 21:7, he girt his *f.* coat unto him.
See Lk. 5:2.
FIT. Job 34:18, is it *f.* to say to a king?
Lk. 9:62, is *f.* for the kingdom.
14:35, it is not *f.* for the dunghill.
Col. 3:18, submit, as it is *f.* in the Lord.
See Lev. 16:21; Prov. 24:27; Ezek. 15:5; Rom. 9:22.
FITLY. Prov. 25:11; Eph. 2:21; 4:16.
FIXED. Ps. 57:7; 108:1; 112:7; Lk. 16:26.
FLAME. Gen. 3:24, at garden of Eden a *f.* sword.
Jud. 13:20, angel ascended in *f.*
Isa. 5:24, as the *f.* consumeth chaff.
29:6, a *f.* of devouring fire.
43:2, neither shall *f.* kindle.
66:15, rebuke with *f.* of fire.
Ezek. 20:47, the *f.* *f.* shall not be quenched.
Lk. 16:24, tormented in this *f.*
See Ps. 29:7; Heb. 1:7; Rev. 1:14; 2:18.
FLATTER. Job 17:5, he speaketh *f.* to his friends.
32:21, 22, give *f.* titles to man.
Ps. 5:9, they *f.* with their tongue.
12:2, *f.* lips and double heart.
Prov. 20:19, meddle not with him that *f.*

26:28, a *f.* mouth worketh ruin.
1Th. 2:5, neither used we *f.* words.
See Prov. 28:23; 29:5; Dan. 11:21, 32, 34.
LATTERY. Ps. 78:36; Prov. 2:16; 24:24.
LEE. Lev. 26:17, 36, ye shall *f.* when none pursueth.
Num. 10:35, them that hate thee *f.* before thee.
Neh. 6:11, should such a man as I *f.*?
Job 14:2, he *f.* as a shadow.
Ps. 139:7, whither shall I *f.*?
Prov. 28:1, the wicked *f.* when no man pursueth.
17, he shall *f.* to the pit.
Song 2:17; 4:6, till shadows *f.* away.
Isa. 35:10; 51:11, sighing shall *f.* away.
Mt. 3:7; Lk. 3:7, to *f.* from wrath to come.
10:23, in one city, *f.* to another.
24:16; Mk. 13:14; Lk. 21:21, *f.* to mountains.
26:56; Mk. 14:50, forsook him and *f.*
Jn. 10:5, not follow, but will *f.* from him.
13, the hireling *f.*
1Tim. 6:11, *f.* these things.
2Tim. 2:22, *f.* youthful lusts.
Jas. 4:7, he will *f.* from you.
See 1Cor. 6:18; 10:14; Rev. 12:6, 14.
LEECE. Jud. 6:37, I will put a *f.* of wool in the floor.
LESH. Gen. 2:24; Mt. 19:5; Mk. 10:8; 1Cor. 6:16; Eph. 5:31, one *f.*
6:12, all *f.* had corrupted his way.
13, end of all *f.* is come.
7:21, all *f.* died.
Ex. 16:3, when we sat by the *f.* pots.
Lev. 17:14, the life of all *f.* is the blood.
19:28, cuttings in your *f.*
Num. 11:33, while *f.* was between their teeth.
16:22; 27:16, God of spirits of all *f.*
1Ki. 17:6, bread and *f.* in morning and evening.
2Chr. 32:8, with him is an arm of *f.*
Neh. 5:5, our *f.* is as the *f.* of our brethren.
Job 19:26, in my *f.* shall I see God.
33:21, his *f.* is consumed away.
Ps. 16:9; Acts 2:26, my *f.* shall rest in hope.
65:2, to thee shall all *f.* come.
78:20, can he provide *f.*?
Prov. 5:11, mourn, when *f.* consumed.
11:17, the cruel troubleth his own *f.*
23:20, among riotous eaters of *f.*
Eccl. 4:5, the fool eateth his own *f.*
12:12, weariness of the *f.*
Isa. 40:5, all *f.* shall see it.
6; 1Pet. 1:24, all *f.* is grass.
Ezek. 11:19; 36:26, a heart of *f.*
Joel 2:28; Acts 2:17, pour Spirit on all *f.*
Mt. 16:17, *f.* and blood hath not revealed it.
24:22; Mk. 13:20, there should no *f.* be saved.
Mt. 26:41; Mk. 14:38, spirit willing, *f.* weak.
Lk. 24:39, spirit hath not *f.* and bones.
Jn. 1:14, Word made *f.*, and dwelt.
6:51, 54, 55, bread I give is my *f.*
52, can this man give us his *f.*?
63, the *f.* profiteth nothing.
8:15, ye judge after the *f.*
17:2, power over all *f.*
Rom. 6:19, because of the infirmity of your *f.*
8:3, condemned sin in the *f.*
8, they that are in *f.* cannot please God.
9, not in the *f.*, but the Spirit.
12:13, to live after the *f.*
9:3, kinsmen according to the *f.*
5, of whom as concerning the *f.*
13:14, make not provision for the *f.*
1Cor. 1:29, that no *f.* should glory.
15:39, all *f.* not the same *f.*
50, *f.* and blood cannot inherit.
2Cor. 12:7, a thorn in the *f.*
Gal. 1:16, I conferred not with *f.* and blood.
2:20, life I now live in the *f.*
5:17, *f.* lusteth against the Spirit.
Eph. 2:3, lusts of *f.*, desires of *f.*
Phil. 3:3, 4, no confidence in the *f.*
1Tim. 3:16, manifest in the *f.*
1Pet. 3:18, Christ put to death in *f.*
1Jn. 4:2; 2Jn. 7, denieth that Christ is come in *f.*
Jude 8, dreamers defile the *f.*
23, hating garment spotted by *f.*
See Jn. 1:13; 3:6; Gal. 5:19; Heb. 2:14.
FLESHLY. 2Cor. 1:12; 3:3; Col. 2:18; 1Pet. 2:11.
FLIES. Ex. 8:21, I will send swarms of *f.* upon thee.
Ps. 78:45, he sent divers sorts of *f.* among thee.
105:31, he spake, and there came divers sorts of *f.*
FLIGHT. Isa. 52:12; Amos 2:14; Mt. 24:20; Heb. 11:34.
FLINT. Num. 20:11; Dt. 8:15; 32:13; Ps. 114:8; Isa. 5:28; 50:7; Ezek. 3:9; 1Cor. 10:4.
FLOCK. Jer. 13:20, where is the *f.*, thy beautiful *f.*?
Ezek. 34:31, the *f.* of my pasture are men.
Zech. 11:7, the poor of the *f.*
Lk. 12:32, fear not, little *f.*
Acts 20:28, take heed to the *f.*
29, not sparing the *f.*
1Pet. 5:2, feed the *f.* of God.
3, being ensamples to the *f.*
See Ezek. 36:37; Mal. 1:14; Mt. 26:31.
FLOOD. Josh. 24:2, on other side of the *f.*
Job 28:11, he bindeth *f.* from overflowing.
Ps. 32:6, in *f.* of great waters.
Song 8:7, neither can *f.* drown love.
Isa. 44:3, *f.* upon the dry ground.
59:19, enemy come in like a *f.*
Mt. 7:25, *f.* came, and the winds blew.
24:38, in days before the *f.*
39; Lk. 17:27, knew not till *f.* came.
See Gen. 6:17; 7:11; 8; 9:11; Ps. 90:5; 2Pet. 2:5; Rev. 12:15.
FLOOR. 1Sam. 23:1, they rob the threshing-*f.*
2Sam. 24:21, to buy the threshing-*f.* of thee.
Hos. 9:1, loved a reward on every corn-*f.*
Mic. 4:12, gather as sheaves into the *f.*
Mt. 3:12; Lk. 3:17, purge his *f.*
See Dt. 15:14; Dan. 2:35; Joel 2:24.
FLOUR. Ex. 29:2, of wheaten *f.* shalt thou make them.
Lev. 2:2, take thereout his handful of the *f.*
FLOURISH. Ps. 72:7, in his days shall the righteous *f.*
90:6, in the morning it *f.*

92:12, righteous shall *f.* like a palm tree.
103:15, as flower so he *f.*
Prov. 11:28, righteous shall *f.* as branch.
14:11, tabernacle of upright *f.*
Eccl. 12:5, when the almond tree shall *f.*
Song 6:11; 7:12, whether the vine *f.*
Ezek. 17:24, have made dry tree to *f.*
Phil. 4:10, your care of me hath *f.*
See Ps. 92:14; Dan. 4:4.
FLOW. Ps. 147:18, wind to blow, and waters *f.*
Song 4:16, that the spices may *f.* out.
Isa. 2:2, all nations shall *f.* unto it.
64:1, 3, mountains *f.* at thy presence.
Jer. 31:12, shall *f.* to the goodness of the Lord.
Jn. 7:38, shall *f.* living water.
See Job 20:28; Isa. 60:5; Joel 3:18; Mic. 4:1.
FLOWER. 1Sam. 2:33, shall die in *f.* of age.
Job 14:2, cometh forth as a *f.*
Song 2:12, the *f.* appear on earth.
Isa. 28:1, 4, glorious beauty is a fading *f.*
40:6, as the *f.* of the field.
7; Nah. 1:4; Jas. 1:10; 1Pet. 1:24, *f.* fadeth.
See Job 15:33; Isa. 18:5; 1Cor. 7:36.
FLY. Job 5:7, as sparks *f.* upward.
Ps. 55:6, then would I *f.* away.
90:10, and we *f.* away.
Prov. 23:5, riches *f.* away.
Isa. 60:8, that *f.* as a cloud.
See Dan. 9:21; Rev. 14:6; 19:17.
FOAM. Hos. 10:7; Mk. 9:18; Lk. 9:39; Jude 13.
FOES. Ps. 27:2; 30:1; 89:23; Mt. 10:36; Acts 2:35.
FOLD. Prov. 6:10; 24:33, *f.* of the hands to sleep.
Eccl. 4:5, fool *f.* his hands and eateth.
Hab. 3:17, flock cut off from the *f.*
Jn. 10:16, one *f.*, and one shepherd.
See Isa. 13:20; 65:10; Nah. 1:10.
FOLK. Prov. 30:26; Jer. 51:58; Mk. 6:5; Jn. 5:3.
FOLLOW. Num. 14:24, Caleb hath *f.* me fully.
1Ki. 18:21, God, *f.* him.
Ps. 23:6, goodness and mercy shall *f.* me.
63:8, my soul *f.* hard after thee.
68:25, the players *f.* after.
Prov. 12:11; 28:19, that *f.* vain persons.
Isa. 5:11, that they may *f.* strong drink.
Hos. 6:3, if we *f.* on to know the Lord.
Amos. 7:15, took me as I *f.* the flock.
Mt. 4:19; 8:22; 9:9; 16:24; 19:21; Mk. 2:14; 8:34; 10:21; Lk. 5:27; 9:23, 59; Jn. 1:43; 21:22, Jesus said, *f.* me.
8:19; Lk. 9:57, 61, Master, I will *f.* thee.
Mk. 10:28; Lk. 18:28, we left all, and *f.* thee.
32, as they *f.*, they were afraid.
Lk. 22:54, Peter *f.* afar off.
Jn. 10:27, my sheep hear my voice, and *f.* me.
13:36, thou canst not *f.* me now.
Rom. 14:19, *f.* things that make for peace.
1Cor. 10:4, the rock that *f.* them.
14:1, *f.* after charity.
Phil. 3:12, I *f.* after.
1Th. 5:15, ever *f.* that which is good.
1Tim. 5:24, some men they *f.* after.
6:11; 2Tim. 2:22, *f.* righteousness.
Heb. 12:14, *f.* peace with all men.
13:7, whose faith *f.*
1Pet. 1:11, the glory that should *f.*
2:21, that ye should *f.* his steps.
2Pet. 2:15, *f.* the way of Balaam.
Rev. 14:4, they that *f.* the Lamb.
13, their works do *f.* them.
See Mk. 9:38; 1Pet. 3:13; 2Pet. 1:16; Rev. 6:8.
FOLLOWER. Eph. 5:1, *f.* of God, as dear children.
Heb. 6:12, *f.* of them who through faith.
FOLLY. 1Sam. 25:25, and *f.* is with him.
Job 4:18, his angels he charged with *f.*
24:12, yet God layeth not *f.* to them.
42:8, lest I deal with you after your *f.*
Ps. 49:13, this their way is their *f.*
85:8, let them not turn again to *f.*
Prov. 13:16, a fool layeth open his *f.*
14:8, the *f.* of fools is deceit.
18, the simple inherit *f.*
16:22, instruction of fools is *f.*
17:12, rather than a fool in his *f.*
26:4, answer not a fool according to his *f.*
5, answer fool according to his *f.*
Eccl. 1:17, to know wisdom and *f.*
2:13, wisdom excelleth *f.*
7:25, the wickedness of *f.*
Eccl. 10:6, *f.* is set in great dignity.
2Cor. 11:1, bear with me a little in my *f.*
2Tim. 3:9, their *f.* shall be manifest.
See Josh. 7:15; Prov. 14:24; Isa. 9:17.
FOOD. Gen. 3:6, tree good for *f.*
Ex. 21:10, her *f.* shall not be diminished.
Dt. 10:18, in giving him *f.* and raiment.
Job 23:12, more than my necessary *f.*
24:5, wilderness yieldeth *f.*
Ps. 78:25, did eat angels' *f.*
104:14, bring forth *f.* out of the earth.
136:25, giveth *f.* to all flesh.
Prov. 6:8, gathereth her *f.* in harvest.
13:23, much *f.* in tillage of poor.
30:8, with *f.* convenient for me.
31:14, she bringeth her *f.* from far.
2Cor. 9:10, minister bread for your *f.*
1Tim. 6:8, having *f.* and raiment.
Jas. 2:15, destitute of daily *f.*
See Gen. 1:29; 2:9; 6:21; 9:3; 41:35; Lev. 22:7; Ps. 145:16; 147:9.
FOOL. 2Sam. 3:33, died Abner as a *f.* dieth?
Ps. 14:1; 53:1, *f.* said in his heart.
75:4, to *f.*, deal not foolishly.
Prov. 1:7, *f.* despise wisdom.
3:35, shame the promotion of *f.*
10:8, 10, a prating *f.* shall fall.
21, *f.* die for want of wisdom.
23, sport to a *f.* to do mischief.
11:29, the *f.* shall be servant to the wise.
12:15, way of *f.* right in own eyes.
16, *f.* wrath presently known.
13:16, *f.* layeth open his folly.
20, companion of *f.* shall be destroyed.
14:8, folly of *f.* is deceit.
9, *f.* make a mock at sin.
16, the *f.* rageth, and is confident.
15:2, mouth of *f.* poureth out foolishness.

5, a *f.* despiseth his father's instruction.
16:22, the instruction of *f.* is folly.
17:28, a *f.*, when he holdeth his peace, counted wise.
20:3, every *f.* will be meddling.
29:11, a *f.* uttereth all his mind.
Eccl. 2:14, *f.* walketh in darkness.
16, how dieth wise man? as the *f.*
19, who knoweth whether wise or a *f.*?
5:3, a *f.* voice is known by multitude of words.
10:14, a *f.* is full of words.
Isa. 35:8, wayfaring men, though *f.*
Jer. 17:11, at his end he shall be a *f.*
Hos. 9:7, the prophet is a *f.*
Mt. 5:22, shall say, thou *f.*
23:17, ye *f.* and blind.
Lk. 12:20, thou *f.*, this night.
24:25, O *f.*, and slow of heart.
1Cor. 3:18, let him become a *f.*
2Cor. 11:16, let no man think me a *f.*
12:11, I am a *f.* in glorying.
Eph. 5:15, walk not as *f.*, but as wise.
See Prov. 10:18; 19:1; 28:26; Eccl. 10:3

FOOLISH. Dt. 32:6, O *f.* people.
2Sam. 24:10; 1Chr. 21:8, I have done very *f.*
Job 2:10, as one of the *f.* women.
Ps. 73:3, I was envious at the *f.*
Prov. 9:6, forsake the *f.*, and live.
13, a *f.* woman is clamorous.
14:1, the *f.* plucketh it down.
17:25; 19:13, a *f.* son is grief.
Eccl. 7:17, neither be thou *f.*
Jer. 4:22, my people are *f.*
Mt. 7:26, unto a *f.* man.
Rom. 1:21, their *f.* heart was darkened.
1Cor. 1:20, hath not God made *f.*
Gal. 3:1, O *f.* Galatians.
3:3, are ye so *f.*?
Eph. 5:4, nor *f.* talking.
1Tim. 6:9, rich fall into *f.* lusts.
2Tim. 2:23; Ti. 3:9, *f.* questions avoid.
Ti. 3:3, we were sometimes *f.*
1Pet. 2:15, ignorance of *f.* men.
See Job 5:3; Lam. 2:14; Ezek. 13:3.

FOOLISHNESS. Ps. 69:5, thou knowest my *f.*
Prov. 22:15, *f.* is bound in heart of child.
24:9, thought of *f.* is sin.
1Cor. 1:18, to them that perish *f.*
21, by the *f.* of preaching.
23, Christ crucified, to Greeks *f.*
25, the *f.* of God is wiser than men.
2:14, things of Spirit are *f.* to him.
3:19, wisdom of world *f.* with God.
See 2Sam. 15:31; Prov. 27:22.

FOOT. Gen. 41:44, without thee no man lift *f.*
Dt. 2:5, not so much as *f.* breadth.
11:10, wateredst it with thy *f.*
Ps. 38:16, when my *f.* slippeth.
91:12; Mt. 4:6; Lk. 4:11, dash *f.* against stone.
94:18, my *f.* slippeth, thy mercy.
121:3, not suffer *f.* to be moved.
Prov. 3:23, thy *f.* shall not stumble.
25:17, withdraw *f.* from neighbour's house.
Eccl. 5:1, keep thy *f.* when thou goest.
Isa. 1:6, from sole of *f.* to head no soundness.
Mt. 14:13, people followed on *f.*
18:8; Mk. 9:45, if thy *f.* offend thee.
1Cor. 12:15, if the *f.* say, because I am not.
Heb. 10:29, trodden under *f.* the Son of God.
See Jer. 12:5; Mt. 5:35; Jas. 2:3.

FORBADE. Mt. 3:14; Mk. 9:38; Lk. 9:49.

FORBEAR. Ex. 23:5, wouldest *f.* to help.
2Chr. 35:21, *f.* from meddling with God.
Neh. 9:30, many years didst thou *f.* them.
Ezek. 2:5; 3:11, whether hear or *f.*
1Cor. 9:6, power to *f.* working.
Eph. 4:2; Col. 3:13, *f.* one another in love.
6:9, *f.* threatening.
See Prov. 24:11; Ezek. 3:27; Zech. 11:12.

FORBID. Num. 11:28, Joshua said, *f.* them.
Mk. 9:39; Lk. 9:50, *f.* him not.
10:14; Lk. 18:16, children, *f.* them not.
Lk. 6:29, *f.* not to take coat.
23:2, *f.* to give tribute.
Acts 10:47, can any *f.* water?
1Cor. 14:39, *f.* not to speak with tongues.
1Tim. 4:3, *f.* to marry.
See Acts 16:6; 28:31; 1Th. 2:16.

FORCE. Dt. 34:7, nor natural *f.* abated.
Ezra 4:23, made them cease by *f.*
Mt. 11:12, violent take it by *f.*
Jn. 6:15, perceived they would take him by *f.*
Heb. 9:17, a testament is of *f.* after.
See Dt. 20:19; Prov. 30:33; Amos 2:14.

FORCIBLE. Job 6:25.

FOREFATHERS. Jer. 11:10; 2Tim. 1:3.

FOREHEAD. Ex. 28:38, it shall always be on his *f.*
1Sam. 17:49, smote Philistine in his *f.*
Ezek. 3:8, made thy *f.* strong.
9:4, set a mark on *f.* of them that sigh.
Rev. 7:3; 9:4, sealed in their *f.*
22:4, his name shall be in their *f.*
See Rev. 13:16; 14:1; 17:5; 20:4.

FOREIGNER. Ex. 12:45; Dt. 15:3; Eph. 2:19.

FOREKNOW. Rom. 8:29; 11:2; 1Pet. 1:2.

FOREKNOWLEDGE. Acts 2:23, delivered by *f.* of God.

FOREMOST. Gen. 32:17; 33:2; 2Sam. 18:27.

FOREORDAINED. 1Pet. 1:20.

FORERUNNER. Heb. 6:20.

FORESEE. Prov. 22:3; 27:12; Gal. 3:8.

FOREST. Ps. 50:10, every beast of *f.* is mine.
Isa. 29:17; 32:15, field esteemed as *f.*
Jer. 5:6, lion out of *f.* shall slay them.
26:18; Mic. 3:12, high places of the *f.*
46:23, they shall cut down her *f.*
Amos 3:4, will lion roar in the *f.*?
See Ezek. 15:6; 20:46; Hos. 2:12.

FORETELL. Mk. 13:23; Acts 3:24; 2Cor. 13:2.

FOREWARN. Lk. 12:5; 1Th. 4:6.

FORGAT. Jud. 3:7, they *f.* the Lord.
Ps. 78:11, they *f.* his works.
106:13, soon *f.* his works.
Lam. 3:17, I *f.* prosperity.
See Gen. 40:23; Hos. 2:13.

FORGAVE. Mt. 18:27, 32, and *f.* him the debt.

Lk. 7:42, he frankly *f.* them both.
43, he to whom he *f.* most.
2Cor. 2:10, if I *f.* any thing.
Col. 3:13, even as Christ *f.* you.
See Ps. 32:5; 78:38; 99:8.
FORGE. Job 13:4; Ps. 119:69.
FORGET. Dt. 4:9, lest thou *f.* things thine eyes have seen.
23, lest ye *f.* the covenant.
6:12; 8:11, beware lest thou *f.* the Lord.
Job 8:13, so are the paths of all that *f.* God.
Ps. 9:17, all nations that *f.* God.
10:12, *f.* not the humble.
45:10, *f.* thine own people.
50:22, consider, ye that *f.* God.
78:7, that they might not *f.* works of God.
88:12, in the land of *f.*
102:4, I *f.* to eat my bread.
103:2, *f.* not all his benefits.
119:16, I will not *f.* thy word.
137:5, if I *f.* thee, O Jerusalem.
Prov. 2:17, *f.* the covenant of her God.
3:1, *f.* not my law.
31:5, lest they drink and *f.*
7, let him drink, and *f.* his poverty.
Isa. 49:15, can a woman *f.*?
51:13, and *f.* the Lord thy Maker.
65:11, *f.* my holy mountain.
Jer. 2:32, maid *f.* her ornaments.
23:27, cause my people to *f.* my name.
Amos 8:7, I will never *f.* their works.
Phil. 3:13, *f.* those things which are behind.
Heb. 6:10, not unrighteous to *f.*
13:2, not *f.* to entertain.
16, to communicate *f.* not.
Jas. 1:24, *f.* what manner of man.
See Gen. 41:51; Lam. 5:20; Hos. 4:6.
FORGIVE. Ex. 32:32, if thou wilt *f.* their sin.
34:7; Num. 14:18, *f.* iniquity, transgression.
1Ki. 8:30, 39; 2Chr. 6:21, 30, hearest *f.*
2Chr. 7:14, then will I hear and *f.*
Ps. 32:1; Rom. 4:7, whose transgression is *f.*
86:5, good, and ready to *f.*
103:3, who *f.* all thine iniquities.
Mt. 6:12; Lk. 11:4, *f.* us, as we *f.*
14, if ye *f.*
15, if ye *f.* not.
9:6; Mk. 2:10; Lk. 5:24, power to *f.* sin.
18:21, how oft, and I *f.* him?
35, if ye from your hearts *f.*
Mk. 2:7, who can *f.* sins?
11:25, *f.* that your Father may *f.*
26, not *f.*, Father will not *f.*
Lk. 6:37, *f.*, and ye shall be *f.*
7:47, her sins, which are many, are *f.*
49, who is this *f.* sins also?
17:3, 4, if brother repent, *f.* him.
23:34, Father *f.* them, they know not.
Acts 8:22, thought of thine heart may be *f.*
2Cor. 2:7, ye ought rather to *f.*
10, to whom ye *f.*, I *f.* also.
12:13, *f.* me this wrong.
Eph. 4:32, as God for Christ's sake hath *f.*
Col. 2:13, quickened, having *f.*
1Jn. 1:9, faithful and just to *f.*
See Mt. 9:2; 12:31; Mk. 3:28; Lk. 12:10.
FORGIVENESS. Ps. 130:4, *f.* with thee, that thou mayest be feared.
Mk. 3:29, hath never *f.*
Acts 5:31, exalted to give *f.*
Eph. 1:7; Col. 1:14, in whom we have *f.*
See Dan. 9:9; Acts 13:38; 26:18.
FORGOTTEN. Dt. 24:19, and hast *f.* a sheaf.
32:18, *f.* God that formed thee.
Ps. 9:18, needy not always *f.*
10:11, said, God hath *f.*
31:12, *f.* as a dead man.
42:9, why hast thou *f.* me?
44:20, if we have *f.* name of our God.
77:9, hath God *f.* to be gracious?
Eccl. 2:16, in days to come all *f.*
8:10, wicked were *f.* in city.
9:5, the memory of them is *f.*
Isa. 17:10, *f.* the God of thy salvation.
44:21, thou shalt not be *f.* of me.
49:14, my Lord hath *f.* me.
65:16, former troubles are *f.*
Jer. 2:32; 13:25; 18:15, my people have *f.*
3:21, *f.* the Lord their God.
44:9, *f.* the wickedness of your fathers.
50:6, *f.* their restingplace.
Ezek. 22:12; 23:35, thou hast *f.* me.
Mt. 16:5; Mk. 8:14, *f.* to take bread.
Lk. 12:6, not one *f.* before God.
2Pet. 1:9, *f.* that he was purged.
See Lam. 2:6; Hos. 4:6; 8:14; 13:6.
FORM (*n.*). Gen. 1:2; Jer. 4:23, without *f.*, and void.
Job 4:16, could not discern the *f.*
Isa. 52:14, *f.* more than sons of men.
Ezek. 10:8, the *f.* of a man's hand.
Dan. 3:19, *f.* of visage changed.
25, *f.* of fourth like Son of God.
Mk. 16:12, appeared in another *f.*
Rom. 2:20, hast *f.* of knowledge and truth.
Phil. 2:6, being in the *f.* of God.
7, the *f.* of a servant.
2Tim. 1:13, *f.* of sound words.
3:5, having *f.* of godliness.
See 1Sam. 28:14; Ezek. 43:11; Rom. 6:17.
FORM (*v.*). Dt. 32:18, forgotten God that *f.* thee.
2pKi. 19:25; Isa. 37:26, that I have *f.* it.
Job 26:5, dead things are *f.*
13, hath *f.* crooked serpent.
33:6, I also am *f.* of clay.
Ps. 90:2, or ever thou hadst *f.*
94:9, he that *f.* the eye.
Prov. 26:10, great God that *f.* all things.
Isa. 43:1, he that *f.* thee, O Israel.
7; 44:21, I have *f.* him.
10, before me was no God *f.*
21, people have I *f.* for myself.
44:10, who hath *f.* a god?
54:17, no weapon *f.* against thee.
Amos 7:1, he *f.* grasshoppers.
Rom. 9:20, shall thing *f.* say.
Gal. 4:19, till Christ be *f.* in you.

See Gen. 2:7, 19; Ps. 95:5; Jer. 1:5.
ORMER. Ruth 4:7, manner in *f.* time.
Job 8:8, enquire of the *f.* age.
Ps. 89:49, where are they *f.* lovingkindnesses?
Eccl. 1:11, no remembrance of *f.* things.
7:10, *f.* days better than these.
Isa. 43:18, remember not the *f.* things.
46:9, remember the *f.* things of old
48:3, declared *f.* things from beginning.
65:7, measure their *f.* work.
16, *f.* troubles are forgotten.
Jer. 5:24; Hos. 6:3; Joel 2:23, *f.* and latter rain.
10:16; 51:19, the *f.* of all things.
Hag. 2:9, glory of *f.* house.
Zech. 1:4; 7:7, 12, *f.* prophets have cried.
8:11, I will not be as in *f.* days.
14:8, half of them toward *f.* sea.
Mal. 3:4, pleasant as in *f.* years.
Eph. 4:22, concerning the *f.* conversation.
Rev. 21:4, for the *f.* things are passed away.
See Gen. 40:13; Dan. 11:13; Acts 1:1
ORSAKE. Dt. 4:31; 31:6; 1Chr. 28:20, he will not *f.*
12:19, *f.* not the Levite.
32:15, he *f.* God which made him.
Josh. 1:5; Heb. 13:5, I will not fail nor *f.*
Jud. 9:11, *f.* my sweetness and fruit.
1Chr. 28:9, if thou *f.* him, he will cast thee off.
2Chr. 15:2, if ye *f.* him, he will *f.* you.
Neh. 10:39, we will not *f.* house of our God.
13:11, why is house of God *f.*?
Job 6:14, he *f.* the fear of the Almighty.
20:19, oppressed and *f.* the poor.
Ps. 22:1; Mt. 27:46; Mk. 15:34, why hast thou *f.* me?
37:25, yet have I not seen the righteous *f.*
28, the Lord *f.* not his saints.
119:8, *f.* me not utterly.
138:8, *f.* not work of thine own hands.
Prov. 1:8; 6:20, *f.* not law of thy mother.
2:17, *f.* the guide of her youth.
4:6, *f.* her not, and she shall preserve thee.
27:10, thy friend, and father's friend, *f.* not.
Isa. 6:12, a great *f.* in the land.
17:9, as a *f.* bough.
32:14; Jer. 4:29; Ezek. 36:4, a *f.* city.
54:6, as a woman *f.*
7, for a small moment *f.*
62:4, no more be termed *f.*
12, a city not *f.*
Jer. 2:13; 17:13, *f.* fountain of living waters.
Mt. 19:27; Lk. 5:11, we have *f.* all
29, that hath *f.* houses.
26:56; Mk. 14:50, disciples *f.* him, and fled.
Mk. 1:18, they *f.* their nets.
Lk. 14:33, whosoever *f.* not all.
2Cor. 4:9, persecuted, but not *f.*
2Tim. 4:10, Demas hath *f.* me.
16, all men *f.* me.
Heb. 10:25, not *f.* assembling of ourselves.
11:27, but faith Moses *f.* Egypt.
See Ps. 71:11; Isa. 49:14; Jer. 5:7; 22:9; Ezek. 8:12.
FORSWEAR. Mt. 5:33.
FORTRESS. 2Sam. 22:2; Ps. 18:2; Jer. 16:19, Lord is my *f.*
FORTY STRIPES. Dt. 25:3, *f. s.* he may give him.
2Cor. 11:24, of the Jews five times received I *f. s.* save one.
FORTY YEARS. Ex. 16:35, Israel did not eat manna *f. y.*
Num. 14:33, your children shall wander in the wilderness *f. y.*
Ps. 95:10, *f. y.* long was I grieved.
See Jud. 3:11; 5:31; 8:28.
FORWARD. Jer. 7:24, backward, and not *f.*
Zech. 1:15, helped *f.* the affliction.
See 2Cor. 8:8; 9:2; 3Jn. 6.
FOUL. Job 16:16; Mt. 16:3; Mk. 9:25; Rev. 18:2.
FOUND. Gen. 27:20, *f.* it so quickly.
37:2, this have we *f.*
44:16, hat *f.* out iniquity.
1Ki. 20:36, a lion *f.* him.
21:20, hast thou *f.* me?
2Ki. 22:8, I *f.* book of the law.
2Chr. 19:3, good things *f.* in thee.
Job 28:12, 13, where shall wisdom be *f.*?
33:24, I have *f.* a ransom.
Ps. 32:6, where thou mayest be *f.*
36:2, iniquity *f.* to be hateful.
84:3, sparrow hath *f.* an house.
Prov. 25:16, hast thou *f.* honey?
Eccl. 7:28, one among a thousand have I *f.*
29, this only have I *f.*
Song 3:4, but I *f.* him whom my soul loveth.
Isa. 65:1; Rom. 10:20, *f.* of them that sought me not.
Jer. 2:26, thief ashamed when he is *f.*
34, in thy skirts is *f.*
41:8, ten men were *f.*
Ezek. 22:30, I sought for a man, but *f.* none.
Dan. 5:27, weighed, and *f.* wanting.
Mal. 2:6, iniquity not *f.* in his lips.
Mt. 7:25; Lk. 6:48, it was *f.* on a rock.
8:10; Lk. 7:9, have not *f.* so great faith.
Mt. 13:46, *f.* one pearl of great price.
20:6, *f.* others standing idle.
21:19; Mk. 14:40; Lk. 22:45, *f.* nothing thereon.
Mk. 7:2, they *f.* fault.
30, she *f.* the devil gone out.
Lk. 2:46, they *f.* him in the temple.
8:35, they *f.* the man clothed.
15:5, 6, *f.* the sheep.
9, *f.* the piece of money.
24, 32, was lost, and is *f.*
23:14, I have *f.* no fault.
24:2, *f.* the stone rolled away.
3:23, *f.* not the body.
Jn. 1:41, 45, we have *f.* the Messias.
Acts 7:11, our fathers *f.* no sustenance.
9:2, if he *f.* any of this way.
17:23, I *f.* an altar.
Rom. 7:10, I *f.* to be unto death.
Gal. 2:17, we ourselves also are *f.* sinners.
Phil. 2:8, *f.* in fashion as a man.
Heb. 11:5, Enoch was not *f.*

12:17, he *f.* no place of repentance.
Rev. 3:2, not *f.* thy works perfect.
12:8, nor was their place *f.* any more.
16:20, mountains were not *f.*
See Gen. 6:8; 2Chr. 15:4; 2Cor. 5:3; Phil. 3:9.
FOUNDATION. Josh. 6:26; 1Ki. 16:34, lay the *f.* in his firstborn.
Job 4:19, them whose *f.* is in dust.
Ps. 11:3, if *f.* be destroyed.
82:5, all the *f.* of earth out of course.
102:25, of old laid *f.* of earth.
137:7, raise it even to the *f.*
Prov. 10:25, righteous an everlasting *f.*
Isa. 28:16, I lay in Zion a *f.*
Isa. 58:12, the *f.* of many generations.
Lk. 6:48, laid the *f.* on a rock.
49, without a *f.*
Rom. 15:20, on another man's *f.*
1Cor. 3:10, I laid the *f.*
11, other *f.* can no man lay.
12, if any man build on this *f.*
Eph. 2:20, on the *f.* of the apostles and prophets.
1Tim. 6:19, laying up for themselves a good *f.*
2Tim. 2:19, the *f.* of God standeth sure.
Heb. 6:1, not laying the *f.* of repentance.
11:10, a city that hath *f.*
Rev. 21:14, the wall had twelve *f.*
See Mt. 13:35; Jn. 17:24; Acts 16:26.
FOUNTAIN. Gen. 7:11; 8:2, *f.* of great deep.
Dt. 8:7, a land of *f.*
2Chr. 32:3, took counsel to stop *f.* of water.
Ps. 36:9, the *f.* of life.
Prov. 5:16, let thy *f.* be dispersed.
8:24, no *f.* abounding with water.
13:14, law of the wise a *f.* of life
14:27, fear of the Lord a *f.* of life.
25:26, a troubled *f.* and corrupt spring.
Eccl. 12:6, pitcher broken at the *f.*
Song 4:12, a *f.* sealed.
15, a *f.* of gardens.
Jer. 2:13; 17:13, forsaken *f.* of living waters.
9:1, eyes a *f.* of tears.
Hos. 13:15, his *f.* shall be dried up.
Zech. 13:1, in that day shall be a f. opened.
Jas. 3:11, 12, doth a *f.* send forth.
Rev. 7:17, lead them to living *f.*
14:7, worship him that made *f.* of waters.
21:6, of the *f.* of life freely.
See Isa. 12:3; 44:3; 55:1; Jer. 6:7; Joel 3:18; Mk. 5:29; Jn. 5:10.
FOWLS. Gen. 1:20, and *f.* that may fly above the earth.
7:3, of *f.* also of the air by sevens.
Ps. 104:12, the *f.* of heaven have their habitation.
148:10, creeping things, and flying *f.*
FOXES. Song 2:15, take us the *f.*, the little *f.*
Lam. 5:18, the *f.* walk upon it.
Mt. 8:20, the *f.* have holes.
Lk. 13:32, go ye, and tell that *f.*
See Jud. 15:4.
FRAGMENTS. Jn. 6:12, 13, gather up *f.* that remain.
See Mt. 14:20; Mk. 6:43; 8:19; Lk. 9:17.
FRAIL. Ps. 39:4.
FRAME. Jud. 12:6, he could not *f.* to pronounce.
Ps. 94:20, *f.* mischief by a law.
103:14, he knoweth our *f.*
Isa. 29:16, shall thing *f.* say of him that *f.* it?
Eph. 2:21, building fitly *f.* together.
See Ezek. 40:2; Hos. 5:4; Heb. 11:3.
FRANKLY. Lk. 7:42.
FRAUD. Ps. 10:7; Jas. 5:4.
FRAY. Dt. 18:26; Jer. 7:33; Zech. 1:21.
FREE. Gen. 2:16, of every tree thou mayest *f.* eat.
Dt. 24:5, shall be *f.* at home one year.
Josh. 9:23, there shall none of you be *f.*
1Sam. 14:30, if people had eaten *f.*
2Chr. 29:31, of *f.* heart offered.
Ezra 2:68, chief fathers offered *f.*
7:15, king and counsellors offered *f.* to God.
Ps. 51:12, with thy *f.* spirit.
88:5, *f.* among the dead.
Isa. 58:6, let the oppressed go *f.*
Hos. 14:4, I will love them *f.*
Mt. 10:8, *f.* ye have received, *f.* give.
17:26, then are the children *f.*
Mk. 7:11, if a man say Corban, he shall be *f.*
Jn. 8:32, the truth shall make you *f.*
33, how sayest thou, ye shall be f.?
36, Son make you *f.*, ye shall be *f.* indeed.
Acts 22:28, I was *f.* born.
Rom. 3:24, justified *f.* by his grace.
5:15, the *f.* gift.
6:18, 22, being made *f.* from sin.
20, servants of sin, *f.* from righteousness.
8:2, *f.* from the law of sin and death.
32, with him *f.* give us all things.
1Cor. 9:1, am I not *f.*?
19, though *f.* from all men.
12:13; Eph. 6:8, whether bond or *f.*
Gal. 3:28; col. 3:11, there is neither bond nor *f.*
5:1, wherewith Christ hath made us *f.*
2Th. 3:1, word have *f.* course.
1Pet. 2:16, as *f.*, and not using liberty.
Rev. 21:6, give of fountain of life *f.*
22:17, let him take water of life *f.*
See Ex. 21:2; Dt. 15:13; Jer. 34:9; Gal. 4:22.
FREEWILL. Lev. 22:18, and for all his *f.* offerings.
Num. 15:3, or in a *f.* offering.
Dt. 16:10, a tribute of a *f.* offering.
See Ezra 3:5.
FREEWOMAN. Gal. 4:22.
FRESH. Num. 11:8; Job 29:20; 33:25; Jas. 3:12.
FRET. Ps. 37:1, 7, 8; Prov. 24:19, *f.* not thyself.
Prov. 19:3, his heart *f.* against the Lord.
See 1Sam. 1:6; Isa. 8:21; Ezek. 16:43.
FRIEND. Ex. 33:11, as a man to his *f.*
2Sam. 19:6, lovest thine enemies, and hatest *f.*
2Chr. 20:7, Abraham thy *f.* for ever.
Job 6:27, ye dig a pit for your *f.*
42:10, when he prayed for his *f.*
Ps. 35:14, as though he had been my *f.*
41:9, my familiar *f.* hath lifted.
88:18, lover and *f.* hast thou put far from me.
Prov. 6:1, if thou be surety for thy *f.*
3, make sure thy *f.*
14:20, the rich hath many *f.*

16:28; 17:9, whisperer separateth chief *f.*
17:17, *f.* loveth at all times.
18:24, a *f.* that sticketh closer than a brother.
19:4, wealth maketh many *f.*
27:6, faithful are wounds of a *f.*
10, thine own *f.* and father's *f.* forsake not.
17, man sharpeneth countenance of his *f.*
Song 5:16, this is my *f.*
Isa. 41:8, seed of Abraham my *f*
Jer. 20:4, a terror to thy *f*
Mic. 7:5, trust not in a *f.*
Zech. 13:6, wounded in house of my *f.*
Mt. 11:19; Lk. 7:34, a *f.* of publicans.
20:13, *f.* I do thee no wrong.
22:12, *f.*, how camest thou hither?
26:50, *f.*, wherefore art thou come?
Mk. 5:19, go home to thy *f.*,
Lk. 11:5, which of you shall have a *f.*,
8, though he give not because he is his *f.*
14:12, call not thy *f.*
15:6, 9, calleth his *f.* and neighbours.
16:9, *f.* of the mammon.
Jn. 11:11, our *f.* Lazarus sleepeth.
15:13, lay down his life for his *f.*
14, ye are my *f.*, if ye do whatsoever I command.
15, not servants, but *f.*
19:12, thou art not Caesar's *f.*
Jas. 2:23, Abraham was called the *f.* of God.
4:4, a *f.* of the world.
See Prov. 22:24; Lk. 14:10; 3Jn. 14.
FRINGES. Num. 15:37, that they make them *f.*
Dt. 22:12, thou shalt make thee *f.*
See Mt. 23:5.
FROGS. Ex. 8:6; Ps. 78:45; 105:30; Rev. 16:13.
FRONTLETS. Ex. 13:16; Dt. 6:8, for *f.* between thine eyes.
FROWARD. Dt. 32:20, a very *f.* generation.
Prov. 2:12, man that speaketh *f.* things.
3:32, the *f.* is abomination.
4:24, put away *f.* mouth.
11:20; 17:20, of a *f.* heart.
16:28, a *f.* man soweth strife.
21:8, the way of man is *f.*
22:5, snares are in the way of the *f.*
See Prov. 10:32; Isa. 57:17; 1Pet. 2:18.
FRUIT. Num. 13:26, showed them the *f.* of the land.
Dt. 26:2, take the first of all *f.*
33:14, precious *f.* brought forth.
Ps. 107:37, yield *f.* of increase.
127:3, the *f* of the womb is his reward.
Prov. 8:19, my *f.* is better than gold.
11:30, *f.* of the righteous a tree of life.
12:14; 18:20, satisfied by the *f.* of his mouth.
Song 2:3, his *f.* was sweet to my taste.
4:13, 16, orchard with pleasant *f.*
Isa. 3:10; Mic. 7:13, the *f.* of their doings.
27:6, fill face of the world with *f.*
28:4, the hasty *f.* before summer.
57:19, I create the *f.* of the lips.
Jer. 17:10; 21:14; 32:19, according to *f.* of doings.
Hos. 10:13, eaten the *f.* of lies.
Amos 8:1, basket of summer *f.*
Mic. 6:7, *f.* of body for sin of soul.
Hab. 3:17, neither shall *f.* be in vines.
Hag. 1:10, earth is stayed from her *f.*
Mt. 3:8; Lk. 3:8, *f.* meet for repentance.
7:16, 20, by their *f.* ye shall know them.
12:33, make tree good, and his *f.* good.
13:23, is he who beareth *f.*
21:19, let no *f.* grow on thee.
34, when time of *f.* drew near.
26:29; Mk. 14:25, drink of *f.* of vine.
Mk. 4:28, 3 earth bringeth forth *f.* of herself.
12:2, receive the *f.* of the vineyard.
Lk. 13:6, he sought *f.* thereon.
7, I come seeking *f.* on this fig tree.
9, if it bear *f.*, well.
Jn. 4:36, *f.* to life eternal.
15:2, branch that beareth *f.*
4, branch cannot bear *f.* of itself.
8, that ye bear much *f.*
16, ordained that ye should bring forth *f.*
Rom. 1:13, have some *f.* among you.
6:21, what *f.* had ye then.
7:4, bring forth *f.* unto God.
2Cor. 9:10; Phil. 1:11, the *f.* of righteousness.
Gal. 5:22; Eph. 5:9, the *f.* of the Spirit.
Phil. 1:22, this is the *f.* of my labour.
4:17, I desire *f.* that may abound.
Col. 1:6, the gospel bringeth forth *f.* in you.
2Tim. 2:6, first partaker of the *f.*
Heb. 12:11, peaceable *f.* of righteousness.
13:15, the *f.* of our lips.
Jas. 3:17, wisdom full of good *f.*
5:7, waiteth for the precious *f.*
Jude 12, trees whose *f.* withereth, without *f.*
Rev. 22:2, yielded her *f.* every month.
See Gen. 30:2; Ps. 92:14; Jer. 12:2; Col. 1:10.
FRUSTRATE. Ezra 4:5; Isa. 44:25; Gal. 2:21.
FUEL. Isa. 9:5; Ezek. 15:4; 21:32.
FULFIL. Ps. 20:4, the Lord *f.* all thy counsel.
5, *f.* all thy petitions
145:19, he will *f.* the desire of men.
Mt. 3:15, to *f.* all righteousness.
5:17, not to destroy, but to *f.*
18; 24:34, till all be *f.*
Mk. 13:4, what the sign when these shall be *f.*?
Lk. 1:20, my words shall be *f.* in season.
21:24, times of the Gentiles be *f.*
22:16, till it be *f.* in kingdom of God.
Jn. 3:29; 17:13, this my joy is *f.*
Acts 13:25, and as John *f.* his course.
33, God hath *f.* the same unto us.
Rom. 13:10, love is the *f.* of the law.
Gal. 5:14, all the law is *f.* in one word.
6:2, so *f.* the law of Christ.
Eph. 2:3, *f.* the desires of the flesh.
Phil. 2:2, *f.* ye my joy.
Col. 4:17, take heed thou *f.* the ministry.
2Th. 1:11, *f.* good pleasure of his will.
Jas. 2:8, if ye *f.* the royal law.
See Ex. 5:13; 23:26; Gal. 5:16; Rev. 17:17.
FULL. Lev. 19:29, land became *f.* of wickedness.
Dt. 6:11, houses *f.* of good things.
34:9, Joshua was *f* of spirit of wisdom.

Ruth 1:21, I went out *f.*
2Ki. 6:17, mountain was *f.* of horses.
1Chr. 21:22, 24, for the *f.* price.
Job 5:26, come to grave in *f.* age.
11:2, a man *f.* of talk.
14:1, *f.* of trouble.
20:11, *f.* of the sins of youth.
21:23, dieth in his *f* strength.
32:18, I am *f.* of matter.
Ps. 10:7; Rom. 3:14, mouth *f.* of cursing.
65:9, which is *f.* of water.
74:20, *f.* of habitations of cruelty.
88:3, soul *f.* of troubles.
119:64, earth is *f.* of thy mercy.
127:5, happy the man that hath his quiver *f.*
Prov. 27:7, the *f.* soul loatheth an honeycomb.
20, hell and destruction are never *f.*
Prov. 30:9, lest I be *f.*, and deny thee.
Eccl. 1:7, yet the sea is not *f.*
Hab. 3:3, earth *f.* of his praise.
Zech. 8:5, streets *f.* of boys and girls.
Mt. 6:22; Lk. 11:36, *f.* of light.
Lk. 6:25, woe unto you that are *f.*!
11:39, *f.* of ravening.
Jn. 1:14, *f.* of grace and truth.
15:11; 16:24, that your joy may be *f.*
Acts 6:3; 7:55; 11:24, men *f.* of the Holy Ghost.
9:36, *f.* of good works.
Rom. 15:14, ye also are *f.* of goodness.
1Cor. 4:8, now ye are *f.*
Phil. 4:12, I am instructed to be *f.*
18, I am *f.*
2Tim. 4:5, make *f.* proof of thy ministry.
Heb. 5:14, meat to them of *f.* age.
1Pet. 1:8, with joy unspeakable and *f.* of glory.
Rev. 15:7, *f.* of the wrath of God.
See Lev. 2:14; 2Ki. 4:6; 10:21; Amos 2:13.
FULLY. Num. 14:24, Caleb hath followed me *f.*
Eccl. 8:11, heart is *f.* set to do evil.
Rom. 14:5, let every man be *f.* persuaded.
15:19, I have *f.* preached the gospel.
Rev. 14:18, her grapes are *f.* ripe.
See 1Ki. 11:6; Acts 2:1; Rom. 4:21.
FULNESS. Ps. 16:11, *f.* of joy.
Jn. 1:16, of his *f.* have we received.
Rom. 11:25, the *f.* of the Gentiles.
Eph. 1:23, the *f.* of him that filleth all in all.
3:19, filled with the *f.* of God.
4:13, the stature of the *f.* of Christ.
Col. 1:19, in him should all *f.* dwell.
2:9, the *f.* of the Godhead bodily.
See Num. 18:27; Ps. 96:11; Rom. 11:12.
FURIOUS. Prov. 22:24, with a *f.* man thou shalt not go.
29:22, a *f.* man aboundeth in transgression.
Nah. 1:2, the Lord is *f.*
See 2Ki. 9:20; Ezek. 5:15; 23:25.
FURNACE. Dt. 4:20, Lord hath taken you out of *f.*
Ps. 12:6, as silver tried in a *f.*
Isa. 48:10, in the *f.* of affliction.
Mt. 13:42, into a *f.* of fire.
See Gen. 15:17; 19:28; 1Ki. 8:51; Dan. 3:6, 11, 15, etc.;
Ezek. 22:18.
FURNISH. Ps. 78:19; Mt. 22:10; 2Tim. 3:17.
FURROWS. Ps. 65:10; 129:3; Hos. 10:4; 12:11.
FURTHER. Ezra 8:36, they *f.* the people.
Job 38:11, hitherto shalt thou come, but no *f.*
Lk. 24:28, as though he would have gone *f.*
Acts 4:17, that it spread no *f.*
2Tim. 3:9, they shall proceed no *f.*
See Mk. 5:35; Phil. 1:12, 25.
FURY. Gen. 27:44, till thy brother's *f.* turn.
Isa. 27:4, *f.* is not in me.
63:5, my *f.* uphold me.
Jer. 21:5, I will fight against thee in *f.*
25:15, the wine cup of this *f.*
Ezek. 21:17, I will cause my *f.* to rest.
See Dan. 3:13, 19; 8:6; 9:16; 11:44.
GAIN. Job 22:3, is it *g.* to him that thou makest thy ways perfect?
Prov. 1:19; 15:27; Ezek. 22:12, greedy of *g.*
3:14, the *g* thereof better than gold.
28:8, by usury and unjust *g.*
Ezek. 22:13, 27, at thy dishonest *g.*
Dan. 11:39, he shall divide the land for *g.*
Mic. 4:13, consecrate their *g.* to the Lord.
Mt. 16:26; Mk. 8:36; Lk. 9:25, if he *g.* the world.
18:15, thou hast *g.* thy brother.
25:17, 22, had also *g.* other two.
Lk. 19:15, 16, 18, had *g.* by trading.
Acts 16:19, hope of their *g.* was gone.
19:24, no small *g.* to the craftsmen.
1Cor. 9:19, that I might *g.* the more.
20, that I might *g.* the Jews.
2Cor. 12:17, 18, did I make a *g.* of you?
Phil. 1:21, to die is *g.*
3:7, *g.* to me, I counted loss.
1Tim. 6:5, supposing that *g.* is godliness.
6, godliness with contentment is great *g.*
See Jud. 5:19; Job 27:8; Jas. 4:13.
GAINSAY. Lk. 21:15; Ti. 1:9; Jude 11.
GALL. Ps. 69:21; Lam. 3:19; Mt. 27:34; Acts 8:23.
GALLOWS. Est. 7:10, they hanged Haman on the *g.*
GAP. Ezek. 13:5; 22:30.
GARDEN. Gen. 2:8, God planted a *g.* eastward in Eden
13:10, as the *g.* of the Lord.
Dt. 11:10; 1Ki. 21:2, as a *g.* of herbs.
Song 4:12, a *g.* enclosed.
16, blow upon my *g.*
5:1, I am come into my *g.*
6:2, 11, gone down into his *g.*
Isa. 1:8, as a lodge in a *g.*
30, as a *g.* that hath no water.
51:3, her desert like the *g.* of the Lord.
Isa. 58:11; Jer. 31:12, like a watered *g.*
61:11, as the *g.* causeth things sown to spring forth.
Jer. 29:5, plant *g.*, and eat the fruit.
Ezek. 28:13, in Eden the *g.* of God.
31:8, 9, cedars in the *g.* of God.
36:35, is become like the *g.* of Eden.
Joel 2:3, land as the *g.* of Eden before them.
Jn. 18:1, where was a *g.*
26, did not I see thee in the *g.*
19:41, there was a *g.*, and in the *g.*
See Gen. 2:15; Amos 4:9; 9:14; Jn. 20:15.

GARMENT. Gen. 39:12, he left his *g*., and fled.
49:11, washed his *g*. in wine.
Josh. 7:21, a goodly Babylonish *g*.
9:5, Gibeonites took old *g*.
2Ki. 5:26, is it a time to receive *g*.?
7:15, all the way was full of *g*.
Job 37:17, how thy *g*. are warm.
Ps. 22:18, they part my *g*. among them.
102:26; Isa. 50:9; 51:6; Heb. 1:11, wax old as a *g*.
104:2, with light as with a *g*.
6, coveredst it with the deep as with a *g*.
109:18, clothed himself with cursing as with his *g*.
Prov. 20:16, take his *g*. that is surety.
25:20, a *g*. in old weather.
30:4, who hath bound the waters in a *g*.?
Eccl. 9:8, let thy *g*. be always white.
Isa. 52:1, put on thy beautiful *g*.
61:3, *g*. of praise for spirit of heaviness.
10, the *g*. of salvation.
Joel 2:13, rend your heart and not your *g*.
Zech. 13:4, a rough *g*. to deceive.
Mt. 9:16; Mk. 2:21; Lk. 5:36, new cloth, old *g*.
20:14, 36; Mk. 5:27; Lk. 8:44, hem of *g*.
21:8; Mk. 11:8, spread *g*. in way.
22:11, 12, wedding *g*.
23:5, enlarge borders of *g*.
27:35; Mk. 15:24, parted *g*., casting lots.
Mk. 11:7; Lk. 19:35, cast *g*. on colt.
13:16, not turn back again to take *g*.
Lk. 22:36, let him sell his *g*.
24:4, in shining *g*.
Acts 9:39, showing the coats and *g*.
Jas. 5:2, your *g*. are motheaten.
Jude 23, the *g*. spotted by the flesh.
Rev. 3:4, not defiled their *g*.
16:15, that watcheth, and keepeth his *g*.
GARNER. Ps. 144:13; Joel 1:17; Mt. 3:12.
GARNISH. Job 26:13; Mt. 12:44; 23:29.
GATE. Gen. 28:17, the *g*. of heaven.
Dt. 6:9; 11:20, write them on the *g*.
Ps. 9:13, the *g*. of death.
118:19, the *g*. of righteousness.
Prov. 17:19, exalteth *g*. seeketh destruction.
31:23, her husband known in the *g*.
Isa. 26:2, open the *g*., that righteous may enter.
38:10, the *g*. of the grave.
45:1, open the two leaved *g*.
60:11, thy *g*. shall be open continually.
18, walls Salvation, and *g*. Praise.
Mt. 7:13; Lk. 13:24, strait *g*., wide *g*.
16:18, *g*. of hell shall not prevail.
Heb. 13:12, also suffered without the *g*.
Rev. 21:25, *g*. not shut at all by day.
See Ps. 24:7; Isa. 28:6; Nah. 2:6.
GATHER. Gen. 41:35, let them *g*. all the food.
49:10, to him shall *g*. of the people be.
Ex. 16:17, *g*., some more, some less.
Dt. 28:38, carry much out, and *g*. little in.
30:3; Ezek. 36:24, will *g*. thee from all nations.
2Sam. 14:14, spilt which cannot be *g*. up.
Job 11:10, if he *g*. together, who can hinder?
Ps. 26:9, *g*. not my soul with sinners.
39:6, knoweth not who shall *g*. them.
Prov. 6:8, the ant *g*. her food.
10:5, he that *g*. in summer.
13:11, he that *g*. by labour shall increase.
Isa. 27:12, ye shall be *g*. one by one.
40:11, he shall *g*. the lambs.
56:8, yet will I *g*. others.
62:10, *g*. out the stones.
Mt. 3:12; Lk. 3:17, *g*. wheat into garner.
6:26, nor *g*. into barns.
7:16; Lk. 6:44, do men *g*. grapes of thorns?
12:30; Lk. 11:23, he that *g*. not scattereth.
13:28, wilt thou that we *g*. them up?
29, lest while ye *g*. up the tares.
41, shall *g*. out of his kingdom.
25:32, before him shall be *g*. all nations.
Jn. 6:12, *g*. up fragments.
15:6, men *g*. them, and cast.
1Cor. 16:2, that there be no *g*. when I come.
2Th. 2:1, by our *g*. together unto him.
See Mt. 23:37; Jn. 4:36; 11:52.
GAVE. Gen. 3:12, the woman *g*. me.
Josh. 21:44; 2Chr. 15:15; 20:30, Lord *g*. them rest.
1Sam. 10:9, *g*. to Saul another heart.
Neh. 8:8., they read, and *g*. the sense.
Job 1:21, the Lord *g*.
Ps. 21:4, he asked life, and thou *g*. it.
68:11, the Lord *g*. the word.
Eccl. 12:7, to God who *g*. it.
Amos 2:12, ye *g*. the Nazarites wine.
Mt. 21:23; Mk. 11:28; Lk. 20:2, who *g*. thee this authority?
25:35, 42, ye *g*. me meat.
Lk. 15:16, no man *g*. unto him.
Jn. 10:29, my Father, who *g*. them.
Acts 2:4, as the Spirit *g*. them utterance.
26:10, I *g*. my voice against them.
Rom. 1:28, God *g*. them over.
1Cor. 3:6, God *g*. the increase.
Eph. 4:8, *g*. gifts unto men.
11, he *g*. some apostles.
See 2Cor. 8:5; Gal. 1:4; Ti. 2:14.
GAY. Jas. 2:3.
GAZE. Ex. 19:21; Nah. 3:6; Acts 1:11; Heb. 10:33.
GENERATION. Dt. 1:35, not one of this evil *g*.
32:5, 20, a perverse and crooked *g*.
Ps. 14:5, God is in the *g*. of the righteous.
22:30, it shall be accounted for a *g*.
102:18, written for the *g*. to come.
145:4, one *g*. shall praise thy works.
Prov. 27:24, crown endure to every *g*.
30:11, there is a *g*. that curseth.
Eccl. 1:4, one *g*. passeth away.
Isa. 34:10, from *g*. to *g*. it shall lie waste.
Joel 1:3, children tell another *g*.
Mt. 3:7; 12:34; 23:33; Lk. 3:7, *g*. of vipers.
12:41, in judgment with this *g*.
17:17; Mk. 9:19; Lk. 9:41, perverse *g*.
23:36, shall come on this *g*.
24:34; Mk. 13:30; Lk. 21:32, this *g*. shall not

pass.
Lk. 16:8, are in their *g.* wiser.
17:25, rejected of this *g.*
1Pet. 2:9, a chosen *g.*
See Isa. 53:8; Dan. 4:3; Mt. 1:1; Lk. 11:30.
GENTILES. Mt. 10:5, go not in way of the *G.*
Jn. 7:35, to the dispersed among *G.*
Acts 9:15, bear my name before the *G.*
13:42, *G.* besought that these words.
46, we turn to the *G.*
15:3, declaring conversion of the *G.*
18:6, from henceforth I will go to the *G.*
Rom. 3:29, is he not also of the *G.*
11:11, salvation is come to the *G.*
11:13, as the apostle of the *G.*
1Cor. 5:1, not so much as named among *G.*
Eph. 4:17, walk not as other *G.*
2Tim. 1:11, I am ordained a teacher of *G.*
3Jn. 7, taking nothing of the *G.*
See Rom. 2:9; 1Pet. 2:12; Rev. 11:2.
GENTLE. 1Th. 2:7, we were *g.* among you.
2Tim. 2:24, servant of Lord be *g.*
Ti. 3:2, *g.*, showing all meekness.
Jas. 3:17, wisdom is pure and *g.*
1Pet. 2:18, not only to the good and *g.*
See 2Sam. 18:5; 22:36; Gal. 5:22.
GETTETH. Prov. 3:13; 4:7; 19:8; Jer. 17:11.
GIFT. Ex. 23:8; Dt. 16:19, a *g.* blindeth.
2Sam. 19:42, hath he given us any *g.*?
2Chr. 19:7, with the Lord no taking of *g.*
Ps. 68:18; Eph. 4:8, *g.* unto men.
72:10, kings of Sheba and Seba offer *g.*
Prov. 6:35, not content, though many *g.*
15:27, he that hateth *g.* shall live.
17:8, a *g.* is as a precious stone.
18:16, man's *g.* maketh room for him.
21:14, a *g.* in secret pacifieth anger.
Eccl. 3:13; 5:19, enjoy good, it is God's *g.*
7:7, a *g.* destroyeth the heart.
Isa. 1:23, every one loveth *g.*
Mt. 5:23, bring thy *g.* to the altar.
24, leave thy *g.* before the altar.
7:11; Lk. 11:13, know how to give good *g.*
Lk. 21:1, casting *g.* into treasury.
Jn. 4:10, if thou knewest the *g.* of God.
Acts 8:20, though the *g.* of God may be purchased.
Rom. 1:11, some spiritual *g.*
5:15, free *g.*, *g* by grace.
6:23, the *g.* of God is eternal life.
11:29, *g.* of God without repentance.
12:6, *g.* differing according to grace.
1Cor. 7:7, his proper *g.* of God.
12:4, diversities of *g.*
31, covet best *g.*
14:1, 12, desire spiritual *g.*
2Cor. 9:15, unspeakable *g.*
Eph. 2:8, faith the *g.* of God.
Phil. 4:17, not because I desire a *g.*
1Tim. 4:14, neglect not the *g.*
2Tim. 1:6, stir up the *g.*
Jas. 1:17, good and perfect *g.*
See Num. 18:29; Mt. 15:5; Acts 2:38; 10:45; 1Cor. 13:2.
GIRD. 2Sam. 22:40; Ps. 18:39, hast *g.* me with strength.
Isa. 45:5, I *g.* thee, though thou has not.
Joel 1:13, *g.* yourselves, and lament.
Eph. 6:14, having your loins *g.*
See Prov. 31:17; Jn. 13:4; 21:18; Rev. 15:6.
GIRDLE. Ex. 28:4, and a *g*
Jer. 13:1, go and get thee a linen *g.*
See Isa. 11:5; Mt. 3:4; Mk. 1:6.
GIRL. Joel 3:3; Zech. 8:5.
GIVE. Gen. 28:22, I will *g.* the truth.
Ex. 30:15, rich shall not *g.* more, poor not *g.* less
Dt. 15:10, thou shalt *g.* him thine heart.
16:17; Ezek. 46:5, *g.* as he is able.
1Chr. 29:14, of thine own have we *g.* thee.
Ezra 9:9, to *g.* us a reviving.
Ps. 2:8, I shall *g.* thee the heathen.
6:5, in the grave who shall *g.* thanks?
29:11, Lord will *g* strength.
37:4, *g.* thee the desires of thy heart.
21, the righteous showeth mercy, and *g.*
84:11, Lord will *g.* grace and glory.
109:4, I *g.* myself unto prayer.
Prov. 23:26, *g.* me thine heart.
Isa. 55:10, *g.* seed to the sower.
Mt. 5:42, *g.* to him that asketh.
6:11; Lk. 11:3, *g.* daily bread.
7:9, will he *g.* him a stone?
10:8, freely *g.*
13:11; Mk. 4:11, it is *g.* to you to know.
16:26; Mk. 8:37, *g.* in exchange.
19:21; Mk. 10:21, go sell, and *g.* to the poor.
20:23; Mk. 10:40, not mine to *g.*
26:9; Mk. 14:5, sold and *g.* to the poor.
Lk. 6:38, *g.* and it shall be *g.*
Jn. 4:7, 10, *g.* me to drink.
6:37, all that the Father *g.* me.
65, no man can come, except it were *g.* him.
10:28, I *g.* to them eternal life.
Jn. 13:29, that he should *g.* something to poor.
14:27, not as the world *g.*, *g.* I.
Acts 3:6, such as I have *g.* I thee.
6:4, we will *g.* ourselves to prayer.
20:35, more blessed to *g.*
Rom. 12:8, he that *g.*, let him do it.
19, rather *g.* place until wrath.
1Cor. 3:7, God *g.* the increase.
2Cor. 9:7, *g.* not grudgingly, a cheerful *g.*
Phil. 4:15, concerning *g.* and receiving.
1Tim. 4:13, *g.* attendance to reading.
15, *g.* thyself wholly to them.
6:17, who *g.* us richly.
Jas. 1:5, that *g.* to all men liberally.
4:6, *g.* more grace, *g.* grace to humble.
2Pet. 1:5, *g.* all diligence.
See Mk. 12:15; Lk. 12:48; Jn. 3:34.
GLAD. Ex. 4:14, he will be *g.* in heart.
Job 3:22, *g.* when they can find the grave.
Ps. 16:9, therefore my heart is *g.*
34:2; 69:32, humble shall hear, and be *g.*
46:4, make *g.* the city of God.
101:15, maketh *g.* the heart of man.

122:1, I was *g.* when they said.
126:3, whereof we are *g.*
Prov. 10:1; 15:20, wise son maketh a *g.* father.
24:17, let not thine heart be *g.*
Lam. 1:21, they are *g.* that thou hast done it.
Lk. 15:32, make merry, and be *g.*
Jn. 8:56, saw my day, and was *g.*
11:15, I am *g.* for your sakes.
Acts 11:23, when he had seen grace of God, was *g.*
See Mk. 6:20; 12:37; Lk. 1:19; 8:1.
GLADNESS. Num. 10:10, in day of your *g.*
Dt. 18:47, servedst not with *g.* of heart.
Neh. 8:17, there was very great *g.*
Ps. 4:7, thou hast put *g.* in my heart.
45:7; Heb. 1:9, the oil of *g.*
97:11, *g.* is sown for the upright.
Isa. 35:10; 51:11, they shall obtain joy, and *g.*
Acts 2:46, did eat with *g.* of heart.
12:14, opened not for *g.*
14:17, filling our hearts with food and *g.*
See Ps. 100:2; Prov. 10:28; Isa. 51:3.
GLASS. 1Cor. 13:12, we see through a *g.* darkly.
2Cor. 3:18, beholding as in a *g.* the glory of the Lord.
Rev. 4:6; 15:2, a sea of *g.*, like unto crystal.
GLEAN. Lev. 19:10; Jer. 6:9; 49:9.
GLISTERING. 1Chr. 29:2; Lk. 9:29.
GLITTERING. Dt. 32:41; Job 20:25; 39:23; Nah. 3:3.
GLOOMINESS. Joel 2:2; Zeph. 1:15.
GLORIFY. Lev. 10:3, before all people I will be *g.*
Ps. 50:23, whoso offereth praise *g.* me.
86:9, all nations shall *g.* thy name.
12, I will *g.* thy name for evermore.
Isa. 24:15, *g.* the Lord in the fires.
60:7, I will *g.* house of my glory.
Ezek. 28:22, I will be *g.* in midst of thee.
Dan. 5:23, God hast thou not *g.*
Mt. 5:16, *g.* your Father in heaven.
15:31, they *g.* God of Israel.
Lk. 4:15, being *g.* of all.
Jn. 7:39, because Jesus was not yet *g.*
11:4, that the Son of God might be *g.*
12:16, but when Jesus was *g.*, they remembered.
28, Father, *g.* thy name: I have both *g.*
13:32, God shall also *g.* him.
15:8, herein is my Father *g.*
17:1, *g.* thy Son.
4, I have *g.* thee on earth.
21:19, by what death he should *g.* God.
Rom. 1:21, they *g.* him not as God.
8:17, suffer with him, that we may be *g.*
30, them he also *g.*
1Cor. 6:20, *g.* God in body and spirit.
Gal. 1:24, they *g.* God in me.
2Th. 1:10, to be *g.* in his saints.
Heb. 5:5, so Christ *g.* not himself.
See Isa. 25:5; Mt. 9:8; 15:31; Lk. 7:16.
GLORIOUS. Ex. 15:11, *g.* in holiness.
Dt. 28:58; 1Chr. 29:13, this *g.* name.
Ps. 45:13, all *g.* within.
66:2, make his praise *g.*
72:19, blessed be his *g.* name.
87:3, *g.* things are spoken.
Isa. 11:10, his rest shall be *g.*
28:1, whose *g.* beauty is a fading flower.
60:13, place of my feet *g.*
63:1, *g.* in his apparel.
14, to make thyself a *g.* name.
Jer. 17:12, a *g.* high throne.
Dan. 11:16, 41, stand in the *g.* land.
45, in the *g.* holy mountain.
Lk. 13:17, rejoiced for *g.* things done.
Rom. 8:21, *g.* liberty of children of God.
2Cor. 3:7, 8, ministration *g.*
4:4, light of *g.* gospel.
Eph. 5:27, a *g.* church.
Phil. 3:21, like to his *g.* body.
1Tim. 1:11, the *g.* gospel of the blessed God.
Ti. 2:13, the *g.* appearing of the great God.
See Ex. 15:1; 2Sam. 6:20; Isa. 24:23.
GLORY. Ex. 33:18, show me thy *g.*
Num. 14:21; Ps. 72:19; Isa. 6:3, earth filled with *g.*
Ps. 8:1, thy *g.* above the heavens.
16:9, my *g.* rejoiceth.
24:7, 10, the King of *g.*
73:24, afterward receive me to *g.*
84:11, will give grace and *g.*
108:1, will give praise with my *g.*
145:11, the *g.* of thy kingdom.
Prov. 3:35, the wise shall inherit *g.*
17:6, the *g.* of children are their fathers.
20:29, the *g.* of young men is their strength.
25:2, *g.* of God to conceal.
27, for men to search their own *g.* is not *g.*
Isa. 10:2, where will ye leave your *g.*?
24:16, even *g.* to the righteous.
42:8, my *g.* will I not give to another.
43:7, have created him for my *g.*
60:7, will glorify house of my *g.*
Jer. 2:11, my people have changed their *g.*
Ezek. 20:6, 15, the *g.* of all lands.
31:18, to whom art thou thus like in *g.*?
Dan. 2:37; 7:14, God hat given power and *g.*
Hos. 4:7, change *g.* into shame.
Hag. 2:7, I will fill this house with *g.*
Mt. 6:2, that ye may have *g.* of men.
29; Lk. 12:27, Solomon in all his *g.*
16:27; Mk. 8:38, in *g.* of his Father.
19:28; Lk. 9:26, Son of man sit in his *g.*
24:30; Mk. 13:26; Lk. 21:27, power and great *g.*
Lk. 2:14; 19:38, *g.* to God in the highest.
9:31, appeared in *g.*, and spake of his decease.
9:32, they saw his *g.*
24:26, to enter into his *g.*
Jn. 1:14, we beheld his *g.*
2:11, thus did Jesus, and manifested his *g.*
8:50, I seek not mine own *g.*
17:5, the *g.* I had with thee.
24, that they may behold my *g.*
Acts 12:23, he gave not God the *g.*
Rom. 3:23, come short of the *g.* of God.
8:18, not worthy to be compared with *g.*

11:36; Gal. 1:5; 2Tim. 4:18; Heb. 13:21; 1Pet. 5:11, to whom be *g.*
1Cor. 2:8, crucified the Lord of *g.*
10:31, do all to *g.* of God.
11:7, woman is the *g.* of the man.
15, long hair, it is a *g.* to her.
15:40, *g.* of celestial, *g.* of terrestrial.
43, raised in *g.*
2Cor. 3:18, beholding as in a glass the *g.*
4:17, eternal weight of *g.*
Eph. 1:17, the Father of *g.*
3:21, to him be *g.* in the church.
Phil. 3:19, whose *g.* is in their shame.
4:19, according to his riches, in *g.*
Col. 1:27, Christ in you, the hope of *g.*
3:4, appear with him in *g.*
2Th. 1:9, the *g.* of his power.
1Tim. 3:16, received up into *g.*
Heb. 1:3, the brightness of his *g.*
2:10, in bringing many sons to *g.*
3:3, this man was counted worthy of more *g.*
1Pet. 1:8, joy unspeakable and full of *g.*
11, the *g.* that should follow.
24, the *g.* of man as flower of grass.
4:14, the spirit of *g.* and of God.
5:10, called to eternal *g.*
2Pet. 1:17, voice from the excellent *g.*
Rev. 4:11; 5:12, worthy to receive *g.*
7:12, blessing, and *g.*, and wisdom.
18:1, earth lightened with his *g.*
21:23, *g.* of God did lighten it.
See Lk. 17:18; 2Cor. 3:18; Jas. 2:1; Jude 25.

GLORYING. 1Cor. 5:6; 9:15; 2Cor. 7:4; 12:11.

GNASH. Mt. 8:12; 13:42; 22:13; 24:51; 25:30; Lk. 13:28, *g.* of teeth.
Mk. 9:18, he foameth, and *g.* with his teeth.
See Job 16:9; Ps. 35:16; Acts 7:54.

GNAT. Mt. 23:234.

GO. Gen. 32:26, let me *g.*, for the day breaketh.
Ex. 14:15; Job 23:8, *g.* forward.
23:23; 32:34, angel shall *g.* before thee.
33:15, presence *g.* not with me.
Ruth 1:16, whither thou *g.*, I will *g.*
Ps. 139:7, whither shall I *g.*?
Prov. 22:6, the way he should *g.*
30:29, three things which *g.* well.
Mt. 5:41, to *g.* a mile, *g.* twain.
21:30, I *g.* sir, and went not.
Lk. 10:37, *g.* and do likewise.
Jn. 14:12, I *g.* to the Father.
See Mt. 8:9; Lk. 7:8; 1Cor. 9:7; Rev. 14:4.

GOATS. Job 39:1, the wild *g.* of the rock.

GOD. Gen. 5:22; 6:9, walked with *G.*
16:13, thou *G.* seest me.
32:28, hath power with *G.*
48:21, I die, but *G.* shall be with you.
Num. 23:19, *G.* is not a man, that he should lie.
23, what hath *G.* wrought?
Dt. 3:24, what *G.* is there that can do.
33:27, the eternal *G.* is thy refuge.
1Sam. 17:46, may know there is a *G.* in Israel.
1Ki. 18:21, if the Lord be *G.*, follow him.
39, he is the *G.*, he is the *G.*
Job 22:13; Ps. 73:11, how doth *G.* know?
Ps. 14:1; 53:1, hath said, there is no *G.*
22:1; Mt. 27:46, my *G.*, my *G.*, why hast.
56:9, this I know, for *G.* is for me.
86:10; Isa. 37:16, thou art *G.* alone.
Eccl. 5:2, *G.* is in heaven.
Isa. 44:8, is there a *G*, beside me?
45:22; 46:9, I am *G.*, there is none else.
Hos. 11:9, I am *G*, and not man.
Amos 5:27, whose name is the *G*, of hosts.
Jon. 1:6, arise, call upon thy *G.*
Mic. 6:8, walk humbly with thy *G.*
Mt. 1:23, *G*, with us.
22:32, *G*, is not *G.* of dead.
Mk. 12:32, one *G.*, and none other.
Jn. 3:33, that *G.* is true.
4:24, *G.* is a spirit.
13:3, come from *G.*, and went to *G.*
20:17, ascend to my *G.* and your *G.*
Rom. 3:4, let *G.* be true.
8:31, if *G.* be for us.
1Cor. 1:9; 19:13, *G.* is faithful.
14:25, that *G.* is in you.
33, *G.* is not author of confusion.
Gal. 3:20, but *G.* is none.
6:7, *G.* is not mocked.
2Th. 2:4, above all that is called *G.*
1Tim. 3:16, *G.* manifest in the flesh.
Heb. 8:10, I will be to them a *G.*
11:16, not ashamed to be called their *G.*
11:23, but ye are come to *G.*
1Jn. 1:5, *G.* is light.
4:8, 16, *G.* is love.
12, no man hath seen *G.*
5:19, we know that we are of *G.*
Rev. 21:3, *G.* himself shall be with them.
4, *G.* shall wipe away all tears.
7, I will be his *G.*
See Job 33:12; 36:5; Ps. 10:4; 33:12.

GOD *(an idol)*. Gen. 31:30, stolen my *g.*
Ex. 32:1, make us *g.*, which shall go before us.
4, these be thy *g.*
Jud. 5:8, they chose new *g.*
6:31, if he be a *g.*, let him plead.
10:14, go and cry to the *g.* ye have chosen.
17:5, Micah had a house of *g.*
18:24, ye have taken away my *g.*
2Ki. 17:29, every nation made *g.*
33, they feared the Lord, and served own *g.*
Isa. 44:15, maketh a *g.* and worshippeth it.
45:20, pray to a *g.* that cannot save.
Jon. 1:5, cried every man to his *g.*
Acts 12:22, the voice of a *g.*, not a man.
14:11, the *g.* are come down.
1Cor. 8:5, there be *g.* many.
See Ex. 12:12; 20:23; Jer. 2:11; Dan. 3:28.

GODDESS. 1Ki. 11:5; Acts 19:27, 35, 37.

GODHEAD. Acts 17:29; Rom. 1:20; Col. 2:9.

GODLINESS. 1Tim. 3:16, the mystery of *g.*
4:7, exercise thyself to *g.*
8, *g.* is profitable.
6:3, doctrine according to *g.*
5, supposing that gain is *g.*

2Tim. 3:5, a form of *g*.
Ti. 1:1, the truth which is after *g*.
2Pet. 1:3, pertain to life and *g*.
6, and to patience *g*.
3:11, in all holy conversation, and *g*.
See 1Tim. 2:2, 10; 6:6, 11.
GODLY, Ps. 12:1, the *g*. man ceaseth.
Mal. 2:15, seek a *g*. seed.
2Cor. 1:12, in *g*. sincerity.
7:9, 10, *g*. sorrow worketh repentance.
2Tim. 3:12, all that will live *g*. in Christ.
Ti. 2:12, live *g*. in this world.
Heb. 12:28, reverence and *g*. fear.
2Pet. 2:9, how to deliver the *g*.
3Jn. 6, bring forward after a *g*. sort.
See Ps. 4:3; 32:6; 2Cor. 7:9; 11:2.
GOD SAVE THE KING. 2Sam. 16:16, Hushai said unto Absalom, *G*.
GOING. Josh. 23:14, I am *g*. the way of all the earth.
2Sam. 5:24; 1Chr. 14:15, sound of *g*. in trees.
Job 33:24, 28, from *g*. down to pit.
Ps. 17:5, hold up my *g*.
40:2, establish my *g*.
Prov. 5:21, pondereth all his *g*.
20:24, man's *g*. are of the Lord.
Dan. 6:14, laboured till *g*. down of the sun.
Mic. 5:2, whose *g*. forth have been from of old.
Mt. 26:46, rise, let us be *g*.
Rom. 10:3, *g*. about to establish.
1Tim. 5:24, *g*. before to judgment.
See Prov. 7:27; 14:15; Isa. 59:8; Hos. 6:3.
GOLD. Num. 31:22, only *g*., etc., that may abide fire.
Dt. 8:13, when thy *g*. is multiplied.
17:17, nor shall he greatly multiply *g*.
1Ki. 20:3, silver and *g*. is mine.
Job 22:24, then shalt thou lay up *g* as dust.
28:1, a vein for silver, a place for *g*.
19, wisdom not valued with *g*.
Job 31:24, if I made *g*. my hope.
Ps. 19:10, more to be desired than *g*.
21:3, thou settest a crown of pure *g*. upon his head.
Prov. 25:11, like applies of *g*.
Isa. 46:6, they lavish *g*. out of the bag.
60:17, for brass I will bring *g*.
Hag. 2:8, the silver is mine, and the *g*. is mine.
Zech. 4:2, behold, a candlestick all of *g*.
13:9, try them as *g*. is tried.
Mal. 10:9, provide neither *g*. nor silver.
Acts 3:6, silver and *g*. have I none.
17:29, not think Godhead like to *g*.
20:33, coveted no man's *g*.
2Tim. 2:20, in great house not only vessels of *g*
Jas. 2:2, man with a *g*. ring.
5:3, your *g*. is cankered.
1Pet. 1:7, trial more precious than of *g*.
18, not redeemed with *g*.
Rev. 3:18, buy of me *g*. tried in the fire.
21:18, city was pure *g*.
See Gen. 2:11; Eccl. 12:6; Isa. 13:12.
GONE. Dt. 23:23, that which is *g*. out of thy lips.
1Ki. 20:40, busy here and there, he was *g*.
Ps. 42:4, I had *g*. with the multitude.
73:2, my feet were almost *g*.
77:8, mercy clean *g*. for ever.
103:16, wind passeth, and it is *g*.
109:23, I am *g*. like the shadow.
119:176; Isa. 53:6, *g*. astray like sheep.
Eccl. 8:10, come and *g*. from place of the holy.
Jer. 15:9, sun *g*. down while yet day.
Mt. 12:43; Lk. 11:24, spirit *g*. out.
25:8, lamps are *g*. out.
Mk. 5:30; Lk. 8:46, virtue had *g*. out of him.
Jn. 12:19, the world is *g*. after him.
Acts 16:19, hope of their gains *g*.
Rom. 3:12, they are all *g*. out of the way.
Jude 11, *g*. in the way of Cain.
See Ps. 89:34; Song 2:11; Isa. 45:23.
GOOD (*n*.). Gen. 14:21, take the *g*. to thyself.
24:10, the *g*. of his master in his hand.
50:29, God meant it unto *g*.
Neh. 5:19; 13:31, think upon me for *g*.
Job 2:10, shall we receive *g*.
22:21, thereby *g*. shall come.
Ps. 4:6, who will show us any *g*.?
14:1; 53:1; Rom. 3:12, none doeth *g*.
34:12, loveth days that he may see *g*.
39:2, held my peace even from *g*.
86:17, a token for *g*
Prov. 3:27, withhold not *g*
Eccl. 3:12, I know there is no *g*. in them.
5:11, when *g*. increase.
9:18, destroyeth much *g*.
Mt. 12:29; Mk. 3:27, spoil his *g*.
24:27, ruler over all his *g*.
26:24, has been *g*. for that man.
Lk. 6:30, of him that taketh away thy *g*
12:19, much *g*. laid up.
15:12, the portion of *g*.
16:1, accused that he had wasted his *g*.
19:8, half of my *g*. I give.
Acts 10:38, went about doing *g*.
Rom. 8:28, work together for *g*.
13:4, minister of God for *g*.
1Cor. 13:3, bestow all my *g*. to feed.
Heb. 10:34, joyfully the spoiling of your *g*.
1Jn. 3:17, this world's *g*.
Rev. 3:17, rich and increased with *g*.
See Job 5:27; 7:7; Prov. 11:17; 13:21.
GOOD (*adj*.). Gen. 1:4, 10, 12, 18, 21, 25, 31, God saw it was *g*.
2:18, not *g*. that man should be alone.
27:46, what *g*. shall my life do me?
Dt. 2:4; Josh. 23:11, take *g*. heed.
1Sam. 2:24, no *g*. report I hear.
12:23, I will teach you the *g*. way.
25:15, men were very *g*. to us.
Ezra 7:9; Neh. 2:8, the *g*. hand of God on him.
Neh. 9:20, thy *g*. spirit to instruct.
Ps. 34:8, taste and see that the Lord is *g*.
45:1, my heart is inditing a *g*. matter.
112:5, a *g*. man showeth favour.
119:68, thou are *g*., and doest *g*.
145:9, the Lord is *g*. to all.
Prov. 12:25, a *g*. word maketh the heart glad.
15:23, in season, how *g*. is it

20:18, with *g.* advice make war.
22:1, a *g.* name rather to be chosen.
25:25, *g.* news from a far country.
Eccl. 6:12, who knoweth what is *g.*?
Isa. 55:2, eat ye that which is *g.*
Lam. 3:26, it is *g.* that a man hope.
27, *g.* that a man bear yoke.
Zech. 1:13, answered with *g.* words.
Mt. 5:13, it is *g.* for nothing.
7:11; Lk. 11:13, how to give *g.* gifts.
9:22; Lk. 8:48, be of *g.* comfort.
19:16, what *g.* thing shall I do?
17; Lk. 18:19, none *g.*, save one.
20:15, is thine eye evil because I am *g.*?
25:21, *g.* and faithful servant.
Mk. 9:50; Lk. 14:34, salt is *g.*, but.
Lk. 1:53, filled the hungry with *g.* things.
6:38, *g.* measure, pressed down.
10:42, chosen that *g.* part.
12:32, your Father's *g.* pleasure.
16:25, thou in thy lifetime receivedst *g.* things.
23:50, Joseph was a *g.* man, and a just.
Jn. 1:46, can any *g.* thing come out of Nazareth?
2:10, kept *g.* wine until now.
7:12, some said, he is a *g.* man.
10:11, I am the *g.* shepherd.
33, for a *g.* work we stone thee not.
Rom. 7:12, the commandment holy, just, and *g.*
18, in my flesh dwelleth no *g.* thing.
12:2, that *g.* and perfect will of God.
14:21, it is *g.* neither to eat.
1Cor. 7:26, this is *g.* for the present.
15:33, corrupt *g.* manners.
2Cor. 9:8, abound in every *g.* work.
Gal. 6:6, communicate in all *g.* things.
Phil. 1:6, hath begun a *g.* work.
Col. 1:10, fruitful in every *g.* work.
1Th. 5:15; 3Jn. 11, follow that which is *g.*
21, hold fast that which is *g.*
1Tim. 1:8, the law is *g.*
3:1, desireth a *g.* work.
4:4, every creature of God is *g.*
2Tim. 3:3, despisers of *g.*
Ti. 2:7, a pattern in *g.* works.
14, zealous of *g.* works.
Heb. 6:5, tasted the *g.* work of God.
13:9, *g.* thing that the heart be established.
Jas. 1:17, every *g.* gift.
See 2Th. 2:17; Ti. 1:16; 3:8.
GOODLINESS. Isa. 40:6.
GOODLY. Gen. 49:21, giveth *g.* words.
Ex. 2:2, a *g.* child.
Dt. 8:12, when thou hast built *g.* houses.
1Sam. 9:2, a choice young man, and a *g.*
16:12, ruddy, and *g.* to look to.
Ps. 16:6; Jer. 3:19, a *g.* heritage.
Zech. 11:13, a *g.* price I was prized at.
Mt. 13:45, *g.* pearls.
Jas. 2:2, a man in *g.* apparel.
See 1Sam. 8:16; 1Ki. 20:3; Lk. 21:5.
GOODNESS. Ex. 33:19, make all my *g.* pass.
34:6, abundant in *g.* and truth.
Ps. 16:2, my *g.* extendeth not to thee.
23:6, *g.* and mercy shall follow.
27:13, believed to see the *g.* of the Lord.
31:19; Zech. 9:17, how great is thy *g.*
33:5, earth full of thy *g.*
65:11, crownest the year with thy *g.*
Ps. 145:7, the memory of thy *g.*
Prov. 20:6, proclaim every one his own *g.*
Hos. 6:4, your *g.* is as a morning cloud.
Rom. 2:4, the riches of his *g.*
11:22, the *g.* and severity of God.
See Neh. 9:25; Isa. 63:7; Gal. 5:22; Eph. 5:9.
GOSPEL. Rom. 2:16, according to my *g.*
2Cor. 4:3, if our *g.* be hid.
Gal. 1:8, 9, any other *g.*
2:7, the *g.* of uncircumcision, *g.* of circumcision.
Col. 1:23, the hope of the *g.*
1Tim. 1:11, *g.* of the blessed God.
Rev. 14:6, everlasting *g.*
See Mt. 4:23; Mk. 16:15; Acts 20:24.
GOURD. Jon. 4:6, and the Lord God prepared a *g.*
See Jon. 4:7, 9, 10.
GOVERNMENT. Isa. 9:6; 1Cor. 12:28; 2Pet. 2:10.
GRACE. Ps. 45:2, *g.* is poured into thy lips
Prov. 1:9, an ornament of *g.*
3:22, life to thy soul, and *g.* to thy neck.
34; Jas. 4:6, giveth *g.* to the lowly.
Zech. 4:7, crying, *g.*, *g.* unto it.
12:10, spirit of *g.* and supplications.
Jn. 1:14, full of *g.* and truth.
16, all received, and *g.* for *g.*
17, *g.* and truth came by Jesus Christ.
Acts 4:33, great *g.* was upon them all.
11:23, when he had seen the *g.*
14:3, the word of his *g.*
Rom. 1:7; 1Cor. 1:3; 2Cor. 1:2; Gal. 1:3; Eph. 1:2; Phil. 1:2; Col. 1:2; 1Th. 1:1; 2Th. 1:2; Phile. 3; 1Peter 1:2; 2Pet. 1:2; Rev. 1:4, *g.* and peace.
3:24, justified freely by his *g.*
4:4, not reckoned of *g.*, but of debt.
5:2, access into this *g.*
17, abundance of *g.*
20, where sin abounded, *g.* did much more abound.
6:14, 15, under *g.*
11:5, the election of *g.*
2Cor. 8:9, know the *g.* of our Lord.
9:8, able to make all *g.* abound.
12:9, my *g.* is sufficient.
Gal. 1:6, 15, who called you by his *g.*
5:4, ye are fallen from *g.*
Eph. 2:5, 8, by *g.* ye are saved.
3:8, to me is this *g.* given.
4:29, minister *g.* to hearers.
6:24, *g.* be with all that love our Lord.
Col. 4:6, let your speech be alway with *g.*
2Th. 2:16, good hope through *g.*
1Tim. 1:2; 2Tim. 1:2; Ti. 1:4; 2Jn. 3, *g.*, mercy and peace.
Heb. 4:16, the throne of *g.*
10:29, despite to the Spirit of *g.*

12:28, *g.* to serve God acceptably.
13:9, heart established with *g.*
Jas. 1:11, the *g.* of the fashion of it.
4:6, he giveth more *g.*
1Pet. 3:7, heirs of *g.*
5:5, giveth *g.* to the humble.
2Pet. 3:18, grow in *g.*
Jude 4, turning *g.* of God into lasciviousness.
See Acts 20:24; 2Cor. 6:1; Gal. 2:21.

GRACIOUS. Gen. 43:29, God be *g.* to thee.
Ex. 22:27, I will hear, for I am *g.*
33:19, I will be *g.* to whom I will be *g.*
Neh. 9:17, 31, ready to pardon, *g.*, merciful.
Ps. 77:9, hath God forgotten to be *g.*?
Prov. 11:16, a *g.* woman retaineth honour.
Isa. 30:18, wait, that he may be *g.*
Amos 5:15, may be the Lord will be *g.*
Jon. 4:2, I know thou art a *g.* God.
Lk. 4:22, wondered at the *g.* words.
1Pet. 2:3, tasted that the Lord is *g.*
See Ex. 34:6; 2Chr. 30:9; Hos. 14:2.

GRAFT. Rom. 11:17, 19, 23, 24.

GRAIN. Mt. 13:31; 17:20; Mk. 4:31; Lk. 13:19; 17:6, *g.* of mustard seed.
See Amos 9:9; 1Cor. 15:37.

GRANT. Ruth 1:9, *g.* that you may find rest.
1Chr. 4:10, God *g.* him that which he requested.
Job 6:8, *g.* the thing I long for.
Mt. 20:21; Mk. 10:37, *g.* that my two sons.
Rev. 3:21, will I *g.* to sit with me.
See Ps. 20:4; 85:7; Acts 4:29.

GRAPE. Gen. 49:11, washed clothes in the blood of *g.*
Num. 6:3, nor eat moist *g.*, or dried.
Dt. 23:24, then thou mayest eat *g* thy fill.
24:21, when thou gatherest the *g.* of thy vineyard.
32:14, drink the blood of the *g.*
Song 2:13, 15, vines with tender *g.*
Isa. 5:2, looked it should bring forth *g.*
17:6; 24:13, yet gleaning *g.*
Jer. 8:13, there shall be no *g.*
31:29, 20; Ezek. 18:2, have eaten a sour *g.*
Amos 9:13, treader of *g.* shall overtake.
See Lev. 19:10; 25:5; Lk. 6:4; Rev. 14:18.

GRASS. Dt. 32:2, as showers upon the *g.*
2Ki. 19:26; Ps. 129:6, as *g.* on housetops.
Ps. 72:6, like rain upon mown *g.*
90:5, like *g.* which groweth up.
102:4, 11, withered like *g.*
103:15, days are as *g.*
Isa. 40:6; 1Pet. 1:24, all flesh is *g.*
Mt. 6:30; Lk. 12:28, if God so clothe the *g.*
See Prov. 27:25; Jn. 6:10; Rev. 8:7; 9:4.

GRASSHOPPERS. Amos 7:1, and, behold, he formed *g.*

GRAVE (*n.*). Gen. 42:38; 44:31, with sorrow to the *g.*
Ex. 14:11, no *g.* in Egypt.
Num. 19:16, or a *g.*
Job 5:26, come to *g.* in full age.
7:9, he that goeth to the *g.*
14:13, hide me in the *g.*
17:1, the *g.* are ready for me.
13, if I wait, the *g.* is mine house.
33:22, his soul draweth near to the *g.*
Ps. 6:5, in the *g.* who shall give thee thanks?
31:17, let wicked be silent in the *g.*
49:14, like sheep laid in the *g.*
15; Hos. 13:14, the power of the *g.*
Eccl. 9:10, no wisdom in the *g.*
Isa. 38:18, the *g.* cannot praise thee.
53:9, made his *g.* with the wicked.
Hos. 13:14, O *g.*, I will be thy destruction.
Jn. 5:28, all in the *g.* shall hear.
11:31, she goeth to the *g.*
1Cor. 15:55, O *g.*, where is thy victory?
See Mt. 27:52; Lk. 11:44; Rev. 11:9; 20:13.

GRAVE (*v.*). Isa. 49:16, I have *g.* thee upon the palms.
Hab. 2:18, that the maker hat *g.* it.
See Ex. 28:9; 2Chr. 2:7; 3:7.

GRAVE (*adj.*). 1Tim. 3:8; Ti. 2:2.

GRAVEL. Prov. 20:17; Isa. 48:19; Lam. 3:16.

GRAVITY. 1Tim. 3:4; Ti. 2:7.

GRAY. Ps. 71:18; Prov. 20:29; Hos. 7:9.

GREAT. Gen. 12:2; 18:18; 46:3, make a *g.* nation.
48:19, he also shall be *g.*
Dt. 29:24, the heat of his *g.* anger.
1Sam. 12:24, consider how *g* things.
2Ki. 5:13, bid thee do some *g.* thing.
2Chr. 2:5, the house is *g.*, for *g.* is our God.
Neh. 6:3, I am doing a *g.* work.
Job 32:9, *g.* men not always wise.
36:18, a *g.* ransom.
Ps. 14:5; 53:5, there were they in *g.* fear.
19:11, there is *g.* reward.
31:19, how *g.* is thy goodness
92:5, how *g.* are thy works!
139:17, how *g.* is the sum of them!
Prov. 18:16, gift bringeth before *g.* men.
25:6, stand not in place of *g.* men.
Mt. 5:12, *g.* is your reward.
19, called *g.* in kingdom of heaven.
13:46, pearl of *g.* price.
15:28, *g.* is thy faith.
Mt. 20:26, whosoever will be *g.* among you.
22:36, 38, the *g.* commandment.
Lk. 10:2, the harvest is *g.*
16:26, a *g.* gulf fixed.
Acts 8:9, giving out he was some *g.* one.
19:28, 34, *g.* is Diana.
1Tim. 3:16, *g.* is the mystery.
Heb. 2:3, so *g.* salvation.
12:1, so *g.* a cloud of witnesses.
Jas. 3:5, how *g.* a matter a little fire kindleth!
See Dt. 9:2; Eccl. 2:9; Rev. 7:9.

GREATER. Gen. 4:13, punishment *g.* than I can bear.
1Chr. 11:9; Est. 9:4, waxed *g.* and *g.*
Hag. 2:9, glory of latter house *g.*
Mt. 11:11; Lk. 7:28, *g.* than he.
12:6, one *g.* than the temple.
Mk. 12:31, no commandment *g.* than these.
Jn. 1:50; 5:20; 14:12, shalt see *g.* things.
4:12; 8:53, art thou *g.* than our father?

10:29; 14:28, my Father is *g*. than all.
13:16; 15:20, servant not *g*. than his lord.
15:13, *g*. love hath no man.
1Cor. 15:6, the *g*. part remain.
Heb. 6:13, he could swear by no *g*.
1Jn. 3:20, God is *g*. than our hearts.
4:4, *g*. is he in you than he in world.
3Jn. 4, no *g*. joy.
See Gen. 41:40; 48:19; Heb. 9:11.
GREATEST. Mt. 13:32, it is *g*. among herbs.
18:1, 4, who is *g*. in kingdom?
Mk. 9:34; Lk. 9:46, disputed who should be *g*.
1Cor. 13:13, the *g*. of these is charity.
See Job 1:3; Jer. 31:34; Lk. 22:24.
GREATLY. 2Sam. 24:10; 1Chr. 21:8, I have sinned *g*.
1Ki. 18:3, Obadiah feared the Lord *g*.
Ps. 28:7, my heart *g*. rejoiceth.
47:9, God is *g*. exalted.
89:7, *g*. to be feared in the assembly.
116:10, I was *g*. afflicted.
Dan. 9:23; 1:11, thou art *g*. beloved.
Obad. 2, thou art *g*. despised.
Mk. 12:27, ye do *g*. err.
See Ps. 62:2; Mk. 9:15; Acts 3:11; 6:7.
GREATNESS. 1Chr. 29:11, thine is the *g*., power, and glory.
Ps. 145:3, his *g*. is unsearchable.
Prov. 5:23, in the *g*. of his folly.
Isa. 63:1, travelling in the *g*. of his power.
Eph. 1:19, the exceeding *g*. of his power.
See 2Chr. 9:6; Ps. 66:3; 79:11; 150:2.
GREEDILY. Prov. 21:26; Ezek. 22:12.
GREEDINESS. Eph. 4:19.
GREEDY. Prov. 1:19; 15:27, *g*. of gain.
Isa. 56:11, they are *g*. dogs.
See Ps. 17:12; 1Tim. 3:3.
GREEN. Lev. 23:14; Jud. 16:7; Lk. 23:31.
GRIEF. 2Chr. 6:29, every one shall know his own *g*.
Job 6:2, Oh that my *g*. were weighed!
Ps. 31:10, life spent with *g*.
Eccl. 1:18, in much wisdom is much *g*.
Isa. 53:3, acquainted with *g*.
Jer. 10:19, this is a *g*., and I must bear it.
See Jon. 4:6; Heb. 13:17; 1Pet. 2:19.
GRIEVE. Gen. 6:6, it *g*. him at his heart.
45:5, be not *g*. that ye sold me.
1Sam. 2:33, the man shall be to *g*. thine heart.
Ps. 78:40, they *g*. him in the desert.
95:10, forty years was I *g*.
Lam. 3:33, doth not willingly *g*.
Mk. 3:5, being *g*. for the hardness.
10:22, he went away *g*.
Jn. 21:17, Peter was *g*.
Rom. 14:15, brother *g*. with meat.
Eph. 4:30, *g*. not the holy Spirit of God.
See Neh. 2:10; 13:8; Ps. 119:158; 139:21.
GRIEVOUS. Gen. 21:11, thing was *g*. in Abraham's sight.
Gen. 50:11, a *g*. mourning.
Ps. 10:5, his ways are always *g*.
Prov. 15:1, *g*. words stir up anger.
Isa. 15:4, his life shall be *g*.
Jer. 30:12; Nah. 3:19, thy wound is *g*.
Mt. 23:4; Lk. 11:46, burdens *g*. to be borne.
Phil. 3:1, to me is not *g*.
Heb. 12:11, chastening *g*.
1Jn. 5:3, commandments not *g*.
See Eccl. 2:17; Jer. 16:4; Acts 20:29.
GRIND. Isa. 3:15, *g*. faces of the poor.
Lam. 5:13, took young men to *g*.
Mt. 21:44; Lk. 20:18, it will *g*. him to powder.
See Eccl. 12:3; Mt. 24:41; Lk. 17:35.
GROAN. Ex. 2:24, God heard their *g*.
Job 24:12, men *g*. from out the city.
Joel 1:18, how do the beasts *g*.!
Rom. 8:23, we ourselves *g*.
2Cor. 5:2, 4, in this we *g*.
See Job 23:2; Ps. 6:6; Jn. 11:33, 38.
GROPE. Dt. 28:29; Job 5:14; 12:25; Isa. 59:10.
GROSS. Isa. 60:2; Jer. 13:16; Mt. 13:15; Acts 28:27.
GROUND. Ex. 3:5; Acts 7:33, holy *g*.
Job 5:6, nor trouble spring out of the *g*.
Isa. 35:7, parched *g*. become a pool.
Jer. 4:3; Hos. 10:12, break up fallow *g*.
Mt. 13:8; Lk. 8:8, good *g*.
Mk. 4:16, stony *g*.
Lk. 13:7, why cumbereth it the *g*.?
14:18, bought a piece of *g*.
19:44, lay thee even with the *g*.
Jn. 8:6, he wrote on the *g*.
See Zech. 8:12; Mal. 3:11; Jn. 12:24.
GROUNDED. Eph. 3:17; Col. 1:23.
GROW. Gen. 48:16, let them *g*. into a multitude.
2Sam. 23:5, though he make it not to *g*.
Ps. 92:12, *g*. like a cedar.
Isa. 53:2, he shall *g*. up before him.
Hos. 14:5, he shall *g*. as the lily.
Mal. 4:2, *g*. up as calves of the stall.
Mt. 13:30, let both *g*. together.
Mk. 4:27, seed should *g*. up, he knoweth not.
Acts 5:24, whereunto this would *g*
Eph. 2:21, *g*. unto an holy temple.
4:15 may *g*. up into him.
2Th. 1:3, your faith *g*. exceedingly.
1Pet. 2:2, that ye may *g*. thereby.
2Pet. 3:18, *g*. in grace.
See 2Ki. 19:26; Jer. 12:2; Zech. 6:12.
GRUDGE. Lev. 19:18; 2Cor. 9:7; Jas. 5:9; 1Pet. 4:9.
GUESTS. Zeph. 1:7; Mt. 22:10; Lk. 19:7.
GUIDE. Ps. 25:9, meek will he *g*. in judgment.
32:8, I will *g*. thee with mine eye.
48:14, our *g*. even unto death.
73:24, *g*. me with thy counsel.
Prov. 6:7, having no *g*., overseer, or ruler.
Isa. 58:11, the Lord shall *g*. thee.
Jer. 3:4, the *g*. of my youth.
Mt. 23:16, 24, ye blind *g*.
Lk. 1:79, *g*. our feet into the way of peace.
Jn. 16:13, *g*. you into all truth.
See Gen. 48:14; Prov. 11:3; 23:19.
GUILE. Ps. 32:2, in whose spirit is no *g*.
34:13; 1Pet. 3:10, keep lips from speaking *g*.
Jn. 1:47, in whom is no *g*.
2Cor. 12:16, I caught you with *g*.
1Pet. 2:1, laying aside *g*.
22, nor was *g*. found in his mouth.

3:10, and his lips that they speak no *g*.
See Ex. 21:14; 1Th. 2:3; Rev. 14:5.
GUILTLESS. Ex. 20:7; Dt. 5:11, will not hold him *g*.
Josh. 2:19, we will be *g*.
2Sam. 3:28, are *g*. of blood
Mt. 12:7, ye would not have condemned the *g*.
See Num. 5:31; 1Sam. 26:9; 1Ki. 2:9.
GUILTY. Gen. 42:21, verily *g*. concerning our brother.
Ex. 34:7; Num. 14:18, by no means clear the *g*.
Lev. 5:3, when he knoweth of it, he shall be *g*.
Rom. 3:19, all the world *g*. before God.
1Cor. 11:27, *g*. of the body and blood.
Jas. 2:10, he is *g*. of all.
See Num. 35:27; Prov. 30:10; Mt. 26:66.
GULF. Lk. 16:26.
GUSH. 1Ki. 18:28; Ps. 78:20; 105:41; Jer. 9:18.
HABITATION. Ex. 15:13, guided them to thy holy *h*.
2Chr. 6:2, have built an house of *h*.
Ps. 26:8, have loved the *h*.
33:14, from the place of his *h*.
69:25, let their *h*. be desolate.
74:20, full of *h*. of cruelty.
89:14, justice and judgment the *h*. of thy throne.
107:7, 36, a city of *h*.
132:13, the Lord desired it for his *h*.
Prov. 3:33, he blesseth the *h*. of the just.
Isa. 32:18, dwell in a peaceable *h*.
Jer. 21:13, who shall enter into our *h*.
25:37, the peaceable *h*. are cut down.
Lk. 16:9, into everlasting *h*.
Eph. 2:22, an *h*. of God through the Spirit.
Jude 6, angels which left their own *h*.
See Prov. 8:31; Acts 1:20; 17:26; Rev. 18:2.
HAIL. Job 38:22, the treasures of the *h*.
Isa. 28:17, *h*. sweep away refuge of lies.
See Ex. 9:18; Josh. 10:11; Rev. 8:7; 11:19; 16:21.
HAIR. Gen. 42:38; 44:29, bring down gray *h*. with sorrow.
Jud. 20:16, sling stones at *h*. breadth.
Job 4:15, the *h*. of my flesh stood up.
Ps. 40:12, more than the *h*. of my head.
Mt. 3:4; Mk. 1:6, raiment of camel's *h*
5:36, make one *h*. white or black.
10:30, *h*. of head numbered.
1Cor. 11:14, 15, long *h*., it is a shame.
1Tim. 2:9, broided *h*.
1Pet. 3:3, plaiting the *h*.
See 2Sam. 14:26; Hos. 7:9; Jn. 11:2; Rev. 1:14.
HALE. Lk. 12:58; Acts 8:3.
HALL. Jn. 18:28, then led they Jesus from Caiaphas unto the *h*. of judgment.
33; 19:9, then Pilate entered into the judgment *h*.
See Acts 25:23.
HALLOW. Lev. 22:32, I am the Lord which *h*. you.
25:10, shall *h*. the fiftieth year.
Num. 5:10, every man's *h*. things.
1Ki. 9:3, I have *h*. this house.
Jer. 17:22; 24:27, but *h*. ye the sabbath day.
Ezek. 20:20; 44:24, and *h*. my sabbaths.
Mt. 6:9; Lk. 11:2, *h*. be thy name.

HALT. 1Ki. 18:21, how long *h*. ye?
Ps. 38:17, I am ready to *h*.
Jer. 20:10, my familiars watched for my *h*.
See Gen. 32:31; Mic. 4:6; Zeph. 3:19.
HAND. Gen. 16:12, *h*. against every man.
24:2; 47:29, put thy *h*. under my thigh.
27:22, the *h*. are the *h*. of Esau.
31:29, in the power of my *h*. to do you hurt.
Ex. 21:24; Dt. 19:21, *h*. for *h*., foot for foot.
33:22, cover with my *h*. while I pass.
Num. 11:23; Isa. 59:1, Lord's *h*, waxed short.
22:29, would there were sword in mine *h*.
Dt. 8:27, my *h*. hath gotten this wealth.
33:2, from right *h*. went fiery law.
Jud. 7:2, saying, my own *h*. hath saved me.
1Sam. 5:11, *h*. of God was heavy.
6:9, not his *h*. that smote us, but a chance
12:3, of whose *h*. have I received any bribe?
19:5; 28:21, put his life in his *h*.
23:16, Jonathan strengthened his *h*. in God.
26:18, what evil is in mine *h*.?
2Sam. 14:19, is not *h*. of Joab in this?
24:14; 1Chr. 21:13, let us fall into *h*. of Lord.
1Ki. 18:44, cloud like a man's *h*.
2Ki. 5:11, strike his *h*. over the place.
1Chr. 12:2, could use right *h*. and left.
Ezra 7:9; 8:18; Neh. 2:8, good *h*. of God.
10:19, they gave their *h* that they would
Neh. 2:18, strengthened their *h*. for work.
6:5, with open letter in his *h*.
Job 12:10, in whose *h*. is the soul.
19:21, the *h*. of God hath touched me.
40:14, that thine own *h*. can save.
Ps. 16:11, at right *h*. pleasures for evermore.
24:4, clean *h*. and pure heart.
68:31, stretch out her *h* unto God.
90:17, establish thou the work of our *h*.
137:5, let my right *h*. forget her cunning.
Prov. 3:16, in left *h*. riches and honour.
6:10; 24:33, folding of *h*. to sleep.
10:4, that dealeth with slack *h*.
11:21; 16:5, though *h*. join *h*.
12:24, *h*. of diligent shall bear rule.
19:24; 26:15, slothful man hideth his *h*.
22:26, be not of them that strike *h*.
Eccl. 2:24, this I saw was from *h* of God.
9:10, whatsoever thy *h*. findeth.
11:6, in evening withhold not thine *h*.
Isa. 1:12, who hath required this at your *h*.?
5:25; 9:12; 10:4; 14:27, his *h*. stretched out still.
14:26, this is the *h*. that is stretched out.
40:12, measured waters in hollow of *h*.
44:5, subscribe with his *h*. to the Lord.
53:10, pleasure of Lord shall prosper in his *h*.
56:2, keepeth his *h*. from evil.
Jer. 23:14, strengthen *h*. of evil doers.
33:13, shall pass under *h*. of him that telleth.
Lam. 2:4, with his right *h*. as adversary.
4:10, *h*. of pitiful women have sodden.
Ezek. 7:17; 21:7, all *h*. shall be feeble.
10:2, fill *h*. with coals of fire.
17:18, lo, he had given his *h*.

Dan. 4:35, none can stay his *h*.
Hos. 7:5, stretched out *h*. with scorners.
Mic. 7:3, do evil with both *h*. earnestly.
Zeph. 3:16, let not thine *h*. be slack.
Zech. 13:6, what are these wounds in thine *h*.?
Mt. 3:2; 4:17; 10:7, kingdom of heaven at *h*.
12; Lk. 3:17, whose fan is in his *h*.
6:3, let not left *h*. know.
18:8; Mk. 9:43, if thy *h*. or foot offend.
26:18, my time is at *h*.
46; Mk. 14:42, he is at *h*. that doth betray.
Mk. 14:62, sitting on right *h*. of power.
16:19, sat on right *h*. of God.
Lk. 9:44, delivered into *h*. of men.
Jn. 10:28, nor pluck out of my *h*.
29, my Father's *h*.
20:27, reach hither thy *h*.
Acts 20:34, these *h*. have ministered.
2Cor. 5:1, house not made with *h*.
Phil. 4:5, moderation be known, the Lord is at *h*.
1Th. 4:11, work with your own *h*.
2Th. 2:2, the day of Christ is at *h*.
1Tim. 2:8, lifting up holy *h*.
Heb. 10:31, the *h*. of living God.
Jas. 4:8, cleanse your *h*.
1Pet. 4:7, end of all things is at *h*.
1Jn. 1:1, our *h*. have handled of the Word.
See Isa. 49:16; Lk. 9:62; Jn. 18:22; Col. 2:14.

HANDLE. Jud. 5:14, that *h*. pen of the writer.
Ps. 115:7, hands, but the *h*. not.
Prov. 16:20, that *h*. a matter wisely.
Jer. 2:8, they that *h*. the law.
Mk. 12:4, sent away shamefully *h*.
Lk. 24:39, *h*. me, and see.
2Cor. 4:2, not *h*. word deceitfully.
Col. 2:21, taste not, *h*. not.
1Jn. 1:1, have *h*. of Word of life.
See Gen. 4:21; 1Chr. 12:8; Ezek. 27:29.

HANDMAID. Ps. 86:16; 116:16; Prov. 30:23; Lk. 1:38.

HANG. Dt. 21:23; Gal. 3:13, he that is *h*. is accursed.
Job 26:7, *h*. the earth on nothing.
Ps. 137:2, we *h*. our harps upon the willows.
Mt. 18:6; Mk. 9:42; Lk. 17:2, millstone *h*. about neck.
22:40, on these *h*. the law and the prophets.
27:5, went and *h*. himself.
Heb. 12:12, lift up the hands which *h*. down.
See Gen. 40:22; Est. 7:10; Lk. 23:39.

HAPLY. 1Sam. 14:30; Mk. 11:13; Acts 5:39; 17:27.

HAPPEN. 1Sam. 6:9, it was a chance that *h*.
Prov. 12:21, there shall not evil *h*. to the just.
Isa. 41:22, let them show us what shall *h*.
Jer. 44:23, therefore this evil is *h*.
Mk. 10:32, to tell what should *h*.
Lk. 24:14, talked of things that had *h*.
Rom. 11:25, blindness is *h*. to Israel.
1Cor. 10:11, things *h*. for ensamples.
Phil. 1:12, things which *h*. to me.
1Pet. 4:12, as though some strange thing *h*.
2Pet. 2:22, it is *h*. according to proverb.
See Eccl. 2:14; 8:14; 9:11; Acts 3:10.

HAPPY. Gen. 30:13, *h*. am I.
Dt. 33:29, *h*. art thou.
Job 5:17, *h*. is the man whom God correcteth.
Ps. 127:5, *h*. is the man that hath quiver full.
128:2, *h*. shalt thou be.
144:15, *h*. is that people.
Prov. 3:13, 18, *h*. that findeth wisdom.
14:21, he that hath mercy, *h*. is he.
28:14, *h*. is the man that feareth alway.
Jer. 12:1, why are they *h*. that deal treacherously?
Mal. 3:15, now we call proud *h*.
Jn. 13:17, if ye know, *h*. if ye do them.
Rom. 14:22, *h*. is he that condemneth not.
Jas. 5:11, we count them *h*. that endure.
1Pet. 3:14; 4:14, *h*. are ye.
See Ps. 146:5; Prov. 29:18; 1Cor. 7:40.

HARD. Gen. 18:14, is any thing too *h*. for the Lord?
Dt. 1:17; 17:8, cause that is too *h*.
15:18, it shall not seem *h*. to thee.
1Ki. 10:1; 2Chr. 9:1, prove with *h*. questions
Job 41:24, *h*. as piece of nether millstone.
Prov. 13:15, the way of transgressors is *h*.
18:19, brother offended *h*. to be won.
Jer. 32:17, 27, there is nothing too *h*. for thee.
Ezek. 3:5, 6, to a people of *h*. language.
Mt. 25:24, thou art an *h*. man.
Jn. 6:60, this is an *h*. saying.
Acts 9:5; 26:14, *h*. to kick against the pricks.
Heb. 5:11, many things *h*. to be uttered.
2Pet. 3:16, things *h*. to be understood.
See Dt. 15:18; 2Ki. 2:10; Mk. 10:24.

HARDEN. Ex. 4:21; 7:3; 14:4, I will *h*. Pharoah's heart.
14:17, *h*. hearts of Egyptians.
Job 6:10, I would *h*. myself in sorrow.
9:4, who hath *h*. himself against him?
Prov. 21:29, a wicked man *h*. his face.
28:14, he that *h*. his heart.
29:1, he that being often reproved *h*. his neck.
Isa. 63:17, why hast thou *h*. our heart?
Mk. 6:52; 8:17, their heart was *h*.
Jn. 12:40, he hath *h*. their heart.
Acts 19:9, when divers were *h*.
Rom. 9:18, whom he will he *h*.
Heb. 3:13, lest any of you be *h*.
See Dt. 15:7; 2Ki. 17:14; Job 39:16.

HARDLY. Gen. 16:6; Mt. 19:23; Mk. 10:23; Lk. 18:24.

HARDNESS. Mk. 3:5, grieved for *h*. of their hearts.
16:14, upbraided them for *h*. of heart.
2Tim. 2:3, endure *h*., as good soldier.
See Job 38:38; Mt. 19:8; Mk. 10:5; Rom. 2:5.

HARM. Lev. 5:16, make amends for *h*.
Num. 35:23, nor sought his *h*.
1Sam. 26:21, I will no more do thee *h*.
2Ki. 4:41, no *h*. in the pot.
1Chr. 16:22; Ps. 105:15, do prophets no *h*.
Prov. 3:30, if he have done thee no *h*.
Acts 16:28, do thyself no *h*.
28:5, he felt no *h*.
1Pet. 3:13, who will *h*. you?

See Gen. 31:52; Jer. 39:12; Acts 27:21.
HARMLESS. Mt. 10:16; Phil. 2:15; Heb. 7:26.
HARP. 1Sam. 16:16, cunning player on an *h*.
Ps. 49:4, dark sayings on the *h*.
137:2, hanged *h*. on the willows.
Isa. 5:12, *h*. and viol are in their feasts.
24:8, joy of the *h*. ceaseth.
1Cor. 14:7, what is piped or *h*., except they give.
Rev. 14:2, harping with their *h*.
See Gen. 4:21; Ezek. 26:13; Dan. 3:5.
HARROW. 2Sam. 12:31; 1Chr. 20:3; Job 39:10.
HART. Dt. 12:15, and as of the *h*.
1Ki. 4:23, besides *h*. and roebucks.
See Ps. 42:1; Isa. 35:6.
HARVEST. Gen. 8:22, *h*. shall not cease.
Ex. 23:16; 34:22, the feast of *h*.
Lev. 19:19; 23:10; Dt. 24:19, when ye reap *h*.
1Sam. 12:17, is it not wheat *h*. to-day?
Job 5:5, whose *h*. the hungry eateth up.
Prov. 6:8, the ant gathereth food in *h*.
10:5, he that sleepeth in *h*.
25:13, cold of snow in time of *h*.
26:1, as rain in *h*.
Isa. 9:3, according to joy in *h*.
16:9, they *h*. is fallen.
18:4, dew in heat of *h*.
Jer. 5:17, they shall eat up thine *h*.
24, appointed weeks of *h*.
8:20, the *h*. is past, the summer ended.
51:33, the time of her *h*. shall come.
Joel 3:13; Rev. 14:15, the *h*. is ripe.
Mt. 9:37, the *h*. is plenteous.
38; Lk. 10:2, the Lord of the *h*.
13:30, in the time of *h*. I will say.
Mk. 4:29, putteth in sickle, because *h*. is come.
Lk. 10:2, the *h*. truly is great.
Jn. 4:35, the fields are white to *h*.
See Josh. 3:15; Isa. 23:3; Mt. 13:39.
HASTE. Ex. 12:11, shall eat it in *h*.
1Sam. 21:8, king's business required *h*.
Ps. 31:22; 116:11, I said in my *h*.
Prov. 19:2, he that *h*. with feet sinneth.
28:22, he that *h*. to be rich.
Isa. 51:14, captive exile *h*.
60:22, will *h*. it in his time.
Jer. 1:12, I will *h*. my word.
Zeph. 1:14, day of the Lord *h*. greatly.
See 2Ki. 7:15; Ps. 16:4; 55:8; Eccl. 1:5.
HASTILY. Prov. 20:21; 25:8.
HASTY. Prov. 14:29; 21:5; 29:20; Eccl. 5:2; 7:9.
HATE. Gen. 37:4, 5, 8, *h*. Joseph yet the more.
Lev. 19:17, shall not *h*. thy brother.
1Ki. 22:8; 2Chr. 18:7, one man, but I *h*. him.
2Chr. 19:2, and love them that *h*. the Lord.
Ps. 34:21, they that *h*. righteous shall be desolate.
97:10, ye that love the Lord, *h*. evil.
139:21, do not I *h*. them that *h*. thee?
Prov. 1:22, how long will ye *h*. knowledge?
13:24, he that spareth his rod *h*. his son.
14:20, the poor is *h*. of his neighbour.
15:10, he that *h*. reproof shall die.
27, he that *h*. gifts shall live.
Eccl. 2:17, I *h*. life.
3:8, a time to *h*.
Isa. 1:14, your feasts my soul *h*.
61:8, I *h*. robbery for burnt offering.
Amos 5:15, *h*. the evil, and love the good.
Mic. 3:2, who *h*. the good, and love the evil.
Zech. 8:17, these are things that I *h*.
Mal. 1:3; Rom. 9:13, I loved Jacob, and *h*. Esau.
Mt. 5:44; Lk. 6:27, do good to them that *h*. you.
6:24, either he will *h*. the one.
10:22; Mk. 13:13; Lk. 21:17, ye shall be *h*.
24:10, and shall *h*. one another.
Lk. 6:22, blessed are ye when men shall *h*. you.
14:26, and *h*. not his father.
Jn. 3:20, *h*. the light.
7:7, the world cannot *h*. you.
12:25, he that *h*. his life.
15:18; 1Jn. 3:13, marvel not if world *h*. you.
24, they have both seen and *h*.
Eph. 5:29, no man ever yet *h*. his own flesh.
1Jn. 2:9, 11; 3:15; 4:20, *h*. his brother.
See Gen. 27:41; Dt. 1:27; Prov. 6:16; Rev. 2:6.
HATEFUL. Ps. 36:2; Ezek. 23:29; Ti. 3:3.
HATERS. Ps. 81:15; Rom. 1:30.
HAUGHTY. 2Sam. 22:28, thine eyes are upon the *h*.
Ps. 131:1, my heart is not *h*.
Prov. 16:18, a *h*. spirit before a fall.
21:24, proud and *h*. scorner.
Isa. 10:33, the *h*. shall be humbled.
Zeph. 3:11, no more be *h*. because.
See Isa. 2:11; 13:11; 24:4; Ezek. 16:50.
HAWK. Lev. 11:16, and the *h*. after his kind.
Job 39:26, doth the *h*. fly by wisdom?
HEAD. Gen. 3:15, it shall bruise thy *h*.
Josh. 2:19, blood be on his *h*.
Jud. 11:9, shall I be your *h*.?
2Ki. 2:3, take thy master from thy *h*. to-day.
4:19, he said, My *h*., my *h*.
Ps. 24:7, 9, lift up your *h*.
66:12, caused men to ride over our *h*.
110:7, therefore shall he lift up the *h*.
141:5, oil, which shall not break my *h*.
Prov. 10:6, blessings on *h*. of the just.
11:26, on *h*. of him that selleth corn.
25:22; Rom. 12:20, coals of fire on his *h*.
Eccl. 2:14, a wise man's eyes are in his *h*.
Isa. 1:5, the whole *h*. is sick.
35:10; 51:11, everlasting joy upon their *h*.
58:5, to bow down *h*. as bulrush.
59:17; Eph. 6:17, helmet of salvation on *h*.
Jer. 9:1, Oh that my *h*. were waters.
14:3, 4, ashamed, and covered their *h*.
Dan. 3:38, thou art this *h*. of gold.
Amos 2:7, that pant after dust on *h*.
9:1, cut them in the *h*.
Zech. 1:21, no man did lift up his *h*.
4:7, the *h*.-stone with shoutings.
Mt. 5:36, neither swear by *h*.
27:39; Mk. 15:29, reviled, wagging their *h*.
Lk. 7:46, my *h*. thou didst not anoint.
21:18, not hair of *h*. perish.
28, then look up, and lift up your *h*.
Jn. 13:9, also my hands and my *h*.

1Cor. 11:3, the *h*. of every man is Christ.
4, dishonoureth his *h*.
10, woman to have power on her *h*.
Eph. 1:22; 4:15; Col. 1:18, the *h*. of the church.
5:23, husband is *h*. of wife.
Col. 2:19, not holding the *h*.
See Num. 6:5; Josh. 7:6; Acts 18:6; Rev. 13:1.
HEAL. Ex. 15:26, I am the Lord that *h*. thee.
Dt. 32:39, I wound, I *h*.
2Ki. 2:22, waters were *h*.
2Ki. 20:5, 8, I will *h*. the.
Ps. 6:2, O Lord, *h*. me.
41:4, *h*. my soul, for I have sinned.
103:3, who *h*. all thy diseases.
107:20, sent his word, and *h*. them.
Isa. 6:10, lest they convert and be *h*.
53:5, with his stripes we are *h*.
Jer. 6:14; 8:11, they have *h*. the hurt slightly.
15:18, wound refuseth to be *h*.
17:14, *h*. me, and I shall be *h*.
Lam. 2:13, who can *h*. thee?
Hos. 5:13, yet could he not *h*. thee.
6:1, he hath torn, and he will *h*. us.
14:4, I will *h*. their backslidings.
Mt. 8:7, I will come and *h*. him.
8:8, speak, and my servant shall be *h*.
10:1, to *h*. all manner of sickness.
10:8; Lk. 9:2; 10:9, *h*. the sick.
Mt. 12:10; Lk. 14:3, is it lawful to *h*. on sabbath?
Mk. 3:2; Lk. 6:7, whether he would *h*. on the sabbath day.
Lk. 4:18, to *h*. broken-hearted.
23, physician, *h*. thyself.
5:17, power of the Lord present to *h*.
Jn. 5:47, that he would come and *h*.
5:13, he that was *h*. wist not.
Acts. 4:14, beholding the man which was *h*.
5:16, they were *h*. every one.
14:9, he had faith to be *h*.
Heb. 12:13, let it rather be *h*.
Jas. 5:16, pray that ye may be *h*.
1Pet. 2:24, by whose stripes ye were *h*.
Rev. 13:3, his deadly wound was *h*.
See Eccl. 3:3; Isa. 3:7; Mt. 4:21; 14:14.
HEALING. Jer. 14:19, there is no *h*. for us.
Nah. 3:19, no *h*. of thy bruise.
Mal. 4:2, with *h*. in his wings.
Mt. 4:23, went about *h*. all.
Lk. 9:11, that had need of *h*.
1Cor. 12:9, 28, 30, the gift of *h*.
Rev. 22:2, for the *h*. of the nations.
See Jer. 30:13; Lk. 9:6; Acts 4:22; 10:38.
HEALTH. 2Sam. 20:9, art thou in *h*., my brother?
Ps. 42:11; 43:5, the *h*. of my countenance.
67:2, thy saving *h*.
Prov. 3:8, *h*. to thy navel.
4:22, they are *h*. to all their flesh.
16:24, *h*. to the bones.
Isa. 58:8, thy *h*. shall spring forth.
Jer. 8:15, looked for a time of *h*.
22, why is not *h*. recovered?
3Jn. 2, mayest be in *h*.
See Gen. 43:28; Jer. 30:17; Acts 27:34.
HEAP. Dt. 32:23, *h*. mischiefs upon them.
Job 16:4, I could *h*. up words.
27:16, though he *h*. up silver.
Ps. 39:6, he *h*. up riches.
Prov. 25:22; Rom. 12:20, *h*. coals of fire.
Ezek. 24:10, *h*. on wood.
Hab. 1:10, they shall *h*. dust.
Mic. 3:12, Jerusalem shall become *h*.
2Tim. 4:3, *h*. to themselves teachers.
Jas. 5:3, ye have *h*. treasure for last days.
See Jud. 15:16; Neh. 4:2; Eccl. 2:26.
HEAR. Ex. 6:12, how shall Pharaoh *h*. me?
1Sam. 15:14, lowing of oxen which I *h*.
1Ki. 8:42, they shall *h*. of thy great name.
18:26, O Baal, *h*. us.
2Ki. 18:28; Isa. 36:13, *h*. words of the great king.
1Chr. 14:15, when thou *h*. a sound of going.
Neh. 8:2, all that could *h*. with understanding.
Job. 31:35, Oh that one would *h*. me!
Ps. 4:1; 39:12; 54:2; 84:8; 102:1; 143;1; Dan. 9:17, *h*. my prayer.
3; 17:6; Zech. 10:6, the Lord will *h*.
10:17, cause thine ear to *h*.
49:1, *h*. this, all ye people.
59:7, who, say they, doth *h*.?
66:18, if I regard iniquity, the Lord will not *h*. me.
85:8, I will *h*. what God the Lord will speak.
102:20, *h*. groaning of the prisoner.
Prov. 13:8, the poor *h*. not rebuke.
18:13, answereth a matter before he *h*.
22:17, *h*. the words of the wise.
Eccl. 5:1, more ready to *h*. than give.
7:5, better to *h*. rebuke of wise.
12:13, *h*. conclusion of the whole matter.
Isa. 1:2, *h*, O heavens, and give ear.
15; Jer. 7:16; 11:14; 14:12; Ezek. 8:18, make many prayers, I will not *h*.
6:9; Mk. 4:12, *h*. but understand not.
29:18, shall deaf *h*. words of the book.
33:13, *h*., ye that are afar off.
34:1, let the earth *h*.
42:20, opening ears, but he *h*. not.
55:3; Jn. 5:25, *h*., and your soul shall live.
Ezek. 3:27, he that *h*., let him *h*.
33:31, they *h*. words, but will not do them.
Mt. 7:24; Lk. 6:47, whoso *h*. these sayings.
11:4, show things ye do *h*. and see.
5; Mk. 7:37; Lk. 7:22, the deaf *h*.
13:17; Lk. 10:24, those things which ye *h*.
17:5; Mk. 9:7, my beloved Son, *h*. him.
18:16, if he will not *h*. thee.
Mk. 4:24; Lk. 8:18, take heed what ye *h*.
Lk. 9:9, of whom I *h*. such things.
10:16, he that *h*. you, *h*. me.
Jn. 5:25, dead shall *h*. voice of Son of God.
30, as I *h*., I judge.
6:60, who can *h*. it?
8:47, he that is of God *h*. God's words.
9:31, God *h*. not sinners.
11:42, I know thou *h*. me always.
12:47, if any man *h*. my words.
14:24, the word ye *h*. is not mine.

Acts 2:8, how *h.* we every man?
13:44, whole city came to *h.*
Rom. 10:14, *h.* without a preacher.
1Cor. 11:18, I *h.* there be divisions.
1Tim. 4:16, save thyself, and them that *h.*
Jas. 1:19, swift to *h.*
1Jn. 4:5, the world *h.* them.
6, he that knoweth God *h.* us.
5:15, we know that he *h.* us.
Rev. 2:7; 3:6, 13, 22, let him *h.*
3:20, if any man *h.* my voice.
See Dt. 30:17; 2Ki. 19:16; 2Chr. 6:21.
HEARD. Gen. 3:8, they *h.* voice of the Lord.
21:17, God *h.* voice of the lad.
45:2, Joseph wept, and the Egyptians *h.*
Ex. 3:7, I have *h.* their cry.
Num. 11:1; 12:2, the Lord *h.* it.
Dt. 4:12, only he *h.* a voice.
1Ki. 6:7, nor any tool of iron *h.*
10:7; 2Chr. 9:6, exceedeth the fame I *h.*
2Ki. 19:25; Isa. 37:26, hast thou not *h.* long ago?
Ezra 3:13; Neh. 12:43, the noise was *h* afar off.
Job 15:8, hast thou *h.* the secret of God?
16:2, I have *h.* many such things.
19:7, but I am not *h.*
26:14, how little a portion is *h*?
29:11, when the ear *h.* me, it blessed me.
Ps. 6:9, the Lord hat *h.* my supplication.
10:17, has *h.* the desire of the humble.
34:4, I sought the Lord, and he *h.*
38:13, I, as a deaf man, *h.* not.
61:5, thou has *h.* my vows.
81:5, I *h.* language I understood not.
116:1, I love the Lord, because he hath *h.*
Song 2:12, voice of turtle is *h.*
Isa. 40:21, 28, have ye not *h.*?
64:4, not *h.* what he hath prepared.
65:19, weeping no more be *h.*
66:8, who hath *h.* such a thing?
Jer. 7:13, rising early, but ye *h.* not.
8:6, I *h.*, but they spake not aright.
51:46; Obad. 1, a rumour that shall be *h.*
Dan. 12:8, I *h.*, but understood not.
Zech. 8:23, we have *h.* God is with you.
Mal. 3:16, the Lord hearkened, and *h.* it.
Mt. 6:7, *h.* for much speaking.
26:65; Mk. 14:64, ye have *h.* the blasphemy.
Lk. 12:3, shall be *h.* in the light.
Jn. 4:42, we have *h.* him ourselves.
8:36, as though he *h.* them not.
11:41, I thank thee thou has *h.* me.
Acts 4:4, many which *h.* believed.
20, cannot but speak things we have *h.*
16:25, the prisoners *h.* them.
22:15, witness of what thou has seen and *h.*
Rom. 10:14, of whom they have not *h.*
18, have they not *h.*
1Cor. 2:9, eye hath not seen, nor ear *h.*
2Cor. 12:4, *h.* unspeakable words.
Eph. 4:21, if so be ye have *h.* him.
Phil. 4:9, things ye have *h.* and seen in me.
2Tim. 2:2, things thou hast *h.* of me.
Heb. 2:3, confirmed by them that *h.*
4:2, with faith in them that *h.*
5:7, was *h.* in that he feared.
1Jn. 1:1, 3, that which we have *h.* and seen.
Rev. 3:3, remember how thou has *h.*
10:4; 14:2; 18:4, *h.* a voice from heaven.
See Jer. 31:18; Jn. 5:37; Rev. 19:6; 22:8.
HEARER. Rom. 2:13; Eph. 4:29; Jas. 1:23.
HEARING. Dt. 31:11, read this law in their *h.*
2Ki. 4:31, neither voice nor *h.*
Job 42:5, by the *h.* of the ear.
Prov. 20:12, the *h.* ear.
Eccl. 1:8, nor ear filled with *h.*
Amos 8:11, a famine of *h.* the word.
Mt. 13:13, *h.*, they hear not.
Acts 9:7, *h.* a voice, but seeing no man.
Rom. 10:17, faith cometh by *h.*
1Cor. 12:17, where were the *h.*?
Heb. 5:11, ye are dull of *h.*
See Acts 28:27; Gal. 3:2; 2Pet. 2:8.
HEARKEN. Dt. 18:15, unto him ye shall *h.*
Josh. 1:17, so will we *h.* unto thee.
1Sam. 15:22, to *h.* than the fat of rams.
Prov. 29:12, if a ruler *h.* to lies.
Isa. 55:2, *h.* diligently unto me.
Dan. 9:19, O Lord, *h.* and do.
Mk. 7:14, *h.* to me, every one of you.
See Ps. 103:20; Prov. 1:33; 12:15; Acts 4:19.
HEART. Ex. 23:9, ye know the *h.* of a stranger.
Dt. 11:13; Josh. 22:5; 1Sam. 12:20, 24, serve him with all your *h.*
13:3; 30:6; Mt. 22:37; Mk. 12:30, 33; Lk. 10:27, love the Lord with all your *h.*
Jud. 5:16, great searchings of *h.*
1Sam. 10:9, God gave him another *h.*
16:7, the Lord looketh on the *h.*
1Ki. 3:9, 12, give an understanding *h.*
4:29, gave Solomon largeness of *h.*
8:17; 2Chr. 6:7, it was in the *h.* of David.
11:4, not perfect, as was *h.* of David.
14:8, followed me with all his *h.*
1Chr. 12:33, not of double *h.*
29:17; Jer. 11:20, I know thou triest the *h.*
2Chr. 31:21, he did it with all his *h.*
32:25, his *h.* was lifted up.
Neh. 2:2, nothing else but sorrow of *h.*
Job 23:16, maketh my *h.* soft.
29:13, caused the widow's *h.* to sing.
Ps. 10:6; 11:13; 14:1; 53:1, said in his *h.*
19:8, rejoicing the *h.*
27:3, my *h.* shall not fear.
28:7, my *h.* trusted in him.
64:6, the *h.* is deep.
73:7, more than *h.* could wish.
78:37, their *h.* was not right.
97:11, gladness sown for upright in *h.*
119:11, thy word have I hid in my *h.*
80, let my *h.* be sound.
139:23, search me and know my *h.*
Prov. 4:23, keep thy *h.* with all diligence.
14:10, the *h.* knoweth his own bitterness.
21:1, king's *h.* is in the hand of the Lord.
23:7, as he thinketh in his *h.*, so is he.
25:3, king's *h.* is unsearchable.

20, songs to a heavy *h*.
31:11, *h*. of her husband doth trust.
Eccl. 8:5, wise man's *h*. discerneth.
Isa. 35:4, say to them of fearful *h*.
44:20, a deceived *h*.
57:1; Jer. 12:11, no man layeth it to *h*.
15, revive *h*. of contrite.
65:14, sing for joy of *h*.
Jer. 11:20; 20:12, thou triest the *h*.
Jer. 17:9, the *h*. is deceitful above all things.
20:9, in mine *h*. as a burning fire.
24:7, I will give them a *h*. to know me.
30:21, that engaged his *h*. to approach.
49:16; Obad. 3, pride of *h*. deceived thee.
Ezek. 11:19, take stony *h*.
18:31, make you a new *h*.
36:26, will give you a *h*. of flesh.
44:7; Acts 7:51, uncircumcised in *h*.
Dan. 1:8, Daniel purposed in his *h*.
Joel 2:13, rend your *h*.
Zech. 7:12, made *h*. as adamant.
Mal. 2:2, if ye will not lay it to *h*.
4:6, turn *h*. of fathers to children.
Mt. 5:8, blessed are the pure in *h*.
6:21; Lk. 12:34, there will your *h*. be also.
11:29, meek and lowly in *h*.
12:34; Lk. 6:45, out of abundance of the *h*.
15:19, out of the *h*. proceed evil thoughts.
18:35, if ye from your *h*. forgive not.
Mk. 2:8, why reason ye in your *h*.?
8:17, have ye your *h*. yet hardened?
10:5; 16:14, hardness of *h*.
Lk. 2:19, 51, kept them in her *n*.
21:14, settle it in your *h*.
24:25, slow of *h*. to believe.
32, did not our *h*. burn within us?
Jn. 14:1, 27, let not your *h*. be troubled.
Acts 5:23; 7:54, were cut to the *h*.
11:23, with purpose of *h*.
Rom. 10:10, with the *h*. man believeth.
1Cor. 2:9, neither have entered into *h*.
2Cor. 3:3, in fleshy tables of the *h*.
5:12, glory in appearance, not in *h*.
Eph. 3:17, that Christ dwell in your *h*. by faith.
5:19, singing and making melody in your *h*.
6:6, doing will of God from the *h*.
Phil. 4:7, keep your *h*. and minds.
Col. 3:22, in singleness of *h*.
2Th. 3:5, direct your *h*. into love of God.
Heb. 4:12, discerner of intents of the *h*.
10:22, draw near with true *h*.
13:9, good that the *h*. be established.
Jas. 3:14, if ye have strife in your *h*.
4:8, purify your *h*.
1Pet. 3:4, the hidden man of the *h*.
15, sanctify the Lord in your *h*.
See Ps. 57:7; 108:1; Col. 3:15; 2Pet. 1:19.
HEARTH. Gen. 18:6; Ps. 102:3; Isa. 30:14; Jer. 36:22.
HEARTILY. Col. 3:23.
HEAT. Dt. 29:24, the *h*. of this great anger.
Ps. 19:6, nothing hid from *h*. thereof.
Eccl. 4:11, two together, then they have *h*.
Isa. 4:6; 25:4, a shadow from the *h*.
18:4, *h*. upon herbs, dew in *h*. of harvest.
49:10, neither shall *h*. smite them.
Hos. 7:4, as oven *h*. by the baker.
Mt. 20:12, burden and *h*. of the day.
Jas. 1:11, sun no sooner risen with burning *h*.
2Pet. 3:10, melt with fervent *h*.
See Dan. 3:19; Lk. 12:55; Acts 28:3.
HEATH. Jer. 17:6; 48:6.
HEATHEN. Ps. 2:1; Acts 4:25, why do the *h*. rage?
8, give *h*. for inheritance.
102:15, the *h*. shall fear name of the Lord.
Ezek. 36:24, I will take you from among *h*.
Zech. 8:13, ye were a curse among the *h*.
Mt. 6:7, repetitions, as the *h*.
18:17, let him be as *h*. man.
See Lev. 25:44; Dt. 4:27; Neh. 5:8.
HEAVEN. Gen. 28:17, the gate of *h*.
Ex. 20:22, have talked with you from *h*.
Lev. 26:19, make your *h*. as iron.
Dt. 10:14; 1Ki. 8:27; Ps. 115:16, the *h*. and *h*. of heavens.
33:13, the precious things of *h*.
2Ki. 7:2, if the Lord make windows in *h*.
Job 15:15, the *h*. are not clean in his sight.
22:12, is not God in the height of *h*.?
Ps. 8:3, when I consider thy *h*.
14:2; 53:2, had looked down from *h*.
73:25, whom have I in *h*.?
89:6, who in *h*. can be compared to the Lord?
119:89, thy word is settled in *h*.
Prov. 8:27, when he prepared the *h*. I was there.
25:3, the *h*. for height.
Eccl. 5:2, for God is in *h*.
Isa. 13:13; Hag. 2:6, will shake the *h*.
40:12, meted out *h*. with the span.
65:17; Rev. 21:1, new *h*. and new earth.
Jer. 7:18, make cakes to queen of *h*.
23:24, do not I fill *h*. and earth?
31:37, if *h*. can be measured.
Ezek. 1:1; Mt. 3:16; Mk. 1:10, the *h*. were opened.
32:7, I will cover the *h*.
Dan. 7:13, with clouds of *h*.
Hag. 1:10, *h*. over you is stayed from dew.
Mal. 3:10, if I will not open windows of *h*.
Mt. 5:18, till *h*. and earth pass.
11:23, exalted to *h*.
24:29; Mk. 13:25, the powers of *h*.
Mk. 13:32, no, not the angels in *h*.
Lk. 15:18, I have sinned against *h*.
Jn. 1:51, ye shall see *h*. open.
6:31, 32, bread from *h*.
Acts 4:12, none other name under *h*.
Rom. 1:18, wrath of God revealed from *h*.
2Cor. 5:1, eternal in the *h*.
2, our house that is from *h*.
Gal. 1:8, though an angel from *h*. preach.
Eph. 1:10, gather in one, things in *h*.
3:15, whole family in *h*.
6:9; Col. 4:1, your master is in *h*.
Phil. 3:20, our conversation is in *h*.
Heb. 12:23, written in *h*.

1Jn. 5:7, three that bear record in *h*.
Rev. 4:1, door opened in *h*.
2, throne set in *h*.
8:1, silence in *h*.
12:1, 3, a great wonder in *h*.
See 2Cor. 12:2; 1Th. 4:16; 2Th. 1:7.
HEAVENLY. Lk. 2:13, multitude of the *h*. host.
Jn. 3:12, I tell you of *h*. things.
Acts 26:19, the *h*. vision.
1Cor. 15:48, as is the *h*., such are they.
Eph. 1:3; 2:6; 3:10, in *h*. places.
Heb. 3:1, partakers of the *h*. calling.
8:5; 9:23, shadow of *h*. things.
11:16, an *h*. country.
See 2Tim. 4:18; Heb. 6:4; 12:22.
HEAVENLY FATHER. Mt. 6:14, your *h. f.* also will forgive you.
Lk. 11:13, how much more shall your *h. f.* give the Holy Spirit to them that ask him?
HEAVINESS. Ps. 69:20, I am full of *h*.
Prov. 12:25, *h*. in the heart maketh it stoop.
14:13, the end of that mirth is *h*.
Isa. 61:3, garment of praise for spirit of *h*.
Jas. 4:9, let your joy be turned to *h*.
See Ezra 9:5; Prov. 10:1; Rom. 9:2.
HEAVY. Ex. 17:12, Moses' hands were *h*.
1Ki. 14:6, sent with *h*. tidings.
Neh. 5:18, the bondage was *h*.
Job 33:7; Ps. 32:4, hand *h*.
Prov. 25:20, songs to a *h*. heart.
31:6, wine to those of *h*. heart.
Isa. 58:6, to undo the *h*. burdens.
Mt. 11:28, all ye that are *h*. laden.
23:4, they bind *h*. burdens.
26:37, he began to be very *h*.
43; Mk. 14:33, their eyes were *h*.
See Prov. 27:3; Isa. 59:1; Lk. 9:32.
HEDGE. Job 3:23, whom God hat *h*. in.
Prov. 15:19, way of slothful an *h*. of thorns.
Eccl. 10:8, whoso breaketh an *h*.
Lam. 3:7, he hath *h*. me about.
Hos. 2:6, I will *h*. up thy way.
Mk. 12:1, he set a *h*. about it.
Lk. 14:23, the highways and *h*.
See Isa. 5:5; Ezek. 13:5; 22:30; Nah. 3:17.
HEED. 2Sam. 20:10, took no *h*. to the sword.
Ps. 119:9, by taking *h*. thereto.
Eccl. 12:9, preacher gave good *h*.
Isa. 21:7, hearkened diligently with much *h*.
Jer. 18:18, let us not give *h*.
1Tim. 1:4; Ti. 1:14, neither give *h*. to fables.
4:1, giving *h*. to seducing spirits.
Heb. 2:1, give more earnest *h*.
See Prov. 17:4; Acts 3:5; 8:6.
HEEL. Gen. 3:15, thou shalt bruise his *h*.
Ps. 49:5, when the iniquity of my *h*. shall compass me about.
HEIGHT. Ps. 102:19, from *h*. of his sanctuary.
Prov. 25:3, the heaven for *h*.
Isa. 7:11, ask it either in the depth, or in the *h*. above.
Eph. 3:18, 19, the *h*. of the love of Christ.
See Job 22:12; Ps. 148:1; Amos 2:9.
HEIR. 2Sam. 14:7, we will destroy the *h*.
Prov. 30:23, handmaid that is *h*. to her mistress.
Mt. 21:38; Mk. 12:7; Lk. 20:14, this is the *h*.
Rom. 8:17, *h*. of God, joint-*h*. with Christ.
Gal. 3:29, *h*. according to the promise.
4:7, an *h*. of God through Christ.
Eph. 3:6, Gentiles fellow-*h*.
Ti. 3:7, *h*. according to hope of eternal life.
Heb. 1:14, who shall be *h*. of salvation.
6:17, the *h*. of promise.
11:7, *h*. of the righteousness.
Jas. 2:5, *h*. of the kingdom.
1Pet. 3:7, as *h*. together of the grace.
See Jer. 49:1; Mic. 1:15; Rom. 4:13.
HELL. Dt. 32:22, fire shall burn to lowest *h*.
2Sam. 22:6; Ps. 18:5, sorrows of *h*. compassed me.
Job. 11:8, deeper than *h*.
26:6, *h*. is naked before him.
Ps. 9:17, wicked turned into *h*.
16:19; Acts 2:27, not leave soul in *h*.
55:15, let them go down quick into *h*.
139:8, if I make my bed in *h*.
Prov. 5:5, her steps take hold on *h*.
7:27, house is the way to *h*.
9:18, her guests are in the depths of *h*.
15:11, *h*. and destruction before the Lord.
24, that he may depart from *h*. beneath.
23:14, deliver his soul from *h*.
27:20, *h*. and destruction are never full.
Isa. 14:9, *h*. from beneath is moved.
28:15, 18, with *h*. are we at agreement.
Ezek. 31:16, when I cast him down to *h*.
32:21, shall speak out of the midst of *h*.
Amos 9:2, though they dig into *h*.
Jon. 2:2, out of the belly of *h*.
Hab. 2:5, enlargeth his desire as *h*.
Mt. 5:22, in danger of *h*. fire.
29, 30, whole body cast into *h*.
10:28; Lk. 12:5, destroy soul and body in *h*.
11:23; Lk. 10:15, brought down to *h*.
16:18, gates of *h*. shall not prevail.
18:9; Mk. 9:47, having two eyes to be cast into *h*.
23:15, more the child of *h*.
33, now can ye escape the damnation of *h*.?
Lk. 16:23, in *h*. he lift up.
Acts 2:31, soul not left in *h*.
Jas. 3:6, tongue set on fire of *h*.
2Pet. 2:4, cast angels down to *h*.
See Isa. 5:14; Rev. 1:18; 6:8; 20:13.
HELP. Gen. 2:18, 20, an *h*. meet for him.
Dt. 33:29, the shield of thy *h*.
2Chr. 26:15, he was marvellously *h*.
Job 6:13, is not my *h*. in me?
Ps. 22:11, for there is none to *h*.
Ps. 33:20, he is our *h*. and our shield.
42:5, the *h*. of his countenance.
46:1, a very present *h*. in trouble.
60:11; 108:12, vain is the *h*. of man.
89:19, laid *h*. on one that is mighty.
121:1, the hills from whence cometh my *h*.
124:8, our *h*. is in the name of the Lord.

Isa. 10:3, to whom will ye flee for *h.*?
41:6, they *h.* every one his neighbour.
Hos. 13:9, in me is thine *h.*
Mt. 15:25, Lord, *h.* me.
Mk. 9:24, *h.* thou mine unbelief.
Acts 21:28, men of Israel, *h.*
26:22, having obtained *h.* of God.
Heb. 4:16, grace to *h.* in time of need.
See Isa. 31:3; Rom. 8:26; 2Cor. 1:24.
HELPER. Heb. 13:6.
HEM. Mt. 9:20, touched the *h.* of his garment.
14:36, might only touch the *h.* of his garment.
See Num. 15:38, 39; Mt. 23:5.
HEMLOCK. Hos. 10:4, judgment springeth up as *h.*
Amos 6:12, the fruit of righteousness into *h.*
HEN. Mt. 23:37; Lk. 13:34.
HENCEFORTH. 2 Cor. 5:15; Gal. 6:17; 2 Tim. 4:8.
HERITAGE. Job 20:29, *h.* appointed by God.
Ps. 16:6; Jer. 3:19, a goodly *h.*
61:5, the *h.* of those that fear.
127:3, children are an *h.* of the Lord.
Isa. 54:17, this is the *h.* of the servants.
Mic. 7:14, feed flock of thine *h.*
1Pet. 5:3, lords over God's *h.*
See Joel 2:17; 3:2; Mal. 1:3.
HID. 2Ki. 4:27, the Lord hath *h.* it from me.
Job 3:21, more than for *h.* treasures.
Ps. 32:5, mine iniquity have I not *h.*
69:5, my sins are not *h.*
119:11, thy word have I *h.* in mine heart.
Zeph. 2:3, it may be ye shall be *h.*
Mt. 10:26; Mk. 4:22, there is nothing *h.*
Lk. 19:42, now they are *h.* from thine eyes.
1Cor. 2:7, even the *h.* wisdom.
2Cor. 4:3, if our gospel be *h.*
Col. 3:3, your life is *h.* with Christ.
1 Pet. 3:4, the *h.* man of the heart.
Rev. 2:17, to eat of the *h.* manna.
See Gen. 3:8; Mt. 5:14; Mk. 7:24.
HIDE. Gen. 18:17, shall I *h.* from Abraham.
Job 14:13, *h.* me in the grave.
34:29, when he *h.* his face.
Ps. 10:11, he *h* his face.
17:8, *h.* me under the shadow of thy wings.
27:5, *h.* me in pavilion.
31:20, *h.* them in secret of thy presence.
89:46, how long wilt thou *h.* thyself?
139:12, darkness *h.* not from thee.
Isa. 1:15, I will *h.* mine eyes from you.
3:9, they *h.* not their sin.
26:20, *h.* thyself for a little moment.
32:2, a man shall be as an *h.* place.
45:15, thou art a God that *h.* thyself.
Ezek. 28:3, no secret they can *h.* from thee.
Jas. 5:20, *h.* a multitude of sins.
Rev. 6:16, *h.* us from the face of him.
See Job 13:24; Prov. 28:28; Amos 9:3.
HIGH. Job 11:8, it is as *h.* as heaven.
22:12, behold stars, how *h.* they are!
41:34, he beholdeth all *h.* things.
Ps. 62:9, men of *h.* degree are a lie.
68:18, thou hast ascended on *h.*
103:11, as the heaven is *h.* above the earth.
131:1, in things too *h.* for me.
138:6, though the Lord be *h.*
139:6, it is *h.*, I cannot attain unto it.
Eccl. 12:5, afraid of that which is *h.*
Isa. 32:15, spirit poured on us from on *h.*
33:16, he shall dwell on *h.*
35:8, an *h.*-way shall be there.
Isa. 62:10, cast up the *h.*-way.
Jer. 49:16, though thou make thy nest *h.*
Mt. 22:9; Lk. 14:23, go into the *h.*-ways.
Lk. 1:78, dayspring from on *h.*
24:49, power from on *h.*
Rom. 12:16, mind not *h.* things.
13:11, it is *h.* time.
Phil. 3:14, for prize of the *h.* calling.
See Isa. 57:15; 2Cor. 10:5.
HIGHER. Isa. 55:9, heavens *h.* than the earth.
Lk. 14:10, friend, go up *h.*
Heb. 7:26, made *h.* than the heavens.
HILL. Gen. 49:26, the everlasting *h.*
Dt. 11:11, a land of *h.* and valleys.
Ps. 2:6, set my king on holy *h.*
15:1, who shall dwell in thy holy *h.*?
24:3, who shall ascend the *h.* of the Lord?
43:3, bring me to thy holy *h*
50:10, cattle on a thousand *h.*
95:4, strength of the *h.* is his.
121:1, I will lift up mine eyes to the *h.*
Prov. 8:25, before the *h.* was I brought forth.
Isa. 40:12, weighed the *h.* in balance.
Jer. 3:23, salvation hoped for from the *h.*
Hos. 10:8; Lk. 23:30, to the *h.*, fall on us.
Mt. 5:14, city set on an *h.*
See Lk. 4:29; 9:37; Acts 17:22.
HINDER. Gen. 24:56, *h.* me not.
Job 9:12; 11:10, who can *h.* him?
Lk. 11:52, them that were entering ye *h.*
Acts 8:36, what doth *h.* me to be baptized?
1Cor. 9:12, lest we *h.* the gospel
Gal. 5:7, who did *h.* you?
1Th. 2:18, but Satan *h.* us.
1Pet. 3:7, that your prayers be not *h.*
See Num. 22:16; Neh. 4:8; Isa. 14:6.
HIRE. Dt. 24:15, thou shalt give him his *h.*
Mic. 3:11, priests teach for *h.*
Mt. 20:7, no man hat *h.* us.
8, give them their *h.*
Mk. 1:20, in ship with *h.* servants.
Lk. 10:7, labourer worthy of his *h.*
15:17, how many *h.* servants.
Jas. 5:4, *h.* of labourers which is kept back.
See Ex. 12:45; Lev. 25:40; Dt. 15:18.
HIRELING. Job 7:1, like the days of an *h.*
2, as *h.* looketh for reward.
14:6, accomplish, as an *h.*, his day.
Mal. 3:5, that oppress the *h.*
See Isa. 16:14; 21:16; Jn. 10:12.
HITHERTO. Josh. 17:14, the Lord hath blessed me *h.*
1Sam. 7:12, *h.* hath the Lord helped us.
Job 38:11, *h.* shalt thou come.
Jn. 5:17, my Father worketh *h.*
16:24, *h.* have ye asked nothing in my name.

1Cor. 3:2, *h.* ye were not able to bear it.
See Jud. 16:13; 2Sam. 15:34; Isa. 18:2.
HOARY. Job 41:32.
HOLD. Gen. 21:18, *h.* him in thine hand.
Ex. 20:7; Dt. 5:11, will not *h.* him guiltless.
2Ki. 7:9, good tidings and we *h.* our peace.
Est. 4:14, if thou altogether *h.* thy peace.
Job 36:8, *h.* in cords of affliction.
Ps. 18:35, thy right hand hath *h.* me up.
71:6, by thee have I been *h.*
73:23, thou has *h.* me by my right hand.
119:117, *h.* me up, and I shall be safe.
Prov. 11:12, man of understanding *h.* his peace.
17:28, a fool, when he *h.* his peace.
Isa. 41:13, the Lord will *h.* thy hand.
62:1, for Zion's sake will I not *h.* my peace.
Jer. 4:19, I cannot *h.* my peace.
Amos 6:10, *h.* thy tongue.
Mt. 6:14; Lk. 16:13, he will *h.* to the one.
Mk. 1:25; Lk. 4:35, *h.* thy peace, come out.
Rom. 1:18, *h.* the truth in unrighteousness.
1Cor. 14:30, let the first *h.* his peace.
Phil. 2:16, *h.* forth the word of life.
29, *h.* such in reputation.
Col. 2:19, not *h.* the Head.
1Th. 5:21, *h.* fast that which is good.
1Tim. 1:19, *h.* faith and good conscience.
3:9, *h.* the mystery of faith.
2Tim. 1:13, *h.* fast form of sound words.
Ti. 1:9, *h.* fast the faithful word.
Heb. 3:14, *h.* beginning of confidence.
4:14; 10:23, *h.* fast our profession.
Rev. 2:13, thou *h.* fast my name.
25, *h.* fast till I come.
3:3, *h.* fast, and repent.
11, *h.* that fast which thou hast.
See Job 2:3; Jer. 2:13; 51:30; Ezek. 19:9.
HOLE. Isa. 11:8, child shall play on *h.* of the asp.
51:1, *h.* of pit whence ye are digged.
Jer. 13:4, hide in a *h.* of the rock.
Ezek. 8:7, a *h.* in the wall.
Hag. 1:6, a bag with *h.*
Mt. 8:20; Lk. 9:58, foxes have *h.*
See Song 5:4; Mic. 7:17; Nah. 2:12.
HOLIER. Isa. 65:5.
HOLIEST. Heb. 9:3; 10:19.
HOLILY. 1Th. 2:10.
HOLINESS. Ex. 15:11, glorious in *h.*
28:36; 39:30; Zech. 14:20, *h.* to the Lord.
1Chr. 16:29; 2Chr. 20:21; Ps. 29:2; 96:9; 110:3, beauty of *h.*
Ps. 30:4; 97:12, at remembrance of his *h.*
47:8, the throne of his *h.*
60:6; 108:7, God hath spoken in his *h.*
93:5, *h.* becometh thine house.
Isa. 35:8, the way of *h.*
63:15, habitation of thy *h.*
Jer. 23:9, the words of his *h.*
Obad. 17, upon mount Zion there shall be *h.*
Lk. 1:75, might serve him in *h.*
Acts 3:12, as though by our *h.*
Rom. 1:4, according to the spirit of *h.*
6:22, fruit unto *h.*
2Cor. 7:1, perfecting *h.* in fear of God.
Eph. 4:24, created in righteousness and *h.*
1Th. 3:13, unblameable in *h.*
4:7, not called to uncleanness, but *h.*
1Tim. 2:15, continue in faith and *h.*
Ti. 2:3, in behaviour as becometh *h.*
Heb. 12:10, partakes of his *h.*
14, *h.*, without which no man.
See Ps. 89:35; Isa. 23:18; Jer. 2:3.
HOLLOW. Gen. 32:25; Jud. 15:19; Isa. 40:12.
HOLPEN. Ps. 86:17; Isa. 31:3; Dan. 11:34; Lk. 1:54.
HOLY. Ex. 3:5; Josh. 5:15, is *h.* ground.
19:6; 1Pet. 2:9, an *h.* nation.
20:8; 31:14, sabbath day, to keep it *h.*
Lev. 10:10, difference between *h.* and unholy.
20:7, be ye *h.*
Num. 16:5, Lord will show who is *h.*
2Ki. 4:9, this is an *h.* man of God.
Ezra 9:2; Isa. 6:13, the *h.* seed.
Ps. 20:6, hear from his *h.* heaven.
22:3, thou art *h.* that inhabitest.
86:2, preserve my soul, for I am *h.*
98:1, his *h.* arm hath gotten victory.
99:9, worship at his *h.* hill.
145:17, the Lord is *h.* in all his works.
Prov. 20:25, who devoureth that which is *h.*
Isa. 6:3; Rev. 4:8, *h.*, *h.*, *h.*, is the Lord.
52:10, make bare his *h.* arm.
64:10, thy *h.* cities are a wilderness.
11, our *h.* and beautiful house.
Ezek. 22:26, put no difference between *h.* and profane.
Mt. 1:18, 20, with child of the *H.* Ghost.
3:11; Mk. 1:8; Lk. 3:16; Jn. 1:33; Acts 1:5, baptize with the *H.* Ghost.
7:6, give not that which is *h.*
12:31; Mk. 3:29, blasphemy against *H.* Ghost.
Mk. 13:11, not ye that speak, but *H.* Ghost.
Lk. 1:15, shall be filled with the *H.* Ghost.
35, that *h.* thing which shall be born of thee.
3:22, *H.* Ghost descended in bodily shape.
4:1, Jesus being full of the *H.* Ghost.
12:12, *H.* Ghost shall teach you.
Jn. 7:39, the *H.* Ghost was not yet given.
14:26, the Comforter, which is the *H.* Ghost.
17:11, *h.* Father keep those.
20:22, receive ye the *H.* Ghost.
Acts 1:8, after the *H.* Ghost is come.
2:4; 4:31, all filled with *H.* Ghost.
4:27, 30, against thy *h* child Jesus.
5:3, to lie to the *H.* Ghost.
6:3, look out men full of the *H.* Ghost.
7:51, ye do always resist the *H.* Ghost.
8:15, prayed that they might receive *H.* Ghost.
9:31, in comfort of the *H.* Ghost.
10:44, *H.* Ghost fell on all which heard.
47, received *H.* Ghost as well as we.
15:8, giving them *H.* Ghost, as he did unto us.
28, seemed good to the *H.* Ghost.
16:6, forbidden of the *H.* Ghost.
19:2, have ye received the *H.* Ghost?

20:28, *H.* Ghost hath made you overseers.
Rom. 1:2, promised in the *h.* scriptures.
7:12, commandment is *h.*, just, and good.
9:1, bearing witness in *H.* Ghost.
11:16, if firstfruit be *h.*, if root be *h.*
12:1, a living sacrifice, *h.* acceptable to God.
14:17, joy in the *H.* Ghost.
16:16; 1Cor. 16:20; 2Cor. 13:12; 1Th. 5:26; 1Pet. 5:14, with a *h.* kiss.
1Cor. 2:13, words which the *H.* Ghost teacheth.
3:17, the temple of God is *h.*
7:14, now are they *h.*
2Cor. 13:14, communion of the *H.* Ghost.
Eph. 1:4; 5:27, be *h.* and without blame.
2:21, groweth to an *h.* temple in the Lord.
Col. 1:22, present you *h.* and unblameable.
3:12, elect of God, *h.* and beloved.
1Th. 5:27, all the *h.* brethren.
1Tim. 2:8, lifting up *h.* hands.
2Tim. 1:9, called us with an *h.* calling.
Ti. 1:8, bishop must be *h.*
3:5, the renewing of the *H.* Ghost.
Heb. 3:1, *h.* brethren, partakers.
1Pet. 1:12, *H.* Ghost sent down from heaven.
15; 2Pet. 3:11, *h.* in all conversation.
2:5, an *h.* priesthood.
3:5, the *h.* women, who trusted.
2Pet. 1:18, with him in the *h.* mount.
21, *h.* men moved by *H.* Ghost.
Rev. 3:7, saith he that is *h.*
67:10, O lord, *h.* and true.
20:6, *h.* is he that hath part.
21:10, the *h.* Jerusalem.
22:11, he that is *h.*, let him be *h.*
See 2Tim. 3:15; Heb. 2:4; 1Pet. 1:16; 2Pet. 3:2; Jude 20.

HOME. Ex. 9:19, and shall not be brought *h.*
Lev. 18:9, whether born at *h.* or abroad.
Dt. 24:5, free at *h.* one year.
Ruth 1:21, the Lord hath brought me *h.* empty.
2Sam. 14:13, fetch *h.* his banished.
1Ki. 13:7, come *h.* with me.
2Ki. 14:10; 2Chr. 25:19, tarry at *h.*
1 Chr. 13:12, bring ark of God *h.*
Job 39:12, he will bring *h.* thy seed.
Ps. 68:12, she that tarried at *h*
Eccl. 12:5, man goeth to this long *h.*
Lam. 1:20, at *h.* there is as death.
Hag. 1:9, when ye brought it *h.*
Mk. 5:19, go *h.* to thy friends.
Jn. 19:27, took her to his own *h.*
20:10, went away to their own *h.*
1Cor. 11:34, let him eat at *h.*
14:35, ask their husbands at *h.*
2Cor. 5:6, at *h.* in the body.
1Tim. 5:4, show piety at *h.*
Ti. 2:5, keepers at *h.*
See Jer. 2:14; Lk. 9:61; 15:6.

HONEST. Lk. 8:15, an *h.* and good heart.
Acts 6:3, men of *h.* report.
Rom. 12:17; 2Cor. 8:21, provide things *h.*
Rom. 13:13, let us walk *h.*, as in the day.
Phil. 4:8, whatsoever things are *h.*
1Pet. 2:12, conversation *h.* among Gentiles.
See 1Th. 4:12; 1Tim. 2:2; Heb. 13:18.

HONOUR (*n.*). Num. 22:17, I will promote thee to *h.*
24:11, hath kept thee back from *h.*
2Sam. 6:22, of them shall I be had in *h.*
1Ki. 3:13, also given thee riches and *h.*
1Chr. 29:18, died full of riches and *h.*
2Chr. 1:11, 12, thou hast not asked *h.*
26:18, neither shall it be for thy *h.*
Est. 1:20, the wives shall give their husbands *h.*
Job 14:21, his sons come to *h.*
Ps. 7:5, lay mine *h.* in the dust.
8:5; Heb. 2:7, crowned him with *h.*
26:8, place where thine *h.* dwelleth.
49:12, man being in *h.* abideth not.
96:6, *h.* and majesty are before him.
149:9, this *h.* have all his saints.
Prov. 3:16, in left hand riches and *h.*
4:8, she shall bring thee to *h.*
5:9, lest thou give their *h.* to others.
14:28, in multitude of people is king's *h.*
20:3, an *h.* to cease from strife.
25:2, the *h.* of kings to search out.
26:1, 8, *h.* is not seemly for a fool.
31:25, strength and *h.* are her clothing.
Eccl. 6:2, to whom God hath given *h.*
Mal. 1:6, where is mine *h.*?
Mt. 13:57; Mk. 6:4; Jn. 4:44, not without *h.*
Jn. 5:41, I receive not *h.* from men.
44, who receive *h.* one of another.
Rom. 2:7, in well doing seek for *h.*
10, *h.* to every man that worketh good.
12:10, in *h.* preferring one another.
13:7, *h.* to whom *h.*
2Cor. 6:8, by *h.* and dishonour.
Col. 2:23, not in any *h.* to satisfying.
1Th. 4:4, possess his vessel in *h.*
1Tim. 5:17, elders worthy of double *h.*
6:1, count masters worthy of *h.*
16, to whom be *h.* and power everlasting.
2Tim. 2:20, 21, some to *h.*, some to dishonour.
Heb. 3:3, more *h.* than the house.
5:4, no man taketh this *h.* unto himself.
1Pet. 3:7, giving *h.* to the wife.
Rev. 4:11; 5:12, thou art worthy to receive *h.*
See Rev. 5:13; 7:12; 19:1; 21:24.

HONOUR (*v.*). Ex. 14:4, I will be *h.* upon Pharaoh.
Ex. 20:12; Dt. 5:16; Mt. 15:4; 19:19; Mk. 7:10; 10:19; Lk. 18:20; Eph. 6:2, *h.* thy father and mother.
Lev. 19:32, thou shalt *h.* the face of the old man.
1Sam. 2:30, them that *h.* me I will *h.*
15:30, *h.* me now before elders.
Est. 6:6, the king delighteth to *h.*
Ps. 15:4, he *h.* them that fear the Lord.
Prov. 3:9, *h.* the Lord with thy substance.
12:9, better than he that *h.* himself.
Mal. 1:6, a son *h.* his father.
Mt. 15:8; Mk. 7:6, *h.* me with their lips.
Jn. 5:23, *h.* the Son as they *h.* the Father.
1Tim. 5:3, *h.* widows that are widows indeed.
1Pet. 2:17, *h.* all men, *h.* the king.
See Isa. 29:13; 58:13; Acts 28:10.

ONOURABLE. Ps. 45:9, among thy *h*. women.
Isa. 3:3, take away the *h*. man.
9:15, ancient and *h*., he is the head.
42:21, magnify the law, and make it *h*.
See Lk. 14:8; 1Cor. 4:10; 12:23; Heb. 13:4.
OPE (*n*.). Job 7:6, my days are spent without *h*.
Job 8:13, the hypocrite's *h*. shall perish.
Job 17:15, where is now my *h*.?
19:10, my *h*. hath he removed.
Ps. 16:9; Acts 2:26, my flesh also shall rest in *h*.
39:7, my *h*. is in thee.
119:116, let me not be ashamed of my *h*.
Prov. 13:12, *h*. deferred maketh the heart sick.
14:32, hath *h*. in his death.
26:12; 29:20, more *h*. of a fool.
Eccl. 9:4, to all the living there is *h*.
Jer. 17:7, the man whose *h*. the Lord is.
31:17, there is *h*. in thine end.
Hos. 2:15, for a door of *h*.
Zech. 9:12, ye prisoners of *h*.
Acts 28:20, for the *h*. of Israel I am bound.
Rom. 4:18, who against *h*. believed in *h*.
8:24, we are saved by *h*.
12:12, rejoicing in *h*.
1Cor. 13:13, faith, *h*., charity.
15:19, if in this life only we have *h*.
Eph. 1:18, the *h*. of his calling.
2:12, having no *h*., and without God.
Col. 1:27, Christ in you, the *h*. of glory.
1Th. 4:13, even as others who have no *h*.
5:8, for an helmet, the *h*. of salvation.
2Th. 2:16, good *h*. through grace.
Ti. 3:7, the *h*. of eternal life.
Heb. 6:18, lay hold on *h*. set before us.
19, *h*. as an anchor of the soul.
1Pet. 1:3, begotten to a lively *h*.
3:15, a reason of the *h*. that is in you.
See Lam. 3:18; Col. 1:5; 1Jn. 3:3.
OPE (*v*.). Ps. 22:9, thou didst make me *h*.
31:24, all ye that *h*. in the Lord.
42:5, 11; 43:5, *h*. thou in God.
71:14, I will *h*. continually.
Lam. 3:26, good that a man both *h*. and wait.
Rom. 8:25, if we *h*. for that we see not.
1Pet. 1:13, *h*. to the end.
See Jer. 3:23; Acts 24:26; Heb. 11:1.
ORRIBLE. Ps. 11:6; 40:2; Jer. 2:12; Ezek. 32:10.
OSPITALITY. Rom. 12:13; 1Tim. 3:2; Ti. 1:8; 1Pet. 4:9.
OT. Ps. 39:3; Prov. 6:28; 1Tim. 4:2; Rev. 3:15.
OUR. Mt. 10:19; Lk. 12:12, shall be given you in that same *h*.
20:12, have wrought but one *h*.
24:36; Mk. 13:32, that *h*. knoweth no man.
26:40; Mk. 14:37, could ye not watch one *h*.?
Lk. 12:39, what *h*. the thief would come.
22:53, but this is your *h*.
Jn. 5:25; 16:32, the *h*. is coming, and now is.
11:9, are there not twelve *h*. in the day?
12:27, save me from this *h*.
Acts 3:1, at the *h*. of prayer.
Gal. 2:5, give place, no, not for an *h*.
Rev. 3:10, the *h*. of temptation.
See Acts 2:15; 1Cor. 4:11; 15:30; Rev. 3:3.
HOUSE. Gen. 28:17, none other but the *h*. of God.
Dt. 8:12, when thou hast built goodly *h*.
2Ki. 20:1; Isa. 38:1, set thine *h*. in order.
20:15, what have they seen in thine *h*.?
Neh. 13:11, why is the *h*. of God forsaken?
Job 30:23, *h*. appointed for all living.
Ps. 26:8, have loved the habitation of thy *h*.
65:4, satisfied with goodness of thy *h*.
69:9; Jn. 2:17, the zeal of thine *h*.
84:3, the sparrow hath found an *h*.
92:13, planted in the *h*. of the Lord.
118:26, blessed you out of the *h*. of the Lord.
Prov. 2:18, her *h*. inclineth to death.
9:1, wisdom hath builded her *h*.
12:7, *h*. of the righteous shall stand.
19:14, *h*. and riches are inheritance.
Eccl. 7:2, *h*. of mourning, *h*. of feasting.
12:3, when keepers of the *h*. shall tremble.
Isa. 3:14, spoil of poor in your *h*.
5:8, woe unto them that join *h*. to *h*.
64:11, our holy and beautiful *h*. is burned.
Hos. 9:15, I will drive them out of mine *h*.
Hag. 1:4, and this *h*. lie waste.
9, because of mine *h*. that is waste.
Mal. 3:10, that there may be meat in mine *h*.
Mt. 7:25; Lk. 6:48, beat upon that *h*.
10:12, when ye come into an *h*.
12:25; Mk. 3:25, *h*. divided cannot stand.
23:38, your *h*. is left desolate.
24:17; Mk. 13:15, to take anything out of *h*.
Lk. 10:7, go not from *h*. to *h*.
14:23, that my *h*. may be filled.
18:14, went down to his *h*. justified.
Jn. 12:3, *h*. filled with odour.
14:2, in my Father's *h*. are many mansions.
Acts 2:46, breaking bread from *h*. to *h*.
5:42, in every *h*. ceased not to preach.
10:2; 16:34; 18:8, with all his *h*.
20:20, I taught you from *h*. to *h*.
1Cor. 11:22, have ye not *h*. to eat in?
2Cor. 5:1, *h*. not made with hands.
Col. 4:15, church in his *h*.
1Tim. 3:4, 5, 12, ruleth well his own *h*.
5:8, especially for hose of his own *h*.
2Tim. 3:6, which creep into *h*.
Ti. 1:11, subvert whole *h*.
See Mt. 9:6; Lk. 7:44; 19:5, Acts 4:34.
HOUSEHOLD. Gen. 18:19, command his *h*. after him.
1Sam. 17:3; 2Sam. 2:3, every man with his *h*.
2Sam. 6:30, returned to bless his *h*.
Prov. 31:27, looketh well to her *h*.
Mt. 10:36, a man's foes shall be of his own *h*.
Gal. 6:10, the *h*. of faith.
Eph. 2:19, of the *h*. of God.
See Gen. 31:37; 47:12; 2Sam. 17:23.
HUMBLE. Dt. 8:2, to *h*. thee and prove thee.
2Chr. 33:12, *h*. himself greatly.
Ps. 9:12; 10:12, forgetteth not cry of the *h*.
34:2, the *h*. shall hear thereof.
35:13, I *h*. my soul with fasting.
113:6, *h*. himself to behold things in heaven.

Prov. 16:19, better be of *h.* spirit.
Isa. 57:15, of contrite and *h.* spirit.
Mt. 18:4; 23:12; Lk. 14:11; 18:14, *h.* himself.
Phil. 2:8, he *h.* himself.
Jas. 4:6; 1Pet. 5:5, God giveth grace to the *h.*
1Pet. 5:6, *h.* yourselves under mighty hand of God.
See Isa. 2:11; 5:15; Lam. 3:20.
HUMBLY. 2Sam. 16:4; Mic. 6:8.
HUMILITY. Prov. 15:33; 18:12, before honour is *h.*
22:4, by *h.* are riches.
See Acts 20:19; Col. 2:18, 23; 1Pet. 5:5.
HUNGER. Dt. 8:3, he suffered thee to *h.*
Job 18:12, his strength shall be *h.*-bitten.
Ps. 34:10, young lions do lack, and suffer *h.*
Prov. 19:15, an idle soul shall suffer *h.*
Isa. 49:10, shall not *h.* nor thirst.
Jer. 38:9, he is like to die for *h.*
Mt. 5:6; Lk. 6:21, blessed are ye that *h.*
Lk. 6:25, woe unto ye that are full! for ye shall *h.*
Jn. 6:35, he that cometh to me shall never *h.*
Rom. 12:20, if thine enemy *h.*
1Cor. 4:11, we both *h.* and thirst.
11:34, if any man *h.*, let him eat at home.
Rev. 7:16, they shall *h.* no more.
See Mt. 4:2; 12:1; 25:35; Lk. 15:17.
HUNGRY. Job 22:7, withholden bread from *h.*
24:10, they take away the sheaf from the *h.*
Ps. 50:12, if I were *h.*, I would not tell thee.
107:5, *h.* and thirsty, their soul fainted in them.
9, he filled the *h.* soul with goodness.
146:7, which giveth food to the *h.*
Prov. 25:21, if thine enemy be *h.*, give him bread to eat.
27:7, to the *h.* every bitter thing is sweet.
Isa. 29:8, when a *h.* man dreameth.
58:7, is it not to deal thy bread to the *h.*?
65:13, my servants eat, but ye shall be *h.*
Ezek. 18:7, given his bread to the *h.*
Lk. 1:53, he hath filled the *h.* with good things.
Acts. 10:10, and he became very *h.*
1Cor. 11:21, one is *h.*, and another drunken.
Phil. 4:12, instructed both to be full and to be *h.*
See Prov. 6:30; Isa. 8:21; 9:20; Mk. 11:12.
HUNT. 1Sam. 26:20, as when one doth *h.* a partridge.
Jer. 16:16, *h.* them from every mountain.
Ezek. 13:18, *h.* souls of my people.
Mic. 7:2, they *h.* every man his brother.
See Gen. 10:9; 27:5; 1Sam. 24:11.
HUNTING. Prov. 12:27.
HURL. Num. 35:20; 1Chr. 12:2; Job 27:21.
HURT. Ps. 15:4, that sweareth to his own *h.*
Eccl. 8:9, ruleth over another to his own *h.*
Isa. 11:9, shall not *h.* nor destroy.
Jer. 6:14; 8:11, have healed *h.* slightly.
8:21, for the *h.* of my people.
25:6, provoke not, I will do no *h.*
Dan. 3:25, they have no *h.*
6:23, no manner of *h.* found upon him.
Mk. 16:18, deadly thing, it shall not *h.*
Lk. 10:19, nothing shall by any means *h.* you.
Acts 18:10, no man set on thee to *h.* thee.
Rev. 6:6, *h.* not the oil and the wine.
See Rev. 7:2; 9:4; 11:5.
HURTFUL. Ezra 4:15; Ps. 144:10; 1Tim. 6:9.
HUSBAND. Ex. 4:25, a bloody *h.* art thou.
Prov. 12:4, virtuous wife a crown to her *h.*
31:11, 23, 28, her *h.* doth safely trust.
Isa. 54:5, thy Maker is thy *h.*
Jn. 4:16, go, call thy *h.*
1Cor. 7:16, whether thou shalt save thy *h.*
14:35, let them ask their *h.* at home.
Eph. 5:22, submit yourselves to you *h.*
25; Col. 3:19, *h.*, love your wives.
1Tim. 3:12, the *h.* of one wife.
Ti. 2:4, teach young women to love their *h.*
5, obedient to their own *h.*
1Pet. 3:1, be in subjection to your *h.*
7, ye *h.*, dwell with them.
See Gen. 3:6; Ruth 1:11; Est. 1:17, 20.
HYMN. Mt. 26:30; Mk. 14:26; Eph. 5:19; Col. 3:16.
HYPOCRISY. Mt. 23:28, within ye are full of *h.*
Mk. 12:15, he, knowing their *h.*
Lk. 12:1, leaven of Pharisees, which is *h.*
Jas. 3:17, wisdom is pure, and without *h.*
See Isa. 32:6; 1Tim. 4:2
HYPOCRITE. Job 8:13, the *h.* hope shall perish.
20:5, the joy of the *h.* but for a moment.
36:13, the *h.* in heart.
Isa. 9:17, every one is an *h.*
Mt. 6:2, 5, 16, as the *h.* do.
7:5; Lk. 6:42; 13:15, thou *h.*
15:7; 16:3; 22:8; Mk. 7:6; Lk. 12:56, ye *h.*
23:13; Lk. 11:44, woe unto you, *h.*
24:51, appoint his portion with the *h.*
See Job 13:16; 27:8; Prov. 11:9.
HYPOCRITICAL. Ps. 35:16; Isa. 10:6.
IDLE. Ex. 5:8, 17, they be *i.*
Prov. 19:15, an *i.* soul shall hunger.
31:27, she eateth not bread of *i.*
Mt. 12:36, every *i.* word men speak.
20:3, 6, others standing *i.*
See Eccl. 10:18; Ezek. 16:49; 1Tim. 5:13.
IDOL. 1Chr. 16:26; Ps. 96:5, all gods of the people are *i.*
Isa. 66:3, as if he blessed an *i.*
Jer. 50:38, they are mad upon their *i.*
Hos. 4:17, Ephraim is joined to *i.*
Acts 15:20, abstain from pollutions of *i.*
1Cor. 8:4, we know an *i.* is nothing.
7, with conscience of the *i.*
1Th. 1:9, ye turned to God from *i.*
1Jn. 5:21, keep yourselves from *i.*
See Acts 17:16; Gal. 5:20; Col. 3:5.
IGNORANCE. Acts 3:17, through *i.* ye did it.
Acts 17:30, the times of *i.* God winked at.
Eph. 4:18, alienated through *i.*
1Pet. 2:15, put to silence *i.* of foolish men.
See Lev. 4:2, 13, 22, 27; 5:15; Num. 15:24.
IGNORANT. Ps. 73:22, so foolish was I and *i.*
Isa. 63:16, though Abraham be *i.* of us.
Acts 4:13, perceived they were *i.* men.
Rom. 10:3, being *i.* of God's righteousness.
1Cor. 14:38, if any man be *i.*, let him be *i.*

2Cor. 2:11, not *i.* of his devices.
Heb. 5:2, can have compassion on the *i.*
2Pet. 3:5, they willingly are *i.*
See Num. 15:28; Acts 17:23; 1Tim. 1:13.
IAGINATION. Gen. 6:5; 8:21, *i.* of heart evil.
Dt. 29:19; Jer. 23:17, walk in *i.* of heart.
1Chr. 28:9, understandeth all the *i.* of thoughts.
Rom. 1:21, vain in their *i.*
2Cor. 10:5, casting down *i.*
See Dt. 31:21; Prov. 6:18; Lam. 3:60.
IAGINE. Ps. 62:3, how long will ye *i.* mischief?
Nah. 1:9, what do you *i.* against the Lord?
11, there is one that *i.* evil.
See Job 21:27; Ps. 10:2; 21:11; Acts 4:25.
IMORTAL. 1Tim. 1:17.
IMORTALITY. Rom. 2:7; 1Cor. 15:53; 1Tim. 6:16; 2Tim. 1:10.
IPART. Job 39:17; Lk. 3:11; Rom. 1:11; 1Th. 2:8.
IPEDIMENT. Mk. 7:32.
IPENITENT. Rom. 2:5.
IPLACABLE. Rom. 1:31.
IPOSE. Ezra 7:24; Heb. 9:10.
IPOSSIBLE. Mt. 19:26; Mk. 10:27; Lk. 18:27, with men it is *i.*
Lk. 1:37; 18:27, with God nothing *i.*
See Mt. 17:20; Lk. 17:1; Heb. 6:4, 18; 11:6.
IPOTENT. Jn. 5:3; Acts 4:9; 14:8.
IPOVERISH. Jud. 6:6; Isa. 40:20; Jer. 5:17.
IPRISONMENT. Ezra 7:26; 2Cor. 6:5; Heb. 11:36.
IPUDENT. Prov. 7:13; Ezek. 2:4; 3:7.
IPUTE. Lev. 17:4, blood shall be *i.* to that man.
Ps. 32:2; Rom. 4:8, to whom the Lord *i.* not iniquity.
Hab. 1:11, *i.* his power to his god.
Rom. 5:13, sin is not *i.* when there is no law.
See 1Sam. 22:15; 2Sam. 19:19; 2Cor. 5:19.
ICLINE. Josh. 24:23, *i.* your hearts to the Lord.
1Ki. 8:58, that he may *i.* hearts to keep law.
Ps. 40:1; 116:2, he *i.* unto me, and heard my cry.
119:36, *i.* my heart to thy testimonies.
Jer. 7:24; 11:8; 17:23; 34:14, nor *i.* ear.
See Prov. 2:18; Jer. 25:4; 44:5.
ICLOSED. Ps. 17:10; 22:16; Lk. 5:6.
ICONTINENT. 1Cor. 7:5; 2Tim. 3:3.
ICORRUPTIBLE. 1Cor. 9:25, an *i.* crown.
1Pet. 1:4, inheritance *i.*
23, born of *i.* seed.
See Rom. 1:23; 1Cor. 15:42, 50, 52, 53, 54.
ICREASE (*n.*). Lev. 25:36, take no usury or *i.*
26:4, the land shall yield her *i.*
Dt. 14:22, 28, tithe all *i.*
Ps. 67:6; Ezek. 34:27, earth shall yield her *i.*
Prov. 18:20, with the *i.* of his lips.
Eccl. 510, not satisfied with *i.*
Isa. 9:7, *i.* of his government.
1Cor. 3:6, 7, God gave the *i.*
See Jer. 2:3; Eph. 4:16; Col. 2:19.
ICREASE (*v.*). Job 8:7, thy latter end shall greatly *i.*
Ps. 4:7, that their corn and wine *i.*
62:10, if riches *i.*, set not your heart upon them.
115:14, Lord shall *i.* you more and more.
Prov. 1:5; 9:9, a wise man will *i.* learning.
11:24, there is that scattereth, and yet *i.*
Eccl. 1:18, he that *i.* knowledge *i.* sorrow.
Isa. 9:3, multiplied the nation, and not *i.* the joy.
40:29, he *i.* strength.
Ezek. 36:37, *i.* them with men like a flock.
Dan. 12:4, knowledge shall be *i.*
Hos. 12:1, he daily *i.* lies.
Hab. 2:6, that *i.* that which is not his.
Lk. 2:52, Jesus *i.* in wisdom.
Acts 6:7, word of God *i.*
16:5, churches *i.* daily.
Rev. 3:17, I am rich, and *i.* with goods.
See Eccl. 2:9; 5:11; Mk. 4:8; Col. 2:19.
INCREDIBLE. Acts 26:8.
INCURABLE. 2Chr. 21:18; Jer. 15:18; Mic. 1:9.
INDEED. 1Ki. 8:27; 2Chr. 6:18, will God *i.* dwell on the earth?
1Chr. 4:10, bless me *i.*
Mk. 11:32, a prophet *i.*
Lk. 24:34, the Lord is risen *i.*
Jn. 1:47, an Israelite *i.*
6:55, my flesh is meat *i.*, and my blood is drink *i.*
8:36, ye shall be free *i.*
1Tim. 5:3, that are widows *i.*
See Gen. 37:8; Isa. 6:9; Rom. 8:7.
INDIGNATION. Ps. 78:49, wrath, *i.*, and trouble.
Isa. 26:20, till the *i.* be overpast.
Nah. 1:6, who can stand before his *i.*?
Mt. 20:24, moved with *i.*
26:8, they had *i.*
2Cor. 7:11, yea, what *i.*
Heb. 10:27, fearful looking for of fiery *i.*
Rev. 14:10, the cup of his *i.*
See Zech. 1:12; Acts 5:17; Rom. 2:8.
INDITING. Ps. 45:1.
INDUSTRIOUS. 1Ki. 11:28.
INEXCUSABLE. Rom. 2:1.
INFANT. Job 3:16; Isa. 65:20; Lk. 18:15.
INFIDEL. 2Cor. 6:15; 1Tim. 5:8.
INFIRMITY. Ps. 77:10, this is mine *i.*
Prov. 18:14, spirit of man will sustain his *i.*
Mt. 8:17, himself took our *i.*
Rom. 6:19, the *i.* of your flesh.
8:26, the Spirit helpeth our *i.*
15:1, bear the *i.* of the weak.
2Cor. 12:5, 10, glory in mine *i.*
1Tim. 5:23, wine for thin often *i.*
Heb. 4:15, touched with the feeling of our *i.*
See Lk. 5:15; 7:21; Jn. 5:5; Heb. 5:2.
INFLAME. Isa. 5:11; 57:5.
INFLICTED. 2Cor. 2:6.
INFLUENCES. Job 38:31.
INGRAFTED. Jas. 1:21.
INHABIT. Isa. 57:15; 65:21; Amos 9:14.
INHABITANT. Num. 13:32, land eateth up *i.*
Jud. 5:23, curse bitterly the *i.*
Isa. 6:11, cities wasted without *i.*
33:24, *i.* shall not say, I am sick.
40:22, the *i.* thereof are as grasshoppers.
Jer. 44:22, land without an *i.*
See Jer. 2:15; 4:7; Zech. 8:21.

INHERIT. Ex. 32:13, they shall *i*. for ever.
Ps. 25:13, shall *i*. the earth.
37:11, the meek shall *i*. the earth.
Prov. 14:18, the simple *i*. folly.
Mt. 19:29, shall *i*. everlasting life.
25:34, *i*. kingdom prepared.
Mk. 10:17; Lk. 10:25; 18:18, *i*. eternal life.
1Cor. 6:9; 15:50; Gal. 5:21, not *i*. the kingdom.
Heb. 12:17, when he would have *i*. the blessing.
See Heb. 6:12; 1Pet. 3:9; Rev. 21:7.
INHERITANCE. Ps. 16:5, Lord is portion of mine *i*.
47:4, shall choose our *i*. for us.
Prov. 20:21, an *i*. may be gotten hastily.
Eccl. 7:11, wisdom good with an *i*.
Mk. 12:7; Lk. 20:14, the *i*. shall be ours.
Lk. 12:13, that he divide the *i*. with me.
Acts 20:32; 26:18, an *i*. among the sanctified.
Eph. 1:14, earnest of our *i*.
Heb. 9:15, promise of eternal *i*.
See Eph. 5:5; Col. 1:12; Heb. 1:4.
INIQUITY. Ex. 20:5; 34:7; Num. 14:18; Dt. 5:9, visiting the *i*. of the fathers.
34:7; Num. 14:18, forgiving *i*. and transgression.
Job 4:8, they that plow *i*. reap the same.
13:26, to possess the *i*. of my youth.
Job 34:32, if I have done *i*., I will do no more.
Ps. 25:11, pardon mine *i*., for it is great.
32:5, mine *i*. have I not hid.
39:11, when thou dost correct man for *i*.
51:5, I was shapen in *i*.
66:18, if I regard *i*. in my heart.
69:27, add *i*. to their *i*.
79:8, remember not former *i*.
90:8, thou has set our *i*.
103:3, who forgiveth all thine *i*.
10, not rewarded according to *i*.
107:17, fools, because of *i*., are afflicted.
119:3, they also do no *i*.
130:3, if thou shouldest mark *i*.
Prov. 22:8, he that soweth *i*. shall reap vanity.
Isa. 1:4, a people laden with *i*.
6:7, thine *i*. is taken away.
40:2, her *i*. is pardoned.
53:5, he was bruised for our *i*.
59:2, your *i*. separated between you and God.
Jer. 5:25, your *i*. turned away these things.
Ezek. 18:30, repent, so *i*. shall not be your ruin.
Hab. 1:13, canst not look on *i*.
Mt. 24:12 because *i*. shall abound.
Acts 1:18, purchased with reward of *i*.
8:23, in the bond of *i*.
Rom. 6:19, servants to *i*. unto *i*.
2Th. 2:7, the mystery of *i*.
2Tim. 2:19, depart from *i*.
Jas. 3:6, a world of *i*.
See Ps. 36:2; Jer. 31:30; Ezek. 3:18; 18:26.
INJURIOUS. 1Tim. 1:13.
INK. Jer. 36:18; 2Cor. 3:3; 2Jn. 12; 3Jn. 13.
INN. Gen. 42:27; Ex. 4:24; Lk. 2:7; 10:34.
INNOCENT. Job 4:7, who ever perished, being *i*?
9:23, laugh at trial of *i*.
27:17, the *i*. shall divide the silver.
Ps. 19:13, *i*. from the great transgression.
Prov. 28:20, he that maketh haste to be rich sha not be *i*.
Jer. 2:34; 19:4, blood of the *i*.
See Gen. 10:5; Ex. 23:7; Mt. 27:24.
INNUMERABLE. Job 21:33; Ps. 40:12; Heb. 12:22
INORDINATE. Ezek. 23:11; Col. 3:5.
INQUISITION. Dt. 19:18; Est. 2:23; Ps. 9:12.
INSCRIPTION. Acts 17:23.
INSPIRATION. Job 32:8; 2Tim. 3:16.
INSTANT. Rom. 12:12; 2 Tim. 4:2.
INSTRUCT. Neh. 9:20, thy good spirit to *i*. them.
Ps. 16:7, my reins *i*. me in night season.
32:8, I will *i*. thee and teach thee.
Isa. 40:14, who *i*. him?
Mt. 13:52, every scribe *i*. unto the kingdom.
Phil. 4:12, in all things I am *i*.
See Prov. 21:11; Acts 18:25; 2Tim. 2:25.
INSTRUCTION. Ps. 50:17, thou hatest *i*.
Prov. 1:7; 15:5, fools despise *i*.
4:13, take fast hold of *i*.
8:33, hear *i*., and be wise.
12:1, whoso loveth *i*. loveth knowledge.
16:22, the *i*. of fools is folly.
24:32, I looked upon it, and received *i*.
2Tim. 3:16, profitable for *i*.
See Jer. 17:23; 35:15; Zeph. 3:7.
INSTRUMENT. Ps. 7:13, hath prepared *i*. of death.
Isa. 41:15, a new sharp threshing *i*.
Ezek. 33:32, of one that can play on an *i*.
Rom. 6:13, members *i*. of unrighteousness.
See Num. 35:16; Ps. 68:25; 150:4.
INTEGRITY. Job 2:3, he holdeth fast his *i*.
31:6, that God may know my *i*.
Ps. 25:21, let *i*. preserve me.
26:1, I walked in *i*.
Prov. 11:3, the *i*. of the upright.
19:1; 20:7, that walketh in his *i*.
See Gen. 20:5; Ps. 7:8; 41:12; 78:72.
INTENTS. Jer. 30:24; Heb. 4:12.
INTERCESSION. Isa. 53:12, make *i*. for transgressors.
Rom. 8:26, the Spirit itself maketh *i*.
Heb. 7:25, ever liveth to make *i*.
See Jer. 7:16; 27:18; 1Tim. 2:1.
INTERCESSOR. Isa. 59:16.
INTERMEDDLE. Prov. 14:10; 18:1.
INTREAT. Ruth 1:16, *i*. me not to leave thee.
1Sam. 2:25, if a man sin, who shall *i*. for him?
Ps. 119:58, I *i*. thy favour.
Isa. 19:22, he shall be *i*. of them.
1Tim. 5:1, but *i*. him as a father.
Jas. 3:17, wisdom is easy to be *i*.
See Prov. 18:23; Lk. 15:28.
INTRUDING. Col. 2:18.
INVENTIONS. Ps. 106:29; Prov. 8:12; Eccl. 7:29.
INVISIBLE. Col. 1:15; 1Tim. 1:17; Heb. 11:27.
INWARD. Job 38:36, wisdom in the *i*. parts.
Ps. 51:6, truth in the *i*. parts.
64:6, *i*. thought of every one is deep.
Jer. 31:33, I will put my law in their *i*. parts.
Rom. 7:22, delight in law of God after the *i*. mar
2Cor. 4:16, the *i*. man is renewed.

See Ps. 62:4; Mt. 7:15; Rom. 2:29.
SSUES. Ps. 68:20; Prov. 4:23.
TCHING. 2Tim. 4:3.
ACINTH. Rev. 9:17; 21:20.
ANGLING. 1Tim. 1:6.
ASPER. Ex. 28:20; Ezek. 28:13, and a *j.*
Rev. 4:3, he that sat was to look upon like a *j.*
21:11, even like a *j.* stone.
18:, the building of the wall of it was of *j.*
19, the first foundation was *j.*
AVELIN. Num. 25:7, took a *j.* in his hand.
1Sam. 18:10, and there was a *j.* in Saul's hand.
19:10, even to the wall with a *j.*
EALOUS. Ex. 20:5; 34:14; Dt. 4:24; 5:9; 6:15; Josh. 24:19, I am a *j.* God.
1Ki. 19:10, 14, I have been *j.* for the Lord.
Ezek. 39:25, will be *j.* for my holy name.
2Cor. 11:2, I am *j.* over you.
See Num. 5:14; Joel 2:18; Zech. 1:14; 8:2.
EALOUSY. Dt. 32:16; 1Ki. 14:22, they provoked him to *j.*
Prov. 6:34, *j.* is the rage of a man.
Song 8:6, *j.* is cruel as the grave.
Ezek. 36:5, in fire of *j.* have I spoken.
1Cor. 10:22, do we provoke the Lord to *j.*?
See Ps. 78:58; 79:5; Isa. 42:13.
ESTING. Eph. 5:4.
EWELS. Isa. 61:10; Mal. 3:17.
OIN. Prov. 11:21; 16:5, hand *j.* in hand.
Eccl. 9:4, to him *j.* to living there is hope.
Isa. 5:8, that *j.* house to house.
Jer. 50:5, let us *j.* ourselves to the Lord.
Hos. 4:17, Ephraim is *j.* to idols.
Mt. 19:6; Mk. 10:9, what God hath *j.*
Acts 5:13, durst no man *j.* himself.
1Cor. 1:10, perfectly *j.* in same mind.
6:17, *j.* to the Lord.
Eph. 4:16, whole body *j.* together.
See Acts 8:29; 9:26; 18:7; Eph. 5:31.
OINT. Gen. 32:25; Ps. 22:14; Prov. 25:19, out of *j.*
Eph. 4:16, which every *j.* supplieth.
Heb. 4:12, dividing asunder of *j.* and marrow.
See 1Ki. 22:34; Rom. 8:17; Col. 2:19.
OURNEY (*n.*). 1Ki. 18i:27, or he is in a *j.*
Neh. 2:6, for how long shall thy *j.* be?
Mt. 10:10; Mk. 6:8; Lk. 9:3, nor scrip for your *j.*
Jn. 4:6, Jesus wearied with his *j*
OURNEY (*v.*). Num. 10:29, we are *j.* to the place.
See Gen. 12:9; 13:11.
OURNEYINGS. Num. 10:28, thus were the *j.*
2Cor. 11:26, in *j.* often.
OY. Ezra 3:13, nor discern noise of *j.*
Neh. 8:10, *j.* of the Lord is your strength.
Job 20:5, the *j.* of the hypocrite is but a moment.
29:13, widow's heart sing for *j.*
Job 33:26, he will see his face with *j.*
41:22, sorrow is turned into *j.*
Ps. 16:11, fulness of *j.*
30:5, *j.* cometh in the morning.
48:2, the *j.* of the whole earth.
51:12, restore the *j.* of thy salvation.
126:5, they that sow in tears shall reap in *j.*
137:6, prefer Jerusalem above my chief *j.*
Prov. 14:10, not intermeddle with his *j.*
21:15, it is *j.* to the just to do judgment.
Eccl. 2:10, I withheld not my heart from *j.*
9:7, eat thy bread with *j.*
Isa. 9:3, not increased the *j.*
12:3, with *j.* draw water.
24:8, *j.* of the harp ceaseth.
29:19, meek shall increase their *j.*
35:10; 51:11, and everlasting *j.*
65:14, my servants sing for *j.* of heart.
Jer. 15:16, thy word was the *j.* of my heart.
31:13, will turn their mourning into *j.*
49:25, the city of my *j.*
Lam. 2:15, the *j.* of the whole earth.
Mt. 13:20; Lk. 8:13, with *j.* receiveth it.
44, for *j.* goeth and selleth.
25:21, 23, the *j.* of thy Lord.
Lk. 15:7, *j.* in heaven over one sinner.
10, there is *j.* in presence of angels.
24:41, they believed not for *j.*
Jn. 3:29, this my *j.* is fulfilled.
15:11; 16:24, that your *j.* may be full.
Acts 8:8, great *j.* in that city.
20:24, finish my course with *j*
2Cor. 1:24, helpers of your *j.*
Phil. 2:2, fulfil ye my *j.*
Heb. 12:2, for the *j.* that was set before him.
Jas. 1:2, count it all *j.* when ye fall.
1Pet. 1:8, with *j.* unspeakable.
4:13, glad also with exceeding *j.*
2Jn. 12, that our *j.* may be full.
Jude 24, faultless, with exceeding *j.*
See Rom. 14:17; Gal. 5:22; Phil. 1:4.
JOYFUL. Ps. 35:9, my soul shall be *j* in the Lord.
63:5, praise thee with *j.* lips.
66:1; 81:1; 95:1; 98:6, make a *j.* noise.
Eccl. 7:14, in day of prosperity be *j.*
Isa. 56:7, *j.* in my house of prayer.
See 2Cor. 7:4; Col. 1:11; Heb. 10:34.
JUDGE (*n.*). Gen. 18:25; Ps. 94:2, the *j.* of all the earth.
Ps. 50:6, God is *j.* himself.
68:5, a *j.* of the widows.
Mic. 7:3, the *j.* asketh a reward.
Lk. 12:14, who made me a *j.* over you?
18:6, the unjust *j.*
Acts 10:42, the *J.* of quick and dead.
2Tim. 4:8, the Lord, the righteous *j.*
Heb. 12:23, to God the *J.* of all.
Jas. 5:9, the *j.* standeth before the door.
See 2Sam. 15:4; Mt. 5:25; Jas. 4:11.
JUDGE (*v.*). Gen. 16:5, Lord *j.* between me and thee.
Dt. 32:36; Ps. 7:8, Lord *j.* the people.
Ps. 58:11, he is a God that *j.* in the earth.
Isa. 1:17, *j.* the fatherless.
Mt. 7:1, *j.* not, that ye be not *j.*
Lk. 7:43, thou hast rightly *j.*
Jn. 7:24, *j.* righteous judgment.
Rom. 14:4, who are thou that *j.*?
See Jn. 16:11; Rom. 2:16; 3:6; 2Tim. 4:1.
JUDGMENT. Dt. 1:17, the *j.* is God's.
Ps. 1:5, shall not stand in the *j.*
101:1, I will sing of mercy and *j.*

Prov. 29:26, *j.* cometh from the Lord.
Eccl. 11:9; 12:14, God will bring into *j.*
Isa. 28:17, *j.* will I lay to the line.
53:8, taken from prison and from *j.*
Jer. 5:1, if there be any that executeth *j.*
10:24, correct with *j.*, not in anger.
Hos. 12:6, keep mercy and *j.*
Mt. 5:21, in danger of the *j.*
Jn. 5:22, Father committed all *j.* to the Son.
9:39, for *j.* I am come.
16:8, reprove the world of *j.*
Acts 24:25, reasoned of *j.* to come.
Rom. 14:10, we shall all stand before the *j.* seat.
Heb. 9:27, after this the *j.*
1Pet. 4:14, *j.* must begin at house of God.
See Mt. 12:41; Heb. 10:27; Jas. 2:13.
JUST. Job 9:2, how should man be *j.* with God?
Prov. 3:33, God blesseth the habitation of the *j.*
4:18, path of *j.* as shining light.
10:7, memory of *j.* is blessed.
Isa. 26:7, way of the *j.* is uprightness.
Hab. 2:4; Rom. 1:17; Gal. 3:11; Heb. 10:38, the *j.* shall live by faith.
Mt. 5:45, sendeth rain on *j.* and unjust.
Lk. 14:14, recompensed at resurrection of *j.*
15:7, ninety and nine *j.* persons.
Acts 24:15, resurrection both of *j.* and unjust.
Rom. 3:26, that he might be *j.*
Phil. 4:8, whatsoever things are *j.*
Heb. 2:2, a *j.* recompence of reward.
12:23, spirits of *j.* men made perfect.
1Pet. 3:18, the *j.* for the unjust.
See Job 34:17; Acts 3:14; Col. 4:1.
JUSTICE. 2Sam. 15:4, I would do *j.*
Ps. 89:14, *j.* and judgment are the habitation.
Prov. 8:15, by me princes decree *j.*
Isa. 59:4, none calleth for *j.*
Jer. 23:5, execute judgment and *j.* in the earth.
50:7, the habitation of *j.*
See Job 8:3; 36:17; Isa. 9:7; 56:1.
JUSTIFICATION. Rom. 4:25; 5:16, 18.
JUSTIFY. Job 11:2, should a man full of talk be *j.*?
25:4, how then can man be *j.* with God?
Ps. 51:4, be *j.* when thou speakest.
143:2, in thy sight shall no man living be *j.*
Isa. 5:23, which *j.* the wicked for reward.
Mt. 11:19; Lk. 7:35, wisdom is *j.* of her children.
12:37, by thy words thou shalt be *j.*
Lk. 10:29, willing to *j.* himself.
18:14, *j.* rather than the other.
Acts 13:39, all that believe are *j.*
Rom. 3:24; Ti. 3:7, *j.* freely by his grace.
5:1, being *j.* by faith.
9, being now *j.* by his blood.
Gal. 2:16, man is not *j.* by works of the law.
1Tim. 3:16, *j.* in the Spirit.
See Isa. 50:8; Rom. 4:5; 8:33.
JUSTLY. Mic. 6:8; Lk. 23:41; 1Th. 2:10.
KEEP. Gen. 18:19, they shall *k.* the way of the Lord.
Num. 6:24, the Lord bless thee, and *k.* thee.
1Sam. 2:9, he will *k.* the feet of his saints.
25:34, the Lord God hath *k.* me back from hurting thee.
Ps. 17:8, *k.* me as the apple of the eye.
34:13, *k.* thy tongue from evil.
91:11, angels charge to *k.* thee in all thy ways.
121:3, he that *k.* thee will not slumber.
127:1, except the Lord *k.* the city.
141:3, *k.* the door of my lips.
Prov. 4:6, love wisdom, she shall *k.* thee.
21, *k.* my sayings in midst of thine heart.
23, *k.* thy heart with all diligence.
6:20, my son, *k.* thy father's commandments.
Eccl. 3:6, a time to *k.*
5:1, *k.* thy foot when thou goest.
12:13, fear God, and *k.* his commandments.
Isa. 26:3, thou wilt *k.* him in perfect peace.
27:3, I the Lord do *k.* it, I will *k.* it.
Jer. 3:5, 13, will he *k.* his anger?
Hab. 2:20, let the earth *k.* silence.
Mal. 3:14, what profit that we have *k.*
Mt. 19:17, if thou wilt enter life, *k.* the commandments.
Lk. 11:28, blessed are they that *k.*
Lk. 19:43, enemies shall *k.* thee in on every side
Jn. 8:51, 52, *k.* my sayings.
12:25, he that hateth his life shall *k.* it.
14:23, if a man love me, he will *k.* my words.
17:11, holy Father, *k.* through thine own name.
15, that thou shouldest *k.* them from the evil
Acts 16:4, delivered the decrees to *k.*
21:25, *k.* from things offered to idols.
1Cor. 5:8, let us *k.* the feast.
9:27, I *k.* under my body.
Eph. 4:3, *k.* the unity of the Spirit.
Phil. 4:7, the peace of God shall *k.* your hearts.
1Tim. 5:22, *k.* thyself pure.
6:20, *k.* that which is committed.
Jas. 1:27, *k.* himself unspotted.
1Jn. 5:21, *k.* yourselves from idols.
Jude 21, *k.* yourselves in the love of God.
24, him that is able to *k.* you from falling.
Rev. 3:10, I will *k.* thee from hour of temptation.
22:9, which *k.* the sayings of this book.
See 1Pet. 1:5; 4:19; Jude 6; Rev. 3:8.
KEEPER. Ps. 121:5, the Lord is thy *k.*
Eccl. 12:3, when the *k.* of the house shall tremble.
Song 1:6, they made me *k.* of the vineyards.
Ti. 2:5, chaste, *k.* at home.
See Gen. 4:2, 9; Mt. 28:4; Acts 5:23; 16:27.
KEY. Mt. 16:19, the *k.* of kingdom of heaven.
Lk. 11:52, ye have taken away *k.* of knowledge.
Rev. 1:18, the *k.* of hell and of death.
See Isa. 22:22; Rev. 3:7; 9:1.
KICK. Dt. 32:15; 1Sam. 2:29; Acts 9:5.
KILL. Num. 16:13, to *k.* us in the wilderness.
2Ki. 5:7, am I a God to *k.*?
7:4, if they *k.* us, we shall but die.
Eccl. 3:3, a time to *k.*
Mt. 10:28; Lk. 12:4, fear not them that *k.* the body.
Mk. 3:4, is it lawful to save life, or to *k.*?

Jn. 5:18, the Jews sought the more to *k*. him.
7:19, why go ye about to *k*. me?
8:22, will he *k*. himself?
Rom. 8:36, for thy sake we are *k*. all the day.
2Cor. 3:6, the letter *k*.
6:9, chastened, and not *k*.
Jas. 4:2, ye *k*., and desire to have.
5:6, ye condemned and *k*. the just.
See Mt. 23:37; Mk. 12:5; Lk. 22:2.
IND. 2Chr. 10:7, if thou be *k*. to this people.
Mt. 17:21; Mk. 9:29, this *k*. goeth not out.
Lk. 6:35, *k*. to unthankful and evil.
1Cor. 13:4, charity suffereth long, and is *k*.
See Mt. 13:47; Eph. 4:32; Jas. 3:7.
INDLE. Ps. 2:12, his wrath is *k*. but a little.
Prov. 26:21, a contentious man to *k*. strife.
Isa. 50:11, walk in sparks that ye have *k*.
Hos. 11:8, my repentings are *k*. together.
Lk. 12:49, what will I, if it be already *k*.?
Jas. 3:5, how great a matter a little fire *k*.
See Job 19:11; 32:2; Ezek. 20:48.
INDLY. Gen. 24:49; 50:21; Ruth 1:8; Rom. 12:10.
INDNESS. Ruth 3:10, thou hast showed more *k*.
2Sam. 2:6, I will requite you this *k*.
9:1, 7, show him *k*. for Jonathan's sake.
Ps. 17:7; 92:2, thy marvellous loving-*k*.
36:7, how excellent is thy loving-*k*.!
63:3, thy loving-*k*. is better than life.
117:2; 119:76, his merciful *k*.
141:5, righteous smite me, it shall be a *k*.
Prov. 31:26, in her tongue is the law of *k*.
Isa. 54:8, with everlasting *k*.
Jer. 2:2, I remember the *k*. of thy youth.
31:3, with loving-*k*. have I drawn thee.
Col. 3:12, put on *k*., meekness.
2Pet. 1:7, to godliness, brotherly *k*.
See Josh. 2:12; Neh. 9:17; Joel 2:13; Jon. 4:2.
INDRED. Acts 3:25; Rev. 1:7; 5:9; 7:9.
ING. Num. 23:21, the shout of a *k*. is among them.
Jud. 9:8, the trees went forth to anoint a *k*.
Jud. 17:6, no *k*. in Israel.
1Sam. 8:5, now make us a *k*.
19, we will have a *k*.
10:24; 2Sam. 16:16, God save the *k*.
Job 18:14, bring him to the *k*. of terrors.
34:18, is it fit to say to a *k*.?
Ps. 5:2; 84:3, my *K*. and my God.
10:16, the Lord is *K*. for ever.
20:9, let the *k*. hear us when we call.
74:12, God is my *K*. of old.
102:15, the *k*. of the earth shall fear.
Prov. 8:15, by me *k*. reign.
22:29, the diligent shall stand before *k*.
31:3, that which destroyeth *k*.
4, it is not for *k*. to drink wine.
Eccl. 2:12, what can the man do that cometh after the *k*.?
10:16, woe to thee when thy *k*. is a child!
20, curse not the *k*.
Isa. 32:1, a *k*. shall reign in righteousness.
33:17, thine eyes shall see the *k*. in his beauty.
49:23, *k*. shall be thy nursing fathers.
Jer. 10:10, the Lord is an everlasting *k*.
Mt. 22:11, when the *k*. came in to see the guests.
Lk. 19:38, blessed be the *K*. that cometh.
23:2, saying that he himself is Christ a *k*.
Jn. 6:15, by force, to make him a *k*.
19:14, behold your *K*!
15, we have no *k*. but Caesar.
1Tim. 1:17, now unto the *K*. eternal.
6:15, the *K*. of *k*. and Lord of lords.
Rev. 1:6; 5:10, made us *k*. and priests unto God.
15:3, thou *K*. of saints.
See Lk. 10:24; 1Tim. 2:2; 1Pet. 2:17.
KINGDOM. Ex. 19:6, a *k*. of priests.
1Chr. 29:11; Mt. 6:13, thine is the k.
Ps. 22:28, the *k*. is the Lord's.
103:19, his *k*. ruleth over all.
145:12, the glorious majesty of his *k*.
Isa. 14:16, is this the man that did shake *k*.?
Dan. 4:3, his *k*. is an everlasting *k*.
Mt. 4:23; 9:35; 24:14, gospel of the *k*.
8:12, children of the *k*. cast out.
12:25; Mk. 3:24; Lk. 11:17, *k*. divided against itself.
13:38, good seed are children of the *k*.
25:34, inherit the *k*.
Lk. 12:32, Father's good pleasure to give you the *k*.
22:29, I appoint unto you a *k*.
Jn. 18:36, my *k*. is not of this world.
Acts 1:6, wilt thou restore the *k*. to Israel?
1Cor. 15:24, when he shall have delivered *u*p the *k*.
Col. 1:13, into the *k*. of his dear Son.
2Tim. 4:18, to his heavenly *k*.
Jas. 2:5, heirs of the *k*. he hath promised.
2Pet. 1:11, entrance into everlasting *k*.
See Rev. 1:9; 11:15; 16:10; 17:17.
KISS. Ps. 85:10; Prov. 27:6; Lk. 7:38; Rom. 16:16.
KNEW. Gen. 28:16, the Lord is in this place, and I *k*. it not.
Jer. 1:5, before I formed thee I *k*. thee.
Mt. 7:23, I never *k* you, depart.
Jn. 4:10, if thou *k*. the gift of God.
2Cor. 5:21, who *k*. no sin.
See Gen. 3:7; Dt. 34:10; Jn. 1:10; Rom. 1:21.
KNOW. 1Sam. 3:7, Samuel did not yet *k*. the Lord.
1Chr. 28:9, *k*. thou the God of thy father.
Job 5:27, *k*. thou it for thy good.
8:9, we are but of yesterday, and *k*. nothing.
13:23, make me to *k*. my transgression.
19:25, I *k*. that my redeemer liveth.
22:13; Ps. 73:11, how doth God *k*.?
Ps. 39:4, make me to *k*. mine end.
46:10, be still, and *k*. that I am God.
56:9, this I *k*., for God is for me.
103:14, he *k*. our frame.
139:23, *k*. my heart.
Eccl. 9:5, the living *k*. they shall die.
11:9, *k*. that for all these things.
Isa. 1:3, the ox *k*. his owner.
Jer. 17:9, the heart is deceitful, who can *k*. it?
31:34; Heb. 8:11, *k*. the Lord, for all shall *k*. me.
Ezek. 2:5; 33:33, *k*. there hat h been a prophet.

Hos. 2:20, thou shalt *k.* the Lord.
7:9, yet he *k.* it not.
Mt. 6:3, let not thy left hand *k.*
13:11; Mk. 4:11; Lk. 8:10, given to you to *k.*
25:12, I *k.* you not.
Mk. 1:24; Lk. 4:34, I *k.* thee, who thou art.
Lk. 19:42, if thou hadst *k.*
22:57, 60, I *k.* him not.
Jn. 7:17, he shall *k.* of the doctrine.
10:14, I *k.* my sheep, and am *k.* of mine.
13:7, *k.* not now, but shalt *k.* hereafter.
17, if ye *k.* these things.
35, by this shall all men *k.* ye are my disciples.
Acts 1:7, it is not for you to *k.*
Rom. 8:28, we *k.* that all things work.
1Cor. 2:14, neither can he *k.* them.
13:9, 12, we *k.* in part.
Eph. 3:19, and to *k.* the love of Christ.
2Tim. 1:12, I *k.* the love of Christ.
1:12, I *k.* whom I have believed.
3:15, thou hast *k.* the scriptures.
1Jn. 2:4, he that saith, I *k.* him.
3:2, we *k.* that when he shall appear.
Rev. 2:2, 9, 13, 19; 3:1, 8, I *k.* thy works.
See Mt. 6:8; 2Tim. 2:19; 2Pet. 2:9; Rev. 2:17.
KNOWLEDGE. 2Chr. 1:10, 11, 12, give me *k.*
Job 21:14, 23 desire not *k.* of thy ways.
Ps. 94:10, he that teacheth man *k.*
139:6, such *k.* is too wonderful.
144:3, that thou takest *k.* of him.
Prov. 10:14, wise men lay up *k.*
14:6, *k.* is easy to him that understandeth.
17:27, he that hath *k.* spareth words.
24:5, a man of *k.* increaseth strength.
30:3, nor have the *k.* of the holy.
Eccl. 1:18, increaseth *k.* increaseth sorrow.
9:10, nor *k.* in the grave.
Isa. 11:2, the spirit of *k.*
40:14, who taught him *k.*?
53:11, by his *k.* justify many.
Dan. 1:17, God gave them *k.*
12:4, *k.* shall be increased.
Hos. 4:6, destroyed for lack of *k.*
Hab. 2:14, earth shall be filled with the *k.*
Lk. 11:52, taken away key of *k.*
Acts 4:13, took *k.* of them.
24:22, more perfect *k.* of that way.
Rom. 10:2, zeal of God, but not according to *k.*
1Cor. 8:1, *k.* puffeth up.
13:8, *k.* shall vanish away.
15:34, some have not the *k.* of God.
Eph. 3:19, love of Christ, which passeth *k.*
Phil. 3:8, but loss for the *k.* of Christ.
Col. 2:3, treasures of wisdom and *k.*
1Tim. 2:4; 2Tim. 3:7, the *k.* of the truth.
Heb. 10:26, sin after we have received *k.*
2Pet. 1:5, 6, to virtue *k.* and to *k.* temperance.
3:18, grow in grace and *k.*
See Gen. 2:9; 1Sam. 2:3; Prov. 19:2; Hos. 4:1.
LABOUR (*n.*). Ps. 90:10, yet is their strength *l.* and sorrow.
104:23, goeth to his *l.* till evening.
Prov. 13:11, he that gathereth by *l.* shall increase.
14:23, in all *l.* there is profit.
Eccl. 1:8, all things are full of *l.*
2:22, what hath man of all his *l.*
6:7, all the *l.* of man is for his mouth.
Jn. 4:38, are entered into their *l.*
1Cor. 15:58, your *l.* is not in vain.
1Th. 1:3; Heb. 6:10, your *l.* of love.
Rev. 2:2, I know thy *l.* and patience.
14:13, rest from their *l.*
See Gen. 31:42; Isa. 58:3; 2Cor. 6:5; 11:23.
LABOUR (*v.*). Ex. 20:9; Dt. 5:13, six days shalt thou *l.*
Neh. 4:21, so we *l.* in the work.
Ps. 127:1, they *l.* in vain.
144:14, our oxen may be strong to *l.*
Prov. 16:26, he that *l. l.* for himself.
23:4, *l.* not to be rich.
Eccl. 4:8, for whom do I *l.*?
5:12, the sleep of a *l.* man is sweet.
Mt. 11:28, all ye that *l.*
Jn. 6:27, *l.* not for the meat which perisheth.
1Cor. 3:9, we are *l.* together with God.
Eph. 4:28, but rather *l.*, working with his hands.
1Th. 5:12, which *l.*, among you.
1Tim. 5:17, they who *l.* in word and doctrine.
See Mt. 9:37; 20:1; Lk. 10:2.
LACK. Mt. 19:20; Lk. 22:35; Acts 4:34.
LADEN. Isa. 1:4; Mt. 11:28; 2Tim. 3:6.
LAMB. Isa. 5:17, the *l.* feed after their manner.
11:6, the wolf shall dwell with the *l.*
53:7; Jer. 11:19, as *l.* to the slaughter.
Jn. 1:29, 36, behold the *L.* of God.
1Pet. 1:19, as of a *l.* without blemish.
Rev. 5:6; 13:8, stood a *L.* slain.
12:11, by the blood of the *L.*
22:1, the throne of God and of the *L.*
See Isa. 40:11; Lk. 10:3; Jn. 21:15.
LAME. Job 29:15; Prov. 26:7; Isa. 35:6; Heb. 12:13.
LAMENT. Mt. 11:17; Jn. 16:20; Acts 8:2.
LAMP. Ps. 119:105; Prov. 13:9; Isa. 62:1; Mt. 25:1.
LAP. Jud. 7:6; Prov. 16:33.
LAST. Num. 23:10, let my *l.* end be like his.
Prov. 23:32, at the *l.* it biteth like a serpent.
Mt. 12:45; Lk. 11:26, *l.* state of that man.
19:30; 20:16; Mk. 10:31; Lk. 13:30, first shall be *l.*
Jn. 6:39; 11:24; 12:48, the *l.* day.
See Lam. 1:9; 2Tim. 3:1; 1Pet. 1:5; 1Jn. 2:18.
LATTER. Job 19:25; Prov. 19:20; Hag. 2:9.
LAUGH. Prov. 1:26; Eccl. 3:4; Lk. 6:21; Jas. 4:9.
LAW. Josh. 8:34, all the words of the *l.*
Ps. 37:31, the *l.* of his God is in his heart.
40:8, thy *l.* is within my heart.
119:70, 77, 92, 174, I delight in thy *l.*
97:113, 163, 165, how I love thy *l.*
Prov. 13:14, the *l.* of the wise is a fountain of life
Isa. 8:20, to the *l.* and to the testimony.
Mal. 2:6, the *l.* of truth was in his mouth.
Mt. 5:17, not come to destroy the *l.*
23:23, the weightier matters of the *l.*
Jn. 7:51, doth our *l.* judge any man.

19:7 we have a *l.*, and by our *l.*
Rom. 2:14, are a *l.* unto themselves.
3:20, by the deeds of the *l.*
7:12, the *l.* is holy.
14, the *l.* is spiritual.
16; 1Tim. 1:8, the *l.* is good.
8:3, what the *l.* could not do.
Gal. 3:24, the *l.* was our schoolmaster.
5:14, all the *l.* is fulfilled in one word.
23, against such there is no *l.*
6:2, so fulfil the *l.* of Christ.
1Tim. 1:9, the *l.* is not made for a righteous man.
Heb. 7:16, the *l.* of a carnal commandment.
Jas. 1:25; 2:12, perfect *l.* of liberty.
2:8, the royal *l.*
See Ps. 1:2; 19:7; Mt. 7:12; Rom. 10:4.
AWFUL. Mt. 12:2; Jn. 5:10; 1Cor. 6:12.
AWLESS. 1Tim. 1:9.
EAD. Dt. 4:27; 28:37, whither the Lord shall *l.* you.
Ps. 23:2, he *l.* me beside still waters.
27:11, *l.* me in a plain path.
31:3, *l.* me, and guide me.
61:2, *l.* me to the rock that is higher than I.
139:10, there shall thy hand *l.* me.
24, *l.* me in the way everlasting.
Prov. 6:22, when thou goest, it shall *l.* thee.
Isa. 11:6, a little child shall *l.* them.
42:16, I will *l.* them in paths not known.
Isa. 48:17, I am the Lord which *l.* thee.
Mt. 6:13; Lk. 11:4, *l.* us not into temptation.
15:14; Lk. 6:39, if the blind *l.* the blind.
Acts 13:11, seeking some to *l.* him.
1Tim. 2:2, we may *l.* a quiet life.
See Jn. 10:3; 1Cor. 9:5; 2Tim. 3:6; Rev. 7:17.
EAF. Lev. 26:36; Ps. 1:3; Isa. 64:6; Mt. 21:19.
EAN. Prov. 3:5; Amos 5:19; Mic. 3:11; Jn. 13:23; 21:20.
EARN. Dt. 31:13, *l.* to fear the Lord.
Prov. 1:5; 9:9; 16:21, will increase *l.*
22:25, lest thou *l.* his ways.
Isa. 1:17, *l.* to do well.
2:4; Mic. 4:3, neither shall they *l.* war.
29:11, 12, deliver to one that is *l.*
Jn. 6:45, every one that hath *l.* of the Father.
7:15, having never *l.*
Acts 7:22, *l.* in all the wisdom of the Egyptians.
26:24, much *l.* doth make thee mad.
Rom. 15:4, written for our *l.*
Eph. 4:20, ye have not so *l.* Christ.
2Tim. 3:14, in the things thou has *l.*
Heb. 5:8, though a Son, yet *l.* he obedience.
See Mt. 9:13; 11:29; Phil. 4:11; Rev. 14:3.
EAST. Mt. 5:19, one of these *l.* commandments.
11:11; Lk. 7:28, he that is *l.* in kingdom of heaven.
25:40, 45, done it to the *l.* of these.
Lk. 12:26, not able to do that which is *l.*
16:10, faithful in that which is *l.*
Eph. 3:8, less than the *l.* of all saints.
See Gen. 32:10; Jer. 31:34; 1Cor. 6:4.
EAVE. Gen. 2:24; Mt. 19:5; Mk. 10:7; Eph. 5:31, *l.* father and mother, and shall cleave.
Ps. 16:10; Acts 2:27, not *l.* my soul in hell.
27:9; 119:121, *l.* me not.
Mt. 23:23, and not to *l.* the other undone.
Jn. 14:27, peace I *l.* with you.
Heb. 13:5, I will never *l.* thee.
See Ruth 1:16; Mt. 5:24; Jn. 16:28.
LEES. Isa. 25:6; Jer. 48:11; Zeph. 1:12.
LEND. Dt. 15:6, thou shalt *l.* to many nations.
Ps. 37:26; 112:5, ever merciful, and *l.*
Prov. 19:17, he that hath pity on poor *l.* to the Lord.
22:7, the borrower is servant to the *l.*,
Lk. 6:34, if ye *l.* to them of whom.
See 1Sam. 1:28; Isa. 24:2; Lk. 11:5.
LESS. Ex. 30:15; Job 11:6; Isa. 40:17.
LIARS. Ps. 116:11; Jn. 8:44; Ti. 1:12; Rev. 2:2; 21:8.
LIBERAL. Prov. 11:25; Isa. 32:5, 8; Jas. 1:5.
LIBERTY. Ps. 119:45, I will walk at *l.*
Isa. 61:1; Jer. 34:8; Lk. 4:18, to proclaim *l.*
Rom. 8:21, the glorious *l.* of the children of God.
1Cor. 8:9, take heed lest this *l.* of yours.
2Cor. 3:17, where the Spirit is, there is *l.*
Gal. 5:1, stand fast in the *l.*
Jas. 1:25; 2:12, the law of *l.*
See Lev. 25:10; Gal. 5:13; 1Pet. 2:16.
LIFE. Gen. 2:7; 6:17; 7:22, the breath of *l.*
9; 3:24; Rev. 2:7, the tree of *l.*
Dt. 30:15; Jer. 21:8, I have set before thee *l.*
Josh. 2:14, our *l.* for yours.
1Sam. 25:29, bound in the bundle of *l.*
Ps. 16:11, show me the path of *l.*
17:14; Eccl. 9:9, their portion in this *l.*
26:9, gather not my *l.* with bloody men.
27:1, the strength of my *l.*
30:5, in his favour is *l.*
34:12, what man is he that desireth *l.*?
36:9, the fountain of *l.*
91:16, with long *l.* will I satisfy him.
133:3, even *l.* for evermore.
Prov. 3:22, so shall they be *l.* to thy soul.
8:35, whoso findeth me findeth *l.*
15:24, the way of *l.* is above to the wise.
Mt. 6:25; Lk. 12:22, take no thought for your *l.*
18:8; 19:17; Mk. 9:43, to enter into *l.*
Lk. 12:15, a man's *l.* consisteth not.
23, the *l.* is more than meat.
Jn. 1:4, in him was *l.*
5:24; 1Jn. 3:14, passed from death to *l.*
26, as the Father hath *l.* in himself.
40; 10:10, will not come that ye might have *l.*
6:33, 47, 48, 54, the bread of *l.*
10:15, 17; 13:37, I lay down my *l.*
11:25; 14:6, the resurrection and the *l.*
Rom. 6:4, in newness of *l.*
11:15, *l.* from the dead.
2Cor. 2:16, the savour of *l.* unto *l.*
Gal. 2:20, the *l.* that I now live.
Eph. 4:18, alienated from the *l.* of God.
Col. 3:3, your *l.* is hid.
1Tim. 4:8; 2Tim. 1:1, the promise of the *l.*
2Tim. 1:10, brought *l.* to light by gospel.
Jas. 4:14, what is your *l.*?
1Jn. 1:2, the *l.* was manifested.
2:16, the pride of *l.*

5:11, this *l.* is in his Son.
Rev. 22:1, 17, river of water of *l.*
See Mt. 10:39; 20:28; Acts 5:20.

LIGHT. Ex. 10:23, Israel had *l.* in their dwellings.
Job 18:5, the *l.* of the wicked.
37:21, men see not bright *l.* in clouds.
Ps. 4:6; 90:8, the *l.* of thy countenance.
27:1, the Lord is my *l.*
36:9, in thy *l.* shall we see *l.*
97:11, *l.* is sown for the righteous.
119:105, a *l.* to my path.
Eccl. 11:7, the *l.* is sweet.
Isa. 5:20, darkness for *l.*, and *l.* for darkness.
30:26, the *l.* of the moon as *l.* of sun.
59:9, we wait for *l.*
60:1, arise, shine, for thy *l.* is come.
Zech. 14:6, the *l.* shall not be clear.
Mt. 5:15; Jn. 8:12; 9:5, the *l.* of the world.
16, let your *l.* so shine.
6:22, the *l.* of the body is the eye.
Lk. 12:35, your loins girded, and *l.* burning.
16:8, wiser than children of *l.*
Jn. 1:9, that was the true *L.*
3:19, *l.* is come into the world.
20, hateth the *l.*
5:35, burning and shining *l.*
12:35, yet a little while is the *l.* with you.
36, while ye have *l.*, believe in the *l.*
Acts 26:18, turn from darkness to *l.*
1Cor. 4:5, bring to *l.* hidden things.
2Cor. 4:4, *l.* of the gospel.
6, commanded *l.* to shine out of darkness.
11:14, an angel of *l.*
Eph. 5:8, now are ye *l.*, walk as children of *l.*
14, Christ shall give thee *l.*
1Tim. 6:16, in *l.* which no man can approach.
2Pet. 1:19, a *l.* shining in a dark place.
1Jn. 1:5, God is *l.*
7, walk in the *l.*, as he is in the *l.*
Rev. 22:5, they need no candle, neither *l.* of the sun.
See 2Tim. 1:10; Rev. 7:16; 18:23; 21:23.

LIGHTNING. Ex. 19:16; Mt. 24:27; Lk. 10:18.

LIKENESS. Ps. 17:15, when I awake, with thy *l.*
Isa. 40:18, what *l.* will ye compare?
Acts 14:11, gods are come down in *l.* of men.
Rom. 6:5, *l.* of his death, *l.* of his resurrection.
8:3, in the *l.* of sinful flesh.
Phil. 2:7, was made in the *l.* of men.
See Gen. 1:26; 5:1; Ex. 20:4; Dt. 4:16.

LIMIT. Ps. 78:41; Ezek. 43:12; Heb. 4:7.

LINE. Ps. 16:6; Isa. 28:10, 17; 34:11; 2Cor. 10:16.

LINGER. Gen. 19:16; 43:10; 2Pet. 2:3.

LIP. 1Sam. 1:13, only her *l.* moved.
Job 27:4, my *l.* shall not speak wickedness.
33:3, my *l.* shall utter knowledge.
Ps. 12:2, 3, flattering *l.*
4, our *l.* are our own.
17:1, goeth not out of feigned *l.*
31:18; 120:2; Prov. 10:18; 12:22; 17:7, lying *l.*
Prov. 15:7, the *l.* of the wise disperse knowledge.
Eccl. 10:12, the *l.* of a fool will swallow himself.
Song 7:9, causing *l.* of those asleep to speak.
Isa. 6:5, a man of unclean *l.*
Mt. 15:8, honoureth me with their *l.*
See Ps. 51:15; 141:3; Dan. 10:16; Hab. 3:16.

LITTLE. Ezra 9:8, for a *l.* space, a *l.* reviving.
Job 26:14, how *l.* a portion is heard?
Ps. 8:5; Heb. 2:7, a *l.* lower than angels.
37:16, a *l.* that a righteous man hath.
Prov. 6:10; 24:33, a *l.* sleep.
15:16; 16:8, better is a *l.* with fear of Lord.
30:24, four things *l.* on earth.
Isa. 28:10, here a *l.* and there a *l.*
40:15; Ezek. 16:47, as a very *l.* thing.
Hag. 1:6, bring in *l.*
Mt. 6:30; 8:26; 14:31; 16:8; Lk. 12:28, *l.* faith.
10:42; 18:6; Mk. 9:42; Lk. 17:2, *l.* ones.
Lk. 7:47, to whom *l.* is forgiven.
19:3, *l.* of stature.
1Cor. 5:6; Gal. 5:9, a *l.* leaven.
1Tim. 4:8, bodily exercise profiteth *l.*
5:23, use a *l.* wine.
See Jn. 7:33; 14:19; 16:16; Rev. 3:8; 6:11.

LIVE. Gen. 17:18, O that Ishmael might *l.* before thee!
45:3, doth my father yet *l.*?
Lev. 18:5; Neh. 9:29; Ezek. 20:11, if a man do, h shall *l.*
Dt. 8:3; Mt. 4:4; Lk. 4:4, not *l.* by bread alone.
Job. 7:16, I would not *l.* alway.
14:14, shall he *l.* again?
Ps. 118:17, I shall not die, but *l.*
Isa. 38:16, make me to *l.*
55:3, hear, and your soul shall *l.*
Ezek. 3:21; 18:9; 33:13, he shall surely *l.*
16:6, when thou wast in thy blood, *l.*
Hos. 6:2, we shall *l.* in his sight.
Hab. 2:4, the just shall *l.* by faith.
Lk. 10:28, this do, and thou shalt *l.*
Jn. 11:25, though he were dead, yet shall he *l.*
14:19, because I *l.*, ye shall *l.* also.
Acts 17:28, in him we *l.* and move.
Rom. 8:12, *l.* after the flesh.
14:8, whether we *l.*, we *l.* unto the Lord.
1Cor. 9:14, should *l.* of the gospel.
2Cor. 6:9, as dying, and behold we *l.*
Gal. 2:19, that I might *l.* unto God.
5:25, if we *l.* in the Spirit.
Phil. 1:21, for me to *l.* is Christ.
2Tim. 3:12, all that will *l.* godly.
Jas. 4:15, if the Lord will, we shall *l.*
Rev. 1:18, I am he that *l.*, and was dead.
3:1, a name that thou *l.*
See Rom. 6:10; 1Tim. 5:6; Rev. 20:4.

LIVELY. Ex. 1:19; Acts 7:38; 1Pet. 1:3; 2:5.

LIVING. Gen. 2:7, a *l.* soul.
Job 28:13; Ps. 27:13; 52:5; 116:9, the land of the *l.*
33:30; Ps. 27:13, light of *l.*
Ps. 69:28, the book of the *l.*
Eccl. 7:2, the *l.* will lay it to heart.
9:5, the *l.* know they shall die.
Song 4:15; Jer. 2:13; 17:13; Zech. 14:8; Jn. 4:10, water.
Isa. 38:19, the *l.* shall praise thee.

Lam. 3:39, wherefore doth a *l.* man complain?
Mk. 12:44, even all her *l.*
Lk. 8:43, spent all her *l.*
Jn. 6:51, I am the *l.* bread.
Heb. 10:30, a new and *l.* way.
See Mt. 22:32; Mk. 12:27; 1Cor. 15:43.
OADETH. Ps. 68:19.
OAN. 1Sam. 2:20.
OATHE. Num. 21:5; Job 7:16; Ezek. 6:9; 20:43; 36:31.
ODGE. Ruth 1:16; Isa. 1:21; 1Tim. 5:10.
OFTY. Ps. 131:1; Isa. 2:11; 57:15.
ONG. Job 3:21, which *l.* for death.
6:8, that God would grant the thing I *l.* for!
Ps. 63:1, my flesh *l.* for thee in a dry land.
84:2, my soul *l.* for courts of the Lord.
Ps. 119:174, I have *l.* for thy salvation.
See Dt. 12:20; 28:32; 2Sam. 23:15; Phil. 1:8.
OOK. Gen. 19:17, *l.* not behind thee.
Num. 21:8, when he *l.* on the serpent.
Job. 33:27, he *l.* on men.
Ps. 5:3, and will *l.* up.
34:5, they *l.* to him, and were lightened.
84:9, *l.* upon the face of thine anointed.
Isa. 5:7; 59:11, he *l.* for judgment.
17:7, at that day shall a man *l.* to his Maker.
45:22, *l.* unto me, and be saved.
63:5, I *l.*, and there was none to help.
66:2, to this man will I *l.*
Jer. 8:15; 14:19, we *l.* for peace.
39:12, *l.* well to him.
40:4, come with me, and I will *l.* well to thee.
Hag. 1:9, ye *l.* for much.
Mt. 11:3; Lk. 7:19, do we *l.* for another?
24:50, in a day he *l.* not for.
Lk. 9:62, no man *l.* back is fit for the kingdom.
10:32, a Levite came and *l.* on him.
22:61, the Lord turned, and *l.* on Peter.
Jn. 13:22, disciples *l.* one on another.
Acts 3:4, 12, said, *l.* on us.
6:3, *l.* ye out seven men.
2Cor. 4:18, we *l.* not at things seen.
10:7, *l.* upon things after outward appearance.
Phil. 2:4, *l.* not every man on his own things.
Ti. 2:13, *l.* for that blessed hope.
Heb. 11:10, he *l.* for a city.
12:2, *l.* unto Jesus.
1Pet. 1:12, angels desire to *l.* into.
2Jn. 8, *l.* to yourselves.
See Prov. 14:15; Mt. 5:28; 2Pet. 3:12.
OOSE. Job 38:31, canst thou *l.* the bands of Orion?
Ps. 102:20, *l.* those appointed to death.
116:16, thou hast *l.* my bonds.
Eccl. 12:6, or ever the silver cord be *l.*
Mt. 16:19; 18:18, *l.* on earth be *l.* in heaven.
Jn. 11:44, *l.* him, and let him go.
Acts 2:24, having *l.* the pains of death.
1Cor. 7:27, art thou *l.* from a wife?
See Dt. 25:9; Isa. 45:1; 51:14; Lk. 13:12.
ORD. Ex. 34:6, the *L.*, the *L.* God, merciful.
Dt. 4:35; 1Ki. 18:39, the *L.* is God.
6:4, the *L.* our God is one *L.*
Ruth 2:4; 2Chr. 20:17; 2Th. 3:16, the *L.* be with you.
1Sam. 3:18; Jn. 21:7, it is the *L.*
Neh. 9:6; Isa. 37:20, thou art *L.* alone.
Ps. 33:12, whose God is the *L.*
100:3, know that the *L.* he is God.
118:23, this is the *L.* doing.
Zech. 14:9, one *L.*, and his name one.
Mt. 7:21, not every one that saith *L.*, *L.*
26:22, *L.*, is it I?
Mk. 2:28; Lk. 6:5, the *L.* of the sabbath.
Lk. 6:46, why call ye me *L.*, *L.*?
Jn. 9:36, who is he, *L*?
20:25, we have seen the *L.*
Acts 2:36, both *L.* and Christ.
9:5; 26:15, who art thou, *L.*?
Eph. 4:5, one *L.*
See Rom. 10:12; 1Cor. 2:8; 15:47; Rev. 11:15.
LORDSHIP. Mk. 10:42; Lk. 22:25.
LOSE. Mt. 10:39; 16:25; Mk. 8:35; Lk. 9:24, shall *l.* it.
16:26; Mk. 8:36; Lk. 9:25, *l.* his own soul.
Jn. 6:39, Father's will I should *l.* nothing.
See Jud. 18:25; Eccl. 3:6; Lk. 15:4, 8.
LOSS. 1Cor. 3:15; Phil. 3:7, 8.
LOST. Ps. 119:176; Jer. 50:6, like *l.* sheep.
Ezek. 37:11, our hope is *l.*
Mt. 10:6; 15:24, go to *l.* sheep of Israel.
18:18; Lk. 19:10, to save that which was *l.*
Jn. 6:12, that nothing be *l.*
17:12, none of them is *l.*
18:9, have I *l.* none.
See Lev. 6:3; Dt. 22:3; 2Cor. 4:3.
LOT. Ps. 16:5, thou maintainest my *l.*
125:3, not rest on the *l.* of the righteous.
Prov. 1:14, cast in thy *l.* among us.
16:3, *l.* is cast into the lap.
18:18, *l.* causeth contention to cease.
Dan. 12:13, stand in thy *l.*
Acts 8:21, neither part nor *l.* in this matter.
See Num. 26:55; Mt. 27:35; Acts 1:26.
LOUD. Ezra 3:13; Prov. 7:11; 27:14; Lk. 23:23.
LOVE (*n.*). 2Sam. 1:26, wonderful, passing the *l.* of women.
Prov. 10:12, *l.* covereth all sins.
15:17, better a dinner of herbs where *l.* is.
Song 2:4, his banner over me was *l.*
8:6, *l.* is strong as death.
Jer. 31:3, loved thee with everlasting *l.*
Hos. 11:4, the bands of *l.*
Mt. 24:12, *l.* of many shall wax cold.
Jn. 5:42, ye have not the *l.* of God in you.
13:35, if ye have *l.* one to another.
15:13, greater *l.* hath no man than this.
Rom. 13:10, *l.* worketh no ill.
2Cor. 5:14, the *l.* of Christ constraineth us.
13:11, the God of *l.* shall be with you.
Eph. 3:19, the *l.* of Christ, which passeth.
1Tim. 6:10, *l.* of money is the root of all evil.
Heb. 13:1, let brotherly *l.* continue.
1Jn. 4:7, *l.* is of God.
8:16, God is *l.*
10, herein is *l.*, not that we loved God.
18, no fear in *l.*

Rev. 2:4, thou hast left thy first *l*.
See Gen. 29:29; Gal. 5:22; 1Th. 1:3.
LOVE (*v*.). Lev. 19:18; Mt. 19:19; 22:39; Mk. 12:31, thou shalt *l*. thy neighbour.
Dt. 6:5; 10:12; 11:1; 19:9; 30:5; Mt. 22:37; Mk. 12:30; Lk. 10:27, *l*. the Lord thy God.
Ps. 18:1, I will *l*. thee, O Lord, my strength.
26:8, I have *l*. the habitation of thy house.
34:12, what man is he that *l*. many days?
69:36, they that *l*. his name.
97:10, ye that *l*. the Lord.
109:17, as he *l*. cursing.
122:6, they shall prosper that *l*. thee.
Prov. 8:17, I *l*. them that *l*. me.
17:17, a friend *l*. at all times.
Eccl. 3:8, a time to *l*.
Jer. 5:31, my people *l*. to have it so.
31:3, I have *l*. thee with an everlasting *l*.
Hos. 14:4, I will *l*. them freely.
Amos 5:15, hate the evil, and *l*. the good.
Mic. 6:8, but to *l*. mercy, and walk humbly.
Mt. 5:44; Lk. 6:27, I say, *l*. your enemies.
46, if ye *l*. them which *l*. you.
Lk. 7:42, which will *l*. him most?
Jn. 11:3, he whom thou *l*. is sick.
15:12, 17, that ye *l*. one another.
21:15, 16, 17, *l*. thou me?
Rom. 13:8, owe no man any thing, but to *l*.
Eph. 6:24, grace be with all them that *l*. our Lord.
1Pet. 1:8, whom having not seen, ye *l*.
2:17, *l*. the brotherhood.
1Jn. 4:19, we *l*. him, because he first *l*. us.
Rev. 3:19, as many as I *l*. I rebuke.
See Gen. 22:2; Jn. 14:31; 1Jn. 4:20, 21.
LOVELY. 2Sam. 1:23; Song 5:16; Ezek. 33:32; Phil. 4:8.
LOVER. 1Ki. 5:1; Ps. 88:18; 2Tim. 3:4; Ti. 1:8.
LOW. Ps. 136:23; Rom. 12:16; Jas. 1:9, 10.
LOWER. Ps. 8:5; 63:9; Eph. 4:9; Heb. 2:7.
LOWEST. Dt. 32:22; Ps. 86:13; Lk. 14:9.
LOWLINESS. Eph. 4:2; Phil. 2:3.
LOWLY. Prov. 11:2, with the *l*. is wisdom.
Mt. 11:29, I am meek and *l*.
See Ps. 138:6; Prov. 3:34; 16:19; Zech. 9:9.
LUST. Dt. 12:15, 20, 21; 14:26, whatsoever thy soul *l*. after.
Ps. 81:12, gave them up to their own *l*.
Rom. 7:7, I had not known *l*.
Gal. 5:24, Christ's have crucified flesh with *l*.
1Tim. 6:9, rich fall into hurtful *l*.
Ti. 2:12, denying worldly *l*.
Jas. 1:14, when he is drawn of his own *l*.
1Pet. 2:11, abstain from fleshly *l*.
1Jn. 2:16, the *l*. of the flesh.
17, the world passeth away, and the *l*. thereof.
Jude 16, 18, walking after *l*.
See Mt. 5:28; 1Cor. 10:6; Rev. 18:14.
LYING. Ps. 31:18, let the *l*. lips be put to silence.
119:163, I abhor *l*., but thy law I love.
Prov. 6:17, the Lord hateth a *l*. tongue.
12:9, a *l*. tongue is but for a moment.
Jer. 7:4, trust not in *l*. words.
Eph. 4:25, putting away *l*.
See 1Ki. 22:22; 2Chr. 18:21; Dan. 2:9.
MAD. Jn. 10:20; Acts 26:11, 24; 1Cor. 14:23.
MADE. Ex. 2:14, who *m*. thee a prince over us?
Ps. 118:24, this is the day the Lord hath *m*.
Prov. 16:4, the Lord *m*. all things for himself.
Eccl. 3:11, he hath *m*. every thing beautiful.
7:29, God hath *m*. man upright.
Isa. 66:2, all these things hath mine hand *m*.
Jn. 1:3, all things were *m*. by him.
5:6, wilt thou be *m*. whole?
2Cor. 5:21, he hath *m*. him to be sin for us.
Eph. 2:13, *m*. nigh by the blood of Christ.
3:7; Col. 1:23, I was *m*. a minister.
Col. 1:20, having *m*. peace.
Heb. 2:17, to be *m*. like his brethren.
See Ps. 95:5; 149:2; Jn. 19:7; Acts 17:24.
MAGNIFY. Josh. 3:7, this day will I begin to *m*. thee
Job 7:17, what is man, that thou shouldest *m*. him?
Ps. 34:3; 40:16; Lk. 1:46, *m*. the Lord.
35:26; 38:16, that *m*. themselves.
138:2, thou hast *m*. thy word above all.
Isa. 42:21, *m*. the law.
Acts 19:17, the name of Jesus was *m*.
Rom. 11:13, I *m*. mine office.
See Dan. 8:25; 11:36; Acts 5:13; Phil. 1:20.
MAIDSERVANTS. Ex. 20:10, nor thy *m*.
21:7, if a man sell his daughter to be a *m*.
Dt. 15:17, unto thy *m*. thou shalt do likewise.
MAIL. 1Sam. 17:5.
MAINTAIN. 1Ki. 8:45; 49:59; 2Chr. 35:39, *m*. their cause.
Ps. 16:5, thou *m*. my lot.
Ti. 3:8, 14, careful to *m*. good works.
See Job 13:15; Ps. 9:4; 140:12.
MAINTENANCE. Ezra 4:14; Prov. 27:27.
MAKER. Job 4:17, shall a man be more pure than this *m*.?
32:22, my *m*. would soon take me away.
35:10, none saith, where is God my *m*.?
36:3, ascribe righteousness to my *m*.
Ps. 95:6, kneel before the Lord our *m*.
Prov. 14:31; 17:5, reproacheth his *m*.
22:2, the Lord is *m*. of them all.
Isa. 45:9, that striveth with his *m*.
51:13, forgettest the Lord thy *m*.
54:5, thy *m*. is thine husband.
Heb. 11:10, whose builder and *m*. is God.
See Isa. 1:31; 17:7; 22:11; Hab. 2:18.
MALICIOUSNESS. Rom. 1:29; 1Pet. 2:16.
MAN. Gen. 3:22, the *m*. is become as one of us.
8:21, for *m*. sake.
Num. 23:19, God is not a *m*.
Neh. 6:11, should such a *m*. as I flee?
Job. 5:7, *m*. is born to trouble.
10:4, seest thou as *m*. seeth?
11:12, vain *m*. would be wise.
14:1, *m*. that is born of a woman.
15:7, art thou the first *m*. that was born?
25:6, *m*. that is a worm.
33:12, God is greater than *m*.
Ps. 10:18, the *m*. of earth.

49:12, *m.* being in honour abideth not.
89:48, what *m.* is he that liveth?
Ps. 90:3, thou turnest *m.* to destruction.
104:23, *m.* goeth forth to his labour.
118:6, I will not fear, what can *m.* do?
Prov. 12:2, a good *m.* obtaineth favour.
Eccl. 6:12, who knoweth what is good for *m.*?
Isa. 2:22, cease ye from *m.*
Jer. 10:23, it is not in *m.* to direct his steps.
Lam. 3:1, I am the *m.* that hath seen affliction.
Hos. 11:9, I am God, and not *m.*
Mt. 6:24; Lk. 16:13, no *m.* can serve.
8:4; Mk. 8:26, 30; Lk. 5:14; 9:21, tell no *m.*
17:8, they saw no *m.*
Jn. 1:18; 1Jn. 4:12, no *m.* hath seen God.
19:5, behold the *m.*!
1Cor. 2:11, what *m.* knoweth things of a *m.*?
11:8, *m.* is not of the woman.
2Cor. 4:16, though our outward *m.* perish.
Phil. 2:8, in fashion as a *m.*
1Tim. 2:5, the *m.* Christ Jesus.
See Jn. 7:46; 1Cor. 15:47; Eph. 4:24.
MANDRAKES. Gen. 30:14, found *m.* in the field.
Song 7:13, the *m.* give a smell.
MANEH. Ezek. 45:12.
MANGER. Lk. 2:7.
MANIFEST. Mk. 4:22, nothing hid that shall not be *m.*
Jn. 2:11, and *m.* forth his glory.
14:22, how is it thou wilt *m.* thyself?
1Cor. 4:5, who will make *m.* the counsels of the hearts.
2Cor. 2:14, maketh *m.* savour of knowledge.
Gal. 5:19, the works of the flesh are *m.*
2Th. 1:5, a *m.* token of righteous judgment.
1Tim. 3:16, God was *m.* in the flesh.
5:25, good works of some are *m.* beforehand.
Heb. 4:13, no creature that is not *m.*
1Jn. 1:2, the life was *m.*
3:5, he was *m.* to take away our sins.
4:9, in this was *m.* the love of God.
See Rom. 8:19; Jn. 17:6; 1Jn. 3:10.
MANIFOLD. Ps. 104:24, how *m.* are thy works!
Eph. 3:10, the *m.* wisdom of God.
1Pet. 1:6, through *m.* temptations.
4:10, stewards of the *m.* grace of God.
See Neh. 9:19, 27; Amos 5:12; Lk. 18:30.
MANNER. 2Sam. 7:19, is this the *m.* of man?
Ps. 144:13, all *m.* of store.
Isa. 5:17, lambs shall feed after their *m*
Mt. 8:27; Mk. 4:41; Lk. 8:25, what *m.* of man is this!
12:31, all *m.* of sin shall be forgiven.
Acts 26:4, my *m.* of life from my youth.
1Cor. 15:33, evil communications corrupt good *m.*
Heb. 10:25, as the *m.* of some is.
Jas. 1:24, forgetteth what *m.* of man.
1Pet. 1:15, holy in all *m.* of conversation.
2Pet. 3:11, what *m.* of persons ought ye to be?
See Mt. 4:23; 5:11; Lk. 9:55; Rev. 22:2.
MANTLE. 2Ki. 2:8; Job 1:20; Ps. 109:29.
MAR. Lev. 19:27, nor *m.* the corners of thy beard.
1Sam. 6:5, images of your mice that *m.* the land.
Job 30:13, they *m.* my path.
Isa. 52:14, visage *m.* more than any man.
Mk. 2:22, wine spilled, and bottles *m.*
See Ruth 4:6; 2Ki. 3:19; Jer. 13:7; 18:4.
MARBLE. 1Chr. 29:2, and *m.* stones in abundance.
Song 5:15, his legs are as pillars of *m.*
MARK. Gen. 4:15, the Lord set a *m.* on Cain.
Job 22:15, hast thou *m.* the old way?
Ps. 37:37, *m.* the perfect man.
48:13, *m.* well her bulwarks.
130:3, if thou shouldest *m.* iniquities.
Jer. 2:22, thine iniquity is *m.* before me.
23:18, who hath *m.* his word?
Phil. 3:14, I press toward the *m.* for the prize.
17, *m.* them which walk so.
See Lk. 14:7; Rom. 16:17; Rev. 13:16; 20:4.
MARROW. Job 21:24; Ps. 63:5; Prov. 3:8; Heb. 4:12.
MARVEL. Mt. 8:10; Mk. 6:6; Lk. 7:9, Jesus *m.*
Mk. 5:20, all men did *m.*
Jn. 3:7; 5:28; 1Jn. 3:13, *m.* not.
See Eccl. 5:8; Jn. 7:21; Gal. 1:6.
MARVELLOUS. Job 5:9, *m.* things without number.
Ps. 17:7, *m.* lovingkindness.
118:23; Mt. 21:42; Mk. 12:11, *m.* in our eyes.
Jn. 9:30, herein is a *m.* thing.
1Pet. 2:9, into his *m.* light.
See Ps. 105:5; 139:14; Dan. 11:36; Mic. 7:15.
MASTER. 2Ki. 6:32, sound of his *m.* feet behind him.
Mal. 1:6, if I be a *m.*, where is my fear?
2:12, the Lord will cut off the *m.* and the scholar.
Mt. 6:24; Lk. 16:13, no man can serve two *m.*
10:24; Lk. 6:40, disciple not above his *m.*
25, enough for the disciple that he be as his *m.*
17:24, doth not your *m.* pay tribute?
23:8, 10, one is your *M.*, even Christ.
26:25, *M.*, is it I?
Mk. 5:35; Lk. 8:49, why troublest thou the *M.*?
9:5; Lk. 9:33, *M.*, it is good for us to be here.
10:17; Lk. 10:25, good *M.*, what shall I do?
Lk. 13:25, when once the *m.* of the house is risen.
Jn. 3:10, art thou a *m.* of Israel?
11:28, the *m.* is come, and calleth.
13:13, ye call me *M.*, and ye say well.
Rom. 14:4, to his own *m.* he standeth or falleth.
1Cor. 3:10, as a wise *m.*-builder.
Eph. 6:5; Col. 3:22; Ti. 2:9; 1Pet. 2:18, be obedient to *m.*
9; Col. 4:1, *m.*, do the same things to them.
1Tim. 6:1, count their *m.* worthy of honour.
2, that have believing *m.*
Jas. 3:1, be not many *m.*
See Gen. 24:12; 39:8; Prov. 25:13; Eccl. 12:11.
MASTERY. Ex. 32:18; 1Cor. 9:25; 2Tim. 2:5.
MATTER. Ezra 10:4, arise, for this *m.* belongeth to thee.
Job 19:28, the root of the *m.* is found in me.
32:18, I am full of *m.*
Ps. 45:1, my heart is inditing a good *m.*

Prov. 16:20, handleth a *m.* wisely.
18:13, answereth a *m.* before he heareth it.
Eccl. 10:20, that which hath wings shall tell the *m.*
12:13, conclusion of the whole *m.*
Mt. 23:23, the weightier *m.*
Acts 18:14, if it were a *m.* of wrong.
1Cor. 6:2, to judge the smallest *m.*
2Cor. 9:5, as a *m.* of bounty.
Jas. 3:5, how great a *m.* a little fire kindleth!
See Gen. 30:15; Dan. 3:16; Acts 8:21; 71:32.
MAY. Mt. 9:21; 26:42; Acts 8:37.
MEAN. Ex. 12:26; Josh. 4:6, what *m.* ye by this service?
Dt. 6:20, what *m.* the testimonies?
Prov. 22:29, not stand before *m.* men.
Isa. 2:9; 5:15; 31:8, the *m.* man.
Ezek. 17:12, know ye not what these things *m.*?
Mk. 9:10, what the rising from the dead should *m.*
Acts 21:39, citizen of no *m.* city.
See Acts 10:17; 17:20; 21:13.
MEANS. Ex. 34:7; Num. 14:18, by no *m.* clear guilty.
Ps. 49:7, none can by any *m.* redeem.
Mal. 1:9, this hath been by your *m.*
Mt. 5:26, shalt by no *m.* come out.
Lk. 10:19, nothing shall by any *m.* hurt you.
Jn. 9:21, by what *m.* he now seeth.
1Cor. 8:9, lest by any *m.* this liberty.
9:22, that I might by all *m.* save some.
Phil. 3:11, by an *m.* attain.
2Th. 3:16, give you peace always by all *m.*
See Jer. 5:31; 1Cor. 9:27; Gal. 2:2.
MEASURE (*n.*). Dt. 25:14; Prov. 20:10, thou shalt not have divers *m.*
Job 11:9, the *m.* is longer than the earth.
28:25, he weigheth the waters by *m.*
Ps. 39:4, the *m.* of my days.
Isa. 40:12, the dust of the earth in a *m.*
Jer. 30:11; 46:28, I will correct thee in *m.*
Ezek. 4:11, thou shalt drink water by *m.*
Mt. 7:2; Mk. 4:24; Lk. 6:38, with what *m.* ye mete.
13:33; Lk. 13:21, three *m.* of meal.
Mt. 23:32, fill up *m.* of your fathers.
Lk. 6:38, good *m.*, pressed down.
Jn. 3:34, giveth not the Spirit by *m.*
Rom. 12:3, to every man the *m.* of faith.
2Cor. 12:7, exalted above *m.*
Eph. 4:7, the *m.* of the gift of Christ.
13, to the *m.* of the stature.
16, in the *m.* of every part.
Rev. 6:6, a *m.* of wheat for a penny.
21:17, according to the *m.* of a man.
See Ps. 80:5; Isa. 5:14; Mic. 6:10.
MEASURE (*v.*). Isa. 40:12, who hath *m.* the waters?
65:7, I will *m.* former work into bosom.
Jer. 31:37, if heaven can be *m.*
33:22; Hos. 1:10, as the sand cannot be *m.*
2Cor. 10:12, *m.* themselves by themselves.
See Ezek. 40:3; 42:15; Zech. 2:1.
MEAT. Gen. 27:4, make me savoury *m.*
1Ki. 19:8, went in strength of that *m.*
Ps. 59:15, wander up and down for *m.*
69:21, they gave me also gall for my *m.*
78:25, he sent them *m.* to the full.
145:15, *m.* in due season.
Prov. 23:3, dainties for they are deceitful *m.*
30:22, a fool when filled with *m.*
31:15, she giveth *m.* to her household.
Isa. 65:25, dust shall be the serpent's *m.*
Ezek. 4:10, thy *m.* shall be by weight.
47:12, fruit for *m.*
Dan. 1:8, not defile himself with king's *m.*
Hab. 1:16, because their *m.* is plenteous.
3:17, fields yield no *m.*
Mal. 3:10, bring tithes, that there may be *m.*
Mt. 6:25; Lk. 12:23, life more than *m.*?
10:10, workman worthy of his *m.*
15:37; Mk. 8:8, of broken *m.*
25:35, ye gave me *m.*
Lk. 3:11, he that hath *m.* let him do likewise.
24:41; Jn. 21:5, have ye any *m.*?
Jn. 4:32, I have *m.* to eat.
34, my *m.* is to do the will of him that sent me.
6:27, labour not for the *m.* that perisheth.
Acts 2:46, did eat *m.* with gladness.
15:29, abstain from *m.* offered to idols.
Rom. 14:15, destroy not him with thy *m.*
17, kingdom of God is not *m.* and drink.
20, for *m.* destroy not the work of God.
1Cor. 6:13, *m.* for the belly.
8:13, if *m.* make my brother to offend.
10:3, the same spiritual *m.*
1Tim. 4:3, to abstain from *m.*
Heb. 5:12, 14, not of strong *m.*
12:16, who for one morsel of *m.*
See Gen. 1:29; 9:3; Mt. 3:4; Col. 2:16.
MEDDLE. 2Ki. 14:10; 2Chr. 25:19, why *m.* to thy hurt?
Prov. 20:3, every fool will be *m.*
19, *m.* not with him that flattereth.
26:17, that *m.* with strife.
See 2Chr. 35:21; Prov. 17:14; 24:21.
MEDITATE. Gen. 24:63, Isaac went out to *m.*
Josh. 1:8, thou shalt *m.* therein.
Ps. 1:2, in his law doth he *m.*
63:6; 119:148, *m.* in the night watches.
77:12; 143:5, I will *m.* of thy works.
Isa. 33:18, thine heart shall *m.* terror.
Lk. 21:14, not to *m.* before.
1Tim. 4:15, *m.* upon these things.
See Ps. 19:14; 104:34; 119:97, 99.
MEEK. Num. 12:3, Moses was very *m.*
Ps. 22:26, the *m.* shall eat and be satisfied.
25:9, the *m.* will he guide.
37:11; Mt. 5:5, the *m.* shall inherit the earth
149:4, will beautify the *m.*
Isa. 29:19, the *m.* shall increase their joy.
61:1, good tidings to the *m.*
Mt. 11:29, for I am *m.*
1Pet. 3:4, a *m.* and quiet spirit.
See Ps. 76:9; 147:6; Isa. 11:4; Mt. 21:5.
MEEKNESS. 2Cor. 10:1, by the *m.* of Christ.
Gal. 6:1, restore in the spirit of *m.*

1Tim. 6:11, follow after *m*.
2Tim. 2:25, in *m*. instructing.
Ti. 3:2, showing *m*. to all men.
1Pet. 3:15, give reason of hope in you with *m*.
See Zeph. 2:3; Gal. 5:23; Eph. 4:2.
EET. Prov. 11:24, withholdeth more than is *m*.
Mt. 15:26, not *m*. to take children's bread.
25:1, 6, to *m*. the bridegroom.
1Cor. 15:9, not *m*. to be called an apostle.
1Th. 4:17, to *m*. the Lord in the air.
See Prov. 22:2; Amos 4:12; Mt. 8:34.
ELODY. Isa. 23:16; 51:3; Amos 5:23; Eph. 5:19.
ELT. Ps. 46:6, the earth *m*.
97:5, the hills *m*.
107:26, their soul *m*.
147:18, he sendeth his word, and *m*. them.
Isa. 13:7, every man's heart shall *m*.
64:2, as when the *m*. fire burneth.
See Ex. 15:15; Josh. 14:8; Jer. 9:7.
EMBER. Ps. 139:16, all my *m*. were written.
Rom. 6:13, 19, neither yield your *m*.
12:4, as we have many *m*.
1Cor. 6:15, bodies *m*. of Christ.
Jas. 3:5, the tongue is a little *m*.
4:1, lusts which war in your *m*.
See Job 17:7; Mt. 5:29; Eph. 4:24; 5:30.
EMORY. Ps. 109:15; 145:7; Prov. 10:7; Eccl. 9:5.
EN. 2Chr. 6:18, will God dwell with *m*.?
1Sam. 4:9; 1Cor. 16:13, quit yourselves like *m*.
Ps. 9:20, know themselves to be but *m*.
82:7, but ye shall die like *m*.
Eccl. 12:3, strong *m*. shall bow themselves.
Isa. 31:3, the Egyptians are *m*. and not God.
46:8, show yourselves *m*.
Gal. 1:10, do I now persuade *m*.?
1Th. 2:4, not as pleasing *m*., but God.
See Ps. 116:11; 1Tim. 2:4; 1Pet. 2:17.
END. 2Chr. 24:12; 34:10; Mt. 4:21; Mk. 1:19.
ENTION. Gen. 40:14, make *m*. of me to Pharaoh.
Ps. 71:16, I will make *m*. of thy righteousness.
Isa. 12:4, make *m*. that his name is exalted.
63:7, I will *m*. the lovingkindnesses of the Lord.
Rom. 1:9; Eph. 1:16; 1Th. 1:2, *m*. of you in my prayers.
See Isa. 62:6; Ezek. 18:22; 33:16.
ERCHANDISE. Prov. 3:14, *m*. of it better than *m*. of silver.
Isa. 23:18, *m*. shall be holiness to the Lord.
Mt. 22:5, one to his farm, another to his *m*.
Jn. 2:16, my father's house an house of *m*.
2Pet. 2:3, make *m*. of you.
See Dt. 21:14; 24:7; Ezek. 26:12; Rev. 18:11.
ERCHANT. Gen. 23:16, current money with the *m*.
Isa. 23:8, whose *m*. are princes.
47:15, even thy *m*. shall wander.
Rev. 18:3, 11, the *m*. of the earth.
23, thy *m*. were great men of the earth.
See Prov. 31:24; Isa. 23:11; Mt. 13:45.
ERCIFUL. Ps. 37:26, ever *m*., and lendeth.
67:1, God be *m*. to us, and bless us.
Prov. 11:17, the *m*. doeth good to his own soul.
Isa. 57:1, *m*. men are taken away.
Jer. 3:12, return, for I am *m*.
Mt. 5:7, blessed are the *m*.
Lk. 6:36, be ye *m*., as your Father is *m*.
18:13, God be *m*. to me a sinner.
Heb. 2:17, a *m*. High Priest.
See Ex. 34:6; 2Sam. 22:26; 1Ki. 20:31.
MERCY. Gen. 32:10, not worthy the least of the *m*.
Ex. 33:19, will show *m*. on whom I will show *m*.
34:7; Dan. 9:4, keeping *m*. for thousands.
Num. 14:18; Ps. 103:11; 145:8, longsuffering and of great *m*.
1Chr. 16:34, 41; 2Chr. 5:13; 7:3, 6; Ezra 3:11; Ps. 106:1; 107:1; 118:1; 136:1; Jer. 33:11, his *m*. endureth for ever.
Ps. 23:6, surely goodness and *m*. shall follow.
25:7, according to thy *m*. remember me.
Ps. 33:22, let thy *m*. be upon us.
52:8, I trust in the *m*. of God.
59:10, the God of my *m*.
66:20, not turned his *m*. from me.
77:8, is his *m*. clean gone for ever?
85:10, *m*. and truth are met together.
89:2, *m*. shall be built up for ever.
90:14, satisfy us early with thy *m*.
101:1, I will sing of *m*.
108:4, thy *m*. is great above the heavens.
115:1, for thy *m*., and for thy truth's sake.
119:64, the earth is full of thy *m*.
130:7, with the Lord there is *m*.
Prov. 3:3, let not *m*. and truth forsake thee.
14:21, 31, he that hath *m*. on the poor.
16:6; 20:28, *m*. and truth.
Isa. 54:7, with great *m*. will I gather thee.
Jer. 6:23, they are cruel, and have no *m*.
Lam. 3:22, it is of the Lord's *m*.
Hos. 4:1, because there is no *m*. in the land.
6:6; Mt. 9:13, I desired *m*., and not sacrifice.
10:12, sow in righteousness, reap in *m*.
14:3, in thee the fatherless and find *m*.
Mic. 6:8, but to do justly, and love *m*.
7:18, he delighteth in *m*.
Hab. 3:2, in wrath remember *m*.
Mt. 5:7, the merciful shall obtain *m*.
9:27; 15:22; 20:30; Mk. 10:47, 48; 18:38, 39, thou son of David have *m*. on me.
Lk. 10:37, he that showed *m*.
Rom. 9:15, 18, *m*. on whom I will have *m*.
16, of God that showeth *m*.
12:1, beseech you by the *m*. of God.
8, he that showeth *m*., with cheerfulness.
2Cor. 1:3, the Father of *m*.
Eph. 2:4, God, who is rich in *m*.
1Tim. 1:13, 16, I obtained *m*., because.
2Tim. 1:18, that he may find *m*. in that day.
Heb. 4:16, obtain *m*., and find grace.
Jas. 2:13, without *m*., that showed no *m*.
1Pet. 1:3, according to his abundant *m*.
See Prov. 12:10; Dan. 4:27; 1Tim. 1:2.
MERRY. Gen. 43:34, were *m*. with him.
Jud. 16:25, their hearts were *m*.
Prov. 15:13, *m*. heart maketh cheerful countenance.
15, *m*. heart hath a continual feast.

17:22, *m*. heart doeth good like a medicine.
Eccl. 8:15, nothing better than to eat and be *m*.
9:7, drink thy wine with a *m*. heart.
10:19, wine maketh *m*.
Jas. 5:13, is any *m*.?
See Lk. 12:19; 15:23; Rev. 11:10.
MESSENGER. Job 33:23; Prov. 25:13; Isa. 42:19.
METE. Isa. 40:12; Mt. 7:2; Mk. 4:24; Lk. 6:38.
MIDDLE. Ezek. 1:16; Eph. 2:14.
MIDST. Ps. 102:24, in the *m*. of my days.
Prov. 23:34, lieth down in *m*. of the sea.
Dan. 9:27, in the *m*. of the week.
Mt. 18:2; Mk. 9:36, a little child in the *m*.
20, there am I in the *m*.
Lk. 24:36; Jn. 20:19, Jesus himself in the *m*.
Phil. 2:15, in the *m*. of a crooked nation.
Rev. 2:7, in the *m*. of the Paradise of God.
4:6; 5:6; 7:17, in the *m*. of the throne.
See Gen. 2:9; Isa. 12:6; Hos. 11:9.
MIGHT. Dt. 6:5, love God with all thy *m*.
8:17, the *m*. of mine hand hath gotten.
2Sam. 6:14, David danced with all his *m*.
Eccl. 9:10, do it with thy *m*.
Isa. 40:29, to them that have no *m*.
Jer. 9:23, mighty man glory in his *m*.
51:30, their *m*. hath failed.
Zech. 4:6, not by *m*., nor by power.
Eph. 3:16; Col. 1:11, strengthened with *m*.
See Eph. 6:10; 2Pet. 2:11; Rev. 7:12.
MIGHTILY. Jon 3:8; Acts 18:28; 19:20; Col. 1:29.
MIGHTY. Gen. 10:9, he was a *m*. hunter.
Jud. 5:23, to the help of the Lord against the *m*.
2Sam. 1:19, 25, how are the *m*. fallen!
23:8, these be the names of the *m*. men whom David had.
1Chr. 11:10, the chief of the *m*. men.
Job 9:4, wise in heart and *m*. in strength.
Ps. 24:8, strong and *m*., *m*. in battle.
89:13, thou hast a *m*. arm.
19, help upon one that is *m*.
93:4, the *m*. waves of the sea.
Isa. 1:24; 30:29; 49:26; 60:16, the *m*. One of Israel.
5:15, *m*. to drink wine.
63:1, *m*. to save.
Jer. 32:19, *m*. in work.
Amos 2:14, neither shall *m*. deliver himself.
Mt. 11:20; 13:54; 14:2; Mk. 6:2, *m*. works.
Lk. 9:43, the *m*. power of God.
24:19, prophet *m*. in deed and word.
Acts 18:24, *m*. in the scriptures.
1Cor. 1:26, not many *m*.
2Cor. 10:4, weapons *m*. through God.
Eph. 1:19, the working of his *m*. power.
See Num. 14:12; Eccl. 6:10; Mt. 3:11.
MILK. Gen. 49:12, teeth white with *m*.
Prov. 30:33, churning of *m*.
Isa. 55:1, buy wine and *m*.
Lam. 4:7, Nazarites were whiter than *m*.
Ezek. 25:4, shall eat thy fruit and drink thy *m*.
Heb. 5:12, 13, such as have need of *m*.
1Pet. 2:2, the sincere *m*. of the word.
See Jud. 4:19; 5:25; Job 21:24; Joel 3:18.
MIND (*n*.). Neh. 4:6, the people had a *m*. to work.
Job 23:13, he is in one *m*., who can turn him?
34:33, should it be according to thy *m*.?
Ps. 31:12, as a dead man out of *m*.
Prov. 29:11, a fool uttereth all his *m*.
Isa. 26:3, whose *m*. is stayed on thee.
Mk. 5:15; Lk. 8:35, sitting, in his right *m*.
Lk. 12:29, neither be of doubtful *m*.
Rom. 8:7, the carnal *m*. is enmity against God.
12:16, be of the same *m*.
14:5, fully persuaded in his own *m*.
2Cor. 8:12, if there be first a willing *m*.
13:11; Phil. 1:27; 2:2, be of one *m*.
Phil. 2:3, in lowliness of *m*.
5, let this *m*. be in you.
4:7, peace of God keep your *m*.
1Tim. 6:5; 2Tim. 3:8, men of corrupt *m*.
2Tim. 1:7, spirit of sound *m*.
Ti. 3:1, put them in *m*. to be subject.
1Pet. 1:13, the loins of your *m*.
2Pet. 3:1, stir up your pure *m*.
See Rom. 8:6; 11:20; 1Th. 5:14; Jas. 1:8.
MIND (*v*.). Rom. 8:5; 12:16; Phil. 3:16, 19.
MINDFUL. Ps. 8:4; 111:5; Isa. 17:10; 2Pet. 3:2.
MINGLE. Lev. 19:19; Isa. 5:22; Mt. 27:34; Lk. 13:1
MINISTER (*n*.). Ps. 103:21, ye *m*. of his.
104:4; Heb. 1:7, his *m*. a flame of fire.
Isa. 61:6, men shall call you the *m*. of God.
Joel 1:9, the Lord's *m*. mourn.
Mt. 20:26; Mk. 10:43, let him be your *m*.
Rom. 13:4, he is the *m*. of God to thee.
2Cor. 3:6, able *m*. of new testament.
Gal. 2:17, is Christ the *m*. of sin?
Eph. 3:7; Col. 1:23, whereof I was made a *m*.
6:21; Col. 1:7; 4:7, a faithful *m*.
1Tim. 4:6, a good *m*.
See 2Cor. 6:4; 11:23; 1Th. 3:2.
MINISTER (*v*.). 1Sam. 2:11, the child did *m*. unto the Lord.
1Chr. 15:2, chosen to *m*. for ever.
Dan. 7:10, thousand thousands *m*. to him.
Mt. 4:11; Mk. 1:13, angels *m*. to him.
20:28; Mk. 10:45, not to be *m*. unto, but to *m*
Lk. 8:3, which *m*. of their substance.
Acts 20:34, these hands have *m*.
See 2Cor. 9:10; Heb. 1:14; 2Pet. 1:11.
MINISTRATION. Lk. 1:23; Acts 6:1; 2Cor. 3:7; 9:1
MINISTRY. Acts 6:4, give ourselves to the *m*.
2Cor. 4:1, seeing we have this *m*.
5:18, the *m*. of reconciliation.
6:3, that the *m*. be not blamed.
Eph. 4:12, for the work of the *m*.
Col. 4:17, take heed to the *m*.
2Tim. 4:5, make full proof of thy *m*.
See Acts 1:17; 12:25; Rom. 12:7; Heb. 8:6.
MINSTREL. 2Ki. 3:15; Mt. 9:23.
MIRACLE. Jud. 6:13, where be all his *m*.?
Mk. 9:39, no man which shall do a *m*. in my name.
Lk. 23:8, hoped to have seen some *m*.
Jn. 2:11, beginning of *m*.
4:54, this is the second *m*.
10:41, said, John did no *m*.

Acts 2:22, approved of God by *m.* and signs.
1Cor. 12:10, to another, the working of *m.*
See Gal. 3:5; Heb. 2:4; Rev. 13:14; 16:14; 19:20.
IRTH. Ps. 137:3; Prov. 14:13; Eccl. 2:1; 7:4; 8:15.
IRY. Ps. 40:2; Ezek. 47:11; Dan. 2:41.
ISCHIEF. Job 15:35; Ps. 7:14; Isa. 59:4, they conceive *m.*
Ps. 28:3, *m.* is in their hearts.
94:20, frameth *m.* by a law.
Prov. 10:23, it is as sport to a fool to do *m.*
11:27, he that seeketh *m.*
24:2, lips talk of *m.*
Ezek. 7:26, *m.* shall come upon *m.*
Acts 13:10, O full of all subtilty and all *m.*
See Prov. 24:8; Eccl. 10:13; Mic. 7:3.
ISERABLE. Job 16:2; Mt. 21:41; 1Cor. 15:19; Rev. 3:17.
ISERY. Prov. 31:7, drink, and remember his *m.* no more.
Eccl. 8:6, the *m.* of man is great upon him.
Lam. 1:7, remembered in days of her *m.*
Jas. 5:1, howl for your *m.* that shall come.
See Jud. 10:16; Job 3:20; 11:16; Rom. 3:16.
IXED. Prov. 23:30, they seek *m.* wine.
Isa. 1:22, thy wine *m.* with water.
Heb. 4:2, not being *m.* with faith.
See Ex. 12:38; Num. 11:4; Neh. 13:3.
OCK. Gen. 19:14, he seemed as one that *m.*
Num. 22:29; Jud. 16:10, 13, 15, thou hast *m.* me.
1Ki. 18:27, at noon Elijah *m.* them.
2Chr. 36:16, they *m.* the messengers of God.
Prov. 1:26, I will *m.* when your fear cometh.
17:5, whoso *m.* the poor.
30:17, the eye that *m.* at his father.
Gal. 6:7, God is not *m.*
See 2Ki. 2:23; Mt. 2:16; 27:29; Mk. 15:20.
OCKER. Ps. 35:16; Prov. 20:1; Isa. 28:22; Jude 18.
ODERATION. Phil. 4:5.
OISTURE. Ps. 32:4; Lk. 8:6.
OLLIFIED. Isa. 1:16.
OMENT. Num. 16:21, 45, consume them in a *m.*
Job 7:18, try him every *m.*
21:13, and in a *m.* they go down.
Ps. 30:5, his anger endureth but a *m.*
Isa. 26:20, hide thyself as it were a *m.*
27:3, I will water it every *m.*
54:7, for a small *m.* have I forsaken thee.
1Cor. 15:51, 52, we shall all be changed in a *m.*
2Cor. 4:17, affliction, which is but for a *m.*
See Ex. 33:5; Ezek. 26:16; 32:10; Lk. 4:5.
ONEY. 2Ki. 5:26, is it a time to receive *m.*?
Eccl. 7:12, *m.* is a defence.
10:19, *m.* answereth all things.
Isa. 52:3, redeemed without *m.*
55:1, he that hath no *m.*
2, wherefore do ye spend *m.*
Mt. 17:24; 22:19, the tribute *m.*
25:18, hid his lord's *m.*
Acts 8:20, thy *m.* perish with thee.
1Tim. 6:10, the love of *m.*
See Gen. 23:9; Mk. 6:8; Lk. 9:3; Acts 4:37.
ORROW. Prov. 27:1, boast not thyself of to-*m.*
Isa. 22:13; 1Cor. 15:32, for to-*m.* we die.
56:12, to-*m.* shall be as this day.
Mt. 6:34, take no though for the *m.*
Jas. 4:14, ye know not what shall be on the *m.*
See Josh. 5:12; 2Ki. 7:1; Prov. 3:28.
MORSEL. Job 31:17; Ps. 147:17; Prov. 17:1; Heb. 12:16.
MORTAL. Job 4:17, shall *m.* man be more just?
Rom. 6:12; 8:11, in your *m.* body.
1Cor. 15:53, 54, this *m.* must put on immortality.
See Dt. 19:11; 2Cor. 4:11; 5:4.
MORTAR. Prov. 27:22; Ezek. 13:11, 22, 28.
MORTIFY. Rom. 8:13; Col. 3:5.
MOTE. Mt. 7:3; Lk. 6:41.
MOTH. Job 27:18, he buildeth his house as a *m.*
Ps. 39:11, consume away like a *m.*
Isa. 50:9, the *m.* shall eat them up.
Hos. 5:12, unto Ephraim as a *m.*
Mt. 6:10, where *m.* and rust doth corrupt.
MOTHER. Jud. 5:7; 2Sam. 20:19, a *m.* in Israel.
1Ki. 22:52, Ahaziah walked in the way of his *m.*
2Chr. 22:3, his *m.* was his counsellor.
Job 17:14, to the worm, thou art my *m.*
Ps. 113:9, a joyful *m.* of children.
Isa. 66:13, as one whom his *m.* comforteth.
Ezek. 16:44, as is the *m.*, so is her daughter.
Mt. 12:48; Mk. 3:33, who is my *m.*?
Jn. 2:1; Acts 1:14, the *m.* of Jesus.
See Gen. 3:20; 17:16; Gal. 4:26; 1Tim. 1:9; 5:2.
MOULDY. Josh. 9:5, 12.
MOUNT. Ex. 18:5, the *m.* of God.
Ps. 107:26, they *m.* up to heaven.
Isa. 40:31, *m.* with wings, as eagles.
See Job 20:6; 39:27; Isa. 27:13.
MOURN. Gen. 37:35, down to the grave *m.*
Prov. 5:11, and thou *m.* at the last.
Isa. 61:2, to comfort all that *m.*
Jer. 31:13, I will turn their *m.* into joy.
Mt. 5:4, blessed are they that *m.*
24:30, then shall all the tribes of the earth *m.*
Lk. 6:25, woe to you that laugh, for ye shall *m.*
See Neh. 8:9; Zech. 7:5; Jas. 4:9.
MOURNER. 2Sam. 14:2; Eccl. 12:5; Hos. 9:4.
MOURNFULLY. Mal. 3:14.
MOUTH. Job 9:20, mine own *m.* shall condemn me.
40:4, I will lay my hand on my *m.*
Ps. 8:2; Mt. 21:16, out of the *m.* of babes.
39:1, I will keep my *m.* with a bridle.
49:3, my *m.* shall speak of wisdom.
55:21, words of his *m.* smoother than butter.
81:10, open thy *m.* wide.
Prov. 10:14; 14:3; 15:2, the *m.* of the foolish.
13:2, good by the fruit of his *m.*
3; 21:23, he that keepeth his *m.*
Eccl. 6:7, all the labour of a man is for his *m.*
Isa. 29:13; Mt. 15:8, this people draw near with *m.*
Ezek. 33:31, with their *m.* they show much love.
Mal. 2:6, the law of truth was in his *m.*
Mt. 12:34; Lk. 6:45, the *m.* speaketh.
13:35, I will open my *m.* in parables.
Lk. 21:15, I will give you a *m.* and wisdom.
Rom. 10:10, with the *m.* confession is made.
Ti. 1:11, whose *m.* must be stopped.

Jas. 3:10, out of the same *m*. proceedeth.
See Lam. 3:29; Jn. 19:29; 1Pet. 2:22.
MOVE. Ps. 10:6; 16:8; 30:6; 62:2, I shall not be *m*.
Mt. 21:10; Acts 21:30, all the city was *m*.
Jn. 5:3, waiting fro the *m*. of the water.
Acts 17:28, in him we live, and *m*.
20:24, none of these things *m*. me.
See Prov. 23:31; Isa. 7:2; 2Pet. 1:21.
MUCH. Ex. 16:18; 2Cor. 8:15, he that gathered *m*.
Num. 16:3, ye take too *m*. upon you.
Lk. 7:47, for she loved *m*.
12:48, to whom *m*. is given.
16:10, faithful in *m*.
See Prov. 25:16; Eccl. 5:12; Jer. 2:22.
MULTIPLY. Isa. 9:3, thou hast *m*. the nation, and not increased the joy.
Jer. 3:16, when ye be *m*. they shall say.
Dan. 4:1; 6:25; 1 Pet. 1:2; 2 Pet. 1:2; Jude 2, peace be *m*.
Nah. 3:16, thou hast *m*. thy merchants.
See Acts 6:1; 7:17; 9:31; 12:24.
MULTITUDE. Ex. 23:2, a *m*. to do evil.
Job 32:7, *m*. of years should teach wisdom.
Ps. 5:7; 51:1; 69:13; 106:7, in the *m*. of thy mercy.
33:16, no king saved by the *m*. of an host.
94:19, in the *m*. of my thoughts.
Prov. 10:19, in *m*. of words there wanteth not sin.
11:14; 15:22; 24:6, in the *m*. of counsellors.
Eccl. 5:3, through the *m*. of business.
Jas. 5:20; 1Pet. 4:8, hide a *m*. of sins.
See Dt. 1:10; Josh. 11:4; Lk. 2:13.
MURMURINGS. Ex. 16:7; Num. 14:27; Phil. 2:14.
MUSE. Ps. 39:3; 143:5; Lk. 3:15.
MUTTER. Isa. 8:19; 59:3.
MUTUAL. Rom. 1:12.
MYSTERY. Mt. 13:11; 1Cor. 2:7; 15:51; Eph. 5:32.
NAIL. Ezra 9:8, give us a *n*. in his holy place.
Isa. 22:23, fasten as a *n*. in sure place.
Jn. 20:25, put finger into print of *n*.
Col. 2:14, *n*. it to his cross.
See Jud. 4:21; Eccl. 12:11; Dan. 4:33.
NAKED. Ex. 32:25, made *n*. to their shame.
Job 1:21, *n*. came I out, and *n*. shall I return.
Mt. 25:36, *n*., and ye clothed me.
1Cor. 4:11, to this present hour we are *n*.
2Cor. 5:3, we shall not be found *n*.
Heb. 4:13, all things are *n*. to eyes of him.
See Jn. 21:7; Jas. 2:15; Rev. 3:17; 16:15.
NAKEDNESS. Rom. 8:35; 2Cor. 11:27; Rev. 3:18.
NAME (*n*.). Gen. 32:29; Jud. 13:18, wherefore doest thou ask after my *n*.?
Ex. 3:15, this is my *n*. for ever.
23:21, my *n*. is in him.
Josh. 7:9, what wilt thou do to thy great *n*.?
2Chr. 14:11, in thy *n*. we go.
Neh. 9:10, so didst thou get thee a *n*.
Job 18:17, he shall have no *n*. in the street.
Ps. 20:1, the *n*. of God defend thee.
5, in the *n*. of God set up banners.
22:22; Heb. 2:12, I will declare thy *n*.
48:10, according to thy *n*. so is thy praise.
69:36, they that love his *n*.
111:9, holy and reverend is his *n*.
115:1, unto thy *n*. give glory.
138:2, thy word above all thy *n*.
Prov. 10:7, the *n*. of the wicked shall rot.
18:10, the *n*. of the Lord a strong tower.
22:1; Eccl. 7:1, good *n*. rather to be chosen.
Song 1:3, thy *n*. is as ointment poured forth.
Isa. 42:8, I am the Lord, that is my *n*.
55:13, it shall be to the Lord for a *n*.
56:5; 63:12, an everlasting *n*.
57:15, whose *n*. is Holy.
62:2, called by a new *n*.
64:7, there is none that calleth on thy *n*.
Jer. 10:6, thou art great, and thy *n*. is great.
14:14; 23:25; 27:15, prophesy lies in my *n*.
44:26, sworn by my great *n*.
Zech. 10:12, walk up and down in his *n*.
14:9, one Lord, and his *n*. one.
Mal. 1:6, wherein have we despised thy *n*.?
4:2, to you that fear my *n*.
Mt. 6:9; Lk. 11:2, hallowed be thy *n*.
10:22; 19:29; Mk. 13:13; Lk. 21:12; Jn. 15:21
Acts 9:16, for my *n*. sake.
12:21, in his *n*. shall the Gentiles trust.
18:5; Mk. 9:37; Lk. 9:48, receive in my *n*.
20, gathered together in my *n*.
24:5; Mk. 13:6; Lk. 21:8, many shall come in my *n*.
Mk. 5:9; Lk. 8:30, what is thy *n*.?
9:39, do a miracle in my *n*.
Lk. 10:20, *n*. written in heaven.
Jn. 5:43, if another shall come in his own *n*.
14:13; 15:16; 16:23, 24, 26, whatsoever ye ask in my *n*.
Acts 3:16, his *n*. through faith in his *n*.
Acts 4:12, none other *n*. under heaven.
5:28, that ye should not teach in this *n*.
41, worthy to suffer for his *n*.
Eph. 1:21, far above every *n*.
Phil. 2:9, 10, a *n*. above every *n*.
4:3, whose *n*. are in the book of life.
Col. 3:17, do all in the *n*. of the Lord Jesus.
Heb. 1:4, obtained a more excellent *n*.
Jas. 2:7, that worthy *n*.
Rev. 2:13, holdest fast my *n*.
17, a *n*. written, which no man knoweth.
3:1, thou hast a *n*. that thou livest.
4, a few *n*. in Sardis.
13:1, the *n*. of blasphemy.
14:1; 22:4, Father's *n*. in their foreheads.
See Gen. 2:20; Ex. 28:9; Isa. 45:3; Jn. 10:3.
NAME (*v*.). Eccl. 6:10, that which hath been is *n*. already.
Isa. 61:6, ye shall be *n*. Priests of the Lord.
Rom. 15:20, not where Christ was *n*.
2Tim. 2:19, every one that *n*. the name of Christ
See 1Sam. 16:3; Isa. 62:2; Lk. 2:21; 6:13.
NARROW. Isa. 28:20; 49:19; Mt. 7:14.
NATION. Gen. 10:32, by these were the *n*. divided.
20:4, wilt thou slay a righteous *n*.?
Num. 14:12; Dt. 9:14, I will make thee a greater *n*.
2Sam. 7:23; 1Chr. 17:21, what *n*. like thy people

Ps. 33:12, blessed is the *n*. whose God is the Lord.
147:20, he hath not dealt so with any *n*.
Prov. 14:34, righteousness exalteth a *n*.
Isa. 2:4; Mic. 4:3, *n*. shall not lift sword against *n*.
18:2, a *n*. scattered and peeled.
26:2, that the righteous *n*. may enter in.
34:1, come near, ye *n*., to hear.
52:15, so shall he sprinkle many *n*.
Jer. 10:7, O King of *n*.
Zech. 2:11, many *n*. shall be joined to the Lord.
8:22, strong *n*. shall seek the Lord.
Mt. 24:7; Mk. 13:8; Lk. 21:10, *n*. against *n*.
Lk. 7:5, he loveth our *n*.
21:25, distress of *n*.
Jn. 11:50, that the whole *n*. perish not.
Acts 2:5, devout men of every *n*.
10:35, in every *n*. he that feareth.
Phil. 2:15, crooked and perverse *n*.
Rev. 5:9, redeemed out of every *n*.
See Dt. 4:27; 15:6; Jer. 2:11; 4:2; 31:10.
ATIVITY. Gen. 11:28; Jer. 46:16; Ezek. 21:30; 23:15.
ATURAL. Dt. 34:7, nor his *n*. force abated.
Rom. 1:31; 2Tim. 3:3, without *n*. affection.
1Cor. 2:14, the *n*. man receiveth not.
See 1Cor. 15:44; Phil. 2:20; Jas. 1:23.
ATURE. 1Cor. 11:14, doth not even *n*. itself teach?
Eph. 2:3, by *n*. children of wrath.
Heb. 2:16, the *n*. of angels.
2Pet. 1:4, partakers of the divine *n*.
See Rom. 1:26; 2:14, 27; Gal. 2:15; 4:8.
AUGHT. Prov. 20:14, it is *n*., saith the buyer.
Isa. 49:4, spent strength for *n*.
52:3, ye have sold yourselves for *n*.
Mal. 1:10, shut the doors for *n*.
Acts 5:38, if of men, it will come to *n*.
See Dt. 15:9; Job 1:9; Rom. 14:10; 1Cor. 1:28.
AUGHTINESS. 1Sam. 17:28; Prov. 11:6; Jas. 1:21.
AUGHTY. Prov. 6:12; 17:4; Jer. 24:2.
AY. Mt. 5:37; 2Cor. 1:17, 18, 19; Jas. 5:12.
EAR. Jud. 20:34, knew not evil was *n*.
Ps. 22:11, trouble is *n*
148:14, a people *n*. to him.
Prov. 27:10, better a neighbour that is *n*.
Isa. 50:8, he is *n*. that justifieth.
55:6, call upon the Lord while he is *n*.
Obad. 15; Zeph. 1:14, the day of the Lord is *n*.
Mt. 24:33, it is *n*., even at the doors.
Mk. 13:28, ye know that summer is *n*.
See Ezek. 11:3; 22:5; Rom. 13:11.
ECESSARY. Job 23:12; Acts 15:28; 28:10; Ti. 3:14.
ECESSITIES. 2Cor. 6:4, as the ministers of God, in *n*.
ECESSITY. Rom. 12:13, distributing to the *n*. of saints.
1Cor. 9:16, *n*. is laid upon me.
2Cor. 9:7; Phile. 14, give, not grudgingly, or of *n*.
See Acts 20:34; 2Cor. 12:10; Phil. 4:16.
ECK. Prov. 3:3; 6:21, bind them about thy *n*.
Mt. 18:6; Mk. 9:42; Lk. 17:2, millstone about his *n*.
Lk. 15:20; Acts 20:37, fell on his *n*.
Acts 15:10, yoke on the *n*. of disciples.
See Neh. 9:29; Isa. 3:16; Lam. 5:5; Rom. 16:4.
NEED. 2Chr. 20:17, ye shall not *n*. to fight.
Prov. 31:11, he shall have no *n*. of spoil.
Mt. 6:8; Lk. 12:30, what things ye have *n*. of.
9:12; Mk. 2:17; Lk. 5:31, *n*. not a physician.
14:16, they *n*. not depart.
21:3; Mk. 11:3; Lk. 19:31, 34, the Lord hath *n*. of them.
Lk. 11:8, as many as he *n*.
Acts 2:45; 4:35, as every man had *n*.
1Cor. 12:21, cannot say, I have no *n*. of thee.
Phil. 4:12, to abound and to suffer *n*.
19, God shall supply all your *n*.
2Tim. 2:15, that *n*. not to be ashamed.
Heb. 4:16, grace to help in time of *n*.
5:1, ye have *n*. that one teach you.
1Jn. 3:17, seeth his brother have *n*.
Rev. 3:17, rich, and have *n*. of nothing.
21:23; 22:5, city had no *n*. of the sun.
See Dt. 15:8; Lk. 9:11; Jn. 2:25; Acts 17:25.
NEEDFUL. Lk. 10:42; Phil. 1:24; Jas. 2:16.
NEEDY. Dt. 15:11, thou shalt open thine hand to thy *n*.
Job 24:4, they turn the *n*. out of the way.
Ps. 9:18, the *n*. shall not alway be forgotten.
40:17; 70:5; 86:1; 109:22, I am poor and *n*.
74:21, let the poor and *n*. praise thy name.
Prov. 31:9, plead the cause of the poor and *n*.
Isa. 41:17, when the *n*. seek water.
See Ezek. 16:49; 18:12; 22:29; Amos 8:4, 6.
NEGLECT. Mt. 18:17; Acts 6:1; 1Tim. 4:14; Heb. 2:3.
NEGLIGENT. 2Chr. 29:11; 2Pet. 1:12.
NEIGHBOUR. Prov. 3:28, say not to thy *n*., go and come again.
14:20, the poor is hated even of his *n*.
21:10, his *n*. findeth no favour.
Eccl. 4:4, envied of his *n*.
Jer. 22:13, that useth his *n*. service without wages.
Hab. 2:15, that giveth his *n*. drink.
Zech. 8:16; Eph. 4:25, speak every man truth to his *n*.
Lk. 10:29, who is my *n*.?
14:12, call not thy rich *n*.
See Ex. 20:16; Lev. 19:13; Mt. 5:43; Rom. 13:10.
NEST. Num. 24:21, thou puttest thy *n*. in a rock.
Dt. 32:11, as an eagle stirreth up her *n*.
Job 29:18, I shall die in my *n*.
Ps. 84:3, the swallow hath found a *n*.
Mt. 8:20; Lk. 9:58, birds of the air have *n*.
See Prov. 27:8; Isa. 16:2; Jer. 49:16; Obad. 4; Hab. 2:9.
NET. Ps. 141:10, let the wicked fall into their own *n*.
Prov. 1:17, in vain the *n*. is spread.
Eccl. 9:12, as fishes taken in an evil *n*.
Hab. 1:16, they sacrifice unto their *n*.
Mt. 13:47, kingdom of heaven like a *n*.
Mk. 1:18, they forsook their *n*.
Lk. 5:5, at thy word I will let down the *n*.
See Mt. 4:21; Mk. 1:16; Jn. 21:6.
NETHER. Dt. 24:6; Job 41:24.

NEVER. Lev. 6:13, the fire shall *n.* go out.
Job 3:16, as infants which *n.* saw light.
Ps. 10:11, he will *n.* see it.
15:5; 30:6, shall *n.* be moved.
Prov. 27:20; 30:15, *n.* satisfied.
Isa. 56:11, which can *n.* have enough.
Mt. 7:23, I *n.* knew you.
9:33, it was *n.* so seen in Israel.
26:33, yet will I *n.* be offended.
Mk. 2:12, we *n.* saw it on this fashion.
3:29, hath *n.* forgiveness.
14:21, if he had *n.* been born.
Jn. 4:14; 6:35, shall *n.* thirst.
Jn. 7:46, *n.* man spake like this man.
8:51; 10:28; 11:26, shall *n.* see death.
1Cor. 13:8, charity *n.* faileth.
Heb. 13:5, I will *n.* leave thee.
2Pet. 1:10, ye shall *n.* fall.
See Jud. 2:1; Ps. 58:5; Jer. 33:17; Dan. 2:44.
NEW. Num. 16:30, if the Lord make a *n.* thing.
Ps. 33:3; 40:3; 96:1; 98:1; 144:9; 149:1; Isa. 42:10; Rev. 5:9; 14:3, a *n.* song.
Eccl. 1:9, no *n.* thing under the sun.
Isa. 65:17; 66:22; Rev. 21:1, *n.* heavens and *n.* earth.
Lam. 3:23, *n.* every morning.
Mt. 9:16; Mk. 2:21; Lk. 5:36, *n.* cloth to old garment.
13:52, things *n.* and old.
Mk. 1:27; Acts 17:19, what *n.* doctrine is this?
Jn. 13:34; 1Jn. 2:7, 8, a *n.* commandment.
Acts 17:21, to tell or hear some *n.* thing.
2Cor. 5:17; Gal. 6:15, a *n.* creature.
Eph. 2:15; 4:24; Col. 3:10, *n.* man.
Heb. 10:20, *n.* and living way.
Rev. 2:17; 3:12, a *n.* name.
21:5, I make all things *n.*
See Isa. 24:7; 43:19; 65:8; Acts 2:13.
NEWLY. Dt. 32:17; Jud. 7:19.
NEWNESS. Rom. 6:4; 7:6.
NEWS. Prov. 25:25.
NIGH. Num. 24:17, but not *n.*
Dt. 30:14; Rom. 10:8, the word is *n.* unto thee.
Ps. 34:18, *n.* to them of broken heart.
145:18, *n.* to all that call upon him.
Eph. 2:13, made *n.* by the blood of Christ.
See Joel 2:1; Lk. 21:20; Heb. 6:8.
NIGHT. Ex. 12:42, a *n.* to be much observed.
Job 7:4, when shall I arise, and the *n.* be gone?
35:10; Ps. 77:6, songs in the *n.*
Ps. 30:5, weeping may endure for a *n.*
91:5, the terror by *n.*
136:9; Jer. 31:35, moon and stars to rule by *n.*
139:11, then *n.* shall be light about me.
Isa. 21:4, the *n.* of my pleasure.
11, watchman, what of the *n.*?
Lk. 6:12, he continued all *n.* in prayer.
Jn. 9:4, the *n.* cometh, when no man can work.
Jn. 11:10, walk in the *n.*, he stumbleth.
Rom. 13:12, the *n.* is far spent.
1Th. 5:2; 2Pet. 3:10, cometh as a thief in the *n.*
Rev. 21:25; 22:5, no *n.* there.
See Job 7:3; Ps. 121:6; Mt. 27:64; Jn. 3:2.
NOBLE. Neh. 3:5, the *n.* put not their neck.
Job 29:10, the *n.* held their peace.
Jer. 2:21, planted thee a *n.* vine.
14:3, their *n.* sent their little ones to the waters.
Acts 17:11, Bereans were more *n.*
1Cor. 1:26, not many *n.*
See Num. 21:18; Ps. 149:8; Eccl. 10:17.
NOISE. Ezra 3:13, not discern *n.* of joy.
Ps. 66:1; 81:1; 95:1; 98:4; 100:1, joyful *n.*
Ezek. 1:24; 43:2, *n.* of great waters.
2Pet. 3:10, pass away with great *n.*
See Josh. 6:27; Mt. 9:23; Mk. 2:1; Acts 2:6.
NOISOME. Ps. 91:3; Ezek. 14:21; Rev. 16:2.
NOTHING. Dt. 2:7; Neh. 9:21, thou hast lacked *n.*
2Sam. 24:24, neither offer of that which doth cost *n.*
2Chr. 14:11, it is *n.* with thee to help.
Neh. 8:10, portions to them for whom *n.* is prepared.
Job 8:9, but of yesterday, and know *n.*
Ps. 49:17, he shall carry *n.* away.
119:165, *n.* shall offend them.
Prov. 13:4, the sluggard desireth, and hath *n.*
7, there is that maketh himself rich, yet hath *n.*
Lam. 1:12, is it *n.* to you?
Mt. 17:20; Lk. 1:37, *n.* shall be impossible.
21:19; Mk. 11:13, *n.* but leaves.
Lk. 6:35, hoping for *n.* again.
7:42, they had *n.* to pay.
Jn. 15:5, without me ye can do *n.*
1Cor. 4:4, I know *n.* by myself.
2Cor. 6:10, as having *n.*
13:8, we can do *n.* against the truth.
1Tim. 4:4, *n.* to be refused.
6:7, brought *n.* into this world, can carry *n.* out.
See Phil. 4:6; Jas. 1:4; 3Jn. 7.
NOURISH. Isa. 1:2, I have *n.* and brought up children.
1Tim. 4:6, *n.* in words of faith.
Jas. 5:5, have *n.* your hearts.
See Gen. 45:11; 50:21; Acts 12:20; Col. 2:19.
NOW. Job 4:5, *n.* it is come upon thee.
Ps. 119:67, but *n.* have I kept thy word.
Hos. 2:7, then was it better than *n.*
Lk. 14:17, all things are *n.* ready.
Jn. 13:7, thou knowest not *n.*
16:12, ye cannot bear them *n.*
1Cor. 13:12, *n.* I know in part.
Gal. 2:20, the life I *n.* live.
1Tim. 4:8, the life that *n.* is.
1Pet. 1:8, though *n.* ye see him not.
1Jn. 3:2, *n.* are we sons of God.
See Rom. 6:22; Gal. 3:3; Heb. 2:8.
NUMBER (*n.*). Job 5:9; 9:10, marvellous things without *n.*
25:3, is there any *n.* of his armies?
Ps. 139:18, more in *n.* than the sand.
147:4, he telleth the *n.* of the stars.
Acts 11:21, a great *n.* believed.
16:5, the churches increased in *n.* daily.

Rev. 13:17, 18, the *n*. of his name.
See Dt. 7:7; Hos. 1:10; Rom. 9:27.
UMBER (*v*.). Gen. 41:49, gathered corn till he left *n*.
2Sam. 24:2; 1Chr. 21:2, *n*. the people.
Ps. 90:12, so teach us to *n*. our days.
Eccl. 1:15, that which is wanting cannot be *n*.
Isa. 53:12; Mk. 15:28, he was *n*. with transgressors.
Mt. 10:30; Lk. 12:7, hairs are all *n*.
Rev. 7:9, multitude which no man could *n*.
See Ex. 30:12; Job 14:16; Ps. 40:5; Acts 1:17.
URSE. Gen. 35:8, Deborah Rebekah's *n*. died.
2Sam. 4:4, and his *n*. took him up and fled.
1Th. 2:7, even as a *n*. cherisheth her children.
See Ex. 2:7, 9; Isa. 60:4.
URSING. Isa. 49:23, kings shall be thy *n*. fathers, and their queens thy *n*. mothers.
URTURE. Eph. 6:4.
BEDIENCE. Rom. 5:19, by the *o*. of one.
16:26, the *o*. of faith.
Heb. 5:8, yet learned he *o*.
See Rom. 16:19; 2Cor. 10:5; 1Pet. 1:2.
BEDIENT. Ex. 24:7, all will we do, and be *o*.
Prov. 25:12, wise reprover upon an *o*. ear.
Isa. 1:19, if *o*. ye shall eat.
2Cor. 2:9, *o*. in all things.
Eph. 6:5; Ti. 2:9, be *o*. to your masters.
Phil. 2:8, *o*. unto death.
1Pet. 1:14, as *o*. children.
See Num. 27:20; 2Sam. 22:45; Ti. 2:5.
BEISANCE. Gen. 37:7; 43:28; 2Sam. 15:5.
BEY. Dt. 11:27, a blessing if ye *o*.
Josh. 24:24, his voice will we *o*.
1Sam. 15:22, to *o*. is better than sacrifice.
Jer. 7:23, *o*. my voice, and I will be your God.
Acts. 5:29, we ought to *o*. God rather than men.
Rom. 6:16, his servants ye are to whom ye *o*.
Eph. 6:1; Col. 3:20, *o*. your parents in the Lord.
2Th. 1:8; 1Pet. 4:17, that *o*. not the gospel.
Heb. 13:17, *o*. them that have rule over you.
1Pet. 1:22, purified your souls in *o*. the truth.
See Ex. 5:2; 23:21; Dan. 9:10; Mt. 8:27.
BJECT. Acts 24:19.
BSCURE. Prov. 20:20.
BSCURITY. Isa. 29:18; 58:10; 59:9.
BSERVATION. Lk. 17:20.
BSERVE. Gen. 37:11, his father *o*. the saying.
Ps. 107:43, whoso is wise, and will *o*. these things.
Prov. 23:26, let thine eyes *o*. my ways.
Eccl. 11:4, he that *o*. the wind.
Jon. 2:8, that *o*. lying vanities.
Mt. 28:20, teaching them to *o*. all things.
Mk. 6:20, Herod feared John, and *o*. him.
10:20, all these have I *o*.
See Ex. 12:42; 31:16; Ezek. 20:18; Gal. 4:10.
BSERVER. Dt. 18:10.
BSTINATE. Dt. 2:30; Isa. 48:4.
BTAIN. Prov. 8:35, shall *o*. favour of the Lord.
Isa. 35:10; 51:11, shall *o*. joy and gladness.
Lk. 20:35, worthy to *o*. that world.
Acts 26:22, having *o*. help of God.
1Cor. 9:24, so run that ye may *o*.
1Th. 5:9; 2Tim. 2:10, to *o*. salvation.
1Tim. 1:13, I *o*. mercy.
Heb. 4:16, *o*. mercy, and find grace to help.
9:12, having *o*. eternal redemption.
1Pet. 2:10, which had not *o*. mercy, but now have *o*.
2Pet. 1:1, *o*. like precious faith.
See Dan. 11:21; Hos. 2:23; Acts 1:17; 22:28.
OCCASION. 2Sam. 12:14, great *o*. to enemies to blaspheme.
Dan. 6:4, sought to find *o*.
Rom. 7:8, sin, taking *o*. by the commandment.
14:13, an *o*. to fall in his brother's way.
1Tim. 5:14, give none *o*. to the adversary.
See Gen. 43:18; Ezra 7:20; Ezek. 18:3.
OCCUPATION. Gen. 46:33; Jon. 1:8; Acts 18:3; 29:25.
OCCUPY. Ezek. 27:9; Lk. 19:13.
ODOUR. Jn. 12:3; Phil. 4:18; Rev. 5:8.
OFFENCE. Eccl. 10:4, yielding pacifieth great *o*.
Isa. 8:14; Rom. 9:33; 1Pet. 2:8, a rock of *o*.
Mt. 16:23, thou art an *o*. to me.
18:7; Lk. 17:1, woe to the world because of *o*.!
Acts 24:16, conscience void of *o*.
Rom. 14:20, that man who eateth with *o*.
1Cor. 10:32; 2Cor. 6:3, give none *o*.
Phil. 1:10, without *o*. till the day of Christ.
See 1Sam. 25:31; Rom. 5:15; 16:17; Gal. 5:11.
OFFEND. Job 34:31, I will not *o*. any more.
Ps. 119:165, nothing shall *o*. them.
Prov. 18:19, brother *o*. is harder to be won.
Mt. 5:29; 18:9; Mk. 9:47, if thine eye *o*. thee.
13:41, gather all things that *o*.
57; Mk. 6:3, they were *o*. in him.
26:33, though all shall be *o*., yet will I never be.
Rom. 14:21, whereby thy brother is *o*.
Jas. 2:10, yet *o*. in one point.
See Gen. 20:9; Jer. 37:18; 2Cor. 11:29.
OFFENDER. 1Ki. 1:21; Isa. 29:21; Acts 25:11.
OFFER. Jud. 5:2, people willingly *o*. themselves.
Ps. 50:23, whoso *o*. praise.
Mt. 5:24, then come and *o*. thy gift.
Lk. 6:29, one cheek, *o*. also the other.
1Cor. 8:1, 4, 7; 10:19, things *o*. to idols.
Phil. 2:17, *o*. in the service of your faith.
2Tim. 4:6, now ready to be *o*.
Heb. 9:28, Christ once *o*. to bear the sins of many.
See 2Chr. 17:16; Ezra 1:6; 2:68; Mal. 1:8.
OFFICE. 1Sam. 2:36, put me into one of the priests' *o*.
Rom. 11:13, I magnify mine *o*.
1Tim. 3:1, the *o*. of a bishop.
Heb. 7:5, the *o*. of the priesthood.
See Gen. 41:13; Ps. 109:8; Rom. 12:4.
OFFSCOURING. Lam. 3:45; 1Cor. 4:13.
OFFSPRING. Job 27:14; Acts 17:28; Rev. 22:16.
OFTEN. Prov. 29:1, being *o*. reproved.
Mal. 3:16, spake *o*. one to another.
Mt. 23:37; Lk. 13:34, how *o*. would I have

gathered.
1Cor. 11:26, as *o.* as ye eat.
1Tim. 5:23, thine *o.* infirmities.
See 2Cor. 11:26; Heb. 9:25; 10:11.
OIL. Ps. 45:7; Heb. 1:9, with *o.* of gladness.
92:10, be anointed with fresh *o.*
104:15, *o.* to make his face to shine.
Isa. 61:3, *o.* of joy for mourning.
Mt. 25:3, took no *o.* with them.
Lk. 10:34, pouring in *o.* and wine.
See Ex. 27:20; Mic. 6:7; Lk. 7:46.
OLD. Dt. 8:4; 29:5; Neh. 9:21, waxed not *o.*
Josh. 5:11, did eat of the *o.* corn.
Ps. 37:25, I have been young, and now am *o.*
71:18, when I am *o.* forsake me not.
Prov. 22:6, when he is *o.* he will not.
Isa. 58:12, build the *o.* waste places.
Jer. 6:16, ask for the *o.* paths.
Lk. 5:39, he saith, the *o.* is better.
2Cor. 5:17, *o.* things are passed away.
2Pet. 2:5, God spared not the *o.* world.
1Jn. 2:7, the *o.* commandment is the word.
Rev. 12:9; 20:2, that *o.* serpent.
See Job 22:15; Ps. 77:5; Mt. 5:21; Rom. 7:6.
OMITTED. Mt. 23:23.
ONCE. Gen. 18:32, yet but this *o.*
Num. 13:30, let us go up at *o.*
Job 33:14; Ps. 62:11, speaketh *o.*, yea twice.
Isa. 66:8, shall a nation be born at *o.*?
Heb. 6:4, *o.* enlightened.
9:27, *o.* to die.
See Rom. 6:10; Heb. 10:10; 1Pet. 3:18.
ONE. Job 9:3, *o.* of a thousand.
Eccl. 7:27; Isa. 27:12, *o.* by *o.*
Mk. 10:21; LU. 18:22, *o.* thing thou lackest.
Lk. 10:42, *o.* thing is needful.
Jn. 9:25, *o.* thing I know.
17:11, 21, 22, that they may be *o.*
Gal. 3:28, all *o.* in Christ.
Eph. 4:5, *o.* Lord, *o.* faith, *o.* baptism.
See Dt. 6:4; Mk. 12:32; 1Tim. 2:5.
ONYX. Ex. 28:20; 39:13, and an *o.*
OPEN. Num. 16:30, if the earth *o.* her mouth.
Ps. 49:4, I will *o.* my dark saying.
51:15, *o.* thou my lips.
81:10, *o.* thy mouth wide.
104:28; 145:16, thou *o.* thine hand.
119:18, *o.* thou mine eyes.
Prov. 31:8, *o.* thy mouth for the dumb.
Isa. 22:22, he shall *o.*, and none shall shut.
42:7, to *o.* the blind eyes.
60:11, thy gates shall be *o.* continually.
Ezek. 16:63, never *o.* thy mouth.
Mal. 3:10, *o.* windows of heaven.
Mt. 25:11; Lk. 13:25, Lord *o.* to us.
27:52, graves were *o.*
Mk. 7:34, that is, be *o.*
Lk. 24:32, while he *o.* to us the scriptures.
45, then *o.* he their understanding.
Acts 26:18, to *o.* their eyes, and turn them.
1Cor. 16:9, great door and effectual is *o.*
Col. 4:3, *o.* to us a door of utterance.
See Acts 16:14; 2Cor. 2:12; Heb. 4:13; Re. 5:2.
OPERATION. Ps. 28:5; Isa. 5:12; 1Cor. 12:6; Col. 2:12.
OPINION. 1Ki. 18:21; Job 32:6.
OPPORTUNITY. Gal. 6:10; Phil. 4:10; Heb. 11:15.
OPPOSE. Job 30:21; 2Th. 2:4; 2Tim. 2:25.
OPPOSITIONS. 1Tim. 6:20.
OPPRESS. Ex. 22:21; 23:9, *o.* a stranger.
Lev. 25:14, 17, ye shall not *o.* one another.
1Sam. 12:3, whom have I *o.*?
Ps. 10:18, that the man of earth may no more *o.*
Prov. 14:31; 22:16, he that *o.* the poor.
28:3, a poor man that *o.* the poor.
Jer. 7:6, if ye *o.* not the stranger.
Hos. 12:7, he loveth to *o.*
Zech. 7:10, *o.* not the widow.
See Mal. 3:5; Acts 7:24; 10:38; Jas. 2:6.
OPPRESSION. Dt. 26:7, the Lord looked on our *o.*
Ps. 62:10, trust not in *o.*
119:134, deliver me from the *o.* of man.
Eccl. 4:1, I considered the *o.*
7:7, *o.* maketh a wise man mad.
Isa. 30:12, ye trust in *o.*
See Isa. 33:15; Zech. 9:8; 10:4.
ORATOR. Isa. 3:3; Acts 24:1.
ORDAIN. 1Chr. 17:9, I will *o.* a place for my people
Ps. 8:2, hast thou *o.* strength.
81:5, this he *o.* in Joseph.
132:17, I have *o.* a lamp for mine anointed.
Isa. 26:12, thou wilt *o.* peace for us.
30:33, Tophet is *o.* of old.
Jer. 1:5, I *o.* thee a prophet.
Mk. 3:14, Jesus *o.* twelve.
Jn. 15:16, have *o.* you, that ye should bring fort
Acts 1:22, one be *o.* to be a witness.
10:42, *o.* of God to be the Judge.
13:48, *o.* to eternal life.
14:23; Ti. 1:5, *o.* elders.
16:4, decrees that were *o.*
17:31, by that man whom he hath *o.*
Rom. 13:1, the powers that be are *o.* of God.
Gal. 3:19, the law was *o.* by angels.
Eph. 2:10, good works which God hath before *o.*
Jude 4, of old *o.* to this condemnation.
See 1Cor. 2:7; 9:14; 1Tim. 2:7; Heb. 5:1.
ORDER. Jud. 13:12, how shall we *o.* the child?
2Ki. 20:1; Isa. 38:1, set thine house in *o.*
Job 10:22, land without any *o.*
23:4, I would *o.* my cause.
37:19, we cannot *o.* our speech.
Ps. 40:5, they cannot be reckoned in *o.*
50:21, I will set them in *o.*
23, to him that *o.* his conversation aright.
110:4; Heb. 5:6; 6:20; 7:11, the *o.* of Melchisedec.
1Cor. 14:40, decently and in *o.*
Ti. 1:5, that thou shouldest set in *o.*
See Ps. 37:23; Acts 21:24; 1Cor. 15:23.
ORDINANCE. Isa. 58:2; Rom. 13:2, the *o.* of their God.
Mal. 3:14, what profit that we have kept *o.*?
Eph. 2:15, commandments contained in *o.*
Col. 2:14, handwriting of *o.*
Heb. 9:10, in carnal *o.*

See Jer. 31:36; Luke 1:6; 1Pet. 2:13.
RPHANS. Lam. 5:3.
STRICH. Job 39:13, or wings and feathers unto the *o*.
Lam. 4:3, like the *o*. in the wilderness.
UGHT. 1Chr. 12:32, to know what Israel *o*. to do.
Mt. 23:23; Lk. 11:42, these *o*. ye to have done.
Lk. 24:26, *o*. not Christ to have suffered?
Jn. 4:20, the place where men *o*. to worship.
Acts 5:29, we *o*. to obey God.
Rom. 8:26, what we should pray for as we *o*.
Heb. 5:12, when ye *o*. to be teachers.
Jas. 3:10, these things *o*. not so to be.
Pet. 3:11, what manner of persons *o*. ye to be?
See Rom. 12:3; 15:1; 1Tim. 3:15.
URS. Mk. 12:7; Lk. 20:14; 1Cor. 1:2; 2Cor. 1:14.
UT. Num. 32:23, be sure your sin will find you *o*.
Ps. 82:5, are *o*. of course.
Prov. 4:23, *o*. of it are the issues of life.
Mt. 12:34; 15:19, *o*. of abundance of heart the mouth speaketh.
2Tim. 3:11, *o*. of them all the Lord delivered me.
4:2, instant in season, *o*. of season.
See Gen. 2:9, 23; 3:19; Jn. 15:19; Acts 2:5.
UTCAST. Ps. 147:2; Isa. 11:12; 27:13; Jer. 30:17.
UTGOINGS. Josh. 17:18; Ps. 65:8.
UTRAGEOUS. Prov. 27:4.
UTRUN. Jn. 20:4.
UTSIDE. Jud. 7:11; Mt. 23:25; Lk. 11:39.
UTSTRETCHED. Dt. 26:8; Jer. 21:5; 27:5.
UTWARD. 1Sam. 16:7, looketh on *o*. appearance.
Mt. 23:27, appear beautiful *o*.
Rom. 2:28, not a Jew, which is one *o*.
2Cor. 4:16, though our *o*. man perish.
See Mt. 23:28; Rom. 2:28; 1Pet. 3:3.
VERCHARGE. Lk. 21:34; 2Cor. 2:5.
VERCOME. Gen. 49:19, he shall *o*. at last.
Jer. 23:9, like a man whom wine hath *o*.
Jn. 16:33, I have *o*. the world.
Rom. 12:21, be not *o*. of evil, but *o*. evil.
1Jn. 5:4, 5, victory that *o*. the world.
Rev. 2:7, 17, 26; 3:12, 21, to him that *o*.
See Song 6:5; 2Pet. 2:19; Rev. 12:11.
VERMUCH. Eccl. 7:16; 2Cor. 2:7.
VERPAST. Ps. 57:1; Isa. 26:20.
VERPLUS. Lev. 25:27.
VERSEER. Gen. 41:34; Prov. 6:7; Acts 20:28.
VERSHADOW. Mt. 17:5; Mk. 9:7; Lk. 1:35; Acts 5:15.
VERSIGHT. Gen. 43:12; Neh. 11:16; 1Pet. 5:2.
VERSPREAD. Gen. 9:19; Dan. 9:27.
VERTAKE. Amos 9:13, plowman shall *o*. the reaper.
Gal. 6:1, if a man be *o*. in a fault.
1Th. 5:4, day should *o*. you as a thief.
See Dt. 19:6; Isa. 59:9; Jer. 42:16.
VERTHROW. Ex. 23:24, utterly *o*. them.
Job. 19:6, God hath *o*. me.
Ps. 14:4, purposed to *o*. my goings.
Prov. 13:6, wickedness *o*. the sinner.
Jon. 3:4, yet forty days, and Nineveh shall be *o*.
Acts 5:39, if it be of God, ye cannot *o*. it.
See Gen. 19:21; Prov. 29:4; 2Tim. 2:18.
OVERTURN. Job 9:5; 12:15; 28:9; Ezek. 21:27.
OVERWHELM. Job 6:27, ye *o*. the fatherless.
Ps. 61:2, when my heart is *o*.
77:3; 142:3; 143:4, my spirit was *o*.
See Ps. 55:5; 78:53; 124:4.
OVERWISE. Eccl. 7:16.
OWE. Lk. 16:5, 7, how much *o*. thou?
Rom. 13:8, *o*. no man any thing.
See Mt. 18:24, 28; Lk. 7:41; Phile. 18.
OWN. Num. 32:42, called it after his *o*. name.
1Chr. 29:14, of thine *o*. have we given thee.
Ps. 12:4, our lips are our *o*.
Ps. 67:6, even our *o*. God shall bless us.
Mt. 20:15, do what I will with mine *o*.
Jn. 1:11, to his *o*., and his *o*. received him not.
13:1, having loved his *o*.
1Cor. 6:19, ye are not your *o*.
See Acts 5:4; Phil. 3:9; 1Tim. 5:8; Rev. 1:5.
OWNER. Ex. 21:28; 22:11; Eccl. 5:13; Isa. 1:3.
PACIFY. Prov. 16:14; 21:14; Eccl. 10:4; Ezek. 16:63.
PAIN. Ps. 55:4, my heart is sore *p*.
116:3, the *p*. of hell gat hold upon me.
Acts 2:24, having loosed the *p*. of death.
Rom. 8:22, creation travaileth in *p*.
Rev. 21:4, neither shall there be any more *p*.
See Ps. 73:16; Jer. 4:19; 2Cor. 11:27.
PAINTED. 2Ki. 9:30; Jer. 4:30; 22:14; Ezek. 23:40.
PALACE. Ps. 48:13, consider her *p*.
122:7, prosperity within thy *p*.
144:12, the similitude of a *p*.
Jer. 9:21, death is entered into our *p*.
Lk. 11:21, a strong man keepeth his *p*.
Phil. 1:13, manifest in all the *p*.
See 1Chr. 29:1; Neh. 1:1; 2:8; Isa. 25:2.
PALE. Isa. 29:22; Jer. 30:6; Rev. 6:8.
PALM. Isa. 49:16; Mt. 26:67; Mk. 14:65; Rev. 7:9.
PANT. Ps. 38:10; 42:1; 119:131; Amos 2:7.
PARCHMENTS. 2Tim. 4:13, but especially the *p*.
PARDON. Ex. 23:21, he will not *p*.
2Ki. 5:18, the Lord *p*. thy servant.
2Chr. 30:18, the good Lord *p*. every one.
Neh. 9:17, a God ready to *p*.
Isa. 55:7, he will abundantly *p*.
See Jer. 33:8; 50:20; Lam. 3:42; Mic. 7:18.
PARENTS. Mt. 10:21; Mk. 13:12, children rise up against *p*.
Lk. 18:29, no man that hath left *p*.
21:16, ye shall be betrayed by *p*.
Jn. 9:2, who did sin, this man, or his *p*.?
Rom. 1:30; 2Tim. 3:2, disobedient to *p*.
2Cor. 12:14, not to lay up for *p*., but *p*. for children.
Eph. 6:1; Col. 3:20, children, obey your *p*.
See Lk. 2:27; 8:56; 1Tim. 5:4; Heb. 11:23.
PART (*n*.). Josh. 22:25, 27, ye have no *p*. in the Lord.
Ps. 5:9, their inward *p*. is very wickedness.
51:6, in hidden *p*. make me to know.
118:7, the Lord taketh my *p*.
Ps. 139:9, dwell in the uttermost *p*.
Mk. 9:40, he that is not against us is on our *p*.
Lk. 10:42, that good *p*.
Jn. 13:8, thou hast no *p*. with me.
Acts 8:21, neither *p*. nor lot.

2Cor. 6:15, what *p.* hath he that believeth?
See Ti. 2:8; Rev. 20:6; 21:8; 22:19.
PART (*v.*). Ruth 1:17, if ought but death *p.* thee and me.
2Sam. 14:6, there was none to *p.* them.
Ps. 22:18, they *p.* my garments.
Lk. 24:51, while he blessed them he was *p.*
Acts 2:45, *p.* them to all men.
See Mt. 27:35; Mk. 15:24; Lk. 23:34; Jn. 19:24.
PARTAKE. Ps. 50:18, hast been *p.* with adulterers.
Rom. 15:27, *p.* of their spiritual things.
1Cor. 9:10, *p.* of his hope.
13; 10:18, *p.* with the altar.
10:17, *p.* of that one bread.
21, *p.* of the Lord's table.
1Tim. 5:22, neither be *p.* of other men's sins.
Heb. 3:1, *p.* of the heavenly calling.
1Pet. 4:13, *p.* of Christ's sufferings.
5:1, a *p.* of the glory.
2Pet. 1:4, *p.* of the divine nature.
See Eph. 3:6; Phil. 1:7; Col. 1:12; Rev. 18:4.
PARTIAL. Mal. 2:9; 1Tim. 5:21; Jas. 2:4; 3:17.
PARTICULAR. 1Cor. 12:27; Eph. 5:33.
PARTITION. 1Ki. 6:21; Eph. 2:14.
PARTNER. Prov. 29:24; Lk. 5:7; 2Cor. 8:23.
PASS. Ex. 12:13, when I see the blood I will *p.* over.
Isa. 43:2, when thou *p.* through waters.
Mt. 26:39; Mk. 14:36, let this cup *p.*
Lk. 16:26, neither can they *p.* to us.
1Cor. 7:31; 1Jn. 2:17, fashion of this world *p.*
Eph. 3:19, love of Christ, which *p.* knowledge.
Phil. 4:7, which *p.* all understanding.
See Jer. 2:6; LU. 18:37; Rom. 5:12; Rev. 21:1.
PASSION. Acts 1:3; 14:15; Jas. 5:17.
PAST. Job 29:2, as in months *p.*
Eccl. 3:15, God requireth that which is *p.*
Song 2:11, the winter is *p.*
Jer. 8:20, the harvest is *p.*
Rom. 3:25, of sins that are *p.*
11:33, ways *p.* finding out.
2Cor. 5:17, old things *p.* away.
Eph. 4:19, being *p.* feeling.
See Eph. 2:2; 2Tim. 2:18; 1Pet. 2:10.
PASTOR. Jer. 3:15; 17:16; 23:1; Eph. 4:11.
PASTURE. Ps. 95:7; 100:3; Ezek. 34:14; Jn. 10:9.
PATE. Ps. 7:16.
PATH. Job 28:7, there is a *p.* which no fowl knoweth.
Ps. 16:11, show me the *p.* of life.
27:11, lead me in a plain *p.*
65:11, thy *p.* drop fatness.
77:19, thy *p.* is in the great waters.
119:105, a light to my *p.*
Prov. 4:18, the *p.* of the just.
Isa. 2:3; Mic. 4:2, we will walk in his *p.*
42:16, in *p.* they have not known.
58:12, restorer of *p.* to dwell in.
Jer. 6:16, ask for the old *p.*
Mt. 3:3; Mk. 1:3; Lk. 3:4, make his *p.* straight.
See Ps. 139:3; Prov. 3:17; Lam. 3:9; Heb. 12:13.
PATIENCE. Mt. 18:26, 29, have *p.* with me.
Lk. 8:15, bring forth fruit with *p.*
21:19, in your *p.* possess ye your souls.
Rom. 5:3, tribulation worketh *p.*
8:25, with *p.* wait for it.
15:4, through *p.* and comfort.
5, the God of *p.*
2Cor. 6:4, as ministers of God in much *p.*
Col. 1:11, strengthened with all might to all *p.*
1Th. 1:3, your *p.* of hope.
2Th. 1:4, glory in you for your *p.*
1Tim. 6:11, follow after *p.*
Ti. 2:2, sound in faith, charity, *p.*
Heb. 10:36, ye have need of *p.*
Heb. 12:1, run with *p.*
Jas. 1:3, trying of your faith worketh *p.*
1:4, let *p.* have her perfect work.
5:7, the husbandman hath long *p.*
10, for an example of *p.*
11, ye have heard of the *p.* of Job.
2Pet. 1:6, add to temperance *p.*
Rev. 2:2, 19, I know thy *p.*
3:10, thou hast kept word of *p.*
13:10; 14:12, here is the *p.* of saints.
See Eccl. 7:8; Rom. 12:12; 1Th. 5:14.
PATIENTLY. Ps. 37:7; 40:1; Heb. 6:15; 1Pet. 2:20.
PATTERN. 1Tim. 1:16; Ti. 2:7; Heb. 8:5; 9:23.
PAVILION. 2Sam. 22:12, and he made darkness *p.*
See Ps. 18:11; 27:5; 31:20; Jer. 43:10.
PAY. Ex. 22:7, let him *p.* double.
Num. 20:19, water, I will *p.* for it.
2Ki. 4:7, sell the oil, and *p.* thy debt.
Ps. 22:25; 66:13; 116:14, will *p.* my vows.
Prov. 22:27, if thou hast nothing to *p.*
Eccl. 5:4, defer not to *p.* it.
Mt. 18:26, I will *p.* thee all.
18:28, *p.* that thou owest.
23:23, ye *p.* tithe of mint.
See Ex. 21:19; Mt. 17:24; Rom. 13:6; Heb. 7:9.
PEACE. Gen. 41:16, an answer of *p.*
Num. 6:26, the Lord give thee *p.*
25:12, my covenant of *p.*
Dt. 20:10, proclaim *p.* to it.
23:6, thou shalt not seek their *p.*
1Sam. 25:6; Lk. 10:5, *p.* be to this house.
2Ki. 9:19, what hast thou to do with *p.*?
31, had Zimri *p.*, who slew his master?
Job 5:23, beasts shall be at *p.* with thee.
22:21, acquaint thyself with him, and be at *p.*
Ps. 4:8, I will lay me down in *p.*
29:11, the Lord will bless his people with *p.*
34:14; 1Pet. 3:11, seek *p.*, and pursue it.
37:37, the end of that man is *p.*
85:8, will speak *p.* to his people.
122:6, pray for *p.* of Jerusalem.
Eccl. 3:8, a time of *p.*
Isa. 26:3, keep him in perfect *p.*
32:17, work of righteousness shall be *p.*
45:7, I make *p.*, and create evil.
48:18, thy *p.* as a river.
22; 57:21, no *p.* to the wicked.
52:7; Nah. 1:15, that publisheth *p.*
59:8; Rom. 3:17, the way of *p.* they know not
Jer. 6:14; 8:11, saying *p.*, *p.*, when there is no *p.*
8:15; 14:19, we looked for *p.*
34:5, thou shalt die in *p.*
Ezek. 7:25, they shall seek *p.*

Dan. 4:1; 6:25; 1Pet. 1:2; 2Pet. 1:2; Jude 2, *p*. be multiplied.
Hag. 2:9, in this place will I give *p*.
Mt. 10:13, let your *p*. come upon it.
34; Lk. 12:51, to send *p*. on earth.
Mk. 9:50, have *p*. one with another.
Lk. 1:79, to guide our feet into way of *p*.
2:14, on earth *p*.
19:42, things which belong to thy *p*.
Jn. 14:27, *p*. I leave, my *p*. I give you.
16:33, that in me ye might have *p*.
Rom. 1:7; 1Cor. 1:3; 2Cor. 1:2; Gal. 1:3; Eph. 1:2; Phil. 1:2, *p*. from God our Father.
5:1, we have *p*. with God.
10:15; Eph. 6:15, the gospel of *p*.
14:19, follow after the things which make for *p*.
15:33; 16:20; 2Cor. 13:11; Phil. 4:9; 1Th. 5:23; Heb. 13:20, the God of *p*.
1Cor. 14:33, author of *p*.
2Cor. 13:11, live in *p*.
Eph. 2:14, he is our *p*.
17, *p*. to you which were afar off.
4:3, in the bond of *p*.
Phil. 4:7, *p*. of God which passeth all understanding.
Col. 1:2; 1Th. 1:1; 2Th. 1:2; 1Tim. 1:2; 2Tim. 1:2; Ti. 1:4; Phile. 3; 2Jn. 3, grace and *p*. from God.
3:15, let the *p*. of God rule in your hearts.
1Th. 5:13, be at *p*. among yourselves.
2Th. 3:16, Lord of *p*. give you *p*. always.
2Tim. 2:22; Heb. 12:14, follow *p*. with all men.
Heb. 7:2, king of *p*.
Jas. 2:16, depart in *p*.
3:18, fruit of righteousness is sown in *p*.
3:18, fruit of righteousness is sown in *p*.
2Pet. 3:14, found of him in *p*.
See Mt. 5:9; Lk. 24:36; Jn. 20:19; Gal. 6:16.
EACEABLE. Isa. 32:18; 1Tim. 2:2; Heb. 12:11; Jas. 3:17.
EACEABLY. Gen. 37:4; 1Sam. 16:4; Jer. 9:8; Rom. 12:18.
EACOCKS. 2Chr. 9:21, the ships of Tarshish bringing *p*.
Job. 39:13, gavest thou the goodly wings until the *p*.
EELED. Isa. 18:2; Ezek. 29:18.
EEP. Isa. 8:19; 10:14.
ELICAN. Lev. 11:18, and the swan, and the *p*.
Dt. 14:17, the *p*., and the gier eagle.
Ps. 102:6, I am like a *p*. of the wilderness.
EN. Jud. 5:14, they that handle the *p*.
Job 19:24, graven with an iron *p*.
Ps. 45:1, my tongue is the *p*. of a ready writer.
Isa. 8:1, write in it with a man's *p*.
Jer. 8:8, the *p*. of the scribes is in vain.
17:1, is written with a *p*. of iron.
3Jn. 13, I will not with ink and *p*. write.
ENCE. Mt. 18:28; Mk. 14:5; Lk. 7:41; 10:35.
ENNY. Mt. 20:13, didst not thou agree with me for a *p*.?
22:19, they brought him a *p*.
Mk. 12:15, bring me a *p*.
Rev. 6:6, a measure of wheat for a *p*.
PENURY. Prov. 14:23; Lk. 21:4.
PEOPLE. Ex. 6:7; Dt. 4:20; 2Sam. 7:24; Jer. 13:11, I will take you to me for a *p*.
Lev. 20:24, 26, separated from other *p*.
Dt. 4:3, did ever *p*. hear voice of God and live?
33:29, O *p*. saved by the Lord.
2Sam. 22:44; Ps. 18:43, a *p*. I knew not.
Ps. 81:11, my *p*. would not hearken.
144:15, happy is that *p*.
Prov. 30:25, the ants are a *p*. not strong.
Isa. 1:4, a *p*. laden with iniquity.
27:11, a *p*. of no understanding.
43:4, I will give *p*. for thy life.
8, blind *p*. that have eyes.
Jer. 6:22; 50:41, a *p*. cometh from the north.
Jon. 1:8, of what *p*. art thou?
Lk. 1:17, a *p*. prepared for the Lord.
Ti. 2:14, purify unto himself a peculiar *p*.
See Mt. 1:21; Rom. 11:2; Heb. 11:25.
PERCEIVE. Dt. 29:4, a heart to *p*.
Josh. 22:31, we *p*. the Lord is among us.
Job 9:11, I *p*. him not.
23:8, I cannot *p*. him.
Isa. 6:9, see indeed, but *p*. not.
33:19, deeper speech than thou canst *p*.
64:4, nor *p*. by the ear what God hath.
Mt. 22:18, Jesus *p*. their wickedness.
Mk. 8:17, *p*. ye not yet?
Lk. 8:46, I *p* that virtue is gone out.
Jn. 4:19, I *p*. thou art a prophet.
Acts 10:34, I *p*. God is no respecter of persons.
1Jn. 3:16, hereby *p*. we the love of God.
See 1Sam. 3:8; Neh. 6:12; Job 33:14; Mk. 12:28.
PERFECT. Gen. 6:9, Noah was *p*.
17:1, walk before me, and be thou *p*.
Dt. 18:13, thou shalt be *p*. with the Lord.
32:4, his work is *p*.
2Sam. 22:31; Ps. 18:30, his way is *p*.
Ps. 19:7, law of the Lord is *p*.
37:37, mark the *p*. man.
Prov. 4:18, more and more to *p*. day.
Ezek. 28:15, thou wast *p*. in thy ways.
Mt. 5:48; 2Cor. 13:11, be ye *p*.
19:21, if thou wilt be *p*.
Jn. 17:23, be made *p*. in one.
Rom. 12:2, that *p*. will of God.
1Cor. 2:6, wisdom among them that are *p*.
2Cor. 12:9, strength made *p*. in weakness.
Eph. 4:13, unto a *p*. man.
Phil. 3:12, not as though I were already *p*.
15, let us, as many as be *p*.
Col. 1:28, present every man *p*.
4:12, may stand *p*. and complete.
2Tim. 3:17, that the man of God may be *p*.
Heb. 2:10, make *p*. through suffering.
11:40, without us should not be made *p*.
12:23, spirits of just men made *p*.
13:21, make you *p*. in every good work.
Jas. 1:4, patience have her *p*. work.
17, every good and *p*. gift.
25, *p*. law of liberty.

3:2, the same is a *p.* man.
1Jn. 4:18, *p.* love casteth out fear.
See 2Chr. 8:16; Lk. 6:40; 2Cor. 7:1; Eph. 4:12.
PERFECTION. Job 11:7; Ps. 119:96; 2Cor. 13:9; Heb. 6:1.
PERFECTLY. Jer. 23:20; Acts 18:26; 1Cor. 1:10.
PERFECTNESS. Col. 3:14.
PERFORM. Ex. 18:18, not able to *p.* it thyself alone.
Est. 5:6; 7:2, to half of kingdom it shall be *p.*
Job 5:12, cannot *p.* their enterprise.
Ps. 65:1, unto thee shall the vow be *p.*
119:106, I have sworn, and I will *p.* it.
Isa. 9:7, zeal of the Lord will *p.* this.
44:28, shall *p.* all my pleasure.
Jer. 29:10; 33:14, I will *p.* my good word.
Rom. 4:21, able also to *p.*
7:18, how to *p.* that which is good I find not.
Phil. 1:6, *p.* it until day of Christ.
See. Job 23:14; Ps. 57:2; Jer. 35:14; Mt. 5:33.
PERFORMANCE. Lk. 1:45; 2Cor. 8:11.
PERIL. Lam. 5:9; Rom. 8:35; 2Cor. 11:26.
PERILOUS. 2Tim. 3:1.
PERISH. Num. 17:12, we die, we *p.*, we all *p.*
Dt. 26:5, a Syrian ready to *p.*
Job 4:7, who ever *p.*, being innocent?
29:13, blessing of him that was ready to *p.*
34:15, all flesh shall *p.* together.
Ps. 1:6, way of ungodly shall *p.*
37:20, the wicked shall *p.*
49:12, like the beasts that *p.*
80:16, they *p.* at rebuke of thy countenance.
102:26, they shall *p.*, but thou shalt endure.
Prov. 11:10; 28:28, when the wicked *p.*
29:18, no vision, the people *p.*
31:6, strong drink to him that is ready to *p.*
Isa. 27:13, they shall come that were ready to *p.*
Jer. 7:28, truth is *p.*
Jon. 1:6; 3:9, God will think on us, that we *p.* not.
14, let us not *p.* for this man's life.
Mt. 8:25; Lk. 8:24, save us, we *p.*
18:14, that one of these little ones should *p.*
26:52, shall *p.* with the sword.
Mk. 4:38, carest thou not that we *p.*?
Lk. 13:3, 5, ye shall all likewise *p.*
15:17, I *p.* with hunger.
21:18, there shall not an hair of your head *p.*
Jn. 6:27, labour not for the meat which *p.*
Acts 8:20, thy money *p.* with thee.
Col. 2:22, which are to *p.* with the using.
2Pet. 3:9, not willing that any should *p.*
See Ps. 2:12; Jer. 6:21; Jn. 10:28; Rom. 2:12.
PERMISSION. 1Cor. 7:6.
PERMIT. 1Cor. 14:34; 16:7; Heb. 6:3.
PERNICIOUS. 2Pet. 2:2.
PERPETUAL. Ex. 31:16, sabbath for a *p.* covenant.
Lev. 25:34, their *p.* possession.
Ps. 9:6, destructions are come to a *p.* end.
74:3; Jer. 25:9; Ezek. 35:9, the *p.* desolations.
Jer. 8:5, a *p.* backsliding.
15:18, why is my pain *p.*?
Hab. 3:6, the *p.* hills.
See Gen. 9:12; Jer. 5:22; 50:5; 51:39; Ezek. 46:14.
PERPETUALLY. 1Ki. 9:3; 2Chr. 7:16; Amos 1:11.
PERPLEXED. Lk. 9:7; 24:4; 2Cor. 4:8.
PERPLEXITY. Isa. 22:5; Mic. 7:4; Lk. 21:25.
PERSECUTE. Job 19:22, why do ye *p.* me?
Ps. 7:1, save me from them that *p.* me.
10:2, the wicked doth *p.* the poor.
71:11, *p.* and take him, there is none to deliver.
143:3, the enemy hath *p.* my soul.
Mt. 5:11, 12, blessed are ye when men *p.* you.
44, pray for them that *p.* you.
Jn. 15:20, if they have *p.* me.
Acts 9:4; 22:7; 26:14, why *p.* thou me?
22:4, I *p.* this way unto death.
26:11, I *p.* them even to strange cities.
1Cor. 4:12, being *p.*, we suffer it.
15:9; Gal. 1:13, I *p.* the church of God.
2Cor. 4:9, *p.* but not forsaken.
Phil. 3:6, concerning zeal, *p.* the church.
See Jn. 5:16; Acts 7:52; Rom. 12:14; Gal. 1:23; 4:29.
PERSECUTION. Mt. 13:21; Mk. 4:17, when *p.* ariseth.
2Cor. 12:10, take pleasure in *p.*
2Tim. 3:12, all that will live godly shall suffer *p.*
See Lam. 5:5; Acts 8;1; Gal. 6:12; 1Tim. 1:13.
PERSEVERANCE. Eph. 6:18.
PERSON. Dt. 10:17; 2Sam. 14:14, God, which regardeth not *p.*
2Sam. 17:11, go to battle in thine own *p.*
Ps. 15:4; Isa. 32:5, 6, vile *p.*
26:4; Prov. 12:11; 28:19, with vain *p.*
105:37, not one feeble *p.*
Mt. 22:16; Mk. 12:14, regardest not *p.* of men.
2Cor. 2:10, forgave I it in the *p.* of Christ.
Heb. 1:3, the express image of his *p.*
2Pet. 3:11, what manner of *p.* ought ye to be?
See Mal. 1:8; Lk. 15:7; Heb. 12:16; Jude 16.
PERSUADE. 1Ki. 22:20, who shall *p.* Ahab?
Prov. 25:15, by long forbearing is a prince *p.*
Mt. 28:14, we will *p.* him, and secure you.
Acts 26:28, almost thou *p.* me.
Rom. 14:5, let every man be fully *p.*
2Cor. 5:11, we *p.* men.
Gal. 1:10, do I now *p.* men or God?
Heb. 6:9, we are *p.* better things of you.
See 2Ki. 18:32; 2Chr. 18:2; 2Tim. 1:12.
PERTAIN. Rom. 15:17; 1Cor. 6:3; 2Pet. 1:3.
PERVERSE. Dt. 32:5, a *p.* and crooked generation.
Job 6:30, cannot my taste discern *p.* things?
Prov. 4:24, *p.* lips put far from thee.
12:8, *p.* heart shall be despised.
17:20, *p.* tongue falleth into mischief.
23:33, thine heart shall utter *p.* things.
Phil. 2:15, in the midst of a *p.* nation.
See Num. 23:21; Isa. 30:12; 1Tim. 6:5.
PERVERT. Dt. 16:19, a gift doth *p.* words.
Job 8:3, doth God *p.* judgment?
Prov. 10:9, he that *p.* his ways shall be known.
19:3, the foolishness of man *p.* his way.
Jer. 3:21, they have *p.* their way.
23:36, ye have *p.* the words of God.
Acts 13:10, wilt thou not cease to *p.* right ways?
Gal. 1:7, would *p.* the gospel.

See Eccl. 5:8; Mic. 3:9; Lk. 23:2.
ESTILENCE. Ex. 5:3; 9:15; Jer. 42:17; 44:13.
ESTILENT. Acts 24:5.
ETITION. 1Sam. 1:17, God of Israel grant thee thy *p*.
1Ki. 2:20, one small *p*.
Est. 5:6; 7:2; 9:12, what is thy *p*.?
Dan. 6:7, whosoever shall ask a *p*.
13, maketh his *p*. three times a day.
See Est. 7:3; Ps. 20:5; 1Jn. 5:15.
HILOSOPHERS. Acts 17:18, then certain *p*. of the Epicureans.
HILOSOPHY. Col. 2:8.
HYLACTERIES. Mt. 23:5, they make broad their *p*.
See Ex. 13:9, 16; Num. 15:38.
HYSICIAN. Mt. 9:12; Mk. 2:17; Lk. 5:31, they that be whole need not a *p*.
Lk. 4:23, *p*., heal thyself.
See Jer. 8:22.
ICK. Prov. 30:17.
ICTURES. Num. 33:52; Prov. 25:11; Isa. 2:16.
IECE. 1Sam. 2:36; Prov. 6:26; 28:21, a *p*. of bread.
15:33, Samuel hewed Agag in *p*.
Ps. 7:2, rending in *p*. while none to deliver.
50:22, consider, lest I tear you in *p*.
Jer. 23:29, hammer that breaketh rock in *p*.
Amos 4:7, one *p*. was rained upon.
Zech. 11:12, weighed for my price thirty *p*.
13; Mt. 27:6, 9, took thirty *p*. of silver.
See Lk. 14:18; Acts 19:19; 23:10; 27:44.
IERCE. 2Ki. 18:21; Isa. 36:6, into his hand and *p*. it.
Zech. 12:10; Jn. 19:37, they shall look on me whom they have *p*.
1Tim. 6:10, *p*. themselves with many sorrows.
See Isa. 27:1; Lk. 2:35; Heb. 4:12; Rev. 1:7.
IETY. 1Tim. 5:4, let them learn first to show *p*. at home.
ILE. Isa. 30:33; Ezek. 24:9.
ILLAR. Gen. 19:26, a *p*. of salt.
Job 9:6; 26:11, the *p*. thereof tremble.
Prov. 9:1, she hath hewn out her seven *p*.
Gal. 2:9, Cephas and John, who seemed to be *p*.
1Tim. 3:15, the *p*. and ground of the truth.
Rev. 3:12, him that overcometh will I make a *p*.
See Isa. 19:19; Jer. 1:18; Joel 2:30; Lk. 17:32; Rev. 10:1.
ILLOW. Gen. 28:11; 1Sam. 19:13; Ezek. 13:18; Mk. 4:38.
ILOTS. Ezek. 27:8.
IN. Jud. 16:14; Ezek. 15:3.
INE. Lev. 26:39; Lam. 4:9; Isa. 38:12; Ezek. 24:23.
INE TREE. Isa. 41:19; 60:13, and the *p. t*.
IPE. Isa. 5:12, the harp and *p*. are in their feasts.
Mt. 11:17; Lk. 7:32, we have *p*. unto you.
1Cor. 14:7, how shall it be known what is *p*.?
Rev. 18:22, voice of *p*. shall be heard no more.
See 1Sam. 10:5; 1Ki. 1:40; Isa. 30:29.
IT. Gen. 37:20, cast him into some *p*.
Ex. 21:33, 34, if a man dig a *p*.
Num. 16:30, 33, go down quick into the *p*.
Job. 33:24, deliver him from going down to the *p*.
Ps. 28:1; 143:7, like them that go down into the *p*.
40:2, out of an horrible *p*.
Prov. 22:14; 23:27, a deep *p*.
28:10, shall fall into his own *p*.
Isa. 38:17, the *p*. of corruption.
Mt. 12:11; Lk. 14:5, fall into a *p*. on sabbath.
PITCHER. Gen. 24:14, let down thy *p*.
Jud. 7:16, lamps within the *p*.
Eccl. 12:6, or the *p*. be broken.
Lam. 4:2, esteemed as earthen *p*.
Mk. 14:13; Lk. 22:10, a man bearing a *p*. of water.
PITIFUL. Lam. 4:10; Jas. 5:11; 1Pet. 3:8.
PITY. Dt. 7:16; 13:8; 19:13, thine eye shall have no *p*.
2Sam. 12:6, because he had no *p*.
Job 19:21, have *p*. on me, my friends.
Ps. 69:20, I looked for some to take *p*.
Prov. 19:17, that hath *p*. on the poor lendeth.
28:8, gather for him that will *p*. the poor.
Isa. 13:18, they shall have no *p*. on fruit.
63:9, in his *p*. he redeemed them.
Jer. 13:14, I will not *p*. nor spare.
Ezek. 16:5, none eye *p*. thee.
24:21, I will profane what your soul *p*.
Joel 2:18, the Lord will *p*. his people.
Zech. 11:5, their own shepherds *p*. them not.
Mt. 18:33, as I had *p*. on thee.
See Ps. 103:13; Jer. 15:5; Lam. 2:2; Jon. 4:10.
PLACE. Ex. 3:5; Josh. 5:15, *p*. whereon thou standest is holy.
Jud. 18:10, a *p*. where there is no want.
2Ki. 5:11, strike his hand over the *p*.
6:1; Isa. 49:20, the *p*. is too strait for us.
Ps. 26:8, the *p*. where thine honour dwelleth.
32:7; 119:114, thou art my hiding *p*.
37:10, thou shalt diligently consider his *p*.
74:20, the dark *p*. of the earth.
90:1, our dwelling *p*.
Prov. 14:26, his children have a *p*. of refuge.
15:3, the eyes of the Lord in every *p*.
Eccl. 3:20, all go to one *p*.
Isa. 5:8, lay field to field, till there be on *p*.
60:13, the *p*. of my feet.
66:1, where is the *p*. of my rest?
Jer. 6:3, they shall feed every one in his *p*.
Mic. 1:3, the Lord cometh out of his *p*.
Zech. 10:10, *p*. shall not be found for them.
Mal. 1:11, in every *p*. incense shall be offered.
Mt. 28:6; Mk. 16:6, see the *p*. where the Lord lay.
Lk. 10:1, two and two into every *p*.
14:9, give this man *p*.
Jn. 8:37, my word hath no *p*. in you.
18:2, Judas knew the *p*.
Acts 2:1, with one accord in one *p*.
4:31, the *p*. was shaken.
Rom. 12:19, rather give *p*. to wrath.
Eph. 4:27, neither give *p*. to the devil.
Heb. 12:17, found no *p*. of repentance.
Rev. 20:11, there was found no *p*. for them.
See Ps. 16:6; Isa. 40:4; Eph. 1:3; 2:6; 3:10.
PLAGUE. Lev. 26:21, I will bring seven times

more *p*.
Dt. 28:59, will make thy *p*. wonderful.
29:22, when they see the *p*. of that land.
1Ki. 8:38, every man the *p*. of his own heart.
Ps. 73:5, nor are they *p*. like other men.
91:10, nor any *p*. come nigh thy dwelling.
Hos. 13:14, O death, I will be thy *p*.
Rev. 18:4, that ye receive not of her *p*.
22:18, shall add to him the *p*. written.
See Lev. 14:35; Num. 8:19; 16:46; Mk. 3:10.
PLAIN. Gen. 25:27, Jacob was a *p*. man.
Ps. 27:11, lead me in a *p*. path.
Prov. 8:9, they are *p*. to him t hat understandeth.
15:19, the way of the righteous is made *p*.
Isa. 40:4, rough places *p*.
Hab. 2:2, write the vision, make it *p*.
See Gen. 13:10; 19:17; Isa. 28:25; Mk. 7:35.
PLAINLY. Dt. 27:8, write the words very *p*.
Isa. 32:4, stammers shall speak *p*.
Jn. 10:24, tell us *p*.
16:25, I shall show you *p*. of the Father.
29, now speakest thou *p*.
See Ex. 21:5; Ezra 4:18; Jn. 11:14; 2Cor. 3:12.
PLAITING. 1Pet. 3:3.
PLANES. Isa. 44:13.
PLANT (*n*.). Job 14:9, bring forth boughs like a *p*.
Ps. 128:3, children like olive *p*.
144:12, sons as *p*. grown up.
Isa. 5:7; 17:10, his pleasant *p*.
16:8, broken down principal *p*.
53:2, as a tender *p*.
Ezek. 34:29, a *p*. of renown.
Mt. 15:13, every *p*. my Father hath not planted.
See Gen. 2:5; 1Chr. 4:23; Jer. 48:32.
PLANT (*v*.). Num. 24:6, as trees which the Lord hath *p*.
2Sam. 7:10; 1Chr. 17:9, I will *p*. them.
Ps. 1:3; Jer. 17:8, like a tree *p*.
80:15, the vineyard thy right hand hath *p*.
92:13, *p*. in the house of the Lord.
94:9, he that *p*. the ear.
Jer. 2:21, I had *p*. thee a noble vine.
Ezek. 17:10, being *p*. shall it prosper?
Lk. 17:6, be thou *p*. in the sea.
Rom. 6:5, if we have been *p*. together.
1Cor. 3:6, I have *p*.
See Mt. 21:33; Mk. 12:1; Lk. 20:9.
PLATE. Ex. 28:36; 39:30; Jer. 10:9.
PLATTED. Mt. 27:29; Mk. 15:17; Jn. 19:2.
PLATTER. Mt. 23:25; Lk. 11:39.
PLAY. Ex. 32:6; 1Cor. 10:7, people rose up to *p*.
1Sam. 16:17, a man that can *p*. well.
2Sam. 6:21, I will *p*. before the Lord.
10:12, let us *p*. the men.
Job 41:5, wilt thou *p*. with him?
Ps. 33:3, *p*. skilfully with a loud noise.
Isa. 11:8, the sucking child shall *p*.
Ezek. 33:32, can *p*. well on an instrument.
See 2Sam. 2:14; 1Chr. 15:29; Ps. 68:25; Zech. 8:5.
PLEA. Dt. 17:8.
PLEAD. Jud. 6:31, 32, will ye *p*. for Baal?
Job 9:19, who shall set me a time to *p*.?
13:19, who will *p*. with me?
16:21, that one might *p*. for a man.
23:6, will he *p*. against me with his great power?
Isa. 1:17, *p*. for the widow.
3:13, the Lord standeth up to *p*.
43:26, let us *p*. together.
59:4, none *p*. for truth.
Jer. 2:9, I will yet *p*. with you.
Lam. 3:58, thou hast *p*. the causes of my soul.
Joel 3:2, I will *p*. with them for my people.
See 1Sam. 25:39; Job 13:6; Isa. 66:16; Hos. 2:2.
PLEASANT. Gen. 3:6, *p*. to the eyes.
2Sam. 1:23, were *p*. in their lives.
26, very *p*. hast thou been to me.
Ps. 16:6, lines fallen in *p*. places.
106:24, they despised the *p*. land.
133:1, how *p*. for brethren to dwell together.
Prov. 2:10, knowledge is *p*. to thy soul.
15:26, the words of the pure are *p*. words.
16:24, *p*. words are as honeycomb.
Eccl. 11:7, it is *p*. to behold the sun.
Song 4:13, 16; 7:13, with *p*. fruits.
Isa. 64:11, our *p*. things are laid waste.
Jer. 31:20, is Ephraim a *p*. child?
Ezek. 33:32, of one that hath a *p*. voice.
Dan. 10:3, I ate no *p*. bread.
See Amos 5:11; Mic. 2:9; Nah. 2:9; Zech. 7:14.
PLEASANTNESS. Prov. 3:17.
PLEASE. 1Ki. 3:10, the speech *p*. the Lord.
Ps. 51:19, then shalt thou be *p*. with sacrifices.
115:3; 135:6; Jon. 1:14, he hath done whatsoever he *p*.
Prov. 16:7, when a man's ways *p*. the Lord.
Isa. 2:6, they *p*. themselves in children of strangers.
53:10, it *p*. the Lord to bruise him.
55:11, accomplish that which I *p*.
Mic. 6:7, will the Lord be *p*. with rams?
Mal. 1:8, offer it, will he be *p*. with thee?
Jn. 8:29, I do always those thongs that *p*. him.
Rom. 8:8, in the flesh cannot *p*. God.
15:1, to bear, and not to *p*. ourselves.
3, even Christ *p*. not himself.
1Cor. 1:21, it *p*. God by the foolishness of preaching.
10:33, as I *p*. men in all things.
Gal. 1:10, do I seek to *p*. men?
Eph. 6:6; Col. 3:22, as men-*p*.
Heb. 11:6, without faith it is impossible to *p*. God.
See 1Cor. 7:32; Col. 1:19; 1Th. 2:4; 1Jn. 3:22.
PLEASURE. 1Chr. 29:17, hast *p*. in uprightness.
Est. 1:8, do according to every man's *p*.
Job 21:21, what *p*. hath he in his house?
25, another never eateth with *p*.
22:3, is it any *p*. to the Almighty?
Ps. 16:11, *p*. *f*or evermore.
35:27, hath *p*. in the prosperity of his servants.
51:18, do good in thy good *p*.
102:14, thy servants take *p*. in her stones.
103:21, ye ministers of his that do his *p*.
111:2, of all them that hath *p*. therein.

147:11, taketh *p.* in them that fear him.
149:4, the Lord taketh *p.* in his people.
Prov. 21:17, he that loveth *p.* shall be poor.
Eccl. 5:4, he hath no *p.* in fools
12:1, I have no *p.* in them.
Isa. 44:28, Cyrus shall perform all my *p.*
53:10, the *p.* of the Lord shall prosper.
58:3, in the day of your fast ye find *p.*
13, doing thy *p.* on my holy day.
Jer. 22:28; 48:38; Hos. 8:8, a vessel wherein is no *p.*
Ezek. 18:23; 33:11, have I any *p.*?
Mal. 1:10, I have no *p.* in you, saith the Lord.
Lk. 8:14, choked with *p.* of this life.
12:32, Father's good *p.*
Eph. 1:5, the good *p.* of his will.
Phil. 2:13, to will and to do of his good *p.*
1Tim. 5:6, she that liveth in *p.*
2Tim. 3:4, lovers of *p.*
Heb. 10:38, my soul shall have no *p.* in him.
11:25, the *p.* of sin for a season.
12:10, chastened us after their own *p.*
Jas. 5:5, ye have lived in *p.* on earth.
Rev. 4:11, for thy *p.* they were created.
See Gen. 18:12; Ps. 5:4; Eccl. 2:1; Ti. 3:3; 2Pet. 2:13.

PLENTEOUS. Ps. 86:5; 103:8, *p.* in mercy.
130:7, *p.* redemption.
Hab. 1:16, portion fat and meat *p.*
Mt. 9:37, the harvest truly is *p.*
See Gen. 41:34; Dt. 28:11; 30:9; Prov. 21:5; Isa. 30:23.

PLENTIFUL. Ps. 31:23; 68:9; Jer. 2:7; 48:33; Lk. 12:16.

PLENTY. Gen. 27:28, *p.* of corn and wine.
Job 22:26, *p.* of silver.
37:23, *p.* of justice.
Prov. 3:10, barns filled with *p.*
See 2Chr. 31:10; Prov. 28:19; Jer. 44:17; Joel 2:26.

PLOW. Job 4:8 that *p.* iniquity shall reap.
Prov. 20:4, not *p.* by reason of cold.
21:4, the *p.* of the wicked is sin.
Isa. 2:4; Mic. 4:3, beat swords into *p.*-shares.
28:24, doth plowman *p.* all day to sow?
Joel 3:10, beat your *p.*-shares into swords.
Amos 9:13, the *p.*-man overtake the reaper.
See Dt. 22:10; 1Sam. 14:14; Job 1:14; 1Cor. 9:10.

PLUCK. Dt. 23:25, mayest *p.* the ears with thy hand.
2Chr. 7:20, then will I *p.* them up.
Job 24:9, they *p.* the fatherless from the breast.
Ps. 25:15, he shall *p.* my feet out of the net.
74:11, *p.* it out of thy bosom.
Prov. 14:1, foolish *p.* it down with her hands.
Eccl. 3:2, a time to *p.* up.
Isa. 50:6, my cheeks to them that *p.*
Jer. 22:24, yet I would *p.* thee thence.
Amos 4:11; Zech. 3:2, a firebrand *p.* out.
Mt. 5:29; 18:9; Mk. 9:47, offend thee, *p.* it out.
12:1; Mk. 2:23; Lk. 6:1, began to *p.* ears.
Jn. 10:28, nor shall any *p.* out of my hand.
See Gen. 8:11; Lk. 17:6; Gal. 4:15; Jude 12.

POINT. Jer. 17:1, written with the *p.* of a diamond.
Heb. 4:15, in all *p.* tempted.
Jas. 2:10, yet offend in one *p.*
See Gen. 25:32; Eccl. 5:16; Mk. 5:23; Jn. 4:47.

POLE. Num. 21:8.

POLICY. Dan. 8:25.

POLISHED. Ps. 144:12; Isa. 49:2; Lam. 4:7; Dan. 10:6.

POLL. 2Sam. 14:26; Ezek. 44:20; Mic. 1:16.

POMP. Isa. 5:14; 14:11; Ezek. 7:24; 30:18; Acts 25:23.

PONDER. Prov. 4:26, *p.* the path of thy feet.
5:6, lest thou shouldest *p.*
21, the Lord *p.* all his goings.
See Prov. 21:2; 24:12; Lk. 2:19.

POOL. Ps. 84:6; Isa. 35:7; 41:18; Jn. 5:2; 9:7.

POOR. Ex. 30:14, the *p.* shall not give less.
Dt. 15:11, the *p.* shall never cease.
2Ki. 24:14, none remained, save *p.* sort.
Job 24:4, the *p.* of the earth hide.
29:16, I was a father to the *p.*
Ps. 10:14, the *p.* committeth himself to thee.
34:6, this *p.* man cried.
40:17; 69:29; 70:5; 86:1; 109:22, I am *p.*
49:2, rich and *p.* together.
Prov. 10:4, becometh *p.* that dealeth with slack hand.
13:23, food in the tillage of the *p.*
18:23, the *p.* useth entreaties.
22:2, rich and *p.* meet together.
30:9, lest I be *p.* and steal.
Isa. 41:17, when *p.* and needy seek water.
Amos 2:6, they sold the *p.*
Zech. 11:7, 11, I will feed even you, O *p.* of the flock.
Mt. 5:3, blessed are the *p.* in spirit.
2Cor. 6:10, as *p.*, yet making many rich.
8:9, for your sakes he became *p.*
See Lev. 27:8; Jas. 2:2; Rev. 3:17; 13:16.

POPULOUS. Dt. 26:5; Nah. 3:8.

PORTION. Gen. 31:14, is there yet any *p.* for us?
48:22, one *p.* above thy brethren.
Dt. 32:9, the Lord's *p.* is his people.
2Ki. 2:9, a double *p.* of thy spirit.
Neh. 8:10; Est. 9:19, send *p.* to them.
Job 20:29, this is the *p.* of a wicked man.
24:18, their *p.* is cursed.
26:14; 27:13, how little a *p.* is heard of him?
31:2, what *p.* of God is there from above?
Ps. 11:6, this shall be the *p.* of their cup.
16:5, Lord is the *p.* of mine inheritance.
17:14, have their *p.* in this life.
73:26, God is my *p.*
119:57; 142:5, thou art my *p.*, O Lord.
Prov. 31:15, giveth a *p.* to her maidens.
Eccl. 2:10, this was my *p.* of all my labour.
3:22; 5:18; 9:9, rejoice, for that is his *p.*
5:19, God hath given power to take *p.*
9:6, nor have they any more *p.* for ever.
11:2, give a *p.* to seven.
Isa. 53:12, divide a *p.* with the great.
61:7, they shall rejoice in their *p.*
Jer. 10:16; 51:19, *p.* of Jacob not like them.
12:10, my pleasant *p.* a wilderness.

52:34, every day a *p*.
Dan. 1:8, with *p*. of king's meat.
Mic. 2:4, he hath changed the *p*. of my people.
Mt. 24:51, appoint him *p*. with hypocrites.
Lk. 12:42, their *p*. in due season.
46, his *p*. with unbelievers.
15:12, he *p*. of goods that falleth.
See Gen. 47:22; Josh. 17:14; Dan. 4:15; 11:26.
POSSESS. Gen. 22:17; 24:60, thy seed shall *p*. the gate.
Job 7:3, made to *p*. months of vanity.
13:26, *p*. iniquities of my youth.
Prov. 8:22, the Lord *p*. me in beginning.
Lk. 18:12, I give tithes of all I *p*.
21:19, in patience *p*. your souls.
See Lk. 12:15; Acts 4:32; 1Cor. 7:30; 2Cor. 6:10.
POSSESSION. Gen. 17:8; 48:4, an everlasting *p*.
Prov. 28:10, good things in *p*.
Eccl. 2:7; Mt. 19:22; Mk. 10:22, great *p*.
Acts 2:45, and sold their *p*.
Eph. 1:14, redemption of purchased *p*.
See Lev. 25:10; 27:16; 1Ki. 21:15.
POSSIBLE. Mt. 19:26; Mk. 10:27, with God all things are *p*.
24:24; Mk. 13:22, if *p*. deceive elect.
26:39; Mk. 14:35, 36, if *p*. let this cup.
Mk. 9:23, all things are *p*. to him that believeth.
14:36; Lk. 18:27, all things are *p*. to thee.
Rom. 12:18, if *p*. live peaceably.
See Acts 2:24; 20:16; Gal. 4:15; Heb. 10:4.
POST. Dt. 6:9; Job 9:25; Jer. 51:31; Amos 9:1.
POSTERITY. Gen. 45:7; Ps. 49:13; 109:13; Dan. 11:4.
POT. 2Ki. 4:2, not anything save a *p*. of oil.
40, there is death in the *p*.
Job 41:31, maketh the deep boil like a *p*.
Zech. 14:21, every *p*. shall be holiness.
Mk. 7:4, the washing of cups and *p*.
Jn. 2:6, six water-*p*.
See Ex. 16:33; Jer. 1:13; Jn. 4:28; Heb. 9:4.
POTENTATE. 1Tim. 6:15.
POUND. Lk. 19:13; Jn. 12:13.
POUR. Job 10:10, hast thou not *p*. me out as milk.
29:6, rock *p*. out rivers of oil.
30:16, my soul is *p*. out upon me.
Ps. 45:2, grace is *p*. into thy lips.
62:8, *p*. out your heart before him.
Prov. 1:23; Isa. 44:3; Joel 2:28, 29; Acts 2:17, 18, I will *p*. out my Spirit.
Song 1:3, as ointment *p*. forth.
Isa. 26:16, *p*. out prayer when chastening.
32:15, till the spirit be *p*. on us.
44:3, I will *p*. water on thirsty.
53:12, *p*. out his soul unto death.
Jer. 7:20; 42:18, my fury shall be *p*. out.
Lam. 2:19, *p*. out thine heart like water.
Nah. 1:6, fury is *p*. out like fire.
Mal. 3:10, if I will not *p*. out a blessing.
Mt. 26:7; Mk. 14:3, *p*. ointment on his head.
Jn. 2:15, he *p*. out the changers' money.
See 2Sam. 23:16; 2Ki. 3:11; Rev. 14:10; 16:1.
POURTRAY. Ezek. 4:1; 8:10; 23:14.
POVERTY. Gen. 45:11; Prov. 20:13, lest thou come to *p*.
Prov. 6:11; 24:34, thy *p*. come as one that travelleth.
10:15, destruction of poor is *p*.
11:24, it tendeth to *p*.
13:18, *p*. to him that refuseth instruction.
28:19, shall have *p*. enough.
30:8, give me neither *p*. nor riches.
31:7, drink and forget his *p*.
See Prov. 23:21; 2Cor. 8:2; Rev. 2:9.
POWDER. Ex. 32:20; 2Ki. 23:6; Mt. 21:44.
POWER. Gen. 32:28; Hos. 12:3, hast thou *p*. with God.
Ex. 15:6, glorious in *p*.
Lev. 26:19, the pride of your *p*.
Dt. 8:18, he giveth thee *p*. to get wealth.
2Sam. 22:33, God is my strength and *p*.
1Chr. 29:11; Mt. 6:13, thine is the *p*. and glory.
2Chr. 25:8, God hath *p*. to help.
Job 26:2, him that is without *p*.
Ps. 49:15, from the *p*. of the grave.
65:6, being girded with *p*.
90:11, who knoweth *p*. of thine anger.
Prov. 3:27, when it is in *p*. to do it.
18:21, in the *p*. of the tongue.
Eccl. 5:19; 6:2, *p*. to eat thereof.
8:4, where word of king is, there is *p*.
Isa. 40:29, he giveth *p*. to the faint.
Mic. 3:8, full of *p*. by the spirit.
Hab. 3:4, the hiding of his *p*.
Zech. 4:6, not by might, nor by *p*.
Mt. 9:6; Mk. 2:10; Lk. 5:24, *p*. on earth to forgive.
8, who had given such *p*. to men.
24:30; Lk. 21:27, coming in clouds with *p*.
28:18, all *p*. is given to me.
Lk. 1:35, the *p*. of the Highest.
4:6, all this *p*. will I give thee.
14, Jesus returned in the *p*. of the Spirit.
32, his word was with *p*.
5:17, the *p*. of the Lord was present.
9:43, amazed at the mighty *p*. of God.
12:5, that hath *p*. to cast into hell.
11, bring you unto magistrates and *p*.
22:53, your hour and the *p*. of darkness.
24:49, with *p*. from on high.
Jn. 1:12, *p*. to become sons of God.
10:18, I have *p*. to lay it down.
17:2, *p*. over all flesh.
19:10, I have *p*. to crucify thee.
Acts 1:8, *p*. after the Holy Ghost is come.
3:12, as though by our own *p*.
5:4, was it not in thine own *p*.
8:10, this man is the great *p*. of God.
19, give me also this *p*.
26:18, from the *p*. of Satan unto God.
Rom. 1:20, his eternal *p*. and Godhead.
9:17, that I might show my *p*. in thee.
13:2, whosoever resisteth the *p*.
1Cor. 15:43, it is raised in *p*.
Eph. 2:2, prince of the *p*. of the air.
3:7, the effectual working of his *p*.
Phil. 3:10, the *p*. of his resurrection.

2Th. 1:9, from the glory of his *p.*
2Tim. 1:7, spirit of *p.* and love.
3:5, form of godliness, but denying the *p.*
Heb. 2:14, him that had *p.* of death.
6:5, the *p.* of the world to come.
7:16, the *p.* of an endless life.
Rev. 2:26, to him will I give *p.*
4:11, worthy to receive *p.*
See Mt. 22:29; Lk. 22:69; Rom. 1:16.
OWERFUL. Ps. 29:4; 2Cor. 10:10; Heb. 4:12.
RAISE (*n.*). Ex. 15:11, fearful in *p.*
Dt. 10:21, he is thy *p.* and thy God.
Jud. 5:3; Ps. 7:17; 9:2; 57:7; 61:8; 104:33, I will sing *p.*
Neh. 9:5, above all blessing and *p.*
Ps. 22:3, that inhabitest the *p.* of Israel.
25, my *p.* shall be of thee.
33:1; 147:1, *p.* is comely for the upright.
34:1, his *p.* continually be in my mouth.
50:23, whoso offereth *p.* glorifieth me.
65:1, *p.* waiteth for thee.
66:2, make his *p.* glorious.
109:1, O God of my *p.*
148:14, the *p.* of all his saints.
Prov. 27:21, so is a man to his *p.*
Isa. 60:18, call thy gates *P.*
61:3, garment of *p.*
62:7, a *p.* in the earth.
Jer. 13:11, that they might be to me for a *p.*
49:25, how is the city of *p.*
Hab. 3:3, earth was full of his *p.*
Zeph. 3:30, a *p.* among all people.
Jn. 9:24, give God the *p.*
12:43, the *p.* of men.
Rom. 2:29, whose *p.* is not of men.
13:3, thou shalt have *p.*
1Cor. 4:5, every man have *p.* of God.
2Cor. 8:18, whose *p.* is in the gospel.
Eph. 1:6, 12, *p.* of glory of his grace.
Phil. 4:8, if there be any *p.*
Heb. 13:15, offer sacrifice of *p.*
1Pet. 2:14, *p.* of them that do well.
4:11, to whom be *p.* and dominion.
See 2Chr. 29:30; Acts 16:25; 1Pet. 2:9.
RAISE (*v.*). Gen. 49:8, whom thy brethren shall *p.*
2Sam. 14:25, none to be so much *p.*
Ps. 30:9, shall the dust *p.* thee?
42:5, 11; 43:5, I shall yet *p.* him.
45:17, therefore shall the people *p.* thee.
49:18, men will *p.* thee when thou doest well.
63:3, my lips shall *p.* thee.
67:3, 5, let the people *p.* thee.
71:14, I will yet *p.* thee more and more.
72:15, daily shall he be *p.*
76:10, the wrath of man shall *p.* thee.
88:10, shall the dead arise and *p.* thee?
107:32, *p.* him in the assembly.
115:17, the dead *p.* not.
119:164, seven times a day do I *p.* thee.
145:4, one generation shall *p.* thy works.
10, all thy works shall *p.* thee.
Prov. 27:2, let another *p.* thee.
31:31, her own works *p.* her in the gates.
Isa. 38:19, the living shall *p.* thee.
See Lk. 2:13; 24:53; Acts 2:47; 3:8.
PRANCING. Jud. 5:22; Nah. 3:2.
PRATING. Prov. 10:8; 3Jn. 10.
PRAY. Gen. 20:7, a prophet and shall *p.* for thee.
1Sam. 7:5, I will *p.* for you to the Lord.
12:23, sin in ceasing to *p.* for you.
2Chr. 7:14, if my people shall *p.*
Ezra 6:10, *p.* for the life of the king.
Job 21:15, what profit if we *p.* to him.
Ps. 5:2, to thee will I *p.*
55:17, evening, morning, and at noon will I *p.*
122:6, *p.* for the peace of Jerusalem.
Isa. 45:20, *p.* to a god that cannot save.
Jer. 7:16; 11:14; 14:11, *p.* not for this people.
37:3; 42:2, 20, *p.* now to the Lord for us.
Zech. 7:2, they sent men to *p.*
Mt. 5:44, and *p.* for them which despitefully use you.
6:5, they love to *p.* standing.
14:23; Mk. 6:46; Lk. 6:12; 9:28, apart to *p.*
26:36; Mk. 14:32, while I *p.* yonder.
Mk. 11:25, and when ye stand *p.*, forgive.
Lk. 11:1, Lord, teach us to *p.*
18:1, men ought always to *p.*
Jn. 14:16; 16:26, I will *p.* the Father.
17:9, I *p.* for them, I *p.* not for the world.
Jn. 17:20, neither *p.* I for these alone.
Acts. 9:11, behold he *p.*
Rom. 8:26, know not what we should *p.* for.
1Cor. 14:15, I will *p.* with the spirit, and *p.* with understanding also.
Eph. 6:18, *p.* always with all prayer.
1Th. 5:17, *p.* without ceasing.
1Tim. 2:8, that men *p.* everywhere.
Jas. 5:13, is any afflicted? let him *p.*
16, *p.* one for another.
1Jn. 5:16, I do not say he shall *p.* for it.
See Lk. 9:29; 1Cor. 11:4; 14:14; 1Th. 5:25.
PRAYER. 2Chr. 7:15, ears shall be attent to the *p.*
Job 15:4, thou restrainest *p.*
16:17; Ps. 4:1; 5:3; 6:9; 17:1; 35:13; 39:12; 66:19; Lam. 3:8, my *p.*
Ps. 65:2, thou that hearest *p.*
72:15, *p.* shall be made continually.
109:4, I give myself to *p.*
Prov. 15:8, the *p.* of the upright.
Isa. 1:15, when ye make many *p.*
56:7; Mt. 21:13; Mk. 11:17; Lk. 19:46, house of *p.*
Mt. 21:22, whatever ye ask in *p.*, believing.
23:14; Mk. 12:40; Lk. 20:47, long *p.*
Lk. 6:12, all night in *p.* to God.
Acts 3:1, the hour of *p.*
6:4, give ourselves continually to *p.*
12:5, *p.* was made without ceasing.
16:13, where *p.* was wont to be made.
Phil. 4:6, in everything by *p.*
Jas. 5:15, *p.* of faith shall save the sick.
16, effectual fervent *p.* of a righteous man.
1Pet. 4:7, watch unto *p.*
Rev. 5:8; 8:3, the *p.* of the saints.
See Ps. 72:20; Dan. 9:21; Rom. 12:12; Col. 4:2.

PREACH. Neh. 6:7, appointed prophets to *p*. of thee.
Isa. 61:1, to *p*. good tidings.
Jon. 3:2, *p*. the preaching I bid thee.
Mt. 4:17; 10:7, Jesus began to *p*.
11:1, to *p*. in their cities.
5, the poor have the gospel *p*.
Mk. 2:2, he *p*. the word to them.
16:20, and *p*. everywhere.
Lk. 9:60, go thou and *p*. kingdom of God.
Acts 8:5, and *p*. Christ unto them.
10:36, *p*. peace by Jesus Christ.
13:38, through his man is *p*. forgiveness.
17:18, he *p*. Jesus and the resurrection.
Rom. 2:21, thou that *p*. a man should not steal.
10:15, how shall they *p*. except.
1Cor. 1:18, the *p*. of the cross is foolishness.
21, by the foolishness of *p*.
23, but we *p*. Christ crucified.
9:27, lest when I have *p*. to others.
15:11, so we *p*. and so ye believed.
14, then is our *p*. vain.
2Cor. 4:5, we *p*. not ourselves.
Phil. 1:15, some *p*. Christ of envy and strife.
2Tim. 4:2, *p*. the word; be instant.
Heb. 4:2, word *p*. did not profit.
1Pet. 3:19, *p*. to spirits in prison.
See Ps. 40:9; 2Cor. 11:4; Gal. 1:8; Eph. 2:17.
PREACHER. Rom. 10:14, how shall they hear without a *p*.?
1Tim. 2:7, whereunto I am ordained a *p*.
2Pet. 2:5, Noah, a *p*. of righteousness.
See Eccl. 1:1; 7:27; 12:8; 2Tim. 1:11.
PRECEPT. Neh. 9:14, commandedst them *p*.
Isa. 28:10, 13, *p*. must be upon *p*.
29:13, taught by *p*. of men.
Jer. 35:18, ye have kept Jonadab's *p*.
See Ps. 119:4, etc.; Dan. 9:5; Mk. 10:5; Heb. 9:19.
PRECIOUS. Dt. 33:13, 14, 15, 16, *p*. things.
1Sam. 3:1, the word was *p*. in those days.
26:21, my soul was *p*. in thine eyes.
2Ki. 1:13, let my life be *p*.
Ezra 8:27, fine copper, *p*. as gold.
Ps. 49:8, the redemption of their soul is *p*.
Ps. 72:14, *p*. shall their blood be in his sight.
116:15, *p*. in sight of the Lord is death of saints.
126:6, bearing *p*. seed.
133:2, like *p*. ointment upon the head.
139:17, how *p*. are thy thoughts.
Prov. 3:15, wisdom more *p*. than rubies.
Eccl. 7:1, good name better than *p*. ointment.
Isa. 13:12, I will make a man more *p*.
28:16; 1Pet. 2:6, a *p*. corner stone.
43:4, since thou wast *p*. in my sight.
Jer. 15:19, take the *p*. from the vile.
Lam. 4:2, the *p*. sons of Zion.
1Pet. 1:7, trial of faith more *p*. than gold.
19, the *p*. blood of Christ.
2:7, to you which believe he is *p*.
2Pet. 1:1, like *p*. faith.
4, great and *p*. promises.
See Mt. 26:7; Mk. 14:3; Jas. 5:7; Rev. 21:11.
PREEMINENCE. Eccl. 3:19; Col. 1:18; 3Jn. 9.
PREFER. Ps. 137:6; Jn. 1:15; Rom. 12:10; 1Tim. 5:21.
PREMEDITATE. Mk. 13:11.
PREPARATION. Prov. 16:1, *p*. of the heart.
Eph. 6:15, feet shod with *p*. of gospel.
See Mt. 27:62; Mk. 15:42; Lk. 23:54; Jn. 19:14.
PREPARE. 1Sam. 7:3, *p*. your hearts unto the Lor
2Chr. 20:33, as yet the people had not *p*.
Ps. 68:10, thou hast *p*. of thy goodness.
107:36, that they may *p*. a city.
Prov. 8:27, when he *p*. the heavens I was there.
Isa. 40:3; Mal. 3:1; Mt. 3:3; Mk. 1:2; Lk. 1:76, *p* way of the Lord.
62:10, *p*. the way of the people.
Amos 4:12, *p*. to meet thy God.
Jon. 1:17, Lord had *p*. a great fish.
Mt. 20:23; Mk. 10:40, to them for whom *p*.
Jn. 14:2, I go to *p*. a place for you.
Rom. 9:23, afore *p*. to glory.
1Cor. 2:9, things God hath *p*.
Heb. 10:5, a body hast thou *p*. me.
See 1Chr. 22:5; Ps. 23:5; Rev. 21:2.
PRESCRIBE. Ezra 7:22; Isa. 10:1.
PRESENCE. Gen. 4:16, Cain went out from the *p*. the Lord.
47:15, why should we die in thy *p*.
Ex. 33:15, if thy *p*. go not with me.
Job 23:15, I am troubled at his *p*.
Ps. 16:11, in thy *p*. is fulness of joy.
17:2, my sentence come forth from thy *p*.
31:20, in the secret of thy *p*.
51:11, cast me not away from thy *p*.
139:7, whither shall I flee from thy *p*.?
Prov. 14:7, go from *p*. of a foolish man.
Isa. 63:9, angel of his *p*. saved them.
Jer. 23:39; 52:3, I will cast you out of my *p*.
Jon. 1:3, to flee from *p*. of the Lord.
Zeph. 1:7, hold thy peace at *p*. of the Lord.
Lk. 13:26, we have eaten and drunk in thy *p*.
Acts 3:19, times of refreshing from the *p*.
2Cor. 10:1, 10, who in *p*. am base.
2Th. 1:9, destruction from the *p*. of the Lord.
See Gen. 16:12; Ps. 23:5; Prov. 25:6; Lk. 15:10.
PRESENT. 1Sam. 10:27, they brought him no *p*.
Ps. 46:1, a very *p*. help in trouble.
Jn. 14:25, being yet *p*. with you.
Acts 10:33, all here *p*. before God.
Rom. 7:18, to will is *p*. with me.
21, evil is *p*. with me.
8:18, sufferings of this *p*. time.
12:1, *p*. your bodies a living sacrifice.
1Cor. 7:26, good for the *p*. distress.
2Cor. 5:8, to be *p*. with the Lord.
9, whether *p*. or absent.
Gal. 1:4, deliver us from this *p*. world.
Col. 1:28, *p*. every man perfect.
2Tim. 4:10, having loved this *p*. world.
Ti. 2:12, live godly in this *p*. world.
Heb. 12:11, no chastening for *p*. seemeth joyous
2Pet. 1:12, established in the *p*. truth.
Jude 24, able to *p*. you faultless.
See Ps. 72:10; Mt. 2:11; Lk. 2:22.

RESENTLY. Prov. 12:16; Mt. 21:19; 26:53.
RESERVE. Gen. 32:30, I have seen God, and my life is *p*.
45:5, did send me before you to *p*. life.
Job 29:2, as in days when God *p*. me.
Ps. 36:6, thou *p*. man and beast.
121:7, the Lord *p*. thee from evil.
8, *p*. thy going out and coming in.
Prov. 2:8, he *p*. the way of his saints.
11, discretion shall *p*. thee.
20:28, mercy and truth *p*. the king.
Jer. 49:11, I will *p*. them alive.
Lk. 17:33, lose his life shall *p*. it.
See Neh. 9:6; Isa. 49:6; Hos. 12:13; Jude 1.
RESS. Prov. 3:10, *p*. burst with new wine.
Amos 2:13, I am *p*. under you as a cart is *p*.
Mk. 3:10, they *p*. on him to touch him.
Lk. 6:38, good measure, *p*. down.
16:16, every man *p*. into it.
Phil. 3:14, I *p*. toward the mark.
See Mk. 2:4; 5:27; Lk. 8:19; 19:3.
RESUME. Dt. 18:20; Est. 7:5.
RESUMPTUOUS. Num. 15:30; Ps. 19:13; 2Pet. 2:10.
RETENCE. Mt. 23:14; Mk. 12:40; Phil. 1:18.
REVAIL. Gen. 32:28; Hos. 12:4, power with God, and hast *p*.
Ex. 17:11, Moses held up hand, Israel *p*.
1Sam. 2:9, by strength shall no man *p*.
Ps. 9:19, let not man *p*.
65:3, iniquities *p*. against me.
Eccl. 4:12, if one *p*. against him.
Mt. 16:18, gates of hell shall not *p*.
Acts. 19:20, grew word of God and *p*.
See Job 14:20; Jer. 20:7; Lam. 1:16; Jn. 12:19.
REVENT. 2Sam. 22:6; Ps. 18:5, snares of death *p*. me.
Ps. 88:13, in the morning shall my prayer *p*. thee.
119:147, I *p*. the dawning of the morning.
See Ps. 21:3; 79:8; Isa. 21:14; 1Th. 4:15.
REY. Isa. 49:24, shall the *p*. be taken from the mighty?
Jer. 21:9; 38:2; 39:18; 45:5, his life shall be for a *p*.
Ezek. 34:22, my flock shall no more be a *p*.
See Gen. 49:9; Num. 14:3; Neh. 4:4; Amos 3:4.
RICE. Lev. 25:52, the *p*. of his redemption.
2Sam. 24:24; 1Chr. 21:22, I will buy it at a *p*.
Acts 5:2, kept back part of the *p*.
1Cor. 6:20; 7:23, bought with a *p*.
1Pet. 3:4, meek spirit of great *p*.
See Dt. 23:18; Prov. 31:10; Zech. 11:12.
RICKS. Num. 33:55; Acts 9:5; 26:14.
RIDE. Ps. 31:20, hide them from *p*. of man.
Prov. 8:13, *p*. do I hate.
14:3, in mouth of foolish is rod of *p*.
Isa. 28:1, woe to the crown of *p*.
Jer. 49:16, *p*. of thine heart hath deceived thee.
See Mk. 7:22; 1Tim. 3:6; 1Jn. 2:16.
RIEST. Gen. 14:18; Heb. 7:1, *p*. of most high God.
Ex. 19:6, a kingdom of *p*.
1Sam. 2:35, I will raise up a faithful *p*.
2Chr. 6:41; Ps. 132:16, *p*. clothed with salvation.
13:9, *p*. of them that are no gods.
15:3, without a teaching *p*.
Isa. 24:2, as with the people, so with the *p*.
28:7, *p*. and prophet have erred.
61:6, shall be named the *p*. of the Lord.
Jer. 13:13, will fill *p*. with drunkenness.
Mic. 3:11, the *p*. teach for hire.
Mal. 2:7, the *p*. lips should keep knowledge.
Lk. 17:14, show yourselves to the *p*.
Acts 6:7, *p*. were obedient to the faith.
Rev. 1:6; 5:10; 20:6, kings and *p*. to God.
See Heb. 2:17; 3:1; 4:15; 7:26.
PRIESTHOOD. Ex. 40:15; Num. 25:13, an everlasting *p*.
Num. 16:10, seek ye the *p*. also.
Heb. 7:24, an unchangeable *p*.
1Pet. 2:5, an holy *p*.
9, ye are a royal *p*.
See Num. 18:1; Josh. 18:7; Neh. 13:29.
PRINCE. Gen. 32:28, as a *p*. hast thou power.
Ex. 2:14; Num. 16:13, who made thee a *p*. over us?
1Sam. 2:8; Ps. 113:8, to set them among *p*.
2Sam. 3:38, a *p*. fallen in Israel.
Job 12:21; Ps. 107:40, poureth contempt on *p*.
21:28, where is the house of the *p*.?
31:37, as a *p*. would I go near him.
Ps. 45:16, make *p*. in all the earth.
118:9, than to put confidence in *p*.
146:3, put not your trust in *p*.
Prov. 8:15, by me *p*. decree justice.
31:4, nor for *p*. strong drink.
Eccl. 10:7, *p*. walking as servants.
16, when thy *p*. eat in the morning.
17, blessed when *p*. eat in due season.
Isa. 34:12; 40:23, all her *p*. shall be nothing.
Hos. 3:4, abide many days without a *p*.
Mt. 9:34; 12:24; Mk. 3:22, by *p*. of devils.
Jn. 12:31; 14:30; 16:11, the *p*. of this world.
Acts 3:15, and killed the *P*. of life.
5:31, exalted to be a *P.* and Saviour.
1Cor. 2:6, wisdom of the *p*. of this world.
8, which none of *p*. of this world knew.
Eph. 2:2, the *p*. of the power of the air.
See Isa. 3:4; Hos. 7:5; Mt. 20:25.
PRINCIPAL. Prov. 4:7; Isa. 28:25; Acts 25:23.
PRINCIPALITY. Eph. 6:12, we wrestle against *p*. and powers.
Ti. 3:1, to be subject to *p*.
See Rom. 8:38; Eph. 1:21; 3:10; Col. 1:16.
PRINCIPLES. Heb. 5:12; 6:1.
PRINT. Lev. 19:28; Job 13:27; 19:23; Jn. 20:25.
PRISON. Ps. 142:7, bring my soul out of *p*.
Eccl. 4:14, out of *p*. he cometh to reign.
Isa. 53:8, taken from *p*. and from judgment.
61:1, opening of the *p*.
Mt. 5:25; Lk. 12:58, thou be cast into *p*.
11:2, John heard in the *p*.
25:36, 39, in *p*. that ye came unto me.
Lk. 22:33, to go with thee to *p*. and to death.
2Cor. 11:23, in *p*. more frequent.
1Pet. 3:19, spirits in *p*.

See Jer. 32:2; 39:14; Lk. 3:20; Acts 5:18.
PRISONER. Ps. 79:11; Zech. 9:12; Mt. 27:16; Eph. 3:1.
PRIVATE. 2Pet. 1:20.
PRIVATELY. Mt. 24:3; Mk. 9:28; Lk. 10:23; Gal. 2:2.
PRIVILY. Mt. 1:19; 2:7; Acts 16:37; Gal. 2:4; 2Pet. 2:1.
PRIZE. 1Cor. 9:24; Phil. 3:14.
PROCEED. Gen. 24:50, the thing *p.* from the Lord.
Dt. 8:3; Mt. 4:4, that *p.* out of mouth of God.
Job 40:5, I will *p.* no further.
Isa. 29:14, I will *p.* to do a marvellous work.
51:4, a law shall *p.* from me.
Jer. 9:3, they *p.* from evil to evil.
Mt. 15:18; Mk. 7:21, *p.* out of the mouth.
Jn. 8:42, I *p.* forth from God.
Jas. 3:10, *p.* blessing and cursing.
See Lk. 4:22; Jn. 15:26; Eph. 4:29; Rev. 22:1.
PROCLAIM. Ex. 33:19; 34:5, I will *p.* the name of the Lord.
Isa. 61:1, to *p.* liberty to captives.
2, to *p.* acceptable year.
62:11, Lord hath *p.*, thy salvation cometh.
Jer. 34:15, in *p.* liberty every man to his neighbour.
Lk. 12:3, *p.* upon the housetops.
See Dt. 20:10; Prov. 20:6; Jer. 3:12; Joel 3:9.
PROCURE. Prov. 11:27; Jer. 2:17; 4:18; 26:19; 33:9.
PRODUCE. Isa. 41:21.
PROFANE. Lev. 18:21; 19:12; 20:3; 21:6; 22:2, *p.* name of God.
Jer. 23:11, prophet and priest are *p.*
Ezek. 22:26, no difference between holy and *p.*
Mt. 12:5, priests in temple *p.* sabbath.
Acts 24:6, hath gone about to *p.* temple.
1Tim. 1:9, law for unholy and *p.*
4:7, refuse *p.* and old wives' fables.
6:20; 2Tim. 2:16, avoiding *p.* babblings.
Heb. 12:16, any *p.* person.
See Ps. 89:39; Jer. 23:15; Mal. 1:12; 2:10.
PROFESS. Rom. 1:22; 2 Cor. 9:13; 1 Tim. 2:10; 6:12.
PROFIT (*n.*). Gen. 25:32, what *p.* shall birthright do me?
37:26, what *p.* if we slay?
Job 21:15, what *p.* if we pray?
Prov. 14:23, in all labour there is *p.*
Eccl. 1:3; 3:9; 5:16, what *p.* of labour?
2:11, there was no *p.* under the sun.
5:9, *p.* of the earth for all.
7:11, by wisdom there is *p.*
Jer. 16:19, things wherein is no *p.*
Mal. 3:14, what *p.* that we have kept.
1Cor. 10:33, not seeking own *p.*, but *p.* of many.
2Tim. 2:14, about words to no *p.*
Heb. 12:10, he chasteneth us for our *p.*
See Est. 3:8; Ps. 30:9; Isa. 30:5; 1Tim. 4:15.
PROFIT (*v.*). 1Sam. 12:21, vain things which cannot *p.*
Job 33:27, I have sinned, and it *p.* not.
34:9, *p.* nothing to delight in God.
Prov. 10:2, treasures of wickedness *p.* nothing.
11:4, riches *p.* not in the day of wrath.
Isa. 30:5, 6, people that could not *p.*
48:17, the Lord which teacheth thee to *p.*
Jer. 2:11, changed for that which doth not *p.*
23:32, they shall not *p.* this people.
Mt. 16:26; Mk. 8:36, what is a man *p.*?
1Cor. 12:7, to every man to *p.* withal.
Gal. 5:2, Christ shall *p.* you nothing.
1Tim. 4:8, bodily exercise *p.* little.
Heb. 4:2, the word preached did not *p.*
See Mt. 15:5; Rom. 2:25; 1Cor. 13:3; Jas. 2:14.
PROFITABLE. Job 22:2, can a man be *p.* to God?
Eccl. 10:10, wisdom is *p.* to direct.
Acts 20:20, I kept back nothing *p.*
1Tim. 4:8, godliness is *p.* to all things.
2 Tim. 3:16, scripture is *p.* for doctrine.
See Mt. 5:29; 2Tim. 4:11; Ti. 3:8; Phile. 11.
PROLONG. Dt. 4:26; 30:18, ye shall not *p.* your days.
Job 6:11, what is mine end that I should *p.* my life?
Prov. 10:27, fear of the Lord *p.* days.
Eccl. 8:12, though a sinner's days be *p.*
See Ps. 61:6; Prov. 28:2; Isa. 13:22; 53:10.
PROMISE (*n.*). Num. 14:34, ye shall know my breach of *p.*
1Ki. 8:56, hath not failed one word of *p.*
Ps. 77:8, doth his *p.* fail?
Lk. 24:49; Acts 1:4, *p.* of Father.
Acts 2:39, the *p.* is to you and your children.
26:6, for hope of the *p.*
Rom. 4:14, the *p.* made of none effect.
20, staggered not at the *p.*
9:4, to whom pertain the *p.*
8; Gal. 4:28, the children of the *p.*
2Cor. 1:20, *p.* are yea and Amen.
Gal. 3:21, is the law against the *p.* of God?
1Tim. 4:8; 2Tim. 1:1, *p.* of the life that now is.
Heb. 6:12, through faith and patience inherit the *p.*
9:15; 10:36, the *p.* of eternal inheritance.
11:13, died, not having received *p.*
2Pet. 1:4, great and precious *p.*
3:4, where is the *p.* of his coming?
9, not slack concerning his *p.*
See Eph. 1:13; 2:12; 6:2; Heb. 4:1; 11:9.
PROMISE (*v.*). Ex. 12:25, will give you as he hath *p.*
Num. 14:40, will go to place the Lord *p.*
Dt. 1:11; 15:6, the Lord bless you as he hath *p.*
9:28, not able to bring into land *p.*
19:8; 27:3, give the land he *p.* to give.
Josh. 23:15, all good things which the Lord *p.*
2Ki. 8:19; 2Chr. 21:7, he *p.* to give him a light.
Mk. 14:11, they *p.* to give him money.
Rom. 4:21, what he *p.* he was able to perform.
Heb. 10:23; 11:11, he is faithful that *p.*
1Jn. 2:25, he hath *p.* eternal life.
See 1Ki. 8:24; Neh. 9:15; Ezek. 13:22.
PROMOTE. Num. 22:17; 24:11; Prov. 4:8.
PROMOTION. Ps. 75:6; Prov. 3:35.
PRONOUNCE. Jud. 12:6; Jer. 34:5.
PROOF. 2Cor. 2:9; 8:24; 13:3; Phil. 2:22; 2Tim. 4:5.
PROPER. 1Chr. 29:3; 1Cor. 7:7; Heb. 11:23.
PROPHECY. 1Cor. 13:8, whether *p.*, shall fail.

2Pet. 1:19, sure word of *p*.
21, *p*. came not in old time.
Rev. 1:3; 22:7, the words of this *p*.
See Neh. 6:12; Prov. 31:1; 1Tim. 4:14.
PROPHESY. Num. 11:25, they *p*. and did not cease.
2Chr. 18:7, he never *p*. good to me.
Isa. 30:10, *p*. not to us right things.
Jer. 5:31, prophets *p*. falsely.
14:14; 23:25, prophets *p*. lies.
28:9, the prophet which *p*. of peace.
Ezek. 37:9, *p*. to the wind.
Joel 2:28; Acts 2:17, your sons shall *p*.
Amos 3:8, who can but *p*.
7:13, *p*. not again any more.
Mic. 2:11, I will *p*. of wine.
Mt. 26:68; Mk. 14:65; Lk. 22:64, *p*., thou Christ.
Rom. 12:6, let us *p*. according to the proportion.
1Cor. 13:9, we *p*. in part.
14:39, covet to *p*.
1Th. 5:20, despise not *p*.
See Amos 2:12; 1Cor. 11:5; Rev. 10:11; 11:3.
PROPHET. Ex. 7:1, Aaron shall be thy *p*.
Num. 11:29, would all Lord's people were *p*.
12:6, if there be a *p*. among you.
Dt. 13:1, if there arise a *p*. or dreamer.
18:15; Acts 3:22; 7:37, the Lord will raise up a *P*.
34:10, there arose not a *p*. like Moses.
1Sam. 10:12; 19:24, is Saul among *p*.?
1Ki. 13:11, there dwelt an old *p*. in Beth-el.
18:22, I only remain a *p*.
22:7; 2Ki. 3:11, is there not a *p*. besides?
2Ki. 5:8, he shall know there is a *p*.
1Chr. 16:22; Ps. 105:15, do my *p*. no harm.
2Chr. 20:20, believe his *p*., so shall ye prosper.
Ps. 74:9, there is no more any *p*.
Isa. 3:2, the Lord taketh away the *p*.
Jer. 29:26, mad, and maketh himself a *p*.
37:19, where are now your *p*.?
Ezek. 2:5; 33:33, there hath been a *p*. among them.
Hos. 9:7, the *p*. is a fool.
Amos 7:14, I was no *p*., nor *p*. son.
Zech. 1:5, the *p*., do they live for ever?
Mt. 7:15, beware of false *p*.
10:41, that receiveth a *p*. in name of a *p*.
13:57; Mk. 6:4; Lk. 4:24; Jn. 4:44, a *p*. not without honour.
23:29; Lk. 11:47, ye build the tombs of the *p*.
Lk. 1:76, be called the *p*. of the Highest.
7:16, a great *p*. is risen.
28, not a great *p*. than John.
39, if he were a *p*. would have known.
Lk. 13:33, it cannot be that a *p*. perish out of.
24:19, Jesus, who was a *p*. mighty.
Jn. 4:19, I perceive thou art a *p*.
7:40, of a truth this is the *P*.
52, out of Galilee ariseth no *p*.
Acts 26:27, believest thou the *p*.?
1Cor. 12:29, are all *p*.?
14:37, if any man think himself a *p*.
Eph. 2:20, built on foundation of *p*.
4:11, he gave some *p*.
1Pet. 1:10, of which salvation the *p*. enquired.
Rev. 22:9, I am of thy brethren the *p*.
See 1Ki. 20:35; Neh. 6:14; 1Cor. 14:32.
PROPORTION. 1Ki. 7:36; Job 41:12; Rom. 12:6.
PROSPER. Gen. 24:56, the Lord hath *p*. my way.
39:3, the Lord made all Joseph did to *p*.
Num. 14:41, transgress, but it shall not *p*.
Dt. 28:29, thou shalt not *p*. in thy ways.
1Chr. 22:11, *p*. thou, and build.
2Chr. 20:20, believe, so shall ye *p*.
26:5, God made him to *p*.
Ezra 5:8, this work *p*. in their hands.
Neh. 2:20, the God of heaven will *p*. us.
Job 9:4, who hardened himself and *p*.
Ps. 1:3, whatsoever he doeth shall *p*.
Ps. 37:7, fret not because of him who *p*.
73:12, the ungodly who *p*. in the world.
122:6, they shall *p*. that love thee.
Prov. 28:13, he that covereth sins shall not *p*.
Eccl. 11:6, knowest not whether shall *p*.
Isa. 53:10, pleasure of the Lord shall *p*.
54:17, no weapon against thee shall *p*.
55:11, it shall *p*. in the thing.
Jer. 2:37, thou shalt not *p*. in them.
12:1, wherefore doth way of wicked *p*.?
22:30, no man of his seed shall *p*.
Ezek. 17:9, 10, shall it *p*.?
15, shall he *p*., shall he escape?
1Cor. 16:2, lay by as God hath *p*. him.
3Jn. 2, in health, even as thy soul *p*.
See Prov. 17:8; Dan. 6:28; 8:12.
PROSPERITY. Dt. 23:6, thou shalt not seek their *p*.
1Sam. 25:6, say to him that liveth in *p*.
Job 15:21, in *p*. the destroyer shall come.
Ps. 30:6, in my *p*. I said, I shall never.
73:3, when I saw the *p*. of the wicked.
Prov. 1:32, *p*. of fools shall destroy them.
Eccl. 7:14, in day of *p*. be joyful.
Jer. 22:21, I spake to thee in thy *pi*.
See 1Ki. 10:7; Job 36:11; Ps. 35:17; 122:7.
PROSPEROUS. Gen. 39:2, he was a *p*. man.
Josh. 1:8, then thou shalt make thy way *p*.
Job 8:6, make habitation of thy righteousness *p*.
Zech. 8:12, the seed shall be *p*.
See Gen. 24:21; Jud. 18:5; 2Chr. 7:11; Rom. 1:10.
PROTECTION. Dt. 32:38.
PROTEST. Gen. 43:3; Jer. 11:7; Zech. 3:6; 1Cor. 15:31.
PROUD. Job 38:11, here shall thy *p*. waves be stayed.
40:11, every one that is *p*., and abase him.
Ps. 31:23, rewardeth the *p*. doer.
40:4, man that respecteth not the *p*.
94:2, render a reward to the *p*.
101:5, him that hath a *p*. heart will not I suffer.
123:4, soul filled with contempt of the *p*.
138:6, the *p*. he knoweth afar off.
Prov. 6:17, the Lord hateth a *p*. look.
15:25, the Lord will destroy house of the *p*.
16:5, *p*. in heart is abomination.
21:4, a *p*. heart is sin.
Eccl. 7:8, patient better than *p*. in spirit.

Hab. 2:5, he is a *p.* man.
Mal. 3:15, we call the *p.* happy.
Lk. 1:51, scattered the *p.*
1Tim. 6:4, he is *p.*, knowing nothing.
Jas. 4:6; 1Pet. 5:5, God resisteth the *p.*
See Job 9:13; 26:12; Rom. 1:30; 2Tim. 3:2.

PROUDLY. Ex. 18:11; 1Sam. 2:3; Neh. 9:10; Isa. 3:5; Obad. 12.

PROVE. Ex. 15:25, there he *p.* them.
Jud. 6:39, let me *p.* thee but this once.
1Sam. 17:39, I have not *p.* them.
1Ki. 10:1; 2Chr. 9:1, she came to *p.* Solomon.
Ps. 17:3, thou hast *p.* mine heart.
81:7, I *p.* thee at the waters.
95:9; Heb. 3:9, when your fathers *p.* me.
Mal. 3:10, *p.* me now herewith.
Lk. 14:19, I go to *p.* them.
2Cor. 8:22, whom we have often *p.* diligent.
13:5, *p.* your own selves.
1Th. 5:21, *p.* all things.
See Eccl. 2:1; 7:23; Dan. 1:14; Jn. 6:6.

PROVERB. Dt. 28:37, a *p.* and a byword.
Ps. 69:11, I became a *p.* to them.
Eccl. 12:9, set in order many *p.*
Ezek. 16:44, every one that useth *p.*
Lk. 4:23, will surely say this *p.*
Jn. 16:29, speakest plainly, and no *p.*
See Num. 21:27; 1Sam. 10:12; Prov. 1:6.

PROVIDE. Gen. 22:8, God will *p.* himself a lamb.
30:30, when shall I *p.* for mine own house?
Ps. 78:20, can he *p.* flesh?
Mt. 10:9, *p.* neither gold nor silver.
Lk. 12:20, whose shall those things be thou hast *p*?
Lk. 12:33, *p.* bags that wax not old.
Rom. 12:17; 2Cor. 8:21, *p.* things honest.
1Tim. 5:8, if any *p.* not for his own.
Heb. 11:40, having *p.* better thing for us.
See Job 38:41; Prov. 6:8; Acts 23:24.

PROVIDENCE. Acts 24:2.

PROVISION. Gen. 42:25; 45:21, *p.* for the way.
Ps. 132:15, I will abundantly bless her *p.*
Rom. 13:14, make not *p.* for the flesh.
See Josh. 9:5; 1Ki. 4:7; 2Ki. 6:23.

PROVOCATION. Job 17:2; Ps. 95:8; Ezek. 20:28.

PROVOKE. Ex. 23:21, obey his voice and *p.* him not.
Num. 14:11, how long will this people *p.* me?
Dt. 31:20, *p.* me and break my covenant.
Job 12:6, they that *p.* God are secure.
Ps. 106:7, they *p.* him at the sea.
29, they *p.* him with their inventions.
Lk. 11:53, began to urge and *p.* him to speak.
Rom. 10:19; 11:11, I will *p.* to jealousy.
1Cor. 13:5, is not easily *p.*
Gal. 5:26, *p.* one another.
Eph. 6:4, *p.* not your children to wrath.
Heb. 10:24, to *p.* to love and good works.
See Prov. 20:2; Isa. 65:3; Jer. 7:19; 44:8.

PRUDENCE. 2Chr. 2:12; Prov. 8:12; Eph. 1:8.

PRUDENT. Prov. 12:16, a *p.* man covereth shame.
23, a *p.* man concealeth knowledge.
14:15, the *p.* looketh well to his going.
16:21, wise in heart called *p.*
19:14, *p.* wife is from the Lord.
22:3; 27:12, *p.* man forseeth evil.
Isa. 5:21, woe unto them that are *p.* in their own sight.
Jer. 49:7, counsel perished from *p.*
Hos. 14:9, who is *p.*?
Mt. 11:25; Lk. 10:21, hast hid things from *p.*
See Isa. 52:13; Amos 5:13; Acts 13.

PRUNE. Lev. 25:3; Isa. 2:4; Joel 3:10; Mic. 4:3.

PSALTERY. Dan. 3:5, the sound of the cornet, flute *p.*, etc.
See 2Sam. 6:5; 2Chr. 9:11.

PUBLIC. Mt. 1:19; Acts 18:28; 20:20.

PUBLISH. Dt. 32:3, I will *p.* the name of the Lord.
2Sam. 1:20, *p.* it not in Askelon.
Ps. 68:11, great was the company that *p.* it.
Isa. 52:7; Nah. 1:15, that *p.* peace.
Mk. 1:45; 5:20, he began to *p.* it much.
Lk. 8:39, *p.* throughout the whole city.
See Est. 1:20; 3:14; Jon. 3:7; Mk. 13:10.

PUFFED. 1Cor. 4:6; 5:2; 13:4; Col. 2:18.

PUFFETH. Ps. 10:5; 12:5; 1Cor. 8:1.

PULL. Lam. 3:11, *p* me in pieces.
Amos 9:15, shall no more be *p.* up.
Zech. 7:11, they *p.* away the shoulder.
Mt. 7:4; Lk. 6:42, *p.* mote out of thine eye.
Lk. 12:18, will *p.* down barns.
14:5, will not *p.* him out on sabbath.
2Cor. 10:4, to the *p.* down of strong holds.
Jude 23, *p.* them out of the fire.
See Gen. 8:9; Ezra 6:11; Ps. 31:4; Isa. 22:19.

PULPIT. Neh. 8:4.

PULSE. 2Sam. 17:28; Dan. 1:12.

PUNISH. Ezra 9:13, *p.* less than iniquities deserve.
Prov. 17:26, to *p.* the just is not good.
Isa. 13:11, I will *p.* the world for their evil.
26:21, Lord cometh to *p.* inhabitants.
Jer. 13:21, what wilt thou say when he *p.*
Acts 26:11, I *p.* them in every synagogue.
2Th. 1:9, *p.* with everlasting destruction.
2Pet. 2:9, to day of judgment to be *p.*
See Lev. 26:18; Prov. 21:11; 22:3; 27:12.

PUNISHMENT. Gen. 4:13, my *p.* is greater than I can bear.
Lev. 26:41, accept the *p.* of their iniquity.
1Sam. 28:10, no *p.* shall happen to thee.
Lam. 3:39, a man for the *p.* of his sins.
4:6, *p.* greater than *p.* of Sodom.
22, the *p.* is accomplished.
Ezek. 14:10, shall bear *p.* of their iniquity.
Mt. 25:46, everlasting *p.*
Heb. 10:29, of how much sorer *p.*
1Pet. 2:14, the *p.* of evildoers.
See Prov. 19:19; Amos 1:3; 2:1; 2Cor. 2:6.

PURCHASE. Ruth 4:10, have I *p.* to be my wife.
Ps. 74:2, congregation thou hast *p.*
Acts 1:18, *p.* a field with reward of iniquity.
8:20, gift of God *p.* by money.
20:28, he hath *p.* with his own blood.
Eph. 1:14, redemption of *p.* possession.
1Tim. 3:13, *p.* to themselves a good degree.
See Gen. 49:32; Ex. 15:16; Lev. 25:33; Jer. 32:11

URE. Dt. 32:14, the *p*. blood of the grape.
2Sam. 22:27; Ps. 18:26, with *p*. show thyself *p*.
Job 4:17, shall man be more *p*.?
8:6, if thou wert *p*. and upright.
11:4, my doctrine is *p*.
16:17, my prayer is *p*.
25:5, stars are not *p*. in his sight.
Ps. 12:6, the words of the Lord are *p*.
19:8, commandment of the Lord is *p*.
119:140, thy word is very *p*.
Prov. 15:26, words of the *p*. are pleasant.
20:9, who can say, I am *p*.?
Mic. 6:11, shall I count them *p*.?
Zeph. 3:9, turn to the people a *p*. language.
Acts 20:26, *p*. from blood of all men.
Rom. 14:20, all things indeed are *p*.
Phil. 4:8, whatsoever things are *p*.
1Tim. 3:9; 2Tim. 1:3, in a *p*. conscience.
5:22, keep thy self *p*.
Ti. 1:15, to the *p*. all things are *p*.
Jas. 1:27, *p*. religion.
3:17, first *p*., then peaceable.
2Pet. 3:1, stir up your *p*. minds.
1Jn. 3:3, even as he is *p*.
Rev. 22:1, a *p*. river of water of life.
See Ex. 27:20; Ezra 6:20; Mal. 1:11.
URELY. Isa. 1:25.
URENESS. Job 22:30; Prov. 22:11; 2Cor. 6:6.
URER. Lam. 4:7; Hab. 1:13.
URGE. 2Chr. 34:8, when he had *p*. the land.
Ps. 51:7, *p*. me with hyssop.
65:3, transgressions, thou shalt *p*. them.
Isa. 1:25, and purely *p*. away thy dross.
6:7, thy sin is *p*.
22:14, this iniquity shall not be *p*.
Ezek. 24:13, I have *p*. thee and thou wast not *p*.
Mal. 3:3, *p*. them as gold.
Mt. 3:12; Lk. 3:17, *p*. his floor.
Jn. 15:2, he *p*. it, that it may bring forth.
1Cor. 5:7, *p*. out the old leaven.
2Tim. 2:21, if a man *p*. himself from these.
Heb. 9:14, *p*. your conscience.
22, all things are *p*. with blood.
See Prov. 16:6; Heb. 1:3; 10:2; 2Pet. 1:9.
URIFY. Ti. 2:14; Jas. 4:8; 1Pet. 1:22.
URITY. 1Tim. 4:12; 5:2.
URLOINING. Ti. 2:10.
URPOSE. Job 17:11, my *p*. are broken off.
Prov. 20:18, every *p*. established by counsel.
Isa. 14:27, the Lord hath *p*., who shall disannul?
46:11, I have *p*., I will also do it.
Mt. 26:8, to what *p*. is this waste?
Acts 11:23, with *p*. of heart.
Rom. 8:28, called according to his *p*.
9:11, that the *p*. of God might stand.
Eph. 1:11, according to the *p*.
3:11, eternal *p*. in Christ.
See 2Cor. 1:17; 2Tim. 1:9; 1Jn. 3:8.
URSE. Prov. 1:14; Mt. 10:9; Mk. 6:8; Lk. 10:4.
URSUE. Lev. 26:17; Prov. 28:1, shall flee when none *p*.
Dt. 19:6; Josh. 20:5, lest avenger *p*.
Job 13:25, wilt thou *p*. the stubble?
30:15, terrors *p*. my soul.
Ps. 34:14, seek peace and *p*. it.
Prov. 11:19, he that *p*. evil *p*. it to death.
13:21, evil *p*. sinners.
Jer. 48:2, the sword shall *p*. thee.
See Ex. 15:9; 2Sam. 24:13; 1Ki. 18:27.
PUSH. Ex. 21:29; 1Ki. 22:11; Job 30:12.
PUT. Ex. 23:1, *p*. not thine hand with the wicked.
Lev. 26:8; Dt. 32:30, *p*. ten thousand to flight.
Jud. 12:3; 1Sam. 28:21, I *p*. my life in my hands.
1Sam. 2:36, *p*. me into one of priests' offices.
1Ki. 9:3; 14:21, to *p*. my name there.
Eccl. 10:10, must he *p*. to more strength.
Isa. 43:26, *p*. me in remembrance.
Mt. 19:6; Mk. 10:9, let not man *p*. asunder.
Mk. 10:16, *p*. his hands on them and blessed.
Phile. 18, *p*. that on mine account.
2Pet. 1:14, I must *p*. off this tabernacle.
See Lk. 9:62; Jn. 13:2; 1Th. 5:8.
PUTRIFYING. Isa. 1:6.
QUAKE. Joel 2:10; Nah. 1:5; Mt. 27:51; Heb. 12:21.
QUANTITY. Isa. 22:24.
QUARREL. Lev. 26:25; 2Ki. 5:7; Mk. 6:19; Col. 3:13.
QUARTER. Ex. 13:7; Mk. 1:45; Rev. 20:8.
QUATERNIONS. Acts 12:4, delivered him to four *q*.
QUEEN. Jer. 44:17, 25, burn incense unto the *q*.
QUENCH. Num. 11:2, the fire was *q*.
2Sam. 21:17, *q*. not light of Israel.
Song 8:7, many waters cannot *q*. love.
Isa. 34:10, shall not be a *q*. night nor day.
42:3; Mt. 12:20, smoking flax not *q*.
66:24, neither shall their fire be *q*.
Mk. 9:43, 48, fire that never shall be *q*.
Eph. 6:16, able to *q*. fiery darts.
1Th. 5:19, *q*. not the Spirit.
Heb. 11:34, *q*. violence of fire.
See. Ps. 104:11; 118:12; Ezek. 20:27; Amos 5:6.
QUESTION. 1Ki. 10:1; 2Chr. 9:1, to prove him with *q*.
Mt. 22:46, neither durst ask him *q*.
Mk. 9:16, what *q*. ye with them?
11:29, I will ask you one *q*.
1Cor. 10:25, asking no *q*. for conscience.
1Tim. 1:4, which minister *q*. rather.
6:4, doting about *q*.
2Tim. 2:23; Ti. 3:9, unlearned *q*. avoid.
See Mk. 1:27; 9:10; Acts 18:15; 19:40.
QUICK. Num. 16:30; Ps. 55:15, go down *q*.
Isa. 11:3, of *q*. understanding.
Acts 10:42; 2Tim. 4:1; 1Pet. 4:5, Judge of *q*. and dead.
Heb. 4:12, the word is *q*. and powerful.
See Lev. 13:10, 24; Ps. 124:3.
QUICKEN. Ps. 71:20, thou shalt *q*. me again.
80:18, *q*. us and we will call.
119:25, *q*. me according to thy word.
37, *q*. me in thy way.
50, thy word hath *q*. me.
Rom. 8:11, shall also *q*. your bodies.
1Cor. 15:36, that thou sowest is not *q*.
Eph. 2:1, you hath he *q*.

5; Col. 2:13, *q.* us together with Christ.
1Pet. 3:18, to death in flesh, *q.* by Spirit.
See Jn. 5:21; 6:63; Rom. 4:17; 1Tim. 6:13.
QUICKLY. Ex. 32:8; Dt. 9:12, have turned aside *q.*
Num. 16:46, go *q.* to congregation.
Josh. 10:6, come *q.* and save us.
Eccl. 4:12, threefold cord not *q.* broken.
Mt. 5:25, agree with adversary *q.*
Lk. 14:21, go *q.* into streets and lanes.
Jn. 13:27, that thou doest, do *q.*
Rev. 2:5, 16, repent, else I will come *q.*
3:11; 22:7, 12, I come *q.*
22:20, surely I come *q.*
See Gen. 18:6; 27:20; Lk. 16:6; Acts 22:18.
QUICKSANDS. Acts 27:17, fearing lest they should fall into the *q.*
QUIET. Ps. 107:30, then are they glad because *q.*
131:2, I have *q.* myself as a child.
Eccl. 9:17, words of wise are heard in *q.*
Isa. 7:4, be *q.*, fear not.
Isa. 14:7, earth is at rest and *q.*
32:18, in *q.* resting places.
33:20, a *q.* habitation.
Jer. 49:23, sorrow on the sea, it cannot be *q.*
Ezek. 16:42, I will be *q.*
Acts 19:36, ye ought to be *q.*
1Th. 4:11, study to be *q.*
1Tim. 2:2, a *q.* and peaceable life.
1Pet. 3:4, ornament of a meek and *q.* spirit.
See 2Ki. 11:20; 2Chr. 14:1; Job 3:13; 21:23.
QUIETLY. 2Sam. 3:27; Lam. 3:26.
QUIETNESS. Job 34:29, when he giveth *q.*
Prov. 17:1, better a dry morsel and *q.*
Eccl. 4:6, better handful with *q.* than both.
Isa. 30:15, in *q.* and confidence strength.
32:17, effect of righteousness *q.*
See Jud. 8:28; 1Chr. 22:9; 2Th. 3:12.
QUIT. Ex. 21:19; Josh. 2:20; 1Sam. 4:9; 1Cor. 16:13.
QUITE. Gen. 31:15; Job 6:13; Hab. 3:9.
QUIVER. Ps. 127:5; Jer. 5:16; Lam. 3:13.
RACE. Ps. 19:5; Eccl. 9:11; 1Cor. 9:24; Heb. 12:1.
RAGE. 2Ki. 5:12, turned away in a *r.*
Ps. 2:1; Acts 4:25, why do the heathen *r.*
Prov. 14:16, the fool *r.* and is confident.
See Prov. 6:34; 29:9; Dan. 3:13; Hos. 7:16.
RAGGED. Isa. 2:21.
RAGING. Ps. 89:9; Prov. 20:1; Lk. 8:24; Jude 13.
RAGS. Prov. 23:21; Isa. 64:6; Jer. 38:11.
RAIMENT. Gen. 28:20, if the Lord will give me *r.*
Dt. 8:4, thy *r.* waxed not old.
24:13, that he may sleep in his *r.*
17, nor take a widow's *r.* to pledge.
Job 27:16, though he prepare *r.* as the clay.
Isa. 63:3, I will stain all my *r.*
Zech. 3:4, I will clothe thee with *r.*
Mt. 6:25; Lk. 12:23, the body more than *r.*
28, why take though for *r.*
11:8; Lk. 7:25, man clothed in soft *r.*
17:2; Mk. 9:3; Lk. 9:29, his *r.* was white as light.
1Tim. 6:8, having food and *r.*, be content.
Jas. 2:2, poor man in vile *r.*
Rev. 3:18, buy white *r.*
See Mt. 3:4; Lk. 10:30; 23:34; Acts 22:20.
RAIN (*n.*). Lev. 26:4; Dt. 11:14; 28:12, *r.* in due season.
Dt. 11:11, drinketh water of the *r.* of heaven.
32:2, my doctrine shall drop as the *r.*
2Sam. 23:4, clear shining after *r.*
1Ki. 18:41, sound of abundance of *r.*
Ezra 10:13, a time of much *r.*
Job 5:10, who giveth *r.* on earth.
37:6, to small *r.* and to great *r.*
38:28, hath the *r.* a father.
Ps. 72:6, like *r.* on mown grass.
Prov. 25:14, like clouds and wind without *r.*
23, north wind driveth away *r.*
26:1, as *r.* in harvest.
28:3, that oppresseth poor is like sweeping *r*
Eccl. 11:3, if clouds be full of *r.*
12:2, nor clouds return after *r.*
Song 2:11, the *r.* is over and gone.
Isa. 4:6, covert from storm and *r.*
55:10, as the *r.* cometh down.
Ezek. 38:22, I will *r.* an overflowing *r.*
Hos. 6:3, he shall come unto us as the *r.*
Mt. 5:45, *r.* on just and unjust.
7:25, the *r.* descended and floods came.
See Jer. 5:24; Acts 14:17; 28:2; Heb. 6:7.
RAIN (*v.*). Ex. 16:4, I will *r.* bread from heaven.
Job 20:23, God shall *r.* his fury on him.
Ps. 11:6, on wicked he shall *r.* snares.
78:24, 27, and *r.* down manna.
Ezek. 22:24, thou art the land not *r.* upon.
Hos. 10:12, till he come and *r.* righteousness.
See Gen. 2:5; 7:4; Amos 4:7; Rev. 11:6.
RAINY. Prov. 27:15.
RAISE. Dt. 18:15; Acts 3:22, will *r.* up a Prophet.
Jud. 2:16, 18, the Lord *r.* up judges.
1Sam. 2:8; Ps. 113:7, he *r.* poor out of dust.
Job 41:25, when he *r.* himself, mighty are.
Ps. 145:14; 146:8, he *r.* those that be bowed down.
Isa. 45:13, I have *r.* him in righteousness.
Hos. 6:2, in third day he will *r.* us up.
Mt. 10:8; 11:5; Lk. 7:22, *r.* the dead.
16:21; 17:23; Lk. 9:22, be *r.* the third day.
Jn. 2:19, in three days I will *r.* it up.
6:39, 40, 44, 54, I will *r.* him up at the last da
Acts 2:24, 32; 3:15; 4:10; 5:30; 10:40; 13:30, 33, 34; 17:31; Rom. 10:9; 1Cor. 6:14; 2Cor. 4:14; Gal. 1:1; Eph. 1:20, whom God hath *r.* up.
26:8, why incredible that God should *r.* the dead?
Rom. 4:25, *r.* again for our justification.
6:4, like as Christ was *r.* from the dead.
8:11, Spirit of him that *r.* up Jesus.
1Cor. 6:14, and will also *r.* up us by his power.
15:15, *r.* up Christ, whom he *r.* not up.
16, then is not Christ *r.*
17, if Christ be not *r.*
35, how are the dead *r.*
43, it is *r.* in glory, it is *r.* in power.
2Cor. 1:9, trust in God which *r.* the dead.
4:14, he shall *r.* up us also.
Eph. 2:6, and hath *r.* us up together.

Heb. 11:19, accounting God was able to *r.* him.
35, women received dead *r.* to life.
Jas. 5:15, and the Lord shall *r.* him up.
See Lk. 20:37; Jn. 5:21; 2Tim. 2:8.
AN. Ex. 9:23; Num. 16:47; Jer. 23:21.
ANG. 1Sam. 4:5; 1Ki. 1:45.
ANKS. 1Ki. 7:4; Joel 2:7; Mk. 6:40.
ANSOM. Ex. 21:30, give for the *r.* of his life.
30:12, every man a *r.* for his soul.
Job 33:24, I have found a *r.*
36:18, a great *r.* cannot deliver.
Ps. 49:7, nor give a *r.* for him.
Prov. 13:8, the *r.* of a man's life are his riches.
Isa. 35:10, the *r.* of the Lord shall return.
43:3, I gave Egypt for thy *r.*
Hos. 13:14, I will *r.* them from the grave.
Mt. 20:18; Mk. 10:45, to give his life a *r.*
1Tim. 2:6, gave himself a *r.* for all.
See Prov. 6:35; Isa. 51:10; Jer. 31:11.
ARE. Dan. 2:11.
ASE. Ps. 137:7.
ASH. Eccl. 5:2; Acts 19:36.
ATHER. Job 7:15; Jer. 8:3, death *r.* than life.
Ps. 84:10, *r.* be a doorkeeper.
Mt. 10:6, go *r.* to lost sheep
28, *r.* fear him that is able.
25:9, go *r.* to them that sell.
Mk. 5:26, but *r.* grew worse.
Lk. 18:14, justified *r.* than the other.
Jn. 3:19, loved darkness *r.* than light.
Acts 5:29, obey God *r.* than men.
Rom. 8:34, that died, yea *r.*, that is risen.
12:19, *r.* give place to wrath.
1Cor. 6:7, why do ye not *r.* take wrong.
Heb. 11:25, choosing *r.* to suffer.
12:13, let it *r.* be healed.
See Josh. 22:24; 2Ki. 5:13; Phil. 1:12.
AVENING. Ps. 22:13; Ezek. 22:25; Mt. 7:15.
AVENOUS. Isa. 35:9; 46:11; Ezek. 39:4.
EACH. Gen. 11:4; Jn. 20:27; 2Cor. 10:13.
EAD. Dt. 17:19, king shall *r.* his life.
Isa. 34:16, seek out of book of Lord and *r.*
Mt. 12:3; 19:4; 21:16; 22:31; Mk. 2:25; 12:10; Lk. 6:3, have ye not *r.*
Lk. 4:16, Jesus stood up to *r.*
2Cor. 3:2, epistle known and *r.* of all men.
1Tim. 4:13, give attendance to *r.*
See Hab. 2:2; 2Cor. 3:14; Rev. 1:3; 5:4.
EADINESS. Acts 17:11; 2Cor. 8:11; 10:6.
EADY. Num. 32:17, we will go *r.* armed.
Dt. 26:5, a Syrian *r.* to perish.
2Sam. 18:22, wherefore run, no tidings *r.*
Neh. 9:17, thou art a God *r.* to pardon.
Job 12:5, *r.* to slip with is feet.
17:1, the graves are *r.* for me.
29:13, blessing of him *r.* to perish.
Ps. 38:17, I am *r.* to halt.
45:1, pen of a *r.* writer.
86:5, good and *r.* to forgive.
88:15, *r.* to die from my youth.
Prov. 24:11, deliver those *r.* to be slain.
31:6, give strong drink to *r.* to perish.
Eccl. 5:1, be more *r.* to hear.
Isa. 27:13, shall come that were *r.* to perish.
32:4, stammerers *r.* to speak plainly.
38:20, the Lord was *r.* to save me.
Dan. 3:15, if ye be *r.* to fall down.
Mt. 22:4; Lk. 14:17, all things are *r.*
8, the wedding is *r.*
24:44; Lk. 12:40, be ye also *r.*
25:10, they that were *r.* went in.
Mk. 14:38, the spirit is *r.*
Lk. 22:33, I am *r.* to go with thee.
Jn. 7:6, your time is alway *r.*
Acts 21:13, *r.* not to be bound only, but.
Rom. 1:15, I am *r.* to preach at Rome.
2Cor. 8:19, declaration of your *r.* mind.
9:2, Achaia was *r.* a year ago.
1Tim. 6:18, *r.* to distribute.
2Tim. 4:6, *r.* to be offered.
Ti. 3:1, *r.* to every good work.
1Pet. 1:5, *r.* to be revealed.
3:15, *r.* always to give an answer.
5:2, but of a *r.* mind.
Rev. 3:2, things that are *r.* to die.
See Ex. 17:4; 19:11; Ezra 7:6; Job 15:23.
REAP. Lev. 25:11, in jubilee neither sow nor *r.*
Eccl. 11:4, regardeth clouds shall not *r.*
Jer. 12:13, sown wheat, but shall *r.* thorns.
Hos. 8:7, shall *r.* the whirlwind.
10:12, sow in righteousness, *r.* in mercy.
Mic. 6:15, shalt sow, but not *r.*
Mt. 6:26; Lk. 12:24, sow not, neither *r.*
25:26; Lk. 19:21, *r.* where I sowed not.
Jn. 4:38, *r.* whereon ye bestowed no labour.
1Cor. 9:11, if we shall *r.* your carnal things.
2Cor. 9:6, shall *r.* sparingly.
Gal. 6:7, that shall he also *r.*
Jas. 5:4, cried of them which *r.*
See Isa. 17:5; Jn. 4:36, 37; Rev. 14:15.
REASON (*n.*). Job 32:11, I gave ear to your *r.*
Prov. 26:16, seven men that can render a *r.*
Eccl. 7:25, to search out the *r.* of things.
Isa. 41:21, bring forth your strong *r.*
1Pet. 3:15, a *r.* of the hope in you.
See 1Ki. 9:15; Dan. 4:36; Acts 6:2.
REASON (*v.*). Job 9:14, choose words to *r.* with you.
13:3, I desire to *r.* with God.
15:3, should he *r.* with unprofitable talk.
Isa. 1:18, let us *r.* together.
Mt. 16:7; 21:25; Mk. 8:16; 11:31; Lk. 20:5, they *r* among themselves.
Lk. 5:22, what *r.* ye in your hearts.
24:15, while they *r.* Jesus drew near.
Acts 24:25, as he *r.* of righteousness.
See 1Sam. 12:7; Mk. 2:6; 12:28; Acts 28:29.
REASONABLE. Rom. 12:1.
REBEL. Num. 14:9, only *r* not against the Lord.
Josh. 1:18, whosoever doth *r.* he shall die.
Neh. 2:19, will ye *r.* against the king.
Job 24:13, that *r.* against the light.
Ps. 105:28, they *r* not against his word.
Isa. 1:2, have nourished children and they *r.*
63:10, they *r.* and vexed his holy Spirit.
Lam. 3:42, we have *r.*, thou hast not pardoned.
Dan. 9:9, though we have *r.* against him.

See 1Sam. 12:14; Ezek. 2:3; Hos. 7:14; 13:16.
REBELLION. 1Sam. 15:23, *r.* is as the sin of witchcraft.
Job 34:37, he addeth *r.* to his sin.
Prov. 17:11, an evil man seeketh *r.*
Jer. 28:16, thou hast taught *r.*
See Dt. 31:27; Ezra 4:19; Neh. 9:17.
REBELLIOUS. Dt. 21:18, 20, a stubborn and *r.* son.
1Sam. 20:30, son of perverse *r.* woman.
Ps. 66:7, let not the *r.* exalt themselves.
68:6, the *r.* dwell in a dry land.
Isa. 1:23, *r.*, companions of thieves.
Jer. 5:23, this people hath a *r.* heart.
See Ezek. 2:3; 3:9; 12:2; 17:12; 24:3.
REBELS. Num. 17:10; 20:10; Ezek. 20:38.
REBUKE (*n.*). 2Ki. 19:3; Isa. 37:3, this is a day of *r.*
Ps. 39:11, when thou with *r.* doest correct.
80:16, perish at *r.* of thy countenance.
104:7, at thy *r.* they fled.
Prov. 13:8, the poor heareth not *r.*
27:5, open *r.* is better than secret love.
Eccl. 7:5, better to hear *r.* of wise.
Isa. 30:17, thousand flee at *r.* of one.
Jer. 15:15, for thy sake I suffered *r.*
Phil. 2:15, without *r.*
See Dt. 28:20; Isa. 25:8; 50:2.
REBUKE (*v.*). Ps. 6:1; 38:1, *r.* me not in anger.
Prov. 9:7, he that *r.* a wicked man getteth a blot.
8, *r.* a wise man, and he will love thee.
28:23, he that *r.* a man shall find favour
Isa. 2:4; Mic. 4:3, he shall *r.* many nations.
Zech. 3:2; Jude 9, the Lord *r.* thee.
Mal. 3:11, I will *r.* the devourer for your sakes.
Mt. 8:26; Mk. 4:39; Lk. 8:24, he *r.* wind.
16:22; Mk. 8:32, Peter began to *r.* him.
Lk. 4:39, he *r.* the fever.
17:3, if thy brother trespass, *r.* him.
19:39, Master, *r.* thy disciples.
1Tim. 5:1, *r.* not an elder.
20, them that sin, *r.* before all.
2Tim. 4:2, *r.*, exhort, with longsuffering.
Ti. 1:13; 2:15, *r.* them sharply.
Heb. 12:5, nor faint when thou art *r.*
See Ruth 2:16; Neh. 5:7; Amos 5:10.
RECALL. Lam. 3:21.
RECEIPT. Mt. 9:9; Mk. 2:14; Lk. 5:27.
RECEIVE. 2Ki. 5:26, is it a time to *r.* money.
Job 4:12, mine ear *r.* a little.
22:22, *r.* law from his mouth.
Ps. 6:9, the Lord will *r.* my prayer.
49:15, he shall *r.* me.
68:18, hast *r.* gifts for men.
73:24, afterwards *r.* me to glory.
Prov. 2:1, if thou wilt *r.* my words.
Isa. 40:2, she hath *r.* double.
Jer. 2:30, your children *r.* no correction.
Hos. 10:6, Ephraim shall *r.* shame.
14:2, *r.* us graciously.
Mt. 11:5, the blind *r.* their sight.
14, if ye will *r.* it, this is Elias.
18:5, whoso shall *r.* one such little child.
19:12, he that is able let him *r.* it.
21:22, ask, believing ye shall *r.*
Mk. 15:23, but he *r.* it not.
16:19; Acts 1:9, he was *r.* up into heaven.
Lk. 16:9, *r.* you into everlasting habitations.
18:42; Acts 22:13, *r.* thy sight.
Jn. 1:11, his own *r.* him not.
12, to as many as *r.* him.
3:27, can *r.* nothing, except.
5:43, in his own name, he ye will *r.*
44, which *r.* honour one of another.
16:24, ask, and ye shall *r.*
20:22, *r.* ye the Holy Ghost.
Acts 7:59, *r.* my spirit.
8:17, they *r.* the Holy Ghost.
10:43, shall *r.* remission of sins.
19:2, have ye *r.* the Holy Ghost.
20:24, which I have *r.* of the Lord.
Rom. 5:11, by whom we *r.* atonement.
14:3, for God hath *r.* him.
15:7, *r.* ye one another.
1Cor. 3:8, every man shall *r.* his own reward.
11:23, I *r.* of the Lord that which also I delivered.
2Cor. 4:1, as we have *r.* mercy we faint not.
5:10, every one may *r.* things done.
7:2, *r.* us; we have wronged no man.
Phil. 2:29, *r.* him in the Lord.
4:15, as concerning giving and *r.*
Col. 2:6, as ye have *r.* Christ.
1Tim. 3:16, *r.* up into glory.
4:4, if it be *r.* with thanksgiving.
1Jn. 3:22, whatsoever we ask we *r.*
See Ezek. 3:10 Acts 20:35; Jas. 4:3.
RECKON. Lev. 25:50, he shall *r.* with him that bought him.
Ps. 40:5, thy thoughts cannot be *r.* up.
Mt. 18:24, when he had begun to *r.*
25:19, lord of servants *r.* with them.
Rom. 4:4, reward is not *r.* of grace.
6;11, *r.* yourselves dead to sin.
8:18, I *r.* the sufferings of this present time.
See 2Ki. 22:7; Isa. 38:13; Lk. 22:37.
RECOMMENDED. Acts 14:26; 15:40.
RECOMPENCE. Dt. 32:35, to me belongeth *r.*
Job 15:31, vanity shall be his *r.*
Isa. 35:4, God will come with a *r.*
Hos. 9:7, days of *r.* are come.
Joel 3:4, will ye render me a *r.*?
Lk. 14:12, and a *r.* be made thee.
2Cor. 6:13, for a *r.*, be ye also enlarged.
Heb. 2:2; 10:35; 11:26, just *r.* of reward.
See Prov. 12:14; Isa. 34:8; Jer. 51:56.
RECOMPENSE. Num. 5:7, he shall *r.* his trespass.
Ruth 2:12, the Lord *r.* thy work.
2Sam. 19:36, why should the king *r.* me?
Job 34:33, he will *r.* it, whether.
Prov. 20:22, say not, I will *r.* evil.
Isa. 65:6, but will *r.*, even *r.* into their bosom.
Jer. 25:14; Hos. 12:2, will *r.* according to deeds.
Lk. 14:14, for they cannot *r.* thee.
Rom. 11:35, it shall be *r.* to him again.
12:17, *r.* to no man evil for evil.
See 2Chr. 6:23; Jer. 32:18; Heb. 10:30.
RECONCILE. 1Sam. 29:4, wherewith should he *r.*

himself.
Ezek. 45:20, so shall ye *r.* the house.
Mt. 5:24, first be *r.* to thy brother.
Rom. 5:10, if when enemies we were *r.*
Eph. 2:16, that he might *r.* both.
See Lev. 16:20; Rom. 11:15; 2Cor. 5:19.
ECORD. Ex. 20:24, in places where I *r.* my name.
Dt. 30:19; 31:28, I call heaven to *r.*
Job 16:19, my *r.* on high.
Jn. 8:13, thou bearest *r.* of thyself.
Rom. 10:2, I bare them *r.*
Phil. 1:8, God is my *r.* how greatly I long.
1Jn. 5:7, three that bare *r.*
10, he believeth not the *r.*
11, this is the *r.*, that God hath given.
3Jn. 12, we bare *r.*, and our *r.* is true.
See Acts 20:26; Jn. 1:19; Rev. 1:2.
ECOUNT. Nah. 2:5, *r.* his worthies.
ECOVER. 2Ki. 5:3, the prophet would *r.* him.
Ps. 39:13, that I may *r.* strength.
Isa. 11:11, to *r.* remnant of his people.
Hos. 2:9, and I will *r.* my wool and flax.
Mk. 16:18, lay hands on sick, and they shall *r.*
Lk. 4:18, preach *r.* of sight to blind.
See Isa. 38:16; Jer. 8:22; 41:16; 2Tim. 2:16.
ED. Gen. 25:30, *r.* pottage.
49:12, eyes *r.* with wine.
2Ki. 3:22, water *r.* as blood.
Ps. 75:8, wine is *r.*, full of mixture.
Prov. 23:31, look not on wine when *r.*
Isa. 1:18, though your sins be *r.* like crimson.
27:2, a vineyard of *r.* wine.
63:2, *r.* in thine apparel.
Mt. 16:2, fair weather, for the sky is *r.*
See Lev. 13:19; Num. 19:2; Nah. 2:3; Rev. 6:4.
EDEEM. Gen. 48:16, angel which *r.* me.
Ex. 6:6, I will *r.* you.
15:13, people whom thou hast *r.*
Lev. 27:28, no devoted thing, shall be *r.*
2Sam. 4:9, the Lord hath *r.* my soul.
Neh. 5:5, nor is it in our power to *r.* them.
8, after our ability have *r.* Jews.
Job 5:20, in famine he shall *r.* thee.
6:23, to *r.* me from hand of mighty.
Ps. 25:22, *r.* Israel out of all his troubles.
34:22, the Lord *r.* the soul of his servants.
44:26, *r.* us for thy mercies' sake.
49:7, none can *r.* his brother.
15, God will *r.* my soul from the grave.
72:14, he shall *r.* their soul from deceit.
107:2, let the *r.* of the Lord say so.
130:8, he shall *r.* Israel.
Isa. 1:27, Zion shall be *r.* with judgment.
35:9, the *r.* shall walk there.
44:22, return, for I have *r.* thee.
50:2, is my hand shortened, t hat it cannot *r.*
51:11, the *r.* of the Lord shall return.
52:3, *r.* without money.
63:4, the year of my *r.* is come.
Hos. 7:13, though I *r.* them, they have spoken lies.
13:14, I will *r.* them from death.
Lk. 1:68, hath visited, and *r.* his people.
24:21, he who should have *r.* Israel.
Gal. 3:13, *r.* us from curse of the law.
4:5, *r.* them that were under the law.
Ti. 2:14, that he might *r.* us from iniquity.
1 Pet. 1:18, not *r.* with corruptible things.
Rev. 5:9, thou hast *r.* us by thy blood.
See Num. 18:15; 2Sam. 7:23; Eph. 5:16; Col. 4:5.
REDEEMER. Job 19:25, I know that my *r.* liveth.
Ps. 19:14, O Lord, my strength and my *r.*
78:35, God was their *r.*
Prov. 23:11, their *r.* is mighty.
Isa. 47:4, as for our *r.*, the Lord of hosts is his name.
49:26; 60:16, know that I am thy *R.*
59:20, the *R.* shall come to Zion.
63:16, thou art our *r.*
See Isa. 41:14; 44:6; 48:17; 54:5; Jer. 50:34.
REDEMPTION. Lev. 25:24, grant a *r.* for the land.
Ps. 49:8, the *r.* of their soul is precious.
111:9, he sent *r.* to his people.
130:7, plenteous *r.*
Jer. 32:7, the right of *r.* is thine.
Lk. 2:38, that looked for *r.* in Jerusalem.
21:28, your *r.* draweth nigh.
Rom. 8:23, the *r.* of our body.
Eph. 4:30, sealed unto the day of *r.*
See Num. 3:49; Rom. 3:24; 1Cor. 1:30; Heb. 9:12.
REDOUND. 2Cor. 4:15, grace might *r.*
REFORMATION. Heb. 9:10, time of *r.*
REFORMED. Lev. 26:23, if ye will not be *r.*
REFRAIN. Gen. 45:1, Joseph could not *r.* himself.
Job 7:11, I will not *r.* my mouth.
29:9, princes *r.* talking.
Ps. 40:9, I have not *r.* my lips.
119:101, *r.* my feet from every evil way.
Prov. 1:15, *r.* thy foot from their path.
10:19, he that *r.* his lips is wise.
Acts 5:38, *r.* from these men.
See Gen. 43:31; Isa. 64:12; Jer. 31:16; 1Pet. 3:10.
REFRESH. Ex. 31:17, he rested and was *r.*
Job 32:20, I will speak that I may be *r.*
Prov. 25:13, he *r.* the soul of his masters.
Acts 3:19, times of *r.* shall come.
1Cor. 16:18, they *r.* my spirit.
See 1Ki. 13:7; Isa. 28:12; Rom. 15:32; 2Cor. 7:13.
REFUSE (*n.*). 1Sam. 15:9; Lam. 3:45; Amos 8:6.
REFUSE (*v.*). Gen. 37:35, Jacob *r.* to be comforted.
Num. 22:13, the Lord *r.* to give me leave.
1Sam. 16:7, look not on him. for I have *r.* him.
Job 6:7, things my soul *r.* to touch.
Ps. 77:2, my soul *r.* to be comforted.
78:10, they *r.* to walk in his law.
118:22, stone the builders *r.*
Prov. 1:24, I have called and ye *r.*
8:33, be wise and *r.* it not.
10:17, he that *r.* reproof.
13:18, shame to him that *r.* instruction.
15:32, he that *r.* instruction despiseth his soul.
21:25, his hands *r.* to labour.
Isa. 7:15, 16, may know to *r.* the evil.
Jer. 8:5, they *r.* to return.
9:6, they *r.* to know me.

15:18, my wound *r.* to be healed.
25:28, if they *r.* to take the cup.
38:21, if thou *r.* to go forth.
Zech. 7:11, they *r.* to hearken.
Acts 7:35, this Moses whom they *r.*
1Tim. 4:4, nothing to be *r.*
7, *r.* profane and old wives' fables.
5:11, the younger widows *r.*
Heb. 11:24, Moses *r.* to be called.
12:25, *r.* not him that speaketh.
See Ex. 4:23; 10:3; 1Ki. 20:35; 2Ki. 5:16.

REGARD. Gen. 45:20, *r.* not your stuff.
Ex. 5:9, let them not *r.* vain words.
Dt. 10:17, that *r.* not persons.
1Ki. 18:29, neither voice, nor any that *r.*
Job 4:20, they perish without any *r.* it.
34:19, nor *r.* rich more than poor.
39:7, neither *r.* crying of the driver.
Ps. 28:5; Isa. 5:12, they *r.* not works of the Lord.
66:18, if I *r.* iniquity in my heart.
102:17, he will *r.* prayer of the destitute.
106:44, he *r.* their affliction.
Prov. 1:24, and no man *r.*
5:2, that thou mayest *r.* discretion.
6:35, he will not *r.* any ransom.
12:10, *r.* the life of his beast.
13:18; 15:5, he that *r.* reproof.
Eccl. 11:4, he that *r.* the clouds.
Lam. 4:16, the Lord will no more *r.* them.
Dan. 11:37, *r.* God of his fathers, nor *r.* any god.
Mal. 1:9, will he *r.* your persons.
Mt. 22:16; Mk. 12:14, *r.* not the person of men.
Lk. 18:2, neither *r.* man.
Rom. 14:6, he that *r.* the day, *r.* it to the Lord.
See Dt. 28:50; 2Ki. 3:14; Amos 5:22; Phil. 2:30.

REGENERATION. Mt. 19:28, in the *r.*
Ti. 3:5, by the washing of *r.*
See Jn. 1:13; 3:3.

REGISTER. Ezra 2:62; Neh. 7:5, 64.

REHEARSE. Jud. 5:11, *r.* the righteous acts.
Acts 14:27, they *r.* all God has done.
See Ex. 17:14; 1Sam. 8:21; 17:31; Acts 11:4.

REIGN. Gen. 37:8, shalt thou *r.* over us?
Ex. 15:18; Ps. 146:10, Lord shall *r.* for ever.
Lev. 26:17, that hate you shall *r.* over you.
Dt. 15:6, thou shalt *r.* over many nations.
Jud. 9:8, the trees said, *r.* thou over us.
1Sam. 11:12, shall Saul *r.* over us?
12:12, nay, but a king shall *r.* over us.
2Sam. 16:8, in whose stead thou hast *r.*
Job. 34:30, that the hypocrite *r.* not.
Ps. 47:8, God *r* over the heathen.
93:1; 96:10; 97:1; 99:1, the Lord *r.*
Prov. 8:15, by me kings *r.*
30:22, for a servant when he *r.*
Eccl. 4:14, out of prison he cometh to *r.*
Isa. 32:1, a king shall *r.* in righteousness.
52:7, that saith unto Zion, thy God *r.*
Jer. 22:15, shalt thou *r.* because thou closest?
23:5, a king shall *r.* and prosper.
Mic. 4:7, the Lord shall *r.* over them.
Lk. 19:14, not have this man to *r.* over us.
27, that would not I should *r.*
Rom. 5:14, death *r.* from Adam to Moses.
Rom. 5:17, death *r.* by one.
21, as sin hath *r.*, so might grace *r.*
6:12, let not sin *r.* in your bodies.
1Cor. 4:8, ye have *r.* as kings without us.
15:25, for he must *r.*
2Tim. 2:12, if we suffer we shall also *r.* with him
Rev. 5:10, we also shall *r.* on the earth.
11:15, he shall *r.* for ever and ever.
19:6, the Lord God omnipotent *r.*
See Isa. 24:23; Luke 1:33; Rev. 20:4; 22:5.

REINS. Job 16:13, he cleaveth my *r.* asunder.
19:27, though my *r.* be consumed.
Ps. 7:9, God trieth the *r.*
16:7, my *r.* instruct me.
26:2, examine me, try my *r.*
73:21, thus I was pricked in my *r.*
139:13, thou hast possessed my *r.*
Prov. 23:16, my *r.* shall rejoice.
Isa. 11:5, faithfulness the girdle of his *r.*
Rev. 2:23, I am he who searcheth the *r.*
See Jer. 11:20; 12:2; 17:10; 20:12; Lam. 3:13.

REJECT. 1Sam. 8:7, they have not *r.* thee, but they have *r.* me.
10:19, ye have *r.* God who saved you.
15:23, because thou hast *r.* the word of the Lord.
16:1, I have *r.* him from being king.
Isa. 53:3, despised and *r.* of men.
Jer. 2:37, the Lord hath *r.* thy confidence.
7:29, the Lord hath *r.* the generation.
8:9, they have *r.* the word of the Lord.
14:19, thou hast utterly *r.* Judah.
Lam. 5:22, thou has utterly *r.* us.
Hos. 4:6, because thou hast *r.* knowledge, I will thee
Mt. 21:42; Mk. 12:10; Lk. 20:17, the stone whic builders *r.*
Mk. 7:9, full well ye *r.* the commandment.
Lk. 7:30, lawyers *r.* the counsel of God.
17:25, must first be *r.* of this generation.
Ti. 3:10, after admonition *r.*
Heb. 12:17, when he would have inherited was
See Jer. 6:19; Mk. 6:26; 8:31; Lk. 9:22; Jn. 12:48

REJOICE. Dt. 12:7, shall *r.* in all ye put your hand to.
16:14, thou shalt *r.* in thy feast.
26;11, thou shalt *r.* in every good thing.
28:63; 30:9, the Lord will *r.* over you.
30:9, *r.* for good as he *r.* over thy fathers.
1Sam. 2:1, because I *r.* in thy salvation.
1Chr. 16:10, let the heart of them *r.* that seek th Lord.
2Chr. 6:41, let thy saints *r.* in goodness.
Job 21:12, they *r.* at sound of the organ.
31:25, if I *r.* because my wealth was great.
29, if I *r.* at destruction of him that.
39:21, the horse *r.* in his strength.
Ps. 2:11, *r.* with trembling.
5:11, let all that trust in thee *r.*
9:14, I will *r.* in thy salvation.
19:5, *r.* as a strong man to run a race.
33:21, our heart shall *r.* in him.

35:15, in mine adversity they *r*.
26, let them be ashamed that *r*. at my hurt.
38:16, hear me, lest they should *r*. over me.
51:8, bones thou hast broken may *r*.
58:10, righteous shall *r*. when he seeth.
63:7, in shadow of thy wings will I *r*.
68:3, let righteous *r*., yea exceedingly *r*.
85:6, that thy people may *r*. in thee.
89:16, in thy name shall they *r*. all the day.
96:11, let the heavens *r*.
97:11, the Lord reigneth, let the earth *r*.
104:31, the Lord shall *r*. in his works.
107:42, the righteous shall see it and *r*.
109:28, let thy servant *r*.
149:2, let Israel *r*. in him that made him.
Prov. 2:14, who *r*. to do evil.
5:18, *r*. with the wife of thy youth.
23:15, if thine heart be wise, mine shall *r*.
24, father of the righteous shall greatly *r*.
25, she that bare thee shall *r*.
24:17, *r*. not when thine enemy falleth.
Prov. 29:2, when righteous are in authority people *r*.
31:25, she shall *r*. in time to come.
Eccl. 2:10, my heart *r*. in all my labour.
3:12, for a man to *r*. and do good.
22; 5:19, that a man should *r*. in his works.
11:9, *r*. O young man in thy youth.
Isa. 9:3, as men *r*. when they divide the spoil.
24:8, noise of them that *r*. endeth.
29:19, poor among men shall *r*.
35:1, the desert shall *r*.
62:5, as the bridegroom *r*. over the bride.
64:5, him that *r*. and worketh righteousness.
65:13, my servants shall *r*., but ye.
66:14, when ye see this, your heart shall *r*.
Jer. 11:15, when thou doest evil, then thou *r*.
32:41, I will *r*. over them to do them good.
51:39, that they may *r*. and sleep.
Ezek. 7:12, let not buyer *r*.
Amos 6:13, which *r*. in a thing of nought.
Mic. 7:8, *r*. not against me.
Hab. 3:18, yet I will *r*. in the Lord.
Mt. 18:13, he *r*. more of that sheep.
Lk. 1:14, many shall *r*. at his birth.
6:23, *r*. ye in that day, and leap for joy.
10:20, in this *r*. not, but rather *r*. because.
21, in that hour Jesus *r*. in spirit.
15:6, 9, *r*. with me.
Jn. 5:35, willing for a season to *r*. in his light.
8:56, Abraham *r*. to see my day.
14:28, if ye loved me, ye would *r*.
16:20, ye shall weep, but the world shall *r*.
22, I will see you again, and your heart shall *r*.
Rom. 5:2, and *r*. in hope.
12:15, *r*. with them that do *r*.
1Cor. 7:30, they that *r*. as though they *r*. not.
13:6, *r*. not in iniquity, but *r*. in the truth.
Phil. 1:18, I therein do *r*. and will *r*.
2:16, that I may *r*. in the day of Christ.
3:1, finally, *r*. in the Lord.
4:4, *r*. in the Lord alway, and again I say *r*.
1Th. 5:16, *r*. evermore.
Jas. 1:9, let the brother of low degree *r*.
2:13, mercy *r*. against judgment.
1Pet. 1:8, *r*. with joy unspeakable.
See 1Ki. 1:40; 5:7; 2Ki. 11:14; 1Chr. 29:9.
REJOICING. Job 8:21, till he fill thy lips with *r*.
Ps. 107:22, declare his works with *r*.
118:15, voice of *r*. is in tabernacles of the righteous.
119:111, they are the *r*. of my heart.
126:6, shall doubtless come again *r*.
Prov. 8:31, *r*. in the habitable part of his earth.
Isa. 65:18, I create Jerusalem a *r*.
Jer. 15:16, thy word was to me the *r*. of my heart.
Zeph. 2:15, this is the *r*. city.
Acts 5:41, *r*. that they were counted worthy.
Rom. 12:12, *r*. in hope.
2Cor. 6:10, as sorrowful, yet alway *r*.
1Th. 2:19, what is our crown of *r*.
See Hab. 3:14; Acts 8:39; Gal. 6:4; Jas. 4:16.
RELEASE. Est. 2:18; Mt. 27:17; Mk. 15:11; Jn. 19:10.
RELIEVE. Lev. 25:35, then thou shalt *r*. him.
Ps. 146:9, he *r*. the fatherless and widow.
Isa. 1:17, *r*. the oppressed.
Lam. 1:16, comforter that should *r*. my soul is far from me.
See Acts 11:29; 1Tim. 5:10, 16.
RELIGION. Acts 26:5; Gal. 1:13; Jas. 1:26, 27.
RELIGIOUS. Acts 13:43; Jas. 1:26.
RELY. 2Chr. 13:18; 16:7, 8.
REMAIN. Gen. 8:22, while earth *r*.
14:10, they that *r*. fled to the mountain.
Ex. 12:10, let nothing of it *r*. until morning.
Josh. 13:1, there *r*. yet much land to be possessed.
1Ki. 18:22, I only *r*. a prophet.
Job 21:32, yet shall he *r*. in the tomb.
Prov. 2:21, the perfect shall *r*. in the land.
Eccl. 2:9, my wisdom *r*. with me.
Jer. 17:25, this city shall *r*. for ever.
Jer. 37:10, there *r*. but wounded men.
Lam. 2:22, in day of anger none *r*.
Mt. 11:23, would have *r*. until this day.
Jn. 6:12, gather up the fragments that *r*.
9:41, ye say, we see, therefore your sin *r*.
Acts 5:4, whiles it *r*., was it not thine own?
1Cor. 15:6, the greater part *r*. to this present.
1Th. 4:15, we which are alive and *r*. unto coming of the Lord.
Heb. 4:9, there *r*. a rest to the people of God.
10:26, there *r*. no more sacrifice for sins.
Rev. 3:2, things which *r*. ready to die.
See Ps. 76:10; Lam. 5:19; Jn. 1:33; 1Jn. 3:9.
REMEDY. 2Chr. 36:16; Prov. 6:15; 29:1.
REMEMBER. Gen. 40:23, yet did not the butler *r*.
41:9, I do *r*. my faults this day.
Ex. 13:3, *r*. this day ye came out of Egypt.
20:8, *r*. the sabbath day.
Num. 15:39, *r*. all the commandments.
Dt. 5:15; 15:15; 16:12; 24:18, 22, *r*. thou wast a servant.
8:2, *r*. all the way the Lord led thee.

32:7, *r.* the days of old.
1Chr. 16:12, *r.* his marvellous works.
Neh. 13:14, *r.* me, O God, concerning this.
Job 7:7, O *r.* my life is wind.
11:16, *r.* it as waters that pass away.
14:13, appoint me a set time and *r.* me.
24:20, the sinner shall be no more *r.*
Ps. 9:12, when he maketh inquisition he *r.*
20:7, he will *r.* the name of the Lord.
25:6, *r.* thy mercies, they have been ever of old.
7, *r.* not sins of my youth, by mercy *r.* me.
63:6, when I *r.* thee upon my bed.
77:3, I *r.* God and was troubled.
78:39, he *r.* that they were but flesh.
79:8, *r.* not against us former iniquities.
89:47, *r.* how short my time is.
105:8, he hath *r.* his covenant for ever.
119:55, I have *r.* thy name in the night.
136:23, who *r.* us in our low estate.
137:1, we wept when we *r.* Zion.
Prov. 31:7, drink and *r.* his misery no more.
Eccl. 5:20, not much *r.* the days of his life.
11:8, let him *r.* the days of darkness.
12:1, *r.* now thy Creator.
Song 1:4, we will *r.* thy love.
Isa. 23:16, sing songs that thou mayest be *r.*
43:18; 46:9, *r.* ye not the former things.
57:11, thou hast not *r.* me.
65:17, the former heavens shall not be *r.*
Jer. 31:20, I do earnestly *r.* him still.
51:50, ye that have escaped *r.* the Lord.
Lam. 1:9, she *r.* not her last end.
Ezek. 16:61; 20:43; 36:31, then shalt thou *r.* thy ways.
Amos 1:9, and *r.* not the brotherly covenant.
Hab. 3:2, in wrath *r.* mercy.
Zech. 10:9, they shall *r.* me in far countries.
Mt. 26:75, Peter *r.* the word of Jesus.
Lk. 16:25, son, *r.* that thou in thy lifetime.
17:32, *r.* Lot's wife.
23:42, Lord *r.* me when thou comest.
24:8, and they *r.* his words.
Jn. 2:22, when he was risen, they *r.*
15:20, *r.* the word I said unto you.
Acts 11:16, then *r.* I the word of the Lord.
20:35, *r.* the words of the Lord Jesus.
Gal. 2:10, that we should *r.* the poor.
Col. 4:18, *r.* my bonds.
1 Th. 1:3, *r.* your work of faith.
Heb. 13:3, *r.* them that are in bonds.
7, *r.* them that have the rule over you.
Rev. 2:5, *r.* from whence thou art fallen.
3:3, *r.* how thou hast received.
See Ps. 88:5; 103:14; Mt. 5:23; Jn. 16:21.
REMEMBRANCE. Num. 5:15, bringing iniquity to *r.*
2Sam. 18:18, no son to keep my name in *r.*
1Ki. 17:18, art thou come to call my sin to *r.*
Job 18:17, his *r.* shall perish.
Ps. 6:5, in death there is no *r.* of thee.
30:4; 97:12, give thanks at *r.* of his holiness.
77:6, I call to *r.* my song in the night.
112:6, righteous shall be in everlasting *r.*
Eccl. 1:11, there is no *r.* of former things.
2:16, no *r.* of wise more than the fool.
Isa. 43:26, put me in *r.*
57:8, behind doors hast thou set up thy *r.*
Lam. 3:20, my soul hath them still in *r.*
Ezek. 23:19, calling to *r.* days of youth.
Mal. 3:16, a book of *r.*
Lk. 22:19; 1Cor. 11:24, this do in *r.* of me.
Jn. 14:26, bring all things to your *r.*
Acts 10:31, thine alms are had in *r.*
2Tim. 1:3, I have *r.* of thee in my prayers.
2:14, of these things put them in *r.*
See Heb. 10:3; 2Pet. 1:12; 3:1; Jude 5; Rev. 16:1
REMIT. Jn. 20:23, whose soever sins ye *r.*, are *r.*
REMNANT. Lev. 5:13, the *r.* shall be the priest's.
2Ki. 19:4; Isa. 37:4, lift up prayer for the *r.*
Ezra 9:8, grace shewed to leave us a *r.*
Isa. 1:9, unless the Lord had left a *r.*
11:11, to recover the *r.* of his people.
16:14, the *r.* shall be very small and feeble.
Jer. 44:28, *r.* shall know whose words shall stan
Ezek. 6:8, yet will I leave a *r.*
Joel 2:32, the *r.* whom the Lord shall call.
See Mic. 2:12; Hag. 1:12; Rom. 11:5; Rev. 11:13
REMOVE. Dt. 19:14, shall not *r.* landmark.
Job 9:5, *r.* the mountains and they know not.
14:18, the rock is *r.* out of his place.
Ps. 36:11, let not hand of wicked *r.* me.
39:10, *r.* thy stroke away from me.
46:2, not fear though the earth be *r.*
81:6, I *r.* his shoulder from burden.
103:12, so far hath he *r.* our transgressions.
119:22, *r.* from me reproach.
125:1, as mount Zion, which cannot be *r.*
Prov. 4:27, *r.* thy foot from evil.
10:30, the righteous shall never be *r.*
Eccl. 11:10, *r.* sorrow from thy heart.
Isa. 13:13, earth shall *r.* out of her place.
24:20, earth shall be *r.* out of her place.
29:13, have *r.* their heart far from me.
54:10, the hills shall be *r.*
Jer. 4:1, return unto me, then shalt thou not *r.*
Lam. 3:17, thou hast *r.* my soul from peace.
Mt. 17:20, ye shall say, *r.* hence, and it shall *r.*
Lk. 22:42, *r.* this cup from me.
Gal. 1:6, I marvel ye are so soon *r.*
Rev. 2:5, or else I will *r.* thy candlestick.
See Job 19:10; Eccl. 10:9; Ezek. 12:3; Heb. 12:2
REND. 1Ki. 11:11, I will *r.* the kingdom.
Isa. 64:1, that thou wouldest *r.* the heavens.
Hos. 13:8, I will *r.* the caul of their heart.
Joel 2:13, *r.* your heart.
Mt. 7:6, lest they turn again and *r.* you.
See Ps. 7:2; Eccl. 3:7; Jer. 4:30; Jn. 19:24.
RENDER. Dt. 32:41, *r.* vengeance.
1Sam. 26:23, *r.* to every man his faithfulness.
Job 33:26, he will *r.* to man his righteousness.
34:11, the work of a man shall be *r.* to him.
Ps. 28:4, *r.* to them their desert.
38:20, they that *r.* evil for good.
79:12, and *r.* to our neighbour sevenfold.
94:2, *r.* a reward to the proud.
116:12, what shall I *r.* to the Lord.

Prov. 24:12; Rom. 2:6, *r.* to every man according.
26:16, wiser than seven men who can *r.* a reason.
Hos. 14:2, so will we *r.* the calves of our lips.
Joel. 3:4, will ye *r.* me a recompence.
Zech. 9:12, I will *r.* double.
Mt. 21:41, *r.* fruits in their seasons.
22:21; Mk. 12:17; Lk. 20:25, *r.* unto Caesar.
Rom. 13:7, *r.* to all their dues.
1Th. 3:9, what thanks can we *r.*
1Th. 5:15, see that none *r.* evil for evil.
1Pet. 3:9, not *r.* evil for evil, or railing.
See Num. 18:9; Jud. 9:56; Ps. 62:12; Isa. 66:6.
RENEW. Job 10:17, thou *r.* thy witnesses.
29:20, my bow was *r.* in my hand.
Ps. 51:10, and *r.* a right spirit within me.
103:5, thy youth is *r.* like the eagle's
104:30, thou *r.* the face of the earth.
Isa. 40:31, wait on Lord shall *r.* strength.
41:1, let the people *r.* their strength.
Lam. 5:21, *r.* our days as of old.
2Cor. 4:16, the inward man is *r.* day by day.
Eph. 4:23, be *r.* in spirit of your mind.
Col. 3:10, new man which is *r.* in knowledge.
Heb. 6:6, if they fall away, to *r.* them again.
See 2Chr. 15:8; Rom. 12:2; Ti. 3:5.
RENOUNCED. 2Cor. 4:2, have *r.* hidden things.
RENOWN. Gen. 6:4; Num. 16:2, men of *r.*
Num. 1:16, the *r.* of the congregation.
Isa. 14:20, evil doers shall never be *r.*
Ezek. 16:14, thy *r.* went forth among the heathen.
34:29, a plant of *r.*
See Ezek. 23:23; 26:17; 39:13; Dan. 9:15.
RENT. Gen. 37:33, Joseph is *r.* in pieces.
Josh. 9:4, bottles old and *r.*
Jud. 14:5, 6, *r.* lion as he would have *r.* a kid.
1Ki. 13:3, the altar shall be *r.*
Job 26:8, the cloud is not *r.* under them.
Mt. 9:16; Mk. 2:21, the *r.* is made worse.
27:51; Mk. 15:38; Lk. 23:45, veil was *r.* in twain.
See 1Sam. 15:27; Job 1:20; 2:12; Jer. 36:24.
REPAID. Prov. 13:21, to righteous good shall be *r.*
REPAIR. 2Chr. 24:5, gather money to *r.* the house.
Isa. 61:4, they shall *r.* the waste cities.
See 2Ki. 12:5; Ezra 9:9; Neh. 3:4; Isa. 58:12.
REPAY. Dt. 7:10, he will *r.* to his face.
Lk. 10:35, when I come I will *r.* thee.
Rom. 12:19, vengeance is mine, I will *r.*
Phile. 19, I have written it, I will *r.* it.
See Job 21:31; 41:11; Isa. 59:18.
REPEATETH. Prov. 17:9, he that *r.* a matter.
REPENT. Gen. 6:6, it *r.* the Lord.
Ex. 13:17, lest the people *r.*
32:14; 2Sam. 24:16; 1Chr. 21:15; Jer. 26:19, Lord *r.* of evil he thought to do.
Num. 23:19, neither son of man that he should *r.*
Dt. 32:36, Lord shall *r.* for his servants.
1Sam. 15:29, will not *r.*, for he is not a man that he should *r.*
Job 42:6, I *r.* in dust and ashes.
Ps. 90:13, let it *r.* thee concerning thy servants.
106:45, Lord *r.* according to his mercies.
110:4; Heb. 7:21, Lord hath sworn and will not *r.*
Jer. 8:6, no man *r.* of his wickedness.
18:8; 26:13, if that nation turn I will *r.*
31:19, after that I was turned I *r.*
Joel 2:13, he is slow to anger and *r.* him.
Mt. 12:41; Lk. 11:32, they *r.* at the preaching.
21:29, afterward he *r.* and went.
27:3, Judas *r.* himself.
Lk. 13:3, except ye *r.*
15:7, joy over one sinner that *r.*
17:3, if thy brother *r.*, forgive him.
Acts 8:22, *r.* of this thy wickedness.
Rev. 2:21, space to *r.*, and she *r.*, not.
See Acts 2:38; 17:30; Rev. 2:5; 3:3; 16:9.
REPENTANCE. Hos. 13:14, *r.* shall be hid.
Mt. 3:8; Lk. 3:8; Acts 26:2, fruits meet for *r.*
Rom. 2:4, goodness of God leadeth thee to *r.*
11:29, gifts of God are without *r.*
2Cor. 7:10, *r.* not to be repented of.
Heb. 6:1, not laying again the foundation of *r.*
6, to renew them again to *r.*
12:17, no place of *r.*, though he sought it.
See Lk. 15:7; Acts 20:21; 2Tim. 2:25; 2pPet. 3:9.
REPLENISH. Gen. 1:28; 9:1; Jer. 31:25; Ezek. 26:2.
REPLIEST. Rom. 9:20, that *r.* against God.
REPORT (*n.*). Gen. 37:2, their evil. *r.*
Ex. 23:1, thou shalt not *r.* a false *r.*
Num. 13:32, an evil *r.* of the land.
1Sam. 2:24, it is no good *r.* I hear.
1Ki. 10:6; 2Chr. 9:5, it was a true *r.* I heard.
Prov. 15:30, a good *r.* maketh the bones fat.
Isa. 28:19, a vexation only to understand *r.*
53:1, who hath believed our *r.*
Acts 6:3, men of honest *r.*
10:22, of good *r.* among the Jews.
2Cor. 6:8, by evil *r.* and good *r.*
Phil. 4:8, whatsoever things are of good *r.*
1Tim. 3:7, a bishop must have a good *r.*
See Dt. 2:25; Heb. 11:2, 39; 3Jn. 12.
REPORT (*v.*). Neh. 6:6, it is *r.* among heathen.
Jer. 20:10, *r.*, say they, and we will *r.* it.
Mt. 28:15, saying is commonly *r.*
Acts 16:2, well *r.* of by the brethren.
1Cor. 14:25, he will *r.* that God is in you.
See Ezek. 9:11; Rom. 3:8; 1Tim. 5:10; 1Pet. 1:12.
REPROACH (*n.*). Gen. 30:23, hath taken away my *r.*
34:14, that were a *r.* to us.
1Sam. 11:2, lay it for a *r.* upon all Israel.
Neh. 2:17, build that we be no more a *r.*
Ps. 15:3, that taketh not up a *r.*
22:6, a *r.* of men.
31:11, I was a *r.* among mine enemies.
44:13; 79:4; 89:41, a *r.* to our neighbours.
69:9; Rom. 15:3, the *r.* of them that reproached thee.
78:66, put them to a perpetual *r.*
Prov. 6:33, his *r.* shall not be wiped away.
14:34, sin is a *r.* to any people.
18:3, with ignominy cometh *r.*
Isa. 43:28, I have given Israel to *r.*
51:7, fear not the *r.* of men.

Jer. 23:40, I will bring an everlasting *r.*
31:19, I did bear the *r.* of my youth.
Lam. 3:30, he is filled full with *r.*
Ezek. 5:14, I will make thee a *r.* among nations.
15, Jerusalem shall be a *r.* and a taunt.
Mic. 6:16, ye shall bear the *r.* of my people.
2Cor. 11:21, I speak as concerning *r.*
12:10, pleasure in *r.* for Christ's sake.
1Tim. 3:7, good report lest he fall into *r.*
4:10, we labour and suffer *r.*
Heb. 11:26, the *r.* of Christ greater riches.
13:13, without the camp bearing his *r.*
See Ps. 69:10; 119:39; Jer. 6:10; 20:8; 24:9.
REPROACH (*v.*). Num. 15:30, *r.* the Lord.
Ruth 2:15, *r.* her not.
2Ki. 19:22; Isa. 37:23, whom hast thou *r.*
Job 19:3, these ten times have ye *r.* me.
27:6, my heart shall not *r.* me.
Ps. 42:10, as with a sword mine enemies *r.* me.
44:16, the voice of him that *r.*
74:22, how the foolish man *r.* thee.
119:42; Prov. 27:11, to answer him that *r.* me.
Prov. 14:31; 17:5, oppresseth poor *r.* his Maker.
Lk. 6:22, men shall *r.* you for my sake.
1Pet. 4:14, if ye be *r.* for Christ's sake.
See Ps. 55:12; 74:18; 79:12; 89:51; Zeph. 2:8.
REPROACHFULLY. Job 16:10; 1Tim. 5:14.
REPROVE. 1Chr. 16:21, *r.* kings for their sakes.
Job 6:25, what doth your arguing *r.*
13:10, he will *r.* you if ye accept.
22:4, will he *r.* thee for fear.
40:2, he that *r.* God let him answer it.
Ps. 50:8, I will not *r.* thee for burnt offerings.
141:5, let him *r.* me, it shall be excellent oil.
Prov. 9:8, *r.* not a scorner lest he hate thee.
15:12, a scorner loveth not one that *r.*
19:25, *r.* one that hath understanding.
29:1, he that being often *r.*
30:6, lest he *r.* thee and thou be found.
Isa. 11:4, *r.* with equity for the meek.
Jer. 2:19, thy backslidings shall *r.* thee.
Jn. 3:20, lest his deeds should be *r.*
Jn. 16:8, he will *r.* the world of sin.
See Lk. 3:19; Eph. 5:11, 13; 2Tim. 4:2.
REPROVER. Prov. 25:12; Ezek. 3:26.
REPUTATION. Eccl. 10:1, him that is in *r.* for wisdom.
Acts 5:34, had in *r.* among the people.
Phil. 2:7, made himself of no *r.*
29, hold such in *r.*
See Job 18:3; Dan. 4:35; Gal. 2:2.
REQUEST. Jud. 8:24, I would desire a *r.* of thee.
Ezra 7:6, the king granted all his *r.*
Job 6:8, Oh that I might have my *r.*
Ps. 21:2, hast not withholden *r.* of his lips.
106:15, he gave them their *r.*
Phil. 1:4, in every prayer making *r.* with joy.
4:6, let your *r.* be made known.
See 2Sam. 14:15; Neh. 2:4; Est. 4:8; 5:3.
REQUESTED. 1Ki. 19:4, Elijah *r.* that he might die.
REQUIRE. Gen. 9:5, blood of your lives will I *r.*
31:39, of my hand didst thou *r.* it.
Dt. 10:12; Mic. 6:8, what doth the Lord *r.*
Josh. 22:23; 1Sam. 20:16, let the Lord himself *r.* it.
Ruth 3:11, I will do all thou *r.*
1Sam. 21:8, the king's business *r.* haste.
2Sam. 3:13, one thing I *r.* of thee.
19:38, whatsoever thou shalt *r.* I will do.
2Chr. 24:22, the Lord look on it and *r.* it.
Neh. 5:12, we will restore and *r.* nothing of the
Ps. 10:13, he hath said thou wilt not *r.* it.
40:6, sin offering hast thou not *r.*
137:3, they that wasted us *r.* of us mirth.
Prov. 30:7, two things have I *r.* of thee.
Eccl. 3:15, God *r.* that which is past.
Isa. 1:12, who hath *r.* this at your hand?
Ezek. 3:18; 33:6, his blood will I *r.* at thine hand
34:10, I will *r.* my flock at their hand.
Lk. 11:50, may be *r.* of this generation.
12:20, this night thy soul shall be *r.*
48:, of him shall much be *r.*
19:23, I might have *r.* mine own with usury.
1Cor. 1:22, the Jews *r.* a sign.
4:2, it is *r.* in stewards.
See 2Chr. 8:14; Ezra 3:4; Neh. 5:18; Est. 2:15.
REQUITE. Gen. 50:15, Joseph will certainly *r.* us.
Dt. 32:6, do you thus *r.* the Lord.
Jud. 1:7, as I have done so God hath *r.* me.
2Sam. 2:6, I also will *r.* you this kindness.
16:12, it may be the Lord will *r.* good for his
1Tim. 5:4, learn to *r.* their parents.
See Ps. 10:14; 41:10; Jer. 51:56.
REREWARD. Josh. 6:9; Isa. 52:12; 58:8.
RESCUE. Ps. 35:17, *r.* my soul.
Hos. 5:14, none shall *r.* him.
See Dt. 28:31; 1Sam. 14:45; Dan. 6:27; Acts 23:27.
RESEMBLANCE. Zech. 5:6, this is their *r.*
RESEMBLE. Jud. 8:18; Lk. 13:18.
RESERVE. Gen. 27:36, hast thou not *r.* a blessing.
Ruth 2:18, gave her mother in law that she had
Job 21:30, the wicked is *r.* to day of destruction.
38:23, which I have *r.* against time of trouble
Jer. 3:5, will he *r.* anger for ever.
5:24, he *r.* the weeks of harvest.
50:20, I will pardon them whom I *r.*
Nah. 1:2, the Lord *r.* wrath for his enemies.
1Pet. 1:4, an inheritance *r.* in heaven.
2Pet. 2:4, to be *r.* to judgment.
3:7, the heavens and earth are *r.* unto fire.
See Num. 18:9; Rom. 11:4; 2Pet. 2:9; Jude 6:13.
RESIDUE. Ex. 10:5, locusts shall eat the *r.*
Isa. 38:10, I am deprived of the *r.* of my years.
Jer. 15:9, *r.* of them will I deliver to the sword.
Ezek. 9:8, wilt thou destroy all the *r.*
Zech. 8:11, I will not be to the *r.* as in former days.
Mal. 2:15, yet had he the *r.* of the Spirit.
Acts 15:17, that the *r.* might seek the Lord.
See Neh. 11:20; Jer. 8:3; 29:1; 39:3.
RESIST. Zech. 3:1, at his right hand to *r.*
Mt. 5:39, *r.* not evil.
Lk. 21:15, adversaries shall not be able to *r.*
Rom. 9:19, who hath *r.* his will.
13:2, whoso *r.* power, *r.* ordinance of God.

Jas. 4:6; 1Pet. 5:5, God *r.* the proud.
7, *r.* the devil, and he will flee.
1Pet. 5:9, whom *r.* stedfast in the faith.
See Acts 6:10; 7:51; 2Tim. 3:8; Heb. 12:4.
SORT. Neh. 4:20, *r.* hither to us.
Ps. 71:3, whereunto I may continually *r.*
Jn. 18:2, Jesus ofttimes *r.* thither.
See Mk. 2:13; 10:1; Jn. 18:20; Acts 16:13.
SPECT (*n.*). Gen. 4:4, Lord had *r.* to Abel.
Ex. 2:25, God had *r.* unto them.
1Ki. 8:28; 2Chr. 6:19, have *r.* unto their prayer.
2Chr. 19:7; Rom. 2:11; Eph. 6:9; Col. 3:25, there is no *r.* of persons with God.
Ps. 74:20, have *r.* unto thy covenant.
119:15, I will have *r.* unto thy ways.
138:6, yet hath he *r.* to the lowly.
Prov. 24:23; 28:31, not good to have *r.* of persons.
Isa. 17:7, his eyes shall have *r.* to Holy One.
22:11, nor had *r.* to him that fashioned it.
Phil. 4:11, not that I speak in *r.* of want.
See Heb. 11:26; Jas. 2:1, 3, 9; 1Pet. 1:17.
SPECT (*v.*). Lev. 19:15, shalt not *r.* person of poor.
Dt. 1:17, ye shall not *r.* persons in judgment.
Job 37:24, he *r.* not any that are wise of heart.
See Num. 16:15; 2Sam. 14:14; Ps. 40:4; Lam. 4:16.
SPITE. Ex. 8:15; 1Sam. 11:3.
ST (*n.*). Gen. 49:15, Issachar saw that *r.* was good.
Ex. 31:15; 35:2; Lev. 16:31; 23:3, 32; 25:4, the sabbath of *r.*
33:14, my presence shall go with thee, and I will give thee *r.*
Lev. 25:5, a year of *r.* to the land.
Dt. 12:10, when he giveth you *r.* from your enemies.
Jud. 3:30, the land had *r.* fourscore years.
Ruth 3:1, shall not I seek *r.* for thee.
1Chr. 22:9, a man of *r.*, and I will give him *r.*
18, hath he not given you *r.* on every side.
28:2, to build a house of *r.*
Neh. 9:28, after they had *r.* they did evil.
Est. 9:16, the Jews had *r.* from their enemies.
Job 3:17, there the weary be at *r.*
11:18, thou shalt take thy *r.* in safety.
17:16, when our *r.* together is in the dust.
Ps. 55:6, then would I fly away and be at *r.*
95:11; Heb. 3:11, not enter into my *r.*
116:7, return to thy *r.*, O my soul.
132:8, arise into thy *r.*
14, this is my *r.* for ever.
Eccl. 2:23, his heart taketh not *r.* in the night.
Isa. 11:10, his *r.* shall be glorious.
14:7; Zech. 1:11, earth is at *r.* and quiet.
18:4, I will take my *r.*
30:15, in returning and *r.* shall ye be saved.
66:1, where is the place of my *r.*?
Jer. 6:16, ye shall find *r.* for your souls.
Ezek. 38:11, I will go to them that are at *r.*
Mic. 2:10, depart, this is not your *r.*
Mt. 11:28, I will give you *r.*
29, ye shall find *r.* to your souls.
12:43; Lk. 11:24, seeking *r.* and finding none.
26:45; Mk. 14:41, sleep on and take your *r.*
Jn. 11:13, of taking *r.* in sleep.
Acts 9:31, then had the churches *r.*
See Prov. 29:17; Eccl. 6:5; Dan. 4:4; 2Th. 1:7.
REST (*v.*). Gen. 2:2, he *r.* on seventh day.
Num. 11:25, when the Spirit *r.* upon them.
2Chr. 32:8, people *r.* on the words.
Job 3:18, there the prisoners *r.* together.
Ps. 16:9; Acts 2:26, my flesh shall *r.* in hope.
37:7, *r.* in the Lord.
Eccl. 7:9, anger *r.* in bosom of fools.
Isa. 11:2, the spirit of the Lord shall *r.* upon him.
28:12, ye may cause the weary to *r.*
57:20, like the sea when it cannot *r.*
62:1, for Jerusalem's sake I will not *r.*
Isa. 63:14, Spirit of the Lord caused him to *r.*
Jer. 47:6, *r.* and be still.
Dan. 12:13, thou shalt *r.* and stand in thy lot.
Mk. 6:31, come and *r.* awhile.
2Cor. 12:9, power of Christ may *r.* on me.
Rev. 4:8, they *r.* not day and night.
6:11, *r.* yet for a little season.
14:13, that they may *r.* from their labours.
See Prov. 14:33; Song 1:7; Isa. 32:18; Lk. 10:6.
RESTORE. Ex. 22:4, he shall *r.* double.
Lev. 6:4, he shall *r.* that he took away.
Dt. 22:2, things strayed thou shalt *r.* again.
Ps. 23:3, he *r.* my soul.
51:12, *r.* to me the joy of thy salvation.
69:4, I *r.* that which I took not away.
Isa. 1:26, I will *r.* thy judges as at the first.
Jer. 27:22, I will *r.* them to this place.
30:17, I will *r.* health to thee.
Ezek. 33:15, if wicked *r.* pledge.
Mt. 17:11; Mk. 9:12, Elias shall *r.* all things.
Lk. 19:8, I *r.* him fourfold.
Acts 1:6, wilt thou at this time *r.* the kingdom.
Gal. 6:1, *r.* such an one in meekness.
See Ruth 4:15; Isa. 58:12; Joel 2:25; Mk. 8:25.
RESTRAIN. Gen. 11:6, nothing will be *r.*
Ex. 36:6, people were *r.* from bringing.
1Sam. 3:13, his sons made themselves vile, and he *r.* them not.
Job 15:4, thou *r.* prayer before God.
8, dost thou *r.* wisdom to thyself.
Ps. 76:10, remainder of wrath shalt thou *r.*
See Gen. 8:2; Isa. 63:15; Ezek. 31:15; Acts 14:18.
RETAIN. Job 2:9, dost thou still *r.* integrity.
Prov. 3:18, happy is every one that *r.* her.
4:4, let thine heart *r.* my words.
11:16, a gracious woman *r.* honour.
Eccl. 8:8, no man hath power to *r.* the spirit.
Jn. 20:23, whose soever sins ye *r.* they are *r.*
See Mic. 7:18; Rom. 1:28; Phile. 13.
RETIRE. Jud. 20:39; 2Sam. 11:15; Jer. 4:6.
RETURN. Gen. 3:19, to dust shalt thou *r.*
Ex. 14:27, the sea *r.* to his strength.
Jud. 7:3, whosoever is fearful, let him *r.*
Ruth 1:16, entreat me not to leave thee or *r.*
2Sam. 12:23, he shall not *r.* to me.
2Ki. 20:10, let the shadow *r.* backward.

Job 1:21, naked shall I *r.* thither.
7:10, he shall *r.* no more.
10:21; 16:22, I go whence I shall not *r.*
15:22, he believeth not he shall *r.* out of darkness.
33:25, he shall *r.* to the days of his youth.
Ps. 35:13, my prayer *r.* into mine own bosom.
73:10, his people *r.* hither.
90:3, thou sayest, *r.*, ye children of men.
104:29, they die and *r.* to their dust.
116:7, *r.* to thy rest, O my soul.
Prov. 2:19, none that go to her *r.* again.
26:11, as a dog *r.* to his vomit.
27, he that rolleth a stone, it will *r.*
Eccl. 1:7, whence rivers come, thither they *r.* again.
5:15, naked shall he *r.* to go as he came.
12:2, nor the clouds *r.* after the rain.
7, dust *r.* to earth and spirit *r.* to God.
Isa. 21:12, if ye will enquire, enquire ye; *r.*, come.
35:10; 51:11, the ransomed of the Lord shall *r.*
44:22, *r.* unto me, for I have redeemed thee.
45:23, word is gone out and shall not *r.*
55:11, it shall not *r.* to me void.
Jer. 4:1, if thou wilt *r.*, saith the Lord, *r.* unto me.
15:19, let them *r.* unto thee, but *r.* not thou.
24:7, they shall *r.* with whole heart.
31:8, a great company shall *r.* thither.
36:3, *r.* every man from his evil way.
Ezek. 46:9, he shall not *r.* by the way he came.
Hos. 2:7, I will *r.* to my first husband.
5:15, I will *r.* to my place.
7:16, they *r.*, but not to the most High.
Hos. 14:7, they that dwell under his shadow shall *r.*
Amos 4:6, yet have ye not *r.* to me.
Joel 2:14, who knoweth if he will *r.* and repent.
Zech. 1:16, I am *r.* to Jerusalem with mercies.
8:3, I am *r.* to Zion and will dwell.
Mal. 3:7, *r.* to me and I will *r.* to you.
18, then shall ye *r.* and discern.
Mt. 12:44; Lk. 11:24, I will *r.* into my house.
24:18, neither let him in the field *r.* back.
Lk. 9:10, apostles *r.* and told him all.
10:17, the seventy *r.* with joy.
12:36, when he will *r.* from wedding.
17:18, not found that *r.* to give glory.
Acts 13:34, now no more to *r.* to corruption.
Heb. 11:15, might have had opportunity to *r.*
1Pet. 2:25, now *r.* to the Shepherd of your souls.
See Gen. 31:3; Ex. 4:18; Lev. 25:10; Isa. 55:7.
REVEAL. Dt. 29:29, things *r.* belong unto us and to our children.
1Sam. 3:7, nor was word of Lord *r.* to him.
Job 20:27, the heaven shall *r.* his iniquity.
Prov. 11:13; 20:19, a talebearer *r.* secrets.
Isa. 22:14, it was *r.* in mine ears.
40:5, glory of the Lord shall be *r.*
53:1; Jn. 12:38, to whom is arm of Lord *r.*
56:1, my righteousness is near to be *r.*
Jer. 11:20, unto thee have I *r.* my cause.
33:6, I will *r.* abundance of peace.
Dan. 2:22, he *r.* deep and secret things.
28, there is a God that *r.* secrets.
Amos 3:7, he *r.* his secrets to the prophets.
Mt. 10:26; Lk. 12:2, nothing covered that shall not be *r.*
11:25, hast *r.* them unto babes.
16:17, flesh and blood hath not *r.* it.
Lk. 2:35, that thoughts of many hearts may be *r.*
17:30, in day when Son of man is *r.*
Rom. 1:17, righteousness of God *r.*
18, wrath of God is *r.* from heaven.
8:18, glory which shall be *r.* in us.
1Cor. 2:10, God hath *r.* them by his Spirit.
3:13, it shall be *r.* by fire.
14:30, if anything be *r.* to another.
Gal. 1:16, to *r.* his Son in me.
2Th. 1:7, when Lord Jesus shall be *r.*
2:3, man of sin be *r.*
8, that wicked one be *r.*
1Pet. 1:5, ready to be *r.* in last time.
4:13, when his glory shall be *r.*
5:1, partaker of glory that shall be *r.*
See Eph. 3:5; Phil. 3:15; 2Th. 2:6.
REVELATION. Rom. 2:5, *r.* of righteous judgment
16:25, *r.* of the mystery.
1Cor. 14:26, every one hath a *r.*
2Cor. 12:1, to visions and *r.*
See Gal. 2:2; Eph. 1:17; 3:3; 1Pet. 1:13; Rev. 1:1
REVELLINGS. Gal. 5:21; 1Pet. 4:3.
REVENGE. Jer. 15:15, O Lord, *r.* me.
20:10, we shall take our *r.* on him.
Nah. 1:2, the Lord *r.* and is furious.
2Cor. 7:11, what *r.* it wrought in you.
10:6, in readiness to *r.*
See Ps. 79:10; Ezek. 25:12; Rom. 13:4.
REVENUE. Prov. 8:19, my *r.* better than silver.
16:8, better than great *r.* without right.
Jer. 12:13, ashamed of your *r.*
See Ezra 4:13; Prov. 15:6; Isa. 23:3; Jer. 12:13.
REVERENCE. Ps. 89:7; Mt. 21:37; Mk. 12:6; Heb. 12:9.
REVEREND. Ps. 111:9, holy and *r.* is his name.
REVERSE. Num. 23:20; Est. 8:5, 8.
REVILE. Isa. 51:7, neither be afraid of *r.*
Mt. 27:39, they that passed by *r.* him.
Mk. 15:32, they that were crucified *r.* him.
1Cor. 4:12, being *r.* we bless.
1Pet. 2:23, when he was *r.*, *r.* not again.
See Ex. 22:28; Mt. 5:11; Jn. 9:28; Acts 23:4.
REVIVE. Neh. 4:2, will they *r.* the stones.
Ps. 85:6, wilt thou not *r.* us.
Ps. 138:7, thou wilt *r.* me.
Isa. 57:15, to *r.* spirit of the humble.
Hos. 6:2, after two days will he *r.* us.
14:7, they shall *r.* as corn.
Hab. 3:2, *r.* thy work in midst of years.
Rom. 7:9, when commandment came sin *r.*
14:9, Christ both died, rose, and *r.*
See Gen. 45:27; 2Ki. 13:21; Ezra 9:8.
REVOLT. Isa. 1:5; 31:6; 59:13; Jer. 5:23.
REWARD (*n.*). Gen. 15:1, thy exceeding great *r.*
Num. 22:7, *r.* of divination in their hand.
Dt. 10:17, God who taketh not *r.*

Ruth 2:12, full *r.* be given thee of the Lord.
2Sam. 4:10, thought I would have given *r.*
Job 6:22, did I say, give a *r.*
7:2, as an hireling looketh for *r.*
Ps. 19:11, in keeping them there is great *r.*
58:11, there is a *r.* for the righteous.
91:8, thou shalt see the *r.* of the wicked.
127:3, fruit of womb is his *r.*
Prov. 11:18, soweth righteousness a sure *r.*
21:14, a *r.* in the bosom.
24:20, no *r.* to the evil. man.
Eccl. 4:9, they have a good *r.* for labour.
9:5, neither have they any more a *r.*
Isa. 1:23, every one followeth after *r.*
5:23, justify wicked for *r.*
40:10; 62:11, his *r.* is with him.
Ezek. 16:34, thou givest *r.*, and no *r.* is given thee.
Dan. 5:17, give thy *r.* to another.
Hos. 9:1, thou hast loved a *r.*
Mic. 3:11, the heads thereof judge for *r.*
7:3, judge asketh for a *r.*
Mt. 5:12; Lk. 6:23, great is your *r.* in heaven.
46, what *r.* have ye.
6:1, ye have no *r.* of your father.
2, 5, 16, they have their *r.*
10:41, a prophet's *r.*, a righteous man's *r.*
42; Mk. 9:41, in no wise lose *r.*
Lk. 6:35, do good and your *r.* shall be great.
23:41, we receive due *r.* of our deeds.
Acts 1:18, purchased with *r.* of iniquity.
Rom. 4:4, the *r.* is not reckoned.
1Cor. 3:8, every man shall receive his own *r.*
9:18, what is my *r.* then.
Col. 2:18, let no man beguile you of your *r.*
3:24, the *r.* of the inheritance.
1Tim. 5:18, labourer worthy of his *r.*
Heb. 2:2; 10:35; 11:26, recompence of *r.*
2Pet. 2:13, the *r.* of unrighteousness.
See 2Jn. 8; Jude 11; Rev. 11:18; 22:12.

EWARD (*v.*). Gen. 44:4, wherefore have ye *r.*
Dt. 32:41, I will *r.* them that hate me.
1Sam. 24:17, thou hast *r.* me good.
2Chr. 15:7, be strong, and your work shall be *r.*
20:11, behold how they *r.* us.
Job 21:19, he *r.* him and he shall know it.
Ps. 31:23, plentifully *r.* the proud doer.
35:12; 109:5, they *r.* me evil for good.
103:10, nor *r.* us according to our iniquities.
137:8, happy is he that *r.* thee.
Prov. 17:13, whoso *r.* evil, evil shall not depart.
25:22, heap coals, and the Lord shall *r.* thee.
26:10, both *r.* the fool and *r.* transgressors.
Jer. 31:16, thy work shall be *r.*
See 2Sam. 22:21; Mt. 6:4; 16:27; 2Tim. 4:14.

CH. Gen. 13:2, Abram was very *r.*
14:23, lest thou shouldest say, I have made Abram *r.*
Ex. 30:15, the *r.* shall not give more.
Josh. 22:8, return with much *r.* to your tents.
Ruth 3:10, followedst not poor or *r.*
1Sam. 2:7, the Lord maketh poor and *r.*
1Ki. 3:11; 2Chr. 1:11, neither hast asked *r.*
13, I have given thee both *r.* and honour.
10:23; 2Chr. 9:22, Solomon exceeded all for *r.*
1Chr. 29:12, both *r.* and honour come of thee.
Job 15:29, he shall not be *r.*
Job 20:15, he swallowed down *r.*
27:19, *r.* man shall lie down, but shall not be gathered.
36:19, will he esteem thy *r.*
Ps. 37:16, better than *r.* of many wicked.
39:6, he heapeth up *r.*
45:12, the *r.* shall entreat thy favour.
49:16, be not afraid when one is made *r.*
52:7, trusted in abundance of *r.*
62:10, if *r.* increase set not your heart.
73:12, the ungodly increase in *r.*
104:24, the earth is full of thy *r.*
112:3, wealth and *r.* shall be in his house.
Prov. 3:16, in left hand *r.* and honour.
8:18, *r.* and honour are with me.
10:4, hand of diligent maketh *r.*
22, blessing of the Lord maketh *r.*
11:4, *r.* profit not in day of wrath.
13:7, poor yet hath great *r.*
18:23, the *r.* answereth roughly.
21:17, he that loveth wine shall not be *r.*
23:5, *r.* make themselves wings.
28:11, *r.* man is wise in his own conceit.
30:8, give me neither poverty nor *r.*
Eccl. 5:13, *r.* kept for owners to their hurt.
10:20, curse not *r.* in thy bedchamber.
Isa. 45:3, I will give thee hidden *r.*
53:9, with the *r.* in his death.
Jer. 9:23, let not *r.* man glory in his *r.*
17:11, getteth *r.* and not by right.
Ezek. 28:5, heart lifted up because of *r.*
Hos. 12:8, Ephraim said, I am become *r.*
Zech. 11:5, blessed be the Lord, for I am *r.*
Mt. 13:22; Mk. 4:19; Lk. 8:14, deceitfulness of *r.*
Mk. 10:23, hardly shall they that have *r.*
12:41, *r.* cast in much.
Lk. 1:53, *r.* he hath sent empty away.
6:24, woe to you *r.* for ye have received.
12:21, not *r.* toward God.
14:12, call not thy *r.* neighbours.
18:23, sorrowful, for he was very *r.*
Rom. 2:4, the *r.* of his goodness.
9:23, make known the *r.* of his glory.
10:12, the Lord is *r.* to all that call.
11:12, fall of them the *r.* of the world.
33, the depth of the *r.* of the wisdom.
1Cor. 4:8, now ye are full, now ye are *r.*
2Cor. 6:10, poor, yet making many *r.*
8:9, *r.*, yet for your sakes.
Eph. 1:7, redemption according to the *r.* of grace.
2:4, God, who is *r.* in mercy.
7, that he might show the exceeding *r.* of grace.
3:8, unsearchable *r.* of Christ.
Phil. 4:19, according to his *r.* in glory by Christ.
Col. 1:27, *r.* of the glory of this mystery.
2:2, the *r.* of the full assurance.
1Tim. 6:9, they that will be *r.* fall into temptation.
17, nor trust in uncertain *r.*

18, do good and be *r.* in good works.
Heb. 11:26, reproach of Christ greater *r.*
Jas. 1:10, let *r.* rejoice that he is made low.
2:5, hath not God chosen the poor, *r.* in faith.
5:2, your *r.* are corrupted.
Rev. 2:9, but thou art *r.*
3:17, because thou sayest, I am *r.*
18, buy of me gold that thou mayest be *r.*
5:12, worthy is the Lamb to receive *r.*
See Lev. 25:47; Jas. 1:11; 2:6; 5:1; Rev. 6:15.
RICHLY. Col. 3:16; 1Tim. 6:17.
RIDDANCE. Lev. 23:22; Zeph. 1:18.
RIDDLE. Jud. 14:12; Ezek. 17:2.
RIDE. Dt. 32:13, *r.* on high places of the earth.
33:26, who *r.* upon the heaven.
Jud. 5:10, ye that *r.* on white asses.
2Ki. 4:24, slack not thy *r.* for me.
Job 30:22, causest me to *r.* upon the wind.
Ps. 45:4, in thy majesty *r.* prosperously.
66:12, hast caused men to *r.* over our heads.
Ps. 68:4, 33, extol him that *r.* on the heavens.
Isa. 19:1, the Lord *r.* on a swift could.
See Hos. 14:3; Amos 2:15; Hab. 3:8; Hag. 2:22.
RIDER. Gen. 49:17; Ex. 15:1; Job 39:18; Zech. 10:5.
RIDGES. Ps. 65:10, waterest the *r.* thereof.
RIGHT (*n.*). Gen. 18:25, shall not Judge of all do *r.*?
Dt. 6:18; 12:25; 21:9, shalt do that is *r.*
21:17, the *r.* of the firstborn is his.
2Sam. 19:28, what *r.* have I to cry to the king.
Neh. 2:20, ye have no *r.* in Jerusalem.
Job 34:6, should I lie against my *r.*
36:6, he giveth *r.* to the poor.
Ps. 9:4, thou maintainest my *r.*
17:1, hear the *r.*, O Lord.
140:12, Lord will maintain *r.* of the poor.
Prov. 16:8, great revenues without *r.*
Jer. 17:11, that getteth riches and not by *r.*
Ezek. 21:27, till he come whose *r.* it is.
See Amos 5:12; Mal. 3:5; Heb. 13:10.
RIGHT (*adj.*). Gen. 24:48, the Lord led me in *r.* way.
Dt. 32:4, God of truth, just and *r.* is he.
1Sam. 12:23, I will teach you the good and *r.* way.
2Sam. 15:3, thy matters are good and *r.*
Neh. 9:13, thou gavest them *r.* judgments.
Job 6:25, how forcible are *r.* words.
34:23, he will not lay on man more than *r.*
Ps. 19:8, the statutes of the Lord are *r.*
45:6, sceptre is a *r.* sceptre.
51:10, renew a *r.* spirit within me.
107:7, he led them forth by the *r.* way.
119:75, thy judgments are *r.*
Prov. 4:11, I have led thee in *r.* paths.
8:6, opening of my lips shall be *r.* things.
12:5, thoughts of the righteous are *r.*
15:, way of a fool is *r.* in his own eyes.
14:12; 16:25, there is a way that seemeth *r.*
21:2, every way of man is *r.* in his own eyes.
24:26, kiss his lips that giveth a *r.* answer.
Isa. 30:10, prophesy not *r.* things.
Jer. 2:21, planted wholly a *r.* seed.
Ezek. 18:5, if a man do that which is *r.*
19; 21:27; 33:14, that which is lawful and *r.*
Hos. 14:9, the ways of the Lord are *r.*
Amos 3:10, they know not how to do *r.*
Mt. 20:4, whatsoever is *r.* I will give you.
Mk. 5:15; Lk. 8:35, in his *r.* mind.
Lk. 10:28, thou hast answered *r.*
Eph. 6:1, obey your parents, this is *r.*
See Jud. 17:6; Lk. 12:57; Acts 8:21; 2Pet. 2:15.
RIGHTEOUS. Gen. 7:1, thee have I seen *r.* before me.
18:23, wilt thou destroy *r.* with wicked.
20:4, wilt thou slay also a *r.* nation?
38:26, she hath been more *r.* than I.
Ex. 23:8, gift perverteth words of the *r.*
Num. 23:10, let me die the death of the *r.*
Dt. 25:1; 2Chr. 6:23, they shall justify the *r.*
1Sam. 24:17, thou art more *r.* than I.
1Ki. 2:32, two men more *r.* than he.
Job 4:7, where were the *r.* cut off.
9:15, though I were *r.* yet would I not answe
15:14, what is man that he should be *r.*
17:9, *r.* shall hold on his way.
22:3, is it any pleasure that thou art *r.*
23:7, there the *r.* might dispute with him.
34:5, Job hath said, I am *r.*
Ps. 1:5, the congregation of the *r.*
6, the Lord knoweth the way of the *r.*
7:9, the *r.* God trieth the hearts.
11:3, what can the *r.* do.
34:17, the *r.* cry, and the Lord heareth them
19, many are the afflictions of the *r.*
37:16, a little that a *r.* man hath.
21, the *r.* showeth mercy and giveth.
25, have not seen the *r.* forsaken.
29, the *r.* shall inherit the land.
30, mouth of *r.* speaketh wisdom.
39, salvation of *r.* is of the Lord.
Ps. 55:22, never suffer the *r.* to be moved.
58:11, there is a reward for the *r.*
69:28, let them not be written with the *r.*
92:12, the *r.* shall flourish like palm tree.
97:11, light is sown for the *r.*
112:6, *r.* shall be in everlasting remembranc
125:3, rod shall not rest on lot of *r.*
140:13, the *r.* shall give thanks.
141:5, let the *r.* smite me.
146:8, the Lord loveth the *r.*
Prov. 2:7, he layeth up wisdom for the *r.*
3:32, his secret is with the *r.*
10:3, the Lord will not suffer *r.* to famish.
11, the mouth of *r.* is a well of life.
16, labour of *r.* tendeth to life.
21, lips of *r.* feed many.
24, desire of the *r.* shall be granted.
25, the *r.* is an everlasting foundation.
28, hope of the *r.* shall be gladness.
30, the *r.* shall never be removed.
11:8, the *r.* is delivered out of trouble.
10, when it goeth well with the *r.*
21, seed of the *r.* shall be delivered.
12:3, the root of the *r.* shall not be moved.
Prov. 5, thoughts of the *r.* are right.
7, house of the *r.* shall stand.
10, *r.* man regardeth the life of his beast.
26, the *r.* is more excellent than his

neighbour.
13:9, the light of the *r.* rejoiceth.
21, to the *r.* good shall be repaid.
25, *r.* eateth to the satisfying of his soul.
14:9, among the *r.* there is favour.
32, the *r.* hath hope in his death.
15:6, in the house of the *r.* is much treasure.
19, the way of the *r.* is made plain.
28, the heart of the *r.* studieth to answer.
29, he heareth the prayer of the *r.*
16:13, *r.* lips are delight of kings.
18:10, *r.* runneth into it and is safe.
28:1, the *r.* are bold as a lion.
29:2, when the *r.* are in authority, people rejoice.
Eccl. 7:16, be not *r.* overmuch.
9:1, the *r.* and the wise are in the hand of God.
2, one event to *r.* and wicked.
Isa. 3:10, say to *r.* it shall be well.
24:16, songs, even glory to the *r.*
26:2, that the *r.* nation may enter.
41:2, raised up a *r.* man from the east.
53:11, shall my *r.* servant justify.
57:1, *r.* perisheth, and no man layeth it.
60:21, thy people shall be all *r.*
Jer. 23:5, raise to David a *r.* branch.
Ezek. 13:22, with lies ye have made *r.* sad.
16:52, thy sisters are more *r.* than thou.
33:12, the righteousness of the *r.* shall not.
Amos 2:6, they sold the *r.* for silver.
Mal. 3:18, discern between the *r.* and wicked.
Mt. 9:13; Mk. 2:17; Lk. 5:32, not come to call *r.*
13:17, many *r.* men have desired.
43, then shall the *r.* shine forth.
23:28, outwardly appear *r.* to men.
29, garnish sepulchres of the *r.*
25:46, the *r.* unto life eternal.
Lk. 1:6, they were both *r.* before God.
18:9, trusted they were *r.* and despised others.
23:47, certainly this was *r.* man.
Jn. 7:24, judge *r.* judgment.
Rom. 3:10, there is none *r.*, no not one.
5:7, scarcely for a *r.* man will one die.
19, many be *r.*
2Th. 1:6, it is a *r.* thing with God.
2Tim. 4:8, the Lord, the *r.* Judge.
Heb. 11:4, obtained witness that he was *r.*
1Pet. 3:12, eyes of the Lord are over the *r.*
4:18, if the *r.* scarcely be saved.
2Pet. 2:8, Lot vexed his *r.* soul.
1Jn. 2:1, Jesus Christ the *r.*
1 Jn. 3:7, *r.* as he is *r.*
Rev. 22:11, he that is *r.* let him be *r.* still.
See Ezek. 3:20; Mt. 10:41; 1Tim. 1:9; Jas. 5:16.

RIGHTEOUSLY. Dt. 1:16; Prov. 31:9, judge *r.*
Ps. 67:4; 96:10, thou shalt judge the people *r.*
Isa. 33:15, he that walketh *r.* shall dwell on high.
See Jer. 11:20; Ti. 2:12; 1Pet. 2:23.

RIGHTEOUSNESS. Gen. 30:33, so shall my *r.* answer for me.
Dt. 33:19, offer sacrifices of *r.*
1Sam. 26:23; Job 33:26, render to every man his *r.*
Job 6:29, return again, my *r.* is in it.
27:6, my *r.* I hold fast.
29:14, I put on *r.* and it clothed me.
35:2, thou saidst, My *r.* is more than God's?
36:3, I will ascribe *r.* to my Maker.
Ps. 4:1, hear me, O God of my *r.*
5, offer the sacrifice of *r.*
9:8, he shall judge the world in *r.*
15:2, he that worketh *r.* shall never be moved.
17:15, as for me, I will behold thy face in *r.*
23:3, leadeth me in paths of *r.*
24:5, and *r.* from the God of his salvation.
40:9, I have preached *r.*
45:7; Heb. 1:9, thou lovest *r.*
50:6; 97:6, heavens shall declare his *r.*
72:2, he shall judge thy people with *r.*
85:10, *r.* and peace have kissed each other.
94:15, judgment shall return unto *r.*
97:2, *r.* is the habitation of his throne.
111:3; 112:3, 9, his *r.* endureth for ever.
118:19, open to me the gates of *r.*
132:9, let thy priests be clothed with *r.*
Prov. 8:18, durable riches and *r.* are with me.
10:2; 11:4, but *r.* delivereth from death.
11:5, *r.* of the perfect shall direct his way.
6, *r.* of the upright shall deliver.
19, *r.* tendeth to life.
12:28, in the way of *r.* is life.
14:34, *r.* exalteth a nation.
16:8, better is a little with *r.*
12, the throne is established by *r.*
31, crown of glory if found in way of *r.*
Eccl. 7:15, a just man that perisheth in his *r.*
Isa. 11:5, *r.* the girdle of his loins.
26:10, yet will he not learn *r.*
32:1, a king shall reign in *r.*
17, the work of *r.* peace, and the effect of *r.*
41:10, uphold thee with right hand of my *r.*
46:12, ye that are far from *r.*
58:8, thy *r.* shall go before thee.
59:16, his *r.* sustained him.
62:2, the Gentiles shall see thy *r.*
64:6, our *r.* are as filthy rags.
Jer. 23:6; 33:16, this is his name, The Lord our *r.*
33:15, cause the branch of *r.* to grow.
51:10, the Lord hath brought forth our *r.*
Ezek. 3:20; 18:24, righteous man turn from *r.*
14:14, deliver but their own souls by *r.*
18:20, the *r.* of the righteous shall be upon him.
33:13, if he trust to his own *r.*
Dan. 4:27, break off thy sins by *r.*
9:7, *r.* belongeth to thee.
24, to bring in everlasting *r.*
12:3, they that turn many to *r.*
Hos. 10:12, till he rain *r.* upon you.
Amos 5:24, let *r.* run down as a stream.
6:12, turned fruit of *r.* into hemlock.
Zeph. 2:3, ye meek of the earth, seek *r.*
Mal. 4:2, shall the Sun of *r.* arise.

Mt. 3:15, to fulfil all *r.*
5:6, hunger and thirst after *r.*
10, persecuted for *r.* sake.
20, except your *r.* exceed the *r.*
21:32, John came to you in the way of *r.*
Lk. 1:75, in *r.* before him.
Jn. 16:8, reprove the world of *r.*
Acts 10:35, he that worketh *r.*
Acts 13:10, thou enemy of all *r.*
24:25, as he reasoned of *r.*
Rom. 1:17; 3:5; 10:3, the *r.* of God.
4:6, to whom God imputeth *r.*
11, seal of the *r.* of faith.
5:17, which receive the gift of *r.*
18, by the *r.* of one.
21, so might grace reign through *r.*
6:13, yield your members as instruments of *r.*
20, ye were free from *r.*
8:10, the Spirit is life, because of *r.*
9:30, the *r.* which is of faith.
10:3, going about to establish their own *r.*
4, Christ is the end of the law for *r.*
10, with the heart man believeth unto *r.*
14:17, kingdom of God not meat and drink, but *r.*
1Cor. 1:30, Christ is made unto us *r.*
15:34, awake to *r.*
2Cor. 5:21, that we might be made the *r.*
6:7, the armour of *r.*
14, what fellowship hath *r.*
Gal. 2:21, if *r.* come by the law.
5:5, we wait for the hope of *r.*
Eph. 6:14, the breastplate of *r.*
Phil. 1:11, filled with the fruits of *r.*
3:6, touching the *r.* in the law, blameless.
9, not having mine own *r.*, but the *r.* of God.
1Tim. 6:11, follow after *r.*
2Tim. 3:16, for instruction in *r.*
4:8, laid up for me a crown of *r.*
Ti. 3:5, not by works of *r.*
Heb. 1:8, a sceptre of *r.*
5:13, unskilful in the word of *r.*
7:2, by interpretation, King of *r.*
11:7, heir of the *r.* which is by faith.
33, through faith wrought *r.*
12:11, the peaceable fruit of *r.*
Jas. 1:20, wrath of man worketh not *r.* of God.
3:18, the fruit of *r.* is sown in peace.
1Pet. 2:24, dead to sins should live unto *r.*
2Pet. 2:5, a preacher of *r.*
21, better not to have known way of *r.*
3:13, new earth, wherein dwelleth *r.*
1Jn. 2:29, every one that doeth *r.*
See Isa. 54:14; 63:1; Zech. 8:8; Rev. 19:8.
RIGHTLY. Gen. 27:36; Lk. 7:43; 20:21; 2Tim. 2:15.
RIGOUR. Ex. 1:13, 14; Lev. 25:43, 46, 53.
RINGLEADER. Acts 24:5, a *r.* of the sect of the Nazarenes.
RIOT. Rom. 13:13; Ti. 1:6; 1Pet. 4:4; 2Pet. 2:13.
RIPE. Gen. 40:10, brought forth *r.* grapes.
Ex. 22:29, offer the first of thy *r.* fruits.
Num. 18:13, whatsoever is first *r.* be thine.
Joel 3:13, put in sickle, for the harvest is *r.*
Mic. 7:1, my soul desired the first-*r* fruit.
Rev. 14:5, time to reap, for harvest of earth is *r.*
See Num. 13:20; Jer. 24:2; Hos. 9:10; Nah. 3:12.
RISE. Gen. 19:2, ye shall *r.* up early.
23, the sun was *r.* when Lot entered Zoar.
Num. 24:17, a sceptre shall *r.* out of Israel.
32:14, ye are *r.* up in your fathers' stead.
Job 9:7, commandeth the sun and it *r.* not.
14:12, man lieth down and *r.* not.
24:22, he *r.* up, and no man is sure of life.
31:14, what shall I do when God *r.* up.
Ps. 27:3, though war should *r.* up against me.
119:62, at midnight I will *r.* to give thanks.
127:2, it is vain to *r.* up early.
Prov. 31:15, she *r* up while it is yet night.
28, her children *r.* up and call her blessed.
Eccl. 12:4, he shall *r.* at the voice of the bird.
Isa. 33:10, now will I *r.*, saith the Lord.
58:10, then shall thy light *r.* in obscurity.
60:1, the glory of the Lord is *r.* upon thee.
Jer. 7:13; 25:3; 35:14, I spake unto you, *r.* up early.
25; 25:4; 26:5; 29:19; 35:15; 44:4, I sent my servants, *r.* early.
11:7, *r.* early and protesting.
25:27, fall and *r.* no more.
Lam. 3:63, sitting down and *r.* up, I am their music.
Mt. 5:45, maketh sun to *r.* on evil and good.
17:9; Mk. 9:9, until Son of man be *r.*
20:19; Mk. 9:31; 10:34; Lk. 18:33; 24:7, the third day he shall *r.* again.
26:32; Mk. 14:28, after I am *r.* I will go before you.
46, *r.*, let us be going.
Mk. 4:27, should sleep, and *r.* night and day.
9:10, what the *r.* from dead should mean.
10:49, *r.*, he calleth thee.
Lk. 2:34, this child is set for the fall and *r.*
11:7, I cannot *r.* and give thee.
22:46, why sleep ye, *r.* and pray.
24:34, the Lord is *r.* indeed.
Jn. 11:23, thy brother shall *r.* again.
Acts 10:13, *r.*, Peter, kill and eat.
26:16, *r.*, and stand upon thy feet.
23, the first that should *r.* from the dead.
Rom. 8:34, that died, yea rather that is *r.*
1Cor. 15:15, if so be the dead *r.* not.
20, but now is Christ *r.*
Col. 3:1, if ye than be *r.* with Christ.
1Th. 4:16, the dead in Christ shall *r.* first.
See Prov. 30:31; Isa. 60:3; Mk. 16:2; Col. 2:12.
RITES. Num. 9:3, according to all the *r.* of it.
RIVER. Ex. 7:19; 8:5, stretch out hand on *r.*
2Sam. 17:13, that city, and we will draw it into the *r.*
2Ki. 5:12, are the *r.* of Damascus better.
Job 20:17, ye shall not see the *r.* of honey.
28:10, he cutteth out *r.* among the rocks.
29:6, the rock poured out *r.* of oil.
40:23, he drinketh up a *r.*, and hasteth not.
Ps. 1:3, tree planted by the *r.*
36:8, the *r.* of thy pleasures.

46:4, *r.*, the streams whereof make glad.
65:9, enrichest it with *r.* of God.
107:33, turneth *r.* into a wilderness.
119:136, *r.* of waters run down mine eyes.
137:1, by the *r.* of Babylon we sat.
Eccl. 1:7, all the *r.* run into the sea.
Isa. 32:2, shall be as *r.* of water in a dry place.
43:2, through the *r.*, they shall not overflow.
19, I will make *r.* in the desert.
48:18, then had thy peace been as a *r.*
66:12, I will extend peace like a *r.*
Lam. 2:18, let tears run down like *r.*
Mic. 6:7, be pleased with *r.* of oil.
Jn. 7:38, shall flow *r.* of living water.
Rev. 22:1, a pure *r.* of water of life.
See Gen. 41:1; Ex. 1:22; Ezek. 47:9; Mk. 1:5.
ROAD. 1Sam. 27:10, whither have ye made a *r.*
ROAR. 1Chr. 16:32; Ps. 96:11; 98:7, let the sea *r.*
Job 3:24, my *r.* are poured out.
Ps. 46:3, will not fear, though waters *r.*
104:21, young lions *r.* after their prey.
Prov. 19:12; 20:2, king's wrath as the *r.* of a lion.
Isa. 59:11, we *r.* like bears.
Jer. 6:23, their *r.* like the sea.
25:30, the Lord shall *r.* from on high.
Hos. 11:10, he shall *r.* like a lion.
Joel 3:16; Amos 1:2, the Lord shall *r.* out of Zion.
Amos 3:4, will a lion *r.* when he hath no prey?
See Ps. 22:1; 32:3; Zech. 11:3; Rev. 10:3.
ROARING. Prov. 28:15, as a *r.* lion, is a wicked ruler.
Lk. 21:25, distress, the sea and waves *r.*
1Pet. 5:8, the devil as a *r.* lion.
See Ps. 22:13; Isa. 31:4; Ezek. 22:25; Zeph. 3:3.
ROAST. Ex. 12:9, not raw, but *r.* with fire.
Prov. 12:27, slothful man *r.* not that he took.
Isa. 44:16, he *r. r.*, and is satisfied.
See Dt. 16:7; 1Sam. 2:15; 2Chr. 35:13.
ROB. Prov. 22:22, *r.* not the poor.
Isa. 10:2, that they may *r.* the fatherless.
13, I have *r.* their treasures.
42:22, this is a people *r.* and spoiled.
Ezek. 33:15, if he give again that he had *r.*
Mal. 3:8, ye have *r.* me.
2Cor. 11:8, I *r.* other churches.
See Jud. 9:25; 2Sam. 17:8; Ps. 119:61; Prov. 17:12.
ROBBER. Job 12:6, tabernacles of *r.* prosper.
Isa. 42:24, who gave Israel to the *r.*
Jer. 7:11, is this house become a den of *r.*
Jn. 10:1, the same is a thief and a *r.*
8, all that came before me are *r.*
Acts 19:37, these men are not *r.* of churches.
2Cor. 11:26, in perils of *r.*
See Ezek. 7:22; 18:10; Dan. 11:14; Hos. 6:9.
ROBBERY. Phil. 2:6, though it not *r.* to be equal.
ROBE. 1Sam. 24:4, cut off skirt of Saul's *r.*
Job 29:14, my judgment was as a *r.*
Isa. 61:10, covered me with *r.* of righteousness.
Lk. 15:22, bring forth the best *r.*
20:46, desire to walk in long *r.*
See Ex. 28:4; Mic. 2:8; Mt. 27:28; Rev. 6:11.
ROCK. Ex. 33:22, I will put thee in a clift of *r.*
Num. 20:8, speak to the *r.* before their eyes.
10, must we fetch you water out of this *r.*
23:9, from the top of the *r.* I see him.
24:21, thou puttest thy nest in a *r.*
Dt. 8:15, who brought thee water out of the *r.*
32:4, he is the *R.*
15, lightly esteemed the *R.* of his salvation.
18, of the *R.* that begat thee.
30, except their *R.* had sold them.
31, their *r.* is not as our *R.*
37, where is their *r.* in whom they trusted?
1Sam. 2:2, neither is there any *r.* like our God.
2Sam. 22:2; Ps. 18:2; 92:15, the Lord is my *r.*
3, the God of my *r.*
32; Ps. 18:31, who is a *r.*, save our God?
23:3, the *R.* of Israel spake.
1Ki. 19;11, strong wind brake in pieces the *r.*
Job 14:18, the *r.* is removed out of his place.
19:24, graven in the *r.* for ever.
24:8, embrace the *r.* for want of shelter.
Ps. 27:5; 40:2, shall set me up upon a *r.*
31:3; 71:3, thou art my *r.* and my fortress.
61:2, lead me to the *r.* that is higher than I.
81:16, with honey out of the *r.*
Prov. 30:26, yet make their houses in the *r.*
Song 2:14, that art in the clefts of the *r.*
Isa. 8:14, for a *r.* of offence.
17:10, not mindful of the *r.* of thy strength.
32:2, as the shadow of a great *r.*
33:16, defence shall be munitions of *r.*
Jer. 5:3, they made their faces harder than *r.*
23:29, hammer that breaketh the *r.* in pieces.
Nah. 1:6, the *r.* are thrown down by him.
Mt. 7:25; Lk. 6:48, it was founded upon a *r.*
16:18, upon this *r.* I will build my church.
27:51, and the *r.* rent.
Lk. 8:6, some fell upon a *r.*
Rom. 9:33; 1Pet. 2:8, I lay a *r.* of offence.
1Cor. 10:4, spiritual *R.*, and that *R.* was Christ.
Rev. 6:16, said to the *r.*, fall on us.
See Jud. 6:20; 13:19; 1Sam. 14:4; Prov. 30:19.
ROD. Job 9:34, let him take his *r.* from me.
21:9, neither is the *r.* of God upon them.
Ps. 2:9, break them with a *r.* of iron.
23:4, thy *r.* and thy staff comfort me.
Prov. 10:13; 26:3, *r.* for the back of fools.
13:24, he that spareth his *r.*
22:8, the *r.* of his anger shall fail.
23:13, thou shalt beat him with thy *r.*
29:15, the *r.* and reproof give wisdom.
Isa. 10:15, as if the *r.* should shake itself.
11:1, shall come forth a *r.*
Jer. 48:17, how is the beautiful *r.* broken.
Ezek. 20:37, cause you to pass under the *r.*
Mic. 6:9, hear ye the *r.*, and who hath appointed it.
2Cor. 11:25, thrice was I beaten with *r.*
See Gen. 30:37; 1Sam. 14:27; Rev. 2:27; 11:1.
RODE. 2Sam. 18:9; 2Ki. 9:25; Neh. 2:12; Ps. 18:10.
ROLL. Josh. 5:9, I have *r.* away reproach.
Job 30:14, they *r.* themselves on me.
Isa. 9:5, with garments *r.* in blood.
34:4; Rev. 6:14, the heavens shall be *r.* together.
Mk. 16:3, who shall *r.* us away the stone?

Lk. 24:2, they found the stone r. away.
See Gen. 29:8; Prov. 26:27; Isa. 17:13; Mt. 27:60.
ROOF. Gen. 19:8, under the shadow of my r.
Dt. 22:8, make a battlement for thy r.
Job 29:10; Ps. 137:6; Lam. 4:4; Ezek. 3:26, tongue cleaveth to r. of mouth.
Mt. 8:8; Lk. 7:6, I am not worthy that thou shouldest come under my r.
Mk. 2:4, they uncovered the r.
See Josh. 2:6; Jud. 16:27; 2Sam. 11:2; Jer. 19:13.
ROOM. Gen. 24:23, is there r. for us.
26:22, the Lord hath made r. for us.
Ps. 31:8, set my feet in a large r.
80:9, thou preparedst r. before it.
Prov. 18:16, a man's gift maketh r. for him.
Mal. 3:10, there shall not be r. enough.
Mt. 23:6; Mk. 12:39; Lk. 20:46, love uppermost r.
Mk. 2:2, there was no r. to receive them.
Lk. 2:7, no r. for them in the inn.
12:17, no r. to bestow my goods.
14:7, how they chose out the chief r.
9, begin with shame to take the lowest r.
22, it is done, and yet there is r.
See Gen. 6:14; 1Ki. 8:20; 19:16; Mk. 14:15.
ROOT (*n.*). Dt. 29:18, a r. that beareth gall.
2Ki. 19:30, shall again take r. downward.
Job 5:3, I have seen the foolish taking r.
8:17, his r. are wrapped about the heap.
14:8, the r. thereof wax old in the earth.
18:16, his r. shall be dried up.
19:28, the r. of the matter.
29:19, my r. was spread out by the waters.
Prov. 12:3, r. of righteous shall not be moved.
12, r. of righteous yieldeth fruit.
Isa. 5:24, their r. shall be rottenness.
11:1, a Branch shall grow out of his r.
10; Rom. 15:12, there shall be a r. of Jesse.
27:6; 37:31, them that come of Jacob to take r.
53:2, as a r. out of a dry ground.
Ezek. 31:7, his r. was by great waters.
Hos. 14:5, cast forth his r. as Lebanon.
Mal. 4:1, leave them neither r. nor branch.
Mt. 3:10; Lk. 3:9, axe laid to r. of trees.
13:6; Mk. 4:6; Lk. 8:13, because they had no r.
Mk. 11:20, fig tree dried up from the r.
Rom. 11:16, if the r. be holy.
1Tim. 6:10, love of money the r. of all evil.
Heb. 12:15, lest any r. of bitterness.
Jude 12, twice dead, plucked up by the r.
Rev. 22:16, r. and offspring of David.
See 2Chr. 7:20; Dan. 4:15; 7:8; 11:7.
ROOT (*v.*). Dt. 29:28, Lord r. them out.
1Ki. 14:15, he shall r. up Israel.
Job 18:14, confidence shall be r. out.
31:8, let my offspring be r. out.
12, r. out all mine increase.
Ps. 52:5, r. thee out of land of the living.
Mt. 13:29, lest ye r. up also the wheat.
15:13, hath not planted shall be r. up.
Eph. 3:17, being r. and grounded in love.
Col. 2:7, r. and built up in him.
See Prov. 2:22; Jer. 1:10; Zeph. 2:4.
ROSE (*n.*). Song 2:1; Isa. 35:1.
ROSE (*v.*). Gen. 32:31, the sun r. upon him as he passed.
Josh. 3:16, waters r. up on an heap.
Lk. 16:31, though one r. from the dead.
Rom. 14:9, to this end Christ both died and r.
1Cor. 15:4, buried, and r. the third day.
2Cor. 5:15, live to him who died and r.
See Lk. 24:33; Acts 10:41; 1Th. 4:14; Rev. 19:3.
ROT. Num. 5:21; Prov. 10:7; Isa. 40:20.
ROTTEN. Job 41:27; Jer. 38:11; Joel 1:17.
ROTTENNESS. Prov. 12:4; 14:30; Isa. 5:24.
ROUGH. Isa. 27:8, stayeth his r. wind.
40:4; Lk. 3:5, r. places made plain.
Zech. 13:4, wear a r. garment to deceive.
See Dt. 21:4; Jer. 51:27; Dan. 8:21.
ROUGHLY. Gen. 42:7, Joseph spake r.
Prov. 18:23, the rich answereth r.
See 1Sam. 20:10; 1Ki. 12:13; 2Chr. 10:13.
ROUND. Ex. 16:14; Isa. 3:18; Lk. 19:43.
ROWED. Jonah 1:13; Mk. 6:48; Jn. 6:19.
ROYAL. Gen. 49:20, yield r. dainties.
Est. 1:7, r. wine in abundance.
5:1; 6:8; 8:15; Acts 12:21, r. apparel.
Jas. 2:8, fulfil the r. law.
1Pet. 2:9, a r. priesthood.
See 1Chr. 29:25; Isa. 62:3; Jer. 43:10.
RUBIES. Job 28:18; Prov. 8:11; 31:10.
RUDDY. 1Sam. 16:12; Song 5:10; Lam. 4:7.
RUDE. 2Cor. 11:6, r. in speech.
RUDIMENTS. Col. 2:8, 20, r. of the world.
RUIN. 2Chr. 28:23, they were the r. of him.
Ps. 89:40, hast brought his strong holds to r.
Prov. 24:22, who knoweth the r. of both.
26:28, a flattering mouth worketh r.
Ezek. 18:30, so iniquity shall not be your r.
21:15, that their r. may be multiplied.
Lk. 6:49, the r. of that house was great.
See Isa. 3:8; Ezek. 36:35; Amos 9:11; Acts 15:16.
RULE (*n.*). Est. 9:1, Jews had r. over them.
Prov. 17:2, a wise servant shall have r.
19:10, servant to have r. over princes.
25:28, no r. over his own spirit.
Isa. 63:19, thou never barest r. over them.
1Cor. 15:24, when he shall put down all r.
Gal. 6:16, as many as walk according to this r.
Heb. 13:7, 17, them that have the r. over you.
See Eccl. 2:19; Isa. 44:13; 2Cor. 10:13.
RULE (*v.*). Gen. 1:16, to r. the day.
3:16, thy husband shall r. over thee.
Jud. 8:23, I will not r. over you.
2Sam. 23:3, that r. over men must be just.
Ps. 66:7, he r. by his power for ever.
89:9, thou r. the raging of the sea.
103:19, his kingdom r. over all.
Prov. 16:32, that r. his spirit.
22:7, rich r. over the poor.
Eccl. 9:17, him that r. among fools.
Isa. 3:4, babes r. over them.
32:1, princes shall r. in judgment.
40:10, his arm shall r. for him.
Ezek. 29:15, shall no more r. over nations.
Rom. 12:8, he that r. with diligence.

Col. 3:15, peace of God *r.* in your hearts.
1Tim. 3:4, one that *r.* well his own house.
5:17, elders that *r.* well.
See Dan. 5:21; Zech. 6:13; Rev. 2:27; 12:5.
JLER. Num. 13:2, every one a *r.* among them.
Prov. 6:7, ant, having no guide, overseer, or *r.*
23:1, when thou sittest to eat with a *r.*
28:16, a wicked *r.* over the poor.
Isa. 3:6, be thou our *r.*
Mic. 5:2, out of thee shall come *r.*
Mt. 25:21, I will make thee *r.*
Jn. 7:26, do the *r.* know that this is Christ?
48, have any of the *r.* believed.
Rom. 13:3, *r.* not a terror to good works.
See Gen. 41:43; Neh. 5:7; Ps. 2:2; Isa. 1:10.
JMOUR. Jer. 49:14, I have heard a *r.*
Ezek. 7:26, *r.* shall be upon *r.*
Mt. 24:6; Mk. 13:7, wars and *r.* of wars.
See 2Ki. 19:7; Obad. 1; Lk. 7:17.
UN. 2Sam. 18:27, the *r.* of the foremost is like.
2Chr. 16:9, eyes of Lord *r.* to and fro.
Ps. 19:5, as a strong man to *r.* a race.
23:5, my cup *r.* over.
147:15, his word *r.* very swiftly.
Song 1:4, draw me, we will *r.* after thee.
Isa. 40:31, they shall *r.* and not be weary.
Isa. 55:5, nations shall *r.* to thee.
Jer. 12:5, if thou hast *r.* with the footmen.
51:31, one post shall *r.* to meet another.
Dan. 12:4, many shall *r.* to and fro.
Hab. 2:2, that he may *r.* that readeth.
Zech. 2:4, *r.*, speak to this young man.
Lk. 6:38, good measure *r.* over.
Rom. 9:16, nor of him that *r.*
1Cor. 9:24, they which *r.* in a race *r.* all.
26, I therefore so *r.*
Gal. 2:2, lest I should *r.* or had *r.* in vain.
5:7, ye did *r.* well.
Heb. 12:1, let us *r.* with patience.
1Pet. 4:4, that ye *r.* not to same excess.
See Prov. 4:12; Jer. 5:1; Lam. 2:18; Amos 8:12.
USH (*n.*). Job 8:11; Isa. 9:14; 19:15; 35:7.
USH (*v.*). Isa. 17:13; Jer. 8:6; Ezek. 3:12; Acts 2:2.
UST. Mt. 6:19, 20; Jas. 5:3.
ABBATH. Lev. 25:8, number seven *s.* of years.
2Ki. 4:23, it is neither new moon nor *s.*
2Chr. 36:21, as long as desolate she kept *s.*
Ezek. 46:1, on the *s.* it shall be opened.
Amos 8:5, when will the *s.* be gone.
Mk. 2:27, the *s.* was made for man.
28; Lk. 6:5, the Son of man is Lord of the *s.*
Lk. 13:15, doth not each on *s.* loose.
See Isa. 1:13; Lam. 1:7; 2:6; Mt. 28:1; Jn. 5:18.
ACK. Gen. 42:25; 43:21; 44:1, 11, 12; Josh. 9:4.
ACKCLOTH. 2Sam. 3:31, gird you with *s.*
1Ki. 20:32, they girded *s.* on their loins.
Neh. 9:1, assembled with fasting and *s.*
Est. 4:1, put on *s.* with ashes.
Ps. 30:11, thou hast put off my *s.*
35:13, my clothing was *s.*
Jonah 3:5, and put on *s.*
ACRIFICE (*n.*). Gen. 31:54, Jacob offered *s.*
Ex. 5:17, let us go and do *s.* to the Lord.
Num. 25:2, called people to the *s.* of their gods.
1Sam. 2:29, wherefore kick ye at my *s.*
9:13, he doth bless the *s.*
15:22, to obey is better than *s.*
Ps. 4:5, offer the *s.* of righteousness.
27:6, will I offer *s.* of joy.
40:6; 51:16, *s.* thou didst not desire.
51:17, the *s.* of God are a broken spirit.
118:27, bind the *s.* with cords.
Prov. 15:8, *s.* of wicked an abomination.
17:1, than a house full of *s.* with strife.
21:3, to do justice is more acceptable than *s.*
Eccl. 5:1, the *s.* of fools.
Isa. 1:11, to what purpose is multitude of *s.*
Jer. 6:20, nor are your *s.* sweet unto me.
33:18, nor want a man to do *s.*
Dan. 8:11; 9:27; 11:31; daily *s.* taken away.
Hos. 3:4, many days without a *s.*
6:6; Mt. 9:13; 12:7, I desired mercy and not *s.*
Amos 4:4, bring your *s.* every morning.
Zeph. 1:7, the Lord hath prepared a *s.*
Mal. 1:8, ye offer the blind for *s.*
Mk. 9:49, every *s.* shall be salted.
12:33, to love the Lord is more than *s.*
Lk. 13:1, blood Pilate mingled with *s.*
Acts 7:42, have ye offered *s.* forty years.
14:13, and would have done *s.*
Rom. 12:1, present your bodies a living *s.*
1Cor. 8:4; 10:19, 28, offered in *s.* to idols.
Eph. 5:2, a *s.* to God for sweet-smelling savour.
Phil. 2:17, upon the *s.* of your faith.
4:18, a *s.* acceptable, well pleasing.
Heb. 9:26, put away sin by *s.* of himself.
10:12, offered one *s.* for sins.
10:26, there remaineth no more *s.* for sin.
11:4, a more excellent *s.*
13:15, let us offer the *s.* of praise.
16, with such *s.* God is well pleased.
1Pet. 2:5, to offer up spiritual *s.*
See 2Chr. 7:1; Ezra 6:10; Neh. 12:43; Jonah 1:16.
SACRIFICE (*v.*). Ex. 22:20, he that *s.* to any god.
Ezra 4:2, we seek your God, and do *s.* to him.
Neh. 4:2, will they *s.*
Ps. 54:6, I will freely *s.* to thee.
106:37, they *s.* their sons to devils.
107:22, let them *s.* sacrifices of thanksgiving.
Eccl. 9:2, to him that *s.* and that *s.* not.
Isa. 65:3, people that *s.* in gardens.
Hos. 8:13, they *s.*, but the Lord accepteth not.
Heb. 1:16, they *s.* unto their net.
1Cor. 5:7, Christ our passover is *s.* for us.
10:20, things Gentiles *s.*, they *s.* to devils.
See Ex. 8:26; Dt. 15:21; 1Sam. 1:3; 15:15.
SACRILEGE.
Rom. 2:22, dost thou commit *s.*
SAD. 1Ki. 21:5, why is thy spirit so *s.*
Eccl. 7:3, by *s.* of countenance the heart is made better.
Mt. 6:16, be not of a *s.* countenance.
Mk. 10:22, he was *s.* at that saying.
Lk. 24:17, as ye walk and are *s.*
See Gen. 40:6; 1Sam. 1:18; Neh. 2:1; Ezek.

13:22.
SADDLE. 1Sam. 19:26; 1Ki. 13:13.
SAFE. 2Sam. 18:29, is the young man *s.*
Job 21:9, their houses are *s.* from fear.
Ps. 119:117, hold me up and I shall be *s.*
Prov. 18:10, righteous run and are *s.*
29:25, whoso trusteth in the Lord shall be *s.*
Ezek. 34:27, they shall be *s.* in their land.
Acts 27:44, so they escaped all *s.*
See 1Sam. 12:11; Isa. 5:29; Lk. 15:27; Phil. 3:1.
SAFEGUARD. 1Sam. 22:23, with me thou shalt be in *s.*
SAFELY. Ps. 78:53, he led them on *s.*
Prov. 1:33, shall dwell *s.*
3:23, shalt thou walk *s.*
31:11, doth *s.* trust in her.
Hos. 2:18, I will make them to lie down *s.*
See Isa. 41:3; Zech. 14:11; Mk. 14:44; Acts 16:23.
SAFETY. Job 3:26, I was not in *s.*
5:4, his children are far from *s.*
11:18, thou shalt take thy rest in *s.*
Prov. 11:14; 24:6, in the multitude of counsellors is *s.*
21:31, *s.* is of the Lord.
1Th. 5:3, when they say peace and *s.*
See Job 24:23; Ps. 12:5; 33:17; Isa. 14:30.
SAIL. Isa. 33:23; Ezek. 27:7; Lk. 8:23; Acts 27:9.
SAINTS. 1Sam. 2:9, he will keep feet of *s.*
Job 5:1, to which of the *s.* wilt thou turn.
15:15, he putteth no trust in his *s.*
Ps. 16:3, but to the *s.* that are in the earth.
30:4, sing to the Lord, O ye *s.* of his.
37:28, the Lord forsaketh not his *s.*
50:5, gather my *s.* together.
89:5, the congregation of the *s.*
7, to be feared in assembly of *s.*
97:10, preserveth the souls of his *s.*
116:15, precious is the death of his *s.*
132:9, let thy *s.* shout for joy.
149:9, this honour have all his *s.*
Dan. 7:18, but the *s.* shall take the kingdom.
8:13, then I heard one *s.* speaking.
Mt. 27:52, many bodies of *s.* arose.
Acts 9:13, evil he hath done to thy *s.*
Rom. 1:7; 1Cor. 1:2, called to be *s.*
8:27, he maketh intercession for the *s.*
12:13, distributing to the necessity of *s.*
16:2, receive her as becometh *s.*
1Cor. 6:1, dare any go to law, and not before *s.*
2, the *s.* shall judge the world.
16:1, concerning collection for *s.*
16:15, the ministry of *s.*
Eph. 1:18, his inheritance in the *s.*
2:19, fellowcitizens with the *s.*
3:8, less than least of all *s.*
4:12, perfecting of the *s.*
5:3, not named among you, as becometh *s.*
Col. 1:12, the *s.* in light.
1Th. 3:13, at coming of our Lord with *s.*
2Th. 1:10, to be glorified in his *s.*
1Tim. 5:10, if she have washed the *s.* feet.
Jude 3, faith once delivered to *s.*
Rev. 5:8; 8:3, 4, the prayers of *s.*
See Phil. 4:21; Rev. 11:18; 13:7; 14:12; 15:3.
SAKE. Gen. 3:17, cursed for thy *s.*
8:21, not curse ground for man's *s.*
12:13, be well with me for thy *s.*
18:26, I will spare for their *s.*
30:27, the Lord hath blessed me for thy *s.*
Num. 11:29, enviest thou for my *s.*
Dt. 1:37; 3:26; 4:21, angry with me for your *s.*
2Sam. 9:1, shew kindness for Jonathan's *s.*
18:5, deal gently for my *s.*
Neh. 9:31, for thy great mercies' *s.*
Ps. 6:4; 31:16, save me for thy mercies' *s.*
23:3, he leadeth me for his name's *s.*
Ps. 44:22, for thy *s.* are we killed.
106:8, he saved them for his name's *s.*
Mt. 5:10, persecuted for righteousness' *s.*
10:18; Mk. 13:9; Lk. 21:12, for my *s.*
24:22; Mk. 13:20, for the elect's *s.*
Jn. 11:15, I am glad for your *s.*
13:38, wilt thou lay down thy life for my *s.*
Rom. 13:5; 1 Cor. 10:25, for conscience *s.*
Col. 1:24, for his body's *s.* which is the church.
1Th. 5:13, for their work's *s.*
1Tim. 5:23, for thy stomach's *s.*
Ti. 1:11, for lucre's *s.*
2Jn. 2, for the truth's *s.*
See Rom. 11:28; 2Cor. 8:9; 1Th. 3:9.
SALUTATION. Mk. 12:38; Lk. 1:29; Col. 4. 18; 2Th. 3:17.
SALUTE. 1Sam. 10:4; 2Ki. 4:29; Mk. 15:18.
SALVATION. Gen. 49:18, I have waited for thy *s.*
Ex. 14:13; 2Chr. 20:17, see the *s.* of the Lord.
15:2, he is become my *s.*
Dt. 32:15, lightly esteemed the rock of his *s.*
1Sam. 11:13; 19:5, the Lord wrought *s.* in Israel
14:45, Jonathan, who hath wrought this *s.*
2Sam. 22:51, he is the tower of *s.* for his king.
1Chr. 16:23, show forth from day to day his *s.*
2Chr. 6:41, let thy priests be clothed with *s.*
Ps. 3:8, *s.* belongeth to the Lord.
9:14, I will rejoice in thy *s.*
14:7, O that the *s.* of Israel were come.
25:5, thou art the God of my *s.*
27:1; 62:6; Isa. 12:2, my light and my *s.*
35:3, say unto my soul, I am thy *s.*
37:39, the *s.* of the righteous is of the Lord.
40:10, I have declared thy faithfulness and *s.*
50:23, to him will I show the *s.* of God.
51:12; 70:4, restore the joy of thy *s.*
68:20, he that is our God, is the God of *s.*
69:13, hear me in the truth of thy *s.*
29, let thy *s.* set me up on high.
71:15, my mouth shall show forth thy *s.*
74:12, working *s.* in the midst of the earth.
78:22, they trusted not in his *s.*
85:9, his *s.* is nigh them that fear him.
91:16, will satisfy him and show him my *s.*
96:2, show forth his *s.* from day to day.
98:3, ends of the earth have seen the *s.*
116:13, the cup of *s.*
118:14; Isa. 12:2, the Lord is become my *s.*
119:41, let thy *s.* come.
81, my soul fainteth for thy *s.*

123, mine eyes fail for thy *s.*
155, *s.* is far from the wicked.
174, I have longed for thy *s.*
132:16, I will clothe her priests with *s.*
144:10, that giveth *s.* unto kings.
149:4, beautify the meek with *s.*
Isa. 12:3, the wells of *s.*
26:1, *s.* will God appoint for walls.
Isa. 33:2, be thou our *s.* in time of trouble.
45:8, earth open and let them bring forth *s.*
17, saved with an everlasting *s.*
49:8, in a day of *s.* have I helped thee.
51:5, my *s.* is gone forth.
52:7, feet of him that publisheth *s.*
10, ends of the earth shall see *s.*
56:1, my *s.* is near to come.
59:11, we look for *s.*, but it is far off.
16, his arm brought *s.*
17, an helmet of *s.* on his head.
60:18, call thy walls *S.*
61:10, the garments of *s.*
62:1, the *s.* thereof as a lamp.
63:5, mine own arm brought *s.*
Jer. 3:23, in vain is *s.* hoped for.
Lam. 3:26, wait for the *s.* of the Lord.
Jonah 2:9, *s.* is of the Lord.
Hab. 3:8, ride on thy chariots of *s.*
18, I will joy in the God of my *s.*
Zech. 9:9, thy King, just, and having *s.*
Lk. 1:69, an horn of *s.* for us.
77, give knowledge of *s.* to his people.
2:30, mine eyes have seen thy *s.*
3:6, all flesh shall see the *s.* of God.
19:9, this day is *s.* come to this house.
Jn. 4:22, *s.* is of the Jews.
Acts 4:12, neither is there *s.* in any other.
13:26, to you is the word of *s.* sent.
16:17, these men show to us the way of *s.*
Rom. 1:16, the power of God to *s.*
10:10, confession is made to *s.*
13:11, now is our *s.* nearer.
2Cor. 1:6, comforted, it is for your *s.*
6:2, the day of *s.*
7:10, sorrow worketh repentance to *s.*
Eph. 1:13, the Gospel of your *s.*
6:17; 1Th. 5:8, the helmet of *s.* and sword.
Phil. 1:19, this shall turn to my *s.*
28, an evident token of *s.*
2:12, work out your own *s.*
1Th. 5:9, hath appointed us to obtain *s.*
2Th. 2:13, God hath chosen you to *s.*
2Tim. 3:15, wise unto *s.*
Ti. 2:11, grace of God that bringeth *s.*
Heb. 1:14, for them who shall be heirs of *s.*
2:3, if we neglect so great *s.*
10, the captain of their *s.*
5:9, author of eternal *s.*
6:9, things that accompany *s.*
9:28, without sin unto *s.*
1Pet. 1:5, kept through faith unto *s.*
9, end of faith, *s.* of your souls.
10, of which *s.* the prophets enquired.
2Pet. 3:15, longsuffering of the Lord is *s.*
Jude 3, of the common *s.*
Rev. 7:10, saying, *s.* to our God.
See Job 13:16; 1Sam. 2:1; 2Sam. 22:36.
SAME. Job 4:8, sow wickedness, reap the *s.*
Ps. 102:27; Heb. 1:12, thou art the *s.*
Mt. 5:46, do not the publicans the *s.*
Acts 1:11, this *s.* Jesus shall come.
Rom. 10:12, the *s.* Lord over all.
12:16; 1Cor. 1:10; Phil. 4:2, be of *s.* mind.
Heb. 13:8, *s.* yesterday, to-day, and for ever.
See 1Cor. 10:3; 12:4; 15:39; Eph. 4:10.
SANCTIFY. Lev. 11:44; 20:7; Num. 11:18; Josh. 3:5;
7:13; 1Sam. 16:5, *s.* yourselves.
Isa. 5:16, God shall be *s.* in righteousness.
13:3, I have commanded my *s.* ones.
29:23, they shall *s.* the Holy One.
66:17, *s.* themselves in gardens.
Jer. 1:5, I *s.* and ordained thee a prophet.
Ezek. 20:41; 36:23, I will be *s.* in you.
28:25; 39:27, *s.* in them in sight of heathen.
Joel 1:14; 2:15, *s.* yea fast.
Jn. 10:36, him whom the Father *s.*
Jn. 17:17, *s.* them through thy truth.
19, for their sakes I *s.* myself.
Acts 20:32; 26:18, inheritance among them that
are *s.*
Rom. 15:16, being *s.* by the Holy Ghost.
1Cor. 1:2, to them that are *s.*
6:11, but now ye are *s.*
7:14, husband is *s.* by the wife, and the wife
is *s.*
Eph. 5:26, *s.* and cleanse the church.
1Th. 5:23, the very God of peace *s.* you.
1Tim. 4:5, it is *s.* by the word of God.
2Tim. 2:21, a vessel *s.* for the Master's use.
Heb. 2:11, he that *s.* and they who are *s.*
10:10, by the which will we are *s.*
14, perfected for ever them that are *s.*
13:12, that he might *s.* the people.
1Pet. 3:15, *s.* the Lord God in your hearts.
Jude 1, to them that are *s.* by God the Father.
See Gen. 2:3; Ex. 13:2; Job 1:5; Mt. 23:17.
SANCTUARY. Ex. 15:17, plant them in the *s.*
25:8, let them make me a *s.*
36:1; 3:4, work for the *s.*
Num. 7:9, service of *s.* belongeth to them.
Neh. 10:39, where are the vessels of the *s.*
Ps. 74:7, they have cast fire into thy *s.*
Isa. 60:13, beautify the place of my *s.*
Lam. 2:7, the Lord hath abhorred his *s.*
See Dan. 8:11; 9:17; Heb. 8:2; 9:1.
SAND. Gen. 22:17, as the *s.* which is upon the sea
shore.
Hos. 1:10; Rev. 20:8, as the *s.* of the sea.
Heb. 11:12, the *s.* which is by the sea.
See Job 6:3; Prov. 27:3; Mt. 7:26.
SANDALS. Mk. 6:9, be shod with *s.*
Acts 12:8, bind on thy *s.*
SANG. Ex. 15:1; Neh. 12:42; Job 38:7.
SANK. Ex. 15:5, they *s.* into the bottom.
SAP. Ps. 104:16, trees full of *s.*
SAPPHIRE. Ex. 24:10, a paved work of a *s.* stone.
28:18; Ezek. 28:13; Rev. 21:19, and a *s.*

Ezek. 1:26, as the appearance of a *s.* stone.
10:1, as it were a *s.* stone.
SARDINE. Rev. 4:3, like a jasper and *s.* stone.
SARDIUS. Ex. 28:17, the first row shall be a *s.*
Ezek. 28:13; Rev. 21:20, *s.* etc.
SARDONYX. Rev. 21:20, the fifth *s.*
SAT. Jud. 20:26, they *s.* before the Lord.
Job 29:25, I *s.* chief.
Ps. 26:4, have not *s.* with vain persons.
Jer. 15:17, I *s.* alone because of thy hand.
Ezek. 3:15, I *s.* where they *s.*
Mt. 4:16, the people who *s.* in darkness.
Mk. 16:19, he *s.* on the right hand of God.
Lk. 7:15, he that was dead *s.* up.
10:39, Mary *s.* at Jesus' feet.
Jn. 4:6, *s.* thus on the well.
Acts 2:3, cloven tongues *s.* upon each.
See Ezra 10:16; Neh. 1:4; Ps. 137:1; Rev. 4:3.
SATAN. 1Chr. 21:1, *S.* provoked David.
Ps. 109:6, let *S.* stand at his right hand.
Mt. 11:26; Mk. 3:23; Lk. 11:18, if *S.* cast out *S.*
16:23; Mk. 8:33; Lk. 4:8, get behind me, *S.*
Lk. 10:18, I beheld *S.* as lightning fall.
Acts 5:3, why hath *S.* filled thine heart.
26:18, turn them from power of *S.*
2Cor. 12:7, messenger of *S.* to buffet me.
2Th. 2:9, after the working of *S.*
1Tim. 1:20, whom I have delivered unto *S.*
5:15, already turned aside after *S.*
See Rom. 16:20; 1Cor. 5:5; 2Cor. 2:11; 11:14.
SATIATE. Jer. 31:14, 25; 46:10.
SATISFY. Job 38:27, to *s.* the desolate.
Ps. 17:15, I shall be *s.* when I awake.
22:26, the meek shall eat and be *s.*
36:8, they shall be *s.* with fatness.
37:19, in days of famine be *s.*
59:15, and grudge if they be not *s.*
63:5, my soul shall be *s.*
81:16, with honey should I have *s.* thee.
Ps. 90:14, *s.* us early with thy mercy.
91:16, with long life will I *s.* him.
103:5, who *s.* thy mouth with good.
104:13, the earth is *s.*
105:40, he *s.* them with bread from heaven.
107:9, he *s.* the longing soul.
132:15, I will *s.* her poor with bread.
Prov. 6:30, if he steal to *s.* his soul.
12:11, he that tilleth his land shall be *s.*
14:14, a good man shall be *s.* from himself.
19:23, he that hath it shall abide *s.*
20:13, open thine eyes and thou shalt be *s.*
30:15, three things never *s.*
Eccl. 1:8, the eye is not *s.* with seeing.
4:8, neither is his eye *s.* with riches.
5:10, shall not be *s.* with silver.
Isa. 9:20; Mic. 6:14, shall eat and not be *s.*
53:11, travail of his soul and be *s.*
58:10, if thou *s.* the afflicted soul.
11, the Lord shall *s.* thy soul in drought.
Jer. 31:14, shall be *s.* with my goodness.
Ezek. 16:28, yet thou couldest not be *s.*
Amos 4:8, wandered to drink, but were not *s.*
Hab. 2:5, as death and cannot be *s.*
See Ex. 15:9; Dt. 14:29; Job 19:22; 27:14.
SAVE. Gen. 45:7, to *s.* your lives.
47:25, thou hast *s.* our lives.
Dt. 28:29, spoiled and no man shall *s.* thee.
33:29, O people, *s.* by the Lord.
Josh. 10:6, come up quickly and *s.* us.
Jud. 6:15, wherewith shall I *s.* Israel?
1Sam. 4:3, the ark may *s.* us.
10:27, how shall this man *s.* us?
11:3, if there be no man to *s.* us we will come.
14:6, no restraint to *s.* by many or by few.
2Sam. 19:9, the king *s.* us, and now he is fled.
2Ki. 6:10, *s.* himself there, not once nor twice.
Job 2:6, in thine hand, but *s.* his life.
22:29, he shall *s.* the humble.
26:2, how *s.* thou.
Ps. 7:10, God who *s.* the upright.
20:6, the Lord *s.* his anointed.
34:18, he *s.* such as be of a contrite spirit.
44:3, neither did their own arm *s.* them.
60:5, *s.* with thy right hand.
72:4, he shall *s.* the children of the needy.
80:3; Prov. 28:18; Jer. 17:14; Mt. 10:22; 24:13; Mk. 13:13; 16:16; Jn. 10:9; Acts 2:21; 16:31; Rom. 5:9; 9:27; 10:9; 11:26, shall be *s.*
86:2, *s.* thy servant that trusteth.
109:31, *s.* him from those that condemn.
118:25, *s.*, I beseech thee, send prosperity.
119:94, *s.* me, for I have sought.
146, *s.* me, and I shall keep thy testimonies.
138:7, thy right hand shall *s.*
Prov. 20:22, wait on Lord and he shall *s.* thee.
Isa. 35:4, your God will come and *s.* you.
43:12, I have declared and have *s.*
45:20, pray to a god that cannot *s.*
22, look unto me and be ye *s.*
47:15, they shall wander, none shall *s.*
49:25, I will *s.* thy children.
59:1, Lord's hand not shortened, that it cannot *s.*
63:1, mighty to *s.*
Jer. 2:28, let them arise if they can *s.*
8:20, summer is ended, and we are not *s.*
11:12, but they shall not *s.*
14:9, as a mighty man that cannot *s.*
15:20; 30:11; 42:11; 46:27, I am with thee to *s.* thee.
17:14, *s.* me and I shall be *s.*
30:10, I will *s.* thee from afar.
48:6, flee, *s.* your lives.
Lam. 4:17, a nation that could not *s.* us.
Ezek. 3:18, to warn wicked, to *s.* his life.
34:22, therefore will I *s.* my flock.
Hos. 1:7, I will *s.* them by the Lord.
13:10, is there any other that may *s.* thee.
Hab. 1:2, cry to thee and thou wilt not *s.*
Zeph. 3:17, he will *s.*
Mt. 1:21, *s.* his people from their sins.
16:25; Mk. 8:35; Lk. 9:24, will *s.* his life.
18:11; Lk. 19:10, to seek and to *s.* that which was lost.
19:25; Mk. 10:26; Lk. 18:26, who then can

be *s.*?
27:40; Mk. 15:30, *s.* thyself.
42; Mk. 15:31, he *s.* others, himself he cannot *s.*
Mk. 3:4; Lk. 6:9, is it lawful to *s.*
Lk. 7:50; 18:42, thy faith hath *s.* thee.
8:12, lest they should believe and be *s.*
9:56, not to destroy but to *s.*
13:23, are there few that be *s.*?
23:35, let him *s.* himself.
39, if thou be Christ, *s.* thyself and us.
Jn. 3:17, that the world might be *s.*
5:34, these things I say that ye might be *s.*
12:47, not to judge but to *s.*
Acts 2:47, such as should be *s.*
4:12, no other name whereby we must be *s.*
15:1, except ye be circumcised ye cannot be *s.*
16:30, what must I do to be *s.*?
27:43, the centurion willing to *s.* Paul.
Rom. 8:24, we are *s.* by hope.
10:1, my prayer is that they might be *s.*
Rom. 11:14; 1Cor. 9:22, if I might *s.* some.
1Cor. 1:18, to us who are *s.*
21, by foolishness of preaching to *s.* some.
3:15, *s.* yet so as by fire.
5:5, that the spirit may be *s.*
7:16, shalt *s.* thy husband.
2Cor. 2:15, savour in them that are *s.*
Eph. 2:5, 8, by grace ye are *s.*
1Tim. 1:15, came to *s.* sinners.
2:4, who will have all men to be *s.*
4:16, thou shalt *s.* thyself and them.
Heb. 5:7, able to *s.* him from death.
7:25, able to *s.* to the uttermost.
10:39, believe to *s.* of soul.
11:7, an ark to the *s.* of his house.
Jas. 1:21, word which is able to *s.* your souls.
2:14, can faith *s.* him?
4:12, able to *s.* and destroy.
5:15, prayer of faith shall *s.* sick.
20, shall *s.* a soul from death.
1Pet. 3:20, souls were *s.* by water.
4:18, righteous scarcely be *s.*
Jude 23, others *s.* with fear.
See Mt. 14:30; Jn. 12:27; 1Pet. 3:21.
SAVE (*except*). 2Sam. 22:32, who is God, *s.* the Lord?
Mt. 11:27, nor knoweth any *s.* the Son.
13:57, *s.* in his own country.
17:8; Mk. 9:8, *s.* Jesus only.
Lk. 17:18, *s.* this stranger.
18:19, none good *s.* one.
2Cor. 11:24, forty stripes *s.* one.
Gal. 6:14, glory *s.* in the cross.
See Mk. 5:37; Lk. 4:26; Rev. 2:17; 13:17.
SAVIOUR. 2Sam. 22:3, my refuge, my *s.*
2Ki. 13:5, the Lord gave Israel a *s.*
Ps. 106:21, they forgat God their *s.*
Isa. 19:20, he shall send them a *s.*
45:21, a just God and a *S.*
49:26, all shall know I am thy *S.*
63:8, so he was their *S.*
Eph. 5:23, Christ is the *s.* of the body.
1Tim. 4:10, who is the *S.* of all men.
Ti. 2:10, adorn doctrine of God our *S.*
13, glorious appearing of our *S.*
Jude 25, the only wise God our *S.*
See Neh. 9:27; Obad. 21; Jn. 4:42; Acts 5:31.
SAVOUR. Gen. 8:21, Lord smelled a sweet *s.*
Ex. 5:21, have made our *s.* to be abhorred.
Song 1:3, *s.* of thy good ointment.
Joel 2:20, his ill *s.* shall come up.
Mt. 5:13; Lk. 14:34, if salt have lost his *s.*
See Eccl. 10:1; Ezek. 6:13; 20:41; Eph. 5:2.
SAVOUREST. Mt. 16:23; Mk. 8:33.
SAVOURY. Gen. 27:4, 7, 14, 31.
SAW. Gen. 22:4, Abraham *s.* the place.
26:28, we *s.* the Lord was with thee.
Ex. 10:23, they *s.* not one another.
24:10, they *s.* the God of Israel.
2Chr. 25:21, they *s.* one another in the face.
Job 29:11, when the eye *s.* me.
Ps. 77:16, the waters *s.* thee.
Eccl. 2:24, this I *s.*, it was from hand of God.
Song 3:3, *s.* ye him whom my soul loveth.
Mt. 12:22, both spake and *s.*
17:8, they *s.* no man.
Mk. 8:23, if he *s.* ought.
Jn. 1:48, under the fig-tree I *s.* thee.
8:56, Abraham *s.* my day.
20:20, glad when they *s.* the Lord.
See 1Sam. 19:5; Ps. 50:18; Isa. 59:16.
SAY. Ex. 3:13, what shall I *s.* unto them?
4:12, teach thee what thou shalt *s.*
Num. 22:19, know what the Lord will *s.*
Jud. 18:24, what is this ye *s.* to me?
Ezra 9:10, what shall we *s.* after this?
Mt. 3:9, think not to *s.* within yourselves.
7:22, many will *s.* in that day.
16:13; Mk. 8:27, whom do men *s.* that I am?
23:3, they *s.* and do not.
Lk. 7:40, I have somewhat to *s.* to thee.
1Cor. 12:3, no man can *s.* that Jesus.
See Lk. 7:7; Jn. 4:20; 8:26; 16:12.
SAYING. Dt. 1:23, the *s.* pleased me well.
1Ki. 2:38, the *s.* is good.
Ps. 49:4, my dark *s.* upon the harp.
78:2, utter dark *s.* of old.
Prov. 1:6, the dark *s.* of the wise.
Mt. 28:15, this *s.* is commonly reported.
Lk. 2:51, kept all these *s.* in her heart.
Jn. 4:37, herein is that *s.* true.
6:60, an hard *s.*, who can hear it?
See Jn. 21:23; Rom. 13:9; 1Tim. 1:15.
SCAB. Lev. 13:2, a *s.* or bright spot.
Dt. 28:27, and with the *s.*
Isa. 3:17, the Lord will smite with a *s.*
SCANT. Mic. 6:10, *s.* measure.
SCARCE. Gen. 27:30; Acts 14:18.
SCARCELY. Rom. 5:7; 1Pet. 4:18.
SCARCENESS. Dt. 8:9, bread without *s.*
SCAREST. Job 7:14, thou *s.* me with dreams.
SCATTER. Gen. 11:4, lest we be *s.* abroad.
Lev. 26:33, I will *s.* you among the heathen.
Num. 10:35; Ps. 68:1, let thine enemies be *s.*
Job 18:15, brimstone shall be *s.* on his habitation.

37:11, he *s.* his bright cloud.
38:24, which *s.* the east wind.
Ps. 68:30, *s.* thou the people that delight in war.
92:9, the workers of iniquity shall be *s.*
147:16, he *s.* the hoar frost.
Prov. 11:24, there is that *s.* and yet increaseth.
20:8, a king *s.* evil with his eyes.
26, a wise king *s.* the wicked.
Jer. 10:21, all their flocks shall be *s.*
23:1, woe to pastors that *s.* the sheep.
50:17, Israel is a *s.* sheep.
Zech. 13:7; Mt. 26:31; Mk. 14:27, sheep shall be *s.*
Mt. 9:36, *s.* as sheep having no shepherd.
12:30; Lk. 11:23, he that gathereth not with me *s.*
See Jn. 11:52; 16:32; Acts 8:1; Jas. 1:1.
SCENT. Job 14:9; Jer. 48:11; Hos. 14:7.
SCHOLAR. 1Chr. 25:8; Mal. 2:12.
SCHOOLMASTER. Gal. 3:24, the law was our *s.*
SCIENCE. Dan. 1:4; 1Tim. 6:20.
SCOFF. Hab. 1:10; 2Pet. 3:3.
SCORCH. Mt. 13:6; Mk. 4:6; Rev. 16:8.
SCORN. Est. 3:6; Job 16:20; Ps. 44:13; 79:4.
SCORNER. Prov. 9:8, reprove not a *s.*
13:1, a *s.* heareth not rebuke.
19:25, smite a *s.*
Prov. 28, an ungodly witness *s.* judgment.
29, judgments are prepared for *s.*
21:11, when *s.* is punished simple is made wise.
24:9, the *s.* is an abomination.
Isa. 29:20, the *s.* is consumed.
Hos. 7:5, stretched out hands with *s.*
See Ps. 1:1; Prov. 1:22; 3:34; 9:12.
SCORPIONS. Dt. 8:15, fiery serpents and *s.*
Lk. 10:19, power to tread on *s.*
Rev. 9:3, as the *s.* of the earth.
SCOURGE. Job 5:21, the *s.* of the tongue.
9:23, if the *s.* slay suddenly.
Isa. 28:15, the overflowing *s.*
Mt. 10:17; 23:34, they will *s.* you.
Jn. 2:15, a *s.* of small cords.
Acts 22:25, is it lawful to *s.* a Roman.
Heb. 12:6, the Lord *s.* every son.
See Josh. 23:13; Isa. 10:26; Mt. 27:26; Jn. 19:1.
SCRAPE. Lev. 14:41; Job 2:8; Ezek. 26:4.
SCRIBE. 1Chr. 27:32, a wise man and a *s.*
Isa. 33:18, where is the *s.*?
Jer. 8:8, the pen of the *s.* is in vain.
Mt. 5:20, exceed righteousness of the *s.*
7:29, authority, and not as the *s.*
13:52, every *s.* instructed unto kingdom.
Mk. 12:38; Lk. 20:46, beware of the *s.*
See Ezra 4:8; 7:6; Neh. 8:4; Mt. 8:19.
SCRIP. 1Sam. 17:40; Mt. 10:10; Lk. 10:4; 22:35.
SEARCH (*n.*). Ps. 64:6; 77:6; Jer. 2:34.
SEARCH (*v.*). Num. 13:2, that they may *s.* the land.
1Chr. 28:9, the Lord *s.* all hearts.
Job 11:7, canst thou by *s.* find out God?
13:9, is it good that he should *s.* you out?
28:27, he prepared it and *s.* it out.
29:16, the cause I knew not I *s.* out.
32:11, I waited whilst ye *s.* out what to say.
36:26, can number of his years be *s.* out.
Ps. 44:21, shall not God *s.* this out?
139:1, thou hast *s.* me and known me.
23, *s.* me and know my heart.
Prov. 25:2, honour of kings to *s.* out a matter.
27, for men to *s.* out their own glory.
Eccl. 1:13; 7:25, I gave my heart to *s.* wisdom.
Isa. 40:28, no *s.* of his understanding.
Jer. 17:10, I the Lord *s.* the heart.
29:13, when ye shall *s.* for me with all.
31:37, foundations of the earth *s.* out.
Lam. 3:40, let us *s.* our ways, and turn.
Ezek. 34:6, none did *s.* or seek after them.
8, neither did my shepherds *s.* for my flock.
11, I will *s.* my sheep.
Amos 9:3, I will *s.* and take them out thence.
Zeph. 1:12, I will *s.* Jerusalem with candles.
Jn. 5:39; Acts 17:11, *s.* the scriptures.
Rom. 8:27, that *s.* hearts knoweth mind.
1Cor. 2:10, the Spirit *s.* all things.
1Pet. 1:10, which salvation prophets *s.* diligently.
See Job 10:6; 28:3; Prov. 2:4; 1Pet. 1:11.
SEARED. 1Tim. 4:2, conscience *s.*
SEASON. Gen. 1:14, for signs, and *s.*, and days.
Dt. 28:12, give rain in his *s.*
2Chr. 15:3, for long *s.* without true God.
Job 5:26, as a shock of corn in his *s.*
Ps. 1:3, that bringeth forth fruit in his *s.*
22:2, I cry in the night *s.*
104:19, appointed the moon for *s.*
Prov. 15:23, word spoken in due *s.*
Eccl. 3:1, to everything there is a *s.* and a time.
Isa. 50:4, know how to speak a word in *s.*
Jer. 5:24, former and latter rain in his *s.*
33:20, day and night in their *s.*
Ezek. 34:26, cause shower to come down in *s.*
Dan. 2:21, changeth the times and *s.*
7:12, lives prolonged for a *s.*
Hos. 2:9, take away my wine in *s.*
Mt. 21:41, render the fruits in their *s.*
Lk. 1:20, my words shall be fulfilled in *s.*
Lk. 20:10, at the *s.* he sent servant.
23:8, desirous to see him of a long *s.*
Jn. 5:4, angel went down at certain *s.*
35, willing for a *s.* to rejoice.
Acts 1:7, not for you to know times and *s.*
13:11, not seeing the sun for a *s.*
24:25, a convenient *s.*
2Tim. 4:2, be instant in *s.*
Heb. 11:25, pleasure of sin for a *s.*
See 1Th. 5:1; 1Pet. 1:6; Rev. 6:11; 20:3.
SEAT. 1Sam. 20:18, thy *s.* will be empty.
Job 23:3, that I might come even to his *s.*
29:7, when I prepared my *s.* in the street.
Ps. 1:1, the *s.* of the scornful.
Amos 6:3, cause *s.* of violence to come near.
Mt. 21:12, *s.* of them that sold doves.
23:2, scribes sit in Moses' *s.*
6; Mk. 12:39, chief *s.* in synagogues.
See Ezek. 8:3; 28:2; Lk. 1:52; Rev. 2:13; 4:4.
SECRET (*n.*). Gen. 49:6, come not into their *s.*
Job 11:6, the *s.* of wisdom.

15:8, hast thou heard the *s.* of God?
29:4, the *s.* of God was upon my tabernacle.
Ps. 25:14, *s.* of Lord is with them that fear.
27:5, in *s.* of his tabernacle will he hide.
139:15, when I was made in *s.*
Prov. 3:32, his *s.* is with the righteous.
9:17, bread eaten in *s.*
21:14, a gift in *s.* pacifieth anger.
Isa. 45:19; 48:16, I have not spoken in *s.*
Mt. 6:4, thy Father who seeth in *s.*
6, pray to thy Father which is in *s.*
24:26, he is in the *s.* chambers.
Jn. 18:20, in *s.* have I said nothing.
See Prov. 11:13; 20:19; Dan. 2:18; 4:9.
CRET (*adj.*). Dt. 29:29, *s.* things belong to God.
Jud. 3:19, I have a *s.* errand.
13:18, my name, seeing it is *s.*
Ps. 19:12, cleanse thou me from *s.* faults.
90:8, our *s.* sins.
Prov. 27:5, open rebuke better than *s.* love.
See Song 2:14; Isa. 45:3; Jer. 13:17.
CRETLY. Gen. 31:27, flee away *s.*
Dt. 13:6, entice thee *s.*, saying.
1Sam. 18:22, commune with David *s.*
23:9, Saul *s.* practised mischief.
2Sam. 12:12, for thou didst it *s.*
Job 4:12, a thing was *s.* brought to me.
13:10, if you *s.* accept persons.
31:27, my heart hath been *s.* enticed.
Ps. 10:9, he lieth in wait *s.*
31:20, keep them *s.* from the strife.
Jn. 11:28, she called her sister *s.*
19:38, *s.* for fear of the Jews.
See Dt. 27:24; Lev. 28:57; 2Ki. 17:9.
CT. Acts 5:17; 15:5; 24:5; 26:5; 28:22.
CURE. Job 11:18; 12:6; Mt. 28:14.
CURELY. Prov. 3:29; Mic. 2:8.
DUCE. Mk. 13:22, show signs to *s.*
1Jn. 2:26, concerning them that *s.* you.
Rev. 2:20, to *s.* my servants.
See Prov. 12:26; 1Tim. 4:1; 2Tim. 3:13.
E. Gen. 11:5, came down to *s.* the city.
44:23, you shall *s.* my face no more.
45:28, I will go and *s.* him before I die.
Ex. 12:13, when I *s.* the blood.
14:13, *s.* the salvation of the Lord.
33:20, there shall no man *s.* me and live.
Dt. 3:25, let me *s.* the good land.
34:4, I have caused thee to *s.* it.
2Ki. 6:17, open his eyes, that he may *s.*
10:16, *s.* my zeal for the Lord.
Job 7:7, mine eye shall no more *s.* good.
19:26, yet in my flesh shall I *s.* God.
Ps. 27:13, believed to *s.* the goodness.
66:5, come and *s.* the works of God.
94:9, shall he not *s.*
Isa. 6:10, lest they *s.* with their eyes.
32:3, eyes of them that *s.* shall not be dim.
33:17, shall *s.* the king in his beauty.
40:5, all flesh shall *s.* it together.
52:8, they shall *s.* eye to eye.
Jer. 5:21; Ezek. 12:12, eyes and *s.* not.
Mt. 5:8, they shall *s.* God.
12:38, we would *s.* a sign.
13:14; Mk. 4:12; Acts 28:26, *s.* ye shall *s.*
27:4, *s.* thou to that.
28:6, *s.* the place where the Lord lay.
Mk. 8:18, having eyes *s.* ye not.
Lk. 17:23, *s.* here or *s.* there.
Jn. 1:39; 11:34; Rev. 6:1, come and *s.*
50, thou shalt *s.* greater things.
9:25, I was blind, now I *s.*
39, that they who *s.* not might *s.*
Heb. 2:9, but we *s.* Jesus.
1Pet. 1:8, though now we *s.* him not.
1Jn. 3:2, we shall *s.* him as he is.
See Mt. 27:24; Jn. 1:51.
SEED. Gen. 3:15, enmity between thy *s.*
47:19, give us *s.*
Ex. 16:31, manna like coriander *s.*
Lev. 19:19, thou shalt not sow mingled *s.*
26:16, ye shall sow your *s.* in vain.
Num. 20:5, it is no place of *s.*
Dt. 1:8, to give it to their *s.* after them.
11:10, not as Egypt where thou sowedst *s.*
14:22, tithe all the increase of your *s.*
28:38, thou shalt carry much *s.* into field.
Ps. 126:6, bearing precious *s.*
Eccl. 11:6, in the morning sow thy *s.*
Isa. 5:10, the *s.* of an homer shall yield.
17:11, in morning make thy *s.* to flourish.
55:10, give *s.* to the sower.
61:9, the *s.* which the Lord hath blessed.
Jer. 2:21, I had planted thee wholly a right *s.*
Joel 1:17, the *s.* is rotten.
Amos 9:13, overtake him that soweth *s.*
Hag. 2:19, is the *s.* yet in the barn?
Zech. 8:12, the *s.* shall be prosperous.
Mal. 2:15, that he might seek a godly *s.*
See Mt. 13:19; Lk. 8:5; 1Cor. 15:38; 1Pet. 1:23.
SEEK. Gen. 37:15, what *s.* thou?
Num. 15:39, that ye *s.* not after your own heart.
16:10, *s.* ye the priesthood also.
Dt. 4:29, if thou *s.* him with all thy heart.
12:5, even to his habitation shall ye *s.* and come.
23:6; Ezra 9:12, thou shalt not *s.* their peace.
Ruth 3:1, shall I not *s.* rest for thee.
1Chr. 28:9; 2Chr. 15:2, if thou *s.* him, he will be found.
2Chr. 19:3, hast prepared thine heart to *s.* God.
34:3, Josiah began to *s.* after God.
Ezra 4:2, we *s.* your God as ye do.
Neh. 2:10, to *s.* the welfare of Israel.
Job 5:8, I would *s.* unto God.
8:5, *s.* unto God betimes.
20:10, children shall *s.* to please the poor.
39:29, from thence she *s.* the prey.
Ps. 9:10, hast not forsaken them that *s.* thee.
10:4, the wicked will not *s.* after God.
15, *s.* out his wickedness till thou find none.
14:2; 53:2, if there were any that did *s.* God.
24:6, generation of them that *s.* him.
27:4, desired, that will I *s.* after.
8, *s.* ye my face, thy face will I *s.*
34:14; 1Pet. 3:11, *s.* peace and pursue it.

63:1, early will I *s.* thee.
69:32, your heart shall live that *s.* God.
83:16, that they may *s.* thy name.
122:9, I will *s.* thy good.
Prov. 1:28, they shall *s.* me, but not find.
8:17, those that *s.* me early shall find me.
11:27, that diligently *s.* good.
21:6, of them that *s.* death.
Prov. 23:30, they that go to *s.* mixed wine.
35, I will *s.* it yet again.
Eccl. 1:13; 7:25, gave my heart to *s.* wisdom.
Song 3:2, I will *s.* him whom my soul loveth.
Isa. 1:17, learn to do well, *s.* judgment.
8:19, should not a people *s.* unto their God.
19:3, they shall *s.* to charmers.
34:16, *s.* ye out of the book of the Lord.
41:17, when the needy *s.* water.
45:19, I said not, *s.* ye my face in vain.
Jer. 5:1, any that *s.* the truth.
29:13, ye shall *s.* me and find when ye search.
30:17, Zion whom no man *s.* after.
38:4, this man *s.* not welfare of people.
Lam. 3:25, the Lord is good to the soul that *s.* him.
Ezek. 7:25, they shall *s.* peace.
34:16, I will *s.* that which was lost.
Dan. 9:3, I set my face to *s.* by prayer.
Amos 5:4, *s.* me and ye shall live.
Zeph. 2:3, *s.* ye the Lord, all ye meek.
Mal. 2:7, they should *s.* the law at his mouth.
Mt. 6:32, after these things do Gentiles *s.*
33; Lk. 12:21, *s.* first the kingdom of God.
7:7; Lk. 11:9, *s.* and ye shall find.
12:39; 16:4, adulterous generation *s.* a sign.
28:5; Mk. 16:6, I know that ye *s.* Jesus.
Mk. 1:37, all men *s.* for thee.
8:11, *s.* of him a sign from heaven.
Lk. 13:7, I come *s.* fruit.
24, many will *s.* to enter in.
15:8, doth she not *s.* diligently.
19:10, is come to *s.* and to save.
24:5, why *s.* ye the living among the dead?
Jn. 1:38, what *s.* ye?
4:23, the Father *s.* such to worship him.
7:25, is not this he whom they *s.* to kill?
34, ye shall *s.* me and shall not find me.
18:8, if ye *s.* me, let these go their way.
20:15, woman, whom *s.* thou?
Rom. 3:11, there is none that *s.* after God.
1Cor. 1:22, the Greeks *s.* after wisdom.
10:24, let no man *s.* his own.
13:5, charity *s.* not her own.
2Cor. 12:14, I *s.* not yours, but you.
Phil. 2:21, all *s.* their own things.
Col. 3:1, *s.* those things which are above.
Heb. 11:6, a rewarder of them that *s.* him.
14, declare plainly that they *s.* a country.
13:14, but we *s.* one to come.
1Pet. 5:8, *s.* whom he may devour.
Rev. 9:6, in those days shall men *s.* death.
See Jer. 45:5; Mt. 13:45; Jn. 6:24; 1Cor. 10:33.
SEEM. Gen. 19:14, he *s.* as one that mocked.
29:20, they *s.* to him but a few days.
Num. 16:9, *s.* it but a small thing.
Prov. 14:12, there is a way that *s.* right.
Lk. 8:18, taken away that he *s.* to have.
24:11, words *s.* as idle tales.
1Cor. 3:18, if any *s.* to be wise.
11:16, if any man *s.* to be contentious.
Heb. 4:1, lest any *s.* to come short.
12:11, now no chastening *s.* to be joyous.
See Gen. 27:12; Eccl. 9:13; Acts 17:18; Gal. 2:6.
SEEMLY. Prov. 19:10; 26:1.
SEEN. Gen. 32:30, I have *s.* God face to face.
Ex. 14:13, Egyptians whom ye have *s.* to-day.
Jud. 6:22, because I have *s.* an angel.
2Ki. 20:15, what have they *s.*
Job 13:1, mine eye hath *s.* all this.
28:7, a path the vulture's eye hath not *s.*
Ps. 37:25, have I not *s.* righteous forsaken.
90:15, years wherein we have *s.* evil.
Eccl. 6:5, he hath not *s.* the sun.
Isa. 9:2, have *s.* a great light.
64:4; 1Cor. 2:9, neither hath eye *s.*
66:8, who hath *s.* such things.
Mt. 6:1; 23:5, to be *s.* of men.
Mt. 9:33, never so *s.* in Israel.
Mk. 9:1, till they have *s.* the kingdom of God.
Lk. 5:26, we have *s.* strange things to-day.
Jn. 1:18, no man hath *s.* God.
8:57, hast thou *s.* Abraham?
14:9, he that hath *s.* me hath *s.* the Father.
Acts 11:23, when he had *s.* the grace of God.
1Cor. 9:1, have I not *s.* Jesus Christ.
1Tim. 6:16, whom no man hath *s.*, nor can see.
Heb. 11:1, evidence of things not *s.*
1Pet. 1:8, whom having not *s.*, ye love.
See Jn. 5:37; 9:37; 15:24; 20:29; Rom. 1:20.
SEER. 1Sam. 9:9, a prophet was beforetime called a *s.*
2Sam. 24:11, the prophet Gad, David's *s.*
SEETHE. Ex. 23:19; 2Ki. 4:38; Ezek. 24:5.
SEIZE. Job 3:6; Ps. 55:15; Jer. 49:24; Mt. 21:38.
SELF. Ti. 1:7; 2Pet. 2:10.
SELL. Gen. 25:31, *s.* me thy birthright.
37:27, come, let us *s.* him.
1Ki. 21:25, Ahab did *s.* himself to work.
Neh. 5:8, will ye even *s.* your brethren.
Prov. 23:23, buy the truth, and *s.* it not.
Joel 3:8, I will *s.* your sons and daughters.
Amos 8:5, that we may *s.* corn.
6, and *s.* the refuse of the wheat.
Mt. 19:21; Mk. 10:21; Lk. 12:33; 18:22, *s.* that thou hast.
Lk. 22:36, let him *s.* his garment.
Jas. 4:13, we will buy and *s.*, and get gain.
See Ps. 44:12; Prov. 11:26; 31:24; Mt. 13:44.
SELLER. Isa. 24:2; Ezek. 7:12, 13; Acts 16:14.
SEND. Gen. 24:7, God shall *s.* his angel.
12, *s.* me good speed this day.
Ex. 4:13, *s.* by hand of him whom thou wilt *s.*
2Chr. 7:13; Ezek. 14:9, if I *s.* pestilence.
Ps. 20:2, *s.* thee help from the sanctuary.
43:3, *s.* out thy light and truth.
118:25, *s.* now prosperity.
Isa. 6:8, whom shall I *s.*? *s.* me.

Mt. 9:38; Lk. 10:2, *s.* labourers.
12:20, till he *s.* forth judgment.
15:23, *s.* her away, for she crieth after us.
Mk. 3:14, that he might *s.* them to preach.
Jn. 14:26, whom the Father will *s.* in my name
17:8, believed that thou didst *s.* me.
Rom. 8:3, God *s.* his Son in likeness.
See Lk. 10:3; 24:49; Jn. 20:21; 2Th. 2:11.
ENSUAL. Jas. 3:15; Jude 19.
ENT. Gen. 45:5, God *s.* me.
Jud. 6:14, have not I *s.* thee.
Ps. 77:17, the skies *s.* out a sound.
106:15, he *s.* leanness into their soul.
107:20, he *s.* his word and healed them.
Jer. 23:21, I have not *s.* these prophets.
Mt. 15:24, I am not *s.* but to lost sheep.
Jn. 4:34, the will of him that *s.* me.
9:4, work the works of him that *s.* me.
17:3, life eternal to know him whom thou hast *s.*
Acts 10:29, as soon as I was *s.* for.
Rom. 10:15, preach, except they be *s.*
See Isa. 61:1; Jn. 1:6; 3:28; 1Pet. 1:12.
ENTENCE. Ps. 17:2, let my *s.* come forth.
Prov. 16:10, a divine *s.* in the lips of the king.
Eccl. 8:11, because *s.* is not executed speedily.
2Cor. 1:9, *s.* of death in ourselves.
See Dt. 17:9; Jer. 4:12; Dan. 5:12; 8:23.
EPARATE. Gen. 13:9, *s.* thyself from me.
Dt. 19:2, thou shalt *s.* three cities.
Prov. 16:28; 17:9, whisperer *s.* chief friends.
19:4, the poor is *s.* from his neighbour.
Mt. 25:32, he shall *s.* them.
Rom. 8:35, who shall *s.* us from love of God?
2Cor. 6:17, be ye *s.*
Heb. 7:26, *s.* from sinners.
See Num. 6:2; Ezra 10:11; Isa. 56:3; 59:2.
EPARATION. Num. 6:8; 19:9; 31:23; Ezek. 42:20.
ERPENT. Gen. 3:1, the *s.* was more subtil.
49:17, Dan shall be a *s.* by the way.
Job 26:13, his hand formed the crooked *s.*
Ps. 58:4, like the poison of a *s.*
104:3, sharpened their tongues like a *s.*
Prov. 23:32, at last it biteth like a *s.*
Eccl. 10:8, breaketh a hedge, a *s.* shall bite him.
11, *s.* will bite without enchantment.
Isa. 27:1, the Lord shall punish the *s.*
65:25, dust shall be the *s.* meat.
Jer. 8:17, I will send *s.* among you.
Amos 9:3, I will command the *s.*
Mic. 7:17, they shall lick dust like a *s.*
Mt. 7:10; Lk. 11:11, will he give him a *s.*?
10:16, be ye wise as *s.*
23:33, ye *s.*, how can ye escape.
Mk. 16:18, they shall take up *s.*
Jn. 3:14, as Moses lifted up the *s.*
Rev. 12:9; 20:2, that old *s.* called the Devil.
See Ex. 4:3; Num. 21:8; 2Ki. 18:4; Jas. 3:7.
ERVANT. Gen. 9:25, a *s.* of *s.* shall he be.
Job 3:19, the *s.* is free.
7:2, as a *s.* desireth the shadow.
Ps. 116:16; 119:125; 143:12, I am thy *s.*
Prov. 22:7, the borrower is *s.* to the lender.
29:19, a *s.* will not be corrected with words.
Isa. 24:2, as with *s.* so with master.
Mt. 10:25, enough for *s.* to be as his lord.
25:21, good and faithful *s.*
Lk. 12:47, that *s.* which knew his lord's will.
17:10, unprofitable *s.*
Jn. 8:35, *s.* abideth not in house for ever.
15:15, *s.* knoweth not what his lord doeth.
1Cor. 7:21, art thou called, being a *s.*
23, be not ye the *s.* of men.
Eph. 6:5; Col. 3:22; Ti. 2:9; 1Pet. 2:18, *s.* be obedient.
See Rom. 6:16; Col. 4:1; 1Tim. 6:1; Rev. 22:3.
SERVE. Gen. 25:23, elder shall *s.* the younger.
Dt. 6:13; 10:12, 20; 11:13; 13:4; Josh. 22:5; 24:14; 1Sam. 7:3; 12:14, thou shalt fear the Lord and *s.* him.
Josh. 24:15, choose ye whom ye will *s.*
1Chr. 28:9, *s.* him with a perfect heart.
Job 21:15, what is the Almighty, that we should *s.* him?
Ps. 22:30, a seed shall *s.* him.
72:11, all nations shall *s.* him.
Isa. 43:23, I have not caused thee to *s.*
24, thou hast made me to *s.* with thy sins.
Jer. 5:19, so shall ye *s.* strangers.
Dan. 6:16, thy God whom thou *s.* will deliver.
Zeph. 3:9, to *s.* him with one consent.
Mal. 3:17, spareth his son that *s.* him.
18, between him that *s.* God and him that.
Mt. 6:24; Lk. 16:13, no man can *s.* two masters.
Lk. 10:40, hath left me to *s.* alone.
15:29, these many years do I *s.* thee.
Jn. 12:26, if any man *s.* me, let him.
Acts 6:2, leave word of God and *s.* tables.
Rom. 6:6, henceforth we should not *s.* sin.
Gal. 5:13, by love *s.* one another.
Col. 3:24, for ye *s.* the Lord Christ.
1Th. 1:9, from idols to *s.* living God.
Rev. 7:15, they *s.* him day and night.
See Lk. 22:27; Acts 13:36; Heb. 9:14; 12:28.
SERVICE. Ex. 12:26, what mean ye by this *s.*?
1Chr. 29:5, who is willing to consecrate his *s.*
Jn. 16:2, will think he doeth God *s.*
Rom. 12:1, your reasonable *s.*
Eph. 6:7, doing *s.* as to the Lord.
Phil. 2:30, to supply your lack of *s.*
See Ezra 6:18; Ps. 104:14; Jer. 22:13.
SET. Gen. 4:15, the Lord *s.* a mark on Cain.
9:13, I do *s.* my bow in the cloud.
Dt. 1:8, I have *s.* the land before thee.
Job 33:5, *s.* thy words in order.
Ps. 16:8, I have *s.* the Lord before me.
20:5, we will *s.* up our banners.
91:14, he hath *s.* his love upon me.
Eccl. 7:14, hath *s.* the one against the other.
Song 8:6, *s.* me as a seal upon thine heart.
Mt. 5:14, a city *s.* on a hill.
Acts 18:10, no man shall *s.* on thee.
Heb. 6:18, the hope *s.* before us.
See Ps. 75:7; 107:41; Eph. 1:20; Col. 3:2.
SETTLE. Zeph. 1:12; Lk. 21:14; Col. 1:23.
SEVER. Lev. 20:26; Ezek. 39:14; Mt. 13:49.

SEW. Gen. 3:7; Job 14:17; Eccl. 3:7; Mk. 2:21.
SHADE. Ps. 121:5, the Lord is thy *s.*
SHADOW. Gen. 19:8, the *s.* of my roof.
Job 7:2, as servant earnestly desireth the *s.*
14:2, he fleeth as a *s.* and continueth not.
17:7, all my members are as a *s.*
Ps. 91:1, under the *s.* of the Almighty.
102:11, my days are like a *s.*
144:4; Eccl. 8:13, his days are as a *s.*
Eccl. 6:12, life which he spendeth as a *s.*
Song 2:3, under his *s.* with great delight.
17; 4:6, till the *s.* flee away.
Isa. 4:6, for a *s.* in the daytime.
25:4, a *s.* from the heat.
32:2, as the *s.* of a great rock.
49:2; 51:16, in the *s.* of his hand.
Jer. 6:4, the *s.* of evening are stretched out.
Lam. 4:20, under his *s.* we shall live.
Hos. 14:7, they that dwell under his *s.* shall return.
Acts 5:15, the *s.* of Peter might overshadow.
Jas. 1:17, with whom is no *s.* of turning.
See Jud. 9:15, 36; Isa. 38:8; Jonah 4:5.
SHAFT. Ex. 25:31; 37:17; Isa. 49:2.
SHAKE. Jud. 16:20, I will *s.* myself.
Ps. 29:8, voice of Lord *s.* wilderness.
72:16, fruit thereof shall *s.* like Lebanon.
Isa. 2:19, when he ariseth to *s.* the earth.
13:13; Joel 3:16; Hag. 2:6, 21, I will *s.* the heavens.
52:2, *s.* thyself from the dust.
Hag. 2:7, I will *s.* all nations.
Mt. 11:7; Lk. 7:24, a reed *s.* with the wind.
Lk. 6:38, good measure, *s.* together.
2Th. 2:2, be not soon *s.* in mind.
Heb. 12:26, I *s.* not earth only.
27, things which cannot be *s.*
See Job 9:6; Ezek. 37:7; Mt. 24:29.
SHAME. Ps. 4:2, turn my glory into *s.*
40:14; 83:17, let them be put to *s.*
Prov. 10:5; 17:2, a son that causeth *s.*
Isa. 61:7, for your *s.* ye shall have double.
Jer. 51:51, *s.* hath covered our faces.
Ezek. 16:52, bear thine own *s.*
Dan. 12:2, awake, some to *s.*
Zeph. 3:5, the unjust knoweth no *s.*
Lk. 14:9, with *s.* to take lowest room.
Acts 5:41, worthy to suffer *s.*
1Cor. 6:5; 15:34, I speak this to your *s.*
Eph. 5:12, a *s.* to speak of those things.
Phil. 3:19, whose glory is in their *s.*
Heb. 6:6, put him to an open *s.*
12:2, despising the *s.*
See 1Cor. 11:6; 14:35; 1Th. 2:2; 1Tim. 2:9.
SHAPE. Lk. 3:22; Jn. 5:37; Rev. 9:7.
SHARP. 1Sam. 13:20, to *s.* every man his share.
21, a file to *s.* the goads.
Ps. 52:2, tongue like a *s.* razor.
140:3, they *s.* their tongues like a serpent.
Prov. 25:18, false witness is *s.* arrow.
27:17, iron *s.* iron, so a man *s.* his friend.
Isa. 41:15, a *s.* threshing instrument.
Acts 15:39, the contention was so *s.*
Heb. 4:12, *s.* than any two-edged sword.
See Mic. 7:4; 2Cor. 13:10; Rev. 1:16; 14:14.
SHEAF. Dt. 24:19; Ruth 2:7; Ps. 126:6; 129:7.
SHEARERS. Gen. 38:12; 1Sam. 25:7; Isa. 53:7.
SHEATH. 1Sam. 17:51; 1Chr. 21:27; Ezek. 21:3.
SHED. Gen. 9:6, shall his blood be *s.*
Mt. 26:28, *s.* for many for remission of sins.
Rom. 5:5, love of God *s.* in our hearts.
Ti. 3:6, which he *s.* on us abundantly.
Heb. 9:22, without *s.* of blood is no remission.
See Ezek. 18:10; 22:3; Acts 2:33.
SHEEP. Gen. 4:2, Abel was a keeper of *s.*
Num. 27:17; 1Ki. 22:17; 2Chr. 18:16; Mt. 9:36; Mk. 6:34, as *s.* which have no shepherd.
1Sam. 15:14, what meaneth this bleating of *s.*
Ps. 49:14, like *s.* are laid in the grave.
95:7; 100:3, we are the *s.* of his hand.
Isa. 53:6, all we like *s.* have gone astray.
Jer. 12:3, pull them out like *s.* for slaughter.
Ezek. 34:6, my *s.* wandered.
Mt. 7:15, false prophets in *s.* clothing.
10:6, go rather to lost *s.*
12:12, how much is a man better than a *s.*
Jn. 10:2, that entereth by door is shepherd of *s.*
11, good shepherd giveth his life for the *s.*
21:16, feed my *s.*
See Mt. 10:16; 12:11; 18:12; 25:32; Heb. 13:20.
SHEET. Jud. 14:12; Acts 10:11; 11:5.
SHELTER. Job 24:8; Ps. 61:3.
SHEPHERD. Gen. 46:34, *s.* abomination to Egyptians.
Ps. 23:1, the Lord is my *s.*
Isa. 13:20, nor shall *s.* make their fold there.
40:11, he shall feed his flock like a *s.*
56:11, they are *s.* that cannot understand.
Jer. 23:4, I will set *s.* over them who shall feed.
50:6, their *s.* have caused them to go astray.
Amos 3:12, as the *s.* taketh out of the mouth.
Zech. 11:17, woe to the idol *s.*
Jn. 10:14, I am the good *s.*
See Zech. 11:3; Lk. 2:8; 1Pet. 2:25; 5:4.
SHIELD. Jud. 5:8, was there a *s.* seen.
Ps. 5:12, compass him as with a *s.*
33:20; 59:11; 84:9, the Lord is our *s.*
84:11, a sun and *s.*
91:4, truth shall be thy *s.*
Isa. 21:5, anoint the *s.*
Eph. 6:16, taking the *s.* of faith.
See Prov. 30:5; Jer. 51:11; Ezek. 23:24; 39:9.
SHINE. Job 22:28, the light shall *s.* upon thy ways.
29:3, when his candle *s.* upon my head.
Ps. 104:15, oil to make his face *s.*
139:12, the night *s.* as the day.
Prov. 4:18, light that *s.* more and more.
Isa. 9:2, upon them hath the light *s.*
60:1, arise, *s.*, for thy light is come.
Dan. 12:3, wise shall *s.* as the brightness.
Mt. 5:16, let your light so *s.*
13:43, the righteous *s.* as the sun.
2Cor. 4:6, God who commanded the light to *s.*
See Jn. 1:5; 2Pet. 1:19; 1Jn. 2:8; Rev. 1:16.
SHOCK. Jud. 15:5; Job 5:26.
SHOD. Mk. 6:9; Eph. 6:15.

HOOT. Ps. 22:7, they *s.* out the lip.
64:3, to *s.* their arrows, even bitter words.
144:6, *s.* out thine arrows and destroy them.
See 1Chr. 12:2; Mk. 4:32; Lk. 21:30.
HORT. Job 17:12, the light is *s.*
20:5, triumphing of wicked is *s.*
Ps. 89:47, remember how *s.* my time is.
Rom. 3:23, come *s.* of the glory of God.
1Cor. 7:29, the time is *s.*
See Num. 11:23; Isa. 50:2; 59:1; Mt. 24:22.
HORTER. Isa. 28:20, the bed is *s.*
HORTLY. Gen. 41:32; Ezek. 7:8; Rom. 16:20.
HOUT. Ps. 47:5, God is gone up with a *s.*
Lam. 3:8, when I *s.* he shutteth out my prayer.
1Th. 4:16, shall descend with a *s.*
See Num. 23:21; 1Sam. 4:5; Isa. 12:6.
HOWER. Ps. 65:10, makest it soft with *s.*
72:6, like *s.* that water the earth.
Ezek. 34:26, will cause *s.* to come in season.
See Dt. 32:2; Job 24:8; Jer. 3:3; 14:22.
HUN. Acts 20:27; 2Tim. 2:16.
HUT. Gen. 7:16, the Lord *s.* him in.
Isa. 22:22, he shall open and none shall *s.*
60:11, gates shall not be *s.* day nor night.
Jer. 36:5, I am *s.* up, I cannot go to the house of the Lord.
Lam. 3:8, he *s.* out my prayer.
See Gal. 3:23; 1Jn. 3:17; Rev. 3:7; 20:3.
ICK. Prov. 13:12, maketh the heart *s.*
23:35, stricken me and I was not *s.*
Song 2:5, I am *s.* of love.
Isa. 1:5, the whole head is *s.*
Hos. 7:5, made him *s.* with bottles of wine.
Mt. 8:14, wife's mother *s.*
Jas. 5:14, is any *s.*? call elders of the church.
15, prayer of faith shall save the *s.*
ICKNESS. Ps. 41:3; Eccl. 5:17; Mt. 8:17.
IFT. Isa. 30:28; Amos 9:9; Lk. 22:31.
IGHT. Ex. 3:3, this great *s.*
Dt. 28:34, for *s.* of thine eyes.
Eccl. 6:9, better is *s.* of eyes.
Mt. 11:5; 20:34; Lk. 7:21, blind receive *s.*
26; Lk. 10:21, it seemed good in thy *s.*
Lk. 18:42; Acts 22:13, receive thy *s.*
21:11, fearful *s.* and signs from heaven.
Rom. 12:17, things honest in *s.* of all men.
2Cor. 5:7, walk by faith, not by *s.*
See Eccl. 11:9; Isa. 43:4; Dan. 4:11; Heb. 4:13.
IGN. Isa. 7:11, ask thee a *s.* of the Lord.
55:13, for an everlasting *s.*
Ezek. 12:6, I have set thee for a *s.*
Dan. 4:3, how great are his *s.*
Mt. 16:3, *s.* of the times.
Mk. 16:20, with *s.* following.
Lk. 2:34, for a *s.* which shall be spoken against.
Jn. 4:48, except ye see *s.*
Acts 2:22, man approved of God by *s.*
4:30, that *s.* may be done by the name.
See Rom. 4:11; 15:19; 1Cor. 1:22; Rev. 15:1.
IGNIFY. Jn. 12:33; Heb. 9:8; 1Pet. 1:11.
ILENCE. Mt. 22:34; 1Tim. 2:11; 1Pet. 2:15.
ILENT. 1Sam. 2:9, *s.* in darkness.
Ps. 28:1, be not *s.* to me.
31:17, let the wicked be *s.* in the grave.
Zech. 2:13, be *s.*, all flesh, before the Lord.
See Ps. 22:2; 30:12; Isa. 47:5; Jer. 8:14.
SILK. Prov. 31:22, her clothing is *s.* and purple.
Ezek. 16:10, I covered thee with *s.*
SILLY. Job 5:2; Hos. 7:11; 2Tim. 3:6.
SILVER. 1Ki. 10:27, king made *s.* as stones.
Job 22:25, thou shalt have plenty of *s.*
Ps. 12:6; 66:10, as *s.* is tried.
Prov. 8:10, receive instruction and not *s.*
Eccl. 5:10, he that loveth *s.* shall not be satisfied.
Isa. 1:22, thy *s.* is become dross.
Jer. 6:30, reprobate *s.* shall men call them.
Mal. 3:3, sit as a refiner and purifier of *s.*
See Gen. 44:2; Eccl. 12:6; Mt. 27:6; Acts 19:24.
SIMILITUDE. Num. 12:8, the *s.* of the Lord.
Dt. 4:12, saw no *s.*
Ps. 144:12, after the *s.* of a palace.
Rom. 5:14, after the *s.* of Adam's transgression.
Jas. 3:9, made after the *s.* of God.
See Hos. 12:10; Dan. 10:16; Heb. 7:15.
SIMPLE (foolish). Ps. 19:7, making wise the *s.*
116:6, the Lord preserveth the *s.*
119:130, it giveth understanding to the *s.*
Prov. 1:22, how long, ye *s.* ones?
32, the turning away of the *s.*
7:7, and behold among the *s.*
8:5, O ye *s.* understand wisdom.
9:4, whoso is *s.*
14:15, the *s.* believeth every word.
19:25, and the *s.* will beware.
22:3; 27:12, the *s.* pass on, and are punished.
Rom. 16:18, deceive the hearts of the *s.*
SIMPLICITY. 2Cor. 1:12, that in *s.* and godly sincerity.
11:3, from the *s.* that is in Christ.
SIN (*n.*). Gen. 4:7, *s.* lieth at the door.
Num. 27:3, died in his own *s.*
Dt. 24:16; 2Ki. 14:6; 2Chr. 25:4, put to death for his own *s.*
Job 10:6, thou searchest after my *s.*
Ps. 19:13, from presumptuous *s.*
Ps. 25:7, remember not *s.* of my youth.
32:1, blessed is he whose *s.* is covered.
38:18, I will be sorry for my *s.*
51:3, my *s.* is ever before me.
90:8, our secret *s.*
103:10, hath not dealt with us according to our *s.*
Prov. 5:22, holden with cords of *s.*
10:19, in multitude of words wanteth not *s.*
14:9, fools make a mock at *s.*
34, *s.* is a reproach to any people.
Isa. 30:1, to add *s.* to *s.*
43:25; 44:22, not remember *s.*
53:10, offering for *s.*
12, bare the *s.* of many.
Jer. 51:5, land filled with *s.*
Ezek. 33:16, none of his *s.* shall be mentioned.
Hos. 4:8, they eat up *s.* of my people.
Mic. 6:7, fruit of my body for *s.* of my soul.
Mt. 12:31, all manner of *s.* shall be forgiven.
Jn. 1:29, the *s.* of the world.

8:7, he that is without *s.*
16:8, will reprove the world of *s.*
19:11, hath the greater *s.*
Acts 7:60, lay not this *s.* to their charge.
22:16, wash away thy *s.*
Rom. 5:20, where *s.* abounded.
6:1, shall we continue in *s.*
7:7, I had not known *s.*
14:23, whatsoever is not of faith is *s.*
2Cor. 5:21, made him to be *s.* for us.
2Th. 2:3, that man of *s.*
1Pet. 2:24, his own self bare our *s.*
See 1Jn. 1:8; 3:4; 4:10; 5:16; Rev. 1:5.
SIN (*v.*). Gen. 42:22, do not *s.* against the child.
Ex. 9:27; 10:16; Num. 22:34; Josh. 7:20; 1Sam. 15:24; 26:21; 2Sam. 12:13; Job 7:20; Ps. 41:4; Mt. 27:4; Lk. 15:18, I have *s.*
Job 10:14, if I *s.*, thou markest me.
Ps. 4:4, stand in awe and *s.* not.
39:1, that I *s.* not with my tongue.
Prov. 8:36, he that *s.* against me.
Isa. 43:27, thy first father hath *s.*
Ezek. 18:4, the soul that *s.* it shall die.
Hos. 13:2, now they *s.* more and more.
Mt. 18:21, how oft shall my brother *s.*
Jn. 5:14; 8:11, *s.* no more.
Rom. 6:15, shall we *s.* because.
1Cor. 15:34, awake to righteousness and *s.* not.
Eph. 4:26, be ye angry, and *s.* not.
1Jn. 3:9, he cannot *s.* because born of God.
See Num. 15:28; Job 1:5, 22; Rom. 3:23.
SINCERE. Phil. 1:10; 1Pet. 2:2.
SINCERITY. Josh. 24:14; 1Cor. 5:8; Eph. 6:24.
SINFUL. Lk. 5:8; 24:7; Rom. 7:13; 8:3.
SINGING. Ps. 100:2; 126:2; Song 2:12; Eph. 5:19.
SINGLE. Mt. 6:22; Lk. 11:34.
SINGLENESS. Acts 2:46; Eph. 6:5; Col. 3:22.
SINNER. Gen. 13:13, men of Sodom *s.* exceedingly.
Ps. 1:1, standeth not in way of *s.*
25:8, teach *s.* in the way.
26:9, gather not my soul with *s.*
51:13, *s.* shall be converted.
Prov. 1:10, if *s.* entice thee.
13:21, evil pursueth *s.*
Eccl. 9:18, one *s.* destroyeth much good.
Isa. 33:14, the *s.* in Zion are afraid.
Mt. 9:11; Mk. 2:16; Lk. 5:30; 15:2, eat with *s.*
13; Mk. 2:17; Lk. 5:32, call *s.* to repentance.
11:19; Lk. 7:34, a friend of *s.*
Lk. 7:37, woman who was a *s.*
13:2, suppose ye these were *s.* above all?
15:7, 10, joy over one *s.*
18:13, be merciful to me a *s.*
Jn. 9:16, how can a man that is a *s.* do such miracles?
25, whether he be a *s.* I know not.
Rom. 5:8, while we were yet *s.*
Rom. 5:19, many were made *s.*
Heb. 7:26, separate from *s.*
See Jas. 4:8; 5:20; 1Pet. 4:18; Jude 15.
SISTER. Job 17:14; Prov. 7:4; Mt. 12:50; 1Tim. 5:2.
SIT. 2Ki. 7:3, why *s.* we here until we die?
Ps. 69:12, they that *s.* in the gate.
107:10, such as *s.* in darkness.
Isa. 30:7, their strength is to *s.* still.
Jer. 8:14, why do we *s.* still?
Ezek. 33:31, they *s.* before thee as thy people.
Mic. 4:4, they *s.* every man under his vine.
Mal. 3:3, he shall *s.* as a refiner.
Mt. 20:23; Mk. 10:37, to *s.* on my right hand.
See Prov. 23:1; Lam. 3:63; Acts 2:2.
SITUATION. 2Ki. 2:19; Ps. 48:2.
SKILFUL. 1Chr. 28:21; Ps. 33:3; Ezek. 21:31; Dan. 1:4.
SKILL. 2Chr. 2:7; Eccl. 9:11; Dan. 1:17; 9:22.
SKIN. Ex. 34:29, wist not that *s.* of his face shone.
Job 2:4, *s.* for *s.*
10:11, thou hast clothed me with *s.* and flesh.
19:26, though after my *s.* worms destroy.
Jer. 13:23, can the Ethiopian change his *s.*
Ezek. 37:6, I will cover you with *s.*
Heb. 11:37, wandered in sheep-*s.*
See Gen. 3:21; 27:16; Ps. 102:5; Mic. 3:2; Mk. 1:6.
SKIP. Ps. 29:6; 114:4; Jer. 48:27.
SKIRT. Ps. 133:2; Jer. 2:34; Zech. 8:23.
SLACK. Dt. 7:10; Prov. 10:4; Zeph. 3:16; 2Pet. 3:9.
SLAIN. Gen. 4:23, I have *s.* a man.
Prov. 7:26, strong men have been *s.* by her.
22:13, the slothful man saith, I shall be *s.*
24:11, deliver those ready to be *s.*
Isa. 22:2, thy *s.* men are not *s.* with the sword.
26:21, earth shall no more cover her *s.*
66:16, the *s.* of the Lord shall be many.
Jer. 9:1, weep for the *s.* of my people.
Lam. 4:9, *s.* with sword better than *s.* with hunger.
Ezek. 37:9, breathe upon these *s.*
Eph. 2:16, having *s.* the enmity.
Rev. 5:6, a Lamb as it had been *s.*
See 1Sam. 18:7; 22:21; Lk. 9:22; Heb. 11:37.
SLANDEROUSLY. Rom. 3:8, as we be *s.* reported.
SLAUGHTER. Ps. 44:22, as sheep for the *s.*
Isa. 53:7; Jer. 11:19, brought as a lamb to the *s.*
Jer. 7:32; 19:6, valley of *s.*
Ezek. 9:2, every man a *s.* weapon.
See Hos. 5:2; Zech. 11:4; Acts 9:1; Jas. 5:5.
SLAVE. Jer. 2:14; Rev. 18:13.
SLAY. Gen. 18:25, far from thee to *s.* the righteous.
Job 9:23, if scourge *s.* suddenly.
13:15, though he *s.* me.
See Gen. 4:15; Ex. 21:14; Neh. 4:11; Lk. 11:49; 19:27.
SLEEP (*n.*). 1Sam. 26:12, deep *s.* from God.
Job 4:13; 33:15, when deep *s.* falleth.
Ps. 13:3, lest I sleep the *s.* of death.
127:2, giveth his beloved *s.*
Prov. 3:24, thy *s.* shall be sweet.
6:10; 24:33, yet a little *s.*
20:13, love not *s.*, lest.
Eccl. 5:12, the *s.* of a labouring man.
Jer. 51:39, sleep a perpetual *s.*
Lk. 9:32, heavy with *s.*
Jn. 11:13, of taking rest in *s.*
Rom. 13:11, high time to awake out of *s.*
See Dan. 2:1; 6:18; 8:18; Acts 16:27; 20:9.

.EEP (*v.*). Ex. 22:27, raiment, wherein shall he *s.*
Job 7:21, now shall I *s.* in the dust.
Ps. 4:8, I will lay me down and *s.*
121:4, shall neither slumber nor *s.*
Prov. 4:16, they *s.* not, except they have done.
6:22, when thou *s.* it shall keep thee.
10:5, he that *s.* in harvest is a son that causeth shame.
Song 5:2, I *s.*, but my heart waketh.
Dan. 12:2, many that *s.* in the dust.
Mt. 9:24; Mk. 5:39; Lk. 8:52, not dead but *s.*
13:25, while men *s.* the enemy sowed.
26:45; Mk. 14:41, *s.* on now.
Mk. 13:36, coming suddenly he find you *s.*
Lk. 22:46, why *s.* ye? rise and pray.
Jn. 11:11, our friend Lazarus *s.*
1Cor. 11:30, for this cause many *s.*
15:51, we shall not all *s.*
Eph. 5:14, awake thou that *s.*
1Th. 4:14, them which *s.* in Jesus.
5:6, let us not *s.* as do others.
7, they that *s.* *s.* in the night.
10, that whether we wake or *s.*
See Gen. 28:11; 1Ki. 18:27; Acts 12:6; 1Cor. 15:20.
.EIGHT. Eph. 4:14, the *s.* of men.
.EW. Jud. 9:54, a woman *s.* him.
1Sam. 17:36, *s.* both the lion and the bear.
29:5, Saul *s.* his thousands.
2Ki. 10:9, who *s.* all these?
Ps. 78:34, when he *s.* them, then they sought him.
Isa. 66:3, killeth an ox is as if he *s.* a man.
Dan. 5:19, whom he would he *s.*
Mt. 23:35, whom ye *s.* between temple and altar.
Acts 5:30; 10:39, whom ye *s.* and hanged on a tree.
22:20, kept raiment of them that *s.* him.
Rom. 7:11, sin by the commandment *s.* me.
See Gen. 4:8; Ex. 2:12; 13:15; Neh. 9:26; Lam. 2:4.
.IDE. Dt. 32:35; Ps. 26:1; 37:31; Hos. 4:16.
.IGHTLY. Jer. 6:14; 8:11, healed hurt *s.*
.IME. Gen. 11:3; 14:10; Ex. 2:3.
.IP. 2Sam. 22:37; Ps. 18:36, feet did not *s.*
Job 12:5, he that is ready to *s.*
Ps. 17:5, that my footsteps *s.* not.
38:16, when my foot *s.* they magnify.
73:2, my steps had well nigh *s.*
Heb. 2:1, lest we should let them *s.*
See Dt. 19:5; 1Sam. 19:10; Ps. 94:18.
.IPPERY. Ps. 35:6; 73:18; Jer. 23:12.
.OTHFUL. Jud. 18:9, be not *s.* to possess.
Mt. 25:26, thou *s.* servant.
Rom. 12:11, not *s.* in business.
Heb. 6:12, that ye be not *s.*
See Prov. 18:9; 19:24; 24:30; Eccl. 10:18.
.OW. Ex. 4:10, I am *s.* of speech.
Neh. 9:17, a God *s.* to anger.
Prov. 14:29, *s.* to wrath is of great understanding.
Lk. 24:25, *s.* of heart.
See Acts 27:7; Ti. 1:12; Jas. 1:19.
.UGGARD. Prov. 6:6, go to the ant, thou *s.*
10:26, so is the *s.* to them that send him.
13:4, the soul of the *s.* desireth.
20:4, the *s.* will not plow.
26:16, the *s.* is wiser in his own conceit.
SLUMBER. Ps. 121:3, that keepeth thee will not *s.*
Prov. 6:4, give not *s.* to thine eyelids.
10; 24:33, a little more *s.*
Isa. 5:27, none shall *s.* among them.
56:10, loving to *s.*
Nah. 3:18, thy shepherds *s.*
Rom. 11:8, hath given them the spirit of *s.*
See Job 33:15; Mt. 25:5; 2Pet. 2:3.
SMALL. Ex. 16:14, *s.* round thing, *s.* as hoar frost.
18:22, every *s.* matter they shall judge.
Num. 16:9, a *s.* thing that God hath separated.
13, a *s.* thing that thou hast brought us.
Dt. 9:21, I ground the calf *s.*, even as *s.* as dust.
32:2, doctrine distil as *s.* rain.
2Sam. 7:19; 1Chr. 17:17, yet a *s.* thing in thy sight.
1Ki. 2:20, one *s.* petition of thee.
2Ki. 19:26, inhabitants of *s.* power.
Job 8:7, thy beginning was *s.*
15:11, are consolations of God *s.*?
36:27, he maketh *s.* the drops of water.
Ps. 119:141, I am *s.*
Prov. 24:10, thy strength is *s.*
Isa. 7:13, is it a *s.* thing to weary men?
16:14, remnant very *s.* and feeble.
40:15, nations as the *s.* dust.
54:7, for a *s.* moment.
60:22, a *s.* one shall become a strong nation.
Jer. 49:15, I will make thee *s.* among heathen.
Dan. 11:23, strong with a *s.* people.
Amos 7:2, by whom shall Jacob arise? for he is *s.*
Zech. 4:10, the day of *s.* things.
Mk. 8:7; Jn. 6:9, a few *s.* fishes.
Acts 12:18; 19:23, no *s.* stir.
15:2, had no *s.* dissension.
Jas. 3:4, turned with very *s.* helm.
See Jer. 44:28; Ezek. 34:18; 1Cor. 6:2.
SMART. Prov. 11:15, shall *s.* for it.
SMELL. Gen. 27:27, as *s.* of field which the Lord hath blessed.
Deut 4:28, gods that neither see nor *s.*
Job 39:25, he *s.* the battle.
Ps. 45:8, thy garments *s.* of myrrh.
115:6, noses have they, but they *s.* not.
Isa. 3:24, instead of sweet *s.*
Dan. 3:27, nor the *s.* of fire.
1Cor. 12:17, hearing, where were the *s.*?
Eph. 5:2, sacrifice for sweet-*s.* savour.
Phil. 4:18, an odour of a sweet *s.*
See Song 1:12; 2:13; 4:10; 7:8; Amos 5:21.
SMITE. Ex. 2:13, wherefore *s.* thou?
21:12, he that *s.* a man.
1Sam. 26:8, I will not *s.* him the second time.
2Ki. 6:18, *s.* this people with blindness.
21, shall I *s.* them?
Ps. 121:6, the sun shall not *s.* thee by day.
141:5, let the righteous *s.* me.
Prov. 19:25, *s.* a scorner.
Isa. 10:24, he shall *s.* thee with a rod.

49:10, neither shall heat *s.* thee.
50:6, gave my back to the *s.*
58:4, to *s.* with the fist of wickedness.
Jer. 18:18, let us *s.* him with the tongue.
Lam. 3:30, giveth his cheek to him that *s.*
Ezek. 7:9, know that I am the Lord that *s.*
21:14, prophesy, and *s.* thine hands together.
Nah. 2:10, the knees *s.* together.
Zech. 13:7, awake, O sword, and *s.* the shepherd.
Mal. 4:6, lest I *s.* the earth with a curse.
Mt. 5:39, *s.* thee on the right cheek.
24:49, shall begin to *s.* his fellow servants.
Lk. 22:49, shall we *s.* with sword?
Jn. 18:23, why *s.* thou me?
See Lk. 6:29; Acts 23:2; 2Cor. 11:20; Rev. 11:6.
SMITH. 1Sam. 13:19; Isa. 44:12; Jer. 24:1.
SMITTEN. Num. 22:28, that thou hast *s.*
Dt. 28:25, cause thee to be *s.*
1Sam. 4:3, wherefore hath the Lord *s.* us?
2Ki. 13:19, thou shouldest have *s.* five or six times.
Ps. 3:7, thou hast *s.* all mine enemies.
102:4, my heart is *s.*
Isa. 24:12, the gate is *s.* with destruction.
53:4, *s.* of God.
Jer. 2:30, in vain have I *s.* your children.
Hos. 6:1, he hath *s.* and he will bind.
Amos 4:9, I have *s.* you.
See Job 16:10; Ezek. 22:13; Acts 23:3.
SMOKE. Gen. 19:28, as the *s.* of a furnace.
Dt. 29:20, the anger of the Lord shall *s.*
Ps. 37:20, wicked consume into *s.*
68:2, as *s.* is driven away.
74:1, why doth thy anger *s.*?
102:3, my days are consumed like *s.*
104:32; 144:5, he toucheth the hills, and they *s.*
119:83, like a bottle in the *s.*
Prov. 10:26, as *s.* to the eyes.
Isa. 6:4, the house was filled with *s.*
34:10, the *s.* thereof shall go up for ever.
51:6, the heavens shall vanish like *s.*
65:5, these are a *s.* in my nose.
Hos. 13:3, as the *s.* out of a chimney.
See Rev. 9:2; 14:11; 15:8; 18:9; 19:3.
SMOKING. Gen. 15:17; Ex. 20:18; Isa. 42:3; Mt. 12:20.
SMOOTH. Gen. 27:11, I am a *s.* man.
1Sam. 17:40; Isa. 57:6, five *s.* stones.
Isa. 30:10, speak unto us *s.* things.
Lk. 3:5, rough ways shall be made *s.*
See Ps. 55:21; Prov. 5:3; Isa. 41:7.
SMOTE. Num. 20:11, Moses *s.* the rock twice.
Jud. 15:8, Samson *s.* them hip and thigh.
1Sam. 24:5, David's heart *s.* him.
Isa. 60:10, in my wrath I *s.* thee.
Jer. 31:19, I *s.* upon my thigh.
Hag. 2:17, I *s.* you with blasting and mildew.
Mt. 26:68; Lk. 22:64, who is he that *s.* thee?
Lk. 18:13, *s.* upon his breast.
Acts 12:23, immediately angel *s.* him.
See 2Sam. 14:7; Dan. 2:34; Mt. 27:30.
SNARE. Ex. 10:7, this man be a *s.* unto us.
Dt. 7:25, nor take silver of idols, lest thou be *s.*
12:30, take heed that thou be not *s.* by them
Josh. 23:13, they shall be *s.* unto you.
Jud. 8:27, which thing became a *s.* to Gideon.
1Sam. 18:21, that she may be a *s.*
28:9, wherefore layest thou a *s.* for my life?
2Sam. 22:6; Ps. 18:5, *s.* of death prevented me.
Job 18:8, he walketh on a *s.*
22:10, *s.* are round about thee.
Ps. 11:6, upon the wicked he shall rain *s.*
38:12, they lay *s.* for me.
64:5, commune of laying *s.* privily.
69:22, let their table become a *s.*
91:3, deliver thee from *s.* of fowler.
124:7, the *s.* is broken.
Prov. 6:2; 12:13, *s.* with words of thy mouth.
7:23, as a bird hasteth to the *s.*
13:14; 14:27, the *s.* of death.
18:7, a fool's lips are the *s.* of his soul.
22:25, learn his ways, and get a *s.* to thy so
29:8, bring city into *s.*
25, fear of man bringeth a *s.*
Eccl. 9:12, *s.* in an evil time.
Isa. 24:17; Jer. 48:43, the *s.* are upon thee.
Lam. 3:47, fear and a *s.* is come upon us.
Ezek. 12:13, he shall be taken in my *s.*
Hos. 9:8, the prophet is a *s.*
Amos 3:5, can a bird fall in a *s.*?
Lk. 21:35, as a *s.* shall it come.
1Tim. 3:7, lest he fall into the *s.*
6:9, they that will be rich fall into a *s.*
2Tim. 2:26, recover out of the *s.* of the devil.
See Ex. 23:33; Dt. 7:16; Jud. 2:3; Eccl. 7:26.
SNATCH. Isa. 9:20, shall *s.* and be hungry.
SNOW. Ex. 4:6; Num. 12:10; 2Ki. 5:27, leprous as *s*
2Sam. 23:20, slew lion in time of *s.*
Job 6:16, wherein the *s.* is hid.
9:30, wash myself in *s.* water.
24:19, drought and heat consume *s.* waters.
37:6, saith to *s.*, be thou on the earth.
38:22, the treasures of the *s.*
Ps. 51:7, I shall be whiter than *s.*
147:16, he giveth *s.* like wool.
Prov. 25:13, cold of *s.* in harvest.
26:1, as *s.* in summer.
31:21, she is not afraid of the *s.*
Isa. 1:18, your sins shall be white as *s.*
55:10, as the *s.* from heaven returneth not.
Jer. 18:14, will a man leave the *s.* of Lebanon?
Lam. 4:7, Nazarites purer than *s.*
Dan. 7:9; Mt. 28:3; Mk. 9:3, garment white as *s*
See Ps. 68:14; 148:8; Rev. 1:14.
SNUFFED. Jer. 14:6; Mal. 1:13.
SOAKED. Isa. 34:7, land *s.* with blood.
SOAP. Jer. 2:22; Mal. 3:2.
SOBER. 2Cor. 5:13, *s.* for your cause.
1Th. 5:6, let us watch and be *s.*
1Tim. 3:2; Ti. 1:8, a bishop must be *s.*
Ti. 2:2, aged men be *s.*
4, teach young women to be *s.*
1Pet. 4:7, be ye therefore *s.*, and watch.
See Acts 26:25; Rom. 12:3; Ti. 2:6.
SODDEN. Ex. 12:9; 1Sam. 2:15; Lam. 4:10.

)FT. Job 23:16, God maketh my heart *s.*
41:3, will he speak *s.* words?
Ps. 65:10, thou makest it *s.* with showers.
Prov. 15:1, a *s.* answer turneth away wrath.
25:15, a *s.* tongue breaketh the bone.
See Ps. 55:21; Mt. 11:8; Lk. 7:25.
)FTLY. Gen. 33:14; Jud. 4:21; 1Ki. 21:27; Isa. 38:15.
)IL. Ezek. 17:8, planted in a good *s.*
)JOURN. Gen. 19:9, this fellow came in to *s.*
26:3, *s.* in this land, and I will be with thee.
47:4, to *s.* in the land are we come.
Dt. 26:5, *s.* with a few, and became a nation.
Jud. 17:9, I go to *s.* where I may find place.
2Ki. 8:1, *s.* wheresoever thou canst *s.*
Ps. 120:5, woe is me, that I *s.*
Isa. 23:7, feet carry her afar off to *s.*
Jer. 42:22, die in place whither ye desire to *s.*
Lam. 4:15, they shall no more *s.* there.
Heb. 11:9, by faith he *s.* in land of promise.
1Pet. 1:17, pass time of your *s.* here in fear.
)JOURNER. Gen. 23:4; Ps. 39:12.
)LD. Gen. 31:15, our father hath *s.* us.
45:4, whom ye *s.* into Egypt.
Lev. 25:23, the land shall not be *s.* for ever.
42, shall not be *s.* as bondmen.
27:28, no devoted thing shall be *s.*
Dt. 15:12, if thy brother be *s.* unto thee.
32:30, except their Rock had *s.* them.
1Ki. 21:20, thou hast *s.* thyself to work evil.
Neh. 5:8, or shall they be *s.* unto us?
Est. 7:4, for we are *s.* to be slain.
Isa. 50:1, have ye *s.* yourselves?
52:3, ye have *s.* yourselves for nought.
Lam. 5:4, our wood is *s.* unto us.
Joel 3:3, they have *s.* a girl for wine.
Amos 2:6, they *s.* the righteous for silver.
Mt. 10:29, are not two sparrows *s.* for a farthing?
13:46, went and *s.* all that he had.
18:25, his lord commanded him to be *s.*
21:12; Mk. 11:15, cast out them that *s.*
26:9; Mk. 14:5, might have been *s.* for much.
Lk. 17:28, they bought, they *s.*, they planted.
Acts 2:45, and *s.* their possessions.
Rom. 7:14, *s.* under sin.
1Cor. 10:25, whatsoever is *s.* in the shambles.
See Lk. 19:45; Jn. 12:5; Acts 5:1; Heb. 12:16.
)LDIER. Ezra 8:22, ashamed to require *s.*
Mt. 8:9; Lk. 7:8, having *s.* under me.
Lk. 3:14, *s.* demanded, what shall we do?
Acts 10:7, a devout *s.*
2Tim. 2:3, as a good *s.* of Jesus Christ.
See 2Chr. 25:13; Isa. 15:4; Acts 27:31.
)LE. Gen. 8:9, dove found no rest for *s.* of her foot.
2Sam. 14:25; Isa. 1:6, from *s.* of foot to crown.
See Dt. 28:35, 56, 65; Josh. 1:3; Job 2:7.
)LEMN. Ps. 92:3, sing praise with a *s.* sound.
See Num. 10:10; Isa. 1:13; Lam. 2:22; Hos. 9:5.
)LEMNITY. Isa. 30:29, when a holy *s.* is kept.
See Dt. 31:10; Isa. 33:20; Ezek. 45:17; 46:11.
)LEMNLY. Gen. 43:3; 1Sam. 8:9.
)LITARY. Ps. 68:6, God setteth the *s.* in families.
107:4, wandered in a *s.* way.
Isa. 35:1, the wilderness and *s.* place shall be glad.
See Job 3:7; 30:3; Lam. 1:1; Mic. 7:14; Mk. 1:35.
SOME. Gen. 37:20, *s.* evil beast.
Ex. 16:17, gathered, *s.* more, *s.* less.
1Ki. 14:13, found *s.* good thing.
Ps. 20:7, *s.* trust in chariots.
69:20, I looked for *s.* to take pity.
Dan. 12:2, *s.* to life, and *s.* to shame.
Mt. 16:14; Mk. 8:28; Lk. 9:19, *s.* say thou art John the Baptist.
28:17, *s.* doubted.
Jn. 6:64, *s.* of you that believe not.
Acts 19:32; 21:34, *s.* cried one thing, *s.* another.
Rom. 3:3, what if *s.* did not believe?
5:7, *s.* would even dare to die.
1Cor. 6:11, such were *s.* of you.
15:34, *s.* have not knowledge.
Eph. 4:11, *s.* prophets, *s.* evangelists.
1Tim. 5:24, *s.* men's sins are open.
Heb. 10:25, as the manner of *s.* is.
2Pet. 3:9, as *s.* men count slackness.
See 1Tim. 1:19; 2Tim. 2:18; Jude *22*.
SOMEBODY. Lk. 8:46; Acts 5:36.
SOMETIMES. Eph. 2:13, *s.* far off.
5:8, ye were *s.* darkness.
Col. 1:21, *s.* alienated.
See Col. 3:7; Ti. 3:3; 1Pet. 3:20.
SOMEWHAT. 1Ki. 2:14; Gal. 2:6; Rev. 2:4.
SON. Gen. 6:2; Job 1:6; 2:1; 38:7; Jn. 1:12; Phil. 2:15; 1Jn. 3:1, *s.* of God.
Job 14:21, his *s.* come to honour.
Ps. 2:12, kiss the *S.*, lest he be angry.
86:16, save *s.* of thine handmaid.
116:16, I am the *s.* of thine handmaid.
Prov. 10:1; 13:1; 15:20; 17:2; 19:26, a wise *s.*
17:25; 19:13, a foolish *s.*
31:2, *s.* of my womb, *s.* of my vows.
Isa. 9:6, unto us a *s.* is given.
14:12, *s.* of the morning.
Jer. 35:5, *s.* of the Rechabites.
Ezek. 20:31; 23:37, *s.* pass through fire.
Hos. 1:10, the *s.* of the living God.
Mal. 3:17, as a man spareth his *s.*
Mt. 11:27, no man knoweth the *S.*
13:55; Mk. 6:3; Lk. 4:22, the carpenter's *s.*
17:5, this is my beloved *S.*
22:42, Christ, whose *s.* is he?
Lk. 7:12, only *s.* of his mother.
10:6, if the *s.* of peace.
19:9, he also is a *s.* of Abraham.
Jn. 1:18; 3:18, only begotten *S.*
5:21, the *S.* quickeneth whom he will.
8:35, the *S.* abideth ever.
36, if the *S.* make you free.
17:12; 2Th. 2:3, the *s.* of perdition.
Acts 4:36, *s.* of consolation.
Rom. 1:9, serve in the gospel of his *S.*
8:3, God sending his own *S.*
29, conformed to the image of his *S.*
32, spared not his own *S.*
1Cor. 4:14, as my beloved *s.* I warn you.
Gal. 4:5, the adoption of *s.*

7, if a *s.*, then an heir.
Col. 1:13, the kingdom of his dear *S.*
Heb. 2:10, bringing many *s.* to glory.
5:8, though a *S.*, yet learned he obedience.
11:24, refused to be called *s.*
12:6, scourgeth every *s.*
1Jn. 2:22, antichrist denieth the *s.*
5:12, he that hath the *S.* hath life.
See 1Jn. 1:7; 4:9; 5:10, 11; Rev. 21:7.
SONGS. Job 30:9, now am I their *s.*
35:10; Ps. 77:6, who giveth *s.* in the night.
Ps. 32:7, with *s.* of deliverance.
33:3; Isa. 42:10, sing unto him a new *s.*
40:3, he hath put a new *s.* in my mouth.
69:12, I was the *s.* of drunkards.
119:54, my *s.* in house of my pilgrimage.
137:4, the Lord's *s.* in a strange land.
Prov. 25:20, that singeth *s.* to an heavy heart.
Isa. 23:16, sing many *s.*
35:10, the ransomed shall come with *s.*
Ezek. 33:32, as a very lovely *s.*
Amos 8:3, *s.* of the temple.
Eph. 5:19; Col. 3:16, in psalms and spiritual *s.*
See Song 1:1; Rev. 5:9; 14:3; 15:3.
SOON. Ex. 2:18, how is it ye are come so *s.*?
Job 32:22, my Maker would *s.* take me away.
Ps. 37:2, shall *s.* be cut down.
58:3, go astray as *s.* as born.
68:31, Ethiopia shall *s.* stretch out her hands.
90:10, it is *s.* cut off.
Ps. 106:13, they *s.* forgat his works.
Prov. 14:17, he that is *s.* angry.
See Mt. 21:20; Gal. 1:6; 2Th. 2:2; Ti. 1:7.
SORE. 2Chr. 6:29; Isa. 1:6; Lk. 16:20.
SORROW. Gen. 3:16, multiply thy *s.*
42:28, with *s.* to the grave.
Job 6:10, I would harden myself in *s.*
21:17, God distributeth *s.* in his anger.
41:22, *s.* is turned into joy.
Ps. 13:2, having *s.* in my heart daily.
90:10, yet is their strength labour and *s.*
116:3, I found trouble and *s.*
127:2, to eat the bread of *s.*
Prov. 10:22, maketh rich, addeth no *s.*
23:29, who hath *s.*?
Eccl. 2:23, all his days are *s.*
7:3, *s.* is better than laughter.
11:10, remove *s.* from thy heart.
Isa. 17:11, day of desperate *s.*
35:10; 51:11, *s.* and sighing shall flee away.
53:3, a man of *s.*
Jer. 30:15, thy *s.* is incurable.
49:23, there is *s.* on the sea.
Lam. 1:12, any *s.* like unto my *s.*
Mt. 24:8; Mk. 13:8, beginning of *s.*
Lk. 22:45, sleeping for *s.*
Jn. 16:6, *s.* hath filled your heart.
2Cor. 2:7, with overmuch *s.*
7:10, godly *s.* worketh repentance.
1Th. 4:13, *s.* not as others.
1Tim. 6:10, pierced with many *s.*
See Prov. 15:13; Hos. 8:10; Rev. 21:4.
SORROWFUL. 1Sam. 1:15, woman of a *s.* spirit.
Ps. 69:29, I am poor and *s.*
Prov. 14:13, even in laughter the heart is *s.*
Jer. 31, 25, replenished every *s.* soul.
Zeph. 3:18, I will gather them that are *s.*
Mt. 19:22; Lk. 18:23, went away *s.*
26:37, he began to be *s.*
38; Mk. 14:34, my soul is exceeding *s.*
Jn. 16:20, ye shall be *s.*
See Job 6:7; 2Cor. 6:10; Phil. 2:28.
SORRY. Ps. 38:18, I will be *s.* for my sin.
Isa. 51:19, who shall be *s.* for thee?
See 1Sam. 22:8; Neh. 8:10; Mt. 14:9.
SORT. Gen. 6:19, two of every *s.*
1Chr. 29:14, to offer after this *s.*
Dan. 3:29, deliver after this *s.*
Acts 17:5, fellows of the baser *s.*
2Cor. 7:11; 3Jn. 6, after a godly *s.*
2Tim. 3:6, of this *s.* are they.
See Dt. 22:11; Eccl. 2:8; Ezek. 27:24; 38:4.
SOTTISH. Jer. 4:22, they are *s.* children.
SOUGHT. Gen. 43:30, he *s.* where to weep.
Ex. 4:24, the Lord *s.* to kill him.
1Sam. 13:14, the Lord hath *s.* him a man.
1Chr. 15:13, we *s.* him not after due order.
2Chr. 15:4, when they *s.* him he was found.
15, they *s.* him with their whole desire.
16:12, in his disease he *s.* not the Lord.
26:5, as long as he *s.* the Lord.
Ps. 34:4; 77:2, I *s.* the Lord, and he heard me.
111:2, *s.* out of all that have pleasure.
Eccl. 7:29, *s.* out many inventions.
12:10, the preacher *s.* to find acceptable words.
Isa. 62:12, shalt be called, *S.* out.
65:1, *s.* of them that asked not.
Jer. 10:21, pastors have not *s.* the Lord.
Lam. 1:19, they *s.* meat to relieve their souls.
Ezek. 22:30, I *s.* for a man among them.
34:4, neither have ye *s.* that which was lost.
Lk. 11:16, *s.* of him a sign.
13:6, he *s.* fruit thereon.
19:3, *s.* to see Jesus.
Rom. 9:32, *s.* it not by faith.
Heb. 12:17, though he *s.* it carefully with tears.
See Song 3:1; Lk. 2:44; 1Th. 2:6.
SOUL. Gen. 2:7, a living *s.*
Ex. 30:12, a ransom for his *s.*
Dt. 11:13, serve him with all your *s.*
13:6, thy friend, which is as thine own *s.*
30:2; Mt. 22:37, obey with all thy *s.*
Jud. 10:16, his *s.* was grieved.
1Sam. 18:1; 20:17, loved him as his own *s.*
1Ki. 8:48, return with all their *s.*
1Chr. 22:19, set your *s.* to seek the Lord.
Job 3:20, life unto the bitter in *s.*
12:10, in whose hand is the *s.*
16:4, if your *s.* were in my *s.* stead.
23:13, what his *s.* desireth, even that he doeth.
31:30, wishing a curse to his *s.*
33:22, his *s.* draweth near to the grave.
Ps. 33:19, to deliver their *s.* from death.
34:22, redeemeth the *s.* of his servants.

49:8, the redemption of their *s.* is precious.
62:1, my *s.* waiteth upon God.
63:1, my *s.* thirsteth for thee.
74:19, the *s.* of thy turtledove.
103:1; 104:1, bless the Lord, O my *s.*
116:7, return to thy rest, O my *s.*
8, thou hast delivered my *s.* from death.
119:175, let my *s.* live.
142:4, no man cared for my *s.*
Prov. 11:25, the liberal *s.* shall be made fat.
19:2, *s.* without knowledge.
25:25, cold waters to thirsty *s.*
Isa. 55:3, hear, and your *s.* shall live.
58:10, if thou wilt satisfy the afflicted *s.*
Jer. 20:13, hath delivered the *s.* of the poor.
31:12, their *s.* shall be as a watered garden.
Ezek. 18:4, all *s.* are mine.
22:25, they have devoured *s.*
Hab. 2:10, thou hast sinned against thy *s.*
Mt. 10:28, to destroy both *s.* and body.
16:26; Mk. 8:36, lose his own *s.*
26:38; Mk. 14:34, my *s.* is exceeding sorrowful.
Lk. 21:19, in your patience possess ye your *s.*
Acts 4:32, of one heart and *s.*
Rom. 13:1, let every *s.* be subject.
1Th. 5:23, that your *s.* and body be preserved.
Heb. 6:19, an anchor of the *s.*
13:17, they watch for your *s.*
Jas. 5:20, shall save a *s.* from death.
1Pet. 2:11, which war against the *s.*
4:19, commit keeping of *s.* to him.
2Pet. 2:14, beguiling unstable *s.*
3Jn. 2, even as thy *s.* prospereth.
See Prov. 3:22; Ezek. 3:19; Acts 15:24.

OUND (*n.*). Lev. 26:36, the *s.* of a shaken leaf.
1Ki. 18:41, *s.* of abundance of rain.
Job 15:21, a dreadful *s.* is in his ears.
Ps. 89:15, that know the joyful *s.*
92:3, harp with a solemn *s.*
Eccl. 12:4, *s.* of grinding is low.
Jer. 50:22, *s.* of battle in the land.
51:54, *s.* of a cry cometh.
Ezek. 33:5, he heard *s.*, and took not warning.
Jn. 3:8, thou hearest the *s.*, but canst not tell.
Acts 2:2, suddenly a *s.* from heaven.
Rom. 10:18, *s.* went into all the earth.
1Cor. 14:8, an uncertain *s.*
See 2Ki. 6:32; Rev. 1:15; 9:9; 18:22.

OUND (*adj.*). Prov. 2:7; 3:21; 8:14, *s.* wisdom.
Prov. 14:30, a *s.* heart is life of the flesh.
1Tim. 1:10; 2Tim. 4:3; Ti. 1:9; 2:1, *s.* doctrine.
2Tim. 1:7, spirit of a *s.* mind.
13, form of *s.* words.
See Ps. 119:80; Lk. 15:27; Ti. 2:2, 8.

OUND (*v.*). Ex. 19:19, the trumpet *s.* long.
Joel 2:1, *s.* an alarm in holy mountain.
Mt. 6:2, do not *s.* a trumpet before thee.
1Th. 1:8, from you *s.* out word of the Lord.
See Neh. 4:18; 1Cor. 13:1; 15:52; Rev. 8:7.

OUR. Isa. 18:5; Jer. 31:29; Ezek. 18:2; Hos. 4:18.

OW. Job 4:8, they that *s.* wickedness.
Ps. 97:11, light is *s.* for the righteous.
126:5, *s.* in tears.
Prov. 6:16, he that *s.* discord.
Eccl. 11:4, he that observeth the wind shall not *s.*
6, in morning *s.* thy seed.
Isa. 32:20, that *s.* beside all waters.
Jer. 4:3, *s.* not among thorns.
12:13, they have *s.* wheat, but shall reap thorns.
Hos. 10:12, *s.* in righteousness, reap in mercy.
Nah. 1:14, that no more of thy name be *s.*
Hag. 1:6, ye have *s.* much, and bring in little.
Mt. 6:26, they *s.* not.
37, he that *s.* good seed.
Jn. 4:36, both he that *s.* and he that reapeth.
1Cor. 15:36, that which thou *s.* is not quickened.
2Cor. 9:6, he which *s.* sparingly.
Gal. 6:7, whatsoever a man *s.*, that shall he reap.
See Lev. 26:5; Dt. 11:10; Jer. 2:2; Jas. 3:18.

SOWER. Isa. 55:10; Jer. 50:16; Mt. 13:3; Mk. 4:3; Lk. 8:5; 2Cor. 9:10.

SPAKE. Ps. 39:3, then *s.* I with my tongue.
106:33, he *s.* unadvisedly with his lips.
Mal. 3:16, *s.* often one to another.
Jn. 7:46, never man *s.* like this man.
1Cor. 13:11, I *s.* as a child.
Heb. 12:25, refused him that *s.* on earth.
2Pet. 1:21, holy men *s.* as they were moved.
See Gen. 35:15; Jn. 9:29; Heb. 1:1.

SPAN. Ex. 28:16; Isa. 40:12; 48:13; Lam. 2:20.

SPARE. Gen. 18:26, I will *s.* for their sakes.
Neh. 13:22, *s.* me according to thy mercy.
Ps. 39:13, *s.* me, that I may recover strength.
Prov. 13:24, he that *s.* the rod.
19:18, let not thy soul *s.* for his crying.
Joel 2:17, *s.* thy people.
Mal. 3:17, I will *s.* them as a man *s.*
Lk. 15:17, bread enough and to *s.*
Rom. 8:32, *s.* not his own Son.
11:21, if God *s.* not the natural branches.
2Pet. 2:4, if God *s.* not the angels.
See Prov. 17:27; 21:26; Isa. 54, 2; 58:1.

SPARK. Job 5:7; 18:5; Isa. 1:31; 50:11.

SPEAK. Gen. 18:37, to *s.* to God.
Ex. 4:14, I know he can *s.* well.
33:11, spake to Moses as a man *s.* to his friend.
Num. 20:8, *s.* to the rock.
1Sam. 25:17, a man cannot *s.* to him.
Job 11:5, oh that God would *s.* against thee.
13:7, will ye *s.* wickedly for God?
32:7, days should *s.*
33:14, God *s.* once, yea, twice.
37:20, if a man *s.* he shall be swallowed up.
Ps. 85:8, I will hear what the Lord will *s.*
Prov. 23:9, *s.* not in the ears of a fool.
Song 7:9, causing lips of those asleep to *s.*
Isa. 19:18, shall *s.* language of Canaan.
63:1, I that *s.* in righteousness.
65:24, while they are yet *s.*, I will hear.
Jer. 20:9, I will not *s.* any more in his name.
Hab. 2:3, at the end it shall *s.*
Zech. 8:16; Eph. 4:25, *s.* every man the truth.

Mt. 8:8, *s.* the word only, and my servant.
10:19; Mk. 13:11, how or what ye shall *s.*
12:34; Lk. 6:45, of abundance of heart mouth *s.*
36, every idle word that men shall *s.*
Mk. 9:39, can lightly *s.* evil of me.
Lk. 6:26, when all men *s.* well of you.
Jn. 3:11, we *s.* that we do know.
Acts 4:17, that they *s.* to no man in this name.
20, we cannot but *s.*
26:25, I *s.* words of truth and soberness.
1Cor. 1:10, that ye all *s.* the same thing.
14:28, let him *s.* to himself and to God.
2Cor. 4:13, we believe and therefore *s.*
Eph. 4:15, *s.* the truth in love.
Heb. 11:4, he being dead yet *s.*
Heb. 12:24, that *s.* better things than that of Abel.
Jas. 1:19, slow to *s.*
See 1Cor. 14:2; 1Pet. 2:1; 2Pet. 2:12.
SPEAR. Josh. 8:18, stretch out the *s.*
Jud. 5:8, was there a shield or *s.* seen?
1Sam. 13:22, nor *s.* with any but Saul.
17:7, the staff of his *s.*
45, thou comest to me with a *s.*
Ps. 46:9, he cutteth the *s.* in sunder.
Isa. 2:4; Mic. 4:3, beat *s.* into pruninghooks.
See Job 41:29; Jer. 6:23; Hab. 3:11; Jn. 19:34.
SPECIAL. Dt. 7:6; Acts 19:11.
SPECTACLE. 1Cor. 4:9, made a *s.* to the world.
SPEECH. Gen. 11:1, earth was of one *s.*
Ex. 4:10, I am slow of *s.*
Num. 12:8, not in dark *s.*
Dt. 32:2, my *s.* shall distil as dew.
1Ki. 3:10, Solomon's *s.* pleased the Lord.
Job 6:26, the *s.* of one that is desperate.
15:3, or with *s.* wherewith he can do no good.
Ps. 19:2, day unto day uttereth *s.*
3, there is no *s.* where their voice is not heard.
Prov. 17:7, excellent *s.* becometh not a fool.
Song 4:3, thy *s.* is comely.
Isa. 33:19, of deeper *s.* than thou canst perceive.
Mt. 26:73, thy *s.* bewrayeth thee.
1Cor. 2:1, not with excellency of *s.*
4:19, not the *s.*, but the power.
2Cor. 3:12, we use great plainness of *s.*
10:10, his *s.* is contemptible.
Col. 4, 6, let your *s.* be alway with grace.
Ti. 2:8, sound *s.*, that cannot be condemned.
See Ezek. 3:5; Rom. 16:18; 2Cor. 11:6.
SPEECHLESS. Mt. 22:12; Lk. 1:22; Acts 9:7.
SPEED. Gen. 24:12, send me good *s.*
2Jn. 10, receive him not, neither bid him God *s.*
See Ezra 6:12; Isa. 5:26; Acts 17:15.
SPEEDILY. Ps. 31:2, deliver me *s.*
63:17; 143:7, hear me *s.*
Ps. 79:8, let thy mercies *s.* prevent us.
102:2, when I call, answer me *s.*
Eccl. 8:11, because sentence is not executed *s.*
Isa. 58:8, thy health shall spring forth *s.*
Zech. 8:21, let us go *s.* to pray.
Lk. 18:8, he will avenge them *s.*
See 1Sam. 27:1; Ezra 6:13; 7:17; Joel 3:4.
SPEND. Job 21:13, they *s.* their days in wealth.
36:11, they *s.* their days in prosperity.
Ps. 90:9, we *s.* our years as a tale that is told.
Isa. 55:2, why *s.* money for that which is not bread?
2Cor. 12:15, very gladly *s.* and be spent for you.
See Prov. 21:20; Eccl. 6:12; Lk. 10:35.
SPENT. Gen. 21:15, water was *s.* in the bottle.
Job 7:6, days *s.* without hope.
Ps. 31:10, my life is *s.* with grief.
Isa. 49:4, I have *s.* my strength for nought.
Acts 17:21, *s.* their time to tell some new thing.
See Mk. 6:35; Lk. 15:14; 24:29; Rom. 13:12.
SPILT. 2Sam. 14:14, as water *s.*
SPIN. Ex. 35:25; Mt. 6:28; Lk. 12:27.
SPIRIT. Gen. 6:3, my *s.* shall not always strive.
Ex. 35:21, every one whom his *s.* made willing.
Num. 11:17, take of the *s.* that is on thee.
14:24, he had another *s.* with him.
16:22; 27:16, the God of the *s.* of all flesh.
27:18, a man in whom is the *s.*
Josh. 5:1, nor was there any more *s.* in them.
1Ki. 22:21; 2Chr. 18:20, there came forth a *s.*
2Ki. 2:9, let a double portion of thy *s.*
Neh. 9:20, thou gavest thy good *s.* to instruct.
Job 4:15, a *s.* passed before my face.
15:13, thou turnest thy *s.* against God.
26:4, whose *s.* came from thee?
32:8, there is a *s.* in man.
Ps. 31:5; Lk. 23:46, into thine hand I commit my *s.*
32:2, in whose *s.* there is no guile.
51:10, renew a right *s.* within me.
Ps. 78:8, whose *s.* was not stedfast.
104:4; Heb. 1:7, who maketh his angels *s.*
106:33, they provoked his *s.*
139:7, whither shall I go from thy *s.*?
Prov. 16:2, the Lord weigheth the *s.*
18, an haughty *s.* goeth before a fall.
19; 29:23; Isa. 57:15, an humble *s.*
32, he that ruleth his *s.* better than he.
Eccl. 3:21, who knoweth *s.* of man, and *s.* of beast?
7:8, the patient in *s.* better than the proud.
8:8, no man hath power over *s.* to retain *s.*
11:5, the way of the *s.*
12:7, the *s.* shall return to God.
Isa. 4:4; 28:6, *s.* of judgment.
11:2; Eph. 1:17, the *s.* of wisdom.
34:16, his *s.* it hath gathered them.
42:1, I have put my *s.* upon him.
57:16, the *s.* should fail before me.
61:1; Lk. 4:18, the *S.* of the Lord is upon me
Ezek. 3:14; 8:3; 11:1, I went in the heat of my *s.*
11:19; 18:31; 36:26, a new *s.*
Mic. 2:11, a man walking in the *s.* and falsehood
Mt. 14:26; Mk. 6:49, it is a *s.*
26:41; Mk. 14:38, the *s.* is willing.
Mk. 1:10; Jn. 1:32, the *S.* descending on him.
8:12, sighed deeply in his *s.*
Lk. 1:17, go before him in *s.* and power of Elias.
2:27, came by the *S.* into the temple.

8:55, her *s.* came again.
9:55, ye know not what manner of *s.*
10:21, Jesus rejoiced in *s.*
24:39, a *s.* hath not flesh and bones.
Jn. 3:34, God giveth not the *S.* by measure.
4:24, God is a *S.*, worship him in *s.* and in truth.
6:63, it is the *s.* that quickeneth.
14:17; 15:26; 16:13; 1Jn. 4:6, *S.* of truth.
Acts 2:4, begin to speak as the *S.* gave utterance.
6:10, not able to resist the wisdom and *s.*
17:16, his *s.* was stirred within him.
23:8, say that there is neither angel nor *s.*
Rom. 8:1, walk not after the flesh, but after the *S.*
2, the law of the *S.* of life.
11, the *S.* of him that raised up Jesus.
16, the *S.* itself beareth witness.
26, the *S.* maketh intercession.
12:11, fervent in *s.*
1Cor. 2:4, in demonstration of the *S.*
10, the *S.* searcheth all things.
4:21; Gal. 6:1, in the *s.* of meekness.
6:17, he that is joined to the Lord is one *s.*
20, glorify God in body and *s.*
12:4, diversities of gifts, but the same *S.*
10, to another discerning of *s.*
14:2, in the *s.* he speaketh mysteries.
15:45, the last Adam made a quickening *s.*
2Cor. 3:6, the letter killeth, but the *s.* giveth life.
17, where the *S.* of the Lord is, there is liberty.
Gal. 3:3, having begun in the *S.*
5:16, walk in the *S.*
22; Eph. 5:9, the fruit of the *S.*
25, if we live in the *S.*, let us walk in the *S.*
6:8, he that soweth to the *S.* shall of the *S.* reap.
Eph. 2:2, the *s.* that worketh in children of disobedience.
18, access by one *S.*
22, habitation of God through the *S.*
3:16, strengthened by his *S.* in inner man.
4:3, the unity of the *S.*
4, one body and one *S.*
23, renewed in *s.* of your mind.
30, grieve not the holy *S.* of God.
5:18, be filled with the *S.*
6:17, take sword of the *S.*
Phil. 1:27, stand fast in one *s.*
2:1, if any fellowship of the *S.*
Col. 1:8, your love in the *s.*
2:5, absent in flesh, yet with you in the *s.*
1Th. 5:19, quench not the *S.*
2Th. 2:13, chosen through sanctification of the *S.*
1Tim. 3:16, justified in the *S.*
4:1, giving heed to seducing *s.*
12, be thou an example in *s.*
2Tim. 4:22, the Lord Jesus be with thy *s.*
Heb. 1:14, ministering *s.*
4:12, dividing asunder of soul and *s.*
9:14, who through the eternal *S.*
12:9, in subjection to the Father of *s.*
23, to *s.* of just men made perfect.
Jas. 2:26, the body without the *s.* is dead.
4:5, the *s.* lusteth to envy.
1Pet. 1:2, through sanctification of the *S.*
3:4, ornament of a meek and quiet *s.*
18, but quickened by the *S.*
19, preached to *s.* in prison.
4:6, live according to God in the *s.*
1Jn. 3:24, by the *S.* he hath given us.
4:1, believe not every *s.*, but try the *s.*
2, hereby know ye the *S.* of God.
3, every *s.* that confesseth not.
5:6, it is the *S.* that beareth witness.
8, the *s.*, the water, and the blood.
Jude 19, sensual, having not the *S.*
Rev. 1:10, I was in the *S.* on the Lord's day.
2:7, 11, 17, 29; 3:6, 13, 22, hear what the *S.* saith.
4:2, I was in the *s.*, and, behold.
11:11, the *S.* of life from God entered.
14:13, blessed are the dead: Yea, saith the *S.*
22:17, the *S.* and the bride say, Come.
See Mt. 8:16; Jn. 3:5; Acts 7:59; Rom. 7:6.
SPIRITUAL. Hos. 9:7, the *s.* man is mad.
Rom. 1:11, impart some *s.* gift.
7:14, the law is *s.*
15:27, partakers of their *s.* things.
1Cor. 2:13, comparing *s.* things with *s.*
15, he that is *s.* judgeth all things.
3:1, not speak unto you as unto *s.*
10:3, all eat the same *s.* meat.
12:1; 14:1, concerning *s.* gifts.
15:44, it is raised a *s.* body.
46, that was not first which is *s.*
Gal. 6:1, ye. which are *s.*, restore such an one.
Eph. 5:19, in psalms and hymns and *s.* songs.
6:12, *s.* wickedness in high places.
1Pet. 2:5, a *s.* house, to offer up *s.* sacrifices.
See 1Cor. 9:11; Col. 1:9; 3:16.
SPIRITUALLY. Rom. 8:6; 1Cor. 2:14; Rev. 11:8.
SPITE. Ps. 10:14, thou beholdest mischief and *s.*
SPOIL (*n.*). Jud. 5:30, necks of them that take *s.*
1Sam. 14:32, people flew upon the *s.*
2Chr. 15:11, offered to the Lord of the *s.*
20:25, three days gathering the *s.*
28:15, with the *s.* they clothed the naked.
Est. 3:13; 8:11, take the *s.* of them for a prey.
9:10, on the *s.* laid they not their hand.
Job 29:17, I plucked the *s.* out of his teeth.
Ps. 119:162, rejoice as one that findeth great *s.*
Prov. 16:19, than to divide *s.* with the proud.
31:11, he shall have no need of *s.*
Isa. 3:14, the *s.* of the poor is in your houses.
42:24, who gave Jacob for a *s.*?
53:12, divide the *s.* with the strong.
See Isa. 9:3; Ezek. 7:21; 38:13; Nah. 2:9; Zech. 14:1.
SPOIL (*v.*). Ex. 3:22, ye shall *s.* the Egyptians.
Ps. 78:5, the stouthearted are *s.*
Song 2:15, the little foxes that *s.* the vines.
Isa. 33:1, woe to thee that *s.*, and thou wast not *s.*!
42:22, this is a people robbed and *s.*
Jer. 4:30, when *s.*, what wilt thou do?

Hab. 2:8, thou hast *s.* many nations.
Zech. 11:2, howl because the mighty are *s.*
Col. 2:15, having *s.* principalities.
See Ps. 35:10; Isa. 22:4; Col. 2:8; Heb. 10:34.
SPOKEN. Num. 23:19, hath he *s.*, and shall he not make it good?
1Sam. 1:16, out of my grief have I *s.*
1Ki. 18:24, the people said, it is well *s.*
2Ki. 4:13, wouldest thou be *s.* for to the king?
Ps. 62:11, God hath *s.* once.
66:14, my mouth hath *s.* when in trouble.
87:3, glorious things are *s.* of thee.
Prov. 15:23, a word *s.* in due season.
25:11, a word fitly *s.* is like.
Eccl. 7:21, take no heed to all words *s.*
Isa. 48:15, I, even I, have *s.*
Mal. 3:13, what have we *s.* so much against?
Mk. 14:9, shall be *s.* of for a memorial.
Lk. 2:34, for a sign which shall be *s.* against.
Acts 19:36, these things cannot be *s.* against.
Rom. 1:8, your faith is *s.* of.
14:16, let not your good be evil *s.* of.
Heb. 2:2, the word *s.* by angels.
See Heb. 13:7; 1Pet. 4:14; 2Pet. 3:2.
SPOKESMAN. Ex. 4:16, he shall be thy *s.*
SPORT. Gen. 26:8; Isa. 57:4; 2Pet. 2:13.
SPOT. Num. 28:3; 9:11; 29:17, lambs without *s.*
Dt. 32:5, their *s.* is not the *s.* of his children.
Job 11:15, lift up thy face without *s.*
Jer. 13:23, or the leopard his *s.*
Eph. 5:27, glorious church, not having *s.*
1Tim. 6:14, commandment without *s.*
Heb. 9:14, offered himself without *s.*
1Pet. 1:19, lamb without blemish or *s.*
2Pet. 3:14, that ye may be found without *s.*
Jude 12, these are *s.* in your feasts.
See Song 4:7; 2Pet. 2:13; Jude 23.
SPOUSE. Song 4:8; 5:1; Hos. 4:13.
SPRANG. Mk. 4:8; Acts 16:29; Heb. 7:14; 11:12.
SPREAD. Dt. 32:11, eagle *s.* abroad her wings.
2Ki. 19:14; Isa. 37:14, *s.* letter before the Lord.
Job 9:8, God who alone *s.* out the heavens.
26:9, he *s.* his cloud upon it.
29:19, my root was *s.* out by waters.
36:30, he *s.* his light upon it.
37:18, hast thou with him *s.* out the sky?
Ps. 105:39, he *s.* a cloud for a covering.
104:5, they have *s.* a net by the wayside.
Isa. 1:15, when ye *s.* forth your hands I will hide.
33:23, they could not *s.* the sail.
65:2, *s.* out hands to a rebellious people.
Jer. 8:2, they shall *s.* them before the sun.
Ezek. 26:14, a place to *s.* nets upon.
Mt. 21:8; Mk. 11:8; Lk. 19:36, *s.* garments.
Acts 4:17, but that it *s.* no further.
See Jud. 8:25; 1Ki. 8:54; Ezra 9:5.
SPRIGS. Isa. 18:5; Ezek. 17:6.
SPRING. Num. 21:17, *s.* up, O well.
1Sam. 9:26, about the *s.* of the day.
Job 5:6, neither doth trouble *s.* out of the ground.
38:16, hast thou entered into the *s.* of the sea?
Ps. 87:7, all my *s.* are in thee.
104:10, he sendeth the *s.* into valleys.
107:33, he turneth water-*s.* into dry ground.
35, turneth dry ground into water-*s.*
Prov. 25:26, a troubled fountain, and a corrupt *s.*
Isa. 42:9, before they *s.* forth I tell you.
43:19, a new thing, now it shall *s.* forth.
45:8, let righteousness *s.* up together.
58:8, thine health shall *s.* forth.
11, shall be like a *s.* of water.
Mk. 4:27, seed should *s.* he knoweth not how.
See Joel 2:22; Jn. 4:14; Heb. 12:15.
SPRINKLE. Job 2:12; Isa. 52:15; Ezek. 36:25.
SPROUT. Job 14:7, a tree will *s.* again.
SPUNGE. Mt. 27:48; Mk. 15:36; Jn. 19:29.
SPY. Num. 13:16; Josh. 2:1; Gal. 2:4.
STABILITY. Isa. 33:6, the *s.* of thy times.
STABLE. 1Chr. 16:30; Ezek. 25:5.
STAFF. Gen. 32:10, with my *s.* I passed over.
Ex. 12:11, eat it with *s.* in hand.
Num. 13:23, bare grapes between two on a *s.*
Jud. 6:21, the angel put forth end of his *s.*
2Sam. 3:29, not fail one that leaneth on a *s.*
2Ki. 4:29, lay my *s.* on face of the child.
18:21; Isa. 36:6, thou trustest on *s.*
Ps. 23:4, thy rod and *s.* comfort me.
Isa. 3:1, the stay and *s.*, the whole stay of bread.
9:4, thou hast broken the *s.* of his shoulder.
10:5, the *s.* in their hand is mine indignation.
15, as if the *s.* should lift up itself.
14:5, the Lord hath broken the *s.* of the wicked.
Jer. 48:17, how is the strong *s.* broken?
Zech. 11:10, took my *s.*, even Beauty.
Mk. 6:8, take nothing, save *s.* only.
Heb. 11:21, leaning on the top of his *s.*
See Ex. 21:19; Num. 22:27; Isa. 28:27.
STAGGER. Job 12:25; Ps. 107:27, *s.* like a drunken man.
Isa. 29:9, they *s.*, but not with strong drink.
See Isa. 19:14; Rom. 4:20.
STAIN. Job 3:5; Isa. 23:9; 63:3.
STAIRS. 1Ki. 6:8; Neh. 9:4; Song 2:14.
STAKES. Isa. 33:20; 54:2.
STALK. Gen. 41:5; Josh. 2:6; Hos. 8:7.
STALL. Prov. 15:17; Hab. 3:17; Mal. 4:2.
STAMMERING. Isa. 28:11; 32:4; 33:19.
STAMP. Dt. 9:21; 2Sam. 22:43; Jer. 47:3.
STAND. Ex. 14:13; 2Chr. 20:17, *s.* still, and see.
Dt. 29:10, ye *s.* this day all of you before the Lord.
1Sam. 9:27, *s.* thou still a while.
1Ki. 8:11; 2Chr. 5:14, priests could not *s.* to minister.
17:1; 18:15; 2Ki. 3:14; 5:16, the Lord before whom I *s.*
2Ki. 10:4, two kings stood not, how shall we *s.*?
2Chr. 34:32, caused all present to *s.* to it.
Est. 8:11, to *s.* for their life.
Job 8:15, shall lean on his house, but it shall not *s.*
19:25, he shall *s.* at the latter day.
Ps. 1:1, nor *s.* in the way of sinners.
5, the ungodly shall not *s.* in judgment.
4:4, *s.* m awe, and sin not.

10:1, why *s.* thou afar off?
24:3, who shall *s.* in his holy place?
33:11, the counsel of the Lord *s.* for ever.
35:2, *s.* up for my help.
76:7, who may *s.* in thy sight?
94:16, who will *s.* up for me?
109:31, shall *s.* at right hand of the poor.
122:2, our feet shall *s.* within thy gates.
103:3, if thou, Lord, mark iniquities, who shall *s.*?
147:17, who can *s.* before his cold?
Prov. 22:29, shall *s.* before kings.
27:4, who is able to *s.* before envy?
Eccl. 8:3, *s.* not in an evil thing.
Isa. 7:7; 8:10, thus saith the Lord, it shall not *s.*
21:8, I *s.* continually on watchtower.
28:18, your agreement with hell shall not *s.*
40:8, the word of God shall *s.* for ever.
65:5, *s.* by thyself, I am holier than thou.
Jer. 6:16, *s.* ye in the ways, ask for the old paths.
35:19, shall not want a man to *s.* before me.
Dan. 11:16, he shall *s.* in the glorious land.
12:13, and shall *s.* in thy lot.
Mic. 5:4, he shall *s.* and feed in strength.
Nah. 2:8, *s.*, *s.*, shall they cry.
Zech. 3:1, Satan *s.* at his right hand.
Mal. 3:2, who shall *s.* when he appeareth?
Mt. 12:25; Mk. 3:24, 25; Lk. 11:18, house divided shall not*s.*
16:28; Lk. 9:27, there be some *s.* here.
20:3, others *s.* idle in the marketplace.
Rom. 5:2, this grace wherein we *s.*
14:4, God is able to make him *s.*
1Cor. 2:5, faith should not *s.* in wisdom.
16:13, *s.* fast in the faith.
Gal. 4:20, I *s.* in doubt of you.
5:1, *s.* fast in the liberty.
Eph. 6:13, having done all, to *s.*
Phil. 1:27, *s.* fast in one spirit.
4:1; 1Th. 3:8, *s.* fast in the Lord.
1Th. 3:8, we live, if ye *s.* fast.
2Tim. 2:19, the foundation of God *s.* sure.
Jas. 5:9, the judge *s.* before the door.
Rev. 3:20, I *s.* at the door, and knock.
6:17, is come, and who shall be able to *s.*?
20:12, the dead, small and great, *s.* before God.
See Rom. 14:4; 1Cor. 10:12; Rev. 15:2.
TANDARD. Isa. 10:18, as when *s.*-bearer fainteth.
49:22, I will set up my *s.* to the people.
59:19, Spirit of the Lord shall lift up *s.* against.
62:10, go through, lift up a *s.*
Jer. 4:6; 50:2; 51:12, set up a *s.*
See Num. 1:52; 2:3; 10:14.
TATE. Ps. 39:5; Mt. 12:45; Lk. 11:26.
TATURE. Num. 13:32, men of great *s.*
1Sam. 16:7, look not on height of his *s.*
Isa. 10:33, high ones of *s.* hewn down.
45:14, men of *s.* shall come.
Mt. 6:27; Lk. 12:25, not add to *s.*
Lk. 2:52, Jesus increased in *s.*
19:3, little of *s.*

Eph. 4:13, *s.* of the fulness of Christ.
See 2Sam. 21:20; Song 7:7; Ezek. 17:6; 31:3.
STATUTE. Ex. 18:16, the *s.* of God.
Lev. 3:17; 16:34; 24:9, a perpetual *s.*
2Ki. 17:8, *s.* of the heathen.
Neh. 9:14, *s.* and laws.
Ps. 19:8, the *s.* of the Lord are right.
50:16, to declare my *s.*
Ezek. 5:6, hath changed my *s.*
20:25, *s.* that were not good.
33:15, walk in the *s.* of life.
Zech. 1:6, my *s.*, did they not take hold?
See Ps. 18:22; 105:45; 119:12, etc.; Ezek. 18:19.
STAVES. Num. 21:18, nobles digged with *s.*
1Sam. 17:43, am I a dog, that thou comest with *s.*?
Hab. 3:14, strike through with his *s.*
Zech. 11:7, took unto me two *s.*
Mt. 10:10; Lk. 9:3, neither two coats, nor *s.*
See Mt. 26:47; Mk. 14:43; Lk. 22:52.
STAY (*n.*). 2Sam. 22:19; Ps. 18:18, the Lord was my *s.*
Isa. 3:1, take away the *s.* and staff.
See Lev. 13:5; 1Ki. 10:19; Isa. 19:13.
STAY (*v.*). Gen. 19:17, neither *s.* in plain.
Ex. 9:28, ye shall *s.* no longer.
Num. 16:48; 25:8; 2Sam. 24:25; 1Chr. 21:22; Ps. 106:30, the plague was *s.*
2Sam. 24:16; 1Chr. 21:15, *s.* now thine hand.
Job 37:4, he will not *s.* them.
38:11, here shall thy proud waves be *s.*
37, who can *s.* the bottles of heaven?
Prov. 28:17, let no man *s.* him.
Isa. 26:3, whose mind is *s.* on thee.
27:8, he *s.* his rough wind.
29:9, *s.* yourselves, and wonder.
30:12, ye trust m oppression, and *s.* thereon.
50:10, trust in name of the Lord, and *s.* on his God.
Dan. 4:35, none can *s.* his hand.
Hag. 1:10, heaven is *s.*, earth is *s.*
See Josh. 10:13; 1Sam. 24:7; Jer. 4:6; 20:9.
STEAD. Ex. 4:16, be to him in *s.* of God.
Num. 10:31, be to us in *s.* of eyes.
32:14, risen in your fathers's.
Job 16:4, if your soul were in my soul's *s.*
31:40, thistles grow in *s.* of wheat.
34:24, he shall set others in their *s.*
Ps. 45:16, in *s.* of fathers shall be children.
Prov. 11:8., the wicked cometh in his *s.*
Isa. 3:24, In *s.* of girdle a rent.
55:13, in *s.* of the thorn shall come up the fir tree.
2Cor. 5:20, we pray you in Christ's *s.*
See Gen. 30:2; 2Ki. 17:24; 1Chr. 5:22.
STEADY. Ex. 17:12, Moses' hands were *s.*
STEAL. Gen. 31:27, wherefore didst thou *s.* away?
44:8, how then should we *s.* silver or gold?
Prov. 6:30, if he *s.* to satisfy his soul.
30:9, lest I be poor, and *s.*
Jer. 23:30, prophets that *s.* my words.
Mt. 6:19, thieves break through and *s.*
Jn. 10:10, thief cometh not, but to *s.*

See Hos. 4:2; Mt. 27:64; Rom. 2:21.
STEALTH. 2Sam. 19:3, by *s.* into city.
STEDFAST. Ps. 78:8, not *s.* with God.
Dan. 6:26, living God, and *s.* for ever.
Heb. 2:2, word spoken by angels was *s.*
3:14, hold our confidence *s.* to end.
6:19, hope as anchor, sure and *s.*
1Pet. 5:9, resist *s.* in the faith.
See Acts 2:42; Col. 2:5; 2Pet. 3:17.
STEEL. 2Sam. 22:35; Job 20:24; Jer. 15:12.
STEEP. Ezek. 38:20; Mic. 1:4; Mt. 8:32.
STEP. 1Sam. 20:3, but a *s.* between me and death.
Job 14:16, thou numberest my *s.*
23:11, my foot hath held his *s.*
29:6, I washed my *s.* with butter.
31:4, doth not he count my *s.*?
7, if my *s.* hath turned out of the way.
Ps. 37:23, the *s.* of a good man are ordered.
31, none of his *s.* shall slide.
44:18, nor have our *s.* declined.
56:6, they mark my *s.*
73:2, my *s.* had well nigh slipped.
85:13, set us in the way of his *s.*
119:133, order my *s.* in thy word.
Prov. 4:12, thy *s.* shall not be straitened.
5:5, her *s.* take hold on hell.
16:9, the Lord directeth his *s.*
Isa. 26:6, the *s.* of the needy shall tread it down.
Jer. 10:23, not in man to direct his *s.*
Rom. 4:12, walk in *s.* of that faith.
2Cor. 12:18, walked we not in same *s.*?
1Pet. 2:21, that ye should follow his *s.*
See Ex. 20:26; 2Sam. 22:37; Lam. 4:18; Ezek. 40:22.
STEWARD. 1Ki. 16:9, drunk in house of his *s.*
Lk. 12:42, that faithful and wise *s.*
See Gen. 15:2; Lk. 8:3; 1Cor. 4:1; 1Pet. 4:10.
STICK. Num. 15:32, gathered *s.* on sabbath.
1Ki. 17:12, I am gathering two *s.*
Job 33:21, his bones *s.* out.
Ps. 38:2, thine arrows *s.* fast in me.
Prov. 18:24, a friend that *s.* closer than a brother.
Ezek. 37:16, take *s.*, and write on it.
See 2Ki. 6:6; Lam. 4:8; Ezek. 29:4.
STIFF. Ex. 32:9; 33:3; 34:9; Dt. 9:6, 13; 10:16, *s.*-necked people.
Ps. 75:5, speak not with *s.* neck.
Jer. 17:23, obeyed not, but made their neck *s.*
Ezek. 2:4, impudent and *s.*-hearted.
Acts 7:51, ye *s.*-necked, ye do always resist.
See Dt. 31:27; 2Chr. 30:8; 36:13.
STILL. Ex. 15:16, as *s.* as a stone.
Num. 14:38, Joshua and Caleb lived *s.*
Josh. 24:10, Balaam blessed you *s.*
Jud. 18:9, the land is good, and are ye *s.*?
2Sam. 14:32, good to have been there *s.*
2Ki. 7:4, if we sit *s.* here, we die also.
2Chr. 22:9, no power to keep *s.* the kingdom.
Job 2:9, dost thou *s.* retain thine integrity?
Ps. 4:4, commune with thine heart, and be *s.*
8:2, *s.* the enemy and avenger.
23:2, beside the *s.* waters.
46:10, be *s.*, and know that I am God.
76:8, earth feared, and was *s.*
83:1, hold not thy peace, and be not *s.*, O God.
84:4, they will be *s.* praising thee.
107:29, so that the waves thereof are *s.*
139:18, when I awake, I am *s.* with thee.
Eccl. 12:9, he *s.* taught knowledge.
Isa. 5:25; 9:12; 10:4, his hand is stretched out *s.*
30:7, their strength is to sit *s.*
42:14, I have been *s.*, and refrained.
Jer. 8:14, why do we sit *s.*?
31:20, I do earnestly remember him *s.*
Zech. 11:16, nor feed that that standeth *s.*
Mk. 4:39, arose, and said, peace, be *s.*
Rev. 22:11, unjust *s.*, filthy *s.*, holy *s.*
See Num. 13:30; Ps. 65:7; 89:9; 92:14.
STING. Prov. 23:32; 1Cor. 15:55; Rev. 9:10.
STIR. Num. 24:9, who shall *s.* him up?
Dt. 32:11, as an eagle *s.* up her nest.
1Sam. 22:8, my son hath *s.* up my servant.
26:19, if the Lord have *s.* thee up.
1Ki. 11:14, the Lord *s.* up an adversary.
1Chr. 5:26; 2Chr. 36:22; Hag. 1:14, God *s.* up the spirit.
Job 17:8, the innocent shall *s.* up himself.
41:10, none dare *s.* him up.
Ps. 35:23, *s.* up thyself.
39:2, my sorrow was *s.*
Prov. 10:12, hatred *s.* up strifes.
15:18; 29:22, a wrathful man *s.* up strife.
Isa. 10:26, the Lord shall *s.* up a scourge.
14:9, hell from beneath *s.* up the dead.
64:7, none *s.* up himself to take hold.
Lk. 23:5, he *s.* up the people.
Acts 17:16, his spirit was *s.* in him.
19:23, no small *s.* about that way.
2Tim. 1:6, *s.* up gift of God in thee.
2Pet. 1:13, I think it meet to *s.* you up.
See Song 2:7; 3:5; 8:4; Isa. 22:2; Acts 12:18.
STOCK. Job 14:8, though the *s.* thereof die.
Isa. 40:24, their *s.* shall not take root.
44:19, shall I fall down to the *s.* of a tree?
Hos. 4:12, my people ask counsel at their *s.*
Nah. 3:6; Heb. 10:33, a gazing-*s.*
Acts 13:26, children of the *s.* of Abraham.
See Jer. 2:27; 10:8; 20:2; Phil. 3:5.
STOLE. 2Sam. 15:6, Absalom *s.* the hearts.
Eph. 4:28, let him that *s.* steal no more.
See Gen. 31:20; 2Ki. 11:2; 2Chr. 22:11; Mt. 28:13.
STOLEN. Josh. 7:11, they have *s.*, and dissembled.
2Sam. 21:12, men had *s.* the bones of Saul.
Prov. 9:17, *s.* waters are sweet.
Obad. 5, *s.* till they had enough.
See Gen. 30:33; 31:19; Ex. 22:7; 2Sam. 19:41.
STOMACH. 1Tim. 5:23, for thy *s.* sake.
STONE. Gen. 11:3, they had brick for *s.*
28:18, 22; 31:45; 35:14, set up a *s.* for a pillar.
Dt. 8:9, a land whose *s.* are iron.
Josh. 24:27, this *s.* shall be a witness.
2Sam. 17:13, till there be not one small *s.* found there.

2Ki. 3:25, cast every man his *s.*
Job 5:23, in league with *s.* of the field.
6:12, is my strength the strength of *s.*?
14:19, the waters wear the *s.*
28:3, he searcheth out the *s.* of darkness.
41:24, his heart is as firm as a *s.*
Ps. 91:12; Mt. 4:6; Lk. 4:11, lest thou dash thy foot against a *s.*
118:22; Mt. 21:42; Mk. 12:10, the *s.* which the builders refused is become the head *s.*
Prov. 27:3, a *s.* is heavy, a fool's wrath heavier.
Isa. 54:11, I will lay thy *s.* with fair colours.
60:17, bring for *s.* iron.
62:10, gather out the *s.*
Jer. 2:27, and to a *s.*, thou hast brought me forth.
Dan. 2:34, a *s.* was cut out of the mountain.
Hab. 2:11, the *s.* shall cry out of the wall.
19, that saith to the dumb *s.*, arise.
Hag. 2:15, before *s.* was laid upon *s.*
Zech. 3:9, upon one *s.* shall be seven eyes.
4:7, bring forth the head-*s.* thereof.
7:12, they made their hearts as *s.*
Mt. 7:9; Lk. 11:11, will he give him a *s.*?
21:44; Lk. 20:18, whosoever shall fall on this *s.*
24:2; Mk. 13:2; Lk. 19:44; 21:6, not one *s.* upon another.
Mk. 13:1, see what manner of *s.* are here!
16:4; Lk. 24:2, found *s.* rolled away.
Lk. 4:3, command this *s.* that it be made bread.
Jn. 1:42, Cephas, by interpretation a *s.*
8:7, first cast a *s.*
11:39, take ye away the *s.*
Acts 17:29, that the Godhead is like to *s.*
1Pet. 2:5, as lively *s.*, are built up.
See 1Sam. 30:6; 1Cor. 3:12; 2Cor. 3:3; Rev. 2:17.

TONY. Ps. 141:6; Ezek. 11:19; 36:26; Mt. 13:5.

TOOD. Gen. 18:22, *s.* yet before the Lord.
Num. 14:19, *s.* behind them.
Josh. 3:16, waters *s.* up on an heap.
2Ki. 23:3, all the people *s.* to the covenant.
Est. 9:16, Jews *s.* for their lives.
Ps. 33:9, he commanded, and it *s.* fast.
Lk. 24:36, Jesus himself *s.* in the midst.
2Tim. 4:16, no man *s.* with me.
See Gen. 23:3; Job 29:8; Ezek. 37:10; Rev. 7:11.

TOOP. Gen. 49:9, Judah *s.* down.
Prov. 12:25, heaviness maketh the heart *s.*
Jn. 8:6, *s.* down, and wrote on the ground.
See 2Chr. 36:17; Job 9:13; Mk. 1:7; Jn. 20:11.

TOP. Gen. 8:2, windows of heaven were *s.*
1Ki. 18:44, that the rain *s.* thee not.
Ps. 107:42, iniquity shall *s.* her mouth.
Zech. 7:11, refused, and *s.* their ears.
Acts 7:57, *s.* their ears, and ran upon him.
Rom. 3:19, that every mouth may be *s.*
Ti. 1:11, whose mouths must be *s.*
Heb. 11:33, through faith *s.* mouths of lions.
See Gen. 26:15; Job 5:16; Ps. 58:4; Prov. 21:13.

TORE. Lev. 25:22; 26:10, eat of the old *s.*
Dt. 28:5, blessed be thy basket and *s.*
2Ki. 20:17, thy fathers have laid up in *s.*
Ps. 144:13, affording all manner of *s.*
Nah. 2:9, none end of the *s.* and glory.
Mal. 3:10, bring tithes into *s.*-house.
Lk. 12:24, neither have *s.*-house nor barn.
1Cor. 16:2, every one lay by him in *s.*
1Tim. 6:19, laying up in *s.* a good foundation.
2Pet. 3:7, by same word are kept in *s.*
See 1Ki. 10:10; 1Chr. 29:16; Ps. 33:7.

STORK. Ps. 104:17, as for the *s.*, the fir trees are her house.
Jer. 8:7, yea, the *s.* in the heaven.
Zech. 5:9, like the wings of a *s.*

STORM. Ps. 55:8, escape from windy *s.*
83:15, make them afraid with thy *s.*
107:29, he maketh the *s.* a calm.
Isa. 4:6; 25:4, a covert from *s.*
28:2, as a destroying *s.*
Ezek. 38:9, shalt ascend and come like a *s.*
Nah. 1:3, the Lord hath his way in the *s.*
See Job 21:18; 27:21; Mk. 4:37; Lk. 8:23.

STORMY. Ps. 107:25; 148:8; Ezek. 13:11.

STORY. 2Chr. 13:22; 24:27.

STOUT. Dan. 7:20, whose look was more *s.*
Mal. 3:13, words have been *s.* against me.
See Ps. 76:5; Isa. 9:9; 10:12; 46:12.

STRAIGHT. Ps. 5:8, make thy way *s.*
Prov. 4:25, let eyelids look *s.* before thee.
Eccl. 1:15; 7:13, crooked cannot be made *s.*
Isa. 40:3, make *s.* a highway.
4; 42:16; 45:2; Lk. 3:5, crooked shall be made *s.*
Jer. 31:9, cause them to walk in a *s.* way.
Mt. 3:3; Mk. 1:3; Lk. 3:4; Jn. 1:23, make his paths *s.*
Lk. 13:13, she was made *s.*
Acts 9:11, street which is called *S.*
Heb. 12:13, make *s.* paths for your feet.
See Josh. 6:5; 1Sam. 6:12; Ezek. 1:7; 10:22.

STRAIGHTWAY. Prov. 7:22, he goeth after her *s.*
Mt. 4:20; Mk. 1:18, they *s.* left their nets.
Jas. 1:24, *s.* forgetteth what manner of man.
See Lk. 14:5; Jn. 13:32; Acts 9:20; 16:33.

STRAIN. Mt. 23:24, *s.* at a gnat.

STRAIT. 2Sam. 24:14, I am in a great *s.*
Job 20:22, he shall be in *s.*
Isa. 49:20, the place is too *s.* for me, give place.
Mic. 2:7, is spirit of the Lord *s.*?
Mt. 7:13; Lk. 13:24, enter in at the *s.* gate.
Lk. 12:50, how am I *s.* till it be accomplished!
2Cor. 6:12, ye are not *s.* in us.
Phil. 1:23, I am in a *s.* betwixt two.
See 2Ki. 6:1; Job 18:7; 37:10; Jer. 19:9.

STRAITLY. Gen. 43:7; Josh. 6:1; Acts 4:17.

STRAITNESS. Dt. 28:53; Job 36:16.

STRANGE. Gen. 42:7, Joseph made himself *s.*
Ex. 2:22; 18:3; Ps. 137:4, in a *s.* land.
Lev. 10:1; Num. 3:4; 26:61, offered *s.* fire.
1Ki. 11:1, Solomon loved many *s.* women.
Job 19:17, my breath is *s.* to my wife.
31:3, a *s.* punishment to workers.
Prov. 2:16, to deliver thee from the *s.* woman.
5:3, 20, for the lips of a *s.* woman.
21:8, the way of man is froward and *s.*
23:27, a *s.* woman is a narrow pit.

Isa. 28:21, his *s.* work, his *s.* act.
Ezek. 3:5, not sent to people of a *s.* speech.
Zeph. 1:8, clothed with *s.* apparel.
Lk. 5:26, we have seen *s.* things to-day.
Acts 17:20, thou bringest *s.* things to our ears.
26:11, persecuted them even to *s.* cities.
Heb. 13:9, carried about with *s.* doctrines.
1Pet. 4:4, they think it *s.* ye run not.
12, not *s.* concerning the fiery trial.
See Jud. 11:2; Ezra 10:2; Prov. 2:16; Jer. 8:19.
STRANGER. Gen. 23:4; Ps. 39:12, I am a *s.* with you.
Ex. 23:9, ye know the heart of a *s.*
1Chr. 29:15, we are *s.*, as were all our fathers.
Job 15:19, no *s.* passed among them.
31:32, the *s.* did not lodge in the street.
Ps. 54:3, for *s.* are risen up against me.
109:11, let the *s.* spoil his labour.
146:9, the Lord preserveth the *s.*
Prov. 2:16, to deliver thee even from the *s.*
5:10, lest *s.* be filled with thy wealth.
17, let them be thine own, not *s.* with thee.
6:1, stricken thy hand with a *s.*
7:5, from the *s.* which flattereth.
11:15, he that is surety for a *s.* shall smart.
14:10, a *s.* doth not intermeddle.
20:16; 27:13, garment that is surety for a *s.*
27:2, let a *s.* praise thee.
Isa. 1:7, your land, *s.* devour it.
2:6, please themselves in children of *s.*
14:1, the *s.* shall be joined with them.
56:3, neither let the son of the *s.* speak.
Jer. 14:8, why be as a *s.* in the land?
Ezek. 28:10, thou shalt die by the hand of *s.*
Hos. 7:9, *s.* have devoured his strength.
Mt. 25:35, I was a *s.*, and ye took me in.
Lk. 17:18, that returned, save this *s.*
Eph. 2:12, *s.* from the covenant.
19, no more *s.*, but fellowcitizens.
Heb. 11:13, confessed they were *s.*
13:2, be not forgetful to entertain *s.*
See Mt. 17:25; Jn. 10:5; 1Pet. 2:11.
STRANGLED. Nah. 2:12; Acts 15:20; 21:25.
STREAM. Ps. 124:4; Isa. 35:6; 66:12; Amos 5:24.
STREET. Prov. 1:20; Lk. 14:21; Rev. 21:21; 22:2.
STRENGTH. Ex. 15:2; 2Sam. 22:33; Ps. 18:2; 28:7; 118:14; Isa. 12:2, the Lord is my *s.*
Jud. 5:21, thou hast trodden down *s.*
1Sam. 2:9, by *s.* shall no man prevail.
5:29, the *S.* of Israel will not lie.
Job 9:19, if I speak of *s.*, lo, he is strong.
12:13, with him is wisdom and *s.*
Ps. 18:32, girded me with *s.*
27:1, the Lord is the *s.* of my life.
29:11, the Lord will give *s.* to his people.
33:16, mighty not delivered by much *s.*
39:13, spare me, that I may recover *s.*
46:1; 81:1, God is our refuge and *s.*
68:34, ascribe *s.* to God, his *s.* is in the clouds.
35, God giveth *s.* and power.
73:26, God is the *s.* of my heart.
84:5, the man whose *s.* is in thee.
7, they go from *s.* to *s.*
96:6, *s.* and beauty are in his sanctuary.
138:3, strengthenedst me with *s.* in my soul.
Prov. 10:29, the way of the Lord is *s.*
Eccl. 9:16, wisdom is better than *s.*
10:17, princes eat for *s.*
Isa. 25:4, a *s.* to the poor, a *s.* to the needy.
40:29, he increaseth *s.*
51:9, awake, put on *s.*
Hag. 2:22, I will destroy the *s.* of the kingdoms.
Lk. 1:51, he hath showed *s.* with his arm.
Rom. 5:6, when ye were without *s.*
1Cor. 15:56, the *s.* of sin is the law.
Rev. 3:8, thou hast a little *s.*
See Job 21:23; Prov. 20:29; 2Cor. 12:9.
STRENGTHEN. Job 15:25, he *s.* himself against.
Ps. 20:2, *s.* thee out of Zion.
104:15, bread which *s.* man's heart.
Eccl. 7:19, wisdom *s.* the wise.
Isa. 35:3, *s.* ye the weak hands.
Lk. 22:32, when converted, *s.* thy brethren.
Eph. 3:16; Col. 1:11, to be *s.* with might.
Phil. 4:13, all things through Christ who *s.* me.
See Lk. 22:43; 1Pet. 5:10; Rev. 3:2.
STRETCH. Ps. 68:31, *s.* out her hands to God.
Isa. 28:20, shorter than a man can *s.* himself.
Jer. 10:12; 51:15, he *s.* out the heavens.
Ezek. 16:27, I have *s.* out my hand over thee.
Mt. 12:13, *s.* forth thine hand.
See Ps. 104:2; Prov. 1:24; Rom. 10:21; 2Cor. 10:14.
STRIKE. Job 17:3; Prov. 22:26, *s.* hands.
Ps. 110:5, shall *s.* through kings.
Prov. 7:23, till a dart *s.* through his liver.
See Prov. 23:35; Isa. 1:5; 1Tim. 3:3; Ti. 1:7.
STRIPES. Dt. 25:3, forty *s.* he may give.
2Cor. 11:24, five times received I forty *s.*
STRIVE. Gen. 6:3, shall not always *s.*
Prov. 3:30, *s.* not without cause.
Lk. 13:24, *s.* to enter in at strait gate.
2Tim. 2:5, if a man *s.* for mastery.
24, the servant of the Lord must not *s.*
See Isa. 45:9; Jer. 50:24; Mt. 12:19; Heb. 12:4.
STRONG. 1Sam. 4:9; 1Ki. 2:2; 2Chr. 15:7; Isa. 35:4; Dan. 10:19, be *s.*
Job 9:19, if I speak of strength, lo, he is *s.*
Ps. 19:5, as a *s.* man to run a race.
24:8, the Lord is *s.*
31:2, be thou my *s.* rock.
71:7, thou art my *s.* refuge.
Prov. 10:15, the rich man's wealth is his *s.* city.
18:10, the name of the Lord is a *s.* tower.
Eccl. 9:11, the battle is not to the *s.*
Isa. 40:26, for that he is *s.* in power.
Mt. 12:29, first bind the *s.* man.
Rom. 4:20, *s.* in faith.
1Cor. 4:10, we are weak, ye are *s.*
2Th. 2:11, *s.* delusion.
Heb. 5:12, of milk, and not of *s.* meat.
6:18, we have a *s.* consolation.
See Prov. 14:26; Joel 3:10; Rom. 15:1; Rev. 5:2.
STUBBLE. Ps. 83:13, make them as *s.*
Isa. 33:11, conceive chaff, bring forth *s.*

41:2, as driven *s.*
Jer. 13:24, I will scatter them as *s.*
See Joel 2:5; Nah. 1:10; Mal. 4:1; 1Cor. 3:12.
TUDY. Eccl. 12:12, much *s.* is a weariness of the flesh.
See 1Th. 4:11; 2Tim. 2:15.
TUMBLE. Prov. 4:19, know not at what they *s.*
Isa. 28:7, they *s.* in judgment.
59:10, we *s.* at noonday.
Jer. 46:6; Dan. 11:19, *s.* and fall.
Mal. 2:8, have caused many to *s.*
1Pet. 2:8, that *s.* at the word.
See Jn. 11:9; Rom. 9:32; 11:11; 14:21.
UBDUE. Ps. 47:3, he shall *s.* the people.
Mic. 7:19, he will *s.* our iniquities.
Phil. 3:21, able to *s.* all things.
Heb. 11:33, through faith *s.* kingdoms.
See Dan. 2:40; Zech. 9:15; 1 Cor. 15:28.
UBJECT. Lk. 10:17, devils are *s.* unto us.
Rom. 8:7, not *s.* to law of God.
Rom. 8:20, creature *s.* to vanity.
13:1, *s.* to the higher powers.
1Cor. 14:32, spirits of prophets *s.* to prophets.
15:28, then shall the Son also be *s.* to him.
Eph. 5:24, as the church is *s.* to Christ.
Heb. 2:15, all their lifetime *s.* to bondage.
Jas. 5:17, a man *s.* to like passions.
1Pet. 2:18, servants, be *s.* to your masters.
3:22, angels and powers *s.* to him.
5:5, all of you be *s.* one to another.
See Lk. 2:51; Col. 2:20; Ti. 3:1.
UBMIT. 2Sam. 22:45, *s.* themselves.
Ps. 68:30, till every one *s.* himself.
Eph. 5:22, wives *s.* yourselves.
Jas. 4:7, *s.* yourselves to God.
1Pet. 2:13, *s.* yourselves to every ordinance of man.
See Rom. 10:3; Eph. 5:21; Heb. 13:17.
UBSCRIBE. Isa. 44:5; Jer. 32:44.
UBSTANCE. Gen. 13:6, their *s.* was great.
Dt. 33:11, bless his *s.*
Job 30:22, thou dissolvest my *s.*
Ps. 17:14, they leave their *s.* to babes.
139:15, my *s.* was not hid from thee.
Prov. 3:9, honour the Lord with thy *s.*
28:8, he that by usury increaseth his *s.*
Song 8:7, give all his *s.* for love.
Jer. 15:13; 17:3, thy *s.* will I give to spoil.
Hos. 12:8, I have found me out *s.*
Mic. 4:13, I will consecrate their *s.*
Lk. 8:3, ministered to him of their *s.*
15:13, wasted his *s.*
Heb. 10:34, a better *s.*
11:1, the *s.* of things hoped for.
See Prov. 1:13; 6:31; 8:21; 12:27; 29:3.
UBTIL. Gen. 3:1; 2Sam. 13:3; Prov. 7:10.
UBTILTY. Gen. 27:35; Mt. 26:4; Acts 13:10.
UBVERT. Lam. 3:36; 2Tim. 2:14; Ti. 1:11; 3:11.
UCCESS. Josh. 1:8, have good *s.*
UCK. Dt. 32:13, *s.* honey out of rock.
33:19, *s.* abundance of the seas.
Job 20:16, *s.* poison of asps.
Isa. 60:16, *s.* the milk of the Gentiles.
See Mt. 24:19; Mk. 13:17; Lk. 21:23; 23:29.
SUDDEN. Job 22:10; Prov. 3:25; 1Th. 5:3.
SUDDENLY. Prov. 29:1, be *s.* destroyed.
Eccl. 9:12, when it falleth *s.*
Mal. 3:1, shall *s.* come to his temple.
Mk. 13:36, lest coming *s.* he find you sleeping.
1Tim. 5:22, lay hands *s.* on no man.
SUFFER. Job 21:3, *s.* me that I may speak.
Ps. 55:22, never *s.* righteous to be moved.
89:33, nor *s.* my faithfulness to fail.
Prov. 19:15, the idle soul shall *s.* hunger.
Eccl. 5:12, not *s.* him to sleep.
Mt. 3:15, *s.* it to be so now.
8:21; Lk. 9:59, *s.* me first to bury my father.
16:21; 17:12; Mk. 8:31; Lk. 9:22, *s.* many things.
19:14; Mk. 10:14; Lk. 18:16, *s.* little children.
23:13, neither *s.* ye them that are entering to go in.
Lk. 24:46; Acts 3:18, behoved Christ to *s.*
Rom. 8:17, if we *s.* with him.
1Cor. 3:15, he shall *s.* loss.
10:13, will not *s.* you to be tempted.
12:26, whether one member *s.*, all *s.* with it.
Gal. 6:12, lest they should *s.* persecution.
2Tim. 2:12, if we *s.*, we shall also reign.
3:12, shall *s.* persecution.
Heb. 13:3, remember them who *s.*
1Pet. 2:21, *s.* for us, leaving an example.
4:1, he that hath *s.* in the flesh.
See Gal. 3:4; Phil. 3:8; Heb. 2:18; 5:8.
SUFFICIENCY. Job 20:22; 2Cor. 3:5; 9:8.
SUFFICIENT. Isa. 40:16, not *s.* to burn.
Mt. 6:34, *s.* for the day is the evil.
2Cor. 2:16, who is *s.* for these things?
See Dt. 15:8; Jn. 6:7; 2Cor. 3:5; 12:9.
SUM. Ps. 139:17; Acts 22:28; Heb. 8:1.
SUMMER. Gen. 8:22; Ps. 74:17, *s.* and winter.
Prov. 6:8; 30:25, provideth meat in *s.*
10:5, he that gathereth in *s.* is a wise son.
26:1, as snow in *s.*
Jer. 8:20, the *s.* is ended.
Mt. 24:32; Mk. 13:28, ye know *s.* is nigh.
See Dan. 2:35; Zech. 14:8; Lk. 21:30.
SUMPTUOUSLY. Lk. 16:19, fared *s.* every day.
SUN. Josh. 10:12, *s.*, stand thou still.
Jud. 5:31, as the *s.* in his might.
Job 8:16, hypocrite is green before the *s.*
Ps. 58:8, that they may not see the *s.*
84:11, a *s.* and shield.
121:6, the *s.* shall not smite thee.
Eccl. 1:9, no new thing under the *s.*
11:7, a pleasant thing it is to behold the *s.*
12:2, while the *s.* or stars be not darkened.
Song 1:6, because the *s.* hath looked upon me.
6:10, clear as the *s.*
Jer. 15:9, her *s.* is gone down while yet day.
Joel 2:10; 3:15, the *s.* be darkened.
Mal. 4:2, the *S.* of righteousness.
Mt. 5:45, maketh his *s.* to rise on evil.
13:43, then shall righteous shine as *s.*
Eph. 4:26, let not *s.* go down on your wrath.
See 1Cor. 15:41; Jas. 1:11; Rev. 7:16; 21:23.

SUPERFLUITY. Jas. 1:21, *s.* of naughtiness.
SUPPLICATION. 1Ki. 9:3, I have heard thy *s.*
Job 9:15, I would make *s.* to my judge.
Ps. 6:9, the Lord hath heard my *s.*
Dan. 9:3, to seek by prayer and *s.*
Zech. 12:10, spirit of grace and *s.*
Eph. 6:18, with all prayer and *s.*
1Tim. 2:1, that *s.* be made for all men.
See Ps. 28:6; 31:22; Phil. 4:6; Heb. 5:7.
SUPPLY. Phil. 1:19; 2:30; 4:19.
SUPPORT. Acts 20:35; 1 Th. 5:14.
SUPREME. 1Pet. 2:13, to the king as *s.*
SURE. Num. 32:23, be *s.* your sin will find you out.
Job 24:22, no man is *s.* of life.
Prov. 6:3, make *s.* thy friend.
Isa. 55:3; Acts 13:34, the *s.* mercies of David.
2Tim. 2:19, the foundation of God standeth *s.*
See Isa. 33:16; Heb. 6:19; 2Pet. 1:10, 19.
SURFEITING. Lk. 21:34, overcharged with *s.*
SURPRISED. Isa. 33:14; Jer. 48:41; 51:41.
SUSTAIN. Ps. 3:5; 55:22; Prov. 18:14; Isa. 59:16.
SWALLOW. Ps. 84:3, the *s.* a nest for her young.
Prov. 26:2, as the *s.* by flying.
Isa. 38:14, like a crane or a *s.*
Jer. 8:7, the *s.* observe the time.
SWAN. Lev. 11:8; Dt. 14:16, and the *s.*
SWEAR. Ps. 15:4, that *s.* to his hurt.
Eccl. 9:2, he that *s.*, as he that feareth an oath.
Isa. 45:23, to me every tongue shall *s.*
65:16, shall *s.* by the God of truth.
Jer. 4:2, *s.*, the Lord liveth, in truth.
23:10, because of *s.* the land mourneth.
Hos. 4:2, by *s.*, and lying, they break out.
10:4, *s.* falsely in making a covenant.
Zech. 5:3, every one that *s.* shall be cut off.
Mal. 3:5, a witness against false *s.*
See Zeph. 1:5; Mt. 26:74; Heb. 6:13.
SWEAT. Gen. 3:19; Ezek. 44:18; Lk. 22:44.
SWEET. Job 20:12, though wickedness be *s.*
Ps. 55:14, we took *s.* counsel together.
104:34, my meditation shall be *s.*
Prov. 3:24, thy sleep shall be *s.*
9:17, stolen waters are *s.*
13:19, desire accomplished is *s.*
16:24, pleasant words are *s.*
27:7, to the hungry every bitter thing is *s.*
Eccl. 5:12, sleep of labouring man is *s.*
11:7, truly the light is *s.*
Song 2:3, his fruit was *s.* to my taste.
Isa. 5:20, put bitter for *s.*, and *s.* for bitter.
23:16, make *s.* melody.
Jas. 3:11, at same place *s.* water and bitter.
See Jud. 14:18; Mic. 6:15; Mk. 16:1.
SWELLING. Jer. 12:5; 2Pet. 2:18; Jude 16.
SWIFT. Eccl. 9:11, the race is not to the *s.*
Amos 2:15, the *s.* of foot shall not deliver.
Rom. 3:15, feet *s.* to shed blood.
See Job 7:6; 9:25; Jer. 46:6; Mal. 3:5.
SWIM. 2Ki. 6:6, iron did *s.*
Ezek. 47:5, waters to *s.* in.
See Ps. 6:6; Isa. 25:11; Ezek. 32:6; Acts 27:42.
SWOLLEN. Acts 28:6, when he should have *s.*
SWOON. Lam. 2:11, children *s.* in the streets.
SWORD. Ps. 57:4, their tongue a sharp *s.*
Isa. 2:4, nation shall not lift up *s.*
Ezek. 7:15, the *s.* is without, pestilence within.
Mt. 10:34, not to send peace, but a *s.*
Lk. 2:35, a *s.* shall pierce thy own soul.
Rom. 13:4, he beareth not the *s.* in vain.
Eph. 6:17, the *s.* of the Spirit.
Heb. 4:12, sharper than twoedged *s.*
Rev. 1:16; 19:15, out of his mouth a sharp *s.*
13:10, that killeth with *s.* must be killed with *s.*
See Isa. 2:4; Joel 3:10; Mic. 4:3; Lk. 22:38.
TABERNACLE. Ps. 15:1, abide in thy *t.*
27:5, in secret of his *t.* shall he hide me.
84:1, how amiable are thy *t.*!
Isa. 33:20, a *t.* that shall not be taken down.
See Job 5:24; Prov. 14:11; 2Cor. 5:1.
TABLE. Ps. 23:5, thou preparest a *t.*
69:22, let their *t.* become a snare.
78:19, can God furnish a *t.* in the wilderness.
128:3, like olive plants about thy *t.*
Prov. 9:2, wisdom hath furnished her *t.*
Mt. 15:27; Mk. 7:28, from their masters' *t.*
Acts 6:2, leave word of God, and serve *t.*
2Cor. 3:3, fleshy *t.* of the heart.
See Prov. 3:3; Jer. 17:1; Mal. 1:7; 1Cor. 10:21.
TABRET. Gen. 31:27; 1Sam. 18:6; Isa. 5:12, the *t.*
TAKE. Ex. 6:7, I will *t.* you to me for a people.
34:9, *t.* us for thine inheritance.
Jud. 19:30, *t.* advice, and speak your minds.
2Ki. 19:30; Isa. 37:31, shall yet *t.* root.
Job 23:10, he knoweth the way that I *t.*
Ps. 51:11, *t.* not thy holy spirit from me.
116:13, I will *t.* the cup of salvation.
Song 2:15, *t.* us the foxes, the little foxes.
Isa. 33:23, the lame *t.* the prey.
Hos. 14:2, *t.* with you words.
Amos 9:2, thence shall mine hand *t.* them.
Mt. 6:25, 28, 31, 34; 10:19; Mk. 13:11; Lk. 12:11, 22, 26, *t.* no thought.
11:29, *t.* my yoke.
16:5; Mk. 8:14, forgotten to *t.* bread.
18:16, then *t.* with thee one or two more.
20:14, *t.* that thine is, and go thy way.
26:26; Mk. 14:22; 1Cor. 11:24, *t.*, eat; this is my body.
Lk. 6:29, forbid him not to *t.* thy coat also.
12:19, soul, *t.* thine ease.
Jn. 16:15, he shall *t.* of mine.
1Cor. 6:7, why do ye not rather *t.* wrong?
1Tim. 3:5, how shall he *t.* care of the church?
1Pet. 2:20, if yet. it patiently.
Rev. 3:11, that no man *t.* thy crown.
See Jn. 1:29; 10:18; 1 Cor. 10:13; Rev. 22:19.
TALE. Ps. 90:9; Lk. 24:11.
TALK. Dt. 5:24, God doth *t.* with man.
6:7, *t.* of them when thou sittest.
Job 11:2, a man full of *t.*
13:7, will ye *t.* deceitfully for him?
15:3, reason with unprofitable *t.*
Ps. 71:24, *t.* of thy righteousness.
145:11, *t.* of thy power.
Prov. 6:22, it shall *t.* with thee.

Jer. 12:1, let me *t.* with thee of thy judgments.
Ezek. 3:22, arise, and I will *t.* with thee there.
Mt. 22:15, they might entangle him in his *t.*
Lk. 24:32, while he *t.* with us by the way.
Jn. 9:37, it is he that *t.* with thee.
See Prov. 14:23; Jn. 14:30; Eph. 5:4.
ALL. Dt. 1:28; 2:10; 2Ki. 19:23.
AME. Mk. 5:4; Jas. 3:7, 8.
ARE. 2Sam. 13:31; 2Ki. 2:24; Mk. 9:20.
ARRY. Gen. 27:44, and *t.* a few days.
Ex. 12:39, were thrust out, and could not *t.*
2Ki. 7:9, if we *t.* till morning light.
9:3, flee, and *t.* not.
Ps. 68:12, she that *t.* at home divided the spoil.
101:7, he that telleth lies shall not *t.* in my sight.
Prov. 23:30, they that *t.* long at the wine.
Isa. 46:13, my salvation shall not *t.*
Jer. 14:8, that turneth aside to *t.* for a night.
Hab. 2:3, though it *t.*, wait for it.
Mt. 25:5, while the bridegroom *t.*
26:38; Mk. 14:34, *t.* here and watch.
Lk. 24:29, he went in to *t.* with them.
49, *t.* ye in city of Jerusalem until endued.
Jn. 21:22, if I will that he *t.*
Acts 22:16, why *t.* thou, arise, and be baptized.
1Cor. 11:33, *t.* one for another.
Heb. 10:37, will come, and will not *t.*
See 1Sam. 30:24; Mic. 5:7; Jn. 3:22.
ASKMASTERS. Ex. 1:11, they did set over them *t.*
5:6, the *t.* of the people.
ASTE. Num. 11:8, the *t.* of it as *t.* of fresh oil.
Job 6:6, is any *t.* in white of egg?
12:11, doth not the mouth *t.* his meat?
34:3, trieth words as mouth *t.* meat.
Ps. 34:8, *t.* and see that the Lord is good.
119:103, how sweet are thy words to my *t.*!
Jer. 48:11, his *t.* remained in him.
Mt. 16:28; Mk. 9:1; Lk. 9:27, some, which shall not *t.* death.
Lk. 14:24, none bidden shall *t.* of my supper.
Jn. 8:52, keep my saying, shall never *t.* of death.
Col. 2:21, touch not, *t.* not.
Heb. 2:9, *t.* death for every man.
6:4, and have *t.* of the heavenly gift.
1Pet. 2:3, have *t.* that the Lord is gracious.
See 1Sam. 14:43; 2Sam. 19:35; Mt. 27:34.
ATTLERS. 1Tim. 5:13, *t.* and busybodies.
AUGHT. Jud. 8:16, he *t.* the men of Succoth.
2Chr. 6:27, thou hast *t.* them the good way.
23:13, such as *t.* to sing praise.
Ps. 71:17; 119:102, thou hast *t.* me.
Prov. 4:4, he *t.* me also, and said.
11, I have *t.* thee in way of wisdom.
Eccl. 12:9, he still *t.* the people knowledge.
Isa. 29:13, their fear is *t.* by precept of men.
54:13, all thy children shall be *t.* of God.
Jer. 12:16, as they *t.* my people to swear by Baal.
32:33, *t.* them, rising up early.
Zech. 13:5, *t.* me to keep cattle.
Mt. 7:29; Mk. 1:22, *t.* as one having authority.
28:15, and did as they were *t.*
Lk. 13:26, thou hast *t.* in our streets.
Jn. 6:45, they shall be all *t.* of God.
8:28, as my Father hath *t.* me.
Gal. 1:12, nor was I *t.* it, except by revelation.
6:6, let him that is *t.* in the word.
Eph. 4:21, if so be ye have been *t.* by him.
2Th. 2:15, the traditions ye have been *t.*
See Col. 2:7; 1Th. 4:9; Ti. 1:9; 1pJn. 2:27.
TAUNT. Jer. 24:9; Ezek. 5:15; Hab. 2:6.
TEACH. Ex. 4:15, I will *t.* you.
Dt. 4:10, that they may *t.* their children.
6:7; 11:19, *t.* them diligently.
Jud. 13:8, *t.* us what we shall do to the child.
1Sam. 12:23, I will *t.* you the good way.
2Sam. 1:18, bade them *t.* the use of the bow.
2Chr. 15:3, without a *t.* priest.
Job 6:24, *t.* me, and I will hold my tongue.
8:10, thy fathers, shall not they *t.* thee?
Job 12:7, ask the beasts, and they shall *t.* thee.
34:32, that which I see not *t.* thou me.
36:22, God exalteth, who *t.* like him?
Ps. 25:4, *t.* me thy paths.
8, he will *t.* sinners in the way.
27:11; 86:11, *t.* me thy way, and lead me.
34:11, I will *t.* you the fear of the Lord.
51:13, then will I *t.* transgressors.
90:12, so *t.* us to number our days.
94:12, blessed is the man whom thou *t.*
Prov. 6:13, the wicked man *t.* with his finger.
Isa. 2:3; Mic. 4:2, he will *t.* us of his ways.
28:9, whom shall he *t.* knowledge?
26, God doth *t.* him discretion.
48:17, I am thy God which *t.* thee to profit.
Jer. 9:20, and *t.* your daughters wailing.
Ezek. 44:23, *t.* my people the difference.
Mic. 3:11, priests *t.* for hire.
Mt. 28:19, *t.* all nations.
Lk. 11:1, *t.* us to pray.
12:12, the Holy Ghost shall *t.* you.
Jn. 9:34, dost thou *t.* us?
14:26, shall *t.* you all things.
Acts 5:42, they ceased not to *t.* and preach.
Rom. 12:7, he that *t.*, on *t.*
1Cor. 4:17, as I *t.* every where.
11:14, doth not even nature *t.* you?
14:19, that by my voice I might *t.* others.
Col. 1:28, *t.* every man in all wisdom.
3:16, *t.* and admonishing one another.
1Tim. 1:3, charge some that they *t.* no other.
2:12, I suffer not a woman to *t.*
3:2; 2Tim. 2:24, apt to *t.*
4:11, these things command and *t.*
6:2, these things *t.* and exhort.
2Tim. 2:2, faithful men, able to *t.*
Ti. 1:11, *t.* things they ought not.
2:4, *t.* young women to be sober.
12, *t.* us, that denying ungodliness.
Heb. 5:12, ye have need that one *t.* you again.
See Mt. 22:16; Mk. 6:34; 12:14; Rev. 2:20.
TEACHER. 1Chr. 25:8, as well *t.* as scholar.
Ps. 119:99, more understanding than all my *t.*
Prov. 5:13, have not obeyed the voice of my *t.*
Isa. 30:20, thine eyes shall see thy *t.*
Hab. 2:18, a *t.* of lies.

Jn. 3:2, a *t.* come from God.
Rom. 2:20, thou art a *t.* of babes.
1Cor. 12:29, are all *t.*?
Eph. 4:11, evangelists, pastors, and *t.*
1Tim. 1:7, desiring to be *t.* of the law.
Ti. 2:3, aged women, *t.* of good things.
See 1Tim. 2:7; 2Tim. 1:11; Heb. 5:12; 2Pet. 2:1.
TEAR. Job 16:9, he *t.* me in his wrath.
18:4, he *t.* himself in his anger.
Ps. 7:2, lest he *t.* my soul.
35:15, they did *t.* me, and ceased not.
50:22, lest I *t.* you in pieces.
Hos. 5:14, I will *t.* and go away.
See Mic. 5:8; Zech. 11:16; Mk. 9:18; Lk. 9:39.
TEARS. 2Ki. 20:5; Isa. 38:5, I have seen thy *t.*
Job 16:20, mine eye poureth out *t.*
Ps. 6:6, I water my couch with *t.*
39:12, hold not thy peace at my *t.*
42:3, *t.* have been my meat.
56:8, put thou my *t.* into thy bottle.
80:5, the bread of *t.*, and *t.* to drink.
116:8, thou hast delivered mine eyes from *t.*
126:5, they that sow in *t.*
Isa. 16:9, I will water thee with my *t.*
25:8, will wipe away *t.*
Jer. 9:1, oh that mine eyes were a fountain of *t.*!
13:17; 14:17, mine eyes run down with *t.*
31:16, refrain thine eyes from *t.*
Lam. 1:2, her *t.* are on her cheeks.
2:11, mine eyes do fail with *t.*
Ezek. 24:16, neither shall thy *t.* run down.
Mal. 2:13, covering the altar with *t.*
Lk. 7:38, to wash his feet with her *t.*
Acts 20:19, serving the Lord with many *t.*
31, ceased not to warn with *t.*
2Tim. 1:4, being mindful of thy *t.*
See 2Cor. 2:4; Heb. 5:7; 12:17; Rev. 7:17.
TEDIOUS. Acts 24:4, that I be not further *t.*
TEETH. Gen. 49:12, *t.* white with milk.
Num. 11:33, flesh yet between their *t.*
Job 19:20, escaped with the skin of my *t.*
Prov. 10:26, as vinegar to the *t.*
Isa. 41:15, an instrument having *t.*
Jer. 31:29; Ezek. 18:2, *t.* set on edge.
Amos 4:6, cleanness of *t.*
See Mic. 3:5; Zech. 9:7; Mt. 27:44; Rev. 9:8.
TELL. Gen. 15:5, *t.* the stars.
32:29, *t.* me thy name.
2Sam. 1:20, *t.* it not in Gath.
Ps. 48:12, *t.* the towers thereof.
50:12, if I were hungry, I would not *t.* thee.
Eccl. 6:12; 10:14, who can *t.* what shall be after?
10:20, that which hath wings shall *t.*
Jonah 3:9, who can *t.* if God will turn?
Mt. 18:15, *t.* him his fault.
17, *t.* it unto the church.
21:27; Mk. 11:33; Lk. 20:8, neither *t.* I you.
Mk. 5:19, *t.* how great things.
11:33; Lk. 20:7, we cannot *t.*
Lk. 13:32, *t.* that fox.
Jn. 3:8, canst not *t.* whence.
12, if I *t.* you of heavenly things.
4:25, he will *t.* us all things.
18:34, did others *t.* it thee of me?
Acts 17:21, either to *t.* or hear some new thing.
See Ps. 56:8; Isa. 19:12; Mt. 28:7; 2Cor. 12:2.
TEMPER. Ex. 29:2; 30:35; Ezek. 46:14; 1Cor. 12:24.
TEMPEST. Job 9:17, breaketh me with a *t.*
Ps. 11:6, on wicked he shall rain a *t.*
55:8, hasten from windy storm and *t.*
Isa. 32:2, a covert from the *t.*
Heb. 12:18, not come to darkness and *t.*
2Pet. 2:17, clouds carried with a *t.*
TEMPESTUOUS. Ps. 50:3; Jonah 1:11; Acts 27:14.
TEMPLE. 2Sam. 22:7, hear. my voice out of his *t.*
Neh. 6:10, meet together in the *t.*
Ps. 27:4, to enquire in his *t.*
29:9, in his *t.* doth every one speak of his glory.
Isa. 6:1, his train filled the *t.*
Amos 8:3, songs of the *t.* shall be howlings.
Mal. 3:1, the Lord shall suddenly come to his *t.*
Mt. 12:6, one greater than the *t.*
Jn. 2:19, destroy this *t.*
1Cor. 3:16; 6:19; 2Cor. 6:16, ye are the *t.* of God.
See Hos. 8:14; Rev. 7:15; 11:19; 21:22.
TEMPORAL. 2Cor. 4:18, things seen are *t.*
TEMPT. Gen. 22:1, God did *t.* Abraham.
Ex. 17:2, wherefore do ye *t.* the Lord?
Num. 14:22, have *t.* me these ten times.
Dt. 6:16; Mt. 4:7; Lk. 4:12, ye shall not *t.* the Lord your God.
Ps. 78:18, they *t.* God in their heart.
Isa. 7:12, I will not ask, neither *t.* the Lord.
Mal. 3:15, they that *t.* God are delivered.
Mt. 22:18; Mk. 12:15; Lk. 20:23, why *t.* ye me?
Lk. 10:25, a lawyer, *t.* him.
Acts 5:9, agreed together to *t.* the Spirit.
15:10, why *t.* ye God to put a yoke?
1Cor. 10:13, will not suffer you to be *t.*
Gal. 6:1, considering thyself, lest thou be *t.*
Heb. 2:18, hath suffered, being *t.*
4:15, in all points *t.* like as we are.
Jas. 1:13, cannot be *t.*, neither *t.* he any man.
See Mt. 4:1; Mk. 1:13; Lk. 4:2; Jn. 8:6.
TEMPTATION. Mt. 6:13, lead us not into *t.*
26:41; Mk. 14:38; Lk. 22:46, lest ye enter into *t.*
Lk. 8:13, in time of *t.* fall away.
1Cor. 10:13, there hath no *t.* taken you.
Gal. 4:14, my *t.* in flesh ye despised not.
1Tim. 6:9, they that will be rich fall into *t.*
Jas. 1:2, when ye fall into divers *t.*
2Pet. 2:9, how to deliver out of *t.*
See Lk. 11:4; Acts 20:19; 1Pet. 1:6; Rev. 3:10.
TEMPTER. Mt. 4:3, and when the *t.* came to him.
1Th. 3:5, the *t.* have tempted you.
TEND. Prov. 11:19; 14:23; 19:23; 21:5.
TENDER. Dt. 28:54, man that is *t.*
32:2, distil as small rain on *t.* herb.
2Ki. 22:19; 2Chr. 34:27, thy heart was *t.*
Job 14:7, the *t.* branch will not cease.
Prov. 4:3, *t.* in sight of my mother.
Song 2:13, 15; 7:12, vines with *t.* grapes.
Isa. 47:1, no more be called *t.*
53:2, grow up before him as a *t.* plant.

Dan. 1:9, God brought Daniel into *t.* love.
Lk. 1:78, through the *t.* mercy of our God.
Eph. 4:32, be kind and *t.*-hearted.
Jas. 5:11, the Lord is pitiful, and of *t.* mercy.
See 1Chr. 22:5; Ezek. 17:22; Mk. 13:28.
ENOR. Gen. 43:7; Ex. 34:27.
ENT. Gen. 9:21, was uncovered within his *t.*
27, he shall dwell in the *t.* of Shem.
12:8, and pitched his *t.*
25:27, a plain man, dwelling in *t.*
Num. 24:5, how goodly are thy *t.*!
1Sam. 4:10; 2Sam. 18:17, fled every man to his *t.*
1Ki. 12:16, to your *t.*, O Israel.
Ps. 84:10, than to dwell in *t.* of wickedness.
Isa. 38:12, removed as a shepherd's *t.*
54:2, enlarge the place of thy *t.*
Jer. 10:20, there is none to stretch forth my *t.*
Acts 18:3, by occupation they were *t.*-makers.
See Isa. 40:22; Jer. 4:20; 35:7; Zech. 12:7; Heb. 11:9.
ENTH. Gen. 28:22; Lev. 27:32; Isa. 6:13.
ERRIBLE. Ex. 34:10, a *t.* thing I will do.
Dt. 1:19; 8:15, that *t.* wilderness.
7:21; 10:17; Neh. 1:5; 4:14; 9:32, a mighty God and *t.*
10:21, hath done for thee *t.* things.
Jud. 13:6, like an angel of God, very *t.*
Job 37:22, with God is *t.* majesty.
39:20, the glory of his nostrils is *t.*
Ps. 45:4, thy right hand shall teach thee *t.* things.
65:5, by *t.* things in righteousness.
66:3, say unto God, how *t.* art thou!
5, *t.* in his doing.
68:35, *t.* out of thy holy places.
76:12, he is *t.* to the kings of the earth.
99:3, thy great and *t.* name.
145:6, the might of thy *t.* acts.
Song 6:4, *t.* as an army with banners.
Isa. 25:4, blast of the *t.* ones.
64:3, when thou didst *t.* things.
Jer. 15:21, redeem thee out of hand of the *t.*
Joel 2:11, the day of the Lord is very *t.*
Heb. 12:21, so *t.* was the sight.
See Lam. 5:10; Ezek. 1:22; 28:7; Dan. 7:7.
ERRIBLENESS. Dt. 26:8; 1Chr. 17:21; Jer. 49:16.
ERRIBLY. Isa. 2:19, 21; Nah. 2:3.
ERRIFY. Job 9:34, let not his fear *t.*
Lk. 21:9, when ye hear of wars, be not *t.*
24:37, they were *t.* and affrighted.
Phil. 1:28, in nothing *t.* by adversaries.
See Job 7:14; 2Cor. 10:9.
ERROR. Gen. 35:5; Job 6:4, the *t.* of God.
Dt. 32:25, the sword without and *t.* within.
Josh. 2:9, your *t.* is fallen upon us.
Job 18:11, *t.* shall make him afraid.
24:17, in the *t.* of the shadow of death.
31:23, destruction was a *t.* to me.
33:7, my *t.* shall not make thee afraid.
Ps. 55:4, the *t.* of death are fallen upon me.
73:19, utterly consumed with *t.*
91:5, afraid for the *t.* by night.
Jer. 17:17, be not a *t.* to me.
20:4, a *t.* to thyself.
Ezek. 26:21; 27:36; 28:19, I will make thee a *t.*
Rom. 13:3, rulers are not *t.* to good works.
2Cor. 5:11, knowing the *t.* of the Lord.
See Jer. 15:8; Lam. 2:22; Ezek. 21:12; 1Pet. 3:14.
TESTIFY. Num. 35:30, one witness shall not *t.*
Dt. 31:21, this song shall *t.* against them.
Ruth 1:21, seeing the Lord hath *t.* against me.
2Sam. 1:16, thy mouth hath *t.* against thee.
Neh. 9:30, *t.* against them by thy spirit.
Job 15:6, thine own lips *t.* against thee.
Isa. 59:12, our sins *t.* against us.
Hos. 5:5; 7:10, the pride of Israel doth *t.*
Mic. 6:3, what have I done? *t.* against me.
Lk. 16:28, send Lazarus, that he may *t.*
Jn. 2:25, needed not that any should *t.*
3:32, seen and heard, that he *t.*
5:39, they *t.* of me.
7:7, because I *t.* of it.
15:26, he shall *t.* of me.
21:24, the disciple which *t.* of these things.
Acts 23:11, as thou hast *t.* in Jerusalem.
1Tim. 2:6, gave himself to be *t.* in due time.
1Pet. 1:11, it *t.* beforehand the sufferings.
1Jn. 4:14, we have seen and do *t.*
See 1Cor. 15:15; 1Th. 4:6; Rev. 22:16.
TESTIMONY. 2Ki. 17:15, rejected his *t.*
Ps. 93:5, thy *t.* are sure.
119:22, I have kept thy *t.*
24, thy *t.* are my delight.
46, I will speak of thy *t.*
59, I turned my feet to thy *t.*
119, I love thy *t.*
129, thy *t.* are wonderful.
Isa. 8:16, bind up the *t.*
20, to the law and to the *t.*
Mt. 10:18; Mk. 13:9, for a *t.* against them.
Lk. 21:13, it shall turn to you for a *t.*
Jn. 3:32, no man receiveth his *t.*
21:24, we know that his *t.* is true.
Acts 14:3, *t.* to the word of his grace.
1Cor. 2:1, declaring the *t.* of God.
2Cor. 1:12, the *t.* of our conscience.
2Tim. 1:8, be not ashamed of the *t.*
Heb. 11:5, Enoch had this *t.*
See Rev. 1:2; 6:9; 11:7; 12:11; 19:10.
THANK. Mt. 11:25; Lk. 10:21; 18:11; Jn. 11:41, I *t.* thee.
Acts 28:15, *t.* God, and took courage.
1Cor. 1:4, I *t.* God on your behalf.
2Th. 1:3, we are bound to *t.* God.
1Tim. 1:12, I *t.* Jesus Christ.
See 1Chr. 23:30; Dan. 2:23; Rom. 6:17.
THANKS. Neh. 12:31, companies that gave *t.*
Mt. 26:27; Lk. 22:17, took the cup, and gave *t.*
Lk. 2:38, Anna gave *t.* to the Lord.
Rom. 14:6, eateth to the Lord, for he giveth *t.*
1Cor. 15:57, *t.* be to God, who giveth us the victory.
Eph. 5:20, giving *t.* always for all things.
1Th. 3:9, what *t.* can we render?
Rev. 4:9, give *t.* to him that sat on the throne.
See 2Cor. 1:11; 2:14; 8:16; 9:15; Heb. 13:15.
THANKSGIVING. Ps. 26:7, the voice of *t.*

95:2, come before his face with *t.*
Isa. 51:3, *t.* and melody shall be found therein.
Amos 4:5, offer a sacrifice of *t.*
Phil. 4:6, with *t.* let your requests be made.
Col. 4:2, watch in the same with *t.*
1Tim. 4:3, to be received with *t.*
See Neh. 11:17; 12:8; 2Cor. 4:15; 9:11.
THAT. Gen. 18:25, *t.* be far from thee.
Num. 24:13; 1Ki. 22:14, *t.* will I speak.
Job 23:13, even *t.* he doeth.
Ps. 27:4, *t.* will I seek after.
Zech. 11:9, *t. t.* dieth, let it die.
Mt. 10:15; Mk. 6:11, than for *t.* city.
13:12; 25:29; Mk. 4:25, *t.* he hath.
Jn. 1:8, he was not *t.* light.
5:12, what man is *t.* which said?
Jn. 13:27, *t.* thou doest, do quickly.
21:22, what is *t.* to thee?
Rom. 7:19, the evil which I would not, *t.* I do.
Jas. 4:15, we shall live, and do this or *t.*
See Mk. 13:11; 1Cor. 11:23; 2Cor. 8:12; Phile. 18.
THEN. Gen. 4:26, *t.* began men to call.
Josh. 14:12, if the Lord be with me, *t.* I shall be able.
Ps. 27:10, *t.* the Lord will take me up.
55:12, *t.* I could have borne it.
Isa. 58:8, *t.* shall thy light break forth.
Ezek. 39:28, *t.* shall they know.
Mt. 5:24, *t.* come and offer thy gift.
19:25; Mk. 10:26, who *t.* can be saved?
24:14, *t.* shall the end come.
2Cor. 12:10, *t.* am I strong.
See 1Cor. 4:5; 13:12; 1Th. 5:3; 2Th. 2:8.
THESE. Ex. 32:4, *t.* be thy gods, O Israel.
Eccl. 7:10, former days better than *t.*
Isa. 60:8, who are *t.* that fly?
Mt. 5:37, whatsoever is more than *t.*
23:23, *t.* ought ye to have done.
25:40, one of the least of *t.*
Jn. 17:20, neither pray I for *t.* alone.
21:15, lovest thou me more than *t.*?
See Job 26:14; Ps. 73:12; Jer. 7:4.
THICK. Dt. 32:15, thou art grown *t.*
2Sam. 18:9, the mule went under the *t.* boughs.
Ps. 74:5, lifted up axes on the *t.* trees.
Ezek. 31:3, top was among *t.* boughs.
Hab. 2:6, ladeth himself with *t.* clay.
See 1Ki. 12:10; 2Chr. 10:10; Neh. 8:15; Job 15:26.
THICKET. Gen. 22:13; Isa. 9:18; Jer. 4:7, 29.
THIEF. Ps. 50:18, when thou sawest a *t.*
Jer. 2:26, as the *t.* is ashamed.
Joel 2:9, enter at windows like a *t.*
Lk. 12:33, where no *t.* approacheth.
Jn. 10:1, the same is a *t.* and a robber.
1Pet. 4:15, let none suffer as a *t.*
See Prov. 6:30; 29:24; Mt. 24:43.
THIEVES. Isa. 1:23; Lk. 10:30; Jn. 10:8; 1Cor. 6:10.
THIGH. Gen. 24:2; 47:29, put hand under *t.*
32:25, touched hollow of Jacob's *t.*
Jud. 15:8, smote them hip and *t.*
Song 3:8, every man hath sword on his *t.*
See Ps. 45:3; Jer. 31:19; Ezek. 21:12; Rev. 19:16.
THINE. Gen. 31:32, discern what is *t.*
1Sam. 15:28, to a neighbour of *t.*
1Ki. 20:4, I am *t.*, and all I have.
1Chr. 29:11, *t.* is the greatness.
Ps. 74:16, the day is *t.*, the night also is *t.*
119:94, I am *t.*, save me.
Isa. 63:19, we are *t.*
Mt. 20:14, take that is *t.*
Lk. 4:7, worship me, all shall be *t.*
22:42, not my will, but *t.* be done.
Jn. 17:6, *t.* they were, and thou gavest them me.
10, all mine are *t.* and *t.* are mine.
See Gen. 14:23; Josh. 17:18; 1Chr. 12:18; Lk. 15:31.
THING. Gen. 21:11, the *t.* was very grievous.
Ex. 18:17, the *t.* thou doest is not good.
2Sam. 13:33, let not my lord take the *t.* to heart.
2Ki. 20:10, thou hast asked a hard *t.*
Eccl. 1:9, the *t.* that hath been.
Isa. 7:13, is it a small *t.* to weary?
41:12, as a *t.* of nought.
43:19; Jer. 31:22, a new *t.*
Mk. 1:27, what *t.* is this?
Jn. 5:14, lest a worse *t.* come unto thee.
Phil. 3:16, let us mind the same *t.*
See Heb. 10:29; 1Pet. 4:12; 1Jn. 2:8.
THINK. Gen. 40:14, but *t.* on me when it shall be well.
Neh. 5:19, *t.* on me, O my God, for good.
Ps. 40:17, I am poor, yet the Lord *t.* on me.
Prov. 23:7, as he *t.* in his heart, so is he.
Isa. 10:7, nor doth his heart *t.* so.
Jonah 1:6, if God will *t.* upon us.
Mt. 3:9, *t.* not to say within yourselves.
Mt. 6:7, *t.* they shall be heard.
9:4, why *t.* ye evil in your hearts?
17:25; 22:17, what *t.* thou?
22:42; 26:66; Mk. 14:64, what *t.* ye of Christ
Rom. 12:3, more highly than he ought to *t.*
1Cor. 10:12, that *t.* he standeth.
2Cor. 3:5, to *t.* any thing as of ourselves.
Gal. 6:3, if a man *t.* himself to be something.
Eph. 3:20, able to do above all we ask or *t.*
Phil. 4:8, *t.* on these things.
Jas. 1:7, let not that man *t.* he shall receive.
1Pet. 4:12, *t.* it not strange.
See Job 35:2; Jer. 29:11; Ezek. 38:10; Lk. 10:36.
THIRST (*n.*). Ex. 17:3, to kill us with *t.*
Dt. 29:19, to add drunkenness to *t.*
Jud. 15:18, now I shall die for *t.*
2Chr. 32:11, doth persuade you to die by *t.*
Ps. 69:21, in my *t.* they gave me vinegar.
Isa. 41:17, when their tongue faileth for *t.*
Amos 8:11, not a *t.* for water, but of hearing.
2Cor. 11:27, in hunger and *t.* often.
See Dt. 28:48; Job 24:11; Ps. 104:11.
THIRST (*v.*). Ps. 42:2; 63:1; 143:6, my soul *t.* for God.
Isa. 49:10; Rev. 7:16, shall not hunger nor *t.*
55:1, every one that *t.*
Mt. 5:6, *t.* after righteousness.
Jn. 4:14; 6:35, shall never *t.*
7:37, if any man *t.*, let him come unto me.
19:28, I *t.*

See Ex. 17:3; Isa. 48:21; Rom. 12:20; 1Cor. 4:11.
HIRSTY. Ps 63:1; 143:6, in a *t.* land.
Ps. 107:5, hungry and *t.*, their soul fainted.
Prov 25:25, as cold waters to a *t.* soul.
Isa. 21:14, brought water to him that was *t.*
29:8, as when a *t.* man dreameth.
44:3, pour water on him that is *t.*
65:13, but ye shall be *t.*
See Jud. 4:19; Isa. 32:6; Ezek. 19:13; Mt. 25:35.
HISTLE. Gen. 3:18, thorns and *t.* shall it bring forth.
Job 31:40, let *t.* grow instead of wheat.
Mt. 7:16, do men gather figs of *t.*?
See 2Ki. 14:9; 2Chr. 25:18; Hos. 10:8.
HORN. Num. 33:55; Jud. 2:3, *t.* in your sides.
Ps. 118:12, quenched as the fire of *t.*
Prov. 15:19, way of slothful man is as an hedge of *t.*
24:31, it was all grown over with *t.*
26:9, as a *t.* goeth into hand of drunkard.
Eccl. 7:6, crackling of *t.* under a pot.
Song 2:2, as the lily among *t.*
Isa. 33:12, as *t.* cut up shall they be burned.
34:13, and *t.* shall come up in her palaces.
55:13, instead of the *t.* shall come up the fir tree.
Jer. 4:3, sow not among *t.*
12:13, but shall reap *t.*
Hos. 2:6, I will hedge up thy way with *t.*
9:6, *t.* shall be in their tabernacles.
10:8, the *t.* shall come up on their altars.
Mic. 7:4, most upright is sharper than *t.* hedge.
2Cor. 12:7, a *t.* in the flesh.
See Mt. 13:7; 27:29; Mk. 15:17; Jn. 19:2.
HOUGHT (*n.*). 1Chr. 28:9, the Lord understandeth the *t.*
Job 4:13, in *t.* from the visions of the night.
12:5, despised in *t.* of him that is at ease.
42:2, no *t.* can be withholden from thee.
Ps. 10:4, God is not in all his *t.*
40:5, thy *t.* cannot be reckoned.
92:5, thy *t.* are very deep.
94:11, the Lord knoweth the *t.* of man.
19, in the multitude of my *t.*
139:2, thou understandest my *t.* afar off.
17, how precious are thy *t.* to me!
23, try me, and know my *t.*
Prov. 12:5, the *t.* of the righteous are right.
16:3, thy *t.* shall be established.
24:9, the *t.* of foolishness is sin.
Isa. 55:7, and the unrighteous man his *t.*
8, my *t.* are not your *t.*
Isa. 55:9, so are my *t.* higher than your *t.*
Mic. 4:12, they know not the *t.* of the Lord.
Mt. 6:25, 31, 34; 10:19; Mk. 13:11; Lk. 12:11, 22, take no *t.*
9:4; 12:25; Lk. 5:22; 6:8; 9:47; 11:17, Jesus knowing their *t.*
15:19; Mk. 7:21, out of the heart proceed evil *t.*
Lk. 2:35, the *t.* of many hearts may be revealed.
24:38, why do *t.* arise in your hearts?
Acts 8:22, if the *t.* of thine heart may be forgiven.
1Cor. 3:20, the Lord knoweth the *t.* of the wise.
2Cor. 10:5, bringing into captivity every *t.*
Heb. 4:12, the word of God is a discerner of the *t.*
Jas. 2:4, ye are become judges of evil *t.*
See Gen. 6:5; Jer. 4:14; 23:20; Amos 4:13.
THOUGHT (*v.*). Gen. 48:11, I had not *t.* to see thy face.
Num. 24:11, I *t.* to promote thee.
Dt. 19:19, do to him as he *t.* to have done.
2Ki. 5:11, I *t.*, he will surely come out.
Neh. 6:2, they *t.* do me mischief.
Ps. 48:9. we have *t.* of thy lovingkindness.
50:21, thou *t.* I was such an one as thyself.
73:16, when I *t.* to know this.
119:59, I *t.* on my ways.
Prov. 30:32, if thou hast *t.* evil.
Isa. 14:24, as I have *t.*, so shall it come.
Jer. 18:8, I will repent of the evil I *t.* to do.
Zech. 8:14, as *t.* to punish you.
15, I *t.* to do well.
Mal. 3:16, for them that *t.* on his name.
Mt. 1:20, but while he *t.* on these things.
Mk. 14:72, when he *t.* thereon, he wept.
Lk. 12:17, he *t.* within himself, what shall I do?
19:11, *t.* kingdom of God should appear.
Jn. 11:13, they *t.* he had spoken of taking of rest.
Acts 10:19, while Peter *t.* on the vision.
26:8, why should it be *t.* a thing incredible?
1Cor. 13:11, I *t.* as a child.
Phil. 2:6, *t.* it not robbery to be equal with God.
See Gen. 20:11; 50:20; 1Sam. 1:13; Heb. 10:29.
THREAD. Gen. 14:23; Josh. 2:18; Jud. 16:9.
THREATEN. Acts 4:17; 9:1; Eph. 6:9; 1Pet. 2:23.
THREEFOLD. Eccl. 4:12, a *t.* cord.
THRESH. Isa. 41:15, thou shalt *t.* the mountains.
Jer. 51:33, it is time to *t.* her.
Mic. 4:13, arise and *t.*
Hab. 3:12, thou didst *t.* the heathen.
1Cor. 9:10, *t.* in hope.
See Lev. 26:5; 1Chr. 21:20; Isa. 21:10; 28:28
THREW. 2Ki. 9:33; Mk. 12:42; Lk. 9:42; Acts 22:23.
THROAT. Ps. 5:9; 115:7; Prov. 23:2; Mat 18:28.
THRONE. Ps. 11:4, the Lord's *t.* is in heaven.
94:20, shall *t.* of iniquity have fellowship with thee?
122:5, there are set *t.* of judgment.
Prov. 20:28, his *t.* upholden by mercy.
Isa. 66:1; Acts 7:49, heaven is my *t.*
Jer. 17:12, a glorious high *t.* from the beginning.
Dan. 7:9, his *t.* was like the fiery flame.
Mt. 19:28; 25:31, the Son of man shall sit in the *t.*
Col. 1:16, whether they be *t.*
Heb. 4:16, the *t.* of grace.
Rev. 3:21, to him will I grant to sit on my *t.*
4:2, a *t.* was set in heaven.
See Rev. 6:16; 7:9; 14:3; 19:4; 20:11; 22:1.
THRONG. Mk. 3:9; 5:31; Lk. 8:42, 45.
THROW. Mic. 5:11; Mal. 1:4; Mt. 24:2.
THRUST. Job 32:13, God *t.* him down, not man.
Joel 2:8, neither shall one *t.* another.
Lk. 10:15, shall be *t.* down to hell.
13:28, and you yourselves *t.* out.

Jn. 20:25, and *t.* my hand into his side.
Rev. 14:15, *t.* in thy sickle.
See Ex. 11:1; 1Sam. 31:4; Ezek. 34:21.
TIDINGS. Ps. 112:7, afraid of evil *t.*
Jer. 20:15, cursed be the man who brought *t.*
Dan. 11:44, *t.* out of the east.
Lk. 1:19; 2:10; 8:1; Acts 13:32; Rom. 10:15, glad *t.*
See Ex. 33:4; 1Ki. 14:6; Jer. 49:23.
TILL. Gen. 2:5; Prov. 12:11; 28:19; Ezek. 36:9.
TILLAGE. 1Chr. 27:26; Neh. 10:37; Prov. 13:23.
TIME. Gen. 47:29, the *t.* drew nigh.
Job 22:16, cut down out of *t.*
38:23, reserved against the *t.* of trouble.
Ps. 32:6, in a *t.* when thou mayest be found.
37:19, not ashamed in the evil *t.*
41:1, deliver him in *t.* of trouble.
56:3, what *t.* I am afraid.
69:13; Isa. 49:8; 2Cor. 6:2, acceptable *t.*
89:47, remember how short my *t.* is.
Eccl. 3:1, there is a *t.* to very purpose.
9:11, *t.* and chance happeneth to all.
Isa. 60:22, I will hasten it in his *t.*
Jer. 46:21, the *t.* of their visitation.
Ezek. 16:8, thy *t.* was the *t.* of love.
Dan. 7:25, a *t.* and *t.* and the dividing of *t.*
Hos. 10:12, it is *t.* to seek the Lord.
Mal. 3:11, neither shall vine cast fruit before the *t.*
Mt. 16:3, the signs of the *t.*
Lk. 19:44, the *t.* of thy visitation.
Acts 3:19, the *t.* refreshing.
21, the *t.* of restitution.
Rom. 13:11, it is high *t.* to awake.
1Cor. 7:29, the *t.* is short.
Eph. 5:16; Col. 4:5, redeeming the *t.*
Heb. 4:16, help in *t.* of need.
1Pet. 1:11, what manner of *t.*
Rev. 1:3, the *t.* is at hand.
10:6, *t.* no longer.
See Prov. 17:17; Eph. 1:10; 1Tim. 4:1.
TINGLE. 1Sam. 3:11; 2Ki. 21:12; Jer. 19:3.
TINKLING. Isa. 3:16, 18; 1Cor. 13:1.
TOGETHER. Prov. 22:2, meet *t.*
Amos 3:3, can two walk *t.*?
Mt. 18:20, where two or three are gathered *t.*
Rom. 8:28, work *t.* for good.
1Th. 4:17, caught up *t.*
See Mt. 19:6, Eph. 2:21; 2Th. 2:1.
TOIL. Gen. 5:29; 41:51; Mt. 6:28; Lk. 12:27.
TOLERABLE. Mt. 10:15; 11:24; Mk. 6:11; Lk. 10:12.
TONGUE. Job 5:21, hid from scourge of the *t.*
20:12, hide wickedness under his *t.*
Ps. 34:13; 1Pet. 3:10, keep thy *t.* from evil.
Prov. 10:20, *t.* of the just as choice silver.
12:18; 31:26, *t.* of the wise is health.
19, the lying *t.* is but for a moment.
15:4, a wholesome *t.* is a tree of life.
18:21, death and life are in the power of the *t.*
21:23, whoso keepeth his *t.* keepeth his soul.
25:15, a soft *t.* breaketh the bone.
Isa. 30:27, his *t.* as a devouring fire.
50:4, hath given me the *t.* of the learned.
Jer. 9:5, taught their *t.* to speak lies.
18:18, let us smite him with the *t.*
Mk. 7:35, his *t.* was loosed.
Jas. 1:26, and bridleth not his *t.*
3:5, the *t.* is a little member.
6, the *t.* is a fire.
8, the *t.* can no man tame.
1Jn. 3:18, not love in word, neither in *t.*
See Ps. 45:1; Lk. 16:24; Rom. 14:11; Phil. 2:11.
TOOL. Ex. 20:25; 32:4; Dt. 27:5; 1Ki. 6:7.
TOOTH. Ex. 21:24; Prov. 25:19; Mt. 5:38.
TOPAZ. Ex. 28:17; Rev. 21:20.
TORCHES. Nah. 2:3; Zech. 12:6; Jn. 18:3.
TORMENT. Mt. 8:29, to *t.* before the time.
Lk. 16:23, being in *t.*
Heb. 11:37, destitute, afflicted, *t.*
1Jn. 4:18, fear hath *t.*
Rev. 9:5, *t.* as *t.* of a scorpion.
14:11, the smoke of their *t.*
See Mt. 4:24; Mk. 5:7; Lk. 8:28.
TORN. Gen. 44:28, surely he is *t.* in pieces.
Ezek. 4:14, have not eaten of that which is *t.*
Hos. 6:1, he hath *t.*, and he will heal us.
See Isa. 5:25; Mal. 1:13; Mk. 1:26.
TORTOISE. Lev. 11:29, and the *t.* after his kind.
TOSS. Ps. 109:23, I am *t.* up and down.
Isa. 22:18, he will *t.* thee like a ball.
54:11, afflicted, *t.* with tempest.
Eph. 4:14, no more children, *t.* to and fro.
See Mt. 14:24; Acts 27:18; Jas. 1:6.
TOUCH. Gen. 3:3, nor *t.* it, lest ye die.
1Sam. 10:26, a band whose hearts God had *t.*
1Chr. 16:22; Ps. 105:15, *t.* not mine anointed.
Job 5:19, there shall no evil *t.* thee.
6:7, things my soul refused to *t.*
Isa. 6:7, lo, this hath *t.* thy lips.
Jer. 1:9, the Lord *t.* my mouth.
Zech. 2:8, he that *t.* you, *t.* the apple of his eye.
Mt. 9:21; Mk. 5:28, if I may but *t.* his garment.
Mk. 10:13; Lk. 18:15, children, that he should *t.* them.
Jn. 20:17, *t.* me not.
2Cor. 6:17, *t.* not the unclean thing.
Col. 2:21, *t.* not, taste not.
See Job 19:21; Lk. 7:14; 11:46; 1Cor. 7:1.
TOWER. 2Sam. 22:3; Ps. 18:2; 144:2, my high *t.*
Ps. 61:3, a strong *t.* from the enemy.
Prov. 18:10, the name of the Lord is a strong *t.*
Isa. 33:18, where is he that counted the *t.*?
See Isa. 2:15; 5:2; Mic. 4:8; Mt. 21:33.
TRADITION. Mt. 15:2; Mk. 7:3, they disciples transgress the *t.*
Gal. 1:14, zealous of the *t.* of my fathers.
Col. 2:8, after the *t.* of men.
1Pet. 1:18, received by *t.* from your fathers.
TRAFFICK. Gen. 42:34; 1Ki. 10:15; Ezek. 17:4.
TRAIN. 1Ki. 10:2; Prov. 22:6; Isa. 6:1.
TRAITOR. Lk. 6:16; 2Tim. 3:4.
TRAMPLE. Ps. 91:13; Isa. 63:3; Mt. 7:6.
TRANQUILLITY. Dan. 4:27, lengthening of thy *t.*
TRANSFORM. Rom. 12:2; 2Cor. 11:13, 14, 15.
TRANSGRESS. Num. 14:41, wherefore do ye *t.*?

1Sam. 2:24, make the Lord's people to *t.*
Neh. 1:8, if ye *t.*, I will scatter you abroad.
Ps. 17:3, my mouth shall not *t.*
Prov. 28:21, for a piece of bread that man will *t.*
Jer. 2:8, the pastors *t.*
3:13, only acknowledge that thou hast *t.*
Hab. 2:5, he *t.* by wine.
See Mt. 15:2; Rom. 2:27; 1Jn. 3:4; 2Jn. 9.
RANSGRESSION. Ex. 34:7; Num. 14:18, forgiving *t.*
1Chr. 10:13, Saul died for his *t.*
Ezra 10:6, he mourned because of their *t.*
Job 7:21, why dost thou not pardon my *t.*?
13:23, make me to know my *t.*
14:17, my *t.* is sealed up.
31:33, if I covered my *t.*
Ps. 19:13, innocent from the great *t.*
25:7, remember not my *t.*
32:1, blessed is he whose *t.* is forgiven.
51:1, blot out all my *t.*
65:3, as for our *t.*, thou shalt purge them.
107:17, fools because of their *t.* are afflicted.
Prov. 17:9, he that covereth a *t.*
Isa. 43:25; 44:22, blotteth out thy *t.*
53:5, he was wounded for our *t.*
8, for the *t.* of my people was he smitten.
58:1, show my people their *t.*
Ezek. 18:22, his *t.* shall not be mentioned.
Mic. 1:5, what is the *t.* of Jacob?
See Rom. 4:15; 5:14; 1Tim. 2:14; Heb. 2:2.
RANSGRESSOR. Ps. 51:13, teach *t.* thy ways.
59:5, be not merciful to any wicked *t.*
Prov. 13:15, the way of *t.* is hard.
21:18, the *t.* shall be ransom for the upright.
Isa. 48:8, thou wast called a *t.* from the womb.
53:12; Mk. 15:28; Lk. 22:37, numbered with the *t.*
See Dan. 8:23; Hos. 14:9, Gal. 2:18.
RANSLATE. 2Sam. 3:10; Col. 1:13; Heb. 11:5.
RAP. Job 18:10; Ps. 69:22; Jer. 5:26; Rom. 11:9.
RAVAIL. Ps. 7:14, he *t.* with iniquity.
Isa. 23:4, I *t.* not.
53:11, the *t.* of his soul.
Rom. 8:22, the whole creation *t.* in pain.
Gal. 4:19, my children of whom I *t.*
See Job 15:20; Isa. 13:8; Mic. 5:3; Rev. 12:2.
RAVEL. Eccl. 1:13; 2:23; 1Th. 2:9; 2Th. 3:8.
RAVELLER. Jud. 5:6; 2Sam. 12:4; Job 31:32.
REACHEROUS. Isa. 21:2; Jer. 9:2; Zeph. 3:4.
REACHEROUSLY. Isa. 33:1, thou dealest *t.*
Jer. 12:1, why are they happy that deal *t.*?
Lam. 1:2, her friends have dealt *t.* with her.
See Hos. 5:7; 6:7; Mal. 2:10, 15.
READ. Dt. 11:24, whereon soles of feet *t.*
Dt. 25:4; 1Cor. 9:9; 1Tim. 5:18, not muzzle the ox when he *t.*
Ps. 7:5, let him *t.* down my life.
44:5, through thy name will we *t.* them under.
60:12; 108:13, shall *t.* down our enemies.
91:13, thou shalt *t.* upon lion and adder.
Isa. 10:6, to *t.* them down like mire.
16:10, shall *t.* out no wine.
63:3, I will *t.* them in mine anger.
Jer. 48:33, none shall *t.* with shouting.
Ezek. 34:18, but ye must *t.* the residue.
Hos. 10:11, loveth to *t.* out corn.
Mal. 4:3, ye shall *t.* down the wicked.
See Job 9:8; Isa. 41:25; 62:2; Rev. 19:15.
TREASURE. Gen. 43:23, God hath given you *t.*
Ex. 19:5; Ps. 135:4, a peculiar *t.* to me.
Dt. 28:12, open to thee his good *t.*
Job 3:21; Ps. 17:14; Prov. 2:4, for hid *t.*
38:22, the *t.* of the snow.
Prov. 8:21, I will fill *t.* of those that love me.
10:2, *t.* of wickedness profiteth nothing.
15:16, than great *t.* and trouble therewith.
21:20, there is a *t.* to be desired.
Eccl. 2:8, I gathered the peculiar *t.* of kings.
Isa. 2:7, neither is there any end of their *t.*
45:3, I will give thee the *t.* of darkness.
Jer. 41:8, slay us not, for we have *t.*
51:13, waters abundant in *t.*
Dan. 11:43, power over the *t.* of gold.
Mic. 6:10, the *t.* of wickedness.
Mt. 6:21; Lk. 12:34, where your *t.* is.
12:35, out of the good *t.* of the heart.
13:44, like unto *t.* hid in a field.
52, out of his *t.* things new and old.
19:21; Mk. 10:21; Lk. 18:22, thou shalt have *t.* in heaven.
Lk. 12:21, that layeth up *t.* for himself.
Col. 2:3, in whom are hid *t.* of wisdom.
2Cor. 4:7, we have this *t.* in earthen vessels.
Heb. 11:26, greater riches than the *t.* in Egypt.
Jas. 5:3, ye have heaped *t.*
See Dt. 32:34; 33:19; Isa. 33:6; Mt. 2:11.
TREASURER. Neh. 13:13; Isa. 22:15; Dan. 3:2.
TREASURY. Mk. 12:41, the people cast money into the *t.*
Lk. 21:1, rich men casting their gifts into the *t.*
See Josh. 6:19; Jer. 38:11; Mt. 27:6.
TREE. Dt. 20:19, the *t.* is man's life.
Job 14:7, there is hope of a *t.*
24:20, wickedness shall be broken as a *t.*
Ps. 1:3; Jer. 17:8, like a *t.* planted.
104:16, the *t.* of the Lord are full of sap.
Eccl. 11:3, where the *t.* falleth.
Isa. 56:3, I am a dry *t.*
61:3, called *t.* of righteousness.
Ezek. 15:2, what is the vine *t.* more than any *t.*?
31:9, all the *t.* of Eden envied him.
See Mk. 8:24; Lk. 21:29; Jude 12; Rev. 7:3.
TREMBLE. Dt. 2:25, the nations shall *t.*
Jud. 5:4; 2Sam. 22:8; Ps. 18:7; 77:18; 97:4, the earth *t.*
Ezra 9:4, then assembled to me every one that *t.*
Job 9:6, the pillars thereof *t.*
26:11, the pillars of heaven *t.*
Ps. 2:11, rejoice with *t.*
60:2, thou hast made earth to *t.*
99:1, the Lord reigneth, let the people *t.*
104:32, he looketh on the earth, and it *t.*
Eccl. 12:3, the keepers of the house shall *t.*
Isa. 14:16, is this the man that made earth *t.*?
64:2, that the nations may *t.* at thy presence.
66:5, ye that *t.* at his word.

Jer. 5:22, will ye not *t.* at my presence?
33:9, they shall *t.* for all the goodness.
Amos 8:8, shall not the land *t.* for this?
Acts 24:25, Felix *t.*
Jas. 2:19, devils also believe, and *t.*
See Acts 9:6; 16:29; 1Cor. 2:3; Eph. 6:5; Phil. 2:12.
TRENCH. 1Sam. 17:20; 26:5; 1Ki. 18:32; Lk. 19:43.
TRESPASS. Gen. 31:36, what is my *t.*?
50:17, we pray thee forgive the *t.*
Ezra 9:2, rulers have been chief in this *t.*
Ps. 68:21, goeth on still in his *t.*
Mt. 6:14, if ye forgive men their *t.*
18:15, if thy brother *t.*, tell him his fault.
Lk. 17:3, if thy brother *t.* against thee.
2Cor. 5:19, not imputing their *t.*
Eph. 2:1, dead in *t.* and sins.
Col. 2:13, having forgiven you all *t.*
See Num. 5:6; 1Ki. 8:31; Ezek. 17:20; 18:24.
TRIAL. Job 9:23, the *t.* of the innocent.
2Cor. 8:2, a great *t.* of affliction.
See Ezek. 21:13; Heb. 11:36; 1Pet. 1:7; 4:12.
TRIBES. Ps. 105:37, not one feeble person among their *t.*
122:4, whither the *t.* go up.
Isa. 19:13, they that are the stay of the *t.*
49:6, my servant to raise up the *t.*
Hab. 3:9, according to oaths of the *t.*
Mt. 24:30, than shall all *t.* of the earth mourn.
See Num. 24:2; Dt. 1:13; 12:5; 18:5.
TRIBULATION. Dt. 4:30, when thou art in *t.*
Jud. 10:14, let them deliver you in *t.*
Mt. 13:21, when *t.* ariseth.
24:21, then shall be great *t.*
Jn. 16:33, in the world ye shall have *t.*
Acts 14:22, through much *t.*
Rom. 5:3, we glory in *t.* also.
12:12, patient in *t.*
See 2Cor. 1:4; 7:4; Eph. 3:13; Rev. 7:14.
TRIBUTARY. Dt. 20:11; Jud. 1:30; Lam. 1:1.
TRIBUTE. Gen. 49:15, a servant to *t.*
Num. 31:37, the Lord's *t.*
Dt. 16:10, *t.* of freewill offering.
Ezra 7:24, not lawful to impose *t.*
Neh. 5:4, borrowed money for king's *t.*
Prov. 12:24, the slothful shall be under *t.*
See Mat 17:24; 22:17; Lk. 23:2.
TRIM. 2Sam. 19:24; Jer. 2:33; Mt. 25:7.
TRIUMPH. Ex. 15:1, he hath *t.* gloriously.
Ps. 25:2, let not mine enemies *t.*
92:4, I will *t.* in the works of thy hands.
2Cor. 2:14, which always causeth us to *t.*
Col. 2:15, a show of them openly, *t.* over them.
See 2Sam. 20; Job 20:5; Ps. 47:1.
TRODDEN. Job 22:15, the old way which wicked men
have *t.*
Ps. 119:118, thou hast *t.* down all that err.
Isa. 5:5, the vineyard shall be *t.* down.
63:3, I have *t.* the winepress alone.
Mic. 7:10, now shall she be *t.* as mire.
Mt. 5:13, salt to be *t.* under foot.
Lk. 21:24, Jerusalem shall be *t.* down.
Heb. 10:29, hath *t.* under foot the Son of God.
See Deut 1:36; Jud. 5:21; Isa. 18:2.
TRODE. 2Ki. 14:9, 2Chr. 25:18; Lk. 12:1.
TROOP. 2Sam. 22:30; Ps. 18:29; Hos. 7:1.
TROUBLE (*n.*). Dt. 31:17, many *t.* shall befall.
1Chr. 22:14, in my *t.* I prepared for the house.
Neh. 9:32, let not the *t.* seem little.
Job 3:26, yet *t.* came.
5:6, neither doth *t.* spring out of the ground.
7, man is born to *t.*
19, shall deliver thee in six *t.*
14:1, of few days, and full of *t.*
30:25, weep for him that was in *t.*
34:29, he giveth quietness, who can make *t.*?
Job 38:23, I have reserved against the time of *t.*
Ps. 9:9, a refuge in time of *t.*
22:11, for *t.* is near.
25:17, the *t.* of mine heart are enlarged.
22, redeem Israel out of all his *t.*
27:5, in time of *t.* he shall hide me.
46:1, a very present help in *t.*
73:5, they are not in *t.* as other men.
88:3, my soul is full of *t.*
119:143, *t.* and anguish have taken hold on me.
138:7, thou I walk in the midst of *t.*
Isa. 17:14, at eveningtide *t.*
30:6, into the land of *t.* they will carry riches.
65:16, because former *t.* are forgotten.
23, they shall not bring forth for *t.*
Jer. 2:27, in time of *t.* they will say, save us.
8:15, we looked for health, and behold *t.*
1Cor. 7:28, such shall have *t.* in the flesh.
2Cor. 1:4, able to comfort them in *t.*
See Prov. 15:6; 25:19; Jer. 11:12; 30:7; Lam. 1:21
TROUBLE (*v.*). Josh. 7:25, why hast thou *t.* us?
1Ki. 18:17, art thou he that *t.* Israel?
18, I have not *t.* Israel, but thou.
Job 4:5, now it toucheth thee, and thou art *t.*
Ps. 3:1, how are they increased that *t.* me!
77:4, I am so *t.* that I cannot speak.
Prov. 25:26, is as a *t.* fountain.
Isa. 57:20, the wicked are like the *t.* sea.
Dan. 5:10, let not thy thoughts *t.* thee.
11:44, tidings out of the north shall *t.* him.
Mt. 24:6, see that ye be not *t.*
26:10; Mk. 14:6, why *t.* ye the woman?
Jn. 5:4, an angel *t.* the water.
11:33; 12:27; 13:21, Jesus groaned, and was *t*
2Cor. 4:8; 7:5, we are *t.* on every side.
Gal. 1:7, there be some that *t.* you.
6:17, let no man *t.* me.
See 2Th. 1:7; 2:2; Heb. 12:15;1Pet. 3:14.
TROUBLING. Job 3:17; Jn. 5:4.
TRUCE. 2Tim. 3:3, men shall be *t.*-breakers.
TRUE. Gen. 42:11, we are *t.* men.
1Ki. 22:16, tell me nothing but that which is *t.*
2Chr. 15:3, Israel hath been without the *t.* God.
Neh. 9:13, thou gavest them *t.* laws.
Ps. 119:160, thy word is *t.* from the beginning.
Prov. 14:25, a *t.* witness delivereth souls.
Jer. 10:10, the Lord is the *t.* God.
Mt. 22:16; Mk. 12:14, we know that thou art *t.*

Lk. 16:11, the *t.* riches.
Jn. 1:9, that was the *t.* light.
4:23, when the *t.* worshippers.
5:31, if I bear witness of myself, my witness is not *t.*
6:32, the *t.* bread.
10:41, all things that John spake were *t.*
15:1, I am the *t.* vine.
17:3; 1Jn. 5:20, to know thee the only *t.* God.
2Cor. 6:8, as deceivers, and yet *t.*
Eph. 4:24, created in *t.* holiness.
Phil. 4:8, whatsoever things are *t.*
Heb. 10:22, draw near with a *t.* heart.
See Rev. 3:7; 6:10; 15:3; 16:7; 19:9, 11; 21:5.
RUST. Job 13:15, though he slay me, yet will I *t.*
39:11, wilt thou *t.* him, because his strength is great?
Ps. 25:2; 31:6; 55:23; 56:3; 143:8, I *t.* in thee.
37:3; 40:3; 62:8; 115:9; Prov. 3:5; Isa. 26. 4, *t.* in the Lord.
118:8, better to *t.* in the Lord.
144:2, he in whom I *t.*
Prov. 28:26, he that *t.* in his own heart is a fool.
Isa. 50:10, let him *t.* in the name of the Lord.
Jer. 49:11, let thy widows *t.* in me.
Mic. 7:5, *t.* ye not in a friend.
Nah. 1:7, the Lord knoweth them that *t.* in him.
Mt. 27:43, he *t.* in God, let him deliver him.
Lk. 18:9, certain which *t.* in themselves.
See Jer. 17:5; 2Cor. 1:9; 1Tim. 4:10.
RUTH. Dt. 32:4, a God of *t.*
Ps. 15:2, speaketh the *t.* in his heart.
51:6, desirest *t.* in inward parts.
91:4, his *t.* shall be thy shield.
117:2, his *t.* endureth for ever.
119:30, I have chosen the way of *t.*
Prov. 23:23, buy the *t.*
Isa. 59:14, *t.* is fallen in the streets.
Jer. 9:3, they are not valiant for the *t.*
Zech. 8:16, speak every man *t.* to his neighbour.
Mal. 2:6, the law of *t.* was in his mouth.
Jn. 1:14, full of grace and *t.*
8:32, know the *t.*, and the *t.* shall make you free.
14:6, I am the way, the *t.*, and the life.
16:13, Spirit of *t.* will guide you into all *t.*
18:38, what is *t.*?
Rom. 1:18, who hold the *t.* in unrighteousness.
1Cor. 5:8, unleavened bread of sincerity and *t.*
2Cor. 13:8, can do nothing against *t.*, but for the *t.*
Eph. 4:15, speaking the *t.* in love.
1Tim. 3:15, the pillar and ground of *t.*
2Tim. 2:15, rightly dividing the word of *t.*
Jas. 5:19, if any err from the *t.*
See 1Cor. 13:6; 2Tim. 3:7; 1Jn. 3:19; 5:6.
RY. 2Chr. 32:31, God left him to *t.* him.
Job 23:10, when he hath *t.* me.
Ps. 26:2, *t.* my reins and my heart.
Jer. 9:7; Zech. 13:9, I will melt them and *t.* them.
1Cor. 3:13, shall *t.* every man's work.
Jas. 1:12, when *t.* he shall receive the crown.
1Jn. 4:1, *t.* the spirits.
See Prov. 17:3; Isa. 28:16; 1Pet. 4:12; Rev. 3:18.

TURN. Job 23:13, who can *t.* him.
Ps. 7:12, if he *t.* not, he will whet his sword.
Prov. 1:23, *t.* at my reproof.
Jer. 31:18; Lam. 5:21, *t.* thou me, and I shall be *t.*
Ezek. 14:6; 18:30; 33:9; Hos. 12:6; Joel 2:12, repent, and *t.*
Zech. 9:12, *t.* you to the strong hold, ye prisoners.
Mt. 5:39, *t.* the other also.
Acts 26:18, to *t.* them from darkness to light.
2Tim. 3:5, from such *t.* away.
See Prov. 21:1; 26:14; Hos. 7:8; Lk. 22:61; Jas. 1:17.
TWAIN. Isa. 6:2; Mt. 5:41; 19:5; Eph. 2:15.
TWICE. Job 33:14; Mk. 14:30; Lk. 18:12; Jude 12.
TWINKLING. 1Cor. 15:52, in the *t.* of an eye.
UNADVISEDLY. Ps. 106:33, he spake *u.*
UNAWARES. Lk. 21:34; Gal. 2:4; Heb. 13:2; Jude 4.
UNBELIEF. Mk. 9:24, help thou mine *u.*
Rom. 3:3, shall *u.* make faith without effect?
11:32, concluded all in *u.*
Heb. 3:12, evil heart of *u.*
See Mt. 13:58; Mk. 6:6; 1Tim. 1:13; Heb. 4:11.
UMBLAMEABLE. Col. 1:22; 1Th. 3:13.
UNCERTAIN. 1Cor. 9:26; 14:8; 1Tim. 6:7.
UNCLEAN. Acts 10:28; Rom. 14:14; 2Cor. 6:17.
UNCLOTHED. 2Cor. 5:4, not that we would be *u.*
UNCORRUPTNESS. Ti. 2:7, in doctrine showing *u.*
UNCTION. 1Jn. 2:20, an *u.* from the Holy One.
UNDEFILED. Ps. 119:1, blessed are the *u.*
Jas. 1:27, pure religion and *u.*
1Pet. 1:4, an inheritance *u.*
See Song 5:2; 6:9; Heb. 7:26; 13:4.
UNDER. Rom. 3:9; 1Cor. 9:27; Gal. 3:10.
UNDERSTAND. Ps. 19:12, who can *u.* his errors?
73:17, then *u.* I their end.
119:100, I *u.* more than the ancients.
139:2, thou *u.* my thought afar off.
Prov. 8:9, all plain to him that *u.*
20:24, how can a man *u.* his own way?
29:19, though he *u.* he will not answer.
Isa. 6:9, hear ye indeed, but *u.* not.
28:19, a vexation only to *u.* the report.
Jer. 9:24, let him glory in this, that he *u.* me.
Dan. 10:12, thou didst set thine heart to *u.*
12:10, wicked shall not *u.* the wise shall *u.*
Hos. 14:9, who is wise, and he shall *u.* these things?
Mt. 13:51, have ye *u.* all these things?
24:15, whoso readeth, let him *u.*
Lk. 24:45, that they might *u.* the scriptures.
Jn. 8:43, why do ye not *u.* my speech?
Rom. 3:11, there is none that *u.*
15:21, they that have not heard shall *u.*
1Cor. 13:2, though I *u.* all mysteries.
11, I *u.* as a child.
See 1Cor. 14:2; Heb. 11:3; 2Pet. 2:12; 3:16.
UNDERSTANDING. Ex. 31:3; Dt. 4:6, wisdom and *u.*
1Ki. 3:11, hast asked for thyself *u.*
4:29, gave Solomon wisdom and *u.*
7:14, filled with wisdom and *u.*
1Chr. 12:32, men that had *u.* of the times.

2Chr. 26:5, had *u.* in visions.
Job 12:13, he hath counsel and *u.*
20, he taketh away the *u.* of the aged.
17:4, thou hast hid their heart from *u.*
28:12, where is the place of *u.*?
32:8, the Almighty giveth them *u.*
38:36, who hath given *u.* to the heart?
39:17, neither imparted to her *u.*
Ps. 47:7, sing ye praises with *u.*
49:3, the meditation of my heart shall be of *u.*
119:34, 73, 125, 144, 169, give me *u.*
99, I have more *u.* than my teachers.
104, through thy precepts I get *u.*
147:5, his *u.* is infinite.
Prov. 2:2, apply thine heart to *u.*
11, *u.* shall keep thee.
3:5, lean not to thine own *u.*
19, by *u.* hath he established the heavens.
4:5, 7, get wisdom, get *u.*
8:1, doth not *u.* put forth her voice?
9:6, go in the way of *u.*
10, the knowledge of the holy is *u.*
14:29, he that is slow to wrath is of great *u.*
16:22, *u.* is a wellspring of life.
17:24, wisdom is before him that hath *u.*
19:8, he that keepeth *u.* shall find good.
21:30, there is no *u.* against the Lord.
24:3, by *u.* an house is established.
30:2, have not the *u.* of a man.
Eccl. 9:11, nor yet riches to men of *u.*
Isa. 11:2, the spirit of *u.* shall rest on him.
27:11, it is a people of no *u.*
29:14, the *u.* of prudent men shall be hid.
40:14, who showed him the way of *u.*?
28, there is no searching of his *u.*
Jer. 3:15, pastors shall feed you with *u.*
Ezek. 28:4, with thy *u.* thou hast gotten riches.
Dan. 4:34, mine *u.* returned.
Mt. 15:16; Mk. 7:18, are ye also without *u.*?
Mk. 12:33, to love him with all the *u.*
Lk. 2:47, astonished at his *u.*
24:45, then opened he their *u.*
1Cor. 1:19, bring to nothing *u.* of prudent.
14:15, I will pray with the *u.* also.
20, be not children in *u.*
Eph. 4:18, having the *u.* darkened.
Phil. 4:7, peace of God, which passeth all *u.*
See Col. 1:9; 2:2; 2Tim. 2:7; 1Jn. 5:20.
UNDERTAKE. Isa. 38:14, *u.* for me.
UNDONE. Josh. 11:15; Isa. 6:5; Mt. 23:23; Lk. 11:42.
UNEQUAL. Ezek. 18:25, 29; 2Cor. 6:14.
UNFAITHFUL. Ps. 78:57; Prov. 25:19.
UNFEIGNED. 2Cor. 6:6; 1Tim. 1:5; 2Tim. 1:5; 1Pet. 1:22.
UNFRUITFUL. Mt. 13:22; Eph. 5:11; Ti. 3:14; 2Pet. 1:8.
UNGODLINESS. Rom. 1:18; 11:26; 2Tim. 2:16; Ti. 2:12.
UNGODLY. 2Chr. 19:2, shouldest thou help the *u.*?
Job 16:11, God hath delivered me to the *u.*
Ps. 1:1, counsel of *u.*
6, the way of the *u.* shall perish.
43:1, plead my cause against an *u.* nation.
Prov. 16:27, an *u.* man diggeth up evil.
Rom. 5:6, Christ died for the *u.*
1Pet. 4:18, where shall the *u.* appear?
2Pet. 3:7, perdition of *u.* men.
See Rom. 4:5; 1Tim. 1:9; 2Pet. 2:5; Jude 15.
UNHOLY. Lev. 10:10; 1Tim. 1:9; 2Tim. 3:2; Heb. 10:29.
UNICORN. Num. 23:22, he hath as it were the strength of an *u.*
Dt. 33:17, his horns are like the horns of an *u.*
Job 39:9, will the *u.* be willing to serve thee?
Isa. 34:7, the *u.* shall come down with them.
UNITE. Gen. 49:6; Ps. 86:11.
UNITY. Ps. 133:1; Eph. 4:3, 13.
UNJUST. Ps. 43:1; Prov. 11:7; 29:27, *u.* man.
Prov. 28:8, he that by *u.* gain.
Zeph. 3:5, the *u.* knoweth no shame.
Mt. 5:44, he sendeth rain on the just and *u.*
Lk. 18:6, hear what the *u.* judge saith.
11, not as other men, *u.*
Acts 24:15, a resurrection both of the just and *u.*
1Cor. 6:1, go to law before the *u.*
1Pet. 3:18, suffered, the just for the *u.*
Rev. 22:11, he that is *u.*, let him be *u.* still.
See Ps. 82:2; Isa. 26:10; Lk. 16:8; 2Pet. 2:9.
UNKNOWN. Acts 17:23; 1Cor. 14:2; 2Cor. 6:9; Gal. 1:22.
UNLAWFUL. Acts 10:28; 2Pet. 2:8.
UNLEARNED. Acts 4:13; 1Cor. 14:16; 2Tim. 2:23; 2Pet. 3:16.
UNMINDFUL. Dt. 32:18, thou art *u.*
UNMOVEABLE. Acts 27:41; 1Cor. 15:58.
UNPERFECT. Ps. 139:16, yet being *u.*
UNPREPARED. 2Cor. 9:4, find you *u.*
UNPROFITABLE. Job 15:3, *u.* talk.
Mt. 25:30; Lk. 17:10, *u.* servant.
See Rom. 3:12; Ti. 3:9; Phile. 11; Heb. 7:18; 13:17.
UNPUNISHED. Prov. 11:21; 16:5; 17:5; 19:5; Jer. 25:29; 49:12, shall not be *u.*
See Jer. 30:11; 46:28.
UNQUENCHABLE. Mt. 3:12; Lk. 3:17.
UNREASONABLE. Acts 25:27; 2Th. 3:2.
UNREPROVEABLE. Col. 1:22, *u.* in his sight.
UNRIGHTEOUS. Ex. 23:1, an *u.* witness.
Isa. 10:1, decree *u.* decrees.
55:7, let the *u.* man forsake his thoughts.
Rom. 3:5, is God *u?*
Heb. 6:10, God is not *u.* to forget your work.
See Dt. 25:16; Ps. 71:4; Lk. 16:11; 1Cor. 6:9.
UNRIGHTEOUSNESS. Lk. 16:9, mammon of *u.*
Rom. 1:18, hold the truth in *u.*
2:8, to them that obey *u.*
3:5, if our *u.* commend righteousness.
6:13, instruments of *u.*
9:14, is there *u.* with God?
2Cor. 6:14, what fellowship with *u.*?
2Th. 2:12, had pleasure in *u.*
2Pet. 2:13, receive the reward of *u.*
1Jn. 1:9, cleanse us from all *u.*
5:17, all *u.* is sin.
See Lev. 19:15; Ps. 92:15; Jer. 22:13; Jn. 7:18.

NRULY. 1Th. 5:14; Ti. 1:6; Jas. 3:8.
NSAVOURY. Job 6:6, can that which is *u.* be. eaten?
NSEARCHABLE. Job 5:9; Ps. 145:3; Rom. 11:33; Eph. 3:8.
NSEEMLY. Rom. 1:27; 1Cor. 13:5.
NSKILFUL. Heb. 5:13, is *u.* in the word.
NSPEAKABLE. 2Cor. 9:15; 12:4; 1Pet. 1:8.
NSPOTTED. Jas. 1:27, *u.* from the world.
NSTABLE. Gen. 49:4; Jas. 1:8; 2Pet. 2:14.
NTHANKFUL. Lk. 6:35; 2Tim. 3:2.
NWASHEN. Mt. 15:20; Mk. 7:2, 5.
NWISE. Dt. 32:6; Hos. 13:13; Rom. 1:14; Eph. 5:17.
NWORTHY. Acts 13:46; 1Cor. 6:2; 11:27.
PBRAID. Mt. 11:20; Mk. 16:14; Jas. 1:5.
PHOLD. Ps. 51:12, *u.* me with thy free spirit.
54:4, with them that *u.* my soul.
119:116, *u.* me according to thy word.
145:14, the Lord *u.* all that fall.
Isa. 41:10, I will *u.* thee with right hand.
42:1, my servant, whom I *u.*
63:5, wondered there was none to *u.*
Heb. 1:3, *u.* all things by the word of his power.
See Ps. 37:17; 41:12; 63:8; Prov. 20:28.
PPERMOST. Mt. 23:6; Mk. 12:39; Lk. 11:43.
PRIGHT. Job 12:4, the *u.* man is laughed to scorn.
17:8, *u.* men shall be astonied.
Ps. 19:13, then shall I be *u.*
25:8; 92:15, good and *u.* is the Lord.
37:14, such as be of *u.* conversation.
49:14, the *u.* shall have dominion.
111:1, the assembly of the *u.*
112:4, to the *u.* ariseth light.
125:4, that are *u.* in their hearts.
Prov. 2:21, the *u.* shall dwell in the land.
11:3, the integrity of the *u.*
20, such as are *u.* in their way.
14:11, the tabernacle of the *u.*
15:8, the prayer of the *u.* is his delight.
28:10, the *u.* shall have good things.
Eccl. 7:29, God hath made man *u.*
Song 1:4, the *u.* love thee.
See Isa. 26:7; Jer. 10:5; Mic. 7:2; Hab. 2:4.
PRIGHTLY. Ps. 58:1; 75:2, do ye judge *u.*?
84:11, withhold no good from them that walk *u.*
Prov. 10:9; 15:21; 28:18, he that walketh *u.*
Isa. 33:15, he that speaketh *u.*
See Ps. 15:2; Amos 5:10; Mic. 2:7; Gal. 2:14.
PRIGHTNESS. 1Ki. 3:6, in *u.* of heart.
1Chr. 29:17, thou hast pleasure in *u.*
Job 4:6, the *u.* of thy ways.
33:23, to show unto man his *u.*
Ps. 25:21, let *u.* preserve me.
143:10, lead me into the land of *u.*
Prov. 2:13, who leave the paths of *u.*
See Ps. 111:8; Prov. 14:2; 28:6; Isa. 26:7, 10.
PROAR. Mt. 26:5; Mk. 14:2; Acts 17:5; 21:31.
PWARD. Job 5:7; Eccl. 3:21; Isa. 38:14.
RGE. Gen. 33:11; 2Ki. 2:17; Lk. 11:53.
RGENT. Ex. 12:33; Dan. 3:22.
SE. Mt. 6:7, *u.* not vain repetitions.
1Cor. 7:31, they that *u.* this world.
Gal. 5:13, *u.* not liberty for an occasion.
1Tim. 1:8, if a man *u.* it lawfully.
See Ps. 119:132; 1Cor. 9:12; 1Tim. 5:23.
USURP. 1Tim. 2:12, I suffer not a woman to *u.*
USURY. Ex. 22:25, neither shalt thou lay upon him *u.*
Lev. 25:36, take thou no *u.* of him.
Dt. 23:20, thou mayest lend upon *u.*
Neh. 5:7, ye exact *u.*
Ezek. 18:8, not given forth upon *u.*
13, hath given forth upon *u.*
17, that hath not received *u.*
22:12, thou hast taken *u.*
UTTER. Ps. 78:2, I will *u.* dark sayings.
106:2, who can *u.* the mighty acts?
119:171, my lips shall *u.* praise.
Prov. 1:20, wisdom *u.* her voice.
23:33, thine heart shall *u.* perverse things.
29:11, a fool *u.* all his mind.
Eccl. 5:2, let not thine heart be hasty to *u.*
Rom. 8:26, which cannot be *u.*
2Cor. 12:4, not lawful for a man to *u.*
Heb. 5:11, many things hard to be *u.*
See Job 33:3; Isa. 48:20; Joel 2:11; Mt. 13:35.
UTTERANCE. Acts 2:4, as the Spirit gave *u.*
See 1Cor. 1:5; 2Cor. 8:7; Eph. 6:19; Col. 4:3.
UTTERLY. Ps. 119:8, forsake me not *u.*
Jer. 23:39, I will *u.* forget you.
Zeph. 1:2, I will *u.* consume all things.
2Pet. 2:12, these shall *u.* perish.
See Dt. 7:2; Neh. 9:31; Isa. 40:30; Rev. 18:8.
UTTERMOST. Mt. 5:26; 1Th. 2:16; Heb. 7:25.
VAGABOND. Gen. 4:12, a *v.* shalt thou be in the earth.
See Ps. 109:10; Acts 19:13.
VAIL. Mt. 27:51 2Cor. 3:14; Heb. 6:19.
VAIN. Ex. 5:9, not regard *v.* words.
20:7; Dt. 5:11, shalt not take name of the Lord in *v.*
Dt. 32:47, it is not a *v.* thing for you.
2Sam. 6:20, as one of the *v.* fellows.
2Ki. 18:20; Isa. 36:5, they are but *v.* words.
Job 11:12, *v.* man would be wise.
16:3, shall *v.* words have an end?
21:34, how then comfort ye me in *v.*?
Ps. 2:1; Acts 4:25, the people imagine a *v.* thing.
26:4, I have not sat with *v.* persons.
33:17, an horse is a *v.* thing for safety.
39:6, every man walketh in a *v.* show.
60:11; 108:12, *v.* is the help of man.
89:47, wherefore hast thou made men in *v.*?
127:1, labour in *v.*, watchman waketh in *v.*
Prov. 12:11; 28:19, followeth *v.* persons.
31:30, beauty is *v.*
Eccl. 6:12, all the days of his *v.* life.
Isa. 1:13, bring no more *v.* oblations.
45:18, he created it not in *v.*
19, I said not, seek ye me in *v.*
49:4; 65:23, laboured in *v.*
Jer. 3:23, in *v.* is salvation hoped for.
10:3, the customs of the people are *v.*
46:11, in *v.* shalt thou use medicines.

Mal. 3:14, ye have said, it is *v.* to serve God.
Mt. 6:7, use not *v.* repetitions.
15:9; Mk. 7:7, in *v.* do they worship me.
Rom. 13:4, he beareth not the sword in *v.*
1Cor. 15:2, unless ye have believed in *v.*
2Cor. 6:1, receive not the grace of God in *v.*
Gal. 2:2, lest I should run in *v.*
Ti. 1:10, unruly and *v.* talkers.
Jas. 1:26, this man's religion is *v.*
1Pet. 1:18, redeemed from *v.* conversation.
See Prov. 1:17; Rom. 1:21; Gal. 5:26; Phil. 2:3.
VALIANT. 1Sam. 18:17, be *v.* for me.
1Ki. 1:42, for thou art a *v.* man.
Isa. 10:13, put down inhabitants like a *v.* man.
Jer. 9:3, they are not *v.* for truth.
Heb. 11:34, waxed *v.* in fight.
See Ps. 60:12; 118:15; Isa. 33:7; Nah. 2:3.
VALUE. Job 13:4, physicians of no *v.*
Mt. 10:31; Lk. 12:7, of more *v.*
See Lev. 27:16; Job 28:16; Mt. 27:9.
VANISH. Isa. 51:6; 1Cor. 13:8; Heb 8:13.
VANITY. Job 7:3, to possess months of *v.*
15:31, *v.* shall be his recompence.
35:13, God will not hear *v.*
Ps. 12:2, speak *v.* every one with his neighbour.
39:5, every man at his best state is *v.*
62:9, are *v.*, lighter than *v.*
144:4, man is like to *v.*
Prov. 13:11, wealth gotten by *v.*
30:8, remove from me *v.*
Eccl. 6:11, many things increase *v.*
11:10, childhood and youth are *v.*
Isa. 30:28, with the sieve of *v.*
Jer. 18:15, they have burned incense to *v.*
Hab. 2:13, people shall weary themselves for *v.*
Rom. 8:20, the creature was made subject to *v.*
Eph. 4:17, walk in *v.* of mind.
2Pet. 2:18, great swelling words of *v.*
See Eccl. 1:2; Jer. 10:8; 14:22; Acts 14:15.
VAPOURS. Job 36:27, according to the *v.* thereof.
Ps. 135:7; Jer. 10:13, he causeth the *v.* to ascend
148:8, snow and *v.*
VARIABLENESS. Jas. 1:17, with whom is no *v.*
VARIANCE. Mt. 10:35; Gal. 5:20.
VAUNT. Jud. 7:2; 1Cor. 13:4.
VEHEMENT. Song 8:6; Mk. 14:31; 2Cor. 7:11.
VENGEANCE. Dt. 32:35, to me belongeth *v.*
Prov. 6:34; Isa. 34:8; 61:2; Jer. 51:6, the day of *v.*
Isa. 59:17, garments of *v.* for clothing.
Acts 28:4, whom *v.* suffereth not to live.
Jude 7, the *v.* of eternal fire.
See Mic. 5:15; Nah. 1:2; Lk. 21:22; Rom. 12:19.
VENISON. Gen. 25:28, he did eat of his *v.*
27:3, take me some *v.*
VERILY. Gen. 42:21; Ps. 58:11; 73:13; Mk. 9:12.
VERITY. Ps. 111:7; 1Tim. 2:7.
VESSEL. 2Ki. 4:6, there is not a *v.* more.
Ps. 2:9, them in pieces like a potter's *v.*
31:12, I am like a broken *v.*
Isa. 66:20, bring an offering in a clean *v.*
Jer. 22:28, a *v.* wherein is no pleasure.
25:34, fall like a pleasant *v.*
Mt. 13:48, gathered the good into *v.*
25:4, the wise took oil in their *v.*
Acts 9:15, he is a chosen *v.* unto me.
Rom. 9:22, the *v.* of wrath.
23, the *v.* of mercy.
1Th. 4:4, to possess his *v.* in sanctification.
2Tim. 2:21, he shall be a *v.* to honour.
1Pet. 3:7, giving honour to the wife as to weaker *v.*
See Isa. 52:11; 65:4; Jer. 14:3; Mk. 11:16.
VESTRY. 2Ki. 10:22, him that was over the *v.*
VESTURE. Gen. 41:42; Ps. 22:18; 102:26; Mt. 27:35; Heb. 1:12; Rev. 19:13.
VEX. Ex. 22:21; Lev. 19:33, not *v.* a stranger.
Num. 33:55, those ye let remain shall *v.* you.
2Sam. 12:18, how will he *v.* himself?
Job 19:2, how long will ye *v.* my soul?
Isa. 11:13, Judah shall not *v.* Ephraim.
Ezek. 32:9, I will *v.* the hearts of many.
Mt. 15:22, my daughter is grievously *v.*
2Pet. 2:8, *v.* his righteous soul.
See Lev. 18:18; Jud. 16:16; Isa. 63:10; Hab. 2:7.
VEXATION. Eccl. 1:14; 2:22; Isa. 9:1; 28:19; 65:14.
VICTORY. 2Sam. 19:2, *v.* was turned to mourning.
1Chr. 29:11, thine is the *v.*
Ps. 98:1, hath gotten him the *v.*
Mt. 12:20, send forth judgment unto *v.*
1Jn. 5:4, this is the *v.*, even our faith.
See Isa. 25:8; 1Cor. 15:54, 55, 57.
VICTUALS. Ex. 12:39, neither had they prepared *v.*
Josh. 9:14, the men took of their v.
Neh. 10:31, bring *v.* on the sabbath.
13:15, in the day wherein they sold *v.*
Mt. 14:15; Lk. 9:12, into villages to buy *v.*
See Gen. 14:11; Jud. 17:10; 1Sam. 22:10.
VIEW. Josh. 2:7; 7:2; 2Ki. 2:7; Neh. 2:13.
VIGILANT. 1Tim. 3:2; 1Pet. 5:8.
VILE. 1Sam. 3:13, made themselves *v.*
Job 18:3, wherefore are we reputed *v.*?
40:4, I am *v.*, what shall I answer thee?
Ps. 15:4; Isa. 32:5; Dan. 11:21, a *v.* person.
Jer. 15:19, take the precious from the *v.*
Lam. 1:11, see, O Lord, for I am become *v.*
Nah. 3:6, I will make thee *v.*
Rom. 1:26, gave them up to *v.* affections.
Phil. 3:21, shall change our *v.* body.
Jas. 2:2, a poor man in *v.* raiment.
See 2Sam. 1:21; Job 30:8; Ps. 12:8; Nah. 1:14.
VILLANY. Isa. 32:6; Jer. 29:23.
VINE. Dt. 32:32, their *v.* is of the *v.* of Sodom.
Jud. 13:14, may not eat any thing that cometh of the *v.*
1Ki. 4:25, dwelt every man under his *v.*
2Ki. 18:31; Isa. 36:16, eat every man of his own *v.*
Ps. 80:8, a *v.* out of Egypt.
128:3, thy wife as a fruitful *v.*
Isa. 24:7, the new wine mourneth, the *v.* languisheth.
Hos. 10:1, Israel is an empty *v.*
Mic. 4:4, they shall sit every man under his *v.*
Mt. 26:29; Mk. 14:25; Lk. 22:18, this fruit of the *v.*
Jn. 15:1, I am the true *v.*

See Dt. 8:8; Song 2:15; Joel 1:7; Hab. 3:17.
INTAGE. Job 24:6; Isa. 16:10; 32:10; Mic. 7:1.
IOL. Isa. 5:12; 14:11; Amos 5:23; 6:5.
IOLENCE. Gen. 6:11, earth was filled with *v.*
Ps. 11:5, him that loveth *v.*
55:9, I have seen *v.* in the city.
58:2, weigh the *v.* of your hands.
72:14, redeem their soul from *v.*
73:6, *v.* covereth them as a garment.
Prov. 4:17, they drink the wine of *v.*
10:6, *v.* covereth the mouth of the wicked.
Isa. 53:9, because he had done no *v.*
Isa. 60:18, *v.* shall no more be heard.
Ezek. 8:17; 28:16, they have filled the land with *v.*
Amos 3:10, store up *v.* in their palaces.
Hab. 1:3, *v.* is before me.
Mal. 2:16, one covereth *v.* with his garment.
Mt. 11:12, kingdom of heaven suffereth *v.*
Lk. 3:14, do *v.* to no man.
See Mic. 2:2; 6:12; Zeph. 1:9; Heb. 11:34.
IOLENT. Ps. 7:16, his *v.* dealing.
18:48; 140:1; Prov. 16:29, the *v.* man.
See 2Sam. 22:49; Eccl. 5:8; Mt. 11:12.
IOLENTLY. Isa. 22:18; Mt. 8:32; Mk. 5:13.
IRGIN. Isa. 23:12; 47:1; 62:5; Jer. 14:17.
IRTUE. Mk. 5:30; Lk. 6:19; 8:46; Phil. 4:8; 2Pet. 1:5.
IRTUOUS. Ruth 3:11; Prov. 12:4; 31:10, 29.
ISAGE. Isa. 52:14; Lam. 4:8; Dan. 3:19.
ISION. Job 20:8, as a *v.* of the night.
Prov. 29:18, where there is no *v.*, people perish.
Isa. 22:1, the valley of *v.*
28:7, they err in *v.*
Lam. 2:9, prophets find no *v.* from the Lord.
Hos. 12:10, I have multiplied *v.*
Joel 2:28; Acts 2:17, young men shall see *v.*
Zech. 13:4, ashamed every one of his *v.*
Mt. 17:9, tell the *v.* to no man.
Lk. 24:23, had seen a *v.* of angels.
Acts 26:19, not disobedient to heavenly *v.*
See Job 4:13; Ezek. 1:1; 8:3; Mic. 3:6.
ISIT. Gen. 50:24; Ex. 13:19, God will *v.* you.
Ex. 20:5; 34:7; Num. 14:18; Dt. 5:9, *v.* the iniquity of the fathers.
32:34, when I *v.*, I will *v.* their sin upon them.
Ruth 1:6, how the Lord had *v.* his people.
Job 5:24, thou shalt *v.* thy habitation.
7:18, shouldest *v.* him every morning.
Ps. 8:4; Heb. 2:6, the son of man, that thou *v.* him.
106:4, *v.* me with thy salvation.
Jer. 5:9; 9:9, shall I not *v.* for these things?
29:10, I will *v.*, and perform my good word.
Ezek. 38:8, after many days thou shalt be *v.*
Mt. 25:36, I was sick and ye *v.* me.
Acts 15:14, how God did *v.* the Gentiles.
Jas. 1:27, to *v.* the fatherless and widows.
See Job 31:14; Lk. 1:68, 78; 7:16.
ISITATION. Job 10:12, thy *v.* hath preserved.
Isa. 10:3; 1Pet. 2:12, in the day of *v.*
Jer. 8:12; 10:15; 46:21; 50:27; Lk. 19:44, in the time of *v.*

See Num. 16:29; Jer. 11:23; Hos. 9:7.
VOCATION. Eph. 4:1, worthy of the *v.*
VOICE. Gen. 4:10, *v.* of thy brother's blood.
27:22, the *v.* is Jacob's *v.*
Ex. 23:21, obey his *v.*, provoke him not.
24:3, all the people answered with one *v.*
32:18, it is not the *v.* of them that shout.
Dt. 4:33, did ever people hear *v.* of God and live?
Josh. 6:10, nor make any noise with thy *v.*
1Sam. 24:16; 26:17, is this thy *v.*?
1Ki. 19:12, after the fire, a still small *v.*
2Ki. 4:31, there was neither *v.* nor hearing.
Job 3:7, let no joyful *v.* come therein.
30:31, my organ into the *v.* of them that weep.
37:4, a *v.* roareth.
40:9, canst thou thunder with a *v.* like him?
Ps. 5:3, my *v.* shalt thou hear in the morning.
31:22; 86:6, the *v.* of my supplications.
42:4, with the *v.* of joy.
95:7, to day, if ye will hear his *v.*
103:20, the *v.* of his word.
Prov. 1:20, wisdom uttereth her *v.* in the streets.
5:13, not obeyed the *v.* of my teachers.
8:1, doth not understanding put forth her *v.*?
4, my *v.* is to the sons of man.
Eccl. 5:3, a fool's *v.* is known.
12:4, rise up at the *v.* of the bird.
Song 2:8; 5:2, the *v.* of my beloved.
12, the *v.* of the turtle is heard.
14, sweet is thy *v.*
Isa. 13:2, exalt the *v.* unto them.
40:3; Mt. 3:3; Mk. 1:3; Lk. 3:4, *v.* of him that crieth.
6, the *v.* said, cry.
48:20, with a *v.* of singing.
52:8, with the *v.* together shall they sing.
65:19, the *v.* of weeping shall be no more heard.
66:6, a *v.* of noise, a *v.* from the temple.
Jer. 7:34, the *v.* of mirth, and the *v.* of gladness.
30:19, the *v.* of them that make merry.
48:3, a *v.* of crying shall be.
Ezek. 23:42, a *v.* of a multitude at ease.
33:32, one that hath a pleasant *v.*
43:2, *v.* like a noise of many waters.
Nah. 2:7, lead her as with the *v.* of doves.
Mt. 12:19, neither shall any man hear his *v.*
Lk. 23:23, the *v.* of them and of the chief priests prevailed.
Jn. 5:25, the dead shall hear the *v.* of Son of God.
10:4, the sheep follow, for they know his *v.*
5, they know not the *v.* of strangers.
12:30, this *v.* came not because of me.
18:37, every one that is of the truth heareth my *v.*
Acts 12:14, and when she knew Peter's *v.*
26:10, I gave my *v.* against them.
1Cor. 14:10, there are so many *v.* in the world.
19, that by my *v.* I might teach others.
Gal. 4:20, I desire now to change my *v.*
1Th. 4:16, descend with *v.* of archangel.
2Pet. 2:16, the dumb ass speaking with man's *v.*

Rev. 3:20, if any man hear my *v.*
4:5, out of the throne proceeded *v.*
See Gen. 3:17; Ps. 58:5; Jn. 3:29; Acts 12:22.
VOID. Gen. 1:2; Jer. 4:23, without form, and *v.*
Dt. 32:28, a people *v.* of counsel.
Ps. 89:39, made *v.* the covenant.
119:126, they have made *v.* thy law.
Prov. 11:12, *v.* of wisdom.
Isa. 55:11, my word shall not return to me *v.*
Jer. 19:7, make *v.* the counsel of Judah.
Nah. 2:10, empty, *v.* and waste.
Acts 24:16, a conscience *v.* of offense.
See Num. 30:12; Rom. 3:31; 4:14.
VOLUME. Ps. 40:7; Heb. 10:7.
VOLUNTARY. Lev. 1:3; 7:16; Ezek. 46:12; Col. 2:18.
VOMIT. Job 20:15; Prov. 26:11; 2Pet. 2:22.
VOW (*n.*). Gen. 28:20; 31:13, Jacob vowed a *v.*
Num. 29:39, these ye shall do beside your *v.*
Dt. 12:6, thither bring your *v.*
Jud. 11:30, Jephthah vowed a *v.*, and said.
39, her father did with he according to his *v.*
1Sam. 1:21, Elkanah went up to offer his *v.*
Job 22:27, thou shalt pay thy *v.*
Ps. 22:25; 66:13; 116:14, I will pay my *v.*
50:14, pay thy *v.* unto the most High.
Ps. 56:12, thy *v.* are upon me, O God.
61:5, for thou hast heard my *v.*
8, that I may daily perform my *v.*
65:1, to thee shall the *v.* be performed.
Prov. 7:14, this day have I paid my *v.*
20:25, after *v.* to make enquiry.
31:2, the son of my *v.*
Eccl. 5:4, when thou vowest a *v.*, defer not to pay.
Isa. 19:21, they shall vow a *v.* unto the Lord.
Jonah 1:16, feared the Lord, and made *v.*
Acts 18;18, shorn his head, for he had a *v.*
21:23, four men which have a *v.* on them.
See 2Sam. 15:7; Jer. 44:25; Nah. 1:15.
VOW (*v.*). Dt. 23:22, if forbear to *v.*, no sin.
Ps. 76:11, *v.* and pay to the Lord your God.
132:3, and *v.* to the mighty God.
See Num. 21:2; Eccl. 5:5; Jonah 2:9.
VULTURE. Lev. 11:14; Dt. 14:13, and the *v.* after his kind.
Job 28:7, which the *v.* eye hath not seen.
Isa. 34:15, there shall the *v.* be.
WAG. Jer. 18:16; Lam. 2:15; Zeph. 2:15.
WAGES. Gen. 29:15, what shall thy *w.* be?
Gen. 30:28, appoint me thy *w.*
31:7, changed my *w.* ten times.
Ex. 2:9, nurse this child, I will give *w.*
Jer. 33:13, useth neighbour's service without *w.*
Hag. 1:6, earneth *w.* to put in bag with holes.
Lk. 3:14, be content with your *w.*
Jn. 4:36, he that reapeth receiveth *w.*
Rom. 6:23, the *w.* of sin is death.
2Pet. 2:15, the *w.* of unrighteousness.
See Ezek. 29:18; Mal. 3:5; 2Cor. 11:8.
WAGONS. Gen. 45:19; Num. 7:7; Ezek. 23:24.
WAIL. Ezek. 32:18, *w.* for the multitude.
Amos 5:16, *w.* shall be in all streets.
Mic. 1:8, therefore I will *w.* and howl.
Mt. 13:42, there shall be *w.* and gnashing.
Mk. 5:38, he seeth them that *w.* greatly.
Rev. 1:7, all kindreds of the earth shall *w.*
18:15, the merchants shall stand afar off *w.*
See Est. 4:3; Jer. 9:10, 19, 20; Ezek. 7:11.
WAIT. Gen. 49:18, I have *w.* for thy salvation.
Num. 35:20; Jer. 9:8, by laying of *w.*
2Ki. 6:33, should I *w.* for the Lord any longer?
Job 14:14, I will *w.* till my change come.
15:22, he is *w.* for of the sword.
17:13, if I *w.*, the grave is my house.
29:21, to me men *w.*, and kept silence.
23, they *w.* for me as for rain.
30:26, when I *w.* for light, darkness came.
Ps. 25:3; 69:6, let none that *w.* be ashamed.
27:14; 37:34; Prov. 20:22, *w.* on the Lord.
33:20, our soul *w.* for the Lord.
37:7, *w.* patiently.
52:9, I will *w.* on thy name.
62:1; 130:6, my soul *w.* upon God.
5, *w.* only on God.
65:1, praise *w.* for thee in Zion.
69:3, mine eyes fail while I *w.* for God.
104:27, these all *w.* upon thee.
106:13, they *w.* not for counsel.
123:2, so our eyes *w.* on the Lord.
Prov. 27:18, he that *w.* on his master.
Isa. 30:18, the Lord *w.* to be gracious.
40:31, they that *w.* on the Lord shall renew.
42:4, the isles shall *w.* for his law.
59:9, we *w.* for light.
64:4, prepared for him that *w.* for him.
Lam. 3:26, good that a man hope and quietly *w.*
Dan. 12:12, blessed is he that *w.*, and cometh to the days.
Hab. 2:3, though the vision tarry, *w.* for it.
Zech. 11:11, poor of the flock that *w.* upon me.
Mk. 15:43, who also *w.* for the kingdom of God.
Lk. 2:25, *w.* for the consolation of Israel.
12:36, like unto men that *w.* for their lord.
Acts 1:4, but *w.* for promise of the Father.
Rom. 8:23, groan, *w.* for the adoption.
25, then do we with patience *w.* for it.
12:7, let us *w.* on our ministering.
1Cor. 9:13, they which *w.* at the altar are partakers.
Gal. 5:5, we *w.* for the hope.
1Th. 1:10, to *w.* for his Son from heaven.
See Num. 3:10; Neh. 12:44; Isa. 8:17.
WAKE. Ps. 139:18, when I *w.* I am still with thee.
Jer. 51:39, sleep a perpetual sleep, and not *w.*
Joel 3:9, prepare war, *w.* up the mighty men.
Zech. 4:1, the angel came again, and *w.* me.
1Th. 5:10, whether we *w.* or sleep.
See Ps. 77:4; 127:1; Song 5:2; Isa. 50:4.
WALK. Gen. 17:1, *w.* before me, and be perfect.
24:40, the Lord before whom I *w.*
48:15, before whom my fathers did *w.*
Ex. 16:4, whether they will *w.* in my law.
18:20, the way wherein they must *w.*
Lev. 26:12, I will *w.* among you.
Dt. 23:14, God *w.* in midst of the camp.
Jud. 5:10, speak, ye that *w.* by the way.

2Sam. 2:29, Abner and his men *w.* all that night.
Job 18:8, he *w.* on a snare.
Job 22:14, he *w.* in the circuit of heaven.
29:3, when by his light I *w.* through darkness.
Ps. 23:4, though I *w.* through the valley of the shadow of death.
26:11, as for me, I will *w.* in mine integrity.
48:12, *w.* about Zion, and go round about her.
55:14, we *w.* to house of God in company.
56:13, that I may *w.* before God in the light of the living.
84:11, from them that *w.* uprightly.
91:6, the pestilence that *w.* in darkness.
104:3, who *w.* upon wings of the wind.
116:9, I will *w.* before the Lord.
119:45, I will *w.* at liberty.
138:7, though I *w.* in the midst of trouble.
Prov. 10:9; 28:18, he that *w.* uprightly *w.* surely.
13:20, he that *w.* with wise men shall be wise.
19:1; 28:6, better is the poor that *w.* in integrity.
28:26, whoso *w.* wisely shall be delivered.
Eccl. 2:14, the fool *w.* in darkness.
Isa. 2:5, let us *w.* in the light of the Lord.
9:2, the people that *w.* in darkness.
20:3, as my servant hath *w.* naked and barefoot.
30:21, a voice saying, this is the way, *w.* in it.
35:9, the redeemed shall *w.* there.
50:10, that *w.* in darkness, and hath no light.
11, *w.* in the light of your fire.
Jer. 6:16, ask where is the good way, and *w.* therein.
10:23, it is not in man that *w.* to direct his steps.
Ezek. 28:14, hast *w.* in midst of stones of fire.
Dan. 4:37, those that *w.* in pride.
Hos. 14:9, the just shall *w.* in them.
Amos 3:3, can two *w.* together?
Mic. 6:8, to *w.* humbly with thy God.
Nah. 2:11, where the lion *w.*
Zech. 1:11, we have *w.* to and fro through the earth.
Mal. 3:14, what profit that we have *w.* mournfully?
Mt. 9:5; Mk. 2:9; Lk. 5:23; Jn. 5:8, 11, 12; Acts 3:6, arise, and *w.*
12:43; Lk. 11:24, *w.* through dry places.
14:29, he *w.* on the water.
Mk. 16:12, he appeared to two of them, as they *w.*
Lk. 13:33, I must *w.* to day and to morrow.
Jn. 8:12, shall not *w.* in darkness.
11:9, if any man *w.* in the day.
Rom. 4:12, who *w.* in steps of that faith.
6:4, *w.* in newness of life.
8:1, who *w.* not after the flesh, but after the Spirit.
2Cor. 5:7, we *w.* by faith.
Gal. 6:16, as many as *w.* according to this rule.
Eph. 2:2; Col. 3:7, in time past ye *w.*
10, ordained that we should *w.* in them.
4:1, *w.* worthy of the vocation.
17, that ye *w.* not as other Gentiles.
5:15, *w.* circumspectly.
Phil. 3:17, mark them which *w.*
18, many *w.*, of whom I told you.
Col. 1:10; 1Th. 2:12, that ye might *w.* worthy of the Lord.
1Th. 4:1, how ye ought to *w.*
12, ye may *w.* honestly.
2Th. 3:6, from every brother that *w.* disorderly.
1Pet. 4:3, when we *w.* in lasciviousness.
5:8, *w.* about, seeking whom he may devour.
1Jn. 1:7, if we *w.* in the light.
2:6, to *w.*, even as he *w.*
See Gal. 5:16; Eph. 5:2; Phil. 3:16.

WALKING. Dt. 2:7, the Lord knoweth thy *w.*
Job 31:26, the moon *w.* in brightness.
Dan. 3:25, four men loose, *w.* in the fire.
Mt. 14:25, Jesus went to them, *w.* on the sea.
Mk. 8:24, I see men as trees, *w.*
Acts 9:31, *w.* in the fear of the Lord.
See Isa. 3:16; 2Cor. 4:2; 2Pet. 3:3; Jude 16.

WALL. Gen. 49:22, branches run over the *w.*
Ex. 14:22, the waters were a *w.* to them.
Num. 22:24, a *w.* being on this side, a *w.* on that.
2Sam. 22:30; Ps. 18:29, have I leaped over a *w.*
2Ki. 20:2; Isa. 36:11, turned his face to the *w.*
Ezra 5:3, who commanded you to make this *w.*?
Neh. 4:6, so built we the *w.*
Ps. 62:3, a bowing *w.* shall ye be.
122:7, peace be within thy *w.*
Prov. 24:31, the *w.* thereof was broken down.
25:28, like a city without *w.*
Isa. 26:1, salvation will God appoint for *w.*
59:10, we grope for the *w.*
60:18, thou shalt call thy *w.* Salvation.
Ezek. 8:7, a hole in the *w.*
Dan. 5:5, fingers wrote on the *w.*
Amos 5:19, leaned hand on *w.*, and serpent bit him.
Hab. 2:11, the stone shall cry out of the *w.*
Acts 23:3, thou whited *w.*
Eph. 2:14, the middle *w.* of partition.
See Ezek. 38:11; Zech. 2:4; Acts 9:25; Rev. 21:14.

WALLOW. Jer. 6:26; 25:34, *w.* in ashes.
2Pet. 2:22, washed, to her *w.* in the mire.
See 2Sam. 20:12; Ezek. 27:30.

WANDER. Num. 14:33, your children shall *w.*
Dt. 27:18, cursed by he that maketh blind to *w.*
Job 12:24, he causeth them to *w.*
15:23, he w. abroad for bread.
38:41, young ravens *w.* for lack of meat.
Ps. 55:7, then would I *w.* far off.
59:15, let them *w.* up and down.
119:10, let me not *w.* from thy commandments.
Prov. 27:8, as a bird that *w.* from nest.
Isa. 16:3, bewray not him that *w.*
47:15, *w.* every one to his quarter.
Jer. 14:10, thus have they loved to *w.*
Lam. 4:14, they have *w.* as blind men.
Ezek. 34:6, my sheep *w.* through mountains.
Amos 4:8, two cities *w.* to one city to drink.
See Hos. 9:17; 1Tim. 5:13; Heb. 11:37; Jude 13.

WANT (*n.*). Dt. 28:48, thou shalt serve in *w.*
Jud. 18:10, a place where there is no *w.*
19:20, let all thy *w.* lie on me.
Job 24:8, they embrace the rock for *w.*
31:19, if I have seen any perish for *w.*
Ps. 34:9, there is no *w.* to them that fear him.
Amos 4:6, I have given you *w.* of bread.
Mk. 12:44, she of her *w.* cast in all.
Lk. 15:14, he began to be in *w.*
Phil. 2:25, that ministered to my *w.*
See Prov. 6:11; Lam. 4:9; 2Cor. 8:14; Phil. 4:11.
WANT (*v.*). Ps. 23:1, I shall not *w.*
34:10, shall not *w.* any good thing.
Prov. 9:4, for him that *w.* understanding.
10:19, in multitude of words there *w.* not sin.
13:25, the belly of the wicked shall *w.*
Eccl. 6:2, he *w.* nothing for his soul.
Isa. 34:16, none shall *w.* her mate.
Jer. 44:18, we have *w.* all things.
Ezek. 4:17, that they may *w.* bread and water.
Jn. 2:3, when they *w.* vine.
2Cor. 11:9, when I *w.* I was chargeble to no man.
See Eccl. 1:15; Dan. 5:27; Ti. 1:5; Jas. 1:4.
WANTON. Isa. 3:16; Rom. 13:13; 1Tim. 5:11; Jas. 5:5.
WAR (*n.*). Ex. 32:17, there is a noise of *w.*
Num. 32:6, shall your brethren go to *w.*, and shall ye sit here?
Dt. 24:5, taken a wife, he shall not go out to *w.*
Jud. 5:8, then was *w.* in the gates.
1Chr. 5:22, many slain, because the *w.* was of God.
Job 10:17, changes and *w.* are against me.
38:23, reserved against the day of *w.*
Ps. 27:3, though *w.* should rise against me.
46:9, he maketh *w.* to cease.
55:21, *w.* was in his heart.
68:30, scatter the people that delight in *w.*
Prov. 20:18, with good advice make *w.*
Eccl. 3:8, a time of *w.*
8:8, no discharge in that *w.*
Isa. 2:4; Mic. 4:3, nor learn *w.* any more.
Jer. 42:14, to Egypt, where we shall see no *w.*
Mic. 2:8, as men averse from *w.*
Mt. 24:6; Mk. 13:7; Lk. 21:9, *w.* and rumours of *w.*
Lk. 14:31, what king, going to make *w.*?
Jas. 4:1, from whence come *w.*?
Rev. 12:7, there was *w.* in heaven.
See Eccl. 9:18; Ezek. 32:27; Dan. 7:21; 9:26.
WAR (*v.*). 2Sam. 22:35; Ps. 18:34; 144:1, teacheth my hands to *w.*
2Chr. 6:34, if thy people go to *w.*
Isa. 41:12, they that *w.* against thee.
2Cor. 10:3, we do not *w.* after the flesh.
1Tim. 1:18, *w.* a good warfare.
2Tim. 2:4, no man that *w.* entangleth himself.
Jas. 4:1, lusts that *w.* in your members.
2, ye fight and *w.*, yet ye have not.
1Pet. 2:11, from lusts which *w.* against the soul.
See 1Ki. 14:19; Isa. 37:8 Rom. 7:23.
WARDROBE. 2Ki. 22:14; 2Chr. 34:22.
WARE. Mt. 24:50; Lk. 8:27; 2Tim. 4:15.
WARFARE. Isa. 40:2, that her *w.* is accomplished.
2Cor. 10:4, weapons of our *w.* are not carnal.
See 1Sam. 28:1; 1Cor. 9:7; 1Tim. 1:18.
WARM. Eccl. 4:11, how can one be *w.* alone?
Isa. 47:14, there shall not be a coal to *w.* at.
Hag. 1:6, ye clothe you, but there is none *w.*
Mk. 14:54; Jn. 18:18, Peter *w.* himself.
Jas. 2:16, be ye *w.* and filled.
See 2Ki. 4:34; Job 37:17; 39:14; Isa. 44:15.
WARN. Ezek. 3:18; Acts 20:31; 1Th. 5:14.
WASH. 2Ki. 5:10, go, *w.* in Jordan.
12, may I not *w.* in them, and be clean?
Job 9:30, if I *w.* myself with snow water.
14:19, thou *w.* away things which grow.
29:6, when I *w.* my steps with butter.
Ps. 26:6; 73:13, I will *w.* my hands in innocency.
51:2, *w.* me throughly from mine iniquity.
7, *w.* me, and I shall be whiter than snow.
Prov. 30:12, a generation not *w.*
Song 5:12, his eyes are *w.* with milk.
Isa. 1:16, *w.* you, make you clean.
Jer. 2:22, though thou *w.* thee with nitre.
4:14, *w.* thy heart.
Ezek. 16:4, nor wast *w.* in water to supple thee.
Mt. 6:17, when thou fastest, *w.* thy face.
27:24, took water, and *w.* his hands.
Mk. 7:3, except they *w.* oft, eat not.
Lk. 7:38, began to *w.* his feet with tears.
44, she hath *w.* my feet with her tears.
Jn. 9:7, go, *w.* in the pool of Siloam.
Acts 16:33, he *w.* their stripes.
22:16, *w.* away thy sins.
1Cor. 6:11, but ye are *w.*
Heb. 10:22, having our bodies *w.* with pure water.
2Pet. 2:22, the sow that was *w.*
Rev. 1:5, that *w.* us from our sins.
7:14, have *w.* their robes.
See Neh. 4:23; Eph. 5:26; Ti. 3:5; Heb. 9:10.
WASTE. Dt. 32:10; Job 30:3, in *w.* wilderness.
1Ki. 17:14, the barrel of meal shall not *w.*
Ps. 80:13, the boar out of the wood doth *w.* it.
91:6, nor for the destruction that *w.* at noonday.
Isa. 24:1, the Lord maketh the earth *w.*
61:4, they shall build the old *w.*
Joel 1:10, the field is *w.*, the corn is *w.*
See Prov. 18:9; Is. 59:7; Mt. 26:8; Mk. 14:4.
WATCH (*n.*). Ps. 90:4, as a *w.* in the night.
119:148, mine eyes prevent the night *w.*
Jer. 51:12, make the *w.* strong.
Hab. 2:1, I will stand upon my *w.*
See Mt. 14:25; 24:43; 27:65; Lk. 2:8.
WATCH (*v.*). Gen. 31:49, the Lord *w.* between me and thee.
Job 14:16, doest thou not *w.* over my sin?
Ps. 37:32, the wicked *w.* the righteous.
102:7, I *w.* and am as a sparrow.
130:6, more than they that *w.* for morning.
Isa. 29:20, all that *w.* for iniquity are cut off.
Jer. 20:10, my familiars *w.* for my halting.
31:28, so will I *w.* over them, to build.
Jer. 44:27, I will *w.* over them for evil.

Ezek. 7:6, the end is come, it *w.* for thee.
Hab. 2:1, I will *w.* to see what he will say.
Mt. 24:42; 25:13; Mk. 13:35; Lk. 21:36; Acts 20:31, *w.* therefore.
26:41; Mk. 13:33; 14:38, *w.* and pray.
1Th. 5:6; 1Pet. 4:7, let us *w.* and be sober.
Heb. 13:17, for they *w.* for your souls.
See 1Cor. 16:13; 2Tim. 4:5; Rev. 3:2; 16:15.
WATCH TOWER. 2Chr. 20:24; Judah came toward the *w.*
Isa. 21:5, watch in the *w.*
WATER (*n.*). Gen. 26:20, the *w.* is ours.
49:4, unstable as *w.*
Dt. 8:7, a land of brooks of *w.*
11:11, the land drinketh *w.* of rain of heaven.
Josh. 7:5, their hearts melted, and became as *w.*
2Sam. 14:14, as *w.* spilt on the ground.
1Ki. 13:22, eat no bread, and drink no *w.*
22:27; 2Chr. 18:26, *w.* of affliction.
2Ki. 3:11, who poured *w.* on Elijah's hands.
20:20, brought *w.* into the city.
Neh. 9:11, threwest as a stone into mighty *w.*
Job 8:11, can the flag grow without *w.*?
14:9, through the scent of *w.* it will bud.
19, the *w.* wear the stones.
15:16, who drinketh iniquity like *w.*
22:7, thou hast not given *w.* to weary to drink.
26:8, he bindeth up the *w.* in his thick clouds.
38:30, the *w.* are hid as with a stone.
Ps. 22:14, I am poured out like *w.*
23:2, beside the still *w.*
33:7, he gathereth the *w.* of the sea.
46:3, though the *w.* roar and be troubled.
63:1, a dry and thirsty land, where no *w.* is.
73:10, *w.* of a full cup are wrung out to them.
77:16, the *w.* saw thee.
79:3, their blood have they shed like *w.*
124:4, then the *w.* had overwhelmed us.
148:4, praise him, ye *w.* above the heavens.
Prov. 5:15, drink *w.* out of thine own cistern.
9:17, stolen *w.* are sweet.
20:5, counsel is like deep *w.*
25:25, as cold *w.* to a thirsty soul.
27:19, as in *w.* face answereth to face.
30:4, who hath bound the *w.* in a garment?
Eccl. 11:1, cast thy bread upon the *w.*
Song 4:15; Jn. 7:38, well of living *w.*
8:7, many *w.* cannot quench love.
Isa. 1:22, thy wine is mixed with *w.*
3:1, take away the whole stay of *w.*
11:9; Hab. 2:14, as the *w.* cover the seas.
19:5, the *w.* shall fail from the sea.
28:17, *w.* shall overflow the hiding place.
32:20, blessed are ye that sow beside all *w.*
33:16, his *w.* shall be sure.
35:6, in the wilderness shall *w.* break out.
41:17, when the poor seek *w.*
43:2, when thou passest through the *w.*
16, a path in the mighty *w.*
20, I give *w.* in the wilderness.
44:3, I will pour *w.* on him that is thirsty.
55:1, come ye to the *w.*
57:20, whose *w.* cast up mire and dirt.
Jer. 2:13; 17:13, the fountain of living *w.*
9:1, Oh that my head were *w.*!
14:3, their nobles sent little ones to the *w.*
47:2, behold, *w.* rise up out of the north.
Ezek. 4:17, that they may want bread and *w.*
7:17; 21:7, be weak as *w.*
31:4, the *w.* made him great.
36:25, then will I sprinkle clean *w.* upon you.
Amos 8:11, not famine of bread nor thirst for *w.*
Mt. 3:11; Mk. 1:8; Lk. 3:16; Jn. 1:26; Acts 1:5; 11:16, baptize you with *w.*
10:42; Mk. 9:41, whoso giveth a cup of cold *w.*
14:28, bid me come to thee on the *w.*
27:24, Pilate took *w.*, and washed.
Lk. 8:23, ship filled with *w.*
24, and rebuked the raging of the *w.*
16:24, dip the tip of his finger in *w.*
Jn. 3:5, except a man be born of *w.*
23, there was much *w.* there.
4:15, give me this *w.*
5:3, waiting for moving of the *w.*
19:34, forthwith came out blood and *w.*
Acts 10:47, can any forbid *w.*?
2Cor. 11:26, in perils of *w.*
Eph. 5:26, cleanse it with washing of *w.*
1Pet. 3:20, eight souls were saved by *w.*
2Pet. 2:17, wells without *w.*
1Jn. 5:6, this is he that came by *w.*
Rev. 22:17, let him take the *w.* of life freely.
See Ps. 29:3; Jer. 51:13; Ezek. 32:2; 47:1.
WATER (*v.*). Gen. 2:6, mist that *w.* face of ground.
13:10, plain was well *w.*
Dt. 11:10, *w.* it with thy foot, as a garden.
Ps. 6:6, I *w.* my couch with tears.
72:6, as showers that *w.* the earth.
104:13, he *w.* the hills from his chambers.
Prov. 11:25, he that *w.*, shall be *w.*
Isa. 16:9, I will *w.* thee with my tears.
27:3, I will *w.* it every moment.
55:10, returneth not, but *w.* the earth.
58:11; Jer. 31:12, thou shalt be like a *w.* garden.
Ezek. 32:6, I will also *w.* with thy blood.
1Cor. 3:6, Apollos *w.*, but God gave the increase.
See Ps. 65:9; Ezek. 17:7; Joel 3:18.
WAVERING. Heb. 10:23, the profession of our faith without *w.*
Jas. 1:5, ask in faith, nothing *w.*
WAVES. Ps. 42:7, all thy *w.* are gone over me.
65:7; 89:9; 107:29, stilleth noise of *w.*
93:4, the Lord is mightier than mighty *w.*
Isa. 48:18, thy righteousness as the *w.* of the sea.
Jer. 5:22, though the *w.* toss.
Zech. 10:11, shall smite the *w.* in the sea.
Jude 13, raging *w.* of the sea.
See Mt. 8:24; 14:24; Mk. 4:37; Acts 27:41.
WAX (*n.*). Ps. 22:14; 68:2; 97:5; Mic. 1:4.
WAX (*v.*). Ex. 22:24; 32:10, my wrath shall *w.* hot.
Num. 11:23, is the Lord's hand *w.* short?
Dt. 8:4; 29:5; Neh. 9:21, raiment *w.* not old.
32:15, Jeshurun *w.* fat, and kicked.

Ps. 102:26; Isa. 50:9; 51:6; Heb. 1:11, shall *w.* old as doth a garment.
Mt. 24:12, the love of many shall *w.* cold.
Lk. 12:33, bags which *w.* not old.
See Mt. 13:15; 1Tim. 5:11; 2Tim. 3:13.

WAY. Gen. 6:12, all flesh had corrupted his *w.*
28:20, if God will keep me in this *w.*
56, seeing the Lord hath prospered my *w.*
Num. 22:32, thy *w.* is perverse.
Dt. 8:6; 26:17; 28:9; 30:16; 1Ki. 2:3; Ps. 119:3; 128:1; Isa. 42:24, walk in his *w.*
Josh 23:14; 1Ki. 2:2, the *w.* of all the earth.
1Sam. 12:23, teach you the good and right *w.*
2Sam. 22:31; Ps. 18:30, as for God, his *w.* is perfect.
2Ki. 7:15, all the *w.* was full of garments.
2Chr. 6:27, when thou hast taught them the good *w.*
Ezra 8:21, to seek of him a right *w.*
Job 3:23, to a man whose *w.* is hid.
12:24; Ps. 107:40, to wander where there is no *w.*
16:22, I go the *w.* whence I shall not return.
19:8, fenced up my *w.*
22:15, hast thou marked the old *w.*?
23:10, he knoweth the *w.* that I take.
24:13, they know not the *w.* of the light.
31:4, doth not he see my *w.*?
38:19, where is the *w.* where light dwelleth?
Ps. 1:6, the Lord knoweth the *w.* of righteous.
2:12, lest ye perish from the *w.*
25:9, the meek will he teach his *w.*
27:11; 86:11, teach me thy *w.*
36:4, in a *w.* that is not good.
Ps. 37:5, commit thy *w.* unto the Lord.
39:1, I will take heed to my *w.*
49:13, this their *w.* is their folly.
67:2, that thy *w.* may be known.
78:50, he made a *w.* to his anger.
95:10; Heb. 3:10, they have not known my *w.*
101:2, behave wisely in a perfect *w.*
119:5, O that my *w.* were directed.
30, I have chosen the *w.* of truth.
59, I thought on my *w.*
168, all my *w.* are before thee.
139:24, lead me in the *w.* everlasting.
Prov. 2:8, he preserveth the *w.* of his saints.
3:6, in all thy *w.* acknowledge him.
17, her *w.* are *w.* of pleasantness.
5:21, the *w.* of man are before the Lord.
6:6, consider her *w.*, and be wise.
23; 15:24; Jer. 21:8, the *w.* of life.
12:15, the *w.* of a fool is right in his own eyes.
15:19, the *w.* of the slothful man.
16:7, when a man's *w.* please the Lord.
22:6, train up a child in the *w.*
23:19, guide thy heart in the *w.*
26, let thine eyes observe my *w.*
26:13, there is a lion in the *w.*
Eccl. 11:5, the *w.* of the spirit.
12:5, fears shall be in the *w.*
Isa. 2:3; Mic. 4:2, he will teach us of his *w.*
30:21, this is the *w.*, walk ye in it.
35:8, and a *w.*, called the *w.* of holiness.
40:27, my *w.* is hid from the Lord.
42:16, the blind by a *w.* they knew not.
24, they would not walk in his *w.*
45:13, I will direct all his *w.*
55:8, neither are your *w.* my *w.*
58:2, they delight to know my *w.*
Jer. 6:16, where is the good *w.*?
17:10; 32:19, every man according to his *w.*
18:11, make your *w.* and doings good.
32:39, I will give them one heart and one *w.*
50:5, they shall ask the *w.* to Zion.
Ezek. 3:18, to warn the wicked from his *w.*
18:29, are not my *w.* equal? are not your *w.* unequal?
Joel 2:7, march every one on his *w.*
Nah. 1:3, the Lord hath his *w.* in the whirlwind.
Hag. 1:5, consider your *w.*
Mal. 3:1, he shall prepare the *w.* before me.
Mt. 7:13, broad is the *w.* that leadeth.
10:5, go not into *w.* of Gentiles.
22:16; Mk. 12:14; Lk. 20:21, teachest the *w.* of God.
Mk. 8:3, they will faint by the *w.*
11:8; Mt. 21:8; Lk. 19:36, spread garments in the *w.*
Lk. 15:20, when he was yet a great *w.* off.
19:4, he was to pass that *w.*
Jn. 10:1, but climbeth up some other *w.*
14:4, and the *w.* ye know.
6, I am the *w.*, the truth, and the life.
Acts 9:2, if he found any of this *w.*
27, how he had seen the Lord in the *w.*
16:17, which show unto us the *w.* of salvation
18:26, expounded the *w.* of God more perfectly.
19:23, no small stir about that *w.*
24:14, after the *w.* which they call heresy.
Rom. 3:12, they are all gone out of the *w.*
11:33, his *w.* are past finding out.
1Cor. 10:13, will make a *w.* to escape.
12:31, a more excellent *w.*
Col. 2:14, took handwriting of ordinances out of the *w.*
Heb. 5:2, compassion of them out of the *w.*
9:8, the *w.* into the holiest.
10:20, by a new and living *w.*
Jas. 1:8, unstable in all his *w.*
5:20, the sinner from error of his *w.*
2Pet. 2:2, many shall follow their pernicious *w.*
15, which have forsaken the right *w.*
21, better not to have known *w.* of righteousness.
Jude 11, they have gone in the *w.* of Cain.
See Hos. 2:6; Lk. 10:31; Rev. 15:3.

WEAK. Jud. 16:7, *w.* as other men.
2Sam. 3:1, Saul's house waxed *w.* and *w.*
2Chr. 15:7, let not your hands be *w.*
Job 4:3, thou hast strengthened the *w.* hands.
Ps. 6:2, I am *w.*
Isa. 14:10, art thou also become *w.* as we?
35:3, strengthen ye the *w.* hands.
Ezek. 7:17; 21:7, shall be *w.* as water.

16:30, how *w.* is thy heart!
Joel 3:10, let the *w.* say, I am strong.
Mt. 26:41; Mk. 14:38, but the flesh is *w.*
Acts 20:35, ye ought to support the *w.*
Rom. 4:19, being not *w.* in faith.
8:3, for the law was *w.*
1Cor. 1:27, *w.* things to confound the mighty.
11:30, for this cause many are *w.*
2Cor. 10:10, his bodily presence is *w.*
11:29, who is *w.*, and I am not *w.*?
12:10, when I am *w.*, then am I strong.
Gal. 4:9, turn again to *w.* elements.
1Pet. 3:7, giving honour to the wife, as *w.* vessel.
See Job 12:21; Jer. 38:4; Rom. 15:1; 1Th. 5:14.
WEAKNESS. 1Cor. 1:25, the *w.* of God.
2:3, I was with you in *w.*
15:43, it is sown in *w.*, raised in power.
See 2Cor. 12:9; 13:4; Heb. 7:18; 11:34.
WEALTH. Dt. 8:18, Lord giveth power to get *w.*
1Sam. 2:32, thou shalt see an enemy in all the *w.*
2Chr. 1:11, thou hast not asked *w.*
Est. 10:3, seeking the *w.* of his people.
Job 21:13, they spend their days in *w.*
31:25, if I rejoiced because my *w.* was great.
Ps. 44:12, dost not increase *w.* by price.
49:6, they that trust in *w.*
49:10, wise men die, and leave *w.* to others.
112:3, *w.* and riches shall be in his house.
Prov. 5:10, lest strangers be filled with thy *w.*
10:15; 18:11, the rich man's *w.* is his strong city.
13:11, *w.* gotten by vanity.
19:4, *w.* maketh many friends.
Acts 19:25, by this craft we have our *w.*
1Cor. 10:24, seek every man another's *w.*
See Dt. 8:17; Ruth 2:1; Ezra 9:12; Zech. 14:14.
WEALTHY. Ps. 66:12; Jer. 49:31.
WEANED. 1Sam. 1:22; Ps. 131:2; Isa. 11:8; 28:9.
WEAPON. Neh. 4:17, with the other hand held a *w.*
Isa. 13:5; Jer. 50:25, the *w.* of his indignation.
54:17, no *w.* formed against thee shall prosper.
Jer. 22:7, every one with his *w.*
Ezek. 9:1, with destroying *w.* in his hand.
2Cor. 10:4, the *w.* of our warfare.
See Job 20:24; Ezek. 39:9; Jn. 18:3.
WEAR. Job 14:19, the waters *w.* the stones.
Isa. 4:1, we will *w.* our own apparel.
Zech. 13:4, nor shall they *w.* a rough garment.
Mt. 11:8, that *w.* soft clothing.
See Dt. 22:5; Est. 6:8; Lk. 9:12; 1Pet. 3:3.
WEARINESS. Eccl. 12:12; Mal. 1:13; 2Cor. 11:27.
WEARY. Gen. 27:46, I am *w.* of my life.
2Sam. 23:10, he smote till his hand was *w.*
Job 3:17, and the *w.* be at rest.
10:1, my soul is *w.*
16:7, now he hath made me *w.*
22:7, thou hast not given water to the *w.*
Ps. 6:6, I am *w.* with groaning.
Prov. 3:11, be not *w.* of the Lord's correction.
25:17, lest he be *w.* of thee.
Isa. 5:27, none shall be *w.* among them.
7:13, will ye *w.* my God also?
28:12, cause the *w.* to rest.
32:2, as the shadow of a great rock in *w.* land.
40:28, God fainteth not, neither is *w.*
31, they shall run, and not be *w.*
43:22, thou hast been *w.* of me.
46:1, a burden to the *w.* beast.
50:4, a word in season to him that is *w.*
Jer. 6:11, I am *w.* with holding in.
15:6, I am *w.* with repenting.
20:9, I was *w.* with forbearing.
31:25, I have satiated the *w.* soul.
Lk. 18:5, lest she *w.* me.
Gal. 6:9; 2Th. 3:13, be not *w.* in well doing.
See Jud. 4:21; Ps. 68:9; 69:3; Hab. 2:13.
WEARY (*v.*). Isa. 43:24, thou hast *w.* me.
47:13, *w.* in the multitude of counsels.
57:10, *w.* in the greatness of thy way.
Jer. 12:5, with footmen, and they *w.* thee.
Ezek. 24:12, she hat *w.* herself with lies.
Mic. 6:3, wherein have I *w.* thee?
Jn. 4:6, being *w.*, sat thus on the well.
Heb. 12:3, lest ye be *w.* and faint.
See Eccl. 10:10; Jer. 4:31; Mal. 2:17.
WEASEL. Lev. 11:29.
WEATHER. Job 37:22; Prov. 25:20; Mt. 16:2.
WEB. Jud. 16:13; Job 8:14; Isa. 59:5.
WEDGE. Josh. 7:21; Isa. 13:12.
WEEK. Gen. 29:27, fulfil her *w.*
Jer. 5:24, the appointed *w.* of harvest.
Dan. 9:27, in the midst of the *w.*
Mt. 28:1; Mk. 16:2, 9; Lk. 24:1; Jn. 20:1, 19; Acts 20:7; 1Cor. 16:2, the first day of the *w.*
See Num. 28:26; Dan. 10:2; Lk. 18:12.
WEEP. Gen. 43:30, he sought where to *w.*
1Sam. 1:8; Jn. 20:13, why *w.* thou?
11:5, what aileth the people that they *w.*?
30:4, no more power to *w.*
Neh. 8:9, mourn not, nor *w.*
Job 27:15, his widows shall not *w.*
30:25, did not I *w.* for him that was in trouble?
Eccl. 3:4, a time to *w.*
Isa. 15:2, he is gone up to *w.*
22:4, I will *w.* bitterly.
30:19, thou shalt *w.* no more.
Jer. 9:1, that I might *w.* day and night.
22:10, *w.* ye not for the dead.
Joel 1:5, awake, ye drunkards, and *w.*
Mk. 5:39, why make ye this ado, and *w.*?
Lk. 6:21, blessed are ye that *w.* now.
7:13; 8:52; Rev. 5:5, *w.* not.
23:28, *w.* not for me, but *w.* for yourselves.
Jn. 11:31, she goeth to the grave to *w.* there.
Acts 21:13, what mean ye to *w.*?
Rom. 12:15, and *w.* with them that *w.*
See Jn. 16:20; 1Cor. 7:30; Jas. 4:9; 5:1.
WEEPING. 2Sam. 15:30, *w.* as they went.
Ezra 3:13, could not discern noise of joy from *w.*
Job 16:16, my face is foul with *w.*
Ps. 6:8, the Lord hath heard the voice of my *w.*
30:5, *w.* may endure for a night.
102:9, I have mingled my drink with *w.*
Isa. 65:19, the voice of *w.* be no more heard.

Jer. 31:16, refrain thy voice from *w.*
48:5, continual *w.* shall go up.
Joel 2:12, turn to me with fasting and *w.*
Mt. 8:12; 22:13; 24:51; 25:30; Lk. 13:28, *w.* and gnashing of teeth.
Lk. 7:38, stood at his feet behind him *w.*
Jn. 11:33, when Jesus saw her *w.*
20:11, Mary stood without at sepulchre *w.*
Phil. 3:18, now tell you even *w.*
See Num. 25:6; Jer. 31:15; Mal. 2:13; Mt. 2:18; Acts 9:39.

WEIGH. 2Sam. 14:26, *w.* the hair of his head.
Job 6:2, oh that my grief were *w.*!
31:6, let me be *w.* in an even balance.
Isa. 26:7, thou dost *w.* the path of the just.
40:12, who hath *w.* the mountains?
Dan. 5:27, thou art *w.* in the balances.
See Job 28:25; Prov. 16:2; Zech. 11:12.

WEIGHT. Lev. 26:26, deliver your bread by *w.*
Job 28:25, to make the *w.* for the winds.
Ezek. 4:10, thy meat shall be by *w.*
16, they shall eat bread by *w.*
2Cor. 4:17, a more exceeding *w.* of glory.
Heb. 12:1, lay aside every *w.*
See Dt. 25:13; Prov. 16:11; Mic. 6:11.

WEIGHTY. Prov. 27:3; Mt. 23:23; 2Cor. 10:10.

WELFARE. Neh. 2:10, to seek *w.* of Israel.
Job 30:15, my *w.* passeth away.
Ps. 69:22, which should have been for their *w.*
Jer. 38:4, seeketh not the *w.* of this people.
See Gen. 43:27; Ex. 18:7; 1Chr. 18:10.

WELL (*n.*). Num. 21:17, spring up, O *w.*
Dt. 6:11, and *w.* which thou diggedst not.
2Sam. 23:15; 1Chr. 11:17, water of the *w.* of Bethlehem.
Ps. 84:6, through valley of Baca make it a *w.*
Prov. 5:15, waters out of thine own *w.*
10:11, a *w.* of life.
Song 4:15; Jn. 4:14, *w.* of living waters.
Isa. 12:3, the *w.* of salvation.
Jn. 4:6, sat thus on the *w.*
2Pet. 2:17, *w.* without water.
See Gen. 21:19; 49:22; 2Sam. 17:18.

WELL (*adv.*). Gen. 4:7, if thou doest *w.*
12:13, *w.* with me for thy sake.
29:6, is he *w.*? and they said, he is *w.*
40:14, think on me when it shall be *w.* with thee.
Ex. 4:14, I know he can speak *w.*
Num. 11:18, it was *w.* with us in Egypt.
Dt. 4:40; 5:16; 6:3; 12:25; 19:13; 22:7; Ruth 3:1; Eph. 6:3, that it may go *w.* with thee.
1Sam. 20:7, if he say thus, it is *w.*
2Ki. 4:26, is it *w.* with thee, is it *w.*?
2Chr. 12:12, in Judah things went *w.*
Ps. 49:18, when thou doest *w.* to thyself.
Prov. 11:10, when it goeth *w.* with the righteous.
14:15, looketh *w.* with the righteous.
30:29, three things which go *w.*
Eccl. 8:12, it shall be *w.* with them that fear God.
Isa. 3:10, say to the righteous, it shall be *w.*
Ezek. 33:32, one that can play *w.*
Jonah 4:4, doest thou *w.* to be angry?
Mt. 25:21; Lk. 19:17, *w.* done.
Mk. 7:37, he hath done all things *w.*
Lk. 6:26, when all men speak *w.* of you.
Gal. 5:7, ye did run *w.*
See Phil 4:14; 1Tim. 3:5; 5:17; Ti. 2:9.

WENT. Gen. 4:16, Cain *w.* out from the presence.
Dt. 1:31, in all the way ye *w.*
2Ki. 5:26, *w.* not my heart with thee?
Ps. 42:4, I *w.* with them to the house of God.
106:32, it *w.* ill with Moses.
Mt. 21:30, I go, sir, and *w.* not.
Lk. 17:14, as they *w.* they were cleansed.
18:10, two men *w.* up into the temple to pray.
See Mt. 11:7;20:1; Lk. 6:19; Jn. 8:9.

WEPT. 2Ki. 8:11, the man of God *w.*
Ezra 10:1; Neh. 8:9, the people *w.* very sore.
Neh. 1:4, I *w.* before God.
Lk. 7:32, we mourned, and ye have not *w.*
19:41, beheld the city, and *w.* over it.
Jn. 11:35, Jesus *w.*
1Cor. 7:30, that weep as though they *w.* not.
See 2Sam. 12:22 Ps. 69:10; 137:1; Rev. 5:4.

WET. Job 24:8, Dan. 4:15; 5:21.

WHAT. Ex. 16:15, they wist not *w.* it was.
2Sam. 16:10, *w.* have I to do with you?
Ezra 9:10, *w.* shall we say after this?
Job 7:17; 15:14; Ps. 8:4; 144:3, *w.* is man?
Isa. 38:15; Jn. 12:27, *w.* shall I say?
Hos. 6:4, *w.* shall I do unto thee?
Mt. 5:47, *w.* do ye more than others?
Mk. 14:36, not *w.* I will, but *w.* thou wilt.
Jn. 21:22, *w.* is that to thee?
See Acts 9:6; 10:4; 16:30; 1Pet. 1:11.

WHATSOEVER. Ps. 1:3, *w.* he doeth shall prosper.
Eccl. 3:14, *w.* God doeth shall be for ever.
Mt. 5:37, *w.* is more than these cometh of evil.
7:12, *w.* ye would that men should do to you.
20:4, *w.* is right I will give you.
Phil. 4:8, *w.* things are true.
See Jn. 15:16; Rom. 14:23; 1Cor. 10:31.

WHEAT. 1Sam. 12:17, is it not *w.* harvest to-day?
Job 31:40, let thistles grow instead of *w.*
Ps. 81:16; 147:14, the finest of the *w.*
Jer. 12:13, they have sown *w.*, but reap thorns.
23:28, what is the chaff to the *w.*?
Mt. 3:12, gather his *w.* into the garner.
Lk. 22:31, that he may sift you as *w.*
See Jn. 12:24; Acts 27:38; 1Cor. 15:37.

WHEEL. Ex. 14:25, took off their chariot *w.*
Jud. 5:28, why tarry the *w.*?
Ps. 83:13, make them like a *w.*
Prov. 20:26, a wise king bringeth the *w.* over them.
Eccl. 12:6, or the *w.* broken at the cistern.
Isa. 28:28, nor break it with the *w.* of his cart.
Nah. 3:2, the noise of the rattling of the *w.*
See Isa. 5:28; Jer. 18:3; 47:3; Ezek. 1:16.

WHELP. 2Sam. 17:8; Prov. 17:12; Hos. 13:8.

WHEN. 1Sam. 3:12, *w.* I begin, I will also.
1Ki. 8:30, *w.* thou hearest, forgive.
Ps. 94:8, *w.* will ye be wise?
Eccl. 8:7, who can tell him *w.* it shall be?

Mt. 24:3; Mk. 13:4; Lk. 21:7, *w.* shall these things be?
See Dt. 6:7; Jn. 4:25; 16:8; 1Jn. 2:28.
WHENCE. Gen. 42:7; Josh. 9:8, *w.* come ye?
Job 10:21, *w.* I shall not return.
Isa. 51:1, the rock *w.* ye are hewn.
Jas. 4:1, from *w.* come wars?
Rev. 7:13, *w.* came they?
See Mt. 13:54; Jn. 1:48; 7:28; 9:29.
WHERE. Gen. 3:9, *w.* art thou?
Ex. 2:20; 2Sam. 9:4; Job 14:10, *w.* is he?
Job 9:24, if not, *w.* and who is he?
Ps. 42:3, *w.* is thy God?
Jer. 2:6, *w.* is the Lord?
Zech. 1:5, your fathers, *w.* are they?
See Isa. 49:21; Hos. 1:10; Lk. 17:37.
WHEREBY. Lk. 1:18, *w.* shall I know this?
Acts 4:12, none other name *w.* we must be saved.
Rom. 8:15, the spirit of adoption, *w.* we cry.
See Jer. 33:8; Ezek. 18:31; 39:26; Eph. 4:30.
WHEREFORE. 2Sam. 12:23, *w.* should I fast?
Mt. 14:31, *w.* didst thou doubt?
26:50, *w.* art thou come?
See 2Sam. 16:10; Mal. 2:15; Acts 10:21.
WHERETO. Isa. 55:11; Phil. 3:16.
WHEREWITH. Jud. 6:5, *w.* shall I save Israel?
Ps. 119:42, so shall I have *w.* to answer.
Mic. 6:6, *w.* shall I come before the Lord?
See Mt. 5:13; Mk. 9:5; Jn. 17:26; Eph. 2:4.
WHET. Dt. 32:41; Ps. 7:12; 64:3; Eccl. 10:10.
WHETHER. Mt. 21:31, *w.* of them did the will.
Mt. 23:17, *w.* is greater, the gold or the temple?
Rom. 14:8, *w.* we live or die.
2Cor. 12:2, *w.* in the body, or out of the body.
See 1Ki. 20:18; Ezek. 2:5; 3:11; 1Jn. 4:1.
WHILE. 2Chr. 15:2, with you, *w.* ye be with him.
Ps. 49:18, *w.* he lived he blessed his soul.
Isa. 55:6, *w.* he may be found.
Jer. 15:9, her sun is gone down *w.* it was yet day.
Lk. 18:4, he would not for a *w.*
24:44, *w.* I was yet with you.
Jn. 9:4, work *w.* it is day.
1Tim. 5:6, she is dead *w.* she liveth.
See 1Sam. 9:27; 2Sam. 7:19; Acts 20:11.
WHIP. 1Ki. 12:11; Prov. 26:3; Nah. 3:2.
WHIT. 1Sam. 3:18; Jn. 7:23; 13:10; 2Cor. 11:5.
WHITE. Gen. 49:12, his teeth shall be *w.* with milk.
Num. 12:10, leprous, *w.* as snow.
Job 6:6, is any taste in the *w.* of an egg?
Eccl. 9:8, let thy garments be always *w.*
Song 5:10, my beloved is *w.* and ruddy.
Isa. 1:18, they shall be *w.* as snow.
Mt. 5:36, thou canst not make one hair *w.* or black.
Jn. 4:35, *w.* already to harvest.
Rev. 2:17, a *w.* stone.
3:4, walk with me in *w.*
See Dan. 11:35; 12:10; Mt. 17:2; 28:3.
WHITED. Mt. 23:27; Acts 23:3.
WHITER. Ps. 51:7; Lam. 4:7.
WHITHER. 2Ki. 5:25; Song 6:1; Heb. 11:8.
WHOLE. 2Sam. 1:9, my life is yet *w.* in me.
Eccl. 12:13, this is the *w.* duty of man.
Jer. 19:11, a vessel that cannot be made *w.*
Ezek. 15:5, when *w.* it was meet for no work.
Mt. 5:29, not that thy *w.* body be cast into hell.
9:12; Mk. 2:17, the *w.* need not a physician.
13:33; Lk. 13:21, till the *w.* was leavened.
16:26; Mk. 8:36; Lk. 9:25, gain the *w.* world.
Jn. 11:50, expedient that the *w.* nation perish not.
1Cor. 12:17, if the *w.* body were an eye.
1Th. 5:23, I pray God your *w.* spirit.
Jas. 2:10, keep the *w.* law.
1Jn. 2:2, for the sins of the *w.* world.
5:19, the *w.* world lieth in wickedness.
See Mt. 15:31; Jn. 5:6; 7:23; Acts 9:34.
WHOLESOME. Prov. 15:4; 1Tim. 6:3.
WHOLLY. Job 21:23, dieth, being *w.* at ease.
Jer. 2:21, planted thee *w.* a right seed.
46:28, not *w.* unpunished.
Acts 17:16, the city *w.* given to idolatry.
1Th. 5:23, sanctify you *w.*
1Tim. 4:15, give thyself *w.* to them.
See Lev. 19:9; Dt. 1:36; Josh. 14:8.
WHOMSOEVER. Dan. 4:17, 25, 32, to *w.* he will.
Mt. 11:27, to *w.* the Son will reveal him.
21:44; Lk. 20:18, on *w.* it shall fall.
Lk. 4:6, to *w.* I will, I give it.
12:48, to *w.* much is given.
See Gen. 31:32; Jud. 11:24; Acts 8:19.
WHOSE. Gen. 32:17, *w.* art thou, *w.* are these?
Jer. 44:28, shall know *w.* words shall stand.
Mt. 22:20; Mk. 12:16; Lk. 20:24, *w.* is this image?
Lk. 12:20, then *w.* shall these things be?
Acts 27:23, *w.* I am, and whom I serve.
See 1Sam. 12:3; Dan. 5:23; Jn. 20:23.
WHOSOEVER. 1Cor. 11:27, *w.* shall eat this bread.
Gal. 5:10, bear his judgment, *w.* he be.
Rev. 22:17, *w.* will, let him take.
See Mt. 11:6; 13:12; Lk. 8:18; Rom. 2:1.
WHY. 1Sam. 2:23, *w.* do ye such things?
Jer. 8:14, *w.* do we sit still?
27:13; Ezek. 18:31; 33:11, *w.* will ye die?
Mt. 21:25; Mk. 11:31; Lk. 20:5, *w.* did ye not believe?
Mk. 5:39, *w.* make ye this ado?
Acts 9:4; 22:7; 26:14, *w.* persecutest thou me?
Rom. 9:19, *w.* doth he yet find fault?
20, *w.* hast thou made me thus?
See 2Chr. 25:16; Lk. 2:48; Jn. 7:45; 10:20.
WICKED. Gen. 18:23, destroy righteous with *w.*
Dt. 15:9, a thought in thy *w.* heart.
1Sam. 2:9, the *w.* shall be silent.
Job 3:17, there the *w.* cease from troubling.
8:22, dwelling place of the *w.* shall come to nought.
9:29; 10:15, if I be *w.*, why labour I in vain?
21:7, wherefore do the *w.* live?
30, the *w.* is reserved to destruction.
Ps. 7:9, let the wickedness of the *w.* come to an end.
11, God is angry with the *w.*
9:17, the *w.* shall be turned into hell.
10:4, the *w,* will not seek God.

11:2, the *w.* bend their bow.
6, upon the *w.* he shall rain snares.
12:8, the *w.* walk on every side.
26:5, I will not sit with the *w.*
34:21, evil shall slay the *w.*
37:21, the *w.* borroweth, and payeth not.
32, the *w.* watcheth the righteous.
35, I have seen the *w.* in great power.
58:3, the *w.* are estranged from the womb.
68:2, so let the *w.* perish.
94:3, how long shall the *w.* triumph?
139:24, see if there by any *w.* way in me.
145:20, all the *w.* will he destroy.
Prov. 11:5, the *w.* shall fall by his own wickedness.
14:32, the *w.* is driven away.
28:1, the *w.* flee when no man pursueth.
Eccl. 7:17, be not overmuch *w.*
8:10, I saw the *w.* buried.
Isa. 13:11, I will punish the *w.*
53:9, he made his grave with the *w.*
55:7, let the *w.* forsake his way.
57:20, the *w.* are like the troubled sea.
Jer. 17:9, the heart is desperately *w.*
Ezek. 3:18; 33:8, to warn the *w.*
11:2, these men give *w.* counsel.
18:23, have I any pleasure that the *w.* should die?
33:15, if the *w.* restore the pledge.
Dan. 12:10, the *w.* shall do wickedly.
Mic. 6:11, with *w.* balances.
Nah. 1:3, the Lord will not at all acquit the *w.*
Mt. 12:45; Lk. 11:26, more *w.* than himself.
13:49, sever the *w.* from the just.
18:32; 25:26; Lk. 19:22, thou *w.* servant.
Acts 2:23, and by *w.* hands have crucified and slain.
1Cor. 5:13, put away that *w.* person.
Eph. 6:16, the fiery darts of the *w.*
Col. 1:21, enemies in your mind by *w.* works.
2Th. 2:8, then shall that *W.* be revealed.
See Eccl. 9:2; Isa. 48:22; 2Pet. 2:7; 3:17.
WICKEDLY. Job 13:7, will you speak *w.* for God?
34:12, God will not do *w.*
Ps. 73:8; 139:20, they speak *w.*
Dan. 12:10, the wicked shall do *w.*
Mal. 4:1, all that do *w.*
See 2Chr. 6:37; 22:3; Neh. 9:33; Ps. 106:6.
WICKEDNESS. Gen. 39:9, this great *w.*
Jud. 20:3, how was this *w.*?
1Sam. 24:13, *w.* proceedeth from the wicked.
1Ki. 21:25, sold himself to work *w.*
Job 4:8, they that sow *w.*, reap the same.
22:5, is not thy *w.* great?
35:8, thy *w.* may hurt a man.
Ps. 7:9, let the *w.* of the wicked come to an end.
55:11, *w.* is in the midst thereof.
15, *w.* is in their dwellings.
58:2, in heart ye work *w.*
84:10, the tents of *w.*
Prov. 4:17, they eat the bread of *w.*
8:7, *w.* is an abomination to my lips.
11:5, the wicked shall fall by his own *w.*
13:6, *w.* overthroweth the sinner.
26:26, his *w.* shall be shewed.
Eccl. 7:25, the *w.* of folly.
Isa. 9:18, *w.* burneth as the fire.
47:10, thou hast trusted in thy *w.*
Jer. 2:19, thine own *w.* shall correct thee.
6:7, she casteth out her *w.*
8:6, no man repented of his *w.*
44:9, have you forgot the *w.* of your kings?
Ezek. 3:19, if he turn not from his *w.*
7:11, violence is risen up into a rod of *w.*
31:11, I have driven him out for his *w.*
33:12, in the day he turneth from his *w.*
Hos. 9:15, for the *w.* of their doings.
10:13, ye have ploughed *w.*
Mic. 6:10, are treasures of *w.* in house.
Zech. 5:8, he said, this is *w.*
Mal. 1:4, the border of *w.*
3:15, they that work *w.* are set up.
Mk. 7:21, out of the heart proceed *w.*
Lk. 11:39, your inward part is full of *w.*
Rom. 1:29, being filled with all *w.*
1Cor. 5:8, nor with the leaven of *w.*
Eph. 6:12, spiritual *w.* in high places.
1Jn. 5:19, the whole world lieth in *w.*
See Gen. 6:5; Ps. 94:23; Prov. 21:12; Jer. 23:11.
WIDE. Ps. 35:21, they opened their mouth *w.*
104:25, this great and *w.* sea.
Prov. 21:9; 25:24; Jer. 22:14, a *w.* house.
Mt. 7:13, *w.* is the gate that leadeth to destruction.
See Dt. 15:8; Ps. 81:10; Nah. 3:13.
WIFE. Prov. 5:18; Eccl. 9:9, the *w.* of thy youth.
18:22, whoso findeth a *w.* findeth a good thing.
19:14, a prudent *w.* is from the Lord.
Lk. 14:20, I have married a *w.*
17:32, remember Lot's *w.*
1Cor. 7:14, the unbelieving *w.* is sanctified.
Eph. 5:23, the husband is the head of the *w.*
Rev. 21:9, the bride, the Lamb's *w.*
See 1Tim. 3:2; 5:9; Ti. 1:6; 1Pet. 3:7.
WILES. Num. 25:18; Eph. 6:11.
WILFULLY. Heb. 10:26, if we sin *w.*
WILL. Mt. 8:3; Mk. 1:41; Lk. 5:13, I *w.*, be thou clean.
18:14, not the *w.* of your Father.
26:39, not as I *w.*, but as thou wilt.
Mk. 3:35, whosoever shall do the *w.* of God.
Jn. 1:13, born not of the *w.* of the flesh.
4:34, to do the *w.* of him that sent me.
Acts 21:14, the *w.* of the Lord be done.
Rom. 7:18, to *w.* is present with me.
Phil. 2:13, both to *w.* and to do.
1Tim. 2:8, I *w.* that men pray every where.
Rev. 22:17, whosoever *w.*, let him take.
See Rom. 9:16; Eph. 1:11; Heb. 2:4; Jas. 1:18.
WILLING. Ex. 35:5, a *w.* heart.
1Chr. 28:9, serve God with a *w.* mind.
29:5, who is *w.* to consecrate his service?
Ps. 110:3, *w.* in the day of thy power.
Mt. 26:41, the spirit is *w.*
2Cor. 5:8, *w.* rather to be absent.

8:12, if there be first a *w.* mind.
1Tim. 6:18, *w.* to communicate.
2Pet. 3:9, not *w.* that any should perish.
See Lk. 22:42; Jn. 5:35; Phile. 14; 1Pet. 5:2.
WIN. 2Chr. 32:1; Prov. 11:30; Phil. 3:8.
WIND. Job 6:26, reprove speeches which are as *w.*
7:7, remember that my life is *w.*
Prov. 11:29, he shall inherit *w.*
25:23, the north *w.* driveth away rain.
30:4, gathereth the *w.* in his fists.
Eccl. 11:4, he that observeth the *w.*
Isa. 26:18, we have brought forth *w.*
27:8, he stayeth his rough *w.*
Ezek. 37:9, prophesy to the *w.*
Hos. 8:7, they have sown *w.*
Amos 4:13, he that createth the *w.*
Mt. 11:7, a reed shaken with the *w.*
Jn. 3:8, the *w.* bloweth where it listeth.
Eph. 4:14, carried about with every *w.* of doctrine.
See Acts 2:2; Jas. 1:6; Jude 12.
WINDOWS. Gen. 7:11; Eccl. 12:3; Jer. 9:21; Mal. 3:10.
WINGS. Ps. 17:8; 36:7; 57:1; 61:4; 68:13; 91:4, the shadow of thy *w.*
18:10; 104:3, on the *w.* of the wind.
55:6, Oh that I had *w.* like a dove!
139:9, the *w.* of the morning.
Prov. 23:5, riches make themselves *w.*
Mal. 4:2, with healing in his *w.*
See Ezek. 1:6; Zech. 5:9; Mt. 23:37; Lk. 13:34.
WINK. Job 15:12; Ps. 35:19; Prov. 6:13; 10:10; Acts 17:30.
WINTER. Gen. 8:22; Song 2:11; Mt. 24:20; Mk. 13:18.
WIPE. 2Ki. 21:13; Isa. 25:8; Lk. 7:38; Jn. 13:5.
WISDOM. Job 4:21, they die without *w.*
12:2, *w.* shall die with you.
Prov. 4:7, *w.* is the principal thing.
16:16, better to get *w.* than gold.
19:8, he that getteth *w.* loveth his own soul.
23:4, cease from thine own *w.*
Eccl. 1:18, in much *w.* is much grief.
Isa. 10:13, by my *w.* I have done it.
29:14, the *w.* of their wise men shall perish.
Jer. 8:9, they have rejected the word of the Lord; and what *w.* is in them?
Mic. 6:9, the man of *w.* shall see thy name.
Mt. 11:19, *w.* is justified of her children.
1Cor. 1:17, not with *w.* of words.
24, Christ the *w.* of God.
1 Cor. 1:30, who of God is made unto us *w.*
2:6, we speak w. among them that are perfect.
3:19, the *w.* of this world is foolishness with God.
2Cor. 1:12, not with fleshly *w.*
Col. 1:9, that ye might be filled with all *w.*
4:5, walk in *w.* toward them.
Jas. 1:5, if any lack *w.*
3:17, the *w.* from above is pure.
Rev. 5:12, worthy is the Lamb to receive *w.*
13:18, here is *w.*

See Eccl. 1:16; Rom. 11:33; Col. 2:3; 3:16.
WISE. Gen. 3:6, to make one *w.*
Ex. 23:8, the gift blindeth the *w.*
Dt. 4:6, this nation is a *w.* people.
32:29, O that they were *w.*!
1Ki. 3:12, I have given thee a *w.* heart.
Job 9:4, he is *w.* in heart.
11:12, vain man would be *w.*
22:2, he that is *w.* may be profitable.
32:9, great men are not always *w.*
Ps. 2:10, be *w.* now, O ye kings.
19:7, making *w.* the simple.
36:3, he hath left off to be *w.*
94:8, when will ye be *w.*?
107:43, whoso is *w.*, and will observe.
Prov. 1:5, a *w.* man shall attain *w.* counsels.
3:7, be not *w.* in thine own eyes.
6:6; 8:33; 23:19; 27:11, be *w.*
9:12, thou shalt be *w.* for thyself.
11:30, he that winneth souls is *w.*
16:21, the *w.* in heart shall be called prudent.
20:26, a *w.* king scattereth the wicked.
Eccl. 7:23, I said, I will be *w.*
91, the *w.* are in the hands of God.
12:11, the words of the *w.* are as goads.
Isa. 19:11, I am the son of the *w.*
Dan. 12:3, they that be *w.* shall shine.
Mt. 10:16, be *w.* as serpents.
11:25, hid these things from the *w.*
Rom. 1:14, I am debtor to the *w.*
12:16, be not *w.* in your own conceits.
1Cor. 1:20, where is the *w.*?
4:10, ye are *w.* in Christ.
2Tim. 3:15, *w.* unto salvation.
See Isa. 5:21; Jer. 4:22; Mt. 25:2.
WISELY. Ps. 58:5, charmers, charming never so *w.*
101:2, I will behave myself *w.*
Prov. 16:20, that handleth a matter *w.*
See Prov. 21:12; 28:26; Eccl. 7:10; Lk. 16:8.
WISER. 1Ki. 4:31; Lk. 16:8; 1Cor. 1:25.
WISH. Ps. 73:7, more than heart could *w.*
Rom. 9:3, I could *w.* myself accursed.
3Jn. 2, I *w.* above all things.
See Job 33:6; Jonah 4:8; 2Cor. 13:9.
WITCH. Ex. 22:18, thou shalt not suffer a *w.* to live.
Dt. 18:10, or a *w.*
WITHDRAW. Job 9:13; Prov. 25:17; 2Th. 3:6.
WITHER. Ps. 1:3, his leaf shall not *w.*
37:2, they shall *w.* as the green herb.
129:6; Isa. 40:7; 1Pet. 1:24, the grass *w.*
Mt. 21:19; Mk. 11:21, the fig tree *w.* away.
Jude 12, threes whose fruit *w.*
See Joel 1:12; Jn. 15:6; Jas. 1:11
WITHHOLD. Ps. 40:11, *w.* not thy mercies.
84:11, no good thing will he *w.*
Prov. 3:27, *w.* not good from them to whom it is due.
23:13, *w.* not correction.
Eccl. 11:6, *w.* not thy hand.
Jer. 5:25, your sins have *w.* good things.
See Job 22:7; 42:2; Ezek. 18:16; Joel 1:13.
WITHIN. Mt. 23:26, cleanse first what is *w.*
Mk. 7:21, from *w.* proceed evil thoughts.

2Cor. 7:5, *w.* were fears.
See Ps. 45:13; Mt. 3:9; Lk. 12:17; 16:3.
WITHOUT. Gen. 24:31, wherefore standest thou *w.*?
2Chr. 15:3, for a long season *w.* the true God.
Prov. 1:20, wisdom crieth *w.*
Isa. 52:3; 55:1, *w.* money.
Jer. 33:10, *w.* man, *w.* beast *w.* inhabitant.
Hos. 3:4, Israel *w.* king, *w.* prince, *w.* sacrifice.
Eph. 2:12, *w.* God in the world.
Col. 4:5; 1Th. 4:12; 1Tim. 3:7, them that are *w.*
Heb. 13:12, Jesus suffered *w.* the gate.
Rev. 22:15, for *w.* are dogs.
See Prov. 22:12; Mt. 10:29; Lk. 11:40.
WITHSTAND. Eccl. 4:12, two shall *w.* him.
Acts 11:17, what was I that I could *w.* God?
Eph 6:13, able to *w.* in evil day.
See Num. 22:32; 2Chr. 20:6; Est. 9:2.
WITNESS (*n.*). Gen. 31:50, God is *w.* betwixt.
Josh. 24:27, this stone shall be a *w.*
Job 16:19, my *w.* is in heaven.
Ps. 89:37, as a faithful *w.* in heaven.
Prov. 14:5, a faithful *w.* will not lie.
Isa. 55:4, I have given him for a *w.* to the people.
Jer. 42:5, the Lord be a true and faithful *w.*
Mt. 24:14, for a *w.* unto all nations.
Jn. 1:7, the same came for a *w.*
3:11, ye receive not our *w.*
5:36, I have greater *w.* than that of John.
Acts 14:17, he left not himself without *w.*
Rom. 2:15, conscience also bearing them *w.*
1Jn. 5:9, the *w.* of God is greater.
10, hath the *w.* in himself.
See Isa. 43:10; Lk. 24:48; Acts 1:8; 13:31.
WITNESS (*v.*). Dt. 4:26, heaven and earth to *w.*
Isa. 3:9, countenance doth *w.* against them.
Acts 20:23, the Holy Ghost *w.* in every city.
Rom. 3:21, being *w.* by the law and prophets.
1Tim. 6:13, before Pilate *w.* a good confession.
See 1Sam. 12:3; Mt. 26:62; 27:13; Mk. 14:60.
WITS. Ps. 107:27, are at their *w.* end.
WITTY. Prov. 8:12, knowledge of *w.* inventions.
WIZARD. Lev. 20:27, or that is a *w.*
WOEFUL. Jer. 17:16, the *w.* day.
WOMAN. Jud. 9:54, a *w.* slew him.
Ps. 48:6; Isa. 13:8; 21:3; 26:17; Jer. 4:31; 6:24;
13:21, 22, 23; 30:6; 31:8; 48:41; 49:22, 24;
50:43, pain as of a *w.* in travail.
Prov. 6:24, to keep thee from the evil *w.*
9:13, a foolish *w.* is clamorous.
12:4; 31:10, a virtuous *w.*
14:1, every wise *w.* buildeth her house.
21:9, with a brawling *w.* in wide house.
Eccl. 7:28, a *w.* among all those have I not found.
Isa. 54:6, as a *w.* forsaken.
Jer. 31:22, a *w.* shall compass a man.
Mt. 5:28, whoso looketh on a *w.*
15:28, O w. great is thy faith.
22:27; Mk. 12:22; Lk. 20:32, the *w.* died also.
26:10, why trouble ye the *w.*?
13, shall this, that this *w.* hath done, be told.
Jn. 2:4, *w.*, what have I to do with thee?
8:3, a *w.* taken in adultery.
19:26, *w.*, behold thy son.
Acts 9:36, this *w.* was full of good works.
Rom. 1:27, the natural use of the *w.*
1Cor. 7:1, it is good for a man not to touch a *w.*
11:7, the *w.* is the glory of the man.
Gal. 4:4, God sent forth his Son, made of a *w.*
1Tim. 2:12, I suffer not a *w.* to teach.
14, the *w.* being deceived.
See Isa. 49:15; Lk. 7:39; 13:16; Rev. 12:1.
WOMB. Gen. 49:25, blessings of the *w.*
1Sam. 1:5, the Lord had shut up her *w.*
Ps. 22:9, took me out of the *w.*
10, cast upon thee from the *w.*
127:3, the fruit of the *w.* is his reward.
139:13, thou hast covered me in my mother's *w.*
Eccl. 11:5, how bones grow in the *w.*
Isa. 44:2; 49:5, the Lord formed thee from the *w.*
48:8, a transgressor from the *w.*
49:15, compassion on son of her *w.*
Hos. 9:14, give them miscarrying *w.*
Lk. 1:42, blessed is the fruit of thy *w.*
Lk. 11:27, blessed is the *w.* that bare thee.
23:29, blessed are the *w.* that never bare.
See Job 3:11; 24:20; 31:15; Prov. 30:16.
WOMEN. Jud. 5:24, blessed above *w.*
1Sam. 18:7, the *w.* answered one another.
2Sam. 1:26, passing the love of *w.*
Ps. 45:9, among thy honourable *w.*
Prov. 31:3, give not thy strength to *w.*
Lam. 4:10, the pitiful *w.* have sodden their children.
Mt. 11:11; Lk. 7:28, among them that are born of *w.*
24:41; Lk. 17:35, two *w.* grinding at the mill.
Lk. 1:28, blessed art thou among *w.*
1Cor. 14:34, let your *w.* keep silence.
1Tim. 2:9, *w.* adorn themselves.
11, let the *w.* learn in silence.
5:14, that the younger *w.* marry.
2Tim. 3:6, lead captive silly *w.*
Ti. 2:3, the aged *w.* in behaviour as becometh holiness.
Heb. 11:35, *w.* received their dead.
See Acts 16:13; 17:4; Phil. 4:3; 1Pet. 3:5.
WONDER (*n.*). Ps. 71:7, as *w.* unto many.
77:14, thou art the God that doest *w.*
88:12, shall thy *w.* be known in the dark?
96:3, declare his *w.* among all people.
107:24, his *w.* in the deep.
Isa. 20:3, walked barefoot for a sign and a *w.*
29:14, I will do a marvellous work and a *w.*
Joel 2:30; Acts 2:19, I will show *w.* in heaven.
Jn. 4:48, except ye see signs and *w.*
Acts 4:30, that *w.* may be done by the name.
See Rom 15:19; 2Cor. 12:12; 2Th. 2:9.
WONDER (*v.*). Isa. 29:9, stay yourselves, and *w.*
59:16, he *w.* there was no intercessor.
63:5, I *w.* there was none to uphold.
Hab. 1:5, regard, and *w.* marvellously.
Zech. 3:8, they are men *w.* at.
Lk. 4:22, all *w.* at the gracious words.
See Acts 3:11; 8:13; 13:41; Rev. 13:3; 17:6.
WONDERFUL. 2Sam. 1:26, thy love was *w.*

Job 42:3, things too *w.* for me.
Ps. 139:6, such knowledge is too *w.* for me.
Isa. 9:6, his name shall be called *W.*
28:29, who is *w.* in counsel.
See Dt. 28:59; Jer. 5:30; Mt. 21:15.
WONDERFULLY. Ps. 139:14; Lam. 1:9; Dan. 8:24.
WONDROUS. 1Chr. 16:9; Job 37:14; Ps. 26:7; 75:1; 78:32; 105:2; 106:22; 119:27; 145:5; Jer. 21:2, *w.* works.
Ps. 72:18; 86:10; 119:18, *w.* things.
WONT. Ex. 21:29, if the ox were *w.* to push.
Mt. 27:15, the governor was *w.* to release.
Mk. 10:1, as he was *w.*, he taught them.
Lk. 22:39, he went, as he was *w.*
Acts 16:13, where prayer was *w.* to be made.
See Num. 22:30; 2Sam. 20:18; Dan. 3:19.
WOOD. Gen. 22:7, behold the fire and the *w.*
Dt. 29:11; Josh. 9:21; Jer. 46:22, hewer of *w.*
2Sam. 18:8, the *w.* devoured more people.
Ps. 141:7, as one cleaveth *w.*
Prov. 26:20, where no *w.* is, the fire goeth out.
See Jer. 7:18; Hag. 1:8; 1Cor. 3:12.
WOOL. Ps. 147:16, he giveth snow like *w.*
Isa. 1:18, your sins shall be as *w.*
Dan. 7:9; Rev. 1:14, hair like *w.*
See Prov. 31:13; Ezek. 34:3; 44:17; Hos. 9:1.
WORD. Dt. 8:3; Mt. 4:4, every *w.* of God.
30:14; Rom. 10:8, the *w.* is very nigh.
Job 12:11, doth not the ear try *w.*?
35:16, he multiplieth *w.*
38:2, by *w.* without knowledge.
Ps. 19:14, let the *w.* of my mouth be acceptable.
68:11, the Lord gave the *w.*
119:43; 2Cor. 6:7; Eph. 1:13, Col. 1:5; 2Tim. 2:15; Jas. 1:18, the *w.* of truth.
Prov. 15:23, a *w.* spoken in due season.
25:11, a *w.* fitly spoken.
Isa. 29:21, an offender for a *w.*
30:21, thine ears shall hear a *w.* behind thee.
Isa. 50:4, how to speak a *w.* in season.
Jer. 5:13, the *w.* is not in them.
18:18, nor shall the *w.* perish.
4:28, know whose *w.* shall stand.
Hos. 14:2, take with you *w.*
Mt. 8:8, speak the *w.* only.
12:36, every idle *w.* that men shall speak.
18:16, that every *w.* may be established.
24:35, may *w.* shall not pass away.
Mk. 4:14, the sower soweth the *w.*
8:38; Lk. 9:26, ashamed of my *w.*
Lk. 4:22, gracious *w.* which proceeded.
36, amazed, saying, what a *w.* is this!
24:19, a prophet mighty in deed and *w.*
Jn. 6:63, the *w.* I speak are life.
68, thou hast the *w.* of eternal life.
12:48, the *w.* I have spoken shall judge him.
14:24, the *w.* ye hear is not mine.
17:8, I have given them the *w.* thou gavest me.
Acts 13:15, any *w.* of exhortation.
20:35, remember the *w.* of the Lord Jesus.
26:25, the *w.* of truth and soberness.
1Cor. 1:17, not with wisdom of *w.*
4:20, not in *w.*, but in power.
14:9, except ye utter *w.* easy to be understood.
2Cor. 1:18, our *w.* was not yea and nay.
5:19, the *w.* of reconciliation.
Gal. 5:14, all the law is fulfilled in one *w.*
6:6, him that is taught in the *w.*
Eph. 5:6, deceive you with vain *w.*
Phil. 2:16, holding forth the *w.* of life.
Col. 3:16, let the *w.* of Christ dwell in you.
1Th. 1:5, the gospel came not in *w.* only.
4:18, comfort one another with these *w.*
1Tim. 4:6, nourished in *w.* of faith.
5:17, labour in the *w.* and doctrine.
2Tim. 2:14, strive not about *w.*
4:2, preach the *w.*
Ti. 1:3, in due times manifested his *w.*
9, holding fast the faithful *w.*
Heb. 1:3, by the *w.* of his power.
2:2, if the *w.* spoken by angels was stedfast.
4:2, the *w.* preached did not profit.
12, the *w.* of God is quick and powerful.
5:13, is unskilful in the *w.*
6:5, and have tasted the good *w.* of God.
7:28, the *w.* of the oath.
11:3, the worlds were framed by the *w.* of God.
13:7, who have spoken to you the *w.*
Jas. 1:21, the engrafted *w.*
22, be ye doers of the *w.*
23, if any be a hearer of the *w.*
3:2, if any man offend not in *w.*
1Pet. 1:23, being born again by the *w.*
25, this is the *w.* which is preached.
2:2, the sincere milk of the *w.*
8, them that stumble at the *w.*
3:1, if any obey not the *w.*, they also may without the *w.*
2Pet. 1:19, a more sure *w.* of prophecy.
3:2, the *w.* spoken by the prophets.
5, by the *w.* of God the heavens were of old.
7, the heavens by the same *w.* are kept in store.
1Jn. 1:1, hands have handled, of *W.* of life.
2:5, whoso keepeth his *w.*, in him is the love.
3:18, let us not love in *w.*
Rev. 3:8, thou hast kept my *w.*
10, the *w.* of my patience.
6:9, that were slain for the *w.*
22:19, take away from the *w.* of this prophecy.
See Isa. 8:20; Jer. 20:9; Mic. 2:7; Rev. 21:5.
WORK (*n.*). Gen. 2:2, God ended his *w.*
5:29, shall comfort us concerning our *w.*
Ex. 20:9; 23:12; Dt. 5:13, six days thou shalt do all thy *w.*
35:2, six days shall *w.* be done.
Dt. 3:24, what God can do according to thy *w.*?
4:28; 27:15; 2Ki. 19:18; 2Chr. 32:19; Ps. 115:4; 135:15, the *w.* of men's hands.
1Chr. 16:37, as every day's *w.* required.
2Chr. 31:21, in every *w.* he began he did it.
34:12, the men did the *w.* faithfully.
Ezra 5:8, this *w.* goeth fast on.

6:7, let the *w.* alone.
Neh. 3:5, their nobles put not their necks to the *w.*
6:3, why should the *w.* cease?
16, they perceived this *w.* was of God.
Job 1:10, thou hast blessed the *w.* of his hands.
10:3; 14:15; Ps. 143:5, the *w.* of thine hands.
34:11, the *w.* of a man shall he render unto him.
Ps. 8:3, the *w.* of thy fingers.
19:1, his handy-*w.*
33:4, all his *w.* are done in truth.
40:5; 78:4; 107:8; 111:4; Mt. 7:22; Acts 2:11, wonderful *w.*
90:17, establish thou the *w.* of our hands.
101:3, I hate the *w.* of them that turn aside.
104:23, man goeth forth to his *w.*
111:2, the *w.* of the Lord are great.
141:4, to practise wicked *w.*
Prov. 16:3, commit thy *w.* unto the Lord.
20:11, whether his *w.* be pure.
24:12; Mt. 16:27; 2Tim. 4:14, to every man according to his *w.*
31:31, let her own *w.* praise her.
Eccl. 1:14, I have seen all the *w.* that are done.
3:17, there is a time for every *w.*
5:6, wherefore should God destroy the *w.*?
8:9, I applied my heart to every *w.*
9:1, their *w.* are in the hand of God.
7, God now accepteth thy *w.*
10, there is no *w.* in the grave.
12:14, God shall bring every *w.* into judgment.
Isa. 2:8; 37:19; Jer. 1:16; 10:3, 9, 15; 51:18, they worship the *w.* of their own hands.
5:19, let him hasten his *w.*
10:12, when the Lord hath performed his whole *w.*
26:12, thou hast wrought all our *w.* in us.
28:21, do his *w.*, his strange *w.*
29:15, their *w.* are in the dark.
49:4, my *w.* is with my God.
66:18, I know their *w.* and their thoughts.
Jer. 32:19, great in counsel, and mighty in *w.*
48:7, thou hast trusted in thy *w.*
Amos 8:7, I will never for get any of their *w.*
Hab. 1:5, I will work a *w.* in your days.
Mt. 23:3, do not ye after their *w.*
5, all their *w.* they do to be seen of men.
Mk. 6:5, he could there do no mighty *w.*
Jn. 5:20, greater *w.* than these.
6:28, that we might work the *w.* of God.
29, this is the *w.* of God. that ye believe.
7:21, I have done one *w.*, and ye all marvel.
9:3, that the *w.* of God should be made manifest.
10:25, the *w.* I do in my Father's name.
32, for which of those *w.* do ye stone me?
14:12, the *w.* I do shall he do, and greater *w.*
17:4, I have finished the *w.*
Acts 5:38, if this *w.* be of men, it will come to nought.
15:38, who went not with them to the *w.*
Rom. 3:27, by what law? of *w.*?
4:6, imputeth righteousness without *w.*
9:11, not of *w.*, but of him that calleth.
11:6, grace, otherwise *w.* is no more *w.*
13:12, let us therefore cast off the *w.* of darkness.
14:20, for meat destroy not the *w.* of God.
1Cor. 3:13, every man's *w.* shall be made manifest.
9:1, are not ye may *w.* in the Lord?
Gal. 2:16, by *w.* of law shall no flesh be justified.
6:4, let every man prove his own *w.*
Eph. 2:9, not of *w.* lest any man should boast.
4:12, the *w.* of the ministry.
5:11, the unfruitful *w.* of darkness.
Col. 1:21, enemies in your mind by wicked *w.*
1Th. 5:13, esteem them in love for their *w.* sake.
2Th. 2:17, in every good word and *w.*
2Tim. 1:9; Ti. 3:5, saved us, not according to our *w.*
2 Tim. 4:5, do the *w.* of an evangelist.
Ti. 1:16, in *w.* they deny him.
Heb. 6:1; 9:14, from dead *w.*
Jas. 1:4, let patience have her perfect *w.*
2:14, if he have not *w.*, can faith save him?
17, faith, if it hath not *w.*, is dead, being alone.
18, shew me thy faith without thy *w.*
21, was not Abraham justified by *w.*?
22, by *w.* was faith made perfect.
2Pet. 3:10, earth and *w.* therein shall be burnt up.
1Jn. 3:8, destroy the *w.* of the devil.
Rev. 2:2, 9, 13, 19; 3:1, 8, 15, I know thy *w.*
26, he that keepeth my *w.* to the end.
3:2, I have not found thy *w.* perfect.
14:13, and their *w.* do follow them.
See Gal. 5:19; 2Th. 1:11; Rev. 18:6; 20:12.

WORK (*v.*). 1Sam. 14:6, the Lord will *w.* for us.
1Ki. 21:20, sold thyself to *w.* evil.
Neh. 4:6, the people had a mind to the *w.*
Job 23:9, on the left hand, where he doth *w.*
33:29, all these things *w.* God with man.
Ps. 58:2, in heart ye *w.* wickedness.
101:7, he that *w.* deceit.
119:126, it is time for thee to *w.*
Isa. 43:13, I will *w.*, and who shall let it?
Mic. 2:1, woe to them that *w.* evil.
Hag. 2:4, *w.*, for I am with you.
Mal. 3:15, they that *w.* wickedness are set up.
Mt. 21:28, son, go *w.* to day in my vineyard.
Mk. 16:20, the Lord *w.* with them.
Jn. 5:17, my Father *w.* hitherto, and I *w.*
6:28, that we might *w.* the works of God.
30, what dost thou *w.*?
9:4, the night cometh, when no man can *w.*
Acts 10:35, he that *w.* righteousness is accepted.
Rom. 4:15, the law *w.* wrath.
5:3, tribulation *w.* patience.
8:28, all things *w.* together for good.
1Cor. 4:12, and labour, *w.* with our own hands.
12:6, it is the same God which *w.* all in all.
2Cor. 4:12, death *w.* in us.
17, *w.* for us a far more exceeding weight of glory.

Gal. 5:6, faith which *w.* by love.
Eph. 1:11, who *w.* all things after the counsel.
2:2, the spirit that now *w.*
3:20, the power that *w.* in us.
4:28, *w.* with his hands the thing that is good.
Phil. 2:12, *w.* out your own salvation.
1Th. 4:11, *w.* with your own hands.
2Th. 2:7, the mystery of iniquity doth *w.*
3:10, if any would not *w.*, neither should he eat.
Jas. 1:3, the trying of your faith *w.* patience.
See Ezek. 46:1; Prov. 11:18; 31:13; Eccl. 3:9.
WORKMAN. Hos. 8:6; Eph. 2:10; 2Tim. 2:15.
WORLD. Job 18:18, chased out of the *w.*
34:13, who hath disposed the whole *w.*?
37:12, on the face of the *w.*
Ps. 17:14, from men of the *w.*
50:12, the *w.* in mine.
73:12, the ungodly, who prosper in the *w.*
77:18; 97:4, lightnings lightened the *w.*
93:1, the *w.* also is stablished.
Eccl. 3:11, he hath set the *w.* in their heart.
Isa. 14:21, nor fill the face of the *w.* with cities.
24:4, the *w.* languisheth.
34:1, let the *w.* hear.
Mt. 4:8; Lk. 4:5, all the kingdoms of the *w.*
5:14, the light of the *w.*
13:22; Mk. 4:19, the cares of this *w.* choke.
38, the field is the *w.*
40, in the end of the *w.*
16:26; Mk. 8:36; Lk. 9:25, gain the whole *w.*
18:7, woe to the *w.* because of offences.
Mk. 10:30; Lk. 18:30; Heb. 2:5; 6:5, in the *w.* to come.
Lk. 1:70; Acts 3:21, since the *w.* began.
2:1, all the *w.* should be taxed.
16:8, 20:34, children of this *w.*
Lk. 20:35, worthy to obtain that *w.*
Jn. 1:10, he was in the *w.*
29, which taketh away the sin of the *w.*
3:16, God so loved the *w.*
4:42, 1Jn. 4:14, the Saviour of the *w.*
6:33, he that giveth life unto the *w.*
7:4, shew thyself to the *w.*
7, the *w.* cannot hate you.
8:12; 9:5, I am the light of the *w.*
12:19, the whole *w.* is gone after him.
31, now is the judgment of this *w.*
47, not to judge the *w.*, but to save the *w.*
13:1, depart out of this *w.*
14:17, whom the *w.* cannot receive.
22, manifest thyself unto us, and not unto the *w.*
27, not as the *w.* giveth, give I unto you.
30, the prince of this *w.* cometh.
15:18; 1Jn. 3:13, if the *w.* hate you.
19, the *w.* would love his own.
16:33, in the *w.* ye shall have tribulation.
17:9, I pray not for the *w.*
16, they are not of the *w.*
21, that the *w.* may believe.
21:25, the *w.* could not contain the books.
Acts 17:6, turned the *w.* upside down.
Rom. 3:19, that all the *w.* may become guilty.
12:2, be not conformed to this *w.*
1Cor. 1:20, where is the disputer of this *w.*?
2:6, the wisdom of this *w.*
7:31, they that use this *w.* as not abusing it.
2Cor. 4:4, the god of this *w.* hath blinded.
Gal. 1:4, this present evil *w.*
6:14, the *w.* is crucified unto me.
Eph. 2:2, according to the course of this *w.*
12, without God in the *w.*
1Tim. 6:7, we brought nothing into this *w.*
17, them that are rich in this *w.*
2Tim. 4:10, having loved this present *w.*
Heb. 11:38, of whom the *w.* was not worthy.
Jas. 1:27, unspotted from the *w.*
3:6, the tongue is a *w.* of iniquity.
4:4, the friendship of the *w.*
2Pet. 2:5, God spared not the old *w.*
3:6, the *w.* that then was.
1Jn. 2:15, love not the *w.*
3:1, the *w.* knoweth us not.
5:19, the whole *w.* lieth in wickedness.
See 2Sam. 22:16; 1Chr. 16:30; Prov. 8:26.
WORLDLY. Ti. 2:12; Heb. 9:1.
WORM. Job 7:5, my flesh is clothed with *w.*
17:14, I said to the *w.*, thou art my mother.
19:26, though *w.* destroy this body.
21:26, shall lie down, and *w.* shall cover them.
24:20, the *w.* shall feed sweetly on him.
25:6, man, that is a *w.*, etc.
Ps. 22:6, I am a *w.*, and no man.
Isa. 14:11, the *w.* is spread under thee.
41:14, fear not, thou *w.* Jacob.
66:24; Mk. 9:44, 46, 48, their *w.* shall not die.
Mic. 7:17, like *w.* of the earth.
See Jonah 4:7; Acts 12:23.
WORMWOOD. Jer. 9:15; 23:15; Amos 5:7.
WORSE. Mt. 9:16; Mk. 2:21, the rent is made *w.*
12:45:27:64; Lk. 11:26, last state *w.* than the first.
Mk. 5:26, nothing bettered, but grew *w.*
Jn. 5:14, lest a *w.*, thing come unto thee.
1Cor. 11:17, not for the better, but for the *w.*
1Tim. 5:8, he is *w.* than an infidel.
2Tim. 3:13, shall wax *w.* and *w.*
2Pet. 2:20, the latter end is *w.* with them.
See Jer. 7:26; 16:12; Dan. 1:10; Jn. 2:10.
WORSHIP. Ps. 95:6, let us *w.* and bow down.
97:7, *w.* him, all ye gods.
99:5, *w.* at his footstool.
Isa. 27:13, shall *w.* the Lord in the holy mount.
Jer. 44:19, did we *w.* her without our men?
Zeph. 1:5, them that *w.* the host of heaven.
Mt. 4:9; Lk. 4:7, fall down and *w.* me.
15:9, in vain they do *w.* me.
Jn. 4:20, our fathers *w.* in this mountain.
22, ye *w.* ye know not what.
12:20, Greeks came to *w.*
Acts 17:23, whom ye ignorantly *w.*
24:14, so *w.* I the God of my fathers.
Rom. 1:25, *w.* the creature more than the Creator.
1Cor. 14:25, so falling down he will *w.* God.

See Col. 2:18; Heb 1:6; Rev. 4:10; 9:20.
WORTH. Job 24:25; Prov. 10:20; Ezek. 30:2.
WORTHY. Gen. 32:10, I am not *w.* of the least.
1Sam. 26:16, ye are *w.* to die.
1Ki. 1:52, if he shew himself a *w.* man.
Mt. 3:11, whose shoes I am not *w.* to bear.
8:8; Lk. 7:6, I am not *w.* that thou shouldest come.
10:10, the workman is *w.* of his meat.
37, loveth father or mother more than me is not *w.* of me.
22:8, they which were bidden were not *w.*
Mk. 1:7; Lk. 3:16; Jn. 1:27, not *w.* to unloose.
Lk. 3:8, fruits *w.* of repentance.
7:4, that he was *w.* for whom he should do this.
10:7; 1Tim. 5:18, the labourer is *w.* of his hire.
12:48, things *w.* of stripes.
15:19, no more *w.*, to be called thy son.
20:35, *w.* to obtain that world.
Acts 24:2, very *w.* deeds are done.
Rom. 8:18, not *w.* to be compared with the glory.
Eph. 4:1; Col. 1:10; 1Th. 2:12, walk *w.*
Heb. 11:38, of whom the world was not *w.*
Jas. 2:7, that *w.* name.
Rev. 3:4, for they are *w.*
See Nah. 2:5; Rev. 4:11; 5:2; 16:6.
WOULD. Num. 22:29, I *w.* there were a sword.
Ps. 81:11, Israel *w.* none of me.
Prov. 1:25, ye *w.* none of my reproof.
30, they *w.* none of my counsel.
Dan. 5:19, whom he *w.* he slew.
Mt. 7:12; Lk. 6:31, whatsoever ye *w.* that men.
Mk. 3:13, and calleth unto him whom he *w.*
Rom. 7:15, what I *w.* that do I not.
1Cor. 7:7, I *w.* that all men were even as I.
Rev. 3:15, I *w.* thou wert cold or hot.
See Num. 11:29; Acts 26:29; Ga. 5:17.
WOUND (*n.*). Ex. 21:25, give *w.* for *w.*
Job 34:6, my *w.* is incurable.
Ps. 147:3, he bindeth up their *w.*
Prov. 23:29, who hath *w.* without cause?
27:6, faithful are the *w.* of a friend.
Isa. 1:6, but *w.* and bruises.
Jer. 15:18, why is my *w.* incurable?
30:17, I will heal thee of thy *w.*
Zech. 13:6, what are these *w.* in thy hands?
Lk. 10:34, bound up his *w.*
See Prov. 6:33; 20:30; Hos. 5:13; Rev. 13:3.
WOUND (*v.*). Dt. 32:39, I *w.*, and I heal.
1Ki. 22:34; 2Chr. 18:33, carry me out, for I am *w.*
Job 5:18, he *w.*, and his hands make whole.
Ps. 64:7, suddenly shall they be *w.*
109:22, my heart is *w.* within me.
Prov. 7:26, she hath cast down many *w.*
18:14, a *w.* spirit who can bear?
Isa. 53:5, he was *w.* for our transgressions.
Jer. 37:10, there remained but *w.* men.
See Gen. 4:23; Mk. 12:4; Lk. 10:30; Acts 19:16.
WRAP. Isa. 28:10; Mic. 7:3; Jn. 20:7.
WRATH. Gen. 49:7, cursed by their *w.*
Dt. 32:27, were it not I feared the *w.* of the enemy.
Job 21:30; Prov. 11:4; Zeph. 1:15; Rom. 2:5; Rev. 6:17, the day of *w.*
36:18, because there is *w.*, beware.
Ps. 76:10, the *w.* of man shall praise thee.
90:7, by thy *w.* are we troubled.
Prov. 16:14, *w.* of a king is as messengers of death.
19:19, a man of great *w.* shall suffer.
27:3, a fool's *w.* is heavier.
4, *w.* is cruel, and anger outrageous.
Eccl. 5:17, much *w.* with his sickness.
Isa. 13:9, the day of the Lord cometh with *w.*
54:8, in a little *w.* I hid my face.
Nah. 1:2, he reserveth *w.* for his enemies.
Hab. 3:2, in *w.* remember mercy.
Mt. 3:7; Lk. 3:7, from the *w.* to come.
Rom. 2:5, *w.* against the day of *w.*
Eph. 6:4, provoke not your children to *w.*
1Th. 5:9, God hath not appointed us to *w.*
1Tim. 2:8, lifting up holy hands, without *w.*
See Jas. 1:19; Rev. 6:16; 12:12; 14:8.
WRATHFUL. Ps. 69:24; Prov. 15:18.
WREST. Ex. 23:2; Dt. 16:19; Ps. 56:5; 2Pet. 3:16.
WRESTLE. Gen. 32:24; Eph. 6:12.
WRETCHED. Num. 11:15; Rom. 7:24; Rev. 3:17.
WRING. Jud. 6:38; Ps. 75:8; Prov. 30:33.
WRINKLE. Job 16:8; Eph. 5:27.
WRITE. Prov. 3:3; 7:3, *w.* on table of thy heart.
Isa. 10:1, *w.* grievousness which they have prescribed.
19, few, that a child may *w.* them.
Jer. 22:30, *w.* ye this man childless.
31:33; Heb. 8:10, I will *w.* it in their hearts.
Hab. 2:2, *w.* the vision, make it plain.
See Job 13:26; Ps. 87:6; Rev. 3:12.
WRITING. Ex. 32:16; Jn. 5:47; Col. 2:14.
WRITTEN. Job 19:23, Oh that my words were *w.*
Ps. 69:28, let them not be *w.* with the righteous.
Ezek. 2:10, roll was *w.* within and without.
Lk. 10:20, because your names are *w.* in heaven.
Jn. 19:22, what I have *w.* I have *w.*
1Cor. 10:11, *w.* for our admonition.
2Cor. 3:2, ye are our epistle *w.* in our hearts.
See Isa. 4:3; Jer. 17:1; Rev. 2:17; 13:8.
WRONG. Ex. 2:13, to him that did the *w.*
1Chr. 12:17, there is no *w.* in mine hands.
Job 19:7, I cry out of *w.* but am not heard.
Jer. 22:3, do no *w.*
Mt. 20:13, friend, I do thee no *w.*
1Cor. 6:7, why do ye not rather take *w.*?
2Cor. 12:13, forgive me this *w.*
Col. 3:25, he that doeth *w.* shall receive.
Phile. 18, if he hath *w.* thee.
See Prov. 8:36; Acts 25:10; 2Cor. 7:2.
WRONGFULLY. Job 21:27; Ezek. 22:29; 1Pet. 2:19.
WROTE. Dan. 5:5; Jn. 8:6; 19:19; 2Jn. 5.
WROTH. Gen. 4:6, why art thou *w.*?
Dt. 1:34; 3:26; 9:19; 2Sam. 22:8; 2Chr. 28. 9; Ps. 18:7; 78:21, heard your words, and was *w.*
2Ki. 5:11, but Naaman was *w.*, and went away.
Ps. 80:38, thou hast been *w.* with thine anointed.
Isa. 47:6, I was *w.* with my people.

54:9, I have sworn I would not be *w.*
57:16, neither will I be always *w.*
64:9, be not *w.* very sore.
Mt. 18:34, his lord was *w.*, and delivered.
See Num. 16:22; Isa. 28:21; Mt. 2:16.
WROUGHT. Num. 23:23, what hath God *w.*!
1Sam. 6:6, when God had *w.* wonderfully.
14:45, Jonathan hath *w.* with God this day.
Neh. 4:17, with one of his hands *w.* in the work.
6:16, this work was *w.* of our God.
Job 12:9, the hand of the Lord hath *w.* this.
36:23, who can say, thou hast *w.* iniquity?
Ps. 31:19, hast *w.* for them that trust in thee.
68:28, strengthen that which thou hast *w.* for us.
139:15, curiously *w.* in lowest parts of the earth.
Eccl. 2:11, I looked on all my hands had *w.*
Isa. 26:12, thou also hast *w.* all our works in us.
41:4, who hath *w.* and done it?
Jer. 18:3, he *w.* a work on the wheels.
Ezek. 20:9, I *w.* for my name's sake.
Dan. 4:2, the wonders God hath *w.* toward me.
Mt. 20:12, these last have *w.* but one hour.
26:10; Mk. 14:6, she hath *w.* a good work on me.
Jn. 3:21, manifest that they are *w.* in God.
Acts 15:12, what wonders God had *w.*
Acts 18:3, he abode with them, and *w.*
19:11, *w.* special miracles by hands of Paul.
Rom. 7:8, *w.* in me all manner of concupiscence.
15:18, things which Christ hath not *w.*
2Cor. 5:5, he that hath *w.* us for the selfsame thing.
7:11, what carefulness it *w.* in you.
12:12, the signs of an apostle were *w.*
Gal. 2:8, he that *w.* effectually in Peter.
Eph. 1:20, which he *w.* in Christ.
2Th. 3:8, but we *w.* with labour.
Heb. 11:33, through faith *w.* righteousness.
Jas. 2:22, faith *w.* with his works.
1Pet. 4:3, to have *w.* the will of the Gentiles.
2Jn. 8, lose not those things we have *w.*
Rev. 19:20, the false prophet that *w.* miracles.
See Ex. 36:4; 2Sam. 18:13; 1Ki. 16:25.
WRUNG. Lev. 1:15; Ps. 73:10; Isa. 51:17.
YARN. 1Ki. 10:28; 2Chr. 1:16.
YE. 1Cor. 6:11; 2Cor. 3:2; Gal. 6:1.
YEA. Mt. 5:37; Jas. 5:12, let your communication be *y.*, *y.*
2 Cor. 1:17, there should be *y.*, *y.*, and nay, nay.
See 2Cor. 1:18; Phil. 3:8; 2Tim. 3:12.
YEAR. Gen. 1:14, for seasons, days and *y.*
47:9, few and evil have they *y.* of my life been.
Ex. 13:10, keep this ordinance from *y.* to *y.*
23:29, I will not drive them out in one *y.*
Lev. 16:34, make atonement once a *y.*
25:5, it is a *y.* of rest.
Num. 14:34, each day for a *y.* shall ye bear.
Dt. 14:22, thou shalt tithe the increase *y.* by *y.*
15:9, the *y.* of release is a hand.
26:12, the third *y.*, which is the *y.* of tithing.
32:7, consider the *y.* of many generations.
Jud. 11:40, to lament four days in a *y.*
1Sam. 2:19, brought a coat from *y.* to *y.*
7:16, went from *y.* to *y.* in circuit.
2Sam. 14:26, every *y.* he polled it.
1Ki. 17:1, there shall not be dew nor rain these *y.*
2Chr. 14:6, the land had rest, no war in those *y.*
Job 10:5, are thy *y.* as man's days?
15:20, the number of *y.* is hidden.
16:22, when a few *y.* are come.
32:7, multitude of *y.* should teach wisdom.
36:11, they shall spend their *y.* in pleasures.
26, nor can the number of his *y.* be searched out.
Ps. 31:10, my *y.* are spent with sighing.
61:6, prolong his *y.* as many generations.
65:11, thou crownest the *y.* with thy goodness.
77:5, the *y.* of ancient times.
10, I will remember the *y.* of the right hand.
78:33, their *y.* did he consume in trouble.
90:4, a thousand *y.* in thy sight.
9, we spend our *y.* as a tale that is told.
10, the days of our *y.* are threescore and ten.
102:24, they *y.* are throughout all generations.
27, thy *y.* shall have no end.
Prov. 4:10, the *y.* of thy life shall be many.
5:9, lest thou give thy *y.* to the cruel.
10:27, the *y.* of the wicked shall be shortened.
Eccl. 12:1, nor the *y.* draw nigh.
Isa. 21:16, according to the *y.* of an hireling.
29:1, add ye *y.* to *y.*
38:15, go softly all my *y.*
61:2; Lk. 4:10, the acceptable *y.* of the Lord.
63:4, the *y.* of my redeemed is come.
Jer. 11:23; 23:12; 48:44, the *y.* of their visitation.
17:8, shall not be careful in *y.* of drought.
28:16, this *y.* thou shalt die.
51:46, a rumour shall come in one *y.*
Ezek. 4:5, I have laid on thee the *y.* of their iniquity.
22:4, thou art come even unto thy *y.*
38:8, in latter *y.* thou shalt come.
46:17, it shall be his to the *y.* of liberty.
Dan. 11:6, in the end of *y.* they shall join.
Joel 2:2, to the *y.* of many generations.
Mic. 6:6, shall I come with calves of a *y.* old?
Hab. 3:2, revive thy work in the midst of the *y.*
Mal. 3:4, the offering be pleasant, as in former *y.*
Lk. 13:8, let it alone this *y.* also.
Gal. 4:10, ye observe days and *y.*
Rev. 20:2, Satan bound for a thousand *y.*
See Zech. 14:16; Jas. 4:13; Rev. 9:15.
YEARLY. 1Sam. 1:3; 20:6; Est. 9:21.
YEARN. Gen. 43:30; 1Ki. 3:26.
YELL. Jer. 2:15; 51:38.
YESTERDAY. Job 8:9; Ps. 90:4; Heb. 13:8.
YET. Gen. 40:23, *y.* did not the butler remember.
Ex. 10:7, knowest thou not *y.*?
Dt. 9:29, *y.* they are thy people.
12:9, ye are not as *y.* come.
Jud. 7:4, the people are *y.* too many.

1Ki. 19:18, *y.* I have left me.
2Ki. 13:23, nor cast them from his presence as *y.*
Ezra 3:6, the foundation was not *y.* laid.
Job 1:16, while he was *y.* speaking.
13:15, though he slay me, *y.* will I trust in him.
29:5, when the Almighty was *y.* with me.
Ps. 2:6, *y.* have I set my king.
Eccl. 4:3, he which hath not *y.* been.
Isa. 28:4, while it is *y.* in his hand.
49:15, *y.* will I not forget.
Jer. 2:9, I will *y.* plead with you.
23:21, *y.* they ran.
Ezek. 11:16, *y.* will I be to them.
36:37, I will *y.* for this be enquired of.
Dan. 11:35, it is *y.* for a time appointed.
Hos. 7:9, *y.* he knoweth not.
Amos 6:10, is there *y.* any with thee?
Jonah 3:4, *y.* forty days.
Hab. 3:18, *y.* I will rejoice.
Mt. 15:17, do not ye *y.* understand?
19:20, what lack I *y.*?
24:6; Mk. 13:7, the end is not *y.*
Mk. 11:13, the time of figs was not *y.*
Lk. 24:44, while I was *y.* with you.
Jn. 2:4; 7:6; 8:20, hour is not *y.* come.
11:25, though dead, *y.* shall he live.
Rom. 5:6, *y.* without strength.
8:24, why doth he *y.* hope for?
1Cor. 3:15, *y.* so as by fire.
15:17, ye are *y.* in your sins.
Gal. 2:20, *y.* not I, but Christ.
Heb. 4:15, *y.* without sin.
1Jn. 3:2, it doth not *y.* appear.
See Acts 8:16; Rom. 9:19; 1Cor. 3:3.

YIELD. Gen. 4:12, not henceforth *y.* strength.
Lev. 19:25, that it may *y.* the increase.
26:4, the land shall *y.* her increase.
Num. 17:8, the rod *y.* almonds.
2Chr. 30:8, *y.* yourselves to the Lord.
Neh. 9:37, it *y.* much increase to the kings.
Ps. 67:6, the earth *y.* her increase.
107:37, plant vineyards, which may *y.* fruits.
Prov. 7:21, she caused him to *y.*
Eccl. 10:4, *y.* pacifieth great offences.
Hos. 8:7, if it *y.*, the strangers shall swallow it up.
Joel 2:22, the fig tree and vine do *y.* their strength.
Hab. 3:17, though fields shall *y.* no meat.
Mt. 27:50, cried again, and *y.* up the ghost.
Acts 23:21, do not thou *y.* to them.
Rom. 6:13, neither *y.* ye your members, but *y.* yourselves to God.
16, to whom ye *y.* yourselves servants.
Heb. 12:11, *y.* the peaceable fruits of righteousness.
See Gen. 1:29; Isa. 5:10; Dan. 3:28.

YOKE. Gen. 27:40, thou shalt break his *y.*
Lev. 26:13, I have broken the bands of your *y.*
Num. 19:2; 1Sam. 6:7, on which never came *y.*
Dt. 28:48, he shall put a *y.* on thy neck.
1Ki. 12:4, thy father made our *y.* grievous.
Isa. 9:4; 10:27; 14:25, thou hast broken the *y.* of his burden.
58:6, that ye break every *y.*
Jer. 2:20, of old time I have broken thy *y.*
27:2; 28:13, make thee bonds and *y.*
31:18, as a bullock unaccustomed to the *y.*
Lam. 3:27, it is good to bear the *y.* in youth.
Mt. 11:29, take my *y.* upon you.
30, for my *y.* is easy.
Acts 15:10, to put a *y.* upon the neck of the disciples.
2Cor. 6:14, not unequally *y.* with unbelievers.
Gal. 5:1, entangled with the *y.* of bondage.
Phil. 4:3, I entreat thee also, true *y*-fellow.
1Tim. 6:1, as many servants as are under the *y.*
See Job 1:3; 42:12; Lam. 1:14; Lk. 14:19.

YONDER. Gen. 22:5; Num. 23:15; Mt. 17:20.

YOU. Gen. 48:21, God shall be with *y.*
Ruth 2:4, the Lord be with *y.*
1Chr. 22:18, is not the Lord with *y.*?
2Chr. 15:2, the Lord is with *y.*, while ye be with him.
Jer. 19:6, cannot I do with *y.*
42:11; Hag. 1:13; 2:4, for I am with *y.*
Zech. 8:23, we will go with *y.*, God is with *y.*
Mt. 7:12; Lk. 6:21, that men should do to *y.*
28:20, I am with *y.* alway.
Lk. 10:16, he that heareth *y.* heareth me.
13:28, and *y.* yourselves thrust out.
Acts 13:46, seeing ye put it from *y.*
Rom. 16:20; 1Cor. 16:23; Phil. 4:23; Col. 4:18; 1Th. 5:28; 2Th. 3:18; 2Tim. 4:15; Ti. 3:15; Heb. 13:25; 2Jn. 3; Rev. 22:21, grace be with *y.*
1Cor. 6:11, such were some of *y.*
2Cor. 12:14, I seek not yours, but *y.*
Eph. 2:1; Col. 2:13, *y.* hath he quickened.
Col. 1:27, Christ in *y.*
4:9, a brother, who is one of *y.*
1Th. 5:12, know them that are over *y.*
1Jn. 4:4, greater is he that is in *y.*
See Hag. 1:4; Mal. 2:1; 2Cor. 8:13; Phil. 3:1; 1Pet 2:7.

YOUNG. Ex. 23:26, there shall nothing cast their *y.*
Lev. 22:28, ye shall not kill it and her *y.* in one day.
Dt. 22:6, thou shalt not take the dam with the *y.*
28:50, which will not show favour to the *y.*
57, her eyes shall be evil toward her *y.* one.
32:11, as an eagle fluttereth over her *y.*
1Chr. 22:5; 29:1, Solomon my son is *y.*
2Chr. 13:7, when Rehoboam was *y.* and tender.
34:3, while he was yet *y.*, he began to seek God.
Job 38:41, when his *y.* ones cry to God. they wander.
39:16, the ostrich is hardened against her *y.*
Ps. 37:25, I have been *y.*, and now am old.
78:71, from following ewes great with *y.*
84:3, a nest where she may lay her *y.*
147:9, he giveth food to the *y.* ravens which cry.
Prov. 30:17, the *y.* eagles shall eat it.
Song 2:9; 8:14, my beloved is like a *y.* hart.
Isa. 11:7, their *y.* shall lie down together.

40:11, and gently lead those that are with *y.*
Jer. 31:12, flow together for *y.* of the flock.
Ezek. 17:4, cropped off his *y.* twigs.
Jn. 21:18, when *y.* thou girdedst thyself.
Ti. 2:4, teach the *y.* women to be sober.
See Gen. 33:13; Isa. 30:6; Mk. 7:25; Jn. 12:14.
YOUNGER. Gen. 25:23, the elder shall serve the *y.*
Job 30:1, they that are *y.* have me in derision.
Lk. 22:26, he that is greatest, let him be as the *y.*
1Tim. 5:1, intreat the *y.* man as brethren.
1Pet. 5:5, ye *y.*, submit yourselves to the elder
See Gen. 29:18; Lk. 15:12; 1Tim. 5:2, 11.
YOUNGEST. Gen. 42:13; Josh. 6:26; 1Ki. 16:34.
YOURS. 2Chr. 20:15; Lk. 6:20; 1Cor. 3:21.
YOUTH. Gen. 8:21, imagination is evil from *y.*
46:34, about cattle from our *y.* till now.
1Sam. 17:33, he a man of war from his *y.*
55, whose son is this *y.*?
2Sam. 19:7, evil that befell thee from thy *y.*
1Ki. 18:12, I fear the Lord from my *y.*
Job 13:26, to possess the iniquities of my *y.*
20:11, his bones are full of the sin of his *y.*
29:4, as in days of my *y.*
30:12, on my right hand rise the *y.*
33:25, he shall return to the days of his *y.*
36:14, hypocrites die in *y.*
Ps. 25:7, remember not the sins of my *y.*
71:5, thou art my trust from my *y.*
17, thou hast taught me from my *y.*
88:15, ready to die from my *y.* up.
89:45, the days of his *y.* hast thou shortened.
103:5, thy *y.* is renewed like the eagle's.
110:3, the dew of thy *y.*
127:4, the children of thy *y.*
129:1, they have afflicted me from my *y.*
144:12, as plants grown up in *y.*
Prov. 2:17, forsaketh the guide of her *y.*
5:18, rejoice with the wife of thy *y.*
Eccl. 11:9, rejoice, young man, in thy *y.*
10, childhood and *y.* are vanity.
12:1, remember now thy Creator in days of *y.*
Isa. 47:12, wherein thou hast laboured from thy *y.*
54:4, forget the shame of thy *y.*
Jer. 2:2, the kindness of thy *y.*
3:4, thou art the guide of my *y.*
22:21, this hath been thy manner from thy *y.*
31:19, bear the reproach of my *y.*
32:30, have done evil before me from their *y.*
48:11, hath been at ease from his *y.*
Lam. 3:27, it is good that he bear the yoke in his *y.*
Ezek. 4:14, soul not polluted from *y.*
16:22, thou hast not remembered the days of thy *y.*
Hos. 2:15, she shall sing as in the days of her *y.*
Joel 1:8, lament for husband of her *y.*
Zech. 13:5, man taught me to keep cattle from my *y.*
Mt. 19:20; Mk. 10:20; Lk. 18:21, have kept from my *y.*
Acts 26:4, my manner of life from my *y.*
1Tim. 4:12, let no man despise thy *y.*
See Prov. 7:7; Isa. 40:30; Jer. 3:24, 25.
YOUTHFUL. 2Tim. 2:22, flee *y.* lusts.
ZEAL. 2Sam. 21:2, sought to slay them in his *z.*
2Ki. 10:16, come and see my *z.* for the Lord.
Ps. 69:9; Jn. 2:17, the *z.* of thine house.
119:139, my *z.* hath consumed me.
Isa. 9:7, the *z.* of the Lord will perform this.
59:17, clad with *z.* as a cloak.
63:15, where is thy *z.*?
Ezek. 5:13, I have spoken it in my *z.*
Rom. 10:2, they have a *z.* of God.
2Cor. 9:2, your *z.* hath provoked many.
Phil. 3:6, concerning *z.* persecuting the church.
Col. 4:13, he hath a great *z.* for you.
See 2Ki. 19:31; Isa. 37:32; 2Cor. 7:11.
ZEALOUS. Num. 25:11, he was *z.* for my sake.
Acts 21:20, they are all *z.* of the law.
1Cor. 14:12, as ye are *z.* of spiritual gifts.
Ti. 2:14, *z.* of good works.
Rev. 3:19, be *z.* therefore, and repent.
See Num. 25:13; Acts 22:3; Gal. 1:14.
ZEALOUSLY. Gal. 4:18, *z.* affected.

THE NEW OXFORD BIBLE MAPS

1. Jerusalem in Old Testament times
2. Background of the Exodus
3. Israel in Canaan: Joshua to Samuel and Saul
4. The United Monarchy
5. The Near East in the time of the Assyrian Empire
6. Central Palestine in Old Testament times
7. Palestine under the Herods
8. The Background of the New Testament: Rome and the East (including Paul's Journeys)
9. Jerusalem in New Testament times

barim, Mts. of *6,* **Y5**
bdon *3,* **X2**
bel-beth-maacah *4,* **Y2**
bel-keramim *3, 6,* **Y5**
bel-meholah *3, 4, 6,* **X4**
bel-shittim *6,* **Y5**
bila *7,* **Y3**
bilene *7,* **Y1**; *8,* **G4**
cco *3, 4, 6,* **X3**; *5,* **G4**
chaia *8,* **D3**
chor, V. of *3,* **X5**
chshaph *3, 6,* **X3**
chzib: Judah *6,* **W5**
chzib: Phoenicia *3,* **X2**
ctium *8,* **D3**
dadah (Aroer) *3,* **W6**
dam *3,* **Y4**
damah *6,* **X2**
dami-nekeb *6,* **X3**
dhaim, R. *5,* **H4**
diabene *8,* **H3**
dithaim *6,* **X5**
dora *7,* **X5**
dramyttium *8,* **E3**
dria, Sea of *8,* **C2**
dullam *3, 4, 6,* **X5**
dummim *6,* **X5**
egean Sea *8,* **E3**
elana (Aila) *8,* **F5**
elia, Wall of *9*
frica *8,* **C4**
grippa's Wall *9*
grippias (Anthedon) *7,* **V5**
hlab *3,* **X2**
i *3, 6,* **X5**
ijalon: Dan *3, 6,* **X5**
ijalon: Zebulun *6,* **X3**
ila (Aelana) *8,* **F5**
krabbim, Ascent of *3,* **X7**
leppo *5,* **G3**
lexandria: Egypt *8,* **E4**
lexandria Troas *8,* **E3**
lexandrium *7,* **X4**
lmon *6,* **X5**
lmon-diblathaim *6,* **Y5**
malek *4,* **W6**
masea *8,* **G2**
mastris *8,* **F2**
mathus *7,* **Y4**
misus *8,* **G2**
mmon *2 inset; 3, 4,* **Z4**; *5,* **G4**
nab *3,* **W6**
naharath *6,* **X3**
naniah *6,* **X5**

Anathoth *3, 4, 6,* **X5**
Ancona *8,* **B2**
Ancyra *8,* **F3**
Anthedon (Agrippias) *7,* **V5**
Antioch: Galatia *8,* **F3**
Antioch: Syria *8,* **G3**
Antipatris *7,* **W4**
Antium *8,* **B2**
Antonia Tower *9*
Apamea *8,* **G3**
Aphek: Bashan *6,* **Y3**
Aphek: Ephraim *3, 6,* **W4**
Aphekah *6,* **X5**
Aphik (Aphek): Asher *3, 6,* **X3**
Apollonia: Macedonia *8,* **C2**
Apollonia Sozusa *7,* **W4**
Appian Way *8,* **C2**
Appii Forum *8,* **B2**
Aqaba, Gulf of *2,* **T3**
Arabah, The *3, 4, 6,* **Y4**; *2,* **U2**
Arabah, Sea of the *3, 4, 6,* **X5**
Arabia *5,* **H5**
Arabian Desert *8,* **G4**
Arad *3,* **X6**; *2,* **U1**
Aram (Syria) *4,* **Z2**
Ararat (Urartu) *5,* **H3**
Araxes, R. *8,* **H3**
Arbela: Assyria *5, 8,* **H3**
Area *8,* **G4**
Archelais: Cappadocia *8,* **F3**
Archelais: Palestine *7,* **X4**
Argob *4,* **Z3**
Ariminum *8,* **B2**
Armenia, Kingdom of *8,* **H3**
Arnon, R. *3, 4, 7,* **Y6**; *2,* **U1**
Aroer: Moab *3, 4,* **Y6**
Aroer (Adadah): Negeb *3,* **W6**
Arpad *5,* **G3**
Arrapkha *5,* **H3**
Artaxata *8,* **H3**
Arubboth *4, 6,* **X4**
Arumah *3, 6,* **X4**
Aruna *6,* **X4**
Arvad *5,* **G4**
Ascalon *7,* **W5**
Ashan *3,* **W6**
Ashdod *3, 4, 6,* **W5**; *2,* **T1**
Asher: *tribe 3, 4,* **X2**
Ashkelon *3, 4,* **W5**
Ashnah: (nr. Sorek), Judah *6,* **X5**
Ashnah (W. of Hebron), Judah *6,* **W5**
Ashtaroth, *3,* **Z3**
Asia *8,* **E3**

Asor *3, 6,* **W4**
Asphaltitis, L. *7,* **X5**
Asshur *5,* **H3**
Assos *8,* **E3**
Assyria *5,* **H3**
Ataroth: Ephraim *3, 6,* **X4**
Ataroth: Moab *6,* **Y5**
Ataroth-addar *6,* **X5**
Athens *8,* **D3**
Athribis *2,* **Q2**; *5,* **F4**
Attalia *8,* **F3**
Auranitis *7,* **Z3**
Avaris *2,* **Q2**
Azekah *3, 6,* **W5**; *2,* **T1**
Azmon *2,* **T2**
Aznoth-tabor *6,* **X3**
Azotus *7,* **W5**

Baalah (Kiriath-jearim) *3, 6,* **X5**
Baalath *3, 4, 6,* **W5**
Baal-gad *3,* **Y2**
Baal-hazor *4, 6,* **X5**
Baal-meon *6,* **Y5**
Baal-peor *6,* **Y5**
Baal-shalishah *6,* **X4**
Baal-zephon *2,* **R2** *and inset*
Babylon: Egypt *8,* **F5**
Babylon: Mesopotamia *5, 8,* **H4**
Babylonia *5,* **J4**
Balikh, R. *5,* **G3**
Bamoth-baal *6,* **Y5**
Baris: Jerusalem 1
Bashan *3, 4,* **Y3**
Batanaea *7,* **Z3**
Bathyra *7,* **Z2**
Beautiful Gate *9*
Beer *3, 6,* **X3**
Beeroth: Benjamin *3, 4, 6,* **X5**
Beeroth (Bene-jaakan) *2,* **T2**
Beer-sheba *2,* **T1** *and inset; 3, 4, 7,* **W6**
Bene-berak *6,* **W4**
Bene-jaakan (Beeroth) *2,* **T2**
Beneventum *8,* **B2**
Benjamin: *tribe 3, 4,* **X5**
Benjamin, Gate of *1*
Beon *6,* **Y5**
Beroea *8,* **D2**
Bersabe (Beer-sheba) *7,* **W6**
Berytus *5, 8,* **G4**
Besor, Brook *3, 4,* **V6**
Beten *6,* **X3**
Beth-anath *3, 6,* **X3**
Beth-anoth *6,* **X5**

Bethany *7*, **X5**
Betharamphtha *7*, **Y5**
Beth-aven (Bethel) *6*, **X5**
Beth-baal-meon *3, 6*, **Y5**
Beth-dagon *3, 6*, **W5**
Beth-diblathaim *6*, **Y5**
Beth-eden (Bit-adini) *5*, **G3**
Bethel *3, 4, 6*, **X5**
Bethesda, Pool of *9*
Beth-gilgal (Gilgal) *6*, **X5**
Beth-haccherem *6*, **X5**
Beth-haggan *3*, **X2**
Beth-hanan *4*, **X5**
Beth-haram *6*, **Y5**
Beth-hoglah *6*, **Y5**
Beth-horon, Lower *3, 4, 6*, **X5**
Beth-horon, Upper *3, 4, 6* **X5**
Beth-jeshimoth *3, 6*, **Y5**
Bethlehem: Galilee *3, 6*, **X3**
Bethlehem: Judah *3, 4, 6, 7*, **X5**
Beth-meon *6*, **Y5**
Beth-nimrah *3, 6*, **Y5**
Beth-peor *3, 6*, **Y5**
Beth-rehob: *region 4*, **Y2**
Beth-rehob: *town 3, 4*, **Y2**
Bethsaida-Julias *7*, **Y3**
Beth-shan (Beth-shean) *6*, **Y4**
Beth-shean *3, 4, 6*, **X3**
Beth-shemesh: Issachar *6*, **Y3**
Beth-shemesh: Judah *3, 4, 6*, **W5**
Beth-tappuah *6*, **X5**
Bethul (Bethuel) *3*, **W6**
Bethzatha, Pool of *9*
Beth-zur *3, 6*, **X5**
Betogabri *7*, **W5**
Betonim *3, 6*, **Y5**
Bezek *3, 6*, **X4**
Bezer *3*, **Y5**
Bezetha *9*
Bit-adini (Beth-eden) *5*, **G3**
Bithynia & Pontus *8*, **F2**
Black Sea *5*, **F2**
Borim *6*, **X4**
Borsippa *5*, **H4**
Bosphorus *8*, **E2**
Bosporan Kingdom *8*, **G2**
Bozkath *6*, **W5**
Bozrah *2*, **U2**
Brundisium *8*, **C2**
Bubastis *2*, **Q2**
Busiris *2*, **Q2**
Byblos (Gebal) *5*, **G4**
Byzantium *8*, **E2**

Cabbon *6*, **W5**
Cabul *3, 4, 6*, **X3**
Caesarea: Palestine *7*, **W4**; *8*, **F4**
Caesarea (Mazaca) *8*, **G3**
Caesarea Philippi *7*, **Y2**; *8*, **G4**
Calah *5*, **H3**
Callirrhoe *7*, **Y5**
Calno *5*, **G3**
Canaan *2*, **T1**
Canopus *8*, **F4**
Canusium *8*, **C2**
Capernaum *7*, **Y3**
Caphtor (Crete) *5*, **D3**
Cappadocia *8*, **G3**
Capreae (Capri) *8*, **B2**
Capua *8*, **B2**
Carchemish *5, 8*, **G3**
Carmel *4*, **X6**
Carmel, Mt. *3, 4, 6, 7*, **X3**
Carrhae (Haran) *8*, **G3**
Caspian Sea *5*, **K3**
Catana *8*, **C3**
Cauda *8*, **D4**
Cenchreae *8*, **D3**
Chephar-ammoni *6*, **X5**
Chephirah *3, 6*, **X5**
Cherith, Brook *6*, **Y4**
Chersonesus *8*, **F2**
Chesulloth *6*, **X3**
Chezib (Achzib) *6*, **W5**
Chinnereth *3, 6*, **Y3**
Chinnereth, Sea of *3, 4, 6*, **Y3**
Chios *8*, **E3**
Chisloth-tabor *6*, **X3**
Chorazin *7*, **Y3**
Cilicia (Khilakku) *5*, **F3**
Cilicia & Syria *8*, **G3**
Cilicia Trachea *8*, **F3**
City of David *1*
City of Salt *6*, **X5**
Cnidus *8*, **E3**
Colchis *8*, **H2**
Colonia Amasa (Emmaus) *7*, **X5**
Colossae *8*, **E3**
Comana *8*, **G2**
Commagene *5, 8*, **G3**
Corcyra *8*, **C3**
Corinth *8*, **D3**
Cos *8*, **E3**
Court of Gentiles *9*
Court of Israel *9*
Court of Women *9*
Crete *5, 8*, **D3**
Croton *8*, **C3**
Ctesiphon *8*, **H4**
Cuthah *5*, **H4**
Cyprus: *island 5, 8*, **F3**
Cyprus: Palestine *7*, **X5**
Cyrenaica *8*, **D4**
Cyrene *8*, **D4**
Cyzicus *8*, **E2**

Dabbesheth *6*, **X3**
Daberath *6*, **X3**
Dalmatia (Illyricum) *8*, **C2**
Damascus *3, 4, 7*, **Z1**; *5, 8*, **G4**
Damascus Gate *9*
Dan (Laish) *3, 4*, **Y2**
Dan: *tribe 3*, **Y2**
Dan: *tribe 3*, **W5**
Danube, R. *8*, **D2**
Dead Sea *7*, **X6**
Debir: Judah *3, 4*, **W6**; *2*, **T1**
Debir: N.E. Judah *6*. **X5**
Decapolis *7*, **Y3**
Dedan *5*, **G5**
Derbe *8*, **F3**
Dibon *2*, **U1**; *3, 4*, **Y6**
Dion *7*, **Y3**
Diyala, R. *5*, **H4**
Dophkah *2*, **S3** *and inset*
Dor *3, 4, 6*, **W3**
Dora *7*, **W3**
Dorylaeum *8*, **F3**
Dothan *6*, **X4**
Dumah *5, 4*, **G5**
Dura-Europus *8*, **H4**
Dur-sharrukin *5*, **H3**
Dyrrhachium *8*, **C2**

Eastern Sea *5*, **J5**
Ebal, Mt. *3, 4, 6, 7*, **X4**
Eben-ezer *6*, **W4**
Ecbatana *5*, **J4**
Edessa *8*, **G3**
Edom *2*, **U2** *and inset; 3, 4*, **Y7**; *5*, **G4**
Edrei *3*, **Z3**
Eglon *3, 6*, **W5**
Egnatian Way *8*, **D2**
Egypt *2*, **Q2**; *5, 8*, **F5**
Egypt, Brook of *2*, **S1**
Egyptian Port *2*, **S3**
Ekron *3, 4, 6*, **W5**
Elah, V. of *3*, **W5**
Elam *5, 8*, **J4**
Elath *5*, **F5**
Elealeh *6*, **Y5**
Elon *4, 6*, **X5**
Eltekeh *6*, **W5**
Eltekon *6*, **X5**
Emesa *8*, **G4**
Emmaus (Nicopolis or Colonia Amasa) *7*, **W5**
Enam *6*, **X5**
En-dor *3, 6*, **X3**
Engaddi (En-gedi) *7*, **X6**
En-gannim *3, 6*, **X4**
En-gedi *3, 7*, **X6**
En-haddah *6*, **X3**
En-rogel *1*
En-shemesh *6*, **X5**
En-tappuah *6*, **X4**
Ephesus *8*, **E3**
Ephraim: *town 4, 6*, **X5**
Ephraim: *tribe 3, 4*, **X4**
Ephraim, Hill Country of *6*, **X4**
Ephron (Ophrah) *3, 6*, **X5**
Epiphania *8*, **G3**
Erech (Uruk) *5*, **J4**
Eshtaol *6*, **X5**
Eshtemoa *3*, **X6**
Essenes, Gate of *9*
Etam *3, 6*, **X5**
Ether *6*, **W5**

thiopia *5,* **F6**
uphrates, R. *5, 8,* **H3**
uropus (Carchemish) *8,* **G3**
uxine Sea *8,* **F2**
zion-geber *2,* **T3** *and inset; 5,* **F5**

air Heavens *8,* **D4**
arah, Wadi *6,* **X4**
orum of Appius *8,* **B2**
ullers' Tower *9*

abae (Hippeum) *7,* **X3**
abbatha *9*
ad: *tribe 3,* **Y4**
adara: Decapolis *7,* **Y3**
adara: Perea *7,* **Y4**
alatia *8,* **F3**
alilee *6, 7,* **X3**
alilee, Sea of *7,* **Y3**
amala *7,* **Y3**
angra *8,* **F2**
ath: Philistia *3, 4, 6,* **W6**
ath (Gittaim): Benjamin *6,* **W5**
ath of Sharon *6,* **X4**
ath-hepher *6,* **X3**
ath-rimmon *3, 4, 6,* **W4**
aulanitis *7,* **Y3**
aza *2,* **T1** *and inset; 3, 4, 7,* **V6**; *5, 8,* **F4**
azara *7,* **W5**
eba *4, 6,* **X5**
ebal (Byblos) *5,* **G4**
ederah *6,* **W5**
edor *6,* **X5**
ennath Gate *1, 9*
ennesaret *7,* **Y3**
erar *2,* **T1**; *3, 4,* **W6**
erasa *7,* **Y4**
erizim, Mt. *3, 4, 6, 7,* **X4**
eshur *4,* **Y3**
eshur *6,* **Y3**
ethsemane *9*
ezer *3, 4, 5,* **W5**
ibbethon *3, 6,* **W5**
ibeah *3, 4, 6,* **X5**
ibeon *3, 4, 6,* **X5**
ihon Spring *1*
ilboa, Mt. *3, 4, 6,* **X3**
ilead *3, 4, 6,* **Y4**
ilgal (nr. Jericho) *3, 4, 6,* **X5**
ilgal: Ephraim *6,* **X4**
ilgal: Sharon *6,* **W4**
iloh *3, 4, 6,* **X5**
imarrai (Gomer) *5,* **F3**
imzo *6,* **W5**
ittaim (Gath) *6,* **W5**
olan *3,* **Y3**
olgotha: Jerusalem *9*
omer (Gimarrai) *5,* **F3**
ophna *7,* **X5**
ordion (Gordium) *5, 8,* **F3**
ordyene *8,* **H3**

Goshen: Egypt *2,* **Q2**
Goshen: Palestine *3,* **W6**
Gozan *5,* **G3**
Great Bitter Lake *2,* **R2**
Greater Syrtis *8,* **C4**
Great Plain, The *7,* **X3**
Great Sea, The *2,* **S1**; *3, 4,* **W3**; *5,* **E4**

Habor, R. *5,* **H3**
Hadashah *6,* **W5**
Hadid *6,* **W5**
Halhul *6,* **X5**
Halys R. *5, 8,* **G3**
Ham *6,* **Y3**
Hamath *5,* **G3**
Hammath *3, 6,* **Y3**
Hananel: Jerusalem *1*
Hannathon *3, 6,* **X3**
Haran *5, 8,* **G3**
Harim *6,* **W5**
Harod, Spring of *6,* **X3**
Harosheth-ha-goiim *3, 6,* **X3**
Hattina *5,* **G3**
Hauran *5,* **G4**
Havvoth-jair *3, 4,* **Y3**
Hazar-addar *2,* **T2**
Hazar-shual *3,* **W6**
Hazor: Benjamin *6,* **X5**
Hazor: Galilee *3,* **Y2**
Hebron *2,* **U1**; *3, 4, 6, 7,* **X5**
Helam *4,* **Z3**
Helbon *5,* **G4**
Heleph *6,* **X3**
Heliopolis (On) *2,* **Q2** *and inset: 5, 8,* **F4**
Helkath *6,* **X3**
Hepher *3, 4, 6,* **W4**
Heraclea *8,* **F2**
Hermon, Mt. *3, 4,* **Y2**
Hermopolis *5,* **F5**
Hermus, R. *5,* **E3**
Herod, Kingdom of *7*
Herodium *7,* **X5**
Heshbon *3, 4, 6,* **Y5**; *2,* **U1**
Hezekiah's Conduit *1*
High Place *4,* **X5**
Hinnom Valley *1, 9*
Hippeum (Gabae) *7,* **X3**
Hippicus: Jerusalem *9*
Hippos *7,* **Y3**
Holon *6,* **X5**
Horeb, Mt. *2,* **S4**
Hormah *2,* **T1**; *3,* **W6**
Hukkok *6,* **X3**
Hyrcania *7,* **X5**

Iadanna (Cyprus) *5,* **F3**
Ibleam *3, 6,* **X4**
Iconium *8,* **F3**
Idumea *7,* **W6**
Illyricum (Dalmatia) *8,* **C2**
Iphtah *6,* **X5**
Iphtah-el *6,* **X3**
Israel *4, 6,* **X4**; *5,* **G4**
Israel, Hill Country of *3,* **X4**
Issachar: *tribe 3, 4,* **X3**
Istros *8,* **E2**
Italy *8,* **B2**
Ituraea *7,* **Y2**

Jabbok R. *3, 4, 6, 7,* **Y4**
Jabesh-gilead *3, 4, 6,* **Y4**
Jabneel: Galilee *6,* **Y3**
Jabneel (Jamneh, Jamnia): Judah *3, 6, 7,* **W5**
Jahaz *6,* **Y5**
Janoah *6,* **X4**
Japhia *6,* **X3**
Jarmuth (Ramoth): Issachar *6,* **Y3**
Jarmuth: Judah *3, 6,* **W5**
Jattir *3,* **X6**
Javan *5,* **E3**
Jazer *4, 6,* **Y4**
Jebel Helal *2,* **S2**
Jebus (Jerusalem) *3,* **X5**
Jericho *3, 4, 7,* **X5**; *2,* **U1** *and inset*
Jerusalem *3, 4, 6, 7,* **X5** *also 2,* **U1** *and inset;* 5, 8, **G4**
Jerusalem in N.T. times *9*
Jerusalem in O.T. times *1*
Jeshanah *6,* **X4**
Jezreel: V. of Jezreel *3, 4, 6,* **X3**
Jezreel: Judah *3,* **X6**
Jezreel, V. of *3, 4, 6,* **X3**
Jogbehah *3,* **Y4**
Jokneam (Jokmeam) *3, 4, 6,* **X3**
Joppa *3, 4, 6, 7,* **W4**; *8,* **F4**
Jordan, R. *3, 4, 6, 7,* **Y4**
Jotbah *6,* **X3**
Judah: *Kingdom & region 4, 6,* **X5**; *5,* **F4**
Judah: *tribe 3, 4,* **X5**
Judah, Hill Country of *3,* **X5**
Judah, Wilderness of *4, 6,* **X5**
Judea: *region 7,* **X5**; *8,* **G4**
Judea, Wilderness of *7,* **X5**
Juttah *2,* **U1**

Kabul (Cabul) *6,* **X2**
Kabzeel *3, 4,* **W6**
Kadesh *5,* **G4**
Kadesh-barnea *2,* **T2** *and inset*
Kamon *3, 6,* **Y3**
Kanah, Brook of *6,* **W4**
Karkor *3,* **Z6**
Kedar (Qidri) *5,* **G4**
Kedemoth *3,* **Y5**
Kedesh *3,* **Y2**
Keilah *3, 6,* **X5**
Khilakku (Cilicia) *5,* **F3**
Khirbet Qumran *7,* **X5**
Kidron, Brook *6,* **X5**
Kidron Valley *1, 9*
King's Highway *2,* **U3**

Kir-hareseth *2*, **U1**; *4*, **Y6**
Kiriathaim *3, 6*, **Y5**
Kiriath-arba (Hebron) *6*, **X5**
Kiriath-jearim *3, 4, 6*, **X5**
Kishon, R. *3, 4, 6*, **X3**
Kumukhu (Commagene) *5*, **G3**

Lacedaemon (Sparta) *8*, **D3**
Lachish *2*, **T1**; *3, 6*, **W5**
Lahmam *6*, **W5**
Laish (Dan) *3*, **Y2**
Laishah *6*, **X5**
Lakkum *3, 6*, **Y3**
Laodicea *8*, **E3**
Larissa *8*, **D3**
Larsa *5*, **J4**
Lasea *8*, **D3**
Lebanon *5*, **G4**
Lebanon, Mt. *3, 4*, **Y1**
Lebanon, V. of *3*, **Y2**
Lebo-Hamath *5*, **G4**
Lebonah *3, 6*, **X4**
Lehi *6*, **X5**
Leontes, R. *7*, **X2**
Lesbos *8*, **E3**
Lesser Armenia *8*, **G3**
Libnah *3, 4, 6*, **W5**; *2*, **T1**
Libya *5, 8*, **D-E4**
Little Bitter Lake *2*, **R2**
Lo-debar *4, 6*, **Y3**
Lod *6*, **W5**
Lower Beth-horon *3, 4, 6*, **X5**
Lower Sea *5*, **J5**
Lower Zab: R. *5*, **H3**
Lowland, The *3, 4*, **W5**
Lycia *8*, **E3**
Lycopolis (Siut) *5*, **F5**
Lydda *7*, **W5**
Lydia *5*, **E3**
Lystra *8*, **F3**

Maacah *4*, **Y2**
Maarath *6*, **X5**
Macedonia *8*, **D2**
Machaerus *7*, **Y5**
Madia (Medes) *5*, **J3**
Madmannah *3*, **W6**
Madon *3, 6*, **X3**
Maeander R. *5*, **E3**
Magadan (Taricheae) *7*, **Y3**
Mahanaim *4, 6*, **Y4**
Makaz *4, 6*, **W5**
Makkedah *3, 6*, **W5**
Malta *8*, **B3**
Mamre *6*, **X5**
Manasseh: *tribe 3, 4*, **X4**
Manasseh: *tribe 3*, **Y3**
Manasseh's Wall *1*
Mannai (Minni) *5*, **J3**
Maon *3*, **X6**
Mare Internum *7*, **W4**; *8*, **D4**
Mare Nostrum *8*, **D4**
Mareshah *3, 6*, **W5**
Mariamme: Jerusalem *9*
Marisa *7*, **W5**
Masada *7*, **X6**
Mazaca (Caesarea) *8*, **G3**
Medeba *3, 4, 6, 7*, **Y5**; *2*, **U1**
Medes (Madai) *5*, **J3**
Media *8*, **H3**
Media Atropatene *8*, **H3**
Mediterranean Sea *7, 8*
Megiddo *3, 4, 6*, **X3**
Megiddo, Plain of *6*, **X3**
Melita (Malta) *8*, **B3**
Melitene *5,8*, **G3**
Memphis (Noph) *2*, **Q3** *and inset also 5, 8*, **F5**
Menzaleh, L. *2*, **Q1**
Meribah *2*, **T2**
Merom *3, 4*, **X3**
Merom, Waters of *3, 6*, **X3**
Mesembria *8*, **E2**
Meshech (Mushki) *5*, **F3**
Mesopotamia *8*, **H3**
Messana *8*, **C3**
Michmash *3, 6*, **X5**
Middin *3, 6*, **X5**
Midian *2*, **U3**
Migdal *6*, **W4**
Migdol *5*, **F4**
Migron *6*, **X5**
Miletus *8*, **E3**
Milid (Melitene) *5*, **G3**
Millo: Jerusalem *1*
Minni (Mannai) *5*, **J3**
Misrephoth-maim *3*, **X2**
Mitylene *8*, **E3**
Mizpah *3, 6*, **X5**
Mizpeh *6*, **W5**
Moab *2*, **U1** *and inset; 3, 4*, **Y6**; *5*, **G4**
Moab, Plains of *6*, **Y5**
Moesia *8*, **D2**
Mons Casius *2*, **R1**
Moreh, Hill of *3, 6*, **X3**
Moresheth-gath *6*, **W5**
Mount Baalah *3, 6*, **W5**
Mushki (Meshech) *5*, **F3**
Musri *5*, **G3**
Myra *8*, **F3**

Naarah *3, 6*, **X5**
Nabataean Kingdom *7, 8*, **G4**
Nahaliel, R. *4, 6*, **Y5**
Nahalol *3, 6*, **X3**
Nairi *5*, **H3**
Naissus *8*, **D2**
Naphath-Dor *3*, **X3**
Naphtali: *tribe 3, 4*, **X3**
Naucratis *8*, **F4**
Nazareth *7*, **X3**
Neapoils: Italy *8*, **B2**
Neapolis: Macedonia *8*, **D2**
Neapolis: Palestine *7*, **X4**
Neballat *6*, **W5**
Nebo: Judah *6*, **X5**
Nebo: Moab *6*, **Y5**
Nebo, Mt. *3, 6*, **Y5**; *2*, **U1**
Negeb, The *2*, **T1**; *3, 4*, **W6**
Neiel *6*, **X3**
Netophah *4, 6*, **X5**
Nezib *6*, **X5**
Nibshan *3, 6*, **X5**
Nicaea *8*, **E2**
Nicephorum *8*, **G3**
Nicomedia *8*, **E2**
Nicopolis (Emmaus) *7*, **X5**
Nicopolis: Greece *8*, **D3**
Nile, R. *5, 8*, **F5**
Nineveh *5*, **H3**
Ninus *8*, **H3**
Nippur *5*, **J4**
Nisibis *8*, **H3**
Nob *6*, **X5**
Noph (Memphis) *2*, **Q3**; *5*, **F5**

Oboth *2*, **U2**
Odessus *8*, **E2**
Oeseus *8*, **D2**
Olives, Mt. of *1, 9*
Olympia *8*, **D3**
On (Heliopolis) *2*, **Q2**; *5*, **F4**
Ono *6*, **W4**
Ophel: Jerusalem *1*
Ophlas: Jerusalem *9*
Ophrah (Ephron) *3, 6*, **X5**
Orontes, R. *5, 8*, **G3**
Osroëne *8*, **G3**
Ostia *8*, **B2**
Oxyrhynchus *8*, **F5**

Paestum *8*, **B2**
Palace: Jerusalem *1*
Palmyra *8*, **G4**
Pamphylia *8*, **F3**
Paneas *7*, **Y2**
Panormus *8*, **B3**
Paphos *8*, **F4**
Parah *6*, **X5**
Paran, Wilderness of *2*, **T3**
Parthian Empire *8*, **H3**
Patara *8*, **E3**
Pekod (Puqudu) *5*, **J4**
Pella *6, 7*, **Y4**
Pellusium *2*, **R1** *and inset; 5, 8*, **F4**
Peniel (Penuel) *3, 6*, **Y4**
Perea *7*, **Y5**
Perga *8*, **F3**
Pergamum *8*, **E3**
Perusia *8*, **B2**
Pessinus *8*, **F3**
Petra *8*, **G4**
Phasael: Jerusalem *9*
Phasaelis *7*, **X4**
Philadelphia: Asia *8*, **E3**
Philadelphia (Rabbah): E. of R. Jordan *7*, **Y5**
Philippi *8*, **D2**

ıilippopolis *8,* **D2**
ıilistia *6,* **W5**
ıilistia, Plain of 2, **T1**
ıilistines *3, 4,* **W5**
ıoenix *8,* **D3**
ırygia *5,* **F3**
-beseth *2,* **Q2**
ırathon *3, 4, 6,* **X4**
ısgah, Mt. *3, 6,* **Y5**
ısidia *8,* **F3**
ıthom *2,* **Q2**
ɔmpeii *8,* **B2**
ɔntus Euxinus *8,* **F2**
ɔols: Jerusalem *1, 9*
raetorium: Jerusalem *9*
rusa *8,* **E2**
sephinus: Jerusalem *9*
tolemais *7,* **X3**; *8,* **G4**
unon *2,* **U2**
uqudu (Pekod) *5,* **J4**
uteoli *8,* **B2**

antir *2,* **Q2**
arqar *5,* **G4**
idri (Kedar) *5,* **G4**
umran, Khirbet *7,* **X5**

abbah: Judah *6,* **X5**
abbah (Rabbath-ammon): Ammon *3, 4, 7,* **Y5**
akkath *6,* **Y3**
amah: Benjamin *3, 6,* **X5**
amah (Ramathaim-zophim): Ephraim *6,* **X4**
amathaim-zophim *3, 6,* **X4**
amath-mizpeh *6,* **Y4**
ameses *2,* **Q2** *and inset*
amoth *6,* **Y3**
amoth-gilead *3, 4,* **Z4**
aphana *7,* **Z3**
aphia *2,* **T1** *and inset; 5,* **F4**; *7,* **V6**
ed Sea *2,* **R3** & **T4** *and inset; 5, 8,* **F5**
ehob *3, 6,* **X3**
emeth (Ramoth) *6,* **X3**
euben: *tribe 3,* **Y5**
ezeph *5,* **G3**
hegium *8,* **C3**
hodes *5, 8,* **E3**
iblah *5,* **G4**
immon: Benjamin *3, 6,* **X5**
immon: Galilee *3, 6,* **X3**
ogelim *4, 6,* **Y3**
ɔman Empire *8*
ome *8,* **B2**
oyal Porch: Jerusalem *9*
umah *6,* **X3**

aba (Sheba) *5,* **G6**
ais *5, 8,* **F4**
alamis *8,* **F3**
alecah *5,* **G4**

Salmone *8,* **E3**
Salonae *8,* **C2**
Salt, V. of *4,* **X6**
Salt Sea *2,* **U1**; *3, 4, 6,* **X5**
Samal *5,* **G3**
Samaria: *region* 7, **X4**
Samaria: *town* 6, 7, **X4**; *5,* **G4**
Samos *8,* **E3**
Samosata *8,* **G3**
Samothrace *8,* **E2**
Sangarius, R. *5,* **F2**
Sanhedrin: Jerusalem *9*
Saqqarah *2,* **Q3**
Sardica *8,* **D2**
Sardis *5, 8,* **E3**
Sarepta *7,* **X2**
Sarid *6,* **X3**
Scodra *8,* **C2**
Scupi *8,* **D2**
Scythopolis *7,* **X3**
Sebaste (Samaria) *7,* **X4**
Secacah *3, 6,* **X5**
Sela *2,* **U2** *and inset; 5,* **G4**
Selcucia: Asia Minor *8,* **F3**
Seleucia: Mesopotamia *8,* **H4**
Sepharad (Sardis) *5,* **E3**
Sepphoris *7,* **X3**
Serabit el-Khadim *2,* **S3**
Shaalbim *3, 4, 6,* **W5**
Sharon, Plain of *4, 6, 7,* **W4**
Sheba (Saba) *5,* **G6**
Shechem *3, 4, 6,* **X4**
Shephelah *4,* **W5**
Shihor-libnath *6,* **W3**
Shikkeron *3, 6,* **W5**
Shiloh *3, 4, 6,* **X4**
Shimron *3, 6,* **X3**
Shittim *3, 6,* **Y5**; *2,* **U1**
Shunem *3, 6,* **X3**
Shur, Wilderness of *2,* **S2**
Shushan (Susa) *5,* **J4**
Sibmah *6,* **Y5**
Sicily *8,* **B3**
Side *8,* **G2**
Sidon *3, 4, 7,* **X1**; *5, 8,* **G4**
Sidonians *4,* **X2**
Siloam: Jerusalem *1*
Siloam, Pool of *9*
Simeon: *tribe 3,* **W6**
Sin (Pelusium) *2,* **R1**
Sin, Wilderness of *2,* **S3**
Sinai: *region 2,* **S3** *and inset; 5,* **F5**
Sinai, Mt. (?) (Jebel-Helal) *2,* **S2**
Sinai, Mt. (Mt. Horeb) *2,* **S4**; *8,* **F5**
Singidunum *8,* **D2**
Sinope *8,* **G2**
Siphtan *6,* **X4**
Sippar *5,* **H4**
Sirbonis, L. *2,* **S1**
Sirmium *8,* **C2**
Siut (Lycopolis) *5,* **F5**
Smyrna *8,* **E3**

Socoh: Israel *3, 4, 6,* **X4**
Socoh (Soco): Judah *3, 6,* **W5**
Solomon's Pool *9*
Solomon's Porch *9*
Solomon's Wall *1*
Sorek *3, 4, 6,* **W5**
Sparta (Lacedaemon) *8,* **D3**
Strato's Tower *7,* **W3**
Succoth: Egypt *2,* **R2** *and inset*
Succoth: Palestine *3, 4, 6,* **Y4**
Suez, Gulf of 2, **R3**
Susa (Shushan) *5,* **J4**
Sybaris *8,* **C3**
Syene *5,* **F6**
Syracuse *8,* **C3**
Syria *4,* **Z1**; *5,* **G4**
Syria, Province of *7,* **X1**

Taanach *3, 4, 6,* **X3**
Tabal (Tubal) *5,* **G3**
Tabbath *3, 6,* **Y4**
Tabor, Mt. *3, 6,* **X3**
Tadmor (Tadmar) *5,* **G4**
Tahpanhes *5,* **F4**
Tamar *4,* **X7**
Tanis *2,* **Q2**; *5,* **F4**
Tappuah *3, 6,* **X4**
Taralah *6,* **X5**
Tarentum *8,* **C2**
Tarichaea (Magadan) *7,* **Y3**
Tarracina *8,* **B2**
Tarsus *8,* **F3**
Tavium *8,* **F3**
Tekoa *4, 6,* **X5**
Tell el-Yahudiyeh *2,* **Q2**
Tema *5, 8,* **G5**
Teman 2, **U2**
Temple: Jerusalem *1, 9*
Thamna *7,* **X4**
Thebes *5,* **F5**
Thebez *3, 4, 6,* **X4**
Thessalonica *8,* **D2**
Thessaly *8,* **D3**
Thrace *8,* **E2**
Three Taverns *8,* **B2**
Thyatira *8,* **E3**
Tiber, R. *8,* **B2**
Tiberias *8,* **G4**; *7,* **Y3**
Tigranocerta *8,* **H3**
Tigris, R. *5, 8,* **H4**
Til-garimmu *5,* **G3**
Timnah: Hill Country of Judah *3, 6,* **X5**
Timnah: Dan *3, 6,* **W5**
Timnath-serah (Timnath) *3, 6,* **X5**
Timsah, L. *2,* **R2**
Tipsah *5,* **G3**
Tirzah *3, 6,* **X4**
Tishbe *6,* **Y4**
Tjaru (Zilu) *2,* **R2**
Tob *3, 4,* **Z3**
Togarmah *5,* **G3**
Tomi *8,* **E2**

Topheth: Jerusalem *1*
Trachonitis *7,* **Z2**
Trapezus *8,* **G2**
Tripolis *8,* **G4**
Troas (Alexandria Troas) *8,* **E3**
Tubal (Tabal) *5,* **G3**
Turushpa (Tuspar) *5,* **H3**
Tyre *3, 4, 7,* **X2**; *5, 8,* **G4**

Ulatha *7,* **Y2**
Upper Beth horon *3, 4, 6,* **X5**
Upper Sea, The *5,* **E4**
Upper Zab: R. *5,* **H3**
Ur, *5,* **J4**
Urartu (Ararat) *5,* **H3**
Urmia, Lake *5, 8,* **J3**
Uruk (Erech) *5,* **J4**
Ushu *5,* **G4**
Usiana *5,* **F3**

Van, Lake *5, 8,* **H3**
Viminacium *8,* **D2**

Western Sea, The *5,* **E4**

Yarmuk, Wadi *6, 7,* **Y3**
Yazith *6,* **X4**
Yehem *6,* **X4**
Yiron *3,* **X2**

Zaanannim *6,* **X3**
Zab, Upper & Lower *5,* **H3**
Zair (Zior) *6,* **X5**
Zanoah *6,* **X5**
Zaphon *3,* **Y4**
Zarethan *3, 4, 6,* **Y4**
Zebulun: *tribe 3, 4,* **X3**
Zela *3,* **X5**
Zemaraim *6,* **X5**
Zered, Brook *3, 4,* **Y7**
Zeredah: Ephraim *4, 6,* **X4**
Zeredah (Zarethan): Jordan valley *3, 6,* **Y4**
Zererah: Jordan valley *6,* **Y4**
Zeret-shhahar *3, 6,* **Y5**
Zeugma *8,* **G3**
Ziddim *6,* **Y3**
Ziklag *3, 4,* **W6**
Zilu (Tjaru) *2,* **R2**
Zin, Wilderness of *2,* **T2**
Zion, Wall of *1*
Zior (Zair) *6,* **X5**
Ziph: Hill Country of Judah *3,* **X6**
Ziph: Negeb *3,* **W7**
Ziz, Ascent of *6,* **X5**
Zoan *2,* **Q2**; *5,* **F4**
Zobah *4,* **Z1**
Zorah *3, 6,* **W5**

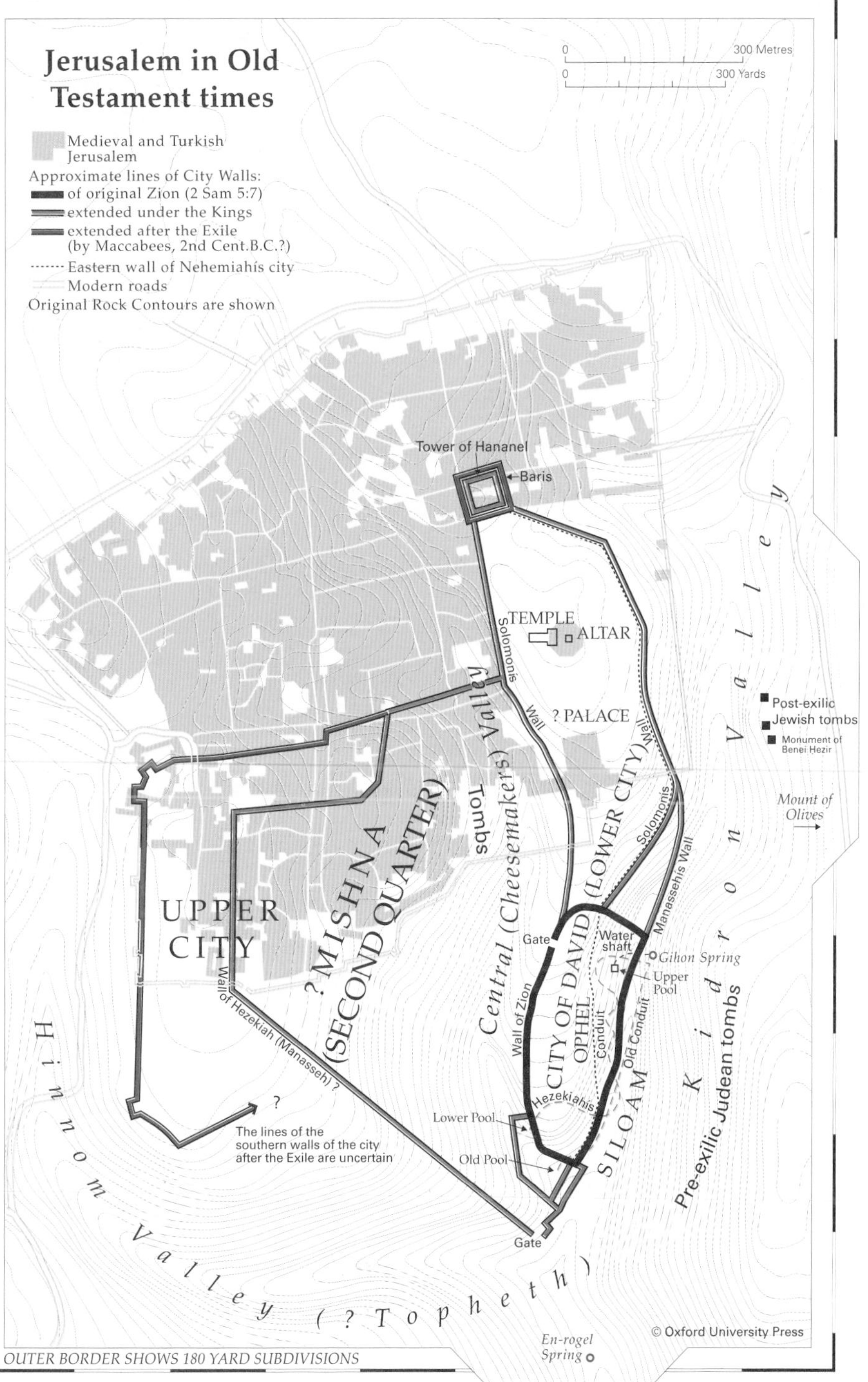
Jerusalem in Old Testament times
Medieval and Turkish Jerusalem
Approximate lines of City Walls:
of original Zion (2 Sam 5:7)
extended under the Kings
extended after the Exile (by Maccabees, 2nd Cent.B.C.?)
Eastern wall of Nehemiahís city
Modern roads
Original Rock Contours are shown
0 300 Metres
0 300 Yards
TURKISH WALL
Tower of Hananel
Baris
TEMPLE
ALTAR
? PALACE
Solomonis Wall
Nehemiahís Wall
Solomonis
Manassehís Wall
Central (Cheesemakers) Valley
Tombs
?MISHNA (SECOND QUARTER)
UPPER CITY
CITY OF DAVID (LOWER CITY)
OPHEL
Gate
Water shaft
Gihon Spring
Upper Pool
Conduit
Old Conduit
Wall of Zion
Wall of Hezekiah (Manasseh) ?
Hezekiahís
SILOAM
Lower Pool
Old Pool
Gate
The lines of the southern walls of the city after the Exile are uncertain
Hinnom Valley (? Topheth)
Kidron Valley
Post-exilic Jewish tombs
Monument of Benei Hezir
Mount of Olives
Pre-exilic Judean tombs
En-rogel Spring
© Oxford University Press
OUTER BORDER SHOWS 180 YARD SUBDIVISIONS

NOBM 11N SW Press

MAP 2

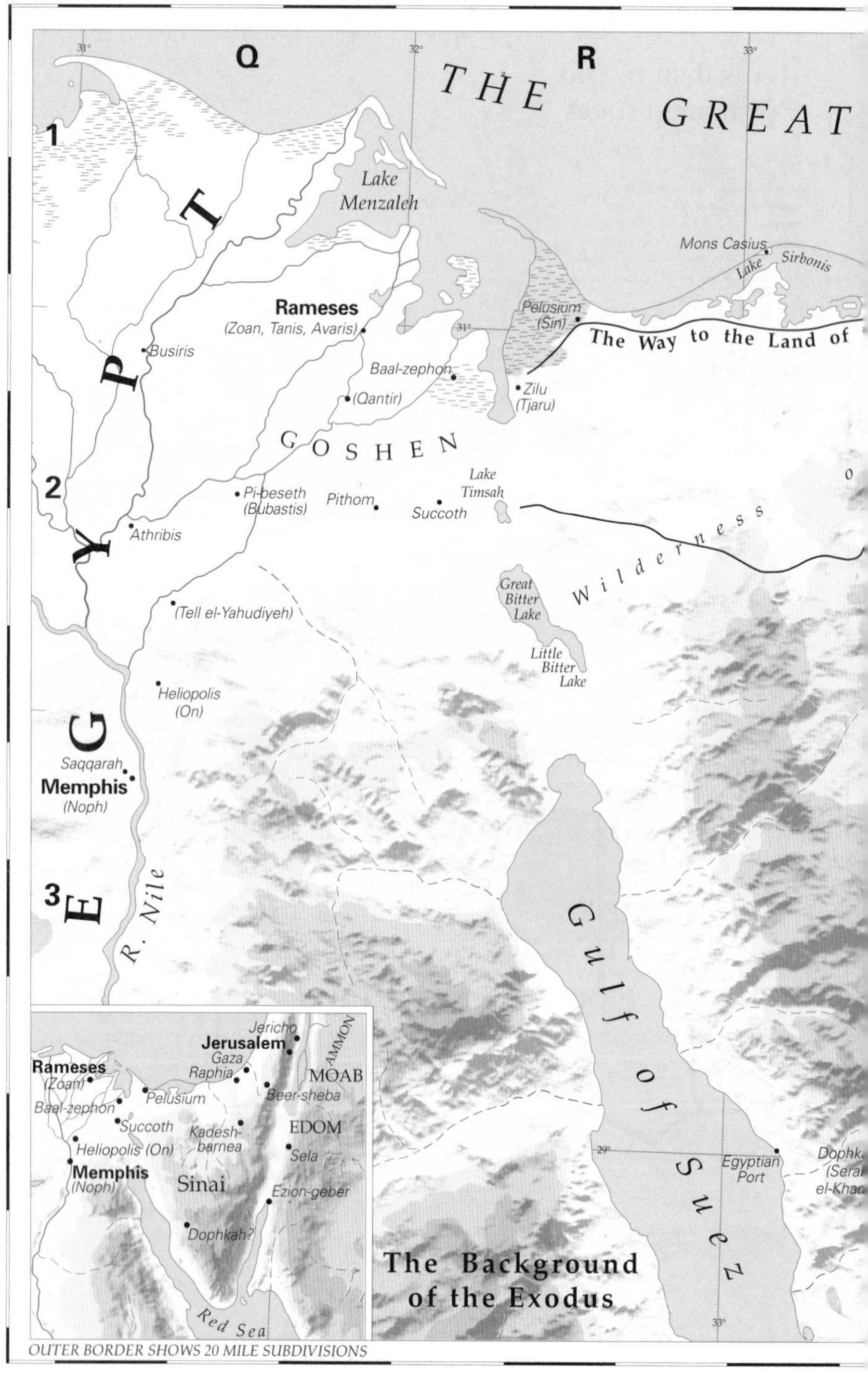

Q
R
31°
32°
33°
1
2
3
THE GREAT
EGYPT
Lake Menzaleh
Mons Casius
Lake Sirbonis
Rameses
(Zoan, Tanis, Avaris)
Pelusium
(Sin)
The Way to the Land of
Busiris
Baal-zephon
Zilu
(Tjaru)
(Qantir)
GOSHEN
Lake Timsah
Pi-beseth
(Bubastis)
Pithom
Succoth
Athribis
Wilderness
Great Bitter Lake
Little Bitter Lake
(Tell el-Yahudiyeh)
Heliopolis
(On)
Saqqarah
Memphis
(Noph)
R. Nile
Gulf of Suez
29°
Egyptian Port
Jericho
Jerusalem
AMMON
Gaza
Raphia
MOAB
Rameses
(Zoan)
Pelusium
Beer-sheba
Baal-zephon
Succoth
Kadesh-barnea
EDOM
Heliopolis (On)
Sela
Memphis
(Noph)
Sinai
Ezion-geber
Dophkah?
Red Sea
The Background of the Exodus
OUTER BORDER SHOWS 20 MILE SUBDIVISIONS

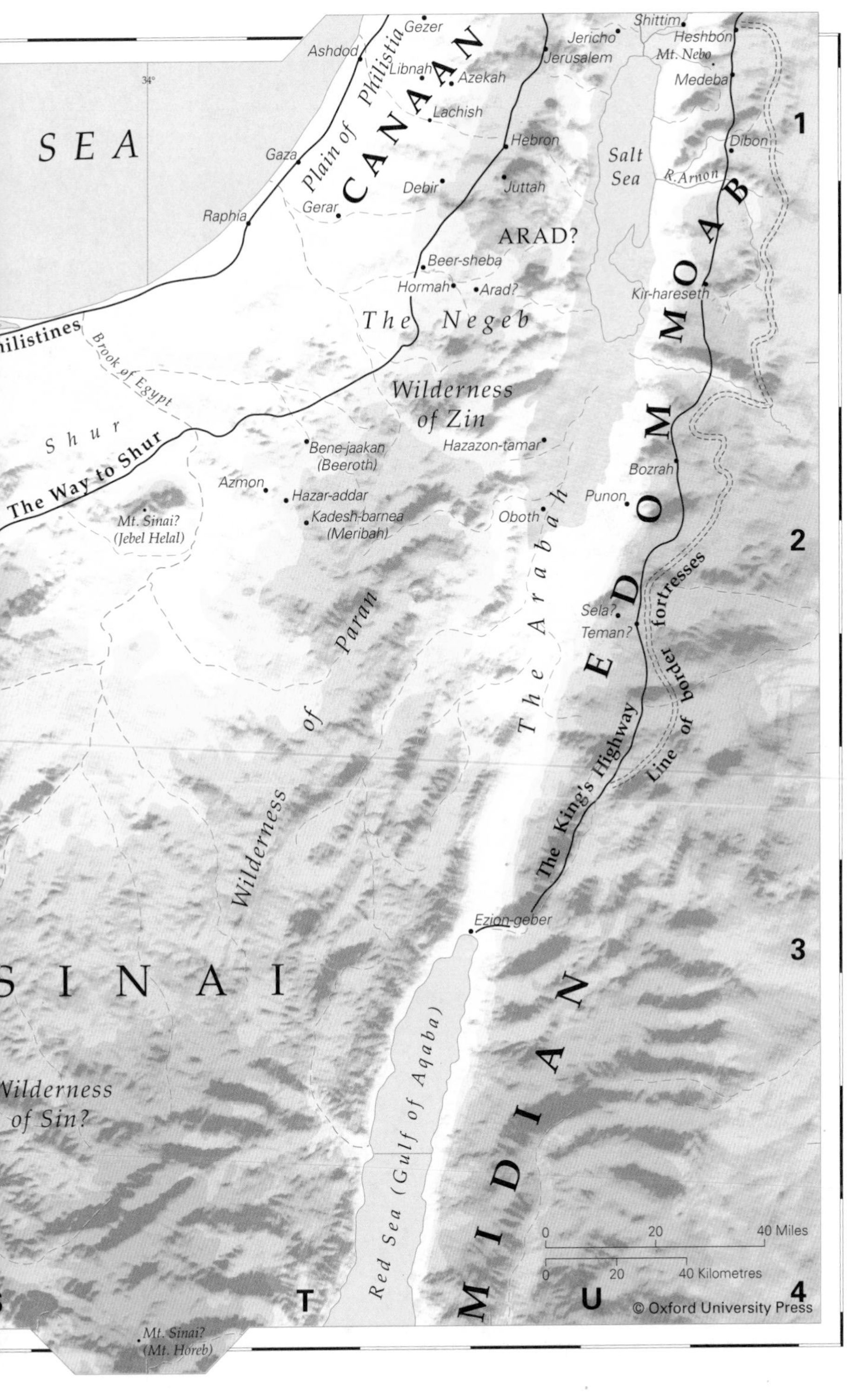
SEA
34°
Gezer
Ashdod
Plain of Philistia
Libnah
Azekah
CANAAN
Lachish
Gaza
Raphia
Gerar
Debir
Hebron
Juttah
ARAD?
Beer-sheba
Hormah
Arad?
The Negeb
Jericho
Jerusalem
Shittim
Heshbon
Mt. Nebo
Medeba
Dibon
Salt Sea
R. Arnon
MOAB
Kir-hareseth
Philistines
Brook of Egypt
Shur
The Way to Shur
Wilderness of Zin
Hazazon-tamar
Bene-jaakan (Beeroth)
Azmon
Hazar-addar
Kadesh-barnea (Meribah)
Mt. Sinai? (Jebel Helal)
Oboth
Punon
Bozrah
EDOM
The Arabah
Sela?
Teman?
fortresses
Line of border
The King's Highway
Wilderness of Paran
Ezion-geber
SINAI
MIDIAN
Wilderness of Sin?
Red Sea (Gulf of Aqaba)
Mt. Sinai? (Mt. Horeb)
0 20 40 Miles
0 20 40 Kilometres
1
2
3
4
T
U
© Oxford University Press

MAP 3

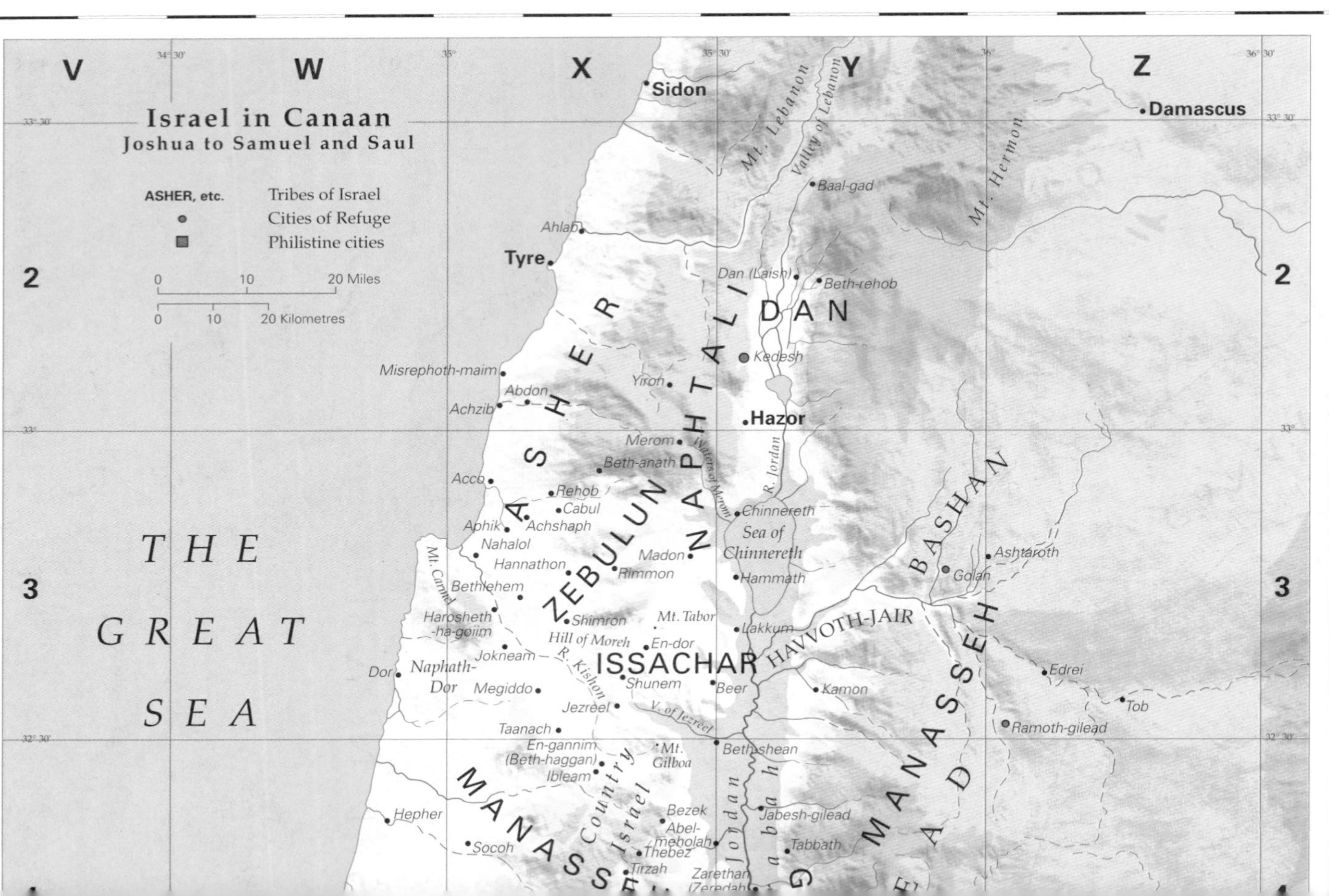

Israel in Canaan
Joshua to Samuel and Saul
ASHER, etc. Tribes of Israel
Cities of Refuge
Philistine cities
0 10 20 Miles
0 10 20 Kilometres
V
W
X
Y
Z
2
3
THE GREAT SEA
Sidon
Damascus
Mt. Lebanon
Valley of Lebanon
Mt. Hermon
Baal-gad
Ahlab
Tyre
Dan (Laish)
Beth-rehob
DAN
Kedesh
Misrephoth-maim
Abdon
Achzib
Yiron
Hazor
Merom
Waters of Merom
R. Jordan
Beth-anath
Acco
Rehob
Cabul
Aphik
Achshaph
Chinnereth
Sea of Chinnereth
Nahalol
Hannathon
Madon
Rimmon
Hammath
Mt. Carmel
Bethlehem
Harosheth-ha-goiim
Shimron
Mt. Tabor
Lakkum
Hill of Moreh
En-dor
Jokneam
R. Kishon
ISSACHAR
HAVVOTH-JAIR
Dor
Naphath-Dor
Megiddo
Shunem
Beer
Kamon
Jezreel
V. of Jezreel
Taanach
En-gannim (Beth-haggan)
Mt. Gilboa
Beth-shean
Ibleam
Country Israel
Hepher
Socoh
Bezek
Abel-meholah
Thebez
Tirzah
Zarethan (Zeredah)
Jordan
Jabesh-gilead
Tabbath
ASHER
NAPHTALI
ZEBULUN
BASHAN
MANASSEH
GAD
Golan
Ashtaroth
Edrei
Tob
Ramoth-gilead

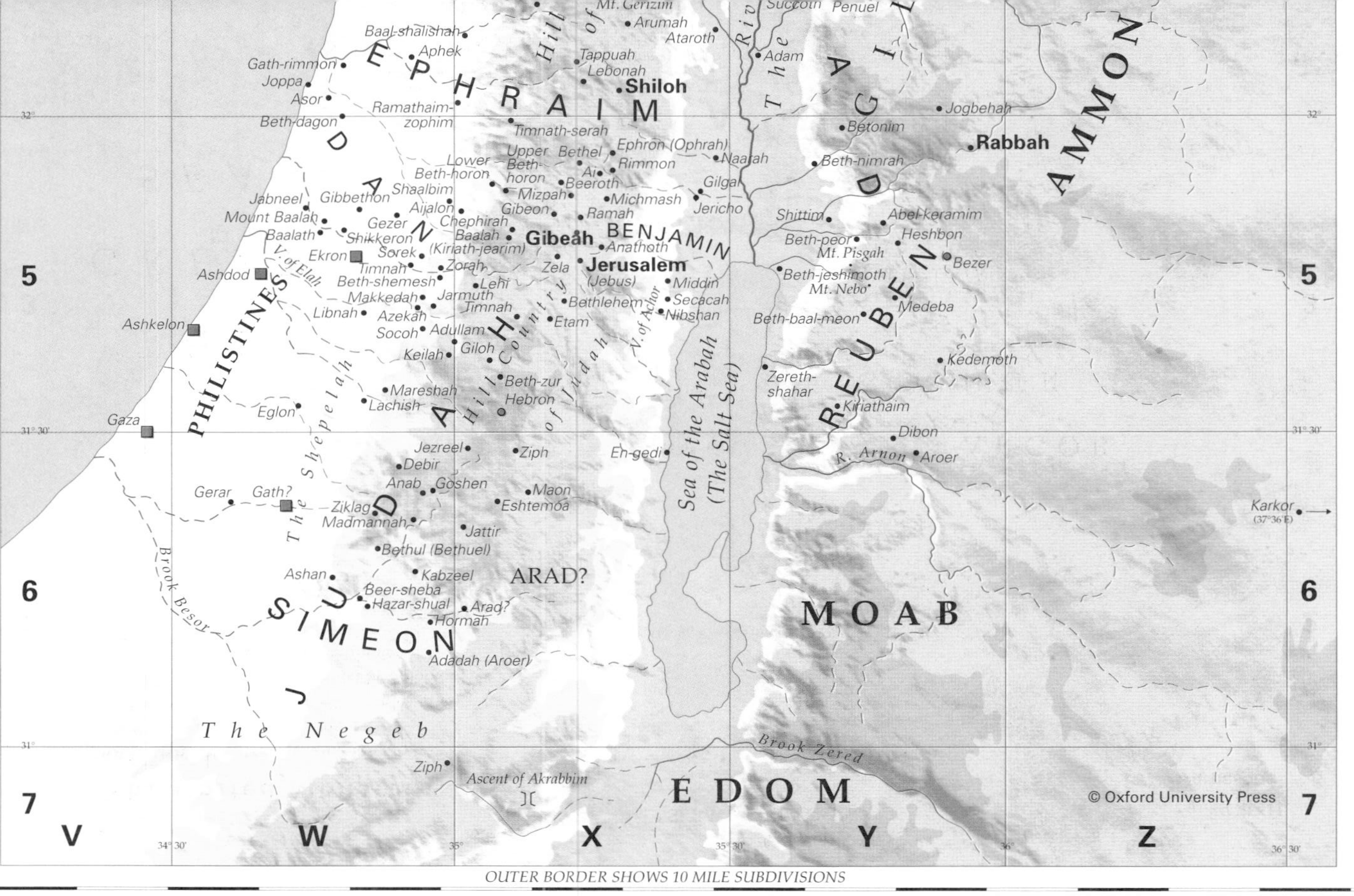

EPHRAIM
DAN
BENJAMIN
JUDAH
SIMEON
PHILISTINES
GAD
REUBEN
AMMON
MOAB
EDOM
Hill of
Mt. Gerizim
Arumah
Ataroth
Succoth
Penuel
Adam
The River
Baal-shalishah
Aphek
Gath-rimmon
Joppa
Asor
Tappuah
Lebonah
Shiloh
Ramathaim-zophim
Beth-dagon
Timnath-serah
Jogbehah
Betonim
Rabbah
Upper Beth-horon
Lower Beth-horon
Bethel
Ephron (Ophrah)
Rimmon
Naarah
Beth-nimrah
Ai
Beeroth
Gilgal
Jericho
Jabneel
Gibbethon
Shaalbim
Mizpah
Michmash
Mount Baalah
Aijalon
Gibeon
Ramah
Shittim
Abel-keramim
Gezer
Chephirah
Baalath
Shikkeron
Baalah (Kiriath-jearim)
Gibeah
Anathoth
Beth-peor
Mt. Pisgah
Heshbon
Ekron
Sorek
Zorah
Zela
Jerusalem (Jebus)
Bezer
Ashdod
V. of Elah
Timnah
Beth-shemesh
Lehi
Middin
Beth-jeshimoth
Mt. Nebo
Makkedah
Jarmuth
Bethlehem
Secacah
Medeba
Libnah
Azekah
Timnah
V. of Achor
Nibshan
Ashkelon
Etam
Beth-baal-meon
Socoh
Adullam
Keilah
Giloh
Kedemoth
Hill Country of Judah
Beth-zur
Zereth-shahar
Mareshah
Hebron
Lachish
Kiriathaim
Eglon
Gaza
Sea of the Arabah (The Salt Sea)
Dibon
Jezreel
Ziph
En-gedi
R. Arnon
Aroer
Debir
The Shephelah
Gerar
Gath?
Anab
Goshen
Maon
Ziklag
Eshtemoa
Karkor (37°36'E)
Madmannah
Jattir
Bethul (Bethuel)
Brook Besor
Ashan
Kabzeel
ARAD?
Beer-sheba
Hazar-shual
Arad?
Hormah
Adadah (Aroer)
The Negeb
Brook Zered
Ziph
Ascent of Akrabbim
© Oxford University Press
32°
31° 30'
31°
34° 30'
35°
35° 30'
36°
36° 30'
5
6
7
V
W
X
Y
Z
OUTER BORDER SHOWS 10 MILE SUBDIVISIONS

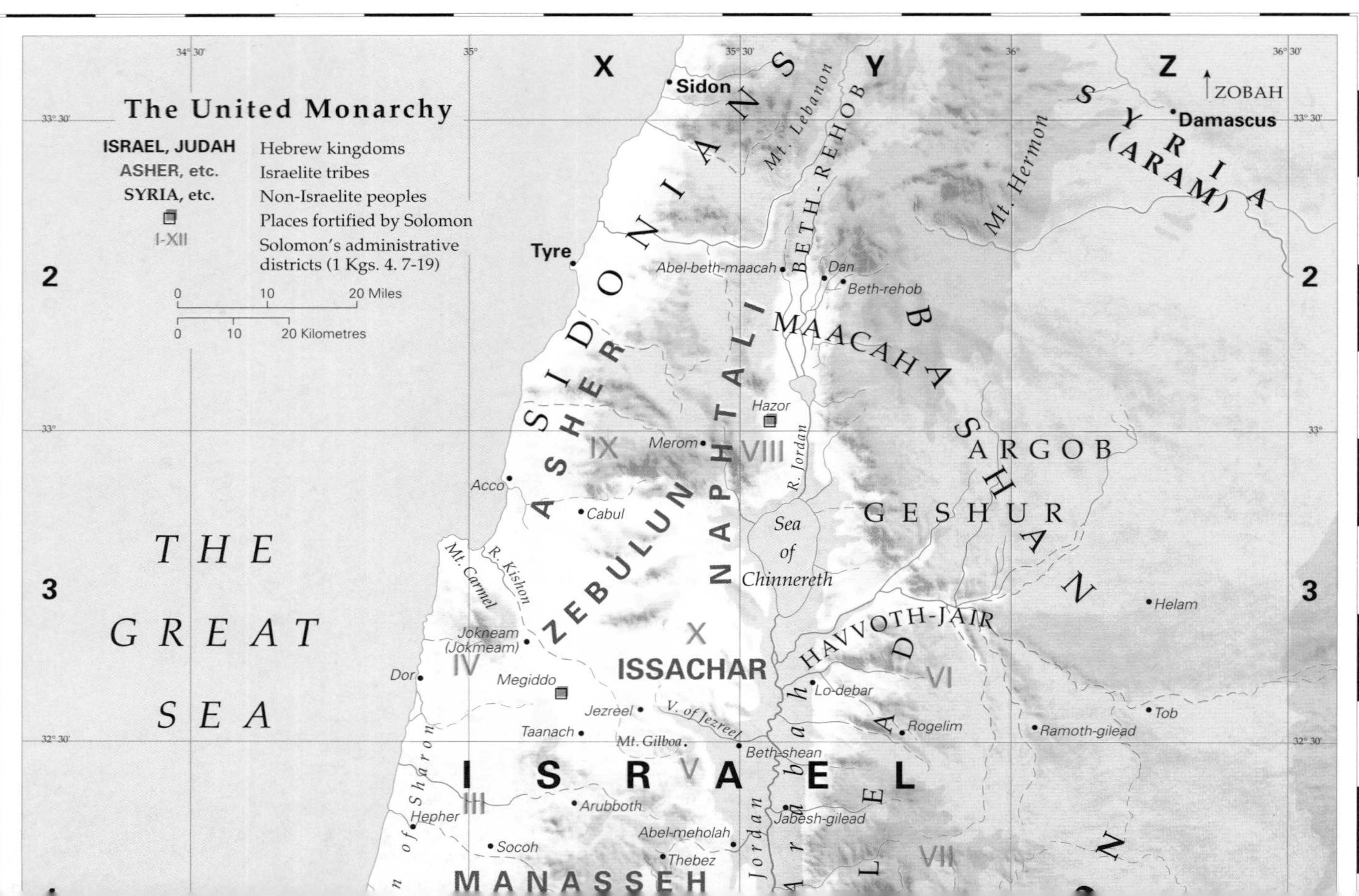
The United Monarchy
ISRAEL, JUDAH Hebrew kingdoms
ASHER, etc. Israelite tribes
SYRIA, etc. Non-Israelite peoples
Places fortified by Solomon
I-XII Solomon's administrative districts (1 Kgs. 4. 7-19)
0 10 20 Miles
0 10 20 Kilometres
THE GREAT SEA
SIDONIANS
Sidon
Tyre
Mt. Lebanon
BETH-REHOB
Mt. Hermon
SYRIA (ARAM)
ZOBAH
Damascus
Abel-beth-maacah
Dan
Beth-rehob
MAACAH
BASHAN
ARGOB
GESHUR
ASHER
NAPHTALI
ZEBULUN
ISSACHAR
Hazor
Merom
R. Jordan
Acco
Cabul
Sea of Chinnereth
Mt. Carmel
R. Kishon
Jokneam (Jokmeam)
Dor
Megiddo
Jezreel
V. of Jezreel
Taanach
Mt. Gilboa
Beth-shean
HAVVOTH-JAIR
GILEAD
Lo-debar
Rogelim
Helam
Tob
Ramoth-gilead
ISRAEL
Arubboth
Hepher
Socoh
Abel-meholah
Thebez
Jabesh-gilead
Jordan
Arabah
Plain of Sharon
MANASSEH
I-XII
IV
IX
VIII
X
VI
V
III
VII
X
Y
Z
2
3
34° 30'
35°
35° 30'
36°
36° 30'
33° 30'
33°
32° 30'

5
6
7
V
W
X
Y
Z
32°
31° 30'
31°
34° 30'
35°
35° 30'
36°
36° 30'
© Oxford University Press
OUTER BORDER SHOWS 10 MILE SUBDIVISIONS
AMMON
Rabbah
(Rabbath-ammon)
Jazer
Heshbon
Medeba
MOAB
Dibon
Aroer
Kir-hareseth
R. Nahaliel
R. Arnon
Brook Zered
EDOM
XII
XI
II
Gilgal
Jericho
BENJAMIN
Jerusalem
Anathoth
Gibeah
High Place
Kiriath-jearim
Salt Sea
(Sea of the Arabah)
Wilderness of Judah
EPHRAIM
Shiloh
Baal-hazor
Ephraim
Bethel
Beeroth
Geba
Upper Beth-horon
Gibeon
Lower Beth-horon
Beth-hanan
Zeredah
Shaalbim
Elon
Gezer
Makaz
Sorek
Beth-shemesh
Gath-rimmon
Joppa
Baalath
Ekron
Ashdod
Ashkelon
Gaza
PHILISTINES
Libnah
Bethlehem
Netophah
Tekoa
JUDAH
Adullam
Giloh
Hebron
Carmel
Arad
Debir
Ziklag
Kabzeel
Valley of Salt
The Shephelah (Lowland)
Gath?
Gerar
Beer-sheba
The Negeb
AMALEK
Brook Besor
Tamar
(30° 48'N)

Black
PHRYGIA
Gomer
(Gimarrai)
Gordion
Meshech
(Mushki)
R. Sangarius
R. Halys
Usiana
Tubal
(Tabal)
LYDIA
R. Hermus
Sardis
(Sepharad)
R. Macander
JAVAN
Musri
CILICIA
(KHILAKKU)
Kue
Crete
(Caphtor)
Rhodes
Cyprus
(Iadanna)
HATTINA
Amanus Mts.
R. Orontes
The Great Sea
(The Upper Sea, the Western Sea)
Arvad
Riblah
Kadesh
Gebal (Byblos)
Berytus
Lebanon
Lebo-Hamath
Helbon
Sidon
Tyre
Damascus
Ushu
Acco
Hauran
ISRAEL
Samaria
Jerusalem
JUDAH
AMMON
MOAB
Raphia
Gaza
Pelusium
Libya
Zoan
(Tanis)
Sais
Tahpanhes
Migdol
Athribis
Memphis
(Noph)
Heliopolis
(On)
EDOM
Sela?
Sinai
Ezion-geber
(Elath)
EGYPT
Hermopolis
Lycopolis
(Siut)
R. Nile
Red Sea
Thebes
Syene
ETHIOPIA
0 100 200 Miles
0 100 200 Kilometres
OUTER BORDER SHO

The Near East in the time of the Assyrian Empire

Approximate extent of Assyrian domination in the latter part of the 8th century.
(Later, under Esarhaddon (681-669), Assyria conquered Egypt.)

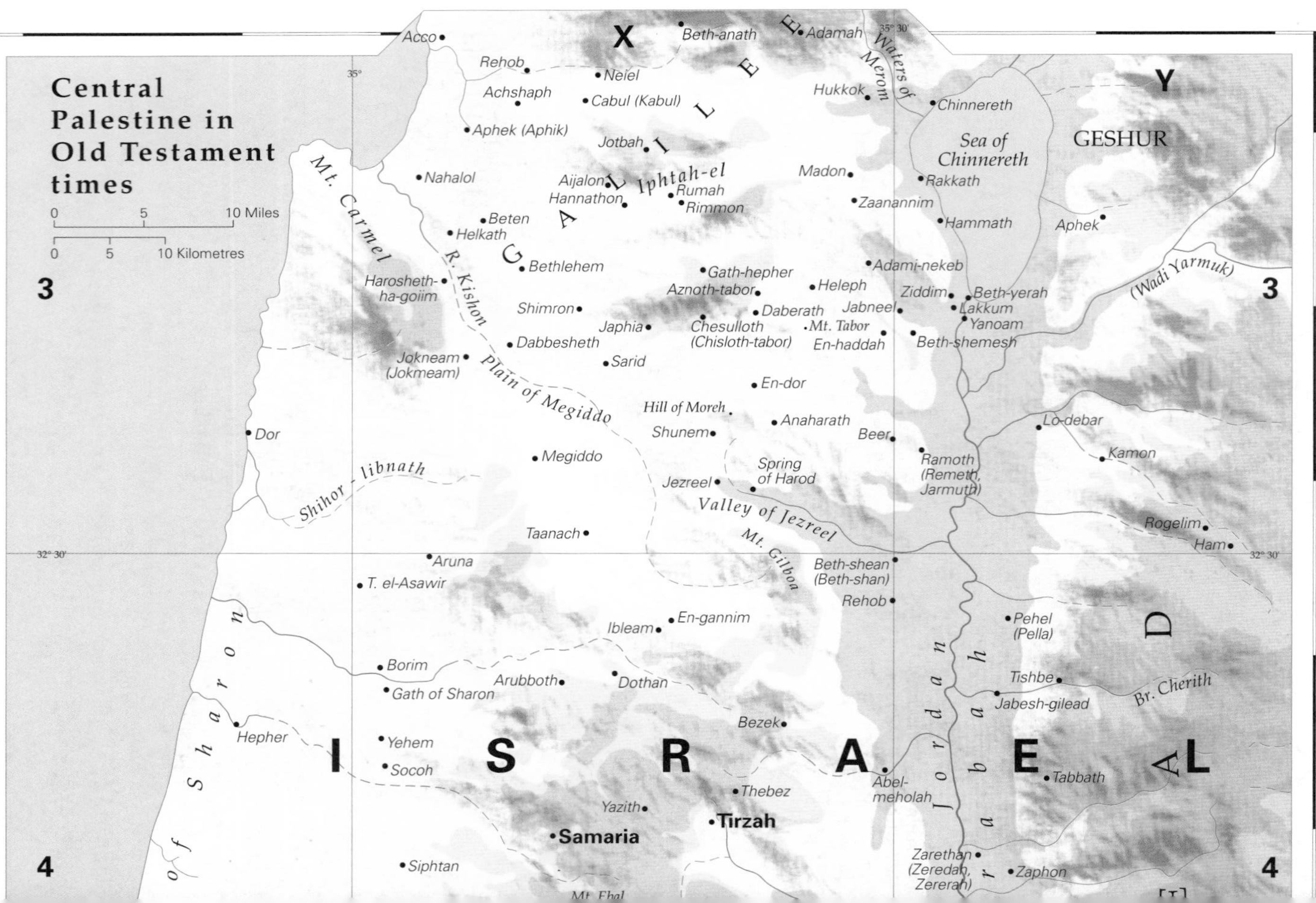
Central Palestine in Old Testament times
0 5 10 Miles
0 5 10 Kilometres
3
4
35°
35° 30'
32° 30'
GALILEE
GESHUR
ISRAEL
Sea of Chinnereth
Waters of Merom
(Wadi Yarmuk)
Br. Cherith
Valley of Jezreel
Mt. Gilboa
Mt. Carmel
R. Kishon
Plain of Megiddo
Shihor-libnath
Plain of Sharon
Jordan
Iphtah-el
Hill of Moreh
Mt. Tabor
Spring of Harod
Acco
Rehob
Achshaph
Aphek (Aphik)
Nahalol
Beten
Helkath
Harosheth-ha-goiim
Jokneam (Jokmeam)
Dor
Neiel
Cabul (Kabul)
Jotbah
Aijalon
Hannathon
Bethlehem
Shimron
Dabbesheth
Japhia
Sarid
Beth-anath
Adamah
Hukkok
Madon
Rumah
Rimmon
Gath-hepher
Aznoth-tabor
Chesulloth (Chisloth-tabor)
Daberath
Heleph
Jabneel
En-haddah
En-dor
Anaharath
Shunem
Jezreel
Megiddo
Taanach
Aruna
T. el-Asawir
Borim
Gath of Sharon
Yehem
Socoh
Siphtan
Hepher
Arubboth
Ibleam
Dothan
En-gannim
Beth-shean (Beth-shan)
Rehob
Bezek
Thebez
Tirzah
Yazith
Samaria
Chinnereth
Rakkath
Hammath
Zaanannim
Adami-nekeb
Ziddim
Beth-yerah
Lakkum
Yanoam
Beth-shemesh
Aphek
Lo-debar
Kamon
Rogelim
Ham
Ramoth (Remeth, Jarmuth)
Beer
Pehel (Pella)
Tishbe
Jabesh-gilead
Tabbath
Zaphon
Zarethan (Zeredah, Zererah)
Abel-meholah

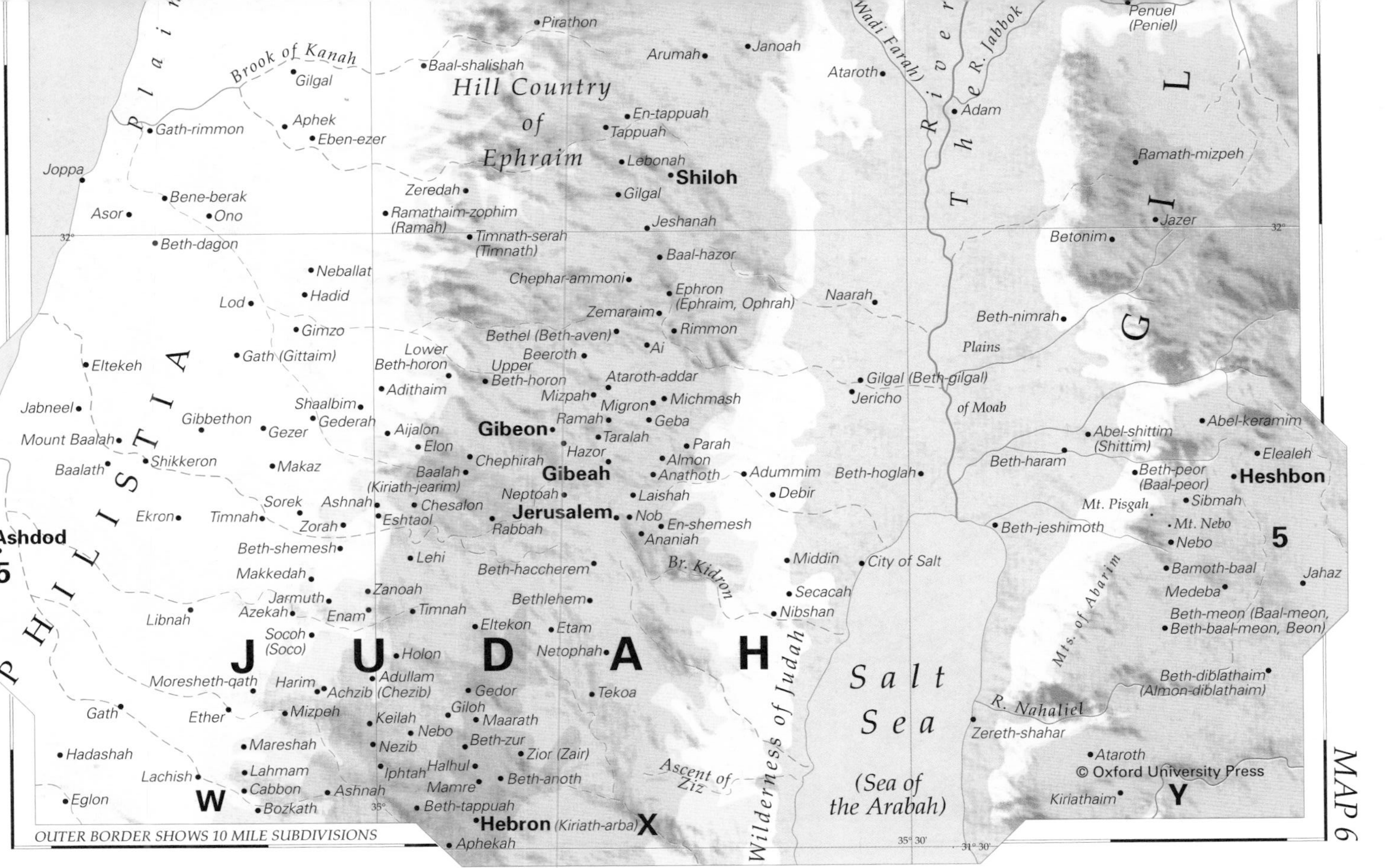
Hill Country of Ephraim
Shiloh
Jerusalem
Gibeah
Gibeon
Hebron (Kiriath-arba)
Heshbon
Ashdod
JUDAH
PHILISTIA
The River Jordan
Salt Sea (Sea of the Arabah)
Wilderness of Judah
Mts. of Abarim
Plains of Moab
R. Jabbok
R. Nahaliel
Br. Kidron
Brook of Kanah
Wadi Farah)
Ascent of Ziz
Joppa
Lod
Gezer
Ekron
Gath
Lachish
Eglon
Jericho
Gilgal (Beth-gilgal)
Bethel (Beth-aven)
Ai
Mizpah
Ramah
Anathoth
Bethlehem
Tekoa
Beth-zur
Adullam
Keilah
Mareshah
Beth-shemesh
Timnah
Zorah
Eshtaol
Azekah
Socoh (Soco)
Libnah
Medeba
Mt. Nebo
Mt. Pisgah
Beth-peor (Baal-peor)
Abel-shittim (Shittim)
Beth-nimrah
Adam
Penuel (Peniel)
Jazer
Ramath-mizpeh
Kiriathaim
Zereth-shahar
Ataroth
OUTER BORDER SHOWS 10 MILE SUBDIVISIONS
© Oxford University Press

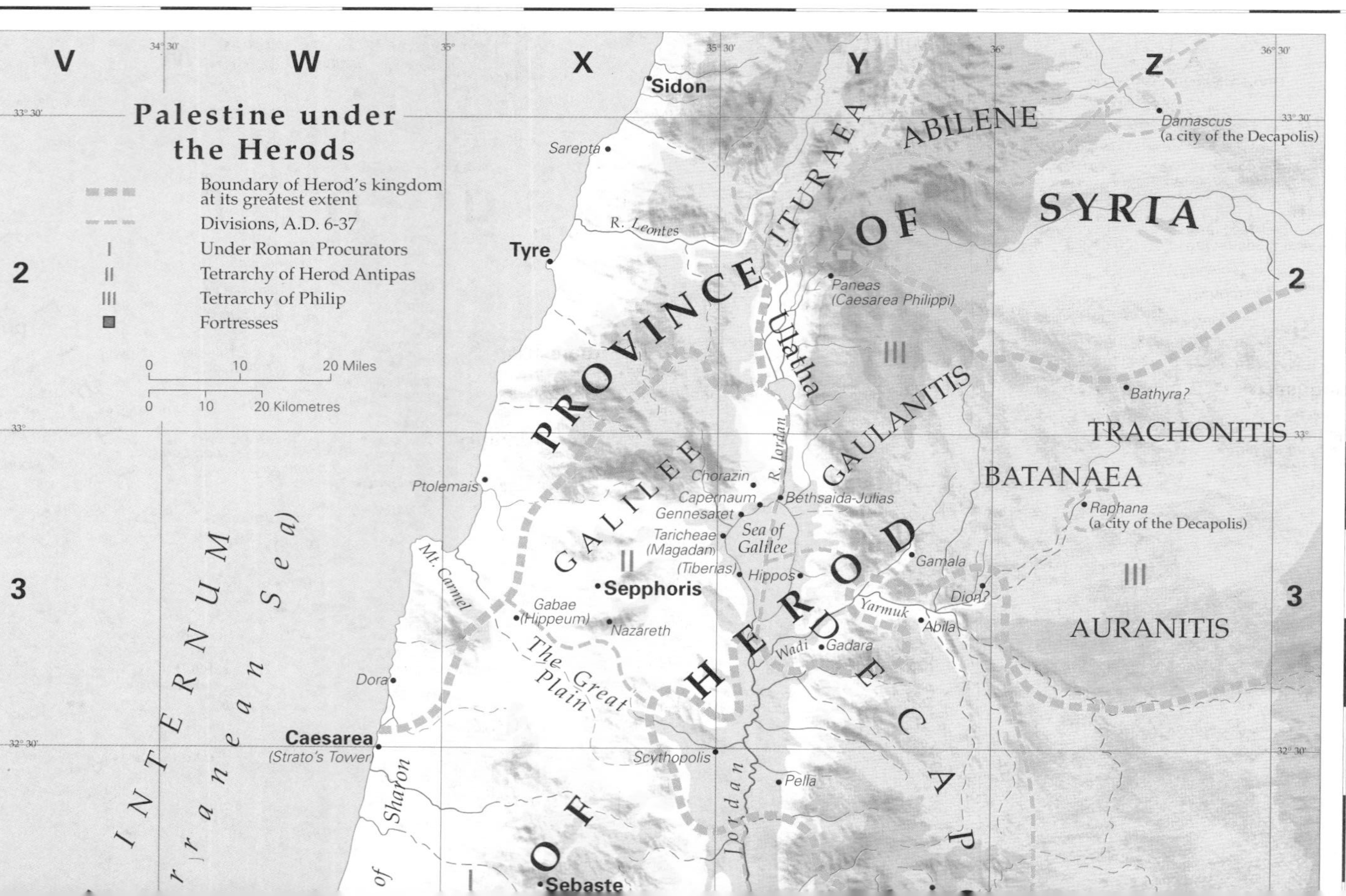
Palestine under the Herods
Boundary of Herod's kingdom at its greatest extent
Divisions, A.D. 6-37
I Under Roman Procurators
II Tetrarchy of Herod Antipas
III Tetrarchy of Philip
Fortresses
0 10 20 Miles
0 10 20 Kilometres
V
W
X
Y
Z
2
3
34° 30'
35°
35° 30'
36°
36° 30'
33° 30'
33°
32° 30'
PROVINCE OF SYRIA
ABILENE
ITURAEA
TRACHONITIS
BATANAEA
AURANITIS
GAULANITIS
GALILEE
HEROD
DECAP
OF
Damascus
(a city of the Decapolis)
Bathyra?
Raphana
(a city of the Decapolis)
Paneas
(Caesarea Philippi)
Ulatha
Sidon
Sarepta
R. Leontes
Tyre
Ptolemais
Mt. Carmel
Dora
Caesarea
(Strato's Tower)
Sharon
Chorazin
Capernaum
Gennesaret
Bethsaida-Julias
R. Jordan
Sea of Galilee
Taricheae
(Magadan)
(Tiberias)
Hippos
Gamala
Dion?
Abila
Yarmuk
Wadi
Gadara
Pella
Jordan
Scythopolis
Sepphoris
Nazareth
Gabae
(Hippeum)
The Great Plain
Sebaste
INTERNUM
rranean Sea)

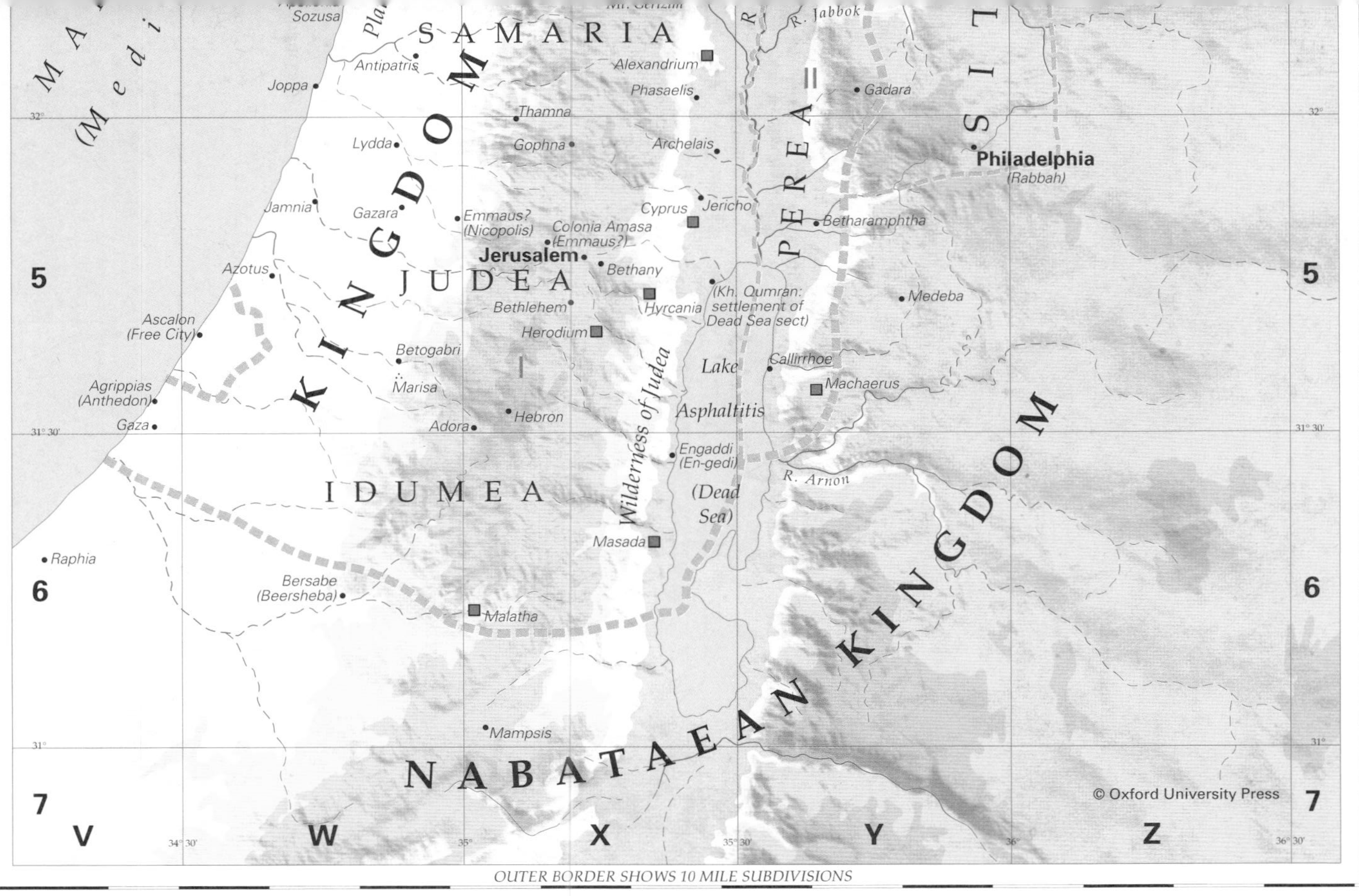

SAMARIA
KINGDOM
JUDEA
IDUMEA
PEREA
NABATAEAN KINGDOM
(Medi
Sozusa
Antipatris
Joppa
Alexandrium
Phasaelis
Gadara
R. Jabbok
Thamna
Lydda
Gophna
Archelais
Philadelphia
(Rabbah)
Jamnia
Gazara
Emmaus?
(Nicopolis)
Colonia Amasa
(Emmaus?)
Cyprus
Jericho
Betharamphtha
Jerusalem
Bethany
Azotus
Bethlehem
Hyrcania
(Kh. Qumran: settlement of Dead Sea sect)
Medeba
Ascalon
(Free City)
Herodium
Betogabri
Marisa
Wilderness of Judea
Lake
Asphaltitis
Callirrhoe
Machaerus
Agrippias
(Anthedon)
Gaza
Hebron
Adora
Engaddi
(En-gedi)
R. Arnon
(Dead
Sea)
Masada
Raphia
Bersabe
(Beersheba)
Malatha
Mampsis
© Oxford University Press
5
6
7
V
W
X
Y
Z
32°
31° 30'
31°
34° 30'
35°
35° 30'
36°
36° 30'
OUTER BORDER SHOWS 10 MILE SUBDIVISIONS

MAP 8

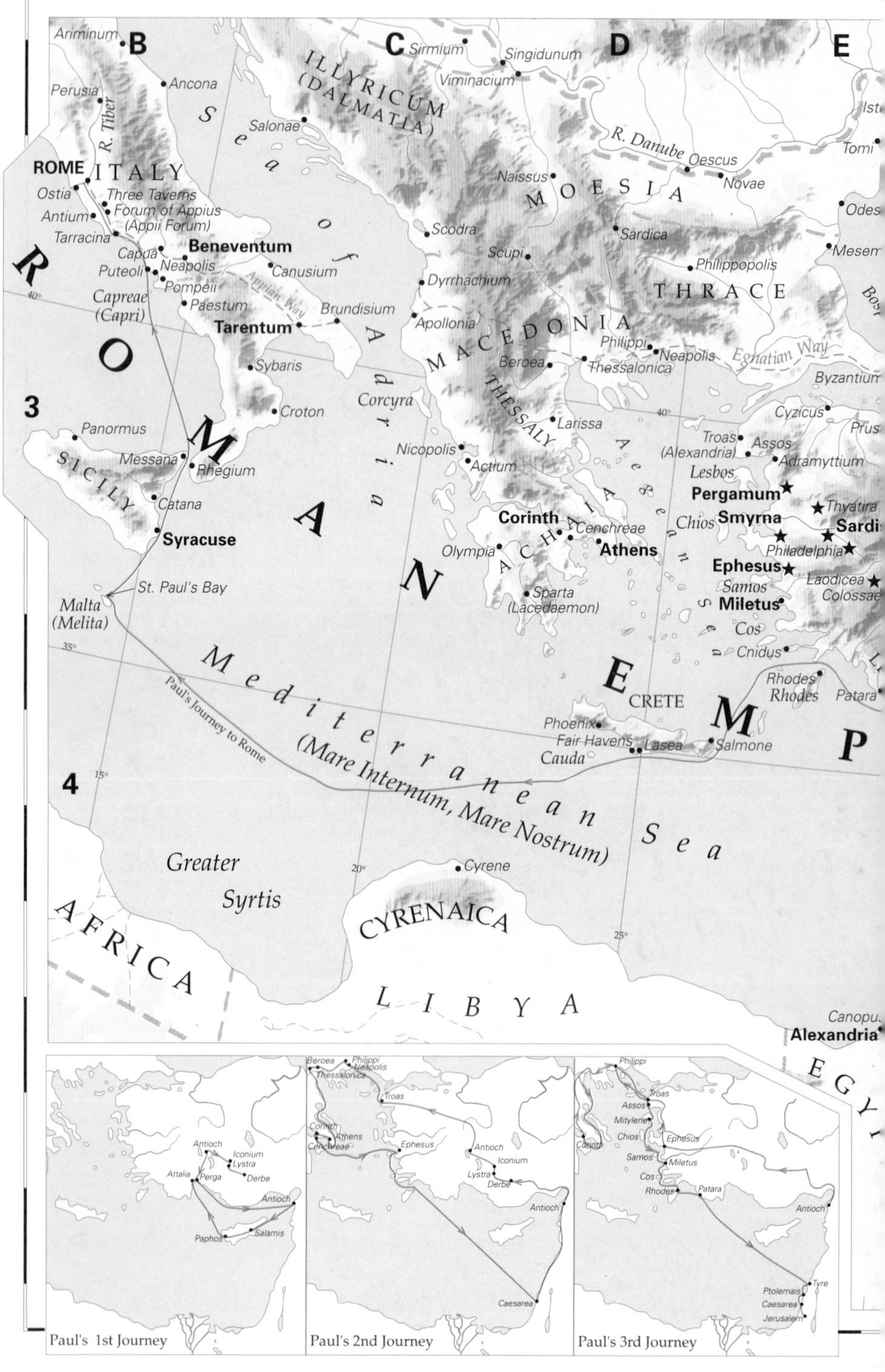

B
C
D
E
3
4
ROME
ITALY
Ariminum
Perusia
Ancona
R. Tiber
Ostia
Three Taverns
Forum of Appius (Appii Forum)
Antium
Tarracina
Capua
Beneventum
Puteoli
Neapolis
Pompeii
Canusium
Appian Way
Capreae (Capri)
Paestum
Brundisium
Tarentum
Sybaris
Croton
Panormus
Messana
Rhegium
SICILY
Catana
Syracuse
St. Paul's Bay
Malta (Melita)
ROMAN EMPIRE
Sea of Adria
Salonae
ILLYRICUM (DALMATIA)
Sirmium
Singidunum
Viminacium
R. Danube
Oescus
Novae
Tomi
Naissus
MOESIA
Odes
Scodra
Sardica
Scupi
Mesem
Philippopolis
Dyrrhachium
THRACE
Apollonia
MACEDONIA
Philippi
Neapolis
Egnatian Way
Beroea
Thessalonica
Byzantium
THESSALY
Corcyra
Larissa
Cyzicus
Nicopolis
Actium
Troas (Alexandria)
Assos
Adramyttium
Lesbos
Pergamum
Thyatira
Aegean Sea
Corinth
Cenchreae
Chios
Smyrna
Sardis
ACHAIA
Olympia
Athens
Philadelphia
Ephesus
Laodicea
Colossae
Sparta (Lacedaemon)
Samos
Miletus
Cos
Cnidus
Rhodes
Rhodes
Patara
CRETE
Phoenix
Fair Havens
Lasea
Salmone
Cauda
Mediterranean Sea
(Mare Internum, Mare Nostrum)
Paul's Journey to Rome
Greater Syrtis
Cyrene
CYRENAICA
AFRICA
LIBYA
Canopus
Alexandria
EGYPT
40°
35°
15°
20°
25°
Paul's 1st Journey
Antioch
Iconium
Lystra
Derbe
Attalia
Perga
Antioch
Paphos
Salamis
Paul's 2nd Journey
Beroea
Philippi
Neapolis
Thessalonica
Troas
Corinth
Athens
Cenchreae
Ephesus
Antioch
Iconium
Lystra
Derbe
Antioch
Caesarea
Paul's 3rd Journey
Philippi
Troas
Assos
Mitylene
Chios
Ephesus
Corinth
Samos
Miletus
Cos
Rhodes
Patara
Antioch
Tyre
Ptolemais
Caesarea
Jerusalem

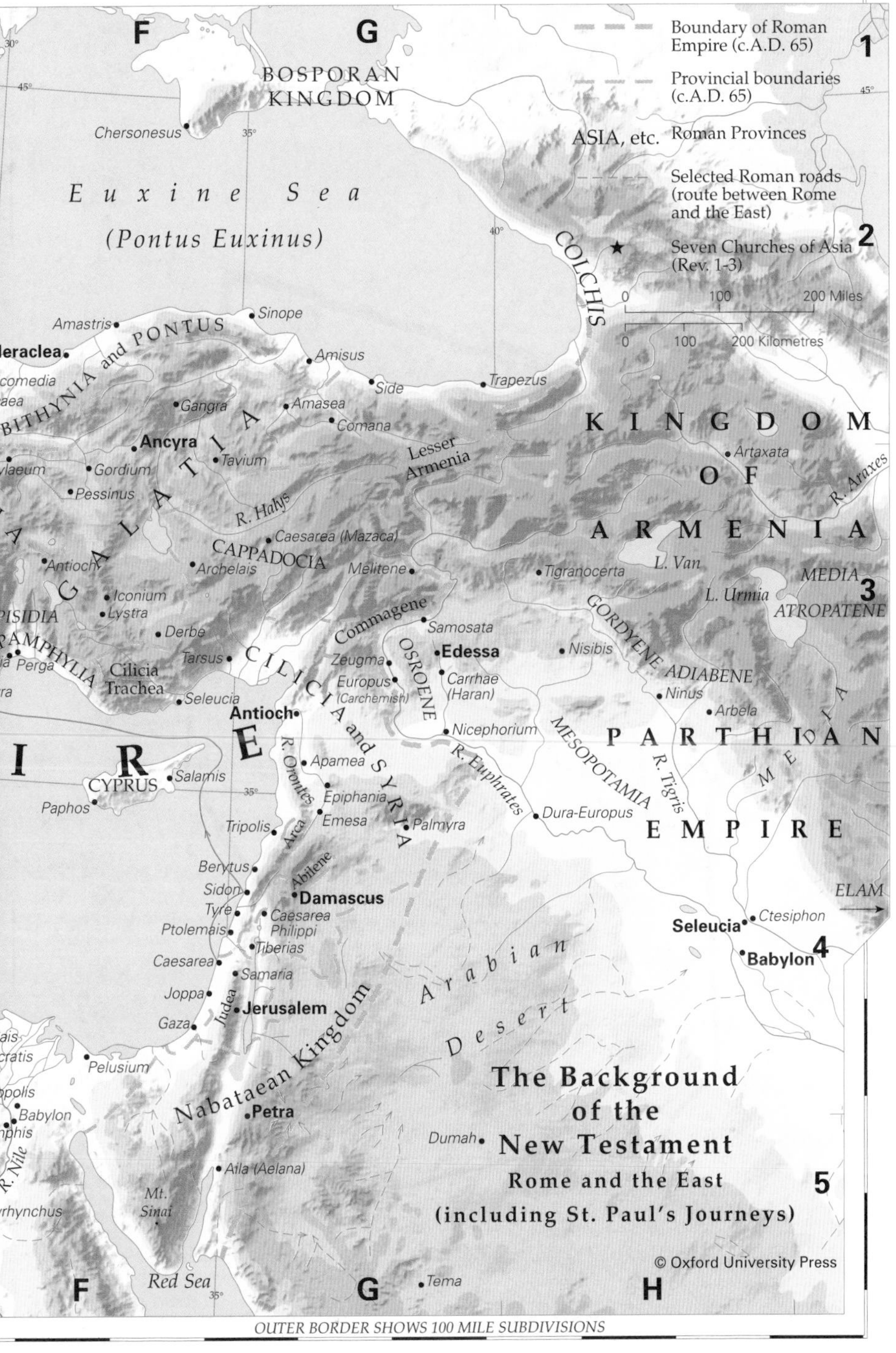

The Background of the New Testament

Rome and the East (including St. Paul's Journeys)

MAP 9

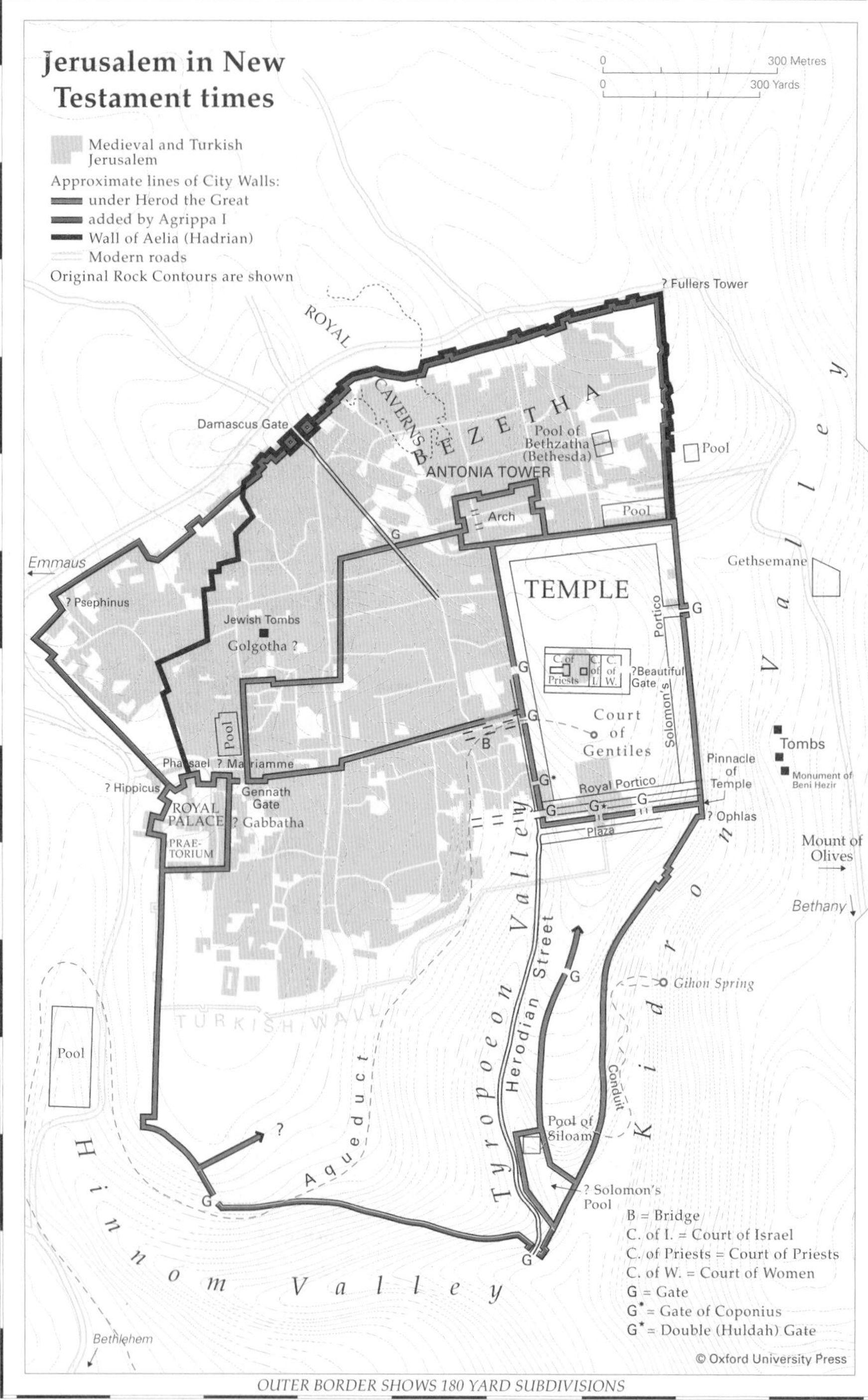
Jerusalem in New Testament times
Medieval and Turkish Jerusalem
Approximate lines of City Walls:
under Herod the Great
added by Agrippa I
Wall of Aelia (Hadrian)
Modern roads
Original Rock Contours are shown
0 300 Metres
0 300 Yards
? Fullers Tower
ROYAL
CAVERNS
BEZETHA
Damascus Gate
Pool of Bethzatha (Bethesda)
Pool
ANTONIA TOWER
Arch
Pool
Emmaus
G
Gethsemane
TEMPLE
Portico
G
? Psephinus
Jewish Tombs
Golgotha ?
C. of Priests
C. of I.
C. of W.
?Beautiful Gate
Solomon's
Court of Gentiles
Pool
B
Tombs
Phasael
? Mariamme
Pinnacle of Temple
Monument of Beni Hezir
? Hippicus
Gennath Gate
Royal Portico
ROYAL PALACE
? Gabbatha
? Ophlas
PRAETORIUM
Plaza
Mount of Olives
Bethany
Kidron Valley
Tyropoeon Valley
Herodian Street
TURKISH WALL
Gihon Spring
Pool
Aqueduct
Conduit
Pool of Siloam
?
? Solomon's Pool
Hinnom Valley
B = Bridge
C. of I. = Court of Israel
C. of Priests = Court of Priests
C. of W. = Court of Women
G = Gate
G* = Gate of Coponius
G* = Double (Huldah) Gate
Bethlehem
© Oxford University Press
OUTER BORDER SHOWS 180 YARD SUBDIVISIONS